Remember When Circulation & Revenue Increases Were Easy?

They Can Be Again!

Circulation and ad revenue growth has been hard to come by these days. It doesn't have to be that way. You can easily add to your circulation and increase ad profits! *Scramblr®* and *Watchword*™ have given a measurable bonus to **over 580 newspapers**.

From Oakland, California to Buffalo, New York, hundreds of newspapers have experienced ...

- An immediate jump in single copy sales
- A sizable increase in new readers
- Increased Advertising Revenues
- Less resistance to price increases
- An amazing increase in "Call Count" on your Information or Audiotex System — up to <u>triple</u> the normal rate

Promotions are adapted to your specific needs. For over 30 years, **Scrambl-Gram, Inc.** has provided newspapers of varying circulations with the quickest way available to boost profits and circulation.

Get started <u>NOW</u> by calling for a **FREE INFORMATION KIT!** You'll receive a complete price quote and valuable marketing information tailored to your paper.

SCRAMBL-GRAM™ INC.

1-800-242-5204

Call Now And Ask For: Chick Elum • Rube Faloon • Mary Elum • Or fax to: 1-800-872-9321

The Name of The Profit Game is Scramblr® and Watchword.™ Call Today!

INTERNATIONAL Year Book®

Published annually by
EDITOR & PUBLISHER,
the oldest publishers' and advertisers'
periodical in the United States

With which has been merged: **The Journalist**, established March 22, 1884; **Newspaperdom**, March 22, 1892; **The Fourth Estate**, March 1, 1894; **Editor & Publisher**, June 29, 1901; **Advertising**, January 22, 1925.

James Wright Brown
Publisher, Chairman of the Board, 1912-1959

Robert U. Brown
President and Editor Emeritus

Year Book Staff
Editor
Ian E. Anderson

Research Staff
Robyn Furman, Myrna Gabriel, Larry Gilbert,
Miriam Rios, Michael Troxler,
Mel Wesenberg, Seth Zupnik

Publishers
D. Colin Phillips
Christopher Phillips

Advertising Vice President
Michael Dardano

Advertising Production Manager
Carol Blum

Art Director
Hector W. Marrero

Production Staff
Lery Chan, Quincee Robinson

Circulation Marketing Director
David Williams

Circulation Fulfillment Manager
Marlene Hazzard

Promotion Manager
Lawrence J. Burnagiel

CD-ROM Sales
Paul Arata

General Office

New York: 11 West 19th St., New York, NY 10011. Phone: (212) 675-4380; FAX: Editorial (212) 691-7287; Advertising (212) 929-1259; Circulation (212) 691-6939. Joan F. Hohauser, Betsy Maloney — sales representatives

Offices

Chicago: 8 South Michigan Ave., Suite 1601, Chicago, IL 60603. Phone: (312) 641-0041; FAX: (312) 641-0043. Mark Fitzgerald — editor; Richard H. Henrichs, Anthony R. George — sales representatives
Long Beach: 369 Seville Way, Long Beach, CA 90814. Phone: (310) 597-1159; FAX: (310) 597-1776. M.L. Stein — editor
Los Angeles: Marshall, McGinley & Doyle Inc., 2001 S. Barrington Ave., Suite 112, Los Angeles, Calif. 90024. Phone: (310) 996-1440; FAX: (310) 996-1446. William Marshall — sales representative
San Francisco: Peter Scott & Associates, 450 Sansome St., Suite 1420, San Francisco, Calif. 94111. Phone: (415) 421-7950; FAX: (415) 398-4156. Peter Scott — sales representative
Washington, DC: National Press Building, Suite 1128, Washington, DC 20045. Phone: (202) 662-7234; FAX: (202) 662-7223. Debra Gersh Hernandez — editor

Copyright ©1996 by the Editor & Publisher Co. All rights reserved. Printed in the United States of America. No part of this publication may be reproduced or distributed in any form or by any means or stored in a data base or retrieval system, without the prior written permission of the publisher.

ISBN 0-9646364-1-7 (Part 1)
ISBN 0-9646364-0-9 (2 Part-Set)

The Editor & Publisher Co. has employed reasonable precautions against errors in the development of this data but does not assume, and hereby disclaims, any liability to any person for any loss or damage caused by errors or omissions whether such errors or omissions result from negligence, accidents, or any other cause.

Memo from the publishers...

The 76th anniversary edition of the Editor & Publisher International Year Book offers a comprehensive view of the newspaper industry in our familiar hard copy and CD-ROM versions.

New for the 1996 Year Book is an expanded Who's Where section. It now includes all daily and weekly newspapers in the United States and Canada plus group personnel in both the U.S. and Canada and all of Section V (News, Picture and Syndicate Services) personnel. The change was in response to user feedback and we look forward to hearing your comments on these additions to, and on other suggestions for, the "Telephone Directory" of the newspaper industry.

Other added features to this year's edition include e-mail and web site information for U.S. and Canadian daily newspapers. Up front is a list of newspaper advertising networks found throughout the U.S., including the newspapers involved, contact information, advertising rates and group circulation.

Our weekly newspaper section (Section II) has added breakdowns of Alternative, Hispanic and Jewish newspapers. Section VII (Other Organizations and Industry Services) now includes Advertising/Circulation Newspaper Promotion Services, State Newspaper Representatives and an expanded Foreign Press & Radio-TV Correspondents in the United States.

This year's survey of daily newspapers in U.S. showed the continued decline of Monday to Friday circulation. Based on the six-month period ended Sept. 30, 1995, circulation dropped from 59,305,436 to 58,193,391, a net loss of 1,112,045. The larger than expected decrease can be partially attributed to the closing of the large circulation *Houston Post,* Baltimore *Evening Sun, New York Newsday* and the evening edition of the new *Milwaukee Journal Sentinel.*

The circulation drop coincides with the number of daily newspapers in the U.S. falling from 1,548 to 1,533 as of Feb. 1, 1996. It was a busy year for U.S. daily newspapers as nine new daily newspapers started up; and six dailies closed outright, five converted into zoned editions of another newspaper, 10 merged into another newspaper and three converted from daily to weekly for a net loss of 15 daily newspapers. These changes and others are detailed in the front of the Year Book on page xxiv.

The trend of evening newspapers converting to morning distribution that started in the mid-1970s continued as 24 evening newspapers converted to morning and seven all-day newspapers converted to morning distribution only. Of the nine new daily newspapers, seven are morning distribution. 14 of the 24 closures had evening distribution.

Sunday trends mirror 1994 as the number of editions increased by two to 888, but circulation declined from 62,294,799 to 61,229,296, a loss of 1,065,503. Again, the high number can be partially attributed to the closing of the large Sunday editions of the *Houston Post* and *New York Newsday.*

In Canada, the total number of daily newspapers stayed at 107. One paper closed, but one started up to offset the loss. The trend of evening to morning continued with four converting from evening to morning and two all-day newspapers converting to morning distribution only. There was one Sunday closure in Canada bringing the total number of Sunday editions down to 27.

The circulation of both the daily and Sunday newspapers continued to decline — daily falling 142,690 (from 5,023,775 to 4,881,085) and Sunday falling 97,118 (from 3,207,046 to 3,109,928). For complete details of U.S. and Canadian circulation and ad rate data, see pages vii to xi in the front of Year Book.

We should also point out the dramatic increase in newspapers offering online services. Newspapers are leveraging their rich content in efforts to expand reach into traditional non-reader population segments, particularly among young people. The number of daily newspapers operating online services grew from only a handful at the start of 1995 to over 250 by the end of the year with continued growth expected. To follow this phenomenon more closely visit our web site at http://www.mediainfo.com/edpub.

Editor & Publisher is grateful to all of the Year Book users who took the time to fill out the short survey we included in the 1995 edition. We hope you like the changes you helped initiate. We also thank our many friends at newspapers and other industry organizations, who have helped us gather the information that is part of this familiar encyclopedia of the newspaper industry.

Sincerely,

D. Colin Phillips
Co-Publisher

Christopher Phillips
Co-Publisher

There's no place like New England

CONNECTICUT
Capital
Hartford
Area
5,018 sq.mi (12,997 sq.km)
Population
3,287,116 (1990)
Largest cities
Bridgeport (141,686)
Hartford (139,739)
Statehood
January 9,1788
Rank: 5th
Principal rivers
Connecticut, Housatonic
Highest point
Mt. Frissell, 2,380ft (726m)
Motto
Qui Transtulit Sustinet
(He Who Transplanted Still Sustains)
Song
"Yankee Doodle"

MAINE
Capital
Augusta
Area
33,265 sq.mi (86,156 sq.km)
Population
1,227,928 (1990)
Largest cities
Portland (64,358)
Lewiston (39,757)
Bangor (33,181)
Statehood
March 15,1820
Rank: 23rd
Principal rivers
Androscoggin,
Kennebec, Penobscot
Highest point
Mt. Katahdin, 5,268ft (1,606m)
Motto
Dirigo (I direct)
Song
"State of Maine Song"

MASSACHUSETTS
Capital
Boston
Area
8,284 sq.mi (21,455 sq.km)
Population
6,016,425 (1990)
Largest cities
Boston (574,283)
Worcester (169,759)
Statehood
February 6, 1788
Rank: 6th
Principal rivers
Connecticut, Charles
Highest point
Mt. Greylock, 3,491ft (1,064m)
Motto
Ense Petit Placidam Sub Libertate Quietem (By the Sword We Seek Peace, but Peace Only Under Liberty)
Song
"All Hail to Massachusetts"

NEW HAMPSHIRE
Capital
Concord
Area
9,279 sq.mi (24,033 sq.km)
Population
1,109,252 (1990)
Largest cities
Manchester (99,567)
Nashua (79,662)
Concord (36,006)
Statehood
June 21, 1788
Rank: 9th
Principal rivers
Connecticut, Merrimark, Androscoggin
Highest point
Mt. Washington, 6,288ft (1, 917m)
Motto
Live Free or Die
Song
"Old New Hampshire"

RHODE ISLAND
Capital
Providence
Area
1,212 sq.mi (3,139 sq.km)
Population
1,003,464 (1990)
Largest cities
Providence (160,728)
Warwick (85,427)
Cranston (76,060)
Statehood
May 29,1790
Rank: 13th
Principal rivers
Providence, Blackstone
Highest point
Jerimoth Hill, 812ft (248m)
Motto
Hope
Song
"Rhode Island"

VERMONT
Capital
Montpelier
Area
9,614 sq.mi (24,900 sq.km)
Population
562,758 (1990)
Largest cities
Burlington (39,127)
Rutland (18,230)
Essex (16,498)
Bennington (16,451)
Statehood
March 4, 1791
Rank: 14th
Principal rivers
Connecticut, West, Otter
Highest point
Mt. Mansfield, 4,393ft (1,340m)
Motto
Freedom and Unity
Song
"Hail, Vermont"

... DEVOTED TO FREEDOM OF THE PRESS SINCE 1704

The American colonies first newspaper, the *Boston News-letter*, published weekly, appeared just two years after the establishment of Britain's first newspaper. The main content of the Boston paper was European news brought by ship captains, with little local news. But colonial newspapers soon grew in number, influence and content.

James Franklin, Benjamin's elder brother, established the *New England Courant* in 1721. This outspoken newspaper so outraged Boston's power elite that James was jailed and, for a time, the paper was printed under Ben Franklin's name. On emerging from jail, James moved his press to free-thinking Rhode Island, where he resumed printing in peace.

The 1735 acquittal of John Peter Zenger of a libel charge–after a year in jail–resulted in reluctance by colonial governments to prosecute printers who published opposing viewpoints. Growing opposition here to British policies insured that there would be no scarcity of these, expressed in many New England newspapers. Samuel Adams' fulminations against the 1765 Stamp Act appeared in many papers over a variety of signatures. His writings were persuasive in making the act ineffectual as a revenue source, and it was repealed the following year.

Today, over fifty New England newspapers–or their direct inheritors- have been published for 100 years or more, the oldest being the *Hartford Courant*, continuously published since 1764. Together, they represent a continuing bulwark against the misuse of power, and a beacon for public enlightenment.

Smart marketing starts with New England daily newspapers

CONNECTICUT
The Advocate (Stamford) (AD&S)
Connecticut Post (M&S)
The Day (New London) (M&S)
Greenwich Time (AD&S)
Hartford Courant (M&S)
The Hour (Norwalk) (E)
Record-Journal (Meridan) (M&S)
New Britain Herald (E)
Waterbury Republican-American (M)
The Sunday Republican (S)

MAINE
Bangor Daily News (M)
Maine Weekend
Sun-Journal (M)
Sunday-Sun journal (S)
Maine Sunday Telegram (S)
Portland Press Herald (M)

MASSACHUSETTS
Boston Globe (M&S)
Boston Herald (M&S)
Cape Cod Times (Hyannis) (M&S)
The Enterprise (Brockton) (E&S)
The Daily Transcript (Dedham) (E)
Gardner News (E)
The Sun (Lowell) (E&S)
Daily Evening Item (Lynn) (E)
The Middlesex News (E&S)
The Standard Times (New Bedford) (E&S)
Daily Hampshire Gazette (Northampton) (E)
The Patriot Ledger (Quincy) (E)
Union-News (Springfield) (AD)
Republican (Springfield) (S)
The News Tribune (Waltham) (E)
Community Newspaper Co. (Needham) (D&W)
Daily Times and Chronicle (Woburn) (E)
Telegram & Gazette (Worcester) (M&S)

NEW HAMPSHIRE
Union Leader (M)
Nashua Telegraph (M&S)
New Hampshire Sunday News (S)

RHODE ISLAND
The Newport Daily News (E)
Providence Journal-Bulletin (M&E)
The Providence Sunday Journal (S)
The Westerly Sun (E)

VERMONT
Rutland Herald (M&S)

SELL NEW ENGLAND WITH NEWSPAPERS

NEWSPAPER ADVERTISING

A SUMMARY OF NEWSPAPER ADVERTISING TRENDS COMPILED BY EDITOR & PUBLISHER FROM MEDIA RECORDS AND NAA REPORTS

LINAGE TOTALS — 1956 to 1970

Note: Figures from 1956 to 1970 are in thousands of lines; department store advertising is included in retail figures.

YEAR	RETAIL	DEPARTMENT STORE	GENERAL	AUTOMOTIVE	FINANCIAL	CLASSIFIED	TOTAL ADVERTISING
1956	1,562,230	577,794	408,645	170,020	45,273	724,610	2,910,780
1957	1,537,032	568,616	377,714	181,339	47,512	685,465	2,829,131
1958	1,507,863	556,663	360,844	141,761	46,400	628,749	2,865,238
1959	1,564,299	568,790	363,580	155,079	54,704	727,574	2,865,238
1960	1,588,269	566,887	345,694	165,208	54,233	735,211	2,888,617
1961	1,549,401	553,332	323,043	147,598	59,175	697,741	2,176,958
1962	1,563,924	551,667	301,495	149,307	58,017	725,507	2,798,250
1963	1,442,817	508,402	261,747	141,877	53,588	695,888	2,595,917
1964	1,673,186	593,476	292,549	159,729	60,867	787,135	2,973,466
1965	1,776,702	627,924	288,528	170,366	63,350	858,631	3,164,577
1966	1,863,633	652,845	310,287	182,894	73,184	924,255	3,354,253
1967	1,897,081	657,266	297,106	158,506	69,946	878,114	3,297,750
1968	1,917,404	625,691	296,134	170,958	72,838	923,724	3,381,058
1969	2,003,022	629,340	300,080	173,623	81,677	1,017,084	3,575,126
1970	2,014,880	613,212	275,156	161,570	74,907	917,262	3,443,775

DOLLAR OUTLAY — 1971 to 1995

Note: On Jan. 1, 1971, the Media Records base was increased to 64 from 52 cities, and the terms of its report from "Total agate lines" to "Dollar outlay". Numbers are in thousands of dollars; department store advertising is included in retail figures.

YEAR	RETAIL	DEPARTMENT STORE	GENERAL	AUTOMOTIVE	FINANCIAL	CLASSIFIED	TOTAL ADVERTISING
1971	1,807,304	536,930	455,356	100,765	103,099	751,652	3,208,176
1972	2,004,666	567,833	504,377	102,514	122,137	914,868	3,648,562
1973		561,770	479,183	99,783	138,898	1,024,153	3,786,112
1974	2,044,095	562,583	491,508	104,191	126,023	966,673	3,767,155
1975	2,078,760	634,965	547,099	93,264	130,810	982,229	4,117,367
1976	2,363,965	733,410	694,595	120,573	139,759	1,255,631	5,068,539
*1977	2,857,981	793,497	752,267	144,538	147,394	1,522,474	5,696,147
1978	3,129,474	871,250	26,614	151,004	201,670	1,884,505	6,643,726
1979	3,579,933	891,902	937,792	192,961	236,771	2,201,717	7,529,043
1980	3,959,802	954,411	1,122,701	183,568	297,962	2,191,773	8,192,234
1981	4,396,320	1,092,674	1,379,698	225,627	387,152	2,514,923	9,575,420
1982	5,067,750	1,151,824	1,419,610	265,013	398,732	2,497,840	9,864,050
1983	5,282,855	1,140,450	1,482,434	248,470	327,427	2,698,155	9,784,751

Note: Since 1984 the dollar volume has been supplied by the Newspaper Advertising bureau, now part of Newspaper Association of America. The large increase in all subsequent years occurs because these figures include all newspapers nationwide.

1984	12,784,000		3,081,000			7,657,000	23,522,000
1985	13,443,000		3,352,000			8,375,000	25,170,000
1986	14,311,000		3,376,000			9,303,000	26,990,000
1987	15,227,000		3,494,000			10,691,000	29,412,000
1988	15,789,000		3,821,000			11,586,000	31,197,000
1989	16,506,000		3,948,000			11,916,000	32,368,000
1990	16,652,000		4,122,000			11,506,000	32,281,000
1991	15,838,803		3,923,565			10,586,586	30,348,954
1992	16,041,371		3,833,786			10,763,627	30,638,784
1993	16,858,982		3,852,817			11,157,262	31,869,061
1994	17,532,142		4,157,728			12,489,824	34,179,694
**1995	18,245,000		4,266,000			13,675,000	36,186,000

* To present a truer picture of advertising trends, all linage carried in the three metropolitan New York City dailies that struck for 90 days August to November 1978 has been excluded from 1978 totals, and 1977 figures have been correspondingly adjusted.

** Newspaper Association of America estimates. Actual figures not available at press time.

BASIC DATA FOR ADVERTISING SPACE BUYERS

Morning

Period ended	Total Number of papers	Total net circulation	Total column inch rate	milinch rate	Relation of 1995 milinch rate to milinch rate for the preceeding 2 years
12/31/95	656	46,382,897 (44,310,252 AM plus 2,072,645 PM through combinations)	$31,948.42	$688.80	increase $101.91 + 14.80%
12/31/94	635	46,094,322 (43,381,578 AM plus 2,712,754 PM through combinations)	$27,895.80	$605.19	increase $65.35 + 10.80%
12/31/93	623	46,092,733 (43,093,866 AM plus 2,998,867 PM through combinations)	$26,208.29	$568.60	increase $59.34 + 10.44%
12/31/92	596	48,616,445 (42,387,813 AM plus 6,228,632 PM through combinations)	$24,846.97	$511.08	increase $25.24 + 4.94%
12/31/91	571	48,480,383 (41,469,756 AM plus 7,010,627 PM through combinations)	$24,600.77	$507.44	increase $69.27 + 13.65%
12/31/90	559	49,593,294 (41,311,167 AM plus 8,282,127 PM through combinations)	$23,023.37	$464.24	increase $63.03 + 13.58%
12/31/89	530	49,134,171 (40,759,016 AM plus 8,375,155 PM through combinations)	$20,252.62	$412.10	increase $59.27 + 14.38%
12/31/88	529	49,442,055 (40,452,815 AM plus 8,989,240 PM through combinations)	$19,298.25	$390.32	increase $33.37 + 8.55%

Afternoon

Period ended	Total Number of papers	Total net circulation	Total column inch rate	milinch rate	Relation of 1995 milinch rate to milinch rate for the preceeding 2 years
12/31/95	891	17,981,520 (13,883,145 PM plus 4,098,375 AM through combinations)	$16,378.72	$910.86	increase $128.04 + 14.06%
12/31/94	935	21,081,183 (15,923,865 PM plus 5,157,318 AM through combinations)	$17,060.22	$809.26	increase $107.20 + 13.25%
12/31/93	954	22,280,381 (16,717,737 PM plus 5,562,644 AM through combinations)	$16,852.57	$756.39	increase $133.36 + 17.63%
12/31/92	996	26,780,596 (17,776,686 PM plus 9,003,910 AM through combinations)	$17,346.54	$647.73	increase $59.99 + 9.26%
12/31/91	1,042	29,893,231 (19,217,369 PM plus 10,675,862 AM through combinations)	$17,886.07	$598.33	increase $53.86 + 9.00%
12/31/90	1,084	33,251,562 (21,016,795 PM plus 12,234,767 AM through combinations)	$19,190.71	$577.14	increase $64.43 + 11.16%
12/31/89	1,125	33,507,635 (21,890,202 PM plus 11,617,433 AM through combinations)	$17,151.89	$511.80	increase $109.22 + 21.34%
12/31/88	1,141	34,518,975 (22,242,001 PM plus 12,276,974 AM through combinations)	$17,730.04	$513.63	increase $99.87 + 19.44%

Sunday

Period ended	Total Number of papers	Total net circulation	Total column inch rate	milinch rate	Relation of 1995 milinch rate to milinch rate for the preceding 2 years
12/31/95	888	64,132,337 (61,229,296 Sunday plus 2,903,041 AM and PM through combinations)	$39,354.48	$613.64	increase $75.46 + 12.30%
12/31/94	886	65,728,260 (62,294,799 Sunday plus 3,433,461 AM and PM through combinations)	$36,939.53	$562.00	increase $64.84 + 11.54%
12/31/93	884	65,982,369 (62,565,574 Sunday plus 3,416,796 AM and PM through combinations)	$33,939.36	$514.37	increase $43.58 + 8.47%
12/31/92	891	65,385,739 (62,159,971 Sunday plus 3,225,768 AM and PM through combinations)	$31,381.86	$479.95	increase $40.07 + 8.35%
12/31/91	875	66,093,415 (62,067,820 Sunday plus 4,025,595 AM and PM through combinations)	$30,511.16	$461.64	increase $64.48 + 13.97%
12/31/90	863	67,985,652 (62,640,947 Sunday plus 5,351,140 AM and PM through combinations)	$28,426.09	$418.12	increase $59.27 + 14.18%
12/31/89	847	73,291,730 (62,008,154 Sunday plus 11,283,576 AM and PM through combinations)	$27,579.15	$376.20	increase $36.86 + 9.80%
12/31/88	840	76,780,594 (61,474,189 Sunday plus 15,306,405 AM and PM through combinations)	$26,219.78	$341.49	increase $14.26 + 4.18%

Copyright ©1996 by the Editor & Publisher Co.

READY RECKONER OF ADVERTISING RATES AND CIRCULATIONS

1,533 daily newspapers (656 morning, 891 evening and including 14 "all-day") and 888 Sunday

Number of newspapers as of Feb. 1, 1996, with circulations mainly as reported for six months ended Sept. 30, 1995

STATE	POPULATION 1996 E&P EST.	NUMBER OF DAILY NEWSPAPERS AMs	PMs	Total	MORNING PAPERS NET CIRCULATION SEPT. 30, 1995 AM circulation	Added PM circulation through combinations	Total circulation serving AM advertisers	Inch rates including all combinations	AFTERNOON PAPERS NET CIRCULATION SEPT. 30, 1995 PM circulation	Added AM circulation through combinations	Total circulation serving PM advertisers	Inch rates including all combinations	TOTALS Total AM & PM circulation	Minimum rates for AM & PM coverage	SUNDAY PAPERS NET CIRCULATION SEPT. 30, 1995 Number of papers	Sunday circulation	Daily combinations circulation	Total circulation secured by advertisers	Total inch rate
Alabama	4,310,435	19	7	26	416,617	246,376	662,993	471.21	326,340	143,435	469,775	256.87	742,957	529.34	18	754,182	160,081	914,263	604.66
Alaska	626,943	4	3	7	99,499	0	99,499	97.36	13,313	0	13,313	31.21	112,812	128.57	4	128,873	0	128,873	115.03
Arizona	4,402,158	9	13	22	548,873	61,549	610,422	430.57	231,771	161,728	393,499	504.07	780,644	772.80	16	916,870	0	916,870	604.89
Arkansas	2,505,877	13	18	31	374,257	0	374,257	271.02	103,674	0	103,674	150.75	477,931	421.77	16	529,664	0	529,664	343.86
†California	34,089,547	67	31	98	5,594,429	136,023	5,730,452	3,545.01	499,120	656,545	1,155,665	882.87	6,093,549	3,968.83	62	6,415,736	18,908	6,434,644	3,714.96
Colorado	3,771,286	17	13	30	924,108	0	924,108	611.72	132,565	0	132,565	134.00	1,056,673	745.72	11	1,253,990	0	1,253,990	714.36
*Connecticut	3,429,499	13	8	18	648,729	0	648,729	585.17	145,423	0	145,423	223.02	794,151	658.78	11	830,894	0	830,894	668.19
*Delaware	718,336	3	1	2	87,639	0	87,639	130.73	62,839	0	62,839	105.18	150,477	130.73	2	183,903	0	183,903	134.86
District of Columbia	607,712	2	0	2	895,041	0	895,041	500.00	0	0	0	0.00	895,041	500.00	2	1,193,396	0	1,193,396	660.00
*Florida	14,806,638	34	7	40	2,934,716	15,819	2,950,535	2,382.64	187,942	194,643	382,585	402.65	3,122,658	2,438.79	35	3,972,247	147,767	4,120,014	3,024.98
Georgia	7,270,154	17	18	35	741,385	136,507	877,892	627.05	327,127	323,778	650,905	504.66	1,068,512	847.04	19	1,293,776	30,344	1,324,120	838.70
Hawaii	1,277,271	3	3	6	135,510	77,535	213,045	157.08	103,292	105,624	208,916	154.04	238,802	184.96	5	260,795	0	260,795	202.08
Idaho	1,101,851	7	5	12	144,817	0	144,817	121.51	80,517	0	80,517	60.98	225,334	182.49	8	240,646	0	240,646	175.88
*Illinois	11,803,846	21	48	68	1,897,970	6,967	1,904,937	1,298.56	589,198	66,870	656,068	700.95	2,487,168	1,941.71	31	2,665,412	0	2,665,412	1,768.84
Indiana	5,697,225	16	55	71	738,774	104,663	843,437	664.96	712,890	183,322	896,212	916.60	1,451,664	1,341.19	21	1,344,117	0	1,344,117	837.45
Iowa	2,757,895	13	25	38	441,474	0	441,474	378.79	235,871	0	235,871	277.18	677,345	655.97	12	710,746	20,066	730,812	501.42
Kansas	2,593,575	8	39	47	285,574	0	285,574	195.16	205,536	0	205,536	266.17	491,110	461.33	15	448,609	6,898	455,507	291.60
Kentucky	3,832,703	8	15	23	454,781	0	454,781	342.50	188,158	0	188,158	193.08	642,939	535.58	12	679,245	0	679,245	450.30
*Louisiana	4,444,987	13	14	26	502,468	0	502,468	433.54	247,587	0	247,587	236.83	750,054	548.67	21	848,956	0	848,956	536.67
Maine	1,297,199	5	2	7	233,095	0	233,095	176.66	25,071	0	25,071	23.50	258,166	200.16	4	222,874	77,631	300,505	182.16
Maryland	5,266,169	10	4	14	562,651	0	562,651	413.01	83,898	0	83,898	104.11	646,549	517.12	7	682,495	0	682,495	387.54
†Massachusetts	6,252,855	10	26	36	1,272,240	0	1,272,240	744.28	552,958	0	552,958	474.29	1,825,198	1,218.57	14	1,450,158	52,055	1,502,213	944.14
†Michigan	9,644,265	11	39	50	746,438	356,048	1,102,486	693.19	1,319,562	533,836	1,853,398	1,250.43	2,066,000	1,436.13	27	2,366,220	0	2,366,220	1,231.99
Minnesota	4,663,826	14	11	25	784,190	0	784,190	467.36	137,596	0	137,596	153.06	921,786	620.42	14	1,184,613	0	1,184,613	574.06
Mississippi	2,762,855	6	16	22	217,087	0	217,087	161.22	185,794	0	185,794	192.43	402,881	353.65	16	395,564	0	395,564	323.56
Missouri	5,376,030	12	32	44	802,150	0	802,150	648.27	205,925	0	205,925	269.77	1,008,075	918.04	23	1,329,618	0	1,329,618	894.53
Montana	853,095	6	5	11	155,120	0	155,120	140.78	40,706	0	40,706	43.39	195,826	184.17	7	201,691	0	201,691	174.93
*Nebraska	1,637,087	5	13	17	252,014	0	252,014	170.42	217,524	0	217,524	195.56	469,538	269.06	6	443,178	0	443,178	206.30
Nevada	1,420,977	4	5	9	227,541	38,497	266,038	186.67	58,013	142,149	200,162	135.39	285,554	220.86	4	317,138	0	317,138	217.10
*New Hampshire	1,265,319	8	5	12	143,609	0	143,609	113.44	93,197	0	93,197	91.56	236,805	167.50	6	200,180	34,607	234,787	145.05
New Jersey	8,208,117	13	7	20	1,199,608	0	1,199,608	775.27	281,579	0	281,579	278.27	1,481,187	1,053.54	16	1,775,966	245,118	2,021,084	1,167.93
New Mexico	1,727,863	7	11	18	200,801	30,012	230,813	162.67	99,607	113,031	212,638	160.54	300,408	250.21	13	299,916	0	299,916	221.28
†New York	18,867,358	26	45	69	5,415,574	128,218	5,543,792	3,675.31	1,160,348	227,939	1,388,287	1,600.66	6,575,921	4,371.32	44	5,440,435	72,371	5,512,806	3,238.05
North Carolina	7,428,803	20	30	50	1,020,959	0	1,020,959	665.72	374,154	0	374,154	341.12	1,395,113	1,006.84	38	1,518,453	239,173	1,757,526	1,004.01
North Dakota	645,896	7	3	10	167,773	0	167,773	136.70	13,655	0	13,655	23.65	181,428	160.35	6	185,400	0	185,400	145.55
Ohio	11,083,040	18	66	84	1,649,567	82,146	1,731,713	1,128.94	971,675	203,158	1,174,833	1,105.13	2,621,242	2,024.47	37	2,877,932	152,211	3,030,143	1,803.80
Oklahoma	3,328,943	11	35	46	480,874	0	480,874	312.23	215,059	0	215,059	258.38	695,933	570.61	39	857,537	212,382	1,069,919	638.79
*Oregon	3,089,876	6	14	19	345,814	0	345,814	246.37	336,907	0	336,907	271.44	682,721	408.91	10	715,767	17,363	733,130	313.54
Pennsylvania	12,160,838	42	45	87	2,144,505	138,602	2,283,107	1,635.04	833,088	191,287	1,024,375	908.45	2,977,593	2,385.45	40	3,331,416	791,346	4,122,762	2,432.54
Rhode Island	1,057,551	3	3	6	228,581	0	228,581	170.47	33,737	0	33,737	37.22	262,318	207.69	3	294,709	0	294,709	188.60
South Carolina	3,851,316	11	4	15	581,841	0	581,841	444.33	56,846	0	56,846	51.64	638,687	495.97	14	758,144	0	758,144	516.43
South Dakota	712,419	6	5	11	133,998	0	133,998	121.80	334,429	0	33,429	40.20	167,427	162.00	4	139,054	9,387	148,441	114.05
Tennessee	5,257,126	12	15	27	661,190	92,788	753,978	585.07	244,974	186,803	431,777	318.34	906,164	715.58	16	1,107,138	0	1,107,138	745.36
Texas	19,083,381	36	53	89	2,613,206	46,647	2,659,853	1,885.45	374,347	187,279	561,626	575.38	2,987,553	2,319.50	85	4,039,961	65,970	4,105,931	2,552.96
Utah	1,904,083	4	4	8	126,076	61,635	187,711	56.14	190,961	126,076	317,037	134.95	317,037	134.95	6	361,052	0	361,052	144.36
Vermont	606,446	4	4	8	95,460	0	95,460	81.97	33,090	0	33,090	37.53	128,550	119.50	5	106,103	0	106,103	67.62
*Virginia	6,734,532	18	12	28	2,389,071	0	2,389,071	1,316.58	214,616	0	214,616	193.91	2,603,686	1,449.64	15	1,010,317	504,185	1,514,502	710.54
†Washington	5,275,295	11	13	24	732,817	232,616	965,433	575.44	470,837	204,544	675,381	408.99	1,203,654	784.79	16	1,285,816	0	1,285,816	772.97
West Virginia	1,770,032	10	12	22	250,648	58,281	308,929	304.91	145,275	59,743	205,018	214.65	395,923	440.97	11	402,010	45,178	447,188	330.20
Wisconsin	5,135,939	10	25	35	539,706	21,716	561,422	424.16	466,084	86,585	552,669	455.72	1,005,790	821.68	18	1,189,928	0	1,189,928	721.60
Wyoming	479,637	6	3	9	69,387	0	69,387	65.97	19,470	0	19,074	27.95	88,857	93.92	4	66,456	0	66,456	54.21
*Totals		656	891	1,533	44,310,252	2,072,645	46,382,897	31,948.42	13,883,145	4,098,375	17,981,520	16,378.72	58,193,391	43,105.98	888	61,229,296	2,903,041	64,132,337	39,354.48

*Indicates population groups including one or more of the 14 "all-day" newspapers counted both in AM & PM columns, but only once in the total.

Circulation for these papers is equally divided between AMs & PMs.

†Indicates states including one of the nationally circulated daily newspapers. Circulation for these newspapers is counted only in the state where indicated. (see section I, page 450 for listing of National Daily Newspapers.)

Copyright © 1996 by the Editor & Publisher Co.

CIRCULATION OF U.S. DAILY NEWSPAPERS BY POPULATION GROUPS BASED ON THE 1990 CENSUS

Based on corporate city limits

POPULATION- 1990 CENSUS	NUMBER OF DAILY NEWSPAPERS				MORNING PAPERS NET CIRCULATION SEPT. 30, 1995				AFTERNOON PAPERS NET CIRCULATION SEPT. 30, 1995				TOTALS		SUNDAY PAPERS NET CIRCULATION SEPT. 30, 1995				
	AMs	PMs	Total		AM circulation	Added PM Circulation through combinations	Total Circulation serving AM advertisers	Inch rates including all combinations	PM circulation	Added AM Circulation through combinations	Total Circulation serving PM advertisers	Inch rates including all combinations	Total AM & PM circulation	Minimum rates for AM & PM coverage	Number of papers	Sunday circulation	Daily combinations circulation	Total Circulation secured by advertisers	Total inch rate
*More than 1,000,000	23	3	25		9,928,745	354,403	10,283,148	6,056.51	674,124	531,825	1,205,949	898.00	10,602,868	6,083.51	15	10,796,742	469,398	11,266,140	5,497.21
500,001 to 1,000,000	20	5	25		5,508,955	385,658	5,894,613	3,382.69	513,943	759,752	1,273,695	878.63	6,022,898	3,776.69	18	7,504,469	254,648	7,759,117	4,122.54
*100,001 to 500,000	140	41	174		17,010,362	1,052,813	18,063,175	12,168.16	2,546,456	1,765,016	4,311,472	3,467.76	19,556,816	12,663.03	144	23,721,672	1,374,132	25,095,804	14,340.91
*50,001 to 100,000	135	69	199		5,580,676	204,186	5,784,862	4,700.79	2,078,044	607,873	2,685,917	2,044.39	7,658,717	6,106.47	168	8,406,490	524,415	8,930,905	5,922.99
*25,000 to 50,000	124	162	285		3,502,013	52,309	3,554,322	2,793.19	2,927,853	60,744	2,988,597	2,991.25	6,429,866	5,699.09	213	6,075,709	175,064	6,250,773	4,961.26
Less than 25,000	214	611	825		2,779,501	23,276	2,802,777	2,847.08	5,142,725	373,165	5,515,890	6,098.69	7,922,226	8,777.19	330	4,724,214	105,384	4,829,598	4,509.57
*Totals	656	891	1,533		44,310,252	2,072,645	46,382,897	31,948.42	13,883,145	4,098,375	17,981,520	16,378.72	58,193,391	43,105.98	888	61,229,296	2,903,041	64,132,337	39,354.48

* Indicates population groups including one or more of the 14 "all-day" newspapers counted both in AM & PM columns, but only once in the total.
Circulation for these papers is equally divided between AMs & PMs.

CIRCULATION OF U.S. DAILY NEWSPAPERS BY POPULATION GROUPS BASED ON 1996 E&P ESTIMATES

Based on corporate city limits

POPULATION- 1995 E&P ESTIMATES	NUMBER OF DAILY NEWSPAPERS				MORNING PAPERS NET CIRCULATION SEPT. 30, 1995				AFTERNOON PAPERS NET CIRCULATION SEPT. 30, 1995				TOTALS		SUNDAY PAPERS NET CIRCULATION SEPT. 30, 1995				
	AMs	PMs	Total		AM circulation	Added PM Circulation through combinations	Total Circulation serving AM advertisers	Inch rates including all combinations	PM circulation	Added AM Circulation through combinations	Total Circulation serving PM advertisers	Inch rates including all combinations	Total AM & PM circulation	Minimum rates for AM & PM coverage	Number of papers	Sunday circulation	Daily combinations circulation	Total Circulation secured by advertisers	Total inch rate
*More than 1,000,000	25	2	27		10,173,133	0	10,173,133	6,046.93	390,037	0	390,037	632.00	10,563,169	6,303.93	16	9,769,480	658,876	10,427,556	5,263.69
500,001 to 1,000,000	22	7	28		5,587,368	792,048	6,379,416	3,736.82	1,016,844	948,805	1,965,649	1,428.16	6,604,212	3,900.82	20	9,301,417	65,970	9,367,387	4,749.51
*100,001 to 500,000	153	45	191		17,213,819	1,021,893	18,235,712	12,292.75	2,528,854	2,390,080	4,918,934	3,401.30	19,742,670	12,918.27	161	23,805,235	1,427,647	25,232,882	14,557.50
*50,001 to 100,000	138	72	206		5,601,749	183,119	5,784,868	4,642.63	2,029,367	325,581	2,354,948	2,092.92	7,631,114	6,183.26	174	8,290,571	470,900	8,761,471	6,007.11
*25,000 to 50,000	115	158	272		3,150,014	52,309	3,202,323	2,558.36	2,819,381	60,744	2,880,125	2,749.79	5,969,395	5,236.95	196	5,550,265	175,064	5,725,329	4,418.38
Less than 25,000	203	606	809		2,584,168	23,276	2,607,445	2,670.93	5,098,662	373,165	5,471,827	6,074.55	7,682,831	8,562.75	321	4,512,328	105,384	4,617,712	4,358.29
*Totals	656	891	1,533		44,310,252	2,072,645	46,382,897	31,948.42	13,883,145	4,098,375	17,981,520	16,378.72	58,193,391	43,105.98	888	61,229,296	2,903,041	64,132,337	39,354.48

* Indicates population groups including one or more of the 14 "all-day" newspapers counted both in AM & PM columns, but only once in the total.
Circulation for these papers is equally divided between AMs & PMs.

Copyright ©1996 by the Editor & Publisher Co.

CIRCULATION OF U.S. DAILY NEWSPAPERS BY CIRCULATION GROUPS

	NUMBER OF DAILY NEWSPAPERS				MORNING PAPERS NET CIRCULATION SEPT. 30, 1995					AFTERNOON PAPERS NET CIRCULATION SEPT. 30, 1995					TOTALS			SUNDAY PAPERS NET CIRCULATION SEPT. 30, 1995				
CIRCULATION-	AMs	PMs	Total		AM circulation	Added PM Circulation through combinations	Total Circulation serving AM advertisers	Inch rates including all combinations		PM circulation	Added AM Circulation through combinations	Total Circulation serving PM advertisers	Inch rates including all combinations		Total AM & PM circulation	Minimum rates for AM & PM coverage	Number of papers	Sunday circulation	Daily combinations circulation	Total Circulation secured by advertisers	Total inch rate
*More than 500,000	11	1	11		9,487,572	354,403	9,841,975	5,503.78		317,314	0	317,314	375.00		9,804,885	5,503.78	19	15,843,944	469,398	16,313,342	7,962.37
*250,001 to 500,000	31	7	34		10,065,306	239,441	10,304,747	6,787.70		1,126,859	837,282	1,964,141	1,554.15		11,192,164	6,963.45	38	13,795,006	906,137	14,701,143	8,295.85
*100,001 to 250,000	62	11	71		9,238,872	671,103	9,909,975	6,337.27		1,190,393	1,155,693	2,346,086	1,571.08		10,429,264	6,391.31	72	11,003,327	827,425	11,830,752	6,260.32
50,001 to 100,000	101	31	130		6,802,910	574,498	7,377,408	4,913.45		1,764,887	670,243	2,435,130	1,765.48		8,567,796	5,806.42	113	8,119,377	573,148	8,692,525	5,581.95
25,001 to 50,000	154	75	226		5,252,605	141,263	5,393,868	4,319.06		2,438,801	532,432	2,971,233	2,612.17		7,691,404	6,333.59	192	6,919,170	30,344	6,949,514	5,502.83
10,001 to 25,000	161	279	438		2,642,397	74,747	2,717,144	2,689.43		4,247,799	680,905	4,928,704	4,476.92		6,890,196	6,746.19	259	4,314,676	80,304	4,394,980	3,986.44
5,000 to 10,000	88	289	377		651,694	15,545	667,239	1,011.29		2,092,369	219,809	2,312,178	2,642.51		2,744,063	3,604.88	143	1,046,303	16,285	1,062,588	1,398.93
Less than 5,000	48	198	246		168,896	1,645	170,541	386.44		704,723	2,011	706,734	1,381.41		873,619	1,756.36	52	187,493	0	187,493	365.79
*Totals	656	891	1,533		44,310,252	2,072,645	46,382,897	31,948.42		13,883,145	4,098,375	17,981,520	16,378.72		58,193,391	43,105.98	888	61,229,296	2,903,041	64,132,337	39,354.48

* Indicates circulation groups including one or more of the 14 "all-day" newspapers counted both in AM & PM columns, but only once in the total.
Circulation for these papers is equally divided between AMs & PMs.

READY RECKONER OF ADVERTISING RATES AND CIRCULATIONS—CANADA

107 DAILY NEWSPAPERS (45 MORNING, 62 EVENING) AND 27 SUNDAY

Number of newspapers as of Feb. 1, 1996, with circulations mainly as reported for six months ended Sept. 30, 1995

	NUMBER OF DAILY NEWSPAPERS				MORNING PAPERS NET CIRCULATION SEPT. 30, 1995					AFTERNOON PAPERS NET CIRCULATION SEPT. 30, 1995					TOTALS			SUNDAY PAPERS NET CIRCULATION SEPT. 30, 1995				
PROVINCE		AMs	PMs	Total	AM circulation	Added PM Circulation through combinations	Total Circulation serving AM advertisers	Line rates including all combinations		PM circulation	Added AM Circulation through combinations	Total Circulation serving PM advertisers	Line rates including all combinations		Total AM & PM circulation	Minimum rates for AM & PM coverage	Number of papers	Sunday circulation	Daily combinations circulation	Total Circulation secured by advertisers	Total line rate
Alberta	2,757,444	4	5	9	401,858	0	401,858	17.62		68,082	0	68,082	5.83		469,940	23.45	5	478,934	0	478,934	20.01
British Columbia	3,662,410	7	10	17	458,745	0	458,745	14.84		64,234	0	64,234	8.36		522,979	23.20	3	279,704	0	279,704	51.05
Manitoba	1,122,834	2	3	5	181,483	0	181,483	7.75		25,953	0	25,953	2.75		207,436	10.50	2	205,570	0	205,570	8.20
New Brunswick	744,550	2	3	5	46,138	0	46,183	3.45		100,467	0	100,467	5.31		146,605	8.76	0	0	0	0	0
Newfoundland	579,835	4	2	2	0	0	0	0		50,047	0	50,047	2.95		50,047	2.95	1	39,202	0	39,202	1.84
Nova Scotia	936,405	4	3	7	157,921	0	157,921	7.56		61,510	0	61,510	6.05		219,431	13.61	1	43,021	0	43,021	1.44
Ontario	10,888,500	13	31	44	1,576,298	0	1,576,298	70.46		566,455	0	566,455	162.36		2,142,753	232.82	9	1,211,211	54,297	1,265,508	35.65
Prince Edward Island	135,695	1	1	2	22,352	0	22,352	1.51		10,868	0	10,868	0.92		33,220	2.43	0	0	0	0	0
Quebec	7,389,500	11	0	11	946,556	0	946,556	41.61		0	0	0	0		946,556	41.61	6	852,286	0	852,286	30.68
Saskatchewan	1,003,108	1	3	4	57,402	0	57,402	3.09		81,946	0	81,946	5.44		139,348	8.53	0	0	0	0	0
Yukon Territory	93,885	0	1	1	0	0	0	0		2,770	0	2,770	1.10		2,770	1.10	0	0	0	0	0
Totals		45	62	107	3,848,753	0	3,848,753	167.89		1,032,332	0	1,032,332	201.07		4,881,085	368.96	27	3,109,928	54,297	3,164,225	148.87

Copyright ©1996 by the Editor & Publisher Co.

IN 112 YEARS WE'VE NEVER MISSED OUR TARGET.

IN today's high speed, information-packed world, there are literally thousands of ways to send and receive the news. But there is only one way to reach those who deliver it... Editor & Publisher magazine.

For 112 years, Editor & Publisher has been the newspaper industry's most widely read trade publication; a tradition we're continuing with our newly redesigned weekly. Only E&P consistently delivers today's most *influential opinion makers* and *powerful decision makers*... as well as more *editors, photographers, ad sales staffers, circulators* and *production personnel* than any other trade publication.

When your product or service advertising must be seen by the news industry, it must be seen in E&P. Because when it comes to hitting your target, close just doesn't count.

For more information on advertising in Editor & Publisher magazine, contact Michael Dardano, V.P. Advertising, at 800-336-4380 x 155 or by e-mail at edpub@mediainfo.com or check out our Web site at http://www.mediainfo.com

When it comes to the newspaper industry, we deliver.

CIRCULATION OF DAILY NEWSPAPERS OF CANADA BY POPULATION GROUPS BASED ON THE 1991 CENSUS

NUMBER OF DAILY PAPERS

POPULATION - 1991 CENSUS	AMs	PMs	Total
More than 1,000,000	4	0	4
500,001 to 1,000,000	9	0	9
100,001 to 500,000	13	6	19
50,001 to 100,000	10	16	26
25,000 to 50,000	5	14	19
Less than 25,000	4	26	30
Totals	45	62	107

MORNING PAPERS — NET CIRCULATION SEPT. 30, 1995

AM circulation	Added PM Circulation through combinations	Total Circulation serving AM advertisers	Line rates including all combinations
629,250	0	629,250	25.92
1,621,834	0	1,621,834	64.14
1,165,123	0	1,165,123	49.20
270,357	0	270,357	18.53
111,132	0	111,132	6.70
51,057	0	51,057	3.40
3,848,753	0	3,848,753	167.89

AFTERNOON PAPERS — NET CIRCULATION SEPT. 30, 1995

PM circulation	Added AM Circulation through combinations	Total Circulation serving PM advertisers	Line rates including all combinations
0	0	0	0
0	0	0	0
319,981	0	319,981	52.14
358,324	0	358,324	22.72
188,288	0	188,288	15.05
165,739	0	165,739	111.16
1,032,332	0	1,032,332	201.07

TOTALS

Total AM & PM circulation	Minimum rates for AM & PM coverage
629,250	25.92
1,621,834	64.14
1,485,104	101.34
628,681	41.25
299,420	21.75
216,796	114.56
4,881,085	368.96

SUNDAY PAPERS — NET CIRCULATION SEPT. 30, 1995

Number of papers	Sunday circulation	Daily combinations circulation	Total Circulation secured by advertisers	Total line rate
3	608,474	0	608,474	22.37
7	1,569,633	0	1,569,633	44.39
8	658,745	54,297	713,042	24.93
8	256,729	0	256,729	56.01
1	16,347	0	16,347	1.17
0	0	0	0	0
27	3,109,928	54,297	3,164,225	148.87

CIRCULATION OF DAILY NEWSPAPERS OF CANADA BY POPULATION GROUPS BASED ON 1996 E&P ESTIMATES

NUMBER OF DAILY PAPERS

POPULATION - 1995 E&P ESTIMATES	AMs	PMs	Total
More than 1,000,000	4	0	4
500,001 to 1,000,000	11	0	11
100,001 to 500,000	11	7	18
50,001 to 100,000	11	15	26
25,001 to 50,000	5	14	19
Less than 25,000	3	26	29
Totals	45	62	107

MORNING PAPERS — NET CIRCULATION SEPT. 30, 1995

AM circulation	Added PM Circulation through combinations	Total Circulation serving AM advertisers	Line rates including all combinations
629,250	0	629,250	25.92
1,961,127	0	1,961,127	73.57
825,830	0	825,830	39.77
316,841	0	316,841	20.98
71,530	0	71,530	4.25
44,175	0	44,175	3.40
3,848,753	0	3,848,753	167.89

AFTERNOON PAPERS — NET CIRCULATION SEPT. 30, 1995

PM circulation	Added AM Circulation through combinations	Total Circulation serving PM advertisers	Line rates including all combinations
0	0	0	0
0	0	0	0
330,051	0	330,051	53.25
348,254	0	348,254	21.61
188,288	0	188,288	15.05
165,739	0	165,739	111.16
1,032,332	0	1,032,332	201.07

TOTALS

Total AM & PM circulation	Minimum rates for AM & PM coverage
629,250	25.92
1,961,127	73.57
1,155,881	93.02
665,095	42.59
259,818	19.30
209,914	114.56
4,881,085	368.96

SUNDAY PAPERS — NET CIRCULATION SEPT. 30, 1995

Number of papers	Sunday circulation	Daily combinations circulation	Total Circulation secured by advertisers	Total line rate
3	608,474	0	608,474	22.37
9	1,759,733	0	1,759,733	49.38
6	468,645	54,297	522,942	19.94
8	256,729	0	256,729	56.01
1	16,347	0	16,347	1.17
0	0	0	0	0
27	3,109,928	54,297	3,164,225	148.87

CIRCULATION OF DAILY NEWSPAPERS OF CANADA BY CIRCULATION GROUPS

NUMBER OF DAILY PAPERS

CIRCULATION	AMs	PMs	Total
More than 500,000	0	0	0
250,001 to 500,000	3	0	3
100,001 to 250,000	12	1	13
50,001 to 100,000	8	4	12
25,001 to 50,000	11	7	18
10,001 to 25,000	7	23	30
5,000 to 10,000	3	13	16
Less than 5,000	1	14	15
Totals	45	62	107

MORNING PAPERS — NET CIRCULATION SEPT. 30, 1995

AM circulation	Added PM Circulation through combinations	Total Circulation serving AM advertisers	Line rates including all combinations
0	0	0	0
1,068,278	0	1,068,278	38.77
1,760,590	0	1,760,590	72.13
544,590	0	544,590	23.35
337,673	0	337,673	23.36
112,656	0	112,656	8.39
20,904	0	20,904	1.20
4,062	0	4,062	0.69
3,848,753	0	3,848,753	167.89

AFTERNOON PAPERS — NET CIRCULATION SEPT. 30, 1995

PM circulation	Added AM Circulation through combinations	Total Circulation serving PM advertisers	Line rates including all combinations
0	0	0	0
0	0	0	0
43,597	0	43,597	4.02
240,883	0	240,883	11.43
226,377	0	226,377	47.38
373,706	0	373,706	26.71
101,164	0	101,164	12.93
46,605	0	46,605	98.60
1,032,332	0	1,032,332	201.07

TOTALS

Total AM & PM circulation	Minimum rates for AM & PM coverage
1,068,278	38.77
1,804,187	76.15
785,473	34.78
564,050	70.74
486,362	35.10
122,068	14.13
50,667	99.29
4,881,085	368.96

SUNDAY PAPERS — NET CIRCULATION SEPT. 30, 1995

Number of papers	Sunday circulation	Daily combinations circulation	Total Circulation secured by advertisers	Total line rate
0	0	0	0	0
3	1,190,419	0	1,190,419	24.21
9	1,251,732	0	1,251,732	53.45
5	392,470	54,297	446,757	56.67
4	160,858	0	160,858	7.27
6	114,449	0	114,449	7.27
0	0	0	0	0
0	0	0	0	0
27	3,109,928	54,297	3,164,225	148.87

Copyright © 1996 by the Editor & Publisher Co.

TOP ONE HUNDRED DAILY NEWSPAPERS IN THE WORLD
ACCORDING TO 1995 CIRCULATION

Newspaper	Circulation
Yomiuri Shimbun (Japan)	**14,573,988**
Asahi Shimbun (Japan)	**12,697,898**
Mainichi Shimbun (Japan)	**5,947,333**
Bild (Germany)	**5,567,100**
Nihon Keizai Shimbun (Japan)	**4,536,561**
Chunichi Shimbun (Japan)	**4,323,142**
Sun (England)	**4,023,548**
Sankei Shimbun (Japan)	**2,882,252**
Renmin Ribao (China)	2,740,000
Daily Mirror (England)	**2,568,957**
Chosun Ilbo (South Korea)	2,225,000
Dong-A Ilbo (South Korea)	2,150,000
Al Ahram (Egypt)	2,117,399
Hokkaido Shimbun (Japan)	**1,964,774**
Yangcheng Evening News (China)	1,900,000
Eleftherotypia (Greece)	1,858,316
Daily Mail (England)	**1,815,507**
Wall Street Journal (United States)	**1,763,140**
Kerala Kaumudi (India)	1,720,000
Joong-Ang Daily News (South Korea)	1,550,000
USA Today (United States)	**1,523,610**
Economic Daily (China)	1,500,000
Guangming Ribao (China)	1,500,000
Kyung-Hyang Daily News (South Korea)	1,478,000
Sports Nippon (Japan)	**1,445,821**
Shizuoka Shimbun (Japan)	**1,421,085**
Sichuan Ribao (China)	1,350,000
NRZ (Germany)	**1,332,800**
West Deutche Allgemeine (Germany)	**1,313,400**
United Daily News (Taiwan)	1,300,000
Wen Hui Bao Daily (China)	1,300,000
China Times (Taiwan)	1,270,000
Daily Express (England)	**1,265,027**
O Estado de Sao Paulo (Brazil)	1,230,160
Jang Daily (Pakistan)	1,200,000
Jang Lahore (Pakistan)	1,200,000
Akhbar El Yom/Al Akhbar (Egypt)	1,159,339
Hankook Ilbo (South Korea)	1,156,000
Tokyo Shimbun (Japan)	**1,137,727**
Hochi Shimbun (Japan)	**1,081,883**
New York Times (United States)	**1,081,541**
Times of India (India)	**1,071,081**
Malayala Manorama (India)	1,070,465
Daily Telegraph (England)	**1,064,717**
Tokyo Sports (Japan)	**1,045,350**
Nishi Nippon Shimbun (Japan)	**1,022,948**
Los Angeles Times (United States)	**1,012,189**
Neue Kronenzeitung (Austria)	1,000,480
Jiefang Ribao (China)	1,000,000
Tianjin Ribao (China)	1,000,000
Nikkan Sports (Japan)	**964,285**
Seoul Shinmun (South Korea)	900,000
Xin Hua Ribao (China)	900,000
Nanfang Ribao (China)	880,000
Jang (Pakistan)	**820,000**
Kyoto Shimbun (Japan)	**813,464**
Chugoku Shimbun (Japan)	**810,506**
Dazhong Ribao (China)	800,000
Kobe Shimbun (Japan)	**799,997**
Washington Post (United States)	**793,660**
Al Akhbar (Egypt)	**789,268**
Ouest-France (France)	784,463
Holos Ukrainy (Ukraine)	768,000
De Telegraaf (Netherlands)	751,400
Dziennik Zachodni (Poland)	750,000
Daily Record (Scotland)	**746,861**
Daily Star (England)	**739,210**
New York Daily News (United States)	**738,091**
Zero Hora (Brazil)	727,188
Diario dos Campos (Brazil)	725,000
Sabah (Turkey)	722,950
Jornal da Tarde (Brazil)	709,793
Hubei Ribao (China)	700,000
Pusan Ilbo (South Korea)	700,000
Thai Rath (Thailand)	700,000
Zhefiang Ribao (China)	700,000
Il Corriere della Sera (Italy)	**691,269**
Chicago Tribune (United States)	**684,366**
Diaro Insular (Portugal)	684,143
Granma (Cuba)	675,000
China Daily News (Taiwan)	670,000
Clarin Daily (Argentina)	670,000
The Times (England)	**667,238**
Al Goumhouryia (Egypt)	650,000
Guanxi Ribao (China)	650,000
Kahoku Shimpo (Japan)	**636,445**
Long Island Newsday (United States)	**634,627**
El Espectador (Colombia)	632,030
La Nacion (Argentina)	630,000
Hurriyet (Turkey)	615,579
Central Daily News (Taiwan)	600,000
Fujian Ribao (China)	600,000
Guangzhou Ribao (China)	600,000
Hurriyet (Pakistan)	600,000
Liaoning Ribao (China)	600,000
Oriental Daily News (Hong Kong)	600,000
Thuringer Allgemeine (Germany)	594,500
Indian Express (India)	576,200
Nawa-e-Waqt (Pakistan)	**573,921**
Herald Sun (Australia)	**568,945**

Note: Bold circulation figure indicates audit available for 1995. Russian newspapers excluded.

TOP ONE HUNDRED DAILY NEWSPAPERS IN THE UNITED STATES ACCORDING TO CIRCULATION SEPTEMBER 30, 1995

Newspaper	Circulation
New York (NY) *Wall Street Journal* (m)	1,763,140
Arlington (VA) *USA Today* (m)	1,523,610
New York (NY) *Times* (m)	1,081,541
Los Angeles (CA) *Times* (m)	1,012,189
Washington (DC) *Post* (m)	793,660
New York (NY) *Daily News* (m)	738,091
Chicago (IL) *Tribune* (m)	684,366
Long Island (NY) *Newsday* (all day)	634,627
Houston (TX) *Chronicle* (m)	541,478
*Detroit (MI) *Free Press* (m)	531,825
Dallas (TX) *Morning News* (m)	500,358
Boston (MA) *Globe* (m)	498,853
San Francisco (CA) *Chronicle* (m)	489,238
Chicago (IL) *Sun-Times* (m)	488,405
Philadelphia (PA) *Inquirer* (m)	469,398
Newark (NJ) *Star-Ledger* (m)	436,634
New York (NY) *Post* (m)	413,705
Cleveland (OH) *Plain Dealer* (m)	396,773
Minneapolis (MN) *Star Tribune* (m)	389,865
Miami (FL) *Herald* (m)	383,212
San Diego (CA) *Union-Tribune* (all day)	379,705
Phoenix (AZ) *Arizona Republic* (m)	365,979
*Detroit (MI) *News* (e)	354,403
Orange County (CA) *Register* (m)	349,874
St. Petersburg (FL) *Times* (m)	349,874
Baltimore (MD) *Sun* (m)	339,493
Portland (OR) *Oregonian* (all day)	333,654
Denver (CO) *Rocky Mountain News* (m)	331,044
St. Louis (MO) *Post-Dispatch* (m)	319,990
Miwaukee (WI) *Journal Sentinel* (m)	309,137
Boston (MA) *Herald* (m)	308,077
Atlanta (GA) *Constitution* (m)	305,457
Denver (CO) *Post* (m)	303,357
San Jose (CA) *Mercury News* (m)	286,935
Kansas City (MO) *Star* (m)	284,675
Sacramento (CA) *Bee* (m)	279,980
Buffalo (NY) *News* (all day)	274,614
Orlando (FL) *Sentinel* (all day)	272,702
New Orleans (LA) *Times-Picayune* (all day)	267,397
Fort Lauderdale (FL) *Sun-Sentinel* (m)	264,863
Tampa (FL) *Tribune* (m)	263,674
Columbus (OH) *Dispatch* (m)	255,390
Pittsburgh (PA) *Post-Gazette* (m)	242,723
Charlotte (NC) *Observer* (m)	239,173
Louisville (KY) *Courier-Journal* (m)	236,465
Seattle (WA) *Times* (e)	232,616
Omaha (NE) *World-Herald* (all day)	232,360
Indianapolis (IN) *Star* (m)	227,535
Fort Worth (TX) *Star-Telegram* (m)	225,080
San Antonio (TX) *Express-News* (m)	221,556
Oklahoma City (OK) *Daily Oklahoman* (m)	212,382
Richmond (VA) *Times-Dispatch* (m)	211,589
Hartford (CT) *Courant* (m)	211,704
St. Paul (MN) *Pioneer Press* (m)	208,807
Seattle (WA) *Post-Intelligencer* (m)	204,544
Cincinnati (OH) *Enquirer* (m)	203,158
Los Angeles (CA) *Daily News* (m)	201,239
Philadelphia (PA) *Daily News* (m)	195,447
Rochester (NY) *Democrat and Chronicle* (m)	194,677
Jacksonville (FL) *Times-Union* (m)	194,643
Los Angeles (CA) *Investor's Business Daily* (m)	193,459
Norfolk (VA) *Virginian-Pilot* (m)	188,678
Providence (RI) *Journal* (m)	185,014
Memphis (TN) *Commercial Appeal* (m)	178,415
Des Moines (IA) *Register* (m)	177,857
Austin (TX) *American-Statesman* (m)	177,704
Little Rock (AR) *Democrat-Gazette* (m)	175,218
West Palm Beach (FL) *Palm Beach Post* (m)	173,699
Tulsa (OK) *World* (m)	168,529
Riverside (CA) *Press-Enterprise* (m)	164,028
Dayton (OH) *Daily News* (m)	163,187
Neptune (NJ) *Asbury Park Press* (e)	161,052
Birmingham (AL) *News* (e)	160,081
Hackensack (NJ) *Record* (m)	156,726
Fresno (CA) *Bee* (m)	152,554
Akron (OH) *Beacon Journal* (m)	152,211
Toledo (OH) *Blade* (m)	147,526
Raleigh (NC) *News & Observer* (m)	146,688
Nashville (TN) *Tennessean* (m)	146,466
Grand Rapids (MI) *Press* (e)	145,521
Las Vegas (NV) *Review-Journal* (m)	142,149
Allentown (PA) *Morning Call* (m)	133,140
Tacoma (WA) *News Tribune* (m)	128,659
Arlington Heights (IL) *Daily Herald* (m)	128,172
Salt Lake City (UT) *Tribune* (m)	126,076
Columbia (SC) *State* (m)	126,074
Wilmington (DE) *News Journal* (all day)	125,677
Atlanta (GA) *Journal* (e)	124,484
Spokane (WA) *Spokesman-Review* (m)	122,961
Knoxville (TN) *News-Sentinel* (m)	116,429
San Francisco Examiner (e)	114,957
Sarasota (FL) *Herald-Tribune* (m)	114,638
Albuquerque (NM) *Journal* (m)	113,031
Lexington (KY) *Herald-Leader* (m)	112,352
Worcester (MA) *Telegram & Gazette* (m)	111,836
Roanoke (VA) *Times & World-News* (m)	110,195
Jackson (MS) *Clarion-Ledger* (m)	110,059
Charleston (SC) *Post & Courier* (m)	109,520
Long Beach (CA) *Press-Telegram* (m)	109,029
Honolulu (HI) *Advertiser* (m)	105,624

*Due to the strike in Detroit, March 31, 1995, figures are used for the two Detroit newspapers.

TOP TEN DAILY NEWSPAPERS IN CANADA ACCORDING TO CIRCULATION SEPTEMBER 30, 1995

Newspaper	Circulation
Toronto (ON) *Star* (m)	491,411
Toronto (ON) *Globe and Mail* (m)	306,260
Montreal (QC) *Le Journal* (m)	270,607
Toronto (ON) *Sun* (m)	240,822
Vancouver (BC) *Sun* (m)	185,535
Montreal (QC) *La Presse* (m)	179,523
Vancouver (BC) *Province* (m)	153,758
Montreal (ON) *Gazette* (m)	148,777
Edmonton (AB) *Journal* (m)	147,060
Ottawa (ON) *Citizen* (all day)	145,952

Copyright ©1996 by the Editor & Publisher Co.

TOP NEWSPAPER ADVERTISING NETWORKS IN THE UNITED STATES

Note: The Top Newspaper Advertising Networks is a new section providing a snap shot of the growing community of advertising networks across the United States. The "Total daily circulation" is based on Sept. 30, 1995, figures where available. Any comments or questions can be sent to edpub@mediainfo.com.

ALABAMA

Alabama Group
2000 Riveredge Pkwy.
Atlanta, GA 30328
tel (770) 955-2335; fax (770) 955-6564
Total daily circulation: 408,252
National column inch rate: $163.00
Network buy includes the following papers:
Birmingham News (e-mon to fri; m-sat; m-S)
Birmingham Post Herald (e-mon to fri; m-sat)
Huntsville News (m-mon to sat)
Huntsville Times (e-mon to sat; m-S)
Mobile Press (e-mon to fri)
Mobile Press Register (m-sat; m-S)
Mobile Register (m-mon to fri)

ARIZONA

Tribune Newspapers
120 W. First Ave.; PO Box 1547
Mesa, AZ 85210
tel (602) 898-6475; fax (602) 898-6463
Total daily circulation: 106,757
National column inch rate: $69.08
Network buy includes the following papers:
Chandler Arizonan-Tribune (m-mon to sat; S)
Gilbert Tribune (m-mon to sat; S)
Mesa Tribune (m-mon to sat; S)
Scottsdale Progress Tribune (e-mon to sat; S)
Tempe Daily News-Tribune (m-mon to sat; S)

CALIFORNIA

Alameda Newspaper Group
116 W. Winton Ave.; PO Box 5050
Hayward, CA 94544
tel (510) 293-2613; fax (510) 293-2605
Total daily circulation: 191,491
National column inch rate: $118.00
Network buy includes the following papers:
Fremont Argus (m-mon to sat; S)
Hayward Daily Review (m-mon to sat; S)
Oakland Tribune (m-mon to sat; S)
Pleasanton Tri-Valley Herald (m-mon to sat; S)

Contra Costa Newspapers Inc.
2640 Shadelands Dr.; PO Box 5088
Walnut Creek, CA 94598
tel (510) 943-8383; fax (510) 977-8410
Total daily circulation: 190,388
National column inch rate: $104.05
Network buy includes the following papers:
Antioch Ledger-Dispatch (e-mon to sat; S)
Pleasanton Valley Times (m-mon to sat; S)
Richmond West County Times (m-mon to sat; S)
Walnut Creek Contra Costa Times (m-mon to sat; S)

Los Angeles ADI USSPI Group
420 Lexington Ave.
New York, NY 10170
tel (212) 687-8425; fax (212) 986-8033
Total daily circulation: 156,401
National column inch rate: $114.75
Network buy includes the following papers:
Glendale News-Press (m-mon to sat)
Pasadena Star-News (m-mon to sat; S)
San Gabriel Valley Tribune (m-mon to sat; S)
Santa Monica Outlook (e-mon to sat)
Whittier Daily News (m-mon to sat; S)

Los Angeles Coastal Combo
5757 Wilshire Blvd.
Los Angeles, CA 90036
tel (213) 936-1069; fax (213) 936-0955
Total daily circulation: 239,191
National column inch rate: $144.68
Network buy includes the following papers:
Long Beach Press-Telegram (m-mon to sat; S)
San Pedro News-Pilot (m-mon to sat; S)
Santa Monica Outlook (m-mon to sat)
Torrance Daily Breeze (m-mon to sat; S)

Southern California Newspaper Network
350 Camino de la Reina; PO Box 191
San Diego, CA 92108-3090
tel (619) 293-1450; fax (619) 293-2368

Total daily circulation: 930,364
National column inch rate: $462.72
Network buy includes the following papers:
Los Angeles Daily News (m-mon to sat; S)
Orange County (Santa Ana) Register (m-mon to sat; S)
San Diego Union-Tribune (m-mon to sat; S)

COLORADO

Colorado Press Service Dailies
1336 Glenarm Pl.
Denver, CO 80204
tel (303) 571-5117; fax (303) 571-1803
Total daily circulation: 999,758
National column inch rate: $674.53
Network buy includes the following 23 papers:
Alamosa Valley Courier (m-tues to sat)
Boulder Daily Camera (m-mon to sat; S)
Canon City Daily Record (e-mon to sat)
Colorado Springs Gazette Telegraph (m-mon to sat; S)
Craig Northwest Colorado Daily Press (e-mon to fri)
Denver Post (m-mon to sat; S)
Denver Rocky Mountain News (m-mon to sat; S)
Durango Herald (m-mon to fri; S)
Fort Collins Coloradoan (m-mon to sat; S)
Fort Morgan Times (e-mon to fri; m-sat)
Glenwood Springs Post (m-mon to sat)
Grand Junction Daily Sentinel (e-mon to sat; S)
Greeley Tribune (e-mon to sat; S)
Gunnison Country Times (m-tues to sat)
La Junta Tribune-Democrat (e-mon to fri)
Lamar Daily News (e-mon to fri)
Longmont Daily Times-Call (e-mon to fri; m-sat; S)
Loveland Daily Reporter-Herald (e-mon to fri; m-sat)
Montrose Daily Press (e-mon to fri)
Pueblo Chieftain (m-mon to sat; S)
Rocky Ford Daily Gazette (e-mon to fri)
Salida Mountain Mail (m-mon to fri)
Sterling Journal-Advocate (e-mon to sat)

CONNECTICUT

Central Connecticut Newspaper Network
S. Braintree Park & 1515 Washington St., Ste. 107
Braintree, MA 02164
tel (617) 356-2772; fax (617) 356-2837
Total daily circulation: 184,050
National column inch rate: $115.50
Network buy includes the following papers:
Bristol Press (all day-mon to sat)
Manchester Journal Inquirer (m-mon to fri; m-sat)
Middletown Press (m-mon to sat)
New Britain Herald (e-mon to fri; m-sat)
New London Day (m-mon to sat; S)
Torrington Register Citizen (m-mon to sat; S)
Willimantic Chronicle (e-mon to fri; m-sat)

Fairfield County Dailies
750 Third Ave.
New York, NY 10017
tel (212) 867-1112; fax (212) 986-4398
Total daily circulation: 100,784
National column inch rate: $96.68
Network buy includes the following papers:
Danbury News Times (m-mon to sat; S)
Greenwich Time (all day-mon to fri; m-sat; S)
Norwalk Hour (e-mon to sat)
Stamford Advocate (all day-mon to fri; m-sat; S)

FLORIDA

Morris Communications Florida Group
3050 Biscayne Blvd.
Miami, FL 33137
tel (305) 573-6768; fax (305) 571-9313
Total daily circulation: 197,845
National column inch rate: $142.50
Network buy includes the following papers:
Jacksonville Florida Times-Union (m-mon to fri; m-sat; S)
St. Augustine Record (e-mon to fri; m-sat; S)

Treasure Coast Group
1000 Cambridge Sq., Ste. D
Alpharetta, GA 30201
tel (770) 667-9366; fax (770) 667-0741
Total daily circulation: 103,213
National column inch rate: $64.47
Network buy includes the following papers:
Fort Pierce Tribune (m-mon to sat; m-S)
Stuart News (m-mon to sat; m-S)
Vero Beach Press-Journal (m-mon to sat; m-S)

GEORGIA

South Georgia Group
1000 Cambridge Sq., Ste. D
Alpharetta, GA 30201-1846
tel (770) 667-9366; fax (770) 667-0741
Total daily circulation: 185,066
National column inch rate: $101.34
Network buy includes the following papers:
Albany Herald (m-mon to sat; S)
Americus Times-Recorder (e-mon to fri; m-sat)
Cordele Dispatch (e-mon to fri)
Moultrie Observer (m-mon to sat)
Thomasville Times-Enterprise (e-mon to fri; S)
Tifton Gazette (e-mon to fri; m-sat)
Valdosta Daily Times (m-mon to sat; S)
Warner Robin Daily Sun (e-mon to fri; S)

HAWAII

Neighbor Island Combo
400 N. St. Paul, Ste. 1300
Dallas, TX 75201-31199
tel (214) 969-0000; fax (214) 754-0421
Total daily circulation: 58,247
National column inch rate: $52.92
Network buy includes the following papers:
Hilo Hawaii Tribune-Herald (m-mon to fri; S)
Kailua-Kona West Hawaii Today (m-mon to fri; S)
Lihue Garden Island (e-mon, wed to fri; S)
Wailuku Maui News (e-mon to fri; S)

IDAHO

Idaho Triangle Group
333 Northgate Mile; PO Box 1800
Idaho Falls, ID 83403
tel (208) 522-1800; fax (208) 529-3142
Total daily circulation: 361,064
National column inch rate: $40.35
Network buy includes the following papers:
Idaho Falls Post Register (e-mon to fri; S)
Pocatello Idaho State Journal (e-mon to fri; S)
Twin Falls Times-News (m-mon to sat; S)

Northwest Newspaper Network (See Oregon listing)

ILLINIOS

Chicago Extended USSPI Group
500 E. Remington Rd., Ste. 104
Schaumburg, IL 60173
tel (708) 490-6000; fax (708) 843-9058
Total daily circulation: 361,064
National column inch rate: $242.39
Network buy includes the following papers:
Aurora Beacon-News (e-mon to fri; m-sat; S)
Chicago Daily Herald (m-mon to sat; S)
Chicago Daily Southtown (m-mon to sat; S)
Crystal Lake Northwest Herald (m-mon to sat; S)
Elgin Courier-News (e-mon to fri; m-sat; S)
Northwest Herald (m-mon to sat; S)
Joliet Herald-News (e-mon to fri; m-sat; S)

Copley Chicago Newspapers
3101 Route 30; PO Box 129
Plainfield, IL 60544
tel (815) 439-5310; fax (815) 439-5357
Total daily circulation: 150,413
National column inch rate: $112.66
Network buy includes the following papers:
Aurora Beacon-News (e-mon to fri; m-sat; m-S)
Elgin Courier-News (e-mon to fri; m-sat; m-S)
Joliet Herald-News (e-mon to fri; m-sat; m-S)
Waukegan News-Sun (e-mon to fri; m-sat)

IOWA

Quad-City Area Newspaper Network
750 Third Ave.
New York, NY 10017
tel (212) 867-1112; fax (212) 986-4398
Total daily circulation: 70,262
National column inch rate: $78.68
Network buy includes the following papers:
Davenport Quad-City Times (m-mon to fri; m-sat; S)
Kewanee (IL) Star-Courier (e-mon to fri; m-sat)
Muscatine Journal (e-mon to fri; m-sat; S)

Metro Iowa Plus Newspaper Network
319 E. Fifth St.
Des Moines, IA 50309
tel (515) 244-2145; fax (515) 244-4855
Total daily circulation: 689,107
National column inch rate: $285.09

Copyright ©1996 by the Editor & Publisher Co.

Newspaper advertising networks

Network buy includes the following papers:
Cedar Rapids-Marion Gazette (m-mon to sat; S)
Davenport Quad City Times (m-mon to fri; m-sat; S)
Des Moines Register (m-mon to sat; S)
Dubuque Telegraph Herald (e-mon to fri; m-sat; S)
Iowa City Press-Citizen (e-mon to sat)
Omaha (NE) World-Herald (all day-mon to fri; m-sat; S)
Sioux City Journal (m-mon to fri; m-sat; S)
Waterloo Courier (e-mon to fri; S)

KANSAS

Kansas City DMA-Plus Newspaper Network
8700 Monrovia, Ste. 310
Lenexa, KS 66215
tel (913) 492-0731; fax (913) 492-0734
Total daily circulation: 158,110
National column inch rate: $150.96
Network buy includes the following 13 papers:
Atchison Daily Globe (e-mon to fri; m-sat)
Blue Springs (MO) Examiner (e-mon to fri; m-sat)
Chillicothe (MO) Constitution-Tribune (e-mon to fri)
Emporia Gazette (e-mon to sat)
Independence (MO) Examiner (e-mon to fri; m-sat)
Kansas City Kansan (e-tues to fri; S)
Lawrence Journal-World (m-mon to fri; m-sat; S)
Leavenworth Times (e-mon to fri; S)
Manhattan Mercury (e-mon to fri; S)
Olathe Daily News (m-mon to sat; S)
Ottawa Herald (e-mon to fri; m-sat)
St. Joseph (MO) News-Press (m-mon to fri; m-sat; S)
Sedalia (MO) Democrat (e-mon to fri; m-sat; S)

KENTUCKY

Kentucky Group
750 Third Ave.
New York, NY 10017
tel (212) 867-1112; fax (212) 986-4398
Total daily circulation: 134,442
National column inch rate: $118.87
Network buy includes the following 10 papers:
Ashland Independent (e-mon to fri; m-S)
Corbin Times-Tribune (e-mon to sat)
Elizabethtown News Enterprise (m-mon to fri; m-S)
Frankfort State Journal (e-mon to fri; m-S)
Harlan Enterprise (m-mon to sat)
Jeffersonville (IN) News (e-mon to fri; m-sat)
Maysville Ledger Independent (m-mon to sat)
Middlesboro News (m-mon to fri; m-sat)
Owensboro Messenger-Inquirer (m-mon to sat; m-S)
Richmond Register (e-mon to fri; m-sat)

MAINE

Maine Newspaper Network
S. Braintree Park & 1515 Washington St., Ste. 107
Braintree, MA 02184
tel (617) 356-2772; fax (617) 356-2837
Total daily circulation: 261,198
National column inch rate: $194.21
Network buy includes the following papers:
Augusta Kennebec Journal (m-mon to sat; S)
Bangor Daily News (m-mon to sat)
Biddeford-Saco Journal Tribune (e-mon to fri)
Brunswick Times Record (e-mon to fri)
Lewiston-Auburn Sun Journal (m-mon to sat; S)
Portland Maine Sunday Telegram (S)
Portland Press Herald (m-mon to sat)
Waterville Central Maine Morning Sentinel (m-mon to sat)

MASSACHUSETTS

BAND-Boston Area Newspaper Dailies
S. Braintree Park & 1515 Washington St., Ste. 107
Braintree, MA 02184
tel (617) 356-2772; fax (617) 356-2837
Total daily circulation: 585,856
National column inch rate: $330.65
Network buy includes the following 21 papers:
Brockton Enterprise (e-mon to fri; m-sat; S)
Concord (NH) Monitor & Sunday Monitor (m-mon to sat; S)
Dedham Daily Transcript (e-mon to fri)
Dover (NH) Foster's Democrat (e-mon to sat)
Fitchburg Sentinel & Enterprise (e-mon to fri; m-sat)
Framingham Middlesex News (e-mon to fri; m-sat; S)
Gloucester Times (e-mon to fri; m-sat)
Haverhill Gazette (e-mon to fri; m-sat)
Hyannis Cape Cod Times (m-mon to sat; S)
Keene (NH) Sentinel (e-mon to fri; m-sat)
Laconia (NH) Citizen (e-mon to fri; m-sat)
Lawrence Eagle-Tribune (e-mon to fri; m-sat)
Lawrence Sunday Eagle-Tribune (S)
Lowell Sun & Sunday Sun (e-mon to fri; m-sat; S)
Lynn Daily Evening Item (e-mon to fri; m-sat)
Milford Daily News (e-mon to fri; m-sat)
Nashua (NH) Telegraph (m-mon to sat; S)
Portsmouth (NH) Herald (m-mon to sat; S)
Quincy Patriot Ledger (e-mon to fri; m-sat)
Salem Evening News (e-mon to fri; m-sat)
Waltham News-Tribune (e-mon to fri)

MICHIGAN

Booth Newspapers Inc.
155 Michigan N.W.; PO Box 2168
Grand Rapids, MI 49501
tel (616) 459-3824; fax (616) 459-1542
Total daily circulation: 550,283
National column inch rate: $235.18
Network buy includes the following papers:
Ann Arbor News (e-mon to sat; S)
Bay City Times (e-mon to sat; S)
Flint Journal (e-mon to sat; S)
Grand Rapids Press (e-mon to sat; S)
Jackson Citizen Patriot (e-mon to sat; S)
Kalamazoo Gazette (e-mon to sat; S)
Muskegon Chronicle (e-mon to sat; S)
Saginaw News (e-mon to sat; S)

Michigan Newspapers Inc.
827 N. Washington Ave.
Lansing, MI 48906
tel (517) 372-2424; fax (517) 372-2429
Total daily circulation: 2,150,370
National column inch rate: $1,537.49
Network buy includes the following 51 papers:
Adrian Daily Telegram (e-mon to fri; m-sat; S)
Albion Recorder (e-mon to sat)
Alpena News (e-mon to fri; m-sat)
Ann Arbor News (e-mon to sat; S)
Bad Axe Huron Daily Tribune (e-mon to fri; S)
Battle Creek Enquirer (e-mon to sat; S)
Bay City Times (e-mon to sat; S)
Benton Harbor-St. Joseph Herald-Palladium (e-mon to sat; S)
Big Rapids Pioneer (m-mon to sat)
Cadillac News (m-mon to sat)
Cheboygan Daily Tribune (m-mon to fri)
Coldwater Daily Reporter (e-mon to fri; m-sat)
Detroit Free Press (m-mon to fri; m-sat; S)
Detroit Legal News (m-mon to fri)
Detroit News (e-mon to fri; m-sat; S)
Dowagiac Daily News (e-mon to fri)
Escanaba Daily Press (e-mon to sat)
Flint Journal (e-mon to fri; m-sat; S)
Grand Haven Tribune (e-mon to sat)
Grand Rapids Press (e-mon to sat; S)
Greenville Daily News (e-mon to sat)
Hillsdale Daily News (e-mon to fri; m-sat)
Holland Sentinel (e-mon to sat; S)
Houghton Daily Mining Gazette (e-mon to sat)
Ionia Sentinel-Standard (m-mon to sat)
Iron Mountain Daily News (e-mon to sat)
Ironwood Daily Globe (e-mon to sat)
Jackson Citizen Patriot (e-mon to fri; m-sat; S)
Kalamazoo Gazette (e-mon to sat; S)
Lansing State Journal (e-mon to sat; S)
Ludington Daily News (e-mon to sat)
Manistee News-Advocate (e-mon to fri; m-sat)
Marquette Mining Journal (e-mon to fri; m-sat; S)
Marshall Chronicle (e-mon to sat; S)
Midland Daily News (e-mon to fri; m-sat; S)
Monroe Evening News (e-mon to fri; m-sat; S)
Mt. Clemens Macomb Daily (e-mon to sat; S)
Mt. Pleasant Morning Sun (e-mon to sat; S)
Muskegon Chronicle (e-mon to sat; S)
Niles Daily Star (e-mon to sat)
Owosso Argus-Press (e-mon to fri; m-sat; S)
Petoskey News-Review (e-mon to fri)
Pontiac Oakland Press (e-mon to sat; S)
Port Huron Times Herald (e-mon to sat; S)
Royal Oak Daily Tribune (e-mon to fri; S)
Saginaw News (e-mon to sat; S)
Sault Ste. Marie Evening News (e-mon to fri; S)
South Haven Daily Tribune (m-mon to fri)
Sturgis Journal (e-mon to sat)
Three Rivers Commercial-News (e-mon to fri; m-sat)
Traverse City Record-Eagle (m-mon to sat; S)

MINNESOTA

Minnesota Newspaper Association
12 S. Sixth St.
Minneapolis, MN 55402
tel (612) 332-8844; fax (612) 342-2958
Total daily circulation: 1,113,676
National column inch rate: $672.42
Network buy includes the following 27 papers:
Albert Lea Tribune (e-mon to fri; S)
Austin Daily Herald (e-mon to fri; S)
Bemidji Pioneer (m-mon to sat; S)
Brainerd Daily Dispatch (e-mon to fri; S)
Breckenridge Daily News (m-tues to fri; S)
Crookston Daily Times (e-mon to fri)
Duluth News-Tribune (m-mon to sat; S)
Fairmont Sentinel (e-mon to sat)
Fargo Forum (m-mon to sat; S)
Faribault Daily News (m-tues to fri; S)
Fergus Falls Daily Journal (e-mon to fri; S)
Hibbing Daily Tribune (m-mon to sat; S)
International Falls Daily Journal (e-mon to fri; S)
Mankato Free Press (m-mon to sat; S)
Marshall Independent (m-mon to sat)
Star-Tribune (m-mon to sat; S)
New Ulm Journal (m-mon to sat; S)
Owatonna People's Press (m-tues to sat; S)
Red Wing Republican Eagle (e-mon to fri; m-sat)
Rochester Post-Bulletin (e-mon to fri; m-sat)
St. Cloud Times (m-mon to fri; m-sat; S)
St. Paul Pioneer Press (m-mon to sat; S)
Stillwater Gazette (e-mon to fri)
Virginia Mesabi Daily News (m-mon to sat; S)
Willmar West Central Tribune (m-mon to sat)
Winona Daily News (m-mon to sat; S)
Worthington Daily Globe (m-mon to sat)

MONTANA

Montana Group
401 N. Broadway; PO Box 36300
Billings, MT 59101
tel (406) 657-1350; fax (406) 657-1345
Total daily circulation: 148,498
National column inch rate: $114.00
Network buy includes the following papers:
Billings Gazette (m-mon to sat; S)
Butte Montana Standard (m-mon to sat; S)
Great Falls Tribune (m-mon to sat; S)
Helena Independent-Record (m-mon to sat; S)
Missoula Missoulian (m-mon to sat; S)

NEBRASKA

Nebraska Group
1120 K St.
Lincoln, NE 68508
tel (402) 476-2851; fax (402) 476-2942
Total daily circulation: 140,791
National column inch rate: $121.80
Network buy includes the following 13 papers:
Beatrice Daily Sun (e-mon to fri; S)
Columbus Telegram (e-mon to fri; S)
Fremont Tribune (e-mon to sat)
Grand Island Independent (m-mon to sat; S)
Holdrege Daily Citizen (e-mon to fri)
Kearney Hub (e-mon to fri; m-sat)
McCook Daily Gazette (e-mon to sat)
Nebraska City News-Press (e-tues to sat)
Norfolk Dail News (e-mon to sat)
North Platte Telegraph (m-tues to sat; S)
Scottsbluff Star-Herald (m-tues to sat; S)
Sidney Telegraph (e-mon to fri)
York News-Times (e-mon to sat)

NEW HAMPSHIRE

Band New Hampshire
S. Braintree Park & 1515 Washington St., Ste. 107
Braintree, MA 02184
tel (617) 356-2772; fax (617) 356-2837
Total daily circulation: 124,952
National column inch rate: $72.72
Network buy includes the following papers:
Concord Monitor & Sunday Monitor (m-mon to sat; S)
Dover Foster's Democrat (e-mon to sat)
Keene Sentinel (e-mon to fri; m-sat)
Laconia Citizen (e-mon to fri; m-sat)
Nashua Telegraph (m-mon to sat; S)
Portsmouth Herald (m-mon to sat; S)

NEW JERSEY

Greater New Jersey Newspaper Network
1 Hoover Way
Woodbridge, NJ 07095
tel (908) 324-7120; fax (908) 442-8705
Total daily circulation: 364,420
National column inch rate: $162.41
Network buy includes the following papers:
Hackensack Bergen County Record (m-mon to sat; S)
Middlesex County Home News & Tribune (m-mon to sat; S)
Neptune Asbury Park Press (e-mon to sat; S)

SOJERN-Southern Jersey Newspaper Network
998 Eagle Rd., Ste. 1204
Wayne, PA 19087
tel (610) 688-5612; fax (610) 688-5615
Total daily circulation: 80,194
National column inch rate: $164.25
Network buy includes the following papers:
Press of Atlantic City (m-mon to sat; S)
Bridgeton Evening News (e-mon to sat)
Salem Today's Sunbeam (m-mon to sat; S)
Toms River Ocean County Observer (m-mon to fri; S)
Trenton Trentonian (m-mon to sat; S)
Vineland Daily Journal (e-mon to sat)
Woodbury Gloucester County Times (e-mon to fri; S)

Newspaper advertising networks

NEW YORK

Albany ADI Newspaper Network
S. Braintree Park & 1515 Washington St., Ste. 107
Braintree, MA 02184
tel (617) 356-2772; fax (617) 356-2837
Total daily circulation: 170,235
National column inch rate: $154.28
Network buy includes the following 11 papers:
Amsterdam Recorder (e-mon to sat; S)
Bennington (VT) Banner (m-mon to sat)
Catskill Daily Mail (e-mon to fri; m-sat)
Glens Falls Post-Star (m-mon to sat; S)
Gloversville Leader-Herald (e-mon to fri; m-sat; S)
Hudson Register-Star (e-mon to fri; S)
North Adams (MA) Transcript (e-mon to fri; m-sat)
Pittsfield (MA) Berkshire Eagle (e-mon to sat)
Saranac Lake Adirondack Daily Enterprise
 (e-mon to fri; m-sat)
Saratoga Springs Saratogian (m-mon to sat; S)
Troy Record & Sunday Record (m-mon to sat; S)

Buffalo DMA Newspaper Network
6964 Promway Ave. N.W.
North Canton, OH 44720
tel (216) 966-8616; fax (216) 966-8717
Total daily circulation: 139,130
National column inch rate: $136.56
Network buy includes the following papers:
Batavia Daily News (e-mon to fri; m-sat)
Dunkirk-Fredonia Evening Observer (e-mon to sat)
Jamestown Post-Journal (e-mon to fri; m-sat; S)
Lockport Union-Sun & Journal (e-mon to sat)
Medina Journal-Register (e-mon to fri)
Niagara Falls Gazette (m-mon to sat; S)
Olean Times-Herald (e-mon to fri; m-sat; S)
Tonawanda News (e-mon to fri; m-sat)

Gannett Suburban Newspapers
One Gannett Dr.
White Plains, NY 10604
tel (914) 694-5384; fax (914) 696-8186
Total daily circulation: 158,795
National column inch rate: $175.00
Network buy includes the following 10 papers:
Mamaroneck Daily Times (e-mon to sat; S)
Mt. Vernon Daily Argus (e-mon to sat; S)
New Rochelle Standard-Star (e-mon to sat; S)
Nyack Rockland Journal-News (e-mon to fri; m-sat; S)
Ossining Citizen Register (e-mon to sat; S)
Peekskill Star (e-mon to sat; S)
Port Chester Daily Item (e-mon to sat; S)
Tarrytown Daily News (e-mon to sat; S)
White Plains Reporter Dispatch (e-mon to sat; S)
Yonkers Herald Statesman (e-mon to sat; S)

UBIE Group
4421 Vestal Pkwy. E.
Vestal, NY 13850
tel (607) 798-1139; fax (607) 798-0261
Total daily circulation: 176,948
National column inch rate: $178.90
Network buy includes the following papers:
Binghamton Press & Sun-Bulletin (m-mon to sat; S)
Elmira Star-Gazette (m-mon to sat; S)
Ithaca Journal (e-mon to sat)
Utica Observer-Dispatch (m-mon to sat; S)

NORTH CAROLINA

Carolinas' Finest Newspaper Group
1000 Cambridge Sq., Ste. D
Alpharetta, GA 30201-1846
tel (770) 667-9366; fax (770) 667-0741
Total daily circulation: 175,140
National column inch rate: $121.25
Network buy includes the following papers:
Concord Tribune (e-mon to fri; S)
Gastonia Gaston Gazette (m-mon to sat; S)
Hickory Record (e-mon to sat; m-sat; S)
Kannapolis Daily Independent (e-mon to fri; S)
Monroe Enquirer-Journal (e-mon to fri; S)
Rock Hill (SC) Herald (m-mon to sat; S)
Salisbury Post (e-mon to sat; S)
Statesville Record & Landmark (e-mon to fri; S)

Raleigh/Durham ADI Newspaper
4488 N. Shallowford Rd., Ste. 101
Dunwoody, GA 30338
tel (404) 399-6407; fax (404) 399-6574
Total daily circulation: 142,501
National column inch rate: $121.58
Network buy includes the following 11 papers:
Clinton Sampson Independent (e-mon to fri; S)
Dunn Daily Record (e-mon to fri)
Elizabeth City Daily Advance (e-mon to fri; S)
Goldsboro News-Argus (e-mon to fri; S)
Henderson Daily Dispatch (e-mon to fri; m-sat)
Kinston Daily Free Press (e-mon to fri; S)
New Bern Sun Journal (e-mon to fri; S)
Roanoke Rapids Daily Herald (e-mon to fri; S)
Rocky Mount Evening & Sunday Telegram (e-mon to sat; S)
Sanford Herald (e-mon to fri; m-sat)
Wilson Daily Times (e-mon to fri; m-sat)

NORTH DAKOTA

North Dakota Newspaper
101 N. 5th St.; PO Box 2020
Fargo, ND 58102
tel (701) 241-5412; fax (701) 241-5487
Total daily circulation: 151,006
National column inch rate: $99.83
Network buy includes the following papers:
Bismarck Tribune (m-mon to sat; S)
Fargo Forum (m-mon to sat; S)
Grand Forks Herald (m-mon to sat; S)
Minot Daily News (m-mon to sat; S)

OHIO

Cleveland DMA Newspaper Network
6964 Promway Ave. N.W.
North Canton, OH 44720
tel (216) 966-8616; fax (216) 966-8717
Total daily circulation: 311,562
National column inch rate: $203.14
Network buy includes the following 12 papers:
Alliance Review (e-mon to sat)
Ashland Times-Gazette (e-mon to fri; m-sat)
Ashtabula Star-Beacon (m-mon to sat; S)
Dover-New Philadelphia Times Reporter (m-mon to sat; S)
Kent-Ravenna Record-Courier (e-mon to sat; S)
Lake County News-Herald (m-mon to sat; S)
Lorain Morning Journal (m-mon to sat; S)
Mansfield News Journal (e-mon to fri; m-sat; S)
Massillon Independent (e-mon to fri; m-sat)
Norwalk Reflector (e-mon to sat)
Sandusky Register (e-mon to sat; S)
Wooster Daily Record (e-mon to sat; S)

Ohio Newspaper Network
6964 Promway Ave. N.W.
North Canton, OH 44720
tel (216) 966-8616; fax (216) 966-8717
Total daily circulation: 703,065
National column inch rate: $633.27
Network buy includes the following 35 papers:
Alliance Review (e-mon to sat)
Ashland Times-Gazette (e-mon to fri; m-sat)
Ashtabula Star-Beacon (m-mon to sat; S)
Bellefontaine Examiner (e-mon to sat; S)
Cambridge Daily Jeffersonian (e-mon to sat)
Canton Repository (e-mon to sat; S)
Dover-New Philadelphia Times Reporter (m-mon to sat; S)
East Liverpool Evening Review (e-mon to fri; m-sat)
Fairborn Daily Herald (e-mon to sat)
Gallipolis Daily Tribune (e-mon to fri; S)
Greenville Daily Advocate (e-mon to fri; m-sat)
Hamilton Journal-News (m-mon to sat; S)
Kent-Ravenna Record-Courier (e-mon to sat; S)
Lake County News-Herald (m-mon to sat; S)
Lisbon Morning Journal (m-mon to sat; S)
Lorain Morning Journal (m-mon to sat; S)
Mansfield News Journal (e-mon to fri; m-sat; S)
Marion Star (e-mon to fri; m-sat; S)
Martins Ferry-Bellaire Times Leader (e-mon to fri; S)
Massillon Independent (e-mon to fri; m-sat)
Middletown Journal (e-mon to fri; m-sat; S)
Mount Vernon News (e-mon to sat)
Newark Advocate (e-mon to fri; m-sat; S)
Norwalk Reflector (e-mon to sat)
Piqua Daily Call (e-mon to sat)
Pomeroy-Middleport Daily Sentinel (e-mon to fri; S)
Portsmouth Daily Times (e-mon to fri; m-sat; S)
Salem News (e-mon to sat)
Sandusky Register (e-mon to sat; S)
Steubenville Herald-Star (e-mon to sat; S)
Troy Daily News (e-mon to sat)
Warren Tribune Chronicle (e-mon to sat; S)
Wooster Daily Record (e-mon to sat; S)
Xenia Daily Gazette (e-mon to fri; m-sat)
Zanesville Times Recorder (m-mon to sat; S)

Target Ohio Network
312 Elm St.
Cincinnati, OH 45202-2754
tel (513) 768-8220; fax (513) 768-8250
Total daily circulation: 711,155
National column inch rate: $406.41
Network buy includes the following papers:
Cincinnati Enquirer (m-mon to sat; S)
Cincinnati Post (e-mon to sat)
Columbus Dispatch (e-mon to sat; S)
Dayton Daily News (m-mon to sat; S)

OREGON

Northwest Newspaper Network
7150 S.W. Hampton St.
Portland, OR 97223-8395
tel (503) 624-6397; fax (503) 639-9009
Total daily circulation: 2,065,120
National column inch rate: $1,322.51
Network buy includes the following 51 papers:
OREGON:
Albany Democrat-Herald (e-mon to sat)
Ashland Daily Tidings (e-mon to sat)
Astoria Daily Astorian (e-mon to fri)
Bend Bulletin (e-mon to fri; S),
Coos Bay-North Bend World (e-mon to fri; m-sat)
Corvallis Gazette-Times (m-mon to sat; S)
Eugene Register-Guard (m-mon to fri; m-sat; S)
Grants Pass Daily Courier (e-mon to fri; m-sat)
Klamath Falls Herald and News (e-mon to fri; S)
La Grande Observer (e-mon to sat)
Medford Mail Tribune (m-mon to fri; m-sat; S)
Ontario Argus Observer (e-mon to fri; S)
Pendleton East Oregonian (e-mon to fri; S)
Portland Oregonian (all day-mon to fri; m-sat; S)
Roseburg News-Review (e-mon to fri; S)
Salem Statesman-Journal (m-mon to sat; S)
The Dalles Chronicle (e-mon to fri; S)
IDAHO:
Blackfoot Morning News (m-mon to sat)
Boise Idaho Stateman (m-mon to sat; S)
Burley South Idaho Press (e-mon to fri; S)
Coeur d'Alene Press (m-mon to sat; S)
Idaho Falls Post Register (e-mon to fri; S)
Kellogg Shoshone News-Press (m-tues to sat; S)
Lewiston Morning Tribune (m-mon to sat; S)
Moscow-Pullman Daily News (e-mon to fri; m-sat)
Nampa-Caldwell Idaho Press-Tribune (e-mon to fri; S)
Pocatello Idaho State Journal (e-mon to fri; S)
Sandpoint Bonner County Daily Bee (m-tues to sat; S)
Twin Falls Times-News (m-mon to sat; S)
WASHINGTON:
Aberdeen Daily World (e-mon to sat; S)
Bellevue Journal American (m-mon to sat; S)
Bellingham Herald (e-mon to fri; m-sat; S)
Bremerton Sun (m-mon to fri; m-sat; S)
Centralia-Chehalis Chronicle (e-mon to fri; m-sat)
Ellensburg Daily Record (e-mon to fri)
Everett Herald (m-mon to sat; S)
Kent Valley Daily News (m-mon to fri; S)
Longview Daily News (e-mon to fri; S)
Moses Lake Columbia Basin Herald (e-mon to fri)
Mount Vernon Skagit Valley Herald (e-mon to fri; m-sat)
Olympia Olympian (m-mon to sat; S)
Pasco-Kennewick-Richland Tri-City Herald (m-mon to sat; S)
Port Angeles Peninsula Daily News (e-mon to fri; S)
Seattle Post-Intelligencer (e-mon to sat; S)
Seattle Times (e-mon to fri; m-sat; S)
Spokane Spokesman-Review (m-mon to fri; m-sat; S)
Sunnyside Daily Sun News (e-mon to fri)
Tacoma News Tribune (m-mon to sat; S)
Vancouver Columbian (e-mon to fri; S)
Walla Walla Union-Bulletin (e-mon to fri; S)
Yakima Herald-Republic (m-mon to sat; S)

PENNSYLVANIA

Central Pennsylvania Newspaper Network
998 Eagle Rd., Ste. 1204
Wayne, PA 19087
tel (610) 688-5612; fax (610) 688-5615
Total daily circulation: 256,564
National column inch rate: $222.58
Network buy includes the following 16 papers:
Altoona Mirror (e-mon to fri; m-sat; S)
Bedford Gazette (m-mon to sat)
Clearfield-Curwensville Progress (e-mon to sat)
Du Bois Courier Express/Tri-County Sunday (e-mon to fri; S)
Franklin-Oil City Derrick (e-mon to sat)
Franklin-Oil City News-Herald (m-mon to sat)
Huntingdon-Mount Union Daily News (e-mon to fri; m-sat)
Indiana Gazette (e-mon to sat; S)
Lewistown Sentinel (m-mon to sat)
Lock Haven-Jersey Shore Express (e-mon to sat)
Meadville Tribune (m-mon to sat; S)
Punxsutawney Spirit (m-mon to sat)
Somerset Daily American (e-mon to sat)
State College Centre Daily Times (m-mon to sat; S)
Tyrone Daily Herald (e-mon to fri; m-sat)
Williamsport Sun-Gazette (e-m,on to fri; m-sat; S)

Pittsburgh DMA Newspaper Network
PO Box 407
Rochester, PA 15074
tel (412) 774-4411; fax (412) 774-5743
Total daily circulation: 360,973
National column inch rate: $238.66
Network buy includes the following 15 papers:
Beaver County Times (e-mon to fri; S)
Butler Eagle (e-mon to sat)
Connellsville Daily Courier (e-mon to fri; m-sat)
Ellwood City Ledger (e-mon to sat)

Greensburg Tribune-Review (m-mon to sat; S)
Indiana Gazette (m-mon to sat)
Irwin Standard Observer (e-mon to fri; m-sat)
Kittanning Leader-Times (e-mon to fri; m-sat)
Latrobe Bulletin (e-mon to fri; m-sat)
McKeesport Daily News (e-mon to fri; m-sat)
Monessen Valley Independent (e-mon to sat)
Morgantown (WV) Dominion Post (m-mon to sat; S)
New Castle News & Weekend (e-mon to fri; m-sat)
Uniontown Herald-Standard (m-mon to fri; S)
Washington Observer-Reporter (m-mon to sat; S)

Greater Philadelphia Network
8400 Route 13
Levittown, PA 19056
tel (215) 949-4151; fax (215) 949-4114
Total daily circulation: 155,326
National column inch rate: $116.00
Network buy includes the following papers:
Levittown Bucks County Courier Times (m-mon to fri; S)
Doylestown Intelligencer/Record (m-mon to fri; S)
Willingboro (NJ) Burlington County Times (e-mon to fri; S)

RHODE ISLAND

RISEM-Rhode Island Southeast Massachusetts
S. Braintree Park & 1515 Washington St., Ste. 107
Braintree, MA 02184
tel (617) 356-2772; fax (617) 356-2837
Total daily circulation: 175,471
National column inch rate: $111.18
Network buy includes the following papers:
Fall River (MA) Herald News (m-mon to sat; S)
New Bedford (MA) Standard Times (e-mon to fri; m-sat)
Newport Daily News (e-mon to fri; m-sat)
Pawtucket Times (m-mon to sat)
Taunton (MA) Daily Gazette (e-mon to fri; m-sat)
West Warwick Kent County Daily Times (e-mon to sat)
Westerly Sun (e-mon to fri; S)
Woonsocket Call (m-mon to sat; S)

SOUTH CAROLINA

South Carolina Metro Plus Network
750 Third Ave.
New York, NY 10017
tel (212) 867-1112; fax (212) 986-4398
Total daily circulation: 532,258
National column inch rate: $377.02
Network buy includes the following papers:
Aiken Standard (e-mon to fri, m-sat; S)
Anderson Independent-Mail (m-mon to sat; S)
Charleston Post and Courier (m-mon to sat; S)
Columbia State (m-mon to sat; S)
Florence Morning News (m-mon to sat; S)
Greenville News (m-mon to fri)
Myrtle Beach Sun News (m-mon to sat; S)
Spartanburg Herald-Journal (m-mon to sat; S)

TENNESSEE

East Tennessee Metro Network
750 Third Ave.
New York, NY 10017
tel (212) 867-1112; fax (212) 986-4398
Total daily circulation: 322,720
National column inch rate: $166.50
Network buy includes the following papers:
Bristol (VA) Herald Courier Virginia-Tennessean (e-mon to fri; m-sat; S)
Chattanooga Free Press (e-mon to sat; S)
Chattanooga Times (m-mon to sat)
Johnson City Press (e-mon to fri; m-sat; S)
Kingsport Times-News (e-mon to fri; m-sat; S)
Knoxville News-Sentinel (e-mon to fri; m-sat; S)

TEXAS

Great State of South Texas
400 N. St. Paul, Ste. 1300
Dallas, TX 75201
tel (214) 969-0000; fax (214) 754-0421
Total daily circulation: 249,200
National column inch rate: $130.19
Network buy includes the following papers:
Brownsville Herald (m-mon to sat; S)
Corpus Christi Caller-Times (m-mon to sat; S)
Harlingen Valley Morning Star (m-mon to sat; S)
Laredo Morning Times (m-mon to sat; S)
McAllen Monitor (m-mon to sat; S)
Victoria Advocate (m-mon to sat; S)

Harte Hanks Newspaper Group
PO Box 120
Wichita Falls, TX 76307
tel (817) 720-3410; fax (817) 720-3453
Total daily circulation: 193,456
National column inch rate: $136.97
Network buy includes the following papers:
Abilene Reporter-News (m-mon to sat; S)
Corpus Christi Caller-Times (m-mon to sat; S)
Plano Star Courier (m-wed to sat; S)
San Angelo Standard-Times (m-mon to sat; S)
Wichita Falls Times Record News (m-mon to sat; S)

Houston USSPI Group
500 E. Remington Rd., Ste. 104
Schaumburg, IL 60173
tel (708) 490-6000; fax (708) 843-9058
Total daily circulation: 62,203
National column inch rate: $92.23
Network buy includes the following papers:
Baytown Sun (e-mon to fri; S)
Brenham Banner-Press (e-mon to fri; S)
Conroe Courier (m-mon to sat; S)
Galveston County Daily News (m-mon to sat; S)
Pasadena Citizen (m-tues to sat; S)
Rosenberg Herald-Coaster (e-mon to fri; S)

Westexan
400 N. St. Paul, Ste. 1300
Dallas, TX 75201
tel (214) 969-0000; fax (214) 754-0421
Total daily circulation: 270,178
National column inch rate: $194.09
Network buy includes the following papers:
Abilene Reporter-News (m-mon to sat; S)
Amarillo Daily News (m-mon to sat; S)
Amarillo Globe Times (e-mon to fri)
Amarillo Sunday News-Globe (S)
Lubbock Avalanche-Journal (m-mon to sat; S)
Midland Reporter-Telegram (m-mon to sat; S)
Odessa American (m-mon to sat; S)
San Angelo Standard-Times (m-mon to sat; S)
Wichita Falls Times Record News (m-mon to sat; S)

VERMONT

Eagle Publishing Group
425 Main St.
Bennington, VT 05201
tel (802) 447-7567; fax (802) 447-0332
Total daily circulation: 50,532
National column inch rate: $35.32
Network buy includes the following papers:
Bennington Banner (m-mon to sat)
Brattleboro Reformer (m-mon to sat)
Pittsfield (MA) Berkshire Eagle (m-mon to sat; S)

PRBM Market Network
27 Wales St.; PO Box 668
Rutland, VT 05702
tel (802) 747-6121; fax (802) 775-2423
Total daily circulation: 57,435
National column inch rate: $47.80
Network buy includes the following papers:
Barre-Montpelier Times Argus (e-mon to fri; m-sat; S)
Plattsburgh (NY) Press-Republican (m-mon to sat; S)
Rutland Herald (m-mon to sat; S)

VIRGINIA

Journal & Express Newspapers
2720 Prosperity Ave.
Fairfax, VA 22034-1010
tel (703) 846-8370; fax (703) 846-8396
Total daily circulation: 112,855
National column inch rate: $158.65
Network buy includes the following papers:
Alexandria Journal (m-mon to fri)
Arlington Journal (m-mon to fri)
Fairfax Journal (m-mon to fri)
Lanham (MD) Prince George's Journal (m-mon to fri)
Manassas Prince William Journal (m-mon to fri)
Rockville (MD) Montgomery Journal (m-mon to fri)

Virginia Newspaper Network
4488 N. Shallowford Rd., Ste. 101
Dunwoody, GA 30338
tel (404) 399-6407; fax (404) 399-6574
Total daily circulation: 228,886
National column inch rate: $218.51
Network buy includes nine weeklies plus the following 12 daily papers:
Covington Virginia Review (e-mon to sat)
Danville Register & Bee (m-mon to sat; S)
Fredericksburg Free Lance-Star (e-mon to sat; S)
Harrisonburg Daily News-Record (m-mon to sat)
Hopewell News (m-mon to sat)
Manassas Journal Messenger (e-mon to fril m-sat)
Martinsville Bulletin (m-mon to sat)
Petersburg Progress-Index (e-mon to fri; m-sat; S)
Staunton Daily and Sunday News Leader (m-mon to sat; S)
Strasburg Northern Virginia Daily (m-mon to sat)
Waynesboro News-Virginian (e-mon to fri; m-sat)
Winchester Star (e-mon to fri; m-sat)

WASHINGTON

Central Washington Newspaper Network
114 N. 4th St.; PO Box 9668
Yakima, WA 98909

Newspaper advertising networks

tel (509) 577-7734; fax (509) 577-7766
Total daily circulation: 125,339
National column inch rate: $109.40
Network buy includes the following papers:
Pasco-Kennewick Tri-City Herald (m-mon to sat; S)
Walla Walla Union-Bulletin (e-mon to fri; S)
Wenatchee World (e-mon to fri; S)
Yakima Herald-Republic (m-mon to sat; S)

Northwest Newspaper Network (See Oregon listing)

WEST VIRGINIA

West Virginia Newspaper Network
4488 N. Shallowford Rd., Ste. 101
Dunwoody, GA 30338
tel (404) 399-6407; fax (404) 399-6574
Total daily circulation: 169,264
National column inch rate: $178.21
Network buy includes the following 11 papers:
Beckley Register Herald (m-mon to sat; S)
Bluefield Daily Telegraph (m-mon to sat; S)
Elkins Inter-Mountain (e-mon to fri; m-sat)
Logan Banner (e-mon to fri; S)
Martinsburg Journal & Sunday Journal (m-mon to sat; S)
Morgantown Dominion Post (m-mon to sat; S)
Parkersburg News (m-mon to sat; S)
Parkersburg Sentinel (e-mon to sat)
Wheeling Intelligencer (m-mon to sat)
Wheeling News-Register (e-mon to fri; S)
Williamson Daily News (e-mon to sat)

WISCONSIN

Gannett Wisconsin Newspapers
435 E. Walnut; PO Box 19430
Green Bay, WI 54307-9430
tel (414) 435-4411; fax (414) 431-8499
Total daily circulation: 86,020
National column inch rate: $57.10
Network buy includes the following papers:
Green Bay Press-Gazette (e-mon to fri; m-sat; S)
Wausau Daily Herald (e-mon to fri; m-sat; S)

Milwaukee DMA Newspaper Network
435 N. Michigan Ave., Ste. 1317
Chicago, IL 55344
tel (312) 644-8270; fax (312) 644-9011
Total daily circulation: 122,047
National column inch rate: $106.08
Network buy includes the following papers:
Kenosha News (m-mon to sat; S)
Racine Journal Times (m-mon to sat; S)
Sheboygan Press (e-mon to fri; m-sat; S)
Waukesha County Freeman (e-mon to fri; m-sat; S)
West Bend Daily News (e-mon to fri; m-sat)

Thomson Wisconsin Newspapers
801 N. Barstow; PO Box 7
Waukesha, WI 53187
tel (414) 542-2501; fax (414) 542-9257
Total daily circulation: 151,955
National column inch rate: $83.77
Network buy includes the following papers:
Appleton Post-Crescent (e-mon to fri; m-sat; S)
Fond du Lac Reporter (e-mon to fri; S)
Manitowoc Herald Times Reporter (e-mon to sat; S)
Sheboygan Press (e-mon to fri; m-sat; S)
Waukesha County Freeman (e-mon to fri; m-sat; S)
West Bend Daily News (e-mon to fri; m-sat)
Wisconsin Rapids Daily Tribune (e-mon to fri; m-sat)

Wausau-Rhinelander DMA Network
435 N. Michigan Ave., Ste. 1317
Chicago, IL 60611
tel (312) 644-8270; fax (312) 644-9011
Total daily circulation: 74,947
National column inch rate: $68.77
Network buy includes the following papers:
Marshfield News-Herald (e-mon to sat)
Rhinelander Daily News (e-mon to fri; S)
Stevens Point Journal (e-mon to sat)
Wausau Daily Herald (e-mon to fri; m-sat; S)
Wisconsin Rapids Daily Tribune (e-mon to fri; m-sat)

La Crosse-Eau Claire DMA Network
250 Prairie Center Dr.
Eden Prairie, MN 55344
tel (612) 944-0245; fax (612) 944-0246
Total daily circulation: 79,943
National column inch rate: $52.31
Network buy includes the following papers:
Eau Claire Leader-Telegram (e-mon to fri; m-sat; S)
La Crosse Tribune (m-mon to sat; S)
Winona (MN) Daily News (m-mon to sat; S)

Copyright ©1996 by the Editor & Publisher Co.

Expanded SAU™ System

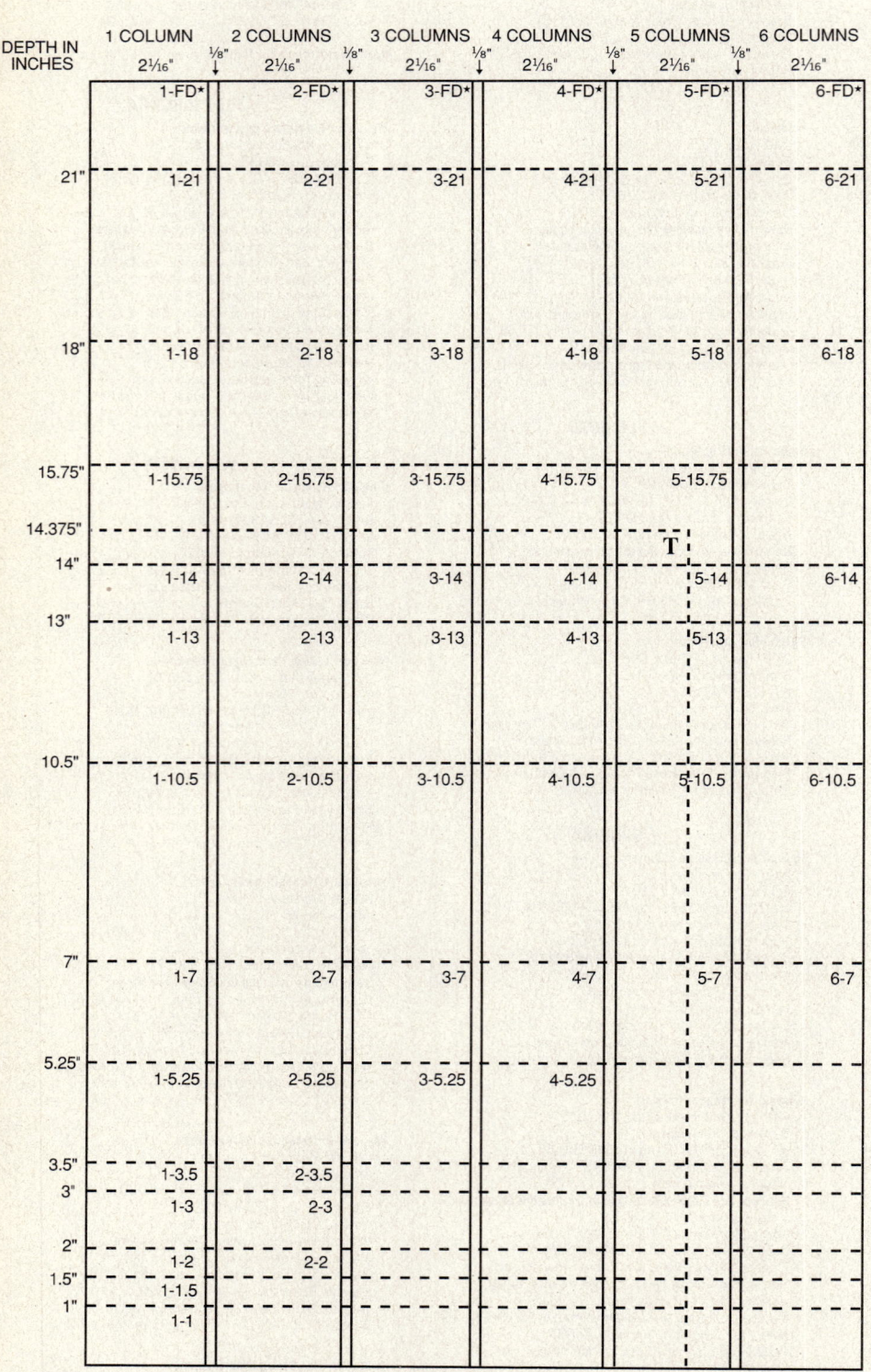

SAU™ Expanded Units

notes:

- 13 inch depths are for tabloid sections of broadsheet newspapers.

- T is a full page size for 21½" cut-off tabloid newspapers. It measures 14⅜" by 9¾".

  1 COLUMN 2 1/16"
  2 COLUMNS 4¼"
  3 COLUMNS 6 7/16"
  4 COLUMNS 8⅝"
  5 COLUMNS 10 13/16"
  6 COLUMNS 13"
  DOUBLE TRUCK 26¾"
  ★FD—FULL DEPTH

★FD = full depth of 21" or longer according to individual newspapers' printed depth as indicated in Standard Rate and Data Service listing. Printed depth generally varies in newspapers from 21" to 22½". All newspapers can accept 21" ads and may float the ad if their printed depth is greater that 21".

The expanded Standard Advertising Unit (SAU) system became effective July 1, 1984, to facilitate placement of newspaper advertising by minimizing format and dimensional differences in order to simplify preparation of advertisements run in a number of newspapers. The system calls for the adoption of a standard column width; the use of the inch as the unit of measurement in place of agate line, and expanding the number of SAU modules from 25 to 57 to provide a wider variety of sizes for advertisers.

Canadian Newspaper Unit
Module standard de publicité

The CNU Grid

1 Column 2 1/16 in.   2 Columns 4 1/4 in.   3 Columns 6 3/8 in.   4 Columns 8 9/16 in.   5 Columns 10 3/4 in.   6 Columns 13 in.

300 Modular Agate Lines

New Canadian Newspaper Units

On October 1, 1985, a standardized advertising system was adopted by most Canadian daily newspapers.

- The basic broadsheet CNU format establishes a 6-column page, each column measuring 2 1/16" (12.4 picas) wide, separated by gutters for a total printed page width of 13" (78.2 picas).

- The basic tabloid CNU format establishes a 5-column page, each column measuring 1 15/16" (11.8 picas) wide, separated by gutters for a total printed page width of 10 1/4" (62 picas).

CNU advertising can be measured and sold by two methods:

- By modular agate lines — for a 9-column broadsheet converting to a 6-column CNU format, the rate for a modular agate line will be 1.5 times the old agate line.

- By modular agate units — to establish modular units, a CNU 6-column format broadsheet with a depth of 300 modular agate lines is divided into 10 equal units per column. Each of these modular units will be 30 lines in depth and each page will contain 60 units.

Copyright ©1996 by the Editor & Publisher Co.

xix

The new streamlined Standard Advertising Invoice (SAI) reproduced here has been developed by the Newspaper Association of America and the International Newspaper Financial Executives in partnership with their retail advertising customers. This new form replaces all previous versions. It is important that the 25 numbered elements (listed on the following page) are not altered because the sequential order of the SAI form is critical to the successful implementation of the standardization process. If adding information to the individual boxes is necessary, do not change the order in which the boxes appear. Below is an example of the SAI, reduced in size. For more information call (703) 620-4-SAI, the SAI Hot Line set up by the INFE.

The 25 elements of the Standard Advertising Invoice (SAI)

LEGEND

1. Billing Period
2. Advertiser-Client Name
3. Terms of Payment
4. Page Number
5. Billing Date
6. Billed Account Number
7. Advertiser-Client Number
8. Billed Account Name and Address
9. Remittance Address
10. Date
11. Newspaper's Reference Number
12. Description-Other Comments, Charges
13. Product, Service Code
14. Other Charges or Credit
15. SAU Size
16. Billed Units
17. Times Run
18. Rate
19. Gross Amount
20. Net Amount
21. Current Net Amount Due
22. Aging of Past Due Amounts
23. Total Amount Due
24. Advertiser Information
25. Invoice Number

1 — Billing Period: Period of time covered by the invoice (week(s), month(s), etc.).

2 — Advertiser-Client Name: If different from account being billed. Applies particularly to advertising agencies.

3 — Terms of Payment: Statement of when payment is due (e.g. net 15). If cash discounts or credit card payments are applicable, they should be designated in the body of the statement.

4 — Page Number: Page number of the invoice.

5 — Billing Date: The date the invoice was generated.

6 — Billed Account Number: The unique identifier assigned to each advertiser or advertising agency by the newspapers. This number would generally be part of the newspaper's accounts receivable control system.

7 — Advertiser-Client Number: If different from account being billed. Applies particularly to advertising placed by advertising agencies.

8 — Billed Account Name and Address: Name of the advertiser or advertising agency that placed the advertising and the complete billing address. This is the field that will show through the envelope window. Note sufficient space is available for newspapers using postal bar coding.

9 — Remittance Address: The name and address to which payment is to be sent.

10 — Date: The insertion date of publication of the advertisement such as month and day(s) or a transaction date for other items such as payments, adjustments, etc.

11 — Newspaper's Reference Number: A newspaper's internal identifier (work order number) assigned for production purposes, document retrieval, cash application and for other purposes.

12 — Description-Other Comments, Charges: (Combined with Elements 13 and 14) Identification of the ad for the advertiser. Description must include the advertiser's or advertising agency's insertion order, control or purchase order number, advertiser's name, key words in the ad or product category advertised.

13 — Product, Service Code: (Combined with Elements 12 and 14) Applicable if you use a numbering system to identify manufacturer and product or service. If not, leave blank and reserve for future universal coding.

14 — Other Charges or Credit: (Combined with Elements 12 and 13) Identification of transaction such as color charges, position charges, production charges, art charges, zone area, service charges and all applicable rate discounts.

15 — SAU Size: (Combined with Element 16) For display ads, the self-descriptive nomenclature of the columns by inches (e.g., 3-x-14 inches would be the SAU number of a 3-column-by-14-inch display ad). For other ads, appropriate dimensions (e.g., 1-by-6 lines for a classified ad).

16 — Billed Units: (Combined with Element 15) The total size of the ads in column inches, lines, number of preprints or other billed units.

17 — Times Run: (Combined with Element 18) The total number of appearances of an ad.

18 — Rate: (Combined with Element 17) The rate per inch, line number of preprints or other billable units charged that are based on the current rate card and contract.

19 — Gross Amount: The extension of total billed amount at the applicable rate before agency commissions and cash discounts. Frequency and other performance discounts should be deducted to arrive at the gross amount. The total gross amount should appear tallied at the bottom of the column. All gross amounts must be printed flush left in the column.

20 — Net Amount: Gross charge minus the agency commission. All net amounts must be printed flush right in the column.

21 — Current Net Amount Due: The total of net charges for advertising, color, production charges, art charges, position charges, etc., appearing on the invoice for the current billing period (Element 1). This field has been relocated to the far left of the invoice for compatibility with the majority of billing systems' software.

22 — Aging of Past Due Amounts: An aging of overdue charges according to billing terms, based on the number of days outstanding from the billing dates, stated in 30-day increments (e.g., 30-60-90). The "unapplied amount" box is optional. If not used it should be left blank.

23 — Total Amount Due: The total of all current net charges plus those charges still outstanding from previous billing periods.

24 — Advertiser Information: A list of the pertinent information needed on file by the advertiser. The following information, if applicable, should be listed in this order: Invoice Number; Billing Period; Billed-Account Number; Advertiser-Client Number; Advertiser-Client Name.

25 — Invoice Number: Invoice number for those newspapers that need to use it for their billing system.

Copyright ©1996 by the Editor & Publisher Co.

TUNED IN.

PLUGGED IN.

For 112 years, the newspaper community has been tuned into Editor & Publisher as *the* primary source of industry information.

Today, a whole new generation involved in online newspaper publishing is also plugged into E&P's Web site Editor & Publisher Interactive.

This industry Web site presents in-depth articles you won't find anywhere else, written by reporters devoted to online newspapering. Included among these is a special daily column - *Stop The Presses* - by renowned online newspaper authority Steve Outing. You can also participate in industry-wide forums and exchange information with interactive publishing experts.

In addition, you won't have to search high and low for research. Because we've already done it for you. In fact, there's a complete section devoted to anything you could possibly need on interactive newspaper publishing.

If you'd like to browse through online newspapers, it's nice to know E&P Interactive has the most comprehensive directory of online newspapers you'll find anywhere - from Alaska to Zambia.

Next time you're on the Web, type in http://www.mediainfo.com. And get plugged in, too.

http://www.mediainfo.com

Nobody delivers to the newspaper industry like Editor & Publisher.

FACTS
Set the Pace.

With the SCC-Conveying System from FERAG.
Controlled flowline processing and individual gripping
with the world's first SCC-Gripper. Consistent, even product pickup;
fast, accurate product release. Maintenance-free; long service life.
Downline processing under control. Step by step.

F·E·R·A·G

FERAG INC., CONVEYING AND PROCESSING SYSTEMS
190 RITTENHOUSE CIRCLE, P.O. BOX 137, BRISTOL, PA 19007-0137
PHONE 215-788-0892; FAX 215-788-7597

TABLE OF CONTENTS

1996 EDITOR & PUBLISHER INTERNATIONAL YEAR BOOK

PART 1

Front Pages
Letter from the publisher ii
Annual newspaper advertising totals vi
Basic data for space buyers vi
Ready reckoners of advertising rates and circulations
    for the United States and Canada vii
NEW! Top one hundred daily newspapers worldwide xii
Top one hundred U.S. daily newspapers xiii
Top ten Canadian daily newspapers xiii
NEW! Newspaper advertising networks xiv
Newspapers Expanded SAU™ System xviii
Canadian Newspaper Unit (CNU) xix
Standard Advertising Invoice xx
Mechanical equipment — abbreviations xxii
New dailies, suspensions xxiv

I — Daily newspapers published in the United States
Daily newspapers 1
National newspapers 454
Tabloid newspapers 454
Newsprint statistics, 1995 454
Groups of newspapers under common ownership 455
Special service newspapers 466

II — Weekly and special newspapers published in the United States
Weekly newspapers 1
NEW! Alternative newspapers 86
Black newspapers 87
Ethnic newspapers 90
Gay & lesbian newspapers 92
NEW! Hispanic newspapers 93
NEW! Jewish newspapers 95
Military newspapers 96
Religious newspapers 98
College and university newspapers 101

III — Newspapers published in Canada
Daily newspapers 1
Weekly newspapers 26
Ethnic newspapers 35
Tabloid newspapers 35
Groups of newspapers under common ownership 36

IV — Newspapers published in foreign countries
The British Press—1995 1
Newspapers of the British Isles 2
Newspapers of Europe 6
Newspapers of Africa 53
Newspapers of Asia and the Far East 59
Newspapers of the Caribbean Region 84
Newspapers of Central America and Mexico 87
Newspapers of the Middle East 101
Newspapers of South America 105
Newspapers of Australia and New Zealand 120
Newspapers of Pacific Ocean Territories 124

V — News and syndicate services
News, picture and syndicate services 1
Comic section groups and networks 12
Newspaper distributed magazine sections 13
Syndicated total market coverage publications 16

VI — Mechanical equipment, supplies and services
Equipment, supplies and services
    Directory of company names 1
    Type of business directory 23
Interactive products and services
    NEW! Directory of company names 45
    NEW! Type of business directory 61
Mechanical forces pay scales 64
Top minimum scales for reporters 67
Starting minimum scales for reporters 68

VII — Other organizations and industry services
NEW! Advertising/Circulation promotion services 1
Association of American Correspondents in London 1
Associations and clubs—national and international 3
Associations and clubs—city, state and regional 6
Clip art services 11
Clipping bureaus 12
Electronic clipping bureaus 12
Foreign newspaper representatives 12
Foreign press and radio-TV correspondents
    in the United States
    New York based correspondents 13
    Washington, DC based correspondents 21
    NEW! California based correspondents 28
    NEW! Chicago based correspondents 31
Foreign Press Association membership directory 32
National newspaper representatives 34
Newspaper Association of America
    membership roster 40
Newspaper brokers and appraisers 45
Organization of News Ombudsmen 46
Schools and departments of journalism 47
NEW! State newspaper representatives 65
Trade unions in the newspaper field 65
United Nations Correspondents Association 66
Index to contents 67
Index to advertisers 68

PART 2

Who's Where
The telephone directory to the
    newspaper industry 3

MECHANICAL EQUIPMENT — ABBREVIATIONS

COMPOSITION

TYPESETTERS

AG —Agfa-Gevaert
AU —Autologic
AX —Automix
Bg —Bobst Graphic
COM —Compugraphic
Dy —Dymo
F —Fairchild
Fi —Filmotype
Fo —Fotosetter
Fr —Friden
HCM —Hell/HCM
Hd —Headliner
HI —Harris
Ik —Itek
Jus —Justowriter
L —Lanston
LC —Linofilm Composer
M —Mergenthaler
Ma —Morisawa
MGD —MGD-Rockwell
MON —Monotype
Ph —Photon
Pr —Protype
Pt —Photo Typositor
So —Simmons-Owega
SP —Star Parts
Sr —Singer
ST —Stripprinter
TC —Titus Communications
V —Varityper
Va —Varisystems
VG —Visual Graphics

FRONT-END HARDWARE & SOFTWARE

ACT —Automated Complete Typesetting
AG —Agfa-Gevaert
Ap —Apple
AP —Associated Press
AT —Atex
AU —Autologic
AX —Automix
BD —Berthold NA
Bee —Beehive
BF —Basic 4
Bg —Bobst Graphic
BR —Bunker Ramo
Bs —Burroughs
C —Chemco
CD —Crosfield Data Systems
CDS —Computer Double Screen
CJ —Collier-Jackson
CM —Cincinnati Milacron
COM —Compugraphic
CPU —Computext
Cp —CompuScan
CS —Computer Services
CSI —Computer Systems Inc.
Cx —Camex
Da —Datapoint
DD —Delta Data
DEC —Digital Equipment Corp.
DL —Data Logic
DS —Data Disc
DTI —Digital Technology International
Dy —Dymo
ECR —ECRM
EKI —Electric Knowledge Inc.
En —Entrex
ES —Evans & Southerland
ESE —Editorial System Engineering Co.
FSI —Freedom Systems Integrators
Gn —Genisis
HAS —Hastech
Hel —Hell
HI —Harris
HP —Hewlett Packard
Hw —Honeywell
Hx —Hendrix
Hz —Hazeltine
IBM —International Business Machines
III —Information International Inc.
Ik —Itek
In —Infotron
INS —Independent Network Services
ISSI —Integrated Software Systems Inc.
KC —Key Corp.
Kk —Kodak
Lf —Leaf Systems
LIP —Logicon-Intercomp
Lk —Lektromedia
LNS —Lee Newspapers Services
LS —Lear-Siegler
M —Mergenthaler
Mac —Macintosh
MD —Micro Data
MeD —Mega Data
MGD —MGD-Rockwell
Mh —Mohr
Mk —Mycro-Tek
MON —Monotype
MPS —Morris Publishing Systems
Mx —Memorex
NEC —Newspaper Electronics Corp.
NW —Neasi-Weber
Omn —Omnitext
Omo —Omron
On —Ontel
Op —Omptimix
OS —One Systems
PBS —Publishing Business Systems
PEP —Perception Electronic Publishing
PS —Peripheral Systems
QPS —Quark Publishing Systems
Ra —Raytheon
RSK —Radio Shack
RZ —Royal Zenith
SCS —Software Consulting Services
SII —System Integrators Inc.
SMS —Stauffer Media Systems
Syc —Sycor
SyD —Systems Development
TC —Titus Communications
Te —Telcom
TI —Texas Instruments
TM —Teleram
Tr —Teleray
TRW —TRW-Fujitsu
TS —Tal-Star
Tt —Teleterm
Tx —Telex
Uni —Univac
V —Varityper
Va —Varisystems
X —Xerox
XIT —Xitron
ZC —Zentec Corp.

AUDIOTEX

DJ —Dow Jones
TEDS —Toronto Star Edition Design System
TMS —Tribune Media Services
VNN —Voice News Network

OCR READERS

Ap —Apple
COM —Compugraphic
Cp —CompuScan
Da —Datatype
Di —Digitek
ECR —ECRM
Hx —Hendrix
M —Mergenthaler
MGD —MGD-Rockwell

PLATE-MAKING

PLATE SYSTEMS

AU —Autologic
B —Brown
CD —Crosfield Data Systems
DiL —DiLitho
DP —DuPont
Dyn —Dynaflex
ECM —EOCOM
F —Fairchild
He —Hercules (Merigraph)
LE —LogEtronics
LP —Laser-Plate
LX —Grace (Letterflex)
Mag —Magnesium
Na —Napp
Nat —National
Rf —Richflex
WL —Western Litho
Z —Zinc

PLATE PROCESSORS

B —Brown
Be —Beach
BM —Ball Metal
CEM —Chemcut
Dow —Dow Chemical
DP —DuPont
Dyn —Dynaflex
He —Hercules (Merigraph)
Ic —Iconics
LG —Laser Graphics
LX —Grace (Letterflex)
MAS —Master
Na —Napp
Nat —National
Nu —nuArc
Ny —Nyloprint
Tas —TasopeSearch
Wd —Wood
WL —Western Litho

CAMERAS

AG —Agfa-Gevaert
B —Brown
Bo —Borrowdale
Br —Bruning
C —Chemco
CL —Clydedale
Co —Consolidated
COM —Compugraphic
DAI —Dainippon
DSA —D.S. America (SCREEN)
ECR —ECRM
Go —Goodkin
Ik —Itek
K —Kenro
Kk —Kodak
Kl —Klimsch
L —Lanston
LE —LogEtronics
MG —ModiGraphic
Nu —nuArc
R —Robertson
Sm —Statmaster
VG —Visual Graphics
W —Western

AUTOMATIC FILM PROCESSORS

AG —Agfa-Gevaert
AU —Autologic
C —Chemo
DP —DuPont
Kk —Kodak
Kr —Kreonite
LE —LogEtronics
P —Pako
WL —Western Litho

COLOR SEPARATION SYSTEMS

AG —Agfa-Gevaert
BKY —Berkey
C —Chemco
Ca —Carlson
Eh —Ehrenreich
Hel —Hell
KFM —K&F Printing Systems International
Kk —Kodak
Lf —Leaf Systems
RZ —Royal Zenith
WDS —Warner MDS

PRESSROOM

DILITHO SYSTEMS

DI —Dahlgren
G —Goss
HI —Harris
In —Inland
RPM —Smith RPM Co.
Ry —Ryco Graphic
T —Taft
Wd —Wood

PRESSES

Bk —Babcock
Cb —Crabtree
FAU —Faustel
Fin —Fincor
FOL —Flex-O-Line
G —Goss
GE —General Electric
H —Hoe
Ha —Hantscho
HAR —Hoe-Aller
HI —Heidleberg-Harris
KB —Koenig & Bauer
KP —King Press
MAN —MAN/Roland USA
MHI —Mitsubishi Heavy Industries
MOT —Motter
SC —Scott
SLN —Solna
TKS —Tokyo Kikai Seisakusho
Tp —Thatcher-Pacer
Wd —Wood
WPC —Web Press Corp.

PRESS CONVERSION SYSTEMS

KDS —Kidder Stacy
KFM —K&F Printing Systems International
PEC —Publishers Equip. Corp.
PMC —Press Machinery Corp.
RKW —Rockwell
RPM —Smith RPM Co.

REPROPORTIONING SYSTEMS

CS —Combined Services
FLS —Flurographic Services

MAILROOM

STACKERS

BG —Baldwin-Gegenheimer
CH —Cutler-Hammer
DG —Didde Glaser
Fg —Ferag
HI —Heidelberg-Harris
HL —Hall
Id —IDAB
KAN —Kansa
MM —Muller-Martini
MRS —Mailroom Systems
NJP —Nolan Jampol
PPK —Pace Pack
QWI —Quipp
RKW —Rockwell
SH —Sta-Hi
St —Stepper

INSERTERS/STUFFERS

D —Dexter
DG —Didde Glaser
Fg —Ferag
G —Goss
Gr —Graphicart
HI —Harris
I —Insertomatic
KAN —Kansa
KR —Kirk-Rudy
LEG —Leger Inc.
M —Mergenthaler
Mc —McCain
Mg —Magnacratt
MM —Muller-Martini
S —Sheridan
SH —Sta-Hi
St —Stepper

BUNDLE TYERS

AMP —Ampag
Bu —Bunn
Ca —Carlson
Cn —Cranston
Cr —Crawford
CYP —Cypack
Eb —Ebby
Gd —Gerrard
Gs —General Strapping
HL —Hall
Id —IDAB
In —Inland
It —Interlake
J —Jampol
Mc —McCain
Md —MidStates
MLN —Signode
MM —Muller-Martini
MVP —Metaveppa
NJP —Nolan Jampol
OVL —Ovalstrapping
PM —Paper Man
QWI —Quipp
S —Sheridan
Sa —Saxmayer
SHt —SatoHit
Si —Parker-Signode
St —Stepper
Ty —Tyler
Us —USSteel
Ws —Walla Star
WT —Wire-Tyer

ADDRESSERS

Am —Addressograph-Multigraph
AVY —Avery
BH —Bell & Howell
Ch —Cheshire
Dm —Dick Mailer
El —Elliott
Gd —Gerrard
GL —Galley List
Gp —Graphotype
Hw —Honeywell
IBM —International Business Machines
KAN —Kansa
KR —Kirk-Rudy
Mg —Magnacraft
Pa —Pollard-Alling
PB —Pitney-Bowes
Rp —Roto-Strip Printer
RSK —Radio Shack
SC —Scriptomatic
Sp —Speedomat
SRC —Standard Register Co.
St —Stepper
Wm —Wing Mailer

DELIVERY SYSTEMS

CBM —Custom Built Machinery
EDS —EDS-IDAB
Fg —Ferag
FMC —FMC Corp.
KAN —Kansa
RKW —Rockwell
SIH —SI Handling

LIBRARY SYSTEMS

AT —Atex
ATT —AT&T
BH —Bell & Howell
CCC —Capital Cities Communications
DDC —Documaster
DEC —Digital Equipment
GE —General Electric
IBM —International Business Machines
IFK —Info-Ky
IXA —Infotex Assoc.
LIP —Logicon-Intercomp
MED —Mead
QLS —QL Systems
SII —System Integrators Inc.
SMS —Stauffer Media Systems

COMMUNICATIONS

FACSIMILE EQUIPMENT

ABD —AB Dick
Ao —Apeco
AP —Associated Press
ATT —AT&T
CD —Crosfield Digital Systems
CP —Canadian Press
DF —Data Fax
Dm —Daycom
ECM —EOCOM
Hel —Hell
Ho —Hogan
IBM —International Business Machines
III —Information International Inc.
LI —Litcom
Mag —Magnavox
Mh —Muirhead
Px —Pressfax
Q —Quickfax
QWI —Quipp
Rem —Remington
SN —Scanatron
SW —Stewart Warner
Uf —Unifax
UPI —United Press International
VI —Vistatype
Wr —Warwick
Wx —Westrex
X —Xerox

DATA COMMUNICATIONS

AMS —American Satellite
DTG —Datalog
EPT —Epic Technology
GAN —Gandalf Data
Mot —Motorola
XIT —Xitron

BUSINESS COMPUTERS

ALR —Advanced Logic Research
Ap —Apple
AT —Atex
ATT —AT&T
Bs —Burroughs
CJ —Collier-Jackson
DEC —Digital Equipment Corp.
DG —Data General
EKI —Electric Knowledge Inc.
HP —Hewlett Packard
Hw —Honeywell
IBM —International Business Machines
Mac —Macintosh
Mk —Mycro-Tek
NEC —Newspaper Electronics Corp.
PBS —Publishing Business Systems
RSK —Radio Shack
TI —Texas Instruments
Uni —Univac
Wa —Wang

The table of abbreviations is for major equipment manufacturers listed in section I & III. Companies not found in the above list are entered in full.

NEW DAILY NEWSPAPERS, SUSPENSIONS, CONVERSIONS, MERGERS

NEW DAILY LISTINGS

Palo Alto (CA) *Daily News* (m-mon to sat) (effective 12/7/95)
Gunnison (CO) *Country Times* (m-tues to sat) (effective 10/29/93)
Telluride (CO) *Daily Planet* (m-mon to fri) (effective 2/93)
Hernando (FL) *Today* (m-mon to sat) **(effective 4/1/96*)**
Lawrenceville (GA) *Gwinnett Daily Post* (m-tues to sat) (effective 7/4/95)
Natchitoches (LA) *Times* (m-tues to fri; S) (effective 7/1/95)
Winnemucca (NV) *Humboldt Sun* (e-mon to fri) (effective 5/2/95)
Laurinburg (NC) *Exchange* (e-mon to fri) (effective 11/1/95)
New York (NY) *Open Air PM* (e-mon to fri; S) **(effective 4/9/96*)**
Pembroke (ON) *Daily News* (e-mon to sat) (effective 12/92)
Grove (OK) *Source* (m-tues to sat) (effective 7/1/95)
Manassas (VA) *Prince William Journal* (m-mon to fri) (effective 9/5/95)

NEW SUNDAY EDITION LISTINGS

Du Quoin (IL) *Evening Call* (e-mon to fri; m-sat; S) (effective 8/25/95)
Harrisburg (IL) *Daily Register* (e-mon to fri; m-sat; S) (effective 7/9/95)
Marshalltown (IA) *Times-Republican* (e-mon to fri; m-sat; S) (effective 7/23/95)
Muscatine (IA) *Journal* (e-mon to fri; m-sat; S) (effective 12/10/95)
Madisonville (KY) *Messenger* (e-tues to sat; S) **(effective 4/2/96*)**
Augusta (ME) *Kennebec Journal* (e-mon to fri; S) (effective 4/2/95)
Waterville (ME) *Central Maine Morning Sentinel* (m-mon to sat; S) (effective 4/2/95)
Branson (MO) *Tri-Lakes Daily News* (m-tues to sat) (effective 5/7/95)
Maryville (MO) *Daily Forum* (e-tues to fri; S) (effective 5/2/95)
Cobleskill (NY) *Daily Editor* (e-mon to fri; S) (reclassification)
Dunkirk (NY) *Evening Observer* (e-mon to sat; S) (effective 5/7/95)
New York (NY) *Post* (e-mon to fri; m-sat; S) **(effective 4/14/96*)**
Henderson (NC) *Daily Dispatch* (m-tues to fri; m-sat; S) (effective 4/2/95)
Wooster (OH) *Daily Record* (e-mon to sat; S) (effective 4/2/95)
Bloomsburg-Berwick (PA) *Press-Enterprise* (m-mon to sat; S) (effective 10/1/95)
Carlisle (PA) *Sentinel* (e-mon to fri; S) **(effective 3/3/96*)**
Hazleton (PA) *Standard-Speaker* (m-mon to sat; S) (effective 6/30/95)
Dyersburg (TN) *State Gazette* (m-tues to sat; S) (effective 10/1/95)
Pecos (TX) *Enterprise* (e-mon to fri; S) (reclassification)

NEW SATURDAY EDITION LISTINGS

Mountain Home (AR) *Daily News* (m-mon to sat) (effective 8/19/95)
Russellville (AR) *Courier* (m-tues to sat; S) (effective 9/1/95)
Tracy (CA) *Press* (e-mon to fri; m-sat) (effective 9/1/95)
Nampa (ID) *Idaho Press-Tribune* (e-mon to fri; m-sat; S) (effective 4/1/95)
Sulphur (LA) *Southwest Daily News* (m-mon to sat; S) (effective 4/24/95)
Laurel (MS) *Leader-Call* (e-mon to sat; S) (effective 11/6/94)
Jefferson City (MO) *Post Tribune* (e-mon to fri; m-sat) (effective 4/93)
Nebraska City (NE) *News-Press* (e-tues to sat) (effective 7/3/95)
Saranac Lake (NY) *Adirondack Daily Enterprise* (e-mon to fri; m-sat) (effective 12/2/95)
New Bern (NC) *Sun Journal* (m-mon to sat; S) (effective 9/1/95)
Beaufort (SC) *Gazette* (m-mon to fri; m-sat; S) (effective 9/2/95)
Hilton Head (SC) *Island Packet* (m-mon to thur; m-fri; m-sat; S) (effective 9/2/95)
Brookings (SD) *Register* (e-mon to fri; m-sat) (effective 5/2/95)
Huron (SD) *Plainsman* (m-tues to sat; S) (effective 3/4/95)
Dyersburg (TN) *State Gazette* (m-tues to sat; S) (effective 10/1/95)
Woodbridge (VA) *Potomac News* (e-mon to fri; m-sat; S) (effective 7/29/95)
Baraboo (WI) *News-Republic/South Central Wisconsin News* (m-mon to sat) (effective 10/14/95)
West Bend (WI) *Daily News* (e-mon to fri; m-sat) (effective 8/26/95)

CEASED DAILY PUBLICATION

Huntsville (AL) *News* (m-mon to fri) (effective 3/15/96*)
Baltimore (MD) *Evening Sun* (e-mon to fri) (effective 9/15/95)
New York (NY) *Newsday* (all day-mon to fri; m-sat; S) (effective 7/16/95)
Charlottetown (PEI) *Evening Patriot* (e-mon to sat) (effective 6/9/95)
Greenville (SC) *Piedmont* (e-mon to fri) (effective 9/29/95)
Houston (TX) *Post* (m-mon to sat; S) (effective 4/18/95)
Tyler (TX) *Courier-Times* (e-mon to fri) (effective 10/31/95)
Norfolk (VA) *Ledger-Star* (e-mon to fri) (effective 8/25/95)

CONVERTED TO ZONED EDITIONS

Alameda (CA) *Times-Star* (m-mon to sat) became a zoned edition of the *Oakland Tribune* (m-mon to sat; S) (effective 7/1/95)
Simi Valley (CA) *Star & Enterprise* (m-mon to sat; S) became a zoned edition of the *Ventura County Star* (m-mon to sat; S) (effective 4/1/95)
Thousand Oaks (CA) *Star & News Chronicle* (m-mon to sat; S) became a zoned edition of the *Ventura County Star* (m-mon to sat; S) (effective 4/1/95)
Valparaiso (IN) *Vidette-Messenger* (e-mon to fri; m-sat; S) became a zoned edition of the *Munster Times* (m-mon to sat; S) (effective 8/1/95)
Shenandoah (PA) *Evening Herald* (e-mon to sat) became a zoned edition of the *Pottsville Republican* (e-mon to sat) (effective 7/31/95)

CEASED SUNDAY PUBLICATION

Mountain Home (AR) *Daily News* (m-mon to sat) (effective 8/19/95)
Olathe (KS) *Daily News* (m-mon to sat) (effective 3/1/95)
Brandon (MB) *Sun* (e-mon to sat) (effective 9/22/95)
Nebraska City (NE) *News-Press* (e-tues to sat) (effective 7/3/95)
Tarboro (NC) *Daily Southerner* (e-tues to fri) (effective 1991)
Cushing (OK) *Daily Citizen* (e-mon to fri) (effective 2/26/95)

Kingsport (TN) *Daily News* (m-tues to fri; wknd) (reclassification)
Baraboo (WI) *News-Republic/South Central Wisconsin News* (m-mon to sat) (effective 10/14/95)

CEASED SATURDAY PUBLICATION

Huntsville (AL) *News* (m-mon to fri) (effective 9/1/95)
El Cajon (CA) *Daily Californian* (e-tues to fri; S) (effective 5/15/95)
South Lake Tahoe (CA) *Tribune* (m-mon to fri) (effective 5/20/95)
Southbridge (MA) *News* (e-mon to fri) (effective 3/94)
Bartlesville (OK) *Examiner-Enterprise* (e-mon to fri; S) (effective 7/30/95)
Pulaski (VA) *Southwest Times* (e-mon to fri; S) (effective 6/94)

MERGERS

Lake Havasu (AZ) *Daily Herald* (m-tues to fri; S) merged with the *Lake Havasu Today's Daily News* (m-tues to fri; S) to form *Today's News-Herald* (m-tues to fri; S) (effective 9/1/95)
Escondido (CA) *Times Advocate* (m-mon to sat; S) merged with the *Oceanside North County Blade-Citizen* (m-mon to sat; S) to form the *Escondido-Oceanside North County Times* (m-mon to sat; S) (effective 12/3/95)
Milford (CT) *Citizen* (e-mon to fri; S) merged with the *New Haven Register* (m-mon to sat; S) (effective 5/26/95)
Beverly (MA) *Times* (e-mon to fri; m-sat) merged with the *Salem Evening News* (e-mon to fri; m-sat; S) (effective 8/21/95)
Peabody (MA) *Times* (e-mon to fri; m-sat) merged with the *Salem Evening News* (e-mon to fri; m-sat; S) (effective 8/21/95)
Menominee (MI) *Herald Leader* (e-mon to sat) merged with the *Marinette (WI) Eagle-Star* to form the *Eagle-Herald* (e-mon to sat) (effective 7/10/95)
Lincoln (NE) *Journal* (e-mon to fri) merged with the *Lincoln Star* (m-mon to fri; S) to form the *Lincoln Journal-Star* (m-mon to fri; S) (effective 8/7/95)
Woodbridge (NJ) *News Tribune* (m-mon to sat; S) merged with the *East Brunswick Home News* (m-mon to sat; S) to form the *Middlesex County Home News & Tribune* (m-mon to sat; S) (effective 10/9/95)
Weirton (WV) *Daily Times* (e-mon to sat) merged with the *Steubenville (OH) Herald-Star* (e-mon to fri; m-sat) (effective 3/94)
Milwaukee (WI) *Sentinel* (m-mon to fri; m-sat; S) merged with the *Milwaukee Journal* (e-mon to fri; m-sat; S) and changed its name to the *Milwaukee Journal Sentinel* (m-mon to sat; S) (effective 4/2/95)

CONVERSIONS/SUSPENSIONS

From Daily To Weekly

Bicknell (IN) *Knox County Daily News* (m-mon to sat) (effective 10/1/95)
Marlboro (MA) *Enterprise-Sun* (e-mon to sat) (effective 9/14/95)
Carrollton (MO) *Democrat* (e-mon to fri) (effective 7/1/95)

From Evening To Morning

Birmingham (AL) *News* (m-mon to fri; S) **(effective 8/5/96*)**
Gadsden (AL) *Times* (m-mon to sat; S) (effective 8/21/95)

Tuscaloosa (AL) *News* (m-mon to sat; S) (effective 10/16/95)
Russellville (AR) *Courier* (m-tues to sat; S) (effective 9/1/95)
Nanaimo (BC) *Daily Free Press* (m-mon to fri) (effective 8/8/95)
Prince George (BC) *Citizen* (m-mon to thur; m-fri; m-sat) (effective 4/1/95)
San Luis Obispo (CA) *Telegram-Tribune* (m-mon to sat) (effective 4/1/95)
San Pedro (CA) *News-Pilot* (m-mon to sat) (effective 9/5/95)
Santa Monica (CA) *Outlook* (m-mon to sat) (effective 9/5/95)
Torrance (CA) *Daily Breeze* (m-mon to sat; S) (effective 9/5/95)
Durango (CO) *Herald* (m-tues to sat; S) (effective 4/4/95)
Winter Haven (FL) *News Chief* (m-mon to sat; S) (effective 10/27/95)
Moline (IL) *Dispatch* (m-mon to sat; S) (effective 9/4/95)
Rock Island (IL) *Argus* (m-mon to sat; S) (effective 9/4/95)
Michigan City (IN) *News Dispatch* (m-mon to fri; m-sat; S) (effective 10/30/95)
Lawrence (KS) *Journal-World* (m-mon to fri; m-sat; S) (effective 8/21/95)
Madisonville (KY) *Messenger* (m-tues to sat; S) **(effective 4/2/96*)**
New Bedford (MA) *Standard Times* (m-mon to fri; m-sat; S) (effective 9/18/95)
Traverse City (MI) *Record-Eagle* (m-mon to sat; S) (effective 4/3/95)
Hannibal (MO) *Courier-Post* (m-mon to sat) (effective 5/1/95)
Bozeman (MT) *Daily Chronicle* (m-mon to fri; S) **(effective 4/1/96*)**
Henderson (NC) *Daily Dispatch* (m-tues to fri; m-sat; S) (effective 4/4/95)
New Bern (NC) *Sun Journal* (m-mon to sat; S) (effective 9/1/95)
Lima (OH) *News* (m-mon to fri; m-sat; S) (effective 7/3/95)
Brantford (ON) *Expositor* (m-mon to sat) (effective 5/15/95)
Hamilton (ON) *Spectator* (m-mon to sat) (effective 10/1/95)
Medford (OR) *Mail Tribune* (m-mon to fri; m-sat; S) (effective 4/3/95)
Sunbury (PA) *Daily Item* (m-mon to sat; S) (effective 7/4/95)
Huron (SD) *Plainsman* (m-tues to sat; S) (effective 5/2/95)
Dyersburg (TN) *State Gazette* (m-tues to sat; S) (effective 10/1/95)
Bremerton (WA) *Sun* (m-mon to fri; S) (effective 5/1/95)

From Morning to Evening

Birmingham (AL) *Post-Herald* (e-mon to fri) **(effective 8/5/96*)**

From All Day To Morning

San Diego (CA) *Union-Tribune* (m-mon to sat) (effective 8/1/94)
San Jose (CA) *Mercury News* (m-mon to fri; m-sat; S) (effective 12/4/95)
Ottawa (ON) *Citizen* (m-mon to fri; m-sat; S) (effective 2/95)
Ottawa (ON) *Le Droit* (m-mon to sat) (reclassification)
Hazleton (PA) *Standard-Speaker* (m-mon to sat; S) (effective 6/30/95)
Providence (RI) *Journal-Bulletin* (m-mon to fri; m-sat; S) (effective 6/5/95)
Kingsport (TN) *Times-News* (m-mon to sat; S) (effective 6/92)
Fort Worth (TX) *Star-Telegram* (m-mon to sat; S) (effective 1/1/95)
San Antonio (TX) *Express-News* (m-mon to thur; m-fri; m-sat; S) (effective 4/28/93)

---

*Bold effective date indicates an anticipated change that is not reflected in the ready reckoner or in the newspaper's listing in the daily newspaper section.

SECTION I

Daily Newspapers Published in the United States

Daily newspapers..1-453
National newspapers..454
Tabloid newspapers 454
Newsprint statistics 454
Newspaper groups under common ownership.........455-465
Special service daily newspapers 466-471

GMA

A straight line to your bottom line with Productivity.

Neil Jackson
Assistant Production Director--Boston Globe

"With more than 20 machines in constant operation at three Globe packaging centers handling both daily and Sunday inserting, we constantly rely upon GMA's advanced technology to address our evolving inserting needs. With advantages like Press-to-Pocket main jacket delivery at press speeds, and the *SLS*2000's ability to run two separate zones simultaneously, GMA's inserting systems offer us a decided edge in accommodating ever-increasing packaging sizes and complexities. We count on GMA to deliver the performance we can count on today and in the 21st century." You can, too.

The SLS2000

Member of the MULLER MARTINI Group

Corporate Headquarters:
2980 Avenue B., Bethlehem, PA 18017
Tel: 610-694-9494 Fax: 610-694-0776

DAILY NEWSPAPERS PUBLISHED IN THE UNITED STATES

ALABAMA

ALEXANDER CITY
Tallapoosa County
'90 U.S. Census- 14,957; E&P '96 Est. 16,289

The Alexander City Outlook
(m-tues to sat)

Alexander City Outlook, 548 Cherokee Rd. (53010); PO Box 999, Alexander City, AL 35011; tel (205) 234-4281; fax (205) 234-6550; e-mail kenneth545@aol.com. Boone Newspapers Inc. group.
Circulation: 5,698(m); 5,698(m-sat); Sworn Oct. 1, 1995.
Price: 25¢(d); 75¢(sat); $7.00/mo; $84.00/yr.
Advertising: Open inch rate $9.89(m); $9.89(m-sat). **Representative:** Landon Associates Inc. **Politics:** Independent. **Established:** 1892.
Not Published: Christmas.
Special Editions: Home Town Business (Jan); Parade (Feb); Spring Fashion (Mar); Bridal Edition (Apr); Wind Creek State Park, Graduation (May); FYI, South Best Kept Secret (July); Back-to-School (Aug); Fall Fashion, Football (Sept); Holiday Cookbook, Gift Guide (Nov); Christmas Greetings (Dec).
Special Weekly Sections: Best Food Day, Automotive, Real Estate, Business (wed); Education (thur); Religion, Lake Martin Fish Wrapper (fri).

GENERAL MANAGEMENT
Publisher	Kenneth Boone

ADVERTISING
Manager	Billy McGhee

CIRCULATION
Manager	Ryan Carter

NEWS EXECUTIVE
Editor	K A Turner

EDITORS AND MANAGERS
Editorial Page Editor	K A Turner
Sports Editor	Lori Dann

PRODUCTION
Manager	Lee Champion

Market Information: TMC.
Mechanical available: Offset; Black and 3 ROP colors; insert accepted — preprinted; page cut-offs — 22¾".
Mechanical specifications: Type page 13" x 21½"; E - 6 cols, 2 1/16", ⅛" between; A - 6 cols, 2 1/16", ⅛" between; C - 9 cols, 2 1/16", ⅛" between.
Commodity consumption: Newsprint 240 short tons; widths 27½", 13¾"; single pages printed 3,696; average pages per issue 12(d); single plates used 2,000.
Equipment: EDITORIAL: Front-end hardware — 7-Ap/Mac; Other equipment — 3-Ap/Mac, 2-Ap/Mac LaserWriter. CLASSIFIED: Front-end hardware — 2-Ap/Mac LaserWriter. PRODUCTION: Typesetters — 2-Ap/Mac LaserWriter; Plate exposures — Nu; Production cameras — CL. PRESSROOM: Line 1 — 5-KP. MAILROOM: Counter stackers — BG/Count-O-Veyor 104A; Bundle tyer — 1-Ca.

ANDALUSIA
Covington County
'90 U.S. Census- 9,269; E&P '96 Est. 8,998

The Andalusia Star News
(m-tues to sat)

Andalusia Star News, 207 Dunson St.; PO Drawer 430, Andalusia, AL 36420-0403; tel (334) 222-2402; fax (334) 222-6597. Boone Newspapers Inc. group.
Circulation: 2,712(m); 2,712(m-sat); Sworn Oct. 16, 1995.
Price: 50¢(d); 50¢(sat); $7.00/mo; $84.00/yr.
Advertising: Open inch rate $6.85(m); $6.85(m-sat).

EXPLANATION OF SYMBOLS AND ABBREVIATIONS FOR U.S. DAILIES

CITY POPULATION, ETC.
Population figures, except where otherwise shown, are from the 1990 U.S. Census. Population estimates for 1996 are provided when available.
ABC definitions follow lines of urban development, trading habit or political boundary. Publishers may report their circulation by **city zone** or **retail trading zone**, or by **newspaper designated market**. These are established with approval of the Audit Bureau of Circulations.
ABC-city zone (ABC-CZ) - Area described as the corporate city center or the target area of circulation.
Newspaper Designated Market (ABC-NDM) - The geographical area which a newspaper considers to be the market it serves. Publisher members have the option of reporting circulation according to just the new NDM or in combination with a City Zone and/or Retail Trading Zone figure.
HH - Households.

NEWSPAPER PUBLICATION AND CIRCULATION
(d) - daily
(m) - morning
(e) - evening
(S) - Sunday
(all day) - several editions published through the day.

CIRCULATION
Figures preceded by "ABC" indicate net paid (excluding bulk) circulation from ABC publisher's statement for period ending Sept. 30, 1995, unless otherwise noted.

All other figures are from newspapers' sworn postal statements of Sept. 30, 1995, unless otherwise noted.

ADVERTISING RATES
Maximum rate per inch (open inch rate) for general (national) display advertising is shown where available for each edition of the paper and for combination between editions and other daily papers.

NEWS SERVICES
AP - Associated Press
AFP - Agence France-Presse
CP - Canadian Press
CN - Capitol News Service
CNS - Copley News Service
CQ - Congressional Quarterly Service
CSM - Christian Science Monitor
DF - Data Features
DJ - Dow Jones
GNS - Gannett News Service
HN - Hearst Newspapers
INS - Independent Network Systems
KRT - Knight-Ridder Tribune
LAT-WP - Los Angeles Times-Washington Post News Service
NEA - Newspaper Enterprises Association
NNS - Newhouse News Service
NYT - New York Times News Service
ONS - Ottaway News Service
PNS - Pacific News Service
RN - Reuters News Agency
SHNS - Scripps-Howard Newspaper Service
SNS - Sterling News Service
THO - Thomson News Service
TMS - Tribune Media Service
UPI - United Press International

For table of abbreviations of equipment and manufacturer, see front pages.
For information on Standard Advertising Units (SAU), and expanded SAUs, see front pages.

News Service: NEA. **Politics:** Independent. **Established:** 1939.
Not Published: New Year; Christmas.
Special Editions: Chamber Guide (Jan); Progress (Feb); Spring Fashion, Home Improvement (Mar); Baseball (Apr); FYI (July); Football (Aug); Fall Fashion, Home Improvement (Sept).
Special Weekly Sections: Education (tues); Agriculture, Best Food Day (wed); Business/Financial Page (thur); Health Page (fri); Lifestyle, Religion, TV (sat).

CORPORATE OFFICER
President	William T Beckner

GENERAL MANAGEMENT
Publisher	William T Beckner

ADVERTISING
Manager	Ruck Ashworth

CIRCULATION
Director	Bill Weaver
Director-Safety	Karen Chavers

NEWS EXECUTIVE
Managing Editor	Art Culpepper

EDITORS AND MANAGERS
Lifestyle Editor	Melissa Kendrick
Sports Editor	Brad Grice

PRODUCTION
Manager	Ray Miller
Systems Operator	Dan Wilson

Market Information: TMC.
Mechanical available: Offset; Black and 3 ROP colors; insert accepted — preprinted, by request; page cut-offs — 21⅞".
Mechanical specifications: Type page 13" x 21½"; E - 6 cols, 2 1/16", ⅛" between; A - 6 cols, 2 1/16", ⅛" between; C - 9 cols, 1 3/8", ⅛" between.

Commodity consumption: Newsprint 600 short tons; width 27½"; black ink 20,000 pounds; color ink 500 pounds; average pages per issue 12(d); single plates used 7,500.
Equipment: EDITORIAL: Front-end hardware — 6-Ap/Mac Quadra 610, 1-Ap/Mac II si; Front-end software — Microsoft/Word, QuarkXPress; Printers — 2-Ap/Mac LaserWriter 810 Pro, Xante/Accel-a-Writer 8200. CLASSIFIED: Front-end hardware — 1-Ap/Mac Quadra 610, 1-Ap/Mac II si; Front-end software — Baseview/Class Manager Plus; Printers — Ap/Mac LaserWriter 810 Pro, Xante/Accel-a-Writer 8200. DISPLAY: Front-end hardware — 1-Ap/Mac Plus, 1-Ap/Mac II si; Front-end software — QuarkXPress 3.31; Printers — Ap/Mac LaserWriter 810 Pro, Xante/Accel-a-Writer 8200. PRODUCTION: Pagination software — QuarkXPress 3.31; OCR software — Caere/OmniPage Professional 5.0; Typesetters — 2-V/3990; Platemaking systems — Nu/Flip Top; Plate exposures — O-240 seconds; Plate processors — Nat/Universal 33 Subtractive; Scanners — 2-HP/ScanJet IIcx, 1-Lf/Leafscan 35; Production cameras — Horizontal/Clyesdale; Automatic film processors — LE/Lins 25.
PRESSROOM: Line 1 — 10-KP/Newsking single width; Press drives — Cutler-Hammer/Responder Drive; Folders — KP/6; Reels and stands — 6-Stands; Press registration system — Compensators/Lateral Register. MAILROOM: Counter stackers — BG/Count-O-Veyor; Inserters and stuffers — KAN/350; Bundle tyer — Wilton; Addressing machine — 2-Dispensa-Matic/16. BUSINESS COMPUTERS: 2-RSK/Tandy 2500XL, 2-RSK/Tandy 1000; Applications: Lotus/PW; PCs & micros networked.

ANNISTON
Calhoun County
'90 U.S. Census- 26,623; E&P '96 Est. 25,471

The Anniston Star
(e-mon to sat; S)

The Anniston Star, 216 W. 10th St.; PO Box 189, Anniston, AL 36202; tel (205) 236-1551; fax (205) 231-0027. Consolidated Publishing Co. group.
Circulation: 30,152(e); 30,152(e-sat); 30,152(S); Sworn Sept. 30, 1995.
Price: 50¢(d); 50¢(sat); $1.00(S); $10.00/mo; $108.00/yr.
Advertising: Open inch rate $22.00(e); $22.00(e-sat); $22.00(S). **Representative:** Papert Companies.
News Services: AP, NYT. **Established:** 1883.
Advertising not accepted: Alcoholic beverages; vending machine copy.
Special Editions: Vacation; Winston 500 Race; Financial; Football; Holiday Cookbook; Band & Cheerleaders; Bride.
Special Weekly Sections: TV Star (sat); Star Homes (S).
Magazine: USA Weekend (S).

CORPORATE OFFICERS
President	Phillip A Sanguinetti
Vice Pres	H Brandt Ayers
Secretary/Treasurer	Almus J Thornton
Consultant	Ralph W Callahan

GENERAL MANAGEMENT
Publisher	H Brandt Ayers
General Manager	Phillip A Sanguinetti
Manager-Credit	Scott Calhoun
Purchasing Agent	Phillip A Sanguinetti
Business Manager	Roger Sawyer

ADVERTISING
Manager-Retail	Ken Warren
Manager-National	Hershel Victory
Manager-Classified	Patricia Flynt

MARKETING AND PROMOTION
Director-Marketing	Pat Taylor

TELECOMMUNICATIONS
Director-Info Systems	Roger Sawyer

CIRCULATION
Director	John Rose

NEWS EXECUTIVES
Editor	H Brandt Ayers
Editor in Chief	Randolph Murray

EDITORS AND MANAGERS
Action Line Editor	Sue Vondracek
Amusements Editor	Michael Stedham
Automotive Editor	Phil Jenkins
Books Editor	Cody Hall
Business/Finance Editor	Fred Burger
Columnist	George Smith
Editorial Page Editor	Chris Waddle
Education Editor	Judy Johnson
Environmental Editor	Richard Coe
Farm/Agriculture Editor	Elizabeth Pezzullo
Fashion/Style Editor	Lauren Peake
Features Editor	Darryal Ray
Graphics Editor/Art Director	David Bone
Health/Medical Editor	Elizabeth Pezzullo
Living/Lifestyle Editor	Darryal Ray
Metro Editor	Phil Jenkins
National Editor	Basil Penny
News Editor	Basil Penny
Photo Editor	Ken Elkins
Political/Government Editor	Tom Spencer
Radio/Television Editor	Michael Stedham
Religion Editor	Eric Larson
Science/Technology Editor	Phil Jenkins
Sports Editor	Ken Patterson
Travel Editor	Darryal Ray
Wire Editor	Basil Penny
Women's Editor	Darryal Ray

MANAGEMENT INFORMATION SERVICES
Data Processing Manager	Roger Sawyer

PRODUCTION
Superintendent	Albert Heard
Foreman-Composing	Jerry Thornton
Foreman-Pressroom	James Weaks
Foreman-Camera Room	Eddie Knighton

Market Information: Split Run; TMC.
Mechanical available: Offset; Black and 3 ROP colors; insert accepted — preprinted; page cut-offs — 22¾".

Copyright ©1996 by the Editor & Publisher Co.

Mechanical specifications: Type page 13" x 21½"; E - 6 cols, 2 1/16", ⅛" between; A - 6 cols, 2 1/16", ⅛" between; C - 9 cols, 1⅜", 1/16" between.
Commodity consumption: Newsprint 2,566 short tons; widths 27½", 13¾"; black ink 49,042 pounds; color ink 7,440 pounds; single pages printed 11,688; average pages per issue 32(d), 64(S); single plates used 19,400.
Equipment: EDITORIAL: Front-end hardware — Ap/Mac, PC/local area Network; Front-end software — Microsoft/Windows Apple Share; Printers — 2-Ap/Mac LaserWriter; Other equipment — Epson/FX-5000. CLASSIFIED: Front-end hardware — Ap/Mac 9150; Front-end software — Baseview/Classified. PRODUCTION: Pagination software — QPS 3.3, Aldus/PageMaker 5.0; OCR software — Caere/OmniPage; Typesetters — NewGen/1200T, Ap/Mac 630 Pro, LaserMaster/1200 XLO; Plate exposures — 1-Nu/Flip Top FT40LNS, 1-Nu/Flip Top FT40V6UPNS; Plate processors — 1-Nat/A-340; Scanners — HP/ScanJet IIcx; Production cameras — 1-R/480, 1-C/Spartan II; Automatic film processors — 1-LE/2600; Reproportion units — ECR/Autokon; Film transporters — 1-C; Shrink lenses — 1-CK Optical/(19", 7.25%); Color separation equipment (conventional) — 1-C/E-Z Color; Digital color separation equipment — ECR/Autokon, Ap/Mac 7100.
PRESSROOM: Line 1 — 6-G; Folders — 1-G; Reels and stands — 6-Cline. MAILROOM: Inserters and stuffers — 2-M; Bundle tyer — 2-Strapack; Other mailroom equipment — MM/Minuteman. LIBRARY: Electronic — Zyindex/Windows. COMMUNICATIONS: Facsimile — Mita/DC 1824ZS, Savinfax/3620, AP/LeFax 35, 5-RSK/100. WIRE SERVICES: News — AP; Photos — AP; Receiving dishes — AP. BUSINESS COMPUTERS: IBM/AS-400; PCs & main system networked.

ATHENS
Limestone County
'90 U.S. Census- 16,901; **E&P '96 Est.** 19,330
ABC-CZ (90): 16,901 (HH 6,662)

The News Courier (m-tues to fri; S)

The News Courier, 410 W. Green St.; PO Box 670, Athens, AL 35611; tel (205) 232-2720; fax (205) 233-7753. Bryan Newspapers group.
Circulation: 6,899(m); 7,848(S); ABC Sept. 30, 1995.
Price: 35¢(d); $1.00(S); $48.40/yr (local), $74.37/yr (elsewhere).
Advertising: Open inch rate $7.25(m); $7.25(S). **News Service:** AP. **Politics:** Independent. **Established:** 1968.
Advertising not accepted: Beer and Liquor.
Special Editions: Football; Spring Fashion; Cattlemen; Agriculture; Home Improvement; Graduation; Tennessee Valley Old Time Fiddlers Convention; Christmas; Santa's Gift Guide; Senior Citizens; Summer Lecture.
Special Weekly Sections: Food Day, Farm Page (wed); Church Page, TV Log (fri); Business (S).
Magazine: TV Tab (Fri).

CORPORATE OFFICERS
President Robert C Bryan
Secretary/Treasurer Betty Bryan

GENERAL MANAGEMENT
Publisher Robert C Bryan
General Manager Mike Jeffreys
Manager-Office Connie Tucker

ADVERTISING
Director Linda Williams
Director-Classified Paula Blakley

CIRCULATION
Manager Randall Wynn

NEWS EXECUTIVE
Editor Sonny Turner

EDITORS AND MANAGERS
Editorial Page Editor Sonny Turner
Librarian Charlotte Fulton
News Editor Sonny Turner
Political Editor Sonny Turner
Sports Editor Neil Chittam
Women's Editor Traci Smith

Market Information: Zoned editions; TMC.
Mechanical available: Offset; Black and 3 ROP colors; insert accepted — preprinted; page cutoffs — 22¾".
Mechanical specifications: Type page 13" x 21½"; E - 6 cols, 2 1/16", ⅛" between; A - 6 cols, 2 1/16", ⅛" between; C - 6 cols, 2 1/16", ⅛" between.
Commodity consumption: Newsprint 44 short tons; widths 28", 14"; black ink 13,000 pounds; color ink 1,750 pounds; single pages printed 4,784; average pages per issue 24(d), 48(S); single plates used 9,000.
Equipment: EDITORIAL: Front-end hardware — COM/Intrepid; Other equipment — 6-ECR/Autokon. CLASSIFIED: Front-end hardware — COM/Intrepid; Other equipment — COM/4961, COM/2414. DISPLAY: Adv layout systems — 1-Ap/Mac; Printers — 1-Ap/Mac LaserPrinter. PRODUCTION: Typesetters — 3-Ap/Mac. BUSINESS COMPUTERS: PCs & micros networked; PCs & main system networked.

AUBURN
See OPELIKA

BIRMINGHAM
Jefferson County
'90 U.S. Census- 265,968; **E&P '96 Est.** 278,575
ABC-CZ (90): 732,331 (HH 280,738)

Birmingham Post-Herald (m-mon to fri)
Birmingham News/ Birmingham Post-Herald (m-sat)

Birmingham Post-Herald, 2200 4th Ave.; PO Box 2553, Birmingham, AL 35202; tel (205) 325-2222; fax (205) 325-2410; e-mail postherald@aol.com; web site http://www.the-matrix.com/ph/ph.html. Scripps Howard group.
Circulation: 58,239(m); 174,081(m-sat); ABC Sept. 30, 1995.
Price: 35¢(d); 35¢(sat); $67.60/yr (mon to fri).
Advertising: Open inch rate $56.04(m); $102.64(m-sat). **Representative:** Newhouse Newspapers/Metro Suburbia.
News Services: AP, SHNS, NYT. **Politics:** Independent. **Established:** 1870 (Herald), 1921 (Post).
Note: The Birmingham Post-Herald and Birmingham News are corporately and editorially separate. The Birmingham News acts as agent for Birmingham Post Co. in printing, circulating and selling advertising space in Birmingham Post-Herald. The Saturday circulation is combined. The combined advertising rate for the Post-Herald & the News is $102.64(d). Effective Aug. 5, 1996, this publication will become an evening paper.
Special Editions: Home & Garden Show (Mar); Summer Fun (May); Apartment & Condo Living (June); Parade of Homes, Football '96 (Aug); Southern Women's Show, Fall Home Show, New Car Show, Holiday Entertainment (Nov).
Special Weekly Sections: Health & Healing, Sports Monday (mon); Business Tuesday (tues); Your Money (thur); Food Day (wed); Your Town (thur); Best Bets, Kudzu (fri).

CORPORATE OFFICERS
President James H Denley
Treasurer E John Wolfzorn
Secretary D J Castellini

TELECOMMUNICATIONS
Audiotex Manager Tom Bailey

CIRCULATION
Director Robert J Dobson
Asst Director Danny J Griffin

NEWS EXECUTIVES
Editor James H Denley
Managing Editor James D Willis

EDITORS AND MANAGERS
Amusements Editor Tabitha Sparkes
Automotive/Aviation Editor Sheila Pinkley
Business/Finance Editor Sheila Pinkley
Columnist Paul Finebaum
Director-Public Service James E Jones Jr
Editorial Page Editor Karl Seltz
Fashion Editor Tabitha Sparkes
Features Editor Tabitha Sparkes
Films/Theater Editor Kathryn Kemp
Graphics Editor Larry Kasperek
Food Editor Rebecca Taylor
Librarian Kay Melcher
Magazine/Music Editor Mitchell Diggs
Metro Editor Stephen D Bell
Asst Metro Editor-State Roderick O Hicks
Asst Metro Editor Sheila Pinkley
News Editor Calvin Beam Jr
Political Editor Ted Bryant
Radio/Television Editor Mitchell Diggs
Real Estate Editor Sheila Pinkley
Sports Editor Donald Kausler Jr
Washington Correspondent Thomas Hargrove
Women's Editor Tabitha Sparkes

MANAGEMENT INFORMATION SERVICES
Data Processing Manager David Farrell

Market Information: Split Run; TMC; Operate audiotex; Electronic edition.
Mechanical available: Offset; Black and 3 ROP colors; insert accepted — preprinted; page cutoffs — 22¾".
Mechanical specifications: Type page 13" x 21¾"; E - 6 cols, 2 1/16", ⅛" between; A - 6 cols, 2 1/16", ⅛" between; C - 10 cols, 1⅜", 1/16" between.
Commodity consumption: widths 54"; 27", 13½"; average pages per issue 36(d).
Equipment: EDITORIAL: Front-end hardware — 2-CSI/1170, 2-Ap/Mac Plus; Other equipment — 15-CSI/Edit-112, 35-CSI/Edit 90, 3-HI/8000 PLS, 2-HI/8900 PLS, 2-HI/2100 PLS. CLASSIFIED: Front-end hardware — CSI/Sys 2400; Other equipment — 54-CSI/112 B. DISPLAY: Adv layout systems — SCS/Layout 8000; Front-end hardware — HI/XP-21. PRODUCTION: Pagination software — HI/XP-21; Typesetters — 3-AU/APS-6 Imaging Sys; Plate exposures — 1-WL/III, 1-BKY, 1-WL/IV; Plate processors — 2-W/38D; Electronic picture desk — Lf/AP Leaf Picture Desk; Direct-to-plate imaging — 1-LE/480; Scanners — 2-ECR/Autokon 1,000, 1-LE/480, Kk/RSF 20354; Production cameras — 2-C/Spartan III, 1-C/Marathon, 1-C/Mod; Automatic film processors — 2-LE/LD24, 1-LE/LD24A, 1-LE/LD24C, 2-LE/24L, Micro/3; Film transporters — 2-C; Color separation equipment (conventional) — 1-CD/646IE.
PRESSROOM: Line 1 — 21-G/Metroliner; Folders — 4-G/3:2; Pasters — 21-G. MAILROOM: Counter stackers — 7-HL/Monitor, 1-HL/AT, 3-RKW/GPS 3000; Inserters and stuffers — 2-S/72P (on-line), 1-S/48P; Bundle tyer — 8-MLN, 2-Power Strap. LIBRARY: Electronic — Nexis/NewsView. COMMUNICATIONS: Facsimile — 2-3M/Remote-copier 600AA, 1-Panafax/MV1200. WIRE SERVICES: News — AP; Stock tables — AP; Syndicates — AP; Receiving dishes — AP, UPI. BUSINESS COMPUTERS: 1-V/8545-II, 2-DEC/Alpha; PCs & main system networked.

The Birmingham News (e-mon to fri; S)
Birmingham News/ Birmingham Post-Herald (m-sat)

The Birmingham News, 2200 N. 4th Ave.; PO Box 2553, Birmingham, AL 35202; tel (205) 325-2222; fax (205) 325-3244. Advance Publications group.
Circulation: 160,081(e); 174,081(m-sat); 202,925(S); ABC Sept. 30, 1995.
Price: 35¢(d); 35¢(sat); $1.25(S); $2.75/wk (d&S); $11.90/mo (d&S); $142.80/yr (d&S).
Advertising: Open inch rate $77.61(e); $102.64(m-sat); $98.86(S); $176.47(e & S); $201.50(m, e & S). **Representative:** Newhouse Newspapers/Metro Suburbia.
News Services: AP, KRT, NNS, Independent News Service. **Politics:** Independent. **Established:** 1888.
Note: The Birmingham News and Birmingham Post-Herald are corporately and editorially separate. The Birmingham News acts as agent for Birmingham Post Co. in printing, circulating and selling advertising space in Birmingham Post-Herald. The Saturday circulation is combined. The combined advertising rate for the Post-Herald & the News is $102.64 (d). Effective Aug. 5, 1996, this publication will become a morning paper.
Advertising not accepted: X-rated movies; NC-17 movies.
Special Editions: Alabama Business (Jan); UAB Medwise, Southern Bridal Affair (Feb); Spring Home & Garden, Auto/Car Care, Gulf Coast Tab (Mar); Winston 500 Race, Lawn & Garden (Apr); Summer Fun, Bruno's Memorial Golf Classic (May); Expo 50 Plus, Summer Olympics (June); Birmingham Barracudas (Canadian Football), Die Hard 500 Race, Summer Olympics (July); Football '96 (Aug); Fall Gulf Coast Tab, Fall Home Show, Outdoors, Job Fair (Sept); Southern Women's Show, Best of Birmingham (Oct); Auto Show '97, Holiday Entertaining (Nov); Birmingham's 125th Anniv. (Dec).
Special Weekly Section: Punch-TV listing (fri).
Magazine: Parade (S).

CORPORATE OFFICERS
President V H Hanson II
Vice Pres V H Hanson III

GENERAL MANAGEMENT
Publisher V H Hanson II
General Manager V H Hanson III
Treasurer William Flick
Manager-Credit Don Larsen
Director-Human Resources Gail Moore
Manager-Purchasing Ken Williams

ADVERTISING
Director-Sales/Marketing Thomas J Lager
Director Bill Ward
Manager-Retail Roger Nelson
Manager-Classified Carl Bates
Manager-Research/Business Development Robert West
Manager-Service Mike West

CIRCULATION
Director Robert J Dobson
Asst Director Danny J Griffin
Manager-South Zone Jim Craig
Manager-Promotion Graham Kimbrough
Manager-West Zone A D Goode Jr
Manager-Northeast Zone Mark Adair

NEWS EXECUTIVES
Editor James E Jacobson
Exec Editor Tom Scarritt
Managing Editor Carol Nunnelley
Asst Managing Editor John Clark

EDITORS AND MANAGERS
Amusements Editor Terri Troncale
Automotive/Aviation Editor Dean Barber
Books Editor Alec Harvey
Business/Finance Editor Dean Barber
Cartoonist Mark Cullum
City Editor Randy Henderson
Editorial Writer Bob Blalock
Editorial Writer Eddie Lard
Editorial Writer Joey Kennedy
Editorial Page Editor Ron Casey
Education Editor Charles Dean
Farm Editor Frank Sikora
Fashion Editor Ingrid Kindred
Films/Theater Editor Bob Carlton
Food Editor Jo Ellen O'Hara
Garden Editor Elma Bell
Graphics Editor/Art Director Ray Brown
Librarian Ann Hobbs
Lively Arts/Music Editor Alec Harvey
Life/Style Editor Terri Troncale
Health Editor Charles McCauley
Metro Editor Wayne Hester
News Editor John Clark
Photo Chief Tom Self
Political/Government Editor Glenn Stephens
Radio/Television Editor Alec Harvey
Real Estate Editor Dean Barber
Religion Editor Greg Garrison
Science Editor Jeff Hansen
State Editor Glenn Stephens
Sports Editor Tom Arenberg
Sunday Editor Rick Frennea
Travel Editor Garland Reeves
Washington Correspondent Michael Brumas
Wire Editor Russ Tate

MANAGEMENT INFORMATION SERVICES
Data Processing Manager David Ferrell

PRODUCTION
Director-Operations James Payton
Asst Director-Operations Thomas P Grillo
Manager-Composing Lajune Mitchell
Manager-Pressroom Alan Pidcock
Manager-Packing/Distribution Steve Johnson
Manager-Maintenance Jackie Nivens
Manager-Newsprint Alan Pidcock
Manager-Dispatch Pam Yarley

Market Information: Zoned editions; Split Run; TMC.
Mechanical available: Offset; Black and 3 ROP colors; insert accepted — preprinted; page cutoffs — 22¾".
Mechanical specifications: Type page 13" x 21¾"; E - 6 cols, 2 1/16", ⅛" between; A - 6 cols, 2 1/16", ⅛" between; C - 10 cols, 1⅜", 1/16" between.
Commodity consumption: Newsprint 33,500 short tons; widths 54", 27", 13½"; black ink 742,000 pounds; color ink 189,000 pounds; single pages printed 39,000; average pages per issue 58(d), 140(S); single plates used 183,219.
Equipment: EDITORIAL: Front-end hardware — 2-CSI/1170, 2-Ap/Mac Plus, 30-HI/Newsmak-

er; Other equipment — 7-HI/Page Layout Sys, 62-CSI/EDIT-112, 41-CSI/EDIT 90. CLASSIFIED: Front-end hardware — CSI/Sys 2400; Other equipment — 54-CSI/112 B. DISPLAY: Adv layout systems — 4-HI/8900 Display Ad Sys, 6-HI/Workstation, 2-HI/2100. PRODUCTION: Typesetters — 3-AU/APS-6 Imaging Sys; Plate exposures — 2-WL/III, 1-BKY, 1-WL/IV; Plate processors — 2-W/38D; Electronic picture desk — Lf/AP Leaf Picture Desk; Scanners — 2-ECR/Autokon 1000, 1-LE/480, Kk/RSF 2035+; Production cameras — 2-C/Spartan III, 1-C/Marathon, 1-C/Mod L; Automatic film processors — 2-LE/LD24, 1-LE/LD24A, 1-LE/LD24AC, 2-LE/24L, Micro/3; Film transporters — 2-C; Color separation equipment (conventional) — 1-CD/646 IE.
PRESSROOM: Line 1 — 21-G/Metroliner; Folders — 4-G/3:2; Pasters — 21-G; Press control system — G/PAR-PCS. MAILROOM: Counter stackers — 4-HL/Monitor, 3-HL/DUK-Carriers, 1-HL/AT, 3-RKW/GPS 3000; Inserters and stuffers — 2-S/72P(on-line), 1-S/72P; Bundle tyer — 8-MLN, 2-Power Strap. LIBRARY: Electronic — Mead Data Central, Nexis/NewsView. COMMUNICATIONS: Facsimile — 2-3M/Remote-copier 600AA, 1-Panafax/MV1200. WIRE SERVICES: News — AP; Stock tables — AP SelectStox, Grand Central Stocks; Syndicates — AP; Receiving dishes — AP, UPI. BUSINESS COMPUTERS: 1-V/8545-II, Dec/Alpha; Applications: Adv billing, Accts receivable, Payroll; CJAIMS; PCs & main system networked.

CULLMAN
Cullman County
'90 U.S. Census- 13,367; E&P '96 Est. 13,945
ABC-CZ (90): 13,367 (HH 5,620)

The Cullman Times
(m-tues to fri; S)
Cullman Times, 300 Fourth Ave. S.E., Cullman, AL 35055; tel (205) 734-2131; fax (205) 734-7310. Bryan Newspapers group.
Circulation: 10,085(m); 11,139(S); ABC Sept. 30, 1995.
Price: 35¢(d); $1.00(S); $48.40/yr.
Advertising: Open inch rate $8.20(m); $8.20(S); $9.55 (wed-TMC).
News Service: AP. **Politics:** Independent. **Established:** 1901, 1961 (daily).
Special Editions: Progress (Mar); Tax (Apr); Graduation (May); Football (Aug); Fall Fashion (Sept).
Special Weekly Sections: Best Food Day-Farm Page, Entertaining Times (TMC), Lifestyle (wed); Business Page (thur); Church Page, TV Spotlight-School Page (fri).

CORPORATE OFFICERS
President .... Robert Bryan
Vice Pres .... Robert Bryan
Secretary/Treasurer .... Betty Bryan
GENERAL MANAGEMENT
Publisher .... Robert Bryan
ADVERTISING
Director .... Robert A Camp
CIRCULATION
Manager .... Sam Mazzara
NEWS EXECUTIVES
Editor .... David Poynor
News Editor .... Jimmy Simms
EDITORS AND MANAGERS
City Editor .... Lionel Green
Special Sections Editor .... Carrie Alexander
Sports Editor .... Lance Griffin
Women's Editor .... Carla Whitaker
PRODUCTION
Manager .... Kenneth Reese

Market Information: TMC; ADS.
Mechanical available: Offset, Black and 3 ROP colors; insert accepted — preprinted, hi-fi; page cut-offs — 22¾".
Mechanical specifications: Type page 13" x 21½"; E - 6 cols, 2¹⁄₁₆", ⅛" between; A - 6 cols, 2¹⁄₁₆", ⅛" between; C - 8 cols, 1¼", ⅛" between.
Commodity consumption: Newsprint 535 short tons; widths 28", 14"; black ink 15,850 pounds; color ink 2,125 pounds; single pages printed 5,216; average pages per issue 16(d), 32(S); single plates used 11,000.
Equipment: EDITORIAL: Front-end hardware — 7-COM/Intrepid, 3-Ap/Mac. CLASSIFIED: Front-end hardware — 4-Ap/Mac. DISPLAY: Adv layout systems — 4-Ap/Mac. PRODUCTION: Pagination software — QPS; Typesetters — 1-COM/8400, Ap/Mac LaserPrinter Plus; Platemaking systems — 1-Nat/A240; Plate

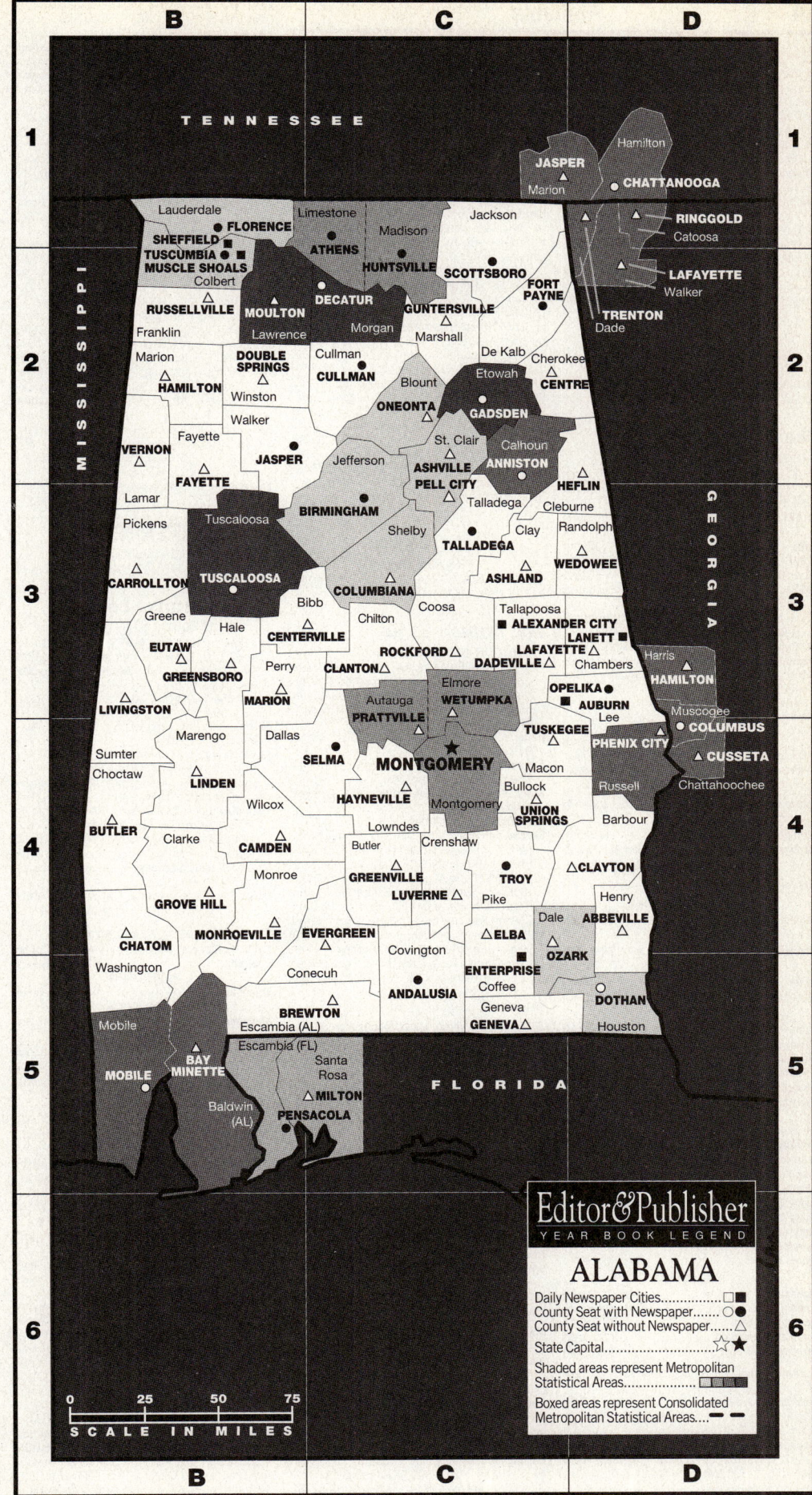

Copyright ©1996 by the Editor & Publisher Co.

I-4 Alabama

exposures — 1-Nu; Plate processors — 1-Nu; Scanners — Ap/Mac II; Production cameras — 1-R, 1-Cl, Kk/Image Maker; Automatic film processors — 1-LE; Color separation equipment (conventional) — 1-BKY, Digi-Colour. PRESSROOM: Line 1 — 10-HI/V-30. MAILROOM: Inserters and stuffers — 1-MM/308 Biliner; Bundle tyer — 1-Bu, 1-Power Strapper; Wrapping singles — 1-St; Addressing machine — 1-Am, 1-KR, 1-KR/4-up head, Prism/Ink Jet. COMMUNICATIONS: Facsimile — 1-AP. WIRE SERVICES: News — AP; Syndicates — AP; Receiving dishes — size-10ft, AP. BUSINESS COMPUTERS: 10-IBM/AS-400; Applications: Accounting, Circ; PCs & micros networked; PCs & main system networked.

DECATUR

Morgan County

'90 U.S. Census- 48,761; E&P '96 Est. 55,768
ABC-CZ (90): 55,794 (HH 21,552)

The Decatur Daily (e-mon to fri; m-sat; S)

The Decatur Daily, 201 1st Ave. S.E.; PO Box 2213-35609, Decatur, AL 35601; tel (205) 353-4612; fax (205) 340-2366.
Circulation: 27,366(e); 29,374(m-sat); 29,445(S); ABC Sept. 30, 1995.
Price: 25¢(d); 25¢(sat); $1.00(S); $9.00/mo; $108.00/yr.
Advertising: Open inch rate $20.30(e); $20.30(m-sat); $21.67(S). **Representative:** Landon Associates Inc.
News Services: AP, NYT. **Politics:** Democrat. **Established:** 1912.
Not Published: Christmas (if it is sat).
Special Weekly Sections: Agriculture (mon); Building Page (tues); Food, Shopping Bag (wed); Church Page, TV Weekly (sat); Business Page (S).
Magazine: USA Weekend (S).

CORPORATE OFFICERS

President Barrett C Shelton Jr
Secretary/Treasurer Georgia T Shelton

GENERAL MANAGEMENT

Controller/Personnel Manager Joe W Perrin

ADVERTISING

Manager Jim Zinn
Manager-Classified Darlene Ziegler

MARKETING AND PROMOTION

Director-Marketing/Sales Don Kincaid

TELECOMMUNICATIONS

Audiotex Manager Clint Shelton

CIRCULATION

Manager John Chapman

NEWS EXECUTIVES

Editor Tom Wright
Managing Editor Doug Mendenhall

EDITORS AND MANAGERS

Automotive Editor Doug Mendenhall
Business Editor Jay Loomis
City Editor Scott Morris
Editorial Page Editor Tom Wright
Education Editor Jan Mendenhall
Entertainment/Amusements Editor Barry H Sublett
Environmental Editor Jay Loomis
Farm/Agriculture Editor R Wright
Features/Travel Editor Barry H Sublett
Graphics Editor/Art Director Cynthia Greene
Health/Medical Editor Ken Retherford
Living Today/Society Editor Barry H Sublett
Photo Department Editor Gary Lloyd
Religion Editor Melanie Smith
Science/Technology Editor Jay Loomis
Sports Editor Bruce McLellan

PRODUCTION

Manager Harold Wright
Foreman-Pressroom Randy Dewberry
Foreman-Camera Judy Counts
Foreman-Composing Don Lovett
Foreman-Mailroom George Dutton

Market Information: Zoned editions; Split Run; TMC; Operate audiotex.
Mechanical available: Offset; Black and 3 ROP colors; insert accepted — preprinted; page cutoffs — $22\frac{3}{4}$".
Mechanical specifications: Type page 13" x $21\frac{1}{2}$"; E - 6 cols, $2\frac{1}{16}$", $\frac{1}{8}$" between; A - 6 cols, $2\frac{1}{16}$", $\frac{1}{8}$" between; C - 10 cols, $1\frac{3}{8}$", $\frac{1}{16}$" between.
Commodity consumption: Newsprint 2,200 short tons; widths $27\frac{1}{2}$", $13\frac{3}{4}$"; black ink 58,000 pounds; color ink 6,000 pounds; single pages printed 12,500; average pages per issue 32(d), 68(S); single plates used 20,000.
Equipment: EDITORIAL: Front-end hardware — 10-Compaq/386, 24-AST/286; Front-end software — Dewar/System III; Other equipment — 2-V/XP 1000, 1-Ultre/4000 imagesetter. CLASSIFIED: Front-end hardware — Dewar/Land Units; Front-end software — Dewar/Sys II; Other equipment — Okidata. AUDIOTEX: Hardware — Brite; Software — Brite; Supplier name — Brite. DISPLAY: Adv layout systems — Dewar; Front-end hardware — 6-Ap/Mac; Front-end software — Dewar, Ap/ Mac; Other equipment — 1-Ultre/4000 imagesetter. PRODUCTION: Typesetters — 2-Tegra/ Varityper XP-1000; Plate exposures — 1-Nu; Plate processors — Nat; Production cameras — SCREEN; Automatic film processors — LE; Color separation equipment (conventional) — BKY; Digital color separation equipment — Lf. PRESSROOM: Line 1 — 7-G/Urbanite. MAILROOM: Counter stackers — Id/EDS; Inserters and stuffers — HI; Bundle tyer — MLN; Addressing machine — KR. WIRE SERVICES: News — AP, NYT; Receiving dishes — size-10ft, AP. BUSINESS COMPUTERS: IBM/Sys 36; Applications: INSI: Circ; PCs & main system networked.

DOTHAN

Houston County

'90 U.S. Census- 53,589; E&P '96 Est. 58,939
ABC-CZ (90): 53,330 (HH 20,595)

The Dothan Eagle (m-mon to sat; S)

Dothan Eagle, 227 N. Oates St.; PO Box 1968, Dothan, AL 36302; tel (334) 792-3141; fax (334) 712-7979. Thomson Newspapers group.
Circulation: 32,385(m); 32,385(m-sat); 36,360(S); ABC Sept. 30, 1995.
Price: 50¢(d); 50¢(sat); $1.25(S); $10.30/mo; $123.60/yr.
Advertising: Open inch rate $18.98(m); $18.98(m-sat); $18.98(S).
News Services: AP, NEA. **Politics:** Independent. **Established:** 1903.
Not Published: Christmas.
Special Editions: Farm; Industry; Brides; Football; Cookbook; National Peanut Festival; Home Improvement; Car Care; College; Football Weekend (Sept-Nov); Golf Section (Spring & Summer); Real Estate Guide, Wire Grass Outdoors (monthly); New Car Section, College Football, Health Section (quarterly).
Special Weekly Sections: Food Section (wed); Health, Parenting, Home & Garden, Wheels (fri); Church Page (sat); Farm Page, Entertainment TV Log, Expanded Business Pages (S); Seniors.
Magazine: Parade (S).

GENERAL MANAGEMENT

Publisher Paul P Seveska
Chief Financial Officer W Roy Aswell

ADVERTISING

Manager-Retail Fred Ellison

MARKETING AND PROMOTION

Manager-Marketing Scott Finch

CIRCULATION

Director Roger Underwood

NEWS EXECUTIVES

Managing Editor Terry Connor
Senior Editor Ramon McPeak

EDITORS AND MANAGERS

Editorial Page Editor Bill Perkins
Focus Editor Mary Abreu-Brown
News Editor Jay Wilson
Sports Editor Jon Johnson

PRODUCTION

Manager-Composing Earl G Hardy
Manager-Pressroom Don Shope

Market Information: Zoned editions; Split Run; TMC; Operate database; Operate audiotex.
Mechanical available: Offset; Black and 3 ROP colors; insert accepted — preprinted; page cutoffs — $22\frac{3}{4}$".
Mechanical specifications: Type page 13" x $21\frac{1}{2}$"; E - 6 cols, $2\frac{1}{16}$", $\frac{3}{16}$" between; A - 6 cols, $2\frac{1}{16}$", $\frac{3}{16}$" between; C - 9 cols, $1\frac{3}{8}$", $\frac{1}{16}$" between.
Commodity consumption: Newsprint 2,100 short tons; widths 27.5", 34"; single pages printed 37,000; average pages per issue 32(d), 68(S).
Equipment: EDITORIAL: Front-end hardware — CText; Printers — V/5300. CLASSIFIED: Front-end hardware — CText; Printers — V/5300. DISPLAY: Adv layout systems — SCS/Layout 8000; Front-end hardware — CText; Printers — V/5300. PRODUCTION: Pagination software — QuarkXPress 3.3; OCR software — Caere/ OmniPage; Typesetters — 2-Tegra/5100, 2-Tegra/5300 Film device; Platemaking systems — 2-Nu/Flip Top FT40UPNS; Plate exposures — 1-Nat/SA250, 1-Subtractive; Electronic picture desk — Lf/AP Leaf Picture Desk, 2-Ap/Mac Quadra 950; Scanners — 2-Umax, 1-Umax/PowerLook; Production cameras — 1-LE/121-V242, 1-R/432; Automatic film processors — 1-LE; Film transporters — 1-LE; Digital color separation equipment — Ap/Mac, Lf. PRESSROOM: Line 1 — 12-G/Urbanite single width (64 page capacity); Press drives — Cleveland. MAILROOM: Counter stackers — 2-Id/2000-4000; Inserters and stuffers — 8-GMA/Station, SLS/1000 (DTP); Bundle tyer — 1-Dynaric/Auto Strapper; Addressing machine — KR/320; Mailroom control system — GMA; Other mailroom equipment — MM/CH4100. LIBRARY: Electronic — Micro-Film. COMMUNICATIONS: Facsimile — 1-Murata, CC Mail, ATT, Toshiba, Canon, Motorola. WIRE SERVICES: News — AP; Photos — AP; Stock tables — AP; Syndicates — UPI, United Media, TMS, LA Times, Creators, King, North America Syndicate, SHNS; Receiving dishes — AP, UPI. BUSINESS COMPUTERS: HP; Applications: Oracle, PBS, ATT, CText, Microsoft/Windows; PCs & main system networked.

ENTERPRISE

Coffee and Dale Counties

'90 U.S. Census- 20,123; E&P '96 Est. 22,407

The Enterprise Ledger (m-tues to fri; S)

The Enterprise Ledger, 106 N. Edwards St.; PO Box 1140, Enterprise, AL 36331; tel (334) 347-9533; fax (334) 347-0825. Thomson Newspapers group.
Circulation: 7,471(m); 10,472(S); Sworn Sept. 30, 1994.
Price: 50¢(d); $1.25(S); $10.30/mo; $123.60/yr (mail).
Advertising: Open inch rate $11.28(m); $11.85(S). **Representatives:** Thomson Newspapers; Papert Companies. **Politics:** Independent. **Established:** 1898.
Special Editions: Brides (Jan); NASCAR Racing (Mar); Fort Rucker Appreciation (Apr); Graduation (May); Progress (June); Women in Business (July); Football (Aug); Cookbook (Oct).
Special Weekly Sections: Food (wed); Automotive, Army Flier (fri).
Magazines: Wednesday TMC; Real Estate (monthly); Apartment Living (quarterly).

GENERAL MANAGEMENT

Publisher/General Manager Mark J Cullen
Controller Kimberly Bell

ADVERTISING

Manager Kelly Speigner

CIRCULATION

Manager Jim Winningham

EDITORS AND MANAGERS

Features Editor Catharine Deon
News Editor Kenneth Tuck
Sports Editor Steve Butterworth

PRODUCTION

Manager Carlton Wallace

Market Information: Zoned editions; Split Run; TMC.
Mechanical available: Offset; Black and 3 ROP colors; insert accepted — preprinted; page cutoffs — $22\frac{3}{4}$".
Mechanical specifications: Type page 13" x $21\frac{1}{2}$"; E - 6 cols, $2\frac{1}{16}$", $\frac{1}{8}$" between; A - 6 cols, $2\frac{1}{16}$", $\frac{1}{8}$" between; C - 9 cols, $1\frac{1}{2}$", $\frac{1}{8}$" between.
Commodity consumption: Newsprint 510 short tons; 70 metric tons; average pages per issue 10(d), 16(S).
Equipment: EDITORIAL: Front-end hardware — Mk/3000, 1-Ap/Mac Centris 610, 1-AG/Arcus Scanner, 1-Nikon/Coolscan, 1-ZyQuest/Power User 88mg; Front-end software — Quark-XPress; Other equipment — Ethernet. CLASSIFIED: Front-end hardware — Mk. PRODUCTION: Pagination software — Adobe/Photoshop; OCR software — Multi-Ad/Creator; Typesetters — 1-Ap/Mac Quadra 630, 1-Ap/Mac IIci, Ap/Mac LaserWriters, V/5100; Production cameras — 1-SCREEN/DT-C240-DST. BUSINESS COMPUTERS: ATT/3B2-500, Oracle; Applications: Lotus, Lotus, WordPerfect: Accounting; PCs & main system networked.

FLORENCE-SHEFFIELD-TUSCUMBIA-MUSCLE SHOALS

Lauderdale and Colbert Counties

'90 U.S. Census- 64,830 (Florence 36,426; Sheffield 10,380; Tuscumbia 8,413; Muscle Shoals 9,611); E&P '96 Est. 65,622 (Florence 37,054; Sheffield 9,970; Tuscumbia 8,162; Muscle Shoals 10,436)
ABC-CZ (90): 64,830 (HH 26,360)

Times Daily (m-mon to sat; S)

Times Daily, 219 W. Tennessee St.; PO Box 797, Florence, AL 35630; tel (205) 766-3434. New York Times Co. group.
Circulation: 33,661(m); 33,661(m-sat); 36,490(S); ABC Sept. 30, 1995.
Price: 50¢(d); 50¢(sat); $1.25(S); $11.25/mo.
Advertising: Open inch rate $30.75(m); $30.75(m-sat); $32.00(S). **Representative:** Landon Associates Inc.
News Service: AP. **Politics:** Independent. **Established:** 1869.
Advertising not accepted: X-rated movies.
Special Editions: Brides Magazine (Jan); Progress (Feb); Home Interiors (Mar); American Home Week (Apr); Graduation, Family-owned Business, Industrial Week (May); Helen Keller Festival (June); Newcomer's Guide (July); W.C. Handy, Football (Aug); Rennaissance Faire (Sept); New Car Section, Senior Citizens (Oct); Holiday Memories (Nov); Christmas Carol Book, NCAA Div. II Championship (Dec).
Special Weekly Sections: Best Food Day (wed); Religion (sat); Valley Life, Business/Agriculture Stock Reports (daily).
Magazines: Parade, TV Week (S).

GENERAL MANAGEMENT

Publisher Frank Helderman
Controller David Caulkins

ADVERTISING

Director Tim Thompson
Manager-Retail Bruce R Davis
Manager-Classified Carole Daniel

TELECOMMUNICATIONS

Audiotex Manager Renita Jimmar

CIRCULATION

Director Aileen Hood

NEWS EXECUTIVES

Exec Editor Kathy Silverberg
Managing Editor Gary Thatcher

EDITORS AND MANAGERS

Amusements/Books Editor Terry Pace
Consumer Interest/Food Editor Teri Thomason
Editorial Page Editor David Palmer
Features Editor Terry Pace
Films/Theater Editor Terry Pace
Graphic Editor Tim Buss
Librarian Valerie Sherer
Music Editor Terry Pace
News Editor Lauren Zuelke
Photo Department Manager Matthew T McKean
Political Editor Mike Goens
Radio/Television Editor Terry Pace
Religion Editor Lucille Prince
Sports Editor Wayne Smith
Teen-Age/Youth Editor Didi Vardaman
Travel Editor Teri Thomason
Women's Editor Teri Thomason

MANAGEMENT INFORMATION SERVICES

Director-ITS/Pre Press Service Arthur P Landry

PRODUCTION

Director Don McGahan
Foreman-Composing Raymond Jeffreys
Foreman-Pressroom Donald Olive

Market Information: TMC; Operate audiotex.
Mechanical available: Offset; Black and 3 ROP colors; insert accepted — preprinted; page cutoffs — $22\frac{3}{4}$".
Mechanical specifications: Type page 13" x $21\frac{1}{2}$"; E - 6 cols, $2\frac{1}{16}$", $\frac{1}{8}$" between; A - 6 cols, $2\frac{1}{16}$", $\frac{1}{8}$" between; C - 9 cols, $1\frac{3}{8}$", $\frac{1}{16}$" between.
Commodity consumption: Newsprint 3,115 short tons; widths 13.5", 27"; black ink 64,000 pounds; color ink 9,000 pounds; single pages printed 12,184; average pages per issue 31(d), 35.3(S); single plates used 24,500.
Equipment: EDITORIAL: Front-end hardware — PC; Front-end software — Dewar. CLASSIFIED: Front-end hardware — PC; Front-end software — Dewar. AUDIOTEX: Hardware — Brite Voice Systems. DISPLAY: Adv layout systems — QuarkXPress; Front-end hardware — Ap/Mac; Printers — VT/1200. PRODUCTION: Typesetters — 1-Tegra/Varityper XM108, V/XP1000, 1-Tegra/Panther Pro, 1-Tegra/Panther Pro/46; Plate exposures — 2-Nu; Plate

processors — 1-Nat; Electronic picture desk — Ap/Mac; Scanners — 1-Umax/UC-200S, 3-Kk/RFS2035, 1-Lf/Leafscan 45, 1-Pixelcraft/8000; Production cameras — 1-C/Spartan III; Automatic film processors — 1-Powermatic/66RA; Color separation equipment (conventional) — 1-C/Color-EZ. PRESSROOM: Line 1 — 8-G/Urbanite; Press drives — 2-Cuttler-Hammer; Reels and stands — 8-Universal. MAILROOM: Counter stackers — 3-Id/2200; Inserters and stuffers — 1-Ha/13/72; Bundle tyer — 2-Power Strap, 6-PSN; Addressing machine — 1-X/Cheshire 515; Other mailroom equipment — 1-MM/Stitcher Trimmer 1528/29. COMMUNICATIONS: Digital ad delivery system — AP AdSend. WIRE SERVICES: News — AP; Photos — AP, ; Stock tables — AP; Receiving dishes — AP. BUSINESS COMPUTERS: 1-IBM/Sys 36, INSI; Applications: INSI: Accts receivable, Circ, Bus, Class; PCs & main system networked.

FORT PAYNE

DeKalb County

'90 U.S. Census- 11,838; E&P '96 Est. 12,454

The Times Journal

(m-tues to sat)

The Times Journal, 811 Greenhill Blvd. N.W.; PO Box 349, Fort Payne, AL 35967; tel (205) 845-2550; fax (205) 845-7459; e-mail bshurett@aol.com. Southern Newspapers Inc. group.

Circulation: 6,711(m); 6,711(m-sat); Sworn Sept. 29, 1994.

Price: 50¢(d); 75¢(sat); $45.00/yr.

Advertising: Open inch rate $7.90(m); $7.90(m-sat). **Politics:** Independent. **Established:** 1878.

Not Published: Thanksgiving; Christmas.

Special Editions: Back-to-School; Salute to High School Bands; Football; Letters to Santa; Progress; June Jam; Basketball; Car Care; Home Owned; National History Week.

Magazines: Senior Lifestyles; DeKalb Homes & Living.

GENERAL MANAGEMENT

Publisher Ben Shurett
Secretary Lissa W Vahldiek

ADVERTISING

Manager Sharon Kyle

CIRCULATION

Manager Larry Anderson

NEWS EXECUTIVES

Editor Ben Shurett
Managing Editor William Bynum

PRODUCTION

Foreman-Composing Sylvia Saferite

Market Information: Zoned editions; TMC.

Mechanical available: Offset; Black and 3 ROP colors; insert accepted — preprinted; page cutoffs — 21½".

Mechanical specifications: Type page 13" x 21½"; E - 6 cols, 2¹⁄₁₆", ⅛" between; A - 6 cols, 2¹⁄₁₆", ⅛" between; C - 6 cols, 2¹⁄₁₆", ⅛" between.

Commodity consumption: Newsprint 250 short tons; width 27½"; black ink 3,600 pounds; color ink 300 pounds; single pages printed 3,600; average pages per issue 16(d); single plates used 2,500.

Equipment: EDITORIAL: Front-end hardware — Mk, Ap/Mac. CLASSIFIED: Front-end hardware — Ap/Mac. DISPLAY: Front-end hardware — Ap/Mac. PRODUCTION: Typesetters — 2-Ap/Mac LaserWriter; Platemaking systems — 1-WL/30A; Plate exposures — 1-Nu; Production cameras — AG/Repromaster/3800; Automatic film processors — 1-P/Pakorol. PRESSROOM: Line 1 — 5-G/Community; Folders — 1-G. MAILROOM: Inserters and stuffers — KAN/320; Addressing machine — 2-Am/1900, 2-El/3101. COMMUNICATIONS: Facsimile — X. WIRE SERVICES: News — AP; Receiving dishes — AP. BUSINESS COMPUTERS: IBM; Applications: Bookkeeping, Billing.

GADSDEN

Etowah County

'90 U.S. Census- 42,523; E&P '96 Est. 41,753

ABC-CZ (90): 70,900 (HH 28,022)

The Gadsden Times

(m-mon to sat; S)

The Gadsden Times, 401 Locust St.; PO Box 188, Gadsden, AL 35999; tel (205) 549-2000; fax (205) 549-2013. New York Times Co. group.

Circulation: 27,626(m); 27,626(m-sat); 29,406(S); ABC Sept. 30, 1995.

Price: 50¢(d); 50¢(sat); $1.25(S); $9.46/mo; $113.52/yr.

Advertising: Open inch rate $25.00(m); $25.00(m-sat); $25.00(S). **Representative:** Landon Associates Inc.

News Services: AP, NYT. **Politics:** Independent. **Established:** 1867.

Note: Effective Aug.21, 1995, this publication changed its publishing plan from (e-mon to fri; m-sat; S) to (m-mon to sat; S)

Special Editions: Football; Graduation; Fashion; County Focus Editions (4); At Home.

Special Weekly Sections: People (mon); Home (tues); Food (wed); Free Times (TMC), Health News, Arts & Entertainment (thur); Religious News (fri); Real Estate (S).

Magazines: TV Week Magazine; Color Comics; Parade.

GENERAL MANAGEMENT

Publisher Roger N Hawkins
Controller Jeff Selsor

ADVERTISING

Director Roger Quinn
Manager-Classified Rita Parrott
Supervisor-Retail Kevin Mathews

CIRCULATION

Director Scot Newcom
Manager-Operations Rufus Manora

NEWS EXECUTIVES

Exec Editor Rusty Starr
Managing Editor Ron Reaves

EDITORS AND MANAGERS

Amusements Editor Leigh Pritchett
Business/Finance Editor Steve Howard
City Editor Randy Johnson
Editorial Page Editor Arthur Shaw
Editorial Writer Arthur Shaw
Fashion/Food Editor Pat Wiggonton
Films/Theater Editor Leigh Pritchett
Garden/Home Furnishings Editor Pat Wiggonton
Music Editor Leigh Pritchett
News Editor Rick Moore
Photo Department Manager Steve Latham
Radio/Television Editor Leigh Pritchett
Real Estate Editor Rick Moore
Religion Editor Sharon Beck
Society Editor Pat Wiggonton
Sports Editor Jimmy Smothers
Travel/Women's Editor Pat Wiggonton

MANAGEMENT INFORMATION SERVICES

Business Systems Manager Richard Davis

PRODUCTION

Director Les Filler
Foreman-Pressroom Bubba Brooks
Foreman-Composing Jay Tysver

Market Information: TMC; Operate audiotex.

Mechanical available: Offset; Black and 3 ROP colors; insert accepted — preprinted; page cutoffs — 22¾".

Mechanical specifications: Type page 13" x 21½"; E - 6 cols, 2¹⁄₁₆", ⅛" between; A - 6 cols, 2¹⁄₁₆", ⅛" between; C - 9 cols, 1¹¹⁄₃₂", ³⁄₃₂" between.

Commodity consumption: Newsprint 2,049 short tons; 1,913 metric tons; widths 27¼", 13⅝", 32½"; black ink 50,500 pounds; color ink 2,500 pounds; single pages printed 10,032; average pages per issue 26(d), 54(S); single plates used 14,000.

Equipment: EDITORIAL: Front-end hardware — Ap/Mac; Front-end software — Baseview; Printers — AU, AG/Accuset. CLASSIFIED: Front-end hardware — Ap/Mac 630; Front-end software — Baseview; Printers — AU, AG/Accuset. AUDIOTEX: Hardware — Brite Voice Systems; Supplier name — Brite Voice Systems. DISPLAY: Adv layout systems — Ap/Mac; Front-end hardware — Ap/Mac Quadra 950; Front-end software — Multi-Ad/Creator 3.6; Printers — AU, AG/Accuset; Other equipment — QMS/Laser Printer 11 x 17. PRODUCTION: Pagination software — QPS 3.31; Typesetters — MAC BASE/AG Accuset; Plate exposures — 2-Nu/Flip Top FT40LNS; Plate processors — 1-Nat/A-340; Electronic picture desk — Ap/Mac; Scanners — Mk/SilverScan, Mk/ScanMaker III, Kk, Nikon/Coolscan; Production cameras — 1-B/24", 1-Goodkin/Vertical; Automatic film processors — 1-LE/LD-20; Shrink lenses — 1-CK Optical; Color separation equipment (conventional) — Ap/Mac, Adobe/Photoshop; Digital color separation equipment — Ap/Mac, Adobe/Photoshop, QPS 3.31. PRESSROOM: Line 1 — 6-G/Urbanite; Folders — 1-G; Reels and stands — 6-G. MAILROOM: Counter stackers — 2-Quipp/200, 1-Quipp/100; Inserters and stuffers — 1-HI/1372; Bundle tyer — 2-Power Strap/PSN6; Addressing machine — 1-PB/730. COMMUNICATIONS: Facsimile — 1-Savin, 2-X. WIRE SERVICES: News — AP, NYT; Stock tables — AP; Receiving dishes — AP. BUSINESS COMPUTERS: IBM/Sys 36; Applications: Adv billing, Accts payable, Accts receivable, Gen ledger, Payroll, Subscriber list, Human resources; PCs & micros networked; PCs & main system networked.

HUNTSVILLE

Madison County

'90 U.S. Census- 159,789; E&P '96 Est. 178,230

ABC-CZ (90): 174,693 (HH 69,025)

Huntsville News (m-mon to fri)

Huntsville News, 2111 W. Clinton Ave.; PO Box 1007, Huntsville, AL 35807; tel (205) 532-4500; fax (205) 532-5530; web site http://www.traveller.com/htimes. Newhouse Newspapers group.

Circulation: 15,087(m); ABC Sept. 30, 1995.

Price: 25¢(d); $5.75/mo; $69.00/yr.

Advertising: Open inch rate $8.34(m). **Representative:** Newhouse Newspapers/Metro Suburbia.

News Services: AP, NYT. **Politics:** Independent. **Established:** 1964.

Note: The Huntsville News (m) has a combination rate of $39.92 with The Huntsville Times (eS). Effective April 1, 1995, this publication ceased publishing its Saturday edition.

Special Editions: Health & Fitness, Bridal, Active Times (Jan); Income Tax Guide, Your Huntsville Board of Realtors, Home & Garden, Auto Leasing, Madison Home Show (Feb); Home Builder/Remodeling, Gulf Coast, Career, Lawn & Garden (Mar); Baseball/Stars Preview, Legal Directory, Design An Ad, American Home Week, Spring Home Show, Nike Alabama Classic, Active Time (Apr); Dental Directory, TABES '96, Golf Guide, Vacation/Summer Fun, Memorial Drive Away (May); Crazy Days, Reader's Choice, Olympic Run, Apartment Guide, 24 Hours (June); Independence Day Drive Away, Active Times, Christmas in July (July); Football, Labor Day Drive Away (Aug); Home & Garden, Gaming Guide, Physicians Directory, Madison Street Festival (Sept); Parade of Homes, All About Madison, Active Times (Oct); Southern Living Cooking School, Holiday Entertaining, Auto Show (Nov); Gift Guide I, Gift Guide II (Last Minute), Letters to Santa, Year End Drive Away, Customer Appreciation (Dec).

Special Weekly Sections: React (tues); Food Pages (wed); Special TV Section, TV Times, Autos (fri); Church Pages (sat).

GENERAL MANAGEMENT

Publisher Robert D Ludwig

ADVERTISING

Director William M Joyner Jr
Manager-Retail Steve Wilson
Manager-Classified Jim Hollenbeck
Manager-Co-op Joe Skipworth
Manager-Services Ron Ragan
Coordinator-General Ken Elmore

MARKETING AND PROMOTION

Manager-Marketing/Promotion Carol Casey

CIRCULATION

Director Carlos R Kirkpatrick

NEWS EXECUTIVE

Editor Lee Woodward

EDITORS AND MANAGERS

Editorial Page Editor David Bowman
Lifestyle Editor Kari Smith
News Editor Bud McLaughlin
Photo Department Manager Jim Taylor
Sports Editor P M Black

Mechanical available: Offset; Black and 3 ROP colors; insert accepted — preprinted; page cutoffs — 21¼".

Mechanical specifications: Type page 13" x 21"; E - 6 cols, 2.03", .17" between; A - 6 cols, 2.03", .17" between; C - 10 cols, 1.23", .14" between.

Commodity consumption: Newsprint 600 short tons; widths 54", 41⅙", 27⅜"; black ink 8,000 pounds; color ink 200 pounds; single pages printed 6,650; average pages per issue 22(d).

Equipment: EDITORIAL: Front-end hardware — Tandem/CLX, 12-PC/286-30, 2-Compaq/386-25; Front-end software — SII/INL System; Printers — Dataproducts/LZR-2600. COMMUNICATIONS: Facsimile — 3-3M/600BB, 4-3M/603BB, 3-3M/856. WIRE SERVICES: News — AP, KRT, LAT-WP, NNS; Photos — AP Laserphoto; Stock tables — AP; Syndicates — AP, KRT, LAT-WP, NNS; Receiving dishes — AP, NNS. BUSINESS COMPUTERS: PCs & micros networked; PCs & main system networked.

The Huntsville Times

(e-mon to fri; m-sat; S)

The Huntsville Times, 2317 S. Memorial Parkway (35801); PO Box 1487 West Station, Huntsville, AL 35807; tel (205) 532-4000; fax (205) 532-4213; web site http://www.traveller.com/htimes. Newhouse Newspapers group.

Circulation: 56,122(e); 67,763(m-sat); 79,723(S); ABC Sept. 30, 1995.

Price: 25¢(d); 25¢(sat); $1.25(S); $10.50/mo (e&S), $6.00/mo (sat/S); $118.20/yr.

Advertising: Open inch rate $35.61(e); $35.61(m-sat); $43.53(S); $51.99 (S & TMC). **Representative:** Newhouse Newspapers/Metro Suburbia.

News Services: AP, LAT-WP, NNS, KRT. **Politics:** Independent. **Established:** 1910.

Note: The Huntsville Times (eS) has a combination rate of $39.92 with the Huntsville News (m).

Special Editions: Health & Fitness, Bridal, Active Times (Jan); Income Tax Guide, Your Huntsville Board of Realtors, Home & Garden Show, President's Day Drive Away, Culture Diversity Section, Auto Leasing, Madison Home Show (Feb); Home Builders/Remodeling, Gulf Coast, Careers, Fashion, Lawn & Garden (Mar); Baseball/Stars Preview, Legal Directory, Design An Ad, American Home Week, Spring Home Show, Nike Alabama Classic, Active Times (Apr); Top Class Event, Dental Directory, TABES '96, Golf Guide, Vacation/Summer Fun, Memorial Day Drive Away, Top 25 (May); Crazy Days, Reader's Choice, Olympic Run, Apartment Guide, 24 Hours (June); Independence Day Drive Away, Active Times, All About Huntsville, Christmas In July (July); Back-to-School, Football, Labor Day Drive Away (Aug); Home and Garden, Gaming Guide, Physician Directory, Madison St. Festival, Big Spring Jam (Sept); Parade of Homes, Fall Fashions, All About Madison, Active Times (Oct); Southern Living Cooking School, Holiday Entertaining, Alabama/Auburn Pre-Game, Alabama/Auburn Post-Game, Auto Show (Nov); Gift Guide, Gift Guide (Last Minute), Letters to Santa, Year End Drive Away, Customer Appreciation (Dec).

Special Weekly Sections: Food Pages (wed); This Week (TMC); Out & About (Thur); Special TV Section (fri); Church Pages, Autos (sat).

Magazines: React (tues); TV Times (fri); Parade (S).

GENERAL MANAGEMENT

Publisher Robert D Ludwig
Controller Kenneth R Faulk
Asst Controller Anita McCain
Asst to Publisher R J (Bob) Ward Jr

ADVERTISING

Director William M Joyner Jr
Manager-Retail Steve Wilson
Manager-Classified Jim Hollenbeck
Manager-Co-op Joe Skipworth
Manager-Services Ron Ragan
Coordinator-General Ken Elmore

MARKETING AND PROMOTION

Manager-Promotion/Research Carol Casey

TELECOMMUNICATIONS

Manager Dale Dayton
Audiotex Manager Cooper Green

CIRCULATION

Director Carlos R Kirkpatrick

NEWS EXECUTIVES

Editor Joe Distelheim
Managing Editor Melinda Joiner

EDITORS AND MANAGERS

Business Editor Ray Garner
City Editor David Prather
Editorial Page Editor John Shringer
Entertainment/Leisure Editor Mike Kaylor
Fashion Editor Michael Rich
Food Editor Mickey Ellis
Health Editor Shawn Windsor
Life Editor Michael Rich

I-6 Alabama

News Editor Joel Duncan
Outdoors Editor Alan Clemons
Chief Photographer Mike Mercier
Photographic Editor Rod Whited
Political Editor John Anderson
Regional Editor Mike Hollis
Religion Editor Yvonne White
Exec Sports Editor Chris Welch
Television/Radio Editor Mike Kaylor
Travel Editor Deborah Storey

PRODUCTION

Director Martha Reichold
Manager-Distribution Center Ed Poe
Superintendent-Pressroom James Stolz

Market Information: Split Run; TMC; ADS; Operate audiotex; Electronic edition.
Mechanical available: Offset; Black and 3 ROP colors; insert accepted — preprinted; page cutoffs — 21¼".
Mechanical specifications: Type page 13" x 21"; E - 6 cols, 2.03", .17" between; A - 6 cols, 2.03", .17" between; C - 10 cols, 1.23", .14" between.
Commodity consumption: Newsprint 8,400 short tons; widths 54, 41 1/16"; black ink 175,600 pounds; color ink 66,300 pounds; single pages printed 19,200; average pages per issue 42(d), 119(S); single plates used 46,800.
Equipment: EDITORIAL: Front-end hardware — Tandem/CLX, 54-IBM/286-30, 6-Compaq/386-25; Front-end software — SII/INL Sys, Decade; Printers — HP/III, HP/IV, Compaq/PageMarq 15. CLASSIFIED: Front-end hardware — Tandem/CLX, 12-IBM/286-30; Front-end software — SII/ICP Sys; Printers — Genicom/LW455 Linewriter. AUDIOTEX: Hardware — Market Link; Software — Market Link 5.08; Supplier name — Voice News Network/Tribune Media Service. DISPLAY: Adv layout systems — 3-SII/Layout 8000; Front-end hardware — Ap/Power Mac; Front-end software — MultiAd/Creator, QuarkXPress, Adobe/Illustrator, IAL/System; Printers — HP/LaserJet III; Other equipment — Epson/ESC P2 LQ-1170. PRODUCTION: Pagination software — HI/NewsMaker; Typesetters — 2-AU/APS-6108, 1-IBM/APS 3850; Plate exposures — WL/Lith-X-poser V; Plate processors — WL/Litho Plater; Scanners — 1-ECR/Autokon 1030, ECR/Autokon 1000, CD/6306 Scanner, Scanmate/Scanview 5000; Production cameras — 1-C/Spartan III Run Film, C/Page Camera; Automatic film processors — DP/Chronality 241; Film transporters — C/OL Conveyor Processor.
PRESSROOM: Line 1 — 8-TKS/M-72 Black Units; Line 2 — 4-TKS/M-72 Half Decks Spot Color Unit; Line 3 — 1-TKS/M-72 4 Color Satellite Unit; Line 4 — 1-TKS/M-72 Standalone Black Unit; Reels and stands — 9-TKS/M-72 Reels & Stands; Press control system — TKS/Press Control Station III. MAILROOM: Counter stackers — 4-QWI/200, 1-Id/440; Inserters and stuffers — 2-HI/1372 Inserters; Bundle tyer — 4-Dynaric/Strapper NP-1; Wrapping singles — 4-QWI/Bottom Wrap; Addressing machine — 2-KR/Label Machine. LIBRARY: Electronic — SII. COMMUNICATIONS: Digital ad delivery system — AP AdSend. WIRE SERVICES: News — AP, NNS, LAT-WP, KRT; Stock tables — AP Grand Central Stocks; Syndicates — AP, LAT-WP, NNS, KRT; Receiving dishes — AP, NNS. BUSINESS COMPUTERS: 1-IBM/400-D35; Applications: INSI/OS400: Ad mgmt, Carrier, Billing, TMC management, Circ, Accts receivable, Payroll; PCs & micros networked; PCs & main system networked.

JASPER

Walker County

'90 U.S. Census- 13,553; E&P '96 Est. 15,306
ABC-CZ (90): 13,553 (HH 5,360)

Daily Mountain Eagle

(e-mon to fri; S)

Daily Mountain Eagle, 1301 E. Viking Dr.; PO Box 1469, Jasper, AL 35501; tel (205) 221-2840; fax (205) 221-2421. Cleveland Newspapers Inc. group.
Circulation: 14,130(e); 14,449(S); ABC Sept. 30, 1995.
Price: 35¢(d); 75¢(S); $9.00/mo; $108.00/yr (county carrier).
Advertising: Open inch rate $9.38(e); $9.38(S). **Representative:** Landon Associates Inc.
News Service: AP. **Politics:** Independent. **Established:** 1872.
Not Published: Christmas.
Special Editions: Progress (Feb); Atlanta Braves, Home, Lawn & Garden (Apr); Graduation (May); Home Folks (June); Senior Citizen (July); Football (Aug); Newcomer's Guide (Sept); Women's World (Oct); Gift Guide (Nov); Letters to Santa (Dec).
Magazines: Business & Industrial Review (tues); Best Food (wed); Church Page, TV Guide (fri).

GENERAL MANAGEMENT

Publisher Douglas Pearson
Manager-Credit Judy Henry
Purchasing Agent Douglas Pearson
Manager-Education Service Steve Cox

ADVERTISING

Director Jerry Geddings
Manager-General Douglas Pearson

MARKETING AND PROMOTION

Manager-Promotion Evelyn Samblin

CIRCULATION

Manager Harold Parrish

NEWS EXECUTIVE

Managing Editor Steve Cox

EDITORS AND MANAGERS

Editorial Page Editor Douglas Pearson
Sports Editor Ty Tyra

PRODUCTION

Superintendent Ken Thornton

Market Information: TMC; ADS.
Mechanical available: Offset; Black and 3 ROP colors; insert accepted — preprinted; page cutoffs — 22¾".
Mechanical specifications: Type page 13" x 21½"; E - 6 cols, 2 1/16", ⅛" between; A - 6 cols, 2 1/16", ⅛" between; C - 8 cols, 1⅜", 1/16" between.
Commodity consumption: Newsprint 600 short tons; width 28"; average pages per issue 20(d), 34(S).
Equipment: EDITORIAL: Front-end hardware — Mk; Other equipment — 12-Mk. PRODUCTION: Typesetters — 2-Mk/Ad Touch, 2-Ap/Mac LaserWriter Plus; Plate exposures — 1-Nu/Flip Top FT40LNS; Plate processors — 1-Nat/340; Production cameras — 1-R/Corsair, 1-DAI/5161; Automatic film processors — 1-LE; Shrink lenses — 1-Ck Optical/SQU 7. PRESSROOM: Line 1 — 8-WPC/Web Leader; Line 2 — 3-WPC/Quadcolor; Folders — 2-WPC/2:1. MAILROOM: Counter stackers — 1-BG/Count-O-Veyor; Inserters and stuffers — 4-DG/320; Bundle tyer — 1-Sa; Addressing machine — 1-Ch/730. WIRE SERVICES: News — AP; Receiving dishes — AP. BUSINESS COMPUTERS: PCs & micros networked.

LANETT, AL-WEST POINT, GA

Chambers County, AL/Troup County, GA

'90 U.S. Census- 12,556 (Lanett, AL 8,985; West Point, GA 3,571); E&P '96 Est. 14,306 (Lanett, AL 11,148; West Point, GA 3,158)

The Valley Times-News

(e-mon to fri)

The Valley Times-News, 220 N. 12th St.; PO Box 850, Lanett, AL 36863; tel (334) 644-1101; fax (334) 644-5587.
Circulation: 8,316(e); Sworn Oct. 1, 1994.
Price: 50¢(d); $1.35/wk; $5.40/mo; $64.80/yr.
Advertising: Open inch rate $6.45(e). **Representative:** Landon Associates Inc.
News Service: AP. **Politics:** Independent. **Established:** 1950.
Not Published: Christmas.
Special Editions: Home Improvement; Little League Football; Senior Citizens; Pre-Vacation; Progress, Graduation (June); Spring Fashion; Fall Fashion (Sept); Car Care, Outdoor, Hunting Edition (Oct); Cookbook, After-Thanksgiving (Nov); Christmas Greetings (Dec).

CORPORATE OFFICERS

President Nell D Walls-Cowart
Vice Pres Cy Wood
Secretary/Treasurer Lawton Cowart

GENERAL MANAGEMENT

Publisher Cy Wood

ADVERTISING

Director Bridge Turner

NEWS EXECUTIVE

Managing Editor Cy Wood

PRODUCTION

Foreman-Pressroom Jerry Bryson
Foreman-Engraving Jerry Hudman

Market Information: TMC.
Mechanical available: Offset; Black and 3 ROP colors; insert accepted — preprinted; page cutoffs — 22¾".
Mechanical specifications: Type page 13" x 21½"; E - 6 cols, 2⅛", ¼" between; A - 6 cols, 2⅛", ¼" between; C - 9 cols, 1½", ⅛" between.
Commodity consumption: Newsprint 460 short tons; widths 28", 14"; black ink 1,800 pounds; color ink 300 pounds; single pages printed 5,300; average pages per issue 16(d); single plates used 5,200.
Equipment: EDITORIAL: Front-end hardware — Mk, PC; Front-end software — Mk, Ap/Mac; Printers — 2-COM/308 Laser. CLASSIFIED: Front-end hardware — Mk, PC, Ap/Mac; Front-end software — Mk; Printers — 2-COM/308 Laser. DISPLAY: Front-end hardware — Ap/Mac, COM, PC; Front-end software — Mk, Ap/Mac; Printers — 2-COM/308. PRODUCTION: OCR software — Mk/Spellcheck; Plate exposures — Nu; Plate processors — 2-Nu; Production cameras — Roconex/1-B; Automatic film processors — 1-LE/LD-1800A; Reproportion units — Richo/DS320. PRESSROOM: Line 1 — 6-G/Community; Folders — G/2:1; Pasters — 1-Handmade. MAILROOM: Counter stackers — 1-BG; Bundle tyer — 1-BG. WIRE SERVICES: News — AP; Syndicates — King Features, Universal Press; Receiving dishes — size-10ft, AP. BUSINESS COMPUTERS: 1-RSK/Model III, 1-Bs/B96-40; Applications: Ap/Mac; PCs & micros networked; PCs & main system networked.

MOBILE

Mobile County

'90 U.S. Census- 196,278; E&P '96 Est. 200,953
ABC-CZ (90): 222,687 (HH 85,822)

The Mobile Register

(m-mon to fri)

The Mobile Press

(e-mon to fri)

The Mobile Press Register

(m-sat; S)

The Mobile Press Register, 304 Government St.; PO Box 2488, Mobile, AL 36652; tel (334) 433-1551; fax (334) 439-7118; e-mail mobile.eds@dibbs.com; web site http://www.mobol.com/. Advance Publications group.
Circulation: 70,109(m); 30,173(e); 93,371(m-sat); 117,328(S); ABC Sept. 30, 1995.
Price: 50¢(d); 50¢(sat); $1.00(S); $9.95/mo (d&S), $5.70/mo (m or e); $119.40/yr.
Advertising: Open inch rate $40.60(m); $40.60(e); $56.71(m-sat); $58.30(S); $56.18(m & e). **Representative:** Newhouse Newspapers/Metro Suburbia.
News Services: AP, LAT-WP, KRT, NEW, SHNS, Religious News. **Politics:** Independent. **Established:** 1813 (Register), 1929 (Press).
Special Weekly Sections: Farm Page (mon); Food Pages (e-wed); Food Pages (e-thur); TV Supplement (fri); Church Pages, College Pages (sat); Garden & Building Page, Travel Page, Business, Women's Section (S).
Magazine: Parade (S).

CORPORATE OFFICERS

Chairman of the Board W J Hearin
President W Howard Bronson
Exec Vice Pres/Treasurer Luis M Williams
Secretary Larry Wooley

GENERAL MANAGEMENT

Publisher W Howard Bronson
Director-Human Resources Lee Stringfellow
Director-New Media John Sellers
Comptroller Luis M Williams

ADVERTISING

Director Larry Wooley
Asst Director Chuck Tallman
Manager-Retail Steve Hall
Manager-Classified Eric Yance
Coordinator-National Elizabeth Knowles

CIRCULATION

Director Michael W Evans
Manager Glen Tabor
Manager-City Wayne Boutwell
Manager-Single Copy Matt Monks
Manager-State Randy Watts

NEWS EXECUTIVES

Editor/Vice Pres-News Stan Tiner
Managing Editor Michael Marshall
Asst Managing Editor-Sports John Cameron
Asst Managing Editor Dewey English
Assoc Editor Bailey Thomson

EDITORS AND MANAGERS

Automotive Editor Ron Colquitt
Business/Finance Editor David Tortorano
City Editor Paul Cloos
Education Reporter Martha Simmons
Editorial Page Editor Bailey Thomson
Environmental Reporter Michael Hardy
Farm/Agriculture Editor Charles Croft
Graphics Editor Thom Dudgeon
Government Editor Gene Owens
Health/Medical Reporter J C Zoghby
Librarian Debbie Stearns
Living Editor Kathy Jumper
Asst Living Editor Bill Finch
News Editor Robert Buchanan
Regional News Editor Steve Mitchell
Outdoors Editor Dave Rainer
Photo Editor Dave Hamby
Religion Editor Parker Holmes
Sports Editor John Cameron

MANAGEMENT INFORMATION SERVICES

Data Processing Manager Wayne Reid

PRODUCTION

Director Melvin R Balch
Asst Director Manuel Rodriguez
Superintendent-Pre Press E L Freeman
Manager-Distribution/Mailroom Rickey Doughty
Manager-Pressroom Robert Jones

Market Information: Zoned editions; Split Run; TMC; ADS; Operate database.
Mechanical available: Letterpress (direct); Black and 3 ROP colors; insert accepted — preprinted; page cut-offs — 21½".
Mechanical specifications: Type page 13" x 20¼"; E - 6 cols, 2 1/16", ⅛" between; A - 6 cols, 2 1/16", ⅛" between; C - 10 cols, 1 9/32" between.
Commodity consumption: Newsprint 17,043 short tons; widths 54¾", 41", 13⅝", 27⅜"; black ink 451,913 pounds; color ink 109,937 pounds; single pages printed 39,573; average pages per issue 60(d), 68(sat), 126(S); single plates used 127,400.
Equipment: EDITORIAL: Front-end hardware — SII/Sys 55, HI/XP-21; Front-end software — Tandem/C30 Operating Sys; Printers — Centronics/351. CLASSIFIED: Front-end hardware — SII/Sys 55; Front-end software — Tandem/C30 Operating Sys, Baseview, ICP; Printers — Centronics/351, Printronix/300. DISPLAY: Adv layout systems — HI/2100; Front-end hardware — Ap/Mac Quadra 950; Front-end software — CJ/Advertising Sys; Printers — HP/3567C. PRODUCTION: Pagination software — HI/XP21; Typesetters — 2-AU/APS-6-10-8C, 1-PS/PIP II, 2-AU/APS-6-80, 3-Alpha RIP, 1-AU/3850; Platemaking systems — 1-Na; Plate exposures — 2-Na/Titan, 2-MAS; Plate processors — 1-NP/80, 1-C/120; Electronic picture desk — Lf/AP Leaf Picture Desk; Scanners — 1-ECR/Autokon DE 1000, Sharp, 1-ECR/Autokon 2045C, 1-ScanView/Scanmate 5000; Production cameras — 1-C/News Pager, 1-C/Marathon; Automatic film processors — Konica, LE, C; Film transporters — 2-C; Digital color separation equipment — Lf/Leafscan 35, Lf/Leafscan 45.
PRESSROOM: Line 1 — 12-G/Mark I(4 half decks); Folders — 2-G/2:1; Pasters — 12-G/RTP; Reels and stands — 12-G; Press registration system — KFM, WPC. MAILROOM: Counter stackers — 6-HL/Monitor; Inserters and stuffers — 2-HI/1372P, 1-HI/1472P; Bundle tyer — 4-Dynaric, 6-MLN; Addressing machine — 2-Ch; Other mailroom equipment — 1-MM/335. LIBRARY: Electronic — SII/LASR system. COMMUNICATIONS: Digital ad delivery system — AdSat. WIRE SERVICES: News — AP Datastream, AP Datafeatures, LAT-WP, KRT, NNS; Photos — KRT, AP, NNS; Stock tables — AP Selectstox; Receiving dishes — AP. BUSINESS COMPUTERS: 1-HP/957; PCs & micros networked; PCs & main system networked.

MONTGOMERY

Montgomery County

'90 U.S. Census- 187,106; E&P '96 Est. 201,615
ABC-CZ (90): 187,106 (HH 69,968)

The Montgomery Advertiser

(m-mon to sat; S)

Montgomery Advertiser, 200 Washington Ave. (36104-4270); PO Box 1000, Montgomery, AL 36101-1000; tel (334) 262-1611; fax (334) 261-1579; e-mail 75151.2602@compuserve.com. Gannett Co. Inc. group.

Circulation: 61,169(m); 61,169(m-sat); 75,132(S); ABC Sept. 30, 1995.
Price: 50¢(d); 50¢(sat); $1.25(S); $3.19/wk (m&S); $13.82/mo (m&S), $7.76/mo (fri, sat & S), $9.10/mo (daily only); $155.48/yr.
Advertising: Open inch rate $64.75(m); $71.25(m-fri); $71.25(m-sat); $71.25(S). **Representative:** Landon Associates Inc.
News Services: AP, SHNS, Knight-Ridder. **Politics:** Independent. **Established:** 1829.
Advertising not accepted: Advertising soliciting products for sale via the U.S. mail with product payment in advance.
Special Editions: Brides Book, Fitness, Martin Luther King, Travel Show (Jan); Boat Show Tab, Black History Festival, College Section (Feb); Crime-Proof Tab, Rodeo, Spring Fashion, Lawn & Garden (Mar); Golf, Montgomery on the Move (Apr); Winston 500, Pet Tab, Health Fair, Tri-County Factbook, Jubilee, The Beach (May); Father's Day, Reader's Choice (June); Summer Fun-Travel, Home Electronics (July); Back-to-School, Kids Expo, Football Section (Aug); Fall Bridal, Fall Fashion, Fall Home & Garden, Sleep Section (Sept); Credit Union, Fall Car Care, Top 100 Businesses, Forestry, Textiles (Oct); Holiday Entertaining, Iron Bowl, Old Newsboys (Nov); Gift Guide, Christmas Greetings, Physicians' Directory (Dec); Alabama Outdoors, Health Monthly, Senior Lifestyles (monthly).
Special Weekly Sections: "Ticket" (weekend entertainment) (thur); Religion, Home & Garden (sat).
Magazine: Parade (S).

CORPORATE OFFICERS

President	Richard H Amberg Jr
Vice Pres-Specialty Products	Lamar Smitherman

GENERAL MANAGEMENT

Publisher	Richard H Amberg Jr
Senior Vice Pres-Operations	John Hollenberger
Vice Pres-Business & Administration	Mike Powell
Vice Pres-News	William B Brown
Personnel Director	John Crawford
General Service Manager	John Khoury
Coordinator-Newspapers in Education	Patricia Frazer

ADVERTISING

Vice Pres-Marketing	Leo Pieri
Manager-Classified	Kathy Cowart
Manager-Retail	Rick Schmidt
Manager-National	Milt Livingston
Manager-Client Services	Glen King
Manager-Audiotex	Pam Summers
Manager-Creative Services	Bob Cantrell

MARKETING AND PROMOTION

Manager-Research	Monica Stephens
Manager-Promotion	Emily Marks

TELECOMMUNICATIONS

Audiotex Manager	Pam Summers

CIRCULATION

Manager	Deborah Rogers

NEWS EXECUTIVE

Vice Pres-News	William B Brown

EDITORS AND MANAGERS

Action Line Editor	Jim Earnhardt
Automotive Editor	David Rountree
Book Editor	Jim Earnhardt
Business/Finance Editor	David Rountree
Cartoonist	Jim Palmer
City Editor	John E Hasselwander
Columnist	Bob Ingram
Columnist	Rick Harmon
Education Editor	John E Hasselwander
Entertainment/Amusements Editor	Rick Harmon
Environmental Editor	Steve Ball
Editorial Page Editor	Kenneth Hare
Asst Editorial Page Editor	Jim Earnhardt
Fashion Editor	Lynn Rollings
Graphic Editor/Art Director	John Helton
Librarian	Peggy Ross
Living/Lifestyles Editor	Ginny Smith
Metro Editor	Nancy Dennis
News Editor	Beth Gribble
Photo Manager	Mickey Welsh
Political/Government Editor	Steve Ball
Religion Editor	Tom Harrison
Society/Women's Editor	Chrys Robbins
Sports Editor	Ragan Ingram
State Editor	Earl Thaxton
Television/Film Editor	Rick Harmon
Theater/Music Editor	M P Wilkerson
Travel Editor	M P Wilkerson
Women's Editor	Ginny Smith

MANAGEMENT INFORMATION SERVICES

Data Processing Manager	Bill Reagan

PRODUCTION

Manager-Pre Press	Mike Bugner
Manager-Press	Desmond Hirst
Manager-Post Press	Deborah Rogers
Superintendent-Pressroom	Wayne Powell
Superintendent-Mailroom	Tommy Talley

Market Information: Zoned editions; Split Run; TMC; Operate audiotex.
Mechanical available: Offset; Black and 3 ROP colors; insert accepted — preprinted, samples; page cut-offs — 21½".
Mechanical specifications: Type page 13" x 21½"; E - 6 cols, 2¹⁄₁₆", ⅛" between; A - 6 cols, 2¹⁄₁₆", ⅛" between; C - 10 cols, 1³⁄₁₆", ⅛" between.
Commodity consumption: Newsprint 10,036 short tons; widths 54", 40½", 27"; black ink 165,000 pounds; color ink 45,000 pounds; single pages printed 24,500; average pages per issue 52(d), 112(S); single plates used 92,000.
Equipment: EDITORIAL: Front-end hardware — HI/XP-21 Newsmaker; Front-end software — Solaris/Newsmaker 2.3; Printers — Genicom, Okidata, LaserMaster/1800. CLASSIFIED: Front-end hardware — HI/CASH; Front-end software — HI/5.1; Printers — Genicom, Okidata. AUDIOTEX: Hardware — Brite Voice Systems; Software — Brite Voice Systems. DISPLAY: Adv layout systems — Ap/Mac; Front-end hardware — 8-Ap/Mac Quadra 800; Front-end software — Multi-Ad/Creator, QuarkXPress, Adobe/Photostop; Printers — 1-Tektronic/300 I, 1-LaserMaster. PRODUCTION: Pagination software — HI/XP-21, Solaris 2.3; Typesetters — 2-V/Pro Panther 36, 1-V/5300-B; Plate exposures — 1-WL, 2-Nu/Flip Top; Plate processors — 1-WL/38D; Electronic picture desk — Lf/Leafscan 35; Scanners — 2-ECR; Production cameras — 1-C; Automatic film processors — 2-LE/121; Film transporters — 2-LE/121; Digital color separation equipment — ScanView/ScanMate 5000.
PRESSROOM: Line 1 — 9-Cosmo double width; Line 2 — 8-Metroliner; Press drives — Fin; Folders — G/3:2 (144 page); Pasters — G/RTP; Reels and stands — 8-G/3-Arm. MAILROOM: Counter stackers — 3-HL, 2-HL/Monitor Stacker, 1-HL/Dual Carrier; Inserters and stuffers — 1-S/72P; Bundle tyer — 3-Dynaric/NP-2; Wrapping singles — 2-TM/45, Ty-Tech, 1-Bu/Tying Machine; Addressing machine — 4-Dispensa-matic/16" Labelling Dispenser; Other mailroom equipment — MM/321 TV Stitcher-Trimmer. LIBRARY: Electronic — Nexis/Lexis. COMMUNICATIONS: Remote imagesetting — Novell/Lan Rover; Digital ad delivery system — AP AdSend. Systems used — satellite. WIRE SERVICES: News — AP, SHNS, KRT; Photos — AP; Stock tables — AP; Syndicates — AP Datafeatures; Receiving dishes — AP. BUSINESS COMPUTERS: IBM/AS 400 9406-300; Applications: Lotus 1-2-3, Word Perfect, Microsoft/Office Pro; PCs & micros networked; PCs & main system networked.

MUSCLE SHOALS

See FLORENCE

OPELIKA-AUBURN

Lee County

'90 U.S. Census- 55,952 (Opelika 22,122; Auburn 33,830); E&P '96 Est. 62,224 (Opelika 22,907; Auburn 39,317)
ABC-CZ (90): 55,952 (HH 21,692)

Opelika-Auburn News

(m-mon to fri; S)

Opelika-Auburn News, 3505 Pepperell Parkway; PO Drawer 2208, Opelika, AL 36802; tel (334) 749-6271; fax (334) 749-1228. Thomson Newspapers group.
Circulation: 13,068(m); 13,631(S); ABC Sept. 30, 1995.
Price: 35¢(d); $1.00(S); $8.00/mo.
Advertising: Open inch rate $14.22(m); $14.50(S). **Representative:** Thomson Newspapers.
News Service: AP. **Politics:** Independent. **Established:** 1904.
Not Published: New Year; Independence Day; Labor Day; Christmas.
Special Weekly Sections: Business Pages, Dining Guide (tues); Best Food Day, Living Pages, Outdoors Page, Education (wed); Business Pages, Farm Pages (thur); Best Automotive Days, Best Real Estate Days, Church Page, Living Pages, Sports Pages (fri); Best Automotive Days, Best Real Estate Days, Living Pages, Sports Pages, Business Pages (S).
Magazine: Parade (S).

GENERAL MANAGEMENT

Publisher/General Manager	Steve F McPhul
Controller	Robert Delaney

ADVERTISING

Manager	Jack Nolan

CIRCULATION

Manager-Sales	Cheryl Smith
Manager-Distribution	Earl Mitchell

NEWS EXECUTIVE

Editor	Richard Walker

EDITORS AND MANAGERS

Columnist	Perry Ballard
Editorial Page Editor	Kim Chandler
Food Editor	William White
Photo Department Manager	Celine Bufkin
Society Editor	William White
Sports Editor	Perry Ballard

PRODUCTION

Manager-Purchasing	Robert Delaney
Foreman-Composing	Dina Lidestri
Foreman-Pressroom	Tim Maxwell

Market Information: TMC.
Mechanical available: Offset; Black and 3 ROP colors; insert accepted — preprinted; page cut-offs — 22".
Mechanical specifications: Type page 13" x 21½"; E - 6 cols, 2¹⁄₁₆", .14" between; A - 6 cols, 2¹⁄₁₆", .14" between; C - 9 cols, 1⁵⁄₁₆", .14" between.
Commodity consumption: Newsprint 675 short tons; width 27½"; average pages per issue 60(d), 122(S).
Equipment: EDITORIAL: Front-end hardware — Mk, Ap/Mac; Front-end software — Mk, QuarkXPress; Printers — V. CLASSIFIED: Front-end hardware — Mk; Front-end software — Mk. DISPLAY: Front-end hardware — Ap/Mac IIcx; Front-end software — Mk/Mycro-Comp AdWriter; Printers — V. PRODUCTION: Typesetters — V/5300E, V/5100; Plate exposures — 1-Nu; Plate processors — NAT/A-250; Production cameras — AMergraph; Color separation equipment (conventional) — Digi-Colour/Sys.
PRESSROOM: Line 1 — 8-G/Community. MAILROOM: Inserters and stuffers — 4-KAN; Bundle tyer — MLN/Sprint. COMMUNICATIONS: Facsimile — Murata/F30. WIRE SERVICES: News — AP; Stock tables — AP; Syndicates — SHNS; Receiving dishes — size-6ft, AP. BUSINESS COMPUTERS: ATT/382-500; Applications: Unix; PCs & micros networked; PCs & main system networked.

SCOTTSBORO

Jackson County

'90 U.S. Census- 13,786; E&P '96 Est. 13,503

The Daily Sentinel

(m-tues to fri; S)

The Daily Sentinel, 701 Veterans Drive; PO Box 220, Scottsboro, AL 35768; tel (205) 259-1020; fax (205) 259-2709. Southern Newspapers Inc. group.
Circulation: 6,803(m); 7,300(S); Sworn Sept. 30, 1994.
Price: 50¢(d); 75¢(S); $57.00/yr; $14.00/3mo, $28.00/6mo.
Advertising: Open inch rate $6.40(m); $6.40(S). **Politics:** Independent. **Established:** 1887.
Not Published: Christmas.
Special Editions: Home Improvement, Lawn & Garden (Mar); Profiles, Car Care (Apr); Graduation (May); Football, Back-to-School (Aug); Car Care (Oct); Cookbook, Industry (Nov); 8 High School Editions.
Special Weekly Section: TV Guide (fri).

CORPORATE OFFICER

President	Rick Loring

GENERAL MANAGEMENT

Publisher	Rick Loring
Business Manager	Faye McBride

ADVERTISING

Manager-Retail	Michelle Whitehead

CIRCULATION

Manager	Helen Chandler

NEWS EXECUTIVES

Editor	Rick Loring
Managing Editor	Carmen Nann

PRODUCTION

Foreman-Pressroom	Helen Chandler

Market Information: Zoned editions; Split Run; TMC.
Mechanical available: Black and 3 ROP colors; insert accepted — preprinted, cards; page cut-offs — 21½".
Mechanical specifications: Type page 13" x 21½"; E - 6 cols, 2¹⁄₁₆", ⅛" between; A - 6 cols, 2¹⁄₁₆", ⅛" between; C - 9 cols, 1½", ¹⁄₁₆" between.
Commodity consumption: Newsprint 280 short tons; widths 27½", 13¾"; black ink 12,000 pounds; color ink 1,158 pounds; average pages per issue 20(d), 38(S).
Equipment: EDITORIAL: Front-end hardware — Ap/Mac Quadra 610; Front-end software — Microsoft/Word, QuarkXPress; Printers — Ap/Mac LaserWriter Pro 810. CLASSIFIED: Front-end hardware — Ap/Mac Quadra 610; Front-end software — Baseview/Class Plus, Baseview/Fraw. DISPLAY: Front-end hardware — Ap/Mac Quadra 610; Front-end software — Multi-Ad/Creator, QuarkXPress; Printers — Ap/Mac LaserWriter Pro 810. PRODUCTION: Production cameras — C/Marathon; Automatic film processors — 1-Portage.
PRESSROOM: Line 1 — 5-KP; Line 2 — 4-KP/Color King. MAILROOM: Counter stackers — 1-BG/Count-O-Veyor; Inserters and stuffers — 3-KR; Bundle tyer — 1-Strapex; Addressing machine — 1-KR. WIRE SERVICES: News — AP. BUSINESS COMPUTERS: IBM, Packard Bell/Force I.

SELMA

Dallas County

'90 U.S. Census- 23,755; E&P '96 Est. 23,052

The Selma Times-Journal

(m-mon to fri; S)

The Selma Times-Journal, 1018 Water Ave.; PO Box 611, Selma, AL 36701; tel (334) 875-2110; fax (334) 875-5896. Boone Newspapers Inc. group.
Circulation: 8,950(m); 8,950(S); Sworn Sept. 30, 1994.
Price: 50¢(d); $1.00(S); $10.75mo; $129.00yr; $25.50/3mo.
Advertising: Open inch rate $11.75(m); $12.15(S). **Representative:** Landon Associates Inc.
News Service: AP. **Politics:** Independent. **Established:** 1827.
Special Editions: Horizons-Progress Edition (Feb); Battle of Selma (Apr); Graduation Edition (May); FYI-For Your Information (July); Kickoff-Football Edition (Aug); Just Say No (Sept).
Magazine: "Time Out" (TV supplement) (fri).

CORPORATE OFFICERS

President	E Wilson Koeppel
Vice Pres	James B Boone Jr
Vice Pres	Robert C Tanner

GENERAL MANAGEMENT

Publisher	E Wilson Koeppel
Business Manager	Jay Davis

ADVERTISING

Manager	George Turner
Manager-Classified	Marcia Caol

CIRCULATION

Manager	Scott Coleman

NEWS EXECUTIVE

Managing Editor	Chuck Chandler

EDITORS AND MANAGERS

Society Editor	Warren Hinson
Sports Editor	Sean Hudson

PRODUCTION

Manager	Jimmy Ruff
Foreman-Composing	Morris Veach
Foreman-Pressroom	John Johnson
Foreman-Mailroom	Fred Scott

Market Information: Zoned editions; Split Run; TMC.
Mechanical available: Offset; Black and 3 ROP colors; insert accepted — preprinted; page cut-offs — 22¾".
Mechanical specifications: Type page 13" x 21½"; E - 6 cols, 2¹⁄₁₆", ⅛" between; A - 6 cols, 2¹⁄₁₆", ⅛" between; C - 9 cols, 1⅜", ¹⁄₁₆" between.
Commodity consumption: Newsprint 960 short tons; widths 27½", 13¾"; black ink 44,000 pounds; color ink 2,000 pounds; single pages printed 6,226; average pages per issue 16(d), 28(S); single plates used 6,400.
Equipment: EDITORIAL: Front-end hardware — Ap/Mac. CLASSIFIED: Front-end hardware — Ap/Mac; Front-end software — Baseview 1;

I-8 Alabama

Other equipment — Ap/Mac. DISPLAY: Adv layout systems — 4-Ap/Mac. PRODUCTION: Typesetters — 4-Ap/Mac LaserWriter; Plate exposures — 1-B, 1-Nu; Plate processors — 1-Nat; Production cameras — 1-SCREEN; Automatic film processors — 1-LE; Digital color separation equipment — Lf/Leafscan. PRESSROOM: Line 1 — 10-KP. MAILROOM: Counter stackers — 1-BG; Inserters and stuffers — 1-DG/5 stations; Bundle tyer — 1-Bu; Addressing machine — 1-KR. WIRE SERVICES: News — AP; Receiving dishes — AP. BUSINESS COMPUTERS: 2-RSK; Applications: Adv billing, Accts receivable, Gen ledger, Payroll; PCs & micros networked; PCs & main system networked.

SHEFFIELD
See FLORENCE

TALLADEGA
Talladega County

'90 U.S. Census- 18,175; E&P '96 Est. 18,005

The Daily Home
(m-mon to sat)

The Daily Home, 4 Sylacauga Hwy.; PO Box 977, Talladega, AL 35160; tel (205) 362-1000; fax (205) 249-4315. Consolidated Publishing Co. group.

Circulation: 9,019(m); 9,019(m-sat); Sworn Sept. 29, 1995.

Price: 50¢(d); 50¢(sat); $9.50/mo (carrier /mail).

Advertising: Open inch rate $9.75(m); $11.75(m-wed); $9.75(m-sat).

News Service: AP. **Politics:** Independent. **Established:** 1867.

Not Published: Christmas.

Special Editions: Bridal Tab, Update '96 (Jan); Vacation Drawing, Tax Time, Medical Registry (Feb); Home & Garden (Mar); Lakeside Living, Winston 500 (Apr); Graduation Tab, Lakeside Living (May); Senior Citizen, Lakeside Living (June); Diehard 500, Lakeside Living (July); Football, Bands, Cheerleaders, Lakeside Living (Aug); Health & Fitness (Sept); Holiday Cookbook, Adopt-A-Pet Classified Promotion (Oct); Christmas Gift Guide (Nov); Spirit of Christmas (Dec).

Special Weekly Sections: Food Page (wed); Business Page (thur); Religion Page (fri); Lifestyle Section, Television (daily).

CORPORATE OFFICERS

President Phillip A Sanguinetti
Vice Pres H Brandt Ayers
Secretary/Treasurer Almus J Thornton

GENERAL MANAGEMENT

Publisher Edgar L Fowler Jr
Asst General Manager Zell S Copeland

ADVERTISING

Director Pam Wright

CIRCULATION

Manager Rickey Garrett

NEWS EXECUTIVES

Editor Edgar L Fowler Jr
Managing Editor Carol Pappas

EDITORS AND MANAGERS

Editorial Page Editor Edgar L Fowler Jr
News Editor Janice Keith
Photo Editor Bob Crisp
Sports Editor Scott Adamson

MANAGEMENT INFORMATION SERVICES

Data Processing Manager Roger Sawyer

PRODUCTION

Foreman Donald Jones

Market Information: Zoned editions; Split Run; TMC; ADS.

Mechanical available: Offset; Black and 3 ROP colors; insert accepted — preprinted; page cutoffs — 22¾".

Mechanical specifications: Type page 13" x 21½"; E - 6 cols, 2¹⁄₁₆", ⅛" between; A - 6 cols, 2¹⁄₁₆", ⅛" between; C - 9 cols, 1⅜", ¹⁄₁₆" between.

Commodity consumption: Newsprint 720 short tons; widths 27½", 13¾"; black ink 25,320 pounds; color ink 4,480 pounds; single pages printed 5,702; average pages per issue 18(d); single plates used 10,460.

Equipment: EDITORIAL: Front-end hardware — Ap/Mac; Front-end software — Aldus/PageMaker, MicroSoft/Word; Printers — Ap/Mac LaserWriter I; Other equipment — HP/Flatbed Photo Scanner, Polaroid/Film Scanner. CLASSIFIED: Front-end hardware — Ap/Mac; Front-end software — Baseview; Printers — Ap/Mac LaserWriter I. DISPLAY: Front-end hardware — Ap/Mac; Front-end software — Aldus/PageMaker, MicroSoft/Word; Printers — Ap/Mac LaserWriter I. PRODUCTION: Plate exposures — 1-Nu; Plate processors — Sandmar/AP 3000; Production cameras — 1-C/19x23; Automatic film processors — 1-LE; Shrink lenses — CK Optical/SQU-7; Color separation equipment (conventional) — COM. PRESSROOM: Line 1 — 6-G/Community, 2-G/Universal Color Unit; Folders — 1-G; Reels and stands — 2-Roll/Stand. MAILROOM: Counter stackers — 1-BG/106; Inserters and stuffers — 6-DG; Bundle tyer — 1-Ty-Tech/Tyer, 3-Bu; Addressing machine — 1-KR. WIRE SERVICES: News — AP; Receiving dishes — AP. BUSINESS COMPUTERS: IBM; Applications: Circ, Bus.

TROY
Pike County

'90 U.S. Census- 13,051; E&P '96 Est. 13,495

The Messenger (m-tues to fri; S)

The Messenger, 918 S. Brundidge St.; PO Box 727, Troy, AL 36081; tel (334) 566-4270; fax (334) 566-4281. Boone Newspapers Inc. group.

Circulation: 3,605(m); 3,605(S); Sworn Sept. 30, 1995.

Price: 50¢(d); $1.00(S); $6.00/mo; $84.00/yr.

Advertising: Open inch rate $9.00(m); $9.00(S).

News Service: NEA. **Established:** 1866.

Note: For printing information see Andalusia Star News.

Special Editions: Bride; Back-to-School; Troy State University Appreciation; Christmas; Graduation; Progress Report.

Magazine: Bonus (TMC) (wed).

CORPORATE OFFICER

President Rick Reynolds

GENERAL MANAGEMENT

Publisher Rick Reynolds

ADVERTISING

Director Deedie Carter

NEWS EXECUTIVES

Editor Chris Day
Managing Editor Huck Tredwell

EDITOR AND MANAGER

Lifestyle Editor Shellie Phillips

Market Information: Zoned editions; TMC.

Mechanical available: Offset; Black and 3 ROP colors; insert accepted — preprinted.

Mechanical specifications: Type page 13½" x 21½"; E - 6 cols, 2", ¼" between; A - 6 cols, 2", ¼" between; C - 9 cols, 1⁵⁄₁₆", ¼" between.

Commodity consumption: average pages per issue 54(S).

Equipment: EDITORIAL: Front-end hardware — Mk/Newswriter. CLASSIFIED: Front-end hardware — Mk. DISPLAY: Adv layout systems — Ap/Mac IIC, Mk/Newswriter. PRODUCTION: Typesetters — Mk/LaserWriter. BUSINESS COMPUTERS: PCs & main system networked.

TUSCALOOSA
Tuscaloosa County

'90 U.S. Census- 77,759; E&P '96 Est. 81,970

ABC-NDM (90): 150,522 (HH 55,354)

The Tuscaloosa News
(m-mon to sat; S)

The Tuscaloosa News, 2001 Sixth St. (35401); PO Box 20587, Tuscaloosa, AL 35402; tel (205) 345-0505; fax (205) 349-0845. New York Times Co. group.

Circulation: 37,320(m); 37,320(m-sat); 39,827(S); ABC Sept. 30, 1995.

Price: 50¢(d); 50¢(sat); $1.50(S); $11.25/mo (eS), $8.50/mo (wknd); $135.00/yr.

Advertising: Open inch rate $30.50(m); $30.50(m-sat); $31.70(S). **Representative:** Papert Companies.

News Services: AP, NYT. **Politics:** Independent. **Established:** 1818.

Note: Effective Oct. 16, 1995 this publication changed its publishing plan from (e-mon to fri; m-sat; S) to (m-mon to sat; S).

Special Editions: Brides (Jan); Focus (Mail away edition) (Feb); Home Improvement, Spring Fashion (Mar); Health Care, Family-owned Business (Apr); Pride in America, Newcomer's Guide (June); Football (Aug); Back-to-School, Fall Fashion, Welcome Back Students (Sept); Home Furnishings, Family-owned Business (Oct).

Special Weekly Sections: Best Food Day (wed); Church Page (fri); Business & Industrial Page (sat); Real Estate, TV & Video, Women's Section (S); Women's Pages (daily).

Magazine: Parade (S).

GENERAL MANAGEMENT

Publisher Ron Sawyer
Controller Steve Shoemaker

ADVERTISING

Director Robert J Gruber
Manager-Retail Henry Burt
Manager-National Linda Carver
Manager-Classified Newell Allen
Manager-Telemarketing Anne Sims

CIRCULATION

Director Paul Hass Jr

NEWS EXECUTIVE

Exec Editor Donald A Brown

EDITORS AND MANAGERS

Automotive Editor Max Heine
Business Editor Max Heine
Editorial Page Editor Ken Stickney
Editorial Writer Ken Stickney
Education Editor Joan Ladd
Entertainment/Amusements Editor Mark Cobb
Environmental Editor Anna Thibodeaux
Farm Editor Ed Watkins
Graphics Editor/Art Director Scott Rogers
Health/Medical Editor Suzanne Henson
Librarian Rachel Durrett
Metro Editor Ben Windham
News Editor Jonathan Austin
Photo Department Manager Neil Brake
Religion Editor Charlotte Voss
Sports Editor Harold Stout
Television/Film Editor Mark Cobb
Theater/Music Editor Mark Cobb
Travel Editor Suzy Fleming
Women's Editor Suzy Fleming

MANAGEMENT INFORMATION SERVICES

Director-Production Technology George Bailey

PRODUCTION

Director Melvin Hunnicutt
Manager-Mailroom T C Bigham

Market Information: TMC; Operate audiotex.

Mechanical available: Offset; Black and 3 ROP colors; insert accepted — preprinted, any size preprints; page cut-offs — 22¾".

Mechanical specifications: Type page 13" x 21½"; E - 6 cols, 2¹⁄₁₆", ⅛" between; A - 6 cols, 2¹⁄₁₆", ⅛" between; C - 9 cols, 1⅜", ¹⁄₁₆" between.

Commodity consumption: Newsprint 4,300 short tons; widths 27", 13½"; black ink 104,000 pounds; color ink 16,000 pounds; single pages printed 15,438; average pages per issue 44(d), 90(S); single plates used 37,000.

Equipment: EDITORIAL: Front-end hardware — AT/Series 60, 40-AT; Printers — Okidata/321. CLASSIFIED: Front-end hardware — AT/series 60, 13-AT; Front-end software — IAS; Printers — Florida Data/OSP 130. AUDIOTEX: Hardware — Brite Voice Systems. DISPLAY: Adv layout systems — Ap/Mac; Front-end hardware — Ap/Mac; Front-end software — QuarkXPress, Adobe/Photoshop; Printers — QMS, HP/Color; Other equipment — X/Scanner, Kk/Scanner. PRODUCTION: Pagination software — QuarkXPress 33.1; Typesetters — 2-COM/9600, 2-Panther Pro/46 5300W; Plate exposures — 2-Nu/Flip Top FT40LNS, 1-Nu/Flip Top FT52UPNS; Plate processors — Nat/A-340; Electronic picture desk — Lf/AP Leaf Picture Desk; Scanners — 2-Kk/RFS 2035+, 2-X/11x17 Flatbed; Production cameras — 1-C/Spartan III, 1-R; Automatic film processors — 1-C/Powermatic 66F; Shrink lenses — 1-Sou/7; Digital color separation equipment — CD/625E. PRESSROOM: Line 1 — 10-G/Urbanite, 1-G/Urbanite (3 color); Press drives — 2-Fin; Pasters — 8-Ebway/H535000; Press control system — 2-Fin; Press registration system — KFM/Pin System. MAILROOM: Counter stackers — 3-HL/Monitor; Inserters and stuffers — 1-S/10-48P; Bundle tyer — 1-MLN/ML, 1-Power Strap, 1-MLN/MLEE, 1-Dynaric/NP-2; Addressing machine — 1-KR. COMMUNICATIONS: Facsimile — Konica/150. WIRE SERVICES: News — AP, NYT; Photos — AP; Stock tables — AP; Syndicates — NYT; Receiving dishes — AP. BUSINESS COMPUTERS: IBM/Sys 36 DIB; Applications: PCs & main system networked.

TUSCUMBIA
See FLORENCE

ALASKA

ANCHORAGE
Anchorage Borough

'90 U.S. Census- 226,338; E&P '96 Est. 250,319

ABC-CZ (90): 226,338 (HH 82,702)

Anchorage Daily News
(m-mon to sat; S)

Anchorage Daily News, 1001 Northway Dr.; PO Box 149001, Anchorage, AK 99514-9001; tel (907) 257-4200; fax (907) 257-4246; e-mail 74220.2560@compuserve.com; web site http://www.adn.com/. McClatchy Newspapers group.

Circulation: 71,574(m); 82,370(m-fri); 71,574(m-sat); 94,356(S); ABC Sept. 30, 1995.

Price: 50¢(d); 50¢(fri); 50¢(sat); $1.50(S); $11.50/mo; $138.00/yr.

Advertising: Open inch rate $59.70(m); $59.70(m-fri); $59.70(m-sat); $71.65(S). **Representative:** Cresmer, Woodward, O'Mara & Ormsbee.

News Services: AP, NYT, LAT-WP, KRT, RN. **Politics:** Independent. **Established:** 1946.

Special Editions: Bridal, Polar Bear, Boat Show (Jan); Fur Rondy, Valentine's Day, Ava (Feb); Home Show, RV Show, Sportsman Show (Mar); Easter, Shorebird Festival, Visitor's Guide, Mother's Day (Apr); Mother's Day, AK Gardening (May); Outdoors, Graduation, Father's Day, Spring Home Improvement (June); Bear Paw Festival, Hunting Permits (July); Back-to-School, Silver Salmon Derby, AK State Fair (Aug); Here's to the Arts, Home Office Technology (Sept); Fall Home Improvement, Permanent Fund Coupon Book (Oct); Alaskan Guide to Winter, Gift Guide (Nov); Last Minute Gifts (Dec).

Special Weekly Sections: Hometown (mon); Your Health (tues); Food (wed); "8" (entertainment) (fri); At Home (sat); We Alaskans, Forum, TV News (S); Outdoors (S, June to Sept); Travel (S, Oct to May).

Magazine: Parade (S).

GENERAL MANAGEMENT

Publisher Fuller A Cowell
Manager-Human Resources Lou Ann Hennig
Coordinator-Community Relations Jola Morris
Controller Mary Hall
Manager-Credit Jim Donahue

ADVERTISING

Director Dave Kuta
Manager-General Sales Todd Webster

MARKETING AND PROMOTION

Manager-Marketing Marj Campbell

TELECOMMUNICATIONS

Audiotex Coordinator Shari Lacy

CIRCULATION

Director John Oates
Asst Director David Crockett

NEWS EXECUTIVES

Editor Kent Pollock
Managing Editor Patrick Dougherty
Asst Managing Editor Michael Campbell

EDITORS AND MANAGERS

Arts Editor Mike Dunham
Books Editor Mike Dunham
Business Editor Bill White
City Editor Rich Mauer
Columnist Mike Doogan
Community News Editor Linda Billington
Copy Desk Chief Jim Macknicki
Editorial Page Editor Michael J Carey
Education Reporter Rosemary Shinohara
Entertainment Editor Kim Severson
Environmental Reporter Kim Fararo
Fashion/Food Editor Linda Sievers
Films/Theater Editor Linda Billington
Health/Medical Editor Kathleen McCoy
Homes Reporter Donna Freedman
Librarian Sharon Palmisamo
Lifestyle Editor Kathleen McCoy
Magazine Editor George Bryson
Oil Reporter Kim Fararo
Photo Editor Richard Murphy
Political Reporter Stan Jones

Radio/Television Editor	Tammy Rychetnik
Real Estate Editor	Bill White
Religion Editorial Asst	Jane Szabo
Science/Technology Editor	Lew Freedman
Sports Editor	Lew Freedman
Travel Editor	Leon Unruh
Weekend Editor	George Bryson
Wire Editor	Eila Brown
Women's Editor	Kathleen McCoy

MANAGEMENT INFORMATION SERVICES
Data Processing Manager .... Lewis (Sandy) Simpson

PRODUCTION
Director	Ken Carter
Asst Director	Kate Baldwin
Manager-Packaging Center	Jon Pearce
Manager-Machine Maintenance	Reggie Ball
Manager-Commercial Printing	Larry Walker
Manager-Commercial Printing/Sales	Cynthia Puig
Director-Newspaper Systems	Sandy Simpson
Manager-Pressroom	Mike Fuller

Market Information: TMC; ADS; Operate audiotex; Electronic edition.
Mechanical available: Offset; Black and 3 ROP colors; insert accepted — preprinted; page cut-offs — 21¼".
Mechanical specifications: Type page 12" x 21"; E - 6 cols, 1⅞", ³⁄₁₆" between; A - 6 cols, 1⅞", ³⁄₁₆" between; C - 10 cols, 1.28", ⅛" between.
Commodity consumption: Newsprint 10,400 metric tons; widths 26⅞", 40³⁄₈", 54"; black ink 187,000 pounds; color ink 47,424 pounds; single pages printed 24,104; average pages per issue 65(d), 120(S); single plates used 91,400.

Equipment: EDITORIAL: Front-end hardware — 57-SII/Coyote, Ap/Mac 55, Tandem/K100 Himalaya; Front-end software — SII/System 66 D20.3, Ap/Mac 55, Ap/Mac II; Printers — 2-COM/8600; Other equipment — 3-Linotronic/530, 1-Linotronic/PTR 60. CLASSIFIED: Front-end hardware — 15-SII/Coyote VDT, 1-X/Telecopier, Tandem/K100 Himalaya, 15-SII Coyote; Front-end software — SII/System 66 (D20.03); Printers — Linotype-Hell/530. AUDIOTEX: Hardware — Brite Voice Systems. DISPLAY: Adv layout systems — Cascade/Dataflow, Mk/Managing Editor/Ad Layout System; Front-end hardware — Ap/Mac Centris 650; Front-end software — Multi-Ad/Creator, QuarkXPress, Aldus/FreeHand, Adobe/Illustrator, Aldus/PageMaker, Microsoft/Excel, Microsoft/Word, Nisus, Cascade/Dataflow; Printers — Prosetter, 3-Linotronic/RIP. PRODUCTION: Pagination software — QPS, Multi-Ad 3.8; Typesetters — 2-COM/8600, 3-Linotype-Hell/5301, 1-Graphic Enterprises/Prosetter; Plate exposures — W, 2-Douthitt, Nu; Plate processors — W, Nat; Electronic picture desk — Ap/Mac Leaf; Scanners — 2-ECR/Autokon, 1-CD/636, 1-Hel/Topaz; Production cameras — 2-C/Spartan III; Automatic film processors — 2-LE/2600, 1-Konica/665, 1-Konica/T-65; Reproportion units — 2-ECR/Autokon, 1-CD; Film transporters — 2-C/Spartan; Shrink lenses — 2-Allen Bradley; Digital color separation equipment — CD/636, Hel/Topaz. PRESSROOM: Line 1 — 9-G/Headliner offset; Line 2 — 8-G/Community; Line 3 — 4-HL/V-30 Heatset; Press drives — 9-GE/Motors, Fin/Controllers, 2-GE Motor/Fin/Control, 1-GE w/ GE/Controllers; Folders — 2-G/3:2 (144 page); Pasters — 9-G; Reels and stands — 9-G/Reel Stands; Press registration system — ⅛" pin system. MAILROOM: Counter stackers — 8-H; Inserters and stuffers — 1-HI, 1-GMA/S-1000, MM/227 5:1; Bundle tyer — 4-MLN, 2-Power Strap, 2-News/90; Addressing machine — X, Ch/525E; Other mailroom equipment — 1-MM/¼ Folder. 1-MM/4head stitcher trimmer. LIBRARY: Electronic — Dialog, Lexus-Nexus, Datatimes; Combination — Clip files. WIRE SERVICES: News — AP, LAT-WP, NYT, KRT; Photos — AP; Stock tables — AP; Syndicates — NYT, LATS, NAS, TMS, King Features, Creators, WP, Chronicle; Receiving dishes — size-6ft, AP. BUSINESS COMPUTERS: 4-HP/3000; Applications: PC/486, PC/386, PC/286; PCs & micros networked; PCs & main system networked.

FAIRBANKS
Fairbanks North Star Borough
'90 U.S. Census- 30,843; E&P '96 Est. 36,063
ABC-NDM (90): 92,111 (HH 31,350)

Fairbanks Daily News-Miner
(m-mon to sat; S)
Fairbanks Daily News-Miner, 200 N. Cushman St. (99701); PO Box 70710, Fairbanks, AK 99707-0710; tel (907) 456-6661; fax (907) 452-5054. MediaNews Inc. group.

Alaska I-9

Circulation: 17,592(m); 17,592(m-sat); 22,993(S); ABC Sept. 30, 1995.
Price: 50¢(d); 50¢(sat); $1.50(S); $13.00/mo; $147.00/yr.
Advertising: Open inch rate $16.01(m); $16.01(m-sat); $16.01(S). **Representative:** Cresmer, Woodward, O'Mara & Ormsbee.
News Services: AP, NYT. **Politics:** Independent. **Established:** 1903.
Not Published: New Year; Memorial Day; Labor Day; Christmas (unless they fall on a Sunday).
Advertising not accepted: Political ads of a negative nature four days prior to election; Advertisements from outside of Market Area, when like products are advertised within Market Area.
Special Editions: Valentine's Day (Feb); Winter Carnival (Mar); Building (Apr); Visitor's Guide, Midnite Sun (June); Golden Days, Hunting (July); Back-to-School (Aug); Football, Car Care (Sept); Mushing Edition (Oct); Christmas Shopper (Nov); Christmas Greeter (Dec); Northland News (monthly).
Special Weekly Sections: Food (wed); Kaleidoscope (arts & entertainment) (thur); Outdoors (fri).
Magazines: Heartland, Weekender Tab (S).

GENERAL MANAGEMENT
Publisher	Paul J Massey
Director-Finance	Virginia N Farmier
Manager-Credit	Diana Osborne
Purchasing Agent	Duane M Snedden
Manager-Education Service (Newspapers in Education)	Joe Wagner

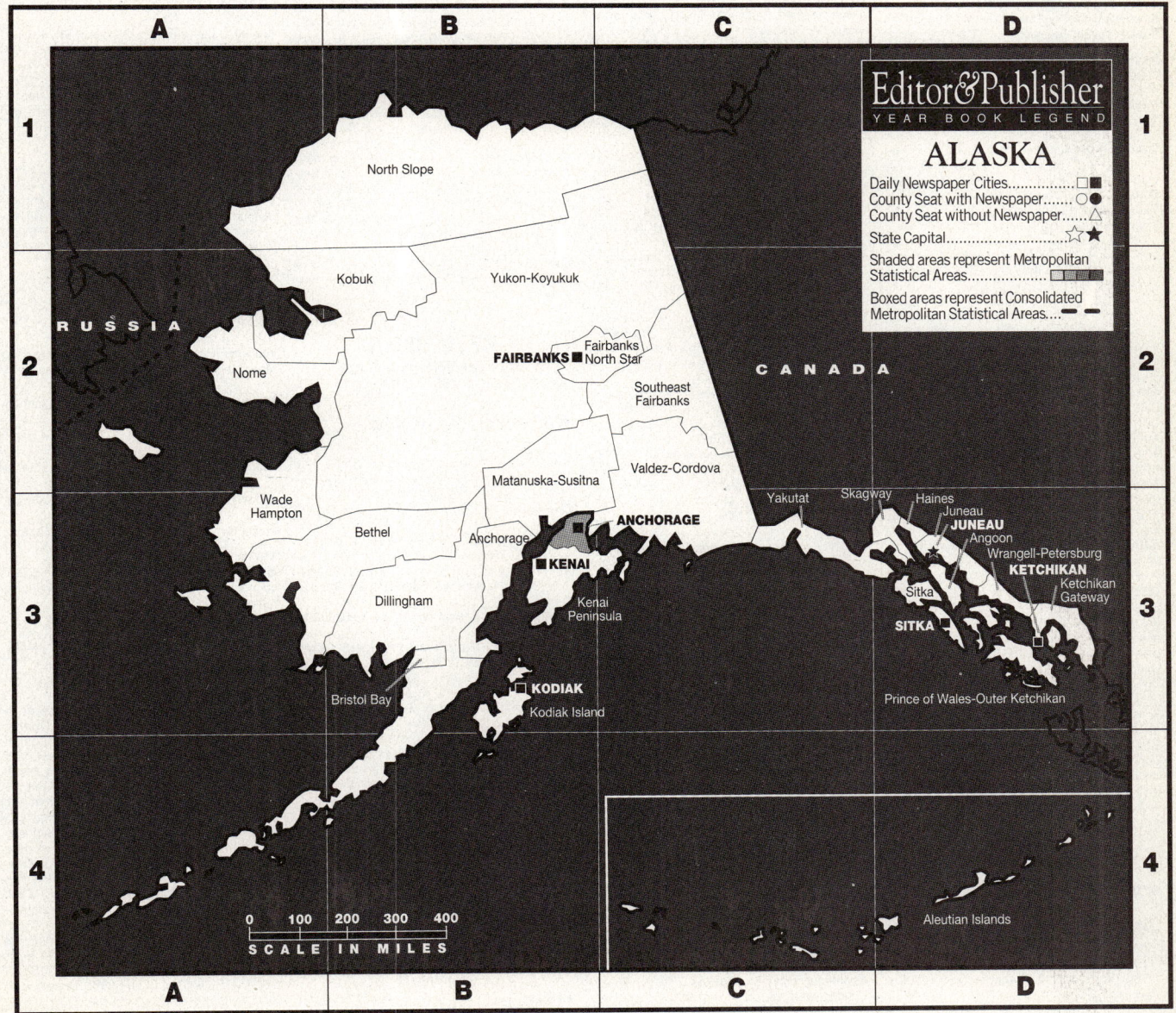

Copyright ©1996 by the Editor & Publisher Co.

ADVERTISING

Director Marilyn Romano
Manager-Retail Louise Satterthwaite
Manager-Promotion Paula Kothe
Manager-Classified Alice Hansen

CIRCULATION

Director Charles Freeman
Manager Dan Foltz

NEWS EXECUTIVE

Editor Kelly Bostian

EDITORS AND MANAGERS

Books Editor Ingrid Martin
Business Editor Patricia Jones
Chief Copy Editor/Weekend Editor Marvin Aronson
Editorial Page Editor Sam Bishop
Editorial Writer Sam Bishop
Education Reporter Wendy Hower
Entertainment/Amusements Editor Ingrid Martin
Features Editor Ingrid Martin
Food Editor Patricia Watts
Graphics Editor Gina Hoppner
Librarian/Northland News Editor/Reporter MaryBeth Smetzer
News Editor Marvin Aronson
Photo Department Manager Mike Mathers
Religion Editor Patricia Watts
Sports Editor Bob Eley
Teen-Age/Youth Editor Carolyn Straub
Travel Editor Marvin Aronson
Wire Editor Marvin Aronson
Women's Editor Carolyn Straub

MANAGEMENT INFORMATION SERVICES

Systems Manager Brian Webster

PRODUCTION

Superintendent-Pressroom Donald Sunderland
Superintendent-Equipment Garth Anderson

Mechanical available: Offset; Black and 3 ROP colors; insert accepted — preprinted; page cut-offs — 22¾".
Mechanical specifications: Type page 12⅞" x 21"; E - 6 cols, 2", ⅛" between; A - 6 cols, 2", ⅛" between; C - 10 cols, 1¼", 1/12" between.
Commodity consumption: Newsprint 1,632 short tons; widths 27¾", 13⅛"; black ink 31,500 pounds; color ink 3,500 pounds; single pages printed 11,472; average pages per issue 30(d), 76(S); single plates used 14,000.
Equipment: EDITORIAL: Front-end hardware — 31-PC/486; Front-end software — HI/PEN System; Printers — Panasonic, 1-Ap/Mac LaserWriter II; Other equipment — 1-Ap/Mac II, 1-Lf/AP Leaf Picture Desk. CLASSIFIED: Front-end hardware — 15-Pentium PC; Front-end software — HI/CASH, Microsoft/Windows 2.0; Printers — 2-Okidata. DISPLAY: Adv layout systems — 2-SCS/Layout 8000, 5-Ap/Power Mac 7100; Front-end hardware — 2-SCS/Layout 8000; Front-end software — Multi-Ad/Creator; Printers — 1-Ap/Mac LaserWriter II. PRODUCTION: Pagination software — HI/XP-21; OCR software — TextBridge; Typesetters — 2-Triple/I 3850; Plate exposures — 1-Nu/Flip Top; Plate processors — 1-Nat/A-250; Electronic picture desk — 1-Lf/AP Leaf Picture Desk; Scanners — 1-RZ/4050, 1-ECR/Autokon 8400; Production cameras — 1-R/16x20, 1-W/20x24; Automatic film processors — Konika; Reproportion units — 1-ECR/Autokon 8400; Shrink lenses — 1-CK Optical; Digital color separation equipment — 1-RZ/4050. PRESSROOM: Line 1 — 7-G/Urbanite, 3-DEV/Horizon (Balloon former); Line 2 — 4-G; Line 3 — 1-G; Line 4 — 2-G; Line 5 — 3-DEV; Folders — 1-G/2:1; Pasters — Manual; Reels and stands — 6-G/Urbanite; Press control system — 2-Fin. MAILROOM: Counter stackers — QWI/108; Inserters and stuffers — 2-MM/227; Bundle tyer — 2-MLN/EE; Addressing machine — 1-IBM/Sys 36. WIRE SERVICES: News — Stock tables — AP; Syndicates — NYT, McClatchy; Receiving dishes — size-16ft, AP. BUSINESS COMPUTERS: 1-IBM/Sys 36, 10-Compaq; Applications: Lotus 1-2-3, Microsoft/Word, Libra: Accts payable; Abra Cadabra: Payroll; Brainworks: Adv; INS; PCs & micros networked; PCs & main system networked.

JUNEAU

Juneau Borough

'90 U.S. Census- 26,751; **E&P '96 Est.** 31,604

Juneau Empire (e-mon to fri; S)

Juneau Empire, 3100 Channel Dr., Juneau, AK 99801-7814; tel (907) 586-3740; fax (907) 586-9097. Morris Communications Corp. group.
Circulation: 7,394(e); 6,852(S); Sworn Oct. 1, 1995.
Price: 50¢(d); $1.25(S); $11.25/mo.
Advertising: Open inch rate $17.12(e); $17.12(S). **Representative:** Papert Companies.
News Services: AP, KRT. **Politics:** Independent. **Established:** 1912.
Not Published: New Year; Memorial Day; Independence Day; Labor Day; Thanksgiving; Christmas.
Advertising not accepted: 900 numbers.
Special Editions: Legislature Edition (Jan); George Washington's Birthday (Feb); Graduation, Juneau Guide (May); Salmon Derby (Aug); Lifestyles (Oct); High School Basketball Preview (Nov); Christmas (Dec).
Special Weekly Sections: Neighbors (wed); Neighbors (fri); Travel Page (S).
Magazines: TV Week, Parade (S).

CORPORATE OFFICER

CEO Will S Morris III

GENERAL MANAGEMENT

Publisher John A Winters

ADVERTISING

Manager Robin Paul

CIRCULATION

Manager Fred B Howard

NEWS EXECUTIVE

Managing Editor Suzanne Downing

EDITORS AND MANAGERS

Business/Finance Editor Lori Thomson
Editorial Page Editor Jim Whitaker
Editorial Writer Jim Whitaker
Entertainment/Amusements Editor Cathy Brown
Health/Medical Editor Jeanine Pohl
News Editor Ed Shoenfeld
Photo Editor Brian Wallace
Sports Editor Mike Stewart
Television/Film Editor Cathy Brown
Theater/Music Editor Cathy Brown
Travel Editor Jim Whitaker

PRODUCTION

Manager David Blumenshine
Foreman-Pressroom Jerry Loesch

Market Information: ADS.
Mechanical available: Offset; Black and 3 ROP colors; insert accepted — preprinted; page cut-offs — 22½".
Mechanical specifications: Type page 13" x 21"; E - 6 cols, 2¹⁄₁₆", ⅛" between; A - 6 cols, 2¹⁄₁₆", ⅛" between; C - 8 cols, 1½", ⅛" between.
Commodity consumption: Newsprint 380 metric tons; widths 27", 13¾"; black ink 6,000 pounds; color ink 300 pounds; average pages per issue 23(d), 76(S); single plates used 6,000.
Equipment: EDITORIAL: Front-end hardware — Gateway; Front-end software — MPS/Tecs 2; Printers — Ap/Mac II NTX; Other equipment — AG/AdFa 1500. CLASSIFIED: Front-end hardware — Gateway; Front-end software — MPS; Printers — Toshiba, Epson. DISPLAY: Front-end hardware — Ap/Macs, Ap/Power Mac; Front-end software — Multi-Ad/Creator, QuarkXPress. PRODUCTION: Typesetters — 2-M/202N; Plate exposures — Nu/Flip Top FT40LNS; Plate processors — Roconex; Production cameras — C/Spartan III; Automatic film processors — C/R650. PRESSROOM: Line 1 — 6-G/Community; Folders — 1-G/Community, G/SC (w/Balloon former). MAILROOM: Inserters and stuffers — KAN/8 units & counter. LIBRARY: Electronic — MPS. COMMUNICATIONS: Digital ad delivery system — AP AdSend. WIRE SERVICES: News — AP, KRT, LAT-WP; Photos — AP; Stock tables — AP, Amex, Nasdaq; Syndicates — KRT; Receiving dishes — size-16ft, AP.

KENAI

Kenai Peninsula Borough

'90 U.S. Census- 6,327; **E&P '96 Est.** 9,136

The Peninsula Clarion

(m-mon to fri)

The Peninsula Clarion, 150 Trading Bay; PO Box 3009, Kenai, AK 99611; tel (907) 283-7551; fax (907) 283-3299. Morris Communications Corp. group.
Circulation: 5,661(m); Sworn Sept. 29, 1995.
Price: 50¢(d); $7.00/mo; $72.00/yr.
Advertising: Open inch rate $11.40(m). **Representative:** Papert Companies.
News Service: AP. **Politics:** Independent. **Established:** 1970, June 1978 (daily).
Not Published: New Year; Independence Day; Thanksgiving; Memorial Day; Labor Day; Christmas.
Advertising not accepted: 900 numbers.
Special Edition: Real Estate (monthly).
Special Weekly Section: Advisor (TMC) (wed).

GENERAL MANAGEMENT

Publisher Susie B Morris
Purchasing Agent/Controller Linda Bell
General Manager Stan Pitlo

ADVERTISING

Director Michelle Glaves

CIRCULATION

Manager Lorrie Carter

NEWS EXECUTIVE

Exec Editor Lori Evans

EDITORS AND MANAGERS

News Editor Andy Hall
Sports Editor J R Rardon

PRODUCTION

Manager Bob Honea

Market Information: TMC; Operate audiotex.
Mechanical available: Offset; Black and 3 ROP colors; insert accepted — preprinted, all; page cut-offs — 21.5".
Mechanical specifications: Type page 13" x 21.5"; E - 6 cols, 2", ⅛" between; A - 6 cols, 2", ⅛" between; C - 6 cols, 2", ⅛" between.
Commodity consumption: Newsprint 294 metric tons; widths 27½", 34"; black ink 3,400 pounds; color ink 2,300 pounds; average pages per issue 20(d); single plates used 8,000.
Equipment: EDITORIAL: Front-end hardware — Ap/Mac. CLASSIFIED: Front-end hardware — Ap/Mac. PRODUCTION: Typesetters — 1-Ap/Mac LaserWriter II NTX, XIT/Cadet, ECR/Imagesetter; Platemaking systems — 2-Nu; Plate exposures — 2-Nu; Plate processors — 2-DP; Production cameras — 1-R; Automatic film processors — 1-Kk, 1-LE, 2-DP. PRESSROOM: Line 1 — 8-G/Offset single width; Press drives — 2-Fin/60 h.p.; Folders — 2-G; Reels and stands — 3-HI; Press registration system — Duarte. MAILROOM: Counter stackers — 1-BG; Inserters and stuffers — 1-St; Bundle tyer — 3-Bu; Wrapping singles — 1-St; Addressing machine — 1-St; Other mailroom equipment — 2-It/Stitchers. 1-Ch/Trimmer. LIBRARY: Electronic — Minolta/Microfilm. WIRE SERVICES: News — AP; Photos — AP; Syndicates — LATS, CT; Receiving dishes — size-10ft, AP. BUSINESS COMPUTERS: 3-HSI/PC; Applications: Adv billing, Accts receivable, Gen ledger, Payroll, Payables; PCs & micros networked; PCs & main system networked.

KETCHIKAN

Ketchikan Gateway Borough

'90 U.S. Census- 8,263; **E&P '96 Est.** 9,210

Ketchikan Daily News

(m-mon to fri; S)

Ketchikan Daily News, 501 Dock St.; PO Box 7900, Ketchikan, AK 99901; tel (907) 225-3157; fax (907) 225-1096.
Circulation: 4,672(m); 4,672(S); Sworn Oct. 1, 1994.
Price: 50¢(d); $1.25(S); $94.00/yr (carrier), $126.00/yr (mail).
Advertising: Open inch rate $10.25(m); $10.25(S). **Representative:** Papert Companies.
News Service: AP. **Politics:** Independent. **Established:** 1935.
Not Published: New Year; President's Day; Memorial Day; Independence Day; Labor Day; Veteran's Day; Thanksgiving; Christmas.
Special Editions: Visitor's Guide; Home; Cooking; Boats; Shopping News; Back-to-School; July 4; Christmas Shopping; Hunting; Outdoor Page; Economy Page; Lifestyle; Walking Tour Map; South East Alaska Explorer.
Special Weekly Sections: Education; Prince of Wales; Waterfront.
Magazines: First City Scene Entertainment (own); TV section; Sunday View Magazine.

CORPORATE OFFICERS

President Lew Williams III
President Tena Williams

GENERAL MANAGEMENT

Publisher Tena Williams
Publisher Lew Williams III
Publisher/Business Manager/Corporate Secretary Kathryn Williams White

ADVERTISING

Manager Lew Williams III

NEWS EXECUTIVE

Editor Belinda Chase

Market Information: TMC; Operate audiotex.
Mechanical available: Offset; Black and 3 ROP colors; insert accepted — preprinted, anything; page cut-offs — 22½".
Mechanical specifications: Type page 13½" x 21"; E - 6 cols, 2¹⁄₁₆", ⅛" between; A - 6 cols, 2¹⁄₁₆", ⅛" between; C - 9 cols, 1½", ¹⁄₁₆" between.
Commodity consumption: Newsprint 212 short tons; width 30"; black ink 7,200 pounds; color ink 1,000 pounds; single pages printed 4,730; average pages per issue 14(d), 72(S); single plates used 11,000.
Equipment: EDITORIAL: Front-end hardware — Ap/Mac. CLASSIFIED: Front-end hardware — Point/4. PRODUCTION: Typesetters — 1-COM/8400, Ap/Mac LaserWriter II, COM/AG/3400 Laserprinter; Plate exposures — 1-Nu/Flip Top; Production cameras — 1-R/Vertical; Automatic film processors — 1-P/Pakonolith.
PRESSROOM: Line 1 — 3-G/Community; Line 2 — 1-G/Universal; Folders — 1-G/2:1. MAILROOM: Addressing machine — 3-Wm. WIRE SERVICES: News — AP. BUSINESS COMPUTERS: Point 4; Applications: Business/Mini Data Software: Mail list, Budgeting, Bus, Adv billing, Accts receivable, Gen ledger, Payroll, Circ.

KODIAK

Kodiak Island

'90 U.S. Census- 7,268; **E&P '96 Est.** 7,422

Kodiak Daily Mirror

(e-mon to fri)

Kodiak Daily Mirror, 1419 Selig St., Kodiak, AK 99615; tel (907) 486-3227; fax (907) 486-3088.
Circulation: 2,953(e); Sworn Sept. 22, 1995.
Price: 50¢(d); $8.00/mo (home delivery), $10.00/mo (mail in state), $15.00/mo (mail out state); $96.00/yr.
Advertising: Open inch rate $6.94(e).
News Service: AP. **Established:** 1940.
Special Editions: ComFish (Mar); Sport Fishing Guide, Crab Festival (May); Hunting Guide (July); Coast Guard Supplement (Aug).
Special Weekly Sections: Sportsweek In Review (mon); Best Food Days, Business Briefs (wed); Best Food Day, TV Section, Harbor Lights (fri).

CORPORATE OFFICERS

Co-Owner Duane Freeman
Co-Owner Nancy Freeman

GENERAL MANAGEMENT

Publisher Nancy Freeman
Manager-Office Karen Tarby

ADVERTISING

Manager-Display Laura Skonberg

CIRCULATION

Manager Jean Heath

NEWS EXECUTIVE

Editor Cecil Ranney

EDITOR AND MANAGER

Sports Editor Ross Courtney

PRODUCTION

Pressman Don Horton

Market Information: TMC.
Mechanical available: Offset; Black and 3 ROP colors; insert accepted — preprinted, any; page cut-offs — 22¾".
Mechanical specifications: Type page 15" x 21"; E - 5 cols, 1¹³⁄₁₆", ⅛" between; A - 5 cols, 1¹³⁄₁₆", ⅛" between; C - 5 cols, 1¹³⁄₁₆", ⅛" between.
Commodity consumption: average pages per issue 20(d).
Equipment: EDITORIAL: Front-end hardware — Ap/Mac SE, Ap/Mac SE30, Ap/Mac IIsi, Ap/Mac II; Front-end software — Microsoft/Word; Printers — Ap/Mac LaserWriter II NT. CLASSIFIED: Front-end hardware — Ap/Mac SE30; Front-end software — Fourth Dimension; Printers — Ap/Mac LaserWriter II NT. DISPLAY: Front-end hardware — Ap/Mac IIcx, Ap/Mac IIsi, CD-Rom/reader; Front-end software — Aldus/PageMaker, Aldus/Deskpaint; Printers — Ap/Mac LaserWriter II NT, NEC/Silentwriter 95. PRODUCTION: Plate processors — Nu/Flip Top FT40UP; Production cameras — SCREEN/Companica 516; Automatic film processors — LE.
PRESSROOM: Line 1 — 3-G/Community; Press control system — Fin. WIRE SERVICES: News — AP; Receiving dishes — AP. BUSINESS COMPUTERS: Synaptic: Epson/Equity 386 Sx; Applications: Synaptic: Accts receivable.

SITKA

Sitka Borough

'90 U.S. Census- 8,588; E&P '96 Est. 9,344

The Daily Sitka Sentinel

(e-mon to fri)

The Daily Sitka Sentinel, 112 Barracks St.; PO Box 799, Sitka, AK 99835; tel (907) 747-3219; fax (907) 747-8898.

Circulation: 2,966(e); Sworn Sept. 30, 1994.

Price: 50¢(d); $75.00/yr.

Advertising: Open inch rate $7.15(e). **Representative:** Papert Companies.

News Service: AP. **Politics:** Independent. **Established:** 1940.

Not Published: New Year; Washington's Birthday; Memorial Day; Independence Day; Labor Day; Alaska Day (Oct 18); Veteran's Day; Thanksgiving; Christmas.

Special Editions: Boat Show (Mar); Summer Visitors Edition (May); Back-to-School (Aug); Alaska Day, Moonlight Madness (Oct); Christmas Shopping Issue (Nov); Christmas Greetings Issue (Dec).

Magazines: Sitka Weekend (TV & Entertainment); Sitka Star (TMC).

CORPORATE OFFICERS

President Thad Poulson
Secretary Sandy Poulson

GENERAL MANAGEMENT

Co-Publisher Sandy Poulson
Co-Publisher Thad Poulson
Business Manager Sandy Poulson

ADVERTISING

Manager Catherine Bagley

CIRCULATION

Manager Margaret Livingston

NEWS EXECUTIVES

Exec Editor Thad Poulson
Managing Editor Thad Poulson

EDITORS AND MANAGERS

Society Editor Sandy Poulson
Sports Editor Heather MacLean
Women's Editor Sandy Poulson

Market Information: TMC.

Mechanical available: Offset; Black and 3 ROP colors; insert accepted — preprinted; page cut-offs — 22¾".

Mechanical specifications: Type page 13½" x 21"; E - 6 cols, 2¹⁄₁₆", ⅛" between; A - 6 cols, 2¹⁄₁₆", ⅛" between; C - 6 cols, 2¹⁄₁₆", ⅛" between.

Commodity consumption: Newsprint 48 short tons; widths 29", 14½"; black ink 900 pounds; color ink 30 pounds; single pages printed 2,600; average pages per issue 10(d); single plates used 1,560.

Equipment: EDITORIAL: Front-end hardware — 9-TC/Titusetter III, Cybertext; Other equipment — Multitech/900, 6-Northgate/286-12, 3-PC/386. DISPLAY: Adv layout systems — Ap/Mac; Front-end software — Aldus/PageMaker; Other equipment — Northgate/286-12, VG. PRODUCTION: Typesetters — 2-Ap/Mac LaserWriter; Plate exposures — 1-Nu/Flip Top; Production cameras — 1-K, 1-SCREEN/640-C.
PRESSROOM: Line 1 — 4-G/Community; Folders — 1-G; Press control system — Fin. MAILROOM: Addressing machine — Wm. WIRE SERVICES: News — AP; Receiving dishes — size-4ft, AP. BUSINESS COMPUTERS: 1-Osborne/1, Tandy/1000 HD, 1-KayPro/4, 2-Northgage/386; Applications: Mail lists, Route lists, Payroll; Peachtree: Gen accounting; PCs & micros networked; PCs & main system networked.

ARIZONA

BISBEE

Cochise County

'90 U.S. Census- 6,288; E&P '96 Est. 5,845

Bisbee Daily Review

(e-mon to fri; S)

Bisbee Daily Review, 12 Main St.; PO Box 127, Bisbee, AZ 85603; tel (520) 432-2231; fax (520) 459-0120. Wick Communications group.

Circulation: 1,081(e); 1,217(S); VAC Mar. 31, 1995.

Price: 50¢(d); $1.25(S); $8.80/mo.

Advertising: Open inch rate $11.26(e); $11.26(S).

News Service: AP. **Politics:** Independent. **Established:** 1896.

Note: For information on printing and production, see the Sierra Vista Daily Herald-Dispatch. Advertisements in the Daily Review (eS) are automatically inserted in the Sierra Vista Herald (eS).

Not Published: New Year; Memorial Day; Independence Day; Labor Day; Christmas.

Special Editions: Progress; Business Report; Back-to-School; Christmas Opening.

Special Weekly Sections: Food Fair (tues); Country Page, Outdoors Page (thur); Real Estate, Religion Page, People Page, Teen Corner (fri); Comics, Entertainment TV, Business Page, People Page (S).

Magazines: Food Fare (tues); Cable Connections; Fort Huachuca; Color Comics (S).

CORPORATE OFFICERS

President Walter M Wick
Vice Pres Robert J Wick

GENERAL MANAGEMENT

General Manager Steve Krehl
Business Manager Sheryll R Bruening

ADVERTISING

Director Dennis Benth

CIRCULATION

Director John Reichard

NEWS EXECUTIVE

Managing Editor Michael Parnell

EDITOR AND MANAGER

Sports Editor Kevin Carolan

PRODUCTION

Manager Ken Murray

Market Information: Zoned editions; TMC.

Mechanical available: Offset; Black and 3 ROP colors; insert accepted — preprinted, all; page cut-offs — 19".

Mechanical specifications: Type page 13" x 21"; E - 6 cols, 2¹⁄₁₆", ⅛" between; A - 6 cols, 2¹⁄₁₆", ⅛" between; C - 9 cols, 1⅜", ¹⁄₁₆" between.

Commodity consumption: Newsprint 800 metric tons; widths 27½", 22"; black ink 5,000 pounds; average pages per issue 24(d), 24(S).

Equipment: EDITORIAL: Front-end hardware — COM/One Sys. MAILROOM: Inserters and stuffers — KAN/480 5-into-1; Bundle tyer — 2-Wilton/Stra Pack 55-80; Addressing machine — Am/1000. WIRE SERVICES: News — AP; Syndicates — NEA; Receiving dishes — size-10m, AP. BUSINESS COMPUTERS: IBM/5120.

BULLHEAD CITY

Mohave County

'90 U.S. Census- 21,951; E&P '96 Est. 27,980

Mohave Valley Daily News

(m-mon to fri; S)

Mohave Valley Daily News, 2435 Miracle Mile (86442); PO Box 21209, Bullhead City, AZ 86439; tel (520) 763-2505; fax (520) 763-7820. Brehm Communications Inc group.

Circulation: 6,748(m); 8,674(m-fri); 6,748(S); VAC June 30, 1995.

Price: 50¢(d); 50¢(fri); 50¢(S); $7.13/mo; $65.99/yr.

Advertising: Open inch rate $18.25(m); $18.25(m-fri); $18.25(S).

News Service: AP. **Established:** 1964 (weekly), 1991 (daily).

Special Editions: Clean Sweep Pages, Today's Women, Turquoise Circuit Finals Rodeo Program (Jan); Seniors Today, Coupon Connection 1, Pet Care (Feb); Southwest Cooking, St. Pat's Lucky Coupons, NCAA Finals, Manuf. Housing-All American Home Show (Mar); Ugliest Pet, Issues of Youth, Weeders Digest, Coupon Connection 2, Route 66 Fun Run (Apr); Life in Colorado, Memorial Day Picnic Page, Golf and R.V. Special Issue (May); Coupon Connection 3, The Picture Book, Fun on the Water (June); Keep the Southwest Beautiful, Fourth of July Picnic Page, Colorado River Dining, Keeping Cool (July); Fall Sports Review, Education in Progress, Discover Laughlin (Aug); Business & Industry, Labor Day Picnic Page, Coupon Connection 4, Weekender Test Drive, Meet Your Merchant (Sept); Newcomer's Guide, Fall is for Planting, Day Trips (Oct); Coupon Connection 5, Holiday Gift Guide, Holiday Theme Pages, Colorado River Migration (Nov); Last Minute Gift Guide, Holiday Recipe Guide, Matador Basketball Tournament, Holidays Happenings on the Colorado (Dec).

Special Weekly Sections: Laughlin Nevada Entertainer Tab, Colorado River Weekender (weekly).

Magazine: Leisure Time (TV tab) (fri).

CORPORATE OFFICERS

President Martin Cody
Secretary Mona Brehm
Asst Secretary/Treasurer Jeff Johnson

GENERAL MANAGEMENT

President/Publisher Martin Cody
Director-Production Nancy Darmofal
Manager-Business Sue Holder

ADVERTISING

Director Steve Paterson
Supervisor-Classified Kathy Jones

MARKETING AND PROMOTION

Director-Marketing/Promotion Steve Paterson

CIRCULATION

Director Rodger Starkey

NEWS EXECUTIVE

Managing Editor Darryle Purcell

EDITORS AND MANAGERS

City Editor Roger Swanson
Editorial Page Editor Darryle Purcell
Education Editor Allen Edwards
Entertainment Editor Alan Marciochi
Features Editor Lewis Clevenger
Living/Lifestyle Editor Lewis Clevenger
Sports Editor Jon Flick

PRODUCTION

Supervisor-Composing Patricia Fisk
Manager-Mailroom Don Kranz
Manager-Pressroom Steve Osborn
Manager-Camera/Stripping Carlos Ruiz

Market Information: Split Run; TMC; ADS.

Mechanical available: Offset; Black and 3 ROP colors; insert accepted — preprinted, most; page cut-offs — 22¾".

Mechanical specifications: Type page 13" x 21½"; E - 6 cols, 2", ⅛" between; A - 6 cols, 2", ⅛" between; C - 8 cols, 1½", ⅛" between.

Commodity consumption: Newsprint 1,281 metric tons; widths 13¾", 27½"; black ink 29,905 pounds; color ink 8,087 pounds; average pages per issue 24(d), 24(S); single plates used 18,000.

Equipment: EDITORIAL: Front-end hardware — Mk; Front-end software — Mk, QPS, Aldus/FreeHand, Adobe/Photoshop, Adobe/Color Access, Baseview; Printers — V, Panasonic; Other equipment — Ap/Mac Color Pagination. CLASSIFIED: Front-end hardware — Ap/Mac; Front-end software — Baseview; Printers — V, Ap/Mac Lasers. DISPLAY: Front-end hardware — Ap/Mac; Front-end software — QPS 3.3, Multi-Ad 3.6.3; PRODUCTION: Pagination software — Baseview 1995; Typesetters — V/400, V/6990, Ap/Mac Laser, V/800, V/5300; Plate exposures — GTS/OLIC; Plate processors — Graham; Scanners — Lf; Production cameras — B; Automatic film processors — P; Digital color separation equipment — V/6990, V/5300.
PRESSROOM: Line 1 — 4-WPC/Web Leader; Line 2 — 4-WPC/Atlas; Folders — WPC/ (¼-½); Reels and stands — 3-WPC; Press control system — Fin. MAILROOM: Counter stackers — KAN/Twin; Inserters and stuffers — 2-KAN; Bundle tyer — MLN/2EE, OVL. COMMUNICATIONS: Systems used — satellite. WIRE SERVICES: News — AP; Receiving dishes — size-12ft, AP. BUSINESS COMPUTERS: Qantel; Applications: Quattro/Pro; PCs & main system networked.

CASA GRANDE

Pinal County

'90 U.S. Census- 19,082; E&P '96 Est. 22,838
ABC-CZ (90): 19,082 (HH 6,495)

Casa Grande Dispatch

(e-mon to fri; m-sat)

Casa Grande Dispatch, 200 W. 2nd St.; PO Box 15002, Casa Grande, AZ 85230-5002; tel (520) 836-7461; fax (520) 836-0343. Kramer Publications group.

Circulation: 8,993(e); 8,993(m-sat); ABC Sept. 30, 1995.

Price: 50¢(d); 50¢(sat); $8.00/mo (carrier), $8.75/mo (motor route); $195.00/yr (out-of-state mail).

Advertising: Open inch rate $10.42(e); $10.42(m-sat). **Representative:** Landon Associates Inc.

News Service: AP. **Politics:** Independent. **Established:** 1912.

Not Published: New Year; Memorial Day; Independence Day; Labor Day; Thanksgiving; Christmas.

Advertising not accepted: Regular newstype faces are not available for advertising; no advertising copy will run upside down.

Special Editions: O'Odham Tash (Indian Days) (Feb); Home Improvement, Spring Fashion, Car Care (Mar); Graduation (May); Customer Appreciation (July); Back-to-School (Aug); Cotton Issue (Oct); Gift Guide (Nov); Christmas (Dec); Progress, Real Estate (monthly).

Special Weekly Section: Tri-Valley Dispatch.

Magazine: Pinal Ways (quarterly).

CORPORATE OFFICERS

President Donovan M Kramer Sr
Vice Pres Ruth A Kramer
Treasurer Donovan M Kramer Jr
Secretary Kara K Bugbee

GENERAL MANAGEMENT

Publisher Donovan M Kramer Sr
Assoc Publisher Donovan M Kramer Jr
Controller E Wayne Cook

ADVERTISING

Director Kara K Bugbee
Director-Promotion/Marketing Kara K Bugbee

CIRCULATION

Director Warren Young

NEWS EXECUTIVES

Editor Donovan M Kramer Sr
Managing Editor Donovan M Kramer Jr

EDITORS AND MANAGERS

Editorial Page Editor Donovan M Kramer Jr
Sports Editor Ed Petruska
Valley Life Editor Patty Machelor

MANAGEMENT INFORMATION SERVICES

Data Processing Manager Rob Williams

PRODUCTION

Director Jeff Bornhorst

Market Information: TMC; ADS.

Mechanical available: Offset; Black and 3 ROP colors; insert accepted — preprinted; page cut-offs — 22¾".

Mechanical specifications: Type page 13" x 21½"; E - 6 cols, 2¹⁄₁₆", ⅛" between; A - 6 cols, 2¹⁄₁₆", ⅛" between; C - 6 cols, 2¹⁄₁₆", ⅛" between.

Commodity consumption: Newsprint 355 short tons; widths 27½", 13¾"; black ink 7,352 pounds; color ink 400 pounds; single pages printed 6,344; average pages per issue 20.66(d); single plates used 3,172.

Equipment: EDITORIAL: Front-end hardware — Ap/Power Mac, Ap/Mac Quadra; Front-end software — Baseview/NewsEdit IQue Pro, Baseview/Wire Manager IQue Pro; Printers — Ap/Mac LaserWriter IIg. CLASSIFIED: Front-end hardware — Ap/Mac Quadra 630; Front-end software — Baseview/ClassManager 3.0.6; Printers — Okidata. DISPLAY: Front-end hardware — Ap/Power Mac; Front-end software — Multi-Ad/Creator 3.7; Printers — Ap/Mac LaserWriter Pro 16/600, Xante/Accel-a-Writer 8200, Tektronix/Phaser 300. PRODUCTION: Pagination software — QuarkXPress 3.1; OCR software — Caere/OmniPage Direct; Typesetters — AG/Accuset 800, AG/Accuset 1500, AG/Viper RIP; Plate exposures — 1-Nu/Flip Top FT32UP, 1-Nu/Flip Top FT32UPNS; Plate processors — Anitec/S-32; Electronic picture desk — Lf/AP Leaf Picture Desk, Ap/Power Mac w/Photoshop 3.0, Ap/Mac Link Transfer; Production cameras — 1-DAI/C-260-D; Automatic film processors — LE/LD-24AQ; Shrink lenses — 1-P/26EL, 1-COM/rep 101; Digital color separation equipment — Kk/RFS 2035 Plus, Polaroid/SprintScan, Umax/Powerlook, Vista/88.
PRESSROOM: Line 1 — 9-G/Community; Folders — 2-G/Suburban (w/balloon). MAILROOM: Counter stackers — 2-BG/105; Inserters and stuffers — 1-KAN/350; Bundle tyer — 2-MLN/ML2EE; Addressing machine — 1-Wm. LIBRARY: Electronic — Baseview/Sonar-text. COMMUNICATIONS: Digital ad delivery system — AP AdSend. WIRE SERVICES: News — AP; Photos — AP; Syndicates — Universal Press, United Media, TMS; Receiving dishes — size-2.7m, AP. BUSINESS COMPUTERS: CJ, Covalent; Applications: Accts payable, Accts receivable, Gen ledger, Payroll, Circ (PIA); PCs & micros networked.

CHANDLER

Maricopa County

'90 U.S. Census- 90,533; E&P '96 Est. 114,208
ABC-CZ (90): 90,533 (HH 31,490)

Chandler Arizonan Tribune

(m-mon to sat; S)

Chandler Arizonan Tribune, 25 S. Arizona Place (Chandler 85240); PO Box 1547, Mesa, AZ 85211; tel (602) 821-7474; fax (602) 821-7480; e-mail coxtrib&@prodigy.com. Cox Newspapers Inc. group.

Circulation: 9,550(m); 9,550(m-sat); 9,763(S); ABC Sept. 30, 1995.

Price: 50¢(d); 50¢(sat); $1.25(S); $2.31/wk; $10.00/mo; $120.00/yr.

Advertising: Open inch rate $69.08(m); $82.65 (m-wed); $69.08(m-sat); $69.08(S). **Representative:** Papert Companies.

News Services: AP, Cox News Service, LAT-WP, SHNS, NYT, GNS, PR Newswire. **Politics:** Independent. **Established:** 1912.

Note: Advertising is sold in combination with Gilbert Tribune (mS), Mesa Tribune (mS), Scottsdale Progress Tribune (eS) and Tempe Daily News Tribune (mS) for $69.08 (d & S) and $82.65 (m-wed). Wednesday rate includes Extended Market Coverage. For detailed equipment information, see the Mesa Tribune.

Special Editions: Senior Living, Super Bowl (Jan); Renaissance Festival, Masterplan Community, Health Directory (Feb); Ostrich Festival, Baseball, Women's Expo, Senior Living/Health (Mar); Good Times, Suns Playoff, Country Thunder (Apr); Home Improvement, Rest Assured (May); Healthy Lifestyles/Seniors (June); Crime Prevention, Health Directory (July); Back-to-School, Football (Aug); Doo Dah Festival, Home Improvement (Sept); East Valley Guide, Balloon Classic, Healthy Lifestyles/Senior/Basketball, Holiday Kick-off (Nov); Last Minute Gifts, Healthy Lifestyles/Seniors, Fiesta Bowl Guide (Dec).

Special Weekly Sections: AZ Tech (mon); Food & Recipes, Entertainment (wed); TGIF (fri); Extended Weekly Stocks Wrap-Up, Homefinder, Religion (sat); Lifestyle, Class Act-Just for Teens, Perspective, Extended Mutual Fund Report, National Manufacturers Coupons, Business, Wheels, Travel (S).

Magazines: Tribune TV, Parade Magazine; Comics (S); Arizona Adventure (thur, bi-wkly).

CORPORATE OFFICERS

President Sanford Schwartz
Vice Pres Belinda Gaudet
Controller Edward Burns

GENERAL MANAGEMENT

Publisher Sanford Schwartz
General Manager Belinda Gaudet
Asst to Publisher Janet Cox
Director-Human Resources Melissa Lows

ADVERTISING

Director H Robert Hirsch
Manager-Classified Tim Thomas
Manager-Retail Tricia Phillips

MARKETING AND PROMOTION

Director-Marketing/Promotion Jody Taylor

TELECOMMUNICATIONS

Director Multimedia Service Bill Roberts

CIRCULATION

Director Michael Romero

NEWS EXECUTIVES

Exec Editor Jeffrey C Bruce
Editor Susan Keaton
Managing Editor Jim Ripley

EDITORS AND MANAGERS

Books/Music Editor Betty Webb
Business/Finance Editor Martha Reinke
Columnist David Leibowitz
Editorial Page Editor Bob Schuster
Entertainment/Amusements Editor Liz B Merritt
Fashion/Style Editor Liz B Merritt
Features Editor Liz B Merritt
Films/Theater Editor Max McQueen
Living/Lifestyle Editor Liz B Merritt
Medical Editor Liz B Merritt
News Editor Bob Netherton
Photo Editor Rick Wiley
Political/Government Editor Mark Flatten
Religion Editor Kelly Ettenborough
Science/Technology Editor Liz B Merritt
Sports Editor Dave Lumia

MANAGEMENT INFORMATION SERVICES

Director-Computer Services Jim Roe

PRODUCTION

Director-Operations Scott Porter
Manager-Pre Press Mark Zawacki
Manager-Press Dave Veno
Manager-Distribution/Packaging Kathy Trappe

Market Information: TMC; Operate database; Operate audiotex.

Mechanical available: Offset; Black and 3 ROP colors; insert accepted — preprinted, product drops; page cut-offs — 22".

Mechanical specifications: Type page 13" x 21"; E - 6 cols, 2.04", 1/6" between; A - 6 cols, 2.04", 1/6" between; C - 9 cols, 1.33", 1/6" between.

Commodity consumption: Newsprint 2,458 short tons; widths 54¾", 41³⁄₁₆", 27⅜"; black ink 39,636 pounds; color ink 21,945 pounds; single pages printed 20,755; average pages per issue 50(d), 90(sat), 100(S); single plates used 156,000.

DOUGLAS

Cochise County

'90 U.S. Census- 12,822; E&P '96 Est. 12,749

The Daily Dispatch

(e-tues to fri; S)

The Daily Dispatch, 530 11th St.; PO Drawer H, Douglas, AZ 85607; tel (520) 364-3424; fax (520) 364-6750. Wick Communications group.

Circulation: 2,464(e); 2,464(S); Sworn Oct. 4, 1994.

Price: 35¢(d); 50¢(S); $102.00/yr.

Advertising: Open inch rate $6.25(e); $8.75(S).

News Service: AP. **Politics:** Independent. **Established:** 1902.

Not Published: New Year; Memorial Day; Independence Day; Labor Day; Thanksgiving; Christmas.

Advertising not accepted: Tobacco.

Special Editions: First Baby, Super Bowl, Customer Appreciation (Jan); High School Sports Calendar, Sweetheart Specials (Feb); Business and Professional (Mar); Vacation Getaway, Horse Races (Apr); Graduation (May); Customer Appreciation (June); Cochise County Fair Premium Book (July); Back-to-School, High School Sports (Aug); County Fair, Mexican Independence Fiesta (Sept); Two Flags Special, Visitor's Guide (Oct); Holiday Shopping Guide, High School Sports Calendar (Nov); Christmas (Dec).

Special Weekly Sections: Health and Fitness (tues); Education (wed); Business (thur); Real Estate, Church Page, Dining and Entertainment (fri); Color Comics, TV Guide, Cochise County Focus, Valley Page, Real Estate, Expanded Classified Section (S).

Magazines: Preview; TMC Viva; Viva Sunday.

GENERAL MANAGEMENT

Publisher Sharilyn Rogers
Bookkeeper Hilda Corella

ADVERTISING

Manager Diane Ramirez

NEWS EXECUTIVE

Editor Sharilyn Rogers

EDITORS AND MANAGERS

Editorial Page Editor Mike Hicks
Sports Editor Bruce Whetten

PRODUCTION

Superintendent Roy Aguirre

Market Information: TMC; ADS.

Mechanical available: Offset; Black and 2 ROP colors; insert accepted — preprinted, cards, single sheets; page cut-offs — 21".

Mechanical specifications: Type page 13" x 21"; E - 6 cols, 2¹⁄₁₆", 1/8" between; A - 6 cols, 2¹⁄₁₆", 1/8" between; C - 6 cols, 2¹⁄₁₆", 1/8" between.

Commodity consumption: widths 27½", 13¾"; average pages per issue 10(d), 16(S).

Equipment: EDITORIAL: Front-end hardware — Ap/Mac II LC; Other equipment — Ap/Mac. CLASSIFIED: Front-end hardware — Ap/Mac II LC. DISPLAY: Adv layout systems — Ap/Mac Centris 610; Front-end hardware — Ap/Mac Centris 610, Ap/Mac; Front-end software — QuarkXPress, Aldus/FreeHand; Printers — QMS/Model 860. PRODUCTION: Typesetters — Ap/Mac LC II; Plate exposures — 1-Nu/Flip Top FT40W; Scanners — Microtek/ScanMaster II; Production cameras — 1-LE/4 Vertical. PRESSROOM: Line 1 — 3-G/Community. WIRE SERVICES: News — AP; Syndicates — NEA. BUSINESS COMPUTERS: Ap/Mac.

FLAGSTAFF

Coconino County

'90 U.S. Census- 45,827; E&P '96 Est. 56,276
ABC-NDM (90): 60,364 (HH 19,820)

The Arizona Daily Sun

(e-mon to fri; m-sat; S)

Arizona Daily Sun, 417 W. Santa Fe; PO Box 1849, Flagstaff, AZ 86001; tel (520) 774-4545; fax (520) 773-1934. Scripps League Newspapers Inc. group.

Circulation: 13,440(e); 13,440(m-sat); 15,116(S); ABC Sept. 30, 1995.

Price: 50¢(d); 50¢(sat); $1.00(S); $9.50/mo.

Advertising: Open inch rate $12.06(e); $12.06(m-sat); $12.06(S).

News Service: AP. **Politics:** Independent. **Established:** 1883.

Special Editions: Women in Business (Jan); Brides (Mar); Progress (Apr); Rodeo, Racing (June); Cardinals (July); Best of Flagstaff, Back-to-School (Aug); Christmas Shopping.

Special Weekly Sections: Best Food Day (tues); TV Listing/Sundial (sat).

Magazine: USA Weekend (S).

CORPORATE OFFICERS

Board Chairman/Treasurer E W Scripps
Vice Chairman/Corporate Secretary Betty Knight Scripps
President/Vice Pres Jack C Morgan
Exec Vice Pres Roger N Warkins
Vice Pres Platt Cline
Vice Pres-Finance Thomas E Wendel

GENERAL MANAGEMENT

Publisher/Personnel Manager Don G Rowley
Manager-Credit Kristi Busch
Purchasing Agent Don G Rowley

ADVERTISING

Director Theresa M Givens

MARKETING AND PROMOTION

Manager-Promotion Don G Rowley

CIRCULATION

Manager Mike Brezina

NEWS EXECUTIVE

Managing Editor Michael Patrick

EDITORS AND MANAGERS

Book Review Editor Becky Blankenship
Business/Finance Editor Randy Wilson
City/Metro Editor Leon Keith
Education Editor Mary Tolan
Entertainment/Amusements Editor Becky Blankenship
Music Editor Becky Blankenship
News Editor Randy Wilson
Photo Editor Sean Openshaw
Sports Editor Matt Wixon
Women's Editor Jan Stevens

PRODUCTION

Manager-Composing Edward D'Hooge
Manager-Pressroom William Smith

Market Information: TMC.

Mechanical available: Offset; Black and 3 ROP colors; insert accepted — preprinted; page cut-offs — 22¾".

Mechanical specifications: Type page 13" x 21½"; E - 6 cols, 2¹⁄₁₆", 1/8" between; A - 6 cols, 2¹⁄₁₆", 1/8" between; C - 8 cols, 1½", 1/8" between.

Commodity consumption: Newsprint 1,120 metric tons; widths 27½", 13²⁵⁄₃₂"; black ink 28,000 pounds; color ink 900 pounds; single pages printed 9,602; average pages per issue 24(d), 34(S); single plates used 8,500.

Equipment: EDITORIAL: Front-end hardware — ScrippSat, PC; Printers — Ap/Mac LaserPrinter; Other equipment — Ap/Mac II-Graphics. CLASSIFIED: Front-end hardware — ScrippSat; Front-end software — Synaptic; Printers — Okidata 393/QMS. DISPLAY: Adv layout systems — ScrippSat; Front-end hardware — 4-PC/ScrippSat; Front-end software — Archetype/Corel Draw, Ami, Aldus/FreeHand, QuarkXPress. PRODUCTION: Pagination software — QPS; Typesetters — 3-QMS/820-Turbo, LaserMaster/1200XLO, ECR/VRL 36, LaserMaster/1800x60; Platemaking systems — 1-Nu; Plate exposures — Amerigraph/437; Plate processors — Nat; Electronic picture desk — Lf/AP Leaf Picture Desk, Lf/Leafscan 35; Scanners — HP/ScanJet IIc; Production cameras — 2-SCREEN/Vertical; Automatic film processors — Kk/65A; Digital color separation equipment — Adobe/Photoshop. PRESSROOM: Line 1 — 8-G/Community (with 2 stacked units); Folders — 1-G/SSC; Press registration system — Duarte. MAILROOM: Counter stackers — 1-BG/Count-O-Veyor 109; Inserters and stuffers — 1-MM/EM10; Bundle tyer — MLN/2MLN; Addressing machine — ScrippSat. COMMUNICATIONS: Systems used — satellite. WIRE SERVICES: News — AP; Photos — AP; Syndicates — SHNS; Receiving dishes — size-10ft, AP. BUSINESS COMPUTERS: ScrippSat; Applications: PBS: Adv, Billing; PBC: Payroll, Accts receivable; PCs & micros networked; PCs & main system networked.

GILBERT

Maricopa County

'90 U.S. Census- 29,188; E&P '96 Est. 39,004
ABC-CZ (90): 29,188 (HH 9,381)

The Gilbert Tribune

(m-mon to sat; S)

Gilbert Tribune, 655 N. Gilbert Rd. 160 (Gilbert 85234); PO Box 1547, Mesa, AZ 85211; tel (602) 898-5611; fax (602) 545-9241; e-mail coxtrib&@prodigy.com. Cox Newspapers Inc. group.

Circulation: 5,227(m); 5,227(m-sat); 5,348(S); ABC Sept. 30, 1995.

Price: 50¢(d); 50¢(sat); $1.25(S); $2.31/wk; $10.00/mo; $120.00/yr.

Advertising: Open inch rate $69.08(m); $82.65 (m-wed); $69.08(m-sat); $69.08(S). **Representative:** Papert Companies.

News Services: AP, Cox News Service, LAT-WP, SHNS, NYT, GNS, PR Newswire, TMS. **Politics:** Independent. **Established:** 1990.

Note: Advertising is sold in combination with Chandler Arizonan Tribune (mS), Mesa Tribune (mS), Scottsdale Progress Tribune (eS) and Tempe Daily News Tribune (mS) for $69.08 (d&S) and $82.65 (m-wed). Wednesday rate includes Extended Market Coverage. For detailed equipment information, see the Mesa Tribune.

Special Editions: Senior Living, Super Bowl (Jan); Renaissance Festival, Masterplan Community, Health Directory (Feb); Women's Expo, Senior Living/Health, Ostrich Festival, Baseball (Mar); Country Thunder, Suns Playoff, Good Times (Apr); Home Improvement, Rest Assured (May); Healthy Lifestyles/Seniors (June); Crime Prevention, Health Directory (July); Back-to-School, Football Preview (Aug); Home Improvement, Doo Dah (Sept); East Valley Guide, Balloon Classic, Healthy Lifestyles/Seniors (Oct); Basketball, Holiday Kickoff (Nov); Last Minute Gifts, Healthy Lifestyles/Seniors, Fiesta Bowl Guide (Dec).

Special Weekly Sections: AZ Tech (mon); Food & Recipes, Entertainment (wed); TGIF (fri); Homefinder, Religion, Extended Weekly Stocks Wrap Up (sat); Lifestyle, Class Act-Just for Teens, Perspectives, Extended Mutual Funds Report, National Manufacturers Coupons, Business, Wheels, Travel (S).

Magazines: Tribune TV, Color Comics, Parade (S); Arizona Adventure (thur, bi-wkly).

CORPORATE OFFICERS

President Sanford Schwartz
Vice Pres Belinda Gaudet
Controller Edward Burns

GENERAL MANAGEMENT

Publisher Sanford Schwartz
General Manager Belinda Gaudet
Asst to Publisher Janet Cox
Director-Human Resources Melissa Lows

ADVERTISING

Director H Robert Hirsch
Manager-Classified Tim Thomas
Manager-Retail Tricia Phillips

MARKETING AND PROMOTION

Director-Marketing/Promotion Jody Taylor

TELECOMMUNICATIONS

Director Multimedia Services Bill Roberts

CIRCULATION

Director Michael Romero

NEWS EXECUTIVES

Exec Editor Jeffrey C Bruce
Editor Kathy Bareiss
Managing Editor Jim Ripley

EDITORS AND MANAGERS

Books/Music Editor Betty Webb
Business/Finance Editor Martha Reinke
Columnist David Leibowitz
Editorial Page Editor Bob Schuster
Entertainment/Amusements Editor Liz B Merritt
Fashion/Style Editor Liz B Merritt
Features Editor Liz B Merritt
Films/Theater Editor Max McQueen
Medical Editor Liz B Merritt

Copyright ©1996 by the Editor & Publisher Co.

News Editor	Bob Netherton
Photo Editor	Rick Wiley
Political/Government Editor	Mark Flatten
Religion Editor	Kelly Ettenborough
Science/Technology Editor	Liz B Merritt
Sports Editor	Dave Lumia

MANAGEMENT INFORMATION SERVICES
Director-Computer Services .... Jim Roe
PRODUCTION
Director-Operations .... Scott Porter
Manager-Pre Press .... Mark Zawacki
Manager-Press .... Dave Veno
Manager-Distribution/Packaging .... Kathy Trappe

Market Information: Operate database; Operate audiotex.
Mechanical available: Offset; Black and 3 ROP colors; insert accepted — preprinted, product drop; page cut-offs — 22".
Mechanical specifications: Type page 13" x 21"; E - 6 cols, 2.04", 1/8" between; A - 6 cols, 2.04", 1/8" between; C - 9 cols, 1.33", 1/8" between.
Commodity consumption: Newsprint 2,458 short tons; widths 54¾", 41³⁄₁₆", 27⅜"; black ink 39,636 pounds; color ink 21,945 pounds; single pages printed 20,755; average pages per issue 50(d), 90(sat), 100(S); single plates used 156,000.

KINGMAN
Mohave County
'90 U.S. Census- 12,722; E&P '96 Est. 16,108
ABC-CZ (90): 24,167 (HH 9,523)

The Kingman Daily Miner
(e-mon to fri; S)

Kingman Daily Miner, 3015 Stockton Hill Road; PO Box 3909, Kingman, AZ 86402; tel (520) 753-6397; fax (520) 753-5661. Western Newspapers Inc. group.
Circulation: 7,348(e); 7,618(e-fri); 7,618(S); ABC Sept. 30, 1995.
Price: 50¢(d); $1.00(S); $6.00/mo (carrier); $12.00/mo (mail); $78.00/yr.
Advertising: Open inch rate $7.70(e); $8.88(e-fri); $8.88(S). **Representative:** Papert Companies.
News Service: AP. **Politics:** Independent. **Established:** 1883.
Special Editions: Top 10 Stories of the Year Section (Miner) (Jan); It's Tax Time (ROP Miner, Prospector, Enterprise) (Feb); No TV Week, Mini Miner Tab (Miner), Spring Home Improvement (Miner, Prospector, Enterprise) (Mar); Rt. 66 Section (Miner, Prospector, Enterprise), Business Fair Section (Miner, Prospector, Enterprise) (Apr); Graduation Section (Miner), Park & Recreation Book (Miner) (May); Welcome to Kingman (Newcomer's Section-Miner) (June); Soap Box Derby Section (Miner) (July); Back-to-School Section (Miner, Prospector) (Aug); Andy Devine Days Section (Miner) (Sept); Home Improvement Section(Miner, Prospector, Enterprise), Destination Kingman (4 sections, Miner) (Oct); Christmas Kick-Off (Miner, Prospector, Enterprise) (Nov); Last Minute Christmas (Miner, Prospector, Enterprise) (Dec).
Special Weekly Sections: Food (tues); Outdoors (wed); Church/Religion (fri); Business (S).
Magazines: Nugget (weekend entertainment); TV Listings.

GENERAL MANAGEMENT
Publisher .... Kit K Atwell
Operations Manager .... Jo Adams
ADVERTISING
Director .... Kathi Wright
MARKETING AND PROMOTION
Director-Special Project .... Jo Adams
CIRCULATION
Manager .... Kandy Cummins
NEWS EXECUTIVE
Editor .... Tim Wiederaenders
PRODUCTION
Director .... Bruce Pedersen
Supervisor-Composing Room ... Colleen Machado

Market Information: TMC; ADS.
Mechanical available: Offset; Black and 3 ROP colors; insert accepted — preprinted; page cut-offs — 22¾".
Mechanical specifications: Type page 13¾" x 22¾"; E - 6 cols, 2.04", .14" between; A - 6 cols, 2.04", .14" between; C - 6 cols, 2.04", .14" between.
Commodity consumption: Newsprint 213 metric tons; widths 27½", 13¾"; black ink 8,674 pounds; color ink 1,785 pounds; single pages printed 5,317; average pages per issue 14(d), 20(S); single plates used 5,304.
Equipment: EDITORIAL: Front-end hardware — Mk. CLASSIFIED: Front-end hardware — 2-Epson/MBM-2095E; Front-end software — Epson/MB80900188; Other equipment — Star/NP10, Royal/9300P. AUDIOTEX: Hardware — Epson/1MBM-20995E. DISPLAY: Front-end hardware — Ap/Mac IIcx; Front-end software — Adobe/Illustrator 2.0, QuarkXPress 3.1, Adobe/Photoshop 2.5; Printers — 2-Ap/Mac LaserWriter Pro; Other equipment — Syquest/tape drive, Mirror/mass storage, Digital/FV540, Quantum/PowerDrive, SupraFax Modem 288, Umax/Scanner w/Caere/OmniPage, Adobe/Photoshop. PRODUCTION: Pagination software — QuarkXPress; OCR software — Caere/OmniPage; Typesetters — Hyphen/Spactra Net 2400 Imagesetter; Plate exposures — OLEC; Plate processors — Nat; Scanners — Umax, Polaroid/SprintScan 35; Production cameras — SCREEN/C-240-D; Automatic film processors — LE; Digital color separation equipment — Ap/Power Mac 8100, Unimax/PowerBook, Polaroid/SprintScan 35. PRESSROOM: Line 1 — 11-G/Suburban; Folders — G/SC, G/Suburban; Press control system — Fin; Press registration system — Duarte. MAILROOM: Counter stackers — 1-IDAB/660, 1-HI/RS10; Inserters and stuffers — 7-Mc, 6-MM; Bundle tyer — 2-MLN/2A; Addressing machine — KR; Other mailroom equipment — MM/221. 6-Pocket/Saddle Stitcher. WIRE SERVICES: News — AP. BUSINESS COMPUTERS: 1-DEC/2000, 5-VT/420, 2-LA/424, 2-VT/220; Applications: Adv billing, Accts receivable, Gen ledger, Payroll; PCs & micros networked; PCs & main system networked.

Arizona
LAKE HAVASU CITY
Mohave County
'90 U.S. Census- 24,363; E&P '96 Est. 31,377

Today's News-Herald
(m-tues to fri; S)

Today's News-Herald, 2225 W. Acoma Blvd., Lake Havasu City, AZ 86403; tel (520) 453-4237; fax (520) 855-9892. River City Newspapers L.L.C. group.
Circulation: 13,500(m); 13,500(S); Estimate Sept. 1995.
Price: 50¢(d); 75¢(S); $6.00/mo; $62.00/yr.
Advertising: Open inch rate $12.98(m); $12.98(S). **Representative:** Papert Companies.
News Service: AP. **Politics:** Independent. **Established:** 1963 (Daily Herald), 1978 (Today's Daily News), 1995 (Today's News-Herald).
Note: Effective Sept. 1, 1995, the Lake Havasu City Daily Herald (m-tues to fri; S) and the Lake Havasu City Today's Daily News (m-tues to fri; S) merged to form Today's News-Herald (m-tues to fri; S). The new paper is equally owned by Western Newspapers Inc. and Wick Communications Co. Inc.
Special Editions: Coupon Connection, Seniors Lifestyle (Jan); Winter Visitor's Guide (Feb); House Builder's Show (Mar); Coupon Connection, Design-An-Ad (Apr); Summer Guide (May); Coupon Connection (July); Football Contest, Fall H.S. Sports (Aug); Meet Your Merchant (Sept); Coupon Connection, London Bridge Days (Oct); Winter Visitor's Guide (Nov); Holiday Shopping Guide (Dec).
Special Weekly Sections: Entertainment Plus (fri); TV Week, Sunday Comics (S).
Magazine: Havasu Home Hunter.

CORPORATE OFFICER
President .... Mike Quinn
GENERAL MANAGEMENT
Publisher .... Mike Quinn
ADVERTISING
Manager .... Kingsley Gerlach
MARKETING AND PROMOTION
Director-Marketing .... Kingsley Gerlach
CIRCULATION
Manager .... Jim Abdon
NEWS EXECUTIVES
Editor .... Mike Quinn
Managing Editor .... Stan Unisowicz
EDITOR AND MANAGER
Features Editor .... Tanya Manus
MANAGEMENT INFORMATION SERVICES
Data Processing Manager ..... Donna Schroeder
PRODUCTION
Manager .... JoAnn Ingrum

Market Information: TMC; ADS.
Mechanical available: Black and 4 ROP colors; insert accepted — preprinted, envelopes, cards; page cut-offs — 21".

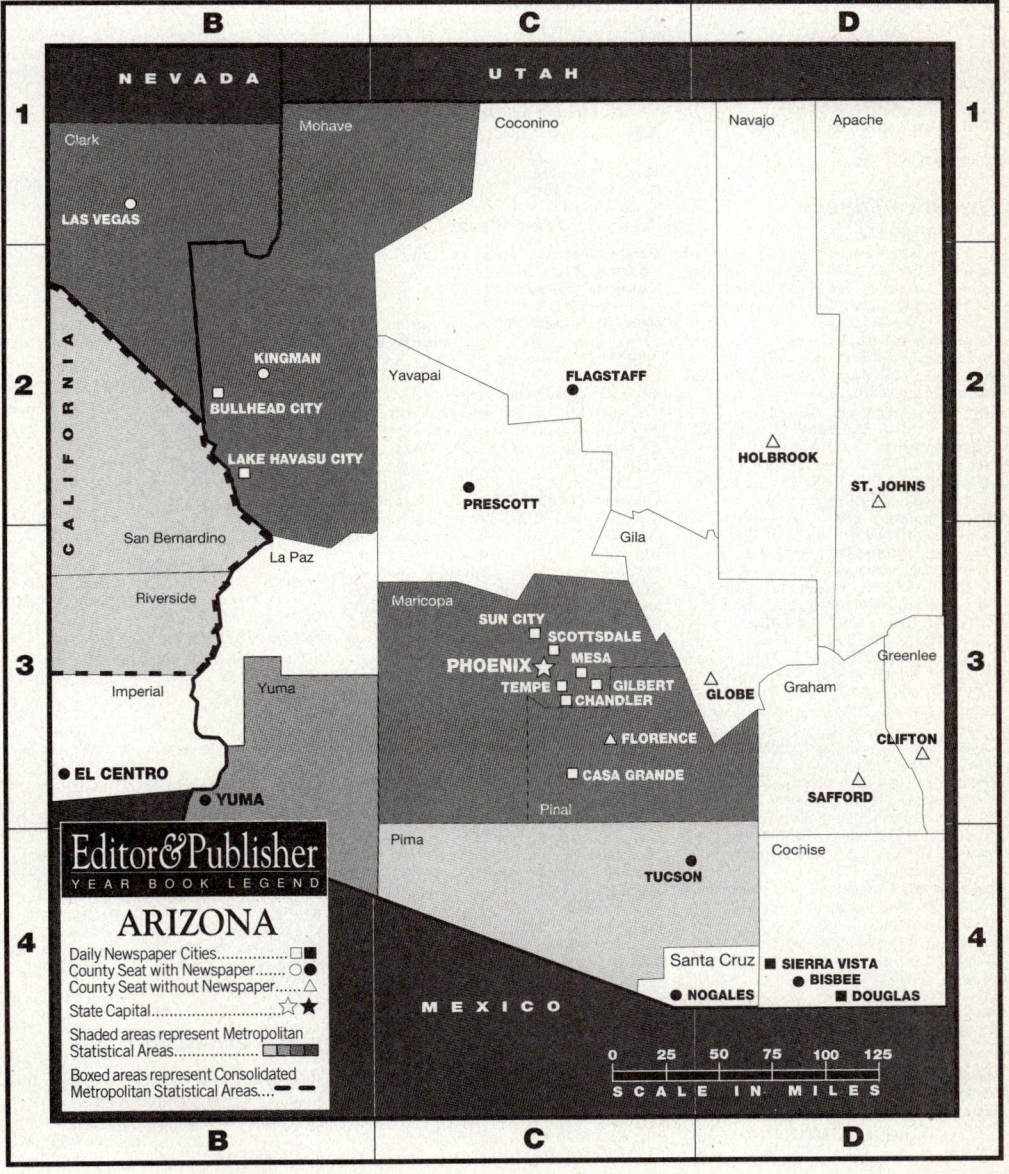

Mechanical specifications: Type page 13" x 21"; E - 6 cols, $2\frac{1}{16}$", $\frac{1}{4}$" between; A - 6 cols, $2\frac{1}{16}$", $\frac{1}{4}$" between; C - 6 cols, $2\frac{1}{16}$", $\frac{1}{4}$" between.
Commodity consumption: Newsprint 6,825 short tons; widths $27\frac{1}{2}$", 34"; black ink 10,400 pounds; color ink 2,600 pounds; single pages printed 6,583; average pages per issue 28(d), 32(S); single plates used 12,880.
Equipment: EDITORIAL: Front-end hardware — 12-Ap/Mac; Front-end software — Microsoft/Word, Aldus/PageMaker, Quark-XPress; Printers — NEC/95. CLASSIFIED: Front-end hardware — 2-Ap/Power Mac; Front-end software — Vision Data, WordPerfect, DataPerfect, Lotus 1-2-3; Printers — Panasonic/KXP4410, Okidata/393 Plus. DISPLAY: Front-end hardware — Ap/Mac; Front-end software — Volk; Printers — NEC/Silentwriter 95. PRODUCTION: Pagination software — Quark-XPress 3.3; Typesetters — Ap/Mac Plus, Ap/Mac Classic II, Ap/Super Mac, NEC/Silentwriter, Ap/Mac w/Radius/monitor, Ap/Mac Radius; Plate exposures — Amerigraph; Plate processors — Anitec/S38; Scanners — Microtek/II SI, Microtek; Production cameras — SCREEN/Auto Companica 516; Automatic film processors — Danagraph; Digital color separation equipment — Microtek.
PRESSROOM: Line 1 — 7-WPC/Atlas Web; Press control system — Marathon. WIRE SERVICES: News — AP; Syndicates — CNS, King Features, TMS, Creators, LATS; Receiving dishes — size-18", AP. BUSINESS COMPUTERS: ATT/Unix PC; Applications: Vision Data; PCs & micros networked; PCs & main system networked.

MESA

Maricopa County

'90 U.S. Census- 288,091; E&P '96 Est. 320,611
ABC-CZ (90):288,091 (HH 107,863)

The Mesa Tribune

(m-mon to sat; S)

Mesa Tribune, 120 W. First Ave. (85210); PO Box 1547, Mesa, AZ 85211; tel (602) 898-6500; fax (602) 898-6463; e-mail coxtrib&@prodigy.com. Cox Newspapers Inc. group.
Circulation: 43,594(m); 43,594(m-sat); 46,528(S); ABC Sept. 30, 1995.
Price: 50¢(d); 50¢(sat); $1.25(S); $2.31/wk; $10.00/mo; $120.00/yr.
Advertising: Open inch rate $69.08(m); $82.65(m-wed); $69.08(m-sat); $69.08(S). **Representative:** Papert Companies.
News Services: AP, Cox News Service, LAT-WP, GNS, NYT, SHNS, PR Newswire. **Politics:** Independent. **Established:** 1949.
Note: Advertising is sold in combination with Chandler Arizonan Tribune (mS), Gilbert Tribune (mS), Scottsdale Progress Tribune (eS) and Tempe Daily News Tribune for $69.08 (d&S) and $82.65 (m-wed). Wednesday rate includes Extended Market Coverage.
Special Editions: Senior Living/Super Bowl (Jan); Health Directory, Renaissance Festival, Masterplan Community (Feb); Ostrich Festival, Senior Living/Health, Baseball, Women's Expo (Mar); Good Times, Suns Playoff, Country Thunder, Home Improvement, Rest Assured (May); Healthy Lifestyles/Seniors (June); Crime Prevention, Health Directory (July); Back-to-School, Football (Aug); Doo-Dah Festival, Home Improvement (Sept); Healthy Lifestyles/Seniors, Balloon Classic, East Valley Guide (Oct); Basketball, Holiday Kickoff (Nov); Last Minute Gifts, Healthy Lifestyles/Seniors, Fiesta Bowl Guide (Dec).
Special Weekly Sections: AZ Tech (mon); Food & Recipes, Entertainment (wed); TGIF (fri); Extended Weekly Stocks Wrap Up, Homefinder, Religion (sat); Perspective, Class Act-Just for Teens, Extended Mutual Fund Report, National Manufacturers Coupons, Business, Wheels, Travel, Lifestyle (S).
Magazines: Tribune TV, Comics, Parade (S); Arizona Adventurer (thur) (bi-wkly).

CORPORATE OFFICERS
President Sanford Schwartz
Vice Pres Belinda Gaudet
Controller Edward Burns

GENERAL MANAGEMENT
Publisher Sanford Schwartz
General Manager Belinda Gaudet
Asst to Publisher Janet Cox
Director-Human Resources Melissa Lows

ADVERTISING
Director H Robert Hirsch
Manager-Classified Tim Thomas
Manager-Retail Tricia Phillips

MARKETING AND PROMOTION
Director-Marketing/Promotion Jody Taylor

TELECOMMUNICATIONS
Director Multimedia Services Bill Roberts

CIRCULATION
Director Michael Romero

NEWS EXECUTIVES
Exec Editor Jeffrey C Bruce
Managing Editor Jim Ripley

EDITORS AND MANAGERS
Books Editor Betty Webb
Business/Finance Editor Martha Reinke
City Editor Phil Boas
Columnist David Leibowitz
Editorial Page Editor Bob Schuster
Education Editor Patty Likens
Fashion/Style Editor Liz B Merritt
Features Editor Liz B Merritt
Films/Theater Editor Max McQueen
Graphics Editor/Art Director Bob Netherton
Living/Lifestyle Editor Liz B Merritt
Medical Editor Liz B Merritt
Metro Editor Phil Boas
Music Editor Betty Webb
News Editor Bob Netherton
Photo Editor Rick Wiley
Political/Government Editor Mark Flatten
Radio/Television Editor Bruce Christian
Religion Editor Kelley Ettenborough
Science/Technology Editor Liz B Merritt
Sports Editor Dave Lumia
Travel Editor Liz B Merritt

MANAGEMENT INFORMATION SERVICES
Director-Computer Services Jim Roe

PRODUCTION
Director-Operations Scott Porter
Manager-Pre Press Mark Zawacki
Manager-Press Dave Veno
Manager-Distribution/Packaging Kathy Trappe

Market Information: Zoned editions; Operate database; Operate audiotex.
Mechanical available: Offset; Black and 3 ROP colors; page cut-offs — 22".
Mechanical specifications: Type page 13" x 21"; E - 6 cols, 2.04", $\frac{1}{6}$" between; A - 6 cols, 2.04", $\frac{1}{6}$" between; C - 9 cols, 1.33", $\frac{1}{6}$" between.
Commodity consumption: Newsprint 2,458 short tons; widths $54\frac{3}{4}$", $41\frac{3}{16}$", $27\frac{3}{8}$"; black ink 39,636 pounds; color ink 21,945 pounds; single pages printed 20,755; average pages per issue 50(d), 90(sat), 100(S); single plates used 156,000.
Equipment: EDITORIAL: Front-end hardware — DEC, 6-Sun/Sparc 20; Front-end software — CCSI, DTI 3.1; Printers — HP/LaserWriter II, HP/LaserWriter III, HP/LaserWriter IV, HP/LaserWriter V. CLASSIFIED: Front-end hardware — 2-DEC/PDP 11-84; Front-end software — CCSI; Printers — Dataproducts, DEC. AUDIOTEX: Hardware — PC/486; Software — Compute/Ease; Supplier name — In-house. DISPLAY: Adv layout systems — DTI; Front-end hardware — Sun/Sprac 10; Front-end software — DTI 3.1; Printers — Ap/Mac LaserWriter, QMS. PRODUCTION: Pagination software — DTI/PageSpeed 3.1, DTI/AdSpeed 3.1; OCR software — Caere/OmniPage 2.1; Typesetters — 2-AU/APS-5, 2-AG/Proset 9800, 2-AU/APS 108-FC; Plate exposures — 2-Nu/Flip Top, 1-OLEC/Light Source; Plate processors — 2-WL; Electronic picture desk — Ap/Mac, Lf/AP Leaf Picture Desk, Iron Mike Software; Production cameras — 1-C/Spartan III, Acti/Horizontal; Automatic film processors — 2-Litex/26, 1-LE/Excel; Digital color separation equipment — AG/Horizon Plus, AG/Focus Color Plus, Nikon/LS-3510 AF, Kk/Film Scanner, Adobe/Photoshop, Sun/PC, Ethernet/network, Ap/Mac.
PRESSROOM: Line 1 — 6-G/Metroliner (3 decks); Line 2 — 2-G/Metroliner (1 deck); Press drives — Fin/100 h.p.(8 Drives, 1 Master); Folders — G/3:2; Reels and stands — 8-G/Reel Stands RTP; Press registration system — KFM. MAILROOM: Counter stackers — 4-Id, 1-HL; Inserters and stuffers — 2-GMA/6-into-2; Bundle tyer — 4-Dynaric; Other mailroom equipment — Mc/¼ Folder Stitcher-Trimmer. COMMUNICATIONS: Facsimile — 10-Cannon/Laser, Thermal; Digital ad delivery system — Digiflex, AP AdSend. WIRE SERVICES: News — AP; Photos — AP; Stock tables — AP; Syndicates — AP, Cox, LAT-WP, NYT, TMS, SHNS, GNS, PR Newswire; Receiving dishes — AP, INS. BUSINESS COMPUTERS: HP/3000-957; Applications: Novell/LAN: Gen ledger; Quattro Pro, Word Perfect, R. Base, Paradox, AOL, Prodigy, Primenet, D-Base, CJ: Accts receivable, Accts payable, Gen ledger, Adv, Circ; PCs & micros networked; PCs & main system networked.

NOGALES

Santa Cruz County

'90 U.S. Census- 19,489; E&P '96 Est. 22,928

Nogales Daily Herald

(e-mon to fri)

Nogales Daily Herald, 87 N. Grand Ave., Nogales, AZ 85621; tel (520) 287-3622.
Circulation: 7,195(e); Sworn Sept. 20, 1993.
Price: 15¢(d); $83.00/yr.
Advertising: Open inch rate $10.00(e). **Politics:** Independent. **Established:** 1914.
Not Published: New Year; Martin Luther King Jr's Birthday; Independence Day; Labor Day; Thanksgiving; Christmas.

GENERAL MANAGEMENT
Publisher Alvin L Sisk

ADVERTISING
Manager Bernie Wilson

NEWS EXECUTIVE
Editor Alvin L Sisk

Market Information: Split Run; TMC; ADS.
Mechanical available: Letterpress; insert accepted — preprinted.
Mechanical specifications: Type page 16" x 19"; E - 8 cols, 2", $\frac{1}{8}$" between; A - 8 cols, 2", $\frac{1}{8}$" between; C - 8 cols, 2", $\frac{1}{8}$" between.
Commodity consumption: Newsprint 500 metric tons; widths 16", 19"; black ink 1,000 pounds; average pages per issue 12(d).
Equipment: PRODUCTION: Typesetters — 5-M/Linotype.
PRESSROOM: Line 1 — Duplex/flatbed letterpress.

PHOENIX

Maricopa County

'90 U.S. Census- 983,403; E&P '96 Est. 1,158,588
ABC-CZ (90): 2,055,713 (HH 782,392)

Phoenix Newspapers Inc.

Phoenix Newspapers Inc., 200 E. Van Buren St. (85004); PO Box 1950, Phoenix, AZ 85001; tel (602) 271-8000; fax (602) 271-8398; web site http://www.azcentral.com. Central Newspapers Inc. group.
Representative: Newspapers First.
News Services: AP, LAT-WP, NYT, SHNS, RN, KRT, HN, BPI. **Politics:** Independent.

CORPORATE OFFICERS
President Eugene S Pulliam
Exec Vice Pres Louis A Weil III
Secretary/Treasurer Frank E Russell
Asst Secretary/Treasurer Donald F Zabek

GENERAL MANAGEMENT
Publisher/CEO Louis A Weil III
Director-Finance Donald F Zabek
Controller Angela Scarcello
Director-Public Affairs William R Shover
Director-Human Resources Mary Ann Matz
Director-Service Sam Young Jr
Director-Property Facilities Bob Guenther
Exec Editor John Oppedahl
Manager-Press Line Amy Ettinger
Senior Editor-Information Technology Howard Finberg
Manager-Research Ellen B Jacobs

ADVERTISING
Director Cathy G Davis
Asst Director David G Alley
Manager-Classified Marilyn Tanious
Manager-General, N.R.S.D. Cathy Zasada

MARKETING AND PROMOTION
Manager-Advertising Sales/Promotion Brad Messer
Manager-Community/Corporate Affairs Gene D'Adamo
Manager-Consumer Marketing Lynn Town

TELECOMMUNICATIONS
Senior Editor-Information Technology Howard Finberg
Audiotex Manager Amy Ettinger

CIRCULATION
Director Richard A Cox
Manager-Metro Mark Mesalam
Manager-Sales Carol Freeman
Manager-Single Copy Sales Mark Weakley
Manager-Support Patricia Moore

MANAGEMENT INFORMATION SERVICES
Manager-Info Service Richard Cunningham
Manager-Client Support Linda Whitney
Manager-Data/Applications Support Jim Lindsey
Manager-Systems Platform Support Bob Frey

PRODUCTION
Director Bob Kotwasinski
Systems Coordinator Jerry Shinaut
Coordinator-Operations Rick Bambauer
Coordinator-Quality Assurance Ric Stone
Training Coordinator Ritch Mitch
Training Coordinator H Michael Rimbey
Unit Manager-Composing Arland Whites
Unit Manager-Packaging (Deer Valley) Judie Greening
Unit Manager-Packaging (Mesa) Norm Rimbey
Unit Manager-Newsprint (Deer Valley) Don Peper
Unit Manager-Newsprint (Mesa) Kyle Skillingstad
Unit Manager-Platemaking (Deer Valley) Kent Greenhalgh
Unit Manager-Platemaking (Mesa) Scott Chamberlain
Unit Manager Pressroom (Deer Valley) Larry Appleby
Unit Manager Pressroom (Mesa) David C George

Market Information: Zoned editions; Split Run; TMC; ADS; Operate database; Operate audiotex; Electronic edition.
Mechanical available: Offset, black; Black and 3 ROP colors; insert accepted — preprinted, samples; page cut-offs — $22\frac{3}{4}$".
Mechanical specifications: Type page 13" x $21\frac{1}{2}$"; E - 6 cols, $2\frac{1}{16}$", $\frac{1}{8}$" between; A - 6 cols, $2\frac{1}{16}$", $\frac{1}{8}$" between; C - 10 cols, $1\frac{3}{16}$", $\frac{1}{16}$" between.
Commodity consumption: Newsprint 104,405 metric tons; widths 54", $40\frac{1}{2}$", 27"; black ink 1,671,000 pounds; color ink 674,000 pounds; single pages printed 59,000; average pages per issue 78(d), 175(S); single plates used 745,300.
Equipment: EDITORIAL: Front-end hardware — SII/Tandem Himalaya, Sun/Sparc 1000; Front-end software — SII, CCI; Other equipment — 35-CE/1010, 319-SII/Coyote. CLASSIFIED: Front-end hardware — SII/Tandem Himalaya, 149-SII/PC Coyote, Sun/Sparc 10; Front-end software — SII/CZAR, CCI; Printers — 1-LP, 6-SLP; Other equipment — 6-SII/Echo. AUDIOTEX: Hardware — AT/2000, Sun/Sparc 100; Software — Micro Voice/Application; Supplier name — AP, VNN. DISPLAY: Adv layout systems — ISSI/Ad Layout; Front-end hardware — SII/Tandem CLX, Ap/Mac, Sun/Sparc 100; Front-end software — SII, III, CCI, QuarkXPress; Printers — 2-HP/Laser; Other equipment — 4-SII/Echo. PRODUCTION: Pagination software — CCI; Typesetters — 6-III/Laser Setter; Plate exposures — 5-WL/Lith-X-Pozer; Plate processors — WL; Electronic picture desk — Lf/AP Leaf Picture Desk, Preserver/photo archive, Ap/Mac; Scanners — 2-Scitex/Smart Scan; Automatic film processors — 6-P/Q-24, 5-LE/2600.
PRESSROOM: Line 1 — 9-G/Metroliner; Line 2 — 9-G/Metroliner; Line 3 — 9-G/Headliner offset; Line 4 — 9-G/Colorliner; Line 5 — 9-G/Colorliner; Line 6 — 9-G/Colorliner; Line 7 — 9-G/Colorliner; Folders — 7-G/3:2; Pasters — 63-G; Reels and stands — 63-G; Press control system — G/PCS, G/APCS. MAILROOM: Counter stackers — 36-HL/Monitor; Inserters and stuffers — 6-AM Graphics/NP2299; Bundle tyer — 32-Power Strap. LIBRARY: Electronic — IBM/RS 6000, Ap/Mac Preserver Image Archive. WIRE SERVICES: News — AP, NYT, KRT, RN, LAT-WP, SHNS; Photos — AP, CRT, RN, Nutimes, All Sports; Stock tables — AP, SelectStox II; Syndicates — AP, INS; Receiving dishes — size-10ft, AP, INS. BUSINESS COMPUTERS: Bull/DPS-8000, Sun/2000; Applications: Circ, Adv billing, Accts receivable, Gen ledger, Payroll;, Microsoft, Cyborg, Lotus Notes; PCs & micros networked; PCs & main system networked.

The Arizona Republic

(m-mon to fri; m-sat; S)

The Arizona Republic, 200 E. Van Buren St. (85004); PO Box 2243, Phoenix, AZ 85001; tel (602) 271-8000; fax (602) 271-8813; web site http://www.azcentral.com. Central Newspapers Inc. group.
Circulation: 365,979(m); 407,874(m-sat); 559,116(S); ABC Sept. 30, 1995.

Price: 50¢(d); 50¢(sat); $1.50(S).
Advertising: Open inch rate $230.00(m); $230.00(m-sat); $308.00(S). **Representative:** Newspapers First.
News Services: AP, LAT-WP, NYT, SHNS, RN, KRT, HN, BPI. **Politics:** Independent. **Established:** 1890.
Note: For additional personnel, production and mechanical information, see Phoenix Newspapers Inc.
Advertising not accepted: X-rated films.
Special Editions: Auto Show, Golf Guide (Jan); 50-Plus (Feb); Spring Fashion, Baseball (Mar); Phoenix Suns Playoff Preview (Apr); Summer Vacation, Arizona Inc./Top 100 (May); Olympics (July); Fall Fashion (Aug); Auto Show, Fall Home Improvement (Sept); Phoenix Suns Preview (Oct); AZ Best, Gift Guide (Nov); Fiesta Bowl (Dec).
Special Weekly Sections: Game-Day Extra, Computing (mon); RV Outdoors (tues); Food, ALT (Teens) (wed); Outdoor Sports (thur); Weekend (fri); Wheels, Religion (sat); Travel, Arts, Life, Perspective (S).
Magazines: Parade (S); AZ Style (monthly).

TELECOMMUNICATIONS

Audiotex Manager Amy Ettinger

NEWS EXECUTIVES

Managing Editor Pam Johnson
Asst Managing Editor Amy Carlilo
Asst Managing Editor Mary Ann Nock
Asst Managing Editor Jeff Dozbaba
Asst Managing Editor/News Operations John Leach
Asst Managing Editor/Administration Jane See White

EDITORS AND MANAGERS

Art Director Tony Bustos
Business Editor Marian Frank
Columnist Steve Wilson
Columnist E J Montini
Editorial Cartoonist Steve Benson
Editorial Page Editor Paul Schatt
Editorial Writer Joel Nilsson
Editorial Writer Linda Valdez
Editorial Writer Jennifer Dokes Garcia
Editorial Writer Ray Archer
Education Editor Hal Mattern
Education/Environment Writer Steve Yozwick
Entertainment Editor Tami Thornton
Farm/Agriculture Writer David Wichner
Fashion Writer Anne Spitza
Features Editor Maren Bingham
Films/Theater Bob Fenster
Fine Arts Writer Richard Nilsen
Food Writer Judy Walker
Garden Writer Thomas Ropp
Health/Medical Writer Jodie Snyder
Librarian Paula Stevens
Metro Editor Steve Knickmeyer
Movie Critic Bob Fenster
Music Editor-Popular Sal Caputo
Exec News Editor Don Nicoson
News Editor Vinton Supplee
Performing Arts Writer Ken La Fave
Perspective Editor Stephanie Robertson
Photo Director Tim Koors
Political Editor Dave Wagner
Political Columnist Keven Willey
Radio/Television Editor Dave Walker
Real Estate Writer Catherine Reagor
Religion Writer Ben Winton
Sports Editor Kathy Brady Tulumello
Sports Columnist David Casstevens
Sports Columnist Bob Jacobsen
Technology Writer Kerry Fehr-Snyder
Teen-Age/Youth Editor Laura Plachecki
Travel Editor Phil Hennessey
Visual Editor Pete Watters

The Phoenix Gazette

(e-mon to fri; e-sat)

The Phoenix Gazette, 200 E. Van Buren St. (85004); PO Box 2245, Phoenix, AZ 85001; tel (602) 271-8000; e-mail phxgazette@aol.com; web site http://www.azcentral.com. Central Newspapers Inc. group.
Circulation: 70,316(e); 75,597(e-sat); ABC Sept. 30, 1995.
Price: 35¢(d); 35¢(sat).
Advertising: Open inch rate $230.00(e); $230.00(e-sat).
News Services: AP, LAT-WP, NYT, RN, KRT. **Politics:** Independent. **Established:** 1880.
Note: For additional personnel, production and mechanical information, see Phoenix Newspapers Inc.
Advertising not accepted: X-rated films.
Special Editions: Auto Show, Golf Guide (Jan); 50-Plus (Feb); Spring Fashion, Arizona Basketball (Mar); Phoenix Suns Playoff Preview (Apr); Summer Vacation, Arizona Inc./Top 100 (May); Olympics (July); Fall Fashion (Aug); Auto Show, Fall Home Improvement (Sept); Phoenix Suns Preview (Oct); AZ Best, Gift Guide (Nov); Fiesta Bowl (Dec).
Special Weekly Sections: Game-Day Extra, Computing (mon); RV Outdoors (tues); Food, ALT (Teens) (wed); Outdoor Sports (thur); Weekend (fri); Wheels, Religion (sat); Travel, Arts, Life, Perspective (S).
Magazines: Parade (S); AZ Style (monthly).

NEWS EXECUTIVES

Managing Editor Pam Johnson
Deputy Managing Editor Don Henninger
Asst Managing Editor Amy Carlilo
Asst Managing Editor Mary Ann Nock
Asst Managing Editor Jeff Dozbaba
Asst Managing Editor/News Operations John Leach
Asst Managing Editor/Administration Jane See White

EDITORS AND MANAGERS

Art Director Tony Bustos
Business Editor Marian Frank
Columnist-Sports Joe Gilmartin
Columnist-Sports Tim Tyers
Columnist Bill Hart
Columnist Sam Lowe
Columnist-Politics John Kolbe
Deputy Editorial Page Editor Mike Genrich
Editorial Page Editor James Hill
Editorial Writer Richard de Uriarte
Editorial Writer Kim Crockett
Education Editor Hal Mattern
Education/Environment Writer Steve Yozwiak
Entertainment Writer Tami Thornton
Farm/Agriculture Editor David Wichner
Fashion Writer Anne Spitza
Features Editor Maren Bingham
Films/Theater Bob Fenster
Fine Arts Writer Richard Nilsen
Food Writer Judy Walker
Garden Writer Thomas Ropp
Health/Medical Writer Jodie Snyder
Librarian Paula Stevens
Metro Editor Steve Knickmeyer
Movie Critic Bob Fenster
Music Editor-Popular Sal Caputo
Exec News Editor Don Nicoson
News Editor Vinton Supplee
Opinion Page Editor Maureen West
Performing Arts Writer Ken La Fave
Photo Director Tim Koors
Political Editor Dave Wagner
Radio/Television Writer Dave Walker
Real Estate Writer Catherine Reagor
Religion Writer Ben Winton
Sports Editor Kathy Brady Tulumello
Technology Writer Kerry Fehr-Snyder
Teen-Age/Youth Editor Laura Plachecki
Travel Editor Phil Hennessey
Visual Editor Pete Watters

PRESCOTT

Yavapai County

'90 U.S. Census- 26,455; E&P '96 Est. 32,489
ABC-NDM (90): 51,536 (HH 21,071)

The Daily Courier

(e-mon to fri; S)

The Daily Courier, 147 N. Cortez; PO Box 312, Prescott, AZ 86302; tel (520) 445-3333. Western Newspapers Inc. group.
Circulation: 16,369(e); 18,476(S); ABC Sept. 30, 1995.
Price: 50¢(d); $1.25(S); $2.10/wk; $109.20/yr.
Advertising: Open inch rate $11.86(e); $13.04(e-fri); $13.04(S). **Representative:** Papert Companies.
News Service: AP. **Politics:** Independent. **Established:** 1882.
Special Editions: Coupon Tab, Super Bowl Preview (broad) (Jan); Who's Who in Business Tab (Feb); Progress '96 (Mar); Home Improvement Tab (Apr); Tourist Treasures (May); Frontier Days (June); Back-to-School (broad) (Aug); Fall Home Improvement (broad) (Sept); Christmas Gift Guide (Nov).
Special Weekly Sections: TV Digest, Real Estate (fri); Entertainment & TV listings.
Magazine: Today's Real Estate (monthly).

CORPORATE OFFICERS

CEO Robert Gilliland
President Donald N Soldwedel
Vice Pres Joseph E Soldwedel
Secretary Lou Edith Soldwedel
Treasurer Ann Buxie

GENERAL MANAGEMENT

Publisher Robert Gilliland
Business Manager Paula Lea Anderson
Personnel Manager Donna Beeson

ADVERTISING

Director Pam Hood

MARKETING AND PROMOTION

Manager-Marketing/Promotion Pam Hood

CIRCULATION

Manager John Harrell

NEWS EXECUTIVES

Editor Jim Garner
Managing Editor Chuck Doud

EDITORS AND MANAGERS

Amusements/Books Editor Lauren Millette
City Editor Karen Despain
Columnist Jim Garner
Editorial Page Editor Jim Garner
Editorial Writer Jim Garner
Films/Theater Editor Lauren Millette
Food Editor Lauren Millette
Metro Editor Chuck Doud
News/Wire Editor Jon L'Hommedieu
Political Editor Jim Garner
Real Estate Editor Mary Woodhouse
Sports Editor Dan Beeson
Teen-age/Youth/Religion Editor Steve Lee

PRODUCTION

Director Tom Bugbee
Manager Armando Rondarte
Asst Manager/Manager-Mailroom Ray Ford

Market Information: TMC; ADS.
Mechanical available: Offset; insert accepted — preprinted.
Mechanical specifications: Type page 13" x 21.5"; E - 6 cols, 2.06", 1/8" between; A - 6 cols, 2.06", 1/8" between; C - 6 cols, 2.06", 1/8" between.
Commodity consumption: Newsprint 839 metric tons; widths 27½", 13¾"; black ink 22,304 pounds; color ink 7,434 pounds; single pages printed 8,748; average pages per issue 28(d), 58(S); single plates used 5,564.
Equipment: EDITORIAL: Front-end hardware — 6-Mk/Touchwriter Plus, 12-Mk/Touchwriter, Ap/Mac Quadra 840 AV, Ap/Mac 19" color monitor, Ap/Mac Performa 200, Ap/Mac Plus, Ap/Mac Club 20MB external drive; Front-end software — Adobe/Photoshop, Lf/AP Leaf Picture Desk 8.3.2, Clarisworks 3.0, QuarkXPress 3.0, Microsoft/Word 5.1, Aldus/FreeHand; Printers — Ap/Mac LaserWriter 16-1600 PS, Ap/Mac Laserphoto; Other equipment — AG/Focus Scanner. DISPLAY: Front-end hardware — 5-Mk/Touchwriter Plus, Ap/Mac Plus; Printers — TI/800 Model DP, Ap/Mac LaserWriter Plus. PRODUCTION: Pagination software — Adobe/Photoshop, Caere/OmniPage, QuarkXPress, Adobe/Illustrator, Broderbund/Typestyler, Adobe/Type Library, Claris/MacDraw Pro; Typesetters — Ap/Mac 16" color monitor, Mirror/19" monitor, Ap/SuperMac Gray Scale monitor, 4-Mirror/Monitor, Ap/Mac Color Plus 14" Display, Ap/Mac Quadra 650, 3-Ap/Mac IIvx, Ap/Mac IIcx, Ap/Mac IIci, Ap/Power Mac 6100-60m server, Ap/Power Mac 6150, Ap/Mac LaserWriter 16-600 PS, 2-Ap/Mac LaserWriter Pro, Ap/Mac LaserWriter II, Mk/Touchwriter Plus; Direct-to-plate imaging — GNS/28 Plate Burner, Nu/Plate Burner; Scanners — Umax/UC1260 Scanner, Canon/FV540 Digital Disk Reader, Mirror/44 Megabyte cartridge reader, Power User/88 MB cartridge reader; Production cameras — Dainippon/Screen Horizontal Camera, Omega/ProLab 4x5 enlarger camera; Automatic film processors — Lf/AP Leafdesk Digital Darkroom, AG/Compugraphic Division 37E14 film developer, Kodak/Ecktamatic processor, AG/CP 380 Processor, LE. PRESSROOM: Line 1 — 10-G/Community; Folders — G/S (w/ upper former), G/Urbanite (w/ upper former). MAILROOM: Counter stackers — MSI/12205; Inserters and stuffers — 8-Mc, 7-Mueller; Bundle tyer — Strap-Pack/Strapper 35-80 AKN, MLN/ML2-EE; Addressing machine — 3-Dispensamatic. COMMUNICATIONS: Facsimile — Mita/C170, HP/900. WIRE SERVICES: News — AP; Receiving dishes — AP. BUSINESS COMPUTERS: DEC/200, 2-DEC/server, 6-DEC/VT-420 monitor, 2-DEC/VT-220 monitor, DEC/LA-424 Desktop printer, C.Itoh/Dot Matrix Printer, AST/PC, Ap/Mac Plus, Ap/Mac LaserWriter Plus, Ap/Mac PowerBook 160, Ap/Mac PowerBook 550, Mk/ScanMaker IIG Scanner, Ap/Mac LaserWriter II NTX; Applications: Vision Data 3.8, Microsoft/Word 6.0, QuarkXPress, Caere/OmniPage Direct, Microsoft/Excel.

SCOTTSDALE

Maricopa County

'90 U.S. Census- 130,069; E&P '96 Est. 172,707
ABC-NDM (90): 219,053 (HH 91,897)

Scottsdale Progress Tribune

(e-mon to fri; m-sat; S)

Scottsdale Progress Tribune, 7525 E. Camelback Rd. (Scottsdale 85252); PO Box 1547, Mesa, AZ 85211; tel (602) 941-2300; fax (602) 970-2360; e-mail coxtrib&@prodigy.com. Cox Newspapers Inc. group.
Circulation: 15,545(e); 17,205(m-sat); 15,739(S); ABC Sept. 30, 1995.
Price: 35¢(d); 35¢(sat); $1.25(S); $1.50/wk; $6.50/mo; $58.44/yr.
Advertising: Open inch rate $59.22(e); $59.22(m-sat); $46.51(S). **Representative:** Papert Companies.
News Services: AP, NYT, SHNS, Cox News Service, LAT-WP, GNS, PR Newswire. **Politics:** Independent. **Established:** 1937.
Note: Advertising is sold in combination with Chandler Arizonan-Tribune (mS), Gilbert Tribune (mS), Mesa Tribune (mS) and Tempe Daily News Tribune (mS) for $69.08 (d&S) and $82.65 (m-wed). Wednesday rate includes Extended Market Coverage. For detailed equipment information, see the Mesa Tribune listing.
Special Editions: Senior Living, Arizona Homes, Parade Del Sol, Super Bowl, Phoenix Open (Jan); Renaissance Festival, Masterplan Community, Health Directory (Feb); Baseball, Senior Living/Health, Women's Expo (Mar); Good Times, Suns Playoff, Country Thunder, Cullinary Festival (Apr); Home Improvement, Rest Assured, Arizona Homes (May); Healthy Lifestyles/Seniors (June); Crime Prevention, 4th of July, Health Directory (July); Back-to-School, Football Preview, Arizona Homes (Aug); Arizona Homes, Home Improvement (Sept); Healthy Lifestyles/Seniors, Scottsdale Valley Guide, Arizona Homes (Nov); Last Minute Gifts, Fiesta Bowl, Healthy Lifestyles/Seniors (Dec).
Special Weekly Sections: AZ Tech (mon); Food & Recipes, Entertainment (wed); Scottsdale Life (thur); Religion, Homefinder, Extended Weekly Stocks Wrap-Up (sat); Lifestyle, Business, Travel, Wheels, Perspectives, Act-Just for Teens, Extended Mutual Fund Report, National Manufacturer's Coupons (S).
Magazines: Parade, Color Comics, Tribune TV (S); Arizona Adventure (thur, bi-wkly).

CORPORATE OFFICERS

President Sanford Schwartz
Vice Pres Belinda Gaudet
Controller Edward Burns

GENERAL MANAGEMENT

Publisher Sanford Schwartz
General Manager Belinda Gaudet
Asst to Publisher Janet Cox
Director Human Resources Melissa Lows

ADVERTISING

Director H Robert Hirsch
Manager-Classified Tim Thomas
Manager-Retail Tricia Phillips

MARKETING AND PROMOTION

Director-Marketing/Promotion Jody Taylor

TELECOMMUNICATIONS

Director Multimedia Service Bill Roberts

CIRCULATION

Director Michael Romero

NEWS EXECUTIVE

Editor Hal Dekeyser

EDITORS AND MANAGERS

Books/Music Editor Betty Webb
Business/Finance Editor Martha Reinke
City Editor Mike Phillips
Columnist David Leibowitz
Editorial Page Editor Bob Schuster
Entertainment/Amusement Editor Liz B Merritt
Features Editor Liz B Merritt
Films/Theater Editor Max McQueen
Living/Lifestyle Editor Liz B Merritt
Medical Editor Liz B Merritt
Photo Editor Rick Wiley
Political/Government Editor Mark Flatten
Real Estate Editor Martha Reinke
Science/Technology Editor Liz B Merritt
Sports Editor Dave Lumia

MANAGEMENT INFORMATION SERVICES

Director Computer Service Jim Roe

PRODUCTION

Operations Director Scott Porter
Manager-Pre Press Mark Zawacki
Manager-Press Dave Veno
Manager-Distribution/Packaging Kathy Trappe

Market Information: Operate database; Operate audiotex.
Mechanical available: Offset; Black and 3 ROP colors; insert accepted — preprinted, any; page cut-offs — 22".
Mechanical specifications: Type page 13" x 21"; E - 6 cols, 2.04", 1/6" between; A - 6 cols, 2.04", 1/6" between; C - 9 cols, 1.33", 1/6" between.
Commodity consumption: Newsprint 1,735 short tons; widths 27 3/8", 41 3/16", 54 3/4"; black ink 27,978 pounds; color ink 15,490 pounds; single pages printed 14,553; average pages per issue 46(d), 86(sat), 96(S); single plates used 156,000.

SIERRA VISTA
Cochise County

'90 U.S. Census- 32,983; E&P '96 Est. 40,580

Sierra Vista Herald
(e-mon to fri; S)

Sierra Vista Herald, 102 Fab Ave., Sierra Vista, AZ 85635; tel (520) 458-9440; fax (520) 459-0120. Wick Communications group.
Circulation: 9,694(e); 11,310(S); VAC Mar. 31, 1995.
Price: 50¢(d); $1.25(S); $8.80/mo.
Advertising: Open inch rate $11.26(e); $11.26(S).
News Service: AP. **Politics:** Independent. **Established:** 1968.
Note: Advertisements in the Sierra Vista Herald (eS) are automatically inserted in the Bisbee Daily Review (eS).
Not Published: New Year; Memorial Day; Independence Day; Labor Day; Christmas.
Special Editions: Progress (Mar); Back-to-School (Aug); Christmas Opening (Nov).
Special Weekly Sections: Food Fair (tues); Country Page, Outdoors Page (thur); Real Estate Section, Religion Page, People Page, Teen Corner (fri); Entertainment TV, Business Page, People Page (S).
Magazines: Tuesday Plus, Food Fare (tues); Fort Huachuca, Cable Connections-TV, Color Comics, Bravo (S).

CORPORATE OFFICERS

President Walter M Wick
Vice Pres Robert J Wick

GENERAL MANAGEMENT

General Manager Steve Krehl
Business Manager Sheryll R Bruening

ADVERTISING

Director Dennis Benth

CIRCULATION

Director John Reichard

NEWS EXECUTIVE

Managing Editor Michael Parnell

EDITORS AND MANAGERS

Entertainment/Amusements Editor Jean King
Sports Editor Kevin Carolan
Sunday News Editor Tim Ellis
Sunday News Editor Lori Maryland

PRODUCTION

Manager Ken Murray
Foreman-Composing Ken Murray
Foreman-Press/Camera Ken Murray

Market Information: Zoned editions; Split Run; TMC.
Mechanical available: Offset; Black and 3 ROP colors; insert accepted — preprinted, all; page cut-offs — 19".
Mechanical specifications: Type page 13" x 21"; E - 6 cols, 2 1/16", 1/8" between; A - 6 cols, 2 1/16", 1/8" between; C - 9 cols, 1 3/8", 1/16" between.
Commodity consumption: Newsprint 800 metric tons; widths 27 1/2", 22"; black ink 5,000 pounds; single pages printed 7,830; average pages per issue 24(d), 32(S).
Equipment: EDITORIAL: Front-end hardware — 1-COM/One, Mk/3500. CLASSIFIED: Front-end hardware — Mk/3500. DISPLAY: Adv layout systems — Mk; Other equipment — 2-COM/One. PRODUCTION: Typesetters — 5-COM/One; Platemaking systems — 1-Nu; Plate exposures — 1-Nu/Flip Top; Plate processors — Nat; Production cameras — 1-B/Commodore; Automatic film processors — 1-P/Pakonolith. PRESSROOM: Line 1 — 6-G/Community; Folders — 1-G. MAILROOM: Inserters and stuffers — 1-KAN/480; Bundle tyer — 1-Ace/Model 50, 2-Wilton/Stra Pack 55-80; Addressing machine — 1-Am/Class 1900. COMMUNICATIONS: Systems used — satellite. WIRE SERVICES: News — AP; Receiving dishes — size-10m, AP. BUSINESS COMPUTERS: DEC.

SUN CITY
Maricopa County

'90 U.S. Census- 44,730; E&P '96 Est. 48,218
ABC-NDM (90): 56,665 (HH 33,215)

Daily News-Sun
(e-mon to fri; m-sat)

Daily News-Sun, 10102 Santa Fe Dr.; PO Box 1779, Sun City, AZ 85372; tel (602) 977-8351; fax (602) 876-3695. Ottaway Newspapers Inc. group.
Circulation: 16,606(e); 16,606(m-sat); ABC Sept. 30, 1995.
Price: 50¢(d); 50¢(sat); $3.00/wk; $8.55/mo; $91.20/yr.
Advertising: Open inch rate $11.35(e); $11.35(m-sat); $21.25 (tues-TMC). **Representatives:** Papert Companies; US Suburban Press.
News Services: AP, DJ, ONS. **Politics:** Independent. **Established:** 1957.
Not Published: New Year; Memorial Day; Independence Day; Labor Day; Thanksgiving; Christmas.
Special Editions: Cooking Recipes and Contest (Mar); Senior Caregivers (May); Fall Home Improvement (Oct).
Special Weekly Sections: Health & Science, Food & Nutrition (tues); Travel (wed); Weekender/Entertainment (thur); Week's End/Business Review (sat).
Magazines: "Extra" (TMC) (tues); View Tab, TV/Entertainment (fri); USA Weekend (sat).

GENERAL MANAGEMENT

President/Publisher Sam L Marocco
Asst General Manager Samuel R Gett Jr
Controller Richard A Ching

ADVERTISING

Manager-Retail Jan E McKinney
Manager-Classified Sandra N Taylor

CIRCULATION

Manager Bill Luicha

NEWS EXECUTIVE

Editor Maryanne Leyshon

EDITORS AND MANAGERS

News Editor Ian Mitchell
Sports Editor Rich Bolas

MANAGEMENT INFORMATION SERVICES

Data Processing Manager Donald J Leyshon

PRODUCTION

Director-Operations Donald J Leyshon
Manager-Press James Dickey
Manager-Composing Kathy Ptak
Manager-Distribution Nicholas J Marocco

Market Information: TMC; ADS.
Mechanical available: Offset; Black and 3 ROP colors; insert accepted — preprinted, all; page cut-offs — 22 3/4".
Mechanical specifications: Type page 13" x 21 1/2"; E - 6 cols, 2 1/16", 1/8" between; A - 6 cols, 2 1/16", 1/8" between; C - 9 cols, 1 11/16", 1/8" between.
Commodity consumption: Newsprint 1,361 metric tons; width 27 1/2"; black ink 25,000 pounds; color ink 4,000 pounds; single pages printed 10,430; average pages per issue 34(d); single plates used 10,500.
Equipment: EDITORIAL: Front-end hardware — Dewar, IBM; Front-end software — Dewar; Printers — Okidata, Ap/Mac LaserWriter Pro 810; Other equipment — Ap/Mac II, Lf/AP Leaf Picture Desk, Lf/Leafscan 35, IBM/Value Point, Ap/Power Mac 8100, Pronex/DXZ-66 Intel. CLASSIFIED: Front-end hardware — Dewar/Disc; Front-end software — Dewar/Disc; Printers — Dataproducts; Other equipment — IBM, Pronex/DX2-66 Intel, HP/ScanJet IIP Scanner. DISPLAY: Adv layout systems — 3-Dewar/Discovery; Front-end hardware — Ap/Mac, Dewar; Front-end software — Dewar; Printers — Okidata, Ap/Mac LaserWriter Pro 810; Other equipment — IBM/Value Point, Ap/PowerMac 8100, Ap/PowerMac 7100, La Cie/Color Scanner. PRODUCTION: Typesetters — V; Plate exposures — Nu; Plate processors — Nat/A-250; Scanners — ECR/Autokon 1030NC; Production cameras — C/Spartan III; Automatic film processors — LE; Color separation equipment (conventional) — Lf/Leafscan 35.
PRESSROOM: Line 2 — 8-G/Urbanite; Press control system — Fin. MAILROOM: Counter stackers — HL/Dual Carrier; Inserters and stuffers — GMA; Bundle tyer — MLN/Spirit. COMMUNICATIONS: Facsimile — 2-Mita/TC-220, 1-RSK/Tandy 1000, 2-Sharp/UX 1200R. WIRE SERVICES: News — AP, DJ, ONS; Stock tables — AP; Receiving dishes — AP. BUSINESS COMPUTERS: IBM/AS400, IBM/Model 60, IBM/AT, 2-IBM/Model 57, IBM/Value Point; Applications: WordPerfect, Multiplan, Microsoft/Word for Windows, Microsoft/Excel; PCs & micros networked.

TEMPE
Maricopa County

'90 U.S. Census- 141,865; E&P '96 Est. 166,500
ABC-CZ (90): 141,865 (HH 55,540)

Tempe Daily News-Tribune
(m-mon to sat; S)

Tempe Daily News Tribune, 51 W. Third St. Suite 106 (Tempe 85281); PO Box 1547, Mesa, AZ 85211; tel (602) 898-5680; fax (602) 968-8030; e-mail coxtrib&@prodigy.com. Cox Newspapers Inc. group.
Circulation: 10,401(m); 10,401(m-sat); 10,589(S); ABC Sept. 30, 1995.
Price: 50¢(d); 50¢(sat); $1.25(S); $2.31/wk; $10.00/mo; $120.00/yr.
Advertising: Open inch rate $69.08(m); $82.65(m-wed); $69.08(m-sat); $69.08(S). **Representative:** Papert Companies.
News Services: AP, Cox News Service, LAT-WP, SHNS, NYT, GNS, PR Newswire, TMS. **Politics:** Independent. **Established:** 1887.
Note: Advertising is sold in combination with Chandler Arizonan-Tribune (mS), Gilbert Tribune (mS), Mesa Tribune (mS) and Scottsdale Progress Tribune (eS) for $69.08 (d&S) and $82.65 (m-wed). Wednesday rate includes Extended Market Coverage. For detailed equipment information, see the Mesa Tribune listing.
Special Editions: Senior Living, Super Bowl (Jan); Renaissance Festival, Masterplan Community, Health Directory (Feb); Ostrich Festival, Baseball, Women's Expo, Senior Living/Health (Mar); Good Times, Suns Playoffs, Country Thunder (Apr); Home Improvement, Rest Assured (May); Healthy Lifestyles/Seniors (June); Crime Prevention, Health Directory (July); Back-to-School, Football Preview (Aug); Home Improvement, Doo Dah Festival (Sept); Healthy Lifestyles/Seniors, East Valley Guide, Balloon Classic (Oct); Basketball, Holiday Kickoff (Nov); Last Minute Gifts, Healthy Lifestyles/Seniors, Fiesta Bowl Guide (Dec).
Special Weekly Sections: AZ Tech (mon); Food & Recipes (wed); TGIF (fri); Religion, Extended Weekly Stock Wrap Up, Homefinder (Real Estate) (sat); Lifestyles, Business, Class Act-Just for Teens, Perspectives, Extended Mutual Fund Report, National Manufacturer's Coupons, Travel, Wheels (S).
Magazines: Tribune TV, Comics, Parade (S); Arizona Adventure (thur, bi-wkly).

CORPORATE OFFICERS

President Sanford Schwartz
Vice Pres Belinda Gaudet
Controller Edward Burns

GENERAL MANAGEMENT

Publisher Sanford Schwartz
General Manager Belinda Gaudet
Asst to Publisher Janet Cox
Director-Human Resources Melissa Lows

ADVERTISING

Director H Robert Hirsch
Manager-Classified Tim Thomas
Manager-Retail Tricia Phillips

MARKETING AND PROMOTION

Director-Marketing/Promotion Jody Taylor

TELECOMMUNICATIONS

Director Multimedia Services Bill Roberts

CIRCULATION

Director Michael Romero

NEWS EXECUTIVES

Exec Editor Jeffrey C Bruce
Editor Dan McCarthy
Managing Editor Jim Ripley

EDITORS AND MANAGERS

Books/Music Editor Betty Webb
Business/Finance Editor Martha Reinke
Columnist David Leibowitz
Editorial Page Editor Bob Schuster
Education Editor Sherry Arpaio
Entertainment/Amusements Editor Liz B Merritt
Fashion/Style Editor Liz B Merritt
Features Editor Liz B Merritt
Films/Theater Editor Max McQueen
Living/Lifestyle Editor Liz B Merritt
Medical Editor Liz B Merritt
News Editor Bob Netherton
Photo Editor Rick Wiley
Political/Government Editor Mark Flatten
Religion Editor Kelly Ettenborough
Science/Technology Editor Liz B Merritt
Sports Editor Dave Lumia
Television/Film Editor Bruce Christian
Women's Editor Liz B Merritt

MANAGEMENT INFORMATION SERVICES

Director-Computer Services Jim Roe

PRODUCTION

Director-Operations Scott Porter
Manager-Pre Press Mark Zawacki
Manager-Press Dave Veno
Manager-Distribution/Packaging Kathy Trappe

Market Information: Operate database; Operate audiotex.
Mechanical available: Offset; Black and 3 ROP colors; insert accepted — preprinted; page cut-offs — 22".
Mechanical specifications: Type page 13" x 21"; E - 6 cols, 2 1/16", 1/8" between; A - 6 cols, 2 1/16", 1/8" between; C - 9 cols, 1 3/8", 1/16" between.
Commodity consumption: Newsprint 2,458 short tons; widths 54 3/4", 41 3/16", 27 3/8"; black ink 39,636 pounds; color ink 21,945 pounds; single pages printed 20,755; average pages per issue 50(d), 90(sat), 100(S); single plates used 156,00.

TUCSON
Pima County

'90 U.S. Census- 405,390; E&P '96 Est. 460,789
ABC-CZ (90): 642,684 (HH 253,791)

Tucson Newspapers Inc.

TNI Partners dba Tucson Newspapers, 4850 S. Park Ave.; PO Box 26887, Tucson, AZ 85726-6887; tel (520) 573-4400; fax (520) 573-4294.
Established: 1940.
Note: The Arizona Daily Star and Tucson Citizen are corporately and editorially separate. Tucson Newspapers is the agent for the merged business, circulation and production functions of the two papers.

CORPORATE OFFICERS

Board Chairman Nicholas G Penniman IV
President-TNI Partners Lawrence J Aldrich
Secretary C Donald Hattfield

GENERAL MANAGEMENT

Vice Pres-Finance/Treasurer Jane Engle
Vice Pres-Human Resources Edith Auslander

ADVERTISING

Vice Pres Terrance C Z Egger
Manager-Retail Sam Adkins
Manager-Major Accounts Brad Clasgens
Manager-Classified Paul Ingeneri

MARKETING AND PROMOTION

Vice Pres-Market Development Michael Soliman

CIRCULATION

Vice Pres Larry T Martin
Manager Gary Carlone
Manager-Single Copy Sales Bernard Hollingsworth
Manager-Home Delivery Barb McGuire
Manager Joanne Phillips
Manager-Operations Mike Welsh

MANAGEMENT INFORMATION SERVICES

Director-Management Info Services Mark T Williams

PRODUCTION

Vice Pres-Operations Wayne Bean
Manager-Operations Bill Hilser
Manager-Special Section/Quality Jerry Bennett
Manager-Service Joann Hardy-Carranza
Manager-Plate/Camera Deryck Burkett
Manager-Pressroom John Lundgren
Manager-Packaging Center Randy Brown
Manager-Production Maintenance Danny Crain
Manager-Physical Resources Bob Ross
Manager-Environmental Lynn Straughn
Manager-Technical Service Dave Dunn

Market Information: Zoned editions; Split Run; TMC; ADS; Electronic edition.
Mechanical available: Offset; Black and 3 ROP colors; insert accepted — preprinted, shingle sheet flyers; page cut-offs — 22 3/4".

Mechanical specifications: Type page 13" x 21½"; E - 6 cols, 2⅟16", ⅛" between; A - 6 cols, 2⅟16", ⅛" between; C - 10 cols, 1¼", ⅟16" between.
Commodity consumption: Newsprint 25,051 metric tons; widths 54½", 40⅞", 27¼"; black ink 457,325 pounds; color ink 201,534 pounds; single pages printed 54,468; average pages per issue 56(d), 150(S); single plates used 256,627.
Equipment: EDITORIAL: Front-end hardware — Proteon/486; Front-end software — III, MPS/Tecs 2 2.39; Printers — HP/LaserJet IV. CLASSIFIED: Front-end hardware — Proteon/386; Front-end software — III, MPS/Tecs 2 2.39; Printers — 3-IBM/Proprint III. DISPLAY: Adv layout systems — SCS/Layout 8000; Front-end hardware — PC/386; Front-end software — SCS/Layout 8000; Printers — DEC/LA 120. PRODUCTION: Pagination software — HI/8900 Classified 7.6; Typesetters — 1-III/3850, 2-III/3810 Imagesetter; Plate exposures — WL/Lith-X-Pozer IV, 2-Nu/FlipTop FT40APRNS; Plate processors — 2-Aqualith/50; Scanners — 1-ECR/Autokon 1000 DE, K&F/Optical Verifier, Pixelcraft/18000 Flatbed 4520 RS; Production cameras — 2-C/Spartan III; Automatic film processors — 2-LD, 1-R/660; Film transporters — 2-C/Spartan; Shrink lenses — 2-CK Optical/SQU-7; Color separation equipment (conventional) — Ap/Mac Power PC, Adobe/Photoshop, Adobe/Color Access. PRESSROOM: Line 1 — 8-G/Metro 3127A (4 half decks); Line 2 — 8-G/Metro 3128A (4 half decks); Press drives — 16-Fin; Folders — 4-G/3:2; Pasters — Automatic Pasters; Reels and stands — G/Hermonic Drive. MAILROOM: Counter stackers — 1-QWI/300, 7-QWI/100, 1-QWI/350; Inserters and stuffers — 1-HI/1472, 1-GMA/SLS-1000-A; Bundle tyer — 6-MLN, 3-Power Strap, 2-HI/RS-25, 2-Dynaric; Wrapping singles — 6-QWI/Bottom Wrap; Addressing machine — 2-Ch/Labeler; Other mailroom equipment — 1-MM/235. WIRE SERVICES: News — AP Datastream, AP Datafeatures; Photos — AP; Stock tables — TMS, AP; Receiving dishes — size-3m, AP. BUSINESS COMPUTERS: IBM/AS400; Applications: Ad Serv/138: Adv; IBM: Circ; PCs & micros networked; PCs & main system networked.

The Arizona Daily Star

(m-mon to sat; S)

The Arizona Daily Star, 4850 S. Park Ave.; PO Box 26807, Tucson, AZ 85726-6807; tel (520) 573-4220; web site http://www.azstarnet.com. Pulitzer Publishing Co. group.
Circulation: 92,956(m); 92,956(m-sat); 173,716(S); ABC Sept. 30, 1995.
Price: 50¢(d); 50¢(sat); $1.50(S); $2.90/wk; $11.60/mo; $150.80/yr.
Representative: Gannett National Newspaper Sales.
News Services: AP, NYT, KRT, SHNS. **Politics:** Independent. **Established:** 1877.
Note: Advertising is sold in combination with Tucson Citizen (e) for $92.76 (d) & $111.50 (S). Individual newspaper rates not made available. For detailed production information, see Tuscon Newspapers listing.
Advertising not accepted: Any judged not to be in the reader's best interests.
Special Editions: Coupon Book; Business Preview/Review; Rodeo; Weddings; Health & Fitness; Home Improvement; Football; Newcomers; Golf; Gift Guide; Seniors; Winter Visitors.
Special Weekly Sections: MoneyPlus, Tucson Inc., Accent/Living, Weekend, Sports Wrapup (mon); Accent/Living (tues); Food & More, Accent/Living (wed); Accent/Living, Weekend (thur); Starlight (entertainment), Sports, Movies (fri); Accent/Living, Movies, Sports (sat); Accent, Home, Comics, TV Week, Sports, Travel (S); Business (daily).
Magazines: Parade, TV-Week, Food & More (wed); Starlight (fri).

CORPORATE OFFICERS

President Michael E Pulitzer
President-TNI Partners Lawrence J Aldrich
Vice Pres Ronald H Ridgway
Treasurer James Vogelpohl
Secretary James Maloney

GENERAL MANAGEMENT

Publisher Michael E Pulitzer
Vice Pres-Finance/Treasurer Jane Engel

ADVERTISING

Vice Pres Terrance C Z Egger
Manager-Retail Sam Adkins
Manager-Major Accounts Brad Clasgens
Manager-Classified Paul Ingeneri

MARKETING AND PROMOTION

Vice Pres-Market Development Michael Soliman

CIRCULATION

Vice Pres Larry T Martin

NEWS EXECUTIVES

Editor Steve Auslander
Managing Editor Bobbie Jo Buel
Asst Managing Editor-News Desk Joe McDermott
Asst Managing Editor-Metro/State John P C Silva

EDITORS AND MANAGERS

Books Editor Colette Bancroft
Business Editor John Bolton
Copy Chief George Campbell
Entertainment Editor Debbie Kornmiller
Editorial Page Editor James M Kiser
Education Editor Maureen O'Connell
Environmental Editor Kieth Bagwell
Fashion Editor Maria Parham
Features Editor Debbie Kornmiller
Films Editor Robert Cauthorn
Food Editor Judith Anderson
Graphics Editor/Art Director Chuck Kramer
Health/Medical Editor Jane Erikson
Home Furnishings Editor Thom Walker
Library Elaine Raines
Outdoors Editor Tom Foust
Photo Editor Mari Schaefer
Science/Technology Editor James Erickson
Sports Editor Robert J Bartlett
Travel Editor Tom Turner

MANAGEMENT INFORMATION SERVICES

Director-Management Info Services Mark T Williams

PRODUCTION

Vice Pres-Operations Wayne Bean
Manager-Operations Bill Hilser
Manager-Special Section/Quality Jerry Bennett
Manager-Service Joann Hardy-Carranza
Manager-Plate/Camera Deryck Burkett
Manager-Pressroom John Lundgren
Manager-Packaging Department Randy Brown
Manager-Production Maintenance Danny Crain
Manager-Physical Resources Bob Ross
Manager-Environmental Lynn Straughn
Manager-Technical Service Dave Dunn

Market Information: Zoned editions; Split Run; TMC; ADS; Electronic edition.
Mechanical available: Offset; Black and 3 ROP colors; insert accepted — preprinted, shingle sheet flyers; page cut-offs — 22¾".
Mechanical specifications: Type page 13" x 21½"; E - 6 cols, 2⅟16", ⅛" between; A - 6 cols, 2⅟16", ⅛" between; C - 10 cols, 1¼", ⅟16" between.
Commodity consumption: Newsprint 25,000 metric tons; widths 54", 54½", 54⅜"; black ink 464,000 pounds; color ink 145,000 pounds; single pages printed 44,135; average pages per issue 60(d), 60(sat), 154(S); single plates used 222,000.
Equipment: EDITORIAL: Front-end hardware — Proteon/486; Front-end software — MPS/Tecs 2 2.39; Printers — HP/LaserJet IV. CLASSIFIED: Front-end hardware — Proteon/386; Front-end software — MPS/Tecs 2 2.39; Printers — IBM/Proprint III. DISPLAY: Adv layout systems — SCS/Layout 8000; Front-end hardware — HI, PC/386; Front-end software — SCS/Layout 8000; Printers — DEC/LA 120. PRODUCTION: Pagination software — HI/8900 Classified 7.6; Typesetters — 1-III/3850, 2-III/3810 Imagesetter; Platemaking systems — 1-WL/Lith-X-Pozer IV-, 2-Nu/Flip Top FT40APRNS; Plate exposures — 2-WL/38D; Scanners — 1-ECR/Autokon 1000 DE, 1-K&F/Optical Verifier; Production cameras — 2-C/Spartan III; Automatic film processors — 2-LD, 1-R/660; Film transporters — 2-C/Spartan; Shrink lenses — 2-CK Optical/SQU-7; Color separation equipment (conventional) — 1-Ap/Mac Power PC, Adobe/Photoshop, Adobe/Color Access; Digital color separation equipment — 1-Pixelcraft/8000 Flatbed 4520 RS Scanner. PRESSROOM: Line 1 — 8-G/Metro 3127A (4 half decks); Line 2 — 8-G/Metro 3128A (4 half decks); Press drives — 16-Fin; Folders — 4-G/3:2; Pasters — Automatic Pasters; Reels and stands — G/Harmonic Drive. MAILROOM: Counter stackers — 1-QWI/300, 7-QWI/100, 2-G/Stackmaster; Inserters and stuffers — 1-HI/1472, 1-GMA/SLS 1000 A; Bundle tyer — 6-MLN, 3-Power Strap, 2-HI/RS-25; Wrapping singles — 6-QWI/Bottom Wrap; Addressing machine — 2-Ch/Labeler. WIRE SERVICES: News — AP Datastream, AP Datafeatures; Photos — AP; Stock tables — AP, TMS; Receiving dishes — size-3m, AP. BUSINESS COMPUTERS: IBM/AS400; Applications: IBM: Circ;, AdServ: Adv; PCs & micros networked; PCs & main system networked.

Tucson Citizen

(e-mon to fri; m-sat)

Tucson Citizen, PO Box 26767, Tucson, AZ 85726; tel (520) 573-4561; fax (520) 573-4569; e-mail tcnews@aol.com. Gannett Co. Inc. group.
Circulation: 46,004(e); 46,004(m-sat); ABC Sept. 30, 1995.
Price: 35¢(d); 35¢(sat).
Representative: Gannett National Newspaper Sales.
News Services: AP, GNS, LAT-WP. **Politics:** Independent. **Established:** 1870.
Note: Advertising is sold in combination with Arizona Daily Star (mS) for $92.76 (d) & $111.50 (S). Individual newspaper rates not made available. For detailed production information, see Tuscon Newspapers listing.
Special Editions: Senior Scene; Hello Tucson; Winter Visitors; Football; Basketball.
Special Weekly Sections: Tucson Inc. (business tab) (mon); Tempo (TMC) (tues); Food (wed); Calender (entertainment tab) (thur).
Magazine: USA Weekend.

CORPORATE OFFICERS

President/Publisher C Donald Hatfield
President-TNI Partners Lawrence J Aldrich
Secretary Thomas L Chapple
Asst Secretary John L Donahue Jr
Asst Treasurer Jimmy L Thomas

GENERAL MANAGEMENT

Publisher C Donald Hatfield

ADVERTISING

Vice Pres Terrance C Z Egger

MARKETING AND PROMOTION

Vice Pres-Market Developement Michael Soliman

CIRCULATION

Vice Pres Larry T Martin

NEWS EXECUTIVES

Editor C Donald Hatfield
Managing Editor Ricardo Pimentel
Asst Managing Editor Judy Lefton

EDITORS AND MANAGERS

Art Director Joel Rochon
Visual Arts Editor Charlotte Lowe
Business Editor Jennifer Boice
City Editor Jim Wyckoff
Columnist John Jennings
Design Editor Paul Schwalbach
Editorial Page Editor Mark Kimble
Films Editor John Jennings
Food Editor Angela Hagen
Librarian Charlotte Kenan
Music Critic Dan Buckley
Outdoors Editor William Quimby
Photo Editor P K Weis
Sports Editor Peter Madrid
Theater Critic Charles D Graham

MANAGEMENT INFORMATION SERVICES

Director-Management Info Services Mark T Williams

PRODUCTION

Vice Pres-Operations Wayne Bean
Manager-Operations Bill Hilser
Manager-Special Section/Quality Jerry Bennett
Manager-Service Joann Hardy-Carranza
Manager-Plate/Camera Deryck Burkett
Manager-Pressroom John Lundgren
Manager-Packaging Department Randy Brown
Manager-Production Maintenance Danny Crain
Manager-Physical Resources Bob Ross
Manager-Environmental Lynn Straughn
Manager-Technical Service Dave Dunn

Market Information: Zoned editions; Split Run; TMC.
Mechanical available: Offset; Black and 3 ROP colors; insert accepted — preprinted, single sheet flyers; page cut-offs — 22¾".
Mechanical specifications: Type page 13" x 21½"; E - 6 cols, 2⅟16", ⅛" between; A - 6 cols, 2⅟16", ⅛" between; C - 10 cols, 1¼", ⅟16" between.
Commodity consumption: Newsprint 24,000 metric tons; widths 54", 54½"; black ink 464,000 pounds; color ink 145,000 pounds; single pages printed 44,135; average pages per issue 58(d); single plates used 222,000.
Equipment: EDITORIAL: Front-end hardware — Proteon/486; Front-end software — MPS/Tecs 2 2.39; Printers — HP/LaserJet IV. CLASSIFIED: Front-end hardware — Proteon/386; Front-end software — MPS/Tecs 2 2.39; Printers — 3-IBM/Proprint III. DISPLAY: Adv layout systems — SCS/Layout 8000; Front-end hardware — PC/386; Front-end software — SCS/Layout 8000; Printers — DEC/LA 120. PRODUCTION: Pagination software — HI/8900 Classified 7.6; Typesetters — 1-III/3850, 2-III/3810 Imagesetter; Platemaking systems — 1-WL/Lith-X-Pozer IV-, 2-Nu/Flip-Top FT40APRNS; Plate exposures — 2-WL/38D; Scanners — 1-ECR/Autokon 1000 DE, 1-K&F/Optical Vertifier; Production cameras — 2-C/Spartan III; Automatic film processors — 2-LD, 1-R/660; Film transporters — 2-C/Spartan; Shrink lenses — 2-CK Optical/SQU-7; Color separation equipment (conventional) — 1-Ap/Mac Power, Adobe/Photoshop, Adobe/Color Access; Digital color separation equipment — 1-Pixelcraft/8000 Flatbed 4520 RS Scanner. PRESSROOM: Line 1 — 8-G/Metro 3127A (4 half-decks); Line 2 — 8-G/Metro 3128A (4 half-decks); Press drives — 16-Fin; Folders — 4-G/3:2; Pasters — Automatic Pasters; Reels and stands — G/Harmonic Drive. MAILROOM: Counter stackers — 1-QWI/300, 7-QWI/100, 2-Goss/Stackmaster; Inserters and stuffers — 1-HI/1472, 1-GMA/SLS 1000; Bundle tyer — 6-MLN, 3-Power Strap, 2-HI/RS-25; Wrapping singles — 6-QWI/Bottom Wrap; Addressing machine — 2-Ch/Labeler. WIRE SERVICES: News — AP Datastream, AP Datafeatures; Photos — AP; Stock tables — AP; Syndicates — LATS; Receiving dishes — size-3m, AP. BUSINESS COMPUTERS: IBM/AS-400; Applications: IBM: Circ; AdServ: Adv; PCs & micros networked; PCs & main system networked.

The Daily Territorial

(m-mon to fri)

The Daily Territorial, 1 W. Orange Grove Rd.; PO Box 35250, Tucson, AZ 85740-5250; tel (520) 297-1107; fax (520) 297-6253. Wick Communications group.
Circulation: 918(m); Sworn Sept. 18, 1995.
Price: 50¢(d); $90.00/yr.
Advertising: Open inch rate $7.50(m). **Representative:** American Newspaper Representatives Inc.
News Services: CNS, CSM. **Politics:** Independent. **Established:** 1930.
Not Published: New Year; Memorial Day; Independence Day; Labor Day; Thanksgiving; Christmas; All postal holidays.

CORPORATE OFFICER

Publisher Stephen E Jewett

ADVERTISING

Manager David Stoler
Manager-Legal Loretta Olguin

CIRCULATION

Manager-Mailing Service Anna Mae Wiersma

NEWS EXECUTIVES

Editor Cheryl Cross-Bushnell
Exec Editor Cheryl Cross-Bushnell

MANAGEMENT INFORMATION SERVICES

Online Manager Jeff Lewis

PRODUCTION

Superintendent George Jenkins

Market Information: Operate database; Electronic edition.
Mechanical available: Offset; Black and 3 ROP colors; insert accepted — preprinted; page cut-offs — 22¾".
Mechanical specifications: Type page 10¼" x 13"; E - 4 cols, 2⅜", ⅛" between; A - 4 cols, 2⅜", ⅛" between; C - 6 cols, 1½", ⅟16" between.
Commodity consumption: Newsprint 39 short tons; widths 27½", 13¾"; black ink 650 pounds; single pages printed 7,000; average pages per issue 24(d); single plates used 1,500.
Equipment: EDITORIAL: Front-end hardware — 1-Mk/3000, 10-PC; Other equipment — Mk. CLASSIFIED: Front-end hardware — Mk/Sys 3000, 1-PC. DISPLAY: Adv layout systems — Mk; Front-end hardware — Ap/Mac; Front-end software — Aldus/PageMaker, Aldus/Free-Hand; Printers — Ap/Mac LaserWriter II. PRODUCTION: Pagination software — Aldus/PageMaker 4.2, Aldus/PageMaker 5.0; OCR software — Postscript; Typesetters — 2-Ap/Mac LaserWriter II NTX, 1-COM/8400; Plate exposures — 1-Nu/Ultra Plus; Plate processors — 1-City Plate/AP-25; Production cameras — 1-SCREEN/Compactica, 1-AG/20 x 24; Automatic film processors — C/Powermatic 65F. PRESSROOM: Line 1 — 6-HI/V-15A; Folders — 1-HI. MAILROOM: Counter stackers — BG/Count-O-Veyor; Bundle tyer — 2-Ace/Tyer; Addressing machine — 1-Ch/612. LIBRARY: Electronic — Territorial/On-Line. WIRE SERVICES: News — Syndicates — LATS. BUSINESS COMPUTERS: NCR/LAN Sys; Applications: Circ, Accts payable, Accts receivable, Gen ledger, Adv; PCs & micros networked; PCs & main system networked.

YUMA

Yuma County

'90 U.S. Census- 54,923; E&P '96 Est. 66,426
ABC-NDM (90): 88,435 (HH 31,369)

The Yuma Daily Sun (e-mon to fri; m-sat; S)

The Yuma Daily Sun, 2055 Arizona Ave.; PO Box 271, Yuma, AZ 85364; tel (520) 783-3333; fax (520) 343-1009; e-mail yuma-sun@primenet.com. Cox Newspapers Inc. group.

Circulation: 16,716(e); 16,716(m-sat); 19,622(S); ABC Sept. 30, 1995.

Price: 50¢(d); 50¢(sat); $1.25(S); $9.00/mo.

Advertising: Open inch rate $18.89(e); $18.89(m-sat); $19.83(S). **Representative:** Papert Companies.

News Service: AP. **Politics:** Independent. **Established:** 1872.

Special Editions: Super Bowl (Jan); ATV Show, Health & Fitness, Home Improvement (Feb); Agriculture, Brides (Mar); Cool Ideas (Apr); Destination: Yuma (May); Discount Tab (June); Back-to-School (July); Summer In Yuma (mail-out) (Aug); Agriculture (Sept); Yuma Home & Style, Wheels (Oct); Health & Fitness, Winter in Yuma, Holiday Gift Guide (Nov).

Special Weekly Sections: Food (tues); Que Pasa (thur).

Magazines: Parade; Television; Color Comics; Bi-monthly Home Book (Rack Only); Monthly Coupon Book.

Cable TV: Operate leased cable TV in circulation area.

GENERAL MANAGEMENT

Publisher	Samuel Pepper
Business Manager	Lee Knapp
Manager-Education Service	Karen Phillips
Director-Accounting	Lisa Miller
Director-Facility	David Fornof
Personnel Director	Muriel Freeman

ADVERTISING

Director	Jerry Collins
Manager-Display	Tim Chaulk
Manager-Classified	Cynthia Marshall
Coordinator-Classified	Lili Imai
Coordinator-Co-op	Heather Rollins

MARKETING AND PROMOTION

Manager-Marketing	Lori Stofft

CIRCULATION

Director	Thomas Agosto

NEWS EXECUTIVES

Editor	Terry L Ross
Managing Editor	Randy Hoeft

EDITORS AND MANAGERS

Automotive Editor	Randy Hoeft
Business Editor	Cathy Richardson
City Editor	John Vaughn
Editorial Page Editor	Terry L Ross
Education Editor	John Vaughn
Entertainment Editor	Tim Chong
Environmental Editor	John Vaughn
Farm/Agriculture Editor	Joyce Christie
Fashion/Style Editor	Lenora Werley
Features Editor	John Vaughn
Foothill's News Editor	Bob Werley
Graphics Editor/Art Director	Randy Hoeft
Health/Medical Editor	Terry L Ross
Home Furnishings/Garden Editor	Lenora Werley
Living/Lifestyle Editor	Lenora Werley
National Editor	Lee Irwin
News Editor	Lee Irwin
Religion Editor	Lenora Werley
Science/Technology Editor	Terry L Ross
Special Sections Editor	Cathy Richardson
Sports Editor	Bob Romantic
Television/Film Editor	Tim Chong
Theater/Music Editor	Tim Chong
Travel Editor	Cathy Richardson
Women's Editor	Lenora Werley

MANAGEMENT INFORMATION SERVICES

Data Processing Manager	Albert Motley

PRODUCTION

Foreman-Pressroom	Richard Zavala
Foreman-Mailroom	Jesse Munoz

Market Information: TMC.

Mechanical available: Offset; Black and 3 ROP colors; insert accepted — preprinted; page cut-offs — 21".

Mechanical specifications: Type page 13" x 21"; E - 6 cols, 2 1/16", 1/8" between; A - 6 cols, 2 1/16", 1/8" between; C - 6 cols, 2 1/16", 1/8" between.

Commodity consumption: Newsprint 1,945 short tons; widths 13 3/4", 19", 27 1/2"; black ink 32,476 pounds; color ink 10,348 pounds; single pages printed 16,576; average pages per issue 23(d), 22(sat), 48(S); single plates used 24,140.

Equipment: EDITORIAL: Front-end hardware — DTI, 17-Ap/Mac II LC, 6-Ap/Mac Quadra; Front-end software — DTI/Pagespeed, DTI/Speedwriter, DTI/Speedplanner; Printers — 1-Ap/Mac LaserWriter, 1-QMS/860; Other equipment — 1-Ap/Mac IIcx, 1-Ap/Mac Plus, SMS/Stauffer Gold, Lf/AP Leaf Picture Desk, Sun/Sparc 5 workstations, Sybase/database, 1-Umax/Scanner, 1-Lf/LeafScanner, 1-Ap/Power Mac 60066, 1-Gateway/7500. CLASSIFIED: Front-end hardware — 5-Ap/Mac III LC; Front-end software — DTI/ClassSpeed, DTI/Class Pagination; Printers — 2-Ultra/94E, V/XP1000; Other equipment — Sun/Sparc 5 IPC, Sybase/database. DISPLAY: Front-end hardware — 1-COM/Dawn, 3-Ap/Mac IIcx, 2-Ap/Mac Quadra 700, 1-Ap/Mac Centris, 1-Ap/Mac Quadra 950; Front-end software — DTI/AdSpeed 3.1; Printers — Ultra/94E, V/XP1000; Other equipment — 1-Umax/Scanner, 1-Ap/Mac Scanner, 1-CD-Rom/Player, Sun/Sparc 5 workstation, Sybase, 1-Storage Dimension/Backup Device. PRODUCTION: Typesetters — 2-Tegra/Varityper/XP1000, 2-Ultra/94; Plate exposures — 1-Nu/Flip Top FT40APNS, 1-Nu/Flip Top FT40V6UPNS; Plate processors — 1-Nat/A-250; Electronic picture desk — Lf/AP Leaf Picture Desk; Scanners — 2-Umax/Scanner, Kurzweil/Discover 7320; Production cameras — 1-C/Spartan II; Automatic film processors — AG/26, 2-P/1800 IS.

PRESSROOM: Line 1 — 9-G/Urbanite; Press registration system — Duarte. MAILROOM: Counter stackers — 2-Id/2100; Inserters and stuffers — GMA/16:1 SLS-1000; Bundle tyer — 3-MLN. LIBRARY: Electronic — SMS/Stauffer Gold. WIRE SERVICES: News — AP; Syndicates — King Features, LATS, AP; AP. BUSINESS COMPUTERS: HP/9000 817S; Applications: CJ: Circ; CJ: Accts receivable; CJ: Gen ledger; CJ: Accts payable; PCs & main system networked.

ARKANSAS

ARKADELPHIA

Clark County

'90 U.S. Census- 10,014; E&P '96 Est. 10,071

Siftings Herald (e-mon to fri)

Arkadelphia Siftings Herald, 205 S. 26th St.; PO Box 10, Arkadelphia, AR 71923; tel (501) 246-5525; fax (501) 246-6556. Donrey Media group.

Circulation: 3,230(e); Sworn Oct. 1, 1994.

Price: 50¢(d); $5.00/mo (home delivery); $60.00/yr (home delivery).

Advertising: Open inch rate $6.37(e). **Representative:** Papert Companies.

News Service: AP. **Politics:** Democrat. **Established:** 1886.

Not Published: New Year; Memorial Day; Independence Day; Labor Day; Thanksgiving Day; Christmas.

Advertising not accepted: Adoption ads; Alcohol.

Special Edition: Progress edition.

CORPORATE OFFICERS

Founder	Donald W Reynolds
President/Chief Operating Officer	Emmett Jones
Exec Vice Pres/Chief Financial Officer	Darrell W Loftin
Vice Pres-Western Newspaper Group	David A Osborn
Vice Pres-Eastern Newspaper Group	Don Schneider

GENERAL MANAGEMENT

Publisher	Judith A Collis

ADVERTISING

Manager	Judith A Collis

CIRCULATION

Manager	Jeri Webb

EDITOR AND MANAGER

News Editor	Steve Fellers

Market Information: TMC.

Mechanical available: Offset; Black and 3 ROP colors; insert accepted — preprinted; page cut-offs — 22 3/4".

Mechanical specifications: Type page 13 1/2" x 21 1/2"; E - 6 cols, 2.06", 1/6" between; A - 6 cols, 2.06", 1/6" between; C - 9 cols, 1.32", 1/6" between.

Commodity consumption: Newsprint 100 short tons; widths 27", 13 3/4"; average pages per issue 10(d).

Equipment: EDITORIAL: Front-end hardware — Ap/Mac; Front-end software — Aldus/PageMaker; Printers — Ap/Mac LaserWriter. CLASSIFIED: Front-end hardware — Ap/Mac; Front-end software — Baseview; Printers — Ap/Mac. DISPLAY: Front-end hardware — Ap/Mac; Front-end software — Multi-Ad/Creator; Printers — Ap/Mac LaserWriter. PRODUCTION: Plate exposures — Nu; Plate processors — Nat/250; Production cameras — SCREEN/Companica 640c.

PRESSROOM: Line 1 — 5-KP/Newsking; Press control system — CH. MAILROOM: Bundle tyer — Ca/Band-Tyer; Addressing machine — Wm. LIBRARY: Combination — DuKane/Micro Reader. WIRE SERVICES: News — AP. BUSINESS COMPUTERS: IBM.

BATESVILLE

Independence County

'90 U.S. Census- 9,187; E&P '96 Est. 9,858

Batesville Guard (e-mon to fri)

Batesville Guard, 258 W. Main (72501); PO Box 2036, Batesville, AR 72503; tel (501) 793-2383; fax (501) 793-9268.

Circulation: 8,919(e); Sworn Oct. 2, 1995.

Price: 35¢(d); $50.00/yr (in state).

Advertising: Open inch rate $8.61(e). **Representative:** Papert Companies.

News Service: AP. **Politics:** Independent-Democrat. **Established:** 1876.

Not Published: Memorial Day; Independence Day; Thanksgiving; Christmas.

Special Weekly Sections: Business (mon); Best Food Day, Cooking, Agriculture, Consumer News (wed); Outdoors (thur); Education, Religion, TV (fri).

Magazine: River Country Tab (fri).

CORPORATE OFFICERS

President	Mrs O E Jones
Vice Pres	O E Jones Jr
Vice Pres	Mrs J P Cargill
Business Manager	Wilson Powell

GENERAL MANAGEMENT

Publisher	O E Jones Jr
General Manager	Pat Jones
Purchasing Agent	Jim Hughes

ADVERTISING

Director	Jim Kemp

MARKETING AND PROMOTION

Manager-Promotion	Jim Kemp

CIRCULATION

Director	Kristy Campbell

NEWS EXECUTIVES

Managing Editor	Jeff Porter
Asst Managing Editor	Debbie Miller

EDITORS AND MANAGERS

Books Editor	Wilson Powell
Business/Finance Editor	Frank Wallace
City Editor	Julie Fidler
Editorial Page Editor	Jeff Porter
Education/Women's Fashion Editor	Julie Fidler
Farm Editor	Frank Wallace
Food/Garden Editor	Sarah Gatling
Historian	Wilson Powell
Home Furnishings Editor	Julie Fidler
Photo Department Manager	Jeff Porter
Photo Editor	J Ross Jones
Outdoor/Sports Editor	Paul Glover
Travel Editor	Larry Strowd

PRODUCTION

Manager-Pressroom	Jim Hughes

Mechanical available: Offset; Black and 2 ROP colors; insert accepted — preprinted; page cut-offs — 22 3/4".

Mechanical specifications: Type page 13" x 21"; E - 6 cols, 2 1/16", 1/8" between; A - 6 cols, 2 1/16", 1/8" between; C - 6 cols, 2 1/16", 1/8" between.

Commodity consumption: average pages per issue 23(d).

Equipment: EDITORIAL: Front-end hardware — 8-TC, 1-XIT/Portable XPT II. CLASSIFIED: Front-end hardware — 1-TC. PRODUCTION: Typesetters — 3-LC; Production cameras — 1-B.

PRESSROOM: Line 1 — 1-F/20-page. MAILROOM: Bundle tyer — 2-Sa. WIRE SERVICES: News — AP; Receiving dishes — AP. BUSINESS COMPUTERS: 3-IBM/Sys 36; Applications: Acct, Circ, Letter writing, Payroll, Accts receivable, Gen ledger, Accts payable.

BENTON

Saline County

'90 U.S. Census- 18,177; E&P '96 Est. 18,534
ABC-CZ (90): 18,177 (HH 6,993)

The Benton Courier (e-mon to fri)

The Benton Courier, 1 Courier Pl.; PO Box 207, Benton, AR 72015; tel (501) 778-8228; fax (501) 776-1230.

Circulation: 9,191(e); ABC Sept. 30, 1995.

Price: 35¢(d); $5.25/wk (carrier); $63.00/yr (carrier), $66.00/yr (mail in-state), $72.00/yr (mail out-state).

Advertising: Open inch rate $9.25(e). **Representative:** Papert Companies.

News Service: AP. **Politics:** Independent. **Established:** 1876.

Not Published: New Year; Christmas.

Special Editions: Business Profile (Feb); Fashion/Bridal Section (Mar); American Home Week/Home Improvement (Apr); Spring Car Care (May); Summer Recreation Guide (June); Football, Back-to-School (Aug); Fall Car Care (Oct); Hunting (Sept); Cooking (Nov); Christmas (Dec).

Special Weekly Sections: Business (tues); Food & Good Health, Home & Garden (wed); Neighbors (Lifestyle) (thur); Religion, Entertainment (fri).

Magazine: TV Magazine (fri).

CORPORATE OFFICER

President	S M Hodges

GENERAL MANAGEMENT

Publisher	Rebecca Hodges Winburn
Controller	Sarah E Causbie

ADVERTISING

Director	Carol Powell

CIRCULATION

Director	T J Sivewright

NEWS EXECUTIVES

Managing Editor	Judy Smith
Assoc Editor	Lynda Hollenback

EDITORS AND MANAGERS

Sports Editor	Robert W Patrick
Women's Editor	Cherie Ward

PRODUCTION

Foreman-Pressroom	Raymond Bermingham

Market Information: TMC.

Mechanical available: Offset; Black and 3 ROP colors; insert accepted — preprinted; page cut-offs — 22 3/4".

Mechanical specifications: Type page 13" x 21 1/2"; E - 6 cols, 2 1/16", 1/8" between; A - 6 cols, 2 1/16", 1/8" between; C - 8 cols, 1 1/2", 1/8" between.

Commodity consumption: Newsprint 27.24 short tons; width 28"; black ink 2,000 pounds; single pages printed 4,160; average pages per issue 12(d); single plates used 2,080.

Equipment: EDITORIAL: Front-end hardware — 9-Ap/Mac; Front-end software — QuarkXPress, Baseview/NewsEdit; Other equipment — V/Imagesetter. CLASSIFIED: Front-end hardware — 2-Ap/Mac; Front-end software — Baseview/Class. DISPLAY: Adv layout systems — Ap/Mac II, Ap/Mac IIcx, Ap/Mac IIfx, Ap/Mac Quadra 700; Front-end hardware — Ap/Mac II NT; Front-end software — QPS, Adobe/Photoshop; Printers — 2-Ap/Mac LaserWriter Plus, V/Imagesetter. PRODUCTION: Typesetters — V/Imagesetter, 2-Ap/Mac Laser, Ap/Mac LaserWriter Plus; Plate exposures — 1-Nu; Plate processors — Nat; Electronic picture desk — Adobe/Photoshop; Scanners — 2-Microtek/Neg. Scanner, Ap/Mac Flatbed Scanner; Production cameras — 1-B; Automatic film processors — 1-Kk; Shrink lenses — Capital Optical; Color separation equipment (conventional) — Adobe/Photoshop, Ap/Mac.

PRESSROOM: Line 1 — 6-KP; Pasters — BG/Acumeter. MAILROOM: Counter stackers — 1-BG; Inserters and stuffers — 1-KAN; Bundle tyer — 2-Bu. WIRE SERVICES: News — AP; Receiving dishes — AP. BUSINESS COMPUTERS: 1-IBM/Sys 36; Applications: All areas of newspaper.

BENTONVILLE

Benton County

'90 U.S. Census- 11,257; E&P '96 Est. 13,293
ABC-CZ (90): 21,307 (HH 8,983)

Benton County Daily Record (m-mon to sat; S)

Benton County Daily Record, 104 S. W. "A" St.; PO Box 1049, Bentonville, AR 72712; tel (501) 271-3700; fax (501) 273-7777; e-mail compub95@aol.com; web site http://nwanews.com/. Community Publishers Inc. group.

Arkansas

I-19

Circulation: 9,268(m); 9,268(m-sat); 10,240(S); ABC Sept. 30, 1995.
Price: 25¢(d); 25¢(sat); 50¢(S); $6.00/mo; $64.80/yr (carrier), $72.00/yr (mail in co) $74.00/yr (mail out co).
Advertising: Open inch rate $9.70(m); $9.70(m-sat); $9.70(S).
News Service: AP. **Politics:** Independent. **Established:** 1886 (weekly), 1978 (daily).
Special Weekly Sections: Health & Fitness (mon); Business (tues); Business, Bella Vista & Education, Best Food Day (wed); Business (thur); Entertainment, Outdoors (fri); Church (sat); Wedding Record, Agriculture, Business, Education, Lifestyle (S).
Magazines: Legal Transactions (mon); Food Section; Westside Benton County (wed); Church Page, Entertainment, Outdoors (fri); Business Section, TV Record, Weddings, Color Comics, School News, Agriculture, Living and PARADE Magazine (S).

CORPORATE OFFICER
President .... Steve Trolinger
GENERAL MANAGEMENT
Publisher .... Mike Brown
ADVERTISING
Manager .... Mike Brown
MARKETING AND PROMOTION
Manager-Marketing & Promotion .... Jean Voyak
CIRCULATION
Manager .... George Loftus
NEWS EXECUTIVE
Editor .... Susan Scantlin
EDITOR AND MANAGER
Photographer .... Kent Marts
MANAGEMENT INFORMATION SERVICES
Online Manager .... Roger Frye
PRODUCTION
Manager .... Charles Lloyd

Market Information: TMC; ADS; Operate database; Electronic edition.
Mechanical available: Offset; Black and 3 ROP colors; insert accepted — preprinted; page cut-offs — 22¾".
Mechanical specifications: Type page 13" x 21"; E - 6 cols, 2 1/16", 1/8" between; A - 6 cols, 2 1/16", 1/8" between; C - 6 cols, 2 1/16", 1/8" between.
Commodity consumption: Newsprint 1,400 short tons; widths 29½", 27¼", 34"; black ink 28,000 pounds; color ink 7,000 pounds; single pages printed 6,500; average pages per issue 22(d), 22(sat), 60(S); single plates used 12,000.
Equipment: EDITORIAL: Front-end hardware — Ap/Mac; Front-end software — Baseview, Novell/Netware, XYQUEST/XyWrite, QPS; Printers — 2-Ap/Mac LaserWriter IIg. CLASSIFIED: Front-end hardware — Baseview; Front-end software — Baseview; Printers — Ap/Mac LaserWriter II NT. DISPLAY: Adv layout systems — Ap/Mac; Front-end hardware — Ap/Mac; Front-end software — Aldus/PageMaker, Canuis, QuarkXPress; Printers — Ap/Mac LaserWriter II NT. PRODUCTION: Typesetters — Ap/Mac LaserWriter II NT; Plate exposures — Nu/Flip Top FT40LNS; Plate processors — Nat/A-250; Production cameras — SCREEN/30x40; Automatic film processors — LE/Tek26; Shrink lenses — 1-CK Optical/SQU-7. PRESSROOM: Line 1 — 8-G/Community; Folders — 1-G/SSC; Press control system — Fin. MAILROOM: Counter stackers — Fg/M-71; Bundle tyer — 2-MLN/Strapper; Addressing machine — KR. LIBRARY: Electronic — SMS/Stuffer Gold. WIRE SERVICES: News — AP; Photos — AP; Stock tables — AP; Receiving dishes — AP. BUSINESS COMPUTERS: PBS; Applications: PBS/MediaPlus; PCs & micros networked; PCs & main system networked.

BLYTHEVILLE
Mississippi County
'90 U.S. Census- 22,906; E&P '96 Est. 22,559

Blytheville Courier News
(e-mon to fri; S)

Blytheville Courier News, Broadway at Moultrie; PO Box 1108, Blytheville, AR 72316; tel (501) 763-4461; fax (501) 763-6874. Rust Communications group.
Circulation: 4,787(e); 4,787(S); Sworn Sept. 26, 1994.
Price: 50¢(d); 50¢(S); $6.25/mo; $90.60/yr.
Advertising: Open inch rate $7.75(e); $7.75(S).
Representative: Papert Companies.
News Service: AP. **Politics:** Independent. **Established:** 1903.
Not Published: New Year; Christmas.
Advertising not accepted: Certain types requiring investments.
Special Editions: Income Tax (Jan); Progress; Family Business; Baseball; Graduation; Back-to-School; Football; Christmas Cookbook.
Special Weekly Sections: Senior Outlook (mon); Health & Environment (tues); Best Food Day, Education, High School Pages (wed); Business (thur); Farm Page, Church Page (fri); Kids Page (S).
Magazines: TV Magazine (fri); Color Comics, USA Weekend (S).

CORPORATE OFFICERS
President .... David Tennyson
Exec Vice Pres .... Wally Lage

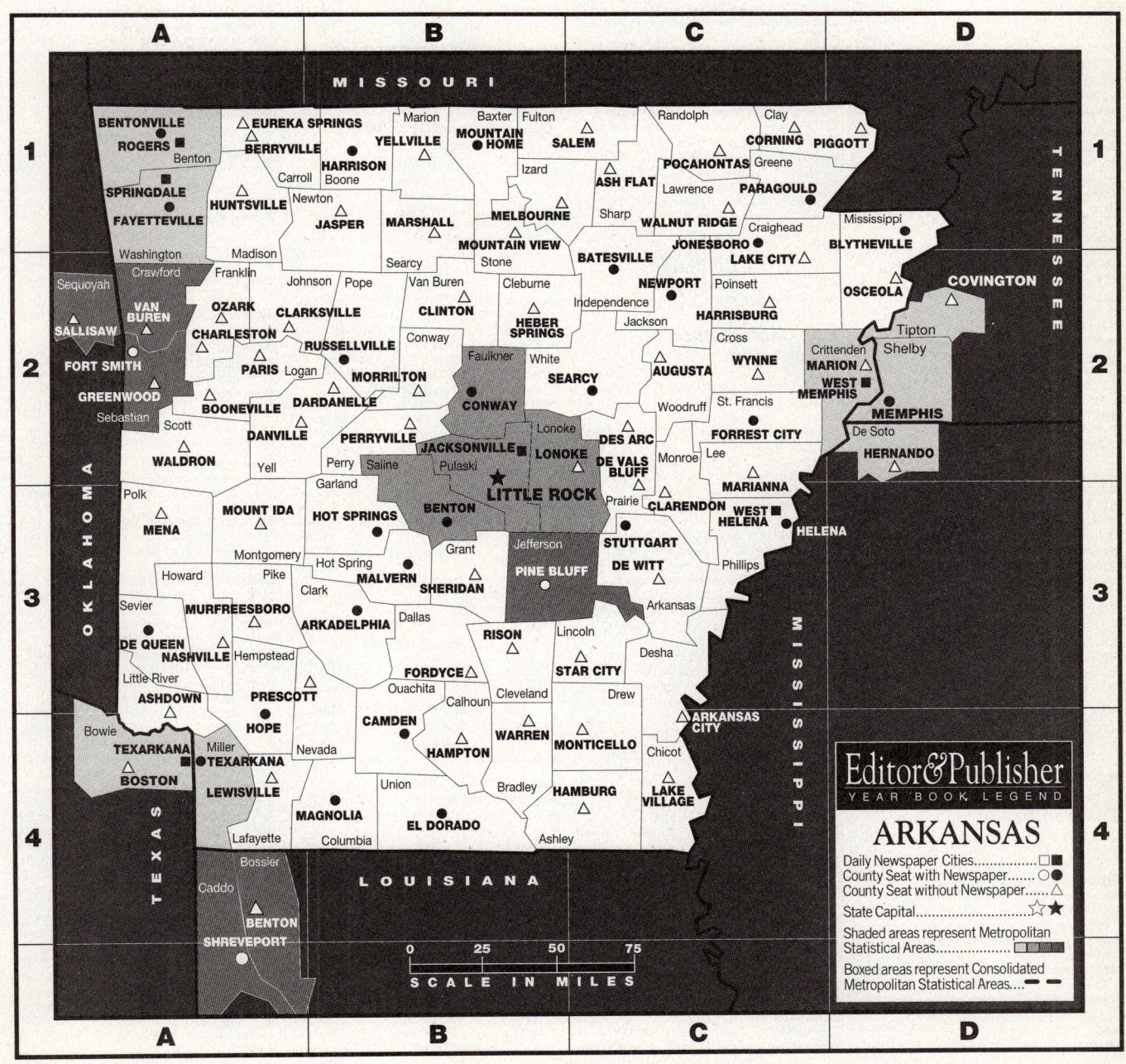

GENERAL MANAGEMENT
Publisher David Tennyson
Purchasing Agent Louis Wyatt

ADVERTISING
Manager Herb Smith

CIRCULATION
Manager Harry Darby

NEWS EXECUTIVES
Editor Sheila McCall
Editor Sandra Tennyson
Managing Editor Cynthia Jardon

EDITORS AND MANAGERS
Business/Finance Editor Larry Dodson
City/Metro Editor Lynn Maples
Editorial Page Editor Cynthia Jardon
Education Editor Cynthia Jardon
Entertainment/Amusements Editor Sheila McCall
Environmental Editor Sheila McCall
Farm/Agriculture Editor Lynn Maples
Features/Travel Editor Sandra Tennyson
Food Editor Sheila McCall
Graphics Editor/Art Director Cynthia Jardon
Health/Medical Editor Sheila McCall
Living/Lifestyle Editor Sheila McCall
National Editor Cynthia Jardon
News Editor Cynthia Jardon
Photo Editor Cynthia Jardon
Political/Government Editor Cynthia Jardon
Religion Editor Sheila McCall
Science/Technology Editor Sheila McCall
Society/Women's Editor Sheila McCall
Sports Editor Ron Chrisco

PRODUCTION
Manager Louis Wyatt
Foreman-Pressroom Susie Robison
Foreman-Composing Louis Wyatt

Market Information: TMC.
Mechanical available: Offset; Black and 3 ROP colors; insert accepted — preprinted, all; page cut-offs — 21½".
Mechanical specifications: Type page 13½" x 21½"; E - 6 cols, 2 1/16", 1/8" between; A - 6 cols, 2 1/16", 1/8" between; C - 9 cols, 1 3/8", 1/8" between.
Commodity consumption: Newsprint 800 short tons; width 27½"; single pages printed 4,368; average pages per issue 14(d), 20(S); single plates used 2,500.
Equipment: EDITORIAL: Front-end hardware — 2-Ap/Mac PowerBook, 3-Ap/Mac Quadra, 2-Ap/Mac Classic; Front-end software — QPS, Baseview/NewsEdit, Multi-Ad/Creator; Printers — Ap/Mac ImageWriter; Other equipment — Microtek/ScanMaker. CLASSIFIED: Front-end hardware — Ap/Mac Quadra 605; Front-end software — Baseview, Microsoft, QPS. DISPLAY: Front-end hardware — 2-Ap/Mac Quadra 610; Front-end software — Multi-Ad/Creator 3.6; Printers — Ap/Mac LaserWriter Pro 810; Other equipment — Microtek/ScanMaker IIG. PRODUCTION: Pagination software — QPS; OCR software — TI/Omni Page; Typesetters — Ap/Mac; Plate exposures — 1-Nu/Flip Top FT40LN5; Plate processors — 1-Nat/250-1391; Production cameras — 1-R/1975, LE/500; Automatic film processors — 1-P/26. PRESSROOM: Line 1 — 8-G/Community; Folders — 1-G/SC, 1-G/Community. MAILROOM: Inserters and stuffers — KAN/320 2-into-1; Bundle tyer — 1-Felin/11313, 1-Us/GMH; Addressing machine — 1-El/300. WIRE SERVICES: News — AP; Receiving dishes — AP. BUSINESS COMPUTERS: Applications: Vision Data, Microsoft/Excel.

CAMDEN
Ouachita County
'90 U.S. Census- 14,380; E&P '96 Est. 13,998

Camden News (e-mon to fri)
Camden News, 113 Madison Ave.; PO Box 798, Camden, AR 71701; tel (501) 836-8192; fax (501) 837-1414. Wehco Media Inc. group.
Circulation: 4,629(e); Sworn Oct. 3, 1995.
Price: 35¢(d); $6.25/mo; $71.00/yr.
Advertising: Open inch rate $8.50(e). **Representative:** Papert Companies.
News Service: AP. **Politics:** Independent. **Established:** 1920.
Not Published: New Year; Independence Day; Christmas.
Special Editions: Industrial Progress Edition (Apr); Football (Aug); Cookbook (Oct).
Magazine: Food (wed).
Broadcast Affiliates: Radio KAMD & KWEH-FM.

CORPORATE OFFICERS
Board Chairman Walter E Hussman Jr
President Walter E Hussman Jr
Vice Pres Eddie J Telford

GENERAL MANAGEMENT
Publisher Walter E Hussman Jr
General Manager Bob Moore

ADVERTISING
Director Susan Parnell

CIRCULATION
Manager Cindy Purifoy

NEWS EXECUTIVE
Editor James Waller

EDITORS AND MANAGERS
Lifestyle Editor Julia Wilson
Sports Editor Lowell Sanders

MANAGEMENT INFORMATION SERVICES
Data Processing Manager Debbye Butt

PRODUCTION
Superintendent Gus Looney

Market Information: TMC.
Mechanical available: Offset; Black and 3 ROP colors; insert accepted — preprinted.
Mechanical specifications: Type page 13" x 21½"; E - 6 cols, 2 1/16", 1/8" between; A - 6 cols, 2 1/16", 1/8" between; C - 8 cols, 1 3/8", 1/16" between.
Commodity consumption: width 27½"; single pages printed 2,642; average pages per issue 12(d).
Equipment: EDITORIAL: Front-end hardware — IBM/PC-AT, IBM/PC-XT; Front-end software — CText; Printers — Epson/DXF 5000. CLASSIFIED: Front-end hardware — IBM/PC-XT; Front-end software — CText; Printers — IBM/Proprinter. DISPLAY: Front-end hardware — Compaq/386-25; Front-end software — Sun/System; Printers — Epson/DFX 5000. WIRE SERVICES: News — Receiving dishes — AP. BUSINESS COMPUTERS: 1-Compaq/386-25, 2-Wyse; Applications: Sun/System; PCs & main system networked.

CONWAY
Faulkner County
'90 U.S. Census- 26,481; E&P '96 Est. 31,504

Log Cabin Democrat
(e-mon to fri; S)
Log Cabin Democrat, 1058 Front St.; PO Box 969, Conway, AR 72033; tel (501) 327-6621; fax (501) 327-6787. Morris Communications Corp. group.
Circulation: 10,189(e); 10,189(S); Sworn Sept. 29, 1995.
Price: 35¢(d); $1.00(S); $7.50/mo; $85.00/yr.
Advertising: Open inch rate $8.40(e); $9.25(S). **Representative:** Papert Companies.
News Service: AP. **Politics:** Democrat. **Established:** 1879.
Special Editions: Red Tag Sale, Recycling Tab (Jan); Bridal Tab, Progress '96 (Feb); Gardening & Home Improvement, Spring Fashion (Mar); Car Dealers Special, Arkansas Furniture Week, Toad Suck Daze (Apr); Mother's Day Gift Guide (May); June Shopping Spree (June); Newcomer's Guide (July); Back-to-School, Football Section (Aug); Fall Fashion, Fall Home Improvement, Hunting Guide '96 (Sept); Women in Business, Auto '97 Car Care (Oct); Christmas Gift Guide (Nov); Christmas Song Book, Last Minute Gift Guide (Dec).
Special Weekly Sections: Best Food Day (tues); Education Page (thur); Church Directory (fri); Business Page, Our Style, TV Log (S).
Magazine: TV Log (TV Guide, Book & Movie Reviews).

CORPORATE OFFICER
President Michael T Hengel

GENERAL MANAGEMENT
Controller Jim Yancey

ADVERTISING
Manager Donna Spears

CIRCULATION
Manager Fern Leslie

NEWS EXECUTIVE
Managing Editor David Keith

EDITORS AND MANAGERS
City Editor David Keith
Editorial Page Editor Colleen Holt
Metro Editor David Keith
Sports Editor David McCollum
Wire Editor Matt Irwin

PRODUCTION
Supervisor Debby Williams

Market Information: TMC.
Mechanical available: Offset; Black and 3 ROP colors; insert accepted — preprinted; page cut-offs — 21½".
Mechanical specifications: Type page 15¼" x 21½"; E - 6 cols, 2 1/16", 1/8" between; A - 6 cols, 2 1/16", 1/8" between; C - 7 cols, 2 1/16", 1/8" between.
Commodity consumption: Newsprint 500 short tons; widths 29", 14½"; black ink 9,000 pounds; color ink 500 pounds; average pages per issue 16(d), 30(S); single plates used 12,000.
Equipment: EDITORIAL: Front-end hardware — Mk; Other equipment — Ap/Mac. CLASSIFIED: Front-end hardware — 2-Mk. DISPLAY: Adv layout systems — Dell/3255X; Printers — HP/LaserJet III; Other equipment — Ap/Mac. PRODUCTION: Platemaking systems — 1-Nu/Flip Top; Plate processors — 1-Nu; Scanners — COM; Production cameras — 1-R/480; Automatic film processors — 1-LE/LD18. PRESSROOM: Line 1 — 6-HI/Cotrell; Folders — 1-HI. MAILROOM: Counter stackers — Stobb/PI; Inserters and stuffers — MM/227-E; Bundle tyer — 1-Bu/63685; Wrapping singles — 1-Sa/EM, 1-St/730; Addressing machine — 1-Wm/28297. LIBRARY: Electronic — SMS/Stauffers Gold. WIRE SERVICES: News — AP; Photos — AP; Receiving dishes — size-3m, AP. BUSINESS COMPUTERS: 1-IBM/Sys 34, Ap/Mac.

DE QUEEN
Sevier County
'90 U.S. Census- 4,633; E&P '96 Est. 4,679

De Queen Daily Citizen
(e-mon to fri)
De Queen Daily Citizen, 404 De Queeen Ave.; PO Box 1000, De Queen, AR 71832; tel (501) 642-2111; fax (501) 642-3138.
Circulation: 2,669(e); Sworn Sept. 28, 1995.
Price: 35¢(d); $4.25/mo (city delivery), $4.50/mo (rural mail), $6.00/mo (outside county); $42.00/yr (city delivery), $44.00/yr (rural mail), $46.00/yr (outside county).
Advertising: Open inch rate $6.75(e).
News Service: AP. **Politics:** Democrat. **Established:** 1933.
Not Published: New Year; Independence Day; Labor Day; Thanksgiving; Christmas.
Special Editions: Spring Car Care (Mar); Back-to-School (Aug); October Festival, Fall Car Care (Oct); Christmas Shopper (Nov).
Special Weekly Sections: Business (mon); Cooking, Agriculture, Consumer News, Best Food Day (wed); Outdoors (thur); Education, Religion, Church Page, TV Section (fri).

CORPORATE OFFICERS
President Ray Kimball
Vice Pres/Secretary Anita Floyd

GENERAL MANAGEMENT
Publisher Ray Kimball

ADVERTISING
Manager Gail Mitchell

CIRCULATION
Manager Betty Snider

NEWS EXECUTIVE
Editor Billy Ray McKelvy

EDITORS AND MANAGERS
Columnist Billy Ray McKelvy
Society Editor Linda Russell
Sports Editor Scott Smith

MANAGEMENT INFORMATION SERVICES
Data Processing Manager Billy Ray McKelvy

PRODUCTION
Superintendent Arlie Frachiseur

Market Information: TMC.
Mechanical available: Offset; Black and 2 ROP colors; insert accepted — preprinted; page cut-offs — 22¾".
Mechanical specifications: Type page 15¼" x 21"; E - 7 cols, 2 1/16", 1/8" between; A - 7 cols, 2 1/16", 1/8" between; C - 7 cols, 2 1/16", 1/8" between.
Commodity consumption: Newsprint 90 short tons; widths 32", 16"; black ink 1,700 pounds; color ink 75 pounds; single pages printed 3,120; average pages per issue 12(d); single plates used 2,100.
Equipment: EDITORIAL: Front-end hardware — HI, Ap/Mac. CLASSIFIED: Front-end hardware — HI, Ap/Mac. DISPLAY: Adv layout systems — 2-Ap/Mac II. PRODUCTION: Typesetters — 2-Ap/Mac Laser, 1-Printware; Plate exposures — 1-Nu/Flip Top FT40V2UP; Plate processors — 1-WL/Litho Plate; Scanners — Dest, Ap, Microtek; Production cameras — 1-R/500; Automatic film processors — 1-LE/17. PRESSROOM: Line 1 — 3-HI/Cottrel V15A; Folders — 1-HI. MAILROOM: Inserters and stuffers — KAN; Bundle tyer — Bu; Addressing machine — 2-St. WIRE SERVICES: News — AP; Receiving dishes — AP. BUSINESS COMPUTERS: 3-TC, Ap/Mac, Ap/Mac II; PCs & micros networked.

EL DORADO
Union County
'90 U.S. Census- 23,146; E&P '96 Est. 22,276
ABC-CZ (90): 23,146 (HH 9,158)

El Dorado News-Times
(m-mon to sat; S)
El Dorado News-Times, 111 N. Madison; PO Box 912, El Dorado, AR 71730; tel (501) 862-6611; fax (501) 862-5226. Wehco Media Inc. group.
Circulation: 10,939(m); 10,939(m-sat); 10,834(S); ABC Sept. 30, 1995.
Price: 35¢(d); 35¢(sat); $1.00(S); $7.75/mo; $93.00/yr.
Advertising: Open inch rate $10.88(m); $10.88(m-sat); $10.88(S). **Representative:** Papert Companies.
News Service: AP. **Politics:** Independent. **Established:** 1889 (Times), 1921 (News).
Advertising not accepted: Fraudulent, misleading copy in poor taste.
Special Editions: Progress Edition (Mar); Spring Fashion (Apr); Graduation (May); Football Edition, Back-to-School, Fair Days (Aug); Fall Fashion (Sept); Recipe Edition (Oct); Christmas Catalogue (Nov).
Magazine: USA Weeekend (S).

CORPORATE OFFICERS
President Walter E Hussman Jr
Vice Pres Eddie J Telford

GENERAL MANAGEMENT
Publisher Walter E Hussman Jr
General Manager Tim LeWallen

ADVERTISING
Director Karen Williams

CIRCULATION
Director Gene Merritt

NEWS EXECUTIVE
Managing Editor George Arnold

EDITORS AND MANAGERS
City Editor Jim Edwards
Entertainment Editor Rod Harrington
Features Editor Shea Wilson
News Editor Chris Qualls
Sports Editor Tony Burns

PRODUCTION
Manager Ernest Looney

Market Information: TMC.
Mechanical available: Offset; Black and 3 ROP colors; insert accepted — preprinted; page cut-offs — 22¾".
Mechanical specifications: Type page 13" x 21½"; E - 6 cols, 2 1/16", 1/8" between; A - 6 cols, 2 1/16", 1/8" between; C - 8 cols, 1½", 1/8" between.
Commodity consumption: Newsprint 457 short tons; widths 27½", 13¾"; black ink 7,772 pounds; color ink 1,206 pounds; single pages printed 6,210; average pages per issue 16(d), 24(S); single plates used 6,074.
Equipment: EDITORIAL: Front-end hardware — 16-IBM/PC, 19-Compaq/PC, 1-Ap/Mac IIfx, 4-Ap/Mac 8100; Front-end software — CText; Printers — 1-Ap/Mac LaserWriter. CLASSIFIED: Front-end hardware — IBM/PC; Front-end software — CText; Printers — Epson/LQ 750. DISPLAY: Front-end hardware — 4-Ap/Mac SE, 5-Ap/Mac 8100; Front-end software — DTI, QuarkXPress; Printers — V/VT 600-W, Ap/Mac Select 360, III/Pagescan. PRODUCTION: Pagination software — Multi-Ad/Creator 6.0; OCR software — Caere/Omni Page; Typesetters — 2-Linotype-Hell/202N, 2-AG/9800 Pro Set; Plate exposures — Nu/Flip Top Double; Plate processors — Nat/240; Production cameras — C/Spartan III; Automatic film processors — LE/Processor; Film transporters — LE/Processor. PRESSROOM: Line 1 — 4-G/Urbanite (8 pgs on each unit); Press control system — MGD, Fin. MAILROOM: Bundle tyer — 1-Ca/Band tyer; Addressing machine — Wm. WIRE SERVICES: News — AP; Photos — AP; Receiving dishes — size-10ft, AP. BUSINESS COMPUTERS: 1-Compaq/Desk Pro, 5-Wyse/W60, 1-Gateway/2000; Applications: PBS; PCs & micros networked; PCs & main system networked.

FAYETTEVILLE

Washington County

'90 U.S. Census- 42,099; E&P '96 Est. 46,178
ABC-CZ (90): 42,099 (HH 16,894)

Northwest Arkansas Times

(m-mon to sat; S)

Northwest Arkansas Times, 212 N. East St.; PO Drawer D, Fayetteville, AR 72701; tel (501) 442-1777; fax (501) 442-5477. Hollinger International Inc. group.

Circulation: 13,938(m); 13,938(m-sat); 14,048(S); ABC Sept. 30, 1995.

Price: 25¢(d); 25¢(sat); $1.00(S); $6.50/mo (carrier); $78.00/yr (mail).

Advertising: Open inch rate $12.76(m); $12.76(m-sat); $13.15(S). **Representative:** Papert Companies.

News Services: AP, SHNS, THO. **Politics:** Independent. **Established:** 1860.

Special Editions: Financial/Banking; Income Tax Tab; Insiders Guide; Progress: Real Estate; Home Improvement; Brides Section; Sr. Citizens Tab; Graduation; Back-to-School; Football Fever (Univ. of Arkansas); Fall Fashion; Hunting & Fishing; Family Business; Autumnfest; Cookbook; Basketball; Christmas Gift Guide; Christmas Carols; 101 Reasons to Love NWA.

Special Weekly Sections: Business Times, Employment Weekly (mon); Education Today (wed); What's Up (fri); Sports Saturday, TV Week (sat); Sports Sunday (S).

Magazines: Parade; Color Comics.

GENERAL MANAGEMENT

Publisher Randy W Cope
Manager-Credit Sandra Thompson

ADVERTISING

Manager Kaye Hunton

MARKETING AND PROMOTION

Manager-Promotion Robert Catlett

TELECOMMUNICATIONS

Manager-Computers and Technology Stan Nelson

CIRCULATION

Manager Mark Benz

NEWS EXECUTIVE

Exec Editor Mike Masterson

EDITORS AND MANAGERS

Amusements Editor Melissa Blouin
Business Editor Taurun Reddy
Columnist Mike Masterson
Columnist Bob Rhodes
Columnist Barry Harrell
Columnist Gwen Rule
Columnist Lorena Anderson
County Editor Julia Wilson
Editorial Page Editor Bob Rhodes
Editorial Writer Mike Masterson
Editorial Writer Bob Rhodes
Education Editor Amanda Fincher
Food Editor Melissa Blouin
Justice Editor Pamela Hill
Living Section Writer Harriet Hamilton
News Editor Barry Harrell
Asst News Editor Lorena Anderson
Photo Department Manager Andy Shupe
Political Editor Rusty Garrett
Religion Editor Melissa Blouin
Sports Editor Dudley E Dawson

PRODUCTION

Foreman-Composing Carla Romere
Foreman-Pressroom Bill Baldwin

Market Information: TMC; ADS.

Mechanical available: Offset; Black and 3 ROP colors; insert accepted — preprinted, cards, coupon books, small items; page cut-offs — 22¾".

Mechanical specifications: Type page 13" x 21½"; E - 6 cols, 2⅟₁₆", ⅛" between; A - 6 cols, 2⅟₁₆", ⅛" between; C - 9 cols, 1⅜", ⅟₁₆" between.

Commodity consumption: Newsprint 952 short tons; width 27½"; black ink 21,000 pounds; color ink 4,200 pounds; single pages printed 10,726; average pages per issue 22(d), 36(S); single plates used 19,600.

Equipment: EDITORIAL: Front-end hardware — Mk, Laptops; Front-end software — Quark-XPress, Mk/Newswriter; Printers — 2-V/400 Towers to 5060W printer; Other equipment — V/6990 negative printer, Lf/AP Leaf Picture Desk. CLASSIFIED: Front-end hardware — Mk; Front-end software — Mk/Ace Classified 2.1; DISPLAY: Adv layout systems — Mk/Master-Planner; Front-end hardware — 2-Mk; Printers — Ap/Mac LaserWriter II. PRODUCTION: Pagination software — QuarkXPress 3.3; Typesetters — 4-Ap/Mac IIci, 2-V/VT6000W, 1-Ap/Mac LaserWriter II NT; Plate exposures — Nu/Flip Top T40V6UPNS; Plate processors — Nat/A-250; Scanners — Companica/680C; Production cameras — B, R; Automatic film processors — LE/LD-220 OT, LE/LD-280 QT; Color separation equipment (conventional) — Digi-Colour.
PRESSROOM: Line 1 — 7-G/Urbanite; Press drives — Fin; Folders — G/Urbanite; Reels and stands — 7-roll stand; Press control system — Fin. MAILROOM: Inserters and stuffers — MM; Bundle tyer — 1-MLN. WIRE SERVICES: News — AP, SHNS, THO; Photos — AP; Stock tables — AP; Receiving dishes — AP. BUSINESS COMPUTERS: ATT/3B2-500 (mainframe), 6-ATT/Monitor; Applications: Unix/OS, Informix; PCs & main system networked.

FORREST CITY

St. Francis County

'90 U.S. Census- 13,364; E&P '96 Est. 13,240

Times-Herald (e-mon to fri)

Times-Herald, 222 N. Izard St. (72335); PO Box 1699, Forrest City, AR 72335-1699; tel (501) 633-3130; fax (501) 633-0599.

Circulation: 4,666(e); Sworn Oct. 8, 1995.

Price: 35¢(d); $82.50/yr (in county).

Advertising: Open inch rate $7.30(e). **Representative:** Landon Associates Inc.

News Service: AP. **Politics:** Independent. **Established:** 1871.

Advertising not accepted: Publisher reserves right to refuse advertising.

Special Editions: Christmas Shopper; Rice; Farm Family Salute; Football.

Magazines: Mini-Page for Children; Weekly Entertainment Guide with mid-South TV Listing.

GENERAL MANAGEMENT

Publisher Trent B McCollum
Assoc Publisher Weston Lewey

ADVERTISING

Director Jim Wirski

CIRCULATION

Director Ronny Barnett

NEWS EXECUTIVE

Managing Editor Kersh Hall

PRODUCTION

Superintendent Arnold Gwathney

Market Information: TMC.

Mechanical available: Offset; Black and 3 ROP colors; insert accepted — preprinted, cards; page cut-offs — 22½".

Mechanical specifications: Type page 13" x 21"; E - 6 cols, 2⅟₁₆", ⅛" between; A - 6 cols, 2⅟₁₆", ⅛" between; C - 9 cols, 1⅜", ⅟₁₆" between.

Commodity consumption: widths 28", 14"; single pages printed 3,400; average pages per issue 20(d).

Equipment: EDITORIAL: Front-end hardware — Mk/3000. CLASSIFIED: Front-end hardware — Ap/Mac IIsi. PRODUCTION: Typesetters — Ap/Mac LaserWriter NTX; Plate exposures — Nu; Plate processors — Nat/Processor; Production cameras — 1-R; Automatic film processors — LE/18.
PRESSROOM: Line 1 — 6-G/Community (w/Ballon Former). MAILROOM: Bundle tyer — Malow. LIBRARY: Electronic — Dukane. WIRE SERVICES: News — AP; Receiving dishes — AP. BUSINESS COMPUTERS: RSK/16; Applications: Accts receivable, Circ; PCs & micros networked; PCs & main system networked.

FORT SMITH

Sebastian County

'90 U.S. Census- 72,798; E&P '96 Est. 73,840
ABC-CZ (90): 94,467 (HH 37,375)

Southwest Times Record

(m-mon to sat; S)

Southwest Times Record, 920 Rogers Ave.; PO Box 1359, Fort Smith, AR 72901; tel (501) 785-7700; fax (501) 785-7741. Donrey Media group.

Circulation: 39,938(m); 39,938(m-sat); 44,180(S); ABC Sept. 30, 1995.

Price: 50¢(d); 50¢(sat); $1.00(S); $8.00/mo (d&S); $96.00/yr.

Advertising: Open inch rate $29.26(m); $29.26(m-sat); $32.77(S). **Representative:** Papert Companies.

News Service: AP. **Politics:** Independent. **Established:** 1832.

Special Editions: Fashions; Car Care; Back-to-School; Home Improvement; Newcomer's Guide; Magic Santa Christmas Opening; Brides; Lawn & Garden; Home Show/Cooking School; Football Preview; Tax Time Tab.

Special Weekly Sections: Food (wed); Entertainment (fri); Business, Religion (sat); Lifestyles (Society), Sports, Travel (S); Entertainment, Sports (daily).

Magazines: TV & Entertainment Focus Magazine (sat); USA Weekend.

CORPORATE OFFICERS

Founder Donald W Reynolds
President/Chief Operating Officer Emmett Jones
Exec Vice Pres/Chief Financial Officer Darrell W Loftin
Vice Pres-Western Newspaper Group David A Osborn
Vice Pres-Eastern Newspaper Group Don Schneider

GENERAL MANAGEMENT

Publisher Gene Kincy
Manager-Credit Phyllis Smallwood

ADVERTISING

Director Ronnie Bell
Manager-Classified Ted McEvoy

CIRCULATION

Director Ted Brannon
Manager-Operations Cecil Garner
Manager-Sales/Promotion Pam Johnson

NEWS EXECUTIVE

Editor Jack Moseley

EDITORS AND MANAGERS

Business/Finance Editor Jennifer Jesse
City Editor Debbye Hughes
Columnist Linda Seubold
Editorial Page Editor Jack Moseley
Education Editor Michael Rowett
Entertainment/Amusements Editor Jay Harshaw
Environmental Editor Debbye Hughes
Farm/Agriculture Editor Jennifer Jesse
Fashion/Style Editor Nancy Steel
Features Editor Nancy Steel
Food Editor Jay Harshaw
Health/Medical Editor Nancy Steel
Lifestyle Editor Nancy Steel
National Editor John Wablay
News Editor Debbye Hughes
Photo Editor Carrol Copeland
Political/Government Editor Jack Moseley
Sports Editor Grant Tolley
Television/Film Editor Donna Payne
Theater/Music Editor Donna Payne
Travel Editor Nancy Steel

PRODUCTION

Manager Kenny Taylor
Supervisor-Composing Marsha Walblay
Superintendent-Pressroom Earl Oxford
Superintendent-Mailroom Dale Boardman

Mechanical available: Offset; Black and 3 ROP colors; insert accepted — preprinted; page cut-offs — 21½".

Mechanical specifications: Type page 13" x 21½"; E - 6 cols, 2⅟₁₆", ⅛" between; A - 6 cols, 2⅟₁₆", ⅛" between; C - 9 cols, 1⅜", ⅟₁₆" between.

Commodity consumption: Newsprint 3,900 metric tons; widths 55", 41¼"; black ink 14,000 pounds; color ink 5,000 pounds; single pages printed 22,000; average pages per issue 38(d), 50(S); single plates used 28,000.

Equipment: EDITORIAL: Front-end hardware — Ap/Mac Quadra 610, Ap/Mac 800, Ap/Mac 950; Front-end software — DTI; Printers — Ap/Mac LaserWriter Plus, Dataproducts/LZR 1560; Other equipment — Ap/Scanner. CLASSIFIED: Front-end hardware — Ap/Mac Quadra 610, Ap/Mac 800, Ap/Mac 950; Front-end software — DTI; Printers — Ap/Mac LaserWriter II NTX, 2-Ap/Mac LaserWriter IIg, Dataproducts/LZR 1560; Other equipment — Ap/Mac cx, Abaton/Scanner, NEC/CD-Rom. DISPLAY: Adv layout systems — DTI; Front-end hardware — Ap/Mac II SE, Ap/Mac CD-Rom, Ap/Mac Scanner, Ap/Mac IIcx; Front-end software — Aldus/FreeHand 3.1, Multi-Ad/Creator 3.0; Printers — Ap/Mac LaserWriter II NTX. PRODUCTION: Pagination software — DTI 3.0 R 4.62; Typesetters — AG/1000, AG/Rapidline 26; Platemaking systems — 3M/Pyrofax; Plate exposures — 2-Nu; Plate processors — Nat/A-250; Scanners — ECR/Autokon 1030C, AG/Arcus Color Scanner; Production cameras — C/Marathon, B; Automatic film processors — LE/2600; Shrink lenses — 19-Nikon; Color separation equipment (conventional) — Digi-Colour, Adobe/Photoshop; Digital color separation equipment — 2-Ap/Mac Quadra 950.
PRESSROOM: Line 1 — G/Cosmo double width 5 floor 1 stacked; Pasters — 6-G/Cosmo; Reels and stands — 6-G/Cosmo. MAILROOM: Counter stackers — 3-HL; Inserters and stuffers — 2-MM/227-Sc 8:1; Bundle tyer — 2-MLN/MLN2A; Wrapping singles — 2-HL/Monarch; Addressing machine — Wm. COMMUNICATIONS: Digital ad delivery system — AP AdSend. WIRE SERVICES: News — AP; Photos — AP; Receiving dishes — size-10ft; 8ft, AP. BUSINESS COMPUTERS: HP/9000-800.

HARRISON

Boone County

'90 U.S. Census- 9,922; E&P '96 Est. 10,179

Harrison Daily Times

(e-mon to fri; S)

Harrison Daily Times, 111 W. Rush Ave.; PO Box 40, Harrison, AR 72601; tel (501) 741-2325; fax (501) 741-5632. Hollinger International Inc. group.

Circulation: 11,121(e); 11,121(S); Sworn Sept. 27, 1995.

Price: 35¢(d); 35¢(S); $5.00/mo (carrier); $75.00/yr.

Advertising: Open inch rate $8.91(e); $8.91(S). **Representative:** Papert Companies.

News Service: AP. **Politics:** Independent. **Established:** 1876.

Special Edition: Farm (monthly).

Special Weekly Section: TV Magazine "Focus" (fri).

CORPORATE OFFICER

Publisher D Jeff Christenson

GENERAL MANAGEMENT

Business Manager Carol Lawson

ADVERTISING

Manager Michelle Kennedy

CIRCULATION

Director-Marketing Dennis Miller

NEWS EXECUTIVE

Editor Dwain Lair

EDITORS AND MANAGERS

Automotive Editor Bob Murphy
Business/Finance Editor Bob Murphy
City/Metro Editor Jeff Dezort
Editorial Page Editor Dwain Lair
Education Editor Jeff Dezort
Entertainment/Amusements Editor Bob Murphy
Farm/Agriculture Editor Jeff Dezort
Fashion/Style Editor Jane Christenson
Food Editor Jane Christenson
Graphics Editor/Art Director Julie Lockett
Living/Lifestyle Editor Linda Callahan
National Editor Jeff Dezort
News Editor Dwain Lair
Photo Editor Shirley Curtis
Political/Government Editor Jeff Dezort
Sports Editor Bennett Horne
Television/Film Editor Linda Callahan
Theater/Music Editor Linda Callahan

PRODUCTION

Manager-Composing Julie Lockett

Market Information: TMC.

Mechanical available: Offset; Black and 3 ROP colors; insert accepted — preprinted; page cut-offs — 22¾".

Mechanical specifications: Type page 13" x 21½"; E - 6 cols, 2⅟₁₆", ⅛" between; A - 6 cols, 2⅟₁₆", ⅛" between; C - 8 cols, 1½", ⅛" between.

Commodity consumption: Newsprint 559 short tons; black ink 2,000 pounds; color ink 250 pounds; single pages printed 5,000; average pages per issue 20(d).

Equipment: EDITORIAL: Front-end hardware — Mk, Ap/Mac; Printers — 2-Ap/Pro 630, 1-Ap/Mac NTX; Other equipment — Ap/Mac II, 10-Mk/400, 3-Ap/Mac. CLASSIFIED: Other equipment — 1-Mk. PRODUCTION: Typesetters — 1-Linotype-Hell/Linotronic 190 RIP 20; Plate processors — Nat; Production cameras — VG/670 C Vertical; Automatic film processors — 1-LE.
PRESSROOM: Line 1 — 7-G/Community(DEV color deck); Folders — 1-G. MAILROOM: Inserters and stuffers — 1-St, 4-KAN/Inserter; Bundle tyer — 2-Bu; Wrapping singles — 1-St/Collator-tyer (ST-3 unit); Addressing machine — 1-Ch. WIRE SERVICES: News — AP; Receiving dishes — AP. BUSINESS COMPUTERS: 5-RSK, APA; PCs & micros networked; PCs & main system networked.

HELENA-WEST HELENA

Phillips County

'90 U.S. Census- 17,186 (Helena 7,491; West Helena 9,695); E&P '96 Est. 15,686 (Helena 6,679; West Helena 9,007)

The Daily World (e-mon to fri; S)

The Daily World, 417 York St.; PO Box 340, Helena, AR 72342; tel (501) 338-9181; fax (501)338-9184. Hollinger International Inc. group.

Circulation: 5,211(e); 5,211(S); Sworn Sept. 29, 1995.

Price: 35¢(d); 35¢(S); $5.50/mo; $66.00/yr (in county), $72.00/yr (out of county).

Advertising: Open inch rate $6.50(e); $6.50(S). **Representative:** Papert Companies.

News Service: AP. **Politics:** Independent. **Established:** 1871.

Not Published: Christmas.

Special Editions: Drug Info Tab (Feb); Farm & Garden, Home Improvement (Mar); Cooking School Tab (Apr); Graduation (May); Baseball (June); Progress (July); Football, Back-to-School (Aug); Blues Festival (Oct); Christmas Wishbook (Nov); Christmas Tab (Dec).

Special Weekly Sections: Grocery Day (tues); Weekly TV Guide; Society Page (S); Comics (daily).

CORPORATE OFFICER

President Larry J Perrotto

GENERAL MANAGEMENT

Publisher Bill Lederman

ADVERTISING

Manager Ann Puckett

CIRCULATION

Director Donna Tanner

NEWS EXECUTIVE

Editor Andy Staten

EDITOR AND MANAGER

Sports Writer Matthew Zabel

PRODUCTION

Manager Steven Montgomery
Foreman-Pressroom Jerry Henry

Market Information: TMC.

Mechanical available: Offset; Black and 3 ROP colors; insert accepted — preprinted, standing cards; page cut-offs — $22\frac{1}{2}$".

Mechanical specifications: Type page $14\frac{3}{4}$" x $21\frac{1}{2}$"; E - 6 cols, $2\frac{1}{16}$", $\frac{1}{8}$" between; A - 6 cols, $2\frac{1}{16}$", $\frac{1}{8}$" between; C - 10 cols, $1\frac{1}{16}$", $\frac{1}{8}$" between.

Commodity consumption: Newsprint 111 short tons; widths 14", 28"; black ink 2,235 pounds; color ink 416 pounds; single pages printed 2,688; average pages per issue 10(d), 14(S); single plates used 2,879.

Equipment: EDITORIAL: Front-end hardware — Ap/Mac; Printers — Ap/Mac LaserWriter Select. CLASSIFIED: Front-end hardware — Ap/Mac; Printers — Ap/Mac LaserWriter Pro. DISPLAY: Adv layout systems — Ap/Mac Quadra 610; Front-end hardware — Ap/Mac; Printers — Ap/Mac LaserWriter Pro. PRODUCTION: Typesetters — Ap/Mac; Platemaking systems — Nu/Flip Top Ft40UP; Scanners — 1-Microtek; Production cameras — 1-SCREEN/640-c Companica; Automatic film processors — 1-LE. PRESSROOM: Line 1 — 5-G/Community; Folders — 1-G/Community. MAILROOM: Counter stackers — BG/Count-O-Veyor; Bundle tyer — Bu/BT-16. LIBRARY: Electronic — Microfiche; Combination — Bound Volumes. WIRE SERVICES: News — AP; Receiving dishes — AP. BUSINESS COMPUTERS: 1-RSK; Applications: Circ, Billing and labels.

HOPE

Hempstead County

'90 U.S. Census- 9,643; E&P '96 Est. 9,390

Hope Star (e-mon to fri)

Hope Star, 522 W. Third; PO Box 648, Hope, AR 71801; tel (501) 777-8841; fax (501) 777-3311. News Co. Inc. group.

Circulation: 4,237(e); Sworn Sept. 29, 1995.

Price: 50¢(d); $5.25/mo; $70.00/yr.

Advertising: Open inch rate $7.00(e). **Representative:** Papert Companies.

News Service: AP. **Politics:** Independent. **Established:** 1899.

Not Published: New Year; Memorial Day; Independence Day; Labor Day; Thanksgiving; Christmas.

Advertising not accepted: Classified offering "home work".

Special Editions: Progress (Mar); Graduation (May); Watermelon Festival (July).

Magazine: Star Time Entertainment (weekly TV section) (fri).

CORPORATE OFFICER

Vice Pres Ronnie Cupstid

GENERAL MANAGEMENT

Publisher Ronnie Cupstid

ADVERTISING

Director Richard Haycox

MARKETING AND PROMOTION

Manager-Promotion Richard Haycox

CIRCULATION

Director Theresa La Growe

EDITOR AND MANAGER

Society/Women's Editor Pat Harris

PRODUCTION

Superintendent Ron Tate

Market Information: TMC; ADS.

Mechanical available: Offset; Black and 3 ROP colors; insert accepted — preprinted, all; page cut-offs — $22\frac{3}{4}$".

Mechanical specifications: Type page 13" x $21\frac{1}{2}$"; E - 6 cols, $2\frac{1}{16}$", $\frac{1}{8}$" between; A - 6 cols, $2\frac{1}{16}$", $\frac{1}{8}$" between; C - 6 cols, $2\frac{1}{16}$", $\frac{1}{8}$" between.

Commodity consumption: Newsprint 270 short tons; width $27\frac{1}{2}$"; black ink 2,500 pounds; color ink 1,500 pounds; single pages printed 3,970; average pages per issue 16(d); single plates used 7,400.

Equipment: EDITORIAL: Front-end hardware — 4-Ap/Mac IIci; Other equipment — 6-HI/1250, 5-COM/Computype, 6-IBM/Model 25. CLASSIFIED: Front-end hardware — Ap/Mac Network. DISPLAY: Adv layout systems — Ap/Mac. PRODUCTION: Typesetters — Ap/Mac LaserWriter NTX; Plate exposures — 2-Nu; Plate processors — Ic; Production cameras — 1-B/Caravelle 18x24; Automatic film processors — P/26EL; Color separation equipment (conventional) — BKY/8x10. PRESSROOM: Line 1 — 5-Web Leader/Marc 25; Reels and stands — 5-F. MAILROOM: Counter stackers — BG/Count-O-Veyor; Bundle tyer — 4-Sa/EM-10755; Wrapping singles — 4-Sa; Addressing machine — 1-Ch/500, 1-Ch/730. WIRE SERVICES: News — AP; Receiving dishes — size-8ft, AP. BUSINESS COMPUTERS: IBM/Sys 34; Applications: Bookkeeping, Payroll, Gen ledger; PCs & micros networked; PCs & main system networked.

HOT SPRINGS

Garland County

'90 U.S. Census- 32,462; E&P '96 Est. 31,090
ABC-CZ (90): 32,462 (HH 14,488)

The Sentinel-Record (m-mon to sat; S)

The Sentinel-Record, 300 Spring St.; PO Box 580, Hot Springs, AR 71902; tel (501) 623-7711; fax (501) 623-2984; e-mail hssr@netc.com. Wehco Media Inc. group.

Circulation: 18,231(m); 18,231(m-sat); 19,308(S); ABC Sept. 30, 1995.

Price: 35¢(d); 35¢(sat); 75¢(S); $8.95/mo; $102.00/yr.

Advertising: Open inch rate $15.70(m); $15.70(m-sat); $15.70(S). **Representative:** Papert Companies.

News Service: AP. **Politics:** Independent. **Established:** 1876.

Advertising not accepted: Ads carrying cash investments, not placed through AAA.

Special Editions: Mail-it-Away (Feb); Christmas (Dec).

Magazine: USA Weekend.

CORPORATE OFFICERS

President Walter E Hussman Jr
Vice Pres Eddie J Telford

GENERAL MANAGEMENT

Publisher Walter E Hussman Jr
General Manager Wallace Ballentine

ADVERTISING

Director Floyd Emerson
Manager-Retail Penny Thornton

CIRCULATION

Director Ted Palmer

NEWS EXECUTIVES

Editor Walter E Hussman Jr
Exec Editor Melinda Gassaway
Assoc Editor Isabelle Peregrin

EDITORS AND MANAGERS

Amusements/Books Editor Karen Erickson
Automotive Editor Janie Dahl
Business/Finance Editor Janie Dahl
City Editor James Gilzow
Columnist Melinda Gassaway
Editorial Page Editor Melinda Gassaway
Education Editor Carol Johnson
Environmental Editor Mark Gregory
Farm/Agriculture Editor Mark Gregory
Fashion/Style Editor Marilyn Holsapple
Features Editor Isabelle Peregrin
Films/Theater Editor Karen Erickson
Food Editor Marilyn Holsapple
Graphic Editor/Art Director Mark Gregory
Health/Medical Editor Mark Gregory
Music Editor Karen Erickson
News Editor/Wire Editor Dawn Hickerson
Photo Editor David Vann
Political Editor Mark Gregory
Political Editor John Howard
Radio/Television Editor Karen Erickson
Real Estate Editor Janie Dahl
Religion Editor John Archibald
Science/Technology Editor Mark Gregory
Sports Editor Robert Wisener
Teen-Age/Youth Editor Carol Johnson
Travel Editor Marilyn Holsapple
Women's Editor Marilyn Holsapple

PRODUCTION

Manager Jimmy Robertson
Foreman-Pressroom Fred McAnally

Market Information: TMC.

Mechanical available: Offset; Black and 3 ROP colors; insert accepted — preprinted; page cut-offs — $22\frac{1}{2}$".

Mechanical specifications: Type page 13" x $21\frac{1}{4}$"; E - 6 cols, $2\frac{1}{6}$", $\frac{1}{8}$" between; A - 6 cols, $2\frac{1}{6}$", $\frac{1}{8}$" between; C - 9 cols, $1\frac{1}{4}$", $\frac{1}{8}$" between.

Commodity consumption: Newsprint 1,250 short tons; width $27\frac{1}{2}$"; black ink 30,000 pounds; color ink 2,550 pounds; single pages printed 10,982; average pages per issue 24(d), 42(S); single plates used 12,000.

Equipment: EDITORIAL: Front-end hardware — PC; Front-end software — XYQUEST/XyWrite. CLASSIFIED: Front-end hardware — IBM; Front-end software — CText. DISPLAY: Adv layout systems — Mk/Ad Manager; Front-end hardware — Ap/Mac; Front-end software — Multi-Ad; Printers — AG/9800. PRODUCTION: Pagination software — QPS 3.3; OCR software — TI/Omni Page; Typesetters — AG/9800; Plate exposures — 1-Nu; Plate processors — W; Production cameras — C; Automatic film processors — LE. PRESSROOM: Line 1 — 7-G/Urbanite; Press drives — Fin; Reels and stands — G/7; Press registration system — D. MAILROOM: Counter stackers — 2-HL/Monitor; Bundle tyer — MLN/MLN2A, OVL; Addressing machine — Ch. COMMUNICATIONS: Digital ad delivery system — AP AdSend. WIRE SERVICES: News — AP; Stock tables — AP; Receiving dishes — size-10ft, AP. BUSINESS COMPUTERS: Compaq; Applications: PBS; PCs & micros networked.

JACKSONVILLE

Pulaski County

'90 U.S. Census- 29,101; E&P '96 Est. 30,399

Jacksonville Patriot (e-mon to fri)

Jacksonville Patriot, 1108B W. Main; PO Box 5329, Jacksonville, AR 72076; tel (501) 982-6506.

Circulation: 2,350(e); Sworn Oct. 31, 1995.

Price: 25¢(d); $36.00/yr (in county); 51.00/yr (outside county); $76.00/yr (out of state).

Advertising: Open inch rate $6.50(e). **Representatives:** National Newspaper Association; American Newspaper Representatives Inc.; Arkansas Press Association; Papert Companies. **Established:** 1958.

Not Published: New Year; Independence Day; Labor Day; Thanksgiving; Christmas.

Special Weekly Sections: Health (mon); Business (tues); Food (wed); Entertainment (thur); Society & Religion (fri).

GENERAL MANAGEMENT

Publisher Cone Magie
Publisher Betty Magie
Assoc Publisher Shelly Moran
Assoc Publisher/General Manager Mark Magie

ADVERTISING

Manager Susie Magie
Manager Shelly Moran

NEWS EXECUTIVE

Editor Bill Rutherford

Market Information: TMC.

Mechanical available: Offset; Black and 3 ROP colors; insert accepted — other; page cut-offs — 21".

Mechanical specifications: Type page $15\frac{1}{4}$" x 21"; E - 7 cols, $2\frac{1}{16}$", $\frac{1}{8}$" between; A - 7 cols, $2\frac{1}{16}$", $\frac{1}{8}$" between; C - 7 cols, $2\frac{1}{16}$", $\frac{1}{8}$" between.

Commodity consumption: Newsprint 25 short tons; width 32"; black ink 300 pounds; color ink 10 pounds; single pages printed 2,340; average pages per issue 8(d); single plates used 2,400.

Equipment: EDITORIAL: Front-end hardware — PC; Front-end software — XYQUEST/XyWrite; Printers — QMS/PS 210. DISPLAY: Front-end hardware — PC; Front-end software — Aldus/PageMaker; Printers — QMS/860. PRODUCTION: Plate processors — Nat; Production cameras — K; Automatic film processors — LE. PRESSROOM: Line 1 — 6-KP. MAILROOM: Addressing machine — Bu.

JONESBORO

Craighead County

'90 U.S. Census- 46,535; E&P '96 Est. 60,700
ABC-CZ (90): 46,535 (HH 17,976)

The Jonesboro Sun (m-mon to sat; S)

The Jonesboro Sun, 518 Carson; PO Box 1249, Jonesboro, AR 72401; tel (501) 935-5525; fax (501) 935-5823.

Circulation: 26,957(m); 26,957(m-sat); 29,467(S); ABC Sept. 30, 1995.

Price: 35¢(d); 35¢(sat); $1.00(S); $8.50/mo; $98.00/yr.

Advertising: Open inch rate $16.25(m); $16.25(m-sat); $16.25(S). **Representative:** Papert Companies.

News Service: AP. **Politics:** Democrat. **Established:** 1903.

Advertising not accepted: Liquor.

Special Weekly Sections: Farm Page (tues); Food Section (wed); Building & Home Improvement (thur); Church Page (sat); Lifescene (S).

Magazines: Re-Act (thur); Parade, TV Guide (S).

GENERAL MANAGEMENT

Publisher John W Troutt Jr
Asst Publisher Robert W Troutt
Asst Publisher John Ed Troutt
General Manager Wade H Martin
Controller Dawn Ginn

ADVERTISING

Director Jerry Donohue
Manager-Classified Pat Hallmark

CIRCULATION

Manager Debbie Gulley

NEWS EXECUTIVES

Editor John W Troutt Jr
Assoc Editor Mike Overall
Assoc Editor Larry Fugate

EDITORS AND MANAGERS

Editorial Page Editor John W Troutt Jr
Films/Theater Editor Mike Overall
Society Editor Myra Buhrmester
Sports Editor Kevin Turbeville

PRODUCTION

Foreman-Composing Roger Brumley
Foreman-Pressroom Dale Lammers

Market Information: Zoned editions; TMC.

Mechanical available: Offset; Black and 3 ROP colors; insert accepted — preprinted; page cut-offs — 21.5".

Mechanical specifications: Type page $13\frac{1}{2}$" x $21\frac{1}{2}$"; E - 6 cols, 2", .14" between; A - 6 cols, 2", .14" between; C - 8 cols, 1.5", .11" between.

Commodity consumption: Newsprint 2,300 short tons; widths $27\frac{1}{2}$", $13\frac{3}{4}$"; single pages printed 13,000; average pages per issue 32(d), 64(S); single plates used 15,000.

Equipment: EDITORIAL: Front-end hardware — 32-Mk, 1-Ap/Mac II, 1-Ap/Mac PowerBook 540c, Ap/Mac ci, Ap/Mac si, Ap/Mac Quadra 800, 1-Ap/Power Mac 6100; Front-end software — Mk; Printers — 1-Ap/Mac LaserWriter Pro 630, 1-HP/LaserWriter, 1-ECR/Autokon 1030, 202 N; Other equipment — Lf/AP Leaf Picture Desk, 2-IBM/Selectric. CLASSIFIED: Front-end hardware — 6-Mk; Front-end software — Mk; Printers — TI/810 impact. DISPLAY: Front-end hardware — 3-MK, 2-Ap/Mac 8100, 1-Ap/Mac 7100, 1-Ap/Mac II, 1-Ap/Power Mac 8100, 2-Ap/Mac Quadra 800, 2-Ap/Mac vx; Front-end software — Mk, Mk/Ad Touch, QuarkXPress, Multi-Ad/Creator 3.5,

Adobe/Photoshop 2.5, Aldus/FreeHand 4.0, ECR/RIP Power Mac; Printers — 1-Ap/Mac LaserWriter 16/600; Other equipment — 1-Mk/VDT, 1-ECR/VR36SS, 1-Fargo/Pictura 310 Color Printer, 1-HP/ScanJet 2 Color Scanner. PRODUCTION: Typesetters — 2-M/Linotron 202W, 1-Ap/Mac LaserWriter NTX, 1-Ap/Mac LaserWriter Pro 630, 1-Ap/Mac LaserWriter 16/600; Platemaking systems — 3M/Pyrofax; Plate exposures — 2-Nu; Plate processors — 1-Nat/Enco; Electronic picture desk — Lf/AP Leaf Picture Desk; Scanners — 1-ECR/1030, 1-HP/ScanJet II; Production cameras — 2-B; Automatic film processors — 1-LE/Excell; Color separation equipment (conventional) — ECR/1030; Digital color separation equipment — Lf, ECR/1030, ECR/VR 36. PRESSROOM: Line 1 — 6-G/Urbanite; Line 6 — 2-Fin; Folders — 1-G/2:1; Reels and stands — 2-G/4 Tier; Press control system — 2-North American Rockwell. MAILROOM: Counter stackers — Newstack, 1-Id/660, 1-Id/2200; Inserters and stuffers — HI/1372, W/ARS; Bundle tyer — 2-MLN; Addressing machine — 1-KR, 2-CYP. COMMUNICATIONS: Digital ad delivery system — AP AdSend, BBS. WIRE SERVICES: News — AP; Stock tables — AP; Syndicates — AP Datafeatures; Receiving dishes — AP. BUSINESS COMPUTERS: 3-Ap/Mac II, 1-ATT/6386-25, 7-WGS/VDT; Applications: ATT/Unix; PCs & micros networked; PCs & main system networked.

LITTLE ROCK

Pulaski County

'90 U.S. Census- 175,695; E&P '96 Est. 188,220
ABC-CZ (90): 323,700 (HH 127,918)

Arkansas Democrat-Gazette (m-mon to sat; S)

Arkansas Democrat-Gazette, Capitol Ave. & Scott; PO Box 2221, Little Rock, AR 72201; tel (501) 378-3400; e-mail news@demgaz.com; web site http://www.ardemgaz.com/. Wehco Media Inc. group.
Circulation: 175,218(m); 175,218(m-sat); 288,250(S); ABC Sept. 30, 1995.
Price: 35¢(d); 35¢(sat); $1.00(S); $10.75/mo; $109.00/yr.
Advertising: Open inch rate $99.50(m); $99.50(m-sat); $141.50(S). **Representative:** Sawyer-Ferguson-Walker Co.
News Services: AP, LAT-WP, SHNS, NYT, KRT. **Politics:** Independent. **Established:** 1878/1819.
Advertising not accepted: Fraudulent, misleading and copy in poor taste; Diet.
Special Editions: Racing (Jan); Spring Fashion (Mar); Fall Fashions, Football (Aug); Basketball (Nov); Christmas Gift (Dec).
Special Weekly Sections: Food (wed); Weekend Arkansas (fri).
Magazine: Parade-TV Magazine (local, offset) (S).
Cable TV: Own cable TV in circulation area.

CORPORATE OFFICERS
President Walter E Hussman Jr
Vice Pres/General Manager Paul Smith
Vice Pres/Operations Manager Lynn Hamilton

GENERAL MANAGEMENT
General Manager Paul Smith
Publisher Walter E Hussman Jr
Controller Allen Berry
Manager-Data Processing/Typeset Geoff George
Manager-Data Processing/Business Judy Nethercutt
Manager-Accounting Terrell Strickland
Personnel Manager Kay Brewer

ADVERTISING
Director John Mobbs
Manager-National Dick Browning
Manager-Retail John White
Manager-Classified Morgan Miller
Manager-Retail Sales Dave Walters
Manager-Retail Sales Jerry Riemenschneider
Manager-Retail Sales Barbara Day

MARKETING AND PROMOTION
Director-Promotion Estel Jeffery

TELECOMMUNICATIONS
Audiotex Manager Morgan Miller

CIRCULATION
Director Larry Graham

NEWS EXECUTIVES
Exec Editor Griffin Smith Jr
Assoc Editor Mary Hargrove
Managing Editor Robert Lutgen
Deputy Managing Editor Frank Fellone
Asst Managing Editor-Administration Rhonda Owen
Asst Managing Editor-Systems Clay Carson
Asst Managing Editor-Night Alyson Hoge
Asst Managing Editor-Sports Wally Hall

EDITORS AND MANAGERS
Automotive Writer James Butta
Business Farm Editor Christi Phelps
Cartoonist John Deering
Cartoonist Vic Harville
Exec City Editor Ray Hobbs
City Editor David Bailey
Columnist John Robert Starr
Columnist Meridith Oakley
Columnist Paul Greenberg
Columnist Frank Fellone
Columnist John Brumett
Editorial Page Editor Paul Greenberg
Education Writer Cynthia Howell
Farm Editor Doug Thompson
Features Editor Jack Schnedler
Health/Medical Writer Karen McAllister
Librarian Alfred Thomas
Photo Editor Barry Arthur
Political Editor Rex Nelson
State Editor Roger Hedges
Television/Film Editor Michael Storey
Theater/Music Editor Ellis Widner
Travel Editor Libby Smith
Wire Editor Ben Pollock
Women's Editor Phyllis Brandon

MANAGEMENT INFORMATION SERVICES
Data Processing Manager Judy Nethercutt

PRODUCTION
Manager-Operations Lynn Hamilton
Manager-Composing Vicki Morgan
Manager-Pressroom Don Mokler
Manager-Mailroom Fred Martin
Manager-Technical Support Jim Shuemake

Market Information: Zoned editions; Split Run; Operate audiotex; Electronic edition.
Mechanical available: Offset; Black and 3 ROP colors; insert accepted — preprinted; page cutoffs — 22".
Mechanical specifications: Type page 13" x 21"; E - 6 cols, 2 1/16", 1/8" between; A - 6 cols, 2 1/16", 1/8" between; C - 9 cols, 1 5/6", 1/8" between.
Commodity consumption: Newsprint 34,588 short tons; widths 55", 41 1/4", 27 1/2"; black ink 535,272 pounds; color ink 290,921 pounds; single pages printed 28,087; average pages per issue 64(d), 134(S); single plates used 260,000.
Equipment: EDITORIAL: Front-end hardware — SII, Novell/LAN; Printers — 2-AU/APS-108S, 2-AG/9800, 2-III/Pagescan; Other equipment — Ap/Mac PCs. CLASSIFIED: Front-end hardware — Novell/LAN, 35-PC; Front-end software — CText; Printers — 2-AU/APS-108S, 2-AG/9800, 2-III/Pagescan. AUDIOTEX: Supplier name — Micro Voice. DISPLAY: Front-end hardware — Novell/LAN, Ap/Mac fx, Ap/Mac Quadra; Front-end software — Multi-Ad/Creator; Printers — 2-AU/APS-108S, 2-AG/9800, 2-III/Pagescan; Other equipment — HP/Sharp 8x10 scanners, CD-Rom. PRODUCTION: Pagination software — QuarkXPress; Plate exposures — 3-WL/Plater; Electronic picture desk — Lf; Scanners — DSA, Nikon, Lf/Leafscan 35-45, HP/Sharp 8x10; Production cameras — C/Spartan III, C/Marathon; Automatic film processors — 3-P; Film transporters — C; Shrink lenses — C.
PRESSROOM: Line 1 — 9-G/Headliner; Line 2 — 9-G/Headliner; Press drives — Allen Bradley; Folders — 4-G/3:2; Pasters — 18-G/C-45; Press control system — Allen Bradley. MAILROOM: Counter stackers — 6-HL/HT, 3-HL/Monitor; Inserters and stuffers — 2-HI/1372, 1-MM/7:1; Bundle tyer — 2-Power Strap/Model 5, 1-MLN/News 90, 4-MLN/MLN2A; Addressing machine — 2-Ch. LIBRARY: Electronic — Mead Data Central Nexis/NewsView. COMMUNICATIONS: Digital ad delivery system — AP AdSend. WIRE SERVICES: News — AP, NYT, KRT, LAT-WP, CT; Photos — AP, PressLink, KRT; Stock tables — AP; Syndicates — Louis Rukeyser Tribune; Receiving dishes — size-3m, AP. BUSINESS COMPUTERS: DEC/VAX, IBM/Sys 36, Novell/LAN; Applications: SCO/Xenix; PCs & micros networked; PCs & main system networked.

MAGNOLIA

Columbia County

'90 U.S. Census- 11,151; E&P '96 Est. 10,854

Banner-News (e-mon to sat)

Banner-News, 134 S. Washington; PO Box 100, Magnolia, AR 71753; tel (501) 234-5130; fax (501) 243-2551. Wehco Media Inc. group.
Circulation: 4,432(e); 4,432(e-sat); Sworn Oct. 2, 1995.
Price: 35¢(d); 35¢(sat); $5.50/mo; $66.00/yr.
Advertising: Open inch rate $17.17(e); $17.17(e-sat).
News Service: AP. **Politics:** Independent. **Established:** 1878.
Note: The Banner-News is printed at El Dorado News-Times. For detailed production information, see the El Dorado News-Times listing.
Not Published: New Year; Independence Day; Thanksgiving; Christmas.
Advertising not accepted: Liquor, beer.
Special Editions: Bride (Apr); Blossom Festival, Progress Edition (May); Football (Sept); Lights Fantastic (Dec).

CORPORATE OFFICER
President Walter E Hussman Jr

GENERAL MANAGEMENT
Publisher Walter E Hussman Jr
General Manager Betty Chatham
Purchasing Agent Betty Chatham

ADVERTISING
Director Susan Carmichael

CIRCULATION
Manager Darlene Bond

NEWS EXECUTIVE
Managing Editor Melissa Butler

EDITOR AND MANAGER
Sports Editor Chris Gilliam

Market Information: TMC.
Mechanical available: Offset; Black and 3 ROP colors; insert accepted — preprinted; page cutoffs — 21 1/2".
Mechanical specifications: Type page 13" x 21"; E - 6 cols, 2 1/16", 1/16" between; A - 6 cols, 2 1/16", 1/16" between; C - 8 cols, 1 3/8", 1/16" between.
Commodity consumption: average pages per issue 10(d).
Equipment: EDITORIAL: Front-end hardware — IBM; Front-end software — CText. CLASSIFIED: Front-end hardware — IBM; Front-end software — CText. DISPLAY: Front-end software — Ap/Mac Display Ad Makeup System; Printers — Ap/Mac LaserWriter II. MAILROOM: Bundle tyer — Cyclone; Addressing machine — Novell/LAN.

MALVERN

Hot Spring County

'90 U.S. Census- 9,256; E&P '96 Est. 8,882

Malvern Daily Record (e-mon to fri)

Malvern Daily Record, 219 Locust St., Malvern, AR 72104; tel (501) 337-7523; fax (501) 337-1226. Hollinger International Inc. group.
Circulation: 5,504(e); Sworn Oct. 2, 1995.
Price: 50¢(d); $4.75/mo (city), $5.25/mo (outside city); $78.00/yr.
Advertising: Open inch rate $8.60(e). **Representative:** Papert Companies.
News Service: AP. **Established:** 1916.
Not Published: Christmas.
Advertising not accepted: X-rated movies.
Special Editions: Progress (Jan); Thanksgiving/Christmas Kick-off (Nov); Christmas Edition (Dec).
Magazines: Food Days (mon, wed); Consumer Review (thur).

GENERAL MANAGEMENT
Publisher Ron Causey
Business Manager Vicki Oden

ADVERTISING
Manager Ron Causey

CIRCULATION
Manager Sandra Joyner

NEWS EXECUTIVE
Editor Steve Brawner

EDITORS AND MANAGERS
Business Editor Keith Davenport
News Editor Don Daily
Reporter Melissa Burrow
Sports Editor Mark Bivens

PRODUCTION
Foreman-Composing Claude Speer

Market Information: TMC.
Mechanical available: Offset; Black and 4 ROP colors; insert accepted — preprinted; page cutoffs — 22 3/4".
Mechanical specifications: Type page 13" x 21 1/2"; E - 6 cols, 2.06", 1/8" between; A - 6 cols, 2.06", 1/8" between; C - 9 cols, 1.33", 1/8" between.
Commodity consumption: Newsprint 165 short tons; widths 28", 27 1/2"; black ink 1,150 pounds; color ink 482 pounds; single pages printed 3,640; average pages per issue 14(d); single plates used 2,393.
Equipment: EDITORIAL: Front-end hardware — Ap/Mac; Front-end software — Baseview, QuarkXPress; Printers — Ap/Mac LaserWriter IIg. CLASSIFIED: Front-end hardware — Ap/Mac; Front-end software — Baseview. DISPLAY: Adv layout systems — Ap/Mac; Front-end software — QuarkXPress; Printers — Ap/Mac LaserWriter IIg. PRODUCTION: Typesetters — Ap/Mac LaserWriter IIg; Plate exposures — 1-Nu; Plate processors — Nat/A-250; Production cameras — B; Automatic film processors — LE; Shrink lenses — CK Optical/6%. PRESSROOM: Line 1 — G. MAILROOM: Counter stackers — BG; Addressing machine — Wm. LIBRARY: Combination — Micro-Film. WIRE SERVICES: News — AP; Receiving dishes — AP. BUSINESS COMPUTERS: 3-Wyse; Applications: Accts receivable, Payroll; PCs & micros networked; PCs & main system networked.

MOUNTAIN HOME

Baxter County

'90 U.S. Census- 9,027; E&P '96 Est. 9,725
ABC-CZ (90): 9,027 (HH 4,253)

The Baxter Bulletin (m-mon to sat)

Baxter Bulletin, 16 W. 6th St.; PO Drawer A, Mountain Home, AR 72653; tel (501) 425-3133; fax (501) 425-5091, (501) 425-5011. Gannett Co. Inc. group.
Circulation: 9,678(m); 9,678(m-sat); ABC Sept. 30, 1995.
Price: 35¢(d); 50¢(sat); $35.88/6mo, $19.75/3mo.
Advertising: Open inch rate $10.76(m); $10.76(m-sat). **Representative:** Landon Associates Inc.
News Service: AP. **Politics:** Independent. **Established:** 1901.
Not Published: Christmas.
Special Editions: Chronology, Income Tax Guide (Jan); Baxter County Fact Book (Feb); Lawn and Garden Edition (Mar); Brides and Fashion Edition (Apr); Mother's Day, Older American's Day (May); Great Outdoors (June); Home Improvement (July); Back-to-School (Aug); Baxter County Fair (Sept); Christmas Gift Guide (Nov); Senior Focus (2nd tues monthly).
Magazine: USA Weekend.

GENERAL MANAGEMENT
Publisher Betty Barker Smith

ADVERTISING
Manager Eddie Majeste

MARKETING AND PROMOTION
Director-Marketing Eddie Majeste

CIRCULATION
Manager Paul Neal

NEWS EXECUTIVE
Editor Bob R Qualls

Market Information: TMC.
Mechanical available: Offset; Black and 3 ROP colors; insert accepted — preprinted; page cutoffs — 22 3/4".
Mechanical specifications: Type page 12 3/4" x 21"; E - 6 cols, 2 1/16", 1/8" between; A - 6 cols, 2 1/16", 1/8" between; C - 6 cols, 2 1/16", 1/8" between.
Commodity consumption: Newsprint 627 short tons; widths 27 1/2", 13 3/4"; black ink 15,000 pounds; color ink 800 pounds; single pages printed 6,865; average pages per issue 19(d); single plates used 7,500.
Equipment: EDITORIAL: Front-end hardware — Mk/3000; Other equipment — 9-Mk/PC. CLASSIFIED: Other equipment — 3-Epson/PC. DISPLAY: Adv layout systems — 3-HI/2221; Other equipment — 3-HI/1420. PRODUCTION:

I-24 Arkansas

Typesetters — 2-COM/8400; Plate exposures — 1-Nu/Flip Top; Plate processors — 1-WL/Platemaker 25; Production cameras — 1-C/Spartan III; Automatic film processors — 1-LE/LD 24 BQ; Color separation equipment (conventional) — 1-BKY.
PRESSROOM: Line 1 — 6-G/Community; Press control system — Fin. MAILROOM: Counter stackers — 1-BG; Inserters and stuffers — 1-MM; Bundle tyer — 2-Bu; Addressing machine — 2-Wm. WIRE SERVICES: News — AP; Receiving dishes — AP. BUSINESS COMPUTERS: 1-IBM/AS400; Applications: Circ, Accts receivable, Budgeting, Payroll, Gen ledger; PCs & micros networked; PCs & main system networked.

The Daily News (m-mon to sat)

The Daily News, Hwy. 62 N.E.; PO Box 1087, Mountain Home, AR 72653; tel (501) 425-6301; fax (501) 424-4488. Phillips Media Inc. group.
Circulation: 2,208(m); 2,208(m-sat); Sworn Sept. 27, 1995.
Price: 35¢(d); 50¢(sat); 96¢/wk; $4.17/mo; $50.00/yr.
Advertising: Open inch rate $6.50(m); $6.50(m-sat). **Representative:** Papert Companies.
News Service: AP. **Politics:** Independent.
Note: Effective Aug. 19, 1995, this publication changed its publishing plan from (m-mon to fri; S) to (m-mon to sat).
Not Published: New Year; Independence Day; Labor Day; Thanksgiving; Christmas.
Advertising not accepted: Classified offering home work.
Special Weekly Sections: Best Food Day (wed); Religion (fri); Entertainment (sat).
Magazine: Senior Views (monthly).

CORPORATE OFFICERS

Owner Rupert E Phillips
Owner Sandra F Phillips

GENERAL MANAGEMENT

Publisher Chuck Pullins

CIRCULATION

Manager Bob Teague

NEWS EXECUTIVES

Editor Joe Dobson
Assoc Editor Laurie Wood

EDITORS AND MANAGERS

Business Editor Laurie Wood
Society/Food Editor Brenda Rose
Sports Editor Gregory Anglin

Market Information: TMC.
Mechanical available: Black and 1 ROP color; insert accepted — preprinted.
Mechanical specifications: Type page 13" x $21\frac{1}{2}$"; E - 6 cols, $2\frac{1}{2}$", $\frac{1}{8}$" between; A - 6 cols, $2\frac{1}{2}$", $\frac{1}{8}$" between; C - 8 cols, $1\frac{21}{32}$", $\frac{1}{12}$" between.
Equipment: EDITORIAL: Front-end hardware — 3-Ap/Mac Color Classic; Front-end software — Baseview/NewsEdit 3.3; CLASSIFIED: Front-end hardware — 1-Ap/Mac Color Classic; Front-end software — QuarkXPress 3.3; Printers — Xante/Accel-a-Writer 8100-A. PRODUCTION: Pagination software — QuarkXPress 3.3; Typesetters — Xante/Accel-a-Writer; Platemaking systems — 1-Nu; Plate exposures — 1-Nu; Plate processors — Nat; Scanners — Nikon/Coolscan, Avec/Color Office 2400 flatbed; Production cameras — Acti; Automatic film processors — LE; Digital color separation equipment — Ap/Mac Quadra 650 w/Photoshop.
PRESSROOM: Line 1 — 7-G/Community; Press drives — Fin; Folders — 1-S/1007 Community. MAILROOM: Wrapping singles — Malow/Straptyper Model 30. WIRE SERVICES: News — AP; Stock tables — AP; Syndicates — Universal Press; Receiving dishes — size-3 ft, AP. BUSINESS COMPUTERS: IBM/386.

NEWPORT

Jackson County

'90 U.S. Census- 7,459; E&P '96 Est. 7,093

Newport Daily Independent (e-mon to fri)

Newport Daily Independent, 2408 Hwy. 67 N.; PO Box 1750, Newport, AR 72112; tel (501) 523-5855; fax (501) 523-6540. Hollinger International Inc. group.
Circulation: 3,021(e); Sworn Sept. 30, 1995.
Price: 50¢(d); $6.00/mo; $68.00/yr.
Advertising: Open inch rate $5.90(e); $7.90(e-tues). **Representative:** Papert Companies.
News Service: AP. **Politics:** Independent. **Established:** 1901.
Not Published: Christmas Day.
Special Editions: Progress (Feb); Farm Family, Summer Clearance, Back-to-School (Aug); Football (Sept); Rice Harvest (Oct).
Special Weekly Sections: Business News (mon); Best Food Day (tues); Church Directory (fri); TV Listings, Lifestyle, Amusements (daily).

CORPORATE OFFICER

President Larry J Perrotto

GENERAL MANAGEMENT

Publisher/General Manager Bill Park
Business Manager Rachelle Poskey

CIRCULATION

Manager Ruth Park

NEWS EXECUTIVE

Editor Patricia Mays

EDITOR AND MANAGER

Sports Editor John Reynolds

Market Information: TMC.
Mechanical available: Offset; Black and 3 ROP colors; insert accepted — preprinted; page cut-offs — $21\frac{1}{2}$".
Mechanical specifications: Type page 13" x $21\frac{1}{2}$"; E - 5 cols, $2\frac{3}{5}$", $\frac{1}{8}$" between; A - 6 cols, $2\frac{1}{16}$", $\frac{1}{8}$" between; C - 6 cols, $2\frac{1}{16}$", $\frac{1}{8}$" between.
Commodity consumption: Newsprint 110 short tons; width 28"; black ink 5,000 pounds; color ink 300 pounds; single pages printed 2,898; average pages per issue 11.5(d); single plates used 4,000.
Equipment: EDITORIAL: Front-end hardware — Ap/Mac; Front-end software — QuarkXPress, Microsoft/Word; Printers — Ap/Mac LaserPrinter, Ap/Mac Pro; Other equipment — HP/Scanner, Ap/Mac CD-Rom. CLASSIFIED: Front-end hardware — Ap/Mac; Front-end software — Baseview/Class Manager Plus; Printers — Ap/Mac LaserPrinter, Ap/Mac ImageWriter, Ap/Mac Pro. DISPLAY: Adv layout systems — Ap/Mac; Front-end hardware — Ap/Mac II, Ap/Super Mac; Front-end software — QuarkXPress, Multi-Ad, Broderbund/TypeStyler; Printers — Ap/Mac LaserPrinter; Other equipment — Ap/Mac CD-Rom, HP/Scanner. PRODUCTION: Scanners — Companica/680c. PRESSROOM: Line 1 — HI/V15A; Line 2 — HI/V15A; Line 3 — HI/V15A; Line 4 — HI/V15A; Folders — HI/JF-7, HI/Quarter; Press control system — Fin/Direct Drive 1800. MAILROOM: Bundle tyer — 1-Bu/23, 1-Bu/119. WIRE SERVICES: News — AP; Receiving dishes — size-10ft, AP. BUSINESS COMPUTERS: 1-Goldstar, 1-Packard Bell; PCs & micros networked; PCs & main system networked.

PARAGOULD

Greene County

'90 U.S. Census- 18,540; E&P '96 Est. 21,094

The Paragould Daily Press (m-tues to sat; S)

Paragould Daily Press, 1401 W. Hunt St. (72450); PO Box 38, Paragould, AR 72451-0038; tel (501) 239-8562; fax (501) 239-8565. Paxton Media group.
Circulation: 5,836(m); 5,836(m-sat); 5,836(S); Sworn Oct. 1, 1994.
Price: 35¢(d); 35¢(sat); 75¢(S); $7.00/mo; $69.00/yr.
Advertising: Open inch rate $8.23(m); $8.23(m-sat); $8.23(S). **Representative:** Papert Companies.
News Service: AP. **Politics:** Independent. **Established:** 1883.
Not Published: New Year; Memorial Day; Labor Day; Thanksgiving; Christmas.
Advertising not accepted: Dating Services; Abortion; Adoption.
Special Editions: Travel (Apr); Spring Fashions (Mar); Family-owned Business (June); Loose Caboose Festival (July); Back-to-School, Fall Fashions (Aug); Progress, Football (Sept); Outdoors (Oct); Thanksgiving (Nov); Christmas (Dec).
Special Weekly Sections: Business (tues); Food (wed); Farm (thur); Entertainment (fri); Religion, Outdoors (sat); Engagement, Weddings (S).
Magazines: Television, Encore!, Sunday Comics, USA Weekend (S).

CORPORATE OFFICER

Chief Financial Officer David M Paxton

GENERAL MANAGEMENT

Publisher/General Manager David Mosesso

ADVERTISING

Manager Dina Mason

CIRCULATION

Manager Tammy Russom

NEWS EXECUTIVE

Editor Chris Day

EDITORS AND MANAGERS

Editorial Page Editor Chris Day
Education Editor Travis Justice
Entertainment/Amusements Editor Sharon Knight
Features Editor Wade Quick
Living/Lifestyle Editor Marie Mitchell
News Editor Sharon Knight
Religion Editor Ronnie Ashhock
Sports Editor Mike McKinney

MANAGEMENT INFORMATION SERVICES

Data Processing Manager Janet Chronister

PRODUCTION

Superintendent-Pressroom Bill Howard

Market Information: TMC.
Mechanical available: Offset; Black and 3 ROP colors; insert accepted — preprinted; page cut-offs — $23\frac{5}{16}$".
Mechanical specifications: Type page 13" x 21"; E - 6 cols, $2\frac{1}{16}$", $\frac{1}{8}$" between; A - 6 cols, $2\frac{1}{16}$", $\frac{1}{8}$" between; C - 9 cols, $1\frac{3}{8}$", $\frac{1}{16}$" between.
Commodity consumption: Newsprint 500 short tons; width 27"; black ink 85,000 pounds; color ink 20,000 pounds; single pages printed 6,000; average pages per issue 20(d), 48(S); single plates used 6,000.
Equipment: EDITORIAL: Front-end hardware — Mk/3000, Ap/Mac; Front-end software — QPS, Microsoft/Word; Printers — QMS/PS2210, ECR/ScriptSetter II; Other equipment — 9-Mk. CLASSIFIED: Front-end hardware — Mk/3000, Ap/Mac; Front-end software — Baseview, QPS; Other equipment — 1-Mk. DISPLAY: Adv layout systems — Ap/Mac; Front-end hardware — 1-Ap/Mac Quadra 630 w/CD-Rom, 1-Ap/Mac IIsi, 1-Ap/Mac II; Front-end software — Multi-Ad/Creator, Adobe/Photoshop, Caere/OmniPage; Printers — QMS/PS2210, Ap/Mac LaserWriter II. PRODUCTION: Typesetters — 2-Ap/Mac Laser Plus; Platemaking systems — 1-Nu/Flip Top; Plate exposures — 1-Nu/Flip Top FT40L; Plate processors — 1-Nat/A-260; Scanners — Nikon/Film Scanner; Production cameras — 1-C/Spartan III; Automatic film processors — 1-LE/LP-18; Color separation equipment (conventional) — Ap/Mac Quadra 950, Pelbox/UR-30.
PRESSROOM: Line 1 — 6-G/Community (1 balloon former); Folders — 1-G. MAILROOM: Inserters and stuffers — KAN/320 4 pocket; Bundle tyer — 1-Sa/4592; Addressing machine — 1-El/3300. LIBRARY: Electronic — BH/Mark II (Microfilm reader). WIRE SERVICES: News — AP; Receiving dishes — size-10ft, AP. BUSINESS COMPUTERS: Leading Edge; Applications: dBase/II.

PINE BLUFF

Jefferson County

'90 U.S. Census- 57,140; E&P '96 Est. 57,720
ABC-CZ (90): 57,140 (HH 20,871)

Pine Bluff Commercial (m-mon to sat; S)

Pine Bluff Commercial, 300 Beech St. (71601); PO Box 6469, Pine Bluff, AR 71611-6469; tel (501) 534-3400; fax (501) 543-1455. Donrey Media group.
Circulation: 19,051(m); 19,051(m-sat); 20,081(S); ABC Sept. 30, 1995.
Price: 50¢(d); 50¢(sat); $1.00(S); $7.50/mo; $90.00/yr (carrier).
Advertising: Open inch rate $15.50(m); $15.50(m-sat); $15.50(S). **Representative:** Papert Companies.
News Services: AP, LAT-WP. **Politics:** Independent. **Established:** 1881.
Special Editions: Chamber of Commerce Tab; Tax Guide Tab; Spring Fashion (full); Lawn; Garden and Home Improvement (full); Wedding Tab; Baseball (full); Vacation Guide Tab; Newcomer's Guide Tab; Football Tab; Fall Fashion (full); Fall Hunting Guide Tab; Cookbook (Holiday) Tab; King Cotton Classic Basketball Tab.
Special Weekly Sections: Food, Business News (wed); Weekend Entertainment, Automotive (fri); Farm Report, TV Section (sat); Real Estate, Business News (S).
Magazine: Parade Magazine.

CORPORATE OFFICERS

Founder Donald W Reynolds
President/Chief Operating Officer Emmett Jones
Exec Vice Pres/Chief Financial Officer Darrell W Loftin
Vice Pres-Western Newspaper Group David A Osborn
Vice Pres-Eastern Newspaper Group Don Schneider

GENERAL MANAGEMENT

Publisher Charles A Berry
Business Manager Jareta Moore

ADVERTISING

Director Nancy Donaldson
Manager-Classified Renee Garcia

CIRCULATION

Director Jerry Hoyt

NEWS EXECUTIVES

Editor Byron Tate
Managing Editor John Henry

EDITORS AND MANAGERS

Accent Editor Eva Marie Pearson
Automotive Editor John Henry
Business/Finance Editor Britt Talent
City/Metro Editor Sandra Hope
Copy Editor John Henry
Editorial Page Editor Byron Tate
Education/School Editor Kay Young
Entertainment/Amusements Editor Eva Marie Pearson
Environmental Editor Britt Talent
Farm Editor Britt Talent
Fashion/Style Editor Eva Marie Pearson
Features Editor Agnes Ross
Films/Theater Editor Eva Marie Pearson
Food Editor Cindy Williams
Graphics Editor/Art Director Frances Solley
Health/Medical Editor John Henry
Home Furnishings Editor Eva Marie Pearson
Librarian Vicki Owen
National Editor John Henry
News Editor John Henry
Photography Editor Andy Marx
Political/Government Editor Donna Mooney
Radio/Television Editor John Henry
Regional Editor Britt Talent
Religion Editor Agnes Ross
Science/Technology Editor Britt Talent
Society Editor Eva Marie Pearson
Sports Editor Scott Loftis
Travel Editor Eva Marie Pearson

PRODUCTION

Foreman-Composing Dickie Northington
Foreman-Pressroom T C Day
Foreman-Mailroom Andrew Elkins

Market Information: TMC.
Mechanical available: Offset; Black and 3 ROP colors; insert accepted — preprinted; page cut-offs — 21".
Mechanical specifications: Type page 13" x 21"; E - 6 cols, $2\frac{1}{16}$", $\frac{1}{8}$" between; A - 6 cols, $2\frac{1}{16}$", $\frac{1}{8}$" between; C - 9 cols, $1\frac{3}{8}$", $\frac{1}{16}$" between.
Commodity consumption: Newsprint 1,212 short tons; 1,100 metric tons; widths $13\frac{3}{4}$", $27\frac{1}{2}$"; black ink 50,000 pounds; color ink 6,000 pounds; single pages printed 10,112; average pages per issue 24(d), 48(S); single plates used 19,000.
Equipment: EDITORIAL: Front-end hardware — 26-Dewar/Disc Net; Front-end software — Dewar/Disc Net; Printers — Okidata/Microline 192; Other equipment — Ap/Mac SE, 5-RSK/Tandy M102. CLASSIFIED: Front-end hardware — 3-Dewar/Disc Net; Front-end software — Dewar/Disc Net; Printers — Okidata/190. DISPLAY: Adv layout systems — Ap/Mac 840 AU; Printers — Panther/Plus. PRODUCTION: Typesetters — Tegra/Genesis, 1-Ap/Mac LaserWriter; Platemaking systems — 3M/Platemaking System, Nu/Flip Top 631; Plate exposures — Nu/631; Plate processors — Nat/A-250; Electronic picture desk — Lf/AP Leaf Picture Desk; Scanners — Nikon/Negative Scanner; Production cameras — Kk/5060B, C/Marathon; Color separation equipment (conventional) — Digi-Colour; Digital color separation equipment — Nikon/LS 3500.
PRESSROOM: Line 1 — 9-G/Urbanite; Folders — 1-G. MAILROOM: Counter stackers — 1-Id/NS440; Inserters and stuffers — 2-MM/227; Bundle tyer — 1-MLN/ML2EE, 1-MLN/2A; Addressing machine — 1-KR/211. WIRE SERVICES: News — AP, LAT-WP; Stock tables — AP SelectStox; Receiving dishes — size-8ft, AP. BUSINESS COMPUTERS: 9-HP/917LX3000, Link/MC5; Applications: Accounting; PCs & main system networked.

ROGERS

See SPRINGDALE

RUSSELLVILLE

Pope County

'90 U.S. Census- 21,260; E&P '96 Est. 28,300

The Courier (m-tues to sat; S)

The Courier, 201 E. 2nd St.; PO Box 887, Russellville, AR 72811; tel (501) 968-5252; fax (501) 968-4037. Paxton Media group.

Circulation: 11,067(m); 11,067(m-sat); 14,151(S); Sworn Sept. 26, 1995.

Price: 35¢(d); 35¢(sat); $1.00(S); $95.40/yr.

Advertising: Open inch rate $10.40(m); $10.40(m-sat); $10.65(S); $14.80 (TMC). **Representative:** Papert Companies.

News Service: AP. **Politics:** Independent. **Established:** 1875, 1924 (daily).

Note: Effective Sept. 1, 1995, this publication (formerly The Courier-Democrat) changed its publishing plan from (e-mon to fri; S) to (m-tues to sat; S).

Special Editions: Salute to Family Business (Jan); Funeral & Death (Feb); Home Improvement (Mar); Welcome to the Valley (Apr); Pet Section (May); The Wheel (June); 55 Plus (July); Football Edition (Aug); Progress Edition (Oct); Christmas Opening (Nov); Christmas Greetings (Dec).

Special Weekly Sections: Business Review (tues); Best Food Day (wed); Church Directory (fri); Business News, Lifestyles (S).

Magazines: TV Spotlight, Color Comics (S); USA Weekend.

GENERAL MANAGEMENT

Publisher Craig Martin

ADVERTISING

Manager Vicki Bowden

MARKETING AND PROMOTION

Manager-Marketing/Promotion Stephen Babb

CIRCULATION

Manager Jim Wade

NEWS EXECUTIVES

Exec Editor Bill Newsom
Managing Editor Roy Ockert

EDITORS AND MANAGERS

Area Editor Sharon Wofford
Society Editor Dianne Edwards
Sports Editor Warren Byrd

MANAGEMENT INFORMATION SERVICES

Business Manager Sandy Williams

PRODUCTION

Manager Harry Brownlee

Market Information: TMC.

Mechanical available: Offset; Black and 3 ROP colors; insert accepted — preprinted; page cut-offs — 22¾".

Mechanical specifications: Type page 13" x 21½"; E - 6 cols, 2", ⅙" between; A - 6 cols, 2", ⅙" between; C - 9 cols, 1 5/16", ⅙" between.

Commodity consumption: Newsprint 1,225 short tons; width 27"; black ink 30,000 pounds; color ink 10,000 pounds; single pages printed 7,400; average pages per issue 20(d), 24(sat), 40(S); single plates used 5,000.

Equipment: EDITORIAL: Front-end hardware — 6-Ap/Mac IIsi, 3-Ap/PowerMac 6100, 1-Ap/PowerMac 7100, 2-Ap/Mac Classic, 3-Ap/Mac Classic II, 1-Ap/Mac Centris 610, 1-Lf/AP Leaf Picture Desk; Front-end software — Baseview/NewsEdit, QuarkXPress 3.3, Adobe/Photoshop; Printers — 1-Ap/Mac LaserWriter II NTX, ECR/Imagesetter; Other equipment — 1-Lf/Leafscan 35, 1-Microtek/300G Flatbed Scanner. CLASSIFIED: Front-end hardware — 1-Ap/Mac Classic, 1-Ap/Mac Quadra 605, 2-Ap/Mac Quadra 610 1-Ap/Mac LC III; Front-end software — Baseview/Classified, QuarkXPress 3.3; Printers — 1-Ap/Mac LaserWriter II NTX, 1-Ap/Mac LaserWriter II NTX, 1-Ap/Mac ImageWriter II, 1-Ap/Mac LaserWriter Plus. DISPLAY: Front-end hardware — 2-Ap/Mac IIcx, 1-Ap/Mac IIsi, 1-CD-Rom, 1-Ap/Mac Quadra 800, 1-Ap/Mac fx, 1-Ap/Mac Classic II, 1-Ap/Mac 8150 Server, 1-Ap/Mac Quadra 610, 1-Ap/Mac Quadra 650; Front-end software — Multi-Ad/Creator 3.8, Adobe/Illustrator 5.5, Abode/Streamline 3.8; Printers — 1-Ap/Mac LaserWriter II NTS, 1-QMS/P2000 Laser printer; Other equipment — 1-Microtek/Scanner. PRODUCTION: Pagination software — QuarkXpress 3.3; OCR software — Caere/OmniPage 3.0; Plate processors — Anitec; Electronic picture desk — Lf/AP Leaf Picture Desk; Production cameras — R; Automatic film processors — DP; Film transporters — PMT; Color separation equipment (conventional) — ECR/Autokon.
PRESSROOM: Line 1 — 8-G/Urbanite; Press drives — Fin; Folders — G/Quarter, G/Half, G/Upper, G/Lower; Press registration system — Burgess. MAILROOM: Counter stackers — 1-BG; Inserters and stuffers — 4-MM; Bundle tyer — 1-Strapex; Wrapping singles — 3-SA; Addressing machine — 2-KR. WIRE SERVICES: News — AP; Photos — Ap Photostream; Receiving dishes — AP. BUSINESS COMPUTERS: 1-Zeos/486 PC, 3-EKI/televideo 286, Ap/Mac; Applications: MSSI: Accts receivable, Circ; Great Plains: Accts payable, Gen ledger; PCs & micros networked.

SEARCY

White County

'90 U.S. Census- 15,180; E&P '96 Est. 16,319

The Daily Citizen (e-mon to fri; S)

Daily Citizen, 3000 E. Race Ave. (72143); PO Box 1379, Searcy, AR 72145; tel (501) 268-8621; fax (501) 268-6277. Paxton Media group.

Circulation: 7,533(e); 7,533(S); Sworn Oct. 1, 1994.

Price: 50¢(d); 75¢(S); $7.25/mo; $81.00/yr.

Advertising: Open inch rate $10.22(e); $10.22(S). **Representative:** Papert Companies.

News Services: AP, NEA. **Politics:** Independent. **Established:** 1854.

Advertising not accepted: Beer; Liquor; Adoption Services; Abortion Services; Personal Relationships.

Special Editions: Home Improvement; Graduation; Bridal; Progress; Car Care; Woman of the Year; Senior Citizens; Back-to-School; Springtime Searcy; Newcomers; Baseball; Lawn & Garden.

Special Weekly Sections: Business Review (mon); Merchant's Market (tues); Best Food Day (wed); Business News (thur); Church Directory, TV Book, Weekend Review (fri); Business News (S); Amusements, Business Directory, Lifestyle (daily).

Magazines: USA Weekend, Color Comics (S).

GENERAL MANAGEMENT

Publisher David McClain
Purchasing Agent Kelly Davis

ADVERTISING

Director Phil Weaver
Office Manager/Bookkeeper Don Lynn

CIRCULATION

Director Richard Pumphrey

NEWS EXECUTIVE

Editor Tommy Jackson

EDITORS AND MANAGERS

Business/Finance Editor Sean Clancy
Columnist Tommy Jackson
Editorial Page Editor Tommy Jackson
Editorial Writer Tommy Jackson
Education Editor Donnie Sewell
Entertainment/Amusements Editor Donnie Sewell
Farm/Agriculture Editor Sean Clancy
Fashion/Style Editor Barbara Cullum
Health/Medical Editor Barbara Cullum
News Editor Kelly Adcock
Religion Editor Barbara Cullum
Television/Film Editor Donnie Sewell
Theater/Music Editor Donnie Sewell
Travel Editor Donnie Sewell

MANAGEMENT INFORMATION SERVICES

Data Processing Manager Kelly Davis

PRODUCTION

Manager Charles Womble

Market Information: TMC.

Mechanical available: Offset; Black and 3 ROP colors; insert accepted — preprinted; page cut-offs — 22⅞".

Mechanical specifications: Type page 13" x 21½"; E - 6 cols, 2 1/16", ⅛" between; A - 6 cols, 2 1/16", ⅛" between; C - 9 cols, 1⅜", 1/16" between.

Commodity consumption: Newsprint 440 short tons; width 27"; black ink 13,200 pounds; color ink 1,000 pounds; single pages printed 5,400; average pages per issue 20(d), 30(S); single plates used 4,500.

Equipment: EDITORIAL: Front-end hardware — Ap/Mac Classics (networked); Front-end software — Baseview; Printers — Ap/Mac LaserPrinters. CLASSIFIED: Front-end hardware — Ap/Mac IIs; Front-end software — Baseview; Printers — Ap/Mac LaserPrinters. DISPLAY: Front-end hardware — Ap/Mac IIs; Front-end software — Multi-Ad/Creator; Printers — Ap/Mac LaserPrinters. PRODUCTION: OCR software — Caere/OmniPage; Plate exposures — 1-Nu; Plate processors — 1-Nat; Production cameras — 1-R; Automatic film processors — 1-LE.
PRESSROOM: Line 1 — 6-HI/V15A. MAILROOM: Bundle tyer — 2-Bu. WIRE SERVICES: News — AP; Syndicates — NEA; Receiving dishes — AP. BUSINESS COMPUTERS: Ap/Mac II, IBM/PCs; PCs & micros networked.

SPRINGDALE-ROGERS

Washington and Benton Counties

'90 U.S. Census- 54,633 (Springdale 29,941; Rogers 24,692); E&P '96 Est. 66,418 (Springdale 35,183; Rogers 31,235)

ABC-CZ (90): 54,633 (HH 21,137)

The Morning News (m-mon to sat; S)

The Morning News of Northwest Arkansas, 2560 N. Lowell Rd.; PO Box 7, Springdale, AR 72764; tel (501) 751-6200. Donrey Media group.

Circulation: 31,928(m); 31,928(m-sat); 34,428(S); ABC Sept. 30, 1995.

Price: 25¢(d); 25¢(sat); $1.00(S); $1.38/wk; $6.00/mo; $72.00/yr.

Advertising: Open inch rate $25.58(m); $25.58(m-sat); $26.90(S). **Representative:** Papert Companies.

News Service: AP. **Politics:** Independent. **Established:** 1887.

Advertising not accepted: X-rated movies.

Special Editions: Rodeo; Football; Spring; Fall Fashion; Christmas; Chamber of Commerce; Basketball; Customer Appreciation; Home Improvement.

Special Weekly Sections: Best Food Day (wed); Entertainment, Weekend in Northwest Arkansas, Business (fri).

Magazine: USA Weekend.

CORPORATE OFFICERS

Founder Donald W Reynolds
President/Chief Operating Officer Emmett Jones
Exec Vice Pres/Chief Financial Officer Darrell W Loftin
Vice Pres-Western Newspaper Group David A Osborn
Vice Pres-Eastern Newspaper Group Don Schneider

GENERAL MANAGEMENT

Publisher Tom Stallbaumer

ADVERTISING

Director Kent Eikenberry
Manager-National/Co-op Lisa Hull

CIRCULATION

Director Keith Sanford
Manager Doug Norwood

NEWS EXECUTIVES

Exec Editor Jim Morriss
Managing Editor Rusty Turner

EDITORS AND MANAGERS

Education Editor Laurinda Joenks
Lifestyle Editor Becca Martin
Metro Editor Leeanna Walker
Metro Editor Charlie Alison
Photo Department Manager Charles Bickford
Political Editor Brenda Blagg
Sports Editor Bob Caudle
Sunday/Wire Editor Steve Linam

MANAGEMENT INFORMATION SERVICES

Data Processing Manager Steve Sparr

PRODUCTION

Superintendent Ed Travis

Mechanical available: Offset; Black and 3 ROP colors; insert accepted — preprinted, single sheets; page cut-offs — 22¾".

Mechanical specifications: Type page 13" x 21¼"; E - 6 cols, 2 1/16", ⅛" between; A - 6 cols, 2 1/16", ⅛" between; C - 9 cols, 1⅜", 1/16" between.

Commodity consumption: Newsprint 2,330 metric tons; width 13½"; black ink 34,000 pounds; color ink 6,500 pounds; single pages printed 22,136; average pages per issue 36(d), 80(S); single plates used 13,200.

Equipment: EDITORIAL: Front-end hardware — Mk/4000, 60-Ap/Power Mac 7100-80 Workstations, Ap/Mac Performa 636 Workstations; Front-end software — Mk/4000, Baseview; Printers — 1-Ap/Mac Laser Pro 600; Other equipment — Canon/Fax 630, 1-Ap/Mac Scanner. CLASSIFIED: Front-end hardware — Mk/4000, 12-Ap/Mac 7100-80 Workstation; Front-end software — Mk/4000, Baseview; Printers — TI, Ap/Mac LaserWriter II NTX; Other equipment — Canon/Facsimile, Minolta/copier, PB/postage meter, 1-Swintec/4040. DISPLAY: Adv layout systems — 2-Ap/Power Mac 7100/80; Front-end hardware — 6-Ap/Mac 7100-80, 1-Ap/Mac 6100-66; Front-end software — Multi-Ad 3.7.1, QuarkXPress 3.31, Adobe/Illustrator 5.5, Adobe/Photoshop 2.5.1; Printers — 1-Xante/8200, 1-Ap/Mac Laser Pro 630, 2-Tegra/Verityper 5300, Panther/Plus. PRODUCTION: Pagination software — Baseview; Typesetters — 3-Ap/Mac LaserWriter II, Xante 8200, Ap/Mac Laser Pro 630, 2-Varityper/5300; Platemaking systems — 2-3M/Deadliner; Plate exposures — 1-Nu/Ultra Plus-Flip Top, B/Ultralite 2500; Plate processors — Nat/Automatic Offset; Electronic picture desk — Ap/Mac 840 AV, P/M 9500; Scanners — Lf/Leafscan 35, Epson/ES-1200C, 4-Ap; Production cameras — SCREEN/C-680-C, LE/Robertson 500; Automatic film processors — LE, Konica/K550; Digital color separation equipment — DC/5000 System, SCREEN/C-680-C.
PRESSROOM: Line 1 — 10-G/Urbanite; Folders — 2-G; Reels and stands — 24-G/High; Press control system — Fin. MAILROOM: Counter stackers — 2-HL, 1-MM/310-20; Inserters and stuffers — 9-MM/227-5; Bundle tyer — 3-MLN/2; Wrapping singles — 2-Monarch/Bottom Wrap; Addressing machine — 4-Wm. LIBRARY: Electronic — Baseview. COMMUNICATIONS: Digital ad delivery system — AP AdSend. WIRE SERVICES: News — AP; Photos — AP; Stock tables — AP; Syndicates — LAT-WP, King Features, United Features, TV Data, Creators, Universal Press, CNS, SHNS; Receiving dishes — size-10ft, AP, UPI, Newspaper Satellite Network. BUSINESS COMPUTERS: 1-HP/927LX(3000), ACR/Provesia (486 DX2); Applications: HP/MPEIX, UDMS, ABII, CJ/Class, DB/General, CJ/AIM: Adv; Progress/4GL, RDBMS: Circ.

STUTTGART

Arkansas County

'90 U.S. Census- 10,420; E&P '96 Est. 10,233

The Stuttgart Daily Leader (e-mon to fri)

Stuttgart Daily Leader, 111 W. 6th St.; PO Box 531, Stuttgart, AR 72160; tel (501) 673-8533; fax (501) 673-3671. Hollinger International Inc. group.

Circulation: 3,430(e); Sworn Sept. 29, 1995.

Price: 50¢(d); $6.50/mo; $78.00/yr.

Advertising: Open inch rate $7.10(e); $8.80(e-tues). **Representative:** Papert Companies.

News Service: AP. **Politics:** Independent. **Established:** 1885.

Not Published: Thanksgiving; Christmas; New Year.

Advertising not accepted: Abortion.

Special Editions: Customer Appreciation; Update; Spring Fashion; Home Improvement; Car Care; June Bride; Back-to-School; Football; Farm Family; Duck; Harvest; Coloring Book; Christmas Gifting; Christmas Greetings; Fact Book; Chamber Directory.

Special Weekly Sections: Business and Review Page (wed); Church Directory (fri).

Magazine: TV (fri, bi-weekly).

Cable TV: Operate leased cable TV in circulation area.

CORPORATE OFFICER

President Larry J Perrotto

GENERAL MANAGEMENT

Publisher Gene Austin
Purchasing Agent Donna Helms

ADVERTISING

Manager Gene Austin

CIRCULATION

Manager Robert Morris

NEWS EXECUTIVE

Editor Bill Bradow

EDITOR AND MANAGER

Sports Editor Chris Pennington

PRODUCTION

Superintendent Dudley Raper

Market Information: TMC.

Mechanical available: Offset; Black and 3 ROP colors; insert accepted — preprinted, any; page cut-offs — 22¾".

Mechanical specifications: Type page 13" x 21½"; E - 6 cols, 2 1/16", ⅛" between; A - 6 cols, 2 1/16", ⅛" between; C - 9 cols, 1⅜", 1/16" between.

Commodity consumption: Newsprint 220 short tons; width 27"; black ink 6,000 pounds; average pages per issue 14(d); single plates used 4,200.

Equipment: EDITORIAL: Front-end hardware — Ap/Mac; Front-end software — WordPerfect; Printers — Ap/Mac NTX. CLASSIFIED: Front-end hardware — Ap/Mac; Front-end software

I-26 Arkansas

— QuarkXPress; Printers — Ap/Mac NTX. DISPLAY: Adv layout systems — Ap/Mac; Front-end hardware — Ap/Mac NTX; Front-end software — QuarkXPress. PRODUCTION: Plate exposures — 1-Nu/Flip Top; Production cameras — 1-SCREEN/Auto film processors.
PRESSROOM: Line 1 — 6-G/Community; Folders — G/Suburban. MAILROOM: Bundle tyer — Felins/Tying. WIRE SERVICES: News — AP. BUSINESS COMPUTERS: PCs & micros networked.

TEXARKANA
See TEXARKANA, TX

WEST HELENA
See HELENA

WEST MEMPHIS
Crittenden County

'90 U.S. Census- 28,259; E&P '96 Est. 28,474
ABC-CZ (90): 28,259 (HH 9,879)

Evening Times (e-mon to fri)

Evening Times, 111 E. Bond St. (72301); PO Box 459, West Memphis, AR 72303; tel (501) 735-1010; fax (501) 735-1020.
Circulation: 8,555(e); ABC Sept. 30, 1995.
Price: 35¢(d); $5.50/mo; $66.00/yr.
Advertising: Open inch rate $9.92(e).
News Service: AP. **Established:** 1957.
Not Published: Christmas.
Special Editions: Financial Preview, Super Bowl Page (Jan); Progress Edition, Valentine Pages (Feb); Lawn and Garden, Bridal Tab (Mar); Agri Section, Victims Advocacy Rally, Egg Hunt Page, Bunny Hop & Easter Coloring Contest, Earle Chamber of Commerce Banquet, Mother's Day Page (Apr); Spring Car Care, Esperanza Bonanza-Marion Community Festival (May); Draw Your Father Contest, Pre-July 4th Specials (June); Back-to-School Tab (July); Farm Family, Pigskin Preview (Aug); Fall Car Care, Annual School Board Elections, Labor Day Coloring Page, Livin' on the Levee (Sept); Crittenden County Women in Business, Halloween Safety Page (Oct); Basketball Preview, Marion Chamber of Commerce, Holiday Gift Guide (Nov); Last Minute Gift Guide, Christmas Lighting Contest, Christmas Greetings, Christmas Coloring Contest (Dec); Golden Times (monthly).
Special Weekly Sections: Business (tues); Best Food Day (wed); Farm News (thur); Church News (fri); Comics, TV (daily).
Cable TV: Operate leased cable TV in circulation area.

CORPORATE OFFICERS
President — Alexander Coulter
Vice Pres — Sherry L Hamilton
Secretary/Treasurer — J Thomas Ricketson

GENERAL MANAGEMENT
Publisher — Alexander Coulter
General Manager — Sherry L Hamilton
Manager-Office — Alice Raines
Manager-Credit — Alice Raines

ADVERTISING
Director — Bob Bruce

CIRCULATION
Manager — Charles Winas

NEWS EXECUTIVE
Editor — Kay Brockwell

PRODUCTION
Foreman-Pressroom — Fred Coon

Market Information: TMC.
Mechanical available: Offset; Black and 3 ROP colors; insert accepted — preprinted; page cut-offs — 23¾".
Mechanical specifications: Type page 13" x 21½"; E - 6 cols, $2\frac{1}{16}$", ⅛" between; A - 6 cols, $2\frac{1}{16}$", ⅛" between; C - 9 cols, 1⅜", $\frac{1}{16}$" between.
Commodity consumption: Newsprint 29,483 short tons; 1,427 metric tons; widths 28", 14", 22.75"; black ink 90,000 pounds; color ink 1,622 pounds; single pages printed 4,194; average pages per issue 24(d); single plates used 4,194.
Equipment: EDITORIAL: Front-end hardware — CText; Front-end software — CText; Printers — COM/8400. CLASSIFIED: Front-end hardware — CText; Front-end software — CText. DISPLAY: Adv layout systems — Ap/Mac; Printers — CG/308, IBM/LaserPrinter LZR158D, Ap/Mac LaserWriter II NTX. PRODUCTION: Typesetters — Ap/Mac, PCs; Plate processors — Nat/25; Scanners — Scan Master/II XE; Production cameras — C/Spartan III; Automatic film processors — P/Pakoblend; Film transporters — C; Shrink lenses — Alan/Anamorphic; Digital color separation equipment — Ap/Mac.
PRESSROOM: Line 1 — 6-KP/Newsking; Press drives — GE; Folders — KP/Newsking; Reels and stands — 6-Roll/Stands; Press control system — GE/SP 200. MAILROOM: Inserters and stuffers — KAN; Bundle tyer — Akebono; Addressing machine — St. WIRE SERVICES: News — Receiving dishes — size-2ft, AP. BUSINESS COMPUTERS: IBM/386-486; PCs & micros networked.

CALIFORNIA

ANTIOCH
Contra Costa County

'90 U.S. Census- 62,195; E&P '96 Est. 80,580
ABC-NDM (90): 165,003 (HH 55,853)

Ledger Dispatch (e-mon to sat; S)

Ledger Dispatch, 1650 Cavallo Rd.; PO Box 2299, Antioch, CA 94509; tel (510) 757-2525. Knight-Ridder Inc. group.
Circulation: 21,066(e); 21,066(e-sat); 21,844(S); ABC Sept. 30, 1995.
Price: 50¢(d); 50¢(sat); $1.25(S); $9.00/mo (carrier).
Representatives: Cresmer, Woodward, O'Mara & Ormsbee; US Suburban Press.
News Service: AP. **Politics:** Independent. **Established:** 1900/1870.
Note: The Contra Costa Daily group includes the following newspapers: Richmond West County Times (mS), Ledger Dispatch (eS), Pleasanton Valley Times (mS) and Walnut Creek Contra Costa Times (mS). The group rates are $104.05 (d) and $114.35 (S). Individual newspaper rates not made available.
Special Editions: Spring and Fall Home and Garden; International Auto; Times Real Estate; Christmas Sections (5); Information Book.
Special Weekly Sections: Automotive (fri); Real Estate (sat); Homes (S).
Magazines: TV Weekly; Time Out (entertainment) (fri); USA Weekend.

GENERAL MANAGEMENT
Publisher/CEO — George Riggs
General Manager — Gloria Thomas

ADVERTISING
Manager — Julie Bouslog

CIRCULATION
Director — Martha Goralka

NEWS EXECUTIVE
Managing Editor — Bob Goll

EDITORS AND MANAGERS
Assoc Editor/Columnist — Clay Kallam
Business Editor — Chris Huesman
City Editor — Ken Maryanski
Editorial Page Editor — Theresa Keegan
Lifestyle Editor — Judith Preive
News Editor — Frank Reichert
Photo/Graphics Editor — Curtis Corlew
Sports Editor — Kerry Young

PRODUCTION
Foreman-Pressroom — Larry Thomas

Market Information: TMC; ADS.
Mechanical available: Offset; Black and 3 ROP colors; insert accepted — preprinted, all; page cut-offs — 22¾".
Mechanical specifications: Type page 13" x 21½"; E - 6 cols, $2\frac{1}{16}$", ⅛" between; A - 6 cols, $2\frac{1}{16}$", ⅛" between; C - 10 cols, $1\frac{7}{32}$", $\frac{1}{16}$" between.
Commodity consumption: average pages per issue 48(d), 72(S).
Equipment: EDITORIAL: Front-end hardware — AT; Front-end software — AT. CLASSIFIED: Front-end hardware — SII; Front-end software — SII. DISPLAY: Front-end hardware — HI; Front-end software — HI. PRODUCTION: Typesetters — AU; Plate exposures — 1-Nu/Flip Top FT40UPNS; Plate processors — 1-Nat; Production cameras — 1-C/Newspager, 1-R; Automatic film processors — P/26RA; Film transporters — C; Shrink lenses — 1-Alan, 1-Rodenstock; Color separation equipment (conventional) — WDS.
PRESSROOM: Line 1 — 9-G/Urbanite; Folders — 1-G. MAILROOM: Counter stackers — 1-Fg, 2-MM/231; Inserters and stuffers — 2-MM/227; Bundle tyer — 4-MLN, 2-Bu. LIBRARY: Combination — Canon/PC80 (microfilm). WIRE SERVICES: News — AP; Syndicates — McClatchy, NYT, NEA, CNS; Receiving dishes — AP. BUSINESS COMPUTERS: 4-Everex/386, 1-Compaq/386 Deskpro; Applications: Novell/Netware, Solomon Software; PCs & micros networked.

AUBURN
Placer County

'90 U.S. Census- 10,592; E&P '96 Est. 13,383
ABC-NDM (90): 56,963 (HH 21,879)

The Auburn Journal (m-mon to fri; S)

The Auburn Journal, 1030 High St.; PO Box 5910, Auburn, CA 95604; tel (916) 885-5656; fax (916) 885-4902. Brehm Communications Inc. group.
Circulation: 12,910(m); 13,689(S); ABC Sept. 30, 1995.
Price: 50¢(d); 75¢(S); $83.66/yr; $22.52/3mo.
Advertising: Open inch rate $15.20(m); $15.20(S). **Representatives:** Landon Associates Inc.; US Suburban Press.
News Service: AP. **Politics:** Independent. **Established:** 1872.
Special Editions: Welcome Edition; Meet Your Merchant; Home Improvement; Spring Fashion; Football; Christmas.
Special Weekly Sections: Food (wed); Seniors Prime Time, Entertainment (thur); Real Estate, Dining, Entertainment, Motoring (fri); Real Estate, Business, Fashion, Dining, Travel (S).
Magazines: TV Journal, Sunday Comics (S); USA Weekend.

CORPORATE OFFICER
Vice Pres — William Brehm Jr

GENERAL MANAGEMENT
Publisher/President — Scott Little
Office Manager — Vicki Booker

ADVERTISING
Manager-Classified — Jeannette Monos

TELECOMMUNICATIONS
Manager-Telecommunications — Larry Risser

CIRCULATION
Director — Jeff Mezzeti

NEWS EXECUTIVE
Editor — Michael Ackley

EDITORS AND MANAGERS
Automotive Editor — Chuck Butler
Business/Finance Editor — Gus Thompson
City/Metro Editor — Robert Miller
Editorial Page Editor — Michael Ackley
Entertainment/Amusements Editor — London Roberts
News Editor — Dirk Werkman
Real Estate Editor — Chuck Butler
Sports Editor — David Kull

MANAGEMENT INFORMATION SERVICES
Data Processing Manager — Vicki Booker

PRODUCTION
Foreman-Pressroom — Keith Bowen

Market Information: TMC.
Mechanical available: Offset; Black and 3 ROP colors; insert accepted — preprinted; page cut-offs — 22".
Mechanical specifications: Type page 13" x 21"; E - 6 cols, $2\frac{1}{16}$", ⅛" between; A - 6 cols, $2\frac{1}{16}$", ⅛" between; C - 9 cols, 1⅜", $\frac{1}{16}$" between.
Commodity consumption: Newsprint 1,400 metric tons; widths 27½", 32", 30"; black ink 12,000 pounds; color ink 4,800 pounds; single pages printed 8,216; average pages per issue 22(d), 48(S); single plates used 12,000.
Equipment: EDITORIAL: Front-end hardware — PC; Front-end software — Dewar; Printers — 2-LaserMaster, 2-Panther/Plus Imagesetter; Other equipment — 25-IBM/PC. CLASSIFIED: Front-end hardware — PC; Front-end software — Dewar; Printers — 2-LaserMaster, 2-Panther/Plus Imagesetter. DISPLAY: Adv layout systems — Multi-Ad; Front-end hardware — Ap/Mac; Front-end software — Multi-Ad/Creator; Other equipment — 4-CD-Rom, 1-SYQUEST, 1-Microtek/Scanner. PRODUCTION: Pagination software — QuarkXPress 3.31; OCR software — Caere/OmniPage Pro; Typesetters — 2-LaserMaster, Panther/Plus; Platemaking systems — 1-3M/Deadliner; Plate exposures — Graham; Plate processors — 1-Nu; Electronic picture desk — Lf/AP Leaf Picture Desk; Scanners — Umax, Polaroid/Sprint Scan; Production cameras — K/3700, SCREEN/5161; Automatic film processors — 2-PermaKwik, 1-LE; Film transporters — AG; Color separation equipment (conventional) — Mk; Digital color separation equipment — Array.
PRESSROOM: Line 1 — 7-G/Community SSC, 1-Universal/Color Unit (3 color). MAILROOM: Counter stackers — 1-BG/105 Count-O-Veyor; Inserters and stuffers — KAN; Bundle tyer — 2-Bu, 1-MLN; Addressing machine — Ch/730S. WIRE SERVICES: News — AP; Photos — AP; Syndicates — AP; Receiving dishes — AP. BUSINESS COMPUTERS: Qantel/Q29BS; PCs & micros networked; PCs & main system networked.

BAKERSFIELD
Kern County

'90 U.S. Census- 174,820; E&P '96 Est. 248,114
ABC-CZ (90): 295,497 (HH 102,861)

The Bakersfield Californian (m-mon to sat; S)

The Bakersfield Californian, 1707 "Eye" St. (93301); PO Box 440, Bakersfield, CA 93302-0440; tel (805) 395-7500; fax (805) 395-7280; e-mail tpc@kern.com; web site http://www.kern.com/tbc.
Circulation: 74,403(m); 74,403(m-sat); 89,240(S); ABC Sept. 30, 1995.
Price: 47¢(d); 47¢(sat); $1.17(S); $10.50/mo (carrier); $126.00/yr (carrier, plus tax); $6.00/mo (sat & S, plus tax).
Advertising: Open inch rate $54.00(m); $55.50(m-fri); $55.50(m-sat); $59.94(S).
Representative: Landon Associates Inc.
News Services: AP, NYT, McClatchy, UPI Photo, CSM. **Established:** 1866.
Special Editions: Health & Fitness, Baby Parade, Financial Outlook (Jan); Home & Garden Show (Feb); Pets & their People (Mar); Lawn, Patio & Garden, The Senior Community (Apr); Expanded Saturday Home, Summer's Best (May); Kern Life (July); Football Season Preview, Kern County Fair Guide, Old Town Kern Arts Fest (Sept); Auto Week '97, Home Furnishings (Oct); The Senior Community, Holiday Gift Guides (Nov).
Special Weekly Sections: Personal Finance (mon); Image/Teens (tues); Automotive (wed); Health/Vintage Years (thur); Your Weekend (fri); On The Go, Auto Mart, At Home, Religion (sat); Travel/Arts, Agriculture, Real Estate, Business, TV Week (S).
Magazines: Parade, TV Week (S).

CORPORATE OFFICERS
President/CEO — Michael J Fisch
Asst to President — Bob Johnson
Publisher/Chairman of the Board — Virginia F Moorhouse
Secretary — Harold F Clifton
Chief Financial Officer/Asst Secretary — Daniel A Lacey

GENERAL MANAGEMENT
Publisher-Emeritus — Donald H Fritts
Controller — Greg Wolff
Director-Human & Organizational Development — Katheleen Q Tandy
Manager/Purchasing Agent-Building Service — Lana Kelsey

ADVERTISING
Director — John Wells
Manager-Display — Marcella Anthony
Manager-Inside Sales — Ellen Rink

MARKETING AND PROMOTION
Manager-Marketing — Kay Ellington
Manager-Promotion/Community Services — Sally Ann Selby

TELECOMMUNICATIONS
Audiotex Manager — John Patton

CIRCULATION
Director — Fred Fedesco
Manager — Larry Riley
Manager-County S/C — John Mihaylo

NEWS EXECUTIVES
Exec Editor — Richard Beene
Managing Editor — Mike Jenner
Asst Managing Editor-Nights — Mike Perry
Asst Managing Editor-Days — Patrick Oster

California I-27

EDITORS AND MANAGERS

Business/Industry Editor	Mike Stepanovich
Design Editor	Glenn Hammett
Editorial Page Editor	Dianne Hardisty
Features Editor	Pat Nolan
Metro Editor	Linda Wienandt
News Editor	John Furtak
Photo Director	Casey Christie
Religion Editor	Ed King
Sports Editor	John Millman

MANAGEMENT INFORMATION SERVICES

Manager-Publishing Systems	Lon Cooper
Network Analyst Programmer	Tracey Davis

PRODUCTION

Director-Operations	Fred Fedesco
Manager	Larry Arnt
Manager-Technical Service	Dennis Birks
Manager-Packaging & Distribution	Mike Bergstrom

Market Information: Split Run; TMC; Operate database; Operate audiotex; Electronic edition.
Mechanical available: Offset; Black and 3 ROP colors; insert accepted — preprinted; page cut-offs — 22.05".
Mechanical specifications: Type page 13" x 21"; E - 6 cols, 2 1/16", 1/8" between; A - 6 cols, 2 1/16", 1/8" between; C - 10 cols, 1 3/8", 1/8" between.
Commodity consumption: Newsprint 10,895 metric tons; widths 54 1/2", 40 7/8", 27 1/2"; black ink 195,000 pounds; color ink 55,000 pounds; single pages printed 21,664; average pages per issue 56(d), 80(S); single plates used 84,000.
Equipment: EDITORIAL: Front-end hardware — SII/Sys 55, Ap/Mac; Front-end software — SII/Sys 55, Microsoft/Word; Printers — 3-TI/810. CLASSIFIED: Front-end hardware — SII/Sys 55; Front-end software — SII/Sys 55; Printers — Okidata. AUDIOTEX: Supplier name — Brite Voice Systems. DISPLAY: Adv layout systems — Mk/Managing Editor, ALS; Front-end hardware — Ap/Power Mac; Front-end software — Multi-Ad/Creator; Printers — QMS/860, AU/6600 Proofers; Other equipment — AG/Focus scanners. PRODUCTION: Pagination software — QuarkXPress; Typesetters — 2-AG/9800, 2-AG/8600, PC/486, AG/Accuset 9000, 2-AU/RIPs, AU/3850; Plate exposures — WL/Lith V; Plate processors — WL/Lithoplate38D; Electronic picture desk — Lf/AP Leaf Picture Desk; Scanners — Nikon, Kk; Production cameras — C/Spartan III, Walzberg, AG/8200; Automatic film processors — LE, SCREEN, P; Film transporters — C; Digital color separation equipment — Adobe/Photoshop.
PRESSROOM: Line 1 — 8-TKS/(4 half decks); Folders — 2-TKS/3:2; Pasters — 8-TKS. MAILROOM: Counter stackers — 3-HL/Monitor; Inserters and stuffers — Fg/(8-into-1); Addressing machine — Domino/Jet Array Ink Jet Printer. COMMUNICATIONS: Digital ad delivery system — AP. WIRE SERVICES: News — AP Datastream, NYT, AP Datafeatures; Photos — AP Photostream; Stock tables — TMS; Receiving dishes — AP. BUSINESS COMPUTERS: Sun/Sparc 10; Applications: PBS: Accounting, Adv, Circ; PCs & micros networked; PCs & main system networked.

BANNING

Riverside County

'90 U.S. Census- 20,570; E&P '96 Est. 26,777

The Record-Gazette (e-mon to fri)

The Record-Gazette, 218 N. Murray; PO Box 727, Banning, CA 92220; tel (909) 849-4586; fax (909) 849-2437. Scripps League Newspapers Inc. group.
Circulation: 2,529(e); Sworn Sept. 29, 1995.
Price: 35¢(d); $5.25/mo; $63.00/yr.
Advertising: Open inch rate $10.25(e).
News Service: AP. **Politics:** Independent. **Established:** 1908.
Not Published: New Year; Memorial Day; Independence Day; Labor Day; Thanksgiving; Christmas.
Special Editions: Pass Progress (Feb); Police & Fire Tab (Mar); Cherry Festival (June); Recipe Tab (Aug); Stagecoach Days (Oct).

CORPORATE OFFICERS

Board Chairman/Treasurer	E W Scripps
Vice Chairman/Corporate Secretary	Betty Knight Scripps
President	Barry H Scripps
Vice Pres-Finance	Thomas E Wendel

GENERAL MANAGEMENT

Publisher	Charles R Freeman

ADVERTISING

Director	Raylene Jackson
Manager-Promotion	Charles R Freeman

CIRCULATION

Manager	Theon Allen

NEWS EXECUTIVE

Managing Editor	Steve Tuckey

EDITORS AND MANAGERS

Amusements/Books Editor	Steve Tuckey
Auto/Aviation Editor	Steve Tuckey
Columnist	Steve Tuckey
Editorial Page Editor	Charles R Freeman
Education Editor	Charles R Freeman
Films/Theater Editor	Charles R Freeman
Food Editor	Charles R Freeman
Sports Editor	Steve Tuckey
Teen-Age/Youth Editor	Catherine Huntington
Women's Editor	Catherine Huntington

PRODUCTION

Manager	Cheri Mitchell

Market Information: TMC.
Mechanical available: Offset; Black and 2 ROP colors; insert accepted — preprinted; page cut-offs — 21 1/2".
Mechanical specifications: Type page 13" x 21 1/2"; E - 6 cols, 2 1/16", 1/8" between; A - 6 cols, 2 1/16", 1/8" between; C - 9 cols, 1 3/8", 1/16" between.
Commodity consumption: Newsprint 130 metric tons; widths 28", 14"; black ink 3,000 pounds; color ink 600 pounds; single pages printed 3,650; average pages per issue 14(d); single plates used 3,200.
Equipment: EDITORIAL: Front-end hardware — ScrippSat. CLASSIFIED: Front-end hardware — ScrippSat. PRODUCTION: Typesetters — 2-ScrippSat/Laser; Plate exposures — 1-Nu; Production cameras — 1-K/Vertical; Automatic film processors — Kk/65 Model.
PRESSROOM: Line 1 — 4-G/Community; Folders — 1-G. MAILROOM: Inserters and stuffers — MM/227; Bundle tyer — 1-CyKlop; Addressing machine — 3-Wm. WIRE SERVICES: News — AP; Syndicates — SHNS; Receiving dishes — size-3ft, AP. BUSINESS COMPUTERS: DEC; Applications: Payroll, Accts receivable.

BARSTOW

San Bernardino County

'90 U.S. Census- 21,472; E&P '96 Est. 24,441

Desert Dispatch (e-mon to fri; m-sat)

Desert Dispatch, 130 Coolwater Lane, Barstow, CA 92311; tel (619) 256-2257; fax (619) 256-0685; e-mail msbro@aol.com. Freedom Communications Inc. group.
Circulation: 6,674(e); 6,674(m-sat); Sworn Oct. 1, 1995.
Price: 25¢(d); 75¢(sat); $1.76/wk; $7.10/mo, $8.00/mo (mail); $85.20/yr.
Advertising: Open inch rate $11.43(e); $11.43(m-sat). **Representative:** Papert Companies.
News Service: AP. **Established:** 1910.
Not Published: New Year; Memorial Day; Independence Day; Labor Day; Thanksgiving; Christmas.
Special Weekly Sections: Business Page (mon); Food Section (wed); TMC Edition (thur); Religion Page, Real Estate (fri); Cover STORY (sat); TV Listings, Comics Section (daily).
Magazine: TV Book.

GENERAL MANAGEMENT

Publisher	Maureen Saltzer Brotherton
Business Manager	Robert Fitzsimmons

ADVERTISING

Manager-Retail	Bea Lint

MARKETING AND PROMOTION

Manager-Marketing	Lynn Tiffany

CIRCULATION

Manager	Mike Belles
Manager-Home Delivery	Jose Blystone

NEWS EXECUTIVES

Exec Editor	Larry Croom D Jr
Managing Editor	Merrill McCarty

EDITORS AND MANAGERS

Business/Finance Editor	Carole Myers
Editorial Page Editor	Steve Williams
Fashion/Style Editor	Carole Myers
Features Editor	Carole Myers
Living/Lifestyle Editor	Carole Myers
National Editor	David Oriard
Religion Editor	Carole Myers
Sports Editor	Russ Lemmon
Women's Editor	Carole Myers

MANAGEMENT INFORMATION SERVICES

Manager Systems	Steve Ryan

PRODUCTION

Manager-Composing	Mike Hochstedler

Market Information: ADS.
Mechanical available: Web offset; Black and 3 ROP colors; insert accepted — preprinted; page cut-offs — 21.5".
Mechanical specifications: Type page 14" x 22 3/4"; E - 6 cols, 2 1/16", .14" between; A - 6 cols, 2 1/16", .14" between; C - 9 cols, 1 1/3", .14" between.
Commodity consumption: Newsprint 270 short tons; widths 27", 13 1/2"; average pages per issue 12(d), 14(sat).
Equipment: EDITORIAL: Front-end hardware — Dewar; Front-end software — Dewar. CLASSIFIED: Front-end hardware — PC; Front-end software — Dewar; Printers — TI/Omni800. DISPLAY: Adv layout systems — Ap/Mac, Dewar; Front-end software — QuarkXPress, Aldus/PageMaker, Aldus/Freehand, Claris/MacDraw, Dewar. PRODUCTION: Pagination software — Dewar; Production cameras — SCREEN/C660C. MAILROOM: Bundle tyer — Akebono/EX415. COMMUNICATIONS: Systems used — satellite. WIRE SERVICES: News — AP; Syndicates — NEA, Universal Press; Receiving dishes — AP. BUSINESS COMPUTERS: PCs & micros networked.

BENICIA

Solano County

'90 U.S. Census- 24,437; E&P '96 Est. 33,691

Benicia Herald (m-tues to fri; S)

Benicia Herald, 544 Curtola Pkwy., Vallejo, CA 94590; tel (707) 643-1706; fax (707) 557-6380. Gibson Publishing group.
Circulation: 4,153(m); 4,153(S); VAC June 30, 1995.
Price: 50¢(d); 50¢(S); $4.50/mo.
Advertising: Open inch rate $5.50(m); $5.50(S). **Representatives:** Papert Companies; US Suburban Press. **Established:** 1877.
Not Published: New Year; Independence Day; Labor Day; Christmas Day.
Special Weekly Section: Entertainment (thur).

GENERAL MANAGEMENT

Publisher	David L Payne
Vice Pres	Jeanne M Payne
Secretary	Heloise C Diricco

ADVERTISING

Manager	Sam Springer

CIRCULATION

Manager	Sam LiRon

NEWS EXECUTIVE

Editor	Richard Hellman

PRODUCTION

Manager	Maureen Compia

Market Information: TMC.
Mechanical available: Offset; Black and 3 ROP colors; insert accepted — preprinted; page cut-offs — 22 1/2".
Mechanical specifications: Type page 12 1/2" x 21 1/2"; E - 6 cols, 2", 1/8" between; A - 6 cols, 2", 1/8" between; C - 8 cols, 1 1/2", 1/8" between.
Commodity consumption: Newsprint 175 metric tons; width 27"; black ink 5,200 pounds; average pages per issue 14(d), 22(S); single plates used 3,500.
Equipment: EDITORIAL: Front-end hardware — COM. CLASSIFIED: Front-end hardware — IBM. PRESSROOM: Line 1 — 8-H. BUSINESS COMPUTERS: IBM/AS 400; PCs & micros networked; PCs & main system networked.

CHICO

Butte County

'90 U.S. Census- 40,079; E&P '96 Est. 53,223
ABC-NDM (90): 160,685 (HH 62,969)

Chico Enterprise-Record (m-mon to sat; S)

Chico Enterprise-Record, 400 E. Park Ave.; PO Box 9, Chico, CA 95927-0009; tel (916) 891-1234; fax (916) 342-3617. Donrey Media group.
Circulation: 29,079(m); 29,079(m-sat); 30,980(S); ABC Sept. 30, 1995.
Price: 47¢(d); 47¢(sat); 93¢(S); $8.00/mo (carrier), $8.50/mo (motor route), $15.00/mo (mail); $96.00/yr (carrier), $102.00/yr (motor route), $180.00/yr (mail).
Advertising: Open inch rate $19.86(m); $19.86(m-sat); $19.86(S). **Representative:** Papert Companies.
News Services: AP, CNS. **Politics:** Independent. **Established:** 1852.
Special Editions: Chamber of Commerce Tab (Jan); Chico Outlook (Feb); Salute to Agriculture Tab (Mar); Home & Garden Issue (Apr); Vacation/Car Care, Silver Dollar Fair Tab (May); University Edition, Hunting Issue (Aug); Chico Expo (Sept); Fall Car Care (Oct); Holiday Gift Guide, Christmas Opening (Nov); Last Minute Gift Guide (Dec).
Special Weekly Sections: Senior's Tab (monthly); Health & Wellness Tab (quarterly).
Magazine: TV Times (sat).

CORPORATE OFFICERS

Founder	Donald W Reynolds
President/Chief Operating Officer	Emmett Jones
Exec Vice Pres/Chief Financial Officer	Darrell W Loftin
Vice Pres-Western Newspaper Group	David A Osborn
Vice Pres-Eastern Newspaper Group	Don Schneider

GENERAL MANAGEMENT

Publisher	James L Dimmitt

ADVERTISING

Director	Milton Moore
Manager-Retail/National	Fred Crosthwaite
Manager-Classified	Gwen Valentine

CIRCULATION

Director	Darren L Jensen

NEWS EXECUTIVE

Editor	Jack Winning

EDITORS AND MANAGERS

Business Editor	Laura Urseny
Farm Editor	Michael Gardner
Lifestyle Editor	Laurie Clifton
News Editor	Ray Kirk
Sports Editor	Skip Reager
Wire Editor	Steve Schoonover

MANAGEMENT INFORMATION SERVICES

Data Processing Manager	Carl Nobel

PRODUCTION

Foreman-Composing	Dave Cowan
Foreman-Pressroom	Steve Knobbe

Market Information: Zoned editions; TMC.
Mechanical available: Offset Press; Black and 3 ROP colors; insert accepted — preprinted; page cut-offs — 22".
Mechanical specifications: Type page 13" x 21"; E - 6 cols, 2 1/16", 1/8" between; A - 6 cols, 2 1/16", 1/8" between; C - 9 cols, 1 5/16", 1/16" between.
Commodity consumption: Newsprint 2,200 metric tons; widths 27 1/2", 44 1/4", 55"; black ink 48,000 pounds; color ink 4,000 pounds; single pages printed 15,000; average pages per issue 36(d), 40(S); single plates used 16,200.
Equipment: EDITORIAL: Front-end hardware — SII/CH1 3230, ET/960, SII/3200 CPO; Other equipment — 6-COM/MDT350 remote, 2-RSK/TRS 80 M-100, 28-SII/ET-960. CLASSIFIED: Front-end hardware — SII/CH1 3230; Other equipment — 7-SII/ET-960. DISPLAY: Other equipment — 3-SII/ET-960 (on-line). PRODUCTION: Typesetters — 2-XIT; Platemaking systems — 3M/Deadliner Pyrofax; Plate exposures — Nu/Flip top; Plate processors — 1-Cookson Graphics; Production cameras — 1-R/LE; Automatic film processors — 1-LE; Color separation equipment (conventional) — 1-C/4x5 Enlarger.
PRESSROOM: Line 1 — 4-MAN/double width/4x2 (2 Color Decks); Folders — 2-MAN; Pasters — 4-MEG. MAILROOM: Counter stackers — 2-HL/Monitor, 1-QWI; Inserters and stuffers — 2-MM; Bundle tyer — 1-MLN, I-It; Addressing machine — 3-Wm. WIRE SERVICES: News — AP; Receiving dishes — AP. BUSINESS COMPUTERS: CJ; Applications: Circ.

COSTA MESA

See ORANGE COUNTY

CRESCENT CITY

Del Norte County

'90 U.S. Census- 4,380; E&P '96 Est. 5,479
ABC-CZ (90): 17,356 (HH 5,683)

The Triplicate (m-tues to sat)

The Triplicate, 312 H St.; PO Box 277, Crescent City, CA 95531; tel (707) 464-2141; fax (707) 464-5102. Western Communications Inc. group.

Copyright ©1996 by the Editor & Publisher Co.

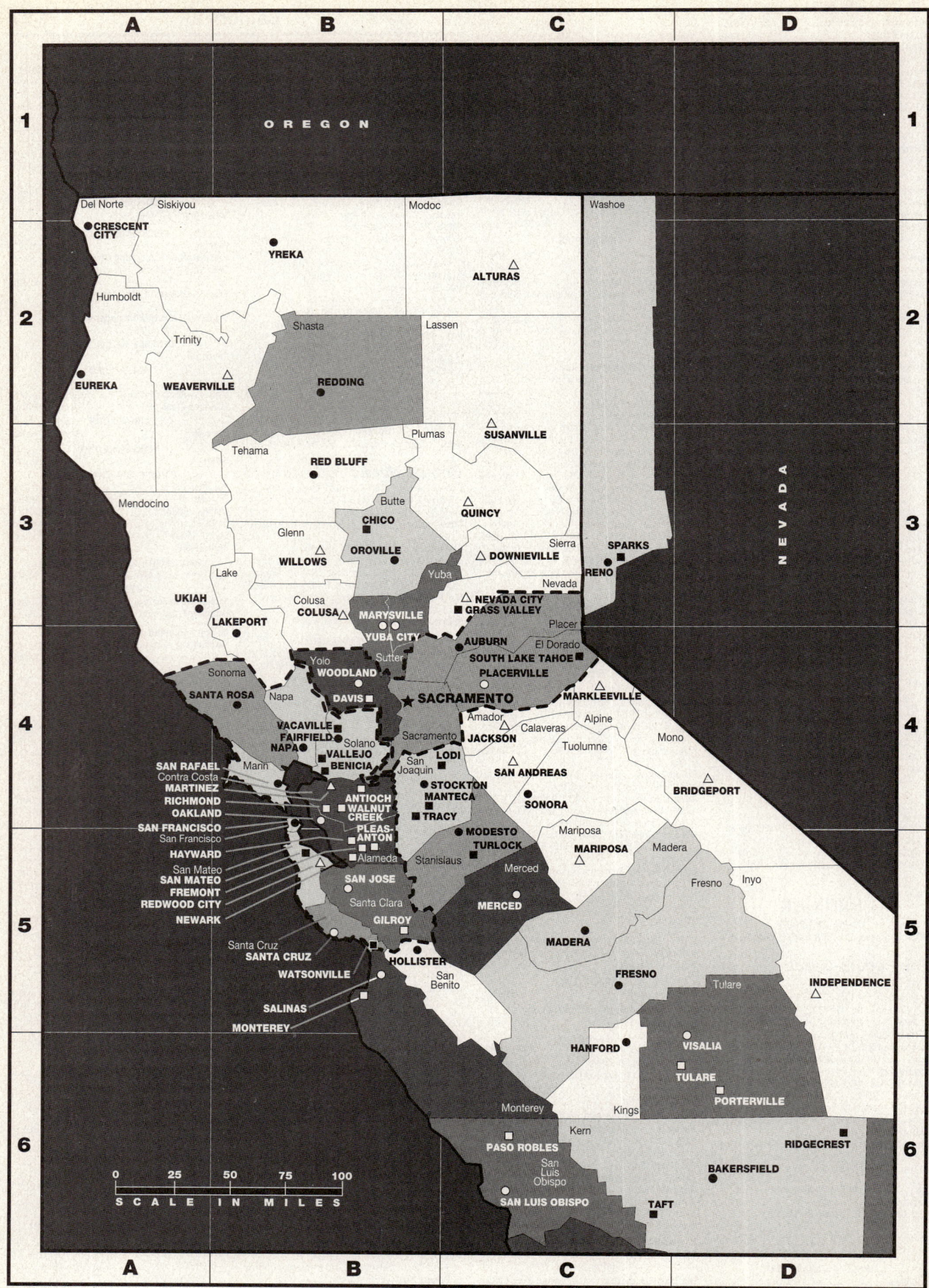

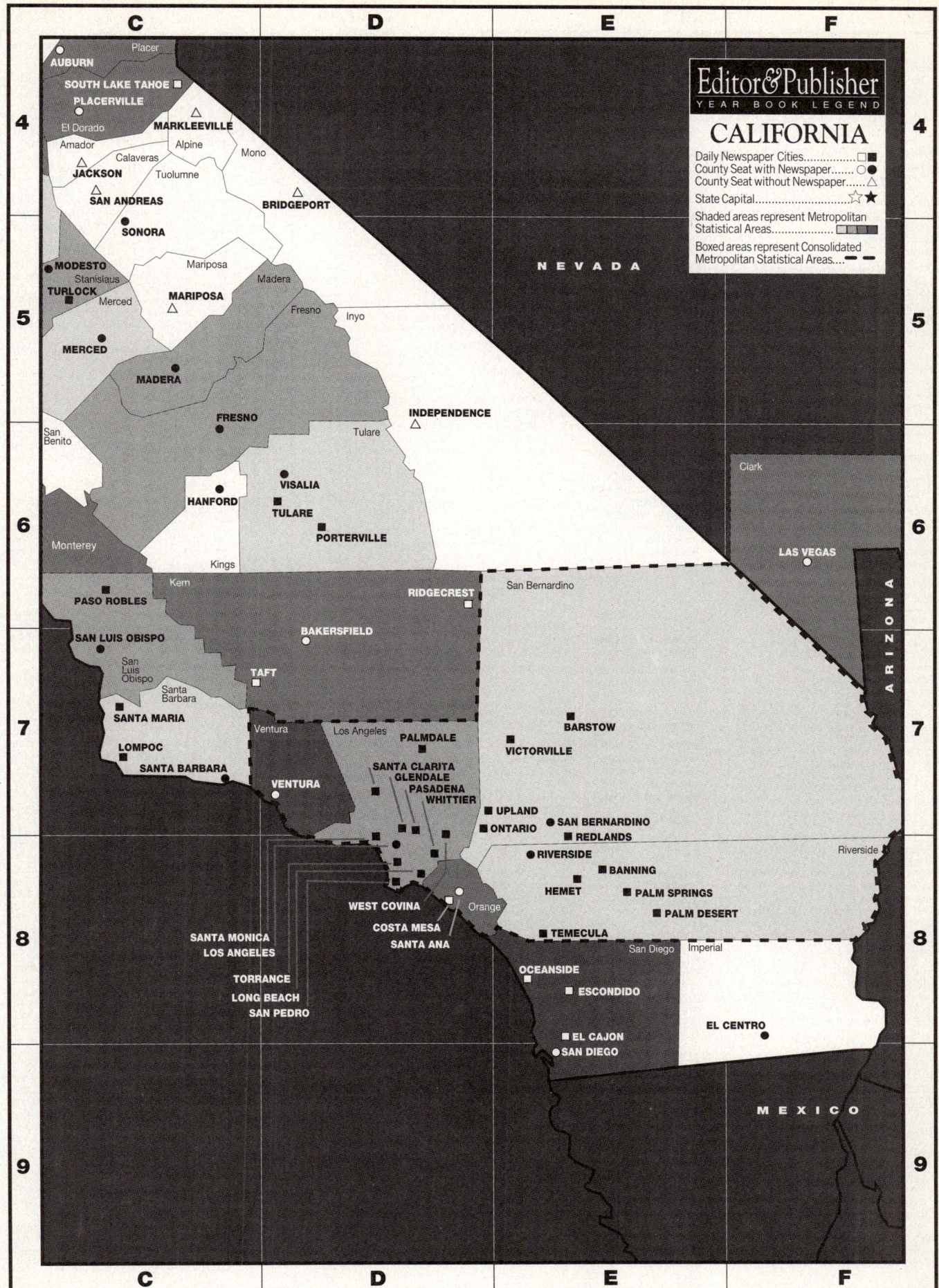

Circulation: 5,039(m); 6,343(m-sat); ABC Sept. 30, 1995.
Price: 35¢(d); 35¢(sat); $1.67/wk; $7.00/mo; $58.19/yr.
Advertising: Open inch rate $10.70(m); $10.70(m-sat). **Representative:** Papert Companies.
News Service: AP. **Politics:** Independent. **Established:** 1879.
Not Published: New Year; Thanksgiving; Christmas.
Special Editions: Bridal (Jan); Vacation (May); July 4 (July); Fair (Aug); Seafood Festival (Sept).
Special Weekly Section: TV Magazine (sat).
Magazine: Television.

CORPORATE OFFICERS

Board Chairman Elizabeth C McCool
President/CEO Gordon Black
Vice Pres Janet Stevens
Vice Pres John Shaver
Vice Pres Robert K Moody
Treasurer Elizabeth C McCool
Secretary Margaret C Cushman
Chief Editorial Officer Robert W Chandler

GENERAL MANAGEMENT

Publisher Geoffrey T White
Manager-Office Ardell Wallen

ADVERTISING

Director Patty Leonard

CIRCULATION

Director Kelly Leibold

NEWS EXECUTIVE

Managing Editor John W Pritchett

MANAGEMENT INFORMATION SERVICES

Data Processing Manager Ardell Wallen

PRODUCTION

Supervisor-Composing Jane Coleman
Supervisor-Press Tom Bosanko
Supervisor-Mailroom Steve Chittock

Market Information: Split Run; TMC; ADS.
Mechanical available: Offset; Black and 3 ROP colors; insert accepted — preprinted; page cut-offs — 22¾".
Mechanical specifications: Type page 13" x 21½"; E - 6 cols, 2", ⅙" between; A - 6 cols, 2", ⅙" between; C - 9 cols, 1⅜", 1/12" between.
Commodity consumption: Newsprint 370 metric tons; widths 13½", 13¾", 27", 27½"; black ink 10,600 pounds; color ink 1,000 pounds; single pages printed 4,238; average pages per issue 16(d); single plates used 7,200.
Equipment: EDITORIAL: Front-end hardware — Ap/Mac; Front-end software — QuarkXPress, Baseview/News; Printers — Ap/Mac LaserWriter IIg; Other equipment — Abaton/Scanner. CLASSIFIED: Front-end hardware — Ap/Mac; Front-end software — QuarkXPress, Baseview; Printers — Ap/Mac LaserWriter IIg. DISPLAY: Front-end hardware — Ap/Mac; Front-end software — QuarkXPress, Adobe/Illustrator; Printers — Ap/Mac LaserWriter IIg; Other equipment — HP/Scanner. PRODUCTION: Typesetters — HP/LaserJet 400 MV; Plate exposures — Nu/Flip Top; Plate processors — Nat; Scanners — HP; Production cameras — SCREEN; Automatic film processors — Konica.
PRESSROOM: Line 1 — 6-G/Community; Folders — SC. MAILROOM: Counter stackers — 1-HL/Monitor; Inserters and stuffers — 1-Mc/5-into-1; Bundle tyer — EAM/Mosca. WIRE SERVICES: News — AP; Receiving dishes — size-10m, AP. BUSINESS COMPUTERS: Packard Bell; Applications: Circ, Accts receivable; PCs & micros networked.

DAVIS

Yolo County

'90 U.S. Census- 46,209; E&P '96 Est. 53,949
ABC-NDM (90): 116,305 (HH 45,800)

The Davis Enterprise

(e-mon to fri; S)

The Davis Enterprise, 315 G St.; PO Box 1078, Davis, CA 95617; tel (916) 756-0800; fax (916) 756-6707. McNaughton Newspapers group.
Circulation: 10,160(e); 10,501(S); ABC Sept. 30, 1995.
Price: 50¢(d); 50¢(S); $1.50/wk (plus tax); $6.50/mo (plus tax); $72.00/yr (plus tax).
Advertising: Open inch rate $13.15(e); $13.15(S). **Representative:** Papert Companies.
News Service: AP. **Established:** 1897.
Not Published: New Year; Memorial Day; Independence Day; Labor Day; Christmas.
Special Editions: Progress (Mar); Picnic Day (Apr); Graduation (June); Yolo County Fair (Aug); Welcome Edition (Sept); Christmas Guide, Cookbook (Nov).
Special Weekly Sections: Business Focus (tues); Best Food Day (wed); Restaurant, TV & Cable Listings (thur); Real Estate (fri); Automotive, Real Estate, Special Features (S).
Magazines: Weekend Magazine (thur); Real Estate Tab (fri).

CORPORATE OFFICERS

President Foy McNaughton
Vice Pres/Secretary Burt McNaughton

GENERAL MANAGEMENT

Publisher Burt McNaughton

ADVERTISING

Director Donna Okinga
Manager-Classified Lisa Zielesch

CIRCULATION

Manager Jess Reiter

NEWS EXECUTIVE

Editor Debbie Davis

EDITORS AND MANAGERS

Arts Editor Debbie Davis
Automotive Editor Jeff Aberbach
Business/Finance Editor Jeff Aberbach
City/Metro Editor Jeff Aberbach
Editorial Page Editor Jeff Aberbach
Education/Schools Editor Sally Ryen
Features Editor Melanie Turner
Living/Lifestyle Editor Gene Fynes
National Editor Jeff Aberbach
News Editor Jeff Aberbach
News Editor Debbie Davis
Photo Editor Todd Hammond
Political/Government Editor Jeff Aberbach
Religion Editor Betsy Schwarzentraub
Real Estate Editor Jennifer Oxley
Society/Women's Editor Gene Fynes
Sports Editor Marek Warszawski
Television/Music Editor Debbie Davis
Theater/Film Editor Debbie Davis

MANAGEMENT INFORMATION SERVICES

Data Processing Manager Pete Huddleson

PRODUCTION

Foreman-Composing Leslie Westergaard
Foreman-Pressroom Richard White

Market Information: Zoned editions; TMC.
Mechanical available: Offset; Black and 4 ROP colors; insert accepted — preprinted; page cut-offs — 21".
Mechanical specifications: Type page 13" x 21"; E - 6 cols, 2 1/16", ⅛" between; A - 6 cols, 2 1/16", ⅛" between; C - 10 cols, 1⅜", 1/16" between.
Commodity consumption: Newsprint 1,300 short tons; width 27"; single pages printed 8,596; average pages per issue 28(d), 48(S).
Equipment: EDITORIAL: Front-end hardware — CText, PC/486; Front-end software — CText, QPS; Printers — AG/Imagesetters, Hyphen/RIP. CLASSIFIED: Front-end hardware — CText, PC/386; Front-end software — CText; Printers — Copal/Postscript, Hyphen/RIP. DISPLAY: Adv layout systems — CText/Adept; Front-end hardware — PC/486; Front-end software — Archetype/Corel Draw, Archetype/Designer, Aldus/FreeHand, Adobe/Photoshop, CText/Adept; Printers — HP/4M, AG/Imagesetters, Copal, Hyphen/RIP. PRODUCTION: Typesetters — AG/9800, AG/Accuset, Hyphen/RIP; Plate exposures — 1-Nu/Ultra Plus; Plate processors — 1-Nat/A-250; Electronic picture desk — Lf/AP Leaf Picture Desk; Scanners — 1-AG/RPS 20-20 Compact, AG/Focus Scanner; Production cameras — 1-Acti/204D; Automatic film processors — AG/Wrex 25; Shrink lenses — Alan/Anamorphic; Color separation equipment (conventional) — Lf/AP Leaf Picture Desk, Adobe/Photoshop.
PRESSROOM: Line 1 — 10-G/S/C; Folders — 1-G. MAILROOM: Counter stackers — BG/108; Inserters and stuffers — 1-KAN; Bundle tyer — 2-MLN/ML2EE. LIBRARY: Electronic — SMS/Stauffer Gold. WIRE SERVICES: News — AP; Photos — AP; Receiving dishes — AP. BUSINESS COMPUTERS: Sun/Sparc II server; Applications: Microsoft/Word, Vision Data, Lotus: Accts, Circ; PCs & micros networked; PCs & main system networked.

EL CAJON

San Diego County

'90 U.S. Census- 88,693; E&P '96 Est. 100,216
ABC-CZ (90): 132,903 (HH 48,581)

The Daily Californian

(e-tues to fri; S)

The Daily Californian, 1000 Pioneer Way; PO Drawer 1565, El Cajon, CA 92022; tel (619) 442-4404; fax (619) 447-6165. Kendell Communications Inc. group.
Circulation: 18,908(e); 22,172(S); ABC Sept. 30, 1995.
Price: 25¢(d); 50¢(S); $6.25/mo (carrier); $69.00/yr (carrier).
Advertising: Open inch rate $33.75(e); $33.75(S); $74.35(e & S); $30.10 (TMC). **Representatives:** US Suburban Press; Landon Associates Inc.
News Service: AP. **Politics:** Independent. **Established:** 1892.
Note: Effective May 15, 1995, this publication dropped its Monday and Saturday editions.
Not Published: New Year; Memorial Day; Independence Day; Labor Day; Christmas.
Special Editions: Senior Lifestyles (Feb); Home Section (Mar); Senior Lifestyles (Apr); Mother's Day, Home Section (May); Senior Lifestyles (July); Football Preview, Home Section (Aug); Automobile Section, Fall Home, New Autos, Home Section, Senior Lifestyles (Oct); Mother Goose Parade Section (Nov); Holiday Shopper (Dec).
Special Weekly Sections: Food, Health (wed); Enjoy Entertainment (thur); Auto (sat); Home (S); Sports, Financial/Business Features (daily).
Magazines: Daily Community Editions (mon-fri); TV Times (S).

CORPORATE OFFICERS

President/Publisher Paul J Zindell
Vice Pres Raymond C Kennedy
Controller Deborah Rico
General Manager James W Schumacher
Operations Manager Antoinette DeVita-Gee

GENERAL MANAGEMENT

Manager-Human Resources Lauri Palermo

ADVERTISING

Manager-Operations Art Phelps
Manager-Classified Lea Hansen
Manager-Sales Jack Lane

CIRCULATION

Manager Catherine Roberts
Coordinator-Newspapers in Education Sandy Puff

NEWS EXECUTIVES

Editor James W Schumacher
Managing Editor Della Elliot

EDITORS AND MANAGERS

Editorial Page Editor Del Hood
Religion Editor Lori Arnold
Sports Editor Bill Dickens
Zone Editor Lori Arnold

PRODUCTION

Manager-Ad Composition Antoinette DeVita-Gee

Market Information: TMC.
Mechanical available: Offset; Black and 3 ROP colors; insert accepted — preprinted, any; page cut-offs — 22¾".
Mechanical specifications: Type page 13" x 21½"; E - 6 cols, 2 1/16", ⅛" between; A - 6 cols, 2 1/16", ⅛" between; C - 6 cols, 2 1/16", ⅛" between.
Commodity consumption: Newsprint 1,500 short tons; widths 27½", 13¾"; black ink 60,000 pounds; color ink 8,000 pounds; single pages printed 9,600; average pages per issue 30(d), 40(S); single plates used 12,000.
Equipment: EDITORIAL: Front-end hardware — 2-CText; Other equipment — 35-CText. CLASSIFIED: Front-end hardware — 20-CText. DISPLAY: Adv layout systems — 5-Ap/Mac; Other equipment — 3-CText. PRODUCTION: Platemaking systems — Nu; Plate exposures — 1-Nu/Ultra Plus, Nu; Plate processors — 1-Dynalith/Dynamatic; Electronic picture desk — Lf/AP Leaf Picture Desk; Scanners — 1-Ap/Mac, 1-HP, 2-Graphic Enterprises/18x24; Production cameras — 1-R/500-OH, 1-LE/Vertical; Automatic film processors — 1-LE/LD-18; Shrink lenses — 1-Kamerak/Scandia I.
PRESSROOM: Line 1 — 8-G/Urbanite; Line 2 — 7-DEV/1400; Press drives — Fin, Westinghouse; Folders — 1-G; Press control system — G. MAILROOM: Counter stackers — 2-Tech/Offset, 1-BG/108, 2-Id/440; Inserters and stuffers — 2-KAN/480; Bundle tyer — 2-MLN, 2-MLN/Spirit; Addressing machine — 1-Am, 1-KR, 3-Wm. WIRE SERVICES: News — AP; Photos — AP; Syndicates — AP; Receiving dishes — size-8ft, AP. BUSINESS COMPUTERS: 1-IBM/Sys 36, 4-PC/linked to AS400; Applications: Adv billing, Accts receivable, Gen ledger, Payroll; PCs & main system networked.

EL CENTRO

Imperial County

'90 U.S. Census- 31,384; E&P '96 Est. 37,585
ABC-NDM (90): 101,933 (HH 29,717)

Imperial Valley Press

(e-mon to fri; S)

Imperial Valley Press, 205 N. 8th St.; PO Box 2770, El Centro, CA 92244; tel (619) 337-3400; fax (619) 353-3003. Schurz Communications Inc. group.
Circulation: 16,629(e); 17,623(S); ABC Sept. 30, 1995.
Price: 50¢(d); $1.00(S); $8.00/mo (carrier); $91.00/yr (carrier).
Advertising: Open inch rate $14.49(e); $14.49(S). **Representative:** Papert Companies.
News Service: AP. **Politics:** Independent. **Established:** 1901.
Advertising not accepted: Contact newspaper advertising dept. for details.
Special Editions: Inland Empire, Business Guide (Jan); California Midwinter Fair (Feb); Sweet Onion Festival, Brawley Progress (May); Graduation (June); County Progress (July); Women of Imperial Valley (Aug); Football Preview (Sept); Cattle Call Tab (Oct).
Special Weekly Sections: Youth Page (tues); Food Page (wed); Farm Page (thur); Church Page (fri); Business Page, Building Page (S).
Magazine: TV Plus (TV Guide) (S).

CORPORATE OFFICERS

President J R (Dick) Fitch
Vice Pres William A Gay
Treasurer Julie Corwin
Secretary A Charles Baker
Asst Secretary Susan Giller

GENERAL MANAGEMENT

Publisher J R (Dick) Fitch
General Manager William A Gay
Controller Julie Corwin

ADVERTISING

Manager-Classified A Charles Baker
Manager-Display John Yanni

MARKETING AND PROMOTION

Manager-Marketing/Promotion Denise Slay

CIRCULATION

Manager Richard Van Duyne

NEWS EXECUTIVES

Editor J R (Dick) Fitch
Managing Editor Susan Giller

EDITORS AND MANAGERS

Action Line/Probe Editor Virginia Horn
Books Editor Peggy Dale
Business Editor Alec Rosenberg
Cartoonist Margaret Chairez
Columnist Virginia Horn
Columnist J R (Dick) Fitch
Columnist Bret Kofford
Consumer Interest Editor Virginia Horn
Couples Editor Angel Rosamond
Editorial Page Editor Susan Giller
Editorial Writer Susan Giller
Education Editor Angel Rosamond
Environmental Editor P A Rice
Features Editor Peggy Dale
Films/Theater Editor Don Quinn
Food/Home Editor Peggy Dale
Graphics Editor Margaret Chairez
Life Page Editor Peggy Dale
Living/Lifestyle Editor Peggy Dale
Metro Editor Bret Kofford
Music Editor Doug Clark
News Editor James Duke
Photo Editor Paul Noden
Political Editor Bret Kofford
Radio/Television Editor Don Quinn
Real Estate Editor Alex Rosenberg
Religion Editor Peggy Dale
Science/Technology Editor Bret Kofford
Special Edition Editor Bret Kofford
Sports Editor Murray Anderson
Teen-Age/Youth Editor Angel Rosamond
Wire Editor Don Quinn

PRODUCTION

Superintendent Clifford James
Foreman-Composing Jeff Schardt
Foreman-Pressroom Clifford James

Market Information: Zoned editions; TMC.
Mechanical available: Offset; Black and 3 ROP colors; insert accepted — preprinted.
Mechanical specifications: Type page 13" x 21½"; E - 6 cols, 2 1/16", ⅛" between; A - 6 cols, 2 1/16", ⅛" between; C - 9 cols, 1⅜", 1/16" between.

Commodity consumption: Newsprint 675 short tons; widths 27½", 13¾"; black ink 21,000 pounds; color ink 10,500 pounds; single pages printed 7,800; average pages per issue 30(d), 40(S); single plates used 52,000.
Equipment: EDITORIAL: Front-end hardware — 30-IBM/PC; Front-end software — ACT, Microsoft/Word 6.0, QuarkXPress 3.3; Printers — 2-Xante/Accel-a-Writer; Other equipment — AG/Accuset 1000 Imagesetter. CLASSIFIED: Front-end hardware — 8-AP/Mac; Front-end software — Baseview; Printers — Dataproducts/LZR 1560, AG/Imagesetter, Graphic Enterprises/Pro Setter 1000. DISPLAY: Front-end hardware — 7-Ap/Mac; Front-end software — Multi-Ad/Creator 3.7, Mk/Managing Editor 2.0; Printers — Dataproducts/LZR 1560, Graphic Enterprises/Pro Setter 1000, Laser-Master/Unity 1800XL-0. PRODUCTION: Pagination software — QuarkXPress 3.31; OCR software — Caere/OmniPage 3.2; Typesetters — 2-Xante/Accel-a-Writer 8200, AG/Accuset 1000; Plate processors — 1-Nat/240; Electronic picture desk — IBM PC, Adobe/Photoshop 3.0 Picture Publisher; Scanners — ECR/Autokon 1000; Automatic film processors — P.
PRESSROOM: Line 1 — G/Urbanite 1061; Folders — 1-G. MAILROOM: Counter stackers — 2-HL; Inserters and stuffers — 2-KAN; Bundle tyer — 2-MLN/ML2EE. LIBRARY: Electronic — ISYS. WIRE SERVICES: News — AP; Photos — AP; Stock tables — AP; Syndicates — AP, United Features, TMS, Creators, King Features, Washington Writer's Group; Receiving dishes — AP. BUSINESS COMPUTERS: DEC, IBM; Applications: Vision Data: Accounting, Circ, Mgmt info; PCs & micros networked; PCs & main system networked.

ESCONDIDO-OCEANSIDE

San Diego County

'90 U.S. Census- 236,725 (Escondido 108,635; Oceanside 128,090) E&P '96 Est. 306,965 (Escondido 154,845; Oceanside 152,120)
ABC-CZ (90): 174,399 (HH 62,672)

North County Times

(m-mon to sat; S)

North County Times, 207 E. Pennsylvania Ave., Escondido, CA 92025; tel (619) 745-6611; fax (619) 741-7370. Howard Publications group.
Circulation: 76,682(m); 76,682(m-sat); 88,285(S); ABC Sept. 30, 1995.
Price: 25¢(d); 25¢(sat); $1.00(S); $2.00/wk (carrier); $104.00/52wk (carrier).
Advertising: Open inch rate $36.62(m); $36.62(m-sat); $37.72(S). **Representative:** Landon Associates Inc.
News Services: AP, KRT, NYT, Cox News Service. **Politics:** Independent.
Note: Effective Dec. 3, 1995, the Escondido Times Advocate (m-mon to sat; S) merged with the Oceanside Blade-Citizen (m-mon to sat; S) to form the Escondido-Oceanside North County Times (m-mon to sat; S). The combined circulation of the two papers is recorded.
Special Editions: % Off (Jan); Jobs on Display, Restaurant Guide, Retirement Living, Spring Fashion Supplement, Torrey Pines Buick Open (Feb); Festival of Homes, Car Care, Bridal Showcase (Mar); Home Improvement, San Diego Auto Show (Apr); California Center for the Arts, Mother's Day (May); Dads & Grads, Del Mar Fair Program (June); % Off, Del Mar Horse Racing, Summer Festival of Homes (July); Back-to-School, California Center for the Arts, Carlsbad 5000, Miramar Air Show, San Diego Chargers Preview (Aug); Women's Opportunity Week (Sept); Car Care, Auto Preview, Fall Fashion Supplement (Oct); Holiday Gift Guide, Last Minute Gift Guide (Dec).
Special Weekly Section: Trips/Places (S).
Magazines: "Preview" entertainment guide (fri); TV Book, Weekend (S).

CORPORATE OFFICERS

President Robert S Howard
President South Coast Newspapers Richard High

GENERAL MANAGEMENT

Director Finance John Knerler
Publisher-Escondido Richard High
Publisher-Fallbrook Don Taylor
Publisher-Oceanside Thomas F Missett
Publisher-Solana Beach Ira Rosenthal
Personnel Manager Peggy Chapman
Manager-Purchasing Ken Griess

ADVERTISING

Director Scott Putnicki
Manager-Retail Kevin Leap
Manager-Classified/Inside Helen Boyd
Manager-Classified/Outside Joan Missett
Manager-Major/National Bob Hess

MARKETING AND PROMOTION

Manager-Marketing/Promotion Laurie Brindle

CIRCULATION

Director Mark Henschen

NEWS EXECUTIVES

Editor Richard K Petersen
Asst Managing Editor W Russell Harris

EDITORS AND MANAGERS

City Editor-Oceanside J Stryker Meyer
City Editor-Carlsbad Jonathan Heller
City Editor-Vista Evan Dreyer
City Editor-Encinitas D Wade Booth
City Editor-Escondido/Valley Center/Ramona Don Stanzlano
City Editor-Poway/Rancho Bernardo David Brown
City Editor-San Marcos Bob Masingale
City Editor-Fallbrook/Bonsall Betty Johnston
City Editor-Temecula Valley James Folmer

PRODUCTION

Director Dutch Greve
Manager-Packaging Stephanie Woodard
Manager-Press Kelly McKeirnan
Manager-Press Andy Powers
Manager-Imaging Richard Sousa
Manager-Imaging Gary Sullivan

Market Information: Zoned editions; TMC; ADS.
Mechanical available: Offset; Black and 3 ROP colors; insert accepted — preprinted; page cut-offs — 22".
Mechanical specifications: Type page 13" x 21"; E - 6 cols, 2.03", ⅙" between; A - 6 cols, 2.03", ⅙" between; C - 10 cols, 1.24", 1/24" between.
Commodity consumption: Newsprint 5,963 metric tons; widths 54", 40½", 27"; black ink 122,206 pounds; color ink 36,238 pounds; single pages printed 19,412; average pages per issue 45(d), 45(sat), 66(S); single plates used 80,000.
Equipment: EDITORIAL: Front-end hardware — SII/CLX740; Front-end software — SII; Printers — 2-DEC/LA 180, 2-DEC/LA 120; Other equipment — 6-Ap/Mac Quadra, 2-Lf/AP Leaf Picture Desk. CLASSIFIED: Front-end hardware — SII/CLX740; Front-end software — SII; Printers — 2-DEC/LA 180. DISPLAY: Adv layout systems — CJ; Front-end hardware — 14-Ap/Mac; Front-end software — Multi-Ad/Creator, QuarkXPress, Adobe/Illustrator. PRODUCTION: Pagination software — QuarkXPress 3.31; Typesetters — 2-V/3000, 3-Hyphen/Plain Paper, HP/IIIsi, QMS/860, 1-V/5000-5510; Plate exposures — 2-Nu; Plate processors — 1-Nat; Electronic picture desk — 3-Lf/AP Leaf Picture Desk; Scanners — 1-ECR/Autokon 1000; Production cameras — 1-C/Spartan III, 2-AG/RPS 6000; Automatic film processors — 2-Litex/26, 1-V; Film transporters — 1-C/Konica; Digital color separation equipment — 2-Ap/Mac.
PRESSROOM: Line 1 — 5-G/HO (3½deck); Press drives — 6-Allen Bradley/Digital; Folders — 2-G/2:1; Pasters — 5-G/CT-45; Press control system — G/MPCS. MAILROOM: Counter stackers — 3-Id/2000, 2-HL/Monitor; Inserters and stuffers — 2-GMA/SLS-1000 6:1; Bundle tyer — 4-Dynaric; Addressing machine — 1-Ch; Other mailroom equipment — Bottom Wrap. 3-IDAB. WIRE SERVICES: News — AP Datastream, AP Datafeatures, AP Stats; Photos — AP; Stock tables — TMS; Receiving dishes — AP. BUSINESS COMPUTERS: Remote processing from Chicago Tribune, IBM/3090, DEC/VAX; Applications: DB: S: Unix-Vision Data: Adv, Circ; Unix-Vision Data; PCs & micros networked; PCs & main system networked.

EUREKA

Humboldt County

'90 U.S. Census- 27,025; E&P '96 Est. 29,131
ABC-CZ (90): 45,834 (HH 18,144)

Times-Standard

(e-mon to sat; S)

Times-Standard, PO Box 3580, Eureka, CA 95502-3580; tel (707) 441-0500; fax (707) 441-0565. Thomson Newspapers group.
Circulation: 21,332(e); 21,332(e-sat); 23,197(S); ABC Sept. 30, 1995.
Price: 50¢(d); 50¢(sat); $1.50(S); $12.75/mo.
Advertising: Open inch rate $19.94(e); $19.94(e-sat); $19.94(S). **Representative:** Papert Companies.
News Service: AP. **Politics:** Independent. **Established:** 1854.
Not Published: New Year; Washington's Birthday; Memorial Day; Independence Day; Labor Day; Christmas.
Special Editions: President's Day Section (Feb); Spring Bridal, Home Improvement, Progress Edition (Mar); Rhododendron Days (Apr); Design-An-Ad, Vacation the North Coast (May); Redwood Acres Fair Tab (June); Back-to-School Section (Aug); Home Edition (Sept); Fall Fashion Tab, New Car Edition, Fact Book (Oct); Gift Guide, Christmas Kick-off (Nov); End of the Year Clearance (Dec).
Special Weekly Sections: North Coast Kids (1st wed/mo); Senior Citizens Tab (alternate thur); Real Estate Tab (alternate sat).
Magazines: Parade (S); Real Estate EXTRA (monthly).

GENERAL MANAGEMENT

Publisher Stephan J Sosinski
Controller Lynn W Johnson

ADVERTISING

Manager Gary Siegel
Manager-National Representative Laurie McBride

CIRCULATION

Manager-Sales Mitchell Lynch

NEWS EXECUTIVE

Managing Editor Rex Wilson

EDITORS AND MANAGERS

Books Editor David Reynolds
Business Editor Charles Winkler
City Editor Charles Winkler
Editorial Writer Jerry Post
Education Editor Kelly Johnson
Features/Food Editor Kathy Dillon
Films/Theater Editor Joel Davis
Music Editor Joel Davis
Political Editor David Anderson
Radio/Television Editor Joel Davis
Religion Editor Joel Davis
Sports Editor Ted Sillanpaa
Women's Editor Kathy Dillon

MANAGEMENT INFORMATION SERVICES

Data Processing Manager Lynn W Johnson

PRODUCTION

Foreman-Composing Bruce Bochetti
Foreman-Pressroom John Pelascini

Market Information: TMC; ADS.
Mechanical available: Offset; Black and 3 ROP colors; insert accepted — preprinted; page cut-offs — 22¾".
Mechanical specifications: Type page 13" x 21½"; E - 6 cols, 2 1/16", ⅛" between; A - 6 cols, 2 1/16", ⅛" between; C - 9 cols, 1⅜", 1/16" between.
Commodity consumption: Newsprint 1,680 short tons; widths 27½", 13¾"; average pages per issue 24(d), 48(S); single plates used 12,000.
Equipment: EDITORIAL: Front-end hardware — 18-Mk; Other equipment — 6-Ap/Mac. CLASSIFIED: Front-end hardware — 4-Mk; Other equipment — 4-Ap/Mac. DISPLAY: Adv layout systems — 2-Ap/Mac Centris. PRODUCTION: Typesetters — 2-V/5900, 1-V/6990, 1-V/6990; Plate exposures — 1-Nu; Plate processors — 2-Nat/A-250; Electronic picture desk — Lf/AP Leaf Picture Desk; Production cameras — 1-R/432 Mark II, 1-LE/121.
PRESSROOM: Line 1 — 8-G/Urbanite; Folders — G/2:1. MAILROOM: Counter stackers — MM; Inserters and stuffers — MM; Bundle tyer — 1-MLN/ML1EE; Wrapping singles — 1-Am/1997B; Addressing machine — ATT; Other mailroom equipment — MM/Stitcher-Trimmer. WIRE SERVICES: News — AP Datastream; Syndicates — NEA, United Features, TMS, Universal Press; Receiving dishes — size-10m, AP. BUSINESS COMPUTERS: ATT; PCs & main system networked.

FAIRFIELD

Solano County

'90 U.S. Census- 77,211; E&P '96 Est. 93,463
ABC-CZ (90): 90,023 (HH 29,966)

Daily Republic (m-mon to sat; S)

Daily Republic, 1250 Texas St.; PO Box 47, Fairfield, CA 94533; tel (707) 425-4646; fax (707) 425-5924. McNaughton Newspapers group.
Circulation: 18,295(m); 18,295(m-sat); 20,121(S); ABC Sept. 30, 1995.
Price: 35¢(d); 35¢(sat); $1.25(S); $96.00/yr (carrier), $108.00/yr (mail).
Advertising: Open inch rate $17.60(m); $17.60(m-sat); $17.60(S). **Representatives:** Papert Companies; US Suburban Press.
News Service: AP. **Politics:** Independent. **Established:** 1855.
Special Editions: Hometown Heroes; Personal Finance; American Home Week (Real Estate); Cookbook; Solano Seniors; Careers & Lifestyles; Solano Summer; Thanksgiving Morning; Christmas Gift; Annual Welcome Edition; Annual Progress.
Special Weekly Sections: Express Line, Best Food Day (wed); Automotive Section, Entertainment/Out & About, Fresh Print (Youth) (fri); Solano Home Life, Religion (sat); Real Estate, Religion (S).
Magazines: Automobile Section (fri); Real Estate Magazine (sat); TV Daily Magazine (local), "Diversions" (local), Color Comics (S).

CORPORATE OFFICERS

President Foy McNaughton
Vice Pres Burt McNaughton
Secretary/Treasurer Burt McNaughton

GENERAL MANAGEMENT

Publisher Foy McNaughton

ADVERTISING

Director Ann Rollin

CIRCULATION

Director-Operations Tom Lucas

NEWS EXECUTIVE

Managing Editor Bill Buchanan

EDITORS AND MANAGERS

City Editor Cathy L'Ecluse
Asst City Editor Catherine Moy
News Editor Maureen Fissolo
Photo Department Manager Mark Pyne
Sports Editor Brad Stanhope

PRODUCTION

Foreman-Pressroom John Polk

Market Information: TMC.
Mechanical available: Offset; Black and 3 ROP colors; insert accepted — preprinted, all types; page cut-offs — 22¾".
Mechanical specifications: Type page 12⅝" x 21⅜"; E - 6 cols, 2 1/16", ⅛" between; A - 6 cols, 2 1/16", ⅛" between; C - 9 cols, 1⅜", ⅛" between.
Commodity consumption: Newsprint 2,134 short tons; width 27"; single pages printed 1,640; average pages per issue 42(d), 68(S); single plates used 8,320.
Equipment: EDITORIAL: Front-end hardware — CText, 36-PC/286-386. CLASSIFIED: Front-end hardware — CText. DISPLAY: Adv layout systems — 3-COM/Dawn (on-line), 5-Ap/Mac Network. PRODUCTION: Typesetters — 2-Birmy/Setter; Platemaking systems — 1-3M/PyroFax Deadliner; Plate exposures — 1-Nu; Plate processors — 1-Nat; Production cameras — 1-Danagraph; Color separation equipment (conventional) — 1-WDS.
PRESSROOM: Line 1 — 9-G/Urbanite; Folders — 1-G. MAILROOM: Counter stackers — 2-BG/Count-O-Veyor; Inserters and stuffers — 2-KAN/480; Bundle tyer — 1-MLN; Addressing machine — 2-Am, 1-Ch/725. COMMUNICATIONS: Facsimile — 1-X. WIRE SERVICES: News — AP; Receiving dishes — AP. BUSINESS COMPUTERS: 1-IBM; Applications: Circ, Payroll, Accts payable, Accts receivable, Gen ledger.

FREMONT-NEWARK

Alameda County

'90 U.S. Census- 211,200 (Fremont 173,339; Newark 37,861); E&P '96 Est. 250,475 (Fremont 208,207; Newark 42,268)
ABC-CZ (90): 264,962 (HH 87,914)

The Argus (m-mon to sat; S)

The Argus, 39737 Paseo Padre, Fremont, CA 94538; tel (510) 661-2600; fax (510) 790-4526. MediaNews Inc. (Alameda Newspapers) group.
Circulation: 31,066(m); 31,066(m-sat); 32,662(S); ABC Sept. 30, 1995.
Price: 50¢(d); 50¢(sat); $1.25(S); $2.80/wk.
Representative: Landon Associates Inc.
News Services: NYT, AP, LAT-WP, SHNS, McClatchy. **Politics:** Independent. **Established:** 1960.
Note: Advertising is sold in combination with Fremont Argus (mS), Haywad Daily Review (mS), Oakland Tribune (mS) and Pleasanton Tri-Valley Herald (mS) for $118.00 (dS).

Individual newspaper rates not made available. For detailed mechanical equipment information, see the Oakland Tribune listing.

Special Editions: East Bay Almanac (Mar); East Bay Leisure Guide (June); "Best" from Valley to Bay (Oct); Auto, Christmas Gifts (Nov); Christmas Gifts (Dec).

Special Weekly Sections: Best Food Day (wed); Automotive (fri); New Homes (sat); Travel (S); CUE (daily).

Magazines: USA Weekend, TV Week (S).

CORPORATE OFFICERS	
President/Publisher	Peter Bernhard
Asst to Publisher/Vice Pres-Administration	Patrick Brown
Senior Vice Pres-Production	Dennis Miller
Senior Vice Pres-Advertising	Roger Grossman
Senior Vice Pres-Circulation	Arthur Farber
Senior Vice Pres/Editor in Chief	David Burgin
Vice Pres-Human Resources	Jim Janiga
GENERAL MANAGEMENT	
Publisher	Peter Bernhard
Assoc Publisher	Joseph Haraburda
Manager-Human Resources	Karen Austin
ADVERTISING	
Director	Melinda Brown
Director-Classified	Pete Laraway
Manager-National	Mary Menard
MARKETING AND PROMOTION	
Director-Marketing/Promotion Service	Deborah Byrum
TELECOMMUNICATIONS	
Manager	Sam Lovato
CIRCULATION	
Director	Wally Tiedemann
Director-Operations	Mary O'Brien
NEWS EXECUTIVES	
Editor	Jack Lyness
Exec Editor	Nancy Conway
Managing Editor	Nancy Debolt
EDITORS AND MANAGERS	
Books Editor	Robert Taylor
Business Editor	David Tong
Asst Business Editor	Scott Ard
Columnist	Ray Orrock
Columnist	Tom Goff
Columnist	Cheryl Gregor-North
Editorial Page Editor	Bob Cuddy
Entertainment Editor	Sharon Betz
Features Editor	Sharon Betz
Food Editor	Catherine Chriss
Director-Libraries	Steve Lavoie
Movie Critic	Barry Caine
Director-News Production	Chris Campos
Director-Photo/Graphics	Rob Lindquist
Sports Editor	Michael Tegner
Sports Columnist	Monte Poole
Sports Columnist	Carl Steward
Sports Columnist	Dave Newhouse
Sacramento CA Bureau Editor	Sam Delson
Television Critic	Susan Young
Travel Editor	Bari Brenner
MANAGEMENT INFORMATION SERVICES	
Data Processing Manager	Ken Marcum
Online Manager	Kevin Hamilton
PRODUCTION	
Director	Dave Boyer
Manager	Pete Salm

Market Information: TMC; Operate database.

Mechanical available: Black and 3 ROP colors; insert accepted — preprinted; page cut-offs — 21.5".

Mechanical specifications: Type page 13" x 21.5"; E - 6 cols, $2\frac{1}{16}$", $\frac{1}{8}$" between; A - 6 cols, $2\frac{1}{16}$", $\frac{1}{8}$" between; C - 10 cols, $1\frac{1}{4}$", $\frac{1}{32}$" between.

Commodity consumption: Newsprint 3,675 metric tons; widths $54\frac{7}{8}$", $41\frac{1}{8}$", $27\frac{3}{8}$"; black ink 72,000 pounds; color ink 7,500 pounds; single pages printed 27,200; average pages per issue 72(d), 96(S); single plates used 28,000.

FRESNO

Fresno County

'90 U.S. Census- 354,202; **E&P '96 Est.** 495,728

ABC-NDM (90): 707,546 (HH 233,067)

The Fresno Bee

(m-mon to sat; S)

The Fresno Bee, 1626 E St., Fresno, CA 93786; tel (209) 441-6111; fax (209) 441-6050. McClatchy Newspapers group.

Circulation: 152,554(m); 152,554(m-sat); 187,273(S); ABC Sept. 30, 1995.

Price: 50¢(d); 50¢(sat); $1.25(S); $10.95/mo; $131.40/yr.

Advertising: Open inch rate $98.95(m); $98.95(m-sat); $122.10(S). **Representative:** Cresmer, Woodward, O'Mara & Ormsbee.

News Services: AP, NYT, LAT-WP, KRT, SHNS. **Politics:** Non-partisan. **Established:** 1922.

Special Editions: ExpressLine Midweek and Weekend Editions (TMC); Farm Equipment Show; Home Improvement (Spring & Fall); Car Care; California Living; Football Preview; Discover Fresno; Fitness; Business & Industry; Super Bowl; Fresno Reads; Pool & Patio.

Special Weekly Sections: Business Monday (mon); Entertainment (fri); Automotive, Religion, Home & Garden, Today's Home (sat); Spotlight (S).

Magazines: Parade, TV Magazine, Color Comics (S).

CORPORATE OFFICERS	
Chairman of the Board/CEO	Erwin Potts
President/Chief Operating Officer	Gary Pruitt
Publisher (McClatchy Newspapers)	James McClatchy
Secretary	Karole Morgan-Prager
Senior Vice Pres	William L Honeysett
Vice Pres-Finance/Treasurer	James P Smith
Controller	Robert Berger
GENERAL MANAGEMENT	
Publisher (Fresno Bee)	Robert J Weil
General Manager	John Ward
Manager-Human Resources	Julie Porter
Director-Finance	Gerald Hug
ADVERTISING	
Director	Alan Truax
Manager-Display	John Coakley
Manager-Classified	Paul Keen
Manager-Operations	Tina Berryman
MARKETING AND PROMOTION	
Manager-Marketing/Research	Darrell Kunken
Manager-Community Relations	Harvey Zimmerman
Manager-Creative Service	William Dick
Manager-Special Sections	Lisa Garabedian
TELECOMMUNICATIONS	
Manager-Technical Service	Frank Lamonski
Audiotex Manager	Paul Keen
CIRCULATION	
Director	Thomas Cullinan
Manager	Ken Hatfield
Manager-Distribution	Barry Budke
Manager-Systems	Jim Fotes
Manager-Sales	Dick Huddleston
NEWS EXECUTIVES	
Exec Editor	J Keith Moyer
Asst Managing Editor/Sports	Rick Vacek
Deputy Managing Editor	Rich Marshall
Editorial Page Editor	James Boren
EDITORS AND MANAGERS	
Art Director	Steven Parra
Art Writer	David Hale
Automotive Editor	Ray Nash
Business Editor	Irwin Speizer
Entertainment/Amusements Editor	Tom Becker
Librarian	Mabel Wilson
Lifestyle Editor	Gail Marshall
Medicine Writer	Jerry Bier
Metro Editor	Cathy Riddick
News Editor	Kris Eldred
Photography Director	Thom Halls
Political Writer	Phoebe Wall Howard
Radio/Television Writer	Lanny Larson
Real Estate Writer	Sanford Nax
Religion Writer	John Taylor
School Writer	Cyndee Fontana
School Writer	Anastasia Hendrix
Sports Writer	John Rich
Travel Editor	Tom Becker
MANAGEMENT INFORMATION SERVICES	
Director-Info Systems	Christopher Caneles
Manager-Info Systems	Maureen King
PRODUCTION	
Director	Janet Owen
Manager-Pre Press	Jerry Carlson
Manager-Pressroom	Dennis Lyall
Manager-Packaging/Distribution	Jack Beacom
Manager-Plant Engineering	Ken Marple

Market Information: Zoned editions; Split Run; TMC; ADS; Operate audiotex.

Mechanical available: Flexographic; Black and 3 ROP colors; insert accepted — preprinted; page cut-offs — 22".

Mechanical specifications: Type page 13" x $20\frac{15}{16}$"; E - 6 cols, 2", .19" between; A - 6 cols, 2", .19" between; C - 10 cols, $1\frac{1}{4}$", $\frac{1}{18}$" between.

Commodity consumption: Newsprint 22,000 metric tons; widths 54", $40\frac{1}{2}$", 27"; black ink 557,000 pounds; color ink 71,247 pounds; single pages printed 25,500; average pages per issue 60(d), 108(S); single plates used 72,500.

Equipment: EDITORIAL: Front-end hardware — SII/Sys 55, 34-SII/Coyote IV, SII/QB, 30-SII, 30-SII/22; Front-end software — SII; Printers — 2-V/600, 3-HP/LaserJet II. CLASSIFIED: Front-end hardware — 33-SII/Coyote IV; Front-end software — SII; Printers — 1-HP/LaserJet I, 1-HP/LaserJet II. AUDIOTEX: Hardware — PEP; Software — Unix, Ingres; Supplier name — BDR. DISPLAY: Adv layout systems — HP/3000, CJ/AIM; Front-end hardware — Sun/Sparc Stations; Front-end software — Cx/Breeze. PRODUCTION: Typesetters — 2-Cx/Super Setters, 2-III/3850; Plate exposures — 2-Na/FPII; Plate processors — 2-Na/FXIV; Scanners — 3-ECR/1000; Production cameras — 1-C/Newspager II, 1-C/Marathon; Automatic film processors — 6-LE; Digital color separation equipment — CD, Diadem/Carat.
PRESSROOM: Line 1 — 6-MAN/Print Couples, 22-MAN/FlexoMan M double width; Line 2 — 6-MAN/Print Couples, 22-MAN/FlexoMan M double width; Line 3 — 6-MAN/Print Couples, 22-MAN/FlexoMan M, 18-FOL double width; Press drives — Allen-Bradley; Folders — MAN/4:3:2; Pasters — 18-HUR/50; Reels and stands — 18-HUR/50; Press control system — MAN/Infoflex; Press registration system — MAN/Infoflex. MAILROOM: Counter stackers — 4-Id/660, 1-Id/2000, 7-HL/HT; Inserters and stuffers — 3-HI/1472P; Bundle tyer — 12-Power Strap/PSN-6; Wrapping singles — 12-HL/Bottom Wrap. LIBRARY: Electronic — SII/Laser. COMMUNICATIONS: Digital ad delivery system — AP AdSend, Digiflex. WIRE SERVICES: News — AP, NYT, AP Datafeatures, LAT-WP, KRT, SHNS; Photos — AP, KRT; Stock tables — AP; Syndicates — AP Datafeatures; Receiving dishes — size-10ft, AP. BUSINESS COMPUTERS: 1-HP/3000 Series 967; Applications: CJ: Accts payable, Adv info mgmt, Payroll, Circ, Gen ledger, Personnel, Accts receivable, Human resources, Newsprint; PCs & micros networked; PCs & main system networked.

GILROY

Santa Clara County

'90 U.S. Census- 31,487; **E&P '96 Est.** 40,753

ABC-CZ (90): 31,487 (HH 9,512)

The Dispatch (m-mon to fri)

The Dispatch, 6400 Monterey; PO Box 22365, Gilroy, CA 95021; tel (408) 842-6400; fax (408) 842-7105. McClatchy Newspapers group.

Circulation: 5,644(m); ABC Sept. 30, 1995.

Price: 50¢(d); $75.00/yr.

Advertising: Open inch rate $14.80(m); comb with Hollister Free Lance(m) $18.40. **Representative:** Papert Companies.

News Service: AP. **Politics:** Independent. **Established:** 1868.

Not Published: New Year; Christmas.

Special Editions: Menus; Home Guide.

Special Weekly Section: TV (thur).

Magazines: Let's Go! (thur); TV.

GENERAL MANAGEMENT	
Publisher	Paula Mabry
ADVERTISING	
Manager-Retail	Arlene Hudson
CIRCULATION	
Manager	Jonathan Hernandez
NEWS EXECUTIVE	
Exec Editor	Mark Derry
EDITORS AND MANAGERS	
City Editor	David Caraccio
Sports Editor	Angi Christensen
MANAGEMENT INFORMATION SERVICES	
Data Processing Manager	Irma Navarro
PRODUCTION	
Supervisor-Composing	Sylvia Myrvold
Manager-Pressroom	Sam Montoya
Manager-Pre Press	Susan Ober
Manager-Packaging Center	Alex Cabezas

Market Information: TMC.

Mechanical available: Offset; Black and 3 ROP colors; insert accepted — preprinted, inserts of any configuration; page cut-offs — $21\frac{1}{2}$".

Mechanical specifications: Type page 13" x $21\frac{1}{2}$"; E - 6 cols, $2\frac{1}{16}$", $\frac{1}{6}$" between; A - 6 cols, $2\frac{1}{16}$", $\frac{1}{6}$" between; C - 10 cols, $1\frac{7}{32}$", $\frac{1}{6}$" between.

Commodity consumption: Newsprint 228 metric tons; widths 27", $13\frac{1}{2}$"; black ink 10,000 pounds; color ink 600 pounds; single pages printed 5,631; average pages per issue 20(d); single plates used 8,014.

Equipment: EDITORIAL: Front-end hardware — Dewar/Sys 4, 21-PC/286-386-SX; Front-end software — Novell; Printers — 1-Okidata; Other equipment — Ap/Mac IIsi. CLASSIFIED: Front-end hardware — Dewar/Sys 4, 4-PC/386-SX; Front-end software — Novell; Printers — 1-Okidata. DISPLAY: Front-end hardware — 2-Ap/Mac SE20, 1-Ap/Mac II, 1-Ap/Mac fx; Front-end software — QuarkXPress, Adobe/Photoshop; Printers — 1-Ap/Mac LaserWriter II NTX. PRODUCTION: Typesetters — 2-Ap/Mac LaserWriter II NTX, 1-Ap/Mac LaserWriter Plus, Printware/1217, 2-Ap/Mac LaserWriter Pro 810, V/3990, V/4000; Plate exposures — 1-Nu; Plate processors — 1-Nat; Electronic picture desk — Ap/Mac 7100; Scanners — Microtek/6002S Flatbed, Kk/RFS 2035; Production cameras — 1-C/Pager, 1-SCREEN/Companica Vertical, 1-VG/Daylighter; Automatic film processors — 1-LE/24AQ, 2-LE/PC3; Film transporters — 1-C; Color separation equipment (conventional) — 1-WDS/(conventional), 1-Microtek/600ZS, 1-Nikon/LS-3510AF.
PRESSROOM: Line 1 — 8-G/Community; Line 2 — 3-DEV/Color Stack Unit; Line 3 — 1-ATF/Davidson-Chief 17 Offset; Folders — 2-G, 1-G/SC (w/upper former). MAILROOM: Counter stackers — 3-BG/Count-O-Veyor, Id/440; Inserters and stuffers — 1-HI/624, 1-KAN/480; Bundle tyer — 1-MLN, 2-MLN/ML-1-EE; Wrapping singles — 1-ID; Other mailroom equipment — Rapid/Trimmer Automatic C. LIBRARY: Electronic — Vu/Text. WIRE SERVICES: News — AP Datafeatures, AP Datastream, AP GraphicsNet, McClatchy News Service; Receiving dishes — size-3m, AP. BUSINESS COMPUTERS: IBM/Sys 36; Applications: Lotus; PCs & main system networked.

GLENDALE

Los Angeles County

'90 U.S. Census- 180,038; **E&P '96 Est.** 214,149

Glendale News-Press

(m-mon to sat)

Glendale News-Press, 425 W. Broadway, Ste. 300; PO Box 991, Glendale, CA 91204; tel (818) 241-4141. Times Mirror Co. group.

Circulation: 10,373(m); 11,065(m-wed); 10,373(m-sat); VAC June 30, 1995.

Price: 25¢(d); $1.25 (wed); 25¢(sat).

Advertising: Open inch rate $17.08(m); $22.50(m-wed); $17.08(m-sat). **Representatives:** Papert Companies; US Suburban Press.

News Services: AP, City News Service. **Politics:** Independent. **Established:** 1905.

Magazine: USA Weekend.

GENERAL MANAGEMENT	
Publisher	Judee Kendall
ADVERTISING	
Director	Erma Hassen
MARKETING AND PROMOTION	
Director-Marketing/Promotion	Erma Hassen
CIRCULATION	
Director	Robert Frank
NEWS EXECUTIVE	
Senior Managing Editor	Dan Bolton
EDITORS AND MANAGERS	
City Editor	Steve Rosenberg
Editorial Page Editor	Marjorie Marks
Entertainment/Amusements Editor	Brian Holquin
Librarian	Denise Burdette
Living/Lifestyle Editor	Cynthia Takano
News Editor	Warren Swil
Chief Photographer	Ray Watt
Religion Editor	Bill Loughlin
Sports Editor	Keith Lair
PRODUCTION	
Director	Troy Feyerabend

Market Information: TMC.

Mechanical available: Offset; Black and 3 ROP colors; insert accepted — preprinted, all preprints; page cut-offs — $22\frac{3}{4}$".

Mechanical specifications: Type page 13" x 21"; E - 6 cols, $2\frac{1}{16}$", $\frac{1}{8}$" between; A - 6 cols, $2\frac{1}{16}$", $\frac{1}{8}$" between; C - 9 cols, $1\frac{3}{8}$", $\frac{1}{16}$" between.

Commodity consumption: Newsprint 410 short tons; width 13"; average pages per issue 20(d).

Equipment: EDITORIAL: Front-end hardware — Ik, Dy. CLASSIFIED: Other equipment — 8-IBM. PRODUCTION: Typesetters — 2-COM/Videosetter, 2-COM/9000; Plate exposures — 1-Nu; Plate processors — 1-Nat; Scanners — 2-Linotype-Hell/Linotron 202N, 2-Mark/V; Production cameras — 1-C/Spartan III;

California I-33

Automatic film processors — LE/LD24; Reproportion units — 1-McBeth/densitometer; Film transporters — 1-C/Spartan III. MAILROOM: Inserters and stuffers — KAN/480-GST; Bundle tyer — 2-MLN/ML2EE; Wrapping singles — 2-MLN, 1-Bu. LIBRARY: Combination — 2-Kodographic. WIRE SERVICES: News — AP, City News Service; Photos — AP; Receiving dishes — size-6ft, AP. BUSINESS COMPUTERS: 1-Bs/B-90; Applications: Bus, Billing, Accts receivable, Accts payable, Circ.

GRASS VALLEY
Nevada County

'90 U.S. Census- 9,048; E&P '96 Est. 11,075
ABC-NDM (90): 69,090 (HH 27,294)

The Union (e-mon to sat)

The Union, 11464 Sutton Way, Grass Valley, CA 95945; tel (916) 273-9561; fax (916) 273-1854. Swift Newspapers group.
Circulation: 15,040(e); 15,040(e-sat); ABC Sept. 30, 1995.
Price: 50¢(d); 50¢(sat); $7.50/mo (city), $8.00/mo (rural); $90.00/yr (city), $96.00/yr (rural).
Advertising: Open inch rate $16.00(e); $16.00(e-sat).
News Service: AP. **Politics:** Independent. **Established:** 1864.
Advertising not accepted: That which requires payment in advance.
Special Editions: Gold Country, Bride (Feb); Home & Garden (Mar); Fair (Aug); Update on Business, Football (Sept).
Special Weekly Sections: Food (tues); Home and Garden (fri); Religious, Community/Society, Business (sat).
Magazines: The Prospector (thur); TV Magazine (sat); Guide to Professional Services (1st wk of the month).

CORPORATE OFFICERS
Chairman Philip E Swift
President Richard K Larson
GENERAL MANAGEMENT
Publisher John Walker
ADVERTISING
Director Matt Bodovrian
CIRCULATION
Manager Lee Mahan
NEWS EXECUTIVE
Managing Editor John Seelmeyer
EDITOR AND MANAGER
Women's Interest Editor Heather MacDonald
PRODUCTION
Supervisor Gary Clelan
Supervisor-Printing Lee Brant

Market Information: Zoned editions; Split Run; TMC.
Mechanical available: Offset; Black and 3 ROP colors; insert accepted — preprinted; page cut-offs — 22¾".
Mechanical specifications: Type page 13" x 21½"; E - 6 cols, 2¹⁄₁₆", ⅛" between; A - 6 cols, 2¹⁄₁₆", ⅛" between; C - 9 cols, 1⅜", ¹⁄₁₆" between.
Commodity consumption: average pages per issue 32(d).
Equipment: EDITORIAL: Front-end hardware — Ap/Mac. CLASSIFIED: Front-end hardware — Ap/Mac. DISPLAY: Adv layout systems — Ap/Mac; Front-end hardware — Ethernet/Ap Talk, 7-Ap/Mac Centris. PRODUCTION: Typesetters — Ap/Mac; Plate exposures — 1-Nu/Flip Top; Plate processors — Nat; Production cameras — 1-SCREEN/Ver; Automatic film processors — 1-P; Color separation equipment (conventional) — WDS.
PRESSROOM: Line 1 — 7-G/Community (2 stack color). MAILROOM: Counter stackers — 1-BG/MFG; Inserters and stuffers — 2-MM, MM/227; Bundle tyer — 1-MLN, 1-Bu. WIRE SERVICES: News — AP; Receiving dishes — size-10ft, AP. BUSINESS COMPUTERS: Sun/Sparc server; Applications: PBS/Media Plus: Gen accounting, Adv accts receivable; Circ; PCs & micros networked.

HANFORD
Kings County

'90 U.S. Census- 30,897; E&P '96 Est. 40,354
ABC-CZ (90): 42,735 (HH 14,457)

The Hanford Sentinel
(e-mon to fri; m-sat; S)

The Hanford Sentinel, 300 W. 6th; PO Box 9, Hanford, CA 93232; tel (209) 582-0471; fax (209) 582-0512. Scripps League Newspapers Inc. group.
Circulation: 13,285(e); 13,285(m-sat); 13,267(S); ABC Sept. 30, 1995.
Price: 50¢(d); 50¢(sat); 75¢(S); $8.50/mo (carrier); $102.00/yr (carrier).
Advertising: Open inch rate $12.48(e); $12.48(m-sat); $12.48(S).
News Service: AP. **Politics:** Independent. **Established:** 1886.
Special Editions: Bridal Tab (Feb); Home Improvement (Mar); Spring Fashion, Carnegie Home Tour Tab (Apr); Old Fashioned Bargain Days, Progress (May); Father's Day, Dairy (June); Year Round School (Aug); Football, Fashion (Sept); Fall Car Care (Oct); Christmas Opening (Nov).
Special Weekly Sections: Business Page, Prime Time (mon); Best Food Day (tues); Farm Page (wed); Farm Page (fri); Church Directory, Church Page (sat); Travel, Health (S).
Magazines: TV Times (sat); Vista Magazine, USA Weekend (S).

CORPORATE OFFICERS
Board Chairman/Treasurer E W Scripps
Vice Chairman/Corporate Secretary Betty Knight Scripps
Exec Vice Pres Roger N Warkins
Vice Pres Jack C Morgan
Vice Pres-Finance Thomas E Wendel
GENERAL MANAGEMENT
Publisher Neil D Williams
Purchasing Agent Lorene Pamley
ADVERTISING
Director Robert Rankin
Manager-Classified Kevin Crawford
CIRCULATION
Director Ron Sears
NEWS EXECUTIVES
Editor Neil D Williams
Managing Editor Leah M Leach
EDITORS AND MANAGERS
Books Editor Leah M Leach
Business Editor Stacy Brouchard
Editorial Page Editor Leah M Leach
Education Editor Amos Fabian
Entertainment Editor Denis Bohannan
Environmental Editor Erik Loyd
Farm Editor Erik Loyd
Fashion/Food Editor Joan Pegues
Features Editor Chet Diestel
Films/Theater Editor Ruth Gomes
Graphics Editor Gary Kazanjian
Lifestyle Editor Joan Pegues
Medical Editor Stacy Brouchard
Military Editor Michele Seaburg
Music Editor Ruth Gomes
Photo Editor Gary Kazanjian
Political Editor Erik Loyd
Radio/Television Editor Ruth Gomes
Religion Editor Pat Browning
Science/Technology Editor Denis Bohannan
Society/Women's Editor Joan Pegues
Sports Editor Jon Earnest
Teen-Age/Youth Editor Amos Fabian
Travel Editor Chet Diestal
Wire Editor Chet Diestal
PRODUCTION
Foreman-Pressroom Doug Wyand
Superintendent Bill Theis

Market Information: Zoned editions; Split Run; TMC.
Mechanical available: Offset; Black and 3 ROP colors; insert accepted — preprinted; page cut-offs — 22¾".
Mechanical specifications: Type page 13" x 21½"; E - 6 cols, 2¹⁄₁₆", ⅛" between; A - 6 cols, 2¹⁄₁₆", ⅛" between; C - 9 cols, 1⅜", ¹⁄₁₆" between.
Commodity consumption: Newsprint 869 metric tons; widths 13¼", 27"; black ink 30,000 pounds; color ink 3,600 pounds; single pages printed 9,374; average pages per issue 26(d), 26(S); single plates used 9,500.
Equipment: EDITORIAL: Front-end hardware — 18-ScrippSat; Front-end software — PC Type; Printers — 2-QMS/810T. CLASSIFIED: Front-end hardware — 4-ScrippSat; Front-end software — Synaptic; Printers — Okidata/393, QMS. DISPLAY: Adv layout systems — 3-ScrippSat/Archetype Designer; Front-end hardware — 3-PCs; Front-end software — Archetype/Corel Draw; Printers — LaserMaster/Unity 1800x60. PRODUCTION: Typesetters — 3-QMS/PS820 Turbo Laserprinter, LaserMaster/1800x60; Plate exposures — 1-Nu/Flip Top FT40; Plate processors — 1-Graham/M-28; Scanners — HP/ScanJet IIc; Production cameras — 1-SCREEN/Companica 660c; Automatic film processors — 1-Kk/65A; Color separation equipment (conventional) — Kk/2035 Plus Film Scanner, Ap/Mac 8100/100, HP/LaserJet Scanner, LaserMaster/Unity 1800x60.
PRESSROOM: Line 1 — 7-G/Community floor, 1-G/Stacked; Folders — 1-SC. MAILROOM: Inserters and stuffers — 1-MM/227E; Bundle tyer — 1-MLN/Spirit, 1-MLN/ML 2EE. WIRE SERVICES: News — AP; Syndicates — SHNS; Receiving dishes — size-10ft, AP. BUSINESS COMPUTERS: 8-Mk/Acer; Applications: Adv billing, Payroll, Pay by mail, Circ accts; PCs & main system networked.

HAYWARD
Alameda County

'90 U.S. Census- 111,498; E&P '96 Est. 124,859
ABC-CZ (90): 257,428 (HH 90,291)

The Daily Review
(m-mon to sat; S)

The Daily Review, 116 W. Winton Ave. (94544); PO Box 5050, Hayward, CA 94540; tel (510) 783-6111; fax (510) 293-2722. MediaNews Inc. (Alameda Newspapers) group.
Circulation: 41,537(m); 41,537(m-sat); 49,536(S); ABC Sept. 30, 1995.
Price: 50¢(d); 50¢(sat); $1.25(S); $2.80/wk.
Representative: Landon Associates Inc.
News Services: NYT, AP, LAT-WP, SHNS, McClatchy. **Politics:** Independent. **Established:** 1891.
Note: Advertising is sold in combination with Fremont Argus (mS), Hayward Daily Review (mS), Oakland Tribune (mS) and Pleasanton Tri-Valley Herald (mS) for $118.00 (dS). Individual newspaper rates not made available. For detailed mechanical equipment information, see the Oakland Tribune listing.
Advertising not accepted: Coin machine buyers; mail orders.
Special Editions: East Bay Almanac (Mar); East Bay Leisure Guide (June); "Best" from Valley to the Bay (Oct); Auto, Christmas Gifts (Nov); Christmas Gifts (Dec).
Special Weekly Sections: Automotive (fri); New Homes (sat); Travel (S); CUE (daily).
Magazines: USA Weekend, TV Week (S).

CORPORATE OFFICERS
President/Publisher Peter Bernhard
Asst to Publisher/Vice Pres-Administration Patrick Brown
Senior Vice Pres-Production Dennis Miller
Senior Vice Pres-Advertising Roger Grossman
Senior Vice Pres-Circulation Arthur Farber
Senior Vice Pres/Editor in Chief David Burgin
Vice Pres-Human Resources Jim Janiga
GENERAL MANAGEMENT
Publisher Peter Bernhard
Assoc Publisher Joseph Haraburda
Manager-Human Resources Karen Austin
ADVERTISING
Director H R Autz
Director-Classified Pete Laraway
Manager-National Mary Menard
MARKETING AND PROMOTION
Director-Marketing/Promotion Service Deborah Byrum
CIRCULATION
Director Wally Tiedemann
Director-Operations Mary O'Brien
NEWS EXECUTIVES
Editor Terry Winckler
Exec Editor Nancy Conway
Managing Editor Mario Dianda
EDITORS AND MANAGERS
Books Editor Robert Taylor
Business Editor David Tong
Asst Business Editor Scott Ard
Asst City Editor Don Buchholtz
Columnist Ray Orrock
Columnist Tom Goff
Editorial Page Editor Bob Cuddy
Entertainment Editor Sharon Betz
Features Editor Sharon Betz
Asst Features Editor Richard Defendorf
Films Editor Barry Caine
Food Editor Catherine Chriss
Director-Libraries Steve Lavoie
Director-News Production Chris Campos
Director-Photo/Graphics Rob Lindquist
Sacramento Bureau Chief Sam Delson
Sports Editor Matthew Schwab
Sports Columnist Monte Poole
Sports Columnist Carl Steward
Sports Columnist Dave Newhouse
Television Editor Susan Young
Travel Editor Bari Brenner
MANAGEMENT INFORMATION SERVICES
Data Processing Manager Ken Marcum
Online Manager Kevin Hamilton
PRODUCTION
Director Dave Boyer
Manager Pete Salm

Market Information: TMC; ADS; Operate database.
Mechanical available: Black and 3 ROP colors; insert accepted — preprinted; page cut-offs — 21.5".
Mechanical specifications: Type page 13" x 21.5"; E - 6 cols, 2¹⁄₁₆"; A - 6 cols, 2¹⁄₁₆"; C - 10 cols, 1¼".
Commodity consumption: Newsprint 6,456 metric tons; widths 55", 41¼", 27⅜"; black ink 136,000 pounds; color ink 9,550 pounds; single pages printed 24,822; average pages per issue 59(d), 89(S); single plates used 27,000.
Equipment: EDITORIAL: Front-end hardware — IBM/PCs, Spear/386; Front-end software — Novell 3.11, XYQUEST/XyWrite 3.54; Printers — Okidata. CLASSIFIED: Front-end hardware — IBM/PCs, Spear/386; Front-end software — HI. DISPLAY: Adv layout systems — SCS/Layout 8000; Front-end hardware — IBM/PCs, Ap/Mac; Front-end software — HI, Multi-Ad 3.7; WIRE SERVICES: News — AP, NYT; Photos — AP; Stock tables — AP Stocks II; Receiving dishes — AP.

HEMET
Riverside County

'90 U.S. Census- 36,094; E&P '96 Est. 50,165
ABC-CZ (90): 78,666 (HH 33,526)

The Hemet News
(m-mon to sat; S)

The Hemet News, 474 W. Esplande Ave. (San Jacinto 92583); PO Box 12003, Hemet, CA 92546-8003; tel (909) 487-2200; fax (909) 487-2250. Donrey Media group.
Circulation: 12,970(m); 12,970(m-sat); 13,137(S); ABC Sept. 30, 1995.
Price: 23¢(d); 23¢(sat); 46¢(S); $1.39/wk (plus tax); $52.00/yr (plus tax).
Advertising: Open inch rate $19.15(m); $19.15(m-sat); $19.15(S). **Representative:** Papert Companies.
News Service: AP. **Politics:** Independent. **Established:** 1893.
Special Editions: Ramona Outdoor Play, Auto Care (Apr); Graduation (June); Football (Sept); Fair (Oct).
Special Weekly Sections: Food Page (wed); Weekend Entertainment (fri); Real Estate Showcase (sat); TV Calendar, Real Estate (S); Financial Pages (daily).
Magazine: 55 and Better (for seniors) (monthly).

CORPORATE OFFICERS
Founder Donald W Reynolds
President/Chief Operating Officer Emmett Jones
Exec Vice Pres/Chief Financial Officer Darrell W Loftin
Vice Pres-Western Newspaper Group David A Osborn
Vice Pres-Eastern Newspaper Group Don Schneider
GENERAL MANAGEMENT
Publisher Jim Fredericks
ADVERTISING
Director Manny Padilla
Manager-Classified Marian Evans
CIRCULATION
Director Amado Gonzalez
NEWS EXECUTIVE
Editor Craig Shultz
EDITOR AND MANAGER
Sports Editor Dan Galvis
MANAGEMENT INFORMATION SERVICES
Data Processing Manager Greg Peterson
PRODUCTION
Manager-Press/Camera George Evans

Market Information: TMC.
Mechanical available: Offset; Black and 3 ROP colors; insert accepted — preprinted; page cut-offs — 22¾".
Mechanical specifications: Type page 13" x 21½"; E - 6 cols, 2¹⁄₁₆", ⅛" between; A - 6 cols, 2¹⁄₁₆", ⅛" between; C - 9 cols, 1⁵⁄₁₆", ⅛" between.
Commodity consumption: Newsprint 165 metric tons; width 27"; black ink 38,880 pounds; color ink 5,400 pounds; average pages per issue 24(d), 89(S); single plates used 9,000.

Equipment: EDITORIAL: Front-end hardware — 23-Mk; Front-end software — Mk. CLASSIFIED: Front-end hardware — 6-Mk, 7-Ap/Mac. PRODUCTION: Pagination software — QPS; Platemaking systems — 3-M/Deadliner; Electronic picture desk — Lf/AP Leaf Picture Desk; Production cameras — Acti/204; Color separation equipment (conventional) — Ap/Mac, Adobe/Photoshop.
PRESSROOM: Line 1 — 10-G/Community 399; Line 2 — 10-G/Community 1; Folders — 1-G/2:1. MAILROOM: Counter stackers — MM; Inserters and stuffers — KAN, MM; Bundle tyer — 1-MLN, 1-Bu; Addressing machine — Ch. LIBRARY: Electronic — Data Times/PLS. WIRE SERVICES: News — AP; Photos — AP; Stock tables — AP; Receiving dishes — size-16ft, AP. BUSINESS COMPUTERS: HP; Applications: Brainworks; PCs & micros networked; PCs & main system networked.

HOLLISTER

San Benito County

'90 U.S. Census- 19,212; **E&P '96 Est.** 27,468
ABC-CZ (90): 19,212 (HH 5,896)

Free Lance (m-mon to fri)

Free Lance, 350 Sixth St. (95023); PO Box 1417, Hollister, CA 95024-1477; tel (408) 637-5566; fax (408) 637-4104. McClatchy Newspapers group.
Circulation: 4,075(m); ABC Sept. 30, 1995.
Price: 50¢(d); $7.70/mo + tax (carrier); $69.28/yr + tax (carrier).
Advertising: Open inch rate $14.80(m); comb with Gilroy Dispatch(m) $18.40. **Representative:** Papert Companies.
News Service: AP. **Politics:** Independent. **Established:** 1873.
Not Published: New Year; Christmas.
Special Weekly Sections: People (tues); Scene (fri).
Magazine: TV (thur).

GENERAL MANAGEMENT
Publisher Paula Mabry
ADVERTISING
Director/Business Manager Brenda Weatherly
MARKETING AND PROMOTION
Director-Marketing/Promotion Brenda Weatherly
CIRCULATION
Director Jonathan Hernandez
NEWS EXECUTIVES
Editor Mark Paxton
Managing Editor Wayne Norton
MANAGEMENT INFORMATION SERVICES
Data Processing Manager Gary Moore
PRODUCTION
Supervisor-Composing Sylvia Myrvold
Manager-Pressroom Sam Montoya
Manager-Pre Press Susan Ober
Manager-Packaging Center Alex Cabezas

Market Information: TMC.
Mechanical available: Offset; Black and 3 ROP colors; insert accepted — preprinted, any; page cut-offs — 22½".
Mechanical specifications: Type page 13" x 21½"; E - 6 cols, $2\frac{1}{16}$", ⅛" between; A - 6 cols, $2\frac{1}{16}$", ⅛" between; C - 10 cols, $1\frac{7}{32}$", ⅛" between.
Commodity consumption: Newsprint 120 metric tons; widths 27", 13½"; black ink 7,500 pounds; color ink 500 pounds; average pages per issue 24(d).
Equipment: EDITORIAL: Front-end hardware — Dewar/Sys IV, 10-PC/286-346 SX, Ap/Mac IIsi; Front-end software — Novell/Network; Printers — 1-Okidata. CLASSIFIED: Front-end hardware — 1-Dewar/Sys IV, 1-PC/386 SX; Printers — 1-Okidata. DISPLAY: Front-end hardware — 1-Ap/Mac SE20; Front-end software — QuarkXPress, Adobe/Photoshop; Printers — 1-Ap/Mac LaserWriter II NTX; Other equipment — 1-Dest/PC Scan 1000. PRODUCTION: Typesetters — 3-Ap/Mac LaserWriter II NTX SMB, 1-Ap/Mac LaserWriter Plus; Production cameras — 1-C/Pager, 1-SCREEN/Companica Vertical, 1-VG/Daylighter; Automatic film processors — 1-LE/24AQ, 2-LE/PC3; Film transporters — 1-C; Color separation equipment (conventional) — 1-WDS.
PRESSROOM: Line 1 — 8-G/Community, 3-DEV/Color Stack; Folders — 2-G. MAILROOM: Counter stackers — 3-BG/Count-O-Veyor, 1-Id/440; Inserters and stuffers — 1-HI/624, 1-KAN/480; Bundle tyer — 2-MLN, 2-MLN/ML1EE. WIRE SERVICES: News — AP Datafeatures, AP Datastream, AP GraphicsNet, AP; Receiving dishes — size-3m, AP. BUSINESS COMPUTERS: IBM/Sys 36; PCs & micros networked; PCs & main system networked.

IMPERIAL VALLEY

See EL CENTRO

LAKE TAHOE

See SOUTH LAKE TAHOE

LAKEPORT

Lake County

'90 U.S. Census- 4,390; **E&P '96 Est.** 4,945

Lake County Record-Bee (m-tues to sat)

Lake County Record-Bee, 2150 S. Main; PO Box 849, Lakeport, CA 95453; tel (707) 263-5636; fax (707) 263-0600. Times Publishing Inc. group.
Circulation: 8,592(m); 8,592(m-sat); Sworn Sept. 30, 1995.
Price: 50¢(d); 50¢(sat); $117.97/yr (mail).
Advertising: Open inch rate $9.98(m); $9.98(m-sat). **Representative:** Papert Companies.
News Service: AP. **Politics:** Independent. **Established:** 1873.
Special Weekly Sections: Business (tues); Best Food Day (wed); Business (thur); Real Estate (fri).
Magazines: USA Weekend, TV Spotlight (sat).

CORPORATE OFFICERS
President Edward M Mead
Vice Pres Michael Mead
GENERAL MANAGEMENT
Business Manager Karen Streim
ADVERTISING
Director Debbie Geissler
CIRCULATION
Supervisor Kim Robbins
NEWS EXECUTIVES
Managing Editor Cliff Larimer
News Editor Greg Bucci
EDITOR AND MANAGER
Sports Editor Brian Sumpter
PRODUCTION
Manager Roy Dufrain Jr

Market Information: TMC.
Mechanical available: Offset; Black and 2 ROP colors; insert accepted — preprinted, 8½" x 11"; page cut-offs — 22¾".
Mechanical specifications: Type page 13" x 21"; E - 6 cols, $2\frac{1}{16}$", ⅛" between; A - 6 cols, $2\frac{1}{16}$", ⅛" between; C - 8 cols, 1½", ⅛" between.
Commodity consumption: Newsprint 900 metric tons; widths 28", 35"; black ink 11,000 pounds; single pages printed 6,500; average pages per issue 16(d); single plates used 8,000.
Equipment: EDITORIAL: Front-end hardware — 6-Ap/Mac, CText; Front-end software — QuarkXPress; Printers — Ap/Mac LaserWriter NTX. CLASSIFIED: Front-end hardware — 2-Synaptic, 2-IBM; Printers — Ap/Mac LaserWriter. DISPLAY: Front-end hardware — 2-Ap/Mac II, 1-Ap/Mac IIci; Front-end software — DTI/Ad Speed 3.0; Printers — Ap/Mac LaserWriter IIg; Other equipment — Microtek/Scanner. PRODUCTION: Typesetters — 2-Ap/Mac LaserWriter; Plate exposures — 1-Nu; Production cameras — SCREEN/250; Automatic film processors — Kk.
PRESSROOM: Line 1 — 6-WPC/Web Leader. MAILROOM: Inserters and stuffers — 6-MM/227; Bundle tyer — 2-Bu; Addressing machine — 1-Ch. WIRE SERVICES: News — AP; Receiving dishes — AP. BUSINESS COMPUTERS: DEC/Micro VAX 3100-40; Applications: Circ, Accts receivable, Gen ledger, Payroll, Spreadsheets, Filing; Word Processing; PCs & micros networked; PCs & main system networked.

LODI

San Joaquin County

'90 U.S. Census- 51,874; **E&P '96 Est.** 67,706
ABC-CZ (90): 51,874 (HH 19,001)

Lodi News-Sentinel

(m-mon to sat)

Lodi News-Sentinel, 125 N. Church St.; PO Box 1360, Lodi, CA 95241; tel (209) 369-2761; fax (209) 369-1084.
Circulation: 17,561(m); 17,561(m-sat); ABC Sept. 30, 1995.
Price: 35¢(d); 35¢(sat); $6.75/mo; $81.00/yr.
Advertising: Open inch rate $13.50(m); $13.50(m-sat). **Representative:** Papert Companies.
News Services: AP, San Joaquin News Service, CNS, McClatchy. **Politics:** Independent. **Established:** 1881.
Not Published: New Year; Memorial Day; Independence Day; Labor Day; Veteran's Day; Christmas.
Advertising not accepted: X-rated.
Special Editions: Brides (Feb); Home Improvement (Mar); California Real Estate (Apr); Grape & Wine Festival (Sept); Christmas (Dec).
Special Weekly Sections: Business/Stock Market (tues); Business/Stock Market, Best Food Day (wed); Business/Stock Market (thur); Business/Stock Market, Farm and Garden, The Entertainer, Entertainment and TV Tab (fri); Real Estate, Church (sat).

CORPORATE OFFICERS
Chairman Fred Weybret
President Marty Weybret
Secretary/Treasurer Jim Weybret
GENERAL MANAGEMENT
Co-Publisher Jim Weybret
Co-Publisher/Editor Marty Weybret
Business Manager Jim Weybret
ADVERTISING
Manager Dan Battilana
Manager-Classified David Phillips
CIRCULATION
Manager Gary Greider
NEWS EXECUTIVE
Editor Marty Weybret
EDITORS AND MANAGERS
Business/Finance Editor Hal Silliman
City Editor Michele Drier
Editorial Page Editor Fred Weybret
Education Editor Toni Mata
Entertainment/Amusements Editor Monique Beeler
Environmental Editor O J Solander
Farm Editor Hal Silliman
Fashion/Style Editor Ellen Chrismer
Features Editor Ellen Chrismer
Graphics Editor/Art Director Eric Johnston
Health/Medical Editor Toni Mata
Living/Lifestyle Editor Ellen Chrismer
Photo Editor Eric Johnson
Political/Government Editor Michele Drier
Religion Editor Monique Beeler
Science/Technology Editor Toni Mata
Sports Editor Richard Myers
Television/Film Editor Monique Beeler
Theater/Music Editor Monique Beeler
Women's Editor Ellen Chrismer
MANAGEMENT INFORMATION SERVICES
Data Processing Manager Jim Broderick
PRODUCTION
Foreman-Composing Bernie Shannon
Foreman-Pressroom Joe Mistretta

Market Information: TMC.
Mechanical available: Offset; Black and 3 ROP colors; insert accepted — preprinted; page cut-offs — 22¾".
Mechanical specifications: Type page 13" x 21½"; E - 6 cols, $2\frac{1}{16}$", ⅛" between; A - 6 cols, $2\frac{1}{16}$", ⅛" between; C - 8 cols, 1½", ⅛" between.
Commodity consumption: Newsprint 877 metric tons; widths 27½", 13¾"; black ink 29,640 pounds; color ink 3,420 pounds; single pages printed 8,496; average pages per issue 26(d), 36(sat); single plates used 7,500.
Equipment: EDITORIAL: Front-end hardware — 17-CText; Front-end software — CText; Printers — XIT/Navigator, XIT/Clipper. CLASSIFIED: Front-end hardware — 6-CText; Front-end software — CText. DISPLAY: Adv layout systems — SCS/Layout 8000; Front-end hardware — 4-PC/486; Front-end software — Archetype/Designer, Archetype/Coral Draw 5.0, Quark XPress. PRODUCTION: OCR software — WordScan/Plus 2.0; Typesetters — ECR/VRL 36; Plate exposures — 1-B/5000; Plate processors — 1-Nat/A-250; Electronic picture desk — Lf/AP Leaf Picture Desk, Adobe Photoshop; Scanners — Microtek/1850 si, HP/ScanJet IIcx; Production cameras — 1-Acti; Automatic film processors — P/2024; Color separation equipment (conventional) — Lf/AP Leaf Picture Desk.
PRESSROOM: Line 1 — 12-RKW, G/Community single width; Folders — 2-G/2:1. MAILROOM: Counter stackers — 1-KAN; Inserters and stuffers — 1-KAN/6 station; Bundle tyer — 1-MLN; Addressing machine — 1-St. LIBRARY: Electronic — SMS/Stauffer Gold, Ap/Mac SE30. COMMUNICATIONS: Systems used — satellite. WIRE SERVICES: News — AP; Photos — AP; Receiving dishes — size-3m, AP. BUSINESS COMPUTERS: 1-MBF/2000; Applications: Payroll, Gen ledger, Accts receivable, Accts payable; PCs & main system networked.

LOMPOC

Santa Barbara County

'90 U.S. Census- 37,649; **E&P '96 Est.** 48,229
ABC-CZ (90): 46,744 (HH 15,794)

The Lompoc Record

(e-mon to fri; S)

The Lompoc Record, 115 N. H St.; PO Box 578, Lompoc, CA 93436; tel (805) 736-2313; fax (805) 736-5654. Donrey Media group.
Circulation: 8,520(e); 8,985(S); ABC Sept. 30, 1995.
Price: 50¢(d); $1.00(S); $7.35/mo (local), $10.97/mo (elsewhere).
Advertising: Open inch rate $11.79(e); $11.79(S). **Representative:** Papert Companies.
News Service: AP. **Politics:** Independent. **Established:** 1875.
Special Editions: Flower Festival Section (June); Welcome to the Central Coast (Aug).
Special Weekly Sections: Business Page (tues); Real Estate (wed); Business Page (thur); Valley Living, Dining Page, Church Page, Best Automobile Days (fri); Lifestyles, Best Automobile Days (S).
Magazines: TV Record (fri); USA Weekend (S).

CORPORATE OFFICERS
Founder Donald W Reynolds
President/Chief Operating Officer Emmett Jones
Exec Vice Pres/Chief Financial Officer Darrell W Loftin
Vice Pres-Western Newspaper Group David A Osborn
Vice Pres-Eastern Newspaper Group Don Schneider
GENERAL MANAGEMENT
Publisher Ron Hoffer
ADVERTISING
Manager Dick Bausman
CIRCULATION
Manager Tom Wilcox
NEWS EXECUTIVE
Editor Rita-Helen Henning
EDITORS AND MANAGERS
Aviation/Space Editor Matt Hoy
Family/Society Editor Margaret Miranda
Health/Schools Editor Katherine McDonald
News Editor Steve Brown
Political Editor Michael Branom
Sports Editor Alan Hunt
Women's Editor Margaret Miranda
PRODUCTION
Supervisor-Pressroom John Gonzales
Supervisor-Composing Room Lorri Schludecker

Market Information: TMC.
Mechanical available: Web Offset; Black and 3 ROP colors; insert accepted — preprinted; page cut-offs — 21½".
Mechanical specifications: Type page 13" x 21½"; E - 6 cols, $2\frac{1}{16}$", .14" between; A - 6 cols, $2\frac{1}{16}$", .14" between; C - 8 cols, 1½", ⅛" between.
Commodity consumption: Newsprint 500 metric tons; width 27"; black ink 10,000 pounds; color ink 396 pounds; single pages printed 6,544; average pages per issue 20(d), 28(S); single plates used 3,272.
Equipment: EDITORIAL: Front-end hardware — Mk/1100 Plus; Front-end software — Mk/1100 Plus; Printers — TI/Omni 800, Ap/Mac LaserWriter II NTX; Other equipment — Ap/Mac Quadra. CLASSIFIED: Front-end hardware — Mk; Front-end software — Mk; Printers — TI/Omni 800. DISPLAY: Front-end hardware — Ap/Mac IIci, Ap/Mac IIcx, Ap/Mac NTX; Front-end software — Mk, Multi-Ad/Creator; Printers — LM/1200. PRODUCTION: Typesetters — 2-COM; Platemaking systems — 3M/Pyrofax (Off-

Copyright ©1996 by the Editor & Publisher Co.

California I-35

set Web); Production cameras — Nu/Horizontal Camera.
PRESSROOM: Line 1 — 5-G/Community; Line 2 — 2-G/Community; Folders — G/Community, G/SC. MAILROOM: Bundle tyer — 1-Cyclone/TM45, 1-Bu, MLN/MS2. WIRE SERVICES: News — AP; Stock tables — AP; Syndicates — NAS, TMS, King Features, United Media, Universal Press, TV Data; Receiving dishes — size-10m, AP. BUSINESS COMPUTERS: HP/System 3000; Applications: CJ/AIM 7.0.

LONG BEACH

Los Angeles County

'90 U.S. Census- 429,433; E&P '96 Est. 482,071
ABC-CZ (90): 516,859 (HH 189,906)

Press-Telegram

(m-mon to fri; m-sat; S)

Press-Telegram, 604 Pine Ave.; PO Box 230, Long Beach, CA 90844; tel (310) 435-1161; fax (310) 435-5415. Knight-Ridder Inc. group.
Circulation: 109,029(m); 106,472(m-sat); 130,979(S); ABC Sept. 25, 1995.
Price: 35¢(d); 35¢(sat); $1.25(S); $2.00/wk (carrier); $104.00/yr (carrier).
Advertising: Open inch rate $82.82(m); $82.82(m-sat); $94.97(S). **Representative:** Sawyer-Ferguson-Walker Co.
News Services: AP, KRT, NYT. **Politics:** Independent. **Established:** 1885.
Advertising not accepted: All advertising subject to approval of management.
Special Weekly Sections: Business Monday (mon); Fitness (tues); Local News (wed); Food (thur); Weekend Plus including Dining (tab) (fri); TV (quarterfold).
Magazine: Parade (S).

CORPORATE OFFICERS

President Richard J Sadowski
Senior Vice Pres/Exec Editor James Crutchfield
Vice Pres/Chief Financial Officer Ray MacLean
Vice Pres-Advertising Margaret Krost
Vice Pres David Stoltler
Vice Pres/Asst Treasurer Ross Jones
Secretary Douglas C Harris
Asst Treasurer Stephen H Sheriff
Asst Secretary Ana Sejeck

GENERAL MANAGEMENT

Publisher Richard J Sadowski
Senior Vice Pres/Exec Editor James Crutchfield
Vice Pres-Human Resources Jack Wilson
Vice Pres-Advertising Margaret Krost
Vice Pres-Circulation David Stotler
Vice Pres/Managing Editor Richard Archbold
Vice Pres-Administration Ray MacLean
Director-Production Harold Davies
Director-Marketing & Promotion Denny Freidenrich
Director-Info & Technical Services Dick Brodowski
Editor Larry Allison

ADVERTISING

Vice Pres Margaret Krost
Manager-Retail Dave Lite
Manager-Classified Gene Pearlman
Director-Marketing/Promotion Denny Freidenrich

CIRCULATION

Vice Pres David Stotler

NEWS EXECUTIVES

Exec Editor James Crutchfield
Exec Editor-News Tim O'Mara
Exec Editor-Sports Jim McCormack
Managing Editor Richard Archbold
Asst Managing Editor Carolyn Roszkiewicz

EDITORS AND MANAGERS

Business Editor Andy Alderette
Computer Assisted Reporting Editor John Zappe
City Editor (Day) Andy Rose
Asst City Editor Julie Gallego
Columnist George Robeson
Columnist Tom Hennessy
Columnist Chris Christensen
Columnist Ralph De la Cruz
Editorial Page Editor Larry Allison
Education Reporter Dan DeVise
Enterprise Editor Jim Robinson
Entertainment Editor Stephanie Goodman
Food Editor Debbie Arrington
Asst News Editor-Graphics Janice Kowalski
Librarian Bob Andrew
Lifestyle Editor Susan Jacobs
Photo Director Hal Wells
Radio/Television Editor Robin Deemer
Restaurant Reviews Editor Al Rudis
Sports Editor Jim Buzinski
Travel Editor Susan Jacobs

MANAGEMENT INFORMATION SERVICES

Data Processing Manager John Joerger

PRODUCTION

Director Harold Davies
Manager-Composing/Engraving Peter Berregard
Manager-Printing/Packaging John Sharp
Manager-Ad Service/Make-Up Joan Sistek
Manager-Maintenance Nick Lincir
Manager-Publishing Systems Paul Borza
Asst Manager-Mailroom Steven Mueller
Asst-Pressroom Robert Louwsma

Market Information: Zoned editions; TMC; Operate audiotex.
Mechanical available: Letterpress/Flexo; Black and 3 ROP colors; insert accepted — preprinted; page cut-offs — 22¾".
Mechanical specifications: Type page 13" x 21½"; E - 6 cols, 2¹⁄₁₆", ⅛" between; A - 6 cols, 2¹⁄₁₆", ⅛" between; C - 10 cols, 1¼", ¹⁄₁₆" between.
Commodity consumption: Newsprint 16,000 metric tons; widths 54", 40½", 27"; black ink 587,000 pounds; color ink 90,000 pounds; single pages printed 23,200; average pages per issue 52(d), 100(S); single plates used 85,000.
Equipment: EDITORIAL: Front-end hardware — SII/Tandem CLX; Front-end software — SII/Editorial. CLASSIFIED: Front-end hardware — SII/Tandem CLX; Front-end software — SII/CZAR. DISPLAY: Adv layout systems — SCS/Layout 8000, SII/IAL; Front-end hardware — 6-Ap/Mac Quadra 800; Front-end software — Ap/Mac AdSpeed, QuarkXPress; Other equipment — 1-SII/Echo, Mac DB Server, CJ/Ad Tracking. PRODUCTION: Typesetters — 2-AU/APS6-108C, AU/Soft PIP RIPS; Platemaking systems — Na; Plate exposures — 2-Na/Starlite, 2-Na/Consolux; Plate processors — 2-Na/NP-80, 1-Na/NP-20, 2-Na/Flex FP II; Electronic picture desk — Lf/AP Leaf Picture Desk; Scanners — ECR/Autokon 1000, AG/Arcus, RZ/210L Scanner, Howtek/D4000; Production cameras — 1-C/Newspager, C/Spartan III; Automatic film processors — Le/XL, Le/Tek26; Film transporters — 2-LE. PRESSROOM: Line 1 — 4-MOT/FX4, 2-MOT/FX4 half decks double width; Line 2 — 11-G/Headliner Mark 1, 7-G/Deck double width; Line 3 — G/Headliner Mark 1, G/Double out 2-to-1; Line 4 — 1-G/Single out; Folders — G/Headliner, G/Headliner 2:1; Pasters — Cline; Reels and stands — G; Press control system — Hurletron. MAILROOM: Counter stackers — 3-HL, 4-Id; Inserters and stuffers — 1-HI/1372, 1-GMA/SLS 1000, 1-OVL; Bundle tyer — 5-MLN, 2-Power Strap; Wrapping singles — 5-Id, 3-Power Strap. LIBRARY: Electronic — 1-Vu/Text SAVE. WIRE SERVICES: News — AP, NYT, KRT, CNS; Photos — AP Photostream; Stock tables — AP SelectStox; Receiving dishes — size-8ft, AP. BUSINESS COMPUTERS: HP/Series 70, HP/3000 Series 967; Applications: CJ/AIM 7.01.G, CJ/Layout 5.01.E, CJ/AD Tracking 5.01.C, CJ/CIS 4.01.H, CJ/Payroll 2.09.M, CJ/Accounts Payable 8.02.D, CJ/General Ledger 7.02.D, MicroSoft/Office Window, MicroSoft/Access Window 2.0, Adobe/Photoshop 3.01, Adobe/Illustrator, QuarkXPress, CJ/AIM: Circ, Adv, Payroll; PCs & micros networked; PCs & main system networked.

LOS ANGELES

Los Angeles County

'90 U.S. Census- 3,485,398; E&P '96 Est. 3,851,616
La Opinion:
ABC-NDM (90): 11,273,720 (HH 3,816,618)
News:
ABC-NDM (90): 2,292,312 (HH 804,456)
Times:
ABC-NDM (90): 11,273,720 (HH 3,816,618)

Daily Commerce (e-mon to fri)

Daily Commerce, 915 E. First St.; PO Box 54026, Los Angeles, CA 90012-4042; tel (213) 229-5300; fax (213) 680-3682. Daily Journal Corp. group.
Circulation: 2,407(e); Sworn Sept. 30, 1994.
Price: $1.00(d); $165.00/yr.
Advertising: Open inch rate $27.00(e).
News Services: AP, LAT-WP, NYT. **Politics:** Independent. **Established:** 1917.
Special Edition: Special Focus (monthly).
Magazine: Real Estate in Review (monthly).

CORPORATE OFFICER

Publisher Nell Fields

ADVERTISING

Representative Joanne McCulloch

CIRCULATION

Manager Eric Lowenback

NEWS EXECUTIVES

Editor Darrell Lippman
Managing Editor Darrell Lippman

Mechanical available: Offset; Black and 4 ROP colors; insert accepted — preprinted; page cut-offs — 11".
Mechanical specifications: Type page 10" x 13½"; E - 4 cols, 2", ¼" between; A - 4 cols, 2⅜", ½" between; C - 3 cols, 3", ½" between.
Commodity consumption: average pages per issue 64(d).
Equipment: EDITORIAL: Front-end hardware — AT, IBM/486, Viewsonic/20 inch monitor; Front-end software — Automated Complete Typesetting, Microsoft 2.1, QPS 3.1; Printers — HP/LaserJet. CLASSIFIED: Front-end hardware — AT. PRODUCTION: Typesetters — 3-COM/8600; Platemaking systems — 3M/Deadliners.

Daily News

(m-mon to fri; m-sat; S)

Daily News, PO Box 4200, Woodland Hills, CA 91365-4200; tel (818) 713-3000; fax (818) 713-0057.
Circulation: 201,239(m); 182,010(m-sat); 219,052(S); ABC Sept. 30, 1995.
Price: 25¢(d); 25¢(sat); $1.00(S); $2.29/wk (plus tax); $9.16/mo (plus tax); $119.00/yr (plus tax).
Advertising: Open inch rate $128.27(m); $137.76(m-fri); $128.27(m-sat); $141.66 (S). **Representative:** Cresmer, Woodward, O'Mara & Ormsbee.
News Services: AP, KRT, NYT, City News Service, McClatchy. **Politics:** Independent. **Established:** 1911.
Advertising not accepted: All advertising subject to publisher's approval.
Special Weekly Sections: Monday Business, Auto-Auto World (mon); Best Food Day (thur); LA Life Weekend, High School Football Special (in season) (fri); High School Football Special (in season) (sat); Travel, Women (S).
Magazines: Real Estate Sections (sat); USA Weekend, TV Book, Real Estate Sections (S).

CORPORATE OFFICERS

Board Chairman Jack Kent Cooke
President/CEO Larry T Beasley

GENERAL MANAGEMENT

Publisher Larry T Beasley
Chief Financial Officer Richard Kasper
Controller Terri Nelson
Manager-Public Relations Bill Vanlaningham

ADVERTISING

Director Kevin E Drolet
Manager-Retail Michael McMullin
Manager-Classified Melene Alfonso
Manager-National Charlene Moerson
Manager-Operations Truman Beasley

MARKETING AND PROMOTION

Director-Marketing Bill Vanlaningham
Manager-Marketing Research/Development Kymberlee Raven

TELECOMMUNICATIONS

Manager-Telecommunications Charles Colby

CIRCULATION

Director Martha J Thompson
Manager-Single Copy Sales David Lack
Manager-Newspapers in Education Joni Roan
Manager-Operations Ron Hasse
Manager-Customer Relations Regina Farmer
Manager-Sales & Marketing Michael Beach

NEWS EXECUTIVES

Editor Robert W Lund
Managing Editor Ron Kaye
Asst Managing Editor Barbara Jones
Asst Managing Editor Mark Barnhill

EDITORS AND MANAGERS

Art Director Gregg Miller
Business Editor Christopher Gessel
City Editor John Corrigan
Columnist Dennis McCarthy
Courts/Police Editor Steve Getzug
Editorial Page Editor Mark Lacter
Entertainment Columnist Phil Rosenthal
Entertainment/Book Editor Robert Lowman
Films Critic Bob Strauss
Food Editor Natalie Haughton
Government/Politics Editor Beth Barrett
LA Life Editor Joe Franco
Chief Librarian Margaret Douglas
Deputy LA Life Editor Lisa Girion
News Editor Rick Quist
Photography Director Dean Musgrove
Restaurant Critic Larry Lipson
Sports Editor Michael Anastasi
Sports Columnist Michael Ventre
Travel Editor Susan Hopkins
Television Columnist Ray Richmond

MANAGEMENT INFORMATION SERVICES

Manager-Management Info Services Charles Colby

PRODUCTION

Director John Webb
Manager-Pressroom Gary Kozlowski
Manager-Mailroom Eduardo Covarrubias

Market Information: Zoned editions; TMC; ADS.
Mechanical available: Offset; Black and 3 ROP colors; insert accepted — preprinted, product samples; page cut-offs — 22".
Mechanical specifications: Type page 13⅝" x 22"; E - 6 cols, 2½", ⅛" between; A - 6 cols, 2½", ⅛" between; C - 10 cols, 1⅜", ¹⁄₁₆" between.
Commodity consumption: Newsprint 47,698.95 short tons; 43,272.20 metric tons; widths 54½", 40¹¹⁄₁₆", 27⅛", 13⅝"; black ink 820,602 pounds; color ink 273,809 pounds; single pages printed 45,251; average pages per issue 86(d), 155(S); single plates used 392,195.
Equipment: EDITORIAL: Front-end hardware — 4-DEC/PDP 11-84, CSI/112B, 25-AT/PC Remote; Front-end software — CCSI. CLASSIFIED: Front-end hardware — 3-DEC/PDP 11-84, CSI/112B; Front-end software — CCSI. DISPLAY: Adv layout systems — SCS/Layout 8000; Printers — Seimens-Nixdorf. PRODUCTION: Pagination software — DTI; Typesetters — 2-AU/APS-6-108, 1-ECR/Scripsetter VR 36, 3-AU/3850; Platemaking systems — WL/Offset; Plate exposures — 2-WL/Lith-X-Pozer 3; Plate processors — 2-Anocoil/XPH36 Processors; Electronic picture desk — 2-Lf/AP Leaf Picture Disk, 6-Ap/Mac Scanning Station, 3-Ap/Mac Picture Disk; Scanners — 1-CD/Page FAX, 2-APS FAX; Production cameras — C/Spartan III; Automatic film processors — 1-P/26"RA, 2-C/OL Conveyor Systems, 2-P, 1-SCREEN/LD-281-Q, 2-Konica/K400, 2-Konica/K550; Shrink lenses — 1-CK Optical/6% Shrink; Color separation equipment (conventional) — DTI.
PRESSROOM: Line 1 — 11-G/Headliner Offset double width; Line 2 — 11-G/Headliner Offset double width; Line 3 — 11-G/Headliner Offset double width; Press drives — Allen Bradley; Folders — 3-G/3:2; Pasters — 10-GH/Digital; Reels and stands — 30-G; Press control system — G/PC; Press registration system — Pin. MAILROOM: Counter stackers — 10-Hall/Monitor HT; Inserters and stuffers — 2-AM Graphics/1472, 1-AM Gaphics/1372; Bundle tyer — 2-MLN/2A, 10-Power Strap/PSN; Wrapping singles — 10-HL/440 Bottom Wrap. LIBRARY: Electronic — Dialog/(File 716), DataTimes/(LAD), Westlaw/(DNLA), AOL/(Mercury Center); Combination — 1-Minolta/Reader-Printer RP 507. COMMUNICATIONS: Facsimile — AU/APS Fax; Remote imagesetting — III/3850's. WIRE SERVICES: News — AP, City News Service, KRT, NYT, TMS, UPI; Receiving dishes — size-10ft, AP. BUSINESS COMPUTERS: DEC/Micro VAX, 4-DEC/VAX 8550; Applications: CJ: Billing; Ross: Finance; In-house: Circ; PCs & micros networked; PCs & main system networked.

Investor's Business Daily

(m-mon to fri)

Investor's Business Daily, 12655 Beatrice St., Los Angeles, CA 90066; tel (310) 448-6700; fax (310) 557-7350; web site http://ibd.ensemble.com (to download access software).
Circulation: 193,459(m); ABC Sept. 30, 1995.
Price: 75¢(d); $189.00/yr; $103.00/6 mos.
Advertising: Open inch rate $89.45(m); $99.29 (m-mon).
News Services: AP, UPI. **Established:** 1984.
Not Published: Jan 1; Feb 19; May 27; July 4; Sept 2; Nov 21; Dec 25.
Special Editions: Retail Sales (monthly); Short Interest (mid month); Mutual Funds Expanded Reports (1st fri/month); Quarterly Winners & Losers, Year End Prices, Annual Reports (six times/yr).
Special Weekly Sections: Management & Leadership; Human Resources; Finance, Taxes &

Accounting; Information Technology; Sales & Marketing-Executive News Summary; In Brief; National Issues; Leaders & Success; News for You; Investor's Corner; Computers & Technology; Washington & The World; Executive Update; The New America; New Issue Update; The Economy; Vital Signs; World Economy Update; Perspective; Business Pulse.

CORPORATE OFFICERS

Chairman William J O'Neil
Publisher W Scott O'Neil

GENERAL MANAGEMENT

Vice Pres Margo Schuster
Manager/Controller Juan Salcedo
Director (Finadco Agency) Jacque Garrison

ADVERTISING

Vice Pres-West Coast Terri L Ayers
Vice Pres-East Coast Sharon Scott

MARKETING AND PROMOTION

Manager-Marketing Harlan B Ratzky

CIRCULATION

Manager-National Ed Levy
Manager-West Coast Doug Stone
Manager-Mid West Joe Devitto
Manager-East Coast Alan Rafal
Manager-Fulfillment Pedro Olivo

NEWS EXECUTIVES

Editor Wesley F Mann
Senior Editor Susan Warfel
Senior Editor Terry Lee Jones
Senior Editor Robert Golum
Senior Editor Michael Woods
Senior Editor Thomas S Gray
Senior Editor Mark Cunningham
Senior Editor Christopher T Warden
Senior Editor Peter K Phabe

EDITORS AND MANAGERS

Computers & Technology Susan Warfel
Economics Christopher T Warden
Editorial Page Editor Mark Cunningham
Financial Markets/New America Michael Woods
Leaders & Success Thomas S Gray
Management Issues Peter K Phabe
News Editor Robert Golum
Political/Government Editor Christopher T Warden

MANAGEMENT INFORMATION SERVICES

Manager-Management Info Services Jim Stateler

PRODUCTION

Manager Harry Weitzel

Market Information: Operate database.
Mechanical available: Web Offset; Black page cut-offs — 22¾".
Mechanical specifications: Type page 14" x 21½"; E - 6 cols, 2¹⁄₁₆", ⅛" between; A - 6 cols, 2¹⁄₁₆", ⅛" between; C - 9 cols, 1½", ¹⁄₁₆" between.
Commodity consumption: Newsprint 4,876 short tons; 4,425 metric tons; widths 27.5", 13.75"; black ink 74,000 pounds; average pages per issue 46(d); single plates used 11,592.
Equipment: EDITORIAL: Front-end hardware — HAS/HS58; Front-end software — HAS/Tops 5 2.4; Printers — Printronix/p600, HP/LaserJet II; Other equipment — Ap/Mac, NewGen/PS660. CLASSIFIED: Front-end hardware — HAS; Front-end software — HAS/Tops 5 2.4; Printers — Printronix/p600. DISPLAY: Adv layout systems — HAS, Ap/Mac; Front-end hardware — HAS, Ap/Mac; Front-end software — Adobe/Pagemaker 5.0, QuarkXPress 3.31, HAS/Tops 5 2.4, Adobe/Photoshop 3.1, Adobe/Illustrator 3.2; Printers — Ap/Mac LaserWriter NTII, Ap/Mac LaserWriter IIg. PRODUCTION: Pagination software — HAS/Tops 5 2.4; Typesetters — MON/Laser, Linotype-Hel/500; Platemaking systems — W; Plate exposures — 1-Nu; Plate processors — W; Direct-to-plate imaging — CD; Scanners — CD, ECR/Autokon, 2-III/3750; Production cameras — SCREEN/Photace DS C 260D; Automatic film processors — 2-P/OC 260; Reproportion units — ECR/Autokon 1000, III/3750, SCREEN/Photace DS C 260D; Film transporters — 2-P/SC 2070; Digital color separation equipment — ECR/Autokon. PRESSROOM: Line 1 — 10-G/Urbanite single width, 10-RKW/U5055 single width, 3-RKW/U5055 single width; Press drives — 2-Fin/SPC 3000, 1-Fin/SPC 3000; Folders — 1-RKW/U5055; Pasters — 3-Jardis/FP4540, 10-Jardis/FP4540; Reels and stands — G; Press control system — G. MAILROOM: Counter stackers — Id/NS660; Bundle tyer — OVL/JP80, OVL/Constellation K-101; Addressing machine — KAN/500 BLZ, Videojet. LIBRARY: Combination — PC/Lexus-Nexus. COMMUNICATIONS: Facsimile — 2-III/3750, Scitex/RKOH Tp-25; Remote imagesetting — III/3810, III/3850; Digital ad delivery system — AdSat, AP AdSend. WIRE SERVICES: News — AP, UPI; Stock tables — AP, UPI; Receiving dishes — size-7m, AP, UPI. BUSINESS COMPUTERS: Bs/A9; Applications: Circ, Editorial; PCs & micros networked; PCs & main system networked.

La Opinion (Spanish)

(m-mon to fri; m-sat; S)

La Opinion, 411 W. 5th St.; PO Box 15093, Los Angeles, CA 90015; tel (213) 622-8332; fax (213) 896-2151.
Circulation: 103,701(m); 87,878(m-sat); 67,106(S); ABC Sept. 30, 1995.
Price: 35¢(d); 35¢(sat); 75¢(S); $22.50/mo; $90.00/yr (carrier), $140.00/yr (mail).
Advertising: Open inch rate $34.96(m); $34.96(m-sat); $34.96(S).
News Services: AP, UPI, EFE, CNS, LAT-WP, AFP, NOTIMEX. **Politics:** Independent. **Established:** 1926.
Advertising not accepted: Immigration (except attorneys); Fortune Tellers; Firearms (except sporting); Abortion.
Special Editions: Special holiday editions on Cinco de Mayo (May 5th); Sept 16 and Christmas.
Special Weekly Sections: Medical Directory, Automotive Directory (wed); Comida (Food Section) (thur); Local Sports Section (fri); Automotive Directory (sat); Vida y Estilo (Life & Style), Comentarios (Commentaries), Teleguia, Color Comics, Espectaculos (Spectaculars), Medical Directory, Acceso (lifestyle section) (S).
Magazines: Esta Semana de Espectaculos (This Week of Spectaculars) (entertainment) (fri); Bienes Raices (Real Estate) (monthly).

GENERAL MANAGEMENT

President/Publisher Jose I Lozano
Chairman/Editor in Chief Ignacio E Lozano Jr
Vice Pres-Sales & Marketing Claudette LaCour
Assoc Publisher/Editor Monica Lozano
General Manager Horacio Martinez
Chief Financial Officer Gil Garcia
Manager-Corporate Affairs Estela Herrera

ADVERTISING

Director-Display Luis Duran
Director-Classified Guillermina Stouwie

MARKETING AND PROMOTION

Director-Marketing Will Mandeville

TELECOMMUNICATIONS

Audiotex Manager Marie Stouwie

CIRCULATION

Director Leslie Smith

NEWS EXECUTIVES

Editor in Chief Ignacio E Lozano Jr
Assoc Editor Gerardo Lopez

EDITORS AND MANAGERS

Assignment Editor Roger Lindo
Business Editor Roger Rivero
Copy Editor Hugo Valicente
Editorial Editor Rapael Buitrago
Entertainment Editor Hugo Quintana
Features Editor Josephina Vidal
Food Editor Katia Ramirez
Latin America Editor Raymundo Reynose
Managing Editor-Entertainment Antonio Mejia
Metro Editor Jesus Hernandez
National Editor Henrik Rehbinder
Special Sections Editor Cruz Alberto Mendez
Sports Editor Fernando Paramo
State Editor Jaime Olivares
TV Guide Editor Blanca Arroyo

MANAGEMENT INFORMATION SERVICES

Director-Management Info Services Paul Mascarella

PRODUCTION

Manager Bill Mumaw
Asst Manager Agustine Rosales

Market Information: Operate audiotex.
Mechanical available: Open Web Offset; Black and 3 ROP colors; insert accepted — upon approval; page cut-offs — 22¾".
Mechanical specifications: Type page 13" x 21½"; E - 6 cols, 2¹⁄₁₆", ³⁄₁₆" between; A - 6 cols, 2¹⁄₁₆", 1¹⁄₁₆" between; C - 10 cols, 1⅜".
Commodity consumption: Newsprint 15,000 metric tons; widths 27½", 13¾"; black ink 321,984 pounds; color ink 42,000 pounds; single pages printed 17,618; average pages per issue 46(d), 40(sat), 60(S); single plates used 40,000.
Equipment: EDITORIAL: Front-end hardware — 52-SII/K-100 Himalaya Risc; Other equipment — RSK/Tandy 2000. CLASSIFIED: Front-end hardware — 52-SII/K-100 Himalaya Risc. PRODUCTION: Typesetters — 2-COM/8600, 1-ECR/VR 36, 1-ECR/VR 30, 1-AG/Arcus; Plate exposures — 2-Magnum/437-D5 7.5 kw; Plate processors — 2-WL/Aqualith 32; Scanners — 1-Nikon/Slide Scanner, 1-Optronics/Prosetter Drum Scanner, 1-Ap/Mac Quadra 950, 1-Ap/Mac Quadra 650; Production cameras — R/500, 1-B/Horizontal; Automatic film processors — 2-P/32 MQ. PRESSROOM: Line 1 — 9-G/Urbanite (s/w U1247); Line 2 — 9-G/Urbanite (s/w U1379); Pasters — 18-Enkel/Autoweb 2500; Press control system — Fin/Consoles. MAILROOM: Counter stackers — 3-NJP, 1-EZ; Bundle tyer — 2-Bu/Tristar 210, 3-OVL/415; Addressing machine — 1-BH, Ap/IIe. LIBRARY: Combination — X. WIRE SERVICES: News — AP Datastream (English), AP (Spanish), UPI (Spanish), EFE, Notimex, CNS, AFP; Syndicates — United Features, Argentine Regional Press, LAT-WP, CNS; Receiving dishes — size-3ft, AP, UPI, AFP, Notimex. BUSINESS COMPUTERS: PBS/Business System, IBM/380 Risc System; Applications: DSI/Papertrack: Accounting, Circ billing, Subscriber billing; PCs & micros networked; PCs & main system networked.

Los Angeles Times

(m-mon to fri; m-sat; S)

Los Angeles Times, Times Mirror Square, Los Angeles, CA 90053; tel (213) 237-5000; e-mail letters@news.latimes.com; web site http://www.latimes.com. Times Mirror Co. group.
Circulation: 1,012,189(m); 954,456(m-sat); 1,410,121(S); ABC Sept. 30, 1995.
Price: 50¢(d); 50¢(sat); $1.50(S); $4.04/wk; $210.08/yr; $16.16/4wk.
Advertising: Open inch rate $584.50(m); $584.50(m-sat); $724.25(S).
News Services: Business Wire, PR Newswire, AP, DF, RN, CSM, DJ, LAT-WP, City News Service, Bloomberg Business News. **Established:** 1881.
Advertising not accepted: Adult video; Hand guns or assault weapons; Illegal or misleading material.
Special Weekly Sections: Food Section (thur); Real Estate, Travel (S).
Magazines: Los Angeles Times Magazine (color, offset), Sunday Calendar (newsprint), Television Times (color, offset), Book Review (newsprint) (S); Traveling in Style (color, offset, 3x/yr).

GENERAL MANAGEMENT

Publisher/CEO Richard T Schlosberg III
Editor/Exec Vice Pres Shelby Coffey III
Senior Vice Pres-Law & Human Resources William A Niese
Senior Vice Pres-Finance William R Isinger
Senior Vice Pres-Operations S Keating Rhoads
Vice Pres-Advertising Marketing & Strategic Planning Robert N Brisco
Vice Pres-LA Times/President-Valley & Ventura Editions Jeffrey S Klein
Vice Pres-LA Times/President-Orange County Edition Judith L Sweeney
Vice Pres-Human Resources R Marilyn Lee
Vice Pres-Advertising Janis Heaphy
Vice Pres-Strategic Alliances Victor A (Chip) Perry III
President/Chief Operating Officer LA Times Syndicate Jesse Levine
Director-Accounting Operations Gary Strong
Director-Administrative Service Colin G Lindsay
Director-Classified Advertising Lawrence M Kline
Director-Advertising Tom Kelley
Director-Advertising Donna Freed
Director-Advertising Marketing & Planning Lisa Morita
Director-National Advertising Mark Wurzer
Director-Strategic Planning/Advertising Marketing Renee LaBran
Director-Business Systems William N Fletcher
Director-Distribution Jack D Klunder
Director-Communications Laura L Morgan
Director-Community Affairs Lisa Cleri Reale
Director-Customer Service Kim McCleary-La France
Director-Employee Relations Tony Franklin
Director-Financial Accounting & Reporting John Beach
Director-Human Resources Michael J Valenti
Director-Medical Joseph M Hughes, MD
Director-Multimedia Publishing Jude Angius
Director-Orange County Operations Thomas J Atkins
Director-San Fernando Valley Operations Richard Horne
Director-Publishing Systems Larry Surratt
Director-Security Service John A Nickols

ADVERTISING

Vice Pres Janis Heaphy
Director-National Mark Wurzer
Manager-Regional Display Jim Maurer

MARKETING AND PROMOTION

Director-Marketing-Valley and Ventura Editions Kay Heitzman
Director-Advertising/Marketing Service Kimberly Greer

TELECOMMUNICATIONS

General Manager-Audiotex/PAC TEL Linda Oubre

CIRCULATION

Director Jack Klunder

NEWS EXECUTIVES

Senior Editor Carol Stogsdill
Editor/Exec Vice Pres Shelby Coffey III
Editor-San Fernando Valley Edition John Arthur
Editor-Ventura County Edition Julie Wilson
Asst to the Editor Frank del Olmo
Managing Editor George J Cotliar
Assoc Editor Narda Zacchino
Deputy Managing Editor Terry Schwardron
Asst Managing Editor-Times Poll/Column One/Special Projects Karen Wada
Asst Managing Editor/Editor (Orange County Edition) Martin Baron

EDITORS AND MANAGERS

MAIN NEWS SECTION

City Editor George Skelton
Columnist-State/Political George Skelton
Columnist-State Peter King
Columnist-Local Robert A Jones
Columnist-Local Bill Boyarsky
Columnist-Local Al Martinez
Columnist-Political Ronald Brownstein
Columnist-Foreign Affairs Jim Mann
Education Editor Sandy Banks
Education Writer-Higher Education Amy Wallace
Education Writer, K-12 Elaine Woo
Education Writer, K-12 Richard Colvin
Education Writer-K-12 Amy Pyle
Environmental Writer Frank Clifford
Environmental Writer Marla Cone
Foreign Editor Simon Li
Health Writer Shari Roan
Health Care Writer Doug Shuit
Legal Affairs Writer Maura Dolan
Legal Affairs Writer Henry Weinstein
Media Critic David Shaw
Medical Writer Terence Monmaney
Medical Writer Tom Maugh
Metro Editor Leo Wolinsky
National Editor Norman C Miller
Obituary Writer Myrna Oliver
Pentagon, DC Richard Serrano
Director of Photography Larry Armstrong
Political Editor-National David Lauter
Political Editor-California Patrick McMahon
Asst Political Editor Don Frederick
Asst Political Editor Lennie La Guire
Political Writer-DC Robert Shogan
Political Writer Cathleen Decker
Political Writer Bill Stall
Religion Editor Sandy Banks
Religion Writer Larry Stammer
Science/Medicine Editor Joel Greenberg
Science Writer Robert Lee Hotz
Science Writer K C Cole
State/Specialist Editor Roxane Arnold
Urban Affairs Writer Sonia Nazario
Urban Affairs Writer Jane Gross

METRO SECTION

Metro Editor Leo Wolinsky
Asst Metro Editor/Specialist Desk Sandy Banks
State Projects Editor Tim Reiterman
City Editor Joel Sappell

EDITORIAL PAGES

Editor of the Editorial Page Janet Clayton
Deputy Editorial Page Editor Nick Williams Jr
Editorial Writer Sergio Munoz
Editorial Writer Andrew Blankstein
Editorial Writer John Needham
Editorial Writer Gayle Pollard Terry
Editorial Writer Robert Reinhold
Editorial Writer Marvin Seid
Editorial Writer Molly Selvin
Editorial Writer Nancy Yoshihara
Opinion Section Editor Allison Silver
Op-Ed Editor Bob Berger
Editorial Page Editor-SF Valley Ronald White
Editorial Page Editor-Orange County Steve Burgard
Voices Editor Judy Dugan
Columnist Thomas Plate

BUSINESS SECTION
Aerospace/Defense Jim Peltz
Aerospace/Defense-DC Ralph Vartabedian
Auto Industry/Steel/Heavy Industry Reporter-Detroit Don Nauss
Business Editor Robert Magnuson
Deputy Editor Bill Sing
Asst Business Editor-Technology/Telecommunication/Multimedia/Cutting Edge Jonathan Weber
Asst Business Editor-Entertainment Industry/Company Town/Film/Records/Radio Mark Saylor
Asst Business Editor-Retail/Marketing/Insurance/Consumer Affairs/Workplace/Tourism/Small Business Pat Benson
Asst Business Editor-California Economy/Real Estate/Agriculture/Airline/Aerospace/Defense/Autos Tom Furlong
Asst Business Editor-Markets Dan Gaines
Asst Business Editor-Mexico/Pacific Rim/Latin America/Europe/Retailing Don Woutat
Business News Editor Mark Yemma
Banking/S&L Insurance Reporter Tom Mulligan
Columnist-Money Talk Carla Lazzareschi
Columnist-Business Computing Richard O'Reilly
Columnist-Financial James Flanigan
Consumer Affairs/Advertising/Marketing Denise Gellene
Economy Reporter DC Robert Rosenblatt
Energy/Economy Patrick Lee
Entertainment Industry Reporter-Broadcast Sallie Hofmeister
Entertainment Industry Reporter-Music Chuck Philips
Entertainment Industry Reporter-Film James Bates
Entertainment Column "The Biz" Claudia Eller
Enterprise Reporter Michael Hiltzik
Health/Drugs David Olmos
Investment "Market Beat" Column Tom Petruno
Pacific Rim/International Trade Evelyn Iritani
Personal Finance Kathy Kristof
Real Estate/Hotels/Gambling Jesus Sanchez
Regional Issues/Southern California Small Business/Travel/Tourism Nancy Rivera-Brooks
Retail George White
Securities-NY Scot Paltrow
Small Business Vicki Torres
Technology/Telecommunications Reporter-Seattle Leslie Helm
Technology (San Francisco) Julie Pitta
Technology/Multimedia Amy Harmon
Telecommunications-DC Jobe Shiver Jr
Trends/Management/Agriculture/General Assignment Martha Groves
Workplace Issues Reporter Stuart Silverstein

LIFE & STYLE SECTION
Auto Care Advice-"Your Wheels" Column Ralph Vartabedian
Columnist Jack Smith
Columnist Robin Abcarian
Columnist Beverly Beyette
Columnist-Consumer (freelance contributor) Lynn Simross
Commitments Editor Doug Adrianson
Design Editor Pamm Higgins
Environment/Consumer Affairs Connie Koenenn
Family Editor Janice Mall
Health/Fitness Editor Michelle Williams
Health Writer (freelance contributor) Kathy Doheny
Involvement Opportunities Aaron Davis
Laugh Lines Editor Charlie Waters
Life/Style Editor Alice Short
Deputy Life/Style Editor Michelle Williams
Medicine Shari Roan
Society News/"Practical View"/"First Person" Editor Janice Mall
Society Writer Jeannine Stein
Writer-54 Hours Laurie Schenden
Writer-The Social City Mary Lou Loper

CALENDAR SECTION (ENTERTAINMENT)
Exec Calendar Editor/Asst Assoc Editor John P Lindsay
Deputy Calendar Editor Sherry Stern
Daily Calendar Editor Oscar Garza
Managing Editor/Sunday Calendar Anne Hurley
News Editor John Thurber
Arts Editor Susan Freudenheim
Art Critic William Wilson
Art Critic Christopher Knight
Art Writer Suzanne Muchnic
Jazz Editor John Thurber
Music and Dance Critic Martin Bernheimer
Pop/Rock Music Critic Robert Hilburn
Dance Writer Lewis Segal
Films Critic Kenneth Turan
"Morning Reporter" Column Shauna Snow
Movie Editor Steve Clow
Movie Industry Writer Robert Welkos
Theater Critic Laurie Winer
Restaurant Critic S Irene Virbila
Radio Writer Judy Michaelson
Television Industry Writer Greg Braxton
Television Industry Writer-NY Jane Hall
Television Editor Mr Lee Margulies
Television Critic Howard Rosenberg
Children's TV Lynn Heffley
TV Times Editor Barbara Saltzman
TV Times Column Nadine Mendoza

MAGAZINE
Los Angeles Times Magazine Editor John Lindsay
Los Angeles Times Magazine Exec Editor (Acting) Kelly Scott
Los Angeles Times Magazine Senior Editor Mr Kit Rachlis
Palm Latitudes Editor Mr Kit Rachlis
Style/Fashion Editor Judy Prouty

OTHER SECTIONS
Editor-Ventura County Edition Julie Wilson
City Editor-Ventura Bureau William Overend
Managing Editor-Valley Edition Ardith Hilliard
Valley Exec News Editor Joe Eckdahl
Valley Editor John Arthur
Editor-Washington Edition Paul Whitefield
Managing Editor-Food Section Russ Parsons
Editor-Online Services Dan Fisher
Book Critic Richard Eder
Book Editor Sonja Bolle
Feature Projects Editor Claudia Luther
Food Editor Laurie Ochoa
Gardening Editor Robert Smaus
Library Director Tom Lutgen
Orange County Editor Martin Baron
Director of Photography Larry Armstrong
Real Estate Editor Richard Barnes
Sacramento Bureau Chief Armando Acuna
San Bernadino/Riverside Bureau Tom Gorman
San Francisco Bureau Maura Dolan
San Francisco Bureau Richard Paddock
Sports Editor Bill Dwyre
Travel Editor Leslie Ward
Wine Columnist Dan Berger

FOREIGN BUREAUS
Beijing Rone Tempest
Berlin Mary Williams Walsh
Brussels Tyler Marshall
Hong Kong Maggie Farley
Jerusalem Marjorie Miller
Johannesburg Bob Drogin
London William D Montalbano
Mexico City Mark Fineman
Moscow Carol J Williams
Nairobi John Balzar
New Dehli John-Thor Dahlburg
Paris Scott Kraft
San Salvador Juanita Darling
Santiago William R Long
Tokyo Sam Jameson
Toronto Craig Turner
Vienna Tracy Wilkinson
Warsaw Dean E Murphy

NATIONAL BUREAUS
Atlanta Eric Harrison
Chicago Stephen Braun
Denver Louis Sahagun
Detroit Don Nauss
Houston Jesse Katz
Miami Anna Virtue
New York John Goldman
Seattle Kim Murphy
Washington, DC Bureau Chief Doyle McManus

MANAGEMENT INFORMATION SERVICES
Director-Business Systems Bill Fletcher
Director Editorial-Systems Wayne Parrack
Director-Publishing Systems Larry Surratt

PRODUCTION
Senior Vice Pres-Operations S Keating Rhoads
Director-Olympic Operations Susan Klutnik
Director-Orange County Operations Thomas J Atkins
Director-San Fernando Valley Operations Richard Horne
Asst Director-Pre Press Operations George A Zambrano

Market Information: Zoned editions; Split Run; TMC; ADS; Operate database; Operate audiotex; Electronic edition.
Mechanical available: Offset; Black and 3 ROP colors; insert accepted — preprinted, preprints $10\frac{1}{4}$" x $13\frac{3}{4}$" maximum; page cut-offs — $22\frac{9}{16}$".
Mechanical specifications: Type page 13" x $21\frac{1}{2}$"; E - 6 cols, $2\frac{1}{16}$", $\frac{3}{16}$" between; A - 6 cols, $2\frac{1}{16}$", $\frac{3}{16}$" between; C - 10 cols, $1\frac{3}{16}$", $\frac{1}{16}$" between.
Commodity consumption: Newsprint 419,533 short tons; 380,598 metric tons; widths 54", $47\frac{1}{4}$", $40\frac{1}{2}$", 27"; black ink 6,946,000 pounds; color ink 1,802,000 pounds; single pages printed 91,122; average pages per issue 111(d), 244(S); single plates used 3,012,000.
Equipment: EDITORIAL: Front-end hardware — Tandem, PCs; Front-end software — SII/Sys 55, Decade; Printers — Genicom, HP/LaserJets, AU/APS 5, AU/APS 6; Other equipment — Ap/Macs. CLASSIFIED: Front-end hardware — IBM/3081GT, Zentec, IBM/Series L; Front-end software — VM, Dos/R34 CSE; Printers — 16-Genicom; Other equipment — IBM/3081G. AUDIOTEX: Hardware — Audio Communications; Software — Audio Communications; Supplier name — Brite, California Lottery, AP Stocks, Dataquick, Mortgage News. DISPLAY: Adv layout systems — SCS/Layout 8000; Front-end hardware — IBM/PCs, 3-Ap/Mac; Front-end software — SCS/Layout 8000, NW/Admarc, Multi-Ad/Creator, Multi-Ad/Services, III/Ad Manager; Printers — Genicom, HP, AU/Proof III; Other equipment — IBM/400J, Sun/Sparc Server. PRODUCTION: OCR software — Caere/OmniPage; Typesetters — 5-AU/APS5, 7-AU/APS6, 4-Hyphen/Imagesetter 3200; Plate exposures — 6-WL/Lith 10, 7-WL/Lith 3; Plate processors — 6-WL/38-G, 7-WL/38-D; Scanners — 3-ECR/Autokon 1000, HP/ScanJet IIP, 1-Magnascan/646, 2-Magnascan/636; Production cameras — 3-C/Spartan III, 1-AG/RPS 6100S; Automatic film processors — 8-P/Pakonolith 24, 4-AG/Litex 25 3; Shrink lenses — 2-CK Optical/SQU-7, 1-CK Optical/SQU 225; Color separation equipment (conventional) — 3-Scitex/Prisma, 1-Scitex/Smart Scan 720, 1-Scitex/Smart Scan 730, 1-Hel/3700 Scanner, 2-Scitex/Dolev 400, 3-Scitex/PS Star.
PRESSROOM: Line 1 — 6-G/Colorliner (Olympic Facility); Line 2 — 4-G/Retrofit Metroliner (San Fernando Facility); Line 3 — 4-G/Colorliner Metroliner (Orange County), 2-G/Retrofit Metroliner (Orange County); Press drives — 16-G; Folders — 32-G; Pasters — 192-G/Surface Sensing RTP; Reels and stands — 72-G/CT 50, 54-G/Static Belt 45, 66-G/CT45; Press control system — G/APCS, G/MPCS; Press registration system — WPC/Color to color registration. MAILROOM: Counter stackers — 4-HL/HT, 46-HL/HTII, 12-HL/Monitor, 1-QWI; Inserters and stuffers — 1-HI/2299, 2-HI/1472; Bundle tyer — 4-Power Strap/PSN-5, 57-Power Strap/PSN-6, 11-Power Strap/PSN-10, 2-HL/Tray System; Wrapping singles — 14-OVL/JP-80, 1-OVL/Constellation; Mailroom control system — 2-Windab/Automated Palletizer. LIBRARY: Electronic — Times/Online, Dataware/BRS Search text retrieval. COMMUNICATIONS: Facsimile — CD/Page fax (6 readers, 12 writers), CD/Page fax (6 readers, 12 writers), CD/Page fax (6 readers, 12 writers); Remote imagesetting — Scitex/Telepress; Digital ad delivery system — First Class/BBS setup, AdSat, AP AdSend, Ad Express, Digiflex; Systems used — fiber optic. WIRE SERVICES: News — AP, RN, DJ, Sports Ticker, AP Datafeatures, PR Newswire, CSM, Business Wire, City News Service; Photos — RN, AFP, AP, Presslink; Stock tables — AP Digital Stocks, AP SelectStox, Bloomberg; Syndicates — LATS, Creators, United Media, Chronicle Features, King Features, TMS, United Features, Universal Press; Receiving dishes — size-3m., AP, AFP, RN, Sp. Ticker. BUSINESS COMPUTERS: IBM/400J; Applications: Microsoft/Windows, Microsoft/Word, Microsoft/Excel, WordPerfect, Lotus, Walker: Accts payable, Purchasing, Stock inventory; Genesys: Payroll, Personnel; Custom Software: Class, Circ, Timekeeping; NW: Display; PCs & micros networked; PCs & main system networked.

MADERA

Madera County

'90 U.S. Census- 29,281; E&P '96 Est. 35,774
ABC-CZ (90): 29,281 (HH 9,159)

Madera Tribune

(e-mon to fri; m-sat)

Madera Tribune, 100 E. 7th St., Madera, CA 93637; tel (209) 674-2424; fax (209) 673-6526. USMedia Inc. group.
Circulation: 8,585(e); 8,585(m-sat); ABC Mar. 30, 1994.
Price: 35¢(d); 35¢(sat); $6.50/mo; $75.00/yr.
Advertising: Open inch rate $8.48(e); $8.48(m-sat). **Representative:** Papert Companies.
News Service: AP. **Politics:** Independent. **Established:** 1892.
Not Published: New Year; Memorial Day; Independence Day; Labor Day; Christmas.
Special Editions: Eye Care, Tax Prep, Health & Fitness Tab, Super Bowl, Welcome to Madera Tab (Jan); Vocational Training Tab, Boy Scout, Valentine, Bridal, President's Day, Future Farmers of America Tab, Tax Prep (Feb); Save your Vision, Girl Scout Birthday, St. Patrick's Day, Campfire, Poison Prevention, Spring Home Improvement, Madera Business Extravaganza, Tax Prep (Mar); Speedway Tab, Church & Worship for Easter, National Library Week, Earth Day Tab, Salute to Volunteers, Tax Prep (Apr); Mother's Day Tab, Cinco De Mayo, Salute to Education, Bike Safety, Vacation/Outdoor, Memorial Day (May); Gifts for Grads, Sober Grad, Top Grads, Flag Day, Father's Day Gift Guide, Salute to Law Enforcement Tab (June); Salute to Agriculture, Start Dining Guide (July); Gathering of the Warbirds, Back-to-School (Aug); Madera District Fair, Football Preview, Fall Home Improvement (Sept); Dining Guide Tab, National 4-H Week, National Fire Prevention, Dental Hygiene Week, Red Ribbon Week Tab (Oct); Veteran's Day, Thanksgiving Turkey Give Away, Yes, We Deliver, Pre Holiday Gift Guide, Coyote Basketball, Thanksgiving/Christmas Kick-off (Nov); Santa's Specials, Christmas Eve Greetings, Safe Driving, Thanks for Another Super Year, New Car Specials 1997 (Dec).
Special Weekly Sections: Financial (mon); Food, Financial, People (tues); Agriculture, Financial, People (wed); Entertainment, Home/Garden, Financial, People (thur); Automotive, Financial, People (fri); Youth/Education, Religion, Real Estate, Automotive (sat).
Magazines: USA Weekend (sat); TV Guide.

CORPORATE OFFICER
President Eugene A Mace

GENERAL MANAGEMENT
Publisher Danny Dean
Business Manager Terry Earls

ADVERTISING
Manager-Retail Armida Roberts

CIRCULATION
Manager Cricket Barow

NEWS EXECUTIVES
Managing Editor Paul Bittick
Asst Editor Robert Adams

EDITORS AND MANAGERS
Business/Finance Editor Paul Bittick
Editorial Page Editor Paul Bittick
Education/School Editor Sabrina McIntosh
Farm Editor Paul Bittick
Food/Women's Editor Paul Bittick
Graphics Editor/Art Director Shirley James
Health/Medical Editor Paul Bittick
Photo Department Mike Chen
Religion Editor Paul Bittick
Science Editor Paul Bittick
Sports Editor Chris Cocoles

Market Information: Zoned editions; TMC.
Mechanical available: Offset; Black and 3 ROP colors; insert accepted — preprinted, 3"x5"; page cut-offs — $22\frac{3}{4}$".
Mechanical specifications: Type page 13" x 21"; E - 6 cols, $2\frac{1}{16}$", $\frac{1}{8}$" between; A - 6 cols, $2\frac{1}{16}$", $\frac{1}{8}$" between; C - 9 cols, $1\frac{3}{8}$", $\frac{1}{16}$" between.
Commodity consumption: Newsprint 300 metric tons; widths 28", 14"; black ink 10,623 pounds; color ink 1,843 pounds; single pages printed 10,510; average pages per issue 32(d); single plates used 10,510.
Equipment: EDITORIAL: Other equipment — IBM/Selectric, 11-HAS. CLASSIFIED: Front-end hardware — COM; Other equipment — 3-HAS. DISPLAY: Other equipment — 1-HAS. PRODUCTION: Typesetters — 2-COM/Videosetter, 1-COM/Unisetter; Plate exposures — 1-Nu; Plate processors — 1-Nat, Anitec; Scanners — 1-COM/Uniscan; Production cameras — 1-C/Spartan II; Automatic film processors — 1-LE; Film transporters — 1-C. PRESSROOM: Line 1 — 8-G/Community; Folders — 2-G. MAILROOM: Inserters and stuffers — 2-MM; Bundle tyer — 1-Bu/16 2X, 1-MLN; Addressing machine — 2-Am/1900. WIRE SERVICES: News — AP; Receiving dishes — size-8ft, AP. BUSINESS COMPUTERS: IBM/Sys 34, HP/Sys; Applications: CJ: Bookkeeping, Payroll, Circ, Adv records; PCs & main system networked.

I-38 California

MANTECA

San Joaquin County

'90 U.S. Census- 40,773; E&P '96 Est. 57,379

Manteca Bulletin

(m-mon to sat; S)

Manteca Bulletin, 531 E. Yosemite Ave.; PO Box 912, Manteca, CA 95336-0912; tel (209) 239-3531; fax (209) 239-1801. Morris Newspaper Corp. group.

Circulation: 5,598(m); 5,598(m-sat); 5,598(S); Sworn Oct. 22, 1995.

Price: 35¢(d); 35¢(sat); 50¢(S); $8.50/mo; $80.00/yr.

Advertising: Open inch rate $9.31(m); $9.31(m-sat); $9.31(S). **Representative:** Papert Companies.

News Service: AP. **Politics:** Independent. **Established:** 1908.

Special Weekly Sections: Best Food Day (wed); Youth Page, Crossroads (local features and entertainment), Bridal (thur); Real Estate Review Tab, Automotive, Medical Directory (fri); Religion (sat); Senior, TV Bulletin, Betty Bear (children's supplement) (S); People, Business, Sports (daily).

Magazines: T-View; Real Estate Weekly Tab.

CORPORATE OFFICER

President Charles H Morris

GENERAL MANAGEMENT

Publisher Darell Phillips
General Manager Laurie Lusk

ADVERTISING

Manager-Retail Rita Hill
Manager-Classified Marge Craig

CIRCULATION

Manager Larry Lusk

NEWS EXECUTIVE

Exec Editor Drew Vooris

EDITOR AND MANAGER

News Editor Karen Hodges

Market Information: TMC.

Mechanical available: Offset; Black and 3 ROP colors; insert accepted — preprinted, all; page cut-offs — 22".

Mechanical specifications: Type page $13\frac{1}{4}$" x 21"; E - 6 cols, $2\frac{1}{16}$", $\frac{1}{8}$" between; A - 6 cols, $1\frac{1}{2}$", $\frac{1}{8}$" between; C - 9 cols, $1\frac{1}{4}$", $\frac{1}{8}$" between.

Commodity consumption: Newsprint 600 metric tons; width 22"; black ink 17,500 pounds; color ink 3,000 pounds; average pages per issue 26(d), 26(S); single plates used 9,000.

Equipment: EDITORIAL: Front-end hardware — 1-Mk/12002, 1-Kwikee ReCas, Ap/Mac Plus. CLASSIFIED: Front-end hardware — 2-Mk; Other equipment — Ap/Mac Plus (LaserPrinter & Scanner). DISPLAY: Adv layout systems — 2-Ap/Mac Plus. PRODUCTION: Typesetters — 2-Ap/Mac Laser; Platemaking systems — 1-Nu; Plate exposures — 1-Nu; Production cameras — 1-B.
PRESSROOM: Line 1 — 4-G/Community, 3-G/Community (6 units); Line 2 — 2-Bu; Line 3 — 1-Am; Folders — 1-G/SC, 1-G/Community. MAILROOM: Counter stackers — 1-BG/Count-O-Veyor; Bundle tyer — 2-Bu; Addressing machine — 1-Am. WIRE SERVICES: News — AP. BUSINESS COMPUTERS: Leading Edge/Model D2.

MARIN COUNTY-SAN RAFAEL

Marin County

'90 U.S. Census- 48,404; E&P '96 Est. 51,077
ABC-NDM (90): 230,096 (HH 95,006)

Marin Independent Journal

(e-mon to fri; m-sat; S)

Marin Independent Journal, 150 Alameda del Prado; PO Box 6150, Novato, CA 94948-6150; tel (415) 883-8600; fax (415) 382-0549; e-mail ij@well.com. Gannett Co. Inc. group.

Circulation: 42,025(e); 42,025(m-sat); 43,420(S); ABC Sept. 30, 1995.

Price: 35¢(d); 35¢(sat); $1.00(S); $16.80/8 wks.

Advertising: Open inch rate $33.82(e); $33.82(m-sat); $34.83(S). **Representatives:** Gannett National Newspaper Sales; Long & Associates.

News Services: AP, Bay City News Service, GNS, KRT, McClatchy. **Politics:** Independent. **Established:** 1861.

Special Editions: Bridal, Super Bowl (Jan); Spring Fashion, Tax Preparation (Feb); Wine & Dine, Home & Garden, Baseball (Mar); Summer Camps (Apr); Bridal (May); Fall Fashion, Football (Aug); Seniors (Sept); Gift Guide (Nov); Last Minute Gift Guide (Dec); Real Estate, Coupon Book (quarterly).

Special Weekly Sections: Weekend (entertainment) (thur); Home & Garden (sat).

Magazines: USA Weekend; TV Book (program guide) (S).

CORPORATE OFFICERS

President Phyllis Pfeiffer
Secretary Thomas Chappel
Treasurer Jimmy L Thomas

GENERAL MANAGEMENT

Publisher Phyllis Pfeiffer
Controller Joe Williams
Director-Human Resources Angela Lusk

ADVERTISING

Director Marty Rubino
Manager-Retail David Dakin
Manager-National Bob Woldmoe

MARKETING AND PROMOTION

Director-Marketing/Promotion Katie Lord

CIRCULATION

Director Bruce Emsley
Manager-Sales Cory Ostos

NEWS EXECUTIVES

Editor Mike Townsend
Managing Editor Jackie Kerwin

EDITORS AND MANAGERS

City Business Editor Pamela Moreland
Editorial Page Editor Jeff Prugh
Graphic Design Editor Beth Renneisen
Lifestyle Editor John Lynch
News Desk Editor Debbie Gump
Photo Editor Scott Henry
Sports Editor Ken Sain
Sunday Editor Joe Konte

PRODUCTION

Director Dan Crisp
Manager-Operations Bob Phillips

Market Information: Split Run; TMC.

Mechanical available: Offset; Black and 3 ROP colors; insert accepted — preprinted; page cut-offs — $22\frac{3}{4}$".

Mechanical specifications: Type page 13" x $21\frac{1}{2}$"; E - 6 cols, $2\frac{1}{16}$", $\frac{1}{8}$" between; A - 6 cols, $2\frac{1}{16}$", $\frac{1}{8}$" between; C - 9 cols, $1\frac{3}{8}$", $\frac{1}{16}$" between.

Commodity consumption: Newsprint 4,813 short tons; widths $54\frac{1}{2}$", $40\frac{7}{8}$", $27\frac{1}{4}$"; black ink 103,250 pounds; color ink 32,500 pounds; single pages printed 18,305; average pages per issue 44(d), 88(S); single plates used 36,980.

Equipment: EDITORIAL: Front-end hardware — 4-AT/Series 60; Front-end software — AT 4.6.8; Printers — 1-Florida Data; Other equipment — 50-AT/ADT. CLASSIFIED: Front-end hardware — 2-AT/Series 60, Sun; Front-end software — AT 4.6.8; Printers — 2-Florida Data; Other equipment — 20-AT. DISPLAY: Adv layout systems — Ap/Mac; Front-end hardware — 4-Ap/Mac, PC/486 fileserver, 3-AT; Front-end software — Multi-Ad/Creator; Printers — Tektronix/III PXi, Ap/Mac LaserWriter 630; Other equipment — Truvell/Color scanner, CD-Rom. PRODUCTION: Typesetters — 2-AU/APS Micro 5, 2-AU/108 FC; Platemaking systems — L/P; Plate exposures — 2-Nu/Flip Top FT40UPNS; Plate processors — 1-WL/30D, 1-WL/38D; Electronic picture desk — 1-Lf/AP Leaf Picture Desk; Scanners — Truvell/Color, RZ/4050E, 1-EC, Kk/RFS 2035, Nikon/AF 3510; Production cameras — 1-SCREEN, 1-C/Spartan III, 1-AG/6000; Automatic film processors — 1-PC/18, 1-PC/13, LD/24 BQ, 1-P; Film transporters — 1-C; Color separation equipment (conventional) — 1-WDS, 1-AG/T42, 1-RZ/1050.
PRESSROOM: Line 1 — 6-H/Lithomatic II double width; Press drives — GE; Folders — 1-H/3:2, 1-H/2:1; Reels and stands — 6-H; Press control system — Wd, H. MAILROOM: Counter stackers — 2-HL/Monitor; Inserters and stuffers — 1-MM/227-E, 1-MM/308; Bundle tyer — 2-MLN/MLN 2, MLN/44, 1-S/1050-2H-28, 1-MLN/EE, 2-MLN/2A; Wrapping singles — 1-St/600; Addressing machine — 1-Ch/542; Other mailroom equipment — MM/321 Stitcher-Trimmer. LIBRARY: Combination — Manual. COMMUNICATIONS: Facsimile — 3-Rapicom/Laser Recorder, 1-Rapicom/3300. WIRE SERVICES: News — AP, Bay City News Service, GNS, KRT, McClatchy; Photos — AP, GNS; Stock tables — AP; Syndicates — KRT, Creators, Jerry Mead Enterprises; Receiving dishes — size-3m, AP, USA Today. BUSINESS COMPUTERS: IBM/AS 400; Applications: Circ, Adv billing, Accts receivable, Gen ledger, Payroll, Accts payable; PCs & main system networked.

MARYSVILLE-YUBA CITY

Yuba and Sutter Counties

'90 U.S. Census- 39,761 (Marysville 12,324; Yuba City 27,437); E&P '96 Est. 49,935 (Marysville 14,256; Yuba City 35,669)
ABC-NDM (90): 122,643 (HH 14,266)

Appeal-Democrat

(m-mon to sat; S)

Appeal-Democrat, 1530 Ellis Lake Dr.; PO Box 431, Marysville, CA 95901; tel (916) 741-2345; fax (916) 741-1195. Freedom Communications Inc. group.

Circulation: 22,508(m); 22,508(m-sat); 23,108(S); ABC Sept. 30, 1995.

Price: 50¢(d); 50¢(sat); $1.00(S); $8.04/mo; $88.75/yr.

Advertising: Open inch rate $18.50(m); $18.50(m-sat); $19.25(S). **Representative:** Papert Companies.

News Service: AP. **Politics:** Libertarian Philosophy. **Established:** 1851.

Special Editions: Brides (Jan); Bokkai, New Neighbors (Feb); Home Improvement, Car Care (Mar); Stampede (May); Health (June); Y-S Fair (July); Beckwourth, Prune Festival (Sept); Seniors, New Car Tab (Oct); X'mas Gift Guide (Nov); Last Minute Gift Guide (Dec).

Special Weekly Sections: Food (wed); Expanded Finance, Religion, Real Estate/Home Page, Outdoors (sat); Teen/Seniors, Farm (S).

Magazines: USA Weekend; TV Preview.

Broadcast Affiliates: WLNE New Bedford, MA; WRGB Schenectady, NY; KTVL Medford, OR; WLNE Providence, RI; WTVC Chattanooga, TN; KFDM Beaumont, TX; KFDM Port Arthur, TX.

CORPORATE OFFICERS

President Jim Rosse
Board Chairman Robert C Hardie
Vice Pres R David Threshie

GENERAL MANAGEMENT

Publisher Robert C Hardie
Manager-Credit Judy Hall
Purchasing Agent Robert C Hardie

ADVERTISING

Director David Kugelman
Manager-National Debbie Baggett
Manager-Classified Debbie Coupe

MARKETING AND PROMOTION

Manager-Marketing/Promotion Shirley Deason

CIRCULATION

Director Donna Perry

NEWS EXECUTIVES

Editor Julie Shirley
Exec Editor Robert C Hardie

EDITORS AND MANAGERS

Assignment Editor Laura Nicholson
Editorial Page Editor Julie Shirley
Entertainment/Amusements Editor Wendy Weitzel
Features Editor Wendy Weitzel
News Editor Jerry Fingal
Photo Editor David Nielsen
Sports Editor Bradley Hall

MANAGEMENT INFORMATION SERVICES

Data Processing Manager Art Clark

PRODUCTION

Director Art Clark
Foreman-Pressroom Jim Thomas
Foreman-Mailroom Troy Simpson
Foreman-Pre Press Gordon Webb

Market Information: TMC.

Mechanical available: Offset; Black and 3 ROP colors; insert accepted — preprinted; page cut-offs — $22\frac{3}{4}$".

Mechanical specifications: Type page 13" x $21\frac{1}{2}$"; E - 6 cols, 2.01", $\frac{1}{8}$" between; A - 6 cols, 2.01", $\frac{1}{8}$" between; C - 9 cols, 1.24", $\frac{1}{16}$" between.

Commodity consumption: Newsprint 1,806.6 metric tons; widths 27.52", 13.74"; black ink 27,270 pounds; color ink 7,326 pounds; single pages printed 12,298; average pages per issue 38(d), 50(S); single plates used 15,000.

Equipment: EDITORIAL: Front-end hardware — Dewar/Sys IV; Front-end software — Dewar/Sys IV; Other equipment — Ap/Mac Quadras, Lf/AP Leaf Picture Desk. CLASSIFIED: Front-end hardware — Dewar/Sys IV; Front-end software — Dewar/Sys IV. DISPLAY: Adv layout systems — Dewar/Sys IV. PRODUCTION: Pagination software — Dewar/SysIV; Typesetters — Tegra/Varityper; Platemaking systems — 1-3M/Deadliner; Plate exposures — 1-Nu; Plate processors — 1-Nat; Electronic picture desk — Lf/AP Leaf Picture Desk; Production cameras — C/Spartan III; Automatic film processors — LE; Digital color separation equipment — Lf/Leafscan 35.
PRESSROOM: Line 1 — 8-G/Urbanite (1 color hump); Pasters — 7-Enkel. MAILROOM: Counter stackers — 1-BG/Count-O-Veyor-108; Inserters and stuffers — 2-MM/227; Bundle tyer — 1-MLN/ML2EE, 1-MLN/Spirit; Wrapping singles — 1-Id. LIBRARY: Electronic — SMS. COMMUNICATIONS: Digital ad delivery system — AP AdSend; Systems used — satellite. WIRE SERVICES: News — AP Datafeatures, NYT, AP Datastream, KRT, Freedom Wire; Photos — AP, KRT; Stock tables — AP; Receiving dishes — AP. BUSINESS COMPUTERS: Compaq; Applications: Southware; PCs & micros networked; PCs & main system networked.

MERCED

Merced County

'90 U.S. Census- 56,216; E&P '96 Est. 75,812
ABC-CZ (90): 83,820 (HH 27,115)

Merced Sun-Star

(m-mon to sat)

Merced Sun-Star, 3033 N. G St.; PO Box 739, Merced, CA 95341-0739; tel (209) 722-1511; fax (209) 384-2226. USMedia Inc. group.

Circulation: 18,284(m); 21,043(m-sat); ABC Sept. 30, 1995.

Price: 50¢(d); 75¢(sat); $9.00/mo; $85.80/yr (carrier), $168.80/yr (mail outside CA).

Advertising: Open inch rate $19.93(m); $19.93(m-sat). **Representative:** Papert Companies.

News Service: AP. **Established:** 1869.

Special Editions: Brides; Vacation; Clearance; Health; Valentines; FFA; President's Day; Auto Red Tag; Meet the Merchants; Tomorrow's Women; Spring Fashions; Parade of Babies; Home & Garden; American Home Week; Medical Directory; Earth Day; Mother's Day; Design an Ad; Auto Show; Memorial Day; Wedding; Meet Your Realtor; Father's Day; Newcomers; July 4; Mecrey Gulch; Fair Tab; Restaurant Tab; Last Chance Sale; Auto Import; Back-to-School; Senior Health; Football; Parade of Homes; Now & Then; Home & Garden; First Aid; Drug Free; New Autos; Holiday Health; Shop November; Gifts for Everyone; Mall Thanksgiving; Letters to Santa; Christmas Countdown; Mall Last Chance; Christmas Greetings; Morning After Christmas.

Magazines: Preview/Entertainment (fri); USA Weekend, TV Update (sat).

CORPORATE OFFICER

President Eugene A Mace

GENERAL MANAGEMENT

Publisher Al Portner
Business Manager Susan Devine

ADVERTISING

Manager-Display Ronald Uecker
Manager-Classified Barbara Ward

CIRCULATION

Manager Dennis Kohn

NEWS EXECUTIVES

Managing Editor Norman Martin Jr
Editor Al Portner

EDITORS AND MANAGERS

City Editor Pat McNally
Editorial Page Editor Mike Conway
Features Editor Barbara Hale
Graphics Editor Edmund P Sciarini
News Editor Darin Bunch
Chief Photographer Roger Wyan
Sports Editor Vern Williams

PRODUCTION

Manager-Pre Press Walt Robbins
Manager-Pressroom Gerald McLendon

Market Information: TMC.

Mechanical available: Offset; Black and 3 ROP colors; insert accepted — preprinted, card inserts; page cut-offs — $22\frac{3}{4}$".

Mechanical specifications: Type page 13" x $21\frac{1}{2}$"; E - 6 cols, $2\frac{1}{16}$", $\frac{1}{8}$" between; A - 6 cols, $2\frac{1}{16}$", $\frac{1}{8}$" between; C - 9 cols, $1\frac{3}{8}$", $\frac{1}{16}$" between.

Copyright ©1996 by the Editor & Publisher Co.

Commodity consumption: Newsprint 930 metric tons; widths 27.5", 13.75"; average pages per issue 26(d).
Equipment: EDITORIAL: Front-end hardware — Ap/Mac; Front-end software — Baseview; Printers — HP/LaserJet. CLASSIFIED: Front-end hardware — Ap/Mac; Front-end software — Baseview; Printers — HP/LaserJet. DISPLAY: Front-end hardware — Ap/Mac; Front-end software — Baseview. PRODUCTION: Pagination software — Baseview, Quark XPress 3.3; Typesetters — 1-Accuset/800, 1-Tegra/Varityper/XP1000; Plate exposures — 1-Nu/2-L, 1-WL; Plate processors — 1-Anitec; Electronic picture desk — Lf/AP Leaf Picture Desk; Scanners — ECR/Autokon, UMAX/1200, Polaroid/Sprint Scan; Production cameras — 1-C/Spartan I, 1-SCREEN/Companica 650 CR (color); Automatic film processors — 1-AG/RAP 28, 2-Konica/K-400; Shrink lenses — 1-CK Optical/K7; Color separation equipment (conventional) — WDS, Lf/AP Leaf Picture Desk, Lf/35 Scanner.
PRESSROOM: Line 1 — 8-G/Urbanite; Folders — 1-G/2:1; Press control system — Fin; Press registration system — Duarte. MAILROOM: Counter stackers — 1-G/Stackmaster; Inserters and stuffers — 4-MM; Bundle tyer — 3-MLN/ML2EE, 1-EAM/Mosca, 2-Timpax; Addressing machine — 1-KR; Other mailroom equipment — 1-MM/3 knife-Trimmer. 1-KR/1/4 folder. COMMUNICATIONS: Facsimile — HI. WIRE SERVICES: News — AP; Syndicates — McClatchy; Receiving dishes — size-3m, Bus Wire. BUSINESS COMPUTERS: 2-IBM/486; Applications: Adv, Accts payable, Gen ledger; PCs & micros networked.

MODESTO

Stanislaus County

'90 U.S. Census- 164,730; E&P '96 Est. 222,664
ABC-CZ (90): 164,730 (HH 57,958)

The Modesto Bee (m-mon to sat; S)

The Modesto Bee, 1325 H St.; PO Box 3928, Modesto, CA 95352; tel (209) 578-2000; fax (209) 578-2095. McClatchy Newspapers group.
Circulation: 83,115(m); 83,115(m-sat); 91,359(S); ABC Sept. 30, 1995.
Price: 50¢(d); 50¢(sat); $1.25(S); $11.25/mo (carrier).
Advertising: Open inch rate $58.05(m); $58.05(m-sat); $64.45(S). **Representative:** Cresmer, Woodward, O'Mara & Ormsbee.
News Services: AP, NYT, LAT-WP, KRT, MNS. **Politics:** Non-partisan. **Established:** 1884.
Special Editions: Agriculture, Business and Industry; Bridal, Spring Home & Garden; Seniors; Discover Modesto; Health; Parade of Homes; Stanislaus County Fair; Football; Women in Business.
Special Weekly Sections: Food Section (wed); Home & Garden, Auto News, Entertainment (fri); Preview (Real Estate) (sat); Real Estate News, Agribusiness, Living Section (S).
Magazines: Parade, TV Week, Comics (S).

CORPORATE OFFICERS

Chairman of the Board/CEO Erwin Potts
President/Chief Operating Officer Gary Pruitt
Publisher (McClatchy Newspapers) James McClatchy
Senior Vice Pres William L Honeysett
Vice Pres-Finance/Treasurer James P Smith
Controller Robert Berger

GENERAL MANAGEMENT

General Manager John W Ward
Director-Finance Walter E Kletke

ADVERTISING

Director Don Wallace
Manager-Retail Don Doud
Manager-Classified Al Autry
Manager-Marketing Debra Kuykendall
Manager-National Larry Dovichi

MARKETING AND PROMOTION

Director-Promotion Sam Gonzalez
Promotion-Manager Michelle Stevenson

TELECOMMUNICATIONS

Audiotex Coordinator Cari Griffin

CIRCULATION

Director Michael Trainor
Manager-Sales Development Patty Tharp
Manager-Single Copy Sales Stephen Foster
Manager-Transportation Craig Mackenzie
Manager-Home Delivery Jim Overton
Manager-Home Delivery Keenen Kroll
Manager-Home Delivery/State Ron Tackett
Manager-Fleet Service Vern Humphrey
Manager-Packaging/Distribution Hank Vander Veen

NEWS EXECUTIVES

Exec Editor Sanders LaMont
Exec Editor-Sports David Lyghtle
Managing Editor Mark Vasche
Asst Managing Editor Susan Windemuth
Assoc Editor Fred Youmans
Assoc Editor Dick LeGrand
Editorial Page Editor Larry McSwain

EDITORS AND MANAGERS

Action Line Editor Judy Sly
Art Director Jim Lawrence
Arts/Theater Editor Leo Stutzin
Auto Editor Mike Dunbar
Business Editor Mike Dunbar
Chief Copy Clerk Evangelina Snuffer
Education Writer Joanne Sbranti
Entertainment/Amusements Editor Carolyn Mann
Environmental Writer Alvie Lindsey
Farm/Agriculture Writer Rich Estrada
Fashion/Style Writer Walt Williams
Features Editor Judy Sly
Health/Medical Reporter Donna Birch
Librarian Kate Roberts
Living/Lifestyle Editor Judy Sly
Asst Metro Editor Alvie Lindsay
Asst Metro Editor John Peters
National Editor Dave Hill
News Editor Dave Hill
Asst News Editor Ed Willhide
Director-Photography Al Golub
Political/Government Editor Alvie Lindsey
Religion Writer Dennis Roberts
Television/Film Writer Leo Stutzin
Theater/Music Writer Leo Stutzin
Travel Writer Walt Williams
Weekend Editor Jack Doo
Women's Editor Judy Sly

MANAGEMENT INFORMATION SERVICES

Director-Management Info Services Allan Six
Manager-Business Systems Gerard Ross
Manager-Publishing Systems C Wayne Jeffries
Manager-Technical Service Terry Winters

PRODUCTION

Director Allan Six
Manager-Composing Room Howard Olson
Manager-Pressroom Roland Ford
Supervisor-Building & Grounds Angela Voigt

Market Information: Zoned editions; Split Run; TMC; ADS; Operate audiotex.
Mechanical available: Flexography; Black and 3 ROP colors; insert accepted — preprinted, tabloids, minis, standards, free standing; page cut-offs — 22".
Mechanical specifications: Type page 13" x 21"; E - 6 cols, 2 1/16", 1/8" between; A - 6 cols, 2 1/16", 1/8" between; C - 10 cols, 1 1/2", 1/16" between.
Commodity consumption: Newsprint 10,777 short tons; widths 54", 40 1/2", 27"; black ink 324,000 pounds; color ink 95,000 pounds; single pages printed 20,535; average pages per issue 55(d), 73(S); single plates used 89,232.
Equipment: EDITORIAL: Front-end hardware — SII/Tandem (4 Tandem TXP processors); Front-end software — SII/Sys 55; Other equipment — 5-Ap/Mac, 63-SII/Coyote, 9-PC. CLASSIFIED: Front-end hardware — SII/Tandem (4 Tandem TXP Processors); Front-end software — SII/Sys 55; Other equipment — 20-SII/Coyote. AUDIOTEX: Hardware — PEP/486 VDN-VSM. DISPLAY: Adv layout systems — Ap/Mac, CJ, SCS/Layout 8000; Front-end hardware — 8-Ap/Mac IIfx, 1-Ap/Mac; Front-end software — DTI/Adspeed; Printers — Hyphen, III; Other equipment — 7-SII/Coyote, 4-DEC/VT320. PRODUCTION: Typesetters — Hyphen/Spectraset, III; Platemaking systems — Na/Flex; Plate exposures — 1-Na/Fx-IV, 2-Consolux; Plate processors — 2-Na/FP-1; Scanners — 2-ECR/Autokon 1000DE, Ap/Mac Quadra 950; Production cameras — 1-C/Spartan III, 1-C/Newspager; Automatic film processors — 2-LE/LD 24A, 2-LE/PC 1800; Film transporters — 2-LE; Color separation equipment (conventional) — CD/645IE; Digital color separation equipment — CD/646 IE.
PRESSROOM: Line 1 — 8-G/Flexoliner; Folders — 2-G; Reels and stands — 8-G/CT-50 RTP; Press control system — G, Allen Bradley. MAILROOM: Counter stackers — 2-HL/HT, 1-HL/Monitor, 1-HL/HTII, 1-HL/HTII dual carrier; Inserters and stuffers — AM Graphics/2299; Bundle tyer — 4-Power Strap/PSN5, 1-Power Strap/PSN6, 1-MLN; Wrapping singles — 3-HL/Monarch, 1-EDS. LIBRARY: Electronic — Vu/Text; Combination — Vu/Text Save. WIRE SERVICES: News — AP Datastream, AP Datafeatures, NYT, LAT-WP, McClatchy; Stock tables — AP SelectStox; Syndicates — TMS; Receiving dishes — size-3m, AP. BUSINESS COMPUTERS: DEC/VAX 4600; Applications: CJ: Adv, Payroll personnel, Class, Accts payable, Gen ledger, Bad debt tracking; In-house-Circ; PCs & micros networked; PCs & main system networked.

MONTEREY

Monterey County

'90 U.S. Census- 31,954; E&P '96 Est. 35,256
ABC-CZ (90): 88,759 (HH 35,690)

The Monterey County Herald (m-mon to sat; S)

The Monterey County Herald, 8 Upper Ragsdale Dr.; PO Box 271, Monterey, CA 93942-0271; tel (408) 372-3311. Scripps Howard group.
Circulation: 34,689(m); 34,698(m-sat); 38,055(S); ABC Sept. 30, 1995.
Price: 50¢(d); 50¢(sat); $1.50(S); $13.00/mo (plus tax); $156.00/yr (plus tax).
Advertising: Open inch rate $29.79(m); $29.79(m-sat); $32.32(S). **Representative:** Cresmer, Woodward, O'Mara & Ormsbee.
News Services: AP, LAT-WP. **Politics:** Independent. **Established:** 1922.
Special Editions: AT&T Pro-Am Golf, Wedding Planner (Feb); Senior 1, Home 1 (Mar); Real Estate, Children (Apr); Automobiles 1, Focus on Salinas (May); Discover Carmel Valley 1, Business Report (June); California Rodeo Salinas (July); Classic Car Weekend, California State University Guide to Monterey Bay, Back-to-School (Aug); Agriculture Report, Seniors 2, California International Air Show (Sept); Automobiles 2, Cherry's Jubliee Car Show & Festival, Home 2, Tourism Report (Oct); Discover Carmel Valley 2 (Nov); Holiday Gift Guides 1 & 2 (Dec).
Special Weekly Sections: Education, Business (mon); Living (tues); Food (wed); Go! (Entertainment Tab), Neighbors (thur); Auto (fri); Real Estate Tab (sat); Family, Home, Travel (S).
Magazines: Parade, Alta Vista Magazine (local), TV Week (S).

GENERAL MANAGEMENT

President Susan H Miller
Chief Financial Officer Nicholas Gagliardo
Manager-Credit Janet Hall

ADVERTISING

Director Jay Palmquist
Manager-Retail Pam Dozier
Manager-National/Co-op Paul Young
Manager-Service Nanette Maysonave

TELECOMMUNICATIONS

Manager-Info Service Michael Elliot

CIRCULATION

Director Mark Olson
Manager-Operations Roy Ulrich

NEWS EXECUTIVES

Editor Susan H Miller
Managing Editor Walter Dawson

EDITORS AND MANAGERS

Alta Vista Magazine Editor Fred Hernandez
Amusements Editor Roslyn White
Art/Books Editor Fred Hernandez
City Editor Mark Whittington
Editorial Page Editor Dennis Sharp
Features Editor Roslyn White
Food Editor Roslyn White
Garden Editor Don Degn
Music Editor Mac McDonald
News Editor Jill Boba
Political Editor Walter Dawson
Radio/Television Editor Marilyn Kirby
Real Estate/Sunday Editor Peter Sigal
Religion Editor Don Degn
Sports Editor Joan Weiner
Travel Editor Roslyn White
Wire Editor Jill Boba
Women's Editor Roslyn White

MANAGEMENT INFORMATION SERVICES

Data Processing Manager Michael A Elliott
Online Manager Jay Palmquist

PRODUCTION

Director Garth Hospers
Foreman-Composing Bill D'Aubin
Foreman-Pressroom/Plate Don Wells
Foreman-Camera Luana Conley
Manager-Packaging Center Chuck Rell

Market Information: TMC; Operate database.
Mechanical available: Flexography; Black and 3 ROP colors; insert accepted — preprinted; page cut-offs — 22 1/4".
Mechanical specifications: Type page 13" x 21"; E - 6 cols, 2 1/16", 1/8" between; A - 6 cols, 2 1/16", 1/8" between; C - 9 cols, 1 3/8", 1/16" between.
Commodity consumption: Newsprint 3,500 short tons; widths 54", 40 1/2", 27 1/2"; black ink 144,480 pounds; color ink 3,780 pounds; single pages printed 16,068; average pages per issue 44(d), 80(S); single plates used 35,000.
Equipment: EDITORIAL: Front-end hardware — 10-PC, 25-Visual Display Terminals; Front-end software — Dewar/Disc Sys III; Printers — 1-Dataproducts/Laser; Other equipment — 2-PrePress Tegra's with 5000 processors & 50001 Imagers. CLASSIFIED: Front-end hardware — 22-PC; Front-end software — Dewar/Disc Sys III. DISPLAY: Adv layout systems — Dewar/Disc Sys III; Front-end hardware — 3-PC/fileserver, 3-Dewar/Discovery, 14-Ap/Mac; Front-end software — CJ/Layout, Dewar/Sys III, QuarkXPress; Printers — HD/401, Storagetex/6024T. PRODUCTION: OCR software — Caere/OmniPage; Typesetters — 2-Tegra/Varityper/XP-1000, 2-Tegra/Varityper 5000 RIP, 1-AG/Avantra 25, 1-Bidco, 2-Cascade/RIP; Platemaking systems — Na; Plate exposures — 2-Consolux/Flexo; Plate processors — 2-Na/Flex FP-II; Electronic picture desk — Lf/AP Leaf Picture Desk, Adobe/Photoshop; Scanners — HP/ScanJet Plus, ECR/Autokon 1000DC; Production cameras — 2-C/Spartan III; Automatic film processors — 2-LE/PC-13, 2-LE/LD-24AQ; Shrink lenses — 1-CK Optical/SQU-7-502; Color separation equipment (conventional) — Ap/Mac, Kk/Film Scanner; Digital color separation equipment — Hel/DC 380.
PRESSROOM: Line 1 — 7-G/Flexoliner; Folders — 2-G. MAILROOM: Counter stackers — 2-MM/310, 1-MM/375; Inserters and stuffers — 2-MM/308 Biliner; Bundle tyer — 2-OVL/JP480, 2-MLN. WIRE SERVICES: News — AP Datastream, AP Datafeatures, AP SelectStox; Photos — AP; Stock tables — Grand Central Stocks; Syndicates — AP Datafeatures; Receiving dishes — size-10ft, AP. BUSINESS COMPUTERS: 1-DEC/VAX-4200, 1-DEC/VAX-4300, 24-IBM, 5-Ap/Mac; Applications: CJ/AIM: Circ, Class; CJ/AIM; PCs & micros networked; PCs & main system networked.

NAPA

Napa County

'90 U.S. Census- 61,842; E&P '96 Est. 70,458
ABC-CZ (90): 62,917 (HH 23,587)

The Napa Valley Register (e-mon to sat; S)

The Napa Valley Register, 1615 2nd St.; PO Box 150, Napa, CA 94559; tel (707) 226-3711; fax (707) 224-3963. Scripps League Newspapers Inc. group.
Circulation: 19,222(e); 19,222(e-sat); 19,682(S); ABC Sept. 30, 1995.
Price: 50¢(d); 50¢(sat); $1.00(S); $9.50/mo; $114.00/yr.
Advertising: Open inch rate $17.43(e); $17.43(e-sat); $17.43(S). **Representative:** Long & Associates.
News Service: AP. **Politics:** Independent. **Established:** 1863.
Special Editions: Health & Fitness (Jan); Bridal Edition, Menu Review (Feb); Spring Home & Garden (Mar); Food & Wine, Design-an-Ad (May); Summer Home Improvement, County Fair (June); Seniors Edition (July); Football '96 (Aug); Fall Home Value, Fall Fashion (Sept); Transamerica Golf Edition (Oct); Gift Guides (Dec).
Special Weekly Sections: Spanish (mon); Food (tues); Senior Citizens (sat); Travel (S).
Magazines: TV Focus, USA Weekend (S).

CORPORATE OFFICERS

Board Chairman/Treasurer E W Scripps
Vice Chairman/Corporate Secretary Betty Knight Scripps
President Jack C Morgan
Exec Vice Pres Roger N Warkins
Vice Pres-Finance Thomas E Wendel

GENERAL MANAGEMENT

Publisher Michael Giangreco
Purchasing Agent/Office Manager Pat Gustafson

ADVERTISING

Director Ian Cooke
Manager-Classified Lani McKay

CIRCULATION

Director Bruce Blackwell

NEWS EXECUTIVE

Managing Editor Doug Ernst

EDITORS AND MANAGERS

Automotive Editor Doug Ernst
Business Editor Kevin Courtney
City Editor Doug Wilks
Editorial Page Editor Doug Ernst
Education Editor Anne Stanley

I-40 California

Entertainment/Amusements Editor L Pierce Carson
Environmental Editor Doug Wilks
Farm Editor Frank Gordon
Features Editor Bruce Baird
Graphics Editor/Art Director Doug Wilks
Health Editor Bruce Baird
Living/Lifestyle Editor Bruce Baird
National Editor Doug Ernst
News Editor Doug Wilks
Photo Department Manager Doug Wilks
Political/Government Editor Doug Ernst
Radio/Television Editor L Pierce Carson
Religion Editor Bruce Baird
Science/Technology Editor Doug Ernst
Sports Editor Marty James
Wire Editor Frank Gordon
Women's Editor Bruce Baird

PRODUCTION

Foreman-Composing George Ness
Foreman-Pressroom/Platemaking Jim Ainsworth

Market Information: Split Run; TMC.
Mechanical available: Offset; Black and 3 ROP colors; insert accepted — preprinted; page cutoffs — 22¾".
Mechanical specifications: Type page 13" x 21½"; E - 6 cols, $2\frac{1}{16}$", ⅛" between; A - 6 cols, $2\frac{1}{16}$", ⅛" between; C - 10 cols, $1\frac{3}{16}$", $\frac{1}{16}$" between.
Commodity consumption: Newsprint 1,447 metric tons; widths 27½", 13¾"; black ink 15,000 pounds; color ink 2,500 pounds; single pages printed 11,668; average pages per issue 30(d), 69(S); single plates used 12,000.
Equipment: EDITORIAL: Front-end hardware — 25-ScrippSat; Front-end software — Synaptic; Printers — 2-LaserMaster/Unity 1800x60. CLASSIFIED: Front-end hardware — 5-ScrippSat; Front-end software — Synaptic; Printers — Okidata/393, LaserMaster/Unity. AUDIOTEX: Supplier name — US Audiotex. DISPLAY: Adv layout systems — ScrippSat; Front-end hardware — 5-ScrippSat; Front-end software — QuarkXPress, QPS, Adobe/Photoshop, Archetype/Corel Draw; Printers — 3-LaserMaster/Unity. PRODUCTION: Pagination software — QuarkXPress 3.31; Typesetters — 5-LaserMaster/Unity; Plate exposures — 1-Nu; Plate processors — 1-Nat; Electronic picture desk — Lf/AP Leaf Picture Desk; Scanners — HP/ScanJet IIc; Production cameras — 1-MG; Automatic film processors — 1-P; Digital color separation equipment — Howtek.
PRESSROOM: Line 1 — 7-G/Urbanite; Folders — 1-G. MAILROOM: Counter stackers — 1-BG; Inserters and stuffers — 2-MM/6-into-1; Bundle tyer — 1-MLN; Addressing machine — American Business Computers. COMMUNICATIONS: Digital ad delivery system — AP AdSend. WIRE SERVICES: News — AP; Stock tables — AP; Syndicates — SHNS; Receiving dishes — size-10ft, AP. BUSINESS COMPUTERS: 6-ScrippSat; Applications: Circ, Adv billing, Accts receivable, Gen Ledger, Payroll; PCs & micros networked; PCs & main system networked.

NEWARK

See FREMONT

OAKLAND

Alameda County

'90 U.S. Census- 372,242; **E&P '96 Est.** 396,117
ABC-NDM (90): 2,082,914 (HH 779,806)

The Oakland Tribune

(m-mon to sat; S)

The Oakland Tribune, 66 Jack London Sq.; PO Box 28884, Oakland, CA 94607; tel (510) 208-6300; fax (510) 208-6404. MediaNews Inc. (Alameda Newspapers) group.
Circulation: 87,066(m); 87,066(m-sat); 85,017(S); ABC Sept. 30, 1995.
Price: 50¢(d); 50¢(sat); $1.25(S); $2.80/wk.
Representative: Landon Associates Inc.
News Services: AP, NYT, LAT-WP, CSM, McClatchy. **Politics:** Independent. **Established:** 1874.
Note: Advertising is sold in combination with Fremont Argus (mS), Hayward Daily Review (mS), Oakland Tribune (mS) and Pleasanton Tri-Valley Herald (mS) for $118.00 (dS). Individual rates not made available.
Special Editions: East Bay Almanac (Mar); East Bay Leisure Guide (June); "Best" from Valley to the Bay (Oct); Auto, Christmas Gifts (Nov); Christmas Gifts (Dec).
Special Weekly Sections: Automotive (fri); New Homes (sat); Travel (S); CUE (daily).
Magazines: TV Week, Parade (S).

CORPORATE OFFICERS

President/Publisher Peter Bernhard
Asst to Publisher/Vice Pres Administration Patrick Brown
Senior Vice Pres-Production Dennis Miller
Senior Vice Pres-Advertising Roger Grossman
Senior Vice Pres-Circulation Arthur Farber
Senior Vice Pres/Editor in Chief David Burgin
Vice Pres-Human Resources Jim Janiga

GENERAL MANAGEMENT

Publisher Peter Bernhard
Assoc Publisher Joseph Haraburda
Manager-Human Resources Karen Austin

ADVERTISING

Director Robert Brown
Director-Classified Pete Laraway
Manager-National Mary Menard

MARKETING AND PROMOTION

Director-Marketing/Promotion Service Deborah Byrum

CIRCULATION

Director Jim Dove
Manager-Operations Mary O'Brien

NEWS EXECUTIVES

Exec Editor Nancy Conway
Editor Tim Graham
Asst Managing Editor-Regional Brian Aronstam
Asst Managing Editor-State/National Jim Jennings

EDITORS AND MANAGERS

Books Editor Robert Taylor
Business Editor David Tong
Asst Business Editor Scott Ard
City Editor Cathy Schutz
Asst City Editor Mark Lowe
Asst City Editor Ed Albro
Asst City Editor Diana Williams
Columnist Tom Goff
Columnist Brenda Payton
Columnist Bill Wong
Editorial Page Editor Bob Cuddy
Features Editor Sharon Betz
Asst Features Editor Richard Defendorf
Films Editor Barry Caine
Food Editor Catherine Chriss
Director-Libraries Steve Lavoie
News Editor Brian Gardner
Director-Photo/Graphics Rob Lindquist
Sacramento, CA Bureau Editor Sam Delson
Sports Editor Don Coulter
Sports Editor-Local Jim Pimental
Deputy Sports Editor Don Drysdate
Sports Columnist Monte Poole
Sports Columnist Carl Steward
Sports Columnist Dave Newhouse
Television Editor Susan Young
Travel Editor Bari Brenner

MANAGEMENT INFORMATION SERVICES

Data Processing Manager Ken Marcum
Online Manager Kevin Hamilton

PRODUCTION

Director Dave Boyer
Manager-Pre Press Pete Salm

Market Information: Zoned editions; Split Run; TMC; ADS; Operate database.
Mechanical available: Offset; Black and 3 ROP colors; insert accepted — preprinted; page cutoffs — 21½".
Mechanical specifications: Type page 13" x 21½"; E - 6 cols, $2\frac{1}{16}$", ⅛" between; A - 6 cols, $2\frac{1}{16}$", ⅛" between; C - 10 cols, 1¼", $\frac{3}{32}$" between.
Commodity consumption: Newsprint 17,000 short tons; widths 55", 41¼", 27⅜"; black ink 700,000 pounds; color ink 45,000 pounds; single pages printed 20,800; average pages per issue 52(d), 100(S); single plates used 90,000.
Equipment: EDITORIAL: Front-end hardware — PC; Front-end software — XYQUEST/XyWrite, HI/XP21; Printers — Okidata/380-OL400. CLASSIFIED: Front-end hardware — PC; Front-end software — HI/XP21; Printers — Okidata/380-OL400. DISPLAY: Adv layout systems — SCS/Layout 8000; Front-end hardware — Dell/386; Front-end software — Xenix, SCS/Layout 8000; Printers — 2-HP/LaserJet III. PRODUCTION: Typesetters — 4-III/Graphix Color Imagers; Plate exposures — 6-Nu, 1-W; Plate processors — 1-MAS, 2-WL, 1-Nat, 1-AN, 1-SL; Scanners — 2-ECR, 4-HP; Production cameras — 4-C; Automatic film processors — 6-C, 2-COM; Film transporters — 2-C; Color separation equipment (conventional) — 1-WDS, 1-Howtek.
PRESSROOM: Line 1 — 5-G/Metro; Line 2 — 12-G/Urbanite; Line 3 — 11-G/Urbanite; Line 4 — 10-G/Urbanite; Line 5 — 7-MAN/Lithomatic II; Line 6 — 7-G/Community; Folders — 5-G/2:1, 2-G/3:2, 1-G/SC, 1-G/Community; Pasters — G, H, Cary, Enkel; Reels and stands — G/Community. MAILROOM: Counter stackers — 10-HL/Monitor; Inserters and stuffers — 2-HI/1372P; Bundle tyer — 10-MLN/2A. COMMUNICATIONS: Remote imagesetting — AdSat; Systems used — satellite. WIRE SERVICES: News — AP; Stock tables — AP; Syndicates — LAT-WP, NYT; Receiving dishes — AP. BUSINESS COMPUTERS: 1-HP/300 957; Applications: CJ: Accts payable, Gen ledger, Payroll, Personnel, Circ, Adv, Newsprint; PCs & main system networked.

OCEANSIDE

See ESCONDIDO

ONTARIO-UPLAND

San Bernardino County

'90 U.S. Census- 196,553 (Ontario 133,179; Upland 63,374); **E&P '96 Est.** 252,753 (Ontario 175,996; Upland 76,757)
ABC-NDM (90): 683,595 (HH 210,585)

Inland Valley Daily Bulletin

(m-mon to sat; S)

Inland Valley Daily Bulletin, 2041 E. 4th St.; PO Box 4000, Ontario, CA 91761; tel (909) 987-6397; fax (909) 948-3197; e-mail ivdb@ix.netcom.com. Donrey Media group.
Circulation: 81,603(m); 81,603(m-sat); 85,524(S); ABC Sept. 30, 1995.
Price: 35¢(d); 35¢(sat); $1.00(S); $7.00/4wk.
Advertising: Open inch rate $47.30(m); $47.30(m-sat); $47.30(S). **Representative:** Papert Companies.
News Services: AP, CNS, KRT, NYT. **Politics:** Independent. **Established:** 1885.
Special Editions: Health & Fitness (Jan); Home & Garden, Seniors (Feb); Baseball (Apr); Seniors, Home & Garden (June); Health & Fitness (July); Football, Fashion (Aug).
Special Weekly Sections: Food (thur); Weekend-Entertainment (fri); Religion, Real Estate (sat); Real Estate, Travel (S); Financial (daily).
Magazines: USA Weekend; The TV Book (TV Magazine).

CORPORATE OFFICERS

Founder Donald W Reynolds
President/Chief Operating Officer Emmett Jones
Exec Vice Pres/Chief Financial Officer Darrell W Loftin
Vice Pres-Eastern Newspaper Group Don Schneider
Vice Pres-Western Newspaper Group David A Osborn

GENERAL MANAGEMENT

Publisher Michael Ferguson
General Manager Don Russell
Manager-Human Resources Elliott Andorko
Director-Creative Service Susan Pate

ADVERTISING

Director-Display John Souza
Director-Classified Peggy del Toro

MARKETING AND PROMOTION

Director-Marketing/Promotion Bill Cortus

TELECOMMUNICATIONS

Audiotex Manager Larry Statti

CIRCULATION

Director Dennis Wagner

NEWS EXECUTIVES

Editor Stephen Trosley
Managing Editor Mike Brossart

EDITORS AND MANAGERS

Automotive Editor Doug Arnold
Business/Finance Editor Randyl Drummer
Columnist Chris Reed
Editorial Page Editor Kevin Chaffee
Entertainment Editor Brian Soergel
Graphics Editor/Art Director Kent Salas
Lifestyles/Business Metro Editor Robert Wagner
Metro Editor-San Bernadino Mike Mahl
Metro Editor David Wert
Metro Editor-Night Laura Farrell
News Editor Michael Lamb
Photo Editor Blair Gallicott
Sports Editor Louis Brewster
Travel Editor Doug Arnold

MANAGEMENT INFORMATION SERVICES

Data Processing Manager Richard Nagey

PRODUCTION

Supervisor-Press Mike Smith
Foreman-Press Dave Millard

Market Information: Zoned editions; TMC; ADS; Operate audiotex.
Mechanical available: Offset; Black and 3 ROP colors; insert accepted — preprinted; page cutoffs — 22¾".
Mechanical specifications: Type page 13" x 21½"; E - 6 cols, $2\frac{1}{16}$", ⅛" between; A - 6 cols, $2\frac{1}{16}$", ⅛" between; C - 10 cols, $1\frac{3}{16}$", $\frac{1}{16}$" between.
Commodity consumption: Newsprint 10,500 metric tons; widths 54", 41¼", 27½"; black ink 300,500 pounds; color ink 37,500 pounds; single pages printed 22,000; average pages per issue 52(d), 68(S); single plates used 80,000.
Equipment: EDITORIAL: Front-end hardware — DTI; Front-end software — DTI; Printers — XIT/486 Clipper, Ap/Mac LaserWriter Plus IIg; Other equipment — Ap/Mac Quadra 950, Ap/Mac IIci, Ap/Mac IIcx, Ap/Mac Plus, Ap/Mac Classic, Ap/Mac SE. CLASSIFIED: Front-end hardware — DTI; Front-end software — DTI; Other equipment — Ap/Mac. AUDIOTEX: Hardware — Micro Voice, AT/2000; Supplier name — Micro Voice, Informix. DISPLAY: Adv layout systems — CJ; Front-end hardware — Ap/Mac IIsi, Ap/Mac IIcx, 2-Ap/Mac SE; Front-end software — Aldus/FreeHand 3.0, Claris/MacDraw II, Microsoft/Excel 3.0, Mk/Ad Director 35g, Microsoft/Word 5.0, Claris/Macwrite II; Printers — Ap/Mac LaserWriter Plus, HP/DeskWriter C. PRODUCTION: Typesetters — Panther/Pro 46; Platemaking systems — 2-KFM/TD-33; Plate processors — 2-XPD-32 Anocoil Subtractive Processors; Electronic picture desk — Lf/AP Leaf Picture Desk; Scanners — ECR/Autokon 1000; Production cameras — C/Spartan III; Automatic film processors — 1-P/26ML, 1-P/26RA; Color separation equipment (conventional) — Lf/AP Leaf Picture Desk.
PRESSROOM: Line 1 — 7-MAN/Uniman 4-2 (4 Colordecks); Line 2 — 7-MAN/Uniman 4-2 (4 Colordecks); Press drives — Fin; Folders — 4-MAN/2:1; Pasters — 14-MEG, 3-DME; Press control system — Fin. MAILROOM: Counter stackers — 4-HL/Monitor; Inserters and stuffers — 2-MM/227-S; Bundle tyer — 5-MLN. LIBRARY: Electronic — Ap/Mac Classic II, Claris/Filemaker Pro. WIRE SERVICES: News — AP, CNS, KRT, NYT, CNS; Photos — AP; Stock tables — AP Grand Central Stocks; Receiving dishes — AP. BUSINESS COMPUTERS: Unisys/6000-70, HP/3000 927-LX; Applications: Unix, Xi/Textspooler, Progress, MPE/XL-IX, Cobol/II-XL, Data General, CJ: Layout, Adv, UDMS/Report Writer; PCs & micros networked; PCs & main system networked.

ORANGE COUNTY-COSTA MESA

'90 U.S. Census- 96,357; **E&P '96 Est.** 106,887

Daily Pilot (m-mon to sat)

Daily Pilot, 330 W. Bay St., Costa Mesa, CA 92627; tel (714) 642-4321; fax (714) 631-5902. Times Mirror Co. group.
Circulation: 25,468(m); 41,821(m-sat); VAC Mar. 30, 1995.
Price: Free.
Advertising: Open inch rate $23.80(m); $23.80(m-sat). **Representatives:** Papert Companies; US Suburban Press. **Politics:** Independent. **Established:** 1923.
Advertising not accepted: Publisher reserves right to refuse objectionable matter.
Special Editions: Health & Fitness (Jan); Brides, International Auto Show (Feb); Home & Garden (Apr); Orange County Fair, Menu Guide (July); Football (Sept); Evenings (Oct); Gift Guide (Nov); Gift Guide (Dec).
Magazine: Real Estate.

CORPORATE OFFICER

President/CEO Jeffrey Klein

GENERAL MANAGEMENT

Publisher Thomas H Johnson

ADVERTISING

Manager-Display Judy Oetting

MARKETING AND PROMOTION

Director-Promotion Lana H Johnson

CIRCULATION

Director Carl Toth

NEWS EXECUTIVES

Editor William S Lobdell
Managing Editor Steve Marble

California I-41

EDITORS AND MANAGERS

Arts/Entertainment Editor Lauri Busby
Sports Editor Roger Carlson
Television/Film Editor Lauri Busby
Theater/Music Editor Lauri Busby

PRODUCTION

Director Hank Knight

Mechanical available: Offset; Black and 3 ROP colors; insert accepted — preprinted, card stock single sheet; page cut-offs — 22¾".
Mechanical specifications: Type page 13" x 21½"; E - 6 cols, 2¹⁄₁₆", ⅛" between; A - 6 cols, 2¹⁄₁₆", ⅛" between; C - 10 cols, 1⅜", ¹⁄₁₆" between.
Commodity consumption: Newsprint 8,000 metric tons; widths 55", 27½", 13¾"; black ink 15,000 pounds; color ink 9,000 pounds; average pages per issue 32(d).
Equipment: EDITORIAL: Front-end hardware — Ik, Dewar/Sys IV, Ap/Mac; Front-end software — QPS. CLASSIFIED: Front-end hardware — Ik, Dewar/Sys IV. DISPLAY: Adv layout systems — Ap/Mac; Front-end software — Multi-Ad. PRODUCTION: Typesetters — 2-V; Plate exposures — 1-Nu/Flip Top FT40V4, 1-Nu/UPNS, 1-BKY/Adlux 5KW; Plate processors — 1-Nat/A-250, 1-WL/38-D; Scanners — AG/6100s Stat Camera, Howtek/Color Scanner; Production cameras — 1-C/Spartan III, 1-R/Loge 500 Proc. Color, 1-Ik/530 Stat camera; Automatic film processors — 2-P/24; Film transporters — LE; Shrink lenses — 1-G&K/10.646%; Color separation equipment (conventional) — CD/625-S.
PRESSROOM: Line 1 — 8-HI/N-1600; Folders — 1-HI/2:1; Pasters — 7-MEG/500; Reels and stands — 7-MEG/500. MAILROOM: Counter stackers — 2-Id/NS440; Inserters and stuffers — 1-S/24P; Bundle tyer — 2-MLN/MLN-2A; Addressing machine — 1-EI/8000-1. WIRE SERVICES: News — AP; Stock tables — AP. BUSINESS COMPUTERS: 1-IBM/Sys 34; Applications: Circ, Adv billing, Accts receivable, Gen ledger, Payroll, Financial statement, Budget comparisons.

ORANGE COUNTY-SANTA ANA

'90 U.S. Census- 293,742; E&P '96 Est. 327,018
ABC-NDM (90): 2,410,556 (HH 827,066)

The Orange County Register (m-mon to sat; S)

The Orange County Register, 625 N. Grand Ave. (92701); PO Box 11626, Santa Ana, CA 92711; tel (714) 835-1234; fax (714) 543-3904; web site http://www.ocregister.com. Freedom Communications Inc. group.
Circulation: 349,874(m); 349,874(m-sat); 412,439(S); ABC Sept. 30, 1995.
Price: 25¢(d); 25¢(sat); $1.25(S); $2.17/wk; $8.68/mo; $112.84/yr.
Advertising: Open inch rate $166.00(m); $166.00(m-sat); $193.00(S). **Representatives:** Cresmer, Woodward, O'Mara & Ormsbee; Hawaiian Media Sales; McGown/Intermac Inc.; Towmar.
News Services: AP, KRT, NYT, McClatchy. **Established:** 1905.
Note: The Orange County Register operates a separate printing facility in Anaheim.
Special Editions: Wedding Book (Jan); Home Beautiful, The Collection (Mar); Hospital & Health (May); Orange County Fair (July); Wedding Book (Aug); Best of Orange County (Sept); Gift Guides, The Collection (Nov); Gift Guides (Dec).
Special Weekly Sections: Business Monday (mon); Food, Preview (thur); Preview (fri); Home & Garden (sat).
Magazines: TV Register, Parade (S).
Cable TV: Own cable TV in circulation area.

GENERAL MANAGEMENT

Publisher R David Threshie
President/Chief Operating Officer John R Schueler
Vice Pres/Chief Financial Officer-Finance Kathy Weiermiller
Vice Pres-Info Services Mark Westling
Vice Pres-Human Resources Peggy Castellano
Vice Pres-Community Relations Ronna Kelly
Vice Pres-Editorial & Commentary Ken Grubbs
Director-Facilities Tom Grochow

ADVERTISING

Senior Vice Pres-Advertiser & Marketing Ron Redfern
Vice Pres Doug Hanes
Director-Display Jim Ryan
Director-Majors/National Tom Marquis
Director-Classified/Telemarketing Michele Marquis
Director-New Media Marketing Virginia Neal

TELECOMMUNICATIONS

Audiotex Manager Lelani Bluner
Audiotex Manager-900 lines Caroline Foxmeyer

CIRCULATION

Vice Pres-Consumer Marketing John Walsh
Senior Director-Consumer Sales Barry Berg
Director-Consumer Services David Johnsmiller
Director-Marketing Joseph Felbab
Director-Consumer Service David Johnsmiller

NEWS EXECUTIVES

Editor/Vice Pres Tonnie L Katz
Exec Editor Ken Brusic
Managing Editor-Strategies & Administration Richard Cheverton
Asst Managing Editor-Topics Larry Burrough
Asst Managing Editor/Art Director Nanette Bisher
Asst Managing Editor-Production Cheryl I Smith
Asst Managing Editor-Features Robin Doussard
Ombudsman Pat Riley
Writing Coach Lucille deView
Director-Administration Catherine Reiland

EDITORS AND MANAGERS

Fashion Writer Lisa Lytle
Graphics Editor Tia Lai
News Director-Research Sharon Ostmann
News Editor-Photos Jodie Steck
News Editor-Copy Desks Marilyn Iturri
News Editor-Wires Blair Charnley
Online Editor Leah Gentry
Sports Editor Mark Tomaszewski
Topics Editor-Special Projects Karlyn Barker
Topics Editor-Education/Science/Government John Doussard
Topics Editor-Show Rich Nordwind
Topics Editor-Money Russ Stanton
Topics Editor-Community News Jeff Light
Topics Editor-Courts Christopher Smith
Topics Editor-So. Cal. Culture Steve Plesa

MANAGEMENT INFORMATION SERVICES

Data Processing Manager Mark Westling

PRODUCTION

Vice Pres-Production Roger Stowell
Vice Pres-Customer Fulfillment Allen Sundstrom
Director-Pre Press Don Bricker
Director-Pressroom Richard Lopez
General Manager-Anaheim Print Facility Rich Blanco
Director-Mailroom/Transportation Mike Burns
Director-Home Delivery Tracy Shannon
Manager-Production Administration Bud Weatherly
Senior Administrative Manager-Mailroom/Transportation Mike Feeney

Market Information: Split Run; TMC; ADS; Operate audiotex.
Mechanical available: Offset; Black and 3 ROP colors; insert accepted — preprinted; page cut-offs — 22¾".
Mechanical specifications: Type page 13" x 21½"; E - 6 cols, 2¹⁄₁₆", ⅛" between; A - 6 cols, 2¹⁄₁₆", ⅛" between; C - 10 cols, 1³⁄₁₆", ⅛" between.
Commodity consumption: Newsprint 120,000 metric tons; widths 54¾", 41¼", 27½"; black ink 1,800,000 pounds; color ink 475,000 pounds; single plates used 850,000.
Equipment: EDITORIAL: Front-end hardware — 14-AT/J-11; Front-end software — AT; Printers — Printronix, Okidata. CLASSIFIED: Front-end hardware — 12-AT/J-11; Front-end software — AT; Printers — Printronix, Okidata; Other equipment — Infoswitch/ACD. AUDIOTEX: Hardware — Centigram/IVR; Software — QNX. DISPLAY: Adv layout systems — III; Front-end hardware — Sun/Microsystems; Front-end software — Unix, III; Other equipment — Infoswitch/ACD. PRODUCTION: Typesetters — 4-M/L-500, 2-M/L-530, 1-ECR/ScriptSetter IV; Plate exposures — 1-Nu, 2-WL/Lith III, 1-WL/Lith 10; Plate processors — 1-B/86; Scanners — 2-ECR/Autokon 1000DE; Production cameras — 1-C/Newspager, R/481, C/Spartan III; Automatic film processors — 2-PC/1800, 1-Kodalith, 2-LE/2600 24AQ; Film transporters — LE; Shrink lenses — 2-CK Optical, 1-Alan; Color separation equipment (conventional) — 1-Hel/Chromacon Sys.
PRESSROOM: Line 1 — 11-G/Metro; Line 2 — 11-G/Metro; Line 3 — 11-G/Metro; Line 4 — 11-G/Headliner; Line 5 — 11-G/Headliner; Line 6 — 11-G/Metro; Press drives — Fin; Folders — 6-G/3:2; Pasters — DEC/Paster Pilot; Reels and stands — G; Press control system — Fin. MAILROOM: Counter stackers — 5-SH/251, 9-GPS/3000, 2-Id/2000; Inserters and stuffers — 1-MM; Bundle tyer — 17-MLN/2E; Wrapping singles — 12-SH, 2-Id; Addressing machine — 3-Ch. LIBRARY: Electronic — 2-DEC/4300. COMMUNICATIONS: Facsimile — PB; Systems used — satellite, microwave, fiber optic. WIRE SERVICES: News — AP Datastream, AP Datafeatures, AP Sports; Stock tables — AP Dataspeed, AP Digital Stocks, AP SelectStox; Receiving dishes — AP. BUSINESS COMPUTERS: HP, IBM; Applications: Accts payable, Accts receivable, Gen ledger, Payroll, Circ; Admarc: Accounting, Distribution, Billing; PCs & micros networked; PCs & main system networked.

OROVILLE

Butte County

'90 U.S. Census- 11,960; E&P '96 Est. 14,832
ABC-CZ (90): 30,329 (HH 11,078)

Oroville Mercury Register (e-mon to sat)

Oroville Mercury Register, 2081 Second St.; PO Box 651, Oroville, CA 95965; tel (916) 533-3131; fax (916) 533-3127. Donrey Media group.
Circulation: 7,696(e); 7,696(e-sat); ABC Sept. 30, 1995.
Price: 50¢(d); $1.00(sat); $7.50/mo.
Advertising: Open inch rate $12.14(e); $12.14(e-sat). **Representative:** Papert Companies.
News Service: AP. **Politics:** Independent. **Established:** 1873.
Not Published: New Year; Memorial Day; Independence Day; Labor Day; Christmas.
Special Editions: Chronology, Health & Fitness (Jan); Progress Edition (Mar); Home and Garden (Apr); Real Estate, Spring Fashion (May); Graduation, Visitor's Guide (June); Real Estate (July); Bingo, Butte Co. Fair, Back-to-School (Aug); Sports Preview (Sept); Oroville Expo, Fall Home Improvement, Careers, "Homemakers" (Oct); Car Care, Shop Oroville First #1 (Nov); Shop Oroville First #2, Real Estate, Shop Oroville First #3 (Dec); Shop Oroville First #4; "Living Better"(Tab for Seniors) (monthly).
Special Weekly Sections: Best Automotive Day (mon); Best Food Day (tues); Entertainment (wed); Business Page, Business Profiles (thur); Best Automotive Day, Best Real Estate Days (fri); Best Real Estate Days (sat).
Magazines: TV Magazine; TV Update; Annual "Our Town" (Mar).

CORPORATE OFFICERS

Founder Donald W Reynolds
President/Chief Operating Officer Emmett Jones
Exec Vice Pres/Chief Financial Officer Darrell W Loftin
Vice Pres-Western Newspaper Group David A Osborn
Vice Pres-Eastern Newspaper Group Don Schneider

GENERAL MANAGEMENT

Publisher John Penrich

ADVERTISING

Manager Milton Moore
Manager-Retail Lorrie Steedman

CIRCULATION

Director Teri Jackson

NEWS EXECUTIVE

Editor Roger Aylworth

PRODUCTION

Foreman-Composing Carl Nobel

Market Information: TMC.
Mechanical available: Offset; Black and 3 ROP colors; insert accepted — preprinted; page cut-offs — 22¾".
Mechanical specifications: Type page 13" x 21½"; E - 6 cols, 2.04", ⅙" between; A - 6 cols, 2.04", ⅙" between; C - 9 cols, 1.38", ⅙" between.
Commodity consumption: Newsprint 361 metric tons; width 27"; black ink 2,000 pounds; color ink 900 pounds; single pages printed 6,797; average pages per issue 20(d); single plates used 3,398.
Equipment: EDITORIAL: Front-end hardware — SII/Sys 22; Front-end software — SII; Printers — XIT/Clipper. CLASSIFIED: Front-end hardware — SII/Sys 22; Front-end software — SII; Printers — XIT/Clipper; Other equipment — 3-COM. PRODUCTION: Typesetters — XIT/Clipper; Plate exposures — 1-Nu; Plate processors — Nat/A-250; Direct-to-plate imaging — 3M/Pyrofax; Production cameras — SCREEN/Companica 680C.
PRESSROOM: Line 1 — 7-G; Folders — 1-G/SC, 1-G/Quarter. MAILROOM: Bundle tyer — MLN. WIRE SERVICES: News — AP; Receiving dishes — size-10ft, AP. BUSINESS COMPUTERS: 15-HP/XL 3000; Applications: CJ.

PALM SPRINGS-PALM DESERT

Riverside County

'90 U.S. Census- 63,433 (Palm Springs 40,181; Palm Desert 23,252); E&P '96 Est. 85,161 (Palm Springs 46,424; Palm Desert 38,737)
ABC-NDM (90): 221,230 (HH 84,838)

The Desert Sun (m-mon to fri; m-sat; S)

The Desert Sun, 750 N. Gene Autry Trail; PO Box 2734, Palm Springs, CA 92263; tel (619) 322-8889; e-mail cchin@palmspri.gannett.com. Gannett Co. Inc. group.
Circulation: 44,167(m); 48,500(m-sat); 45,869(S); ABC Sept. 30, 1995.
Price: 50¢(d); 50¢(sat); $1.00(S); $9.16/mo (includes tax); $109.92/yr (includes tax).
Advertising: Open inch rate $46.00(m); $46.00(m-sat); $49.05(S). **Representative:** Gannett National Newspaper Sales.
News Services: AP, GNS. **Politics:** Independent. **Established:** 1927.
Special Editions: Bob Hope Golf Classic, Riverside County Date Festival (Feb); Dinah Shore Golf Classic (Mar); Home Sweet Home (May); Home Sweet Home (Sept); Newcomer's Guide (Oct); Holiday Gift Guide I (Nov); Holiday Gift Guide II (Dec); Restaurant Guide, Pure Gold Coupons (monthly).
Special Weekly Sections: Rave Youth Page, Consumer Alert, Investment Tips (mon); Restaurant Review, Golf Notes (tues); Prep Sports, Food on the Run Review (wed); Food, Tourism, Dining a la Heart (thur); Weekend Entertainment Guide, Real Estate Section (fri); Viewpoint, Real Estate (sat); Style, Travel, Health (S).
Magazines: Desert Golf Monthly Magazine (thur); "Weekend" Entertainment Guide, USA Weekend (fri); TV Week (sat); Desert Seniors Magazine (S).

CORPORATE OFFICER

President Robert J Dickey

GENERAL MANAGEMENT

President/Publisher Robert J Dickey
Controller Jon Heimerman

ADVERTISING

Director Greg Pedersen
Manager-Retail David Mercier
Manager-Classified Dennis McNamara
Manager-National Holly Brooks

MARKETING AND PROMOTION

Director-Marketing Christine M Chin

TELECOMMUNICATIONS

Audiotex Manager Phil Johns

CIRCULATION

Director Robert Buchheit
Manager-Single Copy Jack Crotty
Manager-Home Delivery Kevin Kreisler

NEWS EXECUTIVES

Exec Editor Joan Behrmann
Managing Editor Ray Griffith
Asst Managing Editor Tom Tait

EDITORS AND MANAGERS

Business Editor Jan Fraser
City Editor Brian Bean
Editorial Page Editor Keith Carter
Education Writer Chris Mahr
Entertainment Editor Bruce Fessier
Real Estate Editor John Hussar
Society Editor Jan Curran
Sports Editor Tom Elliott
Travel Editor T J Marchetti

MANAGEMENT INFORMATION SERVICES

Data Processing Manager Phil Johns

PRODUCTION

Director Donald Kay
Manager-Systems Les Hathaway
Manager-Systems/Business Phil Johns
Manager-Building Ben Baumer
Manager-Camera/Platemaking Darrell Overturf
Manager-Composing Allen Murphy
Manager-Distribution Center Michael Hall

I-42 California

Market Information: TMC; Operate audiotex.
Mechanical available: Offset; Black and 3 ROP colors; insert accepted — preprinted; page cut-offs — 22.08".
Mechanical specifications: Type page 13" x 21"; E - 6 cols, 2 1/16", 1/8" between; A - 6 cols, 2 1/16", 1/8" between; C - 10 cols, 1 3/16", 1/8" between.
Commodity consumption: Newsprint 6,486 metric tons; widths 54 3/8", 40.781", 27.1875"; black ink 122,790 pounds; color ink 18,347 pounds; single pages printed 20,808; average pages per issue 55(d), 72(S); single plates used 65,504.
Equipment: EDITORIAL: Front-end hardware — AT, 55-PC, 4-AT/CPU; Front-end software — AT, IAS/Rev 7.5; Printers — X, LaserMaster. CLASSIFIED: Front-end hardware — 35-AT, 10-PC; Front-end software — IAS/Rev 7.5; AUDIOTEX: Hardware — IBM/PC; Software — Speechmaster. DISPLAY: Adv layout systems — SCS/Layout 8000; Front-end hardware — Dell/286, Dell/386; Front-end software — SCS/Layout 8000; Printers — Dataproducts/LZR1200. PRODUCTION: Typesetters — 2-AU/800 108S, 2-LaserMax/1200, 1-Dataproducts/LZR2600; Plate exposures — 2-Nu/Flip Top FT40; Plate processors — 2-Nat; Scanners — 2-ECR/Autokon 1000; Production cameras — 1-C/Spartan III, 1-C/Newspaper; Automatic film processors — 6-C; Film transporters — 4-C; Shrink lenses — 1-CK Optical; Color separation equipment (conventional) — Lf/AP Leaf Picture Desk.
PRESSROOM: Line 1 — 6-G/HO (3 half decks); Press drives — Fin; Folders — 1-G/Double, G/3:2; Pasters — Automatic Pasters; Reels and stands — 6-G/CT-50; Press control system — G/MPCS. MAILROOM: Counter stackers — Id/NS660, 3-Id/NS2000; Inserters and stuffers — H/14-72; Bundle tyer — Power Strap; Addressing machine — 1-Ch. LIBRARY: Electronic — Ap/Mac. COMMUNICATIONS: Digital ad delivery system — AP AdSend, AdSat. WIRE SERVICES: News — AP Datastream, AP Datafeatures; Stock tables — AP SelectStox; Syndicates — GNS, NYT, CP; Receiving dishes — size-12ft, AP. BUSINESS COMPUTERS: 1-IBM/Sys AS400, 1-IBM/Sys AS400; Applications: Circ, Adv billing, Accts receivable, Gen ledger, Payroll, Accts payable; PCs & main system networked.

PALMDALE

Los Angeles County
'90 U.S. Census- 68,842; E&P '96 Est. 92,574

Antelope Valley Press
(m-tues to sat; S)

Antelope Valley Press, 37404 N. Sierra Hwy.; PO Box 880, Palmdale, CA 93590; tel (805) 273-2700; fax (805) 947-4870; e-mail email@avpress.com.
Circulation: 30,173(m); 30,173(m-sat); 33,871(S); VAC Mar. 31, 1995.
Price: 50¢(d); 50¢(sat); $1.25(S); $2.50/wk; $10.84/mo; $130.00/yr.
Advertising: Open inch rate $33.36(m); $33.36(m-sat); $35.50(S). **Representative:** Landon Associates Inc.
News Services: Metro, AP, TMS, NYT. **Established:** 1915.
Special Editions: Annual People Who Make A Difference (Feb); Annual Fair Edition (Aug); Annual Welcome Edition (Oct).
Special Weekly Sections: Food (thur); Entertainment, Automotive (fri).
Magazines: USA Weekend, Real Estate Magazine, TV Magazine (S).

CORPORATE OFFICERS
President William C Markham
Vice Pres Virginia Markham
Secretary/Treasurer Marilyn Deatherage

GENERAL MANAGEMENT
Controller William E Forhan

ADVERTISING
Director-Retail Linda Rowlee
Director-Classified William Cunningham
Director-National Cherie Bryant

MARKETING AND PROMOTION
Director-Marketing/Promotion Cherie Bryant

TELECOMMUNICATIONS
Audiotex Manager Bill MacKenzie

CIRCULATION
Director Eric Robanske

NEWS EXECUTIVES
Editor Larry Grooms
Managing Editor Vern Lawson
Assoc Managing Editor John Green
Assoc Managing Editor Lynn Dupratt

EDITORS AND MANAGERS
Automotive Editor Shuwana Farmer
Business/Finance Editor Anne Aldrich
City Editor Margo McCall
Design/Graphics Editor Dale Brown
Editorial Page Editor Larry Grooms
Education Editor Linda Lee
Entertainment/Amusements Editor Todd Weiss
Fashion/Style Editor Darlene Phillips
Features Editor Rich Breault
Health/Medical Editor Rich Breault
Living/Lifestyle Editor Rich Breault
People/Outdoor Editor Rich Breault
Photo Editor Gene Breckner
Real Estate Editor Dean MacDonald
Religion Editor Keith Stepro
Science/Technology Editor Margo McCall
Sports Editor Darrin Jones
Television/Film Editor Todd Weiss
Theater/Music Editor Todd Weiss
Travel Editor Linda Lee

MANAGEMENT INFORMATION SERVICES
Data Processing Manager Gary Schneider

PRODUCTION
Manager Carol McCarroll
Manager-Operations Jeff Walter

Market Information: TMC; ADS; Operate audiotex.
Mechanical available: Offset; Black and 4 ROP colors; insert accepted — preprinted; page cut-offs — 22 3/4".
Mechanical specifications: Type page 13" x 21 1/2"; E - 6 cols, 2 1/16", 1/8" between; A - 6 cols, 2 1/16", 1/8" between; C - 9 cols, 1 3/8", 1/16" between.
Commodity consumption: Newsprint 5,200 metric tons; widths 13 3/4", 27 1/2"; black ink 7,000 pounds; color ink 3,200 pounds; single pages printed 21,800; average pages per issue 48(d), 180(S); single plates used 20,100.
Equipment: EDITORIAL: Front-end hardware — 95-IBM/PC, Lf/AP Leaf Picture Desk; Front-end software — MPS 7.03; Printers — 5-IBM/4029; Other equipment — Lf/Leafscan 35, Wing Lynch/Film Processor, 5-Ap/Mac graphics. CLASSIFIED: Front-end hardware — IBM/PCs; Front-end software — MPS 7.03; Printers — 2-IBM/4029. DISPLAY: Front-end hardware — 15-Ap/Mac; Front-end software — Multi-Ad/Creator; Printers — 2-Ap/Mac LaserWriter, 2-Tektronix/Phaser 300. PRODUCTION: Pagination software — QuarkXPress; Typesetters — 2-Tegra/Varityper/5100, 2-XIT/Clipper, 2-XIT/Tartan, 1-Graphic Enterprises/PageScan 3; Plate exposures — 2-Nu/Flip Top; Plate processors — Nat/A-340; Electronic picture desk — Lf/AP Leaf Picture Desk; Scanners — Lf/Leafscan 35, 3-HP/ScanJet IIc; Production cameras — 2-C, R/440, 1-C/Spartan 3; Automatic film processors — P/Processor ML26, DS/American LD 220-QT, 2-LE/In Line Processor; Film transporters — C; Shrink lenses — C.
PRESSROOM: Line 1 — 10-G/Urbanite; Press drives — 3-HP/100; Folders — 1-G/Urbanite 1000 Series; Pasters — 7-Enkel/Automatic; Press control system — G/Console; Press registration system — Duarte/Pin System. MAILROOM: Counter stackers — 3-Id/2100; Inserters and stuffers — Amerigraph/NP 630; Bundle tyer — 2-Dynaric; Addressing machine — KR/Communications; Mailroom control system — Amerigraph/Icon. LIBRARY: Electronic — MPS. COMMUNICATIONS: Systems used — microwave. WIRE SERVICES: News — AP, NYT; Photos — AP, AP GraphicsNet; Stock tables — AP Grand Central Stocks; Receiving dishes — size-3m, AP. BUSINESS COMPUTERS: IBM/Sys 36; Applications: INSI: Circ, Adv; PCs & micros networked; PCs & main system networked.

PALO ALTO

Santa Clara County
'90 U.S. Census- 55,900; E&P '96 Est. 59,303

Palo Alto Daily News
(m-mon to sat)

Palo Alto Daily News, 329 Alma St., Palo Alto, CA 94301; tel (415) 327-6397; fax (415) 327-0676.
Circulation: 3,500(m); 3,500(m-sat); Estimate Dec. 31, 1995.
Price: Free(d); $3.50/wk.
Advertising: Open inch rate $9.50(m); $9.50(m-sat).
News Service: AP. **Politics:** Independent. **Established:** 1995.
Note: Effective Dec. 7, 1995, this publication started publishing. The circulation numbers are the estimates of the president.

CORPORATE OFFICERS
President David N Danforth
Chairman James S Pavelich
Chief Trustee David E Price

GENERAL MANAGEMENT
Publisher James S Pavelich

ADVERTISING
Manager-City Barbara Troy
Manager-Metro Carolyn Bailey

MARKETING AND PROMOTION
Promotion CEO Michelle Bordeaux

CIRCULATION
Manager Amando Mendoza

NEWS EXECUTIVE
Exec Editor David E Price

EDITOR AND MANAGER
Features Editor Pat Carroll

PRODUCTION
Manager Cyn Gabriel

Mechanical available: Offset; Black and 2 ROP colors; page cut-offs — 13".
Mechanical specifications: Type page 10 3/8" x 13"; E - 6 cols, 1 7/12", 1/6" between; A - 6 cols, 1 7/12", 1/6" between; C - 6 cols, 1 7/12", 1/6" between.
Equipment: EDITORIAL: Front-end hardware — 2-Ap/Power Mac 7200/90; Front-end software — Baseview/NewsEdit Pro. CLASSIFIED: Front-end hardware — 2-Ap/Power Mac 7200/90; Front-end software — Baseview/Class Manager Plus; Printers — HP/LaserJet 5mp. DISPLAY: Front-end hardware — 1-Ap/Power Mac 7500/100; Front-end software — QuarkXPress 3.31; Printers — NewGen/Imager Plus 12xf. PRODUCTION: Pagination software — QuarkXPress 3.31; Electronic picture desk — Lf/AP Leaf Picture Desk; Scanners — HP/ScanJet 3C.
PRESSROOM: Line 1 — 3-G/Community; Folders — 4-G. WIRE SERVICES: News — AP; Photos — AP. BUSINESS COMPUTERS: 1-Ap/Power Mac 7200/90; PCs & main system networked.

PASADENA

Los Angeles County
'90 U.S. Census- 131,591; E&P '96 Est. 141,483
ABC-NDM (90): 325,645 (HH 119,601)

Star-News (m-mon to sat; S)

Star-News, 911 E. Colorado Blvd., Pasadena, CA 91101; tel (818) 578-6300; fax (818) 795-3510; web site http://www.earthlink.net/~thomsonla/. Thomson Newspapers group.
Circulation: 42,206(m); 42,206(m-sat); 41,296(S); ABC Sept. 30, 1995.
Price: 35¢(d); 35¢(sat); $1.00(S); $2.50/wk; $10.00/mo; $130.00/yr.
Representative: Cresmer, Woodward, O'Mara & Ormsbee.
News Services: AP, CNS, KRT, McClatchy, NYT. **Politics:** Independent. **Established:** 1886.
Note: The Thomson LA News Group includes the following newspapers: Pasadena Star News (mS), San Gabriel Valley Tribune (mS) and Whittier Daily News (mS). The group combination rate is $63.00 (d) & (S). Individual newspaper rates not made available.
Special Editions: LA Auto Show, New Jobs (Jan); Health File (Feb); Spring Home & Garden, Job Fair (Mar); Careers '96, Bridal Fair (Apr); Spring Fashion Magazine, Mother's Day, Health File, Progress (May); Auto/Summer Wheels, Family-owned Business (June); 4th of July, Careers '96 (July); Health File, Best of Cheers (Aug); Fall Fashion Magazine, LA County Fair Tab (Sept); A Taste of Pasadena, Fall Home & Garden Arboretum, Job Fair Section, New Cars '97 (Oct); Health File, Gift Guide #1 (Nov); Gift Guide #2, Gift Guide #3, The Rose (magazine) (Dec).
Special Weekly Sections: Wheels Automotive, Home Buyer's Guide (sat).
Magazines: Cheers (fri); Parade, TV Magazine (S).

CORPORATE OFFICERS
Group Publisher Joseph A Logan
Exec Editor/Vice Pres John Irby
Director-Circulation Ron L Wood

GENERAL MANAGEMENT
Chief Financial Officer Barry Thompson
Director-Human Resources Ted Barajas

ADVERTISING
Director-Marketing Jan Berk
Manager-Classified Ron Busick
Manager-Retail Janice Jones

CIRCULATION
Director Ron L Wood
Manager-Home Deliveries Joe Robidoux

NEWS EXECUTIVES
Exec Editor/Vice Pres John Irby
Editor Lawrence Wilson
Managing Editor Dorothy Reinhold

EDITORS AND MANAGERS
Automotive Editor Vernon Rodgers
Business Editor Ali Sar
Entertainment Editor Cathie Porrelli
Editorial Page Editor Kevin O'Leary
Fashion/Style Editor Lisa Cooke
Features Editor Catherine Garigh
Graphics Editor Don Sprout
News Editor Michael Coates
Operations Editor Steve O'Sullivan
Photo Editor Tim Berger
Chief Photographer Walt Mancini
Science/Technology Editor Tania Soussan
Sports Editor Sam Pollack
Television Editor Mauricio Minotta

MANAGEMENT INFORMATION SERVICES
Director-Management Info Services Arline King

PRODUCTION
Manager Chuck Previtire

Market Information: Zoned editions; TMC; ADS.
Mechanical available: Offset; Black and 3 ROP colors; insert accepted — preprinted; page cut-offs — 22 3/4".
Mechanical specifications: Type page 13" x 21 1/2"; E - 6 cols, 2 1/16", 1/8" between; A - 6 cols, 2 1/16", 1/8" between; C - 10 cols, 1 1/8", 1/16" between.
Commodity consumption: Newsprint 5,011 metric tons; widths 55", 41 1/4", 27 1/2"; black ink 133,333 pounds; color ink 46,061 pounds; single pages printed 21,170; average pages per issue 70(d), 76(sat), 78(S); single plates used 65,789.
Equipment: EDITORIAL: Front-end hardware — SII/Sys 55; Front-end software — SII/Editorial; Other equipment — 38-SII/Coyote, 2-SII/Coyote 15, 4-SII/PC 22. CLASSIFIED: Front-end hardware — SII/Sys 55; Front-end software — SII/Czar; Other equipment — 27-SII/Coyote 15. DISPLAY: Adv layout systems — SII/IAL; Front-end hardware — 6-Ap/Mac, 3-Compaq; Front-end software — SII/IAL, DTI/AdSpeed; Printers — Proofers. PRODUCTION: Pagination software — SII/INL 9.2; Typesetters — 4-MON/Laser, 2-V/5500, 2-V/5600; Platemaking systems — 2-WL; Electronic picture desk — Lf/AP Leaf Picture Desk; Scanners — 10-Compaq, 2-Lf/Leafscan 35; Production cameras — 1-C/Spartan III, 1-C/Newspaper, 1-C/Spartan III; Automatic film processors — 2-LE; Film transporters — 2-LE; Shrink lenses — 1-Alan; Digital color separation equipment — SII, Ap/Mac, QPS.
PRESSROOM: Line 1 — 7-HO; Line 2 — 7-HO; Press drives — Fin; Folders — 3-HO; Pasters — 14-Enkel; Reels and stands — 14-Enkel; Press control system — G/MPCS; Press registration system — G. MAILROOM: Counter stackers — 5-Id/2000, 2-Id/440; Inserters and stuffers — 4-GMA/SLS 1000; Bundle tyer — 5-Power Strap/PSN5; Addressing machine — 2-Videojet/VMS. WIRE SERVICES: News — AP, KRT, NYT; Photos — AP, KRT, NYT; Stock tables — AP; Syndicates — AP; Receiving dishes — AP. BUSINESS COMPUTERS: HP; Applications: CJ, Ceridian: Payroll; PCs & main system networked.

PASO ROBLES

San Luis Obispo County
'90 U.S. Census- 18,583; E&P '96 Est. 30,809

The Country News-Press
(e-mon to fri)

The Country News-Press, 1414 Park St., Paso Robles, CA 93446; tel (805) 237-6060; fax (805) 237-6066. USMedia Inc. group.
Circulation: 4,983(e); Sworn Oct. 1, 1994.
Price: 35¢(d); $6.50/mo (in county); $78.00/yr (in county).
Advertising: Open inch rate $7.95(e); $9.45 (TMC).

California I-43

News Services: AP, CNS, NEA. **Politics:** Independent. **Established:** 1886.

Note: Effective Feb. 1, 1996, the Paso Robles Daily Press merged with the weekly Paso Robles Country News to form the Paso Robles County News-Press.

Not Published: New Year; Memorial Day; Independence Day; Labor Day; Thanksgiving; Christmas.

Special Editions: Health & Fitness (Jan); Progress (Feb); Home Improvement, Spring Gardener, Paderewski Festival (Mar); Recipe Contest, Food & Appliances (Apr); Wine Festival (May); Outdoor Living, Recreation-Vacation (June); County Fair (July); Back-to-School (Aug); 4-H Week, Football Book (Sept); Pioneer Day, Historical (Oct); Christmas Wish Book (Nov); Year-End Review, Holiday Songbook (Dec).

Special Weekly Sections: Food (wed); Entertainment Guide (fri).

Magazines: TV Forecast (fri); Banner (Senior Citizens) (monthly).

CORPORATE OFFICERS

President Eugene A Mace

GENERAL MANAGEMENT

Publisher Keith Berwick
Business Manager Elizabeth Van Note

ADVERTISING

Director Tim Halbin

CIRCULATION

Manager Lawrence Damme

NEWS EXECUTIVES

Editor Sheena Berwick

Market Information: Split Run; TMC.

Mechanical available: Offset; Black and 1 ROP color; insert accepted — preprinted; page cutoffs — $22\frac{3}{4}$".

Mechanical specifications: Type page 13" x $21\frac{1}{2}$"; E - 6 cols, $2\frac{1}{16}$", $\frac{1}{8}$" between; A - 6 cols, $2\frac{1}{16}$", $\frac{1}{8}$" between; C - 9 cols, $1\frac{3}{8}$", $\frac{1}{16}$" between.

Commodity consumption: Newsprint 257 metric tons; widths $27\frac{1}{2}$", $13\frac{3}{4}$"; black ink 4,200 pounds; color ink 380 pounds; single pages printed 6,100; average pages per issue 16(d); single plates used 3,500.

Equipment: EDITORIAL: Front-end hardware — PC/486, PC/386DX-40, PC/486; Front-end software — Microsoft/Word, QuarkXPress, APT/ACT; Printers — GCC/Select Press 600, HP/LaserJet IV; Other equipment — 1-IBM/Selectric Composer, CD-Rom. CLASSIFIED: Front-end hardware — PC/486; Front-end software — APT; Printers — GCC/Select Press 600; Other equipment — 1-IBM/Selectric Composer. DISPLAY: Adv layout systems — QuarkXPress; Front-end hardware — 3-PC/486DX-33; Front-end software — QuarkXPress, GoldDisk/Professional Draw; Printers — GCC/Select Press 600, HP/LaserJet IV. PRODUCTION: Pagination software — Quark XPress 3.1; OCR software — WinFaxPro; Plate exposures — 1-Nu/Flip top, 1-B/Mercury; Scanners — COM/Uniscan, Microtek; Production cameras — 1-K/24; Automatic film processors — LE.
PRESSROOM: Line 1 — 6-KP/Newsking; Folders — 1-KP/Color King. MAILROOM: Inserters and stuffers — 1-KAN/4 station; Bundle tyer — 1-Bu/16-2X, 1-Bu/P.O.; Addressing machine — 1-Am/1900, 1-Am/1955GC. LIBRARY: Electronic — APT. WIRE SERVICES: News — AP; Photos — AP; Stock tables — AP; Syndicates — AP, CNS, United Features, NEA; Receiving dishes — size-10ft, AP. BUSINESS COMPUTERS: 2-IBM/PC; Applications: Bookkeeping, Circ, Adv sales mgmt; PCs & micros networked; PCs & main system networked.

PLACERVILLE
El Dorado County

'90 U.S. Census- 8,355; E&P '96 Est. 8,838
ABC-CZ (90) : 125,995 (HH 46,845)

Mountain Democrat (m-mon; m-wed to fri)

Mountain Democrat, 1360 Broadway; PO Box 1088, Placerville, CA 95667; tel (916) 622-1255; fax (916) 622-7894. McNaughton Newspapers group.

Circulation: 13,258(m); 11,598(m-thur); ABC Sept. 30, 1995.

Price: 50¢(d); 50¢(thur); $68.00/yr.

Advertising: Open inch rate $13.35(m); $13.35(m-thur). **Representatives:** Papert Companies; US Suburban Press. **Established:** 1851.

Special Weekly Sections: Weekend Sports Wrap-up, Over the Back Fence (mon); Best Food Day (wed); Entertainment, Local Columnists, Foothill Focus (West County News) (thur); Real Estate, Church Directory, Entertainment, Restaurant (fri); Business, Foothill Life, Junior Journal (daily).

GENERAL MANAGEMENT

Publisher James C Webb

ADVERTISING

Manager Laurie Waters

CIRCULATION

Manager Gerry Ulm

NEWS EXECUTIVE

Editor Michael Raffety

MANAGEMENT INFORMATION SERVICES

Director-Management Info Services Scott Coffin

PRODUCTION

Director Scott Coffin

Market Information: TMC.

Mechanical available: Offset; Black and 3 ROP colors; insert accepted — preprinted; page cutoffs — $21\frac{5}{8}$".

Mechanical specifications: Type page 13" x 21"; E - 6 cols, $2\frac{1}{16}$", $\frac{1}{6}$" between; A - 6 cols, $2\frac{1}{16}$", $\frac{1}{16}$" between; C - 9 cols, $1\frac{5}{16}$", $\frac{1}{6}$" between.

Commodity consumption: width 27".

Equipment: EDITORIAL: Front-end hardware — PCs; Front-end software — CText; Printers — AG, HP. CLASSIFIED: Front-end hardware — PCs; Front-end software — CText; Printers — HP, AG. DISPLAY: Adv layout systems — Ap/Mac; Front-end hardware — Ap/Mac; Front-end software — QuarkXPress, Adobe/Photoshop; Printers — Ap/Mac, HP. PRODUCTION: Pagination software — Adobe/Photoshop, QuarkXPress; Automatic film processors — AG. MAILROOM: Inserters and stuffers — KAN; Bundle tyer — MLN. LIBRARY: Electronic — SMS. WIRE SERVICES: News — NYT; Photos — NYT. BUSINESS COMPUTERS: VisionData; Applications: VisionData: Accounting, Circ; PCs & micros networked.

PLEASANTON
Alameda County

'90 U.S. Census- 50,553; E&P '96 Est. 64,897
Tri-Valley Herald:
ABC-NDM (90): 249,197 (HH 87,449)
Valley Times:
ABC-NDM (90): 212,230 (HH 75,303)

Tri-Valley Herald (m-mon to sat; S)

Tri-Valley Herald, 4770 Willow Rd.; PO Box 10367, Pleasanton, CA 94588; tel (510) 734-8600; fax (510) 416-4721. MediaNews Inc. (Alameda Newspapers) group.

Circulation: 37,226(m); 37,226(m-sat); 38,199(S); ABC Sept. 30, 1995.

Price: 50¢(d); 50¢(sat); $1.00(S); $1.61/wk.

Representative: Landon Associates Inc.

News Services: NYT, AP, LAT-WP, SHNS, McClatchy. **Politics:** Independent. **Established:** 1874.

Note: Advertising is sold in combination with Fremont Argus (mS), Hayward Daily Review (mS), Oakland Tribune (mS) and Pleasanton Tri-Valley Herald (mS) for $118.00 (dS). Individual newspaper rates not made available. For detailed mechanical equipment information, see the Oakland Tribune (mS).

Special Editions: East Bay Almanac (Mar); East Bay Leisure Guide (June); "Best" from Valley to Bay (Oct); Auto, Christmas Gifts (Nov); Christmas Gifts (Dec).

Special Weekly Sections: Best Food Day (wed); Automotive (fri); New Homes (sat); Travel (S); CUE (daily).

Magazines: USA Weekend, TV Week (S).

CORPORATE OFFICERS

President/Publisher Peter Bernhard
Asst to Publisher/Vice Pres Administration Patrick Brown
Senior Vice Pres-Production Dennis Miller
Senior Vice Pres-Advertising Roger Grossman
Senior Vice Pres-Circulation Arthur Farber
Senior Vice Pres/Editor in Chief David Burgin
Vice Pres-Human Resources Jim Janiga

GENERAL MANAGEMENT

Publisher Peter Bernhard
Assoc Publisher Joseph Haraburda
Manager-Human Resources Karen Austin

ADVERTISING

Director Jennine Loumena
Director-Classified Pete Laraway
Manager-National Mary Menard

MARKETING AND PROMOTION

Director-Marketing/Promotion Service Deborah Byrum

CIRCULATION

Director Wally Tiedemann
Director-Operations Mary O'Brien

NEWS EXECUTIVES

Exec Editor Nancy Conway
Editor Tim Hunt
Managing Editor Tom Sawyer
Managing Editor-Production Chris Campos

EDITORS AND MANAGERS

Books Editor Robert Taylor
Business Editor David Tong
Asst Business Editor Scott Ard
City Editor Steve Waterhouse
Columnist Ray Orrock
Columnist Tom Goff
Editorial Page Editor Bob Cuddy
Features Editor Sharon Betz
Asst Features Editor Richard Defendorf
Films Editor Barry Caine
Food Editor Catherine Chriss
Director-Libraries Steve Lavoie
Movie Critic Barry Caine
News Editor Brian Gardner
Director-News Production Chris Campos
Director-Photo/Graphics Rob Lindquist
Sacramento CA Bureau Editor Sam Delson
Sports Editor Steve Herendeen
Sports Columnist Dave Newhouse
Sports Columnist Monte Poole
Sports Columnist Carl Stewart
Television Editor Susan Young
Travel Editor Bari Brenner

MANAGEMENT INFORMATION SERVICES

Data Processing Manager Ken Marcum
Online Manager Kevin Hamilton

PRODUCTION

Director Dave Boyer
Superintendent-Pre Press Pete Salm

Market Information: TMC; ADS; Operate database.

Mechanical available: Black and 3 ROP colors; insert accepted — preprinted; page cut-offs — 21.5".

Mechanical specifications: Type page 13" x 21.5"; E - 6 cols, $2\frac{1}{16}$", $\frac{1}{8}$" between; A - 6 cols, $2\frac{1}{16}$", $\frac{1}{8}$" between; C - 10 cols, $1\frac{1}{4}$", $\frac{1}{32}$" between.

Commodity consumption: Newsprint 3,950 metric tons; widths 55", $41\frac{1}{4}$", $27\frac{3}{8}$"; black ink 80,000 pounds; color ink 7,500 pounds; single pages printed 27,632; average pages per issue 72(d), 98(S); single plates used 30,841.

Valley Times (m-mon to sat; S)

Valley Times, 127 Spring St.; PO Box 607, Pleasanton, CA 94566; tel (510) 462-4160; fax (510) 847-2177; e-mail valleytms@aol.com. Knight-Ridder Inc. group.

Circulation: 38,924(m); 38,924(m-sat); 41,287(S); ABC Sept. 30, 1995.

Price: 50¢(d); 50¢(sat); $1.25(S); $7.50/mo (carrier).

Representatives: Cresmer, Woodward, O'Mara & Ormsbee; US Suburban Press.

News Service: AP. **Politics:** Independent. **Established:** 1971.

Note: The Contra Costa Daily Group includes the Antioch Ledger Dispatch (eS), Pleasanton Valley Times (mS), Richmond West County Times (mS) and Walnut Creek Contra Costa Times (mS). The group combination rates are $104.05 (d) and $114.35 (S). Individual newspaper rates not made available.

Special Editions: Spring Home & Garden (Feb); Football Preview (Sept); Fall Home & Garden, Fall Real Estate (Oct); Christmas (5 Sections); Contra Costa/Southern Alameda Counties Info; Book; International Auto; Design-an-Ad.

Special Weekly Section: Auto (fri).

Magazine: USA Weekend.

CORPORATE OFFICER

Publisher/CEO George E Riggs

GENERAL MANAGEMENT

Publisher George E Riggs
General Manager David Rounds

ADVERTISING

Manager Wendy Davidson

NEWS EXECUTIVE

Managing Editor Karen Magnuson

EDITORS AND MANAGERS

Business Editor Patrick Twoey
City Editor Kelly Gust
Editorial Page Editor Linda Seebach
Sports Editor Dan Wood

MANAGEMENT INFORMATION SERVICES

Data Processing Manager Dale Olford

PRODUCTION

Director Donald Jochens
Manager Gordon Brown
Manager-Pressroom Werner Reuper

Market Information: Zoned editions; TMC; ADS.

Mechanical available: Offset; Black and 3 ROP colors; insert accepted — preprinted, min size 6" x 8" on 40lbs stock, max size $13\frac{3}{4}$" x 11 ¼" folded; page cut-offs — $22\frac{3}{4}$".

Mechanical specifications: Type page 13" x 21"; E - 6 cols, $2\frac{1}{16}$", $\frac{1}{8}$" between; A - 6 cols, $2\frac{1}{16}$", $\frac{1}{8}$" between; C - 10 cols, $1\frac{1}{4}$", $\frac{1}{16}$" between.

Commodity consumption: Newsprint 5,322 metric tons; widths 55", $41\frac{1}{4}$", $27\frac{1}{2}$"; black ink 87,278 pounds; color ink 33,316 pounds; single pages printed 35,737; average pages per issue 70(d), 140(S); single plates used 66,769.

Equipment: EDITORIAL: Front-end hardware — AT/9000, PC/486-66. Front-end software — Dewar, AT, Microsoft/Word; Other equipment — 22-AT/Reporter; CLASSIFIED: Front-end hardware — AT/9000; Other equipment — SII, 6-AT/Reporter, DEC/220. DISPLAY: Adv layout systems — SCS/Layout 8000; Front-end hardware — Ap/Power Mac; Front-end software — MultiAd/Creator 3.8; Printers — Ap/Mac LaserWriter; Other equipment — CD-Rom. PRODUCTION: Pagination software — Dewar, Quark XPress. MAILROOM: Counter stackers — 7-QWI/100, 6-QWI/300, 4-MM/288; Inserters and stuffers — 1-HI/1372, 1-HI/1472, 1-HI/2299, 2-MM/275; Bundle tyer — 8-Dynaric, 4-MLN, 3-Bu; Wrapping singles — 1-St/Shanklin; Addressing machine — 1-Ch, 1-St. LIBRARY: Electronic — Condor/Custom Program; Combination — Minolta/Microfiche. WIRE SERVICES: News — AP; Stock tables — Foreign, Futures, US Bonds & Notes, NYSE, American, OTC, Money Market; Syndicates — LATS, NYT. BUSINESS COMPUTERS: PCs, Ap/Mac se; Applications: Lotus, Microsoft/Word, Microsoft/Excel; PCs & micros networked.

PORTERVILLE
Tulare County

'90 U.S. Census- 29,563; E&P '96 Est. 39,080
ABC-CZ (90): 44,837 (HH 14,211)

Recorder (e-mon to fri; m-sat)

Recorder, 115 E. Oak Ave.; PO Box 151, Porterville, CA 93257; tel (209) 784-5000; fax (209) 784-1172. Freedom Communications Inc. group.

Circulation: 12,241(e); 12,241(m-sat); ABC Sept. 30, 1995.

Price: 50¢(d); 75¢(sat); $7.25/mo (plus tax); $87.00/yr (plus tax).

Advertising: Open inch rate $9.80(e); $9.80(m-sat). **Representative:** Papert Companies.

News Service: AP. **Politics:** Independent. **Established:** 1908.

Not Published: New Year; Memorial Day; Independence Day; Labor Day; Thanksgiving; Christmas.

Advertising not accepted: Dubious classified.

Special Editions: Bridal (Jan); Progress Edition (Feb); Spring Home Improvement (Mar); Home Buying Guide, Football Preview (Apr); Fair Tab (May); Classic Car (June); Crazy Days (July); Education Basics (Aug); Customer Appreciation Days (Sept); Red Ribbon Week, Women in Business (Oct); Veteran's Day, Christmas Kick-off (Nov); Christmas Greetings (Dec).

Special Weekly Sections: Food Section (tues); Farm (thur); Business (fri); Religion (sat).

Magazines: TV Week, Vista Magazine, Colored Comics (sat).

CORPORATE OFFICERS

CEO James Rosse
President-West Scott Fischer

GENERAL MANAGEMENT

Publisher James L Lyons

Copyright ©1996 by the Editor & Publisher Co.

ADVERTISING
Director Jonell Webb
CIRCULATION
Manager Paul J Kerrigan
NEWS EXECUTIVE
Managing Editor Rick Elkins
EDITOR AND MANAGER
Sports Editor Charles Whisnand
MANAGEMENT INFORMATION SERVICES
Data Processing Manager Shelley Sailor
PRODUCTION
Manager Kevin Clark

Market Information: Split Run; TMC.
Mechanical available: Offset; Black and 3 ROP colors; insert accepted — preprinted, other; page cut-offs — 22¾".
Mechanical specifications: Type page 13" x 21"; E - 6 cols, 2 1/16", ⅛" between; A - 6 cols, 2 1/16", ⅛" between; C - 8 cols, 1⅝", ⅛" between.
Commodity consumption: Newsprint 629 metric tons; widths 28", 14"; black ink 15,000 pounds; color ink 1,000 pounds; single pages printed 8,000; average pages per issue 26(d), 26(sat); single plates used 5,760.
Equipment: EDITORIAL: Front-end hardware — AST/286's; Front-end software — Microsoft/DOS 3.30, Dewar; Printers — Okidata/Microline 393; Other equipment — 4-SIA/386 file-server. CLASSIFIED: Front-end hardware — 6-AST/286; Front-end software — Microsoft/DOS 3.30, Dewar; Printers — Okidata/Microline 393; Other equipment — 1-Dewar/Discovery, SIA/386. DISPLAY: Adv layout systems — 2-Dewar/Discovery, SIA/386. PRODUCTION: Pagination software — Adobe/Photostop 3.0, QuarkXPress 3.3; Typesetters — 2-Tegra/Varityper 5100, ECR/Scriptsetter II VR36; Plate exposures — 1-Nu; Scanners — Lf/Leafscan 35, AG/Arcus II Flatbed; Production cameras — Acti/225; Automatic film processors — Devotec/20, Ap/Mac Quadra 950; Color separation equipment (conventional) — Ap/Power Mac 7100-80.
PRESSROOM: Line 1 — 8-G/Community; Folders — 1-G/2:1. MAILROOM: Bundle tyer — 2-Us, 1-MLN. WIRE SERVICES: News — AP; Receiving dishes — AP. BUSINESS COMPUTERS: 1-Packard Bell/Novell, 1-Genecom/4440XT, 4-Compaq, 1-Packard Bell/Visionary, 3-IBM/PC 80, 2-IBM/30, Novell; PCs & micros networked.

RED BLUFF

Tehama County

'90 U.S. Census- 12,363; E&P '96 Est. 14,767
ABC-NDM (90): 28,252 (HH 10,863)

Daily News (e-mon to sat)

Daily News, 545 Diamond Ave.; PO Box 220, Red Bluff, CA 96080; tel (916) 527-2151; fax (916) 527-3719. Donrey Media group.
Circulation: 7,948(e); 7,948(e-sat); ABC Sept. 30, 1995.
Price: 47¢(d); 47¢(sat); $6.43/mo (plus tax); $77.16/yr (plus tax).
Advertising: Open inch rate $10.93(e); $10.93(e-sat). **Representative:** Papert Companies.
News Service: AP. **Politics:** Independent. **Established:** 1885.
Not Published: New Year; Memorial Day; Independence Day; Labor Day; Thanksgiving; Christmas.
Special Editions: Bull Sale (Jan); Home Improvement, Spring Celebration (Feb); Health (Mar); Rodeo (Apr); Women (May); Vacation Guide (June); Fair (July); New Faces (Aug); Youth (Sept); County's Past (Oct); Senior Services, Christmas (Nov); Kids Ads (Dec).
Special Weekly Sections: Best Food Day, Senior Citizen Page (tues); Business Page (wed); Farm Page (sat).
Magazine: TV Round-Up (sat).

CORPORATE OFFICERS
Founder Donald W Reynolds
President/Chief Operating Officer Emmett Jones
Exec Vice Pres/Chief Financial Officer Darrell W Loftin
Vice Pres-Western Newspaper Group David A Osborn
Vice Pres-Eastern Newspaper Group Don Schneider

GENERAL MANAGEMENT
Publisher Mel Wagner
Business Manager Daleen Baker
ADVERTISING
Manager Jean Hanson
CIRCULATION
Manager Patrick Scott
NEWS EXECUTIVE
Editor Bill Goodyear
EDITORS AND MANAGERS
News Editor Barbara Beal
Sports Editor John Bohannon
PRODUCTION
Supervisor-Press Max Cavette
Supervisor-Composing Erlyne Savercool

Market Information: TMC.
Mechanical available: Offset; Black and 3 ROP colors; insert accepted — preprinted; page cut-offs — 22½".
Mechanical specifications: Type page 27½" x 22¾"; E - 6 cols, 2", ⅛" between; A - 6 cols, 2 1/16", ⅛" between; C - 9 cols, 1 5/16", 1/12" between.
Commodity consumption: Newsprint 300 metric tons; widths 27½", 27", 13½", 13¾"; black ink 14,975 pounds; color ink 775 pounds; single pages printed 4,496; average pages per issue 14(d), 14(sat); single plates used 5,180.
Equipment: EDITORIAL: Front-end hardware — 5-Mk/1100, 9-Mk/1100 Plus; Front-end software — Mk; Printers — 1-TI/Omni 800. CLASSIFIED: Front-end hardware — 2-Mk/1100 Plus; Front-end software — Mk. PRODUCTION: Typesetters — 2-Ap/Mac LaserPrinter, 2-Mk/Ad Touch; Platemaking systems — 3M/Fuser; Plate exposures — 1-Nu/Flip Top; Production cameras — Acti/Process, 3M/Imager; Shrink lenses — CK Optical.
PRESSROOM: Line 1 — 4-G/Urbanite (Balloon former); Folders — 1-G/2:1; Press control system — CH. MAILROOM: Counter stackers — BG/Count-O-Veyor; Inserters and stuffers — KAN; Bundle tyer — 2-Cyclone. WIRE SERVICES: News — AP; Receiving dishes — AP. BUSINESS COMPUTERS: Applications: IBM: Circ.

REDDING

Shasta County

'90 U.S. Census- 66,462; E&P '96 Est. 91,359
ABC-NDM (90): 166,414 (HH 63,859)

Record Searchlight
(m-mon to sat; S)

Record Searchlight, 1101 Twin View Blvd.; PO Box 492397, Redding, CA 96049-2397; tel (916) 243-2424; fax (916) 225-8212; web site http://www.redding.com/. Scripps Howard group.
Circulation: 37,692(m); 37,692(m-sat); 39,871(S); ABC Sept. 30, 1995.
Price: 50¢(d); 50¢(sat); $1.50(S); $10.75/mo; $129.00/yr.
Advertising: Open inch rate $25.42(m); $25.42(m-sat); $27.25(S). **Representative:** Papert Companies.
News Services: AP, LAT-WP, McClatchy, SHNS. **Politics:** Independent. **Established:** 1852.
Special Editions: Seniors (Jan); Spring Fashion, Home & Garden (Mar); Spring Car Care (Apr); Fall Fashion, Home Beautification (Sept); Fall Car Care (Oct); Christmas; Thanksgiving Day.
Special Weekly Sections: Best Food Day (tues); Entertainment (thur); Automotive (fri); Real Estate (sat); TV Listings, Garden, Building, Travel (S).
Magazines: Business (daily); Best Food Day (tues); Outdoor Sports (thur); Automotive (fri); Real Estate (sat); Building, Garden, Home, Travel (S).

CORPORATE OFFICERS
President Alan M Horton
Vice Pres Jeff Hively
Secretary M Denise Cuprionis
Controller Kim Parks
GENERAL MANAGEMENT
General Manager Larry R Wakefield
ADVERTISING
Director-Marketing William R Dawson
Manager-Retail Bernard Metzger
MARKETING AND PROMOTION
Director-Marketing William R Dawson
CIRCULATION
Manager Leroy Wick
NEWS EXECUTIVE
Editor Robert W Edkin
EDITORS AND MANAGERS
Business/Finance Editor George Winship
City Editor David Waddell
Editorial Page Editor Robert W Edkin
Education Editor Stasia Scarborough
Entertainment/Amusements Editor Betty Lease
Environmental Editor Robert Holquist
Family/Food Editor Betty Lease
Farm/Agriculture Editor David Waddell
Fashion/Style Editor Betty Lease
Features Editor Betty Lease
Graphics Editor/Art Director Greg Clark
Health/Medical Editor Robert Holquist
Living/Lifestyle Editor Betty Lease
Photo Editor Greg Clark
Religion Editor John Crowe
Science/Technology Editor Robert Holquist
Sports Editor David Little
Television/Film Editor Betty Lease
Theater/Music Editor Betty Lease
Travel Editor Steve Moore
Women's Editor Betty Lease
MANAGEMENT INFORMATION SERVICES
Data Processing Manager Paul Anderson
PRODUCTION
Director-Systems William A Wagner
Foreman-Composing W R Guin
Superintendent-Press Dennis McKillop

Market Information: TMC; ADS.
Mechanical available: Offset; Black and 3 ROP colors; insert accepted — preprinted, all; page cut-offs — 22¾".
Mechanical specifications: Type page 13" x 21¼"; E - 6 cols, 2 1/16", ⅛" between; A - 6 cols, 2 1/16", ⅛" between; C - 10 cols, 1⅜", 1/12" between.
Commodity consumption: Newsprint 2,872 metric tons; widths 27", 40½", 54"; black ink 54,116 pounds; color ink 21,000 pounds; single pages printed 14,626; average pages per issue 40(d), 44(S); single plates used 50,400.
Equipment: EDITORIAL: Front-end hardware — PC; Front-end software — Dewar; Printers — V, TB/GUA 5100, TB/GUA 5380E. CLASSIFIED: Front-end software — HI/CASH, HI/CASH for Windows. DISPLAY: Adv layout systems — Dewar/Discovery, Archetype/Corel Draw; Front-end hardware — PC; Front-end software — Dewar. PRODUCTION: Pagination software — Dewar; Typesetters — Dolev/450, Tegra; Plate exposures — 1-BKY, 1-Nu; Plate processors — 2-Nat/A-340-1; Electronic picture desk — Lf; Scanners — Scitex/Smart 540; Production cameras — 1-Acti/504-D; Automatic film processors — Glunz & Jensen; Shrink lenses — CK Optical/Anamorphic 2-25; Color separation equipment (conventional) — Howtek; Digital color separation equipment — Scitex.
PRESSROOM: Line 1 — 7-HI/N1600; Folders — 2-HI; Pasters — 7-MEG; Reels and stands — 7-MEG. MAILROOM: Counter stackers — 4-HL; Inserters and stuffers — GMA/1000; Bundle tyer — 2-MLN/2A; Addressing machine — KR. LIBRARY: Electronic — Mead Data Central/Nexis NewsView. COMMUNICATIONS: Digital ad delivery system — AP AdSend. WIRE SERVICES: News — AP; Photos — AP, LAT-WP, Universal Press Syndicate; Syndicates — SHNS, McClatchy; Receiving dishes — size-10ft, AP. BUSINESS COMPUTERS: 1-IBM/AS400 B30, PBS; Applications: RJE, Circ; PCs & micros networked; PCs & main system networked.

REDLANDS

San Bernardino County

'90 U.S. Census- 60,394; E&P '96 Est. 75,559
ABC-NDM (90): 71,006 (HH 25,964)

Redlands Daily Facts
(e-mon to fri; S)

Redlands Daily Facts, 700 Brookside Ave.; PO Box 2240, Redlands, CA 92373; tel (909) 793-3221; fax (909) 793-9588. Donrey Media group.
Circulation: 7,709(e); 7,755(S); ABC Sept. 30, 1995.
Price: 32¢(d); 93¢(S); $1.50/wk.
Advertising: Open inch rate $13.29(e); $13.29(S). **Representative:** Papert Companies.
News Service: AP. **Established:** 1890.
Advertising not accepted: Vending; Out-of-town employment requiring investment.
Special Weekly Sections: At Your Service, Local Business Features (mon); Church News (tues); Food Advertising, Cultural Arts (wed); Lifestyle, Our Town (thur); Dining Guide, Teen Facts, Church Directory, Our Town (fri); Cultural Arts, Our Town (S); New York Stocks (daily).
Magazines: Parade, TV Facts, Color Comics (S).

CORPORATE OFFICERS
Founder Donald W Reynolds
President/Chief Operating Officer Emmett Jones
Exec Vice Pres/Chief Financial Officer Darrell W Loftin
Vice Pres-Western Newspaper Group David A Osborn
Vice Pres-Eastern Newspaper Group Don Schneider
GENERAL MANAGEMENT
Publisher Toebe Bush
ADVERTISING
Director David Berkowitz
CIRCULATION
Manager Larry Fehrnstrom
Supervisor-Distribution Mike Rust
NEWS EXECUTIVE
Managing Editor Carl Baker
EDITORS AND MANAGERS
Community Editor Nelda Stuck
Sports Editor Obrey Brown
PRODUCTION
Director Augustine J Chavez
Supervisor-Pressroom Ron Munoz

Mechanical available: Offset; Black and 3 ROP colors; insert accepted — preprinted; page cut-offs — 22¾".
Mechanical specifications: Type page 13" x 21½"; E - 6 cols, 2 1/16", ⅛" between; A - 6 cols, 2 1/16", ⅛" between; C - 9 cols, 1⅜", ⅛" between.
Commodity consumption: Newsprint 240 metric tons; widths 27½", 13¾"; black ink 15,500 pounds; color ink 600 pounds; single pages printed 11,000; average pages per issue 16(d), 20(S); single plates used 6,500.
Equipment: EDITORIAL: Front-end hardware — 19-Mk. CLASSIFIED: Front-end hardware — 4-Mk. PRODUCTION: OCR software — Caere/OmniPage Pro 2.12; Typesetters → 2-HP/LaserJet 4M, 2-NewGen/Turbo PS-480; Plate exposures — 1-Nu/Flip Top; Plate processors — 1-Ic/ICM-25; Scanners — 1-Microtek/600-GS; Production cameras — Acti, 1-R/Ll2; Shrink lenses — 1-CK Optical/SQU-7.
PRESSROOM: Line 1 — 5-G/SC; Folders — 1-G. MAILROOM: Counter stackers — BG/Count-O-Veyor; Inserters and stuffers — KAN/320; Bundle tyer — 1-IOA/Strapex; Addressing machine — DPT. WIRE SERVICES: News — AP; Photos — AP; Stock tables — AP; Receiving dishes — size-10ft, AP. BUSINESS COMPUTERS: SSPS/PC-based; Applications: Circ.

RICHMOND

Contra Costa County

'90 U.S. Census- 87,425; E&P '96 Est. 100,528
ABC-NDM (90): 213,268 (HH 79,228)

West County Times
(m-mon to sat; S)

West County Times, 4301 Lakeside Dr. (Richmond 94806); PO Box 100, Pinole, CA 94564; tel (510) 758-8400; fax (510) 262-2719. Knight-Ridder Inc. group.
Circulation: 32,721(m); 32,721(m-sat); 33,029(S); ABC Sept. 30, 1995.
Price: 50¢(d); 50¢(sat); $1.50(S); $9.18/mo (carrier).
Representative: Cresmer, Woodward, O'Mara & Ormsbee.
News Services: AP, LAT-WP, NYT, States News Service, McClatchy. **Politics:** Independent. **Established:** 1899.
Note: The Contra Costa Daily Group includes the following newspapers: Richmond West County Times (mS), Antioch Ledger Dispatch (eS), Pleasanton Valley Times (mS) and Walnut Creek Contra Costa Times (mS). The group combination rates are $104.05(d) and $114.35(S). Individual newspaper rates not made available. For detailed production information, see the Walnut Creek Contra Costa Times listing.
Special Editions: Holiday Recipe; Coupon Section; Home & Garden; California Living; Panorama "Eye on the East Bay"; Time Out; Real Estate; Christmas Sections; International Auto; Occupational Trends; Family Times; Prime Times; Good Times.

Magazines: USA Weekend; Bloomberg Financial (S).

CORPORATE OFFICER

Publisher/CEO George E Riggs

GENERAL MANAGEMENT

General Manager Bill James

ADVERTISING

Manager Jenny Kohler

CIRCULATION

Manager Michael Switzer

NEWS EXECUTIVE

Managing Editor Anthony Marquez

EDITORS AND MANAGERS

City Editor Robin Evans
Education Editor Lisa Reynolds
Environmental Editor Willy Morris
Features Editor John Koopman
Photos Editor Cindi Christie
Religion Editor Tuseda Graggs
Sports Editor Jay Heater

MANAGEMENT INFORMATION SERVICES

Data Processing Manager Dale Oldford

PRODUCTION

Director Donald Jochens
Manager Gordon Brown
Manager-Pressroom Werner Reuper

Market Information: TMC; ADS.
Mechanical available: Offset; Black and 3 ROP colors; insert accepted — preprinted, all; page cut-offs — 22 3/4".
Mechanical specifications: Type page 13" x 21½"; E - 6 cols, 2 1/16", 1/8" between; A - 6 cols, 2 1/16", 1/8" between; C - 10 cols, 1 1/4", 1/16" between.
Commodity consumption: Newsprint 3,038 metric tons; widths 55", 41 1/4", 27½"; black ink 70,000 pounds; color ink 15,000 pounds; average pages per issue 54(d), 70(S).
Equipment: EDITORIAL: Front-end hardware — AT/9000, 3-IBM; Other equipment — 21-IBM/PC, 5-RSK/TRS-100. CLASSIFIED: Front-end hardware — SII. DISPLAY: Adv layout systems — SCS/Layout 8000. LIBRARY: Electronic — NewsView, PhotoView.

RIDGECREST

Kern County

'90 U.S. Census- 27,725; E&P '96 Est. 40,979

The Daily Independent

(e-tues to fri; S)

The Daily Independent, 224 E. Ridgecrest Blvd. (93555); PO Box 7, Ridgecrest, CA 93556; tel (619) 375-4481; fax (619) 375-4880; e-mail daily-i@ridgecrest.ca.us. Swift Newspapers group.
Circulation: 8,392(e); 8,392(S); Sworn Oct. 2, 1994.
Price: 50¢(d); $1.00(S); $7.00/mo; $84.00/yr (carrier).
Advertising: Open inch rate $10.50(e); $10.50(S).
News Service: AP. **Politics:** Independent. **Established:** 1946.
Not Published: Christmas.
Special Editions: Perspective, Independent Babies (Jan); Home Show, Spring Home Improvement (Mar); Sierra View Magazine (Apr); Spring Car Care (May); Graduation Congratulations (June); Fall Sports (Sept); New Car Buyers Guide (Oct); Sierra View Magazine, Holiday Expo, Fall Home Improvement, Christmas Wish List (Nov); Christmas Gift Guide, Christmas Carols & Greetings (Dec).
Special Weekly Sections: Automotive (tues); Best Food Day, Fashion, Clubs (wed); Automotive (thur); Religion, Real Estate (fri); Business, TV (entertainment), Fashion Club (S).
Magazine: Cover Story/TV Guide (S).

CORPORATE OFFICERS

Board Chairman Philip E Swift
President Richard K Larson

GENERAL MANAGEMENT

Publisher W Les Hill
President Richard K Larson

ADVERTISING

Director Matthew Hill

CIRCULATION

Director Brian Voight

NEWS EXECUTIVES

Editor W Les Hill
Managing Editor Scott Farwell

EDITOR AND MANAGER

Sports Editor Tim Allen

PRODUCTION

Manager Betty Jo Heaton

Market Information: Split Run; TMC.
Mechanical available: Offset; Black and 3 ROP colors; insert accepted — preprinted; page cut-offs — 22 3/4".
Mechanical specifications: Type page 13" x 21½"; E - 6 cols, 2 1/16", 1/8" between; A - 6 cols, 2 1/16", 1/8" between; C - 9 cols, 1 1/3", 1/12" between.
Commodity consumption: Newsprint 600 metric tons; widths 27½", 32", 34"; average pages per issue 20(d), 24(S).
Equipment: EDITORIAL: Front-end hardware — Ap/Mac; Other equipment — 2-Ap/Mac ci. CLASSIFIED: Front-end hardware — Ap/Mac Classic II. DISPLAY: Adv layout systems — Ap/Mac Classic II. PRODUCTION: Typesetters — 2-Ap/Mac ci; Plate exposures — 1-Nu; Plate processors — 1-Nat; Production cameras — AG; Automatic film processors — Polychrome; Color separation equipment (conventional) — WDS.
PRESSROOM: Line 1 — 6-G; Folders — 1-G. MAILROOM: Inserters and stuffers — MM; Bundle tyer — MLN. WIRE SERVICES: News — AP; Receiving dishes — AP. BUSINESS COMPUTERS: PBS; Applications: Circ, Payroll, Adv, TMC.

RIVERSIDE

Riverside County

'90 U.S. Census- 226,505; E&P '96 Est. 273,710
ABC-NDM (90): 864,279 (HH 288,211)

The Press-Enterprise

(m-mon to sat; S)

The Press-Enterprise, 3512 14 St. (92501-3878); PO Box 792, Riverside, CA 92502-0792; tel (909) 684-1200; fax (909) 782-7630; web site http://www.pe.net.
Circulation: 164,028(m); 164,028(m-sat); 171,624(S); ABC Sept. 30, 1995.
Price: 25¢(d); 25¢(sat); $1.00(S); $1.97/wk; $102.44/yr.
Advertising: Open inch rate $98.46(m); $98.46(m-sat); $104.36(S). **Representative:** Sawyer-Ferguson-Walker Co.
News Services: AP, NYT, ONS, KRT, SHNS, Cox, McClatchy. **Politics:** Independent. **Established:** 1878.
Special Editions: Auto Show (Feb); Spring Home Furnishings (Mar); Restaurant Reviews (May); Health Care Directory (July); Fall Home Furnishings (Sept); Holiday Home Ent. (Nov); Holiday Gift Guide, Last Minute Gift Guide, Christmas Greetings (Dec).
Special Weekly Sections: Auto-Driving (mon); Health & Fitness (tues); Living (wed); Food (thur); Living, Art & Entertainment, Travel (S).
Magazines: The Guide (weekly entertainment tab) (fri); Parade, TV Week Magazine (S).

CORPORATE OFFICERS

Board Chairman Howard H Hays Jr
Secretary/Treasurer Helen C Hays

GENERAL MANAGEMENT

CEO/President/Publisher Marcia McQuern
Exec Vice Pres Jonathan F Hays
Director-Human Resources Susan Marquez
Director-Operations Howard Owens
Manager-Purchasing Klaus Rombach

ADVERTISING

Director Dave Cornwall
Manager-Display/Asst Director Bob Gray
Manager-Classified Sue Barry
Manager-National Jim Milbourne
Manager-Retail Frances Ruka
Manager-Regional Pam Ayala
Manager-Regional Marlene Placak
Manager-Ad Service Larry Vargas
Manager-Major Accounts Jim Mauer
Asst Manager-Classified Telemarketing Darlene Clayton
Coordinator-Co-op Tom Spearman

MARKETING AND PROMOTION

Director-Marketing Renier van Waesberghe

TELECOMMUNICATIONS

Audiotex Manager David Ober
Manager-New Media/PE.net Michael Quinn

CIRCULATION

Director Robert Perona
Manager Mike Kreiser
Manager Denise Schafer
Manager-Home Delivery Larry Brown
Manager-Transportation Tom Berens
Manager-Single Copy Larry Johnston

Manager-Mailroom Larry Wills
Manager-Customer Service Fred Bryan
Manager-Customer Info Service Systems Ralph Macher
Manager-Subscription Sales Jim Rees

NEWS EXECUTIVES

Editor Marcia McQuern
Managing Editor Mel Opotowsky
Asst Managing Editor-Features/Art Sally Ann Maas
Asst Managing Editor-News Jack Holley

EDITORS AND MANAGERS

Business Editor Andrew McCue
Columnist Dan Bernstein
Editorial Page Editor Joel Blain
Entertainment Editor Richard De Atley
Friday Entertainment Editor Michael Cisneros
Food Editor Orlando Ramirez
Garden Editor Judith Graffam
Health Editor Michael Schwartz
Librarian Jackie Chamberlain
Lifestyle Editor Judith Graffam
Metro Editor Norman Bell
Music Editor Richard De Atley
Director-Photography Jim Edwards
Radio/Television Editor Bob Sokolsky
Sports Editor John Garrett
Theater Editor T E Foreman
TV Week Editor Bob Hirt

MANAGEMENT INFORMATION SERVICES

Manager-Info Systems Cheryl Palmer

PRODUCTION

Director-Operations Howard Owens
Superintendent-Pressroom Paul Wahrman
Manager-Pre Press Charles Jones

Market Information: Zoned editions; Split Run; TMC; ADS; Operate audiotex; Electronic edition.
Mechanical available: Offset; Black and 3 ROP colors; insert accepted — preprinted; page cut-offs — 22".
Mechanical specifications: Type page 13" x 21"; E - 6 cols, 2 1/16", 1/8" between; A - 6 cols, 2 1/16", 1/8" between; C - 10 cols, 1 3/16", 1/16" between.
Commodity consumption: Newsprint 24,372 metric tons; widths 54 7/8", 41 1/4", 27½"; black ink 448,253 pounds; color ink 119,815 pounds; single pages printed 26,227; average pages per issue 66(d), 108(S); single plates used 229,937.
Equipment: EDITORIAL: Front-end hardware — 6-AT/Series 60; Front-end software — AT. CLASSIFIED: Front-end hardware — 4-AT/Series 60; Front-end software — AT; Printers — 9-Epson/(25 pin); Other equipment — 10-IBM/Model 50. AUDIOTEX: Hardware — Micro Voice/Audiotext 2000; Supplier name — VNN, Standard, Comstock. DISPLAY: Adv layout systems — III; Front-end hardware — 10-III/AMS; Front-end software — III; Other equipment — III/3725 Illustration Scanner, III/3650 Info Scanner. PRODUCTION: Typesetters — 3-AU/APS Micro 5, 2-III/3810 Laser, 1-III/3850 Sierra; Plate exposures — 2-WL/Lith-X-Pozer III; Plate processors — 2-WL/Lithoplater 38D; Electronic picture desk — Lf/AP Leaf Picture Desk; Scanners — Scanmate/Scanview 600, 2-ECR/Autokon 1000; Production cameras — 1-C/Marathon, 1-C/Spartan III; Automatic film processors — LE/LD24, LE/2600, LE/PC18, Fuji/FG 660F; Film transporters — 3-AU/APS-35, 2-AU/APS-36, III/Packo SCZ050; Shrink lenses — 1-C; Digital color separation equipment — CD/646 IE.
PRESSROOM: Line 1 — 9-G/HO; Line 2 — 9-G/HO; Line 3 — 9-G/HO; Folders — 6-G; Reels and stands — 24-G, 45-CTS; Press control system — 3-G/MPCS. MAILROOM: Counter stackers — 7-HL; Inserters and stuffers — 6-HI/NP1372, 1-HI/NP1372; Bundle tyer — 7-MLN, 2-Bu; Addressing machine — 2-Ch/Labeler, 2-Ch/Ink Jet; Other mailroom equipment — 1-MM. LIBRARY: Electronic — Data Times. COMMUNICATIONS: Digital ad delivery system — DigiFlex, AP AdSend. WIRE SERVICES: News — AP, NYT, ONS, KRT, SHNS; Photos — AFP, AP, RN, TMS; Stock tables — TMS; Syndicates — AP, NYT, CSM, King Features, United Features, TMS; Receiving dishes — size-3m, AP. BUSINESS COMPUTERS: 2-DEC/VAX 6410; Applications: CJ: Newsprint inventory, Circ info sys, Gen ledger, Class adv, Accts payable, Adv info mgmt, Payroll, Fixed assets; PCs & micros networked; PCs & main system networked.

SACRAMENTO

Sacramento County

'90 U.S. Census- 369,365; E&P '96 Est. 449,506
ABC-NDM (90): 1,427,955 (HH 536,370)

The Sacramento Bee

(m-mon to sat; S)

The Sacramento Bee, 2100 Q St.; PO Box 15779, Sacramento, CA 95852; tel (916) 321-1000; fax (916) 321-1109; e-mail sacbedit@netcom.com. McClatchy Newspapers group.
Circulation: 279,980(m); 279,980(m-sat); 348,735(S); ABC Sept. 30, 1995.
Price: 50¢(d); 50¢(sat); $1.25(S); $10.75/mo; $139.00/yr (carrier).
Advertising: Open inch rate $127.48(m); $152.47(m-sat); $133.82(S). **Representative:** Cresmer, Woodward, O'Mara & Ormsbee.
News Services: AP, Bloomberg, CNS, CT, KRT, LAT-WP, NYT, SHNS. **Politics:** Non-partisan. **Established:** 1857.
Special Weekly Sections: Discovery (mon); Food & Wine, Travel, Entertainment Star (wed); Lifetimes (thur); Automotive, Sidetracks, Ticket (fri); California Life, Family Scene, Real Estate, Travel Sunday (sat); Encore, Real Estate, Time & Money, Travel, TV Today (S).
Magazines: Ticket (fri); Parade, Sunday Star, On TV, Color Comics, Encore (S).

CORPORATE OFFICERS

Chairman of the Board/CEO Erwin Potts
President/Chief Operating Officer Gary B Pruitt
Publisher (McClatchy Newspapers) James McClatchy
Senior Vice Pres William L Honeysett
Vice Pres-Finance/Treasurer James P Smith
Vice Pres-Human Resources Peter CaJacob
Vice Pres-News Gregory E Favre
Secretary Karole Morgan-Prager

GENERAL MANAGEMENT

President/General Manager Frank R J Whittaker
Director-Operations Richard N Frey
Director-Human Resources Denise Longwood
Director-Production Ken Duffield
Controller Dwight Hastings
Manager-Accounts Services Sally Burnham
Editor-Neighbors Kathy Drake
Manager-Neighbors (Advertising) Vern Ingraham

ADVERTISING

Director Gene H Grant
Manager-General Lisa Leonard
Manager-Retail John Kelly
Manager-Classified Scott Whitley

MARKETING AND PROMOTION

Director-Marketing Edward Canale
Manager-Promotion Sharon Blixt
Director-Creative David Flanagan
Manager-Strategic Resources James Green
Manager-Education Service Debra Aban
Manager-Electronic Media Frank Dorf
Manager-Research Ronald Olsen

TELECOMMUNICATIONS

Manager-Telecommunications Susan Rueppel

CIRCULATION

Director Gene Czarny
Manager-Alternative Delivery Systems Gary Pitts

NEWS EXECUTIVES

Exec Editor Gregory E Favre
Managing Editor Rick Rodriguez
Asst Managing Editor-Metro Marje Lundstrom
Asst Managing Editor-Features/Electronic Media Ralph Frattura
Asst Managing Editor-Capitol/Politics/Administration William Endicott
Asst Managing Editor-Sports/Business/Photo/Art Mort Saltzman
Assoc Editor Robert Mott
Assoc Editor Mark Paul
Assoc Editor Ginger Rutland
Assoc Editor Bill Kahrl
Assoc Editor Susanna Cooper

EDITORS AND MANAGERS

Amusements Editor Bruce Dancis
Art Director Howard Shintaku
Automotive Editor Bruce Grant
Exec Business Editor Jack Sirard
Business Editor Bob Shallit
California Life Editor Terry Dvorak
Capitol Bureau Chief Amy Chance
Cartoonist Dennis Renault

Copyright ©1996 by the Editor & Publisher Co.

City Editor	Joyce Terhaar
Columnist	Pete Dexter
Columnist	Dan Walters
Columnist	Diana Griego Erwin
Drama	Peter Haugen
Education (Higher)	Jim Richardson
Education (Lower)	Carlos Alcala
Editorial Page Editor	Peter Schrag
Features Editor	Scott Lebar
Films Editor	Joe Baltake
Food Editor	Mike Dunne
Forum Editor	Bill Moore
Garden Editor	Dick Tracy
Medical	Diana Sugg
Music (Opera)	Bob Masullo
National Editor	Mike Bold
Exec News Editor	Pam Dinsmore
News Graphics Editor	Bob Rebach
Ombudsman	Art Nauman
Photo Director	Mark Morris
Photo Director	John Jacobs
Real Estate	Loretta Kalb
Science/Technology	Deborah Blum
Sports Editor	Steve Blust
Deputy Sports Editor	Jonell McFadden
State Editor	Phil Garcia
Teen-Age/Youth Editor	Jeanne Wong
Theater Editor	Bill Glackin
Travel Editor	Janet Fullwood
TV Magazine Editor	Mike Mattis

MANAGEMENT INFORMATION SERVICES

Director-Info Systems	Sandra Langdale

PRODUCTION

Director	Ken Duffield
Manager-Pre Press	Melanie Bergevin
Manager-Press	Bruce Meissner
Manager-Post Production	Scott Nielsen
Manager-Building/Purchasing	David Fox
Manager-Operations Maintenance	David Leonard

Market Information: Zoned editions; Split Run; TMC; ADS; Operate audiotex.

Mechanical available: Offset; Black and 3 ROP colors; insert accepted — preprinted; page cut-offs — 21".

Mechanical specifications: Type page 13" x 21"; E - 6 cols, 2 1/16", 1/8" between; A - 6 cols, 2 1/16", 1/8" between; C - 10 cols, 1 3/8", 1/16" between.

Commodity consumption: Newsprint 60,162 metric tons; widths 54", 40 1/2", 27"; black ink 908,179 pounds; color ink 346,988 pounds; single pages printed 44,418; average pages per issue 90(d), 176(S); single plates used 344,400.

Equipment: EDITORIAL: Front-end hardware — SII/Sys 55; Front-end software — SII, Guardian/C-30; Printers — HP/LaserJet. CLASSIFIED: Front-end hardware — SII/Sys 55; Front-end software — SII; Printers — HP/LaserJet. AUDIOTEX: Hardware — Brite Voice Systems, Ap/Mac, IBM/PC. DISPLAY: Adv layout systems — Cx; Front-end hardware — 6-Sun/380, 5-Sun/Sparc 360, 9-Sun/Sparc 5; Front-end software — Cx 8.0; Printers — QMS; Other equipment — Linotype-Hell/530, Linotype-Hell/500, 2-III/3850. PRODUCTION: Typesetters — 4-Linotype-Hell/Linotronic 500, 1-Linotype-Hell/Linotronic 530, 1-Hyphen/Spectraset 2200, 2-III/3850; Platemaking systems — WL, KFM; Plate exposures — 1-WL/IV, 2-KFM/Plate Express, 1-KFM/Verifier, 1-Nu/Flip Top; Plate processors — 3-WL/38D, 3-WL/Crimper; Electronic picture desk — CD/Pixielink; Scanners — 2-ECR/Autokon 2000, 2-CD/646; Production cameras — C/Spartan III, C/Newspager; Automatic film processors — 4-AG/2600, 2-Kk/710, 2-LE/1800, 2-PK; Reproportion units — 2-CD/9500C; Film transporters — 2-LE, 2-PK; Shrink lenses — 1-C; Color separation equipment (conventional) — 1-CD/646 I-F, 1-CD/636 M-F; Digital color separation equipment — 2-CD/9500. PRESSROOM: Line 1 — 11-G/Metroliner; Line 2 — 11-G/Metroliner; Line 3 — 11-G/Metroliner; Line 4 — 36-G/Colorliner couples; Pasters — 9-G/RTP; Press control system — G/PCSI, G/APCS, Fin, Allen Bradley. MAILROOM: Counter stackers — 22-QW1/300, 4-Id/200; Inserters and stuffers — 6-Amerigraph/2299; Bundle tyer — 18-Dynaric/NP-1, 24-Dynaric/NP-2, 21-Dynaric/PNP-1; Mailroom control system — Amerigraph/AMCS-Prima. LIBRARY: Electronic — SII/Laser. WIRE SERVICES: News — AP Datafeatures, AP Dataspeed, AP Datafeatures, CNS, KRT, NYT; Photos — AP; Stock tables — AP SelectStox; Syndicates — North America Syndicate; Receiving dishes — size-3m, AP, Bloomberg. BUSINESS COMPUTERS: 3-DEC/8550; Applications: AMS, CMS, Database/Systems, Adabas, DEC/Rdb, Oracle; PCs & micros networked; PCs & main system networked.

SALINAS

Monterey County

'90 U.S. Census- 108,777; E&P '96 Est. 133,183

ABC-NDM (90): 186,565 (HH 53,837)

The Californian (m-mon to sat)

The Californian, 123 W. Alisal St. 93901; PO Box 81091 (93912), Salinas, CA 93901; tel (408) 424-2221; fax (408) 754-4221; e-mail valleynews@aol.com. Gannett Co. Inc. group.

Circulation: 21,517(m); 21,517(m-sat); ABC Sept. 30, 1995.

Price: 35¢(d); 75¢(sat); $9.00/mo.

Advertising: Open inch rate $26.44(m); $26.44(m-sat). **Representative:** Gannett National Newspaper Sales.

News Services: AP, GNS, NYT. **Politics:** Independent. **Established:** 1871.

Special Editions: Welcome (Apr); Economic Outlook (June); Rodeo (July); Cherry's Jubille (Oct).

Special Weekly Sections: Food Day (tues); Entertainment & Dining (thur); Garden, Building, Television, Travel, Religion (sat).

Magazines: USA Weekend; Color Comics; Weekender Living; TV Time Magazine (local, newsprint) (sat).

CORPORATE OFFICER

President	Michael A Chihak

GENERAL MANAGEMENT

Publisher	Michael A Chihak
Personnel Director	Jenine Paul

ADVERTISING

Director	Robert Aguilar
Manager-Retail/Classified	Debbie Clark

MARKETING AND PROMOTION

Marketing Director-Development	Michelle Krans

CIRCULATION

Director	Todd Knapp
Manager	Robert Martin
Manager-Sales & Marketing	Tricia Lucido
Manager-Single Copy Sales	Steve Foerder
Supervisor-Customer Service	Linda Pepper

NEWS EXECUTIVE

Editor	Cindy McCurry-Ross

EDITORS AND MANAGERS

Business Writer	Brandy Tuzon
City Editor (interim)	Larry Parsons
Asst City Editor	Roya Camp
Editorial Page Editor	Roberto Robledo
Features Editor	Sylvia Vilva
Graphics Editor (interim)	Rachel Zents
Living Editor	Sylvia Vilva
News Editor	Jim Albanese
Photo Chief	Clay Peterson
Sports Editor	Richard Martin

MANAGEMENT INFORMATION SERVICES

Data Processing Manager	Ingrid Avila

PRODUCTION

Director	Howard Skirvin

Market Information: Split Run; TMC.

Mechanical available: Web Offset; Black and 3 ROP colors; insert accepted — preprinted, all (3" up to 13 3/4"); page cut-offs — 22.08".

Mechanical specifications: Type page 13" x 21"; E - 6 cols, 2 1/16", 1/6" between; A - 6 cols, 2 1/16", 1/12" between; C - 9 cols, 1 3/8", 1/12" between.

Commodity consumption: Newsprint 1,667 short tons; width 27 3/8"; black ink 58,186 pounds; color ink 9,236 pounds; single pages printed 11,274; average pages per issue 36(d); single plates used 33,280.

Equipment: EDITORIAL: Front-end hardware — SII; Front-end software — SII; Other equipment — Ap/Mac, IBM. CLASSIFIED: Front-end hardware — SII; Front-end software — SII. DISPLAY: Adv layout systems — Ap/Mac IIcx; Printers — QMS/860, Ap/Mac LaserWriter II. PRODUCTION: Typesetters — Advantage II, MDT/350; Plate exposures — 2-Nu; Plate processors — 2-Nat/250; Scanners — ECR/Autokon 1000; Production cameras — C/Spartan III, SCREEN/Companica Vert.; Automatic film processors — LE; Film transporters — LE; Color separation equipment (conventional) — RZ/4050; Digital color separation equipment — Lf/AP Leaf Picture Desk. PRESSROOM: Line 1 — 10-G/Urbanite; Folders — 1-G. MAILROOM: Counter stackers — HI/RS25, QWI; Inserters and stuffers — HI/1372; Bundle tyer — MLN. WIRE SERVICES: News — AP, NYT; Stock tables — AP; Receiving dishes — size-10ft, AP.

SAN BERNARDINO

San Bernardino County

'90 U.S. Census- 164,164; E&P '96 Est. 206,664

ABC-NDM (90): 687,601 (HH 230,565)

The Sun (m-mon to sat; S)

The Sun, 399 N. D St., San Bernardino, CA 92401; tel (909) 889-9666; fax (909) 381-3976. Gannett Co. Inc. group.

Circulation: 81,659(m); 81,659(m-sat); 95,424(S); ABC Sept. 30, 1995.

Price: 35¢(d); 35¢(sat); $1.25(S); $9.70/mo.

Advertising: Open inch rate $57.12(m); $57.12(m-sat); $63.18(S). **Representative:** Gannett National Newspaper Sales.

News Services: AP, NYT, GNS, McClatchy, City News Service. **Politics:** Independent. **Established:** 1873.

Advertising not accepted: Hand guns.

Special Weekly Sections: Health (mon); Gardening (tues); Fashion (wed); Food Section, House and Home (thur); Weekend (fri); Auto Mart, Religion (sat); Business Sunday, Real Estate, Perspective (S); .

Magazines: Homes Magazine (sat); USA Weekend, TV Week (S).

CORPORATE OFFICER

President	Brooks Johnson

GENERAL MANAGEMENT

Publisher	Brooks Johnson
Controller	Bruce Cannady

ADVERTISING

Director	Bob Balzer
Manager-Classified	Mary Lou Wiles
Manager-National	Robert E Teixeira
Manager-Creative Service	Thom Salisbury

MARKETING AND PROMOTION

Director-Marketing Service	Robert Boisson

TELECOMMUNICATIONS

Director-Management Info Services	Gus Ortiz

CIRCULATION

Director	Jack Hogan
Manager-Home Delivery	Rich Robb
Manager-Sales/Marketing	Michael Jelley
Manager-Division	Bill Hildebrand
Manager-Division	Obuse Iweriebor
Manager-Division	Nam Tran

NEWS EXECUTIVES

Editor	Arnold Garson
Managing Editor	Catherine Hamm
Managing Editor-Night	Rosemary McClure
Asst Managing Editor-Features	Maria De Varrenne
Asst Managing Editor-Metro	W Osler McCarthy

EDITORS AND MANAGERS

Arts Editor	Margo Wilson
Copy Editor	Margo Wilson
Editorial Page Editor	Richard S Kimball
Entertainment Editor	Jason Foster
Features Editor	John Weeks
Graphics Director	Betts Griffone
Photo Director	Gary Miller
Political Editor	Cassie MacDuff
Radio/Television Editor	Dan Hendricks
Real Estate Editor	Michael J Murphy
Religion Editor	Carla Wheeler
Special Section Editor	Michael J Murphy
Sports Editor	Paul R Oberjuerge
Travel Editor	John Weeks
Wire Editor	Patrick Olsen

PRODUCTION

Director	William Bogert
Asst Director	Ronald L Coats
Manager-Camera/Plate	Kimberly Moore
Manager-Pressroom	Randy Hackman
Manager-Mailroom	Richard Glasson

Market Information: Zoned editions; Split Run; TMC.

Mechanical available: Offset; Black and 3 ROP colors; insert accepted — preprinted; page cut-offs — 22".

Mechanical specifications: Type page 13" x 21"; E - 6 cols, 2 1/16", 1/8" between; A - 6 cols, 2 1/16", 1/8" between; C - 10 cols, 1 1/4", 1/16" between.

Commodity consumption: Newsprint 18,255 metric tons; width 54 1/2"; black ink 401,610 pounds; color ink 45,455 pounds; single pages printed 21,164; average pages per issue 54(d), 88(S); single plates used 62,000.

Equipment: EDITORIAL: Front-end hardware — 1-AT/Series 60, 1-HAS/News Pro-6 PLT; Front-end software — AT 4.67; Printers — MON/Laser Express; Other equipment — AT, MON/Postscript, Ap/Mac Graphics Systems. CLASSIFIED: Front-end hardware — AT/Series 60; Front-end software — AT 4.67; Printers — MON/Laser Express; Other equipment — MON/Postscript. DISPLAY: Front-end hardware — 12-Ap/Mac; Front-end software — Multi-Ad/Creator; Printers — MON/Postscript. PRODUCTION: Typesetters — 2-MON/Lasercomp Express; Platemaking systems — 2-W; Plate exposures — 2-Na/Newsprinter, 2-Nu; Plate processors — 2-Na/Satellite; Electronic picture desk — Lf/AP Leaf Picture Desk; Scanners — ECR/Autokon 8400, ECR/Autokon 1000; Production cameras — 1-C/Spartan III, 1-C/Pager II; Automatic film processors — 1-LE/LD 2600A, 2-P/26 ML, 2-LE/MTP-26; Film transporters — 2-C/1247; Color separation equipment (conventional) — 1-RZ/4050. PRESSROOM: Line 1 — 6-G/Headliner Offset; Line 2 — 6-G/Headliner Offset; Line 3 — 6-G/Headliner Offset. MAILROOM: Counter stackers — QWI; Inserters and stuffers — 3-Amerigraph/NP 1472; Bundle tyer — 4-MLN/EM1016A; Addressing machine — 2-Ch, 3-Power Strap/PSN-5, 2-Barstrom/on-line Labeler; Mailroom control system — QWI. COMMUNICATIONS: Facsimile — 2-III; Remote imagesetting — 2-III. WIRE SERVICES: News — AP, NYT, GNS, McClatchy; Stock tables — AP; Receiving dishes — size-3m, AP. BUSINESS COMPUTERS: 1-IBM/Sys 38 Model 400; Applications: PCs & micros networked; PCs & main system networked.

SAN DIEGO

San Diego County

'90 U.S. Census- 1,110,549; E&P '96 Est. 1,301,534

ABC-CZ (90): 1,880,399 (HH 673,919)

San Diego Daily Transcript (m-mon to fri)

San Diego Daily Transcript, 2131 Third Ave. (92101); PO Box 85469, San Diego, CA 92816; tel (619) 232-4381; fax (619) 239-5716; e-mail editor@sddt.com; web site http://www.sddt.com.

Circulation: 7,661(m); ABC Sept. 30, 1995.

Price: 75¢(d); $120.68/yr.

Advertising: Open inch rate $32.50(m).

News Service: AP. **Politics:** Independent. **Established:** 1886.

Special Editions: Corporate Profiles (Jan); Health Care (Mar); Law Week (Apr); San Diego By Design (June); Soaring Dimensions (Aug); Driving Decisions (Oct).

Special Weekly Sections: Business Matters, Market Investment/Stock Comment (mon); Technology Today, Money Minders, Marketlink (tues); Law Briefs, Tech Talk (wed); Financial Focus, Leasing Notes (thur); Art-Facts, Food, Booze & Beds, Weekend Watch, Real Estate Roundup (fri).

Magazines: Monday Memo (mon); The Lenders (thur); Business, Financial, Stock Market Quotes (daily).

GENERAL MANAGEMENT

Publisher	Ellen Revelle-Eckis
Editor/Vice Pres	Martin Kruming
General Manager	Robert Loomis
Business Manager	Cynthia Ponath
Personnel Manager	Melanie Potter

ADVERTISING

Manager-Commercial	Thomas Kelleher

CIRCULATION

Manager	Michelle Kawasaki

NEWS EXECUTIVE

Editor	Martin Kruming

EDITORS AND MANAGERS

Bio Medical Editor	Mario Aguilera
Business Editor	Andrew Kleske
City Editor	Andrew Kleske
Finance Editor	Richard Acello
Government Editor	Lynne Carrier
Legal Editor	Susan Gembrowski
News Editor	Manny Cruz
Real Estate Editor	Richard Spaulding

MANAGEMENT INFORMATION SERVICES

Director-Info Systems	Andrew Kleske
Manager-Systems	Cynthia Ponath

PRODUCTION

Director	Roxanne Wyas

California I-49

Director-Human Resources James R Schober
Director-Mercury Center Robert J Ryan
Manager-Purchasing Eric J Merritt

ADVERTISING

Director Steve Weaver
Manager-Retail/Local Accounts Diane Rames
Manager-Retail/Major Accounts Cynthia Barnes
Manager-General Kelvin Blankenship
Director-Creative/Marketing SVC Kate Coleman
Manager-Classified/Auto/Real Estate Louis Alexander
Manager-Employment Sharon Ruwart

MARKETING AND PROMOTION

Director-Marketing Ann Gregs
Manager-Product Development Kate Coleman
Manager-Info Lois Meade
Manager-Marketing Communication Doug Edwards

TELECOMMUNICATIONS

Manager Lynn Frank

CIRCULATION

Director Tom Pounds
Manager-Home Delivery Jim Beck
Manager-Single Copy Rick Biggs
Manager-Marketing Sandy Mastumato

NEWS EXECUTIVES

Exec Editor/Senior Vice Pres Jerry M Ceppos
Vice Pres/Editor Rob Elder
Managing Editor David Yarnold
Deputy Managing Editor-Newsroom Innovation Ann Hurst
Asst Managing Editor-Business/Projects Jonathan Krim
Asst Managing Editor-News Paul Van Slambrouck
Asst Managing Editor-Development Patricia Camp Thompson
Asst Managing Editor-Graphics Bryan Monroe

EDITORS AND MANAGERS

Action Line Editor Andy Bruno
Drive Editor Matthew Nauman
Business/Finance Editor Pete Hillan
Editorial Cartoonist Scott Willis
City Editor Rebecca Salner
Commentary Page Editor James Bray
Chief Editorial Writer Phil Yost
Editorial Columnist Joanne Jacobs
Editorial Columnist Sharon Noguchi
Editorial Page Editor Rob Elder
Assoc Editorial Page Editor Barbara Vroman
Editorial Writer Sarah Bachman
Editorial Writer Patricia Fisher
Editorial Writer Joseph Rodriguez
Education Editor Aleta Watson
Entertainment/Amusements Editor Bruce Manuel
Food Editor Joyce Gemperlein
Home/Garden Editor Joan Jackson
Letters Editor John Swartley
Librarian Gary Lance
National/Foreign Editor Francine Kiefer
Exec News Editor-AM Jeffrey Thomas
Exec News Editor-PM Charles McCollum
News Editor Charan Wollard
Perspective Editor Ed Clendaniel
Director-Photography Geri Migielicz
Political Editor Phil Trounstine
Real Estate Editor Broderick Perkins
Religion Editor Rich Scheinin
Exec Sports Editor David Tepps
Sports Columnist Ann Killion
Sports Columnist Bud Genade
Sports Columnist Mark Purdy
Suburban Editor John Raess
Travel Editor Zeke Wigglesworth

MANAGEMENT INFORMATION SERVICES

Director-Info Systems Jack Schneider
Editorial Systems Editor Jamie Braswell

PRODUCTION

Vice Pres-Operations Gerald H Polk
Director-Info Systems Jack Schneider
Coordinator (Night) Don Dodds
Manager-Pre Press Ed Harris
Manager-Ad Service Heather Bolei
Manager-Composing Doug Vorpahl
Manager-Platemaking Mike Clarke
Manager-Pressroom Alvin Nesmith
Manager-Mailroom Laurie Rogers
Manager-Publishing Systems Tim Benjamin
Manager-Administration Sharon Fowler
Manager-Facilities Jim Thurman
Superintendent-Mechanical Manuel Marquez

Market Information: Zoned editions; Split Run; TMC; ADS; Operate database; Operate audiotex; Electronic edition.
Mechanical available: Offset; Black and 3 ROP colors; insert accepted — preprinted, 2-36 standard pages:, 5 x 7" to $11\frac{1}{2}$ x $13\frac{1}{4}$" finished size; page cut-offs — $22\frac{3}{4}$".
Mechanical specifications: Type page 13" x $21\frac{1}{4}$"; E - 6 cols, $2\frac{1}{16}$", $\frac{1}{8}$" between; A - 6 cols, $2\frac{1}{16}$", $\frac{1}{8}$" between; C - 10 cols, 1.22", $\frac{1}{10}$" between.
Commodity consumption: Newsprint 67,973 metric tons; widths $54\frac{3}{4}$", $27\frac{1}{2}$", $41\frac{1}{2}$"; black ink 1,336,704 pounds; color ink 132,100 pounds; single pages printed 76,405; average pages per issue 100(d), 184(S); single plates used 628,000.
Equipment: EDITORIAL: Front-end hardware — SII; Front-end software — SII; Printers — 3-HP; Other equipment — 300-SII/Coyote, 7-SII/Coyote 22, 16-SII/Coyote PC. CLASSIFIED: Front-end hardware — SII; Printers — 2-Canon, HP; Other equipment — 100-SII/Coyote, 15-SII/Coyote 15, 10-SII/Coyote PC, 65-ET/960. AUDIOTEX: Hardware — PEP/Voice Print. DISPLAY: Adv layout systems — III; Front-end hardware — 4-INP; Front-end software — III/DisplayAd; Printers — III/Proofer; Other equipment — 14-III/AMS-2. PRODUCTION: Typesetters — 2-AU/APS-5G, 2-III/3810 Pagesetter, 1-III/3850 Pagesetter; Plate exposures — 1-WL/Lith III, WL/Lith 10; Plate processors — 2-WL/38D; Electronic picture desk — Lf/AP Leaf Picture Desk; Scanners — 2-ECR/Autokon 1000; Production cameras — C/Newspagers; Automatic film processors — LE, P; Film transporters — C; Shrink lenses — C/95% Anamorphic; Color separation equipment (conventional) — Hel/399ERS, Chromacom/PG Assembly; Digital color separation equipment — 2-Scitex/Prisma, 1-Scitex/Star. PRESSROOM: Line 1 — 10-G/Metro (5 Decks); Line 2 — 10-G/Headliner (5 Decks); Line 3 — 10-G/Headliner (5 Decks); Line 4 — 10-G/Headliner (5 Decks); Folders — 4-G/144 page, 4-G/160 page; Reels and stands — G/45" Static Belt, CT/50 Running Belt; Press control system — G/MPCS. MAILROOM: Counter stackers — 13-HL/HT, 6-HL/Monitor, 2-HL/Dual carriers; Inserters and stuffers — 1-GMA/RESUILT 1572, 1-GMA/SLS 1000 20:2, 1-GMA/SLS 1000 28:2; Bundle tyer — 4-MLN/News 90, 12-MLN/2A, 4-MLN/2, 7-Power Strap, 5-Dynaric. LIBRARY: Electronic — Vu/Text. WIRE SERVICES: News — AP Datafeatures, AP Datastream, NYT, INS, KRT, Weather, TV Data, Bay City News Service, AP SportStats, DJ; Stock tables — AP Digital Stocks, AP SelectStox; Receiving dishes — size-3m. BUSINESS COMPUTERS: 2-HP/960; Applications: CJ/AIM-CIS: Circ, Accts payable, Gen Ledger, Accts receivable; PCs & micros networked; PCs & main system networked.

SAN LUIS OBISPO

San Luis Obispo County

'90 U.S. Census- 41,958; E&P '96 Est. 48,050
ABC-CZ (90): 41,958 (HH 16,952)

Telegram-Tribune

(m-mon to fri; m-sat)

Telegram-Tribune, 3825 S. Higuera; PO Box 112, San Luis Obispo, CA 93406-0112; tel (805) 781-7800; fax (805) 781-7870; e-mail tel.trib@slonet.org; web site http://www.slonet.org/vv//tt. Scripps Howard group.
Circulation: 32,217(m); 37,530(m-sat); ABC Sept. 30, 1995.
Price: 50¢(d); $1.00(sat); $9.75/mo; $108.00/yr.
Advertising: Open inch rate $19.50(m); $21.00(m-sat). **Representative:** Papert Companies.
News Services: AP, McClatchy, SHNS. **Politics:** Independent. **Established:** 1869.
Note: Effective Apr. 1, 1995, this publication changed its publishing plan from (e-mon to fri; m-sat) to (m-mon to sat)
Special Editions: Garden/Home Improvement; American Home Week; Women In Business; Mid-State Fair; Paso Robles Wine Festival; Christmas Opening.
Special Weekly Sections: Business (tues); Business, Food (wed); Business (thur); Business, Agriculture (fri); Religion, Weddings, Business, Real Estate (sat); Entertainment, Television Listings (daily).
Magazines: Focus (own, tab, newsprint); USA Weekend; TV Update (sat).

CORPORATE OFFICERS

Chairman/Editorial Director Paul K Scripps
President/General Manager Julia S Aguilar
Vice Pres Harry Green
Secretary Maurice Watson
Controller Dave Buckey

GENERAL MANAGEMENT

Controller Roger Phillips

ADVERTISING

Director Butch Hughes
Manager-Service Robbie Godfrey
Manager-Retail Devon Goetz
Manager-Classified Sandy Fielder

CIRCULATION

Director Jeff Brinley
Manager-Customer Service Marge Cole
Manager-Single Copy Tranportation Debi Wood
Manager-Zone Cathy Veley
Manager-Zone Robert Moran

NEWS EXECUTIVE

Editor Jeff Fairbanks

EDITORS AND MANAGERS

City Editor Mike Stover
Editorial Page Editor Warren Groshong
Entertainment/Amusements Editor Monica Fiscalini
Graphics Editor Kate Stark
Sports Editor Eric Burdick

MANAGEMENT INFORMATION SERVICES

Data Processing Manager Cindy Tellefsen

PRODUCTION

Director Ron Godfrey
Foreman-Pressroom Jim Babb
Foreman-Composing Cliff Scott
Manager-Mailroom Terry Gardner

Market Information: TMC.
Mechanical available: Offset; Black and 3 ROP colors; insert accepted — preprinted; page cut-offs — $22\frac{3}{4}$".
Mechanical specifications: Type page 13" x 21"; E - 6 cols, $2\frac{1}{16}$", $\frac{1}{8}$" between; A - 6 cols, $2\frac{1}{16}$", $\frac{1}{8}$" between; C - 9 cols, $1\frac{1}{3}$", $\frac{1}{8}$" between.
Commodity consumption: Newsprint 2,300 metric tons; widths $27\frac{1}{4}$", $13\frac{5}{8}$"; black ink 49,900 pounds; color ink 3,110 pounds; single pages printed 11,678; average pages per issue 36(d); single plates used 30,000.
Equipment: EDITORIAL: Front-end hardware — SII/Sys 22, 3-TI/810, 1-IBM/4234, 1-IBM/4224; Front-end software — SII; Printers — 1-Printronix/3121; Other equipment — 1-HP/33491A, 2-Dewar/Disc (for Ad Makeup). CLASSIFIED: Front-end hardware — SII/Sys 22; Front-end software — SII/Sys 22. DISPLAY: Adv layout systems — 2-Dewar/Disc, 3-Ap/Mac; Front-end hardware — PBS; Printers — 1-Ap/Mac LaserWriter Plus. PRODUCTION: Typesetters — 2-Tegra/Varityper, 2-Ap/Mac LaserWriter Plus, AccuSet/1000; Plate exposures — 1-Nu/Flip Top FT40L, 1-BKY; Plate processors — WL/Aqualith; Scanners — ECR/Autokon; Production cameras — Acti/V-24; Automatic film processors — 1-P/524, 1-Powermatic/R650; Shrink lenses — Alan/24" Variable; Color separation equipment (conventional) — Lf/AP Leaf Picture Desk; Digital color separation equipment — Lf/Leafscan 35, ECR/Autokon, ECR/Autokon News Recorder. PRESSROOM: Line 1 — 7-G/Urbanite, 2-DEV; Folders — 1-G. MAILROOM: Counter stackers — 3-Id; Inserters and stuffers — 1-GMA/SLS 1000 (6-into-1); Bundle tyer — 2-Power Strap. COMMUNICATIONS: Systems used — satellite. WIRE SERVICES: News — AP; Photos — AP; Stock tables — AP; Syndicates — AP Datafeatures, SHNS, McClatchy; Receiving dishes — size-10ft, AP. BUSINESS COMPUTERS: PBS; Applications: PBS/MediaPlus; PCs & main system networked.

SAN MATEO

San Mateo County

'90 U.S. Census- 85,486; E&P '96 Est. 91,189
ABC-CZ (90): 195,669 (HH 80,683)

The Times (e-mon to fri; m-sat)

The Times, 1080 S. Amphlett Blvd.; PO Box 5400, San Mateo, CA 94402; tel (415) 348-4321; fax (415) 348-4478; e-mail smtimes@smtimes.com; web site http://www.baynet.com/smtimes/home.html. Amphlett Printing Co. group.
Circulation: 39,376(e); 39,376(m-sat); ABC Sept. 30, 1995.
Price: 50¢(d); 75¢(sat); $97.50/yr; $7.50/4wk.
Advertising: Open inch rate $31.50(e); $31.50(m-sat). **Representative:** Long & Associates.
News Services: AP, NYT, McClatchy, SHNS, CNS, Cox News Service. **Politics:** Independent-Republican. **Established:** 1889.
Special Editions: Real Estate Outlook, Wedding Edition (Feb); Home & Garden (Mar); Baseball Opening (Apr); Summer Fun (May); Best of San Mateo County (June); Best of San Mateo County (July); Fiesta (Aug); NFL & Prep Football, Real Estate Outlook, Wedding Edition (Sept); Home & Garden (Oct); At Your Service Directory, Christmas Gift Guides (Nov); Christmas Gift Guides (Dec); Cruise/Travel (bi-monthly); Parade of Homes (quarterly).
Special Weekly Sections: Expanded Business, Health/Science (mon); Food (tues); Home & Garden, Seniors (thur); Entertainment (fri); Travel (sat).
Magazines: TV Times, USA Weekend (sat).

CORPORATE OFFICERS

President John H Clinton Jr
Secretary Mary Ann Gardner
Treasurer Mary Jane Zirkel

GENERAL MANAGEMENT

Publisher Christopher Scorell Dix
Purchasing Agent Jeff Gummere
Manager-Commercial Printing John Hoffman

ADVERTISING

Director-Sales Robert Miller
Manager-National/Major Accounts Larry Boline
Manager-Classified Nora Jones

MARKETING AND PROMOTION

Manager-Marketing Service Julie Savage

TELECOMMUNICATIONS

Manager-Info Systems Ed Derge

CIRCULATION

Director Tom Weldon
Manager-System/Office Kay Leaman
Asst Manager Bob Lampkin
Asst Manager Paul Gazaway

NEWS EXECUTIVE

Managing Editor Terry Greenberg

EDITORS AND MANAGERS

Automotive Editor Ken Costa
Books Editor Rick Eymer
Business Editor Dave Madden
City Editor Robert Rudy
Editorial Page Editor Terry Robertson
Education Editor Dale Martin
Fashion Editor Mary Jane Clinton
Films/Theater Editor Judy Richter
Films/Theater Editor Karen Petterson
Food Editor Miriam Morgan
Garden Editor Judy Richter
Health/Medical Editor Sandra Burnett
Home Furnishings Editor Mary Jane Clinton
Living/Lifestyle Editor Mary Jane Clinton
Music Editor Sherry Posnick Goodwin
Music Editor Judy Richter
National Editor Karen Petterson
News Editor Alan Quale
Photo Editor Mike Russell
Political/Government Editor Lisa Milligan
Radio/Television Editor Shirley-Anne Owden
Real Estate Editor Will Thomas
Religion Editor Tom Krogstad
Sports Editor John Horgan
"Time Out" Editor Mary Jane Clinton
Transportation Editor Ronna Abramson
Travel/Weekend Editor Christine Delsol
Women's Editor Mary Jane Clinton

MANAGEMENT INFORMATION SERVICES

Data Processing Manager Ed Derge

PRODUCTION

Manager Jeff Gummere
Manager-Technical Service/Facilities Dave Frankovic
Foreman-Composing Gil Peterson
Foreman-Pressroom Jack Murray
Foreman-Mailroom Jim Martinez

Market Information: Zoned editions; TMC; ADS; Operate database; Operate audiotex.
Mechanical available: Offset; Black and 3 ROP colors; insert accepted — preprinted, product samples; page cut-offs — 22".
Mechanical specifications: Type page 13" x $21\frac{1}{2}$"; E - 6 cols, $2\frac{1}{16}$", $\frac{1}{8}$" between; A - 6 cols, $2\frac{1}{16}$", $\frac{1}{8}$" between; C - 10 cols, $1\frac{3}{16}$", $\frac{1}{16}$" between.
Commodity consumption: Newsprint 4,200 metric tons; width $54\frac{3}{4}$"; black ink 156,500 pounds; color ink 18,000 pounds; single pages printed 13,146; average pages per issue 42(d); single plates used 20,000.
Equipment: EDITORIAL: Front-end hardware — CSI/Sys 2400, 29-CSI/112B, 4-IBM, 40-RSK/TRS 80 Model 100; Front-end software — CSI. CLASSIFIED: Front-end hardware — CSI/Sys 2400, 15-CSI/112B, 1-IBM/PC112; Front-end software — CSI. AUDIOTEX: Hardware — ROLM/Phonemail Release 5. DISPLAY: Adv layout systems — SCS/Layout 8000; Front-end hardware — 4-CSI/112B, 3-Cx/Breeze. PRODUCTION: Typesetters — 2-AU/APS-6, 1-Ultre; Plate exposures — 1-Amerigraph, 1-Nu;

I-50 California

Plate processors — 2-WL/30D-38E; Electronic picture desk — Lf/AP Leaf Picture Desk; Scanners — ECR/Autokon 1000DE, 1-Kurtzwil; Production cameras — 2-C/Spartan III; Automatic film processors — 2-P, 2-DP/24L; Color separation equipment (conventional) — Howtek/Colorscan.
PRESSROOM: Line 1 — 5-MAN double width 4 x 2 (3 Color decks); Folders — 2-MAN; Pasters — Automatic Pasters; Reels and stands — MEG; Press control system — MAN, Mavo 11/Color Controls. MAILROOM: Counter stackers — 2-Id/NS660; Inserters and stuffers — 1-KAN/Model 480 (8 Station); Bundle tyer — 4-MLN, 1-Power Strap. LIBRARY: Electronic — SCS/Personal Librarian, Mead Data Central, 1993-Nexis/Newsview. WIRE SERVICES: News — AP Datafeatures, AP Datastream; Stock tables — AP Digital Stocks; Syndicates — AP, NYT, McClatchy, SHNS, Cox, CNS; Receiving dishes — size-2.8m, AP. BUSINESS COMPUTERS: IBM/Sys AS-400, 15-IBM; Applications: Accts receivable, Accts payable, Billing, Fixed assets, Circ, Newsprint inventory, Gen ledger, Financial statements; PCs & main system networked.

SAN PEDRO

Los Angeles County

'90 U.S. Census- N/A; E&P '96 Est. N/A
ABC-CZ (90): 71,433 (HH 26,985)

News-Pilot (m-mon to sat)

News-Pilot, 363 Seventh St., San Pedro, CA 90733-0191; tel (310) 832-0221; fax (310) 833-1540. Copley Press Inc. group.
Circulation: 14,208(m); 14,208(m-sat); ABC Sept. 30, 1995.
Price: 25¢(d); 25¢(sat); $7.00/mo.
Representative: Sawyer-Ferguson-Walker Co.
News Services: AP, CNS, NYT, SHNS, City News Service, McClatchy. **Politics:** Republican. **Established:** 1901.
Note: The News-Pilot is printed and produced by the Torrance Daily Breeze. For commodity consumption, see the Torrance Daily Breeze listing. The Copley Los Angeles Newspapers include the following newspapers: Torrance Daily Breeze (mS), San Pedro News Pilot (m) and the Santa Monica Outlook (m). The group rate is $87.57. Individual newspaper rates not made available. Effective Sept. 5, 1995, this publication changed its publishing plan from (e-mon to sat) to (m-mon to sat).
Advertising not accepted: 900 phone numbers; NC 17 rated movies; X-rated movies.
Special Editions: School Pages (monthly); Wedding Book (Jan); Healthcare, Valentine Restaurant Pages, Valentine Edition (Feb); St. Patrick's Day, Best of the South Bay, Eastern in San Pedro, Eastern Restaurants Pages (Mar); Home & Garden (Apr); Panorama, Mother's Day, Dining Guide (May); Brides Tour, Destination Torrance (June); Football (Aug); School Pages, At Home (Sept); Health & Fitness, Fisherman's Fiesta, Halloween in San Pedro, Ski & Travel, Dining Guide (Oct); Destination Torrance, Holiday Kick-off (Nov); Gift Ideas, 'Tis the Season, Gift Galore, Christmas Services (Churches), Last Minute Gifts, Holiday Greetings, Chronological Boxes (Dec).
Special Weekly Sections: Motion Pictures/Entertainment/TV Pages/Radio, Business News and Stock Quotes (daily); Health (mon); Food, Lifestyle (wed); Home (thur); Entertainment/Restaurants (fri).
Magazines: RAVE! (fri); Television Magazine (S).
Cable TV: Own cable TV in circulation area.

CORPORATE OFFICERS

Board Chairman Helen K Copley
Vice Chairman Hubert L Kaltenbach
President David C Copley
Exec Vice Pres-Finance Charles F Patrick
Vice Pres-Finance Dean P Dwyer

GENERAL MANAGEMENT

Publisher Thomas J Wafer Jr
Business Manager David M Thorne
Buyer Ted Yamada

ADVERTISING

Director Steve Elkins
Manager-Classified Tim Guesman
Manager-Retail Janice Sheldon

MARKETING AND PROMOTION

Manager-Marketing/Promotion Mike Lynn

TELECOMMUNICATIONS

Manager-Info Systems Roland B West

CIRCULATION

Director Charles A McManis Jr
Manager Mike Levine
Manager-Administration Rick Perius

NEWS EXECUTIVES

Editor James M Box
Managing Editor Phillip F Sanfield

EDITORS AND MANAGERS

Automotive Editor Timothy Lemm
City Editor Timothy Lemm
Editorial Page Editor Phillip F Sanfield
Education Editor Richard Redding
Librarian Midori Yasuda
Maritime Editor Carolyn Brady
Photo Editor Bernado Alps
Religion Editor Timothy Lemm
Sports Editor Robert Whitley

MANAGEMENT INFORMATION SERVICES

Manager-Info Systems Roland B West
Manager-Technical Service John Cummins

Market Information: TMC; ADS.
Mechanical available: Offset; Black and 3 ROP colors; insert accepted — preprinted, tab, standard, flexi, products, single sheets; page cutoffs — 22¾".
Mechanical specifications: Type page 13" x 21⅜"; E - 6 cols, 2¹⁄₁₆", ⅛" between; A - 6 cols, 2¹⁄₁₆", ⅛" between; C - 10 cols, 1⁵⁄₁₆", ¹⁄₁₆" between.
Commodity consumption: average pages per issue 32(d).
Equipment: EDITORIAL: Front-end hardware — SII/Sys 55; Other equipment — 15-SII/Coyote. CLASSIFIED: Front-end hardware — SII/Sys 55; Other equipment — 40-SII/Coyote. DISPLAY: Adv layout systems — SCS/Layout 8000. PRODUCTION: Typesetters — 7-AU/APS, AU/3850; Platemaking systems — WL; Plate exposures — 2-WL; Plate processors — 2-WL; Electronic picture desk — AP linked to Ap/Mac Network; Scanners — ECR/Autokon 1000; Production cameras — 2-C/1211; Automatic film processors — 2-LE/LD 18; Film transporters — 2-C; Shrink lenses — 2-CK Optical; Color separation equipment (conventional) — 1-HCM/399ER.
PRESSROOM: Line 1 — 12-G/Metro; Folders — 2-G; Pasters — 12-G; Reels and stands — 12-G. MAILROOM: Counter stackers — 2-HL/Monitor, 4-HL/Monitor HT, 1-QWI/301; Inserters and stuffers — 1-HI/848, 1-MM/227, 1-GMA/SLS 1000; Bundle tyer — 2-MLN/2A, 2-MLN/2EE, 1-MLN/2AHS, 5-Power Strap/2, 3-MLN; Wrapping singles — 1-Shanklin/Plastic Shrinker A22; Addressing machine — 1-Ch/Video Jet Model 9816, 1-St/1200 SDC. LIBRARY: Electronic — 1-DEC/VAX 8800 Basis. WIRE SERVICES: News — AP, AP Datafeatures, NYT, CNS, McClatchy, Race Wire, SHNS; Photos — AP Photostream; Stock tables — AP; Syndicates — NYT, CNS; Receiving dishes — size-3m, AP, NYT. BUSINESS COMPUTERS: DEC/Micro Vax; Applications: PCs & main system networked.

SAN RAFAEL
See MARIN COUNTY

SANTA ANA
See ORANGE COUNTY

SANTA BARBARA

Santa Barbara County

'90 U.S. Census- 85,571; E&P '96 Est. 93,903
ABC-CZ (90): 189,459 (HH 69,883)

Santa Barbara News-Press (m-mon to sat; S)

Santa Barbara News-Press, 715 Anacapa St.; PO Box 1359, Santa Barbara, CA 93102-1359; tel (805) 564-5200; fax (805) 966-6258; web site http://www.independent.com. New York Times Co. group.
Circulation: 46,999(m); 46,999(m-sat); 52,063(S); ABC Sept. 30, 1995.
Price: 50¢(d); 50¢(sat); $1.00(S); $2.59/wk (plus tax); $123.76/yr (plus tax).
Advertising: Open inch rate $33.00(m); $33.00(m-sat); $37.00(S). **Representative:** Cresmer, Woodward, O'Mara & Ormsbee.
News Services: AP, NYT, CNS. **Politics:** Independent. **Established:** 1855.
Special Editions: Business Review and Forecast (Jan); Fashion (Mar); Home and Decorator (Apr); Santa Barbara Fun (May); Fiesta (July); Fashion (Aug); Home and Decorator, Reader's Choice Awards, Performing Arts (Sept); The Season Begins (Nov); Gift Guide (Dec).
Special Weekly Sections: Religion (sat); Sports, Travel, Santa Barbara Real Estate (tab) (S); Business & Financial, Radio/TV, Life (daily).
Magazines: Central Coast Real Estate Weekly, Woman (fri); Coupon Clipper; Scene Magazine; TV Week; Comics.

CORPORATE OFFICERS

Board Chairman Arthur Ochs Sulzberger
President Lance R Primis
Secretary Solomon B Watson IV
Treasurer Richard Thomas
Controller Frank Gatti

GENERAL MANAGEMENT

Publisher P Steven Ainsley
Director-Publishing/Technological Services Jeffrey R Menard
Controller Randy A Alcorn
Manager-Credit Janine Eldridge

ADVERTISING

Director-Retail Lynn Randolph
Director-Classified/National John Leonard

TELECOMMUNICATIONS

Audiotex Manager John Leonard

CIRCULATION

Director Lee Lahargoue
Manager-Home Delivery Mike Lee
Director-Publishing/Technological Services Jeffrey R Menard

NEWS EXECUTIVES

Exec Editor Allen Parsons
Managing Editor Tom Bolton
Asst Managing Editor-News Linda Bowen
Asst Managing Editor-Production Paul Yarbrough

EDITORS AND MANAGERS

Bureau Chief-Lompoc Tad Weber
Business Editor Linda Bowen
City Editor R B Brenner
Asst City Editor Kathy Lawitz
Asst City Editor Jesse Chavarria
Columnist Barney Brantingham
Editorial Page Editor John Lankford
Graphics Editor Michelle Shapiro
Home Furnishings Editor Melinda Johnson
Librarian Sue DeLapa
Lifestyle Editor Melinda Johnson
Lifestyle Production Editor Gary Robb
News Editor Bill Macfayden
Photo Department Manager/Photo Editor Bob Ponce
Sports Editor Mark Patton
Sports Columnist John Zant

MANAGEMENT INFORMATION SERVICES

Data Processing Manager Kim Seward-Goda

PRODUCTION

Director-Publishing/Technological Services Jeffrey R Menard
Manager-Mailroom Steve Kuster
Manager-Pressroom Bob Yznaga
Manager-Pre Press Chris O'Toole
Manager-Plant David D Harvey

Market Information: Zoned editions; Split Run; TMC; Operate audiotex; Electronic edition.
Mechanical available: Offset; Black and 3 ROP colors; insert accepted — preprinted; page cutoffs — 22".
Mechanical specifications: Type page 13" x 21¼"; E - 6 cols, 2¹⁄₁₆", ⅛" between; A - 6 cols, 2¹⁄₁₆", ⅛" between; C - 9 cols, 1⅜", ¹⁄₁₆" between.
Commodity consumption: Newsprint 7,025 short tons; 8,890 metric tons; widths 55", 41¼", 27½", 44"; black ink 209,000 pounds; color ink 21,500 pounds; single pages printed 21,124; average pages per issue 45(d), 84(S); single plates used 30,000.
Equipment: EDITORIAL: Front-end hardware — 1-DEC/PDP 11-84; Front-end software — DEC/TMS-CMS; Printers — DEC, HP, Dataproducts, III/3850. CLASSIFIED: Front-end hardware — Ap/Power Mac, Sun/Sparc; Front-end software — DTI/Class Speed 3.2.1; Printers — HP, Dataproducts, III/3850; Other equipment — Grand Junction/Fast Ethernet Switches. AUDIOTEX: Hardware — Brite Voice Systems; Software — Quantum/Kernel 3.156; Supplier name — VNN. DISPLAY: Adv layout systems — CJ; Front-end hardware — DEC/VAX, DTI/AdSpeed, 30-Ap/Mac Quadra; Front-end software — CJ; Printers — DEC, HP, Dataproducts, Canon/Laser Printer. PRODUCTION: Pagination software — DTI, QuarkXPress 3.3, Adobe/Pagemaker 5.0, Adobe/Freehand 5.0; OCR software — Caere/OmniMax; Typesetters — 3-III/3850; Platemaking systems — 2-WL; Plate exposures — 2-WL; Plate processors — 1-WL; Electronic picture desk — Lf/AP Leaf Picture Desk; Scanners — ECR III/3750, Nikon 35mm, CD, 5-Umax/Flatbed; Production cameras — 2-C; Automatic film processors — 4-LE; Film transporters — 1-C; Shrink lenses — CK Optical; Color separation equipment (conventional) — C, III/Graphic Cobe Imager; Digital color separation equipment — C, QPS, DTI.
PRESSROOM: Line 1 — 4-G/Metrocolor (2 towers; 1 mono; 1 HO w/halfdeck); Press drives — Allen Bradley; Folders — G/3:2 double, single delivery; Pasters — 5-G/CT-45; Reels and stands — 5-G/CT-45; Press control system — G/MCPS-PAR. MAILROOM: Counter stackers — 4-QWI; Inserters and stuffers — 1-HI/AM NP 630; Bundle tyer — 4-Dynaric; Wrapping singles — 3-QWI; Addressing machine — 1-Ch; Mailroom control system — Am/AMCS. MM/Print roll. Davario/Conveyor; Other mailroom equipment — MM/Trimmer-Stitcher. COMMUNICATIONS: Facsimile — III/3750 (w/Telepress); Remote imagesetting — III/3850; Digital ad delivery system — AP AdSend; Systems used — satellite. WIRE SERVICES: News — AP, NYT; Photos — AP; Stock tables — AP; Syndicates — NYT, AP; Receiving dishes — AP. BUSINESS COMPUTERS: DEC/VAX; Applications: CJ, MCBA, Microsoft: Office; PCs & micros networked; PCs & main system networked.

SANTA CLARITA

Los Angeles County

'90 U.S. Census- 110,642; E&P '96 Est. 141,646

The Signal (m-mon to sat; S)

The Signal, 24000 Creekside Rd.; PO Box 801870, Santa Clarita, CA 91380-1870; tel (805) 259-1234; fax (805) 254-8068; e-mail signal@smarlink.net. Morris Newspaper Corp. group.
Circulation: 10,034(m); 10,034(m-sat); 10,034(S); VAC June 30, 1995.
Price: 50¢(d); 50¢(sat); 75¢(S); $6.50/mo.
Advertising: Open inch rate $20.50(m); $20.50(m-sat); $20.50(S). **Representative:** Papert Companies.
News Service: AP. **Politics:** Conservative. **Established:** 1919.
Special Weekly Sections: Softball, Lifestyles/Features (tues); Lifestyles/Features, Outdoors (wed); Food Section (thur); Son of Escape/Dining, Entertainment (fri); Mini Signal/Special Childrens Section, Religion (sat); Medical Directory, Columnists (S); Sports, Business/Finance (daily).
Magazines: Escape (Ent); Real Estate; New Homes.

CORPORATE OFFICER

Owner Charles H Morris

GENERAL MANAGEMENT

Publisher Darell Phillips
General Manager William H Fleet

ADVERTISING

Director Ethel Nakutin

TELECOMMUNICATIONS

Audiotex Manager Ethel Nakutin

CIRCULATION

Director Joe Derfler

NEWS EXECUTIVE

Managing Editor Tim Whyte

EDITORS AND MANAGERS

Business/Finance Editor Cheri Jensen
City Editor David Fox
Editorial Page Editor Tim Whyte
Education Editor Sylvia Oliande
Entertainment/Amusements Editor Eric Harnisch
Fashion/Style Editor Cheri Jensen
Features Editor Cheri Jensen
News Editor Anthony Peck
Photo Editor Kevin Karzin
Sports Editor Dave Shefter
Television/Film Editor Eric Harnisch
Theater/Music Editor Eric Harnisch

PRODUCTION

Director Don Pitts

Market Information: TMC; Operate audiotex.
Mechanical available: Offset; Black and 3 ROP colors; insert accepted — preprinted; page cutoffs — 21¾".

Mechanical specifications: Type page 13" x 21¼"; E - 6 cols, 2 1/16", ⅛" between; A - 6 cols, 2 1/16", ⅛" between; C - 6 cols, 2 1/16", ⅛" between.
Commodity consumption: Newsprint 2,400 metric tons; widths 27", 13¾"; black ink 64,000 pounds; color ink 5,200 pounds; single pages printed 13,000; average pages per issue 30(d), 64(S); single plates used 37,000.
Equipment: EDITORIAL: Front-end hardware — Mk/3500; Front-end software — Mk/Acer II; Printers — Ap/Mac LaserWriter NTX. CLASSIFIED: Front-end hardware — Ap/Mac; Front-end software — Baseview; Printers — TI/Omni 800, Ap/Mac LaserWriter NTX. DISPLAY: Adv layout systems — Baseview; Front-end hardware — Ap/Mac; Front-end software — Baseview. PRODUCTION: Typesetters — Dataproducts/LZR 1260; Plate exposures — 2-Nu/Flip Top FT52; Plate processors — 1-Nat/A-380, 1-MAS/Newspeed; Scanners — Lf/Leafscan 35; Production cameras — 1-Acti; Automatic film processors — AG/Litex 26.
PRESSROOM: Line 1 — 10-G/Urbanite; Folders — 2-G; Pasters — 8-Cary. MAILROOM: Counter stackers — 1-MM/K231, 1-MM/310; Inserters and stuffers — 2-MM/MD227; Bundle tyer — 2-MLN, 1-MLN/MLEE. WIRE SERVICES: News — AP, McClatchy; Stock tables — AP; Syndicates — TMS, NEA, United Features; Receiving dishes — AP. BUSINESS COMPUTERS: PC; Applications: IBM/Acct Mate; PCs & main system networked.

SANTA CRUZ

Santa Cruz County

'90 U.S. Census- 49,040; **E&P '96 Est.** 54,859
ABC-CZ (90): 94,930 (HH 37,351)

Santa Cruz County Sentinel

(m-mon to sat; S)

Santa Cruz County Sentinel, 207 Church St.; PO Box 638, Santa Cruz, CA 95061; tel (408) 423-4242; fax (408) 423-1154; e-mail sentcity@cruzio.com. Ottaway Newspapers Inc. group.
Circulation: 26,983(m); 26,983(m-sat); 26,618(S); ABC Sept. 30, 1995.
Price: 50¢(d); 50¢(sat); $1.25(S); $2.80/wk; $132.80/yr.
Advertising: Open inch rate $23.38(m); $23.38(m-sat); $24.32(S). **Representative:** Papert Companies.
News Services: AP, ONS, McClatchy, NYT. **Politics:** Non-Partisan. **Established:** 1856.
Not Published: New Year; May 27; Independence Day; Sept. 2; Nov. 28; Christmas.
Special Editions: Bride & Groom (Jan); Babies & Alumni (Feb); Progress, Agriculture, Technology, Tourism, Employment, Spring Home Buying Guide (Apr); Almanac, Antiques (June); Wharf to Wharf Race (July); Football (Aug); Home & Garden, Santa Cruz County Fair (Sept); Employment Digest (Oct); Downtown Catalog, Holiday Gift Guide (Nov); Last Minute Gift Guide (Dec).
Special Weekly Sections: Health (tues); Best Food Day (wed); Home & Garden, Sports "Breaking Away" (thur); "Spotlight"-Entertainment & Dining Section, Wheels (fri); Travel, Education, Seniors (S); Bay Living (daily).
Magazines: USA Weekend, TV Magazine (S).

CORPORATE OFFICER

President David B Regan

GENERAL MANAGEMENT

Publisher David B Regan
Asst Publisher John Lindsay
Controller Robert M Hughes

ADVERTISING

Director Karen Carnot
Manager-Sales Dorothy McCoy
Manager-Sales Heather Davis

TELECOMMUNICATIONS

Audiotex Manager Dennis P O'Brien

CIRCULATION

Manager Mardi Browning Douglass

NEWS EXECUTIVES

Editor Tom Honig
Managing Editor Stanley Hojnacki

EDITORS AND MANAGERS

Books Editor Chris Watson
Business Editor Pan White
City Editor William Condy
Editorial Writer Tom Honig
Education Editor Jondi Gumz
Entertainment Editor Tom Long
Fashion Editor Mike Blaesser
Features Editor Mike Blaesser
Films/Theater Editor Tom Long
Food Editor Mike Blaesser
Graphics Editor/Art Director Chris Carothers
Living Editor Mike Blaesser
Photo Editor Bill Lovejoy
Sports Editor Ed Vyeda
Television Editor Tom Long
Travel Editor Melorie Bowen

MANAGEMENT INFORMATION SERVICES

Data Processing Manager Melorie Bowen

PRODUCTION

Director Apolinar Acevedo
Foreman-Composing Wayne Stanton
Foreman-Pressroom Richard Lewis

Market Information: Zoned editions; Split Run; TMC; ADS; Operate audiotex.
Mechanical available: Offset; Black and 3 ROP colors; insert accepted — preprinted, product samples; page cut-offs — 22¾".
Mechanical specifications: Type page 13" x 21½"; E - 6 cols, 2 1/16", ⅛" between; A - 6 cols, 2 1/16", ⅛" between; C - 9 cols, 1⅜", 1/16" between.
Commodity consumption: Newsprint 2,368 short tons; 2,150 metric tons; widths 55", 41¼", 27½"; black ink 90,000 pounds; color ink 1,100 pounds; single pages printed 14,000; average pages per issue 38(d), 36(sat), 60(S); single plates used 35,000.
Equipment: EDITORIAL: Front-end hardware — Tandem, 1-PC/286, 1-PC/386; Front-end software — SII; Printers — Centronics; Other equipment — 35-SII/Coyote, Ap/Power Mac 8100. CLASSIFIED: Front-end hardware — Tandem; Front-end software — SII; Printers — Centronics; Other equipment — 11-SII/Coyote, 1-PC/286. AUDIOTEX: Hardware — PC/486, 4-MB; Software — MNA, BBS, VDC; Supplier name — J H Zerbey Newspaper Inc. DISPLAY: Adv layout systems — Mk/Managing Editor; Front-end hardware — Ap/Power Mac 6100; Front-end software — ALS; Printers — HP/LaserJet 4; Other equipment — 3-SII/Coyote. PRODUCTION: Typesetters — 2-MON/82E; Plate exposures — 2-Nu; Plate processors — 1-WL; Electronic picture desk — Lf; Scanners — RZ/4050; Production cameras — Ik/550, Ik/555; Automatic film processors — Konica; Film transporters — Konica; Color separation equipment (conventional) — RZ.
PRESSROOM: Line 1 — 6-G/Headliner; Pasters — 5-G; Reels and stands — 5-G; Press control system — Fin. MAILROOM: Counter stackers — 3-QWI; Inserters and stuffers — 2-GMA/6:1-8:1; Bundle tyer — 2-Power Strap, 1-OVL. WIRE SERVICES: News — AP, ONI, NYT, McClatchy, Bay City News Service; Photos — Lf/AP Leaf Picture Desk; Stock tables — AP SelectStox, NYSE, Mutual Funds, OTC; Receiving dishes — size-10ft, AP. BUSINESS COMPUTERS: 1-IBM/AS400; Applications: Circ, Adv Billing, Accts receivable, Gen ledger, Payroll; PCs & micros networked; PCs & main system networked.

SANTA MARIA

Santa Barbara County

'90 U.S. Census- 61,284; **E&P '96 Est.** 83,467
ABC-CZ (90): 90,847 (HH 30,265)

Santa Maria Times

(e-mon to fri; m-sat; S)

Santa Maria Times, 3200 Skyway Dr.; PO Box 400, Santa Maria, CA 93454; tel (805) 925-2691; fax (805) 928-5657. Scripps League Newspapers Inc. group.
Circulation: 21,652(e); 21,652(m-sat); 22,463(S); ABC Sept. 30, 1995.
Price: 50¢(d); 25¢(sat); $1.00(S); $8.50/mo; $102.00/yr.
Advertising: Open inch rate $17.25(e); $17.25(m-sat); $17.25(S). **Representative:** Papert Companies.
News Service: AP. **Politics:** Independent. **Established:** 1882.
Special Editions: Brides World (Feb); Home Improvement, Annual Progress Edition (Mar); Mother's Day, Elks Rodeo Tab, Discover the Central Coast (May); Santa Barbara County Fair Tab (June); Women In Business (Oct); Year In Review (Dec); Real Estate Today (monthly).
Special Weekly Sections: Health (tues); Food (wed); Senior (thur); Dining Guide (fri); Garden (sat); Travel (S); Entertainment, Business, Sports, Life, Women's Interest (daily).
Magazines: TV Review, USA Weekend (S).

CORPORATE OFFICERS

Board Chairman/Treasurer E W Scripps
Vice Chairman/Corporate Secretary Betty Knight Scripps
President Barry H Scripps
Vice Pres-Finance Thomas E Wendel

GENERAL MANAGEMENT

Publisher John Shields
Business Manager Karen Keele

ADVERTISING

Manager Bernie Petrich
Manager-Classified Annette Miller

CIRCULATION

Director Bob Roeser

NEWS EXECUTIVE

Managing Editor Wayne Agner

EDITORS AND MANAGERS

Automotive Editor Wayne Agner
Business Editor Michael Todd
City Editor Michael Todd
Editorial Page Editor Wayne Agner
Education Editor Monica Prinzing
Entertainment/Amusements Editor Sherry Wittman
Fashion/Style Editor Sherry Wittman
Graphics Editor/Art Director Chris Gotsill
Living/Lifestyle Editor Sherry Wittman
Missiles/Space Editor Janene Scully
News Editor Michael Todd
Society/Women's Editor Sherry Wittman
Sports Editor Rich Guiremand
Travel Editor Wayne Agner

PRODUCTION

Foreman-Press Ernie Pardo
Foreman-Composing Rudy Galvan

Market Information: Split Run; TMC.
Mechanical available: Offset; Black and 3 ROP colors; insert accepted — preprinted, upon prior quote only; page cut-offs — 22¾".
Mechanical specifications: Type page 13" x 21½"; E - 6 cols, 2 1/16", ⅛" between; A - 6 cols, 2 1/16", ⅛" between; C - 9 cols, 1⅜", 1/16" between.
Commodity consumption: Newsprint 1,526 metric tons; widths 27½", 30"; black ink 40,000 pounds; color ink 3,000 pounds; single pages printed 11,000; average pages per issue 34(d), 52(S); single plates used 4,932.
Equipment: EDITORIAL: Front-end hardware — SII, Ap/Mac; Printers — 2-Ap/LaserWriter IIg; Other equipment — 1-Ap/Mac Quadra 950, 2-Ap/Mac Centris 610, 18-Intel/386. CLASSIFIED: Front-end hardware — SII; Other equipment — 5-Intel/386. DISPLAY: Front-end hardware — 2-Ap/Mac Centris 610, Ap/Mac Centris 650, Ap/Mac Quadra 610; Printers — 1-LaserMaster/Unity 1200XL, 1-LaserMaster/Unity 1800XL. PRODUCTION: Pagination software — QuarkXPress 3.3, Mk/Page Director, Mk/Ad Director, Pongrass; Typesetters — Hyphen/Spectraset 2400, Hyphen/Dash 94; Plate exposures — 1-Nu; Electronic picture desk — Lf/AP Leaf Picture Desk; Scanners — Howtek/Colorscan Sys, Ap/Mac, Polaroid/SprintScan 35, Relisys/4830T; Production cameras — 2-F; Automatic film processors — Wing Lynch.
PRESSROOM: Line 1 — 7-G/Urbanite (1 color deck); Folders — 1-G. MAILROOM: Counter stackers — 1-M, 1-CH; Inserters and stuffers — 2-MM/EMIO-227E; Bundle tyer — 1-MLN; Addressing machine — Wm/from computer lists. WIRE SERVICES: News — AP; Syndicates — KRT; Receiving dishes — size-10ft, AP. BUSINESS COMPUTERS: PBS; Applications: PBS-Circ.

SANTA MONICA

Los Angeles County

'90 U.S. Census- 86,905; **E&P '96 Est.** 86,116
ABC-CZ (90): 86,905 (HH 44,860)

The Outlook (m-mon to sat)

The Outlook, 1920 Colorado Blvd., Santa Monica, CA 90406; tel (310) 829-6811; fax (310) 829-7544. Copley Press Inc. group.
Circulation: 25,127(m); 25,127(m-sat); ABC Sept. 30, 1995.
Price: 25¢(d); 25¢(sat); $7.00/mo.
Representative: Sawyer-Ferguson-Walker Co.
News Services: AP, CNS, NYT, City News Service, McClatchy, SHNS. **Politics:** Republican. **Established:** 1875.
Note: The Outlook is printed and produced by the Daily Breeze. For commodity consumption, see Torrance Daily Breeze listing. The Copley Los Angeles Newspapers includes the following newspapers: Torrance Daily Breeze (mS), San Pedro News Pilot (m) and Santa Monica Outlook (m). The group rate is $87.57. Individual newspaper rates not made available. Effective Sept. 5, 1995, this publication changed its publishing plan from (e-mon to sat) to (m-mon to sat).
Advertising not accepted: 900 Phone numbers; X-rated movies.
Special Editions: School Pages (monthly); Health Care '96, California Home Show, Valentine Boxes, Healthy Kids, President's Day Boxes (Feb); Home & Garden, Jimmy Stewart Relay Marathon (Mar); Best of the West Side (Apr); Health Tab, At Home, Healthy Kids (May); Dining Guide, Santa Monica Chamber Yearly Report (June); California Home Show, Football '96 (Aug); School Pages, Home Improvements (Sept); Health Kids 2000, Health & Fitness, Ski & Travel (Oct); Holiday Kick-off, Gift Ideas, California Home Show (Nov); 'Tis the Season, Gift Galore, Christmas Services (Churches), Last Minute Gifts (Dec).
Special Weekly Sections: Motion Pictures/Entertainment/TV Pages/Radio, Business News and Stock Quotes (daily); Health (mon); Food, Lifestyle (wed); Home (thur); Entertainment, Restaurants (fri).
Magazines: RAVE! (fri); TV Week, USA Weekend (sat).

CORPORATE OFFICERS

Board Chairman Helen K Copley
Vice Chairman Hubert L Kaltenbach
President David C Copley
Exec Vice Pres-Finance Charles F Patrick
Vice Pres-Finance Dean P Dwyer

GENERAL MANAGEMENT

Publisher Thomas J Wafer Jr
Business Manager David M Thorne
Buyer Ted Yamada
Asst Business Manager Thomas M Hellems

ADVERTISING

Director Steve Elkins
Manager-Retail Janice Sheldon
Manager-Classified Tim Guesman

MARKETING AND PROMOTION

Manager-Marketing/Promotion Mike Lynn

TELECOMMUNICATIONS

Manager-Info Systems Roland B West

CIRCULATION

Director Charles A McManis Jr
Manager Dan Sidbury
Manager-Administration Rick Perius

NEWS EXECUTIVES

Editor James M Box
Exec Editor/Asst to Publisher Skip Rimer
Managing Editor Lou Brancaccio

EDITORS AND MANAGERS

Business Editor Ed Moosbrugger
City Editor Patti Wolf
Entertainment Editor Charles Britton
Food Editor Lisa Messinger
Home Furnishings Editor Terry Moore
Photo Department Manager Robert Clark
Real Estate Editor Ed Moosbrugger
Society Editor Gay Goerz
Sports Editor Robert Whitley

MANAGEMENT INFORMATION SERVICES

Manager-Info Systems Roland B West
Manager-Technical Service John Cummins

PRODUCTION

Manager Ronald D Goble
Foreman Larry Robertson
Supervisor-Pressroom Bill Hitt
Foreman-Mailroom Al Cohen

Market Information: Zoned editions; Split Run; TMC; ADS.
Mechanical available: Offset; Black and 3 ROP colors; insert accepted — preprinted, tab, standard, flexi, products, samples, single sheets; page cut-offs — 22¾".
Mechanical specifications: Type page 13" x 21⅜"; E - 6 cols, 2 1/16", ⅛" between; A - 6 cols, 2 1/16", ⅛" between; C - 10 cols, 1 5/16", 1/16" between.
Commodity consumption: average pages per issue 34(d).
Equipment: EDITORIAL: Front-end hardware — SII/Sys 55; Other equipment — Ap/Mac, 30-SII/Coyote. CLASSIFIED: Front-end hardware — SII/Sys 55; Other equipment — DEC/Rainbow, 22-SII/Coyote. DISPLAY: Adv layout systems — SCS/Layout 8000. PRODUCTION: Typesetters — 7-AU/APS, AU/3850; Platemaking systems — WL; Plate exposures — 2-WL; Plate processors — 2-WL; Electronic picture desk — AP linked to Ap/Mac Network; Scanners — ECR/Autokon 1000; Production cameras — 2-C/1211; Automatic film proces-

I-52 California

sors — 2-LE/LD 18; Film transporters — 2-C; Shrink lenses — 2-CK Optical; Color separation equipment (conventional) — 1-HCM/399ER.
PRESSROOM: Line 1 — 12-G/Metro; Folders — 2-G; Pasters — 12-G; Reels and stands — 12-G. MAILROOM: Counter stackers — 2-HL/Monitor, 4-HL/Monitor HT, 1-QUT/XX 5j301; Inserters and stuffers — 1-GMA/SLS 100; Bundle tyer — 2-MLN/2A, 2-MLN/2EE, 1-MLN/2AHS, 5-Power Strap, 3-MLN; Wrapping singles — 1-Shanklin/Plastic Shrinker A22; Addressing machine — 1-ST/1200SDC, 1-Ch/Video Jet Model 9816. LIBRARY: Electronic — DEC/Vax 8800 Basis. WIRE SERVICES: News — AP, CNS, NYT, City News Service, McClatchy, SHNS, Race Wire; Photos — AP Photostream; Stock tables — AP. BUSINESS COMPUTERS: DEC/Micro Vax; Applications: Circ, Payroll, Accts payable, Accts receivable, Gen ledger.

SANTA ROSA

Sonoma County

'90 U.S. Census- 113,313; E&P '96 Est. 139,315
ABC-CZ (90): 165,354 (HH 64,808)

The Press Democrat

(m-mon to sat; S)

The Press Democrat, 427 Mendocino Ave. (95401); PO Box 569, Santa Rosa, CA 95402; tel (707) 546-2020; fax (707) 546-8347 (Adm); web site http://www.pressdemo.com/library/. New York Times Co. group.
Circulation: 93,383(m); 93,383(m-sat); 102,252(S); ABC Sept. 30, 1995.
Price: 50¢(d); 50¢(sat); $1.25(S); $2.75/wk; $128.70/yr.
Advertising: Open inch rate $62.55(m); $62.55(m-sat); $62.55(S). **Representative:** Long & Associates.
News Services: NYT, AP, LAT-WP, McClatchy, Bay City News Service. **Established:** 1857.
Special Editions: Sonoma County Fair Guide (July); Football Preview Pro (Aug); Fall Home & Garden, Fall Cruise, Discover Sonoma County, Harvest Fair (Sept); Travel Mexico, Women (Oct); Sonoma Co. Skiers Info. Guide, Financial Guide, Winter Cruise, Holiday Entertaining (Nov).
Special Weekly Sections: Your Business/Computers (mon); Entertainment Express, Life, Teen Life (tues); Food Life (wed); Weekend Life (thur); Entertainment (fri); Home Life, Church (sat); Sunday Forum, Life (S).
Magazines: TV Week (S); Parade; On Q.

CORPORATE OFFICERS
President Lance R Primis
Vice Pres Michael J Parman

GENERAL MANAGEMENT
Publisher Michael J Parman
Chief Financial Officer W David Foster
Director-Human Resources Kathleen Grant

ADVERTISING
Director Ken Svanum
Manager-Retail Carolyn Brians
Manager-Classified Joanne Davey

MARKETING AND PROMOTION
Manager-Marketing Services Jerry McCartan

CIRCULATION
Director Tim Cambra

NEWS EXECUTIVES
Exec Editor Bruce W Kyse
Managing Editor Robert Swofford
Asst Managing Editor Chuck Buxton
Asst Managing Editor-Design Sharon Roberts
News Editor Jim Fremgen

EDITORS AND MANAGERS
Agriculture Editor Tim Tesconi
Books Editor Peter Golis
Business/Finance Editor Brad Bollinger
City Editor Catherine Barnett
Columnist-Sports Lowell Cohn
Columnist-Sports Bob Padecky
Editorial Director Peter Golis
Editorial Page Editor Peter Golis
Education Editor Catherine Barnett
Features/Fashion Editor Susan Leathers
Films/Theater Editor Dan Taylor
Food Editor Susan Leathers
Home Furnishings Editor Susan Leathers
Librarian Alison Head
Living/Lifestyle Editor Susan Leathers
Music Editor Dan Taylor
Political Editor Paul Ingalls
Radio/Television Editor Dan Taylor
Real Estate Editor Brad Bollinger
Sports Editor Jim Jenks
Travel Editor Susan Leathers
Women's Editor Susan Leathers

MANAGEMENT INFORMATION SERVICES
Data Processing Manager Hormoz Jahansoozi

PRODUCTION
Director-Operations Mike Tobener
Asst Director Chris Dawson
Manager-Building Service (Santa Rosa/Rohnert Park) Peter Stewart
Manager-Pre Press Steve Smedes
Manager-Press/Plate Sam Caddle
Manager-Packaging & Distribution David Springer
Manager-Info Systems Hormoz Jahansoozi

Market Information: Zoned editions; Split Run; TMC; ADS; Operate audiotex.
Mechanical available: Offset; Black and 3 ROP colors; insert accepted — preprinted; page cut-offs — 22".
Mechanical specifications: Type page 12¾" x 20¾"; E - 6 cols, 2$\frac{1}{16}$", $\frac{3}{16}$" between; A - 6 cols, 2$\frac{1}{16}$", $\frac{3}{16}$" between; C - 9 cols, 1⅜", ⅛" between.
Commodity consumption: Newsprint 15,075 short tons; widths 54", 40½", 27"; black ink 270,000 pounds; color ink 56,200 pounds; single pages printed 28,320; average pages per issue 62(d), 124(S); single plates used 108,000.
Equipment: EDITORIAL: Front-end hardware — Tandem/TXP; Front-end software — SII/Sys55 STD; Printers — TI/810; Other equipment — 5-Echo/Page Makeup Terminal, 69-SII/Coyote. CLASSIFIED: Front-end hardware — Tandem/Txp; Front-end software — SII/Decade; Printers — TI/80, HP/Rugged Writer; Other equipment — 34-SII/Coyote Ad Entry Terminal, Dell/486. AUDIOTEX: Hardware — Brite Voice Systems; Software — Brite Voice Systems; Supplier name — Comstock. DISPLAY: Adv layout systems — Cx; Front-end hardware — Ap/Mac, III/Ad Manager; Front-end software — Multi-Ad/Creator III/Ad Manager; Other equipment — SII, Tandem/TXP, SII/Interactive Ad Layout, 1-SII/Tahoe Layout Terminal. PRODUCTION: Typesetters — 2-III/38505, 1-Pelbox/108, 1-Graphic; Platemaking systems — Enterprise/VP 1000; Plate exposures — 1-WL/Lith-X-Pozer; Plate processors — 1-WL/38D; Electronic picture desk — Ap/Mac; Scanners — Nikon, CD, Autokon/1000; Production cameras — 1-C/260D, C/Spartan III-1270; Automatic film processors — 2-P/2624 Series 700; Film transporters — 2-P/SC 250; Color separation equipment (conventional) — CD/635; Digital color separation equipment — 2-ECR/1000, 1-CD/635E.
PRESSROOM: Line 1 — 8-G/Headliner (4 decks); Press drives — Allen Bradley; Folders — 2-G/3:2; Pasters — G/RPT. MAILROOM: Counter stackers — 6-QWI; Inserters and stuffers — 2-AM Graphics/6305 22/24, 1-AMG/NP 630 22 Hopper, 1-AMG/NP 130 26 Hopper; Bundle tyer — 3-MLN/2A, 2-Power Strap/PSN6; Wrapping singles — 1-HI/650 Saddle Binder; Other mailroom equipment — AMG. LIBRARY: Electronic — Vu/Text. COMMUNICATIONS: Facsimile — CD. WIRE SERVICES: News — NYT, AP, LAT-WP, McClatchy, Bay City News Service, KRT; Receiving dishes — AP. BUSINESS COMPUTERS: IBM/AS 400 Model E50; Applications: Admarc: Accts receivable; Lawson: Accts payable; INSI: Circ; PCs & micros networked; PCs & main system networked.

SONORA

Tuolumne County

'90 U.S. Census- 4,153; E&P '96 Est. 4,894

The Union Democrat

(e-mon to fri)

The Union Democrat, 84 S. Washington St., Sonora, CA 95370; tel (209) 532-7151; fax (209) 532-5139.
Circulation: 12,455(e); Sworn Oct. 6, 1995.
Price: 50¢(d); $6.00/mo; $66.00/yr.
Advertising: Open inch rate $10.13(e).
News Service: AP. **Politics:** Independent. **Established:** 1854.
Not Published: New Year; President's Day; Memorial Day; Independence Day; Labor Day; Thanksgiving; Christmas.
Special Editions: Dollars and Sense (Jan); Wedding Planner (Feb); Home & Garden, Wood Cutters Guide (Mar); American Home Week, Spring Fashion, Roundup Queen Review (Apr); MotherLode Roundup, Car Care (May); MotherLode Fair (July); Back-to-School, Prime Time Lifestyle, Tuolumne County Visitors Guide, Know-it-All (Aug); Film Fest Program, Ready for Winter (Sept); Health Fair Guide (Oct); Holiday Treasures Edition, A Taste of the Sierra (Nov); Letters to Santa, Santa's Photo Tour, Year In Review (Dec).
Special Weekly Sections: Business and Building, Best Food Day (tues); Best Food Day (wed); Want Ads Plus, Health and Fitness (thur); Country Living, Business & Building, Restaurants, Weekend (fri).
Magazine: The Weekend (fri).

CORPORATE OFFICERS
President Harvey C McGee
Secretary/Treasurer Helen M McGee

GENERAL MANAGEMENT
Publisher Harvey C McGee
Controller Helen M McGee
Manager-Office Karen Blair

ADVERTISING
Manager-Display Bruce (Bud) Vogel
Manager-Classified Gary Tune

CIRCULATION
Director Sam Pothier

NEWS EXECUTIVES
Editor Harvey C McGee
Managing Editor Buzz Eggleston

EDITORS AND MANAGERS
Business/Finance Editor Amy Nilson
Editorial Page Editor Harvey C McGee
Education Editor Kerry McCray
Environmental Editor John Holland
Fashion/Style Editor Lenore Rutherford
Graphics Editor/Art Director Bonita Clark
News Editor Larry Hashman
Religion Editor Lenore Rutherford
Sports Editor Kevin Sauls
Television/Film Editor Gary Linehan
Theater/Music Editor Gary Linehan
Travel Editor Kathie Waterbury
Women's Editor Kathie Waterbury

MANAGEMENT INFORMATION SERVICES
Manager-Systems David Harden

PRODUCTION
Manager Martha Gibbons

Market Information: Zoned editions; Split Run; TMC.
Mechanical available: Web Offset; Black and 3 ROP colors; insert accepted — preprinted; page cut-offs — 23".
Mechanical specifications: Type page 13" x 21½"; E - 6 cols, 2", ⅙" between; A - 6 cols, 2", ⅙" between; C - 6 cols, 2", ⅙" between.
Commodity consumption: Newsprint 640 metric tons; widths 28", 14"; single pages printed 7,864; average pages per issue 31(d); single plates used 4,700.
Equipment: EDITORIAL: Front-end hardware — Ap/Mac; Front-end software — Baseview, QuarkXPress; Printers — V, Ap/Mac. CLASSIFIED: Front-end hardware — Ap/Mac; Front-end software — Baseview; Printers — V, Ap/Mac. DISPLAY: Adv layout systems — QuarkXPress; Front-end hardware — Ap/Mac; Front-end software — QuarkXPress, Multi-Ad; Printers — V/Imagesetters. PRODUCTION: Typesetters — SII; Plate exposures — 1-Nu/Flip Top FT40V4UP; Plate processors — Nat; Production cameras — SCREEN/Companica 5161; Automatic film processors — 1-LE.
PRESSROOM: Line 1 — 8-G/Community w/Former. MAILROOM: Inserters and stuffers — 6-KAN; Bundle tyer — Bu; Addressing machine — Wm. LIBRARY: Electronic — SMS/Stauffer Gold, Ap/Mac. WIRE SERVICES: News — AP; Receiving dishes — AP. BUSINESS COMPUTERS: 2-Compaq; Applications: In-House.

SOUTH LAKE TAHOE

El Dorado County

'90 U.S. Census- 21,585; E&P '96 Est. 22,219

Tahoe Daily Tribune

(m-mon to fri)

Tahoe Daily Tribune, 3079 Harrison Ave.; PO Box 1358, South Lake Tahoe, CA 95705; tel (916) 541-3880; fax (916) 541-0373; e-mail listproc@www0.cern.ch, tribune@tahoe.com; web site http://www.tahoe.com. Swift Newspapers group.
Circulation: 7,250(m); Sworn Sept. 29,1995.
Price: 50¢(d); $8.50/mo (carrier), $8.75/mo (motor route).
Advertising: Open inch rate $18.00(m).
News Service: AP. **Politics:** Independent. **Established:** 1958.
Note: Effective May 20, 1995, this publication changed its publishing plan from (m-mon to sat) to (m-mon to fri).
Special Editions: Annual Edition, Almanac Series (Oct).
Special Weekly Sections: Entertainment, Real Estate (fri).
Magazines: What's On (TV Book) (thur); Lake Tahoe Action (fri); Best of Tahoe (summer) (June); Sierra Summers (July); Sierra Ski Times (seasonal) (Nov-Apr).

CORPORATE OFFICERS
Chairman Philip E Swift
President Richard K Larson

GENERAL MANAGEMENT
Publisher Loren C Abbott
Business Manager Erin Wiseman

ADVERTISING
Director Steven D Baker
Manager-Retail Jim Smolinski
Manager-Classified Virginia Lindsay

TELECOMMUNICATIONS
Audiotex Manager Virginia Lindsay

CIRCULATION
Director Thomas Erikson

NEWS EXECUTIVE
Managing Editor Claire Fortier

EDITORS AND MANAGERS
Asst Managing Editor-Content Kathy Trissell
Asst Managing Editor-Production Tim Traeger
Editorial Page Editor Claire Fortier
Entertainment/Amusements Editor Denise Sloan
Environmental Reporter Jeff DeLong
Graphics Editor/Art Director Steve Miller
Living/Lifestyle Editor Kathy Trissell
Religion Editor Sally Taylor
Sports Editor Steve Yingling
Tahoe Action Editor Denise Sloan
Theater/Music Editor Denise Sloan
Women's Editor Nancy Oliver Hayden

MANAGEMENT INFORMATION SERVICES
Manager Jim Hemig

PRODUCTION
Manager Patrick Nealy

Market Information: TMC; ADS; Operate audiotex; Electronic edition.
Mechanical available: Web Offset; Black and 3 ROP colors; insert accepted — preprinted, on request; page cut-offs — 22¾".
Mechanical specifications: Type page 12⅞" x 21½"; E - 6 cols, 2", ⅙" between; A - 6 cols, 2", ⅙" between; C - 9 cols, 1⅓", ⅓" between.
Commodity consumption: width 27½"; average pages per issue 20(d), 32(fri).
Equipment: EDITORIAL: Front-end hardware — 1-Ap/Mac; Front-end software — QuarkXPress 3.1; Printers — Ap/Mac LaserWriter II NTX; Other equipment — Lf/AP Leaf Picture Desk. CLASSIFIED: Front-end hardware — Ap/Mac; Front-end software — Fourth Dimension; Printers — Ap/Mac LaserWriter II NTX. DISPLAY: Adv layout systems — 6-Ap/Mac se, 2-Ap/Mac II; Front-end hardware — Ap/Mac; Front-end software — QuarkXPress 3.1, Aldus/FreeHand; Printers — Ap/Mac LaserWriter II NTX; Other equipment — AP AdSend. PRODUCTION: Typesetters — 2-Microcraft/Translator II, Ap/Mac IINTX; Color separation equipment (conventional) — 1-WDS.
PRESSROOM: Line 1 — 10-G/Community; Folders — 1-G. MAILROOM: Counter stackers — 1-BG; Inserters and stuffers — 4-MM; Bundle tyer — 2-MLN. WIRE SERVICES: News — AP Datascreen; Receiving dishes — size-10ft, AP. BUSINESS COMPUTERS: Unisys; Applications: PBS; PCs & micros networked.

STOCKTON

San Joaquin County

'90 U.S. Census- 210,943; E&P '96 Est. 266,991
ABC-CZ (90): 220,343 (HH 72,932)

The Record (m-mon to sat; S)

The Record, 530 E. Market St.; PO Box 900, Stockton, CA 95202; tel (209) 943-6397; fax (209) 546-8246; e-mail e-mail bcox@record.com. Omaha World-Herald Co. group.
Circulation: 54,089(m); 54,089(m-sat); 60,742(S); ABC Sept. 30, 1995.

Copyright ©1996 by the Editor & Publisher Co.

Price: 46¢(d); 46¢(sat); $1.16(S); $10.50/mo.
Advertising: Open inch rate $41.83(m); $41.83(m-sat); $44.80(S).
News Services: AP, KRT, LAT-WP. **Politics:** Independent. **Established:** 1895.
Special Editions: Ag Expo, Wedding Book (Jan); Outlook #1, Outlook #2, Outlook #3, Outlook #4 (Feb); Home & Garden (Mar); Asparagus Festival (Apr); Kid's Day, Outdoors & the Delta (May); Welcome to San Joaquin, County Fair, Honor Roll, Fair Results, Waterfest (June); Su Salud, Parade of Homes (July); Back-to-School (Aug); UOP Football Programs (Sept); Dining Guide (Oct); Holiday Gift Guide I, Holiday Gift Guide II (Nov); Holiday Gift Guide I, Holiday Gift Guide II, Holiday Gift Guide III (Dec).
Special Weekly Sections: BizMonday, Milestones, Community Bulletin Board (mon); Vintage, Health Today, Sports Extra (tues); Food Today, Outdoors (wed); Families Today, Prep Sports (thur); Youth Ink, Automotive (fri); Home & Renter's, Religion (sat); Travel, Lodi/Lode, Valley Values (S).
Magazines: Hot Ticket (TMC) (wed); Time Out-Entertainment Guide (fri); TV Record (S); Parade.

CORPORATE OFFICERS

President/Publisher	Terry Kroeger
Secretary/Treasurer	Steve Peterson
Vice Pres-Advertising	Dave Winegarden
Vice Pres-Circulation	Dave Williams
Vice Pres-Marketing	Ezell Cox

GENERAL MANAGEMENT

Publisher	Terry Kroeger
Director-Administration Service	Steve Peterson
Controller	Ken Ketterling
Manager-Office	Peggy Takahashi
Manager-Credit	Shirley Martin
Manager-Community Service	Carrie Sass

ADVERTISING

Director	Dave Winegarden
Manager-Retail	Chuck Higgs
Manager-Classified	Polly Wright

MARKETING AND PROMOTION

Vice Pres-Marketing	Ezell Cox
Manager-Promotion	Darcy Koster

TELECOMMUNICATIONS

Audiotex Manager	Duffy Ruffin

CIRCULATION

Director	David G Williams
Manager-Operations	Dalton DuVal

NEWS EXECUTIVE

Exec Editor	Betty Liddick

EDITORS AND MANAGERS

Books Editor	Howard Lachtman
Business/Finance Editor	Eric Grunder
Drama Editor	Brian McCoy
Editorial Page Editor	Richard Marsh
Fashion Editor	Joan Simpson
Food Editor	Joan Simpson
Librarian	Thai Strom
Lifestyle Editor	Joan Simpson
Lifestyle Editor	Erin Pasley
Metro Editor	Paul Feist
Asst Metro Editor	Meda Freeman
Music Editor	Brian McCoy
Radio/Television Editor	Sharon Spence
Sports Editor	Joe Pasley

MANAGEMENT INFORMATION SERVICES

Data Processing Manager	Tony Carolla
Director-Systems Info	Rick Henning

PRODUCTION

Director	Gregg Baxter
Manager-Composing	Vip Hale
Manager-Pressroom	Gus Dalsis
Manager-Mailroom	Howard Carter

Market Information: Zoned editions; TMC; ADS; Operate audiotex.
Mechanical available: Letterpress; Black and 3 ROP colors; insert accepted — preprinted, commercial flyers; page cut-offs — 22¾".
Mechanical specifications: Type page 13" x 21½"; E - 6 cols, 2¹⁄₁₆", ⅛" between; A - 6 cols, 2¹⁄₁₆", ⅛" between; C - 10 cols, 1.22", ¹⁄₁₂" between.
Commodity consumption: Newsprint 6,280 short tons; 5,825 metric tons; widths 54⅞", 40", 27⅜"; black ink 195,000 pounds; color ink 22,000 pounds; single pages printed 17,412; average pages per issue 46(d), 62(S); single plates used 35,000.
Equipment: EDITORIAL: Front-end hardware — SII; Front-end software — SII, QuarkXPress; Printers — QMS/810, Ap/LaserWriter II; Other equipment — Ap/Mac, III/Imagesetter. CLASSIFIED: Front-end hardware — Tandem/CLX-R; Front-end software — SII; Printers — QMS/810; Other equipment — Hyphen/Mac RIP, OPI/Hyphen. AUDIOTEX: Hardware — Unix; Software — Brite; Supplier name — Brite. DISPLAY: Front-end hardware — Ap/Mac IIfx; Front-end software — Multi-Ad/Creator; Printers — Hyphen/Dash 600, III/3850; Other equipment — SCS. PRODUCTION: Pagination software — QuarkXPress; OCR software — 1-Nu; Typesetters — III/3850; Platemaking systems — Na/NP40; Plate exposures — Na; Plate processors — Na; Electronic picture desk — Lf/AP Leaf Picture Desk; Scanners — Microtek, Desktop, Graphic Enterprises/PageScan; Production cameras — C/Spartan II; Automatic film processors — 1-P; Film transporters — 1-C; Digital color separation equipment — Desktop, Ap/Mac, Adobe/Photoshop.
PRESSROOM: Line 1 — 8-G/MKI. MAILROOM: Counter stackers — 3-HL; Inserters and stuffers — 1-HI/1472P; Bundle tyer — 3-MLN. LIBRARY: Electronic — SII/CLX R. WIRE SERVICES: News — AP, LAT-WP, KRT; Photos — AP; Stock tables — AP SelectStox; Syndicates — TV Data, United Features, LATS; Receiving dishes — size-12ft, AP. BUSINESS COMPUTERS: IBM/AS400 Model B45; Applications: Circ, Financial, Payroll, Adv; PCs & micros networked; PCs & main system networked.

TAFT
Kern County
'90 U.S. Census- 5,902; E&P '96 Est. 6,330

Daily Midway Driller (e-mon to fri)

Daily Midway Driller, 800 Center St.; PO Bin Z, Taft, CA 93268; tel (805) 763-3171; fax (805) 763-5638. Scripps League Newspapers Inc. group.
Circulation: 3,873(e); Sworn Sept. 29, 1995.
Price: 35¢(d); $5.80/mo.
Advertising: Open inch rate $6.05(e).
News Service: AP. **Politics:** Independent. **Established:** 1910.
Not Published: New Year; Memorial Day; Independence Day; Labor Day; Thanksgiving; Christmas.
Special Weekly Sections: Business (tues); Lifestyle (wed); Opinion (thur); Outdoors, Religion (fri).

CORPORATE OFFICERS

Board Chairman/Treasurer	E W Scripps
Vice Chairman/Corporate Secretary	Betty Knight Scripps
President	Ed Scripps III
Vice Pres-Finance	Thomas E Wendel

GENERAL MANAGEMENT

Publisher	Dorothy G Parsons
Business Manager	Dorothy G Parsons

ADVERTISING

Manager	Caroline Holm

CIRCULATION

Director-Marketing	Sandy Ashmore

NEWS EXECUTIVE

Editor	David Hook

EDITOR AND MANAGER

Sports Editor	David Hook

PRODUCTION

Supervisor	Carrie Cole

Market Information: TMC.
Mechanical available: Offset; Black and 1 ROP color; insert accepted — preprinted; page cut-offs — 21½".
Mechanical specifications: Type page 13" x 21½"; E - 6 cols, 2¹⁄₁₆", ⅛" between; A - 6 cols, 2¹⁄₁₆", ⅛" between; C - 6 cols, 2¹⁄₁₆", ⅛" between.
Commodity consumption: Newsprint 132 metric tons; widths 28", 14"; single pages printed 2,214; average pages per issue 8(d); single plates used 3,500.
Equipment: EDITORIAL: Front-end hardware — 3-IBM/PC, 2-IBM/AT; Printers — 1-HP/Laser Jet Series II Printer. CLASSIFIED: Front-end hardware — 1-IBM/AT; Other equipment — 1-Okidata/99. DISPLAY: Printers — QMS; Other equipment — 1-Mk/Acer 386. PRODUCTION: Typesetters — 1-COM/IV, 1-HP/Laserprinter; Platemaking systems — 1-Nu; Plate exposures — 1-Nu; Production cameras — 1-B; Automatic film processors — 1-PMT.
PRESSROOM: Line 1 — 4-G/Community; Folders — 1-G. MAILROOM: Inserters and stuffers — 1-MM EM10; Bundle tyer — 2-Bu; Addressing machine — 1-Am. WIRE SERVICES: News — AP; Syndicates — ScrippSat. BUSINESS COMPUTERS: 1-IBM/AT, 1-Mk/Acer 486; Applications: Accts receivable, Payroll, Disbursements.

TEMECULA
Riverside County
'90 U.S. Census- 27,099; E&P '96 Est. 55,010
ABC-CZ (90): 53,769 (HH 18,443)

Californian (m-mon to fri; S)

Californian, 27450 Ynez Rd.; PO Box 970, Temecula, CA 92390; tel (909) 676-4315; fax (909) 699-1467. Howard Publications group.
Circulation: 12,411(m); 12,553(S); ABC Sept. 30, 1995.
Price: 25¢(d); 75¢(S); $1.25/wk (plus tax); $56.03/yr (carrier).
Advertising: Open inch rate $11.05(m); $11.05(S). **Representative:** Cresmer, Woodward, O'Mara & Ormsbee.
News Service: AP. **Politics:** Independent. **Established:** 1990 (daily).
Note: For printing and production information, see Escondido Times-Advocate's listing.
Special Edition: Guide to Our Valley (May & Oct).

GENERAL MANAGEMENT

Publisher	Linda Wunderlich

ADVERTISING

Manager	Linda Wunderlich

MARKETING AND PROMOTION

Manager-Marketing/Promotion	Linda Wunderlich

CIRCULATION

Manager	Bette Webster

NEWS EXECUTIVE

Editor	James Folmer

Mechanical available: Offset; Black and 3 ROP colors; insert accepted — preprinted; page cut-offs — 22".
Mechanical specifications: Type page 13" x 21"; E - 6 cols, 2.03", ⅙" between; A - 6 cols, 2.03", ⅙" between; C - 6 cols, 1.24", ⅙" between.
Equipment: EDITORIAL: Front-end hardware — SII; Front-end software — SII; Printers — 2-DEC/LA180; Other equipment — 2-Lf/AP Leaf Picture Desk, 5-Ap/Mac Quadra 700. CLASSIFIED: Front-end hardware — SII; Front-end software — SII; Printers — 2-DEC/LA 180. DISPLAY: Adv layout systems — Homegrown; Front-end hardware — 14-Ap/Mac; Front-end software — Multi-Ad/Creator; Printers — HP/LaserJet IIIsi, HP/Pagescan 3. PRODUCTION: Typesetters — 2-AU/APS Micro 5, 2-V/5000, 2-Hyphen/Plain Paper; Plate exposures — 2-Nu; Plate processors — 1-Nat; Scanners — 1-ECR/Autokon 1000; Production cameras — 1-C/Spartan III, 2-Ag/RPS 6000; Automatic film processors — 2-LITEX/26, 1-V; Color separation equipment (conventional) — 1-RZ/2105; Digital color separation equipment — 2-Ap/Mac.
PRESSROOM: Line 1 — 5-G/HO (3-½ Deck); Folders — 2-G/2:1; Pasters — 5-G/CT-45; Press control system — G/MPCS. MAILROOM: Counter stackers — 3-Id/2000, 1-HL/Monitor; Inserters and stuffers — 2-GMA/SLS-1000 6:1; Bundle tyer — 3-Dynaric; Addressing machine — 1-Ch. WIRE SERVICES: News — AP Datastream, AP Datafeatures, AP Stats; Stock tables — TMS; Receiving dishes — AP. BUSINESS COMPUTERS: PCs & micros networked; PCs & main system networked.

TORRANCE
Los Angeles County
'90 U.S. Census- 133,107; E&P '96 Est. 135,406
ABC-NDM (90): 682,176 (HH 253,912)

Daily Breeze (m-mon to sat; S)

Daily Breeze, 5215 Torrance Blvd., Torrance, CA 90509; tel (310) 540-5511. Copley Press Inc. group.
Circulation: 81,308(m); 81,308(m-sat); 117,109(S); ABC Sept. 30, 1995.
Price: 25¢(d); 25¢(sat); $1.25(S); $7.50/mo.
Representative: Sawyer-Ferguson-Walker Co.
News Services: AP, CNS, NYT, City News Service, McClatchy, SHNS. **Politics:** Republican. **Established:** 1894.
Note: The Copley Los Angeles Newspapers include the following newspapers: Torrance Daily Breeze (mS), San Pedro News Pilot (m) and the Santa Monica Outlook (m). The group rate is $87.57. Individual newspaper rates not made available. Effective Sept. 5, 1995, this publication changed its publishing plan from (e-mon to sat; S) to (m-mon to sat; S).
Advertising not accepted: 900 phone numbers; X-rated movies.
Special Editions: School Pages (monthly); Health & Fitness, Wedding Guide (Feb); Best of South Bay, Home & Garden (Mar); Best of South Bay, Panorama (May); Dining Guide (July); Senior's Tab, Surf Festival (Aug); Football (Sept); At Home (Oct); Health Care, Holiday Kick-off (Nov); Christmas Gift Guides, Christmas Services (Churches), Last Minute Gifts (Dec).
Special Weekly Sections: Motion Pictures/Entertainment/TV Pages/Radio, Business News and Stock Quotes (daily); Health (mon); Food, Life/Arts (wed); Home (thur); Entertainment/Restaurant (fri).
Magazines: RAVE! (fri); Parade, Television Magazine (S).
Cable TV: Own cable TV in circulation area.

CORPORATE OFFICERS

Board Chairman	Helen K Copley
Vice Chairman	Hubert L Kaltenbach
President	David C Copley
Exec Vice Pres-Finance	Charles F Patrick
Vice Pres-Finance	Dean P Dwyer

GENERAL MANAGEMENT

Publisher	Thomas J Wafer Jr
Business Manager	David M Thorne
Asst Business Manager	Thomas M Hellems
Controller	Randy Siegel
Buyer	Ted Yamada
Human Resources Coordinator	Ming Canning
Director-Human Resources	Lisa Henry
Manager-Credit	Patti Tarle

ADVERTISING

Director	Steve Elkins
Manager-Classified	Tim Guesman
Manager-Retail	Janice Sheldon
Manager-National	Steve Lindemann
Coordinator-Co-op	Brian Hicks

MARKETING AND PROMOTION

Manager-Marketing/Promotion	Mike Lynn

TELECOMMUNICATIONS

Manager-Info Systems	Roland B West

CIRCULATION

Director	Charles A McManis Jr
Manager	Michael Levine
Manager-Administration	Rick Perius
Manager-Distribution/Transportation	Russ Humphrey

NEWS EXECUTIVES

Exec Editor	James M Box
Managing Editor	Jean Adelsman
Asst Managing Editor	Lisa Reitzel

EDITORS AND MANAGERS

Amusements/Art Editor	Charles Britton
Automotive Editor	Cyndia Zwahlen
Aviation Editor	Graham Witherall
Books Editor	Don Lechman
City Editor	Frank Suraci
Columnist	John Bogert
Design Editor	Jeannie Grand
Editorial Page Editor	Mike Carrol
Entertainment Editor	Charles Britton
Environment/Ecology Editor	Lee Peterson
Films Editor	Jerry Roberts
Finance Editor	Cyndia Zwahlen
Food Editor	Lisa Messinger
Garden Editor	Meredith Grenier
Home Furnishings Editor	Terry Moore
Librarian	Sam Gnerre
Music Editor	Charlie Britton
News Editor	Kathy Hinson
Chief Photograher	Jack Lardomita
Photo Editor	Robert York
Political Editor	Kathleen Dougherty
Radio/Television Editor	Jim Brooks
Real Estate Editor	Cyndia Zwahlen
Religion Editor	Thom Mead
School/Education Editor	Marie Montgomery
School/Education Editor	Christina LaRussa
Science/Technology Editor	Cyndia Zwahlen
Sports Editor	Robert Whitley
Theater Editor	Jim Farber
Transportation Editor	Jim Radcliffe
Travel Editor	Don Chapman

MANAGEMENT INFORMATION SERVICES

Manager-Info Systems	Roland B West
Manager-Technical Service	John Cummins

PRODUCTION

Director	Ronald D Goble
Supervisor-Camera Platemaking	Ron Propernick
Supervisor-Production Control	Dan McCarthy

I-54 California

Supervisor-Pressroom Bill Hitt
Foreman-Composing Larry Robertson
Foreman-Color Department Norman Poulin
Electronic Technician Nick Glass

Market Information: Zoned editions; TMC; ADS.
Mechanical available: Offset; Black and 3 ROP colors; insert accepted — preprinted, tab, standard, flexi, products samples, single sheets; page cut-offs — 22¾".
Mechanical specifications: Type page 13" x 21¼"; E - 6 cols, 2 1/16", ⅛" between; A - 6 cols, 2 1/16", ⅛" between; C - 10 cols, 1¼", 1/16" between.
Commodity consumption: Newsprint 15,900 short tons; 14,400 metric tons; widths 55", 41¼", 27⅜"; black ink 297,000 pounds; color ink 60,000 pounds; single pages printed 40,980; average pages per issue 120(d), 74(S); single plates used 238,188.
Equipment: EDITORIAL: Front-end hardware — SII; Front-end software — SII; Printers — X/Diablo 630, Centronics/351. CLASSIFIED: Front-end hardware — SII; Front-end software — SII. DISPLAY: Adv layout systems — SCS/Layout 8000; Front-end hardware — PCs; Front-end software — SCS/Layout 8000; Printers — HP/LaserJet II. PRODUCTION: Typesetters — AU/APS-6, AU/3850; Platemaking systems — WL; Plate exposures — 2-WL; Plate processors — 2-WL; Electronic picture desk — AP linked to Ap/Mac Network; Scanners — 2-ECR/Autokon 1000; Production cameras — 2-C; Automatic film processors — 2-LE; Film transporters — 2-C; Shrink lenses — 1-C, 1-CK Optical; Color separation equipment (conventional) — 1-Hel; Digital color separation equipment — 1-Hel.
PRESSROOM: Line 1 — 8-G; Line 2 — 4-G; Pasters — 12-G; Press control system — PEC/Bond. MAILROOM: Counter stackers — 4-HL/Stackers, 2-HL Monitor; Inserters and stuffers — 1-HI/848, 1-GMA/SLS-1000; Bundle tyer — 4-MLN/2A, 6-Power Strap; Addressing machine — 1-Ch/VMS. LIBRARY: Electronic — Proprietary, 1-DEC/VAX 8800 Basis. WIRE SERVICES: News — AP Datastream, AP Datafeatures; Photos — AP Photostream; Stock tables — AP Digital Stocks; Syndicates — NYT, SHNS, TV Data, McClatchy, CNS, City News Service; Receiving dishes — size-8ft, AP. BUSINESS COMPUTERS: DEC/VAX; Applications: Corporate/Sys, CJ: Display adv; PCs & main system networked.

TRACY

San Joaquin County

'90 U.S. Census- 33,558; E&P '96 Est. 51,279

Tracy Press (m-mon to sat)

Tracy Press, 145 W. 10th St. (95376); PO Box 0419, Tracy, CA 95378; tel (209) 835-3030; fax (209) 835-0655.
Circulation: 9,436(m); ABC Sept. 30, 1995.
Price: 25¢(d); 25¢(sat); $40.00/yr; $11.00/3mo, $21.00/6mo.
Advertising: Open inch rate $14.01(m); $14.01(m-sat). **Representative:** Papert Companies.
News Service: AP. **Politics:** Independent. **Established:** 1896.
Note: Effective Sept. 1, 1995, this publication started publishing a Saturday morning edition. Saturday circulation not made available as of press time.
Not Published: Memorial Day; Labor Day.
Special Weekly Sections: Health (mon); Business (tues); Best Food Day (wed); Business (thur); Real Estate, Arts & Entertainment, Marketplace, Travel, Farm, Church, Auto Marketplace, What's On? TV Magazine (fri); Sports, Comics (daily).
Magazines: Business (tues); Food (wed); Home (thur); Entertainment, Church, Farm (fri); Sports, Today's Living (daily).

CORPORATE OFFICERS

President Thomas F Matthews
Vice Pres Samuel H Matthews
Secretary Robert S Matthews

GENERAL MANAGEMENT

Co-Publisher Thomas F Mathews
Co-Publisher Samuel H Mathews
General Manager Robert S Matthews

ADVERTISING

Manager Diane Lopez

NEWS EXECUTIVE

Editor Samuel H Matthews

EDITORS AND MANAGERS

Business Editor Andrew Hamm
Business Editor Kristian Kramer
Education Editor Christy Rinauro
Entertainment Editor Mary McCurley
News Editor John (Jack) Eddy
Photo Editor Enrique Gutierrez
Today's Living Editor Mary McCurley

PRODUCTION

Foreman-Pressroom John Wilson

Market Information: TMC.
Mechanical available: Web Offset; Black and 3 ROP colors; insert accepted — preprinted; page cut-offs — 22¾".
Mechanical specifications: E - 6 cols, 2¼", ⅜" between; A - 6 cols, 2¼", ⅜" between; C - 8 cols, 1⅝", 3/16" between.
Commodity consumption: Newsprint 800 metric tons; width 27½"; black ink 7,123 pounds; color ink 845 pounds; single pages printed 6,760; average pages per issue 26(d); single plates used 2,142.
Equipment: EDITORIAL: Front-end hardware — 2-HAS/HS-52, 2-HI/8900, 13-HAS/Edit III, 2-HAS/Edit VIII. CLASSIFIED: Front-end hardware — HI/Cash PCs; Front-end software — HI/C. DISPLAY: Adv layout systems — Ap/Mac Network; Front-end hardware — Ap/Mac Network; Front-end software — Multi-Ad; Printers — QMS/810, AU/PSII PIP. PRODUCTION: Typesetters — 2-COM/Unisetter, AU/108 APS6; Plate exposures — 1-Nu; Plate processors — Nat; Scanners — X; Production cameras — SCREEN; Automatic film processors — 1-C/Powermatic T65, Kk; Digital color separation equipment — Nikon/Scanner, Microtek.
PRESSROOM: Line 1 — 8-G/Community Offset; Line 2 — G/SC; Line 3 — 7-G/Urbanite Offset; Line 4 — 1-G/Urbanite (3-color); Folders — 1-G/SC, 1-G/Urbanite. MAILROOM: Inserters and stuffers — KAN/480; Bundle tyer — 2-Strapex; Addressing machine — 1-X, Ch/500. WIRE SERVICES: News — AP, McClatchy; Photos — RN; Syndicates — NYT. BUSINESS COMPUTERS: Novell/Network, Ap/Macs; Applications: Adv, Circ, Prod, Billing, Estimates, Ordering; PCs & micros networked.

TULARE

Tulare County

'90 U.S. Census- 33,249; E&P '96 Est. 43,462
ABC-CZ (90): 35,540 (HH 11,578)

Tulare Advance-Register

(e-mon to fri; m-sat)

Tulare Advance-Register, 388 E. Cross Ave.; PO Box 30, Tulare, CA 93275-0030; tel (209) 688-0521; fax (209) 688-7503. Gannett Co. Inc. group.
Circulation: 8,888(e); 8,888(m-sat); ABC Sept. 30, 1995.
Price: 50¢(d); 50¢(sat); $6.75/mo.
Advertising: Open inch rate $11.15(e); $13.64(e-wed); $11.15(m-sat). **Representative:** Gannett National Newspaper Sales.
News Services: AP, GNS. **Politics:** Independent. **Established:** 1882.
Note: Advertising is sold in combination with Visalia Times-Delta (m) for $34.18 (d) and $36.34 (m-sat).
Special Editions: Farm Equipment Show (Feb); Discover Tulare County, Clubs & Organizations (May); Dairy Month (June); Football Kick-off (Sept); Christmas Kick-off, Football Rivalry (Nov).
Special Weekly Sections: Best Food Day (wed); Church Features, TV Times, Real Estate, Money Matters (sat).
Magazines: Choices Magazine-Visalia (fri); USA Weekend (sat); Vista (monthly).

CORPORATE OFFICER

President Amy L Pack

GENERAL MANAGEMENT

Publisher Amy L Pack
Manager-Operations Steve Griffiths

ADVERTISING

Director Tami Crawford
Supervisor Diane Garcia

MARKETING AND PROMOTION

Director-Marketing/Promotion Maryl Cook

CIRCULATION

Director Mel Graul
Supervisor Denise Casey

NEWS EXECUTIVES

Asst Editor Lynda Thullen
Managing Editor Steve Griffiths

MANAGEMENT INFORMATION SERVICES

Data Processing Manager Gary Woodside
Director-Technical Service Gary Dunn

PRODUCTION

Director Fred Conner

Market Information: TMC.
Mechanical available: Offset; Black and 4 ROP colors; insert accepted — preprinted, single sheet; page cut-offs — 21⅜".
Mechanical specifications: Type page 13" x 21½"; E - 6 cols, 2 1/16", ⅛" between; A - 6 cols, 2 1/16", ⅛" between; C - 10 cols, 1¼", 1/16" between.
Commodity consumption: Newsprint 303 metric tons; widths 28", 14"; black ink 4,200 pounds; color ink 1,500 pounds; single pages printed 4,963; average pages per issue 14(d); single plates used 2,600.
Equipment: EDITORIAL: Front-end hardware — SII/System 55, Ap/Mac Quadra, Tandem/TNSI I, 28-SII/Coyote QB; Front-end software — Baseview, SII/System 55; Printers — Centronics/351, Ap/Mac LaserWriter IIf; Other equipment — 3-Ap/Mac. CLASSIFIED: Front-end hardware — SII/System 55, Tandem/TNSII, 7-SII/Coyote QB; Front-end software — SII/System 55; Printers — Centronics/351. DISPLAY: Adv layout systems — Smart Dummy/Ad Layout System; Front-end hardware — PC; Front-end software — Smart Dummy; Printers — HP/LaserJet III. PRODUCTION: Typesetters — 2-COM/8600, 2-Ap/Mac LaserWriter II NTX, ECR/RIP, ECR/Autokon, 1-RZ; Plate exposures — 2-Nu; Plate processors — 2-Nat; Production cameras — 1-C, 1-Nu; Automatic film processors — 2-LPC, 1-L/24, 1-P/26; Film transporters — 1-C; Color separation equipment (conventional) — 1-RZ.
PRESSROOM: Line 1 — 10-G/Urbanite. MAILROOM: Counter stackers — 1-QWI/1000, 1-HI/RS25, 1-G/Overstacker; Inserters and stuffers — 1-HI/848; Bundle tyer — 2-MLN; Wrapping singles — 1-QWI; Addressing machine — 1-Ch. WIRE SERVICES: News — AP, GNS; Photos — AP, GNS; Receiving dishes — size-3m, AP. BUSINESS COMPUTERS: PCs & micros networked; PCs & main system networked.

TURLOCK

Stanislaus County

'90 U.S. Census- 42,198; E&P '96 Est. 58,592
ABC-CZ (90): 42,198 (HH 14,689)

Turlock Journal

(e-mon to fri; m-sat)

Turlock Journal, 138 S. Center St.; PO Box 800, Turlock, CA 95381; tel (209) 634-9141; fax (209) 632-8813. Freedom Communications Inc. group.
Circulation: 8,781(e); 9,446(m-sat); ABC Sept. 30, 1995.
Price: 33¢(d); 47¢(sat); $6.75/mo (plus tax); $81.00/yr (plus tax).
Advertising: Open inch rate $8.88(e); $8.88(m-sat). **Representative:** Papert Companies.
News Services: AP, KRT, Freedom Wire. **Politics:** Libertarian. **Established:** 1904.
Special Editions: Bridal, Best of Turlock (Feb); Fashion, Home Improvement (Mar); Real Estate (Apr); Health & Fitness (May); Real Estate, Graduation (June); Stanislaus County Fair (July); Back-to-School (Aug); Real Estate, Football, Poultry & Dairy Festival, Scandinavian Festival (Sept); Home Improvement, Red Ribbon Week (Oct); Dining Guide, Christmas Gift Guide (Nov).
Special Weekly Sections: Business Pages (tues); Best Food Page (wed); Art Pages, Education (thur); Home Pages, Religion Pages (sat); Entertainment & TV, Lifestyle (daily).
Magazine: USA Weekend (sat).

GENERAL MANAGEMENT

Publisher M Olaf Frandsen
Manager-Accounting Regina Amador

ADVERTISING

Director Christine Hammers

CIRCULATION

Director Tom Anaya

NEWS EXECUTIVE

Editor Niki Miskovich

EDITORS AND MANAGERS

Business/Finance Editor Valerie Wigglesworth
City Editor Valerie Wigglesworth
Editorial Page Editor Niki Miscovich
Education/School Editor Don Hansen
Farm Editor Michelle Wood
Lifestyle Editor Darla Welles
Music Editor Darla Welles
Photo Department Manager Gene Lieb
Picture Editor Gene Lieb
Sports Editor James Silva
Teen-Age/Youth Editor Don Hansen
Travel Editor Don Hansen

MANAGEMENT INFORMATION SERVICES

Data Processing Manager Bob Santos

PRODUCTION

Superintendent Steve Meadows

Market Information: TMC.
Mechanical available: Offset; Black and 3 ROP colors; insert accepted — preprinted, single sheet; page cut-offs — 22¾".
Mechanical specifications: Type page 13" x 21½"; E - 6 cols, 2 1/16", ⅛" between; A - 6 cols, 2 1/16", ⅛" between; C - 9 cols, 1 5/16", ⅛" between.
Commodity consumption: Newsprint 575 metric tons; width 28"; black ink 15,000 pounds; color ink 850 pounds; single pages printed 9,000; average pages per issue 24(d); single plates used 8,520.
Equipment: EDITORIAL: Front-end hardware — SII/386sx PC; Front-end software — Dewar; Printers — Okidata, Ap/Mac LaserWriter II NTX; Other equipment — Ap/Mac IIci, Ap/Mac Scanner. CLASSIFIED: Front-end hardware — SII/386sx PC; Front-end software — Dewar; Printers — Okidata. DISPLAY: Adv layout systems — Dewar/Discovery; Front-end hardware — SII/386sx PC; Front-end software — Dewar; Printers — Tegra/Varityper/XP-1000; Other equipment — Ap/Mac IIci, Ap/Mac Scanner, CD-Rom. PRODUCTION: Typesetters — 2-Tegra/Varityper/5000, 2-Tegra/Varityper/XP-1000; Plate exposures — Ingenuity; Production cameras — Waltzberg.
PRESSROOM: Line 1 — 8-G/Community; Folders — SC. WIRE SERVICES: News — AP, KRT, Freedom Wire; Receiving dishes — size-3m, AP. BUSINESS COMPUTERS: 3-IBM/386sx PC, 1-PC/486, 2-Compaq/386, 1-PC/486; Applications: Southware: Payroll, Accts payable, Gen ledger; Vision Data: Accts receivable, Circ; PCs & micros networked.

UKIAH

Mendocino County

'90 U.S. Census- 14,599; E&P '96 Est. 16,611
ABC-CZ (90): 19,039 (HH 7,130)

Ukiah Daily Journal

(e-mon to fri; S)

Ukiah Daily Journal, 590 S. School St.; PO Box 749, Ukiah, CA 95482; tel (707) 468-3500; fax (707) 468-5780. Donrey Media group.
Circulation: 7,609(e); 7,727(S); ABC Sept. 30, 1995.
Price: 50¢(d); $1.00(S); $7.00/mo (city), $7.50/mo (rural); $84.00/yr (city), $90.00/yr (rural).
Advertising: Open inch rate $11.75(e); $11.75(S). **Representative:** Papert Companies.
News Service: AP. **Politics:** Independent. **Established:** 1864.
Special Weekly Sections: Best Food Day (tues); Business News (wed); Dining and Entertainment (thur).
Magazines: USA Weekend, On TV (S).

CORPORATE OFFICERS

Founder Donald W Reynolds
President/Chief Operating Officer Emmett Jones
Exec Vice Pres/Chief Financial Officer Darrell W Loftin
Vice Pres (Western Newspaper Group) David A Osborn
Vice Pres (Eastern Newspaper Group) Don Schneider

GENERAL MANAGEMENT

Publisher Dennis Wilson

ADVERTISING

Director John Speck
Manager-Local/Display Eddie Sequeira
Manager-Classified Janet Noe

CIRCULATION

Manager Elaine M Grothe

NEWS EXECUTIVES

Editor Randy Foster
Asst Editor Jody Martinez

EDITORS AND MANAGERS

Chief Photographer Jane Freeman
Sports Editor Steve Guertin

PRODUCTION

Manager Vic Martinez

Market Information: TMC; ADS; Electronic edition.
Mechanical available: Offset; Black and 3 ROP colors; insert accepted — preprinted, spadea; page cut-offs — 22¾".

Copyright ©1996 by the Editor & Publisher Co.

California I-55

Mechanical specifications: Type page 13" x 21"; E - 6 cols, $2\frac{1}{16}$", $\frac{1}{8}$" between; A - 6 cols, $2\frac{1}{16}$", $\frac{1}{8}$" between; C - 9 cols, $1\frac{3}{8}$", $\frac{1}{16}$" between.
Commodity consumption: Newsprint 420 metric tons; width $27\frac{1}{2}$"; black ink 6,000 pounds; color ink 500 pounds; average pages per issue 20(d), 28(S); single plates used 6,000.
Equipment: EDITORIAL: Front-end hardware — Mk; Printers — Ap/Mac LaserWriter Plus. CLASSIFIED: Front-end hardware — Mk; Printers — Ap/Mac LaserWriter Plus. DISPLAY: Adv layout systems — 3-Ap/Mac; Front-end software — Multi-Ad/Creator, QuarkXPress 3.314, Microsoft/Word 5.1; Printers — Ap/Mac ImageWriter NTX, Ap/Mac LaserWriter Select 360; Other equipment — Ap/Mac Classic, ReCAs/Co-op system, Ap/Mac Performa, ImMEDIAte Sales Presentation System. PRODUCTION: Pagination software — QuarkXPress 3.31; OCR software — Caere/OmniPage 3.0; Typesetters — 3-Ap/Mac LaserWriter; Platemaking systems — 3M/Deadliner; Scanners — Ap/Mac Scanner; Production cameras — 1-AG. PRESSROOM: Line 1 — 7-G/SC195 Community; Folders — 1-G/Suburban. MAILROOM: Inserters and stuffers — 4-MM; Bundle tyer — MLN/Spirit, It/Power 100; Addressing machine — 3-Avery. LIBRARY: Electronic — 1-Mk. COMMUNICATIONS: Digital ad delivery system — AP AdSend. WIRE SERVICES: News — AP; Syndicates — Creators, Universal Press, King Features, LATS, United Media; Receiving dishes — AP. BUSINESS COMPUTERS: Compaq, Samsung, A/R, HP, CJ; Applications: Lotus 1-2-3; PCs & micros networked; PCs & main system networked.

UPLAND

See ONTARIO

VACAVILLE

Solano County

'90 U.S. Census- 71,479; E&P '96 Est. 101,136
ABC (90): 71,479 (HH 22,627)

Reporter (m-mon to sat; S)

Reporter, 916 Cotting Lane; PO Box 1509, Vacaville, CA 95688; tel (707) 448-6401; fax (707) 447-7405; e-mail newsroom@thereporter.com; web site http://www.thereporter.com.
Circulation: 19,118(m); 19,118(m-sat); 20,922(S); ABC Sept. 30, 1995.
Price: 35¢(d); 35¢(sat); $1.00(S); $10.00/mo; $110.94/yr (carrier), $123.00/yr (mail).
Advertising: Open inch rate $22.00(m); $22.00(m-sat); $22.00(S). **Representative:** Papert Companies.
News Service: AP. **Politics:** Independent. **Established:** 1883.
Special Weekly Sections: Prime Time, The Word (youth) (tues); Food, Business (wed); Billboard, Auto (fri); Marketplace, Religion (sat); Home, Horizon, Business (S).
Magazines: TV Reporter (S); Prime Time Magazine (monthly).

GENERAL MANAGEMENT
Publisher Richard Rico
Asst Publisher Steve Huddleston

ADVERTISING
Director Jerry Billings
Manager-Classified Jane Clark
Manager-Retail Pamela Center

MARKETING AND PROMOTION
Manager-Marketing & Promotion Bruce Gallaudet

CIRCULATION
Manager Bryan L Clark

NEWS EXECUTIVES
Editor Richard Rico
Managing Editor Diane Barney

EDITORS AND MANAGERS
Automotive Editor Pat Rogero
Business/Finance Editor Michael Pulley
City Editor Dan Reichl
Editorial Page Editor Steve Huddleston
Entertainment/Amusements Editor Kathy Thomas-Rico
Features Editor Mary Lou Wilson
Graphics Editor/Art Director Jim Moehrke
News Editor Charles Wilson
Photo Editor Rick Roach
Sports Editor Cecil Conley

PRODUCTION
Manager Gary Davidson

Market Information: TMC; Electronic edition.
Mechanical available: Offset; Black and 3 ROP colors; insert accepted — preprinted; page cut-offs — $22\frac{3}{4}$".
Mechanical specifications: Type page $13\frac{1}{4}$" x 21"; E - 6 cols, $2\frac{1}{16}$", $\frac{1}{8}$" between; A - 6 cols, $2\frac{1}{16}$", $\frac{1}{8}$" between; C - 9 cols, $1\frac{3}{16}$", $\frac{1}{8}$" between.
Commodity consumption: Newsprint 1,320 metric tons; widths 27", $13\frac{1}{2}$"; black ink 5,000 pounds; color ink 1,560 pounds; single pages printed 13,870; average pages per issue 24(d), 92(S); single plates used 5,038.
Equipment: EDITORIAL: Front-end hardware — HI; Printers — Ap/Mac 810, V/6000. CLASSIFIED: Front-end hardware — CText, 12-PC; Front-end software — CText 2.1; Printers — Ap/Mac LaserWriter Plus. DISPLAY: Adv layout systems — 8-Ap/Mac network; Front-end hardware — IBM/486 fileserver, Ap/Mac; Printers — V/6000. PRODUCTION: Pagination software — HI/8900; Typesetters — 1-Ap/Mac LaserWriter NTX, 1-VT/600; Plate exposures — 1-Nu; Plate processors — 2-3M/Deadliner, Nat; Electronic picture desk — Lf/AP Leaf Picture Desk; Scanners — 1-Ap/Mac; Production cameras — SCREEN; Automatic film processors — AG; Digital color separation equipment — Ap/Mac.
PRESSROOM: Line 1 — 7-DEV/Horizon (upper/lower former); Folders — Dev/V50. MAILROOM: Counter stackers — HL/Monitor, Id/Marathoner; Inserters and stuffers — GMA/SLS1000 8:1; Bundle tyer — Ace/50, Power Strap/PSN-6; Mailroom control system — Id/Conveyors, Id/Bottom wrap, Id/Truckloaders. LIBRARY: Electronic — Nexis/Newsview. WIRE SERVICES: News — AP, NYT; Photos — AP; Stock tables — AP SelectStox; Receiving dishes — size-8ft, AP. BUSINESS COMPUTERS: HP/927LX; Applications: CIS 4.01, CJ/AIM 5.01, AP, GL; PCs & micros networked; PCs & main system networked.

VALLEJO

Solano County

'90 U.S. Census- 109,199; E&P '96 Est. 134,248
ABC-CZ (90): 141,342 (HH 49,317)

Vallejo Times-Herald (m-mon to sat; S)

Vallejo Times-Herald, 440 Curtola Pkwy.; PO Box 3188, Vallejo, CA 94590; tel (707) 644-1141; fax (707) 643-4322. Donrey Media Group group.
Circulation: 20,989(m); 20,989(m-sat); 22,409(S); ABC Sept. 30, 1995.
Price: 50¢(d); 50¢(sat); $1.00(S); $8.00/mo; $96.00/yr.
Advertising: Open inch rate $17.85(m); $17.85(m-sat); $17.85(S). **Representative:** Papert Companies.
News Service: AP. **Politics:** Independent. **Established:** 1875.
Special Editions: Bridal Edition (Jan); Spring Fashion, Private Property Week (Apr); Home Improvement (June); Football Section (Sept); Christmas Opening, Christmas in Vallejo (Dec).
Special Weekly Sections: Business (mon); Food (wed); Seniors (thur); Automotive (fri); Church (sat); Real Estate, TV Weekly (S); Financial Pages (daily).
Magazine: Parade (S).
Cable TV: Own cable TV in circulation area.

CORPORATE OFFICERS
Founder Donald W Reynolds
President/Chief Operating Officer Emmett Jones
Exec Vice Pres/Chief Financial Officer Darrell W Loftin
Vice Pres-Western Newspaper Group David A Osborn
Vice Pres (Eastern Newspaper Group) Don Schneider

GENERAL MANAGEMENT
Publisher David R Stringer

ADVERTISING
Director Ron Rhea

MARKETING AND PROMOTION
Director-Marketing/Promotion Lori D Elrod

CIRCULATION
Director Kevin Craig

NEWS EXECUTIVE
Editor Joe Lowell

EDITORS AND MANAGERS
City Editor Mark Mazzafero
Food Editor Mark Mazzafero
Garden Editor Patty Poblete
Home Editor Patty Poblete
Librarian Connie Ramos
News Editor Mike Lerseth
Sports Editor Ted Ward

MANAGEMENT INFORMATION SERVICES
Director-Management Info Services Lisa van Alfen

PRODUCTION
Foreman-Page Production Dick Sexton
Foreman-Pressroom Ron Tilson
Foreman-Creative Services Jim Major

Market Information: TMC.
Mechanical available: Offset; Black and 3 ROP colors; insert accepted — preprinted, other; page cut-offs — $21\frac{1}{2}$".
Mechanical specifications: Type page 13" x $21\frac{1}{2}$"; E - 6 cols, $2\frac{1}{16}$", $\frac{1}{8}$" between; A - 6 cols, $2\frac{1}{16}$", $\frac{1}{8}$" between; C - 10 cols, $1\frac{1}{8}$", $\frac{3}{16}$" between.
Commodity consumption: Newsprint 1,520 metric tons; widths 27", $13\frac{1}{2}$"; black ink 80,000 pounds; color ink 4,800 pounds; single pages printed 16,000; average pages per issue 32(d), 88(S); single plates used 8,000.
Equipment: EDITORIAL: Front-end hardware — 29-AT/Series 6. CLASSIFIED: Front-end hardware — 6-AT. DISPLAY: Adv layout systems — 5-Ap/Mac Workstation; Front-end software — Multi-Ad/Creator 3.6.3; Printers — New-Gen/1200T, NewGen/840E, Panther/ImageSetter. PRODUCTION: Pagination software — AT/Press 2GO (for Classified); OCR software — TI/OmniPage Direct 1.10; Typesetters — 2-NewGen/Laser printer, Panther/ImageSetter; Platemaking systems — 1-3M/Deadliner; Plate exposures — 1-Nu; Plate processors — Anitec; Scanners — OmniScan/Hand-Held, Data-Copy/830 Flat Scanner; Production cameras — 1-C/A2024; Automatic film processors — LD/Loge 1800A; Color separation equipment (conventional) — C/4x5.
PRESSROOM: Line 1 — 9-G/Urbanite; Reels and stands — 2-G. MAILROOM: Counter stackers — 3-QWI/350; Inserters and stuffers — 2-MM/227, 1-MM; Bundle tyer — 1-OVL, 2-Power Strap; Addressing machine — 1-Ch. COMMUNICATIONS: Digital ad delivery system — AP AdSend. WIRE SERVICES: News — AP; Stock tables — AP; Syndicates — NEA; Receiving dishes — size-10ft, AP, NSN. BUSINESS COMPUTERS: 1-Unix/SSPS Progress, 1-HP/400, ALR/Unix; Applications: CJ: Accts receivable; Sco/Unix: Circ; Progress.

VENTURA

Ventura County

'90 U.S. Census- 86,873; E&P '96 Est. 96,334
ABC-NDM (90): 236,181 (HH 81,447)

Ventura County Star (m-mon to sat)
Ventura County Sunday Star (S)

Ventura County Star, 5250 Ralston St.; PO Box 6711, Ventura, CA 93003; tel (805) 650-2900; fax (805) 650-2944. Scripps Howard group.
Circulation: 96,330(m); 96,330(m-sat); 104,035(S); ABC Sept. 30, 1995.
Price: 35¢(d); 35¢(sat); $1.50(S); $2.50/wk; $10.83/mo; $130.00/yr.
Advertising: Open inch rate $67.83(m); $67.83(m-sat); $72.67(S). **Representative:** Cresmer, Woodward, O'Mara & Ormsbee.
News Services: AP, NYT, McClatchy, SHNS. **Politics:** Independent. **Established:** 1925.
Note: Effective Apr. 1, 1995, the Thousand Oaks Star and Simi Valley Star merged to become a zoned edition of the Ventura County Star.
Advertising not accepted: Mail order competitive to local business.
Special Editions: Brides (Feb); Home Show (Mar); County Fair Section, Football Section (Aug); Camarillo Fiesta (Sept); New Car (Oct); Holiday Gift Guides (Nov); Holiday Gift Guides (Dec).
Special Weekly Sections: Food (thur); Time Out (fri); Wheels (sat); Homes & Living (S).
Magazine: TV STAR ($\frac{1}{2}$ tab).

CORPORATE OFFICER
Publisher John P Wilcox

GENERAL MANAGEMENT
Director-Finance Ken J Kraft
Director-Human Resources Joan E Dzuro

ADVERTISING
Director Harvey L Hopkins
Manager-Retail John D Veenstra
Manager-National Robert D Lyon
Manager-Classified Pauline Adams-Mizelle

MARKETING AND PROMOTION
Director-Marketing/Promotion John R Philips

TELECOMMUNICATIONS
Audiotex Manager Ken Radvechel

CIRCULATION
Director Steven A Smith
Manager-Single Copy Maggie Browne
Manager-Home Delivery Edward Griffin
Manager-Office Operations Connie Rose
Manager-Sales/Promotion Jeanne Miller
Manager-Distribution & Mailroom Kevin Oslund

NEWS EXECUTIVES
Editor Tim Gallagher
Managing Editor Joe Howry

EDITORS AND MANAGERS
Business/Finance Editor Frank Moraga
County Editor Burton Swope
Editor-Camarillo Edition Dave Smith
Editor-Thousand Oaks Edition DeAnn Wahl-Justesen
Editor-Simi Valley Edition Michael Hoffman
Editor-Moorpark Edition Debi Ryono
Editor-Oxnard Edtion Mike Craft
Editorial Page Editor Timm Herdt
Life Editor Starley Smith
Asst Managing Editor/News Jim Lawitz
Asst Managing Editor/Photo-Graphics Sheila Schmitz
Chief Photographer Gary Phelps
Sports Editor Mike Blackwell
Writing Coach Steve Chawkins

MANAGEMENT INFORMATION SERVICES
Director-Management Info Services & Technology Todd A Brinker
Manager-Systems Operations Katherine Swanson
Manager-Info Management Judith Pashley

PRODUCTION
Director-Operations Bill Williamson
Director Carl Hiskett
Foreman-Composing David Justesen
Foreman-Pressroom Gary Hillemann

Market Information: Zoned editions; TMC; Operate audiotex; Electronic edition.
Mechanical available: Offset; Black and 3 ROP colors; insert accepted — preprinted; page cut-offs — $22\frac{3}{4}$".
Mechanical specifications: Type page 13" x $21\frac{1}{2}$"; E - 6 cols, $2\frac{1}{16}$", $\frac{1}{8}$" between; A - 6 cols, $2\frac{1}{16}$", $\frac{1}{8}$" between; C - 10 cols, $1\frac{3}{16}$", $\frac{1}{16}$" between.
Commodity consumption: Newsprint 13,183 metric tons; widths 55", $41\frac{1}{4}$", $27\frac{1}{2}$"; black ink 137,000 pounds; color ink 18,000 pounds; single pages printed 22,100; average pages per issue 56.63(d), 81.16(S); single plates used 96,000.
Equipment: EDITORIAL: Front-end hardware — Compaq/Servers; Front-end software — Dewar System 4; Printers — HP/4si mx. CLASSIFIED: Front-end hardware — Compaq/Servers; Front-end software — Dewar System 4; Printers — HP/4si mx. AUDIOTEX: Supplier name — Zimmers Interactive. DISPLAY: Adv layout systems — Multi-Ad/Creator, Dewar/Discovery; Front-end hardware — Ap/Power Mac, PC/386. PRODUCTION: Pagination software — Dewar System 4; Typesetters — 3-AG/Accuset 2400 w/ Harliquin DOS & Window RIPs; Platemaking systems — Offset; Plate exposures — 2-BKY/48; Plate processors — 1-Nat/A-340; Scanners — 1-ECR/Autokon, 1-Scitex/Smart 340L; Production cameras — 1-C/Spartan III; Automatic film processors — 1-C/R-660, 1-P/26EL; Shrink lenses — 1-CK Optical; Color separation equipment (conventional) — 1-WDS; Digital color separation equipment — 1-Howtek.
PRESSROOM: Line 1 — 7-HI/1650; Pasters — 7-MEG/500; Press control system — CH. MAILROOM: Counter stackers — 5-HL/Monitor, Fg; Inserters and stuffers — 1-NP/630, AM Graphics; Bundle tyer — 1-OVL, 4-MLN. LIBRARY: Electronic — FolioViews. COMMUNICATIONS: Digital ad delivery system — AP AdSend, Digiflex. WIRE SERVICES: News — AP; Stock tables — AP; Syndicates — NEA, NYT, McClatchy, LAT-WP, SHNS, ; Receiving dishes — size-8ft, AP. BUSINESS COMPUTERS: 2-SII/2130, INSI, IBM/AS400; Applications: Circ, Adv billing, Accts receivable, Gen ledger.

Copyright ©1996 by the Editor & Publisher Co.

I-56 California

VICTORVILLE

San Bernardino County

'90 U.S. Census- 40,674; E&P '96 Est. 89,777
ABC-NDM (90): 144,310 (HH 48,561)

Daily Press (m-mon to sat; S)

Daily Press, 13891 Park Ave.; PO Box 1389, Victorville, CA 92393-1389; tel (619) 241-7744; fax (619) 241-7145; e-mail dailypress@aol.com. Freedom Communications Inc. group.

Circulation: 27,198(m); 27,198(m-sat); 30,709(S); ABC Sept. 30, 1995.

Price: 30¢(d); 30¢(sat); $1.25(S); $2.15/wk; $8.60/4wk; $111.80/yr.

Advertising: Open inch rate $25.88(m); $25.88(m-sat); $28.15(S). **Representatives:** Papert Companies; The Newspaper National Network; Gannett 4-Color Network.

News Services: AP, KRT. **Politics:** Independent. **Established:** 1937.

Special Editions: Year-in-Review, Bridal & Wedding Guide (Jan); Design-an-Ad, NIE Section (Feb); Your Home (Mar); Home & Garden Show Program, Mavericks Season Guide (Apr); Progress Edition, Family Times (May); Huck Finn Jubilee (June); Graduation, San Bernardino County Fair Program (July); Summer Clearance (Aug); Football Preview, Frontier Days, Family Times (Sept); Auto Show Program, High Desert Opportunity (Oct); Home & Recreation Show Program (Nov); Holiday Shopping Guide, Holiday Gift Guide, Last Minute Gift Guide, Letters to Santa/Christmas Greetings (Dec).

Special Weekly Sections: Teens (mon); Kids (tues); Hobbies & Pets (wed); Cookery (thur); Home & Garden, On Wheels (fri); Health & Fitness, Religion, Real Estate (sat); Travel, Valley People (S); Sports, Money Page, Entertainment Page (daily).

Magazines: React (tues); Daily Press Entertainment Magazine (fri); Parade, TV Update Magazine, Color Comics Section (S).

GENERAL MANAGEMENT

Publisher Maureen Saltzer Brotherton
Business Manager Robert Fitzsimmons

ADVERTISING

Manager-Major Accounts/National Anita Davis
Manager-Retail Ray Marien
Manager-Classified Susan Drake

MARKETING AND PROMOTION

Manager-Promotion Lynn Tiffany

CIRCULATION

Manager Mike Belles

NEWS EXECUTIVES

Exec Editor Larry D Croom Jr.
Managing Editor John Iddings
Managing Editor-Metro Gary West

EDITORS AND MANAGERS

Automotive Editor Lynn Tiffany
Community Editor Joanne Bartholomew
Editorial Page Editor Stephen M Williams
Entertainment/Amusements Editor Veronica Hill
Features Editor Mary Lou Thomas
Magazine Editor Veronica Hill
Religion Editor Dana Pontius
Sports Editor Russ Lemmon
Television/Film Editor Mary Lou Thomas
Theater/Music Editor Veronica Hill

MANAGEMENT INFORMATION SERVICES

Manager-Systems Steve Ryan

PRODUCTION

Director Robert Pendleton

Market Information: TMC; ADS.

Mechanical available: Offset; Black and 3 ROP colors; insert accepted — preprinted, comic spadea, samples, catalogs; page cut-offs — 21½".

Mechanical specifications: Type page 13" x 21½"; E - 6 cols, 2 1/16", 1/8" between; A - 6 cols, 2 1/16", 1/8" between; C - 9 cols, 1 5/16", 1/16" between.

Commodity consumption: Newsprint 2,541 metric tons; widths 27½", 13¾"; black ink 51,042 pounds; color ink 6,613 pounds; single pages printed 14,314; average pages per issue 36(d), 38(sat), 56(S); single plates used 23,854.

Equipment: EDITORIAL: Front-end hardware — 26-Dewar, 3-Ap/Mac; Front-end software — Dewar; Printers — HP/DeskJet 1200c, V/5300B, Panasonic, Ap/Mac LaserWriter II NTX; Other equipment — Lf/Leafscan 45, Ap/Mac Quadra 950, XYQUEST, Lf/AP Leaf Picture Desk. CLASSIFIED: Front-end hardware — 11-Dewar; Front-end software — Dewar; Printers — Okidata. DISPLAY: Adv layout systems — 4-Dewar/Discovery; Front-end hardware — STA/386, 3-Ap/Mac; Front-end software — Dewar/System IV; Printers — Ap/Mac LaserWriter II, Genicom/3410. PRODUCTION: Pagination software — Dewar; Typesetters — V/5300E, V/1000, V/5510; Plate exposures — 2-Nu; Plate processors — 2-Ic; Electronic picture desk — Lf/AP Leaf Picture Desk; Direct-to-plate imaging — 3M/Pyrofax; Scanners — Microtek, X; Production cameras — 1-Nu; Automatic film processors — AG; Color separation equipment (conventional) — Lf/Leafscan 45; Digital color separation equipment — Ap/Mac.
PRESSROOM: Line 1 — 10-G/Urbanite; Folders — 2-G; Reels and stands — 2-G/(5 Position). MAILROOM: Counter stackers — 1-Id; Inserters and stuffers — GMA/SLS 1000 (8 heads); Bundle tyer — 1-Power Strap; Addressing machine — 1-KR. LIBRARY: Electronic — 1-Minolta/RP407E Microfilm Reader, SMS/Stauffer Gold. COMMUNICATIONS: Digital ad delivery system — AP AdSend; Systems used — satellite. WIRE SERVICES: News — AP; Photos — AP, KRT; Stock tables — TMS; Syndicates — KRT, McClatchy, Cox, Freedom Wire; Receiving dishes — size-10ft, AP. BUSINESS COMPUTERS: IBM/Network, AT/11-Station, 3-COM/Network; Applications: PBS; PCs & micros networked.

VISALIA

Tulare County

'90 U.S. Census- 75,636; E&P '96 Est. 101,108
ABC-NDM (90): 90,332 (HH 30,428)

Visalia Times-Delta (m-mon to fri; m-sat)

Visalia Times-Delta, 330 N. West St.; PO Box 31, Visalia, CA 93279; tel (209) 734-5821; fax (209) 733-0826; e-mail apack@sanberna.gannett.com. Gannett Co. Inc. group.

Circulation: 22,231(m); 29,282(m-sat); ABC Sept. 30, 1995.

Price: 50¢(d); $1.00(sat); $2.35/wk; $10.49/mo (plus tax); $125.88/yr (plus tax).

Advertising: Open inch rate $27.11(m); $29.18(m-sat). **Representative:** Gannett National Newspaper Sales.

News Services: AP, GNS, NYT. **Politics:** Independent. **Established:** 1859.

Note: Advertising is sold in combination with Tulare Advance-Register (e) for $34.18 (d) and $36.34 (m-sat)

Special Editions: Year-in-Review, Real Estate Plus, With This Ring (Jan); Farm Equipment Show, Vacation Planner, Auto Tab, Real Estate Plus, Medical Directory (Feb); Great Western, Real Estate Plus, Design-An-Ad (Mar); Real Estate Plus (Apr); Real Estate Plus, BIA, Discover Tulare (May); Dining Guide, Real Estate Plus (June); Vacation Planner, Medical Directory, Real Estate Plus (July); Real Estate Plus (Aug); Real Estate Plus, Football Tab, Tulare County Fair (Sept); Vacation Planner, Women in Business, Real Estate Plus (Oct); Dining Guide, Christmas Catalog, Real Estate Plus (Nov); Real Estate Plus, Christmas Songbook, Vacation Planner, Letters to Santa (Dec).

Special Weekly Sections: Business, Farm (daily); Food (wed); The Shopper (thur); Real Estate, T.V. Times (sat).

Magazines: USA Weekend, TV Book (sat).

CORPORATE OFFICER

President Amy L Pack

GENERAL MANAGEMENT

Publisher Amy L Pack

ADVERTISING

Director Tami Crawford
Manager-Retail Debra Davenport
Manager-Classified Brett Neumann

MARKETING AND PROMOTION

Director-Marketing Maryl Russo

CIRCULATION

Director Mel Graul

NEWS EXECUTIVE

Managing Editor Tom Bray

EDITORS AND MANAGERS

City Editor Amy White
Editorial Page Editor Paul Hurley
Lifestyle Editor T J Marchette
News Editor Bob Elledge
Sports Editor Steve Provost

MANAGEMENT INFORMATION SERVICES

Manager-Systems Gary Woodside

PRODUCTION

Director Fred Conner
Manager-Pressroom Robert Rodriguez
Manager-Distribution/Mailroom Phil Crawford

Market Information: Split Run; TMC.

Mechanical available: Offset; Black and 3 ROP colors; insert accepted — preprinted; page cut-offs — 22".

Mechanical specifications: Type page 13" x 21"; E - 6 cols, 2 1/16", 1/8" between; A - 6 cols, 2 1/16", 1/8" between; C - 10 cols, 1 3/8", 1/16" between.

Commodity consumption: Newsprint 1,600 metric tons; widths 13.5625, 27 1/8"; black ink 48,500 pounds; color ink 14,000 pounds; single pages printed 11,900; average pages per issue 28(d), 34(sat); single plates used 15,600.

Equipment: EDITORIAL: Front-end hardware — Tandem/TNSII, 28-SII/Coyote QB; Front-end software — SII/System 55; Printers — Centronics/351, Ap/Mac LaserWriter IIf; Other equipment — 3-Ap/Mac. CLASSIFIED: Front-end hardware — Tandem/TNSII, 7-SII/Coyote QB; Front-end software — SII/System 55; Printers — Centronics/351. DISPLAY: Adv layout systems — Smart Dummy/Ad Layout System; Front-end hardware — PC; Front-end software — Smart Dummy; Printers — HP/LaserJet III. PRODUCTION: Typesetters — 2-COM/8600, 2-Ap/Mac LaserWriter II NTX, ECR/RIP, ECR/Autokon, 2-Ap/Mac Pro 810, 1-LaserMaster/1120D, 1-AV/APS 6-84ACS; Plate exposures — 2-Nu; Plate processors — 2-Nat; Production cameras — 1-C, 1-Nu; Automatic film processors — 1-LPC, 1-LPC, 1-L/24, 1-P/26; Film transporters — 1-C; Color separation equipment (conventional) — 1-RZ, 1-Hp/ScanJet II, 1-Microtek/Slide-Neg Scanner.
PRESSROOM: Line 1 — 10-G/Urbanite; Folders — 1-Web/5000 Series (¼). MAILROOM: Counter stackers — 1-QWI/1000, 2-HI/RS25, 1-G/Overstacker; Inserters and stuffers — 1-HI/848; Bundle tyer — 2-MLN; Wrapping singles — 1-QWI; Addressing machine — 1-Ch; Other mailroom equipment — Mc/Stitcher-Trimmer. COMMUNICATIONS: Digital ad delivery system — AP AdSend. WIRE SERVICES: News — AP Datastream, AP Datafeatures, AP Dataspeed; Stock tables — AP SelectStox; Receiving dishes — AP. BUSINESS COMPUTERS: IBM/AS400; Applications: Gannett; PCs & micros networked; PCs & main system networked.

WALNUT CREEK

Contra Costa County

'90 U.S. Census- 60,569; E&P '96 Est. 65,678
ABC-NDM (90): 362,585 (HH 143,154)

Contra Costa Times (m-mon to sat; S)

Contra Costa Times, 2640 Shadelands Dr. (94598); PO Box 5088, Walnut Creek, CA 94596; tel (510) 935-2525; web site http://www.infi.net/. Knight-Ridder Inc. group.

Circulation: 95,662(m); 95,662(m-sat); 106,207(S); ABC Sept. 30, 1995.

Price: 50¢(d); 50¢(sat); $1.50(S); $12.85/mo; $144.95/yr.

Representative: Cresmer, Woodward, O'Mara & Ormsbee.

News Services: AP, NYT, Bay City News Service, LAT-WP. **Politics:** Independent. **Established:** 1911.

Note: The Contra Costa Daily group includes the following newspapers: Richmond West County Times (mS), Antioch Ledger-Dispatch (eS), Pleasanton Valley Times (mS) and Walnut Creek Contra Costa Times (mS). The group combination rates are $104.05 (d) and $114.35 (S). Individual newspaper rates not made available.

Special Editions: Football (Prep, College, Pro); Elections.

Special Weekly Sections: Food (wed); Auto, Entertainment (fri).

Magazines: TV Times; USA Weekend.

CORPORATE OFFICER

Publisher/CEO George E Riggs

GENERAL MANAGEMENT

Director-Finance & Administration John Zsenai
Controller Rick Graziano

ADVERTISING

Vice Pres Pamela Henson
Manager-Retail Ruth Maricich
Manager-Classified Patricia Toliver
Manager-Classified Terry Sullivan
Manager-Major Donna Wirtel
Manager-National Jon Edwards

MARKETING AND PROMOTION

Manager-Promotion Peggy Marshburn

NEWS EXECUTIVE

Vice Pres/Exec Editor John Armstrong

EDITORS AND MANAGERS

Business Editor (Acting) Patrick Twohy
Community Editor Donna Pace
Editorial Page Editor Jake Williams
Features/Lifestyle Editor Bev Britton
Asst Features Editor Lisa Wrenn
Graphics Editor Jon Manlove
Exec Metro Editor Cathy Snapp
Exec Metro Editor Dan Hatfield
Exec News Editor Gene Willaims
Exec Photo Editor Jim Vestal
Photo Editor Scott Vlha
Radio/Television Editor Deborah Carvalho
Exec Sports Editor Tod Leonard
Asst Sports Editor Chris DeLuca
Travel Editor Carol Fowler
Wire Editor Jim Day

MANAGEMENT INFORMATION SERVICES

Data Processing Manager Dale Oldford

PRODUCTION

Director Donald Jochens
Manager Gordon Brown
Manager-Pre Press Eileen Hammond-Cuff
Manager-Packaging Center Jim Masingale
Manager-Centralized Maintenance Ron Severn
Manager-Pressroom Werner Reuper

Market Information: Split Run; TMC.

Mechanical available: Offset; Black and 3 ROP colors; insert accepted — preprinted; page cut-offs — 21¼".

Mechanical specifications: Type page 13" x 21"; E - 6 cols, 2.03", 1/6" between; A - 6 cols, 2.03", 1/6" between; C - 10 cols, 1.22", 1/6" between.

Commodity consumption: Newsprint 26,950 metric tons; widths 55", 41¼", 27½"; black ink 232,000 pounds; color ink 60,000 pounds; single pages printed 58,000; average pages per issue 56(d), 80(S); single plates used 44,500.

Equipment: EDITORIAL: Front-end hardware — AT/PC WAN; Front-end software — Dewar, QPS, Microsoft/Word, Microsoft/Windows; Printers — Anzak, Centronics. CLASSIFIED: Front-end hardware — SII/Sys 55, 1-IBM, 1-Evervision/PC, 2-Decision Data, 1-ATT, 2-SII/Tahoe; Front-end software — SII/Sys 55 CPL, SII/CZAR; Printers — Centronics/35, ATT/476, IBM, 2-Anzac/2400, IBM/IIIXL; Other equipment — 3-Swintec/1146 DM, Compaq/DeskPro, 8-IBM/Selectric II, Swintec/1186. PRODUCTION: Pagination software — HI/XP 21, AT/Windows, Microsoft/Word, Dewar, QPS; Typesetters — 2-Cx/Supersetter, 2-Au/APS-108FC; Plate exposures — 2-Nu, 2-WL, WL/Lith 10, Nu/Ultra; Plate processors — 1-WL/Tech 38D, 1-WL/Tech 38G, WL/Lithoplater; Electronic picture desk — 2-Lf/AP Leaf Picture Desk; Scanners — 1-ECR/Autokon 1000, 2-Konica/Newscan 1500 Receiver, 1-III/Diadem/410, 1-III/Diadem/ 410L, ECR/Autokon 2045C, Epson/E 1200C; Production cameras — 1-C/Spartan III; Automatic film processors — 2-P/SC2050; Shrink lenses — CK Optical; Digital color separation equipment — 2-RZ/210L, Carat/500.
PRESSROOM: Line 1 — 8-G/Metro (5 half decks); Line 2 — 8-G/Metro (4 half decks); Line 3 — 5-G/Community (1-3 color unit); Line 4 — 9-G/Colorliner (5 color stacks; 4 mono); Press drives — Allen Bradley/Digital Drive, Fin; Folders — 1-G/Single 3:2, 1-G/Double 3:2, 1-G/Jaw, 2-G/¼, 2-G/3:2 Imperial; Pasters — 16-G/Digital Pilot (w/surface sensing pasters); Reels and stands — G/Stands & wood reel, Martin/reel, G/CT-50s RTP, G/42"RTP; Press control system — RKW, G/APCS; Press registration system — MicroTrak/9500. MAILROOM: Counter stackers — 7-QWI/100, 1-BG, 3-QWI/300, 1-QWI/On-Line System, 1-QWI/Single Belt Distribution System, 1-QWI/Double Belt Over Under Distribution System; Inserters and stuffers — 1-HI/1372, 1-HI/1472, 1-HI/2299, Id; Bundle tyer — 4-Sa, 1-OVL, 3-Dynaric/Strap, 4-Dynaric/Strap, 1-Dynaric/Strap, 3-Bu, Mc; Wrapping singles — 1-St, 3-Bu/String Tyr, 6-QWI, 4-QWI; Addressing machine — 1-Ch; Mailroom control system — 1-Ic. 1-ARS/1372. 1-ARS/1272. LIBRARY: Electronic — NewsView, PhotoView; Combination — IBM. COMMUNICATIONS: Facsimile — 1-Konica/Newscan 1000, 1-Konica/Newscan 1500; Remote imagesetting — 1-Konica/Newscan 1000, 1-Konica/Newscan 1500. WIRE SERVICES: News — AP, NYT, LAT-WP,

Copyright ©1996 by the Editor & Publisher Co.

GNS; Photos — AP; Stock tables — AP, Media General; Syndicates — NYT, GNS, LAT-WP; Receiving dishes — AP. BUSINESS COMPUTERS: IBM/AS-400 F45, IBM/AS-400 E60, 3-PC; Applications: Lawson: Personnel, Payroll; CDS: Financial; PCs & main system networked.

WATSONVILLE
Santa Cruz County
'90 U.S. Census- 31,099; E&P '96 Est. 37,492
ABC-NDM (90): 96,289 (HH 30,597)

Register-Pajaronian
(e-mon to fri; m-sat)

Register-Pajaronian, 1000 Main St.; PO Box 50055, Watsonville, CA 95077; tel (408) 761-7300; fax (408) 722-8386. News Media Corp. group.
Circulation: 10,580(e); 10,580(m-sat); ABC Sept. 30, 1995.
Price: 35¢(d); 35¢(sat); $7.25/mo (home), $9.75/mo (mail); $87.00/yr (home), $117.00/yr (mail).
Advertising: Open inch rate $12.59(e); $12.59(m-sat). **Representative:** Papert Companies.
News Services: AP, SHNS. **Politics:** Independent. **Established:** 1868.
Not Published: New Year; Christmas.
Special Editions: Progress (Mar); Home Improvement (monthly).
Special Weekly Sections: Fashion, Business (mon); Best Food Day, Business (tues); Health, Business (wed); Entertainment, Business (thur); Automotive (fri); Automotive, Home and Garden, Real Estate (sat); TV Log (daily).
Magazines: USA Weekend, Color Comics, TV Weekly (sat).

CORPORATE OFFICERS
President .... John Tompkins
Vice Pres .... Michael Tompkins
GENERAL MANAGEMENT
Publisher .... Douglas M Leifheit
Controller .... Michael Rand
ADVERTISING
Director .... Nancy Moors
Manager-Classified .... Jeanie Johnson
CIRCULATION
Director .... Rob Learn
NEWS EXECUTIVE
Managing Editor .... Bill Watson
EDITORS AND MANAGERS
Amusements/Entertainment Editor
.... Stacey Vreeken
Editorial Page Editor .... Bill Watson
News Editor .... Bob Smith
Sports Editor .... Dave Burge
MANAGEMENT INFORMATION SERVICES
Data Processing Manager .... Denny Klint
PRODUCTION
Manager .... James Borrego

Market Information: TMC.
Mechanical available: Offset; Black and 3 ROP colors; insert accepted — preprinted; page cutoffs — 22¾".
Mechanical specifications: Type page 13" x 21", E - 6 cols, 2¹/₁₆", ⅛" between; A - 6 cols, 2¹/₁₆", ⅛" between; C - 9 cols, 1⅜", ¹/₁₆" between.
Commodity consumption: Newsprint 1,000 metric tons; width 27½"; black ink 24,000 pounds; color ink 3,000 pounds; single pages printed 7,963; average pages per issue 20(d); single plates used 13,000.
Equipment: EDITORIAL: Front-end hardware — 26-SII; Other equipment — 5-RSK/TRS 80 model 100 remote terminal. CLASSIFIED: Front-end hardware — 4-SII. DISPLAY: Adv layout systems — 2-COM. PRODUCTION: Typesetters — 2-COM/Videosetter, 2-COM/Advantage; Plate exposures — 2-Nu/Flip top; Plate processors — 1-Nat; Production cameras — 1-C/Spartan II; Automatic film processors — 1-LE; Shrink lenses — 1-CK Optical.
PRESSROOM: Line 1 — 6-G/Urbanite; Folders — 1-G. MAILROOM: Bundle tyer — 1-MLN. WIRE SERVICES: News — AP; Syndicates — NYT, WP; Receiving dishes — AP. BUSINESS COMPUTERS: INSI; Applications: Class, Display billing; PCs & micros networked; PCs & main system networked.

WEST COVINA
See SAN GABRIEL VALLEY

WHITTIER
Los Angeles County
'90 U.S. Census- 77,671; E&P '96 Est. 83,490
ABC-NDM (90): 188,156 (HH 59,582)

The Whittier Daily News
(m-mon to sat; S)

The Whittier Daily News, 7612 Greenleaf Ave. (90602); PO Box 581, Whittier, CA 90608; tel (310) 698-0955; fax (310) 698-0450; web site http://www.earthlink.net/~thomsonla/. Thomson Newspapers group.
Circulation: 18,622(m); 18,622(m-sat); 17,755(S); ABC Apr. 1, 1995.
Price: 35¢(d); 35¢(sat); $1.00(S); $2.50/wk; $130.00/yr.
Representative: Cresmer, Woodward, O'Mara & Ormsbee.
News Service: AP. **Politics:** Independent. **Established:** 1900.
Note: For detailed production information, see the San Gabriel Valley Tribune. The Thomson LA News Group includes the following newspapers: Pasadena Star-News (mS), San Gabriel Valley Tribune (mS) and Whittier Daily News (mS). The group combination rate is $63.00 (d) & (S). Individual newspaper rates not made available.
Special Editions: LA Auto Show, New Jobs (Jan); Health File (Feb); Spring Home & Garden, Job Fair (Mar); Careers '96, Bridal Faire (Apr); Spring Fashion Magazine, Mother's Day, Health File, Progress (May); Auto/Summer Wheels, Family-owned Business (June); 4th of July, Careers '96 (July); Health File, Best of Cheers (Aug); Fall Fashion Magazine, LA County Fair Tab (Sept); A Taste Of Pasadena, Fall Home & Garden/Aboretum, Job Fair Section, New Cars '97 (Oct); Health File, Gift Guide #1 (Nov); Gift Guide Pages #2, Gift Guide Pages #3, The Rose (magazine) (Dec).
Special Weekly Sections: Wheels, Home Buyers (sat).
Magazines: Cheers (fri); Parade, TV Magazine (S).

CORPORATE OFFICERS
Group Publisher .... Joseph A Logan
Exec Editor/Vice Pres .... John Irby
Director-Circulation .... Ron L Wood
GENERAL MANAGEMENT
Publisher .... Bill Bell
Chief Financial Officer .... Barry Thompson
Director-Human Resources .... Ted Barajas
ADVERTISING
Director-Classified .... Ron Busick
Director-Marketing .... Jan Berk
Manager-Retail .... Ed Loescher
CIRCULATION
Director .... Ron L Wood
Manager-Home Delivery .... Joe Robidoux
Manager-Single Copy .... John Winn
NEWS EXECUTIVES
Editor/Vice Pres .... John Irby
Managing Editor .... Bill Bell
Deputy Editor .... Dorothy Reinhold
EDITORS AND MANAGERS
Automotive Editor .... Vernon Rodgers
Business Editor .... Ali Sar
City Editor .... Kathleen Lund-Seeden
Community Editor .... Val Marrs
Editorial Page Editor .... Kevin O'Leary
Entertainment Editor .... Cathie Lou Porrelli
Fashion/Style Editor .... Lisa Cooke
Features Editor .... Catherine Gaugh
Health/Medical Editor .... Kathleen Lund-Seeden
Librarian .... Bruce Baert
Metro Editor .... Janice Luder
News Editor .... Michael Coates
Operations Editor .... Steve O'Sullivan
Photo Editor .... Tim Berger
Sports Editor .... Sam Pollak
Television Editor .... Mauricio Minotta
MANAGEMENT INFORMATION SERVICES
Director-Management Info Services .... Arline King
PRODUCTION
Manager .... Chuck Previtire

Market Information: Zoned editions; TMC; ADS.
Mechanical available: Offset; Black and 3 ROP colors; insert accepted — preprinted; page cutoffs — 22¾".
Mechanical specifications: Type page 13" x 21½"; E - 6 cols, 2¹/₁₆", ⅛" between; A - 6 cols, 2¹/₁₆", ⅛" between; C - 10 cols, 1⅛", ¹/₁₆" between.
Commodity consumption: Newsprint 2,506 metric tons; widths 55", 14½", 27½"; black ink 51,282 pounds; color ink 17,576 pounds; single pages printed 20,338, average pages per issue 70(d), 76(sat), 78(S); single plates used 25,658.
Equipment: EDITORIAL: Front-end hardware — 1-SII/Sys 55; Front-end software — 1-SII/Editorial; Other equipment — 38-SII/Coyote 15, 2-SII/Coyote 22, 4-SII/PC. CLASSIFIED: Front-end hardware — SII/Sys55; Front-end software — SII/Czar; Other equipment — 27-SII/Coyote 15. DISPLAY: Adv layout systems — SII/IAL; Front-end hardware — 6-Ap/Mac, 3-Compaq; Front-end software — DTI/Ad Speed, SII/IAL; Printers — Proofers. PRODUCTION: Pagination software — SII/INL 9.2; Typesetters — 4-MON/Laser Comp, 2-V/5500, 2-V/5600; Plate-making systems — 2-WL; Electronic picture desk — Lf/AP Leaf Picture Desk; Scanners — 2-Lf/Leafscan 35, 10-Compaq; Production cameras — 1-Spartan/III, 1-C/Newspaper, 1-C/Spartan III; Automatic film processors — 2-LE; Film transporters — 2-LE; Shrink lenses — 1-Alan; Digital color separation equipment — SII, Ap/Mac, QPS.
PRESSROOM: Line 1 — 7-HO; Line 2 — 7-HO; Press drives — Fin; Folders — 3-HO; Pasters — 14-Enkel; Reels and stands — 14-Enkel; Press control system — G/MPCS; Press registration system — G. MAILROOM: Counter stackers — 5-Id/2000, 2-Id/440; Inserters and stuffers — 4-GMA/SLS 1000; Bundle tyer — 5-Power Strap/ PSN5; Addressing machine — 2-Videojet/VMS. WIRE SERVICES: News — AP, NYT, KRT; Stock tables — AP; Syndicates — AP; Receiving dishes — AP. BUSINESS COMPUTERS: HP; Applications: CJ, Ceridian: Payroll; PCs & main system networked.

WOODLAND
Yolo County
'90 U.S. Census- 39,802; E&P '96 Est. 47,874
ABC-CZ (90): 39,802 (HH 14,198)

The Daily Democrat
(e-mon to fri; m-sat; S)

The Daily Democrat, 711 Main St. (95695); PO Box 730, Woodland, CA 95776; tel (916) 662-5421; fax (916) 662-1288. Donrey Media group.
Circulation: 10,404(e); 10,404(m-sat); 10,713(S); ABC Sept. 30, 1995.
Price: 50¢(d); 50¢(sat); 50¢(S); $6.43/mo (plus tax, city), $6.99/mo (plus tax, county).
Advertising: Open inch rate $11.00(e); $11.00(m-sat); $11.00(S). **Representatives:** Papert Companies; US Suburban Press.
News Service: AP. **Politics:** Independent. **Established:** 1857.
Special Editions: Brides Pictorial (Feb); Bridal Show, Car Care, Spring Crops, Healthy Living (Mar); Livestock, Home Improvement (Apr); Vacation, Travel, Pools, Spas, Patios, 4-H Auction (May); Car Care (June); Home Safety & Security (July); Fair Days, County Fair (Aug); Back-to-School (Sept); Halloween Fun, Home Improvement (Oct); Shop at Home, Christmas Preview (Nov); Holiday Entertaining (Dec).
Special Weekly Sections: Food Section (wed); Farm Page, Good Life (thur).
Magazines: Weekly Democrat (TMC) (wed); AG Pages (thur); Business Pages, Real Estate Section, Home & Garden, Automotive (fri).

CORPORATE OFFICERS
Founder .... Donald W Reynolds
President/Chief Operating Officer .... Emmett Jones
Exec Vice Pres/Chief Financial Officer
.... Darrell W Loftin
Vice Pres-Western Newspaper Group
.... David A Osborn
Vice Pres-Eastern Newspaper Group
.... Don Schneider
GENERAL MANAGEMENT
Publisher .... Ted E Dixon
Manager-Office .... Shelby J Downs
ADVERTISING
Director .... Neill Rabon
CIRCULATION
Manager .... Clay Eubank
NEWS EXECUTIVE
Editor .... Jim Smith
EDITORS AND MANAGERS
City Editor .... Robb Hicken
Special Sections Editor .... Mary Goetz
Sports Editor .... Gary Traynham
PRODUCTION
Supervisor-Composing Room .... Sandy Wheeler
Foreman-Pressroom .... Mike Sharp

Market Information: TMC.
Mechanical available: Offset; Black and 3 ROP colors; insert accepted — preprinted; page cutoffs — 22¾".
Mechanical specifications: Type page 13" x 21½"; E - 6 cols, 2¹/₁₆", ⅛" between; A - 6 cols, 2¹/₁₆", ⅛" between; C - 9 cols, 1⅜", ¹/₁₆" between.
Commodity consumption: Newsprint 460 metric tons; width 27"; single pages printed 8,000; average pages per issue 20(d), 24(S); single plates used 10,000.
Equipment: EDITORIAL: Front-end hardware — SII; Printers — 1-TI/Omni 800, 1-Ap/Mac LaserWriter NT; Other equipment — Ap/Mac IIcx. CLASSIFIED: Front-end hardware — SII; Printers — 1-TI/Omni 800. DISPLAY: Adv layout systems — SII; Front-end hardware — 1-Ap/Mac IIcx, 1-Ap/Mac IIci, 1-Ap/Power Mac 6100-66; Front-end software — SII/IAL; Printers — 1-Ap/Mac LaserWriter II, 1-HP/LaserJet; Other equipment — 1-Ap/Mac CD-Rom, 1-Ap/Mac Scan. PRODUCTION: Typesetters — 2-NewGen/Laser printers; Plate-making systems — 3M/Deadliner; Production cameras — Acti/225; Shrink lenses — Nikon.
PRESSROOM: Line 1 — 8-G/Community; Folders — 1-G. MAILROOM: Counter stackers — 1-BG; Inserters and stuffers — 5-KAN; Bundle tyer — 1-MLN. WIRE SERVICES: News — AP; Syndicates — NEA, SHNS, CNS; Receiving dishes — size-10ft, AP. BUSINESS COMPUTERS: ALR/REVQ, 1-HP/3000-917LX.

YREKA
Siskiyou County
'90 U.S. Census- 6,948; E&P '96 Est. 7,739

Siskiyou Daily News
(e-mon to fri)

Siskiyou Daily News, 309 S. Broadway; PO Box 129, Yreka, CA 96097; tel (916) 842-5777; fax (916) 842-6787. Hollinger International Inc. group.
Circulation: 5,194(e); Sworn Sept. 29, 1995.
Price: 50¢(d); $6.50/mo; $67.80/yr (carrier); $73.00/yr (mail).
Advertising: Open inch rate $8.90(e). **Representative:** American Publishing Management Services.
News Service: AP. **Politics:** Independent. **Established:** 1941 (daily), 1859 (weekly).
Not Published: New Year; Memorial Day; Independence Day; Labor Day; Thanksgiving; Christmas.
Special Editions: Progress (Mar); Spring Car Care (Apr); Adventures (June); Siskiyou Golden Fair (Aug); Kick-off '96 (Sept); Holiday Gift Guide (Nov); Year-End Review (Dec).
Special Weekly Section: TV Spotlight (fri).
Magazines: "Siskiyou Spotlight" Tab (fri); TV Section; Siskiyou County Properties (Real Estate) (monthly).

CORPORATE OFFICERS
President/CEO .... Larry J Perrotto
Comptroller .... Roland McBride
GENERAL MANAGEMENT
General Manager & Exec Editor
.... Dale D Andreasen
Bookkeeper .... Sharon Still
Purchasing Agent .... Sharon Still
ADVERTISING
Director .... Eric Grooters
CIRCULATION
Manager .... Paul Shaw
NEWS EXECUTIVES
Managing Editor .... David Kennard
Assoc Editor .... Maggie Maguire
EDITORS AND MANAGERS
Columnist .... Ed Foss
Editorial Page Editor .... Dale D Andreasen
General Reporting .... Lori Sellstrom
General Reporting .... Gene Sheley
Sports Editor .... Renee Casterline
PRODUCTION
Superintendent .... Dale Jerden

Market Information: TMC.
Mechanical available: Offset; Black and 3 ROP colors; insert accepted — preprinted; page cutoffs — 22¾".

I-58 California

Mechanical specifications: Type page 13" x 21½"; E - 6 cols, 2 1/16", 1/8" between; A - 6 cols, 2 1/16", 1/8" between; C - 8 cols, 1½", 1/8" between.
Commodity consumption: Newsprint 365 short tons; 332 metric tons; widths 27½", 35"; black ink 6,000 pounds; color ink 1,500 pounds; single pages printed 3,780; average pages per issue 18(d); single plates used 2,000.
Equipment: EDITORIAL: Front-end hardware — Ap/Mac; Front-end software — Baseview, QuarkXPress; Printers — Ap/Mac LaserWriter Pro 600, Ap/Mac LaserWriter Pro 630; Other equipment — HP/Scanner. CLASSIFIED: Front-end hardware — Ap/Mac; Front-end software — Baseview, QuarkXPress; Printers — Ap/Mac LaserWriter, Dot Matrix. DISPLAY: Adv layout systems — Ap/Mac, QuarkXPress; Front-end hardware — Ap/Mac; Front-end software — Mk/Newswriter Plus, QuarkXPress; Printers — Ap/Mac LaserWriter II, Ap/Mac LaserWriter Pro 600. PRODUCTION: Pagination software — QuarkXPress; OCR software — TI/Omni Page; Typesetters — 2-Ap/Mac LaserWriter II NTX, 1-COM/88, 1-COM/IV, Ap/Mac LaserWriter Pro 600, Ap/Mac LaserWriter Pro 630; Platemaking systems — Amerigraph/Magnum 43; Production cameras — 1-SCREEN/Vertical; Automatic film processors — Glunz & Jensen.
PRESSROOM: Line 1 — 6-G/Community; Folders — 1-G/Community. MAILROOM: Bundle tyer — 1-Us; Addressing machine — 1-Wm. WIRE SERVICES: News — AP; Receiving dishes — size-3ft, AP. BUSINESS COMPUTERS: CompuAdd/386; Applications: Microsoft; PCs & micros networked.

YUBA CITY
See MARYSVILLE

COLORADO

ALAMOSA
Alamosa County
'90 U.S. Census- 7,579; E&P '96 Est. 8,664

The Valley Courier (m-tues to sat)
The Valley Courier, 401 State Ave.; PO Box 1099, Alamosa, CO 81101; tel (719) 589-2553; fax (719) 589-6573. News Media Corp. group.
Circulation: 5,040(m); 5,040(m-sat); Sworn Sept. 29, 1995.
Price: 35¢(d); 35¢(sat); $7.00/mo (carrier); $69.50/yr.
Advertising: Open inch rate $7.90(m); $7.90(m-sat).
News Service: AP. **Established:** 1925.
Not Published: New Year; Memorial Day; Independence Day; Labor Day; Thanksgiving; Christmas.
Special Editions: Home Improvement (Apr); Summer Lifestyle (May); Rodeo (July); Back-to-School (Aug); Hunting (Sept); Ski (Nov); Christmas (Dec).
Special Weekly Sections: Agriculture (thur); Outdoors (fri); TV/Traveller (sat).

CORPORATE OFFICERS
President John Thompkins
Vice Pres Mike Thompkins

GENERAL MANAGEMENT
Publisher Keith R Cerny

ADVERTISING
Director Keith R Cerny
Manager-Classified Diane Mondragon

CIRCULATION
Clerk Linda Brown

NEWS EXECUTIVE
Editor Greg Johnson

EDITORS AND MANAGERS
Action Editor Greg Johnson
Business/Finance Editor Greg Johnson
City/Metro Editor Greg Johnson
Editorial Page Editor Greg Johnson
Education Editor Greg Johnson
Entertainment/Amusement Editor Greg Johnson
Environment Editor Greg Johnson
Features/Travel Editor Greg Johnson
Graphics Editor/Art Director Greg Johnson
Living/Lifestyle Editor Ruth Heide
National Editor Greg Johnson
News Editor Greg Johnson
Photo Editor Greg Johnson
Political/Government Editor Greg Johnson
Religion Editor Ruth Heide
Science/Technology Editor Greg Johnson
Sports Terry Moore
Women's Editor Ruth Heide

PRODUCTION
Manager Vernon Trujillo
Foreman-Pressroom Vernon Trujillo

Market Information: Zoned editions.
Mechanical available: Offset; Black and 3 ROP colors; insert accepted — preprinted; page cut-offs — 21½".
Mechanical specifications: Type page 13" x 21½"; E - 6 cols, 2 1/16", 1/8" between; A - 6 cols, 2 1/16", 1/8" between; C - 8 cols, 1½", 1/8" between.
Commodity consumption: Newsprint 100 short tons; widths 27½", 13¾"; single pages printed 3,598; average pages per issue 14(d), 14(sat); single plates used 2,520.
Equipment: EDITORIAL: Front-end hardware — Ap/Mac; Front-end software — Ap/Mac; Printers — 2-Ap/Mac LaserPrinter. CLASSIFIED: Front-end hardware — Mk, Ap/Mac; Front-end software — Mk; Printers — Ap/Mac. DISPLAY: Adv layout systems — Ap/Mac; Front-end hardware — Ap/Mac; Front-end software — Ap/Mac; Printers — Ap/Mac LaserPrinter. PRODUCTION: Pagination software — Aldus/PageMaker 4.0; Typesetters — 1-COM/4961TL, 1-COM/2961, 1-COM/7200; Platemaking systems — 1-Nu; Plate processors — 1-Nu; Scanners — Ap/Scanner; Production cameras — 1-R.
PRESSROOM: Line 1 — 4-G/Community. WIRE SERVICES: News — AP; Receiving dishes — size-2', AP. BUSINESS COMPUTERS: IBM/PC; Applications: Circ- Interlink.

ASPEN
Pitkin County
'90 U.S. Census- 5,049; E&P '96 Est. 7,021

Aspen Daily News (m-mon to sat)
Aspen Daily News, 517 E. Hopkins Ave.; PO Box DD, Aspen, CO 81611; tel (970) 925-2220; fax (970) 920-2118; e-mail aspend-news@aol.com.
Circulation: 11,500(m); 11,500(m-sat); Sworn Sept. 30, 1992.
Price: Free; $36.00/mo; $400.00/yr.
Advertising: Open inch rate $5.15(m); $5.15(m-sat).
News Service: AP. **Politics:** Independent. **Established:** 1978.
Special Editions: Winterskol (Jan); Winternational (Mar); Spruce Up for Spring (May); Summer Guide (June); Fall Colors (Sept); Fall Home Improvement (Oct); 24 Hours of Aspen (Nov); Winter Guide, Holiday Gift Guide (Dec).
Special Weekly Sections: High Country Real Estate (wed); Time Out (thur).

CORPORATE OFFICER
President David N Danforth

GENERAL MANAGEMENT
Publisher David N Danforth
General Manager John Duffy

ADVERTISING
Manager-Classified Debbie Delk
Manager-Sales Cassandra Davenport

CIRCULATION
Manager Jerry Sleeper

NEWS EXECUTIVE
Exec Editor Curtis Robinson

PRODUCTION
Manager John Mora
Manager-Pressroom Jerry Sleeper

Market Information: Electronic edition.
Mechanical available: Offset web; Black and 3 ROP colors; insert accepted — preprinted, will contract to print inserts; page cut-offs — 14½".
Mechanical specifications: Type page 10¼" x 14"; E - 4 cols, 2.43", 1/3" between; A - 6 cols, 1.57", 1/6" between; C - 6 cols, 1.57", 1/6" between.
Commodity consumption: Newsprint 350 metric tons; width 29½"; single pages printed 12,064; average pages per issue 32(d), 24(sat); single plates used 3,000.
Equipment: EDITORIAL: Front-end hardware — 4-Ap/Mac Quadra 610; Front-end software — QuarkXPress 3.3; Printers — 2-Ap/Mac LaserWriter, GCC/Selectpress 600; Other equipment — 8-Ap/Mac LC III. CLASSIFIED: Front-end hardware — 2-Ap/Mac LC III; Front-end software — Baseview/Class Manager; Printers — GCC/Selectpress 600. DISPLAY: Adv layout systems — QPS; Front-end hardware — 1-Ap/Power Mac; Front-end software — QuarkXPress 3.3; Printers — Ap/Mac LaserWriter 360. PRODUCTION: Pagination software — QuarkXPress 3.3; OCR software — Adobe/Photoshop 3.0; Typesetters — Ap/Mac LaserPrinter NTX, 3-COM/Editwriter 7500, Ap/Mac IIcx, Ap/Mac LaserWriter II NTX; Platemaking systems — Nu/30x40 Platemaker; Scanners — 2-Ap/Mac IIcx, Umax/Vista T630; Production cameras — AG/Repromaster 1100, SCREEN/Auto Companica; Automatic film processors — LE/Rap 20.
PRESSROOM: Line 1 — 5-G/Community; Press drives — Fin; Folders — G/Community; Press registration system — Duarte. WIRE SERVICES: News — AP. BUSINESS COMPUTERS: Ap/Mac SE30, Ap/Mac Classic; Applications: Proprietary: Accts receivable, Runsheets, Gen ledger; PCs & micros networked; PCs & main system networked.

The Aspen Times (m-mon to fri)
The Aspen Times, PO Box E, Aspen, CO 81612; tel (970) 925-3414; fax (970) 925-6240; web site http://www.aspenline.com/clients/aspenonline/ directory/ times /timesindex.html.
Circulation: 7,020(m); Sworn Sept. 30, 1995.
Price: Free.
Advertising: Open inch rate $9.00(m).
News Services: AP, LAT-WP, NYT. **Politics:** Independent. **Established:** 1988.
Special Editions: Style, Restaurant Guide (June); Style (Nov); Restaurant Guide (Dec).
Magazine: Weekend (fri).
Broadcast Affiliates: KMTS-FM; KGLM-AM.

GENERAL MANAGEMENT
Publisher Loren Jenkins

ADVERTISING
Director Candice Welsh

NEWS EXECUTIVE
Editor in Chief Andy Stone

EDITORS AND MANAGERS
Business/Finance Editor Scott Condon
Entertainment/Amusements Editor Stewart Oksenhorn
Graphic Editor/Art Director Bryan Gonzales
Sports Editor Dale Strode

Market Information: TMC; ADS; Operate database.
Mechanical available: Offset; Black insert accepted — preprinted; page cut-offs — 16".
Mechanical specifications: Type page 11½" x 17¼"; E - 5 cols, 1.9", 1/6" between; A - 5 cols, 1.9", 1/6" between; C - 5 cols, 1.9", 1/6" between.
Commodity consumption: average pages per issue 28(d).
Equipment: EDITORIAL: Front-end hardware — 12-Ap/Mac II LC, Ap/Mac ci; Front-end software — Baseview; Printers — LaserMaster, AG. CLASSIFIED: Front-end hardware — 2-Ap/Mac vx, Ap/Mac II LC; Front-end software — Baseview. DISPLAY: Adv layout systems — 2-Ap/Mac ci; Front-end hardware — Ap/Mac; Front-end software — Baseview. PRODUCTION: Typesetters — 3-Ap/Mac LaserPrinter; Plate processors — 1-Nu; Production cameras — LE; Automatic film processors — Kk.
PRESSROOM: Line 1 — 5-WPC/Webheader; Reels and stands — 5-WPC. MAILROOM: Counter stackers — BG; Bundle tyer — Bu. WIRE SERVICES: News — AP; Receiving dishes — AP. BUSINESS COMPUTERS: Osicom; Applications: Billing, Payroll, Accts receivable, Spreadsheets; PCs & micros networked; PCs & main system networked.

BOULDER
Boulder County
'90 U.S. Census- 83,311; E&P '96 Est. 93,459
ABC-CZ (90): 83,312 (HH 34,681)

Daily Camera (m-mon to sat; S)
Daily Camera, 1048 Pearl; PO Box 591, Boulder, CO 80302; tel (303) 442-1202; fax (303) 449-2063. Knight-Ridder Inc. group.
Circulation: 34,733(m); 34,733(m-sat); 43,727(S); ABC Sept. 30, 1995.
Price: 25¢(d); 25¢(sat); 75¢(S); $2.50/wk; $10.82/mo; $130.00/yr.
Advertising: Open inch rate $25.44(m); $25.44(m-sat); $32.87(S). **Representative:** Newspapers First.
News Services: AP, LAT-WP, KRT, NYT. **Politics:** Independent. **Established:** 1890.
Special Editions: Bolder Boulder; Boulder County Almanac; Best of Boulder; Back-to-School; C.U. Preview; Fall Home Furnishings; Ski Section; Holiday Guide; Summer Activities Guide; Bridal Memories (monthly).
Special Weekly Sections: Environment (mon); Business Plus (tues); Food (wed); Discovery (Science & Health) (thur).
Magazines: FIT Magazine (mon); Business Plus, Neighbors (tues); Friday Magazine (fri); TV Times (S).

CORPORATE OFFICERS
Vice Pres Robert F Singleton
Secretary Douglas C Harris
Asst Treasurer Gary Efren

GENERAL MANAGEMENT
President/Publisher Harold Higgins
Vice Pres-Operations Jim Gaasterland
Director-Info Service/Technical Service Roy Schewe
Personnel Director Danielle Ross

ADVERTISING
Director Kelly Mirt
Manager-Retail Bill Sabo
Manager-Classified Cindy Sease
Manager-National/Co-op C J Holloway

MARKETING AND PROMOTION
Manager-Marketing/Promotion Kimberly Harris

TELECOMMUNICATIONS
Audiotex Manager Nora Falvey

CIRCULATION
Director Jaime Naranjo

NEWS EXECUTIVES
Editor-Emeritus Laurence T Paddock
Editor Barrie Hartman
Managing Editor Gary Burns

EDITORS AND MANAGERS
Automotive Editor John Dearrington
Books Editor Juliet Wittman
Business Editor Jerd Smith
Finance Editor Jerd Smith
Environmental Editor Chris Roberts
Editorial Page Editor Glennys McPhilimy
Films/Theater Editor Kathryn Bernheimer
Garden Editor Ronda Haskins
Home Furnishings Editor Ronda Haskins
Librarian Charlotte Smokler
Photo Department Manager Cliff Grassmick
Radio/Television Editor Ronda Haskins
Special Projects Editor Thad Keyes
Special Sections Editor Ronda Haskins
Sports Editor Dan Creedon
Women's Editor Ronda Haskins

MANAGEMENT INFORMATION SERVICES
Data Processing Director Roy Schewe

Market Information: Zoned editions; TMC; ADS; Operate audiotex.
Mechanical available: Offset; Black and 3 ROP colors; insert accepted — preprinted, product samples; page cut-offs — 22¾".
Mechanical specifications: Type page 13" x 21½"; E - 6 cols, 2 1/16", 1/8" between; A - 6 cols, 2 1/16", 1/8" between; C - 9 cols, 1 3/8", 1/16" between.
Commodity consumption: Newsprint 4,112 short tons; 3,730 metric tons; widths 55", 41¼", 27½"; black ink 78,330 pounds; color ink 15,293 pounds; single pages printed 17,286; average pages per issue 40(d), 90(S); single plates used 40,300.
Equipment: EDITORIAL: Front-end hardware — 4-AT/Series 4, 54-AT/ADT; Front-end software — AT 4.5.3; Printers — HP/Rugged Writer, NEC/Pinwriter; Other equipment — Ap/Mac SE30, Ap/Mac LaserWriter, 2-Ap/Mac IIfx, Ap/Power Mac 7100/66, Ap/Power Mac 8100/100. CLASSIFIED: Front-end hardware — 2-Pentium/PC Servers, 18-Pentium/PC Clients; Front-end software — HI/CASH; Printers — NEC/LQ570; Other equipment — 2-Pen-

tium/2100 PC (for pagination). AUDIOTEX: Hardware — Brite Voice Systems/Model B-24 ports; Software — QNX; Supplier name — AP, Brite. DISPLAY: Adv layout systems — SCS; Front-end hardware — 3-PC/386; Front-end software — SCS/Layout 8000; Printers — HP/LaserJet III, HP/2563C. PRODUCTION: Typesetters — 2-AU/APS-6-108C Laser Imaging System, 1-AU/PSII; Platemaking systems — Manual; Plate exposures — 1-Nu/Ultra Plus, 1-Nu/UPNS; Plate processors — 1-WL/30D; Electronic picture desk — Lf/AP Leaf Picture Desk; Scanners — ECR/Autokon 1000-DE; Production cameras — 1-Dt, 1-C/Spartan II; Automatic film processors — 1-Litex/26, 1-Kk/710; Shrink lenses — 1-CK Optical/SQU7, Alan/Reversal Lens; Color separation equipment (conventional) — Screen/SG-608; Digital color separation equipment — SCREEN/SG 608.
PRESSROOM: Line 1 — 5-G/Metro; Line 2 — 5-G/Community (Custom-Built 3-knife trimmer); Press drives — Fin; Folders — 2-G/Metro, 1-G/Community SSC; Pasters — 5-G; Reels and stands — 5-G; Press control system — Fin; Press registration system — Manual. MAILROOM: Counter stackers — 2-Id/NS550, 1-Id/2100, 2-MM/288, 1-QWI/300; Inserters and stuffers — 1-MM/275, Valley Remanufacturing/S-1372; Bundle tyer — 1-MLN/2A, 2-Power Strap/PSN5, Power Strap/PSN6, 1-MLN/2EE. LIBRARY: Electronic — Vu/Text SAVE. WIRE SERVICES: News — AP, WB; Photos — AP; Stock tables — AP; Syndicates — AP Datafeatures, KRT, NYT, LAT-WP, TMS; Receiving dishes — size-4m, AP. BUSINESS COMPUTERS: 1-HP/3000 Series 947; Applications: CJ, CIS, AAP: AGL, PAY, EFA; PCs & micros networked.

CANON CITY
Fremont County
'90 U.S. Census- 12,687; E&P '96 Est. 12,926
ABC-CZ (90): 16,617 (HH 6,682)

Daily Record
(e-mon to fri; m-sat)
Daily Record, 523 Main St.; PO Box 2020, Canon City, CO 81215-2020; tel (719) 275-7565; fax (719) 275-1353. Lehman Communications Corp. group.
Circulation: 8,619(e); 8,619(m-sat); ABC Sept. 30, 1995.
Price: 35¢(d); 35¢(sat); $6.75/mo (carrier), $8.00/mo (mail); $81.00/yr (carrier), $96.00/yr (mail).
Advertising: Open inch rate $9.78(e); $9.78(m-sat). **Representative:** Papert Companies.
News Service: AP. **Politics:** Independent. **Established:** 1875.
Not Published: New Year; Memorial Day; Independence Day; Labor Day; Christmas.
Special Editions: Golden Years; Bridal Guide; Coupon Book; Spring & Fall Home Improvement; Vacation Tourist Guide (Summer); Spring and Fall Car Care; Community Report (Progress Edition); Newcomers Edition; Fall Sports Preview; Woman's Edition; Real Estate Preview (monthly).
Special Weekly Section: Entertainment Weekly (sat).

CORPORATE OFFICERS
Chairman	Edward Lehman
President	Dean G Lehman
Vice Pres-Finance	Richard B Simmons
Secretary/Treasurer	Ruth G Lehman

GENERAL MANAGEMENT
Publisher	Edward Lehman
General Manager	Robert Helsley

ADVERTISING
Manager-Sales	Terry Holloway

CIRCULATION
Manager	Bruce Elliot

NEWS EXECUTIVES
Editor	Robert Helsley
Managing Editor	Tom Swindt

EDITORS AND MANAGERS
Editorial Page Editor	Tom Swindt
Education Editor	Sonya Johnson
Environmental Editor	John Lemons
Fashion/Style Editor	Sonya Johnson
Living/Lifestyle Editor	Sonya Johnson
News Editor	Sonya Johnson
Photo Editor	Tom Pittman
Sports Editor	Evan Lukassen

PRODUCTION
Superintendent	James Thompson
Manager-Business	Glenna Phillips
Sales-Commercial Printing	Mick Croasdell

Market Information: TMC.
Mechanical available: Offset; Black and 4 ROP colors; insert accepted — preprinted; page cutoffs — 22¾".
Mechanical specifications: Type page 13" x 21½"; E - 6 cols, 2¹⁄₁₆", ⅛" between; A - 6 cols, 2¹⁄₁₆", ⅛" between; C - 6 cols, 2¹⁄₁₆", ⅛" between.

Commodity consumption: Newsprint 325 metric tons; widths 27½", 31", 33½"; black ink 8,721 pounds; color ink 925 pounds; single pages printed 5,956; average pages per issue 16(d); single plates used 8,400.
Equipment: EDITORIAL: Front-end hardware — Dewar/Sys II; Front-end software — Dewar/Sys II; Printers — Okidata/MicroLine 192, Ap/Mac LaserWriter II; Other equipment — RSK/Tandy 3000HD PC for OCR use. CLASSIFIED: Front-end hardware — Dewar/Sys; Front-end software — Dewar/Sys; Printers — Okidata/193 Plus. DISPLAY: Front-end hardware — Dewar/Sys II Discovery, Ap/Mac ci, Ap/Mac II; Front-end software — Dewar/Sys II Discovery; Other equipment — 1-Ap/Mac Classic. PRODUCTION: Typesetters — COM/8000(display); Platemaking systems — 1-Nu; Plate exposures — 1-Nu; Plate processors — 1-Nat/A-250; Scanners — 2-HP/ScanJet; Production cameras — AG/Repromaster 3800; Automatic film processors — LE/Tek 26.
PRESSROOM: Line 1 — 6-G/Community single width; Press drives — CH; Folders — 1-SC. MAILROOM: Counter stackers — 1-BG; Inserters and stuffers — KAN/320; Bundle tyer — 1-Malow, 1-Ca, 1-MLN/Strapper; Addressing machine — Automecha/Accufast ST; Other mailroom equipment — Champion/Trimmer. 2-Stitcher. WIRE SERVICES: News — AP; Receiving dishes — AP. BUSINESS COMPUTERS: ATT/Unix PC; Applications: Billing, Inch analysis, Adv, Gen ledger, Accts payable; PCs & micros networked; PCs & main system networked.

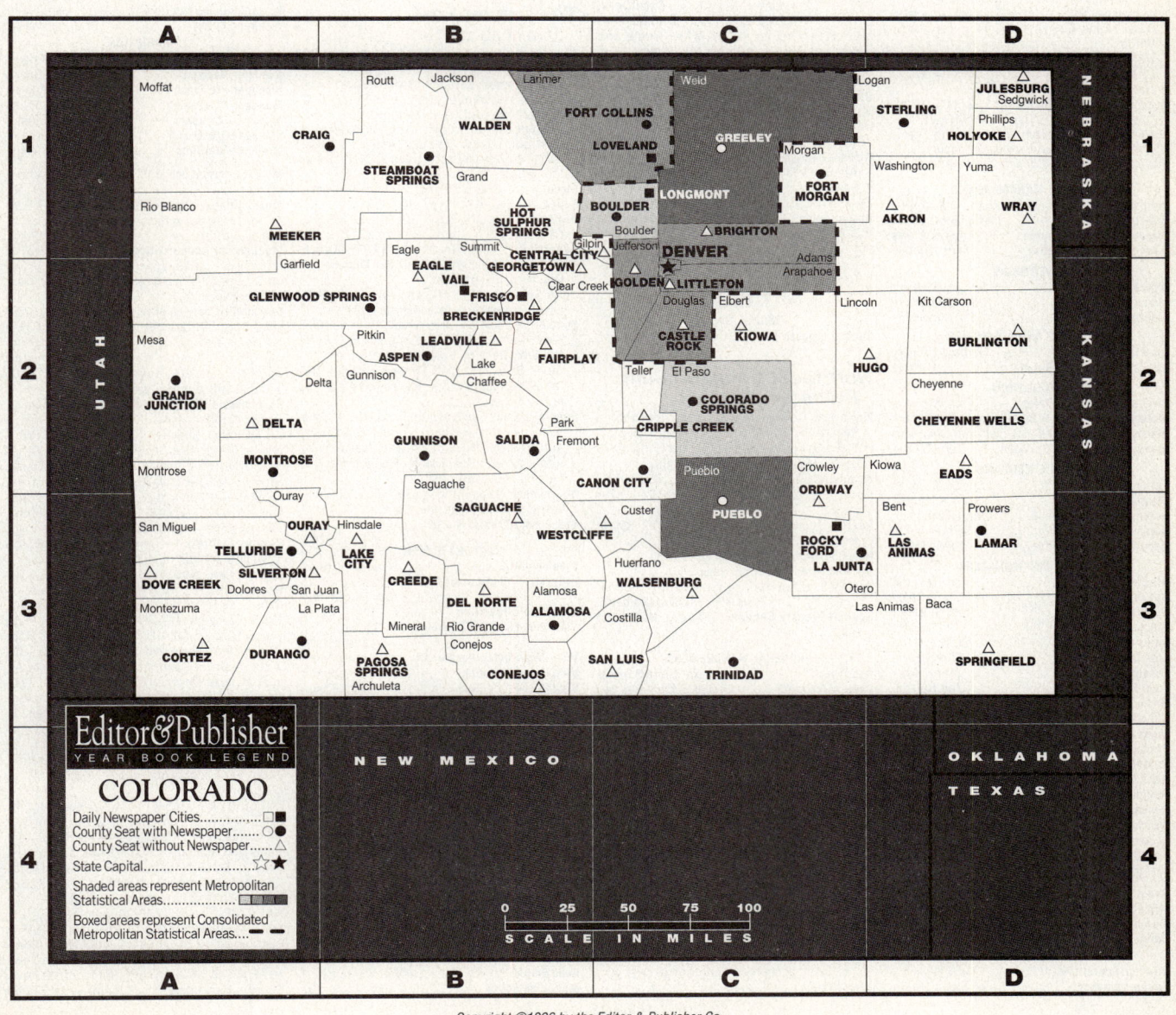

COLORADO SPRINGS

El Paso County

'90 U.S. Census- 281,140; E&P '96 Est. 367,817
ABC-NDM (90): 409,482 (HH 151,685)

Gazette Telegraph

(m-mon to sat; S)

Gazette Telegraph, 30 S. Prospect (80903); PO Box 1779, Colorado Springs, CO 80901; tel (719) 632-5511; fax (719) 636-0333; e-mail gtnews@usa.net; web site http://www.usa/gazette. Freedom Communications Inc. group.

Circulation: 102,298(m); 102,298(m-sat); 123,546(S); ABC Sept. 30, 1995.

Price: 35¢(d); 35¢(sat); $1.00(S); $9.80/mo (carrier).

Advertising: Open inch rate $61.78(m); $61.78(m-sat); $71.23(S). **Representative:** Cresmer, Woodward, O'Mara & Ormsbee.

News Services: AP, NYT, KRT, GNS, SHNS. **Politics:** Independent. **Established:** 1872.

Special Editions: Dining Tab, Bridal, Coupons (Jan); Valentines, Progress (Feb); Spring Car Care, Spring Fashion, Easter Dining (Mar); Home & Design Tab, Mother's Day Dining, Dining Guide, Baseball (Apr); Mother's Day Gift, Careers, Seniors Tab, Medical (May); Vacation, Dining Tab, Father's Day Gift Guide, Spring Spree (June); Answer Book, Rodeo (July); Back-to-School, Fall Fashion, Football Preview Tab (Aug); Fall Home Improvement, Balloon Classic, Hunting (Sept); Salute to Women, Fall Car Care, New Care, Home Furnishing, Dining Tab (Oct); Winter Fun, Thanksgiving Dining, Cookbook, BBB Book (Nov); Gift Guide, Holiday Party Guide, Christmas Greetings, Photo Pages (Dec).

Special Weekly Sections: Food Section (wed); Outdoor, Fashion (thur); Automotive, Entertainment (fri); Home, Gardening (sat); Issues, Travel, Real Estate, Outdoors (S).

Magazines: TV Mag, Comics (S); Parade.

GENERAL MANAGEMENT

Publisher N Christian Anderson III
Director-Finance Michael C Olson
Director-Human Resources Jennifer Burns
Director-Sales/Marketing Mary Jacobus

ADVERTISING

Director Douglas Barnett
Manager-Classified Nicola Myers
Manager-Retail Jane Ellis

MARKETING AND PROMOTION

Director-Marketing Barbara Gregory
Marketing Manager-Database Jeff Potts

CIRCULATION

Director-Subscriber Sales Rich Williams
Manager-Packaging & Distribution Larry Bynum
Manager-Single Copy Sales Jennifer Shephard
Manager-Subscriber Services Terri Clobes

NEWS EXECUTIVES

Editor Steven A Smith
Managing Editor Wayne Stewart
Deputy Managing Editor John Hutchinson
Deputy Managing Editor Terri Fleming
Deputy Managing Editor Todd Hegert

EDITORS AND MANAGERS

Art Director Trich Redman
Books Editor Linda Duval
Business Editor Russell Small
City Editor Cliff Foster
Editorial Page Editor Jon Stepleton
Entertainment Editor Gil Asakawa
Fashion Editor Jane Turnis
Food Editor Jan Spiegel
Home Editor Leslie Weddell
Military Editor Genevieve Anton
News Editor Jim Borden
Photography Director Chuck Bigger
Radio/Television Editor Linda Navarro
Real Estate/Automotive Editor Julie Andrews
Religion Editor Debbie Warhola
Research Center Manager Pula Davis
Sports Editor Scott Smith
Systems Editor Morris Fraser
Travel Editor Linda Duval

MANAGEMENT INFORMATION SERVICES

Senior Manager Info Services Jay Brown
Manager-Business Systems Doug Kellner
Manager-Pre Press Systems Clyde Benson
Online Manager Jeff Potts

PRODUCTION

Director-Operations Gary Blakeley
Senior Manager Glenn Larkin
Operations Manager-Pressroom Bill Hathaway
Operations Foreman-Pressroom Dick Martin
Operations Foreman-Composing George Lewis

Market Information: ADS; Operate database; Electronic edition.

Mechanical available: Offset; Black and 3 ROP colors; insert accepted — preprinted; page cutoffs — 22¾".

Mechanical specifications: Type page 13" x 21½"; E - 6 cols, 2.06", .66" between; A - 6 cols, 2.06", .66" between; C - 10 cols, 1.22", .25" between.

Commodity consumption: Newsprint 13,800 metric tons; widths 55", 41¼", 27½"; black ink 290,880 pounds; color ink 109,055 pounds; single pages printed 22,356; average pages per issue 55(d), 97(S); single plates used 137,796.

Equipment: EDITORIAL: Front-end hardware — DEC, MeD; Front-end software — CSI. CLASSIFIED: Front-end hardware — DEC, MeD; Front-end software — CSI. DISPLAY: Adv layout systems — HI/2100; Front-end hardware — HI/XP 21; Front-end software — HI; Printers — X; Other equipment — 1-SCS/Layout 8000. PRODUCTION: Typesetters — 2-AU/APS-5, 2-AU/APS-108C; Plate exposures — 2-WL/5, Nu/630; Plate processors — 2-WL/38-E, 2-P/on-line; Scanners — 1-Linotype-Hell/Topaz; Production cameras — 2-LE/121; Automatic film processors — 2-LE/18D, 2-Litex/26; Film transporters — 2-SC/2050; Shrink lenses — 1-Kamerak; Color separation equipment (conventional) — 2-Lefex/45; Digital color separation equipment — Lefex/45.
PRESSROOM: Line 1 — 7-MAN/5 Color Deck; Line 2 — 7-MAN/5 Color Deck; Folders — 4-MAN/3:2; Pasters — 14-MAN; Reels and stands — 14-MAN; Press control system — Fin. MAILROOM: Counter stackers — 3-HL/Monitor, 1-HL/HT-2; Inserters and stuffers — 1-GMA/1148P, 1-MM/375-12; Bundle tyer — 4-MLN/2HS, 2-MLN/Portable. LIBRARY: Electronic — Data Times. COMMUNICATIONS: Systems used — satellite. WIRE SERVICES: News — AP, KRT, SHNS, NYT, GNS; Photos — AP; Stock tables — AP SelectStox II; Receiving dishes — size-16ft. BUSINESS COMPUTERS: 1-DEC/VAX 8350, 1-DEC/VAX 4200; Applications: Circ, Financials, Adv receivables; PCs & micros networked; PCs & main system networked.

CRAIG

Moffat County

'90 U.S. Census- 8,091; E&P '96 Est. 8,403

Northwest Colorado Daily Press (e-mon to fri)

Northwest Colorado Daily Press, 466 Yampa Ave. (81625); PO Box 5, Craig, CO 81626-0005; tel (970) 824-7031; fax (970) 824-6810. Howard Publications group.

Circulation: 2,992(e); Sworn Sept. 30, 1995.

Price: 25¢(d); $66.00/yr (carrier), $72.00/yr (mail).

Advertising: Open inch rate $7.00(e). **Representative:** Papert Companies.

News Service: AP. **Established:** 1963.

Not Published: Legal holidays.

Special Editions: Hunting; Summer Recreation; Quarterly "She" (for NW Colorado Women).

Special Weekly Section: Saturday Northwest (sat).

GENERAL MANAGEMENT

Publisher Carol Brett-Beumer
General Manager Carol Brett-Beumer

ADVERTISING

Manager Carol Brett-Beumer

MARKETING AND PROMOTION

Manager-Marketing/Promotion Myrna Pearson

CIRCULATION

Manager Jan Santistevan

NEWS EXECUTIVE

Editor Heather Reiz

EDITORS AND MANAGERS

Editorial Page Editor Chris Mathers
Society Editor Gwen Alexander

PRODUCTION

Manager Roger Beumer

Market Information: TMC.

Mechanical available: Offset; Black and 3 ROP colors; insert accepted — preprinted; page cutoffs — 16".

Mechanical specifications: Type page 10 13/16" x 16"; E - 5 cols, 2 1/16", ⅛" between; A - 5 cols, 2 1/16", ⅛" between; C - 5 cols, 2 1/16", ⅛" between.

Commodity consumption: Newsprint 91 short tons; widths 34", 17"; black ink 2,800 pounds; color ink 100 pounds; single pages printed 5,016; average pages per issue 16(d); single plates used 2,280.

Equipment: EDITORIAL: Front-end hardware — 6-Ap/Mac II, 2-Ap/Mac SE30, 1-Ap/Mac IIci; Front-end software — QuarkXPress; Printers — Hyphen/600. CLASSIFIED: Front-end hardware — 1-Ap/Mac II. DISPLAY: Adv layout systems — 2-Ap/Mac II. PRODUCTION: Typesetters — 1-V/VT600, 1-Ap/Mac LaserWriter, 1-Hyphen/Copal 600; Plate exposures — 1-Nu; Plate processors — 1-Nu; Scanners — 1-Truvell, 1-Ap/Mac Scanner, 1-HP/Scanner; Production cameras — 1-K, Nat; Automatic film processors — 1-P; Color separation equipment (conventional) — 1-WDS.
PRESSROOM: Line 1 — 5-KP; Press control system — CH. MAILROOM: Bundle tyer — 1-Bu, 1-MLN/ML2EE; Addressing machine — 2-Wm. LIBRARY: Combination — 1-ATT/Morge. COMMUNICATIONS: Facsimile — 1-Nefax/II. WIRE SERVICES: News — AP. BUSINESS COMPUTERS: 1-ATT; Applications: Mail, Adv, Bus; PCs & micros networked; PCs & main system networked.

DENVER

Denver County

'90 U.S. Census- 467,610; E&P '96 Est. 496,238
ABC-NDM (90): 1,848,319 (HH 737,806)

The Denver Post

(m-mon to sat; S)

The Denver Post, 1560 Broadway, Denver, CO 80202; tel (303) 820-1010; fax (303) 820-1406; e-mail newsroom@denverpost.com, business@denverpost.com, sports@denverpost.com, living@denverpost.com, arts@denverpost.com, tengdahl@denverpost.com (New Media); web site http://www.denverpost.com/empire. MediaNews Inc. group.

Circulation: 303,357(m); 303,357(m-sat); 456,391(S); ABC Sept. 30, 1995.

Price: 25¢(d); 25¢(sat); 50¢(S); $2.65/wk; $102.96/yr.

Advertising: Open inch rate $177.00(m); $177.00(m-sat); $230.00(S). **Representative:** Newspapers First.

News Services: AP, NYT, LAT-WP, KRT. **Politics:** Independent. **Established:** 1892.

Special Editions: Ski and Snow; Summertime West; Colorado Top 100 Companies; New Car Preview; Best of Summer; Best of Winter; Stock Show; Football Preview; Making the Move Relocation Guide; Hockey on the Edge; Active Times.

Special Weekly Sections: Business (mon); Food (wed); Friday Fashion, Home & Design, Auto/Wheels (fri); Auto/Wheels (sat); Lively Arts, Colorado Real Estate, Home & Design, Perspective, Travel (S).

Magazines: Weekend Magazine (fri); TV/Cable Week, Empire Magazine, Comics (S).

Broadcast Affiliate: KUSA.

CORPORATE OFFICERS

President/Publisher Ryan McKibben
Exec Vice Pres/General Manager Kirk MacDonald
Vice Pres-Circulation Steve Hesse
Vice Pres-Finance/Chief Financial Officer Fritz Anderson
Vice Pres-Human Resources Jim Banman
Vice Pres-Marketing Vernon J Mallinen
Vice Pres-Production Frank Dixon
Vice Pres-Advertising Allen Walters
Vice Pres-Editorial Neil Westergaard

GENERAL MANAGEMENT

Manager-Credit Melinda Dolezal
Manager-Purchasing Kevin Yeaman

ADVERTISING

Vice Pres Allen Walters
Manager-National Gil Borelli

MARKETING AND PROMOTION

Manager-Promotion Tracy Ulmer

CIRCULATION

Manager-City Richard Bradley
Manager-Retention Jack Borland
Manager-Operations April Gauldin
Manager-State Pat O'Neill

NEWS EXECUTIVES

Exec Editor Neil Westergaard
Managing Editor Isabel Spencer
Assoc Editor Jeanette Chavez
Deputy Managing Editor-Photography Steve Larson
Deputy Managing Editor-Sunday Vince Bzdek

EDITORS AND MANAGERS

Art Director Leavett Biles
Automotive Editor John Eaton
Cartoonist Mike Keefe
Drama Editor Jeff Bradley
Editorial Page Editor Sue O'Brien
Education Editor Janet Bingham
Electronic Imaging Editor John Epperson
"Empire" Magazine Editor Edward Smith
Entertainment Editor Diane Carman
Environmental Editor Mark Obmascek
Farm/Agriculture Editor Janet Day
Fashion/Style Editor Francine Parnes
Features Editor Cynthia Pasquale
Films Columnist Howie Movshovitz
Food Editor John Kessler
Investigative Editor Lou Kilzer
Editorial Librarian Vicki Makings
Living/Lifestyle Editor Jeanette Chavez
Metro Editor Frank Scandale
Music Columnist Glenn Giffin
New Media Editor Todd Engdahl
Exec News Editor Jim Bates
Photo Assignment Editor John Sunderland
Political Editor Fred Brown
Radio/Television Editor Joanne Ostrow
Real Estate Editor Steve Raabe
Religion Editor Virginia Culver
Science/Technology Editor Dinah Zeiger
Society Editor Joanne Davidson
Exec Sports Editor Mike Connelly
Sports Editor Mike Bialas
State Editor Mark Harden
Systems Editor Bob Sheue
Travel Editor Mary Ellen Botter
TV Week Editor Giselle Massi
Washington Bureau Chief Adriel Bettelheim
Weekend Editor Tom Walker

PRODUCTION

Manager Larry Frakes
Manager-Newsprint Thomas Cooke
Manager-Pre Press Ric Soulen
Manager-Composing Larry Parks
Manager-Mailroom Derwood Christie
Manager-Pressroom Dan Armand
Manager-Facilities Glenn Vogel

Market Information: Split Run; TMC; Electronic edition.

Mechanical available: Offset; Black and 3 ROP colors; insert accepted — preprinted; page cutoffs — 22".

Mechanical specifications: Type page 13" x 21¼"; E - 6 cols, 2 1/16", ⅛" between; A - 6 cols, 2 1/16", ⅛" between; C - 10 cols, 1 3/16", 1/16" between.

Commodity consumption: Newsprint 61,200 short tons; 55,520 metric tons; widths 54¾", 41 1/16"; black ink 1,082,000 pounds; color ink 325,000 pounds; single pages printed 31,738; average pages per issue 72(d), 177(S); single plates used 235,000.

Equipment: EDITORIAL: Front-end hardware — SII/61 Tandem Risc; Front-end software — SII/Editorial, SII/MTX, SII/MTX Layout; Printers — Centronics/351, DEC/LA 180; Other equipment — Lf/AP Leaf Picture Desk, Bloomberg Financial, Ap/Macs, AP Select, PC with Internet Connections. CLASSIFIED: Front-end hardware — SII/55 Tandem TXP; Front-end software — SII/Classified, SII/Class Pagination; Printers — Centronics/351, DEC/LA 180, HP/LaserJet II. DISPLAY: Adv layout systems — Cx/Breeze; Front-end hardware — 10-Sun/Spacestation; Front-end software — Cx/Breeze; Printers — 1-LZR/26. PRODUCTION: Typesetters — 2-AU/APS-6 1085; Plate exposures — 1-WL/III, 1-NuGraphics, 2-Manual Thiemer; Plate processors — 2-WL/D-38, 1-NuGraphics; Electronic picture desk — Lf/AP Leaf Picture Desk, DIT/Line 303-820-1710; Scanners — QuarkXPress, 3-ECR/Autokon 1000; Production cameras — 1-C/Spartan, 1-C/Newspager; Automatic film processors — 4-LE/3-DS, 1-AG; Film transporters — LE, C; Shrink lenses — 1-Alan; Color separation equipment (conventional) — 1-CD/646, 1-CD/626.
PRESSROOM: Line 1 — 10-G/Headliner Offset; Line 2 — 10-G/Headliner Offset; Line 3 — 11-G/Headliner Offset; Pasters — 30-G/Auto; Reels and stands — 30-G; Press control system — G, G/MPCS-PCSII. MAILROOM: Counter stackers — 4-Id/660, 7-Id/2000; Inserters and stuffers — 1-S/48P, 1-HI/1372P, 1-HI/1472P; Bundle tyer — 11-MLN; Wrapping singles — Manual. LIBRARY: Electronic — 2-Mead Data Central/Nexis; Combination — 1-3M/500. WIRE SERVICES: News — AP, GNS, KRT, LAT-WP, NYT, States News Service, Bloomberg; Stock tables — AP Digital

Stocks; Syndicates — LATS, United Media, TMS, Chronicle, Columbia; Receiving dishes — size-3m, AP, INS. BUSINESS COMPUTERS: 2-HP/3000/960, HP/3000/950, HP/3000/917 LX; Applications: CJ: Accts payable, Gen ledger; PCs & main system networked.

Rocky Mountain News
(m-mon to sat; S)

Rocky Mountain News, 400 W. Colfax Ave., Denver, CO 80204; tel (303) 892-5000; fax (303) 892-2842. Scripps Howard group.
Circulation: 331,044(m); 331,044(m-sat); 436,079(S); ABC Sept. 30, 1995.
Price: 35¢(d); 35¢(sat); 75¢(S); $10.85/mo (mS).
Advertising: Open inch rate $213.50(m); $213.50(m-sat); $227.50(S). **Representative:** Sawyer-Ferguson-Walker Co.
News Services: AP, SHNS, RN, NNS, Deutsche Agency Presse. **Politics:** Independent. **Established:** 1859.
Advertising not accepted: All copy subject to publisher's approval.
Special Weekly Sections: Sports, Suburbs, Business Monday (mon); Business Tuesday, Suburbs (tues); Spotlight on Food, Suburbs (wed); Spotlight on Style, Suburbs (thur); Spotlight on Weekend, Business Friday, Sports-Western Adventure (fri); Automotive & Classified, Colorado Homes (sat); Travel, Las Noticias, Spotlight, TV Daily, Sunday Colorado Times, Careers & Classified, Colorado People (S).
Magazines: Spotlight (mon, tues, fri, sat); TV Dial, Colorado People, Parade, Spotlight, Color Comics (S); Food Fare (broadsheet).

CORPORATE OFFICER

President/CEO Larry D Strutton

GENERAL MANAGEMENT

Publisher Larry D Strutton
Vice Pres-Marketing/Sales Elizabeth Brenner
Vice Pres-Labor/Human Resources Dennis Dressman
Vice Pres-Operations Paul Gledhill
Vice Pres-Technology Info Service Daniel Persiani
Director-General Service John Hilton

ADVERTISING

Vice Pres-Advertising Jerry Dunning
Director-Classified Pat Manginelli
Director-Retail Rick Avery

MARKETING AND PROMOTION

Vice Pres-Marketing/Public Relations Linda Scasc
Director-Marketing Wendy Aro
Director-Research Matt Baldwin
Manager-Research Pamela Michener
Manager-National/New Business Susan Duchin
Manager-Malls/Special Sections Tricia Jorgensen

CIRCULATION

Vice Pres-Circulation Bruce Johnson
Director-Systems Development Lynda Hanshaw
Manager-Consumer Sales and Service Jack Denny
Manager-Metro Hugh McGarry
Manager-Education Service Steve Homolac

NEWS EXECUTIVES

Editor Robert W Burdick
Managing Editor John Temple
Deputy Managing Editor Jack McElroy
Deputy Managing Editor-Graphics Tom DeFeo
Editorial Page Editor Vincent Carroll
Assoc Editor Clifford May
Sunday Editor Linda Droeger
Projects Editor Chris Cubbison

EDITORS AND MANAGERS

Automotive Editor Dick Williamson
Books Editor Marge Carlin
Business Editor Don Knox
Columnist Gene Amole
Columnist Bill Husted
Dining/Wine Writer Bill St John
Editorial Cartoonist Ed Stein
Entertainment Editor Mike Pearson
Education Editor Christopher Broderick
Films Critic Robert Denerstein
Food Editor Marty Meitus
International Editor Holger Jensen
Lifestyle Editor Mary Winter
Metro Editor Deborah Gocken
Music Critic Mark Shulgold
Music Critic-Popular Michael Mehle
Outdoors Editor Ed Dentry
Photo Editor Janet Reeves
Political Columnist Peter Blake
Radio/Television Editor Dusty Saunders
Real Estate Writer John Rebchook
Religion Writer Jean Torkelson
Science Writer Joseph Verrengia
Sports Editor Barry Forbis
Sports Columnist Bob Kravitz
Sports Columnist Norm Clarke
Sports Columnist Mark Wolf
Style/Fashion Editor Suzanne Brown
State Editor Mike Anton
Suburban Editor Steve Krizman
Theater Critic Jackie Campbell
Travel Editor Mim Swartz

PRODUCTION

Manager-Dispatch Jim Davis
Manager-Platemaking Bob Sturms
Manager-Technical Service Dan Custard
Manager-Publishing Systems Dena Greenwalt
Foreman-Composing Dena Greenwalt
Foreman-Pressroom Mark Blancas
Foreman-Mailroom Doug Peper
Foreman-Composing Dena Greenawalt
Foreman-Pressroom Mark Blancas
Foreman-Mailroom Doug Peper

Mechanical available: Offset; Black and 3 ROP colors; insert accepted — preprinted; page cutoffs — 23⁹⁄₁₆".
Mechanical specifications: Type page 10⁵⁄₈" x 13¹⁵⁄₁₆"; E - 5 cols, 2¹⁄₁₆", ⅛" between; A - 5 cols, 2¹⁄₁₆", ⅛" between; C - 8 cols, 1¼", ¹⁄₁₆" between.
Commodity consumption: Newsprint 92,000 short tons; widths 58½", 43⅞", 29¼"; black ink 1,300,000 pounds; color ink 650,000 pounds; single pages printed 74,000; average pages per issue 185(d), 308(S); single plates used 600,000.
Equipment: EDITORIAL: Front-end hardware — Ap/Mac Quadras; Front-end software — AT, QPS. CLASSIFIED: Front-end hardware — AT; Front-end software — AT. AUDIOTEX: Hardware — PC/386; Software — Unix, Teravox; Supplier name — Target Technologies. DISPLAY: Adv layout systems — AT/Architect; Front-end hardware — III/AMS; Front-end software — III/AMS; Printers — VP300/proofers (Xerox engines); Other equipment — Rocky Mountain News/On-Line, AP AdSend. PRODUCTION: Pagination software — AT/Classified Pagination, III/Class Co-Processors, QPS; Typesetters — III/3810 Lasers, III/3850 Lasers, AG/SelectSet 5000; Plate exposures — WL; Plate processors — WL; Electronic picture desk — Lf/AP Leaf Picture Desk; Scanners — III, ECR/Autokon, Scitex, CD, Kk; Production cameras — Konica/Newspager, C/Spartan III; Automatic film processors — LE, P; Film transporters — LE, P; Color separation equipment (conventional) — III, Scitex, CD; Digital color separation equipment — Scitex.
PRESSROOM: Line 1 — 8-G/Colorliner; Line 2 — 8-G/Colorliner; Line 3 — 8-G/Colorliner; Line 4 — 8-G/Colorliner; Line 5 — 8-G/Colorliner; Line 6 — 8-G/Colorliner; Press drives — A/B; Folders — G; Pasters — G/CT-45; Reels and stands — G/CT-45; Press control system — G/APCs. MAILROOM: Counter stackers — 6-Fg/Multicell (5 lines); Inserters and stuffers — Fg/Drum 5 lines; Bundle tyer — PowerStrap; Wrapping singles — Id; Mailroom control system — Burt Technologies. LIBRARY: Electronic — Vu/Text, Datatimes, Newsbank. COMMUNICATIONS: Facsimile — CD/PageFax; Remote imagesetting — III/3850. WIRE SERVICES: News — AP; Photos — AP; Stock tables — AP, Deutsche Agency Presse, NNS, RN; Syndicates — SHNS; Receiving dishes — AP. BUSINESS COMPUTERS: IBM; PCs & micros networked; PCs & main system networked.

DURANGO
La Plata County

'90 U.S. Census- 12,430; **E&P '96 Est.** 13,961
ABC-CZ (90): 12,430 (HH 4,596)

Durango Herald
(m-tues to sat; S)

Durango Herald, 1275 Main Ave.; PO Drawer A, Durango, CO 81302-0950; tel (970) 247-3504; fax (970) 259-5011; e-mail herald-pj@csn.or6.
Circulation: 8,352(m); 8,352(m-sat); 10,488(S); ABC Sept. 30, 1995.
Price: 35¢(d); 35¢(sat); 75¢(S); $7.00/mo (carrier), $14.00/mo (mail); $74.00/yr (carrier), $168.00/yr (mail).
Advertising: Open inch rate $8.10(m); $8.10(m-sat); $9.75(S). **Representative:** Papert Companies.
News Services: AP, NYT, CNS. **Politics:** Independent-Republican. **Established:** 1881.
Note: Effective Apr. 4, 1995, this publication changed its publishing plan from (e-mon to fri; S) to (m-tues to sat; S).
Advertising not accepted: 900 phone numbers, prepay employment opportunity.
Special Editions: Focus on Business (Feb); Southwest Summer (Apr); County Fair (July); Southwest Winter (Oct); Christmas Gift Guide (Nov).
Special Weekly Sections: TV (tues); Business, Education (wed); The Good Earth, Religion (fri); Real Estate (S).
Magazines: USA Weekend (sat); Cross Currents (bi-monthly).

CORPORATE OFFICER

Board Chairman Morley C Ballantine

GENERAL MANAGEMENT

Publisher Richard G Ballantine
Purchasing Agent/Operations Manager Pat Jetton

ADVERTISING

Manager-Sales/Display Sharon Hermes
Manager-Class Pat Jetton

CIRCULATION

Manager Larry Shemely

NEWS EXECUTIVES

Editor Morley C Ballantine
Managing Editor Dan Partridge

EDITORS AND MANAGERS

Arts/Entertainment Editor Chas Langdon
Editorial Page Editor Bill Roberts
News Editor Lewis McCool
Regional Editor Electa Draper
Religion Editor Chas Langdon
Sports Editor John Peel

PRODUCTION

Manager Pat Jetton

Market Information: TMC.
Mechanical available: Offset; Black and 3 ROP colors; insert accepted — preprinted; page cutoffs — 22⅞".
Mechanical specifications: Type page 13" x 21"; E - 6 cols, 2.06", ⅛" between; A - 6 cols, 2.06", ⅛" between; C - 7 cols, 1.75", ⅛" between.
Commodity consumption: Newsprint 483 metric tons; widths 27.5", 13.75"; black ink 7,500 pounds; color ink 600 pounds; single pages printed 6,418; average pages per issue 16(d), 32(S); single plates used 4,184.
Equipment: EDITORIAL: Front-end hardware — 28-Pentium/90 486 PC; Front-end software — QuarkXPress; Printers — NewGen, XIT/Clipper, HP/4MV; Other equipment — Pre Press/Panther 34P Imagesetter, Lf/AP Leaf Picture Desk, Microtek/Scanmaker III. CLASSIFIED: Front-end hardware — 4-Pentium/90 486-PC; Front-end software — QuarkXPress; Printers — TI/500, XIT/Clipper, NewGen; Other equipment — Pre Press/Panther 34P Imagesetter. DISPLAY: Adv layout systems — ACT; Front-end hardware — PC/486; Front-end software — Aldus/FreeHand, Aldus/PageMaker, QuarkXPress; Printers — HP/4MV, XIT/Clipper; Other equipment — Microtek/Scanmaker III. PRODUCTION: Pagination software — QuarkXPress; OCR software — TI/Omni Page; Typesetters — XIT/Clipper, HP/4MV; Plate exposures — 1-Nu; Electronic picture desk — Lf/AP Leaf Picture Desk; Production cameras — B; Automatic film processors — Kk.
PRESSROOM: Line 1 — 5-KP/Newsking single width, 1-Kp/Newsking; Folders — 6-KP. MAILROOM: Inserters and stuffers — KAN/480; Bundle tyer — MLN. LIBRARY: Electronic — SMS. WIRE SERVICES: News — AP; Syndicates — King Features, Universal Press, TMS; Receiving dishes — AP. BUSINESS COMPUTERS: PCs & micros networked; PCs & main system networked.

FORT COLLINS
Larimer County

'90 U.S. Census- 87,758; **E&P '96 Est.** 119,944
ABC-CZ (90): 87,758 (HH 33,689)

The Coloradoan
(m-mon to sat; S)

The Coloradoan, 1212 Riverside Ave.; PO Box 1577, Fort Collins, CO 80522; tel (970) 493-6397; fax (970) 224-7799. Gannett Co. Inc. group.
Circulation: 27,843(m); 27,843(m-sat); 34,627(S); ABC Sept. 30, 1995.
Price: 35¢(d); 35¢(sat); $1.00(S); $2.50/wk (carrier), $2.70/wk (motor route); $130.00/yr (carrier); $140.40/yr (motor route).
Advertising: Open inch rate $25.95(m); $25.95(m-sat); $29.90(S). **Representative:** Gannett National Newspaper Sales.
News Services: AP, GNS, LAT-WP, KRT. **Politics:** Independent. **Established:** 1873.
Advertising not accepted: 900 number personals; Locally brokered.
Special Weekly Sections: Best Food Day (wed); Entertainment Tab (fri).
Magazines: TV Week, USA Weekend (S).

CORPORATE OFFICERS

President Dorothy M Bland
Secretary Thomas L Chapple
Treasurer Lawrence P Gasho

GENERAL MANAGEMENT

Publisher Dorothy M Bland
Controller Ellen Freudenberg
Personnel Director Jean Paben

ADVERTISING

Director Bob Williams
Manager-Retail Sandy Powell
Manager-Classified Shirley Garcia

MARKETING AND PROMOTION

Director-Market Development Libby Rehm

CIRCULATION

Director Fred Foutz
Manager-Sales Craig Hester

NEWS EXECUTIVES

Exec Editor Dave Greiling
Assoc Editor John T Feeley

EDITORS AND MANAGERS

City Editor Mary Benanti
Editorial Page Editor Kathleen Duff
News Editor John T Feeley
Chief Photographer Michael Madrid
Sports Editor Sean Duff

MANAGEMENT INFORMATION SERVICES

Data Processing Manager Dan Searcy

PRODUCTION

Director Kevin R Johnson
Manager-Pressroom Keith Diamond
Manager-Mailroom Jesse Kirchmeier
Manager-Technical Service Robert Romine
Manager-Commercial Printing Marjorie Anderson
Manager-Pre Press Greg Howard

Market Information: TMC.
Mechanical available: Offset; Black and 3 ROP colors; insert accepted — preprinted; page cutoffs — 22¾".
Mechanical specifications: Type page 13" x 21½"; E - 6 cols, 2¹⁄₁₆", ⅛" between; A - 6 cols, 2¹⁄₁₆", ⅛" between; C - 9 cols, 1⅜", ¹⁄₁₆" between.
Commodity consumption: Newsprint 2,692 short tons; widths 27¼", 13⅛"; black ink 41,486 pounds; color ink 7,289 pounds; single pages printed 15,195; average pages per issue 36(d), 75(S); single plates used 61,926.
Equipment: EDITORIAL: Front-end hardware — 15-PC/386-20, 2-PC/386-33, 6-PC/486-20; Front-end software — Dewar/Editorial, Dewar/Layout, Dewar/Pagination; Printers — Okidata/2, Ap/Mac LaserWriter IIg; Other equipment — Ap/Mac graphic mode, Lf/AP Leaf Picture Desk. CLASSIFIED: Front-end hardware — 10-PC/386-20, 2-PC/386-33, PC/486-20; Front-end software — Dewar/Classified pagination; Printers — Okidata/1, Ap/Mac LaserWriter IIg. DISPLAY: Front-end hardware — 5-Ap/Mac Quadra 700, PC/386-33, 1-Ap/Mac Quadra 800, 1-AG/840; Front-end software — Multi-Ad/Creator 3.7; Printers — 1-Ap/Mac LaserWriter IIg, 1-Ap/Mac Pro 350; Other equipment — 1-AG/Scanner, Microtek/Scanner, AU/ Digital. PRODUCTION: Pagination software — Dewar 6.46; Typesetters — 2-V/4000, 2-V/5300E, 1-V/5510, V/5100 Autokon (digital), 2-AccuSet/1000; Plate exposures — 2-Nu/FT40UPNS; Plate processors — KFM/XPA-38; Electronic picture desk — Lf/AP Leaf Picture Desk; Lf/Leafscan 35; Scanners — Microtek; Production cameras — 1-C/Spartan III, C, DSA/620; Automatic film processors — 1-LE/LD2600A, 1-LE/PC1800, 1-LE/LD24AQ, 1-LE/LD24BQ; Film transporters — 1-C/Spartan III.
PRESSROOM: Line 1 — 17-G/Urbanite; Folders — 2-G/2:1; Pasters — 9-Enkel; Press control system — Fin. MAILROOM: Counter stackers — 3-PPK, 1-HL/Monitor, 1-HL/Stackpack, 1-MM/310-25, 2-QWI/351; Inserters and stuffers — GMA/SLS-1000A; Bundle tyer — 1-MLN/ML2E, 2-MLN/9LS, Sp/300, Sterling/MH-40; Addressing machine — 1-Ch, 1-Barstrom/(on-line); Other mailroom equipment

— MM/Fox. LIBRARY: Combination — Microfilm, Microfiche. COMMUNICATIONS: Digital ad delivery system — AP AdSend. WIRE SERVICES: News — GNS, AP, LAT-WP; Stock tables — AP; Syndicates — KRT; Receiving dishes — AP. BUSINESS COMPUTERS: IBM/9406 model; PCs & micros networked; PCs & main system networked.

FORT MORGAN

Morgan County

'90 U.S. Census- 9,068; E&P '96 Est. 9,741

Fort Morgan Times

(e-mon to sat)

Fort Morgan Times, 329 Main; PO Box 4000, Fort Morgan, CO 80701; tel (970) 867-5651; fax (970) 867-7448. Hollinger International Inc. group.

Circulation: 5,183(e); 5,183(e-sat); Sworn Oct. 3, 1995.

Price: 35¢(d); 35¢(sat); $9.00/wk; $77.00/yr.

Advertising: Open inch rate $8.74(e); $8.74(e-sat). **Representative:** Papert Companies.

News Service: AP. **Politics:** Republican. **Established:** 1884.

Not Published: Legal holidays.

Special Editions: Tax Edition, Chamber of Commerce, Soil Conservation (Jan); Earth Day, Car Care (Apr); Festival in the Park (July); Senior Citizen, Sports Preview (Sept); 4-H, Car Care (Oct); Pre Christmas Open House (Nov).

Special Weekly Section: TV Schedule (thur).

GENERAL MANAGEMENT

Publisher Robert W Spencer Jr
General Manager Robert W Spencer
Purchasing Agent Lee Knudson

ADVERTISING

Director Harold E Bohm
Manager-Classified Tammy Nelson

MARKETING AND PROMOTION

Manager-Promotion Harold E Bohm

CIRCULATION

Manager Tammy Nelson

NEWS EXECUTIVES

Editor Robert W Spencer Jr
Managing Editor Robert W Spencer

EDITORS AND MANAGERS

Automotive Editor Harold E Bohm
Books Editor Fern H Spencer
City/Metro Editor Bill Spencer
Editorial Page Editor Robert W Spencer Jr
Entertainment/Amusements Editor John LaPorte
Farm/Agriculture Editor Pamela Dickman
Fashion/Food Editor Fern H Spencer
Home Furnishings Editor Fern H Spencer
Living/Lifestyle Editor Fern H Spencer
Music Editor Fern H Spencer
National Editor Jerod Fiel
News Editor Robert W Spencer Jr
Photo Editor Dan Lassiter
Political/Government Editor Jerod Frel
Sports Editor John LaPorte

PRODUCTION

Foreman Lee Knudson
Foreman-Pressroom Wayne Wacker

Market Information: TMC.

Mechanical available: Offset; Black and 3 ROP colors; insert accepted — preprinted, ½ fold; page cut-offs — 21¼".

Mechanical specifications: Type page 13" x 21½"; E - 4 cols, 3¹⁄₁₆", ⅛" between; A - 6 cols, 2³⁄₁₆", ⅛" between; C - 6 cols, 2³⁄₁₆", ⅛" between.

Commodity consumption: Newsprint 236 short tons; widths 27½", 13¾"; black ink 5,200 pounds; color ink 290 pounds; single pages printed 5,360; average pages per issue 14(d); single plates used 4,564.

Equipment: EDITORIAL: Front-end hardware — 7-IBM/30 Mont & Boads, Mitsuba/Super Modern 2400; Printers — 1-Ap/Mac LaserWriter II, Mitsuba/Super Modern 2400. CLASSIFIED: Front-end hardware — 1-Ap/Mac Plus; Printers — Ap/Mac LaserWriter II. DISPLAY: Adv layout systems — 2-Ap/Mac Plus, 1-Murata/F-32 Fax; Front-end hardware — Ap/Mac Radius, CD-Rom; Front-end software — QuarkXPress; Printers — Ap/Mac LaserWriter II. PRODUCTION: Plate exposures — 1-Nu; Plate processors — 1-Nu/Sink; Production cameras — 1-R, B/Horizontal; Automatic film processors — P/24ML; Shrink lenses — CK Optical; Color separation equipment (conventional) — Light Table.

PRESSROOM: Line 1 — 6-G/Community; Line 2 — 6-G/Community; Folders — 1-G/2:1, 1-G/Community. MAILROOM: Inserters and stuffers — Manual; Bundle tyer — 1-Marlow/Mc; Addressing machine — AKI/Addressograph, AKI/Labeler, AKI/Electronic Labeler. WIRE SERVICES: News — AP; Receiving dishes — AP.

FRISCO

Summit County

'90 U.S. Census- 1,601; E&P '96 Est. 2,131

Summit Daily News

(m-tues to sat)

Summit Daily News, 120 N. 3rd Ave.; PO Box 329, Frisco, CO 80443; tel (970) 668-3998. Swift Newspapers group.

Circulation: 8,300(m); 8,300(m-sat); Sworn Jan. 23, 1995.

Price: Free.

Advertising: Open inch rate $8.65(m); $8.65(m-sat).

News Service: AP. **Established:** 1989.

Note: The Summit Daily News is printed at the Vail Daily Plant. For detailed commodity consumption, advertising & production, see Vail Daily listing. There is a combination rate of $9.50 between the Summit Daily News (m) and Vail Daily (mS).

Special Weekly Section: Real Estate (S).

Magazine: Summit Outdoors (sat).

GENERAL MANAGEMENT

Publisher Robert Brown

ADVERTISING

Manager Mike Kirschbaum

CIRCULATION

Manager Trish Barton

NEWS EXECUTIVES

Editor Kristin North
Weekend Editor Merideth Bloom

EDITOR AND MANAGER

Sports Editor Martin D Hamilton

MANAGEMENT INFORMATION SERVICES

Data Processing Manager A J Grande

PRODUCTION

Manager Nick Marquez
Manager-Pressroom Doug Barton

Market Information: TMC; ADS; Electronic edition.

Mechanical available: Offset; Black insert accepted — page cut-offs — 16¾".

Mechanical specifications: Type page 10⅝" x 16"; E - 5 cols, 2", ⅛" between; A - 5 cols, 2", ⅛" between; C - 5 cols, 2", ⅛" between.

Equipment: EDITORIAL: Front-end hardware — Ap/Mac; Front-end software — QuarkXPress, Adobe/Photoshop; Printers — Panther/3990 Imagesetters. CLASSIFIED: Front-end hardware — Ap/Mac; Printers — Ap/Mac Laser-Writer IIg; Other equipment — Ap/Mac. DISPLAY: Adv layout systems — Ap/Mac; Front-end hardware — Ap/Power Mac PC; Front-end software — QPS, Adobe/Illustrator, Adobe/Photoshop. PRODUCTION: Scanners — Kk, HP. PRESSROOM: Line 1 — 10-KP; Folders — KP/Quarter. MAILROOM: Inserters and stuffers — Manual; Bundle tyer — MLN. WIRE SERVICES: News — AP; Photos — AP; Stock tables — Bloomberg; Receiving dishes — Bloomberg, AP. BUSINESS COMPUTERS: Unix, PBS; PCs & micros networked; PCs & main system networked.

GLENWOOD SPRINGS

Garfield County

'90 U.S. Census- 6,561; E&P '96 Est. 9,393

Glenwood Post (m-mon to sat)

Glenwood Post, 2014 Grand Ave. (81601); PO Box 550, Glenwood Springs, CO 81602; tel (970) 945-8515; fax (970) 945-4487. Morris Communications Corp. group.

Circulation: 5,171(m); 5,171(m-sat); Sworn Sept. 20, 1995.

Price: 35¢(d); 35¢(sat); $8.25/mo; $99.00/yr.

Advertising: Open inch rate $7.25(m); $7.25(m-sat). **Representative:** Papert Companies.

News Service: AP. **Politics:** Independent. **Established:** 1890.

Not Published: New Year; Christmas.

Special Editions: Recreation (Feb); Summer Recreation Guides (May); Hunting (Oct); Holiday Kick-off (Thanksgiving) (Nov); Christmas (Dec).

Special Weekly Sections: Education (tues); Best Food Day (wed); Business (thur); Mountain Leisure (fri); Church (sat).

Magazines: Mountain Leisure (TV & Entertainment); Tourism Magazine (Feb).

CORPORATE OFFICER

President Paul Simon

GENERAL MANAGEMENT

Editor/Publisher Gary Dickson

ADVERTISING

Manager Bob Zanella

TELECOMMUNICATIONS

Audiotex Manager Suzie Evans

CIRCULATION

Manager Alice Nicholson

NEWS EXECUTIVE

Managing Editor Dennis Webb

EDITORS AND MANAGERS

Special Publications Editor Nan Johnson
Sports Editor Kent Mincer

MANAGEMENT INFORMATION SERVICES

Data Processing Manager Tammie Sherman

PRODUCTION

Manager Norm Hephner

Market Information: TMC; Operate audiotex.

Mechanical available: Offset; Black and 3 ROP colors; insert accepted — preprinted; page cut-offs — 22¾".

Mechanical specifications: Type page 13" x 21½"; E - 6 cols, 2¼", ⅙" between; A - 6 cols, 2¼", ⅙" between; C - 6 cols, 2¼", ⅙" between.

Commodity consumption: Newsprint 800 short tons; widths 28", 34"; black ink 10,000 pounds; color ink 1,800 pounds; single pages printed 5,000; average pages per issue 16(d); single plates used 2,500.

Equipment: EDITORIAL: Front-end hardware — Ap/Mac; Front-end software — QuarkXPress, Baseview/Extension; Printers — Ap/Mac Laser-Writers II NTX; Other equipment — Ap/Mac Scanner. CLASSIFIED: Front-end hardware — Ap/Mac IIsi; Front-end software — Baseview, QuarkXPress; Printers — Ap/Mac LaserWriter II NTX. AUDIOTEX: Hardware — Ap/Mac; Software — SMS. DISPLAY: Front-end hardware — Ap/Mac IIsi; Front-end software — Multi-Ad/Creator, QuarkXPress; Printers — Ap/Mac LaserWriter II GS; Other equipment — 2-Ap/Mac CD-Rom. PRODUCTION: Typesetters — MON/1270; Plate exposures — 1-Nu; Plate processors — P/Rapid Access; Production cameras — Acti; Automatic film processors — LE. PRESSROOM: Line 1 — 6-G/Community (w/upper former); Folders — G/2:1. MAILROOM: Bundle tyer — 1-Id, 1-OVL; Addressing machine — Automecha/Accufast, Intermountain. LIBRARY: Electronic — 1-SMS/Stauffer Gold. WIRE SERVICES: News — AP; Syndicates — Universal Press, United Media, Creators; Receiving dishes — size-3m, AP. BUSINESS COMPUTERS: Epson; Applications: Santa Cruz Group.

GRAND JUNCTION

Mesa County

'90 U.S. Census- 29,034; E&P '96 Est. 31,122

ABC-CZ (90): 81,747 (HH 32,230)

The Daily Sentinel

(e-mon to fri; m-sat; S)

The Daily Sentinel, 734 S. 7th St.; PO Box 668, Grand Junction, CO 81502; tel (970) 242-5050; fax (970) 241-6860. Cox Newspapers Inc. group.

Circulation: 30,298(e); 30,298(m-sat); 35,863(S); ABC Sept. 30, 1995.

Price: 35¢(d); 35¢(sat); $1.00(S); $2.25/wk; $117.00/yr (carrier), $156.00/yr (mail).

Advertising: Open inch rate $24.24(e); $24.24(m-sat); $27.63(S). **Representative:** Cresmer, Woodward, O'Mara & Ormsbee.

News Services: AP, Cox News Service, NYT (Pony). **Politics:** Independent. **Established:** 1893.

Special Editions: Financial and Tax Tips, Wedding, Coupon Book (Jan); Indoor Remodeling (Feb); Progress, Ads by Kids, Rookies, Coupon Book (Mar); Home & Gardens, Car Care, Food and Fitness (Apr); Vacation Travel, Juco, Coupon Book (May); Fishing, Country Jam USA (June); Mesa County Fair, Coupon Book (July); Back-to-School, Football (Aug); Coupon Book, Hunting (Sept); Home Improvement, Car Care (Oct); Gift Book, Coupon Book (Nov); Late Shopper's Guide (Dec).

Special Weekly Sections: Best Food Day (wed); Out & About (thur); What's On (fri); Religion (sat).

Magazine: Parade.

CORPORATE OFFICERS

President George Orbanek
Exec Secretary June Reems
Treasurer Larry J DeGolyer

GENERAL MANAGEMENT

Editor/Publisher George Orbanek
General Manager Larry J DeGolyer

ADVERTISING

Director Dennis Mitchell

MARKETING AND PROMOTION

Director-Marketing/Promotion Bill Pewters

CIRCULATION

Manager Bud Windslo

NEWS EXECUTIVE

Managing Editor Dennis Herzog

EDITORS AND MANAGERS

Action Line Editor Michelle Willits
Business Writer Ginger Rice
City Editor Gary Harmon
Editorial Page Editor Bob Silbernagel
Entertainment/Amusements Editor Michelle Willits
Environmental Editor Gary Harmon
Farm/Agriculture Editor Gary Harmon
Fashion/Style Editor Michelle Willits
Features Editor Michelle Willits
Graphics Editor/Art Director Robert Garcia
Health/Medical Editor Michelle Willits
News Editor Steve Stoud
Photo Editor Christopher Tomlinson
Political Writer Gary Harmon
Religion Editor Gary Harmon
Sports Editor Rick M Jussel
Theater/Music Editor Michelle Willits
Travel Editor Michelle Willits

PRODUCTION

Foreman-Composing Sharon Craig
Foreman-Pressroom Vernon Langford

Market Information: Split Run.

Mechanical available: Offset; Black and 3 ROP colors; insert accepted — preprinted; page cut-offs — 22".

Mechanical specifications: Type page 13" x 21"; E - 6 cols, 2", ⅛" between; A - 6 cols, 2¹⁄₁₆", ⅛" between; C - 9 cols, 1⁵⁄₁₆", ¹⁄₁₆" between.

Commodity consumption: Newsprint 2,850 short tons; widths 54", 40½", 27"; single pages printed 11,400; average pages per issue 28(d), 44(S).

Equipment: EDITORIAL: Front-end hardware — Ap/Mac; Front-end software — DTI. CLASSIFIED: Front-end hardware — Ap/Mac; Front-end software — DTI. AUDIOTEX: Supplier name — Micro Voice. DISPLAY: Adv layout systems — Ap/Mac; Front-end hardware — Ap/Mac; Front-end software — DTI. PRODUCTION: Typesetters — 2-Ag/9800; Plate exposures — 1-BKY; Plate processors — 1-Nat/A250; Electronic picture desk — Ap/Mac; Color separation equipment (conventional) — Ap/Mac, DTI; Digital color separation equipment — Ap/Mac, DTI.

PRESSROOM: Line 1 — 5-G/Headliner; Folders — 2-G/2:1. MAILROOM: Counter stackers — 1-Id/660; Inserters and stuffers — 2-MM/(5 to 1); Bundle tyer — 1-CYP/RTV-7-600. WIRE SERVICES: News — AP; Receiving dishes — AP. BUSINESS COMPUTERS: HP/927; Applications: CJ: Circ, General ledger, Accts payable.

GREELEY

Weld County

'90 U.S. Census- 60,536; E&P '96 Est. 71,000

ABC-CZ (90): 71,385 (HH 26,547)

Greeley Tribune

(e-mon to fri; m-sat; S)

Greeley Tribune, PO Box 1138, Greeley, CO 80631; tel (970) 352-0211; fax (970) 356-5780. Swift Newspapers group.

Circulation: 22,798(e); 22,798(m-sat); 23,446(S); ABC Sept. 30, 1995.

Price: 50¢(d); 50¢(sat); 75¢(S); $8.75/mo; $99.00/yr (carrier/mail).

Advertising: Open inch rate $17.55(e); $17.55(m-sat); $17.55(S).

News Service: AP. **Politics:** Independent. **Established:** 1870.

Advertising not accepted: Vending machines; Fortune telling.
Special Editions: Panorama (Mar); Rodeo (June); Stampede Edition (July); Click (Oct).
Special Weekly Sections: People/Senior (tues); People/Senior, Preview TV/Entertainment (thur); Religion (fri); Education (sat); Real Estate, Financial, Agriculture and Business (S); Financial, Entertainment, Sports (daily).
Magazines: Agri Business (tues); Food (wed); Home & Garden (thur); TV & Entertainment (S).

CORPORATE OFFICER

President Richard K Larson

GENERAL MANAGEMENT

Publisher David G Trussell

ADVERTISING

Director John Walker

CIRCULATION

Director Laura Sweep

EDITORS AND MANAGERS

Action Line Editor Mike Peters
City Editor Randall Bangert
Asst City Editor Barry Smith
Farm/Agriculture Editor Bill Jackson

MANAGEMENT INFORMATION SERVICES

Data Processing Manager Carol Veatch

PRODUCTION

Manager Charles Largent
Foreman-Pressroom Mike Meeker

Market Information: Zoned editions; TMC.
Mechanical available: Offset; Black and 3 ROP colors; insert accepted — preprinted; page cutoffs — 22¾".
Mechanical specifications: Type page 13" x 21½"; E - 6 cols, 2 1/16", ⅛" between; A - 6 cols, 2 1/16", ⅛" between; C - 9 cols, 1½", ⅛" between.
Commodity consumption: Newsprint 1,624 metric tons; width 27½"; black ink 32,800 pounds; color ink 9,000 pounds; single pages printed 12,763; average pages per issue 28(d), 44(S).
Equipment: EDITORIAL: Front-end hardware — Ap/Mac IIci, Ap/Mac SE30, Ap/Mac Classic; Front-end software — QuarkXPress, Baseview; Printers — Ap/Mac LaserWriter IIg. CLASSIFIED: Front-end hardware — Ap/Mac SE30, Ap/Mac IIci; Front-end software — Fourth Dimension. DISPLAY: Adv layout systems — Ap/Mac II; Front-end hardware — Ap/Mac II, Ap/Mac SE30; Front-end software — QuarkXPress; Printers — Ap/Mac LaserWriter IIg. PRODUCTION: Pagination software — QuarkXPress; OCR software — TextBridge; Typesetters — Tegra/Varityper, 2-Panther Plus; Plate exposures — 1-Nu; Plate processors — 1-Nat/A250; Electronic picture desk — Lf/AP Leaf Picture Desk; Scanners — Polaroid/Sprint Scan, HP/Color; Production cameras — SCREEN; Automatic film processors — 1-P, 1-DP; Digital color separation equipment — Ap/Mac with Photoshop, Tegra/Varityper Imagesetter.
PRESSROOM: Line 1 — 10-G/Urbanite; Folders — 2-G. MAILROOM: Counter stackers — 2-BG; Inserters and stuffers — 2-KAN/480 (5-to-1); Bundle tyer — MLN; Addressing machine — 1-Ch. LIBRARY: Electronic — Commodore. WIRE SERVICES: News — AP Datastream, AP Datafeatures. BUSINESS COMPUTERS: Sun/Spare Server 670 mp; Applications: PBS: Adv, Circ, Gen accounting; PCs & micros networked; PCs & main system networked.

GUNNISON

Gunnison County

'90 U.S. Census- 4,136 E&P '96 Est. 5,141

The Gunnison Country Times (m-tues to sat)

Gunnison Country Times, 218 N. Wisconsin; PO Box 240, Gunnison, CO 81230; tel (303) 641-1414; fax (303) 641-6515. Ventana Publishing group.
Circulation: 3,800(m); 3,800(m-sat); Estimate Sept. 26, 1995.
Price: 25¢(d); 25¢(sat); $48.00/yr.
Advertising: Open inch rate $6.00(m); $6.00(m-sat). **Established:** 1993.
Special Editions: Mountain Homes, Winter Fun (Jan); Benchmark Progress (Feb); Home & Garden (Apr); Summer Fun (June); Cattleman's Days, Mountain Homes, Summer Fun (July); Hunting, Summer Fun (Aug); Winter Fun (Nov).

GENERAL MANAGEMENT

Publisher Mike Ritchey
Publisher Tony Daranyi

ADVERTISING

Manager David Puddu

CIRCULATION

Manager Elyssa Mears

NEWS EXECUTIVE

Editor Steve Reed

PRODUCTION

Manager Kirsten Stanley
Manager-Press Tom McAndrews

LA JUNTA

Otero County

'90 U.S. Census- 7,637; E&P '96 Est. 7,385

La Junta Tribune-Democrat (e-mon to fri)

La Junta Tribune-Democrat, 422 Colorado Ave.; PO Box 480, La Junta, CO 81050; tel (719) 384-4475.
Circulation: 3,502(e); Sworn Sept. 30, 1992.
Price: 25¢(d); $4.00/mo (local); $62.00/yr (mail).
Advertising: Open inch rate $6.00(e).
News Service: AP. **Politics:** Independent. **Established:** 1897.
Not Published: New Year; Memorial Day; Independence Day; Labor Day; Thanksgiving; Christmas.
Special Editions: Progress (Jan); Spring Fashion (Apr); Kids Rodeo, Back-to-School (Aug); Christmas Shopping (Nov).
Magazine: This Week In La Junta (sat).

CORPORATE OFFICERS

President Wanda Lowe
Secretary John B Lowe

GENERAL MANAGEMENT

Publisher Wanda Lowe
General Manager Jack L Lowe

ADVERTISING

Director John B Lowe
Manager-Classified Adela Licano

CIRCULATION

Manager Barb Romujue

NEWS EXECUTIVE

Editor Wanda Lowe

EDITORS AND MANAGERS

Features Editor Rebecca McMullen
News Editor Wanda Lowe
Society Editor Wanda Lowe
Sports Editor Darian Dudruch

PRODUCTION

Manager Jack L Lowe

Market Information: TMC.
Mechanical available: Offset; Black and 3 ROP colors; insert accepted — preprinted; page cutoffs — 22¾".
Mechanical specifications: Type page 10 13/16" x 14¼"; E - 5 cols, 2 1/16", ⅛" between; A - 5 cols, 2 1/16", ⅛" between; C - 5 cols, 2 1/16", ⅛" between.
Commodity consumption: Newsprint 200 metric tons; widths 29", 14½"; black ink 6,900 pounds; color ink 420 pounds; single pages printed 4,364; average pages per issue 14(d).
Equipment: EDITORIAL: Front-end hardware — 5-Mk/4001. CLASSIFIED: Front-end hardware — 1-Mk/4001. DISPLAY: Adv layout systems — 2-COM/Powerview. PRODUCTION: Typesetters — 1-COM/2961, 1-COM/8400; Plate exposures — 1-Nu; Production cameras — 1-Acti; Automatic film processors — 1-P/24-ML. PRESSROOM: Line 1 — 1-G/Community; Folders — 1-G/2:1. MAILROOM: Bundle tyer — 1-Bu; Addressing machine — 1-KR. WIRE SERVICES: News — AP. BUSINESS COMPUTERS: 1-IMS/International; Applications: Gen ledger, Accts receivable, Accts payable, Payroll, Circ.

LAMAR

Prowers County

'90 U.S. Census- 8,343; E&P '96 Est. 9,323

The Lamar Daily News (e-mon to fri)

Lamar Daily News, 310 S. 5th; PO Box 1217, Lamar, CO 81052-1217; tel (719) 336-2266; fax (719) 336-2526. Hollinger International Inc. group.
Circulation: 3,012(e); Sworn Sept. 28, 1995.
Price: 50¢(d); $6.75/mo; $81.00/yr (tri-state area), $114.00/yr (outside area); $140.00/yr (out of country).
Advertising: Open inch rate $6.55(e).
News Service: AP. **Politics:** Independent-Democrat. **Established:** 1907.
Not Published: New Year; Memorial Day; Independence Day; Labor Day; Thanksgiving; Christmas.
Special Editions: Christmas; Progress; County Fair; Fall Sports; Winter Sports; Graduation.

CORPORATE OFFICERS

President Larry J Perrotto
Comptroller Roland McBride

GENERAL MANAGEMENT

Purchasing Agent Tom Betz

ADVERTISING

Director Sandy Leithty
Manager-Classified Darla Sanders

CIRCULATION

Manager Nikki Betz

NEWS EXECUTIVES

Editor Ava Betz
Managing Editor Tom Betz

EDITORS AND MANAGERS

Agricultural Editor John Contreras
Sports Editor John Contreras

PRODUCTION

Superintendent Ray Sanders

Market Information: TMC.
Mechanical available: Offset; Black and 3 ROP colors; insert accepted — preprinted, preprints accepted in tri-state trader; page cut-offs — 22¾".
Mechanical specifications: Type page 15⅙" x 21"; E - 6 cols, 2 1/16", ⅛" between; A - 6 cols, 2 1/16", ⅛" between; C - 6 cols, 2 1/16", ⅛" between.
Commodity consumption: Newsprint 110 short tons; widths 30", 15"; black ink 2,500 pounds; color ink 300 pounds; single pages printed 2,184; average pages per issue 8.5(d); single plates used 1,910.
Equipment: EDITORIAL: Front-end hardware — Ap/Mac; Front-end software — QuarkXPress; Printers — Ap/Mac LaserPrinter IIfx. CLASSIFIED: Front-end hardware — Ap/Mac; Front-end software — Baseview/Class Ad. DISPLAY: Adv layout systems — Multi-Ad/Creator; Front-end hardware — Ap/Mac. PRODUCTION: Pagination software — QuarkXPress 3.31; Plate exposures — 1-Nu/30x40; Production cameras — 1-B/1822; Shrink lenses — 1-CK Optical/6%.
PRESSROOM: Line 1 — 6-Web Leader. MAILROOM: Bundle tyer — 1-Bu, 1-Cyclops; Addressing machine — 1-St/1200. WIRE SERVICES: News — AP; Receiving dishes — size-3ft, AP. BUSINESS COMPUTERS: RSK/4000; Applications: File Pro 4.1; PCs & micros networked.

LONGMONT

Boulder County

'90 U.S. Census- 51,555; E&P '96 Est. 63,259
ABC-CZ (90): 51,555 (HH 19,570)

Daily Times-Call (e-mon to fri; m-sat; S)

Daily Times-Call, 350 Terry St. (80501); PO Box 299, Longmont, CO 80502; tel (303) 776-2244; fax (303) 678-8615; e-mail tcnews@rmii.com. Lehman Communications Corp. group.
Circulation: 20,393(e); 20,393(m-sat); 22,562(S); ABC Sept. 30, 1995.
Price: 25¢(d); 25¢(sat); 75¢(S); $11.00/mo (mail), $8.50/mo (rural), $8.25/mo (local); $132.00/yr (mail), $102.00/yr (rural), $99.00/yr (local).
Advertising: Open inch rate $15.59(e); $15.59(m-sat); $16.68(S). **Representatives:** Papert Companies; US Suburban Press; The Newspaper Network; Colorado Press Association.
News Service: AP. **Politics:** Independent. **Established:** 1871.
Special Editions: Financial Planning, Health Care (Jan); Longmont Magazine, Parenting Guide (Feb); Annual Community Review (Mar); Home Improvements, Car Care, Fashion, Senior Citizen (Apr); Vacation (May); Longmont Magazine (June); Health Care (July); Fair & Rodeo, Back-to-School, Football (Aug); Literacy Tab (Sept); Home Improvement, Car Care, Senior Citizen, Longmont Magazine, Creative Kids (Oct); Holiday Traditions, Food & Entertainment (Nov); Gift Giving Catalog, Last Minute Gift Guide (Dec); Occasions (Bridal) (monthly).
Special Weekly Sections: Best Food Day (tues); Education (wed); Religion (fri); Home & Design, Outdoor (sat); Carousel (Kids), Travel, Business (S).
Magazines: Day & Night Arts & Entertainment Magazine, Coupon Book (thur); Real Estate (sat); Sunday Color Comics, TV Preview Magazine (S).

CORPORATE OFFICERS

Publisher Edward Lehman
President Dean G Lehman
Vice Pres/Treasurer Ruth G Lehman
Vice Pres-Administration Don Heath
Vice Pres-Finance Richard B Simmons
Director Lauren R Lehman

GENERAL MANAGEMENT

Publisher Edward Lehman
General Manager Mike Gugliotto

ADVERTISING

Director Linda Szaloczi
Manager-Display Karen Stenvall
Manager-Classified Penny Dille

MARKETING AND PROMOTION

Manager-Promotion Connie Coffield

TELECOMMUNICATIONS

Manager-Info Systems John Boone

CIRCULATION

Vice Pres Robert Cook
Manager-District Sean Cavanaugh
Manager-District H Carter Jones Jr
Manager-District Sally Hickman
Manager-District Shelly Morrell

NEWS EXECUTIVES

Editor Dean G Lehman
Managing Editor Keith Briscoe
Assoc Editor Ruth G Lehman

EDITORS AND MANAGERS

Design Director Eric Parker
Features Editor Joyce Davis
Graphics Editor Tom McKay
Local News Editor Pat Ferrier
News Editor John Vahlenkamp
Photo Editor David Harrison
Region Editor Alan Kirkpatrick
Special Sections Editor Andrea Holbrook
Sports Editor Jim Pedley

PRODUCTION

Vice Pres/Manager Dale Carr
Manager-Distribution Randy Sannes
Manager-Pre Press Susan Cappis
Supervisor-Press Don Kerr

Market Information: Zoned editions; Split Run; TMC.
Mechanical available: Offset; Black and 3 ROP colors; insert accepted — preprinted; page cutoffs — 22¾".
Mechanical specifications: Type page 13" x 21½"; E - 6 cols, 2 1/16", ⅛" between; A - 6 cols, 2 1/16", ⅛" between; C - 9 cols, 1⅜", ⅛" between.
Commodity consumption: Newsprint 1,682 metric tons; widths 27½", 13¾", 31", 34", 15½", 17"; black ink 62,853 pounds; color ink 7,390 pounds; single pages printed 15,953; average pages per issue 24(d), 50(sat), 68(S); single plates used 32,500.
Equipment: EDITORIAL: Front-end hardware — SIA/Workstations, Ap/Mac; Front-end software — Dewar/Sys IV; Printers — Ap/Mac LaserWriter NT, HP/LaserJet; Other equipment — 1-Lf/AP Leaf Picture Desk, Lf/Leafscan 35, Kk/RCS Scanner. CLASSIFIED: Front-end hardware — SIA/workstations; Front-end software — Dewar/Sys IV; Printers — Epson. DISPLAY: Adv layout systems — Dewar, Ap/Mac; Front-end hardware — Compaq, Ap/Mac; Front-end software — Dewar/Sys IV, Corel Draw, Adobe/Photoshop, Dewar/Ad Dummy, QuarkXPress, Adobe/Illustrator; Printers — HP/LaserJets; Other equipment — CD-Rom, HP/Scanner, AG/Scanner. PRODUCTION: Pagination software — Dewar Sys 4, QuarkXPress; Typesetters — 2-V/5300E, 1-V/5510, 1-HP/4MV; Plate exposures — Nu/Amerigraph, Nu/FT40APRNS; Plate processors — Nat/A-380; Electronic picture desk — Lf/AP Leaf Picture Desk; Scanners — Kk/RCS, Lf/Leafscan 35; Production cameras — C/Spartan III; Automatic film processors — AG/Super 260; Film transporters — C; Color separation equipment (conventional) — Ap/Mac Network; Digital color separation equipment — 1-ECR/Autokon 1000.
PRESSROOM: Line 1 — 8-G; Press drives — ABB; Folders — 1-G/Urbanite, 1-SU. MAILROOM: Counter stackers — Id/660, BG/Count-O-Veyor 108, HI, PPK; Inserters and stuffers

— GMA/SLS 1000; Bundle tyer — MLN/MLNEE; Addressing machine — Ch/525-E; Other mailroom equipment — Mc/Stitch Trim. LIBRARY: Electronic — SMS/Stauffer Gold. COMMUNICATIONS: Digital ad delivery system — AP AdSend; Systems used — satellite. WIRE SERVICES: News — AP; Photos — AP; Stock tables — AP; Syndicates — LATS; Receiving dishes — AP. BUSINESS COMPUTERS: HP/3000 & 922LX; Applications: Vision Shift, Circ, Accts payable, Payroll, Adv, Gen ledger; PCs & micros networked; PCs & main system networked.

LOVELAND

Larimer County

'90 U.S. Census- 37,352; E&P '96 Est. 47,034
ABC-CZ (90): 37,352 (HH 14,049)

Loveland Daily Reporter-Herald (e-mon to fri; m-sat)

Loveland Daily Reporter-Herald, 201 E. 5th St.; PO Box 59, Loveland, CO 80537; tel (970) 669-5050. Lehman Communications Corp. group.

Circulation: 16,732(e); 18,066(m-sat); ABC Sept. 30, 1995.

Price: 35¢(d); 35¢(sat); $7.50/mo (home delivery), $7.75/mo (motor route), $10.00/mo (mail).

Advertising: Open inch rate $14.13(e); $14.13(m-sat). **Representative:** Papert Companies.

News Services: AP, LAT-WP. **Politics:** Independent. **Established:** 1879.

Special Editions: Loveland Guide, BBB (Jan); Celebrate February Coupon Book (Feb); Community Review, Senior Tab (Mar); Home & Garden, Colorado Home Week (Apr); Vacation Guide (May); Senior Tab (June); Business Window, BBB (July); Celebrate August, Back-to-School, Football (Aug); Fall Home Improvement, Coupon Book (Sept); BBB Tab, Our Creative Kids, Car Care (Oct); Cookbook, Christmas Gifting (Nov); Senior Tab (Dec); Coupon Book (monthly).

Special Weekly Sections: Business, Food Section (wed); School Page (fri); Entertainment, Religion, Business (sat); Community Sports (daily).

Magazine: Valley Window (TV entertainment tab) (sat).

CORPORATE OFFICERS

CEO Edward Lehman
President Dean G Lehman
Vice Pres/Secretary/Treasurer Ruth G Lehman
Director Lauren R Lehman

GENERAL MANAGEMENT

Publisher Edward Lehman
Assoc Publisher Ruth G Lehman
General Manager Robert B Rummel
Personnel Secretary Marjorie Reiber

ADVERTISING

Director Sally Lee

MARKETING AND PROMOTION

Manager-Marketing & Promotion Allison Lockwood

CIRCULATION

Manager John Michael Gunter

NEWS EXECUTIVES

Editor Robert B Rummel
Managing Editor Ken Amundson
Asst Managing Editor Troy Turner

EDITORS AND MANAGERS

City Editor Mark Humbert
Design Editor Mary Snow
Editorial Writer Lauren R Lehman
Editorial Writer Dean G Lehman
Editorial Writer Bob Rummel
Editorial Writer Ken Amundson
Education Editor Scott Yates
Librarian Juanita Cisneros
News Editor Mary Snow
Political Editor Janet Thayer
Regional Editor Phil Tardani
Sports Editor David Krause
Valley Life Editor Felicia Jordan
Valley Window Editor Phillis Walbye
Wire Editor Mary Snow

PRODUCTION

Superintendent-Composition Robert Black
Coordinator-Copy Flow Bill Schmich

Market Information: Split Run; TMC.

Mechanical available: Offset; Black and 3 ROP colors; insert accepted — preprinted, rotos; page cut-offs — 22¾".

Mechanical specifications: Type page 13" x 21½"; E - 6 cols, 2 1/16", ⅛" between; A - 6 cols, 2 1/16", ⅛" between; C - 9 cols, 1⅜", ⅛" between.

Commodity consumption: average pages per issue 36(d).

Equipment: EDITORIAL: Front-end hardware — Dewar; Other equipment — 1-Ap/Mac II, Lf/AP Leaf Picture Desk, Ap/Mac Quadra. CLASSIFIED: Front-end hardware — Dewar. DISPLAY: Adv layout systems — NEC; Front-end hardware — Ap/Mac SE, Dewar/Discovery. PRODUCTION: Typesetters — Tegra/Varityper; Production cameras — AG. MAILROOM: Bundle tyer — 1-Bu; Addressing machine — 1-El. LIBRARY: Electronic — SMS/Stauffer Gold. COMMUNICATIONS: Systems used — satellite, fiber optic. WIRE SERVICES: News — AP, LAT-WP; Receiving dishes — AP. BUSINESS COMPUTERS: 1-HP/3000; Applications: Circ, Payroll, Adv billing, Gen ledger; PCs & main system networked.

MONTROSE

Montrose County

'90 U.S. Census- 8,854; E&P '96 Est. 9,358

The Montrose Daily Press (e-mon to fri)

The Montrose Daily Press, 535 S. 1st St. (81401); PO Box 850, Montrose, CO 81402; tel (970) 249-3444; fax (970) 249-3331.

Circulation: 7,195(e); Sworn Sept. 23, 1994.

Price: 25¢(d); $54.00/yr (in state), $60.00/yr (outside state).

Advertising: Open inch rate $6.50(e).

News Service: AP. **Politics:** Independent. **Established:** 1908.

Not Published: New Year; Memorial Day; Independence Day; Labor Day; Thanksgiving; Christmas.

Special Editions: Brides Edition (Jan); Cook Off (Feb); Easter, St. Patrick's, Baseball, Home and Garden (Mar); Baseball (Apr); Graduation Edition, Mother's Day (May); Handgunner Shoot-off Championship, Father's Day (June); County Fair (July); Back-to-School (Aug); Home Improvement (Sept); Christmas (Nov).

Special Weekly Sections: Best Food Day, Best Real Estate, Best Automotive Day (wed); Best Real Estate, Best Automotive Day (fri).

CORPORATE OFFICER

President William Prescott Allen III

GENERAL MANAGEMENT

Publisher/General Manager William Prescott Allen III

ADVERTISING

Director Charles P Butterbaugh
Manager-Classified Wendy Sims

CIRCULATION

Director William Prescott Allen III

NEWS EXECUTIVE

Managing Editor Richard E Day

EDITOR AND MANAGER

Regional Editor Carol Stolns

PRODUCTION

Manager Dona Freeman

Market Information: Zoned editions; TMC.

Mechanical available: Offset; Black and 3 ROP colors; insert accepted — preprinted, full or part run, quarter folded; page cut-offs — 21½".

Mechanical specifications: Type page 13" x 21"; E - 6 cols, 2 1/16", ⅛" between; A - 6 cols, 2 1/16", ⅛" between; C - 8 cols, 1½", ⅛" between.

Commodity consumption: Newsprint 565 short tons; widths 28", 14"; average pages per issue 18(d); single plates used 6,000.

Equipment: EDITORIAL: Front-end hardware — 2-Mk; Other equipment — 1-Mk/Plus-2. CLASSIFIED: Front-end hardware — 2-Mk. DISPLAY: Adv layout systems — 1-Mk/(Terminal). PRODUCTION: Typesetters — Linotype-Hell/LaserWriter; Platemaking systems — 1-Nu/FT40V6U-PNS; Plate exposures — 1-Nu/FTHOV6U-PNS; Plate processors — Nat/A-250; Production cameras — 1-Nu/2024, 1-AG; Automatic film processors — 1-P/Pakonolith-24.

PRESSROOM: Line 1 — 6-HI/V-15A; Folders — 1-HI; Reels and stands — 6-Hs. MAILROOM: Bundle tyer — 2-Bu; Addressing machine — 1-St/1200. WIRE SERVICES: News — AP. BUSINESS COMPUTERS: 2-RSK/TRS 80, 2-RSK/1000 HD, 2-IBM; Applications: Bookkeeping, Circ, Bad debts, Zoning, Payroll, Inventory; PCs & micros networked; PCs & main system networked.

PUEBLO

Pueblo County

'90 U.S. Census- 98,640; E&P '96 Est. 100,223
ABC-CZ (90): 110,760 (HH 42,751)

The Pueblo Chieftain (m-mon to sat)
The Sunday Chieftain (S)

The Pueblo Chieftain, 825 W. Sixth St.; PO Box 4040, Pueblo, CO 81003; tel (719) 544-3520; fax (719) 546-3235.

Circulation: 50,995(m); 50,995(m-sat); 55,136(S); ABC Sept. 30, 1995.

Price: 25¢(d); 25¢(sat); 50¢(S); $1.85/wk; $8.00/mo; $96.00/yr.

Advertising: Open inch rate $41.35(m); $41.35(m-sat); $42.40(S). **Representative:** Cresmer, Woodward, O'Mara & Ormsbee.

News Service: AP. **Politics:** Independent-Republican. **Established:** 1872.

Special Editions: Senior Lifestyle I, Pueblo Area Economic Outlook (Jan); Health Horizons, Sport, Boat & Recreation Show (Feb); Pueblo Guide Book (Mar); Spring Home & Garden, Senior Lifestyle II (Apr); Car Care, Summer Fest, Classroom Chieftain (May); Women in Business, Senior Lifestyle III (June); Industry Overview (July); Colorado State Fair, Football (Aug); Fall Home Improvement (Sept); Fall Car Care, Senior Lifestyles IV (Oct); Winter Fest (Nov); Christmas Greetings (Dec).

Special Weekly Section: Best Food Day (wed).

Magazines: Pueblo (TMC) (thur); TV Magazine (sat); Parade (S).

CORPORATE OFFICERS

President Robert H Rawlings
Vice Pres Mary G Rawlings
Secretary Mary G Rawlings
Treasurer Robert H Rawlings

GENERAL MANAGEMENT

Publisher Robert H Rawlings
General Manager Barclay Jameson
Manager-Business Office Virginia Neal
Purchasing Agent Virginia Neal

ADVERTISING

Director-Marketing Jack Wyss
Manager-Retail Ron Folkers
Manager-General Service Dorothy Venditti
Manager-Classified Tammy Fern
Manager-Promotion Paulette Moore
Manager-Co-op Celina Garza

MARKETING AND PROMOTION

Director-Marketing/Promotion Jack Wyss

CIRCULATION

Director Marvin Laut

NEWS EXECUTIVES

Editor Robert H Rawlings
Managing Editor Leonard Gregory

EDITORS AND MANAGERS

Business John Norton
City Editor Marvin Read
City Editor Steve Henson
City Editor Chris Woodka
City Editor Larry Lopez
Editorial Page Editor Charles Campbell
Librarian Helene Spitzer
Lifestyle Editor Margie Wood
News Editor Jack Hildner
Photo Director Chris McLean
Radio/Television Editor Charles Campbell
Religion Editor Margie Wood
Sports Editor Judy Hildner

MANAGEMENT INFORMATION SERVICES

Manager-Info Service Phil Ruegg

PRODUCTION

Manager Ned Sutton
Foreman-Pressroom Ralph Garren
Foreman-Composing George Spitzer

Market Information: Split Run; TMC.

Mechanical available: Letterpress; Black and 3 ROP colors; insert accepted — preprinted; page cut-offs — 22¾".

Mechanical specifications: Type page 13" x 21½"; E - 6 cols, 2 1/16", ⅛" between; A - 6 cols, 2 1/16", ⅛" between; C - 9 cols, 1⅜", 1/16" between.

Commodity consumption: Newsprint 4,300 metric tons; widths 55", 41¼", 27½"; black ink 120,000 pounds; color ink 20,000 pounds; single pages printed 13,300; average pages per issue 34(d), 56(S); single plates used 32,000.

Equipment: EDITORIAL: Front-end hardware — HI/Pen Sys, 23-HI/PC, HI/PLS-8300, 5-HI/8860; Front-end software — Crosstalk; Printers — HP/LaserJet II; Other equipment — PC. CLASSIFIED: Front-end hardware — HI/8300, 10-HI/8864; Front-end software — HI/CPS software; Printers — Dataproducts/B600. DISPLAY: Adv layout systems — SCS/Layout 8000, HI/3800; Front-end hardware — 3-HI/8860, 1-HI/8900, IBM/PS2; Front-end software — HI/PLS-SCS; Printers — ALPS/P2100. PRODUCTION: Pagination software — HI/PLS 5.0; Typesetters — 2-MON/Lasercomp 100, 2-MAS; Platemaking systems — Na; Plate processors — Na/NP80, Na/NP20; Electronic picture desk — Lf/AP Leaf Picture Desk; Scanners — 2-ECR/Autokon DE 1000; Production cameras — Co/Precision Camera 31", R/400 Precision Camera 19"; Automatic film processors — AG/Rapidline 43, LE/PC18, LE/LD24, AG/Litex 26; Color separation equipment (conventional) — Lf/AP Leaf Picture Desk.

PRESSROOM: Line 1 — 6-H/Color Convertible; Pasters — Automatic Pasters; Reels and stands — H; Press control system — Fin/3 phase DC controllers; Press registration system — K&F. MAILROOM: Counter stackers — 1-HL/Monitor, 2-HL/Dual Carrier; Inserters and stuffers — 2-HI/1372 R; Bundle tyer — 5-OVL/Typing Machine. LIBRARY: Electronic — SMS/Stauffer Gold; Combination — Minolta/Microfilm. COMMUNICATIONS: Digital ad delivery system — AP AdSend. WIRE SERVICES: News — AP Datastream, AP Datafeatures; Stock tables — AP SelectStox; Receiving dishes — AP. BUSINESS COMPUTERS: 1-IBM/RS6000, 1-IBM/Sys 36, 1-IBM/5225, 1-Decision Data/6708, 19-Dell/PC, 4-IBM/PC; Applications: Payroll, Circ, Accts payable, Retail billing, Class billing; PCs & micros networked; PCs & main system networked.

ROCKY FORD

Otero County

'90 U.S. Census- 4,162; E&P '96 Est. 3,837

Rocky Ford Daily Gazette (e-mon to fri)

Rocky Ford Daily Gazette, 912 Elm Ave.; PO Box 430, Rocky Ford, CO 81067; tel (719) 254-3351.

Circulation: 3,149(e); Sworn Sept. 30, 1994.

Price: 25¢(d); $4.00/mo; $60.00/yr (outside trade area).

Advertising: Open inch rate $4.25(e). **Politics:** Republican. **Established:** 1909.

Not Published: New Year; Memorial Day; Independence Day; Labor Day; Thanksgiving; Christmas.

Special Editions: Arkansas Valley Fair; Bridal; Progress; Christmas Cookbook; Agricultural Review; Spring & Winter Car Care.

Special Weekly Sections: Best Sports Days (mon); Best Food Days, Best Business Day (tues); Best Food Days (wed); Best Area Communities Reach (thur); Best Sports Days, Best Religious Day, Best Entertainment Day (fri).

Magazines: Recreation, Television (fri).

CORPORATE OFFICERS

President Anne Thompson
Secretary/Treasurer J R Thompson

GENERAL MANAGEMENT

Publisher Anne Thompson
Business Manager J R Thompson

ADVERTISING

Manager Laura Thompson

NEWS EXECUTIVE

Managing Editor J R Thompson

EDITOR AND MANAGER

News Editor Julie Malott

Mechanical available: Offset; Black and 3 ROP colors; insert accepted — preprinted; page cut-offs — 22¾".

Mechanical specifications: Type page 13" x 21"; E - 6 cols, 2 1/16", ⅛" between; A - 6 cols, 2 1/16", ⅛" between; C - 6 cols, 2 1/16", ⅛" between.

Commodity consumption: average pages per issue 34(d).

Equipment: EDITORIAL: Front-end hardware — Ap/Mac, Ap/Power Mac; Front-end software — Microsoft/Word, Aldus/SuperPaint, Aldus/PageMaker; Printers — Ap/Mac LaserWriter II NT, Ap/Mac LaserWriter Plus, HP/LaserJet 4V. CLASSIFIED: Front-end hardware — Ap/Mac; Front-end software — Microsoft/Word. DISPLAY: Adv layout systems — Ap/Mac; Front-end hardware — Ap/Power Mac; Front-end software — Aldus/PageMaker 6.0; BUSINESS COMPUTERS: Ap/Mac; Applications: Checkmark; PCs & micros networked.

SALIDA

Chaffee County

'90 U.S. Census- 4,737; E&P '96 Est. 4,824

The Mountain Mail

(m-mon to fri)

The Mountain Mail, 125 E. 2nd; PO Box 189, Salida, CO 81201; tel (719) 539-6691; fax (719) 539-6630. Arkansas Valley Publishing Co. group.

Circulation: 3,095(m); Sworn Sept. 30, 1994.

Price: 25¢(d); $44.00/yr.

Advertising: Open inch rate $5.55(m). **Representative:** Papert Companies. **Established:** 1880.

Not Published: Christmas.

Special Editions: Summer Fun; Fall Fun; Winter Fun; Directions; Visitor's Guide; Mountain Bike Guide.

CORPORATE OFFICERS

Publisher Merle Baranczyk
Vice Pres Sharon A Fatla
Secretary/Treasurer Mary Kay Baranczyk

GENERAL MANAGEMENT

Publisher Merle Baranczyk
Office Manager Karen Hasselbrink

ADVERTISING

Manager Vicki Vigil

CIRCULATION

Manager Joyce Loeffel

NEWS EXECUTIVE

Editor Merle Baranczyk

PRODUCTION

Foreman-Press Morris Christensen

Market Information: TMC.

Mechanical available: Offset; Black and 2 ROP colors; insert accepted — preprinted; page cut-offs — 15¾".

Mechanical specifications: Type page 10$^{13}/_{16}$" x 15¾"; E - 5 cols, 2", ⅛" between; A - 5 cols, 2", ⅛" between; C - 5 cols, 2", ⅛" between.

Commodity consumption: Newsprint 94 short tons; 215 metric tons; widths 27½", 33½"; black ink 2,000 pounds; color ink 100 pounds; single pages printed 3,640; average pages per issue 14(d); single plates used 1,500.

Equipment: EDITORIAL: Front-end hardware — Ap/Mac; Front-end software — QuarkXPress 3.31, Adobe/Photoshop 3.0, Adobe/Illustrator 5.0; Printers — Xante/8100, Xante/8200. CLASSIFIED: Front-end hardware — 2-Ap/Mac. DISPLAY: Adv layout systems — 2-Ap/Mac; Front-end hardware — Ap/Macs; Front-end software — QuarkXPress. PRODUCTION: Pagination software — QuarkXPress 3.31; Typesetters — 2-Ap/Mac; Platemaking systems — 1-Nu; Scanners — LaCie/Silver Scanner II, Polaroid/SprintScan; Production cameras — 1-Acti/183; Automatic film processors — 1-LE.
PRESSROOM: Line 1 — 7-G/Community; Folders — 1-G. MAILROOM: Addressing machine — 2-Wm. BUSINESS COMPUTERS: EPS; Applications: Synaptic: Accts receivable, Gen ledger, Subscriptions, Circ, Payroll; PCs & micros networked; PCs & main sys. networked.

STEAMBOAT SPRINGS

Routt County

'90 U.S. Census- 6,695; E&P '96 Est. 8,926

Steamboat Today

(m-mon to fri)

Steamboat Today, PO Box 774827, Steamboat Springs, CO 80477-4827; tel (970) 879-1502; fax (970) 879-2888. WorldWest Limited Liability Co. group.

Circulation: 6,135(m); Sworn Sept. 22, 1994.

Price: Free.

Advertising: Open inch rate $8.25(m). **Established:** 1989.

Special Editions: Working Women; Business.

GENERAL MANAGEMENT

Publisher Suzanne Antinoro

ADVERTISING

Manager Sandy Lettunich

NEWS EXECUTIVES

Editor Keith Kramer
Manager Tom Ross

PRODUCTION

Director Lisa Present

Mechanical available: Offset; Black and 1 ROP color.

Mechanical specifications: Type page 10½" x 17"; E - 4 cols, 14"; A - 4 cols, 14"; C - 4 cols, 14".

Commodity consumption: average pages per issue 16(d).

Equipment: EDITORIAL: Front-end hardware — IBM. CLASSIFIED: Front-end hardware — IBM. DISPLAY: Adv layout systems — IBM.

STERLING

Logan County

'90 U.S. Census- 10,362; E&P '96 Est. 9,966

Journal-Advocate

(e-mon to sat)

Journal-Advocate, 504 N. 3rd St.; PO Box 1272, Sterling, CO 80751; tel (970) 522-1990; fax (970) 522-2320. Hollinger International Inc. group.

Circulation: 5,168(e); 5,168(e-sat); Sworn Oct. 5, 1995.

Price: 50¢(d); 50¢(sat); $6.25/mo; $71.00/yr (carrier).

Advertising: Open inch rate $9.24(e); $9.24(e-sat). **Representative:** Papert Companies.

News Service: AP. **Politics:** Independent. **Established:** 1884.

Not Published: New Year; Memorial Day; Independence Day; Labor Day; Thanksgiving; Christmas.

Advertising not accepted: Adoptions.

Special Editions: Progress (Mar); Rodeo & Fair, Welcome Jr College Students (Aug); Christmas Greetings (Dec).

Special Weekly Sections: Lifestyles, Agriculture (tues); Food, Lifestyles (wed); Entertainment, Lifestyles (thur); Religion, Business (fri); Television (sat).

CORPORATE OFFICER

Publisher William H Muldoon III

GENERAL MANAGEMENT

Business Manager Julie Tonsing

ADVERTISING

Director Myron House

CIRCULATION

Manager Steve Schneckloth

NEWS EXECUTIVE

Editor Jeff Rice

EDITORS AND MANAGERS

Agriculture Editor Donovan Henderson
Sports Editor Don Miles
Women's Editor Carol Bennett

PRODUCTION

Superintendent Duane Miles
Superintendent-Composing Duane Miles

Market Information: TMC.

Mechanical available: Offset; Black and 3 ROP colors; insert accepted — preprinted, consumer product samples; page cut-offs — 22¾".

Mechanical specifications: Type page 13" x 21½"; E - 6 cols, 2.08", .75" between; A - 6 cols, 2.08", .75" between; C - 9 cols, 1.33", .75" between.

Commodity consumption: Newsprint 206 short tons; width 27½"; average pages per issue 12(d), 20(sat).

Equipment: EDITORIAL: Front-end hardware — Ap/Mac, Ap/Mac Quadra 600; Front-end software — Baseview/NewsEdit, QuarkXPress; Printers — Ap/Mac LaserWriter Plus, Ap/Mac II NTX, HP/LaserJet 4MV. CLASSIFIED: Front-end hardware — Ap/Mac; Front-end software — Baseview; Printers — Ap/Mac LaserWriter Plus, Ap/Mac ImageWriter. DISPLAY: Adv layout systems — Ap/Mac II; Front-end hardware — Ap/Mac; Front-end software — QuarkXPress, Multi-Ad/Creator; Printers — Ap/Mac LaserWriter II NTX; Other equipment — CD-Rom/Reader. PRODUCTION: Typesetters — Ap/Mac LaserWriter II NTX, HP/LaserJet 4MV; Plate exposures — Nu; Plate processors — Roconex/Iconomatic; Production cameras — 1-Acti/125; Automatic film processors — 1-P/24ML.
PRESSROOM: Line 1 — 6-G/Community Offset (24 Page/Broadsheet Capacity); Press control system — Fin. MAILROOM: Bundle tyer — 1-Bu; Addressing machine — Dispensa-Matic. LIBRARY: Combination — Hard cover bound papers. WIRE SERVICES: News — AP. BUSINESS COMPUTERS: IBM; Applications: Nomads/Listmaster.

TELLURIDE

San Miguel County

'90 U.S. Census- 1,339 E&P '96 Est. 2,035

Telluride Daily Planet

(m-mon to fri)

Telluride Daily Planet, 283 S. 1st St.; PO Box 2315, Telluride, CO 81435; tel (970) 728-9788; fax (970) 728-9793; e-mail tdplanet@aol.com; web site http://telluridegateway.com/. Ventana Publishing group.

Circulation: 3,300(m); Sworn Dec. 7, 1995.

Price: Free; $29.00/yr. **Established:** 1993.

Note: This publication is being printed by Cortez Newspapers in Cortez, CO.

CORPORATE OFFICERS

President Mike Ritchey
Secretary Tony Daranyi

GENERAL MANAGEMENT

Publisher Mike Ritchey
Publisher Tony Daranyi
Manager-Office Joni Kozlovski

ADVERTISING

Director John Dourlet

TELECOMMUNICATIONS

Audiotex Manager Audrey Cooper

CIRCULATION

Manager Tom May

NEWS EXECUTIVE

Editor Bob Beer

TRINIDAD

Las Animas County

'90 U.S. Census- 8,580; E&P '96 Est. 8,079
ABC-CZ (90): 8,580 (HH 3,410)

The Chronicle-News

(e-mon to fri)

The Chronicle-News, 200 Church & Convent St.; PO Box 763, Trinidad, CO 80182; tel (719) 846-3311; fax (719) 846-3612. Shearman Newspapers group.

Circulation: 3,524(e); ABC Sept. 30, 1995.

Price: 25¢(d); $44.00/yr (outside county), $42.00/yr (in county).

Advertising: Open inch rate $4.70(e).

News Service: AP. **Politics:** Independent. **Established:** 1877.

Not Published: Christmas.

Special Editions: Rodeo; Christmas; Hunting; Spring Tourism.

CORPORATE OFFICERS

President/Publisher Tom Shearman
Exec Vice Pres William A Shearman

GENERAL MANAGEMENT

Manager Cosette Henritze

ADVERTISING

Director Cosette Henritze

CIRCULATION

Director Bernice Lucero

NEWS EXECUTIVE

Managing Editor Cosette Henritze

EDITORS AND MANAGERS

Features Editor Janet Malin
Sports Editor Jon Pompia

Market Information: Split Run; TMC.

Mechanical available: Offset; and 1 ROP color; insert accepted — preprinted; page cut-offs — 22¾".

Mechanical specifications: Type page 13" x 22"; E - 6 cols, 2$^{1}/_{16}$", ⅛" between; A - 6 cols, 2$^{1}/_{16}$", ⅛" between; C - 8 cols, 1½", ⅛" between.

Commodity consumption: Newsprint 44 short tons; widths 27½", 13¾"; black ink 1,800 pounds; color ink 50 pounds; average pages per issue 8(d).

Equipment: DISPLAY: Adv layout systems — 1-Ap/Mac. PRODUCTION: Typesetters — 1-COM/Videosetter; Plate exposures — 1-Nu; Production cameras — 1-R/500.
PRESSROOM: Line 1 — 2-KP/Color King. MAILROOM: Addressing machine — 1-Am. WIRE SERVICES: News — AP; Receiving dishes — size-2ft, AP. BUSINESS COMPUTERS: PCs & micros networked.

VAIL

Eagle County

'90 U.S. Census- 3,659; E&P '96 Est. 3,914

Vail Daily News

(m-mon to sat; S)

Vail Daily, 143 E. Meadow Dr.; PO Box 81, Vail, CO 81658; tel (970) 476-0555; fax (970) 476-5268; e-mail vaildaily@realinfo.com; web site http://www.vaildaily.com/vail. Swift Newspapers group.

Circulation: 12,125(m); 12,125(m-sat); 12,125(S); Sworn Jan. 23, 1995.

Price: Free.

Advertising: Open inch rate $8.85(m); $8.85(m-sat); $8.85(S).

News Service: AP. **Established:** 1981.

Note: There is a combination rate between the Vail Daily (mS) and Frisco Summit Daily News (mS) for $9.50.

Magazines: Peak Magazine (sat); Mountain Homes and Properties (S).

GENERAL MANAGEMENT

Publisher Robert Brown
Manager-Business Office Rob Schultheis

ADVERTISING

Director Valerie Smith

CIRCULATION

Manager Trish Barton

NEWS EXECUTIVE

Editor Rob Spencer

PRODUCTION

Manager Kurt Desautels
Foreman-Press Doug Barton

Market Information: TMC.

Mechanical available: Offset; Black and 3 ROP colors; insert accepted — preprinted; page cut-offs — 22¾".

Mechanical specifications: Type page 10⅔" x 16"; E - 5 cols, 2", ⅙" between; A - 5 cols, 2", ⅙" between; C - 5 cols, 2", ⅙" between.

Commodity consumption: Newsprint 750 metric tons; width 33.5"; black ink 5,000 pounds; color ink 250 pounds; average pages per issue 48(d), 52(S); single plates used 3,000.

Equipment: EDITORIAL: Front-end hardware — Ap/Mac; Front-end software — Baseview; Printers — Ap/Mac LaserWriter. CLASSIFIED: Front-end hardware — PC; Front-end software — DTI; Printers — HP. DISPLAY: Front-end hardware — Ap/Mac; Front-end software — QuarkXPress, Adobe; Printers — Ap/Mac LaserPrinter. PRODUCTION: Production cameras — AG.
PRESSROOM: Line 1 — 10-KP/Newsking; Folders — 1-KJ/8. WIRE SERVICES: News — AP; Syndicates — Universal Press, United Media, King Features, LATS, TMS.

CONNECTICUT

BRIDGEPORT

See FAIRFIELD COUNTY

BRISTOL

Hartford County

'90 U.S. Census- 61,644; E&P '96 Est. 63,096
ABC-CZ (90): 66,066 (HH 26,099)

The Bristol Press

(all day-mon to sat)

The Bristol Press, 99 Main St.; PO Box 2158, Bristol, CT 06011-2158; tel (860) 584-0501; fax (860) 584-2192. Journal Register Co. group.

Circulation: 20,036(a); 20,036(a-sat); ABC Sept. 30, 1995.

Price: 50¢(d); 50¢(sat); $2.40/wk; $124.80/yr.

Advertising: Open inch rate $20.65(a); $20.65 (a-sat).

News Service: AP. **Politics:** Independent. **Established:** 1871.

Special Editions: Bridal (Jan); Home Show (Feb); Business & Industry Review (Mar); Bridal, Health & Medicine, Home Improvement (Apr); Balloons Over Bristol, Summertime (May); Bridal, Health (June); Back-to-School (Aug); Health (Oct); Gift Guide (Nov); Holiday Celebration (Dec).
Special Weekly Sections: Women (mon); Health (tues); Focus (wed); Tempo (dining guide) (thur); Food (fri); Prime Time, Mini Page, Religion, Real Estate (sat); Business Page, Full Stock Listings (daily).
Magazines: Automotive (fri); USA Weekend (sat).

CORPORATE OFFICERS

President/CEO Robert M Jelenic
Exec Vice Pres/Chief Financial Officer/Treasurer Jean B Clifton

GENERAL MANAGEMENT

Publisher James F Normandin
General Manager Michael R Vanacore
Controller Joseph Mangiameli

ADVERTISING

Director Louis Camporeale

CIRCULATION

Director Jim Clouse

NEWS EXECUTIVE

Editor Robert E Brown

EDITORS AND MANAGERS

Books Editor William Sarno
City Editor Suzanne Simoneau
Editorial Page Editor William Sarno
Education Editor Loretta Waldman
Graphics Editor/Art Director Randy Flaum
Librarian Virginia Rogers
News Editor Doug Hardy
Photo Editor Randy Flaum
Political Editor Steve Collins
Religion Editor Linda Smith
Sports Editor Keith Freeman
Suburban Editor Linda Smith
Teen-Age/Youth Editor Linda Smith
Women's Editor Maureen Hamel

PRODUCTION

Manager-Pre Press James Bousquet
Manager-Systems Jeff Cooper

Market Information: TMC.
Mechanical available: Offset; Black and 3 ROP colors; insert accepted — preprinted; page cutoffs — 22¾".
Mechanical specifications: Type page 13" x 21½"; E - 6 cols, $2\frac{1}{16}$", ⅛" between; A - 6 cols, $2\frac{1}{16}$", ⅛" between; C - 9 cols, 1⅜", $\frac{1}{16}$" between.
Commodity consumption: Newsprint 1,200 short tons; width 27½"; black ink 5,000 pounds; color ink 1,000 pounds; single pages printed 8,200; average pages per issue 28(d); single plates used 10,590.
Equipment: EDITORIAL: Front-end hardware — 18-COM/One Sys w/18 workstation; Front-end software — COM/One Sys; Printers — TI. CLASSIFIED: Front-end hardware — COM/One Sys w/4 workstations; Front-end software — COM/One Sys; Printers — TI. DISPLAY: Front-end hardware — 6-Ap/Mac cx, Ap/Mac ci, Ap/Mac Classic, 1-Ap/Mac SE; Front-end software — Multi-Ad; Other equipment — HP/ScanJet, NewGen/660B. PRODUCTION: Typesetters — NewGen/PS-480; Plate exposures — Burgess/5K3343, 2-Consolux; Plate processors — Nat/Super A-250; Production cameras — C/Spartan II, ECR/8400 Autokon II, AG/Repromaster 2000; Automatic film processors — AG/Lith 26; Film transporters — 24-SQ; Shrink lenses — FLEXCO/Squeeze lens, C/Spartan III. WIRE SERVICES: News — AP; Receiving dishes — AP. BUSINESS COMPUTERS: HP/3000; Applications: CJ: Ad mgmt, Payroll, Circ; INSI: AP/GL; PCs & main system networked.

DANBURY

Fairfield County

'90 U.S. Census- 66,988; **E&P '96 Est.** 69,744
ABC-CZ (90): 83,126 (HH 30,269)

The News-Times

(m-mon to sat; S)

The News-Times, 333 Main St., Danbury, CT 06810; tel (203) 744-5100; web site http://www.danbury.lib.ct.us/media/news/. Ottaway Newspapers Inc. group.
Circulation: 37,371(m); 37,371(m-sat); 44,882(S); ABC Sept. 30, 1995.
Price: 50¢(d); 50¢(sat); $1.50(S).
Advertising: Open inch rate $28.08(m); $28.08(m-sat); $29.79(S). **Representative:** Landon Associates Inc.
News Services: AP, DJ, KRT, ONS. **Politics:** Independent. **Established:** 1883.
Not Published: Christmas.
Special Weekly Sections: Sports Plus (mon); Neighbors (tues); Food (wed); Business Plus (thur); Weekend Entertainment Guide (fri); Religion Page (sat); Travel, Home Improvement, Cookbook, TV Weekly Section, Business Section, Complete Stock Listing (S).
Magazines: Parade; Modern Living (newsprint) (S).

GENERAL MANAGEMENT

Publisher Wayne J Shepperd
General Manager Robert W Parks
Controller Richard Schultz
Manager-Credit Anne Sullivan
Manager-Educational Service Barbara Levitt

ADVERTISING

Director Robert Perk

TELECOMMUNICATIONS

Audiotex Manager Richard Bessel

CIRCULATION

Asst Manager Robert Sypek

NEWS EXECUTIVES

Exec Editor Edward Frede
Editor Paul Steinmetz Jr

EDITORS AND MANAGERS

Amusements Editor Jean Buoy
Automotive Editor Mark Langlois
Business/Finance Editor Mark Langlois
Editorial Page Editor Mary Connolly
Editorial Writer Mary Connolly
Films/Theater Editor Jean Buoy
Food Editor Jean Buoy
Garden/Home Furnishings Editor Jean Buoy
Music Editor Jean Buoy
Photo Editor Robert East
Real Estate Editor Mark Langlois
Society/Fashion Editor Jean Buoy
Sports Editor David Bilmes
Sunday Editor Sarah Passell
Travel Editor Jean Buoy
Women's Editor Jean Buoy

MANAGEMENT INFORMATION SERVICES

Online Manager Dan Wheeler
Data Processing Manager Rich Joudy

PRODUCTION

Director Donald Menzer
Foreman-Composing Robert Nelson
Foreman-Pressroom Walter Gerdauskas
Foreman-Mailroom (Night) Carlos Lopes
Foreman-Mailroom (Day) Helena Kubisek

Market Information: TMC; Operate database; Operate audiotex.
Mechanical available: Offset; Black and 4 ROP colors; insert accepted — preprinted, mini tabs/card/tabs/standards/merchandise; page cut-offs — 22¾".
Mechanical specifications: Type page 13" x 21"; E - 6 cols, $2\frac{1}{16}$", ⅛" between; A - 6 cols, $2\frac{1}{16}$", ⅛" between; C - 9 cols, 1⅜", $\frac{1}{16}$" between.
Commodity consumption: Newsprint 5,500 metric tons; widths 56", 28", 42"; black ink 144,000 pounds; single pages printed 22,000; average pages per issue 44(d), 84(S); single plates used 80,000.
Equipment: EDITORIAL: Front-end hardware — SII/Sys 25. CLASSIFIED: Front-end hardware — SII/Sys 25. PRODUCTION: Typesetters — 2-MON/Express, AG/Accuset 1000; Plate exposures — 2-Nu; Plate processors — Nat/A250; Electronic picture desk — Lf/AP Leaf Picture Desk, Adobe/Photoshop; Production cameras — 1-C/Spartan II; Automatic film processors — 1-LE.
PRESSROOM: Line 1 — 7-G/Metro; Folders — 1-G. MAILROOM: Counter stackers — HL; Inserters and stuffers — 5-Feeder/M275; Bundle tyer — 2-OVL. LIBRARY: Electronic — SII/Sys 25. WIRE SERVICES: News — AP Datastream, ONS; Stock tables — AP Datastream; Syndicates — AP Datafeatures, ONS; Receiving dishes — AP. BUSINESS COMPUTERS: IBM/AS400; PCs & micros networked.

FAIRFIELD COUNTY-BRIDGEPORT

Fairfield County

'90 U.S. Census- 142,322; **E&P '96 Est.** 142,039
ABC-NDM: (90) 438,306 (HH 161,385)

Connecticut Post

(m-mon to sat; S)

Connecticut Post, 410 State St., Bridgeport, CT 06604; tel (203) 333-0161; fax (203) 336-3373. Thomson Newspapers group.
Circulation: 75,583(m); 75,583(m-sat); 93,718(S); ABC Sept. 30, 1995.
Price: 50¢(d); 50¢(sat); $1.50(S); $4.50/wk.
Advertising: Open inch rate $63.00(m); $63.00(m-sat); $70.40(S). **Representative:** Sawyer-Ferguson-Walker Co.
News Services: AP, KRT, LAT-WP. **Politics:** Independent. **Established:** 1883.
Special Weekly Sections: Womanwise (daily); Seniors (mon); Cuisine (wed); Health, Sporting Life (thur); Auto/Truck Section (fri); Religion (sat); Travel (S).
Magazines: Preview/Entertainment Guide (fri); Parade, TV Week, Comics (S).

GENERAL MANAGEMENT

Publisher Robert H Laska
Chief Financial Officer Jeff Hansen
Manager-Business Casper M Zito
Manager-Human Resources Audrey Musco

ADVERTISING

Director Brenda MacDonald
Manager-National/Major Accounts Paul J Ward
Manager-Retail Julie Aliberti
Manager-Retail Susan Chudy
Manager-Retail Bill Couton
Manager-Classified John Marr
Manager-Art Service Ed Packo

MARKETING AND PROMOTION

Director-Marketing John A Arnett
Manager-Promotion Robert DiGioia

TELECOMMUNICATIONS

Audiotex Manager Carol Dauber

CIRCULATION

Director Phillip K Hudson
Manager Louis Cretella

NEWS EXECUTIVES

Editor Rick Sayers
Managing Editor Michael Daly
Asst Managing Editor-News Ann Maria Virzi

EDITORS AND MANAGERS

Business Editor Tom Caruso
Editorial Page Editor Stephen J Winters
Fairfield County Editor Linda Pinto
Magazine/Food Editor Elaine K Ficarra
New Haven County Editor Reg Johnson
Norwalk/Westport Editor James Shay
Operations Editor Todd Hollis
Photo/Graphics Editor Jean Santopatre
Sports Editor Mark Faller
State Editor Paul Sussman

MANAGEMENT INFORMATION SERVICES

Director-Systems Robert Walsh

PRODUCTION

Director Frank Oliva Jr
Manager-Plant Pat Petrino
Manager-Pre Print Ronald Emmerthal

Market Information: Zoned editions; Split Run; TMC; ADS; Operate audiotex.
Mechanical available: Offset; Black and 3 ROP colors; insert accepted — preprinted; page cutoffs — 21½".
Mechanical specifications: Type page 13" x 20¼"; E - 6 cols, $2\frac{1}{16}$", ⅛" between; A - 6 cols, $2\frac{1}{16}$", ⅛" between; C - 10 cols, 1⅜", $\frac{1}{16}$" between.
Commodity consumption: Newsprint 10,675 short tons; 9,682 metric tons; widths 55", 41¼", 27⅜"; black ink 187,880 pounds; color ink 46,970 pounds; single pages printed 20,000; average pages per issue 46(d), 96(S); single plates used 95,000.
Equipment: EDITORIAL: Front-end hardware — Digital/3000 Alpha Chip; Front-end software — Digital/3000 Alpha Chip; Printers — HP/LaserJet 4V, AU/Broadsheet. CLASSIFIED: Front-end hardware — Digital/3000 Alpha Chip; Front-end software — Digital; Printers — Epson. AUDIOTEX: Hardware — Brite Voice Systems; Supplier name — City Line. DISPLAY: Adv layout systems — CJ; Front-end hardware — DEC/VAX 6310, III/4700A; Front-end software — CJ; Printers — DEC/LP25, DEC/LP27, Genicom. PRODUCTION: Pagination software — Dewar/View, Computext/CompoClass; Typesetters — 2-AU/OPI, 2-Digital/RIP, III/3850; Plate exposures — 1-Nu/40-FT/UP, 2-Nu/FTOV6; Plate processors — 1-DP/34S, 2-Nat/A-250; Scanners — 2-ECR/Autokon, 2-ECR/Autokon; Production cameras — 2-C/Spartan III; Film transporters — 4-LE; Color separation equipment (conventional) — Digi-Colour; Digital color separation equipment — Fin.
PRESSROOM: Line 1 — 9-G/Metro offset (5 half decks); Press drives — Fin; Folders — 2-G/3:2; Pasters — 11-Automatic Pasters; Press control system — Fin. MAILROOM: Counter stackers — 3-HL/Monitor HTs, 1-HL/Dual Carrier; Inserters and stuffers — 2-SLS/1000 GMA 18-into-1; Bundle tyer — 4-OVL/JP40, 1-OVL/415, 1-MLN/EE; Addressing machine — 1-Ch/596. COMMUNICATIONS: Digital ad delivery system — AP AdSend, AdSat. WIRE SERVICES: News — AP, THO, KRT, LAT; Stock tables — Tribune Media Stocks; Receiving dishes — AP. BUSINESS COMPUTERS: 2-DEC/VAX, III/6310, III/4700A; Applications: CJ: Class, Personnel, Layout, Circ, Adv; PCs & micros networked; PCs & main system networked.

GREENWICH

Fairfield County

'90 U.S. Census- 58,546; **E&P '96 Est.** 58,083
ABC-NDM (90): 58,411 (HH 22,192)

Greenwich Time

(all day-mon to fri; m-sat; S)

Greenwich Time, 20 E. Elm St., Greenwich, CT 06830; tel (203) 625-4400; fax (203) 625-4419. Times Mirror Co. group.
Circulation: 13,096(a); 12,174(m-sat); 14,263(S); ABC Sept. 30, 1995.
Price: 50¢(d); 50¢(sat); $1.50(S); $3.30/wk; $13.20/mo; $148.20/yr.
Advertising: Open inch rate $50.88(a); $50.88(m-sat); $56.60(S). **Representative:** Landon Associates Inc.
News Services: AP, LAT-WP, KRT. **Politics:** Independent. **Established:** 1877.
Note: Printed at the Stamford Advocate. For detailed mechanical equipment information, see the Stamford Advocate listing.
Not Published: New Year; Christmas.
Advertising not accepted: Publisher reserves the right to reject an advertisement.
Special Editions: Weddings, Education, New Real Estate (Jan); Cruise/Guide, Business & Economic Review, Careers (Feb); Home in Style, Camps, Spring Home Improvement, Bermuda Travel, Showcase of Homes, First Home (Mar); Garden, Home, New York Auto Show, Golf, All About Kids, Canada Travel, Women & Money, Education Outlook, Auto Expo, Real Estate Showcase (Apr); Summer Fun, Our Town, New England Vacations (May); Visit USA, Meet the Merchants, Entertaining, Connecticut's Top 100, Waterfront Real Estate (June); Europe Travel, JAL (July); Survey of Education, Back-to-School, Fall Foliage (Aug); Bahamas Travel, Healthwatch, Weddings, Home Improvement Garden (Sept); Antiques, Arts & Collectibles, Kitchen & Bath, Fall Cruise Guide, Fall Home, Community Sections, Education, Real Estate Showcase, Auto Intro (Oct); Skiing-Private Lessons, Holiday Entertaining, Holiday Countdown, Pilgrim, Florida Travel, Antiques, Real Estate (Nov); Gifts for Every List, Ski Holidays, Great Gift Ideas, Last Minute Gift Guide (Dec).
Special Weekly Sections: Panorama (mon); Panorama/Health (tues); Food (wed); Living (thur); The Guide (TMC), Weekend (fri); Arts, Travel (S); Sports, Business (daily).
Magazines: Parade; Color Comics; TV Magazine (half tab).

CORPORATE OFFICERS

CEO/President William J Rowe
Exec Vice Pres/Editor Kenneth H Brief
Vice Pres/Circulation Director Craig Allen
Vice Pres/Advertising Director John Dunster
Vice Pres/Director-Production/Facility Robert Hughes
Vice Pres/Chief Financial Officer Robert Zikias
Director-Human Resources Terri Flaherty

GENERAL MANAGEMENT

Publisher William J Rowe
Vice Pres/Chief Financial Officer Robert Zikias
Human Resources Director Terri Flaherty

ADVERTISING

Vice Pres/Director John Dunster
Manager-National Marcia Groglio
Manager-Classified Polly Nash

MARKETING AND PROMOTION

Manager-Promotion/Public Affairs Barbara Bind
Manager-Marketing Service Sandra Guss

TELECOMMUNICATIONS

Audiotex Manager Barbara Bind

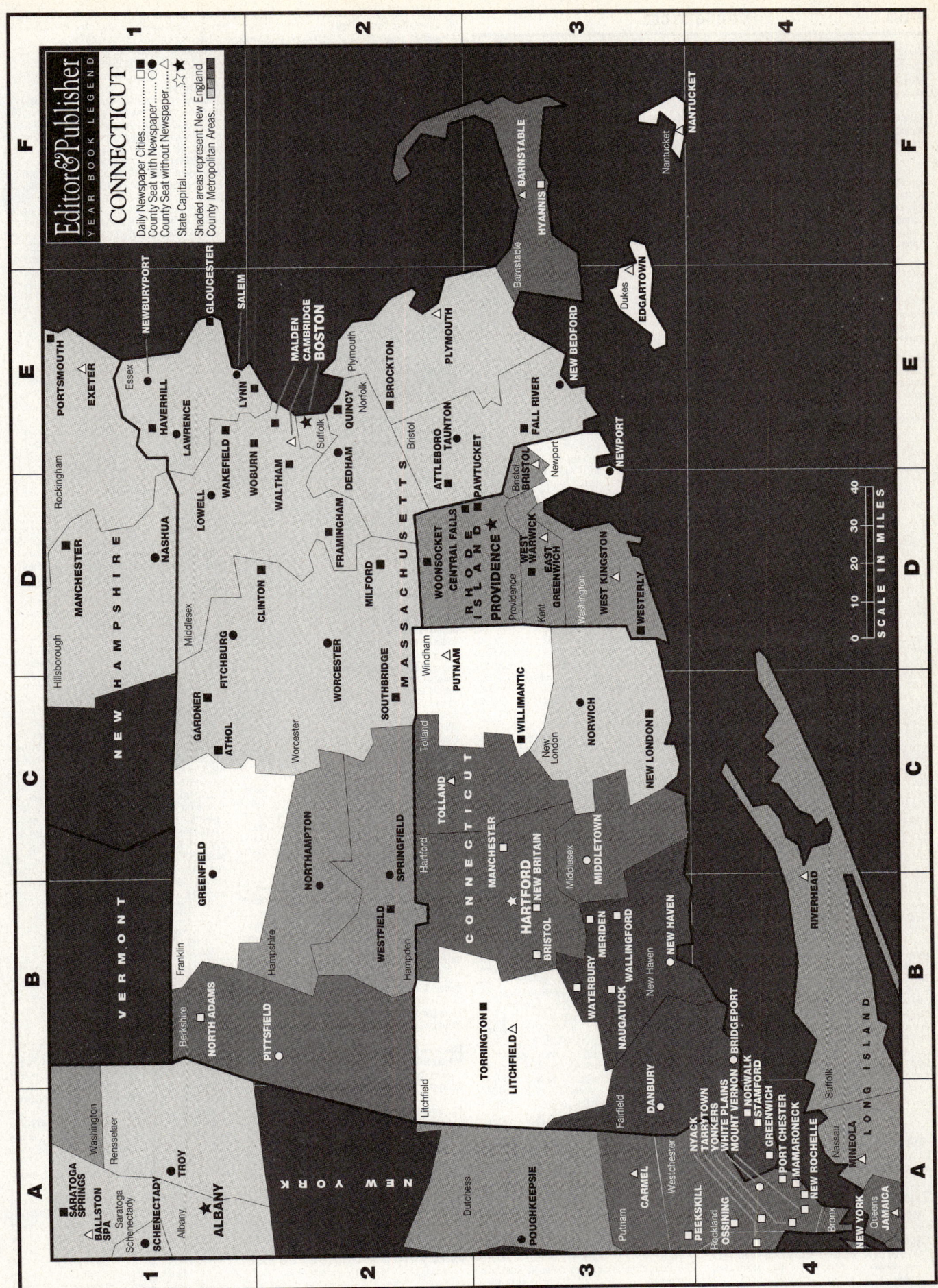

CIRCULATION

Vice Pres/Director Craig Allen
Manager Robert Dance

NEWS EXECUTIVES

Exec Vice Pres/Editor Kenneth H Brief
Managing Editor Joseph Pisani
Asst Managing Editor-Design/Photography Jacqueline Segal

EDITORS AND MANAGERS

Arts Editor Dorothy Friedman
Business Editor Beth Frances Cox
City Editor Bruce Hunter
Editorial Page Editor Mike Sweeney
Features Editor Robert Pellegrino
Sports Editor John Bruening

MANAGEMENT INFORMATION SERVICES

Director-Info Services Steve Harrington

PRODUCTION

Vice Pres/Director Robert T Hughes
Superintendent-Composing Frank Tymula
Superintendent-Pressroom Donald Jordan
Superintendent-Mailroom John Meyer

Market Information: Zoned editions; Split Run; TMC; Operate audiotex.

Mechanical available: Offset; Black and 3 ROP colors; insert accepted — preprinted; page cut-offs — 22¾".

Mechanical specifications: Type page 13" x 21½"; E - 6 cols, 2.48", .22" between; A - 6 cols, 2⅛", ⅛" between; C - 10 cols, 1 3/16", 3/32" between.

Commodity consumption: Newsprint 1,500 metric tons; widths 54", 40½", 27"; black ink 35,505 pounds; color ink 3,000 pounds; single pages printed 17,235; average pages per issue 37(d), 20(sat), 104(S); single plates used 18,000.

Equipment: EDITORIAL: Front-end hardware — 2-CSI/1170, 28-CSI, 12-Ap/Mac; Front-end software — CSI, QuarkXPress, Adobe/Photoshop; Printers — Graphic Enterprises/PS 3, III/3880s; Other equipment — Lf/AP Leaf Picture Desk, Ap/Mac, Kk/Scanners, Lf/45 Scanner. CLASSIFIED: Front-end hardware — 1-CSI/1178, 2-CSI/Terminals; Front-end software — CSI; Printers — AU/APS-5, III/3850s, DEC/LA 120. AUDIOTEX: Hardware — Brite, Unix; Software — Voice; Supplier name — Brite, AP. DISPLAY: Adv layout systems — 8-Ap/Mac; Front-end hardware — Ap/Mac; Front-end software — Multi-Ad/Creator, QuarkXPress; Printers — Ap/Mac LaserWriters, V/600, Graphic Enterprises/PS 3. PRODUCTION: Platemaking systems — KFM/Twin Exposure; Plate exposures — 2-Nu/Flip Top, 1-KFM; Plate processors — 1-KFM, 2-WL/38D; Electronic picture desk — Lf/AP Leaf Picture Desk; Scanners — 1-ECR/AutoKon, Kk/Scanner; Automatic film processors — 3-P/SC 2050; Film transporters — 1-LE, 1-Kk; Shrink lenses — 2-LE/Shrink Lens; Color separation equipment (conventional) — Linotype-Hell. PRESSROOM: Line 1 — 8-HI/1660 offset double width, 2-HI/1660 double width; Press drives — GE; Folders — 2-HI; Pasters — 9-MEG/Automatic; Reels and stands — MEG; Press control system — GE; Press registration system — KFM. MAILROOM: Counter stackers — 3-QWI/SJ100; Inserters and stuffers — 1-HL/1472; Bundle tyer — 4-OVL/JP40; Addressing machine — 1-KR/215; Other mailroom equipment — HI/Stitcher-Trimmer. COMMUNICATIONS: Systems used — satellite. WIRE SERVICES: News — AP, LAT-WP, KRT; Photos — AP, LAT-WP, KRT; Stock tables — AP; Syndicates — LATS, Universal Press, TMS, United Media, Creators, King Features; Receiving dishes — size-3m, AP. BUSINESS COMPUTERS: 1-DEC/VAX 4100, CJ; Applications: Gen ledger, Accts payable, Accts receivable, Adv, Circ, Payroll; PCs & micros networked; PCs & main system networked.

HARTFORD

Hartford County

'90 U.S. Census- 141,210; E&P '96 Est. 143,626
ABC-CZ (90): 303,769 (HH 116,031)

The Hartford Courant

(m-mon to sat; S)

The Hartford Courant, 285 Broad St., Hartford, CT 06115-2510; tel (860) 241-6200; fax (860) 520-3176; web site http://www.courant.com/. Times Mirror Co. group.

Circulation: 211,704(m); 211,704(m-sat); 308,481(S); ABC Sept. 30, 1995.

Price: 50¢(d); 50¢(sat); $1.50(S); $3.90/wk; $16.90/mo; $202.80/yr.

Advertising: Open inch rate $156.07(m); $156.07(m-sat); $224.85(S). **Representatives:** Metropolitan Sunday Network; American Publishers Reps.

News Services: AP, Bloomberg, DJ, Entertainet, KRT, LAT-WP, RN Photo. **Politics:** Independent. **Established:** 1764.

Special Editions: Winter Ski, Caribbean Travel, Weddings Tab, Outlook '96 I, Colossal Classified #1, Florida Travel, Winter Films (Jan); Legislative Tab, Glastonbury Chamber Report Tab, Europe Travel, Washington's Birthday Auto Sales (Feb); Career Choices, NCAA Basketball Play-offs, Spring Fitness Tab, Spring Cruise Travel, Easter Events-Calendar Tab (Mar); Baseball Preview, Bermuda Travel, Let's Talk About Enfield Tab, Cape Cod & The Island Travel, Lawn & Garden, Bristol Savings Stampede Tab, New York State Travel, Manchester Chamber Report Tab, Scholastic Sports Section Tab (Apr); Summer Films, Colossal Classified #2, Virginia/Washington D.C. Travel, National Pet Week, Guide to Education Tab, Windsor Shad Derby, NIE Design-an-Ad Tab, Manchester Parks & Recreation Tab, Parent & Child, Canada Travel, Beach Wear Fashion, Spring Auto Values, Great Chef's Festival Tab, Balloons Over Bristol Tab, Guide to the Connecticut Shoreline II Tab, Berlin Turnpike Tab, Career Choices, Courant Top 100 CT Companies (May); Farmington River Splash Tab, Summer Arts Preview Tab, New England Summer Travel, East Hartford Chamber Report Tab, Celebrate West Hartford Tab, Weddings Tab, Guide to the CT Shoreline II Tab, Colossal Classified #3, Greater Harford Open Tournament, Cape Cod & The Islands Travel, Guide to the Shoreline III Tab, Scholastic Sports Section Tab, Hartford's Camp Courant's 100th Anniv. Tab (June); West Hartford Sale Days Tab, Stay In State Travel, Our Towns (Resident's Guide) Tab, Mt. Carmel Italian Festival Tab (July); Guide to Education Tab, Volvo Tennis Tournament, Parent & Child, Harvest Recipes Cooking Contest, Fall Films, Fall TV Preview (Aug); Fall Arts Preview Tab, Simsbury September-fest Tab, Manchester Parks & Recreation Tab, Glastonbury Apple Festival Tab, Fall Cruise Travel, Career Choices, Focus on Bristol Tab, '97 Auto Preview, Farmington Festival Tab (Sept); Colossal Classified #4, Whalers NHL Preview, Middlesex Expo '96 Tab, New York City Travel, Best of Recipe Exchange (Oct); Voter's Guide Tab, Glastonbury Tab, Holiday Fashion, Holiday Wishes I Tab, Early Ski, International Auto Show, Manchester Road Race Tab, Holiday Events-Calendar Tab, Holiday Films, Holiday Wishes II Tab (Nov); Holiday Books, Holiday Wishes III Tab, Holiday Wishes IV Tab, Guide To Education Tab, Scholastic Sports Section Tab (Dec).

Special Weekly Sections: Outlook '96 II, Education, Jr. Achievement (business wkly tab) (mon); Enter (thur).

Magazines: CT Kids (wed); CT Home Mechanix (fri); Home Remodeling (S, Jan 30); Winter Dining (S, Feb 6); Good Health (S, Feb 13); Personal Finance (S, Feb 27); Vacation Get-Aways (Brochures) (S, Mar 13); Home Show, Northeast Magazine Anniversary (S, Mar 20); Spring Fashions (S, Mar 27); Gardening (S, Apr 10); Spring Travel (S, Apr 24); Spring Dining (S, May 1); Home Design (S, May 15); Summer Dining (S, June 12); Drug & Alcohol Rehabilitation (S, Aug 21); Fall Fashion & Show, Vacation Get-Aways (Brochures) (S, Sept 18); Fall Dining (S, Sept 25); Home Design (S, Oct 2); Home Show (S, Oct 30); Holiday Entertaining (S, Nov 13); Holiday Gift Guide (S, Dec 4).

GENERAL MANAGEMENT

Publisher/CEO Michael E Waller
Asst to Publisher Janett Bailey
Senior Vice Pres/General Manager Marty Petty
Editor/Vice Pres David S Barrett
Vice Pres-Advertising Mark E Aldam
Vice Pres-Marketing & Business Development Louis J Golden
Vice Pres-Administration Richard H King
Vice Pres/Chief Financial Officer Raymond A Koupal
Vice Pres-Circulation, Production & Customer Services Mark H Kurtich
Vice Pres-Employee Services Matthew K Poland
Vice Pres-Info Technology Judith S Kallet
Controller Robert R Rounce
Assoc Publisher-Eastern CT Richard S Feeney
Assoc Publisher-Middlesex County William E Sheedy Jr
Customer Service Manager Colleen Eddy
General Manager-Electronic Publishing Mark S Del Vecchio

ADVERTISING

Manager-General Richard Medeiros Jr
Manager-Retail Kathleen Coddington
Manager-Classified Mary Lou Stoneburner
Manager-Business Development Richard Benner

MARKETING AND PROMOTION

Manager-Marketing Susan Acker
Manager-Research William Hoelzel
Manager-Public Relations Dennis Schain
Manager-Community Affairs Mildred Torres Soto
Creative Director Susan Quirk

TELECOMMUNICATIONS

Audiotex Manager Timothy Nardi

CIRCULATION

Director James A Baldis
Manager-Sales & Marketing Lawrence Newman
Manager-Home Delivery David Bennett

NEWS EXECUTIVES

Managing Editor Clifford L Teutsch
Deputy Managing Editor-Sunday G Claude Albert
Asst Managing Editor-Connecticut Michael Regan
Assoc Editor-Technology Cheryl Magazine
Asst Managing Editor-Nights Paul Spencer
Assoc Editor-Recruiting Jeff Rivers
Reader Representative/Assoc Editor Elissa Papirno
Electronic News Coordinator Christopher Morrill

EDITORS AND MANAGERS

Business Editor George Gombossy
Columnist-Human Interest Denis Horgan
Columnist-Lifestyle Jeff Rivers
Columnist-Urban Affairs Tom Condon
Columnist-Political Don Noel
Columnist Lisa Chedekel
Columnist Stan Simpson
Commentary Editor Carolyn Lumsden
Consumer Affairs Writer Anthony Giorgianni
Deputy CT Editor Bernard Davidow
Deputy CT Editor Paul Stern
Town Editorial Editor Thomas Krazit
Editorial Page Editor John J Zakarian
Deputy Editorial Page Editor Robert Schrepf
Letters Editor Andre Barnett
Letters Editor Jane Gordon
Town Editorial Editor Henry McNulty
Editorial Cartoonist Bob Englehart
Editorial Writer Stephania Davis
Editorial Writer Daryl Perch
Editorial Writer Karen Wagner
Editorial Writer Peter Pach
Editorial Writer Michele Jacklin
Education Writer Robert Frahm
Environmental Writer Daniel Jones
Fashion Writer Donna Larcen
Features Editor Kyrie O'Connor
Films/Theatre Writer Malcolm Johnson
Food Editor Linda Giuca
Government Editor David Fink
Lifestyles/Specialties Editor Stephanie Summers
Magazine Editor Lary Bloom
Manager-News Administration Lori Skoglund
News Librarian Kathy McKula
Religion Writer Gerald Renner
Sports Editor Jeff Otterbein
Television Writer James Endrst

MANAGEMENT INFORMATION SERVICES

Deputy Director-Operations/Telecommunications Robert Sandy
Manager-Publishing Systems Chet Andrews
Manager-Publishing Services Pre Press News Michael Bolduc
Manager-Desktop Services Timothy Aston
Manager-Business Systems Applications Jayaprada Ganta
Manager-Strategic Planning/Administration Jean Barrasso
Manager-Publishing Services Pre Press-Advertising Robert Urillo
Online Manager Mark S Del Vecchio

PRODUCTION

Director Thomas J Anischik
Manager-Press Richard Drapeau
Manager-Transportation Julius Neto
Manager-Engineering Support Bernard Gullotta

Market Information: Zoned editions; Split Run; TMC; Operate database; Operate audiotex; Electronic edition.

Mechanical available: Offset; Black and 3 ROP colors; insert accepted — preprinted, 3"x 7" bumper sticker, shampoo; toothpaste if machine insertable, (other product samples may be delivered via Alternate Delivery capabilities); page cut-offs — 22⅞".

Mechanical specifications: Type page 13" x 21½"; E - 6 cols, 2 1/16", ⅛" between; A - 6 cols, 2 1/16", ⅛" between; C - 10 cols, 1⅜", 1/16" between.

Commodity consumption: Newsprint 36,000 metric tons; widths 53⅞", 40½", 27"; black ink 1,140,000 pounds; color ink 168,000 pounds; single pages printed 30,000; average pages per issue 61(d), 113(S); single plates used 500,000.

Equipment: EDITORIAL: Front-end hardware — 8-AT/9000, 180-AT/9000, 75-Ap/Mac II; Front-end software — AT/9000; Printers — III/3850, III/Postscript Proofers; Other equipment — HP. CLASSIFIED: Front-end hardware — 4-AT/9000, 67-AT/9000 SDT; Front-end software — AT/IAS; Printers — III/3850's, III/Postscript Proofers. AUDIOTEX: Hardware — 2-IBM/RS6000-350; Software — IBM/Direct Talk-6000. DISPLAY: Adv layout systems — 9-Cx/Breeze, 1-ECR/Autokon 1000; Front-end hardware — 2-Cx/Bit, 3-Ap/Mac Quadra, 3-Ap/Mac IIci, 12-Ap/Power Mac; Front-end software — Multi-Ad/Creator, QuarkXPress; Printers — 2-Cx/Bit printers. PRODUCTION: Pagination software — QPS 3.3; OCR software — Caere/ OmniPage; Typesetters — 2-Cx/Bitsetter, 1-AU/APS6, 3-III/3850, 2-Scitex/Dolev 400; Platemaking systems — 2-WL/Lith-X-Pozer; Plate exposures — 2-BKY, Nu/Flip Top DS, 1-KFM/twin drawer; Plate processors — 3-WL/38D; Electronic picture desk — Lf/AP Leaf Picture Desk; Scanners — 2-ECR/Autokon, 2-Scitex/Smartscanner, 1-Scitex/Smartscanner, 1-Hel/Scanner; Production cameras — 2-C/Pager I, 1-SCREEN/Vertical; Automatic film processors — 2-LE/PC-18A, 2-LE/LD24A, 3-LE/LS2600A, 1-LE/CMX2600; Reproportion units — Scitex/Assembler; Film transporters — 2-LE/LD 24A; Shrink lenses — Alan/Anamorphic Adjustable; Color separation equipment (conventional) — Scitex/Smartscanner; Digital color separation equipment — Assembler, Postscript/Gateway, Scitex/Star RS, Scitex/Smart-Scanner. PRESSROOM: Line 1 — 8-G/Metro Offset (4 half decks); Line 2 — 8-G/Metro Offset (4 half decks); Line 4 — 8-G/Metro offset (4 half decks); Line 5 — 8-G/Metro offset (4 half decks); Press drives — Fin; Folders — 6-G/3:2; Pasters — G; Reels and stands — G; Press control system — Fin. MAILROOM: Counter stackers — 7-HL/Monitor; Inserters and stuffers — 3-S/Am 1472, 1-KR; Bundle tyer — 6-Dynaric, 3-Dynaric Offline; Addressing machine — 4-Ch, 2-Domino/On Line Ink Jetting. LIBRARY: Electronic — Vu/Text; Combination — Vu/Text. COMMUNICATIONS: Facsimile — Scitex/TP25, III/3850; Digital ad delivery system — AP AdSend, DIGIFLEX, AdStat, AdExpress, IMAGENET. WIRE SERVICES: News — AP, AP Datafeatures, AP Race Wire, Entertainet, Jai Alai Wire, LAT-WP, Weather; Photos — RN; Stock tables — AP SelectStox; Syndicates — AP Datafeatures; Receiving dishes — size-3m, 5m, AP. BUSINESS COMPUTERS: HP/3000, IBM/4381, Ap/Mac, IBM/RS6000; Applications: Adv, Circ, Fin; PBS/MediaPlus; PCs & micros networked; PCs & main system networked.

MANCHESTER

Hartford County

'90 U.S. Census- 56,048; E&P '96 Est. 72,780
ABC-NDM (90): 264,369 (HH 100,368)

Journal Inquirer

(e-mon to fri; m-sat)

Journal Inquirer, 306 Progress Dr.; PO Box 510, Manchester, CT 06040; tel (860) 646-0500; fax (860) 646-9867; e-mail journal-inq@aol.com.

Circulation: 49,148(e); 49,148(m-sat); ABC Sept. 30, 1995.

Price: 50¢(d); 50¢(sat); $2.40/wk; $124.80/yr.

Advertising: Open inch rate $33.00(e); $33.00(m-sat). **Representative:** Landon Associates Inc.

News Service: AP. **Politics:** Independent. **Established:** 1968.

Special Editions: Brides, Super Sunday, Travel (Jan); Washington's Birthday Auto Section (Feb); Spring Fashions, Business & Industry (Mar); Cook Book, Spring Car Care, Spring Home and Garden (Apr); Dining Out Guide (May); Summer Fun, Fall Brides (June); Discovery (July); Back-to-School, Fall Fashions (Aug); Fall Sports, Home Improvement

Connecticut I-69

(Sept); New Cars, Women's Clubs, Inside Football Report, Fall & Winter Car Care (Oct); Meet the Merchants, Sleighbell (Nov).
Special Weekly Sections: Food Day (wed); Time Out (thur).
Magazines: Food Day; Inside Football.

CORPORATE OFFICER
President Elizabeth S Ellis

GENERAL MANAGEMENT
Publisher Elizabeth S Ellis
Vice Pres-Finance Walter Rucewicz

ADVERTISING
Vice Pres William K Sybert

CIRCULATION
Vice Pres M Andrew Cline
Asst Director Gary Nelson

NEWS EXECUTIVES
Managing Editor/Vice Pres-News Chris Powell
Assoc Editor Lee Giguere

EDITORS AND MANAGERS
Consumer Columnist Cynthia Bercowetz
Editorial Page Editor Keith Burris
Living Section Editor Richard Tambling
News Editor Robert H Boone
Photo Editor Glenn Waterman
Exec Sports Editor Frank Corsoe
Sports Editor Randy Smith

PRODUCTION
Vice Pres Whitney Sutherland
Foreman-Pressroom Timothy Noon

Market Information: Zoned editions; TMC; ADS.
Mechanical available: Offset; Black insert accepted — preprinted, single sheet; page cut-offs — 21⅝".
Mechanical specifications: Type page 10½" x 14"; E - 5 cols, 2.08", ⅙" between; A - 5 cols, 2.08", ⅙" between; C - 8 cols, 1.33", ⅙" between.
Commodity consumption: Newsprint 3,100 short tons; widths 29½", 14¾"; black ink 86,000 pounds; color ink 3,000 pounds; average pages per issue 64(d).
Equipment: EDITORIAL: Front-end hardware — Ik/CPS 1040, 32-Ik/Models 60,61,40; Front-end software — Ik; Printers — 1-DEC/Writer, 1-AIP/ALQ 300, 1-X/Diablo 620, 2-Copal/Laser Writer, 1-ECR/VRL-36; Other equipment — 2-GDT/Astro Series, 22-PC. CLASSIFIED: Front-end hardware — 1-Ik/CPS 1040, 6-Ik/Model 40; Front-end software — Ik. DISPLAY: Front-end hardware — 4-Ap/Mac Quadra 630, 2-Ap/Power Mac; Printers — Ap/Mac LaserWriter II, Ap/Mac LaserWriter Plus; Other equipment — LZR/2080, Typhoon/20. PRODUCTION: Typesetters — 2-Copal/Laser, 1-ECR/VRL-36, 1-ECR/Autokon; Plate exposures — 2-Nu/Flip Top UP; Plate processors — 1-Cookson Graphics; Electronic picture desk — Lf/AP Leaf Picture Desk; Scanners — 2-Lf/Leafscan 35; Production cameras — 1-C; Automatic film processors — DP/24L; Film transporters — C; Digital color separation equipment — Lf/AP Leaf Picture Desk. PRESSROOM: Line 1 — 8-HI/845; Folders — 1-HI; Pasters — 6-MEG; Press control system — Haley/Controls. MAILROOM: Counter stackers — HL/Dual Carrier; Inserters and stuffers — HI/1472; Bundle tyer — 1-MLN, 2-Sterling, 1-Power Strap; Addressing machine — 1-Domino/Ink Jet, 1-St/Paper-Man. WIRE SERVICES: News — AP; Photos — AP; Syndicates — AP; Receiving dishes — size-10ft, AP. BUSINESS COMPUTERS: IBM/Sys 36; Applications: CDS; PCs & main system networked.

MERIDEN-WALLINGFORD
New Haven County

'90 U.S. Census- 105,976 (Meriden 60,294; Wallingford 45,682); E&P '96 Est. 118,773 (Meriden 61,320; Wallingford 57,453)
ABC-CZ (90): 100,301 (HH 38,407)

Record-Journal
(m-mon to sat; S)

Record-Journal, 11 Crown St.; PO Box 915, Meriden, CT 06450; tel (203) 235-1661; fax (203) 639-0210.
Circulation: 29,634(m); 29,634(m-sat); 30,526(S); ABC Sept. 30, 1995.
Price: 50¢(d); 50¢(sat); $1.50(S); $4.00/wk; $208.00/yr.
Advertising: Open inch rate $20.92(m); $20.92(m-sat); $20.92(S). **Representative:** Papert Companies.
News Services: AP, KRT, NYT, CSM. **Established:** 1867.
Not Published: Christmas.
Special Editions: Super Bowl, Bridal (Jan); Washington's Birthday, Automotive, Money (Feb); Spring Auto Care, Design-an-Ad, Cookbook (Mar); American Home, Real Estate Guide, Home Improvement (Apr); Business & Industry (May); Bridal (June); Economy Cars, Economy Trucks (July); Back-to-School, Meet the Merchant (Aug); Car Clearance, Home Improvement (Sept); Restaurant Guide, Fall Auto Care, '97 New Car Section, Home Furnishings (Oct); Shopping Issue, Thanksgiving-Christmas Edition (Nov); Christmas Greetings.
Special Weekly Sections: Living (mon); Teens (tues); Food (wed); Health & Science (thur); Enjoy! (fri); Home & Family (sat); Neighbors, Accent, Perspective (S).
Magazine: Color Comics (S).

CORPORATE OFFICERS
Chairman of the Board Carter H White
Vice Chairman of the Board Barbara C White
President Eliot C White
Senior Vice Pres David T Lucey
Vice Pres-Business Development Michael F Killian
Vice Pres John J Ausanka III
Vice Pres Michael F Killian
Vice Pres Alison W Muschinsky
Vice Pres Timothy E Ryan
Vice Pres James H Smith
Secretary Paul D McKnight
Treasurer Eliot C White

GENERAL MANAGEMENT
Publisher Eliot C White
General Manager David T Lucey
Controller John J Ausanka III

ADVERTISING
Director Raymond U Roy
Manager-Sales Hank Misiak
Manager-Classified Denise Robillard

MARKETING AND PROMOTION
Director-Marketing Service Sandra T Blodgett

CIRCULATION
Director Timothy E Ryan
Asst Director James Ricci

NEWS EXECUTIVES
Editor Eliot C White
Exec Editor James H Smith
Editorial Board Chairman Barbara C White
Managing Editor Donald Schiller
Asst Managing Editor Kenneth H Robinson III
Asst Managing Editor-Sunday Glenn Richter
Asst Managing Editor-Design/Graphics Dorothy Torres

EDITORS AND MANAGERS
Automotive Editor Raymond U Roy
Books Editor Jeff Kurz
Business Editor James Zebora
Cartoonist T Manning
Cartoonist Kevin Mavkowski
Cartoonist Frank A Lamphier Jr
City Editor Ralph Tomaselli
Columnist Warren F Gardner
Community News Editor Sharon Hankin
Copy Desk Chief Jon Korper
Editorial Page Editor Allan S Church
Features Editor Phyllis Donovan
Lifestyle Editor Paul Swan
News Editor Jeffrey Kurz
Picture Editor Rich Mei
Real Estate Editor Raymond U Roy
Sports Editor Robert A Morrissette
Suburban Editor Michael Kelley
Systems Editor Doug Bevins

MANAGEMENT INFORMATION SERVICES
Data Processing Manager Joseph Novak

PRODUCTION
Director-Graphic Service Michael L Scotto
Manager-Systems Daniel Anziano
Foreman-Pressroom Walter T Valunas

Market Information: TMC.
Mechanical available: Offset; Black and 3 ROP colors; insert accepted — preprinted; page cut-offs — 22¾".
Mechanical specifications: Type page 13" x 21½"; E - 6 cols, 2¹⁄₁₆", ⅛" between; A - 6 cols, 2¹⁄₁₆", ⅛" between; C - 10 cols, 1¼", ¹⁄₁₂" between.
Commodity consumption: Newsprint 2,400 metric tons; widths 55", 41¼", 27½"; black ink 25,000 pounds; color ink 2,000 pounds; single pages printed 14,000; average pages per issue 33(d), 70(S); single plates used 24,000.
Equipment: EDITORIAL: Front-end hardware — PC; Front-end software — Hx, Microsoft/Word 6.0A, QuarkXPress 3.31R2; Other equipment — 3-Ap/Mac, 1-Lf/AP Leaf Picture Desk. CLASSIFIED: Front-end hardware — 8-CText; Front-end software — CText. DISPLAY: Adv layout systems — CJ; Front-end hardware — HP, 8-Ap/Mac; Front-end software — Multi-Ad/Creator. PRODUCTION: Pagination software — QuarkXPress; Typesetters — 2-Chelgraph/Laserprinter, ECR, 2-ECR/1245CS; Plate exposures — 2-BKY; Plate processors — 1-Nat/A250; Production cameras — 1-C/Spartan III, 1-AG/2040; Automatic film processors — 1-LE/24; Film transporters — 1-LE; Shrink lenses — Allen Bradley; Digital color separation equipment — Adobe/Photoshop. PRESSROOM: Line 1 — 7-WH/Lithoflex; Folders — 2-WH/2:1; Pasters — 7-Wd. MAILROOM: Counter stackers — 2-Id/440, 2-QWI; Inserters and stuffers — S/1372; Bundle tyer — 2-Power Strap, 1-Sa; Addressing machine — 2-KR. COMMUNICATIONS: Digital ad delivery system — AP AdSend, ISDN. WIRE SERVICES: News — AP, NYT, CSM, KRT; Photos — AP; Stock tables — AP SelectStox; Syndicates — AP Datafeatures; Receiving dishes — AP. BUSINESS COMPUTERS: 1-HP/3000 (Series 937); Applications: CJ: Circ; CJ: Gen ledger; CJ: Payroll; CJ: Accts payable; PCs & micros networked; PCs & main system networked.

MIDDLETOWN
Middlesex County

'90 U.S. Census- 43,755; E&P '96 Est. 45,441
ABC-CZ (90): 63,466 (HH 24,802)

The Middletown Press
(m-mon to sat)

The Middletown Press, 2 Main St.; PO Box 2793, Middletown, CT 06457; tel (860) 347-3331; fax (860) 347-3380. Journal Register Co. group.
Circulation: 13,019(m); 13,019(m-sat); ABC Sept. 30, 1995.
Price: 50¢(d); 50¢(sat).
Advertising: Open inch rate $16.36(m); $16.36(m-sat). **Representative:** Landon Associates Inc.
News Services: AP, NYT, LAT-WP. **Politics:** Independent. **Established:** 1884.
Not Published: Christmas.
Special Editions: Chamber Tab, Super Bowl, Wedding (Jan); President's Day Auto Section, Valentine, Health & Fitness (Feb); Chamber Tab, Home & Garden, March Madness (Mar); Summer Entertaining (Apr); Chamber Tab, Summer Preview (May); Middlesex Summer (June); Chamber Tab, Barbecue Guide (July); Back-to-School, Tennis in CT, College Student's Guide (Aug); Wedding Planner, Home Improvement, Chamber Guide, Car Care (Sept); Regatta, Menu Guide, Hartford Open (Oct); Thanksgiving, Dining Guide, Holiday Gift Guide, Holiday Cookbook, Auto Show, Chamber Guide (Nov); Last Minute Gift Guide, Holiday Count-down, Letters to Santa, Madd Tab (Dec); Coupon Book (monthly).
Special Weekly Sections: Woman (mon); Health & Science (tues); Food (wed); Entertainer (thur); Auto (fri); Real Estate (sat).
Magazines: The Entertainer, USA Today (sat).

CORPORATE OFFICERS
President/CEO Robert M Jelenic
Exec Vice Pres/Chief Financial Officer/Treasurer Jean B Clifton

GENERAL MANAGEMENT
Publisher James F Normandin

ADVERTISING
Director Jamie Tomasic

NEWS EXECUTIVE
Editor Suzanne Simoneau

EDITORS AND MANAGERS
Books Editor Kathy O'Connell
Business Editor Theo Stein
Columnist Sherman Beinhorn
County Editor Ted Funsten
Fashion Editor Julia A Lynch
Features Editor Claudia VanNess
Features Editor Kathy O'Connell
Op-Editorial Page Editor Lucas Held
Society/Women's Editor Julia A Lynch
Sports Editor Paul Augeri

MANAGEMENT INFORMATION SERVICES
Data Processing Manager Michael Manners

PRODUCTION
Superintendent-Pressroom Michael Manners

Market Information: TMC.
Mechanical available: Offset; Black and 3 ROP colors; insert accepted — preprinted, pocket books, free standing stuffers, etc; page cut-offs — 22¾".
Mechanical specifications: Type page 13" x 22½"; E - 6 cols, 2¹⁄₁₆", ⅛" between; A - 6 cols, 2¹⁄₁₆", ⅛" between; C - 8 cols, 1½", ³⁄₁₆" between.
Commodity consumption: Newsprint 1,198 metric tons; widths 27½", 13¾", 27"; black ink 35,007 pounds; color ink 11,162 pounds; single pages printed 10,307; average pages per issue 34(d); single plates used 13,252.
Equipment: EDITORIAL: Front-end hardware — AT. CLASSIFIED: Front-end hardware — AT. DISPLAY: Adv layout systems — 2-AT/GT3X Graphic Display Terminals; Front-end hardware — 4-Ap/Mac Terminal, 2-AT; Front-end software — Mk/Ad Builder. PRODUCTION: Typesetters — 2-Linotype-Hell/Linotronic 101, 2-Ascor/34x33 Vacuum Printer; Plate processors — Nat/A250; Production cameras — 1-AG/RPS 2024, 1-C/1298; Automatic film processors — 1-LE/PC 18, 1-LE/24BQ; Film transporters — 1-C. MAILROOM: Bundle tyer — 1-Sa/Ty. LIBRARY: Electronic — 1-Recordak/MPE. WIRE SERVICES: News — AP, LAT-WP, NYT; Receiving dishes — AP. BUSINESS COMPUTERS: 1-DEC/VAX 11-730, 1-CDC/9715-160 MgB Disk, 2-DEC; Applications: Vision Data: Circ, Adv.

NAUGATUCK
New Haven County

'90 U.S. Census- 31,638; E&P '96 Est. 33,968

Naugatuck Daily News
(e-mon to fri; m-sat)

Naugatuck Daily News, 71 Weid Dr., Naugatuck, CT 06770; tel (203) 729-2228; fax (203) 729-9099. Hollinger International Inc. group.
Circulation: 3,923(e); 3,923(m-sat); Sworn Oct. 1, 1994.
Price: 50¢(d); 50¢(sat); $7.80/mo; $93.60/yr.
Advertising: Open inch rate $7.90(e); $7.90(m-sat). **Representative:** Landon Associates Inc.
News Service: AP. **Politics:** Independent. **Established:** 1885.
Not Published: New Year; Memorial Day; Independence Day; Labor Day; Thanksgiving; Christmas.
Special Editions: Bridal; Fashion; Home Improvement; Car Care; Winter Sports; Health; Weddings.
Magazine: Entertainment Weekend.

GENERAL MANAGEMENT
Publisher Ronald R Waer
Manager-Credit Pat Russo
Manager-Purchasing Pat Russo

ADVERTISING
Manager Cindy Voitavitch

CIRCULATION
Manager Maria Maqalhaes

NEWS EXECUTIVE
Managing Editor John Peritano

EDITORS AND MANAGERS
Features/Ski Editor Julie Martin
Sports Editor Joseph Palladino

PRODUCTION
Superintendent Jackqueline Grande

Market Information: Zoned editions; TMC; ADS.
Mechanical available: Offset; Black and 3 ROP colors; insert accepted — preprinted; page cut-offs — 22¾".
Mechanical specifications: Type page 13" x 21½"; E - 6 cols, 2¹⁄₁₆", ⅛" between; A - 6 cols, 2¹⁄₁₆", ⅛" between; C - 9 cols, 1⅜", ¹⁄₁₆" between.
Commodity consumption: Newsprint 400 short tons; widths 27½", 14", 40"; black ink 10,000 pounds; color ink 40" pounds; single pages printed 5,300; average pages per issue 14(d).
Equipment: EDITORIAL: Front-end hardware — 7-IBM; Other equipment — 8-COM. CLASSIFIED: Front-end hardware — Ap/Mac Plus. DISPLAY: Adv layout systems — Ap/Mac Plus. PRODUCTION: Typesetters — 3-Ap/Mac II Laser; Platemaking systems — 1-BKY; Plate exposures — 1-BKY; Plate processors — Ic/M25-4; Production cameras — SCREEN/Companica 6806; Automatic film processors — SCREEN/LD 220QT. PRESSROOM: Line 1 — 4-G/139 (Grease units), 6-G/Community; Folders — 1-G; Press control system — Fin/SCR. MAILROOM: Counter stackers — BG/108; Bundle tyer — 1-CYP/RO500N, S/14082-B. WIRE SERVICES: News — AP; Receiving dishes — size-2ft, UPI.

I-70 Connecticut

NEW BRITAIN

Hartford County

'90 U.S. Census- 76,254; E&P '96 Est. 77,456
ABC-NDM (90): 109,670 (HH 43,283)

The Herald (e-mon to fri; m-sat)

The Herald, One Herald Sq., New Britain, CT 06050-2050; tel (860) 225-4601; fax (860) 225-4601 ext 238, (860) 229-5718. Journal Register Co. group.

Circulation: 31,344(e); 31,344(m-sat); ABC Sept. 30, 1995.

Price: 50¢(d); 50¢(sat); $2.40/wk (carrier); $30.80/3mo (carrier); $123.20/yr (carrier).

Advertising: Open inch rate $23.15(e); $24.30(m-sat). **Representative:** Landon Associates Inc.

News Service: AP. **Politics:** Independent. **Established:** 1880.

Not Published: Christmas.

Special Editions: Health & Fitness, Senior Lifestyles, Spring Bridal, It's Your Money Coupon Book (Jan); Valentine's Page, President's Sale, Leap Year Section (Feb); Spring Fashion, St. Patrick's Day, Business & Industry, Coupon Book, Spring High School Sports, Spring Car Care, NCAA, Basketball, Poison Prevention (Mar); Home Improvement, Secretaries Page, Senior Citizens, Rock Cats Tab, Coupon Book, Spring Home, Earth Day, Looking Good, Prom Time, Spring Lawn & Garden (Apr); Mother's Day Dining, Boating Promo, Discover Newington, Fun & Leisure, Coupon Book, Summer Preview, Race for the Cure Tab, Senior Health & Fitness, Nursing Home Week (May); Main St. USA, Father's Day Co-op, Congratulations Grads, Greater Hartford Open, Fall Bridal, Summer Discovery (June); Christmas in July, Neighbors, PLV, Crazy Days, Woman's News, Summer Food, Car Care (July); Back-to-School, Show-off Berlin, Business Expo, Education, Vacation Page (Aug); Grandparent's Page, Mum Festival, South Apple Harvest, Home Improvement, Campus Life, Berlin Fair (Sept); Business & Industry, Ready for Winter, Fall Dining, Winter Car Care, Fall Homes, Autumn Values (Oct); Holiday Employment, Thanksgiving Dining, Turkey Give Away Pages, Holiday Edition (Nov); Holiday Gift Guide, Christmas Song Book, New Year's Dining (Dec).

Special Weekly Sections: Suburban Life (mon); Business, Health & Science (tues); Best Food Day (wed); Automotive (thur); The Entertainer, Business (fri); Weekend Auto, Weekend Homes (sat).

Magazine: USA Weekend.

CORPORATE OFFICERS

President/CEO Robert M Jelenic
Exec Vice Pres/Chief Financial Officer/Treasurer Jean B Clifton

GENERAL MANAGEMENT

Publisher James F Normandin
Controller Kurt E Erickson
Manager-Credit Amy Villara
Director-Employee Relations Amy Villara

ADVERTISING

Director Mark Lane
Manager-Classified Kris Eisenlohr

CIRCULATION

Director Greg Campbell

NEWS EXECUTIVES

Exec Editor Robert C Pollack
Editor Judith W Brown

EDITORS AND MANAGERS

Amusements Editor Eugene L Gorlewski
Automotive Editor Bart Fisher
Books Editor Judith W Brown
Business Editor John Kilroy
City Editor Eugene L Gorlewski
Editorial Page Editor Patrick Thibodeau
Education Editor Tracie Mauriello
Fashion Editor Barbara Sobuta
Religion Editor Barbara Sobuta
Style Editor Barbara Sobuta
Travel Editor Jerry Desimas
Wire Editor Thomas Shiel
Women's Editor Barbara Sobuta

PRODUCTION

Foreman-Pressroom Timothy Tighe
Foreman-Mailroom Louis Czarneski Jr
Supervisor-Dispatch Maureen McCarthy

Market Information: Split Run; TMC.

Mechanical available: Offset; Black and 3 ROP colors; insert accepted — preprinted; page cut-offs — 22¾".

Mechanical specifications: Type page 13" x 21½"; E - 6 cols, 2¹⁄₁₆", ⅛" between; A - 6 cols, 2¹⁄₁₆", ⅛" between; C - 9 cols, 1⅜", ¹⁄₁₆" between.

Commodity consumption: Newsprint 1,824 metric tons; widths 55", 41¼", 27½"; black ink 59,000 pounds; color ink 9,780 pounds; single pages printed 8,800; average pages per issue 34(d), 44(sat); single plates used 20,000.

Equipment: EDITORIAL: Front-end hardware — HI/Composition Sys; Front-end software — HI/Composition. CLASSIFIED: Front-end hardware — HI/Composition Sys; Front-end software — HI/Composition 2.0; Other equipment — 9-HI/8860, 1-DEC/LA 180. DISPLAY: Front-end hardware — 6-Ap/Mac; Front-end software — Multi-Ad; Printers — 2-QMS/860. PRODUCTION: Pagination software — HI/PLS 2.0; Typesetters — 3-HI/7450; Plate exposures — 1-BKY/Vertical, 1-Nu/Flip Top; Plate processors — 1-WL, 1-3M/Pyrofax Fuser; Electronic picture desk — Lf/AP Leaf Picture Desk; Scanners — Lf/Leafax 35; Production cameras — 1-C/Marathon; Automatic film processors — 1-LE/PC13.
PRESSROOM: Line 1 — 6-G/Metro 2-half decks; Folders — 1-G; Pasters — 6-G; Reels and stands — 6-G; Press control system — Fin. MAILROOM: Counter stackers — 1-SH; Inserters and stuffers — 2-MM/227; Bundle tyer — 1-CYP, 2-Sa, 2-Bu, 1-MLN, 2-MLN/2A; Addressing machine — 1-Ch. WIRE SERVICES: News — AP; Photos — AP; Syndicates — AP; Receiving dishes — AP. BUSINESS COMPUTERS: Sun/Micro Systems; Applications: Vision Data: Total circ package, all business functions except payroll.

NEW HAVEN

New Haven County

'90 U.S. Census- 132,097; E&P '96 Est. 134,824
ABC-NDM (90): 656,841 (HH 246,096)

New Haven Register (m-mon to sat; S)

New Haven Register, 40 Sargent Dr., New Haven, CT 06511-5918; tel (203) 789-5200; fax (203) 789-5209; e-mail billrush@ichange.com. Journal Register Co. group.

Circulation: 100,226(m); 100,226(m-sat); 122,256(S); ABC Sept. 30, 1995.

Price: 50¢(d); 50¢(sat); $1.75(S); $4.50/wk; $18.00/mo; $234.00/yr.

Advertising: Open inch rate $73.75(m); $73.75(m-sat); $97.90(S). **Representative:** Landon Associates Inc.

News Services: AP, SHNS, LAT-WP, KRT. **Politics:** Independent. **Established:** 1812.

Special Editions: Super Bowl, Outlook '96, Education '96 (Jan); Washington Auto, Dollars & Sense (Feb); Personal Finance, Bride & Bridegroom, Spring Fashions, Home Improvement, Personal Safety (Mar); Lawn & Garden, Especially for Kids, Dining Guide, Raven's Baseball (Apr); Summer Car Care, Newspaper In Education "Design-an-Ad" (May); Bridal (June); Courses and Careers (July); Academia Plus, Volvo Tennis (Aug); House & Home, Reading Tab, Fall Fashions (Sept); Home Improvement, Dining Guide, Cars '97/Car Care (Oct); Holiday Fashion, Holiday Gift Guides (Nov); Holiday Gift Guide (Dec).

Special Weekly Sections: Sports Extra, Today's Woman (mon); Business Extra, Financial/Business (tues); Food, Financial/Business (wed); Science & Health, School Sports Extra (thur); Weekend, Financial Business (fri); Home Furnishings, Financial/Business (sat); Arts/Travel, Home/Real Estates (S); Financial/Business.

Magazines: U.S.A. Weekend, TV Channels (local, newsprint, color) (S).

CORPORATE OFFICERS

President/CEO Robert M Jelenic
Exec Vice Pres/Chief Financial Officer/Treasurer Jean B Clifton

GENERAL MANAGEMENT

Publisher/CEO William J Rush
Manager-Credit Edward Donadio

ADVERTISING

Director-Marketing John Hetzler
Director-Art Val Karnauchov
Manager-National Charlene Chiaro
Manager-Classified Jeryl Parade
Manager-Electronic Publishing Victoria Rodewald
Manager-Research Tina Goodwin
Manager-Retail Gary Bucciero
Manager-Co-op Jim Gibbons
Manager-Preprint Gary Rowland

MARKETING AND PROMOTION

Director-Promotion Jennifer Pomichter

TELECOMMUNICATIONS

Audiotex Manager Jim Gibbons

CIRCULATION

Director Larry King
Manager-Home Delivery Robert Balisciano
Manager-Customer Service Ric Olivia

NEWS EXECUTIVES

Editor David J Butler
Editor-Emeritus Robert J Leeney
Editor-Electronic Publishing Sara Glines
Asst Managing Editor-Design Vern Williams
Sunday Editor David Funkhouser

EDITORS AND MANAGERS

Arts/Travel Editor Mary Colurso
Automotive Editor Raymond Hoye
Business/Finance Editor Paul Jackson
Capitol Bureau Chief Greg Hladky
Education Editor Karla Schuster
Entertainment Editor Fran Fried
Environmental Editor Abe Katz
Editorial Page Editor Charles P Kochakian
Electronic Publishing Graphics Editor Dean Caple
Fashion/Style Editor Richard Sandella
Features Editor Richard Sandella
Health/Medical Editor Abe Katz
Librarian Angel Diggs
Living Editor Richard Sandella
Metro Editor Jack Kramer
News Editor Raymond Hoye
Photo Editor Vern Williams
Political/Government Editor Greg Hladky
Radio/Television Editor Joseph Amarante
Religion Editor Jack Kramer
Science/Tech Editor Abe Katz
Sports Editor Doug Jacobs
Systems Editor Richard Conrad
Travel Editor David Funkhouser
Washington Bureau Chief Tamara Lytle

MANAGEMENT INFORMATION SERVICES

Data Processing Manager Jim Breault

PRODUCTION

Director Gerald Simpkins
Manager Robert Nevola
Manager-Engineering Service Charles Hill
Manager-Ad Service William McKiernan
Manager-Composing Bob Burgarella
Manager-Pressroom Edward Castelli Jr
Manager-Vehicle Maintenance Albert Palmucci
Manager-Mailroom Ella Wilson
Manager-Mailroom Al DeMorro
Manager-Commercial Printing Edward Castelli Jr
Manager-Preprint Packaging/Distribution Mike DiMassa

Market Information: Zoned editions; Split Run; TMC; Operate database; Operate audiotex; Electronic edition.

Mechanical available: Offset; Black and 3 ROP colors; insert accepted — preprinted, die cut, straight edge one side; page cut-offs — 22.08".

Mechanical specifications: Type page 13" x 21"; E - 6 cols, 2¹⁄₁₆", ⅛" between; A - 6 cols, 2¹⁄₁₆", ⅛" between; C - 9 cols, 1⁵⁄₁₆", ¹⁄₁₆" between.

Commodity consumption: Newsprint 15,740 short tons; widths 55", 41¼", 27½"; black ink 388,088 pounds; color ink 107,733 pounds; single pages printed 22,320; average pages per issue 50(d), 112(S); single plates used 115,000.

Equipment: EDITORIAL: Front-end hardware — AT w/80 workstations; Front-end software — AT; Printers — Panasonic/1124, NEC/P5300; Other equipment — 9-Ap/Mac, 40-RSK/100, 24-IBM/PS2, Lf/AP Leaf Picture Desk. CLASSIFIED: Front-end hardware — AT w/30 workstations; Front-end software — AT/Release 4.7.7; Printers — Epson/FX1050, Linotronic, HP/LaserPrinter; Other equipment — 8-Ap/Mac. AUDIOTEX: Hardware — PC/486; Software — Brite Voice Systems/City Line; Supplier name — Brite Voice Systems. DISPLAY: Front-end hardware — Dewar/Discovery IV, 5-PC/FLC20HR; Front-end software — Dewar/Discovery IV; Other equipment — 2-X/765 Flatbed Scanner. PRODUCTION: Typesetters — 2-MON/Express 1200, 2-PPRM-STR/600, 1-MON/6000; Plate exposures — 2-BKY/Ascor 1618-40, 2-Nu/Flip Top FT40, 1-Burgess/Consolux; Plate processors — 2-Nat/A-340; Electronic picture desk — Lf/AP Leaf Picture Desk, 1-Lf/Leafscan 35, 1-Lf/Leafscan 45; Scanners — ECR/Autokon 1000N; Production cameras — 2-C/Spartan III; Automatic film processors — 2-LE/PC 1800, 2-LE/LD24AQ, 1-C/R-660; Digital color separation equipment — Hel/399 ER.
PRESSROOM: Line 1 — 7-G/Metroliner-3272(3 half decks); Line 2 — 7-G/Metroliner-3273(3 half decks); Press drives — Fin; Folders — 2-G/Imperial 3:2; Reels and stands — 14-G/45" RTP 3-arm; Press control system — G/EPCS-PAR; Press registration system — Stoesser. MAILROOM: Counter stackers — 5-MM/388, 1-MM/310, 1-HL/Monitor, 1-HL/Dual Carrier; Inserters and stuffers — 1-GMA/SLS1000-20-1, 4-MM/308 6-1; Bundle tyer — 8-MLN/MLN2, 1-MLN/News90, 2-OVL/JP80; Addressing machine — 2-Ch/525-E. LIBRARY: Electronic — Data Times/MicroVax II. WIRE SERVICES: News — AP, KRT, SHNS, LAT-WP; Stock tables — AP SelectStox; Receiving dishes — size-3m. BUSINESS COMPUTERS: IBM/AS 400E50, DEC/4000, Digital/Micro Vax II; Applications: INSI: Ad mgmt; INSI: Accts payable, Gen ledger, Payroll, Class; CJ: Circ; PCs & micros networked; PCs & main system networked.

NEW LONDON

New London County

'90 U.S. Census- 28,642; E&P '96 Est. 28,720
ABC-CZ (90): 91,614 (HH 32,521)

The Day (m-mon to sat; S)

The Day, 47 Eugene O'Neill Dr.; PO Box 1231, New London, CT 06320-1231; tel (860) 442-2200.

Circulation: 42,366(m); 42,366(m-sat); 48,713(S); ABC Sept. 30, 1995.

Price: 50¢(d); 50¢(sat); $1.00(S); $2.75/wk.

Advertising: Open inch rate $31.48(m); $31.48(m-sat); $34.63(S). **Representative:** Landon Associates Inc.

News Services: AP, NYT, KRT. **Politics:** Independent. **Established:** 1881.

Special Editions: Education, Health & Fitness, Bridal (Jan); Review and Forecast, Washington's Birthday Automotive (Feb); Boating (Mar); Boating, Home & Garden, Car Care (Apr); Education, Vacation Guide (May); Vacation Guide (June); Sailfest, Bridal (July); Home Improvement, Back-to-School, Education (Aug); Fall Sports, Home Furnishings (Sept); Auto Premiere (Oct); Holiday Gift Guide (Nov); Holiday Gift Guide (Dec).

Special Weekly Sections: Health & Fitness (mon); Education, Food (wed); Weekend Entertainment (thur); Real Estate (fri); Church Page, Automotive, Wheels (sat); Business, Travel, Home (S).

Magazines: Health & Science, Small Business (mon); Entertainment This Week (thur); Boating, Garden, Real Estate (fri); Automotive (sat); Travel, Garden, Business, Home (S).

CORPORATE OFFICERS

President Reid MacCluggage
Exec Vice Pres Alcino G Almeida
Secretary/Treasurer Alcino G Almeida

GENERAL MANAGEMENT

Publisher Reid MacCluggage
General Manager Alcino G Almeida
Director-Finance Richard Willis
Controller Vera Cafaro
Manager-Credit Timothy Hinchey
Purchasing Agent Mel Seeger
Director-Human Resources Mary Jane McGinnis

ADVERTISING

Director Thomas P Kasprzak
Manager-Display Timothy Clements
Manager-Classified Paul Sas
Coordinator-Co-op Diane Martin
Coordinator-National Kathleen Bartelli

CIRCULATION

Director Robert E LeQuear
Manager-Delivery Services Robert D Ford
Manager-Sales Matthew R Dery
Manager-Distribution Paul Strecker
Asst Manager Janet M Ballestrini

NEWS EXECUTIVES

Editor Reid MacCluggage
Managing Editor Lance Johnson
Deputy Managing Editor Anthony Cronin
Asst Managing Editor-Operations Ed Murphy

Copyright ©1996 by the Editor & Publisher Co.

Asst Managing Editor-Photography/Graphics	Harold Hanka
Asst Managing Editor-Projects	Maria Hileman
Asst Managing Editor-Reporting/Sunday	Kyn Tolson

EDITORS AND MANAGERS

Arts Editor	Bethe Dufresne
Automotive Editor	Ed Murphy
Business/Finance Editor	Anthony Cronin
City Editor	Rosanne Simborski
City Editor (Night)	Elissa Bass
Editorial Page Editor	Morgan McGinley
Assoc Editorial Page Editor	Maura Casey
Deputy Editorial Page Editor	Gregory N Stone
Education Editor	Vivian Segall
Entertainment/Amusements Editor	Bethe Dufresne
Environmental Editor	Paul Choiniere
Fashion/Style Editor	Vivian Segall
Features	Kyn Tolson
Films/Theater Editor	Bethe Dufresne
Food Editor	Vivian Segall
Health/Medical	Paul Choiniere
Leisure	Kyn Tolson
Librarian	Tammy-Jo Ferdula
Living/Lifestyle Editor	Kyn Tolson
News Editor (Nights)	Tim Cotter
Photo Editor	Tom Toth
Photo Editor	Wayne Begassi
Political Writer	Lisa Hayden
Religion	Kyn Tolson
Science/Technology	Paul Choiniere
Sports Editor	Donald Cawley
Travel Editor	Steve Fagin

PRODUCTION

Director	William R Langman Jr
Manager-Composing Room	Henry Nichols
Manager-Pressroom	James K Coates
Manager-Receiving	Jeff Strother
Supervisor-Mailroom	Colleen Proctor
Coordinator	Lize-Anne Stewart
Electronic Technician	Joe Childs

Mechanical available: Offset; Black and 3 ROP colors; insert accepted — preprinted, product sampling accepted with conditions; page cut-offs — 21".

Mechanical specifications: Type page 13" x 21"; E - 6 cols, 2 1/16", 1/8" between; A - 6 cols, 2 1/16", 1/8" between; C - 10 cols, 1 7/32", 1/16" between.

Commodity consumption: Newsprint 3,770 metric tons; widths 54", 41 1/4", 27 1/2"; black ink 60,700 pounds; color ink 23,676 pounds; single pages printed 17,456; average pages per issue 43(d), 48(sat), 62(S); single plates used 39,018.

Equipment: EDITORIAL: Front-end hardware — 2-Dewar/386 fileserver, 7-Dewar/286, 56-Dewar/Discribe, 11-Compaq/386, 1-Dewar/386, 6-Ap/Mac ci fileserver; Front-end software — CPM; Printers — 1-Okidata/320, 1-Ap/Mac LaserWriter; Other equipment — Lf/AP Leaf Picture Desk, Lf/Leafscan. CLASSIFIED: Front-end hardware — 1-Dewar/286, 1-Compaq/386 fileserver, 9-Dewar/Discribe; Front-end software — CPM, DOS 3.31; Other equipment — 1-Okidata/320. DISPLAY: Adv layout systems — 1-Dewar/386-33 SIA, 1-Compaq/366-20 E, 3-Dewar/Discribe; Front-end hardware — 1-PC/386, 13-Ap/Mac, Unix/fileserver, CD/Jukebox Classic fileserver; Front-end software — Dos 3.31, Ethernet, Appleshare, Multi-Ad/Creator; Printers — 1-NEC/9300 Pinwriter, DTC, 2-Ap/Mac LaserWriter. PRODUCTION: Pagination software — Dewar 2 & 3; Typesetters — AU/3850, 2-DP/600, 1-NewGen/Turbo 660B, 1-LaserMaster/1200, 2-III/3850; Plate exposures — 1-Nu, 1-WL/Lith-X-Pozer; Plate processors — 1-WL; Electronic picture desk — Lf/AP Leaf Picture Desk; Scanners — Newscan, ECR/Autokon 1000, X/7650, AG/Arcus Plus; Production cameras — 1-C/Spartan III, 1-Nu, AG/Rapidline 66; Automatic film processors — AG/Rapidline 66; Film transporters — 1-Konica, 1-C.
PRESSROOM: Line 1 — 7-G/Headliner Offset double width; Press drives — Allen Bradley; Folders — G/Imperial 3:2, 2-G; Pasters — 7-G/Automatic RTP, G/CT-45s; Reels and stands — 7-G; Press control system — G/MPCS. MAILROOM: Counter stackers — 2-QWI/200, 1-QWI/100, 3-QWI/350; Inserters and stuffers — S/NP 630 22-stations; Bundle tyer — 5-Power Strap, 3-Power Strap/3/4Wraps, 3-Matthews/Ink Jet System; Addressing machine — Computer generated; Mailroom control system — Prima Life. QWI/Programmer. ICON/300. WIRE SERVICES: News — AP, NYT, KRT; Stock tables — AP SelectStox I; Receiving dishes — size-8ft, AP. BUSINESS COMPUTERS: 1-DEC/PDP 11-84, 1-DEC/VAX; Applications: Gen ledger, Class transient;, Symphony, WordPerfect, Multimate, FAS/2000: Fixed Assets; PCs & micros networked.

NORWALK

Fairfield County

'90 U.S. Census- 78,892; E&P '96 Est. 79,662
ABC-CZ (90): 78,331 (HH 30,560)

The Hour (e-mon to sat)

The Hour, 346 Main Ave. (06851); PO Box 790, Norwalk, CT 06852-0790; tel (203) 846-3281; fax (203) 846-9897.

Circulation: 19,515(e); 19,515(e-sat); ABC Sept. 30, 1995.

Price: 40¢(d); 75¢(sat); $2.45/wk; $117.60/yr.

Advertising: Open inch rate $20.81(e); $20.81(e-sat). **Representative:** Landon Associates Inc.

News Service: AP. **Politics:** Non-partisan. **Established:** 1871.

Not Published: New Year; Washington's Birthday; Memorial Day; Independence Day; Labor Day; Thanksgiving; Christmas.

Advertising not accepted: Work at home (state law); Mail order.

Special Weekly Sections: Health, Fitness (mon); Travel (tues); Best Food (wed); Entertainment, In the Prime (thur); Weekend (sat).

CORPORATE OFFICERS

Chairman/Finance Officer	Walter E Whitton
President	Jack H Whitton
Secretary	Judith Cunningham
Treasurer	Dorothy Weed

GENERAL MANAGEMENT

Publisher	B J Frazier
Exec Vice Pres/General Manager	Richard E Curran

ADVERTISING

Manager-Retail	Jack H Whitton
Manager-Classified	Linda Guckert
Manager-Sales	Tom Kies

CIRCULATION

Director	John Brennan
Manager	Peter Kish

NEWS EXECUTIVES

Exec Editor	John P Reilly
Managing Editor	Mark Allison
Asst Managing Editor	Mary McGee

EDITORS AND MANAGERS

Automotive Editor	Charles Mitchell
City Editor	Charles Mitchell
Editorial Page Editor	John P Reilly
Education Editor	Keith Hagel
Entertainment/Amusements Editor	William F Torpey
Environmental Editor	David Curran
Fashion/Style Editor	Beth Burgeson
Features/Food Editor	Beth Burgeson
Health/Medical Editor	Willliam F Torpey
Living/Lifestyle Editor	Beth Burgeson
National/State Editor	William F Torpey
News Editor	Jim Honley
Photo Editor	Carol Hofmann
Political/Government Editor	William F Torpey
Religion Editor	Carol Hofmann
Sports Editor	Louis Brodersen
Asst Sports Editor	George Albano
Television/Film Editor	Carol Hofmann
Theater/Music Editor	Carol Hofmann
Travel/Women's Editor	Beth Burgeson
Wire Editor	James R Hanley

MANAGEMENT INFORMATION SERVICES

Data Processing Manager	Mike Dogali

PRODUCTION

Director-Data Processing	Mike Dogali
Foreman-Composing	Eric Feidler
Foreman-Pressroom	L Blackwell

Market Information: TMC.

Mechanical available: Offset; Black and 2 ROP colors; insert accepted — preprinted; page cut-offs — 22 3/4".

Mechanical specifications: Type page 13" x 21 1/2"; E - 6 cols, 2 1/16", 1/8" between; A - 6 cols, 2 1/16", 1/8" between; C - 10 cols, 1 3/8", 1/16" between.

Commodity consumption: Newsprint 1,700 metric tons; widths 54", 40 1/2", 27", 13 1/2"; black ink 37,760 pounds; single pages printed 12,163; average pages per issue 38(d), 44(sat).

Equipment: EDITORIAL: Front-end hardware — 30-AT; Front-end software — AT; Other equipment — Ap/Mac II, Lf/AP Leaf Picture Desk. CLASSIFIED: Front-end hardware — 10-AT; Front-end software — AT. DISPLAY: Adv layout systems — CJ; Front-end software — CJ. PRODUCTION: Typesetters — 2-AU/Micro 5; Plate exposures — 2-BKY; Plate processors — 1-Nat/A340; Electronic picture desk — Lf/AP Leaf Picture Desk; Production cameras — 1-LE/121, 2-R/421, 1-ECR/1030M; Automatic film processors — 1-COM/RCP 101, 2-AG/Rapidline 66; Film transporters — 1-LE/121.
PRESSROOM: Line 1 — 5-G/Cosmo; Folders — 2-G; Reels and stands — 5-G. MAILROOM: Inserters and stuffers — 2-MM/5P; Bundle tyer — 1-Dynaric/1500, 1-MLN. WIRE SERVICES: News — AP; Photos — AP; Receiving dishes — size-10ft, AP. BUSINESS COMPUTERS: 2-HP/3000; Applications: CJ; PCs & micros networked; PCs & main system networked.

NORWICH

New London County

'90 U.S. Census- 37,467; E&P '96 Est. 37,459
ABC-NDM (90): 159,908 (HH 58,726)

Norwich Bulletin (m-mon to sat; S)

Norwich Bulletin, 66 Franklin St., Norwich, CT 06360; tel (860) 887-9211; fax (860) 887-1949; e-mail norbull@q.continuum.net; web site http://www.ctonline.com/cton-line/nbulletin.html. Gannett Co. Inc. group.

Circulation: 32,336(m); 32,336(m-sat); 38,061(S); ABC Sept. 30, 1995.

Price: 50¢(d); 50¢(sat); $1.00(S); $2.75/wk; $11.00/mo; $143.00/yr.

Advertising: Open inch rate $26.25(m); $26.25(m-sat); $26.25(S). **Representative:** Gannett National Newspaper Sales.

News Services: AP, GNS. **Politics:** Independent. **Established:** 1791.

Special Editions: Communique, Education, Bridal (Jan); Regional Guidebook (Feb); Communique, Focus on Future, Health & Fitness (Mar); House & Garden, American Home Week, Spring Motor Care (Apr); Communique, Lawn & Garden, Summertime (May); Summer Bridal, Summertime II (June); Communique, Antique Auto, Prime Time (July); Back-to-School, Community Guidebook, Bus Schedules (Aug); Communique, Football Preview (Sept); Fall Home Improvement, Fall Motor Care, Scary Stories (Oct); Election Tab, Communique, Holiday Gift Guide (Nov); Holiday Who-Dun-It?, Last Minute Gift Guide (Dec).

Special Weekly Sections: Motor Car (sat); TV Bulletin (S).

Magazine: USA Weekend (S).

CORPORATE OFFICER

President	Richard M Bottorf

GENERAL MANAGEMENT

Publisher	Richard M Bottorf
Director-Human Resources	Janine G Dunn
Controller	Linda Rubin

ADVERTISING

Director	William A Baxter Jr

CIRCULATION

Director	Francis J Smith

NEWS EXECUTIVES

Exec Editor	Keith Fontaine
Managing Editor	Randolph Brandt

EDITORS AND MANAGERS

City Editor	Raymond Hackett
Editorial Page Editor	Edward J Dunn
Features Editor	Molly Palmer
Graphics Editor	Wes Rand
News Editor	Sandra L Daine
Photo Editor	Jeff Evans
Sports Editor	Gary Samek

MANAGEMENT INFORMATION SERVICES

Data Processing Manager	Nancy Miclette

PRODUCTION

Director	Myron Breninghouse

Market Information: Zoned editions; Split Run; TMC.

Mechanical available: Offset; Black and 3 ROP colors; insert accepted — preprinted; page cut-offs — 22 3/4".

Mechanical specifications: Type page 13" x 21 1/2"; E - 6 cols, 2 1/16", 1/8" between; A - 6 cols, 2 1/16", 1/8" between; C - 10 cols, 1 3/16", 1/16" between.

Commodity consumption: Newsprint 3,100 short tons; 3,417 metric tons; widths 54", 40 1/2", 27"; black ink 82,000 pounds; color ink 5,500 pounds; single pages printed 14,980; average pages per issue 28(d), 48(S); single plates used 44,000.

Equipment: EDITORIAL: Front-end hardware — SCS, 4-Dell, 35-Falco, 9-Ap/Mac; Front-end software — Multi-Ad/Creator, QuarkXPress; Printers — Tegra/Varityper 5510, 2-Tegra/Varityper 5000. CLASSIFIED: Front-end hardware — SCS, Dell, 8-Falco. DISPLAY: Adv layout systems — SCS/Layout 8000; Front-end hardware — IBM; Printers — IBM. PRODUCTION: Typesetters — Pre-Press/Panther Plus; Platemaking systems — KFM; Plate exposures — Nu/Flip Top; Plate processors — 1-W; Scanners — Kk/RFS 2035 Plus, Microtek; Production cameras — C/Spartan III; Automatic film processors — 1-LE, 1-Litex/26; Digital color separation equipment — Kk/RFS 2035 Plus, Adobe/Photoshop.
PRESSROOM: Line 1 — 5-HI/1650; Folders — 2-HI; Pasters — Handmade. MAILROOM: Counter stackers — 2-QWI; Inserters and stuffers — 1-HI/1372; Bundle tyer — 2-MLN/EE; Addressing machine — Ch. WIRE SERVICES: News — AP, GNS; Stock tables — AP SelectStox; Receiving dishes — AP. BUSINESS COMPUTERS: IBM/AS-400; Applications: Circ, Gen ledger, Accts payable, Adv; PCs & main system networked.

STAMFORD

Fairfield County

'90 U.S. Census- 109,800; E&P '96 Est. 112,947
ABC-CZ (90): 108,056 (HH 41,945)

The Stamford Advocate (all day-mon to fri; m-sat; S)

The Stamford Advocate, 75 Tresser Blvd.; Box 9307, Stamford, CT 06904; tel (203) 964-2200. Times Mirror Co. group.

Circulation: 29,691(a); 28,499(m-sat); 41,125(S); ABC Sept. 30, 1995.

Price: 50¢(d); 50¢(sat); $1.50(S); $3.30/wk; $13.20/mo; $148.20/yr.

Advertising: Open inch rate $50.88(a); $50.88(m-sat); $56.60(S). **Representative:** Landon Associates Inc.

News Services: AP, LAT-WP, KRT. **Politics:** Independent. **Established:** 1829.

Not Published: New Year; Christmas.

Special Editions: Education, Weddings, New Real Estate (Jan); Cruise Guide, Business & Economic Review, Careers (Feb); Home, Camps, Spring Home Improvement, Bermuda Travel, Showcase of Homes, First Home (Mar); Garden, New York Auto Show, Golf, All About Kids, Canada Travel, Education Outlook, Auto Expo, Real Estate Showcase, Women & Money (Apr); Summer Fun, Our Town, New England Vacations (May); Visit USA, Meet the Merchants, Entertaining, Connecticut's Top 100, Waterfront Real Estate (June); Europe, Travel, JAL (July); Survey of Education, Back-to-School, Fall Foliage (Aug); Bahamas Travel, Healthwatch, Weddings, Home Improvement Garden (Sept); Antique Arts & Collectibles, Kitchen & Bath, Fall Cruise Guide, Fall Home, Community Sections, Education, Real Estate Showcase, Auto Intro (Oct); Skiing-Private Lessons, Holiday Entertaining, Holiday Countdown, Pilgrim, Florida Travel, Antique Real Estate (Nov); Gifts for Every List, Ski Holidays, Great Gift Ideas, Last Minute Gift Guide (Dec).

Special Weekly Sections: Panorama (mon); Panorama/Health (tues); Food (wed); Living (thur); The Guide (TMC), Weekend (fri); Arts/Leisure, Travel (S); Sports, Business (daily).

Magazines: Parade Magazine, TV Book, Color Comics (S).

CORPORATE OFFICERS

CEO/President	William J Rowe
Exec Vice Pres/Editor	Kenneth H Brief
Vice Pres/Advertising Director	John Dunster
Vice Pres/Circulation Director	Craig Allen
Vice Pres/Director-Production/Facility	Robert T Hughes
Vice Pres/Controller/Director of Systems	Robert Zikias

GENERAL MANAGEMENT

Publisher	William J Rowe
Vice Pres/Controller/Director of Systems	Robert Zikias
Director-Human Resources	Terri Flaherty

ADVERTISING

Vice Pres/Director	John Dunster
Manager-National	Marcia Groglio
Manager-Classified	Polly Nash

MARKETING AND PROMOTION
Manager-Marketing Service — Sandra Guss
Manager-Promotion/Public Affairs — Barbara Bind
TELECOMMUNICATIONS
Audiotex Manager — Barbara Bind
CIRCULATION
Vice Pres/Director — Craig Allen
NEWS EXECUTIVES
Exec Vice Pres/Editor — Kenneth H Brief
Managing Editor-News — Deirdre Channing
Asst Managing Editor-Design/Photography — Jacqueline Segal
EDITORS AND MANAGERS
Arts Editor — Linda O'Connell
Business Editor — Beth Frances Cox
City Editor — Robin Foster
Senior Editor — Arthur Helms
Editorial Page Editor — Joy Haenlein
Features Editor — Dan Berman
Exec News Editor — Michael Barlow
Photo Editor — Mary Cooney
Sports Editor — Robert Kennedy
MANAGEMENT INFORMATION SERVICES
Director-Info Services — Steve Harrington
PRODUCTION
Vice Pres/Director — Robert T Hughes
Superintendent-Composing — Frank Tymula
Superintendent-Pressroom — Donald Jordan
Superintendent-Mailroom — John Meyer

Market Information: Zoned editions; Split Run; TMC; Operate audiotex.
Mechanical available: Offset; Black and 3 ROP colors; insert accepted — preprinted; page cut-offs — 22 3/4".
Mechanical specifications: Type page 13" x 21 1/2"; E - 6 cols, 2.48", .22" between; A - 6 cols, 2 1/16", 1/8" between; C - 10 cols, 1 3/16", 3/32" between.
Commodity consumption: Newsprint 4,000 metric tons; widths 54", 40 1/2", 27"; black ink 82,846 pounds; color ink 7,000 pounds; single pages printed 19,000; average pages per issue 44(d), 30(sat), 112(S); single plates used 39,000.
Equipment: EDITORIAL: Front-end hardware — 2-CSI/1170, 78-CSI, Ap/Mac, 15-Ap/Mac; Front-end software — CSI, QuarkXPress, Adobe/Photoshop; Printers — Graphic Enterprises/PS 3, III/3880s, AU/APS-5; Other equipment — Lf/AP Leaf Picture Desk, Kk/scanners, Lf/Leaf 45 Scanner. CLASSIFIED: Front-end hardware — 1-CSI/1170, 28-CSI/Terminal; Front-end software — CSI; Printers — AU/APS-5, III/3850, DEC/LA 120. AUDIOTEX: Hardware — Brite, Unix; Software — Voice Print; Supplier name — Brite, AP. DISPLAY: Adv layout systems — 8-Ap/Mac; Front-end hardware — Ap/Mac; Front-end software — Multi-Ad/Creator, QuarkXPress; Printers — Ap/Mac LaserWriters, V/600, Graphic Enterprises/PS 3, III/3850. PRODUCTION: Typesetters — 2-AU/APS-6; Platemaking systems — KFM/Twin-Line; Plate exposures — 1-Nu/Flip Top; Plate processors — 1-WL/38D, 1-KFM; Electronic picture desk — Lf/AP Leaf Picture Desk, 1-KFM; Scanners — 1-ECR/Autokon, Kk/scanner, Linotype-Hell; Production cameras — C/Spartan Upright; Automatic film processors — 3-P/SC 2050; Film transporters — 1-LE, 1-Kk; Shrink lenses — 2-LE/Shrink Lens; Color separation equipment (conventional) — Linotype-Hell.
PRESSROOM: Line 1 — 8-HI/1660 offset double width, 2-HI/1660 Units double width; Press drives — GE; Folders — 2-HI; Pasters — 9-MEG/Automatic; Reels and stands — MEG; Press control system — GE; Press registration system — KFM. MAILROOM: Counter stackers — 3-QWI/SJ100; Inserters and stuffers — 1-HI/1472 On-line; Bundle tyer — 4-OVL/JP40; Addressing machine — 1-KR/215; Other mailroom equipment — HI/Stitch Trimmer. COMMUNICATIONS: Systems used — satellite. WIRE SERVICES: News — AP, LAT-WP, KRT; Photos — AP, KRT, LAT-WP; Stock tables — AP; Syndicates — LATS, Universal Press, TMS, United Media, Creators, King Features; Receiving dishes — size-3m, AP. BUSINESS COMPUTERS: 1-DEC/VAX 4100, CJ; Applications: Gen ledger, Accts payable, Accts receivable, Adv, Circ, Payroll; PCs & micros networked; PCs & main system networked.

TORRINGTON
Litchfield County
'90 U.S. Census- 34,423; E&P '96 Est. 35,857
ABC-CZ (90): 33,687 (HH 13,883)

The Register Citizen
(m-mon to sat; S)
The Register Citizen, 190 Water St.; PO Box 58, Torrington, CT 06790-0058; tel (860) 489-3121; fax (860) 489-6790. Journal Register Co. group.
Circulation: 14,857(m); 14,857(m-sat); 13,936(S); ABC Sept. 30, 1995.
Price: 50¢(d); 50¢(sat); 50¢(S).
Advertising: Open inch rate $15.70(m); $15.70(m-sat); $15.70(S). **Representative:** Landon Associates Inc.
News Services: AP, NYT, CSM. **Politics:** Independent. **Established:** 1874.
Special Editions: Bridal, Education, Coupon Book (Jan); President's Day Auto, Progress (Feb); Health & Fitness, Coupon Book, Medical Directory (Mar); House & Garden, Legal Directory, Car Care (Apr); House & Home, Backyard Living (May); Graduation, Northwest Summer (June); Summer Sales, Community & Community Guide (July); Coupon Book, Education (Aug); Fall Bridal, Home Improvement, Northwest Autumn, Coupon Book (Sept); Coupon Book, Fall Car Care, Home Improvement, New Cars '97 (Oct); Christmas Gift Guide, Holiday Dining, Coupon Book (Nov); Letters to Santa, Last Minute Gift Guide (Dec).
Special Weekly Sections: Entertainment (mon); Entertainment, Health & Science (tues); Arts & Entertainment (wed); Entertainment, Food (thur); TGIF (fri); Business, Entertainment (sat); Real Estate, Travel, Home & Garden (S).
Magazines: TV Preview, USA Weekend, Comics (S).

CORPORATE OFFICERS
President/CEO — Robert M Jelenic
Exec Vice Pres/Chief Financial Officer/Treasurer — Jean B Clifton
GENERAL MANAGEMENT
Publisher — Nancy Cawley
Controller — Lisa DeMarco
ADVERTISING
Manager — Michael O'Sullivan
Manager-Classified — Richard Welch
CIRCULATION
Director — Michael Rafter
NEWS EXECUTIVE
Editor — Don Stacom
EDITORS AND MANAGERS
Features Editor — Melanie O'Brien
News Editor — Patricia Daddona
Sports Editor — Matthew Pepin
PRODUCTION
Foreman-Pressroom — Peter Robustelli

Market Information: Zoned editions; Split Run; TMC.
Mechanical available: Offset; Black and 3 ROP colors; insert accepted — preprinted, single card; page cut-offs — 22 3/4".
Mechanical specifications: Type page 13" x 21 1/4"; E - 6 cols, 2 1/16", 1/8" between; A - 6 cols, 2 1/16", 1/8" between; C - 9 cols, 1 3/8", 1/16" between.
Commodity consumption: Newsprint 1,300 short tons; widths 27 1/2", 13 3/4", 30"; black ink 45,000 pounds; color ink 2,200 pounds; single pages printed 9,300; average pages per issue 30(d); single plates used 18,600.
Equipment: EDITORIAL: Front-end hardware — Dewar Sys; Front-end software — Dewar Sys. CLASSIFIED: Front-end hardware — 1-Dewar Sys; Front-end software — Dewar Sys. DISPLAY: Front-end hardware — Dewar/Discovery; Front-end software — Dewar/Discovery. PRODUCTION: Typesetters — 2-COM/8600, 1-Hyphen/Desk 72E, 1-Hyphen/94E; Plate exposures — 2-Nu; Plate processors — 1-Nat; Electronic picture desk — Lf/AP Leaf Picture Desk; Scanners — Lf/Leafscan 35; Production cameras — 1-C/Spartan III; Automatic film processors — 1-AG, 1-P.
PRESSROOM: Line 1 — 8-G/Urbanite; Folders — 1-G/2:1; Pasters — 2-Enkel/Autoweb, 4-Butler/Auto; Press registration system — Stoesser/Center Pin. MAILROOM: Counter stackers — 1-Fg, 1-HL/Stack Pack, 1-MM/310-20; Inserters and stuffers — 2-MM/227-104; Bundle tyer — 2-MLN/2EE; Addressing machine — 8-Wm. WIRE SERVICES: News — AP; Syndicates — NYT, CSM; Receiving dishes — AP. BUSINESS COMPUTERS: 2-DEC/Micro VAX-3100, IBM/A5400; Applications: INSI: Accts payable/Gen ledger, Adv mgmt, Circ; PCs & micros networked; PCs & main system networked.

WALLINGFORD
See MERIDEN

WATERBURY
New Haven County
'90 U.S. Census- 110,729; E&P '96 Est. 113,923
ABC-CZ (90): 173,075 (HH 66,582)

Waterbury Republican-American (m-mon to sat; S)
Waterbury Republican-American, 389 Meadow St.; PO Box 2090, Waterbury, CT 06722-2090; tel (203) 574-3636; fax (203) 754-0644.
Circulation: 60,221(m); 60,221(m-sat); 74,933(S); ABC Sept. 30, 1995.
Price: 40¢(d); 40¢(sat); $1.50(S); $15.17/mo (d & S); $182.00/yr (d & S).
Advertising: Open inch rate $31.15(m); $31.15(m-sat); $34.55(S). **Representative:** Cresmer, Woodward, O'Mara & Ormsbee.
News Services: AP, KRT, SHNS, SNS, CQ. **Politics:** Independent-Republican. **Established:** 1881 (Republican), 1844 (American).
Not Published: Christmas.
Advertising not accepted: Mail order requiring investment; other mail order at publisher's option.
Special Editions: Meet the Merchants, Health & Fitness (Jan); Bridal (Feb); Auto Servicing (Mar); Gardening, Home Improvement (Apr); Mother's Day, Lifestyles (May); Education, Kids, Career (Aug); Bridal/Fashions, Home Improvement, Restaurants (Sept); Automotive, Kitchen & Bath, Home & Energy (Oct); Travel/Winter, N.W. Holiday Guide (Nov); Downtown Christmas (Dec).
Special Weekly Sections: Your Business (mon); Food Features (wed); The NEWS (West zone tab, local, in-paper and TMC) (thur); The Weekender (fri); Religion Page, Wheels Page (sat); Business News, Commentary, Accent, Travel, Leisure, Antiques Directory, Interiors, Comics (S); Accent, Amusements, Business News (daily).
Magazines: TV Preview (local, offset, full-color, quarter page); Panorama (travel and entertainment, local broadsheet); Today's Woman (local, tab); Home/Real Estate (local, offset, tab); Weekend (local, offset, tab); Cultural Events Preview (local, offset, tab); Connecticut Business (local, offset); Parade (S).

CORPORATE OFFICERS
President/Treasurer — William J Pape II
Vice Pres/Asst Treasurer — Bill Southerland
Vice Pres/Asst Secretary — Benita P Greeley
Secretary — John H Cassidy Jr
Asst Treasurer/Asst Secretary — William B Pape II
Asst Treasurer — Michael J DiVito
Asst Treasurer — Benita P Greeley
GENERAL MANAGEMENT
Publisher — William J Pape II
Business Manager — William B Pape II
Controller — Michael J DiVito
ADVERTISING
Director-Marketing — Fred Hull
Manager — Patrick Cox
Manager-National — Andrew J Pape
Manager-Preprint/Major Accounts — Amy H Cunningham
TELECOMMUNICATIONS
Audiotex Manager — Howard Fielding
CIRCULATION
Director — Edward Winters
Asst Director — Kenneth Collette
Coordinator-Newspapers in Education — Kenneth Collette
NEWS EXECUTIVES
Exec Editor — Bill Southerland
Managing Editor — Bob Veillette
Deputy Managing Editor — Ed Goodman
EDITORS AND MANAGERS
Accent Editor — Tracey O'Shaughnessy
Automotive Editor — Mike Azzara
Business Editor — Howard Fielding
Copy Desk Chief — Mike Griffin
Design Editor — Rob Laszlo
Editorial Writer — Connie Lepore
Editorial Writer — Steve Macoy
Education Editor — Maura Kelly
Entertainment/Amusements Editor — Nancy Van Valkenburg
Environmental Writer — Brigitte Ruthman
Fashion Writer — Kelly Devine
Features Editor — Claire LaFleur
Graphics Editor — James Dean
Health/Medical Writer — Jennifer Gangloff
Metro Editor — Susan Bibisi
News Editor — Greg Hanisek
Local News Editor — Bob Fredricks
News Systems Editor — Chris Feola
Pagination Editor — Andy Saver
Photo Editor — James Staebler
Regional Editor — John Crowell
Regional Editor — Tom Hennick
Science/Technology Editor — Chris Feola
Exec Sports Editor — Lee Lewis
Sports Editor — Tom Talarico
Suburban Editor — Adam Sapiro
Travel Editor — Andy Sauer
Wire Editor — Joe Galbraith
Yes Desk Manager — Breda Bissonnette
MANAGEMENT INFORMATION SERVICES
Data Processing Manager — Steven Volovki
PRODUCTION
Director — Andrea Pape
Manager-Pressroom — Michael Fryette
Superintendent-Composing — E Donald Creighton
Superintendent-Pressroom — Robert Thompson
Foreman-Mailroom — James Gorman

Market Information: Zoned editions; Split Run; TMC; Operate audiotex.
Mechanical available: Offset; Black and 3 ROP colors; insert accepted — preprinted, single sheets; page cut-offs — 22 3/4".
Mechanical specifications: Type page 13" x 21 1/2"; E - 6 cols, 2 1/16", 1/8" between; A - 6 cols, 2 1/16", 1/8" between; C - 9 cols, 1 3/8", 1/16" between.
Commodity consumption: Newsprint 7,500 short tons; 6,804 metric tons; widths 55", 41 1/4", 27 1/2", 13 3/4"; black ink 176,800 pounds; color ink 25,250 pounds; single pages printed 19,372; average pages per issue 41(d), 110(S); single plates used 60,000.
Equipment: EDITORIAL: Front-end hardware — 3-DEC/PDP 11-84, 22-DEC/VT71, 31-DEC/VT173, 6-AST; Front-end software — NSSE, Novell/Network; Printers — 1-HP/Laser-Printer. CLASSIFIED: Front-end hardware — IBM/2RS 6000-370, 17-AST/Workstations; Front-end software — AT/Enterprise; Printers — 2-HP/LaserPrinter 4MS. AUDIOTEX: Hardware — Brite Voice Systems. DISPLAY: Adv layout systems — Managing Editor/Ad Director; Front-end hardware — 5-Xenotron/XVL3, 1-Art-master, 3-Ap/Mac; Front-end software — Xenotron, Multi-Ad/Creator. PRODUCTION: Pagination software — QuarkXPress 3.31; Typesetters — 2-AU/APS-5, 2-Ultre, 1-ECR/VR 36; Plate exposures — 2-Burgess, 1-OLEC; Plate processors — 2-Hoechst; Electronic picture desk — 1-Lf/AP Leaf Picture Desk; Scanners — 1-ECR/Autokon 1000; Production cameras — 1-C/Marathon; Automatic film processors — 1-P/26 RA, 1-AG/Rapidline 66, 1-P/28RA, 1-P/RAII; Shrink lenses — 1-CK Optical/7%; Digital color separation equipment — 2-Kk/2035 plus, 2-Ap/Mac, QPS, Adobe/Photoshop.
PRESSROOM: Line 1 — 6-G/Metro 2 decks; Press drives — Fin; Folders — G/2:1; Pasters — 6-G; Reels and stands — 6-G. MAILROOM: Counter stackers — 5-QWI, 4-SJ/300, SJ/100; Inserters and stuffers — 1-HI/1472 on line, 1-S/1372; Bundle tyer — 7-MLN/2A, 2-Ca/Tyers, 1-MLN/2EE; Wrapping singles — 2-HL/Bottom Wrap, 3-Ap/Mac, 1-QWI; Addressing machine — 1-Ch; Mailroom control system — MM. MM/335 Stitcher-Binder. LIBRARY: Electronic — BH/Microx; Combination — Electronic. WIRE SERVICES: News — AP, KRT, SHNS, CSM, SNS, CQ; Photos — AP; Stock tables — AP SelectStox; Syndicates — AP; Receiving dishes — size-10ft, AP. BUSINESS COMPUTERS: 1-DEC/Micro VAX 3180; Applications: Foxpro/Excel.

WILLIMANTIC
Windham County
'90 U.S. Census- 15,880; E&P '96 Est. 16,399
ABC-NDM (90): 65,515 (HH 20,966)

The Chronicle
(e-mon to fri; m-sat)
The Chronicle, One Chronicle Rd.; PO Box 148, Willimantic, CT 06226; tel (860) 423-8466; fax (860) 423-7641.
Circulation: 10,081(e); 10,081(m-sat); ABC Sept. 30, 1995.

Price: 50¢(d); 50¢(sat); $2.40/wk.
Advertising: Open inch rate $15.75(e); $15.75(m-sat). **Representative:** Landon Associates Inc.
News Service: AP. **Established:** 1877.
Not Published: New Year; Memorial Day; Independence Day; Labor Day; Thanksgiving; Christmas.
Special Editions: Eastbrook Mall Walk, Bridal (Jan); Automotive (Feb); Spring Special (May); Summer Guide (June); Back-to-School (Aug); Sports (Sept); Harvest Values (Oct); Holiday Guide, Christmas (Nov); Gift Gallery (Dec).
Special Weekly Sections: Real Estate (tues); Food (wed); Lifestyle, Home and Garden (thur); Arts, Entertainment (fri); Auto, Religion, Society/Wedding (sat).
Magazines: Regional & Town Pages, Comics Sports, Television, Obituary, Weather (daily).

CORPORATE OFFICERS
President/Treasurer ..... Lucy B Crosbie
Secretary ..... Kevin B Crosbie

GENERAL MANAGEMENT
Publisher ..... Kevin B Crosbie
General Manager ..... Kevin B Crosbie
Purchasing Agent ..... Kevin B Crosbie

ADVERTISING
Director ..... Walter Riley

CIRCULATION
Manager ..... Charles E Burr

NEWS EXECUTIVE
Editorial Director ..... Barry Lewis

EDITORS AND MANAGERS
Automotive/Aviation Editor ..... Kevin B Crosbie
Art/Entertainment Editor ..... T C Karmel
Business/Finance Editor ..... Barry Lewis
Editorial Writer ..... Barry Lewis
Food Editor ..... T C Karmel
Photo Department Manager ..... Fran Funk
Sports Editor ..... Larry Kelley
Suburban Editor ..... Barbara Jordan

MANAGEMENT INFORMATION SERVICES
Data Processing Manager ..... Dan Phelps

PRODUCTION
Manager ..... George Avey
Foreman-Pressroom ..... Peter Linkkila
Foreman-Composing ..... Barbara Kozin
Manager-Distribution Center ..... Charles Straub

Market Information: TMC; ADS.
Mechanical available: Offset; Black and 3 ROP colors; insert accepted — preprinted; page cutoffs — 21½".
Mechanical specifications: Type page 13" x 21½"; E - 6 cols, 2 1/16", 1/8" between; A - 6 cols, 2 1/16", 1/8" between; C - 9 cols, 1 9/16", 1/16" between.
Commodity consumption: Newsprint 375 short tons; width 27½"; single pages printed 9,000; average pages per issue 16(d), 24(sat).
Equipment: EDITORIAL: Front-end hardware — 20-CText, IBM/PCs; Front-end software — CText; Printers — LaserMaster. CLASSIFIED: Front-end hardware — 4-IBM/PC; Front-end software — CText; Printers — Ap/Mac LaserWriter NT. DISPLAY: Front-end hardware — 6-IBM; Front-end software — QuarkXPress; Printers — LaserMaster. PRODUCTION: OCR software — OCR Systems/Read Right; Platemaking systems — Nat; Scanners — HP; Color separation equipment (conventional) — Lf/AP Leaf Picture Desk.
PRESSROOM: Line 1 — 5-WPC/Web Leader; Line 2 — 2-WPC/Web Leader. MAILROOM: Inserters and stuffers — KAN/480; Bundle tyer — MLN. WIRE SERVICES: News — AP; Receiving dishes — size-6ft. BUSINESS COMPUTERS: DEC/Micro VAX II; Applications: Vision Data: Accts payable, Accts receivable, Circ; PCs & micros networked; PCs & main system networked.

DELAWARE

DOVER
Kent County
'90 U.S. Census- 28,454; **E&P '96 Est.** 30,795

Delaware State News
(m-mon to sat)
Daily Whale/Delaware State News (S)
Delaware State News, Webbs Ln. & New Burton Rd.; PO Box 737, Dover, DE 19903; tel (302) 674-3600; fax (302) 674-4752. Independent Newspapers Inc. (DE) group.

Circulation: 21,304(m); 21,304(m-sat); 34,000(S); Sworn Sept. 15, 1995.
Price: 35¢(d); 35¢(sat); $1.00(S); $117.00/yr.
Advertising: Open inch rate $14.75(m); $14.75(m-sat); $17.80(S). **Representative:** Papert Companies.
News Service: Zap News. **Established:** 1901 (weekly), 1953 (daily).
Note: There is a combined (S) circulation and advertising rate between the Delaware State News and the Lewes Daily Whale.
Advertising not accepted: Subject to publisher's approval.
Special Editions: Christmas Greetings; New Year's Greetings.
Magazines: Color Comic (TMC) (thur); Parade, Own TV/Leisure Magazine (S).

CORPORATE OFFICERS
Chairman/CEO ..... Joe Smyth
President ..... Tamra Brittingham
Vice Pres ..... Frank A Fantini
Vice Pres ..... James S Ritch
Treasurer ..... Chris Engel
Secretary ..... Ron Stevens

GENERAL MANAGEMENT
Publisher ..... Tamra Brittingham

ADVERTISING
Manager ..... Frank Pantini
Manager-Classified ..... Bernadette Van Pelt

CIRCULATION
Manager ..... Jim Ritch

NEWS EXECUTIVE
News Exec Editor ..... Michael Pelrine

EDITORS AND MANAGERS
Copy Desk Chief ..... Doug Koesner
Photo Editor ..... Kevin Heslin

PRODUCTION
Manager-Camera Room/Mailroom ..... Don Clendaniel
Manager-Pressroom ..... Dan Breedlove

Mechanical available: Offset; Black and 3 ROP colors; insert accepted — preprinted; page cutoffs — 21½".
Mechanical specifications: Type page 13" x 21½"; E - 6 cols, 2 1/16", 1/8" between; A - 6 cols, 2 1/16", 1/8" between; C - 9 cols, 1 3/8", 1/8" between.
Commodity consumption: average pages per issue 24(d), 110(S).
Equipment: EDITORIAL: Front-end hardware — 2-AT/7000, 31-Gold Star; Front-end software — AT 4.70; Other equipment — Teletype/Model 40. CLASSIFIED: Front-end hardware — III; Front-end software — MPS/Tecs 2; Other equipment — Okidata. AUDIOTEX: Hardware — Brite Voice Systems. DISPLAY: Adv layout systems — SCS/Layout 8000, Ap/Mac IIci, Ap/Mac IIsi, Ap/Mac NTX IIg, Ap/Mac SE, 4-Ap/Mac Plus. PRODUCTION: Typesetters — 2-V/5000; Plate exposures — Nu/631FT40APRNS; Plate processors — Nat/A250; Production cameras — C/Spartan III; Automatic film processors — LE; Film transporters — C; Shrink lenses — Alan/24 Anamorphic.
PRESSROOM: Line 1 — 7-G/Urbanite; Line 2 — 6-G/Community; Folders — 3-G. MAILROOM: Counter stackers — 1-BG/Count-O-Veyor, 1-HL/Monitor 708-724-6100; Bundle tyer — 1-MLN/MI-1-EE, 1-MLN/ML-2-EE; Addressing machine — Ch/596. LIBRARY: Electronic — In-house. WIRE SERVICES: News — AP Datafeatures; Stock tables — AP; Syndicates — LATS, Universal Press, King Features; Receiving dishes — AP. BUSINESS COMPUTERS: IT/90; Applications: DSI/Papertrak: Circ, Adv.

LEWES
Sussex County
'90 U.S. Census- 2,295; **E&P '96 Est.** 2,663

Daily Whale (m-mon to sat)
Daily Whale/Delaware State News (S)
Daily Whale, Rte. 1, Midway Shopping Center; PO Drawer 37, Lewes, DE 19958; tel (302) 645-2265; fax (302) 645-2267; e-mail awested@aol.com. Independent Newspapers Inc. (DE) group.
Circulation: 3,496(m); 3,496(m-sat); 34,000(S); VAC Sept. 15, 1995.
Price: 35¢(d); 35¢(sat); $1.00(S); $100.00/yr (home delivery).
Advertising: Open inch rate $10.80(m); $10.80(m-sat); $17.80(S).
News Services: KRT, LAT-WP, SHNS. **Established:** 1975 (weekly), 1992 (daily).

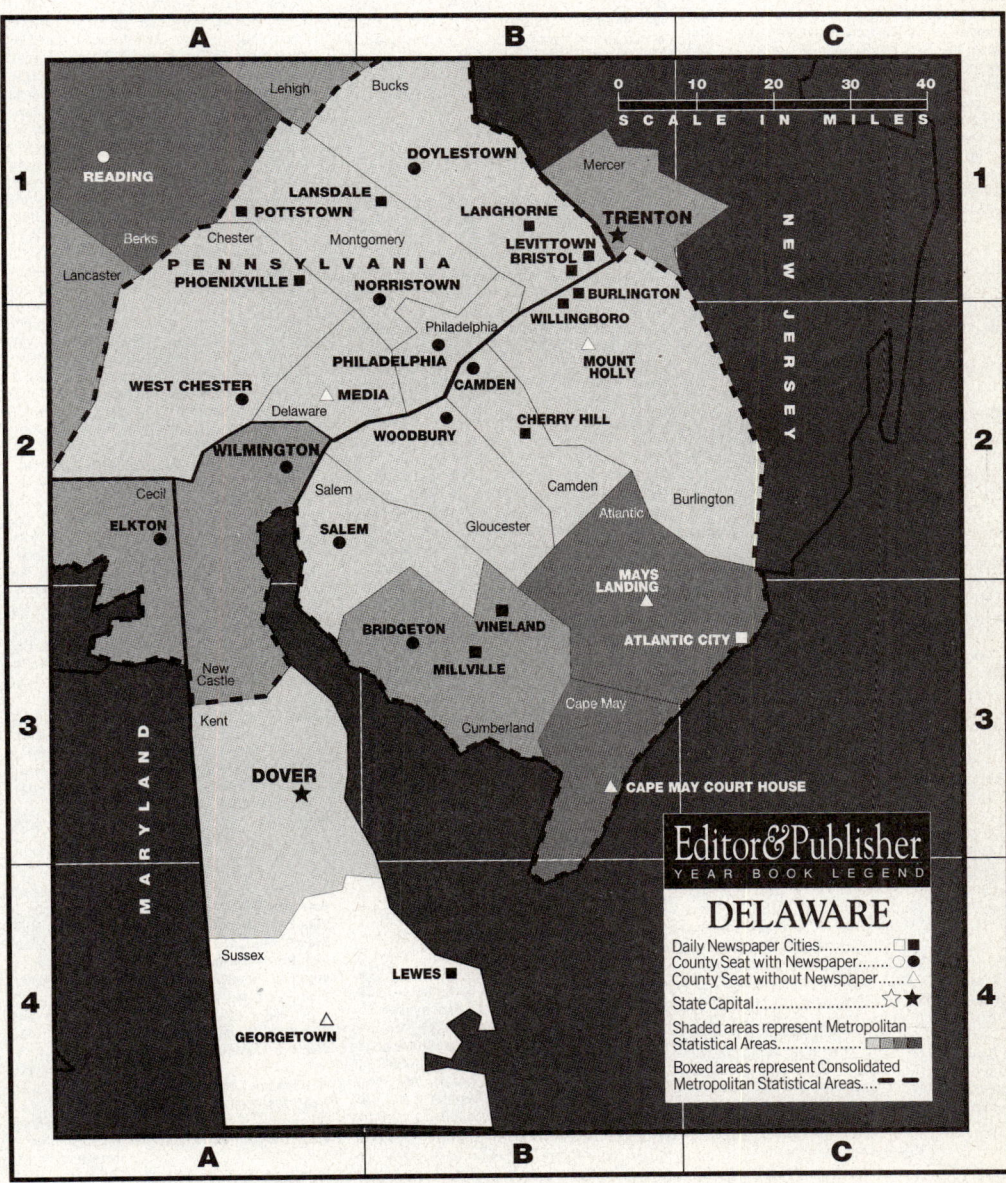

Delaware

Note: There is a combined (S) circulation and advertising rate between the Daily Whale and the Dover Delaware State News. For detailed production information, see the Delaware State News.

Special Editions: Help Wanted-Summer Job Guide (Mar/Apr); Beach Guide (May).

Special Weekly Sections: Senior Scene (tues); Business (wed); Good Times (fri); Entertainment, Real Estate (sat).

Magazine: TV & Leisure Magazine (S).

CORPORATE OFFICERS
CEO	Joe Smyth
President	Tamra Brittingham
Vice Pres	Frank A Fantini
Vice Pres	James S Ritch
Corporate Treasurer	Chris Engel

GENERAL MANAGEMENT
Publisher	Tamra Brittingham

ADVERTISING
Director	Tim Schwab

CIRCULATION
Director	Betsy Marvel

NEWS EXECUTIVE
Editor	Andy West

Mechanical available: Offset; Black and 3 ROP colors; insert accepted — preprinted; page cut-offs — 21½".

Mechanical specifications: Type page 13" x 21½"; E - 6 cols, 2¹⁄₁₆", ⅙" between; A - 6 cols, 2¹⁄₁₆", ⅙" between; C - 9 cols, 1⅜", ⅙" between.

Commodity consumption: average pages per issue 24(d), 110(S).

Equipment: EDITORIAL: Front-end hardware — Ap/Mac; Front-end software — QuarkXPress 4.0; Printers — Ap/Mac; Other equipment — Nikon, Umax/Scanner. CLASSIFIED: Front-end hardware — Ap/Mac; Front-end software — Omni; Printers — Ap/Mac. DISPLAY: Front-end hardware — Ap/Mac; Front-end software — QuarkXPress. WIRE SERVICES: News — KRT, SHNS, LAT-WP, Sports Network.

WILMINGTON
New Castle County

'90 U.S. Census- 71,796; E&P '96 Est. 72,968
ABC-NDM (90): 737,515 (HH 272,222)

The News Journal
(all day-mon to sat)
Sunday News Journal (S)

The News Journal, 950 W. Basin Rd. (New Castle, 19720); PO Box 15505, Wilmington, DE 19850; tel (302) 324-2500; fax (302) 324-5518; e-mail wilmingt@gannett.com. Gannett Co. Inc. group.

Circulation: 125,677(a); 125,677(a-sat); 149,903(S); ABC Sept. 30, 1995.
Price: 50¢(d); 50¢(sat); $1.50(S); $3.30/wk (d&S); $13.20/mo (d&S); $171.60/yr (d&S).
Advertising: Open inch rate $105.18(a); $105.18(a-sat); $117.06(S). **Representative:** Gannett National Newspaper Sales.
News Services: AP, GNS, LAT-WP, Baltimore Sun. **Politics:** Independent. **Established:** 1880 (News), 1871 (Journal).
Advertising not accepted: All ads are subject to publisher's acceptance as to position, size, content and appearance.
Special Editions: Philadelphia Auto Show, Spring Brides (Jan); Health & Fitness (Feb); Business Review, Camp Guide (Mar); Travel, Reader's Choice Restaurant Guide, Home & Garden, Baseball (Apr); Beach Guide, LPGA Official Guide, Career, Child Safety Guide (May); Academic All Stars, Delaware Almanac (June); Football (Aug); Travel (Sept); '97 Auto Show, Home Furnishings, Education, Best of Delaware (Oct); Early Shoppers Guide (Nov); Shopping Guide, Caroling Book, First Night Wilmington (Dec).
Special Weekly Sections: Family, Education, Business Monday (mon); Best Food Day (wed); Crossroads (thur); Garden/Home (fri); Best Food Day, Business, Real Estate, Travel/Resort (S).
Magazines: 55 Hours (Entertainment) (fri); Real Estate (sat); TV Book, USA Weekend (S).

CORPORATE OFFICER
President	W Curtis Riddle

GENERAL MANAGEMENT
Publisher	W Curtis Riddle
Director-Finance	V Rulon Hemingway
Director-Human Resources	Steven Hyatt
Manager-Credit	Nick Choruzy

ADVERTISING
Director	Samuel P Martin
Manager-National	Kitty Burns
Manager-Classified	Bill Janus
Manager-Retail	Bill Seeger

MARKETING AND PROMOTION
Director-Market Development	James P Rowley
Manager-Strategic Marketing	Byron K Roberts
Manager-Research	Kip Cassino

TELECOMMUNICATIONS
Audiotex Manager	James P Rowley

CIRCULATION
Director	John Truitt
Manager-Single Copy	Lynn Davis

NEWS EXECUTIVES
Exec Editor	Bennie L Ivory
Managing Editor	Valerie Bender

EDITORS AND MANAGERS
Business Editor	Peter Frank
City/State Editor	Mark Wert
Features Editor	Gretchen Day-Bryant
Public Editor	John Sweeney

MANAGEMENT INFORMATION SERVICES
Data Processing Manager	John Roselle

PRODUCTION
Director	Antoinette Franceschini
Asst Director	Rob Graham
Manager-Pre Press	Annette Giaco
Manager-Pressroom	Hal Koontz

Market Information: Zoned editions; Split Run; TMC; ADS; Operate audiotex.

Mechanical available: Offset; Black and 3 ROP colors; insert accepted — preprinted, card inserts, custom-designed preprints; page cut-offs — 21⅛".

Mechanical specifications: Type page 13⅛" x 21¼"; E - 6 cols, 2¹⁄₁₆", ⅛" between; A - 6 cols, 2¹⁄₁₆", ⅛" between; C - 10 cols, 1¼", ¹⁄₁₆" between.

Commodity consumption: Newsprint 19,290 short tons; 17,500 metric tons; width 54½"; black ink 405,000 pounds; color ink 44,000 pounds; single pages printed 21,990; average pages per issue 52(d), 120(S); single plates used 95,000.

Equipment: EDITORIAL: Front-end hardware — SII/Sys 55, 73-SII/Coyote QB, 10-SII/Coyote 22, QPS; Front-end software — SII; Printers — SCRM/3850; Other equipment — 1-Colormaster/Plus, GUSS/OPI Spooler. CLASSIFIED: Front-end hardware — SII/Sys 55, 35-SII/Coyote QB; Front-end software — SII; Other equipment — GUSS/OPI Spooler. AUDIOTEX: Hardware — Octel/Aspen. DISPLAY: Adv layout systems — SCS/Layout 8000, Ap/Mac w/QuarkXPress; Printers — HP/LaserJet III, Spectraset, ECR/3850. PRODUCTION: Pagination software — QPS; Typesetters — 2-MON/Express, 1-Spectraset/2200, 1-Copal/Dash 600, SCRM/3850; Platemaking systems — W/Optical Plate Bender; Plate exposures — WL/Lith-X-Pozer III, 2-Nu/Flip Top; Plate processors — WL/Lith-X-Pozer III; Electronic picture desk — Lf/AP Leaf Picture Desk; Scanners — 1-ECR/Autokon 1000; Production cameras — 1-C/Marathon, 1-C/Spartan III; Automatic film processors — 2-LE/LD 2600, 1-LE/Excel, 2-LE/M; Digital color separation equipment — 1-RZ/210L. PRESSROOM: Line 1 — 8-G/Headliner Offset, 1-G/Metro Color Tower; Line 2 — 8-G/Headliner Offset, 1-G/Metro Color Tower; Folders — 4-G; Pasters — 16-G/RTP CT50; Press control system — Fin; Press registration system — 2-G/Quadtech. MAILROOM: Counter stackers — 4-HL/Monitor, 6-QWI; Inserters and stuffers — 1-GE/1372, 2-HI/1472; Bundle tyer — 8-Power Strap; Wrapping singles — 5-Power Strap (¾ wrap); Addressing machine — 1-Ch, 2-Barstrom; Mailroom control system — NCS/Insert Control-Bundle Tracker-Tutalizer. LIBRARY: Electronic — Digital Collections. COMMUNICATIONS: Facsimile — AdSat, AP AdSend. WIRE SERVICES: News — AP; Stock tables — AP; Syndicates — GNS, LAT-WP, SHNS; Receiving dishes — size-12ft, AP. BUSINESS COMPUTERS: IBM/AS-400; PCs & micros networked; PCs & main system networked.

DISTRICT OF COLUMBIA

WASHINGTON

'90 U.S. Census- 621,525; E&P '96 Est. 607,712
Post:
ABC-NDM (90): 3,660,758 (HH 1,370,387)
Times:
ABC-NDM (90): 3,986,843 (HH 1,486,551)

The Washington Post
(m-mon to sat; S)

The Washington Post, 1150 15th St. N.W., Washington, DC 20071; tel (202) 334-6000; fax (202) 334-7126; web site http://www.ichange.com/partners/dink.htm. Washington Post Co. group.

Circulation: 793,660(m); 741,470(m-sat); 1,128,197(S); ABC Sept. 30, 1995.
Price: 25¢(d); 25¢(sat); $1.50(S); $62.40/yr (d); $78.00/yr (S); $127.40/yr (d & S).
Advertising: Open inch rate $450.00(m); $450.00(m-sat); $610.00(S). **Representative:** Sawyer-Ferguson-Walker Co.
News Services: AFP, AP, CT, DJ, KRT, NEA, NNS, RN, UPI. **Politics:** Independent. **Established:** 1877.
Special Editions: Winter High Tech, Seniors, Bridal Feature, Seniors/Retirement Feature (Jan); Homes Showcase, Valentine Section, Maryland, College Directory, Cruise '96, Travel Brochure Pages, Getting Married (Feb); Parent & Child, Europe, Infrastructure, Eastern Canada, Golf-Bannered Pages, Spring Fashion, Spring Travel, Travel Brochure Pages, Home Showcase (Mar); The Education Review: Summer, Apartment Living Update, Environment, Homes Showcase, Golf-Bannered Pages, Post 200, Seniors, Spring Hotel Directory, Cooking Feature, Travel Brochure Pages, Space Cover Story, Home & Design, Fine Homes Spring 1996 (Apr); Homes Showcase, Children's Book World, Spring Adv. Supplement, Local Resorts Features, Outdoor Living Feature, Wolf Trap, Theme Parks, Auto Leasing (May); Home Showcase, High Tech Horizons (June); Homes Showcase, Seniors, Apartment Living Update (July); The Education Review: Fall, High Tech Horizons, Homes Showcase, Football Preview, Living Room Feature (Aug); Fall Fashion, Golf-Bannered Pages, Parent & Child, Auto Leasing, Redskins Cover Story, Fall Fashion, Homes Showcase, Travel Brochure Pages, Dining Guide, Your Next Meeting, Fine Homes Fall 1996 (Sept); Women in Business, Apartment Living Update, Caribbean, Bermuda & The Bahamas, Fall High Tech, Seniors, Fall Hotel Directory, Home & Design, Homes Showcase, Fall Travel, Travel Brochure Pages, The Education Review: Winter (Oct); Open Season to Choose Health Plans, Ski, College Directory, Holiday Entertaining Cover Story, Homes Showcase, Caribbean Vacations-Fall (Nov); Holiday Books/Children's Book World, Holiday Guide Feature, Drunk Driving, Auto Show 1996/1997 (Dec).
Special Weekly Sections: Washington Business Tab (mon); Health Tab (tues); Food Section (broadsheet), Horizons (broadsheet) (wed); WEEKLIES (broadsheet) (thur); Weekend Tab (fri); Bookworld Tab (S); Political Market (monthly).
Magazines: Fast Forward (thur each month); Washington Post Magazine (S).

CORPORATE OFFICERS
Publisher	Donald Graham
President/General Manager	Boisfeuillt Jones Jr
Vice Pres-Advertising	Stephen Hills
Exec Consultant	Jack Patterson
Vice Pres/Counsel	Mary Ann Werner
Vice Pres-Government Affairs	Carol D Melamed
Vice Pres-Circulation/Business Manager	Ted Lutz
Vice Pres-Communications	Vincent Reed
Vice Pres-Advanced Systems/Engineering	Elizabeth Loker
Vice Pres at Large	Benjamin C Bradlee
Vice Pres-Personnel/Industrial Relations	Franklin J Havlicek
Vice Pres/Controller/Personnel Administration	Margaret Schiff
Manager-Labor Relations	Allen Hounshell

ADVERTISING
Director-National	Rick Tippett
Director-Classified	Joyce Richardson
Director-Advertising Operations	Luba Forbes
Publisher Magazine	Anne Karalekas

MARKETING AND PROMOTION
Vice Pres-Marketing/Administration	William Tompkins Jr
Director-Advertising/Promotion	Diana Wallette
Director-Public Relations	Virginia Rodriguez

CIRCULATION
Director-Home Delivery	Steve Reed
Director-Planning/Administration	Victor Capece
Director-Operations	Bennie Whittemore

NEWS EXECUTIVES
Exec Editor	Leonard Downie
Director-Recruiting/News	Jeanne Fox-Alston
Director-Recruiting/News	William Elsen
Managing Editor	Robert Kaiser
Deputy Managing Editor	Michael Getler
Asst Managing Editor	Tom Wilkinson
Asst Managing Editor-Administration/Planning	Shirley Carswell
Asst Managing Editor-Foreign	Jackson Diehl
Asst Managing Editor-National	Karen DeYoung
Asst Managing Editor-Metro	Milton Coleman
Asst Managing Editor-Investigative	Bob Woodward
Asst Managing Editor-Features	Mary Hadar
Asst Managing Editor-Sports	George Solomon
Asst Managing Editor-Finance	David Ignatius
Asst Managing Editor-Photo	Joe Elbert
Asst Managing Editor-News	Wendy Ross
Asst Managing Editor-Art	Michael Keegan
Asst Managing Editor-Style	David von Drehle

EDITORS AND MANAGERS
Architecture Editor (Style)	Ben Forgey
Art Critic (Style)	Paul Richard
Automotive Editor	Warren Brown
Book World Editor	Nina King
Business/Financial Editor	David Ignatius
Cartoonist	Herbert Block
Columnist	Bill Raspberry
Columnist	Richard Cohen
Columnist-Garden	Charles Fenyvesi
Columnist-Local	Bob Levey
Columnist-Local	Judy Mann
Columnist-Politics	David Broder
Columnist-Sports	Kenneth Denlinger
Columnist-Sports	Thomas Boswell
Columnist-Sports	Tony Kornheiser
Assoc Editor	Larry Meyer
Assoc Editor	Lori Miller
Assoc Editor	Sharon Scott
Deputy Editor	Belle Elving
Education Editor	Mary Jordan
Entertainment/Amusements Editor	David von Drehle
Editorial Page Editor	Meg Greenfield
Deputy Editorial Page Editor	Stephen Rosenfeld
Farm/Agriculture Editor	Guy Gugliotta
Fashion Editor (Style)	Robin Givhan
Features Editor	Mary Hadar
Films Editor (Style)	Hal Hinson
Films Editor (Style)	Rita Kempley
Foreign Editor	Gene Robinson
General Manager	Michael Craig
Health Editor	Abigail Trafford
Director-Info Service (Library)	Jennifer Belton
Metro Editor-News District	Jo-Ann Armao
Metro Editor-Virginia	Richard Paxson
Metro Editor-Maryland	Leslie Walker
National Editor	William Hamilton
Publisher/National Weekly	Noel Epstein
Real Estate Editor (Bus/Fin)	Kenneth Bredemeier
Restaurant Critic	Phyllis Chasanow-Richman
Science/Technology Editor	Susan Okie
Sports Deputy Editor	Jeanne McManus
Television Critic (Style)	Tom Shales
Television Columnist (Style)	John Carmody
Theater Critic (Style)	Lloyd Rose
Travel Editor (Style)	Linda Halsey
Washington Business Editor	Todd Beamon
Washington Home Editor	Linda Hales
Washington Post Magazine Senior Editor	Bob Thompson
Washington Post Magazine Editor	Steve Coll

MANAGEMENT INFORMATION SERVICES
Vice Pres-Systems/Engineering	Elizabeth Loker
Online Manager	Jennifer Belton

PRODUCTION
Vice Pres	Michael Clurman
Director-Engineering	Bill Gard
Manager-Pre Press/Makeup	Bob McLane
Manager-Planning/Operations Research	Hugh Price
Manager-Quality Assurance	Kevin Conner
Manager-Springfield Plant	Jim Coley
Manager-Maintenance (NW)	Russ Culver
Manager-Newsprint	Rex Potts
Manager-Post Press (NW)	Ed Alexander
Superintendent-Composing	Sherry Gryder

Superintendent-Engraving (NW) Andrew Hentman
Superintendent-Mailroom (NW) Billy Vanover
Superintendent-Pressroom (NW) Frank Abbott
Manager-Plant (SE) Ed Alexander
Asst Manager-Plant/Mailroom (SE) Joe Rinaldi
Asst Manager-Plant/Mailroom (SE) Les Martin
Superintendent-Engraving (SE) Martin Oberman
Superintendent-Pressroom (SE) Ron Cannon
Superintendent-Engraving (VA) Martin Quinn
Manager-Packaging/Distribution (VA) Richard Hawes
Superintendent-Pressroom (VA) Kent Barnekov

Market Information: Zoned editions; Split Run; TMC; Operate database; Operate audiotex; Electronic edition.
Mechanical available: Letterpress and offset; Black and 3 ROP colors; insert accepted — preprinted; page cut-offs — 23$\frac{9}{16}$".
Mechanical specifications: Type page 13" x 22"; E - 6 cols, 2$\frac{1}{16}$", ⅛" between; A - 6 cols, 2$\frac{1}{16}$", ⅛" between; C - 10 cols, 1$\frac{3}{16}$", $\frac{1}{16}$" between.
Commodity consumption: Newsprint 250,000 short tons; width 54⅞"; black ink 6,050,000 pounds; color ink 570,000 pounds; single pages printed 42,300; average pages per issue 110(d), 200(S); single plates used 1,098,265.
Equipment: EDITORIAL: Front-end hardware — SSI/System Synthesis 66; Other equipment — AU/APS-5. CLASSIFIED: Front-end hardware — SII/System Synthesis 66; Front-end software — SII/Sys 55 Coyote, IBM/3090, IBM/327; Printers — AU/APS-5; Other equipment — Admarc/Amdahl 5990. AUDIOTEX: Hardware — Brite Voice Systems, Micro Voice. DISPLAY: Adv layout systems — Mk/Managing Editor, Mk/Ad Director; Front-end hardware — 50-Ap/Mac; Front-end software — Multi-Ad/Creator; Printers — Harlequin/PEL, III/3850. PRODUCTION: Typesetters — 2-AU/APS-5-100 pica, 2-AU/APS-5-57 pica; Platemaking systems — Na, 6-Titan, 4-C/220, 1-WL/Lith 10, 1-WL/Lith 3, KFM/Auto Benders; Plate exposures — 1-BKY/Ascor-30"x40", 3-Titan/Exposure Unit; Plate processors — 4-C/220, 2-WL/38D; Electronic picture desk — 12-Nat/PC Digital; Scanners — 3-ECR/Autokon 1000; Production cameras — 1-C/Marathon, 1-C/Newspaper; Automatic film processors — 8-LE/processor; Film transporters — 4-C, 4-Mekel; Shrink lenses — 2-CK Optical/SQU-7, 2-Alan/24" variable; Digital color separation equipment — 1-CD/646 IE, 1-CD/870 Studio Sys.
PRESSROOM: Line 1 — 42-G/Mk I (5:G); Line 2 — 18-G/Mk II (3:G); Line 3 — 31-G/Metro (2:G); Line 4 — 10-TKS/Offset (1-TKS); Line 5 — 46-G/MKI (6:G); Press drives — Fin, TKS; Folders — 2-G/2:1, 14-G/3:2; Pasters — 133-G, 10-TKS; Reels and stands — G, TKS; Press registration system — WPC. MAILROOM: Counter stackers — 28-HL/Monitor, 6-Id/330, 5-Id/440, 2-Id/220; Inserters and stuffers — 2-SH/72-P, 3-HI/Collator, 6-GMA/SLS 1000; Bundle tyer — 6-GMA/SLS 1000, 16-MLN/MLN-2, 2-MLN/2A-HS, 24-MLN/2A. LIBRARY: Electronic — Mead Data Central/Nexis, Battelle/Basis IBM 3090. COMMUNICATIONS: Facsimile — III. WIRE SERVICES: News — AFP, AP, RN, UPI; Photos — AFP, AP, RN; Stock tables — AP; Receiving dishes — size-3m, AP. BUSINESS COMPUTERS: Admarc/Amdahl 5990, HP/UX; PCs & micros networked; PCs & main system networked.

The Washington Times
(m-mon to sat; S)

The Washington Times, 3600 New York Ave. N.E., Washington, DC 20002; tel (202) 636-3000; web site http://www.washtimes-weekly.com.
Circulation: 101,381(m); 75,527(m-sat); 65,199(S); ABC Sept. 30, 1995.
Price: 25¢(d); 25¢(sat); $1.00(S); $2.00/wk; $8.00/mo; $104.00/yr.
Advertising: Open inch rate $50.00(m); $50.00(m-sat); $50.00(S). **Representative:** Papert Companies.
News Services: AP, RN. **Politics:** Conservative. **Established:** 1982.
Advertising not accepted: Adult Entertainment/Book Store; Astrology/Palmist (Display).
Special Editions: Dr. Martin Luther King, Jr. Birthday, Business Review & Forecast (Jan); Spring Dining Guide (Mar); Football Preview, Fall Dining (Oct); Auto Show (Dec).
Special Weekly Sections: Island Position/Stock Pages (tues); Food, Island Position/Stock Pages (wed); Today's Home, Washington Weekend and Calendar, Island Position/Stock Pages (thur); Autoweekend, Island Position/Stock Pages (fri); Arts, Books, Comics, Fashion, Television Times (S); Life, Op/Ed (daily).
Magazines: Cable & Network TV Listing (daily); Today's Home (thur); Real Estate (fri); Auto Weekend, Weekly TV Guide, Books, Fashion, Food (S).

CORPORATE OFFICERS
President Dong Moon Joo
Vice Pres/General Manager Geoffrey Edwards

GENERAL MANAGEMENT
Director-Human Resources John Martin
Director-Computer Service Sara Cooperrider
Director-Facilities Paula Gray-Hunker
Director-Operations Chris Ambrosini
Director-Accounting Jan Fukatsu

ADVERTISING
Director Michael R Mahr
Asst Director Marjorie O'Donnell
Manager-Classified Val Kurapka
Manager-Retail Tony Burke
Manager-National Jim Hayden

MARKETING AND PROMOTION
Director-Marketing Peter Courtright

CIRCULATION
Director Craig Simmers
Assoc Director John Tribble
Manager Zos Monzon

NEWS EXECUTIVES
Editor in Chief Wesley Pruden
Editor-Commentary Mary Lou Forbes
Assoc Editor Richard (Woody) West
Managing Editor Josette Shiner
Asst Managing Editor P E Innerst
Asst Managing Editor Ted Agres
Asst Managing Editor Joseph W Scopin
Asst Managing Editor Barbara Taylor
Asst Managing Editor Francis Coombs Jr

EDITORS AND MANAGERS
Automotive Editor Vern Parker
Business Editor Ann Veigle
Editorial Page Editor Tod Lindberg
Fashion/Style Editor Ann Geracimos
Features Editor Deborah Simmons
Foreign Editor David Jones
Inside the Beltway Columnist John McCaslin
Metro Times Editor Ken McIntyre
National Editor Ken Hanner
News Editor Geoff Etnyre
New York Bureau Chief Liz Trotta
Photography Director Glen Stubbe
Deputy Director-Photography Alan Zlotky
Sports Editor Gary Hopkins
Travel Editor Richard Slusser

MANAGEMENT INFORMATION SERVICES
Data Processing Manager Sara Cooperrider

PRODUCTION
Director-Commercial Printing William Langman
Manager-Printing Operations Keith Martin
Manager-Materials Handling James Owens
Manager-Pre Press Operations Dave Coleman

Market Information: Split Run; ADS.
Mechanical available: Offset; Black and 3 ROP colors; insert accepted — preprinted; page cut-offs — 22¾".
Mechanical specifications: Type page 13" x 21½"; E - 6 cols, 2$\frac{1}{16}$", ⅛" between; A - 6 cols, 2$\frac{1}{16}$", ⅛" between; C - 9 cols, 1⅜", $\frac{1}{16}$" between.
Commodity consumption: Newsprint 15,000 metric tons; width 27.5"; black ink 292,626 pounds; color ink 28,000 pounds; single pages printed 23,500; average pages per issue 68(d), 44(sat), 64(S); single plates used 80,000.
Equipment: EDITORIAL: Front-end hardware — 18-DEC/Micro VAX III; Front-end software — SCS/8000; Printers — 4-DEC/LA100, AG/Selectset 5000, 3-M/Linotron 202N; Other equipment — Ap/Mac Page Makeup Workstation. CLASSIFIED: Front-end hardware — SCS/8000 Classified; Front-end software — SCS/Classified 8000; Printers — DEC/LA100, HP/LaserJet. DISPLAY: Adv layout systems — SCS/Layout 8000; Front-end hardware — DEC/VAX 6310, 10-Ap/Mac Quadra; Front-end software — SCS/Layout 8000, QuarkXPress, Adobe/Illustrator; Printers — 2-GCC/Selectpress 600. PRODUCTION: Pagination software — QuarkXPress 3.3; OCR software — TI/Omni Page Professional 5.0; Typesetters — 3-M/Linotron 202N, AG/Selectset 5000; Plate exposures — 2-Nu/Flip Top, 2-WL/Lith-X-Pozer III; Plate processors — 1-W; Electronic picture desk — Lf/AP Leaf Picture Desk; Scanners — AG/Arcus, Lf/Leafscan 35, Nikon/Coolscan, Microtek/ScanMaker II HR, ECR/Autokon 1040, DS/757, Hel/30900; Production cameras — DAI/C250, 1-ECR/Autokon 1000DE, 1-C/Spartan III; Automatic film processors — 2-LE/LD24AQR, LE/LS-26002 On-Line; Film transporters — 1-C/Spartan III; Color separation equipment (conventional) — Lf/Leaf. PRESSROOM: Line 1 — 10-G/Urbanite; Line 2 — 10-G/Urbanite; Line 3 — 9-G/Urbanite (1/3-color Unit); Line 4 — 8-MAN/2x2 (2 color decks); Pasters — 32-Cary/FP4540; Press control system — Fin. MAILROOM: Counter stackers — 4-PPK, 5-G/SH-257S; Inserters and stuffers — 2-HI/1372P; Bundle tyer — 2-MLN/2A, 4-Power Strap; Wrapping singles — 4-G/Bottom Wrap; Addressing machine — 1-KR, 2-Ch; Other mailroom equipment — Mueller/4922FLDR. Prism/Ink Jet. RS/12. LIBRARY: Electronic — SCS/Personal Librarian. WIRE SERVICES: News — AP, RN, DJ, SHNS; Stock tables — AFP; AP. BUSINESS COMPUTERS: 2-DEC/VAX 6310, 250-Ap/Mac, 30-IBM/PC; Applications: Accounting, Circ, Adv billing, Administration; Word Processing; PCs & micros networked; PCs & main system networked.

FLORIDA

BOCA RATON
Palm Beach County

'90 U.S. Census- 61,492; **E&P '96 Est.** 72,310

The News (m-mon to sat; S)

The News, 33 S.E. Third St.; PO Box 580, Boca Raton, FL 33432; tel (407) 395-8300; fax (407) 338-4849. Knight-Ridder Inc. group.
Circulation: 21,897(m); 21,897(m-sat); 25,596(S); VAC Sept. 30, 1994.
Price: 25¢(d); 25¢(sat); 50¢(S); $1.40/wk; $99.00/yr (mail).
Advertising: Open inch rate $23.59(m); $23.59(m-sat); $25.95(S). **Representatives:** US Suburban Press; Newspapers First.
News Services: AP, KRT. **Politics:** Independent. **Established:** 1955.
Special Weekly Sections: Business Extra, Society (mon); Generation X (tues); Health & Nutrition, Motor Cars (thur); Religion, Entertainment, Weekend (fri); Motor Cars, Real Estate News & Review (sat); Religion News, Encore (S).
Magazines: USA Weekend, TV Book (S).

CORPORATE OFFICERS
President Roger W Coover
Vice Pres/Advertising Director Wayne Ezell
Treasurer/Chief Financial Officer Vivian Espinosa

GENERAL MANAGEMENT
Publisher Roger W Coover
Vice Pres/Editor John Futch
Director-Human Resources Carol Martin

ADVERTISING
Vice Pres Wayne Ezell
Manager-National Mark Freindlich
Manager-Retail Robin Prendergast
Manager-Classified/Marketing Judy Green
Manager-Service Michelle Bernzweig

CIRCULATION
Director David Richeson

NEWS EXECUTIVE
Editor John Futch

EDITORS AND MANAGERS
Editorial Page Editor C Randall Murray
Entertainment/Amusements Editor MaryLou Simms
Features/Women's Editor MaryLou Simms
Living/Lifestyle Editor MaryLou Simms
Sports Editor Taylor Scott

MANAGEMENT INFORMATION SERVICES
Data Processing Manager Paula Fontana

PRODUCTION
Vice Pres-Operations Scott Edgerton

Market Information: Zoned editions; Split Run.
Mechanical available: Offset; Black and 3 ROP colors; insert accepted — preprinted, any; page cut-offs — 22.75".
Mechanical specifications: Type page 13" x 21½"; E - 6 cols, 2", $\frac{3}{16}$" between; A - 6 cols, 2", $\frac{3}{16}$" between; C - 10 cols, 1¼", $\frac{1}{16}$" between.
Commodity consumption: Newsprint 5,808 short tons; 5,280 metric tons; width 27½"; black ink 132,000 pounds; color ink 132,000 pounds; average pages per issue 40(d), 215(S); single plates used 140,000.
Equipment: EDITORIAL: Front-end hardware — HI/8900, 14-HI/1420, 8-HI/8000, 12-HI/8860, Ap/Macs; Other equipment — 2-Extel/Extel, 2-Tally/Hi Speed. CLASSIFIED: Front-end hardware — HI/8300, 9-HI/8860, 2-HI/8863; Other equipment — 1-IBM. DISPLAY: Adv layout systems — 7-Ap/Mac; Front-end software — QPS, Aldus/FreeHand, Adobe/Illustrator, Aldus/PageMaker, Adobe/Photostop. PRODUCTION: Typesetters — 3-COM/8600, 3-AU/APS-6, 1-Tegra/Varityper; Platemaking systems — 2-Nu/Amerigraph Burner; Plate exposures — 2-Nu/Plate Burner; Scanners — 1-ECR/Autokon 1000, Lf/Leafscan 45; Production cameras — 1-C/Spartan III, 1-AG/2024; Automatic film processors — 1-LE, 1-AG/Litex 2600; Digital color separation equipment — Lf, Adobe/Photostop, QPS. PRESSROOM: Line 1 — 10-G/Urbanite; Folders — 2-G/2:1; Pasters — WEB/Qwi; Press control system — Fin. MAILROOM: Counter stackers — 1-BG/108, 1-Id/2000; Inserters and stuffers — 2-MM/227; Bundle tyer — 1-MLN, 1-Dynaric; Wrapping singles — Id/Under Crafter; Addressing machine — Convenient/Addressing Sys. LIBRARY: Electronic — Vu/Text SAVE System. WIRE SERVICES: News — AP Datastream; Photos — AP; Stock tables — AP; Receiving dishes — AP. BUSINESS COMPUTERS: 1-HP/3000; Applications: CJ; PCs & micros networked; PCs & main system networked.

BRADENTON
Manatee County

'90 U.S. Census- 43,779; **E&P '96 Est.** 57,703
ABC-CZ (90): 202,078 (HH 88,656)

Bradenton Herald
(m-mon to sat; S)

Bradenton Herald, 102 Manatee Ave. W.; PO Box 921, Bradenton, FL 34206; tel (941) 748-0411; fax (941) 745-7094; web site http://www.gate.net/~savage/. Knight-Ridder Inc. group.
Circulation: 43,798(m); 43,798(m-sat); 56,155(S); ABC circulation average for 12 months ended Sept. 30, 1995.
Price: 25¢(d); 25¢(sat); 75¢(S); $2.60/wk.
Advertising: Open inch rate $27.70(m); $27.70(m-sat); $33.79(S). **Representatives:** Landon Associates Inc.; Newspapers First; Publishers' Representatives of Florida.
News Services: AP, KRT. **Politics:** Independent. **Established:** 1922.
Special Editions: Manatee '96, Boat Show, County Fair (Jan); Senior Lifestyles, Fishing College, The Beach Book, Civic Center Auto Show (Feb); Coupon Book, Bridal Show (Mar); Design-an-Ad, Florida Heritage Celebration (Apr); Coupon Book, Golden Herald Awards (May); Senior Lifestyles (June); Boat Show, Coupon Book (July); School Handbook, Football Facts (Aug); Community Clubs (Sept); RV Showcase, Consumer Guide to Better Business, Arts, Your Health, Wheels '97, Women in Business (Oct); Coupon Book, Junior League Gift Market, Christmas Comes to Manatee, Southern Living Cooking School (Nov); Letters to Santa (Dec).
Special Weekly Sections: Business Extra (mon); Neighbors (tues); Taste (thur); Weekend (fri); Travel (S).
Magazines: Business Extra (own) (mon); Neighbors (own) (tues); Weekend (own) (fri); TV Book (own, local, newsprint), USA Weekend (S).

CORPORATE OFFICERS
President Dorothy S Ridings
Vice Pres Wayne H Poston
Vice Pres Robert G Turner Jr

GENERAL MANAGEMENT
Publisher Dorothy S Ridings
General Manager Robert G Turner Jr
Chief Financial Officer Donald J Watson

ADVERTISING
Director Bruce Faulmann
Manager-Commercial Print Bob Hrycyk
Manager-Classified Jean O'Hara
Manager-Retail Moya Edwards
Supervisor-Inside Phone Shari Couch

MARKETING AND PROMOTION

Coordinator-Marketing Research James K Toomey

CIRCULATION

Director Ed Gruwell
Manager-Home Delivery Jan Brownlee
Manager-Single Copy Mark Wlodarczyk
Manager-Promotion Dave LaBell

NEWS EXECUTIVES

Exec Editor Wayne H Poston
Managing Editor Bruce Lind

EDITORS AND MANAGERS

Agriculture/Garden Editor Teri Grimes
Business Editor Laura Cianci
Deputy City Editor Neil Besougloff
Editorial Page Editor David E Klement
Features Editor Teri Grimes
Food Editor Eydie Cubarrubia
Graphics Editor Lisa Young
Lifestyle Editor Teri Grimes
News Editor Gary Brown
Outdoor Editor Jerry Hill
Photography Chief Al Anderson
Radio/Television Editor Sandy Woolum
Real Estate Editor Laura Cianci
Schools/Education Editor Ellen Moses
Exec Sports Editor Michael Mersch
Women's/Society Editor Christi Villilobos

MANAGEMENT INFORMATION SERVICES

Data Processing Manager Dale Harrell

PRODUCTION

Director-Operations Richard E Chick
Manager Bob Hickman
Manager-Pressroom/Operations Odell Roberts
Manager-Pre Press Jim Stufflebeam
Manager-Mailroom/Bindery Operations Jim Stufflebeam

Mechanical available: Offset; Black and 3 ROP colors; insert accepted — preprinted, printed; page cut-offs — 22¾".
Mechanical specifications: Type page 13" x 21¼"; E - 6 cols, 2 1/16", ⅛" between; A - 6 cols, 2 1/16", ⅛" between; C - 9 cols, 1⅜", 1/16" between.
Commodity consumption: Newsprint 5,237 metric tons; widths 55", 41¼", 27½"; black ink 96,515 pounds; color ink 33,862 pounds; single pages printed 19,340; average pages per issue 46(d), 94(S); single plates used 49,771.
Equipment: EDITORIAL: Front-end hardware — 2-SII/Sys 25, 4-COM/PC Network; Front-end software — SII/Proprietary; Printers — HP/InkJet; Other equipment — Vu/Text Save Library System, AP SelectStox II. CLASSIFIED: Front-end hardware — 2-AT/Standard IAS Series 4, 3-IBM/PC; Front-end software — AT/IAS 4.6.7; Printers — Citizen/120D, MOD/4Q, Florida Data; Other equipment — AT/PC Preference. DISPLAY: Adv layout systems — HI/8300 PLS; Front-end hardware — HI/8300 PLS; Front-end software — HI 6.6. PRODUCTION: Typesetters — 2-AU/APS Micro 5, 1-AU/APS-6 Imager; Plate exposures — 2-Nu/Flip Top; Plate processors — 2-WL/38-D; Electronic picture desk — Lf/AP Leaf Picture Desk; Scanners — ECR; Production cameras — 1-C/Newspager, 1-C/Spartan III; Automatic film processors — 2-LE/2600, 1-C/66F; Film transporters — 3-C; Digital color separation equipment — 1-HL/DC380.
PRESSROOM: Line 1 — 6-MAN/Lithomatic II; Line 2 — 5-G/Suburban; Press drives — GE; Folders — 2-G; Pasters — 6-G; Reels and stands — 6-G; Press control system — GE. MAILROOM: Counter stackers — 4-HL/Monitor; Inserters and stuffers — 3-MM/22 5:1; Bundle tyer — 1-Power Strap/PSN 6, 2-Power Strap/PSN 6; Addressing machine — 1-Ch. LIBRARY: Electronic — Vu/Text SAVE Sys. WIRE SERVICES: News — AP, AP Datafeatures, KRT; Stock tables — AP; Syndicates — TV Data; Receiving dishes — size-10ft, AP. BUSINESS COMPUTERS: 1-HP/3000-922; PCs & micros networked; PCs & main system networked.

CAPE CORAL

Lee County

'90 U.S. Census- 74,991; E&P '96 Est. 90,270

Cape Coral Daily Breeze

(e-mon to fri; m-sat)

Cape Coral Daily Breeze, 2510 Delprado Blvd. (33904); PO Box 846, Cape Coral, FL 33910; tel (941) 574-1110; fax (941) 574-3403. Ogden Newspapers group.
Circulation: 3,675(e); 3,675(m-sat); Sworn Sept. 29, 1995.
Price: 25¢(d); 25¢(sat); $15.00/3mo, $25.00/6mo; $45.00/yr.
Advertising: Open inch rate $7.90(e); $9.90(m-sat). **Representative:** Landon Associates Inc.
News Service: AP. **Politics:** Independent. **Established:** 1975.
Not Published: New Year (unless on a Saturday); Memorial Day; Independence Day; Labor Day; Thanksgiving; Christmas.
Special Editions: Progress & Growth (June); History of Cape Coral (Oct); Real Estate Marketer (every other week).
Special Weekly Section: TV Showtime (fri).
Magazines: Real Estate Section; Travel; Automotive; Health; Business (Local).

CORPORATE OFFICERS

President G Ogden Nutting
Vice Pres Robert M Nutting

GENERAL MANAGEMENT

Publisher Harry Pappas
General Manager Joel Jenkins

ADVERTISING

Director Bonnie Cook

TELECOMMUNICATIONS

Audiotex Manager Robin Gustavuson

CIRCULATION

Director Timothy McIntosh

NEWS EXECUTIVE

Editorial Director Jimmy Espy

EDITORS AND MANAGERS

Photo Department Manager Saul Taffet
Picture Editor Saul Taffet

MANAGEMENT INFORMATION SERVICES

Data Processing Manager Scott Blonde

PRODUCTION

Manager-Press Scott Kelley
Manager-Composing Liz Houston
Manager-Commercial Printing Wanda Lewis

Market Information: TMC; Operate audiotex.
Mechanical available: Offset; Black and 3 ROP colors; insert accepted — preprinted, single sheets; page cut-offs — 22".
Mechanical specifications: Type page 13" x 21½"; E - 6 cols, 2 1/16", ¼" between; A - 8 cols, 1⅝", ¼" between; C - 8 cols, 1⅝", ¼" between.
Commodity consumption: Newsprint 2,100 short tons; widths 34", 29", 27"; average pages per issue 24(d).
Equipment: EDITORIAL: Printers — QMS/650, NewGen/Turbo PS-660-B. CLASSIFIED: Printers — Ap/Mac LaserWriter NTX. DISPLAY: Adv layout systems — Metro/CDs; Printers — Ap/Mac LaserPrinter; Other equipment — 4-RZ/Color Roll Scanner. PRODUCTION: Typesetters — Ap/Mac Radius; Plate exposures — 1-Nu/Flip Top; Plate processors — Nat/A250; Scanners — HP, RZ/4050 Scanner; Production cameras — 1-C/Pager, SCREEN/690D; Automatic film processors — LE/LD1800A.
PRESSROOM: Line 1 — 8-HI/V15; Folders — 1-HI; Pasters — 1-BG/Acumeter SY 1243; Reels and stands — 4-Martin/Splicers. MAILROOM: Counter stackers — 109-BG/Count-O-Veyor, Rima/RS25, Rima/RS10; Inserters and stuffers — HI, S/624, AM Graphics/NP624; Bundle tyer — MLN/Strapper, Ty-Tech/String tyer, Akebono/Strapper; Addressing machine — KR/Labeler; Mailroom control system — MM/Stitcher-Trimmer. WIRE SERVICES: News — AP; Receiving dishes — AP.

CHARLOTTE HARBOR-PORT CHARLOTTE

Charlotte County

'90 U.S. Census- 44,862 (Charlotte Harbor 3,327; Port Charlotte 41,535); E&P '96 Est. 55,455 (Charlotte Harbor 4,161; Port Charlotte 51,294)
ABC-CZ (90): 78,289 (HH 34,545)

Sun Herald (m-mon to sat; S)

Sun Herald, 23170 Harborview Rd. (Charlotte Harbor 33980); PO Box 2390, Port Charlotte, FL 33949; tel (941) 629-2855; fax (941) 629-2085.
Circulation: 27,233(m); 28,955(m-wed); 27,233(m-sat); 32,918(S); ABC circulation average for 12 months ended Sept. 30, 1995.
Price: 35¢(d); 35¢(wed); $1.00(S); $15.42/mo; $155.00/yr (carrier).
Advertising: Open inch rate $18.34(m); $21.79(m-wed); $22.96(S). **Representative:** Landon Associates Inc.
News Services: KRT, AP, RN, Photo Feed. **Politics:** Independent. **Established:** 1893.
Special Editions: Welcome Back Northerners; Ranger Baseball; Health & Fitness; Bluegrass Festival; Hurricane Tab; Home Improvement; Fashion; Parade of Homes; United Way; Income Tax; Recreation; Christmas Gift Guide.
Special Weekly Sections: Weekly Record (mon); Sun Coast Living, Food (wed); Food (thur); Automotive (fri); TV Times, Travel/Leisure, Health/Medicine, Homes (sat); Travel/Leisure, Health/Medicine, Homes, TV Times (S).

GENERAL MANAGEMENT

Publisher Derek Dunn-Rankin
Business Manager Richard A Hackney

ADVERTISING

Director Jim Leatham
Manager-Classified Ron Smith
Manager-Major Account Sales Karen Gammond

CIRCULATION

Director Len Terrell

NEWS EXECUTIVE

Exec Editor Jim Gouvellis

MANAGEMENT INFORMATION SERVICES

Data Processing Manager Debbie Dunn-Rankin

Market Information: Zoned editions; Split Run; TMC.
Mechanical available: Offset; Black; insert accepted — preprinted; page cut-offs — 21".
Mechanical specifications: Type page 13" x 20.75"; E - 6 cols, 2 1/16", ⅛" between; A - 6 cols, 2 1/16", ⅛" between; C - 9 cols, 1⅜", ⅛" between.
Commodity consumption: Newsprint 4,000 short tons; widths 27½", 34"; black ink 12,500 pounds; color ink 7,200 pounds; single pages printed 11,748; average pages per issue 44(d), 40(S); single plates used 46,800.
Equipment: EDITORIAL: Front-end hardware — 19-Ap/Mac; Front-end software — QuarkXPress 3.2; Printers — 2-Dataproducts, 2-LaserMaster/Unity Oversize. CLASSIFIED: Front-end hardware — Ik. PRODUCTION: Typesetters — COM; Platemaking systems — Direct; Plate exposures — 2-Nu; Plate processors — 2-Cookson Graphics/S32; Electronic picture desk — Ap/Mac Quadra 950, Ap/Mac Radius 21" Precision Color Monitor; Scanners — Kk/DFS 2035 Slide Negative Scanner, AG/Arcus Plus, COM; Production cameras — 1-C/Spartan II, 1-AG; Film transporters — C; Color separation equipment (conventional) — Adobe/Photoshop.
PRESSROOM: Line 1 — 12-G/Urbanite-U-5019; Pasters — 5-WPC; Reels and stands — 3-G/Roll Stands; Press control system — 2-Fin/2193E-150-38D, 1-Fin/2193-E-100-38D. MAILROOM: Counter stackers — 1-HI/251017, 1-HL/Monitor, 1-BG/105; Inserters and stuffers — 1-HI/8-48; Bundle tyer — 1-MLN/ML2EE, 1-MLN/A1672A, 1-Bu. WIRE SERVICES: News — AP, KRT; Photos — RN; Stock tables — TMS; Syndicates — LAT-WP, KRT, Universal Press, King Features, Creators; Receiving dishes — AP, RN. BUSINESS COMPUTERS: HP/3000; Applications: CJ: Accounting; Database: Adv, Circ; PCs & main system networked.

CRYSTAL RIVER

Citrus County

'90 U.S. Census- 4,044; E&P '96 Est. 5,617
ABC-NDM (90): 93,515 (HH 40,573)

Citrus County Chronicle

(m-mon to sat; S)

Citrus County Chronicle, 1624 N. Meadowcrest Blvd., Crystal River, FL 34429; tel (904) 563-6363; fax (904) 563-5665; web site http://www.infi.net/chronicle_online/. Landmark Communications Inc. group.
Circulation: 20,392(m); 20,392(m-sat); 24,512(S); ABC circulation average for 12 months ended Sept. 30, 1995.
Price: 25¢(d); 25¢(sat); 75¢(S); $84.00/yr.
Advertising: Open inch rate $14.75(m); $14.75(m-sat); $15.68(S). **Representative:** Landon Associates Inc.
News Service: AP. **Established:** 1892.
Advertising not accepted: Brokered adv.
Special Weekly Sections: Health (tues); Education (wed); Food (thur); Entertainment (fri); Religion (sat); Business, Real Estate Builder (S).

GENERAL MANAGEMENT

Publisher Gerard Mulligan

ADVERTISING

Manager-Sales Leader Dale Bowen

TELECOMMUNICATIONS

Communications Leader Marguerite Ladogana

CIRCULATION

Director R Chris Ordway

NEWS EXECUTIVES

Editor Ken Melton
Editor-Editorial John Bowman

EDITORS AND MANAGERS

Managing Editor Charles Brennan
News Editor Mike Wright

PRODUCTION

Manager Mike Weaver
Manager-Operations Tim Hess
Manager-Composing Room Paul Kempin

Market Information: Zoned editions; TMC; Operate database.
Mechanical available: Web Offset; Black and 3 ROP colors; insert accepted — preprinted; page cut-offs — 21½".
Mechanical specifications: Type page 13" x 21½"; E - 6 cols, 2 1/16", ⅛" between; A - 6 cols, 2 1/16", ⅛" between; C - 10 cols, 1⅛", ⅛" between.
Commodity consumption: Newsprint 1,200 short tons; widths 27½", 34"; black ink 54,000 pounds; color ink 7,000 pounds; single pages printed 22,000; average pages per issue 24(d), 50(S); single plates used 16,000.
Equipment: EDITORIAL: Front-end hardware — CText; Front-end software — XYQUEST/XyWrite, QuarkXPress 3.3; Printers — 2-Birmy/Imagesetter. CLASSIFIED: Front-end hardware — CText. DISPLAY: Adv layout systems — Ap/Mac; Front-end hardware — Ap/Mac; Front-end software — Mk/Ad Touch, Multi-Ad/Creator. PRODUCTION: Pagination software — Layout 8000; Typesetters — Mk/Laser, Printware; Plate exposures — Nu/Flip Top; Plate processors — Anitec; Electronic picture desk — Lf/AP Leaf Picture Desk, Ap/Mac; Scanners — 2-Nikon; Automatic film processors — DP/Chronaflow, LE/2600; Digital color separation equipment — Nikon.
PRESSROOM: Line 1 — 8-G/Community SC (2 color decks, 1 univ offset color); Press drives — Fin; Folders — G/Community SC. MAILROOM: Counter stackers — 2-HL/Monitor; Inserters and stuffers — 1-MM/5-into-1, 1-MM/8-into-1; Bundle tyer — 2-MLN/Strapper; Addressing machine — KR. WIRE SERVICES: News — AP, KRT; Photos — AP; Stock tables — AP; Syndicates — King Features, UPI, Universal Press, LAT-WP, NEA; Receiving dishes — size-8 ft, AP. BUSINESS COMPUTERS: IBM/Sys 36; Applications: Lotus; PCs & micros networked.

DAYTONA BEACH

Volusia County

'90 U.S. Census- 61,921; E&P '96 Est. 68,495
ABC-CZ (90): 223,977 (HH 98,794)

Daytona Beach News-Journal (m-mon to sat; S)

Daytona Beach News-Journal, 901 6th St.; PO Box 2831, Daytona Beach, FL 32120-2831; tel (904) 252-1511; fax (904) 258-8469. Cox Newspapers Inc. group.
Circulation: 99,998(m); 99,998(m-sat); 119,396(S); ABC circulation average for 12 months ended Sept. 30, 1995.
Price: 35¢(d); 35¢(sat); $1.00(S); $66.15/26wk; $10.18/mo; $132.29/yr
Advertising: Open inch rate $70.90(m); $70.90(m-sat); $81.40(S); $94.90(wknd). **Representatives:** Sawyer-Ferguson-Walker Co.; Publishers' Representatives of Florida.
News Services: AP, NYT. **Politics:** Democrat. **Established:** 1904.
Advertising not accepted: Questionable medical ads or obviously misleading ads.
Special Editions: Master Calendar Dining Guide, Almanac Edition (Jan); Spe[illegible]ek's '96 Section, Bride Section, Coupo[illegible]er (Feb); Bike Week Section, Alaska Tra[illegible]ection, Spring Break Section, Garden [illegible]e Lifestyle Show Section, Florida W[illegible]tion, Spring Cruise Travel Secti[illegible]; Master Calendar, Florida Outdoors Section, Caribbean Travel Section, Home Design & Garden Section, LPGA Tournament Section, Vacation USA Travel Section (Apr); Florida's Cookin' Cookbook, NIE Design-an-Ad Section, Coupon Clipper, Graduation Section, Seaside Music Theater Program (May); Dining Guide Section, Summer Cruise Travel

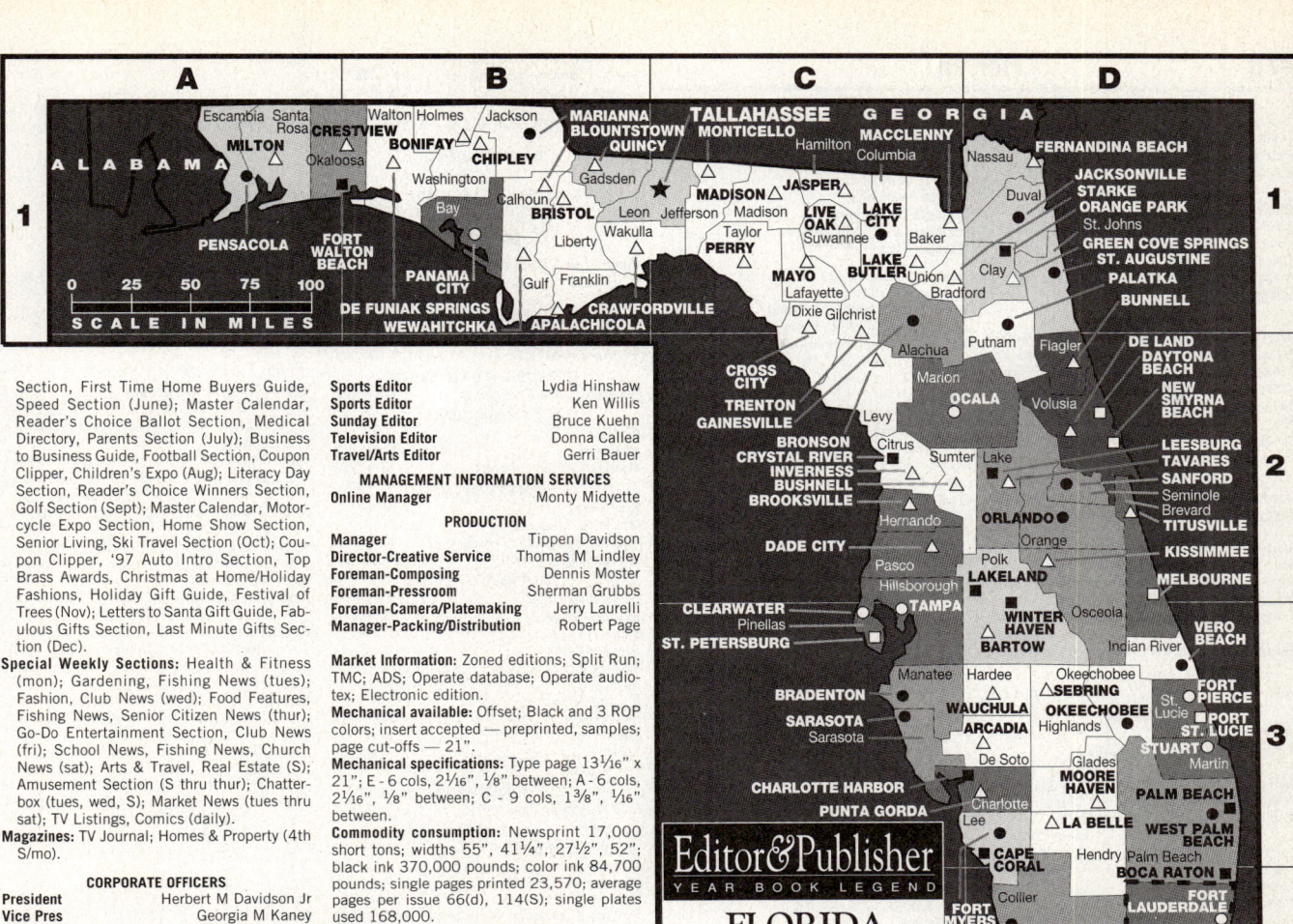

Section, First Time Home Buyers Guide, Speed Section (June); Master Calendar, Reader's Choice Ballot Section, Medical Directory, Parents Section (July); Business to Business Guide, Football Section, Coupon Clipper, Children's Expo (Aug) Literacy Day Section, Reader's Choice Winners Section, Golf Section (Sept); Master Calendar, Motorcycle Expo Section, Home Show Section, Senior Living, Ski Travel Section (Oct); Coupon Clipper, '97 Auto Intro Section, Top Brass Awards, Christmas at Home/Holiday Fashions, Holiday Gift Guide, Festival of Trees (Nov); Letters to Santa Gift Guide, Fabulous Gifts Section, Last Minute Gifts Section (Dec).

Special Weekly Sections: Health & Fitness (mon); Gardening, Fishing News (tues); Fashion, Club News (wed); Food Features, Fishing News, Senior Citizen News (thur); Go-Do Entertainment Section, Club News (fri); School News, Fishing News, Church News (sat); Arts & Travel, Real Estate (S); Amusement Section (S thru thur); Chatterbox (tues, wed, S); Market News (tues thru sat); TV Listings, Comics (daily).

Magazines: TV Journal; Homes & Property (4th S/mo).

CORPORATE OFFICERS
President ..... Herbert M Davidson Jr
Vice Pres ..... Georgia M Kaney
Vice Pres ..... Thomas T Cobb
Chief Financial Officer ..... David R Kendall
Secretary ..... Jonathan D Kaney Jr
Asst Secretary ..... Marc L Davidson
Corporate Director-Circulation/Human Resources ..... Douglas R Davis

GENERAL MANAGEMENT
Publisher ..... Herbert M Davidson Jr
General Manager ..... Georgia M Kaney
Manager-Credit ..... Judith Bennett
Controller ..... Ken Wooten

ADVERTISING
Director-Marketing ..... Robert Hughes
Director ..... Kathy Coughlin
Manager-Classified ..... Bryan Stephens

MARKETING AND PROMOTION
Director-Marketing ..... Robert Hughes
Director-Promotion ..... Katie Carlson

TELECOMMUNICATIONS
Audiotex Manager-Service ..... Bill Stipsits

CIRCULATION
Director ..... Robert Kearley
Manager-Sales ..... John K Shaw
Manager-City ..... Wanda K Ainsworth
Manager-State ..... James L Johnson
Manager-Subscriber Service ..... Ella Miles

NEWS EXECUTIVES
Exec Editor ..... Dick Dunkel
Co-Editor ..... Herbert M Davidson Jr
Managing Editor-News & Editorial ..... Don Lindley
Managing Editor-Operations ..... Lee Moore
Asst Managing Editor ..... Mike Czeczot
Asst Managing Editor ..... Nick Klasne

EDITORS AND MANAGERS
Art Director ..... Steve McLachlin
Business Editor ..... Tom Brown
Editorial Cartoonist ..... Bruce Beattie
Editorial Page Editor ..... Natalie Dix
Education Editor ..... Linda Trimble
Entertainment/Amusements Editor ..... Suzy Kridner
Fashion/Style Editor ..... Judy Liberi
Garden Editor ..... Mary Jane McSwain
Graphics Editor/Asst Managing Editor ..... Troy Moore
Librarian ..... Cathy Harley
Asst Metro Editor ..... Charles D Jackson
Asst Metro Editor ..... Kathy Kelly
Photo Department Manager ..... Jim Tiller
Political Editor ..... Tony Briggs
Regional Editor ..... Barbara Taylor
Special Section Editor ..... Cathy Klasne

Sports Editor ..... Lydia Hinshaw
Sports Editor ..... Ken Willis
Sunday Editor ..... Bruce Kuehn
Television Editor ..... Donna Callea
Travel/Arts Editor ..... Gerri Bauer

MANAGEMENT INFORMATION SERVICES
Online Manager ..... Monty Midyette

PRODUCTION
Manager ..... Tippen Davidson
Director-Creative Service ..... Thomas M Lindley
Foreman-Composing ..... Dennis Moster
Foreman-Pressroom ..... Sherman Grubbs
Foreman-Camera/Platemaking ..... Jerry Laurelli
Manager-Packing/Distribution ..... Robert Page

Market Information: Zoned editions; Split Run; TMC; ADS; Operate database; Operate audiotex; Electronic edition.
Mechanical available: Offset; Black and 3 ROP colors; insert accepted — preprinteds, samples; page cut-offs — 21".
Mechanical specifications: Type page 13 1/16" x 21"; E - 6 cols, 2 1/16", 1/8" between; A - 6 cols, 2 1/16", 1/8" between; C - 9 cols, 1 3/8", 1/16" between.
Commodity consumption: Newsprint 17,000 short tons; widths 55", 41 1/4", 27 1/2", 52"; black ink 370,000 pounds; color ink 84,700 pounds; single pages printed 23,570; average pages per issue 66(d), 114(S); single plates used 168,000.
Equipment: EDITORIAL: Front-end hardware — HI/XP-21, 2-Sun/Sparc 10 Server, Dell/486 33mhz PCs; Front-end software — HI/Newsmaker, XYQUEST/XyWrite, Microsoft/Windows, Microsoft/Windows 3.11; Printers — QMS/860, Okidata/2410. CLASSIFIED: Front-end hardware — VGA; Front-end software — Cx/Intertext; Printers — Okidata/2410, Okidata/Microline 193; Other equipment — Irma/Fastlink, GTE/Trailblazer Modem. AUDIOTEX: Hardware — 2-Intel/486; Software — Unix 3.01; Supplier name — Brite Voice Systems, AP StockQuote II. DISPLAY: Adv layout systems — SCS/Layout HI/XP-21; Front-end hardware — DEC/VAX 8000, SCS/Layout 8000, Dell/66mhz server, Micropolis/Radion Mirrored, Ap/Mac 950s, Ap/Mac 840, Ap/Mac 7100s; Front-end software — SCS/Layout 8000 6.10, Multi-Ad/Creator 3.7, QuarkXPress 3.31, Creator Search 2.0, Aldus/FreeHand 4.0, Novell 3.11; Printers — C.Itoh/TriPrinter, Okidata/2410, QMS/PS-860, NewGen/Turbo 840, Tektonics/Phaser 300; Other equipment — Pinnacle/Micro PMO 16 Stot jukebox, Pinnacle/GB M.O. drive 1.2, XYQUEST/88mb drive, HP/ScanJet Plus scanners, Mirror/CD drives. PRODUCTION: Pagination software — HI/XP-21 2.0, HI/XP-21 1.2; Typesetters — 1-MON/MK IIi, MON/Express Master 25, 2-MON/RIP Express RIP, Sun/Sparc IPXs; Plate exposures — 1-Tasope; Plate processors — 2-Tasope; Electronic picture desk — Lf/AP Leaf Picture Desk, 1-Ap/Mac; Scanners — 3-ECR/Autokon, 1-SCREEN/608 Scanner, HP/ScanJet Plus; Production cameras — 2-C, 1-Payea, 1-C/Spartan; Automatic film processors — 3-P, LE, C/650; Film transporters — 1-C; Color separation equipment (conventional) — SCREEN/DS-608; Digital color separation equipment — Ap/Mac.
PRESSROOM: Line 1 — 14-G/Metroliner units; Folders — 2-G/3:2, 2-G/2:1; Pasters — 12-G; Press control system — G; Press registration system — G. MAILROOM: Counter stackers — 1-QWI/100, 5-QWI/200, 2-QWI/310, 2-MM/CS70-338; Inserters and stuffers — HI/1472, HI/1372; Bundle tyer — 5-Dynaric/NP-2, 2-Dynaric/NP-1; Wrapping singles — 7-QWI, 2-QWI/Cobra (3/4); Addressing machine — Ch/525E, Ch/596; Mailroom control system — Manual. WIRE SERVICES: News — AP Datastream, AP Datafeatures; Stock tables — AP SelectStox, AP SelectStox I; Receiving dishes — AP. BUSINESS COMPUTERS: 2-DEC/Alpha 4610; Applications: CJ, ADP; PCs & micros networked; PCs & main system networked.

FORT LAUDERDALE
Broward County
'90 U.S. Census- 149,377; E&P '96 Est. 146,948
ABC-CZ (90): 1,255,488 (HH 528,442)

Sun-Sentinel (m-mon to sat; S)
Sun-Sentinel, 200 E. Las Olas Blvd., Fort Lauderdale, FL 33301-2293; tel (954) 356-4000; fax (954) 356-4333; e-mail fletters@sunsent.com; web site http: //www.xso.com. Tribune Co. group.
Circulation: 264,863(m); 264,863(m-sat); 369,745(S); ABC circulation average for 12 months ended Sept. 30, 1995.
Price: 35¢(d); 35¢(sat); $1.00(S); $2.60/wk (mS); $33.80/3mo; $128.44/yr.
Advertising: Open inch rate $255.10(m); $255.10(m-sat); $299.70(S). **Representative:** Tribune Newspaper Network.
News Services: AP, NYT, DJ, RN, KRT, LATWP. **Politics:** Independent. **Established:** 1960.
Special Editions: Dining Guide, Super Bowl '96, Ecotourism, Business Outlook (Jan); Alaska/Canada, Retirement Living, Tri-City Fair, Valentine's Day (Feb); Meet Me Downtown, Frozen Food, Home & Design, Boynton Gala, Financial Planning, Disney World (Mar); Home, Lawn & Patio, Caribbean, Easter/Passover, Delray Affair (Apr); Mother's Day, Inside Florida, Cinco de Mayo Festival, Warm Weather Entertaining, Hurricane (May); Florida Vacation Resorts, Bridal Showcase (June); Ice Cream, Sporting Vacations, Boca Festival Days (July); Boca Expo, Education Showcase, Back-to-School, Labor Day, Mexico, United Way, Football '96 (Aug); Apartment Excellence, Meals from the Sea (Sept); Skiing, Our Town, Health Update, Car Care, Seniors, Guide to the Arts, Winter Travel, Halloween (Oct); The Goods, Holiday Entertaining, Florida, Gift Guide (Nov); Holiday Gifts, Busy Person Cooking Guide, Shalom South Palm (Dec); Fall TV Preview (Fall); Cruising (Winter).
Special Weekly Sections: Weekly Business, Business Focus (mon); Back Talk (pre-teen) (tues); Food Section, Lifestyle Focus (thur); Shalom (thur or fri); Garden Pages, Home and Garden, Synagogue, Showtime (fri); Church, Real Estate (sat); Fashion, Business Focus, Travel (S).
Magazines: Sunshine TV Book (S); Exito Magazine, XS Magazine (weekly); Vital Signs Magazine (bi-weekly); South Florida Parenting Magazine (monthly).

CORPORATE OFFICERS
Chairman ..... Thomas P O'Donnell
President/CEO ..... Scott C Smith
Treasurer ..... Walter P Hampton
Vice Pres-Marketing ..... James E Smith
Vice Pres-Operations ..... Richard H Malone
Vice Pres-Advertising ..... Sheldon L Greenberger
Vice Pres-Circulation ..... James Bustraan
Vice Pres-Editorial ..... Earl Maucker
Vice Pres-Development ..... Howard Greenberg
Director-Human Resources ..... Diana L Bonvegna

Copyright ©1996 by the Editor & Publisher Co.

Director-Technology Bob Palermini
Secretary Stanley J Gradowski Jr
Asst Secretary Elsie J Felty

GENERAL MANAGEMENT

Publisher Scott C Smith
Director-Finance Walter P Hampton
Director-Human Resources Diana L Bonvegna
Manager-Purchasing Stephan S Grant
Manager-Public Relations Carol Hobbs
Manager-Facilities Fred W Hubbard

ADVERTISING

Vice Pres/Director Sheldon L Greenberger
Manager-Display Ray Vico
Manager-Display Gayle Blue
Manager-Display (Palm Beach) Lynn Franck
Manager-Classified Ray Daley
Manager-Special Sections Dennis Richardson
Manager-Sales Training/Development Irwin Siegel

MARKETING AND PROMOTION

Vice Pres/Director James E Smith
Manager-Marketing/Communications Mary Riedel
Manager-Public Relations Carol Hobbs
Manager-Consumer Marketing Linda Effinger
Manager-Media Andrea Aleff
Manager-Research Service Dana Franke
Manager-Marketing Service-National/Classified Mitch McKinnon
Manager-Marketing-Retail/Zone Ellen Gibson

TELECOMMUNICATIONS

Editor-Interactive Media Kurt Greenbaum

CIRCULATION

Vice Pres/Director James Bustraan
Manager (North/Central Broward) Karen Fleischer
Manager-Alternate Distribution Chris Cusimano
Manager-Palm Beach County Chuck Rumpf
Manager-Consumer Sales/Marketing Linda Effinger
Manager-Single Copy Sales (North/Central Broward) Paul Heymann
Manager-Sales & Marketing Debbie Meisner
Manager-Circulation & Accounting Steve Forrestal

NEWS EXECUTIVES

Editor Earl Maucker
Managing Editor Ellen Soeteber
Deputy Managing Editor/Palm Beach News Kathy Trumbull
Deputy Managing Editor/Sports & Features Dan Norman
Deputy Managing Editor/Broward News John Christie
Graphics Director John Hall
Exec Editor-News Kurt Franck

EDITORS AND MANAGERS

Art Columnist Roger Hurlburt
Books Editor Chauncey Mabe
Bureau Chief-Tallahassee Linda Kleindeinst
Bureau Chief-Washington William Gibson
Business/Finance Editor Kevin Gale
City/Metro Editor (Broward) Tom Davidson
Classical Music Critic Tim Smith
Columnist Ray Recchi
Columnist Gary Stein
Columnist Dave Hyde
Editorial Page Editor Kingsley Guy
Entertainment Editor John Dolen
Environmental Editor Robert McClure
Fashion Editor Rod Hagwood
Features/Lifestyle Editor John Dolan
Food Editor Deborah Hartz
Foreign Editor Robert Fabricio
Garden Editor Charlyne Varkonyi
Health/Medical Editor Diann Slattery
Horse Racing Editor Dave Joseph
Librarian Bob Isaacs
Motion Pictures Editor Rod Dreher
National Editor Rick Robb
News Editor Jim de Graci
News Editor Jeanne Jordan
Outdoors Editor Steve Waters
Palm Beach Editor Mindy Donnelly
Pop Music Critic Deborah Wilker
Radio/Television Editor Tom Jicha
Religion Editor James Davis
South Broward Editor Joe Jennings
Sports Editor Fred Turner
Stamps/Coins Editor Richard Carr
Sunshine Magazine Editor John Parkyn
Travel Editor Tom Swick
TV Book Editor Paulette Everett

MANAGEMENT INFORMATION SERVICES

General Manager-Interactive Service Mitch Golub
Manager-Sales/Marketing Cathy Stanton
Exec Producer Scott Anderson
Manager-Technology/Business Tom Maffetone

PRODUCTION

Vice Pres/Director Richard H Malone
Director-Technology Bob Palermini
Manager-Pressroom Barry Ferrari
Manager-Quality Assurance Bob Christie
Manager-Packaging Heidi Draper

Market Information: Zoned editions; TMC; ADS; Operate audiotex.
Mechanical available: Offset; Black; insert accepted — preprinted; page cut-offs — 22".
Mechanical specifications: Type page 13" x 21"; E - 6 cols, 2¹⁄₁₆", ⅛" between; A - 6 cols, 2¹⁄₁₆", ⅛" between; C - 10 cols, 1³⁄₁₆", ⅛" between.
Commodity consumption: Newsprint 76,158 short tons; 69,090 metric tons; widths 54¾", 47¹⁵⁄₁₆", 40¾", 27⅛"; black ink 1,340,000 pounds; color ink 327,000 pounds; average pages per issue 102(d), 170(sat), 192(S); single plates used 470,000.
Equipment: EDITORIAL: Front-end hardware — AT, IBM/PC; Front-end software — AT. CLASSIFIED: Front-end hardware — AT, IBM/RS 6000; Front-end software — AT. AUDIOTEX: Hardware — Brite Voice Systems; Supplier name — VNN. DISPLAY: Adv layout systems — SCS/Layout 8000; Front-end hardware — PC; Front-end software — SCS/Layout 8000. PRODUCTION: Typesetters — 3-AU/APS-108 PIPS, 1-Emerald/PS-PIP, 2-AU/APS soft PS-PIP, 4-AU/APS-6; Plate exposures — 3-WL/Lith-X-Pozer III; Plate processors — 3-WL/2-38D, 1-38G; Electronic picture desk — Lf, Scitex; Scanners — 4-ECR/Autokon 1000; Production cameras — 2-C/Spartan III, 2-C/B&W; Automatic film processors — 4-C/66F, 2-C/660; Film transporters — 2-C; Shrink lenses — 2-Alan; Color separation equipment (conventional) — 2-CD/6451E, Scitex; Digital color separation equipment — Scitex. PRESSROOM: Line 1 — 9-G/Colorliner; Line 2 — 9-G/Colorliner; Line 3 — 9-G/Colorliner; Line 4 — 9-G/Colorliner; Line 5 — 9-G/Colorliner; Folders — 5-G/3:2 Single, 1-G/3:2 Double; Pasters — 45-G/Colorliner-CT 50 Belt Tension; Reels and stands — 50-G/Box Columns; Press control system — 12-Fin/AGU. MAILROOM: Counter stackers — 14-HL/Monitor HT; Inserters and stuffers — 4-GMA/SLS 1000, MM; Bundle tyer — 15-Power Strap; Addressing machine — 2-KR/Labeler. LIBRARY: Electronic — Vu/Text SAVE. WIRE SERVICES: News — AP, NYT, RN, DJ, KRT, LAT-WP; Photos — AP, RN; Stock tables — KRT; Syndicates — TMS, LATS, NYT, Universal Press, United Media, Creators, WP, King Features, AP; Receiving dishes — UPI. BUSINESS COMPUTERS: IBM/4381, IBM/RS-6000; Applications: CJ: Circ; SCS/Layout 8000: Preprints; Admarc; PCs & micros networked; PCs & main system networked.

FORT MYERS

Lee County

'90 U.S. Census- 45,206; E&P '96 Est. 52,842
ABC-NDM (90): 335,113 (HH 140,124)

News-Press (m-mon to sat; S)

News-Press, 2442 Dr Martin Luther King Jr Blvd., Fort Myers, FL 33901-3987; tel (941) 335-0200; fax (941) 332-7581. Gannett Co. Inc. group.
Circulation: 95,702(m); 95,702(m-sat); 108,157(S); ABC circulation average for 12 months ended Sept. 30, 1995.
Price: 50¢(d); 50¢(sat); $1.50(S); $3.25/wk.
Advertising: Open inch rate $68.90(m); $85.20(m-sat); $85.20(S). **Representative:** Gannett National Newspaper Sales.
News Services: AP, GNS, KRT. **Politics:** Independent. **Established:** 1884.
Special Editions: Visitors Guide, Bridal Guide, Super Bowl (Jan); Real Estate Floor Plan Guide, Edison Festival, Taste of S.W. Florida (Feb); Spring Training, Parade of Homes, Boaters Bulletin (Mar); Commerce & Growth, Spring Car Care (Apr); Just For Kids, Hurricane, Sandollar Coupons (May); Affordable Homes, Bridal Section, Best Ballots (June); Affordable Living, Back to School, The Best (July); Football, Floor Plan Guide (Aug); Home & Style, Women in Business (Sept); Careers, New Car Preview, Design For Living Expo (Oct); Newcomers Magazine, Holiday Gift Guide 1, Cookbook (Nov); Songbook, Holiday Gift Guide 2, Medical Directory, Holiday Gift Guide 3 (Dec).
Special Weekly Sections: Business Monday (mon); Food (thur); Gulfcoasting Entertainment (fri); Travel (S).
Magazines: USA Weekend, Gulf Coasting (fri).

CORPORATE OFFICER

President Dan A Martin

GENERAL MANAGEMENT

Publisher Dan A Martin
Asst to Publisher Irene Alfieri
Controller Brian A Craig
Director-Human Resources Jo-Ann Bradley

ADVERTISING

Director Ronald Capretta
Manager-General/Co-op Lynn Graniero
Manager-Retail Jeff Bergin
Manager-Classified Michelle Milliken

MARKETING AND PROMOTION

Director-Market Development Leslie Hurst

CIRCULATION

Director Gregory Hafdahl
Manager Michael McKillip
Manager-Customer Affairs George Cook

NEWS EXECUTIVES

Exec Editor Terry Eberle
Managing Editor Vickie Kilgore
Asst Managing Editor-Lifestyles Jill Fredel
Asst Managing Editor-News Maria Lettman

EDITORS AND MANAGERS

Automotive Writer Bill Kilpatrick
Business Editor Harriet Simpson
Editorial Page Editor Gail Pastula
Features Editor Genetta Adams
Graphic Arts Editor Randy Lovely
News Editor Brad Windsor
Outdoors Writer Byron Stout
Photo Editor Garth Francis
Radio/Television Editor Kathy Kinsey
Sports Editor Mike Klocke
Travel Editor Karen Smith

MANAGEMENT INFORMATION SERVICES

Data Processing Manager Dick Ethier

PRODUCTION

Vice Pres-Operations Don Miller
Manager Jean Workman
Manager-Pre Press/Composing Ernie Foxworth
Manager-Camera Steve Olive
Manager-Pressroom William VanDerburgh
Manager-Distribution William Dean
Manager-Computer Systems Greg Helton
Manager-Ad Service Carole Irvine
Engineer-Plant Harry Irvine
Asst Engineer-Plant David Miller

Market Information: Zoned editions; Split Run; TMC; Operate database.
Mechanical available: Offset; Black and 3 ROP colors; insert accepted — preprinted; page cut-offs — 23¾".
Mechanical specifications: Type page 13" x 21½"; E - 6 cols, 2¹⁄₁₆", ⅛" between; A - 6 cols, 2¹⁄₁₆", ⅛" between; C - 10 cols, 1³⁄₁₆", ¹⁄₁₆" between.
Commodity consumption: Newsprint 15,015 short tons; widths 54.5", 40.875"; black ink 360,363 pounds; color ink 89,513 pounds; single pages printed 28,509; average pages per issue 66(d), 152(S); single plates used 135,000.
Equipment: EDITORIAL: Front-end hardware — Tandem/TXP; Front-end software — SII; Printers — Centronics; Other equipment — HAS/Pagination, Lf/AP Leaf Picture Desk. CLASSIFIED: Front-end hardware — Tandem/TXP; Front-end software — SII, SII/Pagination; Printers — Centronics. DISPLAY: Adv layout systems — Realtime/Layout 80; Front-end hardware — DEC/11-73; Front-end software — SCS/Layout 80; Other equipment — Realtime/Ad Tracking, DTI/AdSpeed. PRODUCTION: Pagination software — HAS 2.5; Typesetters — 2-AU/APS-6-108s, 2-AU/APS-800PIP, 4-AU/APS, 2-AU/APS Accuset; Plate exposures — 2-Nu, 1-BKY; Plate processors — 2-Nat; Production cameras — 1-C/Spartan III, 1-C/Spartan II; Automatic film processors — 1-LE/LD1800, 1-LE/LD24A, 1-LE/2600, C/66F; Film transporters — 2-C; Shrink lenses — 1-CK Optical/SQU-7; Color separation equipment (conventional) — 1-RZ/210L. PRESSROOM: Line 1 — 8-G/Metro (4 half decks); Line 2 — 8-G/Metro (4 half decks); Press drives — DC Motors/60 hp; Folders — 4-G/3:2; Pasters — 16-G/Metro; Reels and stands — 16-G/Metro; Press control system — PCS/II; Press registration system — WEB/Micro-Track. MAILROOM: Counter stackers — 6-Id/NS440, 2-PPK, 4-HL/HI, 2-HI/R25; Inserters and stuffers — 2-HI/NP1372; Bundle tyer — 3-MLN, 4-MLN/2A; Wrapping singles — 7-Id; Addressing machine — 2-Ch, 2-Wm, 1-Dispensa-Matic/V-45; Mailroom control system — 1-HL/Stream Scan Bundle Control System. LIBRARY: Electronic — Digital Collections System. WIRE SERVICES: News — AP Datastream, AP Datafeatures, TV Data, KRT; Photos — AP; Receiving dishes — AP. BUSINESS COMPUTERS: IBM/AS-400; PCs & main system networked.

FORT PIERCE-PORT ST. LUCIE

St. Lucie County

'90 U.S. Census- 92,696 (Fort Pierce 36,830; Port St. Lucie 55,866); E&P '96 Est. 113,983 (Fort Pierce 39,341; Port St. Lucie 74,642)
ABC-NDM (90): 150,171 (HH 58,174)

The Tribune (m-mon to sat; S)

The Tribune, 600 Edwards Rd.; PO Box 69, Fort Pierce, FL 34954; tel (407) 461-2050, (407) 467-1953. Freedom Communications Inc. group.
Circulation: 26,619(m); 26,619(m-sat); 29,580(S); ABC circulation average for 12 months ended Sept. 30, 1995.
Price: 25¢(d); 25¢(sat); 75¢(S); $1.60/wk; $6.93/mo; $83.20/yr.
Advertising: Open inch rate $23.31(m); $23.31(m-sat); $24.46(S). **Representative:** Papert Companies.
News Services: AP, UPI, NEA, KRT. **Politics:** Independent. **Established:** 1903.
Special Editions: Back-to-School; Christmas Preview; Christmas; County Fair; Cook Book; Agribusiness; Spring & Fall Car Care; Health & Fitness; Recreation; Home Improvement; Boating & Fishing; Easter; Bridal Tab; Winter Season Mail Away; Advantage Card Directory; Medical Guide; Football.
Special Weekly Sections: Best Food Days (thur); Church Page, Drive Time (sat); Best Food Days, Business, Sports, Real Estate Homes Section (S); Business, Entertainment, Sports, TV Listings (daily).
Magazines: Weekend (Entertainment features) (fri); Sunday Comics, Parade, TV (S).

GENERAL MANAGEMENT

Publisher David T Rutledge
Business Manager Kathy LeClair

ADVERTISING

Director-Marketing Lon Matejczyk
Manager-Major Accounts Frank Harbor
Manager-Display Sales Joe Matessa

MARKETING AND PROMOTION

Director-Marketing/Promotion Jeffrey Rubin
Manager-Promotion Deborah Greene

CIRCULATION

Director George Cogswell

NEWS EXECUTIVE

Exec Editor Harold Muddiman

EDITORS AND MANAGERS

City Editor Cheryl Smith
Life Editor Gloria Weinberg
Photo Editor Bill Mitchell
Sports Editor Mike Graham

MANAGEMENT INFORMATION SERVICES

Data Processing Manager Tim Jernigan

PRODUCTION

Manager Lynn Ferraro
Foreman-Composing (Day) Diane Cooper
Foreman-Composing (Night) Tim Warren
Foreman-Pressroom Jim Mason
Foreman-Mailroom Margaret Townsend

Mechanical available: Offset; Black and 3 ROP colors; insert accepted — preprinted; page cut-offs — 22¾".
Mechanical specifications: Type page 13" x 21½"; E - 6 cols, 2¹⁄₁₆", ⅛" between; A - 6 cols, 2¹⁄₁₆", ⅛" between; C - 9 cols, 1⅜", ¹⁄₁₆" between.
Commodity consumption: Newsprint 3,200 short tons; 2,900 metric tons; widths 27½", 13¾"; black ink 58,000 pounds; color ink 14,763 pounds; single pages printed 17,758; average pages per issue 40(d), 48(sat), 62(S); single plates used 26,043.
Equipment: EDITORIAL: Front-end hardware — 40-Dewar; Front-end software — Dewar; Printers — 1-TI, 2-QMS/860, 2-Xante/Accel-a-Writer 8200; Other equipment — 1-Ap/Mac Quadra, 1-Ap/Mac II, 1-Lf/AP Leaf Picture Desk, 3-Ap/Mac 950 Quadra. CLASSIFIED: Front-end hardware — 7-Compaq; Front-end software — Dewar; Printers — 1-Okidata/Microline 393, 10-Okidata/320, 2-Genicom/4440XT. DISPLAY: Adv layout systems — QuarkXPress, Dewar/Charm Xtension; Front-end hardware — 2-Ap/Mac SE, 4-Compaq; Front-end software — Dewar; Printers — 1-Ap/Mac LaserWriter. PRODUCTION: Pagination software — QuarkXPress 3.31; Typesetters

— 2-Ap/Power Mac RIP, 2-Panther/Pro 36; Plate exposures — 2-Nu; Plate processors — 2-Nat; Electronic picture desk — Lf/AP Leaf Picture Desk; Scanners — 3-HP/IICX flatbed; Production cameras — 1-C/Spartan II; Automatic film processors — 2-LE/26; Shrink lenses — 1-CK Optical; Digital color separation equip. — Lf/Leafscan 35, Kk/2035, HP/2cx. PRESSROOM: Line 1 — 12-G/Urbanite; Press drives — 2-Fin/125 h.p., 1-Fin/150 h.p.; Folders — 2-G/Urbanite; Reels and stands — 8-G; Press control system — 3-Fin; Press registration system — Duarte. MAILROOM: Counter stackers — HL/Monitor, PPK; Bundle tyer — MLN. LIBRARY: Electronic — SMS. WIRE SERVICES: News — AP, NYT, KRT, AP Sports, AP Datastream; Photos — AP, KRT, AP Sports; Stock tables — TMS; size-1m, AP. BUSINESS COMPUTERS: Compaq/486-66, Novell; Applications: Vision Data: Circ; Dewar/Sys IV: Editorial, Class; QuarkXPress, Southware/ Brainworks: Acct; Dewar/Charm Xtension; PCs & micros networked.

FORT WALTON BEACH

Okaloosa County

'90 U.S. Census- 21,471; E&P '96 Est. 21,953
ABC-CZ (90): 110,112 (HH 42,758)

Northwest Florida Daily News (m-mon to sat; S)

Northwest Florida Daily News, 200 Racetrack Rd. (32547); PO Drawer 2949, Fort Walton Beach, FL 32549; tel (904) 863-1111; fax (904) 862-5230. Freedom Communications Inc. group.

Circulation: 37,916(m); 37,916(m-sat); 49,849(S); ABC circulation average for 12 months ended Sept. 30, 1995.

Price: 50¢(d); 50¢(sat); $1.00(S); $9.54/mo; $137.80/yr (d) (mail), $164.30/yr (dS) (mail).

Advertising: Open inch rate $24.15(m); $24.15(m-sat); $24.15(S). **Representative:** Papert Companies.

News Services: AP, NEA, KRT. **Politics:** Independent. **Established:** 1946.

Special Editions: Active Times (Jan); Home Improvement (Mar); Active Times, Spring Fashion (Apr); Vacation Guide (May); Active Times (July); Football (Aug); Active Times (Oct); Recipe Tab (Dec).

Special Weekly Sections: Food (wed); Showcase/Entertainment (fri); Real Estate, Moneyesene (S).

Magazines: Parade Magazine; TV Times.

GENERAL MANAGEMENT

Publisher Marvin DeBolt
Business Manager Jim Bryan
Manager-Education Service Carol Ann DeBolt

ADVERTISING

Director Sam Childs
Manager-Classified Joe Nacchia

MARKETING AND PROMOTION

Manager-Marketing/Promotion Jean Rief

CIRCULATION

Director Darryll Watson
Manager-Promotion Richard Springfield

NEWS EXECUTIVES

Editor Tom Conner
Managing Editor Debbie Lord

EDITORS AND MANAGERS

Artist Craig Terry
Book Editor Marvin DeBolt
Columnist Bill Campbell
News Editor Dan Way
Sports Editor Arnold Feliciano
Wire Editor Del Stone
Women's Editor Debbie Lord

MANAGEMENT INFORMATION SERVICES

Data Processing Manager John Beschler

PRODUCTION

Manager James Lucas
Foreman-Pressroom Ron Rich

Mechanical available: Offset; Black and 3 ROP colors; insert accepted — preprinted, all; page cut-offs — 22¾".

Mechanical specifications: Type page 13" x 21½"; E - 6 cols, 2¹⁄₁₆", ⅛" between; A - 6 cols, 2¹⁄₁₆", ⅛" between; C - 9 cols, 1⅜", ¹⁄₁₆" between.

Commodity consumption: Newsprint 3,000 short tons; 3,500 metric tons; widths 27½", 13¾"; single pages printed 17,438; average pages per issue 42(d), 82(S).

Equipment: EDITORIAL: Front-end hardware — PC; Front-end software — Dewar. CLASSIFIED: Front-end hardware — PC; Front-end software — Dewar. DISPLAY: Adv layout systems — Dewar; Front-end hardware — PC; Front-end software — Dewar. PRODUCTION: Typesetters — V/Plain Paper; Plate exposures — Nu; Plate processors — Nat; Production cameras — C/Spartan III; Automatic film processors — 1-LE/LD-2600A, 1-LE/26; Color separation equipment (conventional) — RZ/210L. PRESSROOM: Line 1 — 9-G/Urbanite (3 color unit); Folders — 1-G; Pasters — 8-Cary. MAILROOM: Counter stackers — 1-HL/Monitor; Inserters and stuffers — GMA; Bundle tyer — 2-MLN/EE, 1-Dynaric. LIBRARY: Electronic — SMS/Stauffer Gold. WIRE SERVICES: News — AP, KRT; Stock tables — AP SelectStox; Syndicates — LATS; Receiving dishes — size-3m, AP. BUSINESS COMPUTERS: PC; Applications: Accts receivable, Accts payable, Gen ledger, Payroll, Circ; PCs & micros networked; PCs & main system networked.

GAINESVILLE

Alachua County

'90 U.S. Census- 84,770; E&P '96 Est. 87,781
ABC-CZ (90): 84,770 (HH 31,924)

The Gainesville Sun (m-mon to sat; S)

The Gainesville Sun, 2700 S.W. 13th St.; PO Box 147147, Gainesville, FL 32608; tel (904) 374-5000; fax (904) 338-3131; e-mail dart@freenet.ufl.edu; web site http://www.jou.ufl.edu/enews/sun. New York Times Co. group.

Circulation: 55,370(m); 55,370(m-sat); 60,303(S); ABC circulation average for 12 months ended Sept. 30, 1995.

Price: 25¢(d); 50¢(sat); 75¢(S); $2.50/wk; $130.00/yr.

Advertising: Open inch rate $43.96(m); $43.96(m-sat); $43.96(S). **Representatives:** Publishers' Representatives of Florida; Sawyer-Ferguson-Walker Co.

News Services: AP, NYT, LAT-WP, KRT. **Politics:** Independent. **Established:** 1875.

Advertising not accepted: Hand guns & assault weapons by private party; Nudity & out-call dancing.

Special Editions: Super Bowl, Travel-Hideaways, Wedding Book (Jan); Almanac '96, Travel-Cruises, Clip-It Coupon Book, Adventures (Feb); Gatornationals, Spring Garden Guide, Design-An-Ad, Travel-Summer in Europe (Mar); Home Improvement, Parent's Guide, Travel-Honeymoon Planner (Apr); Travel-USA and Canada, Chamber Expo '96 Program, Clip-It Coupon Book, Community Section, Careers, Adventures (May); Travel-Exotic Vacations, Health Care, Storms (June); Travel-Caribbean Value Season, Prime Time (July); Back-to-School, Travel-Fall Cruises, Welcome Back, Clip-It Coupon Book, Adventures (Aug); Football '96, Literacy Tab, Travel-Fall Foliage Tours, Readers Choice Awards (Sept); Home Furnishings, Travel-Holiday Hide-aways, 1997 Auto Outlook (Oct); Adventures, Travel-Ski Issue, Clip-It Coupon Book, Basketball '96-'97, Christmas Gift Guide (Nov); Travel-Great Escapes (Dec).

Special Weekly Section: Good Neighbors (thur).

Magazines: Worklife (mon); Scene Entertainment & Arts Magazine; TV Week, Sports Weekend (sat); Parade (S).

CORPORATE OFFICER

President Jim Weeks

GENERAL MANAGEMENT

Publisher John Fitzwater
Controller Dan Friedman
Manager-Credit Bonnie Parker
Manager-Business Office Martha Pattison

ADVERTISING

Director David Minnich
Manager-Retail Sally Galanos
Asst Manager-Classified Naomi Williams
Coordinator-National Dorie Clark
Coordinator-Preprint/Co-op Sharon Garris

TELECOMMUNICATIONS

Audiotex Manager Mike McNell

CIRCULATION

Director Jim Miller
Manager-Operations Bob Carpentieri
Manager-Sales Diane Charette

NEWS EXECUTIVES

Exec Editor Jim Osteen
Managing Editor Curt Pierson
Asst Managing Editor Jacki Levine

EDITORS AND MANAGERS

Action Line Editor Doris Chandler
Business Editor Lillian Castro
City Editor-Night Darell Hartman
Asst City Editor Jeff Moriarity
Editorial Page Editor Ron Cunningham
Education Editor Ray Washington
Education Editor Mary Shedden
Entertainment/Amusements Editor Bill De Young
Environmental Editor Bruce Ritchie
Features/Family/Food Editor Diane Chun
Garden Editor Marina Blomberg
Health/Medical Editor Doris Chandler
Metro Editor Cindy Barnett
News Wire Editor Bill Lever
News Graphic Manager Jean Fleetwood
Photo Department Manager Tim Davis
Radio/Television Editor Bill De Young
Regional Editor Darrell Hartman
Religion/Women's Editor Diane Chun
Scene Magazine Editor Bill De Young
Science/Technology Editor Bruce Ritchie
Sports Editor Noel Nash
Travel Editor Diane Chun

MANAGEMENT INFORMATION SERVICES

Director-Info Technology Mike McNall

PRODUCTION

Director Vern Bean
Manager-Pre Press Allen Baxley
Manager-Pressroom Randy McClellan
Manager-Plant Billy Dean

Market Information: Zoned editions; TMC; Operate audiotex; Electronic edition.

Mechanical available: Offset; Black and 3 ROP colors; insert accepted — preprinted, all; page cut-offs — 22".

Mechanical specifications: Type page 13" x 21"; E - 6 cols, 2¹⁄₁₆", ⅛" between; A - 6 cols, 2¹⁄₁₆", ⅛" between; C - 10 cols, 1³⁄₁₆", ⅛" between.

Commodity consumption: Newsprint 9,414 short tons; widths 55", 41¾", 27½", 13¾"; black ink 151,200 pounds; color ink 52,700 pounds; single pages printed 20,302; average pages per issue 44(d), 80(S); single plates used 71,100.

Equipment: EDITORIAL: Front-end hardware — AT/9000, Ap/Mac; Front-end software — DTI/SpeedWriter, DTI/SpeedPlanner, DTI/PageSpeed 3.1.5; Printers — 2-AU/108c, 1-AU/3850, 1-AU/6600. CLASSIFIED: Front-end hardware — Ap/Mac; Front-end software — DTI/ClassSpeed 3.2; AUDIOTEX: Hardware — Brite. DISPLAY: Adv layout systems — DTI/AdSpeed, DTI/AdManager, DTI/Speed-Planner; Front-end hardware — 6-Ap/Mac Pagination, 2-Ap/Mac Text Input; Front-end software — DTI/AdSpeed, DTI/SpeedPlanner 3.1.5; Printers — 2-AU/APS-6, 1-AU/APS-HS-3850. PRODUCTION: Pagination software — DTI/PageSpeed 3.1.5; OCR software — Caere/OmniPage; Typesetters — 2-AU/APS-6, 1-AU/APS 3850 HS; Plate exposures — 2-Nu/Flip Top; Plate processors — 1-Nat, 1-W; Electronic picture desk — Lf/AP Leaf Picture Desk; Scanners — ECR/Autokon 1030-DE, CD/6461E Color Scanner, Kk/Pro Rfs 2035, Umax/Powerlook, Umax/ Ultra Vision; Production cameras — 1-C/Spartan III, 1-C/Newspager; Automatic film processors — 2-LE/Excel 2600, 1-DP/37-C; Film transporters — 2-C. PRESSROOM: Line 1 — 5-G/Headliner offset (3 half decks); Press drives — Fin; Folders — 2-G/2:1; Pasters — 5-G; Reels and stands — 5-G. MAILROOM: Counter stackers — 2-Id/2200, 3-LI/660; Inserters and stuffers — HI/1472P; Bundle tyer — 1-MLN/2A, 2-Dynaric/NP2; Addressing machine — 1-Ch, 1-KR; Other mailroom equipment — HI/Stitcher-Trimmer. WIRE SERVICES: News — AP, NYT; Stock tables — AP; Syndicates — AP, NYT; Receiving dishes — size-3m, AP. BUSINESS COMPUTERS: 1-IBM/Sys 38; Applications: Microsoft/Excel, Microsoft/Word; PCs & micros networked; PCs & main system networked.

INVERNESS

See CRYSTAL RIVER

JACKSONVILLE

Duval County

'90 U.S. Census- 672,971; E&P '96 Est. 781,851
ABC-CZ (90): 756,125 (HH 287,162)

The Florida Times-Union (m-mon to sat; S)

The Florida Times-Union, One Riverside Ave.; PO Box 1949, Jacksonville, FL 32231; tel (904) 359-4111; fax (904) 359-4400; web site http://newsjobs.com. Morris Communications Corp. group.

Circulation: 194,643(m); 194,643(m-sat); 253,036(S); ABC circulation average for 12 months ended Sept. 30, 1995.

Price: 50¢(d); 50¢(sat); $1.50(S); $2.77/wk; $36.00/13wk; $12.00/mo; $132.91/yr.

Advertising: Open inch rate $131.35(m); $141.30(m-sat); $157.50(S). **Representatives:** Sawyer-Ferguson-Walker Co.; Publishers' Representatives of Florida.

News Services: AP, LAT-WP, NYT. **Politics:** Independent. **Established:** 1864.

Note: Advertising is sold in combination with St. Augustine Record (eS) for $142.50 (d), $150.60 (sat) and $166.15 (S).

Special Editions: Winter Health & Fitness, Super Bowl '96, Beginnings (Jan); Heritage Section, Spring Home & Patio Show, Pool & Spa (Feb); Careers, Spring Cruise Guide (Mar); Spring Fix-Up, Latitudes, Super Sunday (Apr); To Mother With Love, Fine Furnishings, Florida Vacation Guide (May); Summer Health & Fitness (June); Super Sunday, Jaguar Kickoff (July); Back-to-School, Football Preview '96 (Aug); Fall Cruise Guide, Fall Latitudes, Fall Home Improvement (Sept); Southern Women's Show, Florida/Georgia Football (Oct); Fine Furnishings, International Auto Show, Holiday Happenings (Nov); Dear Santa Letters, Last Minute Gift Guide, Bowl Preview '96 (Dec).

Special Weekly Sections: Family (mon); Mind & Body (wed); Food (thur); Religion, Weekend (fri); Digs (sat); Arts & Style, On TV (S); Business, Sports (daily); Easy Living (monthly).

Magazines: First Business (mon); Parade; On TV (Television Magazine).

CORPORATE OFFICERS

Board Chairman W S Morris III
President Paul S Simon

GENERAL MANAGEMENT

Publisher Carl N Cannon
General Manager Robert E Martin
Controller-Division W Mitchel Denning
Personnel Director Donna P Williams
Purchasing Agent/Director-Service Tom Thornton
Manager-Credit Tim Todaro

ADVERTISING

Director-Sales/Marketing Raymond P Dallman
Manager-National/Major Accounts John Lescott
Manager-Display James (Jay) Weimar
Manager-Marketing/Promotion Ginger Rountree
Manager-Classified Geraldine Kotz
Manager-Marketing-Services Wallace Parker

TELECOMMUNICATIONS

Audiotex Manager Steve Cheski

CIRCULATION

Director John Whaley
Director-Distribution Center Robert L Motel
Manager-Promotion Cindy Gonya

NEWS EXECUTIVES

Editor Frederick W Hartmann
Exec Editor Richard T Allport
Assoc Editor Jon Hunt
Managing Editor Mary E Kress
Asst Managing Editor-News Mike Richey
Asst Managing Editor-Projects Mark Middlebrook

EDITORS AND MANAGERS

A-1 Editor Carole Fader
Art Director Vasin Omer Douglas
Books Editor Ann Hyman
Business Editor Robin Clark
Call Box Editor Nicole McGill
Columnist Ron Littlepage
Courts Editor June Bell
Editorial Page Editor Lloyd Brown
Editorial Cartoonist Ed Gamble
Education Editor Jim Saunders
Fashion Editor Linda Hanks
Features Editor Sara Wildberger
Films/Theater Editor Matt Soergel
Food Editor Belinda Hulin
Librarian Maryann Sterzel
Medical Editor Mike Stobbe
Military Editor John Fritz
News Editor John Burr
Night Editor Gary Bell
Outdoors Editor Joe Julavits
Photo Chief Bob Mack
Reader Advocate Mike Clark
Religion Editor Lilla Ross
Sports Editor Joe DeSalvo
Television Editor Charles Patton
Weekend Editor Alison Lucian

MANAGEMENT INFORMATION SERVICES

Data Processing Manager W Mitchel Denning

PRODUCTION

Director Wade H Cason
Asst Director T J Crosby
Director-Advertising/Customer Service Mike Begue
Manager-Pressroom Perry Gann
Manager-Scheduling/Make-Up Mike Begue
Manager-Technical Service Ronald K Petrey
Manager-Technical Service Software Drew Brunson
Superintendent-Engraving Harold Clemons
Superintendent-Bldg Mech A J Bayer Jr
Superintendent-Newsprint Handling Gabriel Hall
Coordinator-Color Mike Horne
Coordinator-Newsprint Tony Taber

Market Information: Zoned editions; Split Run; Operate audiotex.
Mechanical available: DiLitho/Offset; Black and 3 ROP colors; insert accepted — preprinted; page cut-offs — 22¾".
Mechanical specifications: Type page 12¾" x 21½"; E - 6 cols, 2", ⅛" between; A - 6 cols, 2", ⅛" between; C - 10 cols, 1³⁄₁₆", ¹⁄₁₆" between.
Commodity consumption: widths 54", 40½", 27"; average pages per issue 52(d), 76(sat), 120(S); single plates used 285,000.
Equipment: EDITORIAL: Front-end hardware — IBM/AT, IBM/PS-2, Gateway/P5; Front-end software — MPS; Printers — Toshiba, Epson; Other equipment — 4-Ap/Mac Quadra 950, 5-Ap/Mac 8100-80, 1-Ap/Mac 7100. CLASSIFIED: Front-end hardware — 45-Gateway/2000, 15-AT/PS2; Front-end software — MPS; Printers — Toshiba, Epson. AUDIOTEX: Hardware — PEP. DISPLAY: Adv layout systems — III/Advisor; Front-end hardware — 10-III, 4-Ap/Mac fx; Front-end software — III; Printers — Benson, X. PRODUCTION: Pagination software — III; Typesetters — 4-III, Infoset/400 CRT, 2-III/3850H; Platemaking systems — WL; Plate exposures — 2-WL/Lith-X-Pozer 10, 1-WL/Lith-X-Pozer 1; Plate processors — 3-WL/Lithoplates; Electronic picture desk — Lf/AP Leaf Picture Desk, 5-Ap/Mac; Scanners — 2-III, 4-Polaroid; Production cameras — 1-C/Pager, 2-Liberator; Automatic film processors — 2-LE/24-AQ, 1-DR/36, 4-LE/MTP26; Film transporters — 2-Liberator; Digital color separation equipment — Howtek/4500.
PRESSROOM: Line 1 — 22-H/3322; Line 2 — 16-G/Metro 3019,3020; Press drives — Fin; Folders — 4-G/3:2, 6-H/3:2 (DiLitho); Pasters — 22-H/3322, 16-G; Reels and stands — 22-H/3322, 16-G. MAILROOM: Counter stackers — 12-HI/HT; Inserters and stuffers — 3-SLS/1000; Bundle tyer — 12-Power Strap/PSN5; Wrapping singles — Manual. LIBRARY: Combination — Manual. WIRE SERVICES: News — AP; Photos — AP; Stock tables — AP; Syndicates — AP, North America Syndicate; Receiving dishes — size-10ft, AP.

KEY WEST
Monroe County

'90 U.S. Census- 24,832; E&P '96 Est. 25,181
ABC-CZ (90): 24,832 (HH 10,424)

The Key West Citizen
(m-mon to fri; S)

The Key West Citizen, 3420 N. Side Dr.; PO Box 1800, Key West, FL 33041; tel (305) 294-6641; fax (305) 294-0768. Thomson Newspapers group.
Circulation: 10,955(m); 10,921(S); ABC circulation average for 12 months ended Sept. 30, 1995.
Price: 25¢(d); $1.00(S); $1.79/wk; $7.76/mo; $93.09/yr.
Advertising: Open inch rate $12.50(m); $12.50(S). **Representatives:** Papert Companies; The Newspaper National Network; Florida Newspaper Advertising Network.
News Service: AP. **Politics:** Independent. **Established:** 1879.
Not Published: Thanksgiving; Christmas.
Special Editions: Old Island Days (Jan); Arts Festival (Feb); Progress (Mar); Home Improvement, Easter Dining (Apr); Hurricane Tab (June); Hemingway Days (July); Back-to-School (Aug); Football (Sept); Fantasy Fest (Oct); Gift Guide (Nov); Christmas Song Book (Dec); Monthly Real Estate Sections.
Special Weekly Sections: Best Food Day (thur); Church Page (fri); Business Page (S).
Magazines: USA Weekend, Comics (S).

GENERAL MANAGEMENT

Publisher Winston A Burrell

ADVERTISING

Manager Randy Erickson

TELECOMMUNICATIONS

Audiotex Manager Brian Carmen

CIRCULATION

Manager Roger Atkins

NEWS EXECUTIVE

Editor Tim Aten

EDITORS AND MANAGERS

Entertainment/Amusements Editor Michelle Monfort
Lifestyle Editor Rebecca McGowen
News Editor John Guerra
Photo Editor Mike Hentz
Sports Editor Ralph Morrow
Television/Film Editor Michelle Monfort

PRODUCTION

Foreman-Press Larry Martin

Market Information: TMC; ADS; Operate audiotex.
Mechanical available: Offset; Black and 3 ROP colors; insert accepted — preprinted; page cut-offs — 21½".
Mechanical specifications: Type page 13" x 21½"; E - 6 cols, 2¹⁄₁₆", ⅛" between; A - 6 cols, 2¹⁄₁₆", ⅛" between; C - 9 cols, 1⁵⁄₁₆", ¹⁄₁₆" between.
Commodity consumption: Newsprint 399 short tons; widths 27½", 12¾"; black ink 18,047 pounds; color ink 800 pounds; single pages printed 6,099; average pages per issue 18(d), 32(S); single plates used 7,800.
Equipment: EDITORIAL: Front-end hardware — CText, Mk; Front-end software — Novell; Printers — V/5100. CLASSIFIED: Front-end hardware — CText; Front-end software — Novell; Printers — V/5100. AUDIOTEX: Software — Infotext. DISPLAY: Adv layout systems — CText, Ap/Mac; Front-end hardware — Ap/Mac Quadra 8100; Front-end software — Multi-Ad/Creator, Adobe/Photoshop, Adobe/Illustrator, QPS, QuarkXPress; Printers — V/5100, Panther. PRODUCTION: Typesetters — 2-V/5100; Plate exposures — Nu/Flip Top FT40 APRNS; Plate processors — Nat/A-250; Electronic picture desk — Lf/AP Leaf Picture Desk; Scanners — AG/Arcus Plus; Production cameras — SCREEN/Companica 680C; Automatic film processors — SCREEN/220; Color separation equipment (conventional) — Lf/AP Leaf Picture Desk, V/5300.
PRESSROOM: Line 1 — 9-G/1109SS; Folders — 1-G. MAILROOM: Inserters and stuffers — 7-MM; Bundle tyer — 1-OVL; Addressing machine — 1-El. COMMUNICATIONS: Facsimile — AP/Data; Digital ad delivery system — AP AdSend. WIRE SERVICES: News — AP; Photos — AP; Receiving dishes — size-3m, AP. BUSINESS COMPUTERS: ATT.

LAKE CITY
Columbia County

'90 U.S. Census- 10,005; E&P '96 Est. 10,627
ABC-CZ (90): 10,005 (HH 3,903)

Lake City Reporter
(e-mon to fri)

Lake City Reporter, 126 E. Duval St.; PO Box 1709, Lake City, FL 32055; tel (904) 752-1293; fax (904) 752-9400. New York Times Co. group.
Circulation: 9,076(e); ABC circulation average for 12 months ended Sept. 30, 1995.
Price: 25¢(d); $66.00/yr (carrier), $96.00/yr (mail).
Advertising: Open inch rate $15.50(e). **Representative:** Landon Associates Inc.
News Services: AP, NYT. **Established:** 1874.
Special Weekly Sections: Best Food Day (wed); The Entertainer, Real Estate (fri).

CORPORATE OFFICER

President Jim Weeks

GENERAL MANAGEMENT

Publisher Don L Caldwell
Controller Sue Brannon

ADVERTISING

Director Andrew Caldwell

CIRCULATION

Director Bill Hayter

NEWS EXECUTIVE

Exec Editor Tommy Hornsby

PRODUCTION

Director Larry Tucker

Market Information: TMC.
Mechanical available: Offset; Black and 3 ROP colors; insert accepted — preprinted, hand bill size; page cut-offs — 23¾".
Mechanical specifications: Type page 13" x 21½"; E - 6 cols, 2¹⁄₁₆", ⅛" between; A - 6 cols, 2¹⁄₁₆", ⅛" between; C - 8 cols, 1½", ⅛" between.
Commodity consumption: Newsprint 470 short tons; widths 27½", 13¾"; black ink 13,500 pounds; color ink 1,100 pounds; single pages printed 5,300; average pages per issue 20.4(d); single plates used 6,000.
Equipment: EDITORIAL: Front-end hardware — Dewar/Disc Net; Front-end software — Dewar/Disc Net; Printers — Okidata/Microline 190 Plus. CLASSIFIED: Front-end hardware — Dewar/Disc Net; Front-end software — Dewar/Disc Net; Printers — Okidata/Microline 190 Plus. DISPLAY: Adv layout systems — Dewar/Discovery; Front-end hardware — Dewar/Disc Net; Front-end software — Dewar/Disc Net. PRODUCTION: Typesetters — 2-COM/8400; Plate exposures — 1-Nu/FT40; Production cameras — 1-C/Pager, 1-VG/Eskofot 8200; Automatic film processors — LE/24, 1-LE/17A, 1-C/450; Shrink lenses — 1-Alan/Anamorphic(8%); Color separation equipment (conventional) — Lf/AP Leaf Picture Desk; Digital color separation equipment — Lf/Leafscan 35.
PRESSROOM: Line 1 — 6-G/SC; Folders — 1-G. MAILROOM: Counter stackers — 1-BG/105. WIRE SERVICES: News — AP, NYT; Receiving dishes — AP, NYT. BUSINESS COMPUTERS: IBM/Sys 36; PCs & micros networked; PCs & main system networked.

LAKELAND
Polk County

'90 U.S. Census- 70,576; E&P '96 Est. 94,819
ABC-CZ (90): 153,701 (HH 60,416)

The Ledger (m-mon to sat; S)

The Ledger, 401 S. Missouri Ave. (33801); PO Box 408, Lakeland, FL 33802; tel (941) 687-7000; fax (941) 687-7916; web site http://lakeland.tsolv.com/. New York Times Co. group.
Circulation: 80,226(m); 80,226(m-sat); 98,388(S); ABC circulation average for 12 months ended Sept. 30, 1995.
Price: 25¢(d); 25¢(sat); 75¢(S); $2.50/wk (carrier); $130.00/yr.
Advertising: Open inch rate $63.47(m); $63.47(m-sat); $66.66(S). **Representative:** Publishers' Representatives of Florida.
News Services: AP, NYT, KRT, LAT-WP. **Politics:** Independent. **Established:** 1924.
Special Editions: Black History (Feb); A Guide to Polk County, Health Care (Mar); Mayfaire-By-The-Lake, Outdoor Adventure (May); People Who Make A Difference (July); Back-to-School, Football (Aug); Fall Health Care (Sept); Parade of Homes (Oct); Yuletide Reader's Choice (Nov); Santa's Helper, Year In Review (Dec); Today's Senior (monthly).
Special Weekly Sections: Food (thur); Entertainment, Home and Garden (fri); Travel, Seniors (S).
Magazines: Time Out (Entertainment), Real Estate Magazine (sat); TV Book, Parade (S).
Broadcast Affiliates: New York Times Company Broadcast Group.

CORPORATE OFFICERS

President/Chief Operating Officer James C Weeks
Exec Vice Pres-Operations Reginald Davenport
Secretary Solomon B Watson IV
Treasurer Denise Fletcher

GENERAL MANAGEMENT

Publisher/President Don R Whitworth
Controller Tharon L Honeycutt
Personnel Director Cindy C Moates

ADVERTISING

Director Steve Schmidt
Manager-Retail Rob Lee
Manager-Classified Nelson Kirkland

TELECOMMUNICATIONS

Director-Info Systems Michael W Maguire
Audiotex Manager Jeff Wright

CIRCULATION

Director Samuel Diaz

NEWS EXECUTIVES

Exec Editor Louis M Perez
Managing Editor Hunter George
Editorial Page Editor Dave Schultz

EDITORS AND MANAGERS

Action Line Editor Barry Friedman
Amusements/Books Editor Barry Friedman
Art Director Mark Williams
Automotive Editor Lynne Cooke
Business/Real Estate Editor Lynne Cooke
City Editor Lenore Beecken
County Editor Jeff Kline
Deputy City Editor Mary Loftus
Assoc Editorial Page Editor Lonnie Brown
Asst Editorial Page Editor Mark Green
Education Editor Janet Marshall
Farm/Agriculture Editor Lynne Cooke
Fashion Editor Patricia Merritt
Features Editor Barry Friedman
Films/Theater Editor Arthur McCune
Health/Medical Editor Robin Adams
Home/Garden Editor Barry Friedman
Librarian Sandy Kline
Lifestyle/Women's Editor Barry Friedman
Music Editor Marcia Judson
National Editor Bill Rufty
News Editor Tom Arthur
Outdoors Editor Delwin Milligan
Photo Editor Paul Johnson
Political/Government Editor Bill Rufty
Radio/Television Editor Maryemma Bachelder
Religion Editor Maryemma Bachelder
Science/Technology Editor Barry Friedman
Sports Editor John Valerino
Teen-Age/Youth Editor Diane Allen
Travel Editor Barry Friedman

MANAGEMENT INFORMATION SERVICES

Director-Info Technology Michael W Maguire

PRODUCTION

Director Ron Thigpen
Manager-Press Philip Finnigan
Manager-Mailroom Claude Owens

Market Information: Zoned editions; TMC; ADS; Operate audiotex.
Mechanical available: Offset; Black and 3 ROP colors; insert accepted — preprinted, spadea comic wraps; page cut-offs — 22¾".
Mechanical specifications: Type page 13" x 21½"; E - 6 cols, 2¹⁄₁₆", ⅛" between; A - 6 cols, 2¹⁄₁₆", ⅛" between; C - 9 cols, 1⅜".
Commodity consumption: Newsprint 13,500 short tons; widths 54¾", 41⅛", 27½"; black ink 240,940 pounds; color ink 59,512 pounds; single pages printed 27,452; average pages per issue 64(d), 100(S); single plates used 107,523.
Equipment: EDITORIAL: Front-end hardware — AT; Front-end software — AT; Printers — AU/Laserprinter, Okidata; Other equipment — Ap/Mac II, Ap/Mac IIcx, Lf/AP Leaf Picture Desk, AP Leafax, AP Laserphoto. CLASSIFIED: Front-end hardware — AT; Front-end software — AT. AUDIOTEX: Hardware — Brite. DISPLAY: Adv layout systems — SCS/Layout 8000, SCS/LYNX; Front-end hardware — AT/LAS; Front-end software — AT/Classpage FPO. PRODUCTION: Pagination software — AT/Classpage FPO, AT, Press 2go, QuarkXPress; Typesetters — 2-AU/APS 108C, Au/6-82-ACS; Plate exposures — 2-Nu/Flip Top; Plate processors — 1-Nat, 1-WL; Electronic picture desk — Lf/AP Leaf Picture Desk; Scanners — 1-Kk/RFS 2035, 2-PixelCraft/7650X, 1-Howtek/D4000; Production cameras — 1-C/Spartan, 1-C/Marathon; Automatic film processors — 2-LE/26 Excel, 1-LE/2600, 2-C/26; Film transporters — 2-C; Digital color separation equipment — Kk/RFS 2035, 2-Microtek/600, CD/5400.
PRESSROOM: Line 1 — 7-G/Metro(2 Colordecks); Press drives — Fin; Folders — 2-G/3:1; Reels and stands — 7-G; Press control system — Fin. MAILROOM: Counter stackers — 1-Id/550, 4-QWI/J200x; Inserters and stuffers — 1-HI/RS25, 2-HI/NP 1372, 1-HI/NP 1372; Bundle tyer — 4-MLN, Power Strap/PSN-5; Addressing machine — 1-Ch, 1-St. LIBRARY: Electronic — MED/NewsView, MED/PhotoView. WIRE SERVICES: News — AP, NYT, KRT; Photos — AP, RN; Stock tables — AP; Syndicates — AP, NYT, KRT; Receiving dishes — AP. BUSINESS COMPUTERS: IBM/Sys 38 Model 700; Applications: Accts payable, Accts receivable, Gen ledger, Circ, Payroll; PCs & micros networked; PCs & main system networked.

LEESBURG
Lake County

'90 U.S. Census- 14,903; E&P '96 Est. 16,326
ABC-CZ (90): 14,903 (HH 6,348)

The Daily Commercial
(m-mon to sat; S)

The Daily Commercial, 212 E. Main St. (34748); PO Box 490007, Leesburg, FL 34749-0007; tel (904) 365-8200; fax (904) 365-1951. Better Built Media group.

Circulation: 31,290(m); 31,290(m-sat); 34,779(S); ABC circulation average for 12 months ended Sept. 30, 1995.
Price: 25¢(d); 25¢(sat); $1.00(S); $4.95/mo.
Advertising: Open inch rate $20.30(m); $20.30(m-sat); $20.71(S). **Representatives:** Sawyer-Ferguson-Walker Co.; Publishers' Representatives of Florida.
News Services: AP, NYT. **Politics:** Independent. **Established:** 1876.
Special Editions: Super Bowl Preview, The Year In Review (Jan); 1996 Homemakers Show, Focus/Progress '96 (Feb); Fun & Art Festival, For Your Health (Mar); Home Improvement, American Home Week (Apr); Car Care (May); Today's Woman, Summer Cookbook (June); Back-to-School (July); Football Preview (Aug); Home Furnishing, Business Card Directory (Sept); Family Health Month, Chamber of Commerce (Oct); Visitor's Guide, Holiday Recipes (Nov); Holiday Gift Guide, Last Minute Ideas (Dec); Klipper Coupon Book (last wed/mo); Outdoors (3rd thur/mo); Better Living for Seniors (last thur/mo).
Special Weekly Section: Best Food Day (thur).
Magazines: Food (thur); Church (sat); Parade, TV Week (offset), Food (S); Better Living (retirement publication), Real Estate Showcase (monthly).

GENERAL MANAGEMENT
Publisher Jim Perry
Controller Alan Payne

ADVERTISING
Director Carman Cullen

TELECOMMUNICATIONS
Audiotex Manager Jim Perry

CIRCULATION
Director Daisy Burkes

NEWS EXECUTIVE
Editor Jim Perry

EDITORS AND MANAGERS
City Editor Randy Fears
News Editor David Kaminski
News Features Editor David Kaminski
Sports Editor Michael Harris

MANAGEMENT INFORMATION SERVICES
Data Processing Manager Jim Perry

PRODUCTION
Director Jim Perry
Supervisor-Composing Carmen Cullen
Manager-Pressroom Wayne Wicker

Market Information: Operate audiotex.
Mechanical available: Offset; Black and 3 ROP colors; insert accepted — preprinted; page cut-offs — 22¾".
Mechanical specifications: Type page 13" x 21½"; E - 6 cols, $2\frac{1}{16}$", $\frac{3}{16}$" between; A - 6 cols, $2\frac{1}{16}$", $\frac{3}{16}$" between; C - 6 cols, 1¼", ⅛" between.
Commodity consumption: Newsprint 3,780 short tons; width 27½"; black ink 124,000 pounds; color ink 18,000 pounds; single pages printed 20,000; average pages per issue 32(d), 60(S); single plates used 72,000.
Equipment: EDITORIAL: Front-end hardware — AT/7000; Front-end software — AT 4.410; Printers — Teletype/MOD 40. CLASSIFIED: Front-end hardware — AT/7000; Front-end software — AT/7000. AUDIOTEX: Hardware — Brite Voice Systems. PRODUCTION: Typesetters — 2-COM/9600 Laser; Plate exposures — 2-Nu; Plate processors — 1-Nat/A-250; Scanners — ECR/Autokon 1000; Production cameras — 1-C, 1-LE; Automatic film processors — 1-LE/Rapid access, 1-C/80, 1-C/8ORA, 1-Konica/K-550; Film transporters — 1-C; Digital color separation equipment — CD/610 Electronic Dot, 1-Ap/Mac Quadra, V/6990. PRESSROOM: Line 1 — 10-G/Urbanite; Folders — 1-G; Pasters — 6-Webeq. MAILROOM: Counter stackers — 4-QWI, 2-Id; Inserters and stuffers — 1-HI/848; Bundle tyer — 2-MLN, 1-MLN/Spirit; Addressing machine — 1-Ch. WIRE SERVICES: News — AP; Stock tables — AP; Syndicates — AP, NYT, LAT-WP; Receiving dishes — size-8ft, AP. BUSINESS COMPUTERS: IBM/Sys 36; Applications: Circ, Accts receivable, Accts payable, Payroll.

MARIANNA
Jackson County
'90 U.S. Census- 6,852 E&P '96 Est. 5,852

Jackson County Floridan (e-tues to fri; S)
Jackson County Floridan, 4403 Constitution Ln. (32446); PO Box 520, Marianna, FL 32447; tel (904) 526-3614; fax (904) 482-4478. Thomson Newspapers group.
Circulation: 5,915(e); 5,915(S); Sworn Oct. 1, 1995.
Price: 35¢(d); 75¢(S); $7.31/mo; $91.20/yr.
Advertising: Open inch rate $9.62(e); $9.62(S). **Representatives:** Thomson Newspapers; Papert Companies.
News Service: AP. **Politics:** Independent. **Established:** 1922.
Advertising not accepted: Adoption ads.
Special Editions: Health File, Visitor's Guide (supplement) (Jan); Health File, Visitor's Guide (supplement) (Apr); Progress (May); Graduation (June); Health File (July); Football (Aug); Visitor's Guide (supplement) (Sept); Health File (Oct); Holiday Gift Guide (Dec).
Special Weekly Sections: Best Food Day, Business (wed); Entertainment (thur); Religion, TV Log (fri); Business (S).
Magazines: TV Book, Color Comics (S).

GENERAL MANAGEMENT
Publisher/General Manager Jane Benton

ADVERTISING
Director Valeria Roberts

EDITORS AND MANAGERS
Entertainment/Amusements Editor Wendy Gaska
Lifestyle Editor Wendy Gaska
Photo Editor Ed Masterson
Sports Editor Mike Moore

PRODUCTION
Superintendent John Adams

Market Information: TMC.
Mechanical available: Offset; Black and 3 ROP colors; insert accepted — preprinted; page cut-offs — 22¾".
Mechanical specifications: Type page 13" x 21½"; E - 6 cols, $2\frac{1}{16}$", ⅛" between; A - 6 cols, $2\frac{1}{16}$", ⅛" between; C - 8 cols, 1½", ⅛" between.
Commodity consumption: Newsprint 120 short tons; width 27½"; black ink 4,200 pounds; single pages printed 3,288; average pages per issue 12(d), 16(S); single plates used 1,886.
Equipment: EDITORIAL: Front-end hardware — Mk/1100 Plus Sys. CLASSIFIED: Front-end hardware — Mk/1100 Plus Sys; Other equipment — Mk/Plus VDT. PRODUCTION: Typesetters — V/VT600W Imagesetter, 1-Mk/NewsWriter, V/5100; Plate exposures — 1-Nu; Scanners — SCREEN/C-680C. PRESSROOM: Line 1 — 12-G/Urbanite. WIRE SERVICES: News — AP; Receiving dishes — size-10ft, AP. BUSINESS COMPUTERS: 2-Leading Edge, 1-Compaq, 1-Vectra/Business Computer; Applications: Lotus 1-2-3, Microsoft/Works, Wyse, WordPerfect.

MELBOURNE
Brevard County
'90 U.S. Census- 59,646; E&P '96 Est. 71,728
ABC-CZ (90): 398,978 (HH 161,365)

Florida Today (m-mon to sat; S)
Florida Today, One Gannett Plaza; PO Box 419000, Melbourne, FL 32941-9000; tel (407) 242-3500; fax (407) 242-6618; web site http://www.flatoday.com/space/. Gannett Co. Inc. group.
Circulation: 85,200(m); 85,200(m-sat); 112,783(S); ABC circulation average for 12 months ended Sept. 30, 1995.
Price: 50¢(d); 50¢(sat); $1.50(S); $3.25/wk.
Advertising: Open inch rate $64.45(m); $64.45(m-sat); $87.80(S). **Representative:** Gannett National Newspaper Sales.
News Services: AP, UPI, GNS. **Politics:** Independent. **Established:** 1966.
Special Editions: A Year In Review, Space Coast Visitor's Guide, Home Builders, Best of Brevard (Jan); Fact Book, Brevard Boat Show, Marlins Spring Training Guide (Feb); House & Garden Pool (Mar); Spring Parade of Homes, Space Coast Visitor's Guide, Share The Faith, Design-an-Ad, Indian River Festival, Space Congress (Apr); Career Day, Family Activities (May); Palm Bay Day (June); Space Coast Visitor's Guide, Home Builders (July); Back-to-School '96, Football '96 (Aug); Gracious Living (Sept); Fall Parade of Homes, Space Coast Visitor's Guide (Oct); New Car Showcase, Festival of Trees, Space Coast Art Festival, Southern Living Cooking School, Holiday Gift Guide (Nov); Share the Faith, Last Minute Gift Guide (Dec).
Special Weekly Section: Lifelines (tues).
Magazines: Money Monday (mon); Food Guide (thur); TGIF Weekend Magazine, Auto Guide (fri); Home Life (sat); USA Weekend, TV Week, Comics Section, Travel Section, Real Estate (S).

CORPORATE OFFICER
CEO Michael J Coleman

GENERAL MANAGEMENT
Publisher Michael J Coleman
Group Controller Jim Williamson
Asst Controller Deborah Fuller
Director-Human Resources Jay Clark
Director-Management Info Services Dorothy Martini
Manager-Purchasing Spencer Osborne
Manager-Credit Gary Keith

ADVERTISING
Director Michael D Jung
Manager-National Gene Waters
Manager-Classified Kerry Johnson
Manager-Retail Julian Price

MARKETING AND PROMOTION
Director-Market Development Kelly Harville
Manager-Marketing Communications Ann Crane

TELECOMMUNICATIONS
Audiotex Manager Kerry Johnson

CIRCULATION
Director Stan Yoshida
Manager August Fields
Manager-Customer Service Kathy Sanchez
Manager-Budget/Systems David Popp

NEWS EXECUTIVES
Exec Editor Bennie Ivory
Managing Editor Melinda Meers

EDITORS AND MANAGERS
Action Line/Help Editor Jaye Wright
Aerospace/Aviation Editor Todd Halvorson
Amusements Editor Anne Pasko
Columnist Milt Salamon
Editorial Page Editor Pam Platt
Editorial Writer Audie Murphy
Editorial Writer Ralph Bates
Fashion/Features Editor Hanna Krause
Features Editor Robbyn Footlick
Food Editor Hanna Krause
Graphic Editor/Art Director Octavio Diaz
Metro Editor Bob Stover
News Features Editor Robbyn Footlick
Outdoors Editor Bill Sargent
Photo Department Manager Robert McDonald
Radio/Television Editor Holly Martin
Religion Editor Rita Elkins
Science/Technology Editor Todd Halvorson
Sports Editor Tom Squires
Travel/Women's Editor Hanna Krause

MANAGEMENT INFORMATION SERVICES
Director-Management Info Services Dorothy Martini

PRODUCTION
Director Dave Preisser
Asst Director James Burns
Manager-Pressroom Bob Campbell
Manager-Systems George Malone
Manager-Pre Press Sylvia Smith
Manager-Distribution Center Larry Carraway
Manager-Composing Jim Craig
Manager-Building Keith Schnabel

Market Information: Zoned editions; Split Run; TMC; Operate audiotex; Electronic edition.
Mechanical available: Offset; Black and 3 ROP colors; insert accepted — preprinted, printed in-house; page cut-offs — 22".
Mechanical specifications: Type page 13" x 21"; E - 6 cols, $2\frac{1}{16}$", ⅛" between; A - 6 cols, $2\frac{1}{16}$", ⅛" between; C - 10 cols, 1½", $\frac{1}{16}$" between.
Commodity consumption: Newsprint 14,500 short tons; 12,900 metric tons; width 54½"; black ink 306,957 pounds; color ink 183,642 pounds; single pages printed 25,950; average pages per issue 64(d), 118(S); single plates used 160,000.
Equipment: EDITORIAL: Front-end hardware — AT/Series 4; Front-end software — AT 4.65; Printers — Florida Data; Other equipment — HAS/HS58 NewsPro. CLASSIFIED: Front-end hardware — AT/Series 4; Front-end software — AT 4.65; Printers — Florida Data; Other equipment — AT/Claspaq Classified Pagination. DISPLAY: Adv layout systems — HAS, CD; Front-end hardware — HAS/HS58 AdPro, CD/Ad Wizard, Ap/Mac; Front-end software — Aldus/Free-Hand, Multi-Ad/Creator. PRODUCTION: Pagination software — HAS/NewsPro; Typesetters — MON/Lasercom Mark 2i, MON/1000; Plate exposures — 3-Nu; Plate processors — 3-Nat/A340; Scanners — 1-ECR/Autokon 1000, 1-ECR/News Recorder; Production cameras — 2-C/Spartan III; Automatic film processors — 3-LE/2600; Reproportion units — C/Computer; Film transporters — C; Color separation equipment (conventional) — 2-CD/646IE. PRESSROOM: Line 1 — 16-G/Headliner; Folders — 4-G/3:2; Pasters — 16-G/45" RTP; Press control system — Fin/Drive. MAILROOM: Counter stackers — 6-HL/Monitor, 1-MM, HI/RS-25; Inserters and stuffers — 1-Mailstar, 2-Am/630; Bundle tyer — 4-MLN/MLN 2A, 1-MLN/MLZA, 2-Power Strap; Wrapping singles — 6-HL/Bottom Wrap; Addressing machine — 2-Ch, 1-Barstrom. LIBRARY: Electronic — Vu/Text SAVE, Digital Collections; Combination — Lektriever. WIRE SERVICES: News — AP Datastream, AP Datafeatures, AP SportStats; Stock tables — AP Grand Central Stocks; Receiving dishes — AP. BUSINESS COMPUTERS: 1-IBM/AS400 model F45; Applications: Accts payable, Gen ledger, Payroll, Adv, Circ, Newsprint inventory; PCs & micros networked; PCs & main system networked.

MIAMI
Dade County
'90 U.S. Census- 358,548; E&P '96 Est. 369,293
ABC-CZ (90): 1,937,094 (HH 692,355)

Diario Las Americas (Spanish) (m-tues to sat; S)
Diario Las Americas, 2900 N.W. 39th St. (33142); PO Box 593177, Miami, FL 33159; tel (305) 633-3341; fax (305) 635-7668.
Circulation: 68,628(m); 68,628(m-sat); 72,191(S); Sworn Sept. 30, 1994.
Price: 35¢(d); 35¢(sat); 60¢(S); $73.49/yr.
Advertising: Open inch rate $29.00(m); $29.00(m-sat); $29.00(S). **Representative:** Cresmer, Woodward, O'Mara & Ormsbee.
News Services: AFP, EFE, NYT, NYT Spanish. **Politics:** Independent. **Established:** 1953.
Not Published: Day after New Year; Good Friday; Memorial Day; Independence Day; Labor Day; Thanksgiving; Christmas.
Special Editions: Weddings, Carnival Miami (Mar); Cuban Independence Day (May); Nicaraguan Independence Day, Latin Chamber of Commerce (Sept); Hispanic Heritage Festival, "Grito de Vara" (Oct); South Florida Auto Show, Christmas Shopping Guide (Dec).
Special Weekly Sections: Sabado Residencial (Real Estate) (sat); Automobiles (Automotive) (S).

GENERAL MANAGEMENT
Publisher Horacio Aguirre
Asst Publisher Alejandro J Aguirre
Business Manager Victor M Vega
Controller Victor M Vega
Manager-Credit Jorge Consuegra

ADVERTISING
Director Herb Espino
Manager-General Bertha Enriquez
Manager-Classified Jose A Yuste

CIRCULATION
Manager Enrique Sori

NEWS EXECUTIVE
Editor Horacio Aguirre

EDITORS AND MANAGERS
Food Editor Virginia Godoy
Home Editor Luis Gonzalez
News Editor Luis Mario
Society Editor Chichi Aloy
Sports Editor Marino Martinez

MANAGEMENT INFORMATION SERVICES
Data Processing Manager Ariel Martinez

Mechanical available: Offset; Black and 3 ROP colors; insert accepted — preprinted, free-fall, cards, etc; page cut-offs — 21".
Mechanical specifications: Type page 13" x 21"; E - 6 cols, 2.04", ⅛" between; A - 6 cols, $2\frac{1}{16}$", ⅛" between; C - 10 cols, $\frac{13}{16}$", ⅛" between.
Commodity consumption: Newsprint 2,500 short tons; widths 27½", 13¾"; black ink 40,600 pounds; color ink 1,000 pounds; average pages per issue 32(d), 56(S); single plates used 11,500.
Equipment: EDITORIAL: Front-end hardware — Compaq/Pro Liner Servers, Seiko, 30-Compaq; Front-end software — AT/APM4 Pagination, Microsoft/Windows, Microsoft/Word, Novell/Network 4.0, Archetype/Designer, Adobe/Photoshop; Printers — Seiko, 2-QMS/8600; Other equipment — COM. CLASSIFIED: Front-end hardware — 1-HI/CTY; Front-end software — Novell/Network 4.0; DISPLAY: Adv layout sys-

I-82 Florida

tems — 30-Compaq, Compaq/Server; Front-end hardware — Compaq/ ProLiner; Front-end software — Novell/Network 4.0, Archetype/Designer; Printers — Seiko, QMS/860 Printers; Other equipment — Sharp/JX-600 Scanner. PRODUCTION: Pagination software — AT/APM4; Typesetters — 2-COM/Universal, 2-COM/8600, 1-COM/19IN-Dawn; Plate exposures — 2-Nu/Flip Top FT40LNS; Plate processors — 2-W/28; Scanners — Sharp/JX-600; Production cameras — 1-Ik/530, 1-Ik/560, 1-Spartan/1244; Automatic film processors — 1-LE/LD-24; Shrink lenses — 1-SQU/7-335.
PRESSROOM: Line 1 — 8-G/U-686; Folders — 2-G/U-686; Pasters — 8-Cary/Compact Splicer. MAILROOM: Counter stackers — 1-Id; Bundle tyer — 1-Id, 1-Bu/18, 1-MLN/ML2EE; Addressing machine — 1-KR. WIRE SERVICES: News — UPI, AFP, EFE; Syndicates — CNS. BUSINESS COMPUTERS: 6-DEC/CPU 1123; Applications: Circ.

The Miami Herald

(m-mon to sat; S)

The Miami Herald, One Herald Plz., Miami, FL 33132-1693; tel (305) 350-2111; web site http://herald.kri.com/. Knight-Ridder Inc. group.

Circulation: 383,212(m); 383,212(m-sat); 504,555(S); ABC circulation average for 12 months ended Sept. 30, 1995.

Price: 35¢(d); 35¢(sat); $1.00(S); $2.75/wk.

Advertising: Open inch rate $272.50(m); $272.50(m-sat); $321.00(S). **Representative:** Newspapers First.

News Services: AP, DJ, KRT, LAT-WP, SOU, TV Data, UPI. **Established:** 1910.

Special Weekly Sections: Business Monday (mon); Food, Neighbors (12 Zones) (thur); Weekend (2 Zones) (fri); Neighbors (12 Zones), Travel, Home & Design, Arts, View Point (S).

Magazines: Tropic; Parade Magazines (S).

CORPORATE OFFICERS

Chairman of the Board	David Lawrence Jr
President	Joe Natoli
Senior Vice Pres/Exec Editor	Doug Clifton
Vice Pres-Advertising	Larry Wynn
Vice Pres/Chief Financial Officer	Jesus Diaz
Vice Pres-Circulation	Arden Dickey
Vice Pres-Community Relations/Marketing Services	Sam Verdeja
Vice Pres-Operations	Joseph J Bowman
Vice Pres-Human Resources	Jacqui Love Marshall
Vice Pres-Systems & Technology	Dave Bauer
General Counsel	Samuel A Terilli Jr

GENERAL MANAGEMENT

Publisher	David Lawrence Jr
Assoc Publisher-Broward	Chris Mobley
Manager-Credit	Julio Garriga
Manager-Education Service	Carolyn Lavan
Director-Advanced Systems	John Fiedler
Director-Marketing Services	Josie Bacallao
General Manager-Herald Direct/Target Marketing	Bob Elkin

ADVERTISING

Vice Pres	Larry Wynn
Director-Display	Debbie Holzkamp
Director-International	Mark Seibel
Asst Director-Display	Cesar Pizzaro
Manager-Classified	Sabrina Goodson
General Manager-Herald Express	Bob Elkin

MARKETING AND PROMOTION

Vice Pres-Marketing/Promotion	Sam Verdeja
Director-Marketing/Promotion	Josie Bacallao

CIRCULATION

Vice Pres	Arden Dickey

NEWS EXECUTIVES

Vice Pres/Exec Editor	Doug Clifton
Director-Editorial Art	Steve Rice
Editor	Jim Hampton
Editor-Broward	Paul Anger
Editor-El Nuevo	Barbara Gutierrez
Assoc Editor-Editorial Page	Tony Proscio
Assoc Editor-Editorial Page	Martha Musgrove
Assoc Editor-Reporting	Gene Miller
Assoc Editor-Investigations	Jim Savage
Managing Editor	Saundra Keyes
Managing Editor-El Nuevo	Tony Espetia
Asst Managing Editor-Administration	Mike Haggerty
Asst Managing Editor-News	Sue Reisinger
Asst Managing Editor-Staff Development	Christine Morris
Deputy Managing Editor-Broward	Sue Reisinger
Op-Ed Editor-El Nuevo	Luis Aguilar-Leon

EDITORS AND MANAGERS

Action Line Editor	Anne Baumgartner
Books Editor	Margaria Fichtner
Exec Business Editor	Dave Satterfield
Business Monday News Editor	Jim Watters
Cartoonist	Jim Morin
City Editor	Bill Grueskin
City Editor-El Nuevo	Joel Gutierrez
Columnist	Bob Steinback
Columnist	Liz Balmaseda
Columnist	Carl Hiaasen
Dance Critic	Laurie Horn
Drama Critic	Christine Dolen
Assoc Editorial Page Editor-El Nuevo	Araceli Perdomo
Features Editor	Elissa Vanaver
Info Service Editor	Bill Whiting
Library Manager	Gay Nemeti
Music Writer-Classical	Jim Roos
Music Writer-Popular	Leonard Pitts
News Editor-El Nuevo	Manolo Silverio
Palm Beach Bureau Editor	Lori Rocza
Photo Editor-El Nuevo	Jose Iglesias
Research Manager	Liz Donovan
Exec Sports Editor	Dave Wilson
Sports Editor	Edwin Pope
Sports News Editor-El Nuevo	Jose Maldonado
State/Environmental Editor	John Pancake
Sunday Magazine (Tropic) Editor	Tom Shroder
Television Critic	Robin Dougherty
Viernes Editor-El Nuevo	Olga Conner

MANAGEMENT INFORMATION SERVICES

Data Processing Manager	Dave Bauer

PRODUCTION

Vice Pres	Joseph J Bowman
Director-Engineering	Armando Gonzalez
Manager-Packaging	Craig Woishwill
Manager-Quality Assurance/Operations	John Hoover
Manager-Printing	Fran Scarlett
Manager-Electrical	Chuck Dougherty
Manager-Mechanical	Gary Goad
Manager-Imaging/Composing	Peter Birdsall
Asst Manager-Ad Production	Gail Switalski
Asst Manager-Imaging	Shawn Stabell
Asst Manager-Composing	Dorothy Baird

Market Information: Zoned editions; Split Run; TMC; ADS; Operate audiotex.

Mechanical available: Letterpress, offset, flexography; Black and 3 ROP colors; insert accepted — preprinted, single sheets; page cutoffs — 22½".

Mechanical specifications: Type page 13" x 22½"; E - 6 cols, 2 1/16", 3/16" between; A - 6 cols, 2 1/16", 3/16" between; C - 10 cols, 1¼", 3/16" between.

Commodity consumption: Newsprint 121,570 short tons; 110,287 metric tons; widths 54¼", 47⅞", 40⅝", 27⅛", 20⅞", 17"; black ink 3,833,758 pounds; color ink 959,168 pounds; single pages printed 93,810; average pages per issue 85(d), 106(sat), 218(S); single plates used 658,393.

Equipment: EDITORIAL: Front-end hardware — SII; Front-end software — SII/Coyote, SII/MTX. CLASSIFIED: Front-end hardware — PCs. AUDIOTEX: Hardware — PCs, Brite, Intellivoice; Software — Brite, Intellivoice. DISPLAY: Adv layout systems — SCS/Layout 8000; Front-end hardware — PCs, Novell, Unix; Front-end software — SCS/Layout 8000. PRODUCTION: Pagination software — QPS 3.3; Typesetters — 3-AU/APS-5, 2-ECR/3850, 2-Linotype-Hell/530; Platemaking systems — 4-Na/Np-120, 2-WL/38D, Na, WL; Plate exposures — 4-Titan, 2-Na/FX-IU FP II, 1-Va/Starlite, 1-WL/Lith-X-Pozer 3; Plate processors — 4-Na/NP 120, 2-Na/TP, 1-Na/NP40 (DT), 2-WL/38D; Electronic picture desk — Lf/AP Leaf Picture Desk; Scanners — 4-ECR/Autokon, 2-Howtek/D-400, 3-Howtek/Scanner, 1-Ap/Mac interface; Production cameras — 2-C/Pager, 1-C/Spartan, 1-C/Marathon; Automatic film processors — 4-LE/Online, 2-DP, 2-LE; Film transporters — 2-LE/Online Imaging, 2-LE/Online Sys Proc; Color separation equipment (conventional) — 10-Ap/Mac, Adobe/Photoshop; Digital color separation equipment — 1-CD/646, 4-Howtek/Colorscan.
PRESSROOM: Line 1 — 6-MAN/Flexoman (3-half decks), 21-G/Mark II (incl. 12 color humps), 5-G/Newsliner; Line 2 — 6-MAN/Flexoman (3-half decks), 21-G/Mark II (inc. 12 color humps); Line 3 — 4-MAN/Flexoman (2-half decks), 16-G/Mark II (inc. 10 color humps); Line 4 — 18-G/Metroliner (10-half decks); Folders — 10-G/Imperial 3:2, 5-DBL/Del; Pasters — 92-G/Auto; Reels and stands — 74-G/Mark II, 18-G; Press control system — G/PCS (offset). MAILROOM: Counter stackers — 1-Id/330, 7-QWI/300, 7-QWI/200, 6-QWI/100; Inserters and stuffers — 1-S/848, 2-HI/1372P, 2-HI/1472P, 1-HI/1572; Bundle tyer — 9-MLN/MLN2, 13-MLN/MLN2A, 15-Dynaric/NP-2, 4-Dynaric/SSB779; Wrapping singles — 4-Id/60H, 5-QWI/5111, 4-QWI/5112 (¾"), 4-QWI/5111 (¾"), 1-QWI/Cobra (¾"). LIBRARY: Electronic — 13-QLS, 12-IBM/3278, 13-Qume, 12-IBM/3278 terminal. WIRE SERVICES: News — AP, KRT, LAT-WP, SOU, TV Data, UPI; Stock tables — AP, DJ (Digital); Syndicates — AP Datafeatures, Universal Press, NAS, King Features, NYT, Register & Tribune; Receiving dishes — size-11ft, AP, UPI. BUSINESS COMPUTERS: 1-IBM/4381-3, 1-IBM/3081-KX, HP/3000s; Applications: CIS, CJ, Admarc: Local ad receivables; PCs & micros networked; PCs & main system networked.

NAPLES

Collier County

'90 U.S. Census- 19,505; E&P '96 Est. 21,098
ABC-CZ (90): 71,468 (HH 32,127)

Naples Daily News

(m-mon to sat; S)

Naples Daily News, 1075 Central Ave.; PO Box 7009, Naples, FL 33941; tel (941) 262-3161; fax (941) 263-4817; web site http://www.scripps.com/naples.html. Scripps Howard group.

Circulation: 47,769(m); 47,769(m-sat); 61,400(S); ABC circulation average for 12 months ended Sept. 30, 1995.

Price: 35¢(d); 35¢(sat); $1.50(S); $3.30/wk; $14.20/mo; $171.60/yr.

Advertising: Open inch rate $36.07(m); $36.07(m-sat); $42.23(S); $184.60(m & S). **Representative:** Sawyer-Ferguson-Walker Co.

News Services: AP, SHNS, NYT. **Politics:** Independent. **Established:** 1923.

Special Editions: Ambience (fri), New Business, Real Estate Marketplace, Primetime (Jan); Ambience (fri), Newcomers, Naples Art Show, Primetime, Pelican Bay, Home Improvement (Feb); Ambience (fri), Visitor's Edition, Primetime, Estate Planning (S), Portfolio of Homes, Festival of Homes (Mar); Ambience (fri), Condo '96, Great Indoors, Primetime, Tropicool (Apr); Medical Guide, May Real Estate, Primetime, Hurricane (May); Pelican Bay, June Real Estate, Women in Business, Primetime, Pre-Fourth of July (June); Home Improvement, Primetime, July Summer Real Estate (July); Back-to-School, Football, Primetime, August Real Estate (Aug); Naples Nostalgia, September Real Estate, Primetime, Personal Finance (Sept); Philharmonic, Primetime, Portfolio of Homes, Oktoberfest (Oct); Fall Fashion, Primetime, Ambience (fri), Newcomers, Third Street, Thanksgiving (Nov); Ambience, Primetime, Gift-Dining Guide (S), Marco Art Show (Dec); 4/5 Islanders, Marco Real Estate, Real Estate Marketplace (fri) (monthly).

Special Weekly Sections: Business Monday (mon); Health (tues); Food (thur); Fashion, Showcase (fri); Home, Religion (sat); Business, Real Estate, Travel (S).

Magazines: Parade, TV News (in-house), Comics (S).

CORPORATE OFFICERS

President	Corbin A Wyant
Vice Pres	Colleen C Conant
Asst Secretary	Nina D Iverson

GENERAL MANAGEMENT

Publisher	Corbin A Wyant
Director-Finance	Paul M Stephan

ADVERTISING

Director	J Patrick Berling
Asst Director	Robert C Smith
Manager-National/Major	Robert Sandy
Manager-Retail	Rick Kendall
Manager-Co-op	Paula Monty
Manager-Classified	Dennis Sprague
Manager-Marketing & Research	Dan Jacoby

TELECOMMUNICATIONS

Audiotex Manager	Phil Harris

CIRCULATION

Director	Kenneth Tanner

NEWS EXECUTIVES

Editor	Colleen C Conant
Asst to Editor	John Lunsford
Managing Editor	Philip Lewis

EDITORS AND MANAGERS

Business Editor	Jim Lockhart
City Editor	Brent Batten
Editorial Page Editor	Jeffrey Lytle
Education Editor	Maria Cote
Features Editor	Maria Cote
Health/Medical Editor	Maria Cote
News Editor	Chuck Curry
Photo Editor	Eric Strachan
Sports Editor	Tom Rife
Travel Editor	Ken Moore

MANAGEMENT INFORMATION SERVICES

Online Manager	Dan Jacoby

PRODUCTION

Manager-Pre Press	LeRoy Seiler
Manager-Press	Richard Temple
Manager-Mailroom	Glenn Williams

Market Information: Zoned editions; Operate database; Operate audiotex.

Mechanical available: Offset; Black and 3 ROP colors; insert accepted — preprinted; page cutoffs — 23 9/16".

Mechanical specifications: Type page 13" x 22¼"; E - 6 cols, 2 1/16", ⅛" between; A - 6 cols, 2 1/16", ⅛" between; C - 10 cols, 1.19", ⅛" between.

Commodity consumption: Newsprint 8,539 metric tons; widths 27½", 41⅛", 55"; black ink 180,000 pounds; color ink 75,000 pounds; single pages printed 28,748; average pages per issue 63(d), 172(S); single plates used 78,520.

Equipment: EDITORIAL: Front-end hardware — Zenith/386, Zenith/286, Dell, Wyse/286 PC; Front-end software — HI/PEN; Printers — Epson, IBM, Konica. CLASSIFIED: Front-end hardware — Dell/486 PC; Front-end software — HI/CASH; Printers — Epson/DFX 5000, Konica/Laser. AUDIOTEX: Hardware — 1-Brite; Software — Brite Voice Systems; Supplier name — VNN. DISPLAY: Adv layout systems — SCS/Layout 8000; Front-end hardware — 2-PC, Dell/386; Front-end software — SCS; Printers — HP/LaserJet III, C.Itoh/C1400. PRODUCTION: Pagination software — QuarkXPress 3.31, HI/XP-21-2100, HI/XP-21 Newsmaker; Typesetters — 2-AU/APS6, 1-AG/Avantra 25; Plate exposures — 3-Nu; Plate processors — 2-Nat; Electronic picture desk — Lf/AP Leaf Picture Desk; Scanners — Scitex/System, Kk/2035; Production cameras — 2-C; Automatic film processors — 3-LE; Color separation equipment (conventional) — 2-Scitex/System 340, Smart/Scanner, Kk/2035.
PRESSROOM: Line 1 — 9-G/Metro (5½ decks); Press drives — 10-HP/75; Folders — 3-G/3:2 double; Reels and stands — G/reels; Press control system — Fin; Press registration system — G. MAILROOM: Counter stackers — 6-HL/Monitor; Inserters and stuffers — 1-S/1472, 1-S/1272 P; Bundle tyer — 3-MLN/M12E, 1-Power Strap/PSN-2, 2-Power Strap/PSN-6; Wrapping singles — 4-CH, 1-HL/Underwrap. WIRE SERVICES: News — AP, SHNS, NYT; Photos — AP, PressLink; Stock tables — AP; Receiving dishes — size-12½ft, AP. BUSINESS COMPUTERS: IBM/Sys 36 D2K, Sun/Sparc; Applications: PBS: Microsoft/Office: Adv, Circ; PCs & micros networked; PCs & main system networked.

NEW SMYRNA BEACH

Volusia County

'90 U.S. Census- 16,543; E&P '96 Est. 19,186

Observer (m-tues to sat)

Observer, 823 S. Dixie Fwy.; PO Box 10, New Smyrna Beach, FL 32170; tel (904) 427-1000; fax (904) 428-1265. Hollinger International Inc. group.

Circulation: 2,822(m); 2,822(m-sat); Sworn Sept. 29, 1995.

Price: 35¢(d); 35¢(sat); $67.00/yr.

Advertising: Open inch rate $9.50(m); $9.50(m-sat). **Representative:** Papert Companies.

News Service: AP. **Politics:** Independent. **Established:** 1913.

Not Published: New Year; Memorial Day; Independence Day; Labor Day; Thanksgiving; Christmas.

Special Editions: Business & Industry (Jan); Speedweeks, Dining, Spring Fashion (Feb); Art Festival, Spring Exteriors (Mar); Senior Lifestyles, Community Appreciations (Apr); Seaside Fiesta, Dining Guide (June); Progress Edition (July); Fall Fashion, Boat Racing (Aug); Mainstreet Appreciation (Sept); Senior Lifestyles (Oct); Interiors, Christmas Gift Guide (Nov); Holiday Events, Health (Dec).

Special Weekly Sections: North, Central, South Brevard Shopping; News (TMC) (thur).

Magazine: Real Estate (sat).

GENERAL MANAGEMENT

Publisher Larry T (Guy) Beasley
Business Manager Barbara Duck

ADVERTISING

Director Larry T (Guy) Beasley

NEWS EXECUTIVES

Editor James A Jones Jr
Assoc Editor Mark I Johnson

EDITORS AND MANAGERS

Community Editor Sandi Carroll
Sports Editor J M Bennet Jr

PRODUCTION

Manager Carlos Duck

Market Information: TMC.
Mechanical available: Offset; Black and 3 ROP colors; insert accepted — preprinted; page cutoffs — 21½".
Mechanical specifications: Type page 13" x 21½"; E - 6 cols, 2¹⁄₁₆", ⅛" between; A - 6 cols, 2¹⁄₁₆", ⅛" between; C - 8 cols, 1½", ⅛" between.
Commodity consumption: Newsprint 600 short tons; widths 27½", 34"; black ink 12,000 pounds; single pages printed 6,240; average pages per issue 20(d), 24(sat); single plates used 3,300.
Equipment: EDITORIAL: Front-end hardware — IBM, Compaq; Front-end software — TC; Printers — Ap/Mac; Other equipment — Mk. DISPLAY: Adv layout systems — Ap/Mac SE; Front-end hardware — Ap/Mac SE; Front-end software — Aldus/PageMaker; Printers — Ap/Mac LaserWriter II. PRODUCTION: Plate exposures — Nu; Plate processors — Nat/A-340; Scanners — DSA/Companica C690C; Production cameras — Acti; Automatic film processors — SCREEN; Digital color separation equipment — Panther/Plus.
PRESSROOM: Line 1 — 8-KP/Newsking, CH; Folders — 1-KJ/8; Pasters — H&M. MAILROOM: Counter stackers — BG; Bundle tyer — Bu; Addressing machine — Ch. WIRE SERVICES: News — AP; Syndicates — King Features, Universal Press; AP. BUSINESS COMPUTERS: Okidata.

OCALA

Marion County

'90 U.S. Census- 42,045; E&P '96 Est. 46,097
ABC-CZ (90): 42,045 (HH 17,393)

Ocala Star-Banner (m-mon to sat; S)

Ocala Star-Banner, 2121 S.W. 19th Ave. Rd. (34474); PO Box 490, Ocala, FL 34478; tel (904) 867-4010; fax (904) 867-4126. New York Times Co. group.
Circulation: 48,539(m); 48,539(m-sat); 51,212(S); ABC circulation average for 12 months ended Sept. 30, 1995.
Price: 50¢(d); 75¢(sat); $1.25(S); $11.70/mo; $140.40/yr.
Advertising: Open inch rate $35.15(m); $35.15(m-sat); $35.15(S). **Representatives:** Landon Associates Inc.; Publishers' Representatives of Florida.
News Services: AP, NYT, KRT. **Established:** 1866.
Special Editions: Fact Book, Wedding Planner (Jan); Dream 18 Golf Guide, Restaurant Guide (Feb); Lawn & Garden Guide, Parade of Homes, Easter Showcase, Coupon Book (Mar); Home Improvement (Apr); Hometown Business (May); Weather Guide, Father's Day, Coupon Book (June); Back-To-School/Child Care, Football Preview (Aug); Home Furnishings, Health & Heart Show, Showcase of Homes (Oct); Early Bird, Welcome, Gift Guide, Christmas Carol Book (Nov); Christmas in Ocala (Dec).
Special Weekly Sections: Off Campus (Teenage/Parent Feature) (mon); Health Day (tues); Neighbors, Accent on Women (wed); Best Food Day, Business, Stock Listings (thur); On the Go (local travel/entertainment), Wheels (fri); Business, Stock Listings, Religion (sat); Family (S); TV Listings, Sports, Entertainment (daily).
Magazines: Ocala Inc. (Local Business Magazine) (mon); TV Week Magazine, Discovery (environment), Big Sun Homes (sat); Lifestyle/Travel (S).

CORPORATE OFFICERS

President James C Weeks
Vice Pres Charles J Stout

GENERAL MANAGEMENT

Publisher Charles J Stout
Controller Thomas C Garris

ADVERTISING

Director Bob Gruber
Manager-Retail Stan Davis
Manager-Classified Butch Peiker

TELECOMMUNICATIONS

Director-Info Systems Tom Garris
Audiotex Manager (Advertising) Bill Foster
Audiotex Manager (News) Jay McKenzie

CIRCULATION

Director Keith King

NEWS EXECUTIVES

Exec Editor Bruce Gaultney
Managing Editor Jay McKenzie

EDITORS AND MANAGERS

Automotive Editor Jim French
Books Editor Rima Firrone
Business/Real Estate Editor Laura Knight
Asst City Editor Tom McNiff
Asst City Editor Laura Knight
Editorial Page Editor Patti Griffiths
Entertainment Editor David Schlenker
Farm/Agriculture Editor Eric Mitchell
Graphics Editor Steve Antley
News Editor Judy Green
Photo Editor Kyle Danaceau
Researcher Darrell Riley
Sports Editor Larry Savage

MANAGEMENT INFORMATION SERVICES

Online Manager Rich Danielson
Data Processing Manager Tom Garris

PRODUCTION

Director Tom Garris
Manager-Pressroom Rusty Jacobs
Manager-Pre Press Matt Foster

Market Information: Zoned editions; TMC; Operate database; Operate audiotex.
Mechanical available: Offset; Black and 3 ROP colors; insert accepted — preprinted.
Mechanical specifications: Type page 13" x 21.35"; E - 6 cols, 2¹⁄₁₆", ⅛" between; A - 6 cols, 2¹⁄₁₆", ⅛" between; C - 9 cols, 1⅜", ¹⁄₁₆" between.
Commodity consumption: Newsprint 6,474 short tons; widths 27", 40½", 13½", 54"; black ink 107,900 pounds; color ink 32,000 pounds; single pages printed 20,537; average pages per issue 56(d), 76(S); single plates used 56,300.
Equipment: EDITORIAL: Front-end hardware — 2-AT/Series 60, 15-Power PC Pagination editing station; Front-end software — DTI/Page Speed, DTI/SpeedPlanner, DTI/SpeedDriver; Printers — 1-QMS/860; Other equipment — 46-AT. CLASSIFIED: Front-end hardware — 2-AT/Series 60; Other equipment — 14-AT. AUDIOTEX: Hardware — Brite Voice Systems; Software — Brite Voice Systems. DISPLAY: Adv layout systems — 1-AT/Classified Pagination Release 3, DTI/SpeedPlanner; Front-end hardware — 1-IBM, 12-Ap/Mac workstation; Front-end software — DTI/SpeedPlanner, DTI/Ad Speed; Printers — 2-QMS/860, 1-Phaser/300i. PRODUCTION: Pagination software — DTI/SpeedPlanner, DTI/SpeedDriver; Typesetters — 2-AU/APS-6 5-8, 3-Panther/Pro 46; Plate exposures — 1-Nu/Flip Top FT40UPNS, 1-Nu/Flip Top FT40APRNS; Plate processors — 1-WL/D-40, 1-WL/D-48; Electronic picture desk — Lf/AP Leaf Picture Desk; Production cameras — 1-C/Spartan III 1270, 1-C/Newspager; Automatic film processors — 2-AU/APS36, 4-C/66F, 1-C/80RA, 2-P/Online; Color separation equipment (conventional) — 1-CD/645IE; Digital color separation equipment — 2-ECR/Autokon 1000, 6-Ap/Mac Photo workstation.
PRESSROOM: Line 1 — 5-G/Headliner; Press drives — Fin; Folders — 1-G. MAILROOM: Counter stackers — 3-QWI; Inserters and stuffers — 1-HI; Bundle tyer — 3-MLN; Other mailroom equipment — 1-MM/Stitcher-Trimmer. LIBRARY: Electronic — Data Times, DEC/Micro VAX-3100. WIRE SERVICES: News — AP, NYT, KRT, LAT-WP; Stock tables — TMS; Syndicates — KRT, LAT-WP, TMS; Receiving dishes — size-3m, AP, NYT. BUSINESS COMPUTERS: 1-IBM/AS 400 36; Applications: Circ, Adv billing, Accts receivable, Gen ledger, Payroll; PCs & micros networked; PCs & main system networked.

OKEECHOBEE

Okeechobee County

'90 U.S. Census- 4,943; E&P '96 Est. 6,371

The Daily Okeechobee News (m-mon to sat; S)

The Daily Okeechobee News, 107 S.W. 17th St.; PO Box 639, Okeechobee, FL 34974; tel (941) 763-3134; fax (941) 763-5901. Independent Newspapers Inc. (DE) group.
Circulation: 2,642(m); 2,642(m-sat); 2,642 (S); Sworn Sept. 28, 1994.
Price: 35¢(d); 35¢(sat); 50¢(S).
Advertising: Open inch rate $12.67(m); $12.67(m-sat); $12.67(S).
News Service: Zap News. **Established:** 1914 (weekly), 1992 (daily).

GENERAL MANAGEMENT

Publisher Richard Hitt

ADVERTISING

Director Judy Kasteen

CIRCULATION

Director Nick Yackamouih

NEWS EXECUTIVES

Editor Katrina Elsken
Assoc Editor Dick Casselberry
Assoc Editor Kerry Faunce

PRODUCTION

Director Ann Nicoll

ORANGE PARK

Clay County

'90 U.S. Census- 9,488; E&P '96 Est. 10,088

Clay Today (m-tues to sat)

Clay Today, 1564 Kingsley Ave., Orange Park, FL 32073; tel (904) 264-3200; fax (904) 269-6958. ADD Inc. group.
Circulation: 4,769(m); 4,769(m-sat); Sworn Nov. 22, 1994.
Price: Free.
Advertising: Open inch rate $14.00(m); $14.00(m-sat). **Representative:** Cresmer, Woodward, O'Mara & Ormsbee.
News Service: NEA. **Politics:** Independent. **Established:** 1974.
Not Published: New Year; Memorial Day; Independence Day; Labor Day; Thanksgiving; Christmas.
Special Editions: Progress; Resource; Football; Ham Jam; Entertainment/Travel; Home Improvement; Bridal; Auto Care; Medical/Health Care; Real Estate; Christmas Gift Guide; Fashion Guide; Food; Motoring; Women In Business.
Special Weekly Section: Automotive (fri).

GENERAL MANAGEMENT

Publisher Joyce Lydon

ADVERTISING

Manager Scott Nugent

CIRCULATION

Manager Sheri McGraw

NEWS EXECUTIVE

Managing Editor Sandy Mulvihill

PRODUCTION

Foreman-Composing Cathy Roy
Foreman-Press Tony Angelo

Market Information: TMC.
Mechanical available: Offset; Black and 3 ROP colors; insert accepted — preprinted, single sheet cards; page cut-offs — 22¾".
Mechanical specifications: Type page 13" x 21½"; E - 6 cols, 2¹⁄₁₆", ⅛" between; A - 6 cols, 2¹⁄₁₆", ⅛" between; C - 9 cols, 1⅜", ¹⁄₁₆" between.
Commodity consumption: Newsprint 150 short tons; width 27½"; black ink 330 pounds; single pages printed 3,240; average pages per issue 13(d); single plates used 4,335.
Equipment: EDITORIAL: Front-end hardware — 8-CText; Printers — 1-Ap/Mac LaserPrinter II. CLASSIFIED: Front-end hardware — 1-CText; Printers — 1-Panasonic, KX/P1695. DISPLAY: Adv layout systems — 1-CText; Front-end hardware — Adept; Printers — 1-Ap/Mac LaserPrinter II. PRODUCTION: Typesetters — 1-CText; Plate exposures — 1-Nu/ET40L; Production cameras — 1-Acti/204; Automatic film processors — SCREEN/LD-220-QT.
PRESSROOM: Line 1 — 4-KP/Newsking; Folders — 1-KP/Newsking. MAILROOM: Counter stackers — BG/Count-O-Veyor; Bundle tyer — 2-MLN; Addressing machine — 1-PB.

ORLANDO

Orange County

'90 U.S. Census- 164,693; E&P '96 Est. 182,989
ABC-CZ (90): 930,591 (HH 350,724)

The Orlando Sentinel (all day-mon to sat; S)

The Orlando Sentinel, 633 N. Orange Ave. (32801); PO Box 2833, Orlando, FL 32802; tel (407) 420-5000; fax (407) 420-5042. Tribune Co. group.
Circulation: 272,702(a); 272,702(a-sat); 391,130(S); ABC circulation average for 12 months ended Sept. 30, 1995.
Price: 50¢(d); 50¢(sat); $1.50(S); $3.85/wk; $15.40/mo; $184.80/yr (mS).
Advertising: Open inch rate $204.00(a); $204.00(a-sat); $270.00(S). **Representative:** Tribune Newspaper Network.
News Services: NYT, KRT, LAT-WP, AP, DJ, Cox News Service, RN, DJ. **Politics:** Independent. **Established:** 1876.
Special Editions: Florida Forecast (Jan); Spring Parade of Homes, Spring Fashion, Southern Living Cooking School, Arts in April (Mar); Home Fashion, Baseball Preview (Apr); Corporate Scorecard, Senior Resource, Health & Fitness, All Business EXPO Program, At Home, Seasons in the Sun (May); Hot Cars, Health & Fitness (July); Arts Preview (Aug); Fall Parade of Homes, Leadership Orlando, Football, Southern Women's Show, Fall Fashion (Sept); Health & Fitness, New Car Showcase, Senior Resource, Orlando Magic NBA Preview, Southern Women's Show (Oct); Home Design, Gift Guide I, Holiday Gift Guide, Auto Show I, Auto Show II (Nov); Gift Guide II (Dec).
Special Weekly Sections: Central Florida Business (mon); Business (tues, wed); Food, Transportation (thur); Homes (sat); Arts & Entertainment, Homes, Insight, Travel (S).
Magazines: Calendar (fri); TV Time, Florida Magazine (offset), Comics (S).

CORPORATE OFFICERS

President/Publisher John P Puerner
Vice Pres/Director-Business Development F Ashley Allen
Vice Pres/Director-Marketing John H Blexrud
Vice Pres/Director-Finance Richard E Darden
Vice Pres/Director-Circulation Robert W Eickhoff
Vice Pres/Editor L John Haile
Vice Pres/Director-Operations Jeffrey M Johnson
Vice Pres/Director-Advertising William E Steiger
Vice Pres/Director-Human Resources Geraldine White
Asst Controller Harry Amsden

ADVERTISING

Director William E Steiger
Manager-Advertising Administration Joseph P Del Rocco
Manager-Classified Dan Hoag
Manager-General/SDS/Direct Mail/Porch Plus Jack Curtin
Manager-Zoned Publications Ronnie Matthews
Manager-Retail Barry Haselden

MARKETING AND PROMOTION

Director-Marketing/Promotion John H Blexrud
Manager-Community Relations Lisa Warren
Manager-Promotion Terrie Mitchell
Manager-Marketing Service Ray Eckhart
Coordinator-Public Relations Bette Jore
Coordinator-Audiotex Service Janice Graham

TELECOMMUNICATIONS

Audiotex Coordinator-Service (Marketing) Janice Graham

CIRCULATION

Vice Pres/Director Robert W Eickhoff
Manager-Planning/Systems Dianne Crossman
Manager-Operations Jerry Price
Manager-Primary Market Area Deborah Irwin
Manager-Strategic Projects Bill Dafnis
Manager-Consumer Sales/Service Chip Danneker

NEWS EXECUTIVES

Editor L John Haile
Editor-Editorial Technology John Huff
Managing Editor Jane Healy
Assoc Managing Editor-Planning/Design Bill Dunn
Deputy Managing Editor-Features Dana Eagles
Deputy Managing Editor-Local/State Jim Toner
Deputy Managing Editor-Sports Steve Doyle
Deputy Managing Editor-Topics Mike Bales

EDITORS AND MANAGERS

Arts/Entertainment Editor Barry Glenn
Deputy Business Editor Geri Throne
Editorial Page Editor Manning Pynn
Chief Editorial Writer David Porter
Editorial Administration Budget Manager Lee Huber
Editorial Art Manager Mark Williams
Editor-Florida Magazine Sal Recchi
Editor-Lake County Sam Fenton
Health/Science Editor Ned Popkins

Copyright ©1996 by the Editor & Publisher Co.

I-84 Florida

Manager-Library Resources Judy Grimsley
Lifestyle Editor Mick Lochridge
National Editor Ann Hellmuth
News Editor Donna Eyring
Newsphoto Chief Bill Phillips
Orange County Editor Wendy Spirduso
Osceola County Editor Phil Fernandez
Seminole County Editor Lisa Lochridge
Senior Columnist/Sports Larry Guest
Staff Development Editor Jim Clark
State Editor Robert Barker
Sunday Editor Michael Ludden
Topics Editor Mike Lafferty

MANAGEMENT INFORMATION SERVICES

Online Manager Mike Bales

PRODUCTION

Director-Operations Jeffrey M Johnson
Manager Susan Hunt
Manager-Center/RPC/Lake George Burton
Manager-Building Operations Bill Hall
Manager-New Technology Ernie Kuenzli
Manager-Operations Administration Jim Mifflin
Manager-Packaging/OPC Russell Newton
Manager-Pre Press Mark Dial
Manager-Pressroom/OPC Jim Catron
Manager-Quality Assurance Robert Crandall
Manager-Technical Operations Bob Kramer

Market Information: Zoned editions; Split Run; TMC; Operate database; Operate audiotex; Electronic edition.
Mechanical available: Offset; Black and 3 ROP colors; insert accepted — preprinted; page cut-offs — 22".
Mechanical specifications: Type page 13" x 21"; E - 6 cols, 2 1/16", 1/8" between; A - 6 cols, 2 1/16", 1/8" between; C - 10 cols, 1 1/8", 1/8" between.
Commodity consumption: Newsprint 76,394 short tons; width 27.37"; black ink 1,230,000 pounds; single pages printed 61,530; average pages per issue 140(d), 300(S); single plates used 405,000.
Equipment: EDITORIAL: Front-end hardware — 9-AT/9000, 83-Compute Ease/PC; Other equipment — 224-AT. CLASSIFIED: Front-end hardware — SII/Classified System; Other equipment — 68-AT, 6-ATS/Remote Workstation III (PC). AUDIOTEX: Hardware — Automated Voice Information Service. DISPLAY: Adv layout systems — 6-SCS/Layout 8000; Front-end hardware — 17-Ap/Mac; Front-end software — Cx/Breeze. PRODUCTION: Typesetters — 1-Linotype-Hell/Linotronic 300, Hyphen/PC RIP, 2-Linotype-Hell/Linotronic 530, 1-CD/626 1E, 1-CD/646 1E, 2-Linotype-Hell/Linotronic 530, 1-Cx/Bitseller, 2-Scitex/RayStar, Cx/Bitcaster RIP; Platemaking systems — 2-WL/Lith-X-Pozer III; Plate exposures — 2-WL/Lith-X-Pozer III; Plate processors — 2-W/M; Electronic picture desk — 2-Lf/AP Leaf Picture Desk, 9-Ap/Mac; Scanners — 1-CD/Pagefax, 2-ECR/Autokon 1000, 8-X/7650; Production cameras — 1-C/Marathon, 1-C/Spartan, 2-C/Newspager; Automatic film processors — 4-LE/LD2600A, 2-LE/Line 25A, 1-C/R650, 1-C/80RA; Film transporters — 4-Konica, 1-LE; Color separation equipment (conventional) — 1-CD/626 1E, 1-CD/646 1E, 2-Lf/Leafscan 45, 1-Lf/Leafscan 35, 3-Sharp/2X-610; Digital color separation equipment — 1-Scitex/Assembler Plus, 1-Scitex/Micro Assembler. PRESSROOM: Line 1 — 27-G/Metro, 4-G/Imperial; Line 2 — 8-G/Head, 2-G/Imperial; Line 3 — 7-G/Community, 2-DEV/1400; Line 4 — 5-G/Community, 4-DEV/1400; Line 5 — 8-DEV/2400, 1-DEV/H50; Line 6 — 12-Martin/0 speed splicer; Folders — G/3:2, 2-G/SCC, 1-G/600 Urbanite; Pasters — 45-G/RTP; Reels and stands — 45-G, 6-DEV; Press control system — G/MPCS-PACS. MAILROOM: Counter stackers — 11-HL/Monitor, 1-HL/HT2, 4-BG/Count-O-Veyor; Inserters and stuffers — 4-HI/1472, 1-AMG/630; Bundle tyer — 12-MLN/MLN2, 6-Dynaric/MP2; Wrapping singles — 1-St, 2-MM/335; Addressing machine — 1-KR/211, 1-Harlana Simon Press/Mailroom Totalizer; Mailroom control system — Burt Technologies/IPCS (Integrated Pre-Print Control System). WIRE SERVICES: Stock tables — TMS; Receiving dishes — size-3m, AP. BUSINESS COMPUTERS: 392-IBM, 109-Compaq/286-386; Applications: Lotus, Wordstar, Paradox, dBase/IV; PCs & micros networked; PCs & main system networked.

PALATKA

Putnam County

'90 U.S. Census- 10,201; E&P '96 Est. 10,232
ABC-CZ (90): 10,201 (HH 3,949)

Daily News (e-mon to fri)

Daily News, 1825 St. Johns Ave.; PO Box 777, Palatka, FL 32177-0777; tel (904) 328-2721; fax (904) 312-5209. New York Times Co. group.
Circulation: 12,169(e); ABC circulation average for 12 months ended Sept. 30, 1995.
Price: 50¢(d); $5.50/mo; $69.96/yr (carrier), $84.80/yr (mail).
Advertising: Open inch rate $14.70(e). **Representative:** Landon Associates Inc.
News Service: AP. **Politics:** Independent. **Established:** 1885.
Not Published: Christmas.
Special Editions: Meet the Manager (Jan); NASCAR, Fact Book (Feb); Blue Crab Festival (May); Back-to-School (Aug); Businessfest, Football, Industry Appreciation (Sept); Create a Beautiful Home, Fall River Fest (Oct); Gift Guide (Nov).
Special Weekly Sections: Food Day, Health and Fitness Page (wed); Business Page, Church Pages, Currents (fri).
Magazine: Currents (TV/Entertainment) (fri).

CORPORATE OFFICER

President John E Newhouse II

GENERAL MANAGEMENT

Publisher John E Newhouse II
Controller Keith Daniel

ADVERTISING

Manager-Classified Mary Kaye Wells
Manager-Retail Garrett Wallace

CIRCULATION

Director William F Bailey

NEWS EXECUTIVE

Exec Editor Jim Baltzelle

EDITORS AND MANAGERS

Lifestyle Editor Diane Williams
News Editor Mary Doan
Sports Editor Andy Hall

MANAGEMENT INFORMATION SERVICES

Data Processing Manager Mary Kaye Wells

PRODUCTION

Director Charles Gibson

Market Information: Zoned editions; TMC; Operate audiotex.
Mechanical available: Offset; Black and 3 ROP colors; insert accepted — preprinted, small catalogs, cards; page cut-offs — 22 3/4".
Mechanical specifications: Type page 13" x 21 1/2"; E - 6 cols, 2 1/16", 1/8" between; A - 6 cols, 2 1/16", 1/8" between; C - 9 cols, 1 3/8", 1/16" between.
Commodity consumption: Newsprint 780 short tons; width 27 1/2"; black ink 18,400 pounds; color ink 1,500 pounds; single pages printed 6,100; average pages per issue 24(d); single plates used 8,500.
Equipment: EDITORIAL: Front-end hardware — 8-IBM/PC 486, 3-PC/Pagination Station; Front-end software — Computext/AmiPro, QPS; Printers — 1-Ap/Mac LaserWriter IINTX; Other equipment — Ap/Mac IIcx, Ap/Mac 300, Shava/Telebridge, Microcom/9600 Modem, Lf/AP Leaf Picture Desk, Ap/Mac vx. CLASSIFIED: Front-end hardware — Computext/CompuClass; Front-end software — Computext/CompuClass; Printers — Ap/Mac LaserWriter II. AUDIOTEX: Hardware — Brite Voice Systems. DISPLAY: Front-end hardware — 1-Ap/Mac II, 1-Ap/Mac IIci, 1-Ap/Mac Quadra 950; Front-end software — Multi-Ad/Creator, QuarkXPress, Adobe/Photoshop; Printers — 1-DEC/VT 820 Plain Paper, 1-Linotype-Hell/Linotronic LTC-30C, 1-Panther/Plus. PRODUCTION: Pagination software — Computext/Comet; OCR software — TI/Omni Page; Typesetters — 1-Linotype-Hell/Linotron 300, 1-Panther/Plus; Plate exposures — 1-Nu/FT40L-19, 1-Nu/FT 40 APRNS; Plate processors — 1-Nu/A-250; Electronic picture desk — 1-Lf/AP Leaf Picture Desk; Scanners — 2-Microtek/II XE, 1-Kk/RFS 2035; Production cameras — 1-C/Spartan III, 1-3M/Pyrofax; Automatic film processors — 1-C/66F, 1-Konica/K550; Shrink lenses — 1-Alan/24. PRESSROOM: Line 1 — 8-G/Community; Press drives — 1-Fin/75 h.p.; Folders — 1-G. MAILROOM: Counter stackers — QWI; Inserters and stuffers — KAN/5-station 480; Bundle tyer — MLN/MLN-2A; Addressing machine — Ch/586; Mailroom control system — CD. WIRE SERVICES: News — AP, NYT; Syndicates — King Features, NYT, United Features, Cowles, CNS, Crown, Universal Press; Receiving dishes — size-10ft, AP. BUSINESS COMPUTERS: IBM/S-36, PC/Network; Applications: Microsoft/Excel, Microsoft/Word, Symphony, Q&A/PCs, INSI; PCs & micros networked; PCs & main system networked.

PALM BEACH

Palm Beach County

'90 U.S. Census- 9,814; E&P '96 Est. 9,886

Palm Beach Daily News (m-mon to sat; S)

Palm Beach Daily News, 265 Royal Poinciana Way; PO Box 1176, Palm Beach, FL 33480-4063; tel (407) 820-3800; fax (407) 655-4594. Cox Newspapers Inc. group.
Circulation: 9,896(m); 9,896(m-sat); 11,448(S); Sworn Oct. 1, 1995.
Price: 25¢(d); 25¢(sat); 50¢(S); $1.60/wk (home delivery), $3.70/wk (mail); $6.94/mo (home delivery), $14.80/mo (mail); $64.50/yr (home delivery), $149.40/yr (mail); $36.40/yr (S only) (mail).
Advertising: Open inch rate $27.73(m); $27.73(m-sat); $31.01(S). **Politics:** Independent. **Established:** 1897.
Note: All printing and production for the Palm Beach Daily News (mS) is done at the West Palm Beach Post plant. The Palm Beach Daily News is published daily from September through May and twice weekly (thur & S) from June to September.
Not Published: New Year; Christmas (except on a Sunday).
Special Editions: Palm Beach Tropical Flower Show, Grand Estates (Feb); Grand Estates, Fashion Issue (Mar); Season Preview (Sept); Grand Estates, Fashion Issue (Oct); On the Town, Palm Beach Visitor's Guide (Nov); Grand Estates (Dec).
Magazine: Palm Beach Life (Mar & Nov).

CORPORATE OFFICER

President Tom Giuffrida

GENERAL MANAGEMENT

Publisher Joyce Harr

ADVERTISING

Director Donna S Moore

CIRCULATION

Director Therese Christiano

NEWS EXECUTIVES

Editor Linda Rawls
Managing Editor Libby Wells

EDITORS AND MANAGERS

Business Editor Christopher Keidaish
Entertainment Editor Jan Sjostrom
Fashion Editor Laurie Brookins
Food Editor Skippy Harwood
News Editor Lisa Dawson
Chief Photographer Patrick Egan
Society Editor Shannon Donnelly
Sports Editor Michael Strauss

MANAGEMENT INFORMATION SERVICES

Data Processing Manager John Occhipinti

Mechanical available: Offset; Black and 3 ROP colors; insert accepted — preprinted; page cut-offs — 22.5".
Mechanical specifications: Type page 13" x 22 1/4"; E - 6 cols, 2 1/16", 1/8" between; A - 6 cols, 2 1/16", 1/8" between; C - 6 cols, 2 1/16", 1/8" between.
Commodity consumption: average pages per issue 8(d), 6(sat), 34(S).
Equipment: DISPLAY: Adv layout systems — SCS/Layout 8000. MAILROOM: Addressing machine — 1-EDP.

PANAMA CITY

Bay County

'90 U.S. Census- 34,378; E&P '96 Est. 35,153
ABC-NDM (90): 126,994 (HH 48,938)

The News-Herald (m-mon to sat; S)

The News-Herald, 501 W. 11th St.; PO Box 1940, Panama City, FL 32402; tel (904) 747-5000; fax (904) 747-5018. Freedom Communications Inc. group.
Circulation: 35,828(m); 35,828(m-sat); 42,212(S); ABC circulation average for 12 months ended Sept. 30, 1995.
Price: 50¢(d); 50¢(sat); $1.00(S); $9.59/4 wks; $119.28/yr.
Advertising: Open inch rate $24.15(m); $24.15(m-sat); $24.15(S). **Representative:** Papert Companies.
News Services: AP, KRT. **Established:** 1937.
Special Edition: Christmas Edition (Nov).
Special Weekly Sections: Business Monday (mon); Community Review (tues); Food Section, Education Section (wed); Outdoors (thur); The Entertainer (fri); Religion (sat); Lifestyle & Viewpoint (S).
Magazine: The Entertainer (local tab with TV log).

GENERAL MANAGEMENT

Publisher Karen Hanes
Business Manager Karen Taggart

ADVERTISING

Director Kenneth Carpenter
Supervisor-Classified Glenda Vurpillat

MARKETING AND PROMOTION

Director-Marketing/Promotion Nicole Barefield

CIRCULATION

Director Thomas W Byrd

NEWS EXECUTIVES

Editor Stephen Bornhoft
Managing Editor Mike Cazalas

EDITORS AND MANAGERS

Editorial Page Editor Stephen Bornhoft
Entertainment Editor Shirley Courson
Education Editor Tony Simmons
Fashion/Society Editor Debbie Kunkel
Features Editor Douglas Elfman
Food/Women's Editor Debbie Kunkel
Graphics Editor/Art Director John Russo
Sports Editor Pat McCann

MANAGEMENT INFORMATION SERVICES

Manager-Management Info Services Ron Bennett

PRODUCTION

Director Bruce Garner
Manager-Operations Bruce Garner
Foreman-Pressroom David Alcock

Market Information: Split Run; ADS.
Mechanical available: Offset; Black and 3 ROP colors; insert accepted — preprinted; page cut-offs — 22 3/4".
Mechanical specifications: Type page 13" x 21 1/2"; E - 6 cols, 2 1/16", 1/8" between; A - 6 cols, 2 1/16", 1/8" between; C - 9 cols, 1 3/8", 1/16" between.
Commodity consumption: Newsprint 4,200 metric tons; widths 55", 41 3/4", 27", 13 1/2", 34", 17"; black ink 40 pounds; color ink 40 pounds; single pages printed 17,500; average pages per issue 42(d), 70(S); single plates used 27,500.
Equipment: EDITORIAL: Front-end hardware — Compaq; Front-end software — Dewar; Printers — Okidata. CLASSIFIED: Front-end hardware — Compaq; Front-end software — Dewar; Printers — Okidata. DISPLAY: Adv layout systems — Compaq; Front-end hardware — Dewar; Printers — Okidata. PRODUCTION: Pagination software — Dewar/System 4; OCR software — Dest; Typesetters — 1-V/5100, 1-V/5510, 2-Birmy/340; Plate exposures — 2-Nu; Plate processors — Nat; Electronic picture desk — Lf/AP Leaf Picture Desk; Scanners — Linotype-Hell/Topaz, Dest; Production cameras — C/Spartan II; Automatic film processors — 2-LE/LD18, 1-LE/24AQ; Film transporters — 1-C/Spartan III, 1-C/Marathon; Color separation equipment (conventional) — RZ. PRESSROOM: Line 1 — 6-G/C2264; Line 2 — 7-G/Community; Folders — 3-G. MAILROOM: Counter stackers — 2-HL/Monitor; Inserters and stuffers — 1-HI/64-24P; Bundle tyer — 2-MLN; Wrapping singles — 2-Bu; Addressing machine — KAN. LIBRARY: Electronic — SMS. WIRE SERVICES: News — AP; Photos — AP; Stock tables — AP; Receiving dishes — size-8ft, AP, KRT. BUSINESS COMPUTERS: PCs & micros networked; PCs & main system networked.

PENSACOLA

Escambia County

'90 U.S. Census- 58,165; E&P '96 Est. 58,621
ABC-NDM (90): 344,406 (HH 128,508)

Pensacola News Journal (m-mon to fri; m-sat; S)

Pensacola News Journal, 101 E. Romana; PO Box 12710, Pensacola, FL 32574; tel (904) 435-8500. Gannett Co. Inc. group.
Circulation: 61,066(m); 69,685(m-sat); 83,595(S); ABC circulation average for 12 months ended Sept. 30, 1995.
Price: 50¢(d); 50¢(sat); $1.50(S); $13.00/mo; $156.00/yr.
Advertising: Open inch rate $80.87(m); $80.87(m-sat); $93.17(S). **Representative:** Gannett National Newspaper Sales.

News Services: AP, GNS, KRT. **Established:** 1889 (News), 1898 (Journal).
Special Editions: Passport '96 (May); Blue Angels (July); Football Section (Aug); Election (Oct).
Special Weekly Sections: Your Money (mon); Weekender (fri); Homefinder (S).
Magazines: Your Money Tab (mon); Neighbors (thur); Weekender Tab (fri); TV Week listings (local), USA Weekend, Homefinder (S).

CORPORATE OFFICERS
President Denise H Bannister
Vice Pres J Earle Bowden
Secretary Thomas L Chapple

GENERAL MANAGEMENT
Publisher Denise H Bannister
Director-Finance Richard Ottensmeyer
Director-Human Resources James Barnett

ADVERTISING
Director John DiMambro
Manager-Retail Brenda Bohn

MARKETING AND PROMOTION
Director-Market Development Elizabeth Hewey

TELECOMMUNICATIONS
Audiotex Manager Sharon Butler

CIRCULATION
Director Ed Graves

NEWS EXECUTIVES
Editor J Earle Bowden
Managing Editor Michael Ryan
Deputy Managing Editor Susan Ihne
Asst Managing Editor Mike Mika

EDITORS AND MANAGERS
Books Editor Mark Bradley
Business/Finance Editor David Mogollon
Cartoonist J Earle Bowden
Editorial Page Editor Joedy Isert
Education Editor Lori Gaillot
Entertainment/Amusements Editor Cindy Hall
Environmental Editor Dave McFarland
Fashion Editor Susan Catron
Health/Medical Editor Linda Zettler
Librarian Christine McDowell
Life/Features Editor Susan Catron
Metro Editor Dave McFarland
Religion Editor Alice Crann
Sports Editor Gordon Paulus
TV Tab Editor Elizabeth Buchinger

MANAGEMENT INFORMATION SERVICES
Data Processing Manager Terri Trivett

PRODUCTION
Director James M Rife
Manager-Platemaking Tom Harris
Manager-Mailroom Joe Barnhill
Manager-Pressroom Pete Gunn
Manager-Systems Adrian Enfinger
Manager-Composing/Graphic Arts Julie Booher
Chief Technician Sonny McIver

Market Information: Zoned editions; Split Run; TMC; ADS; Operate audiotex.
Mechanical available: Letterpress (direct); Black and 3 ROP colors; insert accepted — preprinted, minimum 4x7-80 lbs stock; page cut-offs — 22¾".
Mechanical specifications: Type page 13" x 21½"; E - 6 cols, 2¹⁄₁₆", ⅛" between; A - 6 cols, 2¹⁄₁₆", ⅛" between; C - 10 cols, 1¼", ¹⁄₁₆" between.
Commodity consumption: Newsprint 7,688 short tons; 6,975 metric tons; widths 54.50", 40.88", 13.625"; black ink 221,000 pounds; color ink 59,000 pounds; single pages printed 17,871; average pages per issue 40(d), 94(S); single plates used 45,000.
Equipment: EDITORIAL: Front-end hardware — 50-SII/Sys 55, Mk/Managing Editor; Front-end software — SII. CLASSIFIED: Front-end hardware — 15-SII/Sys 55; Front-end software — SII. AUDIOTEX: Hardware — Octel. DISPLAY: Adv layout systems — Mk/Ad Director; Front-end hardware — 4-Dewar/Discovery, 2-Dewar/Fileserver, 3-Dewar/110, 7-Ap/Mac; Front-end software — Dewar, Multi-Ad/Creator. PRODUCTION: Pagination software — Pongrass 2.2, Mk/Managing Editor, Mk/Page Director 1.6, QuarkXPress 3.3; Typesetters — 2-AU/APS G/108, 1-AU/APS PIP II; Platemaking systems — Na; Plate exposures — 2-Na/Master 2435FCL; Plate processors — 2-Na/Satellite; Electronic picture desk — Lf/AP Leaf Picture Desk; Scanners — ECR/Autokon; Production cameras — 1-C/Spartan III, 1-C/Newspager II; Automatic film processors — 2-C/66F, 1-LE/DL1800A; Film transporters — 1-C/Newpager II; Color separation equipment (conventional) — 1-RZ/200S; Digital color separation equipment — 1-Lf/Leafscan.
PRESSROOM: Line 1 — 9-G/Mark I; Press drives — 11-GE/60 h.p. Motor; Folders — 2-G/2:1; Pasters — Automatic Pasters; Reels and stands — G; Press control system — Fin. MAILROOM: Counter stackers — 3-Id/2200, 1-HL/Monitor; Inserters and stuffers — Amerigraph/630 inserter w/21 Hopper Heads; Bundle tyer — 2-Dynaric/NP-1, 2-Dynaric/NP-1 Tying Machines; Addressing machine — 1-Ch/525, 1-KR; Mailroom control system — Id/TCP Bundle Control System w/ Traffic Control; Other mailroom equipment — MM/Stitcher-Trimmer 217. WIRE SERVICES: News — AP, GNS, TV Data, AP Datafeatures, KRT; Stock tables — AP; Receiving dishes — AP. BUSINESS COMPUTERS: 1-IBM/AS-400 F45; Applications: Circ, Accts receivable, Gen ledger, Accts payable, Payroll; PCs & micros networked; PCs & main system networked.

PORT ST. LUCIE

See FORT PIERCE

ST. AUGUSTINE

St. Johns County

'90 U.S. Census- 11,692; E&P '96 Est. 11,510
ABC-NDM (90): 62,554 (HH 24,635)

The St. Augustine Record

(e-mon to fri; m-sat; S)

The St. Augustine Record, 158 Cordova St. (32084); PO Box 1630, St. Augustine, FL 32085-1630; tel (904) 829-6562; fax (904) 829-6664. Morris Communications Corp. group.
Circulation: 15,819(e); 15,819(m-sat); 15,851(S); ABC circulation average for 12 months ended Sept. 30, 1995.
Price: 50¢(d); 50¢(sat); $1.00(S); $7.95/mo; $95.40/yr.
Advertising: Open inch rate $13.75(e); $14.26(m-sat); $14.26(S).
News Services: AP, KRT, LAT-WP. **Politics:** Independent. **Established:** 1894.
Note: Advertising is sold in combination with Jacksonville Florida Times Union (mS) for $142.50(d), $150.60(sat) and $166.15(S).
Advertising not accepted: Contrary to paper's publication standards.
Special Editions: Tax Tips (Jan); Bridal (Feb); Just Say No (Mar); Car Care, Real Estate Today, Graduation (May); Back-to-School (Aug); Football (Sept); Christmas Gift Guide, Christmas Greetings (Dec).
Special Weekly Sections: Food Section (wed); Arts & Entertainment (thur); School Page (fri); TV Section, The Welcome Mat, Stock Listings (sat); Lifestyle, Business, Travel (S).
Magazines: TV Book (TMC); Off the Record; EVENTS Magazine.

CORPORATE OFFICERS
COB/CEO W S Morris III
President Paul S Simon

GENERAL MANAGEMENT
Publisher Ronnie J Hughes
Manager-Accounting Zoe Ann Moss

ADVERTISING
Manager Grover Ford

TELECOMMUNICATIONS
Audiotex Manager Steve Carswell

CIRCULATION
Director Lee Hutchins

NEWS EXECUTIVE
Managing Editor Adrian Pratt

EDITORS AND MANAGERS
Business/Finance Editor Brian Thompson
Editorial Page Editor Jim Sutton
Entertainment/Amusements Editor Debra Bokur
Farm/Agriculture Editor Fred Whitley
Fashion/Style Editor Anne Heymen
Features Editor Margo Pope
Health/Medical Editor Colette Trent
Living/Lifestyle Editor Anne Heymen
Photo Department Manager John Studwell
Political/Government Editor Joe Furry
Religion Editor Anne Heymen
Society Editor Anne Heymen
Sports Editor Jim Clark
Television/Film Editor Debra Bokur
Theater/Music Editor Debra Bokur
Travel Editor Colette Trent
Women's Editor Anne Heymen

PRODUCTION
Director Robert E James
Foreman-Pressroom Volker Heigelmann
Foreman-Camera/Platemaking Jeff Taylor
Superintendent-Composing Gail Cumiskey

Market Information: TMC; Operate database; Operate audiotex.
Mechanical available: Offset; Black and 3 ROP colors; insert accepted — preprinted, odd size.
Mechanical specifications: Type page 13" x 21.08"; E - 6 cols, 2¹⁄₁₆", ⅛" between; A - 6 cols, 2¹⁄₁₆", ⅛" between; C - 9 cols, 1⅜", ¹⁄₁₆" between.
Commodity consumption: Newsprint 1,100 short tons; widths 27½", 13¾"; black ink 35,700 pounds; color ink 6,000 pounds; single pages printed 9,048; average pages per issue 28(d), 36(S); single plates used 10,800.
Equipment: EDITORIAL: Front-end hardware — IBM; Front-end software — MPS/4; Printers — Toshiba/321. CLASSIFIED: Front-end hardware — IBM; Front-end software — MPS/4; Printers — Epson. DISPLAY: Front-end hardware — Ap/Mac; Front-end software — Multi-Ad/Creator; Printers — Ap/Mac LaserWriter II; Other equipment — Ap/Mac CD-Rom, Poweruser/ Excerdal Hard Drive. PRODUCTION: Typesetters — XIT; Plate exposures — Nu/Flip Top FT40LHS; Plate processors — 1-WL/38D; Electronic picture desk — Lf/AP Leaf Picture Desk; Production cameras — Liberator/C-473-0, AG/Accuset 1500; Automatic film processors — 1-LE, 1-C/66F, 1-AG/Rapidline 20; Color separation equipment (conventional) — XIT.
PRESSROOM: Line 1 — 12-G/Suburban; Press drives — 3-HP/100; Folders — G/Urbanite Half, SU/Half (w/Quarter); Reels and stands — HI/Roll Stands; Press control system — Fin; Press registration system — Duarte. MAILROOM: Counter stackers — 1-BG/Count-O-Veyor 105, 1-MM; Inserters and stuffers — 1-MM/2275; Bundle tyer — 2-MLN/ML2EE; Addressing machine — 1-Am/1900, KAN. COMMUNICATIONS: Facsimile — ATT/3510 D; Remote imagesetting — XIT. WIRE SERVICES: News — AP, KRT; Receiving dishes — AP. BUSINESS COMPUTERS: IBM; Applications: Morris Comm. Co./On-line; PCs & micros networked; PCs & main system networked.

ST. PETERSBURG-CLEARWATER

Pinellas County

'90 U.S. Census- 337,413 (St. Petersburg 238,629; Clearwater 98,784) E&P '96 Est. 349,008 (St. Petersburg 238,932; Clearwater 110,076)
ABC-NDM (90): 1,110,543 (HH 496,079)

St. Petersburg Times

(m-mon to sat; S)

St. Petersburg Times, 490 1st. Ave. S. (33701-4204); PO Box 1121, St. Petersburg, FL 33731-1121; tel (813) 893-8111; fax (813) 893-8675; e-mail 73174.3344@compuserve.com; web site http://www.sptimes.com.
Circulation: 349,874(m); 349,874(m-sat); 445,800(S); ABC circulation average for 12 months ended Sept. 30, 1995.
Price: 25¢(d); 25¢(sat); $1.00(S); $2.30/wk; $9.20/4wk; $102.85/yr.
Advertising: Open inch rate $240.00(m); $240.00(m-sat); $320.00(S). **Representative:** Cresmer, Woodward, O'Mara & Ormsbee.
News Services: AP, NYT, LAT-WP, RN, SHNS, KRT. **Established:** 1884.
Advertising not accepted: Astrology, Liquor (in color comics).
Special Editions: Pinella Home Search, Action Inserts, Your Home, Business Preview (Jan); Manatee Festival, Auto Racing, N.S. Business Profiles, Home & Garden Show, Seniority (Feb); Spring Training, Your Home, Chasco Fiesta Days, Spring/Summer Cruise, Spring In The Woods (Mar); Oldsmar Days, Fun'n Sun, Odesso Rodeo, Home & Leisure, Seniority (Apr); Your Home, Canada (Toronto), Taste of Pinellas, Hurricane (May); Pinellas Home Search, Golf, Lifebeat, Community & Commerce (June); Pasco Parade of Homes, Price Checker (July); Summer Times, Baby Show, Favorites, Pro & College Football, High School Football (Aug); Tarpon Seafest, Home & Remodeling Show, Fall/Winter Cruise, Orlando/Central Florida, Tampa Bay's Best, New Car Introduction (Sept); Hockey, Clearwater Jazz, Women in Business, Florida Keys, Lifebeat, Community & Commerce, Wedding Book, Carribean, Dunedin Art Harvest (Oct); International Auto Show, Inserts, Hudson Seafest, Winter Travel/Ski, Tampa Gift Guide (Nov); Palm Harbor Art Show, Santa Tracking, First Night (Dec).
Special Weekly Sections: Monday Business (mon); Best Food Day (thur); Weekend (Entertainment) (fri); Travel (S).
Magazines: Parade; TV Dial (quarterfold, local, offset); Sunday comics (standard size).

CORPORATE OFFICERS
President/CEO/Editor Andrew Barnes
Exec Vice Pres Judith Roales
Vice Pres Paul Tash
Vice Pres-Communication & Community Relations Michael F Foley
Vice Pres-Director Affiliates and Planning Andrew P Corty
Vice Pres-Administration/Treasurer/Secretary Catherine Heron
Asst to President Jack Belich

GENERAL MANAGEMENT
General Manager Judith Roales
Manager-Human Resources Lucinda Durning
Manager-Research Steven Kircher
Manager-Credit Mike Ward

ADVERTISING
Director Richard Reeves
Deputy Director-Advertising Administration Jaime Capella
Manager-General Bruce Karlson
Manager-Classified Elaine Myers
Manager-Retail Ralph Scaglione
Manager-Co-op Pam Scheepers
Manager-Ad Operations Barry McIntosh

MARKETING AND PROMOTION
Marketing Service Kristin Brett

TELECOMMUNICATIONS
Audiotex Manager Greg Huffman

CIRCULATION
Director Mike Womack
Manager-Home Delivery Mike Whack
Manager-Marketing Mark Mangone
Manager-Operations Gil Mavro
Manager-Administration Debra Romaine

NEWS EXECUTIVES
Exec Editor Paul Tash
Senior Editor Tom Rawlins
Assoc Editor Lucy Morgan
Assoc Editor Martin Dyckman
Editor-Editorial Philip Gailey
Deputy Editor-Editorial Robert Friedman
Managing Editor Neil Brown
Deputy Managing Editor Susan Taylor Martin
Managing Editor-Tampa Neville Green
Managing Editor-Clearwater Joe Childs
Asst Managing Editor-Copy Desk Anne Glover
Asst Managing Editor-Features Nancy Waclawek
Asst Managing Editor-Sports Jack Sheppard

EDITORS AND MANAGERS
Action Line Editor Judy Garnatz-Harriman
Amusements Editor Dave Scheiber
Auto Editor Kyle Parks
Books Editor Margo Hammond
Business Editor Rob Hooker
Campaign Editor Jeanne Grinstead
City Editor Kim Kleman
Columnist Elijah Gosier
Columnist Jacquin Sanders
Columnist Mary Jo Melone
Editorial Page Editor Philip Gailey
Education Editor James Harper
Environmental Editor David Olinger
Fashion Editor Mary Jane Park
Films Editor Steve Persall
Food Editor Chris Sherman
Garden Editor Jeanne Malmgren
Home Furnishings Editor Judy Stark
Librarian Cary Kenney
Medical Section Editor Sue Landry
Music Editor-Pop Dave Scheiber
Music Editor-Classical John Fleming
National Editor Chris Lavin
Performing Arts Editor Dave Scheiber
Photo Editor Sonya Doctorian
Political Editor Howard Troxler
Radio/Television Editor Monica Yant
Real Estate/Business Editor Kyle Parks
Real Estate/At Home Editor Judy Stark
Religion Editor Mike Wilson
Science/Technology Editor Gretchen Letterman
Systems Editor Karen Dean
Systems Editor Don McBride
Travel Editor Bob Jenkins
World Editor Chris Lavin

MANAGEMENT INFORMATION SERVICES
Online Director Cary Kenney
Data Processing Director Clark Lambert

PRODUCTION
Director Ralph E Imhof

Manager-Production News Greg Steele
Manager-Press David Tallmadge
Manager-Packaging/Distribution Ben Hayes
Manager-Facilities Kent Worrall
Manager-Dispatch Ed Houk
Manager-Composing Bill Satterfield
Manager-Imaging Lorna Borghese
Manager-Distribution Mike Galloway
Manager-Packaging Diane Constantino
Manager-Maintenance Bill Wenzelburger
Engineer-Staff Dale Tillis

Market Information: Zoned editions; Split Run; TMC; ADS; Operate database; Operate audiotex; Electronic edition.
Mechanical available: Offset; Black and 3 ROP colors; insert accepted — preprinted; page cutoffs — 22¾".
Mechanical specifications: Type page 13" x 21¼"; E - 6 cols, 2 1/16", ⅛" between; A - 6 cols, 2 1/16", ⅛" between; C - 10 cols, 1 5/16", 1/16" between.
Commodity consumption: Newsprint 83,846 short tons; widths 27½", 55", 39", 41¼"; black ink 1,500,000 pounds; color ink 540,000 pounds; single pages printed 93,000; average pages per issue 67(d), 84(sat), 141(S); single plates used 700,000.
Equipment: EDITORIAL: Front-end hardware — SII/4 Processor Tandem TXP, 270-SII/Coyote, 110-SII/PC; Front-end software — SII/Editorial Sys; Printers — 3-HP/LaserJet, 2-DS/180, 16-Citizen/180D, 1-Fujitsu/2100. CLASSIFIED: Front-end hardware — Bull/DPS-98-2; Front-end software — In-house. AUDIOTEX: Hardware — 3-PEP/Voice Print Audiotext System; Software — PEP/Voice Print; Supplier name — AP, BDR. DISPLAY: Adv layout systems — III, In-house/Layout Sys, Ap/Macs; Front-end hardware — 1-Bull/DPS6-98, 4-Sun/350-360; Front-end software — In-house; Printers — 2-Ap/Mac LaserWriter. PRODUCTION: Typesetters — 2-III/3810, 4-III/3850; Plate exposures — WL/Lith-X-Pozer; Plate processors — WL; Scanners — ECR/Autokon; Production cameras — C; Automatic film processors — LE; Film transporters — LE; Color separation equipment (conventional) — CD, Ap/Mac; Digital color separation equipment — ECR/Autokon.
PRESSROOM: Line 1 — 21-G/Metro; Line 2 — 21-G/Metro-Metroliner; Line 3 — 21-G/Metroliner; Press drives — Fin; Folders — 6-G/single, 4-G/double; Pasters — 63-MGD; Reels and stands — 63-MGD; Press control system — G/PAR, G/PCS. MAILROOM: Counter stackers — 23-HL, 6-Id; Inserters and stuffers — 2-S/848, 1-S/1372, 5-S/1472, 1-MM/235, 1-MM/335; Bundle tyer — 19-Dynaric, 13-MLN; Wrapping singles — 16-QWI/Wrap, 13-Id/Bottom Wrap. LIBRARY: Electronic — SII/LASR Sys, Photo/AXS. COMMUNICATIONS: Facsimile — 2-Hel, 2-LS/210 PK-100, AdSat; Remote imagesetting — 2-III/3850; Systems used — microwave, fiber optic. WIRE SERVICES: News — AP, RN, NYT, SHNS, LAT-WP, KRT; Photos — AP; Stock tables — AP; Syndicates — LATS, SHNS, NYT; Receiving dishes — size-3m, AP, UPI, RN. BUSINESS COMPUTERS: 1-Bull/DPS 8000-83, 4-Bull/DP6-98; Applications: APU: Billing statistics, Payroll, Personnel; PCs & micros networked; PCs & main system networked.

SANFORD
Seminole County
'90 U.S. Census- 32,387; **E&P '96 Est.** 41,517

Sanford Herald (e-tues to fri; S)

Sanford Herald, 300 N. French Ave., Sanford, FL 32771; tel (407) 322-2611. Haskell Newspapers group.
Circulation: 4,937(e); 4,937(S); Sworn Sept. 29, 1995.
Price: 30¢(d); 75¢(S); $1.50/wk; $6.50/mo; $78.00/yr.
Advertising: Open inch rate $8.43(e); $8.43(S). **Representative:** Landon Associates Inc.
News Service: AP. **Politics:** Independent. **Established:** 1908.
Note: Effective May 22, 1995, this publication changed its publishing plan from (e-mon to fri; S) to (e-tues to fri; S).
Not Published: Christmas.
Special Editions: Positively Tabs; Football; Lk. Mary/Heathrow Art Festival; Fall Car Care; Golden Age; Games; Historic Homes Tour; Christmas Gift Tab; Christmas Greetings.
Special Weekly Sections: Best Food Day (wed); Religion (fri); Health/Fitness, Education, Business (S).
Magazine: Leisure Magazine (TV listings) (fri).

CORPORATE OFFICERS
President Robert H Haskell III
Exec Vice Pres George H Harris
Vice Pres Elizabeth H Haskell
Secretary Ann B Winn
Treasurer Wayne D Doyle

GENERAL MANAGEMENT
Business Manager Odessa Pugh

ADVERTISING
Director Tracy Schneider

CIRCULATION
Asst Manager Tracy Schneider

NEWS EXECUTIVE
Exec Editor Wayne D Doyle

EDITORS AND MANAGERS
Assignment Editor Lacy Doman
People Editor Doris Dietrich
Chief Photographer Thomas Vincent
Religion Editor Susan Wenner
Society Editor Doris Dietrich
Sports Editor Dean Smith

PRODUCTION
Manager Frank Voltoline

Market Information: TMC.
Mechanical available: Offset.
Mechanical specifications: Type page 13" x 21½"; E - 6 cols, 2 1/16", ⅛" between; A - 6 cols, 2 1/16", ⅛" between; C - 8 cols, 1½", ⅛" between.
Commodity consumption: Newsprint 1,058 short tons; widths 27½", 34"; average pages per issue 18(d), 34(S).
Equipment: EDITORIAL: Front-end hardware — COM, IBM; Front-end software — COM; Printers — TI. CLASSIFIED: Front-end hardware — COM; Front-end software — COM; Printers — TI. DISPLAY: Adv layout systems — COM/MCS; Front-end hardware — COM/MCS; Front-end software — COM/MCS; Printers — COM/8400. PRODUCTION: Typesetters — COM/MCS, AP; Plate exposures — Nu; Plate processors — Nat; Production cameras — C; Automatic film processors — LE; Shrink lenses — 1-CK Optical; Color separation equipment (conventional) — 1-BKY.
PRESSROOM: Line 1 — 2-G/Community; Folders — 1-G/Balloon. MAILROOM: Counter stackers — 2-BG; Bundle tyer — 2-Bu. BUSINESS COMPUTERS: DEC/VT 320; Applications: Accts payable, Accts receivable, Payroll, Circ; PCs & micros networked; PCs & main system networked.

SARASOTA
Sarasota County
'90 U.S. Census- 50,961; **E&P '96 Est.** 52,808
ABC-NDM (90): 277,776 (HH 125,493)

Sarasota Herald-Tribune (m-mon to sat; S)

Sarasota Herald-Tribune, 801 S. Tamiami Trl.; PO Box 1719, Sarasota, FL 34230; tel (813) 953-7755. New York Times Co. group.
Circulation: 114,638(m); 114,638(m-sat); 142,373(S); ABC circulation average for 12 months ended Sept. 30, 1995.
Price: 35¢(d); 35¢(sat); $1.00(S); $14.40/5wk, $37.44/13wk, $74.88/26wk; $149.76/yr.
Advertising: Open inch rate $92.04(m); $92.04(m-sat); $105.01(S). **Representative:** Publishers' Representatives of Florida.
News Services: AP, LAT-WP, NYT. **Politics:** Independent. **Established:** 1925.
Special Editions: Jubilee (Jan); Dining Guide, Parade of Homes (Feb); Wine Fest (Mar); Attorney Guide (Apr); Hurricane (May); Suncoast Off-shore Program (June); Dining Guide (July); Back-to-School, Year-end Auto Clearance, Reader's Choice (Aug); Clubs (Sept); Season, Physician Guide (Oct); Holiday Gift Guide (Nov); Auto Showcase (Dec).
Special Weekly Sections: Business Monday (mon); Food (thur); Ticket (Entertainment) (fri); HomeLife, Real Estate Guest (sat); TV Week, Perspective, Arts/Travels (S).
Magazines: Today's Senior; Parade, Comics (S); Sarasota Style; Vitality.
Broadcast Affiliates: Sarasota News Now (SNN6).
Cable TV: Operate leased cable TV in circulation area.

GENERAL MANAGEMENT
Publisher Lynn O Matthews
Publisher-Charlotte (AM) C Steve Hopper
Publisher-Manatee (AM) William Hansen
Director-Operations/Distribution Stanly P Whitty
Personnel Director Nicholas Mastro
Manager-Credit Dick Griffin

ADVERTISING
Director-Marketing/Advertising James Doughton
Manager-Retail Mike Baskin
Manager-National/Co-op Susan DuFour
Manager-Classified Sherry Nixon
Manager-Marketing Stuart Smith

TELECOMMUNICATIONS
Director-Publishing Technology Mike Martin
Audiotex Manager Chris Kelley

CIRCULATION
Director-Operations/Distribution Stanly P Whitty
Manager-Sales/Promotion Paul Staik
Manager-City Rick Harris
Manager-County Nancy Martin
Manager-County Tom Janning
Manager-County Randy White

NEWS EXECUTIVES
Exec Editor Diane H McFarlin
Editor Waldo Proffitt Jr
Managing Editor Bruce Giles
Asst Managing Editor Richard Estrin
General Manager/News Director-News Channel Frank Verdel

EDITORS AND MANAGERS
Business Editor Tom Buckingham
Charlotte County Bureau Chief Deborah Winsor
City Editor Mark Howard
Columnist David Grimes
Columnist Marjorie North
Columnist Tom Lyons
Columnist-Charlotte Eric Ernst
Editorial Page Editor Thomas Lee Tryon
Education Editor Christine Hawes
Environmental Editor Bob King
Farm/Agriculture Editor Tom Buckingham
Features Editor Bill Steiden
Films/Theater Editor Jay Handelman
Food Editor Linda Brandt
Graphics Editor Steve Duckett
Living/Health Editor Diane Tennant
Manatee County Bureau Chief Cindy Kane
Metro Editor Jay Goley
Exec News Editor Kyle Booth
News Research Manager Janice Gehle
Photo Editor William Speer
Real Estate Editor Harold Bubil
Region Editor Eddie Robinette
Radio/Television Editor Joel Welin
Religion Editor Juli Cragg Hillard
Science Editor Linda Brandt
Exec Sports Editor Scott Peterson
Travel Editor Diane Tennant
Venice Bureau Chief Rich Brooks

MANAGEMENT INFORMATION SERVICES
Director-Publishing Technologies Mike Martin

PRODUCTION
Director-Operations/Distribution Stanly P Whitty
Manager-Pressroom James Spear
Manager-Packaging/Distribution Dick Simonson
Manager-Pre Press Charlie Maloney

Market Information: Zoned editions; TMC; Operate audiotex.
Mechanical available: Offset; Black and 4 ROP colors; insert accepted — preprinted; page cutoffs — 22".
Mechanical specifications: Type page 13" x 21"; E - 6 cols, 2 1/16", ⅛" between; A - 6 cols, 2 1/16", ⅛" between; C - 10 cols, 1 1/16", ⅛" between.
Commodity consumption: Newsprint 20,500 short tons; widths 55", 41¼"; black ink 385,000 pounds; color ink 114,400 pounds; single pages printed 29,607; average pages per issue 86(d), 215(S); single plates used 282,500.
Equipment: EDITORIAL: Front-end hardware — AT; Front-end software — AT. CLASSIFIED: Front-end hardware — AT; Front-end software — AT. AUDIOTEX: Hardware — Brite Voice Systems. DISPLAY: Adv layout systems — AT; Front-end hardware — Sun; Front-end software — Cx. PRODUCTION: Typesetters — 2-Bidco/80C Image Setter, 1-III/3850; Platemaking systems — KFM/Plate Express; Plate exposures — WL/Lith-X-Pozer; Plate processors — WL/380; Scanners — ECR/1000, ECR/2000, ECR/8400, Nikon/Scanners; Production cameras — 1-C/Spartan; Automatic film processors — LE/GJ-80RA; Film transporters — LE; Color separation equipment (conventional) — CD/646; Digital color separation equipment — HI/XP-21.
PRESSROOM: Line 1 — 8-G/3 Deck; Line 2 — 2-G (8 unit lines w/1 4-color tower and 3 decks); Pasters — G/RTP 45 DIA; Press control system — Fin; Press registration system — G. MAILROOM: Counter stackers — 2-HL/Monitor HT, 9-HL/Monitor, HL/SH 25; Inserters and stuffers — 3-HI/NP1372; Bundle tyer — 8-MLN/2A, 2-Power Strap/PSN; Wrapping singles — 8-HL/Monarch; Addressing machine — 1-Ch/S42. LIBRARY: Electronic — Vu/Text, Merlin Photo. COMMUNICATIONS: Facsimile — 2-III; Remote imagesetting — 2-HI/3850; Systems used — microwave. WIRE SERVICES: News — AP Datastream, AP Datafeatures, LAT-WP, NYT; Photos — AP; Stock tables — AP SelectStox; Receiving dishes — AP. BUSINESS COMPUTERS: 2-IBM/4381, III/TECS 2; Applications: Accts payable, Gen ledger, Payroll, Circ; Admarc.

STUART
Martin County
'90 U.S. Census- 11,936; **E&P '96 Est.** 14,186
ABC-NDM (90): 100,900 (HH 43,022)

The Stuart News (m-mon to sat; S)

The Stuart News, 1939 S. Federal Hwy.; PO Box 9009, Stuart, FL 34995-9009; tel (407) 287-1550; fax (407) 221-4126. Scripps Howard group.
Circulation: 36,241(m); 36,241(m-sat); 44,586(S); ABC circulation average for 12 months ended Sept. 30, 1995.
Price: 35¢(d); 35¢(sat); $1.00(S); $2.19/wk; $9.50/mo; $106.02/yr.
Advertising: Open inch rate $29.43(m); $29.43(m-sat); $32.16(S). **Representative:** Papert Companies.
News Services: AP, NEA, NYT, SHNS. **Politics:** Independent. **Established:** 1913.
Advertising not accepted: All advertising subject to approval; Upside down ads.
Special Editions: Leisure Time, Dining Out (Jan); Martin County Fair (Mar); Health Matters, Stuart Scene (Apr); Leisure Time, Mother's Day (May); Hurricane Section (June); Leisure Time, Football (Aug); Health Matters, Stuart Scene (Oct); Gift Guide, Treasure Guide (Nov); Stuart Scene (Dec); Coupon Book, Active Times (Quarterly).
Special Weekly Section: Real Estate Preview (fri to S).
Magazines: TV Pastime, Parade (S).

CORPORATE OFFICER
President Thomas E Weber Jr

GENERAL MANAGEMENT
Business Manager Rebecca K Freeman
Controller Theresa Caruthers
Personnel Director Janice Green

ADVERTISING
Director Greg Anderson
Manager-Classified James Dyer
Manager-Retail Jonathan Pat Bridges

MARKETING AND PROMOTION
Director-Marketing/Promotion Elena Lopez
Manager-Home Delivery Molly Hileman

TELECOMMUNICATIONS
Audiotex Manager Greg Anderson

CIRCULATION
Director Michael Manis
Manager-Single Copy John MacMenamin

NEWS EXECUTIVES
Editor Thomas E Weber Jr
Managing Editor Nancy B Smith

EDITORS AND MANAGERS
City Editor Todd J Pratt
Editorial Page Editor Edward (Ted) Burrows
Entertainment/Amusements Editor Martha W Wilson
Health/Medical Editor Martha W Wilson
News Editor Allan Schilling
Photo Editor Henry L Wilson
Religion Editor Martha W Wilson
Science/Technology Editor Martha W Wilson
Sports Editor Jeff Green
Television/Film Editor Robert J Betcher
Theater/Music Editor Robert J Betcher
Travel Editor Martha W Wilson

MANAGEMENT INFORMATION SERVICES
Online Manager Greg Anderson
Data Processing Director Roseann Engelke

PRODUCTION
Manager-Press John (Chip) Dunn
Manager-Mailroom Carl Reibold
Manager-Camera/Plateroom James Smithers

Market Information: Zoned editions; Split Run; TMC; ADS; Operate database; Operate audiotex.

Mechanical available: Offset; Black and 3 ROP colors; insert accepted — preprinted; page cut-offs — 22¾".
Mechanical specifications: Type page 13" x 21½"; E - 6 cols, 2 1/16", ⅛" between; A - 6 cols, 2 1/16", ⅛" between; C - 9 cols, 1⅜", ⅛" between.
Commodity consumption: Newsprint 6,800 metric tons; widths 55", 41¼", 27½", 13¾"; black ink 105,000 pounds; color ink 24,000 pounds; single pages printed 25,452; average pages per issue 61(d), 119(S); single plates used 50,000.
Equipment: EDITORIAL: Front-end hardware — AT/7000, 48-AT; Front-end software — R4 4.49; Printers — 1-Dataproducts/8500; Other equipment — 1-HI/8900, 4-HI/2100, 1-HI/8300, HI/XP-21 Pagination System, 4-Sun. CLASSIFIED: Front-end hardware — 1-AT/7000, 9-AT; Front-end software — R4 4.49; AUDIOTEX: Hardware — PC/486; Software — Micro Voice. DISPLAY: Adv layout systems — 4-Ap/Mac, 5-Ap/Mac Power PC, SCS/Layout 8000; Front-end hardware — PC/386, 5-Ap/Mac Power PC; Front-end software — SCS/Layout 8000, Multi-Ad/Creator, QuarkXPress, Adobe/Photoshop; Printers — HP/LaserJet, QMS/230 Color Printer; Other equipment — Microtek/Scanmaker II XE Color Scanner. PRODUCTION: Pagination software — HI/Release 2; OCR software — Ap/Mac 7.0; Typesetters — 2-MON/Express Series-3, AG/Imagemaster 5000; Plate exposures — Nu/Plate Burner, Nu/ATC FT40APRNS; Plate processors — 2-W, 1-WL; Electronic picture desk — Lf/AP Leaf Picture Desk, HI, Ap/Mac Photoshop; Scanners — Kk/2035, Scitex/Smart 340L; Production cameras — 1-C/Spartan, 1-C/Newspager; Automatic film processors — 2-LE, 1-DP, LE/LD2600A, C/Powermatic 66 RA; Film transporters — 1-LE. PRESSROOM: Line 1 — 5-MAN/Uniman 4x2 (w/4 color decks); Line 2 — ABD/9985 2-color; Line 3 — ABD/11x17; Line 4 — ABD/13x17 1/2; Press drives — GE; Folders — 1-MAN/2:1, MM/335-TV Saddle Stitcher; Pasters — 5-MEG. MAILROOM: Counter stackers — 2-HL/Monitor, 1-HT/Monitor; Inserters and stuffers — 1-GMA/SLS 1000; Bundle tyer — 2-MLN/2A, 1-PSN/5, 1-PSN/25, 1-PSN/6, 1-Newstyer/2000; Wrapping singles — 3-HL/Monarch; Other mailroom equipment — MM/1529. LIBRARY: Electronic — Newsview. COMMUNICATIONS: Digital ad delivery system — AP AdSend. Systems used — satellite. WIRE SERVICES: News — AP, NYT, SHNS, TV Data, Teleram; Photos — AP; Stock tables — AP Stockmaster; Syndicates — United Media; Receiving dishes — size-1m, AP. BUSINESS COMPUTERS: 1-IBM/AS400 B35; Applications: Billing, Adv mgmt; PCs & micros networked; PCs & main system networked.

TALLAHASSEE

Leon County

'90 U.S. Census- 124,773; E&P '96 Est. 149,092
ABC-NDM (90): 192,493 (HH 74,828)

Tallahassee Democrat (m-mon to sat; S)

Tallahassee Democrat, 277 N. Magnolia Dr.; PO Box 990, Tallahassee, FL 32302-0990; tel (904) 599-2100; fax (904) 656-5727; e-mail letters@freenet.fsu.edu. Knight-Ridder Inc. group.
Circulation: 57,044(m); 57,044(m-sat); 78,701(S); ABC circulation average for 12 months ended Sept. 30, 1995.
Price: 50¢(d); 50¢(sat); $1.25(S); $3.18/wk; $13.78/mo; $165.36/yr.
Advertising: Open inch rate $39.90(m); $44.80(m-thur); 44.80(m-fri); $44.80(m-sat); $54.88(S). **Representatives:** Landon Associates Inc.; Publishers' Representatives of Florida.
News Services: KRT, AP, LAT-WP. **Established:** 1905.
Special Editions: Business Outlook, College Student Limelight (Jan); Parade of Homes, Graduation (May); College Student, Limelight (June); Football Preview, School's In, College Student Limelight (Aug); Home Decorating (Oct); Basketball Preview (Nov); Bowl Guide, Football Weekend (Dec); Style Magazine, Money Clip Coupon Book (monthly).
Special Weekly Sections: Your Health (mon); Families (tues); Business (wed); Food & Features (thur); Limelight (Entertainment), Gardening (fri); Religion (sat); Homes, Books, Vacation/Travel, Money & Technology (S).
Magazines: TV Magazine, Parade (S).

CORPORATE OFFICERS

President Carrol Dadisman
Senior Vice Pres Doris Dunlap
Senior Vice Pres Lou Heldman
Vice Pres-Marketing Tom Privett
Secretary Douglas C Harris
Treasurer Samuel Nottage

GENERAL MANAGEMENT

Publisher Carrol Dadisman
Chief Financial Officer Samuel Nottage
Senior Vice Pres/General Manager Doris Dunlap

ADVERTISING

Vice Pres-Marketing Tom Privett
Manager-Retail/National Phyllis McCranie

MARKETING AND PROMOTION

Vice Pres-Marketing Tom Privett

TELECOMMUNICATIONS

Director-Technology Chris Norman
Audiotex Manager Ed Bides

CIRCULATION

Director Tom Bartlett

NEWS EXECUTIVES

Senior Vice Pres/Exec Editor Lou Heldman
Managing Editor Bob Shaw
Asst Managing Editor Janie Nelson

EDITORS AND MANAGERS

Automotive Editor Sue Ray
Books Editor Susan Beason
Business Editor Judy Doyle
City Editor Byron Dobson
Editorial Page Editor Andrea Brunais
Education-Secondary/Higher Bill Berlow
Entertainment/Amusements Editor Zilpha Underwood
Environmental Editor Zannah Lyle
Features Editor Zilpha Underwood
Food Editor Lorrie Guttman
Graphics Editor L K Mirrer
Health/Medical Editor Susan Beason
Librarian Debra Galloway
Living/Lifestyle Editor Zilpha Underwood
Music Editor Zilpha Underwood
News Editor Mark Pudlow
Director-Photography Bob Andres
Political Editor Mark Pankowski
Radio/Television Editor Zilpha Underwood
Real Estate Editor Barbara Laughlin
Religion Editor Martha Brown
Science/Technology Editor Zannah Lyle
Sports Editor Pete Reinwald
Travel Editor Susan Beason
Women's Editor Zilpha Underwood

MANAGEMENT INFORMATION SERVICES

Director-Technology Chris Norman

PRODUCTION

Manager-Press Bruce Erbeck
Manager-Commercial Service Ray Green
Manager-Pre Press Bill Taylor

Market Information: Zoned editions; Split Run; ADS; Operate audiotex.
Mechanical available: Offset; Black and 3 ROP colors; insert accepted — preprinted, catalogs, Bantam books, product samples; page cut-offs — 22¾".
Mechanical specifications: Type page 13" x 21½"; E - 6 cols, 2 1/16", ⅛" between; A - 6 cols, 2 1/16", ⅛" between; C - 9 cols, 1⅜", 1/16" between.
Commodity consumption: Newsprint 10,862 short tons; 9,854 metric tons; widths 54¾", 41 1/16", 27¼", 35", 26⅜", 17½", 34", 17"; black ink 218,787 pounds; color ink 75,426 pounds; single pages printed 24,421; average pages per issue 60(d), 104(S); single plates used 82,500.
Equipment: EDITORIAL: Front-end hardware — 4-AT/7000, 52-AT; Front-end software — AT; Printers — Unity/Lasermaster. CLASSIFIED: Front-end hardware — 2-DEC/File Server, 21-IBM/PC Workstation; Front-end software — Cybergraphics; Printers — Ap/Mac 1600-600. DISPLAY: Adv layout systems — CJ/Layout; Front-end hardware — Ap/Mac, Compaq/PC; Front-end software — QuarkXPress 3.3, Adobe/Photoshop 2.5, Adobe/Illustrator; Printers — Tektronix, HP/Color LaserJet, LaserMaster. PRODUCTION: Typesetters — 2-MON/Express, 1-MON/Prism, 1-Linotype-Hell, 1-APSE/6; Plate exposures — Nu/Flip Top; Plate processors — Anocoil, 1-WL/380, 5-Ap/Mac cx, 1-DEC/LN, 1-Laser Printer, Anocoil/Subtractive, L/Subtractive; Electronic picture desk — Lf/AP Leaf Picture Desk; Scanners — 2-Lf, 2-Kk; Production cameras — 1-C/Spartan, 1-C/Marathon, ECR/Autokon 1000DE; Automatic film processors — 3-LE, 2-C, 1-LE, 1-P; Digital color separation equipment — Ap/Mac w/ Adobe/Photoshop 2.5. PRESSROOM: Line 1 — 7-G/Metro (4 decks); Line 2 — 6-G/Urbanite; Folders — 1-G/Double, 1-SU; Pasters — G/Automatic RTP; Reels and stands — 4-G/Urbanite high roll stand. MAILROOM: Counter stackers — 3-Id/NS-440, 3-MM/310-20; Inserters and stuffers — 3-MM/227; Bundle tyer — 5-MLN/MLN-2, 1-MLN/MLEE, 1-MLN/MLNHS, 1-Icore; Wrapping singles — 3-QWI/50" bottom wrap; Addressing machine — KAN/500 8L2. LIBRARY: Electronic — Vu/Text SAVE. COMMUNICATIONS: Systems used — satellite, fiber optic. WIRE SERVICES: News — AP, AP Datafeatures; Stock tables — AP; Receiving dishes — AP. BUSINESS COMPUTERS: 1-HP/3000-925, CJ, 1-HP/9000; Applications: Payroll, Circ; Word Processing: Adv, Gen ledger, Personnel, Inventory; PCs & micros networked; PCs & main system networked.

TAMPA

Hillsborough County

'90 U.S. Census- 280,015; E&P '96 Est. 287,943
ABC-NDM (90): 933,764 (HH 362,386)

Tampa Tribune (m-mon to sat)
Tampa Tribune and Times (S)

Tampa Tribune and Times, 202 Parker St., Tampa, FL 33606; tel (813) 259-7711; web site http://www.tampatrib.com/. Media General Inc. group.
Circulation: 263,674(m); 263,674(m-sat); 361,048(S); ABC circulation average for 12 months ended Sept. 30, 1995.
Price: 25¢(d); 25¢(sat); 75¢(S)(NDM)/$1.00 (AOZ); $2.50/wk (mS); $130.00/yr (mS).
Advertising: Open inch rate $236.00(m); $236.00(m-sat); $319.00(S). **Representative:** Sawyer-Ferguson-Walker Co.
News Services: AP, UPI, NYT. **Politics:** Independent. **Established:** 1895.
Advertising not accepted: Any deemed objectionable either in its text or illustration.
Special Editions: Florida Brides Book, Newcomer's Guide, Great Britain Travel (Jan); Gasparilla, Valentine's Specials, Financial & Tax Planning, Alaska/Canada Travel, Frozen Food, Frank Sargeant's Outdoor Expo (Feb); Spring Fashion, Spring & Summer Cruise/Tour Issue, Health & Beauty Aids, Future Farmers of America, Financial & Tax Planning Guide, Home Improvement/Spring Garden, Progress Editions, Discover the Nature Coast, Plant City Strawberry Festival, Apartment Living Guide, Frozen Food (Mar); Dining by the Bay, Child Care & Education, Progress Editions, Car Tab, Europe Travel, Art Festival, Home Show Section, Recruitment (Apr); Cruising the Caribbean, Top 50 Business Section, Private Property Week, Plant City Progress, Nat'l Nurses' Day Page, Travel Guide to Florida (May); Gifts for Dad, Hurricane Guides, Summer Cruise (June); Salute to America, Pool & Spa Guide, Ice Cream Novelties, Classified Educational Directory, Apartment Living, Bahamas Travel (July); Back-to-School, Welcome Back USF, Pro & College Football, Apartment Living Tab (Aug); High School Football Section, Newcomer's Guide, Fall & Winter Cruise Tour, Showcase of Homes, Apartment Living, Manufactured Housing, Tampa Bay's Best (Sept); Taste of Florida, Car Show, Home Furnishings, Winter Ski Challenge, Home Improvement, Mexico/Travel, Polk/Heartland Winter Resident's Guide, Discover Tampa Bay (Oct); Fall Dinning & Entertainment, The Bahamas, Christmas Gift Guide, Holiday Spirit Gift Guide (Nov); Brandon Balloon Festival, Last Minute Gift Guides, Hall of Fame Bowl, First Night (Dec).
Special Weekly Sections: Business and Financial Tab, KidsLife (mon); Science & Technology (tues); Outdoors (wed); Food & Health (thur); Friday Extra (fri); Religion, Home & Garden, Automotive (sat); Travel, Real Estate (S).
Magazines: Parade, Television Magazine, Color Comics (S).

CORPORATE OFFICERS

Board Chairman J Stewart Bryan III
Vice Chairman James Evans
President/CEO J Stewart Bryan III
Secretary A J Brent
Vice Pres Jack Butcher

GENERAL MANAGEMENT

Publisher Jack Butcher
Vice Pres/Business Manager Kermit Kauffman
Controller James Gonnering
Asst Controller Robert N Wayne
Manager-Credit Charles Wilson
Director-Human Resources Lloyd DeFrance
Manager-Communications Ric Sierra
Purchasing Agent Lee Groetzinger
Director-Research Ted Stasney
Manager-Education Service Rene Gunter

ADVERTISING

Director Jeffrey Green
Asst Director Tony DiSalvo
Manager-General Joe Gess
Manager-Retail Paul Lindsey
Manager-Retail Mike Osteen
Manager-Classified Pat Jones
Manager-Retail/Major Accounts Larry Boatwright

MARKETING AND PROMOTION

Director-Promotion Michael Kilgore
Asst Director-Promotion Fran Solomon

TELECOMMUNICATIONS

Director-Info Systems John Truffa
Audiotex Manager Pat Jones

CIRCULATION

Director Jim Horton
Manager-Administration Neil Giddens
Manager-Transportation Jim Fernandez
Manager-State Operations Bob Brown
Manager-Customer Relations/Training Lois Kindle
Manager-County Operations Wright Rhodes
Manager-Systems Brian Keena

NEWS EXECUTIVES

Managing Editor Lawrence McConnell
Deputy Managing Editor-Electronic Publishing Carl Crothers
Deputy Managing Editor Al Hutchison
Asst Managing Editor-Content Bill Skutt
Asst Managing Editor-Presentation Patti Breckenridge

EDITORS AND MANAGERS

Archives & Research Center Director Jerry Chambers
Arts Writer Joanne Miliani
BayLife Editor Janice Hall
Books Editor Joe Guidry
Business/Finance Editor Steve Matthews
Columnist Judy Hill
Columnist Leland Hawes
Columnist Steve Otto
Consumer Writer Martha Durrance
Editorial Page Editor Edwin A Roberts
Deputy Editorial Page Editor Joe Guidry
Editorial Writer James Beamguard
Editorial Writer Morris Kennedy
Higher Education Editor Jim Kenyon
Features Editor Martha Durrance
Films Editor Bob Ross
Food Editor Mary Scourtes
Home Editor Beth Dolan
Metro Editor Larry Fletcher
News Editor Dave Hardin
Political Writer Michael Sznajderman
Radio Editor Walt Belcher
Real Estate Editor Beth Dolan
Records Editor-Pop Phillip Booth
Records Editor-Classical Kurt Loft
School Editor Cheryl Schmidt
Science Editor Kurt Loft
Exec Sports Editor Paul C Smith
State Editor Steve Kaylor
Systems Editor Kim Pollard
Tampa Bay Online Editor Bill Prewitt
Travel Editor Karen Long
Theater Editor Maggie Hall
Television Editor Walt Belcher

MANAGEMENT INFORMATION SERVICES

Data Processing Director John Truffa
Online Manager Carl Crothers

PRODUCTION

Director Greg Stewart
Administration Asst Art Kimball
Manager-Pressroom Wally Cosgrove
Manager-Mailroom Danny Garren
Manager-Night Andy Sheppard
Manager-Quality Assurance Ed Eybers

Market Information: Zoned editions; Split Run; TMC; ADS; Operate database; Operate audiotex; Electronic edition.
Mechanical available: Offset; Black and 3 ROP colors; insert accepted — preprinted; page cut-offs — 22".
Mechanical specifications: Type page 13" x 21"; E - 6 cols, 2 1/16", ⅛" between; A - 6 cols, 2 1/16", ⅛" between; C - 10 cols, 1 3/16", ⅛" between.
Commodity consumption: Newsprint 69,322 short tons; widths 27⅜", 41⅛", 55"; black ink 1,381,500 pounds; color ink 480,181 pounds; average pages per issue 76(d), 158(S); single plates used 446,682.

Equipment: EDITORIAL: Front-end hardware — 5-SII/TXP, Tandem; Front-end software — SII/System 55, SII/LASR; Other equipment — 125-PC. CLASSIFIED: Front-end hardware — 5-SII/TXP, Tandem; Front-end software — SII/Turbo Czar, SII/ICP; Printers — 9-Bureau Printers, 7-Ad Proof Printers; Other equipment — 3-Echo/Workstation, 10-PC. DISPLAY: Adv layout systems — HP, CJ/Layout, III/INP-AMS; Front-end hardware — 2-III/INP, HP/957; Front-end software — CJ/Layout, III/INP, QuarkXPress; Other equipment — 10-III/AMS Workstation, 29-Ap/Mac. PRODUCTION: Pagination software — Cascade; Typesetters — 2-AU/APS Micro 5, 3-AU/APS 5, 2-III/385 Grafix Color Imagers; Platemaking systems — WL; Plate exposures — 3-WL/Lith-X-Pozer III; Plate processors — 3-Anocoil/XPH 36; Electronic picture desk — Lf/AP Leaf Picture Desk; Scanners — 2-ECR/Autokon, 2-HP/ScanJet Flatbed; Production cameras — 2-C/Pager, 1-C/Spartan, 1-C/Marathon; Automatic film processors — 4-LE, 3-Konica; Film transporters — 3-C; Shrink lenses — 1-Alan; Digital color separation equipment — 1-CD/895 Studio System, 1-CD/646-M, 1-CD/646-E.
PRESSROOM: Line 1 — 20-TKS/M72 double width; Line 2 — 20-TKS/M72 double width; Folders — 4-TKS/Double; Pasters — 20-TKS, 16-G; Reels and stands — 20-TKS, 16-G; Press control system — TKS/NPC. MAILROOM: Counter stackers — 25-QWI; Inserters and stuffers — 2-HI/1472, 5-GMA/SLS 1000, 1-S; Bundle tyer — 13-Power Strap, 8-MLN, 7-Dynamic; Wrapping singles — 1-NJP, 3-Id, 4-Ch, 8-G, 5-HL, 2-QWI; Addressing machine — 5-Wm. LIBRARY: Electronic — SII; Combination — Rotary file for Clips. WIRE SERVICES: News — AP Datafeatures, AP Datastream, AP Speed, RN, LAT-WP, NYT; Photos — AP, AFP; Stock tables — TMS; Receiving dishes — size-8 ft, AP, AFP, RN. BUSINESS COMPUTERS: 2-HP/957; Applications: CIM: Payroll, Personnel; CJ/AIM, TRN, Microsoft/Word 6.0V, Lotus 1-2-3 4.01V, Novell/Network 3.12; PCs & micros networked; PCs & main system networked.

VERO BEACH

Indian River County

'90 U.S. Census- 17,350; **E&P '96 Est.** 18,332
ABC-NDM (90): 90,208 (HH 38,057)

Vero Beach Press-Journal

(m-mon to sat; S)

Vero Beach Press-Journal, 1801 US 1 (32960); PO Box 1268, Vero Beach, FL 32961-1268; tel (407) 562-2315; fax (407) 978-2365.

Circulation: 32,920(m); 32,920(m-sat); 35,318(S); ABC circulation average for 12 months ended Sept. 30, 1995.

Price: 35¢(d); 50¢(sat); 50¢(S); $1.83/wk; $7.98/mo; $23.92/3mo, $47.83/6mo; $89.88/yr.

Advertising: Open inch rate $18.48(m); $18.48(m-sat); $18.48(S). **Representative:** Papert Companies.

News Services: AP, SHNS. **Politics:** Independent. **Established:** 1919.

Special Editions: Florida Living (Jan); Medical Booklet, Polo (Feb); Dodgers, Rest and Relaxation, Senior Lifestyles (Mar); Today's Home, Business Profile (Apr); Hurricane Coupon Booklet (May); Back-to-School, Chamber's Directory, Naval Air Station 51st Anniversary (Aug); Football, Best in Indian River County (Sept); Coupon Booklet (Oct); Discover Paradise, Gift Guide (Nov); Holiday Guide, Discover Vero (Dec).

Special Weekly Sections: TV Journal, Wheels (sat); Real Estate (S).

Magazines: Parade (S); Wheels.

GENERAL MANAGEMENT

President/Publisher	John J Schumann Jr
Assoc Publisher/General Manager	Darryl K Hicks

ADVERTISING

Manager	Melvin E Adkins
Manager-Classified	Barbara Sprague

MARKETING AND PROMOTION

Manager-Display Advertising	Melvin E Adkins

CIRCULATION

Director	Tom Dickens

NEWS EXECUTIVE

Editor	Larry Reisman

EDITORS AND MANAGERS

Administrative Editor	Cheryl McCloud
Features Editor	Mike Bogin
Lifestyle Editor	Charlotte Atkins
Local News Editor	Jennifer Daniel
News Editor-Night	Dennis Durkee
Opinion Page Editor	Tom Moczydlowski
Sports Editor	Bill Boeding

MANAGEMENT INFORMATION SERVICES

Data Processing Manager	Peggy Ungos

PRODUCTION

Director	Tom Dickens
Manager-Press	Joe Giambalvo
Manager-Composing	Bill Usher

Market Information: TMC; ADS.

Mechanical available: Offset; Black; insert accepted — preprinted; page cut-offs — 22¾".

Mechanical specifications: Type page 13" x 21½"; E - 6 cols, 2.08", ⅛" between; A - 6 cols, 2.08", ⅛" between; C - 6 cols, 2.08", ⅛" between.

Commodity consumption: Newsprint 3,925 short tons; width 27½"; average pages per issue 45(d), 76(S); single plates used 22,000.

Equipment: EDITORIAL: Front-end hardware — HI/XP-21, ISSI/2640 Systems; Front-end software — HI 7.5, ISSI 7.0; Printers — Centronics, AU/Laser 6600; Other equipment — Ap/Mac IIci. CLASSIFIED: Front-end hardware — ISSI/2640 Systems, HI/Class Pag.; Front-end software — ISSI/Rel 7.0, HI/Rel 8.0; Printers — Centronics. DISPLAY: Front-end hardware — HI/8900, X/7650, Sun/Sparc 2; Front-end software — HI 7.5, Sun/Sparc2 MacServer; Other equipment — HI/Pixel Editor. PRODUCTION: Pagination software — HI; OCR software — Calera; Typesetters — AU/Laser; Plate exposures — 1-Nu; Plate processors — Nat; Electronic picture desk — Lf/AP Leaf Picture Desk; Scanners — ISSI/Text Scanning Sub-System, X; Production cameras — C/Spartan III; Automatic film processors — 1-Konica/66F, 1-Konica/K400; Film transporters — 1-LE; Color separation equipment (conventional) — 1-ScanMate/5000, 1-Kk/2035 RFS.
PRESSROOM: Line 1 — 12-HI/NC 450; Folders — 1-HI/RB2; Reels and stands — 9-HI. MAILROOM: Counter stackers — 2-HL/Monitor HT; Inserters and stuffers — 1-GMA/SLS 1000, 1-MM/227 4-1; Bundle tyer — 2-Power Strap/PSN5. LIBRARY: Electronic — SMS/Stauffer Gold. WIRE SERVICES: News — AP, SHNS; Photos — AP, ; Stock tables — AP; Syndicates — LAT-WP, NAS, NEA, CNS, McNaught; Receiving dishes — AP. BUSINESS COMPUTERS: 1-IBM/Sys 36; Applications: Class, Display, Accts receivable, Accts payable, Inventory; PCs & micros networked; PCs & main system networked.

WEST PALM BEACH

Palm Beach County

'90 U.S. Census- 67,643; **E&P '96 Est.** 71,284
ABC-CZ (90): 449,677 (HH 194,493)

The Palm Beach Post

(m-mon to sat; S)

The Palm Beach Post, 2751 S. Dixie Hwy.; PO Box 24700, West Palm Beach, FL 33416-4700; tel (407) 820-4100; fax (407) 820-4136; web site http://www.gate.net/storm95/. Cox Newspapers Inc. group.

Circulation: 173,699(m); 173,699(m-sat); 222,213(S); ABC circulation average for 12 months ended Sept. 30, 1995.

Price: 50¢(d); 50¢(sat); $1.25(S); $2.85/wk.

Advertising: Open inch rate $89.34(m); $92.69(m-sat); $111.54(S). **Representative:** Publishers' Representatives of Florida.

News Services: AP, Bloomberg, CSM, LAT-WP, NYT, PR Newswire, RN, Cox. **Politics:** Independent. **Established:** 1908.

Advertising not accepted: Escort services; Palmists.

Special Editions: Dining Book, Race for the Cure, Super Bowl Guide, Treasure Coast Business Profiles (Jan); Artigras, Guide to the South, South Florida Seniors, Tri County Fair, Voyages, Spring Training/Baseball (Feb); Fact Book, Career Guide, Boynton Gala, Northwood Institute, Auto Show, Guide to the North (Mar); PGA Seniors, Delray Affair, Sunfest (Apr); Florida Travel, Top 50 Companies, Health (May); Guide to the West, Hurricane, Treasure Coast Leaders (June); Guide to the South, Summer Olympics, Boca Festival (July); Football, Guide to Central County (Aug); Family & Home (Sept); South Florida Seniors, Discover the Treasure Coast, Season Preview, Guide to the West (Oct); New Car Buyer's Guide, Guide to the North, Holiday Idea Book (Nov); Zoned Gift Guides (Dec).

Special Weekly Sections: Business Day One Tab (mon); Notables Tab (wed); Food & Dining, Zoned Automotive (thur); TGIF (Entertainment tab), Real Estate Weekend (fri); Travel, Art & Entertainment, Opinion, Home & Garden, Business (S).

Magazines: TV Post, Parade, Color Comics (S).

GENERAL MANAGEMENT

Publisher	Tom Giuffrida
Exec Vice Pres/General Manager	Lon Danielson
Editor	Edward M Sears
Vice Pres/Treasurer	Lawrence E Siedlik
Controller	David Purdom
Manager-Credit	Ted Chittick
Director-Human Resources	Linda Murphy
Manager-Purchasing	Betty Finley
Director-Community Relations/Newspapers in Education	Gale Howden
Manager-Data Processing	John Occhipinti

ADVERTISING

Vice Pres	Alan Ferguson
Director-Classified	Van Esselstyn
Director-Operations	Joe Ernst
Manager-National	Bob Berry
Manager-Major Accounts	Pat Rogell
Manager-TMC/Commercial Printing	Ann Bruffy
Manager-Retail	Rick Beckman

MARKETING AND PROMOTION

Director-Marketing	Ken Walters
Manager-Research	Suzanne Willcox

TELECOMMUNICATIONS

Manager	Ken Steinhoff
Audiotex Manager	Dan Shorter

CIRCULATION

Vice Pres	Thomas G Highfield
Manager-Operations	Gary Evans
Manager-Single Copy	Steve Phillabaum
Manager-Customer Info Service	Linda Campbell

NEWS EXECUTIVES

Manager-Research	Suzanne Willcox
Managing Editor	Tom O'Hara
Asst Managing Editor	John Bartosek
Asst Managing Editor-Features/Graphics	Jan Tuckwood
Asst to Managing Editor	Lynn Kalber

EDITORS AND MANAGERS

Arts/Architecture Editor	Gary Schwan
Books Editor	Scott Eyman
Business Editor	Kevin Miller
Business Columnist	Bob Douglas
Capitol Reporter	Larry Kaplow
Delray Beach Bureau Chief	Susan Garlock
Editorial Page Editor	Randy Schultz
Editorial Cartoonist	Don Wright
Education Editor	Viola Gienger
Environmental Editor	Willie Howard
Farm/Agriculture Editor	Lisa Shuchman
Fashion Editor	Christine Keating
Food Editor	Jan Norris
Features Editor	Pat Morgan
Home/Society Editor	Ava van de Water
Librarian	Mary Kate Leming
Medical Section Editor	Stephanie Jackson
Metro Editor	Fred Zipp
Music Editor-Rock	Scott Benarde
Music Editor-Classical	Charles Passy
News Editor	Bill Greer
Political/Government Editor	Brian Crowley
Photo Department Director	Pete Cross
Reader Representative	Charles Bond
Real Estate Editor	Linus Chua
Religion Editor	Steve Gushee
State Editor	Price Patton
Systems Editor	Chuck Keefer
Travel Editor	Cheryl Blackerby
Washington Bureau Chief	Larry Lipman

PRODUCTION

Manager	Bob Balfe
Manager-Pre Press	Gregg Harr
Superintendent-Composing	Roger Schram
Superintendent-Press	Henry Taylor Jr
Superintendent-Mailroom	Greg Brown
Superintendent-Building	Lex Stinchcomb
Superintendent-Camera/Platemaking	Craig Olson

Market Information: Zoned editions; Split Run; TMC; Operate database; Operate audiotex.

Mechanical available: Offset; Black and 3 ROP colors; insert accepted — preprinted; page cut-offs — 23$\frac{9}{16}$".

Mechanical specifications: Type page 13" x 22½"; E - 6 cols, 2$\frac{1}{16}$", ⅛" between; A - 6 cols, 2$\frac{1}{16}$", ⅛" between; C - 10 cols, 1$\frac{9}{16}$", $\frac{1}{16}$" between.

Commodity consumption: Newsprint 40,298 short tons; widths 54", 40½", 27"; black ink 693,480 pounds; color ink 221,834 pounds; single pages printed 33,773; average pages per issue 78(d), 78(sat), 178(S); single plates used 328,000.

Equipment: EDITORIAL: Front-end hardware — 8-AT/CPU, 200-AT/VDT, 10-Ap/Mac; Front-end software — AT; Other equipment — 3-PC/Networks in Bureaus. CLASSIFIED: Front-end hardware — 4-AT/CPU, 58-AT/VDT; Front-end software — AT; Other equipment — Ricoh/77 Fax, Canon/510 Fax. AUDIOTEX: Hardware — PEP/Voice Print. DISPLAY: Adv layout systems — SCS/Layout 8000, 4-AT/Display Ad Raw Input; Front-end hardware — 12-Ap/Mac, 2-PC/386; Front-end software — ATT/SCO Unix, SCS/Layout 8000, Adobe/Illustrator; Printers — 3-HP/LaserJet III, C.Itoh/CI400Q. PRODUCTION: Typesetters — 3-AU/APS 6, 2-Doley/400; Platemaking systems — 2-WL; Plate exposures — 2-WL; Plate processors — KFM; Electronic picture desk — Lf/AP Leaf Picture Desk; Scanners — 2-ECR/Autokon 1000; Production cameras — 1-C/Spartan, 1-C/Pager; Automatic film processors — LE, Konica; Film transporters — Konica; Shrink lenses — Alan; Color separation equipment (conventional) — CD, Smart/340L; Digital color separation equipment — Scitex.
PRESSROOM: Line 1 — 24-G/Metro (12 color decks); Line 2 — 12-G/Suburban; Line 3 — 6-G/Colorliner; Folders — 3-G; Pasters — 32-G; Reels and stands — 32-G; Press control system — Allen Bradley/Quadtech. MAILROOM: Counter stackers — 1-MM, 1-PPK, 9-HL, 1-Statpak; Inserters and stuffers — 3-SLS/1000; Bundle tyer — 11-Dynaric; Wrapping singles — 4-Constellation; Addressing machine — KR; Mailroom control system — GMA. LIBRARY: Electronic — Vu/Text SAVE. COMMUNICATIONS: Digital ad delivery system — AP AdSend. Systems used — satellite. WIRE SERVICES: News — AP, AP Datafeatures, Bloomberg, LAT-WP, NYT, PR Newswire, RN; Stock tables — AP SelectStox II; Syndicates — AP, RN, North America Syndicate; Receiving dishes — size-5m, AP, RN, INS. BUSINESS COMPUTERS: Unisys/2200; Applications: Circ, Adv, Payroll, Gen ledger; PCs & micros networked; PCs & main system networked.

WINTER HAVEN

Polk County

'90 U.S. Census- 24,725; **E&P '96 Est.** 27,814

News Chief (m-mon to sat; S)

News Chief, 650 6th St. S.W. (33880); PO Box 1440, Winter Haven, FL 33882; tel (941) 294-7731; fax (941) 294-2008. Morris Communications Corp. group.

Circulation: 9,002(m); 9,002(m-sat); 9,002 (S); Sworn Sept. 30, 1994.

Price: 25¢(d); 25¢(sat); 50¢(S); $7.25/mo; $132.08/yr.

Advertising: Open inch rate $17.89(m); $17.89(m-sat); $20.54(S). **Representative:** Papert Companies.

News Services: AP, SHNS. **Politics:** Independent. **Established:** 1911.

Note: Effective Oct. 27, 1995, this publication changed its publishing plan from (e-mon to fri; m-sat; S) to (m-mon to sat; S).

Special Editions: Newcomer's Guide (Jan); Citrus Exposition (Feb); Progress (Mar).

Magazines: Retirement Living (bi-monthly, thur); Accent, Real Estate (fri); Florida Outdoors (sat); TV Showtime (S).

GENERAL MANAGEMENT

Editor/Publisher	Joe Ben Oller
Business Manager	George MacConnell

ADVERTISING

Manager	Tom Duncan

CIRCULATION

Director	Alex Santiago
Manager-Operations	Jim Murray

NEWS EXECUTIVES

Exec Editor	Gary E Maitland
Managing Editor	Bob Sims

EDITORS AND MANAGERS

Books Editor	Velma Daniels
City Editor	Charles Parker
Food Editor	Jennifer Shenkman
Lifestyle Editor	Jennifer Shenkman
Sports Editor	Robert McGinnity

PRODUCTION

Manager	Dennis Wilkinson

Mechanical available: Offset; Black and 3 ROP colors; insert accepted — preprinted; page cut-offs — 22¾".

Mechanical specifications: Type page 13" x 21½"; E - 6 cols, 2 1/16", 1/8" between; A - 6 cols, 2 1/16", 1/8" between; C - 6 cols, 2 1/16", 1/8" between.
Commodity consumption: Newsprint 2,150 short tons; width 27½"; average pages per issue 40(d), 71(S).
Equipment: EDITORIAL: Front-end hardware — 6-Ap/Mac IIcx, 1-Ap/Mac fx fileserver, 12-Ap/Mac Plus; Front-end software — Caere/OmniPage; Other equipment — Ap/Mac Scanner, 2-RSK/TRS 80-1100. CLASSIFIED: Front-end hardware — Ap/Mac IIfx fileserver, 13-Ap/Mac se130. DISPLAY: Adv layout systems — Ap/Mac IIcx, 2-HI/1760; Other equipment — CD-Rom/Scanners. PRODUCTION: Typesetters — 2-V/4000 RIP/5500 Typesetter; Plate exposures — 2-Nu/40; Plate processors — 2-Nat/A250; Scanners — Ap/Mac IIfx, Howtek; Production cameras — 1-C/Spartan II; Automatic film processors — Konica; Reproportion units — 1-ECR/Autokon 8400; Digital color separation equipment — Ap/Mac IIfx, Nikon.
PRESSROOM: Line 1 — 6-G Urbanite/(1-Three Color); Line 2 — 8-HI/V-15A (Color deck); Folders — 1-G, 1-HI. MAILROOM: Counter stackers — 1-MM/1231, 1-QWI/928; Inserters and stuffers — 1-S/NP524, 1-MM/227; Bundle tyer — 2-MLN/MLN; Addressing machine — 1-El, 1-KAN/Labeler. LIBRARY: Electronic — 1-IDI/201-1. WIRE SERVICES: News — AP; Syndicates — North America Syndicate; Receiving dishes — AP. BUSINESS COMPUTERS: ATT/6386 E-33 WGS; Applications: Circ, Adv billing, Accts receivable, Gen ledger, Payroll; PCs & micros networked.

GEORGIA

ALBANY

Dougherty County

'90 U.S. Census- 78,122; E&P '96 Est. 82,034
ABC-CZ (90): 91,749 (HH 32,690)

The Albany Herald

(m-mon to sat; S)

The Albany Herald, 126 N. Washington St. (31701); PO Box 48, Albany, GA 31702-0048; tel (912) 888-9300; fax (912) 888-9357. Gray Communications group.
Circulation: 32,964(m); 32,964(m-sat); 39,409(S); ABC Sept. 30, 1995.
Price: 50¢(d); 50¢(sat); $1.25(S); $10.00/wk; $120.00/yr.
Advertising: Open inch rate $23.25(m); $23.25(m-sat); $26.75(S). **Representative:** Papert Companies.
News Service: AP. **Established:** 1891.
Not Published: Fortune telling.
Special Editions: Kids Quarterly, Outdoors (Jan); Outlook, Football (Feb); Design-an-Ad, Albany Mall (Mar); Kids Quarterly, Outdoors, Artesian Spring Festival, Reader's Choice Awards (Apr); Graduation, Home Builders (May); Family-owned Business (June); Albany Mall (July); Football, Kids Quarterly, Outdoors, Restaurant Guide, Back-to-School, Albany Mall (Aug); Kids Quarterly, Albany Mall, Clean Community Commision (Oct).
Special Weekly Sections: Business in Review (mon); The Herald Express (TMC), Food (wed); TV Times, Automotive (fri); Living, Real Estate Showcase (S); The Lee County Herald; The Worth County Herald; The Calhoun/Clay Herald.
Magazines: Farm & Plantation Magazine (thur); USA Weekend, Comic Section (S).
Broadcast Affiliates: WJHG-TV Panama City, FL; WALB-TV Albany, GA; WYMT Hazard, KY; WKYT Lexington, KY.

CORPORATE OFFICERS

CEO/President John T Williams
Board Chairman William E Mayher III
Chief Financial Officer/Vice Pres William A Fielder III
Secretary Marcie E Crowe

GENERAL MANAGEMENT

Publisher Christian R Schilt
Controller Chris Echols

ADVERTISING

Director Liz Sills
Manager-Retail Michelle Factor
Manager-Classified/Telemarketing Eddie Tyner

MARKETING AND PROMOTION

Manager-Marketing/Promotion Kimberly Heidt

TELECOMMUNICATIONS

Audiotex Manager M C Brooks

CIRCULATION

Director Billy St Clair

NEWS EXECUTIVES

Editor Kay Read
Managing Editor Phil Lucas

EDITORS AND MANAGERS

City Editor Danny Carter
Chief Photographer Denis McElroy
Lifestyle Editor Don Hudson
Sports Editor Steve Ellis
State Editor David Pierce

PRODUCTION

Director-Operations William L Bright
Manager-Info Systems Bill Strickland
Supervisor-Composing Don Kimsey
Supervisor-Pressroom Perry Griggs
Supervisor-Camera Paul Warner
Supervisor-Mailroom David Reed

Market Information: Zoned editions; TMC; Operate audiotex.
Mechanical available: Offset; Black and 3 ROP colors; insert accepted — preprinted; page cutoffs — 22¾".
Mechanical specifications: Type page 13" x 21½"; E - 6 cols, 2 1/16", 1/6" between; A - 6 cols, 2 1/16", 1/6" between; C - 9 cols, 1⅜", 1/8" between.
Commodity consumption: Newsprint 3,400 short tons; width 27½"; black ink 52,500 pounds; color ink 17,900 pounds; single pages printed 13,000; average pages per issue 25(d), 62(S); single plates used 16,492.
Equipment: EDITORIAL: Front-end hardware — SCS, 3-Dell, 40-Falco, 6-Ap/Mac; Front-end software — SCS, QuarkXPress; Printers — 3-Ap/Mac LaserPrinters. CLASSIFIED: Front-end hardware — SCS/Class, 10-Falco/VDT, 2-IBM/PS2, 1-Ap/Mac Quadra, 2-Dell/466XE Networked; Front-end software — SCS/Classified 8000; Printers — 2-PostScript/Laser Printers. AUDIOTEX: Hardware — Texas Micro/486; Software — Info-Connect; Supplier name — Info-Connect. DISPLAY: Adv layout systems — SCS; Front-end hardware — 5-Ap/Mac IIci; Front-end software — Multi-Ad/Creator; Printers — 2-PostScript/Laser Printer; Other equipment — CD-Rom. PRODUCTION: Pagination software — SCS, QuarkXPress; Typesetters — 2-AU/APS-6-84; Plate exposures — 2-Nu; Plate processors — 1-Nat/A340; Electronic picture desk — Lf/AP Leaf Picture Desk; Production cameras — C/Spartan III, C/Newspager; Automatic film processors — 2-P, 2-LE; Color separation equipment (conventional) — WDS.
PRESSROOM: Line 1 — 9-G/Urbanite; Folders — G/2:1; Press control system — 3-Fin/Control Console. MAILROOM: Counter stackers — 3-MM/310, 1-MM/288; Inserters and stuffers — 3-MM/227; Bundle tyer — 2-Dynaric/NP2, 1-MVP; Addressing machine — 3-Wm. WIRE SERVICES: News — AP Datastream, AP Datafeatures; Receiving dishes — size-10ft, AP. BUSINESS COMPUTERS: SCS, 2-Dell, 20-Falco; Applications: Circ, Payroll, Accts payable, Accts receivable, Gen ledger.

AMERICUS

Sumter County

'90 U.S. Census- 16,512; E&P '96 Est. 16,948

Americus Times-Recorder

(e-mon to fri; m-sat)

Americus Times-Recorder, 1612 Vienna Rd.; PO Box 1247, Americus, GA 31709; tel (912) 924-2751; fax (912) 928-6344. Thomson Newspapers group.
Circulation: 7,382(e); 7,382(m-sat); Sworn Sept. 29, 1993.
Price: 35¢(d); 35¢(sat); $7.75/mo; $93.00/yr.
Advertising: Open inch rate $11.16(e); $11.16(m-sat). **Representative:** Thomson Newspapers.
News Services: AP, TNN. **Politics:** Independent. **Established:** 1879.
Not Published: New Year; Memorial Day; Independence Day; Labor Day; Thanksgiving; Christmas.
Special Editions: Tax Section, Insurance Week (Jan); Bride Section, Business & Service Directory (Feb); Lawn & Garden, Spring Fashion (Mar); Lindberg Days, Car Care (Apr); Mother's Day, Community Progress Guide, Private Property Week (May); Father's Day, Summer Recreation (June); Christmas in July (July); Back-to-School, Football (Aug); On Campus GSW (Sept); Fall Harvest, Home-owned Business (Oct); Women in Business, ValueTown-Thanksgiving (Nov); Holiday Cookbook, Home for the Holidays, Gift Ideas, Last Minute Gift Ideas, Christmas Greetings (Dec).
Special Weekly Sections: Best Food Day (tues); Church News (sat); Best Real Estate Day, Best Legal Day (fri).

CORPORATE OFFICER

Group Publisher Keith Blevins

GENERAL MANAGEMENT

Publisher Daryl Henning
Purchasing Agent Mary Camp

ADVERTISING

Manager Jeff Masters

CIRCULATION

Manager Pete McDonald

NEWS EXECUTIVES

Editor M Elizabeth Alston
Managing Editor M Elizabeth Alston

EDITORS AND MANAGERS

Columnist M Elizabeth Alston
Reporter Christopher Sheets
Reporter Hal McKenzie
Society/Women's Editor Leila Barrett
Sports Editor Don Fletcher

PRODUCTION

Manager Jeff Masters
Foreman-Pressroom Robert Murray

Market Information: TMC.
Mechanical available: Offset; Black and 3 ROP colors; insert accepted — preprinted, single sheet; page cut-offs — 22¾".
Mechanical specifications: Type page 13" x 21½"; E - 6 cols, 2 1/16", 1/8" between; A - 6 cols, 2 1/16", 1/8" between; C - 9 cols, 1⅞", 1/16" between.
Commodity consumption: Newsprint 206 short tons; widths 27½", 13¾"; black ink 2,500 pounds; color ink 600 pounds; single pages printed 4,284; average pages per issue 14(d), 14(sat); single plates used 2,650.
Equipment: EDITORIAL: Front-end hardware — 7-Ap/Mac LC III, 2-Ap/Mac Centris 610. CLASSIFIED: Front-end hardware — 1-Ap/Mac Centris 610; Other equipment — 4-ATT. DISPLAY: Adv layout systems — Ap/Mac IIci, Ap/Mac 610 Centris; Front-end hardware — Ap/Mac IIci, Ap/Mac 610 Centris; Front-end software — Multi-Ad/Creator, Aldus/FreeHand, Adobe/Illustrator, QuarkXPress; Printers — 2-Ap/Mac LaserPrinter, Tegra/Varityper/5060W, Tegra/Varityper/600W. PRODUCTION: Typesetters — Ap/Mac IIci, Ap/Mac 610 Centris; Electronic picture desk — Lf/Leafscan 35; Production cameras — B/Horizontal, SCREEN/Vertical; Automatic film processors — SCREEN/220 QT Film processors; Color separation equipment (conventional) — Lf/Leafscan 35; Digital color separation equipment — V/4000 Recorder, V/5300.
PRESSROOM: Line 1 — G/Community (w/upper former); Folders — G/Half, G/Quarter. MAILROOM: Inserters and stuffers — KR/4-pocket; Bundle tyer — MLN/Auto Bundler. COMMUNICATIONS: Facsimile — Murata. WIRE SERVICES: News — TNN, AP; Photos — AP; Receiving dishes — size-3ft, AP. BUSINESS COMPUTERS: 4-ATT, 1-Compaq/PC, 1-ATT/PC-19; PCs & micros networked; PCs & main system networked.

ATHENS

Clarke County

'90 U.S. Census- 45,734; E&P '96 Est. 48,706
ABC-CZ (90): 87,594 (HH 33,170)

Athens Daily News

(m-mon to fri)

Athens Banner-Herald

(e-mon to fri)

Athens Banner-Herald/ Daily News (m-sat; S)

Athens Daily News/Banner-Herald, One Press Pl.; Box 912, Athens, GA 30603-0912; tel (706) 549-0123; fax (706) 543-5234. Morris Communications Corp. group.
Circulation: 18,321(m); 12,023(e); 35,950(m-sat); 36,417(S); ABC Sept. 30, 1995.
Price: 25¢(d); 25¢(sat); $1.00(S); $2.00/wk; $8.67/mo; $104.00/yr.
Advertising: Open inch rate $20.75(m); $20.75(e); $20.75(m-sat); $20.75(S); $10.40(m & e); $7.80(m & S); $7.80(e & S); $13.02(m, e & S); $8.76 (m or e, sat & S), $4.35 (sat & S only). **Representative:** Landon Associates Inc.
News Services: AP, BPI, LAT-WP. **Politics:** Independent. **Established:** 1832 (evening), 1965 (morning).
Special Editions: Brides (Jan); Visitor's Guide (Feb); Golf, Home & Garden (Mar); Earth Day, Design-an-Ad, Little League (Apr); Health, Graduation (May); Auto Leasing, Locally-owned Business (June); Olympic Events Guide (July); Back-to-School, Commemorative Olympic (Aug); Gameday, Hunting (Sept); Gameday (Oct, Nov); Electronics (Dec).
Special Weekly Sections: School Pages (tues); Car & Driver (fri); Health Page (1st tues); Olympic Page (2nd tues); Pet Pages (last sat/month); Lawn & Garden Pages (Spring); Lawn & Garden Pages (Fall).
Magazines: TV Week (local, newsprint); Homefront (Real Estate); Weekend (Entertainment) (fri); Parade (S).

CORPORATE OFFICERS

COB/CEO W S Morris III
President Paul S Simon

GENERAL MANAGEMENT

Publisher Jeffrey A Wilson
Controller-Division Doyle Powell

ADVERTISING

Director Ron Wallace
Manager-Service George James
Manager-Sales Jena Wages

MARKETING AND PROMOTION

Director-Marketing/Promotion Doug Lowry

TELECOMMUNICATIONS

Audiotex Manager Scott Cochran

CIRCULATION

Director Ken Carter

NEWS EXECUTIVES

Exec Editor Adrian Pratt
Managing Editor Rick Parham

EDITORS AND MANAGERS

Amusements Editor (Banner-Herald) Kevin Price
Automotive Editor Bill Stewart
Books Editor Kevin Price
Business/Finance Editor Don Nelson
City Editor (News) Ed McMinn
City Editor (Banner-Herald) Mike Childs
Columnist Hank Johnson
Columnist Rick Parham
Columnist Blake Giles
Editorial Page Editor Hank Johnson
Editorial Writer (Banner-Herald/News) Hank Johnson
Education Editor Jim Thompson
Environmental Editor Lee Shearer
Features Editor Kevin Price
Films/Theater Editor Kevin Price
Food/Garden Editor Kevin Price
Graphics Editor/Art Director Jan Beckley
Lifestyle/Fashion Editor Kevin Price
Metro Editor Betsy Shearron
National Editor Rufus Adair
News Editor Rick Parham
Photo Department Manager Wingate Downs
Political/Government Editor Rufus Adair
Radio/Television Editor Kevin Price
Real Estate Editor Don Nelson
Religion Editor Roger Nielson
Science/Technology Editor Don Nelson
Society/Women's Editor Kevin Price
Sports Editor Blake Giles
Travel Editor Rick Parham

PRODUCTION

Manager Gary Cleveland

Market Information: Zoned editions; Split Run; TMC; ADS; Operate audiotex.
Mechanical available: Offset; Black and 3 ROP colors; insert accepted — preprinted; page cutoffs — 22¾".
Mechanical specifications: Type page 13" x 21¼"; E - 6 cols, 2 1/16", 1/8" between; A - 6 cols, 2 1/16", 1/8" between; C - 8 cols, 1½", 3/16" between.
Commodity consumption: Newsprint 3,000 short tons; widths 27", 13½"; black ink 80,000 pounds; color ink 33,600 pounds; single pages printed 17,954; average pages per issue 28(d), 36(sat), 56(S); single plates used 64,000.
Equipment: EDITORIAL: Front-end hardware — 42-IBM/AT PC, 2-IBM/PS2/50, 2-IBM/PS2/70; Front-end software — MPS; Printers — 3-Toshiba/1351; Other equipment —

Ap/Power Mac 81110, Ap/Mac IIfx. CLASSIFIED: Front-end hardware — 7-IBM/AT PC, 2-IBM/PS-2, 1-Gateway; Front-end software — MPS; Printers — 1-Panasonic/CPX-1123. AUDIOTEX: Hardware — VG/9000; Supplier name — MPS. DISPLAY: Front-end hardware — 3-Ap/Mac IIfx, 3-Ap/Power Mac 8100; Front-end software — Adobe/Photoshop 3.0, Adobe/Illustrator 3.3; Printers — Tecktronix/Color Printer, Ap/Mac LaserWriter II NTX. PRODUCTION: Typesetters — 2-XIT/Clipper, AG/1500; Plate exposures — 2-Nu/FT 140V6UPNS; Plate processors — 2-Nat/A-250; Electronic picture desk — Lf/AP Leaf Picture Desk; Scanners — ECR/1030C; Production cameras — 1-C/Spartan II, 1-C/Spartan III; Automatic film processors — 1-LE/LD24, 1-LE/2600A, Konica/550; Shrink lenses — 1-CK Optical; Color separation equipment (conventional) — Lf/Leafscan, ECR/Autokon 1030C. PRESSROOM: Line 1 — 12-G/Urbanite; Folders — G/2:1, SU; Press control system — Fin. MAILROOM: Counter stackers — 3-HL/HT II, 1-Stackpack; Inserters and stuffers — 2-Amerigraph/048P; Bundle tyer — 2-Power Strap/PSN-6; Wrapping singles — 2-Monarch, 1-QWI; Addressing machine — 2-Ch. COMMUNICATIONS: Digital ad delivery system — AP AdSend. Systems used — satellite. WIRE SERVICES: News — AP, NYT, KRT; Photos — AP; Stock tables — AP; Receiving dishes — AP. BUSINESS COMPUTERS: Applications: WordPerfect, PC/file, Lotus/1-2-3; PCs & micros networked; PCs & main system networked.

ATLANTA

Fulton & DeKalb Counties

'90 U.S. Census- 394,017; E&P '96 Est. 389,993
ABC-NDM (90): 1,001,861 (HH 384,111)

Constitution (m-mon to fri)
Journal (e-mon to fri)
Journal and Constitution (m-sat; S)

Atlanta Journal-Constitution, 72 Marietta St.; PO Box 4689, Atlanta, GA 30303; tel (404) 526-5151; web site http://www.ajc.com/. Cox Newspapers Inc. group.

Circulation: 305,457(m); 124,484(e); 131,192 (m-fri); 53,504 (e-fri); 520,880(m-sat); 692,411(S); ABC Sept. 30, 1995.

Price: 50¢(d); 50¢(sat); $2.00(S); $3.28/wk (7 days); $13.50/mo; $158.62/yr.

Advertising: Open inch rate $319.01(m); $319.01(e); $326.45 (m-fri); $326.45 (e-fri); $326.45(m-sat); $412.18(S); $274.27 (m & e). **Representative:** Newspapers First.

News Services: Cox News Service, AP, UPI, DJ, LAT-WP, NYT, KRT. **Established:** 1868 (Constitution), 1883 (Journal).

Not Published: New Year; Martin Luther King Jr's Birthday; Independence Day; Labor Day; Thanksgiving & Christmas when holiday falls on a weekday.

Special Editions: Nat. Assoc. Home Builders, Kids Guide (Jan); Atlanta Flower Show, Gwinnett Annual Report, Personal Tax Guide (Feb); Brides, Auto Show, Frozen Foods, Springsation, The Real South, Home & Garden (Mar); Home Financing, Health & Fitness, SE Economic Survey (Apr); Georgia 100 The Best of Business, One Day in the Life, Building of the Stadium (May); Health Care, Electronic Appliances, Peachtree Road Race (June); Complete Guide to the Games (July); Atlantans at the Games (Aug); Back-to-School, High School Football, College Football, Pro Football, Southern Living, Cooking School, Home Furnishing, Home & Garden, Wonderfall (Sept); Georgia Top Private Companies, Frozen Foods, Auto Atlanta (Oct); Home Video 500 (Nov); Gift Guide (Dec); Daily 1996 ROP Olympic Section (July 8-Aug 6).

Special Weekly Sections: Gwinnett EXTRA (TMC), Business (Personal Money Management), REACH (mon); Gwinnett EXTRA, Health (tues); Gwinnett EXTRA (TMC) (wed); Food Section, EXTRA/City Life (Community), Outdoors (thur); Olympic Weekly, Gwinnett EXTRA, Preview (Entertainment), Home and Garden, High School Sports, Wheels, Olympic Weekly (fri); Gwinnett EXTRA, Leisure, Wheels (sat); Gwinnett EXTRA, Style, Entertainment, Dixie Living, Travel, Home Finder (S).

Magazines: TV Week, Parade, Color Comics, Sunday Supplements-1996 Olympic Magazine (S).

CORPORATE OFFICERS

Publisher	Dennis Berry
Vice Pres/Business Manager	Paula Grogan
Vice Pres/General Manager	John Mellott
Vice Pres-Circulation	Dick Huguley
Vice Pres-Advertising	Mike Perricone
Vice Pres-Community Affairs/Work Force Diversity	Booker Izell
Vice Pres-Operations	Stan Pantel

GENERAL MANAGEMENT

Director-Classified Advertising	Dean Welch
Personnel Director	George Alford
Director-Purchasing	Ramsey Altman
Director-Training/Development	Marcus Fann
Director-Computer Services	Ed Baer
Controller	Melody Darch
Publisher-Electronic Info Services	David Scott

ADVERTISING

Manager-Retail/Major Account Sales	Roy Sheppard
Manager-Retail/Territory Sales	Hal Greene
Manager-Classified/Telephone Sales	Gigi Bradford
Manager-National/Sales	M A Bleker
Manager-Supplements/Operations	Hugh Gardiner
Manager-Sports Marketing	Molly Padilla
Manager-Direct Marketing	Mark Milversted

MARKETING AND PROMOTION

Director-Marketing/Promotion	Celeste Bottorff
Manager-Advertising Services	Greg Greg
Manager-Marketing Communications	Brenda Reid
Manager- Services	Bill Means
Manager-Creative Services	Charles Riebel
Manager-Events	Forrest Rogers

TELECOMMUNICATIONS

Computer Services Director	Ed Baer
Audiotex Manager	Wendy Donald

CIRCULATION

Director-Distribution	Bill Spyers
Director-Marketing	Michael Parker
Manager-State	Tom Sheppard
Manager-Sales/Promotion	Deborah Pyron
Manager-Single Copy	Bob Ellison
Manager-Systems Operations	Perry Sapp
Manager-Bulk Distribution	Jimmy Easley

NEWS EXECUTIVES

Editor	Ron Martin
Managing Editor	John Walter
Asst Managing Editor-Nation/Local	George Edmonson
Asst Managing Editor-Sports	Don Boykin
Asst Managing Editor-Features	Susan Soper
Asst Managing Editor-Olympics	Thomas Oliver
Asst Managing Editor-Graphics and Photo	Tony Deferia
Asst Managing Editor-Nights	Carolyn Warmbold
Asst Managing Editor-Business	Susan Wells
Asst Managing Editor-Opinion	Susan Stevenson
Asst Managing Editor-Innovation Team	Hyde Post
Administrative Editor	Keith Herndon

EDITORS AND MANAGERS

Automotive Editor	Karl Ritzler
Asst Manager-News Operations	John Reetz
Manager-News Personnel	James Mallory
Manager-News Research	Beverly Shepard
Books Editor	Michael Skube
Cartoonist (Constitution)	Mike Luckovich
City/Metro Editor	Mike King
City Life Editor	Valerie H Y Morgan
Columnist	Rheta Grimsley Johnson
Columnist	Celestine Sibley
Columnist	Colin Cambell
Editorial Page Editor (Constitution)	Cynthia Tucker
Editorial Page Editor (Journal)	James Wooten
Entertainment/Amusements Editor	Tom Sabulis
Education Editor	Cindy Gorley
Films Editor	Eleanor Ringel
Food Editor	Susan Pucket
Foreign Editor	Randall Ashley
Home/Garden Editor	Jill Sabulis
Living/Lifestyle Editor	Ann Morris
Music Editor	Tom Sabulis
Perspective Editor	Larry Conley
Real Estate Editor	Karl Ritzler
Religion Editor	Gayle White
Science/Medicine Editor	Nick Tate
Sports Editor (Journal)	Furman Bisher
Television Editor	Phil Kloer
Travel Editor	Connie Green

PRODUCTION

Vice Pres	Stan Pantell
Manager-Operations	Robert Guthrie
Manager-Reach Operations	Dayton O Flowers
Manager-Gwinnett Printing Facility	Gary Creel
Asst Manager-Gwinnett Printing Facility	Danny Simmons

Market Information: Zoned editions; Split Run; TMC; ADS; Operate database; Operate audiotex; Electronic edition.

Mechanical available: Offset; Black and 3 ROP colors; insert accepted — preprinted, zoned area preprints; page cut-offs — 22.05".

Mechanical specifications: Type page 13" x 21¼"; E - 6 cols, $2\frac{1}{16}$", ⅛" between; A - 6 cols, $2\frac{1}{16}$", ⅛" between; C - 10 cols, $1\frac{3}{16}$", ⅛" between.

Commodity consumption: Newsprint 128,250 short tons; widths 54", 27½", 41¼"; black ink 5,200,000 pounds; color ink 582,200 pounds; single pages printed 85,550; average pages per issue 95(d), 441(S); single plates used 541,400.

Equipment: EDITORIAL: Front-end hardware — 5-AT/9080, 16-AT/9000, 5-IBM/Series 1, 24-IBM/PS2-Model 30; Front-end software — RSK/Tandy, NEC. CLASSIFIED: Front-end hardware — 120-IBM/3192, 1-Ad Star; Front-end software — IBM/Printext. DISPLAY: Adv layout systems — Cx; Front-end hardware — 1-IBM; Printers — 4-Epson. PRODUCTION: Typesetters — 3-AU/APS-4, 3-Cx/Bidco; Platemaking systems — 4-LX/1290A; Plate exposures — 2-WL/Lith-X-Pozer 3, 2-WL/Lith-X-Pozer 4; Plate processors — 4-WL/38D; Scanners — 2-ECR/1800, 4-ECR/Autokon 1000, 1-Scitex/Smartscan; Production cameras — 4-C/Spartan; Automatic film processors — 4-LE; Color separation equipment (conventional) — 1-BKY, 1-WDS, 640-CD, 1-Scitex; Digital color separation equipment — 1-CD. PRESSROOM: Line 1 — 4-TKS/(20 half decks; 4 satellites) (Gwinnett); Line 3 — 4-TKS/(20 half decks; 4 satellites) (Fulton); Folders — 8-TKS/(Fulton), 8-TKS/(Gwinnett). MAILROOM: Counter stackers — 13-SH/257, 12-G/5000; Inserters and stuffers — 6-NP/1472, 1-NP/1372, 3-QWI/201, 4-QWI/301; Bundle tyer — 20-MLN, Power Strap, 8-Dynaric; Addressing machine — 1-Ch. LIBRARY: Electronic — 1-IBM/5890, AT/9000, 12-IBM/3192. WIRE SERVICES: News — AP Datastream, AP Datafeatures, AP SportStats, Weather, DJ; Syndicates — AP, AP Datafeatures; Receiving dishes — size-3m, AP, NIS. BUSINESS COMPUTERS: Amdahl/5890-390 E; Applications: Payroll, Gen ledger, Fixed assets, Accts payable, Adv billing, Circ, Billing & PIA, Ad order entry, Human resources, Elec library; PCs & micros networked.

Atlanta Daily World (m-tues, thur, fri; S)

Atlanta Daily World, 145 Auburn Ave. N.E., Atlanta, GA 30335-1201; tel (404) 659-1110.

Circulation: 16,000(m); 17,000(S); Sworn Sept. 30, 1992.

Price: 25¢(d); 25¢(S); $65.00/yr.

Advertising: Open inch rate $12.74(m); $12.74(S).

News Service: NNPA Service. **Politics:** Independent. **Established:** 1928.

Special Editions: Martin Luther King Jr (Jan); Black History Month/Black Press (Feb); Black History Month/Black Press (Mar); Anniversary Edition (Aug).

CORPORATE OFFICERS

Chairman of the Board	C A Scott
Vice Pres	Ruth P Scott
Secretary	Portia A Scott
Treasurer	Ruth Scott Simmons

GENERAL MANAGEMENT

Publisher	C A Scott
Purchasing Agent	Lloyd C Smith
Bookkeeper	Ruth P Scott

ADVERTISING

Manager-National	Portia A Scott
Manager-Local	J Russell Simmons

CIRCULATION

Manager	Lloyd C Smith

NEWS EXECUTIVES

Exec Editor	C A Scott
Managing Editor	Portia A Scott

EDITORS AND MANAGERS

Business/Finance Editor	William Fowlkes
City/Metro Editor	William Fowlkes
Editorial Page Editor	Portia A Scott
Education Editor	Angela B Sadler
Entertainment/Movie Photographer	Wendell S Scott
Entertainment/Amusements Editor	Angela B Sadler
Fashion/Style Editor	Portia A Scott
Features Editor	Portia A Scott
Food Editor	Ruth Scott Simmons
National Editor	Portia A Scott
Political/Government Editor	Portia A Scott
Political/Government Editor	William Fowlkes
Sports Editor	Darryl E Lassiter
Travel Editor	Portia A Scott
Women's/Lifestyle Editor	Portia A Scott

PRODUCTION

Superintendent	Wendell S Scott
Superintendent	Smith Fleming

Mechanical available: Offset; Black and 3 ROP colors; insert accepted — preprinted.

Mechanical specifications: E - 6 cols, $2\frac{1}{16}$", ⅛" between; A - 6 cols, $2\frac{1}{16}$", ⅛" between; C - 8 cols, $1\frac{3}{8}$", $\frac{1}{16}$" between.

Commodity consumption: average pages per issue 8(d), 8(S).

Equipment: PRODUCTION: Typesetters — 1-COM, 1-V. WIRE SERVICES: News — UPI; Syndicates — National Newspaper Publishers Association.

AUGUSTA

Richmond County

'90 U.S. Census- 44,639; E&P '96 Est. 42,959
ABC-CZ (90): 231,477 (HH 86,502)

The Augusta Chronicle (m-mon to fri; m-sat; S)

The Augusta Chronicle, 725 Broad St. (30901); PO Box 1928, Augusta, GA 30903; tel (706) 724-0851; web site http://www.cris.com/~masters. Morris Communications Corp. group.

Circulation: 74,041(m); 91,634(m-sat); 100,750(S); ABC Sept. 30, 1995.

Price: 50¢(d); 50¢(sat); $1.25(S); $11.00/mo; $132.00/yr.

Advertising: Open inch rate $53.02(m); $53.02(m-sat); $63.06(S). **Representative:** Landon Associates Inc.

News Service: AP. **Politics:** Independent. **Established:** 1785.

Special Editions: Augusta Futurity (Jan); Brides, People In Progress (Feb); Lawn & Garden, Triple Crown (Mar); Masters Golf (Apr); Graduations (May); Back-to-School, Football (Aug); Automotive, Car Care, Barrel Racing (Oct).

Special Weekly Sections: Teen Wrap (tues); Food (wed); Science & Medicine (thur); Applause (fri); Religion (sat).

Magazine: Parade (S).

CORPORATE OFFICERS

COB/CEO	W S Morris III
President	Paul S Simon
Vice Pres-Newspapers	Edward B Skinner
Secretary/Treasurer	William A Herman III

GENERAL MANAGEMENT

Publisher	W S Morris III
General Manager	Julian Miller
Manager-Personnel	Jerilyn Northcutt
Manager-Credit	Kathy Hammons
Controller-Division	Martin Pippin

ADVERTISING

Director	Ron Tennant
Director-Display	Don Bailey
Manager-Delivery	Janet Culver
Manager-Major/National	Bryce Cockerham Jr
Manager-Business Development	Cheryl Williams
Manager-Sales	Sheri Ducharme
Manager-Classified (Outside)	Carey Almond
Manager-Classified (Inside)	Violet Brissey

MARKETING AND PROMOTION

Manager-Marketing/Promotion	Kate Cooper
Manager-Newspapers in Education	Lisa Bryant

TELECOMMUNICATIONS

Audiotex Manager	Lowell Dorn

CIRCULATION

Director	Louis Keith
Director-Technical Development	Denise Harper
Coordinator-CMS	Sheneace Burnett
Manager-Promotion	Howard Timbers

NEWS EXECUTIVES

Exec Editor	Dennis Sodomka
Managing Editor	John Fish

EDITORS AND MANAGERS

Cartoonist	Clyde Wells
Editorial Page Editor	Phil Kent
Editorial Writer	Kirk Weeks
Editorial Writer	Barry Paschal
Features Editor	Les Simpson

Georgia

I-91

Graphics Editor		Rick McKee
Metro Editor		James Folker
Deputy Metro Editor		Bill Kirby
News Editor		Tom Dardenne
Outdoors Editor		William Babb
Director-Photography		Jim Blaylock
Photo Editor		Joey Trotz
Sports Editor		Ward Clayton

PRODUCTION

Director		H J Aaronson
Manager-Ad		Mark Chapin
Manager-Pressroom		David McCoy
Manager-Mailroom		Donnie Harris

Market Information: Zoned editions; Split Run; TMC; ADS; Operate audiotex.

Mechanical available: Offset; Black and 3 ROP colors; insert accepted — preprinted; page cut-offs — 22¾".

Mechanical specifications: Type page 13" x 21½"; E - 6 cols, 2¹⁄₁₆", ⅛" between; A - 6 cols, 2¹⁄₁₆", ⅛" between; C - 10 cols, 1³⁄₁₆", ³⁄₃₂" between.

Commodity consumption: Newsprint 11,785 short tons; widths 55", 41¼", 27½"; black ink 192,000 pounds; color ink 72,159 pounds; single pages printed 29,840; average pages per issue 56(d), 60(sat), 100(S); single plates used 84,000.

Equipment: EDITORIAL: Front-end hardware — 63-IBM/PC-AT, 14-IBM/AT PS2; Front-end software — MPS. CLASSIFIED: Front-end hardware — IBM/AT; Front-end software — MPS. AUDIOTEX: Hardware — DOS/Gateway 2000; Software — PEP/Voice Print, TRT; Supplier name — Morris Information Services. DISPLAY: Adv layout systems — MPS/Ad Layout System; Front-end hardware — Ap/Mac, Ap/Mac NTX; Printers — XIT/Clipper, Tektronix/Phaser; Other equipment — Ap/Mac CD-Rom, Ap/Mac Color Scanner. PRODUCTION: OCR software — Caere/OmniPage; Typesetters — 2-XIT/Clipper, 1-AG/1000, 1-AG/1500; Plate exposures — 2-Nu/Flip Top; Plate processors — 2-DP/3800; Electronic picture desk — Lf/AP Leaf Picture Desk, Ap/Power Mac 8100-80; Scanners — 1-RZ/210 L, Nikon/ScanTouch AX-1200, Kk/Film Scanner RFS-2035; Production cameras — 1-C/Spartan, 1-C/Marathon; Automatic film processors — 2-P/L524, 1-CL/66F; Film transporters — 2-C; Shrink lenses — 1-CK Optical; Color separation equipment (conventional) — RZ/210L. PRESSROOM: Line 1 — 5-G/Metro (2 color decks), 2-G/Metro, 3-G/Metro (3 color decks); Press drives — 10-Fin; Folders — 2-G/3:2, 2-G/2:1; Pasters — 10-G; Reels and stands — 10-G; Press control system — Fin. MAILROOM: Counter stackers — 3-HL/HT2; Inserters and stuffers — 1-Fg, 2-MM/227; Bundle tyer — 5-Dynaric; Addressing machine — 8-Wm, 1-KR. LIBRARY: Electronic — MPS. WIRE SERVICES: News — AP, Datafeatures; Stock tables — AP Stock, KRT/Stock Tables; Receiving dishes — AP. BUSINESS COMPUTERS: 2-IBM/4341.

BRUNSWICK
Glynn County

'90 U.S. Census- 16,433; E&P '96 Est. 15,783

The Brunswick News
(e-mon to sat)

The Brunswick News, 3011 Altama Ave.; PO Box 1557, Brunswick, GA 31521; tel (912) 265-8320; fax (912) 264-4973.
Circulation: 16,115(e); 16,115(e-sat); Sworn Sept. 29, 1995.
Price: 25¢(d); 25¢(sat); $1.14/wk; $5.00/mo; $60.00/yr.
Advertising: Open inch rate $7.77(e); $7.77(e-sat).
News Services: AP, NEA. **Politics:** Independent. **Established:** 1902.
Special Weekly Sections: Wedding & Engagement (mon); Best Food, Business (wed); Business (fri); Religion (sat).

CORPORATE OFFICER
President — C H Leavy III

GENERAL MANAGEMENT
General Manager — W R Maulden

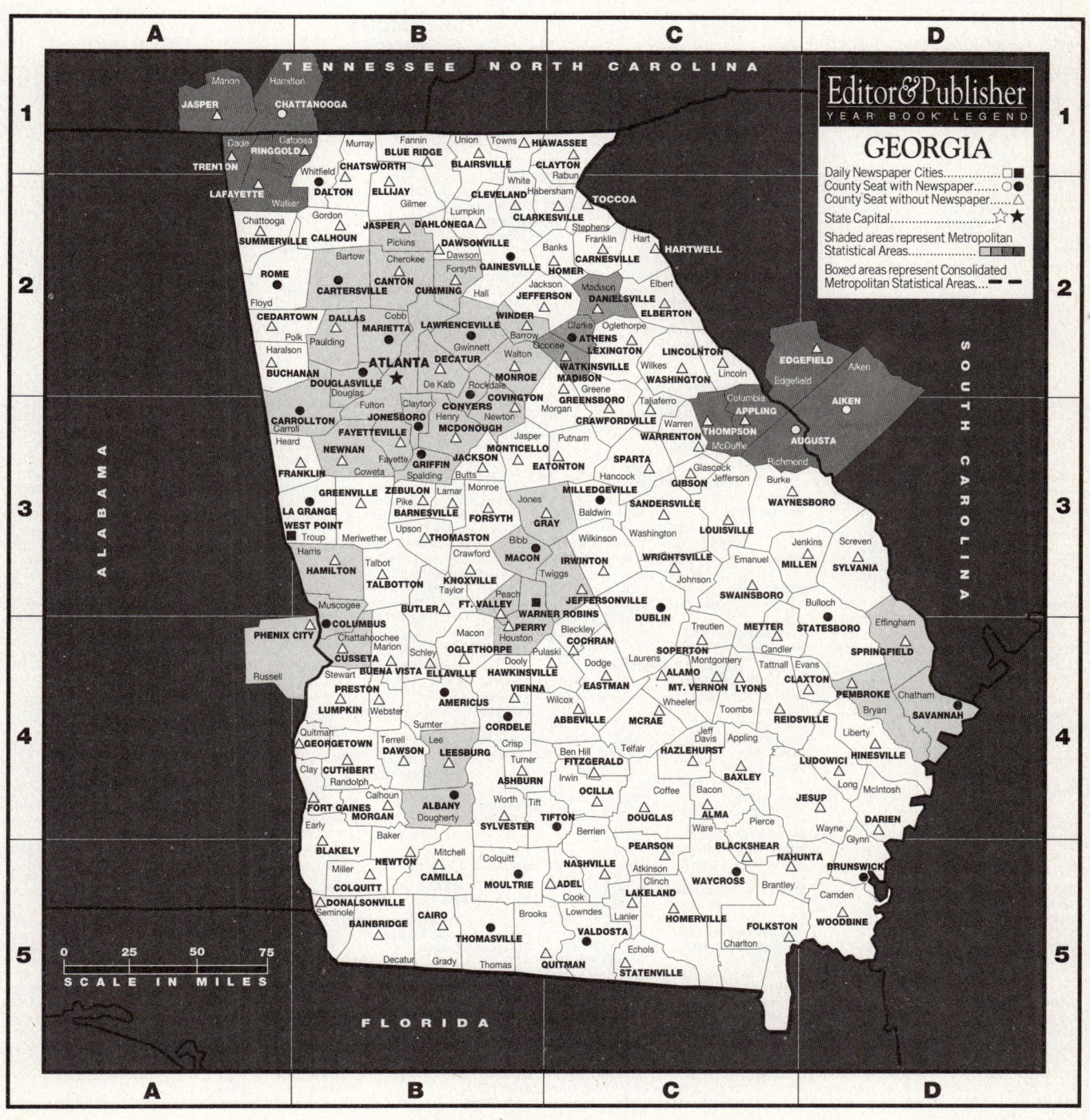

ADVERTISING

Director W R Maulden

CIRCULATION

Manager Wes Oldaker

NEWS EXECUTIVES

Editor C H Leavy III
Managing Editor Hank Rowland

EDITORS AND MANAGERS

Business Editor David Godwin
City Editor Susan Thornton
Lifestyle Editor Joann Pendery
Religion Editor David Godwin
Sports Editor Murray Poole

PRODUCTION

Foreman-Composing Roger Farmer
Foreman-Pressroom Richard Butler

Market Information: Zoned editions.
Mechanical available: Offset; Black and 3 ROP colors; insert accepted — preprinted; page cut-offs — 22¾".
Mechanical specifications: Type page 13" x 21"; E - 6 cols, 2 1/16", 1/8" between; A - 6 cols, 2 1/16", 1/8" between; C - 8 cols, 1½", 1/8" between.
Commodity consumption: Newsprint 1,008 short tons; width 27½"; black ink 24,150 pounds; color ink 2,200 pounds; single pages printed 11,110; average pages per issue 36(d), 36(sat); single plates used 11,110.
Equipment: EDITORIAL: Front-end hardware — COM/One System. CLASSIFIED: Front-end hardware — COM/One System. DISPLAY: Front-end hardware — COM/One System, COM/MCS. PRODUCTION: Typesetters — COM/8600; Plate exposures — Nu/Flip Top; Plate processors — Nat/A-250; Electronic picture desk — Lf/AP Leaf Picture Desk; Production cameras — C/Spartan III; Automatic film processors — 1-LE.
PRESSROOM: Line 1 — 8-G/Community. MAILROOM: Inserters and stuffers — 1-DG; Addressing machine — Papertrack System. WIRE SERVICES: News — AP; Photos — AP; Receiving dishes — AP. BUSINESS COMPUTERS: Papertrak/System.

CARROLLTON

Carroll County

'90 U.S. Census- 16,029; E&P '96 Est. 17,799

Times-Georgian

(m-tues to sat; S)

Times-Georgian, 901 Hayes Mill Rd.; PO Box 460, Carrollton, GA 30117; tel (770) 834-6631; fax (770) 834-9991. Paxton Media group.
Circulation: 10,786(m); 10,786(m-sat); 10,786(S); Sworn Sept. 30, 1994.
Price: 50¢(d); 50¢(sat); $1.00(S); $6.50/mo; $54.65/6mo (mail), $106.45/yr (mail); $75.00/yr.
Advertising: Open inch rate $13.98(m); $13.98(m-sat); $13.98(S). **Representative:** Papert Companies.
News Service: AP. **Politics:** Independent. **Established:** 1945.
Special Edition: Auto (fall).

GENERAL MANAGEMENT

Publisher Dawn Weatherby
Business Manager Joan Brown

ADVERTISING

Director Glenda Hicks

CIRCULATION

Director Dan Demjanek

NEWS EXECUTIVES

Exec Editor Bruce Browning
Managing Editor Frances Long

PRODUCTION

Superintendent-Press Richard Stash

Market Information: TMC.
Mechanical available: Offset; Black and 3 ROP colors; insert accepted — preprinted; page cut-offs — 22¾".
Mechanical specifications: Type page 13" x 21½"; E - 6 cols, 2 1/16", 1/8" between; A - 6 cols, 2 1/16", 1/8" between; C - 9 cols, 1½", 1/8" between.
Commodity consumption: Newsprint 1,500 short tons; widths 28", 30", 16"; black ink 30,000 pounds; color ink 6,000 pounds; single pages printed 6,000; average pages per issue 17(d), 24(S); single plates used 12,000.
Equipment: EDITORIAL: Front-end hardware — 20-EKI/Earth Station; Printers — 1-Ap/Mac LaserWriter II NTX, Ap/Mac Printer; Other equipment — 11-EKI/Televideo. CLASSIFIED: Front-end hardware — 3-EKI/Earth Station, 1-EKI/Televideo & Monitor; Printers — Data South. DISPLAY: Adv layout systems — 2-Ap/Mac II, 1-EKI/Earth Station; Printers — 2-Ap/Mac LaserWriter II NTX. PRODUCTION: Platemaking systems — 1-LE; Plate exposures — 1-Nu/Plateburner; Plate processors — 1-Nat; Production cameras — 1-C/Spartan III; Automatic film processors — 1-Carnfeldt; Film transporters — 1-LE; Color separation equipment (conventional) — 1-Digi-Colour/Sys DC-4000, 1-SCREEN/Companica 680C.
PRESSROOM: Line 1 — 9-G/Community. MAILROOM: Counter stackers — 1-BG/Count-O-Veyor; Inserters and stuffers — 1-MM; Bundle tyer — 2-MLN; Addressing machine — 1-KR. LIBRARY: Electronic — Minolta/Micro-Film/Reader. WIRE SERVICES: News — AP; Syndicates — AP; Receiving dishes — size-2ft, AP. BUSINESS COMPUTERS: 2-IBM/PC-AT, 6-IBM/PC, 1-EKI/Earth Station, 9-Monitor; Applications: Circ, Accts receivable, Gen ledger; PCs & micros networked; PCs & main system networked.

CARTERSVILLE

Bartow County

'90 U.S. Census- 12,035; E&P '96 Est. 14,465

The Daily Tribune News

(e-mon to fri; S)

The Daily Tribune News, 251 Tennessee St.; PO Box 70, Cartersville, GA 30120; tel (770) 382-4545; fax (770) 382-2711. Cleveland Newspapers Inc. group.
Circulation: 9,780(e); 9,780(S); Sworn Oct. 2. 1995.
Price: 50¢(d); $1.00(S); $6.50/mo; $71.00/yr.
Advertising: Open inch rate $8.22(e); $8.22(S). **Representative:** Papert Companies.
News Service: AP. **Established:** 1946.
Not Published: Thanksgiving; Christmas.
Special Editions: Chamber Tab (Jan); Medical Tab (Feb); Earth Day Tab (Apr); Graduation (June); Progress (July); Holiday Cookbook (Nov); Christmas Greetings (Dec).
Special Weekly Sections: Best Food Day (wed); Real Estate Section (fri); Business News Day, Real Estate Section (S).
Magazine: TV Outlook (S).

CORPORATE OFFICER

Vice Pres Charles E Hurley

GENERAL MANAGEMENT

Publisher Charles E Hurley
Manager-Office Johnette Dawson

ADVERTISING

Manager-Classified Barbara Decker
Manager-Retail Jennifer Montes

CIRCULATION

Director Doug Burnette

NEWS EXECUTIVES

Editor Charles E Hurley
Assoc Managing Editor Kevin Atwill
Assoc Editor Lewis Justus

EDITORS AND MANAGERS

Business/Finance Editor Charles Moore
Editorial Page Editor Lewis Justus
Features Editor Susan Sharp
Living/Lifestyle Editor Chris O'Nan
Society Editor Elizabeth Cochran
Sports Editor Jim Jaquish
Women's Editor Elizabeth Cochran

PRODUCTION

Superintendent William Bramlett
Superintendent-Pressroom Charles Simpson

Market Information: Zoned editions; TMC.
Mechanical available: Offset; Black and 3 ROP colors; insert accepted — preprinted, any; page cut-offs — 22¾".
Mechanical specifications: Type page 13" x 21½"; E - 6 cols, 2 1/16", 1/8" between; A - 6 cols, 2 1/16", 1/8" between; C - 6 cols, 2 1/16", 1/8" between.
Commodity consumption: Newsprint 499 short tons; widths 28", 14"; black ink 10,258 pounds; color ink 809 pounds; single pages printed 4,508; average pages per issue 18(d); single plates used 6,400.
Equipment: EDITORIAL: Front-end hardware — Ap/Mac; Front-end software — Baseview; Other equipment — 7-Ap/Mac. CLASSIFIED: Front-end hardware — 2-Ap/Mac; Front-end software — Baseview. DISPLAY: Adv layout systems — Ap/Mac; Front-end hardware — 4-Ap/Mac; Front-end software — Multi-Ad/Creator, QuarkXPress, Aldus/FreeHand. PRODUCTION: Pagination software — Baseview, QuarkXPress; OCR software — QPS; Typesetters — 1-Ap/Mac Laser Pro 630, 2-V/3990 Imagesetter; Plate exposures — 1-Nu; Plate processors — 1-Nat; Electronic picture desk — Adobe/Photoshop; Scanners — 2-AG/Arcus; Production cameras — 1-C/Spartan III; Automatic film processors — C/Powermatic-66F; Shrink lenses — 1-CK Optical/SQU-7; Color separation equipment (conventional) — Ap/Mac Quadra 800, Adobe/Photoshop, V/3990.
PRESSROOM: Line 2 — 7-WPC/Web leader (1-Color quad); Line 3 — 4-WPC/Web leader (1-Color quad); Line 4 — 3-WPC/Web leader; Folders — 5-WPC. MAILROOM: Counter stackers — 1-Mid America Graphics; Inserters and stuffers — MM/5-into-1; Bundle tyer — 2-Bu, 1-Strapex/Solomat; Addressing machine — 3-Dispensa-Matic/16". LIBRARY: Combination — Dukane/MMR 16 & 35. WIRE SERVICES: News — AP; Photos — Graphics; Receiving dishes — size-2½ft, AP. BUSINESS COMPUTERS: 1-Mk/Acer 1100, DEC/PC XL 466D2; Applications: Accts receivable, Accts payable, Payroll, Circ, Gen ledger.

COLUMBUS

Muscogee County

'90 U.S. Census- 178,681; E&P '96 Est. 187,588
ABC-CZ (90): 231,213 (HH 81,971)

Columbus Ledger-Enquirer

(m-mon to sat; S)

Columbus Ledger-Enquirer, 17 W. 12th St.; PO Box 711, Columbus, GA 31901; tel (706) 324-5526; fax (706) 576-6236. Knight-Ridder Inc. group.
Circulation: 52,335(m); 52,335(m-sat); 66,783(S); ABC Sept. 30, 1995.
Price: 35¢(d); 35¢(sat); $1.50(S); $3.25/wk; $14.08/mo; $169.00/yr.
Advertising: Open inch rate $42.35(m); $42.35(m-sat); $48.95(S). **Representative:** Newspapers First.
News Services: AP, KRT. **Politics:** Non-partisan. **Established:** 1828 (Enquirer), 1930 (Sunday Ledger-Enquirer).
Special Editions: Careers (Jan); Bridal, Home and Garden (Feb); Business and Industry, Gulf Coast Section (Mar); GA Coastal Section, Riverfest Guide, Design-an-Ad (Apr); N. GA Mountains (June); Back-to-School, Kick-off '96, Reader's Choice Awards (Aug); Home and Garden, Panama City Beach Seafood Festival (Sept); Colleges and Universities of Georgia and Alabama, Panama City Seafood Festival, Guide to Military Services (Oct); Christmas Open House Directory, Fall Festival of Homes (Nov); Christmas Song and Story Book (Dec).
Special Weekly Sections: Money Today (mon); Friends, Business, Health & Fitness (tues); Food, Business (wed); Business, Excellent Views (thur); Auto Weekend, Arts & Leisure, Business (fri); Homes for Sale, Religion, Business (sat); Business, Vacation/Travel, Living/Society (S).
Magazines: Parade (S); TV Book (quarterfold).

CORPORATE OFFICERS

President John F Greenman
Vice Pres Al Johnson
Vice Pres Robert F Singleton
Vice Pres-Marketing John Kelly
Chief Financial Officer Rita Towler
Secretary Douglas C Harris

GENERAL MANAGEMENT

Publisher John F Greenman
Manager-Business John Kelly
Personnel Manager Margie Watson

ADVERTISING

Director Dick Stone
Manager-New Products David Fletcher

MARKETING AND PROMOTION

Coordinator-Promotion Jenny Collins

TELECOMMUNICATIONS

Director-Electronic Info Systems Bill Jenkins
Manager-Programming Mark Reed

CIRCULATION

Director Jim Lamm
Manager-Distribution Pat Chitwood
Manager-Marketing Dennis Dunn
Manager-Alternate Delivery Robbie Parham

NEWS EXECUTIVES

Exec Editor Al Johnson
Managing Editor Sam Jones
Assoc Editor Mike Owen
Assoc Editor Dusty Nix

EDITORS AND MANAGERS

Business/Finance Editor Carol Hazard
Columnist Tim Chitwood
Editorial Page Editor Billy Winn
Entertainment Editor Sandra Okamoto
Fashion/Style Editor Ben Wright
Features Editor Ben Wright
Food Editor Judith Bethel
Graphics Editor/Art Director Don Coker
Librarian Valerie Pollard
Metro Editor David Dykes
News Editor Chuck Crouch
Photo Editor Allen Horne
Radio/Television Editor Mick Walsh
Sports Editor Chuck Williams

PRODUCTION

Director Pat Stubbs
Manager Leo Shiver
Foreman-Pressroom Roger Rudd
Foreman-Mailroom Dan Fourhman
Foreman-Platemaking Leon Jackson
Foreman-Composing Billy Faircloth

Market Information: Zoned editions; TMC; ADS.
Mechanical available: Offset; Black and 3 ROP colors; insert accepted — preprinted; page cut-offs — 22".
Mechanical specifications: Type page 13" x 21"; E - 6 cols, 2.03", 1/6" between; A - 6 cols, 2.03", 1/6" between; C - 10 cols, 1.19", 1/9" between.
Commodity consumption: Newsprint 6,110 short tons; 5,543 metric tons; widths 54¾", 41 1/16"; black ink 69,898 pounds; color ink 21,874 pounds; single pages printed 14,976; average pages per issue 44(d), 78(S); single plates used 60,000.
Equipment: EDITORIAL: Front-end hardware — Tandem, SII/3; Front-end software — SII/Sys 25; Printers — 1-Centronics; Other equipment — 59-SII/Dakota, 6-SII/22, 2-Lf/AP Leaf Picture Desk, 1-Ap/Mac fx, 3-Ap/Mac Quadra 700. CLASSIFIED: Front-end hardware — Tandem; Front-end software — SII/Sys 25; Printers — 1-Centronics, 1-HP/LaserJet; Other equipment — 13-SII/Dakota, 1-PC/486. AUDIOTEX: Hardware — ATT/Audix; Software — Infinity/G3. DISPLAY: Adv layout systems — Ap/Mac; Front-end hardware — 2-Ap/Mac Quadra 800, 1-Ap/Mac II, 5-Ap/Mac Quadra 700; Front-end software — HI, Aldus/FreeHand, QuarkXPress, Multi-Ad/Creator; Printers — HP/Laser. PRODUCTION: Typesetters — 2-MON/Express, Imagemaster/1200, MON/1270; Electronic picture desk — Lf/AP Leaf Picture Desk, Ap/Mac, Adobe/Photoshop; Scanners — Microtek/Scanmaster Plus III; Automatic film processors — 2-LE/MTP-26.
PRESSROOM: Line 1 — 6-G/Headline Offset; Pasters — Brush; Reels and stands — G/RTP-50; Press control system — G. MAILROOM: Counter stackers — QWI, Id/440, Id/660; Inserters and stuffers — 3-MM/227; Bundle tyer — 5-MLN; Addressing machine — 4-Ch. LIBRARY: Electronic — Vu/Text SAVE. COMMUNICATIONS: Systems used — satellite. WIRE SERVICES: News — AP; Photos — AP; Stock tables — AP SelectStox. BUSINESS COMPUTERS: HP/925; Applications: CJ/AIM-CIS: Gen ledger; PCs & main system networked.

CONYERS

Rockdale County

'90 U.S. Census- 7,380; E&P '96 Est. 8,102
ABC-NDM (90): 54,091 (HH 18,337)

The Rockdale Citizen

(e-mon to fri)

The Rockdale Citizen, 969 S. Main St.; PO Box 136, Conyers, GA 30207; tel (770) 483-7108; fax (770) 483-2955. Gray Communications group.
Circulation: 10,228(e); ABC Sept. 30, 1995.
Price: 50¢(d); $6.60/mo; $72.00/yr.
Advertising: Open inch rate $7.55(e). **Representative:** American Newspaper Representatives Inc.
News Service: AP. **Politics:** Independent. **Established:** 1953 (weekly), 1978 (daily).
Special Editions: Merchants Directory, Tax Supplement (Jan); Brides Tour (Feb); Lawn & Garden (Mar); Home Improvements (Apr); Car Care, Senior Citizen Tab, Small Business Review (May); Graduation (June); Little League (July); Back-to-School, High School Football (Aug); Annual School Report, Home Improvement (Sept); Just the Facts, Arts & Crafts Festival, New Cars (Oct); Gift Guide (Nov); Pre Christmas Shoppers, Old Fashion Christmas (Dec).
Special Weekly Section: East Metro Plus (wed).

Georgia I-93

CORPORATE OFFICER

President Joseph D Cunningham

GENERAL MANAGEMENT

Publisher John Whitman

ADVERTISING

Manager Ernest Yarbrough

CIRCULATION

Director Jim Brumbelow

NEWS EXECUTIVE

Editor Barry King

EDITOR AND MANAGER

News Editor Alice Queen

PRODUCTION

Manager Jeff Norris
Foreman-Composing Vickie Garner

Market Information: TMC.
Mechanical available: Offset; Black and 4 ROP colors; insert accepted — preprinted; page cut-offs — 22¾".
Mechanical specifications: Type page 13" x 21½"; E - 6 cols, $2\frac{1}{16}$", ⅛" between; A - 6 cols, $2\frac{1}{16}$", ⅛" between; C - 8 cols, 1½", ⅛" between.
Commodity consumption: Newsprint 448 short tons; width 28"; black ink 11,310 pounds; color ink 750 pounds; single pages printed 6,650; average pages per issue 40(d); single plates used 3,500.
Equipment: CLASSIFIED: Front-end hardware — Ap/Power Mac 7100; Front-end software — Baseview/ClassFlow 1.1.2; Printers — Xante/8200. DISPLAY: Front-end hardware — 2-Ap/Power Mac 7100, 1-Ap/Mac IIcx; Front-end software — Multi-Ad/Creator, Adobe/Photoshop, QuarkXPress, Aldus/PageMaker; Printers — Xante/8200. PRODUCTION: Typesetters — 1-COM/8400 HS, 3-NewGen/Turbo-PS 480; Platemaking systems — Nu/Flip Top FT40V6UPNS; Plate exposures — 1-Nu; Plate processors — Nat/A-250; Scanners — 1-Nu/2024V-C, 1-Microtek/II HR; Production cameras — SCREEN/C-670-D; Automatic film processors — A, SCREEN/220; Color separation equipment (conventional) — LE/Bessler 45 MXT.
PRESSROOM: Line 1 — 7-G/Community; Press registration system — Stoesser/Pin System through Platebender. MAILROOM: Counter stackers — BG/Count-O-Veyor; Bundle tyer — 3-Bu; Addressing machine — Ch/Mailing Machine 596 Head. WIRE SERVICES: News — AP; Syndicates — Crown, United Media, TMS, Creators, NAS, NYT; Receiving dishes — size-3m, AP.

CORDELE

Crisp County

'90 U.S. Census- 10,321; E&P '96 Est.10,016

Cordele Dispatch (e-mon to fri)

Cordele Dispatch, 306 13th Ave.; PO Box 1058, Cordele, GA 31015-1058; tel (912) 273-2277; fax (912) 273-7239. Thomson Newspapers group.
Circulation: 5,955(e); Sworn Sept. 30, 1994.
Price: 35¢(d).
Advertising: Open inch rate $10.83(e). **Representatives:** Thomson Newspapers; Papert Companies.
News Service: AP. **Politics:** Independent. **Established:** 1908.
Not Published: New Year; Independence Day; Labor Day; Christmas.
Special Editions: Industrial; Progress; Thanksgiving; Watermelon Festival; Tax Guide; Bridal Edition; Progressive Business; Football & Basketball Editions; Home Improvement; Cookbook.
Special Weekly Sections: Business (mon); Best Food Days, Farm Page (tues); Best Food Days (wed); Real Estate, Restaurants (thur); Religious Page (fri).
Magazines: Agribusiness (3rd mon); Cover Story (TMC); Home Magazine.

GENERAL MANAGEMENT

Publisher/General Manager Randy Cox

ADVERTISING

Director Shane Belton
Manager-Classified Cathy Womack

CIRCULATION

Manager Matt Harrell

NEWS EXECUTIVE

Managing Editor Troy Taylor

EDITORS AND MANAGERS

Columnist Harvey Simpson
Columnist Don Howell
Editorial Page Editor Troy Taylor
Editorial Writer Troy Taylor
Fashion/Food Editor Cary McMullen
Home/Garden Editor Cary McMullen
News Editor Troy Taylor
Sports Editor Harvey Simpson
Women's/Society Editor Cary McMullen

PRODUCTION

Compositor Patty Neal
Compositor Betty Ruis

Market Information: TMC; Operate audiotex.
Mechanical available: Offset; Black and 3 ROP colors; insert accepted — preprinted, standing card, specialties; page cut-offs — 22¾".
Mechanical specifications: Type page 13" x 21½"; E - 6 cols, $2\frac{1}{16}$", ⅛" between; A - 6 cols, $2\frac{1}{16}$", ⅛" between; C - 9 cols, 1⅜", $\frac{1}{16}$" between.
Commodity consumption: Newsprint 220 short tons; widths 27½", 13¼", 32", 32"; black ink 10,000 pounds; color ink 1,500 pounds; single pages printed 3,500; average pages per issue 14(d); single plates used 2,990.
Equipment: EDITORIAL: Front-end hardware — 1-Ap/Mac Quadra 950, 4-Ap/Mac LC III, 2-Ap/Mac Centris 610, 1-Ap/Mac IIvx; Front-end software — FSI; Other equipment — TI/Omni 800. CLASSIFIED: Front-end hardware — Ap/Mac Centris 610; Front-end software — FSI. AUDIOTEX: Hardware — Mk/Touch 386 PC; Software — Ads-on-Call. DISPLAY: Adv layout systems — 1-Ap/Mac IIcx; Front-end hardware — Ap/Mac Centris 610; Front-end software — CD-Rom, Multi-Ad/Creator, Aldus/FreeHand, QuarkXPress. PRODUCTION: Pagination software — QuarkXPress 3.3; OCR software — Caere/OmniPage; Typesetters — 1-Ap/Mac LaserPrinter, V/5060, V/5300, DEC/VT-820; Plate exposures — 1-Nu/Flip Top; Plate processors — Nat; Electronic picture desk — 1-Lf/AP Leaf Picture Desk; Scanners — Lf/Leafscan 35, AG/Arcus Plus; Production cameras — 1-R; Automatic film processors — SCREEN/LD-220; Digital color separation equipment — Lf/AP Leaf Picture Desk, Lf/Leafscan.
PRESSROOM: Press registration system — Duarte/Pin Registration System. MAILROOM: Bundle tyer — 1-Midstates, 1-MLN/SP-300; Addressing machine — 1-El, 1-Am. WIRE SERVICES: News — AP, THO, SHNS; Photos — AP; Syndicates — Universal Press, King Features, NAS, WP; Receiving dishes — size-10m, AP. BUSINESS COMPUTERS: ATT; Applications: Lotus 1-2-3: Gen accounting; WordPerfect: Gen accounting; PCs & micros networked; PCs & main system networked.

DALTON

Whitfield County

'90 U.S. Census- 21,761; E&P '96 Est. 22,614
ABC-CZ (90): 21,761 (HH 8,733)

The Daily Citizen-News (m-mon to sat; S)

The Daily Citizen-News, 308 S. Thornton Ave.; PO Box 1167, Dalton, GA 30722-1167; tel (706) 278-1011; fax (706) 275-6641. Thomson Newspapers group.
Circulation: 13,529(m); 15,264(m-wed); 13,529(m-sat); 12,688(S); ABC Sept. 30, 1995.
Price: 50¢(d); 50¢(sat); $1.00(S); $10.45/mo; $125.40/yr.
Advertising: Open inch rate $13.40(m); $13.40(m-sat); $13.40(S). **Representative:** Papert Companies.
News Services: AP, TNI, SHNS. **Politics:** Independent. **Established:** 1962.
Special Edition: Progress (Apr).
Special Weekly Sections: Best Food Day (wed); TV Magazine, Entertainment (sat).

CORPORATE OFFICER

Publisher Ken H Fortenberry

GENERAL MANAGEMENT

Controller Steve Wright

ADVERTISING

Director Peter L Mio
General Manager-Shopper Kathy Burrow

CIRCULATION

Manager Billy Sanford

NEWS EXECUTIVE

Managing Editor Bonnie Williams

EDITORS AND MANAGERS

Books/Lifestyle Editor Suan Morrison
Business Editor Murray Coleman
City Editor Craig Harper
News Editor Wes Chance
Wire Editor Wes Chance

PRODUCTION

Foreman-Composing Fred Collins
Foreman-Pressroom Dwight McElrath

Market Information: TMC.
Mechanical available: Offset; Black and 3 ROP colors; insert accepted — preprinted; page cut-offs — 21½".
Mechanical specifications: Type page 13" x 21½"; E - 6 cols, $2\frac{1}{16}$", ⅛" between; A - 6 cols, $2\frac{1}{16}$", ⅛" between; C - 9 cols, 1⅜", $\frac{1}{16}$" between.
Commodity consumption: Newsprint 620 short tons; width 27½"; black ink 12,000 pounds; color ink 2,000 pounds; single pages printed 7,700; average pages per issue 36(S); single plates used 7,200.
Equipment: EDITORIAL: Front-end hardware — 1-COM, Mk, Ap/Mac; Other equipment — Ap/Mac Graphics Network, Ap/Mac, COM/Intrepid, Mk. CLASSIFIED: Front-end hardware — COM; Other equipment — 3-COM. DISPLAY: Adv layout systems — COM. PRODUCTION: Typesetters — 2-COM/8400; Plate exposures — 1-Nu/Flip Top Plate Burner; Plate processors — Nat/Automatic 250; Production cameras — 1-LE, 1-SCREEN; Automatic film processors — 1-SCREEN; Color separation equipment (conventional) — Lf/AP Leaf Picture Desk.
PRESSROOM: Line 1 — 10-G/Community. MAILROOM: Inserters and stuffers — 1-MM/3-into-1; Bundle tyer — 1-MLN, 1-Bu/String Tying Machine; Addressing machine — 1-KR, 1-KAN. WIRE SERVICES: News — AP; Syndicates — THO, SHNS; Receiving dishes — size-3m, AP. BUSINESS COMPUTERS: ATT; Applications: Accts receivable, Ad scheduling, Accts payable, Payroll; PCs & micros networked; PCs & main system networked.

DOUGLASVILLE

Douglasville

'90 U.S. Census- 11,635; E&P '96 Est. 16,350

Douglas County Sentinel (m-tues to sat)

Douglas County Sentinel, 6405 Fairbyrn Rd. (30134); PO Box 1586, Douglasville, GA 30133; tel (770) 942-6571; fax (770) 949-7556. Paxton Media group.
Circulation: 9,246(m); 9,246(m-sat); Sworn Sept. 20, 1994.
Price: 25¢(d); 25¢(sat).
Advertising: Open inch rate $11.00(m); $11.00(m-sat). **Representative:** Landon Associates Inc.
News Service: AP. **Politics:** Independent. **Established:** 1988.
Special Weekly Section: Food Day (wed).

GENERAL MANAGEMENT

Publisher Dawn Watherby
Business Manager Joan Brown

ADVERTISING

Manager Glenda Hicks

CIRCULATION

Director Dan Demjanik

NEWS EXECUTIVE

Editor Bill Fordham

EDITOR AND MANAGER

Tri-County News Editor Chris Barker

Mechanical available: Offset; Black and 3 ROP colors; insert accepted — preprinted hi-fi.
Mechanical specifications: Type page 13⅝" x 21½"; E - 6 cols, $2\frac{1}{16}$", ⅛" between; A - 6 cols, $2\frac{1}{16}$", ⅛" between; C - 9 cols, 1⅜", $\frac{1}{16}$" between.
Equipment: EDITORIAL: Front-end hardware — 1-EKI, 7-EKI/Televideo. CLASSIFIED: Front-end hardware — 3-PC. WIRE SERVICES: News — AP. BUSINESS COMPUTERS: Applications: Payroll, Billing.

DUBLIN

Laurens County

'90 U.S. Census- 16,312; E&P '96 Est. 16,647
ABC-NDM (90): 61,892 (HH 22,232)

The Courier Herald (e-mon to sat)

The Courier Herald, 115 S. Jefferson St., Dublin, GA 31021-2449; tel (912) 272-5522; fax (912) 272-2189.
Circulation: 12,493(e); 12,493(e-sat); ABC Sept. 30, 1995.
Price: 25¢(d); 25¢(sat); $52.00/yr.
Advertising: Open inch rate $10.00(e); $10.00(e-sat). **Representative:** Landon Associates Inc.
News Service: AP. **Politics:** Independent. **Established:** 1878 (weekly), 1913 (daily).
Not Published: New Year; Independence Day; Labor Day; Thanksgiving; Christmas.
Special Editions: Wedding Planner (Feb); St. Patrick's (Mar); Gardening (Apr); Graduation (May); Back-to-School, Football (Aug); New Car and Auto Guide (Oct); Holiday Gift Guide (Nov).
Special Weekly Sections: Business (mon); Education (tues); Best Food Day (wed); Lifestyles (thur); Legals, Religion (sat).
Magazine: Entertainment (sat).

CORPORATE OFFICERS

President Griffin Lovett
Secretary/Treasurer DuBose Porter

GENERAL MANAGEMENT

Publisher Griffin Lovett
Business Manager Jean Maddox

ADVERTISING

Director Joy Houston
Manager-Classified Donna Phillips

CIRCULATION

Manager Cheryl Gay

NEWS EXECUTIVES

Editor DuBose Porter
Managing Editor Rodney Manley

EDITORS AND MANAGERS

Photographer Joey Wilson
Society/Women's Editor Felicia Christian
Sports Editor Rob Cook

Market Information: TMC.
Mechanical available: Offset; Black and 3 ROP colors; insert accepted — preprinted, maximum size 11"x14"; page cut-offs — 22¾".
Mechanical specifications: Type page 13" x 21½"; E - 6 cols, $2\frac{1}{16}$", ⅛" between; A - 6 cols, $2\frac{1}{16}$", ⅛" between; C - 6 cols, $2\frac{1}{16}$", ⅛" between.
Commodity consumption: Newsprint 496 short tons; widths 27½", 13¾"; black ink 10,450 pounds; color ink 1,565 pounds; single pages printed 5,966; average pages per issue 19(d); single plates used 6,000.
Equipment: EDITORIAL: Front-end hardware — Mk. CLASSIFIED: Front-end hardware — Mk. DISPLAY: Adv layout systems — 2-Ap/Mac IIcx; Front-end hardware — Ap/Mac Radius 19" color monitor. PRODUCTION: Typesetters — 1-Ap/Mac LaserWriter NT, 1-Dataproducts/11 x 17; Plate exposures — 1-Nu; Plate processors — 1-Nat; Scanners — 1-Ap/Mac, 1-Mirror/Color scanner; Production cameras — 1-CL/Horizontal, 1-R/Vertical; Automatic film processors — 2-C; Color separation equipment (conventional) — 1-BKY; Digital color separation equipment — 1-Mirror/Flatbed scanner.
PRESSROOM: Line 6 — 8-G/SC (w/Gev/Flexicolor half deck); Folders — 1-G/SC. MAILROOM: Bundle tyer — 2-AMP, 1-MLN, 1-Bu; Addressing machine — 1-Ch. WIRE SERVICES: News — AP Datafeatures, AP Datastream; Receiving dishes — AP. BUSINESS COMPUTERS: MTI/Micro-Computer; Applications: Circ, Gen ledger, Payroll, Accts payable, Accts receivable.

GAINESVILLE

Hall County

'90 U.S. Census- 17,885; E&P '96 Est. 20,306
ABC-NDM (90): 95,428 (HH 34,721)

The Times (e-mon to sat; S)

The Times, 345 Green St. N.W.; PO Box 838, Gainesville, GA 30503; tel (770) 532-1234; fax (770) 532-0457/7085. Gannett Co. Inc. group.
Circulation: 22,982(e); 22,982(e-sat); 27,196(S); ABC Sept. 30, 1995.
Price: 35¢(d); 35¢(sat); $1.50(S); $2.90/wk; $11.60/mo (4 weeks), $150.80/mo.
Advertising: Open inch rate $20.61(e); $20.61(e-sat); $23.30(S). **Representative:** Gannett National Newspaper Sales.
News Services: AP, AP Sportswire, GNS, AP Photo, AP Graphics. **Politics:** Independent. **Established:** 1947.
Special Editions: Health & You, 1996 Olympics (Jan); Annual Report, 1996 Olympics (Feb); Home & Gardens, 1996 Olympics (Mar); Health & You, Academic All-Stars, Visitor's Guide, 1996 Olympics (Apr); Lake News,

Georgia

1996 Olympics (May); Lake News, Visitor's Guide, 1996 Olympics (June); Lake News, 1996 Olympics (July); Lake News, High School Football, Health & You, 1996 Olympics (Aug); Visitor's Guide (Sept); Home Furnishings (Oct); After Thankgiving Section, Health & You, Visitor's Guide (Nov).
Special Weekly Sections: Educational (mon); Health and Fitness (tues); Growth Report, Cookin' (wed); Teen and Youth Page, Automotives (thur); Church Page (fri); Green Page (sat).
Magazines: Weekends (thur); TV Times, USA Weekend (S).

CORPORATE OFFICERS
Board Chairman	John Curley
President	John Curley
Treasurer	Douglas H McCorkindale

GENERAL MANAGEMENT
Publisher	Sandra S Bailey
Controller	Brad Zimmerman
Manager-Credit	Vickey James
Director-Human Resources	Joyce Ray

ADVERTISING
Director	Brad Hagstrom
Manager-Retail	Donna Montgomery
Manager-Classified	Carol Zimmerman
Manager-Creative	Tom Latos

MARKETING AND PROMOTION
Director-Marketing	Rebecca Johnson

TELECOMMUNICATIONS
Audiotex Manager	Rebecca Johnson

CIRCULATION
Director	Donna Prentice

NEWS EXECUTIVES
Editor	Johnny Vardeman
Managing Editor	John Druckenmiller

EDITORS AND MANAGERS
Education Editor	Keith Strawn
Entertainment/Amusements Editor	Ron Sirmans
Environmental Editor	Rick Lavender
Fashion/Style Editor	Ron Sirmans
Features Editor	Ron Sirmans
Graphics Editor/Art Director	Greg Smith
News Editor	Michael Beard
Photo Editor	Tom Reed
Religion Editor	Ron Sirmans
Sports Editor	Keith Albertson
Television/Film Editor	Ron Sirmans
Theater/Music Editor	Anne Madison

MANAGEMENT INFORMATION SERVICES
Coordinator-Info Systems	Vicki Hope

PRODUCTION
Director	Bob Perini
Superintendent-Mailroom	Phillip Winters

Market Information: Zoned editions; TMC; Operate audiotex.
Mechanical available: Offset; Black and 3 ROP colors; insert accepted — preprinted, minitabs; page cut-offs — 22¾".
Mechanical specifications: Type page 13" x 21½"; E - 6 cols, 2¹⁄₁₆", ⅛" between; A - 6 cols, 2¹⁄₁₆", ⅛" between; C - 10 cols, 1³⁄₁₆", ¹⁄₁₆" between.
Commodity consumption: Newsprint 4,460 metric tons; widths 27", 13½", 33"; black ink 94,750 pounds; color ink 33,548 pounds; single pages printed 33,113, average pages per issue 20(d), 32(S); single plates used 100,000.
Equipment: EDITORIAL: Front-end hardware — Dewar/Sys 3, 27-PC/286, 9-PC/386; Front-end software — Dewar/Disc Net; Printers — 2-Okidata/Dot Matrix; Other equipment — Lf/AP Leaf Picture Desk. CLASSIFIED: Front-end hardware — 5-PC/286, 1-PC/386; Front-end software — Dewar/Class Ad; Printers — 1-Dataproducts/LD 300; Other equipment — SyQuest/Disc Reader. AUDIOTEX: Software — Octel. DISPLAY: Adv layout systems — Dewar/Discovery, 1-Ap/Power Mac 8100, 1-Ap/Power Mac 7100; Front-end hardware — 2-PC/386, 1-PC/286; Front-end software — Dewar/Discovery; Other equipment — SyQuest/Tape Drive. PRODUCTION: Typesetters — 1-Tegra/Varityper/5300E, 2-Tegra/Varityper/5000 RIP, 1-ECR/Autokon 1000 DE, V/Panther Plus; Platemaking systems — NA/A-340; Plate processors — 1-Nu/Flip Top FT40APRNS, 1-Nu/Flip Top FT40APNS; Scanners — ECR/Autokon 1000 DE, AG/Arcus Plus, Umax/Flatbed; Production cameras — C/Spartan III; Automatic film processors — 1-LE/LD 24QA, 1-LE/LD 1800, 2-C/660; Film transporters — 1-C/Spartan Auto Film Transport; Color separation equipment (conventional) — 1-BKY/Separator.
PRESSROOM: Line 1 — 15-G/Urbanite; Press drives — 4-Fin/100 h.p. Drive Motors; Folders — G/Urbanite U775, G/Urbanite U1362; Pasters — 8-Cary; Press control system — Fin. MAILROOM: Counter stackers — 1-QWI/300, 1-PPK; Inserters and stuffers — 2-MM; Bundle tyer — 2-Bu, 2-MLN; Addressing machine — 1-Barstrom/Labeler, 2-Ch. LIBRARY: Combination — Clippings, Minolta/Microfilm. WIRE SERVICES: News — AP, GNS; Photos — AP; Syndicates — GNS, AP; Receiving dishes — size-1.5m, AP. BUSINESS COMPUTERS: IBM/AS 400. Applications: Corporate: Circ, Adv billing, Accts receivable; PCs & main system networked.

GRIFFIN
Spalding County

'90 U.S. Census- 21,347; E&P '96 Est. 21,997
ABC-CZ (90): 21,347 (HH 8,076)

Griffin Daily News
(e-mon to fri; m-sat; S)

Griffin Daily News, 323 E. Solomon; PO Box M, Griffin, GA 30224; tel (770) 227-3276; fax (770) 412-1678. Thomson Newspapers group.
Circulation: 11,473(e); 11,473(m-sat); 11,190(S); ABC Sept. 30, 1995.
Price: 50¢(d); 50¢(sat); $1.00(S); $9.75/mo.
Advertising: Open inch rate $14.47(e); $14.47(m-sat); $14.47(S). **Representative:** Thomson Newspapers.
News Service: AP. **Politics:** Independent. **Established:** 1871.
Not Published: New Year; Independence Day; Labor Day; Christmas.
Special Editions: Super Bowl (Jan); Valentines (Feb); Spring Fashion (Mar); Progress (Apr); Youth Sports (May); Vacation (June); Football, Back-to-School (Aug); Newcomer's Guide (Sept).
Special Weekly Sections: Cover Story (TMC) (wed); TV Notes (sat).
Magazine: Real Estate (sat).

GENERAL MANAGEMENT
Publisher	Otis Raybon Jr
Accountant	Kathy Matthews
Purchasing Agent	Otis Raybon Jr
General Manager	Otis Raybon Jr

ADVERTISING
Manager	Jeff Jones

CIRCULATION
Manager	Dick Beddon

NEWS EXECUTIVE
Managing Editor	Ron Wayne

PRODUCTION
Superintendent	John Davis
Foreman-Composing	David Lachnicht
Foreman-Pressroom	Tim Johnson

Market Information: Zoned editions; TMC; ADS.
Mechanical available: Offset; Black and 3 ROP colors; insert accepted — preprinted, single sheets; page cut-offs — 21½".
Mechanical specifications: Type page 13" x 21½"; E - 6 cols, 2", ⅛" between; A - 6 cols, 2", ⅛" between; C - 9 cols, 1.33", ⅛" between.
Commodity consumption: Newsprint 300 short tons; width 27½"; average pages per issue 18(d), 70(S).
Equipment: EDITORIAL: Front-end hardware — Ap/Mac; Printers — V/5100, V/5300 E. CLASSIFIED: Front-end hardware — Ap/Mac; Printers — 2-V/5100; Other equipment — TI/Omni 800. DISPLAY: Adv layout systems — 1-Ap/Mac IIci, Ap/Mac Radius 2 Page Color Display, Ap/Super Mac 2 Page Display; Front-end software — Aldus/FreeHand; Printers — V/5100; Plate exposures — 2-Ap/One Scanner. PRODUCTION: Typesetters — Mk/Laser printer, 2-V/5100; Plate exposures — 16-Sec; Plate processors — 1-Nat; Electronic picture desk — Lf/AP Leaf Picture Desk; Scanners — 2-Ap/One Scanner; Production cameras — 1-C/Spartan II 1968, 1-SCREEN/Companica 680-C; Automatic film processors — 1-LE, 1-SCREEN; Color separation equipment (conventional) — Digi-Colour/4000, Lf/AP Leaf Picture Desk.
PRESSROOM: Line 1 — 7-G; Press control system — Manual. MAILROOM: Counter stackers — 1-BG/Count-O-Veyor; Inserters and stuffers — 1-MM/5 pockets; Bundle tyer — 1-Bu; Addressing machine — KAN/Zip Code Separator, KAN/Label Applicator. WIRE SERVICES: News — THO, AP; Stock tables — AP Datastream 500; Receiving dishes — size-3m, AP. BUSINESS COMPUTERS: 1-Cumulus/GLC 1220 W; PCs & micros networked; PCs & main system networked.

JONESBORO
Clayton County

'90 U.S. Census- 3,635; E&P '96 Est. 3,342

Clayton News/Daily
(e-mon to fri; m-sat)

Clayton News/Daily, 138 Church St., Jonesboro, GA 30236; tel (770) 478-5753; fax (770) 473-9032; e-mail neelyyou@mindspring.com. Southern Crescent Newspapers group.
Circulation: 6,904(e); 6,904(m-sat); Sworn Sept. 30, 1995.
Price: 35¢(d); 35¢(sat).
Advertising: Open inch rate $10.70(e); $13.55(e-wed); 12.20(e-fri); $10.70(m-sat). **Representative:** American Newspaper Representatives Inc.
News Service: AP. **Politics:** Independent. **Established:** 1971.
Special Editions: Progress (Jan); Bride's Tour (Feb); Spring Car Care (Mar); Spring Tour of Homes, Home Improvement (Apr); Welcome Summer (May); Newcomer's Guide (July); Football Kick-off (Aug); Introduction to New Cars (Sept); Meet the Merchants, Fall Car Care (Oct); Holiday Cookbook, Christmas Gift Guide (Dec).
Special Weekly Sections: Living (thur); Business (fri); Religion (sat).

GENERAL MANAGEMENT
Publisher	Neely Young
Business Manager	Elly Simon

ADVERTISING
Director	Colleen Mitchell

CIRCULATION
Director	Naiomi Jackson

NEWS EXECUTIVES
Editor	Neely Young
Managing Editor	Tom Kerlin

EDITORS AND MANAGERS
Business/Finance	Jeff Whitfield
Columnist	Jeff Whitfield
Editorial Page Editor	Tom Kerlin
Fashion/Women's Editor	Abby Holbert
Religion Editor	Jeff Whitfield
Sports Editor	Don Corbin

PRODUCTION
Foreman-Pressroom	Willie Hines

Market Information: Split Run; TMC.
Mechanical available: Offset; Black and 3 ROP colors; insert accepted — preprinted; page cut-offs — 21½".
Mechanical specifications: Type page 13" x 21½"; E - 6 cols, 2¹⁄₁₆", ⅛" between; A - 6 cols, 2¹⁄₁₆", ⅛" between; C - 6 cols, 2¹⁄₁₆", ⅛" between.
Commodity consumption: Newsprint 540 short tons; width 28"; average pages per issue 22(d).
Equipment: EDITORIAL: Front-end hardware — COM/OS. DISPLAY: Front-end hardware — COM/Power View. PRODUCTION: Typesetters — 11-COM/8400; Plate exposures — 1-Nu/Flip Top; Plate processors — 1-Nat/250; Production cameras — 1-C/17x24, 1-K/Vertical 16x22; Automatic film processors — 1-LE/Max 25.
PRESSROOM: Line 1 — 6-KP/Newsking; Folders — 1-KP; Reels and stands — 6-KP. MAILROOM: Counter stackers — 1-BG; Bundle tyer — 2-Bu; Addressing machine — 1-Ch. WIRE SERVICES: News — AP; Syndicates — King Features, Universal Press, NEA, United Features; Receiving dishes — UPI.

LA GRANGE
Troup County

'90 U.S. Census- 25,597; E&P '96 Est. 26,926

La Grange Daily News
(e-mon to sat)

La Grange Daily News, 105 Ashton St., La Grange, GA 30240; tel (706) 884-7311; fax (706) 884-8712. Mid-South Management Co. Inc. group.
Circulation: 14,765(e); 14,765(e-sat); Sworn Sept. 30, 1994.
Price: 35¢(d); 35¢(sat); $74.16/yr (carrier); $82.00/yr (mail).
Advertising: Open inch rate $9.80(e); $9.80(e-sat). **Representative:** Landon Associates Inc.
News Services: AP, NEA. **Politics:** Independent. **Established:** 1842.
Not Published: Christmas.

GENERAL MANAGEMENT
Publisher	Louis (Lou) P Harvath III
General Manager	Lee West

ADVERTISING
Director	Sue A Long
Manager-Classified	Nick Talley

MARKETING AND PROMOTION
Manager-Promotion	Sue A Long

CIRCULATION
Manager	Stanley Shaw

NEWS EXECUTIVE
Managing Editor	Lee West

EDITORS AND MANAGERS
City Editor	Andrea Lovejoy
TMC Editor	Lean Gannett

Market Information: Zoned editions; TMC.
Mechanical available: Offset; Black and 3 ROP colors; insert accepted — preprinted; page cut-offs — 22".
Mechanical specifications: Type page 13¾" x 21½"; E - 6 cols, 2¹⁄₁₆", ⅛" between; A - 6 cols, 2¹⁄₁₆", ⅛" between; C - 9 cols, 1³⁄₁₆", ¹⁄₁₆" between.
Commodity consumption: Newsprint 575 short tons; width 27½"; single pages printed 7,200; average pages per issue 14(d); single plates used 8,300.
Equipment: EDITORIAL: Front-end hardware — COM/OS. DISPLAY: Adv layout systems — 3-COM/On-line. PRODUCTION: Typesetters — COM/OS; Production cameras — 1-B, 1-C; Automatic film processors — 1-Kk.
PRESSROOM: Line 1 — 7-G; Folders — 2-G. WIRE SERVICES: News — AP; Receiving dishes — AP. BUSINESS COMPUTERS: 1-Bs/90; Applications: Receivables, Payables, Payroll, Ledger; PCs & micros networked; PCs & main system networked.

LAWRENCEVILLE
Gwinnet County

'90 U.S. Census- 17,250 E&P '96 Est. 23,141

Gwinnett Daily Post
(m-tues to sat)

Gwinnett Daily Post, 166 Hwy. 20 (30246); PO Box 603, Lawrenceville, GA 30245; tel (770) 963-9205; fax (770) 339-8081. Gray Communications group.
Circulation: 14,155(m); 14,155(m-sat); ABC Mar. 31, 1995.
Price: 50¢(d); 50¢(sat); $79.95/yr.
Advertising: Open inch rate $14.87(m); $14.87(m-sat).
News Service: AP. **Established:** 1995.
Note: The Post is printed at the Conyers (GA) Rockdale Citizen. The circulation audit is for the three times a week paper that was converted to five days a week effective July 4, 1995. The daily circulation audit was not available at press time.
Special Editions: Home & Garden; Bridal; Graduation; Football; Winter Sports; Real Estate; Jobs.
Special Weekly Sections: Jobs (tues); Real Estate (sat).

CORPORATE OFFICER
CEO	John Williams

GENERAL MANAGEMENT
Publisher	John Whitman Jr

ADVERTISING
Director	Melody Bishop

MARKETING AND PROMOTION
Sales/Marketing Manager	Will Haddock

CIRCULATION
Director	Bill Herbert

NEWS EXECUTIVES
Editor	Norman Baggs
Managing Editor	Howard Reed III

PRODUCTION
Director	Rob LeMaster

Mechanical available: Offset; Black; insert accepted — preprinted.
Mechanical specifications: E - 6 cols, 2¹⁄₃₆", ⅛" between; A - 6 cols, 2³⁄₃₆", ⅛" between; C - 8 cols, 1½", ⅛" between.
Equipment: EDITORIAL: Front-end hardware — Ap/Macs; Front-end software — Baseview. CLASSIFIED: Front-end hardware — Ap/Macs; Front-end software — Baseview. PRODUCTION: Pagination software — Baseview. WIRE SERVICES: News — AP.

MACON
Bibb County

'90 U.S. Census- 106,612; E&P '96 Est. 100,889
ABC-NDM (90): 165,818 (HH 61,847)

The Macon Telegraph
(m-mon to sat; S)

The Macon Telegraph, 120 Broadway (31201); PO Box 4167, Macon, GA 31213; tel (912) 744-4200. Knight-Ridder Inc. group.

Circulation: 74,551(m); 74,551(m-sat); 103,204(S); ABC Sept. 30, 1995.

Price: 50¢(d); 50¢(sat); $1.50(S); $3.23/wk; $14.00/mo; $158.60/yr.

Advertising: Open inch rate $40.77(m); $40.77(m-sat); $53.15(S). **Representative:** Landon Associates Inc.

News Services: AP, KRT, NYT. **Politics:** Independent. **Established:** 1826 (Telegraph), 1884 (News).

Special Editions: Sportsman Connection (Jan); Home Expo, Annual Business Review (Feb); Tax, Cherry Blossom Festival, Home & Garden (Apr); Graduation, Parade of Homes (May); Football, Sportsman Connection (Aug); Coming Up, Fall Home Improvement (Sept); GA National Fair, New Car (Oct); Southern Living Cooking School, Cookbook (Nov).

Special Weekly Sections: Business Plus (mon); Bibb Neighbors (TMC) (tues); Houston/Peach Neighbors (TMC), Best Food Day (wed); Leisure (fri); Travel Guide (S).

Magazines: Mid-Georgia Real Estate (S); Parade; TV Teletime; Entertainment.

CORPORATE OFFICERS

President Carol Hudler
Vice Pres Richard D Thomas
Treasurer Amy Heil Maley

GENERAL MANAGEMENT

Publisher Carol Hudler
Chief Financial Officer Amy Heil Maley
Director-Human Resources Bruce King

ADVERTISING

Manager-Retail Philip Hollen
Manager-ACS Kay Beasley

MARKETING AND PROMOTION

Director-Marketing Dave Wallace
Manager-Promotion Jennifer Chapman
Manager-Research Laura Hemenway

TELECOMMUNICATIONS

Director-Info Systems Mike Cox

CIRCULATION

Director Kaijer Lee
Manager-Customer Service/Retention Jacqueline Ruffini
Manager-Sales/Marketing Jennifer Harding

NEWS EXECUTIVES

Editor Richard D Thomas
Asst Editor Charles Richardson
Managing Editor-Features Barbara Stinson
Managing Editor-News Ron Woodgeard
Asst Managing Editor Phil Dodson
Asst Managing Editor Bill Weaver
Assoc Editor R L Day

EDITORS AND MANAGERS

Book Editor Paul Alexander
Business Editor Steve Bills
Chief Photographer Danny Gilleland
Editorial Page Editor Ed Corson
Entertainment/Amusements Writer Dan Maley
Features Editor James Palmer
Films/Theater Editor Dan Maley
Food Editor Jane Self
Georgia Living Editor James Palmer
Health/Medical Writer Jodi White
Librarian Harriet Comer
Living/Lifestyle Editor James Palmer
Metro Editor Oby Brown
News Editor Nick Russo
Radio/Television Editor Ella Haynes
Religion Editor Jane Self
Sports Editor Kevin Procter

MANAGEMENT INFORMATION SERVICES

Director-Info Systems Mike Cox

PRODUCTION

Director Jim Plunkett
Asst Director Wilbur Wright
Senior Supervisor-Pre Press Rusty Dodd
Manager-Mailroom James K Sutton
Manager-Pressroom Butch Fowler
Manager-Building Service Mike Osborne
Administrative Asst Julie Beck

Market Information: Zoned editions; Split Run; TMC; ADS.

Mechanical available: Flexographic; Black and 3 ROP colors; insert accepted — preprinted; page cut-offs — 22".

Mechanical specifications: Type page 13" x 21¼"; E - 6 cols, 2¹⁄₁₆", ⅛" between; A - 6 cols, 2¹⁄₁₆", ⅛" between; C - 9 cols, 1⅜", ⅛" between.

Commodity consumption: Newsprint 7,702.5 short tons; 6,987.7 metric tons; widths 55", 27½", 41¼"; black ink 240,538 pounds; color ink 87,454 pounds; single pages printed 16,788; average pages per issue 38.5(d), 91.5(S); single plates used 42,771.

Equipment: EDITORIAL: Front-end hardware — 3-SII/Tandem TXP25; Front-end software — SII/Editorial; Printers — Genicom/1040; Other equipment — 63-SII/Dakota. CLASSIFIED: Front-end hardware — 3-SII/Tandem TXP25; Front-end software — SII/Classified, SII/Classified Pagination; Printers — Genicom/1040; Other equipment — 11-SII/Dakota. DISPLAY: Adv layout systems — Ap/Mac Quadra 7 RIP, Ap/Mac ci, CD-Rom; Front-end hardware — Ap/Mac, Ap/Mac IIci; Front-end software — QuarkXPress, Multi-Ad/Creator; Printers — Ap/Mac LaserWriter; Other equipment — MON/Prism Imagesetter, MON, ECR. PRODUCTION: Pagination software — SII/System 25; Typesetters — 2-MON/Laser Express, 1-MON/Laser Prism, 1-MON/Express Master 1270; Platemaking systems — 3-He/SRA-Autocap; Electronic picture desk — Lf/AP Leaf Picture Desk; Scanners — 1-ECR/Autokon 1030; Production cameras — 1-C/Pager II, 1-C/Marathon I; Automatic film processors — 1-LE/LD 24, 1-P/Litex 26, 3-LE/MTP 26; Film transporters — 1-C/Pager II, 3-MON/Laser Express-LE; Shrink lenses — 1-Kamerak/Distorta; Color separation equipment (conventional) — 1-RZ/4050 E.
PRESSROOM: Line 1 — 7-MOT/Flexo double width; Line 2 — 7-H/Colormatic double width; Folders — 1-H/3:2, 1-H/2:1, 1-M/3:2, 1-M/2:1; Pasters — 7-MOT/Automatic, 7-H/Automatic; Reels and stands — 7-MOT, 7-H; Press control system — MOT/Flexo. MAILROOM: Counter stackers — 3-Id/2000, 2-MM/CN 70, 1-MM/20-500; Inserters and stuffers — 2-M/308 Bilner, 1-M/227I; Bundle tyer — 3-PSN/1-MS; Addressing machine — 2-Ch/539. LIBRARY: Electronic — Vu/Text. WIRE SERVICES: News — AP, NYT, KRT; Photos — AP; Stock tables — AP; Syndicates — AP; Receiving dishes — AP. BUSINESS COMPUTERS: 1-HP/3000 Series 957; Applications: Lotus, WordPerfect, Reflections, Monarc, CJ/AIM-CIS: Gen ledger, Accts payable, Payroll, 401K; PCs & micros networked; PCs & main system networked.

MARIETTA
Cobb County

'90 U.S. Census- 44,129; E&P '96 Est. 58,938
ABC-NDM (90): 447,745 (HH 171,288)

Marietta Daily Journal
(m-mon to sat; S)

Marietta Daily Journal, 580 Fairground St.; PO Box 449, Marietta, GA 30061; tel (770) 428-9411; fax (770) 422-9533; e-mail culc43@prodigy.com.

Circulation: 23,873(m); 23,873(m-sat); 23,419(S); ABC Sept. 30, 1995.

Price: 25¢(d); 25¢(sat); 75¢(S); $9.45/mo; $98.28/yr.

Advertising: Open inch rate $19.50(m); $19.50(m-sat); $19.50(S). **Representative:** US Suburban Press.

News Services: AP, SHNS. **Politics:** Independent. **Established:** 1867.

Special Editions: Per Cent Off Savings, Tax Guide (Jan); Progress (Feb); Lawn & Garden, Spring Fashion, Bride's Tour (Mar); Spring Interior, Vacation Get-away (Apr); Spring Car Care, Spring Home Improvement (May); Graduation, Father's Day (June); Newcomer's Guide, Per Cent Off Savings (July); Back-to-School, Football Preview (Aug); Health & Fitness, Fall Home & Garden (Sept); Fall Car Care (Oct); Holiday Cookbook, Thanksgiving Issue (Nov); Christmas Greetings, Gift Guide, First Baby (Dec).

Magazines: "Going Out" (local entertainment) (fri); USA Weekend; TV Times (local).

CORPORATE OFFICERS

President Tom Jones
Vice Pres Stanley Whitaker
Secretary F T Davis

GENERAL MANAGEMENT

Publisher Otis A Brumby Jr
Vice Pres/Director-Operations Harris S Kettles
Assoc Publisher Jay Whorton

ADVERTISING

Director Debra Murray

CIRCULATION

Director Don McGowan

NEWS EXECUTIVE

Editor Rodney Shumake

EDITORS AND MANAGERS

Automotive Editor Luke Johnson
Book Editor Martha Collins
Business Editor Scott Henry
Columnist Bill Kinney
Columnist Joe Kirby
Editorial Page Editor Joe Kirby
Education Editor Jamie Carte
Entertainment/Amusements Editor Suzanne Van Atten
Fashion/Style Editor Martha Collins
Features Editor Martha Collins
Food Editor Martha Collins
Graphics Editor/Art Director Lindell Strong
Living/Lifestyle Editor Martha Collins
Metro Editor Jay Dillon
Newsroom Manager Rodney Shumake
Photo Department Manager Barry Shapiro
Sports Editor Billy Mitchell
Television/Film Editor Suzanne Van Atten
Theater/Music Editor Suzanne Van Atten
Travel Editor Martha Collins

MANAGEMENT INFORMATION SERVICES

Accounting Manager Tammy Bailey

PRODUCTION

Director Jeff Buice

Market Information: TMC; ADS.

Mechanical available: Offset; Black and 3 ROP colors; insert accepted — preprinted; page cut-offs — 21½".

Mechanical specifications: Type page 13" x 21½"; E - 6 cols, 2", .19" between; A - 6 cols, 2", .19" between; C - 10 cols, 1.17", ⅛" between.

Commodity consumption: Newsprint 2,975 short tons; widths 27½", 13¾"; black ink 50,000 pounds; color ink 9,780 pounds; single pages printed 13,536; average pages per issue 36(d), 48(S); single plates used 24,950.

Equipment: EDITORIAL: Front-end hardware — Ik; Front-end software — Ik; Printers — Okidata, Xante. CLASSIFIED: Front-end hardware — Ik; Front-end software — Ik; Printers — Panasonic. PRODUCTION: Typesetters — 3-Ik/Mark IX; Plate exposures — 2-Nu; Plate processors — 1-Nat; Scanners — Lf/Leafscan 45 interfaced to ECR/Autokon; Production cameras — 1-C/Spartan, 1-C/Spartan III; Automatic film processors — 2-LE; Film transporters — 1-LE; Color separation equipment (conventional) — Lf/AP Leaf Picture Desk, 1-C/Easycolor; Digital color separation equipment — Lf/Leafscan 45, ECR/Autokon.
PRESSROOM: Line 1 — 8-G/Urbanite(7 Black; 1 Color); Line 2 — 10-G/Urbanite(9 Black; 1 Color); Folders — 2-G, G/SSC; Press control system — Fin. MAILROOM: Counter stackers — 2-BG/Count-O-Veyor, 1-PPK; Inserters and stuffers — 3-KR; Bundle tyer — 4-Bu. WIRE SERVICES: News — AP; Stock tables — AP; Syndicates — SHNS; Receiving dishes — size-3m, AP. BUSINESS COMPUTERS: 1-IBM/Sys 36; Applications: Circ, Adv, Accts payable, Gen ledger, Payroll, Class; PCs & main system networked.

MILLEDGEVILLE
Baldwin County

'90 U.S. Census- 17,727; E&P '96 Est. 24,085

The Union-Recorder
(m-tues to sat)

The Union-Recorder, Garrett Way; PO Box 520, Milledgeville, GA 31061; tel (912) 452-0567; fax (912) 452-9539. Knight-Ridder Inc. group.

Circulation: 8,547(m); 8,547(m-sat); Sworn Sept. 29, 1995.

Price: 35¢(d); 35¢(sat); $79.30/yr.

Advertising: Open inch rate $11.25(m); $11.25(m-sat). **Representative:** Newspapers First.

News Services: AP, KRT. **Politics:** Independent. **Established:** 1820.

Special Editions: Business & Industry, Home Improvement & Gardening (Mar); Hunting & Fishing, Graduation (May); Focus on Milledgeville (July); Hunting & Fishing, Football (Aug); Basketball, Gift Guide (Nov); Gift Ideas (Dec).

Special Weekly Sections: Teens (tues); Health (wed); Escape (thur); Home (fri); Family (sat).

Magazines: TV Magazine, USA Weekend (sat); I.D. Magazine (college); 50+ Lifestyles (seniors, quarterly).

GENERAL MANAGEMENT

Publisher/Editor Susan L Patterson

ADVERTISING

Director-Marketing John Hall

CIRCULATION

Manager Alton Brown

NEWS EXECUTIVE

Editor Susan L Patterson

EDITORS AND MANAGERS

City Editor Don Schanche Jr
News Editor Debby Durrence
Photo Editor Ed Cottingham

PRODUCTION

Director Ralph Hammock
Director-Creative/Technical Service Keith Barlow

Market Information: TMC; ADS.

Mechanical available: Offset; Black and 3 ROP colors; insert accepted — preprinted; page cut-offs — 22¾".

Mechanical specifications: Type page 13" x 21½"; E - 6 cols, 2¹⁄₁₆", ⅛" between; A - 6 cols, 2¹⁄₁₆", ⅛" between; C - 9 cols, 1⅜", ¹⁄₁₆" between.

Commodity consumption: Newsprint 1,200 metric tons; widths 29", 33½", 27½"; black ink 40,000 pounds; color ink 10,000 pounds; single pages printed 5,500; average pages per issue 16(d); single plates used 10,000.

Equipment: EDITORIAL: Front-end hardware — IBM/PC, 2-Ap/Mac; Front-end software — MPS; Printers — COM/8400, DP/1800, HP/4si, Ap/Mac II NTX. CLASSIFIED: Front-end hardware — IBM/PC, PC; Front-end software — MPS; Printers — HP/IIP. DISPLAY: Front-end hardware — 3-Ap/Mac; Front-end software — QuarkXPress, Aldus/Illustrator, Aldus/FreeHand, Adobe/Photoshop; Printers — Ap/Mac LaserWriter II NT, DP/PPI-1800 Imagesetter, HP/Hsi; Other equipment — Sharp/Scanner, HP/IIcx Scanner, NEC/3xe CD-Rom. PRODUCTION: Pagination software — QuarkXPress 3.3; OCR software — TI/Omni-Page 3.0; Typesetters — COM/8400, DP/PPI-1800 Imagesetter, Ap/Mac LaserWriter, HP/4si; Plate exposures — 2-Nu/Flip Top FT40UPNS; Plate processors — Nat/Super A-250, Nat/A-350; Scanners — Lf/Leafscan 35; Production cameras — C/Spartan III; Automatic film processors — P/Pakonolith 524; Film transporters — C/Spartan; Color separation equipment (conventional) — Lf/AP Leaf Picture Desk; Digital color separation equipment — Lf/Leafscan 35.
PRESSROOM: Line 1 — 7-G/Community; Folders — SC. MAILROOM: Counter stackers — HI/2518; Inserters and stuffers — MM/5 Head; Bundle tyer — Bu/Plastic and string. LIBRARY: Electronic — MPS/Archive System. WIRE SERVICES: News — AP, AP Datafeatures, KRT, AP; Photos — AP; Receiving dishes — size-10ft, AP. BUSINESS COMPUTERS: PCs & main system networked.

MOULTRIE
Colquitt County

'90 U.S. Census- 14,865; E&P '96 Est. 14,433

The Observer (m-mon to sat)

The Observer, 25 N. Main St.; Box 889, Moultrie, GA 31768; tel (912) 985-4545; fax (912) 985-3569. Gannett Co. Inc. group.

Circulation: 7,321(m); 7,321(m-sat); Sworn Oct. 1, 1994.

Price: 35¢(d); 35¢(sat); $8.58/mo; $93.46/yr, $109.20/yr (mail).

Advertising: Open inch rate $11.29(m); $11.29 (m-sat). **Representative:** Landon Associates Inc.

News Service: AP. **Politics:** Independent. **Established:** 1894.

Special Editions: Car Care, Brides Edition, Home, Lawn & Garden, Spring Fashions (Mar); Brides (Apr); Super Mom (May); Colquitt Pride, Grad Tab, Youth Baseball/Softball (June); Progress (July); Football Preview Tab, Back-to-School (Aug); New Car, Fact Book, King Cotton (Sept); Agricultural Exposition (Oct).

Special Weekly Sections: Health Scene (mon); NASCAR Racing Page, Dining Guide (thur); TV Week (sat).

Magazines: Cruising Times (bi-monthly); Chamber of Commerce Guide (annually).

I-96 Georgia

CORPORATE OFFICERS

President	William deB Mebane
Secretary	Thelma Anderson

GENERAL MANAGEMENT

Publisher	Gary W Boley
General Manager/Purchasing Agent	Gary W Boley

ADVERTISING

Director-Marketing	Michael Bortvit
Manager-Retail	Kendra Walden

CIRCULATION

Manager-Sales	Richard Barkley
Supervisor-Customer Service	Loretta Houston

NEWS EXECUTIVES

Editor	Dwain Walden
Managing Editor	Wayne Grandy

EDITORS AND MANAGERS

City Editor	Jodi Scott
Society Editor	Joyce Tyndall
Sports Editor	Cosby Woodruff

MANAGEMENT INFORMATION SERVICES

Data Processing Manager	Bobbie Brigman

PRODUCTION

Director	Dorsey Smith
Foreman-Composing	Glenda Knox
Foreman/Manager-Pressroom	Dorsey Smith

Market Information: TMC.
Mechanical available: Offset; Black and 3 ROP colors; insert accepted — preprinted; page cut-offs — 22 3/4".
Mechanical specifications: Type page 13" x 21 1/2"; E - 6 cols, 2 1/16", 1/8" between; A - 6 cols, 2 1/16", 1/8" between; C - 6 cols, 2 1/16", 1/8" between.
Commodity consumption: Newsprint 330 short tons; widths 27 1/2", 13 3/4"; black ink 8,500 pounds; color ink 500 pounds; single pages printed 6,260; average pages per issue 20(d); single plates used 4,000.
Equipment: EDITORIAL: Front-end hardware — Mk. CLASSIFIED: Front-end hardware — 12-Epson. DISPLAY: Adv layout systems — Mk. PRODUCTION: Typesetters — 2-Dy/Mark 4, 4-COM/4961, 1-COM/2961, 1-COM/7200; Platemaking systems — 3M/Pyrofax; Plate exposures — 1-Nu/Flip Top FT401; Production cameras — 1-C/Spartan II, ECR/Autokon; Automatic film processors — 1-LE/LD18; Shrink lenses — 1-Kamerak.
PRESSROOM: Line 1 — 8-G/SC; Folders — 1-G/2:1. MAILROOM: Bundle tyer — 2-Bu; Addressing machine — 2-Wm. LIBRARY: Combination — 1-Kk. WIRE SERVICES: News — AP; Photos — AP; Stock tables — AP. BUSINESS COMPUTERS: IBM/AS400; PCs & micros networked; PCs & main system networked.

ROME

Floyd County

'90 U.S. Census- 30,326; E&P '96 Est. 31,160

Rome News-Tribune

(e-mon to fri; S)

Rome News-Tribune, 305 E. 6th Ave.; PO Box 1633, Rome, GA 30162-1633; tel (706) 291-6397; fax (706) 232-9632.
Circulation: 20,411(e); 20,411(S); Sworn Sept. 28, 1994.
Price: 50¢(d); $1.50(S); $7.90/mo; $94.80/yr.
Advertising: Open inch rate $15.22(e); $15.22(S). **Representative:** American Newspaper Representatives Inc.
News Services: AP, NEA. **Politics:** Independent. **Established:** 1843.
Not Published: New Year; Independence Day; Labor Day; Thanksgiving; Christmas.
Advertising not accepted: No alcoholic beverage ads accepted for Sunday; No "upside-down" ads.
Special Editions: Bride's World, Coupon Book, Rome, Women's World, Chamber Buyers Guide Book (Jan); Tax Guide (Feb); Rome City Schools, Review and Forecast, Insurance Week (Mar); Realtor Week, Home Improvement, Outdoor/Vacation Leisure Living, Bride's World II (Apr); Car Care, Medical Care, Rome City Schools, Coupon Book II (June); Past Times (Aug); Fair Premium Catalog Book (Sept); Heritage Holidays, Cooking School, Car Care (Oct); Rome Days, Rome City Schools (Nov); Gift Guide (Dec).
Special Weekly Sections: Roman Record (mon); Young Romans (tues); Best Food Guide (wed); Tribune Viewers Guide (fri); Roman Life (S).
Magazines: Business Tab (mon); Youth Tab (tues); TV/Cable Program Magazine (fri); Lifestyle Section (S).

CORPORATE OFFICER

President	Burgett H Mooney III

GENERAL MANAGEMENT

Publisher	Burgett H Mooney III
General Manager	C Dan Mozley
Purchasing Agent	C Dan Mozley

ADVERTISING

Director	Gayle Touchstone
Manager-General	Joyce Yarbrough

CIRCULATION

Manager	Jay A Stone

NEWS EXECUTIVE

Editor	Thomas Toles

EDITORS AND MANAGERS

Lifestyle Editor	Karen Lagow
Sports Editor	James O'Hara

PRODUCTION

Director	Jerry Pollard

Market Information: Split Run; TMC.
Mechanical available: Offset; Black and 3 ROP colors; insert accepted — preprinted; page cut-offs — 22 3/4".
Mechanical specifications: Type page 13" x 21 1/4"; E - 6 cols, 2 1/16", 1/8" between; A - 6 cols, 2 1/16", 1/8" between; C - 9 cols, 1 3/8", 1/16" between.
Commodity consumption: Newsprint 1,200 short tons; widths 27 1/2", 13 3/4", 30"; black ink 17,500 pounds; color ink 4,000 pounds; single pages printed 8,100; average pages per issue 22(d), 42(S); single plates used 21,000.
Equipment: EDITORIAL: Front-end hardware — Ik/CPS 1020, CD/2330, 1-IBM/PC, ACT; Front-end software — Novell/Network 4.1; Other equipment — Ik/VDS-Modem Vadic, 24-Ik/50, 5-Ik/51, 1-Ik/40, 5-Ik/60, 1-HAS/Magician Plus, 1-HAS/Magician. CLASSIFIED: Front-end hardware — CD/2330 Sys; Other equipment — 4-HAS/Magician Plus. DISPLAY: Front-end hardware — PC/486, Archetype. PRODUCTION: Pagination software — ACT; Typesetters — 1-M/202, 1-M/202N, LaserMaster/1200dpi, ECR/Scriptsetter; Plate exposures — 1-Nu/Flip Top FT40APRNS; Plate processors — 1-Nat/A-340; Electronic picture desk — Lf/AP Leaf Picture Desk; Scanners — 1-ECR/Autokon 1000, Lf/Leafscan; Production cameras — 1-C/Spartan III; Automatic film processors — LE, 24-AQ; Film transporters — 1-C; Shrink lenses — 1-Alan/24.
PRESSROOM: Line 1 — 6-G/Urbanite; Folders — 1-G. MAILROOM: Counter stackers — 1-MM/288; Inserters and stuffers — 1-MM/227 1-3 stations, 1-GMA/MM 227 6:1 Jet; Bundle tyer — 1-MLN/MLEE; Addressing machine — 1-Ch/525/E, 1-Prism/InkJet Labeling System. WIRE SERVICES: News — AP Datastream; Syndicates — AP Datafeatures, NEA; Receiving dishes — size-3m, AP. BUSINESS COMPUTERS: 1-IBM/Sys 36-5360, 1-IBM/AS-400; Applications: Accts receivable, Accts payable, Gen ledger, Circ, Direct mail; PCs & main system networked.

SAVANNAH

Chatham County

'90 U.S. Census- 137,560; E&P '96 Est. 137,350
ABC-CZ (90): 183,347 (HH 68,436)

Savannah Morning News

(m-mon to fri)

Savannah Evening Press

(e-mon to fri)

Savannah News-Press

(m-sat; S)

Savannah News-Press, 111 W. Bay St.; PO Box 1088, Savannah, GA 31402; tel (912) 236-9511; fax (912) 236-8909; e-mail ardv38c@prodigy.com. Morris Communications Corp. group.
Circulation: 54,041(m); 13,158(e); 71,616 (m-sat); 77,034(S); ABC Sept. 30, 1995.
Price: 25¢(d); 25¢(sat); $1.25(S); $11.50/mo.
Advertising: Open inch rate $49.40(m); $49.40(e); $49.40(m-sat); $50.75(S). **Representative:** Landon Associates Inc.
News Services: AP, NEA, KRT, LAT. **Politics:** Independent. **Established:** 1850.
Note: Advertising for the Morning News & Evening Press is sold only in combination.
Special Editions: Parenting & Child Care (Jan); Fashion and Bridal (Feb); Southern Home Show, Travel & Vacation Guide (Mar); Heritage Golf, American Home Week (Apr); Mother's Day, Home Decorating (May); Senior Scene (June); Back-to-School, Football (Aug); Children's Section, New Car Issue, Home Improvement (Oct); At Home, Gift Guide (Nov); Holiday Greetings (Dec).
Special Weekly Sections: Our Schools (e-tues); Food (wed); Computers, Accent on Teens (thur); Diversions (fri); Behind the Wheel (sat); Arts and Travel, Review & Opinion (S).
Magazine: Parade (S).

CORPORATE OFFICERS

Chairman of the Board	W S Morris III
President	Paul S Simon
Secretary/Treasurer	William A Herman III

GENERAL MANAGEMENT

Publisher	Frank T Anderson
Manager-Accounting	Augustine Scarboro
Manager-Credit	A V Rocker
Personnel Manager	Frankie Fort

ADVERTISING

Director	Bucky Johnson
Manager-Retail	Buddy L Kuykendall
Manager-Classified	Steve Tuck
Manager-Special Products	Cindy Elliott

MARKETING AND PROMOTION

Manager-Marketing Service	Stacy Jennings

TELECOMMUNICATIONS

Audiotex Manager	Cindy Elliott

CIRCULATION

Director	Linwood Pride
Manager-Alternate Delivery	Don Donley

NEWS EXECUTIVES

Exec Editor	Rexanna Lester
Managing Editor	Dan Suwyn

EDITORS AND MANAGERS

Arts/Books Editor	Doug Wyatt
Business Editor/Public Affairs Editor	Larry Peterson
Community News Editor	Bob Matthews
Copy Desk Chief	Lee Freeman
Editorial Page Editor	Tom Barton
Editorial Writer	Jim Halbe
Environment Editor	Doug Wyatt
Features Planning Editor	Claudia Ortega
Health/Education Editor	Doug Wyatt
Librarian	Julia Muller
News Planning Editor	Steve Thomas
Outdoors Editor	John Burke
Photo Department Manager	Steve Bisson
South Carolina Editor	Kyle Poplin
Sports Editor	Tony Stastny
State Editor	Tuck Thompson
Television Editor	Doug Wyatt

PRODUCTION

Director	Michael Traynor
Manager-Pre Press	David Meadows
Supervisor-Electronics	Mark Goldwire
Supervisor-Building	Tink Cole
Asst Supervisor-Pressroom	Randolph Nettles
Superintendent-Mailroom	Freeman Stone
Chief Machinist	David Folmar

Market Information: Zoned editions; TMC; ADS; Operate audiotex.
Mechanical available: Offset; Black and 3 ROP colors; insert accepted — preprinted, odd sizes subject to approval; page cut-offs — 22 3/4".
Mechanical specifications: Type page 13" x 21 1/2"; E - 6 cols, 2 1/16", 1/8" between; A - 6 cols, 2 1/16", 1/8" between; C - 9 cols, 1 3/8", 1/16" between.
Commodity consumption: Newsprint 8,070 short tons; widths 55", 41 1/4", 27 1/2"; black ink 159,000 pounds; color ink 62,208 pounds; single pages printed 26,000; average pages per issue 36(d), 44(sat), 84(S); single plates used 60,000.
Equipment: EDITORIAL: Front-end hardware — IBM/PC-AT, Ap/Mac 8100/80, Ap/Mac IIfx, Ap/Mac SE; Front-end software — MPS/Tecs 2, QuarkXPress, Adobe/Illustrator, Aldus/FreeHand; Printers — HP/4, III/Xitron, Clipper/Navigator; Other equipment — IBM/Selectric. CLASSIFIED: Front-end hardware — IBM/PC-AT; Front-end software — MPS/Tecs 2. AUDIOTEX: Hardware — 1-BDR/Voicegate, 1-Zephyrus/down converter, 1-Wyse, 1-Panasonic/P1180. DISPLAY: Adv layout systems — Ap/Mac IIfx, Ap/Mac Quadra 950, Ap/Mac 8100/80; Front-end hardware — Ap/Mac; Front-end software — Multi-Ad/Creator, Aldus/FreeHand, Adobe/Illustrator, QuarkXPress; Printers — Ap/Mac LaserWriter IIg, Tectronix/Phaser III, III/Xitron, Clipper/Navigator; Other equipment — Ap/Mac CD-Rom, Micronet/Tape Backups, PLI/128 Meg Optical Drive. PRODUCTION: Pagination software — QuarkXPress; Typesetters — XIT/Clipper, XIT/Navigator; Plate exposures — 2-Nu/Flip Top FT40UPNS, 1-B, Nu/Vacuum plate burner; Plate processors — 1-Nat/A340; Electronic picture desk — 1-Lf/AP Leaf Picture Desk; Scanners — RZ/210L, Kk/RFS-2035, Polaroid/SprintScan, Nikon/Scan Touch; Production cameras — 2-C/Spartan III; Automatic film processors — 1-P/26 EL, 1-C/Powermatic 66F, 1-C/Powermatic 66RA; Film transporters — 2-C; Shrink lenses — CK Optical; Color separation equipment (conventional) — RZ/210L; Digital color separation equipment — 2-Kk/RFS 2035, Polaroid/SprintScan, Nikon/Scan Touch.
PRESSROOM: Line 1 — 7-G/3176; Press drives — Fin; Folders — 2-G/2:1; Pasters — 7-G; Reels and stands — 7-G. MAILROOM: Counter stackers — 2-Id/NS660; Inserters and stuffers — MM/227 (3-MM 6:1); Bundle tyer — Dynaric/NP-4; Addressing machine — 2-Ch, 1-KR; Other mailroom equipment — QWI/Bottom Wrap. Fg/Single Gripper Conveyor. COMMUNICATIONS: Digital ad delivery system — AP AdSend. Systems used — satellite. WIRE SERVICES: News — AP; Photos — AP; Stock tables — AP SelectStox, AP Grand Junction; Syndicates — KRT; Receiving dishes — AP, Press Release. BUSINESS COMPUTERS: IBM/PS2, Gateway 2000/P5-90; Applications: Lotus 1-2-3, Microsoft; PCs & micros networked.

STATESBORO

Bulloch County

'90 U.S. Census- 15,854; E&P '96 Est. 16,756

Statesboro Herald

(m-mon to sat; S)

Statesboro Herald, One Herald Sq.; PO Box 888, Statesboro, GA 30458; tel (912) 764-9031; fax (912) 489-8181. Morris Newspaper Corp. group.
Circulation: 7,093(m); 7,093(m-sat); 7,093(S); Sworn Sept. 30, 1995.
Price: 35¢(d); 35¢(sat); 75¢(S); $9.50/mo; $114.00/yr.
Advertising: Open inch rate $10.80(m); $10.80(m-sat); $10.80(S). **Representatives:** Landon Associates Inc.; Morris Newspaper Corp. Advertising Sales.
News Service: AP. **Politics:** Independent. **Established:** 1937.
Special Editions: Back-to-School; Football; Bridal; Pride; Newcomer's Guide; Home Improvement; Gift Guide; Halloween Spooktacular; 11th Hour Santa; Cookbook; Today's Woman.
Magazines: Entertainment Guide; Sunday Comics.

CORPORATE OFFICERS

Board Chairman	Charles H Morris
President	Joe McGlamery

GENERAL MANAGEMENT

Publisher	Randy Morton

ADVERTISING

Manager-Retail	Jan Melton

CIRCULATION

Manager	Jim Purdon
Manager-District	Carl Bensley
Manager-District	Marty Herrin

NEWS EXECUTIVE

Editor	Larry Anderson

EDITORS AND MANAGERS

Sports Editor	Anthony Dasher
Women's Editor	Nancy Welch

MANAGEMENT INFORMATION SERVICES

Data Processing Manager	Edra Street

PRODUCTION

Manager	Charles Joiner
Supervisor-Camera	William Edwards
Foreman-Mailroom	William Tidwell
Foreman-Composing	Constance Parker
Supervisor-Press	Henry Westberry

Market Information: TMC.
Mechanical available: Offset; Black and 3 ROP colors; insert accepted — preprinted; page cut-offs — 22".
Mechanical specifications: Type page 13" x 21 1/2"; E - 6 cols, 2", 1/8" between; A - 6 cols, 2", 1/8" between; C - 9 cols, 1 3/8", 1/16" between.
Commodity consumption: Newsprint 1,800 short tons; width 27 1/2"; black ink 38,000 pounds; color ink 9,600 pounds; single pages printed 7,200; average pages per issue 18(d), 36(S); single plates used 22,000.

Georgia I-97

Equipment: EDITORIAL: Front-end hardware — 8-Ap/Mac Centris 610 4-80, 1-Ap/Mac Duo 230 8-80; Front-end software — Baseview/NewsEdit IQ 1.1.2, QuarkXPress 3.3, AppleShare 4.0; Printers — 1-Ap/Mac LaserPrinter NTX; Other equipment — Kk/RFS 2035 Scanner, 1-Ap/Mac Quadra 840 32-500, Ap/Mac Quadra 950 32-1500 Fileserver. CLASSIFIED: Front-end hardware — Mk, 3-Ap/Mac Centris 610 4-80; Front-end software — Mk, Baseview/Class Manager 3.2.1; Printers — Okidata/320. DISPLAY: Adv layout systems — 1-Ap/Mac Quadra 800 24-500; Front-end software — QuarkXPress 3.3, Mk/Ad Director 1.5.2; Other equipment — CD-Rom, Mk/Scan Maker IIG. PRODUCTION: Pagination software — QuarkXPress 3.3, Baseview/News Edit IQueX 1.1.2, QTools 2.0.2; OCR software — PLI/88mb, XYQUEST, AppleShare/Pro 40 3.7.68; Typesetters — IIV/3850 Film Recorder, IIV/3850 Film Recorder, QMS/860, 5-Ap/Mac Quadra 800-25-500, Ap/Mac Server; Plate exposures — 1-Nu, Nu/Flip Top FT 40 APRNs; Plate processors — Nat/A-250; Scanners — MK/Scan Maker IIxe, Sharp/JX 610; Production cameras — 1-DAI, 1-SCREEN/DSC-24-D; Automatic film processors — 1-LE, 1-LE/LD24 AQ, 1-Clunz & Jenson; Film transporters — 1-Clunz & Jenson, ECR/Imager 3850.
PRESSROOM: Line 1 — 12-G/Community; Folders — 12-ISSC; Pasters — 9-Enkel. MAILROOM: Addressing machine — KR. WIRE SERVICES: News — AP; Photos — AP; Syndicates — AP; Receiving dishes — AP. BUSINESS COMPUTERS: Applications: Peachtree.

THOMASVILLE
Thomas County
'90 U.S. Census- 17,457; E&P '96 Est. 16,921
ABC-CZ (90): 17,457 (HH 6,718)

Thomasville Times-Enterprise (e-mon to fri; S)
Thomasville Times-Enterprise, 106 South St.; PO Box 650, Thomasville, GA 31799; tel (912) 226-2400; fax (912) 228-5863. Thomson Newspapers group.
Circulation: 10,147(e); 9,992(S); ABC Sept. 30, 1995.
Price: 50¢(d); $1.00(S); $8.25/mo; $99.00/yr.
Advertising: Open inch rate $12.50(e); $12.50(S). **Representative:** Papert Companies.
News Service: AP. **Politics:** Independent. **Established:** 1889.
Not Published: New Year; Independence Day; Labor Day; Christmas .
Advertising not accepted: Vending machine; Stuffing envelopes.
Special Editions: Back-to-School; Football Kick-off; Christmas Gift Guide; Mature Living; George Washington's Birthday Sale; Rose Festival; Women of the 90's; Salute to Area Churches; Home-owned Business; Home Improvement; Cookbook; Spring & Fall Fashion Tabs; Progress.
Special Weekly Sections: Agriculture, Best Food Days (tues); Best Food Days (wed); Best Auto Day, Weekend Page (thur); Church Pages, School News, Best Real Estate Day (fri); Business (S).
Magazines: TV Listings, Entertainment, Color Comics (S).

CORPORATE OFFICER
Group Publisher Keith Blevins
GENERAL MANAGEMENT
Publisher Wallace Goodman
ADVERTISING
Manager Norman Bankston
CIRCULATION
Manager Rob Morrell
NEWS EXECUTIVE
Managing Editor Steven Meadows
EDITORS AND MANAGERS
City Editor Patti Ward
Editorial Page Editor Steven Meadows
Lifestyle Editor Patti Ward
Sports Editor Ira Schoffel
Wire Editor Tami Mott
PRODUCTION
Foreman-Composing Everette Reeves
Foreman-Pressroom Vince Cribb

Market Information: Zoned editions; Split Run; TMC; ADS.
Mechanical available: Offset; Black and 3 ROP colors; insert accepted — preprinted, free standing; page cut-offs — 22½".
Mechanical specifications: Type page 13" x 21½"; E - 6 cols, 2¹⁄₁₆", ⅛" between; A - 6 cols, 2¹⁄₁₆", ⅛" between; C - 9 cols, 1⁵⁄₁₆", ⅛" between.
Commodity consumption: Newsprint 375 short tons; width 27½"; black ink 8,200 pounds; color ink 500 pounds; single pages printed 6,038; average pages per issue 18(d), 40(S); single plates used 3,717.
Equipment: EDITORIAL: Front-end hardware — FSI, Ap/Mac; Front-end software — QuarkXPress, FSI; Other equipment — Ap/Mac. CLASSIFIED: Front-end hardware — Ap/Mac. DISPLAY: Other equipment — Ap/Mac. PRODUCTION: Typesetters — 1-Ap/Mac Laser-Writer, Tegra/Varityper, 2-Ap/Mac, 1-Mk/AdComp; Plate exposures — 1-Nu/Flip Top FT40L; Plate processors — 1-Nat/A-250; Scanners — Lf/Leafscan; Production cameras — SCREEN/Vertical; Automatic film processors — 1-SCREEN.
PRESSROOM: Line 1 — 8-G, 7-G/Community (1 color unit). MAILROOM: Inserters and stuffers — 5-MM; Bundle tyer — 1-OVL; Addressing machine — 3-Wm/5. WIRE SERVICES: News — AP; Syndicates — SHNS, THO, NEA; Receiving dishes — size-3m, AP. BUSINESS COMPUTERS: 6-ATT/Business Sys; Applications: WordPerfect 6.0, Lotus 4.1; PCs & micros networked.

TIFTON
Tift County
'90 U.S. Census- 14,215; E&P '96 Est. 14,720

The Tifton Gazette (e-mon to fri; m-sat)
The Tifton Gazette, 211 N. Tift Ave.; PO Box 708, Tifton, GA 31793; tel (912) 382-4321; fax (912) 387-7322. Thomson Newspapers group.
Circulation: 9,058(e); 9,058(m-sat); Sworn Sept. 29, 1995.
Price: 50¢(d); 50¢(sat); $8.50/mo; $96.00/yr.
Advertising: Open inch rate $10.31(e); $10.31(m-sat). **Representative:** Thomson Newspapers.
News Service: AP. **Politics:** Independent. **Established:** 1888 (weekly), 1914 (daily).
Not Published: New Year; Memorial Day; Independence Day; Labor Day; Christmas.
Advertising not accepted: Right reserved to reject any objectionable copy.
Special Editions: Moonlight Madness Edition, Bridal Section, Health & Fitness (Jan); Valentine's Gift Gallery, Customer Appreciation (Feb); Insurance Feature, Home and Garden Section (Mar); Spring Fashion, Tiftarea Progress Edition, Love Affair Tab (Apr); Senior Citizens Edition, Mother's Day (May); Beach Party, Progress (June); Home-owned Business, Christmas in July (July); Football Preview Section, Back-to-School (Aug); Hunting, Fishing, Oktoberfest (Sept); Women in Business, Lay-Away-Early for Christmas (Oct); T.G. Christmas "Bucks", Holiday Gift Guide (Nov); Countdown to Christmas, Christmas Greetings (Dec).
Special Weekly Sections: Business (mon); Farm Page (tues); Best Food Day (wed); Education (thur); Church Page (fri); Entertainment (sat).

CORPORATE OFFICER
Group Publisher Keith Blevins
GENERAL MANAGEMENT
Publisher James S McKee
Purchasing Agent James S McKee
ADVERTISING
Manager-Display Randy Blalock
Manager-Classified Randy Blalock
CIRCULATION
Manager Phil Jones
NEWS EXECUTIVE
Managing Editor Mike Jones
PRODUCTION
Foreman-Pressroom/Camera Jeff Blease

Market Information: TMC.
Mechanical available: Offset; Black and 3 ROP colors; insert accepted — preprinted, any; page cut-offs — 22¾".
Mechanical specifications: Type page 13" x 21½"; E - 6 cols, 2¹⁄₁₆", ⅛" between; A - 6 cols, 2¹⁄₁₆", ⅛" between; C - 9 cols, 1⅜", ¹⁄₁₆" between.
Commodity consumption: Newsprint 280 short tons; width 27"; black ink 11,800 pounds; single pages printed 5,200; average pages per issue 17(d); single plates used 4,400.
Equipment: EDITORIAL: Front-end hardware — Mk/1100. CLASSIFIED: Front-end hardware — Mk/1100. PRODUCTION: Typesetters — 2-Mk/Laserwriter; Plate exposures — 1-Nu/Flip Top; Production cameras — 1-III/Newsprint; Automatic film processors — LE/LD-220 QT (Table Top Film Processor).
PRESSROOM: Line 1 — 6-G/Community; Folders — 1-G. MAILROOM: Counter stackers — BG; Bundle tyer — 1-Bu, 1-Staplex; Addressing machine — 2-Wm. WIRE SERVICES: News — AP; Receiving dishes — AP. BUSINESS COMPUTERS: ATT.

VALDOSTA
Lowndes County
'90 U.S. Census- 39,806; E&P '96 Est. 41,907
ABC-CZ (90): 39,806 (HH 14,143)

The Valdosta Daily Times (m-mon to sat; S)
Valdosta Daily Times, 201 N. Troup St. (31601); PO Box 968, Valdosta, GA 31603; tel (912) 244-1880; fax (912) 247-2560. Thomson Newspapers group.
Circulation: 19,125(m); 19,125(m-sat); 19,726(S); ABC Sept. 30, 1995.
Price: 50¢(d); 50¢(sat); $1.00(S); $108.00/yr (home delivery), $98.00/yr (mail).
Advertising: Open inch rate $14.76(m); $14.76(m-sat); $14.76(S). **Representative:** Papert Companies.
News Service: AP. **Politics:** Independent. **Established:** 1867.
Special Editions: Spring Fashion (Mar); Progress (Apr); Cookbook (June); Back-to-School, Football (Aug); Fall Fashion, Valdosta Guide (Sept); Gift Guide (Nov); Health & Fitness; Full Maturity; Youth in Schools; Monthly Motoring Guide.
Special Weekly Sections: Food Page (wed); Church Page, TV Section (sat); Business Page (S).
Magazine: Parade.

CORPORATE OFFICER
Group Publisher Keith Blevins-Valdosta
GENERAL MANAGEMENT
Publisher/General Manager Keith Blevins-Valdosta
ADVERTISING
Manager Bill Wallace
CIRCULATION
Director Richard Weisbach
NEWS EXECUTIVE
Editor Gerald Guy
EDITORS AND MANAGERS
Society Editor Elizabeth Butler
Sports Editor Randy Kennedy
PRODUCTION
Director Hubby Brooks
Foreman-Composing Hubby Brooks
Foreman-Pressroom Edwin Cribbs

Market Information: Zoned editions; TMC.
Mechanical available: Offset; Black and 3 ROP colors; insert accepted — preprinted; page cut-offs — 22¾".
Mechanical specifications: Type page 13" x 21½"; E - 6 cols, 2¹⁄₁₆", ⅛" between; A - 6 cols, 2¹⁄₁₆", ⅛" between; C - 9 cols, 1½", ⅛" between.
Commodity consumption: Newsprint 1,300 short tons; widths 27½", 13¾"; single pages printed 9,800; average pages per issue 24(d), 48(S); single plates used 12,500.
Equipment: EDITORIAL: Front-end hardware — CD/2300. CLASSIFIED: Front-end hardware — 1-COM/40. PRODUCTION: Typesetters — 2-Tegra/Varityper/XP-1000; Plate exposures — Nu/FT40V6; Plate processors — Nat/A-250; Production cameras — 1-LE/121, C, SCREEN/C 680; Automatic film processors — 1-LE/LD-24BQ; Digital color separation equipment — Digi-Colour.
PRESSROOM: Line 1 — 7-G/Urbanite; Folders — 1-G. MAILROOM: Counter stackers — 2-MM/(3 station automatic inserter); Bundle tyer — 1-Md; Addressing machine — 1-ATT. COMMUNICATIONS: Systems used — satellite. WIRE SERVICES: News — AP; Stock tables — AP; Syndicates — TNI; Receiving dishes — AP. BUSINESS COMPUTERS: AT/3B2-500; Applications: Payroll, Adv, Circ; PCs & micros networked.

WARNER ROBINS
Houston County
'90 U.S. Census- 43,726; E&P '96 Est. 47,204
ABC-NDM (90): 71,598 (HH 26,160)

The Daily Sun (e-mon to fri)
The Sunday Sun (S)
The Daily Sun, 1553 Watson Blvd.; Box 6129, Warner Robins, GA 31095-6129; tel (912) 923-6432; fax (912) 328-7682. Park Communications Inc. group.
Circulation: 7,693(e); 8,487(S); ABC Sept. 30, 1995.
Price: 35¢(d); $1.00(S); $2.20/wk; $9.55/mo; $114.60/yr.
Advertising: Open inch rate $11.95(e); $11.95(S). **Representative:** Papert Companies.
News Service: AP. **Politics:** Independent. **Established:** 1969.
Not Published: Christmas.
Special Editions: Chamber of Commerce (Jan); Brides (Feb); Clean Community (Mar); City Festival (Apr); Graduates (May); Football Preview, Back-to-School (Aug); International City Championship, Christmas Gift Guide (Nov); Health Journal, Real Estate (monthly).
Special Weekly Sections: Business (mon); Food (wed); Entertainment (thur); Outdoors, Today's Home (S).
Magazines: Family Section, TV Guide (S); USA Weekend.

CORPORATE OFFICERS
President Wright M Thomas
Vice Pres-Newspapers Ralph J Martin
GENERAL MANAGEMENT
General Manager H Thomas Reed Jr
Purchasing Agent Molly Mills
ADVERTISING
Manager Donald Baumgart
Supervisor-Classified Sara Colbert
CIRCULATION
Manager Sherry Denk
NEWS EXECUTIVE
Managing Editor Rex Sanders
EDITORS AND MANAGERS
Action Line Editor Rex Sanders
Automotive Editor Rex Sanders
Business/Finance Editor Brigette Loudermilk
City/Metro Editor Rex Sanders
Editorial Page Editor Rex Sanders
Education Reporter Karen Stroble
Entertainment/Amusements Editor Brigette Loudermilk
Environmental Writer Billy Faires
Farm/Agriculture Writer Billy Faires
Fashion/Style Editor Marilyn Teal
Features Editor Brigette Loudermilk
Fishing Editor Tom Reed
Graphics Editor/Art Director Dee McLelland
Health/Medical Writer Kimberly Cassel Pritchett
Living/Lifestyle Editor Marilyn Teal
National Writer Kimberly Cassel Pritchett
News Editor Dee McLelland
Photo Editor Norman Hosch
Political/Government Writer Kimberly Cassel Pritchett
Religion Writer Kimberly Cassel Pritchett
Special Sections Editor Brigette Loudermilk
Sports Editor Jimmy Simpson
Television/Film Editor Brigette Loudermilk
Theater/Music Editor Brigette Loudermilk
Women's Editor Marilyn Teal
MANAGEMENT INFORMATION SERVICES
Data Processing Manager Dan Yochem
PRODUCTION
Manager Ronnie Zimerle
Foreman-Pressroom Brent O'Reilly

Market Information: TMC.
Mechanical available: Offset; Black and 3 ROP colors; insert accepted — preprinted, all; page cut-offs — 22¾".
Mechanical specifications: Type page 13" x 21½"; E - 6 cols, 2.08", ⅙" between; A - 6 cols, 2.08", ⅙" between; C - 10 cols, 1.17", ⅙" between.
Commodity consumption: Newsprint 591 short tons; widths 28", 14"; single pages printed 6,994; average pages per issue 18(d), 36(S).
Equipment: EDITORIAL: Front-end hardware — Ap/Mac; Front-end software — Baseview; Printers — LaserMaster/Unity 1200XL. CLASSIFIED: Front-end hardware — Ap/Mac; Front-end software — Baseview; Printers — Ap/Mac

LaserWriter IIg. DISPLAY: Adv layout systems — Ap/Mac; Front-end hardware — Ap/Mac Centris 650; Front-end software — QuarkXPress 3.3; Printers — LaserMaster/Unity 1200XL. PRODUCTION: Plate exposures — Nu/Flip Top FTNS 631; Plate processors — 1-Nat/A-250; Production cameras — SCREEN/Companica 670C; Automatic film processors — SCREEN/LD-260-L; Digital color separation equipment — PrePress Solutions, Panther/Plus.
PRESSROOM: Line 1 — 8-G/Community; Folders — 1-G. MAILROOM: Inserters and stuffers — Manual; Bundle tyer — Strapex, Bu/Tyer. WIRE SERVICES: News — AP; Receiving dishes — size-8ft, AP. BUSINESS COMPUTERS: 3-Vision Data/Unix PC; Applications: Vision Data.

WAYCROSS
Ware County
'90 U.S. Census- 16,410; E&P '96 Est. 14,683

Waycross Journal-Herald
(e-mon to sat)

Waycross Journal-Herald, 402 Isabella St.; PO Box 219, Waycross, GA 31502; tel (912) 283-2244; fax (912) 283-0740.
Circulation: 12,076(e); 12,076(e-sat); Sworn Oct. 1, 1994.
Price: 35¢(d); 35¢(sat); $8.00/mo; $96.00/yr.
Advertising: Open inch rate $9.50(e); $9.50(e-sat).
News Service: AP. **Politics:** Democrat. **Established:** 1914.
Not Published: Independence Day; Labor Day; Thanksgiving; Christmas.
Advertising not accepted: Alcoholic beverage, fortune tellers.
Special Editions: Tax (Jan); Bridal (Feb); Spring (Mar); Forest (Apr); Back-to-School, Football (Aug); Fair Edition (Sept); Cookbook (Oct); Christmas (Dec).
Special Weekly Section: TV (sat).

CORPORATE OFFICER
President Roger L Williams

GENERAL MANAGEMENT
Publisher Roger L Williams
Business Manager Donnie Carter
Manager-Credit Donnie Carter
Personnel Manager Van Mock

ADVERTISING
Manager David Tanner
Manager-National David Tanner
Manager-Classified Pat Roundtree

MARKETING AND PROMOTION
Manager-Promotion Donnie Carter

CIRCULATION
Manager Stanley Morgan

NEWS EXECUTIVES
Editor Jack Williams III
Managing Editor Gary Griffin

EDITORS AND MANAGERS
Amusements Editor Rick Head
Books Editor Jack Williams III
Editorial Page Editor Jack Williams III
Education/Religion Editor Martha Davis
Farm/Picture Editor Jack Williams III
Fashion Editor Nickie Carter
Films/Theater Editor Gary Griffin
Food/Garden Editor Nickie Carter
Photo Department Manager James Hooks
School/Science Editor Martha Davis
Society/Women's Editor Nickie Carter
Wire Editor Rick Head

PRODUCTION
Superintendent James Hooks
Foreman-Composing James Hooks
Asst Foreman-Composing Charles Adams
Foreman-Pressroom Danny Stone
Superintendent-Press/Plateroom Danny Stone

Market Information: Split Run; TMC.
Mechanical available: Letterpress (direct) Dynaflex; Black and 3 ROP colors; insert accepted — preprinted; page cut-offs — 22¾".
Mechanical specifications: Type page 13" x 21½"; E - 6 cols, 2 1/16", ⅛" between; A - 6 cols, 2 1/16", ⅛" between; C - 9 cols, 1⅜", 1/16" between.
Commodity consumption: Newsprint 460 short tons; width 27½"; black ink 40,000 pounds; color ink 3,000 pounds; average pages per issue 24(d); single plates used 13,000.
Equipment: EDITORIAL: Front-end hardware — Ap/Mac, Mk/1100 Plus; Front-end software — QPS 3.31; Printers — Ap/Mac LaserPrinter; Other equipment — 1-COM/7200H. CLASSIFIED: Front-end hardware — 2-Mk/Touchwriter Plus; Printers — Ap/Mac LaserPrinter. DISPLAY: Adv layout systems — Ap/Mac; Front-end hardware — Ap/Mac; Front-end software — Multi-Ad/Creator 3.6.1; Printers — Ap/Mac LaserPrinter. PRODUCTION: Pagination software — QPS 3.31; OCR software — TI/OmniPage 3.1; Typesetters — SelectPress/600; Platemaking systems — 1-Na; Plate processors — 1-Dynalite, 1-BKY; Production cameras — 1-C/Spartan III; Automatic film processors — 1-LE/24; Film transporters — 1-LE.
PRESSROOM: Line 1 — 5-G/Universal 175. MAILROOM: Inserters and stuffers — KAN/402; Addressing machine — IBM/Sys 36. WIRE SERVICES: News — AP; Photos — AP; Receiving dishes — size-10ft, AP. BUSINESS COMPUTERS: 1-IBM/Sys 54; PCs & micros networked; PCs & main system networked.

WEST POINT
See LANETT, AL

HAWAII

HILO
Hawaii County
'90 U.S. Census- 45,723; E&P '96 Est. 58,546
ABC-NDM (90): 76,944 (HH 26,526)

Hawaii Tribune-Herald
(m-mon to fri; S)

Hawaii Tribune-Herald, 355 Kinoole St.; PO Box 767, Hilo, HI 96720; tel (808) 935-6621; fax (808) 961-0098. Donrey Media Group group.
Circulation: 19,419(m); 23,304(S); ABC Sept. 30, 1995.
Price: 50¢(d); $1.00(S); $8.50/mo, $102.00/yr.
Advertising: Open inch rate $18.76(m); $18.76(S). **Representative:** Papert Companies.
News Service: AP. **Politics:** Independent. **Established:** 1895 (Tribune), 1923 (Tribune-Herald).
Special Editions: New Auto Show (Feb); Home and Garden, Bride (Apr); Fall Savings (Aug); Electronics (Nov); Christmas Gift Guide (Dec).
Special Weekly Sections: Best Food Day (tues); Best Food Day (wed); Church (fri); Best Food Day (S).
Magazines: Orchid Isle; Own newprint Tab, incl. TV listing (S).

CORPORATE OFFICERS
Founder Donald W Reynolds
President/Chief Operating Officer Emmett Jones
Exec Vice Pres/Chief Financial Officer Darrell W Loftin
Vice Pres-Western Newspaper Group David A Osborn
Vice Pres-Eastern Newspaper Group Don Schneider

GENERAL MANAGEMENT
Publisher Jim D Wilson

ADVERTISING
Manager Sandy Ault

CIRCULATION
Manager-Subscriber Service Darrell Snyder

NEWS EXECUTIVE
Editor Eugene Tao

EDITORS AND MANAGERS
Science Editor F Stapleton
Sports Editor Bill O'Rear

PRODUCTION
Foreman-Composing Larry Jarneski
Foreman-Pressroom Clay Jensen

Market Information: TMC.
Mechanical available: Offset; Black and 3 ROP colors; insert accepted — preprinted; page cut-offs — 21½".
Mechanical specifications: Type page 13" x 21½"; E - 6 cols, 2 1/16", ⅛" between; A - 6 cols, 2 1/16", ⅛" between; C - 9 cols, 1⅜", 1/16" between.
Commodity consumption: Newsprint 13,500 metric tons; widths 27½", 13½"; single pages printed 10,500; average pages per issue 24(d), 44(S).
Equipment: EDITORIAL: Front-end hardware — Mk. CLASSIFIED: Front-end hardware — Mk. PRODUCTION: Typesetters — Mk; Plate exposures — 1-Nu; Production cameras — 1-C.
PRESSROOM: Line 1 — 7-G/Urbanite; Folders — 1-G. MAILROOM: Inserters and stuffers — KAN/320 Inserter; Bundle tyer — 1-St, MLN; Wrapping singles — 1-St; Addressing machine — KAN/Labeler. COMMUNICATIONS: Facsimile — NEC. WIRE SERVICES: News — AP. BUSINESS COMPUTERS: CJ; Applications: CJ.

HONOLULU
Honolulu County
'90 U.S. Census- 399,166; E&P '96 Est. 444,172
ABC-NDM (90): 836,231 (HH 265,304)

Hawaii Newspaper Agency Inc.

Hawaii Newspaper Agency Inc., 605 Kapiolani Blvd.; PO Box 3350, Honolulu, HI 96801; tel (808) 525-8000; fax (808) 525-8685.
Note: The Honolulu Star-Bulletin (e) and the Honolulu Advertiser (mS) are independent and competitive newspapers, published by separate corporations, which publish jointly the Sunday Advertiser. Hawaii Newspaper Agency Inc., agent for Gannett Pacific Corp. and Liberty Newspapers Ltd. Partnership operates the newspapers' advertising, circulation, accounting and production depts.
Special Weekly Sections: Dining Out; Hawaii Real Estate Showcase.

CORPORATE OFFICERS
President Lawrence R Fuller
Senior Vice Pres-Marketing Howard L Griffin
Vice Pres-Production James A Granata
Vice Pres-Finance Richard Fuke
Vice Pres-Circulation Dennis E Francis
Vice Pres-Systems Gary L Wild
Vice Pres-Human Resources Carole Medeiros
Vice Pres-Market Development James George
Secretary/Treasurer Douglas H McCorkindale

GENERAL MANAGEMENT
Controller Carney Hogan
Director-Analysis & Reporting Arthur Li
Manager-Human Resources Julie Davies
Manager-Safety Cee Peterson

ADVERTISING
Vice Pres Howard L Griffin
Director Rebecca Bradner
Manager-Classified Gail Roberts
Manager-Display Randall Brant

MARKETING AND PROMOTION
Vice Pres-Market Development James George
Director-Promotion David Maszak
Director-Research Alvin Katahara

CIRCULATION
Vice Pres Dennis E Francis
Director Steve Mills
Manager-Suburban Home Delivery Steve Tomino
Manager-Operations Mark Thompson
Manager-Customer Service Merrilee Lucas
Manager-Sales Bob Marciel
Manager-Single Copy Lester Kodama

PRODUCTION
Vice Pres James A Granata
Vice Pres-Systems Gary L Wild
Manager-Pree Press Adam Horwitz
Manager-Press Terrence Derby Sr
Manager-Nights Gary Dishman
Manager-Camera/Quality Leonard Rapozo
Manager-Mailroom Dennis Tsukamoto
Manager-Commercial/Systems Darcy Bellows
Manager-Composing Andy Lai Hipp
Librarian Beatrice Kaya

Market Information: Split Run.
Mechanical available: Letterpress (direct); Black and 3 ROP colors; insert accepted — preprinted, minimum size by negotiation; maximum size; page cut-offs — 22¾".
Mechanical specifications: Type page 13" x 21½"; E - 6 cols, 2 1/16", ⅛" between; A - 6 cols, 2 1/16", ⅛" between; C - 10 cols, 1¼", 1/16" between.
Commodity consumption: Newsprint 28,000 short tons; widths 54½", 41", 27¼"; black ink 920,000 pounds; color ink 120,000 pounds; single pages printed 38,800; average pages per issue 50(d), 156(S); single plates used 120,840.
Equipment: EDITORIAL: Front-end hardware — 1-SII/CLX, 1-Ap/Mac. CLASSIFIED: Front-end hardware — 1-SII/CLX. DISPLAY: Adv layout systems — Dewar/Disc, QuarkXPress; Front-end hardware — PC, Ap/Mac; Front-end software — QuarkXPress, Dewar/Disc. PRODUCTION: Typesetters — 2-AU/108; Platemaking systems — Na; Plate exposures — Na; Plate processors — Na/80; Scanners — 1-ECR/Autokon; Production cameras — 3-C/Marathon; Automatic film processors — 2-LE/LD24, 1-C/650; Film transporters — 2-C/1246; Shrink lenses — 2-CK Optical/SQU-912 & 918; Color separation equipment (conventional) — DTI; Digital color separation equipment — SCREEN/2010.
PRESSROOM: Line 1 — 8-G/Mark II; Line 2 — 8-H/Colormatic; Line 3 — 12-G/Urbanite; Folders — 5-G; Pasters — 8-H, 8-G; Reels and stands — 8-H, 8-G; Press control system — Hurletron. MAILROOM: Counter stackers — 6-HL; Inserters and stuffers — 2-HI/1372P; Bundle tyer — 4-Power Strap; Wrapping singles — 1-Gd. LIBRARY: Electronic — Digital Collections Paper Desk Archive. WIRE SERVICES: News — AP, NYT, BW, LAT-WP, PR Newswire; Stock tables — AP SelectStox; Syndicates — LATS; Receiving dishes — size-6m/7m, AP, AP Stocks. BUSINESS COMPUTERS: 1-IBM/4361 Model 5, 1-IBM/AS 400 B50; Applications: Circ, Adv billing, Gen ledger, Payroll, Accts payable, Fixed assets; PCs & main system networked.

The Honolulu Advertiser
(m-mon to sat)
Sunday Advertiser (S)

The Honolulu Advertiser, 605 Kapiolani Blvd.; PO Box 3110, Honolulu, HI 96802; tel (808) 525-8000. Gannett Co. Inc. group.
Circulation: 105,624(m); 105,624(m-sat); 192,849(S); ABC Sept. 30, 1995.
Price: 50¢(d); 50¢(sat); $1.50(S).
Advertising: Open inch rate $98.40(m); $98.40(m-sat); $137.76(S); $126.16(m & e); comb with Honolulu Star-Bulletin. **Representative:** Gannett National Newspaper Sales.
News Services: AP, LAT-WP, KRT. **Politics:** Independent. **Established:** 1856.
Note: For advertising, circulation, production personnel and mechanical specifications, see Hawaii Newspaper Agency listing. For Sunday News Executives, Editors and Managers, see listing for Honolulu Advertiser which is responsible for news and editorial copy.
Special Editions: Hawaiian Open Golf (Jan); Home Improvements & Garden (Feb); Annual Edition (Mar); Summer School (Apr); Bridal Section, Classified Job Market (May); Island Fresh (June); Fall School (July); Parade of Homes Tab (Sept); Football Tab, Island Home Style (Aug); Political Tab (Sept); General Election Tab, First Hawaiian Auto Show (Oct); Gift Guide I (Nov); Gift Guide II, Last Minute Gift Guide (Dec).
Magazine: USA Weekend.

CORPORATE OFFICER
President/CEO Lawrence R Fuller

GENERAL MANAGEMENT
Publisher Lawrence R Fuller

ADVERTISING
Senior Vice Pres-Marketing Howard Griffin

MARKETING AND PROMOTION
Vice Pres-Marketing James George

CIRCULATION
Vice Pres Dennis E Francis

NEWS EXECUTIVES
Editor at Large George Chaplin
Exec Editor John Hollon
Managing Editor-News Presentation/Operations M J Smith

EDITORS AND MANAGERS
Arts/Entertainment Editor Wayne Harada
Business/Finance Editor Ilene Aleshire
Cartoonist Dick Adair
City Editor Dan Nakaso
Colleges Editor William Kresnak
Columnist Robert Krauss
Consumer Affairs Editor Susan Hooper
Editorial Page Editor Jerry Burris
Editorial Writer David Polhemus
Education Esme Infante
Fashion/Features Editor Wanda Adams
Food Editor Joan Clarke
Garden Editor Sandra Oshiro
Graphics Editor Rob Dudley

Hawaii

Home Furnishings/Improvement Editor
  Sandra Oshiro
Labor Editor Tom Kaser
Money Editor Ilene Aleshire
News Editor John Strobel
Religion Editor Dan Nakaso
Sports Editor Jamie Turner
Travel Editor Ed Kennedy
  MANAGEMENT INFORMATION SERVICES
Data Processing Manager Gary Wild

Market Information: Split Run.

Honolulu Star-Bulletin
(e-mon to sat)

Honolulu Star-Bulletin, 605 Kapiolani Blvd. (96813); PO Box 3080, Honolulu, HI 96802; tel (808) 525-8000; fax (808) 523-8509; e-mail starbull@pixi.com. Liberty Newspapers Limited Partnership group.
Circulation: 77,535(e); 77,535(e-sat); ABC Sept. 30, 1995.
Price: 50¢(d); 50¢(sat); $6.50/4 wks (d).
Advertising: Open inch rate $75.71(e); $75.71(e-sat); $126.16(m & e); comb with The Honolulu Advertiser. **Representative:** Gannett National Newspaper Sales.
News Services: AP, NYT, RN, SHNS, ASAHI. **Politics:** Independent. **Established:** 1882.
Note: For advertising, circulation, production personnel and mechanical specifications, see Hawaii Newspaper Agency listing.
Special Editions: Hawaiian Open Golf (Jan); Summer School (Apr); Classified Job Market (May); Fall School (July); Parade of Homes (Sept); Football Tab (Aug); Political Tab (Sept); General Election Tab (Oct); First Hawaiian Auto Show, Gift Guide I (Nov); Gift Guide II (Dec).
Magazine: USA Weekend (S).
  CORPORATE OFFICER
President/CEO Rupert E Phillips
  GENERAL MANAGEMENT
Editor/Publisher John M Flanagan
  NEWS EXECUTIVES
Senior Editor/Editorial Page Editor Diane Chang
Managing Editor David Shapiro
Asst Managing Editor Frank Bridgewater
Asst Managing Editor Michael Rovner
  EDITORS AND MANAGERS
Action Line Editor (Kukoa Line)
  Hildegaard Verploegen
Auto/Aviation Editor Russ Lynch
Books Editor Cynthia S Oi
Business Editor Ed Lynch
City Editor Lucy Young-Oda
Asst City Editor Peter Wagner
Asst City Editor Lila Fujimoto
Columnist Charles Memminger
Columnist Dave Donnelly
Contributing Editor A A (Bud) Smyser
Editorial Writer Mary Poole-Burlingame
Editorial Writer Carl Zimmerman
Education Christine Donnelly
Features Editor Cynthia S Oi
Films/Theater Editor Cynthia S Oi
Food Editor Catherine Enomoto
Graphics Editor Betty Shimakuhuro
Health Writer Helen Altonn
Librarian Beatrice Kaya
Music/Women's Editor Cynthia S Oi
News Editor Steve Petranik
Political Editor Mike Yuen
Radio/Television Editor Cynthia S Oi
Real Estate/Planning Writer Rob Perez
Science/Technology Writer Helen Altonn
Sports Editor Paul Carvalho
Teen-Age/Youth Editor Cynthia S Oi
Wire Editor Steve Petranik
  MANAGEMENT INFORMATION SERVICES
Data Processing Manager Gary Wild
Equipment: LIBRARY: Electronic — 1995-Digital Collection Paper Desk.

KAILUA-KONA
Hawaii County
'90 U.S. Census- 17,823; E&P '96 Est. 22,457
ABC-NDM (90): 44,342 (HH 15,363)

West Hawaii Today
(m-mon to thur; m-fri; S)

West Hawaii Today, 75-5580 Kuakini Hwy.; PO Box 789, Kailua-Kona, HI 96740; tel (808) 329-9311; fax (808) 329-3659. Donrey Media Group group.
Circulation: 10,467(m); 12,141 (m-fri); 13,181(S); ABC Sept. 30, 1995.

Price: 50¢(d); 50¢(fri); $1.00(S); $7.75/mo; $88.00/yr.
Advertising: Open inch rate $12.16(m); $12.16(m-fri); $12.16(S). **Representative:** Papert Companies.
News Service: AP. **Politics:** Independent. **Established:** 1968.
Special Editions: Aloha; Dining Guide; Health & Fitness; Fashion; Real Estate Review.
Special Weekly Sections: Food (wed); Entertainment, Real Estate (fri); Church, Travel, Food (S).
Magazine: USA Weekend (S).
  CORPORATE OFFICERS
Founder Donald W Reynolds
President/Chief Operating Officer Emmett Jones
Exec Vice Pres/Chief Financial Officer
  Darrell W Loftin
Vice Pres-Western Newspaper Group
  David A Osborn
Vice Pres-Eastern Newspaper Group
  Don Schneider
  GENERAL MANAGEMENT
Publisher Richard M Asbach
  ADVERTISING
Manager Debbie Ward
  CIRCULATION
Manager Daryl Dickens
  NEWS EXECUTIVES
Editor Reed Flickinger
Asst Editor Dan Breeden
  EDITORS AND MANAGERS
Agriculture Editor Reed Flickinger
Business Editor Brenda Jensen
Child-Rearing Columnist Margie Wong
Club News Editor Lillian Towata
Editorial Page Editor Reed Flickinger
Fishing Editor Paul Young
Food Editor Brenda Jensen
Home/Family Editor Brenda Jensen
Marine Activities Editor Paul Young
Outdoors/Sports Editor Paul Young
Real Estate Editor Brenda Jensen
  MANAGEMENT INFORMATION SERVICES
Data Processing Manager Lana Taira
  PRODUCTION
Manager-System/Composing Peter Rosenstern
Supervisor-Press Greg Covey

Market Information: TMC.
Mechanical available: Offset; Black and 3 ROP colors; insert accepted — preprinted, Card-70 lb Bound Stock; page cut-offs — 15".
Mechanical specifications: Type page 10 13/16" x 15 13/16"; E - 5 cols, 2.07", 1/8" between; A - 5 cols, 2.07", 1/8" between; C - 6 cols, 1.67", 1/8" between.
Commodity consumption: Newsprint 750 metric tons; widths 32", 27½"; black ink 20,160 pounds; color ink 2,350 pounds; single pages printed 21,424; average pages per issue 48(d), 100(S); single plates used 9,000.
Equipment: EDITORIAL: Front-end hardware — 1-Mk/1100 Plus, Mk/Touchwriter, 3-Mk/Touchwriter Plus; Front-end software — WordPerfect, Aldus/FreeHand, Adobe/Photoshop; Other equipment — Ap/Mac, IBM/PC. CLASSIFIED: Front-end hardware — 1-Mk/ Printers — 5-Mk/Touchwriter Plus. DISPLAY: Adv layout systems — 1-Ap/Mac II; Front-end hardware — 3-PC/486DX-33; Front-end software — QuarkXPress; Printers — 1-Ap/Mac LaserWriter I Layout, 1-Mk/Touchwriter Plus Two, 2-Mk/Touchwriter. PRODUCTION: Typesetters — 2-NewGen/840 Turbo PS, 2-LaserMaster/Unity 1200XL-O; Platemaking systems — 1-3M/Deadliner; Plate exposures — 1-Nu; Scanners — 1-Umax/OA-1; Production cameras — 1-Acti/204, 1-LE/490 vertical; Automatic film processors — 1-N/P1400. PRESSROOM: Line 1 — 8-G/Community; Press drives — 2-Fin/60 h.p.; Folders — 1-G/SC. MAILROOM: Bundle tyer — 2-MLN/Strapper; Addressing machine — 3-Wm. WIRE SERVICES: News — AP; Stock tables — AP; Syndicates — Chronicle, CT, King Features, LAT-WP, NAS, United Features, Universal Press; Receiving dishes — size-7m, AP. BUSINESS COMPUTERS: Unisys/5000, HP/3000; Applications: Circ, Bookkeeping, Billing, TMC addressing, Adv billing; PCs & micros networked.

LIHUE
Kauai County
'90 U.S. Census- 5,202; E&P '96 Est. 6,662
ABC-NDM (90): 51,177 (HH 16,295)

The Garden Island
(e-mon to fri; S)

The Garden Island, 3137 Kuhio Hwy.; PO Box 231, Lihue, HI 96766; tel (808) 245-3681; fax (808) 245-5286; e-mail ginews@aloha.net. Scripps League Newspapers Inc. group.
Circulation: 7,640(e); 8,050(S); ABC Sept. 30, 1995.
Price: 35¢(d); 50¢(S); $7.00/mo (carrier); $12.00/mo (mail); $78.00/yr (carrier); $144.00/yr (mail).
Advertising: Open inch rate $12.53(e); $15.70(S). **Representatives:** US Suburban Press; Papert Companies.
News Service: AP. **Politics:** Independent. **Established:** 1902.
Advertising not accepted: X-rated movies.
Special Edition: Progress (Feb).
Special Weekly Sections: TV Times (S); Island Times.
  CORPORATE OFFICERS
Board Chairman/Treasurer E W Scripps
Vice Chairman/Corporate Secretary
  Betty Knight Scripps
President Jack C Morgan
President/Exec Vice Pres Roger N Warkins
Vice Pres-Finance Thomas E Wendel
  GENERAL MANAGEMENT
Publisher Roy Callaway
Manager-Office/Business Manager Linda Jordan
  ADVERTISING
Director Chris Myrvall
  MARKETING AND PROMOTION
Manager-Marketing/Promotion Chris Myrvall
  CIRCULATION
Manager Brett Weaver
  NEWS EXECUTIVE
Managing Editor Rita DeSilva
  PRODUCTION
Superintendent-Shop James Oyadomari
Superintendent-Mechanical Art Tsuha

Market Information: Zoned editions; Split Run; TMC; ADS.
Mechanical available: Offset; Black and 3 ROP colors; insert accepted — preprinted; page cut-offs — 22¾".
Mechanical specifications: Type page 13" x 21½"; E - 6 cols, 2", 1/8" between; A - 6 cols, 2", 1/8" between; C - 6 cols, 2", 1/8" between.
Commodity consumption: average pages per issue 40(d), 80(S).
Equipment: EDITORIAL: Front-end hardware — 10-ScrippSat/PC; Printers — 2-QMS/820 Turbo. CLASSIFIED: Front-end hardware — 3-ScrippSat/PC; Front-end software — Synaptic/ScrippSat; Printers — Okidata/Microline, QMS/393. DISPLAY: Adv layout systems — ScrippSat; Front-end hardware — 2-ScrippSat; Front-end software — Archetype/Designer, Archetype/Corel Draw; Printers — QMS, LaserMaster/1800x60. PRODUCTION: Typesetters — QMS/820 Turbo; Plate exposures — Nu/Flip Top FT40UP; Plate processors — Nat/A-250; Production cameras — SCREEN/Companica 690 E; Automatic film processors — Kk/Kodamatic 65A; Digital color separation equipment — Microsoft/Windows, Adobe/Photoshop 3.0.
PRESSROOM: Line 1 — 12-G/Community; Folders — 1-G. MAILROOM: Counter stackers — 1-B/108; Inserters and stuffers — MM/221-E; Bundle tyer — Bu/String Tyer and Plastic Strap; Other mailroom equipment — 1-MM/235. WIRE SERVICES: News — AP; Syndicates — Creators, SHNS; Receiving dishes — size-1 1/4m, AP, SLNI News. BUSINESS COMPUTERS: PCs & micros networked; PCs & main system networked.

WAILUKU
Maui County
'90 U.S. Census- 14,985; E&P '96 Est. 20,023
ABC-CZ (90): 27,577 (HH 8,692)

The Maui News
(e-mon to thur; e-fri; S)

The Maui News, 100 Mahalani St.; PO Box 550, Wailuku, HI 96793; tel (808) 244-3981; fax (808) 242-6390; web site http://www.maui.net/~mauinews/news.htm.
Circulation: 18,117(e); 20,865(e-fri); 23,411(S); ABC Sept. 30, 1995.
Price: 35¢(d); 35¢(fri); $1.25(S).

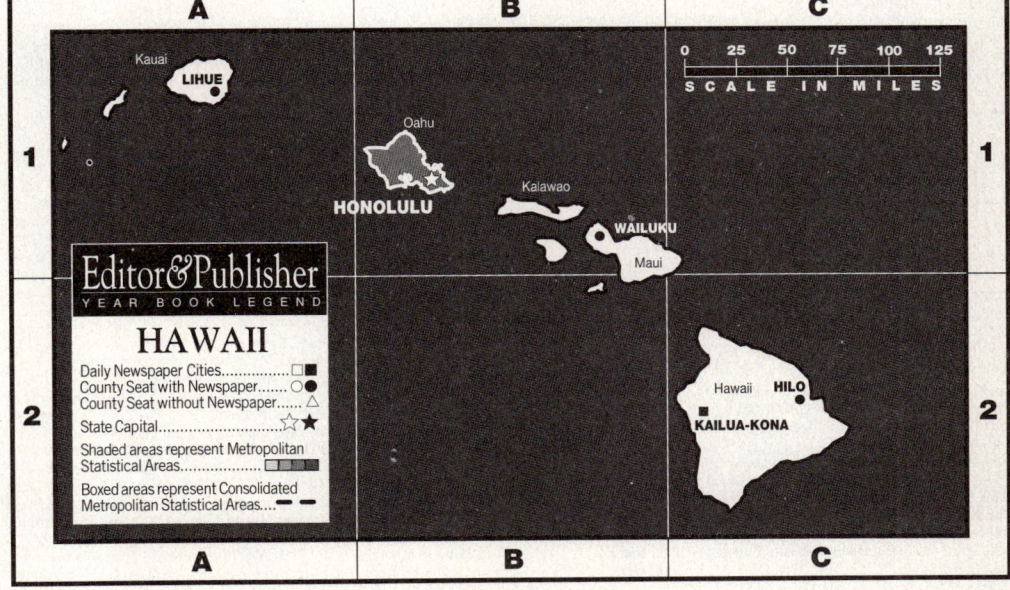

Advertising: Open inch rate $15.35(e); $15.35(e-fri); $17.70(S). **Representatives:** Papert Companies; US Suburban Press.
News Services: AP, NYT, LAT-WP. **Established:** 1900.
Special Editions: Seniors Today (monthly); Outlook '96 (Economic Outlook Tab) (Jan); Bridal Fair (Mar); Women of Maui, Barrio Fiesta, Graduation Section (May); Maui Contractors Assoc.-Building & Materials Expo (June); Annual JAYCEE Carnival, Pet Parade (July); Football '96, Back-to-School (Aug); Parade of Homes (Sept); Maui County Fair, Fire Prevention Week, Aloha Festivals (Oct); Kapalua International, First Hawaiian Auto Show, Retail Christmas Sections (includes Maui Mall & Kaahumanu Center) (Nov); Kahului Industrial Area Christmas '96 (Dec); Seniors Today (monthly).
Special Weekly Sections: Financial (daily); Automotive (mon); Super Market Aids (tues); Food, Maui Living Section (wed); Maui Scene (thur); Real Estate, Land Transactions, Entertainment, Week in Review, Mainland Air Shipped Edition, Religion (fri); Comics, Weekly TV Tab, Sports, Travel, Light Life, Maui Living Section (S).

GENERAL MANAGEMENT

Publisher Mary C Sanford
General Manager Mae McCarter

ADVERTISING

Manager Dawne Miguel

CIRCULATION

Manager Elmer Kanoholani

NEWS EXECUTIVE

Editor David Hoff

EDITORS AND MANAGERS

City Editor Christy Wilson
Entertainment Editor Rick Chatenever
Features Editor Rick Chatenever
News Editor Lee Imada
Sports Editor Rick Hoff

MANAGEMENT INFORMATION SERVICES

Data Processing Manager Richard Allen

Market Information: Zoned editions; TMC.
Mechanical available: Offset; Black and 3 ROP colors; insert accepted — preprinted; page cut-offs — 22¾".
Mechanical specifications: Type page 13¼" x 21½"; E - 6 cols, 2 1/16", ⅛" between; A - 6 cols, 2 1/16", ⅛" between; C - 9 cols, 1⅜", 1/16" between.
Commodity consumption: Newsprint 1,800 metric tons; widths 28", 14"; average pages per issue 40(d), 80(S).
Equipment: EDITORIAL: Front-end hardware — TC, PC; Other equipment — IBM/PC, AT/XT 386 Clone. CLASSIFIED: Front-end hardware — TC, PC; Other equipment — IBM/PC, AT/XT Clone. DISPLAY: Adv layout systems — TC, PC. PRODUCTION: Typesetters — TC, PC/386; Platemaking systems — 3M/Sys; Scanners — Diadem/750 Color Scanner; Production cameras — AG/6100s Daylight Camera. PRESSROOM: Line 1 — 9-G/Community. MAILROOM: Counter stackers — MM/TYP 267; Inserters and stuffers — St; Bundle tyer — MLN/Wilton. WIRE SERVICES: News — AP; Syndicates — NYT. BUSINESS COMPUTERS: IBM; Applications: Accounting, Circ, Adv Order Entry, Billing.

IDAHO

BLACKFOOT

Bingham County

'90 U.S. Census- 9,646; E&P '96 Est. 9,433

The Morning News

(m-mon to sat)

The Morning News, 34 N. Ash; PO Box 70, Blackfoot, ID 83221; tel (208) 785-1100; fax (208) 785-4239. Hollinger International Inc. group.
Circulation: 3,903(m); 3,903(m-sat); Sworn Sept. 29, 1995.
Price: 50¢(d); 50¢(sat); $72.00/yr (carrier), $83.00/yr (mail).
Advertising: Open inch rate $8.25(m); $8.25(m-sat). **Representative:** Landon Associates Inc.
News Service: AP. **Politics:** Independent. **Established:** 1904.
Not Published: Labor Day; Christmas.
Special Editions: Financial Planning (Feb); Progress (Mar); Brides, Home (Apr); Outdoors (May); Back-to-School (July); State Fair, Seniors, Outdoors (Sept); Harvest, Auto (Oct).
Special Weekly Sections: Food Day (wed); Agriculture (sat); Religion News (fri).
Magazines: Food (wed); Weekend West (TV & Leisure), Church (fri); Farm (sat).

CORPORATE OFFICERS

President Larry J Perrotto
Comptroller Roland McBride

GENERAL MANAGEMENT

Publisher Kaye Moses

ADVERTISING

Director Leslie Bare
Director Kaye Moses

CIRCULATION

Director Barry Goodyear

NEWS EXECUTIVE

Editor Michael O'Donnell

PRODUCTION

Manager Leslie Bare

Market Information: TMC.
Mechanical available: Offset; Black and 3 ROP colors; insert accepted — preprinted; page cut-offs — 22¾".
Mechanical specifications: Type page 13" x 21½"; E - 6 cols, 2 1/16", ⅛" between; A - 6 cols, 2 1/16", ⅛" between; C - 9 cols, 1⅜", 1/16" between.
Commodity consumption: width 27½"; average pages per issue 13(d).
Equipment: EDITORIAL: Front-end hardware — Ap/Macs. CLASSIFIED: Front-end hardware — Ap/Mac II LC. DISPLAY: Adv layout systems — 1-COM/Advantage; Front-end software — QuarkXPress. PRODUCTION: Typesetters — Ap/Mac; Plate exposures — B; Plate processors — 1-Nat; Production cameras — 1-Acti; Automatic film processors — 1-P. PRESSROOM: Line 1 — 4-KP. MAILROOM: Counter stackers — 1-BG/Count-O-Veyor; Inserters and stuffers — MM/227E (2-into-1); Bundle tyer — 1-Bu; Addressing machine — 1-Sp. WIRE SERVICES: News — AP Datastream; Receiving dishes — size-3ft, AP. BUSINESS COMPUTERS: Corsair/List Master Systems.

BOISE

Ada County

'90 U.S. Census- 125,738; E&P '96 Est. 145,457
ABC-NDM (90): 205,775 (HH 77,471)

The Idaho Statesman

(m-mon to sat; S)

The Idaho Statesman, 1200 N. Curtis Rd.; PO Box 40, Boise, ID 83707; tel (208) 377-6200; e-mail 76424.3356@compuserve.com. Gannett Co. Inc. group.
Circulation: 66,376(m); 66,376(m-sat); 88,406(S); ABC Sept. 30, 1995.
Price: 50¢(d); 50¢(sat); $1.50(S); $3.00/wk; $12.00/4wk; $24.00/8wk (m & S), $16.40/8wk (daily only), $14.00/8wk (S & holiday); $156.00/yr.
Advertising: Open inch rate $49.80(m); $49.80(m-sat); $64.79(S). **Representative:** Gannett National Newspaper Sales.
News Services: AP, GNS, NYT. **Politics:** Independent. **Established:** 1864.
Advertising not accepted: All copy is screened for approval.
Special Editions: Boise River Festival (June); Discover Treasure Valley (Sept).
Special Weekly Sections: Family Life Std (tues); Food Std (wed); Home Std, "Rec" (Outdoor Tab) (thur); "Scene" (Entertainment Tab) (fri); Automotive-Classified Std, Real Estate Classified Tab (sat); Business Std (S).
Magazines: TV Idaho (sat); USA Weekend (S).
Cable TV: Operate leased cable TV in circulation area.

CORPORATE OFFICERS

President Pamela F Meals
Treasurer Jimmy L Thomas
Secretary Thomas Chapple

GENERAL MANAGEMENT

Publisher Pamela F Meals
Controller J Linden Edmund
Manager-Credit Becky Reddy
Director-Personnel Keith D Bulling

ADVERTISING

Director Deborah Pantenburg
Manager-Classified Gene Fulton

MARKETING AND PROMOTION

Director-Marketing Services Nancy S McKinnon

CIRCULATION

Director Robert L Pedersen
Manager Rick Hardy
Manager-State Steve Devore
Manager-Sales/Promotion Paul Peterson
Manager-Single Copy Gary Jaeger
Manager-Home Delivery Allen Green
Manager-Customer Service Shirley Lamun
Manager-Transportation Beverly Barnes
Manager-Customer Info Systems Donna Johnson

NEWS EXECUTIVES

Exec Editor John A Costa
Managing Editor Karen Baker

EDITORS AND MANAGERS

Art Director Patrick Davis
Automotive Editor Paul Beebe
Books Editor Michael Deeds
Business Editor Paul Beebe
Columnist Tim Woodward
Editorial Page Editor Ralph Poore
Education Editor David Woolsey
Entertainment/Amusements Editor Michael Deeds
Environmental Editor Jonathan Brinkman
Farm/Agriculture Editor Paul Beebe
Fashion/Features Editor Michael Deeds
Food/Home Editor Michael Deeds
Graphics Editor Patrick Davis
Health/Medical Editor Colleen LaMay
Librarian Althea Orvis
Metro Editor Dennis Joyce
News Editor Holly Anderson
Photographer Tom Shanahan
Political Editor Dan Popkey
Radio/Television Editor Lucinda Doolittle
Real Estate Editor Paul Beebe
Religion Editor Bill Roberts
Science/Technology Editor Michael Deeds
Special Projects Editor Jim Hopkins
Sports Editor Art Lawler
Travel Editor Michael Deeds
Wire Editor Jim Bowers
Women's Editor Michael Deeds

MANAGEMENT INFORMATION SERVICES

Data Processing Manager Dan Stevens

PRODUCTION

Director Mike Tomasieski
Manager-Systems Pete Greco
Manager-Pressroom Rick Mayer
Manager-Distribution Center Ed Allen
Manager-Pre Press Tom Meister
Manager-Technichal Service David Dinger

Market Information: Zoned editions; Split Run; TMC; Electronic edition.
Mechanical available: Offset; Black and 3 ROP colors; insert accepted — preprinted, pre-printed; page cut-offs — 23 9/16".
Mechanical specifications: Type page 13" x 22"; E - 6 cols, 2.04", ⅙" between; A - 6 cols, 2", ¼" between; C - 10 cols, 1.21", 1/12" between.
Commodity consumption: Newsprint 8,455 short tons; 7,670 metric tons; width 54½"; black ink 113,920 pounds; color ink 31,583 pounds; single pages printed 19,147; average pages per issue 48(d), 78(S); single plates used 64,900.
Equipment: EDITORIAL: Front-end hardware — 1-AT/1170; Front-end software — AT; Printers — Florida Data; Other equipment — Newsview. CLASSIFIED: Front-end hardware — AT/1170; Front-end software — AT; Printers — Florida Data; Other equipment — Celera/OCR and scanner for legals. DISPLAY: Adv layout systems — DTI; Front-end hardware — Ap/Mac; Front-end software — DTI/AdSpeed; Other equipment — Hyphen/OPI; AG/Imagers. PRODUCTION: Pagination software — AT/R4; Typesetters — MON/84E Class-News, Hyphen/Advertising, AG/Select 1000; Plate exposures — 2-Nu; Plate processors — 1-Nat, 1-WL; Electronic picture desk — Lf/AP Leaf Picture Desk; Scanners — 1-Microtek/ScanMaker II;Horizon/Scanner; Production cameras — 2-C; Automatic film processors — 2-LE, 1-P; Film transporters — 2-LE; Color separation equipment (conventional) — 1-RZ, 1-AP, 1-AG; Digital color separation equipment — Lf/AP Leaf Picture Desk, Canon, Adobe/Photoshop. PRESSROOM: Line 1 — 9-G/Metro; Folders — 1-G; Pasters — 9-G/Automatic. MAILROOM: Counter stackers — 2-Id/440, 1-Id/550; Inserters and stuffers — 1-HI/1472P; Bundle tyer — 3-MLN/2A; Addressing machine — 1-Ch, 1-HL/On-line labeler; Other mailroom equipment — MM/TV Quarterfolder/s/t. LIBRARY: Electronic — Mead Data Central/Nexis NewsView; Combination — NewsView (electronic). COMMUNICATIONS: Digital ad delivery system — AP AdSend. WIRE SERVICES: News — AP, GNS, NYT; Photos — AP, GNS; Stock tables — AP; Syndicates — AP; Receiving dishes — size-3m, AP. BUSINESS COMPUTERS: 1-IBM/AS-400 Model 45; Applications: Gannet & Business Applications; PCs & micros networked; PCs & main system networked.

BURLEY

Cassia and Minidoka Counties

'90 U.S. Census- 8,702; E&P '96 Est. 8,709

South Idaho Press

(e-mon to fri; S)

South Idaho Press, 230 E. Main St.; PO Box 190, Burley, ID 83318; tel (208) 678-2201; fax (208) 678-0412. Park Communications Inc. group.
Circulation: 5,604(e); 5,604(S); Sworn Sept. 27, 1995.
Price: 50¢(d); 75¢(S); $6.85/mo (city), $7.70/mo (motor route).
Advertising: Open inch rate $8.63(e); $8.63(S).
News Services: AP, NEA. **Politics:** Independent. **Established:** 1904.
Not Published: Christmas.
Special Editions: Bridal (Apr); Car Care (Aug); Homemaker Cookbook (Oct); Christmas Greetings (Dec).
Special Weekly Sections: Farm (thur); Church (fri).

CORPORATE OFFICERS

President Tommy Thomas
Vice Pres Ralph Martin

GENERAL MANAGEMENT

Business Manager Edward Fenton
General Manager Kary Miller

ADVERTISING

Manager Marva Osterhout

CIRCULATION

Manager Chris Sutliff

EDITORS AND MANAGERS

Books/Education Editor LaRue Cheney
City Editor Ken Leuy
Columnist Rob Mayer
Editorial Page Editor Kary Miller
Food Editor LaRue Cheney
Librarian/Music Editor LaRue Cheney
Photo Department Kay Moore
Political Editor Paul Allen
Radio/Television Editor LaRue Cheney
Real Estate Editor Renee Wells
Religion Editor Renee Wells
Science/Technology Editor Renee Wells
Society/Women's Editor LaRue Cheney
Sports Editor Brian Mortenson
Teen-Age/Youth Editor LaRue Cheney

MANAGEMENT INFORMATION SERVICES

Data Processing Manager Kelly Solomon

PRODUCTION

Superintendent Kay Moore

Market Information: Zoned editions; TMC.
Mechanical available: Offset; Black and 3 ROP colors; insert accepted — preprinted, ROP Inserts; page cut-offs — 22¾".
Mechanical specifications: Type page 13" x 21½"; E - 6 cols, 2 1/16", ⅛" between; A - 6 cols, 2 1/16", ⅛" between; C - 10 cols, 1⅜", 1/16" between.
Commodity consumption: Newsprint 520 short tons; widths 27½", 34"; average pages per issue 18(d), 24(S); single plates used 9600.
Equipment: EDITORIAL: Front-end hardware — Ap/Mac; Front-end software — QuarkXPress 3.3; Other equipment — 1-Umax/630 scanner. CLASSIFIED: Front-end hardware — Ap/Mac Centris 650; Front-end software — QuarkXPress 3.3; Printers — 2-Ap/Mac LaserWriter; Other equipment — 1-Umax/840 scanner, CD-Rom. DISPLAY: Front-end hardware — Ap/Mac Centris 650; Front-end software — QuarkXPress 3.3; Printers — 2-Ap/Mac LaserWriter. PRODUCTION: Pagination software — QuarkXPress 3.3; Typesetters — 2-Ap/Mac LaserWriter; Plate exposures — B/Ultra-Lite 5000; Plate processors — Nat/A-250; Scanners — 1-Umax/840, 1-Umax/630; Production cameras — 1-C/H-134; Automatic film processors — 1-P/24; Color separation equipment (conventional) — WDS/Plano III. PRESSROOM: Line 1 — 8-G; Folders — G. MAILROOM: Counter stackers — 1-BG/Count-O-Veyor; Bundle tyer — 1-Ace; Addressing machine — 2-Multilith. WIRE SERVICES: News — AP; Receiving dishes — size-2½ft, AP. BUSINESS COMPUTERS: IBM/AT, ATT/6300; Applications: Gen ledger, Budgeting.

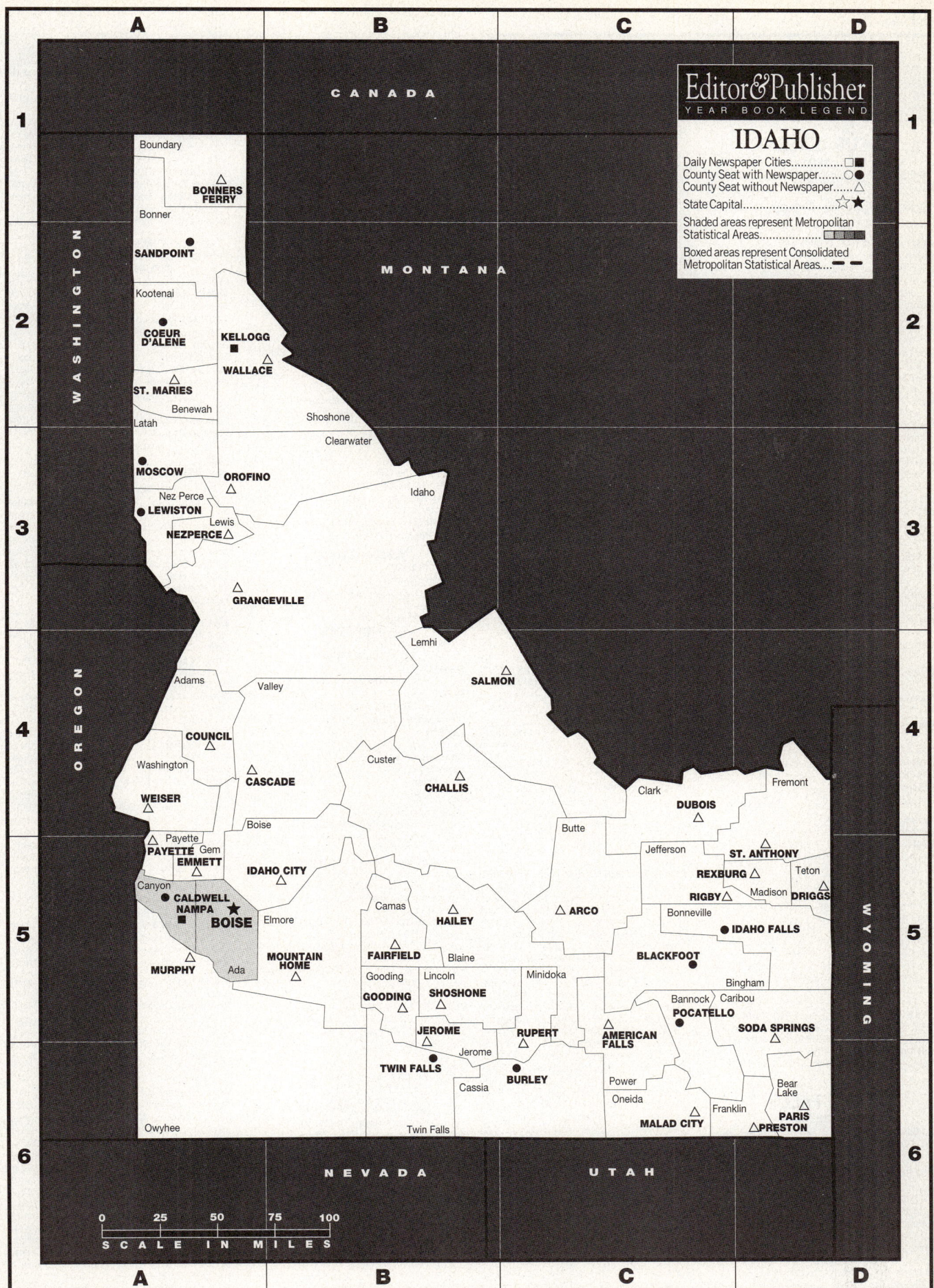

CALDWELL
See NAMPA

COEUR d'ALENE
Kootenai County

'90 U.S. Census- 24,563; E&P '96 Est. 28,378

Coeur d'Alene Press
(m-mon to sat)
North Idaho Sunday (S)

Coeur d'Alene Press, 201 2nd Ave.; PO Box 7000, Coeur d'Alene, ID 83814; tel (208) 664-8176; fax (208) 664-0212. Hagadone Corp. group.

Circulation: 16,559(m); 16,559(m-sat); 28,500(S); Sworn Oct. 1, 1995.

Price: 50¢(d); 50¢(sat); $1.00(S); $9.00/mo, $9.50/mo (motor route).

Advertising: Open inch rate $15.34(m); $15.34(m-sat); $25.76(S).

News Services: AP, NEA. **Politics:** Independent. **Established:** 1903.

Note: The North Idaho Sunday serves the five northern counties in Idaho and is a combined effort of three dailies and three weeklies: Coeur d'Alene Press (m), Sandpoint Bonner County Daily Bee (m), Kellogg Shoshone News-Press (m), Priest River Times (w), Bonners Ferry Herald and Post Falls Tribune (w). Founded November 1984. The Sunday circulation figure is an estimate.

Not Published: New Year; Memorial Day; Independence Day; Labor Day; Christmas.

CORPORATE OFFICERS

President Duane B Hagadone
Secretary/Treasurer Arthur S Flagan

GENERAL MANAGEMENT

Publisher James Thompson
Business Manager Frank Granier
Purchasing Agent Frank Granier

ADVERTISING

Director Paul Burke

MARKETING AND PROMOTION

Manager-Promotion Paul Burke

CIRCULATION

Manager Bob Weber

NEWS EXECUTIVE

Editor Mike Feiler

EDITORS AND MANAGERS

Auto Editor Bob Abbot
Cartoonist John Firehammer
City Editor Mike Feiler
Editorial Page Editor Mike Feiler
Real Estate Editor Dave Gunter

Market Information: TMC.

Mechanical available: Offset; Black and 3 ROP colors; insert accepted — preprinted.

Mechanical specifications: Type page 13" x 21½"; E - 6 cols, 2 1/16", ⅛" between; A - 6 cols, 2 1/16", ⅛" between; C - 8 cols, 1⅜", ⅛" between.

Commodity consumption: average pages per issue 40(d), 72(S).

Equipment: EDITORIAL: Front-end hardware — 1-Dy/Cps 300. CLASSIFIED: Front-end hardware — 1-Dy/Cps 300. PRODUCTION: Typesetters — 2-Dy/CPS 300; Platemaking systems — 1-Nu/Flip Top FT4CUP; Plate processors — 1-Ic/ICM-1; Production cameras — 1-K/Vertical 24.
PRESSROOM: Line 1 — 4-G/Community. MAILROOM: Inserters and stuffers — 3-M; Bundle tyer — 1-Bu/PP8-6; Addressing machine — 1-Ch/500PM. WIRE SERVICES: News — AP; Receiving dishes — size-1ft, AP.

IDAHO FALLS
Bonneville County

'90 U.S. Census- 43,929; E&P '96 Est. 47,526
ABC-CZ (90): 43,929 (HH 16,017)

Post Register (e-mon to fri; S)

Post Register, 333 Northgate Mile (83401); PO Box 1800, Idaho Falls, ID 83403; tel (208) 522-1800; fax (208) 529-3142.

Circulation: 30,005(e) 30,003(S); ABC Mar. 31, 1995.

Price: 50¢(d); $1.50(S); $9.50/mo (carrier), $9.75/mo (motor route), $11.00/mo (mail).

Advertising: Open inch rate $16.10(e); $16.30(S).

News Services: AP, SHNS, LAT-WP. **Politics:** Independent. **Established:** 1880.

Special Editions: Home Improvement/Home & Garden (Mar); Home Improvement/Home & Garden, E. Idaho Guide (Apr); Progress, Football (Aug); Hunting (Sept); Home Improvement/Home & Garden, E. Idaho Guide, Idaho Family (Oct); El Sol (monthly).

Special Weekly Sections: Food (tues); Community (wed); Let's Go (thur); Farm & Ranch (weekly).

Magazines: Parade (S); Intermountain Hunting & Fishing; Intermountain Farm & Ranch.

Broadcast Affiliate: KIFI-TV, (NBC) Idaho.

CORPORATE OFFICERS

President Jerry M Brady
Vice Pres Jim Wilson
Controller Lee Schumway

GENERAL MANAGEMENT

Publisher/Editor Jerry M Brady
Vice Pres-Marketing and Development Jim Wilson
Director-Circulation Mike Lowe
Director-Advertising David Gilchrist
Business Manager Lee Schumway
Exec Editor Mei Mei Chan

ADVERTISING

Director David Gilchrist

MARKETING AND PROMOTION

Vice Pres-Marketing/Development Jim Wilson

CIRCULATION

Director Mike Lowe

NEWS EXECUTIVES

Editor Jerry M Brady
Exec Editor Mei Mei Chan

EDITORS AND MANAGERS

City Editor Dean S Miller
Editorial Page Editor Gene Fadness
Features Editor Margaret Wimborne
Food/Community Editor Margaret Wimborne
Graphics Editor Jerry Painter
Hunting & Fishing Editor Rob Thornberry
News Editor Bill Hathaway
Photo Editor Monte LaOrange
Political Editor Kevin Richert
Special Section Editor Kristie Jones
Sports Editor Rob Thornberry
Sunday Editor Paul Menser

MANAGEMENT INFORMATION SERVICES

Online Manager Mike Lowe
Data Processing Manager Doug Evans

PRODUCTION

Foreman-Composing Bob Bright
Foreman-Pressroom Dan Fursteneau

Market Information: TMC; ADS; Operate database.

Mechanical available: Offset; Black and 3 ROP colors; insert accepted — preprinted, free standing cards; page cut-offs — 22¾".

Mechanical specifications: Type page 13" x 21½"; E - 6 cols, 2.04", ⅙" between; A - 6 cols, 2 1/16", ⅛" between; C - 9 cols, 1¾", 1/16" between.

Commodity consumption: Newsprint 1,800 metric tons; widths 27½", 24", 13¾"; black ink 49,000 pounds; single pages printed 11,500; average pages per issue 36(d), 68(S); single plates used 20,000.

Equipment: EDITORIAL: Front-end hardware — Cx/Magician; Front-end software — Cx/Magician, Cx/2390; Printers — Dataproducts/LZR 960, Dataproducts/1150, LaserMax/1000dpi, HP/LaserJet 4. CLASSIFIED: Front-end hardware — Cx/Magician; Front-end software — Cx/Magician, Cx/CAP-6. AUDIOTEX: Hardware — Bigmouth. DISPLAY: Front-end hardware — Sun/360, Sun/380, Ap/Mac Quadra, Ap/Mac cx, Ap/Mac ci, 3-Ap/Mac Quadra 800; Front-end software — Multi-Ad/Creator 3.5.4, QPS, Adobe/Illustrator; Other equipment — Cricket Draw. PRODUCTION: Typesetters — 2-Ultre/Studiosetter; Plate exposures — 1-BKY/Ascor 5K-Watt, 1-Nu/3000 Watt; Plate processors — 1-Star International; Scanners — Lf/Leafscan 35, Microtek/300dpi, 1-SCREEN/Laser Drum Scanner, HP/C105 Flatbed Color Scanner; Production cameras — 1-B/Page Camera, 1-AG/Vertical camera, 1-ECR/Autokon 1000D; Automatic film processors — 1-P/G, 1-AG; Color separation equipment (conventional) — Lf/AP Leaf Picture Desk, Lf/Leafscan.
PRESSROOM: Line 1 — 10-G/Urbanite; Press drives — 3-Fin; Folders — 1-G; Press control system — Fin. MAILROOM: Counter stackers — 1-BG; Inserters and stuffers — 2-MM/227E; Bundle tyer — 1-MLN/ML2EE; Addressing machine — 2-Am, Wm. LIBRARY: Electronic — Mead Data Central/Nexis NewsView. COMMUNICATIONS: Systems used — satellite. WIRE SERVICES: News — AP, LAT-WP; Photos — AP; Stock tables — AP, TMS; Syndicates — LATS, SHNS; Receiving dishes — AP. BUSINESS COMPUTERS: 24-Data Sciences/PC; Applications: Data Sciences; PCs & micros networked; PCs & main system networked.

KELLOGG
Shoshone County

'90 U.S. Census- 2,591; E&P '96 Est. 2,227

Shoshone News-Press
(m-tues to sat)
North Idaho Sunday (S)

Shoshone News-Press, 401 Main St., Kellogg, ID 83837; tel (208) 783-1107; fax (208) 784-6791. Hagadone Corp. group.

Circulation: 4,294(m); 4,294(m-sat); 28,500 (S); Sworn Oct. 1, 1993.

Price: 35¢(d); 35¢(sat); $1.00(S); $6.00/mo (carrier), $6.50/mo (motor route).

Advertising: Open inch rate $7.56(m); $7.56(m-sat); $25.76(S).

News Services: AP, NEA. **Politics:** Independent. **Established:** 1897 (Press), 1985 (News-Press).

Note: The Sunday edition serves the five northern counties in Idaho and is a combined effort of three dailies and three weeklies: Coeur d'Alene Press (m), Sandpoint Bonner County Daily Bee (m), Shoshone News-Press (m), Priest River Times (w), Bonners Ferry Herald (w) and Post Falls Tribunes (w). Founded November 1984. The Sunday circulation figure is an estimate.

Not Published: Legal holidays.

Special Editions: Football; Christmas; Progress; Winter Sports.

Magazines: Visitor's Guide Tab (thur); The North Idaho Advertiser.

CORPORATE OFFICERS

Board Chairman Duane B Hagadone
Secretary/Treasurer Art Flagan

GENERAL MANAGEMENT

Publisher Dan Drewry
Business Manager Regina Mason

ADVERTISING

Director Judi Binkley

CIRCULATION

Manager Hans Gallert

NEWS EXECUTIVE

Editor Darrel Beehner

EDITORS AND MANAGERS

Business/Mining Editor Darrel Beehner
City Editor Don Sauer
Columnist Darrel Beehner
Classified Editor Deborah Mellon
Education Editor Darrel Beehner
News Editor Darrel Beehner
Sports Editor Patrick Ryan

Market Information: TMC.

Mechanical available: Offset; Black and 3 ROP colors; insert accepted — preprinted, any; page cut-offs — 22¾".

Mechanical specifications: Type page 13" x 21½"; E - 6 cols, 2 1/16", ⅛" between; A - 6 cols, 2 1/16", ⅛" between; C - 8 cols, 1½", 1/16" between.

Commodity consumption: average pages per issue 18(d), 72(S).

Equipment: EDITORIAL: Front-end hardware — Ap/Mac SE30. CLASSIFIED: Front-end hardware — 1-Ap/Mac SE30. PRODUCTION: Plate exposures — 1-Nu.
PRESSROOM: Line 1 — 4-G/Community; Folders — 1-G/Community. MAILROOM: Bundle tyer — 1-It; Addressing machine — 2-Am. WIRE SERVICES: News — AP; Receiving dishes — AP. BUSINESS COMPUTERS: 2-DEC/UT220 B2; Applications: Accounting, Circ, Payroll.

LEWISTON, ID-CLARKSTON, WA
Nez Perce County, ID
Asotin County, WA

'90 U.S. Census- 34,835 (Lewiston, ID 28,082; Clarkston, WA 6,753); E&P '96 Est. 35,066 (Lewiston, ID 28,391; Clarkston, WA 6,675)

Lewiston Morning Tribune
(m-mon to sat; S)

Lewiston Morning Tribune, 505 C St.; PO Box 957, Lewiston, ID 83501; tel (208) 743-9411; e-mail alajr@lmtribune.com; web site http://www.lmtribune.com. Kearns-Tribune Corp. group.

Circulation: 24,723(m); 24,723(m-sat); 24,723(S); Sworn Oct. 10, 1995.

Price: 50¢(d); 50¢(sat); $1.25(S); $9.50/mo (d&S), $4.75/mo (S only).

Advertising: Open inch rate $17.00(m); $17.00(m-sat); $17.00(S). **Representative:** Papert Companies.

News Services: AP, NYT. **Politics:** Independent-Democrat. **Established:** 1892.

Special Editions: Brides (Jan); Neighbors (Feb); Home & Garden, Spring Car Care, Vacation/Recreation (Mar); Roundup (Sept); Home Improvement, Fall Car Care (Oct); Christmas Greetings (Dec).

Special Weekly Sections: Agriculture (mon); Food (wed); Outdoors (thur); Entertainment (fri); Business (S).

Magazines: React (mon); Parade, TV Today (S).

CORPORATE OFFICER

President A L Alford Jr

GENERAL MANAGEMENT

Publisher A L Alford Jr
General Manager Wayne Hollingshead
Manager-Credit Frank Hoyt
Business Manager Ray Rosch

ADVERTISING

Director Rob Minervini
Manager-Retail Kristi Schlottman
Manager-Classified Yvette Crosby
Manager-National Rob Minervini

CIRCULATION

Manager Michael McBride
Manager-Customer Service Teri Nitey
Manager-Operations Sue Roberts

NEWS EXECUTIVES

Editor A L Alford Jr
Managing Editor Paul Emerson

EDITORS AND MANAGERS

Automotive Editor Melodie Maller
Books Editor Jeanne DePaul
Business/Finance Editor Todd Adams
City Editor Diane Pettit
Columnist David Johnson
Editorial Page Editor Bill Hall
Editorial Writer James Fisher
Education Editor Sandra Lee
Entertainment/Amusements Editor Rebecca Huntington
Environmental Editor Paul Emerson
Farm/Agriculture Editor Sandra Lee
Fashion/Style Editor Jeanne DePaul
Features Editor Diane Petit
Food Editor Jeanne DePaul
Garden Editor Jeanne DePaul
Graphics Editor/Art Director Todd Adams
Health/Medical Editor Diane Pettit
Librarian Phillis Collins
News Editor Bill Furstenau
Outdoor Editor Bill Loftus
Photo Editor Barry Kough
Political Editor Mike Wickline
Radio/Television Editor Jeanne DePaul
Religion Editor Jeanne DePaul
Science/Technology Editor Diane Pettit
Sports Editor Bert Sahlberg
Teen-Age/Youth Editor Diane Pettit
Travel Editor Todd Adams
Wire Editor Michael Crater
Women's Editor Jeanne DePaul

MANAGEMENT INFORMATION SERVICES

Manager-Info Systems Glenn Cruickshank

PRODUCTION

Manager-Press Operations Ron Turner
Manager-Pressroom Junior Stockwell
Foreman-Mailroom Linda King
Manager-Electronic Processing Marcia Johnson

Market Information: TMC; Operate audiotex; Electronic edition.

Mechanical available: Offset; Black and 3 ROP colors; insert accepted — preprinted, card stock, sample packets; page cut-offs — 22¾".

Mechanical specifications: Type page 13" x 21.5"; E - 6 cols, 2 1/16", ⅛" between; A - 6 cols, 2 1/16", ⅛" between; C - 9 cols, 1⅜", 1/16" between.

Commodity consumption: Newsprint 2,140 metric tons; widths 27½", 34"; black ink 105,000 pounds; color ink 12,200 pounds; single pages printed 12,600; average pages per issue 34.9(d), 59(S); single plates used 36,500.

Equipment: EDITORIAL: Front-end hardware — 2-IBM/RISC 6000, 8-Micron/486 Pagination PC, 21-Micron/486 workstation, AT; Front-end software — QPS 3.3, Microsoft/Windows 3.1, Dewar/DewarView, Microsoft/Word 6.0, Sybase 4.95, AIX 3.51, Novell/Netware 3.11; Printers — Compaq/PageMark 20; Other equipment — 1-Micron/486, Archetype/OPI, 1-PC 486/Digital NT Server. CLASSIFIED: Front-end hardware — 5-Micron/486 workstation, 1-Ap/Power Mac; Front-end software — Sybase 4.95, AIX 3.5, AT/Enterprise, Microsoft/Word 3.11,

Microsoft/Word 6.0, AT/Press; Printers — IBM/4039. AUDIOTEX: Hardware — PC/386-SX; Software — DOS Vicki 7.2; DISPLAY: Adv layout systems — 13-Gateway/workstation, SCS/Layout 8000; Front-end software — Microsoft/Windows 3.11, Aldus/PageMaker 5.0, Archetype/Corel Draw 3.0, Microsoft/Word 6.0, Adobe/Photoshop; Printers — Compaq/PageMark 20; Other equipment — Ap/Mac IIcx, Immediate/Ad Director. PRODUCTION: Pagination software — Aldus/Page Maker 5.0, Adobe; Typesetters — 2-AG/9800, 2-Hyphen/RIP 10.0; Plate exposures — 1-B/5KW, 1-Nu/Flip Top; Plate processors — Nat/34; Scanners — AG/9800, AG/2000, 6-HP/Scanner, Howtek/Colorscan Sys, Kk/Scan; Production cameras — 1-C/Spartan III, 1-Nu/Flip Top FT; Automatic film processors — 1-LE, 1-SCREEN; Film transporters — 1-LE. PRESSROOM: Line 1 — 9-G/Urbanite; Press drives — 2-Westinghouse/150 h.p.; Folders — 2-G; Pasters — 4-WPC; Reels and stands — 4-Roll/Stand. MAILROOM: Counter stackers — 2-BG/104; Inserters and stuffers — 2-MM/227-E; Bundle tyer — 1-MLN/ML-2EE; Addressing machine — 1-MG. LIBRARY: Electronic — Lexis-Nexis/NewsView Connections, PhotoView/Photo Library Sys. WIRE SERVICES: News — AP, NYT, SHNS, McClatchy; Photos — AP; Stock tables — AP; Syndicates — NYT; Receiving dishes — size-3m/1m, AP. BUSINESS COMPUTERS: IBM/AS 400 Advance 36; Applications: Payroll, Circ mail billing, Budgets, Accts receivable, Accts payable, Gen ledger, Subscribers and non-Subscribers; PCs & micros networked; PCs & main system networked.

MOSCOW, ID-PULLMAN, WA

Latah County, ID/Whitman County, WA

'90 U.S. Census- 41,997 (Moscow, ID 18,519; Pullman, WA 23,478); E&P '96 Est. 43,600 (Moscow, ID 20,175; Pullman, WA 23,425)

The Moscow-Pullman Daily News (e-mon to fri; m-sat)

The Moscow-Pullman Daily News, 409 S. Jackson; PO Box 8187, Moscow, ID 83843; tel (208) 882-5561; fax (208) 883-8205. Kearns-Tribune Corp. group.

Circulation: 7,192(e); 7,192(m-sat); VAC March 31,1995.

Price: 50¢(d); $1.00(sat); $9.41/mo; $112.92/yr.

Advertising: Open inch rate $10.00(e); $10.00(m-sat). **Representative:** Papert Companies.

News Services: AP, NYT. **Politics:** Independent. **Established:** 1911.

Not Published: New Year; Memorial Day; Labor Day.

Special Editions: Brides, Back-to-School (Jan); Bridal (Feb); Agriculture, Spring Ag, Brides, University of Idaho, Washington State University, Football, Car Care (Mar); Home Improvement, Tax Help (Apr); Mother's Day (May); Agriculture, Fall Ag (Aug); Football (Sept); Car Care, Back-to-School, Brides, University of Idaho, Washington State University, Football (Oct); Winter Recreation, Christmas Opening (Nov).

Special Weekly Sections: Business, Palouse Palate (tues); Arts & Entertainment (thur); Slice of Life (sat).

Magazines: TV Listings; Book; Weekend Color Comics.

Broadcast Affiliate: Cablevision.

Cable TV: Operate leased cable TV in circulation area; Own cable TV in circulation area.

CORPORATE OFFICER

President	A L Alford Jr

GENERAL MANAGEMENT

Publisher	Randy C Frisch
Business Manager	Ray Rosch

ADVERTISING

Director-Marketing	Randy Pressnall
Manager-Sales	Randy Pressnall

CIRCULATION

Manager	Vickie Carr

NEWS EXECUTIVES

Editor	Randy C Frisch
Managing Editor	Rick Hoover

EDITORS AND MANAGERS

Business/Finance Editor	Vera White
Editorial Page Editor	Randy C Frisch
Higher Education Editor	Tina Crinite
Environment/Ecology Editor	Greg Burton
Farm Editor	Tina Crinite
Films/Music Editor	Vera White
Food/Garden Editor	Vera White
Health Editor	Vera White
Picture Editor	Brian Kratzer
School Editor	Greg Burton
Science Editor	Greg Burton
Sports Editor	Laurence Miedema
Sports Writer	Tim Sullivan

MANAGEMENT INFORMATION SERVICES

Data Processing Manager	Randy Pressnall

PRODUCTION

Manager	Jeanette Hites
Foreman-Computers	Jeff Eickhoff

Market Information: TMC; ADS.

Mechanical available: Offset; Black and 3 ROP colors; insert accepted — preprinted, all; page cut-offs — 22¾".

Mechanical specifications: Type page 13" x 21½"; E - 6 cols, 2 1/16", 1/8" between; A - 6 cols, 2 1/16", 1/8" between; C - 9 cols, 1 3/8", 1/16" between.

Commodity consumption: Newsprint 511 metric tons; widths 27½", 13¾"; black ink 20,000 pounds; color ink 2,000 pounds; single pages printed 6,700; average pages per issue 22(d), 32(sat); single plates used 8,500.

Equipment: EDITORIAL: Front-end hardware — Ap/Macs; Front-end software — QPS; Printers — QMS, HP, Xante. CLASSIFIED: Front-end hardware — Ap/Macs; Front-end software — Baseview; Printers — Sony, HP. DISPLAY: Adv layout systems — Ap/Macs; Front-end hardware — Ap/Macs; Front-end software — QPS; Printers — QMS/Laser Printers. PRODUCTION: Pagination software — QPS; Typesetters — QMS, HP; Platemaking systems — Dyn; Plate exposures — 2-Dyn; Plate processors — Nat; Electronic picture desk — Ap/Mac, Adobe/Photoshop; Scanners — Lf, Microtek; Production cameras — SCREEN; Automatic film processors — Dyn; LE; Shrink lenses — CQ; Color separation equipment (conventional) — Ap/Mac, Adobe/Photoshop.
PRESSROOM: Line 1 — 5-HI/Cotrell V-25; Folders — 1-HI; Reels and stands — 4-HI/Cotrell. MAILROOM: Counter stackers — 7-KAN/480; Bundle tyer — 1-MLN/ML2EE. WIRE SERVICES: News — AP, NYT; Syndicates — WP, NYT, Universal Press, King Features, Creators, TMS, United Features; Receiving dishes — AP. BUSINESS COMPUTERS: CDS; Applications: P&L statements, Accts receivable, Accts payable, Subscriber/non-subscriber lists, Payroll; PCs & micros networked; PCs & main system networked.

NAMPA-CALDWELL

Canyon County

'90 U.S. Census- 46,765 (Nampa 28,365; Caldwell 18,400); E&P '96 Est. 50,080 (Nampa 31,046; Caldwell 19,034)

ABC-CZ (90): 65,198 (HH 22,932)

Idaho Press-Tribune (e-mon to fri; m-sat; S)

Idaho Press-Tribune, 1618 N. Midland Blvd.; PO Box 9399, Nampa, ID 83652; tel (208) 467-9251; fax (208) 467-9252; e-mail ipt2001@aol.com. Pioneer Newspapers group.

Circulation: 20,173(e); 20,173(m-sat); 20,458(S); ABC Sept. 30, 1995.

Price: 50¢(d); 50¢(sat); $1.00(S); $8.50/mo (city carrier), $9.00/mo (motor route).

Advertising: Open inch rate $12.25(e); $12.25(m-sat); $12.25(S).

News Service: AP. **Politics:** Independent. **Established:** 1883.

Note: Effective Apr. 1, 1995, the Press-Tribune started publishing on Saturday.

Special Editions: 13th Annual High School Wrestling, NAIA Basketball Championship, 12th Annual Spring Home Show (Mar); Spring Car Care, Spring Home & Garden (Apr); Mom of the Year, On the Move (May); Customer Appreciation, Summer Discoveries, Dad of the Year (June); Snake River Stampede, Newcomer's Guide (July); Caldwell Night Rodeo, High School Football (Aug); Club Directory, Kids Section (Sept); Fall Car Care, 3rd Annual Fall Home Show, Get Ready for Winter (Oct); Holiday Delights, Holiday Gift Guide (Dec).

Special Weekly Sections: Health Page, Bubble Gum Wrapper (for young readers) (mon); Food (tues); People, Ag Features (wed); M.O.R.E., Movie Review, Home Decor (thur); Religion (fri); TV Preview, Travel, Real Estate Showcase (sat); Stock Page, Family, Senior Calendar (S).

Magazines: Parade, Color Comics (S).

GENERAL MANAGEMENT

Publisher/President	James T Barnes Jr
Business Manager	Daniel J Jones

ADVERTISING

Director	John F Rybarczyk
Manager-Retail	Mike Vinson

MARKETING AND PROMOTION

Director-Marketing/Promotion	Carolyn Sinnard

TELECOMMUNICATIONS

Audiotex Manager	Laurie Kiester

CIRCULATION

Director	James Lindholm

NEWS EXECUTIVE

Managing Editor	Wayne Cornell

EDITORS AND MANAGERS

Business Editor	Steve Martin
City Editor	Vickie Holbrook
Recreation/Entertainment Editor	Allison Westfall
Religion Editor	Sandy Roberts
Sports Editor	Aarron Knox
Women's Editor	Marie Galyean

PRODUCTION

Manager	Michael W Stout
Pre Press-Pagination	Bonnie Ward
Pre Press-Composing	Gary Barr
Manager-Press	Eric Alfred

Market Information: TMC; Operate audiotex.

Mechanical available: Offset; Black and 3 ROP colors; insert accepted — preprinted, almost all (please call); page cut-offs — 22¾".

Mechanical specifications: Type page 13" x 21½"; E - 6 cols, 2 1/16", 1/8" between; A - 6 cols, 2 1/16", 1/8" between; C - 9 cols, 1 3/8", 1/16" between.

Commodity consumption: Newsprint 1,500 metric tons; widths 27", 30", 33"; black ink 4,000 pounds; color ink 1,100 pounds; single pages printed 10,790; average pages per issue 30(d), 40(S); single plates used 12,000.

Equipment: EDITORIAL: Front-end hardware — Ap/Power Mac 8100-80, Ap/Mac Quadra 605s, Ap/Mac Quadra 660s, Ap/Mac Quadra 840s; Front-end software — Baseview/NewsEdit Pro 2.0; Printers — 2-Accuset/1100. CLASSIFIED: Front-end hardware — Ap/Mac Quadra 630S; Front-end software — Baseview/Class Manager 3.2; Printers — Ap/Mac ImageWriter, Okidata/320. AUDIOTEX: Hardware — ZEOS/486DX/Pantera; Software — The Vital System 5.04.05; Supplier name — Market Link. DISPLAY: Adv layout systems — QuarkXPress 3.31; Front-end hardware — 4-Ap/Mac IIci, 1-Ap/Mac IIfx, 3-Ap/Mac Classic, 1-Sun/Sparc ELC. PRODUCTION: Pagination software — QuarkXPress 3.31; OCR software — TI/OmniPage; Typesetters — 2-COM, AG/P-3400, PS/Laserprinter, 2-Accuset/Imagesetters; Plate exposures — 1-Nu/Flip Top FT 40LNS; Plate processors — 1-Ic/ICM252; Electronic picture desk — Lf/AP Leaf Picture Desk; Scanners — Ap/Mac, Polaroid/Neg Scanner; Production cameras — 2-SCREEN/680C, Sony/MVC-2000 Digital, Canon/RV301-Digital, QuickTake 150; Automatic film processors — 1-P/524; Digital color separation equipment — Lf/AP Leaf Picture Desk.
PRESSROOM: Line 1 — 11-G/Community; Line 2 — Consolidated/225, 3-Knife Trimmer/Stitcher; Folders — 1-G/Urbanite. MAILROOM: Inserters and stuffers — 2-KAN/480 (5-into-1 inserters); Bundle tyer — 1-MLN/ML2-EE. WIRE SERVICES: News — AP; Photos — AP; Receiving dishes — size-8ft, AP. BUSINESS COMPUTERS: 1-Olympic/386, 1-AIC/286, Sun/Sparc Server 10-40; Applications: Media Plus, PBS: Advertising, Gen ledger, Accts payable, Payroll, Circ; PCs & micros networked; PCs & main system networked.

POCATELLO

Bannock County

'90 U.S. Census- 46,100; E&P '96 Est. 46,183

ABC-CZ (90): 53,818 (HH 19,587)

Idaho State Journal (e-mon to fri; S)

Idaho State Journal, 305 S. Arthur; PO Box 431, Pocatello, ID 83204; tel (208) 232-4161; fax (208) 233-8007. Pioneer Newspapers group.

Circulation: 17,543(e); 19,141(S); ABC Sept. 30, 1995.

Price: 50¢(d); $1.25(S); $9.00/mo; $108.00/yr; $14.00/mo (mail).

Advertising: Open inch rate $14.00(e); $14.40 (S). **Representative:** Papert Companies.

News Services: AP, KRT. **Politics:** Independent. **Established:** 1892.

Special Editions: Dodge National Circuit Finals Rodeo; Outdoor Idaho; Home Improvement; Back-to-School; Hunting; Football Kick-off; Winter Car Care; Spring Car Care; Lawn & Garden; Design-an-Ad Contest; Christmas Opening; Real Dairy Centennial Bowl Tab; Journal of Homes; Simplot Games; Progress.

Special Weekly Sections: Best Food Day (tues); Business Pulse, Agricultural News (wed); Entertainment, Escapes (thur); Church (fri).

Magazines: Parade, TV Journal (S).

GENERAL MANAGEMENT

President/Publisher	Donald J Byrne
Manager-Office	Jeri Larsen

ADVERTISING

Director	Leonard C Martin
Manager-Classified	Rich Ballou

TELECOMMUNICATIONS

Audiotex Manager	Julie Goebel

CIRCULATION

Director	James Smith

NEWS EXECUTIVES

Managing Editor	Don Black
Asst Managing Editor	Mark Mendiola

EDITORS AND MANAGERS

Editorial Page Editor	Don Black
Entertainment Editor	Shauna Lund
Food Editor	Joy Morrison
Photo Department Manager	Doug Lindley
Sports Editor	Robert Brundage
Women's Editor	Joy Morrison

MANAGEMENT INFORMATION SERVICES

Data Processing Manager	Jeri Larsen

PRODUCTION

Supervisor	Shanna Cunning
Foreman-Pressroom	Kerry Johnson

Market Information: Zoned editions; TMC; Operate audiotex.

Mechanical available: Offset; Black and 3 ROP colors; insert accepted — preprinted; page cut-offs — 22¾".

Mechanical specifications: Type page 13" x 21½"; E - 6 cols, 2 1/16", 1/8" between; A - 6 cols, 2 1/16", 1/8" between; C - 9 cols, 1 3/8", 1/16" between.

Commodity consumption: Newsprint 1,307 metric tons; widths 27½", 13¾"; black ink 56,032 pounds; color ink 4,482 pounds; single pages printed 12,078; average pages per issue 32(d), 62(S); single plates used 9,000.

Equipment: EDITORIAL: Front-end hardware — Ap/Mac; Front-end software — Baseview/NewsEdit, QuarkXPress 3.31; Printers — HP/4M-2. CLASSIFIED: Front-end hardware — Baseview, Ap/Mac; Front-end software — Baseview; Printers — Ap/Mac ImageWriter II. AUDIOTEX: Hardware — Pony/486-66; Software — Vital System 5.04.05; Supplier name — Market Link. DISPLAY: Adv layout systems — 4-Ap/Mac Quadra 660AV; Front-end software — QuarkXPress 3.31, Adobe/Illustrator 5.5; Printers — Ap/Mac ImageWriter IIg, Ap/Mac ImageWriter II NTX; Other equipment — Power CD-Rom, Umax/Scanners, Nikon/Coolscan. PRODUCTION: Pagination software — QuarkXPress 3.31; OCR software — Caere/OmniPage Professional; Typesetters — Hyphen, Spectraset/2400; Platemaking systems — 1-Nu/Fliptop; Plate exposures — 12-Nu; Plate processors — 1-Ic, Dynalith/M28 Dynamatic; Electronic picture desk — Lf/AP Leaf Picture Desk; Scanners — Nikon; Production cameras — 1-K, 1-Argile/16 x 23; Automatic film processors — 1-P/24; Color separation equipment (conventional) — Nikon/LS 3510AF Scanner, Epson/300C Flatbed Scanner; Digital color separation equipment — Adobe/Photoshop.
PRESSROOM: Line 1 — 7-G/Urbanite single width; Press control system — Fin; Press registration system — Duarte/Punch System. MAILROOM: Counter stackers — 1-BG; Inserters and stuffers — 2-MM/217E; Addressing machine — 1-Am. WIRE SERVICES: News — AP; Photos — AP; Syndicates — TV Data; Receiving dishes — AP. BUSINESS COMPUTERS: Sun/Sparc fileserver; Applications: PBS, Adv billing, Accts receivable, Gen ledger, Payroll; PCs & micros networked; PCs & main system networked.

SANDPOINT
Bonner County

'90 U.S. Census- 5,203; E&P '96 Est. 5,821

Bonner County Daily Bee
(m-tues to sat)
North Idaho Sunday (S)

Bonner County Daily Bee, 310 Church St.; PO Box 159, Sandpoint, ID 83864; tel (208) 263-9534. Hagadone Corp. group.
Circulation: 6,441(m); 6,441(m-sat); 28,500(S); Sworn Sept. 29, 1995.
Price: 50¢(d); 50¢(sat); $1.00(S); $8.00/mo.
Advertising: Open inch rate $7.31(m); $7.31(m-sat); $25.76(S).
News Service: AP. **Politics:** Independent. **Established:** 1966.
Note: The North Idaho Sunday serves the five northern counties in Idaho and is a combined effort of three dailies and three weeklies: Coeur d'Alene Press (m), Bonner County Daily Bee (m), Kellogg Shoshone News-Press (m), Priest River Times (w), Bonners Ferry Herald (w) and the Post Falls Tribune (w). The Sunday circulation figure is an estimate.
Not Published: Legal holidays.
Special Editions: Spring; Progress (Mar); Fishing, North Idaho Tourist Guide (May); Winter Sports, Hunting (Nov).
Special Weekly Section: Best Food Day (tues).
Magazines: Weekly TV Guide; Spotlight (TMC).

CORPORATE OFFICERS
President (Hagadone Communications Division) Roy C Wellman
Treasurer Art Flagan

GENERAL MANAGEMENT
Publisher Joe Grimes
Manager-Credit Carolyn Goodnight-Inge

ADVERTISING
Director Herb Offermann

CIRCULATION
Director Jack Howell

NEWS EXECUTIVE
Managing Editor Bill Buley

Market Information: TMC.
Mechanical available: Offset; Black and 3 ROP colors; insert accepted — preprinted; page cut-offs — 22 3/4".
Mechanical specifications: Type page 13" x 21 1/2"; E - 6 cols, 2 1/16", 1/8" between; A - 6 cols, 2 1/16", 1/8" between; C - 8 cols, 1 5/8", 1/8" between.
Commodity consumption: average pages per issue 14(d), 72(S).
Equipment: EDITORIAL: Front-end hardware — Ap/Mac SE. CLASSIFIED: Front-end hardware — Ap/Mac SE. PRODUCTION: Automatic film processors — DP; Film transporters — DP; Color separation equipment (conventional) — Reflection. MAILROOM: Addressing machine — 1-St. COMMUNICATIONS: Facsimile — Nefax/Bit 1. WIRE SERVICES: News — AP. BUSINESS COMPUTERS: CIT; Applications: Circulation; PCs & micros networked; PCs & main system networked.

TWIN FALLS
Twin Falls County

'90 U.S. Census- 27,591; E&P '96 Est. 28,774
ABC-CZ (90): 32,811 (HH 12,332)

The Times-News
(m-mon to sat; S)

The Times-News, 132 3rd St. W. (83301); PO Box 548, Twin Falls, ID 83303-0548; tel (208) 733-0931; fax (208) 734-5538. Howard Publications group.
Circulation: 22,521(m); 22,521(m-sat); 23,511(S); ABC Sept. 30, 1995.
Price: 50¢(d); 50¢(sat); $1.50(S); $3.15/wk.
Advertising: Open inch rate $16.25(m); $16.25(m-sat); $16.75(S). **Representative:** Papert Companies.
News Services: AP, LAT-WP. **Politics:** Independent. **Established:** 1904.
Special Editions: Summer Fun Guide (May); Fair & Farm (Aug); Home (Sept).
Special Weekly Sections: Health/Fitness/Fashion (mon); Magic Values (TMC) (tues); Food & Home (wed); Money, Outdoors (thur); TV/Entertainment (fri); Agriculture, Church Page (sat); Valley Life, Business (S).
Magazines: TV Magazine (fri); Parade (S).

CORPORATE OFFICER
President Robert S Howard

GENERAL MANAGEMENT
Publisher Stephen Hartgen
Business Manager Allen Wilson

ADVERTISING
Director Peter York
Manager-Sales Janet Goffin
Manager-Classified Kim Patterson

TELECOMMUNICATIONS
Audiotex Manager Peter York

CIRCULATION
Manager Ty Ransdell

NEWS EXECUTIVE
Managing Editor Clark Walworth

EDITORS AND MANAGERS
Business Editor Bruce Whiting
City Editor Mark Kind
Editorial Writer Clark Walworth
News Editor Dale Stewart
Photo Department Manager Mike Salsburg
Society Editor Steve Crump
Sports Editor Brad Bowlin

PRODUCTION
Foreman-Composing William Rosenbaum
Foreman-Press Paul Kurowski

Market Information: Zoned editions; Split Run; TMC; ADS; Operate audiotex.
Mechanical available: Offset; Black and 3 ROP colors; insert accepted — preprinted; page cut-offs — 21 1/2".
Mechanical specifications: Type page 13" x 21 1/2"; E - 6 cols, 2 1/16", 1/8" between; A - 6 cols, 2 1/16", 1/8" between; C - 9 cols, 1 3/8", 1/16" between.
Commodity consumption: Newsprint 2,015 short tons; widths 14", 28"; single pages printed 14,000; average pages per issue 33(d), 50(S).
Equipment: EDITORIAL: Front-end hardware — Sun, Mk, CText; Front-end software — Arbortext; Printers — 2-Linotype-Hell/Linotronic 500, ECR/Pellbox, Ap/Mac LaserPrinter. CLASSIFIED: Front-end hardware — DG/Dasher 286; Front-end software — CText; Printers — Ap/Mac LaserPrinters; Other equipment — PC/4-286DG. AUDIOTEX: Hardware — IBM/486; Software — Tribune Publishing Company/Vicki; Supplier name — In-house. DISPLAY: Adv layout systems — Ap/Mac II; Front-end hardware — Ap/Mac II; Front-end software — QuarkXPress; Printers — 1-Linotype-Hell/Linotronic 500, ECR/Pellbox, Ap/Mac LaserWriters. PRODUCTION: Typesetters — ECR/Pellbox, Linotype-Hell/Linotronic 500, Ap/Mac LaserWriter; Scanners — Truvell, Nikon; Production cameras — Canon; Automatic film processors — LE; Color separation equipment (conventional) — Ap/Mac IIci, Adobe/Photoshop; Digital color separation equipment — Nikon/LS3500 SR1 Digital Scanner.
PRESSROOM: Line 1 — 7-G/Urbanite (Cole/3 Knife trimmer); Line 2 — 1-G/Urbanite Color Deck; Folders — 1-G, 1-G/quarter folder; Press control system — 2-Fin/control, 2-DC/Motors 100 h.p.. MAILROOM: Counter stackers — 1-HL/Monitors; Inserters and stuffers — MM/227; Bundle tyer — MLN; Wrapping singles — Id; Other mailroom equipment — Mueller/Stitcher. WIRE SERVICES: News — AP; Syndicates — North America Syndicate; Receiving dishes — AP. BUSINESS COMPUTERS: Sun/Sparc, DG/286, Compaq; PCs & micros networked; PCs & main system networked.

ILLINOIS

ALTON-EAST ALTON-WOOD RIVER
Madison County

'90 U.S. Census- 51,458 (Alton 32,905; East Alton 7,063; Wood River 11,490); E&P '96 Est. 50,249 (Alton 32,099; East Alton 7,244; Wood River 10,906)
ABC-CZ (90): 89,711 (HH 34,668)

The Telegraph (m-mon to sat; S)

The Telegraph, 111 E. Broadway; PO Box 278, Alton, IL 62002; tel (618) 463-2500; fax (618) 463-9829. Journal Register Co. group.
Circulation: 31,325(m); 31,325(m-sat); 33,228(S); ABC Sept. 30, 1995.
Price: 50¢(d); 50¢(sat); $1.50(S); $2.80/wk; $11.95/mo; $143.40/yr.
Advertising: Open inch rate $26.02(m); $26.02(m-sat); $27.01(S). **Representative:** Papert Companies.
News Services: AP, NEA, SHNS. **Politics:** Independent. **Established:** 1836.
Note: The Telegraph cross sells with the Suburban Journals of Greater St. Louis, a Journal-Register Company. The Telegraph also prints 16 Suburban Journal publications.
Advertising not accepted: Ads requesting readers to send money for any reason; 900 numbers, unless they publish fee per call.
Special Editions: Brides & Groom, Active Times (Jan); Health & Fitness (Feb); Investment Guide, Home Safety, Home Builders, Farm & Garden (Mar); Home Decor, Active Times, Home Improvement, Car Care (Apr); Religion Tab, Heroes, Summer Fun/Vacation Guide (May); The Guide, Main Event Auto, Fireworks on the Mississippi (June); Summer Guide, The Great Outdoors, Salute to Family Business, Active Times (July); Back-to-School, Football (Aug); Fall Home Improvement, New Car Intro, Parents Today (Sept); Car Care, Active Times (Oct); Holiday Dining, Cooking School, Wish Book, Medical Directory, Holiday Entertaining, Basketball-HS & College (Nov); Wrap It Up (Dec).
Special Weekly Sections: County Edition (tues); Food (wed); Cover Story, Entertainment (thur); County Edition, Lifestyles, Business (fri); Wheels and Deals, Travel (S); Stock Summaries (tues-fri; S).
Magazines: USA Weekend, TV Week (quarter-fold magazine) (S); Coupon Book (half quarterfold).

CORPORATE OFFICERS
President/CEO Robert M Jelenic
Exec Vice Pres/Chief Financial Officer/Treasurer Jean B Clifton

GENERAL MANAGEMENT
Publisher Thomas E Rice
Controller Julie Yost

ADVERTISING
Director Doug Cooper
Manager-Classified Bret Mayberry

CIRCULATION
Director Thomas G Norton

NEWS EXECUTIVE
Managing Editor Walt Sharp

EDITORS AND MANAGERS
Amusements/Entertainment Editor Mike Leathers
Books Editor Mike Leathers
Business/Finance Editor Dennis Grubaugh
City Editor Jack Farmer
Editorial Writer Walt Sharp
Education/Schools Editor Jack Farmer
Environment/Ecology Editor Dennis Grubaugh
Family/Fashion Editor Mary Ann Mazenko
Features Editor Mike Leathers
Films/Theater Editor Mike Leathers
Food/Garden Editor Mike Leathers
Medical/Hospital Editor Mary Ann Mazenko
Music Editor Mike Leathers
Photo Department Manager Russ Smith
Political Editor Walt Sharp
Radio/Television Editor Mike Leathers
Real Estate Editor Dennis Grubaugh
Religion Editor Mike Leathers
Sports Editor Steve Porter
Wire Editor Vickie Kinney
Women's Editor Mary Ann Mazenko

PRODUCTION
Manager Karla Suttles
Foreman-Pressroom Dave Sweetman

Market Information: Zoned editions.
Mechanical available: Offset; Black and 3 ROP colors; insert accepted — preprinted, Spadeas, FSI; page cut-offs — 22 3/4".
Mechanical specifications: Type page 13" x 21.75"; E - 6 cols, 2 1/16", 1/8" between; A - 6 cols, 2 1/16", 1/8" between; C - 10 cols, 1 3/16", 1/16" between.
Commodity consumption: Newsprint 5,500 short tons; widths 54", 40 1/2", 27"; black ink 102,000 pounds; color ink 21,000 pounds; single pages printed 41,000; average pages per issue 28(d), 40(S); single plates used 110,000.
Equipment: EDITORIAL: Front-end hardware — 1-SII/Sys 25, 29-SII, 7-IBM/AT; Front-end software — SII; Printers — 1-Panasonic/KX-P1624; Other equipment — Lf/AP Leaf Picture Desk. CLASSIFIED: Front-end hardware — SII/Sys 55, 10-SII/Coyote; Front-end software — SII; Printers — 1-Centronics/Printstation 351. DISPLAY: Adv layout systems — 2-Dewar/Discovery Sys; Front-end hardware — Dewar; Front-end software — Dewar; Printers — 1-Okidata/Microline 320. PRODUCTION: Typesetters — 2-Tegra/XP-1000, 2-Tegra/Varityper/XP-1000, 1-Hyphen/Dash 72E; Platemaking systems — Nu, Nat; Plate exposures — 2-Nu/Flip Top FT40V6UPNS; Plate processors — 2-Nat/A250; Production cameras — 1-Commodore/2638; Automatic film processors — 1-LE/Excel 26.
PRESSROOM: Line 1 — 7-MAN/Uniman 4/2; Press drives — 3-GE/DC 300; Folders — 2-Wd-H; Pasters — 6-MEG; Reels and stands — 7-MEG. MAILROOM: Counter stackers — 2-HL/Monitor; Inserters and stuffers — 1-MM/4 bay, Amerigraph/NP 848; Bundle tyer — 1-MLN/ML2EE, 1-MLN/ML 2CC; Wrapping singles — Manual; Addressing machine — 1-Cheshire/525-E. LIBRARY: Combination — Manual, 1-3M/Reader Printer. WIRE SERVICES: News — AP; Photos — AP; Stock tables — AP; Syndicates — NEA, AP, SHNS; Receiving dishes — size-8ft, AP. BUSINESS COMPUTERS: IBM/AS400; Applications: INSI: Ad mgmt; Transient Management Systems: Circ, Accts payable, Gen ledger, Credit Management; PCs & main system networked.

ARLINGTON HEIGHTS
See CHICAGO

AURORA
Kane County

'90 U.S. Census- 99,581; E&P '96 Est. 105,616
ABC-CZ (96): 118,735 (HH 40,681)

The Beacon-News
(e-mon to fri; m-sat; S)

The Beacon-News, 101 S. River St., Aurora, IL 60506; tel (708) 844-5844; fax (708) 844-5818. Copley Press Inc. group.
Circulation: 37,964(e); 37,964(m-sat); 40,038(S); ABC Sept. 30, 1995.
Price: 35¢(d); 35¢(sat); $1.00(S).
Advertising: Open inch rate $35.87(e); $35.87(m-sat); $35.87(S). **Representative:** Sawyer-Ferguson-Walker Co.
News Services: CNS, AP, NEA, NYT, SHNS. **Politics:** Independent-Republican. **Established:** 1846.
Special Editions: Money Matters, Town Section-Oswego, Coupon Book, Bridal (Jan); Automobile Show, Customer Appreciation (Feb); Spring Car Care, Spring Home Improvement, Annual Progress, Holy Week Church (Mar); School/Business Partnership, Golf Section, Home Improvement, Travel, Coupon Book (Apr); Town Section-Naperville, Graduation Section, Fox Valley Summer (May); Bridal, Town-Fox Festival (June); Health & Services Directory, Town Sections-Aurora, North Aurora & Montgomery (July); Back-to-School, Fall Sports (Aug); Home Furnishings/Improvements, Travel (Sept); Town Section-Yorkville, Piano & Sandwich, Coupon Book, Discover Book (Oct); Holiday Gift Guides (b), Basketball, Holiday Dining, Thanksgiving, Town Section-Batavia, Geneva & St. Charles (Nov); Gift Guides, Holiday Church Services, Top Stories of 1996 (Dec).
Special Weekly Sections: Health & Fitness (mon); Teens Day (tues); Food Section (wed); Night & Day Section (thur); Automotive (fri); Faith & Family, New Homes (sat); Keepsakes, Real Estate Showcase (S); Sports, Communities, Business Page (daily); Pro Football Weekend (fri, Sept to Jan).
Magazines: USA Weekend, Television (sat); TV Program Guide (S).

CORPORATE OFFICERS
Board Chairman Helen K Copley
President David C Copley
Secretary/Treasurer Charles F Patrick

GENERAL MANAGEMENT
Publisher David M Stamps
General Manager Peggy Kirby

ADVERTISING
Manager-Sales Jeffrey A Thilgen
Asst Manager-Sales Dave Nash

MARKETING AND PROMOTION
Manager-Promotion Christine Weber

CIRCULATION
Manager Curtis L Moon

NEWS EXECUTIVES
Managing Editor Michael W Chapin
Assoc Editor Jeff Kuczora
Assoc Editor Jim King

EDITORS AND MANAGERS
Automotive Editor Tom Johnson
Business/Finance Editor Jim Peters

City Editor John Russell
Editorial Page Editor P Joseph Gillette
Education Editor John Russell
Entertainment/Amusements Editor Jim King
Farm/Agriculture Editor John Russell
Fashion/Food Editor Jim King
Features Editor Jim King
Graphics Editor/Art Director Joyce Bassett
Health/Medical Editor Marcia Nelson
National Editor Jeff Kuczosa
News Editor Jeff Kuczosa
Photo Editor David Stephenson
Political/Government Editor Jeff Kuczosa
Religion Editor Marcia Nelson
Sports Editor Joe Halpern
Television/Film Editor Jim King
Theater/Music Editor Jim King
Travel/Women's Editor Jim King

PRODUCTION

Manager Don L Voss
Foreman-Composing Stephen Gamble
Foreman-Pressroom Charles Layfield
Foreman-Camera Rob Cordes

Market Information: Zoned editions; Split Run; TMC.

Mechanical available: Offset; Black and 3 ROP colors; insert accepted — preprinted; page cut-offs — 22¾".

Mechanical specifications: Type page 13" x 21"; E - 6 cols, 2.04", 1/6" between; A - 6 cols, 2.04", 1/6" between; C - 10 cols, 1 3/16", 1/16" between.

Commodity consumption: Newsprint 2,817 metric tons; widths 55", 41¼", 27½"; black ink 97,500 pounds; color ink 18,000 pounds; single pages printed 11,800; average pages per issue 30(d), 44(S); single plates used 28,000.

Equipment: EDITORIAL: Front-end hardware — SII, Ap/Mac; Front-end software — SII; Printers — HP. CLASSIFIED: Front-end hardware — SII; Front-end software — SII; Printers — HP. DISPLAY: Adv layout systems — DTI; Front-end hardware — Ap/Mac; Front-end software — DTI; Printers — HP. PRODUCTION: Typesetters — AU/APS-6-108; Plate exposures — WL/3, WL/4; Plate processors — WL/Pcat; Scanners — ECR/Autokon 1000; Production cameras — C/Spartan III; Automatic film processors — LE; Reproportion units — ECR/Autokon; Film transporters — C; Shrink lenses — III; Color separation equipment (conventional) — Diadem/Caret; Digital color separation equipment — RZ/210-S, Howtek/D-4000. PRESSROOM: Line 1 — G/Colorliner (38 couples); Line 2 — 8-G/CT50; Line 3 — 8-G; Press control system — Allen Bradley. MAILROOM: Counter stackers — HL; Inserters and stuffers — AMA; Bundle tyer — Power Strap; Addressing machine — 2-AVY, 1-Ch. LIBRARY: Electronic — SII; Combination — electronic. WIRE SERVICES: News — AP; Photos — AP; Stock tables — AP; Syndicates — CNS; Receiving dishes — size-10ft, AP. BUSINESS COMPUTERS: DEC/VAX; Applications:

BELLEVILLE

St. Clair County

'90 U.S. Census- 42,785; E&P '96 Est. 43,810
ABC-NDM (90): 129,679 (HH 50,943)

Belleville News-Democrat

(m-mon to sat; S)

Belleville News-Democrat, 120 S. Illinois St.; PO Box 427, Belleville, IL 62222-0427; tel (618) 234-1000; fax (618) 234-7782. Capital Cities/ABC Inc. group.

Circulation: 50,252(m); 50,252(m-sat); 61,605(S); ABC Sept. 30, 1995.

Price: 50¢(d); 50¢(sat); $1.25(S); $3.25/7 days (home delivery); $169.00/yr; $42.25/quarterly.

Advertising: Open inch rate $32.51(m); $32.51(m-sat); $32.51(S). **Representative:** Sawyer-Ferguson-Walker Co.

News Services: NYT, AP. **Politics:** Independent. **Established:** 1858.

Special Editions: Auto Show Tab (Jan); Income Tax/Finance Tab, Home Builders Show Tab (Feb); Health & Fitness, Home Improvements Tab (Mar); Baseball (Apr); Metro East Information Tab (May); Senior Citizens Tab (June); County Fair Tab (July); Fall Bridal (Aug); Football Tab, Home Improvement (Sept); Wheels '97, Auto Care Tab (Oct); Christmas Wishbook (Nov); Holiday Songbook, Wrap-it-Up (Dec).

Special Weekly Sections: Senior Citizen, Parenting/School (mon); Medicine/Science (tues); Food (wed); Entertainment (thur); Etiquette, Home/Fashion (fri); Religion (sat); Wedding/Engagement, Real Estate, Farm News (S); Business, Financial, Consumer News, Weather Map (daily).

Magazine: Parade (S).

CORPORATE OFFICER

President Gary Berkley

GENERAL MANAGEMENT

Vice Pres/Chief Financial Officer Randy Atkisson
Publisher Gary Berkley
Publisher-Sunday Magazine Greg Edwards

ADVERTISING

Director David Baur
Manager-Classified Cathy Wymer

MARKETING AND PROMOTION

Vice Pres-Marketing Frank Duke

CIRCULATION

Director Jay Tebbe
Manager Ken Holdener

NEWS EXECUTIVE

Editor Greg Edwards

EDITORS AND MANAGERS

Business Editor Fred Ehrlich
City Editor Gary Dotson
Editorial Page Editor Lori Browning
Librarian Debbie Miller
Lifestyle Editor Pat Kuhl
News Editor Candice Mount
Chief Photographer Tim Vizer
Sports Editor Joseph Ostermeier

MANAGEMENT INFORMATION SERVICES

Data Processing Manager David Rosenberg

PRODUCTION

Manager Charlie George
Foreman-Composing Bob Sax
Foreman-Pressroom Larry Hofmeister

Market Information: Zoned editions; Split Run; TMC.

Mechanical available: Offset; Black and 4 ROP colors; insert accepted — preprinted; page cut-offs — 21½".

Mechanical specifications: Type page 13" x 21½"; E - 6 cols, 2 1/32", 1/6" between; A - 6 cols, 2 1/32", 1/6" between; C - 9 cols, 1.29", 1/6" between.

Commodity consumption: Newsprint 4,999 short tons; widths 27.5", 13.75"; black ink 132,600 pounds; color ink 10,200 pounds; single pages printed 16,310; average pages per issue 36(d), 40(sat), 64(S); single plates used 27,458.

Equipment: EDITORIAL: Front-end hardware — Ap/Mac; Front-end software — Baseview 1.04; Printers — 1-Ap/Mac LaserWriter, 1-Dataproducts/LZR2080; Other equipment — AG/Arcus Scanner, Kk/Slide Scanner. CLASSIFIED: Front-end hardware — IBM/PC; Front-end software — Dewar; Printers — 2-Okidata, 1-HP/4L. DISPLAY: Front-end hardware — Ap/Mac; Front-end software — Multi-Ad/Creator; Printers — Typhoon 20; Other equipment — AG/Arcus Scanner, Kk/Slide Scanner. PRODUCTION: Pagination software — QuarkXPress; Typesetters — XIT, Dataproducts, AG/SelectSet 5000, QMS, LZR/1560 Laser Printers, Panther/Pro-46; Platemaking systems — Newark; Plate exposures — 2-Nu; Plate processors — 1-Nat; Electronic picture desk — Lf/AP Leaf Picture Desk; Scanners — AG/Arcus, 2-Kk/Slide; Production cameras — C/Spartan II, C/Spartan III; Automatic film processors — 1-LE/LD24AQ, AG/Rapidline 28, Olenta/2275L; Film transporters — 2-C; Color separation equipment (conventional) — WDS. PRESSROOM: Line 2 — 10-G/Urbanite (3 color); Line 4 — 7-G/Community; Folders — 2-G; Reels and stands — G; Press control system — Fin. MAILROOM: Counter stackers — 2-HL, 2-HL; Inserters and stuffers — S/9-48, GMA/SC1000 8-into-1; Bundle tyer — 2-Dynaric/NP1, Dynaric/NP2; Addressing machine — 1-Automecha/Accufast P4M, 1-BH/1530. LIBRARY: Electronic — Sonar. COMMUNICATIONS: Digital ad delivery system — AP AdSend. Systems used — satellite. WIRE SERVICES: News — AP Datastream, AP Datafeatures; Stock tables — AP SelectStox; Receiving dishes — AP. BUSINESS COMPUTERS: DEC/Micro VAX II, 40-DEC/VAX 3100; Applications: JADTEC: Accts receivable, Gen ledger, Accts payable, Payroll; PCs & micros networked; PCs & main system networked.

BELVIDERE

Boone County

'90 U.S. Census- 15,958; E&P '96 Est. 16,640

Belvidere Daily Republican

(e-mon to sat)

Belvidere Daily Republican, 401 Whitney Blvd., Belvidere, IL 61008; tel (815) 544-9811; fax (815) 544-6334.

Circulation: 4,822(e); 4,822(e-sat); Sworn Oct. 1, 1995.

Price: 35¢(d); 35¢(sat); $85.00/mo.

Advertising: Open inch rate $12.50(e); $12.50(e-sat). **Representative:** Landon Associates Inc.

News Services: AP, NEA. **Politics:** Republican. **Established:** 1892.

Not Published: New Year; Memorial Day; Independence Day; Labor Day; Thanksgiving; Christmas.

Special Editions: Progress (Jan); Tax Guide (Feb); Bridal, Spring, Health & Fitness (Mar); Farming Section (Apr); Drug & Alcohol Series, Senior (May); Information Guide (July); Fair Section (Aug); Fall, Sports Section (Sept); Fall Section, Health & Fitness (Oct); Early Christmas Gift (Nov); Christmas Gift, Christmas Greetings (Dec); Super Saver Coupons (monthly).

Special Weekly Sections: Youth Page (mon); Health, Business (tues); Best Food Day (wed).

CORPORATE OFFICER

President Patrick Mattison

GENERAL MANAGEMENT

Publisher Nancy S Mattison
Assoc Publisher Patrick Mattison
General Manager Steven Steinke

ADVERTISING

Director Sherron Aspenson

CIRCULATION

Manager Mary Alice Larson

NEWS EXECUTIVE

Managing Editor Kathy Sterbenc

EDITORS AND MANAGERS

Editorial Page Editor Patrick Mattison
Editorial Writer Kathy Sterbenc

PRODUCTION

Manager Steven Steinke

Market Information: Zoned editions; Split Run; TMC.

Mechanical available: Offset; Black and 3 ROP colors; insert accepted — preprinted, any; page cut-offs — 22¾".

Mechanical specifications: Type page 13¼" x 21"; E - 6 cols, 2.07", 1/12" between; A - 6 cols, 2.07", 1/12" between; C - 9 cols, 1.36", 1/8" between.

Commodity consumption: average pages per issue 18(d).

Equipment: EDITORIAL: Front-end hardware — Ap/Mac; Front-end software — QuarkXPress, Baseview/NewsEdit; Printers — NewGen/Imager Plus 12. CLASSIFIED: Front-end hardware — IBM/Compatible; Printers — Ap/Mac LaserWriter Plus. AUDIOTEX: Hardware — Synaptic; Software — Computer Group/Ads-on-call. DISPLAY: Front-end hardware — Ap/Mac. PRODUCTION: Pagination software — Baseview/NewsEdit; Typesetters — 3-Ap/Mac si; Plate exposures — 1-B; Plate processors — 1-Ic; Scanners — Ap/Mac; Production cameras — 1-R. PRESSROOM: Line 1 — 8-G/Suburban. MAILROOM: Counter stackers — 1-BG/Count-O-Veyor; Inserters and stuffers — 1-Mc; Bundle tyer — 4-Bu; Addressing machine — 1-Am, 1-MG. LIBRARY: Electronic — SMS/Stauffer Gold. COMMUNICATIONS: Facsimile — 1-3M/2110. WIRE SERVICES: News — AP; Syndicates — United Media, Newspaper Interfuse Association, TMS; Receiving dishes — size-2ft, AP. BUSINESS COMPUTERS: 3-TC; Applications: QPS, Baseview/NewsEdit; PCs & micros networked; PCs & main system networked.

BENTON

Franklin County

'90 U.S. Census- 7,216; E&P '96 Est. 7,054

Benton Evening News

(e-mon to thur; m-sat; S)

Benton Evening News, 111 E. Church St.; PO Box 877, Benton, IL 62812; tel (618) 438-5611; fax (618) 435-2413. Hollinger International Inc. group.

Circulation: 3,907(e); 3,907(m-sat); 3,907(S); VAC June 30, 1995.

Price: 50¢(d); 75¢(sat); $1.00(S); $2.20/wk; $9.50/mo; $114.00/yr.

Advertising: Open inch rate $7.25(e); $7.25(m-sat); $7.25(S).

News Service: AP. **Established:** 1926.

Not Published: Independence Day; Christmas.

Special Edition: Progress edition (Mar).

Special Weekly Section: American Weekend (S).

Magazine: USA Weekend.

GENERAL MANAGEMENT

Publisher Roby Robards

ADVERTISING

Manager-Retail Nancy Winter
Manager-Classified Lea Kays

CIRCULATION

Manager Doug Dunmeyer

NEWS EXECUTIVE

Managing Editor Danny Malkovich

EDITORS AND MANAGERS

Entertainment Editor Jo Anne Malkovich
Reporter Phil Pearson
Reporter Jim Muir
Sports Editor Diana Winson

PRODUCTION

Manager Alice Bedokis

Mechanical available: Laser; Black and 3 ROP colors; insert accepted — preprinted, all; page cut-offs — 21½".

Mechanical specifications: Type page 13" x 21½"; E - 6 cols, 2", 1/6" between; A - 6 cols, 2", 1/6" between; C - 8 cols, 1½", 1/6" between.

Commodity consumption: average pages per issue 14(d), 20(sat).

Equipment: EDITORIAL: Front-end hardware — Ap/Mac; Front-end software — Microsoft/Word; Printers — Ap/Mac LaserWriter II. CLASSIFIED: Front-end hardware — Ap/Mac; Printers — Ap/Mac LaserWriter II. DISPLAY: Front-end hardware — Ap/Mac. PRODUCTION: Pagination software — QuarkXPress 3.31; OCR software — Adobe/Photoshop 2.5; Platemaking systems — Nu/Flip Top FT40U3UP; Plate exposures — 1-Nu; Plate processors — RoConex Fully Auto ICM 25-2; Scanners — Nikon/Coolscan, Scanmaker II XE; Production cameras — SCREEN/Companica 680C; Automatic film processors — SCREEN/LD-220-QT. MAILROOM: Bundle tyer — 1-Bu. WIRE SERVICES: News — AP; Syndicates — Creators, Chicago Sun Times, Chicago Tribune; Receiving dishes — size-10ft, AP. BUSINESS COMPUTERS: Club America; Applications: Nomads/Listmaster.

BLOOMINGTON-NORMAL

McLean County

'90 U.S. Census- 91,995 (Bloomington 19,989; Normal 15,393); E&P '96 Est. 102,634 (Bloomington 58,849; Normal 43,785)
ABC-CZ (90): 96,256 (HH 34,928)

The Pantagraph

(m-mon to sat; S)

The Pantagraph, 301 W. Washington; PO Box 2907, Bloomington, IL 61701; tel (309) 829-9411; fax (309) 829-9104. Chronicle Publishing Co. group.

Circulation: 50,670(m); 50,670(m-sat); 55,129(S); ABC Sept. 30, 1995.

Price: 50¢(d); 50¢(sat); $1.25(S).

Advertising: Open inch rate $35.10(m); $35.10(m-sat); $36.45(S).

News Services: AP, SHNS, KRT. **Politics:** Independent. **Established:** 1837.

Special Editions: Health & Fitness, Seniors (Jan); Agribusiness (Feb); Progress (Mar); Homes, Seniors (Apr); Vacation, Travel (June); Fairtime, Seniors (July); Homes (Sept); New Cars, Seniors (Oct); Holiday Shopping (Nov); Holiday Shopping (Dec).

Special Weekly Sections: Health, Fitness (mon); Today's Woman (tues); Food (wed); People (thur); Weekend Entertainment (fri); Travel, Leisure (S).

Magazines: TV Magazine (local, offset) (sat); USA Weekend, Sunday Comics (spot and full color) (S).

GENERAL MANAGEMENT

Publisher Donald R Skaggs
Director-Finance Barry L Winterland
Human Resources Director Michael L Meece

ADVERTISING

Director Mary E Keogh
Manager-Display John F Hoffman
Manager- Operations Loretta Vance

MARKETING AND PROMOTION

Director-Marketing Service Sharen M Kardon

TELECOMMUNICATIONS

Audiotex Manager Sharen Kardon

CIRCULATION

Director William R Hertter
Manager-Home Delivery Paul McNamee

Copyright ©1996 by the Editor & Publisher Co.

NEWS EXECUTIVES

Exec Editor Fred Kardon
Managing Editor-News Jan Dennis
Managing Editor-Editorial Bill Wills

EDITORS AND MANAGERS

Business Editor Jane Pickering
Business Writer Kathy McKinney
Business Writer Paul Swiech
Columnist Bill Flick
Chief Editorial Writer Lenore Sobota
Education Writer Victoria Pierce
Education Writer Randy Gleason
Entertainment Writer Dan Craft
Farm Editor Christine Anderson
Features Editor Steve Gleason
Food Editor Nancy Gordon
Health/Medical Writer Gary Mays
Librarian Diane Logsdon
Metro Editor Mark Pickering
Photo Editor David Proeber
Political Writer Don Thompson
Radio/Television Editor Steve Gleason
Sports Editor Bryan Bloodworth

MANAGEMENT INFORMATION SERVICES

Finance Director Barry L Winterland

PRODUCTION

Director Dan O'Brien
Supervisor-Composing Tim Morris
Supervisor-Pressroom Jack Bolender
Supervisor-Mailroom David Brannan

Market Information: TMC; Operate audiotex.
Mechanical available: Offset; Black and 3 ROP colors; insert accepted — preprinted; page cut-offs — 21½".
Mechanical specifications: Type page 13" x 21¼"; E - 6 cols, 2", 1/8" between; A - 6 cols, 2.07", 1/8" between; C - 9 cols, 1.33", 1/16" between.
Commodity consumption: Newsprint 5,200 short tons; 4,718 metric tons; widths 54", 40½", 27"; black ink 110,000 pounds; color ink 32,000 pounds; single pages printed 15,350; average pages per issue 38(d), 60(S); single plates used 80,000.
Equipment: EDITORIAL: Front-end hardware — 41-AST/PC 286 Discribe; Front-end software — Dewar/Sys III Editorial; Other equipment — Ap/Mac II, Lf/AP Leaf Picture Desk. CLASSIFIED: Front-end hardware — 15-PPI/Advertising Management System; Front-end software — Dewar/Sys II; Printers — HP/4M Plus. AUDIOTEX: Hardware — Brite. DISPLAY: Adv layout systems — AD-Tracker; Front-end hardware — 11-Ap/Mac, Pentium/90MH2 w/Novell 3.12; Front-end software — Multi-Ad/Creator 3.7.1; Printers — HP/1600 cm, HP/MV4 Accelawriter 8100, HP/CPS 1200, HP/MV4. PRODUCTION: Pagination software — Ap/Mac w/CNI/Open; Typesetters — 2-V/5100, Hyphen/94E, MON/Rip Express ImageMaster 1000, MON/Rip Express Imagemaster 1500, 2-HP/MV4; Plate exposures — Nu/Flip Top; Plate processors — Nat/A-340; Scanners — Sharp/JX 325, Sharp/JX 610, Kk/RFS 2035; Production cameras — ATF/24, C/Marathon; Automatic film processors — 2-Konica/720; Color separation equipment (conventional) — Ap/Mac, 2-Ap/Mac Quadra 950, Lf, Ap/Power Mac 8100, Adobe/Photoshop 3.01. PRESSROOM: Line 1 — 9-G/Cosmo 3516; Folders — 1-G/3:2; Reels and stands — 7-G/3516. MAILROOM: Counter stackers — 1-Id/NS660, 1-HL/Monitor, HT/II; Inserters and stuffers — 1-SLS/1000, 1-GMA/42P 8-into-1; Bundle tyer — 2-MLN, 2-MLN/A; Wrapping singles — 1-QWI/Underwrap, 1-SH/Underwrap; Addressing machine — 1-Ch/596. LIBRARY: Electronic — Data Times, 4-DEC/Micro VAX II; Combination — Microfiche: Microfilm. WIRE SERVICES: News — AP Datastream, AP Datafeatures, SHNS, KRT; Receiving dishes — size-7ft, AP. BUSINESS COMPUTERS: 1-IBM/AS-400; Applications: INSI; PCs & micros networked; PCs & main system networked.

CANTON

Fulton County

'90 U.S. Census- 13,922; E&P '96 Est. 13,473

Daily Ledger (e-mon to fri; m-sat)

Daily Ledger, 53 W. Elm St., Canton, IL 61520; tel (309) 647-5100; fax (309) 647-4665. Hollinger International Inc. group.
Circulation: 5,851(e); 5,851(m-sat); Sworn Sept. 28, 1995.
Price: 50¢(d); 50¢(sat); $101.00/yr.
Advertising: Open inch rate $7.68(e); $7.68(m-sat).
News Service: AP. **Politics:** Independent. **Established:** 1849.
Not Published: New Year; Memorial Day; Independence Day; Labor Day; Thanksgiving; Christmas.
Special Editions: Bridal, Income Tax (Jan); Agriculture (Feb); Car Care (Mar); Lawn & Garden (Apr); Home Improvement (May); Father's Day (June); Bridal (July); Back-to-School, Agriculture (Aug); Pre-Labor Day (Sept); Car Care, Cookbook, Home Improvement (Oct); Turkey Give-away (Nov); Christmas Wishbook (Dec).
Magazine: Channel Guide (fri).

CORPORATE OFFICER

Publisher Scott Koon

GENERAL MANAGEMENT

Business Manager Carla Shawgo

ADVERTISING

Manager Jackie Caulkins

CIRCULATION

Manager Rick Bybee

NEWS EXECUTIVE

Editor Linda Woods

EDITOR AND MANAGER

Sports Editor Steve Shank

MANAGEMENT INFORMATION SERVICES

Data Processing Manager Carla Shawgo

PRODUCTION

Manager Darin Smith
Manager-Composing Vicky Waughtel

Market Information: TMC.
Mechanical available: Offset; Black and 3 ROP colors; insert accepted — preprinted; page cut-offs — 22¾".
Mechanical specifications: Type page 13" x 21½"; E - 6 cols, 2 1/16", 1/8" between; A - 6 cols, 2 1/16", 1/8" between; C - 8 cols, 1 9/16", 1/16" between.
Commodity consumption: Newsprint 458 short tons; widths 34", 27", 13½", 27"; black ink 19,500 pounds; color ink 3,900 pounds; single pages printed 4,770; average pages per issue 14(d); single plates used 3,500.
Equipment: EDITORIAL: Front-end hardware — Ap/Mac. CLASSIFIED: Front-end hardware — Ap/Mac Classic. PRODUCTION: Typesetters — 3-Ap/Mac LaserWriter NT; Platemaking systems — BKY/Offset platemaking; Plate exposures — 1-B; Plate processors — Roconex/Troy Ohio; Scanners — SCREEN C/680, C; Production cameras — 1-SCREEN; Automatic film processors — Ultramatic/Diffusion Transfer. PRESSROOM: Line 1 — 6-G/Community; Folders — 1-G; Press control system — G/Community 50DC (Suburban Control). MAILROOM: Bundle tyer — Bu/67590; Addressing machine — Dispensa-Matic/16"; Other mailroom equipment — 3-K/Trimmer. COMMUNICATIONS: Systems used — satellite. WIRE SERVICES: News — AP; Stock tables — AP; Receiving dishes — size-6ft, AP. BUSINESS COMPUTERS: 2-IBM/PC; Applications: Adv billing, Accts receivable.

CARBONDALE-HERRIN-MURPHYSBORO

Jackson and Williamson Counties

'90 U.S. Census- 47,066 (Carbondale 27,033; Herrin 10,857; Murphysboro 9,176); E&P '96 Est. 47,545 (Carbondale 27,670; Herrin 11,119; Murphysboro 8,756)
ABC-NDM (90): 233,719 (HH 90,175)

Southern Illinoisan

(m-mon to sat; S)

Southern Illinoisan, 710 N. Illinois Ave. (62901); PO Box 2108, Carbondale, IL 62902; tel (618) 529-5454; fax (618) 457-2935. Lee Enterprises Inc. group.
Circulation: 29,626(m); 29,626(m-sat); 34,258(S); ABC Sept. 30, 1995.
Price: 50¢(d); 50¢(sat); $1.50(S); $2.95/wk; $11.80/4wk; $153.40/yr.
Advertising: Open inch rate $26.10(m); $26.10(m-sat); $28.15(S). **Representative:** Landon Associates Inc.
News Services: AP, KRT. **Politics:** Independent. **Established:** 1947.
Not Published: Christmas.
Special Editions: Brides (Jan); Nutrition & Health, House Plans (Mar); Home and Garden (Apr); Tourism (May); Football, Progress (Sept); Basketball, Gift Guide (Nov); Gift Guide (Dec).
Magazine: Parade (S).

GENERAL MANAGEMENT

Publisher Richard R Johnston

ADVERTISING

Coordinator-National Jennifer Hayes
Manager Jeff Barr
Manager-Classified Mary Mechler

MARKETING AND PROMOTION

Manager-Marketing/Promotion Kevin Bishop

CIRCULATION

Manager Richard Davis

NEWS EXECUTIVE

Editor Carl Rexroad

EDITORS AND MANAGERS

Business/Finance Editor Tom Wolfe
City/Metro Editor Tom Wolfe
Editorial Page Editor Joe Beck
Education Editor Tracy James
Entertainment/Amusements Editor Linda Sickler
Environmental Editor Cindy Humphreys
Farm/Agriculture Editor Tom Wolfe
Features Editor Tom Wolfe
Graphics Editor/Art Director Pam Kellerman
Health/Medical Editor Cindy Humphreys
News Editor Gary Marx
Photo Editor Dick Carter
Sports Editor Rick Underwood
Television/Film Editor Linda Sickler
Theater/Music Editor Linda Sickler

MANAGEMENT INFORMATION SERVICES

Data Processing Manager Charles Rich

PRODUCTION

Manager Paul Parson
Supervisor-Pre Press Ray Taylor
Supervisor-Press Claude Stearns
Supervisor-Distribution Kent Buckles

Market Information: Zoned editions; Split Run; TMC; Operate database.
Mechanical available: Offset; Black and 3 ROP colors; insert accepted — preprinted; page cut-offs — 22¾".
Mechanical specifications: Type page 13" x 21½"; E - 6 cols, 2", 1/8" between; A - 6 cols, 2", 1/8" between; C - 9 cols, 1 5/16", 1/16" between.
Commodity consumption: Newsprint 2,865 short tons; 1,930 metric tons; widths 27½", 26"; black ink 90,000 pounds; color ink 25,000 pounds; single pages printed 10,432; average pages per issue 24.2(d), 54(S); single plates used 41,000.
Equipment: EDITORIAL: Front-end hardware — HI; Other equipment — Ad Sys/8860. CLASSIFIED: Front-end hardware — HI; Other equipment — Ad Sys/8860, Ad Sys/8300. DISPLAY: Adv layout systems — HI/8300; Front-end hardware — Ap/Mac. PRODUCTION: Typesetters — AU/Laser; Plate exposures — 1-Nu/Double Flip Top; Plate processors — 1-Nat/A250; Scanners — AU, Nikon/Scanner; Production cameras — 1-C/Spartan III, 1-Ik/530; Automatic film processors — 1-LE; Color separation equipment (conventional) — Digi-Colour, Lf/AP Leaf Picture Desk, HI. PRESSROOM: Line 1 — 8-G/Urbanite (balloon former); Folders — 2-G/2:1, 1-G/1:4; Reels and stands — 8-G/Stands. MAILROOM: Counter stackers — MM/321; Inserters and stuffers — 2-MM/270; Bundle tyer — 1-Sa, 2-MLN; Addressing machine — Cheshire. LIBRARY: Electronic — 1-Sys. WIRE SERVICES: News — AP, KRT; Photos — AP; Stock tables — NYSE; Receiving dishes — size-2½ft, AP, KNT. BUSINESS COMPUTERS: 2-IBM/Sys 38; Applications: Adv, Circ billing, Gen accounting, Payroll; PCs & micros networked; PCs & main system networked.

CARMI

White County

'90 U.S. Census- 5,564; E&P '96 Est. 5,290

Carmi Times

(e-mon to fri; m-sat)

Carmi Times, 323-325 E. Main St.; PO Box 190, Carmi, IL 62821; tel (618) 382-4176; fax (618) 384-2163. Hollinger International Inc. group.
Circulation: 2,612(e); 2,612(m-sat); Sworn Sept. 30, 1995.
Price: 50¢(d); 50¢(sat); $8.15/mo; $75.00/yr.
Advertising: Open inch rate $6.05(e); $6.05(m-sat).
News Service: AP. **Politics:** Independent. **Established:** 1950.
Not Published: New Year; Memorial Day; Independence Day; Labor Day; Thanksgiving; Christmas.

CORPORATE OFFICERS

President Larry Perrotto
Secretary/Treasurer Charles G Cowan

GENERAL MANAGEMENT

Publisher Barry Cleveland

ADVERTISING

Manager Linda Devoy

CIRCULATION

Manager Brenda Pennington

NEWS EXECUTIVE

Editor Barry Cleveland

EDITORS AND MANAGERS

City News Editor Rob Wick
Society/Women's Editor Lori Allen
Sports Editor Bryan Weaver

PRODUCTION

Manager Rosemary Aud
Foreman Joe Maughan

Market Information: TMC.
Mechanical available: Offset; Black and 3 ROP colors; insert accepted — preprinted; page cut-offs — 21½".
Mechanical specifications: Type page 13" x 21½"; E - 6 cols, 2", 1/8" between; A - 6 cols, 2", 1/8" between; C - 8 cols, 1½", 1/16" between.
Commodity consumption: Newsprint 200 metric tons; widths 27½", 13¾"; single pages printed 3,000; average pages per issue 10(d).
Equipment: EDITORIAL: Front-end hardware — 5-Ap/Mac Plus, 1-Ap/Mac Classic, 1-Ap/Mac Classic II; Front-end software — Microsoft/Word, Aldus/PageMaker; Printers — Ap/Mac LaserWriter II, Ap/Mac ImageWriter. DISPLAY: Adv layout systems — 2-Ap/Mac SE, 1-Ap/Mac IIsi; Front-end software — Aldus/PageMaker, Aldus/FreeHand; Printers — 1-Ap/Mac LaserWriter II NTX. PRODUCTION: Typesetters — 6-L, 1-LU; Plate exposures — X; Plate processors — X. PRESSROOM: Line 1 — 1-G; Line 2 — G. MAILROOM: Addressing machine — 1-Am, 1-Ap/Mac ImageWriter. WIRE SERVICES: News — AP; Syndicates — TMS; Receiving dishes — AP.

CENTRALIA-CENTRAL CITY-WAMAC

Marion

'90 U.S. Census- 17,165 (Centralia 14,274; Central City 1,390; Wamac 1,501); E&P '96 Est. 16,784 (Centralia 13,762; Central City 1,427; Wamac 1,595)

Centralia Sentinel

(m-mon to fri; S)

Centralia Sentinel, 232 E. Broadway; PO Box 627, Centralia, IL 62801; tel (618) 532-5604; fax (618) 532-1212.
Circulation: 15,772(m); 15,772(S); Sworn Oct. 1, 1994.
Price: 35¢(d); 75¢(S); $1.50/wk; $78.00/yr (carrier).
Advertising: Open inch rate $8.25(m); $8.25(S). **Representative:** Papert Companies.
News Service: AP. **Politics:** Independent. **Established:** 1863.
Not Published: New Year; Memorial Day; Independence Day; Labor Day; Thanksgiving; Christmas.
Special Editions: Food; School; Fall Fashions; Christmas Edition; Spring & Easter; Christmas Greetings; Centralia Days; Sidewalk Sale; Veteran's Day; Moonlight Madness; Last Minute Gifts; Baby; 3 Stooges; Can-O-Rama; Draw-an-Ad; Cooking School; Derby; President's Day Sale; Mother's Day; Father's Day; Labor Day; Early Bird Specials; Summer's Evening Opening; Fall Sunday Opening; Dollar Days; Halloween; Football; Car Care; Design-an-Ad.
Special Weekly Sections: Food, Society (wed); Entertainment, Church (fri); Society, Farm, Business (S); Sports, Stocks, Society (daily).
Magazines: Telly Times (fri); Parade, Comics (S).

CORPORATE OFFICERS

President John Perrine
Secretary/Treasurer William Perrine

GENERAL MANAGEMENT

General Manager Dan Nichols
Manager-Office Julie Copple
Purchasing Agent Gary E Sprehe

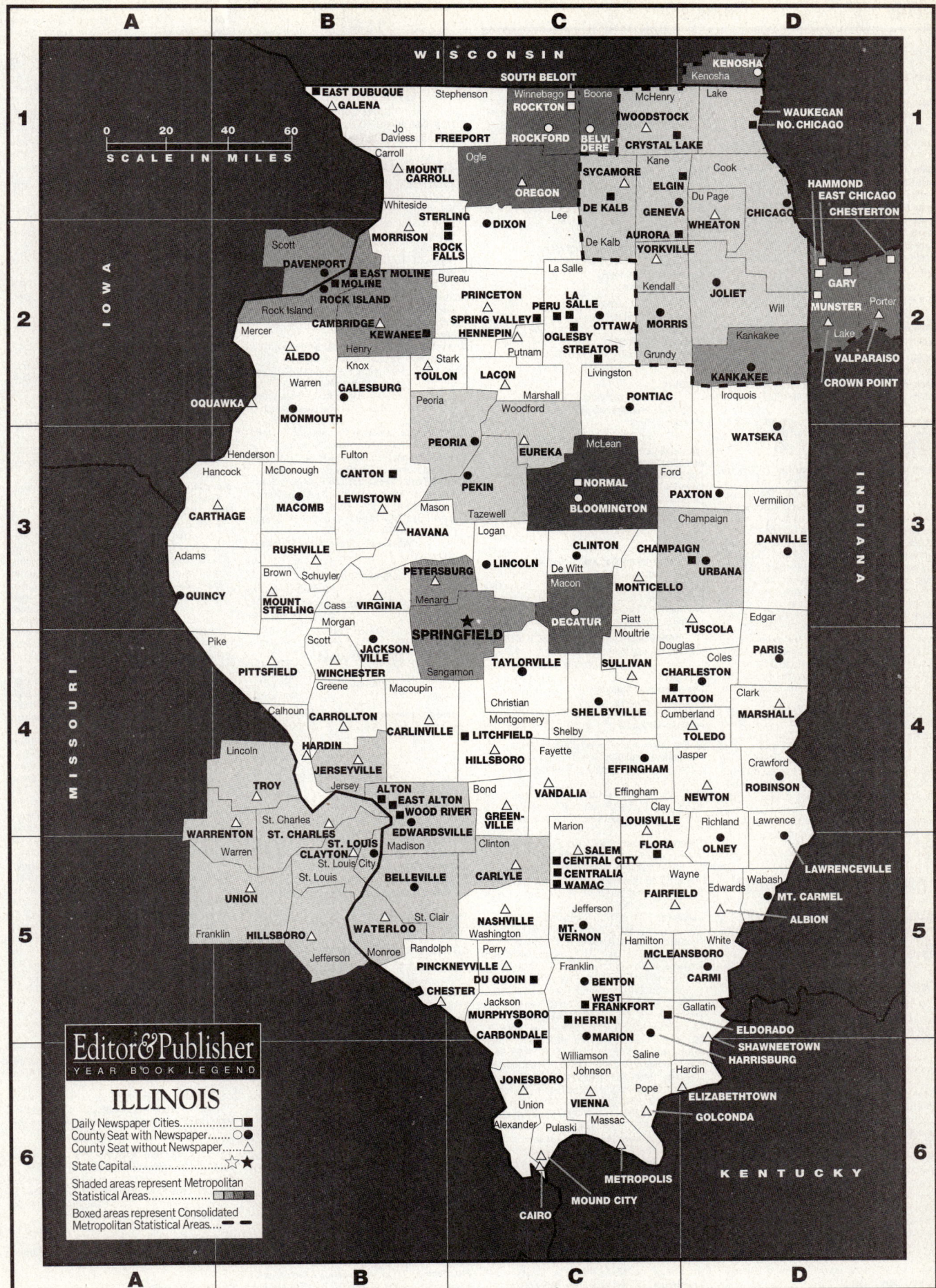

I-108 Illinois

ADVERTISING

Manager Dan Nichols

CIRCULATION

Director Randy Brooks

NEWS EXECUTIVES

Managing Editor David Felts
Assoc Editor Mark Hodapp

EDITORS AND MANAGERS

Editorial Page Editor David Felts
Farm Editor Judith Joy
Feature Editor Judith Joy
Photo Department Manager Will Pennington
Political Editor Mark Hodapp
Sports Editor Randy List
State Editor Mike Jones
West Counties Editor Mark Hodapp
Wire Editor David Felts

MANAGEMENT INFORMATION SERVICES

Data Processing Manager Teri Kelley

PRODUCTION

Manager Gary E Sprehe
Supervisor-Composing Terry Kelly

Market Information: Zoned editions; Split Run; TMC; Operate audiotex.

Mechanical available: Offset; Black and 3 ROP colors; insert accepted — preprinted, 3x5" in size to 15x11.5; page cut-offs — $22\frac{3}{4}$".

Mechanical specifications: Type page 13" x $21\frac{1}{4}$"; E - 6 cols, $2\frac{3}{16}$", $\frac{1}{16}$" between; A - 6 cols, $2\frac{3}{16}$", $\frac{1}{16}$" between; C - 8 cols, $2\frac{1}{16}$", $\frac{1}{16}$" between.

Commodity consumption: Newsprint 750 metric tons; widths 33", $16\frac{1}{2}$"; black ink 6,000 pounds; color ink 100 pounds; single pages printed 9,354; average pages per issue 23(d), 64(S); single plates used 5,614.

Equipment: EDITORIAL: Front-end hardware — 13-Mk, 1-Ap/Mac. CLASSIFIED: Front-end hardware — Mk/1100 Plus, 2-Mk. DISPLAY: Adv layout systems — 2-Mk/Ad Comp, Ap/Mac Quadra 650, Ap/Mac; Front-end software — QuarkXPress, Adobe/Illustrator; Printers — QMS/860, Ap/Mac LaserWriter II. PRODUCTION: Typesetters — 2-M/202, Ap/Mac LaserWriter, Ap/Mac LaserWriter II, QMS/860, Hyphen/Spectraset 2400; Plate exposures — 1-Nu; Plate processors — 1-Nat; Electronic picture desk — Adobe/Photoshop; Scanners — AG/Arcus, Kk/RFS Film Scanner; Production cameras — 1-R/481; Automatic film processors — 1-LE/LD 1800A. PRESSROOM: Line 1 — 6-G/Urbanite (offset); Press drives — MGD, Fin; Folders — 1-G; Reels and stands — 6-G/Roll Stand; Press control system — G. MAILROOM: Inserters and stuffers — 1-MM; Bundle tyer — 2-Bu; Addressing machine — Ultra Comp/PC (w/Panasonic Printer for Labels). WIRE SERVICES: News — AP; Stock tables — AP; Receiving dishes — size-3m, AP, NYT. BUSINESS COMPUTERS: 2-Novell; Applications: Circ, Payroll, Bookkeeping, Accts receivable; PCs & micros networked; PCs & main system networked.

CHAMPAIGN-URBANA

Champaign County

'90 U.S. Census- 99,846 (Champaign 63,502; Urbana 36,344); E&P '96 Est. 104,746 (Champaign 68,096; Urbana 36,650)
ABC-CZ (90): 118,512 (HH 44,719)

The News-Gazette (e-mon to fri; m-sat; S)

The News-Gazette, 15 Main St.; PO Box 677, Champaign, IL 61820; tel (217) 351-5252; fax (217) 351-5291; e-mail gazette@prairienet.org.

Circulation: 45,425(e); 45,600(m-sat); 52,143(S); ABC Sept. 30, 1994.

Price: 35¢(d); 35¢(sat); $1.50(S); $2.90/wk.

Advertising: Open inch rate $25.76(e); $25.76(m-sat); $27.39(S).

News Service: AP. **Politics:** Independent. **Established:** 1852.

Not Published: Christmas.

Special Editions: Money Matters (Jan); Farm Edition (Feb); Design-an-Ad, Outdoors (Mar); Home & Garden (Apr); Car Care, Summer Fun Guide (May); People In Business, Danville Balloon Classic (June); Answer Book, Football (Aug); Fall TV Preview, Home & Garden (Sept); Fall/Winter Fun Guide, Help Book (Oct); Window Shopping (Holiday Gift Guides) (Nov); Window Shopping (Holiday Gift Guides) (Dec).

Special Weekly Sections: Weekend Sports Wrap-up (mon); Beginnings Engagement/Wedding (tues); Best Food Day (wed); Anniversaries/Birth Announcements (thur); Religion Page, Pet Column (fri); Real Estate, Home Improvement (sat); Sports; Farm/Business; Travel/Vacation.

Magazines: Entertainment Magazine, Television Magazine (fri); USA Weekend (S).

Broadcast Affiliates: WDWS-AM; WHMS-FM.

CORPORATE OFFICERS

Board Chairman Marajen Stevick Chinigo
President/CEO John C Hirschfeld
Secretary/Treasurer Michael S Ovca

GENERAL MANAGEMENT

Publisher Marajen Stevick Chinigo
Chief Financial Officer Michael S Ovca
Purchasing Agent Michael S Ovca

ADVERTISING

Vice Pres-Marketing Ronald A Wilcox
Director Sue Trippiedi
Manager-Classified Sue Trippiedi
Manager-National Denny Santarelli

CIRCULATION

Manager Pete Jones

NEWS EXECUTIVES

Editor/Vice Pres-Newspapers John R Foreman
Managing Editor John Beck

EDITORS AND MANAGERS

Amusements Editor Tom Kacich
Business Editor Don Dodson
City Editor Scott Koenemann
Editorial Page Editor Rosemary T Garhart
Editorial Writer Jim Dey
Education Editor Julie Wurth
Food Editor Tom Kacich
Librarian Carolyn Vance
News Editor Dan Corkery
Photo Department Manager Darrell Hoemann
Political Editor Scott Koenemann
Exec Sports Editor Loren Tate
Sports Editor Jean McDonald
Television Editor Pete Wetmore
Women's Editor Tom Kacich

MANAGEMENT INFORMATION SERVICES

Info Technology Manager Linda Bauer

PRODUCTION

Manager Fred Richards
Superintendent-Building Steve Farruggia
Foreman-Composing Greg Durbin
Foreman-Pressroom Fred Richards
Foreman-Mailroom Floyd Bundy

Market Information: Zoned editions; TMC.

Mechanical available: Offset; Black and 3 ROP colors; insert accepted — preprinted; page cut-offs — $21\frac{1}{2}$".

Mechanical specifications: Type page 13" x $21\frac{1}{2}$"; E - 6 cols, $2\frac{1}{16}$", $\frac{1}{8}$" between; A - 6 cols, $2\frac{1}{16}$", $\frac{1}{8}$" between; C - 9 cols, $1\frac{3}{8}$", $\frac{1}{8}$" between.

Commodity consumption: Newsprint 5,644 short tons; 5,149 metric tons; widths 55", $41\frac{1}{4}$", $27\frac{1}{2}$", $13\frac{3}{4}$"; black ink 76,698 pounds; color ink 20,668 pounds; single pages printed 14,648; average pages per issue 35(d), 70(S); single plates used 25,823.

Equipment: EDITORIAL: Front-end hardware — 3-SII/Tandem TXP Sys 55; Front-end software — SII/Editorial. CLASSIFIED: Front-end hardware — 3-SII/Tandem TxP Sys 55; Front-end software — SII/Editorial. DISPLAY: Adv layout systems — PPC, Ap/Mac; Front-end hardware — Xenotron/XVC 3s, Xenotron/XVC 4s, Ap/Mac II, PPC, AP Adsend; Front-end software — QuarkXPress 3.3, Multi-Ad/Creator 3.7, Adobe/Photoshop 3.0; Printers — AU/Soft PIP, AG/Accuset 1000, Hyphen/PC RIP; Other equipment — ECR/Autokon 1000 DE, Tektronix/Phaser III Pxi, HP, Umax, Epson/Flatbed Scanners, Bernoulli/Drivers, XYQUEST/Drivers. PRODUCTION: Pagination software — QuarkXPress 3.3; Typesetters — AU/Soft PIP, AG/Accuset 1000, 2-QMS/860 plain paper, 1-Hyphen/PC RIP; Plate exposures — 2-Nu/Flip Top; Plate processors — 1-WL/30D; Scanners — 2-ECR/Autokon 1000 DE, 1-Umax/1200 flat bed color; Production cameras — C/Newspager II; Automatic film processors — LE/PC13, 1-LS/2600, 1-LS/210JRL. PRESSROOM: Line 1 — 8-G/Cosmo; Folders — 2-G/2:1; Pasters — 6-G; Reels and stands — 6-G; Press control system — 2-Hurletron. MAILROOM: Counter stackers — 3-QWI; Inserters and stuffers — HI/1476; Bundle tyer — 4-OS/JP80; Addressing machine — 1-Ch/Labeler. WIRE SERVICES: News — AP Datastream, AP Datafeatures; Stock tables — AP SelectStox I; Receiving dishes — AP. BUSINESS COMPUTERS: 2-DEC/Micro VAX 3100; Applications: CJ: Adv, Circ, Classified, Layout, Accts receivable, Gen ledger, Accts payable, Payroll; PCs & main system networked.

CHARLESTON

Coles County

'90 U.S. Census- 20,398; E&P '96 Est. 21,303
ABC-CZ (90): 20,398 (HH 6,358)

Coles County Daily Times-Courier (m-mon to sat)

Coles County Daily Times-Courier, 307 6th St.; Box 650, Charleston, IL 61920; tel (217) 345-7085; fax (217) 345-7090. Howard Publications group.

Circulation: 7,472(m); 7,472(m-sat); ABC Sept. 30, 1995.

Price: 50¢(d); 50¢(sat); $98.80/yr (carrier), $104.00/yr (mail).

Advertising: Open inch rate $8.50(m); $8.50(m-sat); comb with Mattoon Journal Gazette $12.70. **Representative:** Landon Associates Inc.

News Service: AP. **Politics:** Independent-Republican. **Established:** 1840.

Note: The Coles County Daily Times-Courier is being printed at the Mattoon Journal-Gazette. For detailed mechanical equipment information, see the Mattoon Journal-Gazette listing.

Not Published: New Year; Memorial Day; Independence Day; Labor Day; Christmas.

Special Editions: Annual Farm Section (Jan); Annual Thanksgiving Day Edition (Nov).

Special Weekly Sections: Business News, Newspapers in Education (mon); About People (tues); Lifestyle/Food (wed); Farm Features, Best Food Day (thur); Church, TV Section (fri); Sports/Lifestyle (sat).

Magazines: Weekly Food; Business; Entertainment; TV.

CORPORATE OFFICER

President Robert S Howard

GENERAL MANAGEMENT

Publisher Betty Boyer

ADVERTISING

Director Robert S Yamamoto

NEWS EXECUTIVE

Editor William Lair

PRODUCTION

Manager Robert S Yamamoto

Commodity consumption: width $27\frac{1}{2}$"; average pages per issue 24(d).

CHICAGO

Cook County

'90 U.S. Census- 2,783,726; E&P '96 Est. 2,776,653
Daily Herald:
ABC-NDM (90): 1,214,083 (HH 436,530)
Defender:
ABC-NDM (90): 2,782,632 (HH 1,018,729)
Southtown:
ABC-NDM (90): 883,901 (HH 314,522)
Sun-Times and Tribune:
ABC-NDM (90): 2,837,374 (HH 1,047,781)

Chicago Defender (m-mon to thur; wknd)

Chicago Defender, 2400 S. Michigan, Chicago, IL 60616; tel (312) 225-2400; fax (312) 225-5659.

Circulation: 19,541(m); 27,981(wknd); ABC Sept. 30, 1994.

Price: 35¢(d); 50¢(wknd); $99.00/yr (carrier), $112.84/yr (mail).

Advertising: Open inch rate $20.72(m); $22.30(wknd).

News Service: UPI. **Politics:** Independent. **Established:** 1905 (weekend), 1956 (daily).

Special Editions: Dr. Martin Luther King (Jan); African American History Month, Auto Show (Feb); Career Week (Mar); Easter Special (Apr); Health & Fitness (June); Bud Billiken Section, Back-to-School Section, Education Guides (Aug); Financial Section (Sept); Healthcare & Wellness (Nov); Education Guide, Shopping Guide (Christmas-Kwanzaa) (Dec).

Special Weekly Section: Auto (tues).

CORPORATE OFFICERS

Board Chairman John H Sengstacke
President Fredrick D Sengstacke
Secretary Robert Sengstacke

GENERAL MANAGEMENT

Publisher Fredrick D Sengstacke
General Manager Eugene Scott

ADVERTISING

Director Harriett H Diles

MARKETING AND PROMOTION

Manager-Marketing Michael Brown

NEWS EXECUTIVE

Editor John H Sengstacke

EDITOR AND MANAGER

City Editor Ken Green

PRODUCTION

Manager Betty Furcron

Mechanical available: Offset; Black and 3 ROP colors.

Mechanical specifications: Type page $10\frac{13}{16}$" x 14"; E - 5 cols, $2\frac{1}{16}$", $\frac{1}{8}$" between; A - 5 cols, $2\frac{1}{16}$", $\frac{1}{8}$" between; C - 5 cols, $2\frac{1}{16}$", $\frac{1}{8}$" between.

Commodity consumption: average pages per issue 23(d).

Equipment: WIRE SERVICES: News — UPI; Receiving dishes — UPI. BUSINESS COMPUTERS: PCs & main system networked.

Daily Herald (m-mon to sat; S)

Daily Herald, 155 E. Algonquin Rd.; PO Box 280, Arlington Heights, IL 60006; tel (847) 427-4300; fax (847) 427-1550.

Circulation: 128,172(m); 128,172(m-sat); 125,849(S); ABC Sept. 30, 1995.

Price: 50¢(d); 50¢(sat); $1.25(S); $3.80/wk; $30.40/8wk; $197.60/yr.

Advertising: Open inch rate $54.70(m); $54.70(m-sat); $54.70(S). **Representatives:** US Suburban Press; Papert Companies.

News Services: AP, CSM. **Politics:** Independent. **Established:** 1872.

Note: Listing covers 19 editions of the Daily Herald serving Elgin/South Elgin, Carpentersville, East Dundee, West Dundee, Gilberts, Sleepy Hollow, Algonquin, Fox River Grove, Lake in the Hills, Libertyville, Mundelein, Vernon Hills, Mettawa, Green Oaks, Hawthorn Woods, Kildeer, Island Lake, Lake Zurich, Wauconda, Bloomingdale, Itasca, Medinah, Roselle, Wood Dale, Wheaton, Glen Ellyn, Carol Stream, Glendale Heights, Warrenville, West Chicago, Winfield, Lisle, Naperville, Lombard, Oak Brook, Oakbrook Terrace, Villa Park, Mount Prospect, Prospect Heights; Des Plaines, Barrington Hills, Deer Park, Lake Barrington, North Barrington, South Barrington, Tower Lakes, Buffalo Grove, Long Grove, Wheeling, Hoffman Estates, Schaumberg, Arlington Heights, Rolling Meadows.

Special Editions: Wedding Planner, Elk Grove 40th Anniversary (Jan); Spring Home Furnishings and Improvement, 1996 New Home Preview, Valentine's Gift Guide, Auto Show Preview, Woodfield (Feb); DuPage '96, Home Furnishings and Improvement, Pet Pizzaz, Action Adults (Mar); Baseball Preview, Spring Lawn & Garden, Spring Dining and Entertainment Guide (Apr); Mother's Day Gift Guide, Health & Fitness (May); Father's Day Gift Guide, Summer in Arlington Heights, Cavalcade of Homes (June); Parade of Homes, Taste & Touch of Palatine (July); Cardunal Jamboree Days, Fall Fashion & Back-to-School, Autumn Dining & Entertainment Guide, Wedding Planner, Elgin Fine Arts, Arlington Million, Buffalo Grove Days (Aug); PRO Football '96 Preview (Sept); Woodfield Mall-Fall Edition, Fall Home Furnishings and Improvement, Fall Home Furnishings and Improvement-DuPage (Oct); Toys & Electronics Gift Guide, Early Birds Gift Guide, Gift Guide I (Nov); Gift Guide II, Holiday Dining and Entertainment Guide (Dec).

Special Weekly Sections: Flair (tues); Food (wed); Time Out, Real Estate, Sports Extra High School (fri); Weekend Leisure, Auto Showcase, Home Styles (New Homes) (sat); TV Magazine, Home Styles (New Homes), Discovery, Home & Garden, USA Weekend (S).

Magazines: Showcase (Entertainment) (daily); TV Magazine, Color Comics (S).

CORPORATE OFFICERS

Board Chairman/Publisher/CEO Stuart R Paddock Jr
Vice Chairman/Exec Vice Pres-Administration Robert Y Paddock
President/Chief Operating Officer Daniel E Baumann
Vice Pres-Finance/Secretary/Treasurer Robert F Donahue
Vice Pres/Asst Secretary/Treasurer Margie S Flanders
Vice Pres-Production William F Schoepke

Illinois I-109

GENERAL MANAGEMENT

Vice Pres-Advertising James F Walsh
Vice Pres-Circulation James J Galetano
Vice Pres/Editor Douglas K Ray
Vice Pres-Human Resources Judith A Orgell
Asst Vice Pres/Asst to Exec Vice Pres Robert Y Paddock Jr

ADVERTISING

Director James F Walsh
Manager-Classified Donald J Longacre
Manager-Co-op Bonnie J Reicks
Manager-Legals Margie S Flanders
Manager-Division Sales Jon C Rutherford
Manager-Division Sales James J McCambridge
Manager-Division Sales Robert C Strasser
Manager-National Jon C Rutehrford

MARKETING AND PROMOTION

Asst Vice Pres/Manager-Marketing/Promotion Karin E Guy

TELECOMMUNICATIONS

Asst Vice Pres/New Media Coordinator Stuart R Paddock III

CIRCULATION

Director James J Galetano
Manager John G Janos
Manager-Single Copy Sales Joseph M Marek
Manager-Promotion Wayne S Gebis

NEWS EXECUTIVES

Editor Douglas K Ray
Asst Vice Pres/Managing Editor John A Lampinen

EDITORS AND MANAGERS

Assoc Editor James E Slusher
Business Editor James Kane
City Editor Renee C Trappe
DuPage Editor James S Davis
Editorial Page Editor David L Beery
Fashion Editor Cheryl A TerHorst
Features Editor Jean L Rudolph
Films Editor Dann P Gire
Graphics Editor Robert E Finch
Health/Environment Editor Daniel G Rozek
Home Furnishings Patricia A Gerlach
Librarian Mary Tomasello
Metropolitan Editor Tom E Quinlan
News Editor Richard Klicki
Director-Photography Michael Seeling
Political Madeleine L Doubek
Sports Editor James A Cook
Television Theodore J Cox
Theater Editor Thomas A Valeo
Travel Editor M Eileen Brown
Weekend Editor Colin O'Donnell

MANAGEMENT INFORMATION SERVICES

Data Processing Manager Michael P Schoepke
Online Manager John Graham

PRODUCTION

Director William F Schoepke
Asst Vice Pres/ Manager Jerome A Schur
Manager-Pressroom/Mailroom Edward V Domain
Manager-Newspaper Processing Center Neil Clark

Market Information: Zoned editions; Split Run; TMC; Operate database; Electronic edition.
Mechanical available: Offset; Black and 3 ROP colors; insert accepted — preprinted, advertising, editorial; page cut-offs — 22".
Mechanical specifications: Type page 13" x 21"; E - 6 cols, 2", ⅙" between; A - 6 cols, 2", ⅙" between; C - 9 cols, 1⅜", 1/16" between.
Commodity consumption: Newsprint 16,000 metric tons; widths 54", 40½", 27", 13½"; black ink 300,000 pounds; color ink 150,000 pounds; single pages printed 46,800; average pages per issue 63(d), 76(S); single plates used 220,000.
Equipment: EDITORIAL: Front-end hardware — DEC/VAX 4700; Front-end software — Dewar/View 1.13F; Printers — III/Postscript. CLASSIFIED: Front-end hardware — DEC/VAX 4700; Front-end software — Computext; Printers — III/Postscript. DISPLAY: Adv layout systems — SCS/Layout 8000; Front-end hardware — DEC/VAX 4700; Front-end software — Internal; Printers — DEC/LA 180. PRODUCTION: Pagination software — Dewar/View 1.4; Typesetters — 3-III/ImageCenters; Platemaking systems — Hoechst/Plate Processors; Plate exposures — 3-Nu/6000; Plate processors — 2-Hoechst; Electronic picture desk — Lf/AP Leaf Picture Desk; Scanners — Optronics/Colorgetter; Production cameras — 1-C/Spartan III Color; Automatic film processors — 3-LE/LDQ-24; Film transporters — 1-C; Shrink lenses — 1-CK Optical/Variable 2%-5%; Digital color separation equipment — PCS/100. PRESSROOM: Line 1 — KBA/Commander 48 pages; Line 2 — KBA/Commander 48 pages; Line 3 — KBA/Commander 48 pages; Press drives — Ewert Ahrensburg Electronics; Folders — 3-KFM/80; Pasters — 9-KBA/Pastomat; Press control system — Ewert Ahrensburg Electronics; Press registration system — Automatic/Film Punch. MAILROOM: Counter stackers — 9-HT; Inserters and stuffers — 3-AMG/630 20 into 1; Bundle tyer — 5-Dynaric/Plastic; Addressing machine — 3-Am. LIBRARY: Electronic — Datatimes/PLS. COMMUNICATIONS: Digital ad delivery system — AP AdSend. WIRE SERVICES: News — AP, UPI, RN; Photos — AP; Stock tables — Ap Grand Central Stocks; Receiving dishes — size-10ft, AP, UPI. BUSINESS COMPUTERS: 2-DEC/VAX 4000-700; Applications: CJ; PCs & micros networked; PCs & main system networked.

Daily Southtown

(m-mon to sat; S)

Daily Southtown, 5959 S. Harlem Ave., Chicago, IL 60638; tel (312) 586-8800; fax (312) 229-2555. Hollinger International Inc. group.
Circulation: 58,034(m); 46,784(m-sat); 65,621(S); ABC Sept. 30, 1995.
Price: 35¢(d); 35¢(sat); $1.25(S); $116.00/yr; $22.00/8wk.
Advertising: Open inch rate $45.38(m); $45.38(m-sat); $50.82(S). **Representative:** Papert Companies.
News Services: AP, CNS, NYT, NEA, DJ, Entertainment News Wire, Wall Street Journal. **Politics:** Independent. **Established:** 1906.
Special Editions: Educational Opportunities; Weddings; Home Improvement; Health & Fitness; Auto Show; Golden Opportunities; Dining; Christmas Gift Guides; Western Open; Home Furnishings; Golf; Baseball Preview; Dining Guide.
Special Weekly Sections: Dollar$ense (mon); Food (wed); Your Town Extra, Pro Football This Week (thur); Home Guide, TGIF!, Real Estate (fri); Auto Guide (sat); Home Guide, Your Town Extra (S).
Magazine: TV Magazine (S).

GENERAL MANAGEMENT

Publisher Norman A Rosinski
Vice Pres-Operations Gerald Smith
Controller George Voleta

ADVERTISING

Director Mike Beatty
Manager-Retail Andrew Walter
Manager-Classified Rita Hendren Feigl

MARKETING AND PROMOTION

Manager- Marketing Thaine Shetter
Manager- Marketing Jim DeSeno

TELECOMMUNICATIONS

Manager-Electronic Info Jody Carmack

CIRCULATION

Director John Novosel

NEWS EXECUTIVE

Editor Michael J Kelley

EDITORS AND MANAGERS

Business/Real Estate Editor John Obrecht
Columnist Phil Kadner
Community News Editor Bill Padjen
Editorial Page Editor Ed Koziarski
Education Writer Annie Sweeney
Features/Entertainment Editor George Haas
Asst Features Editor Monica Eng
Food/Society Writer Eloise Valadez
Health/Environment Writer Kevin Carmody
Metro Editor Douglas R Williams
Deputy Metro Editor John Hector
Asst Metro Editor Anita Huslin
Asst Metro Editor Thomas Finn
News Editor Tim Sheil
Political Writer Rick Bryant
Sports Editor Michael Waters
Sports Columnist Paul Ladewski
Sports Columnist Phil Arvia
Television Writer Joel Brown

MANAGEMENT INFORMATION SERVICES

Data Processing Manager Patrick Kennedy

PRODUCTION

Director Robert Moyer
Manager Thomas Gannon
Manager-Pre Press Joanne Stavola
Manager-Post Press Don Stamper

Market Information: Zoned editions; Split Run; TMC; Operate audiotex.
Mechanical available: Offset; Black and 3 ROP colors; insert accepted — preprinted; page cut-offs — 22¾".
Mechanical specifications: Type page 13" x 21½"; E - 6 cols, 2 1/16", ⅛" between; A - 6 cols, 2 1/16", ⅛" between; C - 10 cols, 1⅜", 1/16" between.
Commodity consumption: Newsprint 10,000 metric tons; width 54"; average pages per issue 64(d), 76(S).
Equipment: EDITORIAL: Front-end hardware — PC/286 8Mhz; Front-end software — III/Tecs 2. CLASSIFIED: Front-end hardware — PC/286 8Mhz; Front-end software — III/Tecs 2. DISPLAY: Adv layout systems — Ap/Mac, CJ; Front-end hardware — HI/8300, HI/8900; Front-end software — HI; Printers — 3-Tegra/Varityper 5510, 2-Tegra/Varityper 1000P, 1-Hyphen/Dash, 1-SLS/SelectPress. PRODUCTION: OCR software — Kurzweil; Typesetters — 2-Tegra/Varityper XP-1000, 3-Tegra/Varityper/XP-5500, Bidco/80C; Platemaking systems — 2-KFM; Electronic picture desk — Lf/AP Leaf Picture Desk; Scanners — X, Howtek/Colorscan, 2-X, 2-ImageTex, Kk/2035; Production cameras — 1-C/Spartan II, 1-C/Newspager, 1-B; Automatic film processors — 2-LE, 1-P, 1-C; Film transporters — 2-LE, 1-P; Shrink lenses — Alan/Anamorphic; Color separation equipment (conventional) — Howtek, Ap/Mac; Digital color separation equipment — Howtek, Ap/Mac. PRESSROOM: Line 1 — 17-G/Metro; Line 2 — 9-G/Urbanite; Press drives — Fin; Folders — 3-G, G/2:1, 1-G/3:2; Pasters — G, R&P. MAILROOM: Counter stackers — 2-QWI/300, 3-Monitor/HT, 2-HL/Sta-Hi; Inserters and stuffers — 2-SLS/6:1, 1-SLS/4:1; Bundle tyer — 3-MLN, 10-MLN/2A, 1-Spirit, 2-News/90; Addressing machine — 3-Ch. WIRE SERVICES: News — AP Datastream, AP Datafeatures; Stock tables — AP Digital Stocks; Receiving dishes — size-12ft, AP, NYT, IBD, USA Today. BUSINESS COMPUTERS: 4-DEC/VAX; Applications: CJ: Circ, Adv billing, Accts receivable, Gen ledger, Payroll; PCs & micros networked; PCs & main system networked.

Chicago Sun-Times

(m-mon to fri; m-sat; S)

Chicago Sun-Times, 401 N. Wabash Ave., Chicago, IL 60611; tel (312) 321-3000; fax (312) 321-2920 (Corporate Comm.); web site http://www.suntimes.com. Hollinger International Inc. group.
Circulation: 488,405(m); 347,397(m-sat); 462,803(S); ABC Sept. 30, 1995.
Price: 35¢(d); 35¢(sat); $1.25(S).
Advertising: Open inch rate $351.00(m); $351.00(m-sat); $351.00(S). **Representative:** Cresmer, Woodward, O'Mara & Ormsbee.
News Services: AP, UPI, DJ, LAT-WP, RN, Chicago City News Bureau. **Politics:** Independent. **Established:** 1948 (Chicago Sun: 1941).
Advertising not accepted: Handgun and handgun ammunition.
Special Editions: Education Guide, Active Times, Bride & Groom, Health & Fitness (Jan); Valentine's Day Greeting Ads, Black History Month, 1996 Auto Show, Valentine's Day Gift Guide, Off-Price Guide (Feb); Education Guide, Your Home (Mar); Active Times, Health & Fitness, Spring Dining Guide, Baseball Preview, Our Best Friends, Spring Home, Lawn & Garden, Mother's Day Gift Guide (Apr); Education Guide, Welcome to Chicago, Mother's Day Greeting Ads (May); Off-Price Guide, Graduation Greeting Ads, Father's Day Greeting Ads (June); Bride & Groom, Black Expo, Health & Fitness, Active Times, Old Style Softball Classic (July); Education Guide, Sun-Times Grand Prix/USPRO Criterium (Aug); Bears/NFL Review, Commercial & Real Estate Report, Energy & Home Improvement, Nightlife Chicago (Sept); College Bound, Fall Auto Care, Pet Care, Bulls/NBA Preview (Oct); Early Bird Gift Guide, Holiday Dining Guide, Holiday Gift Guide, Education Guide (Nov); Last Minute Gift Guide, 10 Days & Counting (Dec).
Special Weekly Sections: Auto Times (mon); Food Guide (wed); Home Life, Weekend Plus (fri); Showcase, Travel, Med Life, Book Week, Homelife (S).
Magazines: TV Prevue, USA Weekend (S); Bloomberg Financial (Select Sundays).

CORPORATE OFFICERS

Chairman F David Radler
President/CEO Larry J Perrotto
Exec Vice Pres/Chief Financial Officer J David Dodd

GENERAL MANAGEMENT

Chicago Group
Exec Vice Pres/Editor (Chicago Sun-Times) Dennis A Britton
Exec Vice Pres-Legal Counsel & Chief Legal Counsel James W Artz
Exec Vice Pres-Sales/Marketing (Chicago Sun-Times) Joseph Sherman
Exec Vice Pres/Publisher (Daily Southtown & Star Newspapers) Norman A Rosinski
Exec Vice Pres/Publisher (Pioneer Press) Thomas J Neri
Vice Pres-Labor Relations (Chicago Sun-Times/ Chicago Group) Ted Rilea
President (Sun Times Features Inc.) Andrew B Davis

Chicago Sun-Times
Vice Pres-Production Frank Marcangelo
Vice Pres-Advertising Joseph J Sherman Sr
Director-Human Resources Boni Fine
Director-Marketing Mark F Mulholland
Managing Editor Julia D Wallace
Asst Controller Helen McCarthy

ADVERTISING

Vice Pres Joseph J Sherman
Director-Administration John Sullivan
Director-Classified Larry Green
Director-Display Entertainment/Amusement Casey Ladowski
Director-General Robin Ingle
Director-Network Advertising Susan Herzog
Director-Planning & Strategy William A Southern
Director-Retail Sales Kenneth DePaola
Director-Voice Info Service John M Stump

MARKETING AND PROMOTION

Asst to Exec Vice Pres Marketing Peter Belluomini
Director-Advertising Marketing Mark Mulholland
Director-Special Events George Berger
Manager-Community/Client Service Patricia Dudek
Manager-Market Research Frank Such
Manager-Corporate Communications Joanne Kitsos

TELECOMMUNICATIONS

Audiotex Manager John M Stump

CIRCULATION

Director of Distribution Mark Hornung
Exec Asst to Director of Distribution Peter Belluomini
Operations Manager Tom Spatz
Home Delivery Sales Manager Larry Blake
Manager-Single Copy Sales & Marketing Mike DiMaria
Suburban Manager Nick Manzie
Home Delivery Manager Nick Manzie

NEWS EXECUTIVES

Editor/Exec Vice Pres Dennis A Britton
Managing Editor Julia D Wallace
Deputy Managing Editor Steve Duke
Deputy Managing Editor-Sports/Graphics/Photo Rick Jaffe
Deputy Managing Editor-Sunday/Business Mark Miller
Deputy Managing Editor/Special Projects Lynn Roberts

EDITORS AND MANAGERS

ART
Editorial Art Director-Days Char Searl
Editorial Art Director-Nights Toby Roberts
News Room Administration David Lyons
BUSINESS
Auto Industry Dan Jedlicka
Baseball Writer Dan Bickley
Baseball Writer Toni Ginnetti
Baseball Writer Joe Goddard
Baseball Writer Dave Van Dyck
Bears/NFL Columnist Mike Mulligan
Bears/NFL Columnist Dan Pompei
Bulls/NBA Writer Lacy Banks
Bulls/NBA Writer John Jackson
Asst Finance Editor Michael Arnold
Columnist-Sports Rick Telander
College Sports Toni Ginnetti
College Sports Herb Gould
Consumer Products/Labor Pat Moore
General Assignment Daryl Van Schouwen
Health Care/Computers Della de Lafuente
High School Mark Potash
High School David Southwell
High School Steve Tucker
Horse Racing Dave Feldman
Manufacturing/Telecommunications John Barron
Media/Advertising/Entertainment/Sports Business John Barron
Notre Dame Sports/Golf Brian Hewitt
Personal Finance/Banking Lisa Holton
Real Estate Markets William Smith
Real Estate Writer Larry Finley

Copyright ©1996 by the Editor & Publisher Co.

I-110 Illinois

Real Estate Writer Bill Rumbler
Retail/Transportation Mary Ellen Podmolik
Small Business/Women in Business/Minority Business Francine Knowles
Sports Active Page Bob Richards
Sports Active Page-Golf/Tennis Len Ziehm

CITY DESK
Asst Managing Editor-Metro Steven Huntley
Deputy Metro Editor Michael Cordts
Asst Metro Editor Mike Cordts
Asst Metro Editor John Erickson
Asst Metro Editor Roger Flaherty
Asst Metro Editor Celeste Garrett
Asst Metro Editor Don Hayner
Asst Metro Editor Nancy Moffett

CITY NEWS BEATS
City Hall Reporter Fran Spielman
City Hall Reporter Mary Mitchell
Columnist-Advice Jeffrey Zaslow
Columnist-Celebrities Bill Zwecker
Columnist-General Raymond Coffey
Columnist-General Irv Kupcinet
Columnist-General Judy Markey
Columnist-General Richard Roeper
Columnist-General Michael Sneed
Columnist-Society Mary Cameron Frey
Criminal Courts Dan Lehmann
Education Writer Rosalind Rossi
Education Writer Rosalind Rossi
Environment/Science Writer Jim Ritter
Federal Building Mary Mitchell
Foundation/Charities/Social Service Maudlyn Ihejrika
General Assignment Leon Pitt
General Assignment Scott Fornek
General Assignment Charles Nicodemus
General Assignment Phillip O'Connor
General Assignment Maureen O'Donnell
General Assignment Lori Rotenberk
General Assignment Neil Steinberg
Housing Gil Jimenez
Immigration/Consulates Jorge Oclander
Investigative Reporter Charles Neubauer
MedLife Medical Writer Howard Wolinsky
Multicultural Affairs Jorge Oclander
Museums/Libraries/Cultural Institutions Adrienne Drell
Obituaries Chuck McWhinnie
Police Beat-Days Jim Casey
Public Health/Medical Writer Tom McNamee
Religion Andrew Herrmann
Suburban Writer Sharon Cotliar
Suburban Writer Phil Franchine
Suburban Writer Alex Rodriquez
Suburban Writer John Carpenter
Suburban Writer Michelle Campbell
Transportation Tamara Kerrill
Washington, DC Bureau Chief Lynn Sweet
Washington, DC Bureau Michael Briggs
Washington, DC Bureau Basil Talbott

EDITORIAL BOARD/EDITORIAL PAGES
Editorial Page Editor Michelle Stevens
Deputy Editorial Page Editor Michelle Stevens
Editorial Board Member/Editorial Writer Leslie Baldacci
Editorial Board Member/Editorial Writer Dennis Byrne
Editorial Board Member/Editorial Writer Cindy Richards
Editorial Board Member/Editorial Writer Tom Sheridan
Editorial Board Member/Editorial Writer Michelle Stevens
Editorial Cartoonist Jack Higgins
Political Columnist Steve Neal

FEATURES
Books Editor Henry Kisor
Comedy Ernest Tucker
Dance/Arts Lynn Voedisch
Fashion Maureen Jenkins
Deputy Features Editor/Administration Don Snider
Deputy Features Editor/Content Cristi Kempf
Asst Features Editor Laura Emerick
Asst Features Editor Darel Jevins
Features Reporter Celeste Busk
Features Reporter Mary Cameron Frey
Features Reporter Bob Herguth
Features Reporter Jae-Ha Kim
Features Reporter Delia O'Hara
Features Reporter Susy Schultz
Food Editor Beverly Bennett
Guide Listings Denise O'Neal
Movie Criticism Roger Ebert
Music Editor-Classical Wynne Delacoma
Music Editor-Pop/Country Dave Hoekstra
Music Editor-Jazz Lloyd Sachs
Nutrition Olivia Wu
Radio/Television Columnist Robert Feder
Theater Critic Hedy Weiss
Television Critic Lon Grahnke
Television Prevue Martha Flores
Television Prevue Mary Skilton
Television Prevue Jim Wagner
Travel Writer Brenda Rotzell
WeekendPlus Editor Kaarin Tisue
Asst Weekend Plus Editor Avis Weathersbee

NEWS DESK
Exec News Editor Joyce Winnecke
Asst Managing Editor-Production John McDonough

MANAGEMENT INFORMATION SERVICES
Data Processing Manager Verlin Wiley

PRODUCTION
Vice Pres Frank Marcangelo
Manager Randall Ridge
Asst Manager James Burklow

Market Information: Zoned editions; Split Run; TMC; Operate audiotex; Electronic edition.
Mechanical available: Letterpress; Black and 3 ROP colors; insert accepted — preprinted, preprinted; page cut-offs — $23\frac{9}{16}$".
Mechanical specifications: Type page $10\frac{9}{16}$" x $13\frac{7}{8}$"; E - 5 cols, $2\frac{1}{16}$", $\frac{1}{8}$" between; A - 5 cols, $2\frac{1}{16}$", $\frac{1}{8}$" between; C - 8 cols, $1\frac{1}{4}$", $\frac{1}{8}$" between.
Commodity consumption: Newsprint 115,000 metric tons; widths 58", $43\frac{1}{2}$", 29"; black ink 2,800,000 pounds; color ink 300,000 pounds; single pages printed 38,000,000; average pages per issue 128(d), 144(S); single plates used 500,000.
Equipment: EDITORIAL: Front-end hardware — 8-AT/J-11, 200-IBM/486 DX-2; Front-end software — AT 7.0; Other equipment — 25-AT, IBM/RS 6000, 15-IBM/Power PC. CLASSIFIED: Front-end hardware — 4-AT/J-11, 60-IBM/486 DX-2; Front-end software — AT 7.0; Other equipment — 2-AT, 2-IBM/RS 6000 pagination. DISPLAY: Front-end hardware — 12-Ap/Mac; Front-end software — Multi-Ad/Creator; Printers — 3-AU/6600. PRODUCTION: Typesetters — 3-AU/APS-5, 3-AU/6600; Platemaking systems — LX, Na; Plate exposures — 4-PR2/120; Scanners — 1-SCREEN/608G Color Scanner; Production cameras — 2-C/Newspager, 1-C/Marathon, 1-C/Spartan III; Automatic film processors — 2-LE/LD24, 2-LE/RA26, 1-Kk/Kodamatic 24, 1-P/Lith; Film transporters — 3-C; Shrink lenses — 1-Alan/24; Digital color separation equipment — 2-ECR/Autokon.
PRESSROOM: Line 1 — 21-G/Mark I Headliner; Line 2 — 21-G/Mark I Headliner; Line 3 — 24-G/Mark I Headliners; Folders — 10-G; Reels and stands — 8-W/C-SE-5B, 1-W/CFP, 12-G/Digital Pilot, 21-G/Amplidine, 12-G/Selsyn. MAILROOM: Counter stackers — 12-HL/Sta-Hi ZS7S, 2-HL/Dual Carrier; Inserters and stuffers — 2-S/272P, 1-AM Graphics/2299; Bundle tyer — 12-MLN/MLN-2A, 9-It/PSN6; Addressing machine — PC/Systems. LIBRARY: Electronic — Battelle/Basis Software. WIRE SERVICES: News — AP Digital stocks, RN; Photos — AP, RN, AFP; Stock tables — AP; Syndicates — NAS; Receiving dishes — AP. BUSINESS COMPUTERS: 1-IBM/370; Applications: PCs & micros networked; PCs & main system networked.

Chicago Tribune

(m-mon to fri; m-sat; S)

Chicago Tribune, 435 N. Michigan Ave., Chicago, IL 60611; tel (312) 222-3232; e-mail tribletter@aol.com; web site http://www.chicago.tribune.com. Tribune Co. group.

Circulation: 684,366(m); 609,731(m-sat); 1,083,963(S); ABC Sept. 30, 1995.
Price: 50¢(d); 50¢(sat); \$1.75(S); \$3.80/wk; \$197.60/yr.
Advertising: Open inch rate \$424.00(m); \$424.00(m-sat); \$594.00(S). **Representative:** Western States Associates.
News Services: AP, RN, NYT, TMS, DJ, KRT. **Politics:** Independent. **Established:** 1847.
Advertising not accepted: Handguns and handgun ammunition.
Special Editions: Employment Outlook, Education Today-Mid Winter, Cruise Planner, Winter Breaker (Jan); Europe, Auto Show I & II (Feb); Education Today-Spring, Spring/Summer Cruises, Chicago Flower & Garden, Technology and the Workplace, Spring Fashion, Spring/Summer Travel (Mar); Spring Home Design, Baseball '96, Small Business, Education Today-Summer (Apr); Spring Dining Out, Midwest Vacations, Chicago Top 100 Companies (May); Golf '96 (June); Mid-Year Employment Outlook, Heartland Air Show, Education Today-Fall (July); Football '96, Fall Fashion, Fall Home Design, Fall/Winter Cruises, Follow the Sun (Sept); Fall Dining Guide, Ski Time, Education Today-Graduates, Technology and the Workplace, Small Business, Fall/Winter Travel (Oct); Basketball '96, Education Today-Winter, Holiday Gift Guide-I, Local Values Wrap-I (Nov); Holiday Celebration Guide, Holiday Gift Guide-II, Local Values Wrap-II, Year in Pictures (Dec).
Special Weekly Sections: Kidnews (tues); Good Eating (wed); Friday, Your Place (fri); Home Guide (sat); Arts & Entertainment, Books, Business, Home, Real Estate, Perspective, Sports, Tempo, Transportation, Travel, Womannews (S).
Magazines: Chicago Tribune Magazine, TV Week, Color Comics (S).
Broadcast Affiliates: KTLA-TV Los Angeles; KCTC-AM/KYMX-FM Sacramento, CA; KWGN-TV Denver; WGN Chicago; WGN-TV Chicago; KWGN-TV Denver; WGNO-TV New Orleans, LA; WQCD-FM New York; WPIX-TV New York.

CORPORATE OFFICERS
Publisher Jack Fuller
President/CEO Jack Fuller
Vice Pres-Operations James O'Dell
Vice Pres-Advertising Dennis Grant
Vice Pres-Circulation Howard Hay
Vice Pres-Developing Business Kathleen M Waltz
Vice Pres/Editor Howard A Tyner
Vice Pres-Marketing & Development Tim Landon
Director-Finance Denise E Palmer

ADVERTISING
Director Dennis Grant
Director-Sales David Murphy
Director-General Gerald McCarthy
Director-Classified Jane Migely
Manager-Make-Up Robert McDonald
Manager-Supplements Robert Reese

MARKETING AND PROMOTION
Director-Promotion/Public Relations Kathy Manilla
Director-Marketing Research/Service Bruce Kramer

CIRCULATION
Director Howard Hay
Director-Metro Rick Surkamer
Director-Consumer Sales/Service Tom Buttel
Director-National Fred Hunter
Director-Operations John Donnelly
Director-Alternate Delivery Jeffrey A Elliott
Manager-Distribution Kevin King
Manager-South Metro Sheila Davidson
Manager-North Metro Tony Hunter
Manager-Systems Ed Wolfe
Manager-Customer Service Cherly Brewer
Manager-Single Copy Bob Thomas

NEWS EXECUTIVES
Editor Howard A Tyner
Senior Editor John Twohey
Senior Editor Tony Majeri
Assoc Editor-Operations Joseph Leonard
Managing Editor-News Ann Marie Lipinski
Assoc Managing Editor-Metropolitan News Gerould Kern
Assoc Managing Editor-Sports Tim Franklin
Assoc Managing Editor-News Editing Randall Weismann
Assoc Editor-Op-Ed Page Marcia Lythcott
Chief of Correspondents George de Lama
Assoc Managing Editor-Features Janet Franz

EDITORS AND MANAGERS
Arts & Entertainment Editor Rebecca Brown
Art Critic Alan Artner
Architecture Critic Blair Kamin
Auto Writer James Mateja
Careers Writer Carol Kleiman
Cartoonist Jeff MacNelly
Cartoonist Richard Locher
Chief Critic Richard Christiansen
City/Metro Editor Gerould Kern
Columnist Andrew Leckey
Columnist Judy Heurdejs
Columnist Mike Conklin
Columnist Steve Johnson
Columnist Bob Verdi
Columnist John Husar
Columnist George Lazarus
Columnist Mike Royko
Columnist William Rice
Columnist Michael Kilian
Columnist Bob Greene
Columnist Bernie Lincicome
Columnist Steve Daley
Columnist Eric Zorn
Columnist William Gruber
Columnist Barbara Brotman
Editorial Writer Bruce Dold
Editorial Writer Richard Liefer
Editorial Writer Terry Brown
Editorial Writer Ken Knox
Editorial Writer/Columnist Clarence Page
Editorial Writer/Columnist John McCarron
Editorial Writer/Columnist Steve Chapman
Editorial Page Editor Don Wycliff
Environmental Writer Casey Bukro
Environmental Writer Stevenson Swanson
Fashion Writer Teresa Wiltz
Finance Editor Pat Widder
Food Guide Editor Carol Haddix
Food/Wine Columnist William Rice
Foreign & National Editor Judy Peres
Deputy Foreign & National Editor Marshall Froker
Friday Editor Kevin Moore
Magazine Editor Denis Gosselin
Movie Critic Michael Wilmington
Movie Columnist Gene Siskel
Music Critic-Classical John Von Rhein
Music Critic-Country Jack Hurst
Music Critic-Rock Greg Kot
Online Editor John Lux
Director-Photography Mark Hinojosa
Photo/Graphic Sales Ken Widelka
Public Editor George Langford
Public Health Writer Jean Latz Griffin
Religion Writer Paul Galloway
Restaurant Critic Phil Vettel
Sections Editor Karen Callaway
Science Writer Ronald Kotulak
Sports Editor John Cherwa
Sunday Magazine Editor Denis Gosselin
Tempo Editor Rebecca Brown
Television Critic Steve Johnson
Television Critic Steve Johnson
Television Editor Karen Olson
Theater/Dance Critic Sid Smith
Transportation Writer Gary Washburn
Travel Editor Randy Curwen
Tribune Books Editor Larry Kart
Urban Affairs Writer Patrick Reardon
Womanews Editor Marla Krause
Writing Coach Mary Knoblasch

PRODUCTION
Director James O'Dell
Manager-Composing Service Mark Thomas
Director-Technical Operations/Pre Press Barbara Boyer
Manager-Printing Operations Ron Hank
Manager-Operations (Night) Art Costello
Manager-Technical Training Paul Lynch
Director-Engineering John Hazen
Manager-Operations Service Dean Gerdes
Manager-Packaging Steve Weisser
Director-Printing Operations Tom Hojnicki
Manager-Newsprint Operations Steven Aguina

Market Information: Zoned editions; Split Run; TMC; ADS; Electronic edition.
Mechanical available: Offset; Black and 3 ROP colors; insert accepted — preprinted; page cut-offs — 22".
Mechanical specifications: Type page 13" x 21"; E - 6 cols, $2\frac{1}{16}$", $\frac{1}{8}$" between; A - 6 cols, $2\frac{1}{16}$", $\frac{1}{8}$" between; C - 9 cols, $1\frac{3}{8}$", $\frac{1}{16}$" between.
Commodity consumption: Newsprint 200,000 metric tons; widths 55", $41\frac{1}{4}$"; black ink 4,000,000 pounds; color ink 1,000,000 pounds; average pages per issue 56(d), 80(S); single plates used 1,300,000.
Equipment: EDITORIAL: Front-end hardware — CText; Front-end software — Lf/Ap Leaf Picture Desk, Ap/Mac Appleserver; Printers — HP/LaserJet. CLASSIFIED: Front-end hardware — 2-On/OPR. DISPLAY: Adv layout systems — Xenotron, Ap/Mac. PRODUCTION: Typesetters — 3-Mk/Lasercompll, 3-Xenotron/UX 90, 2-L/300, 1-L/500, 2-AU/APS V; Platemaking systems — Hel/Pressfax; Plate exposures — 4-WL/Lith-X-Pozer III; Plate processors — 5-WL/Lithoplater; Production cameras — 1-SCREEN/Rollmatic 475; Automatic film processors — 7-DP/RA2, 2-DP/44c; Reproportion units — 6-ECR/Autokon, 2-ECR/Autokon 1000 Electronic Camera; Color separation equipment (conventional) — 1-Hel/DC 300B, 2-SCREEN/608, 1-Scitex, 1-Imager/2, 1-Pixet, 1-Lynart.
PRESSROOM: Line 1 — 90-G/Metroliner offset presses (2 Color Decks per press); Line 2 — 10-RKW/Metrocolor Press Units(Added to end of existing presses); Pasters — 90-G; Reels and stands — 90-G; Press control system — G/PCS. MAILROOM: Counter stackers — 25-Sh/257S, HL/HT; Inserters and stuffers — 5-Sh/72P, 1-HI/1372 P, AM Graphics/NP2299, AM Graphics/NP100; Bundle tyer — 38-MLN/2A, 9-Dynamic; Wrapping singles — 2-St/Collator. LIBRARY: Electronic — Vu/Text SAVE. WIRE SERVICES: News — AP, RN, KRT, NYT, DJ, RN, SHNS, Telex; Stock tables — AP;

Copyright ©1996 by the Editor & Publisher Co.

Illinois I-111

Syndicates — CT, KRT. BUSINESS COMPUTERS: 4-DEC/KL 10, IBM/3083 JX3, IBM/3090-18 E, IBM/4381-R14; Applications: Circ, Adv billing, Accts receivable, Gen ledger, Payroll, Accts payable; PCs & micros networked; PCs & main system networked.

CLINTON

De Witt County

'90 U.S. Census- 7,437; E&P '96 Est. 7,272

Clinton Daily Journal

(e-mon to fri)

Clinton Daily Journal, Rt. 54 W.; PO Box 615, Clinton, IL 61727; tel (217) 935-3171; fax (217) 935-6086. News Media Corp. group.

Circulation: 3,593(e); Sworn Oct. 3, 1994.

Price: 35¢(d); $60.00/yr; $4.00/2wk. (carrier).

Advertising: Open inch rate $8.24(e). **Representative:** Landon Associates Inc.

News Service: UPI. **Politics:** Independent. **Established:** 1904.

Special Editions: Progress; New Car Guide; Home Improvement; Apple 'n Pork Festival Edition; Dollars & Sense; DeWitt County Cookbook.

Special Weekly Sections: Grocery Stores (mon); Travel Tips (tues); Theatre (entertainment) (thur); Car Dealers, Real Estate (fri); Lifestyles, Sports, Service Directory (daily).

Magazines: Weekly TMC (tues); Farm Bureau (wed).

GENERAL MANAGEMENT

Publisher Terrie Baker
Purchasing Agent Terrie Baker

ADVERTISING

Director Terrie Baker

CIRCULATION

Director Sue Smith

NEWS EXECUTIVE

Editor Camaron Maun

PRODUCTION

Manager Paul Fabris

Market Information: Zoned editions; TMC.

Mechanical available: Offset; Black and 1 ROP color; insert accepted — preprinted; page cut-offs — 22¾".

Mechanical specifications: Type page 15" x 21½"; E - 8 cols, 1¾", ⅙" between; A - 8 cols, 1¾", ⅙" between; C - 8 cols, 1¾", ⅙" between.

Commodity consumption: average pages per issue 23(d).

Equipment: PRODUCTION: Typesetters — 1-COM/IV, 2-COM/JR, 1-COM/7200; Plate exposures — 1-B/1500; Production cameras — 1-N/V-2024.

PRESSROOM: Line 1 — 3-MGD/Community; Folders — 1-MGD. MAILROOM: Bundle tyer — 1-Bu; Addressing machine — 1-PB. LIBRARY: Electronic — 1-Kodagraph. WIRE SERVICES: News — UPI.

CRYSTAL LAKE

McHenry County

'90 U.S. Census- 24,512; E&P '96 Est. 30,298
ABC-NDM (90): 227,174 (HH 76,948)

The Northwest Herald

(m-mon to sat; S)

The Northwest Herald, 7717 S. Rt. 31; PO Box 250, Crystal Lake, IL 60014; tel (815) 459-4040; fax (815) 477-4960. Shaw Newspapers group.

Circulation: 31,025(m); 31,025(m-sat); 32,731(S); ABC Sept. 30, 1995.

Price: 50¢(d); 50¢(sat); $1.25(S); $2.90/wk, $12.57/mo; $130.00/yr.

Advertising: Open inch rate $22.06(m); $22.06(m-sat); $22.06(S). **Representative:** US Suburban Press.

News Services: AP, NEA, SHNS. **Politics:** Independent. **Established:** 1856.

Special Weekly Sections: Food, Style (mon); Style (tues, wed); Entertainment, Style (thur); Automotive (fri); Real Estate (sat); Variety (S); Community (daily).

Magazines: Television, USA Weekend (S).

CORPORATE OFFICER

President Robert A Shaw

GENERAL MANAGEMENT

Publisher Robert A Shaw

ADVERTISING

Director Christopher L Golbeck
Manager-Classified Kathy Smith

MARKETING AND PROMOTION

Director-Marketing Jim Powers

TELECOMMUNICATIONS

Audiotex Manager Christopher L Golbeck

CIRCULATION

Director Walt Heskett

NEWS EXECUTIVES

Editor Mark M Sweetwood
Editor-McHenry Cyndi Wyss
Editor-Crystal Lake Gerard Dziuba
Editor-Woodstock Peter Gill
Managing Editor Cliff Ward
Managing Editor Dennis McNamara

EDITORS AND MANAGERS

Auto Editor Jerry Kuyper
Business Editor Kevin Polzin
Editorial Page Editor Dick Peterson
Features Editor Mary De Pietro
News Editor Rich Carter
Photo Editor Scott Dalzell
Political Reporter Kurt Begalka
Sidetrack Copy Editor Stacy Sabadash-Kalas
Sports Editor Kevin Ball

PRODUCTION

Manager Kevin Elder

Market Information: Zoned editions; Split Run; TMC; ADS; Operate audiotex.

Mechanical available: Offset; Black and 3 ROP colors; insert accepted — preprinted; page cut-offs — 22".

Mechanical specifications: Type page 13" x 21"; E - 6 cols, 2⅟₁₆", ⅛" between; A - 6 cols, 2⅟₁₆", ⅛" between; C - 9 cols, 1⅜", ⅛" between.

Commodity consumption: Newsprint 3,500 metric tons; widths 27½", 34"; black ink 53,100 pounds; color ink 9,000 pounds; single pages printed 19,820; average pages per issue 42(d); single plates used 14,000.

Equipment: EDITORIAL: Front-end hardware — 1-AT/Dual Sys 4. CLASSIFIED: Front-end hardware — 1-AT/Dual Sys 4. DISPLAY: Front-end hardware — 13-Ap/Mac Quadra 700; Front-end software — Multi-Ad/Creator. PRODUCTION: Typesetters — 2-AU/Micro 5; Platemaking systems — 1-BKY; Plate exposures — 2-Nu; Plate processors — 1-Nat/A-250, 1-MAS; Scanners — 1-COM/VTS5; Production cameras — 1-B; Color separation equipment (conventional) — WDS.

PRESSROOM: Line 1 — 8-G/Urbanite; Folders — 1-G/Urbanite; Pasters — 6-Enkel; Press registration system — Stoesser. MAILROOM: Counter stackers — 2-QWI; Inserters and stuffers — 1-Amerigraph/1372; Bundle tyer — 2-MLN/Spirit; Addressing machine — 1-KR; Mailroom control system — Ic. COMMUNICATIONS: Facsimile — 1-Canon/Ambassador 220. WIRE SERVICES: News — AP; Stock tables — AP; Receiving dishes — AP. BUSINESS COMPUTERS: 1-IBM/RISC-6000; Applications: Vision Data.

DANVILLE

Vermilion County

'90 U.S. Census- 33,828; E&P '96 Est. 30,616
ABC-CZ (90): 55,129 (HH 21,674)

Commercial-News

(e-mon to fri; m-sat; S)

Commercial News, 17 W. North, Danville, IL 61832; tel (217) 446-1000; fax (217) 446-9825. Gannett Co. Inc. group.

Circulation: 20,099(e); 20,099(m-sat); 22,612(S); ABC Sept. 24, 1995.

Price: 35¢(d); 35¢(sat); $1.00(S); $2.60/wk.

Advertising: Open inch rate $39.52(e); $39.52(m-sat); $45.34(S). **Representative:** Gannett National Newspaper Sales.

News Services: AP, GNS. **Politics:** Independent. **Established:** 1866.

Special Weekly Sections: Best Food Day (wed); Church (sat); Farm Page (S); Stock Listings, Sports, TV Listing (daily).

Magazines: Teleview (sat); USA Weekend, Color Comics (S).

CORPORATE OFFICER

President Charles Morris

GENERAL MANAGEMENT

Publisher Charles Morris
Manager-Credit Margaret Lynne Elston
Controller Robert J Moore

ADVERTISING

Manager-Ad Service Robert Fretty

CIRCULATION

Director Dennis Floyd

NEWS EXECUTIVE

Managing Editor Richard Farrant

EDITORS AND MANAGERS

Business Editor Jim Sonnenberg
City Editor Doug Haddix
Editorial Page Editor Larry Smith
Education Editor Linda Busche
Farm Editor Dennis Bartlow
Features Editor Doug Haddix
Food Editor Margie Yee
Graphics Editor Rich Stefaniak
Health Editor Margie Yee
Librarian Janet Leisch
News Editor Stephanie Angel
Photo Editor Rich Stefaniak
Sports Editor Chad Roberts

MANAGEMENT INFORMATION SERVICES

Data Processing Manager Susan Pohl

PRODUCTION

Director Edison S Amachree
Foreman-Composing Duane Sandmeyer
Foreman-Press Mike Latoz
Foreman-Mailroom Wanda Hamm

Market Information: Zoned editions; Split Run; TMC.

Mechanical available: Offset; Black and 3 ROP colors; insert accepted — preprinted, 3" x 5" cards, single sheets 8 ½" x 11"; page cut-offs — 22.77".

Mechanical specifications: Type page 13" x 21½"; E - 6 cols, 2⅟₁₆", ⅛" between; A - 6 cols, 2⅟₁₆", ⅛" between; C - 9 cols, 1⅜", ⅛" between.

Commodity consumption: Newsprint 1,384 short tons; 1,256 metric tons; widths 27", 13½"; black ink 30,449 pounds; color ink 10,319 pounds; single pages printed 9,360; average pages per issue 22(d), 48(S); single plates used 52,196.

Equipment: EDITORIAL: Front-end hardware — Dewar/Discribe; Front-end software — Dewar; Printers — 2-Okidata. CLASSIFIED: Front-end hardware — Dewar/Discovery; Front-end software — Dewar. DISPLAY: Adv layout systems — Dewar; Front-end hardware — 2-Ap/Mac IIci, Ap/Mac Quadra 950; Printers — 1-Okidata, HP/PaintJet XL 300; Other equipment — Kensington/Masterpiece, TECMAR/QT-525es Drive. PRODUCTION: Typesetters — 1-V/5500, 1-V/5100, 2-V/5000; Plate exposures — 1-Nu; Plate processors — 1-Nu, 1-Nat; Scanners — 1-ECR/Autokon, XRS/6C 24bit Color Scanner; Production cameras — 1-C/Spartan III; Automatic film processors — 1-LE/2600A, 1-LE/PC13, 1-LS/2600R; Color separation equipment (conventional) — Lf/AP Leaf Picture Desk, Lf/Leafscan.

PRESSROOM: Line 1 — 6-HI/845; Folders — 1-HI/2:1; Pasters — Manual; Reels and stands — 6-Cline, 6-CW/Reel; Press control system — Hurletron. MAILROOM: Counter stackers — 1-MSI/1220, 1-Fg/H 501, 1-MSI/841; Inserters and stuffers — 1-Mc; Bundle tyer — 2-MLN, 1-HITT/String Tyer; Addressing machine — 1-KAN. WIRE SERVICES: News — AP, GNS; Stock tables — AP; Syndicates — AP; Receiving dishes — size-10ft, AP, NSN. BUSINESS COMPUTERS: 1-IBM/AS-400 CE-10, 1-DEC/PDP 11-70; Applications: Circ, Adv, Billing, Accts receivable, Accts payable, Gen ledger; PCs & main system networked.

DECATUR

Macon County

'90 U.S. Census- 83,885; E&P '96 Est. 77,377
ABC-CZ (90): 99,389 (HH 39,654)

Herald & Review

(m-mon to fri; m-sat; S)

Herald & Review, 601 E. William St.; PO Box 311, Decatur, IL 62525; tel (217) 429-5151; fax (217) 421-6913. Lee Enterprises Inc. group.

Circulation: 40,830(m); 48,453(m-sat); 51,916(S); ABC Sept. 30, 1995.

Price: 50¢(d); 50¢(sat); $1.75(S); $3.60/wk (daily & S), $1.75/wk (sat & S); $187.20/yr (daily & S), $91.00/yr (sat & S).

Advertising: Open inch rate $35.58(m); $35.58(m-sat); $37.00(S). **Representative:** Landon Associates Inc.

News Services: AP, KRT. **Politics:** Independent. **Established:** 1878 (Review), 1880 (Herald).

Special Editions: Basketball Tab; Last Minute Gift Catalog; Christmas Storybook; Brides; Outlook; Design-an-Ad; Lawn & Garden; Earth Day; Home Show; Summerfest; Substance Abuse; All Eyes on St. Louis; Decatur Celebration; Answer Book; Football Tab; All Eyes on Chicago.

Special Weekly Sections: Food/Health (wed); Teens (thur); Entertainment (fri); TV Review, Religion/Family (sat); Business, Outdoors, At Home (S).

GENERAL MANAGEMENT

Publisher William K Johnston
Controller Terre T Engleton
Manager-Human Resources Terri Kuhle

ADVERTISING

Manager-Retail Kevin Haezebroeck
Manager-Classified Gordon Schrader
Manager-National/Major Accounts Fred W Whobrey
Special Projects Editor Carol Alexander

TELECOMMUNICATIONS

Audiotex Manager-New Ventures Marilyn Andriesen

CIRCULATION

Manager Greg B Sloan

NEWS EXECUTIVE

Editor George Althoff

EDITORS AND MANAGERS

City Editor Jan Touney
Community News Editor Robert Fallstrom
Lifestyle Editor Theresa Churchill
Opinion Writer Richard Icen
Sports Editor Mark Tupper

MANAGEMENT INFORMATION SERVICES

Data Processing Supervisor Karen Woare

PRODUCTION

Manager-Product Service Robert W Strabala
Manager-Distribution James Knierim
Manager-Commercial Printing Paul Rickman
Supervisor-Press Bill Tyus
Supervisor-Press Bret Waddington

Market Information: Zoned editions; Split Run; TMC; ADS; Operate database; Operate audiotex.

Mechanical available: Flexography; Black and 3 ROP colors; insert accepted — preprinted.

Mechanical specifications: Type page 13" x 21½"; E - 6 cols, 2⅟₁₆", ⅛" between; A - 6 cols, 2⅟₁₆", ⅛" between; C - 9 cols, 1⅜", ⅟₁₆" between.

Commodity consumption: Newsprint 3,486 metric tons; widths 54", 40½", 27"; black ink 98,100 pounds; color ink 35,974 pounds; single pages printed 12,198; average pages per issue 28(d), 68(S); single plates used 37,005.

Equipment: EDITORIAL: Front-end hardware — HI/8900; Front-end software — HI/PLS. CLASSIFIED: Front-end hardware — HI/CASH; Front-end software — HI/CASH. AUDIOTEX: Hardware — VNN. DISPLAY: Adv layout systems — SCS/Layout 8000, Ap/Mac; Front-end hardware — Cascade Dataflow/Image Flow; Front-end software — QuarkXPress, Multi-Ad/Creator. PRODUCTION: Typesetters — 2-COM/8600, 2-AG/Avantra 25 Laser Drum Imager; Plate exposures — 1-FX/VIII, 1-Consolux; Plate processors — 2-FP/II; Electronic picture desk — Lf/AP Leaf Picture Desk, CD/Newsline; Scanners — Kk/2035, Pixel; Production cameras — C/Spartan III; Automatic film processors — AG/Litex 26; Film transporters — 1-C; Color separation equipment (conventional) — CD/Newsline; Digital color separation equipment — Adobe/Photoshop.

PRESSROOM: Line 2 — KBA/Colormax; Press drives — KBA, MOT; Folders — H/Double 3:2; Pasters — Automatic Pasters. MAILROOM: Counter stackers — 2-QWI/300, 1-HL/Monitor; Inserters and stuffers — 1-MM/227 5-into-1, HI/1372; Bundle tyer — 2-Power Strap/PSN6, 3-MLN/2A, 2-Bu/String Tyer; Wrapping singles — 2-Bu; Addressing machine — 2-BH/Mg 1530. LIBRARY: Electronic — ISYS. COMMUNICATIONS: Digital ad delivery system — AP AdSend. WIRE SERVICES: News — AP, KRT; Photos — AP; Stock tables — AP; Receiving dishes — size-10ft, AP. BUSINESS COMPUTERS: IBM/AS-400; PCs & micros networked.

DE KALB

De Kalb County

'90 U.S. Census- 34,925; E&P '96 Est. 36,506
ABC-CZ (90): 44,633 (HH 14,388)

The Daily Chronicle

(e-mon to fri; S)

The Daily Chronicle, 1586 Barber Greene Rd.; PO Box 587, De Kalb, IL 60115; tel (815) 756-4841; fax (815) 756-2079. Scripps League Newspapers Inc. group.

Circulation: 10,384(e); 11,404(S); ABC Sept. 30, 1995.
Price: 50¢(d); $1.00(S); $8.25/mo; $108.00/yr.
Advertising: Open inch rate $14.38(e); $14.38(S). **Representative:** Landon Associates Inc.
News Service: AP. **Politics:** Independent. **Established:** 1879.
Not Published: New Year; Memorial Day; Independence Day; Labor Day; Thanksgiving; Christmas.
Special Editions: First Baby Contest, Chronological Calendar, Tax Guide, Farm Forecast (Jan); Valentine's Day Section, Clubs and Organizations Tab, FFA Week (Feb); Spring Opening, Spring Home Improvement, Spring Car Care (Mar); Spring Farm Edition, Annual Brochure, Easter Section (Apr); Mother's Day Gift Guide, Pet Tab, Graduation Section, Home Improvement-Lawn & Garden (May); Just for Summer, Father's Day Gift Section, Baseball (June); Senior Living Guide, Great Gasoline Give-away, Mid-Summer Farm Edition (July); Back-to-School, Soccer, Fall Sports, De Kalb Comfest, NIU/Kish Registration (Aug); Fall Opening, National Farm Safety Week, Fall Home Improvement, Car Care (Sept); 4-H Week Tab, Sycamore Pumpkin Festival, Fall Farm Edition, Women in Business (Oct); Dollar and Sense, De Kalb Business Directory, Christmas Edition, Winter Sports (Nov); Gift Guide, Fun in the Snow, Letters to Santa, After Christmas Sale, Holiday Beauty Guide (Dec).

CORPORATE OFFICERS
Board Chairman/Treasurer E W Scripps
Vice Chairman/Corporate Secretary Betty Knight Scripps
President/Exec Vice Pres Roger N Warkins
Vice Pres-Finance Thomas E Wendel

GENERAL MANAGEMENT
Publisher Paul Senft
Business Manager Nancy Coffman

ADVERTISING
Manager-Sales James Horn
Director Reino Riippi

CIRCULATION
Manager Jason Luebke

NEWS EXECUTIVES
Editor Paul Senft
Managing Editor John Secor

EDITORS AND MANAGERS
Business Editor Paul Senft
Lifestyle Editor Kurt Guessler
Photo Editor Kathy Fox
Sports Editor Bill Wesselhoff

PRODUCTION
Foreman-Composing Bert Hale
Foreman-Press Brian Hume

Market Information: TMC; ADS.
Mechanical available: Offset; Black and 3 ROP colors; insert accepted — preprinted, any size; page cut-offs — 21½".
Mechanical specifications: Type page 13" x 21½"; E - 6 cols, 2⅟₁₆", ⅛" between; A - 6 cols, 2⅟₁₆", ⅛" between; C - 8 cols, 1⅜", ⅟₁₆" between.
Commodity consumption: Newsprint 631 metric tons; width 27½"; black ink 12,482 pounds; color ink 1,549 pounds; single pages printed 6,855; average pages per issue 20(d), 44(S); single plates used 3,352.
Equipment: EDITORIAL: Front-end hardware — ScrippSat; Front-end software — ScrippSat; Printers — 2-QMS/820 T. CLASSIFIED: Front-end hardware — 3-ScrippSat/PC; Front-end software — Synaptic; Printers — Okidata/393, QMS. DISPLAY: Front-end hardware — 2-Mk/Acer; Front-end software — Archetype/Corel Draw; Printers — 2-QMS/820 T. PRODUCTION: Typesetters — QMS/PS 820 TurboLazer; Plate exposures — Nu; Plate processors — Graham; Production cameras — SCREEN/Companica 6500 D; Automatic film processors — KN/4800; Color separation equipment (conventional) — Lf/Leafscan 35. PRESSROOM: Line 1 — 5-G/Urbanite 813; Folders — G/1:4; Press registration system — Duarte Register Systems. MAILROOM: Inserters and stuffers — 1-MM/227 E; Bundle tyer — 1-MLN; Addressing machine — 3-Wm; Other mailroom equipment — 1-MM/235 Stitcher Trimmer. WIRE SERVICES: News — AP; Photos — AP; Syndicates — SHNS; Receiving dishes — size-10ft, AP. BUSINESS COMPUTERS: DEC/RX02; Applications: Mk/ACER: Adv billing, Payroll, Circ; PCs & micros networked; PCs & main system networked.

DIXON
Lee County
'90 U.S. Census- 15,144; E&P '96 Est. 14,790
ABC-CZ (90): 15,144 (HH 5,541)

The Telegraph
(e-mon to fri; m-sat)

The Telegraph, 113-115 Peoria Ave.; Box 409, Dixon, IL 61021-0409; tel (815) 284-2222; fax (815) 284-2870. Shaw Newspapers group.
Circulation: 10,360(e); 10,360(m-sat); ABC Sept. 30, 1995.
Price: 50¢(d); $1.00(sat); $2.00/wk; $98.00/yr.
Advertising: Open inch rate $9.17(e); $9.17(m-sat). **Representative:** Papert Companies.
News Service: AP. **Politics:** Republican. **Established:** 1851.
Not Published: New Year; Memorial Day; Independence Day; Labor Day; Thanksgiving; Christmas.
Advertising not accepted: At publisher's discretion.
Special Editions: Health & Fitness (Jan); Brides, Economic Development (Feb); Car Care, Tourism (May); Football, Home Improvement (Sept); Women, Car Care, 4-H (Oct); Basketball, Christmas Gift Guide (Nov).
Special Weekly Sections: Grocery Days (mon, tues, wed); Church News, TV Tab, Real Estate (fri); Automotive, Entertainment Section (sat).
Magazine: USA Weekend (sat).

CORPORATE OFFICERS
Chairman of the Board E K Shaw
President/CEO Thomas D Shaw
Chief Financial Officer Phillip E Metka
Vice Pres/Treasurer Robert A Shaw
Vice Pres William E Shaw
Secretary Phillip E Metka

GENERAL MANAGEMENT
Publisher William E Shaw
General Manager J W Nelson

ADVERTISING
Manager-Retail Ed Bushman
Manager-Classified Linda Ross

CIRCULATION
Manager Geoff Vanderlin

NEWS EXECUTIVE
Managing Editor Mike Chapman

EDITORS AND MANAGERS
Amusements Editor Jim Dunn
Automotive/Aviation Editor Ken Brown
Business/Finance Editor Ken Brown
City Editor Ken Brown
Editorial Page Editor Mike Chapman
Education Editor Clark Kelly
Farm Editor Jim Dunn
Fashion/Women's Editor Paula Sherman
Food/Home Furnishings Editor Paula Sherman
Living/Lifestyle Editor Paula Sherman
Photo Editor Mark Sauer
Political Editor Clark Kelly
Radio/Television Editor Mike Chapman
School Editor Clark Kelly
Society Editor Paula Sherman
Sports Editor Ron Warnick
Travel Editor Paula Sherman
Wire Editor Tim O'Brien

PRODUCTION
Foreman Gunars Kulikovskis

Market Information: TMC.
Mechanical available: Offset; Black and 3 ROP colors; insert accepted — preprinted, all; page cut-offs — 22¾".
Mechanical specifications: Type page 13" x 21½"; E - 6 cols, 2⅟₁₆", ⅛" between; A - 6 cols, 2⅟₁₆", ⅛" between; C - 9 cols, 1⅜", ⅟₁₆" between.
Commodity consumption: Newsprint 1,000 short tons; widths 27½", 13¾"; black ink 16,000 pounds; color ink 2,500 pounds; single pages printed 7,500; average pages per issue 22(d), 36(sat); single plates used 10,700.
Equipment: EDITORIAL: Front-end hardware — 11-Ap/Mac; Front-end software — Baseview; Printers — HP/LaserJet 4; Other equipment — Lf/AP Leaf Picture Desk. CLASSIFIED: Front-end hardware — Ap/Mac; Front-end software — Baseview. DISPLAY: Front-end hardware — Ap/Mac; Printers — HP/Laser 5MP. PRODUCTION: Pagination software — Baseview; Typesetters — 2-AU/APS 6-82; Plate exposures — 1-Nu/Flip Top FT40L; Plate processors — 1-Ic/TCM25-1; Electronic picture desk — Lf/AP Leaf Picture Desk; Production cameras — 1-B/4000-C, Nu/SSTE 2024SB; Automatic film processors — 1-P/524; Color separation equipment (conventional) — Adobe/Photoshop. PRESSROOM: Line 1 — 5-G/Urbanite; Folders — 1-G. MAILROOM: Inserters and stuffers — 1-Kansa/480 5:1; Bundle tyer — 3-B/18; Addressing machine — 1-Dispensa-Matic. COMMUNICATIONS: Systems used — satellite. WIRE SERVICES: News — AP; Photos — AP; Receiving dishes — size-10ft, AP. BUSINESS COMPUTERS: ATT, Ap/Mac, Convergent/S480; Applications: Circ, Adv billing, Accts receivable, Gen ledger, Payroll; PCs & micros networked.

DU QUOIN
Perry County
'90 U.S. Census- 6,697; E&P '96 Est. 7,005

Du Quoin Evening Call
(e-mon to fri; m-sat; S)

Du Quoin Evening Call, 9 N. Division St.; PO Box 184, Du Quoin, IL 62832; tel (618) 542-2133; fax (618) 542-2726. Hollinger International Inc. group.
Circulation: 4,035(e); 4,035(m-sat); 4,646(S); VAC June 30, 1995.
Price: 50¢(d); 75¢(sat); $1.00(S); $7.50/wk; $21.00/mo; $75.00/yr.
Advertising: Open inch rate $8.51(e); $8.51(m-sat); $8.51(S). **Representative:** Hollinger International Inc.
News Service: AP. **Politics:** Independent. **Established:** 1895.
Note: Effective Aug. 25, 1995, this publication started publishing a Sunday edition. The Sunday circulation reported is an estimate.
Not Published: Independence Day; Christmas.
Special Editions: Tax Guide Tab (Feb); Progress (Mar); Spring Home Improvements (Apr); Du Quoin State Fair (Aug); Fall Home Improvements (Oct); Christmas Preview (Nov).
Special Weekly Sections: Farm (fri); Business, American Weekend (sat).
Magazine: USA Weekend (sat).

CORPORATE OFFICERS
President Larry J Perotto
Comptroller Roland McBride

GENERAL MANAGEMENT
Publisher Steve Fisher
General Manager Steve Fisher

ADVERTISING
Director Doris Hottes
Director-National Classified Leigh Ann Kristiansen

CIRCULATION
Director Dan Klein

NEWS EXECUTIVE
Managing Editor John H Croessman

EDITORS AND MANAGERS
Action Line Editor John H Croessman
Business/Finance Editor John H Croessman
Editorial Page Editor John H Croessman
Education/Travel Editor John H Croessman
National Editor John H Croessman
Science/Technology Editor John H Croessman
Sports Editor Tim Petrowich
Television/Film Editor John H Croessman
Theater/Music Editor John H Croessman

PRODUCTION
Manager Eugene Gallmeister

Market Information: TMC.
Mechanical available: Offset; Black and 4 ROP colors; insert accepted — preprinted; page cut-offs — 21½".
Mechanical specifications: Type page 13.8" x 23"; E - 6 cols, 2⅟₁₆", ⅛" between; A - 6 cols, 2⅟₁₆", ⅛" between; C - 8 cols, 1⁴⁄₁₆", ⅛" between.
Commodity consumption: single pages printed 5,000; average pages per issue 14(d), 28(sat); single plates used 3,600.
Equipment: EDITORIAL: Front-end hardware — Ap/Mac Plus; Front-end software — Microsoft/Word 4.0, MK/NewsWriter; Printers — Ap/Mac LaserWriter II NT. CLASSIFIED: Front-end hardware — IBM/PC; Front-end software — MK/Newscraft; Printers — Ap/Mac LaserWriter II NT. DISPLAY: Front-end hardware — Ap/Mac LC II, Ap/Mac IIsi; Front-end software — Aldus/PageMaker 4.0; Printers — Ap/Mac LaserWriter II NT; Other equipment — CD-Rom. PRODUCTION: Pagination software — QuarkXPress; Typesetters — Ap/Mac LC III, Ap/Mac LC III, Ap/Mac LC III, Quantra/610; Platemaking systems — Ic/Roconex; Plate exposures — Theimer; Plate processors — Ic/Roconex; Scanners — Microtek/Image Scanner, TI/OMNI Page Professional; Production cameras — SCREEN/C-680-C Vertical; Automatic film processors — C/Pm R650. MAILROOM: Bundle tyer — 1-Bu; Addressing machine — IBM/Listmaster. COMMUNICATIONS: Systems used — satellite. WIRE SERVICES: News — AP; Syndicates — King Features, TMS, TV Data, NEA, United Media; Receiving dishes — AP. BUSINESS COMPUTERS: Ap/Mac IIe, IBM/XT, Hyundai/386, Club America/286.

EAST ALTON
See ALTON

EAST DUBUQUE
See DUBUQUE, IA

EAST MOLINE
See MOLINE

EDWARDSVILLE
Madison County
'90 U.S. Census- 14,579; E&P '96 Est. 16,409
ABC-NDM (90): 53,651 (HH 20,060)

Edwardsville Intelligencer
(e-mon to fri; m-sat)

Edwardsville Intelligencer, 117 N. 2nd St.; PO Box 70, Edwardsville, IL 62025; tel (618) 656-4700; fax (618) 656-7618; e-mail mminton@edwpub.com. Hearst Newspapers group.
Circulation: 6,894(e); 6,894(m-sat); ABC Sept. 30, 1995.
Price: 50¢(d); 50¢(sat); $2.25/wk; $111.00/yr.
Advertising: Open inch rate $11.55(e); $11.55 (m-sat). **Representative:** Papert Companies.
News Services: AP, HN. **Politics:** Independent. **Established:** 1862.
Not Published: New Year; Thanksgiving; Christmas.
Special Editions: Economic Outlook, Auto Show (Jan); Draw-an-Ad (Feb); Home & Garden (Mar); Good News (Apr); Customer Appreciation, Bride & Groom (June); Fall Sports (Aug); Spotlight/Madison Co. (Sept); Harvest Homefest, Customer Appreciation (Oct); Christmas Opening (Nov); Christmas Greetings, Last Minute Gift Guide (Dec).
Special Weekly Sections: Real Estate, Family, Preview of the Week, Best Food Day (mon); Best Food Day (wed); Real Estate, Religion (fri); Real Estate (sat).
Magazine: Weekender (entertainment) (sat).

CORPORATE OFFICERS
Vice Pres Bruce E Coury
Asst Treasurer Gail L Salantai

GENERAL MANAGEMENT
Publisher Bruce E Coury
Controller Gail L Salantai

ADVERTISING
Director Michelle Loftus

TELECOMMUNICATIONS
Audiotex Manager Marcel Brown

CIRCULATION
Manager Barbara Jurgena-Stamer

NEWS EXECUTIVE
Editor Meta Minton

EDITORS AND MANAGERS
News Editor Shay Wessol
Sports Editor Bill Tucker

MANAGEMENT INFORMATION SERVICES
Online Manager Marcel Brown

PRODUCTION
Director-Advertising Design Service Jennifer Gerdes
Manager-Systems Justin Makler
Foreman-Press/Camera Rodney D Wink

Market Information: TMC; Operate database; Operate audiotex; Electronic edition.
Mechanical available: Offset; Black and 3 ROP colors; insert accepted — preprinted; page cut-offs — 22½".
Mechanical specifications: Type page 12⅞" x 21½"; E - 6 cols, 2⅟₁₆", ⅛" between; A - 6 cols, 2⅟₁₆", ⅛" between; C - 9 cols, 1⅜", ⅟₁₆" between.
Commodity consumption: Newsprint 615 short tons; widths 27½", 29", 34"; black ink 8,100 pounds; color ink 1,000 pounds; single pages printed 4,606; average pages per issue 15(d); single plates used 9,500.

Illinois I-113

Equipment: EDITORIAL: Front-end hardware — Ap/Mac Quadras, Ap/Mac LC IIIs; Front-end software — QuarkXPress; Other equipment — 4-RSK/Tandy TRS 100. CLASSIFIED: Front-end hardware — 2-Ap/Mac Quadra 605; Front-end software — FSI/Classified; Printers — 1-TI. AUDIOTEX: Hardware — Zimmers; Supplier name — VNN. DISPLAY: Adv layout systems — 2-Mk; Front-end hardware — Ap/Mac IIci, Ap/Mac fx, Ap/Mac Quadras; Front-end software — Multi-Ad/Creator, Ap/Mac System 7.1, QuarkXPress 3.3; Printers — Ap/Mac LaserWriter IIg, Lynx/Image Setter, Imager/Plus 12. PRODUCTION: Pagination software — FSI; Typesetters — 4-Ap/Mac LaserWriter, LZR/1560, Ap/Mac LaserWriter IIg, Lynx/ImageSetter; Plate exposures — 1-Nu; Plate processors — 1-Nat; Scanners — 1-Ap/Mac Scanner, Nikon; Production cameras — 1-R; Automatic film processors — 1-LE, AG/Rapidline.
PRESSROOM: Line 1 — 7-KP single; Press drives — CH; Folders — 1-KJ/6. MAILROOM: Counter stackers — 1-BG; Inserters and stuffers — 1-KAN/320, 4-KAN/Station inserter; Bundle tyer — 2-Bu/String Tying Machine; Addressing machine — 1-Automecha/Accufast PL-M. COMMUNICATIONS: Facsimile — Brother/Intelefax 710M; Digital ad delivery system — AP AdSend. Systems used — satellite. WIRE SERVICES: News — HN, AP; Photos — AP; Syndicates — NEA; Receiving dishes — AP. BUSINESS COMPUTERS: 3-IBM/486 DX2, 2-ALR/Powerflex, 3-Packard Bell/486-DX2, Compaq/286, 1-IBM/AST 486 DX2; Applications: Lotus 1-2-3, Peachtree: Accounting; WordPerfect 5.0; PCs & micros networked.

EFFINGHAM

Effingham County

'90 U.S. Census- 11,651; E&P '96 Est. 11,969
ABC-CZ (90): 14,260 (HH 5,538)

Effingham Daily News

(e-mon to fri; m-sat)

Effingham Daily News, 201 N. Banker St.; PO Box 370, Effingham, IL 62401; tel (217) 347-7151; fax (217) 342-9315. Park Communications Inc. group.

Circulation: 12,815(e); 12,815(m-sat); ABC Sept. 30, 1995.

Price: 50¢(d); 50¢(sat); $1.75/wk; $7.40/mo; $78.00/yr.

Advertising: Open inch rate $9.10(e); $9.10(m-sat).

News Service: AP. **Politics:** Independent. **Established:** 1899 (Daily Record), 1946 (Daily News).

Not Published: New Year; Memorial Day; Independence Day; Labor Day; Thanksgiving; Christmas.

Special Editions: Progress Edition, Discount Days, Health & Fitness (Jan); Washington Birthday Sale, FFA, Bridal Tab (Feb); Student Create-An-Ad, Girl Scout (Mar); Spring Car Care, Spring Home Improvement, Parenting (Apr); Graduation, Senior Citizens (May); Focus, Youth League Baseball (June); Christmas in July, Bowling (July); Back-to-School, Farm Fair Edition (Aug); Fall Home Improvement, Transportation Fest, Fall Car Care (Sept); Restaurant Month, What's Cookin' (Oct); Basketball, Christmas Opening (Nov).

Special Weekly Sections: Food Page (mon); Builders Pages (tues); The Mini Page (wed); Farm/Business, County Farm Bureau Bulletin (thur); Health Page, Church Page (fri); Outdoors, Senior Page, Weekend, School Page (sat).

GENERAL MANAGEMENT
General Manager Paul E Semple

ADVERTISING
Director Carl Thoele
Manager-Classified N Jean Voelker

CIRCULATION
Manager Diana Barr

NEWS EXECUTIVES
Editor Paul E Semple
Managing Editor Susan Duncan

EDITOR AND MANAGER
Sports Editor Sam Rickelman

MANAGEMENT INFORMATION SERVICES
Data Processing Manager Paul E Semple

PRODUCTION
Manager Robert Jackson
Manager-Systems Ken Joslyn

Market Information: TMC; ADS.

Mechanical available: Offset; Black and 3 ROP colors; insert accepted — preprinted; page cutoffs — 22¾".

Mechanical specifications: Type page 13" x 21½"; E - 6 cols, 2.07", ⅛" between; A - 6 cols, 2.07", ⅛" between; C - 9 cols, 1⅜", ⅛" between.

Commodity consumption: Newsprint 475 metric tons; width 27½"; black ink 27,132 pounds; color ink 2,035 pounds; single pages printed 7,368; average pages per issue 24(d), 22(sat); single plates used 5,000.

Equipment: EDITORIAL: Front-end hardware — Ap/Mac; Front-end software — Baseview/Managing Editor. CLASSIFIED: Front-end hardware — 3-Ap/Mac; Front-end software — Baseview/Class Manager Plus. DISPLAY: Adv layout systems — QuarkXPress 3.1; Front-end hardware — Ap/Mac; Front-end software — Multi-Ad/Creator 2.5; PRODUCTION: Typesetters — 1-M/Linotronic 300, M/Linotronic RIP-4, 1-LaserMaster/400XL, 1-ECR/Imagesetter; Plate exposures — 1-Nu/FT46V6UPNS; Plate processors — 1-Graham/S3-27; Electronic picture desk — Lf/Leafscan 35; Scanners — Sharp/JX-600; Production cameras — 1-B/4000C, 1-SCREEN/670D; Automatic film processors — 1-LE/DSLD281L; Digital color separation equipment — Lf/Leafscan 35, Sharp/JX-600, Adobe/Photoshop.
PRESSROOM: Line 1 — 12-G/SC; Folders — 1-G/SC; Press control system — Fin. MAILROOM: Counter stackers — 1-MM; Inserters and stuffers — 5-MM/267; Bundle tyer — 1-MM/TABA 310-20, 2-MLN/ML2EE, 1-MLN/Spirit; Addressing machine — 1-CH. LIBRARY: Combination — 1-Recordak/MPE-1. WIRE SERVICES: News — AP; Receiving dishes — size-10ft, AP. BUSINESS COMPUTERS: Vision Data, 1-Ap/Mac; Applications: Circ, Adv billing, Accts receivable, Gen ledger, Payroll; PCs & micros networked.

ELDORADO

Saline County

'90 U.S. Census- 4,536; E&P '96 Est. 4,261

Eldorado Daily Journal

(e-mon to fri; m-sat)

Eldorado Daily Journal, 1200 Locust St., Eldorado, IL 62930; tel (618) 273-3379; fax (618) 273-3738. Hollinger International Inc. group.

Circulation: 1,254(e); 1,254(m-sat); Sworn Sept. 29, 1995.

Price: 50¢(d); 75¢(sat).

Advertising: Open inch rate $8.25(e); $8.25(m-sat).

News Service: AP. **Established:** 1911.

Not Published: New Year; Independence Day; Christmas.

Magazines: Weekender, TV Guide (fri).

GENERAL MANAGEMENT
Publisher George Q Wilson
Office Manager Charleen Soper

ADVERTISING
Manager Sally Wofford

CIRCULATION
Manager Scott Dunn

NEWS EXECUTIVE
Managing Editor Scott Hines

EDITORS AND MANAGERS
Sports Editor Phil Knapper

Mechanical available: Offset; Black and 1 ROP color; insert accepted — preprinted.

Mechanical specifications: Type page 13¾" x 21½"; E - 6 cols, 2¹⁄₁₆", ⅛" between; A - 6 cols, 2¹⁄₁₆", ⅛" between; C - 8 cols, 1⅔", ⅛" between.

Commodity consumption: average pages per issue 26(d).

Equipment: EDITORIAL: Front-end hardware — 2-Ap/Mac. MAILROOM: Bundle tyer — 1-Bu. WIRE SERVICES: News — AP. BUSINESS COMPUTERS: PCs & micros networked; PCs & main system networked.

ELGIN

Cook and Kane Counties

'90 U.S. Census- 77,010; E&P '96 Est. 89,333
ABC-CZ (90): 84,484 (HH 29,318)

The Courier-News

(e-mon to fri; m-sat; S)

The Courier-News, 300 Lake St.; PO Box 531, Elgin, IL 60121; tel (847) 888-7800; fax (847) 888-7714. Copley Press Inc. group.

Circulation: 25,609(e); 25,069(m-sat); 22,612(S); ABC Sept. 30, 1995.

Price: 30¢(d); 30¢(sat); 75¢(S); $2.10/wk; $102.90/yr.

Advertising: Open inch rate $34.38(e); $34.38(m-sat); $34.38(S). **Representative:** Sawyer-Ferguson-Walker Co.

News Services: AP, CNS, NYT, SHNS. **Politics:** Independent-Republican. **Established:** 1874.

Special Editions: Business & Industry (Mar); Gift Guides; Home Improvement; Back-to-School.

Special Weekly Sections: Business (mon); Best Food Day (wed); Auto (fri); Real Estate (sat); Travel (S).

Magazines: Entertainment (thur); TV Week (sat); Weekend Magazine.

CORPORATE OFFICER
Board Chairman Helen K Copley

GENERAL MANAGEMENT
General Manager Peggy Kirby
Business Manager Peggy Kirby

ADVERTISING
Director-Sales Richard Ballschmiede
Supervisor-Classified Bonnie Isom

CIRCULATION
Director Douglas Phares
Manager-Home Delivery Colleen Bennett
Manager-Distribution Steve Gardner

NEWS EXECUTIVE
Managing Editor Mike Bailey

EDITORS AND MANAGERS
Assignment Editor Scott Stone
Business Editor Nick Petersen
Copy Desk Chief Marty O'Mara
Editorial Writer Chris Bailey
Entertainment/Amusements Editor Betsey Guzior
Features Editor Betsey Guzior
Graphics Editor/Art Director Bob Ahrens
Living/Lifestyle Editor Betsey Guzior
News Editor Mike Smith
Photo Editor Darrell Goemaat
Sports Editor Don Wojciechowski
Travel Editor Jack Biesterfield
Women's Editor Betsey Guzior

PRODUCTION
Foreman-Composing Robert Branick

Market Information: Zoned editions; Split Run; TMC.

Mechanical available: Offset; Black and 3 ROP colors; insert accepted — preprinted; page cutoffs — 22⅞".

Mechanical specifications: Type page 13" x 21¼"; E - 6 cols, 2¹⁄₁₆", ⅛" between; A - 6 cols, 2¹⁄₁₆", ⅛" between; C - 10 cols, 1⅜", ¹⁄₁₆" between.

Commodity consumption: Newsprint 3,103 metric tons; widths 55", 41.25", 27.5"; black ink 106,500 pounds; color ink 12,400 pounds; single pages printed 10,911; average pages per issue 22(d), 66(S); single plates used 38,000.

Equipment: EDITORIAL: Front-end hardware — AST/386; Front-end software — Dewar; Printers — Okidata. CLASSIFIED: Front-end hardware — AST/386; Front-end software — Dewar; Printers — Dataproducts. DISPLAY: Adv layout systems — CJ; Front-end hardware — Dewar; Front-end software — CJ. PRODUCTION: Typesetters — AU/APS 6-108; Plate exposures — BASF; Production cameras — C/Spartan III; Automatic film processors — LE; Film transporters — 1-C; Color separation equipment (conventional) — Lf; Digital color separation equipment — Lf. WIRE SERVICES: News — AP; Syndicates — Creators; Receiving dishes — size-3m, AP. BUSINESS COMPUTERS: CJ; Applications: Adv billing, Accts receivable, Gen ledger, Payroll, Circ; PCs & micros networked; PCs & main system networked.

FLORA

Clay County

'90 U.S. Census- 5,054; E&P '96 Est. 4,984

The Daily Clay County Advocate-Press

(e-mon to fri)

The Daily Clay County Advocate-Press, 105 W. North Ave.; PO Box 519, Flora, IL 62839; tel (618) 662-2108. Hollinger International Inc. group.

Circulation: 3,725(e); Sworn Sept. 22, 1995.

Price: 50¢(d); $1.50/wk; $70.50/yr (in county), $84.50/yr (out of county).

Advertising: Open inch rate $5.70(e). **Representative:** Landon Associates Inc.

News Services: NEA, AP. **Politics:** Independent. **Established:** 1886 (weekly), 1930 (daily).

Not Published: New Year; Memorial Day; Independence Day; Labor Day; Columbus Day; Veteran's Day; Thanksgiving; Christmas.

Special Edition: Progress Edition (June).

CORPORATE OFFICERS
President Larry J Perrotto
Comptroller Roland McBride

GENERAL MANAGEMENT
General Manager Jack L Thatcher

ADVERTISING
Manager Shirley Garrett

CIRCULATION
Manager Deanita Phillips

NEWS EXECUTIVE
Editor Jack L Thatcher

EDITORS AND MANAGERS
City Editor Duane Crays
Sports Editor Lindell Smith

PRODUCTION
Manager Bonnie Thatcher

Market Information: Zoned editions; TMC.

Mechanical available: Offset; Black and 2 ROP colors; insert accepted — preprinted, require quarter fold size; page cut-offs — 21".

Mechanical specifications: Type page 13¾" x 21"; E - 6 cols, 2¹⁄₁₆", ⅛" between; A - 6 cols, 2¹⁄₁₆", ⅛" between; C - 6 cols, 2¹⁄₁₆", ⅛" between.

Commodity consumption: average pages per issue 12(d).

Equipment: WIRE SERVICES: News — AP; Receiving dishes — AP.

FREEPORT

Stephenson County

'90 U.S. Census- 25,840; E&P '96 Est. 25,584
ABC-CZ (90): 25,840 (HH 10,843)

The Journal-Standard

(e-mon to fri; m-sat)

The Journal-Standard, 27 S. State Ave.; PO Box 330, Freeport, IL 61032; tel (815) 232-1171; fax (815) 232-3601. Howard Publications group.

Circulation: 16,555(e); 16,555(m-sat); ABC Sept. 30, 1995.

Price: 35¢(d); $1.00(sat).

Advertising: Open inch rate $15.00(e); $15.00(m-sat). **Representative:** Papert Companies.

News Service: AP. **Politics:** Independent. **Established:** 1847.

Not Published: Christmas.

Advertising not accepted: Mail order; Work at home; 900 lines.

Special Editions: Bridal (Jan); Agri-Business (Feb); Home & Garden, Chamber Directory (Mar); Dream Homes (Apr); Summer Calendar (May); Agri-Business (June); Senior Citizens (July); Tutty Baker Days, Football Tab (Aug); Home Furnishings (Sept); Agri-Business (Oct); Basketball Tab, Christmas Gift Guide (Nov); Holiday Songbook (Dec).

Special Weekly Sections: Best Food Day (wed); Entertainment, Lifestyle, Health, Religion (sat).

Magazines: Weekender (newsprint); TV Talk.

CORPORATE OFFICER
President Robert S Howard

GENERAL MANAGEMENT
Publisher Gary S Quinn
Manager-Business Robert Sahm

ADVERTISING
Director Mike Aurand

CIRCULATION
Manager Gino Amodeo
Manager-Classified Ann Young

NEWS EXECUTIVES
Editor John Plevka
Asst Managing Editor Olga Gize Carlile

EDITORS AND MANAGERS
City Editor Randy Keho
Sports Editor Jeff Rogers

PRODUCTION
Foreman-Press Dick Kerr
Manager-Systems Angie Olson

Market Information: TMC.

Mechanical available: Offset; Black and 3 ROP colors; insert accepted — preprinted, machine insertable; page cut-offs — 22¾".

I-114 Illinois

Mechanical specifications: Type page 13" x 21¼"; E - 6 cols, 2 1/16", ⅛" between; A - 6 cols, 2 1/16", ⅛" between; C - 8 cols, 1½", ⅛" between.
Commodity consumption: Newsprint 850 metric tons; widths 27½", 13¾", 34"; black ink 24,000 pounds; color ink 6,000 pounds; single pages printed 9,200; average pages per issue 32(d); single plates used 13,500.
Equipment: EDITORIAL: Front-end hardware — 3-Compaq/386, 15-Amdek/VDT, 2-Sun/4-110, 3-Ap/Mac II, 3-Ap/Mac IIci, Sun/Storage System 2gig; Front-end software — QuarkXPress; Printers — 1-Ap/Mac LaserWriter, Ap/Mac Personal LaserWriter; Other equipment — NEC/CD-Rom. CLASSIFIED: Front-end hardware — 6-Amdek/Database, t.p.; Front-end software — Ctext; Printers — Ap/Mac Personal LaserWriter, RSK/Tandy DMP440. DISPLAY: Adv layout systems — Compaq/286e, HP/LaserJet, SCS/Layout 8000, Sun/Storage System 2gig; Front-end hardware — 5-Ap/Mac II, 1-Ap/Mac IIci, Ap/Mac w/Radius monitors; Front-end software — QuarkXPress, Adobe/Illustrator; Printers — Ap/Mac LaserWriter, Imager/1200L, Hyphen; Other equipment — Ap/Mac Scanner, 2-Ap/Mac CD-Rom, 1-NEC/CD-Rom. PRODUCTION: Typesetters — ECR/Pelbox, Sun/Storage System 4gig, OPI; Scanners — AG/7A Flatbed-Slide Scanner, Ap/Mac Scanner, Lf/Leafscan Slide-Negative Scanner; Digital color separation equipment — Adobe/Illustrator.
PRESSROOM: Line 1 — H; Line 2 — 7-G/Urbanite; Press control system — Hurletron. MAILROOM: Counter stackers — 1-BG/Count-O-Veyor; Inserters and stuffers — 1-MM/227; Bundle tyer — OVL. WIRE SERVICES: News — AP; Photos — AP; Syndicates — KRT; Receiving dishes — size-12ft, AP. BUSINESS COMPUTERS: Sun/Micro, ATT; PCs & micros networked; PCs & main system networked.

GALESBURG
Knox County

'90 U.S. Census- 33,530; E&P '96 Est. 32,471
ABC-CZ (90): 34,343 (HH 13,573)

The Register-Mail
(e-mon to fri; m-sat)

The Register-Mail, 140 S. Prairie St.; PO Box 310, Galesburg, IL 61401; tel (309) 343-7181; fax (309) 342-5171. Peoria Journal Star Inc. group.
Circulation: 17,518(e); 17,971(m-sat); ABC Sept. 30, 1995.
Price: 50¢(d); 50¢(sat); $7.00/mo; $76.00/yr.
Advertising: Open inch rate $15.30(e); $15.30(m-sat). **Representative:** Cresmer, Woodward, O'Mara & Ormsbee.
News Service: AP. **Politics:** Independent. **Established:** 1879.
Not Published: New Year; Memorial Day; Independence Day; Labor Day; Thanksgiving; Christmas.
Special Editions: Income Tax (Jan); Home Improvement (Mar); Brides Tab, Lawn and Garden (Apr); Car Care (May); Health Care, Railroad Days (June); Progress Edition, Football (Sept); Winterize Home/Car (Oct); Basketball (Nov).
Special Weekly Section: TV (fri).
Magazine: Welcome (Visitor's Guide) (Mar & Aug).

CORPORATE OFFICERS
President John T McConnell
Secretary Jan Meyer

GENERAL MANAGEMENT
Publisher Don Cooper
Business Manager Joan Potts

ADVERTISING
Manager-Classified Carol A Uhlmann
Manager-Retail Doris Medhurst

CIRCULATION
Manager Terry Welty

NEWS EXECUTIVE
Editor Robert F Harrison

EDITORS AND MANAGERS
City/Metro Editor John Pulliam
Editorial Page Editor Robert F Harrison
Editorial Writer Robert F Harrison
Education Editor Geri Reynolds
Farm Robert F Harrison
Fashion/Style Editor Janet Saunders
Features Editor Janet Saunders
Living/Lifestyle Editor Janet Saunders
News Editor Mike Homco
Photo Department Manager Randy Squiers
Radio/Television Editor Robert F Harrison
Sports Editor Mike Trueblood
Women's Editor Janet Saunders

PRODUCTION
Manager Lyle Fawer
Foreman-Composing Ron McGarry

Market Information: TMC.
Mechanical available: Offset; Black and 3 ROP colors; insert accepted — preprinted; page cutoffs — 22⅝".
Mechanical specifications: Type page 13¾" x 22⅝"; E - 6 cols, 2.03", ⅛" between; A - 6 cols, 2.03", ⅛" between; C - 9 cols, 1.38".
Commodity consumption: Newsprint 1,040 short tons; widths 13¾", 27½", 55"; black ink 28,000 pounds; color ink 1,500 pounds; single pages printed 8,350; average pages per issue 27(d); single plates used 8,600.
Equipment: EDITORIAL: Front-end hardware — Dewar; Front-end software — Dewar; Printers — T/300, Okidata/182; Other equipment — Mac/Photo System, Lf/AP Leaf Picture Desk. CLASSIFIED: Front-end hardware — Dewar; Front-end software — Dewar. DISPLAY: Adv layout systems — Multi-Ad/Creator; Front-end hardware — Ap/Mac; Front-end software — Multi-Ad Creator; Printers — Ap/Mac; Other equipment — Dewar/DiscNet. PRODUCTION: Typesetters — 3-Printware/720 IQ; Plate exposures — 2-Nu; Plate processors — 1-Wd/Lithoflex, 1-Nat; Production cameras — 1-SCREEN; Automatic film processors — AG/Raffin Access.
PRESSROOM: Line 1 — 4-Wd/double-width, Wd/Lithoflex; Line 2 — 3-G/Community; Line 3 — 10-WPC/Atlas (w/2-Quadra-color unit); Folders — 2-G; Press control system — GE. MAILROOM: Inserters and stuffers — MM/228E 5-into-1; Bundle tyer — Strapper; Addressing machine — KAN/500. LIBRARY: Electronic — SMS/Stauffer Gold. COMMUNICATIONS: Systems used — satellite. WIRE SERVICES: News — AP; Photos — AP; Syndicates — AP Datafeatures; Receiving dishes — size-10ft, AP. BUSINESS COMPUTERS: ATT, Vision Data; Applications: Vision Data; PCs & micros networked; PCs & main system networked.

GENEVA
Kane County

'90 U.S. Census- 12,617; E&P '96 Est. 14,219

Kane County Chronicle
(m-tues to sat)

Kane County Chronicle, 1000 Randall Rd., Geneva, IL 60134; tel (708) 232-9222; fax (708) 232-4976. Shaw Newspapers group.
Circulation: 13,774(m); 13,774(m-sat); Sworn Oct. 2, 1995.
Price: 50¢(d); 50¢(sat); $64.35/yr.
Advertising: Open inch rate $18.64(m); $18.64(m-sat).
News Service: AP. **Established:** 1991.
Special Weekly Sections: Lifestyle (wed); Real Estate (thur); Auto (fri); TV Watch (sat).

GENERAL MANAGEMENT
Publisher Roger F Coleman

ADVERTISING
Director James W Holm

CIRCULATION
Director Frank Piller

NEWS EXECUTIVES
Editor Dave Heun
Managing Editor Lee Husfeldt

EDITORS AND MANAGERS
Business Editor Roald Haase
Entertainment Editor Cindy DiDonna
Sports Editor Darryl Mellema

PRODUCTION
Director James Comiskey
Plant Manager Ted Robinson

Market Information: TMC.
Mechanical available: Offset; Black and 3 ROP colors; insert accepted — preprinted, minimum overall size 8½" x 11"; single sheets must be, thicker than .004"; page cut-offs — 22¾".
Mechanical specifications: Type page 13" x 21"; E - 6 cols, 2 1/16", ⅛" between; A - 6 cols, 2 1/16", ⅛" between; C - 9 cols, 1 5/16", ⅛" between.
Commodity consumption: average pages per issue 24(d).
Equipment: EDITORIAL: Front-end hardware — Baseview; Front-end software — Baseview/NewsEdit, QuarkXPress; Printers — Compaq/PageMarq 15. CLASSIFIED: Front-end hardware — Dewar/Sys II, Baseview; Front-end software — Dewar/Custom Software, Baseview; Printers — Lanier/Laser printer M-2008. DISPLAY: Front-end hardware — Ap/Mac, Dewar/Discovery, 1-Ap/Power Mac; Front-end software — Multi-Ad/Creator, Dewar/Custom, Multi-Ad, QuarkXPress, Adobe/Illustrator; Other equipment — Horizon/Plus Scanner, AP AdSend. PRODUCTION: Pagination software — QuarkXPress; Typesetters — Ap/Mac Laser-Writer, 2-AU/APS 6-84ACS; Plate exposures — Nu; Plate processors — Southern Litho; Scanners — AG/Horizon Plus, Ap/Mac One Scan; Production cameras — B; Automatic film processors — 1-LE, 2-AG; Film transporters — AG; Digital color separation equipment — AGFA Horizon, Microtek Scanmaker II SP, Nikon Coolscan-Photoshop Software.
PRESSROOM: Line 1 — 8-G/Urbanite single width; Press drives — Baldor; Folders — G/1000 Series; Reels and stands — G; Press control system — G; Press registration system — G. MAILROOM: Counter stackers — BG/167, MM; Inserters and stuffers — MM/227; Bundle tyer — MLN, Bu. LIBRARY: Electronic — Claris/Filemaker Pro. COMMUNICATIONS: Digital ad delivery system — AP AdSend. WIRE SERVICES: News — AP; Photos — AP; Syndicates — United Media, Universal Press, Creators Syndicate, King Features, L.A. Times; Receiving dishes — AP. BUSINESS COMPUTERS: Ap/Mac; Applications: Baseview: Class, Editorial; QuarkXPress, Multi-Ad; PCs & micros networked; PCs & main system networked.

HARRISBURG
Saline County

'90 U.S. Census- 9,289; E&P '96 Est. 8,573

The Daily Register
(e-mon to fri; m-sat; S)

The Daily Register, 35 S. Vine; PO Box 248, Harrisburg, IL 62946; tel (618) 253-7146; fax (618) 252-0863; e-mail gwilson@ampub.com. Hollinger International Inc. group.
Circulation: 5,643(e); 5,643(m-sat); 5,643(S); Sworn Sept. 29, 1995.
Price: 50¢(d); 50¢(sat); $1.00(S); $2.10/wk.
Advertising: Open inch rate $8.25(e); $8.25(m-sat); $8.25(S).
News Service: AP. **Politics:** Independent. **Established:** 1915.
Note: Effective July 9, 1995, this publication changed its publishing plan from (e-mon to fri; m-sat) to (e-mon to fri; m-sat; S). Sunday circulation figure is an estimate
Not Published: New Year; Independence Day; Christmas.
Magazines: American Weekend, Sports Saturday (sat); Sports Sunday (S).

CORPORATE OFFICERS
President Larry J Perrotto
Comptroller Roland McBride

GENERAL MANAGEMENT
Publisher George Q Wilson

ADVERTISING
Director Sally Wofford

CIRCULATION
Director Scott Dunn

NEWS EXECUTIVE
Managing Editor Lee Smith

EDITOR AND MANAGER
County Editor Gregory Norfleet

PRODUCTION
Manager Jack L Larkin

Market Information: Operate audiotex.
Mechanical available: Offset; Black and 2 ROP colors; insert accepted — preprinted; page cut-offs — 21¾".
Mechanical specifications: Type page 13" x 21½"; E - 6 cols, 2 1/16", ⅛" between; A - 6 cols, 2 1/16", ⅛" between; C - 9 cols, 1⅜", 1/16" between.
Commodity consumption: Newsprint 268 short tons; width 27½"; black ink 8,350 pounds; color ink 750 pounds; single pages printed 5,475; average pages per issue 14(d); single plates used 5,600.
Equipment: EDITORIAL: Front-end hardware — Ap/Mac; Other equipment — 2-Ap/Mac Powerbook 140B. CLASSIFIED: Front-end hardware — IBM/PC Compatible. PRODUCTION: Typesetters — 2-Ap/Mac Laser; Production cameras — 1-R; Automatic film processors — 1-LE.
PRESSROOM: Line 1 — 5-G. MAILROOM: Bundle tyer — 1-Bu; Addressing machine — 2-Wm. WIRE SERVICES: News — AP; Receiving dishes — size-3m, AP. BUSINESS COMPUTERS: IBM; Applications: Full accounting, Circ.

HERRIN
See CARBONDALE

JACKSONVILLE
Morgan County

'90 U.S. Census- 19,324; E&P '96 Est. 18,711
ABC-CZ (90): 22,511 (HH 8,801)

Jacksonville Journal-Courier
(m-mon to sat; S)

Jacksonville Journal-Courier, 235 W. State St.; PO Box 1048, Jacksonville, IL 62651-1048; tel (217) 245-6121; fax (217) 245-1226. Freedom Communications Inc. group.
Circulation: 14,457(m); 14,457(m-sat); 14,543(S); ABC Sept. 30, 1995.
Price: 50¢(d); 50¢(sat); $1.25(S); $2.55/wk; $11.95/mo, $132.60/yr (carrier), $130.00/yr (mail).
Advertising: Open inch rate $14.00(m); $14.00(m-sat); $14.00(S). **Representative:** Landon Associates Inc.
News Service: AP. **Politics:** Independent. **Established:** 1830.
Not Published: Jan 2; May 25; Sept 7; Nov 27; Dec 26.
Advertising not accepted: Abortion clinics.
Special Editions: Bridal Tab; Tax Preparation; Valentine Idea; Saving of the Green; Spring Agriculture Tab; Spring Fashion; Investment Tab; Realtors' Tab; Moonlite Madness; Spring Auto Tab; Mother's Day Gift; Living Indoors & Out; Lawn & Garden; Graduation Tab; Morgan County Fair Tab; Summer Cooking Tab; Father's Day; Pre-4th of July Sale; July $ Days; Summer Bridal Tab; Progress Edition; Sidewalk Days; Back-to-School; Jacksonville A to Z; Football Tab; Fall Home Improvement; New Car Showing; Harvest Tab; Fall Auto Care Tab; Fire Prevention Week; Spring Home Improvement Tab; Holiday Cookbook; Christmas Kick-off; Christmas Gifts; Basketball Tab; New Year's Eve; Christmas Wish Book; 12 Days of Christmas; Late Shoppers; Christmas Greetings; New Year's Greetings; Modern Farmer.
Special Weekly Sections: Food Section (wed); Senior Citizen Page, Fling (thur); Church Page (sat); Farm Section, Society Section (S).
Magazines: Business Page, Movie Page, Sports Section, TV Listings (daily); 'Diversions' Section, Travel Page, Outdoor Page (S).

GENERAL MANAGEMENT
Publisher/General Manager John R Power

ADVERTISING
Director Randy Lohrenz

CIRCULATION
Manager Rusty Hall

NEWS EXECUTIVE
Editor John R Power

EDITORS AND MANAGERS
Books Editor John R Power
Editorial Page Editor John R Power
Farm Editor Christy Nies
Fashion/Society Editor Pamela Olson
Food Editor Pamela Olson
Home Furnishings/Women's Editor Pamela Olson
Photo Department Manager Abel Uribe
Sports Editor Craig Wack

PRODUCTION
Superintendent Lloyd Summers
Foreman-Mailroom Jim Van Hyning

Market Information: Zoned editions; Split Run; TMC.
Mechanical available: Offset; Black and 3 ROP colors; insert accepted — preprinted; page cut-offs — 22¾".
Mechanical specifications: Type page 13" x 21"; E - 6 cols, 2 1/16", ⅛" between; A - 6 cols, 2 1/16", ⅛" between; C - 9 cols, 1⅜", 1/16" between.

Equipment: PRESSROOM: Line 1 — 8-G/Urbanite. WIRE SERVICES: News — AP; Photos — AP; Syndicates — NEA, NAS, King Features, United Media, LATS, CT, Creators; Receiving dishes — AP.

JOLIET

Will County

'90 U.S. Census- 76,836; E&P '96 Est. 76,173
ABC-CZ (90): 147,721 (HH 50,445)

Herald-News

(e-mon to fri; m-sat; S)

Herald-News, 300 Caterpillar Dr., Joliet, IL 60436; tel (815) 729-6161. Copley Press Inc. group.
Circulation: 49,390(e); 49,390(m-sat); 49,390(S); Sworn Oct. 1, 1995.
Price: 35¢(d); 35¢(sat); $1.25(S); $2.75/wk.
Advertising: Open inch rate $36.56(e); $36.56(m-sat); $36.56(S). **Representative:** Sawyer-Ferguson-Walker Co.
News Services: AP, CNS, SHNS, NYT. **Politics:** Independent-Republican. **Established:** 1839.
Special Editions: Progress (Mar); Building & Auto.
Special Weekly Sections: Sports, Community Calendar (mon); Consumer Page (tues); Food Page (wed); Weekend (thur); Automotive, Homes (fri); Saturday Living, Church (sat); Health (S).
Magazines: TV Update (sat); USA Weekend (S).

CORPORATE OFFICER
Board Chairman Helen K Copley

GENERAL MANAGEMENT
General Manager Marx Gibson
Controller Karen Kuma
Manager-Education Service Mary Ingram

ADVERTISING
Manager-Sales Cory Bollinger

CIRCULATION
Manager James Briscoe

NEWS EXECUTIVE
Managing Editor (Interim) Bill Wimbiscus

EDITOR AND MANAGER
City Editor John Whiteside

PRODUCTION
Manager-Prepress Ron Likovic

Market Information: Zoned editions; Split Run; TMC; ADS; Electronic edition.
Mechanical available: Offset; Black and 3 ROP colors; insert accepted — preprinted, any; page cut-offs — 21".
Mechanical specifications: Type page 13" x 21"; E - 6 cols, 2 1/16", 3/16" between; A - 6 cols, 2 5/32", 1/16" between; C - 10 cols, 1 3/8", 1/16" between.
Commodity consumption: Newsprint 3,600 metric tons; widths 55", 27 1/2", 13 3/4"; black ink 155,000 pounds; color ink 30,000 pounds; single pages printed 12,500; average pages per issue 30(d), 56(S); single plates used 21,200.
Equipment: EDITORIAL: Front-end hardware — SII/Sys 55, 25-SII/Coyote; Front-end software — SII; Printers — 1-TI/810, Ap/Mac LaserWriter NTX; Other equipment — 1-Ap/Mac II, 1-Ap/Mac IIci, 1-Ap/Mac SE. CLASSIFIED: Front-end hardware — SII/Sys 55; Front-end software — CLS, SII/Coyote Standard, SII. DISPLAY: Front-end hardware — DEC; Front-end software — CJ; Printers — OMS/Laser Printer. PRODUCTION: Typesetters — 2-AU/APS Micro 5; Plate exposures — 2-WL/Lith-X-PozerIII; Plate processors — 2-WL; Scanners — 1-ECR/Autokon 1000; Production cameras — C/Spartan III; Automatic film processors — LE/XL 32, LE/2600; Color separation equipment (conventional) — Zenith/210L; Digital color separation equipment — RZ/ Diadem. PRESSROOM: Line 1 — 21-G/Colorliner couples; Line 2 — 18-G/Colorliner couples; Pasters — 10-G/CT50; Reels and stands — 10-G/CT50; Press control system — Allen Bradley. MAILROOM: Counter stackers — 6-QWI, 2-HL; Inserters and stuffers — 2-GMA/SLS1000 (14-into-1); Bundle tyer — 8-Power Strap; Addressing machine — 2-AVY, 1-Ch. LIBRARY: Electronic — SII/GetNet News Library. WIRE SERVICES: News — AP, CNS, NYT, SHNS; Photos — AP; Syndicates — CNS, NYT, SHNS; Receiving dishes — AP, NYT, SHNS. BUSINESS COMPUTERS: DEC; Applications: Archetype/Corel Draw, MicroGraphics/Designer; PCs & micros networked; PCs & main system networked.

KANKAKEE

Kankakee County

'90 U.S. Census- 27,575; E&P '96 Est. 26,013
ABC-CZ (90): 54,761 (HH 19,945)

The Daily Journal

(e-mon to fri)

The Sunday Journal (S)

The Daily Journal, 8 Dearborn Sq.; PO Box 632, Kankakee, IL 60901; tel (815) 937-3300; fax (815) 937-3301. Small Newspaper Group Inc. group.
Circulation: 29,162(e); 33,400(S); ABC Sept. 30, 1995.
Price: 35¢(d); $1.25(S); $2.15/wk (carrier), $2.25/wk (motor route); $106.60/yr (carrier), $111.80/yr (motor route).
Advertising: Open inch rate $16.98(e); $16.98(S). **Representative:** Landon Associates Inc.
News Services: AP, NYT. **Politics:** Independent. **Established:** 1853.
Not Published: New Year; Memorial Day; Independence Day; Labor Day; Thanksgiving; Christmas.
Special Editions: Bridal Tab (Jan); Progress Editions (Feb); Newspaper in Education Tab, Farm Section (Mar); House & Garden Section, Realtor Tab, Area Chambers Annual Showcase Tab (Apr); Graduation Tab, Summertime Tab (May); Bourbonnais Friendship Festival, Air Festival Tab (June); Iroquois Fair Tab, Senior Citizen Living, % Off Tab (July); Football Tab, Kankakee Fair Tab, Homes on Parade, River Regatta Tab (Aug); Fall Home & Yard Section, Auto Section (Sept); Cookbook Tab (Oct); Basketball, Gift Guide (Nov); Gift Guide (Second Run), Last Minute Gift Ideas, After Christmas Sale (Dec).
Special Weekly Section: Weddings (2nd & 4th mon, bi-wkly).
Magazine: USA Weekend (S).

CORPORATE OFFICERS
Board Chairman Jean Alice Small
President Len Robert Small
Senior Vice Pres/Secretary Thomas P Small
Treasurer/Asst Secretary Joseph E Lacaeyse

GENERAL MANAGEMENT
Publisher Jean Alice Small
Vice Pres-Operations/General Manager Mario Sebastiani
Vice Pres-Finance Joseph E Lacaeyse
Vice Pres-Administration Donald U des Lauriers
Personnel Officer Christine Huffman
Business Manager Brenda Albers

ADVERTISING
Director Pam Dunlap

CIRCULATION
Manager Weldon Greeneberg

NEWS EXECUTIVES
Editor Jean Alice Small
Managing Editor Phil Angelo

EDITORS AND MANAGERS
Agriculture Editor Bob Themer
Business/Finance Editor Roy Bernard
City/Metro Editor Phil Angelo
Editorial Phil Angelo
Editorial Page Editor Bob Thomas
Education Editor Karen Mellen
Environmental Editor Bob Themer
Fashion/Style Editor Mary Lu Laffey
Food Editor Martha Purdy
Health/Medical Editor Lee Provost
Home Furnishings Editor Mary Lu Laffey
News Editor Ray Bachar
Outdoors Editor Bob Themer
Photo Editor Bill Jurevich
Picture Editor Bill Jurevich
Religion Editor Bill Norman
Sports Editor Tim Yonke
Teen-Age/Youth Editor Sherry Weiler
Television/Film Editor Sherry Weiler
Theater/Music Editor John Stewart
Women's Editor Mary Lu Laffey

MANAGEMENT INFORMATION SERVICES
Data Processing Manager Tom Steele

PRODUCTION
Foreman-Composing Ross Bertrand
Foreman-Press (Day) Leonard Bydalek
Foreman-Press (Night) David Decker

Market Information: Split Run; TMC.
Mechanical available: Offset; Black and 3 ROP colors; insert accepted — preprinted; page cut-offs — 22 1/2".
Mechanical specifications: Type page 13" x 21 1/2"; E - 6 cols, 2 1/16", 1/8" between; A - 6 cols, 2 1/16", 1/8" between; C - 8 cols, 1 3/8", 1/16" between.
Commodity consumption: Newsprint 1,800 metric tons; widths 55", 41 1/4", 27 1/2"; black ink 53,000 pounds; color ink 10,500 pounds; single pages printed 12,000; average pages per issue 30(d), 56(S); single plates used 22,000.
Equipment: EDITORIAL: Front-end hardware — AT/7000; Front-end software — AT. CLASSIFIED: Front-end hardware — PC/052/Novell. DISPLAY: Adv layout systems — 3-Ap/Mac 7100, 3-Ap/Mac 6100, 1-Ap/Mac IIcx, Ap/Mac IIfx; Printers — Ap/Mac LaserWriter II NT, HP/LaserJet 4MV. PRODUCTION: Pagination software — QPS 3.3; Typesetters — 1-AU/APS Micro 5, 2-AG/Selectset 5000; Plate exposures — 1-B, 1-Nu; Plate processors — 1-WL; Electronic picture desk — Lf/AP Leaf Picture Desk; Scanners — Umax/1260, 2-Polaroid/ SprintScan, 1-Nikon/Scantouch; Production cameras — 2-R; Automatic film processors — 2-LD/18; Digital color separation equipment — 1-Z/4050. PRESSROOM: Line 1 — 6-G/Metro-2 Color Deck (2 Tol); Folders — 2-G; Pasters — 6-G; Reels and stands — 6-G; Press control system — Fin. MAILROOM: Counter stackers — 1-HL/Sta-Hi 257-S, 1-Id/2000; Inserters and stuffers — 2-MM/Model 227; Bundle tyer — Dynaric; Addressing machine — Ch/525E. WIRE SERVICES: News — AP, NYT; Receiving dishes — AP. BUSINESS COMPUTERS: PC/486 DX-50; Applications: Lotus, Javelin; PCs & micros networked; PCs & main system networked.

KEWANEE

Henry County

'90 U.S. Census- 12,969; E&P '96 Est. 11,984
ABC-CZ (90): 12,969 (HH 5,376)

Star-Courier (e-mon to fri; m-sat)

Star-Courier, 105 E. Central Blvd. (61443); PO Box A, Kewanee, IL 61443-0836; tel (309) 852-2181; fax (309) 852-0010. Lee Enterprises Inc. group.
Circulation: 6,547(e); 6,547(m-sat); ABC Sept. 30, 1995.
Price: 50¢(d); 50¢(sat); $2.15/wk; $8.45/mo; $92.25/yr.
Advertising: Open inch rate $10.64(e); $10.64(m-sat). **Representative:** Landon Associates Inc.
News Service: AP. **Politics:** Independent. **Established:** 1893.
Not Published: New Year; Memorial Day; Independence Day; Labor Day; Thanksgiving; Christmas.
Special Editions: Bridal (Jan); Farm Tab (Mar); Home Improvement (Apr); 101 Things To Do In Henry County (May); Fair Tab (June); People Making A Difference (July); Hogsmopolitan (Aug).

GENERAL MANAGEMENT
General Manager Anita Bird

ADVERTISING
Manager-Sales Janice Nugent

NEWS EXECUTIVE
Editor Anita Bird

EDITORS AND MANAGERS
City/Education Editor Mike Berry
Photo Department Manager Mike Berry
Regional Editor Dave Clarke
Sports Editor Robert Westlund

PRODUCTION
Foreman-Composing Janell Smith

Market Information: TMC.
Mechanical available: Offset; Black and 3 ROP colors; insert accepted — preprinted; page cut-offs — 22 3/4".
Mechanical specifications: Type page 13" x 21 1/2"; E - 6 cols, 2 1/16", 1/8" between; A - 6 cols, 2 1/16", 1/8" between; C - 8 cols, 1 1/2", 1/16" between.
Commodity consumption: Newsprint 308.3 metric tons; widths 13 3/4", 27 1/2"; black ink 4,500 pounds; color ink 500 pounds; single pages printed 5,591; average pages per issue 16(d); single plates used 9,500.
Equipment: EDITORIAL: Front-end hardware — Ap/Macs; Other equipment — 8-COM/Compugraphic, 1-TC. CLASSIFIED: Other equipment — Baseview. PRODUCTION: Typesetters — Ap/Macs; Scanners — 1-GMS/E-Z-Scan II. PRESSROOM: Line 1 — 4-G/Colorliner; Press control system — Cline. MAILROOM: Bundle tyer — 2-Bu. WIRE SERVICES: News — AP; Receiving dishes — AP. BUSINESS COMPUTERS: 3-IBM/PC-KT, 2-Compaq/386-S; Applications: Circ, Adv billing, Accts receivable, Gen ledger.

LA SALLE-PERU-OGLESBY-SPRING VALLEY

La Salle and Bureau Counties

'90 U.S. Census- 27,884 (La Salle 9,717; Peru 9,302; Oglesby 3,619; Spring Valley 5,246); E&P '96 Est. 26,203 (La Salle 9,337; Peru 8,329; Oglesby 3,498; Spring Valley 5,039)
ABC-CZ (90): 29,927 (HH 12,421)

News-Tribune

(e-mon to sat)

News-Tribune, 426 Second St., La Salle, IL 61301; tel (815) 223-3200.
Circulation: 19,416(e); 19,416(e-sat); ABC Sept. 30, 1995.
Price: 50¢(d); 50¢(sat).
Advertising: Open inch rate $16.50(e); $16.50(e-sat).
News Service: AP. **Established:** 1891.
Magazines: TV Update, USA Weekend (S).

CORPORATE OFFICERS
President Peter Miller
Vice Pres-Sales/Marketing Robert Vickrey
Vice Pres/General Manager Joyce McCullough
Vice Pres-Operations Peter Miller III
Secretary Frederick C Miller
Asst Secretary Peter Miller III
Treasurer Peter Miller

GENERAL MANAGEMENT
Publisher Peter Miller III
Co-Publisher Mary Miller
Manager-Credit Craig Baker
Personnel Manager Joyce McCullough
Manager-Mailroom Fort Miller

ADVERTISING
Vice Pres Robert Vickrey

MARKETING AND PROMOTION
Manager-Marketing/Sales Robert Vickrey

CIRCULATION
Director Pat Nemeth

NEWS EXECUTIVE
Managing Editor Linda Kleczewski

EDITORS AND MANAGERS
City Editor Lori Edwards
Picture Editor Kemp Smith
Society/Women's Editor Beverly Sons
Sports Editor David Elsessor

PRODUCTION
Manager Lynn Ridder
Manager-Pressroom Jeff Hoos

Market Information: Split Run; TMC.
Mechanical available: Offset; Black and 3 ROP colors; insert accepted — preprinted; page cut-offs — 22 3/4".
Mechanical specifications: Type page 13" x 21 1/2"; E - 6 cols, 2.09", 1/8" between; A - 6 cols, 2.09", 1/8" between; C - 9 cols, 1.37", 1/8" between.
Commodity consumption: Newsprint 880 short tons; widths 28", 14"; black ink 20,000 pounds; color ink 6,000 pounds; single pages printed 7,500; average pages per issue 24(d); single plates used 21,000.
Equipment: EDITORIAL: Front-end hardware — Dewar; Front-end software — Dewar; Printers — Okidata. CLASSIFIED: Front-end hardware — PC; Front-end software — PPI/Advertising Management Systems; Printers — Accuset/ 1000. DISPLAY: Adv layout systems — Dewar/Discovery; Front-end hardware — Dewar/Discovery; Front-end software — Dewar/Discovery; Printers — Okidata. PRODUCTION: Pagination software — Informatel; Typesetters — 2-COM, Accuset/1000; Plate exposures — Nu; Plate processors — 1-Nat; Production cameras — R; Automatic film processors — LE; Color separation equipment (conventional) — Digi-Colour. PRESSROOM: Line 1 — 8-G/Urbanite; Press control system — Fin. MAILROOM: Bundle tyer — 2-MLN/ML2EE; Addressing machine — Ch. WIRE SERVICES: News — AP; Receiving dishes — AP. BUSINESS COMPUTERS: HDW/Dell; Applications: MSSI: Circ, Adv, Manifest, Gen ledger, Accts payable, TMC, Payroll; PCs & micros networked; PCs & main system networked.

I-116 Illinois

LAWRENCEVILLE

Lawrence County

'90 U.S. Census- 4,897; E&P '96 Est. 4,556

Daily Record (e-mon to fri)

Daily Record, 1209 State St.; PO Box 559, Lawrenceville, IL 62439; tel (618) 943-2331; fax (618) 943-3976. Lewis Newspapers group.

Circulation: 3,947(e); Sworn Sept. 30, 1995.

Price: 25¢(d); $1.25/wk; $59.00/yr; $38.00/yr.

Advertising: Open inch rate $4.90(e); comb with Robinson Daily News (e) 12.50.

News Service: AP. **Politics:** Independent. **Established:** 1847.

Not Published: Christmas; New Year; Memorial Day; Independence Day; Labor Day; Thanksgiving Day.

Advertising not accepted: 900 numbers; massage parlors.

Special Editions: Tax Guide (Feb); Spring Ag Salute (Mar); Kreative Kids (Apr); American Home Week (May); Senior Citizen Salute (June); Summer Savings, Country 4-H Fair (July); Back-to-School (Aug); Fall Festival, Home Improvement, Car Care (Sept); Working Women, Chamber of Commerce Directory (Oct); Christmas Opening (Nov); Christmas Greetings (Dec).

Magazines: TV Section (fri); What's On.

GENERAL MANAGEMENT

Owner Larry H Lewis
Assoc Publisher John Peterson

ADVERTISING

Director Sandie Stafford

CIRCULATION

Manager Joyce Tredway

NEWS EXECUTIVE

Managing Editor Michael Van Dorn

EDITORS AND MANAGERS

Action Line Editor Michael Van Dorn
Books Editor Ray Cronin
Business Editor John Peterson
City Editor Michael Van Dorn
Editorial Page Editor Michael Van Dorn
Education Editor Beverly Johnson
Films/Theater Editor Ray Cronin
Food/Religion Editor Beverly Johnson
Librarian/Music Beverly Johnson
Political Editor Ray Cronin
Radio/Television Editor Beverly Johnson
Real Estate Editor John Peterson
Science/Technology Editor Michael Van Dorn
Sports Editor Joe Jones
Women's Editor Beverly Johnson

MANAGEMENT INFORMATION SERVICES

Manager-Management Info Services Renee Goff

PRODUCTION

Manager Beverly Johnson

Market Information: Zoned editions; TMC; ADS.

Mechanical available: Offset; Black and 4 ROP colors; insert accepted — preprinted, all-quarter folded (max. size 7x11); page cut-offs — 22¾".

Mechanical specifications: Type page 13" x 21"; E - 6 cols, 2¹⁄₁₆", ⅛" between; A - 6 cols, 2¹⁄₁₆", ⅛" between; C - 9 cols, 1½", ¹⁄₁₆" between.

Commodity consumption: average pages per issue 10(d).

Equipment: EDITORIAL: Front-end hardware — Ap/Mac; Front-end software — Baseview NewsPro 1.1; Printers — 2-Xante/Accel-a-Writer 8100; Other equipment — Nikon/Coolscan film scanner. CLASSIFIED: Front-end hardware — Ap/Mac; Front-end software — Hypercard; Printers — Xante/Accel-a-Writer 8100A. DISPLAY: Adv layout systems — Ap/Mac ci, Xante/Accel-a-Writer 8100A; Front-end hardware — Ap/Mac; Front-end software — Adobe/Illustrator; Printers — Xante/Accel-a-Writer 8100A; Other equipment — Mk/Scan-Maker print scanner. PRODUCTION: Pagination software — QuarkXPress 3.3; Typesetters — 1-Ap/Mac LaserWriter. MAILROOM: Bundle tyer — 1-US; Addressing machine — 1-Am. COMMUNICATIONS: Facsimile — Canon/630. WIRE SERVICES: News — AP; Receiving dishes — AP. BUSINESS COMPUTERS: Ap/Mac; Applications: Microsoft/Word, Microsoft/Excel; PCs & micros networked; PCs & main system networked.

LINCOLN

Logan County

'90 U.S. Census- 15,418; E&P '96 Est. 14,872
ABC-CZ (90): 15,418 (HH 5,963)

The Courier (e-mon to fri; m-sat)

The Courier, 601 Pulaski St.; PO Box 740, Lincoln, IL 62656-0740; tel (217) 732-2101; fax (217) 732-7039. Copley Press Inc. group.

Circulation: 6,967(e); 6,967(m-sat); ABC Sept. 30, 1995.

Price: 35¢(d); 35¢(sat); $2.10/wk; $9.10/mo; $100.36/yr.

Advertising: Open inch rate $9.09(e); $9.09(m-sat); comb with Springfield State Journal-Register $44.77.

News Services: AP, CNS, SHNS. **Politics:** Independent. **Established:** 1856.

Not Published: New Year; Memorial Day; Independence Day; Labor Day; Thanksgiving; Christmas.

Special Weekly Sections: Lifestyles (wed); Entertainment (sat).

GENERAL MANAGEMENT

Publisher John P Clarke
Purchasing Agent Billie Cheek
Office Manager Billie Cheek

CIRCULATION

Manager Chris Slack

NEWS EXECUTIVE

Managing Editor Jeff Nelson

EDITORS AND MANAGERS

Church Editor Paul Ayars
City Editor Dan Tackett
Lifestyle Editor Nancy Saul
Photo Editor Ann Klose
Sports Editor Jeff Grieser

MANAGEMENT INFORMATION SERVICES

Online Manager Ed Richardson

PRODUCTION

Foreman-Composing Ed Richardson
Foreman-Press Matthew Mason

Market Information: TMC; Operate database.

Mechanical available: Offset; Black and 3 ROP colors; insert accepted — preprinted; page cut-offs — 21¼".

Mechanical specifications: Type page 13" x 21"; E - 6 cols, 2¹⁄₁₆", ⅛" between; A - 6 cols, 2¹⁄₁₆", ⅛" between; C - 9 cols, 1⅜", ¹⁄₁₆" between.

Commodity consumption: Newsprint 277 short tons; width 13¾"; black ink 5,280 pounds; color ink 650 pounds; average pages per issue 28(d); single plates used 10,400.

Equipment: EDITORIAL: Front-end software — Dewar/Disc Net, Dewar/Sys 2, Dewar/Sys 4, Dewar/Discovery; Printers — XIT/Clipper; Other equipment — Lf/AP Leaf Picture Desk. CLASSIFIED: Front-end software — Dewar/Disc Net; Printers — XIT/Clipper. DISPLAY: Front-end hardware — 1-Dewar/Discovery; Front-end software — Dewar/Disc Net, Dewar/Sys 2, Dewar/Sys 4, Dewar/Discovery. PRODUCTION: Typesetters — XIT/Clipper; Plate processors — Nat; Production cameras — R/500, C/Marathon; Automatic film processors — Polychrome/26". PRESSROOM: Line 1 — 7-G/Community. MAILROOM: Bundle tyer — MLN. WIRE SERVICES: News — AP, CNS, SHNS; Photos — AP; Syndicates — Universal Press, King Features, Creators; Receiving dishes — size-12ft, AP.

LITCHFIELD

Montgomery County

'90 U.S. Census- 6,883; E&P '96 Est. 6,865

News-Herald (e-mon to fri)

News-Herald, 112 E. Ryder; PO Box 160, Litchfield, IL 62056; tel (217) 324-2121; fax (217) 324-2122.

Circulation: 5,800(e); Sworn Sept. 30, 1992.

Price: 20¢(d); $16.00/yr (mail, local), $20.00/yr (mail).

Advertising: Open inch rate $2.80(e).

News Service: AP. **Politics:** Independent-Democrat. **Established:** 1856.

Not Published: New Year; Memorial Day; Independence Day; Labor Day; Veteran's Day; Thanksgiving; Christmas.

Special Editions: Dollar Day (Feb); Dollar Day (Aug); Christmas (Nov); Fashions, Home Improvement, Great Outdoors (Spring); Fashions, Home Improvement, Back-to-School (Fall).

CORPORATE OFFICER

Publisher John C Hanafin

GENERAL MANAGEMENT

Business Manager John C Hanafin

ADVERTISING

Director Fred W Jones
Asst Manager Barbara Harms

NEWS EXECUTIVE

Editor Michelle Romanus

EDITOR AND MANAGER

Wire Editor Michelle Romanus

PRODUCTION

Superintendent James Keith

Mechanical available: Offset; Black and 3 ROP colors; insert accepted — preprinted; page cut-offs — 22¾".

Mechanical specifications: Type page 14" x E - 8 cols, 1.67", ⅛" between; A - 8 cols, 1.67", ⅛" between; C - 8 cols, 1.67", ⅛" between.

Commodity consumption: average pages per issue 28(d).

Equipment: EDITORIAL: Front-end hardware — 4-COM/MDT 350. PRODUCTION: Typesetters — 2-COM/2961HS, 1-COM/ACM9000; Plate exposures — 1-Nu; Production cameras — 1-DSA/Companica-640C; Automatic film processors — 1-Kk/324M. PRESSROOM: Line 1 — 4-G/Community. MAILROOM: Bundle tyer — 1-B; Addressing machine — 1-Am/1900. WIRE SERVICES: News — AP; Syndicates — NEA.

MACOMB

McDonough County

'90 U.S. Census- 19,952; E&P '96 Est. 20,041

Macomb Journal (e-mon to fri; S)

Macomb Journal, 120 N. Lafayette St., Macomb, IL 61455; tel (309) 833-2114; fax (309) 833-2346. Park Communications Inc. group.

Circulation: 7,450(e); 7,450(S); Sworn Sept. 29, 1995.

Price: 35¢(d); 75¢(S); $1.90/wk.

Advertising: Open inch rate $10.13(e); $10.13(S). **Representative:** Landon Associates Inc.

News Services: AP, LAT-WP, Sports Ticker. **Politics:** Independent. **Established:** 1855.

Not Published: Christmas Day (unless a Sunday).

Special Edition: Business News.

Special Weekly Sections: Best Food Day (wed); Entertainment (Happenings) (thur); Church (fri); Lifestyles, TV Section (Channels) (S).

GENERAL MANAGEMENT

General Manager Thomas E Hutson

ADVERTISING

Manager Lisa Maxwell

TELECOMMUNICATIONS

Audiotex Manager Tom Hutson

CIRCULATION

Manager Diane Moore

NEWS EXECUTIVE

Editor Thomas E Hutson

EDITOR AND MANAGER

News Editor Craig Kibler

PRODUCTION

Foreman-Pressroom Terry Roley

Market Information: TMC; Operate audiotex.

Mechanical available: Offset; Black and 3 ROP colors; insert accepted — preprinted; page cut-offs — 22¾".

Mechanical specifications: Type page 13" x 21½"; E - 6 cols, 2¹⁄₁₆", ⅛" between; A - 6 cols, 2¹⁄₁₆", ⅛" between; C - 10 cols, 1¼", ¹⁄₁₆" between.

Commodity consumption: Newsprint 427 metric tons; width 27½"; single pages printed 4,884; average pages per issue 14(d), 28(S).

Equipment: EDITORIAL: Front-end hardware — Mk, Ap/Power Mac 7100; Front-end software — Mk/NewsTouch AT, QuarkXPress, Microsoft/Word; Printers — Ap/Mac LaserWriter NTX, HP/LaserJet. CLASSIFIED: Front-end hardware — Mk; Printers — Ap/Mac LaserWriter NTX, TI/Omni 800. DISPLAY: Front-end hardware — Ap/Mac IIcs, Ap/Power Mac 70; Front-end software — Mk/Mycro-Comp AdWriter, Mycrolink, QuarkXPress, Multi-Ad/Creator; Printers — Ap/Mac LaserWriter NTX, Ap/Mac Pro 810; Other equipment — HP/ScanJet II cx. PRODUCTION: Pagination software — QuarkXPress 3.31; OCR software — TI/OmniPage Professional; Typesetters — Mk, Ap/Mac LaserWriter NTX, Ap/Mac Pro 810; Plate exposures — Ultra-Lite/5000; Scanners — HP/ScanJet IIcx; Production cameras — R; Automatic film processors — LD/220-QT; Color separation equipment (conventional) — Adobe/Photoshop. PRESSROOM: Line 1 — 7-G/Community. MAILROOM: Bundle tyer — 2-Bu. WIRE SERVICES: News — AP, LAT-WP, Sports Ticker; Receiving dishes — size-1m, AP, Sports Ticker. BUSINESS COMPUTERS: Applications: Vision Data; PCs & main system networked.

MARION

Williamson County

'90 U.S. Census- 19,952; E&P '96 Est. 20,041

The Marion Daily Republican (e-mon to fri; m-sat; S)

The Marion Daily Republican, 111-115 Franklin Ave.; PO Box 490, Marion, IL 62959; tel (618) 993-2626; fax (618) 993-8326. Hollinger International Inc. group.

Circulation: 4,545(e); 4,545(m-sat); Sworn Oct. 3, 1994.

Price: 50¢(d); 50¢(sat); $1.00(S); $116.40/yr.

Advertising: Open inch rate $11.95(e); $11.95(m-sat). **Representative:** Landon Associates Inc.

News Service: UPI. **Established:** 1913.

Note: The Marion Daily Republican is printed at American Publishing, West Frankfort, IL. Effective Mar. 14, 1995, this publication added a Sunday edition. Sunday circulation figure not made available at press time.

Not Published: New Year; Independence Day; Thanksgiving; Christmas.

Magazine: Buyer's Guide.

CORPORATE OFFICERS

President Larry J Perrotto
Comptroller Roland McBride

GENERAL MANAGEMENT

Publisher Sam Shelton
General Manager Nancy Sims

CIRCULATION

Manager Scott Shelton

NEWS EXECUTIVES

Managing Editor Wanda Brandon
Assoc Editor Bill Grimes

EDITOR AND MANAGER

City/News Editor Bill Grimes

PRODUCTION

Manager Steve Shelton

Market Information: TMC.

Mechanical available: Offset; Black and 4 ROP colors; insert accepted — preprinted, minimum 8 1/2" x 11"; page cut-offs — 21½".

Mechanical specifications: Type page 13" x 21½"; E - 6 cols, 2¹⁄₁₆", ⅛" between; A - 6 cols, 2¹⁄₁₆", ⅛" between; C - 8 cols, 1⅝", ¹⁄₁₆" between.

Commodity consumption: average pages per issue 16(d).

Equipment: EDITORIAL: Front-end hardware — 1-Ap/Mac II; Front-end software — Microsoft/Word; Printers — Ap/Mac LaserWriter II. CLASSIFIED: Front-end hardware — Ap/Mac; Front-end software — Baseview; Printers — Ap/Mac LaserWriter II. DISPLAY: Adv layout systems — Ap/Mac; Front-end hardware — 4-Ap/Mac; Front-end software — Aldus/PageMaker; Printers — Ap/Mac LaserWriter IIg; Other equipment — CD-Rom. PRODUCTION: Plate exposures — Nu/FT40U3VP; Plate processors — Roconex; Production cameras — B; Automatic film processors — AG/Rapidline 43; Color separation equipment (conventional) — Digi-Colour. MAILROOM: Bundle tyer — 2-Bu. LIBRARY: Combination — Recordak/Microfilm machine. WIRE SERVICES: News — AP; Syndicates — CT, United Media, TV Listings, King Features, Creators; Receiving dishes — size-3m, AP. BUSINESS COMPUTERS: 2-Club America/486; Applications: Nomads/Listmaster: Accts receivable, Circ.

MATTOON

Coles County

'90 U.S. Census- 18,441; E&P '96 Est. 18,052
ABC-CZ (90): 18,441 (HH 7,824)

Mattoon Journal-Gazette (m-mon to sat)

Mattoon Journal-Gazette, 100 Broadway, Mattoon, IL 61938; tel (217) 235-5656; fax (217) 235-1925. Howard Publications group.

Circulation: 11,969(m); 11,969(m-sat); ABC Sept. 30, 1995.

Illinois I-117

Price: 50¢(d); 50¢(sat); $2.05/wk; $26.65/13wk; $106.60/yr.
Advertising: Open inch rate $9.65(m); $9.65(m-sat); comb with Charleston Times Courier $12.70. **Representative:** Landon Associates Inc.
News Service: AP. **Politics:** Independent. **Established:** 1905.
Not Published: New Year; Memorial Day; Independence Day; Labor Day; Christmas.
Special Editions: Annual Farm Section (Jan); Annual Thanksgiving Day Edition (Nov).
Special Weekly Sections: Business News, Newspapers in Education (mon); About People (tues); Lifestyle-Food (wed); Farm Feature (thur); TV Section (fri); School News-Sports-Lifestyle (sat).
Magazine: TV.

CORPORATE OFFICER
President Robert S Howard
GENERAL MANAGEMENT
Publisher William B Hamel Jr
ADVERTISING
Director Robert S Yamamoto
CIRCULATION
Director Kolby Jensen
NEWS EXECUTIVE
News Editor Bill Lair
PRODUCTION
Manager Robert S Yamamoto
Foreman-Press Lonnie Gerrie

Mechanical available: Offset; Black and 3 ROP colors; insert accepted — preprinted; page cut-offs — 22¾".
Mechanical specifications: Type page 13" x 21½"; E - 6 cols, 2 1/16", .17" between; A - 6 cols, 2 1/16", .17" between; C - 9 cols, 1⅜", .12" between.
Commodity consumption: width 27½"; average pages per issue 26(d).
Equipment: EDITORIAL: Front-end hardware — 16-Sun/SLC, 4-Sun/Sparc II; Front-end software — Sun/Micro Sys, Unix/Arbotext; Printers — Copal/600, Ap/Mac LaserWriter NTX, ECR/1085. CLASSIFIED: Front-end hardware — 2-Sun/Sparc II, 3-NCD, 2-Sun/ECL; Front-end software — Island Write; Printers — 1-HP/IIIP. DISPLAY: Adv layout systems — SCS/Layout 8000; Front-end hardware — 7-Ap/Mac II, 2-Ap/Mac SE30, 1-Ap/Mac ci; Front-end software — QuarkXPress, Adobe/Photoshop; Printers — ECR/1085; Other equipment — 2-Ap/Mac CD-Rom. PRODUCTION: Pagination software — Quark XPress 3.3, SCS/Lynx 3.1; OCR software — Caere/OmniPro 5.0; Plate exposures — 1-Nu/FT40LNS; Plate processors — 1-Nat/A-250; Scanners — 2-HP/ScanJet Plus, 1-Truvell/Color, AG/Horizon; Production cameras — SCREEN/Companica 680C; Automatic film processors — 1-LE; Color separation equipment (conventional) — Nikon/3500, Lf/Leafscan 35.
PRESSROOM: Line 1 — 8-G/Community; Folders — 1-G. MAILROOM: Counter stackers — 1-BG/Count-O-Veyor 106; Inserters and stuffers — 2-MM/227E; Bundle tyer — 1-Bu/BT16, 2-MLN/ML2EE; Addressing machine — 2-Wm/5. WIRE SERVICES: News — AP; Stock tables — AP; Receiving dishes — size-10ft, AP. BUSINESS COMPUTERS: 1-Compaq/386, Sun/4110.

MOLINE-EAST MOLINE
Rock Island County
'90 U.S. Census- 63,349 (Moline 43,202; East Moline 20,147); E&P '96 Est. 61,362 (Moline 41,698; East Moline 19,664)
ABC-CZ (90): 140,203 (HH 56,269)

The Dispatch (m-mon to sat; S)
The Dispatch, 1720 5th Ave., Moline, IL 61265; tel (309) 764-4344; fax (309) 797-0311; web site http://www.qconline.com. Small Newspaper Group Inc. group.
Circulation: 28,247(m); 28,247(m-sat); 34,813(S); ABC Sept. 30, 1995.
Price: 50¢(d); 50¢(sat); $1.50(S); $2.70/wk; $10.80/mo; $140.40/yr.
Representative: Papert Companies.
News Services: KRT, INS, NYT, AP, IPS, NEA. **Politics:** Independent. **Established:** 1878.
Note: The Moline Dispatch (mS) has a combination rate of $38.25 (d) & $39.95 (S) with the Rock Island Argus (eS). Individual newspaper rates not made available. Effective Sept. 4, 1995, this publication changed its publishing plan from (e-mon to fri; m-sat; S) to (m-mon to sat; S).
Not Published: New Year; Memorial Day; Independence Day; Labor Day; Thanksgiving; Christmas.
Special Editions: Progress (Feb); Home Improvement (Apr); Vacation (May); Football Tab (Aug); Bridal Guide, College Opportunities (Sept); Car Care, Home Improvement (Oct); Holiday Cookbook (Nov); Holiday Gift Guide (Dec).
Special Weekly Sections: Best Food Day (wed, S); Entertainment Section (thur); Religion (sat); Business, Entertainment, Farm Page, Travel Page (S); TV Listings, Financial, Business (daily).
Magazines: TV Week (local, offset, quarterfold, combined with the Rock Island Argus); USA Weekend.

CORPORATE OFFICERS
Board Chairman Len Robert Small
Senior Vice Pres/Secretary Thomas P Small
Treasurer/Asst Secretary Joseph E Lacaeyse
GENERAL MANAGEMENT
Publisher Gerald J Taylor
Business Manager Scott Aswege
Personnel Officer Donna Herbig
Director-Special Projects Steve Flatt
ADVERTISING
Director-Marketing Al Roels
Director-Sales Tony Shelton
Manager-Inside Sales Val Yazbec
Manager-National Jon Melin
Coordinator-Classified Mike Ward
MARKETING AND PROMOTION
Manager-Promotion Sandy Percy
TELECOMMUNICATIONS
Audiotex Manager Steve Flatt
CIRCULATION
Director Joseph M Luethmers
Subscriber Service Manager Bob Moran
NEWS EXECUTIVES
Editor Gerald J Taylor
Managing Editor Russell A Scott
EDITORS AND MANAGERS
Agriculture Editor Pam Berenger
Auto Editor Rita Pearson
Business Editor Rita Pearson
Consumer Affairs Editor Joe Payne
Editorial Page Editor Kenda Burrows
Education Editor Judy Norris
Entertainment Editor Sean Leary
Environmental Editor Carolyn Hardin
Fashion/Style Editor Joe Payne
Features Editor Joe Payne
Films/Music Editor Sean Leary
Food Editor Elizabeth Meegan
Government Editor Carolyn Hardin
Graphics Editor/Art Director Kathy Bush
Health/Medical Editor Carolyn Hardin
Helping Hand Editor Barb Vandewiele
Librarian JoAnn Parmley
Lifestyle/Society Editor Joe Payne
Metro Editor Ron Sutton
News Editor Mike Romkey
Photo Director Terry Herbig
Radio/Television Editor Sean Leary
Religion Editor Judy Meirhaeghe
Science/Technology Editor Carolyn Hardin
Sports Editor Marc Nesseler
Travel Editor Sean Leary
Women's Editor Joe Payne
MANAGEMENT INFORMATION SERVICES
Data Processing Manager Sue Gramling
Online Manager Greg Booras
PRODUCTION
Director Daniel Wahlheim

Market Information: Zoned editions; Split Run; Operate database; Operate audiotex.
Mechanical available: Offset; Black and 3 ROP colors; insert accepted — preprinted; page cut-offs — 22¾".
Mechanical specifications: Type page 13" x 21½"; E - 6 cols, 2 1/16", ⅛" between; A - 6 cols, 2 1/16", ⅛" between; C - 9 cols, 1⅜", ⅛" between.
Commodity consumption: Newsprint 2,932 short tons; widths 55", 41¼", 27½", 13¾"; black ink 51,481 pounds; color ink 13,842 pounds; single pages printed 6,912; average pages per issue 39(d), 86(S); single plates used 27,442.
Equipment: EDITORIAL: Front-end hardware — 1-CText, 1-IBM; Front-end software — XYQUEST/XyWrite, QuarkXPress 3.3; Printers — Epson/Laser II; Other equipment — HP/ScanJet, PC/486. CLASSIFIED: Front-end hardware — 66-PC/486, 2-Gig/HD 16 Mega-Ram; Printers — Copal/600, Compex/420. AUDIOTEX: Hardware — Brite Voice Systems. DISPLAY: Adv layout systems — SCSI; Front-end hardware — PC/486-66; Front-end software — SCS/Layout 8000 6.6; Printers — HP/Laser II; Other equipment — 8-Ap/Mac. PRODUCTION: Pagination software — QuarkXPress 3.3; Typesetters — 2-Copal, 1-AG/Film 5000 Drum Recorder, CK Optical/6%, 1-Graphics Enterprises/Page Scan 18x24; Plate exposures — 1-B/5000, 1-Nu/FT; Plate processors — 1-Milart; Scanners — Lf/AP Leaf Picture Desk, AG; Production cameras — 2-C/Spartan, 1-Nu/V, 1-ECR/Autokon; Automatic film processors — 2-LE/24A, 1-LE/13; Color separation equipment (conventional) — 2-PC/486-66, Adobe/Photoshop 2.51; Digital color separation equipment — 2-PC/486-66, Adobe/Photoshop 2.51.
PRESSROOM: Line 1 — 7-HI/1650; Folders — 1-HI/3:2; Pasters — 6-HI/Registron; Reels and stands — 6-HI/Registron. MAILROOM: Counter stackers — 1-St/257; Bundle tyer — 3-MLN, 1-Md/Plastic Strapper; Addressing machine — 1-Ch/715. WIRE SERVICES: News — AP; Stock tables — AP; Syndicates — KRT, NYT; Receiving dishes — AP. BUSINESS COMPUTERS: 1-IBM/400, 10-IBM/PC; PCs & micros networked; PCs & main system networked.

MONMOUTH
Warren County
'90 U.S. Census- 9,489; E&P '96 Est. 8,715

Daily Review Atlas (e-mon to fri; m-sat)
Daily Review Atlas, 400 S. Main; PO Box 650, Monmouth, IL 61462; tel (309) 734-3176; fax (309) 734-7649. Hollinger International Inc. group.
Circulation: 3,416(e); 3,416(m-sat); Sworn Sept. 27, 1995.
Price: 50¢(d); 50¢(sat); $70.00/yr.
Advertising: Open inch rate $7.95(e); $7.95(m-sat). **Representative:** American Publishing Co.
News Service: AP. **Politics:** Independent. **Established:** 1924.
Not Published: New Year; Memorial Day; Independence Day; Labor Day; Christmas.
Special Editions: Farm; Bridal; Automotive; Lifetimes.
Magazines: Weekend Up Date (sat); Channel Guide-Television Guide Section (weekly); Senior Citizens Magazine (monthly).

CORPORATE OFFICERS
President Larry J Perrotto
Comptroller Roland McBride
GENERAL MANAGEMENT
Publisher/General Manager Scott Champion
ADVERTISING
Manager Scott Champion
CIRCULATION
Manager Gary Tomlin
NEWS EXECUTIVE
Editor John Stiles
PRODUCTION
Manager Barb Simmons

Market Information: TMC.
Mechanical available: Offset; Black and 3 ROP colors; insert accepted — preprinted; page cut-offs — 22¾".
Mechanical specifications: Type page 13" x 21½"; E - 6 cols, 2 1/16", ⅛" between; A - 6 cols, 1⅜", ⅛" between; C - 9 cols, 1⅜", 1/16" between.
Commodity consumption: Newsprint 103 short tons; widths 27½", 34"; black ink 14,000 pounds; color ink 2,600 pounds; single pages printed 3,696; average pages per issue 10(d); single plates used 3,696.
Equipment: EDITORIAL: Front-end hardware — 6-Mk. CLASSIFIED: Front-end hardware — 4-Ap/Mac. DISPLAY: Adv layout systems — Ap/Mac Desktop, Ap/Mac Plus. PRODUCTION: Pagination software — Baseview; Platemaking systems — LE; Plate processors — Dyn; Production cameras — 1-B. MAILROOM: Bundle tyer — 2-Bu; Addressing machine — 2-Am. WIRE SERVICES: News — AP; Syndicates — AP, NEA; Receiving dishes — size-10in, AP. BUSINESS COMPUTERS: 2-IBM/PC, AT; Applications: Accts receivable, Accts payable, Payroll, Gen ledger, Circ data base.

MORRIS
Grundy County
'90 U.S. Census- 10,270; E&P '96 Est. 11,521

Daily Herald (e-mon to fri)
Daily Herald, 1804 Division St.; PO Box 749, Morris, IL 60450-0749; tel (815) 942-3221; fax (815) 942-0988. Shaw Newspapers group.
Circulation: 7,173(e); Sworn Sept. 29, 1995.
Price: 50¢(d); $61.00/yr.
Advertising: Open inch rate $9.35(e).
News Service: AP. **Politics:** Republican. **Established:** 1878.
Not Published: New Year; Memorial Day; Independence Day; Labor Day; Thanksgiving; Christmas.
Special Editions: Football (Aug); Baketball (Nov).
Special Weekly Section: Sports Plus (mon).

GENERAL MANAGEMENT
Publisher Timothy J West
ADVERTISING
Manager Jon Ringer
CIRCULATION
Manager Lori Carlson
NEWS EXECUTIVES
Editor Timothy J West
Managing Editor Pete C Resler
EDITOR AND MANAGER
City Editor Pete C Resler

Market Information: TMC.
Mechanical available: Offset; Black and 3 ROP colors; insert accepted — preprinted, any; page cut-offs — 22¾".
Mechanical specifications: Type page 13" x 21½"; E - 6 cols, 2 1/16", ⅛" between; A - 6 cols, 2 1/16", ⅛" between; C - 8 cols, 1½", ⅛" between.
Commodity consumption: Newsprint 750 metric tons; widths 27½", 32", 34"; black ink 7,000 pounds; color ink 1,750 pounds; single pages printed 6,300; average pages per issue 24(d); single plates used 7,500.
Equipment: EDITORIAL: Front-end hardware — 1-Mk, Ap/Mac Scanner, 8-Ap/Mac; Front-end software — Baseview; Printers — 4-Ap/Mac LaserPrinter. CLASSIFIED: Front-end hardware — 3-Ap/Mac; Front-end software — Baseview. DISPLAY: Adv layout systems — 5-Ap/Mac; Front-end hardware — Ap/Mac; Front-end software — Multi-Ad/Creator; Printers — 1-Ap/Mac LaserPrinter. PRODUCTION: Pagination software — Baseview; Typesetters — 1-Ap/Mac LaserPrinter; Plate processors — 1-Ic; Production cameras — B.
PRESSROOM: Line 1 — 12-G; Folders — 2-G. MAILROOM: Counter stackers — 2-BG; Bundle tyer — 3-BU; Addressing machine — 3-Wm. WIRE SERVICES: News — AP; Receiving dishes — size-9m, AP. BUSINESS COMPUTERS: 3-Bs, Dell, 3-Ap/Mac; Applications: Circ, Accounting; PCs & micros networked.

MOUNT CARMEL
Wabash County
'90 U.S. Census- 8,287; E&P '96 Est. 8,117

Daily Republican Register (e-mon to fri)
Daily Republican Register, 115 E. 4th St.; PO Box 550, Mount Carmel, IL 62863; tel (618) 262-5144; fax (618) 263-4437. Brehm Communications Inc group.
Circulation: 4,192(e); Sworn Sept. 30, 1995.
Price: 50¢(d); $53.50/yr.
Advertising: Open inch rate $6.55(e). **Representative:** American Newspaper Representatives Inc.
News Service: AP. **Politics:** Independent. **Established:** 1839.
Not Published: New Year; Memorial Day; Independence Day; Labor Day; Thanksgiving; Christmas.
Special Editions: Progress, Soil Conservation (Jan); Sports (Feb); Spring Car Care (Mar); Home Improvement, Moonlight Madness, Lawn & Garden, Graduation (May); Brides, Little League (June); 4-H Edition (July); Ag Days, Wabash Valley College, Back-to-School (Aug); Fall Car Care, Today's Homes (Sept); Meet Your Merchant (Oct); Football, Grade School (Nov); Letters to Santa, Christmas Specials (Dec).

CORPORATE OFFICER

President — Jack Rodgers

GENERAL MANAGEMENT

Publisher — Jack Rodgers

ADVERTISING

Director — Sally Voigt

CIRCULATION

Manager — Linda Collins

NEWS EXECUTIVE

Editor — Phil Gower

Mechanical available: Offset; Black and 3 ROP colors; insert accepted — preprinted; page cut-offs — 22¾".

Mechanical specifications: Type page 13" x 21"; E - 6 cols, 2", 3/16" between; A - 6 cols, 2", 3/16" between; C - 8 cols, 1½", 1/9" between.

Commodity consumption: Newsprint 250 short tons; widths 27½", 13¾", 30"; black ink 10,000 pounds; color ink 500 pounds; single pages printed 9,000; average pages per issue 13(d); single plates used 5,500.

Equipment: EDITORIAL: Front-end hardware — Mk; Printers — 2-Ap/Mac LaserWriter. CLASSIFIED: Front-end hardware — Mk. DISPLAY: Front-end hardware — 2-Ap/Mac; Front-end software — Multi-Ad/Creator; Printers — Ap/Mac LaserWriter. PRODUCTION: Plate exposures — 1-Nu/Flip Top FT40LNS; Plate processors — 1-Ic; Production cameras — SCREEN; Automatic film processors — 1-LE. PRESSROOM: Line 1 — 4-G/C-141; Folders — 1-G/2:1. MAILROOM: Bundle tyer — 1-Sa/50; Addressing machine — Wm. WIRE SERVICES: News — AP; Receiving dishes — AP. BUSINESS COMPUTERS: 1-Qantel/232; Applications: Payroll, Accts payable, Accts receivable, Report Generator; PCs & micros networked; PCs & main system networked.

MOUNT VERNON

Jefferson County

'90 U.S. Census- 16,988; E&P '96 Est. 16,870
ABC-CZ (90): 16,988 (HH 7,127)

Register-News (e-mon to sat)

Register-News, 118 N. 9th St.; PO Box 489, Mount Vernon, IL 62864; tel (618) 242-0117; fax (618) 242-8286. Thomson Newspapers group.

Circulation: 11,904(e); 11,109 (e-tues to fri); 11,109(e-sat); ABC Sept. 30, 1995.

Price: 35¢(d); 35¢(sat); $7.50/mo; $22.00/3mo; $84.00/yr (mail).

Advertising: Open inch rate $11.50(e); $11.50(e-sat). **Representative:** Thomson Newspapers.

News Service: AP. **Politics:** Independent. **Established:** 1870.

Special Editions: Bridal Edition (Jan); Focus Edition (Feb); Home Improvement (Mar); Lawn & Garden (Apr); Mother's Day (May); Father's Day (June); Illinois Engine Show (July); Sweetcorn/Watermelon Festival (Aug); Cedar Craft Fair (Sept); Fall Home Improvement (Oct); Christmas Openings (Nov); Christmas (Dec).

Special Weekly Sections: Best Food Day (wed); TV Booklet, Business Section (fri); Church Page (sat); Comic Page, Lifestyle (daily).

GENERAL MANAGEMENT

General Manager — Charles E Deitz

ADVERTISING

Manager — Sarah Sledge

CIRCULATION

Manager — Mary Hodges

NEWS EXECUTIVE

Managing Editor — Terry Geese

EDITORS AND MANAGERS

City Editor — Paul Lorenz
Sports Editor — William Looby

PRODUCTION

Manager — Robert D Deitz

Market Information: Zoned editions; TMC.

Mechanical available: Offset; Black and 3 ROP colors; insert accepted — preprinted; page cut-offs — 22¾".

Mechanical specifications: Type page 13" x 21½"; E - 6 cols, 2 1/16", 1/8" between; A - 6 cols, 2 1/16", 1/8" between; C - 9 cols, 1⅜", 1/16" between.

Commodity consumption: average pages per issue 28(d).

Equipment: EDITORIAL: Front-end hardware — Mk/3000; Front-end software — Mk; Printers — Ap/Mac; Other equipment — Ap/Mac. CLASSIFIED: Front-end hardware — Mk/3000; Front-end software — Mk. PRODUCTION: Pagination software — Mk/Page 2.2; Typesetters — 2-V/4000; Plate exposures — 1-Nu; Plate processors — 1-Nu; Electronic picture desk — Lf/AP Leaf Picture Desk; Scanners — Lf/Leafscan 35, Ap/Mac, AVR; Production cameras — 1-A/V24; Automatic film processors — 1-P/24. PRESSROOM: Line 1 — 9-G/Community; Press drives — Fin; Folders — 1-G. MAILROOM: Bundle tyer — 1-Bu, 1-Malow; Addressing machine — 2-Am/1900. WIRE SERVICES: News — AP; Photos — AP; Receiving dishes — size-11ft, AP. BUSINESS COMPUTERS: HP; Applications: Accts payable, Accts receivable, Adv, Circ.

MURPHYSBORO

See CARBONDALE

NORMAL

See BLOOMINGTON

NORTH CHICAGO

See WAUKEGAN

OGLESBY

See LA SALLE

OLNEY

Richland County

'90 U.S. Census- 8,664; E&P '96 Est. 8,669

Olney Daily Mail (e-mon to fri; m-sat)

Olney Daily Mail, 206 Whittle Ave.; PO Box 340, Olney, IL 62450; tel (618) 393-2931; fax (618) 392-2953. Hollinger International Inc. group.

Circulation: 4,183(e); 4,183(m-sat); Sworn Sept. 20, 1994.

Price: 50¢(d); 50¢(sat); $9.00/mo; $90.00/yr.

Advertising: Open inch rate $10.20(e); $10.20(m-sat). **Representative:** American Publishing Co.

News Service: AP. **Politics:** Independent. **Established:** 1847.

Not Published: New Year; Memorial Day; Independence Day; Labor Day; Thanksgiving; Christmas.

Special Weekly Section: School Life (tues).

CORPORATE OFFICERS

President — Larry J Perrotto
Comptroller — Roland McBride

GENERAL MANAGEMENT

Publisher — Steve Raymond
Manager-Office — Cindy Brown
Manager-Composition — Alice Smith

ADVERTISING

Manager — Carol Lydle
Manager-Classified — Sherry Snyder

CIRCULATION

Manager — Joe Gardner

NEWS EXECUTIVE

Editor — Perry Dable

PRODUCTION

Foreman-Press — Tony Childers

Market Information: TMC.

Mechanical available: Offset; Black and 3 ROP colors; insert accepted — preprinted; page cut-offs — 21½".

Mechanical specifications: Type page 13" x 21½"; E - 6 cols, 2", 1/6" between; A - 6 cols, 2", 1/6" between; C - 8 cols, 1⅓-3/5-27/32-4⅔", 1/6" between.

Commodity consumption: Newsprint 200 short tons; widths 28", 22¾"; black ink 4,840 pounds; color ink 700 pounds; single pages printed 6,000; average pages per issue 14(d); single plates used 3,600.

Equipment: EDITORIAL: Front-end hardware — Ap/Mac Quadra 6100; Front-end software — Microsoft/Word, Aldus/PageMaker; Printers — Ap/Mac LaserWriter II. CLASSIFIED: Front-end hardware — IBM; Front-end software — TC; Printers — IBM. DISPLAY: Front-end hardware — Ap/Mac Quadra 6100; Front-end software — Aldus/PageMaker, Multi-Ad/Creator; Printers — Ap/Mac LaserPro 810. PRODUCTION: Production cameras — SCREEN. PRESSROOM: Line 1 — 5-G/Community. WIRE SERVICES: News — AP; Receiving dishes — AP. BUSINESS COMPUTERS: IBM.

OTTAWA

La Salle County

'90 U.S. Census- 17,451; E&P '96 Est. 16,995
ABC-CZ (90): 26,090 (HH 10,426)

The Daily Times (e-mon to fri; m-sat)

The Daily Times, 110 W. Jefferson St., Ottawa, IL 61350; tel (815) 433-2000. Small Newspaper Group Inc. group.

Circulation: 12,580(e); 12,580(m-sat); ABC Sept. 30, 1995.

Price: 35¢(d); 35¢(sat); $78.00/yr (carrier), $65.00/yr (mail).

Advertising: Open inch rate $10.10(e); $10.10(m-sat). **Representative:** Landon Associates Inc.

News Services: NEA, AP. **Politics:** Republican. **Established:** 1844.

Not Published: New Year; Memorial Day; Independence Day; Labor Day; Thanksgiving; Christmas.

Special Edition: Annual Progress Edition (Mar).

CORPORATE OFFICERS

Board Chairman — Len R Small
Senior Vice Pres/Secretary — Thomas P Small
Treasurer/Asst Secretary — Joseph E Lacaeyse

GENERAL MANAGEMENT

General Manager — James Malley
Asst General Manager — Joan A Heyers
Manager-Business — Gayle Elias

ADVERTISING

Director — Joan A Heyers

CIRCULATION

Director — Cynthia Liptak
Asst Manager — Ken McDonald

NEWS EXECUTIVE

Managing Editor — Lonny Cain

EDITORS AND MANAGERS

City Editor — Patrick Harrison
Farm Editor — Paul Carpenter
Photo Department Manager — Paul Carpenter
Sports Editor — Mike Cunniff
Wire Editor — Paul Carpenter

PRODUCTION

Foreman-Composing — Allen Stone
Foreman-Press — Richard Todd
Coordinator — Joe Briel

Market Information: TMC; ADS.

Mechanical available: Offset; Black and 3 ROP colors; insert accepted — preprinted, all; page cut-offs — 22¾".

Mechanical specifications: Type page 13" x 21½"; E - 6 cols, 2 1/16", 1/8" between; A - 6 cols, 2 1/16", 1/8" between; C - 10 cols, 1 3/16", 1/16" between.

Commodity consumption: Newsprint 850 metric tons; widths 27½", 13¾"; black ink 27,000 pounds; color ink 2,000 pounds; single pages printed 6,997; average pages per issue 23(d); single plates used 10,000.

Equipment: EDITORIAL: Front-end hardware — 13-Mk/Touchwriter, 2-Mk/Touchwriter Plus, Mk/1100 Plus, 3-Ap/Mac Quadra; Front-end software — Mk, TI/Omni Pace; Printers — TI/810; Other equipment — Ap/Mac LC III, Abaton/Scanner. CLASSIFIED: Front-end hardware — 2-Mk/Touchwriter Plus; Front-end software — Mk/Touchwriter Plus; Printers — TI/810. DISPLAY: Adv layout systems — Ap/Mac; Front-end hardware — 1-Ap/Mac IIfx, 2-Ap/Mac Quadra, 2-Ap/Mac Pro 630, 1-Ap/Mac Centris 610; Front-end software — Multi-Ad/Creator; Printers — 1-Ap/Mac Pro 630; Other equipment — CD-Rom, 6-Ap/Mac 630 Scanner, Nikon/3510 Slide Film Scanner, Pioneer/6 CD Player. PRODUCTION: Pagination software — QuarkXPress 3.3, Mk/Page 3.1.2; OCR software — TI/OmniPage 3.0; Typesetters — 2-CG/8400, 1-CG/9400, 2-Lynx/Ultra 94E, 1-QMS/2210, 1-Ap/Mac IIg, 2-Ap/Mac Laser Pro 630, 1-Lynx/Proofer 11 x 17; Plate exposures — Nu/Flip Top; Plate processors — Nat/250; Electronic picture desk — Lf/AP Leaf Picture Desk, Ap/Power Mac 8100; Scanners — 1-Abaton/Scanner, 2-Ap/Mac 630, 1-Nikon/3510 Slide Film Scanner; Production cameras — R/480, R/432; Automatic film processors — WL/Model 4, LE/LP 2600A. PRESSROOM: Line 1 — 6-G/Urbanite (Balloon former); Folders — 1-G/2:1; Press control system — Ch. MAILROOM: Bundle tyer — Bu/16", MLN/ML2; Wrapping singles — CH/Bottom Wrap; Addressing machine — 2-Sp/2605. WIRE SERVICES: News — AP Datafeatures, AP Datastream, AP Graphics; Photos — AP; Receiving dishes — size-3m, AP. BUSINESS COMPUTERS: 1-Magitronic, PC/386, 7-Wyse/Model 50; Applications: Adv billing, Accts receivable, Gen ledger, Payroll; PCs & micros networked; PCs & main system networked.

PARIS

Edgar County

'90 U.S. Census- 8,987; E&P '96 Est. 8,685

The Paris Daily Beacon-News (e-mon to sat)

Paris Daily Beacon-News, 218 N. Main St.; PO Box 100, Paris, IL 61944-0100; tel (217) 465-6424; fax (217) 463-1232.

Circulation: 5,542(e); 5,542(e-sat); Sworn Oct. 1, 1995.

Price: 40¢(d); 40¢(sat); $50.00/yr (mail).

Advertising: Open inch rate $5.80(e); $5.80(e-sat). **Representative:** Landon Associates Inc.

News Services: UPI, CNS. **Politics:** Independent-Republican. **Established:** 1848.

Not Published: New Year; Memorial Day; Independence Day; Labor Day; Thanksgiving; Christmas.

Special Editions: Christmas; Spring Opening; Back-to-School; Vacation.

CORPORATE OFFICERS

President — Edward H Jenison
Exec Vice Pres/Assoc Publisher — Ned Jenison
Treasurer — Marguerite J Pease

GENERAL MANAGEMENT

Publisher — Edward H Jenison
Assoc Publisher — Ned Jenison
Assoc Publisher — Kevin Jenison
General Manager — Elizabeth Brown
Purchasing Agent — Ned Jenison

ADVERTISING

Manager-General — Edward H Jenison

CIRCULATION

Director — Elizabeth Brown

NEWS EXECUTIVES

Editor — Edward H Jenison
Managing Editor — Nancy Garrett

EDITORS AND MANAGERS

Aviation Editor — Barbara Jenison
Farm Editor — Ned Jenison
News Editor — Ned Jenison
Photo Department Manager — Ned Jenison
School Editor — Ned Jenison
Sports Editor — Kevin Jenison

PRODUCTION

Foreman-Composing — Albert Hickman
Foreman-Press — William Graham
Foreman-Camera — Harry Perry

Mechanical available: Offset; Black and 3 ROP colors; insert accepted — preprinted; page cut-offs — 22¾".

Mechanical specifications: Type page 13¾" x 21"; E - 6 cols, 2 1/16", 1/8" between; A - 6 cols, 2 1/16", 1/8" between; C - 8 cols, 1⅜", 1/16" between.

Commodity consumption: Newsprint 170 short tons; width 30"; black ink 5,700 pounds; color ink 250 pounds; average pages per issue 12(d).

Equipment: EDITORIAL: Front-end hardware — Mk/550. CLASSIFIED: Front-end hardware — Mk/Touchwriter. PRODUCTION: Typesetters — COM/7900 Universal, Ap/Mac LaserWriter; Plate exposures — Nu/FT40L; Production cameras — 1-B, R, LE/500. PRESSROOM: Line 1 — 6-G/Community w/double former. MAILROOM: Counter stackers — 1-BG/Count-O-Veyor; Bundle tyer — 1-Bu; Addressing machine — 1-Dispensa-Matic. WIRE SERVICES: News — UPI; Syndicates — King Features, CNS; Receiving dishes — UPI.

PAXTON

Ford County

'90 U.S. Census- 4,289; E&P '96 Est. 4,461

Paxton Daily Record (e-mon to fri)

Paxton Daily Record, 218 N. Market St., Paxton, IL 60957; tel (217) 379-4313; fax (217) 379-3104.

Circulation: 1,245(e); Sworn Sept. 27, 1995.

Price: 25¢(d); $1.00/wk; $46.00/yr (carrier), $54.00/yr (mail in county).

Advertising: Open inch rate $6.10(e). **Politics:** Independent. **Established:** 1865.

Special Edition: Back-to-School (Aug).

Illinois I-119

CORPORATE OFFICERS

President William E Frye
Vice Pres Toni Swan
Secretary Darlos Phillips

GENERAL MANAGEMENT

Publisher Paul E Anderson
Purchasing Agent Tom McQuinn

ADVERTISING

Manager Toni Swan

CIRCULATION

Manager Cathy Younker

NEWS EXECUTIVES

Editor Robert Maney
News Editor David Hinton

PRODUCTION

Superintendent William E Frye

Mechanical available: Offset; Black and 1 ROP color; insert accepted — preprinted; page cut-offs — 21".
Mechanical specifications: Type page 13" x 21"; E - 6 cols, 2⅟16", ⅛" between; A - 6 cols, 2⅟16", ⅛" between; C - 5 cols, 1⅔", ⅙" between.
Commodity consumption: Newsprint 60 metric tons; widths 28", 14"; black ink 1,200 pounds; color ink 20 pounds; average pages per issue 6(d); single plates used 1,300.
Equipment: PRODUCTION: Typesetters — 1-COM/7900, 2-COM/2750, 1-COM/9000, Ap/Mac SE20; Platemaking systems — 1-Nu/Flip top; Production cameras — 1-Nu/20x24; Automatic film processors — AG/66.
PRESSROOM: Line 1 — 6-HI/V15A; Folders — 1-HI. MAILROOM: Counter stackers — 1-HI/Count-O-Veyor; Bundle tyer — 2-Bu; Addressing machine — 2-Am, KR. COMMUNICATIONS: Facsimile — Toshiba.

PEKIN

Tazewell County

'90 U.S. Census- 32,254; E&P '96 Est. 31,232
ABC-CZ (90): 32,254 (HH 13,078)

Pekin Daily Times

(e-mon to fri; m-sat)

Pekin Daily Times, 22 S. 4th St.; PO Box 430, Pekin, IL 61555; tel (309) 346-1111; fax (309) 346-9815. Howard Publications group.
Circulation: 14,565(e); 14,565(m-sat); ABC Sept. 30, 1995.
Price: 50¢(d); 50¢(sat); $1.85/wk; $89.00/yr.
Advertising: Open inch rate $12.40(e); $12.40(m-sat). **Representative:** Landon Associates Inc.
News Service: AP. **Politics:** Independent. **Established:** 1881.
Not Published: New Year; Memorial Day; Independence Day; Labor Day; Christmas.
Special Weekly Sections: Kid's Page (tues); Best Food Day, Home and Garden (wed); Religion, Farm Page (fri); Senior Citizens, Local Features (sat).

GENERAL MANAGEMENT

Publisher David C Simpson

ADVERTISING

Director Eleanor Gibbons
Manager-National Eleanor Gibbons

CIRCULATION

Manager Mike Vetroczky

NEWS EXECUTIVE

Managing Editor Tamara O'Shaughnessy

EDITORS AND MANAGERS

City Editor Terry O'Conner
Graphics Editor/Art Director Roland Millington
Sports Editor Jim Haas

MANAGEMENT INFORMATION SERVICES

Data Processing Manager Bonnie Boyd

PRODUCTION

Foreman-Press Brian Luckring
Manager-Systems Don Holder
Manager-Plant David C Simpson

Market Information: TMC.
Mechanical available: Offset; Black and 3 ROP colors; insert accepted — preprinted; page cut-offs — 22¾".
Mechanical specifications: Type page 13" x 21½"; E - 6 cols, 2⅟16", ⅛" between; A - 6 cols, 2⅟16", ⅛" between; C - 9 cols, 1⅜", ⅟16" between.
Commodity consumption: Newsprint 800 metric tons; width 27¼"; black ink 18,000 pounds; color ink 1,500 pounds; single pages printed 7,800; average pages per issue 25(d); single plates used 4,200.
Equipment: EDITORIAL: Front-end hardware — Sun/Sparc Station, 3-Ap/Mac IIci, Ap/Mac II. CLASSIFIED: Front-end hardware — 1-OS/40. DISPLAY: Adv layout systems — 5-Ap/Mac II. PRODUCTION: Typesetters — 1-COM/Universal, 2-Ap/Mac LaserWriter, Hyphen, ECR/Autokon, PelBox/1085; Plate exposures — 1-Nu; Plate processors — Nat; Scanners — Truvell/Scanner; Production cameras — 1-R/580; Automatic film processors — 2-LE/18; Digital color separation equipment — Nikon/Mac IIci. PRESSROOM: Line 1 — 7-G/Urbanite; Folders — 1-G; Reels and stands — 1-G/8. MAILROOM: Counter stackers — 2-Id/Marathon; Inserters and stuffers — 1-MM; Bundle tyer — 2-Bu/201; Wrapping singles — 1-Cr; Addressing machine — 1-Am, 1-Ch/527. WIRE SERVICES: News — NYT, AP; Photos — AP; Receiving dishes — size-8ft. BUSINESS COMPUTERS: 2-ATT/3B1, 1-Sun/Sparc 402; Applications: Circ, Adv billing, Accts receivable, Gen ledger, Payroll, Accts payable; PCs & micros networked; PCs & main system networked.

PEORIA

Peoria County

'90 U.S. Census- 113,504; E&P '96 Est. 107,020
ABC-CZ (90): 220,501 (HH 85,639)

Journal Star

(all day-mon to fri; m-sat; S)

Journal Star, 1 News Plz., Peoria, IL 61643; tel (309) 686-3000; e-mail xxnews@heartland.bradley.edu. Peoria Journal Star Inc. group.
Circulation: 76,724(a); 96,959(m-sat); 105,870(S); ABC Sept. 30, 1995.
Price: 50¢(d); 50¢(sat); $1.50(S); $3.80/wk; $187.20/yr.
Advertising: Open inch rate $57.80(a); $57.80(m-sat); $57.80(S). **Representative:** Cresmer, Woodward, O'Mara & Ormsbee.
News Services: AP, LAT-WP, SNS. **Politics:** Independent. **Established:** 1855.
Not Published: Christmas.
Special Weekly Sections: Kids (mon); Business (tues); Best Food Day (wed); Home Builder.
Magazines: Stock Listings (tues to thur); "Cue" Entertainment/Leisure Guide, Stock Listings (fri); Religion, Stock Listings (sat); Resort, Travel, Home Builders, TV Listings, Theater (S).

CORPORATE OFFICERS

Board Chairman Henry P Slane
President John T McConnell
Vice Pres Fred L Bergia
Treasurer Fred L Bergia

GENERAL MANAGEMENT

Publisher John T McConnell
Controller Ken Mauser
Business Manager Ken Mauser
Manager-Credit Jon Dunlap
Coordinator-Newspapers in Education Barbara Pierce
Personnel Manager John J Swingle
Purchasing Agent Jack Boatman

ADVERTISING

Director Carl Arrenius
Manager-Retail Dave Auer
Manager-Classified Becky Miller
Coordinator-National Lynn Thurman

MARKETING AND PROMOTION

Manager-Marketing Janet S Peterson

TELECOMMUNICATIONS

Manager-Info Systems Lynn Kavelman

CIRCULATION

Manager Lyle Andrews

NEWS EXECUTIVES

Managing Editor Jack Brimeyer
Asst Managing Editor Bonnie Vance
Asst Managing Editor-Photo/Graphic/Design Christine McNeal
Editor of Editorial Page Barb Mantz-Drake
Assoc Editor Shelley Epstein
Assoc Editor Mike Bailey

EDITORS AND MANAGERS

Action Line Editor Brenda Story
Arts Reporter Gary Panetta
Automotive Editor Paul Gordon
Business Editor Paul Gordon
City Editor-Day Jerry McDowell
City Editor-Night Bill Peak
Editorial Systems Editor Dennis Diamond
Education Editor Clare Howard
Entertainment/Amusements Editor Lori Timm
Environmental Editor Elaine Hopkins
Farm/Agriculture Editor Doug Freuhling
Fashion/Style Editor Sally McKee
Films/Theater Editor Gary Panetta
Health/Medical Editor Dean Olsen
Librarian Judy Howard
Living/Lifestyle Editor Sally McKee
Music Editor Gary Panetta
National Editor Toby Eckert
News Editor Kelly VanLaningham
Photo Editor Eric Behrens
Political/Government Editor Toby Eckert
Radio/Television Editor Mike Miller
Religion Editor Mike Miller
Science Technology Editor Tim Jamiolkowski
Sports Editor Kirk Wessler
Sunday Editor Nancy Trueblood
Travel Editor Nancy Trueblood

MANAGEMENT INFORMATION SERVICES

Data Processing Manager Lynn Kavelman

PRODUCTION

Manager Robert C Lane
Foreman-Press John Mason
Foreman-Mailroom Walt Adams
Foreman-Transportation Rick McDonald
Foreman-Composing John Johnson

Market Information: Zoned editions; Split Run; TMC; Operate audiotex.
Mechanical available: Letterpress; Black and 3 ROP colors; insert accepted — preprinted; page cut-offs — 22¾".
Mechanical specifications: Type page 13" x 21⅞"; E - 6 cols, 2⅟16", ⅛" between; A - 6 cols, 2⅟16", ⅛" between; C - 9 cols, 1⅜", ⅟16" between.
Commodity consumption: Newsprint 9,100 metric tons; widths 55", 41¼", 27½", 13¾"; black ink 275,000 pounds; color ink 50,500 pounds; single pages printed 17,331; average pages per issue 44(d), 67(S); single plates used 61,000.
Equipment: EDITORIAL: Front-end hardware — HI/NewsMaker; Front-end software — Newsmaker 2.44; CLASSIFIED: Front-end hardware — DEC/PDP 11-36, III/PPI TECS 2 Class Systems; Front-end software — HI: TECS 2. AUDIOTEX: Hardware — Brite; Supplier name — Brite, Accu-Weather, AP Stockquote II. DISPLAY: Adv layout systems — III; Front-end hardware — Sun/360, Sun/Sparc, Ap/Mac, Ap/Mac Centris; Front-end software — III, Multi-Ad/Creator. PRODUCTION: Pagination software — HI/2100 2.5; Typesetters — 2-III/3810P; Plate exposures — 1-MAS, 1-Na/Newsprinter; Electronic picture desk — Lf/AP Leaf Picture Desk; Scanners — 1-III, 5-Nikon; Production cameras — 1-B/24, 1-C/Newspager II; Automatic film processors — 2-LE/24, 1-AG; Film transporters — 1-C, 2-LE; Color separation equipment (conventional) — Ap/Mac Quadra, Adobe/Photoshop; Digital color separation equipment — 1-III.
PRESSROOM: Line 1 — 8-G/Headliner; Line 2 — 4-G/Headliner Mark I; Line 3 — 2-G/Color; Folders — 2-G/2:1, 1-G/3:2 Imperial; Pasters — Arco/conversion paster & tension; Reels and stands — G; Press control system — GE, Fin, Incom Inter Inc; Press registration system — Web Tech. MAILROOM: Counter stackers — 2-QWI/100, 3-QWI/300; Inserters and stuffers — 2-GMA/14-into-1, PTP; Bundle tyer — 4-Dynaric. LIBRARY: Electronic — Data Times. WIRE SERVICES: News — AP, States News Service, KRT; Photos — AP; Stock tables — AP; Receiving dishes — AP. BUSINESS COMPUTERS: IBM/AS-400 E-50; Applications: Circ, Payroll, Accts payable, Accts receivable; PCs & micros networked; PCs & main system networked.

PERU

See LA SALLE

PONTIAC

Livingston County

'90 U.S. Census- 11,428; E&P '96 Est. 11,585

The Daily Leader

(e-mon to fri; m-sat)

The Daily Leader, 318 N. Main St.; PO Box 170, Pontiac, IL 61764; tel (815) 842-1153; e-mail pontiacdl@aol.com. Hollinger International Inc. group.
Circulation: 6,545(e); 6,545(m-sat); Sworn Oct. 1, 1995.
Price: 50¢(d); 50¢(sat); $106.60/yr.
Advertising: Open inch rate $8.35(e); $8.35(m-sat). **Representative:** American Publishing Co.
News Service: AP. **Politics:** Independent. **Established:** 1880.
Not Published: New Year; Memorial Day; 4th of July; Labor Day; Christmas.
Special Edition: Progress (Mar).
Special Weekly Sections: Agriculture Page (tues); Business Page (thur).
Magazines: Weekly TV; Weekly Leisuretime.

GENERAL MANAGEMENT

Publisher R A Westerfield
Business Manager Linda Blair

ADVERTISING

Director Beth Nolan

CIRCULATION

Manager Roger Swearingen

NEWS EXECUTIVE

Managing Editor Pat Graziano

EDITOR AND MANAGER

Sports Editor Erich Murphy

PRODUCTION

Foreman-Composing Jeff Rushin
Foreman-Press/Camera Department Troy Eden

Market Information: TMC.
Mechanical available: Offset; Black and 3 ROP colors; insert accepted — preprinted; page cut-offs — 22¾".
Mechanical specifications: Type page 13" x 21½"; E - 6 cols, 2⅟16", ⅛" between; A - 6 cols, 2⅟16", ⅛" between; C - 8 cols, 1½", ¼" between.
Commodity consumption: Newsprint 700 short tons; widths 27", 34"; black ink 20,000 pounds; color ink 3,000 pounds; single pages printed 10,000; average pages per issue 14(d), 10(sat); single plates used 6,000.
Equipment: EDITORIAL: Front-end hardware — Ap/Mac; Front-end software — Baseview; Printers — 2-Ap/Mac LaserWriter NTX; Other equipment — 2-Ap/Mac IIsi. CLASSIFIED: Front-end hardware — 2-Ap/Mac III, Mk; Front-end software — CAMS, Multi-Ad. DISPLAY: Front-end hardware — 2-Ap/Mac Centris 610; Front-end software — Multi-Ad/Creator, QuarkXPress; Printers — Ap/Mac LaserWriter Pro 630. PRODUCTION: Plate exposures — 2-B/2332; Plate processors — 1-Nat; Production cameras — 1-R/580, 1-VG/POS-1-CPS; Automatic film processors — 1-AG/Rapidline 66.
PRESSROOM: Line 1 — 6-G/Community; Line 2 — Cole/Rotary Trimmer; Folders — 1-G, 1-Cole. MAILROOM: Counter stackers — 1-BG/Count-O-Veyor; Bundle tyer — 2-Bu, 2-Malow; Addressing machine — 1-MG/1530. COMMUNICATIONS: Systems used — satellite. WIRE SERVICES: News — AP; Stock tables — AP; Receiving dishes — AP. BUSINESS COMPUTERS: Wa, Bs.

QUINCY

Adams County

'90 U.S. Census- 39,681; E&P '96 Est. 37,944
ABC-CZ (90): 50,591 (HH 19,923)

The Quincy Herald-Whig

(e-mon to fri; m-sat; S)

The Quincy Herald-Whig, 130-38 S. 5th; PO Box 909, Quincy, IL 62306-0909; tel (217) 223-5100; fax (217) 223-9757; e-mail whig@cis.net; web site http://www.cis.net/~whig. Quincy Newspapers Inc. group.
Circulation: 25,074(e); 25,074(m-sat); 29,313(S); ABC Sept. 30, 1995.
Price: 50¢(d); 50¢(sat); $1.25(S); $10.30/mo; $13.65/3mo (S only); $112.00/yr.
Advertising: Open inch rate $25.03(e); $25.03(m-sat); $25.76(S). **Representative:** Landon Associates Inc.
News Service: AP. **Politics:** Independent. **Established:** 1835.
Not Published: New Year; Memorial Day; Independence Day; Labor Day; Thanksgiving; Christmas.
Advertising not accepted: All advertising subject to publisher's approval.
Special Editions: Car Care, Focus on the Future (Mar); Home Improvement (Apr); Football, Home Improvement, Fashion (Sept); Car Care (Oct); Basketball (Nov); Business Extra (monthly); Blueprints (quarterly).
Special Weekly Sections: Food (wed); Entertainment, Comics (S).
Magazines: TV Week Mini Book (sat); Parade (S).

I-120 Illinois

Broadcast Affiliates: KTIV-TV Sioux City, IA; WGEM-AM/WGEM-FM Quincy, IL; WGEM-TV Quincy, IL; WSJV-TV Elkhart, IN; WSJV-TV South Bend, IN; KTTC-TV Rochester, MN; WVVA-TV Bluefield, WV.

CORPORATE OFFICERS

President/Publisher Thomas A Oakley
Vice Pres-Newspaper Operations James W Collins
Asst Treasurer David A Graff

GENERAL MANAGEMENT

Publisher Thomas A Oakley
Business Manager Julian Boone
Controller David A Graff
Manager-Education Service Sue Welch

ADVERTISING

Manager-Classified Randi Smith
Manager-Retail Mel Envanoff

MARKETING AND PROMOTION

Manager-Promotion/Research Bruce Tomlinson

CIRCULATION

Manager P A Oakley

NEWS EXECUTIVES

Editor Joseph I Conover
Managing Editor Michael B Hilfrink

EDITORS AND MANAGERS

Amusements Editor Holly Wagner
Business Editor Tom Saul
Farm Editor Debbie Gertz
Fashion/Style Editor Betty Moritz
Films/Theater Editor Holly Wagner
Health/Medical Editor Kelly Wilson
Home Section/Food Editor Betty Moritz
Librarian Judy Nelson
News Editor Doug Wilson
Photo Department Manager Joe Liesen
Political (Senior Writer, Editorial Asst) John Webber
Radio/Television Editor Holly Wagner
Sports Editor Don Crim
Sunday Editor Michael B Hilfrink
Women's Editor Betty Moritz
Youth Page Editor Helen Warning

PRODUCTION

Superintendent Rudie Schappat
Foreman-Composing Led Luttrell
Foreman-Press Robert Romeo
Foreman-Mailroom Rick Rose

Market Information: Split Run; TMC; Operate audiotex; Electronic edition.
Mechanical available: Offset; Black and 3 ROP colors; insert accepted — preprinted; page cut-offs — 22.05".
Mechanical specifications: Type page 13" x 21"; E - 6 cols, 2¹⁄₁₆", ⅛" between; A - 6 cols, 2¹⁄₁₆", ⅛" between; C - 9 cols, 1⅜", ¹⁄₁₆" between.
Commodity consumption: Newsprint 1,550 metric tons; widths 27", 13.25"; black ink 42,000 pounds; color ink 16,500 pounds; single pages printed 9,900; average pages per issue 22(d), 52(S); single plates used 20,500.
Equipment: EDITORIAL: Front-end hardware — Dewar; Front-end software — Dewar; Printers — Panasonic/1180; Other equipment — Ap/Mac. CLASSIFIED: Front-end hardware — Dewar; Front-end software — Dewar; Printers — Okidata/192; Other equipment — 6-Dewar. AUDIOTEX: Hardware — SMS; Supplier name — Voice News Network. DISPLAY: Adv layout systems — Ap/Mac; Front-end hardware — 5-Ap/Mac 650 Centris; Front-end software — Multi-Ad/Creator, QuarkXPress; Printers — 2-LaserMaster/1000, Compaq/20. PRODUCTION: Typesetters — Compaq/Plain Paper, 2-Compaq/PageMark 20; Platemaking systems — Nu; Plate exposures — Nu; Plate processors — Nat; Electronic picture desk — Lf/AP Leaf Picture Desk; Scanners — Microtek, Microtek/600ZS Scanner; Production cameras — R; Automatic film processors — LE/PC13; Reproportion units — R; Color separation equipment (conventional) — WDS.
PRESSROOM: Line 1 — 8-G/Urbanite; Press drives — Fin; Folders — 1-G; Press control system — HL. MAILROOM: Counter stackers — BG/109; Inserters and stuffers — KAN/480; Bundle tyer — MLN/330, MLN/LS 300; Mailroom control system — 1-MM/Stitcher Trimmer 948125. LIBRARY: Electronic — SMS/Electronic Library. COMMUNICATIONS: Digital ad delivery system — AP Fast Fax. Systems used — satellite. WIRE SERVICES: News — AP; Receiving dishes — size-10ft, AP. BUSINESS COMPUTERS: IBM/Sys 36; Applications: INSI; PCs & micros networked; PCs & main system networked.

ROBINSON

Crawford County

'90 U.S. Census- 6,740; E&P '96 Est. 6,577

Robinson Daily News

(e-mon to fri; m-sat)

Robinson Daily News, 302 S. Cross St.; PO Box 639, Robinson, IL 62454; tel (618) 544-2101; fax (618) 544-9533. Lewis Newspapers group.
Circulation: 6,877(e); 6,877(m-sat); Sworn Sept. 30, 1995.
Price: 35¢(d); 35¢(sat); $1.25/wk; $5.00/mo; $59.00/yr.
Advertising: Open inch rate $7.50(e); $7.50(m-sat); comb with Lawrenceville Daily Record (e) $12.50.
News Service: AP. **Established:** 1919.
Not Published: New Year; Memorial Day; Independence Day; Labor Day; Thanksgiving; Christmas.
Advertising not accepted: Vending machine; work at home.
Special Editions: Bridal Pages (Jan); Tax Guide (Feb); Agriculture (Mar); America Home (Apr); Heath Toffee Festival (May); 4-H Fair (July); LTC Section (Aug); Robinson Fall Festival (Sept); Working Woman (Oct); Christmas Gift, Veterans Salute (Nov); Holiday Recipe Guide (Dec).
Special Weekly Section: What's On (TV Listing) (fri).

CORPORATE OFFICERS

President Larry H Lewis
Secretary/Treasurer Kathy Lewis

GENERAL MANAGEMENT

Publisher Larry H Lewis
Business Manager Kathy Lewis

ADVERTISING

Director Wally Dean
Manager-Classified Dinah Corder
Manager-National Larry Gullett

CIRCULATION

Manager-Promotion Bob Fox

NEWS EXECUTIVE

Managing Editor Byron Tracy

EDITORS AND MANAGERS

Picture Editor Byron Tracy
Sports Editor Tim Brooks

MANAGEMENT INFORMATION SERVICES

Data Processing Manager Winnie Piper

PRODUCTION

Foreman-Press Bill Holloway

Mechanical available: Offset; Black and 4 ROP colors; insert accepted — preprinted; page cut-offs — 22¾".
Mechanical specifications: Type page 13" x 21"; E - 6 cols, 2¹⁄₁₆", ⅛" between; A - 6 cols, 2¹⁄₁₆", ⅛" between; C - 9 cols, 1½", ⅛" between.
Commodity consumption: average pages per issue 16(d).
Equipment: EDITORIAL: Front-end hardware — 7-Mk, 7-Ap/Mac; Front-end software — Baseview, QuarkXPress, Adobe/Photoshop; Printers — Xante, LaserMaster/Unity. CLASSIFIED: Front-end hardware — Ap/Mac; Printers — Xante, LaserMaster/Unity, QMS. DISPLAY: Adv layout systems — Ap/Mac; Front-end hardware — Ap/Mac; Front-end software — Multi-Ad/Creator, QPS, Adobe/Photoshop, Adobe/Illustrator; Printers — Xante, LaserMaster/Unity. PRODUCTION: Typesetters — 2-COM/Unisetter, 1-COM/4961, 1-COM/7200; Plate exposures — 1-Nu/FT40; Production cameras — 1-B/Caravel; Automatic film processors — 1-LE.
PRESSROOM: Line 1 — 6-G/Community; Folders — 1-G/2:1. MAILROOM: Counter stackers — 1-BG/Count-O-Veyor; Bundle tyer — 2-Bu; Addressing machine — 1-Am/Speed-umat 2600. WIRE SERVICES: News — AP; Syndicates — CNS; Receiving dishes — AP. BUSINESS COMPUTERS: Mk, Ap/Mac; Applications: Bookkeeping, Circ, Billing; Baseview; PCs & micros networked; PCs & main system networked.

ROCK FALLS
See STERLING

ROCK ISLAND

Rock Island County

'90 U.S. Census- 40,552; E&P '96 Est. 36,538
ABC-CZ (90): 140,703 (HH 56,269)

The Rock Island Argus

(m-mon to sat; S)

The Rock Island Argus, 1724 4th Ave.; PO Box 3160, Rock Island, IL 61204-3160; tel (309) 786-6441; fax (309) 786-7639; web site http://www.qconline.com. Small Newspaper Group Inc. group.
Circulation: 13,583(m); 13,583(m-sat); 16,269(S); ABC Sept. 30, 1995.
Price: 50¢(d); 50¢(sat); $1.50(S); $2.70/wk; $10.80/mo; $140.40/yr.
Representative: Papert Companies.
News Services: AP, NEA, NYT, KRT, Bloomberg. **Politics:** Independent. **Established:** 1851.
Note: Effective Sept. 4, 1995, this publicaton changed its publishing plan from (e-mon to fri; m-sat; S) to (m-mon t sat; S). The Rock Island Argus (mS) has a combination rate of $38.25 (d) & $39.95 (S) with the Moline Dispatch (mS). Individual newspaper rates not made available.
Not Published: Christmas.
Special Editions: Progress (Feb); Home Improvement (Apr); Vacation (May); Football (Aug); College Opportunities, Bridal Guide (Sept); Car Care, Home Improvement (Oct); Holiday Cookbook (Nov); Gift Guide (Dec).
Special Weekly Sections: Best Food Day (wed); Entertainment (thur); Church Page (sat); Farm Page, Best Food Days, Television Section, Travel Page, Entertainment (S); Financial Page, Business Section (daily).
Magazines: "TV Week" (combined with Moline Dispatch), USA Weekend (S).

CORPORATE OFFICERS

Board Chairman Len R Small
Senior Vice Pres/Secretary Thomas P Small
Treasurer/Asst Secretary Joseph E Lacaeyse

GENERAL MANAGEMENT

Publisher Gerald J Taylor
Business Manager Scott Aswege
Personnel Officer Donna Herbig

ADVERTISING

Director-Marketing Al Roels
Director-Sales Tony Shelton
Manager-National Jon Melin
Coordinator-Classified Val Yazbec

MARKETING AND PROMOTION

Manager-Promotion Sandy Percy

TELECOMMUNICATIONS

Audiotex Manager Steve Flatt

CIRCULATION

Director Joseph M Luethmers
Subscriber Service Manager Bob Moran

NEWS EXECUTIVE

Managing Editor Roger Ruthhart

EDITORS AND MANAGERS

Action Line Editor Barb Vandewiele
Auto/Aviation Editor Rita Pearson
Business Editor Steve Jagler
Columnist John Mark
Editorial Page Editor Murray Hancks
Education Editor Judy Norris
Entertainment/Amusements Editor Sean Leary
Environmental Writer Katie Schallert
Farm Editor Pam Berenger
Fashion/Features Editor Joe Payne
Films/Theater Editor Sean Leary
Finance Editor Steve Jagler
Food Editor Elizabeth Meegan
Garden/Women's Editor Joe Payne
Graphics Editor Kathy Bush
Librarian JoAnn Parmley
Living/Lifestyle Editor Joe Payne
Medical Editor John Kanthak
Metro Editor Ron Sutton
Asst Metro Editor Carolyn Hardin
Asst Metro Editor Steve Jagler
Music Editor Sean Leary
Photo Department Manager Terry Herbig
Religion Editor Judy Meirhaeghe
Sports Editor Marc Nesseler
State Editor Judy Norris
Travel Editor Joe Payne

MANAGEMENT INFORMATION SERVICES

Data Processing Manager Sue Gramling
Online Manager Greg Booras

PRODUCTION

Director Daniel Wahlheim

Market Information: Split Run; ADS; Operate database; Operate audiotex.
Mechanical available: Offset; Black; insert accepted — preprinted; page cut-offs — 22¾".
Mechanical specifications: Type page 13" x 21½"; E - 6 cols, 2¹⁄₁₆", ⅛" between; A - 6 cols, 2¹⁄₁₆", ⅛" between; C - 9 cols, 1⅜", ⅛" between.
Commodity consumption: Newsprint 1,420 short tons; widths 41¼", 27½"; black ink 24,785 pounds; color ink 6,318 pounds; single pages printed 16,912; average pages per issue 39(d), 86(S); single plates used 18,920.
Equipment: EDITORIAL: Front-end hardware — 1-CText; Front-end software — XYQUEST/XyWrite, QuarkXPress 3.3; Printers — Epson/Laser II; Other equipment — HP/ScanJet, PC/486-66. CLASSIFIED: Front-end hardware — PC/486-66; Front-end software — Ward-Vision; Other equipment — Copal/600, Comrex/420. AUDIOTEX: Hardware — Brite Voice Systems. DISPLAY: Adv layout systems — SCS; Front-end hardware — PC/486-66; Front-end software — SCS/Layout 8000 6.60; Printers — HP/Laser II; Other equipment — 9-Ap/Mac. PRODUCTION: Pagination software — QPS 3.3; OCR software — Adobe/Photoshop 2.5.1; Typesetters — 2-Copal, 2-AG/Film 500; Plate exposures — 1-B/5000, 1-Nu/FT; Plate processors — 1-Milart; Scanners — Lf/Leafscan 35, AG/Horizon; Production cameras — 2-C/Spartan, 1-Nu/V, 1-ECR/Autokon; Automatic film processors — 2-LE/24A, 1-LE/13; Shrink lenses — CK Optical/6%; Color separation equipment (conventional) — 2-PC/486-66; Digital color separation equipment — 2-PC/486-66.
PRESSROOM: Line 1 — 7-HI/1650; Folders — 2-HI/3:2; Pasters — 6-HI/Registron; Reels and stands — 6-HI/Registron. MAILROOM: Counter stackers — 1-ST/257; Bundle tyer — 3-MLN, 1-Md/Plastic Strapper; Addressing machine — 1-Ch/715. WIRE SERVICES: News — AP; Photos — AP; Stock tables — AP; Syndicates — KRT, NYT, NEA, Bloomberg; Receiving dishes — AP. BUSINESS COMPUTERS: 1-IBM/400, 10-IBM; PCs & micros networked; PCs & main system networked.

ROCKFORD

Winnebago County

'90 U.S. Census- 139,426; E&P '96 Est. 139,417
ABC-NDM (90): 287,940 (HH 109,200)

Rockford Register Star

(m-mon to sat; S)

Rockford Register Star, 99 E. State St., Rockford, IL 61104; tel (815) 987-1200; fax (815) 962-6578/961-5820; web site http://sinnfree.org/sinnfreetree/rrs/rrshp.html. Gannett Co. Inc. group.
Circulation: 75,218(m); 75,218(m-sat); 87,833(S); ABC Sept. 30, 1995.
Price: 50¢(d); 50¢(sat); $1.50(S); $3.25/wk (carrier); $169.00/yr.
Advertising: Open inch rate $66.10(m); $66.10(m-sat); $79.82(S). **Representative:** Gannett National Newspaper Sales.
News Services: AP, GNS, Times Mirror, KRT. **Politics:** Independent.
Special Editions: 55 Plus, Real Estate Marketplace (monthly).
Special Weekly Sections: Business Monday (mon); Food and Fitness (wed); Wheels, Go (fri); Saturday At Home (sat); Escape-Travel & Entertainment, Real Estate, What's On TV, Insight, Business (S).
Magazine: Rockford Magazine.

CORPORATE OFFICERS

President John J Curley
Secretary Thomas L Chapple
Treasurer Jimmy L Thomas

GENERAL MANAGEMENT

Publisher Mary P Stier
Controller Michael Seeber
Director-Human Resources Diane Killion
Manager-Data Systems Allen Goodman

ADVERTISING

Director Margaret Buchanan
Manager-Retail Michele Massoth
Manager-Classified/National Reginald Cowie

CIRCULATION

Director Rufus Friday
Manager Jim Robertson
Manager-Home Delivery Esther Martin
Manager-Single Copy Sales Steve Costello

NEWS EXECUTIVES

Exec Editor Linda G Cunningham
Managing Editor C W Johnson
Asst Managing Editor/Operations Wally Haas
Asst Managing Editor Scott Faust

EDITORS AND MANAGERS

City Editor Belinda Stewart

Illinois I-121

Editorial Page Editor Wayne Peterson
Features Editor Doug Gaff
Graphics Editor Keith Grace
News Editor Bob Satnan
Neighbors Editor Dave Shultz
Sports Editor Randy Ruef

MANAGEMENT INFORMATION SERVICES

Data Processing Manager Allen Goodman

PRODUCTION

Director-Operations Paul Mollway
Manager-Building Service Jim O'Connell
Manager-Pressroom Larry Cramer
Manager-Distribution Center Tom Hickey
Manager-Technical Service Brian Harrington
Manager-Pre Press Kris Smith
Coordinator Jay Casey

Market Information: Zoned editions; TMC.
Mechanical available: Letterpress (direct); Black and 3 ROP colors; insert accepted — preprinted; page cut-offs — 22¾".
Mechanical specifications: Type page 13" x 21½"; E - 6 cols, 2¹⁄₁₆", ⅛" between; A - 6 cols, 2¹⁄₁₆", ⅛" between; C - 10 cols, 1³⁄₁₆", ³⁄₃₂" between.
Commodity consumption: Newsprint 8,267 short tons; 7,500 metric tons; widths 54¾", 41¼", 27½"; black ink 270,000 pounds; color ink 54,500 pounds; single pages printed 17,300; average pages per issue 40(d), 80(S); single plates used 48,800.
Equipment: EDITORIAL: Front-end hardware — SII/Synthesis 66XR; Front-end software — SII. CLASSIFIED: Front-end hardware — CSI/DEC 1184; Front-end software — CSI. DISPLAY: Adv layout systems — Ap/Mac; Front-end hardware — 13-Ap/Mac; Front-end software — QuarkXPress, Multi-Ad/Creator; Printers — QMS/2210, Tektronics/Phaser 300I; Other equipment — 8-Logitech/Scan Man Scanners. PRODUCTION: Typesetters — 2-MON/82E, 1-Hyphen/3100; Platemaking systems — Na; Plate exposures — Na/Starlite; Plate processors — Na/NP40; Electronic picture desk — Lf/AP Leaf Picture Desk; Scanners — AG/Arcus, DS/SG737, Nikon; Production cameras — C/Spartan II, C/Spartan III; Automatic film processors — 2-LE/2600A, 1-LE/1800A; Digital color separation equipment — SCREEN/DS 737, Nikon/3510 AF, Microtek/60.
PRESSROOM: Line 1 — 8-H/Colormatic; Folders — 2-H; Reels and stands — 8-H; Press control system — Fin. MAILROOM: Counter stackers — 2-HL/Monitor HT, 1-Id/NS440; Inserters and stuffers — HI/1372 (14 heads); Bundle tyer — 2-Dynaric; Wrapping singles — Bu; Addressing machine — Ch/525E. LIBRARY: Electronic — Alpha/4 3.0. WIRE SERVICES: News — LAT-WP, AP, GNS, CNS, KRT; Photos — AP, GNS; Stock tables — AP SelectStox I; Receiving dishes — AP. BUSINESS COMPUTERS: 11-IBM/AS-400; Applications: Lotus 5.0; PCs & micros networked; PCs & main system networked.

ROCKTON
See BELOIT, WI

SHELBYVILLE
Shelby County

'90 U.S. Census- 4,943; E&P '96 Est. 4,875

Daily Union (e-mon to fri)

Daily Union, 100 W. Main St., Shelbyville, IL 62565; tel (217) 774-2161; fax (217) 774-5732.
Circulation: 4,295(e); Sworn Oct. 20, 1994.
Price: 25¢(d); $50.00/yr.
Advertising: Open inch rate $6.80(e).
News Service: AP. **Politics:** Independent. **Established:** 1864.
Not Published: New Year; Independence Day; Labor Day; Thanksgiving; Christmas.
Special Edition: Recreation Sections (Apr to Aug).

GENERAL MANAGEMENT

Publisher George Frazier

CIRCULATION

Manager George Frazier

NEWS EXECUTIVE

Editor George Frazier

Market Information: TMC.
Mechanical available: Offset; Black; insert accepted — preprinted; page cut-offs — 22½".
Mechanical specifications: Type page 15½" x 21½"; E - 7 cols, 2¹⁄₁₆", ⅛" between; A - 7 cols, 2¹⁄₁₆", ⅛" between; C - 7 cols, 1⅝", ⅛" between.
Commodity consumption: average pages per issue 28(d).
Equipment: EDITORIAL: Front-end hardware — PC; Front-end software — CText; Printers — Ap/Mac. CLASSIFIED: Front-end hardware — PC; Front-end software — CText; Printers — Ap/Mac. DISPLAY: Adv layout systems — 1-Ap/Mac; Front-end hardware — Ap/Power Mac; Front-end software — Multi-Ad/Creator; Printers — Ap/Mac. PRODUCTION: Plate exposures — 1-Nu; Production cameras — 1-K, 1-C. PRESSROOM: Line 1 — 3-G/Community; Folders — 1-G/Community. MAILROOM: Bundle tyer — 2-Bu. WIRE SERVICES: News — AP; Receiving dishes — AP. BUSINESS COMPUTERS: IBM; Applications: Accts receivable, Billing; PCs & micros networked.

SOUTH BELOIT
See BELOIT, WI

SPRING VALLEY
See LA SALLE

SPRINGFIELD
Sangamon County

'90 U.S. Census- 105,227; E&P '96 Est. 110,058
ABC-CZ (90): 127,696 (HH 54,329)

The State Journal-Register
(m-mon to sat; S)

The State Journal Register, 1 Copley Plz.; PO Box 219, Springfield, IL 62705-0219; tel (217) 788-1300; fax (217) 788-1352. Copley Press Inc. group.
Circulation: 66,870(m); 66,870(m-sat); 76,184(S); ABC Sept. 30, 1995.
Price: 35¢(d); 35¢(sat); $1.25(S); $2.85/wk; $12.35/mo; $136.24/yr.
News Services: CNS, AP, NYT, SHNS. **Politics:** Independent. **Established:** 1831.
Note: The State Journal-Register (mS) has a combination rate of $44.77 with the Lincoln Courier (e). Individual newspaper rate for State Journal Register not made available.
Special Editions: Business Outlook (Jan); Active Times (Feb); Home Builders Tab, Spring Home Improvement (Mar); Lawn & Garden Tab (Apr); Mother's Day Tab, Active Times (May); Academic Excellence, Father's Day Tab, Corvette Tab, Visitor's Guide (June); Percent Off Tab, Active Times (July); State Fair Tab, State Farm Rail Classic (Aug); Fall Home Improvement (Sept); Active Times (Oct); Wrap It Up Early, Festival of Trees, Christmas Gifts (Nov); Last Minute Gifts, First Night Springfield (Dec).
Special Weekly Section: Best Food Day (wed).
Magazines: Entertainment (thur); Heartland (fri); TV Update (sat); Travel, Parade (S); Puck, The Comic Weekly (weekly).

GENERAL MANAGEMENT

Publisher John P Clarke
Business Manager David Adami

ADVERTISING

Manager Gary Kreppert
Manager-Display Charles Choate
Manager-Classified William Charlton
Manager-General Joe Fitzgerald

MARKETING AND PROMOTION

Manager-Promotion Nancy F Evans

CIRCULATION

Manager Robert Titone

NEWS EXECUTIVES

Editor J Stephan Fagan
Managing Editor Patrick Coburn
Deputy Managing Editor Barry J Locher

EDITORS AND MANAGERS

Business Editor Chris Dettro
City Editor Dana Heupel
Assoc City Editor Mike Kienzler
Asst City Editor Gary Schieffer
Features Editor Paul Povse
Food Editor Charlyn Fargo
Senior News Editor Ted Wolf
Chief Photographer Bill Hagen
Director-Photography Robert Pope
Radio/Television Editor Matt Dietrich
Sports Editor Jim Ruppert

MANAGEMENT INFORMATION SERVICES

Data Processing Manager Ron Bird

PRODUCTION

Manager J Robert Pavich
Foreman-Composing Pete Rooney
Foreman-Press Al Meier
Foreman-Camera/Platemaking Marvin Mantei
Foreman-Mailroom Del Van Dyke

Market Information: Split Run; TMC; Electronic edition.
Mechanical available: Offset; Black and 3 ROP colors; insert accepted — preprinted; page cut-offs — 22¾".
Mechanical specifications: Type page 13" x 21¼"; E - 6 cols, 2¹⁄₁₆", ⅛" between; A - 6 cols, 2¹⁄₁₆", ⅛" between; C - 9 cols, 1⅜", ¹⁄₁₆" between.
Commodity consumption: Newsprint 5,400 metric tons; width 55"; black ink 130,000 pounds; color ink 55,000 pounds; single pages printed 4,400; average pages per issue 28(d), 72(S); single plates used 57,000.
Equipment: EDITORIAL: Front-end hardware — AT/Series 60; Front-end software — AT/Series 60; Printers — 1-Florida Data. CLASSIFIED: Front-end hardware — AT/Series 60; Front-end software — AT/Series 60; Printers — 1-Florida Data. DISPLAY: Adv layout systems — AT/Architect; Front-end hardware — Sun; Front-end software — AT/Series 60; Printers — AST. PRODUCTION: Pagination software — AT/ Classified Pagination; Typesetters — 2-Express Master/1200; Plate exposures — WL/Lithoflex-X-Pozer V; Plate processors — 1-W/Plate Processor, 1-Polychrome/48; Electronic picture desk — Lf/AP Leaf Picture Desk; Scanners — 2-ECR/Autokon 1000; Production cameras — 1-C/Spartan, 1-C/Marathon; Automatic film processors — 1-Polychrome/37, 1-Polychrome/26, 1-LE/F64, 1-Glunz & Jensen/ 26"; Film transporters — 1-III/3850; Digital color separation equipment — 2-Diadem/ 210S, 1-Diadem/410.
PRESSROOM: Line 1 — 9-G/Metro (5 color deck); Folders — 2-G/3:2; Pasters — 9-G; Reels and stands — 9-G; Press control system — 1-G/PCS. MAILROOM: Counter stackers — 2-QWI; Inserters and stuffers — 1-Fg/10:1; Bundle tyer — 4-Power Strap; Addressing machine — 2-AVY/On-line. COMMUNICATIONS: Digital ad delivery system — AP AdSend. WIRE SERVICES: News — AP; Stock tables — AP; Syndicates — CNS, NYT, Cox, SHNS; AP. BUSINESS COMPUTERS: 3-DEC/VAX 8650; Applications: Adv, Class, Newsprint, Circ, Payroll.

STERLING-ROCK FALLS
Whiteside County

'90 U.S. Census- 24,786 (Sterling 15,132; Rock Falls 9,654); E&P '96 Est. 23,491 (Sterling 14,432; Rock Falls 9,059)
ABC-CZ (90): 30,412 (HH 11,883)

The Daily Gazette
(e-mon to fri; m-sat)
Sauk Valley Sunday (S)

The Daily Gazette, 312 2nd Ave; PO Box 498, Sterling, IL 61081; tel (815) 625-3600; fax (815) 625-9390. Shaw Newspapers group.
Circulation: 14,423(e); 14,423(m-sat); 13,813(S); ABC Sept. 30, 1995.
Price: 35¢(d); 35¢(sat); $1.00(S); $2.25/wk; $9.75/mo; $112.50/yr.
Advertising: Open inch rate $12.25(e); $12.25(m-sat); $12.25(S). **Representative:** Landon Associates Inc.
News Services: AP, United Media Service, SHNS. **Politics:** Independent. **Established:** 1854.
Not Published: New Year; Memorial Day; Independence Day; Labor Day; Thanksgiving; Christmas.
Special Editions: Car Care, Home Improvement (Fall & Spring); Brides; Tax Guide; Graduation; Progress Edition; Industrial Expo; Low Riders; Christmas Recipe; Welcome Spring; Whiteside County Fair; Football-Basketball Season Previews; Mexican Fiesta; Senior Echo; Ask the Expert; Preparing for Death; Today's Farm (quarterly).
Special Weekly Sections: Women's Page (tues); Best Food Day (wed); Farm Page, Auto (thur); Outdoor Look (sat); Expanded Lifestyles, Sports & Business (S).
Magazines: "Channels" (TV listings, etc.) (fri); Color Comics (S).

GENERAL MANAGEMENT

Publisher William E Shaw
Accountant Dianna Johnson
General Manager J W Nelson

ADVERTISING

Director Gary Bright

MARKETING AND PROMOTION

Director-Marketing John Rung

CIRCULATION

Manager Doug Maxwell

NEWS EXECUTIVES

Exec Editor Mike Chapman
Managing Editor Jonie Larson

EDITORS AND MANAGERS

Business/Finance Editor Bill Inks
Lifestyle Editor Maggie Rohwer
News Editor Mike Egenes
Photo Editor Barry Blitzsten
Sports Editor Mike Renkes

PRODUCTION

Foreman-Composing Norman Day
Foreman-Press Larry Bowlin

Market Information: TMC.
Mechanical available: Offset; Black and 3 ROP colors; insert accepted — preprinted, any; page cut-offs — 22.75".
Mechanical specifications: Type page 13" x 21½"; E - 6 cols, 2.06", .15" between; A - 6 cols, 2.06", .15" between; C - 6 cols, 2.06", .15" between.
Commodity consumption: Newsprint 1,020 short tons; widths 27½", 14"; black ink 30,800 pounds; color ink 5,400 pounds; single pages printed 8,780; average pages per issue 22(d), 26(S); single plates used 5,100.
Equipment: EDITORIAL: Front-end hardware — CD; Front-end software — CD; Printers — V; Other equipment — CD, Ap/Mac. CLASSIFIED: Front-end hardware — CD; Front-end software — CD; Printers — V. DISPLAY: Adv layout systems — Ap/Mac; Front-end hardware — Ap/Mac Centris 610; Front-end software — Multi-Ad/Creator. PRODUCTION: Typesetters — LaserMaster/Unity 1200XLO; Plate exposures — 2-B/Ultra-Lite 5000; Plate processors — Nat/A-250; Electronic picture desk — Lf/AP Leaf Picture Desk; Production cameras — Nu/SST 1822 LC; Automatic film processors — Carnfeldt, SCREEN/LD220QT.
PRESSROOM: Line 1 — 4-WPC; Line 2 — 4-WPC; Folders — 2-WPC; Reels and stands — Web Leader; Press control system — Avtek. MAILROOM: Bundle tyer — MLN/ML1-EE. WIRE SERVICES: News — THO, AP; Stock tables — AP; Syndicates — AP, United Media; Receiving dishes — size-3ft, AP. BUSINESS COMPUTERS: ATT/3B2500; Applications: Unix.

STREATOR
La Salle County

'90 U.S. Census- 14,121; E&P '96 Est. 13,694
ABC-CZ (90): 18,571 (HH 7,381)

Streator Times-Press
(e-mon to sat)

Streator Times-Press, 115 Oak St., Streator, IL 61364; tel (815) 673-3771; fax (815) 672-9332. Small Newspaper Group Inc. group.
Circulation: 8,897(e); 8,897(e-sat); ABC Sept. 30, 1995.
Price: 35¢(d); 35¢(sat).
Advertising: Open inch rate $9.69(e); $10.47(e-wed); $9.69(e-sat). **Representative:** Landon Associates Inc.
News Service: AP. **Politics:** Republican. **Established:** 1873.
Not Published: New Year; Memorial Day; Independence Day; Labor Day; Thanksgiving; Christmas.

CORPORATE OFFICERS

Board Chairman Len R Small
Senior Vice Pres/Secretary Thomas P Small
Treasurer/Asst Secretary Joseph E Lacaeyse

GENERAL MANAGEMENT

General Manager Cynthia J Liptak

ADVERTISING

Director Joan A Heyers
Manager-Sales Anne Hinterlong

CIRCULATION

Manager John Babczak

NEWS EXECUTIVE

Managing Editor James Russell

EDITORS AND MANAGERS

City Editor Don Hrabal
Editorial Page Editor James Russell
Photo Department Manager Paula Gillman
Sports Editor Harold Olson
Women's Editor Delia Hillyer

Market Information: TMC.

I-122 Illinois

Mechanical available: Offset (Printed in Ottawa, IL); Black and 3 ROP colors; insert accepted — preprinted; page cut-offs — 22¾".
Mechanical specifications: Type page 12.17" x 21½"; E - 6 cols, 2¹⁄₁₆", ⅛" between; A - 6 cols, 2¹⁄₁₆", ⅛" between; C - 10 cols, 1⅛", ⅛" between.
Equipment: EDITORIAL: Front-end hardware — 12-Mk; Printers — TI/810. CLASSIFIED: Front-end hardware — 2-Mk; Printers — TI/810. DISPLAY: Adv layout systems — Ap/Mac; Front-end hardware — 1-Ap/Mac IIfx, Ap/Mac IIsi; Front-end software — Multi-Ad/Creator, QuarkXPress, Broderbund/Typestyler; Printers — OMS/2210 LaserPrinter 11x17. PRODUCTION: Electronic picture desk — Lf/AP Leaf Picture Desk; Scanners — Epson, Abaton; Production cameras — 1-B/500L, R/500L; Automatic film processors — LE/LD 2600A-Loopline. MAILROOM: Bundle tyer — 2-Bu; Wrapping singles — 1-Cr/1255-263L; Addressing machine — 1-Am/2605, 1-Am/2600. WIRE SERVICES: News — AP. BUSINESS COMPUTERS: 1-IMS/Televideo.

TAYLORVILLE
Christian County
'90 U.S. Census- 11,133; E&P '96 Est. 10,976
ABC-CZ (90): 12,769 (HH 5,299)

The Taylorville Daily Breeze-Courier
(e-mon to fri; S)

The Taylorville Daily Breeze-Courier, 212 S. Main St.; PO Box 440, Taylorville, IL 62568; tel (217) 842-2233; fax (217) 824-2026.
Circulation: 6,941(e); 6,966(S); ABC Sept. 30, 1995.
Price: 35¢(d); 75¢(S); $6.50/mo; $65.00/yr.
Advertising: Open inch rate $7.50(e); $7.50(S). **Representative:** Landon Associates Inc.
News Service: AP. **Politics:** Independent. **Established:** 1894.
Not Published: New Year; Thanksgiving; Christmas.
Advertising not accepted: Publisher reserves the right to reject any questionable ads.
Special Editions: Tax Tab (Jan); Senior Citizens (Feb); Agriculture (Mar); Home Improvement, Lawn & Garden (Apr); Bridal (June); County Fair (July); Back-to-School (Aug); Fall Home Improvement (Sept); Car Care, Bridal (Oct); Winter Sports, Antique Tab (Nov); Christmas, First Baby (Dec).
Special Weekly Sections: Entertainment, TV Tab (S).
Magazine: TV Guide (12 page tab) (fri).

CORPORATE OFFICERS
President — James F Cooper
Exec Vice Pres — Wilda Quinn Cooper
Secretary — John Robert Cooper

GENERAL MANAGEMENT
Publisher — James F Cooper
Business Manager — Marylee Lasswell
General Manager-Treasurer — Marylee Lasswell
Manager-Credit — Cleo E Thacker
Personnel Manager — John Robert Cooper
Purchasing Agent — Marylee Lasswell

ADVERTISING
Director — Joe Dorr

TELECOMMUNICATIONS
Audiotex Manager — Cindy Emrick

CIRCULATION
Director — John Broux

NEWS EXECUTIVE
Editor — John Robert Cooper

EDITORS AND MANAGERS
City Editor — John Robert Cooper
Features Editor — Elizabeth Bergsteid
News Editor — John Robert Cooper
Sports Editor — Jeff Hill

PRODUCTION
Manager — Richard Thacker

Market Information: Zoned editions; Split Run; Operate audiotex.
Mechanical available: Offset; Black and 3 ROP colors; insert accepted — preprinted, any size; page cut-offs — 21".
Mechanical specifications: Type page 13" x 21"; E - 6 cols, 2¹⁄₁₆", ⅛" between; A - 6 cols, 2¹⁄₁₆", ⅛" between; C - 9 cols, 1¾", ⅛" between.
Commodity consumption: average pages per issue 28(d), 62(S).
Equipment: EDITORIAL: Front-end hardware — Ap/Mac; Front-end software — Baseview, QPS, Adobe/Photoshop; Printers — MON, Ap/Mac LaserWriters; Other equipment — Microtek/Scanner, Nikon/Coolscan, Kk/DCS200 Digital camera. CLASSIFIED: Front-end hardware — Ap/Mac; Front-end software — Baseview; Printers — MON. AUDIOTEX: Hardware — Samsung; Software — SMS/Stauffer Gold. DISPLAY: Adv layout systems — Ap/Mac; Front-end hardware — Ap/Mac; Front-end software — QPS; Printers — Ap/Mac LaserWriter II NTX; Other equipment — Ap/Mac CD-Rom, Ap/Mac Scanner. PRODUCTION: Typesetters — 1-COM; Platemaking systems — 1-B/1500; Plate exposures — 1-B/1500; Electronic picture desk — Lf/AP Leaf Picture Desk; Production cameras — 1-B/Caravel; Automatic film processors — 1-LE; Color separation equipment (conventional) — 1-lc.
PRESSROOM: Line 1 — 4-G/Community; Folders — 1-G. MAILROOM: Inserters and stuffers — 2-MM/227-E, 2-MM/277; Bundle tyer — 1-Bu/7; Addressing machine — 1-Am. WIRE SERVICES: News — AP; Photos — AP; Receiving dishes — AP. BUSINESS COMPUTERS: Ap/Mac; Applications: QPS, Adobe/Photoshop, TI/OmniPage, Baseview.

URBANA
See CHAMPAIGN

WAMAC
See CENTRALIA

WATSEKA
Iroquois County
'90 U.S. Census- 5,424; E&P '96 Est. 5,513

Iroquois County's Times-Republic (e-mon to fri)

Iroquois County's Times-Republic, 1492 E. Walnut St.; PO Box 250, Watseka, IL 60970; tel (815) 432-5227; fax (815) 432-5159. Nixon Newspapers Inc. group.
Circulation: 3,001(e); Sworn Sept. 29,1995.
Price: 50¢(d); $91.00/yr (carrier), $72.50/yr (mail in county), $91.00/yr (mail in state), $104.00/yr (mail out of state).
Advertising: Open inch rate $5.76(e). **Representative:** Nixon Newspapers.
News Service: AP. **Politics:** Independent-Republican. **Established:** 1870.
Not Published: New Year; Memorial Day; Independence Day; Labor Day; Thanksgiving; Christmas.
Advertising not accepted: Adoptions unless by a laywer.
Special Editions: Twin State Farmer; Twin State News & Views (quarterly); Bridal Edition (3x/yr).

CORPORATE OFFICER
President — John R Nixon

GENERAL MANAGEMENT
Publisher — Bette D Schmid
General Manager — Carol M Christy

ADVERTISING
Director — Randy Jones
Manager-Classified — Randy Jones

CIRCULATION
Director — Don Trammell

NEWS EXECUTIVE
Editor — Carla Waters

EDITOR AND MANAGER
News Editor — Charles Schuttrow

PRODUCTION
Manager — Carol Christy

Market Information: Zoned editions; Split Run; TMC.
Mechanical available: Offset; Black and 2 ROP colors; insert accepted — preprinted, single sheets; page cut-offs — 15".
Mechanical specifications: Type page 10¼" x 14"; E - 6 cols, 1.58", ⅙" between; A - 6 cols, 1.58", ⅙" between; C - 6 cols, 1.58", ⅙" between.
Commodity consumption: Newsprint 340 metric tons; widths 30", 35", 17½", 15"; black ink 12,000 pounds; color ink 500 pounds; single pages printed 3,820; average pages per issue 20(d); single plates used 6,000.
Equipment: EDITORIAL: Front-end hardware — 6-Ap/Mac; Front-end software — Ap/Mac, Baseview/NewsEdit; Printers — 1-Xante/Accel-a-Writer 8200, 1-Compaq/Pagemark. CLASSIFIED: Front-end hardware — 1-Ap/Mac, 1-Ap/Mac; Front-end software — Ap/Mac, Baseview/Class Manager Plus, QuarkXPress; Printers — 1-Ap/Mac Laser, 1-Compaq/Pagemark. DISPLAY: Adv layout systems — 4-Ap/Mac, 2-Ap/Mac Centris 610, 1-Ap/Mac Centris 650, 1-Ap/Mac IIcx; Front-end hardware — Ap/Mac II; Front-end software — Multi-Ad/Creator, Microsoft/Word; Printers — 1-Xante/Accel-a-Writer 8200, 1-Compaq/Pagemark; Other equipment — CD-Rom, HP/Scanner. PRODUCTION: Pagination software — QuarkXPress 3.3; OCR software — TI/OmniPage 2.12; Typesetters — 1-Xante/Accel-a-Writer 8200, 1-Compaq/PageMark; Plate exposures — 1-Nu; Plate processors — 1-Nat; Production cameras — 1-Nu, 1-R; Automatic film processors — 1-LE.
PRESSROOM: Line 1 — 4-KP/Newsking; Folders — 1-R. MAILROOM: Counter stackers — 1-CH; Bundle tyer — 4-Bu; Addressing machine — 1-Ch. LIBRARY: Electronic — 1-Multi-Ad, 1-Metro, 1-Classified, Dynamics. COMMUNICATIONS: Facsimile — 1-DEC/VAX 460, 1-Sharp. WIRE SERVICES: News — AP; Receiving dishes — size-2ft, AP. BUSINESS COMPUTERS: 2-IBM/Sys 36; Applications: Bookkeeping.

WAUKEGAN-NORTH CHICAGO
Lake County
'90 U.S. Census- 104,370 (Waukegan 69,392; North Chicago 34,978); E&P '96 Est. 103,424 (Waukegan 70,898; North Chicago 32,526)
ABC-CZ (90): 82,207 (HH 29,279)

The News-Sun
(e-mon to fri; wknd)

The News-Sun, 100 W. Madison St., Waukegan, IL 60085; tel (708) 336-7000; fax (708) 249-7246. Copley Press Inc. group.
Circulation: 34,319(e); 38,555(wknd); ABC Sept. 30, 1995.
Price: 35¢(d); $1.00(wknd); $2.50/wk (carrier); $130.00/yr (carrier).
Advertising: Open inch rate $35.53(e); $35.53(wknd). **Representative:** Sawyer-Ferguson-Walker Co.
News Services: AP, CNS, SHNS, NYT. **Politics:** Independent. **Established:** 1892.
Special Editions: Wedding Planner, Money Matters (Jan); Customer Appreciation, Chicago Auto Show Guide, Valentine's Messages, Health and Fitness, Coupon Book (Feb); 1996 Lake County Progress Edition, Spring Car Care, Spring Home Improvement, Baseball/Softball, Spring Dining Guide (Mar); Home Energy Guide, Easter Church Directory I & II, Spring Home and Garden Section (Apr); 1996 Salmon Classic, Summer Fun Guide, In Memoriams (May); Libertyville Days, Mundelein Days (June); Zion Nostalgia Days, Vernon Hills Days, Grayslake Centennial, Jet Ski, Customer Appreciation (July); Back-to-School, Gurnee Days, 1996 Prep Football Guide (Aug); Fall Homes & Furnishings, Health & Fitness, Fall Coupon Book (Sept); Fall Car Care Guide, Natural Gas Tab, National Business Women's Week (Oct); Holiday Gift Guide, 1996 Prep Basketball Guide, Coupon Book (Nov); Last Minute Gift Guide, Holiday Traditions, Spirit of Christmas, 1996 Year in Review (Dec).
Special Weekly Sections: Night & Day (thur); Auto Showcase, Football Weekend (fri).
Magazines: Weekend Color Comics (sat); Television Magazine; USA Weekend Magazine.

CORPORATE OFFICERS
Chairman of the Board/CEO (Copley Press Inc.) — Helen K Copley
President/Exec Comm/Director (Copley Press Inc.) — David C Copley
Exec Vice Pres/Chief Financial Officer (Copley Press Inc.) — Charles F Patrick
President (Fox Valley Press Inc.) — Arthur E Wible

GENERAL MANAGEMENT
Publisher (The News-Sun) — Robert C Propernick

ADVERTISING
Manager-Sales — John Rung
Manager-Classified — Gail Robinson

MARKETING AND PROMOTION
Manager-Marketing & Promotion — John Belmont

CIRCULATION
Manager — Lynne Schaefer

NEWS EXECUTIVES
Editor — Donald G Asher
Exec Editor — D G Schumacher
Managing Editor — Charles Selle
Asst Managing Editor-Lake County — Roxann Marshburn
Asst Managing Editor-Systems/Administration — Chris Cashman
Asst Managing Editor-News — Jon Drummond

EDITORS AND MANAGERS
City Editor — Chris Brenner
Education Editor — Chris Brenner
Entertainment/Amusements Editor — Wendy Fox Weber
Fashion/Style Editor — Wendy Fox Weber
Features Editor — Wendy Fox Weber
Librarian — Barbara Apple
Living/Lifestyle Editor — Wendy Fox Weber
News Editor — Dick Walter
Opinion Page Editor — D G Schumacher
Sports Editor — Dan O'Shea
Television/Film Editor — Dan Moran
Theater/Music Editor — Dan Moran
Women's Editor — Wendy Fox Weber

PRODUCTION
Manager-Prepress — Frank Zorc

Market Information: Zoned editions; TMC.
Mechanical available: Offset; Black and 3 ROP colors; insert accepted — preprinted, single sheet flyers; page cut-offs — 22".
Mechanical specifications: Type page 13" x 21"; E - 6 cols, 2¹⁄₁₆", ⅛" between; A - 6 cols, 2¹⁄₁₆", ⅛" between; C - 10 cols, 1³⁄₁₆", ⅛" between.
Equipment: EDITORIAL: Front-end hardware — SII/CLX Non-Stop; Front-end software — Tandem, SII/EDIT; Printers — 4-Centronics/351; Other equipment — 3-RSK/TRS 1000, 3-SII/Coyote PC, 46-SII/Coyote terminal, Ap/Mac 8100, Howtek/Scanner. CLASSIFIED: Front-end hardware — SII/CLX Non-Stop; Front-end software — SII/Class, Tandem; Printers — 1-CText/515; Other equipment — 10-SII/Coyote terminal. DISPLAY: Adv layout systems — CJ; Front-end hardware — CJ; Front-end software — CJ 7.01G; Printers — DEC/Server 17; Other equipment — Data/Plus PC. PRODUCTION: Typesetters — 2-AU/APS-Micro 5, 2-AU/APS-Micro 6, 2-AU/APS-6000 Proofers; Electronic picture desk — 1-Lf/AP Leaf Picture Desk; Scanners — 1-ECR/Autokon 1000, 1-ECR/Autokon 2030, 1-Howtek/4500; Production cameras — 2-B; Automatic film processors — 3-C, 2-P/OL260; Film transporters — 2-P/JC2050; Digital color separation equipment — 1-RZ/220S. LIBRARY: Electronic — 1-DEC/8800. COMMUNICATIONS: Facsimile — 1-III/3750 InfoScan Laser Scanner; Digital ad delivery system — AP AdSend. WIRE SERVICES: News — AP, CNS, NYT, SHNS; Photos — AP, AP Graphics; Syndicates — NEA, Universal Press, CNS, United Media, Creators; Receiving dishes — size-12ft, AP. BUSINESS COMPUTERS: 1-DEC/6610, 1-DEC/7610; Applications: DEC/VAX-VMS, CJ: Circ; CJ: Adv; CJ: Layout; PCs & micros networked; PCs & main system networked.

WEST FRANKFORT
Franklin County
'90 U.S. Census- 8,526; E&P '96 Est. 8,204

The Daily American
(e-mon to sat)

The Daily American, 101-115 S. Emma St.; PO Box 617, West Frankfort, IL 62896; tel (618) 932-2146; fax (618) 937-6006. Hollinger International Inc. group.
Circulation: 3,375(e); 3,375(e-sat); Sworn Oct. 31, 1995.
Price: 50¢(d); 75¢(sat); $2.40/wk; $9.50/mo.
Advertising: Open inch rate $7.00(e); $7.00(e-sat). **Representative:** American Publishing Co.
News Service: AP. **Politics:** Independent. **Established:** 1916.
Not Published: Christmas; Independence Day.
Special Editions: Bridal (Jan); Progress (Feb); Old King Coal (June); Home Improvement (Oct); Homes (monthly).
Special Weekly Section: TV Guide.
Magazines: American Weekend, USA Weekend, Sports Saturday (sat).

CORPORATE OFFICERS
President — Larry J Perrotto
Comptroller — Roland McBride

GENERAL MANAGEMENT
Publisher — G David Green

ADVERTISING
Manager — Diann Walthes

CIRCULATION
Manager — Donna Pearson

NEWS EXECUTIVE
Editor — Bob Ellis

Indiana　　　　　　　　　　　　　　　　　　　　　I-123

PRODUCTION
Manager — Steve Triest
Market Information: TMC; ADS.
Mechanical available: Offset; Black and 4 ROP colors; insert accepted — preprinted; page cut-offs — 21½".
Mechanical specifications: Type page 13¾" x 21½"; E - 6 cols, 2¹⁄₁₆", ⅛" between; A - 6 cols, 2¹⁄₁₆", ⅛" between; C - 8 cols, 1½", ⅛" between.
Commodity consumption: average pages per issue 28(d), 28(sat).
Equipment: EDITORIAL: Front-end hardware — Ap/Mac 610, Ap/Mac 605; Front-end software — QPS, Multi-Ad Creator, Microsoft, Adobe/Photoshop; Printers — Ap/Mac 630. CLASSIFIED: Front-end hardware — IBM. DISPLAY: Adv layout systems — Ap/Mac 650, Ap/Mac 800; Front-end software — QPS, Multi-Ad/Creator, Adobe/Photoshop; Printers — Ap/Mac 630; Other equipment — Ap/Mac Scanner, V/ImageSetter. PRODUCTION: Pagination software — QPS 3.3; Typesetters — V. PRESSROOM: Line 1 — 11-G/Community; Folders — G/Suburban. MAILROOM: Inserters and stuffers — St. WIRE SERVICES: News — AP; Receiving dishes — AP.

WOOD RIVER
See ALTON

INDIANA

ANDERSON
Madison County
'90 U.S. Census- 59,459; E&P '96 Est. 56,537
ABC-CZ (90): 61,692 (HH 25,245)

The Herald Bulletin
(m-mon to sat; S)
The Herald Bulletin, 1133 Jackson St. (46016); PO Box 1090, Anderson, IN 46015-1090; tel (317) 622-1212; fax (317) 640-4820; e-mail hb@internetmci.com; web site http://www.indol.com. Thomson Newspapers group.
Circulation: 31,669(m); 31,669(m-sat); 32,908(S); ABC Sept. 30, 1995.
Price: 50¢(d); 50¢(sat); $1.50(S); $3.00/wk (m&S); $156.00/yr.
Advertising: Open inch rate $28.50(m); $28.50(m-sat); $28.50(S). **Representative:** Papert Companies.
News Services: AP, THO. **Politics:** Independent. **Established:** 1868 (Herald), 1885 (Bulletin), 1987 (The Herald Bulletin).
Magazine: USA Weekend.

GENERAL MANAGEMENT
Publisher — Henry Bird
Director-Finance — Dean Bannon
Director-Operations — Jeffrey Evans
ADVERTISING
Manager — Connie Alexander
Manager-National — Cindy Croke
Manager-Major Accounts — Gayle Jones Burris
Manager-Classified — Cindy Morgan
MARKETING AND PROMOTION
Director-Marketing — Steve Elkins
Manager-Marketing Services — De Anna May
TELECOMMUNICATIONS
Audiotex Manager — Susan Lutz
CIRCULATION
Director — Clif Blossom
Manager-Customer Service — Kim Geiger
Manager-Sales — Dorian DuPlain
NEWS EXECUTIVES
Editor — Elliot Tompkin
Managing Editor — Tom Schuman
EDITORS AND MANAGERS
Action Line Editor — Tammy Everitt
Art Director — Rick Madewell
Automotive Editor — Marilyn Young
Books/Music Editor — Marilyn Young
Business/Labor Editor — Anita Munson
City/Courts Editor — Phil Miller
City Government Editor — Ken de la Bastide
Columnist — James Bannon
Columnist — Jim Bailey
Distribution Manager — Susan Brooks
Editorial Page Editor — James Bannon
Education — Amy Starnes
Entertainment/Amusements Editor — Marilyn Young
Farm/Agriculture Editor — Phil Miller
Fashion/Style Editor — Theresa Campbell
Features Editor — Marilyn Young
Food Editor — Theresa Campbell
Graphics Editor — Rick Madewell
Health/Medical Editor — Janice Chavers
Librarian — Beverly Suelean
Photography — John Cleary
Police — Ron Wilkins
Political — Ken De la Bastide
Radio/Television Editor — Tammy Everitt
Religion Editor — Phil Miller
Sports Editor — Scott Underwood
Teen-Age/Youth Editor — Janice Chavers
Travel Editor — Janice Chavers
Wire Editor — Paula Bivens
MANAGEMENT INFORMATION SERVICES
Data Processing Manager — John Anderson
Online Manager — Clif Blossom
PRODUCTION
Coordinator — Anna Hiuvon

Market Information: Split Run; TMC; ADS; Operate database; Operate audiotex; Electronic edition.
Mechanical available: Offset; Black and 3 ROP colors; insert accepted — preprinted; page cut-offs — 22¾".
Mechanical specifications: Type page 13.3" x 22.0"; E - 6 cols, 2¹⁄₁₆", ⅛" between; A - 6 cols, 2¹⁄₁₆", ⅛" between; C - 9 cols, 1⅜", ¹⁄₁₆" between.
Commodity consumption: Newsprint 2,907 short tons; 2,616 metric tons; widths 27½", 13¾", 35"; black ink 52,675 pounds; color ink 2,515 pounds; single pages printed 13,000; average pages per issue 30(d), 52(S); single plates used 11,200.
Equipment: EDITORIAL: Front-end hardware — CText, 2-DEC/386DX2; Front-end software — CText; Printers — V/4000-5300E; Other equipment — 23-DEC/333C, 6-DEC/420SX. CLASSIFIED: Front-end hardware — 2-DEC/386DX2; Front-end software — CText; Printers — 1-C.Itoh; Other equipment — 10-DEC/333C. AUDIOTEX: Hardware — PC/486; Software — Zimmers Interactive, IBS; Supplier name — UNN, Tribune Media. DISPLAY: Front-end hardware — 2-IBM/PS2, 2-IBM/3196; Front-end software — SCS/Layout 8000; Printers — 1-C.Itoh; Other equipment — 2-IBM/PS-2, 2-IBM/3196, 2-DEC/466 D2LP66, 1-DEC/420SX. PRODUCTION: Pagination software — QPS 3.312; Typesetters — 2-V/4000-5300 E; Plate exposures — Nu/Ultra Violet burner; Plate processors — Nat; Electronic picture desk — Lf/AP Leaf Picture Desk; Scanners — 1-Sharp/1200R, 1-Lf/AP Leaf 35mm, ECR/Autokon; Production cameras — 2-SCREEN/6500C; Automatic film processors — SCREEN/480; Reproportion units — ECR/Autokon, Adobe/Photoshop; Color separation equipment (conventional) — Ap/Mac, Adobe/Photoshop, Color Access; Digital color separation equipment — 1-Sharp/1200R. PRESSROOM: Line 1 — 8-G/Urbanite single width; Folders — 1-G; Reels and stands — 6-G/Stands; Press control system — RKW, Fin. MAILROOM: Counter stackers — HL; Inserters and stuffers — 1-Mc; Bundle tyer — 1-MLN, 1-Bu; Addressing machine — KR, FMC; Other mailroom equipment — 1-MM/Fox Saddle Stitcher-Trimmer. LIBRARY: Electronic — 1-SMS/Stauffer Gold, DEC. COMMUNICATIONS: Digital ad delivery system — AP AdSend. WIRE SERVICES: News — AP; Photos — AP; Stock tables — AP; Syndicates — THO; Receiving dishes — size-3m, AP. BUSINESS COMPUTERS: IBM/AS400; Applications: Payroll, Payables, Billing, Receivables, Gen ledger; PCs & micros networked; PCs & main system networked.

AUBURN
De Kalb County
'90 U.S. Census- 9,379; E&P '96 Est. 10,598
ABC-NDM (90): 36,193 (HH 13,065)

The Evening Star
(e-mon to fri; m-sat)
The Evening Star, 118 W. 9th St.; PO Box 431, Auburn, IN 46706; tel (219) 925-2611; fax (219) 925-2625. Witwer Newspapers group.
Circulation: 8,556(e); 8,556(m-sat); ABC Sept. 30, 1995.
Price: 50¢(d); 50¢(sat); $2.25/wk; $10.00/mo, $108.00/yr.
Advertising: Open inch rate $8.75(e); $8.75(m-sat).
News Services: AP, NEA, CSM. **Politics:** Republican. **Established:** 1870.
Note: All production of the Auburn Evening Star is done at the central plant in Kendallville.
Not Published: New Year; Memorial Day; Independence Day; Labor Day; Thanksgiving; Christmas.
Special Editions: De Kalb County Progress, Spring Bridal Planner, Noble County Focus (Jan); Family/Health & Fitness, Mature Living, Sectional Basketball Preview (Feb); Coupon Book, Home & Garden, Agriculture, Design-an-Ad (Mar); Spring Car Care, Look At Lagrange, Spring Homes For You (Apr); Family, Look At Lagrange, Graduation (May); Discover De Kalb, Noble County Progress (June); Noble County 4-H Scrapbook, Lagrange County 4-H Scrapbook (July); Chautauqua Days, Butler Days, Coupon, Fall Bridal Planner, Scouting, Marshmallow Days, ACD Festival (Aug); Great Outdoors, Literacy Days, Home Improvement, Corn School (Sept); Apple Festival, De Kalb County 4-H Scrapbook, Family, Fall Car Care, Dining Guide, Fall Homes For You (Oct); 1997 Calendar, Basketball Preview, Holiday Shopping (Nov); Last Minute Shopping (Dec); Mature Living (monthly).
Special Weekly Sections: Best Food Day (mon); Entertainment Page (thur); Church Page (fri); Business Page, Agri-Business (sat).
Magazine: TV Weekly (sat).

CORPORATE OFFICERS
President — James D Kroemer
Board Chairman — George O Witwer
GENERAL MANAGEMENT
Publisher — George O Witwer
General Manager — James D Kroemer
ADVERTISING
Manager — Martin Alexander
Director-Inserts — Karen Elliott
Director-Marketing — Ron Ensley
CIRCULATION
Manager — Donna Eggeman
NEWS EXECUTIVES
Editor — James D Kroemer
Managing Editor — Dave Kurtz
EDITORS AND MANAGERS
Sports Editor — Mark Murdock
Women's Editor — Sheryl Prentice
PRODUCTION
Manager — Phil Markward

Market Information: TMC; ADS.
Mechanical available: Offset; Black and 3 ROP colors; insert accepted — preprinted, product samples; page cut-offs — 22¾".
Mechanical specifications: Type page 13" x 21½"; E - 6 cols, 2¹⁄₁₆", ⅛" between; A - 6 cols, 2¹⁄₁₆", ⅛" between; C - 6 cols, 2¹⁄₁₆", ⅛" between.
Commodity consumption: Newsprint 1,600 metric tons; widths 27½", 14", 32"; black ink 6,000 pounds; color ink 1,500 pounds; single pages printed 6,200; average pages per issue 14(d); single plates used 14,400.
Equipment: EDITORIAL: Front-end hardware — 12-Ap/Mac; Front-end software — Baseview, QuarkXPress; Printers — 2-Ap/Mac Laser-Writer; Other equipment — 6-RSK/TRS 80 Model 100. CLASSIFIED: Front-end hardware — 3-Ap/Mac; Front-end software — Baseview, QuarkXPress; Printers — 2-Ap/Mac Laser-Writer. DISPLAY: Front-end hardware — 9-Ap/Mac; Front-end software — QuarkXPress, Multi-Ad; Printers — 2-Ap/Mac LaserWriter. PRODUCTION: Pagination software — QuarkXPress 3.3; Typesetters — 2-AG/Imagesetter 1200, 8-Ap/Mac LaserWriter, 1-Tek Color/4C Printer; Plate exposures — 1-Nu/Flip Top FT40UPNS, 1-Nu/OH 631; Plate processors — 1-Nat/250; Electronic picture desk — Lf/AP Leaf Picture Desk; Scanners — Ap/Mac, Ap/Mac Scanner, 1-AG/Arcus, 2-AG/Arcus Plus, 1-Kk/RFS 2035; Production cameras — 1-B, 1-Kk/Image Maker IM600; Automatic film processors — 2-DP/Rapid Access; Color separation equipment (conventional) — CSAF/DSSK. PRESSROOM: Line 1 — 11-G/Community; Folders — 2-G/SSC; Pasters — 1-KTI/Splicer; Press control system — 1-Ebway/Industries Pneumatic Master Control. MAILROOM: Counter stackers — 1-The Stacker Machine Co/S-N 316-19, 1-BG/Count-O-Veyor; Inserters and stuffers — 1-KAN/5-pocket inserter, KAN/Twin Stacker, Macey/Saddlebinder 4-pocket, 1-Challenge/Single-knife cutter; Bundle tyer — 4-Bu, 1-Akebond/Strapper. COMMUNICATIONS: Facsimile — 1-X/Telecopier 7020, 1-Toshiba/TF-341M. WIRE SERVICES: News — AP; Photos — AP; Syndicates — AP; Receiving dishes — size-3m, AP. BUSINESS COMPUTERS: 1-Convergent/580; Applications: Adv billing, Accts receivable, Accts payable, Payroll, Gen ledger, Circ; PCs & micros networked.

BEDFORD
Lawrence County
'90 U.S. Census- 13,817; E&P '96 Est. 13,712
ABC-CZ (90): 20,136 (HH 8,023)

The Times-Mail
(e-mon to fri; m-sat)
Sunday Herald-Times (S)
The Times-Mail, 813 16th St.; PO Box 849, Bedford, IN 47421; tel (812) 275-3355; fax (812) 275-4191; e-mail tmnews@tima.com; web site http://www.tmnews.com. Schurz Communications Inc. group.
Circulation: 14,386(e); 14,386(m-sat); 44,291(S); ABC Sept. 30, 1995.
Price: 50¢(d); 50¢(sat); $1.50(S); $10.50/mo (foot), $11.05 (motor route); $126.00/yr (foot), $132.60 (motor route).
Advertising: Open inch rate $16.65(e); $16.65(m-sat); $32.05(S) comb with Bloomington Herald-Times (mS) $32.05. **Representative:** Landon Associates Inc.
News Service: AP. **Politics:** Independent. **Established:** 1942.
Note: Sunday Herald-Times is published jointly with Bloomington Herald-Times and printed in Bloomington plant. For more information, see Bloomington listing. The two daily papers have a combined (S) publication.
Not Published: New Year; Memorial Day; Independence Day; Labor Day; Christmas.
Special Editions: The Baby Book, Another Year For Area Businesses, Money, Money, Money (Jan); Girls Basketball Sectional Preview, The Spring Bride, Area Dining Out Guide (Feb); Boys Basketball Sectional Preview, Area Church Directory, Kitchen, Bath and Furniture, Spring Fashion (Mar); Spring Home and Garden, 1996 Business Expo (Apr); Just For Mom, Graduation and Careers, Summer Fun, The Summer Bride (May); Father's Day Salute, Women in Business, Limestone Heritage Festival (June); 4-H Fair Tab, City-Wide Sidewalk Sale (July); Back-to-School, Fall Sports Preview, Fall Fashion, The Fall Bride (Aug); Persimmon Festival, Spotlight '96 (Sept); The Winter Bride, Senior Citizen and Retirement Living, Homemaker's Cooking School (Oct); Area Basketball Preview, Thanksgiving Edition, Holiday Cooking (Nov); Christmas Ideas, Holiday Gift Guide, Christmas Greetings, First Baby of 1997 (Dec); Prime Advantage, Family, Health Update (monthly); Yellow Pages (quarterly).
Magazines: Parade Prime Advantage (S); Family (monthly).

CORPORATE OFFICERS
President — Scott C Schurz
Vice Pres — Michael J Hefron
Treasurer/Secretary — Mark P Wozniak
Asst Secretary — Linda L Breeden
GENERAL MANAGEMENT
Publisher — Scott C Schurz
General Manager — Debbie Demitroulas
Controller — Mark P Wozniak
Purchasing Agent — Vicki Fields
ADVERTISING
Director — Ellen Ware
Manager-Retail — Ellen Ware
Manager-Classified — Bruce A Montavon
TELECOMMUNICATIONS
Audiotex Manager — Ellen Ware
CIRCULATION
Manager — Cathy Byers
NEWS EXECUTIVES
Editor in Chief — Scott C Schurz
Editor — Debbie Demitroulas
Managing Editor — Carol Johnson
EDITORS AND MANAGERS
Business/Finance Editor — Doug Bennett
City/Metro Editor — Carol Johnson
Editorial Page Editor — Carol Johnson
Education Editor — Missy Adams
Entertainment/Amusements Editor — Jamie Wildman

Copyright ©1996 by the Editor & Publisher Co.

I-124 Indiana

Environmental Editor Mary Johnson
Farm Editor Roger Moon
Fashion Editor Eleanor Himebaugh
Features Editor Eleanor Himebaugh
Graphics Editor/Art Director Mark Hardman
Health/Medical Editor Troy Guthrie
Living/Lifestyle Editor Eleanor Himebaugh
National Editor Roger Moon
News Editor Roger Moon
Photo Department Manager A J Mast
Political/Government Editor Doug Bennett
Religion Editor Glendora Goodwin
School Editor Carol Johnson
Sports Editor Bob Bridge
Television/Film Editor John Hughey
Theater/Music Editor John Hughey
Travel Editor Eleanor Himebaugh
Women's Editor Eleanor Himebaugh

MANAGEMENT INFORMATION SERVICES

Data Processing/Online Manager A J Mast

PRODUCTION

Manager Randy White
Foreman-Press Robert Neal
Foreman-Composing Randy White
Foreman-Mailroom Gary Sanders
Foreman-Electronic Pre Press Sanford Gentry

Market Information: Split Run; TMC; Operate database; Operate audiotex; Electronic edition.
Mechanical available: Offset; Black and 3 ROP colors; insert accepted — preprinted, standing card; page cut-offs — $22\frac{3}{4}$".
Mechanical specifications: Type page 13" x 21"; E - 6 cols, $2\frac{1}{16}$", $\frac{1}{8}$" between; A - 6 cols, $2\frac{1}{16}$", $\frac{1}{8}$" between; C - 9 cols, $1\frac{3}{8}$", $\frac{1}{16}$" between.
Commodity consumption: Newsprint 1,386 short tons; widths 34", $27\frac{1}{2}$", 32"; single pages printed 7,828; average pages per issue 28(d), 64(S).
Equipment: EDITORIAL: Front-end hardware — 21-Dewar/Disc Net; Printers — Dataproducts/LaserPrinter 1580; Other equipment — 1-XIT/XPT. CLASSIFIED: Front-end hardware — 5-Dewar/Disc Net, 5-IBM/PC; Front-end software — Dewar/System IV; Printers — Dataproducts/LZR 1580. DISPLAY: Adv layout systems — 2-AU/APS5, Ap/Mac; Front-end hardware — 3-Ap/Mac ci, 1-Ap/Mac SE30 server, 1-Ap/Mac IIsi, 2-Ap/Mac Quadra, 1-Ap/Mac 650; Front-end software — Adobe/Photoshop, Aldus/PageMaker, Multi-Ad/Creator, QuarkXPress, Aldus/FreeHand; Printers — Dataproducts/LaserPrinter 1580; Other equipment — 3-HI/1420. PRODUCTION: OCR software — Multi-Ad, Aldus/PageMaker, QPS; Typesetters — 2-Hardot/14" Imagesetter; Plate exposures — 2-Nu/Flip Top FT40UP; Plate processors — 1-Nat/Subtractive; Electronic picture desk — Lf/AP Leaf Picture Desk; Scanners — 1-Lf/Leafscan 45, 2-Kk/RFE 2035, Ap/Mac; Production cameras — 1-K/241E, 1-LE/500, 1-Ik/530, R/500, 1-Ik/550; Automatic film processors — 1-LE/LD18, 1-LE/PC18; Color separation equipment (conventional) — 2-Ap/Mac 950, Adobe/Photoshop; Digital color separation equipment — 2-Hardot/RIP.
PRESSROOM: Line 1 — 15-G/Community single width (Color); Folders — 1-G/SC1045 Balloon Double Former, 1-G/SC1045; Pasters — MM/Minute Man Stitcher Trimmers-4-Heads Plus Cover Feeder. MAILROOM: Counter stackers — 1-BG/Count-O-Veyor, 1-BG/Stabb Brick; Inserters and stuffers — 2-KAN/480; Bundle tyer — 1-FMC/APM2A, 1-Sa/SR2A, 2-Dynaric, 2-Bu, 1-Interlake, Sterling; Addressing machine — Ch. LIBRARY: Electronic — Ap/Mac. WIRE SERVICES: News — AP; Photos — AP; Syndicates — NEA, LATS; Receiving dishes — size-2ft, AP. BUSINESS COMPUTERS: 1-DEC/VAX, 1-DEC/Rainbow, IBM; Applications: Accts receivable, Accts payable, Payroll, Circ, Gen ledger; PCs & micros networked; PCs & main system networked.

BLOOMFIELD

Greene County

'90 U.S. Census- 2,592; E&P '96 Est. 2,571

The Evening World

(e-mon to fri)

The Evening World, 29-31 W. Main St.; PO Box 311, Bloomfield, IN 47424-0311; tel (812) 384-3501; fax (812) 384-3741.
Circulation: 3,479(e); Sworn Sept. 28, 1995.
Price: 35¢(d); $1.25/wk.
Advertising: Open inch rate $4.70(e).
News Service: AP. **Politics:** Democrat. **Established:** 1930.
Not Published: Memorial Day; Independence Day; Labor Day; Thanksgiving; Christmas.

GENERAL MANAGEMENT

Publisher/General Manager William C Miles

ADVERTISING

Manager Richard A Hamlin

CIRCULATION

Manager Richard A Hamlin

NEWS EXECUTIVE

Managing Editor Gayle R Robbins

PRODUCTION

Superintendent Richard A Hamlin

Market Information: Split Run.
Mechanical available: Offset; Black and 3 ROP colors; insert accepted — preprinted; page cut-offs — $22\frac{3}{4}$".
Mechanical specifications: Type page 13" x $21\frac{1}{2}$"; E - 6 cols, $2\frac{1}{16}$", $\frac{1}{8}$" between; A - 6 cols, $2\frac{1}{16}$", $\frac{1}{8}$" between; C - 8 cols, $1\frac{1}{2}$", $\frac{1}{8}$" between.
Commodity consumption: Newsprint 55 short tons; width 28"; black ink 2,000 pounds; color ink 50 pounds; average pages per issue 10(d); single plates used 1,664.
Equipment: EDITORIAL: Front-end hardware — Ap/Macs; Front-end software — Claris/MacWrite; Printers — Ap/Mac LaserWriter; Other equipment — Smith-Corona. CLASSIFIED: Front-end hardware — Ap/Macs; Front-end software — Claris/MacWrite, Microsoft/Word; Printers — Ap/Mac ImageWriter II; Other equipment — 3-Ro. DISPLAY: Front-end hardware — Ap/Mac IIci; Front-end software — QuarkXPress; Printers — LaserMaster/1000; Other equipment — HP/Scanner. PRODUCTION: Plate exposures — 1-B; Scanners — HP/Flatbed; Production cameras — 1-R.
PRESSROOM: Line 1 — 4-G/Community; Line 2 — 1-ABD/360; Folders — G/C. COMMUNICATIONS: Facsimile — Canon. WIRE SERVICES: News — AP; Receiving dishes — AP. BUSINESS COMPUTERS: Ap/Mac LCII; Applications: Peachtree: Accounting; PCs & micros networked; PCs & main system networked.

BLOOMINGTON

Monroe County

'90 U.S. Census- 60,633; E&P '96 Est. 68,942
Herald Times:
ABC-CZ (90): 81,708 (HH 29,413)
Sunday Herald-Times:
ABC-NDM (90): 198,409 (HH 73,320)

Herald-Times(m-mon to sat)
Sunday Herald-Times (S)

Herald-Times Inc, 1900 S. Walnut St. (47401); PO Box 909, Bloomington, IN 47402; tel (812) 332-4401; fax (812) 331-4285; web site http://www.intersource.com/~bcmag. Schurz Communications Inc. group.
Circulation: 29,779(m); 29,779(m-sat); 44,291(S); ABC Sept. 30, 1995.
Price: 50¢(d); 50¢(sat); $1.50(S); $10.95/mo; $131.40/yr.
Advertising: Open inch rate $32.05(m); $32.05(m-sat); $32.05(S) comb with Bedford Times (eS) $32.05. **Representatives:** Landon Associates Inc.; Papert Companies.
News Service: AP. **Politics:** Independent-Republican. **Established:** 1877.
Note: The Bloomington Herald Times and the Bedford Times-Mail have a combined (S) publication.
Not Published: New Year; Memorial Day; Independence Day; Labor Day; Christmas (unless on Sunday).
Special Editions: College Mall, New Car Care, Two Day Business Focus, Dining Out, Bridal (Jan); Valentine's Gift Guide, Apartment and Condominium Guide, Progress Edition, Senior Times, The Herald-Times Homeshow Edition (Feb); NCAA Souvenir Edition, Creative Kids (Mar); Spring Car Care, Spring Home and Garden Edition, American Home Week, Parents & Kids (Apr); Mother's Day Edition, Senior Times, Graduation '96, Indy 500 Race (May); Summer Bridal Edition, Greatest Dad Contest (June); Fourth of July Page, Downtown Sidewalk Sale, Medical Guide '96, Monroe County Fair Edition (July); 1996 IU Six Day Package, Brickyard 400 (Aug); 1996 "I" Edition, Fall Bridal Edition (Sept); Fall Home Improvement Edition, Fall Car Care, New Car Preview, Senior Times (Oct); Tip-off Basketball Preview, Thanksgiving Day, Christmas Opener (Nov); Calendar, Season's Greetings, A Year In Review (Dec).
Special Weekly Sections: Consumers, Neighbors (mon); School Tab (tues); Best Food Day, Senior Citizens (wed); Leisure, Home (thur); Entertainment, Sports (fri); Religion (sat); Arts & Entertainment, Travel, Auto (S).
Magazines: Fun (fri); TV Tab (mini-page) (sat); Parade (S).

CORPORATE OFFICERS

President Scott C Schurz
Vice Pres Michael J Hefron
Vice Pres Bill Schrader
Asst Secretary Linda L Breeden
Treasurer/Secretary Mark P Wozniak

GENERAL MANAGEMENT

Publisher Scott C Schurz
General Manager Michael J Hefron
Director-Personnel/Community Service Allan R Murphy
Controller Mark P Wozniak
Purchasing Agent Scott C Schurz
Manager-Education Service Allan R Murphy

ADVERTISING

Director Lori Grass
Manager-Retail Kim Sutton
Manager-National Lori Grass

MARKETING AND PROMOTION

Manager-Marketing Laura Inman

TELECOMMUNICATIONS

Audiotex Manager Bill Kline

CIRCULATION

Manager Jay Westerfield

NEWS EXECUTIVES

Editor in Chief Scott C Schurz
Editor Robert Zaltsberg
Managing Editor Rob Schorman

EDITORS AND MANAGERS

Business Editor Brian Werth
City Editor William Strother
Editorial Page Editor Robert Zaltsberg
Features/Lifestyle Editor Kay Long
News Editor Barbara Ralls
Photo Department Manager David Snodgress
Sports Editor Bob Hammel

MANAGEMENT INFORMATION SERVICES

Data Processing Manager Jerry Keller

PRODUCTION

Director-Technical Jerry Keller
Manager-Graphic Arts Danny Wagoner
Superintendent Brad Clarke
Superintendent-Pressroom Tom Miller
Superintendent-Mailroom Fred Dugan
Superintendent-Composing John Matson
Foreman-Composing Richard Johnson

Market Information: Operate audiotex.
Mechanical available: Offset; Black and 3 ROP colors; insert accepted — preprinted; page cut-offs — 22".
Mechanical specifications: Type page 13" x 21"; E - 6 cols, 2.06", .14" between; A - 6 cols, 2.06", .14" between; C - 9 cols, 1.39", $\frac{1}{10}$" between.
Commodity consumption: Newsprint 2,750 short tons; widths 55", $41\frac{1}{4}$", $27\frac{1}{2}$"; black ink 80,000 pounds; color ink 20,900 pounds; single pages printed 14,190; average pages per issue 36(d), 64(S); single plates used 22,000.
Equipment: EDITORIAL: Front-end hardware — DEC/Micro VAX; Front-end software — Dewar/View, Microsoft/Windows, Microsoft/Word 2.0, QuarkXPress 3.2; Printers — NewGen/11x19 600 dpi Laser, NewGen/8.5x11 Laser Printer. CLASSIFIED: Front-end hardware — CD/HJ58, DEC; Front-end software — CD/Tops 3.1. DISPLAY: Adv layout systems — Ap/Mac; Front-end hardware — Ap/Mac file-server; Front-end software — Multi-Ad, SCS/Layout 8000. PRODUCTION: Pagination software — Dewar; Typesetters — 1-MON/MK2I; Plate exposures — 1-Nu/Flip Top FT40V20P, 1-Nu/Flip Top FT40V6UPNS; Plate processors — 1-Antec/SN32, 1-Antec/SN32; Electronic picture desk — Lf/AP Leaf Picture Desk; Scanners — ECR/Autokon 1000DG; Production cameras — Nu/Horizontal; Automatic film processors — DP/26C, LD/281-Q; Color separation equipment (conventional) — RZ/210-L; Digital color separation equipment — RZ/210-L.
PRESSROOM: Line 1 — 5-KB/(3 color humps) double width; Folders — 3-KB/3:2 KF 80 Jaw; Reels and stands — 5-MEG; Press control system — Hurletron; Press registration system — Hurletron. MAILROOM: Counter stackers — 1-QWI/300, 1-Rima/RS30, 2-HL/Dual Carrier; Inserters and stuffers — 1-KAN/480 6-into-1, 1-AmGraphics/NP630 13-into-1; Bundle tyer — 2-Power Strap/PSN20; Addressing machine — 1-KR, 1-Ch. LIBRARY: Electronic — Inhouse. WIRE SERVICES: News — AP Datafeatures; Stock tables — AP SelectStox; Receiving dishes — AP. BUSINESS COMPUTERS: 2-DEC/VAX 3900, 4-IBM; PCs & micros networked; PCs & main system networked.

BLUFFTON

Wells County

'90 U.S. Census- 9,020; E&P '96 Est. 9,413

News-Banner (e-mon to fri)

News-Banner, 125 N. Johnson St.; PO Box 436, Bluffton, IN 46714; tel (219) 824-0224; fax (219) 824-0700. News-Banner Publications Inc. group.
Circulation: 5,056(e); Sworn Sept. 27, 1994.
Price: 50¢(d); $2.10/wk; $96.00/yr.
Advertising: Open inch rate $8.35(e).
News Service: AP. **Politics:** Independent. **Established:** 1892.
Not Published: New Year; Memorial Day; Independence Day; Labor Day; Thanksgiving; Christmas.
Advertising not accepted: Beer; Liquor; Cigarettes.
Special Editions: Christmas Greetings; Dollar Days; Sidewalk Sales Day; Washington's Birthday; Progress Edition.
Special Weekly Sections: Food Day (mon); ECHO (tues); Entertainment Guide, Weekender, Farm Day (sat).
Magazine: USA Weekend (sat).

CORPORATE OFFICERS

President/Treasurer James C Barbieri
Vice Pres/Secretary George B Witwer

GENERAL MANAGEMENT

Publisher/General Manager James C Barbieri
Manager-Office Robin Minnear
Purchasing Agent James C Barbieri
Controller Michelle A Moore

ADVERTISING

Director Connie Edington
Manager-General Robin Minniear
Manager-Classified Robin Minniear

MARKETING AND PROMOTION

Director-Marketing George B Witwer

CIRCULATION

Manager Brenda Holloway

NEWS EXECUTIVES

Editor James C Barbieri
Managing Editor Joel Smekens

EDITORS AND MANAGERS

News Editor Joel Smekens
Society Editor Barbara Barbieri
Sports Editor Paul Beitler

PRODUCTION

Superintendent Tim Gregg

Market Information: TMC.
Mechanical available: Offset; Black and 2 ROP colors; insert accepted — preprinted; page cut-offs — $22\frac{3}{4}$".
Mechanical specifications: Type page 13" x $21\frac{1}{2}$"; E - 6 cols, $2\frac{1}{16}$", $\frac{1}{16}$" between; A - 6 cols, $2\frac{1}{16}$", $\frac{1}{16}$" between; C - 6 cols, $2\frac{1}{16}$", $\frac{1}{16}$" between.
Commodity consumption: Newsprint 270 short tons; widths $27\frac{1}{2}$", $13\frac{3}{4}$", 32", 16"; average pages per issue 14(d).
Equipment: EDITORIAL: Front-end hardware — 6-Ap/Mac IIe; Front-end software — Concept Publishing. DISPLAY: Front-end hardware — 3-Ap/Mac; Front-end software — Multi-Ad, QuarkXPress. PRODUCTION: Typesetters — 2-Ap/Mac; Plate processors — 1-Nu; Production cameras — 1-Nu.
PRESSROOM: Line 1 — 4-G/Community. MAILROOM: Bundle tyer — 2-Bs. WIRE SERVICES: News — AP; Receiving dishes — AP. BUSINESS COMPUTERS: Applications: Vision Data.

BRAZIL

Clay County

'90 U.S. Census- 7,640; E&P '96 Est. 7,659

The Brazil Times

(e-mon to fri; m-sat)

The Brazil Times, 100 N. Meridian St.; PO Box 429, Brazil, IN 47834; tel (812) 446-2216; fax (812) 446-0938. Nixon Newspapers Inc. group.
Circulation: 5,386(e); 5,386(m-sat); Sworn Oct. 2, 1995.
Price: 50¢(d); 50¢(sat); $1.45/wk (carrier); $75.00/yr.
Advertising: Open inch rate $5.25(e); $5.25(m-sat). **Representative:** Nixon Newspapers.
News Service: AP. **Politics:** Republican. **Established:** 1888.
Not Published: Memorial Day; Independence Day; Labor Day; Veteran's Day; Thanksgiving; Christmas; New Year.
Special Editions: Dollar Days; Basketball; Home Show; Graduation; Business & Industry; County Fair; Summer Sidewalk Sale; Foot-

Copyright ©1996 by the Editor & Publisher Co.

ball; Christmas Greetings; New Year's Greeting; New Year's Baby.
Special Weekly Sections: Best Food Day (mon); Agri-Business (tues); TV Times (fri); Religion Page, School News Page (sat).

CORPORATE OFFICERS
President .... John R Nixon
Vice Pres .... William Harper
Treasurer .... John W Stackhouse
Secretary .... Debbie Huff

GENERAL MANAGEMENT
Publisher .... William Harper

ADVERTISING
Director .... Larry Knight

CIRCULATION
Director .... Earl Hutcheson

NEWS EXECUTIVE
Managing Editor .... James Dressler

EDITORS AND MANAGERS
Editorial Page Editor .... James Dressler
News Editor .... Richard Green
Seen 'n Heard Editor .... James Dressler
Sports Editor .... Cecil Davis
Women's Editor .... Caryn Shinske

PRODUCTION
Manager .... Earl Hutcheson

Mechanical available: Offset; Black and 3 ROP colors; insert accepted — preprinted; page cut-offs — 22¾".
Mechanical specifications: Type page 13" x 21½"; E - 6 cols, 2¹/₁₆", ⅛" between; A - 6 cols, 2¹/₁₆", ⅛" between; C - 9 cols, 1½", ¹/₁₆" between.
Commodity consumption: Newsprint 101 metric tons; width 21½"; single pages printed 3,084; average pages per issue 10(d).
Equipment: PRODUCTION: Typesetters — Ap/Mac LaserWriter 630 Pro's; Plate exposures — 1-Nu/FT 40L; Production cameras — 1-R/480; Automatic film processors — 1-LE/LD-18; Color separation equipment (conventional) — 1-LE/Bessler. PRESSROOM: Line 1 — 5-G/Community; Folders — G. MAILROOM: Bundle tyer — 1-Malow. COMMUNICATIONS: Facsimile — 1-Minolta/Beta 450Z. WIRE SERVICES: News — AP; Receiving dishes — UPI. BUSINESS COMPUTERS: IBM.

CHESTERTON
Porter County
'90 U.S. Census- 9,124; E&P '96 Est. 9,765

Chesterton Tribune
(e-mon to fri)
Chesterton Tribune, 193 S. Calumet Rd.; PO Box 558, Chesterton, IN 46304; tel (219) 926-1131; fax (219) 926-6389.
Circulation: 4,930(e); Sworn Sept. 29, 1995.
Price: 35¢(d); $5.00/mo.
Advertising: Open inch rate $6.08(e).
News Service: AP. **Politics:** Republican. **Established:** 1884.
Not Published: New Year; Memorial Day; Independence Day; Labor Day; Thanksgiving; Christmas.
Advertising not accepted: Beer; Liquor; Cigarettes.
Special Editions: Sidewalk Sale, Festival of Dunes (July); Oz Festival (Sept); Christmas Shopping Guide (Nov).
Magazine: TV (tues).

CORPORATE OFFICER
President .... Warren H Canright

GENERAL MANAGEMENT
Publisher .... Warren H Canright

ADVERTISING
Director .... Bill Mathe

CIRCULATION
Manager .... Alma Rabe

NEWS EXECUTIVE
Editor .... David Canright

Mechanical available: Offset; insert accepted — preprinted; page cut-offs — 22".
Mechanical specifications: Type page 13" x 21"; E - 6 cols, 2¹/₁₆", ⅛" between; A - 6 cols, 2¹/₁₆", ⅛" between; C - 6 cols, 2¹/₁₆", ⅛" between.
Commodity consumption: Newsprint 80 metric tons; widths 28", 14"; black ink 2,375 pounds; single pages printed 3,048; average pages per issue 12(d); single plates used 1,524.
Equipment: EDITORIAL: Front-end hardware — Ap/Mac Plus; Front-end software — Lorenz, Baseview; Printers — Ap/Mac LaserWriter, Ap/Mac LaserWriter Plus. CLASSIFIED: Front-end hardware — Ap/Mac Plus, Ap/Mac Quadra; Front-end software — Lorenz, Baseview; Printers — Ap/Mac LaserWriter, Ap/Mac LaserWriter Plus. DISPLAY: Adv layout systems — Aldus/PageMaker; Front-end hardware — Ap/Mac; Front-end software — Aldus/PageMaker; Printers — Ap/Mac LaserWriter. PRODUCTION: Typesetters — Ap/Mac LaserWriter; Plate exposures — B; Production cameras — R.
PRESSROOM: Line 1 — 3-G/Community; Folders — 1-G. MAILROOM: Addressing machine — Am. WIRE SERVICES: News — AP; Photos — AP; Receiving dishes — size-3m, AP.

CLINTON
Vermillion County
'90 U.S. Census- 5,040; E&P '96 Est. 4,995

The Daily Clintonian
(e-mon to fri)
The Daily Clintonian, 422 S. Main St.; PO Box 309, Clinton, IN 47842-0309; tel (317) 832-2443.
Circulation: 5,491(e); Sworn Oct. 2, 1995.
Price: 50¢(d); $1.85/wk.
Advertising: Open inch rate $4.20(e).

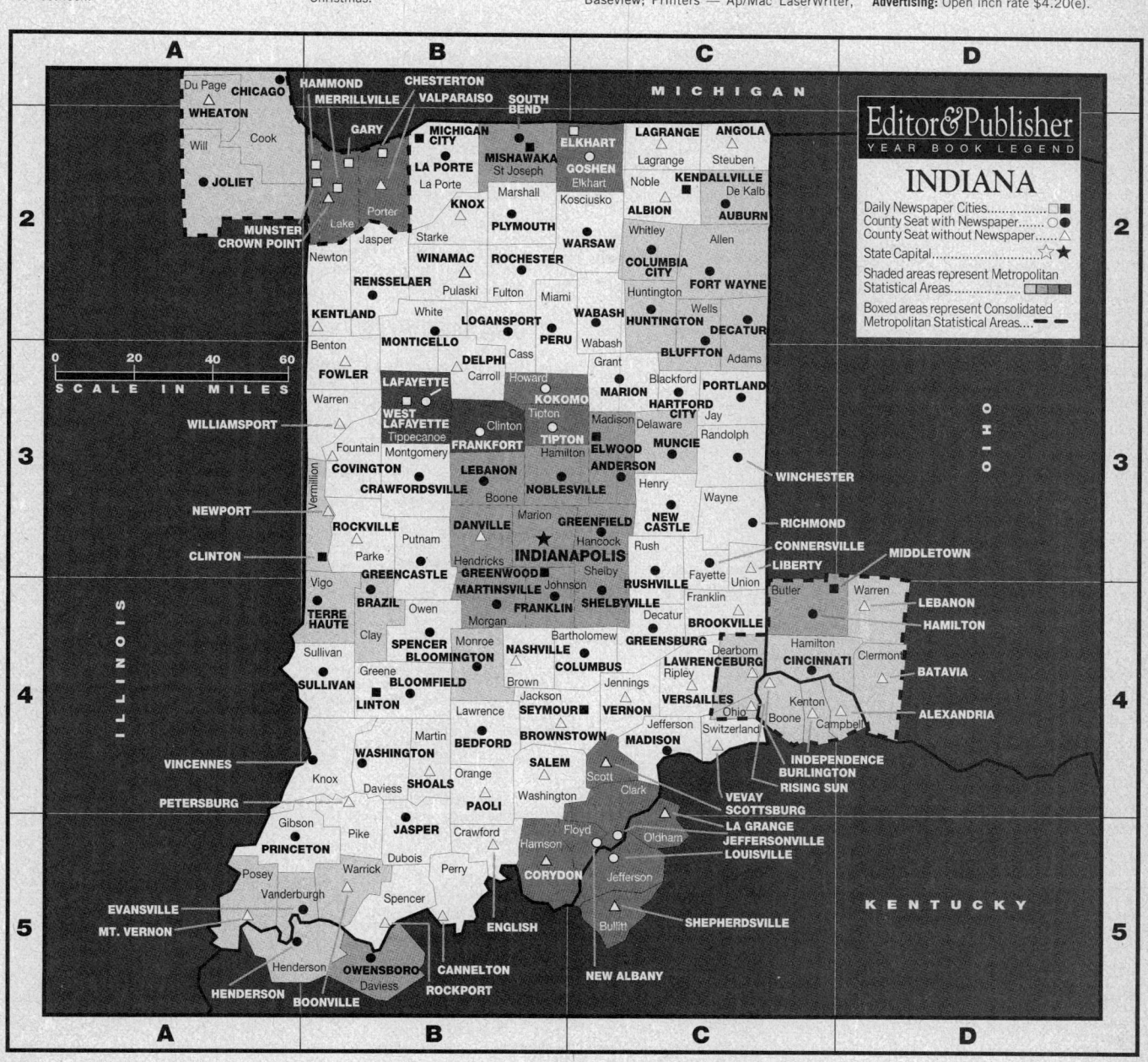

I-126 Indiana

News Service: AP. **Politics:** Republican. **Established:** 1912.
Not Published: New Year; Thanksgiving; Christmas.
Advertising not accepted: 900 numbers (to be called and then to order a book).
Special Editions: Graduation (May); Il Bollettino (Sept); Christmas (Dec).

CORPORATE OFFICERS
President George L Carey
Vice Pres George B Carey
Secretary/Treasurer Diane E Waugh

GENERAL MANAGEMENT
Publisher George L Carey
Business Manager George B Carey
Purchasing Agent George B Carey

ADVERTISING
Manager C R Bartlett

CIRCULATION
Manager C Krapesh

NEWS EXECUTIVE
Editor J F Carey

EDITOR AND MANAGER
Columnist George L Carey

PRODUCTION
Foreman-Composing George B Carey
Foreman-Pressroom George B Carey

Mechanical available: Offset; Black and 2 ROP colors; insert accepted — preprinted, hand stuffing in-plant; page cut-offs — 22¾".
Mechanical specifications: Type page 15.5" x 21"; E - 7 cols, 2¹⁄₁₆", ⅛" between; A - 7 cols, 2¹⁄₁₆", ⅛" between; C - 7 cols, 1½", ⅛" between.
Commodity consumption: Newsprint 265 short tons; widths 17½", 35"; black ink 8,800 pounds; color ink 980 pounds; single pages printed 3,445; average pages per issue 10(d); single plates used 6,835.
Equipment: EDITORIAL: Front-end hardware — 10-Synaptic/PC; Front-end software — Novell/LAN; Other equipment — Lf/AP Leaf Picture Desk, Microtek/Scanner, 8-DD/5200G. CLASSIFIED: Front-end hardware — 1-PC. DISPLAY: Adv layout systems — Panasonic/1395; Other equipment — 5-DD/5200G. PRODUCTION: Typesetters — 2-M/202 N, LaserMaster/1000; Plate exposures — 1-Nu/30x40 UP; Scanners — Microtek; Production cameras — 1-B/Caravelle; Automatic film processors — 1-AG/Super 260(Pako); Reproportion units — LE/LD-18.
PRESSROOM: Line 1 — 4-KP/Color King; Folders — 1-KP. MAILROOM: Counter stackers — 1-BG/Count-O-Veyor; Bundle tyer — 2-Bu; Addressing machine — 1-KR/215. LIBRARY: Electronic — 1-Folio. WIRE SERVICES: News — AP; Photos — AP; Receiving dishes — size-3m, AP. BUSINESS COMPUTERS: 1-Centurion; Applications: Adv billing, Accts receivable, Accts payable, Gen ledger, Payroll, Annual comparisons; PCs & micros networked; PCs & main system networked.

COLUMBIA CITY
Whitley County
'90 U.S. Census- 5,706; E&P '96 Est. 6,314

The Post & Mail
(e-mon to fri; m-sat)
The Post & Mail, 116 N. Chauncey St., Columbia City, IN 46725; tel (219) 244-5153; fax (219) 244-7598. Hollinger International Inc. group.
Circulation: 4,018(e); 4,018(m-sat); Sworn Sept. 25, 1995.
Price: 50¢(d); 50¢(sat); $2.30/wk; $9.20/mo; $103.20/yr.
Advertising: Open inch rate $6.25(e); $8.80(e-tues); $6.25(m-sat).
News Service: UPI. **Politics:** Independent. **Established:** 1905 (Mail), 1853 (Post).
Not Published: New Year; Memorial Day; Independence Day; Labor Day; Thanksgiving; Christmas.
Special Editions: Taxes & Finances Tab (Jan); Progress Edition (Feb); Home & Garden Tab, High School Sports Tab (Apr); High School Commencement Tab, Car Care Tab (May); Old Settlers Day (Community Festival) Program (July); High School Sports Tab, 4-H Tab (Aug); High School Sports Tab (Nov); Senior Citizens Tab (monthly).
Special Weekly Section: Whitley TV Weekly (fri).

GENERAL MANAGEMENT
Publisher Doug Driscoll
General Manager Rick Kreps

CIRCULATION
Manager Joan Gaff

NEWS EXECUTIVE
Editor Doug Driscoll

Market Information: TMC.
Mechanical available: Offset; Black and 3 ROP colors; insert accepted — preprinted, maximum 29"; page cut-offs — 21½".
Mechanical specifications: Type page 13" x 21½"; E - 6 cols, 2¹⁄₁₆", ⅛" between; A - 6 cols, 2¹⁄₁₆", ⅛" between; C - 8 cols, 1½", ⅛" between.
Commodity consumption: widths 27½", 34"; average pages per issue 16(d).
Equipment: EDITORIAL: Front-end hardware — Mk, Ap/Mac; Printers — Ap/Mac; Other equipment — 5-Mk. CLASSIFIED: Front-end hardware — 1-Mk. DISPLAY: Front-end hardware — Ap/Mac; Printers — Ap/Mac LaserPrinter. PRODUCTION: Plate exposures — 1-Nu; Plate processors — 1-Ic; Scanners — Microtek; Production cameras — 1-SCREEN; Automatic film processors — 1-SCREEN; Color separation equipment (conventional) — AG. MAILROOM: Bundle tyer — 2-Bu. WIRE SERVICES: News — AP; Receiving dishes — AP.

COLUMBUS
Bartholomew County
'90 U.S. Census- 31,802; E&P '96 Est. 33,247
ABC-CZ (90): 37,466 (HH 14,935)

The Republic (e-mon to sat; S)
The Republic, 333 2nd St., Columbus, IN 47201; tel (812) 372-7811; fax (812) 379-5608. Home News Enterprises group.
Circulation: 21,890(e); 21,890(e-sat); 25,572(S); ABC Sept. 30, 1995.
Price: 50¢(d); 50¢(sat); $1.50(S); $9.50/mo (carrier), $10.50/mo (home delivery).
Advertising: Open inch rate $18.10(e); $18.10(e-sat); $18.95(S). **Representative:** Papert Companies.
News Services: AP, NEA, SHNS, KRT. **Politics:** Independent-Republican. **Established:** 1872.
Special Editions: Tourism, Wedding (Feb); AgriBusiness, Fashion, Spring Sports (Mar); Home Improvement, Business Profiles (Apr); Garden, Outdoors (May); Fitness, Answer Book (June); 4-H (July); Education, Football (Aug); Home Improvement (Sept); People, Cookbook (Oct); Basketball, Gift Guide (Nov); Yuletide, Year In Review (Dec).
Special Weekly Sections: Food, Family (mon); Entertainment, Best Bets for the Weekend, Arts, Socially Speaking, School (thur); Health, Consumer News (fri); Religion, Auto, Homes (sat); TV, Nature/Environment, Kids Page, Outdoors, Business, Religion, Weddings/ Engagements, Travel, Entertainment (S).
Magazines: USA Weekend; Sunday Color Comics (Sullivan Graphics).

GENERAL MANAGEMENT
Publisher Don R Bucknam
Business Manager Cindy Owens
Controller Robert Carothers
Manager-Human Resources Harleen Cutrell

ADVERTISING
Director Joel Cardwell
Manager-Special Publications Pamela Wells-Lego
Manager-Classified Amy Lutheran

TELECOMMUNICATIONS
Audiotex Manager Joel Cardwell

CIRCULATION
Director David Walters
Director-Operations Lynne Klamo

NEWS EXECUTIVES
Editor John Harmon
Assoc Editor Harry McCawley
Managing Editor J K Murphy

EDITORS AND MANAGERS
City Editor Mike Martoccia
Editorial Page John Harmon
Features Editor Doug Showalter
Librarian Jane Peabody
Photo Editor Darron Cummings
Region Editor Doug Showalter
Sports Editor Dan Courtney

PRODUCTION
Director Neil Thompson
Manager Randy Reeves

Market Information: TMC; Operate audiotex.
Mechanical available: Offset; Black and 3 ROP colors; insert accepted — preprinted, product sampling bags; page cut-offs — 22¾".
Mechanical specifications: Type page 13" x 21½"; E - 6 cols, 2¹⁄₁₆", ⅛" between; A - 6 cols, 2¹⁄₁₆", ⅛" between; C - 9 cols, 1⅜", ¹⁄₁₆" between.
Commodity consumption: Newsprint 1,439 short tons; widths 34", 30", 27½"; black ink 17,273 pounds; color ink 4,102 pounds; single pages printed 10,327; average pages per issue 27(d), 40(S); single plates used 13,148.
Equipment: EDITORIAL: Front-end hardware — Dewar/Disc Net, 24-VG/55, 4-AST, HP/PCs, Sun/Sparc Servers; Front-end software — Hyphen/HES; Printers — 1-Panasonic/KX-P1595, 1-Ap/Mac LaserWriter II; Other equipment — 2-Ap/Mac IIci, 1-Ap/Mac SE. CLASSIFIED: Front-end hardware — Dewar/Disc Net, 5-AST, 7-HP/PC; Front-end software — PPI; Printers — 1-Okidata/321. AUDIOTEX: Supplier name — Info-Connect/Pottsville Republican. DISPLAY: Adv layout systems — Mk/Ad Director, Ap/Mac; Front-end hardware — 7-Ap/Mac; Front-end software — QuarkXPress, Multi-Ad/Creator; Printers — 2-NewGen/Turbo 660. PRODUCTION: Pagination software — Hyphen; OCR software — TI/OmniPage 5.0, Ap/Mac; Typesetters — Hyphen/Spectraset 3000-100, ECR/ScriptSetter II, Hyphen/RIPs; Plate exposures — 1-Nu/Flip Top FT40LNS; Plate processors — 1-Nat/A-250; Electronic picture desk — Lf/AP Leaf Picture Desk; Scanners — 1-ECR/1030, 3-Umax, 1-Lf/AP Leafscan 45, 3-Kk/2035; Production cameras — 1-C/Spartan II; Automatic film processors — 1-LE/LD-24, Konica/K-400; Film transporters — 1-C; Color separation equipment (conventional) — RZ/210L; Digital color separation equipment — Ap/Mac w/Adobe/Photoshop.
PRESSROOM: Line 1 — 7-G/U-823; Press drives — 2-Reliance Electric; Folders — 1-G; Reels and stands — 8-G; Press registration system — Duarte. MAILROOM: Counter stackers — 1-Id/NS660; Inserters and stuffers — 2-KAN/460; Bundle tyer — 2-Si/MLN, 1-OVL/410. WIRE SERVICES: News — AP, KRT, SHNS, TMS; Photos — AP; Syndicates — NEA; Receiving dishes — size-10m, AP. BUSINESS COMPUTERS: 1-Bs/B920; Applications: PBS/MediaPlus: Circ, Adv billing.

CONNERSVILLE
Fayette County
'90 U.S. Census- 15,550; E&P '96 Est. 14,724

Connersville News-Examiner (e-mon to fri; m-sat)
Connersville News-Examiner, 406 Central Ave.; PO Box 287, Connersville, IN 47331-0287; tel (317) 825-0581; fax (317) 825-4599. Nixon Newspapers Inc. group.
Circulation: 9,078(e); 9,078(m-sat); Sworn Sept. 30, 1995.
Price: 50¢(d); 50¢(sat); $7.25/mo; $87.00/yr.
Advertising: Open inch rate $10.00(e); $10.00(m-sat). **Representative:** Landon Associates Inc.
News Service: AP. **Politics:** Independent-Republican. **Established:** 1887.
Not Published: New York; Memorial Day; Independence Day; Labor Day; Thanksgiving; Christmas.
Special Editions: Basketball; Football; Car Care; Bridal; Home Improvement; Christmas Kick-off; Christmas Greetings; NIE (Newspaper in Education) TV.
Special Weekly Sections: Best Food Day (mon); Best Real Estate Days (thur); Best Real Estate Days, Church Page (fri).
Magazine: Our Town (quarterly).

CORPORATE OFFICERS
Chairman of the Board John R Nixon
President John Claxton
Vice Pres Ken Bronson
Secretary Deborah M Huff
Treasurer John W Stackhouse

GENERAL MANAGEMENT
General Manager John Claxton
Coordinator-Plant Sherry Roberts
Manager-Business Office Rosalie Mills

ADVERTISING
Manager-Classified/Retail Diane Howell

CIRCULATION
Manager William Savoy

NEWS EXECUTIVE
Managing Editor Robert L Powers

EDITORS AND MANAGERS
Amusements Editor Robert L Powers
Copy Editor Gary Hufferd
Automotive Editor Robert L Powers
Editorial Page Editor Robert L Powers
Sports Editor Randy Huggler

PRODUCTION
Manager Sherry Roberts
Foreman-Composing Gloria Potters
Foreman-Pressroom Greg Jeffries
Foreman-Camera Room Steve Cooney

Market Information: Zoned editions; Split Run; TMC.
Mechanical available: Offset; Black and 3 ROP colors; insert accepted — preprinted, free standing; page cut-offs — 22¾".
Mechanical specifications: Type page 13" x 21"; E - 6 cols, 2¹⁄₁₆", ⅛" between; A - 6 cols, 2¹⁄₁₆", ⅛" between; C - 9 cols, 1⁵⁄₁₆", ⅛" between.
Commodity consumption: Newsprint 400 short tons; widths 27½", 13¾"; black ink 9,209 pounds; color ink 614 pounds; single pages printed 5,756; average pages per issue 18(d); single plates used 12,000.
Equipment: EDITORIAL: Front-end hardware — Ap/Mac, 1-IBM, 3-RSK/Tandy 102, 6-Ap/Mac, 3-Ap/Super Mac; Front-end software — QuarkXPress; Printers — 1-LaserMaster/1200, Ap/Mac LaserWriter II. CLASSIFIED: Front-end hardware — 3-Ap/Mac; Front-end software — Baseview; Printers — NEC/Silentwriter LC 890. DISPLAY: Adv layout systems — Ap/Mac; Front-end hardware — Ap/Mac II, Ap/Mac; Front-end software — QuarkXPress; Printers — Ap/Mac LaserWriter II, LaserMaster/1200; Other equipment — CD-Rom, HP/Scanner, AG/Scanner. PRODUCTION: Pagination software — Ap/Mac, QPS; Typesetters — Ap/Mac LaserWriterII, LaserMaster/1200; Plate exposures — 1-Montakomp; Plate processors — 1-Nat/Universal 26; Electronic picture desk — Lf/AP Leaf Picture Desk; Production cameras — 1-SCREEN; Automatic film processors — 2-LE.
PRESSROOM: Line 1 — 6-G/Suburban; Line 2 — 4-G/Community; Press drives — Fin; Folders — G/SSC, G/SC; Reels and stands — 6-G/Suburban Rollstand; Press control system — Fin; Press registration system — Duarte. MAILROOM: Counter stackers — 1-Mid America Graphics, 1-BG; Bundle tyer — 1-Bu/String, 1-Bu/Strap; Addressing machine — 1-Mk. WIRE SERVICES: News — AP; Photos — AP; Syndicates — TV Data, AP Laserphoto; Receiving dishes — size-10ft, AP. BUSINESS COMPUTERS: 2-Synaptic/Micro Solutions Workstation; Applications: Synaptic/Micro Solutions: Class billing, Accts receivable; PCs & micros networked; PCs & main system networked.

CRAWFORDSVILLE
Montgomery County
'90 U.S. Census- 13,584; E&P '96 Est. 14,048
ABC-CZ (90): 13,584 (HH 5,500)

Journal Review
(m-mon to sat)
Journal Review, 119 N. Green; PO Box 512, Crawfordsville, IN 47933-0512; tel (317) 362-1200; fax (317) 364-5427. Freedom Communications Inc. group.
Circulation: 10,922(m); 10,922(m-sat); ABC Sept. 30, 1995.
Price: 50¢(d); 75¢(sat); $10.00/mo; $120.00/yr.
Advertising: Open inch rate $10.00(m); $10.00(m-sat). **Representative:** Papert Companies.
News Services: AP, KRT. **Politics:** Independent. **Established:** 1841.
Not Published: Christmas.
Special Editions: Just Say No Drugs Tab, Bridal (Jan); Silver Salute (Feb); Home Improvement, Car Care (Mar); Crawfordsville Directory (Apr); Silver Salute (June); Bridal (July); Fall Sports, Silver Salute, 4-H Section (Aug); Car Care, Silver Salute, Home Improvement (Oct); Winter Sports, Christmas Opening (Nov); Last Minute Christmas (Dec).
Special Weekly Sections: Best Food Day, Agriculture (tues); Business (wed); Business, Church (sat).
Magazines: "TV & More" (TV & Entertainment Section) (sat); Montgomery Magazine (historical) (1st day/mo).

GENERAL MANAGEMENT
Publisher James J McMillen

ADVERTISING
Manager-General Randy List
Director-Sales/Marketing Randy List

Indiana I-127

TELECOMMUNICATIONS

Audiotex Manager Randy List

CIRCULATION

Director Brent Harris

NEWS EXECUTIVE

Managing Editor Gaildene Hamilton

EDITORS AND MANAGERS

Business Editor Tim McGrady
City/Metro Editor David Tomaro
Civic Affairs Editor Joanne Zuhl
Education Editor Doug Hunt
Editorial Page Editor Gaildene Hamilton
Entertainment/Amusements Editor Glen Cumbarelis
Environment Editor Glen Cumbarelis
Farm/Agriculture Editor Glen Cumbarelis
Fashion/Style Editor Susan Brook
Features Editor David Tomaro
Films/Theater Editor Glen Cumbarelis
Food Editor Susan Brook
Graphics Editor David Tomaro
Health/Medical Editor Susan Brook
Living/Lifestyle Editor Susan Brook
Music Editor Glen Cumbarelis
News Editor David Tomaro
Photo Editor Steve Rosenberg
Political Editor Joanne Zuhl
Radio/Television Editor Glen Cumbarelis
Religion Editor Susan Brook
Sports Editor Barry Lewis
Travel Editor Glen Cumbarelis
Women's Editor Susan Brook

MANAGEMENT INFORMATION SERVICES

Data Processing Manager Kay Shelton

PRODUCTION

Manager Richard Keller
Manager-Composing Room Jim Rankin
Foreman-Pressroom Ronald Cooley

Market Information: TMC; Operate audiotex.
Mechanical available: Offset; Black and 3 ROP colors; insert accepted — preprinted; page cut-offs — $22\frac{3}{4}$".
Mechanical specifications: Type page 13" x $21\frac{1}{2}$"; E - 6 cols, $2\frac{1}{16}$", $\frac{1}{8}$" between; A - 6 cols, $2\frac{1}{16}$", $\frac{1}{8}$" between; C - 9 cols, $1\frac{11}{32}$", $\frac{1}{8}$" between.
Commodity consumption: Newsprint 590 short tons; widths $27\frac{1}{2}$", $13\frac{3}{4}$"; black ink 12,500 pounds; color ink 1,750 pounds; single pages printed 6,770; average pages per issue 22(d), 32(sat); single plates used 7,300.
Equipment: EDITORIAL: Front-end hardware — Ap/Mac; Front-end software — Baseview. CLASSIFIED: Front-end hardware — Ap/Mac; Front-end software — Baseview; Printers — Epson. DISPLAY: Adv layout systems — 3-Ap/Mac; Front-end hardware — Ap/Mac IIcx, Ap/Mac IIci, Ap/Mac II SE; Front-end software — Multi-Ad; Printers — Ap/Mac LaserWriter. PRODUCTION: Pagination software — QuarkXPress 3.3; Typesetters — Linotype-Hell/Lino 190B, GCC/Select Press 600, QMS/860 Print System; Plate exposures — 1-Nu; Plate processors — 1-Nat/A-250; Electronic picture desk — Ap/Mac, Adobe/Photoshop; Scanners — AG/Arcus Flatbed, Nikon/Film; Production cameras — 1-B; Automatic film processors — 1-SCREEN.
PRESSROOM: Line 1 — 9-HI/V-15D; Folders — 1-HI. MAILROOM: Inserters and stuffers — KAN/480; Bundle tyer — Bu. LIBRARY: Electronic — SMS/Stauffer Gold. WIRE SERVICES: News — AP, KRT; Stock tables — AP; Syndicates — Creators, Roll Call Reports, Universal Press, King Features, LATS, NAS, United Media, Freedom Wire; Receiving dishes — size-10ft, AP. BUSINESS COMPUTERS: 6-IBM; Applications: Southware; PCs & micros networked; PCs & main system networked.

DECATUR

Adams County

'90 U.S. Census- 8,644; E&P '96 Est. 8,740

Decatur Daily Democrat

(e-mon to fri; m-sat)

Decatur Daily Democrat, 141 S. 2nd St.; PO Box 1001, Decatur, IN 46733-5001; tel (219) 724-2121; fax (219) 724-7981; e-mail ddd@madman.com. Hollinger International Inc. group.
Circulation: 5,916(e); 5,916(m-sat); Sworn Sept. 30, 1995.
Price: 50¢(d); 50¢(sat); $2.25/wk; $9.00/mo; $106.00/yr.
Advertising: Open inch rate $8.14(e); $8.14(m-sat).
News Service: AP. **Politics:** Independent. **Established:** 1857.
Not Published: New Year; Memorial Day; Independence Day; Labor Day; Thanksgiving; Christmas.
Special Editions: Basketball, Progress (Feb); Callithumpian (Oct); Christmas Opening (Nov).
Special Weekly Sections: Best Food Day (mon); School Scene (wed); Entertainment (thur); Agri-News (thurs); Business News, Church Page (fri); Church Page (sat); Society, Community, Obituaries, Local News, Comics, Sports (daily).
Magazines: Extra (TMC) (tues); Weekly TV Section (fri).

GENERAL MANAGEMENT

Publisher Mark F Miller
Business Manager/Purchasing Agent Mark F Miller
Manager-Education Service Sue Casebeer

ADVERTISING

Manager Ron Platt
Manager-Classified Karel Long

CIRCULATION

Manager Bob Crowell

NEWS EXECUTIVES

Editor Mark F Miller
Managing Editor Robert W Shraluka

EDITORS AND MANAGERS

Business/Finance Editor Edith Voltz
Education Editor Melanie McCullough
Living/Lifestyle Editor Helen Walters
Sports Editor James Hopkins
Women's Editor Helen Walters

MANAGEMENT INFORMATION SERVICES

Systems Manager Howard Jones Jr

PRODUCTION

Manager Howard Jones Jr

Market Information: TMC.
Mechanical available: Offset; Black and 3 ROP colors; insert accepted — preprinted, all inserts accepted; page cut-offs — $22\frac{3}{4}$".
Mechanical specifications: Type page 13" x $21\frac{1}{2}$"; E - 6 cols, $2\frac{1}{8}$", $\frac{1}{8}$" between; A - 6 cols, $2\frac{1}{8}$", $\frac{1}{8}$" between; C - 6 cols, $2\frac{1}{8}$", $\frac{1}{8}$" between.
Commodity consumption: Newsprint 260 short tons; width $27\frac{1}{2}$"; black ink 8,500 pounds; color ink 680 pounds; single pages printed 5,440; average pages per issue 16.1(d); single plates used 3,700.
Equipment: EDITORIAL: Front-end hardware — 4-Ap/Mac Quadra 605, Ap/Mac Quadra 630, 2-Ap/Mac Quadra 610; Front-end software — Baseview/NewsEdit; Printers — Ap/Mac Pro 630. CLASSIFIED: Front-end hardware — Ap/Mac Quadra 610; Front-end software — Claris/File Maker Pro. PRODUCTION: Pagination software — QuarkXPress 3.31; OCR software — Caere/OmniPage Pro 5.0; Typesetters — 2-Ap/Power Mac, 1-Ap/Mac Pro 630; Plate exposures — 1-Nu/Double Flip top; Scanners — Mk; Production cameras — 1-R/400.
PRESSROOM: Line 1 — 8-G/Community (w/2 stacks); Folders — 1-SC. MAILROOM: Bundle tyer — 1-Bu/162X; Addressing machine — 1-Am/CL 1900. COMMUNICATIONS: Digital ad delivery system — AP AdSend. WIRE SERVICES: News — AP; Receiving dishes — AP.

ELKHART

Elkhart County

'90 U.S. Census- 43,627; E&P '96 Est. 46,137
ABC-CZ (90): 86,061 (HH 32,532)

The Elkhart Truth

(e-mon to fri; m-sat; S)

The Elkhart Truth, Communicana Bldg.; PO Box 487, Elkhart, IN 46515; tel (219) 294-1661; fax (219) 294-4014. Federated Media Corp. group.
Circulation: 27,750(e); 27,750(m-sat); 32,751(S); ABC Sept. 30, 1995.
Price: 50¢(d); 50¢(sat); $1.25(S); $9.75/mo (carrier); $10.00/mo (motor route), $111.00/yr.
Advertising: Open inch rate $19.90(e); $19.90(m-sat); $19.90(S). **Representative:** Landon Associates Inc.
News Services: AP, SHNS. **Politics:** Independent. **Established:** 1889.
Special Editions: Business and Industry (Jan); Brides, Basketball (Feb); Garden, Spring Fashion, R.V. Show Edition (Mar); Home Improvement, Spring Car Care (Apr); New Car, Great Race (May); Newcomers (June); 4-H Fair (July); Mobile Home Show (Aug); New Car Intro, Fall Home Improvement & Energy (Sept); Furniture, Clubs (Oct); Fall Car Care (Nov).
Special Weekly Sections: Vittles (Food) (mon); The Truth Business Report (tues); Stock Page (sat); AM/Entertainer, Travel Page, Habitat (S).
Magazines: USA Weekend; TViewing.
Broadcast Affiliates: WTMM Elkhart, IN; WQHK-FM/AM Fort Wayne, IN; WBYT-FM South Bend, IN; WKLZ-FM Grand Rapids, MI; WCKY.

CORPORATE OFFICERS

President John F Dille III
Vice Pres Anthony H Biggs
Secretary/Treasurer Robert A Watson

GENERAL MANAGEMENT

Publisher Anthony H Biggs
Controller Dallas K Johnston

ADVERTISING

Director David L Ogle

MARKETING AND PROMOTION

Director-Marketing Service Ronald Schmanske

CIRCULATION

Manager David Conwell

NEWS EXECUTIVE

Managing Editor John J Gillaspy

EDITORS AND MANAGERS

City Editor Steve Bibler
Columnist Jim McNeile
Editorial Page Editor Larry Murphy
Education Editor Stephanie Gattman
Home Furnishings Editor Barb Dodson
News Editor William Wilson
Photo Department Manager Fred Flury
Radio/Television Editor Marcia Fulmer
Religion Editor Tom Price
Society Editor Mike Knaack
Sports Editor Dennis Kraft
State Editor Sherrie Leonard
Wire Editor Robert Mast

MANAGEMENT INFORMATION SERVICES

Data Processing Manager Dallas K Johnston

PRODUCTION

Director Cliff Stuck
Manager-Composing Steve Samson
Manager-Pressroom John Platt
Manager-Mailroom Lorna Long

Market Information: Split Run; TMC.
Mechanical available: Web Offset; Black and 3 ROP colors; insert accepted — preprinted; page cut-offs — $22\frac{3}{4}$".
Mechanical specifications: Type page 13" x $21\frac{1}{2}$"; E - 6 cols, $2\frac{1}{16}$", $\frac{5}{32}$" between; A - 6 cols, $2\frac{1}{16}$", $\frac{5}{32}$" between; C - 10 cols, $1\frac{3}{8}$", $\frac{1}{32}$" between.
Commodity consumption: Newsprint 2,600 short tons; 2,300 metric tons; widths 56", 42", 28"; black ink 46,500 pounds; color ink 7,200 pounds; single pages printed 13,955; average pages per issue 28(d), 65(S); single plates used 33,432.
Equipment: EDITORIAL: Front-end hardware — CD/2330, 34-HAS/VDT, 7-RSK/10V, 1-XIT/Portable; Front-end software — CD; Printers — Okidata; Other equipment — Ap/Mac Quadra 950, PM/8100 Photo. CLASSIFIED: Front-end hardware — CD/2330, 7-HAS/VDT; Front-end software — CD; Printers — Okidata. DISPLAY: Adv layout systems — 1-SCS/Layout 8000; Front-end hardware — Dell, Ap/Mac Centris 650-CD, 2-PM/7100 CD; Front-end software — SCS; Printers — CI/300, HP/550C, Ap/Mac Laser Pro 630; Other equipment — Ap/Mac One color scanner. PRODUCTION: Typesetters — 2-COM/8400, 2-Ap/Mac LaserPrinter NTX 300 DPI, 2-COM/8400, 2-Ap/Mac LaserPrinter NTX, Ap/Mac 810, AG/1000 Imagesetter; Plate exposures — 2-Nu/Flip Top FT52UPNS; Plate processors — WL/30C; Production cameras — C/Spartan III, K/Vert; Automatic film processors — LE/LD24AQ; Film transporters — C; Shrink lenses — 1-CK Optical/SQU-7; Color separation equipment (conventional) — 1-BKY; Digital color separation equipment — Kk/2035+ (35mm), Ap/Power Mac 8100.
PRESSROOM: Line 1 — 5-HI/N1650; Folders — 2-HI/2:1; Reels and stands — 4-HI/Registron Reel Stand. MAILROOM: Counter stackers — 2-MRS; Inserters and stuffers — 3-Mc/N660, 2-Mc/N660; Bundle tyer — 2-Power Strap; Addressing machine — 1-KR. WIRE SERVICES: News — AP; Stock tables — AP; Syndicates — SHNS, AP; Receiving dishes — AP. BUSINESS COMPUTERS: 1-HP/922LX; Applications: CJ; PCs & micros networked; PCs & main system networked.

ELWOOD

Madison County

'90 U.S. Census- 9,494; E&P '96 Est. 8,910

The Call-Leader

(e-mon to fri; m-sat)

Elwood Call-Leader, 317 S. Anderson St.; PO Box 85, Elwood, IN 46036-2018; tel (317) 552-3355; fax (317) 552-3358. Ray Barnes Newspapers Inc. group.
Circulation: 3,612(e); 3,612(m-sat); Sworn Jan. 29, 1996.
Price: 35¢(d); 35¢(sat); $6.00/mo (carrier), $7.00/mo (motor route); $64.80/yr (carrier), $75.60/yr (motor route).
Advertising: Open inch rate $5.80(e); $5.80(m-sat); comb with Tipton County Tribune (e) $8.00.
News Service: AP. **Politics:** Independent-Republican. **Established:** 1891 (Call), 1891 Leader, 1894 (Call-Leader).
Not Published: New Year; Memorial Day; Independence Day; Labor Day; Thanksgiving; Christmas.
Special Editions: Mature Years (Jan); Cookbook, Basketball Sectional Edition (Feb); Spring Brides, Spring Opening (Mar); Farm & Garden (Apr); Spring Home Improvement (May); Welcome to Elwood (June); Madison Co., 4-H, Fair Wrap-up, Elwood Glass Festival Edition, Football Preview Edition (Aug); Frankton Heritage Days Festival Edition (Sept); Women in Business, Fall Car Care, Fall Brides (Oct); Basketball Preview Edition, Holiday Cookbook, Christmas Opening (Nov).
Special Weekly Section: Best Food Day (mon).
Magazines: The Mini-Page for Kids (tues); What's on TV (fri).

CORPORATE OFFICERS

President Jack L Barnes
Vice Pres Charles G Barnes
Secretary Judith K Barnes

GENERAL MANAGEMENT

Publisher Jack L Barnes
Business Manager Robert L Nash
Asst Publisher Brian Barnes

ADVERTISING

Director Robert L Nash

CIRCULATION

Director Chris Idlewine

NEWS EXECUTIVES

Editor Neil Johnson
Managing Editor Saundra Burton

EDITORS AND MANAGERS

Photo Department Manager Tim Waymire
Sports Editor Ed Hamilton

PRODUCTION

Foreman Melvin Fry

Market Information: TMC.
Mechanical available: Web Offset; Black and 3 ROP colors; insert accepted — preprinted; page cut-offs — $22\frac{3}{4}$".
Mechanical specifications: Type page 13" x $21\frac{1}{2}$"; E - 6 cols, $2\frac{1}{16}$", $\frac{1}{8}$" between; A - 6 cols, $2\frac{1}{16}$", $\frac{1}{8}$" between; C - 8 cols, $1\frac{1}{2}$", .15" between.
Commodity consumption: Newsprint 98 short tons; 90 metric tons; widths 27.5", 13.75"; black ink 2,880 pounds; color ink 360 pounds; single pages printed 3,766; average pages per issue 10(d); single plates used 2,150.
Equipment: EDITORIAL: Front-end hardware — Mk/1000; Front-end software — Mk/Mycro-Comp. CLASSIFIED: Front-end hardware — Mk/1000; Front-end software — Mk/Mycro-Comp. DISPLAY: Adv layout systems — 2-Ap/Mac SE. PRODUCTION: Typesetters — 2-Ap/Mac LaserWriter II NT/NTX; Plate exposures — 1-Nu/Flip Top; Production cameras — 1-R/Commodore; Automatic film processors — 1-LE/LD-24.
PRESSROOM: Line 1 — 4-G/Community; Folders — 1-G. MAILROOM: Bundle tyer — 2-Malow; Addressing machine — 2-Am. LIBRARY: Combination — 1-Recordak/Micro-Film reader. WIRE SERVICES: News — AP; Receiving dishes — AP. BUSINESS COMPUTERS: 1-BS/B-20, 1-RSK/TRS 80 model 4; Applications: Display billing, Sales reports, Subscriber billing, Subscriber/non-subscriber lists.

Copyright ©1996 by the Editor & Publisher Co.

I-128 Indiana

EVANSVILLE

Vanderburgh County

'90 U.S. Census- 126,272; E&P '96 Est. 126,098
ABC-CZ (90): 158,241 (HH 64,356)

Evansville Courier Company Inc.

Evansville Courier Co. Inc., 300 E. Walnut St.; PO Box 268, Evansville, IN 47702-0268; tel (812) 424-7711; fax (812) 464-7487. Scripps Howard group.

Representative: Sawyer-Ferguson-Walker Co.

Note: The Evansville Courier and the Evansville Press are corporately and editorially separate. The Evansville Courier Co., publisher of the Evansville Courier and the Sunday Courier acts as agent for the Evansville Press in their business, advertising, circulation and production functions.

CORPORATE OFFICERS

President (Courier) Thomas W Tuley
President (Press) Bill D Jackson

GENERAL MANAGEMENT

Business Manager/Controller Susanne A Brauer
Manager-Credit Gary Kelley
Personnel Director Thomas Mominee

ADVERTISING

Director Jack Pate
Manager-Display Robert Savage
Manager-Territory Sales Ron Obermeier
Manager-Territory Sales Delores Mason
Manager-Territory Sales Tina Corey St Clair

MARKETING AND PROMOTION

Manager-Promotion/Research Carolyn Franklin

TELECOMMUNICATIONS

Audiotex Manager Terri Woolen

CIRCULATION

Director Jerry Liddle

MANAGEMENT INFORMATION SERVICES

Director-Info Systems Charley Johnson

PRODUCTION

Director-Operations Dennis Ray
Asst Director Carl Dassel

Market Information: Zoned editions; Split Run; TMC; ADS; Operate audiotex.

Mechanical available: Flexography; Black and 3 ROP colors; insert accepted — preprinted; page cut-offs — 22".

Mechanical specifications: Type page 13" x 21.125"; E - 6 cols, $2\frac{1}{16}$", $\frac{1}{6}$" between; A - 6 cols, $2\frac{1}{16}$", $\frac{1}{6}$" between; C - 10 cols, $1\frac{1}{4}$", $\frac{1}{6}$" between.

Commodity consumption: Newsprint 9,294 short tons; widths 54", 27", $13\frac{1}{2}$", 40.5"; average pages per issue 35(d), 82(S).

Equipment: EDITORIAL: Front-end hardware — AT/ESP II; Front-end software — AT; Printers — Florida Data. CLASSIFIED: Front-end hardware — AT/ESP II; Front-end software — AT; Printers — Florida Data. AUDIOTEX: Hardware — PEP. DISPLAY: Adv layout systems — Ap/Mac; Front-end hardware — Sun/3160, Ap/Mac; Front-end software — QuarkXPress. PRODUCTION: Pagination software — AT/Class Page 5.0, P. INK/Pagination; Typesetters — III/Laser, Dolev/800, Dolev 450; Platemaking systems — Na; Plate exposures — 4-Na; Plate processors — 2-Na; Electronic picture desk — Lf/AP Leaf Picture Desk; Scanners — 2-ECR, Scitex/Smartscan; Production cameras — C, Nu; Automatic film processors — 2-P, 3-LE; Film transporters — C; Color separation equipment (conventional) — Scitex; Digital color separation equipment — Scitex. PRESSROOM: Line 1 — 12-MOT/FX 4 (6-Half decks, 2-Three color decks); Press drives — MOT; Folders — 2-MOT/2:1, 1-MOT/3:2; Pasters — MOT/Auto; Reels and stands — 12-MOT; Press control system — MOT; Press registration system — Hurletron. MAILROOM: Counter stackers — 3-HL/HT, 1-HL/HT2, 2-HL/Monitor, 3-HI/Commercial; Inserters and stuffers — 1-HI/72P-1372P, HI/NP-2299; Bundle tyer — 10-Power Strap; Wrapping singles — 3-HL/Bottom, 2-Power Strap; Addressing machine — 1-Ch, 1-Automecha/Accufast; Mailroom control system — HL; Other mailroom equipment — MM/355 Saddle Stitcher; MM/Quarter Folder. LIBRARY: Electronic — Vu/Text. WIRE SERVICES: News — AP; Photos — AP; Stock tables — AP; Syndicates — LAT-WP, NYT, SHNS; Receiving dishes — AP. BUSINESS COMPUTERS: 1-DEC/VAX 6310, 1-DEC/ 3100, Sun/System 10-512, IBM/RS6000; Applications: CJ: Circ; WordPerfect, Quattro, In-house, Microsoft/Word, Microsoft/Excel; PCs & micros networked; PCs & main system networked.

The Evansville Courier

(m-mon to sat; S)

The Evansville Courier, 300 E. Walnut St.; PO Box 268, Evansville, IN 47702-0268; tel (812) 424-7711; fax (812) 464-7487; web site http://www.evansville.net/. Scripps Howard group.

Circulation: 61,792(m); 61,792(m-sat); 114,002(S); ABC Sept. 30, 1995.

Price: 50¢(d); 50¢(sat); $1.75(S); $16.40/mo.

Advertising: Open inch rate $57.41(m); $57.41(m-sat); $70.20(S) comb with The Evansville Press (e) $66.31. **Representative:** Sawyer-Ferguson-Walker Co.

News Services: AP, NYT, SHNS. **Politics:** Independent. **Established:** 1845.

Note: The Evansville Courier and the Evansville Press are corporately and editorially separate. The Evansville Courier Co., publisher of the Evansville Courier and the Sunday Courier acts as agent for the Evansville Press in their business, advertising, circulation and production functions. For detailed production and printing functions, see the Evansville Courier Co. listing.

Special Editions: E-Qual Quality (Feb); Home & Garden (Mar); Home Show, Summer Vacation (Apr); Progress (July); Progress (Aug); Gift Guide, Holiday Cookbook (Nov).

Special Weekly Sections: Church and Religion, Star Watch (sat); Family (sat, 2x/mo); Sunday TV Video (S).

Magazine: Parade.

TELECOMMUNICATIONS

Audiotex Manager Nancee Simms

NEWS EXECUTIVES

Editor Thomas W Tuley
Exec Editor Paul McAuliffe
Asst Managing Editor-News Kathleen Wagner
Asst Managing Editor-Sunday Thomas Ryder

EDITORS AND MANAGERS

Business Editor Tim D Barker
Columnist Garrett Mathews
Director-Community Service Carol Wersich
Director-Photography/Color Graphic Input Jimmy Bye
Editorial Page Editor Chuck Leach
Education Reporter Byron Rohrig
Entertainment Editor Roger McBain
Features Editor John Reiter
Asst Features Editor Jim Michels
Food Editor Anne Schleper
Librarian Roseann Derk
Metro Editor Mark Kroeger
Asst Metro Editor-City Barry Rose
News Editor L D Seits
Special Assignments Editor Roberta Heiman
Exec Sports Editor Dave Johnson
Asst Sports Editor Jay Stockman
Asst Sports Editor Tim Kaiser
Television Editor Rebecca Coudret

MANAGEMENT INFORMATION SERVICES

Data Processing Manager Charley Johnson
Online Manager Vickie Hempfling

PRODUCTION

Director-Operations Dennis Ray
Asst Director Carl Dassel

Market Information: Zoned editions; Split Run; TMC; ADS; Operate database; Operate audiotex; Electronic edition.

Mechanical available: Flexo; Black and 3 ROP colors; insert accepted — preprinted; page cut-offs — 22.047".

Mechanical specifications: Type page 13" x 21.125"; E - 6 cols, $2\frac{1}{16}$", $\frac{1}{6}$" between; A - 6 cols, $2\frac{1}{16}$", $\frac{1}{6}$" between; C - 10 cols, $1\frac{1}{4}$", $\frac{1}{6}$" between.

Commodity consumption: Newsprint 9,294 metric tons; widths 53.875", 40.40675", 26.9375", 13.46895"; black ink 386,807 pounds; color ink 156,296 pounds; single pages printed 25,724; average pages per issue 35(d), 30(sat), 81(S); single plates used 142,000.

The Evansville Press

(e-mon to sat)

The Evansville Press, 300 E. Walnut St.; PO Box 454, Evansville, IN 47703; tel (812) 464-7614; fax (812) 464-7641.

Circulation: 24,666(e); 24,666(e-sat); ABC Sept. 30, 1995.

Price: 50¢(d); 50¢(sat); $8.35/mo; $100.20/yr.

Advertising: Open inch rate $56.74(e); $56.74(e-sat) comb with The Evansville Courier (m) $66.31. **Representative:** Sawyer-Ferguson-Walker Co.

News Services: KRT, NEA, AP. **Politics:** Independent. **Established:** 1906.

Note: The Evansville Courier and the Evansville Press are corporately and editorially separate. The Evansville Courier Co., publisher of the Evansville Courier and Sunday Courier, acts as agent for the Evansville Press in their business, advertising, circulation and production functions. For detailed production and printing functions, see the Evansville Courier Co. listing.

Not Published: Memorial Day; Independence Day; Labor Day.

Special Weekly Sections: Best Food Days (wed); Best Food Days (thur); Church and Religion (sat); Sunday TVideo (S).

CORPORATE OFFICERS

President Bill D Jackson
Publisher Robert H Hartmann

ADVERTISING

Director Jack Pate

NEWS EXECUTIVE

Editor Bill D Jackson

EDITORS AND MANAGERS

Amusements/Entertainment Editor Sandra Knipe
Auto/Aviation Editor Mel Runge
Books Editor Chris Gustin
Business/Finance Editor Mel Runge
Education Editor Patricia Swanson
Editorial Page Editor Bill D Jackson
Family/Leisure Editor Rick Mark
Food Editor Sara Corrigan
Films Editor Sandra Knipe
Librarian Ellen Sprepski
Metro Editor Bob Gustin
Music/Radio Editor Sandra Knipe
News Editor Rick Mark
Photography Editor Lou Bloss
Real Estate Editor Mel Runge
Religion/Schools Editor Patricia Swanson
Sports Editor Tim Ethridge
Television Editor Bob Hall
Women's Editor Rick Mark

MANAGEMENT INFORMATION SERVICES

Office Administrator Debbie Mauck

Mechanical specifications: Type page $13\frac{1}{16}$" x 22"; E - 6 cols, $2\frac{1}{16}$", $\frac{1}{8}$" between; A - 6 cols, $2\frac{1}{16}$", $\frac{1}{8}$" between; C - 10 cols, $1\frac{1}{4}$", $\frac{1}{16}$" between.

Commodity consumption: average pages per issue 34(d).

FORT WAYNE

Allen County

'90 U.S. Census- 173,072; E&P '96 Est. 177,245
ABC-NDM (90): 271,775 (HH 103,805)

Fort Wayne Newspapers Inc.

Fort Wayne Newspapers Inc., 600 W. Main St.; PO Box 100, Fort Wayne, IN 46801; tel (219) 461-8444; fax (219) 461-8749.

Note: The News-Sentinel (e) and the Journal-Gazette (mS) operate their business, advertising, circulation and mechanical departments under a joint publishing company. They are corporately and editorially separate.

CORPORATE OFFICERS

President/CEO Scott McGehee
Vice Pres-Sales/Marketing Carolyn Pictor Hughes
Chief Financial Officer John Kovatch

GENERAL MANAGEMENT

Manager-Credit Dan Dougan
Manager-Purchasing Doe Bell
Personnel Director James Bentley

ADVERTISING

Director Lisa Goodman
Senior Manager-Product Development Sue Crouch
Senior Manager-Sales Tom Eason
Manager-Sales Mark Sumney
Manager-Sales Gene Villarreal
Manager-Operations Laura Coon
Manager-Specialty Publications Chris Vosmeier
Manager-Strategic Initiatives Dennis Robinson

MARKETING AND PROMOTION

Director-Marketing Service Andy Candor
Manager-Promotion Steve Cebalt

TELECOMMUNICATIONS

Director-Info Systems Dawn Bonfiglio
Manager-Operations Lee Dickerson
Manager-Programming Rod Custer
Audiotex Manager Gordon Given

CIRCULATION

Director John Murray
Manager-Sales/Promotion Shellie Nice
Manager-The Journal Gazette Kathy Fetsch
Manager-Administration Mark Gidley
Manager-The News-Sentinel Betty Robbins Lentz

MANAGEMENT INFORMATION SERVICES

Data Processing Manager Dawn Bonfiglio

PRODUCTION

Director Phil Haggerty
Asst Director Betty Forehand
Manager-Composing Dave Tappy
Manager-Building Bob Havener
Manager-Budget/Warehouse Kathy Dobbins
Manager-Packaging/Distribution Gene Kline
Manager-Technology Steve Yoho
Manager-Press/Plate Tanya Jarvis
Supervisor-Electronic Imaging Nancy Walker

Market Information: Zoned editions; Split Run; TMC; ADS; Operate audiotex.

Mechanical available: Flexo, Letterpress; Black; insert accepted — preprinted; page cut-offs — $23\frac{9}{16}$".

Mechanical specifications: Type page 13" x 22"; E - 6 cols, $2\frac{1}{16}$", $\frac{1}{8}$" between; A - 6 cols, $2\frac{1}{16}$", $\frac{1}{8}$" between; C - 10 cols, $1\frac{1}{4}$", $\frac{1}{16}$" between.

Commodity consumption: Newsprint 12,686 metric tons; widths $54\frac{3}{4}$", 41", $27\frac{1}{4}$"; black; ink 433,370 pounds; color ink 114,430 pounds; single pages printed 35,254; average pages per issue 42(d), 104(S); single plates used 92,496.

Equipment: EDITORIAL: Front-end hardware — Dell; Front-end software — III/Tecs 2; Printers — Epson, HP/LaserJet. CLASSIFIED: Front-end hardware — Dell/PC-compatible; Front-end software — III/Tecs 2; Printers — Epson, HP/LaserJet. AUDIOTEX: Hardware — Brite Voice Systems; Supplier name — City Line. DISPLAY: Adv layout systems — HP/3000 Series 967 CJ, CJ; Front-end hardware — 2-Ap/Mac, HP; Front-end software — Quark-XPress, Aldus/FreeHand; Printers — HP, QMS, Ap/Mac LaserPrinter. PRODUCTION: Pagination software — Baseview/Managing Editor, Mk/Page Director CLS 1.7.3; Typesetters — 1-AU/Micro5, 1-AU/APS-6-80, 1-AU/APS-82-ACS, 1-AU/APS-9800, 1-AU/APS-7-3850-ES; Plate exposures — 2-He/SRA; Plate processors — 2-He/SRB; Scanners — ECR/Autokon 1000, RZ/200S, 3-Howtek/ Scanmaster 3 Plus, 1-Lf/AP Leafscan 35; Production cameras — 1-C/Newspager II, 1-C/Marathon; Automatic film processors — 2-LE/Systems 2600; Film transporters — 1-C; Shrink lenses — 1-C; Color separation equipment (conventional) — 1-Ap/Mac Quadra 800, 2-Ap/Mac Quadra 900. PRESSROOM: Line 1 — 4-MAN/Flexoman 1 (2-four color, 2-half decks), 8-G/Mark I (2-black; 6-color); Press drives — PEC/James Bond; Folders — G/2:1; Pasters — PEC/Automatics; Reels and stands — G; Press control system — PEC/James Bond. MAILROOM: Counter stackers — 2-MSI/1220s, HI, 1-QWI/SJ20X, 2-QWI/300, 1-HL/Dual Carrier; Inserters and stuffers — 1-HI/1472, 1-HI/1372; Bundle tyer — 2-Power Strap/PSN6, 1-Power Strap/PSN5, 1-Dynaric/NP-2, 1-MLN/Spirit; Addressing machine — 2-Ch/529; Other mailroom equipment — 1-MM/22-Saddle Stitcher. LIBRARY: Electronic — III, Vu/Text. WIRE SERVICES: News — UPI, AP; Stock tables — UPI, AP; Receiving dishes — size-3m, AP. BUSINESS COMPUTERS: 1-HP/967; Applications: CJ; PCs & micros networked; PCs & main system networked.

The Journal Gazette

(m-mon to sat; S)

Journal Gazette, 600 W. Main St.; PO Box 88, Fort Wayne, IN 46801; tel (219) 461-8333; fax (219) 461-8648, (219) 461-8893; e-mail jgletters@plink.qels.com.

Circulation: 62,222(m); 62,222(m-sat); 139,012(S); ABC Sept. 30, 1995.

Price: 50¢(d); 50¢(sat); $1.50(S); $3.15/wk; $163.80/yr.

Advertising: Open inch rate $65.26(m); $65.26(m-sat); $77.26(S); comb with Fort Wayne News-Sentinel(e) $109.56. **Representative:** Landon Associates Inc.

News Services: AP, SHNS, RN, LAT-WP, BPI. **Politics:** Independent. **Established:** 1863 (Gazette), 1868 (Journal), 1869 (Journal-Gazette).

Note: For detailed advertising, circulation, production and mechanical information, see Ft. Wayne Newspaper Inc. listing.

Copyright ©1996 by the Editor & Publisher Co.

Indiana I-129

Advertising not accepted: Right reserved to reject any copy or illustration.
Special Editions: Auto Show (Jan); Passport to Saving, Auto Leasing, Bride's Guide (Feb); Design-an-Ad, Spring Car Care Guide (Mar); Town & Country, American Cancer, Home & Lawn (Apr); Guide to Fort Wayne, Passport to Saving, Auto Leasing, Indy 500 (May); Three Rivers Festival, Swiss Days (July); Passport to Saving, Auto Leasing (Aug); Parade of Homes (Sept); News Haven, New Cars, Diner's Guide, Fall Car Care (Oct); Early Holiday Gift Guide, Passport to Saving (Nov); Holiday Gift Guide, Last Minute Gift Guide, Letters to Santa (Dec).
Special Weekly Sections: Business, Living For Kids (mon); Next (young adult) (tues); Restaurant Reviews, Food/Best Food Day, Next (young adult) (wed); Restaurant News, Next (young adult) (thur); Religion (sat); Outdoor Page, Real Estate, Agriculture, TV Listings, Book/Music Reviews, Kids Stories & Puzzles, Travel & Arts (S); Entertainment/Restaurants/Theatres, Financial, Living, Sports, State/Regional (daily).
Magazines: People (TMC) (tues); Parade (S); New Homes & Remodeling Magazine (monthly).

CORPORATE OFFICERS
President Richard G Inskeep
Secretary/Corporate Treasurer Jerry Fox
Vice Pres Julie Inskeep Walda
Vice Pres-Finance Stephen S Inskeep

GENERAL MANAGEMENT
Publisher Richard G Inskeep
Asst Publisher Julie Inskeep Walda

ADVERTISING
Vice Pres Sales/Marketing Carolyn Pictor Hughes
Director Lisa Goodman

MARKETING AND PROMOTION
Director-Marketing/Promotion Andy Candor

TELECOMMUNICATIONS
Audiotex Manager Gordon Given

CIRCULATION
Director John Murray
Manager Kathy Fetsch

NEWS EXECUTIVES
Editor Craig Klugman
Managing Editor Sherry Skufca

EDITORS AND MANAGERS
Asst Managing Editor-Features Sandy Thorn Clark
Asst Managing Editor-News Keith Elchert
Business Editor Tom Pellegrene
Cartoonist Dan Lynch
Editorial Page Editor Larry Hayes
Food Editor Sandy Thorn Clark
Graphic Editor Ed Breen
Librarian Jody Habayeb
Metro Editor Tracy Warner
Chief Photographer Dean Musser Jr
Sports Editor Justice Hill
Travel/Arts Editor Harriet Heithaus
Television Editor Dean Robinson

MANAGEMENT INFORMATION SERVICES
Data Processing Manager Dawn Bonfiglio

PRODUCTION
Director Phil Haggerty

Market Information: Zoned editions; TMC; ADS; Operate audiotex.
Mechanical available: Flexo, Letterpress; Black; insert accepted — preprinted; page cut-offs — 23⁹⁄₁₆".
Mechanical specifications: Type page 13" x 22"; E - 6 cols, A - 6 cols, C - 10 cols.
Commodity consumption: average pages per issue 42(d), 104(S).
Equipment: EDITORIAL: Front-end hardware — Dell; Front-end software — III/Tecs 2. CLASSIFIED: Front-end hardware — Dell; Front-end software — III/Tecs 2. AUDIOTEX: Hardware — Brite; Software — Brite; Supplier name — City Line. DISPLAY: Adv layout systems — CJ; Front-end hardware — Ap/Mac; Front-end software — Multi-Ad/Creator. LIBRARY: Electronic — III/Tecs 2. WIRE SERVICES: News — AP; Photos — AP; Stock tables — AP; Syndicates — LATS. BUSINESS COMPUTERS: HP/3000-967; Applications: WordPerfect, Quattro; PCs & micros networked; PCs & main system networked.

The News-Sentinel (e-mon to sat)

The News-Sentinel, PO Box 100, Fort Wayne, IN 46801; tel (219) 461-8222; fax (219) 461-8649. Knight-Ridder Inc. group.
Circulation: 52,910(e); 52,910(e-sat); ABC Sept. 30, 1995.
Price: 50¢(d); 50¢(sat); $1.65/wk; $85.80/yr.
Advertising: Open inch rate $65.26(e); $65.26(e-sat); comb with Fort Wayne Journal-Gazette(m) $109.56. **Representatives:** Landon Associates Inc.; Newspapers First.
News Services: AP, KRT. **Politics:** Independent. **Established:** 1833 (Sentinel), 1874 (News), 1918 (News-Sentinel).
Note: For detailed advertising, circulation, production and mechanical information, see Fort Wayne Newspapers Inc. listing.
Advertising not accepted: Right reserved to reject any copy or illustration.
Special Editions: Auto Show, ½ Off Customer Appreciation (Jan); Brides Guide (Feb); Design-An-Ad, Spring Car Care Guide, Town & Country, American Cancer (Mar); Home & Lawn, Passport to Savings, New Haven Open House (Apr); Guide to Fort Wayne, Indy 500 (May); Family Owned Business (June); Three Rivers Festival, Swiss Days (July); Fort Wayne Answer Book, Parade of Homes, Passport to Savings (Sept); Diner's Guide, Fall Car Care (Oct); Holiday Gift Guide, Holiday Home Entertaining (Nov); Letters to Santa (Dec).
Special Weekly Sections: Farming (mon); Food/Best Food Day (tues); Book/Music Reviews, Home Decorating, TV Listings, Entertainment, Gardening (sat); Entertainment/Restaurants/Theatres, Financial, Living/Lifestyle, Sports, State/Regional (daily).
Magazine: New Homes & Remodeling Magazine (monthly).

GENERAL MANAGEMENT
Publisher Scott McGehee

CIRCULATION
Manager Betty Robins Lentz
Manager-Single Copy Sales David Gearet

NEWS EXECUTIVES
Exec Editor Joe Weiler
Managing Editor Richard Battin
Asst Managing Editor Carolyn Di Paolo

EDITORS AND MANAGERS
Business Editor Marilyn Karst
Copy Desk Chief Rick Rimelspach
Editorial Page Editor Leo Morris
Metro Editor Michael Johnson
Neighbors Editor Constance Haas Zuber
Director-Photography Keith Hitchens
Exec Sports Editor Kerry Hubartt

Market Information: TMC; ADS.
Mechanical available: Flexo, Letterpress; Black; insert accepted — preprinted; page cut-offs — 23⁹⁄₁₆".
Mechanical specifications: Type page 13" x 22"; E - 6 cols, 2¹⁄₁₆", ⅛" between; A - 6 cols, 2¹⁄₁₆", ⅛" between; C - 10 cols, 1¼", ¹⁄₁₆" between.
Equipment: EDITORIAL: Front-end hardware — Dell; Front-end software — III/Tecs 2; Printers — Epson, HP/LaserJet. CLASSIFIED: Front-end hardware — Dell; Front-end software — III/Tecs 2; Printers — Epson, HP/LaserJet. WIRE SERVICES: News — Photos — AP.

FRANKFORT
Clinton County
'90 U.S. Census- 14,754; E&P '96 Est. 14,787

The Times (e-mon to fri; m-sat)

The Times, 251 E. Clinton St.; PO Box 9, Frankfort, IN 46041-0009; tel (317) 659-4622; fax (317) 654-7031. Nixon Newspapers Inc. group.
Circulation: 7,632(e); 7,632(m-sat); Sworn Oct. 2, 1995.
Price: 50¢(d); 50¢(sat); $6.25/mo (city), $6.75/mo (motor route).
Advertising: Open inch rate $11.48(e); $11.48 (m-sat). **Representative:** Nixon Newspapers.
News Service: AP. **Politics:** Independent. **Established:** 1877.
Not Published: New Year; Memorial Day; Independence Day; Labor Day; Thanksgiving; Christmas.
Special Editions: Spring Bridal; Home Show; Spring Home Improvement; Spring Car Care; Mother's Day; Graduation; National Restaurant Month; Father's Day; Fall Sports Section; Fall Bridal; Fall Farm Section; Fall Home Improvement; Fall Car Care; 4-H tab; Winter Sports; Christmas; Antique Tab; Golf Guide; Favorite Brands; Meet the Merchant; Herds & Plowshares.
Special Weekly Sections: Business Directory (tues); TV Listing (fri).
Magazines: Senior Times; Clinton County TV/Cable Guide.
Cable TV: Own cable TV in circulation area.

CORPORATE OFFICERS
President John R Nixon
Vice Pres Ken Bronson
Secretary Deborah M Huff

GENERAL MANAGEMENT
Publisher J Mark Ingels

ADVERTISING
Director Greg Ludlow
Manager-Classified Dave Wood

CIRCULATION
Manager Tammy Janz

NEWS EXECUTIVE
Managing Editor Howard Hewitt

EDITORS AND MANAGERS
Copy Editor Peggy Miller
Education Editor Alan Girton
Government Editor Matt Mora
News Editor Brian Zink
Photographer Steve Harmon
Sports Editor Jim Bush

PRODUCTION
Manager Ken Koppelmann

Market Information: Zoned editions; TMC.
Mechanical available: Offset; Black and 3 ROP colors; insert accepted — preprinted, single sheets, booklets; page cut-offs — 22¾".
Mechanical specifications: Type page 13" x 21½"; E - 6 cols, 2¹⁄₁₆", ⅛" between; A - 6 cols, 2¹⁄₁₆", ⅛" between; C - 6 cols, 2¹⁄₁₆", ⅛" between.
Commodity consumption: Newsprint 600 metric tons; widths 30", 27½", 24"; black ink 3,175 pounds; color ink 1,160 pounds; single pages printed 4,150; average pages per issue 13.6(d); single plates used 3,013.
Equipment: EDITORIAL: Front-end hardware — Ap/Mac; Front-end software — Baseview, QuarkXPress; Printers — Ap/Mac LaserWriter NTX, Ap/Mac LaserWriter IIf; Other equipment — Ap/Mac Scanner. CLASSIFIED: Front-end hardware — Ap/Mac; Front-end software — Baseview; Printers — Ap/Mac LaserWriter NTX. DISPLAY: Front-end hardware — 1-Dewar/Discovery, 2-Ap/Mac Classic; Front-end software — Multi-Ad/Creator. PRODUCTION: Typesetters — 1-COM/8400, 1-Ap/Mac LaserWriter II; Plate exposures — 1-Nu; Plate processors — 1-Nat/A-250; Production cameras — 1-R/400; Automatic film processors — 1-LE/18. PRESSROOM: Line 1 — 10-G/Community; Folders — 1-G. MAILROOM: Counter stackers — 1-BG; Inserters and stuffers — 1-KAN/320; Bundle tyer — 1-Bu/20-2-1-E4, 1-Bu/Tristar 210; Addressing machine — 1-Ch/515. COMMUNICATIONS: Digital ad delivery system — AP AdSend. WIRE SERVICES: News — AP; Receiving dishes — AP. BUSINESS COMPUTERS: 1-IBM/Sys 36.

FRANKLIN-GREENWOOD
Johnson County
'90 U.S. Census- 39,172 (Franklin 12,907; Greenwood 26,265); E&P '96 Est. 43,000 (Franklin 14,242; Greenwood 29,314)
ABC-NDM (90): 88,109 (HH 31,354)

Daily Journal (e-mon to fri; m-sat)

Daily Journal, 2575 N. Morton St.; PO Box 699, Franklin, IN 46131; tel (317) 736-7101; fax (317) 736-2713. Home News Enterprises group.
Circulation: 17,230(e); 17,230(m-sat); ABC Sept. 30, 1995.
Price: 50¢(d); 75¢(sat); $7.50/mo (carrier/motor route); $90.00/yr.
Advertising: Open inch rate $15.05(e); $15.05(m-sat).
News Service: AP. **Politics:** Independent. **Established:** 1963.
Not Published: New Year; Memorial Day; Independence Day; Labor Day; Christmas.
Special Editions: Taxes, Bridal, Coupon Plus, Auto Tax Guide (Jan); Central 9, Home Improvement, Progress Edition (Feb); Agriculture, Junior Journal, Lawn & Garden (Mar); American Home Week, Coupon Plus, Car Care (Apr); Mother's Day, Indy 500 (May); Business Profile (June); Johnson County 4-H Fair (July); Fall Sports, School Preview (Aug); Fall Home Care (Sept); Car Care (Oct); Winter Sports (Nov); Last Minute Christmas Gift Guide (Dec).
Special Weekly Sections: School Page (mon); Business Pages (tues); Best Food Day (wed); TV Book, Church Page (sat).
Magazines: TV Section; Parade of Homes; Coupons Plus; Local Adv. Newsprint; USA Weekend; Real Estate (monthly).

GENERAL MANAGEMENT
Publisher Howard Herron

ADVERTISING
Director J Fred Mattingly
Manager-Ad Sales Mary Crouch

CIRCULATION
Director Robert Blue

NEWS EXECUTIVES
Editor Jeff Owen
Managing Editor David Hackett

EDITORS AND MANAGERS
Editorial Page Editor Jeff Owen
Sports Editor Jeff Madsen

PRODUCTION
Director Merrill Eddy
Manager-Graphic Arts Kris Lewis
Manager-Computer Systems Kathy McDermott
Manager-Post Press Joe Saba

Market Information: TMC.
Mechanical available: Offset; Black and 3 ROP colors; insert accepted — preprinted, call (317) 736-2750 re. other inserts accepted; page cut-offs — 22¾".
Mechanical specifications: Type page 13" x 21½"; E - 6 cols, 2.07", ⅙" between; A - 6 cols, 2.07", ⅙" between; C - 9 cols, 1⅓", ⅙" between.
Commodity consumption: Newsprint 613 short tons; width 27½"; black ink 21,850 pounds; color ink 4,650 pounds; single pages printed 6,330; average pages per issue 21(d), 30(sat); single plates used 12,000.
Equipment: EDITORIAL: Front-end hardware — Ap/Mac, PC, CNI/PC fileservers, Novell/Betrieve, Dewar; Front-end software — Dewar, QuarkXPress 3.31, Microsoft/Word 2.0; Printers — Ap/Mac LaserWriter II, ECR/VR36, Unity/1200 XLO, Ap/Mac LaserWriter IIq, Ap/Mac LaserWriter II NT; Other equipment — Ap/Mac Quadra 650, Ap/Mac Quadra 950, Lf/Leafscan 35, Umax/UC1260. CLASSIFIED: Front-end hardware — Dewar; Front-end software — Dewar; Printers — Ap/Mac LaserWriter II, Unity/1200 XLO. DISPLAY: Adv layout systems — Ap/Mac Quadra 650, Ap/Mac IIci, Multi-Ad, CNI/Ad Database; Front-end hardware — Ap/Mac Quadra 650, Ap/Mac IIci; Front-end software — Multi-Ad/Creator 3.6, CNI/Ad Database; Printers — Unity/1200 XLO, Ap/Mac LaserWriter II NT, Ap/Mac LaserWriter IIg, ECR/VR 36. PRODUCTION: Pagination software — Dewar, QuarkXPress 3.31; Typesetters — Ap/Mac LaserWriter II NT, ECR/VR 36, Unity/1200 XLO, Ap/Mac LaserWriter IIg; Plate exposures — 1-Nu; Plate processors — Nat; Electronic picture desk — Lf/AP Leaf Picture Desk; Scanners — Lf/Leafscan 35, Umax/1260; Production cameras — SCREEN/Companica; Automatic film processors — Litex/26 C-660-C, LE/500; Color separation equipment (conventional) — Ap/Mac Quadra 650, Ap/Mac Quadra 950, Adobe/Photoshop 3.0.
PRESSROOM: Line 1 — 12-G/Community SSC; Press drives — 3-G/Community SSC; Folders — 2-G/Community SSC; Reels and stands — 10-G/Roll Stand; Press control system — Fin. MAILROOM: Counter stackers — HI; Inserters and stuffers — 2-KAN; Bundle tyer — 3-Bu, 1-MLN; Wrapping singles — Power Strap/Bottom-Wrapper; Addressing machine — MG. WIRE SERVICES: News — AP, SHNS; Syndicates — NEA, TMS, Universal Press; Receiving dishes — AP. BUSINESS COMPUTERS: 2-Sun/workstation, 5-Teck Tronix, 2-Wyse; Applications: PBS: Circ, Adv billing.

GARY
Lake County
'90 U.S. Census- 116,646; E&P '96 Est. 100,076
ABC-CZ (90): 239,445 (HH 84,607)

Post-Tribune (m-mon to sat; S)

Post-Tribune, 1065 Broadway, Gary, IN 46402-2998; tel (219) 881-3000; e-mail gpt@crown.net. Knight-Ridder Inc. group.
Circulation: 67,680(m); 67,680(m-sat); 78,623(S); ABC Sept. 30, 1995.
Price: 50¢(d); 50¢(sat); $1.50(S); $3.00/wk; $13.00/mo; $156.00/yr.
Advertising: Open inch rate $46.90(m); $46.90(m-sat); $53.00(S). **Representative:** Landon Associates Inc.

News Services: AP, KRT, LAT-WP. **Politics:** Independent. **Established:** 1909.
Special Editions: Bridal (Jan); Chicago Auto Show (Feb); Spring Home Improvement, Porter County Home & Garden Show, Employment Access (Mar); Communities (June); Porter County Fair (July); Lake County Fair (Aug); Health Services/Leisure, Popcorn Festival, Pork Fest (Sept); Auto Preview, Business/Health Expo (Oct); Holiday Catalog (Nov); Downtown Valparaiso Holiday Tab, Holiday Songbook (Dec).
Special Weekly Sections: On the Money (mon); Health & Fitness (tues); Edibles (wed); Bravo!, Gary Neighbors (thur); Time Out, Weekend (fri); Home Owner, Families (sat); Northwest Indiana, Real Estate, Lifestyle (S).
Magazines: Parade (newsprint, regional), TV (quarterfold) (S).

CORPORATE OFFICERS
President Scott Bosley
Vice Pres Ross Jones
Vice Pres William W Sutton Jr
Secretary Douglas C Harris
Treasurer Stephen H Sheriff

GENERAL MANAGEMENT
Publisher Scott Bosley
Director-Finance Jan Pallares
Director-Human Resources Charles Cammack

ADVERTISING
Director Lawrence A Leibengood
Manager-Display Thomas Sanders
Manager-Inside Sales Terry Weaver
Manager-Customer Service Paula Knight

MARKETING AND PROMOTION
Director-Marketing/Community Relations Diane Schoon

CIRCULATION
Director Mike Burlingame
Manager-Marketing Jim Nelson
Manager-Home Delivery Lawrence Smith
Coordinator-Newspapers in Education Alicia McGill

NEWS EXECUTIVES
Editor William W Sutton Jr
Managing Editor Kay Manning
Asst Managing Editor Linda Williams

EDITORS AND MANAGERS
Daily Magazine Editor Sharon Wilmore
Design Editor Mark Emmert
Editorial Page Editor Peter Blum
News Editor William W Sutton Jr
Photography Editor Kenneth Walker
Porter County Editor Patrick Webb
Southlake Editor Chris Celek

MANAGEMENT INFORMATION SERVICES
Data Processing Manager Larry Mellman

PRODUCTION
Director George Shown
Manager-Pressroom John Martin
Manager-Mailroom Tom Trakas
Engineer-Plant David Farley

Market Information: Zoned editions; Split Run; TMC.
Mechanical available: Offset; Black and 3 ROP colors; insert accepted — preprinted, other inserts on request; page cut-offs — 22".
Mechanical specifications: Type page 13" x 21"; E - 6 cols, $2\frac{1}{16}$", $\frac{1}{8}$" between; A - 6 cols, $2\frac{1}{16}$", $\frac{1}{8}$" between; C - 10 cols, $1\frac{1}{4}$", $\frac{1}{16}$" between.
Commodity consumption: Newsprint 7,580 metric tons; widths 55", $41\frac{1}{4}$", $27\frac{1}{2}$"; black ink 192,000 pounds; color ink 33,981 pounds; single pages printed 25,802; average pages per issue 40(d), 92(S); single plates used 96,000.
Equipment: EDITORIAL: Front-end hardware — 6-AT/J-11; Front-end software — AT. CLASSIFIED: Front-end hardware — AT/IAS; Front-end software — AT/IAS. DISPLAY: Adv layout systems — CJ, HP; Front-end hardware — Ap/Mac; Front-end software — QuarkXPress 3.3, Adobe/Photoshop 3.0, Adobe/Illustrator 5.5; PRODUCTION: Typesetters — 2-MON/Series 3, 1-MON/Laserpress; Plate exposures — 2-Nu; Plate processors — 2-G/Imperial; Electronic picture desk — Lf/AP Leaf Picture Desk; Scanners — 2-ECR/Autokon, 2-Lf/Leafscan 35; Production cameras — 1-C/Spartan III, 2-C/Marathon; Automatic film processors — 4-LE, C.
PRESSROOM: Line 1 — 3-PEC/Eagle 3 Color, 6-PEC/Spectrum B&W; Folders — 2-G; Pasters — 6-G/Automatic, 3-PEC/Automatic; Reels and stands — 9-G/Mark II; Press control system — GE. MAILROOM: Counter stackers — 2-QWI/3000, 2-Id/440, 2-QWI/200; Inserters and stuffers — 1-GMA/14-72p, 1-S/48p; Bundle tyer — 2-MLN/2A, 2-MLN/News 90; Addressing machine — 2-Ch. LIBRARY: Electronic — Vu/Text. COMMUNICATIONS: Digital ad delivery system — AP AdSend. Systems used — satellite. WIRE SERVICES: News — Stock tables — AP Grand Central Stocks; Receiving dishes — AP. BUSINESS COMPUTERS: HP/3000-947; Applications: Accts payable, Gen ledger, Payroll, Adv, Circ, Personnel, Budget; PCs & micros networked; PCs & main system networked.

GOSHEN
Elkhart County
'90 U.S. Census- 23,797; E&P '96 Est. 27,924
ABC-CZ (90): 28,342 (HH 10,477)

The Goshen News
(e-mon to sat)

The Goshen News, 114 S. Main St. (46526); PO Box 569, Goshen, IN 46527; tel (219) 533-2151; fax (219) 533-0839.
Circulation: 16,840(e); 16,840(e-sat); ABC Sept. 30, 1995.
Price: 50¢(d); 50¢(sat).
Advertising: Open inch rate $10.12(e); $10.12 (e-sat). **Representative:** Landon Associates Inc.
News Service: AP. **Politics:** Republican-Independent. **Established:** 1837.
Not Published: New Year; Memorial Day; Independence Day; Labor Day; Christmas.
Special Editions: Bride Tab; 4-H Week; Basketball Tourney Time; Agriculture; Business & Industry; Home Improvement, Car Care Tab (Spring & Fall); Elkhart Co. Fair Tab; Fall & Winter Sports Tab.
Special Weekly Sections: Food Section (full color recipes on front cover) (tues); Viewer's Choice (TV Listings) (fri).

CORPORATE OFFICERS
President/Treasurer Jane Gemmer
Exec Vice Pres/Secretary John Gemmer

GENERAL MANAGEMENT
Publisher John Gemmer

ADVERTISING
Director James Young

CIRCULATION
Director Terry Bauer

NEWS EXECUTIVE
Editor Gerry Hertzler

EDITOR AND MANAGER
City Editor Roger Schneider

Market Information: TMC.
Mechanical available: Offset; Black and 3 ROP colors; insert accepted — preprinted; page cut-offs — $22\frac{3}{4}$".
Mechanical specifications: Type page 13" x $21\frac{1}{2}$"; E - 6 cols, $2\frac{1}{16}$", $\frac{1}{8}$" between; A - 6 cols, $2\frac{1}{16}$", $\frac{1}{8}$" between; C - 8 cols, $1\frac{1}{2}$", $\frac{1}{8}$" between.
Commodity consumption: Newsprint 750 metric tons; widths $27\frac{1}{2}$", $13\frac{3}{4}$"; black ink 30,000 pounds; color ink 1,800 pounds; single pages printed 8,500; average pages per issue 25(d); single plates used 8,500.
Equipment: EDITORIAL: Front-end hardware — Mk; Front-end software — Mk; Other equipment — AP GraphicsNet, Lf/AP Leaf Picture Desk. CLASSIFIED: Front-end hardware — Mk; Front-end software — Mk. DISPLAY: Front-end hardware — Ap/Mac; Front-end software — Scan, Multi-Ad/Creator; Other equipment — CD-Rom. PRODUCTION: Typesetters — Ap/Mac LaserWriter NTX, XIT/Clipper; Plate exposures — 2-Nu/Flip Top; Electronic picture desk — Lf/AP Leaf Picture Desk; Scanners — AG/B-W; Automatic film processors — 1-LE; Shrink lenses — Alan/24 Squeeze.
PRESSROOM: Line 1 — G/Community (32 pg w/2 Stack units). MAILROOM: Inserters and stuffers — KAN; Bundle tyer — 3-Bu; Addressing machine — Am. WIRE SERVICES: News — AP; Photos — AP; Receiving dishes — size-12ft, AP. BUSINESS COMPUTERS: DEC; Applications: Vision Data: Circ, Accts payable, Accts receivable.

GREENCASTLE
Putnam County
'90 U.S. Census- 8,984; E&P '96 Est. 9,612

Banner-Graphic (e-mon to sat)

Banner-Graphic, 100 N. Jackson St.; PO Box 509, Greencastle, IN 46135; tel (317) 653-5151; fax (317) 653-2063. Federated Media Corp. group.
Circulation: 5,843(e); 5,843(e-sat); Sworn Sept. 30, 1995.
Price: 50¢(d); 50¢(sat); $1.50/wk; $6.50/mo; $83.50/yr.
Advertising: Open inch rate $9.57(e); $9.57(e-sat).
News Service: AP. **Politics:** Independent. **Established:** 1969.
Not Published: New Year; Memorial Day; Independence Day; Labor Day; Thanksgiving; Christmas.
Advertising not accepted: Material not considered in best interests of readers.
Special Editions: Agriculture Day; Boys & Girls Basketball; Football; Christmas Gift Guide; Annual Progress & Industry; New Cars; Car Care; 4-H Fair Section; Bride & Groom; Spring Home Improvement.
Special Weekly Sections: Farm News (wed); Senior Citizens (thur); Church (fri).
Magazines: Weekly TV Section; USA Weekend; Weekly Spectrum TMC.
Broadcast Affiliates: WTRC & WYEZ (FM) Elkhart, IN; WMEE & WMEF (FM) Fort Wayne, IN; WCUZ & WFFX (FM) Grand Rapids, MI; WCKY & WWEZ (FM) Cincinnati, OH.

GENERAL MANAGEMENT
General Manager Steve Hendershot
Controller Gib Farmer

ADVERTISING
Director Steve Hendershot

CIRCULATION
Manager June Leer

NEWS EXECUTIVE
Editor Eric Bernsee

EDITORS AND MANAGERS
Columnist/Sports Writer Todd Zellars
Columnist Lisa Meyer-Trigg
Editorial Page Editor Eric Bernsee
Family Editor Lisa Meyer-Trigg
Political/Religion Editor Joe Thomas
Radio/Television Eric Bernsee
Sports Editor Steve Fields
Wire Editor Joe Thomas

PRODUCTION
Manager Wilbur C Kendall

Market Information: TMC.
Mechanical available: Offset; Black and 3 ROP colors; insert accepted — preprinted; page cut-offs — $22\frac{3}{4}$".
Mechanical specifications: Type page 13" x 21"; E - 6 cols, $2\frac{1}{16}$", $\frac{1}{8}$" between; A - 6 cols, $2\frac{1}{16}$", $\frac{1}{8}$" between; C - 8 cols, $1\frac{3}{4}$", $\frac{1}{8}$" between.
Commodity consumption: Newsprint 168 short tons; widths 28", $13\frac{3}{4}$"; black ink 4,815 pounds; color ink 180 pounds; single pages printed 4,000; average pages per issue 12(d); single plates used 4,800.
Equipment: EDITORIAL: Front-end hardware — 6-Ap/Mac Plus; Front-end software — Baseview; Printers — Ap/Mac LaserWriter NT II. CLASSIFIED: Front-end hardware — Ap/Mac Plus; Front-end software — Baseview; Printers — Ap/Mac LaserWriter NT II. DISPLAY: Front-end hardware — Ap/Mac SE; Front-end software — Multi-Ad/Creator; Printers — Ap/Mac LaserWriter NT II. PRODUCTION: Typesetters — 2-Ap/Mac LaserWriter; Plate exposures — Nu/Flip Top; Production cameras — LE, R/500; Automatic film processors — LE/Flo-CD-24A.
PRESSROOM: Line 1 — 5-G/Community; Folders — 1-G/2:1. MAILROOM: Bundle tyer — 2-BN; Addressing machine — 1-Wm. WIRE SERVICES: News — AP; Receiving dishes — size-10ft, AP. BUSINESS COMPUTERS: 2-Epson/Equity II; Applications: Billing.

GREENFIELD
Hancock County
'90 U.S. Census- 11,657; E&P '96 Est. 12,052
ABC-CZ (90): 11,657 (HH 4,249)

Daily Reporter
(e-mon to fri; m-sat)

Daily Reporter, 22 W. New Road; PO Box 279, Greenfield, IN 46140; tel (317) 462-5528; fax (317) 467-6009. Home News Enterprises group.
Circulation: 8,863(e); 8,863(m-sat); ABC Sept. 30, 1995.
Price: 50¢(d); 50¢(sat); $7.50/mo; $90.00/yr.
Advertising: Open inch rate $10.18(e); $10.18(m-sat).
News Service: AP. **Politics:** Republican. **Established:** 1908.
Not Published: New Year; Memorial Day; Independence Day; Labor Day; Thanksgiving; Christmas.
Special Editions: Weddings, Proms (Jan); Meet Your Merchants (Feb); Design-An-Ad, Agriculture Day, Spring Sports (Mar); Home Improvement, Lawn & Garden, Car Care (Apr); Indy 500 Preview (May); Health & Fitness (June); 4-H Fair (July); Fall Sports, Back-to-School (Aug); Riley Festival (Sept); Fall Home Improvement, Car Care (Oct); Winter Sports, Christmas Gift Guide (Nov); Holiday Recipes & Carol Book, Last Minute Gift Ideas (Dec).
Special Weekly Sections: Best Food Day (mon); Education (tues); Ag (wed); Arts/Entertainment, Business News (thur); Religion (sat).
Magazines: TV Section, USA Weekend (sat).

CORPORATE OFFICERS
Chairman Robert N Brown
President Ned Bradley

GENERAL MANAGEMENT
Publisher Larry W Brown
Administrative Manager Judy Williams

ADVERTISING
Director Jeff Fawbush
Manager-Commercial Sales Michael Butt

CIRCULATION
Manager Ronald Rayburn

NEWS EXECUTIVE
Editor Paul Fedorchak

EDITORS AND MANAGERS
Agriculture Editor Jeff Stanton
Business Editor Paul Fedorchak
Editorial Page Editor Paul Fedorchak
Education Editor Anne Durham
Entertainment Editor Dave Scott
Finance Editor Paul Fedorchak
Lifestyle Editor Karen Kuhn
News Editor Dave Scott
Photo Editor Dave Scott
Religion Editor Eric North
Sports Editor Steve Brooks
Travel Editor Dave Scott

MANAGEMENT INFORMATION SERVICES
Data Processing Manager Judy Williams

PRODUCTION
Director Gary George
Manager-Press & Plate Larry Ham
Manager-Post Press Mike Brandenburg
Manager-Pre Press Tracy Hunt
Manager-Building Services Al Horton

Market Information: TMC.
Mechanical available: Offset; Black and 3 ROP colors; insert accepted — preprinted, max. size 11"x 13"; page cut-offs — $22\frac{3}{4}$".
Mechanical specifications: Type page 13" x $21\frac{1}{2}$"; E - 6 cols, $2\frac{1}{16}$", $\frac{1}{8}$" between; A - 6 cols, $2\frac{1}{16}$", $\frac{1}{8}$" between; C - 9 cols, $1\frac{3}{8}$", $\frac{1}{16}$" between.
Commodity consumption: Newsprint 300 short tons; width 55"; black ink 3,000 pounds; color ink 520 pounds; single pages printed 4,012; average pages per issue 13(d); single plates used 3,400.
Equipment: EDITORIAL: Front-end hardware — 1-Dewar, 2-Ap/Mac Quadra 650; Front-end software — Dewar; Printers — 1-HP/ScanJet Flatbed OCR Scanner; Other equipment — 2-Supra Fax/Modem. CLASSIFIED: Front-end hardware — Dewar; Front-end software — Dewar. DISPLAY: Adv layout systems — 1-Ap/Mac IIci; Front-end hardware — Dewar; Front-end software — Dewar; Other equipment — 1-CD-Rom, 1-PLI/Removable Drive. PRODUCTION: OCR software — TI/OmniPage Professional 5.0; Typesetters — Ap/Mac LaserWriter II NT, Ap/Mac LaserWriter II NTX, Ap/Mac LaserWriter IIg, NewGen/Imager Plus 12, 1-Linotype-Hell/L190-B Imagesetter, 1-ECR/VR-36; Plate exposures — 2-Nu/Flip Top FT40APRNS; Plate processors — Nat/A-250; Scanners — 1-Ap/Mac Centris 650, 5-PLI/Removable Drives, 1-Ap/Mac IIvx, 5-CD-Rom, 1-AG/Arcus Color Scanner, 2-Ap/Mac IIci, 1-Polaroid/SprintScan 35mm, 1-Umax, 1-AG/Arcus, 1-Ap/Power Mac 7100, Ap/Power Mac 6100 Server; Production cameras — SCREEN/C-270D; Automatic film processors — SCREEN/LD-281Q, Devotec/2D RA Processor; Digital color separation equipment — Ag/Arcus Plus Flatbed, Adobe/Photoshop.
PRESSROOM: Line 1 — 8-G/Community; Line 2 — 4-G/Community; Press drives — 2-Fin/75 h.p., 1-Fin/75 h.p.; Folders — 1-G/Community SSC Half, 1-G/Community SSC Quarter, 1-G/Community SSC Half, 1-G/Community SSC Quarter; Pasters — 2-Enkel/Zero Speed Splicer, 2-Enkel/Zero Speed Splicer; Press control system — Fin/Control System; Press registration system — Quad-Tech/Motorized Registration System. MAILROOM: Counter stackers — QWI/Model 1000, BG/Count-O-Veyor Model 108, Rima/25 105; Bundle tyer — 1-MLN/Spirit, 3-Bu/BT-18; Addressing machine — Automecha/Accufast PL. WIRE SERVICES: News — AP; Syndicates — Universal Press,

NEA, TV Data Technologies; Receiving dishes — size-2½ft, AP. BUSINESS COMPUTERS: Sun, Gateway 12000, Microsoft; Applications: PBS; PCs & micros networked; PCs & main system networked.

GREENSBURG
Decatur County
'90 U.S. Census- 9,286; E&P '96 Est. 9,499

Greensburg Daily News
(e-mon to sat)

Greensburg Daily News, 135 S. Franklin St.; PO Box 106, Greensburg, IN 47240; tel (812) 663-3111; fax (812) 663-2985. Hollinger International Inc. group.
Circulation: 5,977(e); 5,977(e-sat); Sworn Oct. 1, 1995.
Price: 50¢(d); 50¢(sat); $2.00/wk; $8.07/mo; $104.00/yr (carrier/motor route), $110.00/yr (mail).
Advertising: Open inch rate $9.00(e); $9.00(e-sat).
News Service: AP. **Established:** 1894.
Not Published: Christmas.
Special Editions: Customer Appreciation Day, Tax Tips Tab, Soil & Water Conservation Tab (Jan); 4-H Tab, Chamber of Commerce Tab, Progress Edition (Feb); Basketball Section, Ag Week Tab, "Who's Who" Contest (Mar); Spring Spectacular (Apr); Wedding Tab (Jan); Mother's Day Gang Page, Graduation Section (May); Chamber Tab, Mini Progress (June); Weddings of Yesteryear Tab, Fair Tab, "After Fair" Tab (July); Baseball Section, Football Section, Parade of Honor (Aug); Senior Citizens Lifestyles, Fall Section Tab, Say Nope to Dope Drug Tab (Oct); Christmas Club Check Tab, Basketball Section (Nov); Carol Book/Holiday Cookbook, Christmas Greetings Section, New Year's Greetings, First Baby Contest (Dec).
Special Weekly Sections: Agri-News (wed); Commerce News (tues); Pastimes (thur); Church News (fri); School News (sat).

GENERAL MANAGEMENT
Publisher Phillip Hart
Business Manager Lisa Roseberry

ADVERTISING
Manager-Retail Pamela Jackson Abel
Manager-Classified Patty Clark

MARKETING AND PROMOTION
Director-Marketing/Promotion Phillip Hart

CIRCULATION
Manager Lisa Huff

NEWS EXECUTIVE
Editor Jeff Emsweller

EDITORS AND MANAGERS
Sports Editor Joe Frollo
Women's Editor Jeff Emsweller

PRODUCTION
Superintendent-Pressroom Randy Jester
Manager-Composing Susan Peters

Market Information: TMC.
Mechanical available: Offset; Black and 3 ROP colors; insert accepted — preprinted, all; page cut-offs — 23".
Mechanical specifications: Type page 13" x 21½"; E - 6 cols, 2¹⁄₁₆", ⅛" between; A - 6 cols, 2¹⁄₁₆", ⅛" between; C - 8 cols, 1⁷⁄₁₆", ⅛" between.
Commodity consumption: Newsprint 385 short tons; widths 27½", 13¾"; black ink 7,300 pounds; color ink 1,500 pounds; single pages printed 3,670; average pages per issue 14.5(d), 14.5(sat); single plates used 4,000.
Equipment: EDITORIAL: Front-end hardware — Ap/Mac; Front-end software — QuarkXPress; Printers — 1-NewGen/Imager 12 Plus, 2-Ap/Mac LaserWriter IIg; Other equipment — Umax/12x12 scanner, 2-Microtek/CD 300 Drives, Nikon/CoolScan. CLASSIFIED: Front-end hardware — Ap/Mac SE30; Front-end software — Baseview/Class Manager Plus; Printers — Ap/Mac LaserWriter. AUDIOTEX: Hardware — 1-Recordak/MPE. PRODUCTION: Pagination software — QuarkXPress; Typesetters — 1-NewGen/Imager 12 Plus, 2-Ap/Mac LaserWriter IIg; Plate exposures — 1-Nu; Plate processors — 1-Nat; Production cameras — 1-CL; Automatic film processors — 1-LE; Reproportion units — 1-GL; Color separation equipment (conventional) — Ap/Mac Centris 650, Adobe/Photoshop.
PRESSROOM: Line 1 — 1-G; Line 2 — G/Community, 1-G/Community; Folders — 1-G. MAILROOM: Bundle tyer — 1-Bu; Addressing machine — 2-Wm/Labels. LIBRARY: Electronic — Recordak/MPE. COMMUNICATIONS: Facsimile — Ricoh; Systems used — satellite. WIRE SERVICES: News — AP; Receiving dishes — size-1m, AP. BUSINESS COMPUTERS: PC/486-DXZ-50, PC/486-DX2-66; Applications: Microsoft/Excel: Accts receivable, Spreadsheets; Word processing; PCs & micros networked.

HAMMOND
See MUNSTER

HARTFORD CITY
Blackford County
'90 U.S. Census- 6,960; E&P 96 Est. 6,589

News-Times
(e-mon to fri; m-sat)

News-Times, 123 S. Jefferson St., Hartford City, IN 47348; tel (317) 348-0110; fax (317) 348-0112. Hollinger International Inc. group.
Circulation: 2,210(e); 2,210(m-sat); Sworn Sept. 30, 1994.
Price: 50¢(d); 50¢(sat); $2.20/wk (in county); $9.45/mo (in county); $105.00/yr (in county).
Advertising: Open inch rate $6.01(e); $6.01(m-sat).
News Service: AP. **Politics:** Independent. **Established:** 1892 (News), 1898 (Times).
Not Published: New Year; Memorial Day; Independence Day; Labor Day; Thanksgiving; Christmas.
Special Editions: New Year's Baby (Jan); Progress (Feb); Home & Garden (Mar); Spring Car Care (Apr); Senior Citizen, Graduation (May); 4-H (July); Fall Home Yard Garden (Oct); Christmas Tab (Nov).
Magazine: Market Basket (TMC) (tues).

CORPORATE OFFICERS
President Larry J Perrotto
Comptroller Roland McBride

GENERAL MANAGEMENT
Publisher Beverly Everhart
General Manager Beverly Everhart

ADVERTISING
Manager Connie Murray

CIRCULATION
Manager Doug Gilland

NEWS EXECUTIVE
Editor William Laney

EDITORS AND MANAGERS
News Editor William Laney
Sports Editor William Laney

Market Information: TMC.
Mechanical available: Offset; Black and 3 ROP colors; insert accepted — preprinted; page cut-offs — 22½".
Mechanical specifications: Type page 13" x 21½"; E - 6 cols, 2", ⅙" between; A - 6 cols, 2", ⅙" between; C - 8 cols, 2" ⅙" between.
Commodity consumption: widths 27½", 13¾"; average pages per issue 12(d).
Equipment: EDITORIAL: Front-end hardware — 2-Ap/Mac Classic II, 1-Ap/Mac Plus, 2-Ap/Mac Quadra 630; Front-end software — Microsoft/Word 4.0; Printers — Ap/Mac LaserWriter II NT. CLASSIFIED: Front-end hardware — 1-Ap/Mac Plus, 2-Ap/Mac SE-SE30, 2-Ap/Mac II; Front-end software — Microsoft/Word 4.0, Multi-Ad; Printers — Ap/Mac LaserWriter II NT, Ap/Mac LaserWriter Pro. DISPLAY: Front-end hardware — 1-Ap/Mac LC, 2-Ap/Mac SE, 3-Ap/Mac Radius Full Page Display; Front-end software — Multi-Ad; Printers — Ap/Mac LaserWriter II NTX; Other equipment — Microtek/II XE scanner, Panasonic/CD-Rom. PRODUCTION: Plate exposures — Nu/Flip Top; Production cameras — SCREEN/Companica 680C. MAILROOM: Bundle tyer — Bu. COMMUNICATIONS: Digital ad delivery system — AP AdSend. WIRE SERVICES: News — AP; Receiving dishes — AP. BUSINESS COMPUTERS: Arche Triumph/386SX; Applications: Aged acct only; PCs & micros networked.

HUNTINGTON
Huntington County
'90 U.S. Census- 16,389; E&P '96 Est. 16,858

Huntington Herald-Press
(e-mon to fri; S)

Huntington Herald-Press, 7 N. Jefferson St.; PO Box 860, Huntington, IN 46750; tel (219) 356-6700; fax (219) 356-9026.
Circulation: 7,737(e); 7,737(S); Sworn Sept. 25, 1995.
Price: 50¢(d); $1.50(S); $1.95/wk; $11.70/6wk, $25.35/13wk, $50.70/26wk, $101.40/52wk.
Advertising: Open inch rate $8.40(e); $8.40(S).
News Service: AP. **Politics:** Independent-Republican. **Established:** 1848.
Advertising not accepted: Lottery.
Special Editions: Sectional/Spring Sports (Feb); Farm (Mar); Home Improvement (Apr); Heritage Days (June); Back-to-School/Fall Sports, 4-H Fair (Aug); Sidewalk Day (Sept); Car Care, Huntington College (Oct); Christmas Opening Winter Sports (Nov).
Special Weekly Sections: Best Food Days, Business Page (tues); Farm Page (wed); School Page, Business (thur); Church Page (fri); Best Food Days (S).
Magazine: Comics (S).

CORPORATE OFFICERS
President James C Quayle
Vice Pres Michael E Quayle
Secretary/Treasurer Corinne Quayle

GENERAL MANAGEMENT
Vice Pres-Operations/General Manager Steven K Kimmel

ADVERTISING
Manager Claude Good
Manager-Classified Brenda Ross

MARKETING AND PROMOTION
Coordinator-Promotion John Klingenberger

CIRCULATION
Manager Bonnie Hall

NEWS EXECUTIVE
Editor Michael Perkins

EDITORS AND MANAGERS
Automotive Editor Tom Hernes
Books/Music Editor Cindy Klepper
Business Editor Tom Hernes
Columnist Michael Perkins
Editorial Page Editor Michael Perkins
Editorial Writer Michael Perkins
Education Editor Cindy Klepper
Fashion Editor Pam Knepper
Features Editor Michael Perkins
Films/Theater Editor Cindy Klepper
Food Editor Pam Knepper
Photo Department Manager Matt Farmer
Political Editor Michael Perkins
Radio/Television Editor Cindy Klepper
Religion Editor Cindy Klepper
Sports Editor Paul Siegfried
Wire Editor Cindy Klepper
Women's Editor Pam Knepper

MANAGEMENT INFORMATION SERVICES
Data Processing Manager Steven K Kimmel

PRODUCTION
Foreman Gary Kimmel

Market Information: Zoned editions; Split Run.
Mechanical available: Offset; Black and 3 ROP colors; insert accepted — preprinted; page cut-offs — 22¾".
Mechanical specifications: Type page 13" x 21"; E - 6 cols, 2¹⁄₁₆", ⅛" between; A - 6 cols, 2¹⁄₁₆", ⅛" between; C - 9 cols, 1⅜", ¹⁄₁₆" between.
Commodity consumption: Newsprint 265 short tons; widths 27½", 13¾"; black ink 9,800 pounds; color ink 600 pounds; single pages printed 4,984; average pages per issue 14(d), 25(S); single plates used 4,584.
Equipment: EDITORIAL: Front-end hardware — Ap/Mac SE30, Ap/Mac ci, Ap/Mac si; Front-end software — Baseview/NewsEdit, QuarkXPress, Adobe/Photoshop, Aldus/FreeHand, Multi-Ad; Printers — Ap/Mac LaserWriter NT, Ap/Mac LaserWriter NTX. CLASSIFIED: Front-end hardware — Ap/Mac SE30; Front-end software — Baseview/Class Manager; Printers — Ap/Mac LaserWriter NTX. DISPLAY: Front-end hardware — Ap/Mac II, Ap/Mac IIfx, Ap/Mac ci; Front-end software — QuarkXPress, Multi-Ad, Aldus/FreeHand, Adobe/Illustrator; Printers — Ap/Mac LaserWriter II NTX. PRODUCTION: Pagination software — QuarkXPress 3.0; OCR software — TI/OmniPage 2.0; Typesetters — AG/Secsect Set 5000; Plate exposures — 1-Nu; Plate processors — Nat/250; Electronic picture desk — Lf/AP Leaf Picture Desk; Scanners — 1-HP, HP/JetScan, 2-Microtek/Flatbed; Production cameras — 1-B/Caravelle; Automatic film processors — 1-LE/BG 24; Color separation equipment (conventional) — Adobe/Photoshop; Digital color separation equipment — Nikon/LS-3510 AF, Mk/MSF 300.
PRESSROOM: Line 1 — 3-G/Urbanite (1-3 color unit); Press control system — Fin. MAILROOM: Inserters and stuffers — KAN/4 Station 320; Bundle tyer — Dynaric. COMMUNICATIONS: Systems used — satellite. WIRE SERVICES: News — AP; Receiving dishes — size-10ft, AP. BUSINESS COMPUTERS: IBM/PC; Applications: Custom Software: Adv billing, Accts receivable, Accts payable, Gen ledger, Circ.

INDIANAPOLIS
Marion County
'90 U.S. Census- 731,327; E&P '96 Est. 766,966
ABC-NDM (90): 1,249,822 (HH 480,010)

The Indianapolis Star
(m-mon to sat; S)

The Indianapolis News
(e-mon to sat)

The Indianapolis Star/News, 307 N. Pennsylvania St., Indianapolis, IN 46204; tel (317) 633-1240; fax (317) 633-1174; web site http://www.starnews.com. Central Newspapers Inc. group.
Circulation: 227,535(m); 73,788(e); 227,535 (m-sat); 73,788(e-sat); 398,322(S); ABC Sept. 30, 1995.
Price: 50¢(d); 50¢(sat); $1.50(S); $2.75/wk (mS), $2.75/wk (eS), $4.25/wk (m,eS).
Advertising: Open inch rate $164.00(m); $164.00(e); $164.00(m-sat); $164.00(e-sat); $175.00(S). **Representative:** Newspapers First.
News Services: AP, NANA, CNS. **Politics:** Independent. **Established:** 1869 (News), 1903 (Star).
Special Edition: 500-mile Auto Race Souvenir (May).
Special Weekly Section: Weekend (m & e-fri).
Magazines: TV (e-sat); Parade Magazine, TV Week (S).

CORPORATE OFFICERS
President/General Manager Malcolm W Applegate
Senior Vice Pres Eugene S Pulliam
Secretary/Treasurer Frank E Russell

GENERAL MANAGEMENT
Publisher Eugene S Pulliam
Director-Transportation/Safety Kenneth R Todd
Manager-Transportation Larry R Killion
Manager-Safety Tim Hahn
Business Manager Jeffery B Rogers
Manager-Credit Gary W Gray
Personnel Director Larry Roberts
Manager-Purchasing Scott Peglow

ADVERTISING
Director Kimberly J Parker
Director-Operations Ron Morgan
Manager-Major Kevin Bridgewater
Manager-Retail Abby Clark
Manager-General/Co-op Robert Widner

MARKETING AND PROMOTION
Director-Community Relations Carolyn Pugh Foust
Asst Director-Marketing Service & Community Relations Janet Campbell Baker

TELECOMMUNICATIONS
Audiotex Manager Shawn Powell

CIRCULATION
Director Michael Kujawa
Asst Director Jerry Zakes
Manager-City Robert Penick
Manager-Recruitment Carol Dahl
Manager-State Carol Butrum
Manager-Administration Jay Harmon
Manager-Marketing Lee Richardson
Manager-Single Copy Bryan Sturgeon
Manager-Customer Service/Quality Assurance Carol Randall-Grier
Supervisor-Transportation Ron Smith

NEWS EXECUTIVES
Editor (Star) John H Lyst
Editor (News) Russel B Pulliam

EDITORS AND MANAGERS
Star/News
Exec Editor Frank Caperton
Managing Editor-Features/Photo/Graphics Nancy Comiskey
Managing Editor-News Ted Daniels
Asst Managing Editor-Administration Lyle Mannweiler
Asst Managing Editor-Local News Vic Caleca
Asst Managing Editor-Business Pamela Klein
Asst Managing Editor-Sports Steve Greenberg
Asst Managing Editor-Photo/Graphics Charlie Nye

I-132 Indiana

Asst Managing Editor-PM Cycle Jack Sales
Asst Managing Editor-AM Cycle Curt Wellman
Art Director Tom Peyton
Arts & Entertainment Editor Zoch Dunkin
City Editor Jon Schwantes
Columnist John Shaughnessy
Columnist Dick Cady
Environment Writer Kyle Niederpruem
Food Editor Patti Denton
Health & Fitness Writer Abe Aamidor
Home & Garden Writer Betsy Harris
Lifestyle Editor Ruth Holladay
Medicine Writer Eric Schoch
News Editor-AM Alex Waddell
News Editor-PM Tom Swenson
Outdoor Life Writer Skip Hess
Projects Editor Mark Rochester
Director of Photography Chip Maury
Religion Writer Judith Cebula
Suburban Editor Liz Brown
Television/Radio Editor Steve Hall
Travel/Books Editor David Mannweiler

Star
Editorial Page Editor John H Lyst
Editorial Writer James Patterson
Editorial Writer Andrea Neal
Editorial Writer Richard R Roberts
Editorial Writer Woolsey Teller

News
Editorial Page Editor Russel B Pulliam
Editorial Writer David Rohn
Editorial Writer Bill McCleery
Editorial Writer Lisa Coffey
Editorial Writer Bonnie Harris

MANAGEMENT INFORMATION SERVICES
Director-Electronic News/Info Myrta Pulliam
Online Manager Sandra E Fitzgerald
Data Processing Manager Donald L Prestel

PRODUCTION
Director Chuck Blevins
Asst to Director Richard Dawson
Manager William R Grider
Asst Manager-Building Maintenance Martine Thibo
Asst Manager Steve Covert
Asst Manager/Engineer Richard Rinehart
Asst Tim Ruse
Asst Phil Maus
Manager-Electronic Production Systems Hershell Sandlin
Superintendent-Pressroom (Day) Richard Bales
Superintendent-Pressroom (Night) Steve Trout
Foreman-Composing Donald J Sullivan
Foreman-Mailroom John Rossman
Foreman-Platemaking Tom Lund

Market Information: Split Run; TMC; ADS; Operate database; Operate audiotex; Electronic edition.

Mechanical available: Offset; Black and 3 ROP colors; insert accepted — preprinted; page cut-offs — 22¾".

Mechanical specifications: Type page 13" x 22"; E - 6 cols, 2", 3/16" between; A - 6 cols, 2", 3/16" between; C - 10 cols, 1 5/32", 5/32" between.

Commodity consumption: Newsprint 50,000 metric tons; width 54"; black ink 1,029,680 pounds; color ink 223,778 pounds; single pages printed 39,726; average pages per issue 58(d), 180(S); single plates used 260,000.

Equipment: EDITORIAL: Front-end hardware — AT; Front-end software — AT 4.74; Printers — 25-Epson, TI, NEC, HP/LaserPrinter. CLASSIFIED: Front-end hardware — AT; Front-end software — AT/Class Ad; Printers — 5-Genicom, Epson. AUDIOTEX: Hardware — 2-PC/386, Brite Voice Systems/48-line; Supplier name — Brite. DISPLAY: Adv layout systems — Mk/Managing Editor; Front-end hardware — Ap/Mac; Front-end software — Mk/Ad Director 2.0; Printers — 1-Lips, 1-HP/LaserJet; Other equipment — AP AdSend. PRODUCTION: Typesetters — 3-AU/APS5, 2-AU/APS6, 1-III/3850; Plate exposures — 2-WL; Plate processors — 2-Anacoil/XPH 36; Electronic picture desk — Lf/AP Leaf Picture Desk; Scanners — 2-Ik/420; Production cameras — 2-C/NP-1, 1-C/Spartan, 1-C/Marathon, 2-ECR/Autokon 10; Automatic film processors — 1-LE/24, 2-AG/Litex, 1-LE/Line 17A, 1-C/R660, 1-AG/Rap, 1-AG/380; Film transporters — 2-C; Color separation equipment (conventional) — 2-RZ; Digital color separation equipment — 1-RZ/320-I, 1-RZ/210L.
PRESSROOM: Line 1 — 9-G/HO double width; Line 2 — 9-G/HO double width; Line 3 — 9-G/HO double width; Line 4 — 7-G/HO double width; Line 5 — 9-G/HO double width; Line 6 — 8-G/HO double width; Press drives — Allen Bradley; Folders — 6-G/144-3:2; Pasters — 24-Static Belt/40 RTP, 27-Static Belt/42 RTP; Press control system — G/MPCS Level 5. MAILROOM: Counter stackers — 6-HL/HTII, 9-HPS/Dual carrier, 3-Prim/Hail Commmercial; Inserters and stuffers — 3-HI/1472P, 1-Na/NP2299, 1-Na/NP 630; Bundle tyer — 1-MLN/2A, 2-MLN/EE, 2-Malow, 25-Power Strap, 3-Sterling; Wrapping singles — 2-Felins; Addressing machine — 5-AVY, 1-Ch. LIBRARY: Electronic — 1-DEC/VAX; Combination — Minolta/Microfilm. WIRE SERVICES: News — AP; Stock tables — AP; Syndicates — AP; Receiving dishes — size-3m, AP. BUSINESS COMPUTERS: IBM/ ES9000-170, IBM/AS400; Applications: DUS/VSE, ESA: Circ, Accts payable, Payroll, Gen ledger, Credit, Ad order entry; PCs & micros networked; PCs & main system networked.

JASPER

DuBois County

'90 U.S. Census- 10,030; **E&P '96 Est.** 10,969

The Herald (e-mon to sat)

The Herald, 216 E. 4th St.; PO Box 31, Jasper, IN 47546; tel (812) 482-2424; fax (812) 482-4104; e-mail dcherald@aol.com.

Circulation: 12,723(e); 12,723(e-sat); Sworn Sept. 30, 1995.

Price: 50¢(d); 50¢(sat); $8.00/mo (carrier), $8.25/mo (motor route).

Advertising: Open inch rate $9.00(e); $9.00(e-sat). **Representative:** Papert Companies.

News Service: AP. **Politics:** Democrat. **Established:** 1895.

Not Published: New Year; Memorial Day; Independence Day; Labor Day; Thanksgiving; Christmas.

Special Editions: Brides & Weddings (Jan); Boys Basketball Sectional, Newspaper in Education, Agriculture Salute (Mar); Home, Lawn & Garden, Spring Car Care, Senior Citizen Salute (Apr); Patoka Playground, Graduation (May); 4-Fair Kick-off, Back-to-School (July); Fall Home Improvement, Literacy Week (Sept); Winter Car Care (Oct); Christmas Opening, Christmas Greetings (Nov).

Special Weekly Sections: Farm (mon); Food (tues); Outdoors (thur); Business (sat).

CORPORATE OFFICERS
Co-President John A Rumbach
Co-President Dan E Rumbach
Vice Pres Edwin J Rumbach
Secretary John A Rumbach
Treasurer Dan E Rumbach

GENERAL MANAGEMENT
Co-Publisher John A Rumbach
Co-Publisher Dan E Rumbach
Manager-Operations Jill Oeding
Controller Mark Fierst

ADVERTISING
Director Edwin J Rumbach
Manager Donald L Shreve

TELECOMMUNICATIONS
Director-Electronic News Service Hak Haskins

CIRCULATION
Manager James Wuchner

NEWS EXECUTIVE
Editor John Rumbach

EDITORS AND MANAGERS
City Editor Fred Smith
Editorial Page Editor John A Rumbach
Farm Editor Dawn Mazur
People Editor Janet Epple
Sports Editor Robert Denbo
Wire Editor Dawn Mazur

PRODUCTION
Manager Earl R Epple

Market Information: Split Run; TMC; Operate audiotex.

Mechanical available: Offset; Black and 3 ROP colors; insert accepted — preprinted, subject to approval; page cut-offs — 16".

Mechanical specifications: Type page 10 3/16" x 16"; E - 5 cols, 1 7/8", 1/8" between; A - 5 cols, 1 7/8", 1/8" between; C - 5 cols, 1 15/16", 1/16" between.

Commodity consumption: Newsprint 654 metric tons; widths 35", 17½"; black ink 19,020 pounds; color ink 1,815 pounds; single pages printed 11,052; average pages per issue 36(d); single plates used 4,457.

Equipment: EDITORIAL: Front-end hardware — 15-AT; Front-end software — AT; Other equipment — 1-Ap/Mac IIci, 1-Ap/Mac LC II, 1-Ap/Mac 7100-80. CLASSIFIED: Front-end hardware — AT; Front-end software — AT. AUDIOTEX: Hardware — Zimmers Interactive; Software — Zimmers Interactive; Supplier name — VNN. DISPLAY: Front-end hardware — Ap/Mac Quadra 650, Ap/Mac Quadra 700, Ap/Mac Quadra 950, 1-Ap/Mac 7100-80; Front-end software — DTI/AdSpeed, Multi-Ad/Creator. PRODUCTION: Typesetters — COM/8400, XIT/Clipper; Plate exposures — Nu; Plate processors — 1-Nat; Production cameras — DSA; Automatic film processors — LE. PRESSROOM: Line 1 — 6-G/w/hump; Press registration system — Duarte. MAILROOM: Inserters and stuffers — KAN/480; Bundle tyer — 3-Bu/60-71; Addressing machine — 1-Am/57. WIRE SERVICES: News — AP; Photos — AP; Receiving dishes — AP. BUSINESS COMPUTERS: 4-Samsung; Applications: MSI; PCs & micros networked; PCs & main system networked.

JEFFERSONVILLE

Clark County

'90 U.S. Census- 21,841; **E&P '96 Est.** 22,738

The Evening News (e-mon to sat)

The Evening News, 221 Spring St.; PO Box 867, Jeffersonville, IN 47130; tel (812) 283-6636; fax (812) 284-7080. Park Communications Inc. group.

Circulation: 10,838(e); 10,838(e-sat); Sworn Sept. 26, 1995.

Price: 50¢(d); 50¢(sat); $7.80/mo; $84.24/yr.

Advertising: Open inch rate $10.50(e); $10.50(e-sat). **Representative:** Landon Associates Inc.

News Service: AP. **Politics:** Democrat-Independent. **Established:** 1872.

Special Editions: Cook Book (Jan); Basketball (Feb); Progress (Mar); Spring Fashion (Apr); Bridal (May); Travel (June); Back-to-School (Aug); Fall Fashion, Football (Sept); New Car Preview (Oct); Thanksgiving (Nov); Christmas Style (Dec).

Magazine: TV News/Golden Opportunity (3rd wed of month).

CORPORATE OFFICER
President Wright M Thomas

GENERAL MANAGEMENT
General Manager Tom Lindley III
Manager-Business Jean Gibson

ADVERTISING
Manager Donna Barrett

CIRCULATION
Manager Freda Minton

NEWS EXECUTIVES
Editor Tom Lindley III
Managing Editor John Gilkey

EDITORS AND MANAGERS
Editorial Page Editor John Gilkey
Education Editor Brenda Dorman
Farm/Agriculture Editor Tim Gobel
Fashion/Style Editor Jim Nichols
Lifestyle Editor Jim Nichols
News Editor Marc Meyer
Photo Editor Thom Whittinghill
Sports Editor Bryce Meyer
Wire Editor Marc Meyer

PRODUCTION
Foreman-Composing Doug Duvall
Foreman-Press John Vissing

Market Information: TMC.

Mechanical available: Offset; Black and 3 ROP colors; insert accepted — preprinted; page cut-offs — 21½".

Mechanical specifications: Type page 13" x 21½"; E - 6 cols, 2.08", 1/12" between; A - 6 cols, 2.08", 1/8" between; C - 10 cols, 1 1/3", 1/12" between.

Commodity consumption: Newsprint 640 short tons; width 27½"; black ink 17,000 pounds; color ink 1,800 pounds; single pages printed 5,136; average pages per issue 16(d), 16(sat); single plates used 6,000.

Equipment: EDITORIAL: Front-end hardware — Ap/Mac Quadra 800; Front-end software — QuarkXPress, Baseview/NewsEdit; Printers — LaserMaster/Unity 1200XL, Ap/Mac LaserWriter IIg. CLASSIFIED: Front-end hardware — Ap/Mac Quadra 800; Front-end software — QuarkXPress, Baseview/NewsEdit; Printers — LaserMaster/Unity 1200XL, Ap/Mac LaserWriter IIg. PRODUCTION: Pagination software — QuarkXPress 3.3; OCR software — TI/OmniPage 2.1; Typesetters — Ap/Mac LaserWriter IIg, LaserMaster/Unity 1200 XLO; Plate exposures — BKY/Ascor; Plate processors — Nat; Electronic picture desk — Lf/AP Leaf Picture Desk; Scanners — Umax/840; Production cameras — SCREEN/C-690-C; Automatic film processors — SCREEN/LD-281-Q; Color separation equipment (conventional) — Ap/Mac IIfx; Digital color separation equipment — Ap/Mac One Scanner.
PRESSROOM: Line 1 — 19-G/Urbanite IF 6507; Line 2 — 20-G/Urbanite IF 6507; Line 3 — 21-G/Urbanite IF 6507; Line 4 — 22-G/Urbanite IF 6507; Line 5 — 23-G/Urbanite IF 6507; Folders — G/U-1280-1D29054; Reels and stands — 1-G/2 Tier, 1-G/3 Tier; Press control system — 2-Fin/2193A-100-40F; Press registration system — Duarte/Pin Register. MAILROOM: Counter stackers — BG; Inserters and stuffers — Mc/60-40; Bundle tyer — 2-Bu; Addressing machine — Wm. WIRE SERVICES: News — AP; Syndicates — NEA, King Features, TV Data; Receiving dishes — size-2ft, AP. BUSINESS COMPUTERS: DEC/VT320; Applications: Vision Data; PCs & micros networked; PCs & main system networked.

KENDALLVILLE

Noble County

'90 U.S. Census- 7,773; **E&P '96 Est.** 8,294
ABC-NDM (90): 39,602 (HH 14,051)

The News-Sun (e-mon to fri; m-sat)

The News-Sun, 102 N. Main St.; PO Box 39, Kendallville, IN 46755; tel (219) 347-0400; fax (219) 347-2693. Witwer Newspapers group.

Circulation: 8,223(e); 8,223(m-sat); ABC Sept. 30, 1995.

Price: 50¢(d); 50¢(sat); $2.25/wk; $10.00/mo; $108.00/yr.

Advertising: Open inch rate $8.75(e); $8.75(m-sat).

News Services: AP, NEA, CSM. **Politics:** Independent. **Established:** 1911.

Not Published: New Year; Memorial Day; Independence Day; Labor Day; Thanksgiving; Christmas.

Advertising not accepted: Cigarettes.

Special Editions: Noble County in Focus, Spring Bridal Planner, De Kalb County Focus (Jan); Family/Health & Fitness, Sectional Basketball Preview (Feb); Agriculture, Design-An-Ad, Home & Garden, Coupon Book (Mar); Spring Car Care, Spring Homes for You, Look at Lagrange (Apr); Family, Graduation, Great Outdoors (May); Discover De Kalb, Noble County Progress (June); Lagrange County 4-H Scrapbook, Noble Co. 4-H Scrapbook (July); Fall Bridal Planner, Scouting, Coupon Book II, Butler Days, Chautaqua Days, Marshmallow Days, ACD Festival (Aug); National Literacy Day, Home Improvement, Corn School (Sept); Apple Festival, De Kalb County 4-H Scrapbook, Fall Homes for You, Family, Fall Car Care, Dining Guide (Oct); Basketball Preview, Holiday Shopping, 1997 Calendar (Nov); Last Minute Christmas Shopping (Dec); Mature Living (monthly).

Special Weekly Sections: Best Food Day (mon); Church Page (fri); Business Page, Agri-Business Page (sat).

Magazines: Best Food Day (mon); Entertainment Page (thur); TV Weekly (sat).

CORPORATE OFFICERS
Chairman George O Witwer
President James D Kroemer
Vice Pres George B Witwer

GENERAL MANAGEMENT
Publisher George O Witwer
General Manager James D Kroemer

ADVERTISING
Director Ron Ensley
Manager Debbie Ensley
Director-Inserts Nancy Rogers

MARKETING AND PROMOTION
Director-Marketing Ron Ensley

CIRCULATION
Manager Mark Gaines

NEWS EXECUTIVE
Managing Editor Terry Housholder

EDITORS AND MANAGERS
Business/Finance Editor Joe Potter
Columnist Cleon Point
Columnist Grace Housholder
Columnist Terry Housholder
Columnist Margaret Tarney
Editorial Page Editor Terry Housholder
Entertainment/Amusements Editor Dennis Nartker
Features Editor Terry Housholder
Food Editor Margaret Tarney

Indiana I-133

Sports Editor Adam Kroemer
Wire Editor George Haynes
Women's Editor Margaret Tarney

PRODUCTION

Manager Phil Markward
Foreman-Pressroom Phil Yates

Market Information: TMC; ADS; Operate audiotex.
Mechanical available: Offset; Black and 3 ROP colors; insert accepted — preprinted, product samples; page cut-offs — 22¾".
Mechanical specifications: Type page 13" x 21½"; E - 6 cols, 2$\frac{1}{16}$", ⅛" between; A - 6 cols, 2$\frac{1}{16}$", ⅛" between; C - 6 cols, 2$\frac{1}{16}$", ⅛" between.
Commodity consumption: Newsprint 1,600 metric tons; widths 14", 27.5", 32"; black ink 6,000 pounds; color ink 1,500 pounds; single pages printed 6,200; average pages per issue 16(d); single plates used 15,000.
Equipment: EDITORIAL: Front-end hardware — 12-Ap/Mac; Front-end software — Baseview, QuarkXPress; Printers — 2-Ap/Mac LaserWriter; Other equipment — 6-RSK/TRS 80 Model 100. CLASSIFIED: Front-end hardware — 3-Ap/Mac; Front-end software — Baseview, QuarkXPress; Printers — 1-Ap/Mac LaserWriter. DISPLAY: Front-end hardware — 9-Ap/Mac; Front-end software — QuarkXPress, Multi-Ad; Printers — 2-Ap/Mac LaserWriter. PRODUCTION: Typesetters — 1-Ap/Mac LaserWriter, ALFA/Imagesetter 1200; Plate exposures — 1-Nu/Flip Top FT40UPNS; Plate processors — 1-Nat/250; Electronic picture desk — 1-Lf/AP Leaf Picture Desk; Scanners — 1-Kk, 2-AG; Production cameras — 1-B; Automatic film processors — 1-DP/Rapid Access; Color separation equipment (conventional) — CSAF DSSK, 1-ALFA/Imagesetter 1200. PRESSROOM: Line 1 — 1-G/Floor SSC Units, 1-Stalk/Pathfinder; Line 2 — 1-G/4-High; Pasters — 1-KTI. MAILROOM: Counter stackers — 1-The Stacker Machine Co./S-N 316-19, 1-BG/Count-O-Veyor; Inserters and stuffers — 1-KAN/5 Pocket Inserter, KAN/Twin Stacker, Macey/Saddle Binds-4 Pocket, 1-Challenge/Single Knife; Bundle tyer — 4-Bu. WIRE SERVICES: News — AP; Syndicates — AP; Receiving dishes — size-3m, AP. BUSINESS COMPUTERS: 1-Covircint/580; Applications: Adv billing, Accts receivable, Accts payable, Gen ledger, Payroll, Circ; PCs & micros networked.

KOKOMO

Howard County

'90 U.S. Census- 44,962; E&P '96 Est. 43,434
ABC-CZ (90): 49,915 (HH 20,596)

The Kokomo Tribune

(e-mon to fri; m-sat; S)

The Kokomo Tribune, 300 N. Union (46901); PO Box 9014, Kokomo, IN 46904-9014; tel (317) 459-3121; e-mail ktonline@aol.com. Thomson Newspapers group.
Circulation: 27,869(e); 27,869(m-sat); 29,076(S); ABC Sept. 30, 1995.
Price: 50¢(d); 50¢(sat); $1.50(S); $2.50/wk, $2.75/wk (motor route).
Advertising: Open inch rate $23.05(e); $23.05(m-sat); $23.05(S). **Representatives:** Thomson Newspapers; Papert Companies.
News Service: AP. **Politics:** Independent-Republican. **Established:** 1850.
Not Published: New Year; Memorial Day; Labor Day; Christmas.
Magazines: Parade; TV Update.

GENERAL MANAGEMENT

Publisher/General Manager Arden A Draeger

ADVERTISING

Manager-Classified Nancy Blackwood

TELECOMMUNICATIONS

Audiotex Manager Jack Bezzano

CIRCULATION

Manager-Sales Richard Schram

NEWS EXECUTIVE

Editor John Wiles

EDITORS AND MANAGERS

Agriculture Editor Ann Hubbard
Automotive Editor Jerri Jensen
Business Editor Jerri Jensen
City Editor Julie McClure
Editorial Page Editor John Wiles
Education Editor Valerie Kiger
Entertainment/Amusements Editor Susan Goff
Living Section Editor Tom Carey
Photo Editor Brian Reynolds
Radio/Television Editor Susan Goff
Sports Editor David Kitchell
Travel Editor Tom Carey
Wire Editor James Langenschied

MANAGEMENT INFORMATION SERVICES

Data Processing Manager Steve Smith

PRODUCTION

Director Gerald Radel
Foreman-Composing Jim Christie
Foreman-Pressroom Larry Clark

Market Information: TMC; Operate audiotex; Electronic edition.
Mechanical available: Offset; Black and 3 ROP colors; insert accepted — preprinted, any; page cut-offs — 22¾".
Mechanical specifications: Type page 13" x 21½"; E - 6 cols, 2$\frac{1}{16}$", ⅛" between; A - 6 cols, 2$\frac{1}{16}$", ⅛" between; C - 9 cols, 1⅜", $\frac{1}{16}$" between.
Commodity consumption: Newsprint 1,800 metric tons; widths 54", 40½", 27"; average pages per issue 28(d), 176(S).
Equipment: EDITORIAL: Front-end hardware — DEC; Front-end software — CText; Printers — Tegra/Varityper; Other equipment — Ap/Mac. CLASSIFIED: Front-end hardware — DEC; Front-end software — CText; Printers — Tegra/Varityper. DISPLAY: Front-end hardware — DEC; Front-end software — CText; Printers — Tegra/Varityper. PRODUCTION: Plate exposures — 1-Nu; Plate processors — SCREEN; Production cameras — Ik/530, SCREEN; Automatic film processors — 1-LE/LD-24. MAILROOM: Counter stackers — 1-HI; Inserters and stuffers — KAN/480 7-into-1 Double Out; Bundle tyer — 1-MLN. WIRE SERVICES: News — AP; Syndicates — AP; Receiving dishes — AP. BUSINESS COMPUTERS: 1-DEC/1170; Applications: Circ, Adv billing, Accts receivable, Gen ledger, Payroll.

LAFAYETTE-WEST LAFAYETTE

Tippecanoe County

'90 U.S. Census- 69,671 (Lafayette 43,764; West Lafayette 25,907); E&P '96 Est. 75,764 (Lafayette 45,201; West Lafayette 30,563)
ABC-NDM (90): 197,802 (HH 71,093)

Journal and Courier

(m-mon to sat; S)

Journal and Courier, 217 N. 6th St., Lafayette, IN 47901-1448; tel (317) 423-5511; fax (317) 742-5633; e-mail postmaster @jandc.mdn.com; web site http://www.mdn.com/jconline. Gannett Co. Inc. group.
Circulation: 37,488(m); 37,488(m-sat); 44,704(S); ABC Sept. 30, 1995.
Price: 50¢(d); 50¢(sat); $1.50(S); $3.25/wk; $169.00/yr.
Advertising: Open inch rate $35.12(m); $36.28(m-fri); $36.28(m-sat); $40.28(S). **Representative:** Gannett National Newspaper Sales.
News Services: AP, GNS. **Politics:** Independent. **Established:** 1829.
Special Editions: Junior Achievement (Jan); Farm, Home Improvement (Feb); Lawn & Garden, Business Industry (Mar); Indy 500 (May); Community Connections, Football, Welcome to Purdue, Brickyard 400 (Aug); Home Improvement (Oct); Basketball (Nov).
Special Weekly Sections: Food (mon); 4 Kidz Only (tues); Amateur Sports (thur); TGIF (fri); Home Place (sat); TV Journal, Business Review, Wheels Automotive (S); Market/Commodities (daily).
Magazines: Homeplace, USA Weekend (sat); New Horizons TV Journal (½ tab) (monthly).

CORPORATE OFFICERS

Exec Board Chairman Robert B Miller
President John Curley
Vice Pres/Treasurer Larry F Miller

GENERAL MANAGEMENT

Publisher Richard L Holtz
Manager-Credit Andy S Muinzer
Controller Mathew Ramsey
Human Resource Director Angelyn R Rizzo

ADVERTISING

Director Ted Taylor
Manager-Classified Cheryl Smith
Manager-Retail Jim Kaczmarek

MARKETING AND PROMOTION

Director-Marketing Development Arvid Olson

TELECOMMUNICATIONS

Audiotex Manager Cheryl Smith

CIRCULATION

Director Gary F Ruhberg
Manager-Home Delivery Glen Vick

NEWS EXECUTIVES

Exec Editor/Chief News Exec George Benge
Managing Editor Denise Richter

EDITORS AND MANAGERS

Business Writer Greg Hall
Editorial Page Editor Shirley Ragsdale
Features Editor Dave Baugert
Films/Theater Editor Kathy Matter
Food Editor Dave Baugert
Graphics Editor James Jackson
Librarian Rita Owens
Local/Regional Editor Phillip Fiorini
Chief Photographer Tom Campbell
Religion Editor Byron Parvis
Sports Editor Jim Lefko
Asst Sports Editor Jim D Stafford

MANAGEMENT INFORMATION SERVICES

Data Processing Manager Michael Kearney
Online Manager James Jackson

PRODUCTION

Director Robert Yost
Coordinator Garry Swaney

Market Information: TMC; Operate database; Operate audiotex; Electronic edition.
Mechanical available: Letterpress; Black and 3 ROP colors; insert accepted — preprinted; page cut-offs — 22¾".
Mechanical specifications: Type page 13" x 21½"; E - 6 cols, 2.06", ⅛" between; A - 6 cols, 2.06", ⅛" between; C - 9 cols, 1.38", ⅛" between.
Commodity consumption: Newsprint 3,210 short tons; 2,912 metric tons; widths 54.75", 40$\frac{15}{16}$"; black ink 94,590 pounds; color ink 11,800 pounds; single pages printed 12,872; average pages per issue 32(d), 52(S); single plates used 35,000.
Equipment: EDITORIAL: Front-end hardware — 5-Dewar, 32-VG/55, 6-SIA; Front-end software — Dewar; Printers — DEC/LA 180, OC-E/Proof Express; Other equipment — Ap/Mac SE, Ap/Mac IIci, Ap/Mac fx, Ap/Mac Quadra 950, IBM/PC 486, Ap/Mac 650, Ap/Mac 630. CLASSIFIED: Front-end hardware — SII/Tandem; Front-end software — SII; Printers — Panasonic. AUDIOTEX: Hardware — Octel. DISPLAY: Adv layout systems — Ap/Mac; Front-end hardware — Ap/Mac, 9-Ap/Mac; Front-end software — Multi-Ad; Printers — 2-Linotype-Hell/Linotronic 530. PRODUCTION: Pagination software — 9-Dewar/System 3; Typesetters — 2-Linotype-Hell/ Linotronic 530; Platemaking systems — Na; Plate exposures — 1-Na/Starlite; Plate processors — 1-Na/NP-40; Electronic picture desk — 1-Lf; Scanners — ECR/Autokon; Production cameras — 2-C/Spartan III; Color separation equipment (conventional) — Lf/AP Leaf Picture Desk. PRESSROOM: Line 1 — 6-G/Mark (2 half decks; 1 hump); Folders — G/2:1; Press control system — Fin; Press registration system — KFM/Pin Registration. MAILROOM: Counter stackers — 2-HL, 1-QWI; Inserters and stuffers — 1-HI/848; Bundle tyer — 2-Power Strap; Addressing machine — Ch. WIRE SERVICES: News — AP, GNS; Stock tables — AP SelectStox; Receiving dishes — size-6ft, AP, GNS. BUSINESS COMPUTERS: 1-IBM/AS-400-F35; PCs & micros networked; PCs & main system networked.

LA PORTE

La Porte County

'90 U.S. Census- 21,507; E&P '96 Est. 21,556
ABC-CZ (90): 21,507 (HH 8,675)

The La Porte Herald-Argus

(e-mon to sat)

La Porte Herald-Argus, 701 State St., La Porte, IN 46350-3328; tel (219) 362-2161; fax (219) 362-2166. Small Newspaper Group Inc. group.
Circulation: 13,170(e); 13,170(e-sat); ABC Sept. 30, 1995.
Price: 35¢(d); 35¢(sat); $1.60/wk (carrier); $7.15/mo (motor route); $108.00/yr (mail).
Advertising: Open inch rate $9.00(e); $9.00(e-sat).
News Services: AP, SHNS. **Politics:** Independent-Republican. **Established:** 1880.
Not Published: New Year; Memorial Day; Independence Day; Labor Day; Thanksgiving; Christmas.
Special Editions: Finance (Feb); Farm Section (Mar); Home Improvement/Gardening (Apr); Car Care Section (Oct); Christmas, X'mas Lay-Away (Nov).
Special Weekly Sections: Best Food Day (mon); Agriculture (tues); Business/Industry (wed); Homes (thur); Senior (fri); Religion (sat).
Magazine: TV Viewer (television listings) (sat).

CORPORATE OFFICERS

Chairman of the Board Len R Small
Secretary Thomas P Small
Asst Secretary Joseph E Lacaeyse

GENERAL MANAGEMENT

Publisher C T Otolski
Business Manager Robert Rehlander
Purchasing Agent Robert Rehlander

ADVERTISING

Manager Thos P Avery
Manager-Retail Carol Kuta
Manager-Classified Donna Maglio

MARKETING AND PROMOTION

Manager-Promotion Thos P Avery

CIRCULATION

Manager John Schulz

NEWS EXECUTIVE

Managing Editor Mark Johnson

EDITORS AND MANAGERS

Action/Hot Line Editor Jason Scales
Books Editor Mark Johnson
Business/Finance Editor Mark Harper
City Editor Mark Harper
Editorial Page Editor Beth Boardman
Education Editor Carol Druga
Farm Editor Jason Scales
Features Editor Sandra Provan
Films/Theater Editor Mark Johnson
Food/Home Furnishings Editor Sandra Provan
Librarian Mark Kreag
Music Editor Julie Kessler
Political Editor Beth Boardman
Radio/Television Editor Julie Kessler
Real Estate Editor Mark Harper
Religion Editor Julie Kessler
Science/Technology Editor Mark Johnson
Sports Editor Dan Knott
Teen-Age/Youth Editor Sandra Provan
Wire Editor Julie Kessler
Women's/Society Editor Sandra Provan

MANAGEMENT INFORMATION SERVICES

Data Processing Manager Robert Rehlander

PRODUCTION

Foreman-Composing Ronnie Haberman
Foreman-Pressroom Ronald G Ulrich

Mechanical available: Offset; Black and 3 ROP colors; insert accepted — preprinted; page cut-offs — 22¾".
Mechanical specifications: Type page 13" x 21½"; E - 6 cols, 2$\frac{1}{16}$", ⅛" between; A - 6 cols, 2$\frac{1}{16}$", ⅛" between; C - 9 cols, 1⅜", $\frac{1}{16}$" between.
Commodity consumption: Newsprint 557 short tons; 506 metric tons; widths 27½", 13¾"; black ink 11,570 pounds; color ink 1,150 pounds; single pages printed 6,926; average pages per issue 22(d); single plates used 9,450.
Equipment: EDITORIAL: Front-end hardware — Dewar/Sys 2; Front-end software — Dewar/Disc Net; Other equipment — 16-Dewar/Discribe. CLASSIFIED: Front-end hardware — Dewar/Sys 2; Front-end software — Dewar/Disc Net; Other equipment — 5-Dewar/Discribe. DISPLAY: Adv layout systems — 2-Dewar/Sys IV; Front-end hardware — 2-Dewar/AST. PRODUCTION: Typesetters — 2-Tegra/Varityper XP-1000, M/1000; Plate exposures — 1-B; Electronic picture desk — 1-Lf/AP Leaf Picture Desk; Production cameras — 1-Nu/2024-V, 1-R/580; Automatic film processors — 1-AG/Rapidline 66; Digital color separation equipment — Ap/Power Mac 8100 w/Adobe/PhotoShop. PRESSROOM: Line 1 — 6-G/Urbanite, 1-G/3-Color single width; Press drives — 2-Baldor; Folders — 1-G/Universal; Reels and stands — 6-G; Press control system — Fin; Press registration system — Stoesser System. MAILROOM: Bundle tyer — 1-Bu/String Tyer, 1-MLI/EE. WIRE SERVICES: News — AP; Photos — AP; Syndicates — NEA, King Features, Creators Syndicate, TMS; Receiving dishes — size-12ft, AP. BUSINESS COMPUTERS: Everex/386-33, DTK/Pentium-100; Applications: Adv billing, Accts receivable, Gen ledger, Payroll, Comm sales, Circ billing; PCs & micros networked; PCs & main system networked.

LEBANON

Boone County

'90 U.S. Census- 12,059; E&P '96 Est. 12,723

The Reporter (e-mon to sat)

The Reporter, 117 E. Washington St.; PO Box 1100, Lebanon, IN 46052; tel (317) 482-4650; fax (317) 482-4652.

Copyright ©1996 by the Editor & Publisher Co.

Circulation: 7,156(e); 7,156(e-sat); Sworn Sept. 30, 1995.
Price: 50¢(d); 50¢(sat); $99.00/yr.
Advertising: Open inch rate $6.49(e); $6.49(e-sat). **Representative:** US Suburban Press.
News Service: AP. **Politics:** Independent-Republican. **Established:** 1891.
Not Published: New Year; Memorial Day; Independence Day; Labor Day; Thanksgiving; Christmas.
Special Editions: Auto-Home Show (Apr); Brides (Feb); 500 Specials (May); County 4-H Fair (July); Christmas Opening, Winter Sports (Nov); Christmas Greetings (Dec).
Special Weekly Sections: Senior Citizens (mon); Farm Pages (tues); Best Food (wed); Shopper's Extra (thur); Business Page (fri).
Magazine: TV Times (sat).

CORPORATE OFFICERS

President — Suzanne Murphy
Vice Pres — Michael Quayle
Secretary/Treasurer — James R Mossman

GENERAL MANAGEMENT

Publisher — Michael D Mossman
General Manager — Michael D Mossman
Manager-Credit — Barbara Coe

ADVERTISING

Director — Sharon Loux
Manager-Credit — Barbara Coe

CIRCULATION

Director — Rick Bechtold

NEWS EXECUTIVE

Managing Editor — Owen Hansen

EDITORS AND MANAGERS

Business/Finance Editor — Owen Hansen
City Editor — Rod Rose
Editorial Page Editor — Owen Hansen
Education Editor — Kandi Killin
Lifestyles Editor — Kandi Killin
Farm Editor — Maria Dunbar
Photo Editor — Ron Dulhanty
Sports Editor — Kevin Pompkins
Teen-Age/Youth Editor — Kandi Killin

PRODUCTION

Manager — Ingraham Vancel

Mechanical available: Offset; Black and 3 ROP colors; insert accepted — preprinted; page cut-offs — $22\frac{3}{4}$".
Mechanical specifications: Type page 13" x 21"; E - 6 cols, $2\frac{1}{16}$", $\frac{1}{8}$" between; A - 6 cols, $2\frac{1}{16}$", $\frac{1}{8}$" between; C - 6 cols, $2\frac{1}{16}$", $\frac{1}{8}$" between.
Commodity consumption: Newsprint 250 short tons; widths 28", 14"; black ink 7,500 pounds; color ink 100 pounds; single pages printed 4,796; average pages per issue 14(d); single plates used 2,500.
Equipment: EDITORIAL: Front-end hardware — 1-Ap/Mac; Printers — 1-Ap/Mac; Other equipment — Fotovix. CLASSIFIED: Front-end hardware — 1-Ap/Mac; Front-end software — Baseview/Class Manager; Printers — 1-Ap/Mac. DISPLAY: Adv layout systems — 1-Ap/Mac; Printers — 1-Ap/Mac LaserPrinter. PRODUCTION: Typesetters — 1-Ap/Mac, 1-Printware, 1-Linotype-Hell/Linotronic; Plate exposures — 1-Nu; Plate processors — 1-Nat; Electronic picture desk — Lf/AP Leaf Picture Desk; Scanners — 1-AG/COM, 2-AG; Production cameras — 1-B/Caravel; Automatic film processors — 1-Screen, 1-Devotec, LE/LD-220. PRESSROOM: Line 1 — 7-G/Community; Folders — 1-G. MAILROOM: Bundle tyer — 1-Dynaric; Addressing machine — Wm. WIRE SERVICES: News — AP; Photos — AP; Receiving dishes — size-3m, AP. BUSINESS COMPUTERS: IBM/Sys 60; Applications: Accts receivable, Accts payable, Gen ledger, Payroll, Mail labels; PCs & micros networked; PCs & main system networked.

LINTON

Greene County

'90 U.S. Census- 5,814; E&P '96 Est. 5,535

Linton Daily Citizen

(e-mon to fri)

Linton Daily Citizen, 79 S. Main St., Linton, IN 47441; tel (812) 847-4487; fax (812) 847-9513. Smith Newspapers Inc. group.
Circulation: 4,750(e); Sworn Sept. 27, 1995.
Price: 75¢(d); $95.00/yr.
Advertising: Open inch rate $7.10(e).
News Service: AP. **Politics:** Democrat. **Established:** 1900.
Not Published: New Year; Memorial Day; Labor Day; Thanksgiving; Christmas.
Advertising not accepted: Vending machine.

GENERAL MANAGEMENT

Publisher — Ron Dietz

ADVERTISING

Manager — Ron Dietz

CIRCULATION

Manager — Theresa Slaven

NEWS EXECUTIVE

Managing Editor — Heather Atkinson

PRODUCTION

Foreman — Ron Dietz

Market Information: Zoned editions; Split Run; TMC.
Mechanical available: Offset; Black and 4 ROP colors; insert accepted — preprinted; page cut-offs — $22\frac{3}{4}$".
Mechanical specifications: Type page $12\frac{3}{4}$" x 21"; E - 8 cols, $1\frac{3}{4}$", $\frac{1}{8}$" between; A - 8 cols, $1\frac{3}{4}$", $\frac{1}{8}$" between; C - 8 cols, $1\frac{3}{4}$", $\frac{1}{8}$" between.
Commodity consumption: average pages per issue 41(d).
Equipment: PRODUCTION: Typesetters — 1-COM/2961HS, 1-COM/4961TL, 1-COM/7200, 1-COM/7200L; Platemaking systems — 1-Nu; Production cameras — 1-LE/500; Automatic film processors — 1-Compuquick. PRESSROOM: Line 2 — 3-HI/V-15A; Folders — 1-HI. MAILROOM: Addressing machine — 1-Am.

LOGANSPORT

Cass County

'90 U.S. Census- 16,812; E&P '96 Est. 16,226
ABC-CZ (90): 18,293 (HH 7,443)

Pharos-Tribune

(e-mon to fri; S)

Pharos-Tribune, 517 E. Broadway Ave.; PO Box 210, Logansport, IN 46947; tel (219) 722-5000; fax (219) 722-5238. Thomson Newspapers group.
Circulation: 13,359(e); 14,161(S); ABC Sept. 30, 1995.
Price: 50¢(d); $1.25(S); $2.40/wk; $10.40/mo; $124.80/yr.
Advertising: Open inch rate $12.50(e); $13.25(S). **Representative:** Landon Associates Inc.
News Service: KRT. **Politics:** Independent. **Established:** 1844.
Advertising not accepted: Work at home job opportunities.
Special Editions: 4-H, Football (Aug); Christmas Opening (Nov); Spring Building; Basketball Preview; Senior Citizen; County Government; Bridal; Car Care; Today's Family; Home Furnishing; Year-in-Review.
Special Weekly Sections: Senior Living, Money (wed); Sports Extra, Religion (fri); Lifestyle, Business (S).
Magazine: Parade (S).

GENERAL MANAGEMENT

Publisher — William C Blake
Manager-Business Office — Kim Dillon

ADVERTISING

Director — David A Tucker
Manager-Sales — Robyn Mc Closkey

CIRCULATION

Manager — Wendy Stephens

NEWS EXECUTIVE

Editor — Dave Long

EDITORS AND MANAGERS

Lifestyle Editor — Deb Saine
School Reporter — Heather Nava
Sports Editor — Lewis Bagley

PRODUCTION

Manager — Rich Cox

Market Information: TMC.
Mechanical available: Offset; Black and 3 ROP colors; insert accepted — preprinted; page cut-offs — $22\frac{3}{4}$".
Mechanical specifications: Type page 13" x $21\frac{1}{2}$"; E - 6 cols, $2\frac{1}{16}$", $\frac{1}{8}$" between; A - 6 cols, $2\frac{1}{16}$", $\frac{1}{8}$" between; C - 8 cols, $1\frac{9}{16}$", $\frac{1}{8}$" between.
Commodity consumption: Newsprint 667 short tons; 600 metric tons; widths $27\frac{1}{2}$", $13\frac{3}{4}$"; black ink 19,530 pounds; color ink 6,240 pounds; single pages printed 6,784; average pages per issue 20(d), 28(S); single plates used 3,981.
Equipment: EDITORIAL: Front-end hardware — Sun; Front-end software — ArborText 3.0.4; Printers — 2-Ap/Mac LaserWriter II NTX, 2-Copal/Dash 600; Other equipment — Lf/AP Leaf Picture Desk, Lf/Leafscan 35. CLASSIFIED: Front-end hardware — Sun, NCD; Front-end software — Island Write; Printers — HP/LaserJet, Copal/Dash 600. DISPLAY: Adv layout systems — SCS/Layout 8000; Front-end hardware — Ap/Mac II; Front-end software — QuarkXPress 3.3; Printers — 2-Ap/Mac LaserWriter II NTX, 2-Copal/Dash 600. PRODUCTION: Pagination software — QuarkXPress 3.31; OCR software — TI/OmniPage 2.12; Typesetters — ECR/PelBox 1085; Plate exposures — 11-Nu/Flip Top FT40UPNS; Plate processors — Graham; Production cameras — 1-SCREEN/Companica 680C; Automatic film processors — LE/26R; Film transporters — LE; Digital color separation equipment — 1-Nikon/LS-3500, 1-AG/Focus Color Plus. PRESSROOM: Line 1 — 10-G/SSC; Press control system — CH. MAILROOM: Inserters and stuffers — 4-MM; Bundle tyer — 1-MLN, OVL/415. LIBRARY: Electronic — Verity/Topic. COMMUNICATIONS: Systems used — satellite. WIRE SERVICES: News — AP Datafeatures, AP Datastream; Photos — AP; Syndicates — KRT, King Features, NAS, CT, Creators, Universal Press; Receiving dishes — size-10ft, AP. BUSINESS COMPUTERS: 1-Sun/4-110, 1-Sun/SLC, 1-Compaq/Prolinca 3/25; Applications: Vision Data: Circ, Accts receivable, Class trans; ADP: Payroll; PCs & micros networked; PCs & main system networked.

MADISON

Jefferson County

'90 U.S. Census- 12,006; E&P '96 Est. 11,947

The Madison Courier

(e-mon to fri; m-sat)

The Madison Courier, 310 Courier Sq., Madison, IN 47250; tel (812) 265-3641; fax (812) 273-6903.
Circulation: 9,412(e); 9,412(m-sat); Sworn Oct. 6, 1995.
Price: 35¢(d); 35¢(sat); $5.65/mo (foot), $5.80/mo (motor route), $7.00/mo (mail); $65.10/yr (foot), $67.10/yr (motor route), $88.00/yr (mail).
Advertising: Open inch rate $8.68(e); $8.68(m-sat). **Representative:** Papert Companies.
News Service: AP. **Politics:** Republican. **Established:** 1837.
Not Published: New Year; Memorial Day; Independence Day; Labor Day; Thanksgiving; Christmas.
Special Editions: Wedding Tab, Soil & Water Tab (Jan); Tax Tab (Feb); Lawn & Garden Tab (Mar); Home and Car Improvement Tab (Apr); Graduation Tab (May); Cookbook, Madison Regatta Tab (June); 4-H Fair Tab (July); Basketball Preview Tab, Holiday Guide (Nov); Year-End Tab (Dec).

CORPORATE OFFICER

President — Jane W Jacobs

GENERAL MANAGEMENT

Publisher — Jane W Jacobs

ADVERTISING

Manager-Promotion — Ron Wehner

CIRCULATION

Manager — Curt Jacobs

NEWS EXECUTIVES

Editor-Indiana — Laura Hodges
Editor-Kentucky — Mark Campbell
Managing Editor — Graham Taylor

EDITORS AND MANAGERS

Books Editor — Phil Burton
Sports Editor — Bob Demaree
Teen-Age/Youth Editor — Jennifer Eades
Women's Editor — Jennifer Eades

PRODUCTION

Foreman-Camera/Press — Aaron Bell
Manager — Dale Wilson

Mechanical available: Offset; Black and 3 ROP colors; insert accepted — preprinted, single sheet, booklets; page cut-offs — $22\frac{3}{4}$".
Mechanical specifications: Type page 13" x $21\frac{1}{2}$"; E - 6 cols, $2\frac{1}{16}$", $\frac{1}{8}$" between; A - 6 cols, $2\frac{1}{16}$", $\frac{1}{8}$" between; C - 8 cols, $1\frac{1}{2}$", $\frac{1}{8}$" between.
Commodity consumption: Newsprint 358 short tons; widths $27\frac{1}{2}$", $13\frac{3}{4}$"; single pages printed 7,727; average pages per issue 24(d); single plates used 4,264.
Equipment: EDITORIAL: Front-end hardware — 1-Ap/Mac SE30, 6-Ap/Mac SE, 4-Ap/Mac Plus; Front-end software — Baseview, Jus-Text; Printers — 1-Ap/Mac LaserWriter II NT; Other equipment — 1-RSK/Tandy portable Model 100, 2-RSK/Tandy 1000RL for remote office. CLASSIFIED: Front-end hardware — 3-Ap/Mac SE; Front-end software — Baseview, Jus-Text; Printers — 1-Ap/Mac ImageWriter II NT. DISPLAY: Adv layout systems — COM/One System; Front-end hardware — Ap/Mac Radius; Front-end software — DTI; Printers — Ap/Mac LaserWriter II NT. PRODUCTION: Typesetters — Ap/Mac LaserWriter II NT; Plate exposures — 1-Nu; Production cameras — R/400; Automatic film processors — LE/LD-18; Shrink lenses — CK Optical/SQU7. PRESSROOM: Line 1 — 6-KP/Newsking; Reels and stands — 6-KP; Press control system — 1-CH. MAILROOM: Inserters and stuffers — KAN/4 Station; Bundle tyer — 2-Bu; Addressing machine — 1-St. LIBRARY: Combination — Minolta/Microfilm. WIRE SERVICES: News — AP; Receiving dishes — size-10ft, AP. BUSINESS COMPUTERS: 4-TI/1505.

MARION

Grant County

'90 U.S. Census- 32,618; E&P '96 Est. 31,174
ABC-NDM (90): 101,648 (HH 37,899)

Chronicle-Tribune

(m-mon to sat; S)

Chronicle-Tribune, 610 S. Adams; PO Box 309, Marion, IN 46953; tel (317) 664-5111; fax (317) 664-6292. Gannett Co. Inc. group.
Circulation: 20,464(m); 20,464(m-sat); 24,017(S); ABC Sept. 30, 1995.
Price: 35¢(d); 35¢(sat); $1.50(S); $2.90/wk; $12.56/mo; $150.80/yr.
Advertising: Open inch rate $23.95(m); $23.95(m-sat); $24.75(S). **Representative:** Gannett National Newspaper Sales.
News Services: AP, GNS. **Politics:** Independent. **Established:** 1930.
Special Editions: Progress (Mar); Access Marion (Newcomer's Guide) (Aug); Cook Book (Oct); Spring & Fall Builders; Spring Fashions; Car Care (Spring & Fall); Medical Fitness Health; Famous Front Pages; Summer Travel; Women in Business.
Special Weekly Sections: Best Food Day (mon); Home (thur); Travel (fri); Church, Business (sat); Business (S).
Magazines: USA Weekend, 2nd Sunday Magazine Tab, TeleView (quarter fold booklet), Wabash Sunday (S).

CORPORATE OFFICERS

Exec Board Chairman — R B Miller
President — Louis A Weil Jr
Secretary — Douglas H McCorkindale
Treasurer — Larry F Miller
Asst Secretary/Treasurer — Lucille E Cody

GENERAL MANAGEMENT

Publisher — Victor W Hussey
Controller — Peggy S Crabtree

ADVERTISING

Director — Michael C Casuscelli
Manager-Classified — Annette Burcharts

MARKETING AND PROMOTION

Director-Marketing/Promotion — Sherry French

CIRCULATION

Director — Gary Cooper

NEWS EXECUTIVE

Exec Editor — W Alan Miller

EDITORS AND MANAGERS

Business/Finance Editor — David Nelson
Editorial Page Editor — Alan Miller
Education Editor — Sherie Smith
Entertainment/Amusements Editor — Mike Cline
Fashion/Style Editor — Mike Cline
Features Editor — Mike Cline
Graphics Editor/Art Director — Tammy Kingery
Health/Medical Editor — Shelby Roby
Living/Lifestyle Editor — Mike Cline
News Editor — Bryon Cannon
Photo Editor — Alan Petersime
Sports Editor — Matt Solinsky
Television Editor — Peggy Holmes
Theater/Film Editor — Mike Cline
Women's Editor — Mike Cline

MANAGEMENT INFORMATION SERVICES

Data Processing Manager — Barbara Scott

PRODUCTION

Director — William K Baker
Manager-Composing — Jane Cain
Manager-Pressroom — Robert Rhoades
Manager-Distribution — Ted Shook
Manager-Commercial — Vicki Havens
Manager-Pre Press — Eddie Torres
Manager-Operations — Gary Stoffer

Market Information: Zoned editions; TMC.

Indiana I-135

Mechanical available: Offset; Black and 3 ROP colors; insert accepted — preprinted, 4"x 5" cards to 11 3/8" x 13 3/4" products; page cut-offs — 22 3/4".
Mechanical specifications: Type page 13" x 21 1/2"; E - 6 cols, 2 1/16", 1/8" between; A - 6 cols, 2 1/16", 1/8" between; C - 9 cols, 1 3/8", 1/16" between.
Commodity consumption: Newsprint 1,200 short tons; 1,184 metric tons; widths 27 1/4", 13 5/8"; black ink 25,200 pounds; color ink 11,960 pounds; single pages printed 6,936; average pages per issue 18(d), 30(S).
Equipment: EDITORIAL: Front-end hardware — HAS; Front-end software — CD/TOPS 2.5; Printers — Printronix/P-300. CLASSIFIED: Front-end hardware — HAS; Front-end software — CD/TOPS 2.5; Printers — Printronix/P-300. DISPLAY: Adv layout systems — HAS; Front-end software — CD/Tops 2.5. PRODUCTION: OCR software — QuarkXPress; Typesetters — 2-COM/8600; Platemaking systems — Nat; Plate exposures — Nu/Flip Top FT40UPNS, Nu/Flip Top FT40APRNS; Plate processors — 1-Nat/380; Electronic picture desk — Lf/AP Leaf Picture Desk; Production cameras — 1-C/Spartan III; Automatic film processors — LE/LD24AQ; Film transporters — C/Spartan III; Digital color separation equipment — SCREEN/708.
PRESSROOM: Line 1 — 10-G/Urbanite 845; Line 2 — 6-G/Urbanite 557; Pasters — 7-Jardis; Press control system — Fin/Drive Sys. MAILROOM: Counter stackers — 1-HL/Monitor HI II, 2-HI/RS30; Inserters and stuffers — 1-Mc/660-20; Bundle tyer — 1-MLN/2A, OVL/415, Bu/String; Wrapping singles — Manual; Addressing machine — Ch/596-985. WIRE SERVICES: News — AP; Stock tables — AP SelectStox; Syndicates — GNS; Receiving dishes — size-8ft, AP. BUSINESS COMPUTERS: Time Mgt Sys, IBM/Sys 38; Applications: Accts payable, Payroll, Gen ledger, Circ, Adv; PCs & micros networked; PCs & main system networked.

MARTINSVILLE

Morgan County

'90 U.S. Census- 11,667; E&P '96 Est. 15,057

Daily Reporter (e-mon to sat)

Daily Reporter, 60 S. Jefferson St.; PO Box 1636, Martinsville, IN 46151; tel (317) 342-3311; fax (317) 342-1446.
Circulation: 8,301(e); 8,301(e-sat); CAC Mar. 31, 1994.
Price: 50¢(d); 50¢(sat); $78.00/yr (outside county), $54.00/yr (in county).
Advertising: Open inch rate $8.30(e); $8.30(e-sat). **Representative:** US Suburban Press.
News Service: AP. **Politics:** Republican. **Established:** 1889.
Special Editions: Bridal Show; Boy Scout Page; Valentine's Day; Tax Time Sale; Spring Show; Future Farmers; Girls Scout Page; St. Patrick's Day Party; Clean-up/Paint-up; Race for Values; Graduation; Sidewalk Days; Morgan County Fair; Football Preview; Fall Festival Program; Customer Appreciation Days; Basketball Preview; Holiday Show; Christmas Kick-off; Gift Headquarters; Last Minute Gifts (quarterly); The Better Years/Senior Citizen Newspaper; Car Track.
Broadcast Affiliates: TV W15AY.

CORPORATE OFFICERS	
Board Chairman	Robert S Kendall
President	Mark C Kendall
Exec Vice Pres	Dorothy Kendall
Exec Vice Pres	Wendell Holt
Treasurer	Kathryn Holt
GENERAL MANAGEMENT	
Publisher	R Kay Selch
Purchasing Agent	Rick Morrison
ADVERTISING	
Director	R Kay Selch
Manager	Wayne Kramer
TELECOMMUNICATIONS	
Audiotex Coordinator	John Knerr Jr
CIRCULATION	
Director	Jim Taylor
NEWS EXECUTIVES	
Managing Editor	Bette Nunn
Asst Managing Editor	Jim Asher
EDITORS AND MANAGERS	
Columnist	Robert S Kendall
Society Editor	Gladys Neal
Sports Editor	Darin Kroan
Asst Sports Editor	Hugh Tooley
PRODUCTION	
Superintendent	Rick Morrison

Market Information: TMC; Operate audiotex.
Mechanical available: Offset; Black and 3 ROP colors; insert accepted — preprintec, all; page cut-offs — 22 3/4".
Mechanical specifications: Type page 14 1/4" x 21 1/2"; E - 6 cols, 2 1/4", 1/8" between; A - 6 cols, 2 1/4", 1/8" between; C - 9 cols, 1 1/4", 1/16" between.
Commodity consumption: average pages per issue 15(d), 13(sat).
Equipment: EDITORIAL: Front-end hardware — Ap/Mac; Printers — Ap/Mac LaserWriter. PRESSROOM: Line 1 — 7-G/Community (color unit); Folders — 1-G/2:1. MAILROOM: Bundle tyer — 2-Bu. LIBRARY: Electronic — Morgue System, Ap. WIRE SERVICES: News — AP; Stock tables — AP; Receiving dishes — AP. BUSINESS COMPUTERS: Applications: Baseview: Circ.

MICHIGAN CITY

La Porte County

'90 U.S. Census- 33,822; E&P '96 Est. 32,130

The News Dispatch
(m-mon to sat; S)

The News Dispatch, 121 W. Michigan Blvd., Michigan City, IN 46360; tel (219) 874-7211; fax (219) 872-8511. Nixon Newspapers Inc. group.
Circulation: 13,949(m); 13,949(m-sat); 13,949(S); Sworn Sept. 28, 1995.
Price: 50¢(d); 50¢(sat); $1.00(S); $8.50/mo (carrier), $8.75/mo (motor route); $102.00/yr (mail).
Advertising: Open inch rate $12.78(m); $12.78(m-sat); $14.09(S). **Representative:** Nixon Newspapers.
News Service: AP. **Politics:** Independent-Democrat. **Established:** 1938.
Note: Effective Oct. 30, 1995, this publication changed its publishing plan from (e-mon to fri; m-sat; S) to (m-mon to sat; S).
Not Published: New Year; Memorial Day; Labor Day; Christmas.
Special Editions: Home Builders; Fall & Spring; World of Christmas; Health & Fitness; Real Estate Guide (monthly); Spring Car Care; Bridal; Boat Show.
Special Weekly Sections: Best Food Day, Food Feature (wed); Automotive, Book Review, Lifestyles (thur); Religion (fri); Real Estate (sat); Lifestyles, Business (S).
Magazine: TV Listings (own, local newsprint) (sat).

CORPORATE OFFICERS	
President	John R Nixon
Vice Pres-Finance	John W Stackhouse
Secretary	Deborah M Huff
GENERAL MANAGEMENT	
Publisher	Don J Manaher
Manager-Credit	Kimberly Bremner
Purchasing Agent	Kimberly Bremner
Business Manager	Kimberly Bremner
ADVERTISING	
Manager-Retail	Debra Everly
Manager-National Representative	Cindy Piper
Manager-Classified	Isis Caines
CIRCULATION	
Manager	Doug Wilson
NEWS EXECUTIVE	
Managing Editor	David Hawk
EDITORS AND MANAGERS	
Business/Finance Editor	Henry Lange
City Editor	John Lundy
Columnist	Deborah Sederberg
Columnist	Tim Costello
Columnist	Henry Lange
Columnist	Red Griggs
Consumer Interest Editor	Margaret Humphrey
Education/School Editor	Janet Ortegon
Food Editor	Margaret Humphrey
Lifestyle Editor	Margaret Humphrey
News Editor	Colleen Kuzel
Chief Photographer	Steve Peterka
Sports Editor	Tim Costello
PRODUCTION	
Manager	Doug Wilson
Manager-Press	Bob Yoder
Manager-Distribution	Tony Manns

Market Information: Zoned editions; TMC; ADS.
Mechanical available: Offset; Black and 3 ROP colors; insert accepted — preprinted; page cut-offs — 22 3/4".
Mechanical specifications: Type page 14" x 22 1/2"; E - 6 cols, 2", 1/8" between; A - 6 cols, 2", 1/8" between; C - 9 cols, 1 3/8", 1/8" between.
Commodity consumption: Newsprint 750 metric tons; widths 13 3/4", 27 1/2"; black ink 20,000 pounds; color ink 3,800 pounds; average pages per issue 26(d), 36(S).
Equipment: EDITORIAL: Front-end hardware — Ap/Mac; Front-end software — Baseview, QuarkXPress; Printers — 2-Ap/Mac LaserWriter IINTX. CLASSIFIED: Front-end hardware — Ap/Mac; Front-end software — Baseview/Class Manager; Printers — 2-Ap/Mac LaserWriter IINTX. DISPLAY: Adv layout systems — Ap/Mac; Front-end hardware — AST, PC; Front-end software — Dewar, Multi-Ad/Creator; Printers — AU/Micro 5. PRODUCTION: Plate exposures — 1-B/Ultra 5000; Plate processors — Nat/A-250; Scanners — Microtek/300SZ; Production cameras — R; Automatic film processors — LE/LD18; Color separation equipment (conventional) — Lf/AP Leaf Picture Desk.
PRESSROOM: Line 1 — 8-G/Urbanite (3-Color unit); Folders — G/Half & Quarter; Reels and stands — 8-G/Reel Stand; Press control system — Fin. MAILROOM: Counter stackers — BG/110HB; Inserters and stuffers — 3-KAN/320; Bundle tyer — MLN. WIRE SERVICES: News — AP; Syndicates — NEA; Receiving dishes — size-10ft, AP.

MISHAWAKA

See SOUTH BEND

MONTICELLO

White County

'90 U.S. Census- 5,237; E&P '96 Est. 5,398

Herald Journal (m-mon to sat)

Herald Journal, 114 S. Main St.; PO Box 409, Monticello, IN 47960; tel (219) 583-5121; fax (219) 583-4241. Home News Enterprises group.
Circulation: 6,223(m); 6,223(m-sat); Sworn Sept. 29, 1995.
Price: 50¢(d); 50¢(sat); $69.00/yr, $75.00/yr (outside county), $80.00/yr (outside state).
Advertising: Open inch rate $7.50(m); $7.50(m-sat). **Representative:** Landon Associates Inc.
News Service: AP. **Politics:** Republican. **Established:** 1862.
Not Published: 11 Postal Holidays; New Year; Memorial Day; Independence Day; Labor Day; Thanksgiving; Christmas.
Special Edition: "Where" Vacation Guide.
Special Weekly Sections: Best Food Day (mon); Senior Citizens (tues); Self Help (wed); Agri-Business (thur); Religion, TV (fri); Business & Financial (sat).

GENERAL MANAGEMENT	
Publisher	Don L Hurd
ADVERTISING	
Director	Kevin Lashbrook
NEWS EXECUTIVE	
Editor	David Maroney
EDITOR AND MANAGER	
Sports Editor	Sean Chiszar
PRODUCTION	
Manager	Carol Oliver

Market Information: TMC.
Mechanical available: Offset; Black and 3 ROP colors; insert accepted — preprinted; page cut-offs — 22 3/4".
Mechanical specifications: Type page 13" x 21 1/2"; E - 6 cols, 2 1/16", 1/8" between; A - 6 cols, 2 1/16", 1/8" between; C - 9 cols, 1 5/16", 1/8" between.
Commodity consumption: Newsprint 99 short tons; widths 30", 34"; black ink 5,820 pounds; color ink 2,600 pounds; single pages printed 3,200; average pages per issue 10(d); single plates used 6,000.
Equipment: EDITORIAL: Front-end hardware — 3-Dewar/Disc Net; Printers — Ap/Mac LaserWriter II. CLASSIFIED: Front-end hardware — Dewar/Disc Net; Printers — Ap/Mac LaserWriter II. DISPLAY: Adv layout systems — 2-Ap/Mac; Printers — Ap/Mac LaserWriter II. PRODUCTION: Typesetters — Ap/Mac LaserWriter II; Plate exposures — 1-Nu/Flip Top FT40UPNS; Production cameras — LE, R; Automatic film processors — LE/LD-220-QT, SCREEN.
PRESSROOM: Line 1 — 5-G/Community. WIRE SERVICES: News — AP; Receiving dishes — AP.

MUNCIE

Delaware County

'90 U.S. Census- 71,035; E&P '96 Est. 67,589
ABC-CZ (90): 74,656 (HH 28,456)

The Muncie Star
(m-mon to sat; S)

The Muncie Evening Press
(e-mon to sat)

The Muncie Star/Evening Press, 125 S. High (47305); PO Box 2408, Muncie, IN 47302; tel (317) 747-5700. Central Newspapers Inc. group.
Circulation: 29,529(m); 12,701(e); 29,529 (m-sat); 12,701(e-sat); 36,182(S); ABC Sept. 30, 1995.
Price: 35¢(d); 35¢(sat); $1.50(S); $2.50/wk; $166.40/yr.
Advertising: Open inch rate $30.28(m); $30.28(e); $30.28(m-sat); $30.28(e-sat); $31.10(S); $32.45(m & e). **Representative:** Papert Companies.
News Services: AP, CT, KRT. **Politics:** Independent. **Established:** 1899 (Star), 1905 (Press).
Special Weekly Section: Best Food (thur).
Magazine: Parade.

CORPORATE OFFICERS	
President	Frank E Russell
Senior Vice Pres	Eugene S Pulliam
Vice Pres	Robert G Ellis
Secretary/Treasurer	Marjorie C Tarplee
Secretary/Treasurer	Wayne Wallace
GENERAL MANAGEMENT	
Publisher	Robert G Ellis
ADVERTISING	
Manager	John Rice
Manager-Promotion	Robert Lenhart
MARKETING AND PROMOTION	
Director-Marketing/Promotion	Larry Alexander
CIRCULATION	
Manager	Stuart Cowgill
NEWS EXECUTIVES	
Press	
Editor	Brian Walker
Managing Editor-Features	Sally Mills
Star	
Editor	Larry Shores
Managing Editor	Larry Lough
EDITORS AND MANAGERS	
Press	
Amusements/Music Editor	Keith Roysdon
Aviation Editor	John Carlson
City Editor	John Carlson
Columnist	John Carlson
Editorial Page Editor	Karen Francisco
Fashion/Society Editor	Ellen Ball
Films/Theater Editor	Keith Roysdon
Home Furnishings Editor	Ellen Ball
Librarian	Breena Wysong
Photo Department Manager	Jerry Burney
Pictures Editor	Sally Mills
Religion Editor	Karen Francisco
Sports Editor	Tim Cleland
Star	
Automotive Editor	Ronald Lemasters
Business/Finance Editor	Brian Francisco
City Editor	G K Hawes
Columnist	G K Hawes
Columnist	Larry Lough
Columnist	Larry Shores
Editorial Page Editor	Larry Shores
Editorial Writer	Robert G Imler
Editorial Writer	Larry Shores
Fashion/Food Editor	Donna Penticuff
Films/Theater Editor	Rodney Richey
Garden Editor	Rodney Richey
Home Furnishings Editor	Donna Penticuff
Librarian	Breena Wysong
Music Editor	Larry Shores
News Editor	Kathy Scott
Photo Department Manager	Jerry Burney
Photography Columnist	Ruth Chin
Radio/Television Editor	Rodney Richey
Real Estate Editor	Donna Penticuff
Religion Editor	Greg Maynard
School Editor	Tom Davies
Society Editor	Donna Penticuff
Sports Editor	Randy Benson
PRODUCTION	
Manager	James Baird
Assoc Manager-Automated Systems	Robert Reese
Foreman-Composing	Kenneth Robinson
Foreman-Pressroom	Kenneth Stevens
Foreman-Pressroom	Larry Reinke
Foreman-Mailroom	Noel Graham

Indiana

Market Information: Zoned editions; Split Run; TMC; ADS.
Mechanical available: Letterpress; Black and 3 ROP colors; insert accepted — preprinted; page cut-offs — 22 13/16".
Mechanical specifications: Type page 13" x 22"; E - 6 cols, 2.04", 1/8" between; A - 6 cols, 2.04", 1/6" between; C - 9 cols, 1.38", 1/16" between.
Commodity consumption: Newsprint 2,800 metric tons; widths 55", 27 1/2", 41 3/4"; single pages printed 21,250; average pages per issue 28(d), 60(S); single plates used 24,300.
Equipment: EDITORIAL: Front-end hardware — Ap/Mac; Front-end software — DTI; Printers — Dataproducts, TI, IBM. CLASSIFIED: Front-end hardware — Ap/Mac; Front-end software — DTI; Printers — TI/810. DISPLAY: Adv layout systems — DTI. PRODUCTION: Typesetters — 1-AU/APS H5; Platemaking systems — Na; Scanners — ECR/Autokon, HP, IBM; Production cameras — C/Spartan, KI; Automatic film processors — LE, C; Color separation equipment (conventional) — Ap/Mac, Adobe/Photoshop, Lf; Digital color separation equipment — Microtek, AG.
PRESSROOM: Line 1 — 6-G; Pasters — Auto; Press control system — Fin. MAILROOM: Counter stackers — 1-Id; Inserters and stuffers — 1-GMA; Bundle tyer — 1-Id; Addressing machine — Manual, Topping. WIRE SERVICES: News — AP Datafeatures, AP Datastream, AP; Photos — AP; Stock tables — AP; Receiving dishes — size-15ft, AP. BUSINESS COMPUTERS: 2-IBM/Sys 36; PCs & main system networked.

MUNSTER-HAMMOND-MERRILLVILLE-VALPARAISO
Lake County
Porter County

'90 U.S. Census- 155,856 (Munster 19,949; Hammond 84,236; Merrillville 27,257; Valparaiso 24,414); E&P '96 Est. 153,898 (Munster 18,882; Hammond 80,662; Merrillville 27,802; Valparaiso 26,552)
ABC-CZ (90): 290,456 (HH 109,133)

The Times (m-mon to sat; S)
The Times, 601 45th Ave., Munster, IN 46321; tel (219) 933-3200; e-mail gower@howpubs.com; web site http://www.calunet.com. Howard Publications group.
Circulation: 89,753(m); 89,753(m-sat); 94,815(S); ABC Sept. 30, 1995.
Price: 50¢(d); 50¢(sat); $1.50(S); $3.35/wk; $14.52/mo; $174.20/yr.
Advertising: Open inch rate $51.08(m); $51.08(m-sat); $53.93(S).
News Services: AP, CNS. **Politics:** Independent. **Established:** 1906.
Note: Effective Aug. 1, 1995, the Times absorbed the Valparaiso (IN) Vidette-Messenger (e-mon to fri; m-sat; S).
Advertising not accepted: Sexually explicit.
Special Editions: Bridal (Jan); Auto Show, Best of the Region (Feb); N.I.E., Health & Fitness, Golf (Mar); Home Improvement/Lawn & Garden, Real Estate (Apr); Football (Aug); Regional, Fall Car Care (Oct); Basketball (Nov).
Special Weekly Sections: Your Money, Seniors (mon); Discovery, Prep Extra, 4Kids (tues); Home Section (wed); Best Food/Nutrition Day, Parenting (thur); On the Go, Dining Guide (fri); Outdoors, Religion (sat); Travel, Forum (S).
Magazines: Parade, TV TIMES, Color Comics (S).

CORPORATE OFFICERS
President	Robert S Howard
Vice Pres	William E Howard

GENERAL MANAGEMENT
Publisher	William E Howard
Publisher (Illinois)	Pat Colander
Senior Assoc Publisher	Joseph Pepe
Assoc Publisher (East Lake)	Amy Tuchler
Assoc Publisher (Porter County)	Richard Esposito
Director-Operations	Dan Blom
Director-Production/Manager-Plant	Larry Maas

ADVERTISING
Director	Amy Owens

MARKETING AND PROMOTION
Manager-Marketing	Bob Pinarski
Manager-Promotion	Mike Scamihorn

CIRCULATION
Director	Dan Wright

NEWS EXECUTIVES
Exec Editor	William Nangle
Managing Editor	Tim Harmon
Managing Editor-Eastlake	Sharon Ross
Managing Editor-Westlake	Joe Puchek
Managing Editor-Illinois	Harry Gamble
Managing Editor-Porter County	Don Asher
Asst Managing Editor	Stephan Benzkofer
Asst Managing Editor	Kent Davey

EDITORS AND MANAGERS
Editorial Page Editor	Krishna Gaur
Entertainment/Amusements Editor	Matt Mansfield
Fashion/Style Editor	Nikki Life
Graphics Editor/Art Director	Denise Friant
Health/Medical Editor	Robin Biesen
Living/Lifestyle Editor	Matt Mansfield
Photo Editor	Michael Zajakowski
Sports Editor	David Cambpell
Television/Film Editor	Matt Mansfield
Theater/Music Editor	Matt Mansfield
Women's Editor	Nikki Life

MANAGEMENT INFORMATION SERVICES
Online Manager	Jim Tuchler
Data Processing Manager	Mike Gower

PRODUCTION
Director/Manager-Plant	Larry Maas
Foreman-Mailroom	John Olson
Foreman-Systems Administration	Mike Gower
Foreman-Press	Robin Houle

Market Information: Zoned editions; Split Run; TMC; Operate database; Electronic edition.
Mechanical available: Offset; Black and 3 ROP colors; insert accepted — preprinted, envelope, card; page cut-offs — 21".
Mechanical specifications: Type page 13" x 21"; E - 6 cols, 2.028", .167" between; A - 6 cols, 2.028", .167" between; C - 10 cols, 1.19", .11" between.
Commodity consumption: Newsprint 10,000 metric tons; widths 55", 41 1/4", 27 3/8"; black ink 200,000 pounds; color ink 30,000 pounds; single pages printed 21,944; average pages per issue 52(d), 96(S); single plates used 60,000.
Equipment: EDITORIAL: Front-end hardware — 55-Sun/Sparc; Front-end software — Sun/Abortex, Copal; Printers — HP/Laser, Hyphen/RIP, Hyphen/Dash RIP, Copal. CLASSIFIED: Front-end hardware — 7-Sun/Sparc, 14-NCD; Front-end software — Vision Data; Printers — Ap/Mac Laser, Hyphen/RIP. DISPLAY: Adv layout systems — SCS/Layout 8000; Front-end hardware — 40-Ap/Mac; Front-end software — QuarkXPress; Printers — Hyphen/RIP. PRODUCTION: Typesetters — 2-ECR/PelBox Full-page, 2-Ap/Mac Laser, Hyphen/3100; Platemaking systems — W/Plate Exposers; Plate exposures — 2-Nu; Plate processors — 2-Na/NP80; Electronic picture desk — Lf/AP Leaf Picture Desk; Scanners — 1-Na/NP80, Hyphen/RIP, Kk/2035; Production cameras — WL/Digital Camera, Nikon; Automatic film processors — 3-LE, 2-OD-Line; Film transporters — 3-LE; Color separation equipment (conventional) — WDS, 2-Lf, 4-AG/Horizon.
PRESSROOM: Line 1 — 8-G/Headliner double width; Line 2 — 8-G/Urbanite single width; Press drives — Fin; Folders — G; Pasters — Enkel; Reels and stands — Enkel; Press control system — G. MAILROOM: Counter stackers — 3-MM, 1-MM/388, 3-MM/310, 1-HL; Inserters and stuffers — 4-MM/308; Bundle tyer — 3-MLN, 2-OVL, 1-Sterling; Wrapping singles — 2-KJ; Addressing machine — 2-Barstrom; Other mailroom equipment — MM/335. LIBRARY: Electronic — Newsbank, Telebase, Legis, Tri, Edin, Compuserve, Verity/Topic; Combination — Electronic/Full Text, Clippings, Art Files (w/electronic index). WIRE SERVICES: News — AP, NYT, CNS; Photos — AP; Stock tables — TMS; Receiving dishes — AP. BUSINESS COMPUTERS: Sun/4, COM; Applications: Circ, Adv billing, Accts receivable, Payroll; PCs & micros networked; PCs & main system networked.

NEW ALBANY
Floyd County
'90 U.S. Census- 36,322; E&P '96 Est. 36,206
ABC-CZ (90): 36,322 (HH 14,691)

Tribune (e-mon to fri)
Ledger & Tribune (S)
Tribune/Ledger & Tribune, 303 Scribner Dr., New Albany, IN 47150; tel (812) 944-6481; fax (812) 944-6340. Hollinger International Inc. group.
Circulation: 11,231(e); 11,632(S); ABC Sept. 30, 1995.
Price: 50¢(d); $1.25(S); $2.25/wk.
Advertising: Open inch rate $11.75(e); $11.75(S).
News Service: AP. **Politics:** Independent. **Established:** 1888.
Not Published: New Year; Memorial Day; Independence Day; Labor Day; Thanksgiving; Christmas.
Special Weekly Section: Shopper News.
Magazines: Parade, Color Comics (S).

GENERAL MANAGEMENT
Publisher	Fred Ward
Head Accountant	Cindy Wood

ADVERTISING
Manager-New Products	Dennis Inzer
Manager-Classified	Chris Crum
Manager	Bob Parker

NEWS EXECUTIVE
Managing Editor	Ken Hardin

EDITORS AND MANAGERS
Society Editor	Laurell Smith
Sports Editor	Chris Morris

PRODUCTION
Manager-Commercial Printer	Roland Pinaire
Foreman-Pressroom	Darrell Gibbs

Market Information: TMC.
Mechanical available: Offset; Black and 1 ROP color; insert accepted — preprinted; page cut-offs — 21 1/2".
Mechanical specifications: Type page 13" x 21 1/2"; E - 6 cols, 2 1/16", 1/8" between; A - 6 cols, 2 1/16", 1/8" between; C - 9 cols, 1 5/16", 1/8" between.
Commodity consumption: Newsprint 480 short tons; width 27 1/2"; black ink 22,000 pounds; color ink 400 pounds; single pages printed 5,500; average pages per issue 38(d), 86(S).
Equipment: EDITORIAL: Front-end hardware — 1-COM/One. CLASSIFIED: Front-end hardware — 1-COM/One. PRODUCTION: Plate processors — 1-LE; Production cameras — 1-LE.
PRESSROOM: Line 1 — 8-G; Folders — 1-G/2:1. MAILROOM: Bundle tyer — 1-Bu; Addressing machine — 1-Am. WIRE SERVICES: News — AP; Receiving dishes — AP. BUSINESS COMPUTERS: 2-Auto Tape/9100.

NEW CASTLE
Henry County
'90 U.S. Census- 17,753; E&P '96 Est. 16,813

The Courier-Times
(e-mon to fri; m-sat)
The Courier-Times, 201 S. 14th St.; PO Box 369, New Castle, IN 47362; tel (317) 529-1111; fax (317) 529-1731. Nixon Newspapers Inc. group.
Circulation: 11,553(e); 11,553(m-sat); Sworn Sept. 30, 1994.
Price: 50¢(d); 50¢(sat); $1.65/wk, $1.70/wk (motor route).
Advertising: Open inch rate $8.50(e); $8.50(m-sat). **Representative:** Nixon Newspapers.
News Service: AP. **Politics:** Independent. **Established:** 1841.
Not Published: Christmas.
Special Edition: Cookbook Tab.

CORPORATE OFFICERS
President	John R Nixon
Vice Pres-Finance	John W Stackhouse
Secretary	Emil W Milker

GENERAL MANAGEMENT
Publisher	J Wesley Rowe Jr
Business Manager	David Bundy

ADVERTISING
Director	Gary Books
Manager-Classified	Sandy Moore

CIRCULATION
Director	Tom Thompson

NEWS EXECUTIVE
Managing Editor	Darrel K Radford

EDITORS AND MANAGERS
City Editor	John Head
Society Editor	Donna Cronk
Sports Editor	John Hodge

PRODUCTION
Manager	Jack Ingerman
Foreman-Pressroom	Wade Finney

Market Information: Split Run; TMC.
Mechanical available: Letterpress (direct); Black and 2 ROP colors; insert accepted — preprinted; page cut-offs — 22 3/4".
Mechanical specifications: Type page 13" x 21 1/2"; E - 6 cols, 2 1/16", 1/8" between; A - 6 cols, 2 1/16", 1/8" between; C - 9 cols, 1 3/8", 1/16" between.
Commodity consumption: Newsprint 470 metric tons; widths 27", 13.5", 12"; average pages per issue 20(d).
Equipment: EDITORIAL: Front-end hardware — 1-Mk/1100, 12-Mk; Printers — 1-TI/Printer; Other equipment — AG/COM Focus 5800 GS Scanner, TI/Omni 800-850 XL. CLASSIFIED: Front-end software — Mk/TouchWriter Plus. DISPLAY: Adv layout systems — 2-Ap/Mac IIci; Front-end software — COM/Dawn Ad Make. PRODUCTION: Typesetters — 2-COM/8400; Platemaking systems — 1-Nu/Manual Sys; Plate exposures — 1-Nu/Flip Top FTOV6UPNS; Plate processors — 1-Nat/A-250; Production cameras — 1-R/580; Automatic film processors — 1-LE/18.
PRESSROOM: Line 1 — 5-G/Universal; Folders — 1-G. MAILROOM: Counter stackers — 1-BG/108 Count-O-Veyor; Inserters and stuffers — 2-KAN; Bundle tyer — 1-Bu/20, 1-Bu/String Tyer, 1-Bu/Tape Wrapper; Addressing machine — 1-Am/6341 B. WIRE SERVICES: News — AP Features, AP News; Receiving dishes — size-3m, AP. BUSINESS COMPUTERS: IBM/3600; Applications: Bus office mgmt, Billing.

NOBLESVILLE
Hamilton County
'90 U.S. Census- 17,655; E&P '96 Est. 24,065

Daily Ledger (e-mon to sat)
Daily Ledger, 957 Logan St.; PO Box 1478, Noblesville, IN 46060; tel (317) 773-1210; fax (317) 773-3872. Central Newspapers Inc. group.
Circulation: 10,413(e); 10,413(e-sat); CAC Sept. 29, 1995.
Price: 35¢(d); 35¢(sat); $7.25/mo (carrier), $7.75/mo (motor route).
Advertising: Open inch rate $10.57(e); $10.57(e-sat).
News Service: AP. **Politics:** Republican. **Established:** 1888.
Not Published: Memorial Day; Independence Day; Labor Day; Thanksgiving; Christmas; New Year.
Special Editions: Progress & Review (Mar); Building & Home Improvement (Apr); Vacation (June); Building & Home Improvement (Sept); Women in Business (Oct); Suddenly It's X'mas (Nov); Gift Tab (Dec).
Magazine: USA Today (sat).

CORPORATE OFFICERS
President/CEO	Frank E Russell
Exec Vice Pres	Eugene P Pulliam
Secretary	Marjorie C Tarplee
Treasurer	Wayne D Wallace

GENERAL MANAGEMENT
Publisher	David Lewis
Purchasing Agent	Darrell McConnell

ADVERTISING
Director	Scott Gause

CIRCULATION
Director	Terry Coomer

NEWS EXECUTIVE
Editor	Tom Jekel

EDITORS AND MANAGERS
Local Editor	Laura Musall
News Editor	Gregg Montgomery
Picture Editor	Kelly Huff
Sports Editor	Mike Emery
Women's Editor	Betsy Reason

PRODUCTION
Manager	Darrell McConnell
Asst Supervisor	Patricia Dillon

Market Information: TMC; ADS.
Mechanical available: Offset; Black and 3 ROP colors; insert accepted — preprinted; page cut-offs — 22 3/4".
Mechanical specifications: Type page 13" x 21 1/2"; E - 6 cols, 2 1/16", 1/8" between; A - 6 cols, 2 1/16", 1/8" between; C - 9 cols, 1 11/32", 1/8" between.
Commodity consumption: Newsprint 1,200 metric tons; width 27 1/2"; black ink 38,500 pounds; color ink 1,650 pounds; single pages printed 25,000; average pages per issue 20(d), 20(sat); single plates used 12,500.

Indiana I-137

Equipment: EDITORIAL: Front-end hardware — Ap/Mac; Front-end software — Baseview; Printers — Linotype-Hell/Lino-190. CLASSIFIED: Front-end hardware — Ap/Mac; Front-end software — Baseview; Printers — Linotype-Hell/Lino-190. DISPLAY: Front-end software — Multi-Ad. PRODUCTION: Pagination software — Baseview; OCR software — TI/OmniPage; Typesetters — 2-Linotype-Hell/Lino 190, 2-LaserMaster/1200 XLO; Platemaking systems — 1-Nu/2-sided non-stop; Plate exposures — 1-Nu/2-sided non-stop; Plate processors — Graham/S-3; Electronic picture desk — 1-Lf/AP Leaf Picture Desk, 1-Ap/Mac, Adobe/Photoshop; Scanners — 2-HP/11 x 17 Flat Top color; Production cameras — 1-B/Caravel; Automatic film processors — 1-LE/LD18; Color separation equipment (conventional) — 2-Ap/Mac, Adobe/Photoshop; Digital color separation equipment — Ap/Mac, QuarkXPress. PRESSROOM: Line 1 — 6-G/Community; Folders — 1-G. MAILROOM: Counter stackers — 1-BG/Count-O-Veyor; Bundle tyer — 1-Malow. WIRE SERVICES: News — AP; Photos — AP; Syndicates — AP; Receiving dishes — size-2ft, AP. BUSINESS COMPUTERS: 4-IBM/Sys 36; Applications: Accounting, Circ.

PERU

Miami County

'90 U.S. Census- 12,843; E&P '96 Est. 12,340

The Peru Tribune

(m-mon to sat)

The Peru Tribune, 26 W. Third St.; PO Box 87, Peru, IN 46970; tel (317) 473-6641; fax (317) 472-4438. Nixon Newspapers Inc. group.

Circulation: 7,296(m); 7,296(m-sat); Sworn Sept. 30, 1995.

Price: 50¢(d); 50¢(sat); $8.95/mo; $107.40/yr.

Advertising: Open inch rate $9.87(m); $9.87(m-sat).

News Service: AP. **Politics:** Independent. **Established:** 1921.

Not Published: New Year; Memorial Day; Independence Day; Labor Day; Thanksgiving; Christmas.

Special Editions: Soil & Water, Super Bowl Pages, Year in Review (Jan); Girls Basketball, Health Care Edition (Feb); Basketball Tourney, Spring Farm (Mar); Business Expo (Apr); Recreation Tab, Mother's Day (May); Softball Pages (June); 4-H Fair, Circus (July); This is Miami County (Aug); Back-to-School, Fall Farm, Fall Home Improvement, Heritage Days (Sept); Shopping with Santa, Car Care (Oct); Basketball, Christmas Opening, Miami County Troops (Nov); 1st Baby Contest, Christmas Gift Guides (Dec).

Special Weekly Sections: Business Pages, Food (mon); Real Estate Page (wed); Church Pages (thur); Women's Day (fri); Milestones (Weddings, Engagements, etc) (sat); Next Generation (School Page).

Magazines: Channel Changer (fri-weekly); Miami County Real Estate Guide (quarterfold) (1st mon/mo); Kid's Korner (quarterfold) (2nd mon/mo); Miami County Business & Services Directory (quarterfold) (quarterly); Guide to Living (Audiotext Publication, quarterfold) (3x/yr).

CORPORATE OFFICERS

President	John R Nixon
Vice Pres-Finance	John W Stackhouse
Vice Pres	Raymond Moscowitz
Secretary	Deborah M Huff

GENERAL MANAGEMENT

Publisher	Raymond Moscowitz

ADVERTISING

Director	Ron Storey
Manager-National	Jane Jones

TELECOMMUNICATIONS

Audiotex Manager	Jane Slater
Audiotex Manager	Michelle Wallick

CIRCULATION

Manager	Paul Hart

NEWS EXECUTIVE

Managing Editor	Jeff Ward

EDITORS AND MANAGERS

Agriculture Editor	Marge Donoghue
Editorial Page Editor	Jeff Ward
Librarian	Mary Revelant
Lifestyle Editor	Mike Shaw
News Editor	Andrew Tallackson
Photo Department Manager	Tony Hare
Sports Editor	Brett Anderson

MANAGEMENT INFORMATION SERVICES

Data Processing Manager	Betty Hunter

PRODUCTION

Manager-Pre Press	Ron Storey

Market Information: TMC; Operate audiotex.

Mechanical available: Offset; Black and 3 ROP colors; insert accepted — preprinted, single sheets, DOO sizes; page cut-offs — $22\frac{3}{4}$".

Mechanical specifications: Type page 13" x $21\frac{1}{2}$"; E - 6 cols, $2\frac{1}{16}$", $\frac{1}{8}$" between; A - 6 cols, $2\frac{1}{16}$", $\frac{1}{8}$" between; C - 6 cols, $2\frac{1}{16}$", $\frac{1}{8}$" between.

Commodity consumption: Newsprint 345 metric tons; widths 28", 14"; black ink 6,558 pounds; color ink 1,380 pounds; single pages printed 6,123; average pages per issue 16(d).

Equipment: EDITORIAL: Front-end hardware — Ap/Mac; Front-end software — Baseview/NewsEdit 3.1, QuarkXPress 3.3; Printers — Ap/Mac LaserWriters. CLASSIFIED: Front-end hardware — 2-HI/Micro-Store. AUDIOTEX: Hardware — IBM; Software — SMS/Stauffer Gold; Supplier name — SMS. DISPLAY: Adv layout systems — Ap/Mac; Front-end software — Multi-Ad/Creator 3.5; Printers — Ap/Mac LaserWriter, Xante; Other equipment — AP AdScan, ALS AD Program, Claris/FileMaker Pro. PRODUCTION: Pagination software — QuarkXPress; OCR software — Multi-Ad/Creator 3.5; Typesetters — 2-Ap/Mac LaserPrinter NTX, 2-Ap/Mac; Production cameras — 1-R/480, 1-Ca; Automatic film processors — 1-AG/Rapidline 43. PRESSROOM: Line 1 — 4-G/Urbanite; Folders — 1-G/2:1; Pasters — 2-Enkel. MAILROOM: Bundle tyer — 1-Bu, 1-Plastic Strap; Addressing machine — 1-WM. WIRE SERVICES: News — AP; Syndicates — Universal Press, NEA, King Features, KRT, United Features; Receiving dishes — size-10ft, AP, TMS. BUSINESS COMPUTERS: IBM/5363 Storage Unit, 3-IBM/5291, 1-IBM/Printer-4214; Applications: Bus office, Circ; PCs & micros networked; PCs & main system networked.

PLYMOUTH

Marshall County

'90 U.S. Census- 8,303; E&P '96 Est. 8,947

The Pilot-News

(e-mon to fri; m-sat)

The Pilot-News, 217-223 N. Center St.; PO Box 220, Plymouth, IN 46563; tel (219) 936-3101; fax (219) 936-3844; e-mail pnews@dialn.ind.net. Park Communications Inc. group.

Circulation: 6,845(e); 6,845(m-sat); Sworn Sept. 29, 1995.

Price: 35¢(d); 35¢(sat); $78.00/yr (carrier), $84.00/yr (motor route), $102.00/yr (mail).

Advertising: Open inch rate $9.63(e); $9.63(m-sat).

News Service: AP. **Politics:** Independent-Republican. **Established:** 1851.

Not Published: Christmas.

Special Editions: Christmas Opening; City Wide Dollar Days; Bridal Issue; Old Fashioned Days; 4-H; Progress Edition; Soil Conservation Service Annual Tab; High School Football & Basketball Preview Tabs.

CORPORATE OFFICERS

President	Wright M Thomas
Vice Pres-Newspapers	Ralph J Martin

GENERAL MANAGEMENT

General Manager	Robert E Noren Jr
Manager-Office	Jeanine Grochow

ADVERTISING

Manager	Terri Shirk

EDITOR AND MANAGER

News Editor	Darrin Lyon

PRODUCTION

Foreman-Composing	R William Johnson

Market Information: TMC.

Mechanical available: Offset; Black and 3 ROP colors; insert accepted — preprinted; page cut-offs — $22\frac{3}{4}$".

Mechanical specifications: Type page 13" x $21\frac{1}{2}$"; E - 6 cols, $2\frac{1}{16}$", $\frac{1}{8}$" between; A - 6 cols, $2\frac{1}{16}$", $\frac{1}{8}$" between; C - 10 cols, $1\frac{3}{8}$", $\frac{1}{16}$" between.

Commodity consumption: Newsprint 385 short tons; widths 28", 14"; black ink 8,713 pounds; color ink 1,500 pounds; single pages printed 5,057; average pages per issue 12(d); single plates used 5,057.

Equipment: EDITORIAL: Front-end hardware — Mk/Plus; Other equipment — 6-Mk/12000. CLASSIFIED: Front-end hardware — Mk/Plus; Printers — 1-Mk/Touchwriter Plus. DISPLAY: Adv layout systems — Mk/AdTouch. PRODUCTION: Typesetters — Ap/Mac LaserWriter; Plate exposures — 1-Nu; Production cameras — 1-B/Caravel; Automatic film processors — 1-P. PRESSROOM: Line 1 — 6-G/Community (upper former); Folders — 1-G/Suburban. MAILROOM: Bundle tyer — 1-Bu; Addressing machine — El/3101. WIRE SERVICES: News — AP; Receiving dishes — size-$2\frac{1}{2}$ft, AP.

PORTLAND

Jay County

'90 U.S. Census- 6,483; E&P '96 Est. 6,152

The Commercial Review

(e-mon to fri; m-sat)

The Commercial Review, 309 W. Main St., Portland, IN 47371; tel (219) 726-8141; fax (219) 726-8143.

Circulation: 5,523(e); 5,523(m-sat); Sworn Oct. 2, 1995.

Price: 50¢(d); 50¢(sat); $1.30/wk; $6.30/mo (motor route).

Advertising: Open inch rate $5.10(e); $5.10(m-sat).

News Service: AP. **Politics:** Republican. **Established:** 1871.

Not Published: New Year; Memorial Day; Independence Day; Labor Day; Thanksgiving; Christmas.

Special Editions: Farm & Home (8); Back-to-School; Brides; Beautify Home; Cook Book; Christmas Greetings; Fall Sports; Winter Sports; Basketball; Graduation; Automobiles; Summer Recreation; Tractor Show; High School Band; Jay County Fair.

CORPORATE OFFICERS

Board Chairman	John C Ronald
President	John C Ronald
Treasurer	James E Luginbill

GENERAL MANAGEMENT

Publisher	John C Ronald
Business Manager	Joy Ballard

ADVERTISING

Manager-Retail	Don Gillespie
Manager-Classified	Helen Rouch
Manager-Promotion	Jon Kimmel

CIRCULATION

Manager	Mark Johanning

NEWS EXECUTIVE

Managing Editor	Tom Casey

EDITORS AND MANAGERS

Farm Supplement Editor	Tom Casey
News Editor	Barbara Wilkinson
Photo Department Manager	Dave Marchand
Society Editor	MaryAnn Litton

PRODUCTION

Superintendent	Dave Marchand
Foreman-Composing	Dave Marchand
Foreman-Pressroom	Charles Loper

Market Information: TMC; Operate audiotex.

Mechanical available: Offset; Black and 3 ROP colors; insert accepted — preprinted; page cut-offs — 22".

Mechanical specifications: Type page 13" x $21\frac{1}{4}$"; E - 6 cols, $2\frac{1}{16}$", $\frac{1}{8}$" between; A - 6 cols, $2\frac{1}{16}$", $\frac{1}{8}$" between; C - 8 cols, $1\frac{1}{2}$", $\frac{1}{16}$" between.

Commodity consumption: Newsprint 200 short tons; widths 28", 14"; black ink 5400 pounds; color ink 850 pounds; single pages printed 3,870; average pages per issue 12.6(d); single plates used 2000.

Equipment: EDITORIAL: Front-end hardware — Ap/Mac; Front-end software — Baseview, QuarkXPress; Printers — Ap/Mac. CLASSIFIED: Front-end hardware — Ap/Mac; Front-end software — Baseview; Printers — Ap/Mac. AUDIOTEX: Hardware — Tandy; Software — ABC voice 2.1; Supplier name — Premiere Audiotex. DISPLAY: Front-end hardware — Ap/Mac; Front-end software — QuarkXPress; Printers — Ap/LaserPrinter. PRODUCTION: Typesetters — Ap/Mac LaserPrinters; Plate exposures — 1-Nu/Flip Top FT40, 1-B/30x40; Plate processors — 1-B/Sink; Scanners — HP/ScanJet; Production cameras — 1-R/20x24; Automatic film processors — 1-LE/18; Reproportion units — Minolta/EP470Z. PRESSROOM: Line 1 — 5-G/Community w/DEV Horizon Stack Unit; Folders — 1-SC. MAILROOM: Bundle tyer — 1-Bu; Addressing machine — 1-Am/4000, 1-Am/1900. WIRE SERVICES: News — AP; Photos — AP; Receiving dishes — size-6ft, AP. BUSINESS COMPUTERS: IBM/PC-AT; Applications: BMF; PCs & micros networked; PCs & main system networked.

PRINCETON

Gibson County

'90 U.S. Census- 8,127; E&P '96 Est. 7,817

Princeton Daily Clarion

(m-mon to fri)

Princeton Daily Clarion, 100 N. Gibson St.; Box 321, Princeton, IN 47670; tel (812) 385-2525; fax (812) 386-6199; e-mail gblack2525@aol.com. Brehm Communications Inc. group.

Circulation: 6,052(m); Sworn Oct. 1, 1995.

Price: 50¢(d); $61.00/yr.

Advertising: Open inch rate $8.53(m).

News Service: AP. **Politics:** Republican. **Established:** 1846.

Not Published: Holidays.

Special Weekly Sections: Best Food Day (mon); Farm Page (tues); Business Page (thur); Religion Page, Entertainment Page, TV View, Dining Guide (fri).

Magazine: TV Booklet (fri).

CORPORATE OFFICERS

President	Gary Blackburn
Treasurer	Mona M Brehm

GENERAL MANAGEMENT

Publisher	Gary Blackburn
General Manager	Phil Summers

ADVERTISING

Director	Phil Summers

CIRCULATION

Manager	Vicki Matthews

EDITORS AND MANAGERS

Living/Lifestyle Editor	Sue Ellen Parker
News Editor	Ted Morris
Sports Editor	Pete Swanson
Women's Editor	Sue Ellen Parker

PRODUCTION

Manager	Howard Fields

Market Information: Zoned editions; Split Run; TMC.

Mechanical available: Offset; Black and 3 ROP colors; insert accepted — preprinted; page cut-offs — $22\frac{3}{4}$".

Mechanical specifications: Type page $13\frac{1}{4}$" x $21\frac{1}{2}$"; E - 8 cols, $1\frac{1}{2}$", $\frac{1}{6}$" between; A - 8 cols, $1\frac{1}{2}$", $\frac{1}{6}$" between; C - 8 cols, $1\frac{1}{2}$", $\frac{1}{6}$" between.

Commodity consumption: Newsprint 795 short tons; widths 30", 34", $27\frac{1}{2}$"; average pages per issue 12(d).

Equipment: EDITORIAL: Front-end hardware — Ap/Macs; Front-end software — Baseview; Printers — Panther/Imagesetter for Pre-Press; Other equipment — Gms 860. CLASSIFIED: Front-end hardware — Ap/Macs; Front-end software — Baseview. DISPLAY: Front-end hardware — Ap/Mac; Front-end software — Multi-Ad/Creator. PRODUCTION: Pagination software — QuarkXPress; Typesetters — Ap/Mac LaserWriters, Panther/ImageSetter; Plate exposures — Nu; Production cameras — SCREEN; Automatic film processors — SCREEN. PRESSROOM: Line 1 — 8-G/Community; Press registration system — Duarte. MAILROOM: Inserters and stuffers — 4-KAN. WIRE SERVICES: News — AP; Receiving dishes — AP. BUSINESS COMPUTERS: Qantel.

RENSSELAER

Jasper County

'90 U.S. Census- 5,045; E&P '96 Est. 5,221

Republican (e-mon to fri; m-sat)

Republican, 117 N. Van Rensselaer St.; PO Box 298, Rensselaer, IN 47978; tel (219) 866-5111; fax (219) 866-3775. Hollinger International Inc. group.

Circulation: 2,749(e); 2,749(m-sat); Sworn Oct. 16, 1995.

Price: 50¢(d); 50¢(sat); $1.60/wk.

Advertising: Open inch rate $8.25(e); $8.25(m-sat).

News Service: AP. **Politics:** Republican. **Established:** 1865.

Not Published: New Year; Memorial Day; Independence Day; Labor Day; Thanksgiving; Christmas.

Special Editions: Health Fitness Guide, Business Established (Jan); Basketball Sectional, Spring Bridal (Feb); Ag Day, Spring Edition Home Improvement, Car Care, Fashions (Mar); Progress (June); Football Preview

I-138 Indiana

(Aug); Fall Edition Home Improvement, Car Care, Fashions, Prime Time Senior Citizens Guide (Sept); Basketball Preview, Christmas Tab (Nov); Auto News (monthly); Farm.

Special Weekly Sections: Best Food Day, Youth on the Move (mon); Business News (tues); Farm (wed); Senior Living, Church Page (fri); Youth Focus, TV, Farm (sat).

Magazines: Farm Focus (newsprint tab) (3rd week/month, quarterly); Final Score (2nd thur, school yr).

GENERAL MANAGEMENT

Publisher Douglas S Caldwell
Business Manager William F Hamilton IV

ADVERTISING

Director Frank J Copley

CIRCULATION

Manager Regina Warfel

NEWS EXECUTIVE

Editor John Scheibel

EDITOR AND MANAGER

Sports Editor Harley Tomlinson

PRODUCTION

Manager Derrick M Wachs
Foreman-Press James Byrer

Market Information: Zoned editions; TMC.

Mechanical available: Offset; Black and 2 ROP colors; insert accepted — preprinted; page cut-offs — 22¾".

Mechanical specifications: Type page 13" x 21½"; E - 6 cols, 2", ¼" between; A - 6 cols, 2", ¼" between; C - 9 cols, ⅓", ¼" between.

Commodity consumption: Newsprint 210 short tons; widths 27½", 34"; black ink 10,800 pounds; color ink 750 pounds; single pages printed 7,200; average pages per issue 12(d), 12(sat); single plates used 6,024.

Equipment: EDITORIAL: Front-end hardware — 2-Ap/Mac 610, 9-Ap/Mac LC II; Front-end software — Baseview/Newsedit 3.25, QuarkXPress 3.2; Printers — Ap/Mac LaserWriter Pro, Ap/Mac LaserWriter IIg. CLASSIFIED: Front-end hardware — 2-Ultra/486D-40; Front-end software — Mk/Newscraft; Printers — 2-Epson/LQ 1170. DISPLAY: Adv layout systems — Multi-Ad; Front-end hardware — 3-Ap/Mac Quadra; Front-end software — Multi-Ad 3.8, Adobe/Photoshop 2.5.1, QuarkXPress 3.2, Broderbund/Typestyler 2.0; Printers — Ap/Mac LaserWriter 16 600 PS, Ap/Mac LaserWriter Pro 630; Other equipment — 2-Quicktake/150 Camera, Microtek/ScanMaker IIsp, Microtek/ScanMaker IIxe. PRODUCTION: Pagination software — QuarkXPress 3.2; Platemaking systems — Nu/FT40V2UP; Plate processors — NAT; Scanners — Microtek/ScanMaker IIsp, Microtek/ScanMaker IIIxe; Production cameras — SCREEN/680-C; Automatic film processors — SCREEN/LD200-QT.

PRESSROOM: Line 1 — 5-HI/V-15D single width; Press drives — Powertron; Folders — JF/25; Reels and stands — 5-Roll Stands with rewinder. MAILROOM: Counter stackers — BG/Count-O-Veyor 08; Bundle tyer — 1-EAM/Mosca Strapping machine, 1-Miller Bevco/Strapper; Addressing machine — 2-Address-matic. COMMUNICATIONS: Facsimile — Savin/330; Digital ad delivery system — Acrobat/Exchange. Systems used — satellite. WIRE SERVICES: News — AP; Syndicates — United Media, Universal Press, King Features; Receiving dishes — AP. BUSINESS COMPUTERS: 1-PC/386, 1-PC/486, Ap/Mac LC III; Applications: Lotus 1-2-3, Microsoft/Excell, Microsoft/Office, Listmaster: Circ, Accts receivable.

RICHMOND

Wayne County

'90 U.S. Census- 38,705; E&P '96 Est. 37,269
ABC-NDM (90): 95,409 (HH 36,392)

Palladium-Item

(e-mon to sat; S)

Palladium-Item, 1175 N. A St., Richmond, IN 47374; tel (317) 962-1575; fax (317) 973-4440. Gannett Co. Inc. group.

Circulation: 19,520(e); 19,520(e-sat); 24,375(S); ABC Sept. 30, 1995.

Price: 35¢(d); 35¢(sat); $1.25(S); $2.50/wk; $130.00/yr.

Advertising: Open inch rate $29.86(e); $29.86(e-sat); $35.52(S). **Representative:** Gannett National Newspaper Sales.

News Services: AP, GNS. **Established:** 1831.

Special Weekly Sections: Education (mon); Food, Farm (wed); Business, Entertainment (thur); Business, Religion (sat).

Magazine: USA Weekend.

CORPORATE OFFICERS

President Emmett K Smelser
Secretary Thomas Chapple
Treasurer Jimmy Thomas

GENERAL MANAGEMENT

Publisher Emmett K Smelser
Business Manager James Franovich
Accountant/Manager Pamela Blacker
Personnel Director Marie Thompson

ADVERTISING

Director Al Bonner
Manager-Sales Darin Hein
Manager-Sales Paul Carlson

MARKETING AND PROMOTION

Director-Marketing Susan Plank

CIRCULATION

Director Lon Madarieta
Manager-Office Kristine Atkinson

NEWS EXECUTIVE

Managing Editor Evan Miller

EDITORS AND MANAGERS

Features Editor Scott Hinkley
News Editor Tim Johnson

PRODUCTION

Director Ross Donald
Manager-Commercial Sales Bruce Harris
Manager-Pressroom Jeff Hicks
Manager-Pre Press David Hamilton
Manager-Mailroom Greg Lunsford

Market Information: Zoned editions; Split Run; TMC.

Mechanical available: Offset; Black and 3 ROP colors; insert accepted — preprinted, single sheets; page cut-offs — 22".

Mechanical specifications: Type page 13" x 21"; E - 6 cols, 2 1/16", 1/10" between; A - 6 cols, 2 1/16", 1/10" between; C - 9 cols, 1 5/16", 1/10" between.

Commodity consumption: Newsprint 1,488 short tons; width 27¼"; black ink 32,000 pounds; color ink 12,000 pounds; single pages printed 8,400; average pages per issue 20(d), 57(S); single plates used 38,400.

Equipment: EDITORIAL: Front-end hardware — AS400, HAS/PDP-1144; Front-end software — HAS/TOPS 2.5; Printers — Facit/Documate 3000. CLASSIFIED: Front-end hardware — AS400, HAS/PDP-1144; Front-end software — HAS/TOPS 2.5; Printers — Data Royal/5000-C. DISPLAY: Adv layout systems — COM; Front-end hardware — 2-CG/Advantage II; Front-end software — CG; Other equipment — 3-MDT/350 Input Terminal. PRODUCTION: Typesetters — 2-COM/8600; Plate exposures — 3-Nu/Flip Top FT40V6UPNS; Plate processors — 3-Nat/A-340; Electronic picture desk — Lf/AP Leaf Picture Desk; Scanners — ECR/Autokon 1000, Lf/Leafscan 35; Production cameras — C/Spartan III; Automatic film processors — LE/2600, LE/2400; Film transporters — C; Color separation equipment (conventional) — Lf/Leafscan 35, Lf/AP Leaf Picture Desk.

PRESSROOM: Line 1 — 15-G/Urbanite; Line 2 — 4-HI/VI5A-6%; Press drives — Fin; Folders — 2-G; Pasters — G; Reels and stands — G/2-Arm RTP; Press control system — Fin. MAILROOM: Counter stackers — 1-PPK/Ministack, 1-MM; Inserters and stuffers — 1-MM/308, 1-MM/EM10-2; Bundle tyer — 3-MLN, 1-Sa/Twine; Wrapping singles — 1-Sa; Addressing machine — 1-Barstrom, 1-Ch. WIRE SERVICES: News — AP; Receiving dishes — AP. BUSINESS COMPUTERS: DEC/1144; Applications: Circ, Homeserv, Gen ledger, Budget, Payroll, Accts payable, Adv; PCs & micros networked; PCs & main system networked.

ROCHESTER

Fulton County

'90 U.S. Census- 5,969; E&P '96 Est. 6,889

The Rochester Sentinel

(e-mon to fri; m-sat)

The Rochester Sentinel, 118 E. 8th St.; PO Box 260, Rochester, IN 46975; tel (219) 223-2111, (800) 686-2112; fax (219) 223-5782.

Circulation: 4,481(e); 4,841(m-sat); Sworn Sept. 29, 1995.

Price: 50¢(d); 50¢(sat); $7.50/mo (carrier), $7.75/mo (motor route); $99.00/yr (local), $117.00/yr (out of area).

Advertising: Open inch rate $5.40(e); $5.40(m-sat).

News Service: AP. **Politics:** Independent. **Established:** 1858.

Not Published: New Year; Memorial Day; Independence Day; Labor Day; Thanksgiving; Christmas.

Special Editions: Farm, Taxes (Jan); Bridal (Feb); Basketball, Car Care (Mar); Home Improvement (Apr); Graduates (May); Round Barn Festival, Summer Funtime, Senior Lifestyle (June); 4-H Fair (July); Back-to-School, Bridal (Aug); Trail of Courage, Home Improvement, Living History Festival, Senior Lifestyle (Sept); Car Care (Oct); Christmas Shopping (Nov); Year In Review (Dec).

CORPORATE OFFICERS

President Jack K Overmyer
Vice Pres/Treasurer Margery H Overmyer
Secretary Sarah Overmyer Wilson

GENERAL MANAGEMENT

Publisher-Emeritus Jack K Overmyer
Publisher Sarah Overmyer Wilson

ADVERTISING

Director Ryan N Showley
Manager-Classified Blanche Carter

CIRCULATION

Director Frances Rhodes

NEWS EXECUTIVE

Editor W S Wilson

EDITORS AND MANAGERS

Editorial Page Editor/Writer W S Wilson
Farm Editor W S Wilson
Living/Lifestyle Editor Kellie Ashton
News Editor Stacey Creasy
Photo Department Manager Michael Kenny
Sports Editor Brian Wantuch

PRODUCTION

Manager-Press Craig Shambarger

Market Information: TMC.

Mechanical available: Offset; Black and 3 ROP colors; insert accepted — preprinted; page cut-offs — 22½".

Mechanical specifications: Type page 13¾" x 21½"; E - 6 cols, 2.17", ⅙" between; A - 6 cols, 2.17", ⅙" between; C - 6 cols, 2.17", ⅙" between.

Commodity consumption: Newsprint 200 short tons; widths 29", 14½"; black ink 5,700 pounds; color ink 200 pounds; single pages printed 3,600; average pages per issue 12(d); single plates used 3,000.

Equipment: EDITORIAL: Front-end hardware — 7-Ap/Mac Quadra 630; Front-end software — QuarkXPress 3.3; Printers — Xante/Accel-a-Writer 8200; Other equipment — 2-Ap/Mac PowerBook, Ap/Power Mac 7200 File Server, Ap/Mac Quadra 610 Wire Server. CLASSIFIED: Front-end hardware — Ap/Mac Quadra 610; Front-end software — Multi-Ad/CAMS 4.1; Printers — Ap/Mac LaserWriter NTX. DISPLAY: Front-end hardware — 3-Ap/Mac IIci, 1-Ap/Mac Performa 660CD; Front-end software — Multi-Ad/Creator; Printers — 1-QMS/Laser-Writer 600dpi; Other equipment — 1-Ap/Mac Scanner, 4-Ap/Mac CD-Rom Reader. PRODUCTION: Pagination software — QuarkXPress 3.3; OCR software — Caere/OmniPage; Plate exposures — 1-Nu; Plate processors — Nat; Production cameras — B/Caravel; Reproportion units — Konica/2028.

PRESSROOM: Line 1 — 1-HI/Cotrell V-15A Offset; Line 2 — 1-HI/Cotrell V-15A Offset; Line 3 — 1-HI/Cotrell V-15A Offset; Line 4 — 1-HI/Cotrell V-15A Offset; Folders — 1-HI. MAILROOM: Bundle tyer — 1-Bu/169D. COMMUNICATIONS: Digital ad delivery system — AP AdSend. Systems used — fiber optic. WIRE SERVICES: News — AP; Receiving dishes — size-3ft, AP. BUSINESS COMPUTERS: 3-Epson/Workstations on Novell network, IBM/AT PC; Applications: Mk: Accts receivable, Accts payable, Gen ledger, Display, Class adv, Billing; PCs & micros networked.

RUSHVILLE

Rush County

'90 U.S. Census- 5,533; E&P '96 Est. 5,321

Rushville Republican

(e-mon to sat)

Rushville Republican, PO Box 189, Rushville, IN 46173; tel (317) 932-2222; fax (317) 932-4358. Hollinger International Inc. group.

Circulation: 3,910(e); 3,910(e-sat); Sworn Oct. 10, 1995.

Price: 50¢(d); 50¢(sat); $8.88/mo; $106.56/yr, $112.00/yr (mail in county), $118.00/yr (mail out of county).

Advertising: Open inch rate $8.00(e); $10.25(e-mon); $8.00(e-sat).

News Service: AP. **Politics:** Independent. **Established:** 1840.

Not Published: Memorial Day; Independence Day; Labor Day; Thanksgiving; Christmas.

Special Editions: Progress (Feb); Basketball, Farm Fest (Mar); Graduation (May); Rush County Fair (July); Car Care, Football (Aug); Home Improvement, Rush Co. Guide (Sept); Business Profiles, Women in Business (Oct); Basketball Preview, Christmas Opening (Nov).

Special Weekly Sections: Agriculture (mon); School (thur); Church (fri).

CORPORATE OFFICERS

President Larry J Perrotto
Comptroller Roland McBride

GENERAL MANAGEMENT

Publisher Norman Voiles

ADVERTISING

Director Marilyn Land
Manager-Classified Melody Buckley

CIRCULATION

Manager Christine Wilson

NEWS EXECUTIVE

Editor Charlie Wilson

EDITOR AND MANAGER

Food/Society Editor Charlie Wilson

PRODUCTION

Superintendent Lori Jarboe

Market Information: TMC.

Mechanical available: Offset; Black and 3 ROP colors; insert accepted — preprinted; page cut-offs — 21½".

Mechanical specifications: Type page 13" x 21½"; E - 6 cols, 2 1/16", ⅛" between; A - 6 cols, 2 1/16", ⅛" between; C - 8 cols, 1 17/32", ⅛" between.

Commodity consumption: average pages per issue 12(d).

Equipment: EDITORIAL: Front-end hardware — 4-Ap/Mac; Front-end software — QuarkXPress 2.12, Baseview/NewsEdit; Printers — Ap/Mac LaserPro 630, Ap/Mac LaserWriter, Ap/Mac LaserWriter Plus. CLASSIFIED: Front-end hardware — Ap/Mac se30, Ap/Mac IIsi, Ap/Mac ImageWriter; Front-end software — Baseview/Class Manager, QuarkXPress 3.0; Printers — Ap/Mac LaserWriter. DISPLAY: Adv layout systems — Ap/Mac SE130; Front-end software — Multi-Ad/Creator; Printers — Ap/Mac LaserWriter. PRODUCTION: Pagination software — QuarkXPress, Adobe/Photoshop; OCR software — Caere/Omni Page; Typesetters — Ap/Mac Laser; Plate exposures — 1-Nu; Electronic picture desk — Roconek; Direct-to-plate imaging — Microtek/35T Negative, Microtek/Scanmaker II Flatbed; Production cameras — 1-Nu.

PRESSROOM: Line 1 — G. MAILROOM: Bundle tyer — 2-Bu; Addressing machine — ATT. WIRE SERVICES: News — AP; Syndicates — King Features, TMS, Creators, United Media, Universal Press; Receiving dishes — AP. BUSINESS COMPUTERS: PCs & micros networked.

SEYMOUR

Jackson County

'90 U.S. Census- 15,576; E&P '96 Est. 16,242
ABC-CZ (90): 15,576 (HH 6,071)

The Tribune

(e-mon to fri; m-sat)

The Tribune, 1215 E. Tipton; PO Box 447, Seymour, IN 47274; tel (812) 522-4871; fax (812) 522-7691. Freedom Communications Inc. group.

Circulation: 9,326(e); 9,326(m-sat); ABC Sept. 30, 1995.

Price: 50¢(d); 50¢(sat); $1.75/wk; $81.30/yr.

Advertising: Open inch rate $10.75(e); $10.75(m-sat). **Representative:** Papert Companies.

News Services: AP, KRT. **Politics:** Independent. **Established:** 1879.

Not Published: New Year; Memorial Day; Independence Day; Labor Day; Christmas.

GENERAL MANAGEMENT

Publisher L Thurman Gill

ADVERTISING

Director George N Main

CIRCULATION

Director Lee Upton

NEWS EXECUTIVE

Editor Dan Davis

EDITORS AND MANAGERS

Education/Police Editor Aubrey Woods

Indiana I-139

Farm Editor Aubrey Woods
Home Funishings Editor Joanne Persinger
Society Editor Joanne Persinger
Sports Editor Arv Koontz
Television/Wire Editor Wendy Stein

PRODUCTION

Superintendent Don Bush
Foreman-Photo Greg Surenkanp
Foreman-Pressroom Lynn Sutherland

Mechanical available: Offset; Black and 3 ROP colors; insert accepted — preprinted; page cut-offs — 22¾".

Mechanical specifications: Type page 13" x 21½"; E - 6 cols, $2\frac{1}{16}$", ⅛" between; A - 6 cols, $2\frac{1}{16}$", ⅛" between; C - 6 cols, $2\frac{1}{16}$", ⅛" between.

Commodity consumption: Newsprint 500 short tons; widths 27½", 13¾"; black ink 13,000 pounds; color ink 1,500 pounds; single pages printed 6,018; average pages per issue 20(d); single plates used 12,000.

Equipment: EDITORIAL: Front-end hardware — 1-Mk/4001. CLASSIFIED: Front-end hardware — Ap/Mac; Front-end software — Baseview; Printers — Ap/Mac LaserWriter Pro 810. DISPLAY: Front-end hardware — Ap/Mac; Front-end software — QuarkXPress; Printers — Ap/Mac LaserWriter Pro 810. PRODUCTION: Typesetters — 2-Mk/AdWriter; Plate exposures — 1-Douthitt/L1152; Plate processors — 1-Nat/A-250; Electronic picture desk — Lf/AP Leaf Picture Desk; Production cameras — 1-R/400; Automatic film processors — 2-LD/220-QT; Color separation equipment (conventional) — Digi-Colour; Digital color separation equipment — Digital Darkroom-Ap/Mac workstation w/Photoshop.
PRESSROOM: Line 1 — 4-G/Urbanite; Folders — 1-G. MAILROOM: Counter stackers — 1-BG/Count-O-Veyor; Bundle tyer — 1-Dynaric/SS-80. WIRE SERVICES: News — AP, KRT; Photos — AP; Receiving dishes — size-10ft, AP. BUSINESS COMPUTERS: 5-Compaq/PC, 2-IBM/PC; Applications: Baseview, Brainworks, Southware.

SHELBYVILLE

Shelby County

'90 U.S. Census- 15,336; E&P '96 Est. 15,900
ABC-CZ (90): 15,336 (HH 6,133)

The Shelbyville News

(e-mon to sat)

The Shelbyville News, 123 E. Washington St.; PO Box 750, Shelbyville, IN 46176; tel (317) 398-6631; fax (317) 398-0194; e-mail shelbynews@aol.com.

Circulation: 11,050(e); 11,050(e-sat); ABC Sept. 30, 1995.

Price: 50¢(d); 50¢(sat); $78.00/yr (foot carrier), $84.00/yr (motor route).

Advertising: Open inch rate $11.75(e); $11.75(e-sat). **Representatives:** US Suburban Press; Papert Companies.

News Services: AP Graphics, KRT, NEA, NYT, RN, SHNS. **Politics:** Independent. **Established:** 1947.

Not Published: Christmas.

Special Editions: Basketball (Jan); Basketball (Feb); Progress, N.I.E. Challenge in Creativity, Earth Day, Home Improvement (Apr); 500 Mile Race, Car Care (May); Back-to-School (Aug); Fair, SH Company Profiles (Sept); Home Improvement, Car Care (Oct); Pre Christmas (Thanksgiving), Basketball (Nov); Basketball, Monthly Home Magazine, Monthly Senior Publication, Shopping Gift Guide (Dec).

Magazines: TV (fri); The Extra (weekly).

CORPORATE OFFICERS

President John C DePrez Jr
Vice Pres/Treasurer Peter G DePrez
Secretary Joan C Bowman

GENERAL MANAGEMENT

Controller Tina Hartgrove

ADVERTISING

Director Dee Bonner
Manager-Retail Karen Ragin
Manager-Classified Elizabeth Schooley

CIRCULATION

Director Chris K Cvelbar

NEWS EXECUTIVES

Editor Scarlett Syse
Exec Editor Jim McKinney

EDITORS AND MANAGERS

Automotive/News Editor Doug Kirchberg
Cartoonist Dee Bonner
Farm Editor Doug Kirchberg
Chief Photographer Brett Hampton
Radio/Television Editor Scarlett Syse
Sports Editor Paul Hoffman

MANAGEMENT INFORMATION SERVICES

Systems Manager John Carroll

PRODUCTION

Manager Ronald Mahnke
Foreman-Composing Steve Wells

Market Information: TMC.

Mechanical available: Offset; Black and 3 ROP colors; insert accepted — preprinted; page cut-offs — 22¾".

Mechanical specifications: Type page 13" x 21½"; E - 6 cols, $2\frac{1}{16}$", ⅛" between; A - 6 cols, $2\frac{1}{16}$", ⅛" between; C - 6 cols, $2\frac{1}{16}$", ⅛" between.

Commodity consumption: Newsprint 551 short tons; widths 27½", 31", 34"; black ink 13,132 pounds; color ink 2,007 pounds; single pages printed 6,200; average pages per issue 20(d); single plates used 5,400.

Equipment: EDITORIAL: Front-end hardware — Dewar; Other equipment — Ap/Mac IIcx, Ap/Mac Plus Scanner, HP/ScanJet. CLASSIFIED: Front-end hardware — Dewar/Disc Net. DISPLAY: Front-end hardware — 2-Ap/Mac IIfx 6800, 1-Ap/Mac 840 AV; Front-end software — QPS, Multi-Ad, Aldus/Freehand, Adobe/Photoshop, Adobe/Illustrator. PRODUCTION: Typesetters — 1-Ap/Mac LaserWriter Plus, 2-Printware/720IQ, Ultre/94E, 2-Harlequin/RIP; Plate exposures — 1-Nu/Flip Top FT40UPNS, 1-Douthitt/Genesis; Plate processors — 1-Graham; Electronic picture desk — Ap/Mac 950, Adobe/Photoshop; Scanners — Kk/RSF 2035, AG/Arcus; Production cameras — SCREEN/C680-C; Automatic film processors — 1-SCREEN/LD260L, SCREEN/LD-220 QT.
PRESSROOM: Line 1 — 8-G/SC (Accumeter/gluer); Line 2 — 2-G/SSC; Line 3 — 1-G/SSC UOP; Folders — 2-G/2:1; Pasters — 2-Butler/Automatic. MAILROOM: Counter stackers — 2-BG/105; Inserters and stuffers — 6-KAN/320; Bundle tyer — 3-Bu. LIBRARY: Electronic — SMS. WIRE SERVICES: News — AP, NEA, NYT, RN, SHNS; Photos — AP; Syndicates — NEA, SHNS, Universal Press, NAS, United Media, King Features, Maturity News Service, AP Graphics, KRT; Receiving dishes — size-8ft-6ft, AP, RN, Newstar. BUSINESS COMPUTERS: IBM/PC, 6-Unisys, 1-Dell/PC; Applications: Acct, Circ, Data sciences paper-track, Accts receivable; PCs & micros networked; PCs & main system networked.

SOUTH BEND-MISHAWAKA

St. Joseph County

'90 U.S. Census- 148,119 (South Bend 105,511; Mishawaka 42,608); E&P '96 Est. 150,258 (South Bend 104,912; Mishawaka 45,346)
ABC-CZ (90): 208,926 (HH 79,288)

South Bend Tribune

(e-mon to fri; m-sat; S)

South Bend Tribune, 225 W. Colfax, South Bend, IN 46626; tel (219) 235-6161; e-mail sbtnews@aol.com (News); web site http://www.sbtinfo.com/. Schurz Communications Inc. group.

Circulation: 85,888(e); 85,888(m-sat); 118,316(S); ABC Sept. 30, 1995.

Price: 50¢(d); 50¢(sat); $1.50(S); $10.50/mo (carrier), $11.25/mo (motor route).

Advertising: Open inch rate $46.00(e); $46.00(m-sat); $64.50(S). **Representative:** Cresmer, Woodward, O'Mara & Ormsbee.

News Services: AP, NYT, SHNS, PR Newswire. **Politics:** Independent. **Established:** 1872.

Not Published: Independence Day; Labor Day; Christmas.

Special Weekly Sections: Food Focus (mon); Health (tues); Science & Technology (thur); Religion (fri); Home & Garden, Farming (sat); Automotive, Book, Seniors (S); Entertainment, Obituaries, TV Listings, Business, Features, Sports (daily).

Magazines: Sunday Punch; Parade; TV Magazine.

CORPORATE OFFICERS

President Todd Schurz
Vice Pres David Ray
Secretary Geraldine Dickey
Treasurer Emery L Hirschler

GENERAL MANAGEMENT

Publisher Todd Schurz
Vice Pres-Advertising/Marketing Emery L Hirschler
Vice Pres-Administration Ed Henry
Vice Pres-Operations Keith Russell
Vice Pres-Development & Planning David Ray
Manager-Human Resources Colleen Laderer
Manager-Research Robert Witt
Purchasing Agent Leslie Winey
Controller Mark Hocker

ADVERTISING

Director Carol Smith

MARKETING AND PROMOTION

Manager-Promotion Robert K Greene

TELECOMMUNICATIONS

Audiotex Manager Anita Glenn

CIRCULATION

Director Mike Lee
Asst Director Kevin Shaw
Manager-Operations Al Levy
Manager-Customer Service Bob Emerson
Manager-Special Publications Tina Caparell
Manager-Transportation Mark Clark
Manager-Home Delivery Bill Batteast
Manager-Alternate Delivery Kevin Shaw
Manager-Sales/Promotion Mike O'Neill

NEWS EXECUTIVES

Editor Todd Schurz
Assoc Editor Gayle Dantzler
Assoc Editor James Wensits
Managing Editor-Irish Sports Report David Haugh
Asst Managing Editor-News Janet Marsh
Asst Managing Editor-Operations Ken Klimek

EDITORS AND MANAGERS

Action Line Editor Chris Benninghoff
Amusements Editor Linda McManus
Automotive Editor Phil Vitale
Books Editor Andrew Hughes
Building Editor Phil Vitale
Business/Finance Editor Ray Leliaert Jr
City Editor Greg Swiercz
Copy Desk Chief Susan Kennedy
Farm/Agriculture Writer Wayne Falda
Fashion Editor Kathleen Sechowski
Features Editor Virginia Black
Films/Theater Writer Lisa Bornstein
Food Editor Charlotte Smith
Garden Editor Phil Vitale
Graphics Coordinator Gregg Bender
Librarian Rusty Grauel
Living/Lifestyle Editor Deanna Francis
Music Editor Lisa Bornstein
News Editor Harold Lowe
Photo Editor David Cooper
Political Writer Jack Colwell
Radio/Television Writer Alesia Redding
Religion Writer Kathy Borlik
Science/Technology Editor Harold Lowe
Sports Editor Bill Bilinski
Travel Editor Kathleen McKernan

MANAGEMENT INFORMATION SERVICES

Manager-Management Info Services Ian McLein
Asst Manager Tim Good

PRODUCTION

Director Karen Squibb
Asst Director Charlene Sinn
Manager-Press Operations Don Carlberg
Manager-Training Dwayne Golden
Manager-Pre Press Tina Cohen
Manager-Mailroom Carolyn Prince
Manager-Technical Dave Allen
Manager-Facilities Bill Morey
Manager-Quality Mike Popielski

Market Information: Zoned editions; Split Run; TMC; ADS; Operate audiotex.

Mechanical available: Anilox Keyless Offset; Black and 3 ROP colors; insert accepted — preprinted; page cut-offs — $21\frac{3}{16}$".

Mechanical specifications: Type page 13" x 22¼"; E - 6 cols, $2\frac{1}{16}$", ⅛" between; A - 6 cols, $2\frac{1}{16}$", ⅛" between; C - 10 cols, $1\frac{3}{16}$", $\frac{1}{16}$" between.

Commodity consumption: Newsprint 12,000 short tons; 10,886 metric tons; widths 55", 41¼", 27½"; black ink 440,000 pounds; color ink 15,000 pounds; single pages printed 20,800; average pages per issue 48(d), 114(S); single plates used 72,540.

Equipment: EDITORIAL: Front-end hardware — 3-DEC/PDP 11-84; Front-end software — Phoenix/EMS-CMS. CLASSIFIED: Front-end hardware — 17-DEC/PDP 11-84; Other equipment — Cx/Caps. AUDIOTEX: Supplier name — Brite. DISPLAY: Adv layout systems — III, Ap/Mac Quadra 950; Front-end hardware — 8-Ap/Mac Ad/Makeup Station; Printers — V/600dpi, X/VP300 Proofer, III/VP600 Proofer, Tektronix/Phaser 300, color proofer. PRODUCTION: Pagination software — ECP/News, III/Ad Stacking, QuarkXPress 3.3; Typesetters — 2-III/3810, 2-III/3850 Negative Output Devices, 2-Linotype-Hell/Lino 530; Platemaking systems — 2-Twin Line Units; Scanners — 1-ECR/Autokon 1000, 1-III/Infoscan 3700, 1-X/3650, 1-Scanview/Scanmate 5000, Horizon/Flatbed; Production cameras — 2-C/Marathon, 1-K/v241; Digital color separation equipment — RZ/2005.
PRESSROOM: Line 1 — 20-KBA/Anilox Keyless Offset; Press drives — EAE; Folders — 1-KBA/gear, 2-KBA/jaw; Reels and stands — 8-Von Roll; Press control system — Siemens. MAILROOM: Counter stackers — 4-HL/Monitor; Inserters and stuffers — 2-Fg/Drum 6:1; Bundle tyer — 4-MVP/5000, 4-MVP/2000; Addressing machine — KR, AVY/Labeling Machine. LIBRARY: Electronic — Vu/Text, Mead Data Central/Nexis NewsView. COMMUNICATIONS: Digital ad delivery system — AP AdSend. Systems used — satellite. WIRE SERVICES: News — AP, NYT, SHNS, PR Newswire; Photos — AP; Stock tables — AP Financial, AP SelectStox; Syndicates — AP Datafeatures; Receiving dishes — size-10ft, AP. BUSINESS COMPUTERS: 2-DEC/VAX 4000-300; Applications: Circ, Ad layout, Adv billing, Accts receivable, Gen ledger, Accts payable, Adv scheduling; PCs & micros networked; PCs & main system networked.

SPENCER

Owen County

'90 U.S. Census- 2,609; E&P '96 Est. 2,582

Spencer Evening World

(e-mon to fri)

Spencer Evening World, 114 E. Franklin; PO Box 226, Spencer, IN 47460; tel (812) 829-2255; fax (812) 829-4666.

Circulation: 3,570(e); Sworn Sept. 30, 1994.

Price: 25¢(d); $35.00/yr.

Advertising: Open inch rate $4.45(e). **Politics:** Democrat. **Established:** 1927.

Not Published: New Year; Memorial Day; Independence Day; Labor Day; Thanksgiving; Christmas.

GENERAL MANAGEMENT

Publisher John A Gillaspy
Director-Publication Tom Gillaspy
Asst General Manager John A Gillaspy
Manager-Office Lalla Smith

ADVERTISING

Director Sarah Harrison

CIRCULATION

Manager Bonnie Ervin

NEWS EXECUTIVE

Editor Tom Douglas

PRODUCTION

Manager Philip Gillaspy

Market Information: TMC.

Mechanical available: Offset; Black and 2 ROP colors; insert accepted — preprinted; page cut-offs — 22¾".

Mechanical specifications: Type page 15⅛" x 21"; E - 7 cols, $2\frac{1}{16}$", ⅛" between; A - 7 cols, $2\frac{1}{16}$", ⅛" between; C - 7 cols, $2\frac{1}{16}$", ⅛" between.

Commodity consumption: average pages per issue 8(d).

Equipment: PRODUCTION: Typesetters — 2-Ap/Mac Laser; Plate exposures — 1-Nu/Flip Top FT40, 1-B/2500; Scanners — Microtek; Production cameras — 1-K/240, 1-R.
PRESSROOM: Line 1 — 4-G/Community. MAILROOM: Bundle tyer — 1-Bu/29480; Addressing machine — 1-El/300.

SULLIVAN

Sullivan County

'90 U.S. Census- 4,663; E&P '96 Est. 4,641

The Sullivan Daily Times

(e-mon to fri)

The Sullivan Daily Times, 115 W. Jackson Ave.; PO Box 130, Sullivan, IN 47882-0130; tel (812) 268-6356; fax (812) 268-3110.

Circulation: 4,734(e); Sworn Sept. 29, 1995.

Price: 30¢(d); $1.15/wk (carrier); $6.00/mo (motor route); $42.00/yr (mail).

Advertising: Open inch rate $5.75(e).

News Service: AP. **Politics:** Democrat. **Established:** 1905, 1854 (daily edition of Democrat).

Not Published: New Year; Memorial Day; Independence Day; Labor Day; Thanksgiving; Christmas.

Copyright ©1996 by the Editor & Publisher Co.

I-140 Indiana

Special Editions: Ag Tab (Jan, Feb); Sports Section, Ag Tab (Mar); Car Care, Home & Garden (Apr); Dollar Days, Outdoor Recreation, Careers (May); Sports Section (Aug); Car Care, Home & Garden (Oct); Christmas, Sports Section (Nov); Christmas (Dec).
Special Weekly Sections: Agriculture (mon); Business (tues); Opinion (wed); Nostalgia (thur); Religion (fri).
Magazines: TV Times (thur); Senior (Citizen) Informant (monthly).

CORPORATE OFFICERS

President Nancy Pierce Gettinger
Vice Pres David Pierce
Treasurer Sarah Pierce Geitz

GENERAL MANAGEMENT

General Manager/Managing Editor Tom P Gettinger
Publisher Nancy Pierce Gettinger
Business Manager Patricia Morgan
Purchasing Agent Tom P Gettinger

ADVERTISING

Manager-Retail B J White
Manager-Classified Sandy Maxey

CIRCULATION

Manager Vickie Newman

NEWS EXECUTIVE

News Editor Jeff Salyers

EDITOR AND MANAGER

Sports Editor B J Hargis

PRODUCTION

Supervisor Steph McGhee

Mechanical available: Offset; Black and 2 ROP colors; insert accepted — preprinted; page cutoffs — 21".
Mechanical specifications: Type page $13\frac{3}{8}$" x 21"; E - 6 cols, 2.08", $\frac{1}{6}$" between; A - 6 cols, 2.08", $\frac{1}{6}$" between; C - 6 cols, 2.08", $\frac{1}{6}$" between.
Commodity consumption: Newsprint 1,120 metric tons; widths 28", 14"; black ink 1,056 pounds; color ink 10 pounds; single pages printed 50,000; average pages per issue 10(d); single plates used 1,400.
Equipment: EDITORIAL: Front-end hardware — PC/8088, PC/80286, PC/80386, PC/486, PC/386 DX; Front-end software — Suntype; Printers — 2-NEC/Silentwriter, NEC/1097. CLASSIFIED: Front-end hardware — PC/8088, PC/80286, PC/80386; Front-end software — Suntype. DISPLAY: Adv layout systems — Ap/Mac 7100; Front-end hardware — PC/386 DX, PC/486, Ap/Mac Scanner; Front-end software — Advent/3B2, Archetype/Corel Draw, QuarkXPress, Adobe/Photoshop; Printers — NEC/Silentwriters, NEC/1097; Other equipment — DEST/1000 B&W Scanner. PRODUCTION: Pagination software — QuarkXPress; Scanners — Ap/Mac, Dest; Production cameras — LE, R/500.
PRESSROOM: Line 1 — 4-HI/V-15A; Folders — HI/J-7. MAILROOM: Bundle tyer — Sa. WIRE SERVICES: News — AP; Syndicates — Universal Press, King Features, CNS. BUSINESS COMPUTERS: PC/386 DX, PC/286; Applications: Synaptic/Micro Solutions: Adv, Payroll, Gen ledger; PCs & micros networked; PCs & main system networked.

TERRE HAUTE

Vigo County

'90 U.S. Census- 57,483; E&P '96 Est. 55,528
ABC-CZ (90): 62,237 (HH) 24,187

The Tribune-Star

(m-mon to sat; S)

The Tribune-Star, 721 Wabash Ave.; PO Box 149, Terre Haute, IN 47808-0149; tel (812) 231-4200. Thomson Newspapers group.
Circulation: 36,421(m); 36,421(m-sat); 43,936(S); ABC Sept. 30, 1995.
Price: 50¢(d); 50¢(sat); $1.50(S); $3.00/wk (d & S), $2.05/wk (d only), $1.50/wk (sat & S); $156.00/yr (d & S), $106.00/yr (d only), $78.00/yr (sat & S).
Advertising: Open inch rate $26.36(m); $26.36(m-sat); $29.55(S).
News Services: AP, KRT. **Politics:** Independent. **Established:** 1903 (Star), 1896 (Tribune), 1983 (Tribune-Star).
Special Editions: Cookbook; Business Review; Bridal; Home Improvement; Car Care; Answer Book; Creative Journal; Indy 500; Summer Clearance; Back-to-School; Salute to Labor; Holiday Gift Guide; Year-end Review; Basketball Tournaments Guide; Milestones; Back-to-College.
Special Weekly Sections: Best Food Day (wed); Entertainment (thur); Home Improvement (fri); Farm (sat); Travel (S).
Magazines: Older Living Tab (tues); Cover Story (TMC) (thur); Valley Homes Tab (fri); TV/Entertainment (mini-tab) (S).

CORPORATE OFFICER

Publisher John J Meany

GENERAL MANAGEMENT

Controller Melony Baker

ADVERTISING

Director Rick Schmidt
Manager Jim Swander
Manager Faye Murry

CIRCULATION

Director Scott Daily
Manager-Single Copy Kyle Poorman
Manager-Target Marketing Chris Harter
Manager-Administration Michelle Poorman
Manager-Home Delivery Ron Smith
Manager-Sales & Service Andrea Frizzi

NEWS EXECUTIVES

Editor David H Cox
Asst Editor Trevis Mayfield

EDITORS AND MANAGERS

Business Editor Marilyn Salesman
Editorial Page Editor Max Jones
Features Editor Linda Wolf
News Editor Stephanie Angel
Photo/Graphics Editor Doug McSchooler
Sports Editor Mark Bennett

PRODUCTION

Coordinator Brian Lane
Asst Coordinator Terry Lambert
Foreman-Composing David Bonham

Market Information: Zoned editions; TMC; ADS; Operate audiotex.
Mechanical available: Offset; Black and 3 ROP colors; insert accepted — preprinted; page cutoffs — $22\frac{3}{4}$".
Mechanical specifications: Type page 13" x $21\frac{1}{2}$"; E - 6 cols, $2\frac{1}{16}$", $\frac{1}{8}$" between; A - 6 cols, $2\frac{1}{16}$", $\frac{1}{8}$" between; C - 9 cols, $1\frac{3}{8}$", $\frac{1}{16}$" between.
Commodity consumption: Newsprint 3,250 short tons; widths $27\frac{1}{2}$", $13\frac{3}{4}$"; black ink 86,500 pounds; color ink 13,500 pounds; single pages printed 16,316; average pages per issue 34(d), 114(S); single plates used 48,000.
Equipment: EDITORIAL: Front-end hardware — DEC; Front-end software — CText/AFM. CLASSIFIED: Front-end hardware — DEC; Front-end software — CText/Classified Advertising System. DISPLAY: Adv layout systems — CText/Adept, Ap/Mac; Front-end hardware — DEC; Front-end software — CText/Adept, Multi-Ad/Creator. PRODUCTION: Pagination software — QuarkXPress; Typesetters — 2-V/5300E, 1-V/5100; Plate exposures — 1-Nu/Flip Top FT40; Plate processors — 2-Nat/Super A-250; Production cameras — 1-B/1822, 1-LC/21121; Automatic film processors — 1-LE/LD281Q; Digital color separation equipment — 1-Lf/Leafscan 35, 1-Sharp/JX600.
PRESSROOM: Line 1 — 10-G/Urbanite; Folders — 2-G; Pasters — 3-Cary; Reels and stands — 4-G; Press control system — Fin; Press registration system — Duarte. MAILROOM: Counter stackers — 2-Id/2000; Inserters and stuffers — 1-GMA/SLS 1000; Bundle tyer — 2-Dynaric/NP2; Addressing machine — 1-Ch. LIBRARY: Electronic — SMS/Stauffer Gold. WIRE SERVICES: News — KRT; Photos — AP; Stock tables — Custom Stocks; Receiving dishes — AP. BUSINESS COMPUTERS: IBM/Sys 36; Applications: INSI; PCs & micros networked; PCs & main system networked.

TIPTON

Tipton County

'90 U.S. Census- 4,751; E&P '96 Est. 4,683

Tipton County Tribune

(e-mon to fri; m-sat)

Tipton County Tribune, 110 W. Madison St.; PO Box 48, Tipton, IN 46072; tel (317) 552-3355. Ray Barnes Newspapers Inc. group.
Circulation: 2,714(e); 2,714(m-sat); Sworn Jan. 30, 1996.
Price: 35¢(d); 35¢(sat); $6.00/mo (carrier), $7.00/mo (motor route); $64.80/yr (carrier).
Advertising: Open inch rate $5.30(e); $5.30(m-sat); comb with the Elwood Call-Leader (e) $8.00.
News Service: AP. **Politics:** Independent. **Established:** 1895.
Not Published: New Year; Memorial Day; Independence Day; Labor Day; Thanksgiving; Christmas.
Special Editions: Mature Years (Jan); Cook Book, Basketball Sectional Edition (Feb); Spring Brides, Spring Opening (Mar); Farm & Garden (Apr); Spring Home Improvement, Health Care Edition (May); Welcome to Tipton (June); Mature Years, Tipton 4-H Fair Edition (July); Elwood Glass Festival Edition, Tipton Co. Pork Festival Edition (Aug); Home & Office Technology, Fall Car Care, Fall Brides (Oct); Basketball Preview Edition, Christmas Opening (Nov).
Magazines: What's On TV (fri); The Mini-Page.

CORPORATE OFFICERS

President Jack L Barnes
Vice Pres Charles G Barnes
Secretary Judith K Barnes

GENERAL MANAGEMENT

Publisher Jack L Barnes
Asst Publisher Brian Barnes
Business Manager Robert L Nash

ADVERTISING

Director Robert L Nash
Manager-Retail Jay Puterbaugh

CIRCULATION

Director Chris Idlewine
Manager Wanda Widdup

NEWS EXECUTIVES

Editor Neil Johnson
Managing Editor Neil Johnson

EDITORS AND MANAGERS

News Editor Neil Johnson
Sports Editor Michelle Garmon

PRODUCTION

Foreman Melvin Fry

Market Information: TMC.
Mechanical available: Web offset; Black and 3 ROP colors; insert accepted — preprinted; page cut-offs — $22\frac{3}{4}$".
Mechanical specifications: Type page 13" x $21\frac{1}{2}$"; E - 6 cols, $2\frac{1}{16}$", $\frac{1}{8}$" between; A - 6 cols, $2\frac{1}{16}$", $\frac{1}{8}$" between; C - 8 cols, $\frac{1}{4}$", $\frac{1}{32}$" between.
Commodity consumption: Newsprint 72 short tons; 65 metric tons; widths 27.5", 13.75"; black ink 2,160 pounds; color ink 360 pounds; single pages printed 3,662; average pages per issue 10(d); single plates used 2,150.
Equipment: EDITORIAL: Front-end hardware — Mk/1100; Front-end software — Mk/Mycro-Comp. CLASSIFIED: Front-end hardware — Mk/1100; Front-end software — Mk/Mycro-Comp. DISPLAY: Adv layout systems — 2-Ap/Mac SE. PRODUCTION: Typesetters — 2-Ap/Mac LaserWriter II NT/NTX; Plate exposures — 1-Nu/Flip Top; Production cameras — 1-R/Commodore; Automatic film processors — 1-LE/LD 24.
PRESSROOM: Line 1 — 4-G/Community; Folders — 1-G. MAILROOM: Bundle tyer — 2-Malow; Addressing machine — 2-Am. LIBRARY: Combination — 1-Recordak/Microfilm reader. COMMUNICATIONS: Facsimile — 1-Sharp/FO 330. WIRE SERVICES: News — AP; Receiving dishes — AP. BUSINESS COMPUTERS: 1-Bs/B-20, 1-RSK/TRS 80 model 4; Applications: Display billing, Sales reports, Subscriber billing, Subscriber/non-subscriber lists.

UNION CITY
See WINCHESTER

VALPARAISO
See MUNSTER

VINCENNES

Knox County

'90 U.S. Census- 19,859; E&P '96 Est. 19,613
ABC-CZ (90): 24,940 (HH 9,356)

Vincennes Sun-Commercial (e-mon to fri; S)

Vincennes Sun-Commercial, 702 Main St.; PO Box 396, Vincennes, IN 47591; tel (812) 886-9955; fax (812) 885-2235. Central Newspapers Inc. group.
Circulation: 13,755(e); 15,736(S); ABC Sept. 30, 1995.
Price: 50¢(d); $1.50(S); $1.50/wk; $6.00/mo, $78.00/yr.
Advertising: Open inch rate $11.30(e); $12.42(S). **Representative:** Papert Companies.
News Service: AP. **Politics:** Independent. **Established:** 1804.
Special Editions: Basketball (Feb); Farm (Mar); Back-to-School, County Fair (Aug).
Special Weekly Sections: Best Food Day (wed); Business, Real Estate, Entertainment, Book Reviews, Health, Farm (S).
Magazines: Parade, TV Tab (S).

CORPORATE OFFICERS

President/CEO Frank E Russell
Exec Vice Pres Eugene S Pulliam
Secretary Marjorie C Tarplee
Treasurer Wayne D Wallace

GENERAL MANAGEMENT

Publisher Michael E Quayle

ADVERTISING

Director Veronica A Kopp
Manager-Retail Vickie K Palmer

CIRCULATION

Manager Donnie Williams

NEWS EXECUTIVES

Editor Michael E Quayle
Managing Editor Mikeal N Wright

EDITORS AND MANAGERS

Graphics Editor Mark Crowley
Radio/Television Editor Paula Smith
Religion Editor Deanna Ratts
Sports Editor Dave Staver
Women's Editor Jane Hall

PRODUCTION

Foreman-Pressroom Bob Shepard
Foreman-Composing Paul Blome

Mechanical available: Offset; Black and 3 ROP colors; insert accepted — preprinted; page cutoffs — $22\frac{3}{4}$".
Mechanical specifications: Type page 13" x 21"; E - 6 cols, $2\frac{1}{16}$", $\frac{1}{8}$" between; A - 6 cols, $2\frac{1}{16}$", $\frac{1}{8}$" between; C - 9 cols, $1\frac{3}{8}$", $\frac{1}{16}$" between.
Commodity consumption: Newsprint 860 short tons; 780 metric tons; widths 28", 14"; black ink 16,500 pounds; color ink 2,700 pounds; single pages printed 7,550; average pages per issue 24(d), 44(S); single plates used 9,500.
Equipment: EDITORIAL: Front-end hardware — Ap/Mac; Front-end software — Baseview/NewsEdit-Wire Manager; Other equipment — SCS/Linx. CLASSIFIED: Front-end hardware — Ap/Mac; Front-end software — Baseview/Class Plus Manager. DISPLAY: Front-end hardware — Ap/Mac; Front-end software — Multi-Ad/Creator, QuarkXPress 3.1. PRODUCTION: Typesetters — 2-AU/108-PSPII Laser; Plate exposures — 1-Nu/Flip Top FT40LNS; Plate processors — 1-Nat/330; Production cameras — 1-R/500; Automatic film processors — 1-SCREEN Color separation equipment (conventional) — Ap/Mac, Nikon, Adobe/Photoshop.
PRESSROOM: Line 1 — 5-G/Urbanite (2 Balloon formers); Folders — 1-G. MAILROOM: Inserters and stuffers — Manual; Bundle tyer — Bu. WIRE SERVICES: News — AP; Photos — AP; Receiving dishes — size-12ft, AP. BUSINESS COMPUTERS: 1-IBM/Sys 36; Applications: In-house; PCs & micros networked.

WABASH

Wabash County

'90 U.S. Census- 12,127; E&P '96 Est. 11,659

Wabash Plain Dealer

(e-mon to fri; m-sat)

Wabash Plain Dealer, 123 W. Canal; PO Box 379, Wabash, IN 46992; tel (219) 563-2131; fax (219) 563-0816. Nixon Newspapers Inc. group.
Circulation: 6,967(e); 6,967(m-sat); Sworn Sept. 30, 1995.
Price: 50¢(d); 50¢(sat); $7.05/mo; $82.50/yr.
Advertising: Open inch rate $10.47(e); $10.47(m-sat).
News Service: AP. **Politics:** Independent. **Established:** 1859.
Not Published: New Year; Memorial Day; Independence Day; Labor Day; Christmas.
Special Editions: Industry Review (Jan); Bride (Feb); Basketball, Farm (Mar); Home Improvement, Automotive, Health & Fitness, Earth Day/Recycling (Apr); Graduation (May); 4-H Fair, Little League (July); Canal Days, Back-to-School, Football (Aug); Home Improvement, Farm, Health & Fitness, Industry Review (Sept); Automotive, Women in Business (Oct); Christmas (Nov); Christmas (Dec).

Iowa I-141

Special Weekly Sections: Tastebuds, Cook of the Week, Business (mon); Dollars & Cents (tues); Community (wed); Women & Careers (thur); Women's Health (fri); Romance and Cruisin', Channel Changer TV Listings (sat).

CORPORATE OFFICERS

President John R Nixon
Vice Pres-Finance John W Stackhouse
Vice Pres Gregory S Nixon

GENERAL MANAGEMENT

Publisher James L Widner

ADVERTISING

Manager Rick Welch

CIRCULATION

Manager Paul Hart

NEWS EXECUTIVE

Managing Editor Joe Slacian

EDITORS AND MANAGERS

News Editor Roy Church
Sports Editor Stuart Korfhage

PRODUCTION

Manager Michael Plummer

Market Information: TMC; ADS; Operate audiotex.
Mechanical available: Offset; Black and 3 ROP colors; insert accepted — preprinted; page cut-offs — 22¾".
Mechanical specifications: Type page 21.50" x 21"; E - 6 cols, 2¹⁄₁₆", ⅛" between; A - 6 cols, 2¹⁄₁₆", ⅛" between; C - 6 cols, 1⅜", ⅛" between.
Commodity consumption: Newsprint 229 metric tons; widths 27", 13.50"; black ink 1,500 pounds; color ink 1,000 pounds; average pages per issue 14(d), 16(sat); single plates used 4,800.
Equipment: EDITORIAL: Front-end hardware — Ap/Mac; Front-end software — QuarkXPress. CLASSIFIED: Front-end hardware — Ap/Mac; Front-end software — Baseview; Printers — Ap/Mac. AUDIOTEX: Hardware — IBM; Supplier name — Stauffer Communication. DISPLAY: Front-end hardware — Ap/Mac; Front-end software — QuarkXPress, Multi-Ad. PRODUCTION: Pagination software — QuarkXPress; Typesetters — 4-Ap/Mac, 1-AGFA; Plate exposures — 2-Nu; Plate processors — 1-Nat; Production cameras — 1-R; Automatic film processors — 1-LE; Color separation equipment (conventional) — Kk.
PRESSROOM: Line 1 — 4-G/Urbanite; Folders — 1-G, 1-G/Quarter. MAILROOM: Counter stackers — 1-BG; Bundle tyer — 3-Bu; Addressing machine — 1-Ch. WIRE SERVICES: News — AP; Syndicates — NEA; Receiving dishes — AP. BUSINESS COMPUTERS: IBM/Sys 36; PCs & micros networked.

WARSAW
Kosciusko County

'90 U.S. Census- 10,968; E&P '96 Est. 11,425

Times-Union
(e-mon to fri; m-sat)

Times-Union, Times Bldg.; PO Box 1448, Warsaw, IN 46581-1448; tel (219) 267-3111; fax (219) 267-7784.
Circulation: 12,797(e); 12,797(m-sat); Sworn Oct. 7, 1995.
Price: 50¢(d); 50¢(sat); $11.00/mo (mail out of county); $119.00/yr (mail out of county).
Advertising: Open inch rate $9.00(e); $9.00(m-sat).
News Services: AP, AP Laserphoto. **Politics:** Independent-Republican. **Established:** 1854 (Union), 1856 (Times).
Not Published: New Year; Memorial Day; Independence Day; Labor Day; Thanksgiving; Christmas.
Special Editions: Bridal, Agriculture (Mar); Home Improvement, Spring Fashion (Apr); Graduation Edition (May); Fair Edition, Back-to-School, Home Improvement (Aug); New Car Edition (Oct); Christmas Edition (Nov).
Special Weekly Sections: Best Food Day (mon); Farm Page (wed); Leisure (thur); Auto Section, Home Section, Outdoors, Generations, Business, Spotlight (sat).
Magazines: Best Food Day (mon); Spotlight (TV Section) (sat).
Broadcast Affiliate: WRSW AM & FM.

CORPORATE OFFICERS

President M R Williams
Vice Pres M L Hartle
Secretary/Treasurer M R Williams

GENERAL MANAGEMENT

Publisher M R Williams
General Manager Norman L Hagg
Controller Dennis Plummer
Manager-Credit Dennis Plummer
Personnel Manager C M Williams
Purchasing Agent M R Williams

ADVERTISING

Manager Dean Tucker
Director-Special Editions William Hays

CIRCULATION

Manager Ben White

NEWS EXECUTIVES

Editor in Chief Norman L Hagg
Managing Editor Gary Gerard

EDITORS AND MANAGERS

Automotive/Travel Editor Norman L Hagg
Business/Finance Editor Dan Spalding
Editorial Page Editor Gary Gerard
Education Editor Deb Sprong
Entertainment/Amusements Editor Phil Smith
Farm Editor Laurie Hahn
Features/Food Editor Ruth Anne Long
Films/Theater Editor Joe Felke
Librarian Mary Alice Park
Living/Lifestyle Editor Ruth Anne Long
Music Editor Joe Felke
National Editor Dan Spalding
Photo Department Manager Gary Nieter
Picture Editor Gary Nieter
Political/Government Editor Dan Spalding
Radio/Television Editor Joe Felke
Real Estate Editor Robert Lamirand
Religion Editor Robert Lamirand
Science Editor Phil Smith
Sports Editor Greg Jones
Wire Editor Robert Lamirand
Women's Editor Ruth Anne Long

PRODUCTION

Director Harold Edwards II

Market Information: TMC.
Mechanical available: Offset; Black and 3 ROP colors; insert accepted — preprinted, all; page cut-offs — 21".
Mechanical specifications: Type page 13" x 21"; E - 6 cols, 2¹⁄₁₆", ⅛" between; A - 6 cols, 2¹⁄₁₆", ⅛" between; C - 6 cols, 2¹⁄₁₆", ⅛" between.
Commodity consumption: Newsprint 650 metric tons; widths 27½", 13¾"; black ink 2,100 pounds; color ink 350 pounds; single pages printed 8,200; average pages per issue 24(d); single plates used 4,500.
Equipment: EDITORIAL: Front-end hardware — 13-Mk/1100, 1-Ap/Mac 8100-100, 1-Ap/Mac 7100-80, 1-Ap/Mac II SE; Front-end software — QuarkXPress, Adobe/ Photoshop; Printers — 2-Ap/Mac LaserWriter II, XIT/Clipper; Other equipment — Ultrasetter/94E. CLASSIFIED: Front-end hardware — 4-Ap/Mac 6100-66; Front-end software — Multi-Ad/Cams; Printers — Ultrasetter/94E. DISPLAY: Front-end hardware — 1-Ap/Mac 6100-66, 1-Ap/Mac Quadra 950, 1-Ap/Mac 2CI, 1-Ap/Mac Centris; Front-end software — Multi-Ad/Creator, Aldus/Free-Hand; Printers — XIT/Clipper, TI/MicroLaser Pro 600. PRODUCTION: Pagination software — QuarkXPress, Adobe/PhotoShop; Typesetters — 2-COM/ 8400; Plate exposures — 1-Nu/Ultra-Plus; Production cameras — 1-Nu/2024SST; Automatic film processors — 1-Kk/Versomat 317.
PRESSROOM: Line 1 — 6-G/Urbanite; Folders — 1-G; Press registration system — Dewar. MAILROOM: Inserters and stuffers — MM/227E 5-into-1; Bundle tyer — 2-Bu; Addressing machine — 1-Am, 1-El. WIRE SERVICES: News — AP; Photos — AP; Syndicates — CNS, Universal Press, United Features, NEA; Receiving dishes — size-10ft, AP.

WASHINGTON
Daviess County

'90 U.S. Census- 10,838; E&P '96 Est. 10,741
ABC-CZ (90): 10,838 (HH 4,400)

The Washington Times-Herald (e-mon to sat)

The Washington Times-Herald, 102 E. Vantress St.; PO Box 471, Washington, IN 47501; tel (812) 254-0480; fax (812) 254-0480. Donrey Media Group group.
Circulation: 10,026(e); 10,026(e-sat); ABC Sept. 30, 1995.
Price: 50¢(d); 50¢(sat); $6.00/mo; $72.00/yr.
Advertising: Open inch rate $7.50(e); $7.50(e-sat). **Representative:** Papert Companies.
News Service: AP. **Politics:** Independent. **Established:** 1867.
Not Published: New Year; Memorial Day; Independence Day; Labor Day; Thanksgiving; Christmas.
Advertising not accepted: Mail order.
Special Editions: IRS Income Tax Edition, Customer Appreciation (Jan); Basketball Edition (Mar); Farm Review & Forecast (Apr); Progress (July); Back-to-School (Aug); Sidewalk Sale Days (Sept); Basketball Edition, Christmas (Nov); Christmas (Dec).
Special Weekly Sections: Agriculture Page (mon); Food (wed); Area News (thur); Business Page, Church Page, Entertainment, Real Estate (fri).
Magazines: TV Tab (fri); Tube Times (local, newsprint) (sat).

CORPORATE OFFICERS

Founder Donald W Reynolds
Chairman (Management Committee/Senior Consultant) Fred W Smith
President/Chief Operating Officer Emmett Jones
Exec Vice Pres/Chief Financial Officer Darrell W Loftin
Vice Pres-Western Newspaper Group David A Osborn
Vice Pres-Eastern Newspaper Group Don Schneider

GENERAL MANAGEMENT

Publisher/General Manager Lars Purdue

ADVERTISING

Director Donald Brown
Manager-Retail Donald Brown
Manager-Classified Beverly Briggeman

CIRCULATION

Director Barry Hauser

NEWS EXECUTIVE

Editor Melody Maust

EDITORS AND MANAGERS

Editorial Writer Melody Maust
Education Editor Shannon Yoder
Farm/School Editor Melody Maust
Fashion Editor Nancy Morris
Food/Society Editor Peggy Shake
Librarian Ellen Pride
Photographer Kelly Overton
Radio/Television Editor Donald Brown
Real Estate/Sports Editor Jeff Hayes
Society Editor Peggy Shake

PRODUCTION

Foreman-Composing Roger Pratt

Mechanical available: Offset; Black and 3 ROP colors; insert accepted — preprinted; page cut-offs — 22¾".
Mechanical specifications: Type page 13" x 21½"; E - 6 cols, 2¹⁄₁₆", ⅛" between; A - 6 cols, 2¹⁄₁₆", ⅛" between; C - 8 cols, 1½", ⅛" between.
Commodity consumption: Newsprint 325 metric tons; widths 27½", 13¾"; black ink 10,200 pounds; color ink 1,040 pounds; single pages printed 5,008; average pages per issue 16(d); single plates used 2,500.
Equipment: EDITORIAL: Front-end hardware — 1-Mk/1100; Printers — Ap/Mac LaserWriter II. CLASSIFIED: Front-end hardware — 1-Mk/1100. DISPLAY: Adv layout systems — Ap/Mac SI-II; Front-end software — Multi-Ad/Creator. PRODUCTION: Typesetters — 2-Ap/Mac LaserWriter II NTX; Plate exposures — 1-Nu/FT 40M; Production cameras — 1-LE/R 500; Automatic film processors — 1-Kk/214-K, 1-M/314, C/T-45.
PRESSROOM: Line 1 — 8-Ct/15A; Line 2 — 1-ATF/Chief 15; Line 3 — 1-Townsend/T-51 Color; Folders — 2-Ct. MAILROOM: Bundle tyer — 2-Bu/Package Tie; Addressing machine — Mailing Machine Systems. COMMUNICATIONS: Facsimile — Canon/630. WIRE SERVICES: News — AP; Receiving dishes — UPI.

WEST LAFAYETTE
See LAFAYETTE

WINCHESTER, IN-UNION CITY, OH
Randolph County, IN
Darke County, OH

'90 U.S. Census- 10,691 (Winchester, IN 5,095; Union City, IN 3,612; Union City, OH 1,984); E&P '96 Est. 10,466 (Winchester, IN 4,882; Union City, IN 3,448; Union City, OH 2,116)

The News-Gazette
(e-mon to fri; m-sat)

The News-Gazette, 224 W. Franklin St.; PO Box 429, Winchester, IN 47394; tel (317) 584-4501; fax (317) 584-3066. Hollinger International Inc. group.
Circulation: 4,073(e); 4,073(m-sat); Sworn Oct. 2, 1995.
Price: 50¢(d); 50¢(sat); $6.75/mo; $106.20/yr.
Advertising: Open inch rate $7.30(e); $7.30(m-sat).
News Service: AP. **Politics:** Independent. **Established:** 1858.
Not Published: Thanksgiving; Christmas.
Special Weekly Sections: Business Salute (tues); TV, Church (fri); Farm (sat).
Magazine: TV (fri).

CORPORATE OFFICERS

President Larry J Perrotto
Comptroller Roland McBride

GENERAL MANAGEMENT

Publisher Jack Armstrong

ADVERTISING

Manager Valerie Ashley

CIRCULATION

Manager Kristie Weddell

NEWS EXECUTIVE

Managing Editor Michael Buckmaster

EDITORS AND MANAGERS

Features/Lifestyle Editor Liz Wynn
News Editor Deborah Lilly
Radio/Television Editor Deborah Lilly
Report Photographer Doug Wynn
Sports Editor Kevin Gideon
Wire Editor Michael Buckmaster
Women's Editor Liz Wynn

PRODUCTION

Manager Rick Reed

Market Information: Zoned editions; TMC.
Mechanical available: Offset; Black and 3 ROP colors; insert accepted — preprinted; page cut-offs — 22¾".
Mechanical specifications: Type page 13" x 21½"; E - 6 cols, 2.07", ⅛" between; A - 6 cols, 2.07", ⅛" between; C - 10 cols, 1.17", ⅙" between.
Commodity consumption: Newsprint 153 short tons; widths 28", 14"; black ink 19,500 pounds; color ink 3,000 pounds; single pages printed 3,200; average pages per issue 10(d); single plates used 4,284.
Equipment: EDITORIAL: Front-end hardware — Ap/Mac IIe; Front-end software — CPS; Printers — Ap/Mac LaserWriter II NTX. CLASSIFIED: Front-end hardware — Ap/Mac IIe; Front-end software — CPS; Printers — Ap/Mac LaserWriter II NTX. DISPLAY: Adv layout systems — COM/MCS; Front-end hardware — 2-PowerView/10; Front-end software — CJ; Other equipment — CJ/8400. PRODUCTION: Typesetters — CJ/8400, Ap/Mac LaserWriter Plus, Ap/Mac LaserWriter II NTX; Plate exposures — Nu/Flip Top; Production cameras — R/500; Automatic film processors — LE/LD-18.
PRESSROOM: Line 1 — 5-G/Community; Folders — 1-G. MAILROOM: Bundle tyer — 2-Bu/String Tyer; Addressing machine — 2-Am. WIRE SERVICES: News — AP; Receiving dishes — AP. BUSINESS COMPUTERS: PCs & micros networked; PCs & main system networked.

IOWA

AMES
Story County

'90 U.S. Census- 47,198; E&P '96 Est. 49,079

The Daily Tribune
(e-mon to fri; m-sat)

The Daily Tribune, 317 5th St.; PO Box 380, Ames, IA 50010; tel (515) 232-2160; fax (515) 232-2364. Partnership Press Inc. group.
Circulation: 9,193(e); 9,193(m-sat); VAC Dec. 30, 1994.
Price: 50¢(d); $1.00(sat); $2.30/wk; $25.00/3mo; $107.70/yr.
Advertising: Open inch rate $12.85(e); $12.85(m-sat). **Representatives:** Papert Companies; Iowa Newspaper Assn.
News Services: AP, NYT. **Politics:** Independent. **Established:** 1867.
Not Published: New Year; Memorial Day; Independence Day; Labor Day; Christmas.

Special Editions: Annual Update (Feb); Home (Mar); University (Aug); Engagement Album (bi-monthly); Agri-Times, Auto Spotlight (quarterly).
Special Weekly Sections: Business (mon); Neighbors (tues); Best Food Day (wed); Church (fri); Entertainment, TV Times (sat).
Magazines: Story Today, Boone Today (wed); Nevada Journal (thur); Weekender (sat); TMC.

CORPORATE OFFICERS
Chairman Michael G Gartner
President Gary G Gerlach
Exec Vice Pres Craig S McMullin
Treasurer Craig S McMullin

GENERAL MANAGEMENT
Publisher Gary G Gerlach
President Allen B Weber
General Manager Allen B Weber
Controller Joan Rost

ADVERTISING
Director Don Dauterive

CIRCULATION
Director Jim Wysocki

NEWS EXECUTIVES
Editor Michael G Gartner
Managing Editor Jeff Bruner

EDITORS AND MANAGERS
Business Editor Marc Kovac
Community Life Editor Anne Scott
Editorial Page Editor Drake Mabry
Education Editor Jeff Bruner
Photo Editor Julia Adkisson
Sports Editor Jeff King

MANAGEMENT INFORMATION SERVICES
Data Processing Manager Todd Prins

PRODUCTION
Director Janette Frankel
Commercial Printing Janette Frankel

Market Information: Zoned editions; Split Run; TMC; ADS.
Mechanical available: Offset; Black and 3 ROP colors; insert accepted — preprinted; page cut-offs — $22\frac{3}{4}$".
Mechanical specifications: Type page 13" x $21\frac{1}{2}$"; E - 6 cols, $2\frac{1}{16}$", $\frac{1}{8}$" between; A - 6 cols, $2\frac{1}{16}$", $\frac{1}{8}$" between; C - 9 cols, $1\frac{1}{4}$", $\frac{3}{16}$" between.
Commodity consumption: Newsprint 1,200 short tons; 1,500 metric tons; width $27\frac{1}{2}$"; black ink 26,400 pounds; color ink 8,500 pounds; single pages printed 14,300; average pages per issue 24(d); single plates used 19,200.
Equipment: EDITORIAL: Front-end hardware — 11-CText/Laser Output. CLASSIFIED: Front-end hardware — 4-CText/Laser Output. DISPLAY: Adv layout systems — 8-Ap/Mac Laser Output; Front-end hardware — Ap/Mac; Front-end software — Aldus/PageMaker; Other equipment — Ap/Mac Scanner. PRODUCTION: Typesetters — 5-Ap/Mac LaserWriter; Plate exposures — 1-Nu; Plate processors — 1-Nat/250; Scanners — 1-Ap/Mac; Production cameras — 1-R; Automatic film processors — 1-P/24.
PRESSROOM: Line 1 — 4-G/Urbanite; Folders — 1-G. MAILROOM: Inserters and stuffers — 8-KAN/480; Bundle tyer — 1-Ca, 1-Bu/TS250; Addressing machine — 1-St/1620 QFL. WIRE SERVICES: News — AP, NYT; Receiving dishes — size-10ft, AP. BUSINESS COMPUTERS: 8-IBM; Applications: Circ, Distribution, Gen accounting; PCs & micros networked.

ATLANTIC
Cass County
'90 U.S. Census- 7,432; E&P '96 Est. 7,374

Atlantic News-Telegraph
(e-mon to fri; m-sat)

Atlantic News-Telegraph, 410 Walnut St.; PO Box 230, Atlantic, IA 50022; tel (712) 243-2624. Hollinger International Inc. group.
Circulation: 5,340(e); 5,340(m-sat); Sworn Oct. 30, 1993.
Price: 50¢(d); 50¢(sat); $13.50/mo; $75.00/yr.
Advertising: Open inch rate $11.55(e); $11.55(m-sat). **Representative:** Iowa Newspaper Assn.
News Service: AP. **Politics:** Independent-Republican. **Established:** 1871.
Not Published: New Year; Memorial Day; Independence Day; Labor Day; Thanksgiving; Christmas.
Special Weekly Section: Entertainment (thur).
Magazines: Atlantic Farm (monthly); Today's Action; Senior Courier.

GENERAL MANAGEMENT
Publisher Ken Lingen
General Manager Ken Lingen

ADVERTISING
Manager-Classified LuAnn Combes

CIRCULATION
Director Dixie Pederson

PRODUCTION
Foreman-Composing Kim Jeray

Market Information: TMC; ADS.
Mechanical available: Offset; Black and 4 ROP colors; insert accepted — preprinted, free samples; page cut-offs — $22\frac{3}{4}$".
Mechanical specifications: Type page $13\frac{1}{8}$" x $21\frac{1}{2}$"; E - 6 cols, $2\frac{1}{16}$", $\frac{1}{8}$" between; A - 6 cols, $2\frac{1}{16}$", $\frac{1}{8}$" between; C - 6 cols, $2\frac{1}{16}$", $\frac{1}{8}$" between.
Commodity consumption: Newsprint 410 short tons; widths 28", 14", 30", 34"; black ink 5,000 pounds; color ink 4,000 pounds; average pages per issue 12(d).
Equipment: EDITORIAL: Front-end hardware — 1-Ap/Mac. CLASSIFIED: Front-end hardware — 1-Ap/Mac. PRODUCTION: Plate processors — 1-Ic; Scanners — Ap/Mac One, 1-Ap/Mac LaserPrinter Scanner; Production cameras — 1-Nu; Automatic film processors — 1-P; Digital color separation equipment — Ap/Mac One. PRESSROOM: Line 1 — 6-G; Folders — 1-G/2:1. MAILROOM: Bundle tyer — 3-Bu. WIRE SERVICES: News — AP; Receiving dishes — AP. BUSINESS COMPUTERS: IBM; Applications: Adv, News, Subscriptions, Bookkeeping; PCs & micros networked; PCs & main system networked.

BETTENDORF
See DAVENPORT

BOONE
Boone County
'90 U.S. Census- 12,392; E&P '96 Est. 12,596

Boone News-Republican
(e-mon to fri)

Boone News-Republican, 812 Keeler St.; Box 100, Boone, IA 50036; tel (515) 432-1234; fax (515) 432-7811.
Circulation: 3,826(e); Sworn Sept. 28, 1995.
Price: 50¢(d); $1.63/wk; $6.50/mo; $72.00/yr (in town).
Advertising: Open inch rate $6.70(e); $8.70 (e-tues). **Representative:** Iowa Newspaper Assn.
News Service: AP. **Politics:** Independent. **Established:** 1865.
Not Published: New Year; Memorial Day; Independence Day; Labor Day; Thanksgiving; Christmas.
Special Editions: Chamber of Commerce (Jan); Boone Tourism Guide, Draw-An-Ad (Feb); Home Improvement, Boone Tourism Guide, Draw-An-Ad (Mar); Home Improvement, Salute to Working Women, Little League, Golden Years (Apr); Golden Years, Real Estate Guide (May); Fair, Real Estate Guide (June); Little League, Real Estate Guide (July); Little League, Back-to-School, Football Preview, Real Estate Guide, Pufferbilly Day (Aug); Pufferbilly Day, Autumn Preview, Ag Section, Real Estate Guide (Sept); Real Estate Guide (Oct); Cosmetology, Moonlight Madness (Nov); Christmas Greetings, Shopping Guide/Shopping Hours, Christmas Countdown (Dec).
Special Weekly Sections: Agriculture Page, Engagement/Weddings (tues); Auto Guide, Entertainment (thur); TV, Church Page (fri).
Cable TV: Operate leased cable TV in circulation area.

CORPORATE OFFICERS
President Robert C Schaub
Secretary Jeannine Schaub

GENERAL MANAGEMENT
Publisher Robert C Schaub
Bookkeeper Marilyn Prim

ADVERTISING
Manager Susan E Tolan

CIRCULATION
Manager Mark McDonald

NEWS EXECUTIVE
Managing Editor James A Bachtell

EDITORS AND MANAGERS
Fashion Editor Sandy Hayes
Society/Women's Editor Sandy Hayes
Sports Editor Chuck Hackenmiller

PRODUCTION
Manager Eldon Cunningham

Market Information: TMC; ADS.
Mechanical available: Offset; Black and 3 ROP colors; insert accepted — preprinted, subject to approval; page cut-offs — $22\frac{3}{4}$".
Mechanical specifications: Type page 13" x $21\frac{1}{2}$"; E - 6 cols, $2\frac{1}{16}$", $\frac{1}{8}$" between; A - 6 cols, $2\frac{1}{16}$", $\frac{1}{8}$" between; C - 9 cols, $1\frac{1}{3}$", $\frac{1}{8}$" between.
Commodity consumption: Newsprint 152 short tons; widths 14", 28"; black ink 6,000 pounds; color ink 400 pounds; single pages printed 3,200; average pages per issue 9(d); single plates used 2,000.
Equipment: EDITORIAL: Front-end hardware — 5-Mk/Newswriter; Front-end software — Mk/550; Printers — 1-Ap/Mac LaserWriter Plus. CLASSIFIED: Front-end hardware — 1-Mk/Newswriter, 1-Mk/Touchwriter; Front-end software — Mk. DISPLAY: Front-end hardware — 1-Ap/Mac SE, 1-Ap/Mac SE30; Front-end software — Aldus/PageMaker; Printers — 1-Ap/Mac LaserWriter II NTX. PRODUCTION: Typesetters — Mk/Newswriter, Mk/Touchwriter, 2-Ap/Mac, 1-Ap/Mac LaserWriter II NTX; Plate exposures — Nu.
PRESSROOM: Line 1 — HI/V-15A. MAILROOM: Bundle tyer — 1-Yamada/TM 36; Addressing machine — 3-Wm. WIRE SERVICES: News — AP; Receiving dishes — size-1 1/6ft, AP. BUSINESS COMPUTERS: 1-IBM/PC-XT, 1-Compaq/Proline 4255; Applications: dBase/IV: Bookkeeping; dBase/III Plus: Circ.

BURLINGTON
Des Moines County
'90 U.S. Census- 27,208; E&P '96 Est. 26,075
ABC-CZ (90): 30,291 (HH 12,351)

The Hawk Eye (m-mon to sat; S)

The Hawk Eye, 800 S. Main; PO Box 10, Burlington, IA 52601; tel (319) 754-8461; fax (319) 754-6824. Harris Enterprises Inc. group.
Circulation: 17,267(m); 17,267(m-sat); 18,880(S); ABC Sept. 30, 1995.
Price: 50¢(d); 50¢(sat); $1.25(S); $9.75/mo (carrier), $10.75/mo (motor route); $117.00/yr (carrier), $129.00/yr (motor route).
Advertising: Open inch rate $11.20(m); $11.20(m-sat); $11.20(S). **Representatives:** Papert Companies; Iowa Newspaper Assn.
News Service: AP. **Politics:** Independent. **Established:** 1837.
Advertising not accepted: Vending machines; Cigarette.
Special Editions: Progress (Feb); Progress (Mar); Guide to Hawk Eye Land (May).
Special Weekly Sections: Education (mon); Health (tues); Best Food Day (wed); Entertainment (thur); Religion (fri); Hobbies (sat); Business/Lifestyles, Mutual Funds & Stocks (S).
Magazines: Home Magazine, TV Section, USA Weekend (sat).

CORPORATE OFFICERS
President Bill Mertens
Vice Pres John Lee
Secretary Nelson H Showalter
Treasurer Don L Close

GENERAL MANAGEMENT
Publisher/General Manager Bill Mertens
Assoc Publisher John D Montgomery
Manager-Employee Relations Jan Jaeger

ADVERTISING
Director Nelson H Showalter
Manager-Classified Laurie Trautner
Manager-Promotion Laurie Trautner
Coordinator-Co-op Judi Weinreich
Coordinator-Major Accounts Tim Agnew

CIRCULATION
Director Jay Gillispie

NEWS EXECUTIVES
Editor Bill Mertens
Managing Editor Dale Alison

EDITORS AND MANAGERS
Business/Agriculture Editor Steve Delaney
Editorial Writer Bill Mertens
Photo Department Manager Tony Miller
Radio/Television Editor Larry Lockhart
Sports Editor Craig Sesker
Weekend Editor Dena Bennett

PRODUCTION
Manager-Systems Don L Close
Manager-Mailroom Steve Deggendorf

Market Information: Zoned editions; TMC; Operate audiotex.
Mechanical available: Offset; Black and 3 ROP colors; insert accepted — preprinted; page cut-offs — $22\frac{3}{4}$".
Mechanical specifications: Type page $12\frac{15}{16}$" x $21\frac{1}{2}$"; E - 6 cols, $2\frac{1}{16}$", $\frac{1}{8}$" between; A - 6 cols, $2\frac{1}{16}$", $\frac{1}{8}$" between; C - 8 cols, $1\frac{1}{2}$", $\frac{1}{16}$" between.
Commodity consumption: Newsprint 1,113 metric tons; width $27\frac{1}{2}$"; black ink 25,638 pounds; color ink 2,964 pounds; single pages printed 9,632; average pages per issue 20(d), 18(sat), 44(S); single plates used 14,918.
Equipment: EDITORIAL: Front-end hardware — Dewar/Disc Net, Novell/Netserver; Front-end software — SIA/386-33, SIA/386-33 Ed pag PC. CLASSIFIED: Front-end hardware — Dewar/Disc Net, Ap/Mac 850, Ap/Mac 860; Printers — Dataproducts/Print LB300. DISPLAY: Adv layout systems — 1-Dewar/Disc Net, 1-Dewar/Discovery, 2-Ap/Mac. PRODUCTION: Typesetters — 1-XIT/Clipper, 2-XIT/Yawl Imagesetter; Plate exposures — 1-BKY/30-40, 1-Nu/Flip Top FT40URNS; Plate processors — Nat/Subtractive 33-1; Scanners — 2-AG/Arcus Plus; Production cameras — 1-R; Automatic film processors — LE/24"; Color separation equipment (conventional) — 1-C/E-Z Color 8"x10" Direct Screen Sys.
PRESSROOM: Line 1 — 6-G/1008 (2 formers) single width; Folders — 1-G; Reels and stands — Roll/Stands; Press control system — Fin. MAILROOM: Inserters and stuffers — MM (5 inserter); Bundle tyer — 2-MLN, Power Strap. COMMUNICATIONS: Digital ad delivery system — AP AcSend. Systems used — satellite. WIRE SERVICES: News — AP; Photos — AP; Receiving dishes — size-6ft, AP. BUSINESS COMPUTERS: Data Sciences; Applications: Circ, Adv, Bus; PCs & main system networked.

CARROLL
Carroll County
'90 U.S. Census- 9,579; E&P '96 Est. 9,761

Daily Times Herald
(e-mon to fri)

Daily Times Herald, 508 N. Court St.; PO Box 546, Caroll, IA 51401; tel (712) 792-3573.
Circulation: 5,987(e); Sworn Sept. 29, 1995.
Price: 50¢(d); $1.25/wk.
Advertising: Open inch rate $5.92(e). **Representative:** Iowa Newspaper Assn.
News Service: AP. **Politics:** Independent. **Established:** 1868.
Not Published: New Year; Memorial Day; Independence Day; Labor Day; Thanksgiving; Christmas.
Special Editions: Farm; Progress; Fashion; Graduation; Senior Citizen; Christmas; Car Care; Home Improvement; Spring Recreation; College Guide; Corn & Soybean Issue; First Aid; Bridal; Chamber.
Magazine: TV Magazine (fri).

CORPORATE OFFICERS
President James B Wilson
Vice Pres/Secretary Ann Wilson
Treasurer James B Wilson

GENERAL MANAGEMENT
Publisher James B Wilson
Business Manager James B Wilson

ADVERTISING
Manager-Retail Debra Lucht

CIRCULATION
Manager Daniel Tigges

NEWS EXECUTIVE
Managing Editor James B Wilson

EDITORS AND MANAGERS
News Editor Lawrence Devine
Sports Editor Dennis O'Grady

PRODUCTION
Foreman-Composing Eugene Wagner
Foreman-Press Tim Bohling

Market Information: Zoned editions; TMC.
Mechanical available: Offset; Black and 3 ROP colors; insert accepted — preprinted; page cut-offs — $21\frac{1}{2}$".
Mechanical specifications: Type page $12\frac{15}{16}$" x 21"; E - 6 cols, $2\frac{1}{8}$", $\frac{1}{6}$" between; A - 6 cols, $2\frac{1}{8}$", $\frac{1}{6}$" between; C - 8 cols, $1\frac{1}{2}$", $\frac{1}{6}$" between.
Commodity consumption: Newsprint 287 short tons; width 28".
Equipment: EDITORIAL: Front-end hardware — CText; Printers — Ap/Mac LaserWriter. CLAS-

SIFIED: Front-end hardware — Ap/Mac; Printers — Ap/Mac LaserWriter. DISPLAY: Adv layout systems — Ap/Mac; Printers — Ap/Mac LaserWriter. PRODUCTION: Typesetters — Ap/Mac LaserWriter; Plate exposures — 1-Nu/Flip Top; Plate processors — 1-Homad/25; Production cameras — 1-Nu/SST 1923; Automatic film processors — 1-Kk/Versomat. PRESSROOM: Line 1 — 5-HI/Cotrell-V-15A; Folders — 1-G/2:1. MAILROOM: Bundle tyer — 1-MM/Strap-Tyer. WIRE SERVICES: News — AP; Syndicates — INA; Receiving dishes — AP. BUSINESS COMPUTERS: Synaptic/Circulation Sys.

CEDAR FALLS
See WATERLOO

CEDAR RAPIDS-MARION
Linn County
'90 U.S. Census- 129,154 (Cedar Rapids 108,751; Marion 20,403); E&P '96 Est. 132,154 (Cedar Rapids 110,791; Marion 21,363)
ABC-NDM (90): 168,767 (HH 65,501)

The Gazette (m-mon to sat; S)
The Gazette, 500 3rd Ave. S.E.; PO Box 511, Cedar Rapids, IA 52401; tel (319) 398-8211; e-mail gazette@fyiowa.com; web site http://www.fyiowa.com/gazette.
Circulation: 68,856(m); 68,856(m-sat); 84,046(S); ABC Sept. 30, 1995.

Price: 50¢(d); 75¢(sat); $1.75(S); $4.00/wk; $197.00/yr.
Advertising: Open inch rate $42.55(m); $42.55(m-sat); $47.35(S).
News Services: AP, LAT-WP. Politics: Independent. Established: 1883.
Special Editions: New Baby's News, Stocks & Business Review, Bridal Guide, College Guide (Jan); Home & Building, Financial Future (Feb); Success in Eastern Iowa, Spring Car Care (Mar); Student AD-venture, Explore '96, Springtime in the Amanas (May); Spotlight on Women, Bridal Guide, Freedom Festival Guide (July); Discovery, Football Guide (Aug); Fall Fashions, Fall Leaf Color Guide, College Guide '96, Parade of Homes (Sept); Fall Car Care, Seniors Scene, Reader's Choice (Oct); Recipe Contest, Holiday, Recipe Section, Holiday Wishbook (Nov); Holiday Potpourri (Dec).
Special Weekly Sections: Health & Science (mon); Food (tues); Neighbors (wed); Youth Plus (thur); Weekend (fri); TV Vision, Cue (sat); Milestones, Home & Real Estate, Money, Life & Leisure (S).
Magazines: React (sat); Parade (S).
Broadcast Affiliate: KCRG.

CORPORATE OFFICERS
Board Chairman	Joe F Hladky Jr
President	Joe Hladky III
Vice Pres	Dale Larson
Vice Pres	Ken Slaughter
Secretary	Elizabeth T Barry
Treasurer	Ken Slaughter

GENERAL MANAGEMENT
Publisher	Joe Hladky III
General Manager	Dale Larson
Controller	Mike Campbell
Assoc-Credit	Mary Lou Zenor
Director-Human Resources	Mary Collins

ADVERTISING
Director	David Storey
Manager-Classified	Mary Orth
Manager-National	Curt Woods

MARKETING AND PROMOTION
Manager-Marketing Research	Jeff Wolff
Manager-Promotion/Public Affairs	Terry Bergen

TELECOMMUNICATIONS
Audiotex Manager	Jim Debth

CIRCULATION
Director	Don Michel
Manager-City	Al Battin
Manager-Country	Bill Ruhl
Manager-Sales	Mary Ellen Johnson
Manager-Office	Paula Fries
Manager-Operations	Ted Fries
Manager-Service	Sheryl Steen

NEWS EXECUTIVES
Editor	Joe Hladky III
Managing Editor	Mark Bowden
Asst Managing Editor	Phyllis Fleming

EDITORS AND MANAGERS
Auto Columnist	Tim Banse
Books Editor	Bridget Janus
Columnist	Mike Deupree
Editorial Page Editor	Jerry Elsea
Editorial Writer	Ken Sullivan
Editorial Writer	Jerry Elsea
Editorial Writer	Kurt Rogahn
Entertainment/Amusements Editor	Cindy Cullen Chapman
Environmental Editor	Phyllis Fleming
Family Editor	Dawn Goodlove
Farm/Rural Affairs Writer	Marlene Lucas
Fashion/Home Furnishings Editor	Dawn Goodlove
Features Editor	Dave Morris
Films/Theater Editor	Cindy Cullen Chapman
Food/Garden Editor	Dave Morris
Graphics Director	Duane Crock
Growing Older Editor	Dawn Goodlove
Health Editor	Phyllis Fleming
Interactive Media Editor	Joseph Bauer
Librarian	Bridget Janus
Lifestyle Editor	Dave Morris
Music Editor-Classical/Pop	Rebecca Lindwall
National/Foreign Editor	Don Thompson
Neighbors Editor	Elizabeth Kutter
News Editor	Doug Beach
Outdoor Editor	Orlan Love
Photo Department Manager	Paul Jensen
Picture Editor	Paul Jensen
Political Editor	Ken Sullivan
Radio/Television Editor	Cindy Cullen Chapman
Real Estate Editor	Dawn Goodlove
Religion Editor	Beverley Duffy
Science/Technology Editor	Phyllis Fleming
Sports Editor	Mark Dukes

Iowa I-143

Copyright ©1996 by the Editor & Publisher Co.

I-144 Iowa

Sports Columnist Mike Hlas
Sunday Editor Dan Geiser
Travel/Leisure Editor Dawn Goodlove
Writing/Editing Coach Dale Kueter

MANAGEMENT INFORMATION SERVICES
Director-Management Info Services Steve Hannah

PRODUCTION
Administration Mike Atwood
Administration Tom Happ
Manager-Pressroom John Jenkins
Manager-Processing/Packaging John Jenkins
Manager-Pre Press Peg Schmitz

Market Information: Zoned editions; Split Run; TMC; Operate database; Operate audiotex; Electronic edition.
Mechanical available: Offset; Black and 3 ROP colors; insert accepted — preprinted, preprinted tab, booklets, single sheet 1; page cut-offs — 22¾".
Mechanical specifications: Type page 13" x 21½"; E - 6 cols, 2", ⅙" between; A - 6 cols, 2 1/16", 1/16" between; C - 9 cols, 1⅜", 1/16" between.
Commodity consumption: Newsprint 7,500 short tons; 6,804 metric tons; widths 54⅞", 41⅛", 27⅜"; black ink 150,000 pounds; color ink 42,000 pounds; single pages printed 17,160; average pages per issue 40(d), 88(S); single plates used 75,000.
Equipment: EDITORIAL: Front-end hardware — SII/Sys 55; Front-end software — SII/Sys 55; Printers — HP/LaserJet, Epson, Fujitsu, Okidata; Other equipment — SII/Scoop Pagination. CLASSIFIED: Front-end hardware — SII/Sys 55; Front-end software — SII/Sys 55; Printers — HP/LaserJet, Epson, Fujitsu, Okidata; Other equipment — SII/Scoop Pagination. AUDIOTEX: Hardware — Brite; City Line; Expressway Classifieds. DISPLAY: Adv layout systems — SII/IAL; Front-end hardware — SII; Front-end software — SII; Printers — Okidata, HP/LaserJet, Fujitsu. PRODUCTION: Typesetters — 2-MON/Express, 1-MON/Image Master 5000, MON/Express Master 25; Plate exposures — 3-Nu, 1-Montakomp/95; Plate processors — 1-Nat/Enco, 1-WL/3200; Electronic picture desk — Lf/AP Leaf Picture Desk; Scanners — 1-Howtek/Scanmaster 3 plus, 1-Kk/DCS 200; Production cameras — 1-C/Spartan III, 1-SCREEN/670E; Automatic film processors — 1-LD/260Q, 1-LD/260L, 1-Kk/Kodamatic 710, 2-LE/26 MTP, 1-AG/Avanta 20-25 OLP; Film transporters — 2-C/1274; Shrink lenses — 1-CK Optical; Color separation equipment (conventional) — CD/6355, CD/636IE w/Magna Scan; Digital color separation equipment — 1-Howtek/D4000, 1-CD/636IE.
PRESSROOM: Line 1 — 8-G/Metro (4 Halfdecks); Line 2 — 10-G/Community, 4-G/Community; Press drives — Fin; Folders — 1-G/SSC, 1-G/SSC, 2-G/3:2; Pasters — G/Metro, 3-Enkel/Community; Reels and stands — 8-G/Metro reel, G/Community, 3-Enkel; Press control system — PCS-Par; Press registration system — WPC/Microtrak. MAILROOM: Counter stackers — 1-Id/N3330, 2-QWI/350; Inserters and stuffers — 1-HI/1372P-online; Bundle tyer — 2-MLN/Strapper, 1-ML/2EE Strapper, 2-Dynaric/AM500; Addressing machine — 1-Ch, 2-Dm; Mailroom control system — IC. HI/1372P. LIBRARY: Electronic — SII Laser. COMMUNICATIONS: Digital ad delivery system — AP AdSend. Systems used — fiber optic. WIRE SERVICES: News — AP; Stock tables — AP; Syndicates — AP; Receiving dishes — size-3m, AP. BUSINESS COMPUTERS: 2-DEC/VAX 4,500-300, 4-Sun/Sparc 1000; Applications: Oracle, Microsoft/Windows; PCs & micros networked; PCs & main system networked.

CENTERVILLE

Appanoose County
'90 U.S. Census- 5,936; E&P '96 Est. 5,643

Ad Express & Daily Iowegian (m-mon to fri)

Ad Express & Daily Iowegian, 105 N. Main St.; PO Box 610, Centerville, IA 52544; tel (515) 856-6336. Smith Newspapers Inc. group.
Circulation: 3,029(m); Sworn Sept. 30, 1994.
Price: 50¢(d); $49.00/yr.
Advertising: Open inch rate $6.00(m). **Representative:** Iowa Newspaper Assn.
News Service: AP. **Politics:** Republican. **Established:** 1864.
Not Published: New Year; Washington's Birthday; Memorial Day; Independence Day; Labor Day; Columbus Day; Veteran's Day; Thanksgiving; Christmas.
Special Editions: Progress (Feb); Garden Tab, Farm (Apr); Outdoor Recreation (June); Farm (Oct).
Magazine: Fall-winter sports Tab (Sept & Nov).

CORPORATE OFFICER
President John C Arnold

GENERAL MANAGEMENT
Publisher John C Arnold

ADVERTISING
Director William O Hayes

CIRCULATION
Director Tom Beck

NEWS EXECUTIVES
Editor Steve Dunn
Managing Editor John C Arnold

EDITORS AND MANAGERS
Society Editor Judy Arnold
Sports/City Editor James Cool

PRODUCTION
Superintendent Tom Beck

Market Information: Zoned editions; Split Run; TMC.
Mechanical available: Offset; Black and 3 ROP colors; insert accepted — preprinted; page cut-offs — 22¾".
Mechanical specifications: Type page 13" x 21½"; E - 6 cols, 2 1/16", ⅛" between; A - 6 cols, 2 1/16", ⅛" between; C - 6 cols, 2 1/16", ⅛" between.
Commodity consumption: widths 27½", 34"; black ink 5,000 pounds; color ink 300 pounds; average pages per issue 12(d).
Equipment: EDITORIAL: Front-end hardware — Ap/Mac; Front-end software — QPS, Baseview; Printers — Ap/Mac LaserWriter. DISPLAY: Adv layout systems — Ap/Mac. PRODUCTION: Plate exposures — Nu; Production cameras — Acti; Automatic film processors — AG.
PRESSROOM: Line 1 — G/Community; Line 2 — G/Community; Line 3 — G/Community; Line 4 — G/Community.

CHARLES CITY

Floyd County
'90 U.S. Census- 7,878; E&P '96 Est. 7,460

Charles City Press (e-mon to fri; m-sat)

Charles City Press, 801 Riverside; PO Box 397, Charles City, IA 50616; tel (515) 228-3211; fax (515) 228-2641. Hollinger International Inc. group.
Circulation: 2,828(e); 2,828(m-sat); Sworn Sept. 27, 1995.
Price: 50¢(d); 50¢(sat); $8.50/mo; $72.50/yr.
Advertising: Open inch rate $7.07(e); $7.07(m-sat).
News Services: INA, AP. **Politics:** Independent. **Established:** 1896.
Not Published: New Year; Memorial Day; Independence Day; Labor Day; Thanksgiving; Christmas.
Special Editions: Agriculture (Jan); Agriculture (Feb); Beef (May); Agriculture (July); Pork (Oct).

CORPORATE OFFICERS
President Larry J Perrotto
Comptroller Roland McBride

GENERAL MANAGEMENT
Publisher Gene A Hall

ADVERTISING
Manager Rich Gifford

CIRCULATION
Manager Mike Knox

NEWS EXECUTIVE
Managing Editor David R Ruble

EDITORS AND MANAGERS
Editorial Page Editor David R Ruble
National Editor David R Ruble
News Editor Mark Wicks
Photo Editor Mark Wicks
Political/Government Editor David R Ruble
Sports Editor Dave Smith
Weekend Editor Mark Wicks

PRODUCTION
Foreman-Composing Nancy Eckenrod
Foreman-Press Marvin Ostwald

Market Information: TMC; ADS.
Mechanical available: Offset; Black and 3 ROP colors; insert accepted — preprinted; page cut-offs — 22½".
Mechanical specifications: Type page 13¼" x 21½"; E - 6 cols, 2", ⅙" between; A - 6 cols, 2", ⅙" between; C - 6 cols, 2", ⅙" between.
Commodity consumption: Newsprint 250 metric tons; widths 28", 32"; black ink 12,000 pounds; color ink 4,500 pounds; single pages printed 7,400; average pages per issue 12(d); single plates used 9,000.
Equipment: EDITORIAL: Front-end hardware — Ap/Mac Classic II; Front-end software — Ready-Set-Go/5; Printers — Ap/Mac LaserWriter Plus. CLASSIFIED: Front-end hardware — Ap/Mac Classic II; Front-end software — Ready-Set-Go/5; Printers — Ap/Mac LaserWriter Plus. DISPLAY: Front-end hardware — Ap/Mac IIsi, Ap/Mac IIci; Front-end software — Multi-Ad/Creator, QPS; Printers — Ap/Mac LaserWriter. PRODUCTION: Plate exposures — Nu; Plate processors — Roconex; Scanners — Microtek/Scan Maker 600ZS; Production cameras — SCREEN.
PRESSROOM: Line 1 — 7-G/Community; Folders — 1-G/SC, 1-G/Community. MAILROOM: Counter stackers — BG/Count-O-Veyor; Bundle tyer — Bu; Wrapping singles — El. WIRE SERVICES: News — AP; Syndicates — NEA, King Features, Creators, SHNS; Receiving dishes — size-1m, AP.

CHEROKEE

Cherokee County
'90 U.S. Census- 6,026; E&P '96 Est. 5,670

Cherokee County's Daily Times (m-tues to sat)

Cherokee County's Daily Times, Times Bldg. 111 S. 2nd; PO Box 281, Cherokee, IA 51012; tel (712) 225-5111; fax (712) 225-2910. Edwards Publications group.
Circulation: 3,250(m); 3,250(m-sat); Sworn Sept. 28, 1995.
Price: 50¢(d); 50¢(sat); $10.00/mo; $60.00/yr.
Advertising: Open inch rate $7.55(m); $7.65(m-sat). **Representative:** Iowa Newspaper Assn.
News Service: AP. **Politics:** Independent. **Established:** 1870 (weekly), 1928 (daily)
Not Published: New Year; Thanksgiving; Christmas.
Special Editions: Progress (Feb); Farm (Mar); Car Care, Home Improvement (Apr); Beef Edition, Rodeo (May); Fair Edition (July); Back-to-School (Aug); Fall Sports, Car Care, Home Improvement (Sept); Pork Edition, Winter Fashion (Oct); Winter Sports (Nov).
Special Weekly Sections: Business (thur); Religion (sat).
Magazine: Area Advertiser (TMC) (tues).

GENERAL MANAGEMENT
Publisher John P Kern

ADVERTISING
Manager-Marketing Deb Reynolds

CIRCULATION
Manager-Promotion John P Kern

NEWS EXECUTIVE
Editor Mike Palecek

PRODUCTION
Superintendent Sue Seeley

Market Information: TMC.
Mechanical available: Offset; Black and 3 ROP colors; insert accepted — preprinted; page cut-offs — 22¾".
Mechanical specifications: Type page 13" x 21½"; E - 6 cols, 2 1/16", ⅛" between; A - 6 cols, 2 1/16", ⅛" between; C - 6 cols, 2 1/16", ⅛" between.
Commodity consumption: average pages per issue 12(d).
Equipment: PRODUCTION: Typesetters — 2-Ap/Mac LaserWriter, 1-Ap/Mac LaserPrinter; Plate exposures — 1-Nu; Plate processors — 1-Nat/A-250; Production cameras — SCREEN/250; Automatic film processors — 1-P/524. WIRE SERVICES: News — AP; Receiving dishes — AP. BUSINESS COMPUTERS: Applications: All bus functions, Circ.

CLINTON

Clinton County
'90 U.S. Census- 29,201; E&P '96 Est. 27,813
ABC-CZ (90): 29,201 (HH 11,667)

Clinton Herald (e-mon to fri; m-sat)

Clinton Herald, 221 6th Ave. S.; PO Box 2961, Clinton, IA 52733-2961; tel (319) 242-7101; fax (319) 242-3854. Donrey Media group.
Circulation: 16,617(e); 16,617(m-sat); ABC Sept. 30, 1995.
Price: 50¢(d); 50¢(sat); $6.00/mo; $72.00/yr (carrier).
Advertising: Open inch rate $13.90(e); $13.90(m-sat). **Representatives:** Papert Companies; Iowa Newspaper Assn.
News Service: AP. **Politics:** Independent. **Established:** 1856.
Not Published: Independence Day; Christmas.
Special Editions: Cattlefeeders Edition, Brides & Weddings, Active Times (Jan); Health & Fitness, Financial Edition (Feb); Home Improvement & Yard & Garden (Mar); Active Times (Apr); Art in the Park (May); Riverboat Days (June); Active Times (July); Bazaar Edition (Sept); Active Times (Oct); Christmas Open House (Nov); Holiday Gift Guides (Dec).
Special Weekly Sections: Best Food Day (wed); TV Section (thur); Church Page (fri).
Magazine: TV Tab (thur).

CORPORATE OFFICERS
Founder Donald W Reynolds
President/Chief Operating Officer Emmett Jones
Exec Vice Pres/Chief Financial Officer Darrell W Loftin
Vice Pres-Western Newspaper Group David A Osborn
Vice Pres-Eastern Newspaper Group Don Schneider

GENERAL MANAGEMENT
Publisher Jack Dermody
Manager-Office Marge Terrill

ADVERTISING
Director Gary Bicker
Manager-Classified Sherri Enright

CIRCULATION
Director Robert McCarthy

NEWS EXECUTIVE
Editor William Baker

EDITORS AND MANAGERS
News Editor Dave Overby
Photo Department Manager Jerry Dahl
Sports Editor Ted Schultz
Telegraph Editor Grace Whitten

PRODUCTION
Foreman-Composing Robert Schaefer
Manager A Westphal
Manager-Systems Robert Schaefer

Market Information: TMC.
Mechanical available: Offset; Black and 3 ROP colors; insert accepted — preprinted; page cut-offs — 22¾".
Mechanical specifications: Type page 13" x 21½"; E - 6 cols, 2 1/16", ⅛" between; A - 6 cols, 2 1/16", ⅛" between; C - 9 cols, 1⅜", 1/16" between.
Commodity consumption: width 27½"; black ink 32,611 pounds; color ink 3,500 pounds; single pages printed 9,444; average pages per issue 22(d); single plates used 9,100.
Equipment: EDITORIAL: Front-end hardware — Dewar, 14-PC/286 Workstation, 11-IBM. CLASSIFIED: Front-end hardware — Dewar, 3-PC/286 Workstation; Other equipment — 5-IBM. PRODUCTION: Typesetters — 2-Printware/720IQ; Platemaking systems — 1-Nat/A-250; Plate exposures — 2-Nu; Production cameras — 1-C; Automatic film processors — 1-P/626; Shrink lenses — CK Optical.
PRESSROOM: Line 1 — 4-G/Urbanite; Folders — 1-G/2:1; Pasters — Butler/Automatic. MAILROOM: Counter stackers — 1-BG/108, 1-Id/CS202; Inserters and stuffers — 1-MM; Bundle tyer — 2-MLN/ML-1; Wrapping singles — 1-St/510; Addressing machine — 1-St/1200. WIRE SERVICES: News — AP. BUSINESS COMPUTERS: 1-Hw/L62; Applications: Circ, Bus.

COUNCIL BLUFFS

Pottawattamie County
'90 U.S. Census- 54,315; E&P '96 Est. 54,090
ABC-CZ (90): 54,315 (HH 21,131)

The Daily Nonpareil (e-mon to fri; m-sat; S)

The Daily Nonpareil, 117 Pearl St., Council Bluffs, IA 51503; tel (712) 328-1811; fax (712) 328-1597. Thomson Newspapers group.
Circulation: 17,342(e); 17,342(m-sat); 19,679(S); ABC Sept. 30, 1995.
Price: 35¢(d); 35¢(sat); $1.25(S); $2.00/wk; $8.00/4wk; $104.00/yr.
Advertising: Open inch rate $16.53(e); $16.53(m-sat); $16.53(S). **Representatives:** Thomson Newspapers; Iowa Newspaper Assn.; Papert Companies.
News Service: AP. **Politics:** Independent. **Established:** 1857.

Not Published: New Year; Memorial Day; Independence Day; Labor Day; Christmas; If holiday falls on Sunday no Monday edition will publish.
Special Editions: Bridal Section, President's Day Sale (Feb); Spring Car Care (Mar); Lawn & Garden, Annual Progress, Outdoor Living (Apr); 4-H Fair Section, Working Women (July); Back-to-School, Fall Sports Preview (Aug); Golden Years (Sept); New Car Care, Home & Energy, Fall Car Care (Oct).
Special Weekly Sections: Best Food Day, Direct Mail (tues); Church News (sat); Business and Farm, TV Preview Magazine (S); Lifestyles Pages, Business Page (daily).
Magazine: USA Weekend (S).

GENERAL MANAGEMENT

Publisher/General Manager	M Joseph Craig
Accountant	Carolyn Bell
Purchasing Agent	Carolyn Bell

ADVERTISING

Manager	Denny Koenders

CIRCULATION

Manager	Fred Riedemann

NEWS EXECUTIVE

Managing Editor	Charles M Gates Jr

EDITORS AND MANAGERS

City Editor	Ruth Hall
Features Editor	Carla Chance
Films/Theater Editor	Tammy Coleman
Music Editor	Tammy Coleman
News Editor	Jon Leu
Sports Editor	Steve Sigafoose
Weekend Editor	Dave Coulton

PRODUCTION

Foreman-Composing	Don Torrez
Foreman-Composing	Dan Eshelman
Foreman-Press	Shawn Story
Foreman-Mailroom	Steve Snook

Market Information: TMC; ADS; Operate audiotex.
Mechanical available: Offset; Black and 3 ROP colors; insert accepted — preprinted; page cutoffs — $22\frac{3}{4}$".
Mechanical specifications: Type page 13" x $21\frac{1}{2}$"; E - 6 cols, $2\frac{1}{16}$", $\frac{1}{8}$" between; A - 6 cols, $2\frac{1}{16}$", $\frac{1}{8}$" between; C - 9 cols, $1\frac{3}{8}$", $\frac{1}{16}$" between.
Commodity consumption: Newsprint 925 short tons; widths $27\frac{1}{2}$", 30", 34", $13\frac{3}{4}$"; black ink 25,000 pounds; color ink 5,000 pounds; single pages printed 7,424; average pages per issue 18(d), 40(S); single plates used 7,000.
Equipment: EDITORIAL: Front-end hardware — 15-Cx; Other equipment — Lf/AP Leaf Picture Desk, Ap/Mac Quadra. CLASSIFIED: Front-end hardware — 4-Cx. DISPLAY: Front-end hardware — 2-Ap/Mac; Front-end software — Aldus/FreeHand 3.1, Aldus/PageMaker 5.0, QuarkXPress 3.3, Broderbund/Typestyler 2.1, Ofoto 2.0; Printers — V/5060W, Tegra/Varityper 4990, Ap/Mac Pro 630, HP/LaserJet 4MV, Ap/Mac IIf; Other equipment — 2-Ap/Mac Scanner, Bernouilli/90 Pro, Micronet/Removable 88. PRODUCTION: Pagination software — QuarkXPress 3.3; OCR software — Caere/OmniPage 3.0; Typesetters — 2-V/4000, Tegra/Varityper/4900, 2-Tegra/Varityper/5060W, Ap/Mac LaserWriter Pro 630, HP/4MV; Platemaking systems — Nat/A-250; Plate exposures — 1-Nu/Flip Top FTU6UPNS; Plate processors — 1-Nu, Nat/A-250; Scanners — Ap/Mac Scanners; Production cameras — 1-SCREEN; Automatic film processors — 1-LE/LD 18.
PRESSROOM: Line 1 — 8-G/Community (3-Color Unit & 1-Stack Unit). MAILROOM: Counter stackers — 1-Toledo/Scale #1938; Inserters and stuffers — 1-Mandelli/Star 100 (paper cutter); Bundle tyer — 1-MLN/Spirit, 1-MLN/SP 300; Addressing machine — 1-Ch/595; Mailroom control system — MM/1511 Stitcher-Trimmer. COMMUNICATIONS: Facsimile — Sharp; Systems used — satellite. WIRE SERVICES: News — AP; Receiving dishes — size-3m, AP. BUSINESS COMPUTERS: 1-NCR/I9020; Applications: Adv, Circ, Payroll; Peachtree: Accts receivable, Accts payable.

CRESTON
Union County

'90 U.S. Census- 7,911; E&P '96 Est. 7,791

Creston News-Advertiser
(e-mon to fri)

Creston News-Advertiser, 503 W. Adams St.; PO Box 126, Creston, IA 50801; tel (515) 782-2141; fax (515) 782-6628. Shaw Newspapers group.
Circulation: 5,632(e); Sworn Sept. 28, 1995.
Price: 50¢(d); $116.50/yr.
Advertising: Open inch rate $6.98(e). **Representative:** Iowa Newspaper Assn.
News Service: AP. **Politics:** Independent. **Established:** 1881.
Not Published: New Year; Memorial Day; Independence Day; Labor Day; Thanksgiving; Christmas.
Special Editions: Wedding (Jan); Progress (Mar); Car Care (Apr); Beef, Graduation (May); Pork, Car Care (Oct); Pre-Christmas (Nov).
Special Weekly Sections: Best Food Day, Farm Page, Business Page (wed); Church Page (thur); TV & Entertainment (fri).

CORPORATE OFFICERS

Chairman of the Board	E K Shaw
President/CEO	Thomas D Shaw
Chief Financial Officer	Phillip E Metka
Vice Pres	Robert A Shaw
Vice Pres	William E Shaw

GENERAL MANAGEMENT

Publisher	Arvid E Huisman
Office Manager	Connie White

ADVERTISING

Director	Roger Lanning

CIRCULATION

Director	Cal Tyer

NEWS EXECUTIVE

Managing Editor	Jeff Young

EDITORS AND MANAGERS

Lifestyle Editor	Rita Miller
Sports Editor	Lance Bergeson

MANAGEMENT INFORMATION SERVICES

Data Processing Manager	Connie White

PRODUCTION

Manager-Press	Dan David
Manager-Composing/Darkroom	Ellen Lang

Market Information: TMC.
Mechanical available: Offset; Black and 3 ROP colors; insert accepted — preprinted; page cutoffs — $22\frac{3}{4}$".
Mechanical specifications: Type page 13" x $21\frac{1}{2}$"; E - 6 cols, 2", $\frac{1}{6}$" between; A - 6 cols, 2", $\frac{1}{6}$" between; C - 9 cols, 1.31", .14" between.
Commodity consumption: Newsprint 330 short tons; widths $27\frac{1}{2}$", 29", 32", 34"; black ink 7,200 pounds; color ink 800 pounds; single pages printed 3,965; average pages per issue 15.5(d); single plates used 4,476.
Equipment: EDITORIAL: Front-end hardware — Ap/Mac; Front-end software — Baseview/NewsEdit, Baseview/QXEdit; Printers — Ap/Mac LaserWriter; Other equipment — Polaroid/SprintScan, AG/Flatbed Scanner. CLASSIFIED: Front-end hardware — Ap/Mac; Front-end software — In-house, Claris/Hypercard. DISPLAY: Front-end hardware — Ap/Mac, Ap/Mac Quadra 605, Ap/Mac Quadra 650; Front-end software — Multi-Ad/Creator; Printers — Ap/Mac LaserWriter. PRODUCTION: OCR software — Text-Bridge; Typesetters — Ap/Mac LaserWriter; Plate exposures — Nu; Scanners — Ap/Mac Scanner, Ap/Mac; Production cameras — B/Caravelle.
PRESSROOM: Line 1 — G/Community single width; Line 2 — G/Community single width; Line 3 — G/Community single width; Line 4 — G/Community single width; Line 5 — G/Community single width; Line 6 — G/Community single width; Folders — G. MAILROOM: Bundle tyer — Bu. WIRE SERVICES: News — AP; Receiving dishes — size-1m, AP. BUSINESS COMPUTERS: 1-Dell/486D 50; Applications: Vision Data; PCs & micros networked; PCs & main system networked.

DAVENPORT-BETTENDORF
Scott County

'90 U.S. Census- 123,465 (Davenport 95,333; Bettendorf 28,132); E&P '96 Est. 120,652 (Davenport 91,444; Bettendorf 29,208)
ABC-CZ (90): 266,693 (HH 105,229)

Quad-City Times
(m-mon to fri; m-sat; S)

Quad-City Times, 500 E. 3rd St.; PO Box 3828, Davenport, IA 52808; tel (319) 383-2200; fax (319) 383-2433. Lee Enterprises Inc. group.
Circulation: 52,777(m); 69,772(m-sat); 81,273(S); ABC Sept. 30, 1995.
Price: 50¢(d); 50¢(sat); $2.00(S); $3.95/wk.
Advertising: Open inch rate $40.65(m); $41.08(m-sat); $44.61(S). **Representative:** Landon Associates Inc.
News Services: AP, LAT-WP. **Established:** 1855.

Iowa I-145

Special Editions: Progress; Cookbook; Bridal; Women's Health; Festival of Trees; Readers Choice; Spring & Fall Fashion; Sports Highlights; Spring Around the House; Summer Fun; Answer Book.
Special Weekly Sections: Outdoor Page, Best Food Day (wed); Travel & Style, Entertainment, Business Section, Home, Outdoor Page (S).
Magazines: Parade; TV Times; Go (Entertainment).
Cable TV: Operate leased cable TV in circulation area.

GENERAL MANAGEMENT

Publisher	Robert A Fusie
Personnel Manager	Jill Dekeyser

ADVERTISING

Manager-National	Michael Gulledge
Manager-Classified	Nancy Kluever
Manager-Retail Sales	Michael Gulledge

MARKETING AND PROMOTION

Director-Marketing	Mark Roby
Manager-Database	Michael Gulledge

TELECOMMUNICATIONS

Audiotex Manager	Michael Gulledge

CIRCULATION

Manager	David Enoch

NEWS EXECUTIVES

Editor	Daniel K Hayes
Assoc Editor	William Wundram

EDITORS AND MANAGERS

Features Editor	Jim Renkes
Illinois Editor	Mark Ridolfi
Iowa Editor	Linda Watson
News Editor	Monte Cox
Opinion Page Editor	Deborah Brasier
Photo Editor	Craig Chandler
Regional Editor	Barb Arland-Fye
Sports Editor	Chris Juzwik

MANAGEMENT INFORMATION SERVICES

Data Processing Manager	Harry Greaves

PRODUCTION

Manager	Steve Baker
Manager-Pressroom	Steve Remley
Supervisor-Mailroom	Steve Gilliland

Market Information: Zoned editions; TMC; Operate database; Operate audiotex.
Mechanical available: Offset; Black and 3 ROP colors; insert accepted — preprinted; page cutoffs — 22".
Mechanical specifications: Type page 13" x 21.35"; E - 6 cols, $2\frac{1}{16}$", $\frac{1}{8}$" between; A - 6 cols, $2\frac{1}{16}$", $\frac{1}{8}$" between; C - 9 cols, $1\frac{3}{8}$", $\frac{1}{16}$" between.
Commodity consumption: Newsprint 6,778 metric tons; widths 54", 41", 27"; black ink 281,000 pounds; color ink 50,000 pounds; single pages printed 16,559; average pages per issue 44(d), 90(S); single plates used 65,500.
Equipment: EDITORIAL: Front-end hardware — HI/PEN, 4-HI/8300, 10-HI/8860. CLASSIFIED: Front-end hardware — Zenith/386, Zenith/486; Front-end software — HI/Cash Sys 3.0, HI/Cash Sys 4.6; DISPLAY: Adv layout systems — 4-DEC/VT-220, 4-HI/8300. PRODUCTION: Typesetters — 1-AU/APS-800, 1-AU/APS-800, 2-AU/APS-108; Platemaking systems — WL; Plate exposures — 1-WL/Lith-X-Pozer, V; Plate processors — 1-RZ/210L; Scanners — ECR/Autokon 1000DE; Production cameras — 1-C/19", 1-Nu/19"; Automatic film processors — 1-LE/LD24A; Shrink lenses — 1-CK Optical/SQU-7; Color separation equipment (conventional) — RZ/210-L.
PRESSROOM: Line 1 — 26-G/Color Liner; Line 2 — 10-G/Community, 18-G/Community; Line 3 — 28-G/Color Liner; Press drives — Allen Bradley; Folders — 6-G/3:2, 2-G/SSC; Pasters — G; Reels and stands — 8-H; Press control system — Allen Bradley. MAILROOM: Counter stackers — 4-Id/2000; Inserters and stuffers — 1-MM/227, 2-H/1372; Bundle tyer — 1-MLN/MLN2A, 1-MLN/MLN2, 3-Power Strap/PSN 5; Addressing machine — 2-CH; Mailroom control system — HI; Other mailroom equipment — MM/Stitcher-Trimmer. LIBRARY: Electronic — SMS. COMMUNICATIONS: Facsimile — Lanier/5600. WIRE SERVICES: News — AP, LAT-WP; Photos — AP; Stock tables — AP; Receiving dishes — size-10ft, AP. BUSINESS COMPUTERS: IBM/AS 400; Applications: Gen ledger, Accts receivable, Accts payable, Adv systems; PCs & micros networked; PCs & main system networked.

DES MOINES
Polk County

'90 U.S. Census- 193,187; E&P '96 Est. 198,977
ABC-NDM (90): 761,887 (HH 293,773)

The Des Moines Register
(m-mon to sat; S)

The Des Moines Register, 715 Locust St.; PO Box 957, Des Moines, IA 50304; tel (515) 284-8000; e-mail letters@desmoine.gannett.com. Gannett Co. Inc. group.
Circulation: 177,857(m); 177,857(m-sat); 302,569(S); ABC Sept. 30, 1995.
Price: 35¢(d); 35¢(sat); $1.50(S); $1.75/wk (m), $1.50/wk (S); $7.00/mo (m), $6.00/mo (S); $91.00/yr (m), $78.00/yr (S).
Advertising: Open inch rate $158.17(m); $158.17(m-sat); $197.60(S). **Representatives:** Iowa Newspaper Assn.; Gannett National Newspaper Sales.
News Services: AP, DJ, LAT-WP, KRT, NYT. **Politics:** Independent. **Established:** 1848.
Special Weekly Sections: Metro Business, School Page/Metro (mon); Food/Today, Neighbors (wed); Datebook (thur); Smart Shopper/Today, Metro Home & Real Estate (fri); Weekend Home/Today, Religion Page/Main News (sat); Opinion, The Big Peach (Sports), Diversions (Arts, Travel & Entertainment), Lifestyle, TV & Cable Guide (S); Main News, Metro & Iowa News, Today, Sports, Business, Opinion (daily).
Magazine: USA Weekend (S).

GENERAL MANAGEMENT

President/Publisher	Charles C Edwards Jr
Vice Pres-Human Resources	Sue Tempero
Vice Pres-Finance	Susan A Smith
Manager-Credit	Mary Gilman
Manager-Research	Sharon Pilmer
Manager-Purchasing	David Haman

ADVERTISING

Vice Pres	Henry C Phillips
Manager-Classified	Patty Keuning
Manager-Retail	Jennifer Vanderpool
Manager-Operations	Nancy J Mann
Supervisor-National	Carolyn Tenney

MARKETING AND PROMOTION

Vice Pres-Marketing	Diane Glass

CIRCULATION

Vice Pres	Terry Thompson
Manager-Golden Circle	Staci Molony
Manager-State	Robert Sharp
Manager-Metro	Sheila Mason
Manager-Sales	Julie Bechtel
Manager-Customer Service	Steve Klaus
Manager-Single Copy Sales	Joe Grochala

NEWS EXECUTIVES

Editor	Dennis Ryerson
Managing Editor	Diane Graham
Deputy Managing Editor	David Rhein
Senior Asst Managing Editor	Michael Pauly
Asst Managing Editor	Randy Evans
Asst Managing Editor-Graphics	Lyle Boone
Newsroom Administration	Vernon Brown

EDITORS AND MANAGERS

Agribusiness/Farm Editor	Jerry Perkins
Art Critic	Eliot Nusbaum
Art Director	Matthew Chatterley
Automotive Editor	Jerry Szumski
Books Editor	Joan Bunke
Business/Finance Editor	Rick Jost
Cartoonist	Brian Duffy
City/Metro Editor	Rob Borsellino
Editorial Page Editor	Richard Doak
Education Reporter	Bob Shaw
Entertainment Editor	Kathy Berdan
Environmental Reporter	Perry Beeman
Fashion/Style Editor	Marie McCartan
Features Editor	Jeanne Abbott
Films/Theatre Editor	Joan Bunke
Finance Columnist	Jim Lawless
Health/Medical Reporter	Tom Carney
Librarian	Phyllis Wolfe
Lifestyle Editor	Cynthia Mitchell
Local Columnist	James M Flansburg
Local Columnist	Chuck Offenburger
Outdoors Editor	Larry Stone
Photography Editor	Karen Mitchell
Political Editor	David Yepsen
Religion Editor	William C Simbro
Science Reporter	Mark Seibert
Systems Editor	Marion Love
Exec Sports Editor	David Witke
Sports Columnist	Marc Hansen
Travel Reporter	Pat Denato
Washington Bureau Chief	George Anthan
Wire Editor	Charles Harpster

Copyright ©1996 by the Editor & Publisher Co.

MANAGEMENT INFORMATION SERVICES

Manager-Info Services Dee Wilson

PRODUCTION

Vice Pres J Austin Ryan
Manager-Press/Newsprint Bill J Ghee
Manager-Mailroom Cleon McMahon
Manager-Facility Bill Brown
Manager-Pre Press Michael Morlan

Market Information: Zoned editions; Split Run; TMC.
Mechanical available: Letterpress; Black and 3 ROP colors; insert accepted — preprinted; page cut-offs — $23\frac{9}{16}$".
Mechanical specifications: Type page 13" x $22\frac{1}{4}$"; E - 6 cols, $2\frac{1}{16}$", $\frac{1}{8}$" between; A - 6 cols, $2\frac{1}{16}$", $\frac{1}{8}$" between; C - 10 cols, $1\frac{3}{16}$", $\frac{1}{8}$" between.
Commodity consumption: Newsprint 28,659 short tons; 26,000 metric tons; width $54\frac{1}{2}$"; black ink 1,456,000 pounds; color ink 78,000 pounds; single pages printed 20,097; average pages per issue 46(d), 102(S); single plates used 260,000.
Equipment: EDITORIAL: Front-end hardware — Tandem/CLX 740; Front-end software — SII; Printers — Hyphen/Dash 600, Ap/Mac LaserWriter, HP/LaserJet, X/Diablo 11810; Other equipment — Ap/Mac, SII/Coyote 110. CLASSIFIED: Front-end hardware — Tandem/CLX740; Front-end software — SII; Printers — SII; Other equipment — ROLM. DISPLAY: Adv layout systems — CJ; Front-end hardware — HP/3000 Series 937, Ap/Macs, Sun/630S; Front-end software — CJ/LAYOUT, DTI/AdSpeed, Hyphen; Printers — 2-QMS, Tektronix/Phaser, HP/LaserJet. PRODUCTION: Typesetters — 2-AU/APS Micro 5, 2-Cx/Bitsetter, 1-ECR/Autokon 1000 DE, 2-AG/Accuset 1000, 1-III/3850 Grafix Color Imager; Platemaking systems — Na; Plate exposures — 2-Titan/III, 1-Va/Starlite; Plate processors — 2-Na/NP-120, 1-Na/NP-20; Electronic picture desk — Lf/AP Leaf Picture Desk; Scanners — Horizon/Color, 2-X/7650, Kk, Lf/Leafscan 35, ECR; Production cameras — 1-C/Newspager, 1-C/Spartan III; Automatic film processors — 2-LE/Excel 26, 2-LE/CMX26, 1-LE/LD 2600A, 2-LE/LS-2100RL; Film transporters — 2-Konica, 2-LE; Color separation equipment (conventional) — RZ/200S.
PRESSROOM: Line 1 — 14-G/Mark I; Line 2 — 8-G/Mark I; Line 3 — 8-H/Colormatic; Press drives — 2-Fin, 2-Cline; Folders — 3-G/Double, 1-H/Double; Pasters — 22-G/RPT, 8-H/Automatic; Press control system — Fin, Cline. MAILROOM: Counter stackers — 13-QWI, 3-Id, 7-HL/SH; Inserters and stuffers — 1-S/8-48, 2-HI/13-72, 1-NP/630-26; Bundle tyer — 8-MLN/2A, 2-PowerStrap, 2-Sterling; Addressing machine — 1-AVY/Labler 5209. LIBRARY: Electronic — Data Times/full-text; Combination — CD-Rom/on News Bank. WIRE SERVICES: News — Tribune, LAT-WP, KRT, NYT, GNS, RN, Bloomberg; Photos — AP; Stock tables — TMS; Syndicates — NAS, NYT, Universal Press, Limited Media, TMS, United Media; Receiving dishes — AP, RN. BUSINESS COMPUTERS: 1-HP/3000 Series 937, 1-HP/3000 Series 957; Applications: Circ, Payroll, Personnel, Adv, Accts payable, Gen ledger; PCs & micros networked; PCs & main system networked.

DUBUQUE, IA-EAST DUBUQUE, IL

Dubuque County, IA
Daviess County, IL

'90 U.S. Census- 59,460 (Dubuque, IA 57,546; East Dubuque, IL 1,914); E&P '96 Est. 57,002 (Dubuque, IA 55,204; East Dubuque, IL 1,798)
ABC-CZ (90): 59,460 (HH 22,226)

Telegraph Herald

(e-mon to fri; m-sat; S)

Telegraph Herald, 801 Bluff St.; PO Box 688, Dubuque, IA 52004-0688; tel (319) 588-5611; fax (319) 588-5739; e-mail dubuqueth@ad.com.
Circulation: 30,581(e); 30,581(m-sat); 36,052(S); ABC Sept. 30, 1995.
Price: 50¢(d); 50¢(sat); $1.50(S); $3.25/wk; $156.00/yr.
Advertising: Open inch rate $24.35(e); $24.35(m-sat); $26.30(S). **Representatives:** Papert Companies; Iowa Newspaper Assn.
News Service: AP. **Politics:** Independent. **Established:** 1836.
Special Editions: Chronology (Jan); Baby Register (Feb); Home Builders Show (Mar); Spring Fashion, Home & Garden (Apr); Pets, Vacationland (May); Graduation, Health Care (June); Back-to-School, Fall Football-High School (Aug); Health & Fitness, Home Improvement (Sept); Home Interiors (Oct); Holiday Guide to Gifts & Events (Nov); Downtown Dubuque Gift Guide; Last Minute Gift Guide.
Special Weekly Sections: Your Money, Health (mon); Our World, Family, Nostalgia, Images, Fashion (tues); Food (wed); Arts & Entertainment (thur); Arts & Entertainment, TV Times (fri); Religion (sat); Travel, Business, Agriculture, Home, Garden, Books, Lifestyles (S).
Magazine: USA Weekend (S).
Broadcast Affiliates: KDTH-AM/KATF-FM Dubuque, IA; WHBY-AM/WAPL-FM Appleton, WI.

CORPORATE OFFICERS

Board Chairman F Robert Woodward Jr
President William Skemp
Senior Vice Pres Craig Trongaard
Treasurer Grady Ivy

GENERAL MANAGEMENT

Vice Pres/Publisher Thomas A Yunt

ADVERTISING

Director Jim Hart
Manager-Retail Teri Upstrom
Manager-Classified Michelle Lester

MARKETING AND PROMOTION

Director-Promotion Connie Gibbs

TELECOMMUNICATIONS

Audiotex Manager Dean Millius

CIRCULATION

Director Steven Swails

NEWS EXECUTIVES

Exec Editor Brian Cooper
Managing Editor Soren Nielsen

EDITORS AND MANAGERS

City Editor Amy Gilligan
Asst City Editor Donnelle Eller
Editorial Page Editor Brian Cooper
Features Editor Jim Swenson
Food Editor Gary Dura
Photography Manager Mark Hirsch
Sports Editor Renny Zentz
Television Editor Jon Tibbetts

PRODUCTION

Director-Operations Don Hansen
Manager-Pre Press Ken Smith
Manager-Pressroom Donald McCarthy
Manager-Mailroom Joe Shultz

Market Information: Zoned editions; TMC; Operate audiotex.
Mechanical available: Offset; Black and 3 ROP colors; insert accepted — preprinted, single sheet 60lb minimum weight; page cut-offs — $22\frac{3}{4}$".
Mechanical specifications: Type page $13\frac{1}{2}$" x $21\frac{3}{4}$"; E - 6 cols, $2\frac{1}{16}$", $\frac{1}{8}$" between; A - 6 cols, $2\frac{1}{16}$", $\frac{1}{8}$" between; C - 8 cols, $1\frac{9}{16}$", $\frac{1}{16}$" between.
Commodity consumption: Newsprint 1,910 metric tons; widths 58", 55"; black ink 59,900 pounds; color ink 23,400 pounds; single pages printed 10,639; average pages per issue 26(d), 54(S); single plates used 26,400.
Equipment: EDITORIAL: Front-end hardware — DEC/486 PC Workstations, DEC/VAX 105A servers; Front-end software — Dewar/DewarView, Microsoft/Word 6.0, QuarkXPress 3.3; Printers — QMS/860, Ap/Mac LaserPro 630. CLASSIFIED: Front-end hardware — 2-CSI/1184; Front-end software — CSI; Printers — DEC/LA 120. AUDIOTEX: Supplier name — Interactive Media, Cedar Rapids, IA. DISPLAY: Adv layout systems — Mk/Ad Director; Front-end hardware — Ap/Mac Quadra 800s, 2-DEC/VAX 4000 105A servers, CSI, CJ; Front-end software — QuarkXPress 3.3, Adobe/Illustrator, Adobe/Photoshop; Printers — QMS/860, Tektronics. PRODUCTION: Pagination software — QuarkXPress 3.3; OCR software — Caere/OmniPage 5.0; Typesetters — 2-AU/APS Micro 5, 2-AU/APS-7; Plate exposures — 2-Nu/Flip Top (2pg); Plate processors — 1-WL/30C; Electronic picture desk — Nikon, Kk/Scanners, Adobe/Photoshop 5.0, 4-Ap/Mac Quadra 950; Scanners — Sharp/Flatbed scanner, ECR/ Autokon 1000DE, AG/Horizon Plus, 5-AG/Arcus II; Production cameras — 1-R, 1-C; Automatic film processors — 1-LE; Color separation equipment (conventional) — Adobe/Photoshop 5.0.
PRESSROOM: Line 1 — 4-G/Metro (2 Half decks); Press drives — Fin; Folders — 1-G/2:1; Pasters — 4-G; Reels and stands — 4-G. MAILROOM: Counter stackers — 1-MM, 1-MM; Inserters and stuffers — 1-MM; Bundle tyer — 1-MLN, 1-MLN; Addressing machine — 1-Ch/4-Up. WIRE SERVICES: News — AP; Stock tables — AP; Syndicates — NEA, KRT; Receiving dishes — size-10ft, AP. BUSINESS COMPUTERS: 1-DEC/2060; PCs & micros networked; PCs & main system networked.

ESTHERVILLE

Emmet County

'90 U.S. Census- 6,720; E&P '96 Est. 6,415

Estherville Daily News

(m-mon, wed, thur, sat)

Estherville Daily News, 10 N. 7th St., Estherville, IA 51334; tel (712) 362-2622; fax (712) 362-2624. Ogden Newspapers group.
Circulation: 2,006(m); 2,006(m-sat); Sworn Sept. 30, 1995.
Price: 35¢(d); 35¢(sat); $60.00/yr.
Advertising: Open inch rate $7.55(m); $7.55(m-sat). **Representative:** Iowa Newspaper Assn. **Politics:** Independent. **Established:** 1930.
Not Published: New Year; Memorial Day; Independence Day; Labor Day; Thanksgiving; Christmas.
Special Editions: Home Improvement; Car Care; Agricultural Fair; Weddings; Tax Time; Graduation; Homecoming; Summer Sports Festival; Christmas Gifts; Winter Sports Festival; Farm & Home Show; Medical Directory.
Special Weekly Sections: Business (wed); Best Food Day, Religion, TV Spotlight (thur); Farm (sat); Comics, Entertainment, Family, Sports (daily).
Magazines: Estherville Spirit (TMC) (tues); TV Update (thur).

GENERAL MANAGEMENT

General Manager Ronald L Menendez

ADVERTISING

Director Ronald L Menendez

CIRCULATION

Director Tammy Andrews

NEWS EXECUTIVE

Managing Editor Ronald L Menendez

EDITORS AND MANAGERS

Editorial Page Editor David Swartz
Social Editor Bernice Blom
Sports Editor Greg Nath

Market Information: TMC; ADS.
Mechanical available: Offset; Black and 3 ROP colors; insert accepted — preprinted.
Mechanical specifications: Type page 13" x $21\frac{1}{2}$"; E - 6 cols, $2\frac{1}{16}$", $\frac{1}{8}$" between; A - 6 cols, $2\frac{1}{16}$", $\frac{1}{8}$" between; C - 6 cols, 2", $\frac{1}{16}$" between.
Commodity consumption: average pages per issue 8(d).
Equipment: EDITORIAL: Front-end hardware — Ap/Mac Classic; Front-end software — WriteNow; Printers — Ap/Mac LaserWriter II; Other equipment — 7-COM/MDT 350. CLASSIFIED: Front-end hardware — 2-Ap/Mac LC; Front-end software — QuarkXPress; Printers — Ap/Mac LaserWriter II. DISPLAY: Front-end hardware — 2-Ap/Mac LC; Front-end software — QuarkXPress; Printers — Ap/Mac LaserWriter II. PRODUCTION: Typesetters — Ap/Mac LaserWriter II.
COMMUNICATIONS: Facsimile — Canon. WIRE SERVICES: News — Syndicates — TMS. BUSINESS COMPUTERS: PCs & micros networked.

EVANSDALE

See WATERLOO

FAIRFIELD

Jefferson County

'90 U.S. Census- 9,768; E&P '96 Est. 10,178

The Fairfield Ledger

(e-mon to fri)

The Fairfield Ledger, 112 E. Broadway, Fairfield, IA 52556; tel (515) 472-4129; fax (515) 472-1916. Inland Industries Inc. group.
Circulation: 4,017(e); Sworn Sept. 22, 1995.
Price: 50¢(d); $1.75/wk (carrier).
Advertising: Open inch rate $7.22(e). **Representative:** Iowa Newspaper Assn.
News Service: AP. **Politics:** Independent. **Established:** 1849.
Not Published: New Year; Memorial Day; Independence Day; Labor Day; Thanksgiving; Christmas.
Special Editions: Faces & Places (Jan); Bridal (Feb); Conservation (Mar); Home Improvement (Apr); Beef Month (May); Parsons College Reunion (June); Fiesta Days (July); Back-to-School (Aug); Pork Month (Oct).
Special Weekly Sections: Best Food Day (tues); Farm Page (wed); Business (thur); Religion (fri).

CORPORATE OFFICERS

President Darwin K Sherman
Vice Pres/Secretary Darwin K Sherman
Treasurer Jack Burton

GENERAL MANAGEMENT

Publisher Jeff Wilson

ADVERTISING

Manager Gene Luedtke
Manager-Classified Tara Worley

CIRCULATION

Manager Jeffrey Crile

EDITORS AND MANAGERS

Editorial Page Editor William L Draper
News Editor William L Draper
Society Editor Martha Jacobs
Sports Editor Matt Brindley

PRODUCTION

Superintendent Mark Bradley

Market Information: Zoned editions; TMC.
Mechanical available: Offset; Black and 3 ROP colors; insert accepted — preprinted; page cut-offs — $22\frac{3}{4}$".
Mechanical specifications: Type page 13" x $21\frac{1}{2}$"; E - 6 cols, $2\frac{1}{16}$", $\frac{1}{8}$" between; A - 6 cols, $2\frac{1}{16}$", $\frac{1}{8}$" between; C - 8 cols, $1\frac{1}{2}$", $\frac{1}{8}$" between.
Commodity consumption: Newsprint 190 short tons; widths 28", 34"; black ink 5,400 pounds; color ink 1,000 pounds; single pages printed 5,154; average pages per issue 12(d).
Equipment: EDITORIAL: Front-end hardware — Mk. DISPLAY: Adv layout systems — 2-Page Monitor, 1-Ap/Mac II. PRODUCTION: Typesetters — 3-COM; Plate exposures — 1-Nu; Production cameras — 1-K/241; Automatic film processors — 1-P.
PRESSROOM: Line 1 — 5-G/Community; Folders — 1-G/Community, 1-G/Gregg Plow. MAILROOM: Bundle tyer — 1-Sa; Addressing machine — St/1600 Labeling Machine. WIRE SERVICES: News — AP; Receiving dishes — AP. BUSINESS COMPUTERS: Tandy/3000; Applications: Accounting, Circ.

FORT DODGE

Webster County

'90 U.S. Census- 25,894; E&P '96 Est. 24,682
ABC-CZ (90): 25,894 (HH 10,502)

The Messenger

(m-mon to sat; S)

The Messenger, 713 Central Ave.; PO Box 659, Fort Dodge, IA 50501; tel (515) 573-2141, (800) 622-6613; fax (515) 573-2148. Ogden Newspapers group.
Circulation: 19,696(m); 19,696(m-sat); 21,964(S); ABC Sept. 30, 1995.
Price: 50¢(d); 50¢(sat); $1.00(S); $2.00/wk; $104.00/yr, $39.00/yr (S only).
Advertising: Open inch rate $25.26(m); $25.26(m-sat); $25.26(S). **Representatives:** Papert Companies; Iowa Newspaper Assn.
News Service: AP. **Politics:** Independent-Republican. **Established:** 1856.
Special Editions: Bride Tab, Citywide Clearance, Iowa Corn (Jan); Baby Register, Crime Prevention (Feb); Coupon, Farm Preview (Mar); Golf, Fishing (Apr); Mother's Day Gift Spotter, Fort Dodge Visitor's Guide, Graduation Tab, Transportation (May); Draw Your Dad, Summer Living Tab, Coupon Book, Frontier Days (June); Little League Tab, Health & Fitness, Iowa Soybean, Webster County Fair (July); Girls Softball Tourney, Football Area Tab, Back-to-School (Aug); Progress, Skydiver's Booklet, Weekly Football Contest (Sept); Get Ready For Winter/Car Care, Red Ribbon Week, Coupon Book (Oct); Christmas Countdown, Thanksgiving, Holiday Cookbook, Winter Sports Tab (Nov); Holiday Greetings, The Year in Review (Dec); Senior Citizen Tab, Business Review, Real Estate Buyer's Guide (monthly).
Special Weekly Sections: Education Page (mon); Religion (sat); Best Food Day, Farm, Business (S).
Magazines: This is Entertainment Guide/TV Program Listings, Color Comics (S); Parade.

Copyright ©1996 by the Editor & Publisher Co.

Iowa I-147

CORPORATE OFFICER

President G Ogden Nutting

GENERAL MANAGEMENT

Publisher/General Manager Larry D Bushman

ADVERTISING

Director Tim Craig

CIRCULATION

Director Galen Bremmer

NEWS EXECUTIVES

Editor Larry W Johnson
Editor-Emeritus Walter B Stevens

EDITORS AND MANAGERS

Book/Travel Editor Larry W Johnson
Business Editor Barbara Wallace Hughes
City/Metro Editor Larry W Johnson
Editorial Page Editor Larry W Johnson
Entertainment/Amusements Editor Leslie Drollinger
Environmental Editor Larry W Johnson
Farm Editor Barbara Wallace Hughes
Fashion/Style Editor Kris Hillmer-Pierson
Features Editor Larry W Johnson
Graphics Editor/Art Director Larry W Johnson
Lifestyle Editor Kris Hillmer-Pierson
National Editor Larry W Johnson
News Editor Larry W Johnson
Outdoor Editor Bill McIntyre
Photo Editor Tim Hynds
Political/Government Editor Larry W Johnson
Religion Editor Kara Hildreth
Sports Editor Bill McIntyre
Television/Film Editor Leslie Drollinger
Theater/Music Editor Leslie Drollinger

MANAGEMENT INFORMATION SERVICES

Data Processing Manager Rex Lee

Market Information: TMC; ADS.
Mechanical available: Offset; Black and 3 ROP colors; insert accepted — preprinted; page cut-offs — 22$\frac{3}{4}$".
Mechanical specifications: Type page 13" x 21$\frac{1}{2}$"; E - 6 cols, 2$\frac{1}{16}$", $\frac{1}{8}$" between; A - 6 cols, 2$\frac{1}{16}$", $\frac{1}{8}$" between; C - 9 cols, 1$\frac{3}{8}$", $\frac{1}{16}$" between.
Commodity consumption: Newsprint 1,289 short tons; width 27"; black ink 29,490 pounds; color ink 10,552 pounds; single pages printed 11,039; average pages per issue 26(d), 48(S); single plates used 10,724.
Equipment: EDITORIAL: Front-end hardware — SII, Ap/Power Mac 7100-80, 4-Ap/Power Mac 6100-66, Workgroup Server/6150; Front-end software — QuarkXPress 3.31, Adobe/Photoshop 3.0; Printers — TI/810, 2-HP/LaserJet 4MV; Other equipment — Ap/Mac Classic, Lf/AP Leaf Picture Desk, Lf/Leafscan 35. CLASSIFIED: Front-end hardware — SII; Printers — TI/810. DISPLAY: Adv layout systems — 1-Ap/Mac Quadra 700, 3-Ap/Power Mac 6100-60; Front-end software — Multi-Ad/Creator 3.7; Printers — HP/LaserJet 4MV. PRODUCTION: Pagination software — QuarkXPress 3.31; OCR software — Caere/OmniPage Professional 5.0; Typesetters — 1-Ap/Mac Quadra 700, 3-Ap/Power Mac 6100-60; Plate exposures — 1-Nu; Plate processors — 1-WL; Scanners — HP/ScanJet IIc, Nikon/Coolscan; Production cameras — 1-C/Spartan II, 1-DAT; Automatic film processors — 1-P; Film transporters — 1-C/Spartan II.
PRESSROOM: Line 1 — 12-G/Suburban; Folders — 1-G/3:2, 1-G/SU, 1-G/Quarter; Pasters — 8-Martin/EC Splicer. MAILROOM: Counter stackers — 2-BG/108, 2-Id/NS660, 1-HI/RS25; Inserters and stuffers — HI/1372; Bundle tyer — 2-Bu; Wrapping singles — 3-MLN/ML2EES; Addressing machine — 1-KR, 1-Ch. WIRE SERVICES: News — AP; Photos — AP; Stock tables — TMS; Receiving dishes — AP. BUSINESS COMPUTERS: NCR; Applications: Adv billing, Accts receivable, Gen ledger, Circ; PCs & main system networked.

FORT MADISON

Lee County

'90 U.S. Census- 11,618; E&P '96 Est. 10,926

The Daily Democrat (e-mon to fri)

The Daily Democrat, 1226 Ave. H; PO Box 160, Fort Madison, IA 52627; tel (319) 372-6421; fax (319) 372-3867. Brehm Communications Inc group.
Circulation: 6,238(e); Sworn Sept. 29, 1995.
Price: 50¢(d); $5.75/4wk, $15.75/12wk; $68.25/yr.
Advertising: Open inch rate $8.40(e). **Representative:** Iowa Newspaper Assn.
News Service: AP. **Politics:** Independent. **Established:** 1868.
Not Published: New Year; Memorial Day; Independence Day; Labor Day; Thanksgiving; Christmas.
Special Editions: Bridal Tab, Senior Lifestyles (Jan); Home Improvement, Car Care, Senior Lifestyles (Apr); Vacation, Graduation (May); Fair Tab, Senior Lifestyles (July); Tri-State Rodeo, Octoberfest, Home Improvement (Sept); Industry, Senior Lifestyles, Car Care (Oct).
Special Weekly Sections: Weekend Sports Wrap-Up (mon); Farm Page (tues); Business Page (wed); Entertainment (thur); Weekend Sports Preview (fri).
Magazine: Channels ($\frac{1}{4}$ fold TV booklet).

CORPORATE OFFICER

President William D DeLost

GENERAL MANAGEMENT

Publisher John Lowman
Manager-Accounting Mary Older

ADVERTISING

Director Danna Campbell

CIRCULATION

Manager Pat Kurtz

NEWS EXECUTIVE

Editor Robin Delaney

EDITORS AND MANAGERS

City Government Kris Bernhardt
Photographer Chuck Vanderberg
School Editor Tracey Lamm
Sports Editor Chris Faulkner
Woman's Editor Christie Holtkamp

MANAGEMENT INFORMATION SERVICES

Data Processing Manager Mary Older

PRODUCTION

Superintendent Tom Hazelwood
Foreman-Composing Renee Schofield

Market Information: TMC.
Mechanical available: Offset; Black and 3 ROP colors; insert accepted — preprinted; page cut-offs — 22$\frac{3}{4}$".
Mechanical specifications: Type page 13" x 21$\frac{1}{2}$"; E - 6 cols, 2$\frac{1}{16}$", $\frac{1}{8}$" between; A - 8 cols, 1$\frac{1}{2}$", $\frac{1}{8}$" between; C - 8 cols, 1$\frac{1}{2}$", $\frac{1}{8}$" between.
Commodity consumption: Newsprint 870 metric tons; widths 27$\frac{1}{2}$", 13$\frac{3}{4}$", 34", 17"; black ink 20,000 pounds; color ink 2,000 pounds; single pages printed 4,700; average pages per issue 14(d); single plates used 7,000.
Equipment: EDITORIAL: Front-end hardware — 1-Ap/Mac 7100, Ap/Mac Quadra 630; Front-end software — DragX, QuarkXPress, Baseview/Qtools, Baseview/NewsEdit Pro; Printers — 1-COM/8400, NewGen/Laser Printer. CLASSIFIED: Front-end hardware — Ap/Mac Quadra 630; Front-end software — Baseview/Classmanager; Printers — COM/8400, NewGen/Laser Printer; Other equipment — Okidata/320 Microline Printer. DISPLAY: Adv layout systems — 1-Ap/Power Mac 7100; Front-end hardware — Ap/Mac; Front-end software — QuarkXPress, Baseview, Adobe/Photoshop; Printers — COM/8400, NewGen, Tektronix Phaser III PXI Color. PRODUCTION: Pagination software — QuarkXPress, Baseview/Qtools, DragX; Typesetters — 1-Ap/Power Mac 8150 Fileserver w/Apple Remote Access, NewGen, Panther/Plus, Tektronix/Phaser III, Color Proofer; Platemaking systems — 1-Nu; Plate exposures — 1-Nu; Plate processors — Roconex; Scanners — Lf/Leafscan 35, Umax/Power Look; Production cameras — Acti; Automatic film processors — AG/Rapidline 43; Digital color separation equipment — Ap/Power Mac 8100, Lf/Leafscan, Umax/PowerLook, Tektronix/Phaser III Color Proofer, Panther/Plus Imagesetter.
PRESSROOM: Line 1 — 8-G/Community; Folders — 1-G; Pasters — BG/Acumeter. MAILROOM: Bundle tyer — Bu, MLN/Strappers; Addressing machine — Wm; Other mailroom equipment — Challenge/3 Knife Trimmer. LIBRARY: Electronic — Baseview, Sonar. COMMUNICATIONS: Facsimile — Omnifax/L 140. WIRE SERVICES: News — AP; Stock tables — AP; Syndicates — King Features, Universal Press; Receiving dishes — AP. BUSINESS COMPUTERS: Qantel; Applications: Quatro Pro, Word Prefect, Microsoft/Windows; PCs & micros networked; PCs & main system networked.

IOWA CITY

Johnson County

'90 U.S. Census- 59,734; E&P '96 Est. 65,848
ABC-CZ (90): 71,127 (HH 27,030)

Iowa City Press-Citizen (e-mon to sat)

Iowa City Press-Citizen, 1725 N. Dodge, Iowa City, IA 52245; tel (319) 337-3181; fax (319) 339-7342. Gannett Co. Inc. group.
Circulation: 16,074(e); 16,074(e-sat); ABC Sept. 30, 1995.
Price: 35¢(d); 50¢(sat); $9.00/4wk.
Advertising: Open inch rate $25.31(e); $25.31(e-sat). **Representative:** Gannett National Newspaper Sales.
News Services: AP, GNS. **Politics:** Independent. **Established:** 1841.
Special Editions: Brides, Chamber of Commerce Chronicle (Feb); Fifty Something, Coralville Profile (Mar); Reader's Choice, Spring Decorating and Remodeling, Get-away Travel Guide (Apr); Home Interiors, Discover the Heartland (June); Iowa Festival, Special Report (July); The Key (Aug); Football Weekend, U I Welcome, Iowa Family (Sept); Hospice Pre-Road Race, Fall Home, Careers, Recreation Guide (Oct); Hospice Post Road Race, U I Homecoming, Tune-Up, Holiday Guide I, Holiday Guide II, Holiday Guide III (Nov); Holiday Guide IV.
Special Weekly Sections: Weddings/Engagements, Arts/Entertainment (mon); Travel, Weddings/Engagements (tues); Food, Marketplace, Arts/Entertainment (wed); Health, Info to Go, Real Estate, Outdoor/Recreation (thur); Church News, Arts/Entertainment (fri); Channels (sat); Business (daily).
Magazine: USA Weekend (sat).

CORPORATE OFFICERS

President/Publisher Charles T Wanninger
Secretary Thomas L Chapple
Treasurer Lawrence P Gasho

GENERAL MANAGEMENT

Publisher Charles T Wanninger
Controller Paula L Flom
Director-Human Resources Maria Roth

ADVERTISING

Director Diana White
Manager-Classified Michele McCoy
Manager-Retail Renee Uthoff

MARKETING AND PROMOTION

Director-Marketing Service Dan Brown

CIRCULATION

Director Gary Schmadeke

NEWS EXECUTIVE

Managing Editor Dan Hogan

EDITORS AND MANAGERS

City Editor Susan Gage
Editorial Page Editor Sam Osborne
News Editor Jennifer Kauss
Sports Editor Steve Riley

MANAGEMENT INFORMATION SERVICES

Data Processing Manager Jim Tvedte

PRODUCTION

Director Barb Joseph
Manager-Pressroom David J Cilek
Manager-Service Chris Hayes

Market Information: TMC.
Mechanical available: Offset; Black and 3 ROP colors; insert accepted — preprinted; page cut-offs — 22$\frac{3}{4}$".
Mechanical specifications: Type page 13" x 21$\frac{1}{4}$"; E - 6 cols, 2$\frac{1}{16}$", $\frac{1}{8}$" between; A - 6 cols, 2$\frac{1}{16}$", $\frac{1}{8}$" between; C - 9 cols, 1$\frac{3}{8}$", $\frac{1}{16}$" between.
Commodity consumption: Newsprint 1,055 short tons; width 27$\frac{1}{2}$"; black ink 25,520 pounds; color ink 7,400 pounds; single pages printed 10,406; average pages per issue 30(d); single plates used 14,351.
Equipment: EDITORIAL: Front-end hardware — 1-Dewar/Disc Net. CLASSIFIED: Front-end hardware — 1-Dewar/Disc Net; Other equipment — 4-Dewar/Discribe. DISPLAY: Front-end hardware — 2-Ap/Power Mac 8100, 1-Ap/Mac Quadra 630; Front-end software — QuarkXPress, Multi-Ad/Creator; Printers — HP/LaserJet 4MV. PRODUCTION: Typesetters — 2-COM/8600 S; Plate exposures — Nu/Flip Top FT40APRNS; Plate processors — Nat/A-340; Scanners — Diadem/200S Direct Screen; Production cameras — 1-C/Spartan II, 1-Ik; Automatic film processors — 1-LE/LD18A.
PRESSROOM: Line 1 — 14-G/Urbanite 1000 Series; Folders — 1-G; Reels and stands — Ebway; Press control system — Ross, G/PAR. MAILROOM: Counter stackers — QWI/300 Wall Monitor; Inserters and stuffers — Mueller/227; Bundle tyer — 1-MLN/2EE; Wrapping singles — QWI/Underwrap; Addressing machine — Ch; Other mailroom equipment — MM/1509 Minute Man. WIRE SERVICES: News — AP, GNS; Receiving dishes — AP. BUSINESS COMPUTERS: IBM/AS-400; PCs & micros networked; PCs & main system networked.

KEOKUK

Lee County

'90 U.S. Census- 12,451; E&P '96 Est. 11,924

Daily Gate City (e-mon to fri)

Daily Gate City, 1016 Main St.; PO Box 430, Keokuk, IA 52632; tel (319) 524-8300; fax (319) 524-4363. Brehm Communications Inc group.
Circulation: 5,666(e); Sworn Sept. 29, 1995.
Price: 50¢(d); $68.25/yr (city); $74.00/yr (motor route).
Advertising: Open inch rate $8.80(e). **Representative:** Iowa Newspaper Assn.
News Service: AP. **Politics:** Independent. **Established:** 1847.
Not Published: New Year; Memorial Day; Independence Day; Thanksgiving; Christmas.
Special Editions: Bridal (Jan); Progress (Feb); Farm Section, Spring Car Care (Mar); Real Estate, Home Improvement (Apr); Graduation, Mother's Day, Newcomers and Vacation (May); Father's Day (June); Back-to-School, Labor Day (Aug); Football Tab, Fall Car Care (Sept); Woman, Health and Fitness (Oct); Social Security & 60 Plus, Winter Sports, Early Shopper's Guide (Nov); Last Minute Gift Guide, Chronology, First Baby (Dec).
Magazine: TV Magazine (fri).

CORPORATE OFFICERS

President William D DeLost
Vice Pres W J Brehm
Secretary Mona M Brehm

GENERAL MANAGEMENT

Publisher William D DeLost

ADVERTISING

Director William D DeLost

TELECOMMUNICATIONS

Manager-Telemarketing Debbie Andrews

CIRCULATION

Director Pat Kurtz

NEWS EXECUTIVE

Managing Editor Buzz Ball

Market Information: TMC; ADS.
Mechanical available: Offset; Black and 3 ROP colors; insert accepted — preprinted; page cut-offs — 22$\frac{3}{4}$".
Mechanical specifications: Type page 13$\frac{1}{4}$" x 21$\frac{1}{2}$"; E - 6 cols, 2$\frac{1}{16}$", $\frac{1}{16}$" between; A - 8 cols, 1$\frac{1}{2}$", $\frac{1}{8}$" between; C - 8 cols, 1$\frac{1}{2}$", $\frac{1}{8}$" between.
Commodity consumption: Newsprint 500 short tons; width 27$\frac{1}{2}$"; average pages per issue 13(d).
Equipment: EDITORIAL: Front-end hardware — Ap/Mac; Front-end software — Baseview. CLASSIFIED: Front-end hardware — Ap/Mac; Front-end software — Baseview. DISPLAY: Adv layout systems — 3-Ap/Mac 7100; Front-end hardware — Ap/Mac; Printers — LaserMaster/Unity 1200. PRODUCTION: Pagination software — Baseview; Typesetters — 2-NewGen/Laser, 1-LaserMaster/Unity 1200; Production cameras — 1-R/24580; Automatic film processors — 1-AG/Rapidline 43; Color separation equipment (conventional) — Ap/Mac 8100 w/Photoshop. MAILROOM: Bundle tyer — MLN/2EE. WIRE SERVICES: News — AP; Receiving dishes — size-2ft, AP. BUSINESS COMPUTERS: Qantel; Applications: Circ, TMC, Business; PCs & micros networked; PCs & main system networked.

LE MARS

Plymouth County

'90 U.S. Census- 8,454; E&P '96 Est. 8,745

Le Mars Daily Sentinel (e-mon to fri)

Le Mars Daily Sentinel, 41 First Ave. N.E.; PO Box 930, Le Mars, IA 51031; tel (712) 546-7031; fax (712) 546-7035. USMedia Inc. group.
Circulation: 4,008(e); Sworn Sept. 30, 1994.
Price: 50¢(d); $90.00/yr (in county), $108.00/yr (surrounding states), $175.00/yr (out of state).
Advertising: Open inch rate $6.90(e). **Representative:** Iowa Newspaper Assn.
News Service: AP. **Politics:** Independent. **Established:** 1870, 1958 (daily).
Not Published: Legal holidays.
Special Editions: Bridal, Corn Tab (Jan); Senior Lifestyle (Feb); Family-owned Business

I-148 Iowa

(Mar); Beef & Dairy, Seniors Lifestyle (May); Pride in Plymouth County (June); County Fair (July); Back-to-School, Senior Lifestyle (Aug); America at Work, Pork (Sept); What's in a House, Industry Awarenes (Oct); Senior Lifestyle (Nov).
Magazine: Agriculture (tues).

CORPORATE OFFICER
President Eugene A Mace

GENERAL MANAGEMENT
Publisher Tom Schmitt
Business Manager Joyce Kneip

ADVERTISING
Director Kevin Hook

CIRCULATION
Manager Scott Harwick

EDITOR AND MANAGER
News Editor John Buntsma

MANAGEMENT INFORMATION SERVICES
Data Processing Manager Joyce Kneip

PRODUCTION
Superintendent Gary Jungers

Market Information: TMC.
Mechanical available: Offset; Black and 3 ROP colors; insert accepted — preprinted; page cut-offs — 22¾".
Mechanical specifications: Type page 13" x 21½"; E - 6 cols, 2¹⁄₁₆", ⅛" between; A - 6 cols, 2¹⁄₁₆", ⅛" between; C - 6 cols, 2¹⁄₁₆", ⅛" between.
Commodity consumption: Newsprint 410 short tons; widths 34", 17", 28", 14"; average pages per issue 13(d).
Equipment: EDITORIAL: Front-end hardware — Ap/Mac; Front-end software — Ready-Set-Go; Printers — Ap/Mac LaserWriters, QMS/860. CLASSIFIED: Front-end hardware — Ap/Mac; Front-end software — Ready-Set-Go; Printers — Ap/Mac LaserWriters, QMS/800. DISPLAY: Front-end hardware — Ap/Mac; Front-end software — Ready-Set-Go; Printers — Ap/Mac LaserWriter. PRODUCTION: Typesetters — Ap/Mac LaserWriter; Plate exposures — Nu/Flip Top FT40UPNS; Plate processors — Nat/A-250; Production cameras — 1-SCREEN/C-240-D, Kyoto/Japan; Automatic film processors — 1-P/24.
PRESSROOM: Line 1 — 6-G/Community; Folders — 1-G; Reels and stands — 5-G/Community Stand; Press control system — Fin. MAILROOM: Bundle tyer — Malow/50, Bu; Addressing machine — MG/88002. LIBRARY: Electronic — Go-fer/text retrieval. WIRE SERVICES: News — AP; Syndicates — Universal Press, Extra Newspaper Service; Receiving dishes — size-3½ft, AP. BUSINESS COMPUTERS: 4-Gateway/2000, 3-IBM, 1-Gateway/2000-486; Applications: Ck; PCs & micros networked.

MARION
See CEDAR RAPIDS

MARSHALLTOWN
Marshall County
'90 U.S. Census- 25,178; E&P '96 Est. 24,751
ABC-CZ (90): 25,178 (HH 9,974)

Times-Republican
(e-mon to fri; m-sat; S)

Times-Republican, 135 W. Main St.; PO Box 1300, Marshalltown, IA 50158; tel (515) 753-6611; fax (515) 753-7221. Ogden Newspapers group.
Circulation: 11,323(e); 11,323(m-sat); 11,416(S); ABC Sept. 30, 1995.
Price: 35¢(d); 50¢(sat); 75¢(S); $1.75/wk (carrier), $2.00/wk (mail); $7.50/mo (carrier), $8.65/mo (mail); $91.00/yr (carrier), $104.00/yr (mail).
Advertising: Open inch rate $13.71(e); $13.71(m-sat); $13.71(S). **Representatives:** Papert Companies; Iowa Newspaper Assn.
News Service: AP. **Politics:** Independent. **Established:** 1856.
Note: Effective July 23, 1995, this publication started a Sunday edition. The Sunday circulation reported is Sworn Sept. 24, 1995.
Special Editions: Baby Register, Bridal Tab (Jan); Agribusiness, Financial Planning (Feb); Home Improvement (Mar); Seniors Tab, Visitor's Guide (Apr); High School Graduation, Health Tab (May); Outdoors (June); Progress Edition, Little League Review (July); Fall Sports, Football Contest (Aug); Oktoberfest, Home Improvement/Car Care Salute (Sept); Pork Salute, MFL & Soccer (Oct); Thanksgiving/Christmas Kick-off, Christmas Countdown (Nov); Holiday Greetings, Year in Review (Dec); Business Magazine (monthly).
Special Weekly Sections: Best Food Day (wed); Religion (sat); Best Food Day, Entertainment, TV Times, Color Comics, Business/Farm, Focus, Parade (S).
Cable TV: Operate leased cable TV in circulation area.

CORPORATE OFFICERS
President G Ogden Nutting
Vice Pres William C Nutting
Vice Pres Robert M Nutting
Secretary William O Nutting
Treasurer Duane Wittman

GENERAL MANAGEMENT
Publisher Mike Schlesinger

ADVERTISING
Director Reed Riskedahl
Manager-Classified Reed Riskedahl

CIRCULATION
Director Max Nelson

NEWS EXECUTIVE
Managing Editor Dave Dawson

EDITORS AND MANAGERS
Business/Finance Editor Valerie Milligan
City/Metro Editor Mel Pitzen
Editorial Page Editor Dave Dawson
Education Editor Holly Ivy
Entertainment/Amusements Editor Tim Kenyon
Farm/Agriculture Editor Mel Pitzen
Features Editor Rose Kodet
Graphic Editor/Art Director Steve Plain
Living/Lifestyle Editor Holly Ivy
National Editor Dave Dawson
News Editor Mel Pitzen
Photo Editor Karen Nandell
Political/Government Editor Dave Dawson
Religion Editor Holly Ivy
Sports Editor Bruce Ersland
Television/Film Editor Denise Howie
Women's Editor Holly Ivy

PRODUCTION
Foreman-Composing Steve Plain
Manager-Press Rob Curley

Market Information: Zoned editions; Split Run; TMC; ADS.
Mechanical available: Offset; Black and 3 ROP colors; insert accepted — preprinted, all; no brokered group ads; page cut-offs — 22¾".
Mechanical specifications: Type page 13" x 21½"; E - 6 cols, 2.08", ⅙" between; A - 6 cols, 2.08", ⅙" between; C - 9 cols, 1.33", ⅛" between.
Commodity consumption: Newsprint 2,000 short tons; widths 27", 31", 34"; black ink 60,000 pounds; color ink 30,000 pounds; average pages per issue 19(d), 24(sat), 50(S); single plates used 40,000.
Equipment: EDITORIAL: Front-end hardware — Mk, 7-Ap/Power Mac 6100, 1-Ap/Power Mac 7200; Front-end software — Mk; Printers — 2-Ap/Mac LaserPrinter, 2-HP/600 DPI 4V; Other equipment — 2-Ap/Mac II, 1-Ap/Mac SE, 1-Lf/AP Leaf Picture Desk, 1-Polaroid/SprintScan Film Scanner, 1-Umax/Flatbed Scanner. CLASSIFIED: Front-end hardware — Mk. DISPLAY: Adv layout systems — 3-Ap/Power Mac 6100 w/Multi-Ad/Creator & QuarkXPress; Printers — 1-HP/4V; Other equipment — 1-Umax/Flatbed Scanner. PRODUCTION: Platemaking systems — Nu; Plate exposures — Nu/Flip Top; Plate processors — Nat; Production cameras — AG/RPF.
PRESSROOM: Line 1 — 8-G/Community (upper former); Line 2 — 8-G/Community (upper former); Folders — 8-G. MAILROOM: Counter stackers — HI; Bundle tyer — EAM/Automatic, MLN; Wrapping singles — QWI; Addressing machine — Ch. WIRE SERVICES: News — AP; Photos — AP; Stock tables — AP; Syndicates — AP; Receiving dishes — size-3m, AP. BUSINESS COMPUTERS: NCR.

MASON CITY
Cerro Gordo County
'90 U.S. Census- 29,040; E&P '96 Est. 28,995
ABC-CZ (90): 38,116 (HH 15,744)

Globe-Gazette (m-mon to sat)
Sunday Globe (S)

Globe-Gazette, 300 N. Washington Ave.; PO Box 271, Mason City, IA 50402-0271; tel (515) 421-0500; fax (515) 421-0516. Lee Enterprises Inc. group.
Circulation: 20,066(m); 20,066(m-sat); 23,493(S); ABC Sept. 30, 1995.
Price: 50¢(d); 50¢(sat); $1.50(S); $3.60/wk; $15.60/mo; $177.00/yr.
Advertising: Open inch rate $19.15(m); $19.15(m-sat); $19.15(S); $46.25(m & S). **Representatives:** Landon Associates Inc.; Iowa Newspaper Assn.
News Service: AP. **Politics:** Independent. **Established:** 1893.
Not Published: Christmas.
Special Editions: Bridal, Health & Fitness (Jan); All About Love, Education Directory, Home Directory (Feb); Do it Yourself, Answer Book (Mar); Business Expo, Builder's Tour, Baby Book (Apr); Academics, Lawn & Garden, Summertime, Band Festival, Athletics (May); Brides, Grilling Made Easy (June); Economic Report, North Iowa Fair (July); College Guide, Fall Fashion Show & Section, Fall Sports (Aug); Slice of Life, Fall Lawn & Garden (Sept); Home Energy, Crafts & Parenting, Senior Living (Oct); High School Winter Sports, Holiday Fashion & Entertainment, Gift Guide (Nov); Gifts, Letters to Santa, Newsmakers (Dec); North Iowa Farmer (monthly).
Special Weekly Sections: Teens (mon); Food/Grocery (tues); Entertainment (thur); Religion (sat); Business (S).
Magazines: Sunday TV Magazine, Color Comics (S); North Iowa Farmer (Monthly Farm Publication); Off-Hours (Weekly Entertainment).

GENERAL MANAGEMENT
Publisher Howard Query
Controller William J Meeker

ADVERTISING
Director Byron Wooten
Manager-Classified Byron Wooten
Manager-National/Co-op Sales Linda Halfman

TELECOMMUNICATIONS
Audiotex Manager Greg Wilderman

CIRCULATION
Manager Ken Miller

NEWS EXECUTIVE
Editor Gary Sawyer

EDITORS AND MANAGERS
City Editor Bob Steenson
Editorial Page Editor Gary Sawyer
Librarian Judy Delperdang
Lifestyle Editor Frank Myers
Regional Editor Jane Nelson
Sports Editor Tom Thoma

MANAGEMENT INFORMATION SERVICES
Data Processing Manager Terry Balek

PRODUCTION
Manager Pete Koenigsfeld

Market Information: Zoned editions; Split Run; TMC; Operate database; Operate audiotex.
Mechanical available: Letterpress; Black and 3 ROP colors; insert accepted — preprinted; page cut-offs — 22¾".
Mechanical specifications: Type page 13" x 21½"; E - 6 cols, 2¹⁄₁₆", ⅛" between; A - 6 cols, 2¹⁄₁₆", ⅛" between; C - 9 cols, 1⅜", ¹⁄₁₆" between.
Commodity consumption: Newsprint 1,411 short tons; 1,280 metric tons; widths 56", 42", 28", 14"; black ink 28,000 pounds; color ink 11,000 pounds; single pages printed 9,400; average pages per issue 22(d), 41(S); single plates used 19,637.
Equipment: EDITORIAL: Front-end hardware — 2-IBM/RS-6000, 20-Gateway/2000, PC/4DX-33; Front-end software — CText/Dataline; Printers — Imager/Plus 12, NewGen. CLASSIFIED: Front-end hardware — 2-IBM/RS-6000, 4-Gateway/2000; Front-end software — CText/AdVision; Printers — Imager/Plus 12, NewGen. DISPLAY: Front-end hardware — 4-Ap/Mac IIci, 1-Ap/Power Mac PC 7100-66-500-CD; Front-end software — Multi-Ad/Creator 3.7; Printers — 2-Ap/Mac LaserWriter II NTX, ImageWriter/Plus, NewGen. PRODUCTION: Platemaking systems — 1-Na/NP20-, 1-Na/NP20; Plate exposures — 2-Na/Starlight; Plate processors — 1-Na/NP40, 1-Na/NP20; Electronic picture desk — Lf/AP Leaf Picture Desk; Production cameras — 1-R/480, 1-C/Spartan II, ECR/Autokon 1000; Automatic film processors — 1-P.
PRESSROOM: Line 1 — 4-SC/Super 60; Folders — 1-S. MAILROOM: Inserters and stuffers — 1-MM/227E; Bundle tyer — 2-MLN/ML2EE; Addressing machine — 1-Ch/595-596 Labeler. LIBRARY: Electronic — SMS. WIRE SERVICES: News — AP; Receiving dishes — size-10ft, AP. BUSINESS COMPUTERS: 1-IBM/AS-400; PCs & micros networked; PCs & main system networked.

MOUNT PLEASANT
Henry County
'90 U.S. Census- 8,027; E&P '96 Est. 8,570

Mount Pleasant News
(e-mon to fri)

Mount Pleasant News, 215 W. Monroe; PO Box 240, Mount Pleasant, IA 52641; tel (319) 385-3131; fax (319) 385-8048. Inland Industries Inc. group.
Circulation: 3,730(e); Sworn Oct. 2, 1995.
Price: 50¢(d); $20.50/3mo (carrier), $25.00/3mo (out-of-county).
Advertising: Open inch rate $6.37(e). **Representative:** Iowa Newspaper Assn.
News Service: AP. **Politics:** Independent. **Established:** 1878.
Not Published: New Year; Memorial Day; Independence Day; Labor Day; Thanksgiving; Christmas.
Special Editions: Brides, Taxes (Jan); Agriculture (Mar); Home Show (Apr); Graduation, Summer Fun (May); Little League/Softball (June); Progress, Fair (July); Senior Citizen, Football (Aug); Old Treshers, Make-over (Sept); Women in Business, Chamber of Commerce, Red Ribbon Week (Oct); Christmas Showcase, Christmas Open House (Nov); Basketball (Dec).
Special Weekly Sections: Education (mon); Best Food Day, Agriculture (tues); Editorial Page (wed); Business Page (thur); Church (fri).
Magazine: TV Tab (fri).

CORPORATE OFFICERS
Chairman of the Board Clark O Murray
President Clark O Murray
Exec Vice Pres/Treasurer Jack D Burton

GENERAL MANAGEMENT
Publisher Emery A Styron

ADVERTISING
Director Faith Krause
Manager-National Doug Kofoed
Manager-Classified Stacy Storck

CIRCULATION
Manager Kelly Wallace

EDITORS AND MANAGERS
Business/Finance Editor John Sloca
Editorial Page Editor John Sloca
Education Editor Shelley Doak
Entertainment/Amusements Editor Shelley Doak
Farm/Agriculture Editor John Sloca
Living/Lifestyle Editor Shelley Doak
National Editor John Sloca
News Editor John Sloca
Photo Editor John Sloca
Political/Government Editor John Sloca
Society/Women's Editor Shelley Doak
Sports Editor Keith Kohorst

PRODUCTION
Manager Greg Hoel

Market Information: TMC; ADS.
Mechanical available: Offset; Black and 3 ROP colors; insert accepted — preprinted, any; page cut-offs — 22⅝".
Mechanical specifications: Type page 13" x 21½"; E - 6 cols, 2¹⁄₁₆", ⅛" between; A - 6 cols, 2¹⁄₁₆", ⅛" between; C - 8 cols, 1⁷⁄₁₆", ⅛" between.
Commodity consumption: Newsprint 133 short tons; widths 28", 14", 34", 17"; black ink 3,650 pounds; color ink 795 pounds; single pages printed 3,122; average pages per issue 12(d); single plates used 3,155.
Equipment: EDITORIAL: Front-end hardware — 1-COM/Advantage, 1-Ap/Mac SE. CLASSIFIED: Front-end hardware — Ap/Mac Plus. DISPLAY: Adv layout systems — Ap/Mac IIcx. PRODUCTION: Plate exposures — Nu/Flip Top; Plate processors — 1-Nat/250; Scanners — Ap/Mac; Production cameras — 1-Nu; Automatic film processors — 1-P.
PRESSROOM: Line 1 — 4-G/Community; Folders — 1-G. MAILROOM: Bundle tyer — 1-Bu; Addressing machine — 2-Wm. LIBRARY: Combination — BH/Microfilm Reader (Bound Copies). WIRE SERVICES: News — AP; Receiving dishes — size-3½ft, AP. BUSINESS COMPUTERS: IBM; PCs & micros networked.

MUSCATINE
Muscatine County
'90 U.S. Census- 22,881; E&P '96 Est. 23,170
ABC-CZ (90): 22,881 (HH 8,756)

Muscatine Journal
(e-mon to fri; m-sat; S)

Muscatine Journal, 301 E. 3rd St.; PO Box 809, Muscatine, IA 52761; tel (319) 263-2331; fax (319) 262-8042. Lee Enterprises Inc. group.

Circulation: 9,371(e); 9,371(m-sat); 6,000(S); ABC Sept. 30, 1995.
Price: 50¢(d); 50¢(sat); $2.00(S); $2.25/wk; $9.75/mo; $110.10/yr.
Advertising: Open inch rate $13.00(e); $13.00(m-sat); $13.00(S). Representatives: Landon Associates Inc.; Iowa Newspaper Assn.
News Service: AP. Politics: Independent. Established: 1840.
Note: Effective Dec. 10, 1995, this publication started publishing a Sunday edition. The Sunday circulation figure reported is an estimate.
Not Published: New Year; Christmas.
Special Editions: Annual, Bridal (Jan); Parade of Children (Feb); Progress, Farm (Mar); Home Improvement, Tourism, Spring Car Care (Apr); Design An Ad, Discover Muscatine Co. (May); Graduation Section, Generations (June); Answer Book (July); Family Business, Make-over Section (Aug); Football Preview, Home Improvement (Sept); Auto (Oct); Gift Guide, Home for the Holidays (Nov); Gift Guide (Dec).
Special Weekly Sections: Business (mon); Trends, Food Day (tues).
Magazines: 'Weekender', Entertainment and Travel (thur); Church (fri); Farm (sat).

GENERAL MANAGEMENT
Publisher............................David Fuselier
Controller...........................Lisa Sievers

ADVERTISING
Manager-National...................Jay Lenkersdorfer

MARKETING AND PROMOTION
Coordinator-Promotion..............Jay Lenkersdorfer

CIRCULATION
Manager..............................Brian Stiff

NEWS EXECUTIVES
News Editor........................Tracy Buffington
Managing Editor....................Jeff Tecklanberg

EDITORS AND MANAGERS
Editorial Page Editor...............Jeff Tecklanberg
Photo Department Manager..........Jeff Tecklanberg
Sports Editor......................John Luebbers

PRODUCTION
Manager-Creative Service...........Jay Lenkersdorfer
Manager-Pressroom..................Larry Lichtenwald
Manager-Photo Lab..................Beth Hecht

Market Information: TMC; ADS.
Mechanical available: Offset; Black and 3 ROP colors; insert accepted — preprinted; page cut-offs — 21½".
Mechanical specifications: Type page 13" x 21½"; E - 6 cols, 2¹⁄₁₆", ⅛" between; A - 6 cols, 2¹⁄₁₆", ⅛" between; C - 9 cols, 1³⁄₈", ¹⁄₁₆" between.
Commodity consumption: Newsprint 520 metric tons; widths 34", 27½"; black ink 24,700 pounds; color ink 800 pounds; single pages printed 6,138; average pages per issue 22(d); single plates used 8,000.
Equipment: EDITORIAL: Front-end hardware — DEC; Front-end software — LNS; Printers — DEC/LA 100, Dataproducts/LZR 1560; Other equipment — Ap/Mac IIsi, AP GraphicsNet, Ap/Mac SE, Lf/AP Leaf Picture Desk, Lf/Negative Scanner. CLASSIFIED: Front-end hardware — DEC; Front-end software — LNS; Printers — DEC/LA 100. DISPLAY: Adv layout systems — HI/2221, Ap/Mac IIsi, Ap/Mac IIcx, Ap/Mac 8100, Ap/Mac 650; Front-end hardware — DEC; Front-end software — Multi-Ad/Creator; Printers — DEC/LA 100, Dataproducts/LZR 1560 Laserprinter, HP/PaintWriterXL; Other equipment — HP/Scanner, CD-Rom. PRODUCTION: Typesetters — COM/8400-HS; Platemaking systems — Nat; Plate exposures — 1-Nu; Plate processors — Nat/250 additive; Electronic picture desk — Lf/AP Leaf Picture Desk; Scanners — Ap/Mac One Scanner, HP/ScanJet; Production cameras — 1-Nu, 1-B; Automatic film processors — Eskofot/865A; Shrink lenses — 1-CK Optical/5%; Color separation equipment (conventional) — Lf/AP Leaf Picture Desk.
PRESSROOM: Line 1 — 7-G/Community; Folders — 1-G; Press control system — G. MAILROOM: Bundle tyer — 1-Bu/String, 1-MLN/Spirit-Strapper; Addressing machine — 1-St. LIBRARY: Electronic — ISYS. WIRE SERVICES: News — AP; Photos — AP; Stock tables — AP; Receiving dishes — AP. BUSINESS COMPUTERS: 2-Zeos/386, 2-GIC/386, 1-IBM/AT, 1-Compu Add, 2-Gateway/4 SX-33; Applications: BMF: Accts receivable, Accts payable, Gen ledger, Circ; Microsoft/Excel, Lotus, WordPerfect, Writing Assistant.

NEWTON
Jasper County
'90 U.S. Census- 14,789; E&P '96 Est. 14,955

The Newton Daily News
(e-mon to fri)

The Newton Daily News, 200 First Ave. E.; PO Box 967, Newton, IA 50208; tel (515) 792-3121; fax (515) 792-5505. Shaw Newspapers group.
Circulation: 6,879(e); Sworn Sept. 28, 1995.
Price: 50¢(d); $1.30/wk; $5.59/mo; $66.55/yr.
Advertising: Open inch rate $8.48(e). Representative: Iowa Newspaper Assn.
News Service: AP. Established: 1902.
Not Published: New Year; Memorial Day; Independence Day; Labor Day; Thanksgiving; Christmas.
Special Editions: Year End; Spring Bridal; Fall Football; 55 Plus; Woman's World; Tax Guide.

CORPORATE OFFICERS
Chairman of the Board..............E K Shaw
President/CEO......................Thomas D Shaw
Chief Financial Officer............Phillip E Metka
Vice Pres..........................Robert A Shaw
Vice Pres..........................William E Shaw
Treasurer..........................Robert A Shaw
Secretary..........................Phillip E Metka

GENERAL MANAGEMENT
Publisher..........................Joe McDermott

ADVERTISING
Manager............................Dave Stanley

CIRCULATION
Manager............................Chris Martin

NEWS EXECUTIVE
Editor.............................Peter Hussmann

EDITORS AND MANAGERS
Editorial Writer...................Peter Hussmann
Living/Lifestyle Editor............Shannon Bergman
Picture Editor.....................Peter Hussmann
Sports Editor......................Ed Peck
Women's Editor.....................Shannon Bergman

MANAGEMENT INFORMATION SERVICES
Data Processing Manager............Margaret Modlin

PRODUCTION
Foreman-Composing..................Mari Jo DeGrado
Foreman-Engraving..................Kathy Osborn

Market Information: TMC.
Mechanical available: Offset; Black and 3 ROP colors; insert accepted — preprinted; page cut-offs — 22¾".
Mechanical specifications: Type page 13" x 21½"; E - 6 cols, 2¹⁄₁₆", ⅛" between; A - 6 cols, 2¹⁄₁₆", ⅛" between; C - 9 cols, 1³⁄₈", ¹⁄₁₆" between.
Commodity consumption: Newsprint 590 short tons; widths 29", 31", 34"; black ink 7,600 pounds; color ink 840 pounds; single pages printed 4,111; average pages per issue 12(d); single plates used 10,800.
Equipment: EDITORIAL: Front-end hardware — Ap/Mac; Front-end software — QuarkXPress, Microsoft/Word; Printers — Ap/Mac LaserWriter Plus. CLASSIFIED: Front-end hardware — Ap/Mac LC II; Front-end software — Baseview. PRODUCTION: Typesetters — 2-COM/Unisetter, Ap/Mac; Plate exposures — 1-Nu; Plate processors — Nat; Production cameras — 1-B/Repromaster; Automatic film processors — SCREEN.
PRESSROOM: Line 1 — 6-G/Suburban. MAILROOM: Counter stackers — 1-BG; Bundle tyer — 3-Bu. WIRE SERVICES: News — AP; Receiving dishes — size-3ft, AP. BUSINESS COMPUTERS: 2-BI, ATT; Applications: Circ, Mail lists, Gen ledger, Accts receivable, Accts payable; PCs & micros networked; PCs & main system networked.

OELWEIN
Fayette County
'90 U.S. Census- 6,493; E&P '96 Est. 6,103

The Register (e-mon to fri; m-sat)
The Register, 25 1st St. S.E.; PO Box 511, Oelwein, IA 50662; tel (319) 283-2144; fax (319) 283-3268. Thomson Newspapers group.
Circulation: 5,582(e); 5,582(m-sat); Sworn Oct. 1, 1994.
Price: 35¢(d); 35¢(sat); $1.85/wk (carrier); $96.20/yr (carrier).
Advertising: Open inch rate $11.08(e); $11.08(m-sat). Representative: Iowa Newspaper Assn.
News Service: AP. Established: 1881.

Not Published: New Year; Memorial Day; Independence Day; Labor Day; Thanksgiving; Christmas.
Special Editions: Bridal, Chamber of Commerce, Corn Commitment (Jan); Soil Conservation, Homemaker's School (Feb); Update Edition (Mar); Husky Edition (Apr); Tourism, Mother's Day, Graduation, Beef Editions (May); Dairy, Father's Day (June); Fair, Ridiculous Day, Summer Sports (July); Back-to-School, Pigskin Preview (Aug); Fall-Tourism (Sept); Pork, Fire Prevention (Oct); Christmas Open House, Holiday Cookbook, Winter Sports (Nov); Christmas Promotions, Greeting Cards (Dec).
Special Weekly Sections: Agriculture Edition (wed); Weekly TV Section (fri).

GENERAL MANAGEMENT
Publisher..........................Jody Perrotto
General Manager....................Mark Perrotto
Manager-Credit.....................Janet Hutter

ADVERTISING
Director...........................Cathy Martin

NEWS EXECUTIVE
Managing Editor....................Jim Morrison

EDITORS AND MANAGERS
Amusements/Books Editor............Kenneth Schmith
Editorial Writer...................Kenneth Schmith
Fashion/Food Editor................Kaye Frazer
Librarian..........................Janet Hutter
Picture Editor.....................Kenneth Schmith
Radio/Television Editor............Kaye Frazer
School/Science Editor..............Dave Martin
Society/Women's Editor.............Kaye Frazer
Sports Editor......................Bud Schrader
Teen-Age/Youth Editor..............Kaye Frazer

Market Information: TMC.
Mechanical available: Offset; Black and 3 ROP colors; insert accepted — preprinted; page cut-offs — 22¾".
Mechanical specifications: Type page 14" x 21½"; E - 6 cols, 2.07", ⅛" between; A - 6 cols, 2.07", ⅛" between; C - 9 cols, 1½", ¹⁄₁₂" between.
Commodity consumption: widths 28", 14"; average pages per issue 12(d).
Equipment: PRODUCTION: Typesetters — 2-COM/Unisetter, 1-COM/Area Unified Composer; Plate exposures — 1-Nu/FT-40LNS.
PRESSROOM: Line 1 — 7-G/C901; Folders — 2-G. MAILROOM: Bundle tyer — 1-Bu, 1-Sa, 1-Malow/MC-50; Addressing machine — 1-SC/labeler. WIRE SERVICES: News — AP; Receiving dishes — AP.

OSKALOOSA
Mahaska County
'90 U.S. Census- 10,632; E&P '96 Est. 10,753

Oskaloosa Herald
(e-mon to sat)
Oskaloosa Herald, 1901 A Ave E.; PO Box 530, Oskaloosa, IA 52577-0530; tel (515) 672-2581; fax (515) 672-2294. Donrey Media Group group.
Circulation: 4,615(e); 4,615(e-sat); Sworn Sept. 30, 1994.
Price: 50¢(d); 50¢(sat); $5.50/mo (in county).
Advertising: Open inch rate $6.40(e); $6.40(e-sat). Representative: Papert Companies.
News Services: NEA, INA, AP. Established: 1850.
Not Published: New Year; Memorial Day; Independence Day; Labor Day; Thanksgiving; Christmas.
Special Editions: Progress (Mar); Holiday Recipes (Nov).
Special Weekly Sections: Senior Citizens (mon); Agriculture (tues); Business (wed); Church News (fri); TV Listings (sat).

CORPORATE OFFICERS
Founder............................Donald W Reynolds
President/Chief Operating Officer..Emmett Jones
Exec Vice Pres/Chief Financial Officer
...................................Darrell W Loftin
Vice Pres-Western Newspaper Group
...................................David A Osborn
Vice Pres-Eastern Newspaper Group
...................................Don Schneider

GENERAL MANAGEMENT
Publisher..........................Keith Ponder

ADVERTISING
Director...........................Deb Van Engelenhoven

CIRCULATION
Manager............................Keith Camp

NEWS EXECUTIVE
Editor.............................Kimberly Walker

EDITORS AND MANAGERS
City Editor........................Gene Murphy
Sports Editor......................R D Keep

PRODUCTION
Manager............................Charles Roberts

Market Information: TMC.
Mechanical available: Offset; Black and 3 ROP colors; insert accepted — preprinted, all; page cut-offs — 22¾".
Mechanical specifications: Type page 13" x 21½"; E - 6 cols, 2¹⁄₁₆", ⅛" between; A - 6 cols, 2¹⁄₁₆", ⅛" between; C - 6 cols, 2¹⁄₁₆", ¹⁄₁₆" between.
Commodity consumption: black ink 6,000 pounds; average pages per issue 12(d).
Equipment: EDITORIAL: Front-end hardware — Mk/Touchwriter Plus. CLASSIFIED: Front-end hardware — 6-HI. DISPLAY: Adv layout systems — Ap/Mac. PRODUCTION: Typesetters — 2-Mk/Touchwriter Plus, Mk/Ad Touch, 2-Ap/Mac LaserWriter; Plate exposures — 1-Nu/Flip Top FT40L; Scanners — Ap/Mac; Production cameras — Acti/S 25; Automatic film processors — 1-P/G-24-1, LE/24AQ.
PRESSROOM: Line 1 — 6-Web Leader; Folders — Web Leader. MAILROOM: Bundle tyer — 1-Bu/182XE4, 1-Sa/SR2CTAN; Addressing machine — 1-Am/1950-B. WIRE SERVICES: News — Syndicates — NEA. BUSINESS COMPUTERS: IBM; Applications: Circ.

OTTUMWA
Wapello County
'90 U.S. Census- 24,488; E&P '96 Est. 23,382
ABC-CZ (90): 24,488 (HH 10,280)

The Ottumwa Courier
(m-mon to sat)
The Ottumwa Courier, 213 E. Second St., Ottumwa, IA 52501; tel (515) 684-4611; fax (515) 684-7834. Lee Enterprises Inc. group.
Circulation: 18,959(m); 18,959(m-sat); ABC Sept. 30, 1995.
Price: 50¢(d); 50¢(sat); $2.44/wk; $9.75/mo; $113.55/yr.
Advertising: Open inch rate $17.56(m); $17.56(m-sat). Representatives: Landon Associates Inc.; Iowa Newspaper Assn.
News Service: AP. Politics: Independent. Established: 1847.
Not Published: Christmas.
Special Editions: Taxes & Finance, Healthy Living, Corn, Super Bowl (Jan); Bridal Tab, Homemakers Festival, Cow-Calf-Corn, Design-An-Ad (Feb); Home Expo, Progress (Mar); Home Improvement (Apr); Salute to Graduates, Beef Produces (May); Little League (June); Back-to-School, Fair (Aug); Football Preview, Home Improvement, Answer Book (Sept); Pork Producers, ROP, Fall and Winter Car Care (Oct); IHCC Warrior Preview, Citywide Open House, Cookbook, Winter Sports Preview (Nov); Gift Guide, Santa Tracking, Year End (Dec).
Special Weekly Sections: Business (mon); Food (wed); Outdoor Sportsman (thur); Weekender (fri); Religion (sat).
Cable TV: Operate leased cable TV in circulation area.

GENERAL MANAGEMENT
Publisher..........................Martha Wells

ADVERTISING
Director-Retail....................Mary Kay Hopson
Manager-Classified.................Glenda Campbell

MARKETING AND PROMOTION
Promotion Marketing Specialist.....Tim Kurtz

TELECOMMUNICATIONS
Audiotex Manager...................Tim Kurtz

CIRCULATION
Manager............................Doug Techel

NEWS EXECUTIVE
Editor.............................Rusty Cunningham

EDITORS AND MANAGERS
City Editor........................Dave Pitt
Editorial Page Editor..............Sally Finder-Koziol
News Editor........................Sally Finder-Koziol
Photo Department Manager..........M Scott Mahaskey
Sports Editor......................Bob Fenske

MANAGEMENT INFORMATION SERVICES
Systems Specialist.................Steve Welker

I-150 Iowa

PRODUCTION
Foreman-Composing — Barb Coop
Foreman-Press — Steve Reed
Foreman-Mailroom — Louise Wheaton

Market Information: Split Run; TMC; ADS; Operate audiotex.
Mechanical available: Offset; Black and 3 ROP colors; insert accepted — preprinted; page cut-offs — 22¾".
Mechanical specifications: Type page 13" x 21½"; E - 6 cols, 2 1/16", 1/8" between; A - 6 cols, 2 1/16", 1/8" between; C - 9 cols, 1 3/8", 1/16" between.
Commodity consumption: Newsprint 750 metric tons; width 27½"; black ink 25,980 pounds; color ink 4,261 pounds; single pages printed 7,100; average pages per issue 22(d); single plates used 10,000.
Equipment: EDITORIAL: Front-end hardware — DEC/PDP 11-80; Front-end software — LNS; Printers — 3-DEC/LaserWriter, 2-COM/8400; Other equipment — 15-DEC/VT 220. CLASSIFIED: Front-end hardware — DEC/PDP 11-80; Front-end software — LNS; Printers — 2-COM/8400; Other equipment — 2-DEC/VT 2-20. AUDIOTEX: Software — LNS/Voice Response. DISPLAY: Adv layout systems — 2-HI/2221(on-line); Front-end hardware — 2-Ap/Mac IIcx, Ap/Mac IIsi, Ap/Mac Quadra 610; Front-end software — Multi-Ad/Creator, Aldus/FreeHand, Aldus/PageMaker; Printers — QMS/PS-410, HP/LaserJet IIIsi; Other equipment — 2-DEC/VT 220, HP/ScanJet IIp, 2-CD-Rom/reader. PRODUCTION: OCR software — Caere/OmniPage, Caere/OmniPage Direct; Typesetters — 2-Ap/Mac IIcx, 2-COM/8400, HP/LaserJet IIIsi, QMS/PS-410; Platemaking systems — LE/LD 2600A; Plate processors — Nat/A-250; Electronic picture desk — Lf/Leafscan 35; Scanners — HP/ScanJet Plus, HP/ScanJet IIp; Production cameras — 1-C/Spartan II, 1-SCREEN; Automatic film processors — 1-P/24-1, 1-COM/894; Digital color separation equipment — Digi-Colour, Lf/Leafscan 35.
PRESSROOM: Line 1 — 5-G/Urbanite 850; Folders — 1-G/2:1; Press registration system — Duarte. MAILROOM: Counter stackers — 1-HL/Monitor; Inserters and stuffers — Mueller/227E 5:1; Bundle tyer — 1-Cyclops, 1-MLN; Addressing machine — 1-Ch/582N, 1-VideoJet/569 Labeler. LIBRARY: Electronic — ISYS. WIRE SERVICES: News — AP; Photos — AP; Receiving dishes — AP. BUSINESS COMPUTERS: 1-IBM/Sys 38, IBM/PC-XT, IBM/PS2, Ap/Mac SE, PC/Support; Applications: Lotus 1-2-3, Microsoft/Excel: Circ, Adv billing, Accts receivable, Gen ledger, Payroll; WordPerfect, PC Support: Microsoft/Works; PCs & micros networked; PCs & main system networked.

SHENANDOAH
Page County
'90 U.S. Census- 5,572; E&P '96 Est. 5,303

Valley News Today-Daily Sentinel (e-tues to sat)
Valley News Today-Daily Sentinel, 702 W. Sheridan Ave.; PO Box 369, Shenandoah, IA 51601; tel (712) 246-3097; fax (712) 246-3099. Gleason Knowles Communications Inc. group.
Circulation: 3,399(e); 3,399(e-sat); Sworn Sept. 30, 1995.
Price: 50¢(d); 50¢(sat); $96.00/yr.
Advertising: Open inch rate $7.28(e); $7.28(e-sat). **Representative:** American Newspaper Representatives Inc.
News Service: Iowa Media Link. **Established:** 1989.
Special Editions: Health, Travel, Sr. Lifestyles (Jan); Progress Edition, Bridal (Feb); Home Improvement, Gardening, Car (Mar); Spring Sports (Apr); Beef, Travel/Tourism (May); Summer Sports (June); Southwest Iowa Fairs (July); Back-to-School (Aug); High School Sports Preview, Fall Home Improvement, Car Care (Sept); Christmas Kick-off (Nov); Christmas Gift Booklet (Dec).

CORPORATE OFFICER
President — Gregg K Knowles
GENERAL MANAGEMENT
Publisher — Gregg K Knowles
ADVERTISING
Director — Gregg K Knowles
Manager-Classified — Becky Streitenberger

CIRCULATION
Manager — Benjamin McCoy
EDITOR AND MANAGER
News Editor — Julia Dinville
PRODUCTION
Manager-Composing — Mary Fielder

Market Information: Split Run; TMC.
Mechanical available: Offset; Black and 3 ROP colors; insert accepted — preprinted; page cut-offs — 22 5/8".
Mechanical specifications: Type page 13" x 21½"; E - 6 cols, 2", 1/8" between; A - 6 cols, 2", 1/8" between; C - 6 cols, 2", 1/8" between.
Commodity consumption: Newsprint 200 short tons; widths 28", 32"; black ink 9,000 pounds; color ink 1,500 pounds; single pages printed 3,500; average pages per issue 14(d), 32(sat); single plates used 2,200.
Equipment: EDITORIAL: Front-end hardware — Ap/Mac; Front-end software — Microsoft/Word; Printers — Ap/Mac LaserWriter Pro 600. CLASSIFIED: Front-end hardware — Ap/Mac; Front-end software — Microsoft/Word. DISPLAY: Front-end hardware — Ap/Mac; Front-end software — Aldus/PageMaker; Printers — Ap/Mac LaserWriter Pro 800. PRODUCTION: Scanners — HP. WIRE SERVICES: News — Iowa Media Link; Syndicates — Universal Press, LATS, Creators, NAS. BUSINESS COMPUTERS: Compaq.

SIOUX CITY
Woodbury County
'90 U.S. Census- 80,505; E&P '96 Est. 81,770
ABC-CZ (90): 96,443 (HH 36,244)

Sioux City Journal
(m-mon to fri; m-sat; S)
Sioux City Journal, 515 Pavonia St. (51101); PO Box 118, Sioux City, IA 51102; tel (712) 279-5019; fax (712) 279-5099; e-mail scjrnl@pionet.com; web site http://www1.trib.com/scjournal/. Hagadone Corp. group.
Circulation: 49,347(m); 49,079(m-sat); 50,548(S); ABC Sept. 30, 1995.
Price: 50¢(d); 50¢(sat); $1.50(S); $12.25/mo (carrier); $147.00/yr (carrier).
Advertising: Open inch rate $29.00(m); $29.00(m-sat); $29.00(S). **Representative:** Landon Associates Inc.
News Service: AP. **Politics:** Independent. **Established:** 1870.
Not Published: New Year; Christmas.
Special Edition: Progress (Mar).
Special Weekly Sections: Food (wed); Entertainment, TV Log (fri); Business, Travel (S).
Magazine: Parade (S).

CORPORATE OFFICER
President — Duane B Hagadone
GENERAL MANAGEMENT
Publisher — Tom Kurdy
Business Manager/Credit Manager — Ken Brandvold
ADVERTISING
Manager — Steve Griffith
Manager-Classified — Lynda Allen
Manager-Promotion — Margi Griffith
MARKETING AND PROMOTION
Director-Marketing/Promotion — Margi Weiss
Manager-Marketing/Promotion — Tami Breeden
CIRCULATION
Director — Roger Kann
NEWS EXECUTIVES
Editor — Larry Myhre
Managing Editor — Karen Luken
EDITORS AND MANAGERS
Amusements Editor — Bruce Miller
City Editor — Glen Olson
Editorial Page Editor — Larry Myhre
Fashion Editor — Marcia Poole
Food Editor — Marcia Poole
Films/Theater Editor — Bruce Miller
Librarian — Deb Murphey
Living Editor — Bruce Miller
Music Editor — Bruce Miller
News Editor-Night — Jim Jenkins
Photo Department Manager — Mark Fageol
Society/Women's Editor — Marcia Poole
Sports Editor — Terry Hersom

PRODUCTION
Foreman-Composing Room — Robert Olkiewicz
Foreman-Press — Lawrence James
Foreman-Mailroom — Brad Christopherson

Market Information: Zoned editions.
Mechanical available: Offset; Black and 3 ROP colors; insert accepted — preprinted; page cut-offs — 22¾".
Mechanical specifications: Type page 13" x 21½"; E - 6 cols, 2 1/16", 1/8" between; A - 6 cols, 2 1/16", 1/8" between; C - 9 cols, 1.33", 1/8" between.
Commodity consumption: Newsprint 3,000 metric tons; widths 27½", 13¾"; single pages printed 11,400; average pages per issue 24(d), 48(S); single plates used 13,000.
Equipment: EDITORIAL: Front-end hardware — COM/Intrepid 48; Front-end software — COM/One System; Printers — NewGen. CLASSIFIED: Front-end hardware — COM/Intrepid 48; Front-end software — COM/One System; Printers — Okidata/192. DISPLAY: Adv layout systems — 5-Archetype; Front-end hardware — PC/486; Front-end software — Archetype/Corel Draw; Printers — NewGen; Other equipment — Panasonic/Image Scanner 256. PRODUCTION: Typesetters — 2-NewGen; Scanners — Panasonic/Image Scanner 16; Digital color separation equipment — Lf/AP Leaf Picture Desk.
PRESSROOM: Line 1 — 10-G/Urbanite (2 Stacked). MAILROOM: Counter stackers — 1-Id; Inserters and stuffers — MM. WIRE SERVICES: News — AP; Stock tables — AP; Receiving dishes — AP.

SPENCER
Clay County
'90 U.S. Census- 11,066; E&P '96 Est. 10,925

The Daily Reporter
(m-tues to sat)
The Daily Reporter, 416 1st Ave. W.; PO Box 7920, Spencer, IA 51301; tel (712) 262-6610; fax (712) 262-3044. Edwards Publications group.
Circulation: 4,006(m); 4,006(m-sat); Sworn Sept. 26, 1995.
Price: 75¢(d); 75¢(sat); $6.50/mo; $60.00/yr.
Advertising: Open inch rate $5.40(m); $5.40(m-sat). **Representative:** Iowa Newspaper Assn.
News Services: AP, NEA. **Politics:** Independent. **Established:** 1874.
Not Published: New Year; Memorial Day; Independence Day; Labor Day; Thanksgiving Christmas.
Advertising not accepted: All advertising subject to publisher's approval.
Special Weekly Sections: Best Food Day (wed); TV (thur); Religion, Education (fri).
Magazine: TV Update (thur).

GENERAL MANAGEMENT
Publisher — Joni Weerheim
ADVERTISING
Director — Chris Swanson
CIRCULATION
Manager — Ron Courtney
NEWS EXECUTIVE
Editor — John Payne
MANAGEMENT INFORMATION SERVICES
Data Processing Manager — Terri Rolfes
PRODUCTION
Manager — Mary Britton

Market Information: Zoned editions; Split Run; TMC.
Mechanical available: Offset; Black and 3 ROP colors; insert accepted — preprinted, any; page cut-offs — 22 5/8".
Mechanical specifications: Type page 13" x 21½"; E - 6 cols, 2 1/16", 1/8" between; A - 6 cols, 2 1/16", 1/8" between; C - 6 cols, 2 1/16", 1/8" between.
Commodity consumption: Newsprint 650 short tons; widths 27", 31"; black ink 10,000 pounds; color ink 3,000 pounds; single pages printed 12; average pages per issue 10(d).
Equipment: EDITORIAL: Front-end hardware — Mk. CLASSIFIED: Front-end hardware — Mk. DISPLAY: Adv layout systems — 4-Ap/Mac. PRODUCTION: Typesetters — 2-Ap/Mac LaserWriter; Plate exposures — Nu; Plate processors — Nat/A-250; Scanners — Gam; Production cameras — SCREEN/Companica; Automatic film processors — P.
PRESSROOM: Line 1 — 5-G/Community. MAILROOM: Bundle tyer — Bu; Addressing machine — Am. WIRE SERVICES: News — AP; Syndicates — TMS, UPS, TV Data, United Media; Receiving dishes — AP. BUSINESS COMPUTERS: Ap/Mac; Applications: Circ, Payroll, Gen ledger.

STORM LAKE
Buena Vista County
'90 U.S. Census- 8,769; E&P '96 Est. 9,081

Pilot Tribune (m-tues to sat)
Pilot Tribune, 111 W. 7th St.; PO Box 1187, Storm Lake, IA 50588; tel (712) 732-3130; fax (712) 732-3152. Edwards Publications group.
Circulation: 4,358(m); 4,358(m-sat); Sworn Oct. 10, 1995.
Price: 50¢(d); 50¢(sat); $1.50/wk; $5.00/mo; $50.00/yr.
Advertising: Open inch rate $8.65(m); $8.65(m-sat). **Representative:** Iowa Newspaper Assn.
News Service: AP. **Politics:** Independent. **Established:** 1870.
Not Published: New Year; Independence Day; Thanksgiving; Christmas.
Special Editions: Bridal Tab, Iowa Corn Tab (Jan); College Coupon Tab, Progress Section (Feb); Winter Sports Tab, Ag Tab, Easter Bunny Giveaway (Mar); Spring Car Care Tab, Lawn/Home Tab, Spring Sports Tab (Apr); Beef/Critters Tab, Graduation Tab, Mug Shot (13-wk promotion), Travel Guide (May); Summer Sports Tab, Ecology Tab, Golden Years Tab, Star Spangled Spectacular Tab (June); Fair Preview/Review Tab, Ridiculous Day Tab (July); Thersheman Tab, Behind the Business Tab, Balloon Days Tab, Football Contest (12 wks) (Aug); Fall Sports Tab, Home Improvement Tab, Sailing in Storm Lake Tab, Fall Car Care Section (Sept); Pork Tab, Women in Business Tab (Oct); Open House Tab, X'mas Gift Tab, Thanksgiving Section, Winter Sports Tab, Layaway/Restaurant/Sunday (Sections) (Nov); X'mas Gift Tab, Greetings Sections, 1st Baby of the Year Contest (Dec).
Special Weekly Section: Television (sat).

CORPORATE OFFICER
Publisher — Michael K Harmon
GENERAL MANAGEMENT
Business Manager — Kari Vanderwoude
ADVERTISING
Manager — Teresa Rae
CIRCULATION
Manager — Phil Stough
NEWS EXECUTIVE
Managing Editor — Dana Larsen
EDITOR AND MANAGER
Sports Editor — Jamie Knapp
PRODUCTION
Manager-Composing — Lisa Harmon

Market Information: TMC; ADS.
Mechanical available: Web offset; Black and 3 ROP colors; insert accepted — preprinted; page cut-offs — 21".
Mechanical specifications: Type page 13" x 21½"; E - 6 cols, 2", 3/16" between; A - 8 cols, 1½", 3/16" between; C - 8 cols, 1½", 3/16" between.
Commodity consumption: Newsprint 428 short tons; widths 31", 27"; black ink 8,190 pounds; color ink 2,000 pounds; average pages per issue 14(d); single plates used 9,059.
Equipment: EDITORIAL: Front-end hardware — Ap/Mac; Front-end software — Baseview; Printers — Ap/Mac LaserPrinter. CLASSIFIED: Front-end hardware — Ap/Mac; Front-end software — Baseview; Printers — Ap/Mac LaserPrinter; Other equipment — Ap/Mac Imagesetter. DISPLAY: Front-end hardware — Ap/Mac Centris; Front-end software — QPS, Multi-Ad/Creator; Printers — 2-Ap/Mac LaserPrinter; Other equipment — 1-Lynx/Photo Imagesetter. PRODUCTION: OCR software — Caere/OmniPage; Typesetters — 1-Lynx/Imagesetter; Platemaking systems — Nu/Ultra Plus Flip Top; Plate processors — Nat/Automatic Plate Processor; Scanners — Microtek; Production cameras — Ca/Exposure Computer, SCREEN/DS C-250-D; Automatic film processors — AG/Rapidline 28; Digital color separation equipment — Adobe/Photoshop, Ap/Mac Centris, Lynx/Imagesetter.
PRESSROOM: Line 1 — 6-G/Community; Folders — 1-G/Community. MAILROOM: Bundle tyer — 2-Bu; Addressing machine — Ch/542 Base-532 Labeling head. WIRE SERVICES: News — AP, Iowa Link; Syndicates — NEA, NYT, CT; Receiving dishes — AP. BUSINESS COMPUTERS: Ap/Mac SE30; Applications: SBT; PCs & micros networked.

Copyright ©1996 by the Editor & Publisher Co.

VINTON

Benton County

'90 U.S. Census- 5,103; E&P '96 Est. 5,258

Cedar Valley Daily Times

(e-mon to fri)

Cedar Valley Daily Times, 108 E. Fifth St.; PO Box 468, Vinton, IA 52349; tel (319) 472-2311; fax (319) 472-4811. Mid-America Publishing group.

Circulation: 2,639(e); Sworn Aug. 28, 1995.

Price: 50¢(d); $60.00/yr (carrier), $49.00/yr (mail).

Advertising: Open inch rate $4.15(e). **Representatives:** American Newspaper Representatives Inc.; Iowa Newspaper Assn.

News Services: LAT-WP, Iowa Newspaper Media Link. **Politics:** Independent. **Established:** 1886.

Not Published: New Year; Memorial Day; Independence Day; Labor Day; Thanksgiving; Christmas.

Magazines: Monthly Farm editions; Pork and Beef.

GENERAL MANAGEMENT

Publisher — Doug Lindner

ADVERTISING

Manager — Merlin Alpers

CIRCULATION

Manager — Beverly Albert

NEWS EXECUTIVE

Editor — Doug Lindner

EDITOR AND MANAGER

Sports Editor — Jeff Holmes

PRODUCTION

Manager — Gene Deterding

Mechanical available: Offset; Black and 3 ROP colors; insert accepted — preprinted, mostly all; page cut-offs — $22\frac{3}{4}$".

Mechanical specifications: Type page $13\frac{7}{8}$" x 21"; E - 6 cols, $2\frac{3}{8}$", $\frac{3}{16}$" between; A - 6 cols, $2\frac{1}{8}$", $\frac{3}{16}$" between; C - 8 cols, $1\frac{5}{8}$", $\frac{1}{8}$" between.

Commodity consumption: Newsprint 250 short tons; widths 34", 30", 17", 15"; black ink 7,500 pounds; color ink 200 pounds; average pages per issue 8-10(d); single plates used 5,200.

Equipment: EDITORIAL: Front-end hardware — COM; Printers — 1-Ap/Mac LaserPrinter. CLASSIFIED: Front-end hardware — Ap/Mac; Printers — Ap/Mac ImageWriter. DISPLAY: Adv layout systems — Ap/Mac; Front-end software — Aldus/PageMaker. PRODUCTION: Pagination software — Aldus/PageMaker 4.2; Typesetters — 2-V/430; Plate exposures — 1-Nu; Production cameras — 1-B/17423; Automatic film processors — 1-P.
PRESSROOM: Line 1 — G/C-869; Folders — 1-G. MAILROOM: Counter stackers — 1-BG/Count-O-Veyor; Bundle tyer — 2-Bu; Addressing machine — 1-Am/500. BUSINESS COMPUTERS: PCs & micros networked; PCs & main system networked.

WASHINGTON

Washington County

'90 U.S. Census- 7,074; E&P '96 Est. 7,487

The Washington Evening Journal (e-mon to fri)

The Washington Evening Journal, 111 N. Marion Ave.; PO Box 471, Washington, IA 52353; tel (319) 653-2191; fax (319) 653-7524. Inland Industries Inc. group.

Circulation: 4,286(e); Sworn Oct. 2, 1995.

Price: 50¢(d); $69.00/yr.

Advertising: Open inch rate $5.79(e). **Representative:** Iowa Newspaper Assn.

News Service: AP. **Politics:** Independent. **Established:** 1893.

Not Published: New Year; Memorial Day; Independence Day; Labor Day; Thanksgiving; Christmas.

Special Editions: Beef Issue (May); Pork Production (Oct); Spring & Fall Opening; Christmas.

Special Weekly Sections: Business (mon); Best Food Day (tues); Farm Page (thur); Church Page, Week in Review (fri).

CORPORATE OFFICERS

Chairman — Clark O Murray
President — Darwin K Sherman
Exec Vice Pres — Jack D Burton

GENERAL MANAGEMENT

Publisher/General Manager — Darwin K Sherman
Purchasing Agent — Darwin K Sherman

ADVERTISING

Manager — Arnold Smith
Manager-Classified — Arnold Smith

EDITORS AND MANAGERS

City Editor — Brooks Taylor
Editorial Page Editor — Brooks Taylor
Chief Photographer — Brooks Taylor

PRODUCTION

Manager — Mark Bradley

Market Information: Split Run; TMC; ADS.

Mechanical available: Offset; Black and 3 ROP colors; insert accepted — preprinted; page cut-offs — $22\frac{3}{4}$".

Mechanical specifications: Type page 13" x $21\frac{1}{2}$"; E - 6 cols, $2\frac{1}{16}$", $\frac{1}{16}$" between; A - 6 cols, $2\frac{1}{16}$", $\frac{1}{16}$" between; C - 8 cols, $1\frac{9}{16}$", $\frac{1}{8}$" between.

Commodity consumption: Newsprint 180 metric tons; widths $13\frac{3}{4}$", $16\frac{3}{4}$", $27\frac{1}{2}$", $33\frac{1}{2}$"; single pages printed 2,540; average pages per issue 10(d).

Equipment: EDITORIAL: Front-end hardware — Ap/Mac; Front-end software — Microsoft/Word; Printers — Ap/Mac LaserWriter II NT. CLASSIFIED: Front-end hardware — Ap/Mac; Front-end software — Microsoft/Word, Aldus/PageMaker. DISPLAY: Front-end hardware — Ap/Mac; Front-end software — Aldus/PageMaker; Printers — Ap/Mac LaserWriter II NT. PRODUCTION: Typesetters — Ap/Mac NT; Plate exposures — Nu; Automatic film processors — P.
PRESSROOM: Line 1 — HI/V-15A. WIRE SERVICES: News — AP; Syndicates — UPS. BUSINESS COMPUTERS: PC; Applications: BMF; PCs & micros networked; PCs & main system networked.

WATERLOO-CEDAR FALLS-EVANSDALE

Black Hawk County

'90 U.S. Census- 105,403 (Waterloo 66,467; Cedar Falls 34,298; Evansdale 4,638); E&P '96 Est. 101,585 (Waterloo 63,025; Cedar Falls 33,871; Evansdale 4,689)

ABC-CZ (90): 107,110 (HH 41,012)

Waterloo Courier

(e-mon to fri; S)

Waterloo Courier, 501 Commercial St.; PO Box 540, Waterloo, IA 50704; tel (319) 291-1400; fax (319) 234-6405. Howard Publications group.

Circulation: 47,065(e); 54,826(S); ABC Sept. 30, 1995.

Price: 50¢(d); $1.75(S); $3.00/wk; $156.00/yr.

Advertising: Open inch rate $30.32(e); $30.61(S). **Representatives:** Landon Associates Inc.; Iowa Newspaper Assn.

News Service: AP. **Politics:** Independent. **Established:** 1858.

Special Weekly Sections: Fashion (mon); Food (tues); Arts (wed); People (thur); Health, FRIDAY (weekend) (fri); Travel Pages (S).

Magazines: Parade, Color Comics, TV Showtime (S).

CORPORATE OFFICER

Secretary/Treasurer — Richard Newell

GENERAL MANAGEMENT

Publisher/General Manager — James W Lewis
Business Manager — Jerald W Zeiner
Asst to Publisher — David Tansey

ADVERTISING

Director — David Tansey
Manager-General — David Tansey
Manager-Classified — Sharon Jordan

CIRCULATION

Exec Director — Virgil Dahl

NEWS EXECUTIVES

Editor — Saul Shapiro
Managing Editor — Eric Woolson

EDITORS AND MANAGERS

Books Editor — Carolyn Cole
Business/Finance Editor — Pat Kinney
Business Editor — Pat Kinney
City Editor — Patt Johnson
Copy Editor — Dave Martin
Editorial Page Editor — Eric Woolson
Editorial Writer — Eric Woolson
Education Editor — Jim Stanton
Fashion Editor — Carolyn Cole
Films Editor — Melody Parker
Food/Garden Editor — Curt Glenn
Home Furnishings Editor — Melody Parker
Music Editor — Melody Parker
Photo Department Manager — Dan Nierling
Radio/Television Editor — Curt Glenn
Religion Editor — Carolyn Cole
School Editor — Jim Stanton
Society/Women's Editor — Carolyn Cole
Sports Editor — Kevin Evans
Teen-Age/Youth Editor — Lisa Cosmillo
Travel Editor — Carolyn Cole

PRODUCTION

Foreman-Composing — Brian Lewis
Foreman-Press — Joe Snyder
Foreman-Mailroom — Greg Schmitz

Market Information: Zoned editions; Split Run; TMC.

Mechanical available: Offset; Black and 3 ROP colors; insert accepted — preprinted; page cut-offs — $22\frac{3}{4}$".

Mechanical specifications: Type page 13" x $21\frac{1}{2}$"; E - 6 cols, $2\frac{1}{8}$", $\frac{1}{6}$" between; A - 6 cols, $2\frac{1}{8}$", $\frac{1}{6}$" between; C - 9 cols, $1\frac{3}{8}$", $\frac{1}{6}$" between.

Commodity consumption: Newsprint 3,750 metric tons; widths 55", $41\frac{1}{4}$", $27\frac{1}{2}$", $13\frac{3}{4}$"; black ink 120,000 pounds; color ink 12,000 pounds; single pages printed 13,200; average pages per issue 36(d), 82(S); single plates used 20,500.

Equipment: EDITORIAL: Front-end hardware — Sun; Front-end software — Arbortext, QuarkXPress; Printers — ECR/PelBox, Ap/Mac LaserWriters. CLASSIFIED: Front-end hardware — Sun; Front-end software — Unify, Island Write; Printers — Ap/Mac LaserWriters, ECR/PelBox. DISPLAY: Adv layout systems — SCS; Front-end hardware — Ap/Mac; Front-end software — QuarkXPress; Printers — Ap/Mac LaserWriters, ECR/PelBox. PRODUCTION: Pagination software — QPS; Typesetters — 2-ECR/Autokon PelBox; Plate exposures — Nu; Plate processors — W; Electronic picture desk — Lf/AP Leaf Picture Desk; Scanners — Lf, AG/Horizon; Production cameras — B; Automatic film processors — LE; Shrink lenses — B; Color separation equipment (conventional) — Nikon; Digital color separation equipment — Nikon, AG.
PRESSROOM: Line 1 — 5-PEC (3-Black; 2-Color); Press drives — Hurletron; Folders — G; Pasters — G, G; Reels and stands — G; Press control system — Hurletron. MAILROOM: Counter stackers — 3-Id/440; Inserters and stuffers — 2-MM/308; Bundle tyer — 2-MLN/Hi speed; Addressing machine — 1-KR. LIBRARY: Electronic — Sun, Topic. WIRE SERVICES: News — AP; Photos — AP; Stock tables — AP; Syndicates — LAT-WP, NAS, Creators, TMS, Universal Press; Receiving dishes — size-10ft, AP. BUSINESS COMPUTERS: 1-Sun/Sparc; Applications: Vision Data, Access Technology: 2.54; PCs & micros networked; PCs & main system networked.

WEBSTER CITY

Hamilton County

'90 U.S. Census- 7,894; E&P '96 Est. 7,564

ABC-CZ (90): 7,894 (HH 3,205)

The Daily Freeman-Journal

(e-mon to fri)

The Daily Freeman-Journal, 720 Second St.; PO Box 490, Webster City, IA 50595; tel (515) 832-4350; fax (515) 832-2314. Ogden Newspapers group.

Circulation: 3,633(e); ABC Sept. 30, 1995.

Price: 35¢(d); $59.80/yr.

Advertising: Open inch rate $8.12(e); comb with Ft. Dodge Messenger (m) $25.26. **Representatives:** Papert Companies; Iowa Newspaper Assn.

News Service: AP. **Politics:** Independent-Republican. **Established:** 1847.

Not Published: New Year; Memorial Day; Independence Day; Labor Day; Thanksgiving; Christmas.

Advertising not accepted: Schemes requiring under $1,000 investment.

Special Editions: Dollar Days; Back-to-School; County Fair; X'mas Countdown; Christmas Shopping; Medical Directory; Spring Agriculture Supplement.

Special Weekly Section: TV Journal (fri).

CORPORATE OFFICER

President — G Ogden Nutting

GENERAL MANAGEMENT

Publisher — Daniel Corrow
General Manager — Mike Fertiz

ADVERTISING

Manager — Jay Ouverson

CIRCULATION

Manager — Lori Fischels

NEWS EXECUTIVE

Editor — Lori Nilles

PRODUCTION

Foreman-Press — Jeff Morris

Market Information: TMC.

Mechanical available: Offset; Black and 3 ROP colors; insert accepted — preprinted; page cut-offs — $22\frac{3}{4}$".

Mechanical specifications: Type page 13" x $21\frac{1}{2}$"; E - 6 cols, $2\frac{1}{16}$", $\frac{1}{8}$" between; A - 6 cols, $2\frac{1}{16}$", $\frac{1}{8}$" between; C - 9 cols, $1\frac{5}{16}$", $\frac{1}{8}$" between.

Commodity consumption: Newsprint 78 short tons; width 27"; black ink 1,410 pounds; color ink 250 pounds; single pages printed 2,570; average pages per issue 10(d); single plates used 3,302.

Equipment: EDITORIAL: Front-end hardware — 6-COM/MDT 350. PRODUCTION: Typesetters — 2-COM/7900, 3-COM/2750; Plate exposures — 1-Nu; Plate processors — 1-WL; Production cameras — 1-B, 1-DAI; Automatic film processors — 1-P.
PRESSROOM: Line 1 — 12-G/Urbanite; Folders — 2-G/3:2. MAILROOM: Counter stackers — 2-BG/108; Bundle tyer — 2-Bu; Addressing machine — 1-Kr. LIBRARY: Electronic — 1-Recordak/MPG 1; Combination — 1-X. WIRE SERVICES: News — AP; Receiving dishes — size-10ft, AP.

KANSAS

ABILENE

Dickinson County

'90 U.S. Census- 6,242; E&P '96 Est. 6,178

Abilene Reflector-Chronicle

(e-mon to sat)

Abilene Reflector-Chronicle, 303 Broadway; PO Box 8, Abilene, KS 67410; tel (913) 263-1000. Cleveland Newspapers Inc. group.

Circulation: 4,252(e); 4,252(e-sat); Sworn Oct. 2, 1995.

Price: 50¢(d); 50¢(sat); $6.10/mo; $72.00/yr.

Advertising: Open inch rate $6.30(e); $6.30(e-sat).

News Service: AP. **Politics:** Republican. **Established:** 1872.

Not Published: New Year; Memorial Day; Independence Day; Labor Day; Thanksgiving; Christmas.

Special Editions: Progress; Graduation; Christmas; Education; Enrolment Edition; Fair & Rodeo; Dairy; Soil Conservation; Basketball; Football; Wrestling; Vacation Tab; Recipe Tab; Fall Home Tour Tab.

Magazine: TV Guide.

CORPORATE OFFICERS

President — Vivien L Sadowski
Secretary/Treasurer — Yvonne Walls

GENERAL MANAGEMENT

Publisher — Vivien L Sadowski

ADVERTISING

Manager — Janelle Gantenbein

CIRCULATION

Manager — Ronald Hostetler

NEWS EXECUTIVE

Managing Editor — Dave Bergmeier

EDITORS AND MANAGERS

City/County Editor — Ericka Breckenridge
Society Editor — Marge Moore
Sports Editor — Julie Perry

Market Information: Zoned editions; TMC.

Mechanical available: Offset; Black and 3 ROP colors; insert accepted — preprinted; page cut-offs — $21\frac{1}{2}$".

Mechanical specifications: Type page 13" x $21\frac{1}{2}$"; E - 6 cols, $2\frac{1}{16}$", $\frac{1}{8}$" between; A - 6 cols, $2\frac{1}{16}$", $\frac{1}{8}$" between; C - 6 cols, $2\frac{1}{16}$", $\frac{1}{8}$" between.

Commodity consumption: Newsprint 135 short tons; widths 28", 14"; black ink 10 barrels pounds; single pages printed 3,250; average pages per issue 12(d); single plates used 2,800.

Equipment: CLASSIFIED: Other equipment — 2-IBM/Typewriter. PRODUCTION: Platemaking systems — 1-B/Ultra-Lite Plate Burner; Plate processors — 1-Nat/A-250; Production cameras — 1-Acti; Automatic film processors — 1-Kk.

Copyright ©1996 by the Editor & Publisher Co.

PRESSROOM: Line 1 — 4-G; Folders — 1-G/2:1. MAILROOM: Bundle tyer — 1-Sa; Addressing machine — 1-Am. WIRE SERVICES: News — AP; Receiving dishes — AP. BUSINESS COMPUTERS: Applications: Accts receivable, Gen ledger, Payroll.

ARKANSAS CITY

Cowley County

'90 U.S. Census- 12,762; E&P '96 Est. 12,762

Arkansas City Traveler

(e-mon to fri; m-sat)

Arkansas City Traveler, 200 E. 5th Ave.; PO Box 988, Arkansas City, KS 67005; tel (316) 442-4200; fax (316) 442-7483. Morris Communications Corp. group.

Circulation: 5,478(e); 5,478(m-sat); Sworn Sept. 30, 1994.

Price: 50¢(d); 50¢(sat); $97.00/yr.

Advertising: Open inch rate $6.80(e); $6.80(m-sat). **Representative:** Papert Companies.

News Service: AP. **Politics:** Independent. **Established:** 1870.

Not Published: New Year; Memorial Day; Independence Day; Labor Day; Thanksgiving; Christmas.

Special Weekly Sections: Education (mon); Business (tues); Food (wed); Farm Page (thur); Church, Health (fri); Weddings/Engagements (sat).

CORPORATE OFFICERS

Chairman of the Board	W S Morris III
President	Paul S Simon
Secretary/Treasurer	William A Herman III

GENERAL MANAGEMENT

Publisher	Kim Benedict

ADVERTISING

Manager	Lisa Froese

CIRCULATION

Manager	Barbara Babcock

NEWS EXECUTIVES

Editor	Kim Benedict
Managing Editor	Rick Horn

EDITORS AND MANAGERS

Farm/City Editor	Jeff Guy
Society Editor	Rick Horn
Sports Editor	Rick Horn

PRODUCTION

Manager	Kip Wedel

Market Information: Zoned editions; Split Run; TMC.

Mechanical available: Offset; Black and 3 ROP colors; insert accepted — preprinted, all.

Mechanical specifications: Type page 13" x 21½"; E - 6 cols, 2", 3/16" between; A - 6 cols, 2", 3/16" between; C - 6 cols, 2", 3/16" between.

Commodity consumption: Newsprint 322 short tons; width 28"; single pages printed 4,340; average pages per issue 12(d).

Equipment: EDITORIAL: Front-end hardware — Ap/Mac, 3-Ap/Mac IIsi, 5-Ap/Mac Classic, 6-Ap/Mac SE, 1-Ap/Mac IIci; Other equipment — SMS/Stauffer Gold, Ap/Mac SE Super Drive. CLASSIFIED: Front-end hardware — 1-Ap/Mac; Printers — Ap/Mac LaserPrinter. DISPLAY: Printers — Ap/Mac LaserWriter II, Ap/Mac LaserWriter II NTX. PRODUCTION: Typesetters — Ap/Mac LaserWriter II, Ap/Mac LaserWriter II NTX; Platemaking systems — 1-B/Acti; Plate exposures — B/5000; Plate processors — Nat/A-250; Production cameras — 1-B, Acti; Automatic film processors — SCREEN.

PRESSROOM: Line 1 — 7-G/Community; Folders — 1-G. MAILROOM: Bundle tyer — 1-Sa; Addressing machine — 2-Am. LIBRARY: Electronic — SMS/Stauffer Gold. WIRE SERVICES: News — AP; Receiving dishes — size-3ft, AP. BUSINESS COMPUTERS: ATT; Applications: Accts receivable, Accts payable, Payroll, Circ billing, Gen Ledger.

ATCHISON

Atchison County

'90 U.S. Census- 10,656; E&P '96 Est. 10,444

Atchison Daily Globe

(e-mon to fri; m-sat)

Atchison Daily Globe, 1015-25 Main St.; PO Box 247, Atchison, KS 66002; tel (913) 367-0583; fax (913) 367-7531. Hollinger International Inc. group.

Circulation: 4,226(e); 4,226(m-sat); Sworn Sept. 27, 1995.

Price: 50¢(d); $1.00(sat); $7.45/mo (carrier), $8.65/mo (mail); $89.40/yr (carrier), $96.00/yr (mail).

Advertising: Open inch rate $8.55(e); $8.55(m-sat). **Representative:** American Publishers Reps.

News Service: AP. **Politics:** Independent. **Established:** 1877.

Not Published: New Year; Memorial Day; Independence Day; Labor Day; Thanksgiving; Christmas.

Special Editions: Brides; Farm; Progress; Graduation; County Fair; Back-to-School; Fall Sports; Christmas Gift; Medical Guide; College Life; Winter Sports.

GENERAL MANAGEMENT

Publisher	Stan Wilson
Accountant	Marilyn Andre

CIRCULATION

Manager	Dave Delk

NEWS EXECUTIVE

Editor	James Headley

EDITORS AND MANAGERS

Business/Finance Editor	James Headley
Photo Department Manager	Chris Taylor
Sports Editor	Reuben Mosqueda
Women's Editor	Phyllis Bomberger

PRODUCTION

Foreman-Paste-Up	Emogene Kautz

Market Information: TMC.

Mechanical available: Offset; Black and 3 ROP colors; insert accepted — preprinted; page cut-offs — 22¾".

Mechanical specifications: Type page 13" x 21½"; E - 6 cols, 2 1/16", ⅛" between; A - 6 cols, 2 1/16", ⅛" between; C - 8 cols, 1½", ⅛" between.

Commodity consumption: Newsprint 220 short tons; width 27½"; single pages printed 3,963; average pages per issue 12(d).

Equipment: EDITORIAL: Front-end hardware — Ap/Mac; Front-end software — Microsoft/Word; Printers — 2-Ap/Mac LaserWriter Plus. CLASSIFIED: Front-end hardware — Ap/Mac; Front-end software — CAMS; Printers — Ap/Mac LaserWriter Plus. DISPLAY: Adv layout systems — Ap/Mac; Front-end hardware — Ap/Mac; Front-end software — Multi-Ad/Creator; Printers — Ap/Mac LaserWriter Plus. PRODUCTION: Plate exposures — Nu/UP; Production cameras — SCREEN/Companica 680 C; Automatic film processors — LE/LD-220-QT.

PRESSROOM: Line 1 — 5-HI/V-15-A. MAILROOM: Bundle tyer — OVL. WIRE SERVICES: News — AP; Receiving dishes — AP. BUSINESS COMPUTERS: MIS/486; Applications: Lotus 1-2-3: Accounting.

AUGUSTA

Butler County

'90 U.S. Census- 7,876; E&P '96 Est. 8,617

Augusta Daily Gazette

(e-mon to fri)

Augusta Daily Gazette, 204 E. 5th St.; PO Box 9, Augusta, KS 67010; tel (316) 775-2218; fax (316) 775-3220. Hollinger International Inc. group.

Circulation: 2,686(e); Sworn Oct. 2, 1995.

Price: 50¢(d); $6.20/mo (carrier); $61.27/yr (in county).

Advertising: Open inch rate $6.80(e).

News Service: AP. **Politics:** Independent. **Established:** 1893.

Note: For printing and production information see the El Dorado Times.

Not Published: New Year; President's Day; Memorial Day; Independence Day; Labor Day; Thanksgiving; Christmas.

Special Editions: Yearly Review Section (Jan); Women's Section (Apr); Spring Opening, Graduation (May); Get Ready for School (Aug); Football (Sept); Cookbook, Progress (Nov); Christmas (Dec).

CORPORATE OFFICERS

President/CEO	Larry J Perrotto
Comptroller	Roland McBride

ADVERTISING

Director	Len Hudson

CIRCULATION

Manager	Bill Kincaid

NEWS EXECUTIVE

Editor	Michael McDermott

EDITORS AND MANAGERS

Action Line Editor	Michael McDermott
Business/Finance Editor	Michael McDermott
City/Metro Editor	Michael McDermott
Columnist	Anita Johnson
Editorial Page Editor	Michael McDermott
Education Editor	Robert Clausing
Entertainment/Amusements Editor	Mike Wallace
Fashion/Style Editor	Mike Wallace
Graphics Editor/Art Director	Rhonda Zinn
Living/Lifestyles Editor	Gayla Bonnell
News Editor	Michael McDermott
Photo Editor	Chris Strunk
Religion Editor	Chris Strunk
School Editor	Robert Clausing
Science Editor	Michael McDermott
Society Editor	Mike Wallace
Sports Editor	Chris Strunk
Teen-Age/Youth Editor	Mike Wallace
Women's Editor	Mike Wallace

MANAGEMENT INFORMATION SERVICES

Data Processing Manager	Becky Cryderman

PRODUCTION

Manager-Commercial Printing	Gene Sowers

Market Information: Split Run; TMC.

Mechanical available: Offset; Black and 2 ROP colors; insert accepted — preprinted; page cut-offs — 22¾".

Mechanical specifications: Type page 13" x 21"; E - 6 cols, 2¼", ⅛" between; A - 6 cols, 2¼", ⅛" between; C - 6 cols, 2¼", ⅛" between.

Commodity consumption: Newsprint 217 short tons; widths 28", 14"; black ink 5,806 pounds; color ink 1,076 pounds; single pages printed 1,785; average pages per issue 7(d); single plates used 1,972.

Equipment: EDITORIAL: Front-end hardware — Mk; Printers — Ap/Mac LaserPrinter.

PRESSROOM: Line 1 — 1-Chief/17, 1-Chief/117; Line 2 — Solm 17x22. MAILROOM: Bundle tyer — Bu. WIRE SERVICES: News — AP; Syndicates — Creators, Cowles, NEA; Receiving dishes — AP. BUSINESS COMPUTERS: IBM.

BELOIT

Mitchell County

'90 U.S. Census- 4,066; E&P '96 Est. 3,977

Beloit Daily Call & Post

(e-mon to fri)

Beloit Daily Call & Post, 122 E. Court; PO Box 366, Beloit, KS 67420; tel (913) 738-3537; fax (913) 738-6442.

Circulation: 2,706(e); Sworn Sept. 30, 1992.

Price: 35¢(d); $31.57/yr (carrier).

Advertising: Open inch rate $5.82(e).

News Service: AP. **Politics:** Independent. **Established:** 1872 (weekly), 1901 (daily).

Not Published: New Year; Memorial Day; Independence Day; Veteran's Day; Labor Day; Thanksgiving; Christmas.

Special Editions: Spring Lake Edition; Fall Hunting Edition; Soil Conservation Edition, ½ Day Sale (Jan); Progress Edition, President's Day Sale (Feb); Home Improvement & Lawn & Garden (Apr); Mother's Day (May); Father's Day (June); Back-to-School, Sidewalk Sale (Aug); Moonlight Madness (Oct); Christmas Edition (Nov/Dec).

Magazine: TV Schedule (fri).

Cable TV: Operate leased cable TV in circulation area.

GENERAL MANAGEMENT

Publisher	Joe Beach

ADVERTISING

Manager	Stacy Frost

CIRCULATION

Manager	Jennifer Kresin

NEWS EXECUTIVE

Editor	Linda Wellman

EDITOR AND MANAGER

Sports Editor	Bobbi Gati

PRODUCTION

Manager	Robert Milburn
Foreman-Press	Robert Milburn

Market Information: Zoned editions; TMC.

Mechanical available: Offset; Black and 1 ROP color; insert accepted — preprinted; page cut-offs — 22¾".

Mechanical specifications: Type page 13" x 21"; E - 6 cols, 2 1/16", ⅛" between; A - 6 cols, 2 1/16", ⅛" between; C - 6 cols, 2 1/16", ⅛" between.

Commodity consumption: Newsprint 70 short tons; widths 27½", 13¾"; black ink 825 pounds; color ink 20 pounds; average pages per issue 10(d); single plates used 3,120.

Equipment: EDITORIAL: Front-end hardware — COM, RSK. DISPLAY: Adv layout systems — 1-RSK/TRS-80. PRODUCTION: Typesetters — COM/Trendsetter; Plate exposures — 1-B; Production cameras — B.

PRESSROOM: Line 1 — 3-G/Community. MAILROOM: Addressing machine — 1-Am, 1-Pressure Sensitive/Labeling. WIRE SERVICES: News — AP; Receiving dishes — AP. BUSINESS COMPUTERS: IBM/Main frame 36.

CHANUTE

Neosho County

'90 U.S. Census- 9,488; E&P '96 Est. 9,115

The Chanute Tribune

(e-mon to fri; m-sat)

The Chanute Tribune, 15 N. Evergreen; PO Box 559, Chanute, KS 66720; tel (316) 431-4100; fax (316) 431-2635. Harris Enterprises Inc. group.

Circulation: 4,595(e); 4,595(m-sat); Sworn Oct. 1, 1995.

Price: 50¢(d); 50¢(sat); $84.46/yr.

Advertising: Open inch rate $6.75(e); $6.75(m-sat). **Representative:** Papert Companies.

News Service: AP. **Politics:** Independent. **Established:** 1892.

Not Published: New Year; Memorial Day; Independence Day; Labor Day; Thanksgiving; Christmas.

Special Editions: Tax Tab (Feb); Bridal Tab (Mar); Basketball, Progress, Lawn, Garden & Home (Apr); Summer Fun (June); Medical Tab (July); Back-to-School (Aug); Football (Sept); Christmas, Holiday Recipe, Gift Guide (Dec).

Special Weekly Sections: Business, Agriculture (mon); Best Food Day, Community News, Anniversaries (tues); Farm News, Seniors (wed); Education (thur); Entertainment, Religion, Family (fri); Weddings, Engagements (sat).

Magazine: `This Week' (local, newsprint) (sat).

CORPORATE OFFICERS

President	Thomas N Bell
Vice Pres	Lloyd Ballhagen
Secretary/Treasurer	Bruce A Royse

GENERAL MANAGEMENT

Publisher	Thomas N Bell
Purchasing Agent	Thomas N Bell

ADVERTISING

Director	JoAnne D Johnson

CIRCULATION

Manager	Brenda Peck

NEWS EXECUTIVES

Editor	Thomas N Bell
Managing Editor	Stuart Butcher

EDITORS AND MANAGERS

Business/Finance Editor	Stuart Butcher
Editorial Page Editor	Thomas N Bell
Fashion/School Editor	Connie Woodard
News Editor	Stuart Butcher
Picture Editor	Mark Colson
Religion Editor	Stuart Butcher
Sports Editor	Mack McClure
Teen-Age/Youth Editor	Connie Woodard
Travel Editor	Stuart Butcher

MANAGEMENT INFORMATION SERVICES

Data Processing Manager	Bruce A Royse

PRODUCTION

Foreman-Pressroom	Vester Reed

Market Information: Split Run; TMC.

Mechanical available: Offset; Black and 3 ROP colors; insert accepted — preprinted; page cut-offs — 22¾".

Mechanical specifications: Type page 13" x 21½"; E - 6 cols, 2 1/16", ⅛" between; A - 6 cols, 2 1/16", ⅛" between; C - 8 cols, 1⅜", 1/16" between.

Commodity consumption: Newsprint 230 short tons; width 27"; average pages per issue 12(d).

Equipment: EDITORIAL: Front-end hardware — Mk; Front-end software — Mk; Printers — Ap/Mac LaserWriters. CLASSIFIED: Front-end hardware — Mk; Front-end software — Mk; Printers — TI. PRODUCTION: Typesetters — 2-Ap/Mac LaserWriter NT, 2-Ap/Mac Plus; Plate exposures — 1-Nu; Production cameras — 1-R; Automatic film processors — 1-Kk.

PRESSROOM: Line 1 — 5-G/Community; Folders — 1-G/Suburban. MAILROOM: Inserters and stuffers — KAN; Bundle tyer — 1-Bu; Addressing machine — 2-Wm. WIRE SERVICES: News — AP; Syndicates — King Features, NAS, United Media, Creators; Receiving dishes — AP. BUSINESS COMPUTERS: 1-

Copyright ©1996 by the Editor & Publisher Co.

TI/1500; Applications: PaperTrak: Circ, Accts receivable, Accts payable, Payroll; PCs & micros networked; PCs & main system networked.

CLAY CENTER
Clay County
'90 U.S. Census- 4,613; E&P '96 Est. 4,516

The Clay Center Dispatch
(e-mon to fri)

The Clay Center Dispatch, 805 5th St.; Box 519, Clay Center, KS 67432; tel (913) 632-2127.
Circulation: 2,957(e); Sworn Oct. 1, 1994.
Price: 35¢(d).
Advertising: Open inch rate $4.66(e). **Representative:** Landon Associates Inc.
News Service: AP. **Politics:** Independent. **Established:** 1873.
Not Published: New Year; Memorial Day; Independence Day; Labor Day; Columbus Day; Veteran's Day; Thanksgiving; Christmas.
Advertising not accepted: Liquor.
Special Editions: Conservation Edition, Social Security/Tax (Jan); F.F.A. Edition, Boy Scouts Edition (Feb); Gardening, Car Care, Girl Scouts Edition (Mar); Home & Garden (Apr); Graduation (May); Fair Preview Tab (July); Back-to-School (Aug); Car Care, 4-H Edition (Oct); Auto Care, Christmas, Recipe (Nov).

CORPORATE OFFICER
President/Treasurer .... H E Valentine Jr
GENERAL MANAGEMENT
Publisher/General Manager .... H E Valentine Jr
Purchasing Agent/Business Manager
.... H E Valentine Jr
ADVERTISING
Director .... Jamie Bloom
CIRCULATION
Director .... Shari Huffman
NEWS EXECUTIVE
Editor .... Wayne Culley
EDITORS AND MANAGERS
Auto Editor .... Jeannine Anderson
Columnist .... H E Valentine Jr
Editorial Page Editor .... H E Valentine Jr
Fashion/Home Furnishings Editor .. Diane Rickley
Society Editor .... Diane Rickley
Sports Editor .... Dave Berggren
PRODUCTION
Superintendent/Foreman-Composing
.... Robert Dankenbring
Market Information: TMC.
Mechanical available: Offset; Black and 3 ROP colors; insert accepted — preprinted; page cutoffs — 22¾".
Mechanical specifications: Type page 13" x 21"; E – 6 cols, 2 1/16", 1/8" between; A – 6 cols, 2 1/16", 1/8" between; C – 6 cols, 2 1/16", 1/8" between.
Commodity consumption: Newsprint 80 short tons; widths 28", 14"; average pages per issue 9(d).
Equipment: EDITORIAL: Front-end hardware — PC; Printers — HP/LaserJet. CLASSIFIED: Front-end hardware — PC; Printers — HP/LaserJet. DISPLAY: Adv layout systems — Archetype/Corel Draw; Front-end hardware — PC. PRODUCTION: Typesetters — HP; Plate exposures — 1-Nu/Flip Top; Production cameras — 1-K/240V.
PRESSROOM: Line 1 — G/Community; Folders — 1-G/3:1. MAILROOM: Addressing machine — 1-Ch. WIRE SERVICES: News — AP; Receiving dishes — AP. BUSINESS COMPUTERS: Epson/386, Acer/486; Applications: Business.

COFFEYVILLE
Montgomery County
'90 U.S. Census- 12,917; E&P '96 Est. 11,970

The Coffeyville Journal
(e-tues to fri; S)

The Coffeyville Journal, Eighth & Elm St.; PO Box 849, Coffeyville, KS 67337-0849; tel (316) 251-3300; fax (316) 251-1905. Hometown Communications group.
Circulation: 5,841(e); 5,841(S); Sworn Sept. 27, 1993.
Price: 35¢(d); 75¢(S); $6.70/mo; $74.00/yr.
Advertising: Open inch rate $8.72(e); $8.72(S). **Representative:** Papert Companies.
News Service: AP. **Politics:** Independent. **Established:** 1875.
Advertising not accepted: Vending machine routes; Work at home; Astrology.
Special Editions: Recipe (Mar); Graduation (May); Fair, Back-to-School (Aug); Fashion (Sept).
Magazine: TV Watch (own) (S).

CORPORATE OFFICER
President .... Jim McGinnis
GENERAL MANAGEMENT
Publisher .... Mike Thornberry
ADVERTISING
Director .... Chris Zimmerman
CIRCULATION
Manager .... Dee Kitterman
NEWS EXECUTIVE
Editor .... Tim Flowers

Kansas

I-153

EDITORS AND MANAGERS
City Editor .... Glenn Craven
Sports Editor .... Allen Twichell
Women's Editor .... Carol Eli
PRODUCTION
Supervisor-Composing .... Juanita Flowers
Market Information: TMC.
Mechanical available: Offset; Black and 3 ROP colors; insert accepted — preprinted; page cutoffs — 22¾".
Mechanical specifications: Type page 13" x 21½"; E – 6 cols, 2 1/16", 1/8" between; A – 6 cols, 2 1/16", 1/8" between; C – 9 cols, 1 3/8", 1/8" between.
Commodity consumption: Newsprint 225 short tons; widths 27", 13½"; black ink 8,700 pounds; color ink 775 pounds; single pages printed 4,200; average pages per issue 10(d), 22(S); single plates used 5,600.
Equipment: EDITORIAL: Front-end hardware — 2-DEC/PDP 11-34, Hx/Hs 46. CLASSIFIED: Front-end hardware — 1-Hx. DISPLAY: Adv layout systems — 1-Hx. PRODUCTION: Typesetters — 2-COM/Universal Videosetter; Plate exposures — 1-B/5000; Plate processors — 1-Nat/A-250; Production cameras — 1-R/480; Automatic film processors — 1-LE/LD24AQ; Color separation equipment (conventional) — 1-BKY.
PRESSROOM: Line 1 — 6-HI/Cotrell V-22; Folders — 1-HI/2:1. MAILROOM: Counter stackers — HI/RS 25; Bundle tyer — 2-Bu. WIRE SERVICES: News — AP Datastream; Receiving dishes — size-3m, AP. BUSINESS COMPUTERS: DPT; Applications: All bus office transactions.

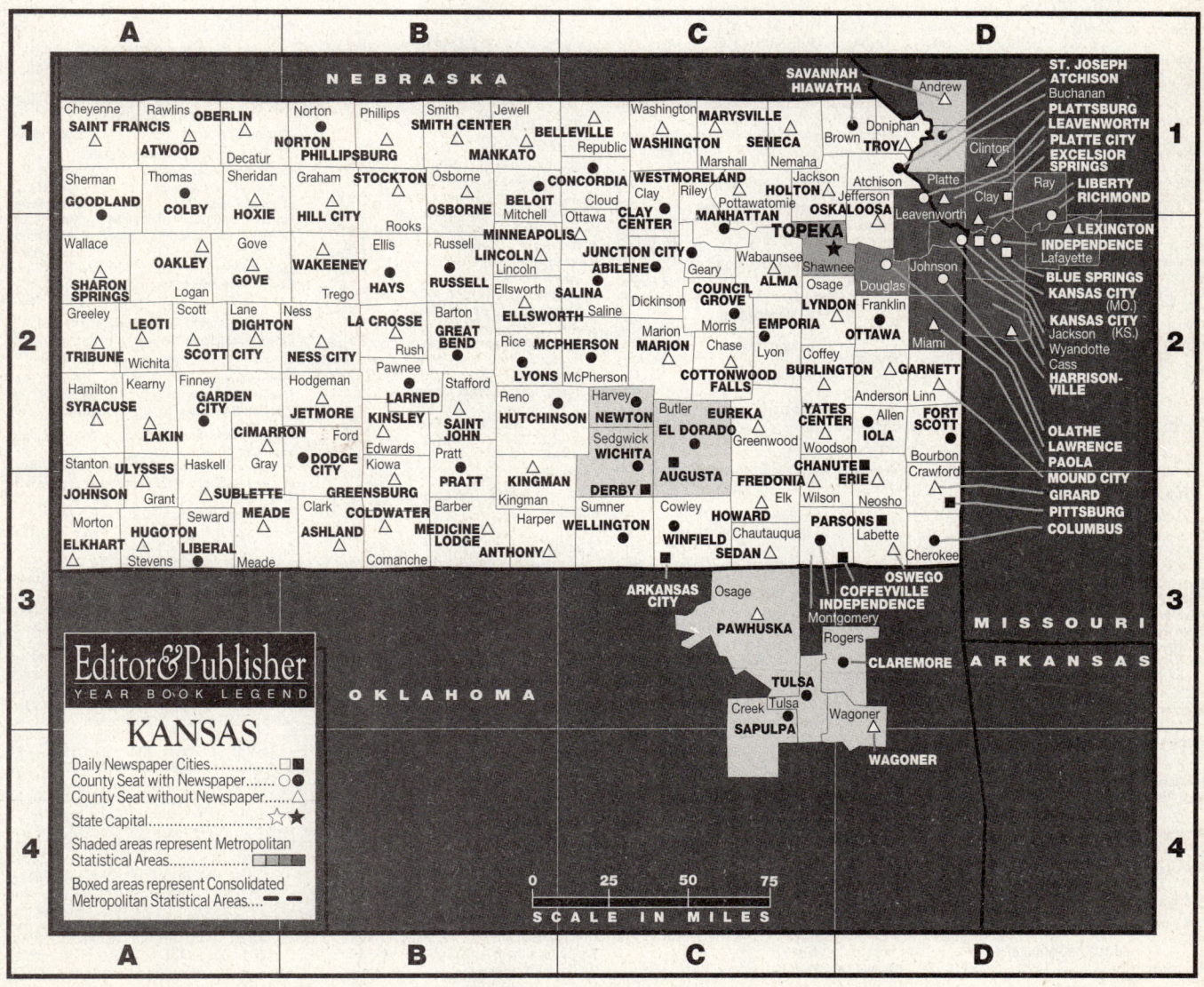

Copyright ©1996 by the Editor & Publisher Co.

COLBY
Thomas County
'90 U.S. Census- 5,396; E&P '96 Est. 5,417

Colby Free Press
(e-mon to thur; m-sat)

Colby Free Press, 155 W. 5th St.; PO Box 806, Colby, KS 67701; tel (913) 462-3963; fax (913) 462-7749. USMedia Inc. group.
Circulation: 2,757(e); 2,757(m-sat); Sworn Oct. 1, 1992.
Price: 50¢(d); 50¢(sat); $60.00/yr (outside state), $50.00/yr (local).
Advertising: Open inch rate $7.00(e); $7.00(m-sat).
News Service: AP. **Politics:** Independent. **Established:** 1888.
Not Published: New Year; Independence Day; Thanksgiving; Christmas.
Special Editions: Travel Guide; Progress; Newcomers; Spring Fashions; Car Care; Conservation; Back-to-School; Christmas Season Opening.

GENERAL MANAGEMENT
Publisher Patty Decker
Business Manager Debbie Denton
ADVERTISING
Manager Patty Decker
CIRCULATION
Manager Annisa Mercurio
NEWS EXECUTIVE
Managing Editor Patty Decker
PRODUCTION
Manager Larry Hiller

Market Information: TMC.
Mechanical available: Offset; Black and 2 ROP colors; insert accepted — preprinted; page cut-offs — 21½".
Mechanical specifications: Type page 13" x 21½"; E - 6 cols, 2¹⁄₁₆", ⅛" between; A - 6 cols, 2¹⁄₁₆", ⅛" between; C - 6 cols, 2¹⁄₁₆", ⅛" between.
Commodity consumption: Newsprint 90 short tons; widths 28", 14"; black ink 2,400 pounds; single pages printed 2,600; average pages per issue 10(d); single plates used 2,000.
Equipment: EDITORIAL: Front-end hardware — 1-Ap/Mac. CLASSIFIED: Front-end hardware — 1-Ap/Mac. DISPLAY: Adv layout systems — 1-Ap/Mac. PRODUCTION: Typesetters — 1-Ap/Mac LaserPrinter; Plate processors — 1-Ic; Production cameras — 1-Acti; Automatic film processors — Kk/Kodalith Processor. PRESSROOM: Line 1 — 3-HI/Cottrell. MAILROOM: Bundle tyer — 1-Bu; Addressing machine — IBM/PC Labels. WIRE SERVICES: News — AP; Receiving dishes — size-2½ft, AP. BUSINESS COMPUTERS: IBM/AT, IBM/PC-2.

COLUMBUS
Cherokee County
'90 U.S. Census- 3,268; E&P '96 Est. 3,242

The Columbus Daily Advocate (e-mon to fri)

Columbus Daily Advocate, 215 S. Kansas; PO Box 231, Columbus, KS 66725; tel (316) 429-2773; fax (316) 429-3223.
Circulation: 2,474(e); Sworn Sept. 29, 1995.
Price: 25¢(d); $38.48/yr (city).
Advertising: Open inch rate $4.00(e).
News Service: AP. **Politics:** Independent. **Established:** 1874.
Not Published: New Year; Memorial Day; Independence Day; Labor Day; Thanksgiving; Christmas.
Special Editions: Fair (July); Car Care, Columbus Day (Oct); Christmas (Dec).
Magazine: TV Listing (City only).

CORPORATE OFFICERS
President/Treasurer Haskell Carter
Vice Pres/Secretary Jay Lacy
GENERAL MANAGEMENT
Business Manager/Purchasing Agent Jay Lacy
ADVERTISING
Manager Jay Lacy
CIRCULATION
Manager Francine Miller
NEWS EXECUTIVE
Editor Alan Storey
EDITOR AND MANAGER
Wire Editor Alan Storey
PRODUCTION
Superintendent Haskell Carter

Market Information: TMC.
Mechanical available: Offset; insert accepted — preprinted; page cut-offs — 22¾".
Mechanical specifications: Type page 14" x 21"; E - 6 cols, 2.17", ⅙" between; A - 6 cols, 2.17", ⅙" between; C - 6 cols, 2.17", ⅙" between.
Commodity consumption: Newsprint 60 short tons; widths 30", 15"; black ink 275 pounds; single pages printed 1,800; average pages per issue 8(d); single plates used 3,000.
Equipment: EDITORIAL: Front-end hardware — 2-AT/PC, 2-PC, I/486, I/386; Front-end software — Alpha-Pi; Printers — HP/LaserJet II, HP/LaserJet III. CLASSIFIED: Front-end hardware — AT. DISPLAY: Adv layout systems — Aldus/PageMaker; Front-end hardware — PC/Pentium; Printers — HP/LaserJet 4MV. PRODUCTION: Typesetters — HP/LaserJet 4MV; Plate exposures — B; Scanners — Microtek; Production cameras — Acti. PRESSROOM: Line 1 — 2-KP/Newsking. MAILROOM: Bundle tyer — Strap Tyer; Addressing machine — Automecha/Accufast PUM. WIRE SERVICES: News — AP, AP Phone In. BUSINESS COMPUTERS: AT/286 Executive; Applications: ListMaster: Subscriptions, Accts receivable.

CONCORDIA
Cloud County
'90 U.S. Census- 6,167; E&P '96 Est. 5,916

Blade-Empire (e-mon to fri)

Blade-Empire, 510 Washington St.; PO Box 309, Concordia, KS 66901; tel (913) 243-2424; fax (913) 243-4407.
Circulation: 3,400(e); Sworn Sept. 30, 1992.
Price: 50¢(d); $47.36/yr (in trade area).
Advertising: Open inch rate $4.65(e).
News Service: AP. **Politics:** Independent. **Established:** 1902.
Not Published: New Year; Memorial Day; Independence Day; Labor Day; Thanksgiving; Christmas.
Magazines: Weekly Supplement; The Advertiser.

CORPORATE OFFICERS
President Brad Lowell
Vice Pres Art Lowell
GENERAL MANAGEMENT
Publisher Brad Lowell
Business Manager Mana Roberts
ADVERTISING
Manager Jonie Reignier
CIRCULATION
Director Pat Scott
NEWS EXECUTIVE
Editor Brad Lowell
EDITORS AND MANAGERS
City/People Editor Brad Lowell
Sports Editor Jim Lowell

Mechanical available: Offset; Black and 3 ROP colors; insert accepted — preprinted; page cut-offs — 22½".
Mechanical specifications: Type page 14"; E - 6 cols, 2.03", ⅙" between; A - 6 cols, 2.03", ⅙" between; C - 6 cols, 2.03", ⅙" between.
Commodity consumption: average pages per issue 16(d).
Equipment: EDITORIAL: Front-end hardware — Mk; Front-end software — Mk/Mycro-Comp AdWriter. CLASSIFIED: Front-end hardware — Mk; Front-end software — Mk/Mycro-Comp AdWriter. PRODUCTION: Plate exposures — 1-Nu; Plate processors — WL; Production cameras — DAI. PRESSROOM: Line 1 — 4-KP. MAILROOM: Bundle tyer — Bu. WIRE SERVICES: News — AP; Receiving dishes — AP. BUSINESS COMPUTERS: RSK/Tandy; Applications: Redwing.

COUNCIL GROVE
Morris County
'90 U.S. Census- 2,228; E&P '96 Est. 2,186

Council Grove Republican
(e-mon to fri)

Council Grove Republican, 208 W. Main St.; PO Box E, Council Grove, KS 66846; tel (316) 767-5123.
Circulation: 2,448(e); Sworn Oct. 1, 1994.
Price: 25¢(d); $38.98/yr (local), $71.65/yr (outside state).
Advertising: Open inch rate $3.50(e).
News Service: AP. **Politics:** Republican. **Established:** 1872.
Not Published: New Year; Memorial Day; Independence Day; Labor Day; Thanksgiving; Christmas.
Special Editions: Bridal (Feb); Tourism (Apr).

GENERAL MANAGEMENT
Publisher/Editor Craig A McNeal
ADVERTISING
Manager Don A McNeal
MARKETING AND PROMOTION
Manager-Marketing/Promotion Craig A McNeal
CIRCULATION
Manager Christy Jimerson

Mechanical available: Offset; Black and 3 ROP colors; insert accepted — preprinted; page cut-offs — 22¾".
Mechanical specifications: Type page 15" x 21½"; E - 7 cols, 2½", ⅙" between; A - 7 cols, 2½", ⅙" between.
Commodity consumption: width 33"; single pages printed 1,316; average pages per issue 6(d).
Equipment: EDITORIAL: Front-end hardware — 3-Ap/Mac; Front-end software — Microsoft/Word 3.0; Printers — Ap/Mac LaserWriter II NT. CLASSIFIED: Front-end hardware — 1-Ap/Power Mac Performa; Front-end software — Microsoft/Word 6.0, PageMaker 5.0; Printers — Ap/Mac LaserWriter II NT. DISPLAY: Front-end hardware — 1-Ap/Power Mac Performa; Front-end software — PageMaker 5.0; Printers — Ap/Mac LaserWriter II NT. PRODUCTION: Typesetters — 1-Ap/Mac LaserWriter II NT. MAILROOM: Addressing machine — 1-Am. WIRE SERVICES: News — AP; Receiving dishes — AP.

DERBY
Sedgwick County
'90 U.S. Census- 14,699; E&P '96 Est. 15,138

The Daily Reporter
(e-mon to fri)

The Daily Reporter, PO Box 190, Derby, KS 67037; tel (316) 788-2835; fax (316) 788-0854. Hollinger International Inc. group.
Circulation: 1,672(e); Sworn Sept. 28, 1995.
Price: 50¢(d); $6.50/mo; $78.00/yr (carrier).
Advertising: Open inch rate $6.73(e).
News Service: AP. **Politics:** Independent. **Established:** 1960.
Not Published: New Year; Memorial Day; Independence Day; Labor Day; Thanksgiving; Christmas.
Special Editions: Progress (Feb); Home Improvement (Apr); Newcomer's Guide (July); Back-to-School (Aug); Sports, Home Improvement (Sept); Sports (Oct).

CORPORATE OFFICERS
President/CEO Larry J Perrotto
Vice Pres Ken Cope
Comptroller Roland McBride
GENERAL MANAGEMENT
Publisher Jim Stephenson
ADVERTISING
Manager Faye Osenbaugh
CIRCULATION
Manager Tim Mello
EDITOR AND MANAGER
Editor Sam Foster
PRODUCTION
Manager Renee Browing

Market Information: TMC.
Mechanical available: Offset; Black and 3 ROP colors; insert accepted — preprinted; page cut-offs — 22¾".
Mechanical specifications: Type page 13" x 21"; E - 6 cols, 2¹⁄₁₆", ⅛" between; A - 6 cols, 2¹⁄₁₆", ⅛" between; C - 6 cols, 2¹⁄₁₆", ⅛" between.
Commodity consumption: single pages printed 3,200; average pages per issue 12(d).
Equipment: EDITORIAL: Front-end hardware — IBM; Front-end software — TC; Printers — HP, AP; Other equipment — HP, Ap/Mac Scanner. DISPLAY: Front-end hardware — Ap/Mac Plus, Ap/Mac IIci; Front-end software — Quark-XPress; Printers — Ap/Mac LaserPrinter. PRODUCTION: Scanners — Ap/Mac. MAILROOM: Wrapping singles — 2-Bu/Tyers. WIRE SERVICES: News — AP.

DODGE CITY
Ford County
'90 U.S. Census- 21,129; E&P '96 Est. 23,618

Dodge City Daily Globe
(m-mon to sat)

Dodge City Daily Globe, 705 Second; PO Box 820, Dodge City, KS 67801; tel (316) 225-4151; fax (316) 225-4154. Morris Communications Corp. group.
Circulation: 8,611(m); 8,611(m-sat); Sworn Oct. 1, 1994.
Price: 50¢(d); 50¢(sat); $7.50/mo; $90.00/yr.
Advertising: Open inch rate $7.65(m); $7.65(m-sat).
News Service: AP. **Politics:** Independent. **Established:** 1911.
Not Published: New Year; Memorial Day; Labor Day; Christmas; Independence Day.
Special Editions: Bridal Tab (Jan); Home Building, 1880 Tourist (Mar); Bridal Tab, Dodge City Days (July); Fall Fashion (Sept); Senior Citizens, Home Improvement, Car Care (Oct); Christmas Kick-off (Thanksgiving Day) (Nov); Holiday Cookbook, Christmas Song Book (Dec).
Special Weekly Sections: Health Page (tues); Best Food Day (wed); Youth Page, Religion Page, Real Estate (fri); Business Page, Farm and Agriculture Page, Outlook TV Tab (sat).

CORPORATE OFFICERS
Chairman of the Board W S Morris III
President Paul S Simon
Secretary/Treasurer William A Herman III
GENERAL MANAGEMENT
Publisher Terry Cochran
Manager-Credit Linda Berry
Personnel Manager Linda Berry
ADVERTISING
Director Linda Livingston
Manager-Retail Linda Livingston
Manager-Marketing Linda Livingston
TELECOMMUNICATIONS
Audiotex Manager Linda Livingston
CIRCULATION
Manager Les Tresner
NEWS EXECUTIVE
Managing Editor Gary Reber
EDITORS AND MANAGERS
Automotive/Books Editor Gary Reber
Business/Finance Editor Gary Reber
Editorial Page Editor Gary Reber
Editorial Writer/Education Editor Gary Reber
Fashion/Home Furnishings Editor Anne Zohner
News Editor Gary Reber
Picture Editor Garrett McClure
Society/Women's Editor Anne Zohner
Sports Editor Brian Reetz
MANAGEMENT INFORMATION SERVICES
Data Processing Manager Linda Berry
PRODUCTION
Superintendent Edward O'Neil
Foreman-Mailroom Roger Hedgecoth
Foreman-Pressroom Edward O'Neil

Market Information: Split Run; TMC; Operate audiotex.
Mechanical available: Offset; Black and 3 ROP colors; insert accepted — preprinted; page cut-offs — 22¾".
Mechanical specifications: Type page 13" x 21½"; E - 6 cols, 2¹⁄₁₆", ¹⁄₁₆" between; A - 6 cols, 2¹⁄₁₆", ¹⁄₁₆" between; C - 6 cols, 2¹⁄₁₆", ¹⁄₁₆" between.
Commodity consumption: Newsprint 475 short tons; widths 13½", 27"; black ink 10,400 pounds; color ink 1,650 pounds; single pages printed 6,466; average pages per issue 18(d); single plates used 6,000.
Equipment: EDITORIAL: Front-end hardware — 6-Ap/Mac si, 3-Ap/Mac SE, 4-Ap/Mac Classic; Front-end software — Baseview, QuarkXPress; Printers — Ap/Mac LaserWriter NTX, MON. CLASSIFIED: Front-end hardware — Ap/Mac SE; Front-end software — Baseview; Printers — Ap/Mac LaserWriter NTX. AUDIOTEX: Hardware — Samsung/486; Software — SMS/Stauffer Gold. DISPLAY: Front-end hardware — 3-Ap/Mac IIsi; Front-end software — Aldus/PageMaker, Aldus/FreeHand. PRODUCTION: Typesetters — Ap/Mac LaserWriter NTX, Ap/Mac LaserWriter NT, MON, HP/LaserJet 4MV. PRESSROOM: Line 1 — 7-G/Community; Folders — 1-G. MAILROOM: Inserters and stuffers — KAN/480; Addressing machine — Ch/705. LIBRARY: Electronic — Ap/Mac, SMS/Stauffer Gold. WIRE SERVICES: News — AP; Receiving dishes — size-6ft, AP. BUSINESS COMPUTERS: Epson/486, Wyse/terminals, Unix; Applications: SMS/Business Software, Unix.

Kansas I-155

EL DORADO
Butler County
'90 U.S. Census- 11,504; E&P '96 Est. 12,358

The El Dorado Times
(e-mon to sat)

The El Dorado Times, 114 N. Vine; PO Box 694, El Dorado, KS 67042; tel (316) 321-1120; fax (316) 321-7722. Hollinger International Inc. group.
Circulation: 4,131(e); 4,131(e-sat); Sworn Oct. 1, 1994.
Price: 50¢(d); 50¢(sat); $8.10/mo; $78.75/yr.
Advertising: Open inch rate $8.00(e); $8.00(e-sat).
News Service: AP. **Politics:** Independent. **Established:** 1882.
Not Published: New Year; Memorial Day; Independence Day; Labor Day; Thanksgiving Day; Christmas.
Advertising not accepted: Abortion; Investments.
Magazine: TV Section (thur).

GENERAL MANAGEMENT
Publisher Guy P Russell
ADVERTISING
Manager Guy P Russell
CIRCULATION
Manager Alberta Gardner
NEWS EXECUTIVE
Editor Mike Boucher
EDITORS AND MANAGERS
Editorial Writer Mike Boucher
Home Furnishings Editor Kenna Bruner Pierce
Science Editor Steve Smith
Sports Editor Bob Mings
PRODUCTION
Superintendent Bruce Lacey

Market Information: TMC; ADS.
Mechanical available: Offset; Black and 3 ROP colors; insert accepted — preprinted; page cut-offs — 22¾".
Mechanical specifications: Type page 13" x 21½"; E - 6 cols, 2 1/16", ⅛" between; A - 6 cols, 2 1/16", ⅛" between; C - 6 cols, 2 1/16", ⅛" between.
Commodity consumption: Newsprint 414 short tons; widths 28", 32"; single pages printed 3,881; average pages per issue 12(d); single plates used 9,600.
Equipment: EDITORIAL: Front-end hardware — Ap/Mac; Front-end software — QPS 3.2; Printers — Ap/Mac LaserPrinter. CLASSIFIED: Front-end hardware — Ap/Mac; Front-end software — QPS 3.2; Printers — Ap/Mac LaserPrinter. DISPLAY: Front-end hardware — Ap/Mac II; Front-end software — QuarkXPress; Printers — Ap/Mac LaserWriter. PRODUCTION: Typesetters — 2-COM/4961, 2-COM/7200; Plate exposures — 1-B/MP2; Plate processors — 1-Nat; Production cameras — 1-Acti/225; Automatic film processors — Glunz & Jensen/550RA.
PRESSROOM: Line 1 — 6-HI/Cotrell V-25 & V-22; Folders — 1-HI. MAILROOM: Counter stackers — 1-BG; Bundle tyer — 1-Bu; Wrapping singles — 1-Bu; Addressing machine — 1-Am/6381, 1-KR. WIRE SERVICES: News — AP; Receiving dishes — AP. BUSINESS COMPUTERS: IBM/386; Applications: NoMads.

EMPORIA
Lyon County
'90 U.S. Census- 25,512; E&P '96 Est. 26,152
ABC-CZ (90): 25,512 (HH 9,753)

The Emporia Gazette
(e-mon to sat)

The Emporia Gazette, 517 Merchant St.; PO Drawer C, Emporia, KS 66801; tel (316) 342-4800; fax (316) 342-8108; e-mail egazette@aol.com.
Circulation: 9,690(e); 9,690(e-sat); ABC Sept. 30, 1995.
Price: 35¢(d); 50¢(sat); $6.00/mo (carrier), $9.90/mo (mail); $72.00/yr (carrier), $118.80/yr (mail).
Advertising: Open inch rate $10.25(e); $10.25(e-sat).
News Services: AP, NYT. **Politics:** Independent. **Established:** 1890.
Not Published: New Year; Memorial Day; Independence Day; Labor Day; Christmas.
Advertising not accepted: Work at home; Astrology; All 900 telephone number ads.
Special Editions: Get Away Emporia (Jan); Ads by Kids (Mar); Just Say No (May); Coloring Book, Discover Emporia (June); Back-to-School (Aug); Football (Sept); Christmas Gift Guide (Nov); Christmas Greetings, New Year's Greetings, Basketball (Dec).
Magazine: TV Week.

CORPORATE OFFICERS
President Paul David Walker
Vice Pres Barbara White Walker
Secretary/Treasurer Christopher White Walker
GENERAL MANAGEMENT
Publisher Paul David Walker
Asst Publisher Christopher White Walker
General Manager Ray J Beals
ADVERTISING
Manager-Display R Bruce Knaak
Manager-National R Bruce Knaak
CIRCULATION
Manager Gary D Warner
NEWS EXECUTIVES
Editor Barbara White Walker
Managing Editor Patrick S Kelley
EDITORS AND MANAGERS
Book Review Editor Patrick S Kelley
City Editor Susan Hess
Copy Editor Kay Lingenfelter
Lifestyle Editor Gwen Larson
Photo Department Manager Michael Dakota
Sports Editor Brent D Maycock
Travel Editor Barbara White Walker
Wire Editor Katherine Wood
PRODUCTION
Manager Dallas Sedgwick

Market Information: Split Run.
Mechanical available: Offset; Black and 3 ROP colors; insert accepted — preprinted, single sheets, 8½" x 11" min; page cut-offs — 22¾".
Mechanical specifications: Type page 13" x 21"; E - 6 cols, 2 1/16", ⅛" between; A - 6 cols, 2 1/16", ⅛" between; C - 6 cols, 2 1/16", ⅛" between.
Commodity consumption: Newsprint 400 short tons; widths 28", 14"; black ink 13,000 pounds; color ink 350 pounds; single pages printed 7,450; average pages per issue 23(d); single plates used 4,200.
Equipment: EDITORIAL: Front-end hardware — Mk/Touchwriter Plus, Mk/Newstouch AT; Front-end software — Mk; Printers — TI/810. CLASSIFIED: Front-end hardware — Mk/Touchwriter; Front-end software — Mk. DISPLAY: Front-end hardware — Ap/Mac II; Front-end software — Mk/Mycro-Comp AdWriter; Printers — GCC/Select Press 600. PRODUCTION: Typesetters — GCC/Select Press 600; Plate exposures — 1-BKY/30x40, Burgess/Light Source; Plate processors — 1-Nat; Production cameras — 1-Acti/183; Automatic film processors — 1-Glunz-Jensen/Multi-line 550.
PRESSROOM: Line 1 — 7-G/Community; Folders — 1-G. MAILROOM: Inserters and stuffers — 5-KAN/480; Bundle tyer — 2-Bu/23; Addressing machine — 1-KAN/Labeler. WIRE SERVICES: News — NYT, AP; Syndicates — NYT; Receiving dishes — size-10ft, AP. BUSINESS COMPUTERS: 5-ATT/WGS 386; Applications: Circ, Billing, Adv; PCs & micros networked.

FORT SCOTT
Bourbon County
'90 U.S. Census- 8,362; E&P '96 Est. 8,227

The Fort Scott Tribune
(e-mon to fri; m-sat)

The Fort Scott Tribune, 6 E. Wall St.; PO Box 150, Fort Scott, KS 66701-0150; tel (316) 223-1460; fax (316) 223-1469.
Circulation: 4,452(e); 4,452(m-sat); Sworn Oct. 1, 1995.
Price: 35¢(d); 35¢(sat); $6.35/mo; $64.10/yr.
Advertising: Open inch rate $4.60(e); $4.60(m-sat). **Representative:** Papert Companies.
News Service: AP. **Politics:** Independent. **Established:** 1884.
Not Published: New Year; Memorial Day; Independence Day; Labor Day; Thanksgiving; Christmas.
Special Editions: Conservation; Wedding; Home Show; Chamber; Good Ol' Days; Graduation; Home Fix-up; Fair; Back-to-School; Football; Basketball; Pioneer Harvest Fiesta; Car Care; Christmas.
Special Weekly Sections: Best Food Day (wed); Business (thur); Church (fri); Agriculture, TV (sat).

CORPORATE OFFICER
President Frank E Emery
GENERAL MANAGEMENT
Publisher Frank E Emery
ADVERTISING
Director Tammie Braznell
CIRCULATION
Manager Kenneth Lyon
NEWS EXECUTIVE
Managing Editor Melinda Rhodes
EDITORS AND MANAGERS
Business/Finance Editor Melinda Rhodes
City/Metro Editor Melinda Rhodes
Editorial Page Editor Melinda Rhodes
Education Editor Gerard Hauser
Features Editor Nell Dikeman
Living/Lifestyle Editor Nell Dikeman
Sports Editor Scott Aust
Women's Editor Nell Dikeman
PRODUCTION
Foreman-Pressroom Charles Bolling

Market Information: TMC.
Mechanical available: Offset; Black and 1 ROP color; insert accepted — preprinted; page cut-offs — 22¾".
Mechanical specifications: Type page 13" x 21"; E - 6 cols, 2 1/16", ⅛" between; A - 6 cols, 2 1/16", ⅛" between; C - 8 cols, 1½", ⅛" between.
Commodity consumption: Newsprint 202 short tons; widths 30", 27½", 15", 13¾"; black ink 3,600 pounds; color ink 248 pounds; single pages printed 3,355; average pages per issue 11(d); single plates used 2,750.
Equipment: EDITORIAL: Front-end hardware — Ap/Mac; Printers — Ap/Mac LaserWriter II; Other equipment — Ap/Mac Scanner, 5-Ap/Mac, 1-Radius. CLASSIFIED: Front-end hardware — Ap/Mac; Printers — Ap/Mac LaserWriter II; Other equipment — 1-Ap/Mac, 1-Radius. PRODUCTION: Typesetters — 2-Ap/Mac LaserWriter II; Plate exposures — B/Ultra-Lite 1500; Production cameras — 1-Acti; Automatic film processors — LE/Flo LD-18, LE/Line 17.
PRESSROOM: Line 1 — 4-G/Community. MAILROOM: Bundle tyer — 1-Bu/BT-17; Addressing machine — Compudyne/486SX-25. WIRE SERVICES: News — AP; Syndicates — NEA; Receiving dishes — size-1⅔ft, AP. BUSINESS COMPUTERS: 1-Compudyne/386DN-25, 1-Compudyne/486DN; Applications: Circ, Labeling, Mail delivery, Accts receivable.

GARDEN CITY
Finney County
'90 U.S. Census- 24,097; E&P '96 Est. 28,794

The Garden City Telegram
(e-mon to sat)

The Garden City Telegram, 310 N. 7th St.; PO Box 958, Garden City, KS 67846; tel (316) 275-8500; fax (316) 275-5165. Harris Enterprises Inc. group.
Circulation: 10,895(e); 10,895(e-sat); Sworn Sept. 26, 1995.
Price: 50¢(d); 75¢(sat); $6.95/mo; $104.52/yr.
Advertising: Open inch rate $7.50(e); $7.50(e-sat).
News Services: AP, Harris. **Politics:** Independent. **Established:** 1929.
Not Published: New Year; Memorial Day; Independence Day; Labor Day; Thanksgiving; Christmas.
Special Weekly Sections: Best Food Day, Weddings/Engagements (wed); Farm Pages (thur); TV Tab (fri); Business News (sat).

CORPORATE OFFICERS
President James E Bloom
Vice Pres Lloyd Ballhagen
Secretary/Treasurer Carol Crupper
Asst Secretary/Treasurer Tom E Brungardt
GENERAL MANAGEMENT
Publisher James E Bloom
Business Manager Janet Born
ADVERTISING
Manager Kent O'Toole
CIRCULATION
Manager Tom E Brungardt
NEWS EXECUTIVES
Editor James E Bloom
Managing Editor Carol Crupper
EDITORS AND MANAGERS
Editorial Page Editor James E Bloom
Photo Department Manager Carol Crupper
Society Editor Tomari Quinn
Sports Editor Kevin Krier
Teen-Age/Youth Editor Tomari Quinn
Women's Editor Tomari Quinn
MANAGEMENT INFORMATION SERVICES
Data Processing Manager Janet Born
PRODUCTION
Foreman-Composing Kenneth Allen
Foreman-Pressroom Victor McCart

Market Information: TMC.
Mechanical available: Offset; Black and 3 ROP colors; insert accepted — preprinted, We Prints-Telegram prints; page cut-offs — 22¾".
Mechanical specifications: Type page 13" x 21½"; E - 6 cols, 2⅛", ⅜" between; A - 6 cols, 2⅛", ⅜" between; C - 8 cols, 1½", 1/16" between.
Commodity consumption: Newsprint 480 metric tons; widths 13¾", 27½"; black ink 2,400 pounds; color ink 500 pounds; single pages printed 6,490; average pages per issue 22(d); single plates used 3,245.
Equipment: EDITORIAL: Front-end hardware — Ap/Mac Centris 610, Ap/Mac Centris 650, Ap/Mac Centris 660, Ap/Mac Centris 800, Ap/Mac Quadra 610, Ap/Mac Quadra 650, Ap/Mac Quadra 660, Ap/Mac Quadra 800; Front-end software — Baseview/IQX Edit, QuarkXPress w/library system; Printers — NewGen/1200B Laser Printer. CLASSIFIED: Front-end hardware — Ap/Mac Centris 610s, Ap/Mac Quadra 800, 2-COM; Front-end software — Multi-Ad/Creator, QuarkXPress, Baseview; Printers — NewGen/1200B Laser Printer. DISPLAY: Adv layout systems — Ap/Mac Centris 610s, Ap/Mac Quadra 800; Front-end hardware — Ap/Mac IIsx, Ap/Mac Centris 610, Ap/Mac Centris 650, Ap/Mac Centris 800, Ap/Mac Quadra 610, Ap/Mac Quadra 650, Ap/Mac Quadra 800; Front-end software — Multi-Ad/Creator, QuarkXPress, Baseview; Printers — NewGen/1200B Laser Printer. PRODUCTION: Pagination software — QuarkXPress 3.3; OCR software — Caere/OmniPage Pro; Typesetters — NewGen/1200B Laser-Printers, ECR/VR-14 Imagesetter; Plate exposures — 1-Nu/Flip Top FT40C; Plate processors — 1-Ic/ICM25; Electronic picture desk — Lf/AP Leaf Picture Desk, Adobe/Photoshop, Ap/Mac Quadra 800; Production cameras — 1-R/580; Automatic film processors — 1-LE/LD-18; Color separation equipment (conventional) — Adobe/Photoshop, Ap/Mac Quadra 800.
PRESSROOM: Line 1 — 8-G/SC-578; Folders — 1-G. MAILROOM: Inserters and stuffers — 4-KAN; Bundle tyer — 1-Bu/66858, 1-Bu/32133; Addressing machine — 1-Am/1900, 1-Ch. WIRE SERVICES: News — AP, HI; Photos — AP; Stock tables — AP; Receiving dishes — AP. BUSINESS COMPUTERS: 2-DEC/PC LPV 433 DX, 7-TI/DSI Digital Venturis; Applications: Microsoft/Windows, Microsoft/Office: Budgeting, Management information, Circ, Adv, Accts payable, Gen ledger, Accts receivable, Newsprint; Informix/Smart II; PCs & micros networked; PCs & main system networked.

GOODLAND
Sherman County
'90 U.S. Census- 4,983; E&P '96 Est. 4,691

The Goodland Daily News
(e-tues to fri; m-sat)

The Goodland Daily News, 1205 Main St.; PO Box 500, Goodland, KS 67735; tel (913) 899-2338; fax (913) 899-6186. USMedia Inc. group.
Circulation: 2,468(e); 2,468(m-sat); Sworn Sept. 29, 1995.
Price: 50¢(d); 50¢(sat); $5.30/mo; $56.18/yr.
Advertising: Open inch rate $4.90(e); $4.90(m-sat); $6.75(tues & sat).
News Service: AP. **Politics:** Independent. **Established:** 1932.
Not Published: New Year; Memorial Day; Independence Day; Labor Day; Thanksgiving; Christmas.

CORPORATE OFFICER
President Eugene A Mace
GENERAL MANAGEMENT
Publisher Randy McCants
Business Manager Terri Mace
ADVERTISING
Manager Gennifer House
CIRCULATION
Manager Sheila Smith

Copyright ©1996 by the Editor & Publisher Co.

NEWS EXECUTIVE

Editor — Steven Lincoln

MANAGEMENT INFORMATION SERVICES

Data Processing Manager — Sheila Smith

PRODUCTION

Director — Jim Bowker

Mechanical available: Offset; Black and 2 ROP colors; insert accepted — preprinted; page cut-offs — 21½".
Mechanical specifications: Type page 13" x 21½"; E - 6 cols, 2¹⁄₁₆", ⅛" between; A - 6 cols, 2¹⁄₁₆", ⅛" between; C - 6 cols, 2¹⁄₁₆", ⅛" between.
Commodity consumption: Newsprint 140 short tons; widths 28", 14"; black ink 2,000 pounds; color ink 200 pounds; single pages printed 3,000; average pages per issue 10(d); single plates used 3,110.
Equipment: EDITORIAL: Front-end hardware — 3-Ap/Mac; Front-end software — QuarkXPress. CLASSIFIED: Front-end hardware — 1-Ap/Mac. DISPLAY: Adv layout systems — 3-Ap/Mac. PRODUCTION: Pagination software — QuarkXPress, Aldus/PageMaker; Typesetters — 2-Ap/Mac LaserWriter; Plate exposures — B/Ultra-lite 1500; Scanners — Ap/Mac Scanner, Umax/Scanner; Production cameras — Acti/204; Automatic film processors — 1-P/Pakonolith 24.
PRESSROOM: Line 1 — 3-HI/V15A. MAILROOM: Bundle tyer — Bu. WIRE SERVICES: News — AP; Stock tables — AP; Receiving dishes — AP. BUSINESS COMPUTERS: IBM, Compudrive; Applications: Circ, Billing, Gen ledger, Payroll; PCs & micros networked; PCs & main system networked.

GREAT BEND

Barton County

'90 U.S. Census- 15,427; E&P '96 Est. 15,069

Great Bend Tribune

(e-mon to fri; S)

Great Bend Tribune, 2012 Forest St.; PO Box 228, Great Bend, KS 67530-0228; tel (316) 792-1211; fax (316) 792-3441. Morris Newspaper Corp. group.
Circulation: 8,156(e); 8,156(S); Sworn Sept. 29, 1994.
Price: 50¢(d); $1.00(S); $8.03/mo; $96.39/yr.
Advertising: Open inch rate $8.36(e); $8.36 (S). **Representative:** Papert Companies.
News Service: AP. **Politics:** Independent. **Established:** 1876.
Not Published: Christmas.
Advertising not accepted: Liquor in Sunday editions.
Special Editions: Progress (Feb); Spring Opening (Mar); Back-to-School (Aug); Annual Cookbook (Oct); Christmas Shopping (Nov).
Special Weekly Sections: Food Day (wed); 50+ (thur); Church Page, TV (fri); Health (S).
Magazines: What's On (TV Listing) (fri); "Waggin' Tales" (monthly).

CORPORATE OFFICER

President — Charles H Morris

GENERAL MANAGEMENT

Publisher — Bob Werner
Manager-Credit — Mary Holsington

ADVERTISING

Manager — Debbie Piland

TELECOMMUNICATIONS

Audiotex Manager — Debbie Piland

CIRCULATION

Manager — Ginger Riordan

NEWS EXECUTIVE

Managing Editor — Cleon Rickel

EDITORS AND MANAGERS

Farm Editor — Susan Thacker
News Editor — Chuck Smith
Religion/Society Editor — Rosanna Padilla
Sports Editor — John Mesh

PRODUCTION

Foreman-Composing — Karma Byers
Foreman-Pressroom — Dale Marbut
Foreman-Mailroom — Mike Staab

Market Information: Zoned editions; TMC; Operate audiotex.
Mechanical available: Offset; Black and 3 ROP colors; insert accepted — preprinted, all; page cut-offs — 22½".
Mechanical specifications: Type page 13" x 21½"; E - 6 cols, 2¹⁄₁₆", ⅛" between; A - 6 cols, 2¹⁄₁₆", ⅛" between; C - 8 cols, 1⅜", ⅛" between.
Commodity consumption: Newsprint 400 short tons; widths 27½", 13⅝"; black ink 7,800 pounds; color ink 1,500 pounds; single pages printed 5,968; average pages per issue 17(d), 34(S); single plates used 3,282.
Equipment: CLASSIFIED: Front-end hardware — Ap/Mac; Printers — TI/Omni 800. AUDIOTEX: Supplier name — SMS. PRODUCTION: Typesetters — Mk, Ap/Mac Plus, Ap/Mac IIci printer, 2-Ap/Mac; Plate exposures — 1-B/Ultra-lite 5000; Scanners — Ap/Mac LC III; Production cameras — 1-Op; Automatic film processors — C.
PRESSROOM: Line 1 — 8-G/Community. MAILROOM: Counter stackers — BG/Count-O-Veyor; Bundle tyer — 2-Bu/Tyer; Addressing machine — KR. WIRE SERVICES: News — AP; Photos — AP; Receiving dishes — size-8ft, AP. BUSINESS COMPUTERS: IBM/PC; Applications: Circ, Mail labels.

HAYS

Ellis County

'90 U.S. Census- 17,767; E&P '96 Est. 19,039

The Hays Daily News

(e-mon to fri; S)

The Hays Daily News, 507 Main St., Hays, KS 67601; tel (913) 628-1081; fax (913) 628-8186. Harris Enterprises Inc. group.
Circulation: 12,884(e); 12,884(S); Sworn Sept. 22, 1995.
Price: 50¢(d); $1.00(S); $8.25/mo; $91.60/yr.
Advertising: Open inch rate $9.50(e); $9.50(S).
News Services: AP, Harris, NYT. **Politics:** Independent. **Established:** 1929.
Not Published: Memorial Day; Labor Day.
Special Editions: Tax Guide (Jan); Bridal Fair, State Wrestling (Feb); State Basketball, Outdoor Living (Mar); Home Improvement (Apr); Travel & Tourism (May); Wild West Festival (June); Back-to-School (Aug); Area Football (Sept); Oktoberfest, Winter Car Care (Oct); Hunting & Fishing (Nov).
Special Weekly Sections: Best Food Day (wed); Church Services (fri); Business, Wedding/Engagement, Real Estate (S).
Magazines: TV Guide (fri); Comics, USA Weekend (S).

CORPORATE OFFICERS

Chairman — Lloyd Ballhagen
President — John Lee

GENERAL MANAGEMENT

Publisher — Kay Berenson
Business Manager — Janice Tinkel

ADVERTISING

Director — Michael H Haas

CIRCULATION

Manager — Bob Weigel

NEWS EXECUTIVES

Editor — Kay Berenson
Managing Editor — Gregory Halling
Asst Managing Editor — Doug Weller

EDITORS AND MANAGERS

Editorial Writer — Kay Berenson
Editorial Writer — Gregory Halling
News Editor — Rebecca Leudders
Photo Editor — Charlie Riedel
Regional Editor — Mike Corn
Sports Editor — Diane Gasper O'Brien
Asst Sports Editor — Randy Gonzales

PRODUCTION

Manager-Systems — Howard K Droegemeier
Manager-Pre Press — Norman Matal
Manager-Mailroom — Jonathan DeLaConcepcion
Foreman-Pressroom — Glen Windholz

Market Information: TMC.
Mechanical available: Offset; Black and 3 ROP colors; insert accepted — preprinted, all; page cut-offs — 22¾".
Mechanical specifications: Type page 13" x 21½"; E - 6 cols, 2¹⁄₁₆", ⅛" between; A - 6 cols, 2¹⁄₁₆", ⅛" between; C - 8 cols, 1⁹⁄₁₆", ¹⁄₁₆" between.
Commodity consumption: Newsprint 599.53 metric tons; widths 27½", 13¾"; black ink 17,205 pounds; color ink 2,264 pounds; single pages printed 6,571; average pages per issue 17(d), 43(S); single plates used 16,766.
Equipment: EDITORIAL: Front-end hardware — Ap/Mac; Front-end software — FSI/Editor, QuarkXPress 3.3; CLASSIFIED: Front-end hardware — Ap/Mac; Front-end software — QuarkXPress 3.3, FSI/Advance Pro; Printers — Epson, LQ/1170. DISPLAY: Adv layout systems — Multi-Ad/Creator, FSI/Series ROP Ad Layout; Front-end hardware — 2-Ap/Mac Classic, 1-Ap/Power Mac, 2-Ap/Mac Quadra 650; Front-end software — Microsoft/Word; Printers — NewGen 880B. PRODUCTION: Pagination software — QuarkXPress 3.3; OCR software — Caere/OmniPage 5.0; Typesetters — ECR/ScriptPrinter, ECR/VR36; Plate exposures — 1-Nu/Flip Top FT40LNS; Plate processors — 1-Nat/A340; Electronic picture desk — Lf/AP Leaf Picture Desk, Ap/Mac 840, AU, Adobe/Photoshop 5.0; Scanners — AG/Arcus Plus, 2-Lf/Leafscan 35; Production cameras — 1-R/580; Automatic film processors — 1-LE/L2100MPS, P/1800 IS; Color separation equipment (conventional) — Ap/Mac, Adobe/Photoshop.
PRESSROOM: Line 1 — 8-G/SC650; Folders — 1-G/3:2. MAILROOM: Inserters and stuffers — 1-KAN/480 (6 station); Bundle tyer — 2-Bu; Addressing machine — Ch/525 E. LIBRARY: Combination — Minolta/Microfilm. WIRE SERVICES: News — AP, Harris News Service, NYT; Photos — AP; Stock tables — AP; Receiving dishes — size-10ft, AP. BUSINESS COMPUTERS: TI/941; Applications: Microsoft/Office, DSI; PCs & micros networked; PCs & main system networked.

HIAWATHA

Brown County

'90 U.S. Census- 3,603; E&P '96 Est. 3,617

Hiawatha Daily World

(e-mon to fri)

Hiawatha Daily World, 607 Utah St., Hiawatha, KS 66434; tel (913) 742-2111; fax (913) 742-2276. Cleveland Newspapers Inc. group.
Circulation: 2,263(e); Sworn Sept. 30, 1995.
Price: 50¢(d); $59.02/yr (mail).
Advertising: Open inch rate $4.75(e). **Politics:** Republican. **Established:** 1908.
Not Published: New Year; Memorial Day; Independence Day; Labor Day; Thanksgiving; Christmas.
Special Edition: Community Spotlight.
Magazines: Agri-Business Report (mon); Best Food Day (wed).

GENERAL MANAGEMENT

Publisher — Barry A Stokes
Manager-Education Service — Barry A Stokes

ADVERTISING

Manager — Barry A Stokes

CIRCULATION

Manager — Ron Carron

NEWS EXECUTIVE

Managing Editor — Denise La Roe-West

EDITOR AND MANAGER

Lifestyle Editor — Liza Zubler

PRODUCTION

Manager — Donald Dodds

Market Information: TMC.
Mechanical available: Offset; Black and 2 ROP colors; insert accepted — preprinted; page cut-offs — 22½".
Mechanical specifications: Type page 13" x 21"; E - 6 cols, 2¹⁄₁₆", ⅛" between; A - 6 cols, 2¹⁄₁₆", ⅛" between; C - 6 cols, 2¹⁄₁₆", ⅛" between.
Commodity consumption: Newsprint 92 short tons; width 28"; black ink 2,500 pounds; single pages printed 7,500; average pages per issue 8(d).
Equipment: EDITORIAL: Front-end hardware — IBM/PC Juniors, Ap/Mac, RZ, IBM. CLASSIFIED: Front-end hardware — RZ; Other equipment — IBM. PRODUCTION: Typesetters — IBM/PC; Platemaking systems — 1-Nu; Plate exposures — 1-Nu; Production cameras — 1-R/401; Automatic film processors — LE.
PRESSROOM: Line 1 — 4-HI/Cotrell V-15-A. MAILROOM: Bundle tyer — 1-Bu; Addressing machine — RSK/Labels, PC. BUSINESS COMPUTERS: 1-RSK/TRS 80 II, 1-RSK/4000; Applications: Payroll, Gen ledger, Accts receivable; PCs & micros networked.

HUTCHINSON

Reno County

'90 U.S. Census- 39,308; E&P '96 Est. 39,521
ABC-CZ (90): 46,724 (HH 18,484)

The Hutchinson News

(m-mon to sat; S)

The Hutchinson News, 300 W. Second St. (67501); PO Box 190, Hutchinson, KS 67504-0190; tel (316) 694-5700; fax (316) 694-5767. Harris Enterprises Inc. group.
Circulation: 37,828(m); 37,828(m-sat); 41,935(S); ABC Sept. 30, 1995.
Price: 50¢(d); 50¢(sat); $1.25(S); $9.94/mo (carrier); $119.28/yr (carrier).
Advertising: Open inch rate $21.25(m); $21.25(m-sat); $21.25(S).
News Services: AP, NYT, LAT-WP. **Politics:** Independent. **Established:** 1872.
Advertising not accepted: 900 Numbers; Pornographic; We reserve the right to refuse.
Special Editions: Pulse, Flatlanders (monthly).
Special Weekly Section: TV Mag (S).
Magazine: USA Weekend (S).

CORPORATE OFFICERS

President — Wayne Lee
Vice Pres — John Lee
Vice Pres — Lloyd Ballhagen
Vice Pres — John G Harris
Secretary/Treasurer — Rex Christner

GENERAL MANAGEMENT

Publisher — Wayne Lee
Business Office Manager — Rex Christner
Human Resources Director — Kathy Beshears

ADVERTISING

Director — Lori Beck
Coordinator-Classified — Tammy Milligan
Coordinator-National — Anita Stuckey

MARKETING AND PROMOTION

Director-Marketing/Promotion — Debbie Lemen

TELECOMMUNICATIONS

Audiotex Manager — Ken Willard

CIRCULATION

Manager — Kevin McCarthy

NEWS EXECUTIVES

Editor — Wayne Lee
Managing Editor — Steve Whitmore

EDITORS AND MANAGERS

Business/Finance Editor — Steve Whitmore
City Editor — Mary Rintoul
Columnist — Dwight Jurgens
Editorial Page Editor — Steve Whitmore
Editorial Writer/Travel Editor — Steve Whitmore
Education/School Editor — Don Hart
Farm Editor — Ray Hemman
Hospitals Editor — Anna Hostutler
Lifestyle Editor — Joyce Hall
Oil & Gas/Political Editor — Steve Whitmore
Religion Editor — Joyce Hall
Sports Editor — Steve Carpenter

MANAGEMENT INFORMATION SERVICES

Systems Director — Jim Beasley

PRODUCTION

Foreman-Composing — George Friesen
Foreman-Press — Darrel Mangels
Foreman-Mailroom — Gregg Beals

Market Information: Zoned editions; TMC; Operate audiotex.
Mechanical available: Offset; Black and 3 ROP colors; insert accepted — preprinted; page cut-offs — 21½".
Mechanical specifications: Type page 13" x 21½"; E - 6 cols, 2¹⁄₁₆", ⅛" between; A - 6 cols, 2¹⁄₁₆", ⅛" between; C - 9 cols, 1⅜", ¹⁄₁₆" between.
Commodity consumption: Newsprint 2,532,852 metric tons; width 27½"; black ink 58,087 pounds; single pages printed 9,592; average pages per issue 24(d), 40(S); single plates used 19,100.
Equipment: EDITORIAL: Front-end hardware — 39-Dewar/Disc Net System II; Front-end software — Dewar/Disc Net; Printers — DEC/LA 36. CLASSIFIED: Front-end hardware — 5-VGA/55, Dewar/Disc Net; Front-end software — Dewar/Disc Net; Printers — Okidata/390. AUDIOTEX: Hardware — Brite; Software — Brite; Supplier name — Brite. DISPLAY: Front-end hardware — 4-Ap/Mac Centris 650, 4-Ap/Power Mac PC 7100; Front-end software — Adobe/Illustrator 5.0, Multi-Ad/Creator 3.7; Printers — Phaser/440 color printer. PRODUCTION: Pagination software — QuarkXPress; Typesetters — 2-COM/8600, 1-QMS/860, 1-QMS/Clipper 11x17 plain paper, 2-V/5300 M; Plate exposures — 1-Nu/FT40UPNS; Plate processors — 1-WL/32-1; Production cameras — 1-C/1211; Automatic film processors — 1-DP/24L; Film transporters — 1-C; Digital color separation equipment — Ap/Mac, Adobe/Photoshop, Lf/Leafscan.
PRESSROOM: Line 1 — 8-G/1018-4-72; Folders — 2-G. MAILROOM: Counter stackers — QWI, HL/DC, HL/Monitor; Inserters and stuffers — 1-MM/227-E, GMA/1000-A; Bundle tyer — 2-MLN, 1-Sterling/MR45CH; Addressing machine — 1-KR/227. LIBRARY: Electronic — IBM/Corp proprietary. WIRE SERVICES: News — AP, NYT, LAT-WP, SHNS; Photos — AP; Stock tables — AP SelectStox II;

Syndicates — AP Satellite Earth Station; Receiving dishes — size-10ft, AP. BUSINESS COMPUTERS: 1-IBM/Sys 3, 1-TI/DX990; Applications: Circ, Adv billing, Accts receivable, Gen ledger, Payroll.

INDEPENDENCE

Montgomery County

'90 U.S. Census- 9,942; E&P '96 Est. 9,768
ABC-NDM (90): 155,625 (HH 62,496)

Independence Daily Reporter (e-mon to fri; S)

Independence Daily Reporter, 320 N. 6th St.; Box 869, Independence, KS 67301; tel (316) 331-3550; fax (316) 331-3550 ext. 66.

Circulation: 8,181(e); 8,181(S); Sworn Sept. 30, 1994.
Price: 35¢(d); 75¢(S); $7.75/mo; $73.95/yr.
Advertising: Open inch rate $5.93(e); $5.93(S). **Representative:** Papert Companies.
News Service: AP. **Politics:** Independent. **Established:** 1881.
Not Published: Independence Day; Christmas.
Advertising not accepted: Mail order.
Magazine: View (TV Listing Guide).

CORPORATE OFFICERS

President	Herbert A Meyer III
Vice Pres	Georgia High
Vice Pres	Steve McBride
Treasurer	Micha Millis
Secretary	Kristin Meyer

GENERAL MANAGEMENT

Publisher	Herbert A Meyer III
General Manager	Herbert A Meyer III
Controller/Credit Manager	Micha Millis
Personnel Manager	Herbert A Meyer III
Manager-Education Service	Herbert A Meyer III

ADVERTISING

Manager	Steve McBride
Manager-Classified	Deanna Stewart

MARKETING AND PROMOTION

Manager-Promotion	Steve McBride

CIRCULATION

Director	James Tracy

NEWS EXECUTIVES

Editor	Herbert A Meyer III
Managing Editor	Georgia High

EDITORS AND MANAGERS

Amusements Editor	Georgia High
Aviation Editor	Ken Garner
Books/Science Editor	Herbert A Meyer III
Business/Finance Editor	Herbert A Meyer III
Columnist	Ken Garner
Editorial Page Editor	Herbert A Meyer III
Education Editor	Jennifer Beals
Fashion/Food Editor	Angela Greer
Films/Theater Editor	Georgia High
Home Furnishings Editor/Librarian	Angela Greer
News Editor	Georgia High
Religion Editor	Georgia High
School Editor	Jennifer Beals
Society/Women's Editor	Angela Greer
Sports Editor	Ken Garner
Teen-Age/Youth Editor	Herbert A Meyer III
Travel Editor	Herbert A Meyer III

PRODUCTION

Superintendent	Robert Burris

Market Information: Split Run.
Mechanical available: Offset; Black and 3 ROP colors; insert accepted — preprinted; page cutoffs — $22\frac{3}{4}$".
Mechanical specifications: Type page 13" x 21"; E - 6 cols, $2\frac{1}{16}$", $\frac{1}{8}$" between; A - 6 cols, $2\frac{1}{16}$", $\frac{1}{8}$" between; C - 6 cols, $2\frac{1}{16}$", $\frac{1}{8}$" between.
Commodity consumption: Newsprint 220 short tons; widths $27\frac{1}{2}$", $13\frac{3}{4}$"; black ink 4,536 pounds; color ink 577 pounds; single pages printed 5,500; average pages per issue 20(d), 60(S); single plates used 3,600.
Equipment: EDITORIAL: Front-end hardware — Mk/1100; Front-end software — Mk/1100. CLASSIFIED: Front-end hardware — Mk/1100; Front-end software — Mk/1100. PRODUCTION: Typesetters — 2-Ap/Mac LaserWriter II; Plate exposures — 1-Nu/Flip Top FT40; Production cameras — 1-Acti/183; Automatic film processors — 1-LE/LD18; Color separation equipment (conventional) — 1-BKY/4901-71. PRESSROOM: Line 1 — 6-G/SC. MAILROOM: Inserters and stuffers — 1-DG/320; Bundle tyer — 1-Malow/51; Wrapping singles — 2-St/510W. WIRE SERVICES: News — Receiving dishes — size-3m, AP. BUSINESS COMPUTERS: 5-Unix/U5000-30C; Applications: Unix, R&D Systems; PCs & main system networked.

IOLA

Allen County

'90 U.S. Census- 6,351; E&P '96 Est. 5,977

Iola Register (e-mon to fri; m-sat)

Iola Register, 302 S. Washington St.; PO Box 767, Iola, KS 66749; tel (316) 365-2111; fax (316) 365-6289.

Circulation: 4,155(e); 4,155(m-sat); Sworn Oct. 3, 1994.
Price: 35¢(d); 35¢(sat); $6.00/mo; $56.00/yr.
Advertising: Open inch rate $5.00(e); $5.00(m-sat).
News Service: AP. **Politics:** Independent-Republican. **Established:** 1865.
Not Published: New Year; Memorial Day; Independence Day; Labor Day; Thanksgiving; Christmas.
Special Editions: Spring (Mar); Fair, Sports Tab (July); Business & Professional Tab (Oct).
Special Weekly Sections: Farm Page (mon); Best Food Day (tues); TV Guide (fri).

CORPORATE OFFICERS

President	Mickey J Lynn
Secretary/Treasurer	Jack E Hastings

GENERAL MANAGEMENT

Publisher/General Manager	Emerson E Lynn Jr
Manager-Office	Glenda Aikins

ADVERTISING

Manager	Jack E Hastings
Manager-Display	Mark Hastings
Manager-Classified	Jeanie Malloy

CIRCULATION

Manager	Spring Sutterby

EDITORS AND MANAGERS

Action Line Editor	Bruce Symes
Automotive Editor	Bob Johnson
Business/Finance Editor	Emerson E Lynn Jr
City Editor	Robert Johnson
Editorial Page Editor	Emerson E Lynn Jr
Education Editor	Jenelle Johnson
Entertainment/Amusements Editor	Jenelle Johnson
Environmental Editor	Bruce Symes
Farm/Agriculture Editor	Bruce Symes
Fashion/Style Editor	Jenelle Johnson
Features Editor	Bruce Symes
Graphics Editor/Art Director	Jack E Hastings
Health/Medical Editor	Jenelle Johnson
National Editor	Emerson E Lynn Jr
News Editor	Bob Johnson
Photo Editor	Jocelyn Sheets
Political/Government Editor	Emerson E Lynn Jr
Science/Technology Editor	Bruce Symes
Society Editor	Jenelle Johnson
Sports Editor	Jocelyn Sheets
Travel/Women's Editor	Jenelle Johnson

PRODUCTION

Superintendent	Emerson E Lynn Jr

Market Information: TMC.
Mechanical available: Offset; Black and 1 ROP color; insert accepted — preprinted; page cutoffs — $21\frac{1}{2}$".
Mechanical specifications: Type page 13" x $21\frac{1}{2}$"; E - 6 cols, $2\frac{1}{16}$", $\frac{3}{16}$" between; A - 6 cols, $2\frac{1}{16}$", $\frac{3}{16}$" between; C - 8 cols, $2\frac{1}{16}$", $\frac{3}{16}$" between.
Commodity consumption: Newsprint 160 short tons; widths $27\frac{1}{2}$", $13\frac{3}{4}$"; black ink 5,000 pounds; color ink 200 pounds; single pages printed 4,283; average pages per issue 12(d), 6(sat).
Equipment: EDITORIAL: Front-end hardware — 6-Mk/Mycro-Comp; Front-end software — Mk/1100; Printers — Ap/Mac LaserWriter II; Other equipment — Mk/Mycro-Comp 550 OLI, Mk/Mycro-Comp 400 DD, Mk/Mycro-Comp 410 DD, Mk/Mycro-Comp 80C Controller, Equatorial/5100 Controller. CLASSIFIED: Front-end hardware — 6-Mk/Mycro-Comp. DISPLAY: Front-end hardware — Ap/Mac IIsi; Front-end software — Ap/Mac Sys 6.0.7, Multi-Ad/Creator; Printers — Ap/Mac LaserWriter II. PRODUCTION: Plate exposures — B/Ultra-lite 1500; Production cameras — Acti/183; Automatic film processors — LE/LD18; Reproportion units — TI/Q-700 Data Center. PRESSROOM: Press control system — HI. MAILROOM: Bundle tyer — Strapping. WIRE SERVICES: News — AP; Receiving dishes — size-5ft, AP. BUSINESS COMPUTERS: 3-SAMTRON/SM-460; Applications: Novell/Western: Circ, Accts receivable, Accts payable, Gen ledger; Pachioli: Payroll; Microsoft; PCs & micros networked.

JUNCTION CITY

Geary County

'90 U.S. Census- 20,604; E&P '96 Est. 21,816
ABC-CZ (90): 21,837 (HH 8,337)

The Daily Union (e-mon to fri; S)

The Daily Union, 222 W. Sixth St.; PO Box 129, Junction City, KS 66441; tel (913) 762-5000; fax (913) 762-4584.

Circulation: 6,851(e); 7,607(S); ABC Sept. 30, 1995.
Price: 35¢(d); $1.00(S); $7.00/mo; $75.50/yr.
Advertising: Open inch rate $8.85(e); $8.85(S); $12.15(e-wed). **Representative:** Papert Companies.
News Service: AP. **Politics:** Independent. **Established:** 1861.
Not Published: New Year; Memorial Day; Independence Day; Labor Day; Thanksgiving; Christmas.
Special Editions: Bridal (Jan); Progress (Feb); Home & Garden (Mar); Cooking School (Apr); Seniors, Recreation, Health & Fitness (May); JC Guide (July); Back-to-School, Football (Aug); Home Improvement/Furniture, Football (Sept); Christmas, Automotive (Nov); Basketball (Dec).
Special Weekly Sections: Coping with Life (mon); Home & Farm (tues); Best Food Day (wed); Seniors, Regional (thur); Faith, Entertainment-Leisure (fri); Business Page, TV Listings, Wedding Page, Youth, Regional, USA Weekend (S).
Magazines: Way to Grow, Kid! (local, newsprint) (mon); TV Channel Cues (local, newsprint) (S).
Broadcast Affiliate: KTMJ.

CORPORATE OFFICERS

President	John Grey Montgomery
Vice Pres/Secretary	Roland E Waechter

GENERAL MANAGEMENT

Publisher	John Grey Montgomery
General Manager	Roland E Waechter
Purchasing Agent	Roland E Waechter

ADVERTISING

Manager	Steve Stevens

CIRCULATION

Director	Mike Massek

NEWS EXECUTIVES

Editor	John Grey Montgomery
Managing Editor	Ronald W Hosie

EDITORS AND MANAGERS

Editorial Page Editor	Ronald W Hosie
Local Editor	Rob Roberts
Photo Editor	Valerie Bontrager
Political/Government	Bill Shea
Sports Editor	Rod Shetler
Wire Editor	Kerrey Britt

PRODUCTION

Manager	Ron Maley
Foreman-Composing	Debbie Glessner
Foreman-Pressroom	Jeff Knaak
Superintendent-Maintenance	Art Malsbury

Market Information: TMC.
Mechanical available: Offset; Black and 3 ROP colors; insert accepted — preprinted; page cutoffs — $22\frac{3}{4}$".
Mechanical specifications: Type page 13" x $21\frac{1}{2}$"; E - 6 cols, $2\frac{1}{16}$", $\frac{1}{8}$" between; A - 6 cols, $2\frac{1}{16}$", $\frac{1}{8}$" between; C - 6 cols, $2\frac{1}{16}$", $\frac{1}{8}$" between.
Commodity consumption: Newsprint 315 short tons; widths 34", 28", 17", 14"; black ink 13,820 pounds; color ink 2,010 pounds; single pages printed 6,054; average pages per issue 15(d), 42(S); single plates used 3,810.
Equipment: EDITORIAL: Front-end hardware — 23-RSK/Tandy 3000 NL; Front-end software — CText; Other equipment — 1-Ap/Mac. CLASSIFIED: Front-end hardware — 5-Multitech/700; Front-end software — CText; Printers — 1-IBM/Proprinter. DISPLAY: Front-end software — Multi-Ad/Creator 3.8, QuarkXPress 3.31; Printers — HP/4MV; Other equipment — Scanner, Digital Cameras. PRODUCTION: Typesetters — 1-Ap/Mac LaserWriter Plus, 1-Tegra/Varityper Genesis; Plate exposures — 1-Nu; Electronic picture desk — 1-Lf/AP Leaf Picture Desk; Scanners — 1-Lf/Leafscan 35; Production cameras — 1-Acti; Automatic film processors — 1-SCREEN/LD-220-QT; Digital color separation equipment — 1-ECR/Autokon. PRESSROOM: Line 1 — 6-G/Community; Folders — 1-G/Suburban; Press control system — Fin. MAILROOM: Inserters and stuffers — 1-KAN/480; Bundle tyer — 1-Bu, 1-Malow/MC Straptyer. COMMUNICATIONS: Digital ad delivery system — AP AdSend. WIRE SERVICES: News — AP; Photos — AP; Receiving dishes — size-3m, AP. BUSINESS COMPUTERS: 10-IBM/3151; Applications: IBM/RISC-6000-PBS: Adv, Accounting, Circ, Payroll, Gen ledger; PBS/MediaPlus.

KANSAS CITY

Wyandotte County

'90 U.S. Census- 149,767; E&P '96 Est. 148,583

Kansas City Kansan (e-tues to fri; S)

Kansas City Kansan, 901 N. 8th St., Kansas City, KS 66101; tel (913) 371-4300; fax (913) 342-8620. Inland Industries Inc. group.

Circulation: 12,305(e); 12,305(S); Sworn Sept. 29, 1995.
Price: 35¢(d); $1.00(S); $67.35/yr.
Advertising: Open inch rate $11.25(e); $11.25(S). **Representative:** Landon Associates Inc.
News Service: AP. **Politics:** Independent. **Established:** 1921.
Not Published: New Year; Memorial Day; Independence Day; Labor Day; Christmas.
Special Editions: Senior's Tab, Bank Statement, Black History Page, Winter Bridal (Jan); KCK Chamber of Commerce Tab, Tax Guide #1 Tab, Progress Edition (Feb); Spring Automotive, Tax Guide #2, Senior's Tab, Easter (Mar); Lawn & Garden, Minority Business Guide Tab, Bank Statements, Rental Guide (Apr); Lawn & Garden, Summer Education Guide, Mother's Day, Senior's Tab, Memorial Day - Don't Drink & Drive (May); Summer Automotive, Summer Bridal '96, Father's Day (June); Lawn & Garden, Banks Statements, Senior's Tab (July); Fall Education Guide, Back-to-School, Coupon Pages (Aug); High School Football, Labor Day, Senior's Tab, Home Improvement, Autumn, Central Avenue Parade (Sept); Fall Automotive, Bank Statements, Living Guide (Oct); High School Basketball, Senior's Tab, Christmas Gift Guide #1, American Royal Page (Nov); Spring Education Guide, Christmas Gift Guide #2, Christmas Greetings, News Year's Greetings (Dec).
Magazine: TV This Week in Wyandotte County (S).

CORPORATE OFFICERS

Chairman	Clark O Murray
President	William Epperheimer
Exec Vice Pres	Jack D Burton

GENERAL MANAGEMENT

Publisher	William Epperheimer
Controller	Patricia Monteleone

ADVERTISING

Director	Joie Mellenbruch
Manager-National	Joie Mellenbruch

CIRCULATION

Manager	Jeff Charpentier

NEWS EXECUTIVE

Editor	Patrick Lowry

EDITOR AND MANAGER

Sports Editor	Phil Ellenbecker

PRODUCTION

Manager	Lori Steele
Foreman-Pressroom	Buddy Black

Market Information: TMC.
Mechanical available: Offset; Black and 3 ROP colors; insert accepted — preprinted; page cutoffs — $21\frac{1}{2}$".
Mechanical specifications: Type page $12\frac{3}{4}$" x $21\frac{1}{2}$"; E - 6 cols, 2", $\frac{1}{4}$" between; A - 6 cols, 2", $\frac{1}{4}$" between; C - 9 cols, $1\frac{5}{16}$", $\frac{1}{6}$" between.
Commodity consumption: average pages per issue 12(d), 24(S).
Equipment: EDITORIAL: Front-end hardware — Ap/Mac; Front-end software — Microsoft/Word, QuarkXPress; Printers — 2-Dataproducts/LZR 1560. CLASSIFIED: Front-end hardware — Ap/Mac; Front-end software — Baseview. DISPLAY: Front-end hardware — Ap/Mac; Front-

end software — QuarkXPress, Multi-Ad/Creator; Printers — Dataproducts/LZR 1560. PRODUCTION: Plate exposures — Nu/Flip Top; Plate processors — WL; Production cameras — DAI; Automatic film processors — LE. PRESSROOM: Line 1 — 5-G/Urbanite. MAILROOM: Counter stackers — Fg; Inserters and stuffers — KAN/480; Bundle tyer — MLN. WIRE SERVICES: News — AP; Receiving dishes — AP. BUSINESS COMPUTERS: 3-IBM/PC; Applications: BMF: Circ, Accts receivable, Accts payable, Gen ledger.

LARNED

Pawnee County

'90 U.S. Census- 4,490; E&P '96 Est. 4,398

The Tiller & Toiler

(e-mon to fri)

The Tiller & Toiler, 115 W. 5th St.; PO Box 206, Larned, KS 67550; tel (316) 285-3111; fax (316) 285-6062. Kansas Press Association group.

Circulation: 1,798(e); Sworn Oct. 2, 1995.

Price: 50¢(d); $52.95/yr.

Advertising: Open inch rate $3.96(e); $5.50 (e-tues TMC).

News Service: AP. **Politics:** Republican. **Established:** 1879.

Not Published: New Year; Memorial Day; Independence Day; Labor Day; Thanksgiving; Day after Thanksgiving; Christmas.

Magazine: The Tuesday Issue of the Paper (TMC).

CORPORATE OFFICER

President Marshall Settle

GENERAL MANAGEMENT

Publisher Marshall Settle
Assoc Publisher John M Settle
Managing Editor Dennis Martin

ADVERTISING

Manager Dennis Martin
Representative Susan White

CIRCULATION

Manager Rhonda Gabel

NEWS EXECUTIVE

Managing Editor Dennis Martin

EDITOR AND MANAGER

News/Sports Editor Mark Zwink

Market Information: TMC.

Mechanical available: Offset; Black and 3 ROP colors; insert accepted — preprinted.

Mechanical specifications: Type page 12⅞" x 21½"; E - 6 cols, 2¹⁄₁₆", ⅛" between; A - 6 cols, 2¹⁄₁₆", ⅛" between; C - 6 cols, 2¹⁄₁₆", ⅛" between.

Commodity consumption: average pages per issue 12(d).

Equipment: PRODUCTION: Typesetters — 4-P, 2-COM, 1-F; Plate processors — 1-Stereotype Platecaster, 1-HA, 1-H; Production cameras — 1-DAI.

PRESSROOM: Line 1 — 3-HI/Cotrell. MAILROOM: Addressing machine — 1-Am. WIRE SERVICES: News — AP.

LAWRENCE

Douglas County

'90 U.S. Census- 65,608; E&P '96 Est. 75,799

ABC-CZ (90): 65,608 (HH 24,513)

Journal-World

(m-mon to sat; S)

Journal-World, 609 New Hampshire St.; PO Box 888, Lawrence, KS 66044; tel (913) 843-1000; fax (913) 843-4512; e-mail ljworld@aol.com; web site http://www.ljworld.com/.

Circulation: 18,418(m); 18,418(m-sat); 19,481(S); ABC Sept. 30, 1995.

Price: 50¢(d); 50¢(sat); $1.00(S); $116.35/yr.

Advertising: Open inch rate $14.60(m); $14.60(m-sat); $14.60(S). **Representative:** Papert Companies.

News Services: AP, NYT. **Politics:** Independent. **Established:** 1854.

Note: Effective Aug. 21, 1995, this publication changed its publishing plan from (e-mon to fri; m-sat; S) to (m-mon to sat; S).

Special Editions: Conservation, Tax Tab (Jan); Bridal, Lawn & Garden (Feb); Spring Fashion, Spring Home Improvement (Mar); Progress (Apr); Graduation (May); Kansas University, Fair, Fall Fashion (Aug); City Scene, Fall Home Improvement (Sept); Basketball, Holiday Gift Guide (Nov); Christmas Greetings (Dec).

Special Weekly Section: Travel (S).

Magazines: USA Weekend; Sunday Comics; TV Update.

Cable TV: Own cable TV in circulation area.

CORPORATE OFFICERS

President Dolph C Simons Jr
Secretary/Treasurer Marie N Simons

GENERAL MANAGEMENT

Publisher Dolph C Simons Jr
Manager-Operations Dolph C Simons III
General Manager Ralph Gage
Controller Donna Wiley
New Ventures Dan Simons

ADVERTISING

Director Tom Fisher
Manager-National Tom Fisher

TELECOMMUNICATIONS

Audiotex Manager Dan Simons

CIRCULATION

Manager Mark Chaney

NEWS EXECUTIVES

Editor Dolph C Simons Jr
Deputy Editor Bill Snead

EDITORS AND MANAGERS

Business Editor Tom Gress
Editorial Page Editor Ann Gardner
Education Editor Caroline Trowbridge
Entertainment Editor Jan Biles
News Editor John Taylor
Photo Department Manager Mike Yoder
Sunday Editor Kurt Caywood
Sports Editor Chuck Woodling

MANAGEMENT INFORMATION SERVICES

Data Processing Manager Tom Hitt
Online Manager Dan Simons

PRODUCTION

Manager Dallas Dolan

Market Information: TMC; ADS; Operate database; Operate audiotex; Electronic edition.

Mechanical available: Offset; Black and 3 ROP colors; insert accepted — preprinted; page cut-offs — 22".

Mechanical specifications: Type page 13" x 20⅞"; E - 6 cols, 2", ⅛" between; A - 6 cols, 2", ⅛" between; C - 9 cols, 1⁵⁄₁₆", ¼" between.

Commodity consumption: Newsprint 1,890 short tons; widths 27", 13½"; black ink 33,400 pounds; color ink 13,180 pounds; single pages printed 15,185; average pages per issue 36(d), 62(S); single plates used 41,520.

Equipment: EDITORIAL: Front-end hardware — Ap/Mac; Front-end software — QuarkXPress, Baseview/NewsEdit; Printers — Ap/Mac; Other equipment — Lf/AP Leaf Picture Desk, Nikon/Scanners. CLASSIFIED: Front-end hardware — Ap/Mac; Front-end software — Baseview, QuarkXPress; Printers — Okidata. AUDIOTEX: Hardware — Brite Voice Systems; Supplier name — Brite Voice Systems. DISPLAY: Adv layout systems — CJ; Front-end hardware — Ap/Mac, HP; Front-end software — Baseview, Multi-Ad/Creator, QuarkXPress, Adobe/RIP; Printers — HP, Ap/Mac Laser-Printer. PRODUCTION: Typesetters — 2-ECR/Expressmaster 1270, 1-Imagemaster/1200; Plate exposures — 1-BKY, 1-Nu; Plate processors — 1-WL/30, 1-Nat; Scanners — AG/Horizon, Ap/Mac Scanner; Production cameras — 1-B, 1-C; Automatic film processors — 1-P; Film transporters — 1-C.

PRESSROOM: Line 1 — 15-G/Urbanite; Line 2 — 12-G/Urbanite; Press drives — Fin; Pasters — 14-Enkel. MAILROOM: Counter stackers — 1-BG/Count-O-Veyor, 1-Id/660; Inserters and stuffers — 1-MM, 1-MM; Bundle tyer — 2-MLN; Addressing machine — 2-Ch. LIBRARY: Electronic — SMS. WIRE SERVICES: News — AP Datafeatures, AP Datastream; Photos — AP; Stock tables — AP; Syndicates — NYT; Receiving dishes — size-3m, AP, USA Today. BUSINESS COMPUTERS: HP; Applications: CJ: Circ, Circ billing, Accts payable, Accts receivable, Payroll, Ad processing;, SCS/Layout 8000; PCs & micros networked; PCs & main system networked.

LEAVENWORTH

Leavenworth County

'90 U.S. Census- 38,495; E&P '96 Est. 42,401

ABC-CZ (90): 38,495 (HH 11,475)

The Leavenworth Times

(e-mon to fri; S)

The Leavenworth Times, 422 Seneca; PO Box 144, Leavenworth, KS 66048; tel (913) 682-0305; fax (913) 682-1114. Hollinger International Inc. group.

Circulation: 8,578(e); 9,352(S); ABC Sept. 30, 1994.

Price: 50¢(d); $1.00(S); $7.95/mo.

Advertising: Open inch rate $11.34(e); $11.34(S).

News Service: AP. **Politics:** Independent. **Established:** 1857.

Not Published: National holidays.

Special Edition: Homes Guide.

Magazines: Color Comics, TV Scene (S); USA Weekend.

GENERAL MANAGEMENT

Publisher/General Manager Barbara Trimble

ADVERTISING

Manager Todd Franz
Supervisor-Classified Kelvin Ross
Major Accounts Representative Don Alexander

CIRCULATION

Manager Susan Kirwin

NEWS EXECUTIVE

Editor Keith Robison

EDITORS AND MANAGERS

Family Page Editor Heather Swan
Sports Editor Mike Goens
Sunday Editor Cathy Trowbridge

PRODUCTION

Foreman Lenny Peters
Foreman-Press Barbara Trimble

Market Information: TMC.

Mechanical available: Offset; Black and 3 ROP colors; insert accepted — preprinted, free standing cards; page cut-offs — 22¾".

Mechanical specifications: Type page 13" x 21½"; E - 6 cols, 2⅛", ⅛" between; A - 6 cols, 2⅛", ⅛" between; C - 9 cols, 1⁵⁄₁₆", ⅛" between.

Commodity consumption: Newsprint 263 metric tons; widths 27½", 30", 34"; single pages printed 48,864; average pages per issue 20(d), 44(S).

Equipment: EDITORIAL: Front-end hardware — Mk; Printers — Tegra/Varityper. CLASSIFIED: Front-end hardware — Mk. DISPLAY: Adv layout systems — Ap/Mac. PRODUCTION: Typesetters — Mk/10, 1-COM/8400, 2-Ap/Mac; Platemaking systems — 1-Nu/Flip Top FT40LNS; Plate exposures — 1-Nu/2024V; Electronic picture desk — Lf/AP Leaf Picture Desk; Production cameras — 1-Nu; Color separation equipment (conventional) — Lf/Leafscan.

PRESSROOM: Line 1 — 8-G/Community; Folders — 1-G/1/4, 1-G; Press registration system — Duarte. MAILROOM: Bundle tyer — 3-Malow/Strap-Tyer, 1-Bu/BT 18; Addressing machine — 1-Am. LIBRARY: Electronic — Minolta/Microfilm. WIRE SERVICES: News — AP, THO; Photos — AP; Receiving dishes — size-3m, AP. BUSINESS COMPUTERS: ATT; Applications: Billing, Circ; PCs & main system networked.

LIBERAL

Seward County

'90 U.S. Census- 16,959; E&P '96 Est. 17,959

Southwest Daily Times

(e-mon to fri; S)

Southwest Daily Times, 16 S. Kansas Ave.; PO Box 889 (67905), Liberal, KS 67901; tel (316) 624-2541; fax (316) 624-0735; e-mail swdtbettis@aol.com (adv), swdtwalker@aol.com (edit). Southern Newspapers Inc. group.

Circulation: 6,898(e); 6,898(S); Sworn Oct. 2, 1995.

Price: 50¢(d); $1.00(S); $7.75/mo; $84.00/yr.

Advertising: Open inch rate $8.75(e); $8.75(S); $7.75(e & S). **Representative:** Papert Companies.

News Service: AP. **Politics:** Independent. **Established:** 1886.

Special Edition: Life & Times (Mar & Sept).

Special Weekly Sections: Business Day (tues); Leisure Times, Best Food Day (wed); Farm & Ranch (thur); Entertainment (fri); Leisure Times, Entertainment (S).

Magazine: FYI (S).

CORPORATE OFFICER

President Jeff A Burkhead

GENERAL MANAGEMENT

Publisher Jeff Burkhead
Purchasing Agent Tawana Earnest

ADVERTISING

Manager Mitch Bettis

CIRCULATION

Manager John Tucker

NEWS EXECUTIVES

Editor Ken Walker
Managing Editor Ken Walker
Asst Managing Editor Lane Allison

EDITORS AND MANAGERS

Editorial Page Editor Charlie Hayes
Features Editor Rachel Coleman
Sports Editor Steve Brisendine

PRODUCTION

Superintendent Earl Watt

Market Information: Zoned editions; Split Run; TMC.

Mechanical available: Offset; Black and 3 ROP colors; insert accepted — preprinted, cards, catalogs; page cut-offs — 21½".

Mechanical specifications: Type page 12½" x 20"; E - 6 cols, 2", ⅛" between; A - 6 cols, 2", ⅛" between; C - 8 cols, 1⅜", ¹⁄₁₆" between.

Commodity consumption: Newsprint 420 short tons; widths 27", 13½"; black ink color ink 400 pounds; single pages printed 6,254; average pages per issue 20(d), 36(S); single plates used 3,500.

Equipment: EDITORIAL: Front-end hardware — 7-Ap/Mac II; Front-end software — Baseview/NewsEdit, QuarkXPress 3.31, Adobe/Photoshop 2.5.1; Printers — 2-Ap/Mac Laser-Printer; Other equipment — 2-Flatbed Scanners, Lf/Leafscan Negative Scanner, Panther/Imagesetter. CLASSIFIED: Front-end hardware — 1-Ap/Mac SE, 1-Ap/Mac SE30, Ap/Mac LC III-Color Monitor; Front-end software — Baseview/Class Manager; Printers — Ap/Mac ImageWriter II. DISPLAY: Adv layout systems — Ap/Mac; Front-end hardware — 1-Ap/Mac Classic, 2-Ap/Mac II, 1-Ap/Mac Classic, Ap/Mac Centris 660AV; Front-end software — Aldus/PageMaker, Broderbund/TypeStyler, QuarkXPress, Adobe/Photoshop 2.5; Printers — Pre-Press/ImageSetter; Other equipment — Umax/Scanner, Lf/Leafscan Negative Scanner. PRODUCTION: Pagination software — QuarkXPress 3.31; OCR software — Caere/Omni Page 2.1; Typesetters — 2-Ap/Mac Laserwriter II, 1-Pre-Press/ImageSetter; Electronic picture desk — 1-Ap/Mac Quadra 800; Scanners — 1-Umax/UC-1200 SE Color Scanner, 1-Lf/Leafscan 35mm Negative Scanner; Production cameras — Acti/Horizontal Full Frame; Automatic film processors — 3-P/Bath-developer-wash, P, Konica/7200; Digital color separation equipment — GAM.

PRESSROOM: Line 1 — 5-WPC/Atlas (1-Quadra color; 4 color & up); Folders — 1-WPC; Press control system — Marathon; Press registration system — Pin System. MAILROOM: Inserters and stuffers — 1-KAN/4-station; Bundle tyer — 2-Bu. COMMUNICATIONS: Facsimile — X/Telecopier 7033. WIRE SERVICES: News — AP; Syndicates — North America Syndicate, Creators, King Features. BUSINESS COMPUTERS: Zenith/Z-386, Panasonic/KXP 1595, Zenith/Z-386, Panasonic/KXP1180; PCs & micros networked.

LYONS

Rice County

'90 U.S. Census- 3,688; E&P '96 Est. 3,508

The Lyons Daily News

(e-mon to fri)

The Lyons Daily News, 210 W. Commercial, Lyons, KS 67554; tel (316) 257-2368; fax (316) 257-2369.

Circulation: 2,457(e); Sworn Sept. 30, 1995.

Price: 25¢(d); $38.00/yr.

Advertising: Open inch rate $4.40(e).

News Service: AP. **Politics:** Independent. **Established:** 1906.

Not Published: New Year; Memorial Day; Independence Day; Labor Day; Thanksgiving; Christmas.

Special Editions: Back-to-School; Christmas Kick-off; Farm.

GENERAL MANAGEMENT

Publisher Paul E Jones

ADVERTISING

Director Paul E Jones

CIRCULATION

Director Shirley Kelley

NEWS EXECUTIVE

Editor — John Sayler

EDITORS AND MANAGERS

Home Furnishings/Society Editor — Judy Jones
Sports Editor — John Sayler
Wire Editor — Mrs John Sayler

PRODUCTION

Manager — Leo Schemm

Market Information: TMC.
Mechanical available: Offset; Black and 1 ROP color; insert accepted — preprinted; page cut-offs — 22⅜".
Mechanical specifications: Type page 13" x 21"; E - 6 cols, 2", ⅛" between; A - 6 cols, 2", ⅛" between; C - 6 cols, 2", ⅛" between.
Commodity consumption: Newsprint 80 short tons; widths 28", 14"; single pages printed 2,288; average pages per issue 8(d); single plates used 1,700.
Equipment: EDITORIAL: Front-end hardware — 6-Ap/Mac; Front-end software — Aldus/PageMaker; Printers — Ap/Mac LaserWriter II. CLASSIFIED: Front-end hardware — 6-Ap/Mac; Front-end software — Aldus/PageMaker; Printers — Ap/Mac LaserWriter II. PRODUCTION: Plate exposures — 1-B; Production cameras — 1-Acti.
PRESSROOM: Line 1 — 3-HI/15A; Folders — 1-HI. MAILROOM: Bundle tyer — 1-Bu. WIRE SERVICES: News — AP; Receiving dishes — AP. BUSINESS COMPUTERS: 1-Ap/Mac; PCs & micros networked.

MANHATTAN

Riley and Pottawatomie Counties

'90 U.S. Census- 37,712; E&P '96 Est. 41,775
ABC-CZ (90): 46,903 (HH 16,679)

The Manhattan Mercury

(e-mon to fri; S)

The Manhattan Mercury, 318 N. Fifth St. (66502); PO Box 787, Manhattan, KS 66505-0787; tel (913) 776-2200; fax (913) 776-8807. Seaton group.
Circulation: 11,573(e); 13,089(S); ABC Sept. 30, 1995.
Price: 35¢(d); 75¢(S); $8.00/mo; $96.00/yr (carrier).
Advertising: Open inch rate $9.86(e); $9.86 (S). **Representative:** Landon Associates Inc.
News Services: AP, NYT, LAT-WP. **Politics:** Independent. **Established:** 1884.
Not Published: New Year; Labor Day; Christmas.
Special Editions: Back-to-School; Home Improvement; Football; Christmas Season Opening; Kansas State University; Guide to Manhattan; Home & Business Show; Parade of Homes.
Broadcast Affiliate: KMAN; KMKF.

CORPORATE OFFICERS

Board Chairman — R M Seaton
President — Edward L Seaton
Vice Pres — Donald R Seaton

GENERAL MANAGEMENT

Publisher/General Manager — Edward L Seaton

ADVERTISING

Manager-National — Steve Stallwitz

CIRCULATION

Director — Joyce Kirkendall

NEWS EXECUTIVES

Editor in Chief — Edward L Seaton
Exec Editor — Bill Felber
Senior Editor — W A Colvin

EDITORS AND MANAGERS

Editorial Page Editor — Walter Braun
Fashion/Home Furnishings Editor — Paul Branson
Living/Lifestyle Editor — Paul Branson
News Editor — Joe Bathke
Photo Editor — Rod Mikinski
Religion Editor — Amy Gunnerson
Society Editor — Paul Branson
Sports Editor — Mark Janssen

PRODUCTION

Coordinator-Quality — Bob Wilburn
Coordinator-Systems — Brian Carter
Foreman-Pressroom/Stereo — Larry Funk
Foreman-Mailroom — Tom Sugg

Market Information: TMC; ADS.
Mechanical available: Offset; Black and 3 ROP colors; insert accepted — preprinted, all; page cut-offs — 22¾".
Mechanical specifications: Type page 13" x 21½"; E - 6 cols, 2$\frac{1}{16}$", ⅛" between; A - 6 cols, 2$\frac{1}{16}$", ⅛" between; C - 6 cols, 2$\frac{1}{16}$", ⅛" between.
Commodity consumption: Newsprint 800 short tons; widths 28", 14"; black ink 35,000 pounds; color ink 1,200 pounds; single pages printed 8,476; average pages per issue 23(d), 52(S); single plates used 20,500.
Equipment: EDITORIAL: Front-end hardware — 1-Mk/1100 Plus, IBM, 14-RSK/TRS 80-100, 4-Ap/Mac, 10-Mk; Front-end software — Mk/Page, QuarkXPress; Printers — XIT/Clipper, Ap/Mac LaserWriter NTX, TI, HP/LaserJet. CLASSIFIED: Front-end hardware — 3-Mk/1100 Plus, 1-Ap/Mac; Front-end software — Mk, Mk/Page; Printers — XIT/Clipper, Ap/Mac LaserWriter NTX, TI, HP/LaserJet; Other equipment — IBM. DISPLAY: Adv layout systems — 1-Mk/MasterPlanner, Ap/Mac; Front-end hardware — Mk, 1-Ap/Mac; Front-end software — Mk/Mycro-Comp AdWriter, Acrobat; Printers — XIT/Clipper, HP/LaserJet. PRODUCTION: OCR software — Caere/OmniPage Pro 5.0; Typesetters — XIT/Clipper, Ap/Mac LaserWriter NTX; Plate exposures — 1-Nu; Plate processors — 1-WL/38C; Electronic picture desk — Lf/AP Leaf Picture Desk; Scanners — Umax/UG80; Production cameras — 1-R/580; Automatic film processors — 1-P/Super G2; Color separation equipment (conventional) — 1-BKY.
PRESSROOM: Line 1 — 4-HI/845; Folders — 1-HI/2:1; Reels and stands — 1-HI; Press control system — Haley/Controller. MAILROOM: Counter stackers — 1-BG/Count-O-Veyor 107; Inserters and stuffers — 5-KAN/480; Bundle tyer — 1-Bu/Constellation K101; Addressing machine — 1-KAN. COMMUNICATIONS: Digital ad delivery system — AP AdSend. Systems used — satellite. WIRE SERVICES: News — AP Datastream, LAT-WP, AP, NYT; Receiving dishes — size-3m, AP. BUSINESS COMPUTERS: IBM/5360; Applications: CDS: Accts receivable, Accts payable, Payroll.

McPHERSON

McPherson County

'90 U.S. Census- 12,422; E&P '96 Est. 13,079

McPherson Sentinel

(e-mon to sat)

McPherson Sentinel, 301 S. Main; PO Box 926, McPherson, KS 67460; tel (316) 241-2422; fax (316) 241-2425. Hollinger International Inc. group.
Circulation: 5,369(e); 5,369(e-sat); Sworn Oct. 20, 1995.
Price: 50¢(d); 50¢(sat); $ 8.25/mo; $90.00/yr.
Advertising: Open inch rate $8.00(e); $8.00(e-sat).
News Service: AP. **Politics:** Independent. **Established:** 1887.
Not Published: New Year; Memorial Day; Independence Day; Labor Day; Thanksgiving; Christmas.
Special Editions: Soil Conservation (Feb); Progress (Mar); Industrial Appreciation (June); 4-H Fair (July); Back-to-School, Mac Facts (Aug); Football (Sept); Christmas (Nov); Christmas (Dec).
Magazines: Food & Farm (tues); Food & Farm (wed); Church (fri).

CORPORATE OFFICERS

President — Larry J Perrotto
Comptroller — Roland McBride

GENERAL MANAGEMENT

Publisher — Tom Throne

ADVERTISING

Director — Gary Mehl

CIRCULATION

Manager — Jim Price

NEWS EXECUTIVES

Editor — Tom Throne
Managing Editor — Kathy Hackleman

PRODUCTION

Superintendent — Janell Dreiling

Market Information: Zoned editions; TMC.
Mechanical available: Offset; Black and 3 ROP colors; insert accepted — preprinted; page cut-offs — 21½".
Mechanical specifications: Type page 13" x 21½"; E - 6 cols, 2.03", ⅙" between; A - 6 cols, 2.03", ⅙" between; C - 6 cols, 2.03", ⅙" between.
Commodity consumption: Newsprint 244 short tons; widths 13¾", 27½"; black ink 2,700 pounds; color ink 150 pounds; single pages printed 4,106; average pages per issue 14(d); single plates used 10,000.
Equipment: EDITORIAL: Front-end hardware — IBM/30-286; Front-end software — TC; Printers — Ap/Mac LaserWriter NT. CLASSIFIED: Front-end hardware — Packard-Bell; Front-end software — Nomad. DISPLAY: Front-end hardware — 3-Ap/Mac; Front-end software — QuarkXPress; Other equipment — Umax/Scanner. PRODUCTION: Typesetters — Ap/Mac LaserWriter 360; Plate exposures — Nu/Flip Top FT4OUPNS; Automatic film processors — AG/Rapidline 43.
PRESSROOM: Line 1 — 5-G/Community; Line 2 — 1-G/Community; Folders — 1-G/SC. MAILROOM: Bundle tyer — 1-Marlo. WIRE SERVICES: News — AP; Receiving dishes — size-2ft, AP. BUSINESS COMPUTERS: 1-AT, 1-Corsair/386; Applications: Nomads: Accts payable, Accts receivable, Gen ledger, Circ.

NEWTON

Harvey County

'90 U.S. Census- 16,700; E&P '96 Est. 17,252

The Newton Kansan

(e-mon to fri; m-sat)

The Newton Kansan, 121 W. 6th; PO Box 268, Newton, KS 67114; tel (316) 283-1500; fax (316) 283-2471. Morris Communications Corp. group.
Circulation: 7,645(e); 7,645(m-sat); Sworn Sept. 29, 1995.
Price: 50¢(d); 50¢(sat); $7.50/mo; $84.00/yr.
Advertising: Open inch rate $7.74(e); $7.74(m-sat). **Representative:** Papert Companies.
News Service: AP. **Politics:** Independent. **Established:** 1872.
Not Published: New Year; Memorial Day; Independence Day; Labor Day; Thanksgiving; Christmas.
Special Editions: Bridal Tab (Jan); Home Improvement (Mar); Car Care Tab (Apr); Welcome to Harvey County (June); Winterizing Tab (Oct); Christmas Kick-off (Nov).
Magazine: Leisure Times (TV Section) (fri).

CORPORATE OFFICERS

Chairman of the Board — W S Morris III
President — Paul S Simon
Secretary/Treasurer — William A Herman III

GENERAL MANAGEMENT

Publisher — Douglas J Anstaett
Business Manager — Janice Nesser

ADVERTISING

Manager — Dennis Garrison

TELECOMMUNICATIONS

Audiotex Manager — Mark Schnabel

CIRCULATION

Manager — Larry Sadowski

NEWS EXECUTIVES

Editor — Douglas J Anstaett
Managing Editor — Connie White

EDITORS AND MANAGERS

Editorial Page Editor — Douglas J Anstaett
Editorial Writer — Douglas J Anstaett
Education/Features Editor — Brian Bowman
Food/Lifestyle Editor — Wendy Nugent
News Editor — Bill Wilson
Photographer — Eric Rathke
Reporter — Keturah Truesdell Austin
Sports Editor — Mark Schnabel

MANAGEMENT INFORMATION SERVICES

Data Processing Manager — Janice Nesser

PRODUCTION

Manager-Press — Kevin Almond
Supervisor-Press — Ken Driskill

Market Information: TMC; Operate audiotex.
Mechanical available: Offset; Black and 3 ROP colors; insert accepted — preprinted; page cut-offs — 22¾".
Mechanical specifications: Type page 13" x 21½"; E - 6 cols, 2.04", ⅙" between; A - 6 cols, 2.04", ⅙" between; C - 6 cols, 2.04", ⅙" between.
Commodity consumption: Newsprint 295 short tons; widths 28", 14"; black ink 8,000 pounds; color ink 1,800 pounds; single pages printed 4,698; average pages per issue 15.3(d); single plates used 3,300.
Equipment: EDITORIAL: Front-end hardware — 5-Ap/Mac II, 3-Ap/Mac Classic, Ap/Mac Quadra; Front-end software — QuarkXPress, Baseview/News; Printers — Ap/Mac LaserWriter II NTX, MON/Imagesetter. CLASSIFIED: Front-end hardware — 1-Ap/Mac II; Front-end software — QuarkXPress, Baseview/Classified; Printers — Ap/Mac LaserWriter II NTX. AUDIOTEX: Supplier name — SMS/Stauffer Gold Audiotext. DISPLAY: Front-end hardware — 1-Ap/Mac SE, 2-Ap/Mac II, Ap/Mac Quadra; Front-end software — Aldus/PageMaker, QuarkXPress; Printers — Ap/Mac LaserWriter II NTX, MON/Imagesetter. PRODUCTION: Pagination software — QuarkXPress; Typesetters — 2-Ap/Mac LaserWriter II NTX, 1-Ap/Mac LaserWriter Plus; Plate exposures — Nu; Plate processors — Nat; Production cameras — DAI/DS; Automatic film processors — 1-LE/24; Color separation equipment (conventional) — Ap/Mac Quadra.
PRESSROOM: Line 1 — 7-G; Folders — 1-G/SC. MAILROOM: Bundle tyer — 2-Bu; Addressing machine — 1-Ch. LIBRARY: Electronic — SMS/Stauffer Gold. WIRE SERVICES: News — AP; Receiving dishes — size-2ft, AP. BUSINESS COMPUTERS: NCR/System 3230; Applications: Accts receivable, Circ, Accts payable, Payroll; PCs & micros networked; PCs & main system networked.

NORTON

Norton County

'90 U.S. Census- 3,017; E&P '96 Est. 2,868

The Norton Daily Telegram

(e-mon to fri)

The Norton Daily Telegram, 215 S. Kansas St.; PO Box 320, Norton, KS 67654; tel (913) 877-3361.
Circulation: 2,061(e); Sworn Sept. 30, 1994.
Price: 15¢(d); $43.01/yr (mail).
Advertising: Open inch rate $4.20(e).
News Service: AP. **Politics:** Independent. **Established:** 1906.
Not Published: New Year; Memorial Day; Independence Day; Labor Day; Thanksgiving; Christmas.
Advertising not accepted: Alcoholic beverages.
Special Weekly Sections: Best Food Day (mon); TV Time (thur); Religion (fri).

CORPORATE OFFICER

President — Richard D Boyd

GENERAL MANAGEMENT

Publisher — Richard D Boyd

ADVERTISING

Manager — Victor Randolph

CIRCULATION

Manager-Bookkeeping — Larry Boyd
Manager-Carrier — Mary Jan Van Patton

NEWS EXECUTIVE

Editor — Richard D Boyd

EDITORS AND MANAGERS

Editorial Page Editor — Richard D Boyd
Society/Women's Editor — Von Fowler

Mechanical available: Offset; Black and 1 ROP color; insert accepted — preprinted; page cut-offs — 22¾".
Mechanical specifications: Type page 13¾" x 22¾"; E - 6 cols, 2$\frac{1}{16}$", $\frac{3}{16}$" between; A - 6 cols, 2$\frac{1}{16}$", $\frac{3}{16}$" between; C - 6 cols, 2$\frac{1}{16}$", $\frac{3}{16}$" between.
Commodity consumption: average pages per issue 20(d).
Equipment: EDITORIAL: Front-end hardware — Hyundai/Super 386SE-40M; Front-end software — IBM/Prof Write, IBM/Arts & Letters; Printers — HP/LaserJet III. CLASSIFIED: Front-end hardware — Hyundai/Super 386SE-40M; Front-end software — IBM/Prof Write, IBM/Arts & Letters. DISPLAY: Front-end hardware — Ap/Mac SE-40M, Hyundai/Super 386; Front-end software — IBM/Prof Write, IBM/Arts & Letters; Printers — HP/LaserJet III. PRODUCTION: Plate exposures — 1-B/5000; Plate processors — 1-Nat/A-250; Production cameras — 1-Acti. MAILROOM: Addressing machine — Am.

OLATHE

Johnson County

'90 U.S. Census- 63,352; E&P '96 Est. 79,184
ABC-CZ (90): 63,352 (HH 21,445)

The Olathe Daily News

(m-mon to fri; m-sat)

The Olathe Daily News, 514 S. Kansas; PO Box 130, Olathe, KS 66051; tel (913) 764-2211; fax (913) 764-3672.
Circulation: 8,478(m); 8,972(m-sat); ABC Sept. 30, 1995.
Price: 35¢(d); $1.00(sat); $6.85/mo (carrier); $76.20/yr (carrier).
Advertising: Open inch rate $9.80(m); $9.80(m-sat).
News Services: AP, Harris, NYT. **Politics:** Independent. **Established:** 1859.
Note: Effective Mar. 1, 1995, this publication changed its publishing plan from (m-mon to sat; S) to (m-mon to fri; m-sat).
Special Editions: Wedding Guide (Jan); Progress (Mar); Homes (Apr); Answer Book (July);

Back-to-School/Education, Fall Sports (Aug); Senior Lifestyle (Sept); Homes (Oct); Holiday Gift Guide (Nov); Health Care (Dec).
Special Weekly Sections: Business (mon); Cruisin' (Youth) (tues); Flavor (wed); Home Teams (thur); Weekend (fri); Focus (Features) (S).
Magazines: TV Week, Real Estate & Rental Guide, USA Weekend (S).

CORPORATE OFFICER

President/CEO Timothy P O'Donnell

GENERAL MANAGEMENT

Publisher Timothy P O'Donnell
General Manager Scott Smith

ADVERTISING

Director Rick J Brown
Manager-Classified Judy Leary

NEWS EXECUTIVE

Editor Laird McGregor

EDITORS AND MANAGERS

Managing Editor Laird McGregor
News Editor Gerald Hay
Photo Editor Dave Kaup
Sports Editor Scott Hollister

PRODUCTION

Manager Ken Chubb
Manager-Composing Brice Bickford

Market Information: Zoned editions; TMC.
Mechanical available: Offset; Black and 3 ROP colors; insert accepted — preprinted; page cut-offs — 22¾".
Mechanical specifications: Type page 13" x 21½"; E - 6 cols, 2¹⁄₁₆", ⅛" between; A - 6 cols, 2¹⁄₁₆", ⅛" between; C - 9 cols, 1½", ³⁄₃₂" between.
Commodity consumption: Newsprint 1,430 short tons; 1,300 metric tons; widths 27", 34", 30"; black ink 27,400 pounds; color ink 420 pounds; single pages printed 16,800; average pages per issue 20(d), 36(sat); single plates used 19,100.
Equipment: EDITORIAL: Front-end hardware — 26-Ap/Mac; Front-end software — Baseview 1.1.2; CLASSIFIED: Front-end hardware — 5-Ap/Mac; Front-end software — Baseview 3.2; DISPLAY: Adv layout systems — 6-Ap/Mac; Front-end hardware — Ap/Mac; Front-end software — Baseview 1.5.1, Aldus/FreeHand 4.0; PRODUCTION: Pagination software — Baseview 1.1.2; Typesetters — 1-Ap/Mac LaserWriter, 2-QMS/820, 1-AU/APS-6-82 ACS, 1-Ap/Mac LaserWriter Pro 810; Plate exposures — 1-Nu/FT40V6UPNS; Plate processors — 1-Glunz Jensen/Multiplater 88; Electronic picture desk — Lf/AP Leaf Picture Desk; Scanners — Lf/Leafscan 35, Umax/1260, HP/ScanJet Plus; Production cameras — 1-R/500; Automatic film processors — 1-Glunz Jensen/MLSS, 1-Kk/Imagemate 55DT. PRESSROOM: Line 1 — 6-G/Urbanite; Folders — 1-G/2:1. MAILROOM: Counter stackers — 1-BG/Count-O-Veyor, 1-Id/440, 1-Fg; Inserters and stuffers — 1-Mc/660 7 Station; Bundle tyer — 2-Bu/String, 1-MLN/ML2EE. COMMUNICATIONS: Remote imagesetting — satellite. WIRE SERVICES: News — AP Datafeatures, Harris News Service, AP, NYT; Photos — AP; Syndicates — United Media, Universal Press, Creators, King Features, TMS, LATS, NAS; Receiving dishes — size-3m, AP. BUSINESS COMPUTERS: 8-TI/800, 1-DEC/PC, 1-PC; Applications: Data Sciences Inc: Circ, Business, Accts receivable, Gen ledger, Payroll, Newsprint Inventory; PCs & micros networked; PCs & main system networked.

OTTAWA

Franklin County

'90 U.S. Census- 10,667; **E&P '96 Est.** 10,667

Herald (e-mon to fri; m-sat)

Herald, 104 S. Cedar St., Ottawa, KS 66067; tel (913) 242-4700; fax (913) 242-9420. Harris Enterprises Inc. group.
Circulation: 5,718(e); 5,718(m-sat); Sworn Sept. 30, 1995.
Price: 50¢(d); 50¢(sat); $6.38/mo; $70.56/yr (carrier).
Advertising: Open inch rate $6.30(e); $7.15(e-tues); $6.30(m-sat).
News Service: AP. **Politics:** Independent. **Established:** 1896.
Not Published: New Year; Memorial Day; Independence Day; Labor Day; Thanksgiving; Christmas.
Advertising not accepted: Tobacco.
Special Edition: Progress Edition (Jan).
Special Weekly Sections: Best Food Day (tues); Weddings/Engagements (wed); Farm (thur); Youth/Health (fri).
Magazines: Society (wed); TV Scene, Out & About (entertainment) (fri).

CORPORATE OFFICERS

President Jim Hitch
Vice Pres Lloyd Ballhagen
Secretary/Treasurer Tom Love

GENERAL MANAGEMENT

Publisher Jim Hitch
Purchasing Agent Jim Hitch

ADVERTISING

Director Tom Love
Manager-Classified Karen Wooge

CIRCULATION

Manager Gene Kelsey

NEWS EXECUTIVE

Editor Jim Hitch

EDITORS AND MANAGERS

Amusements/Auto Editor Jay Bemis
Books Editor Jay Bemis
Business/Finance Editor David Bartowski
City Editor Jay Bemis
Editorial Page Editor Jim Hitch
Education Editor Greg Mast
Farm Editor David Bartowski
Fashion/Food Editor David Bartowski
Features Editor Jay Bemis
Health/Medical Editor David Bartowski
Lifestyle Editor David Bartowski
National Editor Jim Hitch
News Editor Jay Bemis
Political/Government Editor Jim Hitch
Religion Editor Jim Hitch
Sports Editor Greg Mast

PRODUCTION

Foreman-Composing Jeanie Rossman
Foreman-Pressroom Wayne Snow

Market Information: TMC.
Mechanical available: Offset; Black and 3 ROP colors; insert accepted — preprinted; page cut-offs — 22¾".
Mechanical specifications: Type page 12¹³⁄₁₆" x 21½"; E - 6 cols, 2", ³⁄₁₆" between; A - 6 cols, 2", ³⁄₁₆" between; C - 6 cols, 1¹⁵⁄₁₆", ³⁄₁₆" between.
Commodity consumption: Newsprint 210 short tons; widths 27", 13½"; black ink 6,600 pounds; color ink 715 pounds; single pages printed 4,057; average pages per issue 12(d); single plates used 5,480.
Equipment: EDITORIAL: Front-end hardware — Ap/Mac Centris 610, Ap/Mac 650; Front-end software — Baseview, QuarkXPress; Printers — Ap/Mac LaserWriter NTX, QMS/PS-860 11" x 17"; Other equipment — Microtek/Scanner Flatbed. CLASSIFIED: Front-end hardware — Ap/Mac Centris 610; Front-end software — Baseview, QuarkXPress; Printers — Ap/Mac LaserWriter II, QMS/PS 860. DISPLAY: Front-end hardware — Ap/Mac Centris 610s; Front-end software — Aldus/PageMaker, Aldus/FreeHand; Printers — Ap/Mac LaserWriter Plus; Other equipment — CD-Rom, Microtek/Scanner. PRODUCTION: OCR software — Caere/OmniPage Direct; Typesetters — Ap/Mac LaserWriter Plus, QMS/PS 860; Plate exposures — Nu; Plate processors — Roconex; Scanners — Microtek/Scanner; Production cameras — C/260-S St; Automatic film processors — LE. PRESSROOM: Line 1 — 6-HI/V15-A; Line 2 — 6-HI/V15-A; Line 3 — 6-HI/V15-A; Line 4 — 6-HI/V15-A; Line 5 — 6-HI/V15-A; Line 6 — 6-HI/V15-A. MAILROOM: Inserters and stuffers — KAN/320 3-sleeve; Bundle tyer — Bu. WIRE SERVICES: News — AP; Receiving dishes — size-8ft, AP. BUSINESS COMPUTERS: 6-TI; Applications: Amdek; PCs & micros networked; PCs & main system networked.

PARSONS

Labette County

'90 U.S. Census- 11,924; **E&P '96 Est.** 11,615

Parsons Sun

(e-mon to fri; m-sat)

Parsons Sun, 220 S. 18th St.; PO Box 836, Parsons, KS 67357; tel (316) 421-2000; fax (316) 421-2217. Harris Enterprises Inc. group.
Circulation: 7,006(e); 7,006(m-sat); Sworn Sept. 22, 1995.
Price: 50¢(d); 50¢(sat); $6.95/mo; $75.06/yr.
Advertising: Open inch rate $7.69(e); $7.69(m-sat). **Representative:** Papert Companies.
News Services: AP, Harris. **Politics:** Independent. **Established:** 1871.
Not Published: New Year; Thanksgiving; Christmas.
Special Editions: Bridal, Gardening (Mar); Fishing and Outdoors, Mother's Day Edition (May); Why My Dad's the Greatest (June); Back-to-School, Senior Citizens (Aug); Home Improvement (Sept); Recipe, Christmas Opening (Nov).
Special Weekly Sections: Business (mon); Best Food Day, Farm, County Line (wed); TV Scene (fri).

CORPORATE OFFICERS

President Ann K Charles
Vice Pres Lloyd Ballhagen
Secretary/Treasurer Shirley Moore

GENERAL MANAGEMENT

Publisher Ann K Charles

ADVERTISING

Director Carolyn Kennett
Manager-Classified Carolyn Kennett

CIRCULATION

Manager Carolyn Phillips

NEWS EXECUTIVES

Editor Ann K Charles
Managing Editor Jim Cook

EDITORS AND MANAGERS

Business Editor Ray Nolting
Education Robert Hite
Farm/Regional Editor Jim Cook
Fashion/Food Editor Connie Brown
News Editor Jean Teller
Photography Editor Dennis Lungren
Religion Editor Connie Brown
Sports Editor Jack Harris
Television Editor Jean Teller

PRODUCTION

Foreman-Pressroom Dale Conrad
Manager-Graphic Arts Donna Blackburn

Market Information: TMC.
Mechanical available: Offset; Black and 3 ROP colors; insert accepted — preprinted; page cut-offs — 22¾".
Mechanical specifications: Type page 13" x 21"; E - 5 cols, 2¹⁄₁₆", ⅛" between; A - 6 cols, 2¹⁄₁₆", ⅛" between; C - 6 cols, 2¹⁄₁₆", ⅛" between.
Commodity consumption: Newsprint 424 short tons; widths 27½", 30"; black ink 6,710 pounds; color ink 1,100 pounds; single pages printed 5,000; average pages per issue 14(d); single plates used 4,760.
Equipment: EDITORIAL: Front-end hardware — Ap/Mac; Front-end software — Aldus/FreeHand, QPS, Multi-Ad/Creator, Baseview; Printers — NewGen/Turbo PS-1200B. CLASSIFIED: Front-end hardware — Ap/Mac; Front-end software — Baseview; Printers — Okidata, NewGen/Turbo PS-1200B. DISPLAY: Adv layout systems — Ap/Mac; Front-end software — QPS, Baseview, Multi-Ad/Creator; Printers — Ap/Mac LaserWriter II, NewGen/Turbo PS-1200B. PRODUCTION: Pagination software — Baseview; Plate exposures — Nu; Plate processors — W; Scanners — Ap/Mac One, Ap/Mac, Umax/UC1260; Production cameras — 1-Acti; Automatic film processors — 1-LE. PRESSROOM: Line 1 — 7-G; Folders — 1-G/2:1. MAILROOM: Inserters and stuffers — MM; Bundle tyer — 2-Bu. COMMUNICATIONS: Systems used — satellite. WIRE SERVICES: News — AP, HN; Stock tables — AP; Receiving dishes — size-10ft, AP. BUSINESS COMPUTERS: DS /PaperTrak; Applications: Microsoft/Word, Microsoft/Excel.

PITTSBURG

Crawford County

'90 U.S. Census- 17,775; **E&P '96 Est.** 17,561

The Morning Sun

(m-mon to sat; S)

The Morning Sun, 701 N. Locust St.; PO Box H, Pittsburg, KS 66762; tel (316) 231-2600; fax (316) 231-0645. Morris Communications Corp. group.
Circulation: 10,962(m); 10,962(m-sat); 13,962(S); Sworn Sept. 30, 1995.
Price: 50¢(d); 50¢(sat); $1.00(S); $8.50/mo; $81.00/yr.
Advertising: Open inch rate $7.10(m); $7.10(m-sat); $7.10(S). **Representative:** Papert Companies.
News Service: AP. **Politics:** Independent. **Established:** 1887.
Not Published: Day following: New Year; Memorial Day; Independence Day; Labor Day; Thanksgiving; Christmas.
Special Weekly Sections: Best Food Day (wed); Church Page (sat); Business Page, Market Page, Bridal Pages, Mini-Kids (S); Entertainment Page (daily).
Magazines: Sun Profile TV Magazine (sat); Comics (S); Parade.

GENERAL MANAGEMENT

Publisher Tom H Collinson
Manager-Business Billie Casella

ADVERTISING

Manager Karen VanLeeuwen

CIRCULATION

Manager Shari Redd

NEWS EXECUTIVES

Editor Tom H Collinson
Managing Editor Tom Farmer

EDITORS AND MANAGERS

Amusements/Books Editor Nikki Patrick
Columnist Ken Simons
Fashion/Food Editor Nikki Patrick
Films/Theater Editor Nikki Patrick
Radio/Televison Editor Nikki Patrick
Sports Editor Bill McMillen

MANAGEMENT INFORMATION SERVICES

Data Processing Manager Billie Casella

PRODUCTION

Superintendent Charles Booe

Market Information: TMC; Operate audiotex.
Mechanical available: Offset; Black and 3 ROP colors; insert accepted — preprinted; page cut-offs — 22¾".
Mechanical specifications: Type page 13" x 21½"; E - 6 cols, 2¹⁄₁₆", ⅛" between; A - 6 cols, 2¹⁄₁₆", ⅛" between; C - 8 cols, 1½", ⅛" between.
Commodity consumption: Newsprint 650 short tons; widths 27½", 13¾"; black ink 4,400 pounds; color ink 1,200 pounds; single pages printed 7,000; average pages per issue 20(d), 36(S); single plates used 10,000.
Equipment: EDITORIAL: Front-end hardware — Ap/Mac, 10-Ap/Mac SE, 2-Ap/Mac ci, 1-Ap/Mac SE30; Printers — 1-STAR/X-15. CLASSIFIED: Front-end hardware — 4-Ap/Mac SE, 1-Ap/Mac IIci; Printers — Ap/Mac LaserWriter II NTX. PRODUCTION: Typesetters — 2-COM/Advantage II, 1-Translator/II, 1-Ap/Mac IIci; Plate exposures — 1-B/500-255; Plate processors — 1-WL/30B 64007; Production cameras — 1-B/Commodore 241305; Automatic film processors — 1-LD/24-AQ. PRESSROOM: Line 1 — 5-G/Urbanite; Folders — 1-G/2:1. MAILROOM: Inserters and stuffers — 1-MM/5 heads; Bundle tyer — 1-MLN/ML2EE; Addressing machine — 1-Ch; Other mailroom equipment — MM/Minuteman. LIBRARY: Electronic — SMS/Stauffer Gold. WIRE SERVICES: News — AP; Syndicates — NEA; Receiving dishes — AP. BUSINESS COMPUTERS: ATT/WGS; Applications: Circ, Adv billing, Accts receivable, Payroll, Accts payable; PCs & micros networked; PCs & main system networked.

PRATT

Pratt County

'90 U.S. Census- 6,687; **E&P '96 Est.** 6,705

The Pratt Tribune

(e-mon to fri)

The Pratt Tribune, 320 S. Main, Pratt, KS 67124; tel (316) 672-5511; fax (316) 672-5514. Hometown Communications group.
Circulation: 2,730(e); Sworn Sept. 30, 1994.
Price: 50¢(d).
Advertising: Open inch rate $6.30(e). **Representative:** Papert Companies. **Politics:** Independent. **Established:** 1917.
Not Published: New Year; Memorial Day; Independence Day; Labor Day; Thanksgiving; Christmas.
Special Editions: ½ Day Sale (Jan); Tax Guide, Progress Edition (Feb); City-Farm Festival, Bridal (Mar); Lawn & Garden, Home Improvement, Car Care (Apr); Leisure Time, Mother's Day, Graduation (May); Oil % Gas, 4-H Sale, Miss Kansas (June); Sidewalk Sale, 4-H Fair Results (July); Football Kick-off, Back-to-School (Aug); Senior Citizens, Fall Car Care (Sept); Moonlight Madness, Hunting (Oct); Shop Early, Christmas (Nov); Christmas Gift Guide, 13 Month (Dec).
Special Weekly Sections: Business (mon); Farm (tues); Seniors (wed); Church, Kids, Farm (thur); Outdoors (fri).
Magazines: Total TV (tues); The Sunflower (TMC).

GENERAL MANAGEMENT

Publisher Jim Phillips
Controller Virginia Watkins

ADVERTISING

Manager Ronda Brown
Manager-Classified Susan Iparra

NEWS EXECUTIVE

Editor Conrad Easterday

PRODUCTION

Manager K Don Kutz

Market Information: Split Run; TMC.
Mechanical available: Offset; Black and 3 ROP colors; insert accepted — preprinted; page cut-offs — 22¾".
Mechanical specifications: Type page 13¾" x 21½"; E - 6 cols, 2 1/16", 1/8" between; A - 6 cols, 2 1/16", 1/8" between; C - 8 cols, 2 1/16", 1/8" between.
Commodity consumption: average pages per issue 12(d).
Equipment: EDITORIAL: Front-end hardware — 6-Mk. CLASSIFIED: Front-end hardware — 1-Mk. PRODUCTION: Typesetters — 3-COM; Plate exposures — 1-Nu; Production cameras — 1-R.
PRESSROOM: Line 1 — 4-G/Community. MAILROOM: Bundle tyer — 1-Bu; Addressing machine — 1-Am. BUSINESS COMPUTERS: 1-Bs.

RUSSELL

Russell County

'90 U.S. Census- 4,781; E&P '96 Est. 4,525

The Russell Daily News

(e-mon to sat)

The Russell Daily News, 802 N. Maple St., Russell, KS 67665; tel (913) 483-2116; fax (913) 483-4012.
Circulation: 2,700(e); 2,700(e-sat); Sworn Oct. 2, 1995.
Price: 50¢(d); 50¢(sat); $4.75/mo.
Advertising: Open inch rate $6.30(e); $6.53(e-sat). **Representative:** Landon Associates Inc.
News Service: UPI. **Politics:** Independent. **Established:** 1930.
Not Published: New Year; Memorial Day; Independence Day; Labor Day; Thanksgiving; Christmas.
Special Editions: Jan 1; Progress; Graduation; Fair; Oil; Christmas Opening; Christmas Greetings.

CORPORATE OFFICER

President Allan D Evans

GENERAL MANAGEMENT

Publisher/General Manager Allan D Evans
Assoc Publisher David A Evans

ADVERTISING

Director Allan D Evans

NEWS EXECUTIVE

Editor Jim Joule

EDITORS AND MANAGERS

City Editor Albert Linn
Features Editor Irene Jepsen

PRODUCTION

Manager Allan D Evans

Market Information: TMC.
Mechanical available: Offset; Black and 3 ROP colors; insert accepted — preprinted.
Mechanical specifications: Type page 15¼" x 21½"; E - 8 cols, 1.83", .14" between; A - 8 cols, 1.83", .14" between; C - 8 cols, 1.83", .14" between.
Commodity consumption: average pages per issue 20(d).
Equipment: PRODUCTION: Typesetters — 1-COM/7200, 3-COM/Comp II; Platemaking systems — 1-Nu; Scanners — 1-M, 1-Lu; Production cameras — 1-R/500; Automatic film processors — 1-P/Pakonolith.
PRESSROOM: Line 1 — 3-KP/Newsking; Folders — 1-KP. MAILROOM: Bundle tyer — 1-Cyclone; Addressing machine — 1-Am/Class 1900.

SALINA

Saline County

'90 U.S. Census- 42,303; E&P '96 Est. 43,417
ABC-CZ (90): 42,303 (HH 17,287)

The Salina Journal

(m-mon to sat; S)

The Salina Journal, 333 S. 4th St.; PO Box 740, Salina, KS 67401; tel (913) 823-6363; fax (913) 823-3207. Harris Enterprises Inc. group.
Circulation: 31,184(m); 31,184(m-sat); 32,314(S); ABC Sept. 30, 1995.
Price: 50¢(d); 50¢(sat); $1.50(S); $3.46/wk (In Salina); $15.00/mo (In Salina); $140.00/yr (In Salina).
Advertising: Open inch rate $19.80(m); $19.80(m-sat); $21.24(S).
News Services: AP, NYT, Cox News Service, SHNS, Harris. **Politics:** Independent. **Established:** 1871.
Advertising not accepted: Cigarette.
Special Editions: Bridal (Jan); Progress (Feb); Farm Show, Dream Homes, Progress (Mar); Fashion, Medical Directory (Apr); Travel, Professional Women/Careers (May); Senior Citizen, River Festival (June); Back-to-School (July); Guide to Salina, Football, Craft & Hobby (Sept); Fashion, Car Care, Hunting & Fishing (Oct); Basketball, Holiday Cookbook (Nov); Christmas Gift Guide (Dec).
Special Weekly Sections: Neighbors, Health (mon); Applause (TMC), Best Food Day (wed); Encore/Entertainment, Home/Garden (fri); Church, TV Week, Fashion (sat).
Magazines: TV Week (TV Listings) (S); Dream Homes (quarterly).

CORPORATE OFFICERS

President Harris Rayl
Vice Pres Lloyd Ballhagen
Secretary/Treasurer George Pyle

GENERAL MANAGEMENT

Publisher Harris Rayl
Business Manager Dave Martin
Manager-Human Resources Jane Glenn

ADVERTISING

Director Jeanny Sharp
Manager-Sales Kim Norwood

TELECOMMUNICATIONS

Audiotex Manager Janet Lancaster

CIRCULATION

Manager Bryan Sandmeier
Manager-City Brian Walter
Manager-State Brent Walter
Customer Service Rebecca Tucker

NEWS EXECUTIVES

Exec Editor Scott Seirer
Asst Editor Jim Haag
Deputy Editor Ben Wearing

EDITORS AND MANAGERS

Amusements Editor Jim Haag
Auto Editor Scott Seirer
Books Editor Jim Haag
Editorial Page Editor George Pyle
Fashion/Food Editor Sherida Warner
Films/Theater Editor Jim Haag
Home Furnishings Editor Sherida Warner
Photo Department Manager Fritz Mendell
Radio/Television Editor Jim Haag
Society Editor Sherida Warner
Sports Editor Bob Davidson

MANAGEMENT INFORMATION SERVICES

Data Processing Manager Roxy Belden

PRODUCTION

Director-Safety Dave Atkinson
Manager Dave Atkinson
Manager-Systems Bob Kelly
Supervisor-Pre Press Ronuge Webb
Foreman-Pressroom Buster Base
Foreman-Mailroom Norbert Laue

Market Information: Zoned editions; Split Run; TMC; Operate audiotex.
Mechanical available: Offset; Black and 3 ROP colors; insert accepted — preprinted, other; page cut-offs — 22¾".
Mechanical specifications: Type page 13" x 21½"; E - 6 cols, 2 1/16", 1/8" between; A - 6 cols, 2 1/16", 1/8" between; C - 9 cols, 1 3/8", 1/16" between.
Commodity consumption: Newsprint 1,876 metric tons; widths 27½", 13¾"; black ink 43,084.2 pounds; color ink 4,618 pounds; single pages printed 10,238; average pages per issue 26(d), 43(S); single plates used 16,340.
Equipment: EDITORIAL: Front-end hardware — Ap/Mac Quadra 650s, Ap/Mac Quadra 610s; Front-end software — QuarkXPress/QED, QuarkXPress/Q-Edit, QuarkXPress/Q-View, 2-QuarkXPress/Q-Gather, QuarkXPress/Q-Wire; Printers — Ap/Mac LaserWriter II, Ap/Mac Pro 630, Printware/1217, Ap/Mac LaserWriter 16-600. CLASSIFIED: Front-end software — QuarkXPress/QED, QuarkXPress/Q-Sales, QuarkXPress/Q-Plan, QuarkXPress/Q-Class Act; Printers — Okidata/393. AUDIOTEX: Hardware — Brite, Wyse, Okidata/Microline, Zephyrus/300 Series Satellite. DISPLAY: Front-end hardware — 6-Ap/Mac Quadra, Novell/Netware 486 DX fileservers; Front-end software — Multi-Ad/Creator; Printers — Tektronix/Phaser III Printware 1217; Other equipment — Micronet/Optical Drive. PRODUCTION: Typesetters — 2-XIT/YAWL; Plate exposures — 1-Nu/Flip Top FT40V6UPNS, 1-Nu/Flip Top FT40APRNS; Plate processors — WL/30D, Nat/A-340; Electronic picture desk — Lf/AP Leaf Picture Desk; Scanners — 2-AG/Arcus Scanner; Production cameras — 1-Nu/SST 1418, 1-C/Spartan II; Automatic film processors — 1-LE/24Q, 1-LE/16; Film transporters — 1-C/1247; Color separation equipment (conventional) — Ap/Mac Quadra 950, Lf/AP Leaf Picture Desk; Digital color separation equipment — Lf/Leafscan 35, Sharp/320.
PRESSROOM: Line 1 — 8-G/Urbanite (3-Color Unit;5-Black Unit); Folders — 1-G/2:1; Reels and stands — 6-Cline, 2-G/Stands, 2-G/Rolls. MAILROOM: Inserters and stuffers — MM/9-head; Bundle tyer — MLN; Wrapping singles — MLN; Addressing machine — MM. LIBRARY: Electronic — In-House; Combination — Electronic. WIRE SERVICES: News — AP, NYT, SHNS, HNS; Photos — AP; Stock tables — AP; Syndicates — AP; Receiving dishes — size-12ft, AP. BUSINESS COMPUTERS: TI, Data Sciences; Applications: Circ, Billing, Subscriber, Non-subscriber, Payables, Gen ledger, Production; PCs & main system networked.

TOPEKA

Shawnee County

'90 U.S. Census- 119,883; E&P '96 Est. 125,066
ABC-CZ (90): 160,976 (HH 63,768)

The Topeka Capital-Journal

(m-mon to sat; S)

The Topeka Capital-Journal, 616 S.E. Jefferson St., Topeka, KS 66607-1120; tel (913) 295-1111; fax (913) 295-1198. Morris Communications Corp. group.
Circulation: 64,486(m); 64,486(m-sat); 71,325(S); ABC Sept. 30, 1995.
Price: 25¢(d); 25¢(sat); $1.25(S); $10.00/mo (carrier), $24.00/mo (mail); $120.00/yr (carrier), $169.00/yr (mail).
Advertising: Open inch rate $45.70(m); $57.05(m-sat); $57.05(S). **Representative:** Cresmer, Woodward, O'Mara & Ormsbee.
News Services: AP, LAT-WP. **Established:** 1874 (State Journal), 1879 (Capital).
Special Editions: Weddings (Jan); Flower, Lawn & Garden, Capitalizing on Topeka (Feb); THBA Home Show Tab, Northeast Kansas Golf Directory (Mar); Earth Day, Buy Kansas Expo (Apr); Pet Tab, Design-An-Ad Tab, Parade of Homes, Lakes & Recreation, Guide to Retirement Living, Best of Topeka, Mustang Celebration (May); Governor's Health Fair, Heartland Grand Nationals, Weddings (June); Safe & Sound, Rowing Tab, 4-H Fair Tab (July); USD 501 Tab, Topeka Life, Railroad Days (Aug); Football Tab (Sept); Parade of Homes (Oct); Women's Show, Veteran's Day, Christmas Gift Guides 1 & 2 (Nov); Basketball Tab, Christmas Gift Guides 3, 4, 5 & 6 (Dec); Age (monthly).
Special Weekly Sections: Government, Health & Environment (mon); Youth (tues); Good Taste (wed); Weekender (fri); Religion (sat); Arts & Leisure, Real Estate (S).
Magazines: Parade, TV Magazine (local, offset) (S).

CORPORATE OFFICERS

Chairman of the Board W S Morris III
President Paul S Simon
Secretary/Treasurer William A Herman III

GENERAL MANAGEMENT

Editor/Publisher P Scott McKibben
Business Manager Randy Magee
Coordinator-Human Resources Randy Magee

ADVERTISING

Director Ron Burns
Manager Leslie Palace

MARKETING AND PROMOTION

Director-Marketing Service Nancy Burkhardt

TELECOMMUNICATIONS

Audiotex Manager Ron Burns

CIRCULATION

Manager Garran Allison
Manager-City Ron House

NEWS EXECUTIVES

Exec Editor Mark Nusbaum
Managing Editor-News Anita Miller
Managing Editor-Photo Jeff Jacobsen
Managing Editor-Sports Pete Goering

EDITORS AND MANAGERS

Business Editor Anita Miller
Editorial Page Writer Mike Ryan
Education Editor Kristen Hays
Farm Editor Jim Suber
Features Page Mark Sommer
Librarian Patricia Johnston
Metro Editor Fred Johnson
News Editor Cynthia McGowan
Political Editor Roger Myers
State Editor Steve Swartz
Television Editor Billie Padilla

MANAGEMENT INFORMATION SERVICES

Online Manager Mike Forman

PRODUCTION

Director Larry Rogers
Manager-Technical Service Mike Blankenship
Manager-Systems Larry Bunton
Asst Manager Ed Robertson
Foreman-Composing (Day) Tom Bridson
Foreman-Composing (Night) George Doss
Foreman-Photo/Plate (Day) Harold Hypse
Foreman-Photo/Plate (Night) Brian Bronson
Superintendent-Press Craig Kane
Foreman-Pressroom (Day) Don Bennett
Foreman-Pressroom (Night) Royce Dial

Market Information: Split Run; TMC; Operate database; Operate audiotex.
Mechanical available: Offset; Black and 3 ROP colors; insert accepted — preprinted, cards; page cut-offs — 23 9/16".
Mechanical specifications: Type page 13¾" x 22"; E - 6 cols, 2 1/16", 1/8" between; A - 6 cols, 2 1/16", 1/8" between; C - 9 cols, 1 5/16", 1/8" between.
Commodity consumption: Newsprint 7,981 short tons; 7,241 metric tons; widths 27⅜", 41¼", 55"; black ink 168,000 pounds; color ink 27,478 pounds; single pages printed 13,992; average pages per issue 40(d), 75(S); single plates used 30,000.
Equipment: EDITORIAL: Front-end hardware — 1-Lf/Leafscan 35, 1-SII/TNS1, 1-Ap/Mac ci, 1-Ap/Mac II, 1-Ap/Mac Quadra 900; Front-end software — SII, QuarkXPress, Adobe/Photoshop, Aldus/FreeHand; Printers — Ap/Mac LaserWriter NTX, AU/APS-108; Other equipment — 1-Microtek/Flatbed scanner 600ZS, Lf/AP Leaf Picture Desk. CLASSIFIED: Front-end hardware — 1-SII/TNS1; Front-end software — SII. DISPLAY: Adv layout systems — SCS/Layout 8000; Front-end hardware — 1-Ap/Mac Quadra 700, 1-Ap/Mac Quadra 900, 3-Ap/Mac cx, 2-Ap/Mac fx, 1-Ap/Mac ci; Front-end software — Aldus/PageMaker, QuarkXPress, Adobe/Illustrator, Multi-Ad/Creator; Printers — 1-Ap/Mac LaserPrinter, 1-V/VT600W, AU/APS6-108; Other equipment — 1-Ap/Mac Scanner, 3-Ap/Mac CD-Rom. PRODUCTION: Typesetters — 2-AU/APS Micro 5, 1-AU/APS6-108; Platemaking systems — Offset; Plate exposures — 2-Nu/Flip Top; Plate processors — 2-WL/Lithoplater, 1-WL/Lithotech; Production cameras — 2-C/Spartan, 1-C/Marathon; Automatic film processors — 1-LE, 1-AG/litex, 1-P; Film transporters — 1-C; Shrink lenses — 1-C; Color separation equipment (conventional) — RZ/4050; Digital color separation equipment — ECR/Autokon 1000.
PRESSROOM: Line 1 — 6-G/Mark II, 2-G/Color half decks; Folders — 2-G; Pasters — G; Reels and stands — G; Press control system — Fin. MAILROOM: Counter stackers — 1-Id/2000, 1-Id/Marathoner, 1-Id/660; Inserters and stuffers — 1-S/72p; Bundle tyer — 1-MLN, 1-MLN, 1-MLN, 1-Power Strap; Wrapping singles — 4-Bu; Addressing machine — 1-Ch, 2-AVY. LIBRARY: Electronic — SMS/Stauffer Gold. WIRE SERVICES: News — AP; Stock tables — AP; Syndicates — LAT-WP; Receiving dishes — size-10ft, AP, AP Stocks, Weather. BUSINESS COMPUTERS: 1-Unisys/6000-50, ATT/6386E; Applications: Adv billing, Accts receivable, Gen ledger, Mailroom/Label printing, Accts payable, Online circ; PCs & micros networked; PCs & main system networked.

WELLINGTON

Sumner County

'90 U.S. Census- 8,411; E&P '96 Est. 8,697

Wellington Daily News

(e-mon to wed; e-fri)

Wellington Daily News, 113 W. Harvey; Box 368, Wellington, KS 67152; tel (316) 326-3326.
Circulation: 3,512(e); Sworn Oct. 12, 1995.
Price: 50¢(d).
Advertising: Open inch rate $6.20(e). **Representative:** Landon Associates Inc.

News Service: AP. **Politics:** Republican. **Established:** 1901.
Note: Effective June 1, 1995, this publication changed its publishing plan from (e-mon to fri) to (e-mon to wed; e-fri).
Not Published: New Year; Memorial Day; Independence Day; Labor Day; Thanksgiving; Christmas.
Special Editions: Spring Tab (Mar); Back-to-School Tab, Football Tab (Aug); Fall Tab (Sept); Christmas Tab (Nov).
Special Weekly Sections: Church Directory, TV Guide (fri).

CORPORATE OFFICER
President Jackson C Mitchell

GENERAL MANAGEMENT
Publisher Jackson C Mitchell
Manager-Office Beverly Stallbaumer
Bookkeeper Chad Ward

ADVERTISING
Director Bill Newland
Exec Alda Boyd
Manager-Classified Chad Ward

CIRCULATION
Manager-Subscriptions Beverly Stallbaumer

NEWS EXECUTIVE
Editor Janet Johnson

EDITORS AND MANAGERS
Action Line Editor Janet Johnson
Automotive Editor Tracy McCue
Business/Finance Editor Janet Johnson
City Editor Linda Stinnett
Editorial Page Editor Janet Johnson
Editorial Writer Jackson C Mitchell
Education Editor Linda Stinnett
Entertainment/Amusements Editor Janet Johnson
Features Editor Linda Stinnett
Graphics Editor/Art Director Janet Johnson
Living/Lifestyle Editor Janet Johnson
News Editor Janet Johnson
Photo Editor Janet Johnson
Political/Government Editor Janet Johnson
Radio/Television Editor Tracy McCue
Sports Editor Tracy McCue

PRODUCTION
Superintendent Terry Craig

Market Information: TMC.
Mechanical available: Offset; Black and 2 ROP colors; insert accepted — preprinted; page cut-offs — 21".
Mechanical specifications: Type page 13⅜" x 21"; E - 6 cols, 2¹⁄₁₆", ⅛" between; A - 6 cols, 2¹⁄₁₆", ⅛" between; C - 6 cols, 2¹⁄₁₆", ⅛" between.
Commodity consumption: Newsprint 100 short tons; width 28"; black ink 2,200 pounds; color ink 50 pounds; single pages printed 2,540; average pages per issue 10(d); single plates used 1,270.
Equipment: EDITORIAL: Front-end hardware — 6-Ap/Mac Classic II, Ap/Mac IIci; Front-end software — Baseview/NewsEdit, QuarkXPress; Printers — Ap/Mac LaserWriter II NTX, Ap/Mac LaserWriter 630 Pro. CLASSIFIED: Front-end hardware — Ap/Mac Classic; Printers — Ap/Mac LaserWriter II NTX, Ap/Mac LaserWriter 630 Pro. DISPLAY: Adv layout systems — 2-Ap/Mac Classic II; Front-end software — QuarkXPress, Aldus/PageMaker; Printers — Ap/Mac LaserWriter II NTX, Ap/Mac LaserWriter 630 Pro. PRODUCTION: Plate exposures — 1-Nu; Production cameras — SCREEN; Automatic film processors — Kodalith. PRESSROOM: Line 1 — G/Community; Press drives — Fin. MAILROOM: Inserters and stuffers — Manual; Bundle tyer — Manual; Addressing machine — Dispensa-Matic.

WICHITA
Sedgwick County
'90 U.S. Census- 304,011; **E&P '96 Est.** 325,552
ABC-NDM (90): 403,662 (HH 156,571)

The Wichita Eagle
(m-mon to sat; S)

The Wichita Eagle, 825 E. Douglas Ave.; PO Box 820, Wichita, KS 67201-0820; tel (316) 268-6000; fax (316) 268-6673; e-mail eaglenws@aol.com. Knight-Ridder Inc. group.
Circulation: 105,607(m); 105,607(m-sat); 185,279(S); ABC Sept. 30, 1995.
Price: 50¢(d); 50¢(sat); $1.50(S); $3.69/wk; $16.03/mo; $163.80/yr (carrier), $235.04/yr (mail).
Advertising: Open inch rate $69.26(m); $69.26(m-sat); $88.80(S). **Representative:** Newspapers First.
News Services: AP, KRT, NYT, CNS (Commodity), LAT-WP. **Politics:** Independent. **Established:** 1872.
Special Editions: Brides Guide, Home Show, Wichita Women's Show (Jan); Sports, Boat & Travel Show, Kansas Economy (Feb); Spring Fashion '96, Lawn, Flower & Garden Show, Spring Parade of Homes (Mar); Voter's Guide (Apr); Beer Festival, Football '96 (Aug); Fall Parade of Homes, Literacy Tab (Sept); 41th Annual Holiday Cookbook, Holiday Shopping Catalog, Christmas Gift Guide, Basketball '96 (Nov).
Special Weekly Sections: Business Plus (mon); Business, Farm News (tues); Business, Farm News, Living, Food (wed); Business, Farm News (thur); Business, Farm News, Living (Entertainment), Go Entertainment (fri); Travel, TV Week, Real Estate Weekly (S).
Magazines: Employment Weekly (wed); Parade, TV Week (local) (S); First Friday (monthly).

CORPORATE OFFICERS
President Reid Ashe
Senior Vice Pres/Editor Davis Merritt Jr
Vice Pres/Assoc Publisher Sheri Dill
Vice Pres-Advertising Ronald Davidson
Vice Pres-Operations Kevin Desmond
Vice Pres-Circulation Doug Sumrell
Chief Financial Officer Dan Moehle

GENERAL MANAGEMENT
Director-Employee Relations James Spangler
Director-Development William Handy
Controller Mark Bjordahl

ADVERTISING
Vice Pres-Marketing Ronald Davidson
Manager-Classified Bob Clinger

MARKETING AND PROMOTION
Manager-Promotion Laurie Thomas

TELECOMMUNICATIONS
Audiotex Manager Tod Myers

CIRCULATION
Director Doug Sumrell
Manager-Home Delivery Bob Hilton
Manager-Marketing & Distribution Keith Petty
Manager-State Lynne Frazier

NEWS EXECUTIVES
Editor Davis Merritt Jr
Managing Editor Janet Weaver
Administrative Editor Fran Kentling

EDITORS AND MANAGERS
Body and Soul Editor Tom Schaefer
Crime/Safety Editor Grace Hobson
Editorial Page Editor David Awbrey
Kansas Roots Editor Sherry Johnson
Learning Editor Suzanne Perez Tobias
Leisure Editor Kevin Sheedy
Librarian Allan Tanner
Nation/World Editor Tom Green
News Assoc Editor Glenda Elliott
Photo Editor Bo Rader
Presentation Editor Sara Quinn
Presentation Editor Jeff Rush
Public Life Editor Mark Ivancic
Relationships Editor Tom Koetting
Sports Editor Tom Shine

MANAGEMENT INFORMATION SERVICES
Data Processing Manager Denis Brown

PRODUCTION
Operations Director Kevin Desmond
Operations Manager-Technology Denis Brown
Operations Manager-Pressroom Joe Anderson
Operations Manager-Assembly & Distribution Debbie Franks
Operations Manager-Systems Bob Hoch
Operations Manager-Composing Marcia Franklin

Market Information: Zoned editions; Split Run; TMC; Operate audiotex.
Mechanical available: Letterpress; Black and 3 ROP colors; insert accepted — preprinted; page cut-offs — 23⁹⁄₁₆".
Mechanical specifications: Type page 13" x 22¼"; E - 6 cols, 2¹⁄₁₆", ⅛" between; A - 6 cols, 2¹⁄₁₆", ⅛" between; C - 10 cols, 1¼", ¹⁄₁₆" between.
Commodity consumption: Newsprint 17,816 short tons; 16,163 metric tons; widths 54", 40½", 27"; black ink 708,160 pounds; color ink 53,822 pounds; single pages printed 22,743; average pages per issue 55(d), 108(S); single plates used 82,000.
Equipment: EDITORIAL: Front-end hardware — DEC/Alpha Servers, HP/Desktop PCs; Front-end software — DewarView; Printers — HP/LaserJet II; Other equipment — Lf/AP Leaf Picture Desk. CLASSIFIED: Front-end hardware — IBM/Servers, HP/Desktop PCs; Front-end software — AT/Enterprise; Printers — HP/LaserJet; Other equipment — Edgil/Edg-Capture Credit Card Authorization Server. AUDIOTEX: Supplier name — Brite Voice Systems. DISPLAY: Adv layout systems — AT/Architect; Front-end hardware — 7-Ap/Power Mac 8100-100; Front-end software — Multi-Ad/Creator 3.7; Printers — III, Cannon, OCE; Other equipment — Pixelcraft, Umax/Scanners. PRODUCTION: Typesetters — 2-AU/APS-5U, 2-Cx/Bitsetter, 1-Hyphen/Spectraset 2000, 3-III/3850; Platemaking systems — Na; Plate exposures — 1-Na/StarLite, 2-Na; Plate processors — 1-Na/FPC, 1-Na/NP-80, 1-Na/NP-20, 1-Na/FPII; Electronic picture desk — Lf/AP Leaf Picture Desk; Scanners — ECR/1000 DE, 2-Kk/RFS 20-354; Production cameras — 1-C/Marathon; Automatic film processors — 3-Glunz & Jensen; Digital color separation equipment — Ap/Mac w/Adobe/Photoshop 3.0. PRESSROOM: Line 1 — 6-H/Convertible double width, 2-MAN/Flexo double width; Line 2 — 6-H/Colormatic double width, 2-H/Convertible double width, 2-MAN/Flexo double width; Folders — 2-H/Double 2:1; Pasters — 8-H/Semi-auto, 8-H/Auto; Press control system — 1-CH, 1-Hurletron. MAILROOM: Counter stackers — 4-QWI/300, 3-Id/660; Inserters and stuffers — 3-S/72P; Bundle tyer — 4-Dynaric/NP-2, 1-OVL/JP-40, 3-MLN/MLN-2-HS; Wrapping singles — 2-OVL/415; Addressing machine — 1-MG, 1-KR. LIBRARY: Electronic — Vu/Text, Vu/Text Save. COMMUNICATIONS: Digital ad delivery system — AP AdSend. WIRE SERVICES: News — KRT, AP; Photos — AP, KRT, PressLink; Stock tables — AP Grand Central Stox; Receiving dishes — AP. BUSINESS COMPUTERS: HP/3000 957; Applications: CJ/CIS 4.01H: Gen ledger;, CJ/CIS 0.601D: Gen ledger; CJ/CIS 2.09E: Payroll; PCs & micros networked; PCs & main system networked.

WINFIELD
Cowley County
'90 U.S. Census- 11,931; **E&P '96 Est.** 12,928
ABC-CZ (90): 11,931 (HH 4,456)

Winfield Daily Courier
(e-mon to fri; m-sat)

Winfield Daily Courier, 201 E. 9th St.; PO Box 543, Winfield, KS 67156; tel (316) 221-1050; fax (316) 221-1101. Seaton group.
Circulation: 5,568(e); 5,568(m-sat); ABC Sept. 30, 1995.
Price: 50¢(d); 50¢(sat); $5.69/mo; $63.80/yr (carrier/mail).
Advertising: Open inch rate $5.96(e); $5.96(m-sat). **Representative:** Landon Associates Inc.
News Service: AP. **Politics:** Independent. **Established:** 1871.
Not Published: Independence Day; Christmas.
Special Editions: Achievement Edition (Feb); Spring Clean Up Tab (Mar); Kanza Edition (May); Cowley County Fair Edition, Making Tracks (Aug); Football Tab Edition (Sept); Getting Ready for Winter (Oct).

CORPORATE OFFICERS
President Frederick D Seaton
Secretary/Treasurer Frederick D Seaton

GENERAL MANAGEMENT
Publisher Frederick D Seaton
Business Manager Lloyd Craig

ADVERTISING
Manager Lloyd Craig
Manager-Classified Lloyd Craig

TELECOMMUNICATIONS
Audiotex Manager Frederick D Seaton

CIRCULATION
Manager Kenneth Jennings

NEWS EXECUTIVES
Editor Frederick D Seaton
Managing Editor Tod Megredy

EDITORS AND MANAGERS
Editorial Writer Frederick D Seaton
Lifestyle Editor Judy Zaccaria
News Editor Jane Sandbulte
Sports Editor Jeff Adkins

PRODUCTION
Manager Tom Porter

Market Information: TMC; Operate audiotex.
Mechanical available: Offset; Black and 3 ROP colors; insert accepted — preprinted, will consider any requests; page cut-offs — 22".
Mechanical specifications: Type page 13⅝" x 21"; E - 6 cols, 2¹⁄₁₆", ⅛" between; A - 6 cols, 2¹⁄₁₆", ⅛" between; C - 8 cols, 1½", ⅛" between.
Commodity consumption: Newsprint 184 metric tons; widths 27½", 13¾"; single pages printed 4,354; average pages per issue 14(d); single plates used 2,177.
Equipment: EDITORIAL: Front-end hardware — 9-Mk; Front-end software — FSI, Multi-Ad/Creator, QuarkXPress; Printers — LaserMaster; Other equipment — Ap/Mac One Scanner. CLASSIFIED: Front-end hardware — 1-IBM; Front-end software — BMF. AUDIOTEX: Hardware — 1-IBM; Software — TCS; Supplier name — Tele Computer Service. DISPLAY: Adv layout systems — Multi-Ad/Creator, Aldus/PageMaker, Canvas; Front-end hardware — Ap/Power Mac; Printers — LaserMaster, Ap/Mac PS; Other equipment — Ap/Mac One Scanner, CD-Rom. PRODUCTION: Typesetters — 2-COM/4961TL, 2-COM/Unisetter, 2-Ap/Mac Laserwriter; Platemaking systems — B; Plate exposures — 1-B; Production cameras — 1-Acti; Automatic film processors — 1-LE, 1-Kk/Ektamatic. PRESSROOM: Line 1 — 4-G/Community. MAILROOM: Inserters and stuffers — 1-KAN/3 Station; Bundle tyer — 1-Miller-Bevco; Addressing machine — 2-Am/1900. WIRE SERVICES: News — AP; Receiving dishes — AP. BUSINESS COMPUTERS: Cumulus/IBM compatible; Applications: TMC, Circ, Accts receivable, Accts payable, Gen ledger; PCs & micros networked; PCs & main system networked.

KENTUCKY

ASHLAND
Boyd
'90 U.S. Census- 23,622; **E&P '96 Est.** 21,200
ABC-CZ (90): 60,977 (HH 23,568)

The Daily Independent
(e-mon to sat; S)

The Daily Independent, 226 17th St.; PO Box 311, Ashland, KY 41101; tel (606) 329-1717; fax (606) 329-0935. Ottaway Newspapers Inc. group.
Circulation: 22,274(e); 22,274(e-sat); 25,317(S); ABC Sept. 30, 1995.
Price: 50¢(d); 50¢(sat); $1.25(S); $2.90/wk (carrier), $2.95/wk (motor route); $12.60/mo (carrier), $12.80/mo (motor route); $142.50/yr (carrier), $154.40/yr (motor route).
Advertising: Open inch rate $15.91(e); $15.91(e-sat); $16.66(S). **Representative:** Landon Associates Inc.
News Services: AP, ONS, SHNS. **Politics:** Independent. **Established:** 1896.
Not Published: Evening edition on Christmas.
Special Editions: Religion, Taxes & Investing, Primetime (Jan); Religion, To Your Health, Parents & Kids (Feb); Home Improvement, Fashion & Bridal, Religion, Entertainment (Mar); Religion, Primetime, Design-An-Ad (Apr); Religion, Southern Living, Greenup County Salute, VE Day, Great Outdoors (May); Salute to Grads, Religion, US Open, Carter County Salute, Regatta (June); Primetime, Religion, Home Security (July); ACC Tab, Religion, Fashion & Bridal, VJ Day, Answer Book (Aug); Home Improvement, Religion, Annual Arts, Entertainment (Sept); Insight (Oct); Religion, Boys Basketball (Nov); Religion, Girls Basketball, Santa Letters (Dec).
Special Weekly Sections: Best Food Day (wed); Best Food Day (S); Business Page, Society, Today's Living, Entertainment Page (daily).
Magazines: TV Magazine, Comic Page (S).

CORPORATE OFFICER
President John Del Santo

GENERAL MANAGEMENT
Publisher John Del Santo
Controller Rick Rakes

ADVERTISING
Manager Kelly Voiers
Manager-Classified Willard (Skip) Reinhard
Manager-National Coordinator Paula Cornette

CIRCULATION
Manager Donald Shaw

NEWS EXECUTIVE
Editor Wickliff R Powell

EDITORS AND MANAGERS
Business/Finance Editor Kenneth A Hart
City Editor Paul Gottbrath

Editorial Page Editor John Cannon
Education Editor George Wolfford
Living/Leisure Editor Cathie Shaffer
Environmental Editor San Adams
Graphics Editor/Art Director William E Martin
Photo Dept Manager John Flavell
Sports Editor Mark Maynard
Wire Editor Stan Champer
Women's News Editor Cathie Shaffer

PRODUCTION

Manager-Composing Carl Vance
Manager-Pressroom Francis Porter Jr
Manager-Mailroom Steve Conley

Market Information: Split Run; TMC.
Mechanical available: Offset; Black and 3 ROP colors; insert accepted — preprinted; page cutoffs — 22¾".
Mechanical specifications: Type page 13" x 21"; E - 6 cols, 2 1/16", ⅛" between; A - 6 cols, 2 1/16", ⅛" between; C - 8 cols, 1 9/16", 1/16" between.
Commodity consumption: Newsprint 1,719 short tons; 1,540 metric tons; width 27½"; black ink 40,000 pounds; color ink 3,400 pounds; single pages printed 12,100; average pages per issue 28(d), 16(sat), 68(S); single plates used 12,500.
Equipment: EDITORIAL: Front-end hardware — IBM; Front-end software — Dewar; Printers — Okidata; Other equipment — SIA/Pagination Terminals. CLASSIFIED: Front-end hardware — Dewar; Front-end software — Dewar; Printers — Okidata, Ap/Mac LaserWriter IIg. DISPLAY: Adv layout systems — Dewar/Ad Pagination; Front-end hardware — IBM/386-DOS 5, Ap/Mac IIsi; Front-end software — Dewar; Printers — Okidata/Microline 395 Plus, Ap/Mac LaserWriter IIg. PRODUCTION: Pagination software — Dewar 6.46; Typesetters — 2-COM/8600, AU/APS-6-84-ACS, AU/APS-6600 Plain Paper; Plate exposures — 1-Nu; Plate processors — Nat; Electronic picture desk — 2-Lf/AP Leaf Picture Desk; Scanners — ECR/Autokon, Lf/Leafscan 35; Production cameras — 1-Nu, 1-B, 1-LE; Automatic film processors — 2-LE, Konica/K-400; Digital color separation equipment — ECR/Autokon. PRESSROOM: Line 1 — 7-HI/Cotrell 845; Folders — 1-HI/2:1. MAILROOM: Counter stackers — 2-HL; Inserters and stuffers — 1-GMA; Bundle tyer — Power Strap/PSN-6E. COMMUNICATIONS: Systems used — satellite. WIRE SERVICES: News — AP, ONS, SHNS; Syndicates — Universal Press, WP, NEA, McNaught; Receiving dishes — size-10ft, AP. BUSINESS COMPUTERS: IBM/AS400-D80; Applications: Adv, Circ, Gen ledger, Payroll, Accts payable, PCs & micros networked; PCs & main system networked.

BOWLING GREEN

Warren County

'90 U.S. Census- 40,641; E&P '96 Est. 40,821
ABC-CZ (90): 40,641 (HH 15,973)

Daily News (e-mon to fri; S)

Daily News, 813 College St. (42101); PO Box 90012, Bowling Green, KY 42102-9012; tel (502) 781-1700; fax (502) 781-0726; e-mail dailynews1@aol.com.
Circulation: 21,591(e); 25,942(S); ABC Sept. 30, 1995.
Price: 50¢(d); $1.25(S); $2.30/wk; $9.97/mo; $119.60/yr.
Advertising: Open inch rate $12.54(e); $14.42 (S). **Representative:** Papert Companies.
News Service: AP. **Politics:** Independent. **Established:** 1854.
Not Published: Independence Day; Labor Day; Thanksgiving; Christmas.
Advertising not accepted: Sunday liquor ads.
Special Editions: Valentine Tab (Feb); Chamber Update (Mar); Bowling Green Tab (May); Chamber Update (July); Welcome Western (Aug); Fountain Square, Chamber Update, Health & Fitness Tab (Sept); Homemakers School Tab (Oct); Holiday Gift Wrap-Up, Chamber Update, Greenwood Mall Tab (Dec).
Magazines: Daily News TV Entertainer (fri); Parade (S).
Broadcast Affiliates: WKCT-AM; WDNS-FM.

CORPORATE OFFICERS

President/Treasurer John B Gaines
Vice Pres/Secretary Pipes Gaines

GENERAL MANAGEMENT

Publisher John B Gaines
Co-Publisher Pipes Gaines
Manager-Education Service Vicki Enoch
General Manager Mark Van Patten

ADVERTISING

Manager Roger Jones
Manager-National Mary Gaines
Manager-Classified Holly Sanger

MARKETING AND PROMOTION

Manager-Promotion Mary Gaines

CIRCULATION

Manager Charles Theis

NEWS EXECUTIVES

Exec Editor/Managing Editor Don Stringer
Asst Managing Editor David Bauer

EDITORS AND MANAGERS

Business/Finance Editor David Bauer
City Editor Robyn Minor
Editorial Page Editor Don Stringer
Entertainment/Amusements Editor Angela Bauer
Food Editor Angela Bauer
Living/Lifestyle Editor Angela Bauer
News/Wire Editor Andy Dennis
Photo Editor Joe Imel
Religion Editor Ann Marie Smedley
Sports Editor Joe Medley

PRODUCTION

Manager Larry Simpson
Foreman-Pressroom Glen Spear

Market Information: Zoned editions; TMC; ADS.
Mechanical available: Offset; Black and 3 ROP colors; insert accepted — preprinted; page cutoffs — 22¾".
Mechanical specifications: Type page 13" x 21"; E - 6 cols, 2 1/16", ⅛" between; A - 6 cols, 2 1/16", ⅛" between; C - 9 cols, 1 5/16", ⅛" between.
Commodity consumption: Newsprint 1,675 short tons; widths 27½", 13¾"; black ink 26,960 pounds; color ink 6,300 pounds; single pages printed 9,123; average pages per issue 23(d), 59(S); single plates used 32,400.
Equipment: EDITORIAL: Front-end hardware — COM/One System; Front-end software — COM; Printers — Ap/Mac LaserWriter NT; Other equipment — Ap/Mac II. CLASSIFIED: Front-end hardware — COM/One Sys; Front-end software — COM. DISPLAY: Front-end hardware — 2-Ap/Mac IIcx, 4-Ap/Power Mac 7100-66; Front-end software — Multi-Ad Creator; Printers — 2-QMS/860; Other equipment — 1-AG/Focus scanner, Ap/Mac Plus scanner, 1-Howtek, 1-Ap/Mac Workgroup Server 80. PRODUCTION: Typesetters — Birmy/400 Imagesetter; Plate exposures — 1-Nu/Flip Top FT401, 1-Nu/Flip Top FT40V6UPNS; Plate processors — 1-Nat/A-250; Production cameras — 1-C/Spartan III; Automatic film processors — 1-P/Pakonolith-24, 1-Vastech/DT-22; Color separation equipment (conventional) — Lf/AP Leaf Picture Desk; Digital color separation equipment — Lf/Leafscan 35, Polaroid/SprintScan 35, 1-Ap/Power Mac 9500-132. PRESSROOM: Line 1 — 9-G/Urbanite single width; Folders — 1-G. MAILROOM: Counter stackers — MM; Inserters and stuffers — 10-MM, MLN/MLN 2E, Akebono/415; Bundle tyer — Tytech. WIRE SERVICES: News — AP; Photos — AP; Syndicates — AP Datafeatures; Receiving dishes — size-10ft, AP. BUSINESS COMPUTERS: IBM/AS-400, 6-CRT.

CORBIN

Whitley County

'90 U.S. Census- 7,419; E&P '96 Est. 6,904

Times-Tribune (e-mon to sat)

Times-Tribune, 201 N. Kentucky St. (40701); PO Box 516, Corbin, KY 40702; tel (606) 528-2464; fax (606) 528-9850. Hollinger International Inc. group.
Circulation: 7,576(e); 7,576(e-sat); Sworn Oct. 1, 1994.
Price: 50¢(d); 50¢(sat); $8.50/mo; $102.00/yr.
Advertising: Open inch rate $11.41(e); $11.41 (e-sat). **Representative:** Landon Associates Inc.
News Services: AP, THO. **Established:** 1892.
Not Published: New Year; Memorial Day; Independence Day; Labor Day; Christmas.
Special Editions: Christmas Greetings; Graduation; Football Preview; Basketball Preview; Community Guide; Progress; Cookbook; Spring Fashion; Fall Fashion; Fall Home Improvement; Home-Owned Business.
Special Weekly Sections: Best Food Day (wed); Business Page (thur); Church Page (sat).
Magazine: TV Guide (sat).

GENERAL MANAGEMENT

Publisher Joseph Hardwick
Accountant Lee C Johnson
Purchasing Agent Lee C Johnson

ADVERTISING

Manager Rochell Stidham
Manager-Classified Shirley Clark

MARKETING AND PROMOTION

Manager-Marketing & Promotion Sam Milwee

CIRCULATION

Manager Jerry H Adkins

NEWS EXECUTIVE

Managing Editor Debra Legg

EDITORS AND MANAGERS

City/Metro Editor John T Whitlock
Editorial Page Editor Debra Legg
Living/Lifestyle Editor Cheryl Meadows
Society/Women's Editor Cheryl Meadows
Sports Editor D Wade Holland

MANAGEMENT INFORMATION SERVICES

Data Processing Manager Lee C Johnson

PRODUCTION

Foreman-Composing Ray Frye
Foreman-Pressroom Glenn Hensley

Market Information: TMC; ADS.
Mechanical available: Offset; Black and 3 ROP colors; insert accepted — preprinted; page cutoffs — 22¾".
Mechanical specifications: Type page 13" x 21½"; E - 6 cols, 2 1/16", ⅛" between; A - 6 cols, 2 1/16", ⅛" between; C - 9 cols, 1⅜", ⅛" between.
Commodity consumption: Newsprint 450 short tons; widths 27½", 32"; black ink 4,000 pounds; single pages printed 4,646; average pages per issue 16(d); single plates used 6,000.
Equipment: EDITORIAL: Front-end hardware — Mk, Ap/Mac IIci, Ap/Mac IIcx; Front-end software — Mk, Aldus/FreeHand, Adobe/Photoshop, QuarkXPress, Aldus/PageMaker, Multi-Ad/Creator; Printers — 2-Ap/Mac LaserWriter, 2-Tegra/Varityper VT600W, 1-Tegra/Varityper 4990T Imagesetter. CLASSIFIED: Front-end hardware — Mk; Front-end software — Mk; Printers — 2-Ap/Mac LaserWriter, 2-Tegra/Varityper VT600W, 1-Tegra/Varityper 4990T Imagesetter. DISPLAY: Adv layout systems — Multi-Ad/Creator; Front-end hardware — Mk, Ap/Mac IIcx, Ap/Mac IIci; Front-end software — Mk, Aldus/FreeHand, Adobe/Photoshop, QuarkXPress, Aldus/PageMaker, Multi-Ad/Creator; Printers — 2-Ap/Mac LaserWriter, 2-Tegra/Varityper VT600W, 1-Tegra/Varityper 4990T Imagesetter. PRODUCTION: OCR software — Caere/OmniPage; Typesetters — 1-Tegra/Varityper 4990T Imagesetter; Plate exposures — 1-Nu; Plate processors — 1-Nu/LT40L; Electronic picture desk — Lf/AP Leaf Picture Desk; Scanners — Lf/Leafscan 35, AVR; Production cameras — 1-Nu, 1-SCREEN/680C; Automatic film processors — SCREEN/220QT. PRESSROOM: Line 1 — 4-G/Community; Line 2 — 2-G/Community. MAILROOM: Inserters and stuffers — MM/227 E; Bundle tyer — Strapex; Addressing machine — Ch. WIRE SERVICES: News — AP; Photos — AP; Syndicates — NEA; Receiving dishes — size-3m, AP. BUSINESS COMPUTERS: ATT/3B2; Applications: Gen ledger, Adv, Accts payable, Payroll, Circ.

COVINGTON

Kenton

'90 U.S. Census- 43,264; E&P '96 Est. 38,873

The Kentucky Post (e-mon to fri; m-sat)

The Kentucky Post, 421 Madison Ave.; PO Box 2678, Covington, KY 41011; tel (606) 292-2600; fax (606) 291-2525. Scripps Howard group.
Circulation: 35,056(e); 35,056(m-sat); Sworn Oct. 1, 1995.
Price: 35¢(d); 75¢(sat); $96.20/yr.
Advertising: Open inch rate $42.65(e); $42.65(m-sat). **Representative:** Gannett National Newspaper Sales.
News Service: AP. **Politics:** Independent. **Established:** 1890.
Note: For detailed information on production, printing, advertising, circulation and general management personnel see Cincinnati (OH) Enquirer & Post listing. The Kentucky Post is an edition of the Cincinnati Post.

ADVERTISING

Vice Pres David Hunke
Director-Sales Carol Hahn
Manager Connie Cooper

TELECOMMUNICATIONS

Audiotex Manager Chuck Cornelius

CIRCULATION

Vice Pres William Hunsberger
Manager Michael Knollman

NEWS EXECUTIVES

Editor Paul F Knue
Managing Editor Mike Farrell

EDITORS AND MANAGERS

City Editor Mark Neikirk
Editorial Page Editor Shirl Short
Education Editor Debra Vance
Features Editor Michele Day
Librarian Barbara Herzog
Director-Photography Randy Dieter
Sports Editor Mark Tomasik

MANAGEMENT INFORMATION SERVICES

Data Processing Manager Bette M Kinder

Market Information: TMC; Operate audiotex.
Mechanical available: Offset; Black and 1 ROP color; insert accepted — preprinted; page cutoffs — 21½".
Mechanical specifications: Type page 13" x 21½"; E - 6 cols, 2 1/16", ⅛" between; A - 6 cols, 2 1/16", ⅛" between; C - 10 cols, 1 3/16", ⅛" between.
Commodity consumption: average pages per issue 28(d).
Equipment: LIBRARY: Electronic — Vu/Text. WIRE SERVICES: News — AP.

DANVILLE

Boyle County

'90 U.S. Census- 12,420; E&P '96 Est. 11,993
ABC-CZ (90): 12,420 (HH 4,895)

The Advocate-Messenger (e-mon to fri)
The Kentucky Advocate (S)

The Advocate-Messenger, 330 S. Fourth St.; PO Box 149, Danville, KY 40423-0149; tel (606) 236-2551; fax (606) 236-9566; e-mail advocate@searnet.com. Schurz Communications Inc. group.
Circulation: 11,493(e); 13,162(S); ABC Sept. 30, 1995.
Price: 50¢(d); $1.00(S); $9.60/mo (carrier/motor route); $115.20/yr (home delivery).
Advertising: Open inch rate $12.11(e); $12.41(e-wed); $12.71(S). **Representative:** Papert Companies.
News Service: AP. **Politics:** Independent. **Established:** 1865.
Not Published: New Year; Memorial Day; Independence Day; Labor Day; Christmas.
Special Editions: Kids' Press (Apr); Football Preview (Aug); Season's Greetings (Dec); Prime Time (monthly).
Special Weekly Sections: Country Life (tues); Church Page (fri); Business Page (S).
Magazine: TV Parade (S).

CORPORATE OFFICERS

President/Treasurer Mary Schurz
Vice Pres John T Davis
Secretary Barbara Anderson

GENERAL MANAGEMENT

Editor/Publisher Mary Schurz

ADVERTISING

Manager-National Jerry Dunn
Manager Michael G Elliott

CIRCULATION

Manager Pat Prendergrist

NEWS EXECUTIVE

Managing Editor John Davis

EDITORS AND MANAGERS

Copy Editor Joyce West
Copy Editor Ken Bledsoe
Features Editor Emily Morse
Sports Editor Bill Vaught

PRODUCTION

Foreman-Press Troy Maddox

Market Information: TMC.
Mechanical available: Offset; Black and 3 ROP colors; insert accepted — preprinted; page cutoffs — 22¾".
Mechanical specifications: Type page 13¾" x 21½"; E - 6 cols, 2 1/16", ⅛" between; A - 6 cols, 2 1/16", ⅛" between; C - 9 cols, 1⅜", 1/16" between.
Commodity consumption: Newsprint 625 short tons; widths 27½", 13¾"; black ink 17,020 pounds; color ink 2,705 pounds; single pages printed 8,180; average pages per issue 21(d), 55(S); single plates used 9,429.
Equipment: EDITORIAL: Front-end hardware — CText; Other equipment — 17-RSK/Tandy

I-164 Kentucky

3000. CLASSIFIED: Front-end hardware — Baseview. DISPLAY: Adv layout systems — SCS/Layout 8000; Front-end hardware — Ap/Mac. PRODUCTION: Pagination software — QuarkXPress 3.3; Typesetters — Ap/Mac Laser-printers, 3-Ultra/94 Imagesetter; Platemaking systems — Nu/Flip Top Ultra Plus; Plate exposures — 2-Nu/Ultra Plus; Plate processors — 1-Nat/A-250; Electronic picture desk — Lf/AP Leaf Picture Desk; Scanners — Data Copy/730 GS, Microtek/Scanmaker IIXE; Production cameras — 1-LE, 1-R; Automatic film processors — 1-LE/Log E saver; Color separation equipment (conventional) — C/Color 45 Enlarger; Digital color separation equipment — Lf/Leafscan 45, Adobe/Photoshop.
PRESSROOM: Line 1 — 5-Uniman/2 (1/2 color decks); Folders — 3-Uniman. MAILROOM: Counter stackers — 2-HI/Graphics Model 2512; Inserters and stuffers — MM/227E; Bundle tyer — 1-Bu/TSZ10, 1-Bu/AS210A; Addressing machine — KR/515 Base w/211 Head; Mailroom control system — HL/Conveyor; Other mailroom equipment — Accuwrap/25 Bottom Wrap. COMMUNICATIONS: Facsimile — Savin/3620; Digital ad delivery system — AP AdSend. WIRE SERVICES: News — AP; Stock tables — AP; Receiving dishes — AP. BUSINESS COMPUTERS: IBM/RISC Sys 6000 CIO; PCs & main system networked.

ELIZABETHTOWN

Hardin County

'90 U.S. Census- 18,167; E&P '96 Est. 20,762
ABC-NDM (90): 72,598 (HH 26,597)

The News Enterprise

(m-mon to fri; S)

The News Enterprise, 408 W. Dixie, Elizabethtown, KY 42701; tel (502) 769-2312; fax (502) 765-7318. Landmark Communications Inc. group.
Circulation: 16,031(m); 18,067(S); ABC Sept. 30, 1995.
Price: 50¢(d); $1.00(S); $9.50/mo, $26.00/3mo, $50.00/6mo; $97.00/yr.
Advertising: Open inch rate $8.75(m); $9.99(S). **Representative:** Landon Associates Inc.
News Service: AP. **Politics:** Independent. **Established:** 1869, 1974 (daily).
Not Published: New Year; Memorial Day; Labor Day; Christmas.
Advertising not accepted: Brokered advertising.
Special Weekly Sections: Mini Page, Senior Living (mon); Farm Pages (tues); Real Estate Section (wed); Best Food Day (thur); Religion, Entertainment, Auto Weekly Section (fri); Business Pages (S).
Magazines: TV Guide/Times, Comics (S).

GENERAL MANAGEMENT
Publisher Mike Anders
Manager-Business Office Lisa D'Alessio
ADVERTISING
Manager Jamie Sizemore
Outside Sales Team Leader Cindy Smith
Classified Sales Team Leader Monica Ruehling
Graphic Design Team Leader Lydia Leasor
MARKETING AND PROMOTION
Manager-Marketing Lisa Robertson
TELECOMMUNICATIONS
Audiotex Manager Lisa Robertson
CIRCULATION
Manager Kathy Helm
Sales Team Leader Carol Underdonk
NEWS EXECUTIVE
Editor David Greer
EDITORS AND MANAGERS
Asst Editor Darrell Bird
Copy Desk Chief Steven Paul
Sports Editor Jeff D'Alessio
PRODUCTION
Manager Bob Loving
Manager-Post Press David Dickens
Press Team Leader Charles Love
Camera Team Leader Duane McClure

Market Information: TMC; Operate audiotex; Electronic edition.
Mechanical available: Offset; Black and 3 ROP colors; insert accepted — preprinted, all; page cut-offs — 22¾".
Mechanical specifications: Type page 13" x 21½"; E - 6 cols, 2 1/16", ⅛" between; A - 6 cols, 2 1/16", ⅛" between; C - 8 cols, 1½", ⅛" between.
Commodity consumption: widths 27½", 13¾"; average pages per issue 30(d), 60(S); single plates used 20,000.
Equipment: EDITORIAL: Front-end hardware — CText; Other equipment — 1-Turbo/XT, 2-Dell/220, SCS/Layout 8000. CLASSIFIED: Front-end hardware — CText; Front-end software — CText, Novell 4.0; Printers — C.Itoh/CI 5000. AUDIOTEX: Hardware — Brite; Supplier name — Brite. DISPLAY: Adv layout systems — 11-Ap/Mac II; Front-end hardware — Dell/220; Front-end software — SCS/Layout 8000 6.08; Printers — HP/LaserJet IVP. PRODUCTION: Pagination software — QuarkXPress 3.31 R5; OCR software — Caere/OmniPage; Typesetters — 2-VHreSetter/94E, PageScan/3, Ap/Mac LaserWriter II NTX, Compaq/LaserWriter; Plate exposures — 1-Nu/Flip Top FT40, 1-Nu/Flip Top FT40L; Plate processors — 1-MAS/Model W-26; Scanners — Kk/2035RFS, Microtek/Scanmaker IIXE; Production cameras — DST/240C; Automatic film processors — 1-Kk/710, 1-LE/PC13 RC, Devotec/20.
PRESSROOM: Line 1 — 11-G/Community Single; Folders — 2-G. MAILROOM: Counter stackers — 2-BG, 1-MM/310-20, 1-MM/231; Inserters and stuffers — 3-MM; Bundle tyer — 3-Bu, 3-MLN; Addressing machine — 1-Ch, 1-KR. WIRE SERVICES: News — AP Datafeatures, AP Datastream; Receiving dishes — size-10ft, AP. BUSINESS COMPUTERS: 8-IBM/5251 terminal, Papertrak; Applications: Lotus: Accts receivable, Gen ledger, Payroll, Circ; Microsoft/Works; PCs & micros networked; PCs & main system networked.

FRANKFORT

Franklin County

'90 U.S. Census- 25,968; E&P '96 Est. 26,016

The State Journal

(e-mon to fri; S)

The State Journal, 321 W. Main St.; PO Box 368, Frankfort, KY 40601; tel (502) 227-4556; fax (502) 227-2831. Dix Communications Inc. group.
Circulation: 10,609(e); 10,609(S); Sworn Oct. 1, 1995.
Price: 50¢(d); $1.00(S); $8.75/mo.
Advertising: Open inch rate $6.50(e); $6.50(S). **Representative:** Landon Associates Inc.
News Services: AP, NYT. **Politics:** Independent. **Established:** 1901.
Not Published: New Year; Memorial Day; Independence Day; Labor Day; Thanksgiving; Christmas.
Advertising not accepted: Pinball; Palm readers; Fortune tellers; etc.
Special Weekly Section: Main Street (TV, videos, books, etc).
Magazine: Main Street (S).

CORPORATE OFFICER
President Albert E Dix
GENERAL MANAGEMENT
Publisher Albert E Dix
ADVERTISING
Director Wayne Dominick
Manager-Classified Gene Flynn
TELECOMMUNICATIONS
Audiotex Manager Ann D Maenza
CIRCULATION
Manager Lloyd Lynch
Manager Doug Patrick
NEWS EXECUTIVE
Editor Carl West
EDITORS AND MANAGERS
Amusements Editor Phillip Case
Automotive Editor Dave Baker
Books/Real Estate Editor Todd Duvall
City Editor Ron Herron
Columnist Todd Duvall
Editorial Page Editor Todd Duvall
Education Editor Phillip Case
Films/Theater Editor Phillip Case
Food Editor Phillip Case
News Editor Carl West
Radio/Television Editor Ron Herron
Sports Editor Brian Rickard
Sports Editor Linda Younkin
Wire Editor Mary Branham
Women's Editor Phillip Case
PRODUCTION
Foreman-Composing Ron Martin
Foreman-Pressroom Scotty Willard

Market Information: TMC; Operate audiotex.
Mechanical available: Offset; Black and 3 ROP colors; insert accepted — preprinted, all; page cut-offs — 21½".
Mechanical specifications: Type page 13" x 21½"; E - 6 cols, 2", ⅑" between; A - 6 cols, 2", ⅑" between; C - 8 cols, 1½", ⅑" between.
Commodity consumption: Newsprint 700 short tons; widths 28", 14"; black ink 23,250 pounds; color ink 3,350 pounds; single pages printed 8,960; average pages per issue 20(d), 58(S); single plates used 10,135.
Equipment: EDITORIAL: Front-end hardware — Ap/Mac Quadra 950, Ap/Mac Quadra 840, 11-Ap/Power Mac 6100, 1-Ap/Power Mac 8100, 1-Ap/Mac Quadra 700; Front-end software — Microsoft/Word, PowerShare, QuarkXPress, AppleShare; Printers — 1-Ap/Mac LaserPrinter IIg, 1-TI/810; Other equipment — Lf/AP Leaf Picture Desk, 2-Nikon/Scanner. CLASSIFIED: Front-end hardware — 3-Mk; Front-end software — Mk. DISPLAY: Adv layout systems — Ap/Mac IIci, Ap/Power Mac 6100; Front-end software — Aldus/PageMaker, QuarkXPress. PRODUCTION: Pagination software — QuarkXPress 3.31; Typesetters — 2-Ap/Mac ci, 1-XIT/Clipper, 2-Ap/Mac LaserPrinter, 3-QMax/ImageSetter, 4-Ap/Power Mac 7100, 1-Ap/Power Mac 8100; Plate exposures — 1-Nu; Electronic picture desk — Ap/Mac Quadra 840, AppleShare 4.0; Scanners — 2-Nikon/Scanner; Production cameras — 2-B/Vertical; Automatic film processors — 1-Vastec/D22, 1-Konica/500; Color separation equipment (conventional) — Lf/AP Leaf Picture Desk, Ap/Mac 8100; Digital color separation equipment — Adobe/Photoshop 3.0.
PRESSROOM: Line 1 — 8-G/Community w/Colordeck. MAILROOM: Inserters and stuffers — 3-MM; Bundle tyer — 2-Bu; Addressing machine — 1-KR. COMMUNICATIONS: Remote imagesetting — Ap/ARA; Systems used — satellite, microwave. WIRE SERVICES: News — AP; Photos — AP; Syndicates — LATWP; Receiving dishes — size-10ft, AP. BUSINESS COMPUTERS: DSI.

GLASGOW

Barren County

'90 U.S. Census- 12,351; E&P '96 Est. 11,831

Glasgow Daily Times

(e-mon to fri; S)

Glasgow Daily Times, 100 Commerce Dr.; PO Box 1179, Glasgow, KY 42142-1179; tel (502) 678-5171; fax (502) 678-5052. Donrey Media group.
Circulation: 9,417(e); 9,417(S); Sworn Oct. 1, 1995.
Price: 50¢(d); $1.00(S); $6.00/mo (in-state); $72.00/yr (in-state), $95.00/yr (out-of-state).
Advertising: Open inch rate $9.52(e); $9.52(S). **Representative:** Papert Companies.
News Service: AP. **Politics:** Independent-Democrat. **Established:** 1865.
Not Published: New Year; Memorial Day; Independence Day; Labor Day; Thanksgiving; Christmas.
Special Editions: Tax Preparation (Feb); Times Community Review (Mar); Spring Home Improvement (Apr); Mother's Day Tab, Baseball Tab, Car Care (May); Today's Bride (June); Sidewalk Days (Aug); Senior Citizens Tab (Sept); Fall Home Improvement, Car Care (Oct); Tobacco (Nov); Christmas Greetings (Dec).
Special Weekly Sections: Best Food Day, Farming (wed); TV Screen (fri); Church (S).

CORPORATE OFFICERS
Founder Donald W Reynolds
President/Chief Operating Officer Emmett Jones
Exec Vice Pres/Chief Financial Officer Darrell W Loftin
Vice Pres-Western Newspaper Group David A Osborn
Vice Pres-Eastern Newspaper Group Don Schneider
GENERAL MANAGEMENT
Publisher William J Tinsley
Purchasing Agent William J Tinsley
ADVERTISING
Director Harold Spear
Manager-Classified Mary Fletcher
CIRCULATION
Manager Clyde T Harlow
NEWS EXECUTIVE
Managing Editor Joel Wilson
EDITORS AND MANAGERS
Editorial Page Editor Joel Wilson
School/Women's Editor Connie Pickett
Society Editor Francis Bastien
Sports Editor Loy Milam
PRODUCTION
Superintendent Martha Thomas
Supervisor-Composing Martha Thomas
Foreman-Pressroom Ralph Lynn
Supervisor-Commercial Martha Thomas

Market Information: TMC.
Mechanical available: Offset; Black and 3 ROP colors; insert accepted — preprinted; page cut-offs — 21½".
Mechanical specifications: Type page 13" x 21½"; E - 6 cols, 2 1/16", ⅛" between; A - 6 cols, 2 1/16", ⅛" between; C - 8 cols, 1 5/16", ⅛" between.
Commodity consumption: Newsprint 425 metric tons; widths 27", 30", 15", 13½"; black ink 12,000 pounds; color ink 1,200 pounds; average pages per issue 20(d), 28(S); single plates used 4,000.
Equipment: EDITORIAL: Front-end hardware — 1-Mk, 1-M; Front-end software — Mk/Mycro-Comp; Printers — Ap/Mac LaserWriter IIg; Other equipment — IBM/Selectric. CLASSIFIED: Front-end hardware — Mk; Printers — TI/Omni 800. DISPLAY: Adv layout systems — 2-Ap/Mac SE, Ap/Mac SE30, 1-Ap/Mac Radius Big Screen; Printers — 2-Ap/Mac LaserWriter II. PRODUCTION: OCR software — Mk/Mycro-Comp 1100; Typesetters — 2-Ap/Mac Laser-Writer II; Plate processors — 1-Nu; Direct-to-plate imaging — 1-3M/Deadliner; Scanners — 1-Ap/Mac Scanner; Production cameras — 1-B; Automatic film processors — 1-LE.
PRESSROOM: Line 1 — 1-KP; Folders — 1-KP/2:1. MAILROOM: Counter stackers — 1-BG/Count-O-Veyor; Inserters and stuffers — 1-KAN/480; Bundle tyer — 4-Bu, 2-Sa; Addressing machine — 3-Ch. WIRE SERVICES: News — AP; Receiving dishes — AP. BUSINESS COMPUTERS: 1-Unisys, 3-Link/Console, Brain Works. Applications: Circ.

HARLAN

Harlan County

'90 U.S. Census- 2,686; E&P '96 Est. 2,437

The Harlan Daily Enterprise

(m-mon to sat)

The Harlan Daily Enterprise, Hwy. 421 S.; PO Box E, Harlan, KY 40831; tel (606) 573-4510; fax (606) 573-0042. Hollinger International Inc. group.
Circulation: 6,652(m); 6,652(m-sat); Sworn Oct. 2, 1995.
Price: 50¢(d); 50¢(sat); $7.25/mo; $87.00/yr.
Advertising: Open inch rate $8.70(m); $8.70(m-sat). **Representative:** Landon Associates Inc.
News Service: AP. **Politics:** Independent. **Established:** 1901.
Not Published: Christmas.
Special Editions: Harlan County Heritage Tab (Feb); Home Improvement (Apr); Home Improvement (Sept); Fall Car Care Tab (Oct); Christmas Shopping Guide (Nov); Christmas Shopping Guide, Christmas Greetings (Dec); Football Section; Basketball Section.

CORPORATE OFFICERS
President Larry J Perrotto
Comptroller Roland McBride
ADVERTISING
Manager Bill Combs
CIRCULATION
Manager Brenda Hunter
NEWS EXECUTIVE
Exec Editor John Henson
EDITORS AND MANAGERS
City/Metro Editor Rick Howell
Editorial Page Editor John Henson
Education Editor Pat Rigney
Fashion/Style Editor Pat Rigney
Living/Lifestyle Editor Pat Rigney
Photo Editor Lori Howell
Religion Editor Pat Rigney
Sports Editor Jeff Drummond
Women's Editor Pat Rigney
MANAGEMENT INFORMATION SERVICES
Data Processing Manager Pat Lay

Market Information: TMC.
Mechanical available: Offset; Black and 3 ROP colors; insert accepted — preprinted, catalogs; page cut-offs — 22½".
Mechanical specifications: Type page 13" x 21½"; E - 6 cols, 2 1/16", ⅛" between; A - 6 cols, 2 1/16", ⅛" between; C - 8 cols, 1¾", 1/16" between.
Commodity consumption: Newsprint 330 short tons; width 27½"; black ink 9,680 pounds; color ink 4,804 pounds; single pages printed 4,382; average pages per issue 14(d); single plates used 2,503.

Equipment: EDITORIAL: Front-end hardware — 6-Ap/Mac; Front-end software — QuarkXPress, Baseview/NewsEdit; Printers — 2-Ap/Mac LaserWriter II; Other equipment — Ap/Mac Scanner. CLASSIFIED: Front-end hardware — 1-Ap/Mac; Front-end software — Fox; Printers — Okidata. DISPLAY: Front-end hardware — 2-Ap/Mac; Front-end software — Multi-Ad/Creator. PRODUCTION: Typesetters — 2-Ap/Mac LaserWriter II; Plate exposures — 1-Nu; Plate processors — 1-Nat; Scanners — Ca/Sharpshooter Densi-Probe; Production cameras — 1-C/Spartan III; Automatic film processors — 1-LE. MAILROOM: Bundle tyer — 2-Bu; Addressing machine — KR. WIRE SERVICES: News — AP; Receiving dishes — size-10ft, AP. BUSINESS COMPUTERS: IBM/Sys 36, IBM/PC; Applications: Accts receivable, Accts payable, Gen ledger.

HENDERSON
Henderson County
'90 U.S. Census- 25,945; E&P '96 Est. 26,956
ABC-CZ (90): 25,945 (HH 10,548)

The Gleaner (m-tues to sat; S)
The Gleaner, 455 Klutey Park Plz.; PO Box 4, Henderson, KY 42420; tel (502) 827-2000; fax (502) 827-2765; e-mail austin@evansville.com. Gleaner & Journal Publishing Co. group.
Circulation: 11,364(m); 11,364(m-sat); 13,690(S); ABC Sept. 30, 1995.
Price: 50¢(d); 50¢(sat); $1.50(S); $98.45/yr.
Advertising: Open inch rate $9.13(m); $9.13(m-sat); $10.06(S). **Representative:** Papert Companies.
News Service: AP. **Established:** 1885.
Special Editions: Progress Edition (Mar); Lawn & Garden/Home Improvement (Apr); Fair Edition (July); Car Care (Oct); Home for the Holidays (Nov).
Special Weekly Sections: Food, etc (thur); Youth News & Views (fri).
Magazines: TV Showcase (local, newsprint); Sunday Comics; USA Weekend.

CORPORATE OFFICERS
President	Walter M Dear II
Secretary/Treasurer	Martha C Dear

GENERAL MANAGEMENT
Publisher	Steve Austin
Controller	William J Barthel

ADVERTISING
Director-Display	Nancy R Pippin

TELECOMMUNICATIONS
Audiotex Manager	Lee Ann Oliver

CIRCULATION
Manager	Mark Potts

NEWS EXECUTIVES
Editor	Ron Jenkins
Managing Editor	David Dixon

EDITORS AND MANAGERS
Action Line Editor	Libby Lautzenheiser
Automotive Editor	Chuck Stinnett
Business/Finance Editor	Chuck Stinnett
City Editor	Doug White
Editorial Page Editor	Ron Jenkins
Education Editor	Sharon Wright
Entertainment/Amusements Editor	Donna Stinnett
Environmental Editor	Chuck Stinnett
Farm/Agriculture Editor	Chuck Stinnett
Fashions/Style Editor	Donna Stinnett
Features Editor	Donna Stinnett
Graphics Editor/Art Director	Kathy Meadows
Health/Medical Editor	Judy Jenkins
Lifestyle Editor	Donna Stinnett
National Editor	Frank Boyett
News Editor	Doug White
Photo Editor	Mike Lawrence
Political/Government Editor	Frank Boyett
Religion Editor	Frank Boyett
Science/Technology Editor	Chuck Stinnett
Sports Editor	Jim Kurk
Television/Film Editor	Roger Mossburger
Theater/Music Editor	Roger Mossburger
Travel Editor	Donna Stinnett

PRODUCTION
Manager	Buddy Morgan
Foreman-Pressroom	Walter Campbell

Market Information: Split Run; TMC; Operate audiotex.
Mechanical available: Offset; Black and 3 ROP colors; insert accepted — preprinted, any; page cut-offs — 21½".
Mechanical specifications: Type page 13" x 21½"; E - 6 cols, 2 1/16", 1/8" between; A - 6 cols, 2 1/16", 1/8" between; C - 9 cols, 1½", 1/16" between.
Commodity consumption: Newsprint 1,800 short

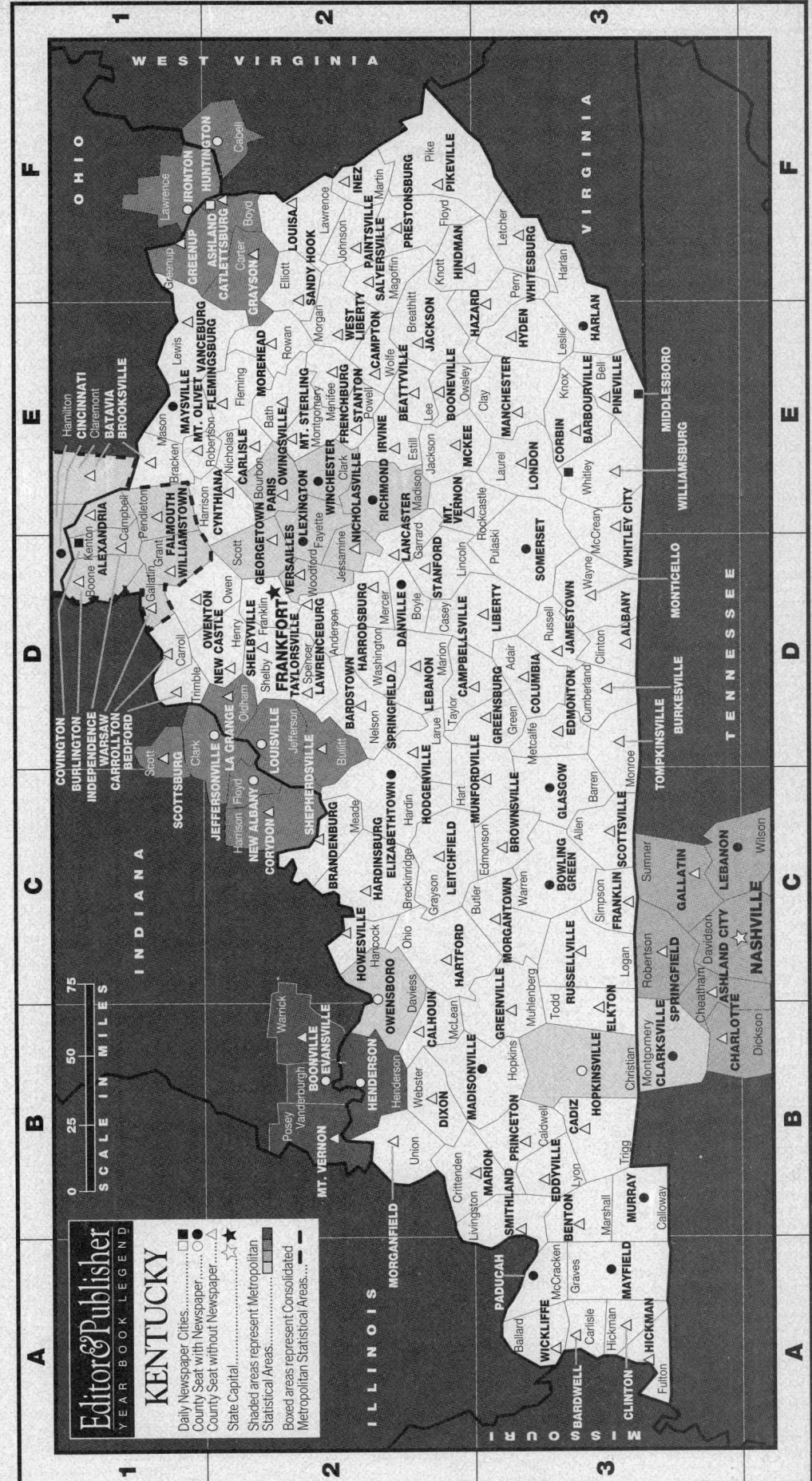

Copyright ©1996 by the Editor & Publisher Co.

tons; widths 27.5", 34"; black ink 45,000 pounds; color ink 7,150 pounds; single pages printed 8,800; average pages per issue 28(d), 49(S); single plates used 5,200.

Equipment: EDITORIAL: Front-end hardware — 1-HI; Other equipment — Lf/AP Leaf Picture Desk, 20-HI. CLASSIFIED: Front-end hardware — 1-HI; Other equipment — 4-HI. DISPLAY: Adv layout systems — 1-HI/8600. PRODUCTION: Typesetters — 1-ECR; Plate exposures — 2-Nu/Flip Top; Plate processors — 1-MAS; Electronic picture desk — Lf/AP Leaf Picture Desk; Production cameras — 1-SCREEN; Automatic film processors — 1-P. PRESSROOM: Line 1 — 9-WPC. MAILROOM: Inserters and stuffers — 6-MM/227; Bundle tyer — 2-Bu/202xE4; Addressing machine — 2-Wm, 1-MMS. WIRE SERVICES: News — AP; Photos — AP; Receiving dishes — AP. BUSINESS COMPUTERS: TI/1500; Applications: Circ, Adv billing, Accts receivable, Gen ledger, Payroll.

HOPKINSVILLE

Christian County

'90 U.S. Census- 29,809; E&P '96 Est. 31,948
ABC-NDM (90): 47,238 (HH 17,766)

Kentucky New Era

(e-mon to sat)

Kentucky New Era, 1618 E. 9th St.; PO Box 729, Hopkinsville, KY 42240; tel (502) 886-4444.

Circulation: 13,721(e); 13,721(e-sat); ABC Sept. 30, 1995.

Price: 50¢(d); 50¢(sat); $8.00/mo; $96.00/yr.

Advertising: Open inch rate $16.75(e); $16.75(e-sat). **Representative:** Papert Companies.

News Service: AP. **Politics:** Independent. **Established:** 1869.

Not Published: New Year; Independence Day; Labor Day; Thanksgiving; Christmas.

Special Editions: January Clearance, Tax Tips (Jan); Brides Edition (Feb); Design-An-Ad (Mar); Outdoor Edition, Homes/Building Pages (Apr); Senior Scene, Homes/Building Pages (May); Homes/Building Page (June); Back-to-School, Football Edition (Aug); Football Contest (Sept); Football Contest (Oct); Football Contest, Christmas Gift Guide, Basketball Edition, Christmas Gift Spotter-Classified (Nov); Christmas Gift Spotter-Classified (Dec).

Special Weekly Sections: Building Page (mon); Best Food Day (wed); Farm Page (thur); TV and Amusement Page, Business Page (daily).

Broadcast Affiliates: W43AG-Low power television.

CORPORATE OFFICERS

President	Robert C Carter
Secretary/Treasurer	Charles Henderson

GENERAL MANAGEMENT

Publisher	Robert C Carter
Manager-Retail	Taylor Hayes
Personnel Manager	Sheryl Ellis
Purchasing Agent	Robert C Carter
Manager-Education Service	Bill Renshaw

ADVERTISING

Director-Marketing	Bill Renshaw
Director	Taylor Hayes

MARKETING AND PROMOTION

Manager-Promotion	Bill Renshaw

CIRCULATION

Director	George McCouch
Supervisor-Mailroom	Dorris Wilson

NEWS EXECUTIVES

Managing Editor	Mike Herndon
Assoc Editor-News	La Mar Bryan
Assoc Editor-News Operations	Rob Dollar

EDITORS AND MANAGERS

Amusements Editor	David Jennings
Columnist	Cecil Herndon
Editorial Page Editor	Mike Herndon
Farm Editor	La Mar Bryan
Lifestyles Editor	Laura Field
Photo Department Manager	Patrick Harding
Sports Editor	Ray Duckworth

PRODUCTION

Superintendent	Tom White
Foreman-Pressroom	Harold Rose

Market Information: TMC.

Mechanical available: Offset; Black and 3 ROP colors; insert accepted — preprinted; page cut-offs — 22¾".

Mechanical specifications: Type page 13" x 21½"; E - 6 cols, 2.03", ⅛" between; A - 6 cols, 2.03", ⅛" between; C - 9 cols, 1.33", ⅛" between.

Commodity consumption: Newsprint 1,200 short tons; widths 27¼", 13⅛"; black ink 27,145 pounds; color ink 6,600 pounds; average pages per issue 24(d); single plates used 14,400.

Equipment: EDITORIAL: Front-end hardware — 25-Dewar/M45; Front-end software — Dewar; Printers — 2-Okidata. CLASSIFIED: Front-end hardware — 3-Dewar/M45; Front-end software — Dewar. DISPLAY: Adv layout systems — Dewar; Front-end hardware — 3-Dewar/Discovery M340; Front-end software — Dewar/Discovery. PRODUCTION: Typesetters — 2-Tegra/Varityper/5100, 3-Ultra/Imagesetter; Plate exposures — 1-Nu/Flip Top; Plate processors — 1-Nat/250; Scanners — 1-HP/Scanner, 1-Microtek/ScanMaker II; Production cameras — 1-B/Caravel; Automatic film processors — LE/LD-18; Color separation equipment (conventional) — 2-Ap/Mac Quadra 800; Digital color separation equipment — 1-Lf/Leafscan 45, 1-Kk/Scanner. PRESSROOM: Line 1 — 7-G/Urbanite U864(Upper former); Folders — 1-G. MAILROOM: Inserters and stuffers — 6-KAN/480; Bundle tyer — 2-OVL, 1-OVL; Wrapping singles — 3-Dri wrap; Addressing machine — 1-St/mailing label. WIRE SERVICES: News — AP; Syndicates — AP; Receiving dishes — size-10ft, AP. BUSINESS COMPUTERS: DEC/PDP 1144; Applications: RSTS/7-2; PCs & micros networked; PCs & main system networked.

LEXINGTON

Fayette County

'90 U.S. Census- 225,366; E&P '96 Est. 243,481
ABC-CZ (90): 225,366 (HH 89,529)

Lexington Herald-Leader

(m-mon to sat; S)

Lexington Herald-Leader, 100 Midland Ave., Lexington, KY 40508-1999; tel (606) 231-3100; fax (606) 231-3454, (606) 231-3155; web site http://www.kentuckyconnect.com/heraldleader/. Knight-Ridder Inc. group.

Circulation: 112,352(m); 135,170 (m-fri); 128,135(m-sat); 163,091(S); ABC Sept. 30, 1995.

Price: 50¢(d); 50¢(sat); $1.50(S); $4.35/wk.

Advertising: Open inch rate $67.49(m); $67.49 (m-fri); $67.49(m-sat); $89.41(S). **Representative:** Newspapers First.

News Services: AP, NYT, KRT, LAT-WP. **Established:** 1860 (Herald), 1888 (Leader), 1983 (Herald-Leader).

Special Editions: Visitor's Guide, Wedding (Jan); Outlook '96 (Mar); Gardening, Travel (Apr); Derby '96 (May); Summer Activities, Health & Fitness (June); Parenting (July); College Football Fever (Aug); Senior Golf Classic, College Guide (Sept); Holiday Catalog (Oct); College Basketball Preview (Nov).

Special Weekly Sections: Your Money/Personal Finance (mon); Today (tues); Community, Best Food Day (wed); You/Female Topics (thur); Weekender (fri); At Home (sat); Outdoors Page, Travel Directory, Business Sunday (S).

Magazine: Parade Magazine.

CORPORATE OFFICERS

President	Lewis Owens
Secretary	Douglas C Harris
Treasurer	Mike McCord

GENERAL MANAGEMENT

Publisher	Lewis Owens
Chief Financial Officer	Mike McCord
Director-Human Resources	James R Green

ADVERTISING

Director	Don Nunes
Manager-Classified	Brenda Waybright
Manager-Display	Larry Brooks
Asst Manager-Display	Anna Stipp
Manager-Customer Service	Sue Knauss
Coordinator-Co-op	Cathy Kane

MARKETING AND PROMOTION

Director-Promotion	David Wilkinson
Director-Market Research	Jeffrey Liles

CIRCULATION

Director	Gregg Greer
Manager-Marketing	Delight Ducker
Manager-Home Delivery (City)	Bobby Fulks
Manager-Subscriber Outreach	Joe Mitchell
Manager-Single Copy/State Home Delivery/ Operations	Don Hargis
Manager-Customer Service	Tammy Osborne

NEWS EXECUTIVES

Editor	Tim Kelly
Managing Editor	David Holwerk
Asst Managing Editor-News	Jerry Wakefield
Asst Managing Editor-Lifestyles/Sports/News-room Artist	Mike Johnson
Asst Managing Editor-Local News	Tom Caudill
Asst Managing Editor-Projects	Carol Hanner
Administrative Editor	David Reed

EDITORS AND MANAGERS

Business Editor	Cheryl Truman
Cartoonist	Joel Pett
Chief Librarian	LuAnn Farrar
City Editor	John Winn Miller
Community Editor	Jim Durham
Editorial Page Editor	Pam Luecke
Lifestyle Editor	Paula Anderson
Radio/Television Editor	Howard Snyder
State Editor	Liz Petros
Sports Editor	Gene Abell
Story Editor/Writing Coach	Harry Merritt

MANAGEMENT INFORMATION SERVICES

Director-Technology/Info Systems	Mel C Caswell

PRODUCTION

Director-Operations	David Stone
Director-Technology/Info Service	Mel C Caswell
Manager-Pre Press	Jim Wills
Manager-Plant Operations	R D Sexton
Manager-Mailroom	Joel Allen
Manager-Pressroom	John Royse
Manager-Environmental/Safety	Deborah Taylor
Manager-Advanced Systems	Tony Moyer
Manager-Business Systems	Mike Serraglio
Manager-Systems Operations	Mark Webster
Manager-Technology	Mechealle Hanks

Market Information: Zoned editions; Split Run; TMC; ADS.

Mechanical available: Offset; Black and 3 ROP colors; insert accepted — preprinted, cata books for topping; page cut-offs — 22¾".

Mechanical specifications: Type page 13" x 21½"; E - 6 cols, 2¹⁄₁₆", ⅛" between; A - 6 cols, 2¹⁄₁₆", ⅛" between; C - 10 cols, 1¼", ¹⁄₁₆" between.

Commodity consumption: Newsprint 16,474 short tons; 14,945 metric tons; width 54"; black ink 304,769 pounds; color ink 60,130 pounds; single pages printed 21,562; average pages per issue 47(d), 131(S); single plates used 140,000.

Equipment: EDITORIAL: Front-end hardware — 6-AT/Series 6, 112-Ap/Mac; Front-end software — Microsoft/Word 5.0; Printers — Linotype-Hell/Linotype 530, LaserMaster/Unity. CLASSIFIED: Front-end software — Cybergraphics 5.0, Caere/OmniPage; Printers — Linotype-Hell/Linotype 530; Other equipment — Ap/Mac IIcx, HP/Scanner. DISPLAY: Adv layout systems — Mk/Ad Director, Mk/Managing Editor; Front-end hardware — Ap/Mac; Front-end software — Multi-Ad/Creator; Printers — Linotype-Hell/Linotype 530, LaserMaster/Unity; Other equipment — Flatbed Scanners. PRODUCTION: Pagination software — QuarkXPress; Typesetters — 3-MON/Lasercomp express, 1-VT/600W, 2-MON/4000 RIP, 2-Linotype-Hell/Linotype 530, RIP/50XMO, 2-LaserMaster/Unity 1200; Platemaking systems — 2-W/NuGraphic Plate Bender-, 1-W/Automatic Punch-Coater; Plate exposures — 3-Nu, 3-Nu/FT Flip Top; Plate processors — 2-MAS; Electronic picture desk — Adobe/Photoshop, Lf/AP Leaf Picture Desk; Scanners — Ap/Mac, 1-Nikon/3500, Microtek/600ZS, 2-ECR/Autokon 1000, 2-Howtek/D4000; Production cameras — 1-C/Pager, 1-C/Spartan III; Automatic film processors — 2-LE, 1-P, 2-Kk; Reproportion units — 1-C/Variable; Film transporters — 1-C; Shrink lenses — 1-Class. PRESSROOM: Line 1 — 7-G/Metro (3½ decks); Line 2 — 7-G/Metro (3½ decks); Press drives — Fin; Folders — 3-G/Imperial 3:2; Pasters — 14-G/Digital; Reels and stands — 14-G/Reels; Press control system — G; Press registration system — Standard/Pin Register. MAILROOM: Counter stackers — 1-QWI, 2-MM, 4-ID/2100; Inserters and stuffers — 2-Fg; Bundle tyer — 5-MLN/HS, 1-MLN/EE, 1-Bu; Wrapping singles — 4-QWI; Addressing machine — 2-KAN/AVY Labeler. LIBRARY: Electronic — Dialog, Vu/Text. WIRE SERVICES: News — AP, AP Datafeatures, KRT, NYT, LAT-WP; Stock tables — TMS; Receiving dishes — AP. BUSINESS COMPUTERS: 1-HP/3000 Series 955; Applications: Circ, Adv, Inventory, Human resources, Personnel, Gen ledger; PCs & micros networked; PCs & main system networked.

LOUISVILLE

Jefferson County

'90 U.S. Census- 269,063; E&P '96 Est. 256,105
ABC-CZ (90): 758,544 (HH 301,136)

The Courier-Journal

(m-mon to sat; S)

The Courier-Journal, 525 W. Broadway; PO Box 740031, Louisville, KY 40201-7431; tel (502) 582-4011; fax (502) 582-4075; web site http://iglou.com/gizweb. Gannett Co. Inc. group.

Circulation: 236,465(m); 236,465(m-sat); 325,354(S); ABC Sept. 30, 1995.

Price: 50¢(d); 50¢(sat); $1.50(S); $3.35/wk; $14.50/mo, $7.85/mo (d), $8.85/mo (weekend package); $174.00/yr.

Advertising: Open inch rate $192.99(m); $192.99(m-sat); $222.23(S).

News Services: AP, NYT, LAT-WP. **Politics:** Independent-Democrat. **Established:** 1868.

Special Editions: Outlook '96 (Feb); Home, Garden & Flower Show, Spring Home Improvement (Mar); Women Today, Kentucky Derby Festival, New Car Show (Apr); Derby Wrap, Mini Marathon, Homerama (June); PGA Championship Guide, Remodeled Home Tour, State Fair, Arts Preview (Aug); Fall Home Improvement (Sept); Women Today, Your Doctor and You (Oct); Headstart to Holidays, Best Christmas Ever, Thanksgiving Issue (Nov); Holiday Gift Guide (Dec).

Special Weekly Sections: $avvy (Financial) (mon); Neighborhoods, Food (wed); Autos, Weekend (fri); Scene (sat); Business, Real Estate, Recruitment, Arts, Features, Forum (S).

Magazines: Weekend Magazine (sat); TV Week & Cable Guide (S); Lifetime (55+ adult product, 6 issues).

CORPORATE OFFICERS

President	Edward E Manassah
Exec Vice Pres	Bernard Block
Vice Pres-Operations	Ralph Drury
Vice Pres-Advertising	Stephen W Bernard
Vice Pres-Market Development	Linda Pursell
Vice Pres-Circulation	Larry Gray
Vice Pres-Human Resources	Larry Vonderhaar

GENERAL MANAGEMENT

Publisher	Edward E Manassah
Manager-Public Service	Joanna Gnau
Director-Procurement	Tom Thompson
Controller	Marybeth Evans
Director-Finance	Jack Willenbrink
Director-Operations	Ralph Drury
Manager-Research	Mark Schneider

ADVERTISING

Director	Stephen W Bernard
Director-Classified	Cathy Melton
Coordinator-Acceptance	Kim Becker
Manager-Major Accounts	Susan Cantrell
Manager-Metro	Deborah Schroeder
Manager-National	Nancy Busath

MARKETING AND PROMOTION

Manager-Marketing Communications	Annette Merritt Cummings
Director-Market Development	Linda Pursell

CIRCULATION

Director	Larry Gray
Director-Operations	Stevan Ecken

NEWS EXECUTIVES

Editor/Vice Pres	David Hawpe
Assoc Editor-Administration	William Ellison
Assoc Editor-Development	Mervin Aubespin
Managing Editor	Stephen Ford
Asst Managing Editor	Ben Post
Asst Managing Editor	Sandra Duerr
Deputy Managing Editor	Rochelle Riley
Ombudsman	John Long

EDITORS AND MANAGERS

Action Line Editor	Ken Neuhauser
Amusements Editor	Maureen McNerney
Arts/Entertainment Editor	Maureen McNerney
Assoc Editor-Forum	Fletcher Clarke
Automotive Editor	Greg Otolski
Books Editor	Keith Runyon
Business/Finance Editor	Linda Raymond
Cartoonist	Hugh Haynie
Cartoonist	Nick Anderson
Consumer Editor	Leslie Ellis
Chief Editorial Writer	Bert Emke
Editorial Editor	Ed Bennett
Opinion Page Editor	Keith Runyon
Editorial Writer	Laurel Shackelford
Editorial Writer	Jill Keeney
Editorial Writer	Betty Baye
Education Editor	Mark Schaver
Environmental Editor	Andrew Melnykovych
Fashion/Style Editor	Greg Johnson
Features Editor	Greg Johnson

Food Editor Sarah Fritschner
Garden Editor Diane Heilenman
Health/Medicine Editor Dick Kaukas
Librarian Sharon Bidwell
Living/Lifestyle Editor Greg Johnson
Metro Editor Hunt Helm
Asst Metro Editor-Indiana Jean Porter
Music Editor Jeffrey Puckett
Music Editor Andrew Adler
National Editor Alan Player
Neighborhoods Editor Fran Jeffries
News Editor Marie Geary
Chief Photographer Bill Luster
Photo Editor Rob King
Political/Government Editor Al Cross
Radio/Television Editor Tom Dorsey
Real Estate Editor Greg Otolski
Regional Editor Mark Provano
Religion Editor Leslie Scanlon
Scene Editor Greg Johnson
Sports Editor Harry Bryan
Theater Editor Judy Egerton
Travel Editor Larry Pellegrino
Washington Bureau Mike Brown
Women's Editor Greg Johnson

MANAGEMENT INFORMATION SERVICES
Data Processing Manager John Thompson

PRODUCTION
General Supervisor-Composing Howard Roller
Superintendent-Pressroom Louis Evans
General Supervisor-Engraving Joseph Wantland
Superintendent-Mailroom Steve Eichberger
General Supervisor-Transportation George Wathen

Market Information: Zoned editions; Split Run; TMC.
Mechanical available: Letterpress; Black and 3 ROP colors; insert accepted — preprinted, samples; page cut-offs — 22¾".
Mechanical specifications: Type page 13" x 21½"; E - 6 cols, 2 1/16", 1/8" between; A - 6 cols, 2 1/16", 1/8" between; C - 10 cols, 1 1/8", 3/16" between.
Commodity consumption: Newsprint 36,556 short tons; widths 54½", 40⅞", 27¼"; black ink 1,005,629 pounds; color ink 119,125 pounds; single pages printed 21,460; average pages per issue 48(d), 125(S); single plates used 236,813.
Equipment: EDITORIAL: Front-end hardware — 12-AT; Front-end software — AT 4.7.6; CLASSIFIED: Front-end hardware — 2-AT; Front-end software — AT 4.7.6; DISPLAY: Adv layout systems — 2-III; Front-end hardware — III; Front-end software — III 9.3.3.35; PRODUCTION: Pagination software — AT/News Layout 2 Plus; Typesetters — 3-III/3810; Platemaking systems — Na; Plate exposures — 2-NAPP Flex-FX-IV, 2-NAPP Titans; Plate processors — 2-NAPP Flex-FP-II, 2-NAPP C-120; Electronic picture desk — Lf/AP Leaf Picture Desk; Scanners — 3-ECR/Autokon; Production cameras — 2-C/Pager II, 2-C/Spartan; Automatic film processors — 6-P, 1-C; Film transporters — 4-C; Digital color separation equipment — 1-Diadem/2205.
PRESSROOM: Line 1 — 8-G/Mark I, 1-KBA/MOT 5 color; Line 2 — 8-G/Mark I, 1-KBA/MOT 5 color; Line 3 — 7-H/Color Convertible, 1-KBA/MOT 5 color; Line 4 — 8-G/Mark II, 1-KBA/MOT 5 color; Folders — 3-G/3:2, 1-H/2:1; Pasters — G, H; Reels and stands — G, H; Press control system — GE, Cline. MAILROOM: Counter stackers — 4-St/257S, 3-QWI/SJ201, 2-QWI/301B; Inserters and stuffers — 3-HI/72P; Bundle tyer — 5-MLN/2A, 2-EAM/Mosca RO-TA-500PA, 2-Power Strap/PSN-5, 1-Power Strap/PSN-6, 2-MLN/90; Addressing machine — 1-Ch/AMS Sys, 1-Ch/596, 1-Ch/569, 1-Ch/594. LIBRARY: Electronic — IFK, Battelle/Basis, Digital Collections. COMMUNICATIONS: Facsimile — AP, AP AdSend; Digital ad delivery system — AdSat, AP AdSend. Systems used — satellite. WIRE SERVICES: News — AP, NYT, LAT-WP, GNS, DJ; Photos — AP, GNS; Receiving dishes — size-10ft, AP. BUSINESS COMPUTERS: 2-DEC/6410, 1-DEC/VAX 3100; Applications: Circ, Adv billing, Accts receivable, Gen ledger, Payroll, Personnel, Cost; PCs & micros networked; PCs & main system networked.

MADISONVILLE

Hopkins County

'90 U.S. Census- 16,200; E&P '96 Est. 15,597
ABC-CZ (90): 16,200 (HH 6,532)

The Messenger (e-mon to sat)

The Messenger, 221 S. Main St.; PO Box 529, Madisonville, KY 42431; tel (502) 821-6833; fax (502) 821-6855. Paxton Media group.
Circulation: 10,971(e); 10,971(e-sat); ABC Sept. 30, 1995.
Price: 50¢(d); 50¢(sat); $6.75/mo; $79.00/yr.
Advertising: Open inch rate $13.05(e); $13.05(e-sat). **Representative:** Papert Companies.
News Service: AP. **Politics:** Independent. **Established:** 1914.
Note: Effective Apr. 2, 1996, this publication will change its publishing plan from (e-mon to sat) to (m-tues to sat; S).
Not Published: New Year; Memorial Day; Independence Day; Labor Day; Thanksgiving; Christmas.
Advertising not accepted: X-rated movies.
Special Editions: Bridal Tour (Jan); Progress (Feb); Progress (May); Fair Tab (July); Football (Aug); Progress (Sept); Women in Business (Oct); Christmas Sections (Nov); Christmas Sections (Dec).
Magazines: TV and Leisure Magazine (sat); Maturing Messenger (monthly-last tues).

GENERAL MANAGEMENT
Publisher Robert Morris
Controller Wayne Smith

ADVERTISING
Director Beth Baggerly

CIRCULATION
Director Beverly Cullen

NEWS EXECUTIVE
Editor Tom Clinton

EDITORS AND MANAGERS
Business/Finance Editor Mike Heronemus
City Editor Mike Heronemus
Editorial Page Editor Tom Clinton
Farm/Agriculture Editor Garth Gramblin
Photo Editor Lowell Mendyk
Society/Women's Editor Martha May
Sports Editor Brad Schneider

MANAGEMENT INFORMATION SERVICES
Coordinator-Systems Lisa Cain

PRODUCTION
Manager-Composing Room Bill Patterson
Foreman-Pressroom John Faulk
Supervisor-Mailroom Gloria Lamb

Market Information: TMC.
Mechanical available: Offset; Black and 3 ROP colors; insert accepted — preprinted; page cut-offs — 22¾".
Mechanical specifications: Type page 13" x 21½"; E - 6 cols, 2 1/16", 1/4" between; A - 6 cols, 2 1/16", 1/8" between; C - 8 cols, 1½", 1/16" between.
Commodity consumption: Newsprint 525 short tons; width 14"; black ink 15,000 pounds; color ink 1,300 pounds; single pages printed 5,800; average pages per issue 22(d); single plates used 5,800.
Equipment: EDITORIAL: Front-end hardware — 14-AT/5000; Other equipment — 3-Ap/Mac SE, Lf/AP Leaf Picture Desk. CLASSIFIED: Front-end hardware — 4-AT/5000. DISPLAY: Adv layout systems — 2-Ap/Mac Centris 650; Front-end hardware — 6-Ap/Mac PowerBook 160; Front-end software — Multi-Ad/Creator, Broderbund/TypeStyler, Claris/MacDraw Pro, Adobe/Photoshop, Adobe/Illustrator; Printers — Ap/Mac LaserWriter 650, Dataproducts/LZR1560; Other equipment — Ap/Mac Color One Scanner, Microtek/Scanmaker IIXE. PRODUCTION: Typesetters — 2-COM/8400; Plate exposures — 1-Nu; Production cameras — 1-Nu; Automatic film processors — 1-LE.
PRESSROOM: Line 1 — 8-G/Community. MAILROOM: Inserters and stuffers — KAN/480; Bundle tyer — 1-MLN/Spirit; Addressing machine — 3-Wm, KR/215. WIRE SERVICES: News — AP Datastream, NYT; Photos — AP; Receiving dishes — size-8ft, AP. BUSINESS COMPUTERS: IBM/3600; Applications: Payroll, Accts receivable, Circ, Accts payable, Gen ledger.

MAYFIELD

Graves County

'90 U.S. Census- 9,935; E&P '96 Est. 9,299

Mayfield Messenger

(e-mon to fri; m-sat)

Mayfield Messenger, 201 N. 8th St.; PO Box 709, Mayfield, KY 42066; tel (502) 247-5223; fax (502) 247-6336. Haskell Newspapers group.
Circulation: 7,072(e); 7,072(m-sat); Sworn Sept. 30, 1995.
Price: 50¢(d); 50¢(sat); $5.00/mo.
Advertising: Open inch rate $6.00(e); $6.00(m-sat). **Representative:** Papert Companies.
News Service: AP. **Politics:** Independent. **Established:** 1900.
Not Published: New Year; Independence Day; Thanksgiving; Christmas.

CORPORATE OFFICERS
President Robert H Haskell
Exec Vice Pres George H Harris
Vice Pres Elizabeth H Haskell
Secretary/Treasurer Carolyn Williams

GENERAL MANAGEMENT
General Manager Eric Hoffman
Business Manager Carolyn Williams

ADVERTISING
Director Susan B Seay
Director-National Clay McClain

CIRCULATION
Manager Jeff Fike

NEWS EXECUTIVE
Editor Michael E Turley

PRODUCTION
Superintendent Don Herring

Market Information: TMC.
Mechanical available: Offset; Black and 3 ROP colors; insert accepted — preprinted, free-standing inserts; page cut-offs — 22¾".
Mechanical specifications: Type page 12⅞" x 21½"; E - 6 cols, 2 1/16", 1/8" between; A - 6 cols, 2 1/16", 1/8" between; C - 9 cols, 1½", 1/16" between.
Commodity consumption: Newsprint 300 short tons; widths 27.5", 13.75"; black ink 10,000 pounds; color ink 400 pounds; single pages printed 6,500; average pages per issue 20(d); single plates used 6,000.
Equipment: EDITORIAL: Front-end hardware — 3-Ap/Mac 7200 w/CD-Rom, 3-Ap/Mac 7500 w/CD-Rom, 1-Ap/Mac PowerBook 540c; Front-end software — Baseview/Newsedit Pro, DragX, QuarkXPress; Printers — 2-Ap/Mac LaserWriter, 1-NewGen/Image Plus 11x17. CLASSIFIED: Front-end hardware — 1-Ap/Mac Performa 425, 1-Ap/Mac 7200 w/CD-Rom; Printers — 1-Ap/Mac LaserPrinter. DISPLAY: Front-end hardware — 3-Ap/Mac 7500 w/CD-Rom; Front-end software — Multi-Ad/Creator; Other equipment — 1-Ap/Mac 7500 w/CD-Rom color workstation, 2-Mk/Scanmaker II. PRODUCTION: Typesetters — 2-Ap/Mac Plus; Plate exposures — 2-Nu; Plate processors — Nu; Production cameras — 1-B; Automatic film processors — AG/Rapidline 28.
PRESSROOM: Line 1 — 7-G/Community; Folders — 1-G/SC. MAILROOM: Bundle tyer — 2-Bu; Addressing machine — 1-Am. WIRE SERVICES: News — AP. BUSINESS COMPUTERS: 1-Ap/Mac SE, 1-Ap/Mac; PCs & micros networked; PCs & main system networked.

MAYSVILLE

Mason County

'90 U.S. Census- 7,169; E&P '96 Est. 6,582

The Ledger Independent

(m-mon to sat)

The Ledger Independent, 41-43 W. Second St.; PO Box 518, Maysville, KY 41056; tel (606) 564-9091; fax (606) 564-6893. Howard Publications group.
Circulation: 9,639(m); 9,639(m-sat); Sworn Oct. 2, 1995.
Price: 50¢(d); 75¢(sat); $2.25/wk; $9.00/mo; $117.00/yr (carrier), $148.20/yr (mail).
Advertising: Open inch rate $9.50(m); $9.50(m-sat). **Representative:** Landon Associates Inc.
News Service: AP. **Politics:** Independent. **Established:** 1968.
Not Published: Christmas.
Special Editions: Income Tax Guide (Jan); Bridal, Cookbook (Feb); Spring Fashion, Basketball (Mar); Car Care, Gardening, Home Improvement, Farm & Garden (Apr); Homemakers Section (May); Dairy Month (June); Back-to-School (Aug); Home Improvement, Car Care (Sept); 4-H (Oct); Progress Edition, Tobacco, Basketball (Nov); Christmas Greetings (Dec).
Special Weekly Sections: Food (mon); Food (tues); Food (wed); Home and Garden (thur); Lifestyles/TV (sat).

CORPORATE OFFICER
President Robert S Howard

GENERAL MANAGEMENT
Publisher Robert L Hendrickson
Business Manager Margaret F Wallingford

ADVERTISING
Manager Patty Moore
Manager-Advertising Service Rita Kinder

CIRCULATION
Manager Marsha Fritz

NEWS EXECUTIVE
Editor Matt Stahl

EDITOR AND MANAGER
Design Editor James Mulcahy

PRODUCTION
Supervisor John Arn Jr

Market Information: TMC; ADS.
Mechanical available: Offset; Black and 3 ROP colors; insert accepted — preprinted; page cut-offs — 22¾".
Mechanical specifications: Type page 13" x 21½"; E - 6 cols, 2 1/16", 1/8" between; A - 6 cols, 2 1/16", 1/8" between; C - 8 cols, 1½", 1/8" between.
Commodity consumption: Newsprint 625 short tons; width 27½"; single pages printed 6,500; average pages per issue 20(d).
Equipment: EDITORIAL: Front-end hardware — CText. CLASSIFIED: Front-end hardware — CText. DISPLAY: Adv layout systems — DEC/Layout 8000. PRODUCTION: Typesetters — Ap/Mac NXT, VT/600; Plate exposures — 1-B; Plate processors — 1-Nat; Production cameras — 1-DAI; Automatic film processors — 1-LE.
PRESSROOM: Line 1 — 5-HI/Cotrell V-15A; Folders — 1-HI/Cotrell. MAILROOM: Counter stackers — 1-BG; Inserters and stuffers — MM; Bundle tyer — MLN; Addressing machine — 1-Ch. COMMUNICATIONS: Facsimile — AP/Fax. WIRE SERVICES: News — AP; Photos — AP; Receiving dishes — AP. BUSINESS COMPUTERS: 2-ATT, ATT/7300, BI; Applications: Accts receivable, Circ, Accts payable, Payroll; PCs & micros networked; PCs & main system networked.

MIDDLESBORO

Bell County

'90 U.S. Census- 11,328; E&P '96 Est. 10,588

The Daily News

(e-mon to fri; m-sat)

The Daily News, 120 N. 11th St.; PO Box 579, Middlesboro, KY 40965; tel (606) 248-1010; fax (606) 248-7614. Hollinger International Inc. group.
Circulation: 6,447(e); 6,447(m-sat); Sworn Oct. 1, 1995.
Price: 50¢(d); 50¢(sat); $7.25/mo (home delivery).
Advertising: Open inch rate $10.57(e); $10.57(m-sat). **Representative:** Hollinger International Inc.
News Service: AP. **Politics:** Independent. **Established:** 1911.
Not Published: Christmas.
Special Editions: Christmas; Spring Home Improvement; July 4th; Mt. Laurel Festival; Back-to-School; Graduation; Lawn & Garden; Progress.
Special Weekly Sections: Best Food Day, Food Page (wed); Business Page (thur); Religion Page (fri).
Magazine: TV & Leisure (sat).

GENERAL MANAGEMENT
Publisher J T Hurst
Bookkeeper Gina Short

ADVERTISING
Director Pat Cheek

CIRCULATION
Supervisor Gina Short

NEWS EXECUTIVE
Managing Editor Raymond Short

EDITORS AND MANAGERS
Automotive/Books Editor Donna Greene
Farm/Food Editor Donna Greene
Fashion Editor Donna Greene
Home Furnishings Editor Donna Greene
News Editor Niki Lockhart
Society/Women's Editor Donna Greene
Sports Editor Neil Morgan
Teen-Age/Youth Editor Donna Greene

PRODUCTION
Director J T Hurst

Market Information: TMC.
Mechanical available: Offset; Black and 3 ROP colors; insert accepted — preprinted; page cut-offs — 22¾".

Mechanical specifications: Type page 13" x 21½"; E - 6 cols, 2 1/16", 1/8" between; A - 6 cols, 2 1/16", 1/8" between; C - 8 cols, 1½", 1/8" between.
Commodity consumption: Newsprint 790 short tons; widths 27½", 13¾"; black ink 24,000 pounds; color ink 2,500 pounds; single pages printed 4,567; average pages per issue 14(d); single plates used 8,000.
Equipment: EDITORIAL: Front-end hardware — Ap/Mac; Front-end software — Baseview; Printers — Ap/Mac LaserPrinter. CLASSIFIED: Front-end hardware — Ap/Mac; Front-end software — Baseview; Printers — Ap/Mac LaserPrinter. DISPLAY: Front-end hardware — 2-Ap/Mac; Front-end software — Baseview; Printers — Ap/Mac LaserPrinter. PRODUCTION: Typesetters — Ap/Macs; Plate exposures — Nu/Flip Top; Plate processors — Nat; Production cameras — Acti; Automatic film processors — P. PRESSROOM: Line 1 — 5-G/Community; Press control system — Fin. MAILROOM: Bundle tyer — 3-Bu; Addressing machine — KR. COMMUNICATIONS: Facsimile — Mita. WIRE SERVICES: News — AP. BUSINESS COMPUTERS: IBM/Sys 36; Applications: Gen ledger, Accts payable, Accts receivable.

MURRAY

Calloway County

'90 U.S. Census- 14,439; E&P '96 Est. 14,589

The Murray Ledger & Times (e-mon to sat)

The Murray Ledger & Times, 1001 Whitnell; PO Box 1040, Murray, KY 42071; tel (502) 753-1916; fax (502) 753-1927. Lancaster Management Inc. group.
Circulation: 7,845(e); 7,845(e-sat); Sworn Sept. 29, 1995.
Price: 50¢(d); 50¢(sat); $6.00/mo; $72.00/yr.
Advertising: Open inch rate $7.75(e); $7.75(e-sat). **Representative:** Papert Companies.
News Services: AP, CNS. **Politics:** Independent. **Established:** 1879.
Not Published: New Year; Independence Day; Thanksgiving; Christmas.
Special Editions: Brides (Jan); Profile (Mar); Home Improvement (Apr); Miss Spring, Car Care (May); June Dairy (June); Great Outdoors (July); Back-to-School (Aug); Fall Fashion, Hunting Guide, Homecoming (Sept); Restaurant Menu Section, Fall Car Care (Oct); Holiday Cookbook (Nov); Christmas Gift Guide, Songbook (Dec).
Special Weekly Sections: Farm Page (mon); Best Food Day (wed); Arts & Entertainment (thur); Church Page (fri); Outdoor Page, TV Guide (sat).
Magazine: TV Week (sat).

CORPORATE OFFICER

President Walter L Apperson

GENERAL MANAGEMENT

Publisher Walter L Apperson
General Manager Alice Rouse

ADVERTISING

Manager-Retail Mary Ann Orr
Manager-Classified Karen Covert

CIRCULATION

Manager Jeff Duncan

NEWS EXECUTIVES

Editor Walter L Apperson
Managing Editor Gina Hancock

EDITORS AND MANAGERS

Business/Finance Editor Walter L Apperson
Editorial Page Editor Walter L Apperson
Editorial Writer Gina Hancock
Education Editor Amy Wilson
Fashion/Style Editor Rainey Apperson
Living/Lifestyle Editor Jo B Burkeen
National Editor Walter L Apperson
Political/Government Editor Walter L Apperson
Religion Editor Jo B Burkeen
Society Editor Jo B Burkeen
Sports Editor Steve Parker

PRODUCTION

Foreman-Pressroom R J McDougal
Foreman-Composing Bryan O'Neill

Market Information: Zoned editions; Split Run; TMC; ADS.
Mechanical available: Offset; Black and 3 ROP colors; insert accepted — preprinted, all; page cut-offs — 21".
Mechanical specifications: Type page 13" x 21½"; E - 6 cols, 2", 1/8" between; A - 6 cols, 2", 1/8" between; C - 9 cols, 1 3/8", 1/16" between.
Commodity consumption: Newsprint 550 short tons; widths 42", 27½"; black ink 12,000 pounds; color ink 500 pounds; single pages printed 6,076; average pages per issue 20(d); single plates used 8,000.
Equipment: EDITORIAL: Front-end hardware — 1-Mk/3000, 6-Mk; Printers — 1-TI/Omni 800. CLASSIFIED: Front-end hardware — 2-AT/NewsTouch. DISPLAY: Adv layout systems — Mk/Mycro-Comp AdWriter. PRODUCTION: Typesetters — 2-Ap/Mac LaserWriter II NTX; Plate exposures — 1-Nu/Flip Top FT40U3UPNS; Production cameras — 1-DAI/Vertical; Automatic film processors — 1-P. PRESSROOM: Line 1 — 8-G/Community (w/upper former); Folders — 1-G. MAILROOM: Counter stackers — 1-KAN; Inserters and stuffers — 2-Bu; Wrapping singles — 1-Ch. WIRE SERVICES: News — AP; Receiving dishes — size-10ft, AP. BUSINESS COMPUTERS: PCs & micros networked; PCs & main system networked.

OWENSBORO

Daviess County

'90 U.S. Census- 53,549; E&P '96 Est. 52,607
ABC-CZ (90): 54,332 (HH 21,979)

Messenger-Inquirer (m-mon to sat; S)

Messenger-Inquirer, 1401 Frederica St.; PO Box 1480 (42302), Owensboro, KY 42301; tel (502) 926-0123; fax (502) 685-3446. A H Belo Corp. group.
Circulation: 32,363(m); 32,363(m-sat); 33,398(S); ABC Sept. 30, 1995.
Price: 50¢(d); 50¢(sat); $1.50(S); $2.85/wk; $12.35/mo; $140.75/yr (d & S).
Advertising: Open inch rate $24.19(m); $24.19(m-sat); $25.81(S). **Representative:** Landon Associates Inc.
News Services: AP, KRT, LAT-WP. **Politics:** Independent. **Established:** 1875 (Messenger), 1884 (Inquirer).
Advertising not accepted: Mail order; Fortune tellers.
Special Editions: Brides, Coupon Quarterly, Prime, Chamber, Agriculture (Jan); Women, Home Builders, Parenting, Cabin Fever, NASCAR (Feb); Design-An-Ad, Home & Garden (Mar); Prime, Coupon Quarterly (Apr); Grief & Memorials, Parenting, Moms/Dads/Grads, Vacation Guide (May); Chamber, Parade of Homes (June); Daviess County Fair, Prime, Coupon Quarterly (July); Parenting, End of Summer, Football (Aug); Home Interiors, Bluegrass, Olympics (Sept); Women's Escapade, Winter Energy Guide, Prime (Oct); Holiday Entertaining, Parenting, Holiday Gift Guide, Basketball (Nov); Photo Review (Dec).
Special Weekly Sections: Community (tues); Food (wed); Senior Citizens, Health (thur); Entertainment (fri); Sports Weekend, Religion/Values (sat); Business, Style, Travel, Agriculture, Education (S).
Magazines: React (tues); Parade, Television Magazine, Color Comics (S).

CORPORATE OFFICERS

Board Chairman John S Hager
President/CEO John S Hager
Corporate Secretary Sue Trautwein
Vice Pres T Edward Riney
Treasurer T Edward Riney

GENERAL MANAGEMENT

Publisher John S Hager
General Manager T Edward Riney
Director-Human Resources Linda Heath
Director-Community Relations/Market Research Sue Trautwein
Controller Doug Robinson

ADVERTISING

Director Frank Leto
Manager-Display Elaine Morgan
Manager-Classified Maggie Rollins

CIRCULATION

Director-Packaging Tony Maddox
Manager-Operations Barry Carden

NEWS EXECUTIVES

Editor Robert Ashley
Editor-City Paul Raupp
Asst Editor-City Dianna Borsi

EDITORS AND MANAGERS

Librarian Sherri Heckel
News Editor Hunter Reigler
Photography Editor Gary Emord-Netzley
Sports Editor Rich Suwanski
Sunday Editor Tommy Newton
Systems Editor Jim Baumgarten
Wire Editor Mike Hall

MANAGEMENT INFORMATION SERVICES

Data Processing Manager-CORE/Info Service Terri Kenitzer

PRODUCTION

Manager Mike Weafer
Manager-Pressroom Pat Head
Coordinator-Composing/Commercial Phil Trivett

Market Information: Split Run; TMC.
Mechanical available: Offset; Black and 3 ROP colors; insert accepted — preprinted, sizes up to 14"x10½" large; 3"x 5" small; page cut-offs — 22¾".
Mechanical specifications: Type page 13" x 21"; E - 5 cols, 2 1/16", 1/6" between; A - 6 cols, 2 1/16", 1/6" between; C - 10 cols, 1¼", 1/6" between.
Commodity consumption: Newsprint 3,303 short tons; widths 55", 41¼", 27½"; black ink 69,805 pounds; color ink 21,924 pounds; single pages printed 14,981; average pages per issue 33.9(d), 83.9(S); single plates used 16,000.
Equipment: EDITORIAL: Front-end hardware — 30-SII/Synthesis 66, 3-Ap/Mac Quadra 950, 3-Ap/Mac Quadra 800, Ap/Power Macs; Front-end software — SII/Synthesis 66, QuarkXPress, Ap/Mac 55; Printers — 2-Hyphen/D600 Plain Paper, 2-Hyphen/Imagesetter SelectSet 5000; Other equipment — 1-Lf/AP Leaf Picture Desk, 5-Cascade/OPI Server, Sun/Spare 20, Cascade/Dataflow Server. CLASSIFIED: Front-end hardware — CText, P/590 Servers; Front-end software — CText, Novell 3.11, CText/Adform 5.0; Printers — C.Itoh/Billing printer, Hyphen/D600 Plain Paper. DISPLAY: Adv layout systems — MK/Managing Editor, Mk/Ad Director; Front-end hardware — Ap/Mac Centris 650, 1-Ap/Mac fx, 4-Ap/Mac Quadra 950, 3-Ap/Power Mac 8100; Front-end software — QuarkXPress, Adobe/Illustrator; Printers — Hyphen/D600 Plain Paper, Hyphen/Imagesetter SelectSet 5000. PRODUCTION: Pagination software — QuarkXPress 3.3; Typesetters — Hyphen/D-600, Hyphen/Imagesetter 3100, Hyphen/D-600; Plate exposures — 1-Douthitt, Nu; Scanners — ECR/8400 Line & halftone camera, 1-Howtek/D-400 drum scanner, 1-Howtek/Flatbed scanner; Production cameras — 1-C/Spartan, 1-SCREEN/Vertical; Film transporters — LE/26; Shrink lenses — R, C. PRESSROOM: Line 1 — 4-G/Metro 3033; Line 2 — 4-G/Metro 3033; Folders — 2-G/2:1 double width; Pasters — 3-G/Auto; Reels and stands — 6-RKW; Press control system — Fin. MAILROOM: Counter stackers — 1-HL/stackpack, 1-HL/Monitor, 1-Id/550, 1-HL/Dual Carrier; Inserters and stuffers — 1-Sh/848; Bundle tyer — 2-IT/PSN6, 1-MLN/ML 2EE; Addressing machine — 1-Ch; Other mailroom equipment — MM/Minuteman Stitcher Trimmer. LIBRARY: Electronic — SII/LASR, Info/KY Personal Librarian. WIRE SERVICES: News — AP, TV Data, LAT-WP, KRT, PR Newswire, Graphic Net; Photos — AP, KRT; Receiving dishes — AP. BUSINESS COMPUTERS: HP/937LX; Applications: CJ/AIM: Accts payable, Gen ledger, Circ; PCs & micros networked; PCs & main system networked.

PADUCAH

McCracken County

'90 U.S. Census- 27,256; E&P '96 Est. 25,544
ABC-CZ (90): 57,113 (HH 23,482)

The Paducah Sun (m-mon to sat; S)

The Paducah Sun, 408 Kentucky Ave.; PO Box 2300, Paducah, KY 42002-2300; tel (502) 443-1771; fax (502) 443-1771. Paxton Media group.
Circulation: 29,915(m); 29,915(m-sat); 32,683(S); ABC Sept. 30, 1995.
Price: 50¢(d); 50¢(sat); $1.25(S); $11.90/mo; $142.80/yr.
Advertising: Open inch rate $21.75(m); $21.75(m-sat); $22.84(S). **Representative:** Papert Companies.
News Services: AP, LAT-WP. **Established:** 1929.
Advertising not accepted: Mail order.
Special Editions: Wedding (Jan); NASCAR, Children's Ad Craft (Feb); Fashion, Home Improvement, Fishing, Auto Care, Lawn & Garden (Mar); American Quilters (Apr); Lakeland (May); NASCAR, Back-to-School, Fall Fashion (July); Hunting, Progress, Edition, Auto Care (Sept); Christmas Gift Guide (Nov); Sun Age (monthly).
Special Weekly Sections: Health (mon); Food Day (tues); Food Days, Outdoor (wed); Church (fri); Outdoor, Travel (S); Business, Style, Entertainment (daily).
Magazine: Investment (S).
Broadcast Affiliates: WPSD-TV, NBC.

CORPORATE OFFICERS

President Fred Paxton
Vice Pres/Secretary Jim Paxton
Vice Pres/Asst Secretary Richard Paxton
Vice Pres/Treasurer/Chief Financial Officer David M Paxton

GENERAL MANAGEMENT

Publisher Fred Paxton
Controller/Asst Treasurer David Mathis
General Manager Jay Frizzo
Asst General Manager Jana Moore

ADVERTISING

Director-Classified Jana Thomasson
Coordinator-National Talmadge Martin
Manager-Retail Jana Moore

MARKETING AND PROMOTION

Manager-Promotion Steve Rich

CIRCULATION

Director Jeff Scott

NEWS EXECUTIVES

Editor Jim Paxton
Exec Editor Karl Harrison

EDITORS AND MANAGERS

Business/Finance Editor Bruce Gardner
City/Metro Editor Ron Clark
Editorial Page Editor Don Gordon
Entertainment/Amusements Editor Glenn Cochrum
Environmental Editor Kevin Simpson
Farm/Agriculture Editor Ron Clark
Features Editor Leigh Landini
Food Editor Pat Brockenborough
Health/Medical Editor Mark Hultman
Home Furnishings Editor Ron Clark
National Editor Bill Oakley
News Editor Mark Hultman
Photo Editor Lyn McDaniel
Political/Government Editor Bill Bartleman
Radio/Television Editor Glenn Cochrum
Religion Editor Ron Clark
Science/Technology Editor Kevin Simpson
Sports Editor Steve Millizer
Travel Editor Lyn McDaniel
Women's Editor Leigh Landini

PRODUCTION

Manager Larry Sholar
Foreman-Pressroom Hap Siress
Foreman-Mailroom Gary McElrath
Foreman-Engraving Hap Siress

Market Information: Zoned editions; Split Run; TMC.
Mechanical available: Offset; Black and 3 ROP colors; insert accepted — preprinted; page cut-offs — 22¾".
Mechanical specifications: Type page 13 1/8" x 21¼"; E - 6 cols, 2 1/16", 1/8" between; A - 6 cols, 2 1/16", 1/8" between; C - 9 cols, 1¼", 1/8" between.
Commodity consumption: Newsprint 2,800 short tons; width 27"; black ink 16,000 pounds; color ink 5,000 pounds; single pages printed 13,400; average pages per issue 38(d), 62(S); single plates used 25,000.
Equipment: EDITORIAL: Front-end hardware — Ap/Power Macs, Ap/Mac Quadra 605s; Front-end software — DTI, Ap/Mac Sys 7.5; Printers — QMS/1660, MON, Ap/Mac LaserWriter 16-600, Ap/Mac LaserWriter, ECR/3850. CLASSIFIED: Front-end hardware — 3-Ap/Mac 650, 1-Ap/Mac IIsi; Front-end software — Multi-Ad, Baseview; Printers — Ap/Mac Personal LaserWriter, Ap/Mac Imagewriter; Other equipment — Ap/Mac Centris 610 fileserver. DISPLAY: Adv layout systems — SCS/Layout 8000; Front-end hardware — Sun/River, Dell/fileservers; Front-end software — SCS; Printers — QMS 2220; Other equipment — Ap/Mac LaserWriter II, 5-Ap/Mac. PRODUCTION: Pagination software — QPS; OCR software — Caere/OmniPage, Publish Pac; Typesetters — Ap/Mac LaserWriter 16-600, Ap/Mac LaserWriter 16-600, QMS/660, 2-ECR/3850-1085; Plate exposures — 1-Nu; Plate processors — 2-Nat; Electronic picture desk — Lf/AP Leaf Picture Desk; Scanners — ECR/Autokon 1030, Lf/Leafscan 45, Mk/IIXE, Dest, Nikon/3510AF; Production cameras — C/Spartan II, AG/20 x 24; Automatic film processors — 1-LE, Powermatic/R660, LE/24AQ, C/R660, Konica/K550; Shrink lenses — 1-CK Optical; Color separation equipment (conventional) — Lf/AP Leaf Picture Desk, ECR/Autokon Newsrecorder, Nikon/Scanner.
PRESSROOM: Line 1 — 10-G/Urbanite; Press drives — Fin; Folders — G/Urbanite; Reels and stands — Universal; Press control system — G; Press registration system — Duarte. MAIL-

ROOM: Counter stackers — 2-Id; Inserters and stuffers — 1-HI; Bundle tyer — 2-Bu, 1-Id; Addressing machine — 1-KAN. WIRE SERVICES: News — AP Datastream, AP Datafeatures, TV Data; Photos — AP Photostream; Stock tables — AP; Receiving dishes — AP. BUSINESS COMPUTERS: IBM/Sys 36, Ap/Mac LAN; Applications: Circ; Great Plains, Baseview, SCS: Billing; PCs & micros networked; PCs & main system networked.

RICHMOND

Madison County

'90 U.S. Census- 21,155; E&P '96 Est. 20,655

The Richmond Register

(e-mon to fri; m-sat)

The Richmond Register, 380 Big Hill Ave:; PO Box 99, Richmond, KY 40475; tel (606) 623-1669; fax (606) 623-2337. Hollinger International Inc. group.

Circulation: 8,634(e); 8,634(m-sat); Sworn Sept. 30, 1995.

Price: 50¢(d); 50¢(sat); $8.00/mo; $96.00/yr.

Advertising: Open inch rate $10.17(e); $10.17(m-sat). **Representative:** Landon Associates Inc.

News Service: AP. **Politics:** Independent. **Established:** 1808.

Not Published: Independence Day; Christmas.

Special Editions: Progress; Car Care; Football; Basketball; Health File; Home Improvement; EKU Football & Basketball Programs; Businesss Profiles; Christmas Greetings; Healthfiles; Super Bowl; Tax Guide; Spring & Fall; Graduation; Father's Day; Mother's Day.

Special Weekly Sections: Health & Fitness (mon); Farm Page, Food (wed); Outdoors (thur); Church, Real Estate (fri); TV Supplement (sat).

Magazines: Showcase of Homes; Showcase of Autos.

GENERAL MANAGEMENT

Publisher David N Harrison
Accountant Sandy Miller

ADVERTISING

Director Teresa Scenters

CIRCULATION

Manager Robert Parks

NEWS EXECUTIVES

Editor Terri Blackwell
Asst Editor Lea Shultz

EDITOR AND MANAGER

Sports Editor Nick Nicholas

PRODUCTION

Manager Joyce Rose

Market Information: Zoned editions; TMC.

Mechanical available: Offset; Black and 3 ROP colors; insert accepted — preprinted; page cutoffs — 23".

Mechanical specifications: Type page 13" x 21½"; E - 6 cols, 2 1/16", ⅛" between; A - 6 cols, 2 1/16", ⅛" between; C - 9 cols, 1 3/8", 1/16" between.

Commodity consumption: Newsprint 550 short tons; width 13¾"; average pages per issue 16(d).

Equipment: EDITORIAL: Front-end hardware — 6-Mk/4003; Front-end software — HI/Compuedit, HI/1420. CLASSIFIED: Front-end hardware — 2-Mk/4010. DISPLAY: Adv layout systems — Mk/AdComp. PRODUCTION: Typesetters — 2-COM/2961 HS, 1-COM/Unisetter, 1-M/101; Plate exposures — 1-BKY/1601-48, 1-B/MP2; Plate processors — 1-Ic/ICM25-1; Production cameras — 1-R/500; Automatic film processors — 1-P/Pakonolith. PRESSROOM: Line 1 — 6-G/Community; Folders — 2-G/2:1. MAILROOM: Inserters and stuffers — MM/3 bay; Bundle tyer — 1-MLN, 1-MLN/MLIEE; Addressing machine — 1-Am/1900. WIRE SERVICES: News — AP; Receiving dishes — size-8ft, AP.

SOMERSET

Pulaski County

'90 U.S. Census- 10,733; E&P '96 Est. 10,804

The Commonwealth-Journal (e-mon to fri; S)

The Commonwealth-Journal, 110-112 E. Mt. Vernon St.; PO Box 859, Somerset, KY 42502-0859; tel (606) 678-8191; fax (606) 679-9225. Park Communications Inc. group.

Circulation: 8,515(e); 8,515(S); Sworn Sept. 29, 1995.

Price: 50¢(d); $1.00(S); $7.50/mo (carrier); $90.00/yr (home delivery).

Advertising: Open inch rate $10.15(e); $10.15(S). **Representative:** Papert Companies.

News Services: AP, NEA. **Politics:** Independent. **Established:** 1895.

Not Published: Christmas.

Special Editions: Bridal Fair, Chamber Annual Report (Jan); Winter Clearance (Feb); Agriculture Week (Mar); Home & Garden, Baby Week (Apr); Summertime Fun, Grads of '96 (May); Summer Clearance (June); Back-to-School (July); High School Football (Aug); Football Contest (Sept); Auto Guide, Professional Businesswomen (Oct); Regional Basketball Preview, Cooking Guide (Nov); Christmas Songbook (Dec).

Special Weekly Sections: Best Food Days, Business, Engagements, Weddings (wed); Best Food Days, TV Listings, Business, Engagements, Farm, Weddings (S).

Magazine: Lake Cumberland Shopper (TMC) (mon).

CORPORATE OFFICER

President Gary Knapp

GENERAL MANAGEMENT

General Manager Tim Stratton
Business Manager Judy Handcock

ADVERTISING

Manager Kathy Gregory

MARKETING AND PROMOTION

Manager-Marketing & Promotion Kathy Gregory

CIRCULATION

Manager Aaron Glover

NEWS EXECUTIVES

Editor Tim Stratton
Managing Editor Bill Mardis

EDITOR AND MANAGER

Sports Editor Jeff Neal

MANAGEMENT INFORMATION SERVICES

Data Processing Manager Carol Lafavers

PRODUCTION

Manager Mike Burdine

Market Information: TMC; ADS.

Mechanical available: Offset; Black and 3 ROP colors; insert accepted — preprinted, half-fold, quarter-fold; page cut-offs — 22¾".

Mechanical specifications: Type page 13" x 21½"; E - 6 cols, 2 1/16", ⅛" between; A - 6 cols, 2 1/16", ⅛" between; C - 10 cols, 1 3/16", 1/12" between.

Commodity consumption: Newsprint 440 short tons; widths 27.5", 13.75"; black ink 24,000 pounds; color ink 2,600 pounds; single pages printed 5,810; average pages per issue 20(d), 36(S); single plates used 7,020.

Equipment: EDITORIAL: Front-end hardware — Ap/Mac Quadra 650, Ap/Mac Quadra 610, Ap/Mac Quadra 605; Front-end software — QuarkXPress; Printers — HP/LaserJet. CLASSIFIED: Other equipment — 2-Ap/Mac Quadra 605. DISPLAY: Adv layout systems — 2-Ap/Mac Quadra 650; Printers — 1-Ap/Mac LaserWriter. PRODUCTION: Typesetters — 2-Ap/Mac Quadra 650; Plate exposures — 1-Nu/Flip Top FT401; Procuction cameras — 1-BKY/Omega 20x24; Autcmatic film processors — 1-P/24-1; Color separation equipment (conventional) — 1-Kk. PRESSROOM: Line 1 — 6-G/Community SC157; Folders — 1-G. MAILROOM: Counter stackers — 4-MM; Inserters and stuffers — 4-MM; Bundle tyer — 2-Felins/Paktyer F10-F12; Addressing machine — 2-Am/1800-1900. LIBRARY: Combination — Tomlison. WIRE SERVICES: News — AP; Syndicates — NEA; Receiving dishes — size-10ft, AP. BUSINESS COMPUTERS: Vision Data/486; Applications: Circ, Accts receivable; PCs & micros networked; PCs & main system networked.

WINCHESTER

Clark County

'90 U.S. Census- 15,799; E&P '96 Est. 16,363

The Winchester Sun

(e-mon to fri; m-sat)

The Winchester Sun, 20 Wall St. (40391); PO Box 4300, Winchester, KY 40392; tel (606) 744-3132; fax (606) 745-0638.

Circulation: 6,937(e); 6,937(m-sat); Sworn Sept. 30, 1995.

Price: 50¢(d); 50¢(sat); $8.00/mo; $96.00/yr.

Advertising: Open inch rate $8.00(e); $8.00(m-sat). **Representative:** Papert Companies.

News Service: AP. **Politics:** Democrat. **Established:** 1878.

Not Published: New Year; Memorial Day; Independence Day; Labor Day; Thanksgiving; Christmas.

Special Editions: Baby Tab (Jan); Auto Leasing (Feb); Computers (Mar); Home & Garden (Apr); Graduation, Senior Citizens (May); Nutrition & Health, Kids Today (June); Back-to-School, Pioneer Festival (Aug); Energy Awareness, Car Care (Oct); Holiday Gift Guide (Nov); Christmas Greetings (Dec).

Special Weekly Sections: Health & Fitness (mon); Food, Business (wed); Church (sat).

CORPORATE OFFICERS

President George S Tatman Jr
Exec Vice Pres Betty Berryman
Secretary Sharon Tuminski
Treasurer Vera Smith

GENERAL MANAGEMENT

Publisher Betty Berryman
Manager-Finance Sharon Tuminski

ADVERTISING

Director Ann Laurence

CIRCULATION

Director Bob Martin

NEWS EXECUTIVE

Editor William S Blakeman

EDITORS AND MANAGERS

Design Editor Jared Peck
Editorial Writer William S Blakeman
Food Editor Betty Smith
Sports Editor Jeff Kerr
Women's Editor Betty Smith

PRODUCTION

Manager-Pre Press Steve Berryman
Superintendent-Plant Fred Baber

Market Information: Zoned editions; TMC.

Mechanical available: Offset; Black and 3 ROP colors; insert accepted — preprinted; page cutoffs — 22¾".

Mechanical specifications: Type page 13½" x 21½"; E - 6 cols, 1 15/16", ⅛" between; A - 6 cols, 1 15/16", ⅛" between; C - 9 cols, 1 5/16", 1/16" between.

Commodity consumption: Newsprint 1,008 short tons; width 28"; black ink 31,746 pounds; color ink 16,202 pounds; single pages printed 11,898; average pages per issue 16(d); single plates used 5,949.

Equipment: EDITORIAL: Front-end hardware — 9-Ap/Mac; Front-end software — Baseview/News Edit 3.2.5, QuarkXPress 3.3; Printers — Compac. CLASSIFIED: Front-end hardware — 2-Ap/Mac; Front-end software — Baseview/Class Ad System 3.2.1; Printers — Okidata/Microline 321. PRODUCTION: Typesetters — 4-Ap/Mac, Ultre/Setter 94E; Plate exposures — 2-Nu; Plate processors — 1-Nat; Electronic picture desk — Adobe/Photoshop, Lf/AP Leaf Picture Desk; Scanners — 3-Microtek/Scanmaker IIxe; Production cameras — 1-LE; Automatic film processors — 1-LE. PRESSROOM: Line 1 — 9-WPC; Folders — 2-WPC. MAILROOM: Counter stackers — Stacker/652; Inserters and stuffers — MM; Bundle tyer — 2-Bu; Addressing machine — 1-KR; Other mailroom equipment — 2-Ap/Mac Quadra 630. Baseview/Circulation Pro 1.9.2, Ap/Mac LaserWriter, Okidata/Pacemark 3410. WIRE SERVICES: News — AP; Receiving dishes — size-10ft, AP. BUSINESS COMPUTERS: IBM/Sys 36; Applications: Accts receivable, Billing, Gen ledger, Payroll; PCs & micros networked; PCs & main system networked.

LOUISIANA

ABBEVILLE

Vermilion Parish

'90 U.S. Census- 11,187; E&P '96 Est. 10,338

Abbeville Meridional

(m-tues to fri; S)

Abbeville Meridional, 318 N. Main; PO Box 400, Abbeville, LA 70510; tel (318) 893-4223; fax (318) 898-9022.

Circulation: 5,486(m); 5,486(S); Sworn Oct. 1, 1995.

Price: 50¢(d); 75¢(S).

Advertising: Open inch rate $6.89(m); $6.89(S).

News Service: AP. **Politics:** Independent. **Established:** 1856.

GENERAL MANAGEMENT

Publisher David Clevenger

ADVERTISING

Manager Mike Hebert

CIRCULATION

Manager Ben Boulet

NEWS EXECUTIVE

Managing Editor Gwen Broussard

Market Information: TMC.

Mechanical available: Offset; Black and 3 ROP colors; insert accepted — preprinted; page cutoffs — 22⅞".

Mechanical specifications: Type page 13" x 21½"; E - 6 cols, 2 1/16", ⅛" between; A - 6 cols, 2 1/16", ⅛" between; C - 8 cols, 1 9/16", 1/16" between.

Commodity consumption: Newsprint 260 short tons; width 27"; black ink 5,915 pounds; color ink 800 pounds; single pages printed 9,209; average pages per issue 14(d), 24(S); single plates used 11,940.

Equipment: EDITORIAL: Front-end hardware — Mk; Other equipment — 9-COM. CLASSIFIED: Front-end hardware — Mk; Other equipment — 1-COM. DISPLAY: Adv layout systems — Ap/Mac. PRODUCTION: Typesetters — 2-Ap/Mac LaserWriter; Plate exposures — 1-3M/Deadliner; Production cameras — SCREEN/Companica Horizontal. PRESSROOM: Line 1 — 6-KP/Newsking. MAILROOM: Bundle tyer — 1-Bu; Addressing machine — IBM/Sys (w/printer for labeling). WIRE SERVICES: News — UPI; Syndicates — Louisiana State Newspapers; Receiving dishes — size-2ft, AP. BUSINESS COMPUTERS: PCs.

ALEXANDRIA-PINEVILLE

Rapides Parish

'90 U.S. Census- 61,439 (Alexandria 49,188; Pineville 12,251); E&P '96 Est. 59,912 (Alexandria 47,433; Pineville 12,479)

ABC-CZ (90): 68,593 (HH 24,863)

Alexandria Daily Town Talk

(m-mon to sat; S)

Alexandria Daily Town Talk, 1201 Third St. (71301); PO Box 7558, Alexandria, LA 71306; tel (318) 487-6397; fax (318) 487-6315.

Circulation: 40,001(m); 40,001(m-sat); 41,020(S); ABC Sept. 30, 1995.

Price: 35¢(d); 35¢(sat); $1.00(S); $12.00/mo.; $144.00/yr, $168.00/yr (mail).

Advertising: Open inch rate $23.76(m); $23.76(m-sat); $24.69(S). **Representative:** Papert Companies.

News Services: AP, NYT. **Politics:** Independent. **Established:** 1883.

Not Published: Christmas.

Special Editions: Annual Report (Jan); Brides, Spring Fashion, Religion (Mar); Lawn & Garden (Apr); Back-to-School, Fall Fashion (Aug); Civic Clubs (Sept); Cookbook (Nov).

Special Weekly Sections: Business (tues); Best Food Day, Express Line (wed); Church (sat); Amusement Page (S).

Magazines: TV (Channels) (sat); Color Comics, USA Weekend (S).

CORPORATE OFFICERS

Board Chairman Joe D Smith Jr
President/CEO Larry D Smith
Vice Pres Thomas Jarreau O'Quin
Secretary/Treasurer Tom Jarreau Hardin

GENERAL MANAGEMENT

Publisher Tom Jarreau Hardin
General Manager Larry D Smith
Director-Personnel Joy L Williford
Director-Data Processing Roger Davis
Manager-Cityline Jim Smilie

ADVERTISING

Manager-General/Retail William C (Bill) Heirtzler Jr
Manager-Classified O D Gray

MARKETING AND PROMOTION

Manager-Promotion/Marketing William C (Bill) Heirtzler Jr

TELECOMMUNICATIONS

Audiotex Manager Jim Smilie

CIRCULATION

Director Gary McKay

NEWS EXECUTIVES

Managing Editor Jim Butler
Asst Managing Editor Ron Grant

EDITORS AND MANAGERS

Amusements Editor Jim Dagar

I-170 Louisiana

Automotive Editor Mark Watson
Business/Finance Editor Mark Watson
Editorial Page Editor Jim Butler
Fashion/Focus Editor Jim Dagar
Food/Home Furnishings Editor Jim Dagar
Living Editor Jim Dagar
Photo Department Manager Leandro (Lee) Huebner
Religion Editor Jim Dagar
Science Editor Jim Butler
Sports Editor Gaylen Duskey
Travel Editor Jim Dagar
Women's Editor Jim Dagar

MANAGEMENT INFORMATION SERVICES
Data Processing Manager Roger Davis

PRODUCTION
Director Joe M Blackwell
Director-Engineering Maintenance John Choate
Superintendent-Composing Mike Branigan
Superintendent-Mailroom Stanley DeSelle
Superintendent-Pressroom Charles Humphreys

Market Information: Zoned editions; Split Run; TMC; Operate audiotex.
Mechanical available: Offset; Black and 3 ROP colors; insert accepted — preprinted; page cut-offs — 21".
Mechanical specifications: Type page 13" x 21"; E - 6 cols, 2 1/16", 1/8" between; A - 6 cols, 2 1/16", 1/8" between; C - 9 cols, 1 3/8", 1/16" between.
Commodity consumption: Newsprint 3,482 short tons; widths 27 1/2", 41 1/4", 55"; black ink 52,000 pounds; color ink 22,169 pounds; single pages printed 14,615; average pages per issue 36(d), 56(S); single plates used 36,548.
Equipment: EDITORIAL: Front-end hardware — 59-Compaq, 1-Ap/Mac Quadra 950, 8-RSK/TRS 80-100, 1-Ap/Mac, 1-Ap/Power Mac 7100-80, 1-Ap/Mac Quadra 650; Front-end software — Computext, Comet/II, QuarkXPress 3.3; Printers — HP/IV SI. CLASSIFIED: Front-end hardware — 11-Compaq; Front-end software — Computext/Classified; Printers — 1-Epson. AUDIOTEX: Hardware — 1-Brite. DISPLAY: Adv layout systems — SCS/Layout 8000; Front-end hardware — 5-Ap/Mac fx, 2-Ap/Mac Quadra 950, 1-Ap/Mac Quadra 840; Front-end software — CompuText, CAT; Printers — 1-Dataproducts. PRODUCTION: Pagination software — Computext, QPS 3.3; OCR software — HP/Accuscan; Typesetters — 1-ECR/1245, 2-ECR/3850; Plate exposures — 2-Nu; Plate processors — 2-Nat/A-250; Scanners — ECR/Autokon 1030, ECR/2045, 1-AG, 2-HP; Production cameras — 1-C/Spartan II, 1-LE/Pagemaker; Automatic film processors — 2-LE/LD24AQ, 1-LE/1800A, 3-Konica/OL; Film transporters — 1-LE/121, 3-C/OL System; Digital color separation equipment — ECR/1245CS, Lf/Leafscan 35, Kk/RFS 2035. PRESSROOM: Line 1 — 6-G/Headliner offset (4-color decks); Folders — 1-G/Double 2:1; Press control system — Fin. MAILROOM: Counter stackers — 4-Id/660; Inserters and stuffers — 2-H/624; Bundle tyer — 2-MLN/2A, 1-MLN/Spirit; Wrapping singles — 2-NJP. COMMUNICATIONS: Remote imagesetting — Net Blazer; Digital ad delivery system — AP AdSend. WIRE SERVICES: News — AP, SHNS, NYT; Photos — AP; Stock tables — AP; Receiving dishes — size-10ft, AP. BUSINESS COMPUTERS: 2-DEC/Micro VAX 4300; Applications: SCS/Layout, Compushare; PCs & micros networked; PCs & main system networked.

BASTROP
Morehouse Parish
'90 U.S. Census- 13,916; E&P '96 Est. 12,795

Bastrop Daily Enterprise
(e-mon to fri)

Bastrop Daily Enterprise, 119 E. Hickory; PO Box 311, Bastrop, LA 71220; tel (318) 281-4421; fax (318) 283-1699. Smith Newspapers Inc. group.
Circulation: 5,812(e); Sworn Oct. 1, 1993.
Price: 35¢(d); $5.00/mo.
Advertising: Open inch rate $6.47(e).
News Service: AP. **Politics:** Independent. **Established:** 1901.
Not Published: New Year; Independence Day; Labor Day; Thanksgiving; Christmas.
Special Editions: Bridal (Feb); Pride (Apr); Graduation (May); Gin Whistle (Sept); Quarterly (Oct); Gift Guide (Nov).
Special Weekly Sections: Food (wed); Farm (thur).
Magazine: TV Preview.

CORPORATE OFFICER
President Wally Gallian

ADVERTISING
Director Pam Glenn

CIRCULATION
Manager Mark Glenn

NEWS EXECUTIVE
Managing Editor Tim Franklin

MANAGEMENT INFORMATION SERVICES
Data Processing Manager Mark Glenn

PRODUCTION
Superintendent Phillip Patterson

Market Information: TMC.
Mechanical available: Offset; Black and 3 ROP colors; insert accepted — preprinted, any; page cut-offs — 22 3/4".
Mechanical specifications: Type page 13" x 21"; E - 6 cols, 2 1/16", 1/8" between; A - 6 cols, 2 1/16", 1/8" between; C - 9 cols, 1 5/16", 1/8" between.
Commodity consumption: Newsprint 220 short tons; width 27 1/2"; black ink 6,000 pounds; color ink 1,000 pounds; single pages printed 4,000; average pages per issue 14(d); single plates used 4,200.
Equipment: EDITORIAL: Front-end hardware — Mk. CLASSIFIED: Front-end hardware — Mk. DISPLAY: Adv layout systems — Ap/Mac. PRODUCTION: Typesetters — Ap/Mac LaserWriter; Plate exposures — 1-Nu, 1-B; Plate processors — 1-Nat; Production cameras — 1-C/Model T, 1-CL; Automatic film processors — 1-P. PRESSROOM: Line 1 — 5-G/Suburban. MAILROOM: Inserters and stuffers — 1-KR; Bundle tyer — 2-Bu; Addressing machine — 3-Dispensa-Matic. WIRE SERVICES: News — AP. BUSINESS COMPUTERS: 2-RSK/II-TRS-80; Applications: Circ, Records, Operations & label generation, Payroll, Bookkeeping; Word Processing.

BATON ROUGE
East Baton Rouge Parish
'90 U.S. Census- 219,531; E&P '96 Est. 220,962
ABC-NDM (90): 380,105 (HH 138,620)

The Advocate
(m-mon to fri; m-sat)
Sunday Advocate (S)

The Advocate, 525 Lafayette St. (70802); PO Box 588, Baton Rouge, LA 70821-0588; tel (504) 383-1111.
Circulation: 97,153(m); 112,346(m-sat); 134,407(S); ABC Sept. 30, 1995.
Price: 50¢(d); 50¢(sat); $1.25(S); $2.15/wk; $9.71/mo; $116.48/yr.
Advertising: Open inch rate $51.36(m); $51.36(m-sat); $56.25(S). **Representative:** Sawyer-Ferguson-Walker Co.
News Services: AP, LAT-WP, KRT. **Politics:** Independent. **Established:** 1842.
Not Published: Christmas.
Special Weekly Sections: Food (thur); Wheels (Class), Entertainment (fri); Business (S); TV Page (daily).
Magazines: Fun (fri); TV Week (quarter fold, tab) (sat); Parade, Sunday Advocate Magazine (own) (S).
Broadcast Affiliates: WBRZ-TV Baton Rouge, LA; KRGV-TV Weslaco, TX.

CORPORATE OFFICER
President Douglas L Manship

GENERAL MANAGEMENT
Publisher David Manship
Manager-Credit Kay Rice
Manager-Human Resources Betty Jo Baker
Director-Accounting Curtis Hatcher
Manager-Education Service Steve Fitzgerald

ADVERTISING
Director Don Stewart
Director-Display Mike Nola
Manager-Classified James Conner

MARKETING AND PROMOTION
Director-Marketing/Promotion Linda Wunstel

TELECOMMUNICATIONS
Director-Info Systems Richard Shurley
Audiotex Manager Ty Whitley

CIRCULATION
Manager James Prince

NEWS EXECUTIVES
Exec Editor Linda Lightfoot
Managing Editor Jim Whittum

EDITORS AND MANAGERS
Amusements Editor Tim Belehrad
Books Editor Sarah Sue Goldsmith
City Editor Katheryn Flownoy
Editorial Page Editor Douglas L Manship Jr
Home Furnishings Editor Madelyn Lamb
Librarian Jill Arnold
News Editor Tom Herline
News/Features Editor Freda Dunne
Photo Department Manager Ron Bell
Radio/Television Editor Tim Belehrad
Sunday Editor Arthur J Adams
Sports Editor Butch Muir
Women's Editor Madelyn Lamb

MANAGEMENT INFORMATION SERVICES
Director-Info Service Systems Richard Shurley
Online Manager Dusty Kling
Online Manager Jill Arnold

PRODUCTION
Director Fred Weimer
Manager-Blue Bonnet Plant Aubry Linder
Co-Manager-Creative Service Hoot Gipson
Co-Manager-Creative Service Vicky Nola
Superintendent-Pressroom Frank Dantzler
Superintendent-Platemaking Kenny Fontenot
Superintendent-Mailroom John Tinkler

Market Information: Zoned editions; TMC; ADS; Operate database; Operate audiotex; Electronic edition.
Mechanical available: Letterpress; Black and 3 ROP colors; insert accepted — preprinted; page cut-offs — 22 1/2".
Mechanical specifications: Type page 13" x 21 1/2"; E - 6 cols, 2", 1/8" between; A - 6 cols, 2", 1/8" between; C - 9 cols, 1 1/3", 1/8" between.
Commodity consumption: Newsprint 20,456 short tons; widths 55", 27 1/2", 41 1/4"; black ink 895,000 pounds; color ink 198,600 pounds; single pages printed 27,340; average pages per issue 65(d), 65(sat), 135(S); single plates used 104,000.
Equipment: EDITORIAL: Front-end hardware — DEC/VAX 4300/4700 servers, PC/486, PC/386, 2-Celebris/590, 5-Pentium PC; Front-end software — DEC/Dewarview; Other equipment — 3-Ap/Power Mac 8100-80. CLASSIFIED: Front-end hardware — DEC/VAX 4300 servers, 30-PC/386; Front-end software — DEC/CompuClass. AUDIOTEX: Hardware — 1-IBUS/4820/R-1939; Software — QNX 3.21, Software Application 2.06; Supplier name — Brite. DISPLAY: Adv layout systems — CJ/Layout; Front-end hardware — 1-DEC/VAX 4300 server, 20-Ap/Power Mac 8100-80, 1-PC/workgroup server 8150; Front-end software — DEC/CAT Computext, QuarkXPress, Multi-Ad/Creator; Other equipment — 3-AU/APS 108C imagers, AU/APS 200 OPI. PRODUCTION: Pagination software — Dewar/Pagination 1.40; Typesetters — 3-AU/APS-108C; Platemaking systems — 2-LX/200; Plate exposures — 1-Nu, 1-BKY; Electronic picture desk — Lf/AP Leaf Picture Desk; Production cameras — 2-C/Spartan II, 1-C/Spartan III, 1-B; Automatic film processors — 6-LE/Processor; Film transporters — 3-Konica/film transport; Shrink lenses — 1-CK Optical/SQU-7; Color separation equipment (conventional) — 2-WDS; Digital color separation equipment — 1-ECR/Autokon, 1-Lf/AP Leaf Picture Desk. PRESSROOM: Line 1 — 11-G/Mark I, 1-G/Mark II; Line 2 — 4-G/Mark II, 8-G/Mark I; Folders — 2-G/3:2; Pasters — 24-G; Reels and stands — 24-G; Press control system — GE. MAILROOM: Counter stackers — 6-RKW/257, 2-G/Processing 5000; Inserters and stuffers — 2-Fg/ETR-3 Drums, 2-MM/227; Bundle tyer — 7-OVL/JP80, 1-MLN/2A; Wrapping singles — 1-OVL/K-101 Constellation. LIBRARY: Electronic — Data Times. COMMUNICATIONS: Facsimile — Konica/News-scan; Digital ad delivery system — AP AdSend. WIRE SERVICES: News — AP Datafeatures, AP Datastream; Photos — AP; Stock tables — TMS; Syndicates — LATS, TMS, AP, KRT, Creators, Universal Press; Receiving dishes — AP. BUSINESS COMPUTERS: 2-DEC/VAX 4300; Applications: CJ: Pub rel, Accts payable, Personnel, Accts receivable, Circ; PCs & micros networked; PCs & main system networked.

BOGALUSA
Washington Parish
'90 U.S. Census- 14,280; E&P '96 Est. 12,330

Daily News (e-mon to fri; S)

Daily News, 525 Ave. V (70427); PO Box 820, Bogalusa, LA 70429; tel (504) 732-2565; fax (504) 732-4006. Wick Communications group.
Circulation: 6,918(e); 6,918(S); VAC June 30, 1995.
Price: 50¢(d); $1.00(S); $8.50/mo; $101.97/yr.
Advertising: Open inch rate $7.75(e); $8.15(S).
News Service: AP. **Politics:** Independent. **Established:** 1947.
Not Published: Independence Day; Labor Day.
Special Editions: Mardi Gras (Feb); Progress (Apr, May); Parish Fair (Oct).
Special Weekly Sections: Best Food Days (wed); TV Focus (fri); Best Food Days (S).
Magazines: TV Update (fri); USA Weekend.

CORPORATE OFFICERS
President Walter Wick
Exec Vice Pres Lou Major Sr
Treasurer Bob Wick

GENERAL MANAGEMENT
Publisher Lou Major Sr
General Manager Lou Major Jr

ADVERTISING
Director Linda Clements
Manager-Classified Debbie Netherland

CIRCULATION
Director Gary Verbois

NEWS EXECUTIVES
Editor Lou Major Jr
Managing Editor Sandy Seal

EDITORS AND MANAGERS
Action Line/Hot Line Editor Sheila Hughes
Columnist-Consumerism Bob Ann Breland
Home Furnishings Editor/Librarian Bob Ann Breland
Religion/Society Editor Bob Ann Breland
Science/Sunday Editor Danny Nowlin
Sports Editor Mike Byrd
Teen-Age/Youth Editor Erin Moore

PRODUCTION
Manager Cindy Slocum
Foreman-Pressroom Herb Travis

Market Information: TMC.
Mechanical available: Offset; Black and 3 ROP colors; insert accepted — preprinted; page cut-offs — 22 3/4".
Mechanical specifications: Type page 13" x 21 1/2"; E - 6 cols, 2", 1/6" between; A - 6 cols, 2", 1/6" between; C - 9 cols.
Commodity consumption: Newsprint 500 short tons; widths 27", 13 1/2"; black ink 15,000 pounds; color ink 600 pounds; single pages printed 6,980; average pages per issue 18(d), 32(S); single plates used 7,300.
Equipment: EDITORIAL: Front-end hardware — Mk; Printers — Ap/Mac LaserWriter II. CLASSIFIED: Front-end hardware — Mk; Printers — Ap/Mac LaserWriter II. DISPLAY: Front-end hardware — Ap/Mac IIci; Front-end software — QuarkXPress; Printers — NewGen/Turbo PS 800. PRODUCTION: Typesetters — Ap/Mac LaserWriter, Ap/Mac LaserWriter II; Scanners — Microtek/Scanmaker 600Z; Automatic film processors — 1-P. PRESSROOM: Line 1 — 8-WPC/Atlas; Line 2 — 7-WPC/Atlas; Folders — 1-WPC/Marc 25, 1-WPC/Atlas, 1-WPC/Gate; Press control system — 2-Marathon. MAILROOM: Counter stackers — 1-BG/Count-O-Veyor, 1-Mid America Graphics. WIRE SERVICES: News — AP; Syndicates — King Features, United Features; Receiving dishes — AP. BUSINESS COMPUTERS: DEC/Micro VAX; PCs & micros networked; PCs & main system networked.

CROWLEY
Acadia Parish
'90 U.S. Census- 13,983; E&P '96 Est. 12,617

The Crowley Post-Signal
(e-tues to fri; S)

The Crowley Post-Signal, 602 N. Parkerson Ave.; PO Box 1589, Crowley, LA 70526; tel (318) 783-3450; fax (318) 788-0949.
Circulation: 5,354(e); 5,354(S); Sworn Sept. 29, 1995.
Price: 50¢(d); 75¢(S).
Advertising: Open inch rate $6.50(e); $6.50(S).
News Services: UPI, NEA. **Politics:** Conservative. **Established:** 1898.
Special Editions: Football Tab; International Rice Festival Cookbook; 4-H Edition; Auto.

CORPORATE OFFICERS
Co-owner B I Moody
President R H Fackelman
Vice Pres-Operations Marc A Richard
Secretary Ann Fackelman
Treasurer Broward E Ratliff

GENERAL MANAGEMENT
Publisher Milo A Nickel
Business Manager Doug Cart

ADVERTISING
Director Glen Boudreaux

CIRCULATION
Manager Dean Harris

NEWS EXECUTIVE
Editor Harold Gonzales

Louisiana — I-171

EDITORS AND MANAGERS
Action Line/Hot Line Editor .... Harold Gonzales
Columnist .... Harold Gonzales
Fashion Editor .... Janet Sarver
Photo Department Manager .... Tanny Smith
Society Editor .... Janet Sarver

MANAGEMENT INFORMATION SERVICES
Data Processing Manager .... Hazel Nolan

PRODUCTION
Superintendent .... Roland Domingue
Foreman-Composing .... Hazel Nolan
Foreman-Mailroom .... Dean Harris

Mechanical available: Offset; Black and 4 ROP colors; insert accepted — preprinted; page cut-offs — 21½".
Mechanical specifications: Type page 13" x 21½"; E - 6 cols, 2 1/16", 1/8" between; A - 6 cols, 2 1/16", 1/8" between; C - 6 cols, 2 1/16", 1/8" between.
Commodity consumption: average pages per issue 18(d), 28(S).
Equipment: MAILROOM: Bundle tyer — 1-Wilton/Stra Pack; Addressing machine — 2-Dispensa-Matic.

DE RIDDER
Beauregard Parish
'90 U.S. Census- 9,868; E&P '96 Est. 9,047

Beauregard Daily News
(m-tues to fri; S)

Beauregard Daily News, 903 W. 1st St.; PO Box 698, De Ridder, LA 70634; tel (318) 462-0616; fax (318) 463-5347. News Leader Inc. group.

Circulation: 6,450(m); 6,450(S); Sworn Sept. 30, 1994.
Price: 25¢(d); 50¢(S); $41.20/yr.
Advertising: Open inch rate $10.05(m); $10.05(S).
News Services: AP, NEA. **Established:** 1945.
Special Editions: Income Tax (Jan); Bridal Section (Feb); Business Review (July); Football (Aug); Home Improvement (Sept); Car Care, Holiday Cookbook (Oct); Christmas Carol Song Book (Nov).
Magazines: Color Comics (S); USA Weekend.

CORPORATE OFFICER
President .... E C Gensheimer

GENERAL MANAGEMENT
Publisher .... Erbon W Wise
General Manager .... George Jinks

ADVERTISING
Manager .... Beaux Victor

CIRCULATION
Manager .... James Brown

NEWS EXECUTIVE
Editor .... Bob Houston

EDITORS AND MANAGERS
News Editor .... Jerry Gaulding
Photo Editor .... Krista Duhon
Sports Editor .... Gary Christenson

PRODUCTION
Manager .... Pat Brown

Market Information: TMC.
Mechanical available: Web Offset; Black and 3 ROP colors; insert accepted — preprinted; page cut-offs — 22¾".
Mechanical specifications: Type page 13" x 21"; E - 6 cols, 2 1/16", 1/8" between; A - 6 cols, 2 1/16", 1/8" between; C - 8 cols, 1 7/16", 1/8" between.
Commodity consumption: average pages per issue 18(d), 28(S).
Equipment: EDITORIAL: Front-end hardware — Mk/1100 Plus, Ap/Mac; Other equipment — 5-Mk. CLASSIFIED: Front-end hardware — 2-Mk/Plus II; Other equipment — Mk. DISPLAY: Adv layout systems — 1-Mk/Ad Touch, Ap/Mac; Other equipment — 1-Mk. PRODUCTION: Typesetters — 2-Ap/Mac LaserPrinter; Production cameras — Portage/DPS 80, Argyle/23; Automatic film processors — 2-Ektamatic; Reproduction units — Minolta/EP450. WIRE SERVICES: News — AP.

FRANKLIN
St. Mary Parish
'90 U.S. Census- 9,004; E&P '96 Est. 8,571

The Franklin Banner-Tribune (e-mon to fri)

The Franklin Banner-Tribune, 115 Wilson St.; PO Box 566, Franklin, LA 70538-0566; tel (318) 828-3706; fax (318) 828-2874. Morgan City Newspapers Inc. group.
Circulation: 3,203(e); Sworn Sept. 30, 1994.
Price: 25¢(d); $30.00/yr.
Advertising: Open inch rate $4.76(e).
News Service: AP. **Politics:** Independent. **Established:** 1884.
Not Published: New Year; Christmas.

Special Editions: Bridal (Jan); Profile Edition (Apr); Football (Aug); Drug Free (Oct); Christmas (Dec).

CORPORATE OFFICER
President .... Doyle E Shirley

GENERAL MANAGEMENT
Publisher .... Allan Von Werder

ADVERTISING
Manager .... Debbie Von Werder
Manager-Classified .... Geri Williams

CIRCULATION
Manager .... Kathy Boudreaux

NEWS EXECUTIVE
Managing Editor .... Paul Godfrey

MANAGEMENT INFORMATION SERVICES
Online Manager .... Allan Von Werder
Data Processing Manager .... Judith Colon

Market Information: TMC; Operate database; Electronic edition.
Mechanical available: Offset; Black and 3 ROP colors; insert accepted — preprinted, all types, small booklets to response cards; page cut-offs — 22¾".
Mechanical specifications: Type page 13" x 21"; E - 6 cols, 2", 1/6" between; A - 6 cols, 2", 1/6" between; C - 8 cols, 1 1/2", 1/8" between.
Commodity consumption: Newsprint 100 metric tons; width 29"; black ink 2,000 pounds; color ink 150 pounds; single pages printed 3,000; average pages per issue 20(d); single plates used 2,400.

Equipment: EDITORIAL: Front-end hardware — COM/RTR One System; Front-end software — COM/RTR Edit; Printers — 2-NewGen/Turbo Laser; Other equipment — Panasonic. CLASSIFIED: Front-end hardware — COM/RTR One System; Front-end software — COM/RTR Translator III. DISPLAY: Front-end hardware — PC/486, PC/486 (w/CD-Rom); Front-end software — Archetype/Corel Draw; Printers — 2-NewGen/Turbo Laser. PRODUCTION: Typesetters — 2-NewGen/600B Laser Printer.
PRESSROOM: Line 1 — 2-G/Suburban; Folders — 1-G. WIRE SERVICES: News — AP; Receiving dishes — AP. BUSINESS COMPUTERS: 2-PC/386; Applications: In-house: Circ; In-house: Bus.

HAMMOND

Tangipahoa Parish

'90 U.S. Census- 15,871; E&P '96 Est. 16,607
ABC-NDM (90): 88,430 (HH 30,729)

The Daily Star (e-mon to fri; S)

The Daily Star, 725 S. Morrison Blvd. (70403); PO Box 1149, Hammond, LA 70404; tel (504) 345-2333; fax (504) 542-0242. Nixon Newspapers Inc. group.
Circulation: 11,882(e); 13,203(S); ABC Sept. 30, 1995.
Price: 50¢(d); $1.00(S); $8.00/mo; $96.00/yr.
Advertising: Open inch rate $10.44(e); $10.44 (S). **Representative:** Papert Companies.
News Service: AP. **Politics:** Independent. **Established:** 1959.
Not Published: New Year; Memorial Day; Independence Day; Labor Day; Christmas; Memorial Day.
Special Editions: Profile Progress (Feb); Home Improvement & Gardening, Kids Beat (Mar); Strawberry Festival (Apr); Recreation (May); Medical (July); Football (Aug); Women in Business (Sept); Basketball Tourney (Dec).
Special Weekly Sections: Best Food Days (wed); Church (fri); Best Food Days, Business (S).
Magazines: TV Update (S); The Mini Page; USA Weekend.

CORPORATE OFFICERS
President John R Nixon
Vice Pres David K Frazer
Secretary Debbie Huff
Vice Pres-Finance John W Stackhouse

GENERAL MANAGEMENT
Publisher David K Frazer

ADVERTISING
Manager Liz Black
Manager-Classified Mike Smith

MARKETING AND PROMOTION
Manager-Promotion David K Frazer

CIRCULATION
Manager Patsy Atkins

NEWS EXECUTIVE
Managing Editor Lillian K Mirando

EDITORS AND MANAGERS
News Editor Cindy Fletcher
Society Editor Joan Davis
Sports Editor John Lenz

MANAGEMENT INFORMATION SERVICES
Data Processing Manager Joseph P Davis

PRODUCTION
Manager Art Graziano

Market Information: Zoned editions; TMC; Operate audiotex.
Mechanical available: Offset; Black and 3 ROP colors; insert accepted — preprinted; page cut-offs — 22¾".
Mechanical specifications: Type page 13" x 21½"; E - 6 cols, 2.03", ⅙" between; A - 6 cols, 2.03", ⅙" between; C - 9 cols, 1.38", ⅛" between.
Commodity consumption: Newsprint 1,617 metric tons; widths 27½", 30"; black ink 25,955 pounds; color ink 2,689 pounds; average pages per issue 15(d), 38(S); single plates used 34,519.
Equipment: EDITORIAL: Front-end hardware — Ap/Mac; Front-end software — Baseview, QuarkXPress; Printers — 2-Compaq/Page Marq 20; Other equipment — HP/ScanJet 2C, CD-Rom. CLASSIFIED: Front-end hardware — Ap/Mac; Front-end software — Baseview/Class Manager; Printers — Okidata, Ap/Mac LaserWriter. DISPLAY: Adv layout systems — Ap/Mac Centris 650, Ap/Mac Quadra 650, Ap/Power Mac 8100, Ap/Mac LC 475; Front-end software — Broderbund/Typestyler 2.0, Multi-Ad/Creator, QuarkXPress, Aldus/FreeHand; Printers — 2-Compaq/Page Marq 20; Other equipment — Ap/Mac CD-Rom, Micronet/Optical 650 drive. PRODUCTION: Pagination software — QuarkXPress; Plate exposures — Nu/Double Sided, Douthitt/3040; Plate processors — Nat/A-250, Nat/A-250; Scanners — HP/ScanJet 2C; Production cameras — Acti/Horizontal; Automatic film processors — LE/LD-24B.
PRESSROOM: Line 1 — 7-G/Urbanite, 1-G/Urbanite Color Unit; Folders — 1-G/2:1; Press control system — Fin. MAILROOM: Counter stackers — 1-BG/Count-O-Veyor, HH/3017S; Bundle tyer — 1-MLN/Strapper, 1-MLN/Strapper; Other mailroom equipment — Ideal/Shrink wrapper & Tunnel. COMMUNICATIONS: Digital ad delivery system — AP AdSend. WIRE SERVICES: News — AP; Receiving dishes — size-12ft. BUSINESS COMPUTERS: IBM/Sys 36; Applications: Microsoft/Windows, Microsoft/Excel, Microsoft/Word; PCs & micros networked.

HOUMA

Terrebonne Parish

'90 U.S. Census- 30,495; E&P '96 Est. 28,943
ABC-NDM (90): 96,982 (HH 31,837)

The Courier (e-mon to fri; S)

The Courier, 3030 Barrow St.; PO Box 2717, Houma, LA 70361; tel (504) 850-1100; fax (504) 857-2233 (Pub). New York Times Co. group.
Circulation: 19,396(e); 21,264(S); ABC Sept. 30, 1995.
Price: 50¢(d); $1.00(S); $8.25/mo; $99.00/yr.
Advertising: Open inch rate $15.17(e); $15.17 (S). **Representative:** Papert Companies.
News Services: AP, NYT. **Established:** 1878.
Not Published: Christmas.
Special Editions: Tax Guide, Progress Edition (Jan); Mardi Gras Tab (Feb); Easter Bayou Gourmet Cook Book, Bridal Section (Apr); Graduation (May); Football Tab (Aug); Oil & Industry (Sept); Bridal Section (Oct); Thanksgiving Cookbook (Nov); Christmas Greetings (Dec).
Special Weekly Sections: Health & Fitness (mon); Home & Family (tues); Bon Amis (Bayou Correspondents), Bon Appetit (wed); Preview (Entertainment, What's Happening), Outdoors (thur); Religion, TV Update (fri); Louisiana Style, Op-Ed (S); Business, Community Calendar, Sports Calendar (daily).
Magazines: Parade; Color Comics; TV Update.

GENERAL MANAGEMENT
Publisher H Miles Forrest
Controller Wayne Dupre
Personnel Manager Flo Jeanice
Purchasing Agent Wayne Dupre

ADVERTISING
Director-Retail Lisa Ferrell
Manager-Classified Peggy Bougard
Manager-Promotion Lisa Ferrell

TELECOMMUNICATIONS
Audiotex Manager Peggy Bougard

CIRCULATION
Manager S Wade Peak

NEWS EXECUTIVE
Exec Editor Mike M Slaughter

EDITORS AND MANAGERS
Business/Finance Editor Brent St Germaine
City Editor Keith Magill
Editorial Page Editor H Miles Forrest
Education Editor Marty Authement
Features Editor Marty Authement
Sports Editor George Becnel Jr
Women's Editor Marty Authement

MANAGEMENT INFORMATION SERVICES
Data Processing Manager Mark Gray

PRODUCTION
Director-Operations Mark Gray

Market Information: TMC; ADS; Operate audiotex.
Mechanical available: Offset; Black and 3 ROP colors; insert accepted — preprinted, zoned inserts; page cut-offs — 22".
Mechanical specifications: Type page 13" x 21"; E - 6 cols, 2$\frac{1}{16}$", ⅛" between; A - 6 cols, 2$\frac{1}{16}$", ⅛" between; C - 9 cols, 1⅜", ⅛" between.
Commodity consumption: Newsprint 3,000 short tons; width 27½"; black ink 48,000 pounds; color ink 7,800 pounds; single pages printed 10,400; average pages per issue 26(d), 60(S); single plates used 45,000.
Equipment: EDITORIAL: Front-end hardware — 21-Computext/PC; Front-end software — AT/7000 4.4, Caere/OmniPage, Computext/Comet II; Printers — Ap/Mac LaserWriter NTX, 2-Pre-press/Pro, Pre-press/5000; Other equipment — Ap/Mac II, Nikon/Scanner, HP/Scanner, Kk/3510, Umax. CLASSIFIED: Front-end hardware — 9-IBM/PC; Front-end software — CPU/Compuclass. AUDIOTEX: Hardware — Brite Voice Systems; Software — Brite Voice Systems; Supplier name — City Line. DISPLAY: Adv layout systems — 6-Ap/Mac; Front-end hardware — 6-Ap/Mac; Front-end software — QuarkXPress 3.3, CPU/Cats, Adobe/Photoshop 2.5; Printers — Ap/Mac LaserWriter, 2-Prepress/Pro 46, Prepress/5000; Other equipment — Kk/Scanner, Umax/Scanner. PRODUCTION: Pagination software — CPU; Typesetters — 2-V/5000, 2-V/5100, 1-V/5300, 1-Ap/Mac LaserWriter, 2-V/Panther Pro 46; Platemaking systems — 1-Nu, 1-Nat, 1-LE, 2-3M/Pyrofax; Plate exposures — 2-Nu; Plate processors — Anitec; Electronic picture desk — Lf/AP Leaf Picture Desk; Scanners — Umax, Nikon; Production cameras — 2-C/Spartan; Automatic film processors — 1-Konica; Digital color separation equipment — Ap/Mac.
PRESSROOM: Line 1 — 3-G/Headliner with ½ deck; Press drives — 1-Fin; Folders — 1-Regency/2:1; Pasters — 3-G/Paster 5003; Reels and stands — 3 stands, 9 reels; Press control system — Fin/5003. MAILROOM: Counter stackers — 3-Id/660; Inserters and stuffers — GMA/SLS 1000; Bundle tyer — 1-Bu, 2-MLN/2; Addressing machine — 2-El, KR/211; Other mailroom equipment — MLN/Stitcher-Trimmer. LIBRARY: Electronic — SMS/Stauffer Gold. COMMUNICATIONS: Digital ad delivery system — AP AdSend. Systems used — satellite. WIRE SERVICES: News — AP, NYT; Photos — AP, Wick; Receiving dishes — size-15ft, AP. BUSINESS COMPUTERS: IBM/Sys 36; Applications: INSI: Gen ledger, Accts payable, Accts receivable, Payroll; PCs & micros networked; PCs & main system networked.

JENNINGS

Jefferson Davis Parish

'90 U.S. Census- 11,305; E&P '96 Est. 10,542

Jennings Daily News (e-tues to fri; S)

Jennings Daily News, 238 Market St.; PO Box 910, Jennings, LA 70546; tel (318) 824-3011; fax (318) 824-3019. Fackelman Newspapers group.
Circulation: 5,443(e); 5,443(S); Sworn Sept. 29, 1995.
Price: 50¢(d); 75¢(S); $6.00/mo; $72.00/yr.
Advertising: Open inch rate $6.50(e); $6.85(S).
News Service: AP. **Politics:** Independent. **Established:** 1896.
Advertising not accepted: 900 numbers.
Special Editions: Income Tax (Jan); Business Focus (Feb); Spring Lawn & Garden, Who's Who (Mar); Graduation (May); Jeff Davis Tourism Guide (June); Rice Harvest (July); Football (Aug); Drug Awareness, Basketball, Christmas Gift (Nov).
Magazine: Television Magazine Weekly (TMC) (wed).

CORPORATE OFFICERS
President Ann Nixon
Vice Pres-Operations Marc A Richard
Secretary Anna L Fackelman
Treasurer Broward E Ratliff

GENERAL MANAGEMENT
Publisher Marc A Richard
General Manager Dona Smith

ADVERTISING
Director Paula Richard

CIRCULATION
Manager Sandra Miller

NEWS EXECUTIVE
Editor Jack Giovo

EDITORS AND MANAGERS
Family/Living Editor Janet Doucet
Sports Editor Brian Trahan

PRODUCTION
Foreman-Pressroom Ron Romero

Market Information: TMC.
Mechanical available: Offset; Black and 3 ROP colors; insert accepted — preprinted, all; page cut-offs — 21½".
Mechanical specifications: Type page 13" x 21½"; E - 6 cols, 2$\frac{1}{16}$", ⅛" between; A - 6 cols, 2$\frac{1}{16}$", ⅛" between; C - 8 cols, 1½", ⅛" between.
Commodity consumption: Newsprint 300 short tons; widths 27", 13½"; black ink 7,000 pounds; color ink 750 pounds; single pages printed 5,000; average pages per issue 12(d), 18(S); single plates used 2,500.
Equipment: EDITORIAL: Front-end hardware — Ap/Mac Performa 630/475; Printers — Ap/Mac LaserWriter IIf. CLASSIFIED: Front-end hardware — Mk, Ap/Mac LC III; Printers — Ap/Mac LaserWriter; Other equipment — 5-Ap/Mac. DISPLAY: Adv layout systems — Ap/Mac Quadra 650; Other equipment — Mk. PRODUCTION: Typesetters — 2-Ap/Mac LaserWriter IIf, Ap/Mac Pro Edit 600; Plate exposures — 1-Nu/Flip Top FT40, 1-Nu/Flip Top FT40L; Electronic picture desk — Ap/Mac Quadra 650; Scanners — Nikon/Negative scanner; Production cameras — Nikon; Automatic film processors — Portage.
PRESSROOM: Line 1 — 4-HI/Cotrell V-15A. MAILROOM: Addressing machine — IBM/486. WIRE SERVICES: News — AP; Receiving dishes — AP. BUSINESS COMPUTERS: IBM/486.

LAFAYETTE

Lafayette Parish

'90 U.S. Census- 94,440; E&P '96 Est. 105,251
ABC-CZ (90): 120,055 (HH 45,046)

The Advertiser (m-mon to sat; S)

The Advertiser, 221 Jefferson St.; PO Box 3268, Lafayette, LA 70502; tel (318) 289-6300; fax (318) 289-6443; e-mail acasmg@acol.com. Thomson Newspapers group.
Circulation: 39,289(m); 39,289(m-sat); 46,446(S); ABC Sept. 30, 1995.
Price: 35¢(d); 35¢(sat); $1.00(S).
Advertising: Open inch rate $26.42(m); $26.42(m-sat); $27.62(S). **Representative:** Papert Companies.
News Service: AP. **Established:** 1865.
Special Edition: Real Estate (monthly).
Special Weekly Section: Church Page (weekly).

GENERAL MANAGEMENT
Publisher/General Manager R E D'Aquin
Accountant Jim Mitchell

ADVERTISING
Manager John Meche

CIRCULATION
Manager Larry Boggs

NEWS EXECUTIVE
Managing Editor Charles Lenox

EDITORS AND MANAGERS
Action Line/Action Corner Editor Jim Bradshaw
Business Editor Robert Wolf
City Editor Jim Bradshaw
Oil News Editor Jim Bradshaw
Radio/Television Editor Druann Domangue
Religion Editor John Sullivan
Sports Editor Bruce Brown
Teen-Age/Youth Editor Karen Naumann

PRODUCTION
Superintendent Sherman Trahan
Foreman-Pressroom Edward Habetz

Market Information: Zoned editions; TMC; ADS.
Mechanical available: Offset; Black and 3 ROP colors; insert accepted — preprinted, any; page cut-offs — 22¾".
Mechanical specifications: Type page 13" x 21½"; E - 6 cols, 2.04", ⅑" between; A - 6 cols, 2.04", ⅑" between; C - 9 cols, 1⅓", ⅑" between.
Equipment: EDITORIAL: Front-end hardware — CD, Ap/Mac; Front-end software — CD 3.1, QuarkXPress; Printers — 2-V/5000, 2-V/5100 plain pager, V/5300E, Ap/Mac LaserWriter II NTX. CLASSIFIED: Front-end hardware — CD; Front-end software — CD 3.1; Printers — Okidata/Microline 393. DISPLAY: Adv layout systems — COM/MCS 100, Ap/Mac; Front-end hardware — CD, Ap/Mac Quadra 950; Front-end software — MCS/Series G, CD/V3.1, QuarkXPress/3.1; Printers — 2-V/5000, 2-V/5100. PRODUCTION: OCR software — Caere/OmniPage; Typesetters — 2-V/5000, 2-V/5100 plain paper, CIS/Color Access; Plate exposures — 2-Nu/Flip Top; Plate processors — 2-WL/Litho-plate; Electronic picture desk — Lf/AP Leaf Picture Desk; Scanners — Lf/Leafscan 35; Production cameras — Liberator, COM/680C; Automatic film processors — LE/Flo LD-24, LE/220-QT; Shrink lenses — Kamerak/Distorta; Digital color separation equipment — Lf/AP Leaf Picture Desk v. 8.1, CIS/Color Access.
PRESSROOM: Line 1 — 10-G/Urbanite; Folders — G/U 1320; Pasters — 8-Cary/Pasters; Press control system — Fin. MAILROOM: Counter stackers — 2-Id/2000-1; Inserters and

stuffers — GMA/SLS 1000; Bundle tyer — Dynaric/NP2, OVL/415; Wrapping singles — Id. WIRE SERVICES: News — AP; Stock tables — AP; Syndicates — Creators, TMS, LATS; Receiving dishes — AP. BUSINESS COMPUTERS: ATT/3B2-500; Applications: Unix; PCs & micros networked; PCs & main system networked.

LAKE CHARLES

Calcasieu Parish

'90 U.S. Census- 70,580; E&P '96 Est. 67,128
ABC-CZ (90): 110,881 (HH 41,115)

Lake Charles American Press (m-mon to sat; S)

Lake Charles American Press, 4900 Hwy. 90 E.; PO Box 2893, Lake Charles, LA 70602; tel (318) 433-3000; fax (318) 494-4008. Shearman Newspapers group.
Circulation: 36,779(m); 36,779(m-sat); 40,543(S); ABC Sept. 30, 1995.
Price: 35¢(d); 35¢(sat); $1.00(S); $9.00/mo; $108.00/yr.
Advertising: Open inch rate $21.00(m); $21.00(m-sat); $22.50(S).
News Service: AP. **Politics:** Independent. **Established:** 1895.
Special Editions: Outdoor (Feb); Brides, Care for Your Car (May); Back-to-School (Aug); Football (Sept); Hunting & Fishing, Care for Your Car (Oct); Christmas Gift Guide (Nov).
Magazines: Marquee (fri); Focus (sat); Parade (S).

CORPORATE OFFICERS

President	Thomas B Shearman III
Vice Pres	Thomas B Shearman Jr
Secretary/Treasurer	Maynard Woodhatch

GENERAL MANAGEMENT

Publisher	Thomas B Shearman III
Business Manager/Purchasing Agent	Terri Simpson
Manager-Credit	Anita Tinsley

ADVERTISING

Director	Gwen Dugas
Manager-Retail/National	Gwen Dugas

CIRCULATION

Manager	C L Woods Jr

NEWS EXECUTIVE

Editor	James C Beam

EDITORS AND MANAGERS

Books Editor	Michael Jones
Metro Editor	Brett Downer
Metro Editor	Edward Alderman
Music Editor	Edward Alderman
News Editor	Bobby Dower
Sports Editor	Scooter Hobbs
State Editor	Linda Young

MANAGEMENT INFORMATION SERVICES

Data Processing Manager	Sarah Young

PRODUCTION

Manager-Computer	Gary Fletcher
Foreman-Pressroom	Robert Craft
Foreman-Camera/Platemaking	Ray Vinson
Foreman-Mailroom	Dennis Bresnahan

Market Information: TMC.
Mechanical available: Offset; Black and 3 ROP colors; insert accepted — preprinted; page cutoffs — 22¾".
Mechanical specifications: Type page 13" x 22"; E - 6 cols, 2¹⁄₁₆", ⅛" between; A - 6 cols, 2¹⁄₁₆", ⅛" between; C - 10 cols, 1⅛", ⅙" between.
Commodity consumption: Newsprint 3,409 short tons; widths 55", 41¼", 27½"; black ink 43,080 pounds; color ink 28,644 pounds; single pages printed 13,176; average pages per issue 34(d), 51(S); single plates used 24,000.
Equipment: EDITORIAL: Front-end hardware — Tandem; Front-end software — SII. CLASSIFIED: Front-end hardware — Ap/Mac; Front-end software — Baseview. DISPLAY: Adv layout systems — SCS/Layout 8000; Front-end hardware — Ap/Mac; Front-end software — DTI, QPS, Multi-Ad/Creator. PRODUCTION: Pagination software — QuarkXPress; OCR software — Caere/OmniPage; Typesetters — V; Plate exposures — Nu; Plate processors — Nat; Electronic picture desk — Lf/AP Leaf Picture Desk; Scanners — HP, Ap/Mac, Sharp, Lf/Leafscan 35; Production cameras — C/Spartan III; Automatic film processors — LE; Film transporters — C; Color separation equipment (conventional) — V; Digital color separation equipment — Lf/Leafscan 35, Sharp/600. PRESSROOM: Line 1 — 8-HI/1660; Pasters — 7-MEG/2-ARM. MAILROOM: Counter stackers — 3-QWI; Inserters and stuffers — 2-S/P-72; Bundle tyer — 2-MLN, 1-Dynaric; Wrapping singles — 2-Sa; Addressing machine — 1-Ch. LIBRARY: Electronic — SII. WIRE SERVICES: News — AP; Stock tables — AP; Receiving dishes — AP. BUSINESS COMPUTERS: HP/3000-922; Applications: CJ: Circ, Adv, Gen ledger, Accts payable, Payroll; PCs & micros networked; PCs & main system networked.

LEESVILLE

Vernon Parish

'90 U.S. Census- 7,638; E&P '96 Est. 6,608

The Leesville Daily Leader (m-tues to fri; S)

The Leesville Daily Leader, 206 E. Texas; PO Box 619, Leesville, LA 71446; tel (318) 239-3444; fax (318) 238-1152, (318) 528-3044. News Leader Inc. group.
Circulation: 6,487(m); 6,487(S); Sworn Oct. 3, 1994.
Price: 25¢(d); 50¢(S); $41.00/yr.
Advertising: Open inch rate $10.05(m); $10.05(S).
News Service: AP. **Established:** 1898 (weekly), 1984 (daily).
Advertising not accepted: Publisher reserves right to refuse.
Special Editions: White Goods, $$Dollar Days$$, Tax Guide (Jan); Bridal Tab, Valentine's Special, Love Lines, Business in Review (Feb); Business Card, St. Patrick's Day, Spring & Easter Fashions (Mar); Secretary's Week, Spring Home & Garden (Apr); Contraband Days, Arts & Crafts, Mother's Day, Armed Forces, Graduation (tentative date), Memorial Day, Astroworld (May); Travel Guide, Bridal, Father's Day, Flag Day (June); July 4th Sales, Dining Out, Car Care, Back-to-School, Coupon Tab (July); Real Estate Page, Football Tab, Labor Day Sales (Aug); Grandparents Day Sales, Hunting Tab, Fall Home Improvement, New Car Tab, Football Contest Starts (Sept); Cosmetology Page, Columbus Day Specials, Homecoming (tenative date), Halloween, Drug Free America Tab (Oct); Veteran's Day, Christmas Gift Guide, Thanksgiving Specials, Songbook, Coupon Tab (Nov); Christmas Gift Guide & Santa's Letters, Last Minute Ideas, Christmas Greetings, New Year's & 1st Baby of the Year (Dec).
Magazines: TV Guide (S); USA Weekend.

CORPORATE OFFICER

President	E C Gensheimer

GENERAL MANAGEMENT

Publisher	Erbon W Wise
General Manager	George Jinks

ADVERTISING

Director	Cindy Petersen

CIRCULATION

Director	Billy Douga

NEWS EXECUTIVE

Editor	Shannon Duhon

EDITOR AND MANAGER

Sports Editor	Ben Barkley

MANAGEMENT INFORMATION SERVICES

Data Processing Manager	Lewis Cain

PRODUCTION

Manager	Jeanne Hugley

Market Information: TMC; Electronic edition.
Mechanical available: Offset; Black and 3 ROP colors; insert accepted — preprinted; page cutoffs — 22¾".
Mechanical specifications: Type page 12½" x 21"; E - 6 cols, 2¹⁄₁₆", ⅛" between; A - 6 cols, 2¹⁄₁₆", ⅛" between; C - 8 cols, 1½", ⅛" between.
Commodity consumption: Newsprint 900 short tons; width 27½"; black ink 71,000 pounds; color ink 1,000 pounds; average pages per issue 16(d), 20(S); single plates used 9,000.
Equipment: EDITORIAL: Front-end hardware — 5-Mk. CLASSIFIED: Front-end hardware — 2-Mk. DISPLAY: Adv layout systems — Ap/Mac. PRODUCTION: Pagination software — Ap/Mac; OCR software — HP. PRESSROOM: Line 1 — 3-WL/Color Quad; Line 2 — 5-WL/Regular. WIRE SERVICES: News — AP; Stock tables — AP; Receiving dishes — AP.

MINDEN

Webster Parish

'90 U.S. Census- 13,661; E&P '96 Est. 12,651

Minden Press-Herald (e-mon to fri)

Minden Press-Herald, 203 Gleason; PO Box 1339, Minden, LA 71055; tel (318) 377-1866; fax (318) 377-1895. Specht Newspapers Inc. group.
Circulation: 4,918(e); Sworn Sept. 26, 1995.
Price: 50¢(d); $7.00/mo; $84.00/yr.
Advertising: Open inch rate $8.00(e). **Representative:** The Newspaper Network.
News Service: AP. **Politics:** Independent. **Established:** 1848.
Special Editions: Progress; Spring Fashion; Cookbook; Car-Care (Spring & Fall); Cattlemen; Agri-business; Gift Guide; Church; Kids Design-An-Ad; Business Card Directory; Football; Basketball; Christmas Greetings; Dirt Traxx.
Special Weekly Sections: Press-Herald Xtra (wed); Entertainment, Religion, Remote Control (TV) (fri).

CORPORATE OFFICERS

President	David A Specht
Vice Pres	David Specht Jr

GENERAL MANAGEMENT

Asst Publisher	David Specht Jr
Manager-Credit	Richard McCranie
Business Manager	Nila Johnson

ADVERTISING

Manager-Retail	Billy Walker
Manager-Classified	Nila Johnson

CIRCULATION

Director	Tina Specht

NEWS EXECUTIVE

Managing Editor	Bonnie Koskie

EDITORS AND MANAGERS

Action Line Editor	Allen Smith
Business/Finance Editor	Allen Smith
City Editor	Allen Smith
Environmental Editor	Allen Smith
Graphics Editor/Art Director	David Specht Jr
National Editor	Allen Smith
News Editor	Allen Smith
Photo Editor	Allen Smith
Political/Government Editor	Allen Smith
Science/Technology Editor	Allen Smith
Sports Editor	Mike Hinton
Theater/Music Editor	Allen Smith

PRODUCTION

Foreman	Cody Richard

Market Information: TMC.
Mechanical available: Offset; Black and 3 ROP colors; insert accepted — preprinted; page cutoffs — 21".
Mechanical specifications: Type page 13¹⁄₁₆" x 21"; E - 6 cols, 2¹⁄₁₆", ⅛" between; A - 6 cols, 2¹⁄₁₆", ⅛" between; C - 9 cols, 1⅜", ⅛" between.
Commodity consumption: Newsprint 450 short tons; width 27½"; black ink 17,000 pounds; color ink 5,200 pounds; single pages printed 6,200; average pages per issue 16(d); single plates used 6,500.
Equipment: EDITORIAL: Front-end hardware — Ap/Mac; Front-end software — QPS 3.3; Printers — HP/4MV. CLASSIFIED: Front-end hardware — PC; Front-end software — BMF. DISPLAY: Front-end hardware — Ap/Mac. PRODUCTION: OCR software — WordScan 1.0; Typesetters — HP/4MV; Plate exposures — 1-Nu/Flip Top; Plate processors — 1-Nat/A250-2Z206A; Production cameras — 1-Argyle/23-G23; Automatic film processors — 1-Powermatic/T-45. PRESSROOM: Line 1 — 6-WPC/Leader; Folders — 1-WPC. MAILROOM: Bundle tyer — 1-Felins/Pack Tyer; Addressing machine — Wm. WIRE SERVICES: News — AP; Syndicates — King Features, Universal Press; Receiving dishes — AP. BUSINESS COMPUTERS: IBM/Sys 36 PC LINV; Applications: Circ, Billing, Payroll, Accts receivable, Accts payable.

MONROE

Ouachita Parish

'90 U.S. Census- 54,909; E&P '96 Est. 53,499
ABC-NDM (90): 183,213 (HH 64,916)

The News-Star (m-mon to sat; S)

The News-Star, 411 N. 4th St. (71201); PO Box 1502, Monroe, LA 71210; tel (318) 322-5161; fax (318) 362-0311; e-mail emajor@jackson.gannett.com. Gannett Co. Inc. group.
Circulation: 38,713(m); 38,713(m-sat); 45,162(S); ABC Sept. 30, 1995.
Price: 35¢(d); 35¢(sat); $1.50(S); $12.00/mo; $144.00/yr (carrier), $161.40/yr (mail).
Advertising: Open inch rate $51.21(m); $51.21(m-sat); $59.80(S). **Representative:** Gannett National Newspaper Sales.
News Services: AP, GNS, KRT, LAT-WP. **Politics:** Independent. **Established:** 1892 (News-Star), 1929 (Morning World).
Advertising not accepted: Vending machines.
Special Editions: Auto; Home Improvement; Brides; Football; Parade of Homes; Cooking School; Spring Fashions; Home Furnishings; Outdoor Living; Hunting; Car Care; Back-to-School; Outlook; Clubs; Home Improvement & Gardening; Auto Show; Fall Fashions; Father's Day; Mother's Day.
Special Weekly Sections: Best Food Edition (wed); TV Viewing, Entertainment, Travel (S).
Magazine: TV/Cable (S).

GENERAL MANAGEMENT

Publisher	Edgar A Major
Controller	Delinda Renner

ADVERTISING

Director	Roy Heatherly
Manager-National	Patty Anderson
Manager-Classified	Sheila Runnels
Manager-Retail	Jimmy Skeen

MARKETING AND PROMOTION

Director-Market Development	Audrey Stevenson

CIRCULATION

Director	T Don Sage

NEWS EXECUTIVE

Editor	Cathy Spurlock

EDITORS AND MANAGERS

Business Editor	Cecil Brumley
City Editor	Greg Hilburn
Editorial Page Editor	Jimmy Hatten
Exec News Editor	Mark Henderson
Photo Department Manager	Margaret Croft
Sports Editor	Jeff Duncan

MANAGEMENT INFORMATION SERVICES

Data Processing Manager	Robert Boyd

PRODUCTION

Director	Doug Nobles
Manager-Pressroom	Jerry Ford
Manager-Camera/Platemaking	Charles Hatten
Manager-Mailroom	John Coronado
Manager-Computer Systems	Robert Boyd

Market Information: Zoned editions; TMC; ADS; Operate audiotex.
Mechanical available: Letterpress; Black and 3 ROP colors; insert accepted — preprinted; page cut-offs — 22½".
Mechanical specifications: Type page 13.08" x 22.5"; E - 6 cols, 2.04", ⅙" between; A - 6 cols, 2.04", ⅙" between; C - 9 cols, 1.38", .08" between.
Commodity consumption: Newsprint 3,375 short tons; widths 27", 41", 54½"; black ink 68,000 pounds; color ink 9,800 pounds; single pages printed 13,650; average pages per issue 32(d), 72(S); single plates used 20,500.
Equipment: EDITORIAL: Front-end hardware — AT/JII Series 60; Front-end software — AT/Editorial 4.6.5; Printers — 1-AU/LZR-1200 Laser printer; Other equipment — 2-AT/ADT video terminal, 32-IBM/PS-2-50. CLASSIFIED: Front-end hardware — AT/JII Series 60; Front-end software — AT/IAS 4.6.5; Printers — Florida Digital/model 130 dot matrix; Other equipment — 10-AT/ADT video terminal, 2-IBM/PS-2-50. DISPLAY: Adv layout systems — COM; Front-end hardware — 2-Ap/Mac Quadra 840 AV, 2-Ap/Mac Quadra 610, 1-Ap/Mac Quadra 950 fileserver; Printers — AU/APS-6-84-ACS, AU/APS-1560 LaserPrinter. PRODUCTION: Typesetters — AU/APS 684 ACS, 2-AU/APS 108; Platemaking systems — Na; Plate exposures — 2-Na/News Printer; Plate processors — 2-Na/Processor; Electronic picture desk — Lf/AP Leaf Picture Desk; Scanners — 1-ECR/Autokon; Production cameras — 1-C/Spartan III, 1-C/Newpager; Automatic film processors — 2-LE/PC-13, 2-LE/APS-36, 2-P/EL26, 1-C/P66F; Film transporters — 2-LE/APS-36; Color separation equipment (conventional) — 1-Lf/AP Leaf Picture Desk; Digital color separation equipment — 1-Lf/Leafscan 35. PRESSROOM: Line 1 — 1-G/2138 Headliner Letterpress (8 units; 3 half-deck); Press drives — Fin; Folders — 1-G/Double; Press control system — 8-Fin/3122 60hp DC drives; Press registration system — WL/Magnetic Saddles. MAILROOM: Counter stackers — 2-HL/HT, 1-Id/NS-440; Inserters and stuffers — 1-HI/NP-624; Bundle tyer — MLN; Wrapping singles — Id. WIRE SERVICES: News — AP, GNS, KRT, LAT-WP; Photos — AP, GNS; Stock tables — AP SelectStox I; Receiving dishes — size-12ft, AP. BUSINESS COMPUTERS: DEC/PDP 11-84; Applications: DEC/RSTS (10); PCs & micros networked; PCs & main system networked.

I-174 Louisiana

MORGAN CITY
St. Mary Parish
'90 U.S. Census- 14,531; E&P '96 Est. 13,417

The Daily Review
(e-mon to fri)

The Daily Review, 1014 Front St.; PO Box 948, Morgan City, LA 70381; tel (504) 384-8370; fax (504) 384-4255. Morgan City Newspapers Inc. group.
Circulation: 6,127(e); Sworn Sept. 29, 1995.
Price: 35¢(d); $35.00/yr (local), $80.00/yr (mail).
Advertising: Open inch rate $5.60(e).
News Service: AP. **Politics:** Independent. **Established:** 1872.
Not Published: Christmas.
Special Editions: Chamber of Commerce (Jan); Progress (Apr); Dixie Youth-Little League Baseball (July); Shrimp & Petroleum Festival-Oil (Sept, fri prior to Labor Day); Energy Coastal; Christmas (Dec 24).
Special Weekly Section: Real Estate (fri).

GENERAL MANAGEMENT
Publisher Doyle E Shirley
Assoc Publisher Steve Shirley

ADVERTISING
Manager Andy Shirley

CIRCULATION
Director Kevin Fernandez

NEWS EXECUTIVE
Managing Editor Steve Shirley

EDITORS AND MANAGERS
City/Metro Editor Ted McManus
Editorial Page Editor Steve Shirley
Fashion/Style Editor Diane Fears
Photo Editor Christine Provost
Sports Editor Chris Landry
Women's Editor Diane Fears

MANAGEMENT INFORMATION SERVICES
Manager Steve Shirley

PRODUCTION
Manager Carol LeBlanc

Market Information: TMC.
Mechanical available: Offset; Black and 3 ROP colors; insert accepted — preprinted, $8\frac{1}{2}$x11 card or single sheet; page cut-offs — $22\frac{15}{16}$".
Mechanical specifications: Type page 13" x $21\frac{1}{2}$"; E - 6 cols, $2\frac{1}{16}$", $\frac{1}{8}$" between; A - 6 cols, $2\frac{1}{16}$", $\frac{1}{8}$" between; C - 8 cols, $1\frac{1}{2}$", $\frac{1}{8}$" between.
Commodity consumption: Newsprint 450 short tons; width 28"; black ink 1,120 pounds; color ink 40 pounds; single pages printed 4,980; average pages per issue 16(d); single plates used 3,000.
Equipment: EDITORIAL: Front-end hardware — 1-COM/One 26; Printers — NewGen/Laser PS 840E. CLASSIFIED: Front-end hardware — 1-COM/One 26; Printers — NewGen/Laser PS-840E; Other equipment — IBM. DISPLAY: Adv layout systems — 2-Cornerstone Technology/486. PRODUCTION: Typesetters — 6-COM, 2-NewGen/Turbo PS-840E; Platemaking systems — 3-Nu; Scanners — Translator/11; Production cameras — 1-B.
PRESSROOM: Line 1 — 4-G; Folders — 1-G. MAILROOM: Addressing machine — 1-Hyundai/286. WIRE SERVICES: News — AP; Receiving dishes — size-1m, AP. BUSINESS COMPUTERS: DEC.

NATCHITOCHES
Natchitoches County
'90 U.S. Census- 16,609 E&P '96 Est. 16,821

Natchitoches Times
(m-tues to fri; S)

Natchitoches Times, 904 Hwy. 1 S.; PO Box 448, Natchitoches, LA 71457; tel (318) 352-5501; fax (318) 352-7842.
Circulation: 7,500(m); 7,500(S); Estimate Sept. 26, 1995.
Price: 50¢(d); 50¢(S); $6.50/mo; $65.00/yr.
Advertising: Open inch rate $6.00(m); $6.00(S). **Established:** 1995.
Note: This is a new daily paper. Publisher's sworn statement of circulation not made available as of press time.
Special Edition: Bridal (June).

CORPORATE OFFICER
President Lovan Thomas

GENERAL MANAGEMENT
Publisher Lovan Thomas

ADVERTISING
Manager Charles Norman

MARKETING AND PROMOTION
Manager-Marketing/Promotion Charles Norman

CIRCULATION
Manager Jerry Hooper

NEWS EXECUTIVE
Editor Carolyn Roy

PRODUCTION
Manager Charles Norman

Market Information: TMC; ADS.
Mechanical available: Black; insert accepted — preprinted; page cut-offs — $22\frac{3}{4}$".
Commodity consumption: width $27\frac{1}{2}$"; single pages printed 23,400; average pages per issue 18(d).
Equipment: EDITORIAL: Front-end hardware — Ap/Power Mac, Linotype-Hell/Linotron 190; Front-end software — QuarkXPress; Printers — Ap/Mac LaserWriter 810. CLASSIFIED: Front-end software — Multi-Ad. PRODUCTION: Color separation equipment (conventional) — Linotype-Hell/Linotron 190; Digital color separation equipment — SCREEN.
PRESSROOM: Line 1 — 10-G.

NEW IBERIA
Iberia Parish
'90 U.S. Census- 31,828; E&P '96 Est. 31,077

The Daily Iberian
(e-mon to fri; m-sat; S)

The Daily Iberian, 926 E. Main St.; PO Box 9290, New Iberia, LA 70562; tel (318) 365-6773; fax (318) 367-9640. Wick Communications group.
Circulation: 14,301(e); 14,301(m-sat); 15,159(S); VAC June 30, 1995.
Price: 50¢(d); 50¢(sat); $1.00(S); $8.00/mo; $98.64/yr (carrier), $143.52/yr (mail).
Advertising: Open inch rate $12.00(e); $12.00(m-sat); $12.00(S). **Representative:** Papert Companies.
News Service: AP. **Politics:** Independent. **Established:** 1893.
Special Editions: Bridal (Jan); Business Report (Feb); Health, Lawn & Garden (Mar); Home Improvement, Outdoors (Apr); Mother's Day, Bridal Section, HS Graduation (May); Father's Day, Dining (June); Football (Aug); Sugar Cane Festival, Cookbook (Sept); Car Care, Farm Edition, Home Furnishings, Drug Awareness Coloring Book (Oct); Gift Guide (Nov).
Special Weekly Sections: Health News (tues); Food (wed); Business News (thur); Church Page, Business Spotlight (sat); Outdoor, Family Section, Business (S).
Magazines: TMC (wed); TV Listings (fri); Color Comics, USA Weekend (S).

CORPORATE OFFICER
President Walter M Wick

GENERAL MANAGEMENT
Publisher Will Chapman

ADVERTISING
Manager Jim Hornbeck

CIRCULATION
Director Sandy Schimweg

NEWS EXECUTIVE
Editor Ted Truby

EDITORS AND MANAGERS
Action Line Editor Jennifer May
Amusements Editor Don Shoopman
Automotive/Aviation Editor Lisa Hurt
Business/Finance Editor Connie Lewis
Columnist Will Chapman
Editorial Page Editor Will Chapman
Education Editor John Cummins
Environmental Editor Bernard Chaillot
Farm/Agriculture Editor Connie Lewis
Fashion/Style Editor Jennifer May
Features Editor Jennifer May
Films/Theater Editor Don Shoopman
Food Editor Jennifer May
Graphics Editor/Art Director Don Shoopman
Health/Medical Editor Don Shoopman
Living/Lifestyle Editor Jennifer May
National Editor Ted Truby
News Editor Fred Bandy
Photo Editor Lee Ball
Political/Government Editor Ted Truby
Radio/Television Editor Ted Truby
Real Estate Editor Connie Lewis
Religion Editor Lori LeBlanc
Sports Editor Don Shoopman
Wire Editor Don Shoopman
Women's Editor Jennifer May

PRODUCTION
Manager Ted Uhall Sr

Market Information: TMC; ADS.
Mechanical available: Offset; Black and 3 ROP colors; insert accepted — preprinted; page cut-offs — $22\frac{3}{4}$".
Mechanical specifications: Type page 13" x $21\frac{1}{2}$"; E - 6 cols, $2\frac{1}{32}$", $\frac{1}{8}$" between; A - 6 cols, $2\frac{1}{32}$", $\frac{1}{8}$" between; C - 9 cols, $1\frac{5}{16}$", $\frac{1}{16}$" between.
Commodity consumption: Newsprint 871 short tons; widths 27", $13\frac{1}{2}$"; black ink 21,300 pounds; color ink 1,000 pounds; single pages printed 9,968; average pages per issue 20(d), 16(sat), 36(S); single plates used 4,984.
Equipment: EDITORIAL: Front-end hardware — Mk; Front-end software — Mk; Printers — TI/810. CLASSIFIED: Front-end hardware — Mk; Front-end software — Mk; Printers — TI/810. DISPLAY: Adv layout systems — Ap/Mac; Front-end hardware — 5-Ap/Mac IIci; Front-end software — Aldus/PageMaker, Multi-Ad/Creator, Lotus; Printers — Xante, Ap/Mac. PRODUCTION: OCR software — Caere/OmniPage; Typesetters — XIT/Clipper, 2-Ap/Mac, Ap/Mac LaserWriter NT, Ap/Mac LaserWriter NTX, Ap/Mac LaserWriter, WDS, Ap/Mac Asante; Platemaking systems — 3M/Pyrofax; Plate exposures — Nu; Plate processors — WL; Scanners — Ap/Mac Scanner; Production cameras — Acti/183; Automatic film processors — AG/Rapidline 17; Digital color separation equipment — Nikon/Coolscan.
PRESSROOM: Line 1 — 5-G/Urbanite; Press drives — 1-Fin; Folders — G/Urbanite U521; Press control system — G; Press registration system — Duarte. MAILROOM: Counter stackers — MRS; Bundle tyer — MLN. COMMUNICATIONS: Systems used — satellite. WIRE SERVICES: News — AP; Photos — AP; Receiving dishes — AP. BUSINESS COMPUTERS: IBM/Sys 34; Applications: Payroll, Accts payable, TMC mailings, Circ, Best buy.

NEW ORLEANS
Orleans Parish
'90 U.S. Census- 496,938; E&P '96 Est. 494,371
ABC-CZ (90): 1,264,391 (HH 463,391)

The Times-Picayune
(all day-mon to fri; m-sat; S)

Times-Picayune, 3800 Howard Ave., New Orleans, LA 70140; tel (504) 826-3279; fax (504) 826-3636; web site http://www.neworlens.net/. Advance Publications group.
Circulation: 267,397(a); 260,049(m-sat); 317,046(S); ABC Sept. 30, 1995.
Price: 50¢(d); 50¢(sat); $1.50(S); $11.00/mo (mS), $6.20/mo (m), $7.00/mo (S).
Advertising: Open inch rate $121.70(a); $121.70(m-sat); $124.61(S). **Representative:** Newhouse Newspapers/Metro Suburbia.
News Services: AP, CNS, DJ, LAT-WP, NNA, NYT. **Politics:** Independent-Democrat. **Established:** 1837.
Special Editions: Bridal Tab, St. Tammany Bridal Tab (H), Money & Banking, Information Guide (Jan); Mardi Gras Tab, Your Money, Winter/Spring Cruise, West Bank Health (Feb); St. Tammany Home Show, Frozen Food Festival, Coupon Book (D,E), Chef's Soiree, Home, Garden & Outdoor Living, WB Home Improvement, Auto Show, Northshore Wheels Tab (Mar); St. Bernhard Progress, New Orleans East Update, Coupon Book (Apr); LA Inc., Primelife Tab (May); Summer Dining (D,E), Slidell Summer Dining (H3,H4), St. Tammany Dining (H1) (June); Summer Dining (A1), Summer Dining (B1), Coupon Book (A,B,C), Money & Economy, Physician's Guide, Business River Parishes (July); St. Tammany Back-to-School Tab (HI), Slidell Back-to-School (H3,H4), Metro Prep (A-C), Metro Prep (D,E), Metro Prep (F), Metro Prep (G), Metro Prep (H), Metro Prep (I) (Aug); Fall Cruise Feature, Overture, St. Tammany Health, Coupon Book (D,E) (Sept); Restaurant, Ski Vacation Feature, Your Home, Kenner Business (D,E), Coupon Book (H1,H3,H4) (Oct); River Parishes Christmas Tab (I), St. Bernard Christmas Tab (G) (Nov); Slidell Christmas (H3,H4), St. Tammany Christmas (H1), West Bank, Christmas Wish, Brok (F) (Dec).
Special Weekly Sections: Best Food Day (thur); Weekend Entertainment (fri); Travel Feature (S).
Magazines: TV Focus Magazine, Parade (S).

CORPORATE OFFICERS
President Ashton Phelps Jr
Vice Pres/Treasurer Linda Dennery
Vice Pres/Secretary Ray Massett

GENERAL MANAGEMENT
Publisher Ashton Phelps Jr
General Manager Linda Dennery
Business Manager Ray Massett
Controller Arthur Anzalone
Manager-Credit Hiram Torres
Personnel Manager Beth Adams
Purchasing Agent Wayne Benjamin

ADVERTISING
Director Robert G O'Neill
Manager-Sales & Development Greig Smith
Asst Director Randy Trahan
Manager-Copy/Art Service Rick Martin
Manager-National Alex Wimberly
Manager-Retail Wensel Ballard Conroy
Manager-Retail Nancy Carroll
Manager-Retail Jack D Lagarde
Manager-Retail Deborah Loviza
Manager-Retail Kelly Rose
Manager-Retail Mark Rose
Manager-Retail Bob Charlet
Manager-Classified JoAnn Chiasson
Manager-Special Sections Dawn Buckley

MARKETING AND PROMOTION
Director-Marketing Crawford C Carroll

CIRCULATION
Director Morris Schneider

NEWS EXECUTIVES
Editor Jim Amoss
Exec Editor-News Dan Shea
Assoc Editor-News Peter Kovacs
Assoc Editor-Editorial Malcolm Forsyth
Asst to Editor Lynn Cunningham

EDITORS AND MANAGERS
Action Line Editor Jeannie Blake
Business/Finance News Editor Charley Blaine
City Editor Jed Horne
Columnist Jack Wardlaw
Columnist James Gill
Columnist Betty Guillaud
Columnist Angus Lind
Columnist Nell Nolan
Columnist Edgar Poe
Columnist Iris Kelso
Columnist Sheila Stroup
Columnist Lolis Elie
Coordinator-News Production Thomas Perrien
Editorial Page Editor Malcolm Forsyth
Editorial Writer Joe Massa
Editorial Writer Sara Pagones
Education Editor Leslie Williams
Energy Editor Mary Judice
Entertainment/Amusements Editor Karen Taylor Gist
Environment Editor Paul Bartels
Fashion Editor Chris Bynum
Features/Lifestyle Editor Bettye Anding
Films/Theater Editor Richard Dodds
Food Editor Dale Curry
Health/Medical Writer John Pope
Librarian Nancy Burris
Metro Editor Peter Kovacs
Music Writer-Classical Ted Mahne
Music Writer-Popular Scott Aiges
National Editor Paul Bartels
News Editor O J Valeton Jr
News Editor Ray Lincoln
Night Metro Editor Tim Morris
Page One Editor Paula Devlin
Chief Photographer G Andrew Boyd
Photo Editor Dinah Rogers
Photo Editor Doug Parker
Political/Government Editor Paul Bartels
Radio/Television Editor Tammy Carter
Real Estate Editor Greg Thomas
Religion Editor Bruce Nolan
Sports Managing Editor Tim Ellerbee
Sports Editor Peter Finney
Suburban Editor David Meeks
Travel Editor Millie Ball
Women's Editor M L Atkinson

MANAGEMENT INFORMATION SERVICES
Data Processing Manager Chris Ruppert

PRODUCTION
Director Ray Maly
Asst Manager Pat Achor
Manager-Pressroom Carl Knoblauch
Manager-Facility Harley Bonham
Manager-Mailroom Lewis (Woody) Schuler
Manager-Pre Press Michael Caminita
Manager-Mechanical/Building Maintenance Paul Voisin

Market Information: Zoned editions; Split Run; TMC; Operate audiotex; Electronic edition.
Mechanical available: Offset; Black and 3 ROP colors; insert accepted — preprinted, 3x5 & above; page cut-offs — 22.06".
Mechanical specifications: Type page 13" x $21\frac{1}{8}$"; E - 6 cols, $2\frac{1}{16}$", $\frac{1}{8}$" between; A - 6 cols, $2\frac{1}{16}$", $\frac{1}{8}$" between; C - 10 cols, $1\frac{3}{16}$", $\frac{1}{16}$" between.
Commodity consumption: width $54\frac{7}{8}$"; average pages per issue 18(d), 22(S).

Equipment: EDITORIAL: Front-end hardware — 2-DEC/VAX 750, 4-DEC/11-84; Front-end software — CSI; Printers — 2-DEC/LA 75. CLASSIFIED: Front-end hardware — 2-Intel/XLXBASE 8TE 8F Fileservers; Front-end software — HI/Metro Cash; Printers — 4-Epson/DFX-5000, 3-Epson/LX810, 3-Epson/LX3000. DISPLAY: Adv layout systems — HI, Sun, Ap/Mac, 13-HI/2100; Front-end hardware — 2-HI/8000, 2-HI/8002, Sun/ GDM-1662B, Ap/Mac Quadra, Timer/AI-950X; Front-end software — HI/Pagination System, Sun/Conton Scanner software, Ap/Mac, Deltagraph, Timer/AI-950X; Printers — Mercury/N1000 Instant Printer, Ap/Mac LaserWriter Plus; Other equipment — X/7650 scanner HA-1, LE/24" Processor, LE/MicroDigital 480 Vertical Camera, Olix/Integrator. PRODUCTION: Pagination software — HI 2.1; Typesetters — 4-AU/APG; Plate exposures — 5-WL, 5-WL, 5-WL; Plate processors — 5-WL/38D, 5-WL/38D, 5-WL/38D; Scanners — 2-ECR/Autokon 1000; Production cameras — 2-C/Spartan III, 2-C/Newspager, 1-C/Spartan I; Automatic film processors — 5-LE/LD24, 2-LE/PC 1800, 1-Konica, 4-LE/APS36; Film transporters — 4-C, 4-LE/APS36; Shrink lenses — 3-C; Color separation equipment (conventional) — CD, DP/645E, DP/645M; Digital color separation equipment — CD/870 Studio System.
PRESSROOM: Line 1 — 9-G/HO; Line 2 — 9-G/HO; Line 3 — 9-G/HO; Line 4 — 10-G/HO; Line 5 — 10-G/HO; Folders — 2-G/3:2, 6-H/3:2, 2-H/2:1; Press control system — G/MPCS. MAILROOM: Counter stackers — 7-HL/Monitor, 4-HL/H-T, 2-Rima/RS-25; Inserters and stuffers — 3-HI/1372, 2-HI/1472; Bundle tyer — 5-Dynaric/NPI, 9-Dynaric/NP2, 6-MLN, 7-MLN/2A; Addressing machine — Dm. LIBRARY: Electronic — Vu/Text. WIRE SERVICES: News — AP, LAT-WP, NNS, NYT; Photos — AP; Stock tables — AP DataStox; Syndicates — North America Syndicate; Receiving dishes — AP, DJ. BUSINESS COMPUTERS: IBM/9370 Model-150, Novell/Network; Applications: Circ, Accts receivable, Adv, Payroll, Accts payable; PCs & micros networked.

OPELOUSAS

St. Landry Parish

'90 U.S. Census- 18,151; E&P '96 Est. 17,583
ABC-NDM (90): 107,586 (HH 36,967)

The Daily World

(e-mon to fri; S)

The Daily World, I 49 S. Frontage Rd. (70570); PO Box 1179, Opelousas, LA 70571-1179; tel (318) 942-4971; fax (318) 948-6572. New York Times Co. group.
Circulation: 12,676(e); 13,949(S); ABC Sept. 30, 1995.
Price: 50¢(d); 75¢(S); $7.50/mo.
Advertising: Open inch rate $12.25(e); $12.25(S). **Representative:** Papert Companies.
News Service: AP. **Politics:** Independent. **Established:** 1939.
Not Published: Christmas.
Special Editions: Progress (Feb); Spring Car Care, Home Improvement (Mar); Brides (Apr); Father's Day (June); Woman's World (July); Football Roundup (Aug); Yambilee, Cooking Section (Oct); Fall Car Care (Nov); Senior World, Real Estate Magazine (monthly).
Special Weekly Sections: Farm Page (mon); Medical Page (tues); Food Page (wed); Acadiana TV Listings (thur); Church Page (fri); Business Section (S); Sports (daily).
Magazine: TV Week.

CORPORATE OFFICER
President Aaron Parsons

GENERAL MANAGEMENT
Publisher Aaron Parsons

ADVERTISING
Director Bill Brownlee
Manager-Classified Al Andrepont

CIRCULATION
Manager John Poirier

NEWS EXECUTIVE
Editor Harlan Kirgan

EDITORS AND MANAGERS
Books/Education Editor Harlan Kirgan
Business/Finance Editor Harlan Kirgan
Columnist Jeff Zeringue
Films/Theater Editor Jeff Zeringue
Religion Editor Harlan Kirgan
Sports Editor Herman Fuselier
Women's Editor Jeff Zeringue

PRODUCTION
Superintendent Gary Messner
Foreman-Composing/Mailroom Gary Messner

Market Information: Zoned editions; TMC; Operate audiotex.
Mechanical available: Offset; Black and 3 ROP colors; insert accepted — preprinted; page cutoffs — 23½".
Mechanical specifications: Type page 13" x 21½"; E - 6 cols, 2¹⁄₁₆", ³⁄₁₆" between; A - 6 cols, 2¹⁄₁₆", ³⁄₁₆" between; C - 9 cols, 1⅜", ⅛" between.
Commodity consumption: Newsprint 640 short tons; width 27½"; black ink 24,000 pounds; color ink 1,000 pounds; single pages printed 7,506; average pages per issue 20(d), 32(S); single plates used 3,670.
Equipment: EDITORIAL: Front-end hardware — 2-AT/5000, IBM; Other equipment — 21-AT. CLASSIFIED: Front-end hardware — 1-AT/5000; Other equipment — 4-AT, IBM. DISPLAY: Adv layout systems — 1-AT; Other equipment — 2-Softsetter/ATE GED3. PRODUCTION: Typesetters — 2-COM/8600; Plate exposures — 1-Nu/52; Plate processors — 1-LG/25, 1-Nat, 1-Nu/52; Production cameras — 1-C/Spartan II; Automatic film processors — 1-LE, 1-C.
PRESSROOM: Line 1 — 8-G/Community; Folders — 2-G. MAILROOM: Counter stackers — BG; Inserters and stuffers — 3-MM; Bundle tyer — 2-Bu; Addressing machine — 1-Ch. LIBRARY: Electronic — 2-BH/Microfilm. WIRE SERVICES: News — NYT, AP; Receiving dishes — size-12ft, AP. BUSINESS COMPUTERS: DPT/8200, IBM/3600, IBM/PC-Model 50, IBM/PC-Model 25; Applications: Adv billing, Accts receivable, Payroll, Gen ledger, Circ; PCs & micros networked; PCs & main system networked.

PINEVILLE

See ALEXANDRIA

RUSTON

Lincoln Parish

'90 U.S. Census- 20,027; E&P '96 Est. 19,575

Ruston Daily Leader

(e-mon to fri; S)

Ruston Daily Leader, 208 W. Park Ave. (71270); PO Box 520, Ruston, LA 71273-0520; tel (318) 255-4353; fax (318) 255-4006. Fackelman Newspapers group.
Circulation: 6,146(e); 6,146(S); Sworn Oct. 1, 1995.
Price: 50¢(d); 75¢(S); $6.00/mo; $78.00/yr.
Advertising: Open inch rate $7.25(e); $7.25(S).
News Service: AP. **Politics:** Independent. **Established:** 1894.
Not Published: Christmas.
Special Editions: Progress (Jan); Spring Bride & Fashion, Financial Focus (Feb); Mini Grand Prix, Piney Hills, Hello Ruston (Mar); Mother's Day Salute (Apr); Graduation (May); Peach Festival, Anniversary Edition (June); Back-to-School, Football (Aug); Welcome Edition for LA Tech, Fall Fashion (Sept); Christmas Gift Guide (Nov); Christmas Greetings (Dec).
Magazine: TV Magazine (tues).
Broadcast Affiliates: KIX-FM; KPCH-FM Ruston, LA.

CORPORATE OFFICERS
President Ann Nixon
Vice Pres-Operations Marc A Richard
Secretary Ann Fackelman
Treasurer Broward E Ratliff

GENERAL MANAGEMENT
Publisher Rick Hohlt
General Manager-Credit Mary Hurst

ADVERTISING
Director Jeanie McCartney
Manager-Classified Jeanie McCartney

MARKETING AND PROMOTION
Manager-Marketing/Promotion Jeanie McCartney

CIRCULATION
Manager Terri Cooper

NEWS EXECUTIVES
Editor Melanie Stone-Heyen
Managing Editor Jeff Benson

EDITORS AND MANAGERS
Business/Finance Editor Melanie Stone-Heyen
City/Metro Editor Jeff Benson
Editorial Page Editor Jeff Benson
Education Editor Melanie Stone-Heyen
Entertainment/Amusements Editor Julie Yoder
Farm/Agriculture Editor Donna Bernard
Fashion/Style Editor Julie Yoder
Features Editor Julie Yoder
Living/Lifestyle Editor Julie Yoder
National Editor Jeff Benson
News Editor Melanie Stone-Heyen
Photo Editor Susan Porter
Political/Government Editor Jeff Benson
Publications Manager Terri Cooper
Religion Editor Julie Yoder
Sports Editor O K Davis
Women's Editor Julie Yoder

MANAGEMENT INFORMATION SERVICES
Data Processing Manager Mary Hurst

PRODUCTION
Manager Darryl Crawford

Market Information: TMC; Operate database.
Mechanical available: Offset; Black and 3 ROP colors; insert accepted — preprinted; page cutoffs — 21½".
Mechanical specifications: Type page 13" x 21½"; E - 6 cols, 2¹⁄₁₆", ⅛" between; A - 6 cols, 2¹⁄₁₆", ⅛" between; C - 9 cols, 1⅜", ¹⁄₁₆" between.
Commodity consumption: Newsprint 298 metric tons; widths 27½", 13¾"; black ink 1,400 pounds; color ink 725 pounds; single pages printed 5,300; average pages per issue 16(d), 24(S).
Equipment: EDITORIAL: Front-end hardware — Ap/Mac IIsi, Ap/Mac Classic; Front-end software — Aldus/PageMaker, Microsoft/Word, Microsoft/Excel, Caere/OmniPage, Broderbund/TypeStyler. CLASSIFIED: Front-end hardware — Ap/Mac; Front-end software — Baseview/Class Manager. DISPLAY: Adv layout systems — Ap/Mac SE, Ap/Mac Plus; Front-end hardware — Ap/Mac; Front-end software — Aldus/PageMaker. PRODUCTION: Platemaking systems — 1-Nu; Plate processors — 1-Nat; Scanners — Abaton/Scanner; Production cameras — 1-AG; Automatic film processors — LE.
PRESSROOM: Line 1 — 6-WPC/Leader; Folders — 1-WPC. MAILROOM: Bundle tyer — 2-Bu; Addressing machine — 1-Am. WIRE SERVICES: News — AP; Syndicates — CSM; Receiving dishes — AP. BUSINESS COMPUTERS: 1-RSK/80; PCs & micros networked.

SHREVEPORT

Caddo Parish

'90 U.S. Census- 198,525; E&P '96 Est. 194,426
ABC-NDM (90): 334,341 (HH 123,966)

The Times (m-mon to sat; S)

The Times, 222 Lake St.; PO Box 30222, Shreveport, LA 71130; tel (318) 459-3200; fax (318) 459-3301. Gannett Co. Inc. group.
Circulation: 79,223(m); 79,223(m-sat); 99,285(S); ABC Sept. 30, 1995.
Price: 50¢(d); 50¢(sat); $1.50(S); $12.25/mo; $147.00/yr.
Advertising: Open inch rate $85.90(m); $85.90(m-sat); $90.40(S). **Representative:** Gannett National Newspaper Sales.
News Services: AP, GNS. **Established:** 1839.
Special Editions: Outlook (Jan); Nike Shreveport Open, Louisiana Downs (Apr); Parade of Homes, Answer Book (June); Red River Hot Air Balloon Rally (July); Super Derby Festival, Red River Revel (Sept); Independence Bowl (Dec); Good Business (monthly); Destination (quarterly).
Special Weekly Sections: Food (wed); Preview (Entertainment) (fri); Lifestyles, Travel, Business, Automotive, Real Estate (S); Entertainment, Lifestyle (daily).
Magazines: TV Magazine (local, letterpress) (S); This Week (Extra).

CORPORATE OFFICER
President Richard Stone

GENERAL MANAGEMENT
Publisher Richard Stone
Controller Ron Johnson
Director-Human Resources Barbara Deane

ADVERTISING
Director Dan Mills
Manager-Retail Linda Traweek
Manager-Telemarketing Marilyn Rech
Manager-Classified Donna Currey
Manager-Sales Development Wendy Bencoster
Manager-Operations Roy May

MARKETING AND PROMOTION
Director-Marketing Service Bob Faricy

TELECOMMUNICATIONS
Audiotex Manager Robert Wright

CIRCULATION
Director Judith Skinner

NEWS EXECUTIVES
Editor Judy Pace Christie
Managing Editor Bob Bryan
Asst Managing Editor-News Craig Durrett
Asst Managing Editor-Presentation Martha H Fitzgerald
Asst Managing Editor-Night Eleanor Ransburg

EDITORS AND MANAGERS
Amusements Editor Lane Crockett
Business/Finance Editor Tom Haywood
Business Writer Bill Cooksey
Columnist Teddy Allen
Columnist Wiley Hilburn
Editorial Page Editor Frank May
Education/School Editor Gayla Moore
Environmental Editor Stacy Sullivan
Farm/Agriculture Editor Tom Haywood
Fashion Editor Margaret Martin
Features Editor Kathie Rowell
Films/Theater Editor Lane Crockett
Food/Garden Editor Kathie Rowell
Graphics Editor/Art Director Roger Coley
Health/Medical Editor Tom Haywood
Leisure/Culture Editor Kathie Rowell
Librarian Martha Matlock
Living/Lifestyle Editor Kathie Rowell
Music Editor John Floyd
National Editor Stacy Sullivan
News Editor Don Walker
Photo Department Manager Tom Stanford
Political/Government Editor Stacy Sullivan
Radio/Television Editor Kathie Rowell
Real Estate Editor Tom Haywood
Religion Editor Gayla Moore
Science/Technology Editor Tom Haywood
Society/Women's Editor Kathie Rowell
Sports Editor Mikel LeFort
Teen-Age/Youth Editor Gayla Moore
This Week Editor Kathie Rowell
Travel Editor Kathie Rowell
Wire Editor Bill Beene

MANAGEMENT INFORMATION SERVICES
Data Processing Manager Cilla Trenado

PRODUCTION
Director J C Zagone

Market Information: Zoned editions; Split Run; TMC; Operate audiotex.
Mechanical available: Letterpress; Black and 3 ROP colors; insert accepted — preprinted; page cut-offs — 22¾".
Mechanical specifications: Type page 13" x 21½"; E - 6 cols, 2¹⁄₁₆", ⅛" between; A - 6 cols, 2¹⁄₁₆", ⅛" between; C - 10 cols, 1³⁄₁₆", ⅛" between.
Commodity consumption: Newsprint 9,809 short tons; widths 54.5", 41", 27.25", 13.625"; black ink 98,336 pounds; color ink 37,833 pounds; single pages printed 17,554; average pages per issue 42(d), 90(S).
Equipment: EDITORIAL: Front-end hardware — SII/CLX 840; Front-end software — SII/Guardian 90; Printers — Tandem/5212, Ap/Mac LaserWriter II NT. CLASSIFIED: Front-end hardware — SII/CLX 840; Front-end software — SII/Guardian 90; Printers — Tandem/5212. DISPLAY: Adv layout systems — Multi-Ad/Creator 3.7.1. SL; Front-end hardware — Ap/Mac; Front-end software — Mk 3.0.16; Printers — Dataproducts/LZR-1560, Shinko CHC 746. PRODUCTION: Pagination software — QuarkXPress 3.31; Typesetters — AU/APS6-108S, AU/Pagescan 3; Platemaking systems — Na/Titan; Plate exposures — Na/Starlite; Plate processors — Na/NP80; Electronic picture desk — Lf/AP Leaf Picture Desk; Scanners — Lf/Leafscan 35, AG, AG/Arcus; Production cameras — C/Spartan III; Automatic film processors — P/On line, OL/260; Film transporters — P/SC2050.
PRESSROOM: Line 1 — 8-G, 5-8-G/Headliner; Press drives — CH; Folders — 1-G/2:1, 1-G/3:2; Pasters — G; Reels and stands — G; Press control system — CH; Press registration system — W. MAILROOM: Counter stackers — 3-HL; Inserters and stuffers — 1-S/24P, 1-S/72P, 1-MM/227; Bundle tyer — 3-MLN. LIBRARY: Electronic — Digital Collection Archive. COMMUNICATIONS: Systems used — satellite, fiber optic. WIRE SERVICES: News — AP Datastream, AP Datafeatures; Photos — AP Photostream; Stock tables — AP Stocks; Syndicates — AP Datafeatures; Receiving dishes — size-10ft, AP. BUSINESS COMPUTERS: IBM/AS-400; Applications: Lotus, WordPerfect, Lotus for Windows; PCs & micros networked; PCs & main system networked.

I-176 Louisiana

SLIDELL

St. Tammany Parish

'90 U.S. Census- 24,124; E&P '96 Est. 22,294

Slidell Sentry-News

(m-tues to sat; S)

Slidell Sentry-News, 3648 Pontchartrain Dr., Hwy. 11 S.; PO Box 910, Slidell, LA 70459; tel (504) 643-4918; fax (504) 643-4966. Wick Communications group.

Circulation: 4,699(m); 4,699(m-sat); 4,699(S); VAC Dec. 31, 1994.

Price: 50¢(d); 50¢(sat); $1.00(S); $8.75/mo.

Advertising: Open inch rate $8.25(m); $8.25(m-sat); $8.25(S). **Representative:** US Suburban Press.

News Services: AP, NEA. **Established:** 1965.

Not Published: Independence Day; Labor Day.

Special Editions: Med Fax (Health Care) (Jan); Home & Garden (Mar); Progress (May); Graduation Tab (June); Back-to-School (July); Football (Aug); Cookbook (Nov).

Special Weekly Sections: Spotlight (tues); Business Review Page, Spotlight (wed); Spotlight (thur); Spotlight, Church Page (sat); Spotlight (S).

Magazines: Tempo (Leisure & Entertainment) (fri); Broker East (Real Estate) (S).

CORPORATE OFFICERS

President Walter Wick
Exec Vice Pres Lou Major
Secretary/Treasurer Robert J Wick

GENERAL MANAGEMENT

Publisher Terry Maddox
Controller Ann McGehee
Personnel Manager Terry Maddox

ADVERTISING

Director Charles LaFerrara
Manager-Classified Ron McCall

CIRCULATION

Director Lou Sabatini

NEWS EXECUTIVES

Exec Editor Terry Maddox
Managing Editor Kevin Chirie

EDITORS AND MANAGERS

Amusements Editor John Perkins
Books/Education Editor Shannon McDaniel
Columnist Terry Maddox
Columnist Gilda Perkins
Fashion/Food Editor Shannon McDaniel
Home Furnishings Editor Shannon McDaniel
Real Estate Editor Ron McCall
Religion Editor Shannon McDaniel
Society/Women's Editor Shannon McDaniel
Sports Editor Renn Pravata

PRODUCTION

Manager Jane White
Foreman-Pressroom Herb Travis

Market Information: Split Run; TMC.

Mechanical available: Offset; Black and 3 ROP colors; insert accepted — preprinted; page cutoffs — 21½".

Mechanical specifications: Type page 13" x 21½"; E - 6 cols, 2 1/16", 1/8" between; A - 6 cols, 2 1/16", 1/8" between; C - 8 cols, 1 9/16", 1/16" between.

Equipment: EDITORIAL: Front-end hardware — Mk; Printers — Ap/Mac. CLASSIFIED: Front-end hardware — Mk; Printers — Ap/Mac. DISPLAY: Front-end hardware — Ap/Mac; Printers — NewGen. PRODUCTION: Typesetters — 8-COM/UTS; Platemaking systems — 1-3M/Pyrofax; Production cameras — Argyle/23. PRESSROOM: Line 1 — 4-KP/Newsking. MAILROOM: Bundle tyer — 2-Bu; Addressing machine — Am. WIRE SERVICES: News — Syndicates — AP; Receiving dishes — AP. BUSINESS COMPUTERS: 2-IBM; Applications: Bills, Payroll, Lineage reports.

SULPHUR

Calcasieu Parish

'90 U.S. Census- 20,125; E&P '96 Est. 20,542

Southwest Daily News

(m-mon to sat; S)

Southwest Daily News, 716 E. Napoleon; PO Box 1999, Sulphur, LA 70663; tel (318) 527-7075; fax (318) 528-3044. News Leader Inc. group.

Circulation: 6,989(m); 6,989(m-sat); 6,989(S); Sworn Oct. 3, 1994.

Price: 25¢(d); 25¢(sat); 50¢(S); $26.00/yr.

Advertising: Open inch rate $10.95(m); $10.95(m-sat); $10.95(S). **Representative:** Papert Companies. **Established:** 1929.

Note: Effective Apr. 24, 1995, this publication changed its publishing plan from (m-tues to fri; S) to (m-mon to sat; S).

Special Editions: New Year's Greetings, First Baby, Super Bowl, Bridal Tab (Jan); Chamber Annual Report, Valentine's Day Specials (Feb); Business Review (Mar); Contraband Day Tab, Home Improvement, Secretary's Day, Easter Specials (Apr); Astroworld, Mother's Day Specials, Graduate Specials (May); Brides Tab, Father's Day Specials (June); July 4th Special, Christmas Carol/Songbook Kick-off, School Supply List Pages, Back-to-School (July); Football Tab, Labor Day Specials (Aug); Christmas Greetings Kick-off, Football Contest Begins, Sports Fest '96 Tab (Sept); Cal-Cam Fair Section Tab, Holiday Cookbook Contest Tab (Oct); Turkeyology, Christmas Carol Songbook, Christmas Gift Guide (Nov); Last Minute Gifts, Christmas Greetings (Dec).

Magazines: TV Weekend (fri); USA Weekend (S).

CORPORATE OFFICERS

Chairman of the Board E W Wise
President/CEO E C Gensheimer
Secretary/Controller Lewis Cain
Vice Pres-Marketing Ophelia Hayes

GENERAL MANAGEMENT

Publisher Erbon W Wise

ADVERTISING

Director Susane Peveto

MARKETING AND PROMOTION

Manager-Marketing/Promotion Billy Douga

CIRCULATION

Manager Billy Douga

NEWS EXECUTIVE

Editor Ophelia Hayes

EDITOR AND MANAGER

Sports Editor Jerry Cormier

PRODUCTION

Manager Jeanne Hugley

Market Information: TMC.

Mechanical available: Offset; Black and 3 ROP colors; insert accepted — preprinted; page cutoffs — 22¾".

Mechanical specifications: Type page 13" x 21"; E - 6 cols, 2 1/16", 1/8" between; A - 6 cols, 2 1/16", 1/8" between; C - 8 cols, 1½", 1/8" between.

Commodity consumption: Newsprint 950 short tons; width 27½"; black ink 22,000 pounds; color ink 3,000 pounds; average pages per issue 18(d), 22(S); single plates used 9,000.

Equipment: EDITORIAL: Front-end hardware — Mk, Ap/Mac; Front-end software — QPS, Adobe/Illustrator, Adobe/Photoshop. CLASSIFIED: Front-end hardware — Mk. DISPLAY: Adv layout systems — Ap/Mac; Front-end hardware — Ap/Mac; Front-end software — Ap/Mac. PRODUCTION: Pagination software — Mk/Page Director; OCR software — Caere/OmniPage; Typesetters — TI/Page Scan 3, QMS/860; Platemaking systems — 3M/Pyrofax; Plate processors — 3M; Scanners — Nikon, HP/ScanJets; Production cameras — Kk; Shrink lenses — Kk. PRESSROOM: Line 1 — 3-WL/Color Quad; Line 2 — 5-WL/Regular. MAILROOM: Counter stackers — BG; Bundle tyer — OVL; Addressing machine — Ch. WIRE SERVICES: News — AP; Stock tables — AP. BUSINESS COMPUTERS: HP; Applications: MSSI; PCs & micros networked; PCs & main system networked.

THIBODAUX

Lafourche Parish

'90 U.S. Census- 14,035; E&P '96 Est. 12,821

ABC-NDM (90): 60,455 (HH 20,461)

Daily Comet (e-mon to fri)

The Daily Comet, 705 W. Fifth St.; PO Box 5238, Thibodaux, LA 70302; tel (504) 447-4055; fax (504) 448-7606. New York Times Co. group.

Circulation: 11,712(e); ABC Sept. 30, 1995.

Price: 50¢(d); $63.00/yr (carrier), $71.50/yr (mail).

Advertising: Open inch rate $12.44(e). **Representative:** Papert Companies.

News Services: AP, NYT. **Politics:** Independent. **Established:** 1888.

Not Published: Christmas.

Special Editions: FYI (Jan); Farm & Progress, Wedding, Dollar Days (Feb); Graduation (May); Wedding (July); Dollar Days, Back-to-School (Aug); Football (Sept); Christmas Opening (Nov).

Special Weekly Sections: Business/Agriculture Page, Bridal Announcements (mon); Health Page (tues); Best Food Day, Local Club News (wed); Mes Amis (thur); Religion Page (fri).

Magazine: TV UP-DATE (TV magazine) (fri).

GENERAL MANAGEMENT

Publisher Chris Band

ADVERTISING

Director Alan Rini
Manager-Classified Brent Madere

TELECOMMUNICATIONS

Audiotex Manager Robin Naquin

CIRCULATION

Director David Simon

NEWS EXECUTIVE

Managing Editor Colley Charpentier

EDITORS AND MANAGERS

Business/Farm Editor Colley Charpentier
Sports Editor Alex Songe

Market Information: TMC; Operate audiotex.

Mechanical available: Offset; Black and 3 ROP colors; insert accepted — preprinted; page cutoffs — 22".

Mechanical specifications: Type page 13" x 21"; E - 6 cols, 2 1/16", 1/8" between; A - 6 cols, 2 1/16", 1/8" between; C - 9 cols, 1 3/8", 1/16" between.

Commodity consumption: Newsprint 900 metric tons; width 27½"; black ink 22,440 pounds; single pages printed 7,300; average pages per issue 28(d); single plates used 16,790.

Equipment: EDITORIAL: Front-end hardware — Dewar. DISPLAY: Adv layout systems — Dewar/Discovery. PRODUCTION: Typesetters — 2-COM/8400; Plate exposures — Nu; Plate processors — Nat; Production cameras — 1-B; Automatic film processors — 1-LE. PRESSROOM: Line 1 — 3-G/Headliner. MAILROOM: Bundle tyer — 1-Wilton. WIRE SERVICES: News — AP, NYT; Syndicates — NEA, Universal Press; Receiving dishes — AP. BUSINESS COMPUTERS: Bs, 7-IBM/AT-Network; Applications: Payroll, Accts receivable, Accts payable, Gen ledger, Circ, TMC; PCs & micros networked; PCs & main system networked.

MAINE

AUBURN

See LEWISTON

AUGUSTA

Kennebec County

'90 U.S. Census- 21,325; E&P '96 Est. 20,953

ABC-CZ (90): 23,859 (HH 9,936)

Kennebec Journal

(m-mon to sat)

Kennebec Journal Sunday (S)

Kennebec Journal, 274 Western Ave.; PO Box 1052, Augusta, ME 04330; tel (207) 623-3811; fax (207) 623-2167. Guy Gannett Communications group.

Circulation: 17,486(m); 17,486(m-sat); 15,008(S); ABC Sept. 30, 1995.

Price: 50¢(d); 50¢(sat); $1.25(S); $3.00/wk (carrier & motor route).

Advertising: Open inch rate $19.59(m); $19.59(m-sat); $20.57(S). **Representative:** Landon Associates Inc.

News Services: AP, NYT. **Established:** 1825.

Note: On Apr. 2, 1995, the Kennebec Journal started publishing on Sunday.

Not Published: Christmas.

Special Editions: Bridal Tab, Baby Parade (Jan); Cabin Fever, Family Expo, Outlook '96, President's Day Auto Section (Feb); Great Outdoors Tab, Do It Yourself Tab (Mar); Baseball/Softball Section, Lawn & Garden (Apr); Crafted in Maine, Ideas for Kids, Dining Guide, Start Your Engines (May); Summer in Maine, Whatever Week, June Brides (June); Skowhegan Fair (July); Miracle Mile (Aug); Home Decorating, Fall Sports (Sept); Home Energy Guide, Fall Car Care (Oct); Let It Snow, Countdown to Christmas, Crafted in Maine (Nov); Countdown to Christmas (Dec).

Special Weekly Sections: What's Happening (entertainment) (fri); What's on TV (S).

GENERAL MANAGEMENT

President/Central Maine Newspapers Michael J Sexton
Manager-Business Gary Zemrak

ADVERTISING

Director Molly Evans
Manager-Retail Sales David Cousins
Manager-Classified Susan Colfer

MARKETING AND PROMOTION

Manager-Marketing & Promotion Cindy Stevens

CIRCULATION

Director Bruce Bourgoine

NEWS EXECUTIVE

Exec Editor Warren Watson

EDITORS AND MANAGERS

Books Editor Maryann Brooke
City Editor Patricia Ammons
Social Editor Tedda Henry
Sports Editor Jerry Lauzon

MANAGEMENT INFORMATION SERVICES

Data Processing Manager Christine Solloway

PRODUCTION

Director John L Maxwell
Director-Post Press Robert Gagne
Supervisor-Composing John Merrill
Supervisor-Press Steve Rote

Market Information: Split Run; TMC.

Mechanical available: Offset; Black and 3 ROP colors; insert accepted — preprinted; page cutoffs — 22¾".

Mechanical specifications: Type page 13" x 21½"; E - 6 cols, 2 1/16", 1/8" between; A - 6 cols, 2 1/16", 1/8" between; C - 9 cols, 1 3/8", 1/16" between.

Commodity consumption: Newsprint 1,337 short tons; widths 27.5", 34", 33", 13.75", 16.5"; black ink 34,718 pounds; color ink 4,783 pounds; single pages printed 10,640; average pages per issue 34(d); single plates used 26,250.

Equipment: EDITORIAL: Front-end hardware — 2-DEC/PDP 11-44, SCS. CLASSIFIED: Front-end hardware — DEC/PDP 11-44, SCS; Front-end software — SCS. DISPLAY: Adv layout systems — SCS/Layout 8000; Front-end hardware — SCS; Other equipment — Ap/Mac PowerBook. PRODUCTION: Typesetters — 2-COM/8600; Plate exposures — 2-BKY/5k, 1-Nu/FT40; Plate processors — 1-WL/30A, 1-Nat/A340; Production cameras — 1-C/Spartan III, 1-C/Spartan II, 1-AG/RPS; Automatic film processors — 2-AG/660; Film transporters — 1-C/In-Line; Shrink lenses — 1-CK Optical/SQU 7. PRESSROOM: Line 1 — 14-G/Urbanite; Line 2 — 1-Custom-Built/384 4 Knife Trimmer; Line 3 — 1-D&R/(on Press Glue Sys); Press drives — 4-HP/100, Fin; Folders — 2-G/Urbanite, 2-G/Quarterfolder; Pasters — 6-KTI/Splicers; Press registration system — Duarte. MAILROOM: Counter stackers — 1-HI/RS25, 3-HL/Monitor, 1-HL/Stackpack; Inserters and stuffers — 1-HI/1372, 1-Mc; Bundle tyer — 1-Sa/BMIA, 2-CYP/Plast tyer, 1-MLN/MS-B, 1-MLN/ML-OAE; Mailroom control system — HI/Icon System. COMMUNICATIONS: Facsimile — Ricoh/60, Fujitsu/dex 730; Remote imagesetting — AP (via telephone lines). WIRE SERVICES: News — AP, NYT; Stock tables — AP, Media General; Receiving dishes — size-3m, AP. BUSINESS COMPUTERS: IBM/4331 II, Bs/1860, DEC/VAX 8250; Applications: Circ, Adv billing, Accts receivable, Gen ledger, Payroll, Payables; Microsoft/Excel, Microsoft/Word.

BANGOR

Penobscot County

'90 U.S. Census- 33,181; E&P '96 Est. 35,097

ABC-CZ (90): 75,652 (HH 28,033)

Bangor Daily News

(m-mon to fri; wknd)

Bangor Daily News, 491 Main St.; PO Box 1329, Bangor, ME 04402-1329; tel (207) 990-8000; fax (207) 941-9476; e-mail bangornews@aol.com.

Circulation: 72,769(m); 89,255 (wknd); ABC Sept. 30, 1995.

Price: 50¢(d); $1.25 (wknd); $2.90/wk (carrier), $3.10/wk (motor route); $182.00/yr.

Advertising: Open inch rate $48.50(m); $60.63 (wknd). **Representative:** Sawyer-Ferguson-Walker Co.

News Services: AP, NYT, LAT-WP. **Politics:** Independent. **Established:** 1889.

Advertising not accepted: Tobacco.

Special Editions: Progressive Business Firms, Money Matters, Planning Your Wedding (Jan); Engineers Week, Basketball Tournament Time, Washington's Birthday Autorama, Report '96, Home Furnishings (Feb); Funeral and Estate Planning Guide, Health Care, Maine's Way of Boating, Newspaper in Education Week (Mar); Home & Garden, Bangor Spring Home Show, Earth Day, Northeast Loggers Show, Mainely Motorsports (Apr); Contractor's Outlook, On the Move, Nat'l Nurses & Hospitals Week (May); Experience Maine, Health Care Quarterly (June); Mainely Motorsports, Belfast Bay Festival, Planning Your Wedding, Open Farm Days (July); Back-to-School, Mainely Motorsports, Home Furnishings (Aug); Football Preview, Fall Home Improvement, Hunting in Maine, Health Care (Sept); New Designs in Kitchens & Baths, Maine Forest Products Week, 1997 New Car Preview, Doing Business (Oct); Power Play: UMaine Hockey Preview, Holiday Gift Guide, Maine 2000: Annual Report (Nov); High School Basketball, The Good News of Christmas (Dec).

Special Weekly Section: Maine Style (S).

Magazines: Food (mon); USA Weekend, TV Update, Color Comics (sat); Color Comics (S).

CORPORATE OFFICERS

Chairman Joanne J Van Namee
President Richard J Warren
Chairman-Exec Committee Richard K Warren
Treasurer Arthur E McKenzie
Vice Pres/Secretary Carolyn Mowers

GENERAL MANAGEMENT

Publisher Richard J Warren
Vice Pres-Administration Robert W Stairs
Vice Pres-Operations John Bishop
Controller Timothy Reynolds
Manager-Credit David Small
Manager-Education Service Donna E Fransen
Personnel Manager Eloise McLaughlin
Director-Community Affairs Thomas (Skip) Chappelle

ADVERTISING

Director Wayne A Lawton
Manager-General Roger Choquet
Manager-Retail Nancy J Golding
Asst Manager-Retail Dana B Leeman
Manager-Classified Andrew J Constantine
Manager-Portland Office Edward Hryrhor

MARKETING AND PROMOTION

Manager-Marketing Administration James M Spox

TELECOMMUNICATIONS

Manager-Computer Service Carol A Raymond

CIRCULATION

Manager Cornelius Noddin
Asst Manager James P Hayes

NEWS EXECUTIVES

Editor Richard J Warren
Exec Editor Robert A Kelleter

EDITORS AND MANAGERS

Business Editor Carroll Astbury
Business Editor Mike Dowd
Editorial Page Editor A Mark Woodward
Graphics/Design Director Eric Zelz
Librarian Charles Campo
Maine Style Editor Jeanne Curran
Maine Style Editor Jeff Strout
News Editor Jim Emple
Outdoor Columnist Tom Hennessey
Political Editor Julie Murchison
Political Editor Rick Levasseur
Projects Editor Greg McManus
Projects Editor Wayne Reilly
Photography Editor Scott Haskell
Sports Editor Robert Haskell

MANAGEMENT INFORMATION SERVICES

Manager Carol A Raymond

PRODUCTION

Manager Donald D Darkis
Foreman-Composing Alston Wildes
Foreman-Pressroom Charles E Villard
Foreman-Mailroom Eric E Baron

Market Information: Zoned editions; Split Run; TMC.

Mechanical available: Flexography; Black and 3 ROP colors; insert accepted — preprinted, free-standing, single sheet, product samples; page cut-offs — 22".

Mechanical specifications: Type page 13" x 21"; E - 6 cols, 2", 1/8" between; A - 6 cols, 2 1/16", 1/8" between; C - 9 cols, 1 3/8", 1/8" between.

Commodity consumption: Newsprint 5,845 short tons; widths 54", 40½", 27"; black ink 212,600 pounds; color ink 9,483 pounds; single pages printed 12,516; average pages per issue 36(d), 64(wknd); single plates used 35,500.

Equipment: EDITORIAL: Front-end hardware — AT/7000; Front-end software — AT/7000 3.4; Printers — Brother/1709, NEC/97; Other equipment — PC/Bureau Dial-up Network. CLASSIFIED: Front-end hardware — AT/IAS; Front-end software — AT/IAS; Printers — Brother/1709. DISPLAY: Adv layout systems — IBM/AS-400, 6-Ap/Mac. PRODUCTION: Typesetters — 1-LaserMaster/1200, 2-Select-Set/5000, 2-Rapid, ECR/Autokon 1000, BYSO/Color Separation II; Plate exposures — 1-Na/Consolux, 1-Na/Newsprinter II; Plate processors — 2-Na/PP-1; Scanners — 1-SCREEN/DS-1030, 1-Arcus Plus; Production cameras — 1-C/Spartan III, 1-C/Newspager I; Automatic film processors — 1-Kodamatic/425, 1-C/R650, 1-Kk/710; Color separation equipment (conventional) — ECR/Autokon 1000, BYSO/Color Separation. PRESSROOM: Line 1 — 8-H/PEC; Folders — 1-H/3:2; Pasters — Automatic Pasters. MAILROOM: Counter stackers — 4-HL, 2-Id/4400; Inserters and stuffers — 1-HI/1472, 1-GMA/SLS 1000; Bundle tyer — 2-Power Strap/PSN5, 4-Power Strap/PSN6; Wrapping singles — 6-Monarch/Bottom wrap; Addressing machine — 1-KAN/Labeling System. LIBRARY: Electronic — Data Times, Nexis; Combination — Microfiche. COMMUNICATIONS: Digital ad delivery system — AP AdSend. WIRE SERVICES: News — AP, NYT, LAT-WP; Photos — AP Photostream; Stock tables — AP SelectStox I; Receiving dishes — size-3m, AP. BUSINESS COMPUTERS: IBM/AS-400; Applications: In-house: Adv, Circ, Gen ledger, Accts payable, Payroll; PCs & main system networked.

BIDDEFORD-SACO

York County

'90 U.S. Census- 35,891 (Biddeford 20,710; Saco 15,181); E&P '96 Est. 38,852 (Biddeford 21,576; Saco 17,276)
ABC-CZ (90): 35,891 (HH 13,934)

Journal Tribune

(e-mon to fri; m-sat)

Journal Tribune, PO Box 627, Biddeford, ME 04005; tel (207) 282-1535; fax (207) 282-3138; e-mail jtribune@biddeford.com. Alta Group Newspapers group.

Circulation: 12,702(e); 12,702(m-sat); ABC Sept. 30, 1995.

Price: 50¢(d); 75¢(sat); $111.80/yr (carrier), $160.00/yr (mail).

Advertising: Open inch rate $14.50(e); $14.50(m-sat). **Representative:** Landon Associates Inc.

News Service: AP. **Politics:** Independent. **Established:** 1884.

Not Published: New Year; Memorial Day; Independence Day; Labor Day; Christmas.

Advertising not accepted: 900 numbers; Offers requiring cash or prepayment of materials ordered.

Special Weekly Sections: Best Food Day (mon); TV Week, Bridal/Engagements/Anniversaries, Religion, Seniors, Books, Weekend Edition (sat); Business (daily).

Magazines: Best Food Day (tues); Weekend Edition (sat); Entertainment (daily).

GENERAL MANAGEMENT

Publisher Dennis J Flaherty
Purchasing Agent Chet Garron

ADVERTISING

Manager-National/Retail Donald Lauzier
Manager-Classified Kim Crepeau

MARKETING AND PROMOTION

Manager-Marketing/Promotion Frank De Francesco

CIRCULATION

Manager Charles Osbon Jr

NEWS EXECUTIVE

Managing Editor Robert Saunders

EDITORS AND MANAGERS

Business Editor Morris Mehlsak
City Editor Richard Buhr
Editorial Page Editor Gail Lemley
Sports Editor Karen Hanson

PRODUCTION

Manager Chet Garron
Supervisor-Composing Denise Dube

Market Information: Zoned editions; Split Run; TMC.

Mechanical available: Offset; Black and 3 ROP colors; insert accepted — preprinted; page cut-offs — 22¾".

Mechanical specifications: Type page 13" x 21½"; E - 6 cols, 2 1/16", 1/8" between; A - 6 cols, 2 1/16", 1/8" between; C - 9 cols, 1 3/8", 1/16" between.

Commodity consumption: Newsprint 780 short tons; widths 27", 13.5", 32", 16"; black ink 24,050 pounds; color ink 1,100 pounds; single pages printed 9,150; average pages per issue 28(d), 40(sat); single plates used 8,000.

Equipment: EDITORIAL: Front-end hardware — Ik/Minitek I, 1-Ap/Mac SE, 1-Ap/Mac IIcx. CLASSIFIED: Front-end hardware — Ik/Minitek I; Printers — NewGen/Turbo 600, Design Express lo, MicroLaser 600. DISPLAY: Adv layout systems — 5-Ap/Mac IIcx, 3-Ap/Mac SE, 1-NewGen/630, 1-NewGen/660, 2-Ap/Power Mac 6100, 1-Ap/Mac LC 520; Printers — 1-Ap/Mac, Micro Laser 600. PRODUCTION: Plate exposures — 2-Nu/Flip Top; Plate processors — 1-Nat/A-250; Scanners — Umax, Ap/Mac; Production cameras — 1-R/5000; Automatic film processors — 1-DAI, LD/260-L; Shrink lenses — 1-CK Optical/SQU-7; Color separation equipment (conventional) — Lf/Leafscan 35. PRESSROOM: Line 1 — 6-G/U-553; Folders — 1-G. MAILROOM: Inserters and stuffers — 1-MM/227; Bundle tyer — 2-Sa, 1-MLN; Addressing machine — 1-Ch/525E. WIRE SERVICES: News — AP; Photos — AP; Receiving dishes — size-10ft, AP. BUSINESS COMPUTERS: 1-TI/690; Applications: Payroll, Adv, Circ, Accts payable, Gen ledger; PCs & micros networked; PCs & main system networked.

BRUNSWICK

Cumberland County

'90 U.S. Census- 14,683; E&P '96 Est. 13,509
ABC- NDM (90): 41,167 (HH 15,374)

The Times Record

(e-mon to fri)

The Times Record, 6 Industry Rd.; PO Box 10, Brunswick, ME 04011-1302; tel (207) 729-3311; fax (207) 729-5728.

Circulation: 12,369(e); 14,908(e-fri); ABC Sept. 30, 1995.

Price: 50¢(d); 75¢(fri); $2.10/wk (jr. carrier), $2.25 (motor route); $98.30/yr (carrier), $124.70/yr (mail), $105.30/yr (motor route).

Advertising: Open inch rate $9.00(e); $9.00 (e-fri). **Representative:** Landon Associates Inc.

News Services: AP, NYT. **Politics:** Democrat. **Established:** 1967.

Not Published: New Year; Memorial Day; Independence Day; Labor Day; Thanksgiving; Christmas.

Special Editions: Money (Jan); Automotive (Feb); NIE (Mar); Home & Garden (Apr); Summer Lifestyles (May); Saltwater Fishing (July); Back-to-School (Aug); Home Improvement (Sept); Car Care, U.S. Navy (Oct); Holiday Gift Guide (Nov).

Special Weekly Sections: Sports Monday, Best Food Day (mon); Home & Family, Kids Tuesday, Milestones (Weddings & Engagements) (tues); Business (wed); Ticket, Sights & Sounds (thur); Living (fri).

Magazine: "What's On" TV Section (fri).

CORPORATE OFFICERS

President Campbell B Niven
Vice Pres/General Manager Daniel H Snow
Vice Pres/Controller Rick Guillerault
Vice Pres-Human Resources Phyllis A Thiboutot
Vice Pres/Asst Publisher Douglas M Niven

GENERAL MANAGEMENT

Publisher Campbell B Niven
Asst Publisher Douglas M Niven
General Manager Daniel H Snow
Controller Richard R Guillerault
Purchasing Agent Richard R Guillerault
Human Resources Phyllis A Thiboutot

ADVERTISING

Director John Bamford
Manager Jennifer Geiger

CIRCULATION

Manager George Reichert
Asst Manager Paula Cornelio

NEWS EXECUTIVE

Managing Editor Martin P McKenna

EDITORS AND MANAGERS

Amusements Editor Barbara Bartels
Arts/Entertainment Editor Barbara Bartels
Arts/Entertainment Editor Hilary Nangle
Automotive Editor Mark A Shankland
Business Editor James McCarthy
City Editor Bernie Monegain
Community Service Laura Mosqueda
Editorial Page Editor Mark A Shankland
Fashion/Style Editor Barbara Bartels
Feature Editor Hilary Nangle
Feature Editor Barbara Bartels
Librarian Laura Mosqueda
Living/Lifestyle Editor Hilary Nangle
News Editor James McCarthy
Photo Editor Gary Bonaccorso
Radio/Television Editor Hilary Nangle
Religion Editor William Cutlip
Science/Technology Editor James McCarthy
Sports Editor David Bourque
Travel Editor Barbara Bartels
Wire Editor James McCarthy

PRODUCTION

Manager-Pressroom/Post Press Carl DesRochers
Manager-Pre Press Herbert Thompson
Manager-Maintenance Scott Wight
Supervisor-Composing Room Peter Michaud
Systems Technician Michael Johnson

Market Information: TMC.

Mechanical available: Offset; Black and 2 ROP colors; insert accepted — preprinted; page cut-offs — 22¾".

Mechanical specifications: Type page 28" x 21½"; E - 6 cols, 2.08", 1/6" between; A - 6 cols, 2.08", 1/6" between; C - 8 cols, 1.57", 1/8" between.

Commodity consumption: Newsprint 850 short tons; width 28"; black ink 22,200 pounds; color ink 2,780 pounds; single pages printed 7,085; average pages per issue 28(d); single plates used 4,070.

Equipment: EDITORIAL: Front-end hardware — Ap/Mac; Front-end software — Xenotron/7600 Editorial-Classified, Baseview/Server IQue; Printers — 2-HP/4MV, 2-Compaq/PageMarq, 1-MON; Other equipment — 2-Linotype-Hell/L530 ImageSetter w/RIP50. CLASSIFIED: Front-end hardware — Ap/Mac; Front-end software — Xenotron/7600 Classified, Caere/OmniPage Plus, Baseview. DISPLAY: Adv layout systems — Ap/Mac w/QuarkXPress; Front-end hardware — Sun, Ap/Mac; Front-end software — QuarkXPress; Printers — MON/Imagemaster 1200, Compaq/PageMarq 20, 2-Linotype-Hell/L530 Imagesetter w/RIP50; Other equipment — ECR/Autokon 1000, Desktop/Scanner. PRODUCTION: Pagination software — QuarkXPress 3.31; OCR software — Caere/OmniPage; Typesetters — 2-L/530; Plate exposures — 1-Nu; Plate processors — Nat; Electronic picture desk — 2-Lf/AP Leaf Picture Desk; Scanners — ECR/Autokon 1000, AG/Arcus Scanner, 1-Ap/Mac; Production cameras — C/Spartan III; Automatic film processors — LE/LD 1800, LE/PC 1800, LE/Excel 26; Color separation equipment (conventional) — ECR/Autokon, 4-Digi-Colour; Digital color separation equipment — Lf/Leafscan 35, Adobe/Photoshop. PRESSROOM: Line 1 — G/Community (2-4HI, 1-2HI); Line 2 — G/Community (6, 1 VOP); Pasters — 3-Enkel/"O"Spud. MAILROOM: Counter stackers — 1-PPK/Ministack, 1-PPK/Novas; Inserters and stuffers — 1-MM/227E; Bundle tyer — 2-Strapex/330, 1-EAM/Mosca Rom; Addressing machine — 1-Ch/539, KR/512. WIRE SERVICES: Receiving dishes — size-3m. BUSINESS COMPUTERS: Sun/4-110; Applications: Vision Data; PCs & micros networked; PCs & main system networked.

LEWISTON-AUBURN

Androscoggin County

'90 U.S. Census- 64,066 (Lewiston 39,757; Auburn 24,309); E&P '96 Est. 64,481 (Lewiston 39,236; Auburn 25,245)
ABC-CZ (90): 64,066 (HH 25,370)

Sun-Journal (m-mon to sat)
Sunday Sun-Journal (S)

Sun-Journal, 104 Park St.; PO Box 4400, Lewiston, ME 04240; tel (207) 784-5411; fax (207) 777-3436.

Circulation: 41,551(m); 41,551(m-sat); 44,889(S); ABC Sept. 30, 1995.

Price: 50¢(d); 50¢(sat); $1.00(S); $2.95/wk; $153.39/yr (carrier), $222.00/yr (mail).

Advertising: Open inch rate $32.19(m); $32.19(m-sat); $32.19(S). **Representative:** Landon Associates Inc.

News Services: AP, CSM, KRT. **Politics:** Independent. **Established:** 1893 (Sun), 1861 (Journal), 1983 (Sun-Journal).

Not Published: Christmas.

Special Editions: Bundles of Joy (Jan); Annual

Review, Social Security, Washington's Birthday (Feb); Bridal, Fishing & Boating, Home Show (Mar); Home Improvement, Car Care, Tasty Take Out (Apr); Landscaping & Gardening, Summer in Maine, Police, Graduation (May); Vacationland Dining, True Value 250 (June); Agricultural Festival (July); Welcome to Lewiston-Auburn, Working Parents (Aug); Fall Sports, Hunting in Maine, Bridal (Sept); Fall Home Improvement, Fall Car Care, Cookbook (Oct); Ski (Nov); Holiday Gift Guide, Winter Recreation, Winter Sports, Christmas Greetings, Business Review (Dec).

Special Weekly Sections: Spotlight, Economy/Business, Travel (S); Advocate (daily).

Magazines: TV Preview (local, newsprint), Color Comics (S).

CORPORATE OFFICER

Treasurer Edward M Snook

GENERAL MANAGEMENT

Publisher/General Manager James R Costello Sr
Controller James A Thornton

ADVERTISING

Manager-Marketing Stephen M Costello
Manager-Classified Marianne Ireland
Manager-Retail Sales Stephen M Costello

MARKETING AND PROMOTION

Manager-Marketing Stephen M Costello

CIRCULATION

Director Robert T Snyder

NEWS EXECUTIVES

Exec Editor Thomas E Kelsch
Asst Exec Editor David Ehrenfried
Managing Editor Greg LaFreniere
Managing Editor-Graphics Heather McCarthy

EDITORS AND MANAGERS

Action Line Editor Tim McCloskey
Advocate Editor Linda Galway
Assignment Editor Mark Mogensen
Automotive Editor Susan Bean
Business/Finance Editor Lisa Giguere
City Editor Wendy Watkins
Chief Editorial Writer Mary Lynn Kelsch
Community News Ben Stackhouse
Editorial Page Editor Ben Stackhouse
Education Editor Mary Lou Wendell
Entertainment/Amusements Editor Polly Ouimet
Farm/Agriculture Editor Susan Bean
Fashion/Style Editor Susan Bean
Features Editor Ursula Albert
Films/Theater Editor Susan Bean
Graphics Editor/Art Director Heather McCarthy
Health/Medical Editor Leal BailairGeon
Living Page Editor Ursula Albert
Music Editor Polly Ouimet
National Editor Heather McCarthy
Photo Editor Russel Dillingham
Political/Government Editor Ben Stackhouse
Society Editor Sue Littlefield
Special Section Editor Susan Bean
Sports Editor Doug Clawson
Television Editor Polly Quimet
Travel Editor Ursula Albert

MANAGEMENT INFORMATION SERVICES

Data Processing Manager Gisele Lamontagne

PRODUCTION

Manager-Press James R Costello Jr
Manager-Pre Press David Costello
Foreman-Mailroom Robert McCarthy

Market Information: Zoned editions; ADS.

Mechanical available: Offset; Black and 3 ROP colors; insert accepted — preprinted; page cutoffs — $22\frac{3}{4}$".

Mechanical specifications: Type page 13" x 21"; E - 6 cols, $2\frac{1}{16}$", 1/8" between; A - 6 cols, $2\frac{1}{16}$", 1/8" between; C - 9 cols, $1\frac{3}{8}$", 1/16" between.

Commodity consumption: Newsprint 4,500 short tons; width $27\frac{1}{4}$"; black ink 76,000 pounds; color ink 10,000 pounds; average pages per issue 102(S); single plates used 36,500.

Equipment: EDITORIAL: Front-end hardware — 1-HAS/HS-55, 1-PC/Server, 13-HAS, 33-PC, 3-Ap/Mac; Front-end software — CD/TOPS 2.5, Novell 3.11, QuarkXPress, XYQUEST/XyWrite III; Printers — 1-Hyphen/11x17, Ap/Mac LaserWriter Plus, 1-NewGen, 1-XIT/Schooner; Other equipment — Ap/Mac Plus Agaton Scanner, CD. CLASSIFIED: Front-end hardware — 1-HAS/2330, 1-HAS/HS-55, 3-IBM, 11-HAS; Front-end software — CD/TOPS 2.5; Other equipment — 7-IBM/Selectric. DISPLAY: Adv layout systems — 8-PC, 2-IBM/PC, AT; Front-end hardware — 8-PC; Front-end software — Archetype/Designer, XYQUEST/XyWrite III, Archetype/Corel Draw; Printers — 1-XIT/Clipper. PRODUCTION: Plate exposures — 1-Nu/Flip Top FT40UPNS, 1-Nu/Flip Top FT40L, Nu/Flip Top FT40APRNS, Nu/Flip Top; Plate processors — 1-Na/A340; Scanners — ECR/Autokon 1000, AG/RPS 20x24, 1-CD/625E Scanner; Production cameras — 1-R/481, 1-R/432; Automatic film processors — 1-LE/LD 24AQ, AG/660 Rapid Access, C/Rapid Access; Shrink lenses — 1-CK Optical/SQU-7; Color separation equipment (conventional) — 1-C/Color Enlarger. PRESSROOM: Line 1 — 10-G/Urbanite 1283; Press drives — Fin; Folders — G, 1-G/2:1. MAILROOM: Counter stackers — 2-QWI/SJ200; Inserters and stuffers — 1-HI/1372; Bundle tyer — 1-MLN, 2-AHS, 1-MLN/MLIEE, 1-MLN/Spirit. WIRE SERVICES: News — AP Datastream, AP Datafeatures, AP Laserphoto, AP SelectStox I, AP GraphicsNet; Photos — AP; Stock tables — AP Datastream, AP SelectStox I; Syndicates — AP Datafeatures; Receiving dishes — AP. BUSINESS COMPUTERS: 2-IBM/Sys 36; Applications: Accts payable, Payroll, Gen ledger, Accts receivable, Circ; PCs & main system networked.

PORTLAND

Cumberland County

'90 U.S. Census- 64,358; **E&P '96 Est.** 66,427
ABC-CZ (90): 119,015 (HH 49,715)

Portland Press Herald (m-mon to sat)
Maine Sunday Telegram (S)

Portland Press Herald, 390 Congress St. (04101); PO Box 1460, Portland, ME 04112-5277; tel (207) 791-6650; fax (207) 791-6913; e-mail herald@biddford.com; web site http://www.portland.net/ph. Guy Gannett Communications group.

Circulation: 77,631(m); 77,631(m-sat); 143,409(S); ABC Sept. 30, 1995.

Price: 50¢(d); 50¢(sat); $1.50(S); $4.10/wk.

Advertising: Open inch rate $54.94(m); $54.94(m-sat); $77.98(S); $106.89(m & S). **Representative:** Landon Associates Inc.

News Services: AP, NYT, LAT-WP. **Politics:** Independent. **Established:** 1862 (Press Herald).

Special Editions: Brides, Senior Living (Jan); Health Resources, Vacationland, President's Day Auto, Explore York County (Feb); American Lung, Explore Greater Portland, NIE (Mar); Seniority, Summer Camp, Home & Garden, Spring Home Show (Apr); Insurance, Health Resources, Vacationland (May); Vacationland, South Coast Visitor's Guide, White Mountain Visitor's Guide (June); Vacationland (July); Careers, Back-to-School (Aug); Fall Home Improvement, Vacationland, Mt. Washington Valley Visitor's Guide (Sept); Health Resources, New Car Guide, Winter Warmth (Oct); Winter Recreation, Holiday Shopping Guide, Seniority (Nov); Winter Sports, Mt. Washington Visitor's Guide, White Mountain Visitor's Guide (Dec).

Special Weekly Sections: Food & Health (mon); Business (tues); Style (wed); Go (thur); Real Estate, Wheels (fri); Religion (sat); Home & Family, Maine/New England, Travel, Insight (S).

Magazines: GO (entertainment & recreation planner) (thur); TV Week, Audience, Comics (S); Parade.

Broadcast Affiliates: WGME.

GENERAL MANAGEMENT

President Bruce J Gensmer
Chief Financial Officer Thomas A Pellegriti
Vice Pres-Operations Robert R Rowell
Vice Pres-Marketing Angus H Twombly
Vice Pres/Editor Louis A Ureneck
Director-Human Resources Grace Noonan-Kaye
Director-Labor Relations Maryann Kelly

ADVERTISING

Director Gary R Gagne
Co-Director Amanda Schumaker
Manager-Operations Carl A Johnson
Manager-Group Sales Timothy J Hooper
Manager-Group Sales James S McNeil
Manager-Group Sales Lee Hews
Manager-Group Sales Carol Jordon
Manager-Group Sales Janet Ketchum

MARKETING AND PROMOTION

Director-Research & Market Info Rodd Wagner
Manager-Non-Subscriber Operations William S Plumley
Manager-Marketing & Communications Monique Spina

CIRCULATION

Director Peter O Starren
Asst Director-Home Delivery Timothy J Crilley
Asst Director-Single Copy Ed Beck
Customer Service & Info Manager Jodie Krueger

NEWS EXECUTIVES

Vice Pres/Editor Louis A Ureneck
Managing Editor-Reporting Jeannine Guttman
Asst Managing Editor/Reporter Thomas Ferriter
Asst Managing Editor-Sports David McNabb

EDITORS AND MANAGERS

Arts/Books Editor Jane P Lord
Business Editor John Gormley
City Editor-Night Steve Greenlee
Copy Desk Chief Robert J Dixon
Design Editor Andrea Philbrick
Editorial Page Editor George Neavoll
Entertainment/Amusements Editor Jane P Lord
Environment Editor Dieter Bradbury
Fashion/Style Editor Jane P Lord
Features Editor Jane P Lord
Graphics Editor Rick Wakely
Living/Lifestyle Editor Jane P Lord
Metro Editor Jeff Ham
Music Editor Jane P Lord
Exec News Editor Curt Hazlett
Online Editor Joseph A Michaud
Radio/Television Editor Jane P Lord
Manager-Reader Service Marcia MacVane
Sports Editor Operations Steve Dandy
Travel Editor Tom Atwell

MANAGEMENT INFORMATION SERVICES

Online Manager Marcia MacVane
Data Processing Manager-Software Bill Ridden
Data Processing Manager-Hardware Ray Lewis

PRODUCTION

Advertising Operations Manager James Sanville
Operations Manager-Printing & Distribution Paul Brawn
Operations Manager-Technical Service/Plant Maintenance Michael Laberge
Operations Manager-Facilities (390 Congress St) Amory Houghton
Operations Manager-Distribution (South Portland) David Miller
Operations Manager-Distribution (South Portland) Dennis Rockwell
Operations Supervisor-Control Point Louise Cliche
Operations Supervisor-Advertising Graphics Elizabeth Torraca
Operations Camera Supervisor-Days Frederick Clancy
Operations Camera Supervisor-Nights Charles Butler
Operations Supervisor-Pressroom/Platemaking Mark Bragdon
Operations Supervisor-Pressroom/Platemaking Keith Toothaker
Operations Page Build Supervisor-Days Philip Noyes
Operations Page Build Supervisor-Nights Daniel Presby
Operations Ad Build Supervisor-Days Wayne Bailey Sr
Operations Page Ad Build Supervisor-Nights Gerald Vaillancourt

Market Information: Zoned editions; Split Run; TMC; ADS; Operate database; Electronic edition.

Mechanical available: Flexographic; Black and 3 ROP colors; insert accepted — preprinted, all; page cut-offs — 22".

Mechanical specifications: Type page 13" x $21\frac{1}{8}$"; E - 6 cols, $2\frac{1}{16}$", 1/8" between; A - 6 cols, $2\frac{1}{16}$", 1/8" between; C - 9 cols, $1\frac{3}{8}$", 1/16" between.

Commodity consumption: Newsprint 11,000 short tons; widths 54", 40.50", 26.78"; black ink 336,000 pounds; color ink 132,000 pounds; single pages printed 25,000; average pages per issue 44(d), 124(S); single plates used 90,000.

Equipment: EDITORIAL: Front-end hardware — CD, 12-RSK/100, 90-Mk/Edit 112B, 15-PC; Front-end software — CD; Printers — 5-DEC/LA 210; Other equipment — 6-Ap/Mac. CLASSIFIED: Front-end hardware — CD, 38-Mk/Edit 112B; Front-end software — CD; Printers — 5-NEC, 2-LP/25. DISPLAY: Adv layout systems — SCS/Layout 8000; Front-end hardware — 8-HI/8300; Front-end software — HI/8300; Other equipment — 1-RZ/210L, 1-ECR/1000, 2-Hel/Pressfax. PRODUCTION: Typesetters — Tegra/Varityper/XM108, AU/3850T; Platemaking systems — 1-Hercules/Merigraph, Na; Plate exposures — 2-He, 1-Consulux; Plate processors — 2-He, KFM/Model 100 P.T.B., 1-Na/Flex Processor Unit; Electronic picture desk — Lf/AP Leaf Picture Desk; Scanners — ECR, 2-HP/3C, 1-Kk/2035; Production cameras — 1-C/Spartan III, 1-C/Newspager II, 1-Co; Automatic film processors — 1-P/Super G, 1-P/PakoQuick, 1-Co, 1-DP, 1-GJ/Online, 1-LE/MTP26; Film transporters — 1-C/Spartan III, 1-C/Newspager II; Digital color separation equipment — RZ/210L. PRESSROOM: Line 1 — 6-G/Flexoliner; Line 2 — 6-G/Flexoliner; Press drives — Allen Bradley; Folders — 2-G/160 Page Sovereign, G/Double Delivery; Pasters — 12-G/CT 50; Press control system — Allen Bradley. MAILROOM: Counter stackers — 6-HL/HT2, QWI; Inserters and stuffers — 1-HI/2299, 1-HI/1372; Bundle tyer — 10-OVL/JP40, 2-MLN, 1-Dynaric; Addressing machine — IBM/Computer Product; Mailroom control system — HL/Dock console. LIBRARY: Combination — Vu/Text Save, Vu/Text Lektriever for clippings. COMMUNICATIONS: Facsimile — HEL/Press Fax; Digital ad delivery system — AdSat. Systems used — satellite. WIRE SERVICES: News — AP; Photos — AP; Stock tables — AP; Syndicates — AP; Receiving dishes — size-2.8ft. BUSINESS COMPUTERS: IBM/4381; Applications: Microsoft/Office 4.3: Acctg; Great Plains Dynamics C/S, Microsoft/Office 4.3: Circ; PCs & micros networked; PCs & main system networked.

SACO

See BIDDEFORD

WATERVILLE

Kennebec County

'90 U.S. Census- 17,173; **E&P '96 Est.** 16,710
ABC-CZ (90): 25,403 (HH 9,942)

Central Maine Morning Sentinel (m-mon to sat)
Sunday Sentinel (S)

Central Maine Morning Sentinel, 25 Silver St., Waterville, ME 04901; tel (207) 873-3341; fax (207) 873-3341. Guy Gannett Communications group.

Circulation: 23,658(m); 23,658(m-sat); 19,568(S); ABC Sept. 30, 1995.

Price: 50¢(d); 50¢(sat); $1.25(S); $3.00/wk; $148.00/yr (carrier), $168.00/yr (mail).

Advertising: Open inch rate $21.44(m); $21.44(m-sat); $22.51(S). **Representative:** Landon Associates Inc.

News Service: AP. **Politics:** Independent. **Established:** 1904.

Note: On Apr. 2, 1995, the Central Maine Morning Sentinel started publishing on Sunday.

Not Published: Christmas.

Special Editions: Baby, Tax Time (Jan); Bridal (Feb); Progress, Outdoor (Mar); Real Estate, Home and Garden (Apr); Spring Car Care, Summer in Maine (May); Home Design, Family Business (June); Artfest (July); Football (Aug); Interior-Exterior, Hunting (Sept); Fall Automotive, Nat'l. Home Week, Women in Business (Oct); Winter Lifestyles, Holiday Cookbook, Thanksgiving (Nov); Christmas Gifts, Basketball/Hockey (Dec).

Special Weekly Sections: What's Happening (entertainment) (fri); What's on TV (S).

GENERAL MANAGEMENT

President/Central Maine Newspapers Michael J Sexton
Business Manager Gary Zemrak
Director-Human Resources Nancy Manes

ADVERTISING

Director Molly Evans
Manager-Retail David Cousins
Manager-Classified Susan Colfer

MARKETING AND PROMOTION

Manager-Marketing/Promotion Cindy Stevens

CIRCULATION

Director Bruce Bourgoine

NEWS EXECUTIVES

Exec Editor Warren Watson
Asst Managing Editor-News Ann McGowan
Asst Managing Editor-Operations Glenn Turner

EDITORS AND MANAGERS

Columnist C Clayton LaVerdiere
Columnist Gerard Boyle
Editorial Writer Gerard Boyle
Editorial Director Davis Rawson
Fashion/Food Editor Darlene T Sanborn
News Editor Thomas Lizotte
Photo Department Manager Ronald Maxwell
Sports Editor Larry Grand
Wire Edition Editor Philip Norvish
Women's Editor Lynn Ascrizzi

MANAGEMENT INFORMATION SERVICES

Data Processing Manager Christine Solloway

Copyright ©1996 by the Editor & Publisher Co.

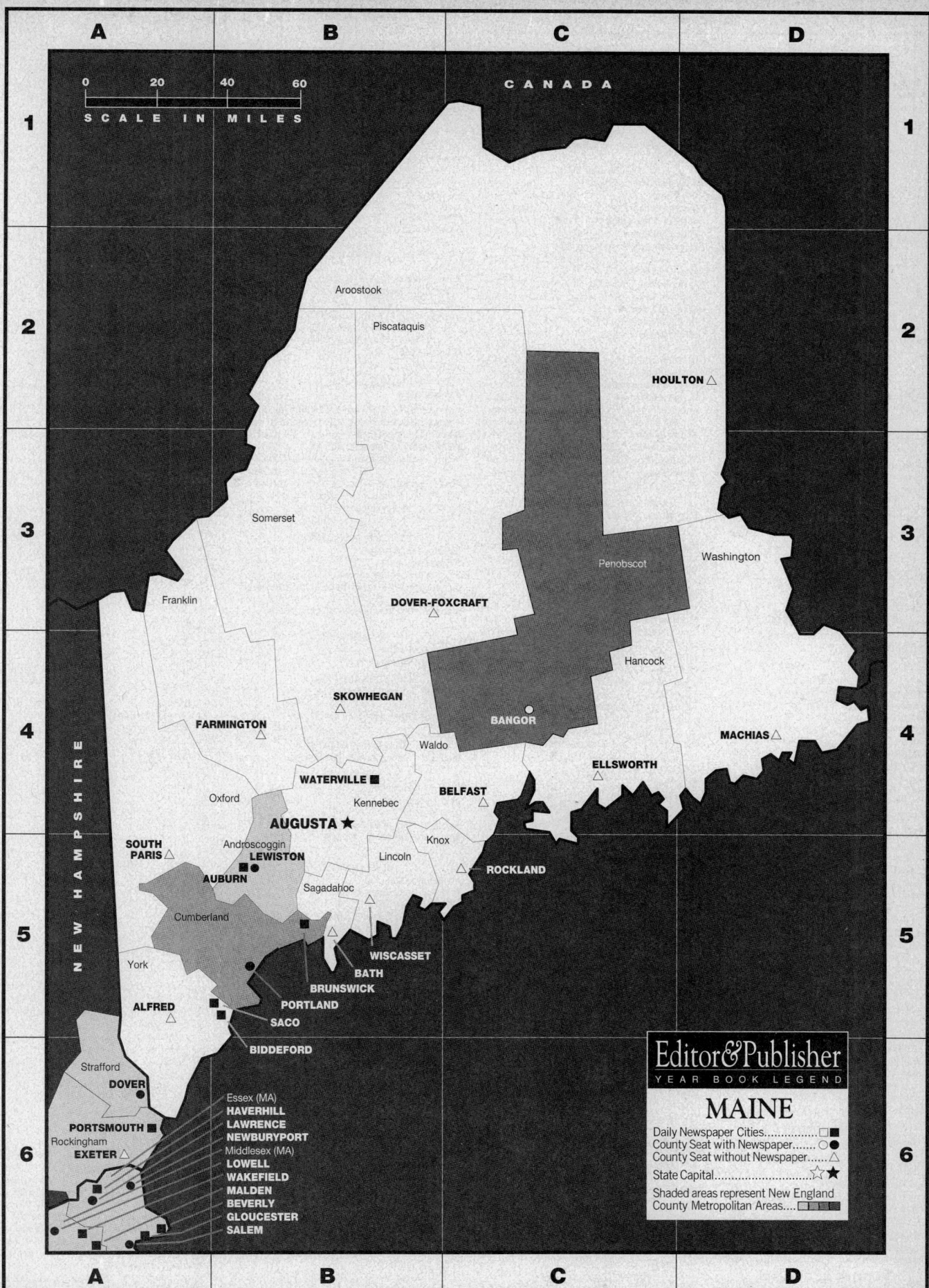

I-180 Maine

PRODUCTION
Director — John L Maxwell
Foreman-Night Composing — Jack Merrill
Supervisor-Pressroom — Steve Rote

Market Information: Zoned editions; Split Run; TMC.
Mechanical available: Offset; Black and 3 ROP colors; insert accepted — preprinted; page cut-offs — 22¾".
Mechanical specifications: Type page 13" x 21½"; E - 6 cols, 2¹⁄₃₂", ⁵⁄₃₂" between; A - 6 cols, 2¹⁄₃₂", ⁵⁄₃₂" between; C - 9 cols, 1⁵⁄₁₆", ¹⁄₁₆" between.
Commodity consumption: Newsprint 1,774 short tons; widths 27.5", 13.75"; black ink 46,087 pounds; color ink 6,350 pounds; single pages printed 10,851; average pages per issue 32(d); single plates used 35,000.
Equipment: EDITORIAL: Front-end hardware — 3-Dell; Front-end software — SCS; Printers — HP/Laser Printers. CLASSIFIED: Front-end software — SCS. DISPLAY: Adv layout systems — 4-Ap/Mac IIcx; Front-end hardware — 3-Dell; Front-end software — SCS; Printers — HP, C.Itoh; Other equipment — Ap/Mac PowerBooks. COMMUNICATIONS: Facsimile — 4-Ricoh/20E; Remote imagesetting — AP/(via telephone lines). WIRE SERVICES: News — AP; Photos — AP; Stock tables — AP; Receiving dishes — size-3m, AP. BUSINESS COMPUTERS: Dell/486; Applications: Microsoft/Excel, Microsoft/Word: Circ, Adv, Billing, Payroll, Gen ledger; PCs & micros networked; PCs & main system networked.

MARYLAND

ANNAPOLIS
Anne Arundel County
'90 U.S. Census- 33,187; E&P '96 Est. 34,507
ABC-CZ (90): 67,407 (HH 24,572)

The Capital (e-mon to sat; S)
The Capital, 2000 Capital Dr.; PO Box 911, Annapolis, MD 21404; tel (410) 268-5000; fax (410) 268-4643; web site http://www.infi.net/capital/.
Circulation: 47,225(e); 47,225(e-sat); 49,114(S); ABC Sept. 30, 1995.
Price: 35¢(d); 35¢(sat); 75¢(S); $2.50/wk; $121.50/yr.
Advertising: Open inch rate $45.94(e); $45.94(e-sat); $45.94(S). **Representative:** Landon Associates Inc.
News Service: AP. **Politics:** Independent. **Established:** 1884.
Not Published: New Year; Memorial Day; Independence Day; Labor Day; Christmas (unless holiday falls on a Sunday).
Advertising not accepted: Cash investment ads; 900 numbers.
Special Editions: Bridal Tab, Newcomer, Recruitment (Jan); Boating, Home & Garden (Apr); Real Estate (May); Football (Aug); Home & Garden (Sept); Real Estate (Oct); Menu (Nov); Gift Guide (Dec).
Special Weekly Sections: Arundel Report, Sports (mon); Commercial, Industrial & Business Real Estate, Sports (tues); Food, Sports (wed); Living, Home & Real Estate, Sports (thur); Annapolis, Entertainment Guide, Sports (fri); Sports, Religion, Stock Home & Real Estate (sat); Commercial, Industrial & Business Real Estate, Boating Marketplace, Lifestyle, Sports, TV Week (S).
Magazine: Entertainment Guide (Tab).

CORPORATE OFFICER
President/Publisher — Philip Merrill
GENERAL MANAGEMENT
Assoc Publisher — Eleanor Merrill
Chief Financial Officer — James Brown
Business Manager — George R Cruze Jr
Director-Technology — Fred P Glennie
ADVERTISING
Director — Bernard C Hoff III
Manager-Classified — Kimberly Welty
Manager-Retail — Sue Murphy
MARKETING AND PROMOTION
Manager-Promotion — Austin Bachmann

TELECOMMUNICATIONS
Audiotex Manager — Brian Henley
CIRCULATION
Director — John R Bieberich
NEWS EXECUTIVES
Exec Editor — Edward D Casey
Managing Editor — Tom Marquardt
EDITORS AND MANAGERS
Business/Finance Editor — Rick Hutzell
City Editor — Stuart Samuels
City Government Editor — Bart Jansen
Editorial Page Editor — Gerald Fischman
Education Editor — Leslie Gross
Entertainment/Amusements Editor — Kathy Edwards
Environment Editor — Chris Munsey
Fashion/Style Editor — Kathy Edwards
Features Editor — Kathy Edwards
Graphics Editor — Brian Henley
Health/Medical Editor — Mary Ellen Lloyd
Living/Lifestyle Editor — Kathy Edwards
News Editor — Loretta Haring
National Editor — Jay Votel
Photo Editor — Brian Henley
Political/Government Editor — Stu Samuels
Religion Editor — Fran Jaques
Science/Technology Editor — Kathy Edwards
Society Editor — Mary Felter
Sports Editor — Joe Gross
Television/Film Editor — Elayne Hopkins
Theater/Music Editor — Elayne Hopkins
Travel Editor — Kathy Edwards
Women's Editor — Mary Felter
MANAGEMENT INFORMATION SERVICES
Data Processing Manager — Gary Choulis
PRODUCTION
Director-Operations — Richard P Murchake
Manager — James Murchake
Superintendent-Pressroom — Bill Hope

Market Information: Operate audiotex; Electronic edition.
Mechanical available: Offset; Black and 3 ROP colors; insert accepted — preprinted; page cut-offs — 22".
Mechanical specifications: Type page 13" x 21"; E - 6 cols, 2¹⁄₁₆", ¹⁄₈" between; A - 6 cols, 2¹⁄₁₆", ¹⁄₈" between; C - 9 cols, 1³⁄₈", ¹⁄₁₆" between.
Commodity consumption: Newsprint 6,800 short tons; widths 54", 40¾", 27"; black ink 21,000 pounds, color ink 5,250 pounds; single pages printed 33,460; average pages per issue 40(d), 52(sat), 84(S); single plates used 82,000.
Equipment: EDITORIAL: Front-end hardware — 86-DEC/VAX 6000; Front-end software — Cybergraphics; Printers — 4-Panasonic/2624; Other equipment — 1-HP/ScanJet. CLASSIFIED: Front-end hardware — 35-DEC/VAX 6000 Terminals; Front-end software — Cybergraphics; Printers — 2-Panasonic/2624, 2-TI/850. DISPLAY: Adv layout systems — SCS/Layout 8000; Front-end hardware — DEC/VAX 6000; Front-end software — Cybergraphics from Ap/Mac w/Multi-Ad; Printers — 4-HP/LaserJet IV. PRODUCTION: Pagination software — Cybergraphics; Typesetters — 3-III/3850; Plate exposures — 2-Nu/631; Plate processors — Cookson Graphics/Subtractive; Electronic picture desk — 2-Kk/RFS 2035; Scanners — 2-ECR/Autokon 1000, 1-ECR/Autokon 2040, 4-AG/Argus II; Production cameras — 1-C/Spartan III; Automatic film processors — 3-Glunz & Jensen, 1-AG; Film transporters — 1-LE; Shrink lenses — 1-CK Optical; Color separation equipment (conventional) — RZ/200S; Digital color separation equipment — 4-AG/Arcus II.
PRESSROOM: Line 1 — 5-G/Headliner Offset double width (3 color decks); Folders — 3-G/2:1; Pasters — 5-G/RTP. MAILROOM: Counter stackers — 4-RKW, 1-HL; Inserters and stuffers — 1-HI/1372; Bundle tyer — 4-MLN/2A; Addressing machine — 2-KR/15W-211 Head. LIBRARY: Electronic — Mead Data Central/Nexis NewsView. COMMUNICATIONS: Digital ad delivery system — AP AdSend, Imagenet. WIRE SERVICES: News — AP; Photos — AP; Stock tables — AP; Receiving dishes — AP. BUSINESS COMPUTERS: 2-DEC/VAX 6000; Applications: Data Sciences: Circ; Neasi Weber Ad Marc: Accts receivable; Mcba: Payroll, Accts payable, Gen ledger; PCs & micros networked; PCs & main system networked.

BALTIMORE
An Independent City
'90 U.S. Census- 736,014; E&P '96 Est. 720,642
ABC-NDM (90): 2,348,219 (HH 867,656)

The Sun (m-mon to fri; m-sat)
The Sunday Sun (S)
The Sun, 501 N. Calvert St., Baltimore, MD 21278; tel (410) 332-6000; fax (410) 783-2583; e-mail baltsun@clark.net; web site http://www.sunstore.com/sunsource/. Times Mirror Co. group.
Circulation: 339,493(m); 367,189(m-sat); 486,844(S); ABC Sept. 30, 1995.
Price: 50¢(d); 50¢(sat); $1.50(S).
Advertising: Open inch rate $210.70(m); $206.70(m-sat); $237.10(S). **Representative:** Cresmer, Woodward, O'Mara & Ormsbee.
News Services: AP, RN, KRT, NYT, DJ, LAT-WP, INS. **Politics:** Independent. **Established:** 1837.
Note: Effective Sept. 15, 1995, the Evening Sun (e-mon to fri) ceased publication.
Advertising not accepted: Upon review.
Magazines: Sun Magazine (local roto); TV Week, Parade Magazine (S).

CORPORATE OFFICERS
Publisher/CEO — Mary Junck
President/CEO-Baltimore Community Newspapers/Homestead Publ. Co. — John Patinella
Senior Vice Pres/Editor — John Carroll
Vice Pres/Chief Financial Officer — Jean Halle
Vice Pres/Director-Marketing/Communications — Regina Swearingen
Vice Pres/Director-Sales — Hilary Schneider
Vice Pres-Circulation — Robert T O'Sullivan
Vice Pres-Employee/Labor Relations — Howard G Weinstein
GENERAL MANAGEMENT
Director-Purchasing — Robert Amos
Purchasing Agent — Paula Haas
Director-Human Resources — Barbara Jones
Director-New Business Development/Business Manager — Karen Stabley
Manager-New Business Development/Sales — Scott Miller
ADVERTISING
Manager-Division — Jack Ross
Manager-Division — S Dwight Hanna
MARKETING AND PROMOTION
Manager-Communication/Research — Michael Shultz
Manager-Product & Sales Development — Miriam Tillman
TELECOMMUNICATIONS
Manager-Telecommunications — Michael Thomas
CIRCULATION
Director-Distribution — Bruce McEntee
Asst Director — J Mike Hughes
Asst Director — W Scott Moores
Manager-Packaging Operations — Jack Conaboy
Manager-Fleet Distributions Operations — Richard Donati
NEWS EXECUTIVES
Managing Editor — William Marimow
Asst Managing Editor-Graphics — Joseph Hutchinson
Asst Managing Editor-Metro — Gilbert L Watson III
Asst Managing Editor-Projects — Rebecca Corbett
Asst Managing Editor-Features — Steve Proctor
Asst Managing Editor-News — Tony Barbieri
Asst Managing Editor-Sports — Jack Gibbons
EDITORS AND MANAGERS
Administrative Editor — Edward D Hewitt
Administrative Editor — Thomas Linthicum Jr
Book Editor — Michael Packenham
Business Editor — Gerald Merrell
Columnist-Features — Alice Steinbach
Columnist-Features — Kevin Cowherd
Columnist-Features — Mike Littwin
Columnist-Features — Susan Reimer
Columnist-Local — Gregory Kane
Columnist-Local — Daniel Rodricks
Columnist-Local — Michael Olesker
Columnist-Political — Bill Zorzi
Editorial Cartoonist — Kevin Kallaugher
Editorial Cartoonist — Michael J Lane
Education Editor — Bill Salganik
Editorial Page Editor — Joseph RL Sterne
Editorial Page Director — Barry Rascovar
Editorial Page Director — Sara Engram
Editor-Baltimore City Sun — Jim Asher
Editor-Arundel Sun — Candy Thomson
Editor-Harford Sun — Bill McCauley
Editor-Baltimore County Sun — David Rosenthal
Editor-Carroll Sun — Chris Guy
Editor-Howard Sun — Robert Benjamin
Fashion Editor — Vida Roberts

Features Editor — Kim Marcum
Director-Electronic News/Info Service — Lisa LoVullo
National Editor — Lee Horwich
Perspective Editor — Michael Adams
Washington Bureau Chief — Paul West
MANAGEMENT INFORMATION SERVICES
Director-Info Systems — Donald P Ruthig
PRODUCTION
Director — Robert M Crocco
Manager-Pre Press Operations — Francis X Przybylek
Manager-Press Operations — Edwin Foard III
Manager-Graphics — Shelley Cuffee
Manager-Sun Park — John Hallameyer

Market Information: Zoned editions; TMC; Operate audiotex; Electronic edition.
Mechanical available: Offset; Black and 3 ROP colors; insert accepted — preprinted, all; page cut-offs — 22".
Mechanical specifications: Type page 13" x 21⅛"; E - 6 cols, 2¹⁄₁₆", ¹⁄₈" between; A - 6 cols, 2¹⁄₁₆", ¹⁄₈" between; C - 10 cols, 1³⁄₁₆", ¹⁄₈" between.
Commodity consumption: Newsprint 72,215 metric tons; width 54¾"; black ink 1,372,000 pounds; color ink 300,000 pounds; single pages printed 43,662; average pages per issue 68(d), 170(S); single plates used 624,000.
Equipment: EDITORIAL: Front-end hardware — SII/Sys 55 6TXP, 191-SII/Coyote QB, 6-Dakota/XW, 26-SII/Coyote 22, 4-SII/Coyote 15, 7-SII/Coyote R, 7-Dakota/R; Front-end software — SII/Editorial Sys; Printers — 4-MON; Other equipment — 4-CD/Electronic Darkroom, RSK/TRS-100, 40-RSK/TRS-200, RZ, 50-Gateway/Handbook, 30-Ap/Mac. CLASSIFIED: Front-end hardware — SII/Sys 55, 4-TNS/II 3TXP, 96-SII/Coyote; Other equipment — 1-TDD/TYY C-Phone 1-A. AUDIOTEX: Hardware — Brite Voice Systems, Audiofax; Supplier name — AP, DI, Voice Info, Accu-Weather. DISPLAY: Adv layout systems — SCS/Layout 8000, SII/Coyote; Front-end hardware — 3-PC; Front-end software — SCS/Layout 8000. PRODUCTION: Typesetters — 4-III/3850, 2-Linotype-Hell/Linotronic 530; Platemaking systems — 3-WL/10, 1-WL/3; Plate exposures — 2-Roconex; Plate processors — 4-AG/650; Electronic picture desk — Lf/AP Leaf Picture Desk; Scanners — Cd/Magnascan 6451E Eskofot; Production cameras — 1-C/Pager II, 1-C/Spartan III; Automatic film processors — 6-LE/LS2600, 2-AG/650; Color separation equipment (conventional) — CD/Studio 9500. PRESSROOM: Line 1 — 12-G/Colorliner; Line 2 — 12-G/Colorliner; Line 3 — 12-G/Colorliner; Line 4 — 12-G/Colorliner; Press drives — Allen Bradley; Folders — 3-G/Double 3:2, 1-G/Single 3:2; Press control system — G/PAR-APCS. MAILROOM: Counter stackers — 2-HL/Commerical, 2-Rimas, 20-HL/HT II, 6-HL/HT; Inserters and stuffers — 4-SLS/1000 8-into-2, 1-SLS/1000 16-into-2, 2-SLS/1000 24-into-2; Bundle tyer — 4-MLN/2A, 30-Power Strap/5,6,6E; Wrapping singles — 13-HL/Monarch, 11-Power Strap; Addressing machine — 6-Dm/Hand; Mailroom control system — HL/Traymatic II. LIBRARY: Electronic — SII/Library Archive Search and Retrieval Sys, Novell, LAN CD-Rom Sys, Lf/AP Leaf Preserver Sys; Combination — 3-Realist/KR-3343, 2-Mark II, 3-Realist, 1-Minolta/Reader-Printer. COMMUNICATIONS: Facsimile — 3-CD/Pagefax; Systems used — fiber optic. WIRE SERVICES: News — AP, Weather, RN, Race Wire, Federal News Services, PR Newswire, NYT, Sports Ticker, Bloomberg; Stock tables — AP; Syndicates — AP, LAT-WP, WYT, KRT, TMS, CSM; Receiving dishes — size-10ft, AP, RN, INS, Weather. BUSINESS COMPUTERS: IBM/3090-E16, IBM, AdMarc; Applications: Circ, Adminstration, Personnel, Adv, Payroll, Accts payable; PCs & micros networked; PCs & main system networked.

CAMBRIDGE
Dorchester County
'90 U.S. Census- 11,514; E&P '96 Est. 11,347

The Daily Banner (e-mon to fri)
The Daily Banner, 1000 Goodwill Rd.; PO Box 580, Cambridge, MD 21613; tel (410) 228-3131; fax (410) 228-6547; e-mail Shorenews@aol.com, DAFB@aol.com (editor). Independent Newspapers Inc. (DE) group.
Circulation: 5,688(e); ABC Dec. 31, 1994.
Price: 35¢(d); $64.00/yr.
Advertising: Open inch rate $11.90(e). **Representative:** Landon Associates Inc.
News Service: LAT-WP. **Politics:** Independent. **Established:** 1897.

Special Editions: Black History Month; Outdoor Snow (Feb); Discover Dorchester (Mar); Waterways (May); Summer Fun (June); Dorchester Showcase (Sept); Grand National Waterfowl Hunt (Dec).

CORPORATE OFFICERS
Board Chairman	Joe Smyth
President	Tamra Brittingham
Vice Pres	Frank A Fantini
Vice Pres	James S Ritch

GENERAL MANAGEMENT
Office Manager	Sandi Stokes

ADVERTISING
Manager	Craig McGines

MARKETING AND PROMOTION
Manager-Promotions	Teresa Stokes

CIRCULATION
Manager	Debby McGrath

NEWS EXECUTIVES
Editor	Debra Bierbaum
Asst Editor	Craig McGines

EDITORS AND MANAGERS
Editor	Debra Bierbaum
Sports Editor	Dean Wells

PRODUCTION
Manager	Raye Brohawn
Cameraman	Ricky Smith

Market Information: Split Run; TMC.
Mechanical available: Offset; Black and 3 ROP colors; insert accepted — preprinted, 8 ½" x 10" up to 11" x 15"; page cut-offs — 22¾".
Mechanical specifications: Type page 13" x 21"; E - 6 cols, 2¹⁄₁₆", ⅛" between; A - 6 cols, 2¹⁄₁₆", ⅛" between; C - 9 cols, 1½", ¹⁄₁₆" between.
Commodity consumption: Newsprint 325 short tons; width 27½"; black ink 24,000 pounds; color ink 1,000 pounds; single pages printed 5,200; average pages per issue 20(d).
Equipment: EDITORIAL: Front-end hardware — Ap/Mac SE, Ap/Mac II. CLASSIFIED: Front-end hardware — Ap/Mac SE, Ap/Mac II. DISPLAY: Adv layout systems — Ap/Mac. PRODUCTION: Typesetters — 3-Ap/Mac NTX; Plate exposures — 1-Nu/Flip Top FT40UP; Plate processors — 1-Nat/A250; Production cameras — 1-R/400; Automatic film processors — 1-P/Pakonolith 24; Shrink lenses — 1-CK Optical/SQU-7, 1-CK Optical, S, N/104.
PRESSROOM: Line 1 — 5-G/Community; Folders — 2-G. MAILROOM: Inserters and stuffers — 1-MM/EM-102; Bundle tyer — 2-Bu/18; Addressing machine — 2-EI/Dymatic 3301.
WIRE SERVICES: News — AP, LAT-WP; UPI. BUSINESS COMPUTERS: 3-DEC/VT220; Applications: Adv, Bookkeeping, Circ.

CUMBERLAND
Allegany County
'90 U.S. Census- 23,706; **E&P '96 Est.** 22,106
ABC-CZ (90): 40,005 (HH 16,752)

The Cumberland Times-News (m-mon to sat; S)
The Cumberland Times-News, 19 Baltimore St.; PO Box 1662, Cumberland, MD 21502; tel (301) 722-4600; fax (301) 722-4870. Thomson Newspapers group.
Circulation: 31,442(m); 31,442(m-sat); 33,979(S); ABC Sept. 30, 1995.
Price: 50¢(d); 50¢(sat); $1.25(S); $2.75/wk; $11.75/mo; $141.00/yr.
Advertising: Open inch rate $28.04(m); $28.04(m-sat); $28.04(S). **Representative:** Papert Companies.
News Service: AP. **Politics:** Independent. **Established:** 1870.
Not Published: New Year; Memorial Day; Independence Day; Labor Day; Day after Thanksgiving; Christmas.
Special Editions: Tax Tips Tab (Jan); Bridal Tab (Feb); Progress Edition (Mar); Senior Citizens, Home Improvement (May); Back-to-School (Aug); Local Footbal Tab, Home Improvement (Sept); Car Care Tab (Oct); Cover Story, Health & Medicine Journal, Sports Magazine, Winston Cup Magazine (monthly).
Special Weekly Sections: Food (wed); Automotive Section (thur); Real Estate (sat); Color Comics, Food (S).
Magazines: USA Weekend; Sport Magazine, Cover Story, Health & Medicine Journal (monthly); On Tracks (NASCAR) (10 issues).

GENERAL MANAGEMENT
Publisher	Terry Horne
General Manager	George J Griffin
Manager-Finance	Thomas Snyder
Manager-Credit	Harriet Grove

ADVERTISING
Director	Steve Stouffer
Manager-Retail	Steve Stouffer
Manager-Classified	Marion Richardson

CIRCULATION
Manager	George J Griffin

NEWS EXECUTIVES
Managing Editor	Lance White
Editorial Page Editor	Jan Alderton

EDITORS AND MANAGERS
Automotive Editor	Rick Twigg
City Editor	Robert Likens
Copy Desk Chief	John Smith
Fashion/Style Editor	Mike Sawyer
Graphics Editor/Art Director	William Burkey
Lifestyle Editor	Mike Sawyer
Sports Editor	Michael Burke

PRODUCTION
Manager-Systems	Robert McDonald
Foreman-Pressroom	James Bell
Foreman-Composing	Ronald Straw
Foreman-Mailroom	Michael Wolfe
Supervisor-Plant Maintenance	Leo Evans

Market Information: TMC.
Mechanical available: Offset; Black and 3 ROP colors; insert accepted — preprinted; page cut-offs — 22¾".
Mechanical specifications: Type page 13" x 21½"; E - 6 cols, 2¹⁄₁₆", ⅛" between; A - 6 cols, 2¹⁄₁₆", ⅛" between; C - 9 cols, 1½", ⅛" between.
Commodity consumption: Newsprint 2,500 short tons; widths 55", 41¼", 27½", 13¾"; black ink 50,000 pounds; color ink 3,500 pounds; average pages per issue 30(d), 68(S); single plates used 20,000.
Equipment: EDITORIAL: Front-end hardware — PC/IBM Compatible; Front-end software — COM/One System, CText; Printers — Genicom, Tegra/4000, Panther/Pro, V/5100, DEC/1152; Other equipment — 14-COM, Ap/Mac Quadra 950, X/1200 R Scanner, Lf/AP Leaf Picture Desk, Lf/Leaf Scan 35. CLASSIFIED: Front-end hardware — PC/IBM Compatible; Front-end software — COM/One System, CText; Printers — Genicom, Tegra/4000, Panther/Pro, V/5100, DEC/1152; Other equipment — 4-COM. DISPLAY: Adv layout systems — SCS/Layout 8000; Front-end hardware — PC/IBM-compatible; Front-end software — CText; Printers — DEC/Laser 1152. PRODUCTION: Pagination software — QuarkXPress 3.12, QuarkXPress 3.1; Typesetters — 2-V/5000, 2-V/5100, 1-V/4000, 1-V/5300E; Platemaking systems — 1-Nu/Flip Top FT40V4UP; Plate exposures — WL; Plate processors — 1-Nu/Flip Top FT40V4UP, 1-WL/Lithoplater; Electronic picture desk — Lf/AP leaf Picture Desk, Lf/Leaf Scan 35; Scanners — Sharp/Color, X/B-W; Production cameras — 1-C/Spartan II; Automatic film processors — AG/Rapidline 43, DuPont/Easy Compact 72; Shrink lenses — 1-C.
PRESSROOM: Line 1 — 8-G/Cosmo. MAILROOM: Counter stackers — 1-Id/2000; Inserters and stuffers — GMA/8 pocket, GMA/SLS-1000; Bundle tyer — 1-MLN/NPS 80, OVL/JP-40; Addressing machine — KR. LIBRARY: Electronic — SMS/Stauffer Gold. WIRE SERVICES: News — AP; Photos — AP; Stock tables — AP; Receiving dishes — size-10ft, AP. BUSINESS COMPUTERS: IBM/Sys 36.

EASTON
Talbot County
'90 U.S. Census- 9,372; **E&P '96 Est.** 11,057

The Star-Democrat (m-mon to fri)
The Sunday Star (S)
The Star-Democrat, 29088 Airpark Dr.; PO Box 600, Easton, MD 21601; tel (410) 822-1500; fax (410) 820-6519. Chesapeake Publishing Corp. group.
Circulation: 16,339(m); 15,960(S); CAC Mar. 31, 1995.
Price: 50¢(d); $1.25(S); $24.15/3mo; $92.40/yr.
Advertising: Open inch rate $14.90(m); $14.90(S). **Representatives:** Landon Associates Inc.; US Suburban Press.
News Service: AP. **Politics:** Independent. **Established:** 1799.
Not Published: New Year; Christmas.
Special Edition: Healthwise (monthly).
Special Weekly Sections: Family Page (mon); Life on the Shore (wed); Church Page (fri); Life on the Shore, Channels (S); Youth Sports; Public Service.
Magazine: Home Magazine (monthly).

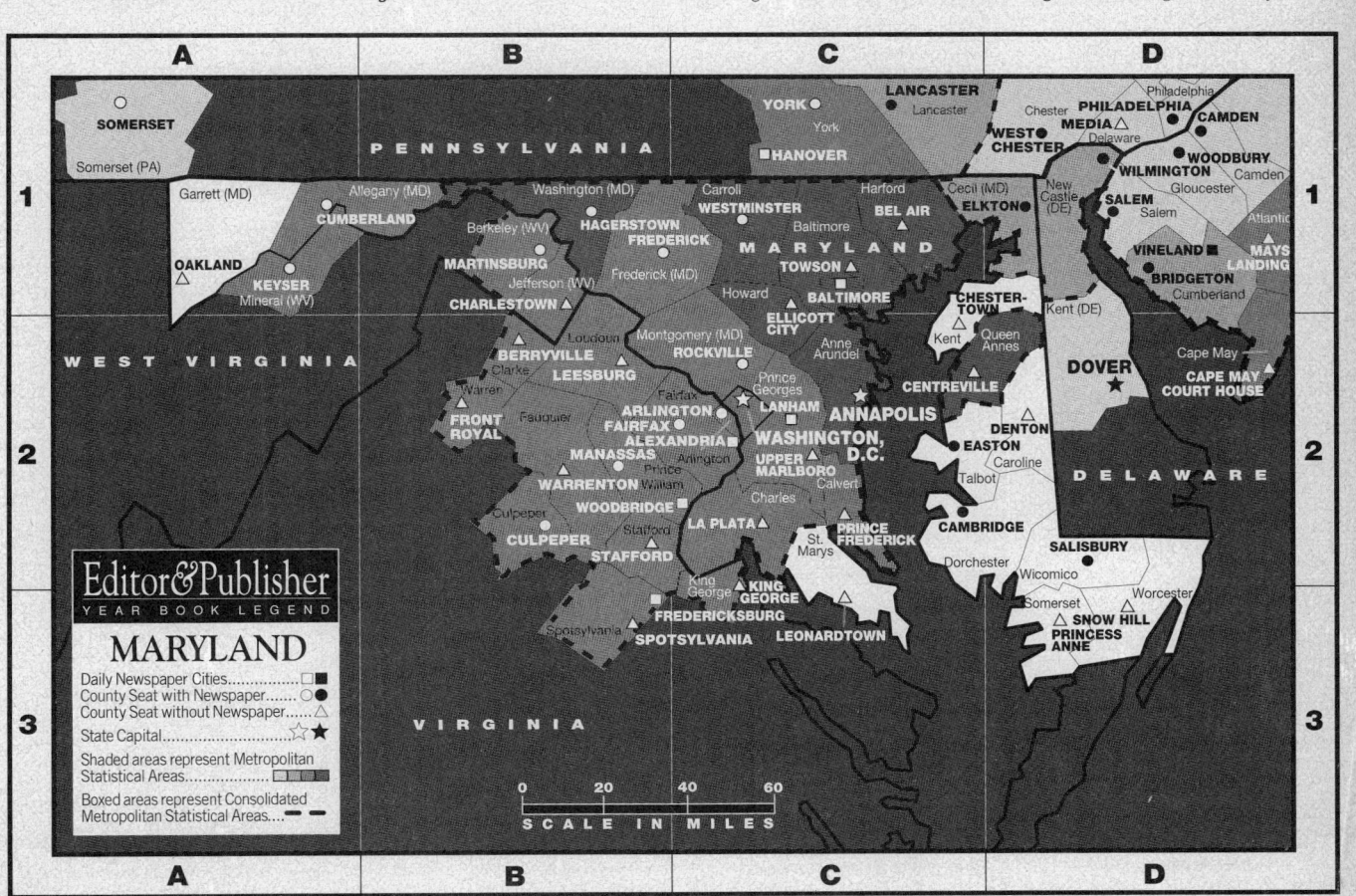

I-182 Maryland

CORPORATE OFFICERS

President Thomas Bradlee
Chairman Charles A Calka

GENERAL MANAGEMENT

Publisher Larry Effingham

ADVERTISING

Director David Fike
Manager-Classified Diane Ferguson

CIRCULATION

Manager Leon Rebuck

NEWS EXECUTIVE

Editor Denise Riley

PRODUCTION

Manager Mike Allison

Mechanical available: Offset; Black and 3 ROP colors; insert accepted — preprinted; page cut-offs — $22\frac{3}{4}$".

Mechanical specifications: Type page 13" x 21"; E - 6 cols, $2\frac{1}{16}$", $\frac{1}{8}$" between; A - 6 cols, $2\frac{1}{16}$", $\frac{1}{8}$" between; C - 9 cols, $1\frac{3}{8}$", $\frac{1}{8}$" between.

Commodity consumption: Newsprint 688 short tons; width $27\frac{1}{2}$"; black ink 14,735 pounds; color ink 1,956 pounds; single pages printed 8,927; average pages per issue 25(d), 36(S); single plates used 5,463.

Equipment: EDITORIAL: Front-end hardware — Ap/Mac; Front-end software — DTI/PageSpeed, DTI/SpeedWriter; Printers — Ap/Mac Laser, Birmy/Page Scan 3; Other equipment — Ap/Mac Scanner, Sun/Sparc, Sun/Sparc Station, AP Satellite Data Sys, Lf/AP Leaf Picture Desk. CLASSIFIED: Front-end hardware — Ap/Mac; Front-end software — DTI/Classified; Printers — Ap/Mac Laser, Birmy/Page Scan 3. DISPLAY: Adv layout systems — DTI; Front-end hardware — Ap/Mac; Front-end software — DTI/AdSpeed; Printers — Ap/Mac Laser, Birmy/Page Scan; Other equipment — Microtek/MSF-300G Image Scanner. PRODUCTION: Plate exposures — 2-Nu/Flip Top FTUPNS; Plate processors — Nat/A250; Scanners — RDS/6100S, Microtek/MSF-300G; Production cameras — D, C/260; Automatic film processors — LE/LD24; Shrink lenses — 1-Alan/Anamorphic; Color separation equipment (conventional) — CD.
PRESSROOM: Line 1 — 1-G/Community; Line 2 — 8-G/Community; Folders — 1-G/SC, 1-G/SSC. MAILROOM: Counter stackers — MM, MM/CN-25, GMA/AF-100; Inserters and stuffers — 2-MM, GMA/10:1, GMA/SG-1000; Bundle tyer — 2-MLN; Addressing machine — 2-Ch/Labeler. WIRE SERVICES: News — AP; Receiving dishes — AP. BUSINESS COMPUTERS: TI/990, AST/386, AST/286; Applications: ICIS, Lotus, Prologic/PR, Xenix, Aware.

ELKTON

Cecil County

'90 U.S. Census- 9,073; E&P '96 Est. 10,527

Cecil Whig (m-mon to fri)

Cecil Whig, 601 Bridge St. (21921); PO Box 429, Elkton, MD 21922-0429; tel (410) 398-3311; fax (410) 398-4044. Chesapeake Publishing Corp. group.

Circulation: 13,696(m); Sworn Oct. 1, 1994.

Price: 35¢(d); $57.00/yr.

Advertising: Open inch rate $13.80(m). **Representatives:** Landon Associates Inc.; US Suburban Press; American Newspaper Representatives Inc.

News Service: AP. **Politics:** Independent. **Established:** 1841 (weekly), 1989 (daily).

Not Published: New Year; Christmas.

Special Editions: Visions, Pulse (Jan); Home Improvement (Mar); Home Improvement (Sept).

Special Weekly Sections: Accent Feature (wed); Automotive (thur); Real Estate, TV (fri).

GENERAL MANAGEMENT

Publisher/President/CEO Thomas Bradlee
General Manager Jeff Mezzatesta

ADVERTISING

Director Tina Winmill

CIRCULATION

Director Bill Sims

NEWS EXECUTIVE

Editor Terry Peddicord

EDITORS AND MANAGERS

Features Editor Becky Reigel
News Editor David Healey
Sports Editor Marty Valania

PRODUCTION

Manager Patty Hutton

Market Information: Zoned editions; TMC.

Mechanical available: Offset; Black.

Mechanical specifications: Type page 21" x 13"; E - 6 cols, $2\frac{1}{16}$", $\frac{1}{8}$" between; A - 6 cols, $2\frac{1}{16}$", $\frac{1}{8}$" between; C - 9 cols, $1\frac{3}{8}$", $\frac{1}{8}$" between.

Commodity consumption: average pages per issue 24(d).

Equipment: EDITORIAL: Front-end hardware — Mk, Ap/Mac; Front-end software — QuarkXPress, Claris/MacWrite II. CLASSIFIED: Front-end hardware — Mk. DISPLAY: Adv layout systems — Mk, Ap/Mac; Front-end hardware — Ap/Mac; Front-end software — Multi-Ad/Creator, QuarkXPress, Ap/Mac Write II; Printers — Birmy/RIPs, Ultre, Cannon/11x17. PRODUCTION: Plate exposures — Nu/Flip Top; Plate processors — WL/30D; Production cameras — Photo Ace/260 D; Automatic film processors — LE/XL26.
PRESSROOM: Line 1 — 18-G/Community (One Line; 3 Power Drives); Folders — 2-G. MAILROOM: Counter stackers — 2-MM; Inserters and stuffers — MM/227; Bundle tyer — MLN/ML-EE; Addressing machine — Cheshire/4UP (One Line, one off-line). WIRE SERVICES: News — AP; Photos — AP; Stock tables — AP SelectStox; Receiving dishes — AP.

FREDERICK

Frederick County

'90 U.S. Census- 40,148; E&P '96 Est. 48,269
ABC-CZ (90): 40,148 (HH 15,671)

The Frederick Post (m-mon to sat)
The News (e-mon to sat)

The Frederick Post/The News, 200 E. Patrick St.; PO Box 578, Frederick, MD 21705; tel (301) 662-1177; fax (301) 662-1615.

Circulation: 30,907(m); 13,776(e); 30,907 (m-sat); 13,776(e-sat); ABC Sept. 30, 1995.

Price: 50¢(d); 50¢(sat); $1.50/wk; $7.20/mo (carrier); $79.75/yr (carrier).

Advertising: Open inch rate $18.88(m); $18.88(e); $18.88(m-sat); $18.88(e-sat). **Representatives:** US Suburban Press; Landon Associates Inc.

News Service: AP. **Politics:** Independent. **Established:** 1883 (News), 1910 (Post).

Not Published: New Year; Memorial Day; Independence Day; Labor Day; Thanksgiving; Christmas.

Special Editions: Wedding Planner (Jan); Business/Tax Guide (Feb); Guide to Recreation & Leisure (Mar); Frederick Keys Supplement, Home, Lawn & Garden (Apr); NIE/Design-An-Ad, Spring Car Care, Guide to Area Golf (May); Agriculture & Dairy Digest (June); Hello Frederick County, Senior Citizens Guide (July); Pets On Parade (Aug); Fall Football Guide, Home Design & Decor (Sept); Fall Auto Guide, The 1996 Great Frederick Fair Issue (Oct); Holiday Magazine (Nov); Holiday Gift Guide, Christmas Carol Collection (Dec).

Special Weekly Sections: Travel, Family Section, Sports Section (mon); Agriculture Section, Business/Finance Section, Sports Section (tues); Food Section, Family Section, Business/Finance Section, Sports Section (wed); Garden Pages, Business/Finance Section, Sports Section (thur); Entertainment Section, Real Estate Section, Business/Finance Section, Sports Section (fri); Religion Section, Real Estate Section, Business/Finance Section, Sports Section (sat).

Magazine: TV Update.

Cable TV: Own cable TV in circulation area.

CORPORATE OFFICERS

President/Publisher George B Delaplaine Jr
Vice Pres George E Randall Esq
Corporate Director-Advertising/Marketing James P Enright
Secretary Marlene B Young
Controller Philip W Hammond CPA
General Counsel George E Randall Esq
Purchasing Agent Cheryl Pryor

GENERAL MANAGEMENT

General Manager George E Randall Esq

ADVERTISING

Corporate Director-Advertising/Marketing James P Enright
Manager-Display Lisa Williams
Manager-Classified Pauline Saloukas
Manager-National Donna Ausherman
Coordinator-Co-op Art Kester

MARKETING AND PROMOTION

Corporate Director-Advertising/Marketing James P Enright

TELECOMMUNICATIONS

Manager-Voice Info Systems Patricia Chambers

CIRCULATION

Director Ervin Hagy
Asst Director Mary May
Manager-Customer Service Becky Ketterman

NEWS EXECUTIVES

Editor George B Delaplaine Jr
Managing Editor Michael S Powell
Asst Managing Editor Robert Harper

EDITORS AND MANAGERS

Automotive Editor Betty Lester
Business Editor Ed Waters Jr
City Editor Nancy Luse
Courts George Dorsey
Editorial/Op-Editor Pages William Pritchard
Education Editor Tamara Hatch
Entertainment/Amusements Editor Linda B Gregory
Family Editor Linda B Gregory
Farm/Agriculture Editor Susan G Summers
Fashion/Style Editor Sue Guynn
Features Editor Linda B Gregory
Food Editor Gail Cissna
Health/Medical Editor Matthew Barakat
News Editor (News) Joan Candy
News Editor (Post) Neil Crowner
Chief Photographer Sam Yu
Photo Editor Sam Yu
Real Estate Editor Ed Waters Jr
Religion Editor Gail Cissna
Science/Technology Editor Matthew Barakat
Sports Editor Stan Goldberg
Travel Editor Linda B Gregory

MANAGEMENT INFORMATION SERVICES

Manager-Info Systems Paul LaPlante

PRODUCTION

Manager-Pressroom (Day & Night) Onyx Barker
Supervisor-Pressroom (Night) Phil Gange
Supervisor-Composing (Day & Night) Woody Stottlemyer
Supervisor-Composing (Night) Bob Brashears

Market Information: TMC; ADS; Operate database; Operate audiotex.

Mechanical available: Offset; Black and 3 ROP colors; insert accepted — preprinted, all; page cut-offs — $22\frac{3}{4}$".

Mechanical specifications: Type page 13" x 21"; E - 6 cols, $2\frac{1}{16}$", $\frac{1}{8}$" between; A - 6 cols, $2\frac{1}{16}$", $\frac{1}{8}$" between; C - 8 cols, $1\frac{1}{2}$", $\frac{1}{8}$" between.

Commodity consumption: Newsprint 3,100 short tons; widths $27\frac{1}{2}$", $13\frac{3}{4}$"; black ink 75,000 pounds; color ink 2,500 pounds; single pages printed 13,672; average pages per issue 44(d); single plates used 20,000.

Equipment: EDITORIAL: Front-end hardware — 4-Ap/Mac Centris 610; Front-end software — Baseview/NewsEdit Pro, QuarkXPress, DD; Printers — Ap/Mac LaserWriter 16/600. CLASSIFIED: Front-end hardware — 14-Ap/Power Mac 6100/66; Front-end software — Baseview/ClassManager; Printers — 1-Ap/Mac LaserPrinter; Other equipment — 2-ECR/Autokon. AUDIOTEX: Hardware — Micro Voice; Supplier name — VNN, AP. DISPLAY: Adv layout systems — 3-Ap/Mac Quadra, 4-Ap/Mac Classic II; Front-end hardware — 4-Ap/Mac Classic; Front-end software — Multi-Ad/Creator 3.7; Printers — 3-Ap/Mac Printer; Other equipment — 2-AG/Horizon Scanners, 2-Graphic Enterprises/Pro Setter 1000, 1-NewGen/ImagePlus 12. PRODUCTION: Pagination software — Baseview; Typesetters — 2-Konica, ECR/Autokon, 1-NewGen, 3-Ap/Mac Quadra 700, 2-Ap/Mac Centris 610, 2-Ap/Mac Quadra 800, 1-Ap/Mac IIsi, 1-Ap/Mac Quadra 950 fileserver, 4-Ap/Mac Centris 610, 4-Ap/Mac Classic II, 2-Graphic Enterprises/Pro Setter 1000; Plate exposures — 2-Nu/Flip Top; Plate processors — 1-Nat/A-250; Electronic picture desk — Lf/AP Leaf Picture Desk; Scanners — ECR/Autokon, 2-Konica, 2-Graphic Enterprises/PageScan, 1-AG/Horizon; Production cameras — 1-C/Spartan III, 1-C/Spartan II; Automatic film processors — 2-LE; Film transporters — 1-C/Spartan; Color separation equipment (conventional) — Adobe/Photoshop 2.5; Digital color separation equipment — Adobe/Photoshop 2.5.
PRESSROOM: Line 1 — 6-G/Urbanite; Folders — 2-G; Press control system — Fin. MAILROOM: Counter stackers — 1-HL/Monitor; Bundle tyer — 2-Sa, 1-OVL/JP40, 1-OVL/Constellation; Wrapping singles — 1-HL/Monarch; Addressing machine — 2-MD/Computer Printer. COMMUNICATIONS: Digital ad delivery system — AP AdSend. WIRE SERVICES: News — AP News and Features; Photos — AP; Receiving dishes — size-3m, AP. BUSINESS COMPUTERS: Microdata/M6000, Baseview; Applications: Billing, Bus functions; PCs & micros networked; PCs & main system networked.

HAGERSTOWN

Washington County

'90 U.S. Census- 35,445; E&P '96 Est. 36,681
ABC-CZ (90): 76,733 (HH 30,114)

The Morning Herald (m-mon to fri)
The Daily Mail (e-mon to fri)
The Herald Mail (m-sat; S)

The Morning Herald, 100 Summit Ave.; PO Box 439, Hagerstown, MD 21740; tel (301) 733-5131; fax (301) 733-7264; e-mail herldmail@aol.com. Schurz Communications Inc. group.

Circulation: 20,922(m); 17,209(e); 37,991 (m-sat); 41,208(S); ABC Sept. 30, 1995.

Price: 50¢(d); 50¢(sat); $1.25(S); $10.00/mo (carrier), $10.75/mo (motor route); $111.00/yr (carrier), $119.40/yr (motor route).

Advertising: Open inch rate $27.39(m); $27.39(e); $27.39(m-sat); $27.39(S). **Representative:** Papert Companies.

News Service: AP. **Politics:** Independent. **Established:** 1828 (Mail), 1873 (Herald).

Note: Advertising is sold only in combination.

Not Published: New Year; Memorial Day; Independence Day; Labor Day; Christmas.

Special Editions: National Food Month (Feb); Lawn & Garden Pages (Mar); Easter Dining (Apr); Home Fashions, May Get Away (May); Father's Day (June); Picnic Pages, Back-to-School, Fall Home Improvement, Hunting & Fishing (Aug); Fall Fashions, National Restaurant Month, Fall Get-away (Sept); New Year's Banner Pages (Dec).

Special Weekly Sections: Farm Page (tues); Food Pages and Recipes (wed); Weekend: Entertainment and Activities (thur); Growing Older (fri); Real Estate, Weddings, Engagements, Church News, Church Directory, Sports Saturday (sat); Life Style, Money, NewsPlus, Transportation (S).

Magazines: Sunday TV Weekly (S); Parade.

CORPORATE OFFICERS

President John League
Secretary Marlene Russell
Vice Pres Terry McDaniel
Treasurer Joseph O' Toole

GENERAL MANAGEMENT

Publisher John League
Personnel Director David Elliott
Controller Marlene L Russell

ADVERTISING

Director-Sales Terry McDaniel
Manager-Territory Sales Gail Petry
Manager-Territory Sales Craig Reichard

MARKETING AND PROMOTION

Director-Marketing & Promotion Cathy Mesares

TELECOMMUNICATIONS

Audiotex Manager Alicia Blake

CIRCULATION

Director Joseph O'Toole
Manager-Home Delivery Chris Miller
Manager-Single Copy Mac Elser
Manager-Promotion Rod Sova

NEWS EXECUTIVES

Editor John W League
Exec Editor Gloria George
Managing Editor (Herald) Linda Duffield
Managing Editor (Mail) Anthony Mulieri

EDITORS AND MANAGERS

Action Line Editor Franca Lewis
City/Metro Editor Elizabeth Douglas
Editorial Page Editor Bob Maginnis
Food/Women's Editor Lisa Prejean
Lifestyle Editor Lisa Prejean
Photo Department Manager Kevin Gilbert
Religion Editor Marlo Barnhart
Sports Editor Bill Callen
Sports Editor Larry Yanos
Television/Film Editor Lisa Prejean
Theater/Music Editor Lisa Prejean

MANAGEMENT INFORMATION SERVICES

Data Processing Manager Dave Foster

PRODUCTION

Foreman-Pressroom Doug Hoffman
Foreman-Mailroom Ed Clopper
Foreman-Composing Sam Turnbull
Foreman-Maintenance Zane Oberhalzer
Manager-Data Processing Dave Foster

Market Information: Operate audiotex.

Mechanical available: Offset; Black and 3 ROP colors; insert accepted — preprinted; page cut-offs — $21\frac{1}{2}$".

Mechanical specifications: Type page 13" x $21\frac{1}{2}$"; E - 6 cols, $2\frac{1}{16}$", $\frac{1}{6}$" between; A - 6 cols, $2\frac{1}{16}$", $\frac{1}{6}$" between; C - 9 cols, $1\frac{7}{16}$", $\frac{1}{12}$" between.

Maryland I-183

Commodity consumption: Newsprint 4,200 short tons; widths 27½", 41¼", 55", 13¾"; black ink 102,000 pounds; color ink 8,000 pounds; average pages per issue 36(d), 40(sat), 64(S); single plates used 32,000.

Equipment: EDITORIAL: Front-end hardware — Ap/Mac 8150 Server; Front-end software — Baseview; Printers — Xante/Accel-a-Writer; Other equipment — MON/Imagesetters. CLASSIFIED: Front-end hardware — DEC/VAX 4000-100; Front-end software — Cybergraphics; Printers — DEC/LA 75. AUDIOTEX: Hardware — Brite; Software — Brite/Perception. DISPLAY: Adv layout systems — Ap/Mac 6100/60; Front-end hardware — CD-Rom; Front-end software — Multi-Ad/Creator, Aldus/FreeHand, Aldus/PageMaker, QuarkXPress; Printers — MON/RIP, Xante/Accel-a-Writer; Other equipment — Umax/Color Scanner, SyQuest/Drive. PRODUCTION: Pagination software — Baseview/NewsEdit Pro/Que 1.0.4, QuarkXPress 3.1; OCR software — Caere/OmniPage Pro; Typesetters — 2-MON/Series III, 2-HI/7450; Platemaking systems — Nat, KFM; Plate exposures — 2-Nu; Plate processors — Nat, WL/Subtractive; Electronic picture desk — Lf/AP Leaf Picture Desk; Scanners — HP/ScanJet IIP; Production cameras — C/Spartan III; Automatic film processors — LE; Film transporters — LE; Shrink lenses — 1-C; Color separation equipment (conventional) — CD; Digital color separation equipment — 2-ECR/Autokon B&W. PRESSROOM: Line 1 — 8-G/Cosmo; Press control system — 150 h.p. motor, 2-Fin; Press registration system — KFM. MAILROOM: Counter stackers — HL, Id; Inserters and stuffers — HI; Bundle tyer — Power Strap; Addressing machine — Domino/Amjet. LIBRARY: Electronic — Minolta/Microfilm. WIRE SERVICES: News — AP, KRT, Regional Bureaus; Stock tables — AP SelectStox; Syndicates — AP, CSM, KRT; Receiving dishes — size-10ft, AP. BUSINESS COMPUTERS: 2-DEC/VAX Server-3400, 2-DEC/PDP 11-70, DEC/VAX 4000-100; Applications: Lotus 1-2-3, WordPerfect; PCs & micros networked; PCs & main system networked.

LANHAM
Prince George's County

'90 U.S. Census- 16,792; **E&P '96 Est.** 12,418
ABC-NDM (90): 729,268 (HH 258,011)

The Prince George's Journal (m-mon to fri)

The Prince George's Journal, 9410 Annapolis Rd., Lanham, MD 20706; tel (301) 459-3131; fax (301) 731-8363; e-mail journal-exp@aol.com, journal@infi.net; web site http://www.infi.net/journal/. Journal Newspapers Inc. group.

Circulation: 29,735(m); ABC Sept. 30, 1995.
Price: 25¢(d); $65.00/yr.
Advertising: Open inch rate $32.00(m). **Representative:** Cresmer, Woodward, O'Mara & Ormsbee.
News Services: AP, SHNS. **Established:** 1972 (weekly), 1981 (daily).
Note: For detailed production and printing information, see Alexandria (VA) Journal listing.
Not Published: Postal holidays.
Special Weekly Sections: Home PC (mon); Food & Home (wed); Fashion (thur); Cover Story, Home Report, Auto Report (fri).
Magazine: USA Weekend.

CORPORATE OFFICERS
Chairman — Rupert Phillips
President — Karl Spain

GENERAL MANAGEMENT
Publisher — Ryan E Phillips
Assoc Publisher — Lisa Evans

TELECOMMUNICATIONS
Director-Telecommunications — Jim Reeves

CIRCULATION
Director — Michael Wynn

NEWS EXECUTIVES
Senior Editor — James Farrell
Managing Editor — Lon Slepicka

EDITORS AND MANAGERS
City/Metro Editor — Christopher Dolan
Editorial Page Editor — Jo Ann Goslin
Living/Lifestyle Editor — Linda Schubert
News Editor — Nancy Wykle
Real Estate Editor — James McCormcik
Sports Editor — Mark Stewart
Television/Film Editor — Mary Ellen Webb

MANAGEMENT INFORMATION SERVICES
Data Processing Manager — Jim Reeves

PRODUCTION
Director-Operations — Jim Reeves

Market Information: Zoned editions; TMC; Electronic edition.
Mechanical available: Offset; Black and 3 ROP colors; insert accepted — preprinted; page cutoffs — 22¾".
Mechanical specifications: Type page 13" x 21½"; E - 6 cols, 2 1/16", ⅛" between; A - 6 cols, 2 1/16", ⅛" between; C - 10 cols, 1¼", 1/16" between.
Commodity consumption: average pages per issue 24(d).
Equipment: EDITORIAL: Front-end hardware — AT, Euromax; Front-end software — AT, Euromax. CLASSIFIED: Front-end hardware — AT; Front-end software — AT; Printers — Teletype. DISPLAY: Adv layout systems — SCS/Layout 8000; Front-end hardware — Dell/310; Front-end software — SCS/Layout 8000; Printers — HP/LaserJet II; Other equipment — Falco/Terminals, Penril/Modem 400 Watt UPS Mouse. WIRE SERVICES: News — AP, SHNS; Receiving dishes — AP. BUSINESS COMPUTERS: NCR/3447; Applications: Vision Data, Lotus, WordPerfect: Accts payable, Accts receivable, Circ.

ROCKVILLE
Montgomery County

'90 U.S. Census- 44,835; **E&P '96 Est.** 45,782
ABC-NDM (90): 757,027 (HH 282,228)

The Montgomery Journal (m-mon to fri)

The Montgomery Journal, 2 Research Ct., Rockville, MD 20850; tel (301) 670-1400; fax (301) 670-1421; e-mail journalexp@aol.com, journal@infi.net; web site http://www.infi.net/journal. Journal Newspapers Inc. group.

Circulation: 29,906(m); ABC Sept. 30, 1995.
Price: 25¢(d); $65.00/yr.
Advertising: Open inch rate $33.50(m). **Representative:** Cresmer, Woodward, O'Mara & Ormsbee.
News Services: AP, SHNS. **Established:** 1972 (weekly), 1981 (daily).
Note: For detailed production and printing information, see Alexandria (VA) Journal listing.
Not Published: Postal holidays.
Advertising not accepted: X-rated movies.
Special Weekly Sections: Home PC (mon); Food, Home (wed); Fashion (thur); Cover Story, Home Report, Auto Report (fri).
Magazine: USA Weekend.

CORPORATE OFFICERS
CEO — Ryan E Phillips
President — Karl Spain

GENERAL MANAGEMENT
Publisher — Ryan E Phillips
Assoc Publisher — Sherri Divver

ADVERTISING
Manager — Nikki Rasnic
Manager-Classified — Donald Farrier

TELECOMMUNICATIONS
Director-Telecommunications — Jim Reeves

CIRCULATION
Manager — Michael Wynn

NEWS EXECUTIVE
Managing Editor — Julie Rasicott

EDITORS AND MANAGERS
Chief Photographer/Graphics Editor — Jeff Taylor
City Editor — Erik Fatemi
Editorial Page Editor — Matt Hamblen
News Editor — Kellie M McIntyre
Real Estate Editor — James McCormick
Sports Editor — Dan Shepherd
Tempo Editor — Linda Schubert

MANAGEMENT INFORMATION SERVICES
Data Processing Manager — Jim Reeves

Market Information: TMC; Electronic edition.
Mechanical available: Offset; Black and 3 ROP colors; insert accepted — preprinted; page cutoffs — 21½".
Mechanical specifications: Type page 13" x 21½"; E - 6 cols, 2 1/16", ⅛" between; A - 6 cols, 2 1/16", ⅛" between; C - 10 cols, 1¼", 1/16" between.
Commodity consumption: average pages per issue 24(d).
Equipment: EDITORIAL: Front-end hardware — AT, Euromax; Front-end software — AT, Euromax. CLASSIFIED: Front-end hardware — AT; Front-end software — AT; Printers — Teletype. DISPLAY: Adv layout systems — SCS/Layout 8000; Front-end hardware — Dell/310; Front-end software — SCS/Layout 8000; Printers — HP/LaserJet II; Other equipment — Falco/Terminals, Penril/Modem 400 Watt UPS Mouse. PRODUCTION: Pagination software — Euromax. WIRE SERVICES: News — AP, SHNS; Receiving dishes — AP. BUSINESS COMPUTERS: NCR/3447; Applications: Vision Data, Lotus, WordPerfect: Accts payable, Accts receivable, Circ.

SALISBURY
Wicomico County

'90 U.S. Census- 20,592; **E&P '96 Est.** 24,487
ABC-CZ (90): 46,998 (HH 17,841)

The Daily Times (m-mon to sat; S)

The Daily Times, 115 E. Carroll St. (21801); PO Box 1937, Salisbury, MD 21802; tel (410) 749-7171; fax (410) 543-8736; e-mail thetimes@shore.intercom.net, toadvine@shore.intercom.net; web site http://www.intercom.net/dailytimes. Thomson Newspapers group.

Circulation: 27,889(m); 27,889(m-sat); 31,894(S); ABC Sept. 30, 1995.
Price: 50¢(d); 50¢(sat); $1.25(S); $2.76/wk; $11.95/mo; $143.52/yr.
Advertising: Open inch rate $20.01(m); $20.01(m-sat); $20.38(S). **Representative:** Landon Associates Inc.
News Services: AP, NEA. **Politics:** Independent. **Established:** 1923.
Special Editions: Progress, Boat Show, Health Guide (Feb); Car Care (Mar); Visitor's Guide (Apr); Visitor's Guide (Sept); Home Building, Car Care (Oct); Home (Nov); Eastern Shore Real Estate, Photo Auto Club, Business Magazine (monthly).
Special Weekly Sections: Times Express, Best Food Days (wed); Delmarva Home (thur); Weekend, O C Weekend (fri); TV, Religion, Real Estate Mag (sat); Best Food Days, Bridal Guide (S).
Magazines: Delmarva Home (thur); Weekend (fri); Delmarva-TV (sat).

GENERAL MANAGEMENT
General Manager — Edward C White
Controller — William Johnston

MARKETING AND PROMOTION
Director-Marketing/Promotion — Earl J Roberts

TELECOMMUNICATIONS
Manager-Systems — Dwayne Kilgo
Audiotex Manager — Arvell Kiah

CIRCULATION
Director — Ted Stazak

NEWS EXECUTIVE
Managing Editor — Mel Toadvine

EDITORS AND MANAGERS
Editorial Page Editor — Cliff Mister
News Editor — Dick Fleming
News/Design Editor — Bill See
Sports Editor — Richard L Cullen

PRODUCTION
Foreman-Composing — Joe Shaffer
Foreman-Pressroom — Michael Alexander

Market Information: Zoned editions; TMC; Operate audiotex; Electronic edition.
Mechanical available: Offset; Black and 3 ROP colors; insert accepted — preprinted; page cutoffs — 22¾".
Mechanical specifications: Type page 13" x 21½"; E - 6 cols, 2 1/16", ⅛" between; A - 6 cols, 2 1/16", ⅛" between; C - 9 cols, 1⅜", 1/16" between.
Commodity consumption: Newsprint 2,600 short tons; widths 55", 41¼"; black ink 6,700 pounds; color ink 9,600 pounds; single pages printed 12,560; average pages per issue 30(d), 58(S); single plates used 29,851.
Equipment: EDITORIAL: Front-end hardware — CD/2330, Ap/Mac LC III, Ap/Mac Quadra 650; Front-end software — WordPerfect; Printers — Ap/Mac LaserWriter IIg, QMS/815. CLASSIFIED: Front-end hardware — CD. AUDIOTEX: Hardware — TI/Micro; Software — Info-Connect 4.20; DISPLAY: Adv layout systems — Ap/Mac; Front-end hardware — CD/Artex. PRODUCTION: Pagination software — CD; Platemaking systems — 2-Nat; Plate exposures — 2-Nu; Electronic picture desk — Lf/AP Leaf Picture Desk; Scanners — 1-Microtek, 1-Umax/Scanner, 1-Kurzweil/Scanner, AG, Tegra/Varityper; Production cameras — 1-R, 1-LE; Automatic film processors — 2-LE; Color separation equipment (conventional) — Konica, ECR/Autokon, Lf/AP Leaf Picture Desk. PRESSROOM: Line 1 — 9-G/Cosmo; Press drives — Fin; Folders — 1-G/2:1; Reels and stands — 5-G, 1-Enkel. MAILROOM: Counter stackers — 1-HL; Inserters and stuffers — 1-GMA/8-into-1; Bundle tyer — 1-Gd, OVL; Wrapping singles — I, Id, OVL; Addressing machine — KR; Other mailroom equipment — MM/1529. WIRE SERVICES: News — AP; Photos — AP; Stock tables — AP; Syndicates — TMS; Receiving dishes — AP. BUSINESS COMPUTERS: HP; Applications: PBS: Adv, Circ; PCs & micros networked.

WESTMINSTER
Carroll County

'90 U.S. Census- 13,068; **E&P '96 Est.** 17,925
ABC-NDM (90): 123,372 (HH 42,248)

Carroll County Times (m-mon to sat; S)

Carroll County Times, 201 Railroad Ave.; PO Box 346, Westminster, MD 21157; tel (410) 848-4400; fax (410) 857-8749. Landmark Communications Inc. group.

Circulation: 22,322(m); 22,322(m-sat); 23,496(S); ABC Sept. 30, 1995.
Price: 50¢(d); 50¢(sat); $1.00(S); $10.50/mo; $96.60/yr.
Advertising: Open inch rate $13.79(m); $13.79(m-sat); $13.79(S). **Representatives:** Landon Associates Inc.; US Suburban Press.
News Services: AP, GNS. **Politics:** Independent. **Established:** 1911.
Not Published: Thanksgiving; Christmas.
Special Editions: Bride's Guide; Home & Garden; Focus; Back-to-School; Wine Festival; Holiday Lifestyles; Last Minute Shopper; Thanksgiving Sample Edition; Auto; Christmas Songbook; Book Covers; 4-H Fair Guides; Christmas Greetings Coupon Book.
Special Weekly Sections: Stock Pages, Best Food Day, Carroll Life Section (wed); Auto Page, Prep Sports, School Page (thur); Weekend, Religion, Church Directory (fri); Homes, TV Guide, Carroll Life Section (S).
Magazines: TV Week, USA Weekend (S).

CORPORATE OFFICER
Secretary — Charles W Baker

GENERAL MANAGEMENT
Publisher — Robin A Saul

ADVERTISING
Director — Charles W Baker

MARKETING AND PROMOTION
Manager-Marketing/Promotion — Kim Myers

TELECOMMUNICATIONS
Audiotex Manager — Kim Myers

CIRCULATION
Director — Robert Trazkovich

NEWS EXECUTIVES
Editor — Ed Shamy
Managing Editor — David Ammenheuser

EDITORS AND MANAGERS
Librarian — Robin Sealover
Lifestyle Editor — Ellen Cornelius
Photo/Production Editor — George Welty
Sports Editor — Scott Blanchard

MANAGEMENT INFORMATION SERVICES
Data Processing Manager — Sandy Mornung

PRODUCTION
Director — Greg Linard

Market Information: Zoned editions; TMC; Operate audiotex; Electronic edition.
Mechanical available: Offset; Black and 3 ROP colors; insert accepted — preprinted; page cutoffs — 22¾".
Mechanical specifications: Type page 13" x 21½"; E - 6 cols, 2 1/16", ⅛" between; A - 6 cols, 2 1/16", ⅛" between; C - 6 cols, 2 1/16", ⅛" between.
Commodity consumption: Newsprint 1,837 short tons; widths 27½", 27¼", 13¾", 13⅝"; black ink 47,524 pounds; color ink 12,650 pounds; single pages printed 12,298; average pages per issue 38(d), 52(S).
Equipment: EDITORIAL: Front-end hardware — Novell/486 50 MHZ File Server; Front-end software — CText/AFM Editorial System, QPS 3.3; Printers — Graphic Enterprises/18x24, HP/LaserJet IV, PelBox/3850, PelBox/1245CX. CLASSIFIED: Front-end hardware — Novell/486 50 MHZ File Server; Front-end software — CText/Classified System; Printers — PelBox/3850, PelBox/1245CX, Graphics Enterprises/18x24, HP/LaserJet IV. DISPLAY:

Copyright ©1996 by the Editor & Publisher Co.

I-184 Maryland

Adv layout systems — SCS/Layout 8000; Front-end hardware — 13-Ap/Mac, 2-Ap/Power Mac 7100; Front-end software — Multi-Ad/Creator 3.7.1.; Printers — HP/LaserJet, Canon/11x17, Graphic Enterprises/18x24, PelBox/3850, PelBox 1245CX; Other equipment — QuarkXPress, Adobe/Photoshop, DTI/AdSend. PRODUCTION: Pagination software — QuarkXPress 3.3; OCR software — Caere/OmniType; Typesetters — PelBox/245CS, PelBox/3850; Platemaking systems — Dal/THITT w/OLEC Lamp Source, Teaneck; Plate processors — Polychrome; Electronic picture desk — Lf/AP Leaf Picture Desk; Scanners — AG/Arcus, Microtek/35mm, Microtek/Flatbed, Lf/AP Leaf Picture Desk; Production cameras — C/Spartan III, AG/2024; Automatic film processors — LE/Maxim 26, Konica/550, Konica/OL Conyevor System; Digital color separation equipment — Microtek/Scanmaker IIsp, Microtek/Scanmaker 35T. PRESSROOM: Line 1 — 9-G/Super Community; Line 2 — 5-G/Community; Line 3 — 8-G/Urbanite; Press drives — Fin; Folders — 4-G; Pasters — 6-Cary, 1-Martin; Reels and stands — Mill/Stands; Press control system — Fin; Press registration system — Duarte. MAILROOM: Counter stackers — 2-HI/RS-3010, 1-HI/RS, LD, 1-BG/Count-O-Veyor 1055MM; Inserters and stuffers — 1-MM/7:1, 1-HI/1372 (Dual Delivery Lines), 1-MM/Stacker, 2-Id/Stacker; Bundle tyer — 2-Bu, 2-OVL, 1-OVL/Semi-automatic, 1-Ty/Tech; Addressing machine — 1-KR, 1-Ch; Other mailroom equipment — Ch/Box Trimmer; Mc/4-Pocket Stitcher w/destra Stacker; Ch/Flatbed; Wohlenberg/Automatic Trimmer 3-Knife; Stahl/Semi-Automatic-3 Knife. LIBRARY: Combination — 1-Microfilm/reader. WIRE SERVICES: News — AP Datastream, AP Datafeatures; Receiving dishes — size-10ft, AP. BUSINESS COMPUTERS: IBM/Sys 36, 3-Convergent/AWS, 3-PC; Applications: Circ, Accts receivable, Gen ledger, Financial statement; PCs & micros networked; PCs & main system networked.

MASSACHUSETTS

ATHOL

Worcester County

'90 U.S. Census- 11,451; E&P '96 Est. 12,197

Athol Daily News

(e-mon to fri; m-sat)

Athol Daily News, 225 Exchange St.; PO Box 1000, Athol, MA 01331; tel (508) 249-3535; fax (508) 249-9630.

Circulation: 5,049(e); 5,049(m-sat); Sworn Sept. 30, 1995.

Price: 35¢(d); 35¢(sat); $1.80/wk; $7.00/mo; $81.00/yr (carrier).

Advertising: Open inch rate $6.00(e); $6.00(m-sat).

News Service: AP. **Politics:** Independent-Republican. **Established:** 1934.

Not Published: New Year; Memorial Day; Independence Day; Labor Day; Thanksgiving; Christmas.

Special Editions: Bridal Supplement (Jan); Business Review, Boy Scout Page (Feb); River Rat Review (Apr); Memorial Day, Graduation Pages (May); Graduation Pages (June); Back-to-School, Football Pages (Sept); Fire Prevention (Oct); Thanksgiving Greetings (Nov); Christmas Greetings, First Baby Contest (Dec).

Special Weekly Sections: Best Food Day (mon); Amusements (fri); Amusements (sat).

Magazine: TV Guide (sat).

CORPORATE OFFICERS

President Richard J Chase Jr
Treasurer Stephen F Chase

GENERAL MANAGEMENT

Publisher Richard J Chase Jr
General Manager Richard J Chase Jr
Purchasing Agent Richard J Chase Jr

ADVERTISING

Director Bernard R Cunningham
Manager-Classified Cynthia Mallet

MARKETING AND PROMOTION

Director-Marketing/Promotion Richard J Chase Jr

CIRCULATION

Manager Susan Peters

NEWS EXECUTIVES

Editor Barney B Cummings
Managing Editor Cindy Jack

EDITORS AND MANAGERS

Automotive Editor Bernard R Cunningham
Books Editor Richard J Chase
City Editor Barney B Cummings
Editorial Writer Barney B Cummings
Food Editor Kelly L Chase
Librarian Kelly L Chase
Radio/Television Editor Richard J Chase Jr
Real Estate Editor Richard J Chase Jr
Society Editor Deborrah Porter
Sports Editor Barney B Cummings
Wire Editor Barney B Cummings
Women's Editor Kelly L Chase
Women's Editor Jennifer Chase

MANAGEMENT INFORMATION SERVICES

Director-Operations Robert A Perkins

PRODUCTION

Superintendent Harley L Smith

Market Information: Zoned editions; Split Run; TMC.

Mechanical available: Offset; Black and 3 ROP colors; insert accepted — preprinted, single sheet $8\frac{1}{2}$"x11" minimum; page cut-offs — $22\frac{3}{4}$".

Mechanical specifications: Type page 13" x 21"; E - 6 cols, $2\frac{1}{16}$", $\frac{1}{4}$" between; A - 6 cols, $2\frac{1}{16}$", $\frac{1}{4}$" between; C - 8 cols, $1\frac{1}{2}$", $\frac{1}{8}$" between.

Commodity consumption: Newsprint 280 short tons; width 28"; black ink 12,000 pounds; color ink 1,300 pounds; single pages printed 7,368; average pages per issue 14(d); single plates used 3,684.

Equipment: EDITORIAL: Front-end hardware — Ap/Mac; Front-end software — Baseview; Printers — MON/PageScan. CLASSIFIED: Front-end hardware — Ap/Mac; Front-end software — Baseview; Other equipment — 2-Texas Line/Facit Punches. DISPLAY: Adv layout systems — Ap/Mac. PRODUCTION: Typesetters — MON/PageScan; Plate exposures — 1-Nu; Plate processors — 1-Ic; Electronic picture desk — Lf/AP Leaf Picture Desk; Production cameras — 1-Nu/20x24; Automatic film processors — 1-DP/20x24.

PRESSROOM: Line 1 — 4-G. MAILROOM: Bundle tyer — 1-Strapex; Addressing machine — 1-RSK/TRS-80, Vision Data/Circulation Sys, 1-Ch. LIBRARY: Electronic — Minolta/Microfilm. WIRE SERVICES: News — AP; Photos — AP; Receiving dishes — size-3m, AP. BUSINESS COMPUTERS: RSK/TRS-80, Vision Data/Business Sys, Ap/Mac Desktop Pub Sys; Applications: Circ, Adv billing, Accts receivable, Payroll, Gen ledger, TMC; PCs & micros networked; PCs & main system networked.

ATTLEBORO

Bristol County

'90 U.S. Census- 38,383; E&P '96 Est. 40,597

ABC-CZ (90): 63,421 (HH 23,415)

The Sun Chronicle

(e-mon to fri; m-sat; S)

The Sun Chronicle, 34 S. Main St.; PO Box 600, Attleboro, MA 02703-0600; tel (508) 222-7000; fax (508) 226-5851. United Communications Corp. group.

Circulation: 23,195(e); 23,195(m-sat); 24,193(S); ABC Sept. 30, 1995.

Price: 50¢(d); 50¢(sat); $1.25(S); $3.25/wk (home delivery); $13.00/mo (home delivery); $169.00/yr (home delivery).

Advertising: Open inch rate $12.95(e); $12.95(m-sat); $12.95(S). **Representative:** Landon Associates Inc.

News Services: NEA, AP, WP. **Politics:** Republican-Independent. **Established:** 1888 (The Chronicle), 1889 (The Sun), 1971 (The Sun Chronicle).

Not Published: New Year; Memorial Day; Independence Day; Labor Day; Thanksgiving; Christmas.

Special Editions: Financial, Furniture (Jan); Bridal (Feb); Spring Fashions (Mar); Home Improvement, Pawtucket Red Sox (Apr); Summer Showcase (May); Answer Book (July); Back-to-School, School Bus Routes (Aug); Football '96 (Sept); Winter '96 (Oct); Christmas Gift Guide (Nov); Last Minute Gift Guide (Dec).

Special Weekly Sections: Lifestyle (tues); Best Food Day, Financial/Business (wed); Lifestyle (fri); Home, Leisure/Travel, Money, Senior Citizens, Schools, Best Food Day, Channels (S).

Magazines: TV Magazine, Channels (S).

CORPORATE OFFICERS

President Howard J Brown
Senior Vice Pres Eugene W Schulte
Vice Pres Paul A Rixon
Clerk/Treasurer Eugene W Schulte

GENERAL MANAGEMENT

Publisher Paul A Rixon
General Manager Oreste P D'Arconte
Business Manager Roy Belcher

ADVERTISING

Director Paul J Morrissey
Manager-Classified Charles H Miles Jr
Manager-Retail Roland A Demers
Asst Classified Manager Patrica Bailey

CIRCULATION

Manager Arleen McGlone

NEWS EXECUTIVES

Managing Editor Ned Bristol
Asst Managing Editor Mark Flanagan
Asst Managing Editor Mike Kirby

EDITORS AND MANAGERS

Area Editor Don Ross
Community Editor Nancy Sylvestre
Entertainment Editor Don Wilding
Lifestyle Editor Betsy Johnson
Local Editor Larry Kessler
Sports Editor Bill Stedman
Sunday Sports Editor Mark Farinella
Sunday Editor Mike Kirby
Wire Editor Rick Foster

PRODUCTION

Manager Kendall Nye
Manager-Systems Joseph Previty
Manager-Graphics Michael Forgette
Supervisor-Graphics Donna Handel
Foreman-Pressroom Maurice Marcoux

Market Information: Zoned editions; Split Run; TMC.

Mechanical available: Offset; Black and 4 ROP colors; insert accepted — preprinted; page cut-offs — $22\frac{3}{4}$".

Mechanical specifications: Type page 13" x $21\frac{1}{2}$"; E - 6 cols, $2\frac{1}{16}$", $\frac{1}{8}$" between; A - 6 cols, $2\frac{1}{16}$", $\frac{1}{8}$" between; C - 9 cols, $1\frac{3}{8}$", $\frac{1}{16}$" between.

Commodity consumption: Newsprint 2,100 metric tons; widths 28", 14"; black ink 40,000 pounds; color ink 7,000 pounds; single pages printed 14,466; average pages per issue 32.8(d), 81.3(S); single plates used 18,500.

Equipment: EDITORIAL: Front-end hardware — Novell/Netserver; Front-end software — CText/OS-2 Dateline; Printers — Typhoon/800 DPI, Hyphen/600 DPI; Other equipment — AU/APS 6/84 ACS. CLASSIFIED: Front-end hardware — Novell/Netserver; Front-end software — CText/OS-2 Advision; Printers — Hyphen/600 DPI, Typhoon/800 DPI. DISPLAY: Adv layout systems — 3-PC; Front-end hardware — PC/fileserver; Front-end software — Archetype, Novell; Printers — Hyphen/600 DPI, Typhoon/800 DPI; Other equipment — 3-Umax/840 scanners. PRODUCTION: Pagination software — QuarkXPress 3.1; Typesetters — 2-AU/APS 6/84 ACS, 3-Ap/Mac LaserWriter NTX, Hyphen/600 DPI, Typhoon/800 DPI; Plate exposures — 2-Nu/Ultra Plus; Plate processors — 1-Nat/A-340; Electronic picture desk — Lf/AP Leaf Picture Desk, 2-Ap/Mac Quadras, 1-Ap/Power Mac; Scanners — 2-Kk/2035+, 2-Microtek/flatbeds, 4-Umax/flatbeds; Production cameras — 1-C/Spartan III, 1-R/Vertical; Automatic film processors — 2-LE/LD18 & 24; Film transporters — 1-C; Shrink lenses — 1-CK Optical/SQU-7, 1-CK Optical/SQU-7.

PRESSROOM: Line 1 — 10-G/Urbanite; Folders — 1-G; Press control system — Fin. MAILROOM: Counter stackers — 2-HL/Monitor II; Inserters and stuffers — GMA/Model SLS-1000 (8 pockets); Bundle tyer — 1-MLN, 2-MLN/ML2EE, Power Strap. LIBRARY: Electronic — SMS/Stauffer Gold. WIRE SERVICES: News — AP, LAT-WP; Photos — AP; Receiving dishes — size-12ft, AP. BUSINESS COMPUTERS: HP/3000 Model 927; Applications: CJ.

BOSTON

Suffolk County

'90 U.S. Census- 574,283; E&P '96 Est. 586,951

ABC-CZ (90): 1,948,025 (HH 758,605)

The Christian Science Monitor

(m-mon to fri)

The Christian Science Monitor, One Norway St., Boston, MA 02115; tel (617) 450-2000; web site http://freerange.com/csmonitor.

Circulation: 77,410(m); ABC Sept. 30, 1995.

Price: 75¢(d); $159.00/yr. **Representatives:** The Magazine Group Ltd.; Robert J Flahive Co.; Tolbert/Sheridan; Neese and Associates; Russell Palmer Inc.; Media Marketplace.

News Services: RN, AFP, AP. **Politics:** Independent. **Established:** 1908.

Note: The Christian Science Monitor is printed at Gannett Corp. plants in Norwood, MA and Phoenix, AZ. Only full-page advertising is sold for $5,000 (4-color) and $4,000 (b&w) respectively. Frequency discounts and fractional rates are also available.

Not Published: New Year; Martin Luther King Day; President's Day; Memorial Day; Independence Day; Labor Day; Columbus Day; Veteran's Day; Thanksgiving; Christmas.

Advertising not accepted: Liquor; Tobacco; Medicine; Gambling; Caffeine Product.

Special Weekly Sections: Arts; Home Forum (TMC); Habitat; Books; Food; Sports; Media; Now; Science & Technology; Points of the Compass; Images; Cover Story; Justice; Community; Profile.

Broadcast Affiliates: Monitor Radio; Broadcast daily on American Public Radio.

GENERAL MANAGEMENT

Director-Publishing Brian McCauley
General Manager William Hill
Controller Harley Gates

ADVERTISING

Manager Nick Drinker

MARKETING AND PROMOTION

Manager-Business Development David Creagh

NEWS EXECUTIVES

Editor David T Cook
Managing Editor John Dillin

EDITORS AND MANAGERS

Business/Finance Editor David R Francis
Columnist Marilyn Gardner
Design Director John Van Pelt
Economy Editor David R Francis
Editorial Cartoonist Jeff Danziger
Editorial Page Editor Earl Foell
Entertainment/Amusements Editor April Austin
Environmental Editor Elizabeth Ross
Fashion/Style Editor April Austin
Features Editor Jane Lampmann
Films Editor April Austin
Graphic Editor/Art Director Jewel B Simmons
Home Forum Editor (TMC) Elizabeth Lund
International News Editor Clay Jones
Living/Lifestyle Editor Jane Lampmann
Music Editor April Austin
National/News Editor Scott Armstrong
Natural Science Editor Eric Evarts
Page One Editor Ruth J Wales
Religion Editor Jane Lampmann
Science/Technology Editor Eric Evarts
Senior Writer Keith Henderson
Sports Writer Ross Atkin
Theater/Arts Editor April Austin
Travel Editor Elizabeth Ross

PRODUCTION

Manager Jane Atencio
Director-Operations David Stormont
Manager-Distribution Deborah Scavotto

Market Information: Split Run; Electronic edition.

Mechanical available: Offset; Black and 3 ROP colors; insert accepted — preprinted, stuffers; page cut-offs — $12\frac{3}{4}$".

Mechanical specifications: Type page $10\frac{7}{16}$" x $13\frac{7}{8}$"; E - 5 cols, 1.83", $\frac{1}{8}$" between; A - 5 cols, 1.83", $\frac{1}{8}$" between.

Commodity consumption: Newsprint 600 short tons; 661 metric tons; widths 28", 14"; black ink 46,200 pounds; color ink 32,760 pounds; single pages printed 5,200; average pages per issue 20(d); single plates used 58,680.

Equipment: EDITORIAL: Front-end hardware — 8-A/9000, 156-AT, Ap/Mac; Front-end software — QuarkXPress 3.3, QPS/Copy Desk, QPS; Printers — HP/LaserJet 4N Plus; Other equipment — 8-Ap/Mac fx, 1-Ap/Mac Quadra 950, Nikon/LS-3510 Scanner. DISPLAY: Front-end software — QuarkXPress 3.3; PRODUCTION: Pagination software — QuarkXPress 3.3; Typesetters — Scitex, Raystar, Dolev; Scanners — Scitex/Smart Scanner, X; Automatic film processors — 2-LE/24; Reproduction units — Scitex/Response Sys; Color separation equipment (conventional) — Scitex/Response Sys. LIBRARY: Combination — Nexis. WIRE SERVICES: News — AP, RN; Photos — AFP, RN; Syndicates — LATS; Receiving dishes — size-5.5m, Christian Science Monitor. BUSINESS COMPUTERS: 2-DEC/Sys 10, 1-IBM/4361; Applications: Circ, Adv billing, Accts receivable, Gen ledger, Payroll; PCs & micros networked; PCs & main system networked.

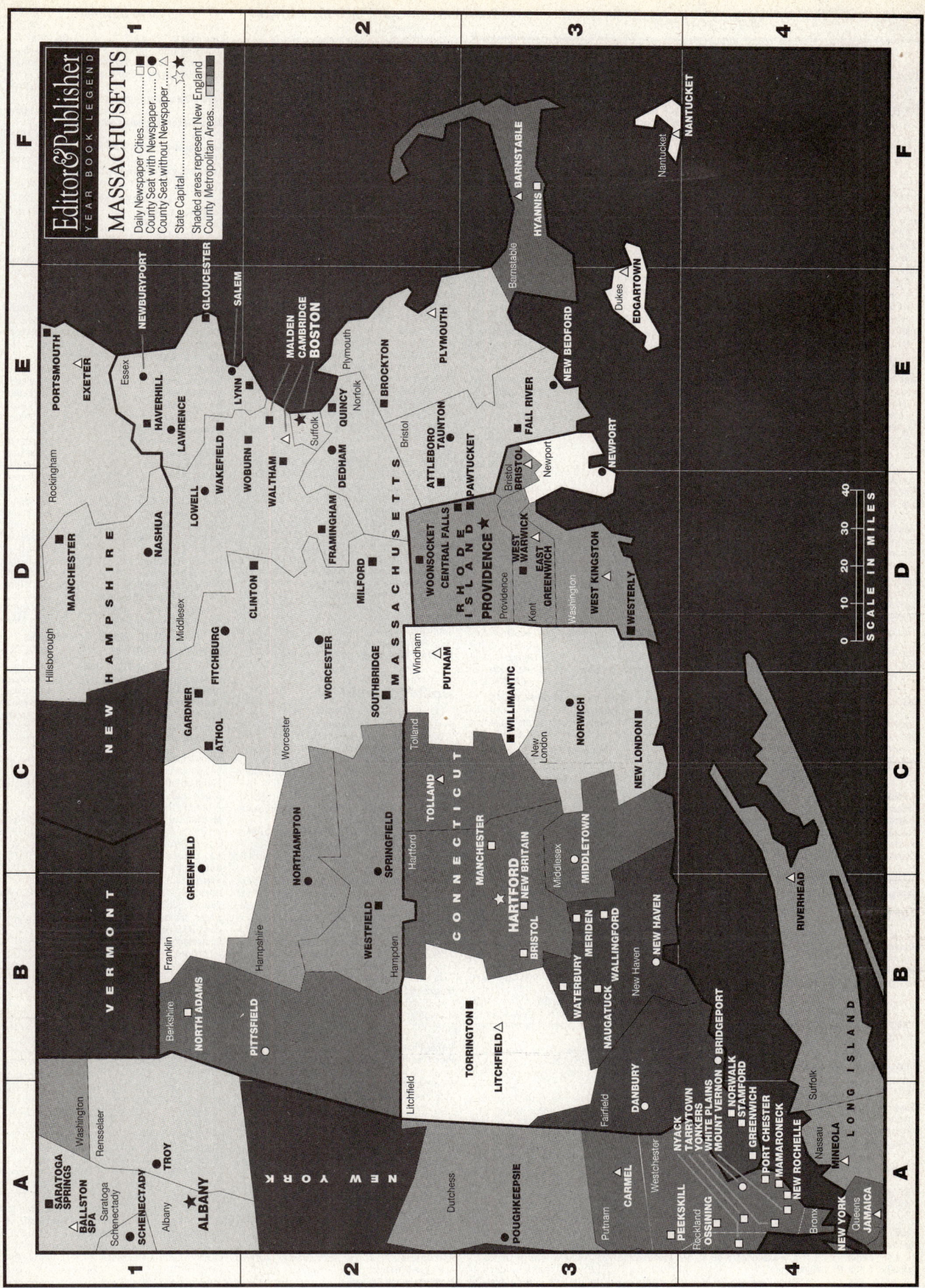

I-186 Massachusetts

The Boston Globe
(m-mon to fri; m-sat)
Boston Sunday Globe (S)

The Boston Globe, 135 Morrissey Blvd. (02107); PO Box 2378, Boston, MA 02109; tel (617) 929-2000; fax (617) 929-3318; e-mail news@globe.com; web site http://www.boston.com. New York Times Co. group.

Circulation: 498,853(m); 475,387(m-sat); 493,672(S); ABC Sept. 30, 1995.

Price: 50¢(d); 50¢(sat); $2.00(S); $27.00/mo, $35.50/mo (outside N.E.); $324.00/yr.

Advertising: Open inch rate $268.60(m); $268.60(m-sat); $313.75(S). **Representatives:** Newspapers First; The Newspaper National Network; Gannett National Newspaper Sales.

News Services: AP, DJ, LAT-WP. **Politics:** Independent. **Established:** 1872.

Special Editions: Adventures in Travel, Your Home (Mar); Your Health (Apr); Your Home (Sept); Adventures in Travel, Your Health (Oct).

Special Weekly Sections: Health & Science (mon); Business Extra (tues); Food (wed); At Home, Calendar (thur); Sports Plus (fri); Real Estate (sat).

Magazines: Calendar Magazine Tab (thur); The Boston Globe Magazine (local, roto), Parade (S).

CORPORATE OFFICERS

Chairman of the Board/CEO William O Taylor
President Benjamin B Taylor
Chief Financial Officer/Exec Vice Pres William B Huff
Treasurer William F Connolly Jr
Controller Paul R Norman
Corporate Counsel/Clerk Catherine E C Henn

GENERAL MANAGEMENT

Publisher William O Taylor
Chief Operating Officer Benjamin B Taylor
Exec Vice Pres Stephen B Taylor
Vice Pres/Asst to Publisher Timothy Leland
Vice Pres-Corporate & Legal Affairs Catherine E C Henn
Vice Pres-Sales & Marketing Mary Jane Patrone
Vice Pres-Circulation Godfrey W Kauffmann Jr
Vice Pres-Human Resources Frank E Grundstrom Jr
Vice Pres-Employee Relations Gregory L Thornton
Vice Pres-Production Michael A Ide
Vice Pres-Info Services Robert T Murphy
Vice Pres-Strategic Planning Richard J Daniels
Vice Pres-New Media Lincoln Millstein
Vice Pres-Electronic Publishing Lincoln Millstein
Director-Public Affairs Leslie F Griffin Jr
Director-Benefits Cathryn C Lewis
Director-Public Relations Richard P Gulla
Director-Research Susan DiManno
Director-Training Robert Henderson
Director-Administration Services Douglas J Dwyer
Director-Employee Relations Harriet Gould
Manager-Electronic Publishing David L Margulius
Asst Treasurer Mary E Marty

ADVERTISING

Director Robert Manning
Manager-Display George Harden
Manager-Classified Marilyn Won
Manager-Classified/Recruitment Advertising Kimberly C Green

MARKETING AND PROMOTION

Director-Sales Promotion/Public Relations James Regan

TELECOMMUNICATIONS

Manager-Telecommunications Tammy McFarland

CIRCULATION

Vice Pres Godfrey W Kauffmann Jr
Director Steve Cahow
Manager-Sales Thomas O'Neil
Manager-Transportation/Distribution Richard Yankun
Manager-Planning/Market Development Rolf Arend
Manager-Data Management James Burbine
Superintendent-Delivery James Pitt

NEWS EXECUTIVES

Editor Matthew V Storin
Exec Editor Helen W Donovan
Managing Editor Gregory L Moore
Managing Editor-News/Operations Thomas F Mulvoy Jr
Managing Editor-Administration Alfred S Larkin Jr
Managing Editor-New Media Lincoln Millstein
Deputy Managing Editor Thomas Ashbrook
Asst Managing Editor Michael Larkin
Asst Managing Editor-Features Mary Jane Wilkinson
Asst Managing Editor-Design Lucy Bartholomay
Asst Managing Editor-Zones John Burke
Assoc Editor Ellen Goodman
Assoc Editor David Nyhan
Assoc Editor Martin F Nolan
Assoc Editor Stanley Grossfeld
Exec Editor-Sports Don Skwar
Ombudsman Mark Jurkowitz
Bureau Chief-Berlin Elizabeth Neuffer
Bureau Chief-Jerusalem Ethan Bronner
Bureau Chief-Tokyo Charles Radin
Bureau Chief-Washington David Shribman

EDITORS AND MANAGERS

Automotive Editor John White
Arts Editor Scott Powers
Book Editor Gail Caldwell
Business Editor Lawrence Edelman
Calendar Editor Julie Michaels
Drama Editor Edward Siegel
Editorial Page Editor H D S Greenway
Education Editor Alice Dembner
Fashion Editor Pamela T Reynolds
Food Editor Sheryl Julian
Foreign Editor Philip Bennett
Garden Editor Carol Stocker
Librarian Elizabeth D Tuite
Living Editor Nick King
Medical Editor Richard Knox
Metro Editor Walter Robinson
Music Editor-Classical Richard Dyer
Music Editor-Contemporary Steve Morse
National Editor James T Concannon
Night Editor Douglas M Warren
Page One Editor Charles Mansbach
Director-Photography Peter A Southwick
Radio/Television Editor Frederick M Biddle
Real Estate Editor Matthew Carroll
Religion Editor Diego F Ribadeneira
Restaurants Editor Alison Arnett
Science/Technology Editor Nils Bruzelius
Special Sections Editor Robert Cutting
Spotlight Editor Gerard O'Neill
Sunday Magazine Editor Evelynne H Kramer
Travel Editor Jerry Morris

MANAGEMENT INFORMATION SERVICES

Vice Pres-Info Services Robert T Murphy
Director-Info Services Christopher M Mayer
Asst Director-Info Services Robert D Sylvester

PRODUCTION

Vice Pres Michael A Ide
Director John Bopp
Manager Joe Dillon
Manager George Munroe
Manager Tom Coveney
Superintendent-Composing Robert Bletzer
Superintendent-Engraving Steve Sferrazza
Superintendent-Pressroom Paul O'Brien
Superintendent-Mailroom Richard Kerrigan
Manager-Plant (Billerica) Neil A Jackson
General Foreman-Mailroom (Billerica) Robert McCoy
General Foreman-Pressroom (Billerica) Richard Staples
General Foreman-Westwood Jack Snyder
Manager-Plant (Westwood) Richard Kerrigan
Manager-Plant (Boston) Steve Cate

Market Information: Zoned editions; Split Run; TMC; ADS; Operate audiotex.

Mechanical available: Offset; Black and 3 ROP colors; insert accepted — preprinted, preprinted advertising sections, product samples; page cut-offs — 22".

Mechanical specifications: Type page 13" x 21"; E - 6 cols, $2\frac{1}{16}$", $\frac{1}{8}$" between; A - 6 cols, $2\frac{1}{16}$", $\frac{1}{8}$" between; C - 10 cols, $1\frac{1}{4}$", $\frac{1}{16}$" between.

Commodity consumption: Newsprint 130,000 short tons; 116,000 metric tons; widths 54", $40\frac{1}{2}$", 27"; black ink 3,000,000 pounds; color ink 126,250 pounds; single pages printed 37,856; average pages per issue 84(d), 84(sat), 272(S); single plates used 710,000.

Equipment: EDITORIAL: Front-end hardware — AT; Front-end software — AT 4.7.10; Printers — DEC/LNO3s. CLASSIFIED: Front-end hardware — AT; Front-end software — AT 4.7.5; Printers — DEC/LNO3s, LP/27; Other equipment — Pti/ADSTAR, Edgil/credit card processing, MCT/AdFax, MCT/AdFast, Ad Express, Tele-Magic. AUDIOTEX: Supplier name — Micro Voice. DISPLAY: Adv layout systems — 2-Sun/360, 2-Sun/110 at class page, 5-Cx/360, 3-Cx/380, 3-Cx/Sparc IFC, Ap/Mac, Cascade/Image, Data Flow; Front-end hardware — 2-ECR/Autokon; Front-end software — Cx, AT; Printers — Cx/Bitcasters; Other equipment — AT/RS6000 (Makeup). PRODUCTION: Pagination software — AT/Ed Page 1.6.2, Press To Go; OCR software — TextBridge; Typesetters — 2-MON, 4-Bidco, 4-LB/Printer (proofers), ECR/Autokon, 2-Full-Page Proofers; Platemaking systems — 2-WL; Plate exposures — 6-WL, 6-W, 2-Nu; Plate processors — 5-WL, 6-W; Scanners — 4-III/Scanner, 1-CD, 2-Scitex; Production cameras — 2-C/Camera; Automatic film processors — 6-LE, 4-AG/Processor; Reproportion units — ECR/Autokon, C/Camera; Film transporters — 6-LE, 4-AG, 1-SCREEN; Shrink lenses — C; Digital color separation equipment — Scitex, CD. PRESSROOM: Line 1 — 16-G/Metroliner, 4-G/Metro Color (4/4 color towers) double width; Line 2 — 18-G/Metroliner, 4-G/Metro Color (4/4 color towers) double width; Line 3 — 24-G/Metroliner, 6-G/Metro Color (4/4 color tower) double width; Line 4 — 10-G/Metroliner, 2-G/Metro Color (4/4 color tower) double width; Press drives — Fin, Allen Bradley; Folders — 8-G/Imperial (144pg); Pasters — 80-G/Reel tension paster; Reels and stands — 82-G; Press control system — 8-Globe/press control sys, MPCS II; Press registration system — Quad Tech System (on Metro Color Towers). MAILROOM: Counter stackers — 35-HL/HT, 21-QWI/301; Inserters and stuffers — 15-GMA/MM 6-into-1; Bundle tyer — Dynaric/30, Power Strap/13; Wrapping singles — 43-Power Strap/MP2; Addressing machine — 1-Matthews, 19-Domino. LIBRARY: Electronic — Vytex, Data Times, Mead Data Central/Nexis. COMMUNICATIONS: Facsimile — 3-III/Scanner 3750, 3-III/3800 Recorder; Remote imagesetting — 3-III/3800 Recorder; Digital ad delivery system — AP AdSend, AP AdExpress, AP AdFast, Digiflex, AdSat. Systems used — satellite, fiber optic. WIRE SERVICES: News — AP Day Book, NES, DJ, AP Day Book, Mass Election Wire, DJ, AP SportStats, Mass Election Wire; Stock tables — AP SelectStox; Syndicates — North America Syndicate; Receiving dishes — size-3m, AP. BUSINESS COMPUTERS: 2-DEC/VAX 6520, 2-DEC/VAX 8650, 1-DEC/VAX 8700, 4-DEC/Micro VAX 2; Applications: Circ, Mailroom, Adv billing, Accts receivable, Gen ledger; PCs & micros networked; PCs & main system networked.

Boston Herald
(m-mon to fri; m-sat; S)

Boston Herald, One Herald Sq., Boston, MA 02106; tel (617) 426-3000.

Circulation: 308,077(m); 248,797(m-sat); 216,290(S); ABC Sept. 30, 1995.

Price: 50¢(d); 50¢(sat); $1.50(S); $18.60/mo (d) (mail), $28.20/mo (dS) (mail).

Advertising: Open inch rate $216.50(m); $216.50(m-sat); $216.50(S). **Representative:** Sawyer-Ferguson-Walker Co.

News Services: AP, RN, Business Wire, DJ. **Politics:** Independent. **Established:** 1903.

Special Editions: Careers Extra (monthly); Health (2x/yr).

Special Weekly Sections: Careers, Business Extra (mon); Tuesday Business (tues); Food (wed); Travel & Recreation (thur); Scene, Real Estate (fri); Super Saturday Classifieds (sat); Sports Pull-Out, Travel, Bloomberg-personal, Forum, Arts & Leisure, Tech Talk, Weddings, Comics, Your Style, Health & Fitness, Home Style, Informed, Coupons (S); Arts & Lifestyle (daily).

Magazines: Style, Home Style, Health & Fitness, Informed (S-monthly); TVPlus (TV Magazine).

GENERAL MANAGEMENT

Owner/Publisher Patrick J Purcell
Vice Pres-Finance/General Manager Jean Eichenbaum
Vice Pres-Advertising Jack Breed
Vice Pres-Human Resources David St Mary

ADVERTISING

Manager-National Randy Hano
Manager-Retail Kathleen Rush
Manager-Classified Paul Gulya
Manager-Classified Joseph J LoPilato
Manager-Marketing Research/Administration Dianne Chin

MARKETING AND PROMOTION

Vice Pres-Promotion Gwen Gage

CIRCULATION

Vice Pres John Hoarty
Asst Director James DeSalvo
Manager-Marketing Amanda Anderson
Manager-Home Delivery Gerald Sher

NEWS EXECUTIVES

Editor Andrew F Costello Jr
Exec Asst to Editor Bert MacNeil
Managing Editor-News Andrew Gully
Managing Editor-Sunday Features Kevin Convey
Deputy Managing Editor-News Andrew Tomolonis
Deputy Managing Editor-News James MacLaughlin
Deputy Managing Editor-Arts/Lifestyle Sonia Turek
Asst Managing Editor-Business Mary Helen Gillespie
Asst Managing Editor-Arts/Entertainment Bill Weber

EDITORS AND MANAGERS

Art/Graphics Editor Ed Barrett
Chief Editorial Writer Guy Darst
Exec City Editor Mike Bello
Editor/Columnist Joe Sciacca
Editorial Columnist Don Feder
Editorial Page Editor Shelly Cohen
Environmental Editor Jules Crittendon
Fashion Editor Sarah Wright
Films Critic Editor Jim Verniere
Food Editor Jane Dornbusch
Health/Medical Editor Mike Lasalandra
Investigative/Politics Editor Walter Roche
Lifestyle Editor Stephanie Schorow
Music Editor Larry Katz
News Columnist Peter Gelzinis
News Columnist Joe Fitzgerald
News Columnist Margery Eagan
News Columnist Leonard Greene
Director-Photography Kevin Cole
Political Columnist Wayne Woodlief
Political Columnist Howie Carr
Real Estate Editor Jim Matte
Sports Editor Mark Torpey
Sports Columnist George Kimball
Sports Columnist Jim Baker
Sports Columnist Steve Buckley
Sports Columnist Steve Bulpett
State House Bureau Chief Robert Connolly
Sunday Editor Eric Norment
Sunday Magazine Stephanie Schorow
Sunday Magazine Sarah Wright
Television Columnist Monica Collins
The Inside Track Columnist Gayle Fee
The Inside Track Columnist Laura Raposa
Washington Bureau Chief Andrew Miga

MANAGEMENT INFORMATION SERVICES

Director-Info Technology Tom Libby

PRODUCTION

Director-Operations Thomas J Connors
Asst Manager Michael Donovan
Superintendent-Composing Domenic Ferrante
Superintendent-Engraving Stanley Sampson
Superintendent-Pressroom Robert Reilly
Superintendent-Mailroom Robert Johnson

Market Information: Split Run; Operate audiotex; Electronic edition.

Mechanical available: Letterpress (direct); Black and 1 ROP color; insert accepted — preprinted; page cut-offs — $22\frac{3}{4}$".

Mechanical specifications: Type page $10\frac{13}{16}$" x $14\frac{1}{4}$"; E - 5 cols, $2\frac{1}{16}$", $\frac{3}{32}$" between; A - 5 cols, $2\frac{1}{16}$", $\frac{3}{32}$" between; C - 8 cols, $1\frac{1}{4}$", $\frac{1}{8}$" between.

Commodity consumption: Newsprint 45,000 metric tons; widths $58\frac{1}{2}$", $43\frac{7}{8}$", $29\frac{1}{4}$"; black ink 1,100,000 pounds; color ink 28,000 pounds; single pages printed 41,000; average pages per issue 104(d), 168(S); single plates used 350,000.

Equipment: EDITORIAL: Front-end hardware — AT/9000; Front-end software — AT/7000; Printers — 2-Panasonic/1180, 3-Canon/Laser, 3-LaserMaster/1800 DAF, QMS/2210, 1-QMS/860; Other equipment — 124-AT/Terminal, 3-Ap/Mac Radius, 4-Ap/Mac IIfx, 1-Ap/Super Mac, 1-Ap/Mac, 10-PC/486. CLASSIFIED: Front-end hardware — AT/9000; Front-end software — AT/7000; Printers — Panasonic/1180, 1-C.Itoh/8000, 2-HP/DeskJet 520, 1-HP/LaserJet IIP, 1-KXP/1826, 1-KXP/1624, 1-KXP/2124; Other equipment — 32-AT/terminal. DISPLAY: Adv layout systems — Mk/Managing Editor ALS; Front-end hardware — 1-Ap/Mac IIfx, 1-Ap/Super Mac; Printers — 1-QMS/2200; Other equipment — 2-Ap/Mac Classic, 2-PC/486. PRODUCTION: Pagination software — Editorial System Engineering/Editorial News Layout; Typesetters — 2-AU/APS5U, 1-AG/A; Platemaking systems — Na; Plate exposures — 3-Na/Titan III; Plate processors — 3-Na/C-220; Scanners — 1-ECR/Autokon 1030, 1-ECR/Autokon 1000; Production cameras — 1-C/Pager, 1-C/Spartan III, 2-C/F; Automatic film processors — 1-LE/1800, 1-LE/2600, 1-C/66F, Rapiddoprint/AG1 DD6400; Shrink lenses — 2-CK Optical/5.4%. PRESSROOM: Line 1 — 21-H/Color Convertible; Line 2 — 20-H/Color Convertible; Folders

Massachusetts I-187

— 6-H/3:2, 1-H/2:1; Pasters — 30-Eaton Dynamatic/SCR Mark 3; Reels and stands — 30-Wd, 11-H/Reels; Press control system — 14-Walco/Solid State, 27-GE/Control, CH. MAILROOM: Counter stackers — 10-HL, 2-S/2200-2; Inserters and stuffers — HI, 2-HI/1372, S/NP630 26:1; Bundle tyer — 16-MLN/2A, 6-Dynaric; Wrapping singles — 1-J, 2-CH, 4-HL/SH, 2-Id. COMMUNICATIONS: Digital ad delivery system — AP AdSend, Digiflex, BBS. WIRE SERVICES: News — AP, RN, DJ, TV Data; Photos — AP; Stock tables — AP Grand Central Stocks; Syndicates — SHNS, GNS; Receiving dishes — size-10ft, AP. BUSINESS COMPUTERS: 1-NT C/S System w/ Microsoft/Windows, 1-Unisys/V340, 1-Sco/Unix; Applications: Class adv billing, Adv billing; PCs & micros networked; PCs & main system networked.

BROCKTON
Plymouth County

'90 U.S. Census- 92,788; E&P '96 Est. 90,609
ABC-CZ (90): 199,521 (HH 69,288)

The Enterprise
(e-mon to fri; m-sat; S)

The Enterprise, 60 Main St.; PO Box 1450, Brockton, MA 02403; tel (508) 586-7200; fax (508) 586-7903; e-mail enternews@aol.com.

Circulation: 50,111(e); 49,915(m-sat); 62,585(S); ABC Sept. 30, 1995.

Price: 50¢(d); 50¢(sat); $1.50(S); $3.05/wk (eS); $12.20/mo; $143.60/yr.

Advertising: Open inch rate $28.10(e); $28.10(m-sat); $28.10(S). **Representative:** Landon Associates Inc.

News Services: AP, LAT-WP, SHNS. **Politics:** Independent. **Established:** 1880.

Not Published: New Year; Memorial Day; Independence Day; Labor Day; Christmas.

Special Editions: Education (Jan); Love Lines, Brides, Washington's Birthday, Auto Special, Tax Special (Feb); Spring Home & Garden, Education (Apr); Real Estate (May); Leisure Living/Outdoors, Best of Summer (June); Education (Aug); Fall Bridal, Football '96, Neighbors (Sept); Fall Home Improvement (Oct); Chronology Pages (Dec).

Special Weekly Sections: Best Food Day (wed); Home & Garden (thur); Stock/Financial/Bank, Home & Garden, Travel, Hobbies, Fashion, Books, Health & Fitness, Senior Citizens (S); Business (daily).

Magazines: USA Weekend, TV Times (S).

Broadcast Affiliates: WBET-AM, WCAV-FM.

CORPORATE OFFICERS

President Myron F Fuller
Secretary Charles N Fuller

GENERAL MANAGEMENT

Publisher Charles N Fuller
Business Manager David F Meade Jr
Controller Harry E Nelson

ADVERTISING

Director Roy Vallatini
Manager Richard E Ferreira
Manager-Classified Paula J Walker
Coordinator-National & Preprint Laura Hogan

CIRCULATION

Director David M Jameson
Manager Scott Murdoch

NEWS EXECUTIVE

Exec Editor Bruce P Smith

EDITORS AND MANAGERS

Action Line Editor June Jurek
Amusements Editor Joseph Sherman
Automotive Editor Leigh Carlson
Books Editor Fred Nobles
Business/Finance Editor Terry Downing
City Editor Stephen Damish
Editorial Page Editor Gary Finkelstein
Education Editor Marilyn Hancock
Environmental Editor Gil Bliss
Farms/Agriculture Editor Paul Salters
Fashion/Style Editor Louise Anderson
Features Editor Joseph Sherman
Films/Theater Editor Martha Raber
Food Editor Louise Anderson
Graphics Editor/Art Director David Laferriere
Health/Medical Editor Kent Jones
Librarian Steve Sharp
Lifestyle Editor Fred Nobles
Music Editor Martha Raber
National Editor Garry Leppanen
News Editor Michael H Allain
Photo Editor Craig Murray
Political/Government Editor John Hoey
Radio/Television Editor Martha Raber
Real Estate Editor Terry Downing
Religion Editor Shirley Rajala
Science/Technology Editor Fred Nobles
Sports Editor William Abramson
Suburban Editor Robert Richards
Sunday Editor Joseph Sherman
Travel Editor Fred Nobles
Wire Editor Garry Leppanen
Women's Editor Louise Anderson

PRODUCTION

Foreman-Composing Room Jack Richardson
Foreman-Pressroom D Dmitruk
Manager-Systems/Composing Frank Gabriele

Market Information: Zoned editions; Split Run; TMC; Operate audiotex.

Mechanical available: Letterpress and Flexo combined; Black and 3 ROP colors; insert accepted — preprinted; page cut-offs — $22\frac{3}{4}$".

Mechanical specifications: Type page 13" x 21"; E - 6 cols, $2\frac{1}{16}$", $\frac{1}{8}$" between; A - 6 cols, $2\frac{1}{16}$", $\frac{1}{8}$" between; C - 9 cols, $1\frac{3}{8}$", $\frac{1}{16}$" between.

Commodity consumption: Newsprint 5,537 short tons; widths 55", $41\frac{1}{4}$", 27.5; black ink 193,418 pounds; color ink 24,033 pounds; single pages printed 17,269; average pages per issue 41.7(d), 85.6(S); single plates used 27,067.

Equipment: EDITORIAL: Front-end hardware — 2-Sun/Sparc Station, 1-Sun/Sparc 20 Server, 1-Sun/Sparc 10 Client, 2-Dell/PC 486 Wire Server, 44-Dell/PC 486; Front-end software — HI/Newsmaker 2.22, HI/XP21 2.5, HI/2100 2.1; Printers — HP/LaserJet 4si; Other equipment — 1-Ap/Mac Quadra 950, 1-Ap/Power Mac 8100-80, 1-Ap/Mac II. CLASSIFIED: Front-end hardware — 2-Dell/PC 486, 11-Dell/PC 486 Workstation; Front-end software — HI/CASH 5.0; Printers — Epson. AUDIOTEX: Supplier name — Tele-Publishing Inc. DISPLAY: Adv layout systems — CJ, HI/2100, Ap/Mac; Front-end hardware — DEC/VAX 4100, 4-Dell/PC 486, 2-Ap/Mac Quadra 800; Front-end software — CJ, HI/2100 PLS 2.1; Printers — Dataproducts/B600, Dataproducts/B1000, 2-Toshiba/TN-7270. PRODUCTION: Pagination software — HI/XP21 2.1; Typesetters — 2-HI/7700, 2-MON/RipExpress RIP, 2-PelBox/108C, 1-III/3850; Platemaking systems — Na; Plate exposures — 1-Burgess, 1-News Printer/II, Master; Plate processors — 2-Na/NP-80, 2-Na/FP1; Electronic picture desk — Lf/AP Leaf Picture Desk, HI/Image System; Scanners — 1-ECR/Autokon 1000, X/7650, Umax; Production cameras — 1-C/Spartan III, 1-P/Pager; Automatic film processors — 1-LE/Excel 26, 1-P/Pakonolith processor; Reproportion units — C/Image Reverser; Film transporters — 1-C/Spartan, 1-C/Pager; Shrink lenses — 1-C/Spartan, 1-C/Prime Squeeze Lens; Digital color separation equipment — HI/Images, 1-RZ. PRESSROOM: Line 1 — G/Mark I, MAN/Flexoman; Pasters — G/Automatic. MAILROOM: Counter stackers — 1-HL/Monitor HT; Inserters and stuffers — 1-GMA/SLS 1000; Bundle tyer — 3-OVL/JP-80, OVL/K101. WIRE SERVICES: News — AP, LAT-WP, SHNS; Photos — AP; Stock tables — AP; Syndicates — LATS, NEA, Register & Tribune, Universal Press, Chronicle; Receiving dishes — size-10ft, AP. BUSINESS COMPUTERS: DEC/VAX 4100; Applications: CJ, Circ, Accts receivable, Accts payable, Gen ledger, Adv layout, Adv tracking; PCs & main system networked.

CAPE COD
See HYANNIS

CLINTON
Worcester County

'90 U.S. Census- 13,222; E&P '96 Est. 13,672

Daily Item (e-mon to fri)

Daily Item, 156 Church St.; PO Box 710, Clinton, MA 01510; tel (508) 368-0176; fax (508) 368-1151. Chronicle Publishing Co. group.

Circulation: 3,906(e); Sworn Sept. 29, 1995.

Price: 50¢(d); $1.85/wk (carrier); $8.00/mo (Worcester County).

Advertising: Open inch rate $8.60(e). **Representative:** Landon Associates Inc.

News Service: AP. **Politics:** Independent. **Established:** 1893.

Not Published: New Year; Memorial Day; Independence Day; Labor Day; Thanksgiving; Christmas.

Advertising not accepted: Objectionable copy.

Special Editions: Bridal (Jan); Community Guide (Feb); Senior Salute (Mar); Homes & Real Estate (Apr); Spring into Summer (May); Guide to Professionals (June); Summer Eats & Treats (July); Back-to-School, Fall Fashion (Aug); Fall Home Improvement (Sept); Car Care (Oct); Gift Guide (Nov); Season's Best (Dec); Bridal (Spring); Bridal (Summer).

Special Weekly Sections: Health, Seniors (mon); Business & Weekly Business Review (tues); Food, Kids (wed); Entertainment & Weekend (thur); Homes (fri).

CORPORATE OFFICER

CEO John Sias

GENERAL MANAGEMENT

Publisher Frank Hewitt

ADVERTISING

Manager Ron Chapdelain
Manager-Classified Theresa Tierney
Manager-Classified Sandra Hisman

CIRCULATION

Manager Chris Parker

NEWS EXECUTIVE

Managing Editor Jan Gottesman

EDITORS AND MANAGERS

News Editor Lisa Drueke
Sports Editor Susan Wessling

PRODUCTION

Manager Patricia Houck

Market Information: ADS.

Mechanical available: Flexo; Black and 3 ROP colors; insert accepted — preprinted; page cut-offs — $22\frac{3}{4}$".

Mechanical specifications: Type page 13" x 21"; E - 6 cols, 2.07", $\frac{1}{8}$" between; A - 6 cols, 2.07", $\frac{1}{8}$" between; C - 6 cols, 2.07", $\frac{1}{8}$" between.

Commodity consumption: Newsprint 140 short tons; width $27\frac{5}{16}$"; black ink 4,100 pounds; color ink 320 pounds; single pages printed 2,978; average pages per issue 12(d); single plates used 1,640.

Equipment: EDITORIAL: Front-end hardware — COM/Intrepid. CLASSIFIED: Front-end hardware — COM/Intrepid. DISPLAY: Front-end hardware — Ap/Mac IIsi; Front-end software — QuarkXPress, Multi-Ad/Creator; Printers — NEC/Silent Writer Model 95 Laser Printer; Other equipment — Ap/Mac One Scanner. PRODUCTION: Typesetters — NEC/Silent Writer 95 Laser Printer. LIBRARY: Combination — COM/Intrepid PC-based index. WIRE SERVICES: News — AP; Syndicates — NEA. BUSINESS COMPUTERS: AST/VGA-286; Applications: Accts receivable, Accts payable.

DEDHAM
Norfolk County

'90 U.S. Census- 23,782; E&P '96 Est. 22,651
ABC-NDM (90): 65,039 (HH 23,952)

Daily Transcript (e-mon to fri)

Daily Transcript, 33 New York Ave.; PO Box 9149, Framingham, MA 01701; tel (617) 329-5008; fax (617) 326-9675. Community Newspaper Co. (Middlesex Community Newspapers) group.

Circulation: 7,761(e); ABC Sept. 30, 1995.

Price: 50¢(d); $2.00/wk; $104.00/yr.

Advertising: Open inch rate $12.35(e). **Representatives:** Landon Associates Inc.; US Suburban Press.

News Service: AP. **Politics:** Independent. **Established:** 1973.

Note: For detailed information on production, see the Framingham Middlesex News.

Not Published: New Year; Christmas.

Special Editions: Bridal '96 (Jan); New Construction, President's Day, Auto Showcase (Feb); Progress '96 (Mar); Outdoors, Spring Home & Garden, Home Buyers Guide (Apr); Nursing '96, Parenting, Health & Lifestyles, Your Child, Senior Lifestyles (May); Guide to Metro West (June); Community Guides (July); Back-to-School (Aug); Bridal, Fall Home Improvement, New Construction (Sept); Outdoors, Wheels, Working Women, Interiors (Oct); Holiday Dining, Holiday Gift Guide (Nov); Home for the Holidays, Last Minute Gift Guide (Dec).

Special Weekly Sections: Sports Monday (mon); Autoweekly, Best Food Day (wed); Business, Expanded Entertainment (thur); This Week in Real Estate (fri).

Magazines: Weekend Guide; Auto Weekly.

CORPORATE OFFICER

President Larry Franklin

GENERAL MANAGEMENT

Publisher Asa Cole
Controller Jeffrey Feingold
Manager-Credit Dianne Nordstrom

ADVERTISING

Director Paul M Farrell

MARKETING AND PROMOTION

Manager-Marketing/Promotion Paula Bubello

TELECOMMUNICATIONS

Manager-Telecommunications Debra Freeman

CIRCULATION

Manager Brian Hanify

NEWS EXECUTIVE

Editor William Finucane

EDITORS AND MANAGERS

Action Line Editor Joseph Gibbs
Automotive Editor Karen Buckley
Business Editor Robert Dickson
City/Metro Editor Joseph Gibbs
Editorial Page Editor Joseph Gibbs
Education Editor Joseph Gibbs
Environmental Editor Joseph Gibbs
Features/Travel Editor Joseph Gibbs
Finance Editor Robert Dickson
Graphics Editor/Art Director Joseph Gibbs
Living/Lifestyle Editor Joseph Gibbs
National Editor Joseph Gibbs
News Editor Joseph Gibbs
Photo Editor Joseph Gibbs
Political/Government Editor Joseph Gibbs
Religion Editor Joseph Gibbs
Sports Editor Craig Larson
Television/Film Editor Joseph Gibbs
Theater/Music Editor Joseph Gibbs

PRODUCTION

Manager Nancy McNiff

Market Information: Zoned editions.

Mechanical available: Offset; Black and 3 ROP colors; insert accepted — preprinted; page cut-offs — 15".

Mechanical specifications: Type page $10\frac{13}{16}$" x $13\frac{1}{2}$"; E - 5 cols, $2\frac{1}{16}$", $\frac{1}{8}$" between; A - 5 cols, $2\frac{1}{16}$", $\frac{1}{8}$" between; C - 7 cols, $1\frac{3}{8}$", $\frac{1}{16}$" between.

Commodity consumption: Newsprint 7,500 short tons; widths 30", 15"; black ink 160,000 pounds; color ink 21,000 pounds; single pages printed 9,796; average pages per issue 40(d); single plates used 67,600.

Equipment: EDITORIAL: Front-end hardware — PC/286, PC/386, PC/486; Front-end software — III/Editorial System; Printers — Toshiba; Other equipment — Microcom/Modems. CLASSIFIED: Front-end hardware — PC; Front-end software — III/Classified Software; Printers — HP/Ruggedwriters, Toshiba; Other equipment — Microcom/Modems. DISPLAY: Adv layout systems — 2-HI/2002, 2-HI/2220, 2-HI/1420, 1-MDT/350, 2-HI/1250, 2-Vecra. PRODUCTION: Pagination software — QuarkXPress 3.3; Typesetters — Tegra/Varityper/ 5000, 1-Tegra/Varityper/5100, 2-III/3850; Plate exposures — 2-Nu/Ultra Plus; Plate processors — 2-Nat/A340; Electronic picture desk — Lf/AP Leaf Picture Desk; Scanners — 3-Kk/ 2035 Film Scanner, 1-AG Arcus Plus Color Scanner; Production cameras — 2-Image Maker/ 506A, 2-C/News Pager; Automatic film processors — 2-LE/Excel 26, 1-P/Film Processor; Film transporters — 2-C, P/Film Transport; Shrink lenses — 1-CK Optical $9\frac{1}{4}$, 2-CK Optical/5%. PRESSROOM: Line 1 — 12-G/Urbanite; Line 2 — 12-G/Urbanite; Line 3 — 1-G/HV; Pasters — 20-G/Automatic 2 am; Reels and stands — 20-G/Automatic 2-arm; Press control system — 2-Fin. MAILROOM: Counter stackers — 2-Id, 1-RIMA, 4-HL/Monitor HT2; Inserters and stuffers — 1-S/948P, 1-KR, 1-GMA/SLS 1000; Bundle tyer — 6-MLN; Addressing machine — 2-Ch, 1-KR, 1-Domino/Ink Jet Printer. WIRE SERVICES: News — AP. BUSINESS COMPUTERS: HP/3000-935 Series 935; Applications: Gen ledger, Accounting, Customer invoicing.

FALL RIVER
Bristol County

'90 U.S. Census- 92,703; E&P '96 Est. 93,238
ABC-CZ (90): 151,991 (HH 58,659)

The Herald News (m-mon to sat)
Sunday Herald News (S)

The Herald News, 207 Pocasset St., Fall River, MA 02722-3010; tel (508) 676-8211; fax (508) 673-3375. Journal Register Co. group.

I-188 Massachusetts

Circulation: 31,827(m); 31,827(m-sat); 34,924(S); ABC Sept. 30, 1995.
Price: 50¢(d); 50¢(sat); $1.25(S); $2.85/wk; $148.20/yr.
Advertising: Open inch rate $25.85(m); $25.85(m-sat); $25.85(S). **Representative:** Landon Associates Inc.
News Service: AP. **Politics:** Independent. **Established:** 1872.
Note: The Herald News also prints the Pawtucket (RI) Times, a Journal Register publication.
Not Published: Christmas.
Special Editions: Bridal, Year in Review, Super Bowl (Jan); Auto, Health & Fitness (Feb); Progress (Mar); Domestic Violence (March); Home & Garden, Car Care, Employment Quarterly (Apr); Home & Garden (May); Summer Guide, Bridal, Chamber Guide, Employment Quarterly (June); Business Review (July); Back-to-School, Employment Quarterly, Fall River Celebrates America (Aug); Football Preview, Fall Car Care, Auto Show (Sept); Readers Choice, Car Care, Home Improvement, New Car Intro (Oct); Home Furnishings, Gift Guide, Employment Quarterly, Christmas in Fall River (Nov); Hockey & Basketball Preview, Christmas Gift Guide (Dec).
Special Weekly Sections: Wheels (tues); Best Food Day (wed); Friday (Entertainment Guide) (fri); Real Estate Guide (sat); Travel, Lifestyle (S); Business (daily).
Magazines: USA Weekend, TV Preview, Comics (S).

CORPORATE OFFICERS

President/CEO	Robert M Jelenic
Exec Vice Pres/Chief Financial Officer/Treasurer	Jean B Clifton

GENERAL MANAGEMENT

Publisher	Tracy R Greene
Publisher-Emeritus	Edward F St John
Controller	Joseph P Cavanna

ADVERTISING

Director	William T Murray

CIRCULATION

Director	Neil Moran
Manager	Craig Kauffmann

NEWS EXECUTIVE

Managing Editor	Paul V Palange

EDITORS AND MANAGERS

Asst Managing Editor	Bianca Pavoncello
Editorial Page Editor	Lisa Strattan
Entertainment	Tom Ward
Librarian	Judy Rebello
Lifestyles Editor	Arthur Jones
Exec Sports Editor	Michael Silva
Sports Editor	George Darmondy

PRODUCTION

Foreman-Composing	William Benevides
Foreman-Mailroom	Robert Pacheco

Market Information: Split Run; TMC.
Mechanical available: Offset; Black and 3 ROP colors; insert accepted — preprinted; page cutoffs — $22\frac{3}{4}$".
Mechanical specifications: Type page 13" x $21\frac{3}{8}$"; E - 6 cols, $2\frac{1}{16}$", $\frac{1}{8}$" between; A - 6 cols, $2\frac{1}{16}$", $\frac{1}{8}$" between; C - 9 cols, $1\frac{3}{8}$", $\frac{1}{16}$" between.
Commodity consumption: Newsprint 3,819 short tons; widths $13\frac{3}{4}$", $27\frac{1}{2}$"; black ink 70,651 pounds; color ink 17,185 pounds; single pages printed 21,001; average pages per issue 32(d), 62(S); single plates used 26,880.
Equipment: EDITORIAL: Front-end hardware — Dewar/Information System, PC Network; Front-end software — Dewar/View; Printers — MON. CLASSIFIED: Front-end hardware — Dewar/Information System, PC Network; Front-end software — Dewar/System IV. DISPLAY: Adv layout systems — Dewar; Front-end hardware — Ap/Mac Centris 650; Front-end software — Multi-Ad/Creator; Printers — MON. PRODUCTION: Pagination software — Dewar/View, QPS; Typesetters — 2-MON/ExpressMaster 1200, 1-MON/PaperMaster 600; Plate exposures — 2-Amerigraph/433 DS; Plate processors — 1-Graham; Electronic picture desk — Lf/AP Leaf Picture Desk; Scanners — Lf/Leafscan 35; Production cameras — 1-C/Spartan III; Automatic film processors — 3-Konica/K550; Film transporters — 1-C/Spartan III; Digital color separation equipment — Umax.
PRESSROOM: Line 1 — 9-G/Urbanite; Press drives — Fin; Folders — G/Urbanite 2:1; Pasters — 8-Jardis/Automatic 4540; Press registration system — Stoesser. MAILROOM: Counter stackers — 1-HL/Monitor, 1-MM/CN70 (388); Inserters and stuffers — 1-MM/227; Bundle tyer — 3-MLN/EE, 1-MLN/2A; Addressing machine — 1-Ch/515010. WIRE SERVICES: News — AP. BUSINESS COMPUTERS: 1-Bs/92, IBM/AS400; Applications: INSI: Circ, Adv, Payroll, Gen ledger, Accts payable, Credit mgmt; PCs & micros networked; PCs & main system networked.

FITCHBURG

Worcester County

'90 U.S. Census- 41,194; **E&P '96 Est.** 42,752
ABC-CZ (90): 79,339 (HH 30,197)

Sentinel & Enterprise

(e-mon to fri; m-sat; S)

Sentinel & Enterprise, 808 Main St.; PO Box 730, Fitchburg, MA 01420; tel (508) 343-6911; fax (508) 342-1158. Thomson Newspapers group.
Circulation: 20,125(e); 20,125(m-sat); 20,181(S); ABC Sept. 30, 1995.
Price: 50¢(d); 50¢(sat); 75¢(S); $2.50/wk.
Advertising: Open inch rate $18.92(e); $18.92 (m-sat); $18.92(S). **Representatives:** Thomson Newspapers; Landon Associates Inc.
News Service: AP. **Politics:** Independent. **Established:** 1838.
Not Published: Christmas.
Special Editions: Bride and Groom (Jan); Washington's Birthday (Feb); Spring Home Improvement, Progress (Mar); Mother's Day Gifts, Graduation (May); Longs Jo Bike Race (July); Back-to-School (Aug); Fall Home Improvement (Sept); Fall Car Care (Oct); Thanksgiving Edition (Nov); Holiday Gift Guide (Dec).
Special Weekly Sections: Today's Woman (mon); Well-Being (tues); Food & Nutrition (wed); Auto Weekender (thur); Homes (fri); "As Time Goes By" (Seniors) (sat); Pursuit (travel & hobbies) (S).

GENERAL MANAGEMENT

Publisher/General Manager	William A White
Asst General Manager	Bernie Stephens
Manager-Credit	Leo Niro

ADVERTISING

Director-Sales/Marketing	Janet Banville

TELECOMMUNICATIONS

Audiotex Manager	Janet Banville

CIRCULATION

Director	Bernie Stephens

NEWS EXECUTIVES

Exec Editor	Ann Connery Frantz
Managing Editor	Michael Cleveland

EDITORS AND MANAGERS

Arts Editor	S DiGeronimo
Automotive Editor	Al Tuttle
Business/Finance Editor	Bruce Phillips
City Editor	Brian Milligan
Editorial Page Editor	Michael Fallon
Education Editor	Tracy Seelye
Entertainment/Amusements Editor	S DiGeronimo
Fashion/Style Editor	Michele Babineau
Features Editor	Keith Shaw
Food Editor	J Selwyn
Health/Medical Editor	Keith Shaw
Living/Lifestyle Editor	Keith Shaw
National Editor	Tracy Seelye
News Editor	Michael Cleveland
Photo Editor	Richard Sowers
Political/Government Editor	Tracy Seelye
Science/Technology Editor	Bruce Phillips
Sports Editor	Jim Clark
Television/Film Editor	S DiGeronimo
Theater/Music Editor	S DiGeronimo
Travel Editor	Keith Shaw

MANAGEMENT INFORMATION SERVICES

Manager-Systems	Michele Babineau
Online Manager	John Shaw

PRODUCTION

Director	Normajean Dupuis

Market Information: Split Run; TMC; ADS; Operate database; Operate audiotex.
Mechanical available: Offset; Black and 3 ROP colors; insert accepted — preprinted, single sheet; page cut-offs — $22\frac{3}{4}$".
Mechanical specifications: Type page 13" x $21\frac{1}{2}$"; E - 6 cols, $2\frac{1}{16}$", $\frac{1}{8}$" between; A - 6 cols, $2\frac{1}{16}$", $\frac{1}{8}$" between; C - 9 cols, $1\frac{3}{8}$", $\frac{1}{16}$" between.
Commodity consumption: Newsprint 1,071 short tons; width 27"; black ink 26,158 pounds; color ink 3,350 pounds; single pages printed 10,800; average pages per issue 28(d), 28(S); single plates used 9,744.
Equipment: EDITORIAL: Front-end hardware — CText; Front-end software — CText; Printers — 1-Tegra/Varityper 5100, 1-Tegra/Varityper 5300, 1-Tegra/Varityper 4000. CLASSIFIED: Front-end hardware — CText; Front-end software — CText; Printers — 1-Tegra/Varityper 5100, 1-Tegra/Varityper 5300, 1-Tegra/Varityper 4000. DISPLAY: Adv layout systems — CText/Adept, Ap/Macs; Front-end hardware — CText/Adept, Ap/Mac cx, Ap/Mac ci; Front-end software — QuarkXPress, Adobe/Photoshop; Printers — Tegra/Varityper 5100, Tegra/Varityper 5300, Tegra/Varityper 4000, Ap/Mac Personal LaserWriter II. PRODUCTION: Typesetters — 1-Tegra/Varityper 5300E, 2-Tegra/Varityper 5100, Tegra/Varityper 4000, 2-Ap/Mac LaserWriter; Plate exposures — Nu/Flip Top FT40V6UPNS; Plate processors — Nat/A-250; Electronic picture desk — Lf/AP Leaf Picture Desk; Scanners — Lf/Leafscan 45; Production cameras — LE/121; Automatic film processors — Jobo, Screen/CD-281-Q; Film transporters — LE; Color separation equipment (conventional) — Lf/AP Leaf Picture Desk, Lf/Leafscan 45; Digital color separation equipment — Lf/AP Leaf Picture Desk, Lf/Leafscan 45.
PRESSROOM: Line 1 — 7-G/Urbanite; Press drives — W/House Motors; Folders — 1-G/2:1; Press control system — Thin Core; Press registration system — Pin Registration System. MAILROOM: Bundle tyer — OVL; Addressing machine — Domino. WIRE SERVICES: News — AP Laserphoto, NEA, THO, United Features, SHNS; Stock tables — AP; Syndicates — THO. BUSINESS COMPUTERS: PBS; Applications: PBS/MediaPlus; PCs & micros networked; PCs & main system networked.

FRAMINGHAM

Middlesex County

'90 U.S. Census- 64,989; **E&P '96 Est.** 64,720
ABC-NDM (90): 198,344 (HH 73,926)

The Middlesex News

(e-mon to fri; m-sat; S)

The Middlesex News, 33 New York Ave.; PO Box 9149, Framingham, MA 01701-9157; tel (508) 626-3800; e-mail mnews@world.std.com; web site http://www.harvard-net.com/marathon/ & gopher://ftp.std.com. Community Newspaper Co. (Middlesex Community Newspapers) group.
Circulation: 33,992(e); 33,992(m-sat); 42,569(S); ABC Sept. 30, 1995.
Price: 50¢(d); 50¢(sat); $1.50(S); $2.75/wk; $143.00/yr (carrier), $208.00/yr (mail).
Advertising: Open inch rate $36.15(e); $36.15(m-sat); $36.15(S). **Representatives:** Landon Associates Inc.; US Suburban Press.
News Services: AP, SHNS. **Politics:** Independent. **Established:** 1897.
Special Editions: Weddings (Jan); President's Day, Auto Showcase, New Construction (Feb); Business (Mar); Spring Home & Garden, Home Buyer's Guide (Apr); Parenting, Health & Lifestyles (May); MetroWest Community Guide (June); Community Guides (July); Back-to-School/College (Aug); Bridal Section, Fall Home Improvement, New Construction (Sept); Wheels, Interiors (Oct); Holiday Gift Guide, Holiday Dining (Nov); Home for the Holidays, Last Minute Gift Guide (Dec).
Special Weekly Sections: Metrowest Classroom, Sports Monday (mon); Autoweekly, Best Food Day (wed); This Week in Real Estate (fri); Mutual Fund Listing (sat); Expanded Business, Expanded Entertainment, Working, Cyberspace (S).
Magazines: USA Weekend, TV Viewer (own), Comic Section (S).

GENERAL MANAGEMENT

Publisher	Asa Cole
Controller	Greg Weaver

ADVERTISING

Director-Sales/Marketing	Paul Farrell
Manager-Major Accounts	Karen Aloia
Manager-Retail	David Geiger
Manager-Retail	Susan Robinson
Manager-Auto/Real Estate	David Kampner
Manager-Print & Delivery	Diane Nordstrom
Manager-Special Sections	David Kampner
Analyst	Susan Bleiweiss

MARKETING AND PROMOTION

Director-Promotion	Paula Bubello

TELECOMMUNICATIONS

Manager-Info Service	Emily Greenwood

CIRCULATION

Director	Brian Hanify
Manager-Transportation	Gary Burnell

NEWS EXECUTIVE

Editor	Andrea Haynes

EDITORS AND MANAGERS

Business/Finance Editor	Maureen McLellan
Design Director	Patricia Capobianco
Education Page Editor	Vanessa Parks
Fashion/Theater Editor	Virginia Lucier
Features/Special Sections Editor	Karen Buckley
News Editor	Rus Lodi
Op-Editor/Editorial Page Editor	Rick Holmes
Photo Department Manager	Art Illman
Regional Editor-South	William Finucane
Regional Editor-Central	Neil Swidey
Regional Editor-West	Brian Milligan
Sports Editor	Mark Murphy
Sunday Editor	Joe Dwinell
Technology Editor	Eric Bauer

MANAGEMENT INFORMATION SERVICES

Data Processing Manager	Barbara Bell

PRODUCTION

Director-Operations	Nancy McNiff

Market Information: Zoned editions; Split Run; TMC; ADS; Operate database.
Mechanical available: Offset; Black and 3 ROP colors; insert accepted — preprinted; page cutoffs — $27\frac{3}{8}$".
Mechanical specifications: Type page 13" x 21"; E - 6 cols, $2\frac{1}{16}$", $\frac{1}{8}$" between; A - 6 cols, $2\frac{1}{16}$", $\frac{1}{8}$" between; C - 9 cols, $1\frac{3}{8}$", $\frac{1}{16}$" between.
Commodity consumption: Newsprint 7,500 short tons; widths $27\frac{3}{8}$", $13\frac{1}{2}$"; black ink 160,000 pounds; color ink 21,000 pounds; single pages printed 9,796; average pages per issue 32(d), 32(sat), 76(S); single plates used 67,600.
Equipment: EDITORIAL: Front-end hardware — PC/286, PC/386, PC/486; Front-end software — III/Editorial System; Printers — Toshiba; Other equipment — Microcom/Modems. CLASSIFIED: Front-end hardware — PC; Front-end software — III/Classified Software; Printers — HP/Ruggedwriters, Toshiba; Other equipment — Microcom/Modems. DISPLAY: Adv layout systems — 2-HI/2002, 2-HI/2220, 2-HI/1420, 1-MDT/350, 2-HI/1250, 2-Vecra. PRODUCTION: Pagination software — QuarkXPress 3.3; Typesetters — 1-Tegra/Varityper 5000, 1-Tegra/Varityper 5100, 2-III/3850; Plate exposures — 2-Nu/Ultra-Plus; Plate processors — 2-Nat/A340; Electronic picture desk — Lf/AP Leaf Picture Desk; Scanners — 3-Kk/2035 Film Scanner, 1-AG/Arcus Plus Color Scanner; Production cameras — 2-Image Maker/506A, 2-C/News Pager; Automatic film processors — 2-LE/Excel 26, P/Film Processor; Film transporters — 2-C, P/Film Transport; Shrink lenses — 1-CK Optical/$9\frac{1}{4}$%, 2-CK Optical/5%.
PRESSROOM: Line 1 — 12-G/Urbanite; Line 2 — 12-G/Urbanite; Line 3 — 1-G/HV; Pasters — 20-G/Automatic 2 arm; Reels and stands — 20-G/Automatic 2 arm; Press control system — 2-Fin. MAILROOM: Counter stackers — 2-Id, 1-RIMA, 4-HL/Monitor HT2; Inserters and stuffers — 1-S/948P, 1-KR, 1-GMA/SLS 1000; Bundle tyer — 6-MLN; Addressing machine — 2-Ch, 1-KR, 1-Domino/Ink Jet Printer. WIRE SERVICES: News — AP; Receiving dishes — AP. BUSINESS COMPUTERS: HP/3000-935 Series 935; Applications: Circ, Accts receivable, Adv, Gen ledger, Accts payable; PCs & main system networked.

GARDNER

Worcester County

'90 U.S. Census- 20,125; **E&P '96 Est.** 22,150
ABC-CZ (90): 20,125 (HH 7,979)

The Gardner News

(e-mon to fri; m-sat)

The Gardner News, 309 Central St., Gardner, MA 01440; tel (508) 632-8000; fax (508) 630-2231.
Circulation: 8,109(e); 8,109(m-sat); ABC Sept. 30, 1995.
Price: 35¢(d); 35¢(sat); $128.00/yr (mail), $85.00/yr (carrier).
Advertising: Open inch rate $9.55(e); $9.55(m-sat). **Representative:** Landon Associates Inc.
News Service: AP. **Politics:** Independent. **Established:** 1869.
Not Published: New Year; Memorial Day; Independence Day; Labor Day; Thanksgiving; Christmas.
Special Editions: NIE Supplement; Spring Home Improvement; Graduation Supplement; Fall Home Improvement.
Special Weekly Sections: Business (tues); Best Food Day, Lifestyle (wed); Lifestyle, Arts & Area Functions Page (thur); Kids Page, Lifestyle (sat); Sports, Local Entertainment (daily).

CORPORATE OFFICERS

President/Publisher	Alberta Bell
Controller	Walter Park

Massachusetts I-189

GENERAL MANAGEMENT
Manager-Operations Randy Mitchell
ADVERTISING
Manager Donna Watson
CIRCULATION
Director Randy Mitchell
NEWS EXECUTIVE
Editor Rob Heenan
EDITOR AND MANAGER
Sports Editor Brian Carter
PRODUCTION
Manager Charles Gouin Jr

Mechanical available: Offset; Black and 2 ROP colors; insert accepted — preprinted; page cut-offs — 22$\frac{1}{4}$".
Mechanical specifications: Type page 12$\frac{5}{8}$" x 21$\frac{1}{4}$"; E - 7 cols, 1$\frac{5}{8}$", $\frac{1}{6}$" between; A - 7 cols, 1$\frac{5}{8}$", $\frac{1}{6}$" between; C - 7 cols, 1$\frac{5}{8}$", $\frac{1}{6}$" between.
Commodity consumption: Newsprint 306 short tons; width 28"; single pages printed 4,960; average pages per issue 16(d); single plates used 2,600.
Equipment: EDITORIAL: Front-end hardware — 4-COM/Intrepid 4, COM/Power Editors-28A; Front-end software — COM/One System. CLASSIFIED: Front-end hardware — 4-Ap/Mac LC 4-40; Front-end software — Baseview/Class Manager; Printers — 1-Ap/Mac ImageWriter II, 1-Okidata/293, 1-NEC/90 LaserPrinter; Other equipment — 1-IBM/Selectric III. DISPLAY: Front-end hardware — 3-Ap/Mac ci 8-160; Front-end software — Ap/Mac w/Multi-Ad; Printers — 2-NEC/90 LaserPrinter. PRODUCTION: Typesetters — 2-NEC/90 LaserPrinter; Plate exposures — Nu/Flip Top FT40UNS; Plate processors — 1-WL; Scanners — Typist/3.0, Konica, ECR/Autokon 1040; Production cameras — Acti/Process; Automatic film processors — DP/28C.
PRESSROOM: Line 1 — KP/Color King F-11; Line 2 — KP/Color King F-11; Line 3 — KP/Color King F-11; Line 4 — KP/Color King F-11; Folders — 1-KP. MAILROOM: Bundle tyer — 1-Akebond/Oval Strapping. LIBRARY: Electronic — Minolta/Microfilm. WIRE SERVICES: News — Receiving dishes — AP. BUSINESS COMPUTERS: 1-Samsung/Monochrome Display Monitor, 1-IBM/PC; Applications: Armor/Premier.

GLOUCESTER

Essex County
'90 U.S. Census- 28,716; **E&P '96 Est.** 29,671
ABC-CZ (90): 36,198 (HH 14,933)

Gloucester Times
(e-mon to fri; m-sat)

Gloucester Times, 32 Dunham Rd., Beverly, MA 01915; tel (508) 922-1234; fax (508) 922-4330. Ottaway Newspapers Inc. group.
Circulation: 12,132(e); 12,132(m-sat); ABC Sept. 30, 1995.
Price: 35¢(d); 35¢(sat); $1.80/wk (carrier).
Advertising: Open inch rate $14.50(e); $14.50(m-sat). **Representatives:** US Suburban Press; Landon Associates Inc.
News Services: AP, ONS, Quincy, Patriot Ledger Sports Service. **Politics:** Independent. **Established:** 1856.
Note: The Gloucester Daily Times is printed at the Beverly Times. For detailed production and printing information, other than in editorial department, see Beverly (MA) Times listing.
Not Published: New Year; Memorial Day; Independence Day; Labor Day; Christmas.
Special Editions: Business Update (Jan); Washington's Birthday Auto Section (Feb); Spring Bride Edition, Spring Car Care, North Shore Boat Show (Mar); Spring Home Improvement (Apr); Spring Real Estate Review (May); Guide to the North Shore Edition (June); Fall Fashions, Fall Real Estate Review (Sept); Fall Car Care, Fall Home & Garden (Oct).
Special Weekly Section: Food (wed).
Magazines: USA Weekend; North Shore (own, newsprint) (thur).

CORPORATE OFFICER
President John P Kinney
GENERAL MANAGEMENT
Publisher John P Kinney
General Manager Peter Watson
ADVERTISING
Director-Sales/Marketing Brent M Connolly
Manager Linda Burke
Manager-Classified Margo A Wagner
CIRCULATION
Manager Charles Kearns
Manager-Sales Rino Vitolo
NEWS EXECUTIVE
Editor Mary Wessling
EDITORS AND MANAGERS
City Editor David Leeco
Chief Photographer Cristel Bradley
PRODUCTION
Manager Bradley M Koltz
Manager-Systems Richard H Cook

Market Information: TMC.
Mechanical available: Offset; Black and 3 ROP colors; insert accepted — preprinted, any; page cut-offs — 21".
Mechanical specifications: Type page 13" x 21$\frac{1}{2}$"; E - 6 cols, 2$\frac{1}{16}$", $\frac{5}{16}$" between; A - 6 cols, 2$\frac{1}{16}$", $\frac{5}{16}$" between; C - 9 cols, 1$\frac{1}{2}$", $\frac{5}{16}$" between.
Commodity consumption: Newsprint 620 metric tons; average pages per issue 36(d).
Equipment: EDITORIAL: Front-end hardware — 2-AT/9080; Other equipment — 4-IBM/Selectric. CLASSIFIED: Front-end hardware — 1-AT/2. WIRE SERVICES: News — ONS, AP. BUSINESS COMPUTERS: IBM/AS 400; Applications: Billing, Payroll; PCs & micros networked; PCs & main system networked.

GREENFIELD

Franklin County
'90 U.S. Census- 18,666; **E&P '96 Est.** 18,916
ABC-CZ (90): 31,144 (HH 12,774)

The Recorder (m-mon to sat)

The Recorder, 14 Hope St.; Box 273, Greenfield, MA 01302; tel (413) 772-0261. Newspapers of New England group.
Circulation: 15,181(m); 15,181(m-sat); ABC Sept. 30, 1995.
Price: 40¢(d); 40¢(sat); $2.10/wk (carrier); $9.10/mo; $109.20/yr.
Advertising: Open inch rate $14.00(m); $14.00(m-sat). **Representative:** Landon Associates Inc.
News Services: AP, LAT-WP. **Politics:** Independent. **Established:** 1792.
Not Published: New Year; Christmas.
Special Editions: Bridal (Jan); Car Care, Finance (Feb); Spring, Business (Apr); Summer Edition (June); Back-to-School (Aug); Fair Section, Fall Section, Fall Sports (Sept); Winter Edition (Oct); First Snow, Christmas (Nov); Gift Guide II, Holiday Recipes (Dec).
Special Weekly Sections: Sports Wrap-up, Child Services (mon); Classes, Courses & Workshops, Business (tues); Food (wed); Arts/Entertainment (thur); Money, Real Estate, Rental Property Page, Tag Sales (fri); Weddings, Home & Garden, TV Recorder, Religion Page, Used Vehicle Lot (sat).
Magazines: TV Update, USA Weekend (sat).
Broadcast Affiliates: WFSB (CBS) Hartford, CT; WCVB (ABC) Boston; WHDH (CBS) Boston; WBZ (NBC) Boston; WGGB (ABC) Springfield, MA; WWLP (NBC) Springfield, MA; WGBY (PBS).

CORPORATE OFFICERS
Chairman of the Board Donald R Dwight
President George Wilson
GENERAL MANAGEMENT
Publisher Michael P Kapusta
Controller Rebecca J Vortherms
Business Manager Jane A Kane
Director-Operations Douglas W Hillman
ADVERTISING
Director Richard Fahey
Manager-Classified Jeanne Martin
CIRCULATION
Director Charles Apicella
Manager-Customer Service Curtis Panlilio
NEWS EXECUTIVES
Editor Timothy A Blagg
Editorial Board Timothy A Blagg
Editorial Board Michael P Kapusta
Editorial Board Charles McChesney
Managing Editor George Forcier
EDITORS AND MANAGERS
Books Editor Roger Bowman
Business Editor Bob York
Copy Desk Chief Jane McChesney
Entertainment Editor Roger Bowman
Food/Home/Garden Editor Jane McChesney
Librarian Diane Poirier
Sports Editor Gary Sanderson
MANAGEMENT INFORMATION SERVICES
Data Processing Manager Douglas W Hillman

Market Information: TMC; ADS.
Mechanical available: Offset; Black and 3 ROP colors; insert accepted — preprinted, all; page cut-offs — 22$\frac{3}{4}$".
Mechanical specifications: Type page 13" x 21$\frac{3}{8}$"; E - 6 cols, 2.04", $\frac{1}{6}$" between; A - 6 cols, 2.04", $\frac{1}{6}$" between; C - 9 cols, 1$\frac{5}{16}$", $\frac{3}{32}$" between.
Commodity consumption: Newsprint 838 short tons; 760 metric tons; widths 27$\frac{1}{2}$", 13$\frac{3}{4}$"; black ink 17,700 pounds; color ink 1,500 pounds; single pages printed 9,000; average pages per issue 27.07(d); single plates used 10,000.
Equipment: EDITORIAL: Front-end hardware — 16-AT, 9-IBM/PC; Front-end software — MPS; Printers — Epson. CLASSIFIED: Front-end hardware — PC, 5-IBM/PC; Front-end software — CText; Printers — IBM/Graphics, IBM/Proprinters. DISPLAY: Front-end hardware — 4-PC/486 DX66; Front-end software — Archetype/Designer, Microsoft/Windows; Printers — 2-NewGen/660B. PRODUCTION: Typesetters — 2-NewGen; Plate exposures — Nu, BKY; Plate processors — Nat; Electronic picture desk — Lf/AP Leaf Picture Desk; Production cameras — C/Spartan I, ECR/Autokon 1000; Automatic film processors — AG.
PRESSROOM: Line 1 — 5-G/Urbanite, DEV/2400; Press drives — 2-Allen Bradley/100 Horse Power; Folders — 1-G/Urbanite; Press control system — 1-Allen Bradley. MAILROOM: Counter stackers — QWI; Inserters and stuffers — HI/624; Bundle tyer — EAM/Mosca, Strapex; Addressing machine — KR. LIBRARY: Combination — IBM/PC. WIRE SERVICES: News — AP; Photos — AP; Syndicates — King Features, LATS, Tribune Media, United Media, Universal Press; Receiving dishes — size-3m, AP. BUSINESS COMPUTERS: HP/3000; Applications: Payroll, Gen ledger, Circ, Adv, Accts payable; PCs & micros networked; PCs & main system networked.

HAVERHILL

Essex County
'90 U.S. Census- 51,418; **E&P '96 Est.** 55,484
ABC-CZ (90): 51,418 (HH 19,575)

The Haverhill Gazette
(e-mon to fri; m-sat)

The Haverhill Gazette, 447 W. Lowell Ave.; PO Box 991, Haverhill, MA 01831-2499; tel (508) 374-0321; fax (508) 521-6790. Scripps League Newspapers Inc. group.
Circulation: 9,608(e); 9,608(m-sat); ABC Sept. 30, 1995.
Price: 50¢(d); 50¢(sat); $2.40/wk (carrier); $9.60/mo (carrier); $124.80/yr (carrier).
Advertising: Open inch rate $19.37(e); $19.37(m-sat). **Representatives:** Landon Associates Inc.; US Suburban Press.
News Service: AP. **Politics:** Independent. **Established:** 1821.
Not Published: New Year; Christmas.
Special Editions: Financial Forecast, Bridal Section, Super Bowl, Health & Fitness (Jan); Spring Drug Tab, Car Care (Feb); Home Improvement (Apr); Progress Edition, Used Car Tab (May); Dance School, Little League, Pet Tab (Aug); Home Improvement, Football (Sept); Dining Guide, New Car (Oct); Holiday Gift Guide (Nov); Holiday Gift Guide (Dec); Senior Circuit (monthly).
Special Weekly Sections: Senior Citizens (mon); Real Estate (tues); Food, Georgetown/Groveland Page (wed); Wheels, Bumper to Bumper, Pubs, Clubs, Eateries, Entertainment, Lifestyle (thur); Real Estate (fri); Bridal Directory, Business (sat).
Magazine: USA Weekend.
Broadcast Affiliates: WHAV.
Cable TV: Operate leased cable TV in circulation area.

CORPORATE OFFICERS
Board Chairman/Treasurer E W Scripps
Vice Chairman/Corporate Secretary Betty Knight Scripps
President Barry H Scripps
President/Exec Vice Pres Roger N Warkins
Vice Pres-Finance Thomas E Wendel
GENERAL MANAGEMENT
General Manager Paul Ryan
Business Manager Denise Langlois
ADVERTISING
Manager Paul Ryan
CIRCULATION
Manager Randy Mitchell
NEWS EXECUTIVE
Managing Editor Robert J Gates
EDITORS AND MANAGERS
City Editor William Smith
Community Editor Molly Hartle
Sports Editor Mike Ryan
Suburbs Editor Molly Hartle
PRODUCTION
Superintendent-Composing Robert Stabile
Foreman-Pressroom Larry Inman

Market Information: TMC.
Mechanical available: Offset; Black and 3 ROP colors; insert accepted — preprinted, odd size 8$\frac{1}{2}$" x 11"; page cut-offs — 22$\frac{3}{4}$".
Mechanical specifications: Type page 13" x 21$\frac{1}{2}$"; E - 6 cols, 2$\frac{1}{16}$", $\frac{1}{8}$" between; A - 6 cols, 2$\frac{1}{16}$", $\frac{1}{8}$" between; C - 9 cols, $\frac{15}{16}$", $\frac{1}{16}$" between.
Commodity consumption: widths 13.5"; 27"; average pages per issue 24(d), 24(sat).
Equipment: EDITORIAL: Front-end hardware — 15-ScrippSat/PC; Front-end software — Synaptic; Printers — QMS. CLASSIFIED: Front-end hardware — 3-ScrippSat; Front-end software — Synaptic; Printers — QMS/Okidata 393. DISPLAY: Adv layout systems — Ap/Mac Centris 650; Front-end hardware — 2-ScrippSat; Front-end software — Archetype/Corel Draw; Printers — QMS. PRODUCTION: Typesetters — 2-QMS/1700; Plate exposures — 1-Amerigraph; Plate processors — 1-Nat; Production cameras — 1-R, 1-DAI; Automatic film processors — 1-LE/LD 18.
PRESSROOM: Line 1 — 8-G/Community; Folders — 1-G; Pasters — 6-Amal/25. MAILROOM: Counter stackers — 1-MM/231; Inserters and stuffers — 1-MM/227E, HAS; Bundle tyer — 1-MLN/ML2EE, 1-Sa/SR 1A. WIRE SERVICES: News — AP; Photos — AP; Syndicates — SHNS; Receiving dishes — size-10ft, AP. BUSINESS COMPUTERS: 6-IBM/PC; Applications: Payroll, Circ, Accts receivable, Accts payable; PCs & micros networked; PCs & main system networked.

HYANNIS-CAPE COD

Barnstable County
'90 U.S. Census- 14,120; **E&P '96 Est.** 15,785
ABC-NDM (90): 186,605 (HH 77,586)

Cape Cod Times
(m-mon to sat; S)

Cape Cod Times, 319 Main St., Hyannis, MA 02601; tel (508) 775-1200; fax (508) 771-8924; e-mail cctimes@delphi.com (editorial). Ottaway Newspapers Inc. group.
Circulation: 51,846(m); 51,846(m-sat); 64,246(S); ABC Sept. 30, 1995.
Price: 50¢(d); 50¢(sat); $1.75(S); $3.50/wk.
Advertising: Open inch rate $27.98(m); $27.98(m-sat); $27.98(S). **Representative:** Landon Associates Inc.
News Services: AP, DJ, ONS, NYT, LAT-WP. **Politics:** Independent. **Established:** 1936.
Special Editions: Your Wedding (Jan); Automobiles (Feb); Arts & Antiques, Classroom Times, Spring Home Improvement (Mar); Lawn & Garden, Travel Times (Apr); Arts & Antiques (June); Summer Times (eight editions), Barnstable County Fair (July); Back-to-School (Aug); Arts & Antiques, Fall Home Improvement (Sept); Gift Guide, Holiday Song Book (Nov); First Night (Dec); Prime Time (monthly).
Special Weekly Sections: Health & Science, Business, Tuesday (tues); Best Food Day (wed); Arts & Entertainment (sat); Travel, At Home, Home Improvement, Economy (S).
Magazines: CapeWeek Magazine (fri); Parade, TV Times (S).

GENERAL MANAGEMENT
President/Publisher Scott Himstead
General Manager Peter D Meyer
Controller David Hautanen
Manager-Credit Mary Jane Taylor
Manager-Education Service Michael Garvan
Manager-Human Resources Leslie Terry
ADVERTISING
Manager-Retail Joseph Gallant
Manager-Classified Julie Kaminsky
Manager-Service Kenneth Borden
CIRCULATION
Director Donald Waterman
NEWS EXECUTIVES
Editor Cliff Schectman
Managing Editor Timothy White
EDITORS AND MANAGERS
Action Line Editor (Write to Know) Ann Smith
Business Editor James Kinsella
Capestyle Editor Alicia Blaisdell-Bannon

I-190 Massachusetts

Cape Week Editor Amy Sharpe
Copy Desk Chief Charles Hibbert
Editorial Page Editor William Smith
Features Editor Deborah Forman
Graphics Editor Manuel Lopez
News Desk Chief Mark Sullivan
Sports Editor William Higgins
Sunday Editor James Kershner

PRODUCTION

Manager-Composing Robert Fellows
Manager-Mailroom Joseph Allen
Manager-Pressroom Michael Fabia

Market Information: Split Run; TMC.
Mechanical available: Offset; Black and 3 ROP colors; insert accepted — preprinted; page cut-offs — 22¾".
Mechanical specifications: Type page 13" x 21½"; E - 6 cols, 2", ⅓" between; A - 6 cols, 2 1/16", ⅓" between; C - 9 cols, 1⅖", ⅙" between.
Commodity consumption: Newsprint 5,300 metric tons; widths 55", 41¼"; black ink 120,000 pounds; color ink 21,000 pounds; single pages printed 17,640; average pages per issue 42(d), 96(S); single plates used 42,000.
Equipment: EDITORIAL: Front-end hardware — AT; Front-end software — AT. CLASSIFIED: Front-end hardware — AT; Front-end software — AT. PRODUCTION: Typesetters — Cx; Plate exposures — 2-Nu; Plate processors — 2-Nat; Scanners — 1-ECR/Autokon; Production cameras — C/Spartan; Automatic film processors — LE; Color separation equipment (conventional) — CD.
PRESSROOM: Line 1 — 12-G/Metro; Folders — 2-G/3:2; Press control system — DJ. MAILROOM: Counter stackers — 4-HL; Inserters and stuffers — 2-GMA/6-to-1, 1-GMA/14-to-1; Bundle tyer — 4-OVL; Addressing machine — 1-Ch. WIRE SERVICES: News — NYT, LAT-WP, DJ, AP; Stock tables — AP; Syndicates — South-North, TV Data; Receiving dishes — AP. BUSINESS COMPUTERS: IBM/AS-400.

LAWRENCE

Essex County

'90 U.S. Census- 70,207; E&P '96 Est. 76,648
ABC-NDM (90): 209,390 (HH 73,613)

The Eagle-Tribune
(e-mon to fri; m-sat)
The Sunday Eagle-Tribune (S)

The Eagle-Tribune, 100 Turnpike St., North Andover, MA 01845; tel (508) 685-1000; fax (508) 685-1588; e-mail news@eagletribune.com.
Circulation: 52,698(e); 52,698(m-sat); 58,355(S); ABC Sept. 30, 1995.
Price: 50¢(d); 50¢(sat); $1.50(S); $3.50/wk.
Advertising: Open inch rate $28.46(e); $28.46(m-sat); $28.46(S). **Representative:** Landon Associates Inc.
News Services: AP, SHNS. **Politics:** Independent. **Established:** 1867.
Not Published: Christmas.
Special Weekly Sections: Entertainment (thur); Engagements, Weddings, TV Update, Books, Travel (S).
Magazine: USA Weekend.
Broadcast Affiliates: WHAV Haverhill, MA; WNNW Lawrence, MA.

CORPORATE OFFICERS

President/Treasurer Irving E Rogers Jr
Vice Pres William F Lucey Jr
Vice Pres Chip Rogers

GENERAL MANAGEMENT

Publisher Irving E Rogers Jr
Business Manager William F Lucey Jr
General Manager Chip Rogers
Controller Ronald Pollina
Manager-Credit Allen Naffah
Personnel Manager Ellen Howard
Purchasing Agent William F Lucey Jr

ADVERTISING

Director Vincent Cottone
Manager-Retail Jeanne Noah
Manager-Classified Phillip Pelletier

MARKETING AND PROMOTION

Director-Marketing Ellen Howard

CIRCULATION

Director W Frank Gennarelli
Asst Director Andy Eick

NEWS EXECUTIVES

Editor Daniel Warner
Managing Editor Gerry Molina

EDITORS AND MANAGERS

Action Line Editor Daniel Warner
Amusements Editor Judy Wakefield
Books Editor Daniel Warner
Business/Finance Editor Ken Johnson
City Editor Allen White
Columnist Mike Tempesta
Editorial Page Editor Edward Achorn
Education Editor Al Lara
Features Editor Mary Fitzgerald
Films/Theater Editor Judy Wakefield
Food Editor Mary Fitzgerald
Librarian Linda Baron
Metro Editor Allen White
Exec News Editor Greg Lang
Photo Department Manager Marc McGeehan
Political Editor John Gill
Radio/Television Editor Judy Wakefield
Sports Editor Russ Conway
State Editor Susan Scully
Women's Editor Mary Fitzgerald

MANAGEMENT INFORMATION SERVICES

Data Processing Manager John Gregory

PRODUCTION

Manager Dennis Turmel
Superintendent-Composing James Robson
Foreman-Pressroom Sam Solomon
Foreman-Mailroom Frank Tridenti
Engineer-Plant Dana Scholtz

Market Information: Zoned editions; TMC.
Mechanical available: Offset; Black and 3 ROP colors; insert accepted — preprinted; page cut-offs — 22¾".
Mechanical specifications: Type page 13" x 21½"; E - 6 cols, 2 1/16", ⅛" between; A - 6 cols, 2 1/16", ⅛" between; C - 10 cols, 1¼", 1/16" between.
Commodity consumption: Newsprint 5,700 short tons; widths 55", 41¼", 27½"; black ink 160,000 pounds; color ink 15,000 pounds; single pages printed 16,000; average pages per issue 38(d), 82(S); single plates used 25,000.
Equipment: EDITORIAL: Front-end hardware — HAS/5800; Front-end software — HAS/5800; Printers — Epson. CLASSIFIED: Front-end hardware — PPI/PC-Based; Front-end software — PPI/PC-Based; Printers — Epson/Laser-Writer. DISPLAY: Adv layout systems — Mk/Managing Editor; Front-end hardware — Ap/Mac, PC; Front-end software — Archetype; Printers — MON/Image Master 600DPI. PRODUCTION: Pagination software — QuarkXPress; OCR software — Caere/OmniPage; Typesetters — 2-ECR/1045; Plate exposures — Nu/Flip Top; Plate processors — 1-Stark; Electronic picture desk — Lf/AP Leaf Picture Desk; Scanners — Microtek, ECR/1000, RZ/200B Scanner; Production cameras — C/Marathon Galley; Automatic film processors — P, LE, Kk; Film transporters — LE/Processor, Kk; Digital color separation equipment — Kk/PCS100, Optronics/4000.
PRESSROOM: Line 1 — 8-G/Metro (w/3 color decks); Press drives — Fin; Folders — 1-G/Double 2:1; Pasters — Automatic Pasters; Press control system — Fin. MAILROOM: Counter stackers — 4-Id/2200-2; Inserters and stuffers — 2-HI/72P; Bundle tyer — 4-Power Strap; Addressing machine — AVY. LIBRARY: Electronic — Meade. COMMUNICATIONS: Systems used — satellite. WIRE SERVICES: News — AP; Stock tables — AP; Receiving dishes — size-8ft, AP. BUSINESS COMPUTERS: IBM/System 38; Applications: Accts payable, Accts receivable, Payroll, Gen ledger, Circ; PCs & micros networked; PCs & main system networked.

LOWELL

Middlesex County

'90 U.S. Census- 103,439; E&P '96 Est. 113,491
ABC-CZ (90): 251,325 (HH 86,042)

The Sun (e-mon to fri; m-sat)
The Sunday Sun (S)

The Sun, 15 Kearney Sq.; PO Box 1477, Lowell, MA 01853; tel (508) 458-7100; fax (508) 970-4700.
Circulation: 52,055(e); 52,021(m-sat); 56,060(S); ABC Sept. 30, 1995.
Price: 50¢(d); 50¢(sat); $1.50(S); $2.10/wk (e), $1.40/wk (S); $9.10/mo (e), $7.00/mo (S); $107.80/yr (e), $72.80/yr (S).
Advertising: Open inch rate $29.25(e); $29.25(m-sat); $29.25(S); $46.80(e & S).
Representatives: US Suburban Press; The Newspaper National Network.
News Services: AP, NYT, CNS, SHNS, NEA. **Politics:** Independent. **Established:** 1878.
Not Published: New Year; Memorial Day; Independence Day; Labor Day; Christmas.
Special Editions: Bridal (Jan); Washington's Birthday, "55 Plus" (Feb); Auto Leasing (Mar); Home & Garden (Apr); Neighbors, Profile (May); Summer Living (June); Folk Festival (July); Back-to-School (Aug); Home Design, Auto Leasing (Sept); Health (Oct); Cookbook (Nov); Christmas Gift Guide (Dec).
Special Weekly Sections: Food (wed); Going Out (thur); Restaurant Guide, Religious Pages, Real Estate (sat); Travel, Style, Sports, Business, Leisure, TV Week, Real Estate, Education, Help Wanted (S); Sports, TV Listing, Lifestyle, Business (daily).
Magazines: USA Weekend; TV Week, Color Comics, Sunday (S).

CORPORATE OFFICERS

Publisher John H Costello Jr
President Alexander Costello
Vice Pres Thomas Costello
Treasurer Kendall M Wallace
Secretary Kendall M Wallace

GENERAL MANAGEMENT

General Manager Kendall M Wallace
Asst to Publisher James I O'Hearn
Controller Carmen Bellerose
Business Manager-Credit Jim Wright

ADVERTISING

Director-Sales/Marketing Paul A Schwabe
Manager-Retail Edward J Madden
Manager-Classified Thomas Littlefield
Manager-National Frank D Standley
Coordinator-National Patricia Hamm
Director-Special Service Charlotte Lapierre
Manager-Sales Development Andrea Mendes
Manager-Major Accounts Lynda Vallatini
Manager-Co-op/Special Projects Kenneth E Hughes

MARKETING AND PROMOTION

Director-Special Service Charlotte LaPierre
Manager-Community Relations Meg Buckley

TELECOMMUNICATIONS

Audiotex Manager Paul A Schwabe

CIRCULATION

Manager James Bukala

NEWS EXECUTIVES

Editor John H Costello Jr
Exec Editor Jonathan Kellogg
Managing Editor Malcolm Gibson
Assoc Editor Alexander Costello
Asst Managing Editor-Sunday John Greenwald
Asst Managing Editor-Lifestyle Carol McQuaid

EDITORS AND MANAGERS

Automotive Editor Donna O'Rourke
Business Editor Cromwell Schubarth
City Editor Charles St Amand
Editorial Page Editor Alexander Costello
Food Editor Carol McQuaid
Features Editor Carol McQuaid
Graphics Editor Jeffrey Walsh
Living/Lifestyle Editor Carol McQuaid
National News Editor David McArdle
Exec News Editor James Campanini
Director-Photography David Gregory
Radio/Television Editor Carol McQuaid
Society Editor Carol McQuaid
Sports Editor Dennis Whitton
Style Editor Carol McQuaid
Suburban Editor Thomas Zuppa
Travel Editor Nicholas Caraganis
Women's Editor Carol McQuaid

MANAGEMENT INFORMATION SERVICES

Online Manager James Bukala
Data Processing Manager Lorraine Rodrigues

PRODUCTION

Director Thomas Costello
Manager Robert Moore
Superintendent Theodore Litzkow
Foreman-Composing Don Bourassa
Foreman-Pressroom Charles Delaney

Market Information: Zoned editions; Split Run; TMC; ADS; Operate database; Operate audiotex.
Mechanical available: DiLitho; Black and 3 ROP colors; insert accepted — preprinted, spadeas; page cut-offs — 21½".
Mechanical specifications: Type page 13" x 21½"; E - 6 cols, 2 1/16", ⅛" between; A - 6 cols, 2 1/16", ⅛" between; C - 9 cols, 1⅜", 1/16" between.
Commodity consumption: Newsprint 5,842 short tons; widths 54", 40½", 27"; black ink 200,000 pounds; color ink 30,000 pounds; single pages printed 19,500; average pages per issue 44(d), 32(sat), 120(S); single plates used 48,000.
Equipment: EDITORIAL: Front-end hardware — 1-Xenotron/7800, 1-Ap/Mac PC LAN; Front-end software — QuarkXPress, Baseview/Qtools, Baseview/QXedit, Baseview/NewsEdit, Novell 3.1, Appleshare; Printers — Compaq/Page Marq 15, V/5100 Typesetters, AG/Accuser 1500, HP/4M4. CLASSIFIED: Front-end hardware — CText/Sys IV; Front-end software — XYQUEST/XyWrite, Novell; Printers — V/5100 Typesetter. DISPLAY: Adv layout systems — 1-PC/486, 8-Ap/Mac; Front-end hardware — 8-Ap/Mac; Front-end software — Multi-Ad/Creator; Printers — 2-QMS/PS410, 1-Compaq/Page Marq 15; Other equipment — 3-Mikrotek/Scanner. PRODUCTION: Pagination software — QuarkXPress 3.1, QuarkXPress 3.2, Baseview/Qtools, Baseview/QXedit; OCR software — Mk, Caere/OmniPage Professional; Typesetters — 2-V/5100, 2-AG/Accuser 1500 w/Xitron RIP; Plate exposures — 2-Nu/FT40; Plate processors — 1-Nat/A340; Electronic picture desk — Lf/AP Leaf Picture Desk; Scanners — 2-ECR/Autokon 1000, 1-C/Marathon, 1-C/NewsPager; Production cameras — 2-ECR/Autokon 1000, 1-C/Marathon, 1-C/NewsPager; Automatic film processors — 1-LE/PC18, 1-LE/LD24, Konica/K400; Film transporters — 1-C; Shrink lenses — 1-C/NewsPager; Color separation equipment (conventional) — 1-BKY.
PRESSROOM: Line 1 — 9-H/Colormatic, H/double width; Press drives — GE/Tenetrol; Folders — H/2:1; Pasters — 9-H/Auto; Reels and stands — 9-H; Press control system — GE/SCR; Press registration system — Pin. MAILROOM: Counter stackers — 3-LD/NS440; Inserters and stuffers — 2-S/848P; Bundle tyer — OVL/JP80; Addressing machine — 1-Am/431, 1-Am/500, 1-Ch/528. WIRE SERVICES: News — AP, PR Newswire, NYT, AP Datafeatures, RN; Photos — AP; Stock tables — AP; Receiving dishes — AP. BUSINESS COMPUTERS: IBM/AS-400 Advanced 36; Applications: Payroll, Accts payable, Accts receivable, Circ, Gen ledger; PCs & micros networked; PCs & main system networked.

LYNN

Essex County

'90 U.S. Census- 81,245; E&P '96 Est. 84,014
ABC-CZ (90): 124,272 (HH 47,670)

Daily Evening Item
(e-mon to fri; m-sat)

Daily Evening Item, 38 Exchange St.; PO Box 951, Lynn, MA 01903; tel (617) 593-7700; fax (617) 581-3178.
Circulation: 23,500(e); 22,175(m-sat); ABC Sept. 30, 1995.
Price: 35¢(d); 35¢(sat); $1.80/wk.
Advertising: Open inch rate $23.00(e); $23.00(m-sat). **Representatives:** Landon Associates Inc.; US Suburban Press.
News Services: AP, SHNS. **Politics:** Independent. **Established:** 1877.
Not Published: New Year; Washington's Birthday; Patriot's Day; Memorial Day; Independence Day; Labor Day; Columbus Day; Veteran's Day; Thanksgiving; Christmas.
Special Editions: Income Tax Tab, Brides Tab (Jan); Business Profile, Washington's Birthday Auto (Feb); Health & Fitness, Spring Home Improvement (Apr); Real Estate Review, Financial Planning, Spring Car Care (May); Summer Thing, Dining Guide (June); Back-to-School, Campus (Aug); Fall Car Care, Topsfield Fair (Sept); New Car Preview (Oct); Fall Dining Guide, Holiday Gift Guide (Nov); Christmas Song Book (Dec).
Special Weekly Sections: Super Saver Specials (mon); Food, Healthlines (wed); Entertainment, Coming Up (thur); Dining Guide (fri); Brides, Travel (sat).

CORPORATE OFFICERS

President/Treasurer Peter Gamage
Vice Pres/Asst Treasurer Peter H Gamage

GENERAL MANAGEMENT

Publisher/General Manager Peter H Gamage
Asst General Manager Peter L Chipman
Manager-Credit Paul Guinivan Jr
Manager-Education Service Kay Leary

ADVERTISING

Director Kevin Kelly
Manager-Retail Sean Brackett
Manager-Classified Sharon Ruchalski

CIRCULATION

Director Brian Lacy

NEWS EXECUTIVES

Managing Editor Allan T Kort
Assoc Editor Fred H Goddard

EDITORS AND MANAGERS

City Editor Earle Stern

Massachusetts I-191

Radio/Television Editor Sandra Stanger
Regional Editor Ralph Nelson
Sports Editor Paul Halloran
Travel Editor Fred H Goddard

PRODUCTION

Manager Peter L Chipman
Foreman-Composing Robert Owyer
Foreman-Pressroom Charles Payne
Foreman-Stereo Mel Blomster
Foreman-Mailroom Michael Sullivan

Market Information: Zoned editions; Split Run; TMC.
Mechanical available: Letterpress (direct); Black and 3 ROP colors; insert accepted — preprinted, any; page cut-offs — 22 3/4".
Mechanical specifications: Type page 13" x 21"; E - 6 cols, 2 1/16", 1/8" between; A - 6 cols, 2 1/16", 1/8" between; C - 9 cols, 1 5/16", 1/8" between.
Commodity consumption: Newsprint 1,400 short tons; widths 55", 41 1/4"; black ink 12,050 pounds; color ink 1,000 pounds; single pages printed 9,550; average pages per issue 32(d); single plates used 13,458.
Equipment: EDITORIAL: Front-end hardware — Ik/cps 1020, 31-ZC/50; Other equipment — Ap/Mac IIci. CLASSIFIED: Front-end hardware — Cx, 8-IBM/PS-2. DISPLAY: Adv layout systems — 2-Cx/Breeze, Sun/3-60, 2-Epson, 2-IBM/PS. PRODUCTION: Typesetters — 2-Cx/Bitcaster, W/Ultra Recorders, 2-Ik/Mark IX; Platemaking systems — 2-LX/135; Plate exposures — 2-MAS; Plate processors — 2-MAS; Scanners — ECR/Autokon 1000; Automatic film processors — 2-LE, 3-Kk, 1-C/R660; Digital color separation equipment — ECR/Autokon 1000.
PRESSROOM: Line 1 — 5-H/Color-Conv; Folders — 2-H; Pasters — 5-Wd/Semi-Auto. MAILROOM: Counter stackers — 1-BG/Count-O-Veyor; Inserters and stuffers — 1-P/24S; Bundle tyer — 1-MLN; Wrapping singles — 2-Bu. WIRE SERVICES: News — AP; Syndicates — AP, SHNS, NEA; Receiving dishes — size-10ft, UPI. BUSINESS COMPUTERS: 1-IBM/Sys 36; Applications: Invoices, Payables, Gen ledger, Circ; PCs & main system networked.

MALDEN

Middlesex County

'90 U.S. Census- 53,884; E&P '96 Est. 54,490

The Daily News-Mercury

(e-mon to fri)

The Daily News-Mercury, 277 Commercial St., Malden, MA 02148; tel (617) 321-8000; fax (617) 321-8008; e-mail newsmer@user1.ch1.com.
Circulation: 15,585(e); Sworn Sept. 30, 1992.
Price: 35¢(d); $13.00/mo; $120.00/yr.
Advertising: Open inch rate $12.00(e). **Representatives:** Landon Associates Inc.; US Suburban Press.
News Service: UPI. **Politics:** Independent. **Established:** 1880 (Mercury), 1892 (News), 1989 (News-Mercury).
Not Published: New Year; Memorial Day; Independence Day; Labor Day; Columbus Day; Thanksgiving; Christmas.
Special Editions: Progress (Jan); Bridal, Washington's Birthday Auto (Feb); Money (Mar); Home & Car Care (Apr); Social Security (July); Golf (Sept); Chamber of Commerce (Oct); Holiday Recipe (Nov); Holiday Recipe (Dec).
Special Weekly Section: Tempo (thur).

NEWS EXECUTIVES

Editor Steve Freker
Exec Editor T John Daily

EDITOR AND MANAGER

Sports Editor Steve Freker

PRODUCTION

Foreman-Pressroom Christopher Dellolusso
Foreman-Composing Steve Freker

Market Information: TMC.
Mechanical available: Offset; Black and 3 ROP colors; insert accepted — preprinted, single card stock; all tab or standard-size inserts; page cut-offs — 22 3/4".
Mechanical specifications: Type page 13" x 21 1/2"; E - 6 cols, 2 1/16", 1/8" between; A - 6 cols, 2 1/16", 1/8" between; C - 9 cols, 1 3/8", 1/8" between.
Commodity consumption: Newsprint 710 short tons; widths 28", 14"; black ink 19,400 pounds; color ink 180 pounds; average pages per issue 28(d).
Equipment: EDITORIAL: Front-end hardware — 26-COM/Intrepid. CLASSIFIED: Front-end hardware — 26-COM/Intrepid. PRODUCTION: Typesetters — 2-COM/8400, 2-COM/Lasermaster 1200; Platemaking systems — 1-3M/Pyrofax; Production cameras — 1-Nu/Horizontal, 1-K/Vertical.
PRESSROOM: Line 1 — 6-HI/V-15-A; Folders — 1-HI. MAILROOM: Inserters and stuffers — 1-S/P-24; Bundle tyer — 2-Sa; Addressing machine — 1-Am. BUSINESS COMPUTERS: Compaq/386, Accpac; Applications: Accounting.

MILFORD

Worcester County

'90 U.S. Census- 25,355; E&P '96 Est. 27,132
ABC-NDM (90): 94,224 (HH 32,984)

Milford Daily News

(e-mon to fri; m-sat)

Milford Daily News, 159 S. Main St., Milford, MA 01757; tel (508) 473-1111; fax (508) 478-8769. Alta Group Newspapers group.
Circulation: 14,013(e); 14,013(m-sat); ABC Sept. 30, 1995.
Price: 50¢(d); 50¢(sat); $2.70/wk (home delivery); $140.40/yr.
Advertising: Open inch rate $12.42(e); $12.42(m-sat). **Representative:** Landon Associates Inc.
News Services: NYT, AP. **Established:** 1887.
Not Published: New Year; Memorial Day; Independence Day; Labor Day; Christmas.
Advertising not accepted: Work at home; 900 number sex calls.
Special Editions: Business Biography, Bargain Blockbuster Pages, Tax Column (Jan); Spring Bridal Tab, Valentine's Gift Page, Valentine's Love Lines & Pix, Washington's Birthday Auto Section, Terrific Sale Pages, Dentist Page, Boy Scout Page (Feb); Physical Fitness Page, St. Patrick's Day Page, Yard Sales Promo, Home & Garden Tab (Mar); Physical Fitness Page, Spring Car Care Tab, Secretary's Week Pages, Easter Ham Pages, Earth Day Page (Apr); Summer Fun Tab #1, Mother's Day Page, Pet Care Page (May); Summer Fun Tab #2, Father's Day Page, Graduation Tab, Summer Cookbook (June); Sidewalk Sale Days, Antique Page (July); Bus Schedule Tab, Pawtucket Red Sox Night, Doctor's Directory, Pre-School Directory (Aug); Fall Bridal Tab (Sept); Fall Car Care Tab, Business & Industry Review (Oct); Thanksgiving 1/2 Price Special, Gift Spotter, Thanksgiving Turkey Pages, Holiday Cookbook (Nov); Christmas Cards, Christmas Turkey Pages, Christmas Tree Directory (Dec).
Special Weekly Sections: Bridal Registry (mon); Coupon Page, Business Card Page (2nd tues).
Magazines: Sports Extra (tab) (fri); USA Weekender (sat); "Neighbors" (local weekend TMC); "TV Scene".

GENERAL MANAGEMENT

Publisher Thomas C Sawyer Sr
Manager-Office Marie Dicampo

ADVERTISING

Director/Asst Publisher Richard P Rae
Manager Arthur Lucca
Manager-Classified Dennis Fitzgerald

CIRCULATION

Director Armando Larouco

NEWS EXECUTIVE

Editor Nicholas J Tosches

EDITORS AND MANAGERS

Business Editor Peter J Tosches
Science Editor Nicholas J Tosches
Sports Editor David Maril
Wire Editor Peter J Tosches

MANAGEMENT INFORMATION SERVICES

Manager-Info Systems Brian J Bodio

PRODUCTION

Foreman-Composing Michael J Deluca
Foreman-Pressroom Agostino Lancia

Market Information: TMC; ADS.
Mechanical available: Offset; Black and 3 ROP colors; insert accepted — preprinted, minimum size 5" x 8"; page cut-offs — 21 1/2".
Mechanical specifications: Type page 13" x 21 1/2"; E - 6 cols, 2 1/16", 1/8" between; A - 6 cols, 2 1/16", 1/8" between; C - 9 cols, 1 3/8", 1/16" between.
Commodity consumption: Newsprint 704 short tons; width 27 1/2"; black ink 21,375 pounds; color ink 2,480 pounds; single pages printed 7,603; average pages per issue 24.75(d); single plates used 6,581.
Equipment: EDITORIAL: Front-end hardware — 25-PC; Front-end software — III 3.9; Printers — Toshiba/P351 SQ, Ap/Mac LaserWriter, 2-QMS/860, HP/4M Plus; Other equipment — 18-RSK/TRS-80 Model 100, RSK/TRS-80 Model 200, Lf/Leafscan 35. CLASSIFIED: Front-end hardware — 4-PC; Front-end software — III 3.9; Printers — Toshiba/P351 SX. DISPLAY: Front-end hardware — 10-Ap/Mac; Front-end software — DTI/AdSpeed, QuarkXPress; Printers — 2-Ap/Mac LaserWriter, 2-QMS/860, HP/4M Plus. PRODUCTION: Pagination software — QuarkXPress 3.3, Microsoft/Windows, Ap/Mac; OCR software — Caere/OmniPage Pro; Typesetters — 2-QMS/860; Plate exposures — Nu/Flip Top FT40APRNS-631; Plate processors — 1-Nat/A250; Electronic picture desk — Lf/AP Leaf Picture Desk; Scanners — Lf/Leafscan 35, Microtek, HP/Scanner; Production cameras — 1-R, 1-LE/R, AG/RPS 6100S; Automatic film processors — 1-Litex/25, AG; Color separation equipment (conventional) — Ca/Pin Register Sys; Digital color separation equipment — Lf/AP Leaf Picture Desk, Lf/Leafscan.
PRESSROOM: Line 1 — 8-G/U1224; Folders — 1-G. MAILROOM: Counter stackers — 1-BG, MM/3 pocket plus main; Inserters and stuffers — DG/320 4 stations; Bundle tyer — 1-MLN, 1-Bu; Addressing machine — KR/215 mailer & quarter folder. LIBRARY: Electronic — III; Combination — Dukane/Explorer 14 Microfilm. WIRE SERVICES: News — AP; Photos — AP; Syndicates — NYT; Receiving dishes — size-8ft, AP. BUSINESS COMPUTERS: TI/990-12R; Applications: DSI: Adv billing, Accts receivable, Gen ledger, Payroll, Circ, TMC; PCs & micros networked; PCs & main system networked.

NEW BEDFORD

Bristol County

'90 U.S. Census- 99,922; E&P '96 Est. 101,567
ABC-CZ (90): 136,985 (HH 53,148)

The Standard Times

(m-mon to fri; m-sat; S)

The Standard Times, 25 Elm St.; PO Box 5912, New Bedford, MA 02742; tel (508) 997-7411; fax (508) 997-7852; e-mail jstevens@s-t.com; web site http://www.s-t.com/newstandard. Ottaway Newspapers Inc. group.
Circulation: 42,226(m); 42,810(m-sat); 48,307(S); ABC Sept. 30, 1995.
Price: 50¢(d); 50¢(sat); $1.75(S); $2.00/wk (d), $1.65/wk (S), $3.05/wk (dS); $13.22/mo; $152.60/yr.
Advertising: Open inch rate $22.25(m); $22.25(m-sat); $23.65(S). **Representative:** Papert Companies.
News Services: AP, NYT, DJ, ONS. **Politics:** Independent. **Established:** 1850.
Note: Effective Sept. 18, 1995, this publication changed its publishing plan from (e-mon to fri; m-sat; S) to (m-mon to fri; m-sat; S).
Advertising not accepted: Fortune tellers.
Special Editions: Bridal, Parenting (Jan); Golfing, Washington's Birthday Auto (Feb); Spring Home & Garden, Home Show, Cookbook (Mar); Spring Auto Service, Best Read Guide (Entertainment) (Apr); Factory Outlet Guide, Seaside Summer Recreation, Best Read Guide (May); Seaside Summer Recreation, Seniors (June); Parenting, Summerfest, Seaside Summer Recreation (July); Area Menus, Health & Medicine (Aug); Fall Home & Garden, Bridal, High School Football (Sept); Fall Auto Service (Oct); Holiday Planner, Toward 2000, Holiday Shopping Guide (Nov); Holiday Song Book, High School Basketball, Last Minute Gift Guide (Dec).
Special Weekly Sections: Real Estate Today Tab (sat); At Home (S).
Magazines: Parade, Color Comics, TV Update (S).

GENERAL MANAGEMENT

Publisher William T Kennedy
General Manager John F Stevens
Controller Patricia Yost
Manager-Human Resources Joel E Burns

ADVERTISING

Director Sheila Parker
Manager Coralia S Merritt
Manager Madhu McKenzie
Manager-Advertising Service Theresa Pereira

MARKETING AND PROMOTION

Director-Marketing/Promotion Rita K Thieme
Coordinator-Educational Service B Jean Bessette

TELECOMMUNICATIONS

Supervisor James A Knox

CIRCULATION

Director Peter L Eschauzier
Manager-Sales Leon Long

NEWS EXECUTIVES

Editor Ken Hartnett
Managing Editor-Operations Neil Roiter
Managing Editor-News Dave Humphrey

EDITORS AND MANAGERS

Action Line Editor Claudia Simpson
Amusements Editor Ann Humphrey
Automotive Editor Steven DeCosta
Books Editor Steven DeCosta
Business Editor Patricia O'Connor
Editorial Page Editor Stephen F Urbon
Education Editor Sue Pawlak-Seaman
Environment Editor Michael Connery
Fashion Editor Anne Humphrey
Features Editor Steven DeCosta
Films Editor Bob Lovinger
Food Editor Joanna McQuillen Weeks
Graphics Editor George Heath
Health/Medical Editor Steven DeCosta
Librarian Gail Couture
Lifestyle Editor Steven DeCosta
Metro Editor Chris Gonsalves
Real Estate Editor Jim Vincent
Religion Editor Robert Bercellos
Science/Technology Editor Steven DeCosta
Sports Editor Steve DeCosta
Suburban Editor Jeff Burt
Systems Editor Norman Cloutier
Teen-Age/Youth Editor Paula Demers
Theater/Music Editor Dan O'Brien
Travel Editor Carlos Cunha

MANAGEMENT INFORMATION SERVICES

Director-Management Info Services David Marujo
Manager-Production Systems John Enos

PRODUCTION

Manager-Distribution Kim A Cabral
Foreman-Pre Press David Marujo
Foreman-Press/Plate Alcido Fernandes

Market Information: Zoned editions; Split Run; TMC; Electronic edition.
Mechanical available: Offset; Black and 3 ROP colors; insert accepted — preprinted, single sheets, catabooks; page cut-offs — 22 3/4".
Mechanical specifications: Type page 13" x 21 1/2"; E - 6 cols, 2 1/16", 1/8" between; A - 6 cols, 2 1/16", 1/8" between; C - 9 cols, 1 3/8", 1/16" between.
Commodity consumption: Newsprint 3,520 metric tons; widths 55", 41 1/4"; black ink 60,170 pounds; color ink 18,086 pounds; single pages printed 14,666; average pages per issue 32(d), 78(S); single plates used 35,200.
Equipment: EDITORIAL: Front-end hardware — 45-Dell/486 66MHS (14 w/32 MB RAM, 10 w/16 MB RAM); Front-end software — Dewar/Unixaix Network; Printers — 2-HP/4M, 1-HP/44" Color Plotter, 1-NewGen/11x17 Laser Printer. CLASSIFIED: Front-end hardware — 15-CSI; Front-end software — CSI/112B; Printers — 1-DEC/LA 120. DISPLAY: Front-end hardware — 6-PC/486-66, Novell; Front-end software — Archetype, Microsoft/Windows, Adobe/Photoshop, Dewar/View, Oracle; Printers — 2-HP/4M, 2-QMS/860. PRODUCTION: Pagination software — QuarkXPress 3.3; Typesetters — 2-AU/Micro 5, 2-AU/APS 1000, 2-AG/On Line Processors; Plate exposures — 2-Nu; Plate processors — 1-Nat/A-300; Electronic picture desk — 1-Lf/AP Leaf Picture Desk; Scanners — 1-ECR/Autokon 1000DE; Production cameras — 1-C/Spartan III, 1-C/Marathon; Automatic film processors — 1-Wing Lynch/Color, 2-LE; Film transporters — 1-C; Shrink lenses — 1-Alan/squeeze-stretch, 1-ECR/Autokon; Color separation equipment (conventional) — 1-C/Enlarger, 1-Lf/Leafscan 45.
PRESSROOM: Line 1 — 8-G/Metro double width (w/3 process Color Units); Folders — 2-G; Pasters — 8-G; Reels and stands — 8-G. MAILROOM: Counter stackers — 2-QWI; Inserters and stuffers — 1-GMA/SLA 100 (8 stations); Bundle tyer — 2-MLN/MLN-2; Addressing machine — 1-KR. WIRE SERVICES: News — AP Datafeatures, DJ, ONS, NYT, SHNS; Receiving dishes — size-3m, AP. BUSINESS COMPUTERS: IBM/AS400; Applications: INSI, Software Plus: Payroll; Computer Associates: Gen ledger; Lawson: Fixed assets; Lawson: In-house development, Class billing; PCs & micros networked; PCs & main system networked.

I-192 Massachusetts

NEWBURYPORT
Essex County
'90 U.S. Census- 16,317; E&P '96 Est. 16,746
ABC-CZ (90): 31,314 (HH 12,276)

The Daily News of Newburyport (e-mon to fri; m-sat)
The Daily News of Newburyport, 32 Dunham Rd., Beverly, MA 01915; tel (508) 922-1234. Ottaway Newspapers Inc. group.
Circulation: 13,368(e); 13,368(m-sat); ABC Sept. 30, 1995.
Price: 35¢(d); 35¢(sat); $1.80/wk.
Advertising: Open inch rate $15.25(e); $15.25(m-sat). **Representatives:** US Suburban Press; Landon Associates Inc.
News Services: UPI, ONS. **Politics:** Independent-Republican. **Established:** 1887.
Not Published: New Year; Memorial Day; Independence Day; Labor Day; Christmas.
Special Editions: Auto (Feb); Back-to-School; Christmas; Spring Clean & Paint-Up.
Special Weekly Section: Food (wed).
Magazines: North Shore Magazine (local, offset tab) (Newburyport, Beverly, Gloucester, Peabody) (thur); USA Weekend.

CORPORATE OFFICER
President John P Kinney
GENERAL MANAGEMENT
Publisher John P Kinney
General Manager Peter Watson
ADVERTISING
Director-Sales/Marketing Brent M Connolly
Manager Michael Eramo
CIRCULATION
Manager Mark Lingerman
Manager-Sales Rino Vitolo
NEWS EXECUTIVE
Managing Editor Calhoun J Killeen Jr
EDITORS AND MANAGERS
City Editor Victor Tyne
Sports Editor Kevin Doyle

Market Information: TMC.
Mechanical available: Offset; Black and 3 ROP colors; insert accepted — preprinted; page cut-offs — 21".
Mechanical specifications: Type page 13" x 21½"; E - 6 cols, 2 1/16", 5/16" between; A - 6 cols, 2 1/16", 5/16" between; C - 9 cols, 1½", 5/16" between.
Commodity consumption: Newsprint 620 metric tons; average pages per issue 32(d).
Equipment: EDITORIAL: Front-end hardware — AT, 16-IBM/Perry 199. CLASSIFIED: Other equipment — 16-IBM/Perry 199. DISPLAY: Adv layout systems — 1-Cp. PRODUCTION: Typesetters — 2-COM/2961HS; Production cameras — 1-lk. WIRE SERVICES: News — ONS, AP.

NORTH ADAMS
Berkshire County
'90 U.S. Census- 16,797; E&P '96 Est. 15,879

The Transcript (e-mon to fri; m-sat)
The Transcript, 124 American Legion Dr.; PO Box 473, North Adams, MA 01247; tel (413) 663-3741; fax (413) 662-2792. Hollinger International Inc. group.
Circulation: 8,850(e); 8,850(m-sat); Sworn Oct. 1, 1995.
Price: 35¢(d); 35¢(sat); $127.40/yr, $121.80/yr (motor route), $144.00/yr (mail).
Advertising: Open inch rate $10.64(e); $10.64 (m-sat). **Representative:** Landon Associates Inc.
News Service: AP. **Politics:** Independent. **Established:** 1843.
Not Published: New Year; Christmas.
Special Weekly Sections: Consumer (Health), Consumer (Fashion) (tues); Food, Best Food Coupon Day (wed); Recreation, Outdoors (thur); Arts (fri); Bridal, Business, Churches (sat).

GENERAL MANAGEMENT
Publisher David Nahan
Business Manager Doreen Kozak
ADVERTISING
Manager Mellissa Tower
CIRCULATION
Director Patricia Sanpelli
NEWS EXECUTIVE
Managing Editor David Nahan
EDITORS AND MANAGERS
Editorial Page Editor David Nahan
Sports Editor Kris Dufour
PRODUCTION
Foreman-Composing Philip A Ouimet
Foreman-Pressroom Philip A Ouimet

Market Information: TMC.
Mechanical available: Offset; Black and 3 ROP colors; insert accepted — preprinted; page cut-offs — 22¾".
Mechanical specifications: Type page 13" x 21½"; E - 6 cols, 2 1/16", ⅛" between; A - 6 cols, 2 1/16", ⅛" between; C - 9 cols, 1⅜", 1/16" between.
Commodity consumption: Newsprint 400 short tons; widths 28", 30", 27½"; black ink 17,024 pounds; color ink 600 pounds; single pages printed 6,111; average pages per issue 16(d); single plates used 3,500.
Equipment: EDITORIAL: Front-end hardware — 2-HI/1420. CLASSIFIED: Front-end hardware — 2-HI/1420. PRODUCTION: Typesetters — 1-COM/24-14, 2-COM/Universal Videosetter; Platemaking systems — 1-Nat/250; Plate exposures — 1-BKY, 1-Nu; Production cameras — 1-AG/3000, 1-AG/RPS 2024; Automatic film processors — 1-P/24". PRESSROOM: Line 1 — 8-G/Community; Folders — G/SC. MAILROOM: Counter stackers — 1-BG/Count-O-Veyor; Bundle tyer — 1-Ty-Tech/Tyer, 2-CYP/RO-500-N-S; Addressing machine — 1-DEC/310. COMMUNICATIONS: Facsimile — 1-ABD/321. WIRE SERVICES: News — AP; Receiving dishes — AP. BUSINESS COMPUTERS: 1-DEC/310; Applications: Accts payable, Payroll, Circ, Accts receivable.

NORTHAMPTON
Hampshire County
'90 U.S. Census- 29,289; E&P '96 Est. 29,432
ABC-NDM (90): 103,539 (HH 34,422)

Daily Hampshire Gazette (e-mon to fri; m-sat)
Daily Hampshire Gazette, 115 Conz St.; PO Box 299, Northampton, MA 01060; tel (413) 584-5000; fax (413) 585-5222.
Circulation: 22,357(e); 22,357(m-sat); ABC Sept. 30, 1995.
Price: 50¢(d); 50¢(sat); $2.70/wk; $10.80/mo; $128.50/yr.
Advertising: Open inch rate $19.34(e); $19.34 (m-sat). **Representative:** Papert Companies.
News Services: AP, LAT-WP. **Politics:** Independent. **Established:** 1786.
Not Published: New Year; Memorial Day; Independence Day; Labor Day; Thanksgiving; Christmas.
Special Editions: Business & Industry (Jan); Bridal, Auto Section (Feb); Spring Fashion (Mar); Spring Home & Garden (Apr); Create-An-Ad (May); Summer Guide (June); Back-to-School (Aug); Valley Almanac (Sept); Fall Home, Fall Fashion, Menu Guide (Oct); Christmas Shopping Bag, Christmas Gift Guide (Nov).
Special Weekly Sections: Business (mon); Health (tues); Lifestyle Features, Food, Books (wed); Home & Garden, Business, Arts & Entertainment (thur); Hampshire Life, Social Announcements (fri); Weekend (sat); Travel; Seniors; Family; Children's Events & Stories; Automobile News; Features.
Magazines: "Hampshire Life", "Amherst Bulletin" (local TMC, Amherst area) (fri); USA Weekend, "Television" (weekly TV log) (sat).

CORPORATE OFFICER
President Peter L DeRose
GENERAL MANAGEMENT
Co-Publisher Charles W DeRose
Co-Publisher Peter L DeRose
Business Manager James V Frustere
ADVERTISING
Director John Ebbets
Manager-Classified David A Sikop
Manager-Retail William Knittle
Manager-Co-op Patty Masure
TELECOMMUNICATIONS
Audiotex Manager Patty Masure
CIRCULATION
Manager Dennis Skoglund
NEWS EXECUTIVES
Editor James T Foudy
Managing Editor Louis Groccia
EDITORS AND MANAGERS
Books/Films Editor Elise Gibson
Business Editor Kay Moran
Editorial Page Editor Kay Moran
Entertainment Editor Elise Gibson
Librarian Nancy Rhodes
Music Editor Elise Gibson
News Editor Larry Parnass
Real Estate Editor Kay Moran
Religion Editor Kay Moran
Sports Editor Deborah Oakley
Wire Editor Louis Groccia
Women's Editor Elise Gibson
MANAGEMENT INFORMATION SERVICES
Data Processing Technician Heather Moore
PRODUCTION
Manager-Pre Press Peter Soderberg
Manager-Pressroom John Raymer

Market Information: Split Run; TMC; Operate audiotex.
Mechanical available: Offset; Black and 3 ROP colors; insert accepted — preprinted, product samples; page cut-offs — 22¾".
Mechanical specifications: Type page 13" x 21½"; E - 6 cols, 2 1/16", ⅛" between; A - 6 cols, 2 1/16", ⅛" between; C - 9 cols, 1⅜", 3/32" between.
Commodity consumption: Newsprint 1,509 short tons; widths 27¼", 13⅝"; black ink 41,300 pounds; color ink 1,200 pounds; single pages printed 12,775; average pages per issue 41.5(d); single plates used 13,127.
Equipment: EDITORIAL: Front-end hardware — SII/22 STD; Front-end software — SII/22 STD; Printers — NewGen/840E Laser; Other equipment — 41-SII/E7-960, 10-RSK/TRS-100, 14-RSK/TRS-1000 SX. CLASSIFIED: Front-end hardware — SII/22STD; Front-end software — SII/22STD; Printers — NewGen/840E Laser; Other equipment — 8-SII/ET-960. AUDIOTEX: Hardware — Northgate/PC-386; Software — Info-Connect/Pottsville Republican. DISPLAY: Adv layout systems — 2-Pentium w/File Server; Front-end hardware — 2-IBM/PC-386, 3-Gateway/2000 4DX2-66; Front-end software — Archetype/Designer 3.2, Archetype/Corel Draw, Adobe/Photoshop; Printers — 2-NewGen/840E, ECR/Scriptsetter 3; Other equipment — 4-SII/ET-960, 1-Data-Master/PC-286 Datalink. PRODUCTION: Pagination software — Archetype/Designer 3.2; Typesetters — 3-NewGen/Turbo PS-840E, ECR/Scriptsetter 3; Platemaking systems — 2-3M/Deadliner; Electronic picture desk — Lf/AP Leaf Picture Desk; Scanners — Microtek/Scanmaker 3; Production cameras — B/Caravelle; Color separation equipment (conventional) — Lf/AP Leaf Picture Desk; Digital color separation equipment — Lf/AP Leaf Picture Desk. PRESSROOM: Line 1 — 8-G/Urbanite w/3-Color Satellite Unit; Press drives — 2-Fin, 100-HP/Westinghouse, 100-HP/GE; Folders — 1-G/Urbanite; Reels and stands — 2-G/3-High Stands; Press registration system — Duarte/Pin Register System. MAILROOM: Bundle tyer — 3-MLN/ML2-EE; Addressing machine — 1-Ch, 1-Ch. LIBRARY: Electronic — Mead Data/Central, Nexis/NewsView. COMMUNICATIONS: Digital ad delivery system — AP AdSend. WIRE SERVICES: News — AP; Photos — AP; Syndicates — LATS; Receiving dishes — size-3m, AP. BUSINESS COMPUTERS: 1-DEC/Prioris HX 590 System, Papertrack/2000; Applications: Circ, Accts payable, Gen ledger, Display adv, Scheduling, Billing; PCs & micros networked; PCs & main system networked.

PITTSFIELD
Berkshire County
'90 U.S. Census- 48,622; E&P '96 Est. 46,154
ABC-NDM (90): 73,363 (HH 29,145)

The Berkshire Eagle (m-mon to sat; S)
The Berkshire Eagle, 75 S. Church St.; PO Box 1171, Pittsfield, MA 01202; tel (413) 447-7311; fax (413) 499-3419; e-mail eaglelinks@aol.com. MediaNews Inc. (New England Newspapers) group.
Circulation: 30,768(m); 30,768(m-sat); 34,678(S); ABC Sept. 30, 1995.
Price: 50¢(d); 50¢(sat); $1.50(S); $13.75/mo, $17.25/mo (postal); $134.20/yr.
Advertising: Open inch rate $24.05(m); $24.05(m-sat); $24.05(S). **Representative:** Landon Associates Inc.
News Services: AP, NYT, CSM, LAT-WP. **Politics:** Independent. **Established:** 1789.
Not Published: Christmas.
Special Editions: Wedding Planner (Jan); Presidents' Auto, Business & Industry (Feb); Coupon Booklet (Mar); Dining Guide, Spring Home & Garden (Apr); Menus To Go, Pool & Patio, Berkshire Preview (May); Wedding Planner II (June); Health Living, Answer Book (Aug); Dining Guide II, Josh Billings (Sept); Fall Home Improvement, Fall Car Care (Oct); Holiday Coupon Booklet, Holiday Gift Guide (Nov); Last Minute Gift Guide (Dec).
Special Weekly Sections: Sports Monday (mon); Berkshire This Weekend (fri); Berkshire Saturday (sat); Opinion, Sports, Business, TV Week, Social, Life (S).
Magazines: Berkshires Week (thur, June-Oct); TV Week, Sunday Magazine, Comics (S).

CORPORATE OFFICERS
President/CEO Jim Wall
Exec Vice Pres/Chief Operating Officer Martin C Langeveld
Vice Pres/Chief Financial Officer Martin D Terrien
GENERAL MANAGEMENT
Publisher Martin C Langeveld
Director-Systems Wayne A Eastwood
Director-Operations & Facilities John Richardson
Manager-Human Resources Alinda Shank
Purchasing Agent Ronald T Kinnas
ADVERTISING
Manager-Sales John J Gallacher
Manager-Classified Susan Burtchell
CIRCULATION
Director Joseph Sheehy
NEWS EXECUTIVES
Editor David Scribner
Assoc Editor Grier Horner
EDITORS AND MANAGERS
Boston Bureau Carol Sliwa
City Editor Debra A DiMassimo
Columnist Nancy Q Keefe
Columnist Bonner McAllester
Columnist Richard Nunley
Columnist Alan Chartock
Columnist Theodore Giddings
Columnist Molly Gordon
Columnist Ruth Bass
Columnist Mary Potter
Columnist Michelle Gillett
Editorial Page Editor Bill Everhart
Entertainment Editor Jeffrey Borak
Features Ruth Bass
Food Editor Charles Bonenti
Librarian Grace McMahon
News Editor Clarence Fanto
Asst News Editor Brian Sullivan
Sports Editor Robert McDonough
PRODUCTION
Manager-Press Scott Craig

Market Information: TMC.
Mechanical available: Offset; Black and 3 ROP colors; insert accepted — preprinted, product samples, sample packs; page cut-offs — 22¾".
Mechanical specifications: Type page 13" x 21.5"; E - 6 cols, 2 1/16", ⅛" between; A - 6 cols, 2 1/16", ⅛" between; C - 9 cols, 1⅜", 1/16" between.
Commodity consumption: Newsprint 2,825 short tons; widths 27", 13.5"; black ink 67,900 pounds; color ink 13,890 pounds; single pages printed 14,332; average pages per issue 33(d), 77(S); single plates used 7,500.
Equipment: EDITORIAL: Front-end hardware — Dewar; Front-end software — Dewar/Disc Net II; Printers — Okidata 320. CLASSIFIED: Front-end hardware — Dewar; Front-end software — Dewar/Disc Net II; Printers — Okidata/320. DISPLAY: Adv layout systems — SCS/Layout 8000; Front-end hardware — Ap/Mac Quadra 950, 8-Ap/Mac Quadra 650; Front-end software — Multi-Ad 3.63, Multi-Ad/Search 3.0; Printers — CI/300; Other equipment — V/VT800, LaserMaster/1800XL-O. PRODUCTION: Typesetters — Tegra/Varityper 5100; Platemaking systems — Amerigraph; Plate exposures — Amerigraph; Plate processors — Anitec/538; Electronic picture desk — Lf/AP Leaf Picture Desk; Scanners — X/7650; Production cameras — C/Spartan, C/Pager; Automatic film processors — 2-AG/Lith 26; Shrink lenses — CK Optical; Color separation equipment (conventional) — Lf/AP Leaf Picture Desk, ECR/Autokon 1000 Laser-Graphic; Digital color separation equipment — Lf/Leafscan 35.
PRESSROOM: Line 1 — 11-G/Urbanite; Folders — G/Urbanite, Hantscho/F10W839; Pasters — 8-Enkel/Auto Paster; Press control system — Fin. MAILROOM: Counter stackers — 2-HL/Monitor HT; Inserters and stuffers —

GMA/SLS 1000 (8-into-1); Bundle tyer — Power Strap, Bu; Addressing machine — Ch; Other mailroom equipment — MM/4-Pocket Stitcher-Trimmer. LIBRARY: Electronic — KMC/Engineering. WIRE SERVICES: News — AP; Photos — AP; Stock tables — AP; Receiving dishes — size-2ft, AP. BUSINESS COMPUTERS: DEC/Micro VA 3600; Applications: Circ, Gen ledger, Accts receivable, Accts payable; PCs & micros networked; PCs & main system networked.

QUINCY
Norfolk County

'90 U.S. Census- 84,985; E&P '96 Est. 85,561
ABC-CZ (90): 172,884 (HH 68,403)

The Patriot Ledger
(e-mon to fri; m-sat)

The Patriot Ledger, 400 Crown Colony Dr. (02169); PO Box 9159, Quincy, MA 02269-9159; tel (617) 786-7000; fax (617) 786-7120.

Circulation: 87,973(e); 102,375(m-sat); ABC Sept. 30, 1995.

Price: 75¢(d); $1.00(sat); $3.00/wk, $1.00/wk (sat only).

Advertising: Open inch rate $47.39(e); $47.39(m-sat). **Representative:** Landon Associates Inc.

News Services: NYT, AP, SHNS, TMS. **Established:** 1837.

Not Published: New Year; Memorial Day; Independence Day; Labor Day; Christmas.

Special Editions: Education Guide, People in Business (Jan); Auto Section I, Auto Section II, Your Wedding Day, The Coupon Source, Financial Planning (Feb); Your Health, Red Sox Preview (Mar); Dining Guide, Educational Guide, Spring Gardening And Home Improvement, Auto Section I (Apr); Auto Section II, The Coupon Source, Employment Opportunities, Guide to Summer Fun (May); Your Wedding Day (June); Education Guide I (July); Education Guide II, Football, The Coupon Source (Aug); Answer Book, Employment Opportunities, Your Health (Sept); Your Home, 1997 Auto Buyer's Guide, Buying a car in the 90's, Your Wedding Day, Dining Guide (Oct); Holiday Recipes, The Coupon Source (Nov); Holiday Gift Guide (Dec).

Special Weekly Sections: Living (mon); Health/Science, Arts (tues); Food (wed); Home, Driving (Auto Section) (thur); Music/Movies, Housing Extra (Real Estate Section) (fri); Family, Business Plus, TV Ledger, Travel, For Kids Only (sat).

Magazines: Weekly TV Ledger, USA Weekend (wkly).

CORPORATE OFFICERS

Board Chairman K Prescott Low
Chief Financial Officer Frank Grueter

GENERAL MANAGEMENT

Publisher K Prescott Low
General Manager Patrick J DeGiso
Director-Administration Karen Dobbyn
Director-Finance Service Marshall Fine
Manager-Human Resources Cyndi Papile
Manager-Purchasing Communications Jan Johnson

ADVERTISING

Director-National/Retail Ed Feldman
Director-Classified David A Benoy
Manager-Classified Linda Siemers
Manager-Retail/National Sharron McCarthy
Manager-Operations Retail Edward J Siemers
Manager-Operations-Classified Helen Taylor
Manager-Systems/Classified Holly Warshaw

MARKETING AND PROMOTION

Director-Administration Karen Dobbyn

TELECOMMUNICATIONS

Audiotex Manager Linda Siemers

CIRCULATION

Director Paul D DeLorey
Director-Distribution Richard Lakus
Manager-Distribution David Hamilton
Manager George Rosenfield

NEWS EXECUTIVES

Editor William B Ketter
Managing Editor Terry Ryan
Assoc Editor Bernard W Caughey

EDITORS AND MANAGERS

Action Line Editor Bill Flynn
Automotive Editor Colin Stewart
Books Editor Jon L Lehman
Business/Finance Editor Colin Stewart
City Editor Randy Keith
City/Suburban Final Edition Editor Linda Bliss
Editorial Page Editor Peter M Knapp
Education Editor Kate Zernike
Entertainment/Amusements Editor Jon L Lehman
Fashion Editor Jon L Lehman
Feature/TV Ledger Editor Jon L Lehman
Films/Theater Editor Jon L Lehman
Food Editor Vicky Fitzgerald
Graphics Editor Tony Lanier
Health/Medical Editor Ann Doyle
Living/Lifestyle Editor Jon L Lehman
Manager-Electronic Library Info Systems Linda Chapman
National Editor Carolyn Ryan
News Editor Warren Talbot
News Editor-Night Steve Shepherd
Photo Editor Joe Lippincott
Political/Government Editor Carolyn Ryan
Reader Representative Bill Flynn
Religion Editor Ann Doyle
Science/Technology Editor Ann Doyle
South Edition Editor Ken Johnson
Sports Editor Earl LaChance
Systems Editor Paul Williams
Travel Editor Vera Vida

MANAGEMENT INFORMATION SERVICES

Online Manager Linda Chapman
Data Processing Manager Gary Smith

PRODUCTION

Director-Printing/Distribution Richard Lakus
Manager-Composing Richard Boyer
Foreman-Pressroom Greg Carney

Market Information: Zoned editions; Split Run; TMC; Operate database; Operate audiotex.

Mechanical available: Letterpress (direct); Black and 3 ROP colors; insert accepted — preprinted; page cut-offs — 23 9/16".

Mechanical specifications: Type page 13" x 22"; E - 6 cols, 2.03", 1/6" between; A - 6 cols, 2.03", 1/6" between; C - 9 cols, 1.39", .07" between.

Commodity consumption: Newsprint 8,531 metric tons; widths 54", 40½", 27"; black ink 328,500 pounds; color ink 26,000 pounds; single pages printed 17,602; average pages per issue 50(d), 88(sat); single plates used 44,176.

Equipment: EDITORIAL: Front-end hardware — AT/7000; Front-end software — AT 4; Other equipment — 60-PC, 3-Ap/Mac, Lf/AP Leaf Picture Desk, Novell/Staffer Library System. CLASSIFIED: Front-end hardware — AT/7000, 2-Leading Edge/PC; Front-end software — AT 4; Printers — 1-Florida Data; Other equipment — 27-AT/7000 VDT, 2-Leading Edge /PC. DISPLAY: Adv layout systems — SCS/Layout 8000, 3-Xenotron; Front-end hardware — 3-AT/7000VDT, 6-Ap/Mac Quadra 840, 1-Ap/Mac 7100, 2-Sun/Sparc 20, PCS Limited/386, AP AdSend Ambra; Front-end software — SCS/Layout 8000, Adobe/Illustrator, Acrobat, Aldus/PageMaker, QuarkXPress, Multi-Ad/Creator, Aldus/FreeHand, Ap/Mac Ad Assistant; Printers — C.Itoh, Lips/10 Plus Laser, LaserMaster/1800-XL, GCC/Select Press 1200, QMS/860, QMS/860 Plus, 1-Epson/FX 870, 1-Epson/LQ 850; Other equipment — AG/Arcus Scanner, Syquest/Tape, Pixelcraft/Scanner. PRODUCTION: Typesetters — 2-AU/Micro 5, AdSat (Matsushita) LED Scanner-Recorder; Plate exposures — 2-LX/135; Plate processors — 2-LX/135; Electronic picture desk — Lf/AP Leaf Picture Desk; Scanners — 1-ECR/Autokon 1000, 2-AU/APS-44 Logo Scanners; Production cameras — 1-C/Pager, 1-R/432 Mic II; Automatic film processors — 2-P, 2-DP/RAII; Film transporters — 1-C; Shrink lenses — Alan/2 1/2%. PRESSROOM: Line 1 — 7-Sc, 3-Wd; Line 2 — 8-H/Colormatic; Press drives — 5-PEC/Custom Made 100 Horse Power; Folders — 2-SC, 1-H; Pasters — Wd, 6-Cline, H; Reels and stands — Wd, 6-Cline, H; Press control system — GE, PEC/Bond; Press registration system — Kiam/3-Color Registration System. MAILROOM: Counter stackers — 2-HL/HT-2, 2-HL/Monitor; Inserters and stuffers — 2-GMA/SLS-1000(8-into-1); Bundle tyer — 4-OVL/JP-80, 1-OVL/Constellation; Wrapping singles — 2-HL/Bottom Wraps; Addressing machine — 1-IBM/Sys 36. LIBRARY: Electronic — SMS, Novell. WIRE SERVICES: News — AP Datastream, AP Datafeatures, NYT, SHNS; Photos — AP; Stock tables — TMS; Syndicates — United Media, TMS; Receiving dishes — size-3m, AP. BUSINESS COMPUTERS: 2-IBM/Sys 36-5360; Applications: Circ, Adv billing, Accts receivable, Accts payable, Gen ledger, Payroll, Credit processing; PCs & micros networked; PCs & main system networked.

Massachusetts I-193

SALEM
Essex County

'90 U.S. Census- 38,091; E&P '96 Est. 37,895
ABC-CZ (90): 129,275 (HH 50,400)

The Salem Evening News
(e-mon to fri; m-sat)

The Salem Evening News, 155 Washington St., Salem, MA 01970; tel (508) 744-0600; fax (508) 744-1010. Ottaway Newspapers Inc. group.

Circulation: 36,759(e); 36,759(m-sat); ABC Sept. 30, 1995.

Price: 35¢(d); 35¢(sat); $2.20/wk.

Advertising: Open inch rate $36.75(e); $36.75 (m-sat). **Representative:** Landon Associates Inc.

News Service: AP. **Politics:** Independent. **Established:** 1880.

Note: On Aug. 21, 1995, the Beverly Times (e-mon to fri; m-sat) & the Peabody Times (e-mon to fri; m-sat) merged with the Salem Evening News (e-mon to fri; m-sat).

Not Published: New Year; Memorial Day; Independence Day; Labor Day; Christmas.

Special Editions: Bridal, Washington's Birthday (Feb); Financial & Industrial (Mar); Home & Garden (Apr); Real Estate (May); Summer Living (June); Heritage Days, Back-to-School (Aug); H.S. Football, Fall Home Improvement (Sept); North Shore Restaurants, Cars '97 (Oct); Fall Real Estate, Holiday Recipes (Nov); Christmas Gift Guide (Dec).

Special Weekly Sections: Education (mon); Health & Fitness (tues); Food, Wedding (wed); Business (thur); Calendar, Living (fri); Food, Wedding (sat).

Magazines: North Shore Magazine (thur); USA Weekend (fri).

CORPORATE OFFICERS

President/Publisher John P Kinney
General Manager Peter Watson
Asst to the Publisher Paul Briand

GENERAL MANAGEMENT

Controller Gary Your
Director-Human Resources John Maihos

ADVERTISING

Director Brent Connolly
Director-Classified Margo Wagner
Manager Robert Babcock

CIRCULATION

Director Rino Vitolo

NEWS EXECUTIVE

Editor David Marcus

EDITORS AND MANAGERS

Assignment Editor Lisa Kosan
Editorial Page Editor Nelson K Benton III
News Editor John Mackenna
Sports Editor Paul Leighton

PRODUCTION

Director-Systems Brad Koltz
Systems Manager-Pressroom Joe Wilcox
Systems-Manager-Mailroom George Silva

Market Information: Zoned editions; TMC; ADS.

Mechanical available: Offset; Black and 3 ROP colors; insert accepted — preprinted; page cut-offs — 21½".

Mechanical specifications: Type page 13" x 21½"; E - 6 cols, 2 1/16", 1/8" between; A - 6 cols, 2 1/16", 1/8" between; C - 9 cols, 1 3/8", 1/16" between.

Commodity consumption: Newsprint 1,734 short tons; widths 55", 41¼"; black ink 55,000 pounds; average pages per issue 40(d); single plates used 24,000.

Equipment: EDITORIAL: Front-end hardware — PC. CLASSIFIED: Front-end hardware — CD. DISPLAY: Adv layout systems — PC. PRODUCTION: Pagination software — QuarkXPress. MAILROOM: Inserters and stuffers — HI. WIRE SERVICES: News — AP, ONS; Photos — AP; Receiving dishes — AP. BUSINESS COMPUTERS: IBM/AS 400; PCs & micros networked; PCs & main system networked.

SOUTHBRIDGE
Worcester County

'90 U.S. Census- 17,816; E&P '96 Est. 18,859

The News (e-mon to fri)

The News, 25 Elm St.; PO Box 90, Southbridge, MA 01550; tel (508) 764-4325; fax (508) 764-6743. Worcester County Newspapers group.

Circulation: 4,951(e); Sworn Sept. 15, 1995.

Price: 45¢(d); $1.55/wk; $6.20/mo; $80.60/yr.

Advertising: Open inch rate $10.55(e). **Established:** 1923.

Note: In March 1994, this publication ceased publishing its m-sat edition.

Not Published: New Year; Memorial Day; Independence Day; Labor Day; Thanksgiving; Christmas.

Advertising not accepted: Cigarette ads.

Special Editions: Wedding Guide, Brimfielder (Jan); Industrial & Business Review, President's Day Auto Care (Feb); The Villager, Summertime (May); Graduation, Meet your Professionals (June); Community Guide, Fall Home Improvement, Healthy Living (Sept); Organization Guide (Oct); Christmas Gift Guide (Nov); The Villager, Restaurant Guide, Last Minute Gift Guide (Dec).

Special Weekly Section: Regionally Speaking (1st wed-monthly).

CORPORATE OFFICERS

President Loren Ghiglione
Publisher Loren Ghiglione
Vice Pres Nancy Ghiglione
Vice Pres Fran Boutilier

ADVERTISING

Director Jean Ashton

CIRCULATION

Manager Gail Utakis

NEWS EXECUTIVES

Exec Editor Malcolm Donahoo
Editor Loren Ghiglione
Managing Editor Joe Capillo
Assoc Editor-News Joe Capillo

EDITORS AND MANAGERS

Amusements Editor Malcolm Donahoo
Books Editor Jean Ashton
Editorial Page Editor Malcolm Donahoo
Films/Theater Editor Malcolm Donahoo
Director-Photography Donald Cadoret
Radio/Television Editor Malcolm Donahoo
Sports Editor Tom Gaudet

MANAGEMENT INFORMATION SERVICES

Data Processing Manager Alan Lacasse

PRODUCTION

Manager John Agnew

Mechanical available: Offset; Black and 3 ROP colors; insert accepted — preprinted; page cut-offs — 17".

Mechanical specifications: Type page 9 5/8" x 16"; E - 6 cols, 1½", 3/16" between; A - 6 cols, 1½", 1/10" between; C - 7 cols, 1 3/8", 1/10" between.

Commodity consumption: Newsprint 181 short tons; widths 28", 14"; black ink 8,190 pounds; color ink 156 pounds; single pages printed 6,120; average pages per issue 24(d); single plates used 1,530.

Equipment: EDITORIAL: Front-end hardware — 2-Sperry/8, 2-Mpf/Pc 700. DISPLAY: Adv layout systems — 2-Ap/Mac Centris 610. PRODUCTION: Typesetters — LaserMaster/1200, 2-Ap/Mac LaserWriter; Production cameras — 1-B/3 N1, 1-B/E224, SCREEN/620DL, SCREEN/670E. WIRE SERVICES: News — United Features II; Syndicates — McNaught, King Features, LAT-WP, United Media, Universal Press; Receiving dishes — size-12ft, AP. BUSINESS COMPUTERS: Epson/III Plus; Applications: Word Processing: Accts receivable, Accts payable, Gen ledger, Circ, Mailing; PCs & micros networked; PCs & main system networked.

SPRINGFIELD
Hampden County

'90 U.S. Census- 156,983; E&P '96 Est. 161,590
ABC-CZ (90): 371,845 (HH 139,215)

Union-News (m-mon to sat)
Sunday Republican (S)

Union-News, 1860 Main St., Springfield, MA 01101; tel (413) 788-1000; e-mail general:mail@union-news.com. Advance Publications group.

Circulation: 104,216(m); 104,216(m-sat); 152,376(S); ABC Sept. 30, 1995.

Price: 50¢(d); 50¢(sat); $1.50(S).

Advertising: Open inch rate $56.05(m); $56.05(m-sat); $65.68(S). **Representative:** Newhouse Newspapers/Metro Suburbia.

News Services: AP, NYT, LAT-WP, NNS. **Politics:** Independent. **Established:** 1864.

I-194 Massachusetts

Special Editions: Bride & Bridegroom, Outlook '96 (Jan); Washington's Birthday Auto (Feb); Create-an-Ad, Home Show (Mar); Parade of Homes, Auto Show (Apr); Mother's Day, Summer Living (May); Back-to-School (Aug); Kielbasa Fest, Fall Home Improvement (Sept); Newcomers' Guide; Parade of Homes.
Special Weekly Sections: Business (mon); Consumer (tues); Best Food Day (wed); Weekend Section (thur); Health & Science (fri); TV Time Section (S).
Magazines: Color Comics, Parade, Leisure Time (S).

CORPORATE OFFICERS

President David Starr
Vice Pres Theodore Newhouse
Treasurer David B Evans

GENERAL MANAGEMENT

Publisher David Starr
Assoc Publisher Richard C Garvey
Asst to Publisher Robyn A Newhouse
General Manager Brian J Long
Personnel Director Judy Fraser
Purchasing Agent Michael Demarinis
Controller David B Evans

ADVERTISING

Director Dwight L Brouillard
Manager-Classified Maureen Thorpe
Manager-General Joseph A Ascioti
Manager-Major Accounts Rita J Martin

CIRCULATION

Director Michael P Fay

NEWS EXECUTIVES

Exec Editor Larry A McDermott
(Union News/Sunday Republican
Managing Editor-Features Romola Mimi Rigali
Managing Editor-News Wayne E Phaneuf
Managing Editor-Production Thomas F Haggerty
Managing Editor-Sunday Robert A Perkins

EDITORS AND MANAGERS

Art Director Michael Nasuti
Art Critic Gloria Russell
Business Editor Carolyn Robbins
Boston Bureau John O'Connell
City Editor-Day Larry Rivais
City Editor-Night Steven D Smith
Columnist Garry P Brown
Columnist Tom Shea
Columnist Robert Chipkin
Columnist Ron Chimelis
Columnist Zedra Aranow
Editorial Page Editor Joseph Hopkins
Editorial Page Editor Patricia Delo
Editorial Page Editor Janet Davenport
Entertainment/Arts Editor Doris Schmidt
Metro Editor James Gillen
Metro Editor Michael Brault
Metro Editor Robert Chipkin
Metro Editor William Whitney
Metro Editor Lu Feorino
Metro Editor John Bart
Metro Editor Marie Grady
Music Critic-Popular Kevin O'Hare
Music Critic-Classical Clifton J Noble Jr
News Editor Vernon Hill
Religion Editor Beatrice O'Quinn Dewberry
Photo Editor Dale Ruff
Sports Editor Richard Lord
Outdoors Editor Frank Sousa
Theater Critic Fred Sokol
Dance Editor H B Kronen
Theater Editor Ronni Gordon
Washington Bureau Jo-Ann Moriarty
Librarian Ellen Turner

PRODUCTION

Director Jim Foley
Manager-Systems Michael D Siciliano
Supervisor-Composing Michael D Siciliano
Supervisor-Press Paul Boissy

Market Information: Zoned editions; Split Run; TMC; ADS.
Mechanical available: DiLitho; Black and 3 ROP colors; insert accepted — preprinted, BFD inserts; page cut-offs — 22¾".
Mechanical specifications: Type page 13" x 21½"; E - 6 cols, 2$\frac{1}{16}$", ⅛" between; A - 6 cols, 2$\frac{1}{16}$", ⅛" between; C - 10 cols, 1$\frac{3}{16}$", $\frac{1}{16}$" between.
Commodity consumption: Newsprint 20,000 short tons; widths 54", 40.5", 27", 13.5"; black ink 505,000 pounds; color ink 48,000 pounds; average pages per issue 48(d), 140(S).
Equipment: EDITORIAL: Front-end hardware — DEC; Front-end software — CSI; Printers — 3-DEC/LA 75, AU/6600; Other equipment — CSI/103, CSI/112B, 3-HI/8300, 7-HI/8900, HI/Pagination Systems. CLASSIFIED: Front-end hardware — DEC; Front-end software — CSI; Printers — DataProducts, DEC/LA 75, DEC/LA 120; Other equipment — 28-CSI/C112. DISPLAY: Adv layout systems — CJ; Front-end hardware — HP; Front-end software — CJ; Other equipment — 5-HI/8000, 1-HI/8900 Classified Pagination, 1-HI/8900 Pixel Editing. PRODUCTION: Pagination software — HI/8300-8900; Typesetters — 2-AU/APS-6, 1-AU/APS Micro 5; Plate exposures — 2-Nat; Plate processors — 2-Nat; Electronic picture desk — Lf/AP Leaf Picture Desk; Scanners — 1-ECR/Autokon, 2-X/Flatbed, 1-Nikon 35mm Scanner; Production cameras — 1-C/Marathon, 2-Ik, 1-C/Pager, 1-C/Spartan II; Automatic film processors — 2-P, 2-LE/PC18, 1-P, 1-LE/2600, 2-LE/PC-18, 2-LE/APS-36; Film transporters — 2-C; Digital color separation equipment — 1-RZ/200S, 1-Ap/Mac, Adobe/Photoshop.
PRESSROOM: Line 1 — 6-H/Colormatic-Dilitho; Line 2 — 7-H/Colormatic-Dilitho; Folders — 2-H/2:1, 2-H/3:2. MAILROOM: Counter stackers — 4-QWI, 2-QWI/300; Inserters and stuffers — 2-S/1372P, 1-S/1272 On-Line; Bundle tyer — 5-MLN/MLN2A, 3-Strapex, 2-Dynaric, 1-EAM/Mosca; Addressing machine — 3-Ch/525E Labeler, 1-Ch/596 Labeler. LIBRARY: Electronic — Data Times. WIRE SERVICES: News — AP; Stock tables — AP; Syndicates — NYT, LAT-WP, NNS; Receiving dishes — AP. BUSINESS COMPUTERS: IBM/AS-400, IBM/AS-400, IBM/AS-400; Applications: IBM/AS-400: Payroll, Gen ledger, Accts payable.

TAUNTON

Bristol County

'90 U.S. Census- 49,832; E&P '96 Est. 54,269
ABC-CZ (90): 49,832 (HH 18,849)

Taunton Daily Gazette

(e-mon to fri; m-sat)

Taunton Daily Gazette, 5 Cohannet St.; PO Box 111, Taunton, MA 02780; tel (508) 880-9000; fax (508) 880-9049. Thomson Newspapers group.
Circulation: 15,180(e); 15,180(m-sat); ABC Sept. 30, 1995.
Price: 50¢(d); 50¢(sat); $2.35/wk; $10.00/mo; $110.00/yr.
Advertising: Open inch rate $14.75(e); $14.75(m-sat). **Representatives:** Thomson Newspapers; Landon Associates Inc.
News Service: AP. **Politics:** Independent. **Established:** 1848.
Not Published: New Year; Memorial Day; Independence Day; Labor Day; Christmas.
Special Editions: Progress; Washington's Birthday; Home Improvement; Spring Fashion; Car Care; Bride; Mother's Day; Father's Day; Graduation Gift Guide; Back-to-School; Football; Christmas Gift; Milestones (monthly).
Special Weekly Sections: Dine Out (wed); Medical Directory (thur); Bridal (sat).
Magazines: Cover Story (TMC, local newsprint); Coupons! (1st wed); Your Home (3rd wed).

GENERAL MANAGEMENT

Publisher Jean Scarborough

ADVERTISING

Manager Ginger Vieira

MARKETING AND PROMOTION

Manager-Marketing/Promotion Dana De Barras

CIRCULATION

Manager J William Dean

NEWS EXECUTIVE

Managing Editor Eva Gaffney

EDITORS AND MANAGERS

City Editor Craig Borges
Sports Editor Michael Mimoso
Suburban Editor Paul Kandarian

PRODUCTION

Manager Nancy L Porter
Supervisor-Pressroom Robert Silvia
Supervisor-Composing Room Nancy Rego

Market Information: TMC; ADS.
Mechanical available: Offset; Black and 3 ROP colors; insert accepted — preprinted, all; page cut-offs — 22¾".
Mechanical specifications: Type page 13" x 21½"; E - 6 cols, 2", ⅙" between; A - 6 cols, 2", ⅙" between; C - 9 cols, 1⅓", .13" between.
Commodity consumption: Newsprint 580 short tons; widths 27½", 13¾"; black ink 16,000 pounds; color ink 1,320 pounds; single pages printed 7,000; average pages per issue 24(d); single plates used 8,200.
Equipment: EDITORIAL: Front-end hardware — Mk; Front-end software — Mk; Printers — Okidata. CLASSIFIED: Front-end hardware — Mk; Front-end software — Mk; Printers — Okidata. DISPLAY: Adv layout systems — Mk/MasterPlanner; Front-end hardware — Mk; Front-end software — Mk/MasterPlanner. PRODUCTION: Typesetters — Tegra/Varityper/VT-600; Plate exposures — 1-Nu; Plate processors — Nat; Electronic picture desk — Lf/AP Leaf Picture Desk; Scanners — The Complete Page Scanner; Production cameras — SCREEN, R; Automatic film processors — SCREEN; Color separation equipment (conventional) — Lf/AP Leaf Picture Desk.
PRESSROOM: Line 1 — 10-G/Community. MAILROOM: Bundle tyer — MLN/ML2E, MLN/Suretyer. COMMUNICATIONS: Facsimile — Brother. WIRE SERVICES: News — AP; Receiving dishes — size-3m, AP. BUSINESS COMPUTERS: CCPS.

WAKEFIELD

Middlesex County

'90 U.S. Census- 24,825; E&P '96 Est. 24,707

Wakefield Daily Item

(e-mon to fri)

Wakefield Daily Item, 26 Albion St., Wakefield, MA 01880; tel (617) 245-0080; fax (617) 246-0061.
Circulation: 4,182(e); Sworn Oct. 3, 1994.
Price: 35¢(d); $115.00/yr (mail), $190.00/yr (home delivery).
Advertising: Open inch rate $12.00(e). **Politics:** Independent. **Established:** 1894.
Not Published: New Year; President's Day; Memorial Day; Independence Day; Labor Day; Columbus Day; Veteran's Day; Thanksgiving; Christmas.
Special Editions: Bridal Supplement (Jan); Valentine's Page (Feb); St. Patrick's Page, Spring Home & Garden Page, Easter Page (Mar); Mother's Day Page (Apr); Memorial Day Page, Graduation Pages (May); Father's Day Page (June); 4th of July (July); Back-to-School (Aug); Football, Columbus Day (Sept); Thanksgiving Day, Holiday Gift Guide (Nov); Christmas Gift, New Baby (Dec).

CORPORATE OFFICERS

President Glenn D Dolbeare
Treasurer Cortland B Bacall

GENERAL MANAGEMENT

Publisher Robert P Dolbeare
General Manager Glenn D Dolbeare
Controller/Personnel Manager Glenn D Dolbeare
Purchasing Agent Robert Moores

ADVERTISING

Manager Steve Leahy
Manager-Classified Mary McNulty

CIRCULATION

Manager Glenn D Dolbeare

NEWS EXECUTIVES

Editor Peter Rossi
Asst Editor Robert Burgess

EDITORS AND MANAGERS

School Editor Robert Keohan
Sports Editor John Alabiso

PRODUCTION

Foreman Glenn D Dolbeare

Mechanical available: Offset.
Mechanical specifications: Type page 13" x 21"; E - 6 cols, 2$\frac{1}{16}$", ⅛" between; A - 9 cols, 1¼", ⅛" between; C - 9 cols, 1¼", ⅛" between.
Commodity consumption: average pages per issue 41(d).
Equipment: EDITORIAL: Front-end software — Baseview/NewsEdit.

WALTHAM

Middlesex County

'90 U.S. Census- 57,878; E&P '96 Est. 57,494

News-Tribune (e-mon to fri)

Waltham News-Tribune, 580 Winter St.; Box 69, Waltham, MA 02154; tel (617) 487-7200; fax (617) 890-9008. Community Newspaper Co. (Middlesex Community Newspapers) group.
Circulation: 8,845(e); CAC June 30, 1993.
Price: 50¢(d); $1.75/wk; $91.00/yr.
Advertising: Open inch rate $12.35(e). **Representatives:** Landon Associates Inc.; US Suburban Press.
News Services: AP, SHNS. **Politics:** Independent. **Established:** 1862.
Note: For detailed production information, see the Framingham Middlesex News listing.
Not Published: New Year; Christmas.
Special Editions: Wedding (Jan); President's Day Auto Showcase (Feb); Progress '96 (Mar); Spring Home & Garden, Home Buyers Guide (Apr); Nursing '96, Your Child, Senior Lifestyles (May); Metro West Community Guide (June); Community Guides (July); Bridal Section, Fall Home Improvement (Sept); Wheels, Working Women, Interiors (Oct); Holiday Gift Guide (Nov); Home for the Holidays, Last Minute Gift Guide (Dec).
Special Weekly Sections: Sports Monday (mon); Best Food Day (wed); Expanded Business, Expanded Entertainment (thur); This Week in Real Estate (fri).
Magazines: Weekend Guide; Auto Weekly.

GENERAL MANAGEMENT

Publisher Asa Cole
Controller Jeffrey Feingold
Manager-Credit Vincent Alphonse

ADVERTISING

Director-Sales/Marketing Paul M Farrell

MARKETING AND PROMOTION

Manager-Marketing/Promotion Paula Bubello

TELECOMMUNICATIONS

Manager-Telecommunications Debra Freeman

CIRCULATION

Manager Brian Hanify

NEWS EXECUTIVE

Editor Ellen Ishkanian

EDITORS AND MANAGERS

Business Editor Robert Dickson
Design Director Patricia Capabianco
Editorial Page Editor Ellen Ishkanian
News Editor Ellen Ishkanian
Photo Editor Art Illman
Religion Editor Jeanne Washington
Sports Editor Jerry Spar
Weekend Guide Editor Karen Buckley

PRODUCTION

Manager Nancy McNiff

Market Information: Zoned editions.
Mechanical available: Offset; Black and 3 ROP colors; insert accepted — preprinted; page cut-offs — 15".
Mechanical specifications: Type page 10$\frac{13}{16}$" x 13½"; E - 5 cols, 2$\frac{1}{16}$", ⅛" between; A - 5 cols, 2$\frac{1}{16}$", ⅛" between; C - 7 cols, 1⅜", $\frac{1}{16}$" between.
Commodity consumption: Newsprint 7,500 short tons; width 30"; black ink 160,00 pounds; color ink 21,000 pounds; single pages printed 7,264; average pages per issue 32(d).
Equipment: EDITORIAL: Front-end hardware — IBM, 36-HP, 1-Ap/Mac II, Ap/Mac Quadra, 16-Austin; Front-end software — III/Tecs 2; Printers — 1-Ap/Mac LaserPrinter, 1-HP/Rugged-Writer; Other equipment — 2-Microtek/ScanMaker II. CLASSIFIED: Front-end hardware — IBMs; Front-end software — III/Tecs 2; Printers — Toshiba, HP/RuggedWriter. DISPLAY: Adv layout systems — Ap/Mac, 1-SCS/Layout 8000, 7-Ap/Mac II; Front-end hardware — Ap/Mac, IBMs; Front-end software — SCS/Layout 8000, Multi-Ad. PRODUCTION: Pagination software — QuarkXPress 3.3; Plate exposures — 2-Nu/Ultra-Plus; Plate processors — 2-Nat/A340; Electronic picture desk — Lf/AP Leaf Picture Desk; Scanners — 3-Kk/2035 Film Scanner, 1-AG/Arcus Plus Color Scanner; Production cameras — 2-Image Maker/5060A, 2-C/NewsPager; Automatic film processors — 2-LE/Excel 26, P/Film Processor; Film transporters — 2-C, P/Film Transport; Shrink lenses — 1-CK Optical (9¼%), 2-CK Optical/(5%).
PRESSROOM: Line 1 — 12-G/Urbanite; Line 2 — 12-G/Urbanite; Line 3 — 1-G/HV; Pasters — 20-G/Automatic 2 arm; Reels and stands — 20-G/Automatic 2 arm; Press control system — 2-Fin. MAILROOM: Counter stackers — 2-Id, 1-RIMA, 4-HL/Monitor HT2; Inserters and stuffers — 1-S/948P, 1-KR, 1-GMA/SLS 1000; Bundle tyer — 6-MLN; Addressing machine — 2-Ch, 1-KR, 1-Domino/Ink Jet Printer. LIBRARY: Electronic — III/Archive System. WIRE SERVICES: News — AP; Photos — AP; Syndicates — SHNS. BUSINESS COMPUTERS: HP/3000-935 Series 935; Applications: Gen ledger, Accounting, Customer invoicing.

WESTFIELD

Hampden County

'90 U.S. Census- 38,372; E&P '96 Est. 40,127

Westfield Evening News

(e-mon to fri; m-sat)

Westfield Evening News, 62-64 School St., Westfield, MA 01085; tel (413) 562-4181; fax (413) 562-4185. Allbritton Communications group.

Circulation: 5,226(e); 5,226(m-sat); Sworn Sept. 29, 1995.

Price: 50¢(d); 50¢(sat); $9.00/mo (mail), $7.00/mo (in county).

Advertising: Open inch rate $10.25(e); $10.25 (m-sat). **Representative:** Landon Associates Inc.

News Service: AP. **Politics:** Independent. **Established:** 1931.

Not Published: New Year; Memorial Day; Independence Day; Labor Day; Thanksgiving; Christmas.

Special Weekly Sections: Food (wed); Business, Arts & Leisure (thur); At Home (fri); Bridal (sat).

Magazines: Food Day (wed); Money Day, Business (thur); Real Estate, Wheels (fri).

CORPORATE OFFICERS

President Joe L Allbritton
Vice Pres E Carol Mazza
Secretary Virginia White
Treasurer Bernard Gaarsoe

GENERAL MANAGEMENT

Publisher E Carol Mazza
Business Manager Marie Gianchetti

ADVERTISING

Director Martha Baillargeon

CIRCULATION

Manager Adam Liptak

NEWS EXECUTIVE

Managing Editor George O'Brien

EDITORS AND MANAGERS

City Editor Dan McCormick
Sports Editor Ted Syron

PRODUCTION

Foreman Norman LePage

Market Information: TMC.

Mechanical available: Offset; Black and 1 ROP color; insert accepted — preprinted; page cutoffs — 22$\frac{3}{4}$".

Mechanical specifications: Type page 13" x 21$\frac{1}{4}$"; E - 6 cols, 2$\frac{1}{16}$", $\frac{1}{8}$" between; A - 6 cols, 2$\frac{1}{16}$", $\frac{1}{8}$" between; C - 6 cols, 2$\frac{1}{16}$", $\frac{1}{8}$" between.

Commodity consumption: Newsprint 600 metric tons; widths 28", 34"; black ink 23,000 pounds; color ink 2,600 pounds; average pages per issue 20(d); single plates used 2,500.

Equipment: EDITORIAL: Front-end hardware — Mk. PRODUCTION: Typesetters — 1-COM/2961HS, 1-COM/7200, 1-COM/2961TL, Ap/Mac; Plate processors — 1-AG; Scanners — COM/Computwriter, Ap/Mac Scanner; Production cameras — AG/1600. MAILROOM: Inserters and stuffers — KAN; Bundle tyer — 2-Bu; Addressing machine — Ch/labeller. COMMUNICATIONS: Facsimile — Ricoh. WIRE SERVICES: News — AP; Receiving dishes — AP. BUSINESS COMPUTERS: 1-ATT.

WOBURN

Middlesex County

'90 U.S. Census- 35,943; E&P '96 Est. 35,381

Daily Times Chronicle

(e-mon to fri)

Daily Times Chronicle, 1 Arrow Dr., Woburn, MA 01801; tel (617) 933-3700; fax (617) 932-3321.

Circulation: 13,428(e); CAC Mar. 31, 1995.

Price: 45¢(d); $2.25/wk; $10.00/mo; $122.50/yr.

Advertising: Open inch rate $13.40(e). **Representatives:** US Suburban Press; American Newspaper Representatives Inc.

News Services: AP, NEA, SHNS, LAT-WP. **Politics:** Independent. **Established:** 1901.

Not Published: New Year; Memorial Day; Independence Day; Labor Day; Thanksgiving; Christmas.

Special Editions: Cars, Bridal (Feb); Spring Home Improvement (Mar); Graduation (June); Pre-Season Football (Aug); Bridal, Fall Home Improvement (Sept); Football, Thanksgiving (Nov); Christmas (Dec).

Special Weekly Sections: Medical Directory (mon); Business Guide (tues); Bridal Directory, Medical Directory (wed); Business Guide (thur); Bridal Directory (fri).

Magazine: Middlesex East (wed).

CORPORATE OFFICERS

President Peter M Haggerty
Secretary Joel Haggerty
Treasurer James D Haggerty III

GENERAL MANAGEMENT

Publisher Peter M Haggerty
Business Manager Richard P Haggerty
Controller Chris Campbell
Manager-Credit Carol Carlson
Personnel Manager Peter M Haggerty
Purchasing Agent Peter M Haggerty

ADVERTISING

Manager Thomas Kirk
Manager-Classified Mary Haggerty
Manager-National Marcia Santarpio

MARKETING AND PROMOTION

Manager-Promotion Mark Haggerty

CIRCULATION

Manager Peter Curran

NEWS EXECUTIVES

Editor James D Haggerty III
Managing Editor James D Haggerty IV

EDITORS AND MANAGERS

Action Line Editor James D Haggerty III
Amusements Editor Laurie Haggerty
Auto/Aviation Editor William Sullivan
Book Editor James D Haggerty III
Business/Finance Editor James D Haggerty III
City Editor James Haggerty IV
Columnist Dan Kennedy
Editorial Page Editor James D Haggerty III
Editorial Writer William Sullivan
Education Editor Pamela Mieth
Environmental Editor Charles Ryan
Farm Editor Charles Ryan
Fashion/Women's Editor Nancy Halliday
Features Editor James D Haggerty III
Films/Theater Editor James D Haggerty III
Food Editor Nancy Halliday
Garden Editor Laurie Haggerty
Graphics Editor/Art Director Laurie Haggerty
Health/Medical Editor James D Haggerty III
Home Furnishings Editor Laurie Haggerty
Librarian Charles Ryan
Living/Lifestyle Editor Nancy Halliday
Music Editor Laurie Haggerty
National Editor James D Haggerty III
News Editor James D Haggerty IV
News Editor John White
News Editor Ken Maguire
Photo Department Manager Joseph Brown
Picture Editor John Peterson
Political/Government Editor James D Haggerty III
Radio/Television Editor James D Haggerty III
Real Estate Editor James D Haggerty III
Religion/School Editor Charles Ryan
Science/Technology Editor Nancy Halliday
Sports Editor Rick Pearl
Travel Editor James D Haggerty III

PRODUCTION

Manager Jay M Haggerty
Foreman-Ad Composing Italo Galante
Foreman-Composing James Corduck
Foreman-Pressroom Bertel Franson
Foreman-Mailroom Peter Curran

Market Information: Zoned editions; Split Run; TMC; ADS.

Mechanical available: Offset; Black and 2 ROP colors; insert accepted — preprinted; page cutoffs — 21".

Mechanical specifications: Type page 27$\frac{1}{2}$" x 21"; E - 6 cols, 2$\frac{1}{16}$", $\frac{1}{8}$" between; A - 6 cols, 2$\frac{1}{16}$", $\frac{1}{8}$" between; C - 9 cols, 1$\frac{3}{8}$", $\frac{1}{16}$" between.

Commodity consumption: Newsprint 836 short tons; width 28"; black ink 20,900 pounds; color ink 1,050 pounds; single pages printed 8,820; average pages per issue 34(d); single plates used 11,400.

Equipment: EDITORIAL: Front-end hardware — COM/One Sys, 8-CK, 5-PC/486, 2-PC/386; Front-end software — COM/One Sys, XYQUEST/XyWrite, Azimoth, Novell; Printers — Novell, 2-COM/8400, 2-COM/Videosetters, 2-HP/LaserJet 4. CLASSIFIED: Front-end hardware — COM/One Sys, 8-CK; Front-end software — COM/One Sys, CK; Printers — 2-COM/8400, 2-COM/Videosetter. DISPLAY: Adv layout systems — 2-COM/105, 6-Ap/Mac SE, 2-Ap/Mac 7100-80; Front-end software — COM/8400, COM/Intrepid. PRODUCTION: Typesetters — 2-COM/8400, 2-COM/Intrepid, 6-Ap/Mac SE; Plate exposures — 1-BKY; Plate processors — 1-Nu/Plateprocessor; Production cameras — 2-DSA; Automatic film processors — 1-DP/24L; Shrink lenses — 1-Kamerak; Color separation equipment (conventional) — 1-GAM, 1-Ca. PRESSROOM: Line 1 — 8-G/Community. MAILROOM: Inserters and stuffers — MM; Bundle tyer — 1-CYP, 2-Sa; Wrapping singles — Am; Addressing machine — 2-Am/1800. COMMUNICATIONS: Systems used — satellite. WIRE SERVICES: News — AP, SHNS; Photos — AP; Syndicates — NEA, LATS, United Media; Receiving dishes — AP. BUSINESS COMPUTERS: 6-Vision Data; Applications: Mailing, Accts receivable, Accts payable, Circ; PCs & micros networked; PCs & main system networked.

WORCESTER

Worcester County

'90 U.S. Census- 169,759; E&P '96 Est. 177,162

ABC-CZ (90): 273,167 (HH 101,876)

Telegram & Gazette

(m-mon to sat)

Sunday Telegram (S)

Telegram & Gazette, Box 15012, Worcester, MA 01615-0012; tel (508) 793-9100; fax (508) 793-9313. Chronicle Publishing Co. group.

Circulation: 111,836(m); 111,836(m-sat); 141,722(S); ABC Sept. 30, 1995.

Price: 50¢(d); 50¢(sat); $1.50(S); $4.00/wk.

Advertising: Open inch rate $89.00(m); $89.00(m-sat); $92.85(S).

News Services: AP, NYT. **Politics:** Independent. **Established:** 1866 (Gazette), 1884 (Telegram), 1989 (Telegram & Gazette).

Special Editions: Bridal Section (Jan); Business Review, Washington's Birthday (Feb); Home Show, Spring & Summer Travel, Spring Home Improvement (Apr); Fall Home Improvement (Sept); Business Expo '96 (Oct); New Cars, Ski Section (Nov).

Special Weekly Sections: Time Out (thur); Homes, Travel (S).

Magazines: Datebook (Entertainment Tab); Parade (S).

CORPORATE OFFICERS

Chairman/President John Sias
President/Massachusetts Operations Donald R Skaggs

GENERAL MANAGEMENT

Publisher Bruce S Bennett
Director-Human Resources Peter H Horstmann
Director-Finance Robert R Beatty
Personnel Manager Sheila Battles
Manager-Credit Robert L Meunier
Manager-Purchasing Jane L Simpson
Controller Joseph E Sgro

ADVERTISING

Director Robert N Recore
Asst Director Nancy Cahalen Bayley
Manager-Operations Anthony J Simollardes
Manager-National Maurice J Guarini
Manager-Zone Sales Division Reinhold Wolfram

MARKETING AND PROMOTION

Director-Marketing Service Thomas F X Cole
Director-Research Averil Capers
Special Sections Editor Kathleen Pierce

TELECOMMUNICATIONS

Manager-Info Systems Valerie Winer
Audiotex Manager Cheryl E Haskins

CIRCULATION

Director Barry LaRoche
Manager-Transportation Steven A Erikson
Manager-Single Copy Sales Joel Houde
Manager-Sales Kimberly Cicero
Manager-Customer Service Carole Heywood

NEWS EXECUTIVES

Editor Harry T Whitin
Managing Editor-Local News Leah Lamson
Asst Managing Editor James B Donham

EDITORS AND MANAGERS

Arts Editor Frank Magiera
Business Editor Anne N Esposito
Editorial Page Editor Robert Z Nemeth
Education Editor Clive McFarlane
Education Editor Mark Melody
Environment Editor John J Monahan
Features Editor David Mawson
Asst Features Editor Karen Webber
Food Editor Barbara Houle
Librarian George R LaBonte
News Editor Lee Merkel
Photo/Graphics Editor Leonard J Lazure
Sports Editor David E Nathan
Sunday News Editor Thomas W Bergstrand
Travel Editor Diana Scott

MANAGEMENT INFORMATION SERVICES

Manager-Info Systems Valerie Winer
Online Manager George R LaBonte

PRODUCTION

Manager-Plant Charles R Pickens
Manager-Pre Press Robert P Dupuis
Superintendent-Pressroom David H Johnson
Superintendent-Plant (Night) Ronald G Corriveau
Manager-Mailroom Wayne Shepard
Manager-Equipment Maintenance Dennis McArthur
Manager-Transportation/Warehouse Steven A Erikson
Manager-Facilities James Denman
Supervisor-Alternate Delivery Gerald Reed

Market Information: Zoned editions; Split Run; TMC; ADS; Operate database; Operate audiotex.

Mechanical available: Flexography; Black and 3 ROP colors; insert accepted — preprinted, partials d & S; page cut-offs — 22".

Mechanical specifications: Type page 13" x 21"; E - 6 cols, 2$\frac{1}{16}$", $\frac{1}{8}$" between; A - 6 cols, 2$\frac{1}{16}$", $\frac{1}{8}$" between; C - 9 cols, 1$\frac{3}{8}$", $\frac{1}{16}$" between.

Commodity consumption: Newsprint 15,216 short tons; 13,803 metric tons; width 54$\frac{1}{2}$"; black ink 490,773 pounds; color ink 104,544 pounds; single pages printed 18,616; average pages per issue 42(d), 124(S); single plates used 142,673.

Equipment: EDITORIAL: Front-end hardware — 2-DEC/PDP 11-84, 35-DEC/VT71, 12-DEC/VT72, 16-DEC/VT173R, 40-PC/486; Printers — Epson/DFX 5000; Other equipment — 24-NSSE/200. CLASSIFIED: Front-end hardware — 1-Mentor, 6-PC/386, 24-PC/486. AUDIOTEX: Hardware — Brite; Software — Brite; Supplier name — Brite, AP, DJ. DISPLAY: Adv layout systems — 4-Cx, Ap/Mac, SCS/Layout 8000. PRODUCTION: Typesetters — 3-Tegra/Varityper/5000, 1-Tegra/Varityper/5300E, 3-Xante/Laser Printers, 1-Konica/News-Scan facsimile system; Platemaking systems — Na/Flexo; Plate exposures — 3-MAS, 1-FX/4, 2-Burgess/Consolux; Plate processors — 2-Na/FP2; Electronic picture desk — Lf/AP Leaf Picture Desk; Scanners — 2-ECR/Autokon, Sharp/JX600, UMax/840; Production cameras — 1-C/Marathon, 1-C/Pager; Automatic film processors — 4-F; Film transporters — 1-C; Shrink lenses — 1-Alan; Color separation equipment (conventional) — Ap/Mac Desktop, Adobe/Photoshop, Color Acess, ECR/Autokon; Digital color separation equipment — 1-ECR/3850, 1-ECR/1045 HS. PRESSROOM: Line 1 — 7-G/Flexoliner double width; Line 2 — 7-G/Flexoliner double width; Press drives — Allen Bradley; Folders — 2-Sovereign/3:2, 1-G/3:2 double, 1-G/3:2 single; Pasters — 14-G/CT50; Reels and stands — 6-Wd, 6-Sc, 14-G; Press control system — Allen Bradley/PLC-5. MAILROOM: Counter stackers — 3-Id/NS440, 1-Id/NS550, 6-HL/HT; Inserters and stuffers — 4-GMA; Bundle tyer — 4-OVL/Constellation, 5-Power Strap; Addressing machine — 2-Ch; Mailroom control system — GMA/SLS1000 PMS. LIBRARY: Electronic — Data Times, DEC/VAX. WIRE SERVICES: News — AP, NYT; Stock tables — AP; Syndicates — AP; Receiving dishes — size-3m, AP. BUSINESS COMPUTERS: 1-DEC/VAX 4000-100, 1-IBM/AS-400; Applications: Circ, Adv billing, Accts receivable, Payroll, Media & market research; PCs & micros networked; PCs & main system networked.

MICHIGAN

ADRIAN

Lenawee County

'90 U.S. Census- 22,097; E&P '96 Est. 23,355

ABC-CZ (90): 22,097 (HH 7,479)

The Daily Telegram

(e-mon to fri; m-sat; S)

The Daily Telegram, 133 N. Winter St.; PO Box 647, Adrian, MI 49221; tel (517) 265-5111; fax (517) 263-4152. Thomson Newspapers group.

Circulation: 17,376(e); 17,382(m-sat); 17,376(S); ABC Sept. 30, 1995.
Price: 50¢(d); 50¢(sat); $1.25(S); $2.90/wk (carrier); $13.00/mo (motor route); $156.00/yr.
Advertising: Open inch rate $15.55(e); $15.55(m-sat); $15.55(S). **Representatives:** Thomson Newspapers; Landon Associates Inc.
News Services: AP, LAT-WP. **Politics:** Independent. **Established:** 1892.
Not Published: New Year; Independence Day; Labor Day; Thanksgiving; Christmas.
Special Weekly Sections: Church Page, Farm Page (sat); Entertainment TV Log, Outdoor Page (S).
Magazines: Ultra (Publication for the Senior Citizen); Real Estate Resource; Lenawee's Real Country.

GENERAL MANAGEMENT
Publisher Robert L Krout
ADVERTISING
Manager Michelle Micklewright
MARKETING AND PROMOTION
Manager-Marketing & Promotion Michelle Micklewright
TELECOMMUNICATIONS
Manager-Telecommunications Michelle Micklewright
CIRCULATION
Manager Tammy Hanson
NEWS EXECUTIVE
Editor Robert Jodon
EDITORS AND MANAGERS
Business/Finance Editor Joseph Kieta
Editorial Page Editor Robert Jodon
Farm/County Editor John Shiemo
Graphics Editor/Art Director John Shiemo
Local News Editor Jim Lyons
News Editor Roger Hart
Photo Editor Lisa Kyle
Religion Editor Roger Ferguson
Outdoor/Sports Editor Dan Daly
Television/Film Editor Marge Furgason
Theater/Music Editor Marge Furgason
Travel Editor Roger Hart
PRODUCTION
Foreman-Composing Mathew Ringkdist
Superintendent-Pressroom Royce Ohlinger

Market Information: Zoned editions; Split Run; TMC; ADS.
Mechanical available: Offset; Black and 3 ROP colors; insert accepted — preprinted; page cut-offs — $22\frac{1}{2}$".
Mechanical specifications: Type page $13\frac{1}{16}$" x $21\frac{1}{2}$"; E - 6 cols, $2\frac{1}{16}$", $\frac{1}{8}$" between; A - 6 cols, $2\frac{1}{16}$", $\frac{1}{8}$" between; C - 9 cols, $\frac{15}{16}$", $\frac{1}{8}$" between.
Commodity consumption: Newsprint 2,047,267 short tons; widths $27\frac{1}{2}$", $13\frac{3}{4}$"; black ink 23,720 pounds; color ink 8,640 pounds; single pages printed 7,172; average pages per issue 18(d), 32(S); single plates used 5,928.
Equipment: EDITORIAL: Front-end hardware — Mk/1100; Front-end software — Mk/1100; Other equipment — 17-Mk/VDT. CLASSIFIED: Front-end hardware — Mk/1100; Front-end software — Mk/1100; Other equipment — 3-Mk/VDT. DISPLAY: Adv layout systems — 4-Ap/Mac IIci; Front-end software — QuarkXPress, Adobe/Photoshop, Multi-Ad/Creator. PRODUCTION: Typesetters — 2-V/4000 Image Controller, 2-V/5100 Laser Printer; Plate exposures — Nu/Flip Top FT40V6UPNS; Plate processors — Nat/A250; Production cameras — R/500, SCREEN/Companica 68C; Automatic film processors — 2-LE/LD-220; Color separation equipment (conventional) — Digi-Colour, ECR/Autokon.
PRESSROOM: Line 1 — 8-G/Community (w/2-color decks; 2 formers); Press drives — 2-Fin; Folders — 1-G/55C; Press registration system — Duarte. WIRE SERVICES: News — AP, LAT-WP; Photos — AP; Stock tables — AP; Syndicates — United Media, King Features, Universal Press; Receiving dishes — size-10ft, AP. BUSINESS COMPUTERS: 6-ATT.

ALBION
Calhoun County
'90 U.S. Census- 10,066; E&P '96 Est. 9,289

Albion Recorder (e-mon to sat)
Albion Recorder, 111 W. Center St., Albion, MI 49224; tel (517) 629-3984; fax (517) 629-5790. Milliman Communications group.
Circulation: 1,645(e); 1,645(e-sat); Sworn Oct. 1, 1994.
Price: 50¢(d); 50¢(sat); $7.50/mo.
Advertising: Open inch rate $7.58(e); $7.58(e-sat); comb with Marshall Chronicle (m) $11.49.
News Service: AP. **Politics:** Independent. **Established:** 1904.
Not Published: New Year; Memorial Day; Independence Day; Labor Day; Thanksgiving; Christmas.
Special Editions: Seniors Unlimited (Feb); High School Graduation, Auto Care, Seniors Unlimited (May); Back-to-School, College, Seniors Unlimited (Aug); College Homecoming, Auto Care, Home Improvement, Women in Business (Oct); Seniors Unlimited (Nov).
Special Weekly Section: Leader (TMC, 5-col tab) (S).

GENERAL MANAGEMENT
Publisher Richard L Milliman II
General Manager Kate Moore
ADVERTISING
Manager Kate Moore
CIRCULATION
Manager John Senger
NEWS EXECUTIVE
Editor Stacey Henson
EDITORS AND MANAGERS
News Editor Stacey Henson
Sports Editor Dave Troppens
PRODUCTION
Manager-Composing Peggy Ellis

Market Information: TMC.
Mechanical available: Offset; Black and 3 ROP colors; insert accepted — preprinted; page cut-offs — $22\frac{3}{4}$".
Mechanical specifications: Type page $13\frac{3}{4}$" x 22"; E - 6 cols, $2\frac{1}{16}$", $\frac{1}{8}$" between; A - 6 cols, $2\frac{1}{16}$", $\frac{1}{8}$" between; C - 6 cols, $2\frac{1}{16}$", $\frac{1}{8}$" between.
Commodity consumption: Newsprint 200 short tons; average pages per issue 12(d); single plates used 12.
Equipment: EDITORIAL: Front-end hardware — Ap/Mac; Front-end software — KE/512, Ap/Mac Plus. CLASSIFIED: Front-end hardware — Ap/Mac Plus. DISPLAY: Adv layout systems — Ap/Mac Plus. PRODUCTION: Typesetters — 2-COM/4961, 1-COM/7200, 1-COM/Comp 4; Plate exposures — 1-Nu/Flip Top; Plate processors — 1-Nat/250; Production cameras — 1-B/Horz; Automatic film processors — 1-P, Kk/42.
PRESSROOM: Line 1 — 5-HI/Cotrell-15A; Folders — 1-HI/Cotrell. MAILROOM: Bundle tyer — 1-Bu; Addressing machine — 1-Am. WIRE SERVICES: News — AP; Receiving dishes — size-3m, UPI. BUSINESS COMPUTERS: 1-IBM, 2-ATT; Applications: Vision Data: Adv billing, Accts receivable, Gen ledger, Payroll, Accts payable; PCs & micros networked; PCs & main system networked.

ALMA
See MOUNT PLEASANT

ALPENA
Alpena County
'90 U.S. Census- 11,354; E&P '96 Est. 10,667
ABC-CZ (90): 20,956 (HH 8,356)

The Alpena News (e-mon to fri)
The News (m-sat)
The Alpena News, 130 Park Pl.; PO Box 367, Alpena, MI 49707; tel (517) 354-3111; fax (517) 354-2096. Ogden Newspapers group.
Circulation: 12,316(e); 12,316(m-sat); ABC Sept. 30, 1995.
Price: 35¢(d); 75¢(sat); $1.95/wk; $7.00/mo; $91.00/yr.
Advertising: Open inch rate $13.17(e); $13.17(m-sat).
News Services: AP, NEA. **Politics:** Independent. **Established:** 1899.
Not Published: New Year; Memorial Day; Labor Day; Thanksgiving; Christmas.
Advertising not accepted: Subject to newspaper's discretion.
Special Editions: Bridal, Money, Money (Feb); Gardening and Outdoor, Home Improvement (Apr); Car Care (May); Back-to-School (Aug); Football (Sept); Car Care, Soil Conservation (Oct); Deer Hunting (Nov).
Special Weekly Sections: Grocery (mon); Business (wed).
Magazines: Entertainment (thur, fri); Weekend Edition, Entertainment (sat); USA.

CORPORATE OFFICERS
President/General Manager G Ogden Nutting
Vice Pres/Asst General Manager Robert M Nutting
GENERAL MANAGEMENT
Publisher Bill Speer
Manager-Business Office Kathryn Burton
Personnel Manager Bill Speer
General Manager Bill Speer
ADVERTISING
Director John Jackowiak
CIRCULATION
Director James Austin
NEWS EXECUTIVE
Editor Bill Speer
EDITORS AND MANAGERS
Action Line Editor Richard Crofton
Automotive Editor John Morris
Business/Finance Editor Richard Crofton
City/Metro Editor Richard Crofton
Editorial Page Editor Richard Crofton
Education Editor Cathy Mason
Entertainment/Amusements Editor Diane Speer
Environmental Editor Connie Allen
Farm/Agriculture Editor Connie Allen
Fashion/Style Editor Diane Speer
Graphics Editor/Art Director Richard Crofton
Health/Medical Editor Cathy Mason
Lifestyle Editor Diane Speer
National Editor Mike Huggler
News Editor Mike Huggler
Photo Editor Christine Malenfont
Political/Government Editor Mike Huggler
Religion Editor Mike Huggler
Science/Technology Editor Richard Crofton
Sports Editor Rodney Hart
Television/Film Editor Diane Speer
Theater/Music Editor Diane Speer
Travel Editor Diane Speer
MANAGEMENT INFORMATION SERVICES
Data Processing Manager Kathryn Burton
PRODUCTION
Manager Andrew Feldhiser
Foreman-Pressroom Keith Weiland

Market Information: Zoned editions; Split Run; TMC; ADS.
Mechanical available: Offset; Black and 3 ROP colors; insert accepted — preprinted; page cut-offs — $22\frac{3}{4}$".
Mechanical specifications: Type page 13" x 21"; E - 6 cols, $2\frac{1}{16}$", $\frac{1}{8}$" between; A - 6 cols, $2\frac{1}{16}$", $\frac{1}{8}$" between; C - 8 cols, $1\frac{3}{8}$", $\frac{1}{16}$" between.
Commodity consumption: Newsprint 511 short tons; widths 27", $13\frac{1}{2}$", 34", 14", 17"; black ink 7,885 pounds; color ink 2,900 pounds; single pages printed 6,223; average pages per issue 16(d), 28(sat); single plates used 13,410.
Equipment: EDITORIAL: Front-end hardware — Ap/Mac; Front-end software — Baseview, Write Now, QuarkXPress, Aldus/FreeHand, Adobe/Photoshop; Printers — HP/4MV. CLASSIFIED: Front-end hardware — 2-Ap/Mac LC; Front-end software — Baseview. DISPLAY: Adv layout systems — Ap/Power Mac; Front-end software — Aldus, QPS, Multi-Ad, Aldus/FreeHand, Adobe/Photoshop; Printers — HP/4MV. PRODUCTION: Plate exposures — 1-Nu/Flip Top FT40L, 1-Nu/Flip Top FT40V6UP; Plate processors — 1-Nat; Production cameras — 1-R/580; Automatic film processors — 1-LE/LD-18.
PRESSROOM: Line 1 — 6-G/U-911; Press drives — Fin; Folders — 1-G; Press control system — Fin. MAILROOM: Bundle tyer — 1-Sa, 2-MLN; Addressing machine — 1-St. COMMUNICATIONS: Systems used — satellite. WIRE SERVICES: News — AP; Receiving dishes — size-3m, AP. BUSINESS COMPUTERS: 1-IBM/34; Applications: Accts, Payroll, Circ billing, Adv billing, Adm reports, Tax, ABC records, Mailing lists; PCs & micros networked; PCs & main system networked.

ANN ARBOR
Washtenaw County
'90 U.S. Census- 109,592; E&P '96 Est. 113,131
ABC-CZ (90): 131,053 (HH 50,266)

The Ann Arbor News (e-mon to sat; S)
The Ann Arbor News, 340 E. Huron St.; PO Box 1147, Ann Arbor, MI 48106; tel (313) 994-6708; fax (313) 994-6989; web site http://www.cic.net/~glew. Advance Publications (Booth Newspapers) group.
Circulation: 57,708(e); 57,708(e-sat); 74,943(S); ABC Sept. 30, 1995.
Price: 35¢(d); 35¢(sat); $1.25(S); $2.54/wk, $11.00/mo; $132.00/yr.
Advertising: Open inch rate $28.05(e); $28.05(e-sat); $36.20(S). **Representative:** Newhouse Newspapers/Metro Suburbia.
News Services: AP, NYT, LAT-WP. **Politics:** Independent. **Established:** 1835.
Special Editions: Southern Travel, Estate Planning, Auto Show, Bridal (Jan); Fine Arts, New Homes Tab, Health/Fitness/Wellness (Feb); Update '96 (Mar); Baseball, Yard & Garden/Home Improvement, Spring Car Care (Apr); Prime Time Tab, Summer Travel (May); Showcase of Homes (June); Prep Football (Aug); M-Edition Univ. of Michigan, Fall Color Tour, Energy/Home Improvements (Sept); Car Care Tab (Oct); Chicago Holidays, Winter Travel (Nov).
Special Weekly Sections: Money Monday, Retail Report (mon); Fashion, Together Tuesday (tues); Food Day, Wheels, Wellness Wednesday (wed); Book Pages, Garden Pages, Tech Thursday, SPOTLIGHT Entertainment, Almanac (thur); Crime Map (fri); Venture Outdoors, Church Pages, Senior Citizens (sat); Book Pages, Arts, Travel, TV Week, At Home (S).
Magazines: TV Mag, Color Comics (S); Parade.

GENERAL MANAGEMENT
Publisher David D Wierman
Manager-Administrative Services David L Busack
Manager-Systems Brian Leonard
ADVERTISING
Director Joe Grech
Manager-Retail Barb Montgomery
Manager-Classified Ken Collica
Manager-National/Co-op Don Kline
MARKETING AND PROMOTION
Manager-Promotion/Community Relations Sandy Eisele
TELECOMMUNICATIONS
Manager-Telecommunications James Tolbert
Audiotex Manager Joe Grech
CIRCULATION
Manager Fred Jahnke
NEWS EXECUTIVES
Editor Ed Petykiewicz
Assoc Editor/Ombudsman David Bishop
EDITORS AND MANAGERS
Automotive Editor Mike Kersmarki
Business/Finance Editor Mike Kersmarki
Connection Editor Julie Wiernik
Editorial Page Editor Kay Semion
Editorial Writer Kay Semion
Entertainment/Amusements Editor Bruce Martin
Environmental Editor Karl Bates
Fashion/Food Editor Steve Cagle
Features Editor Julie Wiernik
Films/Theatre Editor Bruce Martin
Graphics Editor/Art Director Al Bliss
Health/Medical Editor Julie Wiernik
Higher Education Editor Steve Cain
Librarian Grace Purvas
Living/Lifestyle Editor Julie Wiernik
Metro Editor Rick Fitzgerald
National Editor Andy Chapelle
News Editor Andy Chapelle
Photo Editor Judy Nies Tell
Picture Editor Rick Fitzgerald
Political/Government Editor Andy Chapelle
Real Estate Editor Mike Kersmarki
Religion Editor Don Faber
School Editor Pat Windsor
Science Editor Julie Wiernik
Sports Editor Geoff Larcom
Travel Editor Steve Cagle
Women's Editor Julie Wiernik
MANAGEMENT INFORMATION SERVICES
Data Processing Manager Brian Leonard
Online Manager Karl Bates
PRODUCTION
Manager Jeff Frank
Supervisor-Pre Press Don Miller
Supervisor-Press Plate Vern Aungst

Market Information: Zoned editions; Split Run; TMC; Operate database; Operate audiotex.
Mechanical available: Letterpress (direct); Black and 3 ROP colors; insert accepted — preprinted; page cut-offs — $23\frac{9}{16}$".
Mechanical specifications: Type page 13" x 22"; E - 6 cols, $2\frac{1}{16}$", $\frac{1}{8}$" between; A - 6 cols, $2\frac{1}{16}$", $\frac{1}{8}$" between; C - 10 cols, $1\frac{1}{4}$", $\frac{1}{16}$" between.
Commodity consumption: Newsprint 8,068 short tons; 7,319 metric tons; width 55"; black ink 221,000 pounds; color ink 42,000 pounds; single pages printed 19,374; average pages per issue 45(d), 102(S); single plates used 41,200.

Equipment: EDITORIAL: Front-end hardware — 44-AT; Front-end software — AT; Printers — Fujitsu/DL5600. CLASSIFIED: Front-end hardware — AT; Front-end software — AT; Printers — Fujitsu/DL5600. DISPLAY: Adv layout systems — 4-AT, 4-Ap/Mac; Front-end hardware — Cx, 5-Sun/3-80, 2-Sun/3-60; Front-end software — CT, Cx 7.0; Printers — Bideo/Imagesetter; Other equipment — Teltronix/Color Printer, ECR/Autokon. PRODUCTION: Pagination software — QuarkXPress 3.3; Typesetters — 1-AU/APS/6, 2-Cx; Platemaking systems — Na; Plate exposures — 2-Va/Starlite; Plate processors — 1-NP/40, 1-C/50; Electronic picture desk — 1-Lf, 3-Ap/Mac; Scanners — 2-ECR/Autokon, 1-Microtek, 1-Polaroid; Production cameras — 2-C/Spartan III; Automatic film processors — 1-P, 1-Kk/324; Film transporters — 2-C; Shrink lenses — 1-CK Optical/SQU-7; Digital color separation equipment — 1-Lf, Adobe/Photoshop. PRESSROOM: Line 1 — 6-G/Mark II, Line 2 — 6-G/Mark II; Folders — 4-G/3:2; Pasters — G/Automatic. MAILROOM: Counter stackers — 4-HL/Monitor; Inserters and stuffers — 2-SLS/1000 (10-into-2); Bundle tyer — 4-Dynaric/NP2. COMMUNICATIONS: Digital ad delivery system — AP AdSend. Systems used — satellite. WIRE SERVICES: News — AP; Photos — AP; Stock tables — AP; Syndicates — NYT, LAT-WP; Receiving dishes — size-3 ½m,

AP. BUSINESS COMPUTERS: 1-TI/990, 1-Sun/Sparc 2, 1-Sun/Sparc 20; PCs & micros networked; PCs & main system networked.

BAD AXE
Huron County

'90 U.S. Census- 3,484; E&P '96 Est. 3,840
ABC-CZ (90): 3,484 (HH 1,356)

The Huron Daily Tribune
(e-mon to fri; S)

The Huron Daily Tribune, 211 N. Heisterman, Bad Axe, MI 48413; tel (517) 269-6461; fax (517) 269-9893; e-mail hdtmng@aol.com. Hearst Newspapers group.
Circulation: 8,145(e); 7,761(S); ABC Sept. 30, 1995.
Price: 35¢(d); $1.00(S); $8.50/mo; $102.00/yr.
Advertising: Open inch rate $10.90(e); $12.50(S). **Representative:** Papert Companies.
News Service: AP. **Politics:** Independent. **Established:** 1955.
Not Published: Memorial Day; Independence Day; Labor Day; Thanksgiving; Christmas; New Year.
Magazines: Thumb Farmer (1st tues each mo); TV in the Thumb (wed).

Michigan

I-197

GENERAL MANAGEMENT
Publisher .... H Allen Wamsley
ADVERTISING
Manager .... Helen J Kopack
TELECOMMUNICATIONS
Audiotex Manager .... Aileen Shedd
CIRCULATION
Manager-Service .... Thomas A Shedd
NEWS EXECUTIVE
Editor .... Sandra T Sutton
MANAGEMENT INFORMATION SERVICES
Online/New Media Manager .... Aileen Shedd
PRODUCTION
Manager .... Larry Schelke

Market Information: TMC; Operate database; Operate audiotex.
Mechanical available: Offset; Black and 3 ROP colors; insert accepted — preprinted, subject to approval; page cut-offs — 22¾".
Mechanical specifications: Type page 13¾" x 21½"; E - 6 cols, 2 1/16", 1/8" between; A - 6 cols, 2 1/16", 1/8" between; C - 9 cols, 1 3/8", 1/16" between.

Commodity consumption: Newsprint 851 short tons; width 27½"; black ink 24,480 pounds; color ink 2,680 pounds; single pages printed 5,004; average pages per issue 20(d); single plates used 8,900.
Equipment: EDITORIAL: Front-end hardware — Ap/Mac; Front-end software — Mk/NewsEdit 3.3, Baseview; Printers — Ap/Mac LaserWriter II, Ap/Mac LaserWriter 810, AG/800 Imagesetter; Other equipment — Ap/Mac Scanner, Lf/AP Leaf Picture Desk, Ap/Power Mac, Ap/Power Mac/7100 Photo Desk. CLASSIFIED: Front-end hardware — Ap/Mac; Front-end software — Baseview, Mk/Class Manager 3.2; Printers — Ap/Mac LaserWriter II; Other equipment — Ap/Mac Scanner. DISPLAY: Front-end hardware — Ap/Power Mac, Ap/Power Mac PC 7100; Front-end software — QuarkXPress 3.3; Printers — Ap/Mac LaserWriter II, Ap/Mac LaserWriter 810; Other equipment — NEC, CD-Rom. PRODUCTION: Pagination software — AG, QuarkXPress 3.3; OCR software — Caere/OmniPage 3.0; Typesetters — AG/800 ImageSetter, Power PC/8100; Plate processors — 1-Nu; Production cameras — C/Spartan III, C/Marathon; Automatic film processors — LE; Film transporters — LE.

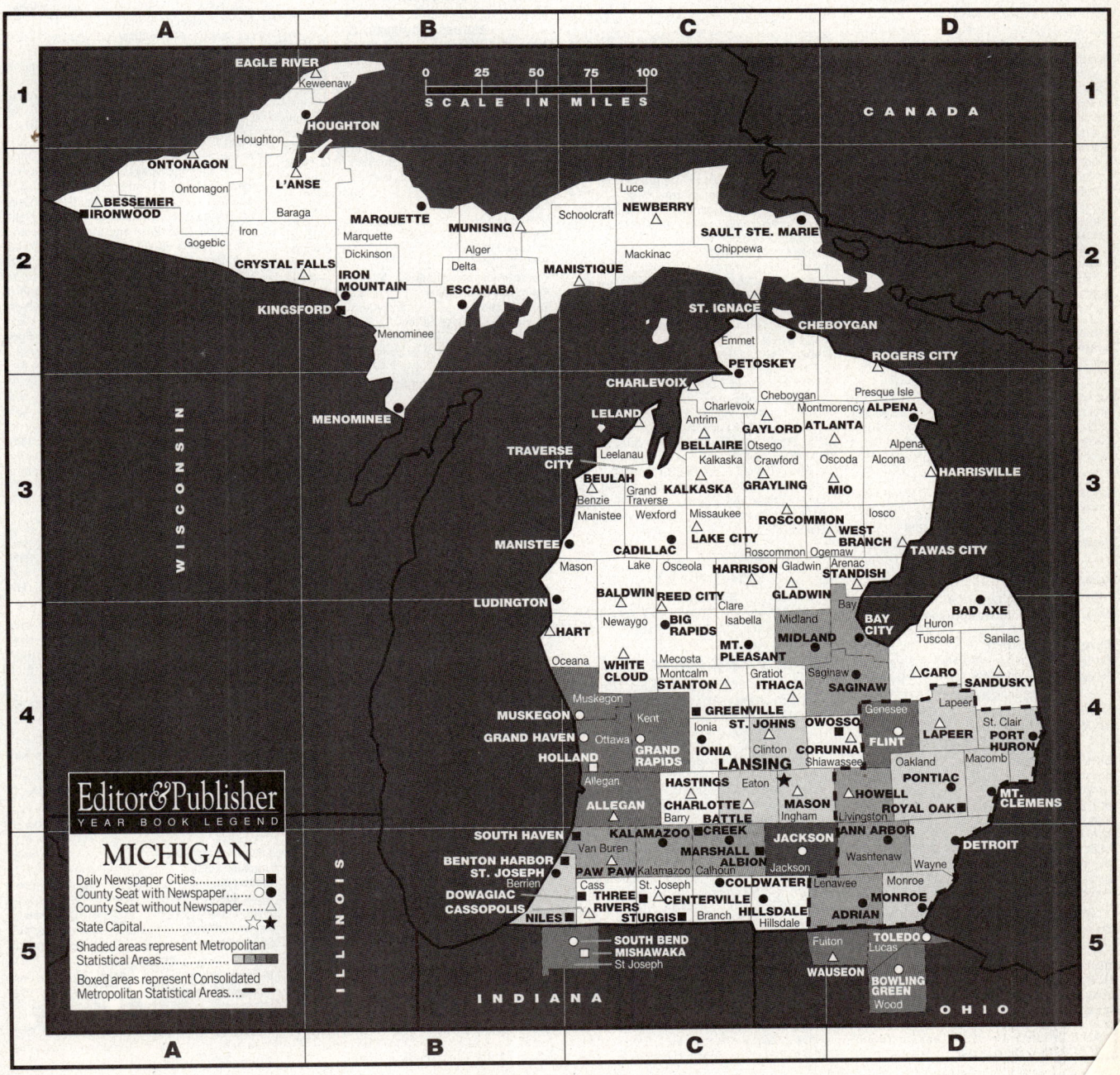

PRESSROOM: Line 1 — 9-KP/Newsking; Folders — 1-KP; Pasters — BG/Acumeter. MAILROOM: Bundle tyer — 2-Bu, 2-MLN; Addressing machine — Ch. WIRE SERVICES: News — AP; Receiving dishes — AP, HN. BUSINESS COMPUTERS: IBM/Sys 36; Applications: CDS; PCs & micros networked; PCs & main system networked.

BATTLE CREEK

Calhoun County

'90 U.S. Census- 53,540; E&P '96 Est. 51,255
ABC-NDM (90): 162,272 (HH 61,353)

Battle Creek Enquirer

(e-mon to fri; m-sat; S)

Battle Creek Enquirer, 155 W. Van Buren St., Battle Creek, MI 49017-3093; tel (616) 964-7161; fax (616) 964-0299. Gannett Co. Inc. group.

Circulation: 27,955(e); 27,955(m-sat); 36,780(S); ABC Sept. 30, 1995.

Price: 35¢(d); 35¢(sat); $1.50(S); $2.75/wk; $11.00/mo (carrier); $143.00/yr (carrier).

Advertising: Open inch rate $34.86(e); $34.86(m-sat); $38.17(S). **Representative:** Gannett National Newspaper Sales.

News Services: AP, GNS. **Politics:** Independent. **Established:** 1900.

Advertising not accepted: 900 numbers; Any ad of discriminatory nature.

Special Editions: Bridal Tab (Jan); Progress, Home Show (Mar); Think Spring, Car Care (Apr); Mother of the Year (May); Cereal Festival, Balloon Championships (June); Discover Southwest Michigan, Taste of Battle Creek (July); Back-to-School, International Festival, Football 1996 (Aug); Marshall Home Tour (Sept); Car Care, Funeral Guide, Credit Union (Oct); Festival of Lights, Christmas Gift Catalogs (Dec).

Special Weekly Sections: Neighbors (mon); Planet 'Kid' Pull-out (tues); Business Journal (wed); WOW (What's On Weekends) (thur); Health Today (fri).

Magazines: Home, Auto (S).

CORPORATE OFFICERS

President/CEO — John J Curley
Treasurer — Larry F Miller
Secretary — Thomas L Chapple

GENERAL MANAGEMENT

Publisher — Randy N Miller
Director-Human Resources — Cynthia Spencer
Controller — Thomas M Ricci
Manager-Credit — Ruth Parks
Purchasing Agent — Thomas M Ricci

ADVERTISING

Manager-Retail — Steve Funk
Manager-Classified — Ann Lyon

MARKETING AND PROMOTION

Director-Marketing Service — Heather Lipp

TELECOMMUNICATIONS

Audiotex Manager — Heather Lipp

CIRCULATION

Manager-Single Copy/Transportation — Don Guilfoyle
Manager-Home Delivery — Tim Hodges
Manager-Regional Home Delivery — Merrie Shina
Manager-Sales/Marketing — Eric Bruce

NEWS EXECUTIVES

Exec Editor — Nan Seelman
Asst Managing Editor — William Church

EDITORS AND MANAGERS

Editorial Page Editor — John Sherwood
Education Editor — Mark Mayes
Living/Lifestyle Editor — Debbie Myers
Local Editor — Steve Morse
News Editor — Merrit Jones
Photo Department Manager — Kevin Hare
Political/Government Reporter — Michele Morin
Religion Editor — Nancy Kaley
Sports Editor — Kim Kaufman
Television Editor — James Styer

MANAGEMENT INFORMATION SERVICES

Data Processing Manager — Mary Purchase

PRODUCTION

Director — Stewart Woodard
Manager-Composing — Sharon Pulsipher
Acting Manager-Pressroom — Lynn Schurig
Manager-Distribution — Susan DeGroat

Market Information: Zoned editions; Split Run; TMC; ADS; Operate audiotex.

Mechanical available: Offset; Black and 3 ROP colors; insert accepted — preprinted, zoned; page cut-offs — 22¾".

Mechanical specifications: Type page 13" x 21¼"; E - 6 cols, 2.04", ⅙" between; A - 6 cols, 2.04", ⅙" between; C - 10 cols, 1¼", .08" between.

Commodity consumption: Newsprint 2,140 short tons; 2,000 metric tons; widths 27¼", 13⅝", 34", 17"; black ink 7,500 pounds; single pages printed 11,580; average pages per issue 26(d), 64(S); single plates used 32,700.

Equipment: EDITORIAL: Front-end hardware — 3-AT/7000, 4-AT/GT-68, 17-AT/94, 9-AT/134, 1-Ap/Mac w/QuarkXPress; Front-end software — AT/7000 4.6.4, QPS; Printers — Ap/Mac LaserWriter II NTX, QMS, Tektronix/Phaser III, HP/DeskJet 1200, AU/APS-6-108C, HP/LaserJet 4MV; Other equipment — Ap/Mac IIci, Ap/Mac IIfx, Lf/Leafscan 35, Ap/Mac Quadras, Ap/Power Macs, SYQUEST, Archivist. CLASSIFIED: Front-end hardware — AT/DEC, 1-AT/7000, 7-AT/134KC, 1-AT/GT68; Front-end software — AT 4.6.4; Printers — AU/APS-Micro 5s. DISPLAY: Adv layout systems — Mk/Managing Editor ALS; Front-end hardware — 4-AT/134KL, Sun, 2-Ap/Mac Quadra 950, 1-Ap/Mac IIfx, Ap/Power Mac PC, SYQUEST; Front-end software — Multi-Ad/Creator 3.8, Aldus/FreeHand 5.0, QuarkXPress, Adobe/Photoshop, Adobe/Illustrator, Broderbund/Typestyler, Aldus/PageMaker, Streamline, Dimensions; Printers — QMS/2220, Tektronix/Phaser III Pxi. PRODUCTION: Pagination software — AT/News Layout 2, QPS; OCR software — OCR Read-H; Typesetters — AU/Micro 5s, AU/6-108C; Platemaking systems — Douthitt/Option X Dual Exposure Unit; Plate exposures — 1-Nu/Flip Top FT 40LNS-90, 1-Nu/Flip Top FT40LNS, 1-Nu/Flip Top FT126L; Plate processors — 2-Nat/A340; Electronic picture desk — Lf/AP Leaf Picture Desk; Scanners — Microtek/Scanmaker II, Microtek/Scanmaker III, Lf/Leafscan 35, Nikon/Coolscan; Production cameras — 1-C/Spartan III, 1-ECR/Autokon 1000; Automatic film processors — 1-LE/LD 18, 2-LE/PC13, 2-C/66F; Color separation equipment (conventional) — RZ/220S LED. PRESSROOM: Line 1 — 15-G/Urbanite single width; Press drives — Fin; Folders — G/U 1098 2:1; Pasters — Webeq; Reels and stands — Webeq; Press control system — Fin. MAILROOM: Counter stackers — 1-QWI/300, BG/Count-O-Veyor; Inserters and stuffers — HI/1372; Bundle tyer — 3-MLN/MLN2. COMMUNICATIONS: Digital ad delivery system — AP AdSend. WIRE SERVICES: News — AP, GNS; Photos — AP, GNS; Stock tables — AP SelectStox; Syndicates — AP, GNS, TV Data; Receiving dishes — AP. BUSINESS COMPUTERS: 1-IBM/AS-400; Applications: GNS/Inhouse: Financials, Payroll, Circ, Gen ledger; PCs & micros networked; PCs & main system networked.

BAY CITY

Bay County

'90 U.S. Census- 38,936; E&P '96 Est. 36,799
ABC-CZ (90): 73,148 (HH 28,716)

The Bay City Times

(e-mon to fri; m-sat; S)

The Bay City Times, 311 Fifth St., Bay City, MI 48708-5853; tel (517) 895-8551; fax (517) 895-5910 (Bus. Office); web site http://www.cic.net/~glew. Advance Publications (Booth Newspapers) group.

Circulation: 39,152(e); 39,152(m-sat); 50,885(S); ABC Sept. 30, 1995.

Price: 35¢(d); 35¢(sat); $1.25(S); $9.50/mo (home delivery), $10.20/mo (motor route), $14.00/mo (mail); $125.00/yr (mail in state).

Advertising: Open inch rate $26.56(e); $26.56(m-sat); $31.47(S). **Representative:** Newhouse Newspapers/Metro Suburbia.

News Services: AP, LAT-WP, NNS. **Politics:** Independent. **Established:** 1873.

Special Editions: Brides '96 Tab, Physical Fitness Tab, Agriculture (Jan); Dining & Entertainment Tab, Personal Finance (Feb); March Madness, Business & Industry, Play Ball (Mar); Child Care, Homes & Gardens, Golf '96 Tab (Apr); Mom's the Greatest, Bay Arts Council, Bay City Urban Feature, Auto Racing '96, Getaway Guide 1 Tab, Academic All Stars Tab (May); Health Care, River Roar '96, Getaway Guide 2 Tab (June); Getaway Guide 3 Tab (July); Getaway Guide 4 Tab, Football '96 Tab (Aug); Rest Assured Tab, Fall Home Improvement, Bazaars '96 Tab (Sept); Auto Preview, Credit Union Tab (Oct); Christmas Gift Catalog (Nov); Last Minute Gift Ideas, Christmas Memories Tab (Dec).

Special Weekly Sections: Food Section (mon); Health & Science, Kids Pages (tues); Outdoor Pages (wed); Arts & Entertainment (thur); Home & Garden Section (fri); Anniversaries, Community, Faith & Family, Senior Citizens (sat); Travel Pages, Wedding, Farm Pages (S).

Magazines: React (tues); TV Times Magazine, Color Comics, Parade (S).

GENERAL MANAGEMENT

Publisher — C Kevin Dykema
Controller — Jerry M Childress

ADVERTISING

Director — Archie W Duncan
Manager-Sales — Michael F Gallagher
Manager-National Representative — Sharon Peloquin

MARKETING AND PROMOTION

Manager-Promotion — Nancy L Clay
Manager-Marketing/Creative — Ed Dombrowski

CIRCULATION

Manager — David Wachowicz

NEWS EXECUTIVE

Editor — Paul M Keep

EDITORS AND MANAGERS

Automotive Editor — Stephen J Sirianni
Business Editor — Stephen J Sirianni
Editorial Page Editor — Irene Portnoy
Education Editor — John P Hiner
Entertainment/Amusements Editor — Elizabeth M Gunther
Environmental Editor — Jenni Laidman
Farm/Agriculture Editor — K Doug Albrecht
Fashion/Style Editor — Elizabeth M Gunther
Features Editor — Elizabeth M Gunther
Health/Medical Editor — Jenni Laidman
Librarian — Ann Sauve
Lifestyle Editor — Elizabeth M Gunther
Metro Editor — John P Hiner
National Editor — David Vizard
News Editor — David Vizard
Political/Government Editor — Michael K Nowlin
Radio/Television Editor — David Phillips
Religion Editor — Elizabeth M Gunther
Science/Technology Editor — Jenni Laidman
Sports Editor — James Deland
Sunday Editor — J Gregory Helmling
Travel Editor — J Gregory Helmling

MANAGEMENT INFORMATION SERVICES

Data Processing Manager — Gerald P Dueweke

PRODUCTION

Manager-Systems — Gerald P Dueweke
Supervisor-Pre Press — Craig Parks
Foreman-Pressroom — Robert B King
Foreman-Mailroom — Todd A Bowker

Market Information: Zoned editions; Split Run; TMC.

Mechanical available: Letterpress (direct); Black and 3 ROP colors; insert accepted — preprinted; page cut-offs — 22¾".

Mechanical specifications: Type page 13" x 21¼"; E - 6 cols, 2¹⁄₁₆", ⅛" between; A - 6 cols, 2¹⁄₁₆", ⅛" between; C - 10 cols, 1⁵⁄₁₆", ¹⁄₁₆" between.

Commodity consumption: Newsprint 3,002 metric tons; widths 55", 41", 27"; black ink 78,091 pounds; color ink 21,766 pounds; single pages printed 13,524; average pages per issue 30(d), 74(S); single plates used 30,000.

Equipment: EDITORIAL: Front-end hardware — AT/9000; Front-end software — AT 4.4.10; Printers — Fujitsu/DL5600, Ap/Mac LaserWriter NTX, HP/LaserJet II; Other equipment — Ap/Mac, Lf/AP Leaf Picture Desk. CLASSIFIED: Front-end hardware — AT/9000; Front-end software — AT 4.4.10; Printers — Fujitsu/DL5600. DISPLAY: Adv layout systems — 3-Ap/Mac; Front-end hardware — Ap/Mac, Dell/486 PC, Ap/Mac 8100-90 RIP; Front-end software — QuarkXPress 3.3, Multi-Ad/Creator 3.7, Adobe/Photoshop 3.0; Printers — Ultre/Setter 94. PRODUCTION: Typesetters — 2-AU/APS-Micro 5, Ultre, 1-Canon/300 (w/Fiery color server), 1-ECR/3850, 1-V/VT600; Plate exposures — 2-Na/Starlite; Plate processors — 1-Na/NP40, 1-Na/C70; Scanners — ECR/Autokon 1000; Production cameras — 1-C/Spartan II; Automatic film processors — 1-P; Film transporters — 1-P; Shrink lenses — C/Hand; Digital color separation equipment — Nikon/25-35 10AF 35mm. PRESSROOM: Line 1 — 6-G/Headliner-Mark I; Folders — 1-G/2:1 double feed; Pasters — 6-G/Semi-Auto; Press control system — GE. MAILROOM: Counter stackers — 2-HL/Monitor; Inserters and stuffers — S/48P, S/72P; Bundle tyer — 2-MLN. WIRE SERVICES: News — AP, LAT-WP, NNS; Photos — AP; Stock tables — AP; Receiving dishes — size-10ft, AP. BUSINESS COMPUTERS: 2-TI/990-12; Applications: DNOS/Customized; PCs & micros networked; PCs & main system networked.

BENTON HARBOR-ST. JOSEPH

Berrien County

'90 U.S. Census- 22,032 (Benton Harbor 12,818; St. Joseph 9,214); E&P '96 Est. 20,280 (Benton Harbor 11,402; St. Joseph 8,878)
ABC-NDM (90): 203,926 (HH 75,677)

The Herald-Palladium

(e-mon to sat; S)

The Herald-Palladium, 3450 Hollywood Rd.; PO Box 128, St. Joseph, MI 49085; tel (616) 429-2400; fax (616) 429-7661. Thomson Newspapers group.

Circulation: 33,295(e); 33,295(e-sat); 33,932(S); ABC Sept. 30, 1995.

Price: 50¢(d); 50¢(sat); $1.25(S); $14.00/mo (mail); $168.00/yr (mail).

Advertising: Open inch rate $26.64(e); $26.64(e-sat); $26.64(S). **Representative:** Landon Associates Inc.

News Service: AP. **Politics:** Independent. **Established:** 1858.

Advertising not accepted: Mediums; Vending machines.

Special Editions: Healthfile, Auto Services Guide (Jan); Spring Brides, Valentine's Gift Guide, Progress Edition (Feb); Design-An-Ad, Spring Car Care, Today's Woman, Home & Garden Pages (Mar); 1996 Tour Guide, Home & Garden Pages, Blossom Time Preview (Apr); 1996 Graduation Tab (May); Service Manager Special, Summer Brides, Golden Years (June); Healthfile, Venetian Festival Guide, Krasl Art Fair Tab (July); Coloma Glad-Punch Festival, Berrien County Youth Fair, Back-to-School, Western Am Tab (Aug); Answer Book, Football Preview, Fall Home Improvement (Sept); Healthfile, Trade-In Sale, Recycling Tab, Home Improvement Pages, Winter Bride, Credit Union Day (Oct); Wishbook/Gift Guide, Thanksgiving Food Section, Reader's Choice Awards, Holiday Recipe/Craft Guide (Nov); Basketball Preview, Holiday Memories/Gift Guide, Christmas Food Section, Letters to Santa, New Year's Pages, Year in Review (Dec); Living in the Southwest (monthly).

Special Weekly Section: Weekend Entertainment (thur).

Magazines: USA Weekend; TV Week; Sunday in Southwest Michigan.

GENERAL MANAGEMENT

Publisher — Charles L Casner
Business Manager — Joseph E Mitchell
Controller — Joseph E Mitchell
Manager-Operations — Larry Hall
Manager-Accounting — Susan Serafin

ADVERTISING

Director — R Douglas Farrell
Manager-Retail — Glen Head
Manager-Classified — Rick M Purcell
Manager-Advertising Service — Rayleen Hart

TELECOMMUNICATIONS

Audiotex Manager — Paul Hicks

CIRCULATION

Director — Tom O'Neil
Manager-Home Delivery — Cary Kirk

NEWS EXECUTIVE

Managing Editor — Steve Pepple

EDITORS AND MANAGERS

Business Editor — Rebecca Burkett
City Editor — Ron Leuty
Editorial Page Editor — Dave Brown
Graphics Editor — Kris Kincaide
Metro Editor — Lisa Snedeker
News Editor — Steve Jewell
Photo Editor — John Madill
Region Editor — Dennis Cogswell
Sports Editor — John Vandenheede

PRODUCTION

Manager-Press — Gary Vanlandingham
Manager-Distribution — Jim Van Huffel

Market Information: TMC; Operate audiotex.

Mechanical available: Offset; Black and 3 ROP colors; insert accepted — preprinted; page cut-offs — 22¾".

Mechanical specifications: Type page 13" x 21½"; E - 6 cols, 2¹⁄₁₆", ⅛" between; A - 6 cols, 2¹⁄₁₆", ⅛" between; C - 6 cols, 2¹⁄₁₆", ⅛" between.
Commodity consumption: Newsprint 2,631 short tons; widths 27½", 41¼", 55"; black ink 53,986 pounds; color ink 10,796 pounds; single pages printed 13,831; average pages per issue 29(d), 64(S); single plates used 21,970.
Equipment: EDITORIAL: Front-end hardware — C/2330, 7-Cx/Magician, 28-Cx/Magician Plus; Other equipment — 1-Ap/Mac IIci, 4-TM, 9-RSK, 5-Falcon, Ap/Mac Quadra 800. CLASSIFIED: Front-end hardware — C/2330, 6-Cx/Magician Plus. AUDIOTEX: Hardware — 2-Mk/NewsTouch. DISPLAY: Front-end hardware — 1-Ap/Mac IIfx, 1-Ap/Mac 700, 1-Ap/Mac 950, 1-Ap/Mac IIci; Front-end software — Multi-Ad/Creator. PRODUCTION: Typesetters — 2-V/5510, 1-V/6990, 1-V/5300; Plate exposures — 1-Nu/Flip Top FT40; Plate processors — 1-Nat/Super A250; Electronic picture desk — Lf/AP Leaf Picture Desk; Production cameras — 1-C/Spartan II, 1-SCREEN/690-C; Automatic film processors — 1-SCREEN/LD220QT, 1-SCREEN/LD281Q; Digital color separation equipment — 2-Lf/AP Leaf Picture Desk, 1-Cx/Newsline, 1-V/600, 1-V/1200. PRESSROOM: Line 1 — 4-G/Cosmo, 2-Graphic Arts Machinery/Vision; Pasters — 4-G/Automatic; Press registration system — Hurletron. MAILROOM: Counter stackers — 1-Id/NS440, 2-Id/Marathoner; Inserters and stuffers — 2-Mc/660; Bundle tyer — 2-Dynaric/NP2. COMMUNICATIONS: Digital ad delivery system — AP AdSend. WIRE SERVICES: News — AP Datastream, SHNS, THO; Photos — AP; Stock tables — AP SelectStox; Receiving dishes — size-10ft, AP. BUSINESS COMPUTERS: 2-HP/9000; Applications: Circ, Adv billing, Accts receivable, Accts payable, Gen ledger, Payroll, TMC; PCs & micros networked; PCs & main system networked.

BIG RAPIDS
Mecosta County
'90 U.S. Census- 12,603; E&P '96 Est. 11,276

Big Rapids Pioneer
(m-mon to sat)

Big Rapids Pioneer, 502 N. State St., Big Rapids, MI 49307; tel (616) 796-4831; fax (616) 796-1152. Pioneer group.
Circulation: 5,185(m); 5,185(m-sat); Sworn Oct. 2, 1994.
Price: 50¢(d); 50¢(sat); $8.00/mo; $80.00/yr; $42.00/6mo.
Advertising: Open inch rate $8.50(m); $8.50(m-sat).
News Service: AP. **Politics:** Independent. **Established:** 1862.
Not Published: New Year; Memorial Day; Independence Day; Thanksgiving; Christmas.
Special Editions: Bridal Issue (Jan); Soil Conservation (Mar); Home Show, Recreation, Michigan Holiday News (Apr); Car Care Tab (Spring); Home & Garden, Graduation (May); Progress (June); Sidewalk Sales, After the Fair (July); Ferris State College Orientation Welcome (Aug); Ferris Dorm, People's Choice Tab (Sept); Car Care Tab (Fall); Michigan Holiday News (Oct); Holiday Edition (Nov); Christmas Recipe Book, Christmas Gift Guide & Songbook (Dec).

CORPORATE OFFICER
President/CEO — John A Batdorff

GENERAL MANAGEMENT
Chief Financial Officer — Ruth Meikle
General Manager — John Batdorff II

ADVERTISING
Manager — Denise Clasen

CIRCULATION
Manager — Anthony S Walker

NEWS EXECUTIVES
Exec Editor — Robert Diehl
Managing Editor — Judy Hale

EDITORS AND MANAGERS
Community Editor — Cynthia Glazier
Night Editor — Dan Stockman
Exec Sports Editor — Tim Syrek
Sports Editor — John Raffel

MANAGEMENT INFORMATION SERVICES
Data Processing Manager — Ruth Meikle

PRODUCTION
Manager — Lora West

Market Information: TMC; ADS.
Mechanical available: Offset; Black and 3 ROP colors; insert accepted — preprinted, all others; page cut-offs — 22¾".
Mechanical specifications: Type page 13" x 21½"; E - 6 cols, 2", ⅙" between; A - 9 cols, 1⅜", ⁷⁄₁₆" between; C - 9 cols, 1⅜", ⁷⁄₁₆" between.
Commodity consumption: Newsprint 480 short tons; widths 34", 17", 28", 14"; black ink 16,000 pounds; color ink 1,000 pounds; single pages printed 16,848; average pages per issue 12(d); single plates used 10,400.
Equipment: EDITORIAL: Front-end hardware — Ap/Mac, POWERUSER/fileserver; Printers — Ap/Mac LaserWriter Plus; Other equipment — 9-Ap/Mac, 1-Ap/Mac II. CLASSIFIED: Front-end hardware — Ap/Mac, POWERUSER/fileserver; Other equipment — 2-Ap/Mac. DISPLAY: Adv layout systems — 4-Ap/Mac IIsi, 1-Ap/Mac IIfx; Printers — Xante/Accel-a-Writer 8100. PRODUCTION: Pagination software — QuarkXPress 3.2; Typesetters — 2-Ap/Mac LaserWriter II, Xante/Accel-a-Writer 8100; Platemaking systems — 2-Ic/24"; Plate exposures — 1-Olea/LTI, 1-Nu/FT40LNS; Plate processors — 1-Graham/GH-28; Scanners — 1-AG/Studio Scan II, 1-Polaroid/Sprint Scan; Production cameras — 1-AG/RPS 2024S, 1-LE/480; Automatic film processors — 1-P/26-EL. PRESSROOM: Line 1 — 4-HI/V-15A; Folders — 1-HI/JF7; Reels and stands — 5-HI. MAILROOM: Bundle tyer — 2-Malow, 1-Bu, 1-Mosco; Addressing machine — Wm. LIBRARY: Combination — Minolta/Microfilm. WIRE SERVICES: News — AP; Receiving dishes — size-2ft, AP. BUSINESS COMPUTERS: IBM/36 5363; Applications: Circ, Adv billing, Accts receivable, Gen ledger, Payroll, Accts payable, Fixed assets, Direct mail; PCs & micros networked; PCs & main system networked.

CADILLAC
Wexford County
'90 U.S. Census- 10,104; E&P '96 Est. 10,023

Cadillac News (m-mon to sat)

Cadillac News, 130 N. Mitchell; PO Box 640, Cadillac, MI 49601-0640; tel (616) 775-6565.
Circulation: 9,739(m); 9,739(m-sat); Sworn Oct. 1, 1994.
Price: 50¢(d); 50¢(sat); $7.69/4wk, $48.48/26wk; $95.46/yr.
Advertising: Open inch rate $15.50(m); $15.50(m-sat). **Representative:** Papert Companies.
News Service: AP. **Politics:** Independent. **Established:** 1872.
Not Published: New Year; Martin Luther King's Birthday; President's Day; Memorial Day; Independence Day; Labor Day; Columbus Day; Veteran's Day; Thanksgiving; Christmas.
Advertising not accepted: Beer; Wine; Liquor.
Special Editions: Brides & Weddings, Generations (50+), North American Snowmobile Festival Guide (Jan); Tax & Investment Guide, Home Show Edition (Feb); Progress Edition (Mar); Spring Car Care, Spring Home Improvement, Generations (50+) (Apr); Brides & Weddings, Summer Recreation I, Graduation Pages (R.O.P.) (May); Summer Recreation II (June); Brides & Weddings, Back-to-School (Aug); Fall Sports Guide, Fall Home Improvement (Sept); Fall Car Care, Generations (50+) (Oct); Holiday Cookbook, Hunting Guide, Thanksgiving Gift Guide (Nov); Holiday Songbook, Christmas Gift Guide, Last Minute Gift Guide (Dec).
Special Weekly Sections: Best Food Day (mon); Seniors (tues); Wedding, 90's Family (wed); Entertainment (thur); Church (fri); Business/Money, Outdoors (sat); Color comics (wknd editions); New Expanded TV Listings (daily).

CORPORATE OFFICERS
President — Thomas C Huckle
Vice Pres/Secretary — R Kaye Huckle
Treasurer — Ronald C Belleville

GENERAL MANAGEMENT
Publisher/General Manager — Thomas C Huckle
Manager-Business/Personnel — Ronald C Belleville
Manager-Credit/Purchasing Agent — Ronald C Belleville

ADVERTISING
Manager-Marketing — James Stevenson

NEWS EXECUTIVES
Editor — Thomas C Huckle
Managing Editor — Mark Lagermey

EDITOR AND MANAGER
Editorial Page Editor — Thomas C Huckle

MANAGEMENT INFORMATION SERVICES
Data Processing Manager — Ronald C Belleville

PRODUCTION
Manager — Thomas C Huckle

Market Information: Zoned editions; TMC.
Mechanical available: Offset; Black and 3 ROP colors; insert accepted — preprinted; page cut-offs — 22¾".
Mechanical specifications: Type page 13" x 22"; E - 6 cols, 2¹⁄₁₆", ⅛" between; A - 6 cols, 2¹⁄₁₆", ⅛" between; C - 6 cols, 2¹⁄₁₆", ⅛" between.
Commodity consumption: Newsprint 409 short tons; widths 28", 14"; black ink 10,933 pounds; color ink 1,091 pounds; single pages printed 5,824; average pages per issue 19.22(d); single plates used 5,824.
Equipment: EDITORIAL: Front-end hardware — Ap/Mac IIci, Ap/Mac SE, Ap/Mac Plus; Front-end software — QuarkXPress, Baseview/NewsEdit; Printers — Ap/Mac LaserWriter Plus. CLASSIFIED: Front-end hardware — Ap/Mac IIsi; Front-end software — Baseview/Classified; Printers — Ap/Mac LaserWriter Plus. DISPLAY: Front-end hardware — Ap/Mac IIfx; Front-end software — Multi-Ad/Creator; Printers — Ap/Mac LaserWriter Plus; Other equipment — Ap/Mac Scanner, NEC/CD-Rom. PRODUCTION: Direct-to-plate imaging — 3M/Deadliner; Production cameras — LE/Vertical MD470. PRESSROOM: Line 1 — 6-HI/V15A. MAILROOM: Bundle tyer — Bu; Addressing machine — Ch. WIRE SERVICES: News — AP; Photos — AP; Receiving dishes — size-3m, AP. BUSINESS COMPUTERS: ATT; Applications: Unix, SMS: Adv, Circ, Gen ledger; PCs & micros networked; PCs & main system networked.

CHEBOYGAN
Cheboygan County
'90 U.S. Census- 4,999; E&P '96 Est. 4,909

Cheboygan Daily Tribune
(m-mon to fri)

Cheboygan Daily Tribune, 308-310 N. Main St.; PO Box 290, Cheboygan, MI 49721; tel (616) 627-7144; fax (616) 627-5331. Hollinger International Inc. group.
Circulation: 4,318(m); Sworn Sept. 30, 1994.
Price: 50¢(d); $78.00/yr; $25.00/3mo, $42.00/6mo.
Advertising: Open inch rate $6.40(m). **Representative:** Landon Associates Inc.
News Service: AP. **Established:** 1875.
Not Published: All legal holidays.
Special Editions: Progress (Feb); Football (Aug).
Special Weekly Sections: Schools (mon); Business (tues); Weddings (wed); Food (thur); Real Estate, Religion, Weekend Edition (fri); Community (daily); Best of Summer (weekly).

GENERAL MANAGEMENT
Publisher — Roy S Trahan II
Business Manager — Ann Wilkinson

ADVERTISING
Manager — Roy S Trahan II

NEWS EXECUTIVE
Editor — Carrie Stiles

Market Information: TMC.
Mechanical available: Offset; Black and 2 ROP colors; insert accepted — preprinted; page cut-offs — 21½".
Mechanical specifications: Type page 13" x 21"; E - 6 cols, 2¹⁄₁₆", ⅛" between; A - 6 cols, 2¹⁄₁₆", ⅛" between; C - 6 cols, 2¹⁄₁₆", ⅛" between.
Commodity consumption: Newsprint 250 short tons; widths 27½", 34"; single pages printed 3,640; average pages per issue 12(d).
Equipment: EDITORIAL: Front-end hardware — Ap/Mac. CLASSIFIED: Front-end hardware — Ap/Mac; Printers — Ap/Mac LaserWriter II NT. DISPLAY: Adv layout systems — Ap/Mac. PRODUCTION: Typesetters — 2-COM; Plate processors — 1-Nu; Production cameras — 2-K. PRESSROOM: Line 1 — 5-G/Community; Folders — 1-G. MAILROOM: Bundle tyer — Bu; Addressing machine — Am. WIRE SERVICES: News — Syndicates — AP. BUSINESS COMPUTERS: PC; Applications: All business functions except payroll; PCs & micros networked.

COLDWATER
Branch County
'90 U.S. Census- 9,607; E&P '96 Est. 9,920

The Daily Reporter
(e-mon to fri; m-sat)

The Daily Reporter, 15 W. Pearl St., Coldwater, MI 49036; tel (517) 278-2318; fax (517) 278-6041. Park Communications Inc. group.
Circulation: 6,358(e); 6,358(m-sat); Sworn Sept. 27, 1994.
Price: 50¢(d); 50¢(sat); $7.00/mo; $77.00/yr, $144.00/yr (mail); $8.00/4wk.
Advertising: Open inch rate $10.08(e); $10.08(m-sat).
News Service: AP. **Politics:** Independent. **Established:** 1895.
Not Published: Christmas.
Special Editions: Graduation; Spring & Fall Fashions; Vacation; Christmas; Football Preview; Car Care; Bridal Section; Progress Report; Homemaker's.
Magazine: Reporter Extra.

CORPORATE OFFICER
Secretary — William M Thomas

GENERAL MANAGEMENT
General Manager — Pamela Ashley
Controller — Michelle Buys
Purchasing Agent — Pamela Ashley

ADVERTISING
Director — Mary Jo Hughes

CIRCULATION
Director — Marilyn Leslie

NEWS EXECUTIVE
Editor — Michelle Reen

EDITOR AND MANAGER
Editorial Page Editor — Michelle Reen

PRODUCTION
Manager — Craig Sowers
Foreman-Pressroom — David Anthony

Market Information: TMC.
Mechanical available: Offset; Black and 3 ROP colors; insert accepted — preprinted, 8" x 11½" & over; page cut-offs — 21½".
Mechanical specifications: Type page 13" x 21½"; E - 6 cols, 2¹⁄₁₆", ⅛" between; A - 6 cols, 2¹⁄₁₆", ⅛" between; C - 10 cols, 1⅛", ¹⁄₁₆" between.
Commodity consumption: Newsprint 218 short tons; width 27½"; single pages printed 4,104; average pages per issue 12(d).
Equipment: EDITORIAL: Front-end hardware — Mk; Front-end software — Mk; Printers — Ap/Mac LaserWriter. CLASSIFIED: Front-end hardware — Mk. DISPLAY: Front-end hardware — Ap/Mac IIci, Ap/Power Mac; Front-end software — Mk/AdWriter, Multi-Ad/Creator; Printers — Ap/Mac Laser. PRODUCTION: Scanners — 1-COM; Production cameras — 1-R/24x24, 1-B/24x24; Automatic film processors — 1-C. PRESSROOM: Line 1 — 1-HI/Cotrell V15A; Folders — 1-HI/2:1. MAILROOM: Bundle tyer — 1-Bu; Addressing machine — 1-Am. COMMUNICATIONS: Facsimile — Canon. WIRE SERVICES: News — AP; Syndicates — NEA; Receiving dishes — size-2ft, AP. BUSINESS COMPUTERS: Vision Data.

DETROIT
Wayne County
'90 U.S. Census- 1,027,974; E&P '96 Est. 906,545
ABC-CZ (90): 1,252,310 (HH 462,271)

Detroit Newspapers

Detroit Newspapers, 615 W. Lafayette Blvd., Detroit, MI 48226; tel (313) 222-6400; fax (313) 222-2230.
Note: The Detroit News, owned by the Gannett Co. Inc., and the Detroit Free Press, owned by the Knight-Ridder Inc., are independent and competitive newspapers, published by separate corporations. On Saturdays, Sundays and major holidays, combined editions of the News and Free Press are produced jointly by the two newspapers, and include sections independently edited by the News and Free Press. The Detroit Newspapers, a joint venture of Gannett and Knight-Ridder, serves as agent for The Detroit News and The Detroit Free Press, and operates the advertising, circulation, accounting and mechanical departments.

CORPORATE OFFICERS

President/CEO Frank J Vega
Senior Vice Pres/Chief Financial Officer Gary L Anderson
Senior Vice Pres-Labor Relations Timothy J Kelleher
Senior Vice Pres-Circulation Robert Althaus
Senior Vice Pres-Marketing Richard J McClennen
Vice Pres-Operations Keith Pierce
Vice Pres-Planning and Development/Human Resources Randi Miller
Vice Pres-Market Development N Suzanne Ellwood
Vice Pres-Info Systems Gasper Genovese

GENERAL MANAGEMENT

Director-Special Projects Alan S Lenhoff
Director-Finance Robert Kuhn
Controller John A Totoraitis
Manager-Accounts Receivable William Monahan
Manager-Credit Virginia Jennings
Director-Purchasing Nicholas P Fonseca
Director-Labor Relations/Senior Legal John A Taylor
Human Resources Dir.-Compensation/Benefits Randall Allison
Manager-HRIS/Compensation Robert Casper
Manager-Benefits Sylvia Garza
Manager-Employee Relations Linda Gray Conroy

ADVERTISING

Vice Pres Robert C Carlson
Director-National George J Kiefer
Senior Sales Director-Major Accounts Retail/National Kristina C Petzer
Director-Sales/Development Jeanine Duvall
Manager-Administration Budgets Edward Murphy
Manager-Major Accounts Joseph P Holt
Manager-Classified/Retail/Telemarketing/Real Estate Chela Dalco-Nixon

MARKETING AND PROMOTION

Director-Community Affairs Laydell Harper
Director-Creative Service Cynthia Andersen
Director-Research Kris McKean
Manager-Promotion Teresa M Lucido
Manager-Events Jill Riddle

TELECOMMUNICATIONS

Manager-Telecommunications Ricardo Vasquez

CIRCULATION

Director-Administration/Operations Jerry Hill
Director-Sales Michael F Quinn
Director-Marketing Paul Thiel
Director-Home Delivery Tommie McLeod
Director-Field Services Richard E Hartnett
Manager-Operations Mark Priesler
Manager-State Mike Crandell
Manager-Customer Service Sandra Donald
Manager-Sales Development James S Martin
Manager-Transportation Pete Savoie

MANAGEMENT INFORMATION SERVICES

Manager-Systems/Programming Janet Niehaus
Manager-Publishing Systems Robert Ross

PRODUCTION

Director D Ashley King
Director-Facilities Thomas McDowell
Manager-Pre Press Systems Larry Ross
Manager-Plant/NP Paul Reiz
Manager-Plant/RF William McLachlan
Manager-Packaging/Distribution Dick Fischer
Manager-Operations Customer Service Bob Emmer
Manager-Special Projects Buck Fife
Manager-Pre Press Pat Izzo
Manager-Planning Karen Zemnickas

Market Information: Zoned editions; Split Run; Operate audiotex.
Mechanical available: Offset; Black and 3 ROP colors; insert accepted — preprinted, Add-A-Cards.
Mechanical specifications: Type page 13" x 21¾"; E - 6 cols, 2¹⁄₁₆", ⅛" between; A - 6 cols, 2¹⁄₁₆", ⅛" between; C - 10 cols, 1⅜", ⅛" between.
Commodity consumption: Newsprint 148,000 metric tons; widths 54¾", 27⅜", 13¹⁵⁄₁₆"; black ink 3,134,000 pounds; color ink 637,000 pounds; single pages printed 39,694; average pages per issue 115(d), 141(S); single plates used 619,500.
Equipment: EDITORIAL: Front-end hardware — AT/Free Press, Raycomp, 146-AT, SII/TNS-2, 20-Ap/Mac II; Front-end software — Tandem/Non-Stop7, SII/Coyote IV, Ap/Mac; Other equipment — 1-Dest, 4-Dakota/XWS, 1-Kennedy/9300 Tape Drive, 6-CDC/Disk Drives 300 mb. CLASSIFIED: Front-end hardware — SII/INS2, 6-Tandem/Non-Stop II; Front-end software — Kennedy/9300, Winchester/Disk Drive 540 mb. DISPLAY: Adv layout systems — 1-Ap/Mac II; Front-end hardware — 2-Mk, 2-ECR/Autokon 1000DE; Front-end software — DTI/AdSpeed; Other equipment — 1-Imagitex/Scanner. PRODUCTION: Typesetters — 2-AU/5 U, 1-AU/s5G, 1-AU/100g, 2-Ultra/94, 2-Adset/1000; Plate exposures — 1-Nu, Ic, 3-WL/Lith-X-Pozer III; Plate processors — 5-LE/LD24 AQ, 4-LE/LD Excell 26, 3-LE/Logeline; Film transporters — 1-C; Color separation equipment (conventional) — 1-C/E-Z Color. PRESSROOM: Line 1 — 42-G/Metro; Line 2 — 10-H/O; Line 3 — 54-TKS/Con offset; Folders — 7-G/3:2, 1-H/3:2, 9-TKS/3:2. MAILROOM: Counter stackers — 4-Id, 6-QWI; Inserters and stuffers — 1-H/1372p, 3-SII/8-48p; Bundle tyer — 9-Ms, 9-MLN, 2-PSN, 5-Power Strap; Addressing machine — 1-Am. LIBRARY: Combination — 1-Kk/QLS-Miracode II. BUSINESS COMPUTERS: IBM/3083JX, IBM/AS400B70; Applications: Circ, Distribution, Accts receivable, Payroll, Financial; PCs & micros networked; PCs & main system networked.

Detroit Free Press (m-mon to fri)
The Detroit News and Free Press (m-sat; S)

Detroit Free Press, 321 W. Lafayette Blvd., Detroit, MI 48226; tel (313) 222-6400; e-mail city@det-freepress.com, business@det-freepress.com; web site gopher://gopher.det-freepress.com:9002/. Knight-Ridder Inc. group.
Circulation: 531,825(m); 823,310(m-sat); 1,107,645(S); ABC Mar. 31, 1995.
Price: 35¢(d); 35¢(sat); $1.25(S).
Advertising: Open inch rate $435.00(m); $435.00(m-sat); $435.00(S); comb with Detroit News (e) $496.00. **Representative:** Newspapers First.
News Services: AP, NYT, KRT, RN, DJ. **Politics:** Independent. **Established:** 1831.
Note: For detailed mechanical specifications, advertising, circulation, production and other business office personnel, see Detroit Newspapers.
Special Editions: Auto Show; Mid-Winter Travel; Economic Outlook; Spring Cruise Vacations; International Travel; Spring Home Improvement; Detroit Boat Show; Ontario Travel; Chicago Travel; Michigan Travel; Tiger Baseball; Toronto Travel; Fall Color Tour; Fall Cruise Vacations; Mexico Travel; Ski/Snow Travel; Caribbean Travel; Builder's Show; Spring Travel; Lawn & Garden; Pistons Basketball; Detroit Grand Prix; Freedom Festival; Lions Football; Entertainment Season; Fall Home Improvement; Michigan State Fair; Fall New Car Buyers' Guide; Red Wings Hockey; Free Press Marathon; Michigan Voters' Guide; Holiday Books & Music; College Basketball; Weddings.
Magazines: Detroit Free Press Magazine (roto, local), TV Book, USA Weekend (S).

GENERAL MANAGEMENT

Vice Pres/Business Manager J Gerard Teagan
Publisher-Emeritus Lee Hills
Publisher Neal Shine
Asst to Publisher Greg Huskisson
Manager-Public Service/Reader Representative Anne Musial

TELECOMMUNICATIONS

Audiotex Manager John Smyntek

NEWS EXECUTIVES

Exec Editor Heath J Meriwether
Editor Joe H Stroud
Assoc Editor David Kushma
Assoc Editor-Children First Jane Daugherty
Managing Editor Robert McGruder
Asst Managing Editor-Administration Ken Clover
Deputy Managing Editor-News Kathy Warbelow
Deputy Managing Editor-News Carole Leigh Hutton
Deputy Managing Editor-Sports & Operations Dave Robinson
Deputy Managing Editor-Features/Business Chip Visci

EDITORS AND MANAGERS

Art Writer Marsha Miro
Auto Writer Joanne Muller
Auto Writer Greg Gardner
Business Editor Tom Walsh
Books Editor Linnea Lannon
Deputy City Editor Angela Tuck
Deputy City Editor Mike Lupo
Columnist-Features Susan Ager
Columnist-Features Bob Talbert
Columnist-News Susan Watson
Columnist-News Jim Fitzgerald
Columnist-News Hugh McDiarmid
Design Director Wayne Kamidoi
Deputy Design Director-News Lee Yarosh
Deputy Design Director-News Steve Anderson
Editorial Page Editor Joe H Stroud
Editorial Cartoonist Bill Day
Education Writer Margaret Trimer-Hartley
Education Writer Joan Richardson
Education Writer Stephen Henderson
Entertainment Editor Leesa Bainbridge
Entertainment Editor Larry Gabriel
Environmental Writer Emilia Askari
Environmental Writer Mike Williams
Fashion Editor Robin Givhan
Features Editor Dale Parry
Films Editor Judy Gerstel
Food Editor Patty LaNoue Stearns
Foreign Editor Charles Mitchell
Director-Free Press Plus John Smyntek
Assoc Director-Free Press Plus Rick Ratliff
Graphics Director Laura Varon Brown
Health/Fitness Writer Bill Laitner
Labor Writer John Lippert
Magazine Editor Brian Dickerson
Medicine Writer Pat Anstett
Music Writer-Classical John Guinn
Music Writer-Pop Gary Graff
Nation/World Editor Nancy Laughlin
Exec News Editor Alex Cruden
Newsroom Technology Director A J Hartley
Director-Photo/Graphics Techonology Mike Smith
Project Editor Ron Dzwonkowski
Recruiting/Development Editor Joe Grimm
Religion Writer David Crumm
Restaurants Critic Molly Abraham
Science Writer Nancy Ross-Flanigan
Sports Columnist Mitch Albom
Sports Columnist Rob Parker
Sports Columnist Charlie Vincent
Television Writer Mike Duffy
Television Writer Mark Gunther
Theater Writer Larry DeVine
Travel Writer Rick Sylvain
Universal Copy Desk Chief Julie Topping

Market Information: Zoned editions; Operate audiotex; Electronic edition.
Equipment: AUDIOTEX: Hardware — VNN, Brite Voice Systems; Supplier name — City Line. WIRE SERVICES: News — AP, NYT, KRT; Stock tables — AP; Syndicates — AP Datafeatures, NAS; Receiving dishes — AP.

The Detroit News (e-mon to fri)
The Detroit News and Free Press (m-sat; S)

The Detroit News, 615 Lafayette Blvd., Detroit, MI 48226; tel (313) 222-2300; web site http://detnews.com/tdnhome/tdnhome.htm. Gannett Co. Inc. group.
Circulation: 354,403(e); 823,310(m-sat); 1,107,645(S); ABC Mar. 31, 1995.
Price: 35¢(d); 35¢(sat); $1.25(S).
Advertising: Open inch rate $435.00(e); $435.00(m-sat); $435.00(S); comb with Detroit Free Press (m) $496.00. **Representative:** Newspapers First.
News Services: AP, UPI, NEA, WNS, LAT-WP, RN, GNS. **Established:** 1873.
Note: For detailed mechanical specifications, advertising, circulation, production and other business office personnel, see Detroit Newspapers.
Special Editions: Auto Show, Economic Outlook (Jan); Michiganians of the Year (Feb); Builders Home & Garden, Spring Fashion, NBA Play-offs (Mar); Tiger Baseball, NHL Play-offs, Fashion, Lawn, Garden & Pools (Apr); Outstanding Seniors, Rosa Parks Scholars, Grand Prix, Senior TPC Golf Championships, US Senior Open (June); Buick Open, Homearama, Fall Fashion (Aug); Football, Fall Home & Garden (Sept); NHL/Red Wings (Oct); NBA/Pistons (Nov).
Magazines: Detroit Free Press Magazine (roto, local) (Free Press Pub), TV Book, USA Weekend (S).

NEWS EXECUTIVES

Editor/Publisher Robert H Giles
Asst to Publisher Lorraine E Needham
Managing Editor Christina Bradford
Deputy Managing Editor James L Gatti
Deputy Managing Editor-News Frank Lovinski
Deputy Managing Editor-Features Julia Heaberlin
Asst Managing Editor-Metro News George Bullard
Asst Managing Editor-National/Business Mark Lett
Asst Managing Editor-Sunday Luther Keith
Asst Managing Editor-Graphics & Design Dale Peskin
Asst Managing Editor-News Desk Susan Burzynski
Bureau Chief-Washington Jacqueline Thomas

EDITORS AND MANAGERS

Automotive Writer Helen Fogel
Automotive Writer Keith Naughton
Automotive Writer David Sedgwick
Books Editor Alan Fisk
Business Editor Nolan Finley
Deputy Business Editor Steve Kaskovich
Budget Manager Linda Brubaker
Cartoonist Larry Wright
Cartoonist Draper Hill
City Editor Judy Diebolt
City Editor-Night James Tittsworth
Deputy City Editor Flora Rathburn
Deputy City Editor N Scott Vance
Columnist Terry Foster
Columnist George Cantor
Columnist Betty DeRamus
Columnist Bob Wojnowski
Columnist Nickie McWhirter
Columnist Jonathon Pepper
Columnist Pete Waldmeir
Columnist George Weeks
Editorial Page Editor Thomas J Bray
Deputy Editorial Page Editor Jeff Hadden
Editorial Writer Tony Snow
Editorial Writer Jeff Hadden
Editorial Writer William Johnson
Editorial Writer Diane Katz
Editorial Writer Richard Burr
Education Editor Ronald Russell
Entertainment/Amusements Editor Pam Shermeyer
Environment Editor Paige St. John
Fashion Editor Julie Hinds
Features Editor Martin Fischhoff
Deputy Features Editor David Good
Films Editor Susan Stark
Food Editor Robin Mather
Graphics Director Felix Grabowski
Lansing Bureau Chief Charles Cain
Librarian Patricia Zacharias
Medical Editor James Tobin
Music Critic Nancy Malitz
News Editor William McMillian
Director-Photography C Thomas Hardin
Production Editor Michael McCormick
Radio Editor Susan Whitall
Readers Representative Robert Pavich
Religion Editor Heidi Mae Bratt
Science/Technology Editor Hugh McCann
Exec Sports Editor Phillip Laciura
Sports Editor Joe Falls
State Editor JoAnna Firestone
Television Editor James McFarlin
Television Editor Tim Kiska
Television Editor Michael McWilliams
Theater Editor Reed Johnson

MANAGEMENT INFORMATION SERVICES

Online Manager Patricia Zacharias
Data Processing Manager Nancy Malitz

Market Information: Operate database; Operate audiotex.
Equipment: WIRE SERVICES: News — AP, UPI, GNS, AP Datafeatures; Stock tables — AP; Receiving dishes — AP.

DOWAGIAC
Cass County

'90 U.S. Census- 6,409; **E&P '96 Est.** 6,622

Dowagiac Daily News (e-mon to fri)

Dowagiac Daily News, 205 Spaulding St.; PO Box 30, Dowagiac, MI 49047; tel (616) 782-2101; fax (616) 782-5290. Boone Newspapers Inc. group.
Circulation: 2,497(e); Sworn Sept. 30, 1995.
Price: 50¢(d); $5.50/mo (carrier), $8.00/mo (mail); $66.00/yr (carrier), $78.00/yr (mail).
Advertising: Open inch rate $9.10(e). **Representative:** American Newspaper Representatives Inc.
News Service: AP. **Politics:** Independent. **Established:** 1897.
Note: For detailed production information, see the Niles Daily Star listing.
Not Published: New Year; Memorial Day; Independence Day; Labor Day; Christmas.
Special Editions: Progress, Bridal (Feb); Home Improvement, Farm & Garden (Mar); Graduation, Waterfront, Summer Fun (May); Waterfront, Summer Fun (July); College

(Aug); Home Improvement, Waterfront, Summer Fun, Farm & Garden (Sept); Cookbook (Nov); Welcome to the Neighborhood (monthly).

Special Weekly Section: TV (fri).

Magazine: F.Y.I. (June).

GENERAL MANAGEMENT

Publisher Thomas J Rattenbury

ADVERTISING

Manager Diana Kingsley

CIRCULATION

Manager Tim Brummer

NEWS EXECUTIVE

Managing Editor John Eby

EDITOR AND MANAGER

Sports/Films Editor Scott Novak

Market Information: Zoned editions; Split Run; TMC.

Mechanical available: Offset; Black and 3 ROP colors; insert accepted — preprinted, all; page cut-offs — 22$\frac{3}{4}$".

Mechanical specifications: Type page 13$\frac{1}{8}$" x 21$\frac{1}{2}$"; E - 8 cols, 1.47", $\frac{1}{6}$" between; A - 8 cols, 1.47", $\frac{1}{6}$" between; C - 8 cols, 1.47", $\frac{1}{6}$" between.

Equipment: EDITORIAL: Front-end hardware — Ap/Mac; Front-end software — QuarkXPress, Microsoft/Write; Printers — Ap/Mac II NTX. CLASSIFIED: Front-end hardware — Ap/Mac; Front-end software — Baseview; Printers — Ap/Mac II NTX. DISPLAY: Front-end hardware — Ap/Mac, Ap/Mac II NTX; Front-end software — DTI/AdSpeed. WIRE SERVICES: News — Syndicates — United Features, NEA; Receiving dishes — size-15m, AP. BUSINESS COMPUTERS: PCs & micros networked; PCs & main system networked.

ESCANABA

Delta County

'90 U.S. Census- 13,659; **E&P '96 Est.** 13,090

ABC-CZ (90): 18,818 (HH 7,464)

The Daily Press

(e-mon to fri; m-sat)

The Daily Press, 600-2 Ludington St., Escanaba, MI 49829; tel (906) 786-2021; fax (906) 786-1491. Thomson Newspapers group.

Circulation: 11,247(e); 11,247(m-sat); ABC Sept. 30, 1995.

Price: 50¢(d); 50¢(sat).

Advertising: Open inch rate $15.61(e); $15.61(m-sat). **Representatives:** Landon Associates Inc.; Thomson Newspapers.

News Service: AP. **Politics:** Independent. **Established:** 1909.

Not Published: New Year; Memorial Day; Independence Day; Labor Day; Thanksgiving; Christmas.

Advertising not accepted: Vending machine; Speculative; Bait.

Special Editions: Bride & Groom (Jan); Spring Fashion (Apr); Fall Back-to-School (Aug); Fashion (Sept).

Magazines: Weekly Grocery Section (TMC) (mon); TV Tab (sat).

GENERAL MANAGEMENT

Publisher Robert B Gregg

Controller C Ettenhofer

ADVERTISING

Manager Jodi Olsen

TELECOMMUNICATIONS

Audiotex Manager Jodi Olsen

CIRCULATION

Manager Laurie Sovey

NEWS EXECUTIVES

Editor Rick Rudden

Managing Editor Dave Andrews

EDITORS AND MANAGERS

Auto/Aviation Editor Brian Rowell

Business/Finance Editor Dave Andrews

Editorial Page Editor Rick Rudden

Editorial Writer Peggy Bryson

Education Editor Lori Rose

Entertainment/Amusements Editor Jennifer McCan

Fashion/Style Editor Jennifer McCan

Features Editor Jennifer McCan

Graphics Editor/Art Director Craig Woerpel

Health/Medical Editor Brian Rowell

Librarian Lori Rose

Lifestyle Editor Jennifer McCan

Music Editor Lori Rose

National Editor Rick Rudden

News Editor Rick Rudden

Photo Editor Doug Brooks

Political/Government Editor Rick Rudden

Religion Editor Jennifer McCan

Science/Technology Editor Brian Rowell

School Editor Lori Rose

Sports Editor Dennis Grall

Teen-Age/Youth Editor Lori Rose

Travel Editor Craig Woerpel

Women's Editor Jennifer McCan

PRODUCTION

Foreman-Composing Len Boudreau

Foreman-Pressroom Jerry Novak

Market Information: TMC; Operate audiotex.

Mechanical available: Offset; Black and 3 ROP colors; insert accepted — preprinted, small booklets; page cut-offs — 22$\frac{3}{4}$".

Mechanical specifications: Type page 13" x 21$\frac{1}{2}$"; E - 6 cols, 2$\frac{1}{16}$", $\frac{1}{16}$" between; A - 6 cols, 2$\frac{1}{16}$", $\frac{1}{16}$" between; C - 9 cols, 1$\frac{3}{8}$", $\frac{1}{16}$" between.

Commodity consumption: Newsprint 800 short tons; width 27$\frac{1}{2}$"; average pages per issue 16(d).

Equipment: EDITORIAL: Front-end hardware — Mk; Printers — TI/KSR Omni Printer; Other equipment — 4-Panasonic. CLASSIFIED: Front-end hardware — Mk; Printers — 2-V. DISPLAY: Adv layout systems — Mk. PRODUCTION: Platemaking systems — 1-Nu/Flip Top FT46UPNS; Plate processors — 1-LE; Production cameras — 1-Nu/SST 20"x24"; Automatic film processors — 1-LE/LD24AC. PRESSROOM: Line 1 — 9-G/Community (Color head); Folders — 2-G. MAILROOM: Bundle tyer — 2-Bu/Strapper, MLN/Spirit Strapper; Addressing machine — SAC/JR. LIBRARY: Electronic — Dukane/microfilm reader Model 27A66. WIRE SERVICES: News — AP; Receiving dishes — size-2m, AP. BUSINESS COMPUTERS: ATT; PCs & micros networked.

FLINT

Genesee County

'90 U.S. Census- 140,761; **E&P '96 Est.** 126,464

ABC-CZ (90): 193,643 (HH 74,003)

The Flint Journal

(e-mon to fri; m-sat; S)

The Flint Journal, 200 E. 1st St., Flint, MI 48502; tel (810) 766-6100; fax (810) 767-9480; e-mail fj@flintj.com; web site http://www.cic.net/~glew. Advance Publications (Booth Newspapers) group.

Circulation: 97,181(e); 97,181(m-sat); 119,762(S); ABC Sept. 30, 1995.

Price: 50¢(d); 50¢(sat); $1.50(S); $2.40/wk (carrier); $10.40/mo (carrier); $124.80/yr (carrier).

Advertising: Open inch rate $46.57(e); $46.57(m-sat); $52.84(S). **Representative:** Newhouse Newspapers/Metro Suburbia.

News Services: AP, NYT, LAT-WP, NNS. **Politics:** Independent. **Established:** 1876.

Special Editions: Weddings, Minding Your Money (Jan); Valentine Pages, Insurance Tab (Feb); Spring Car Care, Builder's Home Show, Lake & Shore, The Answer Book (Mar); Buying Your First Home, Easter Dining Guide, Golf '96, Motorcycles, Home & Yard, Fishing & Tackle (Apr); Manufactured Housing, Design-An-Ad, My Mom's the Greatest, Charter Boats (May); Father's Day Gifts & Dining (2 times), Weddings (June); Buick Open, Bowling, Child Care (2 times), CRIM Review (Aug); Primetime, New Car Review, Focus on Flint, Behind the Scenes, Hunting, GM Car Show (Sept); New Trucks & Vans Review, Fall Fix-up, Hints & Haunts (3 times), Computers & Technology, Winter Car Care, Holiday Cook-Off (Oct); Snow Mobiles, Perfect Holiday Gift Guide (Nov); Holiday Gift Guide, Skiing, New Year's Eve Dining Guide (Dec).

Special Weekly Sections: Primetime-Tempo (mon); Food-Tempo (tues); Fashion-Tempo, Wheels, Word-up (wed); Venture Outdoors (thur); The Entertainer (fri); Health & Technology, People, Etc., Religion (sat); At Home, Travel, Viewpoint (S).

Magazines: React (mon); Coupon Book (wed); Coupon Books, Parade, Color Comics, TV Week (S).

GENERAL MANAGEMENT

Publisher Roger D Samuel

Asst to Publisher Renee Hampton

ADVERTISING

Manager-Classified James G Bronson

Clerk-Pre Print Marilyn Hood

Manager-Display Sales Wendy Brimley

Manager-Sales/Development/National/Co-op Lois Revenaugh

MARKETING AND PROMOTION

Director-Marketing Teresa Calkins

TELECOMMUNICATIONS

Audiotex Manager Mary Ann Chick-Whiteside

CIRCULATION

Director Samuel Harris

NEWS EXECUTIVES

Editor Thomas H Lindley Jr

Managing Editor Roger Van Noord

Asst Managing Editor John Dickson

Assoc Editor Brooke Rausch

EDITORS AND MANAGERS

Automotive Writer Richard Noble

Business Editor Carl Stoddard

Columnist Andrew Heller

Columnist Brenda Brissette-Mata

Columnist Rhonda Sanders

Editorial Page Editor Carlton Winfrey

Features Editor Cookie Wascha

Films/Theater Editor Ed Bradley

Food Editor Ron Krueger

Graphics Editor Michael Robb

Health/Medical Writer Marcia Mattson

Home Section Editor Jennifer Walkling

Librarian David W Larzelere

Metro Editor-AM Michael Riha

Metro Editor-PM John Foren

Music Editor Doug Pullen

New Media Manager Mary Ann Chick-Whiteside

People/Community Events Editor Kathy Greenfield

Photo Editor Tina Beirne

Religion Editor Betty Brenner

Sports Editor David T Poniers

Suburban Editor Jim Larkin

Television Editor Andrea Thornton

MANAGEMENT INFORMATION SERVICES

Data Processing Manager Robert W Pierce

Online Manager Mary Ann Chick-Whiteside

PRODUCTION

Director Robert W Pierce

Manager-Pressroom Max Kuehling

Manager-Platemaking/Camera Dennis Brownrigg

Manager-Mailroom William Ross

Manager-Pre Press Ad Service Sandy Rich

Market Information: Zoned editions; Split Run; TMC; ADS; Operate database; Operate audiotex.

Mechanical available: Letterpress; Black and 3 ROP colors; insert accepted — preprinted, zoned pre-prints, minis; page cut-offs — 23$\frac{9}{16}$".

Mechanical specifications: Type page 13" x 22"; E - 6 cols, 2$\frac{1}{16}$", $\frac{1}{8}$" between; A - 6 cols, 2$\frac{1}{16}$", $\frac{1}{8}$" between; C - 10 cols, 1$\frac{1}{4}$", $\frac{1}{8}$" between.

Commodity consumption: Newsprint 11,848 metric tons; widths 27", 40.5", 54"; black ink 365,670 pounds; color ink 90,449 pounds; single pages printed 20,179; average pages per issue 48(d), 44(sat), 99(S); single plates used 80,715.

Equipment: EDITORIAL: Front-end hardware — AT/J-11; Front-end software — AT. CLASSIFIED: Front-end hardware — AT/JT-11; Front-end software — AT. DISPLAY: Adv layout systems — Cx; Front-end hardware — B/S 360; Front-end software — Cx 80. PRODUCTION: Typesetters — 2-Cx/Bitsetter, 1-AU/APS6, 1-AU/APS108; Platemaking systems — Na; Plate exposures — 2-Na/Starlite; Plate processors — 1-Na/NP120, 1-Na/C-120; Electronic picture desk — Lf/AP Leaf Picture Desk; Scanners — 1-ECR/Autokon 1000, 1-ECR/Autokon 1000DE; Production cameras — 1-C/Spartan III; Automatic film processors — 3-LE/2600; Film transporters — 1-P; Shrink lenses — 1-Allen; Color separation equipment (conventional) — Lf/AP Leaf Picture Desk, Adobe/Photoshop; Digital color separation equipment — Lf/Leafscan 35.
PRESSROOM: Line 1 — 9-G/Mark I double width; Line 2 — 9-G/Mark I double width; Press drives — GE; Folders — 3-G; Pasters — 16-G; Reels and stands — 16-G; Press registration system — WebTech. MAILROOM: Counter stackers — 5-HL/Monitor, 1-HL/Monitor HT, 3-HL/Dual Carrier; Inserters and stuffers — 1-S/1148, 1-GMA/SLS1000, 1-HI/1372; Bundle tyer — 2-Si/MLN2, 4-Si/MLN2A, 5-Power Strap/PSN4, 1-Dynaric/4; Addressing machine — 2-Ch. COMMUNICATIONS: Digital ad delivery system — AdSat. Systems used — satellite. WIRE SERVICES: News — AP, NYT, LAT-WP, NNS; Stock tables — AP; Receiving dishes — size-8ft, AP. BUSINESS COMPUTERS: 3-TI/990, Sun/Sparc 2; Applications: In-house: Adv billing, Accts receivable, Gen ledger, Accts payable, Marketing, Display adv; PBS: Circ; PCs & micros networked; PCs & main system networked.

GRAND HAVEN

Ottawa County

'90 U.S. Census- 11,951; **E&P '96 Est.** 12,347

ABC-CZ (90): 17,407 (HH 7,005)

Grand Haven Tribune

(e-mon to sat)

Grand Haven Tribune, 101 N. Third St., Grand Haven, MI 49417; tel (616) 842-6400; fax (616) 842-9584. Sandusky-Norwalk Newspapers group.

Circulation: 10,680(e); 10,680(e-sat); ABC Sept. 30, 1995.

Price: 35¢(d); 35¢(sat); $95.00/yr (outside county), $110.00/yr (all other points).

Advertising: Open inch rate $10.60(e); $10.60 (e-sat). **Representative:** Landon Associates Inc.

News Service: AP. **Politics:** Independent. **Established:** 1885.

Not Published: New Year; Memorial Day; Independence Day; Labor Day; Thanksgiving; Christmas.

Advertising not accepted: Fortune tellers; Earn money at home.

Special Editions: Bridal (Jan); Cookbook (Feb); Progress (Mar); Gardening & Landscaping, Boating (Apr); Education (May); Coast Guard (Aug); Arts (Sept); New Cars (Nov); Winter Sports (Dec).

Special Weekly Sections: Best Food Day (mon); Lifestyles, Business (thur); Church (sat).

CORPORATE OFFICERS

Board Chairman Dudley A White

President David A Rau

Vice Pres E Mayer Maloney Jr

Treasurer Alice W Rau

Secretary Susan E White

GENERAL MANAGEMENT

Publisher E Mayer Maloney Jr

Purchasing Agent E Mayer Maloney Jr

ADVERTISING

Manager Paul Bedient

CIRCULATION

Manager Carol Barnhill

NEWS EXECUTIVE

Managing Editor Fred VandenBrand

EDITORS AND MANAGERS

News Editor Len Painter

School Editor Marc Fellows

Sports Editor Don Shell

Women's Editor Sheri Benedict

PRODUCTION

Superintendent Arie Boon

Market Information: TMC.

Mechanical available: Offset; Black and 3 ROP colors; insert accepted — preprinted; page cut-offs — 22$\frac{1}{2}$".

Mechanical specifications: Type page 13" x 21$\frac{1}{2}$"; E - 6 cols, 2$\frac{1}{16}$", $\frac{1}{8}$" between; A - 6 cols, 2$\frac{1}{16}$", $\frac{1}{8}$" between; C - 8 cols, 1$\frac{7}{8}$", $\frac{1}{8}$" between.

Commodity consumption: Newsprint 375 short tons; widths 27$\frac{1}{2}$", 13$\frac{3}{4}$", 11$\frac{1}{4}$"; black ink 11,000 pounds; single pages printed 5,700; average pages per issue 18(d).

Equipment: EDITORIAL: Front-end hardware — 2-CD/2330. CLASSIFIED: Front-end hardware — CD/2330s; Printers — 1-Line printer/Tally-1202-CD, Ap/Mac LaserWriter II. PRODUCTION: Typesetters — 3-Ap/Mac LaserWriter; Plate exposures — 1-Nu/FT40LHS; Plate processors — 1-Nat/Super A-250; Production cameras — 1-SCREEN/650C; Automatic film processors — 1-LE/LD24AQ.
PRESSROOM: Line 1 — 5-G/Urbanite; Folders — 1-G. MAILROOM: Bundle tyer — 1-Sa/BM1A. COMMUNICATIONS: Facsimile — Sharp/FO3100. WIRE SERVICES: News — AP, HI/Rosat dish in operation. BUSINESS COMPUTERS: 1-Unisys/5000; Applications: Adv billing, Accts receivable, Gen ledger, Payroll, Circ; PCs & micros networked; PCs & main system networked.

GRAND RAPIDS

Kent County

'90 U.S. Census- 189,126; **E&P '96 Est.** 199,399

ABC-CZ (90): 433,394 (HH 158,267)

The Grand Rapids Press

(e-mon to fri; m-sat; S)

The Grand Rapids Press, 155 Michigan St. N.W., Grand Rapids, MI 49503; tel (616) 222-5400; e-mail editor@GR-press.com; web site http://www.cic.net/~glew. Advance Publications (Booth Newspapers) group.

Circulation: 145,521(e); 145,521(m-sat); 196,553(S); ABC Sept. 30, 1995.
Price: 50¢(d); 50¢(sat); $1.50(S); $12.00/mo (carrier); $216.00/yr (mail).
Advertising: Open inch rate $51.30(e); $51.30(m-sat); $62.10(S). **Representative:** Newhouse Newspapers/Metro Suburbia.
News Services: AP, LAT-WP, NYT, SCM, NNS. **Politics:** Independent. **Established:** 1892.
Special Editions: Business Outlook & Honor Roll, Junior Achievement, Brides, Restaurant Guide, Real Estate Preview, Lakeshore Brides, Health & Fitness (Jan); Lakeshore Home Expo, Grand Center Boat Show, Home Expo (Feb); WCUZ Home Show, Lakeshore Home & Garden, Sports Fishing & RV Show, Lakeshore Spring Fashion, Lakeshore Home & Garden, Auto Leasing, Spring Fashion (Mar); Pro Baseball, Whitecaps Season Opener, Yard & Garden, Golf, Earth Day, Restaurant Guide, Spring Home Improvement, Lakeshore Mother's Day (Apr); Car Care, Careers, Summer Travel, Parade of Homes, Super Star Seniors (May); Toronto Sampler, Northern Michigan Sampler, Grand Guide, Family Owned Businesses (June); Lakeshore Living, Restaurant Guide, Summer Fashion (July); Brides, Back-to-School, Health & Fitness, High School Football (Aug); On Stage...This Fall, Lakeshore Fashion, Fall Travel, Fall Home Improvement, GM Showcase, Lakeshore Remodelers, Custom Builders Showcase, Michigan Colleges & Universities (Sept); Home Idea Expo, Fall Car Care, Credit Unions, New Cars, Parade of Remodeled Homes, Restaurant Guide, Snowmobiles (Oct); Home Decorating, Grand Cook-off, Lakeshore Downtown Christmas, Winter Travel, Holiday Recipe Gift Guide (Nov); Holiday Decorating Gift Guide, Letters to Santa Gift Guide, Christmas Carols Gift Guide (Dec).
Special Weekly Sections: Auto (wed); Outdoors (sat).
Magazines: React (wed); TV Magazine, Comics (S); Parade.

CORPORATE OFFICER

President/Publisher Danny R Gaydon

GENERAL MANAGEMENT

General Manager Richard A Morton
Controller Michael P Ply
Manager-Employment Marietta Lamos

ADVERTISING

Director-Sales/Marketing Monica Benedict
Director-Classified Donald A Edwards
Manager-Co-op Kris Zuhl
Manager-New Media Worth Hanson

MARKETING AND PROMOTION

Manager-Marketing/Promotion Tanya Henderson

CIRCULATION

Manager Chuck St Amour
Manager-State Thomas Hoffman
Manager-Metro South Valerie Van Zomeren
Manager-Metro North Chris Jackson
Manager-City Edwin Tolbert

NEWS EXECUTIVE

Editor Michael S Lloyd

EDITORS AND MANAGERS

Books Editor Sue Thoms
Business Editor Jim Harger
City Editor Andrew Angelo
Columnist Pete DeMaagd
Columnist Tom Rademacher
Columnist John Douglas
Community Editions Editor Jeff Cranson
Editorial Page Editor/Writer Joe Crawford
Education Editor Roland Wilkerson
Entertainment Editor Sue Wallace
Features Editor Sue Schroder
Films Columnist John Douglas
Food Editor Ann Wells
Librarian Ruth Dryer
Music Critic-Classical Jeff Kaczmarczyk
Music Critic-Popular John Gonzalez
News Editor Jim O'Neill
Newspaper in Classroom Editor Bruce Barker
Photo Editor Jim Starkey
Religion Editor Charles Honey
Sports Editor Robert Becker
Sunday Editor April Hunt
Television Editor Ruth Butler
Television Listing Editor Mary Hefferan
Theater Editor David Nicolette
Travel Editor Hank Bornheimer

MANAGEMENT INFORMATION SERVICES

Manager-Info Systems Tony Torreano
Systems Leader Sue Clay

PRODUCTION

Manager Richard A Morton
Manager-Customer Service Ron Clark
Foreman-Plate/Camera Ray Simmons
Foreman-Mailroom Ted Hall
Foreman-Paper Storage Frank Doughty
Foreman-Pressroom Dan Silvernail
Superintendent-Maintenance Jerry Wass

Market Information: Zoned editions; Split Run; TMC.
Mechanical available: Letterpress; Black and 3 ROP colors; insert accepted — preprinted, spadea; page cut-offs — 23$\frac{9}{16}$".
Mechanical specifications: Type page 13" x 22"; E - 6 cols, 2$\frac{1}{16}$", $\frac{1}{8}$" between; A - 6 cols, 2$\frac{1}{16}$", $\frac{1}{8}$" between; C - 10 cols, 1$\frac{3}{8}$", $\frac{1}{16}$" between.
Commodity consumption: Newsprint 23,634 metric tons; widths 54", 40.5", 27"; black ink 696,220 pounds; color ink 134,000 pounds; single pages printed 23,832; average pages per issue 52(d), 148(S); single plates used 132,000.
Equipment: EDITORIAL: Front-end hardware — 4-AT/9000, 68-AT/9000; Front-end software — AT/Editorial. CLASSIFIED: Front-end hardware — 3-AT/9000, 43-AT/9000 VDT; Front-end software — AT/Classified. DISPLAY: Adv layout systems — SCS/Layout 8000; Front-end hardware — 8-AT/9000, 13-Cx/Breeze; Front-end software — HI/Classified Pagination, Cx/Ad Setting. PRODUCTION: Typesetters — 3-Cx/Bitsetter, 3-III/3850; Plate exposures — 2-Na/Starlite; Plate processors — 2-Na/C-120; Electronic picture desk — Lf/AP Leaf Picture Desk; Scanners — 1-ECR/Autokon 1000DE, 1-ECR/Autokon 1000, 1-ECR/2030; Production cameras — 1-C/Spartan III, 2-C/Pager II; Automatic film processors — 3-P/18, LE, 1-P/13, 3-AG/Litex 26; Digital color separation equipment — 1-RZ/210L.
PRESSROOM: Line 1 — 22-G/Mark II Letterpress; Press drives — GE; Folders — 6-G/Imperial 3:2; Pasters — 22-G/Digital paster; Reels and stands — 22-G/3-arm RTP; Press control system — GE/Drive Controls; Press registration system — Hurletron. MAILROOM: Counter stackers — 13-QWI/3001; Inserters and stuffers — 4-GMA/SLS 1000 (16:2); Bundle tyer — 13-Dynaric; Wrapping singles — 5-Dynaric/Single tyer; Addressing machine — 2-Ch/Labeler. LIBRARY: Electronic — Newsview. WIRE SERVICES: News — AP, CSM, NYT, LAT-WP, NNS; Stock tables — AP; Syndicates — King Features, United Media, TV Data, United Features; Receiving dishes — size-10ft, AP. BUSINESS COMPUTERS: 4-TI/990; Applications: Circ, Mailing, Newsprint inventory, Billing, EMC; PCs & micros networked; PCs & main system networked.

GREENVILLE

Montcalm County

'90 U.S. Census- 8,101; E&P '96 Est. 8,328
ABC-CZ (90): 8,101 (HH 3,183)

The Daily News (e-mon to sat)

The Daily News, 109 N. Lafayette St.; PO Box 340, Greenville, MI 48838; tel (616) 754-9301; fax (616) 754-8559.
Circulation: 9,019(e); 9,019(e-sat); ABC Sept. 30, 1995.
Price: 50¢(d); 50¢(sat); $8.00/mo (carrier).
Advertising: Open inch rate $10.55(e); $10.55(e-sat). **Representative:** American Newspaper Representatives Inc.
News Service: AP. **Politics:** Independent. **Established:** 1856.
Not Published: New Year; Memorial Day; Independence Day; Labor Day; Thanksgiving; Christmas.
Advertising not accepted: Tobacco.
Special Editions: Spring Sports, Danish Festival, Farm Tab (Aug); Advanced Christmas (Oct); Back-to-School; Winter Sports; Bridal Tab; Building; Car Care; Fall Sports; Football; Home Improvement; Spring and Fall Fashions; Financial Planning.
Special Weekly Sections: Business Page (mon); Food Page (tues); Agriculture Page (wed); Leisure Page (thur); TV Guide (fri); Home, Business Beat, Celebration Page, Senior & Youth Pages (sat).
Magazines: TV Times; Real Estate Monthly.
Cable TV: Operate leased cable TV in circulation area.

CORPORATE OFFICERS

Chairman of the Board/Publisher John Stafford
Secretary Linda Stafford
Treasurer Richard Ellafrits

GENERAL MANAGEMENT

President Larry Carbonelli
Publisher John Stafford
General Manager John Norton

ADVERTISING

Director Brett Mathis

TELECOMMUNICATIONS

Audiotex Manager Karynne McAndrew

CIRCULATION

Manager Doug McAvoy

NEWS EXECUTIVE

Editor Alan D Blanchard

EDITORS AND MANAGERS

News Editor John Frizzo
Asst News Editor Sandy Main
Chief Photographer Joe Veselenak

PRODUCTION

Manager-Composition Judy Wilson

Market Information: TMC; ADS; Operate audiotex.
Mechanical available: Offset; Black and 3 ROP colors; insert accepted — preprinted; page cut-offs — 22$\frac{3}{4}$".
Mechanical specifications: Type page 13$\frac{3}{4}$" x 21"; E - 8 cols, 1.58", $\frac{1}{6}$" between; A - 8 cols, 1.58", $\frac{1}{6}$" between; C - 8 cols, 1.58", $\frac{1}{6}$" between.
Commodity consumption: Newsprint 275 short tons; widths 27$\frac{1}{2}$", 34"; black ink 6,120 pounds; color ink 1,374 pounds; single pages printed 4,896; average pages per issue 16(d), 14(sat); single plates used 2,784.
Equipment: EDITORIAL: Front-end hardware — Mk; Printers — Ap/Mac LaserWriter IIg; Other equipment — Minolta/RP605Z microfilm reader. CLASSIFIED: Front-end hardware — 3-Mk/1100 Plus Sys; Printers — Ap/Mac LaserWriter IIg. AUDIOTEX: Hardware — TI/Micro 486 Series; Software — Info-Connect/Pottsville Republican; Supplier name — TMS, AP. DISPLAY: Adv layout systems — Ap/Macs; Front-end hardware — Ap/Macs; Front-end software — Aldus/PageMaker 5.0; Printers — 1-LaserMaster/1200, 1-QMS/860, 1-LaserMaster/1200 XO; Other equipment — Ap/Mac Classic. PRODUCTION: Typesetters — 2-Ap/Mac Radius, 1-Ap/Mac II LC, 1-Ap/Mac IIcx, 2-Ap/Mac IIsi, 1-Ap/Mac Classic, 2-Ap/Power Mac 6100-60; Plate exposures — Douthitt; Plate processors — Anitec/SN32; Scanners — HSD/Scan-X Pro, Kk/35mm rapid film scanner; Production cameras — COM/6700; Automatic film processors — Devotec/28D.
PRESSROOM: Line 1 — 8-G/Community (1-4-high); Folders — 1-G/SSC; Reels and stands — FBWAY/HS-35000; Press control system — Manual. MAILROOM: Bundle tyer — 1-MLN, 1-Bu; Addressing machine — 1-KR. WIRE SERVICES: News — AP; Receiving dishes — AP. BUSINESS COMPUTERS: IBM/Sys 36; Applications: Gen ledger, Circ, Accts receivable, Accts payable, Payroll, Sales, Analysis; PCs & micros networked; PCs & main system networked.

HILLSDALE

Hillsdale County

'90 U.S. Census- 8,170; E&P '96 Est. 9,042

The Hillsdale Daily News (e-mon to fri; m-sat)

Hillsdale Daily News, 33 McCollum St.; PO Box 287, Hillsdale, MI 49242-0287; tel (517) 437-7351; fax (517) 437-3963. Morris Communications Corp. group.
Circulation: 7,910(e); 7,910(m-sat); Sworn Sept. 30, 1994.
Price: 50¢(d); 50¢(sat); $7.75/mo; $87.50/yr.
Advertising: Open inch rate $7.85(e); $7.85(m-sat). **Representative:** Papert Companies.
News Service: AP. **Politics:** Independent. **Established:** 1845.
Not Published: New Year; Memorial Day; Independence Day; Labor Day; Thanksgiving; Christmas.
Special Editions: Travel Tab, Progress Edition (Jan); Valentine's Promotion, Bridal Tab (Feb); Spring Fashion Tab, Health & Fitness Tab (Mar); Spring Edition Tab, Weeders Digest, Classified Promotion (Apr); Guide To Hillsdale County Tab, Memoriams (May); Silver Salute Tab, Family Affair (June); Soil Conservation Tab, Hillsdale Sidewalk Days, Back-to-School (July); Back-to-School Tab, Jonesville Sidewalk Sales, Antique Tab, Football Tab (Aug); Fall Fashion Tab, Fair Tab, Grandparent's Day (Sept); Home-care/Car Care Tab, Outdoorsman Tab (Oct); Holiday Cookbook, Pre Christmas Edition (Nov); Santa's Gift Book, New Year's Baby Promotion (Dec).
Special Weekly Section: TV Key (fri).

GENERAL MANAGEMENT

Publisher William Turner
Business Manager David Holcomb

ADVERTISING

Coordinator Marianea Stemen

MARKETING AND PROMOTION

Director-Marketing/Promotion Judy Gabriele

TELECOMMUNICATIONS

Audiotex Manager Marianea Stemen

CIRCULATION

Coordinator Mickey Neukom

NEWS EXECUTIVE

Managing Editor Marcia Loader

EDITORS AND MANAGERS

Home Furnishings Editor Janet Lee
Sports Editor Doug Goodnough

PRODUCTION

Coordinator-Operations Jeff West

Market Information: TMC; ADS; Operate audiotex.
Mechanical available: Offset; Black and 3 ROP colors; insert accepted — preprinted; page cut-offs — 22$\frac{3}{4}$".
Mechanical specifications: Type page 13$\frac{1}{16}$" x 21$\frac{1}{2}$"; E - 6 cols, 2$\frac{1}{16}$", $\frac{1}{8}$" between; A - 6 cols, 2$\frac{1}{16}$", $\frac{1}{8}$" between; C - 6 cols, 2$\frac{1}{16}$", $\frac{1}{8}$" between.
Commodity consumption: Newsprint 275 metric tons; widths 27", 34"; black ink 10,000 pounds; color ink 1,200 pounds; single pages printed 4,420; average pages per issue 14(d); single plates used 4,000.
Equipment: EDITORIAL: Front-end hardware — Ap/Mac; Front-end software — Baseview/NewsEdit; Printers — Ap/Mac LaserWriter NTX. CLASSIFIED: Front-end hardware — Ap/Mac; Front-end software — Baseview/Classified; Printers — Ap/Mac LaserWriter NTX. AUDIOTEX: Hardware — Samsung/486, 33-PC, 2-Dialogic/Cards; Software — SMS. DISPLAY: Front-end hardware — Ap/Mac; Front-end software — QuarkXPress, Multi-Ad/Creator; Printers — Ap/Mac LaserWriter 600; Other equipment — Panasonic/CD-Rom. PRODUCTION: Typesetters — Ap/Mac LaserWriter 600, MON/Imagesetter; Plate exposures — 1-Nu/Flip Top FT40U3UP; Plate processors — Nat/250; Electronic picture desk — Ap/Mac, Adobe/Photoshop; Scanners — Ap/Mac Scanner, Nikon/Photo, Microtek/Scanmaker II; Production cameras — SCREEN/250; Automatic film processors — CP/530N.
PRESSROOM: Line 1 — 5-G/Community; Folders — 1-G. MAILROOM: Bundle tyer — MLN/1100, 1-MLN, 1-Strapex; Addressing machine — Ch/705, Automecha/AccuFast PL. LIBRARY: Electronic — SMS/Stauffer Gold. COMMUNICATIONS: Facsimile — Sharp/FO-3400. WIRE SERVICES: News — AP; Receiving dishes — AP. BUSINESS COMPUTERS: Epson/486SX-25, 4-ATT/610; Applications: SCO/U-386 3.0: Gen ledger, Payroll, Accts payable, Adv billing, Circ; PCs & micros networked; PCs & main system networked.

HOLLAND

Ottawa County

'90 U.S. Census- 30,745; E&P '96 Est. 35,962
ABC-NDM (90): 81,620 (HH 27,947)

The Holland Sentinel (e-mon to sat; S)

The Holland Sentinel, 54 W. 8th St., Holland, MI 49423; tel (616) 392-2311; e-mail hllndsntnl@aol.com; web site http://www.macatawa.org/com/sentinel/home.html. Morris Communications Corp. group.
Circulation: 19,873(e); 19,873(e-sat); 20,268(S); ABC Sept. 30, 1995.
Price: 50¢(d); 50¢(sat); $1.25(S); $10.00/mo; $111.00/yr.
Advertising: Open inch rate $12.18(e); $12.18(e-sat); $12.18(S). **Representative:** Papert Companies.
News Service: AP. **Politics:** Independent. **Established:** 1896.
Not Published: Christmas.
Special Editions: HBA Expo, Brides, Focus (Jan); Taxes (Feb); Holland Home Show, Home & Garden, Spring Fashion (Mar); Spring Car Care (Apr); American Home Week, Tulip Time (May); Parade of Homes, Summer Fun (June); Libertyfest (July); Hope College, Fall Fashion (Aug); RSVP (Restaurant Guide), Women In Business (Sept); Holland Chamber, Auto '97 Car Care (Oct); Song Book

(Nov); Santa's Selection, Last Minute Gifts (Dec); Coupon Tab (monthly).
Special Weekly Sections: In Step (mon); Education (wed); Haps (thur); Outdoor, Open Houses, Religion (fri); Religion, TV Today (sat); Home (S).
Magazine: USA Weekend.

CORPORATE OFFICERS
Chairman of the Board W S Morris III
President Paul S Simon
Vice Pres Edward B Skinner

GENERAL MANAGEMENT
Publisher Clay W Stauffer

ADVERTISING
Manager Susan Temple

TELECOMMUNICATIONS
Audiotex Manager Dawn Edstrom

CIRCULATION
Manager Steve G Knape

NEWS EXECUTIVES
Editor Clay W Stauffer
Managing Editor Sue Sopel

EDITORS AND MANAGERS
City Editor Darin Estep
News Editor Jim Timmerman
Sports Editor Leo Martonosi

PRODUCTION
Manager Steve Lindquist

Market Information: TMC; Operate audiotex.
Mechanical available: Offset; Black and 3 ROP colors; insert accepted — preprinted; page cutoffs — 22¾".
Mechanical specifications: Type page 13" x 21½"; E - 6 cols, 2$\frac{1}{16}$", $\frac{1}{8}$" between; A - 6 cols, 2$\frac{1}{16}$", $\frac{1}{8}$" between; C - 9 cols, 1$\frac{5}{16}$", $\frac{1}{8}$" between.
Commodity consumption: Newsprint 1,569 metric tons; widths 27½", 13¾"; black ink 28,800 pounds; average pages per issue 33(d), 50(S).
Equipment: EDITORIAL: Front-end hardware — Ap/Mac Quadra; Front-end software — Baseview/NewsEdit; Printers — Ap/Mac LaserWriter II NTX. CLASSIFIED: Front-end hardware — Ap/Mac II; Front-end software — Baseview; Printers — Ap/Mac LaserWriter II NTX. AUDIOTEX: Hardware — SMS. PRODUCTION: Typesetters — Ap/Mac LaserWriter II NTX, 2-MON/1270; Plate exposures — 2-Nu; Plate processors — Nat; Scanners — Abaton; Production cameras — R; Automatic film processors — AG/Super 260.
PRESSROOM: Line 1 — 10-G/Urbanite; Folders — 1-G; Reels and stands — G; Press control system — G. MAILROOM: Counter stackers — 1-HL; Inserters and stuffers — 1-HI/NP848; Bundle tyer — 2-Id; Addressing machine — 1-Ch. LIBRARY: Electronic — SMS/Stauffer Gold. WIRE SERVICES: News — AP; Receiving dishes — size-10ft, AP. BUSINESS COMPUTERS: ATT; Applications: SMS; PCs & micros networked; PCs & main system networked.

HOUGHTON
Houghton County
'90 U.S. Census- 7,498; E&P '96 Est. 7,486
ABC-CZ (90): 12,045 (HH 3,812)

The Daily Mining Gazette
(e-mon to sat)

The Daily Mining Gazette, 206 Shelden Ave.; PO Box 368, Houghton, MI 49931; tel (906) 482-1500; fax (906) 482-2726; e-mail gazedt@up.net. Thomson Newspapers group.
Circulation: 12,302(e); 12,302(e-sat); ABC Sept. 30, 1995.
Price: 50¢(d); 50¢(sat); $10.15/mo (carrier), $12.50/mo (mail).
Advertising: Open inch rate $12.56(e); $12.56(e-sat). **Representatives:** Landon Associates Inc.; Thomson Newspapers.
News Service: AP. **Politics:** Independent. **Established:** 1858.
Not Published: New Year; Memorial Day; Independence Day; Labor Day; Thanksgiving; Christmas.
Special Editions: Builders; Spring/Summer Tourism; Back-to-School; Brides; Spring Opening; Christmas; Michigan Technological University Winter Carnival; Community Improvement; Basketball; Football; Year-in-Review; Fall/Winter Tourism; Holiday Cookbook.
Special Weekly Sections: Best Food Day (mon); Outdoors (wed); Religion, Children Today, Entertainment (fri); Business Page (sat).
Magazine: TV Update Magazine (fri).

GENERAL MANAGEMENT
Publisher Brian M McMillan

ADVERTISING
Manager-Retail Karen Callaway
Manager-Classified Sandy Lindblom
Manager-National Lori Baakko

TELECOMMUNICATIONS
Audiotex Manager Sandy Lindblom

CIRCULATION
Manager William Blake

NEWS EXECUTIVE
Editor Cyndi Perkins

EDITORS AND MANAGERS
Regional Editor Kris Manty
Sports Editor Peter Bousu

MANAGEMENT INFORMATION SERVICES
Data Processing Manager Jim Dahl

PRODUCTION
Manager Donald Tervo

Market Information: TMC; ADS; Operate audiotex.
Mechanical available: Offset; Black and 3 ROP colors; insert accepted — preprinted, up to 11"x13"; page cut-offs — 21".
Mechanical specifications: Type page 13" x 21½"; E - 6 cols, 2.03", $\frac{1}{6}$" between; A - 6 cols, 2.03", $\frac{1}{6}$" between; C - 9 cols, 1.33", $\frac{1}{6}$" between.
Commodity consumption: width 27.5"; average pages per issue 16(d).
Equipment: EDITORIAL: Front-end hardware — Mk/1100 Plus; Front-end software — Mk; Printers — TI/810. CLASSIFIED: Front-end hardware — Mk/1100 Plus; Front-end software — Mk; Printers — TI/810. AUDIOTEX: Hardware — PC. DISPLAY: Adv layout systems — Ap/Mac; Front-end hardware — Ap/Mac IIsi; Front-end software — QuarkXPress, Multi-Ad/Creator 3.5; Printers — Ap/Mac LaserWriter II. PRODUCTION: OCR software — Caere/OmniPage; Typesetters — Ap/Mac LaserWriter II NTX, V; Plate exposures — 1-Nu; Plate processors — Nat/A250; Electronic picture desk — Lf; Production cameras — COM/680C; Color separation equipment (conventional) — Tegra/Varityper/4990, Lf; Digital color separation equipment — Lf.
PRESSROOM: Line 1 — 8-G/Offset; Press registration system — Duarte. MAILROOM: Bundle tyer — 4-Bu; Addressing machine — PC. LIBRARY: Electronic — Dukane/Microfilm reader. WIRE SERVICES: News — AP, THO; Photos — AP, THO; Syndicates — AP; Receiving dishes — size-3m, AP. BUSINESS COMPUTERS: 6-IBM/PC network; Applications: Q&A, Lotus, Microsoft/Windows; PCs & micros networked; PCs & main system networked.

IONIA
Ionia County
'90 U.S. Census- 5,935; E&P '96 Est. 6,061

Sentinel-Standard
(m-mon to sat)

Sentinel-Standard, 114 N. Depot, Ionia, MI 48846; tel (616) 527-2100; fax (616) 527-6860. Hollinger International Inc. group.
Circulation: 2,960(m); 2,960(m-sat); Sworn Oct. 2, 1995.
Price: 50¢(d); 50¢(sat); $11.00/mo; $87.00/yr, $78.50/yr (senior citizens).
Advertising: Open inch rate $6.97(m); $10.21 (m-mon); $10.21(m-sat).
News Service: AP. **Politics:** Independent. **Established:** 1866.
Not Published: All legal holidays.
Advertising not accepted: Publisher's discretion.
Special Editions: Back-to-School; Bridal; Christmas; Energy; Free Fair; Graduation; Historical Weekend; Soil Conservation; Spring-Fall-Winter Sports.

CORPORATE OFFICER
President Larry J Perrotto

GENERAL MANAGEMENT
Publisher Jan Anderson
Supervisor-Business Denise Peabody
Purchasing Agent Denise Peabody

ADVERTISING
Manager Duane Suppes

MARKETING AND PROMOTION
Manager-Marketing/Promotion Jan Anderson

CIRCULATION
Manager Kelly McCollar

NEWS EXECUTIVE
Managing Editor Brian Patrick Abbott

PRODUCTION
Manager Robert Zander

Market Information: Zoned editions; Split Run; TMC.
Mechanical available: Offset; Black and 4 ROP colors; insert accepted — preprinted; page cutoffs — 22".
Mechanical specifications: Type page 14¼" x 22"; E - 6 cols, 2$\frac{1}{16}$", $\frac{1}{8}$" between; A - 6 cols, 2$\frac{1}{16}$", $\frac{1}{8}$" between; C - 8 cols, 1$\frac{7}{8}$", $\frac{1}{8}$" between.
Commodity consumption: Newsprint 224 short tons; widths 28", 34"; black ink 9,450 pounds; single pages printed 21,360; average pages per issue 12(d), 10(sat); single plates used 5,000.
Equipment: EDITORIAL: Front-end hardware — 4-Ap/Mac Quadra 630, 2-Ap/Power Mac 6100-60; Front-end software — QuarkXPress, Baseview/NewsEdit Pro; Printers — 1-Ap/Mac LaserWriter 16-600 PS. CLASSIFIED: Front-end hardware — Ap/Mac Plus; Printers — Ap/Mac LaserWriter. DISPLAY: Adv layout systems — Multi-Ad/Creator; Front-end hardware — Ap/Mac IIvx; Printers — HP/Laser. PRODUCTION: Pagination software — QuarkXPress 3.3; Platemaking systems — 1-Nu; Plate processors — 1-Nat, 1-C; Production cameras — 1-B; Automatic film processors — 1-C/Powermatic T65.
PRESSROOM: Line 1 — 4-HI/V15A; Folders — 1-HI. MAILROOM: Inserters and stuffers — 1-MM/227E (4 station); Bundle tyer — 1-Sa, 1-Bu. COMMUNICATIONS: Facsimile — Canon/B140; Systems used — satellite. WIRE SERVICES: News — AP; Receiving dishes — size-3ft. BUSINESS COMPUTERS: 1-IBM/5120, 2-Packard Bell/Legend 401CD; Applications: Accts payable, Accts receivable, Gen ledger, Circ mailing, Labels/billing.

IRON MOUNTAIN-KINGSFORD
Dickinson County
'90 U.S. Census- 14,005 (Iron Mountain 8,525; Kingsford 5,480); E&P '96 Est. 14,611 (Iron Mountain 8,525; Kingsford 5,758)
ABC-CZ (90): 14,005 (HH 5,722)

The Daily News (e-mon to sat)

The Daily News, 215 E. Ludington; PO Box 460, Iron Mountain, MI 49801; tel (906) 774-2772; fax (906) 774-7660. Thomson Newspapers group.
Circulation: 11,029(e); 11,029(e-sat); ABC Sept. 30, 1995.
Price: 50¢(d); 50¢(sat); $2.60/wk (carrier); $11.70/mo; $147.00/yr.
Advertising: Open inch rate $15.02(e); $15.02(e-sat). **Representative:** Landon Associates Inc.
News Service: AP. **Politics:** Independent. **Established:** 1921.
Not Published: New Year; Memorial Day; Independence Day; Labor Day; Thanksgiving; Christmas.
Advertising not accepted: Vending machine routes; 900 numbers.
Special Editions: Ski Jumping (Feb); Bride, Home Improvement (Mar); Spring Fashions, Logging Today (Apr); Vacation Guide (June, July); Vacation Guide, Back-to-School, Progress Edition (Aug); Fall Fashion, Logging Today (Sept); Auto, Fire Prevention, National Furniture (Oct); Deer Hunters, "Huge" Holiday Cookbook (Nov); Christmas (Dec).
Special Weekly Sections: Food (mon); Business (tues, thur); Outdoor, Business, Entertainment (inside TV Preview) (sat).
Cable TV: Own cable TV in circulation area.

CORPORATE OFFICER
Publisher (Great Lakes Group) Jim Gliem

GENERAL MANAGEMENT
Publisher Robert Johnson

ADVERTISING
Director Jon Cantrell
Manager-Classified Carrie Messina

CIRCULATION
Manager Tracy Setner

NEWS EXECUTIVE
Managing Editor Blaine Hyska

EDITORS AND MANAGERS
Business/Finance Editor Linda Lobeck
City/Metro Editor Jim Anderson
Editorial Page Editor Blaine Hyska
Entertainment/Amusements Editor Blaine Hyska
News Editor Jim Anderson
Photo Department Manager Mark Rummel
Sports Editor Burt Angeli
Women's Editor Allyce Westphal

PRODUCTION
Foreman-Composing Gerald Novak

Market Information: TMC.
Mechanical available: Offset; Black and 3 ROP colors; insert accepted — preprinted, all; page cut-offs — 22½".
Mechanical specifications: Type page 13½" x 21½"; E - 6 cols, 2.06", $\frac{1}{8}$" between; A - 6 cols, 2.06", $\frac{1}{8}$" between; C - 9 cols, 1.36", $\frac{1}{9}$" between.
Commodity consumption: width 27"; average pages per issue 16(d).
Equipment: EDITORIAL: Front-end hardware — 10-Mk/Touchwriter; Front-end software — Mk/Touchwriter; Printers — Ap/Mac Laserwriter II NTX; Other equipment — Ap/Power Mac 7100, Polaroid/Sprint Scan, V/4990, 3-Mk/MC 2CI. CLASSIFIED: Front-end hardware — 2-Mk/Touchwriter Plus. DISPLAY: Adv layout systems — Ap/Mac 605Q; Front-end software — Broderbund/TypeStyler; Printers — Stylewriter; Other equipment — Microtek/Scanner. PRODUCTION: Pagination software — Ap/Mac; Typesetters — 2-COM; Electronic picture desk — Lf/AP Leaf Picture Desk, Ap/Power Mac 7100; Scanners — Lf/Leafscan 35, Polaroid/Sprint Scan; Production cameras — R; Automatic film processors — SCREEN/220 QT; Digital color separation equipment — Ap/Mac 7100, V/4990.
PRESSROOM: Line 1 — 11-G/Community; Folders — 2-G. COMMUNICATIONS: Digital ad delivery system — AP AdSend. WIRE SERVICES: News — AP, THO; Photos — AP; Receiving dishes — size-10ft, AP. BUSINESS COMPUTERS: Ap/Mac, IBM; PCs & micros networked.

IRONWOOD
Gogebic County
'90 U.S. Census- 6,849; E&P '96 Est. 6,170

The Ironwood Daily Globe
(e-mon to fri; m-sat)

The Ironwood Daily Globe, 118 E. McLeod Ave.; PO Box 548, Ironwood, MI 49938; tel (906) 932-2211; fax (906) 932-5358. Bliss Communications Inc. group.
Circulation: 7,862(e); 7,862(m-sat); VAC Mar. 31, 1995.
Price: 50¢(d); 50¢(sat); $9.00/mo (carrier); $98.00/yr (carrier).
Advertising: Open inch rate $11.82(e); $11.82(m-sat). **Representative:** Landon Associates Inc.
News Service: AP. **Politics:** Independent. **Established:** 1919.
Not Published: New Year; Memorial Day; Independence Day; Labor Day; Thanksgiving; Christmas.
Special Editions: Progress (Feb); Home Builders, Bridal (Mar); Summer Recreation (May); County Fair (Aug); Early Christmas, Ski, Winter Recreation (various merchandising events) (Nov); Car Care.
Magazine: TV Entertainment (local) (fri).

CORPORATE OFFICERS
President Sidney H Bliss
Vice Pres Gary A Lamberg
Secretary James E Warren
Treasurer Robert J Lisser

GENERAL MANAGEMENT
General Manager Gary A Lamberg
Business Manager Gary Mariani

ADVERTISING
Director Gary Mecum
Manager-Classified Melody Davey

CIRCULATION
Manager Jeff Krone

NEWS EXECUTIVES
Editor Gary A Lamberg
Managing Editor Andy Hill

PRODUCTION
Superintendent Richard Linn

Market Information: TMC.
Mechanical available: Offset; Black and 3 ROP colors; insert accepted — preprinted; page cutoffs — 22¾".
Mechanical specifications: Type page 13" x 21½"; E - 6 cols, 2$\frac{1}{16}$", $\frac{1}{8}$" between; A - 6 cols, 2$\frac{1}{16}$", $\frac{1}{8}$" between; C - 9 cols, 1$\frac{3}{8}$", $\frac{1}{16}$" between.
Commodity consumption: Newsprint 370 short tons; width 27.50"; black ink 5,700 pounds; color ink 813 pounds; single pages printed 5,620; average pages per issue 17(d); single plates used 6,850.

Copyright ©1996 by the Editor & Publisher Co.

Equipment: EDITORIAL: Front-end hardware — 6-CText. CLASSIFIED: Front-end hardware — 1-CText. DISPLAY: Adv layout systems — 3-CText/Adept. PRODUCTION: Plate exposures — 1-Nu; Production cameras — 1-Co/Horizontal 25 CS.
PRESSROOM: Line 1 — 8-G/Community; Folders — 1-G/2:1. MAILROOM: Bundle tyer — 1-Bu; Addressing machine — 2-Am. WIRE SERVICES: News — AP; Photos — AP; Syndicates — NEA; Receiving dishes — AP. BUSINESS COMPUTERS: PCs & micros networked; PCs & main system networked.

JACKSON

Jackson County

'90 U.S. Census- 37,446; **E&P '96 Est.** 35,590
ABC-CZ (90): 81,715 (HH 29,622)

Jackson Citizen Patriot

(e-mon to fri; m-sat; S)

Jackson Citizen Patriot, 214 S. Jackson St., Jackson, MI 49201; tel (517) 787-2300; fax (517) 789-1249; web site http://www.cic.net/~glew. Advance Publications (Booth Newspapers) group.

Circulation: 37,921(e); 37,921(m-sat); 43,573(S); ABC Sept. 30, 1995.

Price: 50¢(d); 50¢(sat); $1.50(S); $9.25/mo (carrier), $9.95/mo (motor route), $17.50/mo (mail).

Advertising: Open inch rate $23.70(e); $23.70(m-sat); $26.25(S). **Representative:** Newhouse Newspapers/Metro Suburbia.

News Services: AP, NNS, Booth. **Politics:** Independent. **Established:** 1837.

Special Editions: Brides, Financial Guide (Jan); Business & Industry, Builders' Show (Mar); Yard & Garden, Spring Car Care, Golf, Summertime Fun (Apr); Graduation, Rose Festival (May); Parade of Homes (June); Seniors Section (July); Jackson-This is Home, Football (Aug); Energy & Home Improvement (Sept); Winter Car Care (Oct); Christmas Gift Guide (Nov); Basketball (Dec).

Special Weekly Sections: Food (mon); Business News (tues); Health & Science, Wheels (wed); At Home, In Town & Around Entertainment (thur); Religious News, Real Estate Properties (fri); Venture Outdoors, Weddings, Community Journal (sat); Travel, Business (S).

Magazines: React (fri); TV Mag (own) (S); Parade; TMC weekly.

GENERAL MANAGEMENT
Publisher F T Weaver
Controller Tim McIntosh

ADVERTISING
Manager-Classified George Otis
Director Jerry Gerdes
Manager-National Jerry Gerdes

MARKETING AND PROMOTION
Manager-Promotion Gerry Lee

TELECOMMUNICATIONS
Audiotex Manager Terry Valentine

CIRCULATION
Manager Gerald J Ludwig

NEWS EXECUTIVE
Editor Sandy Petykiewicz

EDITORS AND MANAGERS
Business/Finance Editor Paul Overeiner
Editorial Writer Ken Wyatt
Features/Entertainment Editor John Piper
Librarian Susanne Weible
Metro Editor Eileen Lehnert
News Editor Thomas Limmer
Sports Editor Jim Knight
TV Magazine Sherri Cauthon

MANAGEMENT INFORMATION SERVICES
Data Processing Manager Tim McIntosh

PRODUCTION
Manager Bill Higdon
Manager-Commercial Printing Jack Gahagan
Manager-Pressroom Keith Broxholm

Market Information: Split Run; TMC; ADS; Operate audiotex.

Mechanical available: Offset; Black and 3 ROP colors; insert accepted — preprinted, any; page cut-offs — 22¾".

Mechanical specifications: Type page 13" x 21¾"; E - 6 cols, 2 1/16", 1/8" between; A - 6 cols, 2 1/16", 1/8" between; C - 10 cols, 1¼", 1/16" between.

Commodity consumption: Newsprint 2,880 short tons; 2,613 metric tons; widths 55", 41¼", 27½"; black ink 51,840 pounds; single pages printed 13,216; average pages per issue 28(d), 58(S).

Equipment: EDITORIAL: Front-end hardware — 3-DEC/PDP 11-75, 44-AT, 1-Ap/Mac fx, 3-Ap/Mac Quadra, 1-Ap/Mac IIsi, Ap/Mac 7100; Front-end software — Adobe/Illustrator, Aldus/FreeHand, Adobe/Photoshop, Claris/MacWrite, QuarkXPress, Microsoft/Fox Pro; Printers — Ap/Mac LaserWriter IIg, Fujitsu/DL5600; Other equipment — 2-Lf/Leafscan 35, 1-Telebit/WorldBlazer Modem. CLASSIFIED: Front-end hardware — 1-DEC/PDP 11-75, 10-AT; Printers — Fujitsu/DL5600. DISPLAY: Front-end hardware — 1-Ap/Mac IIfx, 1-Ap/Mac SE30, 3-Ap/Mac 7100; Front-end software — Adobe/Illustrator, Aldus/FreeHand, QuarkXPress, Adobe/Photoshop, Painter; Printers — Ap/Mac LaserWriter NTX; Other equipment — Microtek/Scanner. PRODUCTION: Typesetters — Ap/Mac Pro 810, 2-MON/3850 Imager w/Sun Express RIP, 2-Konica Film Processor; Plate exposures — 2-Nu/Ultra Plus; Plate processors — 2-Nat; Electronic picture desk — Lf/AP Leaf Picture Desk; Scanners — 2-AG/Arcus Scanner; Production cameras — 1-C/Spartan III, 1-Ik, 1-SCREEN; Automatic film processors — 2-LE; Digital color separation equipment — 1-Ap/Mac Quadra 840, 2-Ap/Mac fx.
PRESSROOM: Line 1 — 8-G/Cosmo; Folders — 2-G; Pasters — 5-G; Reels and stands — 5-G; Press control system — Fin. MAILROOM: Counter stackers — 2-BG/Count-O-Veyor; Inserters and stuffers — 2-MM/E-227; Bundle tyer — 2-Dynaric. WIRE SERVICES: News — AP; Photos — AP, Booth; Stock tables — AP; Syndicates — AP, NNS; Receiving dishes — size-8ft, AP. BUSINESS COMPUTERS: 1-TI/990, 1-Mk/Acer 1030, 2-Mk/Acer 1100sx, 5-Mk/Acer 915, 1-Mk/Acer 1100-33, 2-Dell/425sL, 1-Sun/Sparc2, 12-Link; Applications: Booth Computer Division: Payroll, Accts payable, Accts receivable, Adv billing; PBS: Circ; Lotus, WordPerfect, Microsoft/Windows, Microsoft/Fox Pro; PCs & main system networked.

KALAMAZOO

Kalamazoo County

'90 U.S. Census- 80,277; **E&P '96 Est.** 82,297
ABC-CZ (90): 156,564 (HH 59,598)

Kalamazoo Gazette

(e-mon to fri; m-sat; S)

Kalamazoo Gazette, 401 S. Burdick; PO Box 2007, Kalamazoo, MI 49007; tel (616) 345-3511; fax (616) 388-8427; web site http://www.cic.net/~glew. Advance Publications (Booth Newspapers) group.

Circulation: 62,781(e); 74,387(m-sat); 81,030(S); ABC Sept. 30, 1995.

Price: 50¢(d); 50¢(sat); $1.25(S); $11.30/mo (carrier), $18.25/mo (mail); $8.95/mo (weekends); $129.60/yr.

Advertising: Open inch rate $36.40(e); $39.28(e-fri); $41.13(m-sat); $47.09(S). **Representative:** Newhouse Newspapers/Metro Suburbia.

News Services: AP, NNS, NYT. **Politics:** Independent. **Established:** 1837.

Advertising not accepted: Objectionable medical; mail order; unapproved financial; clairvoyant; matrimonial; palmistry; 900 prefix tel. numbers.

Special Weekly Sections: Best Food Day, Food, Hometown Gazette, Portage Gazette (mon); Health & Science (tues); Every Woman (wed); Family, Mini Page for Kids (thur); Religion (sat); A & E, Auto, Business & Employment, HOMELIFE, Outdoors, Travel (S); GENERATIONS (1st S/month).

Magazines: FRIDAY (entertainment tab) (fri); On TV Magazine (sat); Color Comics (S); Parade.

GENERAL MANAGEMENT
Publisher George E Arwady
Asst to Publisher Terry E Sturgeon
Exec Secretary Janet Herder
Controller Ronald Carpenter

ADVERTISING
Director James Coppinger
Manager-Classified/Administration Diane Day
Supervisor-Classified Elaine Stafford

MARKETING AND PROMOTION
Manager-Marketing/Promotion Rene Johnson

CIRCULATION
Manager Ken Cogswell
Manager-Packaging/Distribution Duane Corstange
Manager-Distribution Steve Raschke
Supervisor-Sales Kyle Odom

NEWS EXECUTIVE
Editor James R Mosby Jr

EDITORS AND MANAGERS
Business/Finance Editor Al Jones
Consumer Interest Editor Al Jones
Editorial Page Editor Mary E Tift
Editorial Writer Mary E Tift
Education Editor Linda Mah
Environment Editor Bill Krasean
Features Editor Joyce Pines
Graphics Editor Scott Harmsen
Health/Medical Editor Bill Krasean
Librarian June Jones
Metro Editor Rebecca Pierce
Music Editor Kathy Doud
News Editor Lane Wick
Photo Editor Bradley S Pines
Political Editor Charlotte Channing
Radio/Television Editor Pat Betwee
Real Estate Editor Al Jones
Religion Editor Thomas Stersic
Science Editor Bill Krasean
Sports Editor Jack Moss
Travel Editor Shirley Bumgardner

PRODUCTION
Manager Thomas Sewall
Foreman-Pressroom Terry L Richards
Foreman-Mailroom Duane Corstange

Market Information: Zoned editions; Split Run; TMC; Operate audiotex.

Mechanical available: Letterpress (direct); Black and 3 ROP colors; insert accepted — preprinted, zoned and TMC inserts; page cut-offs — 23 9/16".

Mechanical specifications: Type page 13" x 22"; E - 6 cols, 2 1/16", 1/8" between; A - 6 cols, 2 1/16", 1/8" between; C - 10 cols, 1¼", 1/16" between.

Commodity consumption: Newsprint 9,573 short tons; 8,685 metric tons; widths 55", 41¼", 27"; black ink 301,555 pounds; color ink 51,747 pounds; single pages printed 23,762; average pages per issue 44(d), 123(S); single plates used 54,280.

Equipment: EDITORIAL: Front-end hardware — 51-AT. CLASSIFIED: Front-end hardware — 19-AT. AUDIOTEX: Hardware — Brite Voice Systems; Software — Brite Voice Systems; Supplier name — Brite Voice Systems, AP. DISPLAY: Adv layout systems — 5-Cx/Breeze; Other equipment — 9-AT. PRODUCTION: Pagination software — QuarkXPress 3.3; Typesetters — 2-Cx, 1-AU/APS-Soft RIP, AU/APS-6; Platemaking systems — 2-Na; Plate exposures — 1-Va/Starlite, 1-Na/Master; Plate processors — 1-Na/NP40, 1-Na/C70; Electronic picture desk — Lf/AP Leaf Picture Desk, 2-Ap/Mac; Scanners — 2-ECR/Autokon 1000; Production cameras — 2-C/SP-3, 1-C/Newspager; Automatic film processors — 2-LE/1800; Digital color separation equipment — 1-Lf/AP Leaf Picture Desk, Ap/Mac.
PRESSROOM: Line 1 — 10-G/M2 (5 Decks, 1 Hump); Press drives — CH, Seamans/Simoreg; Folders — 2-G/3:2; Pasters — 10-G; Reels and stands — 10-G; Press control system — 6-CH/Webmaster, 4-Retrofix; Press registration system — WebTech. MAILROOM: Counter stackers — 4-QWI; Inserters and stuffers — 2-GMA/1148 (Rebuilt); Bundle tyer — 3-Power Strap; Addressing machine — 1-Ch, Imager/Inkjet. LIBRARY: Electronic — Mead Data Central/Nexis NewsView, Photoview. WIRE SERVICES: News — AP, NYT; Stock tables — AP, NYSE; Syndicates — AP, NYT; Receiving dishes — AP. BUSINESS COMPUTERS: 2-TI/990-12; Applications: Adv billing, Accts receivable, Payroll, Circ, Gen ledger, Budgets, Newsprint inventory; PCs & micros networked; PCs & main system networked.

KINGSFORD

See IRON MOUNTAIN

LANSING

Ingham County

'90 U.S. Census- 127,321; **E&P '96 Est.** 130,943
ABC-NDM (90): 409,607 (HH 149,184)

Lansing State Journal

(m-mon to sat; S)

Lansing State Journal, 120 E. Lenawee St., Lansing, MI 48919; tel (517) 377-1000; fax (517) 482-5476. Gannett Co. Inc. group.

Circulation: 71,450(m); 71,450(m-sat); 93,466(S); ABC Sept. 30, 1995.

Price: 35¢(d); 35¢(sat); $1.50(S).

Advertising: Open inch rate $63.24(m); $63.24(m-sat); $78.69(S). **Representative:** Gannett National Newspaper Sales.

News Services: AP, GNS. **Established:** 1855.

Special Editions: Bride, Finance (Jan); Chamber of Commerce, Book of Love (Feb); Home & Landscape, Around Town (Mar); Medical Association, American Home Week, Spring Car Care (Apr); East Lansing Arts Festival, Prime Time/Senior Power Day, LPGA, Great Grads (May); Parade of Homes (June); Michigan Festival (July); Welcome, Riverfest (Aug); Prep Football, College Football (Sept); Credit Union, Fall Car Care (Oct); Holiday Catalog (Nov); Last Minute Gifts (Dec).

Special Weekly Sections: ETC (TMC), Business Monday (mon); Greater Lansing Real Estate Weekly (wed); Auto Focus, What's On (thur); Sunday Real Estate Advertising (S); Today, Flip Side, Sports, Weather Page (daily).

Magazines: Sun TV, TV Week (quarterfold), Comics (S).

CORPORATE OFFICER
President Gary M Suisman

GENERAL MANAGEMENT
Publisher Gary M Suisman
Controller Michael Wieber
Personnel Director Melissa Alford
Manager-Credit Lynn Reik

ADVERTISING
Director W Stan Howard
Manager-Local Sales Patricia Brown
Manager-National/Co-op Bob Powers
Manager-Service Tammy Kearly

MARKETING AND PROMOTION
Director-Marketing/Promotion Sherry Harthnett

CIRCULATION
Director Richard J Ferris

NEWS EXECUTIVES
Editor Zack Binkley
Managing Editor Roni Rucker Waters

EDITORS AND MANAGERS
Automotive Editor Les Smith
Business Editor Les Smith
City Editor Jim McMiller
Editorial Page Editor Mark Nixon
Education Editor Elaine Kulhanek
Entertainment/Amusements Editor Kathleen Lavey
Environmental Editor Elaine Kulhanek
Features Editor Kathleen Lavey
Government Editor Elaine Kulhanek
Health/Medical Editor Kathleen Lavey
Living/Lifestyle Editor Kathleen Lavey
Metro Editor Elaine Kulhanek
News Editor Sharon Buck
Political Editor Elaine Kulhanek
Radio/Television Editor Mike Hughes
Religion Editor Kathleen Lavey
Science/Technology Editor Kathleen Lavey
Sports Editor Jeff Rivers
Women's Editor Kathleen Lavey

PRODUCTION
Director Ken Swanson
Manager-Pressroom Stan Gadulka
Manager-Mailroom Robert Schiffman
Manager-Platemaking Roger A Mattson

Market Information: Split Run; TMC.

Mechanical available: Offset; Black and 3 ROP colors; insert accepted — preprinted; page cut-offs — 23 9/16".

Mechanical specifications: Type page 13" x 22"; E - 6 cols, 2 1/16", 1/8" between; A - 6 cols, 2 1/16", 1/8" between; C - 10 cols, 1 3/8", 1/16" between.

Commodity consumption: Newsprint 7,208 short tons; widths 54¼", 27½"; black ink 235,000 pounds; color ink 20,000 pounds; single pages printed 15,672; average pages per issue 36(d), 90(S); single plates used 47,600.

Equipment: EDITORIAL: Front-end hardware — AT. CLASSIFIED: Front-end hardware — 34-AT; Other equipment — 16-DEC. DISPLAY: Adv layout systems — AT/Architect; Front-end hardware — Ap/Macs, AT; Front-end software — Ap/Mac, Multi-Ad/Creator, QuarkXPress, Adobe/Photoshop; Printers — Linotype-Hell/Linotronic Imagesetter; Other equipment — Sun/Workstation. PRODUCTION: Typesetters — 2-AU/Micro 5; Platemaking systems — He; Plate exposures — 1-He/200, 1-He/SRA; Plate processors — 1-He/200; Production cameras — 1-C/Newspager II, 1-C/Spartan II; Automatic film processors — 1-P/Quick, 1-LE/LD18; Film transporters — 1-C.
PRESSROOM: Line 1 — TKS/Offset (9 units; 5 half decks); Press drives — SCR/DC-55-KW; Folders — 1-TKS/3:2 Double Delivery; Pasters

— G, 3-ARM RTP; Press registration system — ADJ. MAILROOM: Counter stackers — 3-QWI/300, 2-Id/660; Inserters and stuffers — 1-HI/WP 630 (27 Head); Bundle tyer — 2-Power Strap/PSN 6, 3-Power Strap/PSN 6-E; Wrapping singles — Hand; Addressing machine — Ch/525 E. WIRE SERVICES: News — AP, GNS; Stock tables — AP; Receiving dishes — AP, Contel. BUSINESS COMPUTERS: IBM/Sys 38; Applications: Payroll, Accts payable, Circ; PCs & micros networked; PCs & main system networked.

LUDINGTON

Mason County

'90 U.S. Census- 8,507; E&P '96 Est. 8,155
ABC-CZ (90): 8,507 (HH 3,589)

Daily News (e-mon to fri; m-sat)

Daily News, 202 N. Rath Ave.; PO Box 340, Ludington, MI 49431; tel (616) 845-5181; fax (616) 843-4011.

Circulation: 8,408(e); 8,408(m-sat); ABC Sept. 30, 1995.

Price: 50¢(d); 50¢(sat); $8.25/mo; $89.10/yr.

Advertising: Open inch rate $8.49(e); $8.49(m-sat). **Representative:** Michigan Newspapers Inc.

News Service: AP. **Politics:** Independent. **Established:** 1883.

Not Published: New Year; Memorial Day; Independence Day; Labor Day; Thanksgiving; Christmas.

Special Editions: Bridal (Feb); Spring Fashion, Progress Edition (Mar); Clean-up, Local Sports (Apr); Graduation (June); Fair Tab, Back-to-School (Aug); Local Sports (Sept); Christmas Opener (Nov); Local Sports, Christmas Catalogue (4), Christmas Songbook (Dec).

Special Weekly Sections: Best Food Day (mon); Education, Bridal (tues); Business, Agriculture (wed); Church, Outdoor (thur); Entertainment, TV Week (fri); Youth (sat).

CORPORATE OFFICERS

President — David R Jackson
Vice Pres — Susan L McDuffee
Secretary — Alan H Nichols
Treasurer — William R Jackson

GENERAL MANAGEMENT

Publisher/General Manager — David R Jackson
Business Manager — Alan H Nichols

ADVERTISING

Manager — James Frost

TELECOMMUNICATIONS

Audiotex Manager — Brad Pinkerton

CIRCULATION

Manager — Julie Payment

NEWS EXECUTIVE

Managing Editor — Paul S Peterson

EDITORS AND MANAGERS

Amusements Editor — Cheryl Higginson
Agriculture Editor — Patty Boes
Books Editor — Paul S Peterson
Columnist — Ken Case
Columnist — Chuck Stafford
Columnist — Steve Begnoche
Columnist — Bob Scully
Columnist — Eileen Sisko
Columnist — George Wilson
Editorial Page Editor — Paul S Peterson
Features Editor — Steve Begnoche
Food Editor — Jane Grey
Lifestyle Editor — Cheryl Higginson
News Editor — Steve Begnoche
Radio/Television Editor — Paul S Peterson
Religion Editor — Marion Riedl
Sports Editor — Lloyd Wallace
Wire Editor — Paul S Peterson
Women's — Marion Riedl

PRODUCTION

Manager/Foreman — Harold Lovewell
Superintendent — Chris Mapes

Market Information: TMC; ADS; Operate audiotex.

Mechanical available: Offset; Black and 3 ROP colors; insert accepted — preprinted; page cutoffs — 22¾".

Mechanical specifications: Type page 13¼" x 21½"; E - 6 cols, 2.08", ⅙" between; A - 6 cols, 2.08", ⅙" between; C - 6 cols, 2.08", ⅙" between.

Commodity consumption: Newsprint 268 metric tons; width 27½"; black ink 6,123 pounds; color ink 1,051 pounds; single pages printed 6,909; average pages per issue 22.5(d); single plates used 3,453.

Equipment: EDITORIAL: Front-end hardware — 12-Ap/Mac; Front-end software — Baseview, QuarkXPress; Printers — 2-Ap/Mac, NewGen/Imager Plus 12. CLASSIFIED: Front-end hardware — Ap/Mac; Front-end software — Baseview; Printers — Ap/Mac, NewGen/Imager Plus 12. AUDIOTEX: Hardware — IBM; Software — Info-Connect; Supplier name — TMS. DISPLAY: Front-end hardware — Ap/Mac; Front-end software — Aldus/PageMaker, Multi-Ad; Printers — Ap/Mac LaserWriter NTX; Other equipment — Pioneer/CD-Rom 600. PRODUCTION: Typesetters — 4-Ap/Mac; Plate exposures — 1-Nu; Scanners — HP/ScanJet; Automatic film processors — Fuji. PRESSROOM: Line 1 — 6-G/Community. MAILROOM: Inserters and stuffers — KAN/4-station; Bundle tyer — MLN, Bu, Malow. WIRE SERVICES: News — Syndicates — AP; Receiving dishes — size-3m, AP. BUSINESS COMPUTERS: IBM/Sys 36, IBM/PC; Applications: INSI: Gen ledger, Accts payable, Accts receivable, Circ; Lotus, WordPerfect, Query; PCs & micros networked; PCs & main system networked.

MANISTEE

Manistee County

'90 U.S. Census- 6,734; E&P '96 Est. 6,097

Manistee News-Advocate

(e-mon to fri; m-sat)

Manistee News-Advocate, 75 Maple St.; PO Box 317, Manistee, MI 49660; tel (616) 723-3592; fax (616) 723-4733. Pioneer group.

Circulation: 5,064(e); 5,064(m-sat); Sworn Oct. 3, 1994.

Price: 50¢(d); 50¢(sat); $8.50/mo; $86.00/yr.

Advertising: Open inch rate $8.50(e); $8.50(m-sat).

News Service: AP. **Politics:** Independent. **Established:** 1894.

Not Published: New Year; Memorial Day; Independence Day; Labor Day; Thanksgiving; Christmas.

Special Editions: Christmas Opening; Back-to-School; Spring Fashion; Fall Fashion; Spring Sports; Fall Sports; International Days; Forest Festival; New Car; Hunting; Bridal.

CORPORATE OFFICER

President — John A Batdorff

GENERAL MANAGEMENT

Publisher — Terence J Fitzwater
Chief Financial Officer — Ruth Meikle

ADVERTISING

Manager — Marilyn Barker

MARKETING AND PROMOTION

Manager-Marketing/Promotion — Terence J Fitzwater

CIRCULATION

Director — Tony Walker

NEWS EXECUTIVE

Managing Editor — Ken Grabowski

EDITORS AND MANAGERS

Business/Finance Editor — Ken Grabowski
City/Metro Editor — Kristen Asiala
Entertainment/Amusements Editor — Pam Spoor
Environmental Editor — Kim Omarzu
Fashion/Style Editor — Kristen Asiala
Films/Theater Editor — Pam Spoor
Religion Editor — Pam Spoor
Sports Editor — Greg Gielczyk
Women's Editor — Kristen Asiala

MANAGEMENT INFORMATION SERVICES

Data Processing Manager — Ruth Meikle

PRODUCTION

Manager — Shirley Flatten

Market Information: Split Run; TMC; ADS.

Mechanical available: Offset; Black and 3 ROP colors; insert accepted — preprinted, all; page cut-offs — 22½".

Mechanical specifications: Type page 13½" x 21¾"; E - 6 cols, 2 1/16", ⅛" between; A - 6 cols, 2 1/16", ⅛" between; C - 9 cols, 1⅜", ⅛" between.

Commodity consumption: Newsprint 585 short tons; widths 14", 17", 28", 34"; single pages printed 3,800; average pages per issue 36(d); single plates used 2,754.

Equipment: EDITORIAL: Front-end hardware — Ap/Mac; Front-end software — Aldus/PageMaker, QuarkXPress, Claris/MacDraw, Claris/MacPaint, Jus-Text, Microsoft/Word; Printers — HP. CLASSIFIED: Other equipment — 2-Ap/Mac. PRODUCTION: Typesetters — Ap/Mac LaserWriter; Plate exposures — 1-Nu; Plate processors — Nat; Production cameras — R; Automatic film processors — P. PRESSROOM: Line 1 — 4-HI/Cotrell 15; Folders — 1-HI/2:1. MAILROOM: Bundle tyer — Sa; Addressing machine — Wm. WIRE SERVICES: News — AP; Receiving dishes — AP. BUSINESS COMPUTERS: 3-IBM; Applications: Circ, Subscription, Labels, Billing; PCs & micros networked; PCs & main system networked.

MARQUETTE

Marquette County

'90 U.S. Census- 21,977; E&P '96 Est. 20,914
ABC-CZ (90): 21,977 (HH 7,942)

The Mining Journal

(e-mon to fri; m-sat; S)

The Mining Journal, 249 W. Washington St.; PO Box 430, Marquette, MI 49855; tel (906) 228-2500; fax (906) 228-5556. Thomson Newspapers group.

Circulation: 18,619(e); 18,619(m-sat); 20,557(S); ABC Sept. 30, 1995.

Price: 50¢(d); 50¢(sat); $1.00(S); $130.00/yr (carrier), $148.20/yr (mail).

Advertising: Open inch rate $17.99(e); $17.99(m-sat); $17.99(S). **Representatives:** Landon Associates Inc.; Thomson Newspapers.

News Service: AP. **Politics:** Independent. **Established:** 1846.

Not Published: New Year; Memorial Day; Independence Day; Labor Day; Thanksgiving; Christmas.

Special Editions: Bridal, U.P. 200 Sled Dog (Feb); Spring Car Care, Spring Home Improvement (Mar); Lawn & Garden (May); Fall Home Improvement, Fall Car Care (Oct); Cookbook (Nov).

Special Weekly Sections: Builders Page (thur); Outdoor Page, Travel Page (S).

Magazine: TV Week (fri).

GENERAL MANAGEMENT

Publisher — James A Reevs

ADVERTISING

Manager — Gail Englund

MARKETING AND PROMOTION

Director-Marketing — Willie J Peterson

CIRCULATION

Manager — Bill Christensen

NEWS EXECUTIVE

Managing Editor — David Edwards

EDITORS AND MANAGERS

Lifestyle Editor — Renee Prusi
News Editor — Barbara Bannister
Sports Editor — Craig Remsburg

PRODUCTION

Manager — Bob McEachern

Market Information: TMC.

Mechanical available: Offset; Black and 3 ROP colors; insert accepted — preprinted; page cut-offs — 22¾".

Mechanical specifications: Type page 13" x 21½"; E - 6 cols, 2 1/16", ⅛" between; A - 6 cols, 2⅙", ⅛" between; C - 9 cols, 1⅜", ⅛" between.

Commodity consumption: Newsprint 1,000 short tons; widths 27½", 13¾"; black ink 35,000 pounds; color ink 3,000 pounds; single pages printed 8,000; average pages per issue 22(d), 54(S); single plates used 6,400.

Equipment: EDITORIAL: Front-end hardware — Mk/Mycrocomp 1100 Plus, 14-Mk/Mycrocomp Touchwriter, 3-RSK/TRS-102; Front-end software — Mk/Mycrocomp Touchwriter; Printers — V/4990 LaserPrinter. CLASSIFIED: Front-end hardware — 3-Mk/Mycrocomp Touchwriter. DISPLAY: Adv layout systems — COM/MCS 100, 3-Ap/Mac Centris 650, 1-Ap/Mac IIcx. PRODUCTION: Typesetters — 3-V/5100 LaserPrinter; Plate exposures — 1-Nu/Flip Top FT40UPNS; Plate processors — 1-Nat/A-250; Production cameras — 1-SCREEN/Auto Companica 690C; Automatic film processors — 1-SCREEN/LD-220-QT; Color separation equipment (conventional) — 1-Digi-Colour/DC-400; Digital color separation equipment — Lf/Leafscan 35, Ap/Mac Scanner.
PRESSROOM: Line 1 — 8-KP/Daily King; Folders — 1-KP. MAILROOM: Bundle tyer — 2-MLN/ML1EE, 1-MLN/Spirit; Addressing machine — 1-Wm. WIRE SERVICES: News — AP; Photos — AP; Stock tables — AP; Syndicates — TNN; Receiving dishes — size-3m, AP. BUSINESS COMPUTERS: 1-IBM/Sys 34; Applications: Adv billing, Accts receivable, Circ.

MARSHALL

Calhoun County

'90 U.S. Census- 6,891; E&P '96 Est. 6,636

Marshall Chronicle

(m-mon to sat; S)

Marshall Chronicle, 115 S. Grand St., Marshall, MI 49068; tel (616) 781-3943; fax (616) 781-4012. Milliman Communications group.

Circulation: 2,011(m); 2,011(m-sat); 11,287(S); Sworn July 31, 1993.

Price: 35¢(d); 35¢(sat); Free(S); $6.50/mo.

Advertising: Open inch rate $5.25(m); $5.25(m-sat); $6.75(S); comb with Albion Recorder (m) $11.49.

News Service: AP. **Politics:** Independent. **Established:** 1879.

Not Published: New Year; Memorial Day; Independence Day; Labor Day; Thanksgiving; Christmas.

Special Editions: Bridal (Jan); Historic Home Tour Edition (2nd wk Sept); Car Care, Home Improvement (Spring); Car Care, Home Improvement, Sports (Fall); Sports (Winter).

GENERAL MANAGEMENT

Publisher — Richard L Milliman
General Manager — Kurt Madden
Controller — Terence J Fitzwater

ADVERTISING

Manager — Kurt Madden

CIRCULATION

Manager — Richard Dopp

EDITOR AND MANAGER

Editor — James Moses III

Market Information: TMC.

Mechanical available: Offset; Black and 3 ROP colors; insert accepted — preprinted; page cut-offs — 22¾".

Mechanical specifications: Type page 13¾" x 22"; E - 6 cols, 2 1/16", ⅛" between; A - 6 cols, 2 1/16", ⅛" between; C - 6 cols, 2 1/16", ⅛" between.

Commodity consumption: Newsprint 200 short tons; widths 27½", 34"; black ink 600 pounds; color ink 100 pounds; single pages printed 2710; average pages per issue 10(d); single plates used 4,000.

Equipment: EDITORIAL: Front-end hardware — Ap/Mac; Printers — Ap/Mac LaserWriter. CLASSIFIED: Front-end hardware — Ap/Mac. DISPLAY: Adv layout systems — Ap/Mac. PRODUCTION: Typesetters — QMS/PS-810. PRESSROOM: Line 1 — 5-HI/Cotrell V15. MAILROOM: Bundle tyer — 1-Bu. COMMUNICATIONS: Facsimile — HI. WIRE SERVICES: News — AP; Receiving dishes — size-2m, AP. BUSINESS COMPUTERS: ATT; Applications: Labels, Analysis, Financial, Accts receivable; PCs & micros networked; PCs & main system networked.

MENOMINEE

See MARINETTE, WI

MIDLAND

Midland County

'90 U.S. Census- 38,053; E&P '96 Est. 39,500
ABC-CZ (90): 38,053 (HH 14,812)

Midland Daily News

(e-mon to fri; m-sat; S)

Midland Daily News, 124 S. McDonald St., Midland, MI 48640; tel (517) 835-7171; fax (517) 835-9151; e-mail gordonhall@mdnnetlink.com. Hearst Newspapers group.

Circulation: 17,109(e); 17,109(m-sat); 18,457(S); ABC Sept. 30, 1995.

Price: 35¢(d); 35¢(sat); $1.25(S); $2.65/wk; $11.40/mo; $136.80/yr.

Advertising: Open inch rate $19.30(e); $19.30(m-sat); $20.30(S). **Representatives:** Papert Companies; US Suburban Press.

News Services: AP, NYT, HN. **Politics:** Independent. **Established:** 1858.

Special Weekly Sections: Best Food Day (mon); Science Page (tues); Arts Page (wed); Home and Garden, Friends and Neighbors, Agriculture, Outdoor Page, Church Page (thur); Youth Page, Midland Living and Entertainment (fri); Business News, Entertainment

I-206 Michigan

Page, Sports Page, Stock Market, TV Listings (daily).
Magazines: TV Times (own), Color Comics, USA Weekend (S).

GENERAL MANAGEMENT
Publisher/CEO — Gordon Hall
ADVERTISING
Director — Jenny L Anderson
Manager-National — Terry Kenny
Manager-New Projects Development — Kevin Prior
TELECOMMUNICATIONS
Audiotex Manager — Mark Ranzenberger
Audiotex Manager — Kris Orlando
CIRCULATION
Manager — Gary Wamsley
NEWS EXECUTIVE
Editor — John H Telfer II
EDITORS AND MANAGERS
Business Editor — Stu Frohm
Editorial Page Editor — Ralph Wirtz
Education Writer — Renee Reso
Entertainment/Amusements Editor — Lori Qualls
Environmental Writer — Doug Henze
Farm/Agriculture Editor — Dave Shane
Fashion/Style Editor — Lori Qualls
Health/Medical Writer — Lori Qualls
Living/Lifestyle Editor — Lori Qualls
National Writer — Mark Ranzenberger
News Editor — Ralph Wirtz
Photo Editor — Michael Honeywell
Political/Government Writer — Mark Ranzenberger
Religion Editor — Lori Qualls
Science/Technology Editor — Dave Shane
Sports Editor — Don Winger
Television/Film Editor — Lori Qualls
Theater/Music Editor — Lori Qualls
Women's Editor — Lori Qualls
MANAGEMENT INFORMATION SERVICES
Online Manager — Beth Bellor
PRODUCTION
Manager-Systems — Larry Sabourin
Foreman-Pressroom/Camera — Richard Messersmith

Market Information: Split Run; TMC; ADS; Operate database; Operate audiotex;
Mechanical available: Offset; Black and 3 ROP colors; insert accepted — preprinted; page cutoffs — 22¾".
Mechanical specifications: Type page 13" x 21½"; E - 6 cols, 2¹⁄₁₆", ⅛" between; A - 6 cols, 2¹⁄₁₆", ⅛" between; C - 9 cols, 1½", ¹⁄₁₆" between.
Commodity consumption: Newsprint 1,168 short tons; widths 27", 13¾"; black ink 34,000 pounds; color ink 2,500 pounds; single pages printed 11,116; average pages per issue 26(d), 40(S); single plates used 21,000.
Equipment: EDITORIAL: Front-end hardware — 6-RSK/TRS-80-100 Portable, 27-Ap/Mac Quadra 650, 14-Ap/Mac Quadra 605; Front-end software — Baseview/NewsEdit, QuarkXPress 3.3; Printers — 1-Ap/Mac LaserWriter II NTX, 1-Ap/Mac LaserWriter II NT, 1-Ap/Mac LaserWriter Pro; Other equipment — Accuset/800 Imagesetter. CLASSIFIED: Front-end hardware — 5-Ap/Mac Quadra 105; Front-end software — Baseview/Class Ad Mgr; Printers — 1-Ap/Mac LaserWriter II NTX. AUDIOTEX: Hardware — Brite Voice Systems. DISPLAY: Front-end hardware — 3-Ap/Mac IIci, 3-Ap/Mac Quadra 605, 1-Ap/Mac Quadra 650; Front-end software — QuarkXPress 3.3, Adobe/Photoshop 2.5; Printers — 2-HP/LaserJet 4M; Other equipment — 2-CD-Rom. PRODUCTION: Pagination software — QuarkXPress 3.3.1; Typesetters — 2-Accuset/800 Imagesetter; Platemaking systems — 1-3M/Pyrofax; Plate exposures — 1-Nu; Plate processors — 1-Nat; Electronic picture desk — 1-Ap/Mac Quadra 840; Scanners — 1-Nikon/35mm, Epson/800C Flatbed; Production cameras — 1-C/Spartan III, AG/RPS6100S; Automatic film processors — 1-P; Film transporters — 1-LE.
PRESSROOM: Line 1 — 8-G/Urbanite single width; Press drives — G; Folders — 1-G; Reels and stands — 2-Stands; Press control system — Fin; Press registration system — Duarte. MAILROOM: Inserters and stuffers — KAN, HI/38P; Bundle tyer — OVL. WIRE SERVICES: News — AP; Stock tables — AP; Receiving dishes — size-8ft, AP. BUSINESS COMPUTERS: IBM/Sys 36; Applications: Accts receivable, Accts payable, Payroll, Gen ledger, Circ.

MONROE
Monroe County
'90 U.S. Census- 22,902; E&P '96 Est. 22,376
ABC-CZ (90): 32,087 (HH 11,938)

The Monroe Evening News
(e-mon to fri; m-sat)
The Monroe Sunday News (S)

The Monroe Evening News, 20 W. First; PO Box 1176, Monroe, MI 48161; tel (313) 242-1100.
Circulation: 23,096(e); 23,096(m-sat); 24,590(S); ABC Sept. 30, 1995.
Price: 35¢(d); 35¢(sat); $1.00(S); $2.45/wk; $9.80/mo; $127.40/yr.
Advertising: Open inch rate $14.37(e); $14.37(m-sat); $14.37(S).
News Service: AP. **Politics:** Independent. **Established:** 1825.
Not Published: New Year; Independence Day; Thanksgiving; Christmas.
Advertising not accepted: Tobacco; Liquor.
Special Editions: Brides, Soil Conservation (Jan); Car Care, "Prime Times" (Senior Tab) (Mar); Spring Home Improvement, User's Guide to Monroe (Apr); Fair Premium List (May); Cook Book, "Prime Times" (Senior Tab) (June); County Fair (July); Back-to-School (Aug); Fall Home Improvement, Football Preview, "Prime Times" (Senior Tab) (Sept); Car Care (Oct); Christmas, Cookbook (Nov); Christmas, Basketball Preview, Year in Review, "Prime Times" (Senior Tab) (Dec).
Magazines: TV Times; Parade; Comics.

CORPORATE OFFICERS
President — Grattan Gray
Vice Pres — Stephen T Gray
Secretary — Joan Stoner
Treasurer — Rhonda Machcinski
GENERAL MANAGEMENT
General Manager — Grattan Gray
Business Manager — Joan Stoner
ADVERTISING
Director — Robert Simons
Manager-Classified — Beth Salow
MARKETING AND PROMOTION
Director-Sales & Marketing — Lonnie L Peppler
Director-Marketing Development — George W Stoner
TELECOMMUNICATIONS
Audiotex Manager — Jeanine Bragg
CIRCULATION
Director — Lee Hatfield
NEWS EXECUTIVES
Editor — Stephen T Gray
Managing Editor — Deborah Saul
EDITORS AND MANAGERS
Business Editor — Charles Slat
Editorial Page Editor — Thomas Chulski
Local Editor — Robert Stiegel
Sports Editor — Ron Montri
Wire Editor — Harry Orscheln
MANAGEMENT INFORMATION SERVICES
Data Processing Manager — Trent Langton
PRODUCTION
Manager-Pre Press — Mary Goodman
Foreman-Pressroom — Walter Cron

Market Information: TMC; Operate audiotex.
Mechanical available: Letterpress; Black and 3 ROP colors; insert accepted — preprinted; page cut-offs — 22¾".
Mechanical specifications: Type page 13" x 21"; E - 6 cols, 2", ⅛" between; A - 6 cols, 2", ⅛" between; C - 9 cols, 1.33", ⅛" between.
Commodity consumption: Newsprint 1,488 short tons; widths 28", 14"; black ink 38,478 pounds; color ink 500 pounds; single pages printed 11,864; average pages per issue 29(d), 45(S); single plates used 12,686.
Equipment: EDITORIAL: Front-end hardware — PC; Front-end software — QuarkXPress, Adobe/Photoshop, Synaptic 3.01; CLASSIFIED: Front-end hardware — PC; Front-end software — CText, QuarkXPress. AUDIOTEX: Hardware — PC; Software — Info-Connect 4.20C; DISPLAY: Front-end hardware — Ap/Mac; Front-end software — Multi-Ad/Creator, Adobe/Photoshop. PRODUCTION: Pagination software — QuarkXPress 3.3; Typesetters — XIT/Navigator, XIT/Schooner; Platemaking systems — Na; Plate exposures — 2-Na; Electronic picture desk — Lf/AP Leaf Picture Desk; Scanners — Kk, Microtek/ScanMaker II; Production cameras — LE; Automatic film processors — LE; Film transporters — LE.
PRESSROOM: Line 1 — 6-Duplex/Tubular; Line 2 — 6-Duplex/Tubular. MAILROOM: Bundle tyer — 1-OVL, 1-MLN/MLEE. LIBRARY: Electronic — Synaptic/Folio Views 2.1. WIRE SERVICES: News — AP; Photos — AP; Receiving dishes — size-3m, AP. BUSINESS COMPUTERS: 4-PC, IBM/Sys 36; Applications: ACCPAC, CDS; PCs & micros networked; PCs & main system networked.

MOUNT CLEMENS
Macomb County
'90 U.S. Census- 18,405; E&P '96 Est. 18,068
ABC-CZ (90): 262,374 (HH 101,628)

The Macomb Daily
(e-mon to fri; S)

The Macomb Daily, 100 Macomb Daily Dr.; PO Box 707, Mount Clemens, MI 48043; tel (810) 469-4510, (810) 296-0810; fax (810) 469-2892. Independent Newspapers Inc. (MI) group.
Circulation: 49,400(e); 61,331(S); ABC Sept. 30, 1995.
Price: 50¢(d); $1.00(S); $2.10/wk (carrier); $109.20/yr.
Advertising: Open inch rate $46.60(e); $46.60(S). **Representatives:** Papert Companies; US Suburban Press; American Newspaper Representatives Inc.
News Service: AP. **Politics:** Independent. **Established:** 1860.
Advertising not accepted: Abortion clinics; X-rated movies.
Special Editions: 1996 Auto Show, Brides and Grooms, Peace of Mind (Jan); Health Beat, Progress 1996 (Feb); Spring Home Improvement I, Boating, Manufactured Housing (Mar); Spring Home Improvement II, Golf Guide '96 (Apr); To Mom with Love, Home Improvement III (May); Spring/Summer Entertainment, Super Summer Discounts (June); Women in Business, Manufactured Housing (July); Men in Business (Aug); Fall/Winter All Sports, Fall Home Improvement I & II, Trucks & Bucks (Sept); 1997 New Car Preview, Home Interiors, To your Health (Oct); Manufactured Housing, Cookbook, Holiday Gifting (Nov); Holiday Magic, Letters to Santa, Christmas Wrap Up, Student Ad-Craft (Dec).
Special Weekly Sections: Business (mon); Home Improvement, Entertainment (thur); Real Estate (fri); Real Estate, TV Time, Travel (S).

CORPORATE OFFICERS
President/CEO — J Gene Chambers
Chief Financial Officer — William Wenk
Controller — Ken Pranger
GENERAL MANAGEMENT
Publisher — J Gene Chambers
ADVERTISING
Director — Mark Lewis
Director-Marketing — Jerry Ballenger
Manager-Retail — Bob Brisse
CIRCULATION
Director — Bill Heasley
NEWS EXECUTIVE
Editor — Phil Van Hulle
EDITORS AND MANAGERS
Automotive Editor — Sherri Garrett
Business/Finance Editor — Bill Fleming
Editorial Page Editor — Mitch Kehetian
Education Editor — Phil Van Hulle
Entertainment/Amusements Editor — Debbie Komar
Environmental Editor — Mitch Hotts
Farm/Agriculture Editor — Bob Selwa
Fashion/Style Editor — Debbie Komar
Features/Travel Editor — Debbie Komar
Health/Medical Editor — Debbie Komar
Managing Editor-News — Ken Kish
National Editor — Chad Selweski
News Editor — Ken Kish
Photo Department Manager — Dave Posavetz
Political/Government Editor — Chad Selweski
Religion Editor — Bill Fleming
Science/Technology Editor — Bill Fleming
Sports Editor — George Pohly
Television/Film Editor — Debbie Komar
Theater/Music Editor — Debbie Komar
MANAGEMENT INFORMATION SERVICES
Data Processing Manager — Chris Hinton
PRODUCTION
Director-Press Operations — Pat Eagan
Asst — Jackie Grzywacz
Director-Pre Press Operations — Mike McLain
Foreman-Composing — David Austin
Foreman-Mailroom — Gary Peitzsch

Market Information: Zoned editions; TMC.
Mechanical available: Offset; Black and 3 ROP colors; insert accepted — preprinted, card stock, books; page cut-offs — 22¾".
Mechanical specifications: Type page 13¾" x 22¾"; E - 6 cols, 2.04", .14" between; A - 6 cols, 2.04", .14" between; C - 9 cols, 1.33", ⅛" between.
Commodity consumption: Newsprint 4,000 short tons; 3,648 metric tons; widths 55", 41¼", 27½", 13¾"; black ink 90,000 pounds; color ink 8,500 pounds; single pages printed 18,806; average pages per issue 28(d), 64(S); single plates used 48,000.
Equipment: EDITORIAL: Front-end hardware — HAS/HS58; Printers — Okidata. CLASSIFIED: Front-end hardware — HAS/HS58; Front-end software — Cx/Classified Magicians. DISPLAY: Adv layout systems — SCS/Layout 8000; Front-end hardware — Ap/Mac; Front-end software — DTI/AdSpeed 3.01.6; Printers — Ap/Mac LaserWriter IV. PRODUCTION: Pagination software — QPS; Typesetters — AU/APS-108; Plate exposures — Nu/Burner, Douthitt; Plate processors — WL; Scanners — Microtek/ScanMaker 2XE; Production cameras — C/Marathon; Automatic film processors — AU/APS-36; Film transporters — LE; Shrink lenses — Alan; Color separation equipment (conventional) — Kk/RFS 2035.
PRESSROOM: Line 1 — 8-G/Cosmo Offset double width; Press drives — Fin; Folders — 1-G/2:1 Double, 1-G/2:1 Single; Pasters — 8-Automatic Pasters; Press control system — Fin; Press registration system — G/Pin System. MAILROOM: Counter stackers — 4-Id/660, 2-QWI/350; Inserters and stuffers — 2-Mc, 2-SLS/1000A 12:1; Bundle tyer — 3-MLN/2AHS, 3-Sterling; Wrapping singles — 2-QWI, 2-QWI/Bottom Wrapper; Addressing machine — Dm/Hand Held; Mailroom control system — N/Controllers. COMMUNICATIONS: Systems used — satellite. WIRE SERVICES: News — AP; Photos — AP; Stock tables — AP; Receiving dishes — size-10ft, AP. BUSINESS COMPUTERS: IBM/AS-400 F20; Applications: Gen ledger, Accts payable, Accts receivable, Pub relations, Circ; PCs & micros networked; PCs & main system networked.

MOUNT PLEASANT-ALMA
Isabella County
Gratiot County
'90 U.S. Census- 32,819 (Mount Pleasant 23,785; Alma 9,034); E&P '96 Est. 33,555 (Mount Pleasant 24,272; Alma 9,283)
ABC-NDM (90): 82,862 (HH 27,544)

Morning Sun (m-mon to fri; S)

Morning Sun, 215 N. Main; PO Box 447, Mount Pleasant, MI 48804-0447; tel (517) 772-2971; fax (517) 773-0382/772-2971 ext. 222. Brill Media group.
Circulation: 10,595(m); 12,118(S); ABC Sept. 30, 1995.
Price: 50¢(d); $1.25(S); $2.35/wk; $10.18/mo; $122.20/yr.
Advertising: Open inch rate $11.39(m); $11.39(S). **Representative:** Landon Associates Inc.
News Service: AP. **Politics:** Independent. **Established:** 1864.
Not Published: New Year; Memorial Day; Independence Day; Labor Day; Christmas.
Special Editions: Home Show Edition (Mar); Highland Festival Edition (May); Car Care, Yard & Garden, Basketball Tab, All Scholastic/Graduation (Spring); Central Mich. Univ. Welcome Back edition, Football Preview, Progress, Bridal Tab, Car Care, Yard & Garden, Basketball Tab (Fall).
Magazines: TV Book; USA Weekend; CM Business.
Broadcast Affiliates: WEBC-AM/WAVC-FM Duluth, MN; KQWB-AM/FM Moorhead, MN; KLIK-AM/KTXY-FM Jefferson City, MO; KQWB-AM/FM Fargo, ND; WIOV-FM Ephrata, PA; KUAD-FM Windsor, PA; WEBC-AM/WAVC-FM Superior, WI; WBKR-AM/FM Owensboro, KY; WOMI-AM/FM Owensboro, KY.

CORPORATE OFFICER
President — B Ray Pike
GENERAL MANAGEMENT
Publisher — B Ray Pike
Director-Sales/Marketing — Paul Hess
ADVERTISING
Manager-Sales (Alma) — Jo Ann Jacobs
Manager-Classified — Nancy Shackelford
CIRCULATION
Director — Larry Fisher

Michigan I-207

NEWS EXECUTIVES

Editor — Rick Mills
Managing Editor (Alma) — John Ashe

EDITORS AND MANAGERS

Editorial Page Editor — Rick Mills
Librarian — Karen Leuder
News Editor (Mt Pleasant) — Steve Coon
Photo Editor (Mt Pleasant) — Rodney Brazee
Sports — Lee Thompson
Sunday Editor — Mindy Norton

PRODUCTION

Manager-Composing — Cindy McClain
Manager-Pressroom — Gary Ray

Market Information: Zoned editions; TMC; ADS.
Mechanical available: Offset; Black and 3 ROP colors; insert accepted — preprinted; page cut-offs — 22¾".
Mechanical specifications: Type page 13" x 21½"; E - 6 cols, 2 1/16", ⅛" between; A - 6 cols, 2 1/16", ⅛" between; C - 8 cols, 1½", ⅛" between.
Commodity consumption: Newsprint 525 short tons; widths 27½", 13¾"; black ink 7,827 pounds; color ink 710 pounds; single pages printed 5,562; average pages per issue 18(d), 50(S); single plates used 3,454.
Equipment: EDITORIAL: Front-end software — Newscraft/Editorial System; Printers — HP/4P. CLASSIFIED: Front-end hardware — 2-Ultra/486-33 fileserver; Front-end software — NewsCraft/Classified; Printers — 1-Epson/DFX-8000. DISPLAY: Front-end hardware — 1-Ap/Mac Workgroup Server 95, 1-Ap/Mac 7100-80, 1-Ap/Mac Quadra 605, 1-Ap/Mac Quadra 610, 3-Ap/Mac Quadra 650, 2-Ap/Mac Quadra 950, 1-Ap/Mac 8100-100; Front-end software — QuarkXPress 3.1, Adobe/Photoshop 2.5, Adobe/Photoshop 3.0, Adobe/Illustrator 5.5; Printers — 2-HP/4V, 1-NewGen/Imager Plus 12, 1-LaserMaster/Unity 1200XL, 1-AG/Accuset 1000. PRODUCTION: Pagination software — Mk/Ad Director 1.5; OCR software — Caere/OmniPage 2.1, AG/Accuset 1000; Typesetters — 3-M/202 CRT, 1-M/101 Laser, 1-LaserMaster/Unity 1200 XLT; Platemaking systems — 1-Douthitt/Magic 83; Plate exposures — 1-Nu/Flip Top FT40V6UP; Plate processors — 1-W; Electronic picture desk — 1-Ap/Mac Centris 610; Scanners — 1-AG/Arcus Plus, 1-Microtek/Scanmaker IIXE; Production cameras — 1-B/4000, 1-N/VIC-1418, 1-TogeeMD/480, 1-Acti/253; Automatic film processors — 1-Fuji/FG660, 1-P/26RA.
PRESSROOM: Line 1 — 12-G/Community (2 Path finder color decks). MAILROOM: Counter stackers — 2-BG; Inserters and stuffers — 1-MM; Bundle tyer — 6-Bu; Addressing machine — 1-Wa. COMMUNICATIONS: Facsimile — 1-Sharp/FO5300, 1-Sharp/3450T, 1-Sharp/FO300. WIRE SERVICES: News — AP; Receiving dishes — size-2ft, AP. BUSINESS COMPUTERS: 2-Ultra/486-33 File Server; Applications: Accts receivable, Accts payable, Payroll, Gen ledger, Circ; PCs & micros networked; PCs & main system networked.

MUSKEGON

Muskegon County

'90 U.S. Census- 40,283; E&P '96 Est. 39,825
ABC-CZ (90): 94,219 (HH 35,392)

The Muskegon Chronicle

(e-mon to fri; m-sat; S)

The Muskegon Chronicle, 981 Third St.; PO Box 59, Muskegon, MI 49443-0059; tel (616) 722-3161; fax (616) 728-3330; e-mail muskegon@novagate.com; web site http://www.cic.net/~glew. Advance Publications (Booth Newspapers) group.
Circulation: 47,942(e); 47,942(m-sat); 52,282(S); ABC Sept. 30, 1995.
Price: 50¢(d); 50¢(sat); $1.25(S); $12.50/mo (out of state), $10.00/mo (carrier), $10.50/mo (motor route).
Advertising: Open inch rate $25.15(e); $25.15(m-sat); $27.98(S). **Representative:** Newhouse Newspapers/Metro Suburbia.
News Services: AP, NNS. **Politics:** Independent. **Established:** 1857.
Advertising not accepted: NC-17 and X-rated movies.
Special Editions: Living Here, Brides (Feb); Car Care, Health Care, Muskegon Works (Mar); Home Improvement (Apr); Yard-n-Garden (May); Summer Along the Lake, Wheel & Keel (June); Summer Celebration, Retirement, Air Show (Aug); Back-to-School, Fall Fashion, Football (Sept); Home Improvement (Oct); New Car, Fall Car Care, Winter Sports (Nov).
Special Weekly Sections: Best Food Day (mon); Wheels (wed); Venture Outdoors (thur); Church Pages (fri); Kids Pages, What's On TV (sat); Venture Outdoors, Stock Market, Travel and Resorts, Your Home (S).
Magazines: What's On TV (newsprint) (sat); Color Comics (S); Parade (wknd).

GENERAL MANAGEMENT

Publisher — Gary W Ostrom
Controller — Kimberly A Ahrens

ADVERTISING

Director — Kevin M Newton
Manager-Sales — David Kennedy
Supervisor-National — Michele Faust

CIRCULATION

Director — Jay W Wallace

NEWS EXECUTIVE

Editor — Gunnar Carlson

EDITORS AND MANAGERS

Business/Finance Editor — Dave Alexander
City Editor — Jerry Morlock
Editorial Page Editor — David Kolb
Feature Editor — Linda Odette
Librarian — Linda Thompson
Asst News Editor — Stan Harrison
Photo Editor — Greg Dorsett
Sports Editor — Cindy Fairfield

PRODUCTION

Manager — Dale Swartz
Superintendent-Mailroom — Ron Shaw

Market Information: Zoned editions; Split Run; TMC.
Mechanical available: Letterpress; Black and 3 ROP colors; insert accepted — preprinted; page cut-offs — 23 9/16".
Mechanical specifications: Type page 13" x 22"; E - 6 cols, 2 1/16", ⅛" between; A - 6 cols, 2 1/16", ⅛" between; C - 10 cols, 1¼", 1/16" between.
Commodity consumption: Newsprint 4,601 short tons; widths 55", 41¼", 27½"; black ink 115,000 pounds; color ink 11,500 pounds; single pages printed 14,536; average pages per issue 35(d), 68(S); single plates used 30,500.
Equipment: EDITORIAL: Front-end hardware — DEC/PDP 11-34, 4.0-AT/J-11; Front-end software — AT 4.0; Printers — 1-Fujitsu/DL5600; Other equipment — 1-AT/Soft Typsetter, 1-Ap/Mac IIsi. CLASSIFIED: Front-end hardware — DEC/PDP 11-34, AT/J-11; Front-end software — AT 4.0; Printers — 1-Fujitsu/DL5600; Other equipment — Sharp/FO551 Fax. DISPLAY: Adv layout systems — 4-Sun/Breeze 360; Front-end hardware — 4-Sun/Breeze V-AT; Front-end software — Cx 7.0; PRODUCTION: Pagination software — QPS 3.3; Typesetters — 2-AU/APS-5, 2-Ultre/94E; Platemaking systems — Na; Plate exposures — 2-Na/Starlite; Plate processors — 1-Na, 1-C/70; Electronic picture desk — 3-Lf/AP Leaf Picture Desk; Scanners — ECR/Autokon 1000, Umax/Flatbed, Lf/Leafscan 35; Production cameras — 1-C/Spartan III, 1-C/Pager II; Automatic film processors — 1-P/20x24, 1-LE/20x24, 1-P/Super G 1.5; Color separation equipment (conventional) — Ap/Mac, Adobe/Photoshop.
PRESSROOM: Line 1 — 4-G/Headliner (2 humps; 1 deck); Folders — 2-G; Pasters — G/3-arm reels; Press control system — GE; Press registration system — WebTech. MAILROOM: Counter stackers — 1-HL/Monitor, 1-HL/HT, 1-HL/HT, 1-HL/Dual Corrior; Inserters and stuffers — 1-GMA/SLS 1000; Bundle tyer — 1-MLN/Strapper, 1-MLN/Strapper, 1-Dynaric/NP2; Wrapping singles — 1-Bu/String Tyer, 1-Bu/String Tyer; Addressing machine — 1-Ch. LIBRARY: Electronic — Phrasea. COMMUNICATIONS: Digital ad delivery system — AP AdSend. WIRE SERVICES: News — AP, NNS, LAT-WP, NEA, Booth News Service; Photos — AP, NNS; Stock tables — AP Stocks; Receiving dishes — AP. BUSINESS COMPUTERS: 2-TI/990; Applications: Billing, Accts payable, Gen ledger, Payroll, Financial statements; PCs & micros networked; PCs & main system networked.

NILES

Berrien County

'90 U.S. Census- 12,458; E&P '96 Est. 11,922

Niles Daily Star (e-mon to sat)

Niles Daily Star, 217 N. 4th St., Niles, MI 49120; tel (616) 683-2100; fax (616) 683-2175. Boone Newspapers Inc. group.
Circulation: 3,428(e); 3,428(e-sat); Sworn Sept. 30, 1995.
Price: 50¢(d); 50¢(sat); $5.50/mo (carrier), $9.00/mo (mail); $78.00/yr (carrier), $102.00/yr (mail).
Advertising: Open inch rate $9.00(e); $9.00(e-sat). **Politics:** Independent. **Established:** 1886.
Not Published: New Year; Memorial Day; Independence Day; Labor Day; Christmas.
Magazine: F.Y.I. (June).

CORPORATE OFFICERS

President — Jim Boone
Vice Pres — Thomas J Rattenbury

GENERAL MANAGEMENT

Publisher/General Manager — Thomas J Rattenbury

ADVERTISING

Manager-Classified — Hal Shue
Manager — Jim Stevenson

CIRCULATION

Director — Tim Brummer

NEWS EXECUTIVES

Editor — Thomas J Rattenbury
Managing Editor — Jan Griffey

EDITORS AND MANAGERS

News Editor — Jan Griffey
Sports Editor — Joe Howley

PRODUCTION

Foreman-Composing — Sonja Green
Foreman-Pressroom — Allan Tatum

Market Information: TMC.
Mechanical available: Offset; Black and 3 ROP colors; insert accepted — preprinted, all; page cut-offs — 22⅝".
Mechanical specifications: Type page 13¼" x 21½"; E - 8 cols, 1½", ⅙" between; A - 8 cols, 1½", ⅙" between; C - 8 cols, 1½", ⅙" between.
Commodity consumption: Newsprint 1,040 short tons; widths 30", 28", 15", 14"; black ink 22,800 pounds; color ink 4,100 pounds; average pages per issue 29(d); single plates used 7,200.
Equipment: EDITORIAL: Front-end hardware — 12-Ap/Mac. CLASSIFIED: Front-end hardware — COM/Intrepid II, 3-Ap/Mac IIsi. DISPLAY: Adv layout systems — 4-Ap/Mac II. PRODUCTION: OCR software — Caere/OmniPage; Typesetters — Ap/Mac LaserWriter II NTX Plus; Platemaking systems — 1-3M/Pyrofax; Plate exposures — 1-3M/Pyrofax; Plate processors — 1-3M/Pyrofax; Scanners — Ap/Mac Scanner; Production cameras — 1-R.
PRESSROOM: Line 1 — 5-HI/V-22; Folders — 2-HI. MAILROOM: Counter stackers — 1-BG/Count-O-Veyor 108; Inserters and stuffers — MM/3 Station; Bundle tyer — 3-Bu, 1-Sa, 1-MLN; Addressing machine — Dispensa-Matic. WIRE SERVICES: News — Syndicates — United Features, NEA. BUSINESS COMPUTERS: 1-IBM/5364-PC Sys 36, 2-IBM/5150, 2-RSK/1000TL2; Applications: Circ and all bus, TMC; PCs & micros networked; PCs & main system networked.

OWOSSO

Shiawassee County

'90 U.S. Census- 16,322; E&P '96 Est. 16,209

The Argus-Press

(e-mon to fri; m-sat; S)

The Argus-Press, 201 E. Exchange St.; PO Box 399, Owosso, MI 48867; tel (517) 725-5136; fax (517) 725-6376.
Circulation: 11,842(e); 11,842(m-sat); 11,842(S); Sworn Oct. 1, 1994.
Price: 50¢(d); 50¢(sat); 75¢(S); $8.25/mo (carrier), $11.00/mo (MI, mail); $85.00/yr (carrier), $110.00/yr (MI, mail).
Advertising: Open inch rate $10.40(e); $10.40(m-sat); $10.40(S); $12.40 (TMC). **Representative:** Papert Companies.
News Services: AP, AP Graphics Net. **Politics:** Independent. **Established:** 1854.
Not Published: New Year; Memorial Day; Independence Day; Labor Day; Thanksgiving; Christmas.
Advertising not accepted: Mail order.
Special Editions: Bridal; Building-Home Repair; Christmas Opening; Shiawassa Area Football Guide; Christmas Gift Guide; County Fair; Curwood; Energy Conservation; Fall Car Care; Gardening & Lawn Care; Soil Conservation; Spring Fashion; New Car & Truck; Year End.
Special Weekly Section: Entertainment Showcase (US Express from Tribune Media) (wed).
Magazines: Color Comics; USA Weekend; TV Update.

CORPORATE OFFICERS

President/Treasurer — Richard E Campbell
Vice Pres/Secretary — Thomas E Campbell

GENERAL MANAGEMENT

Publisher — Richard E Campbell
General Manager — Thomas E Campbell

ADVERTISING

Director — Thomas E Jacobs
Manager-National — Thomas E Jacobs

MARKETING AND PROMOTION

Director-Marketing/Promotion — Peter J Hinds

CIRCULATION

Manager — G Mark Ludington

NEWS EXECUTIVES

Editor — Richard E Campbell
Managing Editor — Joseph Peacock

EDITORS AND MANAGERS

Business/Finance Editor — Richard E Campbell
City/Metro Editor — Joseph Peacock
Editorial Page Editor — Richard E Campbell
Entertainment/Amusements Editor — Joseph Peacock
Environmental Editor — Richard E Campbell
Farm/Agriculture Editor — Robert J Grank
Fashion/Style Editor — Helen Granger
Features Editor — Richard E Campbell
Films/Theater Editor — Joseph Peacock
Health/Medical Editor — Joseph Peacock
Living/Lifestyle Editor — Helen Granger
National Editor — Richard E Campbell
News Editor — Helene Bough
Photo Editor — Richard E Campbell
Political/Government Editor — Richard E Campbell
Radio/Television Editor — Joseph Peacock
Sports Editor — Gary Webster
Travel Editor — Joseph Peacock
Women's Editor — Helen Granger

PRODUCTION

Manager — Bernard Hanson

Market Information: TMC.
Mechanical available: Offset; Black and 3 ROP colors; insert accepted — preprinted, subject to approval; page cut-offs — 21½".
Mechanical specifications: Type page 13" x 21½"; E - 6 cols, 2 1/16", ⅛" between; A - 6 cols, 2 1/16", ⅛" between; C - 9 cols, 1⅜", 1/16" between.
Commodity consumption: Newsprint 600 short tons; widths 27½", 13¾"; black ink 20,000 pounds; color ink 5,500 pounds; single pages printed 7,800; average pages per issue 16(d), 16(sat), 32(S); single plates used 8,000.
Equipment: EDITORIAL: Front-end hardware — Mk/3000; Front-end software — Mk/Page 1.1.1; Printers — 2-XIT/Clipper; Other equipment — Lf/AP Leaf Picture Desk, Lf/Leafscan 35. CLASSIFIED: Front-end hardware — Mk/3000; Front-end software — Mk/Page 1.1.1; PRODUCTION: Pagination software — Mk/Page 1.1.1; Typesetters — 2-XIT/Clipper Laserprinter; Plate exposures — Nu/Flip Top; Production cameras — DSA; Automatic film processors — LE/LD-2600.
PRESSROOM: Line 1 — 5-G/Urbanite. MAILROOM: Inserters and stuffers — 7-KAN/480; Bundle tyer — EAM/Mosca; Addressing machine — Ch. COMMUNICATIONS: Digital ad delivery system — AP AdSend. WIRE SERVICES: News — AP; Photos — AP; Syndicates — King Features, NEA; Receiving dishes — AP. BUSINESS COMPUTERS: 2-RSK/Tandy 4016; Applications: One Write/Plus.

PETOSKEY

Emmet County

'90 U.S. Census- 6,056; E&P '96 Est. 6,021
ABC-NDM (90): 46,508 (HH 17,759)

Petoskey News-Review

(e-mon to fri)

Petoskey News-Review, 319 State St.; PO Box 528, Petoskey, MI 49770-0528; tel (616) 347-2544; fax (616) 347-6833.
Circulation: 11,704(e); ABC Sept. 30, 1995.
Price: 50¢(d); $2.15/wk (carrier); $12.80/mo (mail).
Advertising: Open inch rate $23.12(e). **Representatives:** American Newspaper Representatives Inc.; US Suburban Press.
News Service: AP. **Politics:** Independent. **Established:** 1875.
Not Published: New Year; Memorial Day; Independence Day; Labor Day; Thanksgiving; Christmas.
Advertising not accepted: X-rated movies and materials.
Special Editions: Estate Planning and Investment Tab, Medical Tab (Jan); Basketball

Tab, Graphic Plus (Tourist Publication) (Mar); Boating Tab, Petoskey Home Show Tab, Spring Car Care Tab, Boating Tab, Business Profiles Tab (Apr); Boating Tab, Spring Fashion, Visitor's Guide, The Graphic Summer Tab (May); Summer Visitor's Guide, The Graphic Summer Tab (July); Football, Back-to-School Tab, Summer Visitor's Guide, The Graphic Summer Tab (Aug); National Home, Kitchen & Bath Week, Fall Color Tours, Visitor's Guide, The Graphic Fall Tab (Sept); Business Expo, Fall Color Tours, Visitor's Guide, The Graphic Fall Tab (Oct); Pre-Christmas Visitor's Guide (Nov); The Graphic Winter Tab, Christmas Tab (Dec); Homes (monthly).

Magazines: Car, Food Pages (mon); Health Page (tues); Outdoor Page (wed); Religion (thur); Entertainment, Real Estate Market, Dining (fri).

CORPORATE OFFICERS

President Kirk Schaller
Vice Pres Ken Winter
Secretary John Schaller

GENERAL MANAGEMENT

Publisher Kirk Schaller
General Manager Ken Winter

ADVERTISING

Manager-Classified Shirley Gibson
Manager-Retail Tari Calouette

CIRCULATION

Manager Carl Redder
Manager-Promotion Ken Winter

NEWS EXECUTIVES

Editor Ken Winter
Managing Editor Ken Stanley

EDITORS AND MANAGERS

Editorial Page Editor Ken Winter
Films/Theater Editor Ken Stanley
Family/Food Editor Babette Stenuis
Librarian Shirley Prall
Music Editor Ken Stanley
People Editor Babette Stenuis
Religion Editor Shirley Prall
Sports Editor Jerry Rosevear
Wire Editor Jim Heil

PRODUCTION

Coordinator Dennis Collins

Market Information: TMC.

Mechanical available: Offset; Black and 3 ROP colors; insert accepted — preprinted, one page flyers, catalog size; page cut-offs — 22¾".

Mechanical specifications: Type page 13" x 21½"; E - 6 cols, 2¹⁄₁₆", ⅛" between; A - 6 cols, 2¹⁄₁₆", ⅛" between; C - 6 cols, 2¹⁄₁₆", ⅛" between.

Commodity consumption: Newsprint 825 short tons; width 28"; black ink 18,000 pounds; color ink 1,000 pounds; single pages printed 6,670; average pages per issue 26(d); single plates used 4,568.

Equipment: EDITORIAL: Front-end hardware — Ap/Mac; Front-end software — QuarkXPress, Baseview/NewsEdit; Printers — Ap/Mac II NTX. CLASSIFIED: Front-end hardware — PC; Front-end software — Baseview/ClassFlow; Printers — Ap/Mac LaserWriter Pro. DISPLAY: Front-end hardware — Ap/Mac; Front-end software — QuarkXPress; Printers — Ap/Mac LaserWriter Pro 810. PRODUCTION: Typesetters — 2-COM/8600; Plate exposures — 2-Nu/Flip-Top; Plate processors — Nat/A250; Production cameras — R/500 OH, Danagraph/Vertical; Automatic film processors — LE/LD24BQ. PRESSROOM: Line 1 — 9-G/Community; Folders — 1-G/SC. MAILROOM: Counter stackers — BG/105; Bundle tyer — 3-Bu. WIRE SERVICES: News — AP; Receiving dishes — size-8ft, AP. BUSINESS COMPUTERS: IBM/Risc 6000; Applications: PBS: Circ, Adv billing.

PONTIAC

Oakland County

'90 U.S. Census- 71,166; E&P '96 Est. 66,743
ABC-NDM (90): 523,775 (HH 188,761)

The Oakland Press (m-mon to sat; S)

The Oakland Press, 48 W. Huron St.; PO Box 436009, Pontiac, MI 48342; tel (810) 332-8181; fax (810) 332-0830; e-mail presslink@aol.com. Capital Cities/ABC Inc. group.

Circulation: 79,623(m); 79,623(m-sat); 91,675(S); ABC Sept. 30, 1995.

Price: 25¢(d); 25¢(sat); $1.25(S); $2.30/wk; $119.60/yr.

Advertising: Open inch rate $47.77(m); $47.77(m-sat); $53.50(S). **Representative:** Sawyer-Ferguson-Walker Co.

News Services: AP, LAT-WP, UPI, SHNS. **Politics:** Independent. **Established:** 1843.

Advertising not accepted: Telephone solicitation from home; vending machine investment; matrimonial offers; palmistry; fortune telling; merchandise for sale from hotel room or rooming house; massage parlors.

Special Editions: International Auto Show, Senior Living, Camper, Travel & RV, Novi Home & Garden (Jan); Bridal Showcase, Boat, Sport & Fishing Show, Cardiac Care Update, Michigan Home & Garden (Feb); Spring Home & Garden/Cobo, Religious Directory, Menu & Entertainment Guide, Oakland in Progress (Mar); Home Improvement, American Home Week #1, Good Health, American Home Week #2 (Apr); Mother's Day Tribute, Fun in the Sun (May); Father's Day Tribute, Menu & Entertainment Guide (June); Senior Living (July); Good Health, 1996 Auto & Truck Grand Finale, Local Business (Aug); Prep, College, Pro Football, Arts & Apple Festival, Fall Home & Garden, Menu & Entertainment Guide, Novi Home Remodeling Show (Sept); Home Improvement, College Guide, Breast Cancer Awareness Update, Bridal Showcase, '97 Automotive Intro, Credit Union Week (Oct); Designing Kids, Diabetes Awareness, Menu & Entertainment Guide, Trucks '97, Religious Directory, Home for the Holidays/Gift Guide (Nov); Annual Holiday Gift Guide, Christmas Songbook (Dec).

Special Weekly Sections: Food (mon); Science & Health (tues); Seniors (wed); Fashion, Check It Out, Wheels (thur); Religion, Marquee Entertainment Tab (fri); Real Estate, Building, Expanded Business/Stock Market, Entertainment, Travel, Metro TV Week (S).

CORPORATE OFFICER

President Dale Duncan

GENERAL MANAGEMENT

Publisher Dale Duncan
Vice Pres-Finance/Production Jack Federspiel
Accounting Manager Sandra Kleven
Manager-Credit Mike Catherincchia

ADVERTISING

Director Alfred Derusha
Manager-Major Accounts Elsie Purtill
Manager-Retail Kerry Davis

MARKETING AND PROMOTION

Director-Marketing Melvin Siler
Manager-Market Development Joseph C Kent

TELECOMMUNICATIONS

Audiotex Manager Joseph C Kent

CIRCULATION

Director Ronald Wood
Manager Floyd Hamilton
Manager-Sales Norrell Nelson
Manager-Distribution Roger Burdette

NEWS EXECUTIVES

Exec Editor William O Thomas Jr
Senior Editor John Cusumano
Editor Neil J Munro
Managing Editor Garry Gilbert
Asst Managing Editor Susan Hood
Asst Managing Editor Roger Wingelaar

EDITORS AND MANAGERS

Automotive Editor Joseph Szczesny
Business Editor Steve Spalding
Entertainment Editor Marylynn Hewitt
Fashion/Food Editor Sybil Little
Features Editor Dan Grantham
News Editor Ken Jones
Chief Photographer Edward R Noble
Photo Editor Edward R Noble
Radio/Television Editor Deb Andersen
Sports Editor Keith Langlois
Travel Editor Dolly Moiseeff

MANAGEMENT INFORMATION SERVICES

Data Processing Manager Len Cote

PRODUCTION

Manager-Engraving Marla Albion
Foreman-Composing Bruce Burmeister
Superintendent-Pressroom Mark Hall
Superintendent-Mailroom Brendan O'Shea
Supervisor-Building Service Roger John

Market Information: Zoned editions; Split Run; TMC; ADS; Operate audiotex.

Mechanical available: Headliner Offset; Black and 3 ROP colors; insert accepted — preprinted, 7 hm books; page cut-offs — 22¼".

Mechanical specifications: Type page 13¼" x 21"; E - 6 cols, 1¾", ⅛" between; A - 6 cols, 1¾"; C - 10 cols, 1³⁄₁₆", ⅛" between.

Commodity consumption: Newsprint 8,944 short tons; 8,114 metric tons; widths 54¾", 41³⁄₁₆", 27⅜"; black ink 180,021 pounds; color ink 46,879 pounds; single pages printed 17,134; average pages per issue 40(d), 100(S); single plates used 62,450.

Equipment: EDITORIAL: Front-end hardware — 2-Ap/Mac 9500, Main/Back-up Server; Front-end software — Baseview/Client Server 2.0; Printers — 10-HP/Deskwriters; Other equipment — 1-Ap/Mac 950 w/Wire Manager, 1-Ap/Mac 950 Library-E-mail. CLASSIFIED: Front-end hardware — Pentium PC/100, 2-Main/Back-up Server; Front-end software — Dewar 6.9.8; Other equipment — 1-Pentium PC/90, 3-PC/386 D10. AUDIOTEX: Hardware — DX2 66; Software — Microvoice; Supplier name — Microvoice. DISPLAY: Adv layout systems — Mk/Managing Editor; Front-end hardware — IBM/590-RISC6000, Ap/Mac II VX, Radius/ZOE Monitor; Front-end software — ALS 2.0; Printers — 1-Ap/Mac II NTX. PRODUCTION: Pagination software — QuarkXPress, Color Central; Typesetters — 2-ECR/3850, 3-XIT/Clipper Plain Paper 11x17; Platemaking systems — WL; Plate exposures — WL; Plate processors — WL; Electronic picture desk — 2-Lf/AP Leaf Picture Desk, 1-MacLan/Leafdesk; Scanners — CD, ECR/Autokon, Kk/2035; Production cameras — C/Spartan III; Automatic film processors — 2-Kk/324; Reproportion units — ECR/Autokon; Film transporters — 1-C/Spartan III; Color separation equipment (conventional) — 1-AG/TCS 1000. PRESSROOM: Line 1 — 7-G/Headliner Offset double width; Line 2 — 7-G/Community single width; Press drives — Allen Bradley; Folders — 1-G/Community 3:2, 1-G/Community SC. MAILROOM: Counter stackers — 3-QWI/300, 1-Id/2000, 2-Id/Marathoner; Inserters and stuffers — 1-GMA/1372, 1-Amerigraph/NP-650, 22-Hopper; Bundle tyer — 3-MLN/MLN-2. LIBRARY: Electronic — 1-Sonar; Combination — 1-Electronic/Library, 1-Minolta/Microfilm & Index. COMMUNICATIONS: Digital ad delivery system — AP AdSend. Systems used — satellite. WIRE SERVICES: News — AP Datafeatures, AP Datastream, UPI, National Weather Service, Horse Race Results, Remote Terminals, TMS TV Grids; Photos — AP; Stock tables — TMS; Syndicates — LAT-WP, SHNS; Receiving dishes — size-10ft, AP, UPI. BUSINESS COMPUTERS: IBM/560 RISC 6000, 1-IBM/590 RISC 6000; Applications: PBS/MediaPlus: Spreadsheet, Circ; Word Processing: Transient billing, Payroll, Payables, Order entry, Polling, Gen ledger; PBS: Adv mgmt; SBS: Accounting; PCs & micros networked; PCs & main system networked.

PORT HURON

St. Clair County

'90 U.S. Census- 33,694; E&P '96 Est. 33,449
ABC-CZ (90): 145,607 (HH 52,882)

Times Herald (e-mon to sat; S)

Times Herald, 911 Military St.; PO Box 5009, Port Huron, MI 48061-5009; tel (810) 985-7171. Gannett Co. Inc. group.

Circulation: 31,602(e); 31,602(e-sat); 41,291(S); ABC Sept. 30, 1995.

Price: 35¢(d); 35¢(sat); $1.50(S); $3.00/wk, $3.20/wk (motor route); $12.00/mo, $12.20/mo (motor route); $156.00/yr, $156.20/yr (motor route).

Advertising: Open inch rate $34.70(e); $34.70(e-sat); $41.40(S). **Representative:** Gannett National Newspaper Sales.

News Services: AP, GNS. **Politics:** Independent. **Established:** 1910.

Special Editions: Health Matters, Bridal (Jan); Outlook (Feb); Home & Builder (Mar); Health Matters, Yard & Garden (Apr); Car Care, Graduation (May); Bridal, Festivals-Tourist (June); Mackinac Event, Health Matters (July); Back-to-School, Football, Gus Macker (Aug); Home & Builder, Health Matters, Car Care (Oct); Answer Book, Main Street, Christmas, Holiday (Nov).

Special Weekly Sections: Express (mon); Living (tues); Outbound (wed); Applause (thur); Religion (S).

Magazines: TV Book (S); USA Weekend.

CORPORATE OFFICERS

President William V Monopoli
Controller Geraldine Adolph

GENERAL MANAGEMENT

Publisher William V Monopoli
Director-Human Resources Cynthia Kovac

ADVERTISING

Director Tim Dowd
Manager-Retail Lori Driscoll
Manager-Classified Robert McFarlane

MARKETING AND PROMOTION

Director-Market Development Sandra Jones

CIRCULATION

Director Lee Warmouth

NEWS EXECUTIVES

Exec Editor Mike Connell
Asst Managing Editor Judith McLean
Asst Managing Editor Garth Kriewall

EDITORS AND MANAGERS

Business Reporter Jeff Karoub
Editorial Page Editor Tom Walker
Features Editor Jill Carlson
Graphics Editor Wes Booher
Librarian Allison Arnold
Photo Department Manager Ralph W Polovich
Religion Editor James Ketchum
Sports Editor Jim Whymer

MANAGEMENT INFORMATION SERVICES

Data Processing Manager Jane Biscorner

PRODUCTION

Director-Operations Pete Zanmiller
Manager-Camera/Plate Don Muir
Manager-Pressroom Tom Bucholtz
Manager-Mailroom Ron Armstrong
Manager-Systems John Loxton

Market Information: Split Run; TMC.

Mechanical available: Offset; Black and 3 ROP colors; insert accepted — preprinted; page cut-offs — 22¾".

Mechanical specifications: Type page 13⅛" x 21½"; E - 6 cols, 2¹⁄₁₆", ⅛" between; A - 6 cols, 2¹⁄₁₆", ⅛" between; C - 9 cols, 1⅜", ¹⁄₁₆" between.

Commodity consumption: Newsprint 2,417 short tons; widths 27¼", 13⅝"; black ink 45,164 pounds; color ink 15,136 pounds; single pages printed 11,099; average pages per issue 25(d), 67(S); single plates used 41,119.

Equipment: EDITORIAL: Front-end hardware — Dewar/Edit 55, SIA; Front-end software — Dewar/System IV, Dewar/System II; Other equipment — Ap/Mac. CLASSIFIED: Front-end hardware — SIA; Front-end software — Dewar/System IV. DISPLAY: Adv layout systems — 4-Dewar/Discovery; Other equipment — Dewar/Edit 55. PRODUCTION: OCR software — Caere/OmniPage Professional; Typesetters — 1-V/5500, 1-V/5510; Plate exposures — 2-Nu/Flip Top 36x48; Plate processors — 2-Nat/A250, 1-DP; Electronic picture desk — 2-Ap/Mac, Lf/AP Leaf Picture Desk; Scanners — Lf/Leafscan 35, Nikon/Coolscan, Microtek/ScanMaker IIXE; Production cameras — 1-C/Spartan III; Automatic film processors — 1-LE, 1-LE/Excel 26; Film transporters — 2-C. PRESSROOM: Line 1 — 15-G/Urbanite; Folders — 2-G, 1-G/Quarter on-line; Pasters — 8-G/RTP. MAILROOM: Counter stackers — 2-QWI/300, 1-QWI/1000, 1-Fg; Inserters and stuffers — 1-GMA/1000; Bundle tyer — 2-MLN/MLN2A, 2-MLN/Spirit; Addressing machine — 2-Ch, 1-Barstrom/on-line 1up labeller. WIRE SERVICES: News — AP; Syndicates — GNS; Receiving dishes — AP, AMS. BUSINESS COMPUTERS: IBM/AS-400; Applications: Payroll, Circ, Billing, Complete business functions; PCs & micros networked; PCs & main system networked.

ROYAL OAK

Oakland County

'90 U.S. Census- 65,410; E&P '96 Est. 61,063
ABC-CZ (90): 65,410 (HH 28,344)

The Daily Tribune (e-mon to fri; S)

The Daily Tribune, 210 E. Third St., Royal Oak, MI 48067; tel (810) 541-3000; fax (810) 541-7041. Independent Newspapers Inc. (MI) group.

Circulation: 23,661(e); 25,909(S); ABC Sept. 30, 1995.

Price: 50¢(d); $1.00(S); $2.00/wk (carrier); $104.00/yr (carrier).

Advertising: Open inch rate $38.85(e); $38.85(S). **Representative:** Papert Companies.

News Service: AP. **Politics:** Independent. **Established:** 1902.

Special Editions: Auto Show, Brides & Grooms (Jan); Progress (Feb); Spring Home Improvement (Mar); Golf, All Sports, Home Improvement (Apr); To Mom with Love, Home

Improvement (May); All Sports (Aug); Fall Home Improvement (2) (Sept); New Car Preview, Home Interior (Oct); Cook Book, To your Health, Holiday Gifting (Nov); Holiday Magic, Letters to Santa, Christmas Countdown, Christmas Wrap-Up, Student Ad-Craft (Dec).

Special Weekly Sections: Business (mon); Schools, Fashion (tues); Food, Auto (wed); Building, Home Improvement (thur); Real Estate, Entertainment (fri); Food, Real Estate (S).

Magazine: TV Time (S).

CORPORATE OFFICERS

President/Chief Operating Officer J Gene Chambers
Chief Financial Officer William Wenk
Controller Ken Pranger
Director-Operations Pat Eagan
Director-Marketing/Advertising Jerry Ballenger
Director-Circulation Bill Heasley

GENERAL MANAGEMENT

Publisher Richard D Isham
General Manager Mary Vellardita

ADVERTISING

Manager Matthew J Fasang
Manager-Classified Janet Patterson

CIRCULATION

Manager Betsy Blower

NEWS EXECUTIVE

Editor Michael A Beeson

EDITORS AND MANAGERS

Business Editor Michael A Beeson
City Editor Steven Finlay
Photo Department Manager Richard Hunt
Political Editor Steven Finley
Sports Editor Jeff Kuehn

PRODUCTION

Manager-Printing Plant Pat Eagan
Asst Jackie Grzywacz
Manager-Pre Press Mike McLain
Foreman-Composing David Austin
Foreman-Pressroom Richard Dalck
Foreman-Mailroom Gary Peitzsch

Market Information: Zoned editions; TMC; ADS.

Mechanical available: Offset; Black and 3 ROP colors; insert accepted — preprinted, card stock; page cut-offs — 21½".

Mechanical specifications: Type page 13" x 21½"; E - 6 cols, 2 1/16", ⅛" between; A - 6 cols, 2 1/16", ⅛" between; C - 10 cols, 1⅜", 1/16" between.

Commodity consumption: Newsprint 6,000 short tons; 5,443 metric tons; widths 55", 41¼", 27½"; black ink 145,284 pounds; color ink 12,468 pounds; single pages printed 7,545; average pages per issue 28(d), 50(S); single plates used 51,600.

Equipment: EDITORIAL: Front-end hardware — 18-PC 486/80; Front-end software — WordPerfect 6.0; CLASSIFIED: Front-end hardware — 2-HAS/Magician. DISPLAY: Adv layout systems — SCS/Layout 8000; Front-end hardware — Ap/Mac; Front-end software — QuarkXPress 3.31; PRODUCTION: Typesetters — AU/APS 6-108S; Plate exposures — 2-Nu; Plate processors — 1-WL; Production cameras — 1-C/Marathon; Automatic film processors — 1-Kk/Kodamatic.
PRESSROOM: Line 1 — 8-G/Cosmo Offset; Pasters — Automatic Pasters; Reels and stands — 8-G. MAILROOM: Counter stackers — 1-St/251, 2-Id/440; Inserters and stuffers — 1-MC, 8-ST/PK; Bundle tyer — 2-MLN/ML2EE. WIRE SERVICES: News — AP; Photos — AP; Syndicates — NEA, King Features; Receiving dishes — size-2½, AP. BUSINESS COMPUTERS: IBM/AS 400; Applications: Accts receivable, Payroll, Gen ledger, Accts payable, Circ.

SAGINAW

Saginaw County

'90 U.S. Census- 69,512; E&P '96 Est. 63,347
ABC-CZ (90): 142,981 (HH 54,388)

The Saginaw News

(e-mon to fri; m-sat; S)

The Saginaw News, 203 S. Washington Ave., Saginaw, MI 48607-1283; tel (517) 752-7171; web site http://www.cic.net/~glew. Advance Publications (Booth Newspapers) group.

Circulation: 55,115(e); 55,115(m-sat); 64,928(S); ABC Sept. 30, 1995.

Price: 35¢(d); 35¢(sat); $1.25(S); $11.50/mo.

Advertising: Open inch rate $31.20(e); $31.20(m-sat); $36.45(S). **Representative:** Newhouse Newspapers/Metro Suburbia.

News Services: LAT-WP, NNA, AP. **Politics:** Independent. **Established:** 1859.

Special Editions: January Coupon Book, Invitation to a Wedding, Valley Magazine, Shiver on the River, Super Bowl Pages, February Coupon Book (Jan); Here's to your Health, March Coupon Book, Financial Planning (Feb); March Madness, Cookbook, Area Business Guide (Mar); April Coupon Book, Auto Spring Clearance, Golf '96, Home & Garden (Apr); May Coupon Book, Mother's Day Special, Vals & Sals, June Coupon Book, Gus Macker (May); Bavarian Festival (June); July Coupon Book, Mid-Michigan '96 Who's Who (July); August Coupon Book, Ethnic Festival Pages, Soap Box Derby, Manufactured Homes, Football '96 (Aug); Fall Arts/TV Preview, September Coupon Book, Fall Color, Auto Clearance, College Bound, Business Expo Pages, Fall Home Fix Up (Sept); October Coupon Book, New Car Preview, Fix Up Pages, Holiday Bazaar Tab, November Coupon Book (Oct); Christmas Gift Shoppe, Holiday Magazine (Nov); Christmas Gift Shoppe, December Coupon Book (Dec).

Special Weekly Sections: Food...Living, Agriculture (mon); Family...Living, The Mini Page, Sports Special (tues); At Home...Living, Business & Labor (wed); Business & Labor, Venture Outdoors, Living it Up, Weekend Activities, Entertainment Calendar (thur); Health...Living, Business & Labor, Dining & Entertainment Guide (fri); Venture Outdoors, Arts & Entertainment, Religion (sat); Travel, Wheels (Automotive), Real Estate, Business & Labor, National Coupons, Neighbors, Senior Neighbors, Mid-Michigan (S).

Magazines: TV Tab (newsprint) (sat); Color Comics, Parade (S).

GENERAL MANAGEMENT

Publisher Rex H Thatcher
Controller Faye V Hutchinson
Manager-Credit Paula Gehoski

ADVERTISING

Director Gene Bobic
Manager-Sales Charles Kretschmer
Manager-Co-op/National Terry Hauger
Manager-Classified Jeri Niederquell

MARKETING AND PROMOTION

Manager-Marketing Service Donn E Cramton

CIRCULATION

Manager James J Siers

NEWS EXECUTIVE

Editor Paul C Chaffee

EDITORS AND MANAGERS

Amusements Editor Janet I Martineau
Automotive Editor Jennifer Pruden-Pruess
Books Editor Fred Garrett
Business/Finance Editor Jennifer Pruden-Pruess
Columnist Maggie Rossiter
Editorial Page Editor John A Puravs
Education Editor Paul Rau
Environmental Editor Geri Rudolf
Farm Editor Fred Garrett
Fashion Editor Ken Tabacsko
Features Editor Ken Tabacsko
Films/Theater Editor Janet I Martineau
Food Editor Mary Foreman
Garden/Home Furnishings Editor Ken Tabacsko
Graphics Editor Stephen Massie
Health/Medical Editor Ken Tabacsko
Metro Editor Robert H Handeyside
Music Editor Janet I Martineau
News Editor Brian Hlavaty
Photo Curtis T Leece
Political Editor Mike Beyer
Radio/Television Editor Janet I Martineau
Real Estate Editor Jennifer Pruden-Pruess
Religion Editor Denise Mitchell
Science/Technology Editor Ken Tabacsko
Sports Editor James T Buckley
Teen-Age/Youth Editor Ken Tabacsko
Wire Editor Brian Hlavaty

PRODUCTION

Manager Robert White
Foreman-Pre Press Edith Sommers
Foreman-Pressroom Ken Rosendall
Foreman-Mailroom Daniel Cramer

Market Information: TMC.

Mechanical available: Letterpress (direct), other; Black and 3 ROP colors; insert accepted — preprinted; page cut-offs — 23 9/16".

Mechanical specifications: Type page 13" x 22¼"; E - 6 cols, 2 1/16", ⅛" between; A - 6 cols, 2 1/16", ⅛" between; C - 10 cols, 1.25", 1/16" between.

Commodity consumption: Newsprint 5,200 metric tons; widths 55", 41¼", 27½"; black ink 235,000 pounds; color ink 27,000 pounds; single pages printed 16,300; average pages per issue 40(d), 80(S); single plates used 26,000.

Equipment: EDITORIAL: Front-end hardware — AT/4-1134; Other equipment — 39-AT. CLASSIFIED: Front-end hardware — AT; Other equipment — QWI/1000 Telecopier, 13-AT. DISPLAY: Adv layout systems — 5-Cx/Breeze, Ap/Mac Ad Builder; Other equipment — 3-AT. PRODUCTION: Typesetters — 2-Cx/Bitsetter; Platemaking systems — Na; Plate exposures — 2-Na/Starlite; Plate processors — 1-Na/C-70; Scanners — 2-ECR/Autokon 1000; Production cameras — 1-C/Spartan II, 1-C/Newspager I; Automatic film processors — 4-LE; Film transporters — 4-LE; Digital color separation equipment — Lf/AP Leaf Picture Desk, Adobe/Photoshop, Nikon/Scanners.
PRESSROOM: Line 1 — 8-G/Mark I; Folders — 2-G. MAILROOM: Counter stackers — 4-QWI; Inserters and stuffers — 2-S/48P (1-9 head single off) (1-11 head double off); Bundle tyer — 3-Si; Addressing machine — 4-Wm. WIRE SERVICES: News — AP; Stock tables — AP; Receiving dishes — AP. BUSINESS COMPUTERS: 2-TI/990, 9-Mk/Acer; Applications: Gen ledger, Inv, Accts receivable, Accts payable, Payroll, Marketing; PCs & micros networked; PCs & main system networked.

ST. JOSEPH

See BENTON HARBOR

SAULT STE. MARIE

Chippewa County

'90 U.S. Census- 14,689; E&P '96 Est. 15,184

The Evening News

(e-mon to fri; S)

The Evening News, 109 Arlington St., Sault Ste. Marie, MI 49783; tel (906) 632-2235; fax (906) 632-1222. Hollinger International Inc. group.

Circulation: 7,085(e); 7,085(S); Sworn Sept. 30, 1994.

Price: 50¢(d); $1.00(S); $3.00/wk; $12.00/mo; $125.00/yr; $68.00/6mo.

Advertising: Open inch rate $9.70(e); $10.35(S). **Representative:** Landon Associates Inc.

News Service: AP. **Politics:** Independent. **Established:** 1879.

Not Published: New Year; Memorial Day; Independence Day; Labor Day; Thanksgiving; Christmas.

Special Editions: Progress, Bridal (Jan); Taxes (Feb); Vacation Guide, Home Repair & Garden (May); Graduation (June); Fall Sports (Aug); Christmas (Nov); Christmas (Dec).

Magazine: TV (fri).

GENERAL MANAGEMENT

Publisher Howard A Kaiser
Business Manager Valerie Rose

ADVERTISING

Manager Richard Beadle

CIRCULATION

Manager Tony Gillespie

NEWS EXECUTIVE

Editor Ken Fazzari

EDITOR AND MANAGER

Sports Editor Chris Marchand

PRODUCTION

Manager Wayne McCuaig

Market Information: TMC.

Mechanical available: Offset; Black and 3 ROP colors; insert accepted — preprinted; page cut-offs — 22¾".

Mechanical specifications: Type page 13" x 21"; E - 6 cols, 2 1/16", ⅛" between; A - 6 cols, 2 1/16", ⅛" between; C - 9 cols, 1⅜", 1/16" between.

Commodity consumption: Newsprint 600 short tons; widths 13¾", 17", 35", 27½"; black ink 24,000 pounds; color ink 500 pounds; single pages printed 5,116; average pages per issue 14(d), 32(S); single plates used 5,116.

Equipment: EDITORIAL: Front-end hardware — Ap/Mac. CLASSIFIED: Front-end hardware — PC/Designs. DISPLAY: Adv layout systems — PC/Designs; Front-end software — Ap/Mac IIsi. PRODUCTION: Typesetters — 5-COM; Platemaking systems — 1-Na; Scanners — 2-COM; Automatic film processors — 1-Na.
PRESSROOM: Line 1 — 7-HI/V-15A; Folders — HI/JF-7. MAILROOM: Bundle tyer — 2-MLN; Addressing machine — 1-Am. WIRE SERVICES: News — AP; Receiving dishes — AP. BUSINESS COMPUTERS: PC/Designs; Applications: Circ, Billing, Receivables, Payables; PCs & micros networked; PCs & main system networked.

SOUTH HAVEN

Van Buren County

'90 U.S. Census- 5,563; E&P '96 Est. 5,257

South Haven Daily Tribune

(m-mon to fri)

South Haven Daily Tribune, 950 Bailey St. #4, South Haven, MI 49090; tel (616) 637-1104; fax (616) 637-8415. Hollinger International Inc. group.

Circulation: 1,828(m); Sworn Oct. 6, 1995.

Price: 50¢(d); $8.00/mo; $79.00/yr.

Advertising: Open inch rate $6.70(m); $8.75(m-mon).

News Service: AP. **Politics:** Independent. **Established:** 1899.

Not Published: New Year; President's Day; Memorial Day; Independence Day; Labor Day; Columbus Day; Veteran's Day; Thanksgiving; Christmas.

Special Edition: Laker Tab (Apr to Aug).

Magazine: TV Tab (fri).

GENERAL MANAGEMENT

Publisher Michael Eastman

ADVERTISING

Manager-Classified Mary Deemer

NEWS EXECUTIVE

Editor Jim Pruitt

MANAGEMENT INFORMATION SERVICES

Data Processing Manager Susan Siewert

Market Information: Split Run; TMC.

Mechanical available: Offset; Black and 3 ROP colors; insert accepted — preprinted; page cut-offs — 22".

Mechanical specifications: Type page 13 13/16" x 22"; E - 6 cols, 2 1/16", ⅛" between; A - 6 cols, 2 1/16", ⅛" between; C - 8 cols, 1½", ⅛" between.

Commodity consumption: average pages per issue 8-10(d).

Equipment: EDITORIAL: Front-end hardware — 4-Ap/Mac; Front-end software — Jus-Text, Microsoft/Word; Printers — Ap/Mac Laser II. CLASSIFIED: Front-end hardware — 1-Ap/Mac; Front-end software — Ap/Mac Caliber Classified; Printers — Ap/Mac Pro 630. DISPLAY: Adv layout systems — Ap/Mac II VX, Ap/Mac LC III; Front-end hardware — Ap/Mac Pro 630; Front-end software — Multi-Ad/Creator, Aldus/PageMaker, QuarkXPress; Other equipment — CD-Rom. PRODUCTION: Typesetters — Ap/Mac Laser. WIRE SERVICES: News — AP; Receiving dishes — AP. BUSINESS COMPUTERS: 1-IBM/5120, 1-IBM/AT; Applications: Circ, Addressing, Billing, Statement print; PCs & micros networked.

STURGIS

St. Joseph County

'90 U.S. Census- 10,130; E&P '96 Est. 10,948

Sturgis Journal (e-mon to sat)

Sturgis Journal, 209 John St.; PO Box 660, Sturgis, MI 49091; tel (616) 651-5407; fax (616) 651-2296. Hometown Communications group.

Circulation: 7,775(e); 7,775(e-sat); Sworn Sept. 22, 1995.

Price: 50¢(d); 50¢(sat); $7.00/mo; $81.00/yr.

Advertising: Open inch rate $8.40(e); $8.40(e-sat).

News Service: AP. **Politics:** Independent. **Established:** 1859.

Not Published: New Year; Memorial Day; Independence Day; Labor Day; Thanksgiving; Christmas.

Special Editions: Progress; Mother's Day; Father's Day; Graduation; Fall Sports; Winter Sports; Christmas Gift Guide; Car Care; Home Improvement.

Special Weekly Sections: Best Food Day (mon); Dining and Entertainment (thur); Church Page, Business, Agriculture (sat).

Magazines: Kid's Mini Page (tues); TV Section (fri).

CORPORATE OFFICER

President Jim McGinnis

GENERAL MANAGEMENT
Publisher Rich Piatt
CIRCULATION
Director Sheila Larsen
NEWS EXECUTIVE
Managing Editor Candice Phelps
EDITOR AND MANAGER
Sports Editor Mike Clutter
PRODUCTION
Manager Dale Peters
Manager-Publications Laura Herman

Market Information: TMC.
Mechanical available: Offset; Black and 3 ROP colors; insert accepted — preprinted; page cut-offs — 22.71".
Mechanical specifications: Type page 13" x 21½"; E - 6 cols, 2¹⁄₁₆", ⅛" between; A - 6 cols, 2¹⁄₁₆", ⅛" between; C - 9 cols, 1⅜", ¹⁄₁₆" between.
Commodity consumption: Newsprint 250 short tons; widths 27¼", 30"; black ink 8,710 pounds; color ink 580 pounds; single pages printed 5,150; average pages per issue 14(d); single plates used 4,400.
Equipment: EDITORIAL: Front-end hardware — Ap/Mac. CLASSIFIED: Front-end hardware — 3-Big Screens/S, 3-Ap/Mac-one double. DISPLAY: Adv layout systems — Ap/Mac. PRODUCTION: Typesetters — 1-Ap/Mac Scanner; Plate exposures — 2-Nu/Flip Top; Plate processors — 1-Nat/A-250; Production cameras — 1-R/Horizontal; Automatic film processors — 1-Kk, 1-LE.
PRESSROOM: Line 1 — 7-G/Community; Line 2 — 7-G/SC665; Folders — 1-G. MAILROOM: Bundle tyer — 1-Bu, 1-Sa, 1-MLN; Addressing machine — 1-Am, KR. WIRE SERVICES: News — AP; Receiving dishes — size-6ft, AP. BUSINESS COMPUTERS: 4-NCR; PCs & micros networked.

THREE RIVERS
St. Joseph County
'90 U.S. Census- 7,413; E&P '96 Est. 7,925

Three Rivers Commercial-News (e-mon to fri; m-sat)
Three Rivers Commercial-News, 124 N. Main St.; PO Box 130, Three Rivers, MI 49093; tel (616) 279-7488. Milliman Communications group.
Circulation: 3,536(e); 3,536(m-sat); Sworn Oct. 1, 1995.
Price: 50¢(d); 50¢(sat); $6.00/mo; $72.00/yr, $86.00/yr (in county).
Advertising: Open inch rate $8.10(e); $8.10(m-sat).
News Service: AP. **Politics:** Independent. **Established:** 1895.
Not Published: New Year; Memorial Day; Independence Day; Labor Day; Thanksgiving; Christmas.
Special Editions: The Way We Were, Seniors, Health & Fitness (broadsheet), White Sale (broadsheet), Bridal (Jan); People's Choice, White Sale (broadsheet) (Feb); Spring Home, Lawn & Garden, NCAA Basketball (grid) (Mar); Spring Car Care, Earth Day/Environmental, Seniors (Apr); Graduation, Summer Recreation (May); Bridal, The Way We Were, Water Festival History (June); Coupon Pages, Michigan Medical Society (July); Back-to-School & College, Seniors, Football Preview (Aug); Football Contest, Grange Fair, Chamber Report, Hunting & Fishing (Sept); Soil Conservation/Farming, Fair In Review, Seniors, Energy Conservation (broadsheet), Women In Business (Oct); Basketball Preview, Christmas Coloring Contest, Gift Guide, Restaurant/Entertainment (broadsheet) (Nov); Gift Guide, Gift Certificate Page, Song Book, Year In Review, Restaurant/Entertainment (broadsheet) (Dec).
Special Weekly Sections: Farm Page; Church Page.
Magazine: Penny Saver.

CORPORATE OFFICER
President Richard L Milliman II
GENERAL MANAGEMENT
Publisher Richard L Milliman II
Publisher Penelope Faber Milliman
General Manager Ronald P Reece
ADVERTISING
Asst Manager Lori Bogda
CIRCULATION
Manager Dan Kile
NEWS EXECUTIVE
Managing Editor Joe Albertson
PRODUCTION
Supervisor-Pressroom Ben Wright

Market Information: TMC.
Mechanical available: Offset; Black and 3 ROP colors; insert accepted — preprinted, any; page cut-offs — 22¾".
Mechanical specifications: Type page 12¾" x 21½"; E - 6 cols, 2.07", ⅙" between; A - 8 cols, 1.57", ⅙" between; C - 8 cols, 1.57", ⅙" between.
Commodity consumption: Newsprint 225 short tons; widths 27½", 27½", 13¾"; black ink 1,600 pounds; color ink 500 pounds; single pages printed 3,744; average pages per issue 12(d); single plates used 1,872.
Equipment: EDITORIAL: Front-end hardware — 3-Mk/1100 plus front-end, 2-COM; Front-end software — Mk/1100. CLASSIFIED: Front-end hardware — 1-Mk/1100 plus (for classifieds). PRODUCTION: Typesetters — 1-COM/8400, 1-COM/Trendsetter; Plate exposures — Nu; Production cameras — 1-B/Caravelle, 1-Cl.
PRESSROOM: Line 1 — 5-HI/Cotrell V-15A; Folders — 1-HI. MAILROOM: Bundle tyer — 2-Bu; Addressing machine — 1-Am. WIRE SERVICES: News — AP; Syndicates — NEA; Receiving dishes — size-2ft, AP. BUSINESS COMPUTERS: Compaq/Deskpro; Applications: All bus sys.

TRAVERSE CITY
Grand Traverse County
'90 U.S. Census- 15,155; E&P '96 Est. 14,852
ABC-NDM (90): 116,943 (HH 44,110)

Traverse City Record-Eagle (m-mon to sat; S)
Record-Eagle, 120 W. Front St.; PO Box 632, Traverse City, MI 49684; tel (616) 946-2000; fax (616) 946-8273. Ottaway Newspapers Inc. group.
Circulation: 26,904(m); 26,904(m-sat); 38,894(S); ABC Sept. 30, 1995.
Price: 50¢(d); 50¢(sat); $1.25(S); $2.90/wk; $10.80/mo; $140.40/yr.
Advertising: Open inch rate $19.23(m); $19.23(m-sat); $20.98(S).
News Services: AP, DJ, ONS. **Politics:** Independent. **Established:** 1897.
Note: Effective Apr. 3, 1995, this publication changed its publishing plan from (e-mon to sat; S) to (m-mon to sat; S).
Special Editions: Winter Home (Jan); Bridal, Spring Car Care, Spring Fashion (Mar); Spring Home, Golf Directory (Apr); Lawn & Garden, Spring Magazine (May); Cherry Festival, Mid Summer Home (July); Back-to-School (Aug); Autumn (Sept); Fall Home, Fall Car Care (Oct); Ski Directory (Nov); Winter Magazine (Dec).
Special Weekly Sections: Food (mon); Outdoor (thur); Bridal, Northern Living Features (fri); Outdoor, Northern Living Features (S).
Magazines: Food, Express Line (mon); TV Guide (S).
Cable TV: Operate leased cable TV in circulation area.

GENERAL MANAGEMENT
Publisher Frank B Senger
Controller Michael C Nau
General Manager Zeke M Fleet
ADVERTISING
Manager-Retail Don Beem
Manager-Retail Patrice Lynch
Manager-Classified Kim Hornyak
Manager-National Zeke M Fleet
TELECOMMUNICATIONS
Audiotex Manager Zeke M Fleet
CIRCULATION
Manager Thomas Bunch
NEWS EXECUTIVE
Editor John Tune
EDITORS AND MANAGERS
Business Editor Bill Echlin
City Editor Loraine Anderson
Community News Editor Teresa Fowler
Editorial Page Editor Michael J Ready
Fashion Editor Kathy Gibbons
Outdoor Editor Gordon Charles
Section Editor Kathy Gibbons
Sports Editor Nick Edson
Sunday Editor David Miller
MANAGEMENT INFORMATION SERVICES
Data Processing Manager Michael C Nau
PRODUCTION
Foreman-Composing Joseph Jamrog
Manager-Pressroom Bill Dixon

Market Information: TMC; ADS; Operate audiotex.
Mechanical available: Offset; Black and 3 ROP colors; insert accepted — preprinted; page cut-offs — 21½".
Mechanical specifications: Type page 13¼" x 21½"; E - 6 cols, 2.08", ⅙" between; A - 6 cols, 2.08", ⅙" between; C - 9 cols, 1.33", ⅙" between.
Commodity consumption: Newsprint 2,549 metric tons; widths 27½", 55", 41¼", 13¾"; black ink 60,000 pounds; color ink 15,000 pounds; single pages printed 14,290; average pages per issue 32(d), 63(S); single plates used 13,900.
Equipment: EDITORIAL: Front-end hardware — 29-Dewar/Sys II; Front-end software — Dewar/Sys II; Printers — 2-Okidata/320. CLASSIFIED: Front-end hardware — Dewar/Sys II; Front-end software — Dewar/Sys II; Printers — Okidata/393. AUDIOTEX: Hardware — Brite, Voice Systems; Supplier name — ITN. DISPLAY: Adv layout systems — Dewar/Discovery; Front-end hardware — 2-PC/386, 2-PC/486; Front-end software — Dewar/Discovery. PRODUCTION: Typesetters — 1-Tegra/Varityper 5100, 1-Tegra/Varityper 5510; Plate processors — Nat/SP326, 1-WL/300; Scanners — HP/ScanJet; Production cameras — C/Spartan III; Automatic film processors — P; Film transporters — P; Color separation equipment (conventional) — Lf/AP Leaf Picture Desk; Digital color separation equipment — ECR/Autokon 1000DE.
PRESSROOM: Line 1 — 5-TKS double width; Pasters — Automatic Pasters; Press control system — TKS; Press registration system — KFM. MAILROOM: Counter stackers — 2-QWI; Inserters and stuffers — 6-MA/SLS100; Bundle tyer — 2-Power Strap. COMMUNICATIONS: Remote imagesetting — AP AdSend; Digital ad delivery system — AP AdSend. Systems used — satellite. WIRE SERVICES: News — AP, ONS; Photos — AP; Receiving dishes — size-6ft, AP. BUSINESS COMPUTERS: IBM/AS 400, Ap/Mac; Applications: Adv; PCs & micros networked; PCs & main system networked.

MINNESOTA

ALBERT LEA
Freeborn County
'90 U.S. Census- 18,310; E&P '96 Est. 17,609
ABC-CZ (90): 19,274 (HH 7,906)

Albert Lea Tribune (e-mon to fri; S)
Albert Lea Tribune, 808 W. Front St.; Box 60, Albert Lea, MN 56007; tel (507) 373-1411; fax (507) 373-0333. Boone Newspapers Inc. group.
Circulation: 7,009(e); 7,671(S); ABC Sept. 30, 1995.
Price: 50¢(d); $1.25(S); $2.45/wk; $10.50/mo; $126.00/yr.
Advertising: Open inch rate $12.91(e); $12.91(S). **Representative:** Papert Companies.
News Service: AP. **Politics:** Independent. **Established:** 1897.
Not Published: New Year; Memorial Day; Independence Day; Labor Day; Christmas.
Advertising not accepted: Vending machines.
Special Editions: Pork (Jan); Progress (Feb); Sports (Apr); Fair (Aug); Farm (Sept); Cookbook, Sports (Nov).
Special Weekly Sections: School (tues); Best Food, Entertainment (thur); Religion (fri); Business, Lifestyles (S).
Magazines: Color Comics, Family Entertainment & TV Magazine (S).

CORPORATE OFFICER
President Robert Brincefield
GENERAL MANAGEMENT
Publisher Robert Brincefield
ADVERTISING
Manager Alan Johnson
CIRCULATION
Manager Mike Schoepf
NEWS EXECUTIVE
Editor Floyd Jennigan
EDITORS AND MANAGERS
Reporter Geri McShane
Sports Editor Jim Lutgens
MANAGEMENT INFORMATION SERVICES
Manager April Habana
PRODUCTION
Foreman Terry Jenson

Market Information: TMC; ADS.
Mechanical available: Offset; Black and 3 ROP colors; insert accepted — preprinted; page cut-offs — 22¾".
Mechanical specifications: Type page 13" x 21½"; E - 6 cols, 2¹⁄₁₆", ⅛" between; A - 6 cols, 2¹⁄₁₆", ⅛" between; C - 9 cols, 1⅜", ⅛" between.
Commodity consumption: Newsprint 274 short tons; widths 27½", 13¾"; black ink 4,500 pounds; color ink 300 pounds; single pages printed 5,000; average pages per issue 14(d), 26(S); single plates used 3,900.
Equipment: EDITORIAL: Front-end hardware — CD, Ap/Mac cx, Ap/Mac Centris; Front-end software — CD, Baseview, QuarkXPress; Printers — NEC/SilentWriter, LaserMaster. CLASSIFIED: Front-end hardware — CD, Ap/Mac Centris; Front-end software — CD, Baseview; Printers — NEC/SilentWriter, LaserMaster. DISPLAY: Adv layout systems — QuarkXPress; Front-end hardware — 2-Ap/Mac Centris; Front-end software — QuarkXPress. PRODUCTION: Typesetters — Laser; Platemaking systems — 1-Nu/FT40L-, Nat; Plate exposures — 1-R/500 Lowbed; Plate processors — 1-LE/LD-24BO; Electronic picture desk — Ap/Mac; Scanners — 2-COM/Unisetter 070, DTI/1200, Ap/Mac, LaCie, Microtek; Automatic film processors — Nikon/CoolScan; Color separation equipment (conventional) — Ap/Mac PowerBook, Adobe/Photoshop. WIRE SERVICES: News — Receiving dishes — AP. BUSINESS COMPUTERS: IBM, TI/LaserWriters; Applications: Quicken, Professional Write, Lotus.

AUSTIN
Mower County
'90 U.S. Census- 21,907; E&P '96 Est. 21,032
ABC-CZ (90): 22,113 (HH 9,436)

Austin Daily Herald (e-mon to fri; S)
Austin Daily Herald, 310 N.E. 2nd St.; PO Box 578, Austin, MN 55912; tel (507) 433-8851; fax (507) 437-8644. Boone Newspapers Inc. group.
Circulation: 8,446(e); 7,677(S); ABC Mar. 31, 1993.
Price: 50¢(d); $1.25(S); $2.05/wk; $101.60/yr.
Advertising: Open inch rate $11.50(e); $11.50(S). **Representative:** Cresmer, Woodward, O'Mara & Ormsbee.
News Service: AP. **Politics:** Independent. **Established:** 1891.
Not Published: New Year; Memorial Day; Independence Day; Labor Day; Thanksgiving; Christmas.
Advertising not accepted: Mail order, vending machines.
Special Editions: Spring & Fall fashions; Cookbook; Farm; Progress; Barrow Show.

GENERAL MANAGEMENT
Publisher Dave Churchill
General Manager Dave Churchill
Manager-Credit Sue Kapaun
ADVERTISING
Supervisor-Classified Bob Mithuen
NEWS EXECUTIVE
Managing Editor Tony Pierskalla
EDITORS AND MANAGERS
Amusements Editor Nicki Merfeld
Business/Finance Editor Chuck Tombarge
Consumer Interest Editor Chuck Tombarge
Editorial Page Editor Tony Pierskalla
Education/School Editor Chuck Tombarge
Environment/Ecology Editor Chuck Tombarge
Reporter Lee Bonordon
Fashion/Food Editor Nicki Merfeld
Home Furnishings/Garden Editor Nicki Merfeld
News Editor Chuck Tombarge
Photo Department Manager Mark Olson
Radio/Television Editor Nicki Merfeld
Science Lee Bonordon
Society/Women's Editor Nicki Merfeld
Teen-Age/Youth Editor Nicki Merfeld
PRODUCTION
Foreman-Composing Jeff Amos
Foreman-Pressroom Jeff Amos

Market Information: TMC.
Mechanical available: Offset; Black and 3 ROP colors; insert accepted — preprinted; page cut-offs — 22¾".

Mechanical specifications: Type page 13" x 21½"; E - 6 cols, 2", ⅛" between; A - 6 cols, 2", ⅛" between; C - 9 cols, 2", ⅛" between.
Equipment: EDITORIAL: Front-end hardware — CD; Front-end software — HAS; Printers — Tegra/Varityper XP-1000. CLASSIFIED: Front-end hardware — CD; Front-end software — HAS; Printers — Tegra/Varityper XP-1000. PRODUCTION: Plate exposures — Nu; Plate processors — Nat/A-250; Production cameras — R, LE; Automatic film processors — LE/LD-220-QT; Color separation equipment (conventional) — Digi-Colour; Digital color separation equipment — Digi-Colour.
PRESSROOM: Line 1 — 8-G/Community. MAILROOM: Bundle tyer — 2-Bu/Tyer. WIRE SERVICES: News — THO, AP.

BEMIDJI
Beltrami County
'90 U.S. Census- 11,245; E&P '96 Est. 11,496

The Daily Pioneer
(m-mon to fri; S)

The Daily Pioneer, 1320 Neilson Ave. S.E., Bemidji, MN 56601; tel (218) 751-3740; fax (218) 751-6914. Park Communications Inc. group.
Circulation: 8,359(m); 8,758(S); VAC Mar. 31, 1995.
Price: 50¢(d); 75¢(S); $8.00/wk; $24.00/mo; $88.00/yr.
Advertising: Open inch rate $9.60(m); $9.60(S). **Representative:** Papert Companies.
News Service: AP. **Politics:** Independent. **Established:** 1896.
Not Published: Christmas (unless falls on Wed or Sun).
Special Editions: President's Day; Create-An-Ad; Agri-Business; Progress Edition; Home Improvement; Bridal; Back-to-School; Car Care; Hunting & Fishing; Summer Tourism Guide; School; Christmas Kick-off; Holiday Recipe Guide; Cooking School; Last Minute Gift Guide; Mardi Gras; Winter Tourism Guide; Christmas Song Book.
Special Weekly Sections: Community (wed); Outdoors, TV Showcase, Church (fri); Best Food Day, Business, Comic (S).
Magazine: Advertiser (TMC) (S).

CORPORATE OFFICERS
President Wright M Thomas
Vice Pres-Newspapers Ralph J Martin
GENERAL MANAGEMENT
General Manager Omar Forberg
Business Manager Tammie Richter
ADVERTISING
Director Jeff Halvorson
Manager-Classified Sherry Wilson
CIRCULATION
Director Gary Newell
NEWS EXECUTIVES
Editor Omar Forberg
Managing Editor Brad Swenson
EDITORS AND MANAGERS
Editorial Page Editor Brad Swenson
Education Editor Monte Draper
Entertainment/Amusements Editor Donna Houser
Family/Religion Editor Donna Houser
Features Editor Brad Swenson
Living/Lifestyle Editor Donna Houser
News Editor Brad Swenson
National Editor Brad Swenson
Photo Editor Monte Draper
Political/Government Editor Brad Swenson
Sports Editor James Carrington
Wire Editor Jerry Madson
Women's Editor Donna Houser
MANAGEMENT INFORMATION SERVICES
Manager Tammie Richter
PRODUCTION
Superintendent-Plant Tim Roline
Foreman-Night Side Tim Miller

Market Information: Zoned editions; TMC.
Mechanical available: Offset; Black and 3 ROP colors; insert accepted — preprinted, free standing cards & envelopes; page cut-offs — 22¾".
Mechanical specifications: Type page 13" x 21½"; E - 6 cols, 2 1/16", ⅛" between; A - 6 cols, 2 1/16", ⅛" between; C - 10 cols, 1½", 1/16" between.
Commodity consumption: Newsprint 1,426 short tons; widths 30", 27.5"; black ink 17,000 pounds; color ink 1,430 pounds; single pages printed 22,915; average pages per issue 32(d), 79(S); single plates used 15,600.
Equipment: EDITORIAL: Front-end hardware — Ap/Mac; Front-end software — Baseview; Printers — Ap/Mac LaserWriter II. CLASSIFIED: Front-end hardware — Ap/Mac; Front-end software — Baseview; Printers — Ap/Mac LaserWriter II. DISPLAY: Front-end hardware — Ap/Mac; Front-end software — Baseview; Printers — 1-Ap/Mac LaserWriter II. PRODUCTION: Typesetters — 1-Ap/Mac LaserWriter II; Plate exposures — 1-Nu/Flip Top FT40LNS; Plate processors — 1-Nat/340; Scanners — 1-HP/ScanJet IIc; Production cameras — 1-B/1822; Automatic film processors — 1-P/24-1; Shrink lenses — 1-CK Optical.
PRESSROOM: Line 1 — 6-G/Community C-1378; Press registration system — Duarte. MAILROOM: Bundle tyer — 1-Bu/20000, 1-MLN/ML2EE; Addressing machine — IBM/36 Label Printer. WIRE SERVICES: News — AP; Receiving dishes — size-1m, AP. BUSINESS COMPUTERS: 1-IBM/Sys 36; Applications: Accts payable, Accts receivable, Billing, Payroll, Circ; PCs & micros networked; PCs & main system networked.

BRAINERD
Crow Wing County
'90 U.S. Census- 12,353; E&P '96 Est. 13,119

The Brainerd Daily Dispatch (e-mon to fri; S)

The Brainerd Daily Dispatch, 506 James St.; PO Box D, Brainerd, MN 56401-0974; tel (218) 829-4705; fax (218) 829-7735. Morris Communications Corp. group.
Circulation: 14,847(e); 14,847(S); Sworn Sept. 30, 1994.
Price: 50¢(d); $1.25(S); $104.00/yr.
Advertising: Open inch rate $11.45(e); $12.35(S). **Representative:** Papert Companies.
News Service: AP. **Politics:** Independent. **Established:** 1881.
Not Published: New Year; Memorial Day; Independence Day; Labor Day; Thanksgiving; Christmas.
Special Editions: Money Page, ½ Price Sale (Jan); Love Lines, Bridal Directory, Nisswa Jubilee, Kid's Ad Contest (Feb); Parenting, MMBA Home Show, Seniors (Mar); Cookbook-Health, Commerce & Industry, Spring Sports, Coupon Book, Golf Guide (Apr); Mother's Day, Great Outdoors, Garden Page, WAVES (sep. distribution), MMBA Bulletin, Parade of Homes, MLS Memorial Day (May); Menu Guide, Bad Bears Baseball, Father's Day, Seniors, Treasure Hunt, July 4th (June); MMBA Bulletin, Crazy Days (July); Nisswa Crazy Days, Back-to-School, Seniors, Chamber Days (Aug); Fall Sports, BAHA Hunters Digest I (Sept); MMBA Bulletin, Hunters Digest II, Do North (Oct); Christmas Catalog, Ski Gull, Christmas Kick-off, Wish Upon Store, Gift Guide, Do North (Nov); Winter Sports, Seniors, Christmas Stories, Roll of Honor (Class), Do North (Dec); MLS (monthly); Medical Quarterly (quarterly).
Special Weekly Sections: Neighbors (wed); Entertainment (thur); Housing Page, Best Food, North County Outdoors (S).
Magazines: Zoned Edition (wed); Entertainment (thur); Best Food Day, Parade, TV Update (S).

CORPORATE OFFICERS
Chairman of the Board W S Morris III
President Paul S Simon
Secretary/Treasurer William A Herman III
GENERAL MANAGEMENT
Publisher Terry McCollough
ADVERTISING
Manager Joe Smart
Asst Manager Mary Panzer
TELECOMMUNICATIONS
Audiotex Manager Carl Specht
CIRCULATION
Manager Greg Guenin
NEWS EXECUTIVE
Editor Roy Miller
EDITORS AND MANAGERS
Automotive Editor Roy Miller
City Editor Mike O'Rourke
Editorial Page Editor Roy Miller
Education Editor Paul Windels
Entertainment/Lifestyle Editor Steve Waller
Photo Department Manager Steve Kohls
Sports Editor Mike Bialka
Television/Film Editor Steve Waller
Theater/Music Editor Steve Waller
Travel Editor Steve Waller
Wire Editor Paul Forsberg
MANAGEMENT INFORMATION SERVICES
Data Processing Manager Joyce Caughey
PRODUCTION
Manager-Pre Press/Systems Denny Newman
Foreman-Pressroom Pat Sprenger

Market Information: Zoned editions; TMC; Operate audiotex.
Mechanical available: Offset; Black and 3 ROP colors; insert accepted — preprinted; page cut-offs — 22¾".
Mechanical specifications: Type page 13" x 21½"; E - 6 cols, 2", .18" between; A - 6 cols, 2", .18" between; C - 6 cols, 2", .18" between.
Commodity consumption: Newsprint 956 short tons; widths 13½", 27"; black ink 18,000 pounds; color ink 2,000 pounds; single pages printed 8,778; average pages per issue 20(d), 52(S); single plates used 7,000.
Equipment: EDITORIAL: Front-end hardware — Ap/Mac; Front-end software — Baseview; Printers — Ap/Mac; Other equipment — Lf/AP Leaf Picture Desk. CLASSIFIED: Front-end hardware — Ap/Mac; Front-end software — Baseview; Printers — Okidata. AUDIOTEX: Hardware — Samsung; Software — SMS. DISPLAY: Adv layout systems — Ap/Mac; Front-end software — Baseview; Printers — 2-Ap/Mac Laser-Printer. PRODUCTION: Typesetters — 2-MON; Electronic picture desk — Ap/Mac; Scanners — 2-Ap/Mac; Production cameras — SCREEN/Companica C-690-D; Color separation equipment (conventional) — Lf/Leafscan 35, Nikon.
PRESSROOM: Line 1 — 8-G/Community (balloon); Folders — 1-G/SSC; Press registration system — Duarte. MAILROOM: Counter stackers — BG; Inserters and stuffers — MM/4; Bundle tyer — 2-MLN; Addressing machine — Ch/525E. LIBRARY: Electronic — SMS/Stauffer Gold. COMMUNICATIONS: Systems used — satellite. WIRE SERVICES: News — AP; Photos — AP; Receiving dishes — size-3m, AP. BUSINESS COMPUTERS: ATT/605; Applications: SMS: Accts payable, Accts receivable, Payroll, Circ; PCs & micros networked.

BRECKINRIDGE
See WAHPETON, ND

CROOKSTON
Polk County
'90 U.S. Census- 8,119; E&P '96 Est. 7,723

Crookston Daily Times
(e-mon to fri)

Crookston Daily Times, 124 S. Broadway; PO Box 615, Crookston, MN 56716; tel (218) 281-2730; fax (218) 281-7234. Hollinger International Inc. group.
Circulation: 4,161(e); Sworn Sept. 29, 1994.
Price: 50¢(d); $1.90/wk (in state); $24.70/mo (in state); $94.00/yr (in state).
Advertising: Open inch rate $6.94(e). **Representative:** Papert Companies.
News Service: AP. **Politics:** Independent. **Established:** 1885.
Special Editions: Winter Shows; Home Sport & Craft Show; Football; University of Minnesota, Crookston.

CORPORATE OFFICERS
President Larry J Perrotto
Comptroller Roland McBride
GENERAL MANAGEMENT
Publisher/General Manager Randal Hultgren
ADVERTISING
Manager Michelle Rupchouck
CIRCULATION
Director Edwin Sylvester
NEWS EXECUTIVE
Editor Twylla Altepeter
EDITOR AND MANAGER
Women's Editor Diane Urness
PRODUCTION
Manager Les Halvorson

Market Information: Zoned editions; TMC.
Mechanical available: Offset; Black and 4 ROP colors; insert accepted — preprinted; page cut-offs — 21½".
Mechanical specifications: Type page 13" x 21½"; E - 6 cols, 2 1/16", ⅛" between; A - 6 cols, 2 1/16", ⅛" between; C - 6 cols, 2 1/16", ⅛" between.
Commodity consumption: Newsprint 300 short tons; width 28"; black ink 600 pounds; color ink 100 pounds; single pages printed 3,300; average pages per issue 10(d); single plates used 1,650.
Equipment: EDITORIAL: Front-end hardware — Mk; Printers — Ap/Mac LaserWriter Plus. DISPLAY: Front-end hardware — Ap/Mac; Front-end software — Aldus/PageMaker; Printers — Ap/Mac Laser. PRODUCTION: Production cameras — B; Automatic film processors — LE.
PRESSROOM: Line 1 — 5-G/Community; Folders — 1-G/2:1. MAILROOM: Bundle tyer — 1-Marlow; Addressing machine — DEC/Line Printer. WIRE SERVICES: News — AP; Receiving dishes — size-1ft, AP. BUSINESS COMPUTERS: 1-Corsair/120 mp; Applications: Nomads/Listmaster: Accts receivable.

DULUTH
St. Louis County
'90 U.S. Census- 85,493; E&P '96 Est. 79,915
ABC-CZ (90): 96,728 (HH 38,413)

Duluth News-Tribune
(m-mon to sat; S)

Duluth News-Tribune, 424 W. 1st St.; PO Box 169000, Duluth, MN 55816-9000; tel (218) 723-5281; fax (218) 723-5295; e-mail mnduh24@plink.geis.com. Knight-Ridder Inc. group.
Circulation: 53,821(m); 53,821(m-sat); 83,089(S); ABC Sept. 30, 1995.
Price: 50¢(d); 50¢(sat); $1.50(S); $3.05/wk (carrier); $12.20/mo (carrier); $158.60/yr (carrier).
Advertising: Open inch rate $37.50(m); $39.38(m-sat); $42.86(S). **Representative:** Landon Associates Inc.
News Services: AP, KRT. **Politics:** Independent. **Established:** 1869.
Special Editions: Weddings (Jan); Outlook (Progress), Active Times (Mar); Fishing, Car Care, Builders & Remodelers (Apr); Home/Garden, Parade of Homes, North Shore Visitor, Northland Summer Visitor, Active Times, Grandma's Marathon (June); Back-to-School (Aug); House & Home, Hunting, Energy (Sept); Health & Fitness, Northland Winter Visitor, Car Care, Energy, Northshore Visitor (Oct); Active Times, Gift Guide (Dec).
Special Weekly Sections: Best Food Days (thur); Weekly TV Log, Radio and Amusement, Travel (S).
Magazine: "Accent" (local, newsprint) (S).

CORPORATE OFFICERS
President James V Gels
Vice Pres Vicki Gowler
GENERAL MANAGEMENT
Publisher James V Gels
Director-Finance Alan R Scherer
Director-Human Resources Karen Rylander-Davis
ADVERTISING
Director Robert Thomson
Manager-Retail Nancie Thomas
Manager-National John Parmeter
Manager-Classified John Parmeter
Supervisor-Classified (Telephone) Mike Raic
MARKETING AND PROMOTION
Director-Marketing/Promotion Sharon Almirall
Manager-Promotion Cindy Nelson
TELECOMMUNICATIONS
Director-Info Systems Roberta Paulson
CIRCULATION
Director Curt Peterson
NEWS EXECUTIVES
Exec Editor Vicki Gowler
Exec Editor-News Holly Gruber
Exec Editor-City Diane Faherty
Managing Editor Craig Gemoules
EDITORS AND MANAGERS
City Editor Connie Wirta
City Editor Andrea Novel
City Editor Linda Hanson
Editorial Page Editor Virgil Swing
Assoc Editorial Page Editor Jim Heffernan
Education Writer Beth Krodel
Education Writer Noam Levey
Entertainment/Arts Writer Dominic Papatola
Environmental Writer John Myers
Features Editor Linda Hanson
Health Writer Kendra Rosencrans
Chief Photographer Bob King
Photo Editor Bob King
Political Writer John Welbes
Outdoors Writer Sam Cook
Sports Editor Joe Bissen
Deputy Sports Editor Chris Miller
MANAGEMENT INFORMATION SERVICES
Manager Roberta Paulson

PRODUCTION

Manager Dan Mastin
Manager-Environmental Ron Brisbin
Foreman-Composing (Gen) Gene Keyser
Foreman-Pressroom (Gen) Dick Christensen
Foreman-Pressroom (Night) Stu Beckett
Foreman-Mailroom/Night Supervisor Oscar Steinhilb
Foreman-Mailroom (Gen) Frank Grandson
Manager-Systems & Services Dean Pyykola
Foreman-Ad Composition Jim Zawislak
Supervisor-Building Ron Brisbin
Ad Manager Tom Walsdorf
Foreman-Maintenance Jerry Lilliberg

Market Information: Zoned editions; Split Run.
Mechanical available: Letterpress,Flexographic; Black and 3 ROP colors; insert accepted — preprinted; page cut-offs — 22 7/8".
Mechanical specifications: Type page 13" x 21"; E - 6 cols, 2 1/16", 1/8" between; A - 6 cols, 2 1/16", 1/8" between; C - 9 cols, 1 3/8", 1/16" between.
Commodity consumption: Newsprint 5,300 short tons; widths 54 3/4", 41 1/4", 27 1/2"; black ink 190,700 pounds; color ink 57,700 pounds; single pages printed 14,000; average pages per issue 32(d), 84(S); single plates used 35,300.
Equipment: EDITORIAL: Front-end hardware — Sun/Sparc 51, PCs; Front-end software — HI/Newsmaker 2.05; Printers — 1-HP/LaserJet IV, 2-Epson/LQ-550. CLASSIFIED: Front-end hardware — 12-AT/Edit V; Front-end software — AT; Printers — 1-Genicom/3000. DISPLAY: Adv layout systems — CJ/Layout (4.01 D); Front-end hardware — 2-Sun/Sparc 51, 2-AT/Edit V; Front-end software — HI/Ad Display, CS/Layout. PRODUCTION: Pagination software — HI/PLS (2); Typesetters — 2-AU/APS-6, 1-AU/APS-5; Platemaking systems — 2-He; Plate exposures — 2-He; Plate processors — 2-He; Electronic picture desk — Lf/AP Leaf Picture Desk; Scanners — 1-Umax/Powerlook, Lf, X/7650, 1-Howtek/D4000; Production cameras — 1-C/Spartan III; Automatic film processors — 4-LE; Film transporters — 1-C, 2-LE; Color separation equipment (conventional) — 1-Howtek/D4000; Digital color separation equipment — HI/PLS (2).
PRESSROOM: Line 1 — G/Headliner Letterpress (w/half deck); Line 2 — G/Headliner Letterpress (w/half deck); Line 3 — G/Headliner Letterpress (w/half deck); Line 4 — 1-G/Headliner Letterpress (w/half deck); Line 5 — 1-MOT/FX4 Flexo (w/half deck & 2-color tower); Line 6 — 1-MOT/FX4 Flexo (w/half deck); Line 7 — 1-MOT/FX4 Flexo (w/half deck); Press drives — PEC/ Bond; Folders — G/2:1; Pasters — G; Reels and stands — G, Cline; Press control system — PEC/James Bond, MOT, PEC/Bond. MAILROOM: Counter stackers — 1-Id/660, 1-Id/440; Inserters and stuffers — 1-MM/Bilinger 308-208, 1-MM 227; Bundle tyer — 2-Power Strap; Wrapping singles — 1-Ca, 1-Maylo; Addressing machine — 1-Ch. LIBRARY: Electronic — Vu/Text Save. COMMUNICATIONS: Digital ad delivery system — AP AdSend. WIRE SERVICES: News — AP Dataspeed, AP Datafeatures, AP Datastream, NYT; Photos — AP; Stock tables — AP SelectStox II; Receiving dishes — size-3m, AP. BUSINESS COMPUTERS: 1-HP/3000-947; Applications: CIS, AAP, AGL, Payroll, Aim; PCs & micros networked; PCs & main system networked.

EAST GRAND FORKS

See GRAND FORKS, ND

FAIRMONT

Martin County

'90 U.S. Census- 11,265; E&P '96 Est. 11,070
ABC-CZ (90): 11,265 (HH 4,717)

Sentinel (m-mon to sat)

Sentinel, 64 Downtown Plz.; PO Box 681, Fairmont, MN 56031; tel (507) 235-3303; fax (507) 235-3718; e-mail sentry@ aol.com. Ogden Newspapers group.
Circulation: 9,654(m); 9,654(m-sat); Sworn Nov. 2, 1995.
Price: 50¢(d); 50¢(sat); $1.50/wk; $6.50/mo (carrier); $85.00/yr (carrier).
Advertising: Open inch rate $12.01(m); $12.01(m-sat). **Representative:** Papert Companies.
News Service: AP. **Established:** 1874.
Not Published: New Year; Independence Day; Labor Day; Thanksgiving; Christmas.
Advertising not accepted: Vending machines.
Special Editions: Tax Guide; Senior Citizen Tab; Bridal Tab; Spring Car Care; Fishing Tab; Agribusiness; City Wide Clean-up Fix-up; Women of Today; Graduation Tab; Moonlight Madness; Dairy and Beef Tab; Crazy Days; 4-H Tab; Football Tab; Farm Safety; Medical Tab; Pork Tab; Christmas Song Book; Boys & Girls Basketball Tab; Area Business Directory.
Special Weekly Section: TV Book (fri).
Broadcast Affiliate: Channel 28 LPTV.

CORPORATE OFFICERS

President G Odgen Nutting
Vice Pres William C Nutting
Vice Pres Robert M Nutting
Secretary William O Nutting
Treasurer Duane D Wittman

GENERAL MANAGEMENT

Publisher Bryan Welch
Manager-Office Mary Rahe

ADVERTISING

Manager Gary Andersen

MARKETING AND PROMOTION

Director-Marketing Gary Andersen

NEWS EXECUTIVE

Editor Russell Roberts

EDITORS AND MANAGERS

Agriculture Reporter Bill Cahalan
Court Reporter Elizabeth Laird
Editorial Writer Russell Roberts
Editorial Writer Bryan Welch
Fashion/Food Editor Judy Juenger
Government Reporter Kevin Featherly
Religion Reporter Bill Cahalan
Sports Editor Charles Sorrells
Wire Editor Anthony Acosta
Women's Editor Judy Juenger

MANAGEMENT INFORMATION SERVICES

Data Processing Manager Russell Roberts

PRODUCTION

Superintendent Lisa Thate

Market Information: TMC; ADS; Operate audiotex.
Mechanical available: Offset; Black and 3 ROP colors; insert accepted — preprinted.
Mechanical specifications: Type page 13" x 21 1/2"; E - 6 cols, 2 1/16", 1/8" between; A - 6 cols, 2 1/16", 1/8" between; C - 9 cols, 1 3/8", 1/16" between.
Commodity consumption: average pages per issue 20(d).
Equipment: EDITORIAL: Front-end hardware — Ap/Mac Pagination Network, 8-Mk/Mycro-Comp, 3-TI/Silent 700, 1-Mk/100 Plus, 2-TI; Front-end software — Mk. CLASSIFIED: Front-end hardware — 1-Mk/Mycro-Comp, 1-Mk/100 Plus; Front-end software — Mk. DISPLAY: Adv layout systems — Ap/Mac, Multi-Ad/Creator; Front-end hardware — Ap/Mac LC, Ap/Mac Quadra, Ap/Mac Centris, Ap/Power Mac 6100, Ap/Mac Server; Front-end software — QPS; Printers — QMS/860; Other equipment — Scanners. PRODUCTION: Pagination software — QuarkXPress 3.31; Typesetters — Ap/Mac Laser, OCU; Electronic picture desk — Lf/AP Leaf Picture Desk; Scanners — Nikon/Coolscan 35mm; Production cameras — 1-B; Automatic film processors — 1-P/Pakonolith; Color separation equipment (conventional) — 1-Tas/Vacuum Printing Unit, Adobe/Photoshop (2.5.1). WIRE SERVICES: News — AP, AP Laserphoto. BUSINESS COMPUTERS: NCR; PCs & micros networked.

FARIBAULT

Rice County

'90 U.S. Census- 17,085; E&P '96 Est. 17,817

Faribault Daily News (m-tues to sat; S)

Faribault Daily News, 514 Central Ave., Faribault, MN 55021; tel (507) 334-1853; fax (507) 334-8569. Huckle Publishing Inc. group.
Circulation: 7,106(m); 7,106(m-sat); 7,106(S); Sworn Sept. 30, 1995.
Price: 50¢(d); 50¢(sat); 50¢(S); $8.75/mo; $95.00/yr.
Advertising: Open inch rate $10.22(m); $10.22(m-sat); $10.22(S). **Representatives:** Minnesota Newspaper Assn.; Papert Companies.
News Service: AP. **Politics:** Independent. **Established:** 1914.
Not Published: New Year; Memorial Day; Independence Day; Labor Day; Christmas.
Special Editions: Brides (Jan); Community Profile (Feb); Spring Farm, Spring Sports, Health & Wellness (Mar); Spring Sports, Home & Garden, Senior Lifestyles (Apr); Graduation, Dining Guide (May); Heritage Festival, Summer Lifestyles (June); County Fair Edition (July); Fall Sports, Fall Farm Scene, Back-to-School (Aug); Car Care, Consumer Information Guide (Sept); It's a Woman's World (Oct); Christmas Kick-off, Winter Sports Preview (Nov); Christmas Gift Guide, Christmas Song Book (Dec).
Magazine: Parade (S).

CORPORATE OFFICERS

President James Huckle
Vice Pres David Balcom
Vice Pres Diana Huckle
Treasurer James Huckle

GENERAL MANAGEMENT

Publisher/Editor David Balcom
Business Manager Lesa Ferguson

MARKETING AND PROMOTION

Director-Marketing Paula Patton

CIRCULATION

Assoc Manager-Sales Sherry Starkenberg
Assoc Manager-Delivery Linda Kaderlik

NEWS EXECUTIVE

Managing Editor Lisa Schwarz

MANAGEMENT INFORMATION SERVICES

Data Processing Manager Lesa Ferguson

Market Information: Split Run; TMC; ADS.
Mechanical available: Offset; Black and 3 ROP colors; insert accepted — preprinted, free-standing; page cut-offs — 22 3/4".
Mechanical specifications: Type page 13" x 21 1/2"; E - 6 cols, 2 1/16", 1/8" between; A - 6 cols, 2 1/16", 1/8" between; C - 6 cols, 2 1/16", 1/8" between.
Commodity consumption: Newsprint 900 metric tons; widths 27", 28", 30"; black ink 15,000 pounds; color ink 3,000 pounds; average pages per issue 18(d), 24(S); single plates used 15,000.
Equipment: EDITORIAL: Front-end hardware — 8-Ap/Mac, 8-Ap/Mac Centris 610; Front-end software — Baseview, QuarkXPress; Printers — Ap/Mac LaserWriters, QMS/860 Hammerhead. CLASSIFIED: Front-end hardware — Ap/Mac, 2-Ap/Mac Centris 610; Front-end software — Baseview. DISPLAY: Adv layout systems — Ap/Mac Quadra 950, Ap/Mac Quadra 700; Front-end hardware — Ap/Mac; Front-end software — Multi-Ad/Creator, CD-Rom; Printers — QMS/860 Hammerhead; Other equipment — CD-Rom, Ap/Mac Scanner. PRODUCTION: Pagination software — Baseview; Typesetters — Graphic Enterprises/Negative Setter; Platemaking systems — 1-Nu; Plate exposures — 1-Nu; Plate processors — 6-NS/28; Electronic picture desk — Adobe/Photoshop; Production cameras — 1-DAI/DS24; Automatic film processors — 1-P/Pakonolith 24; Digital color separation equipment — Lf/Leafscan 35.
PRESSROOM: Line 1 — 7-WPC/Atlas Press; Press registration system — Stausser/Pin Registration System. MAILROOM: Counter stackers — 1-BG/Count-O-Veyor 105; Bundle tyer — 2-Bu, 1-MLN, 2-Spirit; Addressing machine — 1-Ch/525. WIRE SERVICES: News — AP; Photos — AP; Receiving dishes — size-3M, AP. BUSINESS COMPUTERS: 1-IBM/RISC-6000; Applications: PBS, Lotus: Circ, Adv billing, Accts receivable, Gen ledger; PCs & micros networked; PCs & main system networked.

FERGUS FALLS

Otter Tail County

'90 U.S. Census- 12,362; E&P '96 Est. 12,234
ABC-CZ (90): 12,362 (HH 5,080)

Daily Journal (e-mon to fri; m-sat)

Fergus Falls Daily Journal, 914 E. Channing; PO Box 506, Fergus Falls, MN 56537; tel (218) 736-7511; fax (218) 736-5919. Boone Newspapers Inc. group.
Circulation: 9,556(e); 9,556(m-sat); ABC Mar. 31, 1995.
Price: 50¢(d); 50¢(sat); $7.25/mo; $87.00/yr.
Advertising: Open inch rate $10.92(e); $10.92(m-sat). **Representative:** Papert Companies.
News Service: AP. **Established:** 1873.
Not Published: New Year; Memorial Day; Independence Day; Labor Day; Thanksgiving; Christmas.
Special Editions: Progress (Feb); Active Times (Mar); Resorter (May); Resorter, Active Times (June); Resorter (July); Active Times (Aug); Newcomers (Sept); Active Times (Nov).
Magazine: TV Journal.

GENERAL MANAGEMENT

Publisher Jim Morgan

ADVERTISING

Director Doug Phares

CIRCULATION

Manager Connie Knapp

NEWS EXECUTIVE

Managing Editor Richard Hensley

EDITORS AND MANAGERS

Business/Finance Editor Richard Hensley
Education Editor Karla Rose
News Editor Joel Myhre
Photo Editor Matt Baumann
Sports Editor Bridget Buesing

PRODUCTION

Foreman-Composing Eric Bishop
Foreman-Pressroom Terry Scharnberg

Market Information: Zoned editions; Split Run; TMC.
Mechanical available: Web-Offset; Black and 3 ROP colors; insert accepted — preprinted; page cut-offs — 22 3/4".
Mechanical specifications: Type page 13" x 21 1/2"; E - 6 cols, 2 1/16", 1/8" between; A - 6 cols, 2 1/16", 1/8" between; C - 9 cols, 1 1/3", 1/8" between.
Commodity consumption: Newsprint 350 short tons; width 27.5"; single pages printed 3,890; average pages per issue 16(d).
Equipment: EDITORIAL: Front-end hardware — Ap/Mac Centris, 13-Ap/Mac; Front-end software — Baseview; Printers — Ap/Mac LaserWriter 630, Okidata/Microline 182, LaserMaster/1200 XLO. CLASSIFIED: Front-end hardware — 3-Ap/Mac; Front-end software — Baseview; Printers — Okidata/Microline 393. DISPLAY: Front-end hardware — 3-Ap/Mac IIsi; Printers — 3-Ap/Mac LaserWriter 630. PRODUCTION: Pagination software — QPS; Plate exposures — 1-Nu/Flip Top FT40LNS; Plate processors — Nat/A-250; Production cameras — SCREEN/Vertical, SCREEN/Horizontal; Automatic film processors — AG/Rapidline; Shrink lenses — CK Optical/SQU-7.
PRESSROOM: Line 1 — 7-G/Community, 1-G/color unit. MAILROOM: Inserters and stuffers — 1-KAN; Bundle tyer — 1-Bu, 1-Gd; Addressing machine — 1-Ch. WIRE SERVICES: News — AP; Receiving dishes — size-3, AP. BUSINESS COMPUTERS: 3-IBM/VP 486-33 SX; Applications: RPG/II: Accts receivable, Accts payable, Payroll, Circ, Gen ledger; PCs & micros networked; PCs & main system networked.

HIBBING

St. Louis County

'90 U.S. Census- 18,046; E&P '96 Est. 15,818

The Daily Tribune (e-mon to fri; m-sat; S)

The Daily Tribune, 2142 1st Ave., Hibbing, MN 55746; tel (218) 262-1011; fax (218) 262-4318. Murphy Newspaper group.
Circulation: 8,150(e); 8,150(m-sat); 8,150(S); Sworn Sept. 29, 1995.
Price: 50¢(d); 50¢(sat); $1.25(S); $14.50/6wk, $31.46/13wk, $62.92/26wk, $125.84/52wk.
Advertising: Open inch rate $9.45(e); $10.60(m-sat); $10.50(S). **Representative:** Papert Companies.
News Service: AP. **Politics:** Independent. **Established:** 1894.
Note: The Daily Tribune is printed by the Mesabi Publishing Co. at the Mesabi Daily News in Virginia, MN.
Not Published: New Year; Memorial Day; Independence Day; Labor Day; Thanksgiving; Christmas.
Special Editions: Bridal (Jan); Progress (Feb); Home Improvement (Apr); Back-to-School (Aug); Car Fix-up (Sept); Christmas (Nov).
Special Weekly Sections: Food (wed); Stock, Teens, Churches (sat); TV Week (S); Business, Accent, Sports (daily).
Magazines: USA Weekend (S); Real Estate (monthly).

CORPORATE OFFICERS

President John Murphy
Secretary/Treasurer Elizabeth Murphy Burns

GENERAL MANAGEMENT

Publisher John Murphy

Minnesota I-213

General Manager	Terese Almquist
Purchasing Agent	Frank Molich

ADVERTISING
Director	Terry Backstrom
Manager-National	Judy Bonelli

CIRCULATION
Manager	Shawn Weinand

NEWS EXECUTIVE
Managing Editor	Pat Faherty

EDITORS AND MANAGERS
City Editor	John Saccoman
Editorial Page Editor	Pat Faherty
Family Editor	Beth Welden
News Editor	Jack Lynch
Photographer	Michael Lemmons
Sports Editor	Gary Giombetti

MANAGEMENT INFORMATION SERVICES
Data Processing Manager	Judy Bonelli

PRODUCTION
Manager	Frank Molich
Foreman	Jay Parker
Manager-Computer Systems	Frank Molich

Market Information: TMC.
Mechanical available: Offset; Black and 3 ROP colors; insert accepted — preprinted; page cut-offs — 21½".
Mechanical specifications: Type page 13¾" x 21½"; E - 6 cols, 2 1/16", ⅛" between; A - 6 cols, 2 1/16", ⅛" between; C - 8 cols, 1¾", ⅛" between.
Commodity consumption: average pages per issue 16(d), 24(sat), 32(S).
Equipment: EDITORIAL: Front-end hardware — NEC; Front-end software — Mk/Newscraft; Printers — Data South/DS220 Line Printer, 2-Printware/1217, Ap/Mac Laser 630; Other equipment — Lf/AP Leaf Picture Desk, AP Graphics. CLASSIFIED: Front-end hardware — NEC; Front-end software — Mk/Newscraft; Printers — Data South/DS220, 2-Printware/1217, Ap/Mac Laser 630. DISPLAY: Adv layout systems — Multi-Ad/Creator, Quark-XPress; Front-end hardware — 3-Ap/Mac Quadra 650; Front-end software — Quark-XPress; Printers — 2-Printware/1217 Laser, Ap/Mac Laser 630. PRODUCTION: Typesetters — 2-Printware/1217, Ap/Mac Laser 630; Plate exposures — 1-Nu/Flip Top FTUPNS; Plate processors — 1-Nat/A-250; Electronic picture desk — Lf/AP Leaf Picture Desk; Scanners — Lf/Leafscan 35; Production cameras — B/30"x 40"; Automatic film processors — 1-P/24ML; Shrink lenses — 1-CK Optical/SQU-7. MAIL-ROOM: Inserters and stuffers — 1-KAN/320-402; Bundle tyer — 2-Bu; Wrapping singles — 1-Bu; Addressing machine — 1-Am. WIRE SERVICES: News — AP; Photos — AP; Stock tables — AP; Receiving dishes — size-10ft, AP. BUSINESS COMPUTERS: Packard Bell; Applications: Vision Data; PCs & micros networked; PCs & main system networked.

INTERNATIONAL FALLS
Koochiching County
'90 U.S. Census- 8,325; E&P '96 Est. 11,705

The Daily Journal
(e-mon to fri)

The Daily Journal, 500 3rd St.; PO Box 951, International Falls, MN 56649; tel (218) 285-7411; fax (218) 285-7206. Red Wing Publishing Co. group.
Circulation: 4,372(e); Sworn Sept. 28, 1995.
Price: 50¢(d); $7.20/mo; $85.00/yr.
Advertising: Open inch rate $5.90(e).
News Service: AP. **Established:** 1911.
Not Published: New Year; Memorial Day; Independence Day; Labor Day; Thanksgiving; Christmas.
Special Editions: Progress; Car Care; Christmas; Home Improvement; Senior Citizens; Deer Hunting; Fishing.
Special Weekly Sections: Business Page (tues); TV Guide (wed).

CORPORATE OFFICERS
President	Arlin Albrecht
Secretary	Marilyn Albrecht

GENERAL MANAGEMENT
Publisher	Arlin Albrecht
General Manager	Dave Ramnes

ADVERTISING
Manager	Harry Swendsen

CIRCULATION
Manager	Bruce Napper

NEWS EXECUTIVES
Editor	Arlin Albrecht
Managing Editor	Tom Klein

EDITORS AND MANAGERS
City/Metro Editor	Laurel Beager
Editorial Page Editor	Tom Klein
Sports Editor	Chris Todd

PRODUCTION
Foreman	Norm Christiansen

Market Information: Split Run; TMC; ADS.
Mechanical available: Offset; Black and 3 ROP colors; insert accepted — preprinted; page cut-offs — 21½".
Mechanical specifications: Type page 13" x 21½"; E - 6 cols, 2 1/16", ⅛" between; A - 6 cols, 2 1/16", ⅛" between; C - 8 cols, 1½", ⅛" between.
Commodity consumption: Newsprint 160 short tons; widths 14", 14", 28"; black ink 3,450 pounds; color ink 230 pounds; average pages per issue 14(d).

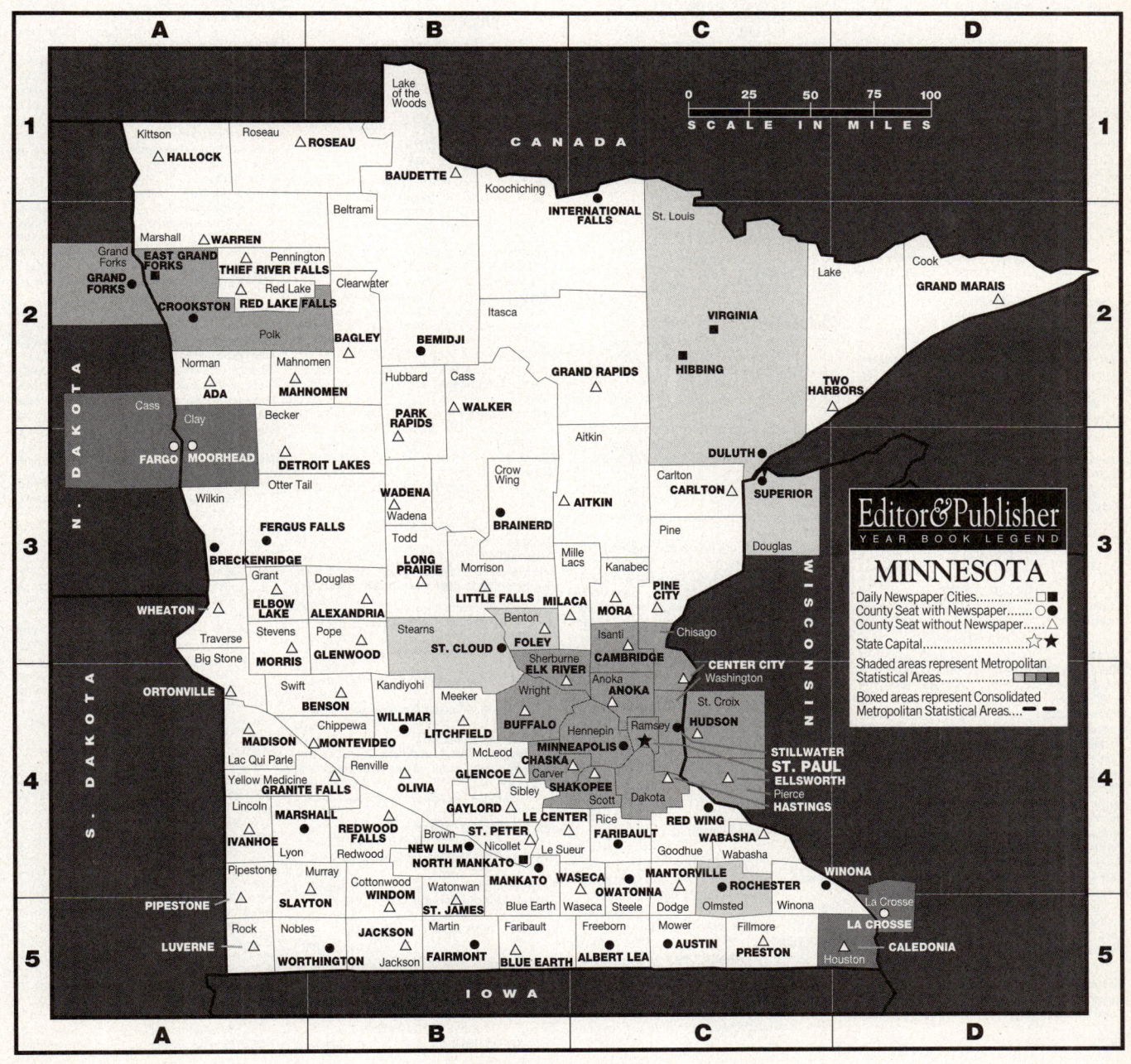

Copyright ©1996 by the Editor & Publisher Co.

Equipment: EDITORIAL: Front-end hardware — Ap/Mac; Front-end software — Aldus/PageMaker; Printers — Ap/Mac. CLASSIFIED: Front-end hardware — Ap/Mac. DISPLAY: Adv layout systems — Ap/Mac; Front-end hardware — Ap/Mac; Front-end software — Aldus/PageMaker; Printers — Ap/Mac LaserPrinter. PRODUCTION: Typesetters — Ap/Mac; Plate exposures — WL; Plate processors — 1-Nu; Scanners — Ap/Mac, HP; Production cameras — SCREEN/Companica 690E.
PRESSROOM: Line 1 — 4-G/Community. MAILROOM: Bundle tyer — Bu; Addressing machine — KR. WIRE SERVICES: News — AP; Receiving dishes — AP. BUSINESS COMPUTERS: IBM/PS-2 Model 50; Applications: MSSI: Adv, Circ; Quattro/Pro.

MANKATO-NORTH MANKATO

Blue Earth and Nicollet Counties

'90 U.S. Census- 41,632 (Mankato 31,468; North Mankato 10,164); E&P '96 Est. 45,116 (Mankato 34,018; North Mankato 11,098)
ABC-CZ (90): 43,428 (HH 15,653)

The Free Press (m-mon to sat)

The Free Press, 418 S. 2nd St., Mankato, MN 56001; tel (507) 625-4451; fax (507) 625-1149; e-mail freepress@ic.mankato.mn.us; web site http://www.ic.mankato.mn.us/news/news/freepress.html. Ottaway Newspapers Inc. group.
Circulation: 26,055(m); 26,055(m-sat); ABC Sept. 30, 1995.
Price: 50¢(d); 50¢(sat); $2.20/wk; $114.40/yr; $8.80/4wk.
Advertising: Open inch rate $14.56(m); $14.56(m-sat).
News Services: AP, ONS. **Politics:** Independent. **Established:** 1887.
Not Published: New Year; Independence Day; Christmas.
Special Editions: Bridal; Tax Guide; Meet Your Area Business People; That's Our Style; Student Guide; Spring Car Care; Fall Car Care; Senior Citizens; Spring Spectacular; Fall Home Improvement; Progress Edition; Mother's Day; Holiday Gift Guide; Crazy Days; Vikings; The Answer Book.
Special Weekly Sections: Business & Financial (mon); Food Section (tues); Arts & Entertainment (thur); Real Estate, TV Section (sat).
Magazines: TV Update (preprint) (sat); Parade.

GENERAL MANAGEMENT

President/Publisher	E Joe Vanderhoof
Controller	Dawn Fazio

ADVERTISING

Director-Marketing	Jay Thompson
Manager	Dan White
Manager-National	Becky Asleson

CIRCULATION

Director	Trish Boeke

NEWS EXECUTIVES

Editor	Deb Flemming
News Editor	Kathy Vos

EDITORS AND MANAGERS

Accent Editor	Michael Lagerquist
After Hours Editor	Michael Lagerquist
Aviation Editor	Michael Lagerquist
Books Editor	Ed Thoma
Business Editor	Joe Spear
Education Editor	Sue Menton
Features Editor	Michael Lagerquist
Films/Theater Editor	Michael Lagerquist
Food Editor	Michael Lagerquist
Librarian	Edie Schmierbach
Music Editor	Joe Tougas
Opinion Page Editor	Michael Larson
Director-Photography	John Cross
Political Editor	Mark Fischenich
Radio/Television Editor	Joe Tougas
Real Estate Editor	Joe Spear
Religion Editor	Michael Lagerquist
Science/Technology Editor	Joe Spear
Sports Editor	Jim Rueda
Teen-Age/Youth Editor	Sue Menton
Women's Editor	Michael Lagerquist

PRODUCTION

Director	Glen Asleson
Foreman-Composing	Jenifer Wendt
Foreman-Pressroom	Lon Youngerberg

Market Information: TMC.
Mechanical available: Offset; Black and 3 ROP colors; insert accepted — preprinted, half-tab, free-standing cards; page cut-offs — 22¾".
Mechanical specifications: Type page 13" x 21½"; E - 6 cols, 2$\frac{1}{16}$", ⅛" between; A - 6 cols, 2$\frac{1}{16}$", ⅛" between; C - 9 cols, 1⅜", $\frac{1}{16}$" between.
Commodity consumption: Newsprint 1,338 metric tons; width 27½"; black ink 30,000 pounds; color ink 5,000 pounds; single pages printed 9,788; average pages per issue 27(d), 28(S); single plates used 12,000.
Equipment: EDITORIAL: Front-end hardware — 27-Dewar/Discribe, 2-Dewar/Discovery; Front-end software — Dewar/Disc Net; Printers — Okidata/193; Other equipment — 1-Lf/AP Leaf Picture Desk, 1-Ap/Power Mac 7100. CLASSIFIED: Front-end hardware — 5-Dewar/Discribe, 1-Dewar/Discovery; Front-end software — Dewar/Disc Net; Printers — Dataproducts/LB300. DISPLAY: Adv layout systems — 8-Dewar/Discribe, 3-Dewar/Discovery; Front-end hardware — Dewar, 3-Ap/Mac IIcx; Front-end software — Dewar/Disc Net, Dewar/Ad Dummy, Multi-Ad/Creator. PRODUCTION: Typesetters — 2-TC/MG 202N, 1-AG/Accuset 1500; Plate exposures — Nu/Flip Top FT40V3UPNS; Plate processors — 1-C; Scanners — 1-ECR/Autokon 1030N; Production cameras — C/Spartan III; Automatic film processors — LE.
PRESSROOM: Line 1 — 6-G/Urbanite; Folders — 1-G. MAILROOM: Counter stackers — Id/2200; Inserters and stuffers — Mc/660; Bundle tyer — 3-MLN/MLNEE, 1-MLN/2EE, 2-MLN/IEE, 1-Power Strap/Newstyer 2000, Power Strap/P-250 A; Addressing machine — 1-Ch, 1-KR. WIRE SERVICES: News — AP, ONS; Photos — AP, ONS; Stock tables — AP; Receiving dishes — AP, ONS. BUSINESS COMPUTERS: 1-IBM/AS-400; Applications: Payroll, Circ, Adv, Accts payable, Gen ledger; PCs & micros networked; PCs & main system networked.

MARSHALL

Lyon County

'90 U.S. Census- 12,023; E&P '96 Est. 12,788
ABC-CZ (90): 12,023 (HH 4,443)

Independent (m-mon to sat)

Independent, 508 W. Main St.; PO Box 411, Marshall, MN 56258; tel (507) 537-1551; fax (507) 537-1557. Ogden Newspapers group.
Circulation: 8,779(m); 8,779(m-sat); ABC Sept. 30, 1995.
Price: 50¢(d); 50¢(sat); $7.50/mo; $85.00/yr.
Advertising: Open inch rate $9.80(m); $9.80(m-sat). **Representative:** Papert Companies.
News Service: AP. **Politics:** Independent. **Established:** 1873.
Not Published: Memorial Day; Labor Day; Christmas.
Special Editions: Pork Products Tab (Jan); Progress, Spring Bridal (Feb); Spring Farm, Home Improvement, Lawn & Garden (Apr); Graduation (May); Crazy Days (July); Back-to-School, Football Preview (Aug); Fall Car Care (Oct); Cook Book, Christmas Opener (Nov).
Special Weekly Sections: Business (mon); Weddings (tues); Education, Best Food Day (wed); Entertainment Page, Farm Focus (thur); TV Book, Church News (fri).
Magazines: Southwestern Minnesota "Peach" Section (Class); TV Program Book (fri).

CORPORATE OFFICER

President	G Ogden Nutting

GENERAL MANAGEMENT

General Manager	Russell Labat
Business Manager	Jane Sovell

ADVERTISING

Manager	Connie Nuese

CIRCULATION

Manager	Glen Caron

NEWS EXECUTIVE

Editor	Jim Tate

EDITOR AND MANAGER

Sports Editor	Per Peterson

PRODUCTION

Manager	Nort Johnson

Market Information: Zoned editions; TMC.
Mechanical available: Offset; Black and 3 ROP colors; insert accepted — preprinted; page cut-offs — 22¾".
Mechanical specifications: Type page 13" x 21½"; E - 6 cols, 2$\frac{1}{16}$", ⅛" between; A - 6 cols, 2$\frac{1}{16}$", ⅛" between; C - 9 cols, 1⅜", ⅛" between.
Commodity consumption: Newsprint 1,931 short tons; widths 27", 34", 32", 23", 34"; black ink 21,305 pounds; color ink 19,649.5 pounds; single pages printed 15,354; average pages per issue 16(d); single plates used 24,181.
Equipment: EDITORIAL: Front-end hardware — 1-Mk/1100 Plus, 7-Mk, 2-Ap/Power Mac 6100. CLASSIFIED: Front-end hardware — 1-Mk/1100 Plus. DISPLAY: Adv layout systems — 3-Ap/Power Mac 6100; Printers — MON/Express Master Imagesetter, HP/LaserJet 4MV. PRODUCTION: Typesetters — HP/LaserJet 4MV; Plate exposures — 1-Nu/FT40NS; Plate processors — 1-WL; Production cameras — 1-SCREEN; Automatic film processors — 1-P/524 Model Type 1.
PRESSROOM: Line 1 — 6-G/Community; Folders — 1-G. MAILROOM: Counter stackers — BG/Count-O-Veyor 108; Inserters and stuffers — MM; Bundle tyer — 1-Malow; Wrapping singles — 1-Wilton/Stra-Pack, MLN; Addressing machine — 1-KR/215, 1-KR/211-215, 4-Wm. LIBRARY: Electronic — 1-Dukane/Microfilm. WIRE SERVICES: News — AP, AP Wirephoto, AP Graphics; Receiving dishes — size-10ft, AP. BUSINESS COMPUTERS: 1-Mk; Applications: Adv billing, Accts receivable, Gen ledger, Payroll, Circ.

MINNEAPOLIS

Hennepin County

'90 U.S. Census- 368,383; E&P '96 Est. 366,279
ABC-NDM (90): 2,579,160 (HH 974,540)

Star Tribune (Newspaper of the Twin Cities) (m-mon to sat; S)

Star Tribune, 425 Portland Ave., Minneapolis, MN 55488; tel (612) 673-4000; fax (612) 673-4359; e-mail opinion@startribune.com; web site http://www.startribune.com/.
Circulation: 389,865(m); 389,865(m-sat); 688,337(S); ABC Sept. 30, 1995.
Price: 35¢(d); 35¢(sat); $1.75(S).
Advertising: Open inch rate $195.68(m); $195.68(m-sat); $247.45(S). **Representatives:** Sawyer-Ferguson-Walker Co.; American Publishers Reps.
News Services: AP, NYT, DJ, LAT-WP, SHNS, RN, States News Service. **Politics:** Independent. **Established:** 1867(Tribune), 1878 (Star).
Special Editions: Bridal (Jan); Thanksgiving Day Edition (Nov); Holiday (Dec); Welcome to the Neighborhood (monthly).
Special Weekly Section: TV Week (S).
Magazines: Comics, USA Weekend (S); TV Week Magazine; Real Estate Extra; Rent Right.

CORPORATE OFFICERS

Chairman of the Board	John Cowless III
President/CEO	David C Cox
Vice Pres/Chief Financial Officer	James J Viera
Vice Pres-Human Resources (Cowles Media Co.)	Pam Sveinson

GENERAL MANAGEMENT

Publisher/President	Joel Kramer
Senior Vice Pres-Marketer Customer Unit	James Diaz
Senior Vice Pres-Leader Strategic Integration Unit	Chris Mahai
Senior Vice Pres-Reader Customer Unit/Editor	Tim J McGuire
Vice Pres-Labor Relations	John Dennison
Vice Pres/Chief Financial Officer	John Grieman
Vice Pres-Sales Leader, Marketer Customer Unit	Charles Hoag
Vice Pres-Human Resources (Star Tribune)	Nancy Koo
Vice Pres/General Counsel	Randy Miller Lebedoff
Vice Pres-Classified/Market Group Leader	Thomas Mohr
Director-Circulation	Lisa Anderson
General Manager-Marketer Customer Unit	James Diaz
General Manager-Reader Customer Unit	Tim J McGuire

ADVERTISING

Director	James Diaz

TELECOMMUNICATIONS

Audiotex Manager	Rick Petersen

NEWS EXECUTIVES

Editor-Reader Customer Unit	Tim J McGuire
Production Editor	Steve Ronald
Asst Managing Editor-Production	Ron Wade
Administration Editor	Kent Gardner
Deputy Managing Editor-Human Resources	Linda Picone
Projects Team Leader	Ron Meador
Projects Team Leader	Larry Werner
News Research Director	Rob Daves
Change Editor	Arnie Robbins
Technology Editor	Tim Bitney
Director-Photography	Darlene Pfister
News Content Editor	Sherrie Marshall
Exec Editor-Sports	Julie Engebrecht
Director-News Budget	Rodgers Adams
Bureau Chief-Washington	Tom Hamburger

EDITORS AND MANAGERS

Books Reporter	Dave Wood
Columnist-Business	Richard Youngblood
Columnist-Gossip	Cheryl Johnson
Columnist-News	Jim Klobuchar
Congressional Editor	Sharon Schmickle
Coordinator Electronic Media	Art Meggitt
Coordinator Electronic News Systems	Bruce Adomeit
Editorial Page Editor	Susan Albright
Deputy Editorial Page Editor	Jim Boyd
Education Reporter-Trends	Mary Jane Smetanka
Features Section Editor	Susie Eaton-Hopper
Asst Features Section Editor	Dennis Branstiter
Food Editor	Ann Burkhardt
General Assignment Reporter	Colin Covert
General Assignment Reporter	Paul McEnroe
Head Librarian	Robert Jansen
Health/Science Editor	Lewis Cope
Home & Garden Editor	Ingrid Sundstrom-Lundegaard
Medical Issues/Research Reporter	Gordon Slovut
Movie Critic	Jeff Strickler
Music Reporter-Classical	Michael Anthony
Natural Resources Reporter	Dean Rebuffoni
Photo Editor	Mike Healy
Reader Representative	Lou Gelfand
Religion/Spiritual Reporter	Martha Allen
Team Leader	Roger Buoen
Team Leader	John Habich
Team Leader	Liz McConnell
Theater Reporter	Peter Vaughan
Theater/Dance Reporter	Michael Steele
Travel Editor	Catherine Watson
TV Critic	Noel Holston
Visual Content Editor	Bill Dunn
Washington Correspondent	Carol Byrne

PRODUCTION

Manager	Tom Hardie
Manager	Dick Ruble
Manager-Mailroom	Ken Larson
Manager-Platemaking	Bernie Weber
Manager-Pre Press	Lisa Anderson
Manager-Pre Press	Pat Weekley
Manager-Graphics	Ron Jasper
Manager-Newsprint	Jerry Kondrak
Manager-Machine Shop	Jim Treeten
Manager-Electric Shop	Chuck Erickson
Manager-Pressroom	Blake Spence

Market Information: Zoned editions; Split Run; TMC; ADS; Operate database; Operate audiotex; Electronic edition.
Mechanical available: Offset; Black and 3 ROP colors; insert accepted — preprinted, free-standing; page cut-offs — 22.07".
Mechanical specifications: Type page 13" x 21"; E - 6 cols, 2$\frac{1}{16}$", ⅛" between; A - 6 cols, 2$\frac{1}{16}$", ⅛" between; C - 10 cols, 1$\frac{3}{16}$", $\frac{1}{16}$" between.
Commodity consumption: Newsprint 92,000 short tons; widths 54", 54", 40⅜", 26⅞"; black ink 1,475,000 pounds; color ink 315,000 pounds; single pages printed 33,950; average pages per issue 73.1(d), 197.4(S); single plates used 600,000.
Equipment: EDITORIAL: Front-end hardware — 10-AT/9000, 190-AT, 30-AT/Remote, 14-AT/Pagination, 60-RSK/Tandy, 9-Panasonic/Portable; Front-end software — AT; Printers — 3-Dataproducts, 2-Florida Data. CLASSIFIED: Front-end hardware — 10-AT; Front-end software — AT; Printers — Dataproducts. AUDIOTEX: Hardware — 3-SpanLink; Software — ATT/Coversat. DISPLAY: Adv layout systems — 6-Ap/Mac Quadra 950, 19-Ap/Mac IIfx; Front-end hardware — 3-Ap/Mac Quadra 950; Front-end software — Adobe/Illustrator 3.2, Adobe/Photoshop 2.0, QuarkXPress 3.1, Multi-Ad/Creator, Ap/Applescan, CD-Rom; Printers — 1-QMS/2210, 1-QMS/Colorscript 100, 1-Ap/Mac LaserWriter II, 1-V/VT600W; Other equipment — 2-X/7650 Scanner, 1-Ap/Mac Applescan, 1-CD-Rom. PRODUCTION: Plate exposures — 4-WL/III; Plate processors — 5-WL; Scanners — 3-LE, 2-P/SC2D50, 1-AU/APS-5-100G, 2-AU/APS-100, 2-AU/APS-5-100; Production cameras — 2-C/Spartan III, 3-ECR/Autokon; Automatic film processors —

5-P/Quick, 2-LE; Reproportion units — 3-Hel/Pressfax; Film transporters — 2-LE, 5-QWI; Shrink lenses — 2-C; Color separation equipment (conventional) — 2-Eikonix Systems; Digital color separation equipment — SCREEN/688.
PRESSROOM: Line 1 — 10-G/Headliner Offset (6 half decks); Line 2 — 10-G/Headliner Offset (6 half decks); Line 3 — 10-G/Headliner Offset (6 half decks); Line 4 — 10-G/Headliner Offset (6 half decks); Line 5 — 10-G/Headliner Offset (6 half decks); Pasters — 1-G/CT50; Press control system — 1-G/MPCS. MAILROOM: Counter stackers — 20-Id/2000; Inserters and stuffers — 4-Fg/8-into-1 drum, 3-HI/72P; Bundle tyer — 10-MLN/2A, 13-Power Strap; Addressing machine — 5-AVY. LIBRARY: Electronic — Data Times, Vu/Text. WIRE SERVICES: News — AP, DJ, RN, AP Datafeatures; Stock tables — TMS; Syndicates — SHNS, NYT, LAT-WP; Receiving dishes — size-3m, AFP. BUSINESS COMPUTERS: 1-IBM/3081, 1-IBM/3090-180J; Applications: Admarc: Payroll, Accts payable, Accts receivable, Gen ledger; PCs & micros networked; PCs & main system networked.

MOORHEAD

See FARGO, ND

NEW ULM

Brown County

'90 U.S. Census- 13,132; **E&P '96 Est.** 12,641
ABC-CZ (90): 13,132 (HH 5,199)

The Journal (m-mon to sat; S)

The Journal, 303 N. Minnesota St.; PO Box 487, New Ulm, MN 56073; tel (507) 359-2911; fax (507) 359-7362. Ogden Newspapers group.
Circulation: 9,999(m); 9,999(m-sat); 10,380(S); ABC Sept. 30, 1995.
Price: 50¢(d); 50¢(sat); 75¢(S); $1.75/wk; $7.60/mo; $86.00/yr.
Advertising: Open inch rate $12.01(m); $12.01(m-sat); $12.01(S). **Representative:** Papert Companies.
News Service: AP. **Politics:** Independent. **Established:** 1898.
Not Published: New Year; Independence Day; Thanksgiving; Christmas.
Special Editions: January Thaw; Winter Sports; Tax Guide; City Progress; President's Day Coupon; Bridal; Shamrock Days; Home & Self Improvement; Spring Car Care; Spring Moonlight Madness; Outdoor Life; Visitor's Guide; Graduation Tab; Farm Progress; Fall Sports; Fall Fashion; Industry Appreciation; Discovery Days; Fall Car Care; Medical Directory; Christmas Kick-off.
Special Weekly Sections: Best Food Day (tues); Agribusiness (fri); Church News (sat); Lifestyle (S).
Magazines: Agribusiness (fri); TV Book, Color Comics, Parade (S).
Broadcast Affiliates: K 22AE-TV New Ulm, MN.

CORPORATE OFFICERS

President G Ogden Nutting
Vice Pres William C Nutting
Vice Pres Robert M Nutting
Secretary William O Nutting
Treasurer Duane D Wittman

GENERAL MANAGEMENT

Publisher Bruce Fenske
Business Manager Debbie Dubberly
General Manager Bruce Fenske

ADVERTISING

Director Michael Stahl

MARKETING AND PROMOTION

Manager-Marketing/Promotion Steve Grosam

TELECOMMUNICATIONS

Manager-Telecommunications Phil Dahlmeier

CIRCULATION

Manager Steve Grosam

NEWS EXECUTIVE

Editor Kevin Sweeney

EDITORS AND MANAGERS

Business/Finance Editor Lee Smith
City Reporter Lee Smith
Columnist Kevin Sweeney
County Reporter Josh Freed
Editorial Page Editor Kevin Sweeney
Editorial Writer Kevin Sweeney
Education/Women's Editor Jody Sailor
Farm/Agriculture Editor Mary Jo Sylwester
Librarian Leah Pockrandt
National Editor Lee Smith
News Editor Donna Weber
Political/Government Editor Lee Smith
Religion Editor Leah Pockrandt
Regional Reporter Mary Jo Sylwester
Sports Editor Blair Meyer

MANAGEMENT INFORMATION SERVICES

Manager Debbie Dubberly

PRODUCTION

Superintendent Gerri Wilfahrt

Market Information: TMC.
Mechanical available: Offset; Black and 3 ROP colors; insert accepted — preprinted; page cut-offs — 21½".
Mechanical specifications: Type page 13" x 21½"; E - 6 cols, 2 1/16", 1/8" between; A - 6 cols, 2 1/16", 1/8" between; C - 9 cols, 1 3/8", 1/16" between.
Commodity consumption: single pages printed 5,906; average pages per issue 19(d), 24(S).
Equipment: EDITORIAL: Front-end hardware — Mk/1100 Plus; Front-end software — QuarkXPress 3.3; Printers — TI; Other equipment — Ap/Mac Classic, Polaroid/Film Scanner, 2-Ap/Mac PC 6100, 1-Ap/Mac PC 7100. CLASSIFIED: Front-end hardware — 1-Mk/1100 Plus; AUDIOTEX: Supplier name — Micro Voice. DISPLAY: Adv layout systems — Ap/Mac, Ap/Mac 6100. Front-end hardware — Ap/Mac; Front-end software — Multi-Ad/Creator 3.3; PRODUCTION: Pagination software — QuarkXPress 3.3; Typesetters — 2-Ap/Mac LaserPrinter; Production cameras — AG/Repromaster 310. WIRE SERVICES: News — AP; Photos — AP; Receiving dishes — size-4.6m, AP. BUSINESS COMPUTERS: NCR/Tower.

NORTH MANKATO

See MANKATO

OWATONNA

Steele County

'90 U.S. Census- 19,386; **E&P '96 Est.** 20,033
ABC-CZ (90): 19,386 (HH 7,382)

Owatonna People's Press (m-tues to sat; S)

Owatonna People's Press, 135 W. Pearl St., Owatonna, MN 55060; tel (507) 451-2840; fax (507) 451-6020. Huckle Publishing Inc. group.
Circulation: 7,484(m); 7,484(m-sat); 7,707 (S); ABC Sept. 30, 1995.
Price: 50¢(d); 50¢(sat); 50¢(S); $8.25/mo; $96.75/yr.
Advertising: Open inch rate $10.53(m); $10.53(m-sat); $10.53(S). **Representatives:** Minnesota Newspaper Assn.; Papert Companies.
News Service: AP. **Politics:** Independent. **Established:** 1874.
Not Published: New Year; Memorial Day; Independence Day; Labor Day; Christmas.
Special Editions: Brides (Jan); Community Profile, Home & Vacation, NIE (Mar); Home & Garden, Spring Sports (Apr); Vacation & Leisure, Graduation, Mother's Day (May); Auto, Father's Day, Area Business (June); Crazy Days (July); County Fair, Back-to-School (Aug); Homes, Service Clubs (Sept); Women In Business (Oct); Christmas Catalog, Cookbook (Nov); Christmas Greetings, Christmas Song Book, Christmas Clearance (Dec).
Special Weekly Section: Photo News (sat).
Magazine: Parade (S).

CORPORATE OFFICERS

President James Huckle
Vice Pres Diana Huckle
Treasurer James Huckle

GENERAL MANAGEMENT

Publisher/Editor Ken Lynam
Business Manager Lesa Ferguson

ADVERTISING

Manager Holly Westercamp

CIRCULATION

Assoc Manager-Sales Carol Harvey
Assoc Manager-Delivery Judy Noble

NEWS EXECUTIVE

Managing Editor John Head

MANAGEMENT INFORMATION SERVICES

Data Processing Manager Lesa Ferguson

Market Information: TMC; ADS.
Mechanical available: Offset; Black and 3 ROP colors; insert accepted — preprinted, free standing; page cut-offs — 22¾".
Mechanical specifications: Type page 13" x 21½"; E - 6 cols, 2 1/16", 1/8" between; A - 6 cols, 2 1/16", 1/8" between; C - 6 cols, 2 1/16", 1/8" between.
Commodity consumption: average pages per issue 18(d), 24(S).
Equipment: EDITORIAL: Front-end hardware — 8-Ap/Mac Centris 610; Front-end software — Baseview, QuarkXPress; Printers — 2-Ap/Mac LaserWriter, QMS/860 Hammerhead. CLASSIFIED: Front-end hardware — 2-Ap/Mac Centris 610; Front-end software — Baseview, QuarkXPress. DISPLAY: Front-end hardware — 1-Ap/Mac Quadra 950, 2-Ap/Mac Quadra 700; Front-end software — Multi-Ad/Creator, CD-Rom; Printers — QMS/860 Hammerhead; Other equipment — CD-Rom, Ap/Mac Scanner. PRODUCTION: Pagination software — Baseview; Typesetters — 2-Graphic Enterprises/Negative Setter; Electronic picture desk — Adobe/Photoshop; Digital color separation equipment — Lf/Leafscan 35. WIRE SERVICES: News — AP; Photos — AP; Receiving dishes — size-6m, AP. BUSINESS COMPUTERS: IBM/RISC-6000; Applications: P.B.S.: Accts payable, Gen ledger, Auto billing; PCs & micros networked; PCs & main system networked.

RED WING

Goodhue County

'90 U.S. Census- 15,134; **E&P '96 Est.** 16,404
ABC-CZ (90): 15,134 (HH 5,973)

Republican Eagle (e-mon to fri; m-sat)

Republican Eagle, 2760 N. Service Dr.; PO Box 82, Red Wing, MN 55066; tel (612) 388-8235; fax (612) 388-8912. Red Wing Publishing Co. group.
Circulation: 7,945(e); 7,945(m-sat); ABC Sept. 30, 1995.
Price: 50¢(d); $1.00(sat); $8.50/mo (carrier); $93.50/yr (carrier).
Advertising: Open inch rate $11.67(e); $11.67 (m-sat). **Representative:** Papert Companies.
News Service: AP. **Politics:** Independent. **Established:** 1857.
Not Published: New Year; Memorial Day; Independence Day; Labor Day; Thanksgiving; Christmas.
Special Editions: Wedding (Jan); Progress (Feb); Health & Wellness, Home Improvement (Apr); Visitor's Guide, Graduation Edition (May); County Fair Edition (Aug); Red Wing Business People (Sept); Christmas Catalog (Nov); Last Minute Gift Guide, Christmas Special (Dec).
Special Weekly Sections: Senior Section; Ask the Professional; Area Business Page.
Magazines: TView (wkly); Connections; Applause (monthly).

CORPORATE OFFICERS

Board Chairman Arlin Albrecht
President Arlin Albrecht
Vice Pres Philip N Duff
Vice Pres Rebecca Albrecht-Poss
Vice Pres Carol Duff
Secretary Marilyn Albrecht
Treasurer James M Becker

GENERAL MANAGEMENT

Publisher Arlin Albrecht
General Manager Pete Baker
Business Manager James M Becker
Purchasing Agent Pete Becker

ADVERTISING

Director Vicki Winge
Manager-Classified Dawn Erickson

MARKETING AND PROMOTION

Manager-Promotion Rebecca Albrecht-Poss

TELECOMMUNICATIONS

Audiotex Manager Mark Poss

CIRCULATION

Director Diane Cedar

NEWS EXECUTIVE

Editor Jim Pumarlo

EDITORS AND MANAGERS

Arts/Entertainment Editor Jim Pumarlo
Automotive Editor Jim Pumarlo
Business/Finance Editor Jim Pumarlo
Editorial Page Editor Jim Pumarlo
Education/School Editor Jim Pumarlo
Farm/Real Estate Editor Jim Pumarlo
Fashion Editor Jim Pumarlo
Food/Home Editor Jim Pumarlo
Photo Editor Bill Pond
Picture Editor Jim Pumarlo
Religion/Science Editor Jim Pumarlo
Sports Editor Jarred Opatz
Teen-Age/Youth Editor Jim Pumarlo
Travel Editor Arlin Albrecht
Women's/Society Editor Jim Pumarlo

MANAGEMENT INFORMATION SERVICES

Data Processing Manager James Becker

PRODUCTION

Manager Bill Stechmann

Market Information: Zoned editions; TMC; ADS; Operate audiotex.
Mechanical available: Offset; Black and 3 ROP colors; insert accepted — preprinted, zoned to specification; page cut-offs — 22¾".
Mechanical specifications: Type page 13" x 21½"; E - 6 cols, 2 1/16", 1/8" between; A - 6 cols, 2 1/16", 1/8" between; C - 8 cols.
Commodity consumption: Newsprint 1,862 short tons; widths 28", 14"; black ink 46,691 pounds; color ink 1,935 pounds; single pages printed 6,827; average pages per issue 14(d); single plates used 22,880.
Equipment: EDITORIAL: Front-end hardware — Ap/Mac; Front-end software — Baseview/NewsEdit, QuarkXPress, Adobe/Photoshop; Printers — Ap/Mac LaserWriter IIg, MON/Expressmaster 1270; Other equipment — HP/ScanJet 3C, AP Photostream, Lf/Leafscan 35. CLASSIFIED: Front-end hardware — Ap/Mac; Front-end software — Baseview/Class Manager Plus, QuarkXPress; Printers — Ap/Mac LaserWriter IIg, Okidata/720. AUDIOTEX: Hardware — SMS/Stauffer; Supplier name — VNN. DISPLAY: Front-end hardware — Ap/Mac; Front-end software — Multi-Ad/Creator, Macromedia/Freehand, Adobe/Pagemaker, Adobe/Photoshop; Printers — Ap/Mac LaserWriter IIg, HP/ScanJet Plus; Other equipment — Pioneer/6-PK CD-Rom, 2-Ap/Mac CD-Rom, 88-MB/removable drive, 200-MB/removable drive. PRODUCTION: Pagination software — QuarkXPress 3.3, Aldus/PageMaker 5.0; OCR software — Caere/OmniPage Pro; Typesetters — MON/ExpressMaster 1270, Ap/Mac LaserWritrer IIg; Plate exposures — 2-Nu/Flip Top FT50V6UPNS; Plate processors — 2-Reconex; Scanners — Lf/Leafscan 35, HP/ScanJet 3C, HP/ScanJet Plus; Production cameras — R/20, LE/Robertson 500; Automatic film processors — LE/LD2600A; Color separation equipment (conventional) — Adobe/Photoshop, Ap/PowerMac 7100; Digital color separation equipment — HP/ScanJet 3C, Lf/Leafscan 35.
PRESSROOM: Line 1 — 10-G/Community, 1-G/SSC four high; Press drives — 2-Fin/75 h.p., 1-Fin/60 h.p.; Folders — 2-G/SSC. MAILROOM: Counter stackers — 1-BG/105, 1-BG/109; Inserters and stuffers — KR/512; Bundle tyer — 2-Bu, 2-EAM/Mosca Rom; Addressing machine — 2-KR/211. COMMUNICATIONS: Digital ad delivery system — AP AdSend. WIRE SERVICES: News — Photos — AP Photostream; Stock tables — AP; Syndicates — AP, Universal Press; Receiving dishes — size-2.8m, AP. BUSINESS COMPUTERS: IBM/Sys 36, Compaq/46; Applications: Custom software: Payroll, Circ, Accts receivable;, Lotus/Smart-Suite 3.0; PCs & micros networked.

ROCHESTER

Olmsted County

'90 U.S. Census- 70,745; **E&P '96 Est.** 83,729
ABC-CZ (90): 84,526 (HH 32,564)

Post-Bulletin (e-mon to fri; wknd)

Post-Bulletin, 18 1st Ave. S.E.; PO Box 6118, Rochester, MN 55903-6118; tel (507) 285-7600. Small Newspaper Group Inc. group.
Circulation: 40,204(e); 44,345 (wknd); ABC Sept. 30, 1995.
Price: 50¢(d); $1.75 (wknd); $2.85/wk; $37.05/13wk; $142.20/yr.
Advertising: Open inch rate $30.29(e); $30.29 (wknd). **Representative:** Papert Companies.
News Services: AP, NYT, KRT. **Politics:** Independent. **Established:** 1859.
Special Editions: Weddings (Jan); Rochester Area Builders Home Show, Home & Lifestyle Magazine (Feb); Drive Magazine (Mar); Senior Scene, Post Bulletin Business Show, Home & Lifestyle Magazine, Earth Day (Apr); Summer Recreation, Spring Home & Garden, Good News (May); Rochesterfest, Home & Lifestyle (June); Honor Roll (July); Education '96, Pigskin Preview, Fall Home Improvement (Aug); Rochester Area Builders Parade of Homes, Golden Generation Trade Show

(Sept); Home & Lifestyle Magazine, Drive Magazine (Oct); Home For the Holidays (Nov); Holiday Greetings (Dec).
Special Weekly Sections: Health, Business (mon); Teen Beat (tues); Food (wed); Prevue, Home (thur); Sports Extra, Real Estate, Marketplace (fri); Money, Leisure, Travel (sat).

CORPORATE OFFICERS
President Len Robert Small
Board Chairman Jean Alice Small
Secretary Thomas P Small
Treasurer Joseph E Lacaeyse

GENERAL MANAGEMENT
Publisher William C Boyne
General Manager Robert Hill
Business Manager Sandra Severson
Director-Human Resources Lynne Miller
Superintendent-Building Ted Perry

ADVERTISING
Director Norm Doty
Manager-Classified Donna Long
Manager-Display Audrey Groteboer

MARKETING AND PROMOTION
Director-Promotion John Withers

TELECOMMUNICATIONS
Manager-Telecommunications Mike Korte

CIRCULATION
Director William Lisser
Manager Todd Heroff
Manager-Customer Service Dawn Molde

NEWS EXECUTIVES
Editor William C Boyne
Managing Editor Jon Losness

EDITORS AND MANAGERS
City Editor Jay Furst
Environment/Ecology Editor John Weiss
Lifestyle Editor Janice McFarland
Medical/Science Editor Jill Burcum
News Editor Amy Morris
Sports Editor Craig Swalboski

MANAGEMENT INFORMATION SERVICES
Director-Management Info Services Sandra Severson
Manager-Management Info Services Victor Denny

PRODUCTION
Manager-Pre Press Joe Long
Manager-Press/Post Press Jeffrey Lansing
Manager-Distribution Center Jereome Ferson
Manager-Pre Press/Quality Robert Sannes
Manager-Pagination Dean Oredson

Market Information: Zoned editions; Split Run; TMC; Operate audiotex.
Mechanical available: Offset; Black and 3 ROP colors; insert accepted — preprinted; page cutoffs — 22".
Mechanical specifications: Type page 13" x 21"; E - 6 cols, $2\frac{1}{16}$", $\frac{1}{8}$" between; A - 6 cols, $2\frac{1}{16}$", $\frac{1}{8}$" between; C - 8 cols, $1\frac{9}{16}$", $\frac{1}{16}$" between.
Commodity consumption: Newsprint 4,400 metric tons; widths 55", $41\frac{1}{4}$", $27\frac{1}{2}$"; black ink 123,000 pounds; color ink 49,000 pounds; single pages printed 18,400; average pages per issue 58(d); single plates used 60,000.
Equipment: EDITORIAL: Front-end hardware — AT, DEC; Front-end software — AT, AT/Atan Express. CLASSIFIED: Front-end hardware — AT, DEC; Front-end software — AT. AUDIOTEX: Hardware — Ap/Mac; Supplier name — Brite. DISPLAY: Adv layout systems — Mk/Ad Director; Front-end hardware — Ap/Mac; Front-end software — QuarkXPress, Adobe/Illustrator; Printers — 2-AG/Selectset 5000, 1-AG/9400PS; Other equipment — 2-AG/Focus Scanner, 2-Hyphen/OP1. PRODUCTION: Pagination software — QPS 3.11; Typesetters — 2-AG/SelectSet 5000, AU/9400 PS; Plate exposures — 1-Nu; Plate processors — WL, WL, Nat/PlateMaker; Electronic picture desk — Lf; Scanners — Polaroid, Umax, Nikon, AG; Production cameras — 1-C/Spartan III; Automatic film processors — 3-AG/RAP66; Color separation equipment (conventional) — Adobe/Photoshop; Digital color separation equipment — Nikon/3510AF, Umax/630. PRESSROOM: Line 1 — 5-G/Headliner Offset (3 decks); Press drives — Allen Bradley; Folders — G/2:1, G/2:1; Pasters — G; Reels and stands — G; Press control system — Allen Bradley; Press registration system — Ternes. MAILROOM: Counter stackers — 2-HL, 2-HL; Inserters and stuffers — GMA, GMA/10 Heads; Bundle tyer — MLN; Wrapping singles — Mosco; Addressing machine — Ch; Other mailroom equipment — 4-MM/Signature Stitcher. COMMUNICATIONS: Digital ad delivery system — AdSat. WIRE SERVICES: News — AP, KRT, NYT; Photos — AP; Stock tables — AP SelectStox; Receiving dishes — size-10ft, AP. BUSINESS COMPUTERS: IBM/AS-400-D35, PCs; Applications: IBM/AS-400: Accts payable, Accts receivable, Payroll, Gen ledger, Circ; Lotus 1-2-3, WordPerfect, Abra/2000, Abrapay: Novell/Personal Netware; PCs & micros networked; PCs & main system networked.

ST. CLOUD

Stearns, Benton & Sherburne Counties
'90 U.S. Census- 37,616; **E&P '96 Est.** 33,988
ABC-CZ (90): 76,772 (HH 27,732)

St. Cloud Times

(e-mon to fri; m-sat; S)

St. Cloud Times, 3000 N. 7th St.; PO Box 768, St. Cloud, MN 56302; tel (612) 255-8700; fax (612) 255-8704. Gannett Co. Inc. group.
Circulation: 28,874(e); 28,874(m-sat); 37,596(S); ABC Sept. 30, 1995.
Price: 35¢(d); 35¢(sat); $1.50(S); $3.00/wk (carrier); $13.00/mo (carrier); $156.00/yr (carrier).
Advertising: Open inch rate $33.87(e); $33.87(m-sat); $45.03(S). **Representative:** Gannett National Newspaper Sales.
News Services: AP, GNS. **Politics:** Independent. **Established:** 1887.
Special Editions: Bridal (Jan); Progress (Mar); Lawn & Garden (Apr); Bridal (July); Football (Sept); Christmas Gift Guide (Dec); Real Estate (monthly).
Special Weekly Sections: "Good Times" (tues); Best Food Day, Hot Ticket (TMC) (wed); Church Page (fri); Travel Page, Money Section (S); Business Page, Weddings/Engagements (daily).
Magazines: Weekend Plus (Entertainment Section) (thur); USA Weekend (S); Home Magazine (Mar); Home Magazine (May); Home Magazine, City Festival (July); Home Magazine (Sept); Home Magazine (Nov).

CORPORATE OFFICERS
President Sonja Sorensen Craig
Vice Pres Don R Casey
Secretary/Corporate Thomas L Chapple
Treasurer/Corporate Lawrence P Gasho

GENERAL MANAGEMENT
Publisher Sonja Sorensen Craig
Controller Berni Hollinger
Manager-Commercial Roger Parmenter
Manager-Systems Duane C Gorman
Director-Human Resources Patricia W Carlson

ADVERTISING
Director Rhonda Barlow
Manager-Sales Celeste P Simon
Manager-Telemarketing Laurie Langen
Coordinator-National Kris Yackley

MARKETING AND PROMOTION
Director-Marketing Development Joan C Karl

TELECOMMUNICATIONS
Audiotex Manager Duane C Gorman

CIRCULATION
Director Geary J Yaeger
Manager-Motor Route/Single Copy Tom Steve
Asst Manager Kathryn R Andersen

NEWS EXECUTIVES
Exec Editor Don R Casey
Managing Editor John L Bodette Jr

EDITORS AND MANAGERS
Assignment Editor Michael Knaak
Copy Desk Chief Randy Krebs
Editorial Page Editor Pia Lopez
Photo Department Manager Michael Knaak
Sports Editor Salary DeLand
Systems Editor Jerry Yadamec
Topic Editor Noreen Kaluza
Topic Editor Lee Rood
Topic Editor Becky Beyers
Topic Editor Michael Nistler

MANAGEMENT INFORMATION SERVICES
Data Processing Manager Duane C Gorman

PRODUCTION
Director Greg Fiorito
Manager-Pressroom Glen Klitsch
Manager-Pre Press Dennis Host
Manager-Packaging/Distribution Center Barb Rosenberger
Manager-Building Service Mark Hessler

Market Information: Split Run; TMC; Operate audiotex.
Mechanical available: Offset; Black and 3 ROP colors; insert accepted — preprinted; page cutoffs — $22\frac{3}{4}$".
Mechanical specifications: Type page 13" x $21\frac{1}{2}$"; E - 6 cols, $2\frac{1}{16}$", $\frac{1}{8}$" between; A - 6 cols, $2\frac{1}{16}$", $\frac{1}{8}$" between; C - 9 cols, $1\frac{3}{8}$", $\frac{1}{16}$" between.
Commodity consumption: Newsprint 2,397 short tons; 2,175 metric tons; widths $27\frac{1}{4}$", $27\frac{1}{4}$", $40\frac{3}{4}$", $54\frac{1}{2}$"; black ink 34,667 pounds; color ink 20,953 pounds; single pages printed 12,738; average pages per issue 32(d), 76(S); single plates used 51,400.
Equipment: EDITORIAL: Front-end hardware — Tandem/KI 22; Front-end software — SII; Printers — HP/LaserJet II; Other equipment — 36-PC, 14-Ap/Mac. CLASSIFIED: Front-end hardware — Tandem/KI 22; Front-end software — SII; Printers — 2-Epson/FX 1050, HP/LaserJet IV; Other equipment — 10-PC. DISPLAY: Front-end hardware — 4-Ap/Mac Quadra 650, 2-Ap/Mac Quadra 610; Front-end software — Multi-Ad Creator. PRODUCTION: Pagination software — QPS 3.3; Typesetters — 2-ECR/3850; Plate exposures — 3-Nu/Flip Top; Plate processors — Graham, WL; Electronic picture desk — CD; Scanners — ECR/Autokon 1000DE, Umax/1260 Scanner, Nikon/3510 Scanner; Production cameras — C/Spartan II Camera; Automatic film processors — 3-LE; Film transporters — C/Spartan II. PRESSROOM: Line 1 — 8-HI/1650; Press drives — Haley/Control (4 GE Drive Motors); Folders — 2-HI/2:1; Pasters — 5-Registron/3 arm RTP. MAILROOM: Counter stackers — 2-HI/2517; Inserters and stuffers — 3-MM/227 (4-pocket), 3-MM/227 (4-pocket); Bundle tyer — 4-MLN; Addressing machine — 3-Ch. LIBRARY: Electronic — Paper Desk. COMMUNICATIONS: Digital ad delivery system — AP AdSend. WIRE SERVICES: News — AP, GNS; Stock tables — AP; Receiving dishes — AP. BUSINESS COMPUTERS: IBM/AS 400; Applications: Circ, Adv, Accts payable, Payroll, Inventory, Gen ledger, Budget.

ST. PAUL

Ramsey County
'90 U.S. Census- 272,235; **E&P '96 Est.** 273,901
ABC-NDM (90): 1,960,876 (HH 741,395)

St. Paul Pioneer Press

(m-mon to fri; m-sat; S)

St. Paul Pioneer Press, 345 Cedar St., St. Paul, MN 55101; tel (612) 222-5011; web site http://www.pioneerplanet.com. Knight-Ridder Inc. group.
Circulation: 208,807(m); 11,386(m-sat); 277,782(S); ABC Sept. 30, 1995.
Price: 25¢(d); 25¢(sat); $1.50(S); $3.30/wk; $14.30/mo; $171.60/yr.
Advertising: Open inch rate $105.73(m); $111.54 (m-fri); $113.86(m-sat); $123.58(S).
News Services: AP, KRT, LAT-WP, KRT News Wire. **Politics:** Independent. **Established:** 1849 (Pioneer Press), 1868 (Dispatch), 1882 (Sunday).
Special Editions: Sports Show, Winter Carnival, Celebration Page: Women's History Month, Home Style, Celebration Page: Black History Month (Jan); Camping Show, Cruises, Home & Patio Show, Frozen Food (Feb); Auto Show (Insert and Program), Frozen Food, Spring Fashion (Mar); Major League Baseball Section, BTC 100 Largest Public Companies, Destinations-Vacation Guide, Metro Golf Guide, Home Style, 1996 Home Tour, Public Service Week Feature (Apr); Cinco de Mayo, Midwest Pet Fair, Walleye Opener (May); Saint Paul Saint Tab, 100 Largest Banks, Guide to Go: Independence Day Fireworks (June); Burnet Senior Golf Classic, Fall Arts Preview, CEO Salary Survey, Destination Vacation Guide, State Fair, Home Style, High School/College Football Preview, Pro Football Preview (Aug); Fall Fashion, Fall TV Preview, Hunting (Sept); Home Style, Savor, Answer Book, Children's Museum (Oct); Home Style, Ski Show, Wolves/NBA, Gift Guide (Nov); Travel: Arizona (Dec).
Special Weekly Sections: Golf Page (Apr 19 - Sept) (wed); Gardening (Apr 27 - June); Fall Gardening (Sept 7 - Oct 12) (thur); Showtime, Sports, Business Twin Cities, Express, Travel, Real Estate, Automotive/Merchandise, Homes/Rentals (S).
Magazines: Color Comics, TV Weekly (S).

CORPORATE OFFICERS
President Peter B Ridder
Senior Vice Pres-Administration Thomas A Stephenson
Vice Pres/Director-Employee Relations Jill Taylor
Vice Pres/Director-Finance Don Bothun

GENERAL MANAGEMENT
Senior Vice Pres Thomas A Stephenson
Publisher Peter B Ridder
Manager-Credit Frank Seidl

ADVERTISING
Vice Pres Mary Altuvilla
Manager-Classified Darrell Rooney
Manager-Display Joan Lane
Manager-Marketing Info Brent Lawrence
Supervisor-Co-op Dick Martens

MARKETING AND PROMOTION
Vice Pres-Consumer Marketing Scott Frantzen
Director-Marketing Services Patrice Bremer

TELECOMMUNICATIONS
Audiotex Manager Lem Lloyd

CIRCULATION
Manager-Metro Sales Barry O'Rourke

NEWS EXECUTIVES
Senior Vice Pres/Editor Walker Lundy
Senior Editor-Minnesota Roots Sue Campbell
Senior Editor-Technology and New Ventures David Fryxell
Senior Editor-Nation/World Martie Malan
Senior Editor-Health & 2000 Pat McMorrow
Senior Editor-Sports Mike O'Malley
Senior Editor-Public Interest Kate Parry
Senior Editor-Education & On-Line Newsroom Liason Dave Peters
Senior Editor-Presentation Hub Dee-Dee Strickland
Senior Editor-Visuals Peter Weinberger
Senior Editor-Minneapolis & Suburbs Don Wyatt
Managing Editor Kenneth Doctor

EDITORS AND MANAGERS
Books Editor Mary Ann Grossmann
Columnist Don Boxmeyer
Columnist Joe Soucheray
Columnist Katherine Lanpher
Editorial Page Editor Ronald D Clark
Editorial Writer Steven Dornfeld
Editorial Writer Glenda Holste
Editorial Writer Denise Johnson
Editorial Writer Doug Tice
Fashion Georgann Koelln
Food Editor Eleanor Ostman
Outdoor Editor Chris Niskanen
Religion Editor Clark Morphew
Television Editor Brian Lambert
Travel Editor Sam Elrod

MANAGEMENT INFORMATION SERVICES
Vice Pres-Pre Press & Technology Harold Hampton
Data Processing Manager Ed Schneider

PRODUCTION
Vice Pres/Director-Operations Larry Barr
Asst Director-Operations Tom Travis
Manager-Machine Shop Chuck Germain
Manager-Composing D C Johnson
Manager-Platemaking Dan Reber
Manager-Electric Shop Jack Anderson
Manager-Mailroom Jim Davies
Coordinator Kathy Johnson

Market Information: Zoned editions; Split Run; TMC; ADS; Operate database; Operate audiotex.
Mechanical available: Offset; Black and 3 ROP colors; insert accepted — preprinted, paper bags, selected product samples; page cut-offs — 22".
Mechanical specifications: Type page 13" x 21"; E - 6 cols, 2", $\frac{3}{8}$" between; A - 6 cols, 2", $\frac{3}{16}$" between; C - 10 cols, $1\frac{1}{4}$", $\frac{1}{16}$" between.
Commodity consumption: Newsprint 32,100 metric tons; widths 54", 54", $40\frac{1}{2}$", $27\frac{1}{8}$", $47\frac{7}{16}$"; black ink 550,000 pounds; color ink 210,000 pounds; single pages printed 26,600; average pages per issue 58(d), 162(S); single plates used 271,000.
Equipment: EDITORIAL: Front-end hardware — SII, 4-CLX; Front-end software — SII; Printers — HP/Lasers; Other equipment — SCS/LinX. CLASSIFIED: Front-end hardware — SII, 4-CLX; Front-end software — SII/Czar, Microsoft/Windows; Other equipment — 55-PC/486-33. AUDIOTEX: Supplier name — Micro Voice. DISPLAY: Adv layout systems — Ap/Mac; Front-end hardware — Ap/Mac, Ap/Mac; Front-end software — QuarkXPress 3.3; PRODUCTION: Typesetters — 2-AU/APS 4, 2-AU/APS 5, 2-ECR/Pelbox; Plate exposures — KFM/Plate Express, Nu; Plate processors — KFM/Plate Express, Nu; Production cameras — 1-C/Spartan III; Automatic film processors — LE, P; Film transporters — LE; Shrink lenses — Ck; Color separation equipment (conven-

Three steps to the BEST information on newspapers today!...

1. GET THE NEWS!

Editor & Publisher

Editor & Publisher Magazine
NEWS ON NEWSPAPERING--
52 times a year. Only $1.25 a week.

YES! Enter a one-year subscription in my name.
❏ Bill me for one year.
❏ My payment for $65 is enclosed.

My name_____
Company_____
Address_____
City_____ State_____ Zip_____

Important! Please tell us about yourself:

A. Your Occupation (Check Only **One** Category)
1. ❏ Daily Newspaper
2. ❏ Weekly Newspaper
3. ❏ Corp./Ind./Assn. Buying Advertising Space
4. ❏ Advertising Agency
5. ❏ Newspaper Rep.
6. ❏ Magazine/Other Publication
7. ❏ Graphic Arts/Printing Service/Newspaper Supplier
8. ❏ News Service/Feature Syndicate
9. ❏ Publicity and Public Relations
10. ❏ Library/Federal/State and Local Governments
11. ❏ Education: Students/Teachers
Other (Please specify)_____

B. Your Occupation (Check Only **One** Category)
A. ❏ Publisher
B. ❏ President
C. ❏ V President
D. ❏ Editor
E. ❏ General Mgr.
F. ❏ Business Mgr.
G. ❏ Controller
H. ❏ Advertising Mgr.
I. ❏ Sales Mgr.
J. ❏ Class Mgr.
K. ❏ Research Mgr.
L. ❏ Promo Mgr
M. ❏ PR Mgr.
O. ❏ Prod Mgr.
P. ❏ Composing Mgr.
Q. ❏ Circulation Mgr.
R. ❏ Editorial Dept.
S. ❏ Advertising Dept.
T. ❏ Circulation Dept.
V. ❏ Production Dept.
W. ❏ Promotion Dept.
X. ❏ Freelance Artist/Writer
Y. ❏ Newspaper Dealer/Distributor
Z. ❏ Retired
AA. ❏ MIS Mgr.
BB. ❏ Prepress Mgr.
CC. ❏ Mailroom Mgr.
Other (Please specify)

EB6Y

2. GET THE MARKETS!

Editor & Publisher Market Guide

In-depth quantitative & qualtitative data on over 1600 US and Canadian newspaper markets. **ONLY $100 postpaid!**

YES! Please ship me the current edition of the Editor & Publisher Market Guide to review. My satisfaction is guaranteed--I may return my copy for a full refund if I'm not satisfied.

❏ Payment enclosed--payable to E&P Market Guide.
  Bill my ❏ MC ❏ VISA: Account #_____
Signature_____ Exp. Date:_____
My name_____
Company_____
Address_____
City_____ State_____ Zip_____

Payment must accompany orders. New York, California, Washington D.C., and Canada residents must add applicable taxes. No delivery to P.O. boxes All remittances must be in U.S. dollars.

MB6Y

3. GET THE FACTS!

Editor & Publisher INTERNATIONAL Year Book

Find all you need to know about US, Canadian and foreign newspapers. Includes: ad rates, circulations, contacts, installed equipment, associations, suppliers and loads more! Now in two easy-to-use, portable volumes!

YES! Please ship me the 1996 edition of the Editor & Publisher International Year Book.

❏ Payment enclosed--payable to E&P Market Guide. **Only $125** (including postage and handling)
  Bill my ❏ MC ❏ VISA: Account #_____
Signature_____ Exp. Date:_____
My name_____
Company_____
Address_____
City_____ State_____ Zip_____

Payment must accompany orders. New York, California, Washington D.C., and Canada residents must add applicable taxes. No delivery to P.O. boxes All remittances must be in U.S. dollars.

YB6Y

QUIK! 800-336-4380 CUSTOMER SERVICE

BUSINESS REPLY MAIL
FIRST-CLASS MAIL   PERMIT NO.20   NEW YORK, NY

POSTAGE WILL BE PAID BY ADDRESSEE

Editor & PUBLISHER

CIRCULATION DEPARTMENT
11 W 19TH ST.
NEW YORK NY 10114 - 0741

NO POSTAGE NECESSARY IF MAILED IN THE UNITED STATES

BUSINESS REPLY MAIL
FIRST-CLASS MAIL   PERMIT NO.20   NEW YORK, NY

POSTAGE WILL BE PAID BY ADDRESSEE

Editor & PUBLISHER

CIRCULATION DEPARTMENT
11 W 19TH ST.
NEW YORK NY 10114 - 0741

NO POSTAGE NECESSARY IF MAILED IN THE UNITED STATES

BUSINESS REPLY MAIL
FIRST-CLASS MAIL   PERMIT NO.20   NEW YORK, NY

POSTAGE WILL BE PAID BY ADDRESSEE

Editor & PUBLISHER

CIRCULATION DEPARTMENT
11 W 19TH ST.
NEW YORK NY 10114 - 0741

NO POSTAGE NECESSARY IF MAILED IN THE UNITED STATES

Minnesota I-217

tional) — Ap/Mac; Digital color separation equipment — X, Lf/Leafscan, Sharp. PRESSROOM: Press drives — Fin; Folders — 3-G/3:2 single; Pasters — G; Reels and stands — G; Press control system — G. MAILROOM: Counter stackers — 7-HL/Monitor, 2-QWI; Inserters and stuffers — 2-Fg/Drum, 1-GMA/SLS 1000 (20:1); Bundle tyer — 4-MLN, 8-Dynaric, 1-Power Strap; Wrapping singles — Bu; Addressing machine — Ch. LIBRARY: Electronic — Vu/Text, Vu/Text Save. COMMUNICATIONS: Facsimile — 2-Hel/Press Fax; Digital ad delivery system — AP AdSend. WIRE SERVICES: News — AP; Stock tables — AP; Syndicates — Accu-Weather, DJ, KRT; Receiving dishes — size-3m, AP. BUSINESS COMPUTERS: 1-HP/3000, Series 947, 1-HP/3000, Series 957; Applications: CJ/AIMCIS: MIS, Gen ledger, Payroll, Accts receivable; PCs & micros networked.

STILLWATER

Washington County

'90 U.S. Census- 13,882; E&P '96 Est. 15,365

Stillwater Evening Gazette

(e-mon to fri)

Stillwater Evening Gazette, 102 S. 2nd St.; PO Box 58, Stillwater, MN 55082; tel (612) 439-3130; fax (612) 439-4713. Hollinger International Inc. group.

Circulation: 4,032(e); Sworn Sept. 29, 1995.

Price: 35¢(d); $94.00/yr (in state), $104.00/yr (out of state).

Advertising: Open inch rate $8.16(e). **Representative:** Papert Companies.

News Service: AP. **Politics:** Independent. **Established:** 1884.

Not Published: New Year; Memorial Day; Independence Day; Labor Day; Thanksgiving; Christmas.

Special Editions: Brides, Jaycee's Sponsor Page (Jan); President's Day Sponsor Page, Who's Who Tab (Feb); United Way Sponsor Page, Spring Sports Tab, Spring Home Improvement Tab (Mar); Earth Day Section, Community Volunteers Sponsor Page (Apr); VE Day Tab, Memorial Day Sponsor Page (May); Graduation Section, Flag Day Sponsor Page (June); Independence Day Sponsor Page, Lumberjacks Days Tab (July); Washington City Fair Sponsor Page, VE Day Tab, Football Tab (Aug); Labor Day Sponsor Page, Fall Sports Tab, Wild West Days Tab (Sept); Fall Home Improvement, Fire Prevention Sponsor Page (Oct); Veteran's Day Sponsor Page, Winter Sports Tab, Thanksgiving Sponsor Page, Holiday Gift Guide, Holiday Lighting Contest (Nov); Christmas Coupon Book, Holiday Lighting Contest, Holiday Photo Greetings, New Year's Don't Drink and Drive Sponsor Page (Dec).

Special Weekly Section: Weekender (wed).

Magazine: Extra edition (TMC) (wed).

GENERAL MANAGEMENT

Publisher/Purchasing Agent	Mike Mahoney

ADVERTISING

Director	John Lund
Manager-Classified	Jean Wilson

EDITORS AND MANAGERS

News Editor	Rod Amlend
Sports Editor	Rod Amlend

PRODUCTION

Foreman-Composing	Wally Gravunder
Foreman-Pressroom	Wally Gravunder

Market Information: TMC.

Mechanical available: Offset; Black and 1 ROP color; insert accepted — preprinted, must be 1/4 folded; no catalogs; page cut-offs — 21⅝".

Mechanical specifications: Type page 13" x 21½"; E - 6 cols, 2 1/16", ⅛" between; A - 6 cols, 2 1/16", ⅛" between; C - 9 cols, 1⅜", 1/16" between.

Commodity consumption: Newsprint 210 short tons; width 28"; single pages printed 4,020; average pages per issue 12(d); single plates used 2,400.

Equipment: EDITORIAL: Front-end hardware — CText. CLASSIFIED: Front-end hardware — CText. DISPLAY: Adv layout systems — Ap/Mac; Front-end software — Aldus/PageMaker. PRODUCTION: Typesetters — 2-Ap/Mac LaserWriter; Platemaking systems — 1-N/FT40L; Production cameras — 1-B/1822. PRESSROOM: Line 1 — 4-HI/V-15A; Folders — 1-HI. MAILROOM: Bundle tyer — 1-Bu; Addressing machine — 1-Am. WIRE SERVICES: News — AP; Receiving dishes — size-2ft, UPI. BUSINESS COMPUTERS: Applications: Ad schedule, Circ, Accts receivable.

VIRGINIA

St. Louis County

'90 U.S. Census- 9,410; E&P '96 Est. 8,245

Mesabi Daily News

(m-mon to sat; S)

Mesabi Daily News, 704 7th Ave. S.; PO Box 956, Virginia, MN 55792; tel (218) 741-5544; fax (218) 741-1005. Murphy Newspaper group.

Circulation: 12,159(m); 12,159(m-sat); 12,159(S); Sworn Sept. 30, 1995.

Price: 50¢(d); 50¢(sat); $1.25(S); $2.65/wk; $137.80/yr.

Advertising: Open inch rate $9.95(m); $9.95(m-sat); $11.10(S). **Representative:** Papert Companies.

News Service: AP. **Politics:** Independent. **Established:** 1893.

Special Editions: Ely Dog Sled, Area Baby Album (Jan); Hockey Tab, Special Year End Edition (Feb); Bridal, Hockey, Basketball, Girl's Basketball, Pet Tab (Mar); Car Tab (Apr); Home Improvement (May); Outdoor Land of Loon Edition (June); Sidewalk Days (July); Football Edition, Senior Citizens (Sept); Home Improvement, Car Tab, Girl's Volleyball (Oct); Mall Home Show (Nov); Thanksgiving Spectacular, 4-Gift Guides (Dec).

Special Weekly Sections: Food (wed); Churches, Teen Page (sat); Outdoor, Food (S); Business, Accent, Sports, Stock Page (daily).

Magazines: TV NEWS Tab; USA Sunday.

CORPORATE OFFICERS

President	John B Murphy
Vice Pres	Elizabeth Murphy Burns
Secretary	Roy H Westman
Treasurer	Lois L Wessman

GENERAL MANAGEMENT

Publisher	John B Murphy
General Manager	Scott Asbach
Business Manager	Nancy Novak
Manager-Operations	Todd Keute
Director-Production	Jeff Asbach

ADVERTISING

Director	Christopher Knight

CIRCULATION

Director-Marketing	Joe Cotner

NEWS EXECUTIVE

Editor	William Hanna

EDITORS AND MANAGERS

News Editor	Linda Tyssen
Regional Editor	Charles Ramsey
Sports Editor	Ron Haggstrom

PRODUCTION

Director	Jeff Asbach
Foreman	Roger Johnston
Foreman-Pressroom	Pete Guski

Market Information: Zoned editions; Split Run; TMC.

Mechanical available: Offset; Black and 3 ROP colors; insert accepted — preprinted, any; page cut-offs — 21½".

Mechanical specifications: Type page 13" x 21½"; E - 6 cols, 2 1/16", 5/16" between; A - 6 cols, 2 1/16", 5/16" between; C - 8 cols, 1¾", 5/16" between.

Commodity consumption: Newsprint 800 short tons; widths 27½", 27½", 13¾"; black ink 12,000 pounds; color ink 2,500 pounds; single pages printed 7,130; average pages per issue 24(d), 36(S); single plates used 7,200.

Equipment: EDITORIAL: Front-end hardware — 14-Cx/Whirlwind 100, 14-COM; Front-end software — PPI, Sun; Printers — 1-Ap/Mac LaserWriter NTX, 2-NewGen/660B, 1-MON/1000. CLASSIFIED: Front-end hardware — 4-Cx/Whirlwind 100; Front-end software — PPI; Printers — 1-Ap/Mac LaserWriter NTX, 1-NewGen/660B. DISPLAY: Adv layout systems — 1-Ap/Mac Quadra 950, 3-Ap/Mac Quadra 700, 3-Ap/Mac cx, 1-Ap/Mac 6100, 1-Ap/Mac 9500; Front-end software — Multi-Ad, QuarkXPress, Aldus/Freehand, Sun; Printers — 2-NewGen/660B, 1-MON/1000. PRODUCTION: Pagination software — PPI, QuarkXPress; OCR software — Caere/OmniPage; Typesetters — 2-Ap/Mac LaserWriter NTX, MON/1000; Plate exposures — 1-Nu; Plate processors — 1-Nat, 1-Ic; Scanners — AG/Arcus; Production cameras — 1-B; Automatic film processors — 1-P; Shrink lenses — 1-CK Optical; Color separation equipment (conventional) — Lf/Leafscan 35; Digital color separation equipment — AP. PRESSROOM: Line 1 — 8-G/Urbanite; Folders — 1-G/2:1. MAILROOM: Counter stackers — 1-HL; Inserters and stuffers — 6-KAN/660; Bundle tyer — 1-Sterling/MR40, 1-Sterling/SSM-Mini; Wrapping singles — 2-Bu; Addressing machine — 1-KAN. WIRE SERVICES: News — AP; Receiving dishes — size-6ft, AP. BUSINESS COMPUTERS: 1-IBM/Risc 6000; PCs & main system networked.

WILLMAR

Kandiyohi County

'90 U.S. Census- 17,561; E&P '96 Est. 19,037

West Central Tribune

(m-mon to sat)

West Central Tribune, 2208 S.W. Trott Ave.; PO Box 839, Willmar, MN 56201; tel (612) 235-1150; fax (612) 235-6769. Forum Communications group.

Circulation: 17,057(m); 17,057(m-sat); VAC June 30, 1995.

Price: 50¢(d); 50¢(sat); $2.25/wk (mail), $2.12/wk (carrier); $9.00/mo (mail), $8.50/mo (carrier); $105.00/yr (mail), $99.00/yr (carrier).

Advertising: Open inch rate $13.95(m); $13.95(m-sat). **Representative:** Landon Associates Inc.

News Service: AP. **Politics:** Independent. **Established:** 1895.

Not Published: New Year; Memorial Day; Independence Day; Labor Day; Thanksgiving; Christmas.

Special Editions: Seniority, Financial (Jan); Bridal I (Feb); Coupon Book, Agriculture (Mar); Spring Home Improvement, Earth Day (Apr); Mother's Day, Tourism (May); Dairy Days, City Festival (June); Bridal II, Seniority, Willmar Mid Summer (July); Back-to-School, Fall Football Preview (Aug); Fall Home Improvement, Hunting (Sept); Fall Car Care, Health Services Directory, Coupon Book (Oct); Food, Holiday Greetings (Nov); Holiday (Dec).

Special Weekly Section: Business (tues).

Magazines: TV Guide (fri); Non-duplicated Shopper (S).

CORPORATE OFFICERS

President	William C Marcil
Exec Vice Pres	Paul E London

GENERAL MANAGEMENT

Publisher/General Manager	Paul E London
Business Manager	Steve Ammermann

ADVERTISING

Director	Marilyn Birkland
Coordinator-National	Marcia Paul

CIRCULATION

Director	Scott Paynter

NEWS EXECUTIVE

Managing Editor	Forrest Peterson

EDITORS AND MANAGERS

Editorial Page Editor	Forrest Peterson
Editorial Page Editor	Paul E London
Farm Editor	David Little
Food/Living Editor	Gary Miller
Photo Department Manager	Bill Zimmer
Regional Editor	Dana Yost
Sports Editor	Bruce Strand
Wire Editor	J D Horning
Women's Editor	Gary Miller

MANAGEMENT INFORMATION SERVICES

Data Processing Manager	Shelby Kingman

PRODUCTION

Foreman-Pressroom	Dennis Swanson
Foreman-Assembly	Forrest Honebrink

Market Information: TMC.

Mechanical available: Offset; Black and 3 ROP colors; insert accepted — preprinted; page cut-offs — 22¾".

Mechanical specifications: Type page 13" x 21"; E - 6 cols, 2 1/16", ⅛" between; A - 6 cols, 2 1/16", ⅛" between; C - 8 cols, 1½", ⅛" between.

Commodity consumption: Newsprint 740 metric tons; widths 27½", 27½", 13¾"; black ink 21,995 pounds; color ink 336 pounds; single pages printed 7,414; average pages per issue 24(d); single plates used 5,815.

Equipment: EDITORIAL: Front-end hardware — SIA; Front-end software — Dewar/System IV; Printers — Okidata/393 Plus; Other equipment — Ap/Mac IIci, Lf/Leafscan 35. CLASSIFIED: Front-end hardware — SIA; Front-end software — Dewar/System IV; Printers — Okidata/320. PRODUCTION: Typesetters — 2-AU/APS 2000 LaserWriter; Plate exposures — 2-Nu/Flip Top; Plate processors — 1-Nat/A-340; Production cameras — 2-C/Spartan III; Automatic film processors — 1-LE/LD24AQ; Film transporters — 1-C. PRESSROOM: Line 1 — BG/Dampening System, 8-G/Community; Folders — 1-G/SCI. MAILROOM: Bundle tyer — OVL; Addressing machine — Ch/596. LIBRARY: Electronic — SMS/Stauffer Gold. WIRE SERVICES: News — AP; Photos — AP Photostream; Stock tables — AP SelectStox; Receiving dishes — size-3m, AP. BUSINESS COMPUTERS: DEC/VAX 6410; Applications: Bookkeeping, Circ.

WINONA

Winona County

'90 U.S. Census- 25,399; E&P '96 Est. 25,670

ABC-CZ (90): 28,277 (HH 10,406)

Winona Daily News

(m-mon to sat; S)

Winona Daily News, 601 Franklin St.; PO Box 5147, Winona, MN 55987-0147; tel (507) 454-6500; fax (507) 454-1440; e-mail staneditor@aol.com; web site http://www.luminet.net/winnet. Lee Enterprises Inc. group.

Circulation: 12,456(m); 12,456(m-sat); 13,354(S); ABC Sept. 30, 1995.

Price: 50¢(d); 50¢(sat); $1.25(S); $2.80/wk; $140.00/yr.

Advertising: Open inch rate $14.42(m); $14.42(m-sat); $14.42(S). **Representatives:** Newspaper Mktg Group; Landon Associates Inc.; Lee Group.

News Service: AP. **Politics:** Independent. **Established:** 1855.

Advertising not accepted: X-rated.

Special Editions: Bridal Showcase (Jan); Home Improvement (Feb); Academic Excellence, Progress (Mar); Golf Guide (Apr); Bowling Review (June); Fall Football Preview, Back-to-School/Campus (Aug); Christmas (Dec).

Special Weekly Sections: Food (wed); Entertainment (thur); TV, TMC (sat); Outdoor, Lifestyle (S).

Magazine: Parade (S).

GENERAL MANAGEMENT

Publisher	Howard Hoffmaster
Controller	Richard Whalen

ADVERTISING

Manager-Retail	Nancy Kortuemo
Manager-Classified	Vicki Peterson

MARKETING AND PROMOTION

Manager-Direct Marketing	Larry Lindsay

CIRCULATION

Manager	Mark Schreiner

NEWS EXECUTIVE

Managing Editor	Jim Galewski

EDITORS AND MANAGERS

Editorial Page Editor	Jim Galewski
News Editor	Jim Galewski
Sports Editor	Jim Kohner

PRODUCTION

Manager-Graphics/Pre Press	Duane Marcotte
Manager-Graphics/Pre Press	Ron Kappmeyer
Manager-Pressroom	James Bethke

Market Information: TMC.

Mechanical available: Offset; Black and 3 ROP colors; insert accepted — preprinted; page cut-offs — 22¾".

Mechanical specifications: Type page 13" x 21½"; E - 6 cols, 2 1/16", ⅛" between; A - 6 cols, 2 1/16", ⅛" between; C - 9 cols, 1⅜", 1/16" between.

Commodity consumption: Newsprint 820 metric tons; widths 27½", 27½", 13¾", 32", 16"; black ink 8,000 pounds; color ink 2,000 pounds; single pages printed 8,068; average pages per issue 20(d), 40(S); single plates used 12,000.

Equipment: EDITORIAL: Front-end hardware — HI, 16-DEC/VT-220. CLASSIFIED: Front-end hardware — 2-DEC/VT-220. DISPLAY: Adv layout systems — COM/ACM 9000, HI/2221, 2-DEC/VT-220; Front-end hardware — Ap/Mac; Front-end software — Multi-Ad/Creator, Aldus/Freehand; Printers — Ap/Mac LaserWriter IIf. PRODUCTION: Typesetters — 2-COM/8300; Platemaking systems — 1-Na; Plate exposures — 1-Nu/Flip Top; Plate processors — 1-Ic/Auto; Production cameras — 1-B; Automatic film processors — 1-P/Pakonolith; Shrink lenses — 1-Ck/Optical. PRESSROOM: Line 1 — 5-G/Urbanite; Folders — 1-G/2:1. MAILROOM: Counter stackers — BG/Count-O-Veyor, MM/4 Station; Inserters and stuffers — 1-DG; Bundle tyer — 3-Bu/20 3XE4, 1-MLN/MLEE plastic strap, SMS/Stauffer Gold; Addressing machine — 1-Ch/525-E. WIRE SERVICES: News — AP; Receiving dishes — size-10ft, AP. BUSINESS COMPUTERS: Bs/800, IBM/PC-XT; Applications: Bus, Circ.

I-218 Minnesota

WORTHINGTON

Nobles County

'90 U.S. Census- 9,977; E&P '96 Est. 9,763
ABC-CZ (90): 9,977 (HH 3,967)

Daily Globe (m-mon to sat)

Daily Globe, 300 11th St.; PO Box 639, Worthington, MN 56187; tel (507) 376-9711; fax (507) 376-5202. Forum Communications group.
Circulation: 12,589(m); 12,589(m-sat); ABC Sept. 30, 1995.
Price: 50¢(d); 50¢(sat); $8.25/mo; $91.85/yr.
Advertising: Open inch rate $11.40(m); $11.40(m-sat). **Representative:** Papert Companies.
News Services: AP, THO, Washington Bureau. **Politics:** Independent. **Established:** 1872.
Not Published: New Year; Memorial Day; Independence Day; Labor Day; Thanksgiving; Christmas.
Special Editions: Bridal Tab, Tax Guide (Jan); College Tab, Health Care (Feb); Spring Farm (Mar); Home Improvement, Car Care (Apr); Progress (June); Builders (Sept); Car Care (Oct).
Special Weekly Sections: Business, Lifestyles, Agriculture (mon); Foods, Business (tues); Agriculture, Business, Looks (wed); Seniors, Business, Fitness (thur); Business, Religion, Outdoors, Time Out (fri); Education, Business, Children (sat).
Magazines: Home Improvement, Farm Report (mon); Farm Report, Food Day (tues); Seniors, Farm Report (wed); Religion, Farm Report (thur); TV Pre-Vu, Outdoors, Farm Report (fri).

GENERAL MANAGEMENT

Publisher	Dennis W Hall
Accountant	Joni Harms

ADVERTISING

Manager	Denise McMillen

CIRCULATION

Manager	Chet Sumstad

NEWS EXECUTIVE

Managing Editor	Carl Gustin

EDITORS AND MANAGERS

Editorial Page Editor	Carl Gustin
Lifestyle Editor	Beth Namanny
Sports Editor	Doug Wolter
News Editor	Bill Evenson

PRODUCTION

Foreman-Pressroom	Rick Kruse

Market Information: TMC.
Mechanical available: Offset; Black and 3 ROP colors; insert accepted — preprinted; page cutoffs — 21½".
Mechanical specifications: Type page 13" x 21½"; E - 6 cols, 2¹⁄₁₆", ⅛" between; A - 6 cols, 2¹⁄₁₆", ⅛" between; C - 8 cols, 1⁷⁄₁₆", ¹⁄₁₆" between.
Commodity consumption: width 27".
Equipment: EDITORIAL: Front-end hardware — CD, HAS/2300; Front-end software — HAS; Printers — NewGen/Imager Plus 12; Other equipment — 4-Ap/Mac. CLASSIFIED: Front-end hardware — CD, HAS/2300; Front-end software — CD, HAS; Printers — NewGen/Imager Plus 12. AUDIOTEX: Hardware — Computer Group/Ads-on-call. DISPLAY: Adv layout systems — CD, Ap/Mac; Front-end hardware — CD/2300, 3-Ap/Mac IIci; Front-end software — CD, QuarkXPress; Printers — Ap/Mac LaserWriter IIf, Ap/Mac LaserWriter IIg; Other equipment — AVR/GS3000 scanner, NEC/CD-Rom. PRODUCTION: OCR software — Caere/OmniPage; Typesetters — V/XP3, Ap/Mac LaserWriter IIg; Plate exposures — Nu/Flip Top FT40V6UPNS; Plate processors — Nat/A-250; Scanners — AVR/scanner; Production cameras — SCREEN; Automatic film processors — 1-P/Pakonolith.
PRESSROOM: Line 1 — 6-HI; Line 2 — 4-HI; Reels and stands — HI; Press control system — HI. MAILROOM: Counter stackers — Manual; Inserters and stuffers — Manual; Bundle tyer — 2-Akebono; Addressing machine — KR. WIRE SERVICES: News — AP, THO; Stock tables — AP; Receiving dishes — size-3m, AP. BUSINESS COMPUTERS: 5-PC, ATT/DB2; Applications: Microsoft/Works, Lotus 1-2-3; PCs & micros networked; PCs & main system networked.

MISSISSIPPI

BILOXI-GULFPORT

Harrison County

'90 U.S. Census- 87,094 (Biloxi 46,319; Gulfport 40,775); E&P '96 Est. 85,990 (Biloxi 44,067; Gulfport 41,923)
ABC-CZ (90): 168,240 (HH 60,993)

The Sun Herald (m-mon to sat; S)

The Sun Herald, 205 DeBuys Rd.; PO Box 4567, Biloxi, MS 39535-4567; tel (601) 896-2100, (601) 896-2441 (circulation); fax (601) 896-2362, (601) 896-2113 (circulation). Knight-Ridder Inc. group.
Circulation: 47,571(m); 47,571(m-sat); 53,895(S); ABC Sept. 30, 1995.
Price: 50¢(d); 50¢(sat); $1.25(S); $11.75/mo, $9.25/mo (mon-fri), $8.25/mo (fri-S); $116.10/yr.
Advertising: Open inch rate $35.70(m); $35.70(m-sat); $38.08(S). **Representative:** Newspapers First.
News Services: AP, KRT, SHNS. **Politics:** Independent. **Established:** 1884 (Herald), 1973 (Sun).
Special Editions: Coast Chamber (Jan); Attractions, Salute to Business & Industry (Feb); ActiveTimes, Inside/Outside (Mar); Nike Classic, Guide to Gulf Coast Living (Apr); Home & Products Show, Leadership Gulf Coast (May); Attractions (June); Wellness/Healthcare Directory (July); Football '96 (Aug); Gulf Coast Women, 17th Annual Salute to the Military (Oct); Christmas Gift Guide, 1997 Auto Showroom (Nov).
Special Weekly Sections: Best Food Day, Business, Star Watch (wed); Church and Religion (sat); Best Food Day, Travel, Business, Real Estate Plus (every other Sunday), Coast Living Section, Arts & Leisure Section (S).
Magazines: Keesler News (14,500 military), Seabee Courier (4,500 military) (thur); Marquee (entertainment tab) (fri); TV Week Magazine, Parade (S).

GENERAL MANAGEMENT

Publisher/President	Roland Weeks Jr
Chief Financial Officer	Flora Point
Coordinator-Credit	Faye Taylor
Director-Human Relations	Toni Dutruch
Manager-Education Service	John McFarland
Controller	Robert Simpson

ADVERTISING

Director	Stone Ellis
Manager-Retail/Classified	Bernie Marinovich

MARKETING AND PROMOTION

Director-Marketing Service	John McFarland
Manager-Marketing Development	Paul Mallery

CIRCULATION

Director	Wanda Howell

NEWS EXECUTIVES

Exec Editor	Mike Tonos
Managing Editor	Andrea Yeger

EDITORS AND MANAGERS

Business Editor	Charles Busby
Editorial Director	Marie Harris
Entertainment Editor	Jean Prescott
Features Editor	Dan Duffey
Librarian	Rhonda Hamrick
Local News Editor	Judy Johnson
Newspapers in Education Coordinator	Beth Walters
News Editor	Trent Roberts
Outdoors Editor	Al Jones
Photo Editor	Tim Isbell
Sports Editor	Slim Smith

MANAGEMENT INFORMATION SERVICES

Data Processing Manager	Carole Brown

PRODUCTION

Director-Operations	Ricky Mathews
Manager-Composing	Gary Rachuba
Manager-Pressroom	Ben Bond
Manager-Distribution	Randy Seib
Asst Director	Randy Jones
Supervisor-Building Service	Randy Ladner

Market Information: Zoned editions; Split Run; TMC; ADS.
Mechanical available: Offset; Black and 3 ROP colors; insert accepted — preprinted; page cutoffs — 22¼".
Mechanical specifications: Type page 13" x 21"; E - 6 cols, 2¹⁄₁₆", ⅛" between; A - 6 cols, 2¹⁄₁₆", ⅛" between; C - 10 cols, 1⅜", ¹⁄₁₆" between.
Commodity consumption: Newsprint 5,288 short tons; widths 55", 55", 41¼", 27½"; black ink 176,265 pounds; color ink 15,000 pounds; single pages printed 18,390; average pages per issue 47(d), 40(S); single plates used 37,900.
Equipment: EDITORIAL: Front-end hardware — AT/Series 4; Front-end software — AT 4.5.3; Printers — Epson, Okidata. CLASSIFIED: Front-end hardware — AT/Series 4; Front-end software — Integrated Adv System; Printers — Okidata, Epson. DISPLAY: Adv layout systems — CJ; Front-end hardware — HP; Front-end software — CJ. PRODUCTION: Pagination software — QuarkXPress 3.31R5; OCR software — Caere/OmniPage; Typesetters — Hyphen/Dash 800, Spectraset/2200, Linotype-Hell/Linotronic 202N; Plate exposures — 2-Nu; Plate processors — 1-WL; Electronic picture desk — Lf/AP Leaf Picture Desk; Scanners — 1-Howtek/4000 Desktop; Production cameras — 1-C/Pager, 1-C/Spartan II, 1-AG/6100; Automatic film processors — 1-LE, 1-C; Film transporters — 1-C; Shrink lenses — 1-C, 1-CK Optical; Color separation equipment (conventional) — 1-BKY; Digital color separation equipment — Ap/Mac Quadra 840, Howtek/4000.
PRESSROOM: Line 1 — 6-G/Headliner Offset; Press drives — Allen Bradley; Folders — 1-G/3:2; Pasters — G/RTP; Reels and stands — CT/50; Press control system — G/MCC-MPCS. MAILROOM: Counter stackers — 2-Id/440, 1-Id/660; Inserters and stuffers — 1-S/6 pocket, 1-HI/8-48, 1-HI/1572; Bundle tyer — 1-MLN/Plastic Strap, 1-JP/80, 2-Md/Plastic; Addressing machine — 1-Ch. LIBRARY: Electronic — Vu/Text. COMMUNICATIONS: Facsimile — Telecopier; Digital ad delivery system — Ap/Mac FX w/Supra Fax Modem 28.8. WIRE SERVICES: News — AP, KRT, SHNS; Photos — AP, KRT; Stock tables — AP SelectStox; Syndicates — AP; Receiving dishes — size-10ft, AP. BUSINESS COMPUTERS: H/3000-925; Applications: CJ; PCs & micros networked; PCs & main system networked.

BROOKHAVEN

Lincoln County

'90 U.S. Census- 10,243; E&P '96 Est. 9,954
ABC-CZ (90): 10,243 (HH 3,845)

Daily Leader (e-mon to fri)

Daily Leader, 129 N. Railroad Ave.; PO Box 551, Brookhaven, MS 39601; tel (601) 833-6961; fax (601) 833-6714.
Circulation: 7,583(e); ABC Sept. 30, 1995.
Price: 50¢(d); $5.25/mo; $60.00/yr (home delivery).
Advertising: Open inch rate $7.85(e). **Representative:** Landon Associates Inc.
News Service: AP. **Politics:** Independent-Republican. **Established:** 1883.
Not Published: New Year; Independence Day; Labor Day; Thanksgiving; Christmas.
Advertising not accepted: Alcohol, Wine.
Special Editions: Cookbook; Gridiron Preview; Car Care; Bridal Preview; Outdoor Section; Holiday Festival; Focus '96; Last Minute Gift Guide; Brookhaven/Lincoln Co. Magazine; Kid's Design-An-Ad; Income Tax; Ole Brook Festival; Easter Fashion Parade.
Special Weekly Sections: Newcomers (mon); Best Food Day, Agriculture Page, Business Page (wed); Outdoors Page, School Page (thur); Church Page, TV Guide (fri).
Magazine: Southwest Magazine (fri).

CORPORATE OFFICERS

President	William O Jacobs
Exec Vice Pres	Amy A Jabocs
Secretary/Treasurer	Amy A Jacobs

GENERAL MANAGEMENT

Publisher	William O Jacobs
Business Manager	William O Jacobs

ADVERTISING

Director	Natalie Davis
Manager-Retail	Francis Gice
Manager-Classified	Lynda Wheat

CIRCULATION

Director	Mitchel Waldon

NEWS EXECUTIVE

Editor	William O Jacobs

EDITORS AND MANAGERS

Action Line Editor (Generally Speaking)	William O Jacobs
Editorial Page Editor	William O Jacobs
News Editor	Nanette Laster
Sports Editor	Tom Goetz
Women's Editor	Joanna Carrol

PRODUCTION

Manager	Bob Ferrell

Market Information: TMC; Operate audiotex.
Mechanical available: Offset; Black and 3 ROP colors; insert accepted — preprinted; page cutoffs — 21½".
Mechanical specifications: Type page 13" x 21½"; E - 6 cols, 2¹⁄₁₆", ⅛" between; A - 6 cols, 2¹⁄₁₆", ⅛" between; C - 6 cols, 2¹⁄₁₆", ⅛" between.
Commodity consumption: Newsprint 300 short tons; width 27½"; black ink 9,500 pounds; color ink 1,000 pounds; single pages printed 4,162; average pages per issue 16(d); single plates used 3,900.
Equipment: EDITORIAL: Front-end hardware — Ap/Mac; Front-end software — Baseview, QuarkXPress. CLASSIFIED: Front-end hardware — Ap/Mac; Front-end software — Mk, Baseview. AUDIOTEX: Hardware — Computer Group/Ads-on-call. DISPLAY: Adv layout systems — Ap/Mac; Front-end hardware — Ap/Mac IIsi, Ap/Mac Quadra; Front-end software — QuarkXPress 3.0; Printers — Ap/Mac LaserWriter II. PRODUCTION: Pagination software — QuarkXPress 3.3; Typesetters — Ap/Mac LaserWriter II; Plate exposures — Nu/Ultra-Plus; Plate processors — Nat/A-250; Scanners — Ap/Mac Scanner; Production cameras — 1-Nu; Automatic film processors — LE.
PRESSROOM: Line 1 — KP/Newsking; Line 2 — KP/Newsking; Line 3 — KP/Newsking; Line 4 — KP/Newsking; Line 5 — KP/Newsking. MAILROOM: Inserters and stuffers — KAN; Addressing machine — Ch. WIRE SERVICES: News — AP; Receiving dishes — AP. BUSINESS COMPUTERS: DEC/PDP 11; Applications: Vision Data: Accts receivable, Accts payable, Gen ledger.

CLARKSDALE

Coahoma County

'90 U.S. Census- 19,717; E&P '96 Est. 18,741
ABC-CZ (90): 19,717 (HH 6,759)

Press Register (e-mon to fri; wknd)

Press Register, 123 2nd St.; PO Box 1119, Clarksdale, MS 38614; tel (601) 627-2201; fax (601) 624-5125. Emmerich Enterprises Inc. group.
Circulation: 7,105(e); 7,279 (wknd); ABC Sept. 30, 1995.
Price: 50¢(d); 50¢(wknd).
Advertising: Open inch rate $7.00(e); $7.00 (wknd). **Representative:** Papert Companies.
News Service: AP. **Politics:** Independent. **Established:** 1865 (weekly), 1908 (daily).
Special Editions: Spring Fashion/Bridal, Economic Profile (Apr); Back-to-School, Football (Aug); Women in Business (Oct); Thanksgiving/Christmas Kick-off (Nov); Christmas Gift Guide (Dec).
Magazines: Delta Outlook-TV, Entertainment Tab (sat).

CORPORATE OFFICER

Publisher	C K Burson

GENERAL MANAGEMENT

General Manager	C K Burson

ADVERTISING

Manager	Joan H Stevens

CIRCULATION

Manager	Ginny Nabors

NEWS EXECUTIVE

Editor	C K Burson

EDITORS AND MANAGERS

News Editor	Gary Perilloux
Sports Editor	Howard Bailey

MANAGEMENT INFORMATION SERVICES

Data Processing Manager	Ginny Nabors

PRODUCTION

Manager	George Wilson

Mechanical available: Offset; Black and 3 ROP colors; insert accepted — preprinted, standing cards, catalogs; page cutoffs — 21½".
Mechanical specifications: Type page 13" x 21½"; E - 6 cols, 2¹⁄₁₆", ⅛" between; A - 6 cols, 2¹⁄₁₆", ⅛" between; C - 8 cols, 1½", ⅛" between.
Commodity consumption: Newsprint 300 short tons; widths 28", 14"; average pages per issue 22(d).
Equipment: EDITORIAL: Front-end hardware — 7-IBM/PC; Front-end software — XYQUEST/XyWrite, Archetype, X-tree; Printers — 2-NewGen/PS-400, QMS/PS410 Laser; Other equipment — Lf/AP Leaf Picture Desk. CLASSIFIED: Front-end hardware — 2-IBM/PC; Front-end software — XYQUEST/XyWrite, Archetype, X-tree; Printers — 1-NewGen/PS-400. DISPLAY:

Mississippi I-219

Adv layout systems — 1-IBM/8507 Terminal; Front-end software — XYQUEST/XyWrite, X-tree, Archetype/Corel Draw, Microsoft/Windows; Printers — NewGen/Turbo PS-400 Laser Printer; Other equipment — Hitachi/CD-Rom, HP/ScanJet II. PRODUCTION: Plate exposures — 1-B; Plate processors — 1-Nat; Production cameras — 1-B; Automatic film processors — 1-P, 1-Kodamatic/425 Processor.
PRESSROOM: Line 1 — 6-F/Daily King; Reels and stands — 6-Vollstands. MAILROOM: Inserters and stuffers — 1-St; Bundle tyer — 3-Bu; Addressing machine — 1-PB. COMMUNICATIONS: Facsimile — 1-AP; Systems used — satellite. WIRE SERVICES: News — AP; Receiving dishes — AP. BUSINESS COMPUTERS: 1-ATT/Unix; Applications: Accts receivable, Payroll, Accts payable, Gen ledger, Circ records & billing.

CLEVELAND
Bolivar County

'90 U.S. Census- 15,384; **E&P '96 Est.** 16,350
ABC-NDM (90): 55,529 (HH 16,996)

The Bolivar Commercial
(e-mon to fri)

The Bolivar Commercial, 821 N. Chrisman; PO Box 1050, Cleveland, MS 38732; tel (601) 843-4241; fax (601) 843-1830. Cleveland Newspapers Inc. group.
Circulation: 7,200(e); ABC Sept. 30, 1995.
Price: 50¢(d); $66.00/yr (in county).
Advertising: Open inch rate $6.96(e). **Representative:** Papert Companies.
News Service: AP. **Politics:** Independent. **Established:** 1916.
Not Published: New Year; Independence Day; Labor Day; Thanksgiving; Christmas.
Special Editions: Delta Agriculture Expo (Jan); Valentine's, Income Tax (Feb); Bridal, Southern Home Ideas Expo (Mar); Crosstie Arts Festival (Apr); Nurses' Week (May); Summer/Outdoor (June); Back-to-School (July); Football (Aug); Fall (Sept); Octoberfest, Business/Professional Women (Oct); Light Up Your Holidays (Nov); Christmas Gift Guide (Dec).
Special Weekly Sections: Sports Wrap-up (mon); Business, Best Food Day (wed); Religious, TV (fri).

CORPORATE OFFICERS
President C Lee Walls
Vice Pres Norman C Van Liew
Secretary/Treasurer Yvonne Walls

GENERAL MANAGEMENT
Publisher/General Manager Norman C Van Liew

ADVERTISING
Manager Ricky Nobile

CIRCULATION
Manager Mark Williams

NEWS EXECUTIVES
Editor Norman C Van Liew
Managing Editor Wayne Nicholas

EDITORS AND MANAGERS
Society Editor Denise Strub
Sports Editor Jeffrey Byrd

PRODUCTION
Foreman-Composing Dorothy C Beck
Foreman-Pressroom Deanna Halliburton

Market Information: Zoned editions; Split Run; TMC.
Mechanical available: Offset; Black and 1 ROP color; insert accepted — preprinted; page cut-offs — 22¾".
Mechanical specifications: Type page 13" x 21½"; E - 6 cols, 2 1/16", 1/8" between; A - 6 cols, 2 1/16", 1/8" between; C - 8 cols, 1½", 1/8" between.
Commodity consumption: Newsprint 180 short tons; widths 13¾", 27½"; black ink 4,750 pounds; color ink 150 pounds; single pages printed 3,664; average pages per issue 14(d); single plates used 3,640.
Equipment: EDITORIAL: Front-end hardware — 8-Ap/Mac Quadra 605; Front-end software — Baseview; Printers — NewGen/1200 Turbo Laser. CLASSIFIED: Front-end hardware — 1-Ap/Mac Quadra; Front-end software — Baseview. DISPLAY: Front-end hardware — 3-Ap/Mac Quadra 650; Front-end software — QuarkXPress, Adobe/Photoshop. PRODUCTION: Pagination software — Baseview; Typesetters — 1-NewGen/1200 Turbo Laser; Plate exposures — 1-Amerigraph; Scanners — 1-HP, Polaroid; Production cameras — 1-B; Automatic film processors — 1-Kk; Color separation equipment (conventional) — AG, Polaroid. PRESSROOM: Line 1 — 5-G/Community; Folders — 1-G. MAILROOM: Bundle tyer — 1-MLN; Addressing machine — 2-Dispensa-Matic/16"; Mailroom control system — RSK/4025 LX. WIRE SERVICES: News — AP; Receiving dishes — size-2ft, AP. BUSINESS COMPUTERS: DEC/XL-466, 2-Genicom/3840P Printer; Applications: PBS: Circ, Adv billing, Accts receivable, Payroll, Gen ledger, P & L.

COLUMBUS
Lowndes County

'90 U.S. Census- 26,689; **E&P '96 Est.** 26,276

The Commercial Dispatch
(e-mon to fri; S)

The Commercial Dispatch, 516 Main St.; PO Box 511, Columbus, MS 39703-0511; tel (601) 328-2424; fax (601) 329-8937.
Circulation: 14,083(e); 15,536(S); VAC Mar. 30, 1995.
Price: 25¢(d); 75¢(S); $8.00/mo.
Advertising: Open inch rate $11.20(e); $11.20(S). **Representative:** Papert Companies.
News Service: AP. **Politics:** Independent. **Established:** 1879 (Dispatch), 1894 (Commercial).
Special Editions: Annual Report (Feb); Pilgrimage Guide (Mar); Football Preview (Aug).
Special Weekly Sections: Best Food Day (wed); Religion and Church Directory (fri); What's on TV Tab (S).
Magazines: Parade; Color Comics (S).
Broadcast Affiliates: KDBC-TV; WBOY-TV; WCBI-TV; WMUR-TV.

CORPORATE OFFICERS
Chairman of the Board Nancy M Imes
President Charles Harmond
Treasurer Doris Bruington

GENERAL MANAGEMENT
Publisher Birney Imes Jr
General Manager Charles Harmond
Director-Operations Jeff Lipsey

ADVERTISING
Director Gary Peeples
Manager-Promotion Cally Finnegan

CIRCULATION
Director Edith Hooker
Director-Promotion Edith Hooker

NEWS EXECUTIVES
Editor Birney Imes Jr
Managing Editor Joseph Ammerman

EDITORS AND MANAGERS
City Editor Andrew Brown
Editorial Page Editor Joseph Ammerman
Fashion/Society Editor Jill O'Bryant
Sports Editor Henry Matuszak
Women's Editor Jill O'Bryant

PRODUCTION
Director-Electronic Systems Tina Perry
Superintendent Jeff Lipsey

Market Information: TMC.
Mechanical available: Offset; Black and 3 ROP colors; insert accepted — preprinted, pocketbook or single card; page cut-offs — 21½".
Mechanical specifications: Type page 13" x 21½"; E - 6 cols, 2 1/16", 1/8" between; A - 6 cols, 2 1/16", 1/8" between; C - 9 cols, 1 3/8", 1/8" between.
Commodity consumption: Newsprint 900 short tons; width 27"; black ink 21,090 pounds; color ink 1,984 pounds; single pages printed 8,542; average pages per issue 22(d), 40(S).
Equipment: EDITORIAL: Front-end hardware — 2-Compaq/386, Dewar; Printers — 2-Tegra/Varityper XP-1000; Other equipment — 6-RSK/Tandy, 3-TM, 18-AST/Bravo-286. CLASSIFIED: Front-end hardware — 4-Pentium PC; Front-end software — Synaptic; Printers — HP/LaserJet 4V; Other equipment — 3-AST/Bravo-286. DISPLAY: Adv layout systems — IBM/486 PC, Ap/Mac; Front-end software — QuarkXPress, Aldus/PageMaker. PRODUCTION: Pagination software — Synaptic, QuarkXPress; Typesetters — 2-Tegra/Varityper 5100; Platemaking systems — 1-Nu/Flip Top FT40LNS-, 1-Nat/A-250; Plate exposures — 1-Nu; Plate processors — 1-Nat; Production cameras — Acti/225; Automatic film processors — 1-AG, 1-Litex 26.
PRESSROOM: Line 1 — 5-G/501(1); Line 2 — 2-HI/Cotrell V15. MAILROOM: Inserters and stuffers — 1-KAN/320; Bundle tyer — 1-MLN/ML2EE; Addressing machine — 1-Am/1957, Ch/515. LIBRARY: Electronic — 1-BH. WIRE SERVICES: News — AP. BUSINESS COMPUTERS: IBM/Sys 400, Ap/Mac LaserWriter; Applications: Adv billing, Accts receivable, Gen ledger, Payroll, Circ, TMC; PCs & micros networked; PCs & main system networked.

CORINTH
Alcorn County

'90 U.S. Census- 11,820; **E&P '96 Est.** 10,486
ABC-NDM (90): 43,905 (HH 17,240)

The Daily Corinthian
(e-mon to fri)

The Daily Corinthian, 1607 S. Harper Rd.; PO Box 1800, Corinth, MS 38834; tel (601) 287-6111; fax (601) 287-3525. Paxton Media group.
Circulation: 8,350(e); ABC Sept. 30, 1995.
Price: 50¢(d); $7.00/mo.
Advertising: Open inch rate $16.30(e). **Representative:** Landon Associates Inc.
News Services: AP, NYT. **Politics:** Independent. **Established:** 1895.
Special Editions: Progress (Feb); Fall Fashion, Back-to-School (Aug); Football, Basketball, Christmas Guide (Nov).
Special Weekly Section: Church Page (fri).

GENERAL MANAGEMENT
Publisher Thomas J Overton
Business Manager Paula Gunn

ADVERTISING
Manager Jim Burnett

TELECOMMUNICATIONS
Audiotex Manager Jim Burnett

CIRCULATION
Manager Willie Walker

NEWS EXECUTIVE
Exec Editor Mark Boehler

EDITOR AND MANAGER
Society Editor Sherry Shawl

PRODUCTION
Foreman-Pressroom Bill Cutshall

Market Information: TMC; Operate audiotex.
Mechanical available: Offset; Black and 3 ROP colors; insert accepted — preprinted; page cut-offs — 21½".
Mechanical specifications: Type page 13" x 21½"; E - 6 cols, 2 1/16", 1/8" between; A - 6 cols, 2 1/16", 1/8" between; C - 9 cols, 1 5/16", 1/8" between.
Commodity consumption: Newsprint 339 short tons; widths 27½", 13¾"; black ink 10,968 pounds; color ink 1,200 pounds; single pages printed 5,408; average pages per issue 22(d); single plates used 6,000.
Equipment: EDITORIAL: Front-end hardware — Dewar/Disc Net; Other equipment — 8-Dewar/Disc Net. CLASSIFIED: Front-end hardware — Dewar/Disc Net; Other equipment — 8-Dewar/Disc Net. AUDIOTEX: Hardware — Brite; Software — AP Stockquote Hotline. DISPLAY: Front-end hardware — 2-Ap/Mac Quadra 950; Front-end software — Multi-Ad/Creator, QuarkXPress; Printers — Xante/8200. PRODUCTION: Typesetters — 2-COM/8400, Dewar/Disc, 2-Dewar/Discribe, Xante/8200; Plate exposures — 1-Nu/Plate Burner; Plate processors — 1-Nat/Plate Marker A250; Electronic picture desk — Lf/AP Leaf Picture Desk, Ap/Mac Quadra 950; Scanners — 2-Microtek/ScanMaker II XE Flatbed, Nikon/Coolscan; Production cameras — 1-B/Caravel; Automatic film processors — 1-LE/LD 24-BQ; Color separation equipment (conventional) — Adobe/Photoshop, Ap/Mac Quadra 950.
PRESSROOM: Line 1 — 7-G/Community. MAILROOM: Inserters and stuffers — KAN/480; Bundle tyer — MLN/Strapper. WIRE SERVICES: News — AP, NYT; Syndicates — NYT; Receiving dishes — size-9m, AP. BUSINESS COMPUTERS: IBM/Sys 36; Applications: INSI; PCs & main system networked.

GREENVILLE
Washington County

'90 U.S. Census- 45,226; **E&P '96 Est.** 49,848
ABC-CZ (90): 45,226 (HH 15,322)

Delta Democrat Times
(e-mon to fri; S)

Delta Democrat Times, 988 N. Broadway; PO Box 1618, Greenville, MS 38701; tel (601) 335-1155; fax (601) 335-2860. Freedom Communications Inc. group.
Circulation: 12,973(e); 14,523(S); ABC Sept. 30, 1995.
Price: 35¢(d); $1.00(S); $9.00/mo; $156.00/yr (mail), $156.00/yr (outside state).
Advertising: Open inch rate $12.68(e); $14.88(e-wed); $13.05(S). **Representative:** Papert Companies.
News Service: AP. **Politics:** Libertarian. **Established:** 1868.
Special Editions: Our Town (Jan); Bridal, Agricultural (Feb).
Special Weekly Sections: Business News and Views (tues); Best Food Day (wed); Church Page (fri).
Magazines: USA Weekend, TV Times, Color Comics (S).

GENERAL MANAGEMENT
Publisher Vernon Lyle DeBolt III

ADVERTISING
Director James Kennedy

CIRCULATION
Director Linda Kellan

NEWS EXECUTIVE
Managing Editor Sullie Gresham

EDITORS AND MANAGERS
Lifestyle Editor Lynn Lafoe
Sports Editor Michel Ariff

MANAGEMENT INFORMATION SERVICES
Operations Director Kent Kilpatrick

PRODUCTION
Foreman-Composing Barbara Dorris
Foreman-Pressroom Doug Maxwell

Market Information: TMC; ADS.
Mechanical available: Offset; Black and 3 ROP colors; insert accepted — preprinted, booklets; page cut-offs — 22¾".
Mechanical specifications: Type page 13" x 21½"; E - 6 cols, 2 1/16", 1/8" between; A - 6 cols, 2 1/16", 1/8" between; C - 8 cols, 1½", 1/16" between.
Commodity consumption: Newsprint 595 metric tons; widths 27½", 13¾"; single pages printed 6,586; average pages per issue 14(d), 40(S).
Equipment: EDITORIAL: Front-end hardware — 13-AST/286; Front-end software — Dewar Sys 3; Other equipment — Ap/Mac 6100. CLASSIFIED: Front-end hardware — 4-Ap/Mac Performa 630-CD; Front-end software — Baseview. DISPLAY: Adv layout systems — 2-Dewar/Discovery, 1-Ap/Mac IIcx, 1-Ap/Mac IIfx, 1-Ap/Mac 630, 1-Ap/Mac 8100, 1-Ap/Mac 7100, 1-Ap/Mac 7200 CD; Front-end hardware — 1-PC/486; Front-end software — Brainworks. PRODUCTION: OCR software — Caere/OmniPage Professional; Typesetters — 2-Tegra/1000, 1-Panther/Pro; Platemaking systems — Nu/FT40APRNS; Plate processors — 1-Nat/A-250; Electronic picture desk — Lf/AP Leaf Picture Desk; Scanners — Nikon/Scantouch; Production cameras — 1-B/24, Spartan/III; Automatic film processors — LE, Konica/K550; Color separation equipment (conventional) — Lf/Leafscan 35.
PRESSROOM: Line 1 — 8-G/Urbanite(1 folder); Press drives — Fin; Press registration system — Duarte. MAILROOM: Bundle tyer — 1-OVL, 1-MLN. COMMUNICATIONS: Digital ad delivery system — AP AdSend. WIRE SERVICES: News — AP, KRT; Photos — AP; Receiving dishes — AP. BUSINESS COMPUTERS: 3-Compac/486; Applications: Southware: Accts;, Brainworks: Adv; Vision Data: Circ; PCs & micros networked.

GREENWOOD
Leflore County

'90 U.S. Census- 18,906; **E&P '96 Est.** 18,093
ABC-CZ (90): 24,006 (HH 8,695)

The Greenwood Commonwealth (e-mon to fri; S)

The Greenwood Commonwealth, 329 Hwy. 82 W.; PO Box 8050, Greenwood, MS 38930; tel (601) 453-5312; fax (601) 453-2908. Emmerich Enterprises Inc. group.
Circulation: 8,854(e); 9,079(S); ABC Sept. 30, 1995.
Price: 35¢(d); $1.00(S); $7.50/mo; $87.00/yr.
Advertising: Open inch rate $8.60(e); $8.60(S). **Representative:** Papert Companies.
News Services: AP, NYT. **Politics:** Independent. **Established:** 1895.
Not Published: Independence Day; Labor Day.
Advertising not accepted: Work at home; credit card or credit repair; publications; offering job or equipment listings.
Special Editions: % Off, Commonwealth Centennial (Jan); Brides (Feb); Profile (Mar); Spring Car Care, Home Improvement (Apr); Senior Scrapbook, Cotton (May); Balloon Classic (June); Crop Day, Football (Aug);

Hunting, Centennial (Sept); Women in Business (Oct); Senior Citizens (Nov); Christmas Song Book, Christmas Greetings (Dec).
Special Weekly Sections: Farm & Business, Family Living (S).
Magazines: TV Week, Parade Magazine (S).

CORPORATE OFFICER
President — J Wyatt Emmerich
GENERAL MANAGEMENT
Publisher — Timothy A Kalich
Business Manager — Pam Downing
ADVERTISING
Manager — Larry Alderman
CIRCULATION
Manager — Andrew McBryde
NEWS EXECUTIVES
Editor — Timothy A Kalich
Managing Editor — Steve Stewart
EDITORS AND MANAGERS
Columnist — Celia Emmerich
Editorial Page Editor — Timothy A Kalich
Sports Editor — Bill Burrus
Women's Reporter — Beth Henderson
PRODUCTION
Manager — Ed Billings

Market Information: TMC.
Mechanical available: Offset; Black and 3 ROP colors; insert accepted — preprinted, all; page cut-offs — 22¾".
Mechanical specifications: Type page 13" x 21½"; E - 6 cols, 2 1/16", 1/8" between; A - 6 cols, 2 1/16", 1/8" between; C - 8 cols, 1½", 1/8" between.
Commodity consumption: Newsprint 564 short tons; width 28"; black ink 29,250 pounds; single pages printed 5,200; average pages per issue 14(d), 30(S); single plates used 6,000.
Equipment: EDITORIAL: Front-end hardware — 3-Sampo/AlphaScan LC, 7-Kenitec/Monitor, 10-PC/Warehouse System 486; Front-end software — QuarkXPress; Printers — 1-TI/Omni 800-810 RO Terminal. CLASSIFIED: Front-end hardware — Mk/1100 TouchWriter Plus; Front-end software — Mk/1100 TouchWriter Plus. DISPLAY: Front-end hardware — 1-IBM/8507, 1-Sampo/TriSync; Front-end software — Archetype; Other equipment — Dest/PC Scan 3000. PRODUCTION: Pagination software — QuarkXPress; Typesetters — 1-NewGen/Turbo PS-800p, 1-NewGen/Turbo PS-400p, 1-HP/LaserJet 4M Plus; Plate exposures — 1-Nu; Plate processors — 1-Nat/A-250; Production cameras — 1-R/580; Automatic film processors — 1-LE/LD 18. PRESSROOM: Line 1 — 6-KP/Newsking (w/Colorking); Folders — 1-KP/K-6. MAILROOM: Counter stackers — 14-KAN/Quadra Cart; Inserters and stuffers — 1-KAN/5-Unit 320; Bundle tyer — CYP/Rotan 500N, MLN/SP-300; Addressing machine — KR/215 Labeler. LIBRARY: Electronic — 1-IBM/Personal Sys 50. WIRE SERVICES: News — AP, NYT; Receiving dishes — AP. BUSINESS COMPUTERS: Compaq/Prosignia, 1-Maxum/386SX; Applications: Vision Data: Accts receivable, Circ; AccPac BPI-GL: Accts payable; PCs & micros networked.

GRENADA

Grenada County
'90 U.S. Census- 10,864; E&P '96 Est. 9,701

The Daily Sentinel-Star
(e-mon to fri)

The Daily Sentinel-Star, 158 Green St. (38901); PO Box 907, Grenada, MS 38902-0907; tel (601) 226-4321; fax (601) 226-8310.
Circulation: 5,093(e); Sworn Sept. 30, 1995.
Price: 35¢(d); $5.75/mo; $69.00/yr.
Advertising: Open inch rate $8.00(e). **Representative:** Papert Companies.
News Service: AP. **Politics:** Independent. **Established:** 1854.
Not Published: New Year; Independence Day; Labor Day; Thanksgiving; Christmas.
Advertising not accepted: Abortion; Adoption.
Special Editions: Tax Tips (Jan); Brides (Feb); Spring Fashion (Mar); Home Improvement (Apr); Graduation (May); Progress (June); Football Preview, Back-to-School (Aug); Fall Fashion (Sept); Basketball (Oct); Thanksgiving Edition (Nov); Christmas Greetings (Dec).
Special Weekly Sections: The Yellow Pages (mon); Business Directory (daily); Monthly Calendar (last wk/mo).
Magazines: TV Guide (daily); The Weekender (thur).

CORPORATE OFFICERS
President — Joseph B Lee III
Secretary/Treasurer — Brenda R Lee
GENERAL MANAGEMENT
Publisher — Joseph B Lee III
ADVERTISING
Director — Jay Lee
MARKETING AND PROMOTION
Creative Services Manager — Jennifer Frazier
CIRCULATION
Manager — Fred Adams
NEWS EXECUTIVE
Managing Editor — Terri Ferguson
EDITORS AND MANAGERS
Action Line Editor — Terri Ferguson
Automotive Editor — Terri Ferguson
Business/Finance Editor — Terri Ferguson
City/Metro Editor — Terri Ferguson
Editorial Page Editor — Terri Ferguson
Education Editor — Terri Ferguson
Entertainment/Amusements Editor — Terri Ferguson
Environmental Editor — Terri Ferguson
Farm/Agriculture Editor — Terri Ferguson
Fashion/Style Editor — Terri Ferguson
Features/Women's Editor — Terri Ferguson
Graphics Editor/Art Director — Terri Ferguson
Health/Medical Editor — Terri Ferguson
Living/Lifestyle Editor — Helen Thomas
National Editor — Terri Ferguson
News Editor — Terri Ferguson
Photo Editor — Terri Ferguson
Political/Government Editor — Terri Ferguson
Religion Editor — Terri Ferguson
Science/Technology Editor — Terri Ferguson
Sports Editor — Chuck Hathcock
Television/Film Editor — Terri Ferguson
Theater/Music Editor — Terri Ferguson
Travel Editor — Terri Ferguson
MANAGEMENT INFORMATION SERVICES
Data Processing Manager — Joyce Provine

Market Information: Zoned editions; Split Run; TMC.
Mechanical available: Offset; Black and 3 ROP colors; insert accepted — preprinted; page cut-offs — 22¾".
Mechanical specifications: Type page 13" x 21½"; E - 6 cols, 2 1/16", 1/8" between; A - 6 cols, 2 1/16", 1/8" between; C - 6 cols, 2 1/16", 1/8" between.
Commodity consumption: average pages per issue 16(d).
Equipment: EDITORIAL: Front-end hardware — ACT, Ap/Mac, Gateway/2000; Front-end software — QPS, Microsoft/Word; Printers — Xante. CLASSIFIED: Front-end hardware — PC; Front-end software — Synaptic. DISPLAY: Adv layout systems — QuarkXPress, Adobe/Photoshop; Front-end hardware — Ap/Mac, PC, Gateway/2000; Front-end software — QuarkXPress 3.31; Printers — Xante/Accel; Other equipment — Quickscan. PRODUCTION: Pagination software — QuarkXPress 3.31; Typesetters — ECR; Plate processors — Nat; Scanners — Quickscan; Production cameras — C/Spartan III; Automatic film processors — LE. PRESSROOM: Line 1 — 6-KP/Newsking. COMMUNICATIONS: Facsimile — Brother/Intellifax. WIRE SERVICES: News — AP; Receiving dishes — AP. BUSINESS COMPUTERS: Applications: Synaptic; PCs & micros networked; PCs & main system networked.

GULFPORT
See BILOXI

HATTIESBURG

Forrest and Lamar Counties
'90 U.S. Census- 39,784; E&P '96 Est. 39,077
ABC-CZ (90): 98,738 (HH 36,033)

Hattiesburg American
(e-mon to fri; m-sat; S)

Hattiesburg American, 825 N. Main St.; PO Box 1111, Hattiesburg, MS 39401; tel (601) 582-4321; fax (601) 583-8244. Gannett Co. Inc. group.
Circulation: 26,111(e); 26,111(m-sat); 29,638(S); ABC Sept. 30, 1995.
Price: 35¢(d); 35¢(sat); $1.25(S); $11.00/mo; $120.00/yr.
Advertising: Open inch rate $28.09(e); $28.09(m-sat); $30.95(S). **Representative:** Gannett National Newspaper Sales.
News Services: AP, GNS. **Politics:** Independent. **Established:** 1917.
Special Editions: Progress, Bridal (Feb); Med Facts (Mar); Bridal (July); Med Facts, Hunting/Fishing (Oct).
Special Weekly Sections: Autos (thur); TV Week (S).
Magazines: USA Weekend; TV Week; American Homes Guide (last thur/mo).

CORPORATE OFFICER
President — David B Petty
GENERAL MANAGEMENT
Publisher — David B Petty
Controller — Greg Lepien
ADVERTISING
Director — Rick Chapman
Manager-Classified — Tracie Fowler
Director-Human Resources — Wanda Naylor
MARKETING AND PROMOTION
Director-Market Development — Erik Smelser
CIRCULATION
Director — Marshall R Andrews
NEWS EXECUTIVES
Exec Editor — Marilyn Mitchell
Managing Editor — Ronny Agnew
EDITORS AND MANAGERS
Editorial Page Editor — Byron McCauley
Asst Features Editor — Molly Pepper
News Editor — Van Arnold
Photo Editor — David Bundy
Religion Editor — Robyn Jackson
Sports Editor — Chuck Abadie
MANAGEMENT INFORMATION SERVICES
Manager-Production Systems — Alfredo Hernandez
Manager-Business Systems — Mark Atteberry
PRODUCTION
Director — Gene Windham
Manager — David Patrick
Manager-Camera/Platemaking — Mary Lair
Manager-Pressroom — Thurman Shows
Manager-Systems — Alfredo Hernandez

Market Information: Zoned editions; TMC.
Mechanical available: Offset; Black and 3 ROP colors; insert accepted — preprinted; page cut-offs — 21½".
Mechanical specifications: Type page 13" x 21½"; E - 6 cols, 2 1/16", 1/8" between; A - 6 cols, 2 1/16", 1/8" between; C - 9 cols, 1 5/16", 1/8" between.
Commodity consumption: Newsprint 2,097 short tons; widths 27¼", 15", 30", 13⅝"; black ink 43,260 pounds; color ink 25,507 pounds; single pages printed 11,580; average pages per issue 26(d), 69(S); single plates used 21,762.
Equipment: EDITORIAL: Front-end hardware — Dewar/Sys 4, Ap/Mac IIcx; Other equipment — X/730 GS Scanner, Lf/AP Leaf Picture Desk. CLASSIFIED: Front-end hardware — 1-Dewar; Front-end software — Dewar 4.0; DISPLAY: Adv layout systems — Ap/Mac IIcx; Front-end hardware — Dewar; Front-end software — Multi-Ad. PRODUCTION: Typesetters — 2-Tegra/Varityper; Platemaking systems — Offset; Plate exposures — 2-Nu; Plate processors — 2-Nat/A-250; Electronic picture desk — Lf/AP Leaf Picture Desk; Production cameras — C/Spartan III; Automatic film processors — 1-LE/LD24AQ, 1-P/2024IS, 1-LE/LD24BQ; Digital color separation equipment — Ap/Mac. PRESSROOM: Line 1 — 8-G/Urbanite; Line 2 — 7-G/Urbanite; Pasters — 8-Cary/Paster; Press control system — 4-Fin/100 h.p. dc drives. MAILROOM: Counter stackers — QWI/300, 1-PP, 1-HI/H-RS125, QWI/350; Inserters and stuffers — HI/1472 II Station; Bundle tyer — 2-Dynaric/NP2, 1-MLN/MLN2A; Addressing machine — 1-Barstrom/On-Line Labeler, 1-Ch/515, 1-Ch/596. WIRE SERVICES: News — AP, GNS; Receiving dishes — size-5m, AP, USA Today. BUSINESS COMPUTERS: DEC/1170; Applications: Gen ledger, Accts receivable, Accts payable, Payroll.

JACKSON

Hinds County
'90 U.S. Census- 195,906; E&P '96 Est. 190,275
ABC-NDM (90): 395,396 (HH 140,157)

The Clarion-Ledger
(m-mon to sat; S)

The Clarion-Ledger, 201 S. Congress St.; PO Box 40, Jackson, MS 39205; tel (601) 961-7000. Gannett Co. Inc. group.
Circulation: 110,059(m); 110,059(m-sat); 127,583(S); ABC Sept. 30, 1995.
Price: 50¢(d); 50¢(sat); $1.50(S); $13.50/mo; $162.00/yr.
Advertising: Open inch rate $79.15(m); $79.15(m-sat); $95.60(S). **Representative:** Gannett National Newspaper Sales.
News Services: AP, NYT, GNS, NNA, Independent Press. **Politics:** Independent. **Established:** 1837.
Special Editions: Spring Fashion (Mar); Mississippi Sports Hall of Fame Grand Opening (Apr); Memorial Day Package (May); Football '96, Fall Fashion (Aug); Southern Living Cooking School (Sept); Holiday Gift Guide (Nov); Last Minute Gift Guide (Dec).
Special Weekly Sections: Business Money, Trends (Lifestyles) (mon); Education (tues); Food (wed); Mississippi Weekend (thur); Autos (fri); Outdoors, Religion (sat); Perspective, Arts & Leisure, Real Estate, Color Comics, TV Week (S).
Magazines: USA Weekend; Mississippi Gaming Guide (monthly).

CORPORATE OFFICER
President — Duane K McCallister
GENERAL MANAGEMENT
Publisher — Duane K McCallister
Director-Finance — Robert Manzi
Comptroller — Angela Andrews
Manager-Credit — Essie Slaughter
Manager-Accounts Receivable — John Blackwell
Director-Human Resources — Nate Ruffin
Personnel Manager — Richard Baxter
ADVERTISING
Manager-Retail — Suzanne Pepper
Manager-Classified — Ken Workman
Manager-Preprint — Brantley Martin
MARKETING AND PROMOTION
Director-Market Development — Susan Sirmons
Manager-Research — Lisa Forbes
Manager-Public Affairs — Judy Foster
Manager-Creative/Promotion — Mike Chesney
Manager-Database Marketing — Lauren Cassel
CIRCULATION
Director — Fred Greer
Manager-Operations — Keith Fountain
Manager-State — David Anderson
Manager-Home Delivery — Mark Lewis
Manager-Single Copy — Lewis Floyd
Manager-Sales — Malcolm Brownell
Newspapers in Education — Terry Turcotte
NEWS EXECUTIVES
Exec Editor — John Johnson
Managing Editor — Margaret Downing
EDITORS AND MANAGERS
Business Editor — Joe Dove
Editorial Director — David Hampton
Education — Ruth Ingram
Editorial Cartoonist — Mark Bolton
Features Editor — Orley Hood
Food/Entertainment Editor — Kim Willis
Director-Graphics — Earnest Hart
Metro Editor — Dan Davis
News Editor — John Hammack
Director-Photography — Chris Todd
Radio/Television & the Arts — Leslie Myers
Religion — Charlotte Graham
Southern Style Editor — Jana John
Sports Editor — Donald Dodd
Travel Editor — Kim Willis
MANAGEMENT INFORMATION SERVICES
Manager-Systems — Scott Davis
PRODUCTION
Director-Operations — Gerry W Riley
Manager-Tech Service — Kirk Martin
Manager-Building Maintenance — Charles Murray
Manager-Pre Press — Buddy White
Manager-Distribution Center — Fred Van Der Meulen
Manager-Press — Mike Huffman

Market Information: Zoned editions; Split Run; TMC.
Mechanical available: Offset; Black and 3 ROP colors; insert accepted — preprinted; page cut-offs — 22".
Mechanical specifications: Type page 13" x 21"; E - 6 cols, 2 1/16", 1/8" between; A - 6 cols, 2 1/16", 1/8" between; C - 10 cols, 1¼", 1/16" between.
Commodity consumption: Newsprint 14,420 short tons; widths 54", 54", 40.5", 27", 13.5"; black ink 283,200 pounds; color ink 136,000 pounds; single pages printed 27,049; average pages per issue 48(d), 112(S); single plates used 131,000.
Equipment: EDITORIAL: Front-end hardware — 60-AT. CLASSIFIED: Front-end hardware — 30-AT. AUDIOTEX: Hardware — Meridian Mail. DISPLAY: Adv layout systems — DTI; Front-

end hardware — Ap/Mac; Front-end software — AU/APS-100; Printers — QMS/860, AU/Broadsheet. PRODUCTION: Typesetters — 2-AU/APS, 2-AU/ACS-84; Platemaking systems — Offset; Plate exposures — 2-Nu; Plate processors — 2-Nat; Electronic picture desk — Lf/AP Leaf Picture Desk; Scanners — 6-Umax/UC-1260 Flatbed, 1-ECR/Autokon 1000 DE; Production cameras — 1-C/Spartan, 1-C/Marathon; Automatic film processors — 2-LE/LD24A, 2-LE; Film transporters — 1-C; Color separation equipment (conventional) — Lf/Leafscan 35, AU/APS Scan, Kk/5035; Digital color separation equipment — Ap/Mac, QuarkXpress 3.3.1, Adobe/Photoshop. PRESSROOM: Line 1 — 8-G/Metroliner; Line 2 — 8-G/Metroliner; Press drives — Fin; Folders — 2-G, 2-G; Pasters — G/3-arm RTP; Press control system — Fin. MAILROOM: Counter stackers — 3-Id, 4-QWI; Inserters and stuffers — 2-S/1372P; Bundle tyer — 2-MLN/News 90, 4-Sterlings; Addressing machine — 1-Ch/Videojet; Other mailroom equipment — MM/Stitcher-Trimmer. COMMUNICATIONS: Digital ad delivery system — AP AdSend. WIRE SERVICES: News — AP, GNS, NYT, KRT; Photos — AP; Stock tables — AP; Receiving dishes — AP. BUSINESS COMPUTERS: IBM/AS-400; Applications: Circ, Adv billing, Accts receivable, Gen ledger, Accts payable, Payroll; PCs & micros networked; PCs & main system networked.

LAUREL
Jones County
'90 U.S. Census- 18,827; E&P '96 Est. 16,707

Laurel Leader-Call
(e-mon to fri; m-sat; S)

Laurel Leader-Call, 130 Beacon St. (39440); PO Box 728, Laurel, MS 39441; tel (601) 428-0551; fax (601) 426-3550. Hollinger International Inc. group.
Circulation: 9,646(e); 9,646(m-sat); 8,896(S); Sworn Sept. 30, 1994.
Price: 35¢(d); 35¢(sat); 35¢(S).
Advertising: Open inch rate $9.94(e); $9.94(m-sat); $9.94(S).
News Service: AP. **Politics:** Independent. **Established:** 1911.
Note: Effective Nov. 4, 1994, this publication started publishing a Sunday editon. The estimated circulation is 8,896.
Not Published: New Year; Independence Day; Labor Day; Christmas.
Special Editions: Financial; Bridal; Home and Garden; Progress; Cookbook; Spring Fashion; Fall Fashion; Graduation; Car Care; Insurance; Football; Senior Citizens; Home Improvement; Christmas Dream Book.
Special Weekly Sections: Best Food Day (wed); Church News, TV Entertainment (sat).

GENERAL MANAGEMENT
Publisher .... Paul Barrett
Business Manager .... Lisa Brown
ADVERTISING
Manager .... Crystal Dupre
CIRCULATION
Manager .... Sean O'Connor
NEWS EXECUTIVE
Managing Editor .... Hal Marx
EDITORS AND MANAGERS
Editorial Page Editor .... Hal Marx
Education Editor .... Murray Tartt
Fashion/Food Editor .... Murray Tartt
Garden/Home Furnishings Editor .. Murray Tartt
Music Editor .... Murray Tartt
Real Estate Editor .... Hal Marx
Society Editor .... Murray Tartt
Sports Editor .... Shawn Wansley

Market Information: Zoned editions; TMC.
Mechanical available: Offset; Black and 3 ROP colors; insert accepted — preprinted; page cutoffs — 22¾".
Mechanical specifications: Type page 13" x 21½"; E - 6 cols, 2 1/16", ⅛" between; A - 6 cols, 2 1/16", ⅛" between; C - 9 cols, 1 3/8", 1/16" between.
Commodity consumption: average pages per issue 16(d).
Equipment: EDITORIAL: Front-end hardware — Mk/Series 3000. CLASSIFIED: Front-end hardware — Mk. PRODUCTION: Typesetters — 2-Ap/Mac LaserPrinter; Plate exposures — 1-Nu; Production cameras — 1-R/500. PRESSROOM: Line 1 — 8-G/Community SFC; Folders — 1-G. MAILROOM: Bundle tyer — 1-Ms; Addressing machine — 1-Am/4000EP.
WIRE SERVICES: News — AP.

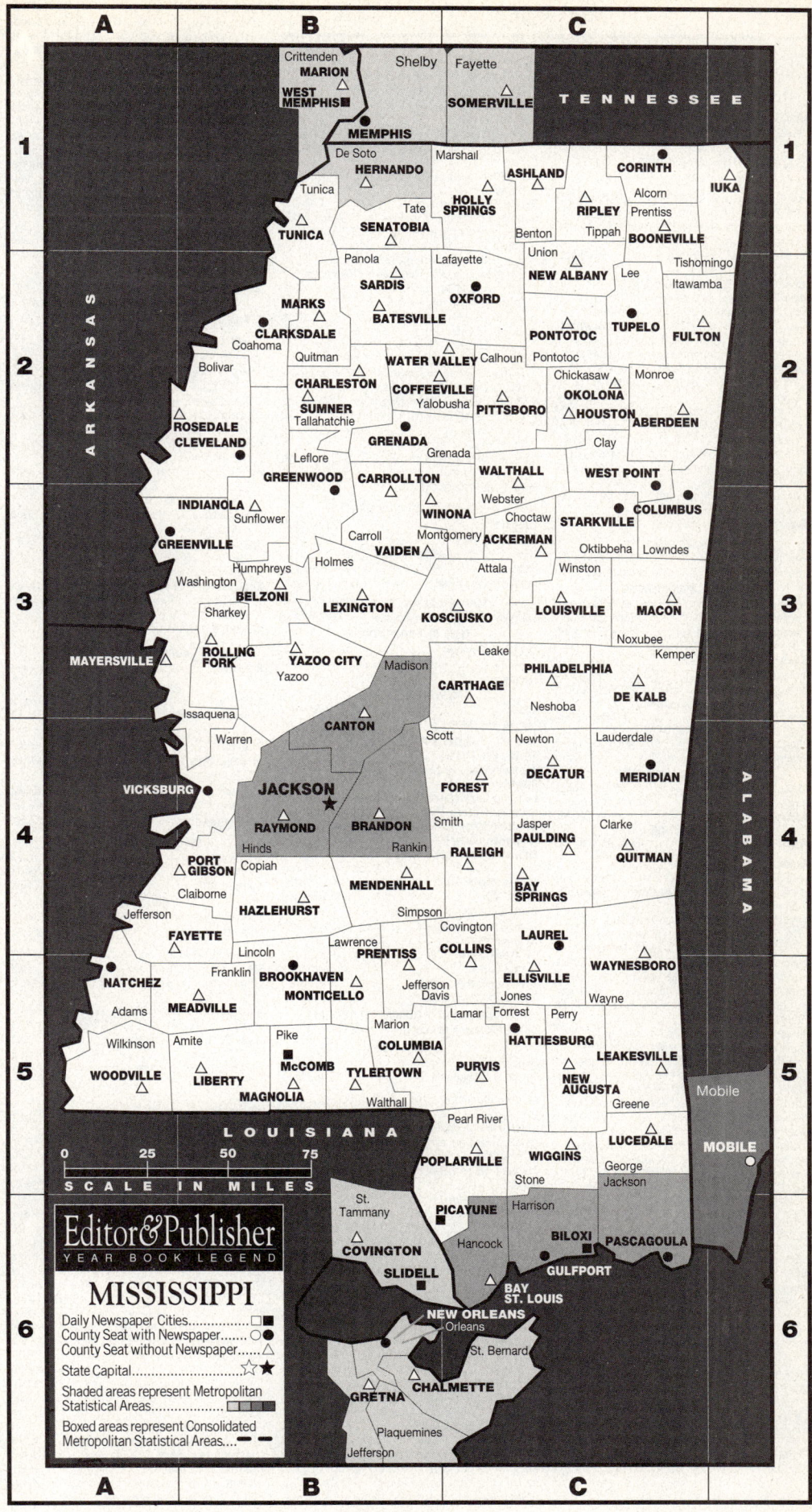

Copyright ©1996 by the Editor & Publisher Co.

McCOMB
Pike County
'90 U.S. Census- 11,591; E&P '96 Est. 11,157
ABC-CZ (90): 17,234 (HH 6,589)

Enterprise-Journal
(e-mon to fri; S)

Enterprise-Journal, 112 Oliver Emmerich Dr.; PO Box 910, McComb, MS 39648; tel (601) 684-2421; fax (601) 684-0836. Emmerich Enterprises Inc. group.
Circulation: 12,141(e); 12,566(S); ABC Sept. 30, 1995.
Price: 50¢(d); $1.00(S); $8.00/mo.
Advertising: Open inch rate $11.00(e); $11.00 (S). **Representative:** Papert Companies.
News Services: AP, CNS, LAT-WP. **Politics:** Independent. **Established:** 1889.
Not Published: Independence Day; Labor Day.
Special Editions: Brides (Jan); Kids Design-An-Ad (Feb); Azalea Section, Perspective (Mar); Spring Fashion, Graduation (Apr); Home and Garden (May); Salute to Industry and Agriculture (June); Back-to-School (July); Fall Fashion, Football (Aug); Outdoor (Sept); Recipe Edition, Women in Business (Oct); Songbook, Gift Guide (Nov); Christmas Promotions, Christmas Greetings (Dec).
Special Weekly Sections: Best Food Day (wed); TV Log (S).
Magazine: Entertainment.

CORPORATE OFFICERS
President Wyatt Emmerich
Treasurer Charles M Dunagin

GENERAL MANAGEMENT
Publisher Charles M Dunagin
Purchasing Agent Mitch Lambuth
Manager-Business Office Alice E Perkins

ADVERTISING
Director Deborah Bean
Manager-Local Deborah Bean
Manager-Classified Vicki Deere

CIRCULATION
Director Freddie Deer

NEWS EXECUTIVES
Editor Charles M Dunagin
Managing Editor Jack Ryan

EDITORS AND MANAGERS
Books Editor Jack Ryan
Sports Editor Randy Hammons
Women's Editor June Gilbert

PRODUCTION
Superintendent Donald Carlisle

Market Information: TMC.
Mechanical available: Offset; Black and 3 ROP colors; insert accepted — preprinted; page cutoffs — 22¾".
Mechanical specifications: Type page 13" x 21½"; E - 6 cols, 2", ⅛" between; A - 6 cols, 2", ⅛" between; C - 8 cols, 1½", ⅛" between.
Commodity consumption: Newsprint 600 short tons; widths 28", 14", 32"; black ink 23,000 pounds; color ink 1,650 pounds; single pages printed 6,256; average pages per issue 17(d), 38(S); single plates used 12,000.
Equipment: EDITORIAL: Front-end hardware — PC; Front-end software — Mk, QuarkXPress, X-tree; Printers — Xante. CLASSIFIED: Front-end hardware — Mk; Front-end software — Mk. DISPLAY: Front-end hardware — IBM/PC; Front-end software — Archetype, QuarkXPress. PRODUCTION: Typesetters — PC; Plate exposures — 2-Nu; Plate processors — 1-Nat; Production cameras — C/Spartan II; Automatic film processors — LE/LD24AQ; Color separation equipment (conventional) — BKY, Lf/AP Leaf Picture Desk.
PRESSROOM: Line 1 — 8-KP; Folders — 1-KP, 1-KP/JK8. MAILROOM: Counter stackers — 2-BG/Count-O-Veyor; Inserters and stuffers — MM; Bundle tyer — 2-MLN; Addressing machine — 1-KR. LIBRARY: Electronic — IBM, SMS/Stauffer Gold. WIRE SERVICES: News — Receiving dishes — AP. BUSINESS COMPUTERS: 4-DEC; Applications: DEC.

MERIDIAN
Lauderdale County
'90 U.S. Census- 43,539; E&P '96 Est. 41,261
ABC-CZ (90): 43,603 (HH 17,100)

The Meridian Star
(e-mon to fri; m-sat; S)

The Meridian Star, 810-12 22nd Ave.; PO Box 1591, Meridian, MS 39301; tel (601) 693-1551; fax (601) 485-1275. Hollinger International Inc. group.
Circulation: 18,916(e); 18,916(m-sat); 21,389(S); ABC Sept. 30, 1995.
Price: 50¢(d); 50¢(sat); $1.25(S); $10.95/mo; $131.40/yr.
Advertising: Open inch rate $16.10(e); $16.10(m-sat); $16.10(S). **Representative:** Papert Companies.
News Service: AP. **Politics:** Independent. **Established:** 1896.
Not Published: Christmas.
Special Editions: Area Progress, Valentine's Theme Page, Profile '96, Income Tax Guide (Feb); Bride & Groom, Outdoors & Recreation, Home & Garden, Brides Section, Fishing & Boating (Mar); Home Improvement, Pet Section, Car Care, Farmers Appreciation Tab (Apr); Jimmie Rogers Days (May); Cookbook, Health & Fitness, Firemen's Appreciation (June); State Games Section (July); Newcomer's Guide (Aug); Football, Sportsman, College Football, Weekly Football Contest, Forestry Section (Sept); Fall Home Improvement, Timber Industry Recognition, Fall Car Care, Outdoor Hunting Tab (Oct); Basketball, Christmas Songbook, Coupon Special, Veteran's Page (Nov); Greet Christmas Section, Christmas Greetings (Dec).
Special Weekly Sections: Best Food Day (wed); TV Viewing (fri).
Magazine: Parade (S).

GENERAL MANAGEMENT
Publisher Jerry Strader
General Manager John Bohl

ADVERTISING
Director Michael Lee
Manager-Classified Judy Taunehill

MARKETING AND PROMOTION
Manager-Marketing/Promotion Michael Lee

TELECOMMUNICATIONS
Audiotex Manager Michael Lee

CIRCULATION
Manager Phil Dupy

NEWS EXECUTIVES
Editor Jerry Strader
Managing Editor Steve Swogetinsky

EDITORS AND MANAGERS
Automotive Editor Judy Tannehill
Business/Finance Editor Stan Torgerson
City/Metro Editor Tom Buckley
Editorial Page Editor Steve Swogetinsky
Editorial Writer Steve Swogetinsky
Editorial Writer Jerry Strader
Education Editor Rachel White
Entertainment/Amusements Editor Dorothy Thompson
Fashion/Style Editor Dorothy Thompson
News Editor Austin Bishop
Photo Department Manager Ray Cook
Radio/Television Editor Dorothy Thompson
Religion Editor Dorothy Thompson
Society/Women's Editor Dorothy Thompson
Sports Editor Austin Bishop
Teen-Age/Youth Editor Ida Brown
Travel Editor Ida Brown

MANAGEMENT INFORMATION SERVICES
Data Processing Manager Marlene Hill

PRODUCTION
Superintendent-Pressroom Joe Fuller
Foreman-Composing Inga Bass

Market Information: TMC; ADS; Operate audiotex.
Mechanical available: Offset; Black and 3 ROP colors; insert accepted — preprinted; page cutoffs — 22¾".
Mechanical specifications: Type page 13¼" x 21½"; E - 6 cols, 2", ⅙" between; A - 6 cols, 2", ⅙" between; C - 9 cols, 1½", ⅙" between.
Commodity consumption: Newsprint 3,900 short tons; width 27"; black ink 99,000 pounds; color ink 20,500 pounds; single pages printed 12,200; average pages per issue 28(d), 40(S); single plates used 29,000.
Equipment: EDITORIAL: Front-end hardware — Ap/Mac; Front-end software — Ap/Mac; Printers — Ap/Mac LaserWriter II NTX, V. CLASSIFIED: Front-end hardware — Vision Data; Front-end software — Vision Data, Baseview; Printers — Ap/Mac LaserWriter II NTX. DISPLAY: Adv layout systems — Ap/Mac; Front-end hardware — Ap/Mac, Ap/Mac II NTX; Front-end software — Aldus/PageMaker. PRODUCTION: Typesetters — Ap/Mac LaserWriter II NTX, V/Imagesetter; Plate exposures — 1-Nu; Plate processors — W; Electronic picture desk — Lf/AP Leaf Picture Desk; Production cameras — C/Spartan III; Automatic film processors — LE; Film transporters — LE; Color separation equipment (conventional) — Ap/Mac.
PRESSROOM: Line 1 — 8-G/Urbanite; Press drives — Fin; Folders — G; Reels and stands — G; Press control system — Fin; Press registration system — Duarte. MAILROOM: Counter stackers — 2-HL; Inserters and stuffers — 2-MM; Bundle tyer — 4-MLN; Addressing machine — El. COMMUNICATIONS: Facsimile — Prepress Unisetters; Remote imagesetting — V; Digital ad delivery system — AP AdSend. Systems used — satellite. WIRE SERVICES: News — AP; Photos — AP; Stock tables — Creators, King Features; Syndicates — NYT, United Media, LATS; Receiving dishes — AP. BUSINESS COMPUTERS: Applications: Vision Data; PCs & micros networked.

NATCHEZ
Adams County
'90 U.S. Census- 19,460; E&P '96 Est. 17,673

The Natchez Democrat
(m-mon to sat; S)

The Natchez Democrat, 503 N. Canal St.; PO Box 1447, Natchez, MS 39120; tel (601) 442-9101; fax (601) 442-7315. Boone Newspapers Inc. group.
Circulation: 12,357(m); 12,357(m-sat); 12,481(S); VAC Mar. 31, 1995.
Price: 50¢(d); 50¢(sat); $1.25(S); $8.00/mo (home delivery).
Advertising: Open inch rate $12.50(m); $12.50(m-sat); $13.40(S). **Representative:** Landon Associates Inc.
News Service: AP. **Politics:** Independent. **Established:** 1863.
Special Editions: Profile (Feb); Spring Pilgrimage (Mar); Natchez & Its Neighbors (July); Fall Pilgrimage (Oct).
Special Weekly Sections: Best Food Day (wed); Real Estate Preview (fri); Religion (sat); Business/Financial, People (S).
Magazine: USA Weekend (S).

CORPORATE OFFICER
President Edward C Darling Jr

GENERAL MANAGEMENT
Publisher Edward C Darling Jr
Business Manager Nicole Doucet

ADVERTISING
Director Bryant Pierpont
Manager-Retail Julie Moss

CIRCULATION
Director Steve Eldridge

NEWS EXECUTIVE
Managing Editor Jimmy Sexton

EDITORS AND MANAGERS
Columnist Edward C Darling Jr
News Editor Scott Morris
Sports Editor Mike Grubb

PRODUCTION
Foreman-Pressroom Johnnie Griffin
Manager-Systems John Lees

Market Information: Zoned editions; TMC.
Mechanical available: Offset; Black and 3 ROP colors; insert accepted — preprinted; page cutoffs — 22¾".
Mechanical specifications: Type page 13" x 21½"; E - 6 cols, 2¹⁄₁₆", ⅛" between; A - 6 cols, 2¹⁄₁₆", ⅛" between; C - 9 cols, 1⅜", ¹⁄₁₆" between.
Commodity consumption: Newsprint 775 short tons; widths 27½", 27½", 13¾"; black ink 45,000 pounds; color ink 4,500 pounds; single pages printed 12,000; average pages per issue 20(d), 40(S); single plates used 10,000.
Equipment: EDITORIAL: Front-end hardware — 8-Ap/Mac Quadra 630, 5-Ap/Mac 7100, Ap/Mac 8150 fileserver, 3-Ap/Mac PowerBook 150; Front-end software — Baseview, QPS/IQ; Printers — 2-Xante/8200, 1-QMS/860. CLASSIFIED: Front-end hardware — 3-Ap/Mac Quadra 630; Front-end software — Baseview; Printers — Xante/8200. DISPLAY: Adv layout systems — 2-Ap/Mac Plus, 2-Ap/Mac SE, 2-Ap/Mac IIcx; Printers — 2-Ap/Mac LaserWriter. PRODUCTION: Typesetters — Ap/Mac Quadra 650; Platemaking systems — 3M/Pyrofax; Plate exposures — 1-Nu; Plate processors — 1-Ic; Production cameras — 1-C; Automatic film processors — 1-LE; Color separation equipment (conventional) — BKY.
PRESSROOM: Line 1 — 10-KP/Newsking; Folders — 1-KP/Balloon former; Reels and stands — 8-Rewinder. MAILROOM: Counter stackers — 1-BG/Count-O-Veyor; Bundle tyer — 1-Md; Addressing machine — 2-El, 2-Am. WIRE SERVICES: News — AP News Wire, AP Datafeatures; Receiving dishes — AP. BUSINESS COMPUTERS: 2-RSK; Applications: Adv billing, Accts receivable, Gen ledger, Payroll; PCs & main system networked.

OXFORD
Lafayette County
'90 U.S. Census- 9,984; E&P '96 Est. 10,247

The Oxford Eagle (e-mon to fri)

The Oxford Eagle, 916 Jackson Ave.; PO Box 866, Oxford, MS 38655; tel (601) 234-4331; fax (601) 234-4351.
Circulation: 5,340(e); Sworn Sept. 30, 1995.
Price: 35¢(d); $4.75/mo; $57.00/yr.
Advertising: Open inch rate $6.94(e). **Representative:** Papert Companies.
News Service: AP. **Established:** 1867.
Not Published: New Year; Independence Day; Labor Day; Friday following Thanksgiving; Christmas.
Special Weekly Sections: Business/Finance Page (mon); Newcomers (tues); Food Day (wed); Farm/Home Page (thur); School News (fri).

GENERAL MANAGEMENT
Publisher Jesse P Phillips
Asst Publisher Dan Phillips
Asst Publisher Tim Phillips
Asst Publisher Rita Vasilyev

ADVERTISING
Director Sandra Leake

CIRCULATION
Manager Gene Hayes

NEWS EXECUTIVE
Editor Nina B Goolsby

EDITORS AND MANAGERS
News Editor Steve Mullen
Sports Editor Don Whitten

Market Information: TMC.
Mechanical available: Offset; Black and 3 ROP colors; insert accepted — preprinted; page cutoffs — 22¾".
Mechanical specifications: Type page 13⅛" x 21"; E - 6 cols, 2¹⁄₁₆", ⅛" between; A - 6 cols, 2¹⁄₁₆", ⅛" between; C - 8 cols, 1½", ⅛" between.
Commodity consumption: Newsprint 315 short tons; width 28"; black ink 15,000 pounds; color ink 210 pounds; single pages printed 3,120; average pages per issue 17(d); single plates used 3,240.
Equipment: EDITORIAL: Front-end hardware — COM; Front-end software — Baseview/NewsEdit. CLASSIFIED: Front-end hardware — COM; Front-end software — Baseview/Class Manager. DISPLAY: Adv layout systems — COM. PRODUCTION: Typesetters — 1-COM/CRT; Plate exposures — 1-Nu; Production cameras — 1-R; Automatic film processors — LE/24AQ.
PRESSROOM: Line 1 — 6-G/Community (upper folder); Folders — SC. MAILROOM: Bundle tyer — 2-Felins; Addressing machine — 1-Am. WIRE SERVICES: News — AP; Syndicates — AP; Receiving dishes — AP. BUSINESS COMPUTERS: 1-RSK/16B, 1-RSK/DT 100, 2-RSK/100; Applications: Accts receivable;, Word processing.

PASCAGOULA
Jackson County
'90 U.S. Census- 25,899; E&P '96 Est. 23,456
ABC-NDM (90): 151,633 (HH 52,585)

The Mississippi Press
(e-mon to fri; S)

The Mississippi Press, 405 Delmas Ave.; PO Box 849, Pascagoula, MS 39568; tel (601) 762-1111; fax (601) 934-1454. Advance Publications group.
Circulation: 21,516(e); 22,208(S); ABC Sept. 30, 1995.
Price: 25¢(d); $1.00(S); $1.65/wk; $7.00/mo; $84.00/yr.
Advertising: Open inch rate $21.20(e); $21.20(S). **Representative:** Newhouse Newspapers/Metro Suburbia.
News Service: AP. **Politics:** Independent. **Established:** 1964.
Special Editions: Insurance (Jan); Bridal (Feb); Industry (Mar); Garden/Home Improvement (Apr); Boat & Fishing (May); Car Care (June); Back-to-School (July); Football (Aug); Home Furnishings (Sept); Cookbook (Nov).
Special Weekly Sections: Business (tues); Food (wed); Entertainment, Religion, TV Week (fri); Travel, Health (S).
Magazine: Parade (S).

CORPORATE OFFICERS
President W Howard Bronson
Secretary Gary Holland
Treasurer Luis M Williams

GENERAL MANAGEMENT
Publisher Wanda Heary Jacobs

ADVERTISING

Director-Marketing Tommy Chelette
Manager-Sales James K Kirklin
Manager-Retail James K Kirklin

CIRCULATION

Director Jim McKeel

NEWS EXECUTIVES

Editor Gary Holland
Senior Managing Editor Donald R Broadus

EDITORS AND MANAGERS

Amusements Editor Charles Brooks
Books Charles Brooks
Business Editor Tom Donnelly
City Editor Michael Wixon
Editorial Page Editor Gary Holland
Education Editor Debbie Wood
Films/Theater Editor Charles Brooks
Food Editor Susan Ruddiman
Librarian Beverly Pike
News Editor Walter Skupien
Political Editor Donald R Broadus
Radio/Television Editor Charles Brooks
Religion Editor Debbie Wood
Sports Editor Mark Bryant
Teen-Age/Youth Editor Debbie Wood
Wire Editor Charles Brooks
Women's Editor Susan Ruddiman

PRODUCTION

Director Doyle R Odom
Asst Superintendent Larry Vann
Foreman-Pressroom Edward R King
Foreman-Mailroom Sheila Vice

Market Information: Zoned editions; Split Run; TMC.

Mechanical available: Offset; Black and 3 ROP colors; insert accepted — preprinted, Mini, Flexi, Spadea; page cut-offs — 22¾".

Mechanical specifications: Type page 13" x 21¼"; E - 6 cols, $2\frac{1}{16}$", ⅛" between; A - 6 cols, $2\frac{1}{16}$", ⅛" between; C - 10 cols, 1⅛", ⅛" between.

Commodity consumption: Newsprint 130 metric tons; width 13⅝"; black ink 25,000 pounds; color ink 4,500 pounds; single pages printed 37,440; average pages per issue 32(d), 48(S); single plates used 20,000.

Equipment: EDITORIAL: Front-end hardware — 5-Ap/Mac (with file server); Front-end software — Baseview; Printers — Linotype-Hell/L190. CLASSIFIED: Front-end hardware — 4-Ap/Mac 800; Front-end software — Baseview, QPS; Printers — QMS/Laserwriter. DISPLAY: Front-end hardware — 4-Ap/Mac 800; Front-end software — Baseview, QPS; Printers — 1-New-Gen/600. PRODUCTION: Pagination software — QPS, Mk/Managing Editor; Typesetters — 2-Linotype-Hell/Ultresetter; Plate exposures — 1-BKY, 1-Nu/Flip Top; Plate processors — 1-Nat/250-A; Electronic picture desk — Ap/Mac, Adobe/Photoshop, Lf/AP Leaf Picture Desk; Scanners — Lf/Leafscan, Microtek; Production cameras — SCREEN/270-D; Automatic film processors — 2-P/18; Color separation equipment (conventional) — Ap/Mac, Adobe/Photoshop.
PRESSROOM: Line 1 — 1-G/1013 full color. MAILROOM: Inserters and stuffers — 2-MM/227; Bundle tyer — 1-Bu/68950, 1-Bu/75094. COMMUNICATIONS: Remote imagesetting — satellite. WIRE SERVICES: News — AP, AP Datafeatures, NNS; Syndicates — AP, North America Syndicate; Receiving dishes — AP. BUSINESS COMPUTERS: 10-IBM/PC2-25, 2-AST/fileserver; Applications: Payroll, Accts receivable, Accts payable, Circ, Gen ledger; PCs & micros networked; PCs & main system networked.

PICAYUNE
Pearl River County

'90 U.S. Census- 10,633; E&P '96 Est. 11,050

Picayune Item (e-tues to fri; S)

Picayune Item, 214 Curran Ave.; PO Box 580, Picayune, MS 39466; tel (601) 798-4766; fax (601) 798-8602. Donrey Media Group group.

Circulation: 6,436(e); 6,436(S); Sworn Sept. 30, 1995.

Price: 50¢(d); 75¢(S); $5.00/mo; $60.00/yr.

Advertising: Open inch rate $8.88(e); $8.88(S). **Representative:** Papert Companies.

News Services: AP, NEA. **Politics:** Independent. **Established:** 1904.

Advertising not accepted: Liquor.

Special Editions: Pearl River County Today; Football; Back-to-School.

Special Weekly Sections: Best Food Day, Farm (wed); Best Food Days, Entertainment (S).

Magazine: Profile Sunday Magazine (S).

CORPORATE OFFICERS

Founder Donald W Reynolds
President/Chief Operating Officer Emmett Jones
Exec Vice Pres/Chief Financial Officer Darrell W Loftin
Vice Pres-Western Newspaper Group David A Osborn
Vice Pres-Eastern Newspaper Group Don Schneider

GENERAL MANAGEMENT

Publisher Dave Sims

ADVERTISING

Director Tom Andrews

CIRCULATION

Director Mike McDougle
Manager Edith Frierson

NEWS EXECUTIVES

Editor Dave Sims
Managing Editor Will Sullivan

EDITORS AND MANAGERS

Editorial Writer Dave Sims
Fashion Editor Reni Winter
Photo Department Manager John Parillo
Society/Women's Editor Reni Winter
Sports Editor Rob Sigler

PRODUCTION

Foreman-Pressroom Clarence Melerine
Foreman-Camera John Parillo

Market Information: TMC.

Mechanical available: Offset; Black and 3 ROP colors; insert accepted — preprinted; page cut-offs — 22¾".

Mechanical specifications: Type page 13" x 21½"; E - 6 cols, $2\frac{1}{16}$", ⅛" between; A - 6 cols, $2\frac{1}{16}$", ⅛" between; C - 8 cols, $1\frac{7}{16}$", $\frac{1}{16}$" between.

Commodity consumption: Newsprint 180 metric tons; widths 13½", 27"; black ink 6,570 pounds; color ink 400 pounds; single pages printed 6,000; average pages per issue 24(d), 48(S); single plates used 3,380.

Equipment: EDITORIAL: Front-end hardware — 5-Mk; Printers — 2-Ap/Mac LaserWriter. CLASSIFIED: Front-end hardware — 2-Mk. DISPLAY: Adv layout systems — 3-Ap/Mac; Front-end software — QuarkXPress; Printers — 1-Ap/Mac LaserWriter II NTX, Dataproducts/LZR 1560. PRODUCTION: Typesetters — 2-Ap/Mac LaserWriter II NTX; Plate exposures — Nu; Plate processors — Ic; Scanners — Ap/Mac Scanner; Production cameras — Goerz/J72; Automatic film processors — P.
PRESSROOM: Line 1 — 4-KP; Folders — 1-KP. MAILROOM: Counter stackers — 1-BG; Bundle tyer — 1-Bu; Addressing machine — Automecha/Accufast. WIRE SERVICES: News — AP; Receiving dishes — size-3ft, AP. BUSINESS COMPUTERS: Unisys.

STARKVILLE
Oktibbeha County

'90 U.S. Census- 18,458; E&P '96 Est. 22,141

Starkville Daily News (m-mon to sat; S)

Starkville Daily News, 316 University Dr.; PO Drawer 1068, Starkville, MS 39759; tel (601) 323-1642; fax (601) 323-6586. Hollinger International Inc. group.

Circulation: 5,399(m); 5,399(S); Sworn Sept. 22, 1995.

Price: 35¢(d); $1.00(S); $86.00/yr.

Advertising: Open inch rate $9.25(m); $9.25(S). **Representative:** Papert Companies.

News Service: AP. **Politics:** Independent. **Established:** 1901.

Note: For detailed production information, see West Point Daily Times Leader.

Not Published: New Year; Memorial Day; Independence Day; Labor Day; Thanksgiving; Christmas.

Special Weekly Sections: Business (tues); Food, Education (wed); Agriculture (thur); Dining, Entertainment (fri); Religion (sat); Lifestyles, Weddings (S).

Magazine: Televisions (TV listing) (S).

GENERAL MANAGEMENT

Publisher Rick L Noffsinger
Business Manager Marcia Deaton

ADVERTISING

Manager Susanne Reed

CIRCULATION

Manager Greg Martin

NEWS EXECUTIVE

Managing Editor Pattye Archer

PRODUCTION

Manager Sandra Hodges

Market Information: TMC.

Mechanical available: Offset; Black and 3 ROP colors; insert accepted — preprinted; page cut-offs — 22¾".

Mechanical specifications: Type page 13" x 21½"; E - 6 cols, $2\frac{1}{16}$", ⅛" between; A - 6 cols, $2\frac{1}{16}$", ⅛" between; C - 9 cols, $1\frac{5}{16}$", ⅛" between.

Commodity consumption: width 27½".

Equipment: EDITORIAL: Front-end hardware — Ap/Mac II, Ap/Mac Quadra 605; Front-end software — Baseview; Printers — Ap/Mac Laser-Writer II. CLASSIFIED: Front-end hardware — Ap/Mac Quadra 605; Front-end software — Baseview. DISPLAY: Adv layout systems — Ap/Mac IIcx, Ap/Mac SE; Front-end software — QuarkXPress, Aldus/PageMaker; Other equipment — Cannon/Scanner. PRODUCTION: Pagination software — QuarkXPress 3.3; WIRE SERVICES: News — AP GraphicsNet; Receiving dishes — AP. BUSINESS COMPUTERS: Applications: PCs & micros networked.

TUPELO
Lee County

'90 U.S. Census- 30,685; E&P '96 Est. 38,502
ABC-CZ (90): 34,624 (HH 13,235)

Northeast Mississippi Daily Journal (m-mon to sat; S)

Northeast Mississippi Daily Journal, 1655 S. Green; PO Box 909, Tupelo, MS 38802-0909; tel (601) 842-2611; fax (601) 842-2233.

Circulation: 38,884(m); 38,884(m-sat); 38,286(S); ABC Sept. 30, 1995.

Price: 50¢(d); 50¢(sat); $1.00(S); $8.90/mo; $24.75/3mo, $49.50/6mo; $99.00/yr.

Advertising: Open inch rate $18.52(m); $18.52(m-sat); $18.52(S). **Representative:** Landon Associates Inc.

News Services: AP, KRT. **Politics:** Independent. **Established:** 1870.

Not Published: Christmas.

Advertising not accepted: Alcoholic beverages; Gaming.

Special Editions: Spring Furn. Market (Jan); Spring Brides '96, Vacation Travel Guide (Feb); Spring Fashion, Home Improvement (Mar); Restaurant Guide (Apr); Oleput (May); Graduation Recognition (June); Fall Furn. Market (July); Back-to-School, Football HS '96, Football College/Pro, Fall Brides '96 (Aug); Home Improvement, Fall Fashion (Sept); Restaurant Guide (Oct); Thanksgiving (Nov); Year-In-Review (Dec).

Special Weekly Sections: Business (mon); Food Day, Lee County Neighbors (wed); Religion (sat).

Magazines: View (local entertainment magazine) (S); TV Week.

CORPORATE OFFICERS

Board Chairman/CEO/President Anna R McLean
Exec Vice Pres William L Crews

GENERAL MANAGEMENT

Publisher William L Crews
Chief Financial Officer Tommy Gilreath
Controller Rosemary Jarrell
General Manager Tom Pittman

ADVERTISING

Director Richard Crenshaw
Manager Cyndi McDurmon

CIRCULATION

Director Tommy Greene
Manager Kelly Cosky

NEWS EXECUTIVES

Editor Lloyd Gray
Managing Editor Charlotte Wolfe

EDITORS AND MANAGERS

Automotive Editor Beth Clements
Business/Finance Editor Glenda Sloan
City/Metro Editor Ginna Parsons
Editorial Page Editor Joe Rutherford
Editorial Writer Lloyd Gray
Editorial Writer Joe Rutherford
Education Editor Monique Harrison
Entertainment/Amusements Editor Terri Tabor
Fashion/Style Editor Beth Clements
Features Editor Beth Clements
Films/Theater Editor Terri Tabor
Food Editor Beth Clements
Health/Medical Editor Beth Clements
Librarian Judy Campbell
Lifestyle Editor Beth Clements
Photo Editor Don Hill
Radio/Television Editor Judy Putt
Religion Editor John Armistead Dr
Sports Editor Gene Phelphs
Teen-Age/Youth Editor Monique Harrison
Wire Editor Charlie Langford

MANAGEMENT INFORMATION SERVICES

Data Processing Manager Clay Foster

PRODUCTION

Director Clay Foster

Market Information: Zoned editions; TMC.

Mechanical available: Offset; Black and 3 ROP colors; insert accepted — preprinted, all; page cut-offs — 22¾".

Mechanical specifications: Type page 13" x 21½"; E - 6 cols, $2\frac{1}{16}$", ⅛" between; A - 6 cols, $2\frac{1}{16}$", ⅛" between; C - 8 cols, 1½", ⅛" between.

Commodity consumption: Newsprint 3,534 short tons; widths 27.5", 27.5", 13¾"; black ink 72,685 pounds; color ink 12,752 pounds; single pages printed 14,505; average pages per issue 32(d), 54(S); single plates used 26,510.

Equipment: EDITORIAL: Front-end hardware — 35-Ap/Mac; Front-end software — Baseview/Editorial System, Baseview/NewsEdit Ique, QuarkXPress; Printers — AG/Avantra 25S. CLASSIFIED: Front-end hardware — AT, Computext/CompuClass; Front-end software — Computext/CompuClass; Printers — Hyphen/Dash 600 BXs, AG/Avantra 25S. DISPLAY: Adv layout systems — SCS/Layout 8000; Front-end hardware — Ap/Mac; Front-end software — Multi-Ad/Creator; Printers — Hyphen/Dash 600 BXs, AG/Avantra 25S. PRODUCTION: Pagination software — QuarkXPress, SCS/Linx; Typesetters — AG/Advantra 25S; Platemaking systems — Nu, Magnum; Plate processors — 1-Nat, Glunz & Jensen; Electronic picture desk — Lf/AP Leaf Picture Desk; Scanners — Lf/Leafscan 35, Nikon/Coolscan, Pixelcraft/7650C; Production cameras — 1-Kyoto/C-260-D; Automatic film processors — 1-GEV/Litex 26, AG/Rapidline 43; Color separation equipment (conventional) — RZ/4050E, Lf/AP Leaf Picture Desk.
PRESSROOM: Line 1 — 12-G/Urbanite Model #U1366; Press drives — Fin; Folders — 1-G/U-1366, 1-G/SU-1708; Pasters — 8-Cary. MAILROOM: Counter stackers — 1-BG/180, 2-HL/Monitor HT II, 1-HL/Monitor; Inserters and stuffers — 1-HI/1472; Bundle tyer — 2-MLN, 2-MLN/News 90; Wrapping singles — 2-HL/Monarch; Addressing machine — 1-Ch. LIBRARY: Electronic — 1-Ap/Mac, SMS/Stauffer Gold Software; Combination — SMS/Stauffer. COMMUNICATIONS: Facsimile — Murata/F-75, Okidata/Okifax 1000; Digital ad delivery system — AP AdSend, Adobe/Aerobot. Systems used — satellite. WIRE SERVICES: News — AP, AP Datanews, KRT; Photos — AP; Stock tables — AP; Syndicates — North America Syndicate, NEA, King Features, United Media, WP; Receiving dishes — AP. BUSINESS COMPUTERS: TI/1500; Applications: Adv billing, Accts receivable, Payroll, Gen ledger, Accts payable; PCs & main system networked.

VICKSBURG
Warren County

'90 U.S. Census- 20,908; E&P '96 Est. 17,845
ABC-CZ (90): 20,908 (HH 8,268)

The Vicksburg Post (e-mon to fri; m-sat; S)

The Vicksburg Post, 920 South St.; PO Box 951, Vicksburg, MS 39180; tel (601) 636-4545; fax (601) 634-0897.

Circulation: 14,447(e); 14,447(m-sat); 14,832(S); ABC Sept. 30, 1995.

Price: 35¢(d); 35¢(sat); $1.00(S); $9.00/mo; $108.00/yr.

Advertising: Open inch rate $11.69(e); $11.69(m-sat); $11.69(S). **Representative:** Papert Companies.

News Service: AP. **Politics:** Independent. **Established:** 1883.

Not Published: Christmas.

Special Editions: Brides (Jan); Engineers (Feb); Pilgrimage (Mar); Car Care, Home Improvement (Apr); Summer Living (May); Cookbook (June); Football (Aug); Fall Outlook Guide (Sept); Car Care, Home & Garden (Oct).

Special Weekly Sections: Best Food Day (wed); TV (S).

CORPORATE OFFICER

President Louis P Cashman III

GENERAL MANAGEMENT

Publisher Louis P Cashman III
General Manager Otis Headley
Purchasing Agent Otis Headley

ADVERTISING

Manager David Gillis

I-224 Mississippi

MARKETING AND PROMOTION

Manager-Marketing/Promotion David Gillis

CIRCULATION

Manager Doug Ducharme

NEWS EXECUTIVES

Editor Louis P Cashman III
Managing Editor Charles D Mitchell

EDITORS AND MANAGERS

Food Editor Mrs Laurin Stamm
Sports Editor Dennis Seid

MANAGEMENT INFORMATION SERVICES

Data Processing Manager Linda Banchetti

PRODUCTION

Foreman-Pressroom Bobby Childers

Market Information: Split Run; TMC.
Mechanical available: Offset; Black and 3 ROP colors; insert accepted — preprinted; page cutoffs — 22¾".
Mechanical specifications: Type page 13" x 21"; E - 6 cols, 2 1/16", ⅛" between; A - 6 cols, 2 1/16", ⅛" between; C - 8 cols, 1⅜", 1/16" between.
Commodity consumption: Newsprint 1,200 short tons; widths 27½", 13¾"; black ink 27,450 pounds; color ink 550 pounds; single pages printed 12,000; average pages per issue 26(d), 44(S); single plates used 11,000.
Equipment: EDITORIAL: Front-end hardware — 20-Mk, 8-Ap/Mac; Front-end software — FSI/QPS; Printers — 3-Xante. CLASSIFIED: Front-end hardware — 2-Ap/Mac; Front-end software — FSI, QPS; Printers — 2-Xante. DISPLAY: Adv layout systems — FSI, QPS; Front-end hardware — 6-Ap/Mac, 6-Ap/Mac; Printers — 2-Xante, HP. PRODUCTION: Typesetters — 2-M/202N; Plate exposures — 2-Nu; Plate processors — 1-Nat; Production cameras — 1-R; Automatic film processors — 1-LE; Color separation equipment (conventional) — Digi-Colour/Direct Screen System.
PRESSROOM: Line 1 — 7-G/Urbanite; Folders — 1-G. MAILROOM: Bundle tyer — 2-MLN. WIRE SERVICES: News — AP; Photos — AP; Receiving dishes — AP. BUSINESS COMPUTERS: 1-DEC/11-21, 5-DEC/101; Applications: Circ, Adv billing, Accts receivable, Gen ledger, Payroll.

WEST POINT

Clay County

'90 U.S. Census- 8,489; E&P '96 Est. 8,390

Daily Times Leader

(m-tues to fri; S)

Daily Times Leader, 227 Court St.; PO Box 1176, West Point, MS 39773; tel (601) 494-1422; fax (601) 494-1414. Hollinger International Inc. group.
Circulation: 2,817(m); 2,817(S); Sworn Sept. 29, 1995.
Price: 35¢(d); 35¢(S); $75.00/yr.
Advertising: Open inch rate $6.10(m); $6.10(S). **Representative:** Papert Companies.
News Service: AP. **Politics:** Independent. **Established:** 1867.
Not Published: New Year; Memorial Day; Independence Day; Labor Day; Thanksgiving; Christmas.
Special Editions: Profile (Feb); Cookbook (Mar); Brides, Sports Edition (Apr); Back-to-School (Aug); Football; Prairie Arts Festival (Sept); Home for the Holidays (Dec).
Magazine: TeleVisions (combined insertion with Starkville Daily News).

GENERAL MANAGEMENT

Publisher/General Manager Rick L Noffsinger
Office Manager Peggy Walls

ADVERTISING

Manager-Local Joyce Pierce

CIRCULATION

Manager Marty Sullivan

NEWS EXECUTIVE

Managing Editor Floyd Ingram

PRODUCTION

Foreman-Pressroom Charles Nail

Market Information: TMC.
Mechanical available: Offset; Black and 3 ROP colors; insert accepted — preprinted; page cutoffs — 22¾".
Mechanical specifications: Type page 13" x 21½"; E - 6 cols, 2 1/16", ⅛" between; A - 6 cols, 2 1/16", ⅛" between; C - 9 cols, 1 5/16", ⅛" between.
Commodity consumption: Newsprint 530 short tons; width 27½"; black ink 13,500 pounds; single plates used 9,540.
Equipment: EDITORIAL: Front-end hardware — Ap/Mac; Front-end software — Baseview; Printers — Ap/Mac LaserWriter. CLASSIFIED: Front-end hardware — Ap/Mac; Front-end software — Baseview. DISPLAY: Adv layout systems — Ap/Mac Radius; Front-end hardware — Ap/Mac Radius. PRODUCTION: Pagination software — QuarkXPress 3.3; Typesetters — Ap/Mac Laser-Writer II; Platemaking systems — Nu; Production cameras — Konica; Automatic film processors — Konica.
PRESSROOM: Line 1 — 6-HI/V-15A. MAILROOM: Counter stackers — BG; Bundle tyer — Bu. WIRE SERVICES: News — AP; Receiving dishes — AP.

MISSOURI

BLUE SPRINGS

Jackson County

'90 U.S. Census- 40,153; E&P '96 Est. 48,803

The Blue Springs Examiner

(e-mon to fri; m-sat)

The Blue Springs Examiner, 500 W. R D Mize Rd. (64014); PO Box 1057, Blue Springs, MO 64013; tel (816) 229-9161; fax (816) 224-7245. Morris Communications Corp. group.
Circulation: 5,406(e); 5,406(m-sat); VAC June 30, 1995.
Price: 50¢(d); 50¢(sat).
Advertising: Open inch rate $10.81(e); $12.61(e-wed); $11.90(m-sat). **Representative:** US Suburban Press.
News Service: AP. **Politics:** Independent. **Established:** 1974.
Note: For detailed production information see the Independence Examiner. Wed. edition has a total free circulation of 22,340.
Not Published: New Year; Memorial Day; Independence Day; Labor Day; Christmas.
Special Editions: Brides, Personal Finance (Jan); Business Review & Forecast (Feb); Health & Fitness (Mar); Kansas City Royals Opening, North Pole Edition (Apr); Brides (May); Senior Citizens (June); Guide to Blue Springs (July); Auto Edition (Oct); Christmas Opening (Nov); Holiday Gift Guide (Dec).
Special Weekly Section: USA Weekend.

GENERAL MANAGEMENT

Publisher Kevin Kampman
Business Manager Becky Ely

ADVERTISING

Director Irene Baltrusaitis

TELECOMMUNICATIONS

Audiotex Manager Harry Stewart

CIRCULATION

Manager Bob Ester

NEWS EXECUTIVE

Managing Editor Dale Brendel

EDITOR AND MANAGER

Sports Editor Huey Counts

Market Information: TMC; Operate audiotex.
Mechanical available: Offset; Black and 3 ROP colors; insert accepted — preprinted.
Mechanical specifications: E - 6 cols, 2.04", ⅙" between; A - 6 cols, 2.04", ⅙" between; C - 1.46", ⅙" between.

BOONVILLE

Cooper County

'90 U.S. Census- 7,095; E&P '96 Est. 7,209

Boonville Daily News

(e-mon to fri)

Boonville Daily News, 412 E. High; PO Box 47, Boonville, MO 65233; tel (816) 882-5335; fax (816) 882-2256. Hollinger International Inc. group.
Circulation: 2,549(e); Sworn Sept. 30, 1994.
Price: 50¢(d); $75.00/yr.
Advertising: Open inch rate $6.75(e).
News Service: AP. **Politics:** Independent. **Established:** 1919.
Not Published: New Year; Independence Day; Memorial Day; Labor Day; Thanksgiving; Christmas.
Special Weekly Sections: Business (wed); Agriculture (thur).
Magazine: Bonville Cable View (TV Guide) (fri).

CORPORATE OFFICERS

President Larry J Perrotto
Comptroller Roland McBride

GENERAL MANAGEMENT

Publisher Scott J Jackson

ADVERTISING

Manager Angela Inscore

CIRCULATION

Director Ernie Pratt

NEWS EXECUTIVE

Editor Steve Thomas

PRODUCTION

Superintendent Flo Hickam

Market Information: TMC.
Mechanical available: Offset; Black and 3 ROP colors; insert accepted — preprinted; page cutoffs — 22¾".
Mechanical specifications: Type page 13" x 21"; E - 6 cols, 2 1/16", ⅛" between; A - 6 cols, 2 1/16", ⅛" between; C - 6 cols, 2 1/16", ⅛" between.
Commodity consumption: Newsprint 200 short tons; widths 27½", 13¾", 30"; black ink 6,500 pounds; color ink 700 pounds; single pages printed 3,200; average pages per issue 12(d); single plates used 3,000.
Equipment: EDITORIAL: Front-end hardware — Ap/Mac Plus, Ap/Mac Classic; Printers — 1-Ap/Mac LaserPrinter. CLASSIFIED: Front-end hardware — Ap/Mac SE. PRODUCTION: Pagination software — QuarkXPress 3.0; Typesetters — 2-Ap/Mac SE, 1-Ap/Mac Laser-Printer; Plate exposures — Nu; Production cameras — SCREEN.
PRESSROOM: Line 1 — 4-G/Community; Folders — 1-G. MAILROOM: Counter stackers — BG; Bundle tyer — 3-Bu; Addressing machine — 2-Dispensa-Matic/16. WIRE SERVICES: News — AP; Receiving dishes — AP. BUSINESS COMPUTERS: IBM, AT; PCs & main system networked.

BRANSON

Taney County

'90 U.S. Census- 3,706; E&P '96 Est. 4,965

Branson Tri-Lakes Daily News

(m-tues to sat; S)

Branson Tri-Lakes Daily News, 114 N. Commercial St. (65616); PO Box 1900, Branson, MO 65615; tel (417) 334-3161; fax (417) 334-4299. Lancaster Management Inc. group.
Circulation: 10,620(m); 10,620(m-sat); 10,620(S); Sworn Oct. 1, 1994.
Price: 50¢(d); 50¢(sat); $1.00(S); $15.00/3mo (carrier/mail); $50.00/yr.
Advertising: Open inch rate $10.90(m); $10.90(m-sat); $14.15(S). **Representative:** Papert Companies.
News Service: AP. **Established:** 1992.
Note: On May 7, 1995, this publication started publishing a Sunday edition. Sunday circulation figure is an estimate
Not Published: New Year; Memorial Day; Independence Day; Labor Day; Thanksgiving.
Special Editions: Tax Series (Jan); Homecoming (Feb); Girl Scout Issue (Mar); Brides, Spring Home Improvement, American Home Week, Kewpiesta (Apr); Mother's Day, Memorial Day Sale, Graduation (May); Father's Day, Safe Boating, Pet Pages (June); July 4th Celebration, Taney County Fair (July); Back-to-School, Arts and Crafts, Rodeo (Aug); Fall Home Improvement, Harvest Moon (Sept); Octoberfest, Football, Restaurants (Oct); Christmas Catalog (Nov); Christmas Greetings, Parade Pages, Basketball (Dec).
Special Weekly Sections: Business (tues); Business, Endearments, Grocery (wed); Business, Education (thur); Business, Entertainment (fri); Business, Entertainment, Religion (sat).
Magazines: Branson TV Take One (TV/Entertainment) (fri); Discover (Real Estate mini tab), Ozark Mountain Visitor (Tourist tab) (monthly).

CORPORATE OFFICER

President/Publisher Dave Reeves

GENERAL MANAGEMENT

General Manager Sandy Schaefer-Wilkinson
Manager-Office Joan Jenkins

ADVERTISING

Director Sandy Schaefer-Wilkinson

CIRCULATION

Manager Gary Camp

NEWS EXECUTIVES

Managing Editor Martha Hoy
Editor-Branson Linda Putman
Editor-Taney County Linda Morgan
Editor-Stone County Mary Jo Fisk

EDITORS AND MANAGERS

Entertainment Editor Jimmy Lancaster
Graphics Manager Carrie Camp
Sports Editor Craig Yuhas

PRODUCTION

Manager Dwain Webb

Mechanical available: Offset; Black and 3 ROP colors; insert accepted — preprinted; page cutoffs — 27¾".
Mechanical specifications: Type page 13" x 21½"; E - 6 cols, 2 1/16", ⅛" between; A - 6 cols, 2 1/16", ⅛" between; C - 6 cols, 2 1/16", ⅛" between.
Equipment: EDITORIAL: Front-end hardware — 1-Ap/Mac LC, 8-Ap/Mac Classic; Front-end software — Baseview/NewsEdit, Baseview/Wire Manager; Printers — 1-Ap/Mac LaserWriter Plus. CLASSIFIED: Front-end hardware — 2-Ap/Mac LC, 2-Ap/Mac Classic II; Front-end software — Baseview/Classified Ad Manager; Printers — Okidata/291. DISPLAY: Front-end hardware — Ap/Mac IIsi, Ap/Mac IIfx fileserver, 4-Ap/Mac Quadra 700; Front-end software — Baseview/Ad Manager, QuarkXPress; Printers — Ap/Mac LaserWriter IIg; Other equipment — Ap/Mac CD-Rom. PRODUCTION: OCR software — Caere/OmniPage; Typesetters — Ap/Mac LaserWriter IIg; Plate exposures — Theimer; Plate processors — Nat; Scanners — Ofoto, Ap/Mac One Scanner; Production cameras — LE; Automatic film processors — LE.
PRESSROOM: Line 1 — 8-KP/Newsking; Folders — 1-KP/KJ8. MAILROOM: Counter stackers — KAN; Inserters and stuffers — KAN/480 5-into-1; Bundle tyer — Bu. COMMUNICATIONS: Facsimile — Toshiba. WIRE SERVICES: News — AP; Syndicates — NEA, TMS, United Features, TV Data; Receiving dishes — AP. BUSINESS COMPUTERS: 5-PC, MSSI; PCs & micros networked; PCs & main system networked.

BROOKFIELD

Linn County

'90 U.S. Census- 4,888; E&P '96 Est. 4,401

Daily News-Bulletin

(e-mon to fri)

Daily News-Bulletin, 107-109 N. Main; PO Box 40, Brookfield, MO 64628; tel (816) 258-7237; fax (816) 258-7238.
Circulation: 3,864(e); Sworn Oct. 13, 1995.
Price: 50¢(d); $69.37/yr (out of state), $56.56/yr (out of county), $38.42/yr (in-county).
Advertising: Open inch rate $5.65(e).
News Services: AP, NEA. **Politics:** Independent. **Established:** 1879 (weekly), 1948 (daily).
Not Published: New Year; Memorial Day; Independence Day; Labor Day; Thanksgiving; Christmas.
Magazine: TV Guide.

CORPORATE OFFICERS

President Susan C Abeln
Secretary/Treasurer Susan C Abeln

GENERAL MANAGEMENT

Publisher/General Manager Richard E Abeln Sr
Publisher/General Manager Susan C Abeln
Purchasing Agent Richard E Abeln Sr

ADVERTISING

Manager Bob Middleton
Manager-Classified Becky O'Brien

CIRCULATION

Manager Ann Banks

NEWS EXECUTIVE

Editor Gregory Orear

EDITORS AND MANAGERS

Automotive Editor Richard E Abeln Sr
Business/Financial Editor Gregory Orear
City/Metro Editor Gregory Orear
Editorial Page Editor Gregory Orear
Features Editor Gregory Orear
Graphics Editor/Art Director Gregory Orear
News Editor Gregory Orear
Photo Editor Gregory Orear

Copyright ©1996 by the Editor & Publisher Co.

Political/Government Editor Gregory Orear
Society Editor Christi Davolt
Sports Editor Gregory Orear

PRODUCTION

Superintendent Richard E Abeln Sr

Mechanical available: Offset; Black and 1 ROP color; insert accepted — preprinted; page cut-offs — 22¾".
Mechanical specifications: E - 6 cols, 2¹⁄₁₆", ⅛" between; A - 6 cols, 2¹⁄₁₆", ⅛" between; C - 6 cols, 2¹⁄₁₆", ⅛" between.
Commodity consumption: Newsprint 80 short tons; widths 29", 14½"; black ink 1,000 pounds; color ink 200 pounds; single pages printed 3,016; average pages per issue 8(d); single plates used 1,010.
Equipment: EDITORIAL: Front-end hardware — 5-Ap/Mac LC III; Printers — LaserMaster/4M. CLASSIFIED: Front-end hardware — 2-Ap/Mac LC III. DISPLAY: Front-end hardware — 2-Ap/Mac LC III; Printers — LaserMaster/4M. PRODUCTION: Typesetters — 2-LaserMaster/4M; Platemaking systems — 1-3M/Deadliner; Plate exposures — 1-3M/Deadliner; Plate processors — 1-3M/Deadliner; Production cameras — K/Vertical, 3M/Deadliner. PRESSROOM: Line 1 — 4-G/Community; Folders — 1-G/2:1. COMMUNICATIONS: Facsimile — Northwestern Bell. WIRE SERVICES: News — AP; Receiving dishes — size-3ft, AP. BUSINESS COMPUTERS: Ap/Mac III LC; Applications: Peachtree: Accounting; PCs & micros networked; PCs & main system networked.

CAMDENTON

Camden County

'90 U.S. Census- 2,561; E&P '96 Est. 2,798

Lake Sun Leader

(m-mon to fri)

Lake Sun Leader, 450 N. Hwy. 5, Camdenton, MO 65020; tel (314) 346-2132; fax (314) 346-4508. Hollinger International Inc. group.
Circulation: 5,342(m); Sworn Oct. 1, 1995.
Price: 50¢(d); $19.12/mo; $80.57/yr.
Advertising: Open inch rate $7.50(m).
News Service: AP. **Politics:** Independent. **Established:** 1879.
Not Published: New Year; Thanksgiving; Christmas.
Special Editions: Home Improvement; Car Care; Christmas; Football; Basketball; Progress.
Magazines: Real Estate Guide; TV Week.

GENERAL MANAGEMENT

General Manager Tom Turner

ADVERTISING

Manager Lisa Miller

CIRCULATION

Manager Debbie Hyman

NEWS EXECUTIVE

Editor Michael Feeback

EDITORS AND MANAGERS

Business/Finance Editor Michael Feeback
City/Metro Editor Michael Feeback
Editorial Page Editor Michael Feeback
Features Editor Michael Feeback
Graphics Editor/Art Director Michael Feeback
News Editor Michael Feeback
Photo Editor Michael Feeback
Political/Government Editor Michael Feeback
Sports Editor Michael Feeback

Market Information: Zoned editions; Split Run; TMC.
Mechanical available: Offset; Black and 2 ROP colors; insert accepted — preprinted.
Mechanical specifications: Type page 13" x 21½"; E - 6 cols, 2¹⁄₁₆", ⅛" between; A - 6 cols, 2¹⁄₁₆", ⅛" between; C - 6 cols, 2¹⁄₁₆", ⅛" between.
Commodity consumption: Newsprint 520 short tons; width 27.5"; black ink 15,620 pounds; color ink 2,160 pounds; single pages printed 5,200; average pages per issue 18(d); single plates used 5,300.
Equipment: EDITORIAL: Front-end hardware — Ap/Macs; Other equipment — IBM, HP. CLASSIFIED: Other equipment — COM/MCS. DISPLAY: Front-end hardware — Ap/Mac. PRODUCTION: Typesetters — HP/LaserJet; Plate exposures — Nu; Scanners — DSA. MAILROOM: Counter stackers — KAN/320; Bundle tyer — Bu; Addressing machine — Ch. WIRE SERVICES: News — AP; Receiving dishes — AP. BUSINESS COMPUTERS: IBM/Sys 36, AmDek/Sys 286A; PCs & micros networked.

CAPE GIRARDEAU

Cape Girardeau County

'90 U.S. Census- 34,438; E&P '96 Est. 34,502

Southeast Missourian

(m-mon to sat; S)

Southeast Missourian, 301 Broadway; PO Box 699, Cape Girardeau, MO 63702-0699; tel (314) 335-6611; fax (314) 334-9258; e-mail capenews@ldd.net. Rust Communications group.
Circulation: 16,276(m); 15,932(m-wed); 16,276(m-sat); 19,311(S); CAC Mar. 31, 1995.
Price: 50¢(d); 50¢; $1.50(S); $2.70/wk (carrier); $130.00/yr (carrier).
Advertising: Open inch rate $15.00(m); $20.00(m-wed); $20.00(m-sat); $21.00(S). **Representative:** Papert Companies.
News Service: AP. **Politics:** Independent. **Established:** 1904.
Not Published: New Year; Memorial Day; Independence Day; Labor Day; Christmas.
Special Editions: Bridal (Jan); Achievement (Feb); Coupon Book, Lawn & Garden (Mar); University Tab (Apr); Vacations, Home Upgrade (May); Vacations, Bridal (June); Back-to-School (Aug); Home Decorating, Family Business, Yell-Newspaper In Education (Sept); Newcomer's Guide, Home Decorating, Best of the Season (Oct); Christmas Opening (Nov); Traditional Christmas (Dec).
Special Weekly Sections: Business (mon); Learning (tues); Home (wed); Arts & Leisure (thur); Church, TV Update (fri); Stocks, Health (sat); Life (S).
Magazines: USA Weekend (S); Business Today, Tipoff Visitor's Guide (Targeted Publications), Homes; TBY: The Best Years (monthly).

CORPORATE OFFICER

President Gary W Rust

GENERAL MANAGEMENT

Publisher Wally Lage
Asst to Publisher Jon K Rust
Assoc Publisher Peter Kinder
Business Manager Richard Caldwell
Director-Systems Brad Hollerbach

ADVERTISING

Manager-Sales Pat Zellmer
Manager-Major Accounts/Preprints Irvin Landewee

MARKETING AND PROMOTION

Director-Marketing/Promotion Mark Kneer

CIRCULATION

Director Mark Kneer

NEWS EXECUTIVES

Editor R Joe Sullivan
Managing Editor Joni Adams

EDITORS AND MANAGERS

Business Editor B Ray Owen
City Editor John Ramey
Entertainment/Amusements Editor Sam Blackwell
News Editor Jay Eastlick
Political/Government Editor Chuck Miller
Region Editor Ralph Wanamaker

MANAGEMENT INFORMATION SERVICES

Data Processing Manager Brad Hollerbach
Online Manager Mark Kneer

PRODUCTION

Manager John Renaud
Foreman-Composing Judy Arnold
Foreman-Pressroom Terry Langston

Market Information: Zoned editions; TMC; ADS; Operate database.
Mechanical available: Offset; Black and 3 ROP colors; insert accepted — preprinted, card 80# stock; page cut-offs — 22¾".
Mechanical specifications: Type page 13" x 21½"; E - 6 cols, 2¹⁄₁₆", ⅛" between; A - 6 cols, 2¹⁄₁₆", ⅛" between; C - 9 cols, 1⅝", ⅛" between.
Commodity consumption: Newsprint 2,200 short tons; width 27"; black ink 50,000 pounds; color ink 5,000 pounds; single pages printed 10,700; average pages per issue 28(d), 60(S); single plates used 5,400.
Equipment: EDITORIAL: Front-end hardware — 21-IBM/AT Class Dos, 6-Ap/Mac; Front-end software — XYQUEST/XyWrite 3.01, QuarkXPress, Baseview/NewsEdit, Aldus/FreeHand; Printers — HP/III, QMS/860, QMS/860+, ECR/ScriptSetter II, ECR/ScriptSetter IV. CLASSIFIED: Front-end hardware — IBM; Front-end software — Synaptic/Classified; Printers — Ap/Mac LaserWriter NTX. DISPLAY: Adv layout systems — 16-Ap/Mac, 1-IBM; Front-end hardware — 16-Ap/Mac, 1-IBM; Front-end software — Multi-Ad/Creator 3.6.3, Adobe/ Photostop 3.0, Adobe/Illustrator, QuarkXPress 3.3; Printers — QMS/860, HP/IV MV, ECR/ScriptSetter II, ECR/ScriptSetter IV. PRODUCTION: OCR software — Caere/Omni-Page; Typesetters — 4-Ap/Mac LaserWriter, 1-Linotype-Hell/Linotronic 300, 1-ECR/Script-Setter II, 1-ECR/ScriptSetter IV, 2-QMS/860+, 1-QMS/860; Plate exposures — Nu/30x40 Flip Top; Plate processors — WL; Electronic picture desk — Lf/AP Leaf Picture Desk; Scanners — Microtek/300 ZS, Data Copy/730, Lf/Leafscan, Nikon/Coolscan, 3-Epson 1200C; Production cameras — R; Automatic film processors — P; Digital color separation equipment — Mk/300 Zs, Lf/AP Leaf Picture Desk. PRESSROOM: Line 1 — 6-WPC/Leader (1-Quad color); Line 2 — 4-WPC/Leader; Folders — 3-WPC/2:1. MAILROOM: Inserters and stuffers — 2-KAN/480; Bundle tyer — 1-Sa/EM9142, 1-Sa/ML2EE, 1-MLN; Wrapping singles — 4-Bu; Addressing machine — Ch/labeler. LIBRARY: Electronic — IBM, Folio Viewer Software. WIRE SERVICES: News — AP; Photos — AP; Syndicates — NEA; Receiving dishes — size-3m, AP. BUSINESS COMPUTERS: 7-IBM/PS2, Bs/B930; Applications: Adv, Circ, Mgmt, Payroll, Class, Spreadsheets; PCs & micros networked; PCs & main system networked.

CARTHAGE

Jasper County

'90 U.S. Census- 10,747; E&P '96 Est. 10,462

The Carthage Press

(e-mon to sat)

The Carthage Press, 527 S. Main; PO Box 678, Carthage, MO 64836; tel (417) 358-2191; fax (417) 358-7428. Hollinger International Inc. group.
Circulation: 3,974(e); 3,974(e-sat); Sworn Oct. 24, 1995.
Price: 50¢(d); 50¢(sat); $7.00/mo.
Advertising: Open inch rate $8.29(e); $8.66(e-sat). **Representative:** Cresmer, Woodward, O'Mara & Ormsbee.
News Service: AP. **Politics:** Independent. **Established:** 1884.
Not Published: New Year; Memorial Day; Independence Day; Labor Day; Thanksgiving; Christmas.
Special Editions: Deal With the Folks You Know, Chamber Tab, National Pizza Week, Brides Tab, Home Owned Business, Kiwanis Sponsor Page, January Clearance (Jan); Restaurants & Entertainment, Boy Scouts Sponsor Page, Valentine Co-op, Income Tax Guide, YMCA Tab, FFA Tab, Jasper FFA, Say No to Drugs, Auto Guide, Say Yes to Better Health (Feb); Progress, Girl Scouts Sponsor, St. Patrick's Day, Spring Fashion, Spring Car Care Tab, Cookbook (Mar); Food Fair, Easter Specials, Easter Dining Guide, Branson Showcase, Realtors Open House Weekend, National Secretaries Day, Main Street (Apr); Mother's Day Special, Jasper/Lockwatch Graduation, YMCA Tab, Lawn & Garden, Carthage Graduation, Memorial Day Co-op, Say Yes to Better Health, Say No to Drugs (May); % OFF Tab, Father's Day Co-op, Flag Day Sponsor, Jasper Fair, July 4th (June); Independence Day, Jasper County Youth Fair, Sidewalk Sale, Farm Safety Sponsor (July); Back-to-School, YMCA Tab, Home Guide, Lamar Fair, Hunting & Fishing, Fall Sports, Pre-Labor Day (Aug); Muscular Dystrophy Sponsor Page, Old Mining Days, Art Tab, Branson Showcase, Historic Tab (Sept); Fire Prevention Tab, 4-H Tab, United Way Tab, Fall Care Care Tab, Friday the 13th, Maple Leaf Tab, Business & Professional Women Sponsor Page, New Comer's Guide, Class of 2008, Pumpkin Safety Sponsor Page (Oct); Lay-away for Christmas, Open House Joplin Christmas, Turkey Contest, Veteran's Day Sponsor Page, Holiday Cookbook, Fix-up for the Holidays, Christmas Kick-off, Happy Thanksgiving Sponsor Page (Nov); Christmas Magazine, True Meaning of Christmas, Last Minute Gift Guide, YMCA Tab, Stocking Stuffers, Christmas Greetings, Don't Drink and Drive (Dec); Professional Guide, We Want Your Business, Car Care Directory, Senior Citizens, Business & Industry, Home Improvement, Community Calendar, Auto Guide, Medical Directory (monthly).
Special Weekly Sections: Business Page (mon); Food (tues); School Page (wed); Farm (thur); Church Page (sat).

GENERAL MANAGEMENT

Publisher/General Manager Jim G Farley
Business Manager Carolyn Baker

ADVERTISING

Director Jim G Farley

CIRCULATION

Manager Clyde Phillips

NEWS EXECUTIVE

Managing Editor Randy Turner

PRODUCTION

Superintendent Jennifer Martin
Foreman-Pressroom Jack Davis

Market Information: TMC.
Mechanical available: Offset; Black and 3 ROP colors; insert accepted — preprinted, card stock; page cut-offs — 22¾".
Mechanical specifications: Type page 13" x 21½"; E - 6 cols, 2¹⁄₁₆", ⅛" between; A - 6 cols, 2¹⁄₁₆", ⅛" between; C - 9 cols, 1⅝", ⅛" between.
Commodity consumption: width 27½"; average pages per issue 12(d).
Equipment: EDITORIAL: Front-end hardware — Mk/1100 Plus. CLASSIFIED: Front-end hardware — Mk/1100 Plus. DISPLAY: Front-end hardware — Ap/Mac; Front-end software — QuarkXPress. PRODUCTION: Typesetters — Ap/Mac LaserWriter II; Platemaking systems — 2-Kk/Ektamatic, 1-COM/Compudry, 1-Kr/110; Plate exposures — 1-Nu/FlipTop40; Production cameras — 1-B/Commodore. PRESSROOM: Line 1 — 4-HI/V-15A; Line 2 — 4-HI/V-15A; Folders — 2-HI. MAILROOM: Bundle tyer — 1-Bu; Addressing machine — 1-Am/1906, 1-Gr/6331. WIRE SERVICES: News — AP; Receiving dishes — size-6ft, AP.

CHILLICOTHE

Livingston County

'90 U.S. Census- 8,804; E&P '96 Est. 8,576

Constitution-Tribune

(e-mon to fri)

Constitution-Tribune, 818 Washington; PO Box 707, Chillicothe, MO 64601; tel (816) 646-2411; fax (816) 646-2028. Hollinger International Inc. group.
Circulation: 4,159(e); Sworn Sept. 29, 1995.
Price: 50¢(d); $10.67/mo; $87.94/yr.
Advertising: Open inch rate $6.25(e); $6.50(e-wed). **Representative:** Landon Associates Inc.
News Service: AP. **Politics:** Independent. **Established:** 1860.
Not Published: New Year; Memorial Day; Independence Day; Labor Day; Thanksgiving; Christmas.
Special Editions: Football; Basketball; Wrestling; Christmas Greetings; Graduation; Christmas Gift Guides; Bridal; Honor Roll of Businesses; Back-to-School Edition; Home Improvement Edition; Tax Guide; Business Spotlight; Hunting Edition; TV Week; Fair Edition; Fishing Edition; Progress Edition.

CORPORATE OFFICERS

Board Chairman Conrad Black
President David Radler

GENERAL MANAGEMENT

Publisher Charles Haney
Business Manager Mardy Moore
Purchasing Agent Charles Haney

ADVERTISING

Manager-General Kevin Haney
Manager-Classified Connie Jones
Manager Rod Dixon

CIRCULATION

Manager Jenetta Keith

NEWS EXECUTIVE

Editor Cathy Stortz

EDITORS AND MANAGERS

Business/Finance Editor Cathy Stortz
City Editor Cathy Stortz
Editorial Page Editor Cathy Stortz
Features Editor Cathy Stortz
Graphics Editor/Art Director Cathy Stortz
News Editor Cathy Stortz
Photo Editor Cathy Stortz
Political/Government Editor Cathy Stortz
Science/Technology Editor Kevin Haney
Sports Editor Bob Carter
Television/Film Editor Kevin Haney
Theater/Music Editor Kevin Haney
Travel Editor Kevin Haney

PRODUCTION

Superintendent Bob Hornsby

Market Information: Zoned editions; TMC; ADS.
Mechanical available: Offset; Black and 2 ROP colors; insert accepted — preprinted, 1-page flyers; page cut-offs — 21½".
Mechanical specifications: Type page 13½" x 21½"; E - 6 cols, 2 1/16", ⅛" between; A - 6 cols, 2 1/16", ⅛" between; C - 6 cols, 2 1/16", ⅛" between.
Commodity consumption: Newsprint 315 short tons; width 27½"; black ink 5,700 pounds; color ink 801 pounds; single pages printed 4,685; average pages per issue 12(d); single plates used 4,019.
Equipment: EDITORIAL: Front-end hardware — 6-CText; Other equipment — CText/Fileserver, CText/AP Wire receiver. DISPLAY: Adv layout systems — 3-Ap/Mac Plus. PRODUCTION: Typesetters — 2-Ap/Mac LaserWriter; Platemaking systems — 1-Nu; Production cameras — 1-Nu; Automatic film processors — 1-C/T-65, 1-COM.
PRESSROOM: Line 1 — 4-G/Community. MAILROOM: Bundle tyer — 1-Malow, 1-Bu; Addressing machine — 3-Rp. WIRE SERVICES: News — AP; Receiving dishes — AP. BUSINESS COMPUTERS: PCs & micros networked.

CLINTON
Henry County
'90 U.S. Census- 8,703; E&P '96 Est. 8,992

Clinton Daily Democrat
(e-mon to fri)

Clinton Daily Democrat, 212 S. Washington; PO Box 586, Clinton, MO 64735; tel (816) 885-2281; fax (816) 885-2265.
Circulation: 4,055(e); Sworn Sept. 29, 1995.
Price: 50¢(d); $3.75/mo (carrier); $37.50/yr (outside county).
Advertising: Open inch rate $5.94(e).
News Service: NEA. **Politics:** Democrat. **Established:** 1868.
Not Published: New Year; Memorial Day; Independence Day; Labor Day; Thanksgiving; Christmas.
Special Editions: Sports, Regional School News (daily).
Special Weekly Sections: Conservation/Outdoors, Regional Military News, Television (thur); Church News (fri).

CORPORATE OFFICERS

President Kathleen White Miles
Secretary Lydia White

GENERAL MANAGEMENT

Publisher Kathleen White Miles
Business Manager Katherine Miles
General Manager Daniel B Miles Jr

ADVERTISING

Manager Katherine Miles
Manager-Classified Mary Jo Witherspoon

CIRCULATION

Manager Mary Jo Witherspoon

NEWS EXECUTIVE

Editor Mahlon White Miles

EDITORS AND MANAGERS

Editorial Page Editor Mahlon White Miles
Sports Editor Brian Hanney

PRODUCTION

Manager Mike Gregory

Market Information: TMC.
Mechanical available: Offset; Black and 2 ROP colors; insert accepted — preprinted; page cut-offs — 22½".
Mechanical specifications: Type page 13" x 21½"; E - 6 cols, 2 1/16", ⅛" between; A - 6 cols, 2 1/16", ⅛" between; C - 6 cols, 2 1/16", ⅛" between.
Commodity consumption: widths 28", 14"; average pages per issue 14(d).
Equipment: EDITORIAL: Front-end hardware — 1-IBM, 1-Ro, 1-U. CLASSIFIED: Other equipment — 1-Ro, 1-IBM. DISPLAY: Adv layout systems — 1-COM/7200, 1-COM/Mark IV. PRODUCTION: Typesetters — 1-HA, 1-EK. MAILROOM: Bundle tyer — 1-Malow; Addressing machine — 1-Am/Mail 5. WIRE SERVICES: News — Receiving dishes — AP. BUSINESS COMPUTERS: Ap/Mac; PCs & micros networked; PCs & main system networked.

COLUMBIA
Boone County
'90 U.S. Census- 69,101; E&P '96 Est. 75,563
ABC-CZ (90): 69,101 (HH 25,841)

Columbia Missourian
(m-mon to fri; S)

Columbia Missourian, 221 S. Eighth St.; PO Box 917, Columbia, MO 65201; tel (314) 882-5700; fax (314) 884-5293; e-mail jour pbh@muccmail.missouri.edu; web site http://digmo.org/.
Circulation: 5,021(m); 5,118(S); CAC July 31, 1994.
Price: 50¢(d); 75¢(S); $9.00/mo; $85.00/yr.
Advertising: Open inch rate $5.65(m); $5.65(S).
News Services: AP, LAT-WP, NYT, SHNS. **Politics:** Independent. **Established:** 1908.
Not Published: Day after Christmas.
Magazine: Weekend Magazine (offset, local) (S).

CORPORATE OFFICERS

President Betty S Spaar
Secretary/Treasurer Patricia B Hoddinott

GENERAL MANAGEMENT

General Manager Patricia B Hoddinott

ADVERTISING

Director Jack Swartz

CIRCULATION

Manager Blanche Campbell

NEWS EXECUTIVE

Managing Editor George Kennedy

EDITORS AND MANAGERS

Food Editor Sharon Harl
Photo Department Manager Bill Kuykendall

PRODUCTION

Superintendent Bob Ludeman

Market Information: Zoned editions; TMC; Electronic edition.
Mechanical available: Offset; Black and 4 ROP colors; insert accepted — preprinted; page cut-offs — 22¾".
Mechanical specifications: Type page 13" x 21½"; E - 6 cols, 2 1/16", ⅛" between; A - 6 cols, 2 1/16", ⅛" between; C - 8 cols, 1½", 1/16" between.
Commodity consumption: Newsprint 1,010 short tons; widths 27", 30"; black ink 33,500 pounds; color ink 3,000 pounds; single pages printed 11,000; average pages per issue 16(d), 49(S); single plates used 14,500.
Equipment: EDITORIAL: Front-end hardware — 2-HAS/H555, IBM/PC; Other equipment — 26-IBM/PC, 7-HAS/Edit 3, 3-HAS/Edit 8, 2-HAS/Magician Layout, 2-HAS/NewsPro. CLASSIFIED: Other equipment — 2-HAS/Edit 8. DISPLAY: Adv layout systems — 5-Ap/Mac; Printers — Birmy. PRODUCTION: Typesetters — 2-Linotype-Hell/Linotronic 100; Plate exposures — 1-Nu/FlipTop 40; Plate processors — Nat/A-250; Scanners — Dest/PC Scan; Production cameras — 1-B/4000; Automatic film processors — 1-LE/18.
PRESSROOM: Line 1 — 6-KP/Newsking (1 balloon); Folders — 1-KP. MAILROOM: Inserters and stuffers — 4-DG; Bundle tyer — 1-Sa, 1-Malow/Strap Tyer; Wrapping singles — 2-Sa; Addressing machine — 1-Am. LIBRARY: Electronic — IBM/PC. COMMUNICATIONS: Facsimile — Sharp/FO 510. WIRE SERVICES: News — AP, LAT-WP, NYT, LAT; Photos — AP; Syndicates — North America Syndicate, NYT, World News Syndicate; Receiving dishes — size-3m, AP. BUSINESS COMPUTERS: PCs & micros networked; PCs & main system networked.

Columbia Daily Tribune
(e-mon to fri; m-sat; S)

Columbia Daily Tribune, 4th & Walnut Sts.; PO Box 798, Columbia, MO 65205; tel (314) 449-3811; fax (314) 874-6413; e-mail cteditr@coin.missouri.edu.
Circulation: 17,494(e); 17,660(m-sat); 22,894(S); ABC Sept. 30, 1995.
Price: 50¢(d); 50¢(sat); $1.00(S); $99.64/yr (carrier).
Advertising: Open inch rate $9.35(e); $11.60(e-wed); $9.35(m-sat); $11.00(S).
Representative: Papert Companies.
News Services: AP, KRT. **Politics:** Independent. **Established:** 1901.
Not Published: New Year; Memorial Day; Independence Day; Labor Day; Thanksgiving; Christmas.
Special Weekly Sections: Best Food Day (wed); Television Listings (thur); Church News, Children's Page, Stock Quotes (sat); Business News (daily).
Magazine: USA Weekend (sat).

CORPORATE OFFICERS

President/Treasurer Henry J Waters III
Vice Pres/Secretary Jack Waters

GENERAL MANAGEMENT

Publisher Henry J Waters III
General Manager Jack Waters
Controller Kevin Coleman

ADVERTISING

Manager Deb Jankowski

CIRCULATION

Manager Charlotte Strawn

NEWS EXECUTIVES

Editor Henry J Waters III
Managing Editor Jim Robertson

EDITORS AND MANAGERS

City Editor John Schneller
Editorial Page Editor Jim Robertson
Editorial Writer Henry J Waters III
Features Editor Donna Pierce
Photo Manager Mike Stewart
Sports Editor Scott Cain
Wire Editor Herron Miller

PRODUCTION

Manager Susan Waters
Manager-Composing Linda Watkins
Manager-Computer Dave Olson
Foreman-Pressroom David Langlais
Foreman-Mailroom Phil Barbee

Market Information: Zoned editions; TMC.
Mechanical available: Offset; Black and 3 ROP colors; insert accepted — preprinted; page cut-offs — 22¾".
Mechanical specifications: Type page 13" x 21"; E - 6 cols, 2", 3/16" between; A - 6 cols, 2", 3/16" between; C - 7 cols, 1¾", ⅛" between.
Commodity consumption: Newsprint 1,775 short tons; widths 27¼", 13⅝"; black ink 74,305 pounds; color ink 29,721 pounds; single pages printed 12,846; average pages per issue 30(d), 62(S); single plates used 9,348.
Equipment: EDITORIAL: Front-end hardware — Novell/Network (PC Based); Front-end software — CText; Printers — Tegra/Varityper Genesis XP 1000, Linotype-Hell/Printer 60, LaserMaster/Unity; Other equipment — Ap/Mac. CLASSIFIED: Front-end hardware — Novell/Network (PC Based); Front-end software — CText/Classified; Printers — Tegra/Varityper Genesis XP-1000. DISPLAY: Adv layout systems — QuarkXPress, Adobe/Photoshop, Adobe/Illustrator; Front-end hardware — Ap/Mac Network; Printers — Linotype-Hell/Printer 60, Linotronic/530; Other equipment — Lf/Leafscan 35, Sharp/Scanner JX600. PRODUCTION: Typesetters — 2-Tegra/Varityper Genesis Laser-Printer, Linotype-Hell/Printer 60L, Linotype-Hell/530; Plate exposures — 1-Nu/Flip Top FT52, 1-Nu/FT52; Plate processors — 1-Milart/AP5055, WL/38D; Scanners — Lf/Leafscan, Sharp/JX 600, ECR/Autokon D1000, Nikon/CoolScan; Production cameras — 1-C/Spartan II; Automatic film processors — 1-Kk/710; Digital color separation equipment — Lf/Leafscan, Sharp/JX 600.
PRESSROOM: Line 1 — 10-HI/845, 1-HI/RBC; Line 2 — 4-HI/845, 1-HI/RBC; Line 3 — 4-G/Community; Folders — 4-HI, 1-HI/ATF, 1-G/Community; Pasters — 8-MEG/246-A; Reels and stands — 3-HI/Stands; Press control system — Allen Bradley/PLC. MAILROOM: Counter stackers — 2-Id/NS 440, 3-BG/Count-O-Veyor model 108; Inserters and stuffers — 2-MM/2275; Bundle tyer — 4-Bu/M127, 2-MLN/ML2EE; Wrapping singles — BeaSealer/Polybagger; Addressing machine — 1-Ch/515, 1-Ch/525. WIRE SERVICES: News — AP, KRT; Receiving dishes — size-8ft, AP. BUSINESS COMPUTERS: PC/Network, Novell/Netware, Everex/486 Unix; Applications: AccuPac: Accounting; PBS: Adv billing; PCs & micros networked; PCs & main system networked.

DEXTER
Stoddard County
'90 U.S. Census- 7,559; E&P '96 Est. 8,015

Daily Statesman
(e-tues to fri; S)

Daily Statesman, 133 S. Walnut St.; PO Box 579, Dexter, MO 63841; tel (314) 624-4545; fax (314) 624-7449. Rust Communications group.
Circulation: 3,597(e); 3,597(S); CAC Oct. 4, 1994.
Price: 50¢(d); 50¢(S); $32.00/yr.
Advertising: Open inch rate $9.25(e); $9.25(S).
Representative: Landon Associates Inc.
News Services: UPI, NEA. **Politics:** Independent. **Established:** 1879, 1973 (daily).
Not Published: New Year; Memorial Day; Independence Day; Labor Day; Thanksgiving; Christmas.
Special Editions: Progress (Feb); Spring Fashion (Apr); Fall Fashion (Sept).
Magazines: Southeast Missouri Farmer, Farm Monthly (Feb-Nov).

CORPORATE OFFICER

President Gary W Rust

GENERAL MANAGEMENT

Publisher Barbara Hill

ADVERTISING

Manager Elaine Pursell

CIRCULATION

Director Vicky Moore

NEWS EXECUTIVE

Editor Debbie Renfro

PRODUCTION

Foreman-Composing Marilyn Tucker
Foreman-Pressroom Bobby Williams

Market Information: Zoned editions; Split Run; TMC.
Mechanical available: Offset; Black and 3 ROP colors; insert accepted — preprinted.
Mechanical specifications: Type page 13" x 22½"; E - 6 cols, 2 1/16", ⅛" between; A - 6 cols, 2 1/16", ⅛" between; C - 8 cols, 1½", ⅛" between.
Commodity consumption: average pages per issue 28(d).
Equipment: EDITORIAL: Front-end hardware — 1-COM/MDT 350. CLASSIFIED: Front-end hardware — 1-COM/MDT 350. PRODUCTION: Typesetters — 1-COM/4961, 1-COM/2961; Production cameras — 1-Acti/140.
PRESSROOM: Line 1 — 3-G/Community; Folders — 1-G/2:1. MAILROOM: Bundle tyer — 1-Strap Tyer; Wrapping singles — 2-Sa; Addressing machine — 1-Am. WIRE SERVICES: News — UPI. BUSINESS COMPUTERS: Applications: Adv billing, Accts receivable.

EXCELSIOR SPRINGS
Clay and Ray Counties
'90 U.S. Census- 10,354; E&P '96 Est. 10,297

The Daily Standard
(e-mon to fri)

The Daily Standard, 417 Thompson St.; PO Box 70, Excelsior Springs, MO 64024; tel (816) 637-6155; fax (816) 637-8411. Fackelman Newspapers group.
Circulation: 2,096(e); Sworn Sept. 27, 1995.
Price: 50¢(d); $.90/wk; $11.75/3mo, $22.50/6mo; $45.00/yr.
Advertising: Open inch rate $8.40(e).
News Service: Missouri Link. **Politics:** Independent. **Established:** 1892.
Not Published: New Year; Memorial Day; Independence Day; Labor Day; Thanksgiving; Christmas.
Advertising not accepted: All advertising taken conditionally.
Special Editions: Progress (Jan); Holiday Gift Guide, Thanksgiving (Nov); Summer Lifestyles; Home Improvement; Car Care; Pride (Community Profile Edition).

CORPORATE OFFICERS

President Ann Nixon
Vice Pres-Operations Mark A Richard
Secretary Ann Fackelman
Treasurer Broward E Ratliff

GENERAL MANAGEMENT

Publisher James F Bouldin
Controller Nancy Elmore

ADVERTISING

Manager Brian Rice

MARKETING AND PROMOTION

Manager-Marketing & Promotion Brian Rice

CIRCULATION

Manager Joan Patton

NEWS EXECUTIVE

Exec Editor Gene Hanson

EDITOR AND MANAGER

Artist Supervisor Janet Brown

MANAGEMENT INFORMATION SERVICES

Data Processing Manager Nancy Elmore

PRODUCTION

Manager-Composing Janet Brown

Market Information: Zoned editions; TMC.
Mechanical available: Offset; Black and 2 ROP colors; insert accepted — preprinted, any free standing inserts; page cut-offs — 21".

Mechanical specifications: Type page 14" x 21"; E - 8 cols, 1¾", 1/12" between; A - 8 cols, 1¾", 1/12" between; C - 8 cols, 1¾", 1/12" between.
Commodity consumption: average pages per issue 8(d).
Equipment: EDITORIAL: Front-end hardware — Ap/Mac; Front-end software — Aldus/PageMaker 4.2; Printers — Ap/LaserWriter II NT; Other equipment — 7-Ap/Mac. **CLASSIFIED:** Front-end hardware — 4-Ap/Mac; Front-end software — Claris/Hypercard; Printers — Ap/Mac LaserWriter Plus. **PRODUCTION:** Typesetters — 7-Ap/Mac LaserWriter, MCS/8400, MCS/10; Production cameras — 1-B/18" x 24". **MAILROOM:** Bundle tyer — 1-Bu; Addressing machine — 2-Am, IBM. **LIBRARY:** Combination — Ap/Mac Plus, Ap/Mac Pro-Printer. **BUSINESS COMPUTERS:** Hyundai/AT Compatible, Ap/Mac IIe; Applications: Circ, Adv billing, Accts receivable, Gen ledger.

FLAT RIVER
See PARK HILLS

FULTON
Callaway County
'90 U.S. Census- 10,033; E&P '96 Est. 9,271

The Fulton Sun (m-tues to sat)
The Fulton Sun, 115 E. 5th St., Fulton, MO 65251; tel (314) 642-7272; fax (314) 642-0656.
Circulation: 4,632(m); 4,632(m-wed); 4,632(m-sat); Sworn Sept. 29, 1994.
Price: 50¢(d); 50¢(sat).

Advertising: Open inch rate $6.85(m); $8.24(m-wed); $6.85(m-sat). **Representative:** Papert Companies.
News Service: AP. **Politics:** Independent. **Established:** 1876.
Not Published: New Year; Memorial Day; Independence Day; Labor Day; Thanksgiving; Christmas.
Special Weekly Section: Food Section (wed).
Magazine: Entertainer (newsprint) (S).

GENERAL MANAGEMENT
General Manager .... Mary Van Orden
ADVERTISING
Manager .... Michael Stauffer
CIRCULATION
Manager .... David Phelps
NEWS EXECUTIVES
Editor .... Mary Van Orden
Managing Editor .... Jennifer Bradley
EDITORS AND MANAGERS
Business/Finance Editor .... Ryan Boland
City/Metro Editor .... Ryan Boland
Editorial Page Editor .... Ryan Boland
Features Editor .... Ryan Boland
Graphics Editor/Art Director .... Ryan Boland
Lifestyle Editor .... Jennifer Bradley
Lifestyle Editor .... Kim Fowler
News Editor .... Ryan Boland
Photo Editor .... Ryan Boland
Political/Government Editor .... Ryan Boland
Sports Editor .... Dylan Carter

Market Information: TMC.
Mechanical available: Offset; Black and 3 ROP colors; insert accepted — preprinted; page cut-offs — 21".
Mechanical specifications: Type page 13" x 21"; E - 6 cols, 2 1/16", 1/8" between; A - 6 cols, 2 1/16", 1/8" between; C - 9 cols, 1 3/8", 1/16" between.
Commodity consumption: average pages per issue 14(d).
Equipment: EDITORIAL: Front-end hardware — CText; Front-end software — CText; Printers — Ap/Mac NTX. **CLASSIFIED:** Front-end hardware — CText; Front-end software — CText. **DISPLAY:** Adv layout systems — CText; Front-end hardware — CText; Front-end software — CText. **PRODUCTION:** Typesetters — Ap/Mac NTX; Plate exposures — Nu; Plate processors — Roconex; Production cameras — R; Automatic film processors — LE/Rap 20. **PRESSROOM:** Line 1 — 4-G/Community; Folders — 1-G. **MAILROOM:** Counter stackers — 1-BG/Count-O-Veyor; Bundle tyer — 1-Bu. **WIRE SERVICES:** News — AP; Receiving dishes — AP. **BUSINESS COMPUTERS:** Novell/LAN; Applications: AccPac.

HANNIBAL
Marion and Ralls Counties
'90 U.S. Census- 18,004; E&P '96 Est. 17,366

Hannibal Courier-Post
(m-mon to sat)
Hannibal Courier-Post, 200 N. 3rd; PO Box A, Hannibal, MO 63401; tel (314) 221-2800; fax (314) 221-1568. Morris Communications Corp. group.
Circulation: 10,033(m); 10,033(m-sat); Sworn Sept. 30, 1994.
Price: 50¢(d); 50¢(sat); $8.00/mo; $81.00/yr, $127.50/yr (mail).
Advertising: Open inch rate $8.50(m); $8.50(m-sat). **Representatives:** Landon Associates Inc.; Missouri Press Service.
News Service: AP. **Politics:** Independent. **Established:** 1838.
Note: Effective May 1, 1995, this publication changed its publishing plan from (e-mon to fri; m-sat) to (m-mon to sat).
Not Published: New Year; Christmas.
Special Editions: Bridal Registry Feature (2x/mo) (Jan); Bridal Edition Tab, Outdoor Edition, Progress Edition (4x/wk) (Feb); Gardening Feature (Weeder's Digest, wkly), Farm Edition, Senior Citizens (Active Times Tab) (Mar); Car Care Edition, Gardening Feature (Weeder's Digest, wkly), Home Improvement Edition (Apr); Outdoor Education, Gardening Feature (Weeder's Digest, wkly) (May); Youth Sports Edition, Bridal (2x), Gardening Feature (Weeder's Digest, wkly), Senior Citizen (Active Times Tab) (June); Youth Sports Edition, Back to School Tab, Gardening Feature (Weeder's Digest, wkly) (July); H.S. Fall Sports Edition, Back-to-School-ROP (Aug); St. Louis Theme Travel Pages (Sept); Senior Citizens (Active Times Tab), Home Improvement (Oct); St. Louis Travel Theme Pages, Youth Sports Edition, Electronics, Christmas Holiday Editions, Winter H.S. Sports Edition (Nov); St. Louis Travel Theme Pages, Christmas Holiday Editions, Education (Career Opportunities) (Dec).
Special Weekly Sections: Best Food Day, Health (mon); Business (tues); Food Feature, Youth, Weddings (wed); Education (thur); T.V. Entertainment, Real Estate (fri); Religion, Weddings (sat).

Magazines: Northeast Missouri Real Estate Guide (1st wed) (monthly); Hannibal Visitor's Guide (last thur) (May to Sept); Active Times (55+ generation) (quarterly).

GENERAL MANAGEMENT
Publisher Robert L Krecklow
ADVERTISING
Manager Bob Hudson
TELECOMMUNICATIONS
Audiotex Manager Jill Sinkclear
CIRCULATION
Manager Jill Sinkclear
NEWS EXECUTIVE
Editor Robert L Krecklow
EDITORS AND MANAGERS
Assignments Editor Mary Lou Montgomery
News Editor Jim Whitaker
News Editor Mary Lou Montgomery
Sports Editor Dan Henley
MANAGEMENT INFORMATION SERVICES
Business Manager Carolyn Taylor
PRODUCTION
Manager-Operations Kenneth Linnenburger
Foreman-Pressroom Joe Gwinner

Market Information: TMC; Operate audiotex.
Mechanical available: Offset; Black and 3 ROP colors; insert accepted — preprinted; page cutoffs — 22¾".
Mechanical specifications: Type page 13" x 21½"; E - 6 cols, 2¹⁄₁₆", ⅛" between; A - 6 cols, 2¹⁄₁₆", ⅛" between; C - 6 cols, 2¹⁄₁₆", ⅛" between.
Commodity consumption: Newsprint 510 short tons; widths 27", 13½"; black ink 12,000 pounds; color ink 500 pounds; single pages printed 4,970; average pages per issue 16(d), 14(sat); single plates used 8,391.
Equipment: EDITORIAL: Front-end hardware — Ap/Mac; Front-end software — QuarkXPress 3.1, Baseview; Printers — Ap/Mac LaserWriter NTX, Ap/Mac LaserWriter Pro (600dpi); Other equipment — 2-Ap/Mac Flatbed scanners, KC/2000 Image Pro Auto Film Processor 35mm. CLASSIFIED: Front-end hardware — Ap/Mac; Front-end software — Baseview; Printers — Ap/Mac IIg. AUDIOTEX: Hardware — Ap/Mac; Software — SMS/Stauffer Media Systems. DISPLAY: Front-end hardware — Ap/Mac Radius 2-page displays, 4-Ap/Mac IIci; Front-end software — Multi-Ad/Creator, QuarkXPress; Printers — 3-Ap/Mac Laser II. PRODUCTION: Pagination software — Caere/OmniPage; Typesetters — 2-Ap/Mac si, MON/1270 Imagesetter w/ Software RIP; Plate exposures — Nu/Flip Top FT40VGUPNS; Plate processors — Anitec/S26; Electronic picture desk — Lf/AP Leaf Picture Desk; Scanners — Scan-Man, Nikon/LS-3510 AF Film Scanner; Production cameras — 1-R/500; Shrink lenses — Lf/Leafscan; Color separation equipment (conventional) — Ap/Mac Quadra 800. PRESSROOM: Line 1 — 9-G/Community; Folders — G/Quarter; Press registration system — Duarte. MAILROOM: Bundle tyer — MLN; Addressing machine — 1-Ch. LIBRARY: Electronic — SMS/Stauffer Gold. COMMUNICATIONS: Digital ad delivery system — AP. WIRE SERVICES: News — AP; Photos — AP; Receiving dishes — size-3m, AP. BUSINESS COMPUTERS: ATT/6386 WGS, SMS; Applications: Unix: Bus office; Microsoft/Excel 4.0: Gen mgmt.

INDEPENDENCE
Jackson County
'90 U.S. Census- 112,301; E&P '96 Est. 112,711

The Examiner
(e-mon to fri; m-sat)

The Examiner, 410 S. Liberty; PO Box 458/459, Independence, MO 64050; tel (816) 254-8600; fax (816) 836-3805. Morris Communications Corp. group.
Circulation: 12,265(e); 12,265(m-sat); VAC June 30, 1995.
Price: 50¢(d); 50¢(sat); $7.99/mo; $85.88/yr.
Advertising: Open inch rate $14.95(e); $14.95(m-sat). **Representatives:** US Suburban Press; Landon Associates Inc.
News Service: AP. **Politics:** Independent. **Established:** 1898.
Not Published: New Year; Memorial Day; Independence Day; Labor Day; Christmas.
Special Editions: Tourist Guide, Chamber Tab (Jan); Brides, Review & Forecast (Feb); Health & Fitness (Mar); Spring Car Care (Apr); Spring Parade of Homes (May); Guide to Independence (June); Football, Santa-Cali-Gon Edition, Senior Citizens (Aug); Boy Scouts, Fall Parade of Homes (Sept); Pets, Car Care (Oct); Christmas Opening (Nov); Kids Original Ads Contest, Holiday Gift Guide (Dec).
Special Weekly Sections: Suburban Shopper, TV (sat).
Magazine: USA Weekend (sat).

CORPORATE OFFICERS
Chairman of the Board/CEO W S Morris III
President Paul S Simon
Asst to the President William S Morris IV
Vice Pres-Community Newspapers Dan P Smith
GENERAL MANAGEMENT
Publisher Ben F Weir Jr
General Manager Dan Potter
Business Manager Becky Ely
Manager-Credit Marsha Leonard
Personnel Manager Becky Ely
ADVERTISING
Director Irene Baltrusaitis
Manager-Classified Dan Potter
Manager-Legal Lou Woods
TELECOMMUNICATIONS
Audiotex Manager Kevin Kampman
CIRCULATION
Manager Kevin Kampman
NEWS EXECUTIVES
Exec Editor Jeff Fox
Managing Editor Kate Lee
EDITORS AND MANAGERS
Community News Editor Frank Haight
Editorial Page Editor Jeff Fox
Food Editor Coral Beach
Garden Editor Coral Beach
Legislative Jeff Fox
News Editor Rob Schlotterbeck
Photo Department Manager Scot Morrissey
Sports Editor Huey Counts
MANAGEMENT INFORMATION SERVICES
Data Processing Manager Dawn Dittmer
PRODUCTION
Superintendent Corwan Akers
Manager-Systems Sandy Turner
Foreman-Pressroom Thad Denzer

Market Information: TMC; Operate audiotex.
Mechanical available: Offset; Black and 3 ROP colors; insert accepted — preprinted, all; page cut-offs — 22¾".
Mechanical specifications: Type page 13" x 21½"; E - 6 cols, 2¹⁄₁₆", ⅛" between; A - 6 cols, 2¹⁄₁₆", ⅛" between; C - 8 cols, 1½", ⅛" between.
Commodity consumption: Newsprint 1,187 short tons; width 27½"; black ink 21,897 pounds; color ink 1,389 pounds; single pages printed 10,540; average pages per issue 24(d), 40(sat); single plates used 8,365.
Equipment: EDITORIAL: Front-end hardware — 1-Mk; Printers — Tegra; Other equipment — SMS/Library System. CLASSIFIED: Front-end hardware — 8-Ap/Mac Performa 630; Front-end software — Baseview; Printers — MON/Express Master 1270. AUDIOTEX: Hardware — SMS/Epson Action Tower 3000; Software — SMS/Stauffer Gold. DISPLAY: Adv layout systems — 1-Ap/Power Mac w/Ad Director; Front-end hardware — Ap/Mac; Front-end software — Multi-Ad/Creator 3.5; Printers — Ap/Mac LaserWriter IIg, Ap/Mac LaserWriter Pro. PRODUCTION: Typesetters — MON/Imagesetter; Platemaking systems — 1-W, Nu/40V6U; Plate exposures — 1-P; Plate processors — 1-Nu, Graham; Production cameras — 1-B; Automatic film processors — 1-P; Color separation equipment (conventional) — Ap/Mac IIci; Digital color separation equipment — Nikon, MON/Prism (output device). PRESSROOM: Line 1 — 7-G/Urbanite; Press drives — Fin, Fin. Folders — 1-G/Urbanite, 1-G/Suburban; MAILROOM: Counter stackers — 1-Id; Inserters and stuffers — 1-HI/NP848; Bundle tyer — 1-MLN; Addressing machine — 1-KR. LIBRARY: Electronic — 1-SMS/Stauffer Gold (full text retrieval). COMMUNICATIONS: Digital ad delivery system — AP AdSend. WIRE SERVICES: News — AP; Photos — Lf/AP Leaf Picture Desk; Syndicates — SHNS, NEA, United Media; Receiving dishes — size-3 m, AP. BUSINESS COMPUTERS: 1-ATT/6386E-WGS; PCs & micros networked.

JEFFERSON CITY
Cole County
'90 U.S. Census- 35,481; E&P '96 Est. 37,101
ABC-CZ (90): 48,356 (HH 18,283)

Daily Capital News
(m-tues to sat)
Jefferson City Post-Tribune
(e-mon to sat)
The Sunday News Tribune (S)

News Tribune, 210 Monroe St., Jefferson City, MO 65102; tel (314) 636-3131; fax (314) 636-7035.
Circulation: 2,660(m); 17,648(e); 2,660(m-sat); 17,648(e-sat); 23,920(S); ABC Sept. 30, 1995.
Price: 25¢(d); 25¢(sat); 75¢(S); $10.00/mo; $120.00/yr (carrier).
Advertising: Open inch rate $10.95(m); $10.95(e); $10.95(m-sat); $10.95(e-sat); $12.00(S). **Representative:** Papert Companies.
News Service: AP. **Politics:** Independent. **Established:** 1865.
Not Published: New Year; Memorial Day; Independence Day; Labor Day; Thanksgiving; Christmas (if on Sunday).
Special Edition: The Statesman (1st tues/mo).
Special Weekly Sections: Business & Finance, Church, TV Week (sat).
Magazine: Parade.

GENERAL MANAGEMENT
Owner/Publisher Mrs William H Weldon
Business Manager Roman Patten
ADVERTISING
Director Jim Ward
CIRCULATION
Manager Doug Herigon
Manager Rob Siebeneck
NEWS EXECUTIVES
Managing Editor Richard McGonegal
Exec Editor Doug Waggoner
EDITOR AND MANAGER
Sports Editor Tom Rackers
MANAGEMENT INFORMATION SERVICES
Data Processing Manager Mike Vivian

Market Information: TMC.
Mechanical available: Offset; Black and 3 ROP colors; insert accepted — preprinted; page cut-offs — 22¾".
Mechanical specifications: Type page 13" x 21½"; E - 6 cols, 2¹⁄₁₆", ⅛" between; A - 6 cols, 2¹⁄₁₆", ⅛" between; C - 6 cols, 2¹⁄₁₆", ⅛" between.
Commodity consumption: Newsprint 1,700 short tons; widths 27½", 13¾", 30"; single pages printed 10,868; average pages per issue 27(d), 74(S).
Equipment: EDITORIAL: Front-end hardware — Dewar/Disc Sys, 8-IBM/Courier 12. CLASSIFIED: Front-end hardware — Dewar/Disc Sys; Other equipment — 3-IBM/II. PRODUCTION: Typesetters — 2-Dewar/Discovery; Platemaking systems — 1-LE; Plate exposures — 1-Nu; Plate processors — E; Production cameras — 1-R; Automatic film processors — 1-LE; Shrink lenses — 1-Kamerak; Color separation equipment (conventional) — 1-BKY. PRESSROOM: Line 1 — 7-G/U909; Folders — 1-G. MAILROOM: Inserters and stuffers — 1-S/624, HI; Bundle tyer — 1-MLN; Addressing machine — 1-Ch. WIRE SERVICES: News — AP; Stock tables — AP; Receiving dishes — AP. BUSINESS COMPUTERS: IBM.

JOPLIN
Jasper and Newton Counties
'90 U.S. Census- 40,961; E&P '96 Est. 42,756
ABC-CZ (90): 62,608 (HH 25,686)

The Joplin Globe
(m-mon to sat; S)

The Joplin Globe, 117 E. Fourth St.; PO Box 7, Joplin, MO 64802-0007; tel (417) 623-3480; fax (417) 623-8450. Ottaway Newspapers Inc. group.
Circulation: 36,797(m); 36,797(m-sat); 45,197(S); ABC Sept. 30, 1995.
Price: 50¢(d); 50¢(sat); $1.50(S); $11.52/mo (carrier).
Advertising: Open inch rate $28.00(m); $28.00(m-sat); $36.00(S). **Representative:** Papert Companies.
News Services: AP, ONS. **Politics:** Independent. **Established:** 1896.
Special Edition: Silver Enquirer (monthly).
Special Weekly Sections: Sports Monday (mon); Business Tuesday (tues); Best Food (wed); Neighbors (thur); Entertainment (fri).
Magazines: Teleview, Comics, Parade (S).

GENERAL MANAGEMENT
Publisher John N Wilcox
General Manager Daniel P Chiodo
Controller Tim Robinson
Manager-Credit Amber Severns
ADVERTISING
Manager-Retail Scott Wright
Manager-Classified Evelyn Brady
TELECOMMUNICATIONS
Manager-Telecommunications Brian Bryan
CIRCULATION
Manager Mike Wittenmyer
NEWS EXECUTIVES
Editor James Ellis
Managing Editor Tom Murray
EDITORS AND MANAGERS
Amusements Editor Brian Hutton
Books Editor Clair Goodwin
Business Editor Richard Polen
Editorial Page Editor Clair Goodwin
Education Editor Wally Kennedy
Farm Editor Mike Surbrugg
Films Editor Brian Hutton
Food Editor Willa Younger
Librarian Bill Caldwell
People/Lifestyle Editor Gloria Turner
Photo Department Manager Mike Gullett
Real Estate Editor Richard Polen
Sports Editor Jim Fryor
PRODUCTION
Manager-Pre Press Bob McFarlin
Manager-Press David Starchman
Foreman-Composing (Night) Bud Russell
Foreman-Mailroom Jeff Seward

Market Information: TMC; ADS; Operate audiotex.
Mechanical available: Offset; Black and 3 ROP colors; insert accepted — preprinted; page cut-offs — 22¾".
Mechanical specifications: Type page 13" x 21¾"; E - 6 cols, 2¹⁄₁₆", ⅛" between; A - 6 cols, 2¹⁄₁₆", ⅛" between; C - 6 cols, 2¹⁄₁₆", ⅛" between.
Commodity consumption: Newsprint 2,602 metric tons; widths 55", 41¼", 27.5", 13.75"; black ink 75,000 pounds; color ink 12,000 pounds; single pages printed 12,898; average pages per issue 28(d), 62(S); single plates used 30,000.
Equipment: EDITORIAL: Front-end hardware — Tandem/TXP; Front-end software — SII; Printers — Centronics/351. CLASSIFIED: Front-end hardware — Tandem/TXP; Front-end software — SII; Printers — Centronics/351. DISPLAY: Adv layout systems — HI/8300; Front-end hardware — HI/8300; Front-end software — HI/8300. PRODUCTION: Typesetters — MON/82E; Plate exposures — 1-BKY, 1-Nu; Plate processors — WL; Scanners — ECR/1000DE, ECR/1030C; Production cameras — 1-C, 1-R; Color separation equipment (conventional) — Lf/AP Leaf Picture Desk; Digital color separation equipment — RZ. PRESSROOM: Line 1 — 5-G/Headliner Unit (2 color decks); Pasters — G/Automatic; Reels and stands — G; Press control system — PEC/Bond Drive. MAILROOM: Counter stackers — 2-QWI, 1-QWI; Inserters and stuffers — 1-MM/227, 1-MM/227; Bundle tyer — 2-OVL/JP80; Wrapping singles — Manual; Addressing machine — 1-Ch. WIRE SERVICES: News — AP Datastream; Stock tables — AP SelectStox; Syndicates — ONS; Receiving dishes — size-10ft, AP. BUSINESS COMPUTERS: IBM/AS-400; PCs & main system networked.

KANSAS CITY
Jackson, Clay and Platte Counties
'90 U.S. Census- 435,146; E&P '96 Est. 433,833
ABC-CZ (90): 1,425,214 (HH 559,962)

The Kansas City Star
(m-mon to fri; m-sat; S)

The Kansas City Star, 1729 Grand Blvd., Kansas City, MO 64108; tel (816) 234-4141. Capital Cities/ABC Inc. group.
Circulation: 284,675(m); 325,093(m-sat); 422,027(S); ABC Sept. 30, 1995.
Price: 50¢(d); 50¢(sat); $1.50(S); $13.95/mo (plus tax).
Advertising: Open inch rate $295.00(m); $300.00(m-sat); $322.00(S). **Representative:** Cresmer, Woodward, O'Mara & Ormsbee.
News Services: AP, KRT, NYT. **Politics:** Independent. **Established:** 1880.

Missouri I-229

Special Editions: Martin Luther King, Active Times, Bridal, American Heart Association (Jan); Remodeling & Decorating Expo, The Auto Show (Feb); Lawn, Garden & Home, Recycling, Family Physicians (Mar); Royals, Lawn, Garden & Home, Easter Religion, Spring Auto Buyer's Guide (Apr); Lawn, Garden & Home; Diaper Days (Mar); Prime Time; Summer Preview (May); Progress Edition Community Newspapers, Women & Heart Disease, Living Guide (June); Active Times, Seniors PGA, Vital Statistics, Education/Back-to-School (July); Cancer, Diaper Days II, Pro & College Football, High School Football (Aug); Fall Fashion, Star Top 50, Fall Lawn, Garden & Home, Breast Cancer (Sept); Active Times, The American Royal, Fall Auto Buyer's Guide (Oct); Holiday Edition, The Star Gift Guide I (Nov); The Star Gift Guide II, Holiday Religion (Dec).

Special Weekly Sections: Sports Extra (mon); Business (tues); Food, Automotive (wed); Preview (fri); Faith, Automotive (sat); Arts, Money Wise, Star Magazine, Star TV, Look, Travel, Real Estate, Arts, Outdoors, Comics (S); FYI (daily).

Magazine: Parade (S).

CORPORATE OFFICERS

Vice Pres/Editor Arthur S Brisbane
Vice Pres-Marketing & Advertising Michael R Petrak
Vice Pres-Circulation/Operations Dell Campbell
Vice Pres-Finance Sharon Lindenbaum
Vice Pres/Editorial Page Editor Rich Hood
Vice Pres-Human Resources Francis E Stowell
Vice Pres-Promotion Ralph W Rowe Jr

GENERAL MANAGEMENT

Publisher Robert C Woodworth
Exec Vice Pres/General Manager Wesley R Turner
Controller Steve Helm
Manager-Credit Lawrence Tigerman
Director-Purchasing Kent McCall
Personnel Director Kent Simcosky

ADVERTISING

Manager-National Jack Hines
Director-Research Hugh Downey
Manager-Magazine Steve Curd
Manager-Classified Tim Kelley

MARKETING AND PROMOTION

Manager-Database Marketing John Mahler

TELECOMMUNICATIONS

Audiotex Manager Nancy Tracewell

CIRCULATION

Manager-Metro Terry Foley
Manager-Home Delivery Roger Minor
Manager-State Chris Hammontree

NEWS EXECUTIVES

Editor Arthur S Brisbane
Managing Editor-News Mark Zieman
Managing Editor-Features & Design Jane Amari
Director-Electronic Media Nancy Tracewell
Editorial Page Editor Rich Hood
Asst Editorial Page Editor Laura Scott
Deputy Editorial Page Editor Steve Win

EDITORS AND MANAGERS

Director-Administration Terrance Thompson
Director-Design Tom Dolphens
Director-Art Jean Moxam
Systems Manager Rob Perschau
Arts Editor Alice Thorson
Book Editor George Gurly
Business Editor Doug Weaver
Cartoonist Lee Judge
Cartoonist Bill Schorr
Columnist G Fred Wickman
Columnist James Fisher
Columnist C W Gusewelle
Columnist Betty Cuniberti
Columnist Jerry Heaster
Consumer Columnist Angela Curry
Humor Columnist Bill Tammeus
Editorial Writer Tom McClanahan
Editorial Writer Robert P Sigman
Editorial Writer Yael Abouhalkah
Environmental Editor Michael Mansur
Entertainment Editor Steve Paul
Fashion Editor Jacqueline White
Features Editor Jeanne Meyer
Films/Theater Editor Robert W Butler
Food Editor Jill Silva
Letters Editor/Editorial Page Editor Jean Haley
Librarian Felicia Moore
Lifestyle Editor Ellen Foley
Magazine Editor Alan Holder
Metro Editor Randall Smith
Mid America/National Editor Darryl Levings
Music Columnist-Classical Scott Cantrell
News Editor Monroe Dodd
Outdoor Editor Brent Frazee
Op-Editor Editor/Editorial Page Editor Rhonda Lokeman
Photo Editor Tim Janicke
Radio/Television Editor Barry Garron
Religion Editor Helen T Gray
Society Editor Laura Hockaday
Sports Columnist Jason Whitlock
Sports Columnist Jonathan Rand
Sports Editor Dale Bye
Sunday Editor/Editorial Page Editor Karen Brown
Travel Editor MaryLou Nolan
Weekend Editor Steve Shirk

MANAGEMENT INFORMATION SERVICES

Data Processing Manager Chet Wakefield
Online Manager Hugh Downey

PRODUCTION

Director-Operations Chet Wakefield
Manager-Operations Bayliss Wikle
Manager-Mailroom Lisa Parks
Manager-Quality Assurance/Pre Press Randy Waters
Manager-Coordinator Denny Billings
Manager-Pressroom David Bibb
Manager-Whitepaper Neil Carr

Market Information: Zoned editions; Split Run; TMC; Operate database; Operate audiotex; Electronic edition.

Mechanical available: Converted Letterpress to Offset; Black and 3 ROP colors; insert accepted — preprinted; page cut-offs — 23$\frac{9}{16}$".

Mechanical specifications: Type page 13" x 22$\frac{1}{4}$"; E - 6 cols, 2$\frac{1}{16}$", $\frac{1}{8}$" between; A - 6 cols, 2$\frac{1}{16}$", $\frac{1}{8}$" between; C - 10 cols, 1$\frac{3}{16}$", $\frac{1}{16}$" between.

Commodity consumption: Newsprint 66,000 short tons; widths 54", 54", 41$\frac{1}{16}$", 27$\frac{3}{8}$"; black ink 1,417,060 pounds; color ink 379,606 pounds; single pages printed 33,673; average pages per issue 69(d), 93(sat), 195(S); single plates used 498,480.

Equipment: EDITORIAL: Front-end hardware — 240-PC/Novell, 25-Ap/Mac, Ap/Power Mac; Front-end software — Dewar/Editing System Disc 4, QuarkXPress 3.3; Printers — Epson/LaserPrinter, HP/LaserPrinter, QMS/LaserPrinters; Other equipment — Lf/AP Leaf Picture Desk, Ap/Mac. CLASSIFIED: Front-end hardware — DEC/VAX; Other equipment — HDS, Northern Telephones. AUDIOTEX: Hardware — PC/486, Unix; Software — Mk/Star-Touch, Brite Voice Systems, PEP. DISPLAY: Adv layout systems — SCS/Layout 8000; Front-end hardware — 1-Ap/Mac IIx, 8-Ap/Mac IIcx, 8-Ap/Mac ci, 1-Ap/Mac IIfx, 2-Ap/Mac Quadra 700, 1-Ap/Mac Quadra 650, 4-Ap/Mac Quadra 800, Ap/Mac Centris 650, 1-Ap/Mac SE, 2-Ap/Mac Power PC 7100, 2-Ap/Mac Quadra 900, 5-Ap/Mac Plus, 2-PC/486, 1-PC/386; Front-end software — QuarkXPress/3.3, Adobe/Streamline, Adobe/Illustrator 5.5, Adobe/Photoshop, SCS/Layout 8000; Printers — 4-Ap/Mac LaserWriter, 4-HP/Scan Jet, 1-AG/Arcus, C.Itoh/Graphic Printer; Other equipment — 1-Nikon/LS-3500, SpectreScan, SpectrePrint, Diadem/Scan-Link. PRODUCTION: Pagination software — Quark XPress 3.3; Typesetters — 3-AU/APS Micro 5, 2-AU/7000 Imagesetters, 2-AU/APS-108 FC Imagesetters; Plate exposures — 2-WL/Lith-X-Pozer III; Plate processors — 2-WL; Scanners — 2-ECR; Production cameras — 2-C/NewsPager; Automatic film processors — 4-LE; Shrink lenses — 2-Alan; Color separation equipment (conventional) — 1-CD.

PRESSROOM: Line 1 — 10-H/Colormatic converted offset; Line 2 — 10-H/Colormatic converted offset; Line 3 — 10-H/Colormatic converted offset; Line 4 — 15-H/Colormatic converted offset; Folders — 9-H; Pasters — Automatic Pasters; Reels and stands — 45-MAN. MAILROOM: Counter stackers — 11-HL/Monitor II; Inserters and stuffers — 5-HI/1372; Bundle tyer — 11-Dynamic/Tying Machines NT-2; Addressing machine — 2-Ch. LIBRARY: Electronic — Data Times. COMMUNICATIONS: Systems used — satellite. WIRE SERVICES: News — AP Newsfeatures, Business Wire, KRT, LAT-WP, NYT, PR Newswire; Photos — AP, KRT; Stock tables — AP SelectStox; Syndicates — KRT, LATS, NYT; Receiving dishes — size-3m, AP, Weather Service. BUSINESS COMPUTERS: PCs, DEC/VAX; PCs & micros networked; PCs & main system networked.

KENNETT

Dunklin County

'90 U.S. Census- 10,941; **E&P '96 Est.** 11,649

The Daily Dunklin Democrat (e-mon to fri; S)

The Daily Dunklin Democrat, 203 1st St.; PO Box 669, Kennett, MO 63857; tel (314) 888-4505; fax (314) 888-5114. Rust Communications group.

Circulation: 4,213(e); 4,059(e-tues); 4,213(S); CAC Mar. 31, 1995.

Price: 50¢(d); 50¢(S); $6.50/mo; $61.00/yr; $63.00/yr (mail in city), $77.70/yr (mail out of city).

Advertising: Open inch rate $9.05(e); $9.05(S). **Representative:** Landon Associates Inc.

News Service: AP. **Politics:** Independent. **Established:** 1888.

Note: Effective July 10, 1995, this publication changed its publishing plan from (e-tues to fri; S) to (e-mon to fri; S).

Not Published: New Year; Memorial Day; Independence Day; Labor Day; Thanksgiving; Christmas.

Special Edition: Progress (Mar).

Special Weekly Sections: Food Pages, Outdoors (tues); Business Page (wed); Food Pages (thur); Entertainment, Church (fri); Agriculture (S).

CORPORATE OFFICER

President Gary W Rust

GENERAL MANAGEMENT

Publisher Bud Hunt
Bookkeeper Tabitha Hyde

ADVERTISING

Manager Terri Coleman
Manager-Classified Kelly Frederick

MARKETING AND PROMOTION

Manager-Marketing/Promotion Bud Hunt

TELECOMMUNICATIONS

Audiotex Manager Bud Hunt

CIRCULATION

Manager Brenda G Crawford

NEWS EXECUTIVES

Editor Steve Gillespie
Assoc Editor Lyman Skyles

EDITOR AND MANAGER

Sports Editor Kyle Smith

PRODUCTION

Foreman-Composing Brenda G Crawford
Foreman-Pressroom John Emerson

Market Information: Zoned editions; Split Run; TMC.

Mechanical available: Offset; Black and 3 ROP colors; insert accepted — preprinted; page cut-offs — 23".

Mechanical specifications: Type page 13" x 21"; E - 6 cols, 2$\frac{1}{16}$", $\frac{1}{16}$" between; A - 6 cols, 2$\frac{1}{16}$", $\frac{1}{16}$" between; C - 8 cols, 1$\frac{1}{2}$", $\frac{1}{16}$" between.

Commodity consumption: Newsprint 242 short tons; width 27"; black ink 2,150 pounds; color ink 918 pounds; single pages printed 10,286; average pages per issue 16(d), 74(S).

Equipment: EDITORIAL: Front-end software — Novell. PRODUCTION: Typesetters — 5-COM; Platemaking systems — 3M; Plate exposures — 3M; Plate processors — 3M. WIRE SERVICES: News — AP; Receiving dishes — AP. BUSINESS COMPUTERS: 1-IBM; Applications: Circ, Adv billing, Accts receivable, Gen ledger, Payroll; PCs & micros networked; PCs & main system networked.

KIRKSVILLE

Adair County

'90 U.S. Census- 17,152; **E&P '96 Est.** 17,140

Kirksville Daily Express & News (e-mon to fri; S)

Kirksville Daily Express & News, 110 E. McPherson St.; PO Box 809, Kirksville, MO 63501; tel (816) 665-2808; fax (816) 665-2608. Hollinger International Inc. group.

Circulation: 6,313(e); 6,313(S); Sworn Sept. 22, 1995.

Price: 50¢(d); 75¢(S); $90.00/yr.

Advertising: Open inch rate $7.00(e); $7.00(S).

News Service: AP. **Politics:** Independent. **Established:** 1915.

Not Published: New Year; Memorial Day; Independence Day; Labor Day; Thanksgiving; Christmas.

Special Edition: Progress (July).

GENERAL MANAGEMENT

Publisher/Business Manager Larry W Freels

ADVERTISING

Director Jon Cook

CIRCULATION

Manager Greg Barns

NEWS EXECUTIVES

Editor Ludy Tritz
Managing Editor Larry W Freels

EDITOR AND MANAGER

Sports Editor Bud Schrader

PRODUCTION

Superintendent Tony Swain

Market Information: Split Run; TMC; ADS.

Mechanical available: Offset; Black and 3 ROP colors; insert accepted — preprinted; page cut-offs — 22$\frac{3}{4}$".

Mechanical specifications: Type page 13" x 21"; E - 6 cols, 2$\frac{1}{16}$", $\frac{1}{8}$" between; A - 6 cols, 2$\frac{1}{16}$", $\frac{1}{8}$" between; C - 6 cols, 2$\frac{1}{16}$", $\frac{1}{8}$" between.

Commodity consumption: Newsprint 312 metric tons; widths 27.5", 13.75"; black ink 17,300 pounds; color ink 900 pounds; single pages printed 8,600; average pages per issue 16(d), 32(S); single plates used 4,000.

Equipment: EDITORIAL: Front-end hardware — Ap/Mac; Front-end software — Ap/Mac. CLASSIFIED: Front-end hardware — 6-Ap/Mac; Printers — 3-Ap/Mac LaserPrinter; Other equipment — CD-Rom. PRODUCTION: Plate exposures — 1-Nu/Double Flip Top; Plate processors — 1-Graphcom/Dateliner 24; Scanners — 1-Linotype-Hell/35, 1-Linotype-Hell/14; Production cameras — 1-R/400; Automatic film processors — 1-LE/18.

PRESSROOM: Line 1 — 6-G/Community; Folders — 1-G. MAILROOM: Bundle tyer — 2-Bu; Addressing machine — 1-Am/4000, 1-Am/2000. WIRE SERVICES: News — AP; Receiving dishes — size-10ft, AP. BUSINESS COMPUTERS: RSK/12, 1-IBM/AT; Applications: Mail list, TMC shopper.

LEBANON

Laclede County

'90 U.S. Census- 9,983; **E&P '96 Est.** 10,395

The Lebanon Daily Record (e-mon to fri; S)

The Lebanon Daily Record, 290 S. Madison St.; PO Box 192, Lebanon, MO 65536; tel (417) 532-9131; fax (417) 532-8140.

Circulation: 4,859(e); 4,859(S); Sworn Sept. 30, 1994.

Price: 50¢(d); 75¢(S); $4.50/mo; $48.00/yr.

Advertising: Open inch rate $6.86(e); $6.86(S).

News Service: AP. **Politics:** Republican. **Established:** 1866.

Special Editions: FFA, Progress (Feb); Trout Talk (Mar); Trout Talk (Apr); Farm Tab, Trout Talk (May); Hillbilly Days, Trout Talk (June); Fair Tab, Trout Talk (July); Back-to-School (Aug); Trout Talk (Sept); Car Care, Trout Talk (Oct); Recipe Cookbook (Nov); Christmas (Dec).

Magazine: Lebanon Area Real Estate & Business Journal (monthly).

CORPORATE OFFICERS

President Dalton C Wright
Vice Pres-Operations Beth Chism

GENERAL MANAGEMENT

Publisher Steve Hilton

ADVERTISING

Manager-Display Rene Barker

CIRCULATION

Director U Dean Foster

NEWS EXECUTIVE

Managing Editor Steve Hilton

EDITORS AND MANAGERS

Business/Finance Editor Matt Decker
City Editor Ed Sisson
Editorial Page Editor Ed Sisson
Education Editor Matt Decker
Health/Medical Director Gary Dedewaldt
Photo Editor Sheila Humphrey
Sports Editor Jim Adair

MANAGEMENT INFORMATION SERVICES

Data Processing Manager Ed Barrett

PRODUCTION

Manager Jeremy Rowland

Market Information: TMC.

Mechanical available: Offset; Black and 3 ROP colors; insert accepted — preprinted; page cut-offs — 22$\frac{3}{4}$".

Mechanical specifications: Type page 13" x 21$\frac{1}{2}$"; E - 6 cols, 2.03", $\frac{1}{6}$" between; A - 6 cols, 2.03", $\frac{1}{6}$" between; C - 6 cols, 2.03", $\frac{1}{6}$" between.

Commodity consumption: Newsprint 290 short tons; widths 27$\frac{1}{2}$", 27"; black ink 1,400 pounds; color ink 1,800 pounds; single pages printed 3,328; average pages per issue 10(d), 16(S); single plates used 6,700.

I-230 Missouri

Equipment: EDITORIAL: Front-end hardware — Dewar/Sys II; Front-end software — Dewar/Sys II. CLASSIFIED: Front-end hardware — PC; Front-end software — Dewar. DISPLAY: Adv layout systems — Archetype/Corel Draw, Aldus/PageMaker, Dewar; Front-end hardware — PC/386; Front-end software — Archetype/Corel Draw, Aldus/PageMaker, Dewar/Discovery; Printers — 2-HP/LaserJet III; Other equipment — Abaton/Scanner, CD-Rom. PRODUCTION: Typesetters — HP/LaserJet III; Plate exposures — Nu/Flip Top FT40 APRNS; Plate processors — Nat/340; Scanners — Abaton/380, Abaton/300; Production cameras — N/Horizontal SSTE2024; Automatic film processors — LE/LD-18.
PRESSROOM: Line 1 — 4-G/Community; Line 2 — 4-G/Community. MAILROOM: Counter stackers — BG; Inserters and stuffers — KAN; Bundle tyer — 2-Bu; Addressing machine — KR/215. WIRE SERVICES: News — AP; size-10ft, AP. BUSINESS COMPUTERS: 3-PC/386; Applications: DAC/Easy, Lotus 1-2-3, Quattro/Pro.

MACON

Macon County

'90 U.S. Census- 5,571; E&P '96 Est. 5,483

Macon Chronicle-Herald (e-tues to fri)

Macon Chronicle-Herald, 217 W. Bourke St.; PO Box 7, Macon, MO 63552; tel (816) 385-3121; fax (816) 385-3082. Hollinger International Inc. group.

Circulation: 2,867(e); Sworn Sept. 29, 1995.

Price: 50¢(d).

Advertising: Open inch rate $6.50(e). **Representative:** Papert Companies.

News Service: AP. **Politics:** Independent. **Established:** 1910.

Not Published: New Year; Memorial Day; Independence Day; Labor Day; Thanksgiving; Christmas.

Special Editions: Customer Appreciation, Year in Review (Jan); President's Birthday Sale, Recipe Edition (Feb); Chamber of Commerce Tab, Lawn & Garden, Spring Fashions (Mar); Bridal, Car Care, Home Improvement (Apr); Graduation, Mother's Day (May); Father's Day, Summer Baseball (June); Back-to-School, Farmer Appreciation (Aug); Football, Home Winterizing, Fall Fashions (Sept); FFA Appreciation, Homecoming Edition, Tiger Days Sale (Oct); Basketball Edition, Christmas Shopping Spree (Nov); Christmas Wrapup (Dec).

Magazine: TV Guide (fri).

GENERAL MANAGEMENT

Publisher Bill Hall
General Manager Janice Wine

ADVERTISING

Director Pat Quinley

MARKETING AND PROMOTION

Manager-Marketing/Promotion Pat Quinley

CIRCULATION

Director Marlene Stuffelbean

NEWS EXECUTIVE

Editor Mark Snow

PRODUCTION

Superintendent Tom Lacas

Market Information: Zoned editions; TMC.

Mechanical available: Offset; Black and 3 ROP colors; insert accepted — preprinted; page cutoffs — 22¾".

Mechanical specifications: Type page 12¾" x 21½"; E - 6 cols, 2", ⅙" between; A - 6 cols, 2", ⅙" between; C - 6 cols, 2", ⅙" between.

Commodity consumption: Newsprint 200 short tons; width 27½"; black ink 6,500 pounds; color ink 400 pounds; single pages printed 20,000; average pages per issue 12(d); single plates used 2,500.

Equipment: EDITORIAL: Front-end hardware — Ap/Mac; Front-end software — Aldus/PageMaker; Printers — Ap/Mac LaserWriter II. CLASSIFIED: Front-end hardware — Ap/Mac; Front-end software — Aldus/PageMaker; Printers — Ap/Mac LaserWriter. DISPLAY: Front-end hardware — Ap/Mac; Front-end software — Aldus/PageMaker; Printers — Ap/Mac LaserWriter II. PRODUCTION: Plate exposures — 1-Nu; Plate processors — Roconex; Production cameras — R; Automatic film processors — LE.
PRESSROOM: Line 1 — 6-KP/Newsking 475. MAILROOM: Bundle tyer — Bu. WIRE SERVICES: News — AP.

MARSHALL

Saline County

'90 U.S. Census- 12,711; E&P '96 Est. 12,654

The Marshall Democrat-News (e-mon to fri)

The Marshall Democrat-News, 121 N. Lafayette; PO Box 100, Marshall, MO 65340; tel (816) 886-2233; fax (816) 886-8544. USMedia Inc. group.

Circulation: 3,896(e); Sworn Sept. 28, 1995.

Price: 50¢(d); $78.54/yr.

Advertising: Open inch rate $6.30(e). **Representative:** Papert Companies.

News Service: AP. **Politics:** Independent. **Established:** 1879.

Not Published: New Year; Memorial Day; Independence Day; Labor Day; Thanksgiving; Christmas.

Advertising not accepted: Investments requested.

Special Weekly Sections: Health, Farm (tues); Food (wed); Business (thur); Religion (fri).

CORPORATE OFFICER

President Eugene A Mace

GENERAL MANAGEMENT

Publisher Shelly Arth
Business Manager Ann Sweigart

CIRCULATION

Manager Pat Marrow

NEWS EXECUTIVE

Managing Editor Mary Jo Rieth

Market Information: TMC.

Mechanical available: Offset; Black and 3 ROP colors; insert accepted — preprinted; page cutoffs — 21½".

Mechanical specifications: Type page 13" x 21½"; E - 6 cols, 2¹⁄₁₆", ⅛" between; A - 6 cols, 2¹⁄₁₆", ⅛" between; C - 6 cols, 2¹⁄₁₆", ⅛" between.

Commodity consumption: Newsprint 204 short tons; width 28"; black ink 5,400 pounds; color ink 200 pounds; single pages printed 3,100; average pages per issue 10(d); single plates used 2,000.

Equipment: EDITORIAL: Front-end hardware — 8-Ap/Mac; Printers — 1-Ap/Mac. CLASSIFIED: Front-end hardware — 1-Ap/Mac. DISPLAY: Front-end hardware — 2-Ap/Mac; Printers — 1-Ap/Mac. PRODUCTION: Platemaking systems — 1-Nu; Plate exposures — 1-Nu; Scanners — Gam/Digital Densitometer; Production cameras — 1-R/500, LE; Automatic film processors — 1-P.
PRESSROOM: Line 1 — 5-KP/Newsking. MAILROOM: Bundle tyer — 1-Bu; Addressing machine — 1-Ch. WIRE SERVICES: News — AP; Receiving dishes — size-2ft, AP. BUSINESS COMPUTERS: 1-Packard/Bell, 2-Acros; PCs & micros networked.

MARYVILLE

Nodaway County

'90 U.S. Census- 10,663; E&P '96 Est. 11,679

Maryville Daily Forum (e-tues to fri; S)

Maryville Daily Forum, 111 E. Jenkins; PO Box 188, Maryville, MO 64468; tel (816) 562-2424; fax (816) 562-2823. Fackelman Newspapers group.

Circulation: 4,129(e); 4,129(S); Sworn Oct. 1, 1995.

Price: 50¢(d); 75¢(S); $6.30/mo; $60.00/yr.

Advertising: Open inch rate $6.75(e); $6.75(S). **Representative:** Papert Companies.

News Service: AP. **Politics:** Independent. **Established:** 1869.

Note: Effective May 7, 1995, this publication started publishing a Sunday edition.

Not Published: New Year; Independence Day; Thanksgiving; Christmas.

Special Editions: Progress (Jan); Bridal, Graduation, Spring Car Care (May); Fair (June); Newcomers (July); Back-to-School, Fall Car Care (Aug); Fall Sports (Football) (Sept); Winter Sports, Christmas Greetings (Dec).

Magazines: Ag News Today (2x/mo) (tues); Weekly Bargain Shopper (TMC), TV Forum (wkly).

CORPORATE OFFICERS

President Ann Nixon
Vice Pres-Operations Marc A Richard
Secretary Ann Fackelman
Treasurer Broward E Ratliff

GENERAL MANAGEMENT

Publisher Jerry Pye
Business Manager Sue Montgomery

ADVERTISING

Director Dirk Allsbury

NEWS EXECUTIVE

Managing Editor Steve Wollfolk

EDITORS AND MANAGERS

Lifestyle Editor Carolyn Elswick
Sports Editor Steve Wollfolk

PRODUCTION

Manager Danny Puckett

Market Information: TMC.

Mechanical available: Offset; Black and 2 ROP colors; insert accepted — preprinted.

Mechanical specifications: Type page 13" x 21½"; E - 6 cols, 2¹⁄₁₆", ⅛" between; A - 6 cols, 2¹⁄₁₆", ⅛" between; C - 6 cols, 2¹⁄₁₆", ⅛" between.

Commodity consumption: Newsprint 360 short tons; width 27½"; black ink 6,800 pounds; color ink 1,600 pounds; single pages printed 5,100; average pages per issue 12(d); single plates used 9,600.

Equipment: EDITORIAL: Front-end hardware — 6-Ap/Mac Plus, 1-Ap/Mac SE30, 1-Ap/Mac II LC; Front-end software — Aldus/PageMaker 4.0; Printers — Ap/Mac LaserWriter; Other equipment — Ap/Mac Scanner. CLASSIFIED: Front-end hardware — Ap/Mac Plus; Front-end software — Class/Act II. DISPLAY: Front-end hardware — 2-Ap/Mac SE30, 1-Ap/Mac Plus; Front-end software — Ready-Set-Go; Printers — Ap/Mac LaserWriter II NT. PRODUCTION: Typesetters — Ap/Mac LaserWriter II NT, Ap/Mac LaserWriter Plus; Plate exposures — Magnum/43DS; Plate processors — Nat/A-250; Production cameras — B/Gammamatic; Automatic film processors — AG/Litex 25.
PRESSROOM: Line 1 — 6-G/Community. MAILROOM: Bundle tyer — Bu/182, Malow/Strap-tyer; Addressing machine — KR/211. WIRE SERVICES: News — AP, Farm Data; Syndicates — NEA, Universal Press; Receiving dishes — AP. BUSINESS COMPUTERS: Cougar Mountain.

MEXICO

Audrain County

'90 U.S. Census- 11,290; E&P '96 Est. 10,540
ABC-CZ (90): 11,290 (HH 4,589)

Mexico Ledger (e-mon to sat)

Mexico Ledger, 300 N. Washington St.; PO Box 8, Mexico, MO 65265; tel (314) 581-1111; fax (314) 581-2029. Hollinger International Inc. group.

Circulation: 8,815(e); 8,815(e-sat); ABC Sept. 30, 1995.

Price: 50¢(d); 50¢(sat).

Advertising: Open inch rate $10.50(e); $10.50(e-sat). **Representative:** Cresmer, Woodward, O'Mara & Ormsbee.

News Service: AP. **Politics:** Independent. **Established:** 1855.

Not Published: New Year; Memorial Day; Independence Day; Labor Day; Thanksgiving; Christmas.

Special Editions: Progress (Feb); Farm Magazines, Car Care (Mar); Home Improvement (Apr); Football (Aug); Hunter's Guide (Oct); Cookbook (Nov).

Special Weekly Sections: Best Food Day (mon, tues); Financial/Business Page (wed); Farm Page (thur); Church Page (fri); TV Tab (sat); Entertainment (daily).

GENERAL MANAGEMENT

Publisher Joe May

ADVERTISING

Director Martin Keller
Manager-Classified Ivan Lewellen
Manager-Promotion Joe May

CIRCULATION

Manager Don Falcone

NEWS EXECUTIVE

Managing Editor Larry Nossaman

EDITORS AND MANAGERS

Business Editor Tracey Berry
City Editor Tracey Berry
Editorial Page Editor Larry Nossaman
Education Editor Larry Nossaman
Entertainment/Amusements Editor Brenda Fike
Farm/Agriculture Editor Larry Nossaman
Fashion/Style Editor Brenda Fike
Features Editor Tracey Berry
Home Furnishings Editor Brenda Fike
Living/Lifestyle Editor Brenda Fike
National Editor Larry Nossaman
News Editor Tracey Berry
Photo Department Manager Dean Patrick
Political/Government Editor Larry Nossaman
Religion Editor Larry Nossaman
Science Editor Larry Nossaman
Sports Editor James Stanley
Television/Film Editor Brenda Fike
Theater/Music Editor Brenda Fike

MANAGEMENT INFORMATION SERVICES

Manager Leslie Van Strien

PRODUCTION

Foreman Lyndell Farrah

Market Information: Split Run; TMC.

Mechanical available: Offset; Black and 3 ROP colors; insert accepted — preprinted; page cutoffs — 21½".

Mechanical specifications: Type page 16½" x 21½"; E - 6 cols, 1.67", ½" between; A - 6 cols, 1.71", ½" between; C - 6 cols, 1.71", ½" between.

Commodity consumption: Newsprint 500 short tons; widths 27½", 13¾"; black ink 6000 pounds; color ink 500 pounds; average pages per issue 14(d).

Equipment: EDITORIAL: Front-end hardware — 12-Mk; Printers — V/5100E; Other equipment — Lf/Leafscan, V/4900 Photos, Ap/Mac. CLASSIFIED: Front-end hardware — 2-Mk. DISPLAY: Adv layout systems — 2-Ap/Mac cx; Front-end software — Multi-Ad/Creator, Aldus/PageMaker; Printers — V/5100E. PRODUCTION: Typesetters — V/5100E; Platemaking systems — 1-Nu; Plate exposures — 1-Nu; Plate processors — 1-Nat/A-250; Electronic picture desk — Lf/AP Leaf Picture Desk; Scanners — Lf/Leafscan, Ap/Mac Scanner; Production cameras — 1-R/580, 1-SCREEN/680C; Automatic film processors — 1-LE; Digital color separation equipment — V/4990.
PRESSROOM: Line 1 — 7-G/Community; Folders — 1-G. MAILROOM: Bundle tyer — 1-Bu; Wrapping singles — 1-Sa/SM; Addressing machine — 1-Ch. COMMUNICATIONS: Facsimile — 1-Canon/8200. WIRE SERVICES: News — AP; Photos — AP; Receiving dishes — size-10ft, AP. BUSINESS COMPUTERS: 500-ATT/3B2; Applications: Bus; PCs & micros networked.

MOBERLY

Randolph County

'90 U.S. Census- 12,839; E&P '96 Est. 12,381

Moberly Monitor-Index & Democrat (e-mon to fri; S)

Moberly Monitor-Index & Democrat, 218 N. Williams; PO Box 697, Moberly, MO 65270; tel (816) 263-4123; fax (816) 263-3626. Donrey Media group.

Circulation: 6,950(e); 6,950(S); Sworn Oct. 1, 1995.

Price: 50¢(d); 75¢(S); $6.00/mo; $72.00/yr.

Advertising: Open inch rate $10.95(e); $9.95(S). **Representative:** Papert Companies.

News Service: AP. **Politics:** Independent. **Established:** 1869.

Advertising not accepted: Adoption Ads.

Special Editions: Chronology, Bridal Edition (Jan); Valentine Hearts, FHA, FFA (Feb); Progress (Mar); Spring Care Care, Spring Farm, Chamber Tab, Spring Home Improvement, Lawn & Garden, Health Care (Apr); Mother's Day, Recreation, Graduation (May); Father's Day, Spring Bridal (June); County Fairs (July); Back-to-School (Aug); Moberly Birthday, Fall Fashion, Fall Home Improvement, Football, United Way, Fall Car Care, Dining Guide (Sept); Cookbook, Basketball, Gift Guides (Nov); Christmas Greetings (Dec).

Special Weekly Sections: Best Food Day, Business Page (tues); Farm Section (wed); Church Guide, Antique Guide (fri).

Magazines: Business Review (every other fri); TV Spotlight (entertainment magazine) (S); 50 Something (1st S/mo).

CORPORATE OFFICERS

Founder Donald W Reynolds
President/Chief Operating Officer Emmett Jones
Exec Vice Pres/Chief Financial Officer Darrell W Loftin
Vice Pres-Western Newspaper Group David A Osborn
Vice Pres-Eastern Newspaper Group Don Schneider

GENERAL MANAGEMENT

Publisher Bob Cunningham

ADVERTISING

Director Judy Orton

MARKETING AND PROMOTION

Manager-Marketing/Promotion Judy Orton

Missouri I-231

CIRCULATION
Director Sam Holder
NEWS EXECUTIVE
Editor Ruth Carr
EDITORS AND MANAGERS
Automotive Editor Sam Holder
Business/Finance Editor Virginia West
City/Metro Editor Scott Loesch
Editorial Page Editor Ruth Carr
Education Editor Jamie P Melchert
Entertainment/Amusements Editor Bob Cunningham
Environmental Editor Scott Loesch
Farm Editor Ruth Carr
Features Editor Scott Loesch
Living/Lifestyle Editor Judy Orton
National Editor Bob Cunningham
News Editor Ruth Carr
Photo Editor Charles Embree
Political/Government Editor Bob Cunningham
Religion Editor Ruth Carr
Society Editor Ruth Carr
Sports Editor Damen Clow
Television/Film Editor Bob Cunningham
Theater/Music Editor Bob Cunningham
Travel Editor Bob Cunningham
Women's Editor Debbie Fitzpatrick
PRODUCTION
Foreman-Composing Viginia Forsyth
Foreman-Pressroom Mark Hisle

Market Information: Zoned editions; Split Run.
Mechanical available: Offset; Black and 3 ROP colors; insert accepted — preprinted; page cut-offs — 22¾".
Mechanical specifications: Type page 13" x 21½"; E - 6 cols, 2 1/16", .17" between; A - 6 cols, 2 1/16", .17" between; C - 8 cols, 1½", .17" between.
Commodity consumption: Newsprint 260 metric tons; widths 13½", 13½", 27"; black ink 10,430 pounds; color ink 400 pounds; single pages printed 6,000; average pages per issue 12(d), 30(S); single plates used 2,900.
Equipment: EDITORIAL: Front-end hardware — Mk, Ap/Mac; Front-end software — Mk, QuarkXpress, Baseview; Printers — Ap/Mac LaserWriter II, Ap/Mac LaserWriter Pro. CLASSIFIED: Front-end hardware — Ap/Mac; Front-end software — Baseview, Fox, Aldus, QuarkXPress; Printers — Ap/Mac LaserWriter II. DISPLAY: Front-end hardware — Ap/Mac; Front-end software — Multi-Ad/Creator, Aldus/FreeHand, QuarkXPress; Printers — Ap/Mac LaserWriter II, Ap/Mac LaserWriter Pro; Other equipment — Ap/Mac Scanner, CD-Rom. PRODUCTION: Platemaking systems — 1-Nu; Plate processors — 1-Nu; Scanners — Ap/Mac; Production cameras — Acti; Automatic film processors — P.
PRESSROOM: Line 1 — 6-G/Suburban. MAILROOM: Bundle tyer — Marlo/Star Tyer, MLN; Addressing machine — Wm. COMMUNICATIONS: Systems used — satellite. WIRE SERVICES: News — AP; Syndicates — TV Data; Receiving dishes — AP. BUSINESS COMPUTERS: Mk, Ap/Mac; PCs & micros networked; PCs & main system networked.

MONETT

Barry and Lawrence Counties
'90 U.S. Census- 6,529; E&P '96 Est. 6,863

Times (e-mon to fri)

Times, 505 Broadway; PO Box 40, Monett, MO 65708; tel (417) 235-3135. Cleveland Newspapers Inc. group.
Circulation: 4,375(e); Sworn Sept. 27, 1995.
Price: 25¢(d); $46.00/yr.
Advertising: Open inch rate $6.50(e). **Politics:** Republican. **Established:** 1908.
Not Published: New Year; Memorial Day; Independence Day; Labor Day; Thanksgiving; Christmas.
Special Editions: Progress; Recipe; Christmas; Football; Basketball; Business Women's Week.

GENERAL MANAGEMENT
Publisher Stephen L Crass
ADVERTISING
Manager-Retail Mike Stubbs
CIRCULATION
Director Kevin Nichols
NEWS EXECUTIVES
Editor Stephen L Crass
Managing Editor Murray Bishoff
EDITORS AND MANAGERS
Columnist Stephen L Crass
Society Editor Lisa Craft
Sports Editor Charles F Brady
MANAGEMENT INFORMATION SERVICES
Data Processing Manager Charlotte Brady

PRODUCTION
Manager Thad Weikal

Market Information: TMC.
Mechanical available: Offset; Black and 3 ROP colors; insert accepted — preprinted; page cut-offs — 22¾".
Mechanical specifications: Type page 13" x 21½"; E - 6 cols, 2", .17" between; A - 6 cols, 2", .17" between; C - 6 cols, 2", .17" between.
Commodity consumption: Newsprint 80 short tons; widths 28", 14"; single pages printed 2,000; average pages per issue 8(d); single plates used 2,400.
Equipment: EDITORIAL: Front-end hardware — Ap/Mac SE; Front-end software — Microsoft/Word, Aldus/PageMaker, Microsoft/Windows; Printers — Ap/Mac LaserWriter. CLASSIFIED: Front-end hardware — Ap/Mac SE; Front-end software — Microsoft/Word, Aldus/PageMaker, Microsoft/Windows; Printers — Ap/Mac LaserWriter. DISPLAY: Adv layout systems — Ap/Mac SE; Front-end software — Aldus/PageMaker; Printers — Ap/Mac LaserWriter, LaserMaster/1200 dpi. PRODUCTION: Typesetters — Ap/Mac SE; Plate exposures — 1-Nu; Scanners — 1-LaCie; Production cameras — CL.
PRESSROOM: Line 1 — 4-WPC/Quadra Color; Press registration system — Carlson. MAILROOM: Bundle tyer — 2-Bu. COMMUNICATIONS: Facsimile — Brother. BUSINESS COMPUTERS: RSK/Tandy 4000; PCs & micros networked; PCs & main system networked.

NEOSHO

Newton County
'90 U.S. Census- 9,254; E&P '96 Est. 9,062

Neosho Daily News (e-mon to fri; S)

Neosho Daily News, 1006 W. Harmony St., Neosho, MO 64850; tel (417) 451-1520; fax (417) 451-6408. Hollinger International Inc. group.
Circulation: 4,775(e); 4,847(S); Sworn Sept. 30, 1995.
Price: 50¢(d); 75¢(S); $7.50/mo; $84.00/yr.
Advertising: Open inch rate $6.50(e); $6.50(S). **Representative:** Hollinger International Inc.
News Service: AP. **Politics:** Republican. **Established:** 1905.
Not Published: New Year; Memorial Day; Independence Day; Labor Day; Thanksgiving; Christmas.
Special Editions: Graduation; Christmas; Fall Festival.

GENERAL MANAGEMENT
Publisher Valerie Prayter
ADVERTISING
Manager Judi Cole
CIRCULATION
Manager Jeff Denefrio
NEWS EXECUTIVE
Editor Christen Jackson
EDITORS AND MANAGERS
Action Line Editor Christen Jackson
Automotive Editor Christen Jackson
Business/Finance Editor Christen Jackson
City/Metro Editor Christen Jackson
Editorial Page Editor Christen Jackson
Education Editor Christen Jackson
Entertainment/Amusements Editor Christen Jackson
Environmental Editor Christen Jackson
Fashion/Style Editor Christen Jackson
Graphics Editor Christen Jackson
Health/Medical Editor Christen Jackson
Home Furnishings Editor Lois Bush
Living/Lifestyle Editor Christen Jackson
National Editor Christen Jackson
News Editor Christen Jackson
Photo Department Manager Jim Burrows
Political/Government Editor Christen Jackson
Religion Editor Christen Jackson
Science/Technology Editor Christen Jackson
Sports Editor Dean Keeling
Travel Editor Christen Jackson
Women's Editor Christen Jackson
PRODUCTION
Manager Bill Lyttle

Market Information: TMC.
Mechanical available: Offset; Black and 3 ROP colors; insert accepted — preprinted; page cut-offs — 22½".
Mechanical specifications: Type page 13" x 21½"; E - 6 cols, 2 1/16", ⅛" between; A - 6 cols, 2 1/16", ⅛" between; C - 6 cols, 2 1/16", ⅛" between.
Commodity consumption: Newsprint 360 short tons; width 13¾"; single pages printed 3,784; average pages per issue 12(d), 18(S).
Equipment: EDITORIAL: Front-end hardware — Ap/Mac; Front-end software — Baseview. CLASSIFIED: Front-end hardware — Ap/Mac; Front-end software — Baseview; Printers — Ap/Mac ImageWriter. PRODUCTION: OCR software — Mk; Typesetters — Ap/Mac LaserWriter IIf, Ap/Mac LaserWriter NTX, Ap/Mac LaserWriter Plus, NEC/SilentWriter 2; Plate exposures — Nu/Flip Top FT40V6UPNS; Plate processors — WL/30C; Production cameras — R; Automatic film processors — LE.
PRESSROOM: Line 1 — 7-G/Community; Folders — 1-G/Community, 1-G/SE. MAILROOM: Bundle tyer — 2-Tri-Star/210; Addressing machine — Ch. LIBRARY: Electronic — Minolta/Microfilm. WIRE SERVICES: News — AP; Receiving dishes — AP. BUSINESS COMPUTERS: PC; Applications: Nomads: Accts receivable.

NEVADA

Vernon County
'90 U.S. Census- 8,597; E&P '96 Est. 8,246

The Nevada Daily Mail (e-tues to fri)
The Nevada Herald (S)

The Nevada Daily Mail, 131 S. Cedar; PO Box 247, Nevada, MO 64772; tel (417) 667-3344; fax (417) 667-8121. USMedia Inc. group.
Circulation: 4,095(e); 4,545(S); Sworn Oct. 9, 1995.
Price: 50¢(d); 50¢(S); $5.15/mo; $72.00/yr.
Advertising: Open inch rate $8.00(e); $8.00(S). **Representative:** Papert Companies.
News Services: AP, NEA. **Politics:** Mail-Democrat, Herald-Republican. **Established:** 1883.
Not Published: New Year; Memorial Day; Independence Day; Labor Day; Thanksgiving; Christmas.
Special Editions: Rural Magazine (monthly); Brides (Jan); Home Improvement (Mar); Graduation (May); Back-to-School (Aug); Brides (Sept); Home Improvement (Oct); Sampler Cookbook (Nov); Christmas Opening, Christmas Shoppers (Dec).
Special Weekly Sections: Senior Living (thur); The Family Entertainer, Special Occassions, Youth (S).
Magazine: Vernon County Rural (3rd wed).

CORPORATE OFFICER
President Eugene A Mace
GENERAL MANAGEMENT
Publisher Tom Larimer
Business Manager Helen Wilkinson
ADVERTISING
Manager Roger Sanders
CIRCULATION
Manager Phil Thompson
NEWS EXECUTIVE
Editor Jerry Curry
EDITORS AND MANAGERS
Columnist Angela Dasbach
Editorial Page Editor Jerry Curry
Real Estate Editor Chris Cluck
Religion Editor Sharyon Duke
Sports Editor Kelly Bradham

Market Information: Zoned editions; Split Run; TMC.
Mechanical available: Offset; Black and 3 ROP colors; insert accepted — preprinted; page cut-offs — 21".
Mechanical specifications: Type page 13" x 21"; E - 6 cols, 2 1/16", ⅛" between; A - 6 cols, 2 1/16", ⅛" between; C - 6 cols, 2 1/16", ⅛" between.
Commodity consumption: Newsprint 310 short tons; 342 metric tons; widths 28", 14", 30"; black ink 15,875 pounds; color ink 1,200 pounds; single pages printed 4,785; average pages per issue 10(d), 20(S); single plates used 6,175.
Equipment: EDITORIAL: Front-end hardware — COM/UTS, Ap/Mac. CLASSIFIED: Front-end hardware — 1-COM/UTS, 1-COM/7500. PRODUCTION: Typesetters — 2-COM/4961, 2-COM/7200; Plate exposures — 1-LE; Production cameras — 1-B; Automatic film processors — 1-LE.
PRESSROOM: Line 1 — 5-G/Community; Folders — 1-G. MAILROOM: Bundle tyer — 1-Bu, 1-St; Wrapping singles — 2-Sa; Addressing machine — 1-Ch. WIRE SERVICES: News — AP.

PARK HILLS

St. Francois County
'90 U.S. Census- 4,823; E&P '96 Est. 5,163

The Daily Journal (e-mon to fri; S)

The Daily Journal, 1513 St. Joe Dr.; PO Box A, Park Hills, MO 63601; tel (314) 431-2010; fax (314) 431-7640. Scripps League Newspapers Inc. group.
Circulation: 9,563(e); 9,563(S); Sworn Sept. 29, 1995.
Price: 50¢(d); 75¢(S); $6.50/mo; $78.00/yr.
Advertising: Open inch rate $12.91(e); $16.51(e-tues); $12.91(S).
News Services: NEA, AP. **Politics:** Independent. **Established:** 1935.
Not Published: New Year; Easter; Memorial Day; Independence Day; Labor Day; Thanksgiving; Christmas.
Special Editions: Vacation (Jan); Bride (Feb); Garden (Mar); Annual Edition (Apr); Summer Fun (May); Home Improvement (June); Newcomer's Guide (July); Back-to-School, Football (Aug); Bonn Terre, Fall Festival, New Car (Sept); Auto Care, Continuity of Care, Farmington Fall Festival (Oct); Christmas (Nov); Christmas Carols, First Baby (Dec).
Special Weekly Sections: Best Food Day (tues); Weekend Living/Entertainment (thur).

CORPORATE OFFICERS
Board Chairman/Treasurer E W Scripps
Vice Chairman/Corporate Secretary Betty Knight Scripps
President/Exec Vice Pres Roger N Warkins
Vice Pres-Finance Thomas E Wendel
GENERAL MANAGEMENT
Publisher/General Manager Ron Weir
Business Manager Dave Buerck
ADVERTISING
Manager-Classified Steve Spence
Manager-Display Steve Spence
CIRCULATION
Manager Kerri Keefel
NEWS EXECUTIVE
Managing Editor Joseph Layden
EDITORS AND MANAGERS
Action Line Editor Joseph Layden
Auto Editor Joseph Layden
Business Manager Dave Buerck
Business/Finance Editor Joseph Layden
City/Metro Editor Sara Heimburger
Editorial Page Editor Joseph Layden
Editorial Writer Joseph Layden
Education Editor Sara Heimburger
Entertainment/Amusements Editor Sara Heimburger
Environmental Editor Sara Heimburger
Farm/Agriculture Editor Joseph Layden
Fashion/Style Editor Sara Heimburger
Features/Religion Editor Sara Heimburger
Food/Women's Editor Sara Heimburger
Health/Medical Editor Sara Heimburger
News Editor Joseph Layden
Political Editor Joseph Layden
Science/Technology Editor Sara Heimburger
Sports Editor Joe Miller
Television/Film Editor Sara Heimburger
Theater/Music Editor Sara Heimburger
Travel Editor Sara Heimburger
Wire Editor Joseph Layden
PRODUCTION
Manager Ronald Breise
Foreman-Pressroom Ronald Breise

Market Information: TMC.
Mechanical available: Offset; Black and 3 ROP colors; insert accepted — preprinted, 7½x11 min; page cut-offs — 22½".
Mechanical specifications: Type page 13" x 21½"; E - 6 cols, 2 1/16", ⅛" between; A - 6 cols, 2 1/16", ⅛" between; C - 9 cols, 1⅜", 1/16" between.
Commodity consumption: Newsprint 483 short tons; 532 metric tons; widths 27½", 13¾"; black ink 18,600 pounds; color ink 2,890 pounds; single pages printed 4,492; average pages per issue 15(d), 12(S); single plates used 2,246.
Equipment: EDITORIAL: Front-end hardware — 13-ScrippSat/PC; Front-end software — PC Type; Printers — QMS/820; Other equipment — Graphic Center. CLASSIFIED: Front-end hardware — 2-ScrippSat/PC; Front-end software — ScrippSat/Synaptic; Printers — QMS/Okidata 393. DISPLAY: Adv layout systems — ScrippSat, 2-Panasonic/M-1900;

I-232 Missouri

Front-end software — Archetype/Corel Draw; Printers — 3-QMS/Turbo, LaserMaster/Unity 1800x60. PRODUCTION: Pagination software — QPS; OCR software — Type Reader; Typesetters — QMS/820 Turbo; Plate exposures — B/Plateburner; Plate processors — Graham; Scanners — HP/ScanJet IIc; Production cameras — K/Vertical; Automatic film processors — LE/LD-18; Color separation equipment (conventional) — Nikon/Coolscan; Digital color separation equipment — Adobe/Photostop.
PRESSROOM: Line 1 — 7-G/Community (1 stack unit); Line 2 — 1-G/Community (stack unit); Folders — 1-G/SC. MAILROOM: Inserters and stuffers — KAN/320; Bundle tyer — Bu, MLN. LIBRARY: Combination — Dukane/ Microfilm, Bound Volume. COMMUNICATIONS: Facsimile — PB/8100. WIRE SERVICES: News — AP; Syndicates — SHNS; Receiving dishes — size-1.5 ft, AP. BUSINESS COMPUTERS: 7-ScrippSat; Applications: Lotus 1-2-3, WordPerfect; PCs & micros networked; PCs & main system networked.

POPLAR BLUFF

Butler County

'90 U.S. Census- 16,996; E&P '96 Est. 16,879

Daily American Republic

(e-mon to fri; S)

Daily American Republic, 206 Poplar St., Poplar Bluff, MO 63901; tel (314) 785-1414; fax (314) 785-2706. Rust Communications group.

Circulation: 13,309(e); 13,293(e-wed); 13,562(S); CAC Sept. 30, 1995.
Price: 50¢(d); 50¢(wed); $1.00(S); $7.00/mo.
Advertising: Open inch rate $11.87(e); $12.36(e-wed); $12.36(S). **Representative:** Papert Companies.
News Services: AP, NYT. **Politics:** Independent. **Established:** 1895.
Not Published: New Year; Memorial Day; Independence Day; Labor Day; Thanksgiving; Christmas.
Magazine: TV Update.

CORPORATE OFFICER

President Gary W Rust

GENERAL MANAGEMENT

Publisher Don Schrieber
Business Manager/Controller Rhonda Fox

ADVERTISING

Director Joe Jordan

CIRCULATION

Director Steve Mercer

NEWS EXECUTIVE

Editor Stan Berry

EDITORS AND MANAGERS

Agriculture Editor Stan Berry
Business Editor John Willy
Lifestyle Editor Michele Frederick
News Editor John Willy
Outdoors Editor Ron Smith
Religion Editor Barbara Horton
Sports Editor Ron Smith

PRODUCTION

Foreman-Pressroom Randy Graves

Market Information: Zoned editions; TMC.
Mechanical available: Offset; Black and 2 ROP colors; insert accepted — preprinted, product samples; page cut-offs — 22¾".
Mechanical specifications: Type page 13" x 21½"; E - 6 cols, 2¹⁄₁₆", ⅛" between; A - 6 cols, 2¹⁄₁₆", ⅛" between; C - 6 cols, 2¹⁄₁₆", ⅛" between.
Commodity consumption: Newsprint 750 short tons; widths 27", 13½"; average pages per issue 23(d), 48(S).
Equipment: EDITORIAL: Front-end hardware — 1-COM/UTS, 1-RSK/TRS 80-Model 100. CLASSIFIED: Front-end hardware — 1-COM/UC. DISPLAY: Adv layout systems — 2-COM/Advantage I. PRODUCTION: Typesetters — 1-COM/8600, 1-COM/Unisetter, 2-COM/7200; Plate exposures — 1-Nu/SP40APNS; Production cameras — 1-B/4000; Automatic film processors — 1-LE/LD-18, 1-DP/Chronaflow.
PRESSROOM: Line 1 — 5-G/Urbanite; Folders — 1-G/2:1. MAILROOM: Bundle tyer — 1-Malow; Addressing machine — RSK/TRS 80. WIRE SERVICES: News — AP, NYT; Receiving dishes — AP. BUSINESS COMPUTERS: 1-RSK/TRS 80-16B; Applications: Payroll, Gen ledger, Accts, Circ, Adv; PCs & micros networked; PCs & main system networked.

RICHMOND

Ray County

'90 U.S. Census- 5,738; E&P '96 Est. 5,944

The Daily News (e-mon to fri)

The Daily News, 204 W. North Main; PO Box 100, Richmond, MO 64085; tel (816) 776-5454; fax (816) 637-1639. Fackelman Newspapers group.

Circulation: 3,113(e); Sworn Sept. 26, 1995.
Price: 50¢(d); $6.75/mo; $51.50/yr, $57.00/yr (mail).
Advertising: Open inch rate $6.75(e). **Politics:** Independent. **Established:** 1914.
Not Published: New Year; Independence Day; Labor Day; Thanksgiving; Christmas.
Special Editions: Year In Review; Bridal Registry; Health & Fitness; Agri-Business; Pillars of Progress, Pharmacy Tab, Drug Tab, Senior Citizen Tab, Doctor's Day (Mar); Spring Home Improvement Guide (Apr); Mushroom Festival Guide, Graduation Tab (May); Agri-Business Tab, Fishing Contest, Ray County Fair Tab, Potato Festival Tab, Back-to-School Savings, Mosquito Fest Tab, Football Contest (Sept); Business Focus, Fall Car Care (Oct); Community Focus, Christmas Gift Guide, Twelve Days of Christmas, Football Forecast (Nov); Greetings and Letters to Santa (Dec).

CORPORATE OFFICERS

President Ann Nixon
Vice Pres-Operations Marc A Richard
Secretary Ann Fackelman
Treasurer Broward E Ratliff

GENERAL MANAGEMENT

Publisher Syd Kibodeaux
Business Manager Colette Kibodeaux

ADVERTISING

Manager Colette Kibodeaux

MARKETING AND PROMOTION

Manager-Marketing/Promotion Colette Kibodeaux

CIRCULATION

Manager Beverly Halloway

NEWS EXECUTIVE

Editor Randy Roberts

EDITORS AND MANAGERS

Aviation/Books Editor Syd Kibodeaux
Columnist Syd Kibodeaux
Editorial Page Editor Syd Kibodeaux
Education Editor Syd Kibodeaux
Features Editor Syd Kibodeaux
Health/Lifestyle Editor Syd Kibodeaux
Librarian Syd Kibodeaux
Radio/Television Editor Syd Kibodeaux
Religion Editor Syd Kibodeaux
Science/Technology Editor Syd Kibodeaux
Sports Editor Syd Kibodeaux

PRODUCTION

Manager Beverly Halloway

Market Information: TMC.
Mechanical available: Offset; Black and 3 ROP colors; insert accepted — preprinted, advertising supplements must have "supplement to Daily News"; page cut-offs — 22¾".
Mechanical specifications: Type page 12¼" x 21½"; E - 7 cols, 2¹⁄₁₆", ⅛" between; A - 7 cols, 2¹⁄₁₆", ⅛" between; C - 8 cols, 2¹⁄₁₆", ⅛" between.
Commodity consumption: Newsprint 120 short tons; widths 27½", 27½", 13¾"; black ink 20,000 pounds; color ink 1,000 pounds; single pages printed 2,000; average pages per issue 10(d); single plates used 1,506.
Equipment: CLASSIFIED: Front-end hardware — 1-Ap/Mac. DISPLAY: Adv layout systems — 1-Ap/Mac. PRODUCTION: Typesetters — 2-Ap/Mac; Platemaking systems — 1-Nu; Plate exposures — 1-Nu/Flip Top; Plate processors — 1-Ic/ICM 25; Production cameras — 1-R/400; Automatic film processors — 1-LE/18 in.
PRESSROOM: Line 1 — 5-G/Community; Folders — 1-G/3:2. MAILROOM: Counter stackers — 1-BG/Count-O-Veyor; Bundle tyer — 1-Bu; Wrapping singles — 2-Sa; Addressing machine — 1-Ch/41. COMMUNICATIONS: Facsimile — 1-Ch. BUSINESS COMPUTERS: IBM/5120, Ap/Mac; PCs & micros networked; PCs & main system networked.

ROLLA

Phelps County

'90 U.S. Census- 14,090; E&P '96 Est. 14,777

Rolla Daily News

(e-mon to fri; S)

Rolla Daily News, 101 W. 7th; PO Box 808, Rolla, MO 65402; tel (314) 364-2468; fax (314) 341-5847. Hollinger International Inc. group.

Circulation: 4,711(e); 4,711(S); Sworn Sept. 25, 1995.
Price: 50¢(d); 75¢(S); $89.00/yr.
Advertising: Open inch rate $8.45(e); $9.65(S).
News Service: AP. **Politics:** Independent. **Established:** 1875.
Note: This publication is printed at the Waynesville Daily Fort Gateway Guide.
Not Published: New Year; Memorial Day; Independence Day; Labor Day; Thanksgiving; Christmas.
Special Editions: Bridal (Jan); Newcomers (Feb); Lawn & Garden, St. Pat's (Mar); Home Building & Improvement, Fashion, Car Care (Apr); Progress (July); Back-to-School (Aug); Football, Welcome Back Students (College) (Sept); Care Care (Oct); Christmas (Nov); Fashion, Car Care, Christmas (Dec).
Magazines: TV Week, TV Guide, Features/Living (S).

GENERAL MANAGEMENT

Publisher Stephen E Sowers

ADVERTISING

Manager Lonna Stephenson

CIRCULATION

Supervisor Joe Shelton

NEWS EXECUTIVE

Editor Stephen E Sowers

EDITOR AND MANAGER

Society Editor R D Hohenfeldt

Market Information: TMC; ADS; Electronic edition.
Mechanical available: Offset; Black and 4 ROP colors; insert accepted — preprinted; page cut-offs — 21".
Mechanical specifications: Type page 13¾" x 21"; E - 6 cols, 2", ⅛" between; A - 6 cols, 2", ⅛" between; C - 6 cols, 2", ⅛" between.
Commodity consumption: average pages per issue 12(d), 40(S).
Equipment: EDITORIAL: Front-end software — TC; Printers — Ap/Mac LaserWriter II; Other equipment — Rem. CLASSIFIED: Front-end software — TC; Printers — Epson. DISPLAY: Front-end hardware — 3-Ap/Mac SE; Front-end software — QuarkXPress; Printers — Ap/Mac LaserWriter II; Other equipment — Ap/Mac Scanner. PRODUCTION: Plate exposures — 1-Nat/A-250; Plate processors — 1-Nat/A-250; Production cameras — 1-Acti/183; Automatic film processors — 1-AG/Rapidline 43. MAILROOM: Bundle tyer — 1-Strapper/Transpak, S/323; Addressing machine — 1-Ch. WIRE SERVICES: News — Syndicates — AP; Receiving dishes — size-11ft, AP. BUSINESS COMPUTERS: 2-Amdek/268A, Nomad.

ST. JOSEPH

Buchanan County

'90 U.S. Census- 71,852; E&P '96 Est. 68,103
ABC-CZ (90): 75,757 (HH 29,840)

St. Joseph News-Press

(m-mon to fri; m-sat; S)

St. Joseph News-Press, 825 Edmond St.; PO Box 29, St. Joseph, MO 64502-0029; tel (816) 271-8500; fax (816) 271-8696.

Circulation: 41,887(m); 41,887(m-sat); 47,040(S); ABC Sept. 30, 1995.
Price: 50¢(d); 75¢(sat); $1.25(S); $10.85/mo; $123.69/yr.
Advertising: Open inch rate $30.42(m); $30.42(m-sat); $31.92(S).
News Services: AP, KRT. **Politics:** Independent. **Established:** 1845 (Gazette).
Special Editions: Tax Tab (Jan); Progress, Home Improvement, Car Care (Apr); Brides (May); Newcomer's Guide (June); Football (Aug); Fall Home Improvement, Health & Fitness (Sept); Fall Car Care, Cookbook (Oct); Gift Guide (Nov); Youth At Heart (monthly).
Special Weekly Sections: Best Food Day (wed); Consumers's Guide (sat); Travel Page, Building and Garden, Business/Financial (S).
Magazine: Parade (S).
Cable TV: Own cable TV in circulation area.

CORPORATE OFFICERS

Board Chairman/Treasurer Hank Bradley
President David R Bradley Jr
Vice Pres-Finance/Secretary Lyle Leimkuhler

GENERAL MANAGEMENT

Publisher David R Bradley Jr
Controller Bruce Kneib

ADVERTISING

Director Richard Heath
Manager-National Richard Thacker
Manager-Retail Martin Novak
Manager-Classified Wilma Goodwin

TELECOMMUNICATIONS

Audiotex Manager Gary Butler

CIRCULATION

Director Lee Sawyer
Manager-Office Nadine Pinzino
Manager-Home Delivery (City) Kevin Smith
Manager-Regional Sales Chris Zey

NEWS EXECUTIVES

Editor David R Bradley Jr
Exec Editor Robert Unger

EDITORS AND MANAGERS

City Editor Ken Newton
Editorial Page Editor Mark Sheenan
Features Editor Preston Filbert
Radio/Television Editor Denise Kerns
Photo Editor Denny Simmons
Sports Editor Paul Suellentrop

MANAGEMENT INFORMATION SERVICES

Data Processing Manager Bruce Kneib

PRODUCTION

Superintendent-Pre Press Charles Fertig
Superintendent-Camera/Plate/Press Michael Kneale
Superintendent-Mailroom Robert Simpson

Market Information: Zoned editions; Split Run; TMC; Operate audiotex.
Mechanical available: Offset; Black and 3 ROP colors; insert accepted — preprinted; page cut-offs — 22¾".
Mechanical specifications: Type page 13" x 21½"; E - 6 cols, 2¹⁄₁₆", ⅛" between; A - 6 cols, 2¹⁄₁₆", ⅛" between; C - 9 cols, 1⅜", ¹⁄₁₆" between.
Commodity consumption: Newsprint 3,419 metric tons; widths 55", 44¼"; black ink 100,000 pounds; color ink 32,000 pounds; single pages printed 17,010; average pages per issue 32(d), 60(S); single plates used 50,000.
Equipment: EDITORIAL: Front-end hardware — Dewar, PC; Front-end software — Dewar; Printers — Okidata/393. CLASSIFIED: Front-end hardware — Dewar, PC; Front-end software — Dewar; Printers — Okidata/393. AUDIOTEX: Hardware — Brite Voice Systems. DISPLAY: Adv layout systems — Dewar; Front-end hardware — Dewar, Sun/Sparc, Ap/Mac Quadra 950; Front-end software — Dewar, AG, Adobe/Photoshop, QuarkXPress, Aldus/Free-Hand; Printers — Okidata/393; Other equipment — Mk/Scanner, Lf/AP Leaf Picture Desk, Caere/OmniPage. PRODUCTION: Pagination software — Dewar; OCR software — Caere/ OmniPage; Typesetters — 2-MON/Laser Comp Mark 2, Sun/Sparc 2, Sun/Sparc 2, MON/ Graphic System 2 (2.7); Plate exposures — 2-Nu/Flip Top FT40; Plate processors — 1-Nu/A-340; Electronic picture desk — Lf/AP Leaf Picture Desk, MGS; Scanners — 1-ECR/Autokon 2000, Pixel/Craft, X/7650, Microtek/600 ZS; Production cameras — 1-SCREEN/510E; Automatic film processors — 2-AG/Litex 26; Reproportion units — MON/Graphic System 2 (2.7); Digital color separation equipment — Ap/Mac Quadra 950, Adobe/Photoshop, Ap/Mac 8100, Ap/Mac 9500 FS.
PRESSROOM: Line 1 — 7-G/Cosmo; Line 2 — 1-G/Metro Color Tower, 11-G; Folders — 1-G/Double; Pasters — G/Automatic; Press control system — Fin. MAILROOM: Counter stackers — 2-CN/70, MM; Inserters and stuffers — MM/319 Print Roll, MM/308 BiLiner; Bundle tyer — 2-MLN/News 90; Wrapping singles — 2-Id/Plastic; Addressing machine — 1-Ch/515; Other mailroom equipment — MM/321 Saddle Stitcher. LIBRARY: Electronic — SMS. WIRE SERVICES: News — AP; Receiving dishes — size-8ft, AP. BUSINESS COMPUTERS: IBM/Sys 36; Applications: Accts receivable, Accts payable, Gen ledger; PCs & micros networked; PCs & main system networked.

ST. LOUIS

An Independent City

'90 U.S. Census- 396,685; E&P '96 Est. 383,758
ABC-NDM (90): 2,117,990 (HH 803,272)

St. Louis Post-Dispatch

(m-mon to fri; m-sat; S)

St. Louis Post-Dispatch, 900 N. Tucker Blvd., St. Louis, MO 63101; tel (314) 340-8000; fax (314) 340-3140; e-mail letters@pd.stlnet.com; web site http://www.stlnet.com/. Pulitzer Publishing Co. group.

Circulation: 319,990(m); 302,867(m-sat); 538,956(S); ABC Sept. 30, 1995.
Price: 50¢(d); 50¢(sat); $1.25(S).
Advertising: Open inch rate $159.00(m); $159.00(m-sat); $217.80(S). **Representative:** Newhouse Newspapers/Metro Suburbia.
News Services: AP, KRT, LAT-WP, NYT, RN, SHNS. **Politics:** Independent. **Established:** 1878.
Advertising not accepted: Any advertising judged not to be in the readers' best interests.
Special Editions: Weddings, Boat and Sport Show (Feb); Working Women's Survival Show, Spring Fashion, Homestyle (Mar); Pools & Patios, Cardinal Baseball, Lawn, Garden and Home Improvement, Dining Out, Golf Guide (Apr); Mother's Day Gift Guide, Top 50 Businesses (May); The Muny, Fair St. Louis (June); Senior Lifestyles (July); Fall Fashion, Football 1996, Fall Home Furnishings (Aug); Symptoms, Fall Homestyle, Home Builders Association Show (Sept); Restaurant Guide (Oct); Christmas in St. Louis, Christmas Gift Guide (Nov).
Special Weekly Sections: Food, Business Plus (mon); Style West (West Zone only) (thur); Style Plus, Travel (S).
Magazines: "Get Out" Entertainment (thur); Television Magazine (S); St. Louis Post-Dispatch Magazine (roto); Parade.
Broadcast Affiliates: KTAR-AM/KKLT-FM Phoenix; WESH Daytona Beach (Orlando ADI), FL; KCCI Des Moines, IA; WLKY Louisville, KY; WXII Winston-Salem, NC; KETV Omaha, NE; KOAT Albuquerque; WGAL Lancaster, PA; WYFF Greenville, SC.

CORPORATE OFFICERS

Board Chairman/President/CEO Michael E Pulitzer
Chairman/Pulitzer 2000 David Lipman
Editor William F Woo
Publisher Nicholas G Penniman IV
Senior Vice Pres-Finance Ronald H Ridgway
Vice Pres-Administration Joseph Pulitzer IV
Vice Pres/Director-Operations Marvin G Kanne
Vice Pres Jeff Edwards

GENERAL MANAGEMENT

Controller Don Zitko
Manager-Credit Gary Voelker
Purchasing Agent Nylin Bathke
Manager-Office Sandy Kay

ADVERTISING

Vice Pres/Director Thomas L Rees
Manager-Display Del Schwinke
Manager-National Gary Plackemeier
Manager-Classified John M Laufer

MARKETING AND PROMOTION

Vice Pres/Director-Marketing Lynne Moeller
Manager-Promotion Debbie Milligan
Manager-Public Relations Nancy Long

TELECOMMUNICATIONS

Director-Info Systems Daniel V Krietemeyer
Audiotex Manager Rebecca Bowman

CIRCULATION

Director Fred Matthias
Manager Bernie Andrews

NEWS EXECUTIVES

Editor William F Woo
Managing Editor Foster Davis
Deputy Managing Editor Ronald Willnow
Asst Managing Editor-News Carolyn Kingcade
Asst Managing Editor-Special Projects Richard Weil Jr
Newsroom Administration John Brophy

EDITORS AND MANAGERS

Art Department Director Tony Lazorko
Arts Editor Robert Duffy
Books Jane Reed
Business/Finance Editor David Nicklaus
City Editor Tim Bross
City Editor-Night Ed Kohn
Commentary Page Editor Donna Korando
Copy Editor Susan Clotfelter
Editorial Page Editor Edward Higgins
Asst Editorial Page Editor Dale Singer
Editorial Cartoonist Thomas A Engelhardt
Editorial Writer William Flannery
Editorial Writer Repps Hudson
Editorial Writer Susan Hegger
Editorial Writer John E Bremner
Editorial Writer Robert Joiner
Entertainment Editor Ellen Futterman
Fashion Editor Becky Homan
Features Director Richard Weiss
Films Editor Harper Barnes
Food Editor Judy Evans
Illinois Editor Mark Peterson
International/National News Editor Margaret Freivogel
Librarian Gerald Brown
Lifestyle Editor Ellen Gardner
Metro Editor Laszlo Domjan
Music/Art Editor Robert Duffy
News Editor Steve Parker
News Editor Steve Kelley
News Editor Vicki Swyers
Photo Department Manager/Photo Editor James B Forbes
Radio/Television Editor Gail Pennington
Religion Editor Pat Rice
Science Bill Allen
Exec Sports Editor Phil Gaitens
Post Dispatch Magazine Mary Leonard
Director-Technology George Landau
Theater Editor Judy Newmark
Travel Editor Kathleen Nelson
Washington Bureau Chief Jon Sawyer
Writing Coach Harry Levins

MANAGEMENT INFORMATION SERVICES

Data Processing Manager Dan Krietemeyer
Online Manager Virgil Tipton

PRODUCTION

Director David Givens
Director-Maintenance Gary Glanzner
Manager-Downtown Plant Thomas Dierzbicki
Manager-Northwest Plant/Color Quality Ralph Snyder
Manager-Offsite Inserting Plant/Mailroom Greg Timme
Manager-Systems Service Glenn Snowert
Asst Manager-Electrician/Systems Dan McGuire
Asst Manager-Newsprint Nick Gentile
Asst Manager-Northwest Plant Tom Atkins
Superintendent-Photomechanical Otto Oberheuser
General Foreman-Composing Room Ron Faveere
General Foreman-Pressroom Teddy Head
General Foreman-Paperhandling Don Stroh
General Foreman-Mailroom Larry Sartori
Foreman-Loading Dock Norvell Stengel
Foreman-Job Printing Curt Kopp
Coordinator-Layout/Schedule John Signorelli
Coordinator-Newsprint Tom Seady

Market Information: Zoned editions; Split Run; TMC; ADS; Operate database; Operate audiotex; Electronic edition.
Mechanical available: Offset; Black and 3 ROP colors; insert accepted — preprinted; page cutoffs — 23 9/16".
Mechanical specifications: Type page 13" x 22 1/2"; E - 6 cols, 2 1/16", 1/8" between; A - 6 cols, 2 1/16", 1/8" between; C - 10 cols, 1 1/2", 1/8" between.
Commodity consumption: Newsprint 88,700 short tons; 80,468 metric tons; widths 54 7/8", 54 7/8", 41 1/4"; black ink 1,500,000 pounds; color ink 320,000 pounds; single pages printed 37,500; average pages per issue 64(d), 110(S); single plates used 400,000.
Equipment: EDITORIAL: Front-end hardware — 10-AT/CPU; Other equipment — 60-IBM/PC, AT/148. CLASSIFIED: Front-end hardware — 5-AT; Other equipment — 80-AT. DISPLAY: Adv layout systems — HI/XP-21 Page Layout System; Front-end hardware — 4-Sun/Sparc 10, Ap/Mac Quadra 800, 1-Ap/Mac Quadra 950, 2-Sun/Sparc 2, 1-Sun/Sparc 5; Front-end software — HI/Page Layout Architecture; Other equipment — 16-HI/2100, 9-HI/8900. PRODUCTION: Pagination software — HI/AT; Typesetters — 3-AU/APS-108-C; Platemaking systems — 3-WL/Lith-X-Pozer; Plate exposures — 4-Nu/Flip Top; Plate processors — 4-W/38, 2-W/38; Electronic picture desk — Lf/AP Leaf Picture Desk; Scanners — 2-Kurzweil/Intelligent Character Recognition Scanner, ECR/Autokon 2045, 1-ECR/Autokon 1000 Scanner, 1-Hel/341 Scanner, 2-X, Scitex/Smartscanner, 2-X/1750, Ik/Digital; Production cameras — 1-C/Newspager, 1-R; Automatic film processors — 5-LE/X-CEL, 3-LE/2600, 1-LE/PC18; Reproportion units — 1-ECR/Autokon 1000, 1-ECR/Autokon 2045; Film transporters — 8-LE/P-D; Digital color separation equipment — Scitex System. PRESSROOM: Line 1 — 8-G/Metro; Line 2 — 8-G/Metro; Line 3 — 8-G/Metro; Line 4 — 8-G/Metro; Line 5 — 8-G/Metro; Line 6 — 8-G/Metro; Folders — 9-G; Reels and stands — 42-G/Metro. MAILROOM: Counter stackers — 2-Sh, 11-QWI, 1-HL, 2-Boss; Inserters and stuffers — 3-HI/1372P, 1-HI/1472A; Bundle tyer — 10-MLN/PD, 5-MLN/MLEE, 6-Power Strap/PSN-5, 8-Power Strap/PSN-6, 3-Sterling/MRCH 40; Wrapping singles — 10-Wm, 4-Dm. LIBRARY: Electronic — SAVE Dialog Information Services, Vu/Text SAVE. COMMUNICATIONS: Facsimile — Hel/PressFax, 2-Eskofot/12636S; Remote imagesetting — 5-Hel/210K Laser Recorders; Digital ad delivery system — AP AdSend. Systems used — microwave, fiber optic. WIRE SERVICES: News — AP, RN; Photos — AP, AFP; Stock tables — AP Dataspeed, AP SelectStox; Syndicates — North America Syndicate, United Media, King Features, United Features, TMS, Creators; Receiving dishes — size-10ft, AP, INS. BUSINESS COMPUTERS: 16-AT, 1-Unisys/110072; PCs & micros networked; PCs & main system networked.

SEDALIA

Pettis County

'90 U.S. Census- 19,800; E&P '96 Est. 18,919
ABC-CZ (90): 19,800 (HH 8,416)

The Sedalia Democrat

(e-mon to fri; m-sat; S)

The Sedalia Democrat, 7th St. and Massachusetts Ave.; PO Box 848, Sedalia, MO 65302; tel (816) 826-1000; fax (816) 826-2413. Freedom Communications Inc. group.
Circulation: 13,400(e); 13,400(m-sat); 14,388(S); ABC Sept. 30, 1995.
Price: 50¢(d); 50¢(sat); $1.25(S); $2.10/wk; $99.20/yr.
Advertising: Open inch rate $11.85(e); $11.85(m-sat); $12.44(S).
News Service: AP. **Politics:** Independent. **Established:** 1868.
Special Editions: Farm, Tax Guide, Bridal (Jan); Progress (Feb); Automotive, Home Improvement, Farm (Mar); Missouri State Fair, Newcomers (June); Back-to-School (Aug).
Special Weekly Section: Best Food Edition (wed).
Magazines: Parade, TV Week Magazine (S).

GENERAL MANAGEMENT

Publisher Frank Lyon
Controller/Purchasing Agent Galen Oehrke

ADVERTISING

Director Lisa Lynn

CIRCULATION

Manager Bill Hackney

NEWS EXECUTIVE

Managing Editor Roger Morton

EDITORS AND MANAGERS

Librarian Milene Mittelhanser
Living/Lifestyle Editor Gail Schneider
News Editor Elaine Garrison
Sports Editor Karl Zinke

PRODUCTION

Foreman-Day Al Cooper
Foreman-Pressroom (Day) John Grimes
Commercial Sales Roger Alewel

Market Information: TMC.
Mechanical available: Offset; Black and 3 ROP colors; insert accepted — preprinted; page cutoffs — 22 3/4".
Mechanical specifications: Type page 11.38" x 21 1/2"; E - 6 cols, 2 1/16", 1/8" between; A - 6 cols, 2 1/16", 1/8" between; C - 9 cols, 1 5/16", 1/8" between.
Commodity consumption: Newsprint 1,600 short tons; width 27 1/2"; single pages printed 7,300; average pages per issue 18(d), 40(S); single plates used 24,000.
Equipment: EDITORIAL: Front-end hardware — CText; Front-end software — CText; Other equipment — Lf/AP Leaf Picture Desk. CLASSIFIED: Front-end hardware — CText; Front-end software — CText; Printers — C.Itoh/On-Line. DISPLAY: Adv layout systems — Ap/Mac; Front-end hardware — Ap/Mac; Front-end software — Ap/Mac; Printers — Ap/Mac Laser-Writer II; Other equipment — Ap/Mac One Scanner. PRODUCTION: Typesetters — Tegra/Varityper; Plate exposures — 1-Nu; Plate processors — W; Production cameras — R; Automatic film processors — AG; Color separation equipment (conventional) — RZ/200S. PRESSROOM: Line 1 — 10-G/Urbanite. MAILROOM: Counter stackers — 1-HL; Inserters and stuffers — 1-MM; Bundle tyer — 2-Ovid; Addressing machine — 1-Ch. WIRE SERVICES: News — AP; Photos — AP; Receiving dishes — size-3m, AP. BUSINESS COMPUTERS: ATT; PCs & micros networked; PCs & main system networked.

SIKESTON

Scott and New Madrid Counties

'90 U.S. Census- 17,641; E&P '96 Est. 17,816

Standard Democrat

(e-mon to fri; S)

Standard Democrat, 205 S. New Madrid, Sikeston, MO 63801; tel (314) 471-1137; fax (314) 471-6277. Hollinger International Inc. group.
Circulation: 9,251(e); 9,251(S); Sworn Sept. 29, 1995.
Price: 50¢(d); $1.00(S); $5.84/mo; $70.10/yr (mail), $68.31/yr (carrier).
Advertising: Open inch rate $9.59(e); $10.90 (e-wed); $10.99(S). **Representative:** Cresmer, Woodward, O'Mara & Ormsbee.
News Service: AP. **Established:** 1913.
Not Published: New Year; Memorial Day; Independence Day; Labor Day; Thanksgiving; Christmas.
Advertising not accepted: Vending machine.
Special Edition: Progress (Feb).

GENERAL MANAGEMENT

Publisher Michael L Jensen
Accountant Lisa Seabaugh

ADVERTISING

Manager-General Deanna Nelson

CIRCULATION

Manager Howard Harper

NEWS EXECUTIVE

Managing Editor Jill Bock

EDITORS AND MANAGERS

Food Editor Tonia Pennington
News Editor John Pillars
Photo Department Manager Jill Bock
Sports Editor Dale Forbis

PRODUCTION

Foreman-Press/Camera/Platemaking Charles Lee
Foreman-Composing/Paste-Up Carolyn Lee

Market Information: Split Run; TMC.
Mechanical available: Offset; Black and 3 ROP colors; insert accepted — preprinted, card inserts; page cut-offs — 22 3/4".
Mechanical specifications: Type page 13" x 21 1/2"; E - 6 cols, 2 1/16", 1/8" between; A - 6 cols, 2 1/16", 1/8" between; C - 9 cols, 1 3/8", 1/16" between.
Commodity consumption: Newsprint 400 short tons; widths 27 1/2", 13 3/4"; average pages per issue 23(d), 67(S).
Equipment: EDITORIAL: Front-end hardware — 2-COM/UTS, Mk. CLASSIFIED: Front-end hardware — COM/UTS. PRODUCTION: Typesetters — 2-COM/Universal Videosetter; Plate exposures — 1-Nu/Flip Top; Plate processors — 1-LE/24; Production cameras — 1-R/400; Automatic film processors — 1-LE/LD24; Shrink lenses — CK Optical/SQU-7. PRESSROOM: Line 1 — 8-G/Suburban (4 + 4 side by side). MAILROOM: Inserters and stuffers — 1-MM/3 station; Bundle tyer — 2-Bu/Packaging Machine; Wrapping singles — 7-Sa/EM; Addressing machine — 1-Am/1900. WIRE SERVICES: News — AP; Receiving dishes — size-1m, AP.

SPRINGFIELD

Greene County

'90 U.S. Census- 140,494; E&P '96 Est. 146,913
ABC-CZ (90): 140,494 (HH 57,353)

Springfield News-Leader

(m-mon to sat; S)

Springfield News-Leader, 651 Boonville (65806); PO Box 798, Springfield, MO 65801; tel (417) 836-1100; fax (417) 837-1335; e-mail ninews@ozarks.sgcl.lib.mo.us. Gannett Co. Inc. group.
Circulation: 64,217(m); 64,217(m-sat); 103,607(S); ABC Sept. 24, 1995.
Price: 50¢(d); 50¢(sat); $1.75(S); $11.95/mo; $143.40/yr.
Advertising: Open inch rate $70.50(m); $70.50(m-sat); $101.30(S). **Representative:** Gannett National Newspaper Sales.
News Services: AP, GNS, NYT. **Politics:** Independent. **Established:** 1933.
Special Editions: Progress (Feb); Visitor's Guide (Mar); Answer Book (July); Nike Open (Aug); Med Facts Tab (quarterly).
Special Weekly Sections: Seniors (tues); Best Food Day (wed); Weekend Tab, Auto News (fri); Real Estate Weekly, Auto News, Church Pages (sat); Travel, Real Estate (S).
Magazines: TV View, USA Weekend (S).

GENERAL MANAGEMENT

President/Publisher Fritz Jacobi
Controller Dan Satchfield

ADVERTISING

Director Larry Whitaker
Manager-Outside Becky Nye
Manager-Outside Pam Browning
Manager-Outside Coreen Fisher
Manager-Inside Carla Powers
Manager-National Ralph Ritter
Supervisor-Tele Sales Theresa Willmann

Missouri

I-234

MARKETING AND PROMOTION
Director-Market Development .... Bruce Deaton

CIRCULATION
Director .... David Brown
Manager-Sales .... Joann Larkee
Manager-Home Delivery .... Tim Alexander
Manager-Single Copy .... Ron Marshall

NEWS EXECUTIVES
Exec Editor .... Randy Hammer
Managing Editor .... Kate Marymount

EDITORS AND MANAGERS
Business Editor .... Louise Whall
City Editor .... Chick Howland
Editorial Page Editor .... Robert Leger
Fashion Editor .... Diane Robinson
Graphics Coordinator .... John Dengler
Home Furnishings Editor .... Diane Robinson
Life/Times Editor .... Diane Robinson
Music Editor .... Ron Sylvester
Outdoor Editor .... Fran Skalicky
Photography Editor .... Dean Curtis
Projects Editor .... Kathleen O'Dell
Real Estate Editor .... Louise Whall
Sports Editor .... James Walker
Suburban Editor .... Sara Hanson
Weekend/Entertainment Editor .... Diane Robinson

MANAGEMENT INFORMATION SERVICES
Director-Info Systems .... Lynn Esser
Data Processing Manager .... Linda Barnett
Manager-Technical Service .... Jim Anton

PRODUCTION
Director .... Jim Eddins
Manager-Pre Press .... Tom Tate
Manager-Pressroom .... Don Lowry
Manager-Mailroom .... Mary Miller

Market Information: Zoned editions; Split Run; TMC.
Mechanical available: Letterpress Direct; Black and 3 ROP colors; insert accepted — preprinted, flexie single sheets; page cut-offs — 22¾".
Mechanical specifications: Type page 13" x 21½"; E - 6 cols, 2½6", ⅛" between; A - 6 cols, 2¹⁄₁₆", ⅛" between; C - 9 cols, 1³⁄₈", ¹⁄₁₆" between.
Commodity consumption: Newsprint 9,100 short tons; widths 27¼", 27¼", 54½", 40¾"; black ink 172,000 pounds; color ink 38,400 pounds; single pages printed 18,270; average pages per issue 40(d), 100(S); single plates used 63,900.
Equipment: EDITORIAL: Front-end hardware — 6-AT/Systems 4; Front-end software — AT 4.62; Printers — MON/Express, Hyphen/Spectraset 2200; Other equipment — 119-AT/VDT, 6-AT/CPU, AT/Pagination. CLASSIFIED: Front-end hardware — AT, SII/Synthesis 66; Front-end software — AT 4.73, AT 4.62, SII/Pongrass Czar; Printers — MON/Express, Hyphen/Spectraset 2200, Hyphen/Spectraset 2400. AUDIOTEX: Hardware — GMT I; Software — AdLink, Novell; Supplier name — GMT I, AdLink. DISPLAY: Adv layout systems — AT, Ap/Mac; Front-end hardware — Sun, Ap/Mac Quadra 950, Ap/Mac Quadra 750, Ap/Mac LC, Ap/Mac cx, Ap/Mac ci; Front-end software — AT/R2, Multi-Ad/Creator, Broderbund/TypeStyler, Adobe/Photoshop, Type/Manager; Printers — MON/Express, AG/2200, Copal/Dash 600, Tektronix/Phaser III; Other equipment — 28-ADT, AT/CLSPAC, 2-AT/Dats. PRODUCTION: Pagination software — AT 4.62, AT/R2, SII/Pongrass Czar; Typesetters — MON/Express, AG/2200, Hyphen/Spectraset 2200, Hyphen/Spectraset 2400; Platemaking systems — Na; Plate exposures — 1-Na/Starlite plate burner; Plate processors — 2-Na/1025000 plate processor; Electronic picture desk — Lf/AP Leaf Picture Desk; Scanners — 1-Microtek/MRS-600zs, 1-Pro Imager/ 8000 Pixelcraft; Production cameras — R/ Comet 500, C/Spartan III; Automatic film processors — C/66F processor; Reproportion units — ECR/Autokon 1000; Film transporters — LE/MTP-26 Sliding Transport; Color separation equipment (conventional) — Lf/AP Leaf Picture Desk, Adobe/Photoshop; Digital color separation equipment — 1-Microtek/MRS-600zs, Lf/AP Leaf Picture Desk, Adobe/Photoshop. PRESSROOM: Line 1 — 8-G/Headliner Mark II; Press drives — Fin; Folders — 2-G; Pasters — G, Fin; Press control system — Fin; Press registration system — G. MAILROOM: Counter stackers — 3-HL/Monitor; Inserters and stuffers — HI/72P; Bundle tyer — 3-MLN/News 90, 2-MLN/1-EE; Wrapping singles — Kraft/Paper; Addressing machine — Ch. LIBRARY: Electronic — Digital Collections Archiving/Picture-

Desk. COMMUNICATIONS: Systems used — satellite. WIRE SERVICES: News — AP, GNS, NYT; Photos — AP; Stock tables — AP SelectStox; Receiving dishes — size-3m, AP, UPI, NSN. BUSINESS COMPUTERS: 1-IBM/AS400; Applications: Lotus R.5: Circ, Class billing, Accts payable, Accts receivable; WordPerfect, Microsoft/Windows; PCs & micros networked; PCs & main system networked.

TRENTON
Grundy County
'90 U.S. Census- 6,129; E&P '96 Est. 5,620

Republican-Times
(e-mon to fri)

Republican-Times, 122 E. 8th St.; PO Box 548, Trenton, MO 64683; tel (816) 359-2212; fax (816) 359-4414.
Circulation: 3,348(e); Sworn Oct. 4, 1995.
Price: 50¢(d); $40.00/yr.
Advertising: Open inch rate $4.65(e).
News Service: AP. **Politics:** Independent. **Established:** 1864.
Not Published: New Year; Memorial Day; Independence Day; Labor Day; Thanksgiving; Christmas.
Advertising not accepted: Alcoholic beverages.
Special Editions: Graduation (May); Fall Sports (Aug); Fall Outdoors (Oct).
Special Weekly Section: TV Guide (thur).
Cable TV: Operate leased cable TV in circulation area.

CORPORATE OFFICERS
President .... Wendell Lenhart
Vice Pres .... Sandra S Alexander
Secretary/Treasurer .... Wendell Lenhart

GENERAL MANAGEMENT
Purchasing Agent .... Wendell Lenhart

ADVERTISING
Director .... DeLane Hein

NEWS EXECUTIVE
Managing Editor .... Wendell Lenhart

EDITOR AND MANAGER
News Editor .... Diane Raynes

MANAGEMENT INFORMATION SERVICES
Data Processing Manager .... Wendell Lenhart

Market Information: TMC; ADS.
Mechanical available: Offset; Black and 3 ROP colors; insert accepted — preprinted; page cut-offs — 21".
Mechanical specifications: Type page 13" x 21"; E - 6 cols, 2¹⁄₁₆", ⅛" between; A - 6 cols, 2¹⁄₁₆", ⅛" between; C - 6 cols, 2¹⁄₁₆", ⅛" between.
Commodity consumption: Newsprint 120 metric tons; widths 28", 28", 14"; black ink 5,000 pounds; color ink 300 pounds; single pages printed 2,700; average pages per issue 10(d); single plates used 1,500.
Equipment: EDITORIAL: Front-end hardware — Ap/Power Mac; Front-end software — QuarkXPress; Printers — Ap/Mac LaserWriter II NTX, HP/LaserJet 4MV. CLASSIFIED: Front-end hardware — Ap/Power Mac; Front-end software — QuarkXPress; Printers — Ap/Power Mac LaserWriter II NTX. DISPLAY: Front-end hardware — Ap/Power Mac 8100; Front-end software — QuarkXpress; Printers — Ap/Mac LaserWriter II NTX. PRODUCTION: Typesetters — Ap/Mac LaserWriter II NTX, HP/LaserJet 4MR; Plate exposures — 1-Nu; Direct-to-plate imaging — HP/ScanJet 3P, Polaroid/Spirit Scan 35; Production cameras — R/Vertical; Automatic film processors — Glunz & Jensen/ML400. PRESSROOM: Line 1 — 4-KP; Press drives — Fin. MAILROOM: Bundle tyer — Bu. WIRE SERVICES: News — AP; Receiving dishes — size-1m, AP. BUSINESS COMPUTERS: PC/486; Applications: Accts receivable, Accts payable, Payroll, Gen ledger, Circ; PCs & micros networked.

WARRENSBURG
Johnson County
'90 U.S. Census- 15,244; E&P '96 Est. 16,552
ABC-CZ (90): 15,244 (HH 5,002)

The Daily Star-Journal
(e-mon to fri)

The Daily Star-Journal, 135 E. Market St.; PO Box 68, Warrensburg, MO 64093; tel (816) 747-8123; fax (816) 747-8110.
Circulation: 4,842(e); ABC Sept. 30, 1995.

Price: 50¢(d); $48.00/yr.
Advertising: Open inch rate $5.00(e).
News Service: AP. **Politics:** Independent. **Established:** 1865.
Not Published: New Year; Independence Day; Labor Day; Thanksgiving; Christmas.
Special Editions: Christmas Shopping; 4-H; Christmas Greetings; Back-to-School; Car Care; Spring and Fall Home Improvement; Spring; Graduation.

CORPORATE OFFICER
President .... Avis G Tucker

GENERAL MANAGEMENT
Publisher .... Avis G Tucker
Business Manager .... Avis G Tucker

ADVERTISING
Manager .... Don W Kirkpatrick
Manager-Promotion .... Don W Kirkpatrick

CIRCULATION
Director .... Russle Kenney

NEWS EXECUTIVE
Editor .... Avis G Tucker

EDITORS AND MANAGERS
Editorial Page Editor .... Avis G Tucker
News Editor .... Nan Cocke
Picture Editor .... David Kopp
Sports Editor .... David Kopp

Market Information: TMC.
Mechanical available: Offset; Black and 3 ROP colors; insert accepted — preprinted; page cut-offs — 22¾".
Mechanical specifications: Type page 13" x 21"; E - 4 cols, 3¹⁄₁₆", ⅛" between; A - 6 cols, 2¹⁄₁₆", ⅛" between; C - 6 cols, 2¹⁄₁₆", ⅛" between.
Commodity consumption: Newsprint 404 short tons; widths 28", 14"; black ink 11,800 pounds; color ink 2,800 pounds; single pages printed 5,800; average pages per issue 20(d); single plates used 4,000.
Equipment: EDITORIAL: Front-end hardware — 7-Mitsuba/PC; Front-end software — Mk. CLASSIFIED: Front-end hardware — 1-Mitsuba/PC; Front-end software — Mk; Printers — 1-Okidata/2410. PRODUCTION: Typesetters — 1-PC, 2-Ap/Mac II; Plate exposures — 1-Nu; Production cameras — 1-DAI; Automatic film processors — 1-P/26EZ. PRESSROOM: Line 1 — 1-HI/Cotrell V150; Line 2 — 1-Ryobi/11x17; Line 3 — 1-HI/L125C(0). MAILROOM: Inserters and stuffers — KAN/480; Bundle tyer — 1-Strap Tyer/50; Addressing machine — Ch/582N Labeler. WIRE SERVICES: News — AP; Receiving dishes — size-3ft, AP. BUSINESS COMPUTERS: 2-IBM/3151; Applications: PBS/MediaPlus; Billing, Booking.

WAYNESVILLE
Pulaski County
'90 U.S. Census- 3,207; E&P '96 Est. 3,508

Daily Fort Gateway Guide
(e-mon to fri)

Daily Guide, 108 Holly Dr. (St. Robert); PO Box 578, Waynesville, MO 65583; tel (314) 336-3711; fax (314) 336-4640. Hollinger International Inc. group.
Circulation: 2,631(e); Sworn Sept. 30, 1994.
Price: 50¢(d); $64.15/yr.
Advertising: Open inch rate $9.20(e). Representative: American Newspaper Representatives Inc.
News Service: AP. **Politics:** Independent. **Established:** 1967.
Not Published: New Year; Memorial Day; Independence Day; Thanksgiving; Christmas.
Special Edition: Progress Edition (Feb to Sept).
Magazines: Own newsprint Mag (fri); Entertainment.

CORPORATE OFFICER
President .... Larry J Perrotto

GENERAL MANAGEMENT
Publisher .... Tim Berrier
Business Manager .... Becky Hendrix

ADVERTISING
Director .... Rendy Conant

CIRCULATION
Manager .... Keith Hatley

EDITORS AND MANAGERS
City Editor .... Carrol Wood
Sports Editor .... Ray Campbell

Market Information: Zoned editions; TMC.
Mechanical available: Offset; Black and 3 ROP colors; insert accepted — preprinted; page cut-offs — 22¾".
Mechanical specifications: Type page 13" x 21½"; E - 6 cols, 2¹⁄₁₆", ⅛" between; A - 6 cols, 2¹⁄₁₆", ⅛" between; C - 6 cols, 2¹⁄₁₆", ⅛" between.

Commodity consumption: Newsprint 960 short tons; widths 27½", 37", 13¾"; black ink 23,000 pounds; color ink 2,000 pounds; single pages printed 2,560; average pages per issue 10(d); single plates used 18,000.
Equipment: EDITORIAL: Printers — Ap/Mac LaserWriter II NT. DISPLAY: Adv layout systems — Ap/Mac SE. PRODUCTION: Typesetters — Ap/Mac LaserWriter II NT; Plate exposures — 1-Nu; Plate processors — 1-Roconex; Scanners — Ap/Mac One; Production cameras — 1-Nu; Automatic film processors — 1-LE, 1-AG/Rapid.
PRESSROOM: Line 1 — 7-G/Community (Balloon former); Folders — 1-G/SC, 1-G/Community. MAILROOM: Counter stackers — BG; Addressing machine — 1-Am. WIRE SERVICES: News — AP; Receiving dishes — size-11ft, AP. BUSINESS COMPUTERS: 1-DEC/W778; Applications: Billing.

WEST PLAINS
Howell County
'90 U.S. Census- 8,913; E&P '96 Est. 10,026

West Plains Daily Quill
(e-mon to fri)

West Plains Daily Quill, 125 N. Jefferson; PO Box 110, West Plains, MO 65775; tel (417) 256-9191; fax (417) 256-9196.
Circulation: 9,363(e); Sworn Sept. 28, 1995.
Price: 30¢(d); $5.50/mo; $60.00/yr.
Advertising: Open inch rate $8.00(e).
News Service: AP. **Politics:** Democrat. **Established:** 1902.
Not Published: New Year; Memorial Day; Independence Day; Labor Day; Thanksgiving; Christmas.
Special Editions: Home Improvement (Mar); Lawn & Garden, Recreation (Apr); Football (Aug).
Special Weekly Sections: Food, Arts, Ag, Outdoors (wed); Real Estate, Auctions (fri).
Magazine: Kaleidoscope (TV Guide) (fri).

CORPORATE OFFICERS
President .... Frank L Martin III
Secretary/Treasurer .... Frank L Martin III

GENERAL MANAGEMENT
Publisher .... Frank L Martin III
General Manager .... Jerry P Womack
Business Manager .... Judy Collins
Purchasing Agent .... Pat Caplinger

ADVERTISING
Manager .... Sunie Pace

CIRCULATION
Manager .... Stacey Moorhead

NEWS EXECUTIVES
Editor .... Frank L Martin III
Managing Editor .... Jerry P Womack

EDITORS AND MANAGERS
Amusements Editor .... Julie Warner
Arts/Theater Editor .... Vickie Taylor
Business/Finance Editor .... Chris White
City Editor .... Carol Bruce
Editorial Page Editor .... Frank L Martin III
Education Editor .... Ron Woolman
Entertainment Editor .... Vickie Taylor
Environmental Editor .... Carol Bruce
Farm Editor .... Dennis Crider
Fashion Editor .... Chris White
Features Editor .... Jerry Womack
Food Editor .... Julie Warner
Health/Medical Editor .... Vickie Taylor
Home Furnishings Editor .... Chris White
National Editor .... Carol Bruce
News Editor .... Carol Bruce
Photo Editor .... Carol Bruce
Political/Government Editor .... Frank L Martin III
Religion Editor .... Carol Bruce
Science Editor .... Frank L Martin III
Society/Women's Editor .... Chris White
Sports Editor .... Dennis Crider
Teen-Age/Youth Editor .... Chris White
Television/Film Editor .... Vickie Taylor
Theater/Music Editor .... Vickie Taylor
Travel Editor .... Carol Bruce

MANAGEMENT INFORMATION SERVICES
Data Processing Manager .... Jerry Womack

PRODUCTION
Manager .... Pat Caplinger

Mechanical available: Offset; Black and 3 ROP colors; insert accepted — preprinted; page cut-offs — 21".
Mechanical specifications: Type page 13" x 21"; E - 6 cols, 2", ⅛" between; A - 6 cols, 2", ⅛" between; C - 6 cols, 2", ⅛" between.
Commodity consumption: Newsprint 2,400 short tons; widths 14", 28", 35"; black ink 11,200 pounds; color ink 500 pounds; single pages printed 3,640; average pages per issue 14(d); single plates used 3,900.

Copyright ©1996 by the Editor & Publisher Co.

Equipment: EDITORIAL: Front-end hardware — 2-Ap/Mac II LC, 6-Ap/Mac Classic, 3-Ap/Mac SE; Front-end software — Claris/MacWriter II; Printers — 3-Ap/Mac LaserPrinter; Other equipment — Ap/Mac Scanner. CLASSIFIED: Front-end hardware — Ap/Mac; Front-end software — Claris/MacWriter, Aldus/PageMaker; Printers — Ap/Mac LaserPrinter; Other equipment — Ap/Mac Scanner. DISPLAY: Front-end hardware — Ap/Mac; Front-end software — Aldus/PageMaker, Claris/MacDraw Pro; Printers — Ap/Mac LaserPrinter; Other equipment — Ap/Mac Scanner. PRODUCTION: Plate exposures — 1-Nu; Plate processors — Nat/A-250; Production cameras — B; Automatic film processors — LE/Line 25.
PRESSROOM: Line 1 — 5-HI; Folders — 1-HI. MAILROOM: Bundle tyer — 1-Miller-Bevco/BMI 80; Addressing machine — 2-Ch/525-E. WIRE SERVICES: News — AP; Receiving dishes — AP. BUSINESS COMPUTERS: IBM/5362; Applications: Bus office, Circ; PCs & micros networked.

MONTANA

ANACONDA
See BUTTE

BILLINGS
Yellowstone County

'90 U.S. Census- 81,151; E&P '96 Est. 94,155
ABC-CZ (90): 89,027 (HH 35,987)

Billings Gazette
(m-mon to sat; S)

Billings Gazette, 401 N. Broadway (59101); PO Box 36300, Billings, MT 59107-6300; tel (406) 657-1200; fax (406) 657-1207. Lee Enterprises Inc. group.
Circulation: 54,234(m); 54,234(m-sat); 59,776(S); ABC Sept. 30, 1995.
Price: 50¢(d); 75¢(sat); $1.75(S); $17.00/4wk; $213.00/yr.
Advertising: Open inch rate $42.50(m); $42.50(m-sat); $47.60(S). **Representative:** Landon Associates Inc.
News Services: AP, KRT. **Established:** 1885.
Special Editions: Financial Planning (Jan); Spring Fashion, Montana Outdoor Recreation Expo, Spring Travel, Winter Games, Travel & Guest Guide (Mar); Car Care, Progress (Apr); Yellowstone Park Daily (May); Answer Book Guide to Billings (June); Big Sky State Games (July); Montana Fair, Fall Fashion (Aug); Travel/Recreation, Hunting, Fall Home & Garden, Fall Car Care (Oct); Holiday Gift Guide (Nov); Holiday Gift Guide (Dec).
Special Weekly Sections: Best Food Day (wed); Outdoors (thur); Auto Plus (fri); Homefront (S).
Magazines: Entertainment Tab (fri); TV Book (sat); Travel Magazine, Sunday Magazine (S).

GENERAL MANAGEMENT
Publisher Wayne Schile
Controller Jim Filiaggi

ADVERTISING
Manager-Display Sales David Payson
Manager-Co-op/Direct Marketing Ron Scoles
Manager-Classified Rita Brehm
Manager-Commercial Print Ron Scoles

TELECOMMUNICATIONS
Audiotex Manager Bob Gibson

CIRCULATION
Manager David Leone

NEWS EXECUTIVE
Editor Richard Wesnick

EDITORS AND MANAGERS
Business/Finance Editor Patricia Bellinghausen
City/Metro Editor Michael Gast
Editorial Page Editor Gary Svee
Education Editor Tom Howard
Entertainment/Amusements Editor Christene Meyers
Farm/Agriculture Editor James Gransbery
Fashion/Style Editor Chris Rubich
Features Editor Chris Rubich
Graphics Editor/Art Director Tim Jones
Health/Medical Editor Sue Olp
National Editor James Oset
Photo Editor Larry Mayer
Political/Government Editor James Gransbery
Radio/Television Editor Christene Meyers
Religion Editor Sue Olp
Sports Editor Warren Rogers
Travel Editor Chris Rubich
Women's Editor Chris Rubich

MANAGEMENT INFORMATION SERVICES
Data Processing Manager Earl Anderson

PRODUCTION
Manager Bob Gibson
Manager-Distribution Lee Vividen
Manager-Press Steve Martin

Market Information: Zoned editions; TMC; ADS; Operate database; Operate audiotex.
Mechanical available: Offset; Black and 3 ROP colors; insert accepted — preprinted; page cut-offs — 22¾".
Mechanical specifications: Type page 13" x 21½"; E - 6 cols, 2 1/32", ⅛" between; A - 6 cols, 2 1/32", ⅛" between; C - 9 cols, 1⅜", 1/16" between.
Commodity consumption: Newsprint 6,673 short tons; 6,054 metric tons; widths 55", 55", 41¼", 27½", 23", 11.5"; black ink 127,000 pounds; color ink 35,000 pounds; single pages printed 14,370; average pages per issue 36(d), 68(S); single plates used 50,000.
Equipment: EDITORIAL: Front-end hardware — HI/Pen-286; Front-end software — Novell, XYQUEST/XyWrite; Printers — Epson/DFX 5000. CLASSIFIED: Front-end hardware — PC/286, Unix; Front-end software — HI/Cash; Printers — Epson/DFX 5000. AUDIOTEX: Hardware — Apex. DISPLAY: Adv layout systems — HI/2100, Ap/Mac; Front-end hardware — Ap/Mac; Front-end software — HI, QPS 3.3, Multi-Ad/Creator, Ap/Mac 7.1; Printers — Tektronix/III PX. PRODUCTION: Pagination software — Ap/Mac, HI/8300, HI/8900, HI/2100; Typesetters — AU/108FC Laser Imagers, V/5500 w/400 PS RIP; Plate exposures — 1-Nu/Flip Top, 1-Nu/Flip Top; Plate processors — 2-Graham; Electronic picture desk — Lf/AP Leaf Picture Desk; Scanners — ECR/Autokon/OOODE, Pixelcraft/8000; Production cameras — 1-C/Spartan II; Automatic film processors — 2-P; Shrink lenses — 1-CK Optical; Digital color separation equipment — Lf/AP Leaf Picture Desk.
PRESSROOM: Line 1 — 6-G/Metro offset; Press control system — Fin. MAILROOM: Counter stackers — 2-Id/550, 1-Id/2000, 1-QWI; Inserters and stuffers — 1-HI/1372, 1-MM/227; Bundle tyer — 2-Power Strap, 2-MLN/MLN; Addressing machine — Ch/labeller. LIBRARY: Electronic — I/Sys. WIRE SERVICES: News — AP, KRT; Photos — AP, KRT; Stock tables — AP SelectStox; Receiving dishes — AP. BUSINESS COMPUTERS: IBM/Sys 38; PCs & micros networked; PCs & main system networked.

BOZEMAN
Gallatin County

'90 U.S. Census- 22,660; E&P '96 Est. 23,637
ABC-CZ (90): 29,656 (HH 11,405)

Bozeman Daily Chronicle
(e-mon to fri; S)

Bozeman Daily Chronicle, 32 S. Rouse; PO Box 1188, Bozeman, MT 59771; tel (406) 587-4491; fax (406) 587-7995. Pioneer Newspapers group.
Circulation: 13,265(e); 15,404(S); ABC Oct. 1, 1995.
Price: 50¢(d); $1.25(S); $11.00/mo.
Advertising: Open inch rate $11.34(e); $11.76(S).
News Services: AP, LAT-WP. **Politics:** Independent. **Established:** 1883.
Note: Effective April 1, 1996, this publication will become a morning paper.
Special Editions: Montana Winter Fair (Jan); Montana Outdoors (May); National College Finals Rodeo (June); Montana State University (Aug); Home Improvement (Sept); Hunting (Oct); Winter Preview (Nov).
Magazines: Entertainment Guide; This Week (newsprint) (fri).

CORPORATE OFFICERS
CEO David Lord
Chief Financial Officer David P Sonnichsen

GENERAL MANAGEMENT
Publisher Rick Coffman
Manager-Office Bob Eichenberger

ADVERTISING
Director Mike Smit

MARKETING AND PROMOTION
Director-Marketing/Promotion Annette Johnson

CIRCULATION
Manager Jerry Olson

NEWS EXECUTIVE
Editor Bill Wilke

EDITORS AND MANAGERS
Books Bill Wilke
News Editor Dan Burkhart
Society/Women's Parker Heinlein
Sports Mike Yawitz

PRODUCTION
Superintendent Tom Diamond

Market Information: Zoned editions; TMC; ADS; Operate audiotex; Electronic edition.
Mechanical available: Offset; Black and 3 ROP colors; insert accepted — preprinted, most; page cut-offs — 22¾".
Mechanical specifications: Type page 13" x 21½"; E - 6 cols, 2 1/16", ⅛" between; A - 6 cols, 2 1/16", ⅛" between; C - 9 cols, 1⅜", 1/16" between.
Commodity consumption: Newsprint 925 metric tons; widths 27½", 13¾"; single pages printed 9,800; average pages per issue 32(d), 46(S).
Equipment: EDITORIAL: Front-end hardware — 17-Ap/Mac, 2-Ap/Mac; Front-end software — Baseview/NewsEdit, QuarkXPress; Printers — Hyphen/RIPS, 2-AG/9800. CLASSIFIED: Front-end hardware — 4-Ap/Mac; Front-end software — Baseview/Class Manager Plus; Printers — Ap/Mac LaserWriter II NTX, Ap/Mac ImageWriter II. AUDIOTEX: Hardware — Tribune Publishing Company/Vicki. DISPLAY: Front-end hardware — 7-Ap/Mac; Front-end software — QuarkXPress; Printers — Hyphen/Rip Dash 600, Ap/Mac LaserWriter II NTX. PRODUCTION: OCR software — Caere/OmniPage; Plate exposures — 1-Nu/Flip Top; Plate processors — Nat; Scanners — Nikon/LS-3510AF; Production cameras — 1-K/240, 1-SCREEN; Automatic film processors — 1-P/524; Color separation equipment (conventional) — 1-Ap/Mac; Digital color separation equipment — Microtek/600ZS.
PRESSROOM: Line 1 — 6-G/Community, 2-G/Community; Folders — 1-G. MAILROOM: Inserters and stuffers — 2-MM/227; Bundle tyer — 1-MLN. WIRE SERVICES: News — AP Datastream, AP Datafeatures; Stock tables — AP SelectStox; Syndicates — AP Datafeatures; Receiving dishes — size-3m, AP. BUSINESS COMPUTERS: PBS; Applications: Payroll, TMC, Mail, Circ, Accts receivable; PCs & micros networked; PCs & main system networked.

BUTTE-ANACONDA
Silver Bow and Deer Lodge Counties

'90 U.S. Census- 43,614 (Butte 33,336; Anaconda 10,278); E&P '96 Est. 40,250 (Butte 30,912; Anaconda 9,338)
ABC-CZ (90): 36,862 (HH 15,408)

The Montana Standard
(m-mon to sat; S)

The Montana Standard, 25 W. Granite St.; PO Box 627, Butte, MT 59703; tel (406) 496-5500; fax (406) 496-5551; e-mail drewvan@aol.com. Lee Enterprises Inc. group.
Circulation: 15,990(m); 15,990(m-sat); 16,809(S); ABC Sept. 30, 1995.
Price: 50¢(d); 75¢(sat); $1.50(S); $3.50/wk (home delivery); $15.20/mo (home delivery); $182.50/yr (home delivery).
Advertising: Open inch rate $21.00(m); $21.00(m-sat); $21.00(S). **Representative:** Landon Associates Inc.
News Services: AP, NYT. **Politics:** Independent. **Established:** 1876.
Special Edition: Back-to-School (Aug).
Special Weekly Sections: Family Focus (mon); Foods (wed); Outdoors (thur); Time Out (sat); Big Sky Living, Health (S).

GENERAL MANAGEMENT
Publisher/Editor Norm Lewis
Comptroller Dennis Morgan

ADVERTISING
Director Bob Barth

TELECOMMUNICATIONS
Audiotex Manager Bob Barth

CIRCULATION
Director Chris Burns

NEWS EXECUTIVE
Managing Editor Drew Van Fossen

EDITORS AND MANAGERS
City Editor Steve Cahalan
Editorial Page Editor Jeffrey Gibson
News Editor Carmen Winslow
Photo Editor Walter Hinick
Sports Editor Hudson Willse

PRODUCTION
Manager-Delivery Services Kris Matteson
Printing Services Team Leader Don McEwen
Electonic Tech Jim Ruark

Market Information: Zoned editions; Operate audiotex.
Mechanical available: Offset; Black and 3 ROP colors; insert accepted — preprinted; page cut-offs — 22¾".
Mechanical specifications: Type page 13" x 21½"; E - 6 cols, 2 1/16", ⅛" between; A - 6 cols, 2 1/16", ⅛" between; C - 9 cols, 1⅜", 1/16" between.
Commodity consumption: Newsprint 1,084 metric tons; widths 27½", 34"; black ink 20,000 pounds; color ink 10,000 pounds; single pages printed 7,910; average pages per issue 20(d), 30(S).
Equipment: EDITORIAL: Front-end hardware — 1-DEC/PDP 11-24, 16-DEC/220; Front-end software — LNS; Printers — DEC/LA 100, DEC/Decwriter III. CLASSIFIED: Front-end hardware — 1-DEC/PDP 11-24, 3-DEC/270; Front-end software — LNS; Printers — DEC/Decwriter III, DEC/LA 100. AUDIOTEX: Hardware — Unix/Inter-Active; Software — Sunsof; Supplier name — Lee Enterprises. DISPLAY: Adv layout systems — 3-HI/2221(on-line); Front-end hardware — 1-DEC/PDP 11-24, 1-DEC/220; Printers — Pre-Press/VT1200, NEC/Silentwriter, Ap/Mac LaserWriter II; Other equipment — Ap/Mac Centris 610, Ap/Mac Quadra 605, Ap/Mac Performa 550, Ap/Mac IIci. PRODUCTION: Pagination software — QuarkXPress 3.31; Typesetters — 2-COM/7400, 1-Pre-Press/Panther Plus Post-script, 1-Pre-Press/VT 1200; Plate exposures — 1-Nu/Flip Top FT40V4LS, 1-Nu/Flip Top FT40L, Nu/Flip Top FT40APRNS; Plate processors — Nat/A-380; Electronic picture desk — Lf/AP Leaf Picture Desk, Ap/Mac Quadra 950; Scanners — Lf/Leafscan 35, 1-HP, Ap/Mac Quadra; Production cameras — 1-C/Spartan II, 1-Nu/2024V, 1-POS/I Daylight Camera, 1-Nu/Horizontal; Automatic film processors — 1-LE, 1-C.
PRESSROOM: Line 1 — 5-G/Urbanite U849; Line 2 — 6-G/Community; Folders — 2-G; Press control system — Fin. MAILROOM: Inserters and stuffers — 2-MM/227-E; Bundle tyer — 1-Malow/50-S, 1-Malow/50, 1-MLN; Other mailroom equipment — Rosback/Stitcher Trimmer, MM/Free Standing Quarter Folder. LIBRARY: Electronic — ISYS. WIRE SERVICES: News — NYT, AP; Photos — AP Photostream; Stock tables — AP SelectStox; Syndicates — NYT, AP; Receiving dishes — size-9ft, AP. BUSINESS COMPUTERS: Gateway/486; Applications: Accounting, Circ; PCs & micros networked; PCs & main system networked.

GREAT FALLS
Cascade County

'90 U.S. Census- 55,097; E&P '96 Est. 54,489
ABC-NDM (90): 161,038 (HH 60,254)

Great Falls Tribune
(m-mon to sat; S)

Great Falls Tribune, 205 River Dr. S.; PO Box 5468, Great Falls, MT 59403-5468; tel (406) 791-1444; fax (406) 791-1431. Gannett Co. Inc. group.
Circulation: 34,401(m); 34,401(m-sat); 40,874(S); ABC Sept. 30, 1995.
Price: 50¢(d); 50¢(sat); $1.25(S); $2.80/wk; $11.20/mo; $145.60/yr.
Advertising: Open inch rate $25.40(m); $25.40(m-sat); $32.50(S). **Representative:** Gannett National Newspaper Sales.
News Services: AP, GNS. **Politics:** Independent. **Established:** 1887.
Advertising not accepted: Brokered Inserts; Offensive; Illegal.
Special Editions: Brides (Jan); Progress Edition (Feb); C.M. Russel Art Auction (Mar); Hunting & Fishing, Spring Fashions (Apr); Montana Vacation Guide, Brides, Home Builders Home Show (May); Guide to Great Falls (June); State Fairs (July); Back-to-School, Fall Fashions (Aug); Football Preview, Medical Directory & Guide (Sept); Interiors, New Car Guide (Oct); X'mas Gift Guide, Greetings (Dec).

Copyright ©1996 by the Editor & Publisher Co.

Special Weekly Section: Weekend Plus (thur).
Magazines: Big Sky Business Review (last mon/month); TV Week (S); Stateside Getaway/Canadian Shopper (S prior to 3-day holidays); USA Weekend.

CORPORATE OFFICER

President Barbara A Henry

GENERAL MANAGEMENT

Publisher Barbara A Henry
Controller Greg Robinson
Personnel Director Terry Oyhamburu
Manager-Technical Services Bruce Kempf
Manager-Credit Mary L Handel

ADVERTISING

Director Kristine Kincaid
Manager-Retail David Gould
Manager-Classified Cyndee F Peil

MARKETING AND PROMOTION

Director-Marketing Ann Snortland

CIRCULATION

Director Ellis Knowles
Manager Marvin Korb

NEWS EXECUTIVES

Exec Editor Dennis Ryerson
Managing Editor Gary Moseman

EDITORS AND MANAGERS

Books Editor Denise Mort
City Editor Linda Caricabura
Editorial Editor Eric Newhouse
Features Editor Steve Shirley
Feature/Travel Editor Steve Shirley
Food Editor Jackie Rice
News Editor Dan Hollow
Deputy News Editor Carrie Koppy
Projects Editor Linda Caricaburu
Regional Editor Bob Gilluly
Sports Editor George Geise

MANAGEMENT INFORMATION SERVICES

Data Processing Manager Cindy Rustad

PRODUCTION

Director Alan Bublitz
Manager-Press Mike Plummer

Market Information: Zoned editions; Split Run; ADS.
Mechanical available: Offset; Black and 3 ROP colors; insert accepted — preprinted; page cutoffs — 22¾".
Mechanical specifications: Type page 13" x 21½"; E - 6 cols, 2 1/16", .14" between; A - 6 cols, 2 1/16", .14" between; C - 9 cols, 1.38", .08" between.
Commodity consumption: Newsprint 2,700 short tons; widths 27.25", 40.875", 54.5"; black ink 56,591 pounds; color ink 20,555 pounds; single pages printed 12,158; average pages per issue 25(d), 68(S); single plates used 34,800.
Equipment: EDITORIAL: Front-end hardware — Dewar, Dewar/System IV, Dewar/Dewarview, QPS/Editorial; Front-end software — Dewar/Disc Net, Dewar/Discovery, Archetype/Corel Draw, Dewar/Discribe, Novell/Netware 3.1; Printers — 2-Tegra/Varityper XP1000, V/5100, Panther/Pro 46; Other equipment — Dewar/Discovery scanner, Lf/AP Leaf Picture Desk. CLASSIFIED: Front-end hardware — Dewar; Front-end software — Dewar/Discovery, Dewar/Discribe, Dewar/System IV. DISPLAY: Adv layout systems — Dewar, Ap/Mac Power PC; Front-end software — Multi-Ad/Creator; Printers — Tegra/Varityper XP1000, V/5100, Panther/Pro 46; Other equipment — X/Flatbed Scanner. PRODUCTION: Typesetters — Tegra/Varityper XP1000, Panther/Pro 46 Imagesetter; Plate exposures — 2-Nu/Flip Top; Plate processors — WL; Scanners — Lf/Leafscan 35; Production cameras — Canon/Xapshot; Automatic film processors — Wing Lynch/Model 5; Color separation equipment (conventional) — Howtek/Colorscan system; Digital color separation equipment — Howtek/35mm, Sharp/8"x10" flatbed. PRESSROOM: Line 1 — 6-G/Metro (2 color decks); Folders — 2-G/2:1; Pasters — 6-G/3-Arm RTP. MAILROOM: Counter stackers — 5-Id/440; Inserters and stuffers — 2-MM/227 5:1; Bundle tyer — 1-OVL/JP80, 1-MLN; Wrapping singles — Manual; Addressing machine — 3-Wm. COMMUNICATIONS: Systems used — satellite. WIRE SERVICES: News — AP, GNS; Stock tables — AP SelectStox; Syndicates — TV Data, AP Datafeatures; Receiving dishes — size-3m, AP, Newspaper Satellite Network. BUSINESS COMPUTERS: 1-IBM/AS-400; Applications: IBM, Gannett; PCs & micros networked; PCs & main system networked.

HAMILTON

Ravalli County

'90 U.S. Census- 2,737; E&P '96 Est. 2,816

Ravalli Republic (m-mon to fri)

Ravalli Republic, 232 Main St.; PO Box 433, Hamilton, MT 59840; tel (406) 363-3300; fax (406) 363-1767. Scripps League Newspapers Inc. group.
Circulation: 5,206(m); Sworn Oct. 2, 1995.
Price: 50¢(d); $7.75/mo (in county); $75.00/yr (in county).
Advertising: Open inch rate $7.85(m). **Politics:** Independent. **Established:** 1889.
Not Published: New Year; Martin Luther King's Birthday; President's Day; Memorial Day; Independence Day; Labor Day; Columbus Day; Veteran's Day; Thanksgiving; Christmas; All other US Postal Service holidays.
Special Editions: Brides (Feb); Agri-business, Progress (Mar); Home Improvement (Apr); Valley Vista (Tourism Publication) (May); Bitterroot Homes, Finance, Summer Fest (July); School, Fair Edition (Aug); Auto Care (Sept); Hunting and Outdoors, Family Health (Oct); Christmas Editions, Winter Recreation Guide (Nov); Christmas Editions (Dec).
Special Weekly Sections: Business, Sports (mon); Editorial (tues); Food Fest, People (wed); Editorial, Business, Sports (thur); Business, Sports (fri).
Magazine: Entertainment Connection/TV (fri).

CORPORATE OFFICERS

Board Chairman/Treasurer E W Scripps
Vice Chairman/Corporate Secretary Betty Knight Scripps
President Ed Scripps III
Vice Pres-Finance Thomas E Wendel

GENERAL MANAGEMENT

Publisher Jo Gmazel-Bartley
Business Manager Julie Collett

ADVERTISING

Manager Cindi Petrusaitis

CIRCULATION

Manager Juanita Anderson

NEWS EXECUTIVE

Managing Editor Drake Kiewit

EDITOR AND MANAGER

Sports Editor John Ebelt

MANAGEMENT INFORMATION SERVICES

Data Processing Manager Lynn Dukelow

PRODUCTION

Manager Frank Serwacki

Market Information: TMC.
Mechanical available: Offset; Black and 3 ROP colors; insert accepted — preprinted; page cutoffs — 22¾".
Mechanical specifications: Type page 13" x 21½"; E - 6 cols, 2 1/16", 1/8" between; A - 6 cols, 2 1/16", 1/8" between; C - 6 cols, 2 1/16", 1/8" between.
Commodity consumption: Newsprint 144 metric tons; widths 28", 28", 27½", 14", 13¾"; black ink 12,000 pounds; color ink 1,500 pounds; single pages printed 2,730; average pages per issue 10(d); single plates used 1,450.
Equipment: EDITORIAL: Front-end hardware — 5-ScrippSat/PC; Front-end software — XYQUEST/XyWrite; Printers — 1-QMS/Laser-Printer. CLASSIFIED: Front-end hardware — 1-IBM/XT, 1-IBM; Front-end software — Synaptic. DISPLAY: Front-end hardware — 1-IBM/386, 1-Gateway/486, 2-Gateway/Pentiums w/CD-Rom; Front-end software — Aldus/PageMaker, Ventura, Signature; Printers — 1-QMS/LaserPrinter. PRODUCTION: Pagination software — Aldus/PageMaker 5.0; OCR software — HP/ScanJet IIc; Plate exposures — 1-Nu; Production cameras — 1-K/241; Automatic film processors — Kk. PRESSROOM: Line 1 — 5-KP/NewsKing; Folders — 1-KP. MAILROOM: Bundle tyer — 1-Bu; Addressing machine — 2-Wm; Other mailroom equipment — 1-Mc. BUSINESS COMPUTERS: 2-PC; PCs & micros networked; PCs & main system networked.

HAVRE

Hill County

'90 U.S. Census- 10,201; E&P '96 Est. 9,911

The Havre Daily News (e-mon to fri)

The Havre Daily News, 119 2nd St.; PO Box 431, Havre, MT 59501; tel (406) 265-6795; fax (406) 265-6798. Pioneer Newspapers group.
Circulation: 4,362(e); Sworn Oct. 1, 1995.
Price: 50¢(d); $8.00/mo (carrier), $9.00/mo (motor route), $10.00/mo (in county), $11.00/mo (mail, in state), $12.00/mo (mail, out of state); $96.00/yr (carrier), $108.00/yr (motor route), $120.00/yr (mail, in county), $132.00/yr (mail, in state), $144.00/yr (mail, out of state).
Advertising: Open inch rate $7.51(e).
News Service: AP. **Politics:** Independent. **Established:** 1914.
Special Editions: Tax Guide (Jan); Senior Citizens (Feb); Farm & Ranch, Who's Who in Northern Montana (Mar); Home & Car Care (Apr); Tourist Guide (May); Bridal Section, Senior Citizens (June); Senior Citizens (July); Fair (Aug); Home & Car Care, MSU/Northern Montana College, Havre Festival Days, Free Sports Preview (Sept); Hunting & Fishing Guide, 4-H (Oct); Thanksgiving Edition (Nov); Christmas Greetings (Dec).
Special Weekly Sections: Sports Wrap-up (mon); Editorial, Grocery (tues); Farm, Ranch (wed); TV & Entertainment, Business (thur); Society, Editorial, Church, Real Estate, Big Sky Living (fri).
Magazine: TV Tab (thur).

GENERAL MANAGEMENT

Publisher Rick V Weaver
Office Manager Val Murri
Controller David P Sonnichsen

ADVERTISING

Manager Paula J Reynolds

CIRCULATION

Director Kenneth H Kihara

NEWS EXECUTIVE

Managing Editor Steve Miller

EDITORS AND MANAGERS

Business/Finance Editor Kathy Lundman
Editorial Page Editor Steve Miller
Education Editor Alan Sorensen
News Editor Steve Miller
Photo Editor Zach Nelson
Religion Editor Alan Sorensen
Sports Editor Boots Gifford

PRODUCTION

Superintendent William R Wagner
Foreman-Pressroom Keith Hanson

Market Information: TMC.
Mechanical available: Offset; Black and 3 ROP colors; insert accepted — preprinted; page cutoffs — 22¾".
Mechanical specifications: Type page 13" x 21½"; E - 6 cols, 2 1/16", 1/8" between; A - 6 cols, 2 1/16", 1/8" between; C - 9 cols, 1 3/8", 1/16" between.
Commodity consumption: Newsprint 130 metric tons; widths 27", 13½"; black ink 3,800 pounds; color ink 270 pounds; single pages printed 4,064; average pages per issue 14(d); single plates used 2,746.
Equipment: EDITORIAL: Front-end hardware — Ap/Mac Sys 7.1; Front-end software — QuarkXPress 3.31; Printers — Data Products/LZR 1560. CLASSIFIED: Front-end hardware — 1-Ap/Mac LC II; Front-end software — Baseview. PRODUCTION: Typesetters — 2-Dataproducts/LZR 1560; Plate exposures — 1-Nu/Flip Top; Plate processors — Roconex; Production cameras — 1-K/24; Shrink lenses — 1-CK Optical/SQU-6. PRESSROOM: Line 1 — 4-G/Community; Folders — 1-G/2:1. MAILROOM: Inserters and stuffers — 3-MM/257; Bundle tyer — 2-Bu/16. WIRE SERVICES: News — AP; Syndicates — United Media, NEA, Creators, King Features, North America Syndicate, TMS, Universal Press; Receiving dishes — AP. BUSINESS COMPUTERS: 3-IBM/386 Compatible, 2-Wyse/370, 1-IBM/486-66 Hz; Applications: PBS/Media Plus: Bookkeeping, Circ; PCs & micros networked; PCs & main system networked.

HELENA

Lewis and Clark County

'90 U.S. Census- 24,569; E&P '96 Est. 25,182
ABC-NDM (90): 42,583 (HH 16,801)

Helena Independent Record (m-mon to sat; S)

Helena Independent Record, 317 Cruse Ave.; PO Box 4249, Helena, MT 59604; tel (406) 447-4000; fax (406) 447-4052. Lee Enterprises Inc. group.
Circulation: 14,371(m); 14,371(m-sat); 14,982(S); ABC Sept. 30, 1995.
Price: 50¢(d); 50¢(sat); $1.25(S); $11.50/mo; $138.00/yr.
Advertising: Open inch rate $16.75(m); $17.75(m-fri); $16.75(m-sat); $17.56(S). **Representative:** Landon Associates Inc.
News Services: AP, NYT, States News Service, Cox News Service. **Established:** 1865.
Magazine: "Your Time" TV Listing tab.

GENERAL MANAGEMENT

Publisher Bruce Whittenberg
Controller Jolene Selby

ADVERTISING

Manager-Classified Kathleen Turdurgon
Manager-Retail Tom Zebrun-Gero

CIRCULATION

Director-Sales Steve Sampson

NEWS EXECUTIVE

Editor Charles Wood

EDITORS AND MANAGERS

City Editor David Shors
Cooking Editor Leah Gilman
Editorial Page Editor Bill Skidmore
Films/Theater Editor Leah Gilman
Music Editor Leah Gilman
Photo Department Manager George Lane
Political Editor Bill Skidmore
Radio/Television Editor Leah Gilman
Sports/Outdoors Editor Roy Pace

PRODUCTION

Supervisor-Pre Press Susie Farr
Supervisor-Pressroom Steve Curran

Market Information: Split Run; TMC; ADS.
Mechanical available: Offset; Black; insert accepted — preprinted; page cut-offs — 22¾".
Mechanical specifications: Type page 12⅞" x 21½"; E - 6 cols, 2.07", 1/6" between; A - 6 cols, 2.07", 1/6" between; C - 9 cols, 1.36", 1/6" between.
Commodity consumption: Newsprint 1,000 metric tons; widths 27½", 34"; black ink 25,000 pounds; color ink 2,700 pounds; single pages printed 12,600; average pages per issue 22(d), 36(S); single plates used 11,000.
Equipment: EDITORIAL: Front-end hardware — DEC/VT 220; Front-end software — LNS/220; Printers — DEC/LetterWriter 100; Other equipment — Lf/AP Leaf Picture Desk, Tegra/Varityper Color-Imagesetter. CLASSIFIED: Front-end hardware — DEC/VT 220; Front-end software — LNS/220; Printers — DEC/Letterwriter 100. DISPLAY: Adv layout systems — Ap/Mac IIci; Front-end hardware — 4-Ap/Mac IIci; Front-end software — Multi-Ad/Creator, Aldus/FreeHand; Printers — LaserMaster/KX 1000, Ap/Mac LaserWriter II NT, HP/PaintJet; Other equipment — Ap/Mac Scanner. PRODUCTION: OCR software — Caere/OmniPage; Typesetters — 2-COM/8400-HS; Scanners — Ap/Mac Scanner, Ap/Mac IIci; Production cameras — 3-Nikon/F2, 1-Nikon/F3. PRESSROOM: Line 1 — 8-G/Suburban (balloon former); Folders — 1-G/Urbanite. MAILROOM: Counter stackers — 1-WPC/Quarter folder; Inserters and stuffers — 1-MM; Bundle tyer — 1-MLN, 1-Malow; Addressing machine — 1-Ch. WIRE SERVICES: News — AP Datastream, AP Datafeatures; Stock tables — AP SelectStox; Syndicates — NYT, AP; Receiving dishes — AP. BUSINESS COMPUTERS: PCs & micros networked; PCs & main system networked.

KALISPELL

Flathead County

'90 U.S. Census- 11,917; E&P '96 Est. 13,020

The Daily Inter Lake (e-mon to fri; S)

The Daily Inter Lake, 727 E. Idaho (59901); PO Box 7610, Kalispell, MT 59904; tel (406) 755-7000; fax (406) 752-6114. Hagadone Corp. group.
Circulation: 15,848(e); 15,848(S); Sworn Sept. 26, 1995.
Price: 50¢(d); $1.00(S); $13.00/mo (Jr carrier), $13.50/mo (rural).
Advertising: Open inch rate $13.00(e); $13.00(S).
News Service: AP. **Politics:** Independent. **Established:** 1907.
Not Published: New Year; Christmas.
Advertising not accepted: Patent medicine.
Special Editions: Home Improvement (wed); Progress; Back-to-School; Fall Opening; Football; Summer Recreation; Winter Recreation; Basketball; Fishing.
Special Weekly Sections: Dream it Do it; Intertainer.
Magazine: TV Listings Magazine (fri).

CORPORATE OFFICERS

President Duane B Hagadone
Secretary/Treasurer Art Flagan

GENERAL MANAGEMENT

Publisher Ronald C Peterson

Business Manager   Jo Ann Burns
Purchasing Agent   Ronald C Peterson
Manager-Education Service Jeffrey W Bain
General Manager   Duane B Hagadone

ADVERTISING
Director   Alan Litchy

TELECOMMUNICATIONS
Audiotex Manager   Victor S Gehlen

CIRCULATION
Director   Jeffrey W Bain

NEWS EXECUTIVE
Managing Editor   Dan Black

EDITORS AND MANAGERS
Editorial Page Editor   Dan Black
News Editor   Jackie Adams
Society Editor   Anne Clark
Sports Editor   Dave Lesnick

PRODUCTION
Superintendent   Victor S Gehlen
Foreman-Pressroom   Ed Dickman
Foreman-Mailroom   T J Archer

Market Information: TMC; ADS; Operate audiotex.
Mechanical available: Offset; Black and 3 ROP colors; insert accepted — preprinted, singles sheet, booklets; page cut-offs — 21".
Mechanical specifications: Type page 12 7/8" x 21"; E - 6 cols, 2", 1/8" between; A - 6 cols, 2", 1/8" between; C - 8 cols, 1 1/2", 1/8" between.
Commodity consumption: Newsprint 900 short tons; width 27 1/2"; black ink 35,000 pounds; average pages per issue 32(d), 48(S); single plates used 12,000.
Equipment: EDITORIAL: Front-end hardware — Ap/Mac; Front-end software — QPS, Baseview, Adobe/Photoshop, Caere/OmniPage; Printers — Ap/Mac LaserWriters, Photo Imagesetter; Other equipment — Lf/Leafscan 35. CLASSIFIED: Front-end hardware — Ap/Mac; Front-end software — Baseview, Ethernet; Printers — Ap/Mac LaserWriters, Ap/Mac ImageWriter. DISPLAY: Front-end hardware — Ap/Mac; Front-end software — Multi-Ad, Adobe/Illustrator, Microsoft/Excel, QuarkXPress, Adobe/Photoshop; Printers — Ap/Mac LaserWriters, LaserMaster/1200, Hyphen/Dash 94EQ Imagesetter, Hyphen/RIP. PRODUCTION: Typesetters — 2-Ap/Mac cx, 1-Ap/Mac ci, 1-Ap/SuperMac, 1-Ap/Mac SE, 1-Ap/Mac SE30, 3-Ap/Mac LaserWriter II NTX, 3-Ap/Mac Radius, Ap/Mac Centris 650, Ap/Mac Quadra 950, Ap/Mac IIsi, Hyphen/Dash 94EQ; Plate-making systems — 1-Nu; Plate processors — Ic/25"; Electronic picture desk — Ap/Mac Centris 650, Adobe/Photoshop, Ofoto; Scanners — Lf/Leafscan 35, Microtek/3002; Production cameras — SCREEN/America 24" vertical; Automatic film processors — LE/1800A; Digital color separation equipment — Adobe/Photoshop.
PRESSROOM: Line 1 — 8-G/Community.
MAILROOM: Inserters and stuffers — MM/227; Bundle tyer — MLN/2EE; Addressing machine — Ch. COMMUNICATIONS: Facsimile — Ricoh; Systems used — satellite. WIRE SERVICES: News — AP; Photos — AP; Receiving dishes — size-10ft, AP. BUSINESS COMPUTERS: DEC/Micro VAX, Ap/Mac; Applications: Microsoft/Word, Microsoft/Excel.

LIVINGSTON
Park County
'90 U.S. Census- 6,701; E&P '96 Est. 6,510

The Livingston Enterprise
(e-mon to fri)

The Livingston Enterprise, 401 S. Main; PO Box 665, Livingston, MT 59047; tel (406) 222-2000; fax (406) 222-8580. Yellowstone Newspapers group.
Circulation: 3,558(e); Sworn Sept. 30, 1995.
Price: 50¢(d); $8.00/mo.
Advertising: Open inch rate $5.10(e). **Representative:** Landon Associates Inc.
News Service: AP. **Politics:** Independent. **Established:** 1883.
Not Published: New Year; Memorial Day; Independence Day; Labor Day; Thanksgiving; Christmas.
Advertising not accepted: Vending machines (cash in advance may be required).
Special Editions: Homemaker School Section (Sept); Clean-up and Painting, Car Care (Spring); Car Care (Winter); Tourist Directory; Hunting; Pioneer Society; Fall Sports; Winter Sports; Back-to-School; Bridal Tab; Christmas Eve.
Magazine: TView Television Guide (thur).

CORPORATE OFFICER
President   John Sullivan

GENERAL MANAGEMENT
Publisher   John Sullivan
Controller   David King

ADVERTISING
Director   Jim Durfey

MARKETING AND PROMOTION
Director   Mark D Bolin

CIRCULATION
Director   Mark D Bolin

NEWS EXECUTIVES
Editor   John Sullivan
Managing Editor   Karin Ronnow

EDITORS AND MANAGERS
Films/Theater Editor   Brenda Binkerd
Food/Women's Editor   Brenda Binkerd
Music Editor   Brenda Binkerd
News Editor   Stephen Matlow
Photo Editor   Ben Danley
Radio/Television Editor   Brenda Binkerd
Sports Editor   Chris Wester

MANAGEMENT INFORMATION SERVICES
Data Processing Manager   Dave King

PRODUCTION
Superintendent   Oron Jacobs

Market Information: Split Run; TMC.
Mechanical available: Offset; Black and 3 ROP colors; insert accepted — preprinted; page cut-offs — 22 3/4".
Mechanical specifications: Type page 13" x 21 1/2"; E - 6 cols, 2 1/16", 1/8" between; A - 6 cols, 2 1/16", 1/8" between; C - 8 cols, 1 1/2", 1/8" between.
Commodity consumption: average pages per issue 14(d).
Equipment: EDITORIAL: Front-end hardware — Ap/Mac; Front-end software — Baseview; Printers — Ap/Mac. DISPLAY: Adv layout systems — QuarkXPress; Front-end hardware — Ap/Mac; Front-end software — QPS; Printers — LaserMaster/Unity, Ap/Mac LaserWriter. PRODUCTION: Typesetters — Ap/Mac LaserWriter, Ap/Mac II, Ap/Mac IIx, Ap/Mac SE; Plate exposures — 1-Nu; Plate processors — 1-C/25-1, Graham/Plate Processor-Model M-28; Scanners — Ap/Mac; Production cameras — 1-Acti, 1-AG/Repromaster; Automatic film processors — 1-Kk.
PRESSROOM: Line 1 — 4-G/Community, 1-DEV/Color unit; Folders — 1-G/Suburban.
MAILROOM: Inserters and stuffers — 1-KR; Addressing machine — 1-Ch; Other mailroom equipment — MM/Stitcher-Trimmer. WIRE SERVICES: News — AP; Receiving dishes — size-2ft, AP. BUSINESS COMPUTERS: IBM; Applications: BMF; PCs & micros networked; PCs & main system networked.

MILES CITY
Custer County
'90 U.S. Census- 8,461; E&P '96 Est. 7,920

Miles City Star (e-mon to fri)
Miles City Star, 13 N. 6th St.; PO Box 1216, Miles City, MT 59301; tel (406) 232-0450; fax (406) 232-6687. Yellowstone Newspapers group.
Circulation: 3,673(e); Sworn Sept. 29, 1995.
Price: 50¢(d); $7.50/mo; $90.00/yr.
Advertising: Open inch rate $6.44(e). **Representative:** Landon Associates Inc.
News Service: AP. **Politics:** Independent. **Established:** 1910.
Not Published: New Year; Memorial Day; Independence Day; Labor Day; Thanksgiving; Christmas.
Special Editions: Back-to-School; Football; Spring Fashion; Spring Home & Garden; Christmas; Hunting; Tourist; Outdoor Sports; Fall Car Care.

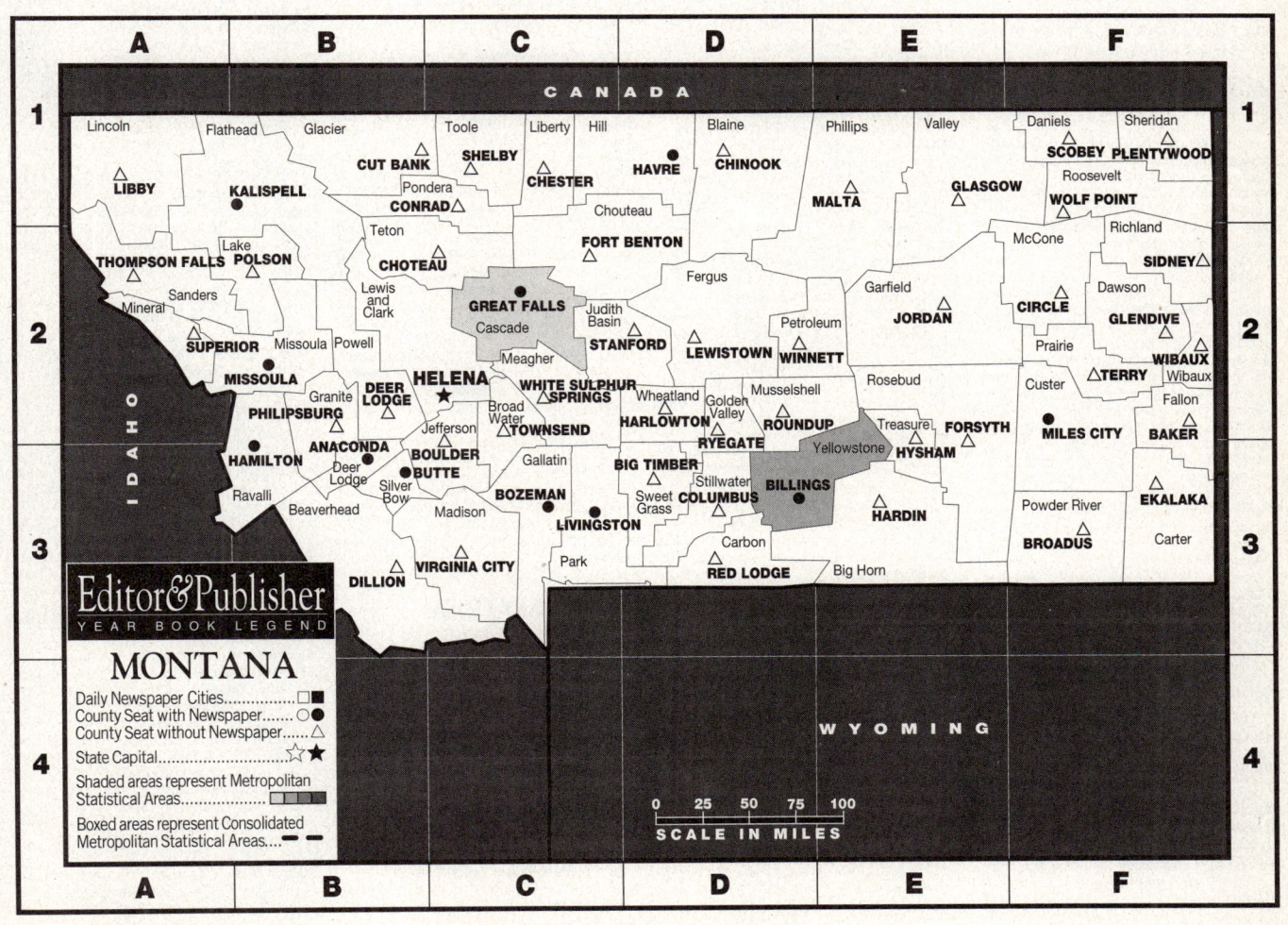

Copyright ©1996 by the Editor & Publisher Co.

Special Weekly Section: Farm & Ranch (TMC) (wed).

GENERAL MANAGEMENT

Publisher/General Manager John Watson

ADVERTISING

Director Giff Wood

CIRCULATION

Director Jeff Virag

NEWS EXECUTIVE

Managing Editor Mark Smidt

MANAGEMENT INFORMATION SERVICES

Data Processing Manager Ann Hilderbrand

Market Information: TMC.
Mechanical available: Offset; Black and 3 ROP colors; insert accepted — preprinted; page cutoffs — 22¾".
Mechanical specifications: Type page 13" x 21½"; E - 6 cols, 2 1/16", ⅛" between; A - 6 cols, 2 1/16", ⅛" between; C - 8 cols, 1½", ⅛" between.
Commodity consumption: Newsprint 260 short tons; width 28"; average pages per issue 13(d).
Equipment: EDITORIAL: Front-end hardware — Ap/Mac; Front-end software — QPS, Baseview/NewsEdit; Printers — Ap/Mac Laser-Printer, LaserMaster/XLO. CLASSIFIED: Front-end hardware — Ap/Mac; Front-end software — Baseview/Class Mgr Plus; Printers — Laser-Master/XLO, Okidata. DISPLAY: Adv layout systems — Ap/Mac; Front-end hardware — Ap/Mac; Front-end software — QPS, Metro Laser/CD-Rom; Printers — Ap/Mac Laser-Printer, LaserMaster. PRODUCTION: Pagination software — Baseview/News Edit; Typesetters — Ap/Mac, LaserMaster, Adobe/Photoshop; Production cameras — 1-K.
PRESSROOM: Line 1 — 4-G/Community. MAILROOM: Bundle tyer — 1-Bu; Addressing machine — 1-Am. WIRE SERVICES: News — AP. BUSINESS COMPUTERS: BEM. Applications: Bus office, Circ.

MISSOULA

Missoula County

'90 U.S. Census- 42,918; **E&P '96 Est.** 51,845
ABC-CZ (90): 54,904 (HH 22,494)

Missoulian (m-mon to sat; S)

Missoulian, PO Box 8029, Missoula, MT 59807; tel (406) 523-5200; e-mail msline@missoulian.com; web site http://www.missoulian.com. Lee Enterprises Inc. group.
Circulation: 30,918(m); 30,918(m-sat); 37,998(S); ABC Sept. 30, 1995.
Price: 50¢(d); 50¢(sat); $1.50(S); $12.60/4wk; $12.25/mo (motor route), $11.75/mo (carrier); $163.70/yr (mail).
Advertising: Open inch rate $27.28(m); $27.28(m-sat); $31.51(S). **Representative:** Cresmer, Woodward, O'Mara & Ormsbee.
News Services: AP, NYT. **Politics:** Independent. **Established:** 1873.
Special Editions: Taxes (Feb); Newspapers in Education, Home Builders Trade Show, Salute to Agriculture, Progress Edition (Mar); Spring Wheels, Montana Designs, Wildlife Film Festival, The Fly Line (Apr); Lawn & Garden, Summer Recreation Guide, Uncover Missoula (May); Picture the Progress, Graduation Section (June); Back-to-School, Western Montana Fair, Fall Sports Preview, University Almanac (Aug); Parade of Homes, Cookbook VIII (Sept); Hunting, New Car/Car Care (Oct); Winter Recreation Guide, Hint Book (Nov); Holiday Foods, Hintbook II (Dec); At-A-Glance; Uniquely Montana; Fish Fax; Special Delivery; Hunting Almanac; Menu of Attractions.
Special Weekly Sections: Pocketbook (mon); Health & Fitness (tues); Best Food Day, Business (wed); Entertainer (fri); On TV, Engagements/Weddings, Business (S).
Magazine: "Entertainer" (arts, events,TV tab).

GENERAL MANAGEMENT

Publisher James E Bell
Controller Karl Finholm
Director-Human Resources Bobbie Engelstad

ADVERTISING

Manager-Retail Steve Trybus
Manager-Classified Janet Taylor

MARKETING AND PROMOTION

Manager-Direct Marketing Sharon Schroeder

CIRCULATION

Director Jim Rickman

NEWS EXECUTIVE

Editor David Rutter

EDITORS AND MANAGERS

Business Editor Jim Ludwick
Local News Editor Michael McInally
Local News Editor Theresa Johnson
Local News Editor Rod Murphy
News Editor David Knadler
Opinion Page Editor Steve Woodruff

MANAGEMENT INFORMATION SERVICES

Online Manager Loren Trebish

PRODUCTION

Manager-Distribution Mike Bailey
Manager-Press Scott Nelson
Manager-Pre Press/Commercial Mike Schroeder

Market Information: Zoned editions; TMC; Operate database; Electronic edition.
Mechanical available: Offset; Black and 3 ROP colors; insert accepted — preprinted; page cutoffs — 22¾".
Mechanical specifications: Type page 13" x 21½"; E - 6 cols, 2 1/16", ⅛" between; A - 6 cols, 2 1/16", ⅛" between; C - 9 cols, 1 5/16", ⅛" between.
Commodity consumption: Newsprint 2,400 metric tons; widths 27½", 27½", 13¾", 34", 17"; single pages printed 12,372; average pages per issue 13(d), 32(S).
Equipment: EDITORIAL: Front-end hardware — 2-HI/8903, 11-HI/8863, 4-HI/8000, 1-DEC/PDP 11-24, 1-HI/8002 Node, 8-DEC/VT2220, 24-Zenith/286, 2-Avcom/306, 1-Ap/Mac fx, 1-Ap/Mac Dash, 1-Ap/Mac ci, 1-Ap/Mac Classic, 2-Ap/Power Mac Featurers 8100, 1-Ap/Power Mac 7100; Front-end software — Novell/100 user 3.2, HI/pen system; Other equipment — 1-Ap/Mac Color One Scanner, 2-Ap/Mac One Scanner. CLASSIFIED: Front-end hardware — 1-HI/CASH Sys, 10-Zenith/286, 2-Zenith/386; Front-end software — HI/CASH; Other equipment — 1-HP/Scanner. DISPLAY: Front-end hardware — 2-Ap/Power Mac, 3-HI/8863, 5-Ap/Mac ci, 1-Ap/Mac Quadra, 3-Ap/Power Mac 7100, 1-Ap/Mac LC; Front-end software — QuarkXPress 3.3, Aldus/FreeHand 4.0, Adobe/Photoshop 3.0; Other equipment — 4-Ap/Mac Color One Scanner, 9-Ap/Mac B&W One Scanner. PRODUCTION: OCR software — Caere/OmniPage; Typesetters — 1-COM/9600, 1-Ap/Mac Laser-Writer, 1-V/5510, 1-V/5300E, 1-V/5100, 1-Panther/Plus Imagesetter; Plate exposures — 2-Nu/Flip Top FT40LNS; Plate processors — 1-Nat/340S, 1-C/650; Electronic picture desk — Lf/AP Leaf Picture Desk; Scanners — 1-PC/386; Production cameras — 1-C/Spartan II, 1-Nu; Automatic film processors — 1-LE/LD-24 AQ; Shrink lenses — 1-CK Optical/SQ-47; Color separation equipment (conventional) — WDS/Color Sys, 1-AG.
PRESSROOM: Line 1 — 9-G/Units; Line 2 — 9-G/Urbanite; Folders — 2-G, 1-G/Quarter, 2-G/Urbanite 707; Reels and stands — G/2 stands 3 high. MAILROOM: Counter stackers — 1-Id/Counter Stacker 660, 1-Id/Counter Stacker 2100; Inserters and stuffers — 1-MM/227-0500 E, HI/1372; Bundle tyer — 2-MLN/Automatic Power Strapping Machines; Addressing machine — 1-AVY, Ch/582 M Base 721 Head; Other mailroom equipment — MM/Minuteman Stitcher Trimmer. Id/Bottom wrap 6114. LIBRARY: Electronic — SMS/Electronic Library System. WIRE SERVICES: News — AP Datastream, Feature Wire, KRT; Photos — AP; Stock tables — AP SelectStox; Receiving dishes — AP. BUSINESS COMPUTERS: 2-IBM/Sys 38; Applications: Acct, Adv, Circ; PCs & micros networked; PCs & main system networked.

NEBRASKA

ALLIANCE

Box Butte County

'90 U.S. Census- 9,765; **E&P '96 Est.** 9,926

The Alliance Times-Herald (e-mon to sat)

The Alliance Times-Herald, 114 E. 4th; PO Box G, Alliance, NE 69301; tel (308) 762-3060. Seaton group.
Circulation: 3,202(e); 3,202(e-sat); Sworn Sept. 29, 1995.
Price: 50¢(d); 50¢(sat); $88.00/yr.
Advertising: Open inch rate $7.35(e); $7.35(e-sat). **Representative:** Nebraska Press Advertising Service.
News Service: AP. **Politics:** Independent. **Established:** 1887.
Not Published: Independence Day; Christmas.
Special Editions: Tax Section (Jan); Bridal, Business & Industry (Feb); AG Progress (Mar); Spring Home & Garden, Students in Print (Apr); Travel Guide, Beef Section (May); Heritage Days Festival, Senior Citizens (July); Fall Sports, Fair Edition, Back-to-School (Aug); Fall Car Care, Iron Rail Days (Sept); Business & Professional Women, Fall Ag & Ranch (Oct); Winter Sports (Nov); Shoppers Guide, Letter to Santa (Dec).
Magazine: TV Spotlight (fri).

CORPORATE OFFICERS

Board Chairman R M Seaton
President Donald R Seaton
Exec Vice Pres/Secretary/Treasurer Fred G Kuhlman
Vice Pres Edward L Seaton

GENERAL MANAGEMENT

Publisher Fred G Kuhlman

ADVERTISING

Manager Fred Aufdembrink

TELECOMMUNICATIONS

Audiotex Manager Fred Kuhlman

NEWS EXECUTIVE

Managing Editor Donna Price

EDITORS AND MANAGERS

Books Editor Donna Price
Editorial Page Editor Donna Price
Features Editor Donna Price
Society Editor Dorothy Kunzman
Sports Editor Rich Headley

PRODUCTION

Manager Mark Sherlock

Market Information: Split Run; TMC; Operate audiotex.
Mechanical available: Offset; Black and 3 ROP colors; insert accepted — preprinted; page cutoffs — 21½".
Mechanical specifications: Type page 14" x 24"; E - 6 cols, 2 1/16", ⅛" between; A - 6 cols, 2 1/16", ⅛" between; C - 7 cols, 1¾", ⅛" between.
Commodity consumption: Newsprint 110 short tons; widths 13½", 27"; black ink 4,200 pounds; color ink 300 pounds; single pages printed 3,584; average pages per issue 12(d); single plates used 2,300.
Equipment: EDITORIAL: Front-end hardware — 1-Ap/Mac SE 30, 1-Ap/Mac Centris, 4-Ap/Mac Classic II, 1-Ap/Mac II; Front-end software — Aldus/PageMaker, Microsoft/Word; Printers — 1-Ap/Mac II NTX, 1-LaserMaster/Unity XL-O. CLASSIFIED: Front-end hardware — 1-Ap/Mac SE20; Front-end software — Baseview; Printers — Ap/Mac ImageWriter II. AUDIOTEX: Supplier name — SMS/Stauffer. DISPLAY: Adv layout systems — Ap/Power Mac 8100; Front-end hardware — Ap/Power Mac 8100; Front-end software — Aldus/PageMaker, Microsoft/Word; Printers — Ap/Mac LaserWriter II NTX, Laser-Master/Unity XL-O. PRODUCTION: Typesetters — 1-Ap/Mac LaserWriter II NTX, LaserMaster/Unity XL-O; Plate processors — 1-Nu; Production cameras — R; Automatic film processors — Kk.
PRESSROOM: Line 1 — 4-G/Community; Folders — 1-G. MAILROOM: Inserters and stuffers — 3-KAN; Bundle tyer — 1-Bu. COMMUNICATIONS: Facsimile — AP/Electronic Carbon. WIRE SERVICES: News — AP; Receiving dishes — size-1ft, AP. BUSINESS COMPUTERS: PCs & micros networked; PCs & main system networked.

BEATRICE

Gage County

'90 U.S. Census- 12,354; **E&P '96 Est.** 12,346

Beatrice Daily Sun (e-mon to fri; m-sat)

Beatrice Daily Sun, 200 N. 7th; PO Box 847, Beatrice, NE 68310; tel (402) 223-5233; fax (402) 228-3571. Hollinger International Inc. group.
Circulation: 9,327(e); 9,327(m-sat); Sworn Sept. 29, 1995.
Price: 50¢(d); 50¢(sat); $90.00/yr.
Advertising: Open inch rate $7.50(e); $7.50(m-sat). **Representative:** Papert Companies.
News Services: AP, NEA. **Politics:** Independent. **Established:** 1902.
Not Published: New Year; Memorial Day; Independence Day; Labor Day; Thanksgiving; Christmas.
Special Editions: Home Show, Progress, Senior Citizens (Feb); Farm, Family Business (Mar); Clean-up, Building, Car Care (Apr); Graduation, Beef, Senior Citizens (May); Homestead Days (June); Sidewalk Sale, County Fair (July); Back-to-School, Sports (Aug); Fall Fashion, Hunting, Senior Citizens (Sept); Moonlight Madness, 4-H (Oct); Senior Citizens, Christmas Shopping, Sports (Nov).
Special Weekly Sections: Business Page (mon); Cooking (wed); Religion (thur); Farm Page (fri); Times & Places, Youth (sat).
Magazines: TV Today (mon); USA Weekend (sat).

GENERAL MANAGEMENT

Publisher Dennis M DeRossett

ADVERTISING

Manager Ronald W Sohl

CIRCULATION

Manager Shannon Kleveland

NEWS EXECUTIVE

Managing Editor Anita Meyer

EDITORS AND MANAGERS

Amusements Editor Anita Meyer
Editorial Page Editor/Writer Anita Meyer
News Editor Diane Vicars
Sports Editor Jane White
State Editor Anita Meyer

Market Information: TMC.
Mechanical available: Offset; Black and 3 ROP colors; insert accepted — preprinted; page cutoffs — 22¾".
Mechanical specifications: Type page 13" x 21½"; E - 6 cols, 2", .17" between; A - 6 cols, 2", .17" between; C - 6 cols, 2", .17" between.
Commodity consumption: Newsprint 600 short tons; widths 27½"; black ink 10,500 pounds; color ink 1,760 pounds; single pages printed 5,700; average pages per issue 18(d), 24(sat); single plates used 13,500.
Equipment: EDITORIAL: Front-end hardware — 13-Ap/Mac Classic II; Front-end software — Baseview/NewsEdit. CLASSIFIED: Front-end hardware — 3-Ap/Mac LC III; Front-end software — Multi-Ad/CAMS. DISPLAY: Front-end hardware — 4-Ap/Mac Classic II; Front-end software — Multi-Ad/Creator 5.1; Printers — 2-Ap/Mac LaserWriter IIg. PRODUCTION: Typesetters — 1-Ap/Mac Plus, 1-Ap/Mac LaserWriter; Plate exposures — 1-Nu/Flip Top FT40; Plate processors — Roconex; Scanners — Microtek/Scanmaker 600GS, Microtek/Scanmaker 660ZS; Production cameras — 1-Nippon/C24DLA; Automatic film processors — AG/Rapidline 17.
PRESSROOM: Line 1 — 7-G/Community. MAILROOM: Bundle tyer — 2-Malow; Addressing machine — 1-Ch/099542090. LIBRARY: Electronic — SMS/Stauffer Gold. WIRE SERVICES: News — AP; Receiving dishes — size-2ft, AP.

COLUMBUS

Platte County

'90 U.S. Census- 19,480; **E&P '96 Est.** 20,876
ABC-CZ (90): 19,480 (HH 7,477)

Columbus Telegram (e-mon to fri; S)

Columbus Telegram, 1254 27th Ave.; PO Box 648, Columbus, NE 68601; tel (402) 564-2741; fax (402) 563-7500. Omaha World-Herald Co. group.
Circulation: 10,918(e); 11,649(S); ABC Sept. 30, 1995.
Price: 50¢(d); 75¢(S); $6.75/mo; $81.00/yr.
Advertising: Open inch rate $10.50(e); $10.50(S). **Representative:** Papert Companies.
News Services: AP, NEA. **Politics:** Independent. **Established:** 1879.
Not Published: Thanksgiving; Christmas.
Special Editions: Senior Salute, Bridal Edition (Jan); Columbus Home Show, Tax Guide (Feb); 1996 Farm Review & Forecast, Senior Salute (Mar); Excellence in Youth, Senior Salute (Apr); AG/Almanac/Beef Edition (May); Farm & Fair Edition, Senior Salute, Sidewalk Sale (July); Back-to-School, Columbus Day, Sports Review (Aug); Power and Progress Edition, Senior Salute (Oct); Recipes, Christmas Opening, Winter Sports (Nov); AG/Almanac/Grain Edition, Last Minute Gift Idea (Dec).
Special Weekly Sections: Top of the Week, Youth (mon); Best Food Day, Pawnee Scout (TMC), Senior (tues); Farm (thur); Cover

Nebraska I-239

Story, Religion/Church (fri); Business, Society, Engagements, Sports, TV Week (S).

CORPORATE OFFICERS
President Keith Haugland
Treasurer A William Kernen

GENERAL MANAGEMENT
Exec Editor Julie Speirs
Business Manager Edward O'Toole

ADVERTISING
Director Jo Sherbo
Manager-Retail Carol Keller
Manager-Classified Renee Ostrander

CIRCULATION
Manager Jackie Regier

NEWS EXECUTIVE
Managing Editor Todd Franko

EDITORS AND MANAGERS
Business/Finance Reporter Andrew Micek
Education Reporter Michelle Flyr
Farm/Agriculture Editor Andrew Micek
Features Editor Susan White
National Editor Susan White
News Editor Mike Auok
Political/Government Editor Todd Franko
Sports Editor Jon Misfeldt

MANAGEMENT INFORMATION SERVICES
Data Processing Manager Edward O'Toole

PRODUCTION
Manager Jerry Gaver
Asst Manager Joe Gaver

Market Information: TMC; ADS.
Mechanical available: Offset; Black and 3 ROP colors; insert accepted — preprinted; page cut-offs — 21½".
Mechanical specifications: Type page 13" x 21½"; E - 6 cols, 2", 1/6" between; A - 6 cols, 2", 1/8" between; C - 8 cols, 1½", 1/8" between.
Commodity consumption: Newsprint 490 short tons; widths 27½", 13¾"; black ink 18,600 pounds; color ink 6,000 pounds; single pages printed 6,508; average pages per issue 18(d), 29(S); single plates used 6,250.
Equipment: EDITORIAL: Front-end hardware — Hyundai/PC, CText/fileserver; Front-end software — CText; Printers — Ap/Mac; Other equipment — Ap/Mac, Lf/AP Leaf Picture Desk. CLASSIFIED: Front-end hardware — Hyundai/PC, CText/fileserver; Front-end software — CText; Printers — Ap/Mac LaserPrinter, C.Itoh/Line Printer. DISPLAY: Adv layout systems — Ap/Mac. PRODUCTION: Typesetters — Ap/Mac LaserWriter; Plate exposures — Nu/Flip Top FT40V6UP; Plate processors — 1-Ic/25; Production cameras — Photo Ace/250D, D, C/250; Automatic film processors — AG/Rapidline 66.
PRESSROOM: Line 1 — 7-HI/V15A; Folders — HI/JF 15. MAILROOM: Counter stackers — BG; Inserters and stuffers — 6-KAN/480; Bundle tyer — MLN/Spirit; Addressing machine — KAN/600. WIRE SERVICES: News — AP; Syndicates — NEA; Receiving dishes — AP. BUSINESS COMPUTERS: DEC/VT 320, DEC/PC, Unix/Platform; Applications: DSI: Gen ledger, Circ, Accts payable, Accts receivable; PCs & micros networked; PCs & main system networked.

FREMONT
Dodge County
'90 U.S. Census- 23,680; E&P '96 Est. 23,852

Fremont Tribune
(e-mon to fri; m-sat)

Fremont Tribune, 135 N. Main St.; PO Box 9, Fremont, NE 68025; tel (402) 721-5000; fax (402) 721-8047. Hometown Communications group.
Circulation: 9,505(e); 9,505(m-sat); Sworn Sept. 30, 1994.
Price: 35¢(d); 35¢(sat).
Advertising: Open inch rate $10.37(e); $10.37(m-sat). **Representative:** Papert Companies.
News Service: AP. **Politics:** Independent. **Established:** 1868.
Not Published: New Year; Memorial Day; Independence Day; Labor Day; Christmas Day.
Special Editions: John C. Freemont Days; Progress Edition; Key to Fremont; Visitor's Guide; Bridal Tab; Fair Tab.
Special Weekly Sections: Best Food Day, Business Day (tues); Agricultural Day (thur); Fremont Living (fri); Church Page (sat).
Magazines: TV Week; TV Section.

GENERAL MANAGEMENT
Publisher Jim Holland
Manager-Credit Rosalie Guenther

ADVERTISING
Director Pam Zoucha

NEWS EXECUTIVE
Managing Editor Brent Wasenius

EDITORS AND MANAGERS
City/Regional Editor Tammy Real-McKeighan
Sports Editor Scott Strenger

Market Information: TMC.
Mechanical available: Offset; Black and 3 ROP colors; insert accepted — preprinted, coupon envelopes; page cut-offs — 22¾".
Mechanical specifications: Type page 13¼" x 21¾"; E - 6 cols, 2 1/16", 1/8" between; A - 6 cols, 2 1/16", 1/8" between; C - 9 cols, 1⅜", 1/16" between.
Commodity consumption: Newsprint 500 short tons; widths 27", 34"; black ink 12,000 pounds; color ink 4,700 pounds; single pages printed 6,320; average pages per issue 16(d); single plates used 5,000.
Equipment: EDITORIAL: Front-end hardware — Dewar/Disc Net; Other equipment — 10-IBM/Sys 71, 15-Dewar/Discribe. CLASSIFIED: Other equipment — 3-IBM/Sys 71, 3-Dewar/Discribe. DISPLAY: Adv layout systems — Ap/Mac. PRODUCTION: Typesetters — Ap/Mac; Plate exposures — 1-Nu/Flip Top FT 40LNS; Plate processors — 1-Ic/M25; Scanners — 2-Cp/Alpha; Production cameras — 1-C/Spartan III; Automatic film processors — 1-C/T45, 1-LE/24BQ; Color separation equipment (conventional) — 1-C/E-Z Color.
PRESSROOM: Line 1 — 4-HI/V22-25; Line 2 — 6-HI/V22-25; Folders — 2-HI/2:1. MAILROOM: Counter stackers — 1-PPK; Bundle tyer — 1-MLN/ML2EES; Addressing machine — 2-Wm/3". WIRE SERVICES: News — AP; Stock tables — AP; Receiving dishes — AP. BUSINESS COMPUTERS: 1-DEC/1144; Applications: Class billing, Gen ledger, Accts payable, Circ PIA, Mail labels.

GRAND ISLAND
Hall County
'90 U.S. Census- 39,386; E&P '96 Est. 43,177

The Grand Island Independent (m-mon to sat; S)

The Grand Island Independent, First & Cedar Sts.; PO Box 1208, Grand Island, NE 68802; tel (308) 382-1000; fax (308) 382-8129. Morris Communications Corp. group.
Circulation: 24,543(m); 24,543(m-sat); 25,881(S); Sworn Sept. 30, 1995.
Price: 50¢(d); 50¢(sat); $1.00(S); $8.50/mo; $102.00/yr.
Advertising: Open inch rate $11.55(m); $11.55(m-sat); $11.55(S). **Representative:** Papert Companies.
News Services: AP, SHNS, KRT. **Politics:** Independent. **Established:** 1870.
Not Published: New Year; Independence Day; Christmas (unless a Sunday).
Advertising not accepted: Vending machines; Direct mail; Certain medical.
Special Editions: Progress and Bridal (Feb); Farm and Tourism, Auto Care/New Cars (Mar); Beef (May); Back-to-School (Aug); Home Improvement (Sept); Salute to Women, Auto Care/New Cars (Oct); Christmas Opening (Nov).
Special Weekly Sections: Building Page, Extra Ordinary People (mon); City Council, School Board, Consumer News (tues); Food, Lifelines, School Sports (wed); Youth, Womens News, Club Calendar (thur); Gardening, Mutual Funds, Entertainment (fri); Farm News, Church News, Weekend Sports (sat); Comics, Business, Weddings/Engagements (S).
Magazine: Parade.

CORPORATE OFFICERS
Chairman of the Board W S Morris III
President Paul S Simon
Secretary/Treasurer William A Herman III

GENERAL MANAGEMENT
Publisher John D Goossen
Office Manager Molly Holcher

ADVERTISING
Manager Gary Loftus

TELECOMMUNICATIONS
Audiotex Manager Justine Wheeler

CIRCULATION
Manager Mike Geiss

NEWS EXECUTIVES
Exec Editor Bill Brennan
Managing Editor Jeff Funk

EDITORS AND MANAGERS
Agriculture Editor Pete Letheby
Business Editor Terri Hahn
Editorial Page Editor Bill Brennen
Entertainment Editor Terri Hahn
Fashion/Home Furnishings Editor Terri Hahn
Features Editor Terri Hahn
Graphics Editor/Art Director Terry Krepel
News Editor Jim Faddis
Photo Editor Eric Gregory
Society Editor Terri Nohn
Sports Editor Jeff Korbelik
Women's Editor Terri Hahn

MANAGEMENT INFORMATION SERVICES
Data Processing Manager Molly Holcher

PRODUCTION
Manager Dennis Kraus
Manager-Pre Press Leroy Fletcher
Superintendent/Pressroom Tom Jakubowski

Market Information: TMC; Operate audiotex.
Mechanical available: Offset; Black and 3 ROP colors; insert accepted — preprinted, all; page cut-offs — 22¾".
Mechanical specifications: Type page 13" x 21½"; E - 6 cols, 2 1/16", 1/8" between; A - 6 cols, 2 1/16", 1/8" between; C - 8 cols, 1 9/16", 1/16" between.
Commodity consumption: Newsprint 2,000 short tons; widths 27", 13½"; black ink 44,963 pounds; color ink 9,958 pounds; single pages printed 13,100; average pages per issue 32(d), 70(S); single plates used 22,500.
Equipment: EDITORIAL: Front-end hardware — Ap/Macs; Front-end software — Baseview, QPS; Printers — Ap/Mac LaserPrinters, V/Imagesetters, Panther/Pro. CLASSIFIED: Front-end hardware — Ap/Mac SE30; Front-end software — Baseview; Printers — Ap/Mac Image Writer. AUDIOTEX: Hardware — Samsung/486-33; Software — Deskmaster. DISPLAY: Adv layout systems — 2-Ap/Mac IIcx, 2-Ap/Mac Quadra 880, 2-Ap/Power Mac 8100; Front-end hardware — 2-Ap/Mac SE; Front-end software — DTI, Multi-Ad/Creator, QPS; Other equipment — 1-Ap/Mac Scanner. PRODUCTION: Pagination software — QPS 3.3; OCR software — Caere/OmniPage, Adobe/Photoshop 2.51; Typesetters — 2-Tegra/Varityper, 1-COM/III, 1-V/53000E, V/6990, 1-Panter/Pro 36; Platemaking systems — 1-Nu; Plate exposures — 1-Nu; Plate processors — 1-WL/30D; Production cameras — 1-DAI/24, 1-Nu/2024U; Automatic film processors — SCREEN/LD-281-Q; Color separation equipment (conventional) — 1-Ap/Mac Quadra, 1-Lf/AP Leaf Picture Desk; Digital color separation equipment — Lf/Leafscan 35.
PRESSROOM: Line 1 — 10-G/Urbanite; Press drives — 2-Fin/100 h.p.; Folders — 1-G/2:1; Press control system — Fin. MAILROOM: Counter stackers — 1-Id/440, 1-Id/Marathoner; Inserters and stuffers — 1-MM/227-S, 6-Pocket; Bundle tyer — 2-MLN/ML2; Addressing machine — 1-Ch/515. LIBRARY: Electronic — 1-SMS/Stauffer Gold (Ap/Mac Configuration). COMMUNICATIONS: Systems used — satellite. WIRE SERVICES: News — AP, AP GraphicsNet, SHNS, KRT; Photos — AP; Syndicates — AP, SHNS, KRT; Receiving dishes — AP. BUSINESS COMPUTERS: 2-ATT/Unix; Applications: Circ, Accts payable, Adv billing, Accts receivable, Payroll; PCs & micros networked; PCs & main system networked.

HASTINGS
Adams County
'90 U.S. Census- 22,837; E&P '96 Est. 23,043
ABC-CZ (90): 22,837 (HH 9,127)

Hastings Tribune
(e-mon to sat)

Hastings Tribune, 908 W. 2nd St.; PO Box 788, Hastings, NE 68901; tel (402) 462-2131; fax (402) 462-2184; e-mail lhavranek@nebland.cnweb.com; web site http://www.cnweb.com/tribune. Seaton group.
Circulation: 13,491(e); 13,491(e-sat); ABC Sept. 30, 1995.
Price: 50¢(d); 50¢(sat); $8.50/mo (carrier); $81.00/yr (carrier).
Advertising: Open inch rate $10.00(e); $10.00(e-sat). **Representative:** Newspaper Mktg Group.
News Services: AP, NEA, SHNS. **Politics:** Independent. **Established:** 1905.
Not Published: New Year; Independence Day; Thanksgiving; Christmas.
Special Editions: Fair; Holiday Gift Guide; Tax Guide; Bridal; Outlook I-II-III; Travel/Transportation; Sports; Cookbook; Home & Garden; Home Improvement; Cottonwood; Senior Citizen; Hastings Guide; Back-to-School; New Car; Business & Professional Women; Holiday Cookbook; Christmas Guide; Spotlight Hastings.
Special Weekly Sections: Best Food Day (tues); Youth Page (thur); TV Section, Farm Pages, Social, Lifestyle Pages, Church Page, Local Business Page (sat).
Magazine: Happenings.

CORPORATE OFFICERS
President Donald R Seaton
Vice Pres Edward L Seaton
Exec Vice Pres Carl Sanders
Secretary/Treasurer Donald L Kissler

GENERAL MANAGEMENT
Publisher Donald R Seaton
General Manager Carl Sanders
Business Manager/Credit Manager Donald L Kissler

ADVERTISING
Director Ken Gettner
Manager-Classified Patti Walton

CIRCULATION
Manager Joseph A Smoljo

NEWS EXECUTIVE
Managing Editor Gary Johansen

EDITORS AND MANAGERS
News Editor Thad Livingston
Asst News Editor Jennifer Kalvelage
Regional Editor Darran Fowler
Sports Editor Todd Henrichs
Wire Editor Tami Humphreys

MANAGEMENT INFORMATION SERVICES
Data Processing Manager Donald L Kissler

PRODUCTION
Manager-Operations Larry Havranek
Ad Services Carla Carda
Manager-Press Scott Carstens

Market Information: Zoned editions; TMC.
Mechanical available: Offset; Black and 3 ROP colors; insert accepted — preprinted; page cut-offs — 22¾".
Mechanical specifications: Type page 13" x 21"; E - 6 cols, 2 1/16", 1/8" between; A - 6 cols, 2 1/16", 1/8" between; C - 8 cols, 1½", 1/8" between.
Commodity consumption: Newsprint 762 short tons; widths 27", 13½"; black ink 17,253 pounds; color ink 2,175 pounds; single pages printed 7,863; average pages per issue 26(d); single plates used 5,970.
Equipment: EDITORIAL: Front-end hardware — Mk/1100 Plus, 8-AT/286, 5-PC/386; Front-end software — Mk/1100Plus, QuarkXPress; Printers — 2-ECR/Scriptsetter II VR36, Ap/Mac LaserWriter 810; Other equipment — Ap/Mac, Microtek/Scanner 600ZS, Lf/Leafscan 35. CLASSIFIED: Front-end hardware — Mk/1100 Plus, 3-AT/286; Front-end software — Mk/1100 Plus; Printers — XIT/Clipper, TI/800, Ap/Mac LaserWriter 810, ECR/Scriptsetter II VR36. DISPLAY: Adv layout systems — Ap/Mac; Front-end hardware — 5-Ap/Mac; Front-end software — Multi-Ad/Creator, QuarkXPress; Printers — Ap/Mac LaserWriter 810, ECR/Scriptsetter II VR36; Other equipment — Microtek/Scanner 6002S, Nikon/Coolscan. PRODUCTION: Pagination software — QuarkXPress; OCR software — Caere/OmniPage 2.0; Typesetters — 2-ECR/Scriptsetter II, IR/Imagesetter; Plate exposures — Nu/Flip Top FT400P; Electronic picture desk — Lf/AP Leaf Picture Desk; Scanners — Lf/Leafscan 35, Microtek/6002S Flatbed, Nikon/Coolscan; Production cameras — R/580; Automatic film processors — P/26RT; Digital color separation equipment — Ap/Mac, Adobe/Photoshop.
PRESSROOM: Line 1 — 6-G/Urbanite 917; Folders — 1-G, 1-G/Cole Quarter; Press control system — Fin. MAILROOM: Counter stackers — BG/Count-O-Veyor 108; Inserters and stuffers — KAN/480, KAN/Twin Stacker; Bundle tyer — MLN/MLEE; Addressing machine — 2-KR/211. WIRE SERVICES: News — AP, SHNS, NEA; Photos — AP; Syndicates — United Media; Receiving dishes — size-3m, AP. BUSINESS COMPUTERS: 9-IBM/RISC 6000; Applications: PBS/MediaPlus: Gen ledger, Payroll, Accts payable, Circ, Ad mgmt.

HOLDREGE
Phelps County
'90 U.S. Census- 5,671; E&P '96 Est. 5,886
ABC-CZ (90): 5,671 (HH 2,356)

Holdrege Daily Citizen
(e-mon to fri)

Holdrege Daily Citizen, 418 Garfield St.; PO Box 344, Holdrege, NE 68949; tel (308) 995-4441; fax (308) 995-5992.
Circulation: 3,438(e); ABC Sept. 30, 1995.
Price: 25¢(d); $3.75/mo; $45.00/yr (carrier), $54.00/yr (mail).
Advertising: Open inch rate $6.00(e). **Representative:** Papert Companies.
News Service: AP. **Politics:** Independent. **Established:** 1885.
Not Published: New Year; Memorial Day; Independence Day; Labor Day; Thanksgiving; Christmas.
Advertising not accepted: Work at Home.
Special Editions: Bridal Section; Football & Basketball Edition; 4-H Section; Beef Section.
Special Weekly Sections: Farm (mon); Best Food Day (wed); Church (thur).

CORPORATE OFFICERS
President/Treasurer H Dwight King
Vice Pres Ruth E King
Secretary Robert D King

GENERAL MANAGEMENT
Publisher H Dwight King
Assoc Publisher Robert D King

ADVERTISING
Manager Barbara Penrod

MARKETING AND PROMOTION
Manager-Marketing/Promotion Barbara Penrod

CIRCULATION
Manager Mary Jensen

NEWS EXECUTIVE
Editor Tunney Price

EDITORS AND MANAGERS
Editorial Writer Robert D King
Home Furnishings Editor Tunney Price
Science Editor Tunney Price
Society Editor Carol Boehler
Sports Editor Jack Donoghue
Teen-Age/Youth Editor Robert D King

Market Information: TMC.
Mechanical available: Offset; Black and 3 ROP colors; insert accepted — preprinted, free standing inserts; page cut-offs — 22¾".
Mechanical specifications: Type page 14¼" x 21"; E - 6 cols, 2¼", ⅛" between; A - 6 cols, 2¼", ⅛" between; C - 8 cols, 1.83", .08" between.
Commodity consumption: Newsprint 141 short tons; widths 30", 15"; black ink 200 pounds; color ink 6,000 pounds; single pages printed 2,616; average pages per issue 10(d); single plates used 1,850.
Equipment: EDITORIAL: Front-end hardware — 5-Mk; Front-end software — Mk/1100 Plus, Mk/NewsTouch; Other equipment — Mk/1100 Plus (2 hard drives). CLASSIFIED: Front-end hardware — Mk. DISPLAY: Adv layout systems — Ap/Mac Radius; Front-end software — Ap/Mac Scanner, Multi-Ad/Creator, Ap/Mac AppleTalk; Printers — Ap/Mac LaserWriter IIf. PRODUCTION: Typesetters — Ap/Mac LaserWriter; Plate exposures — Nu/Flip Top FT40UPNS; Plate processors — Ic; Production cameras — D, C/260, SCREEN; Automatic film processors — LE/Flo LD24BQ.
PRESSROOM: Line 1 — 4-G/Community. MAILROOM: Bundle tyer — Bu; Addressing machine — Am. WIRE SERVICES: News — AP; Receiving dishes — size-3ft, AP.

KEARNEY
Buffalo County
'90 U.S. Census- 24,396; E&P '96 Est. 26,477
ABC-CZ (90): 24,396 (HH 8,973)

Kearney Hub
(e-mon to fri; m-sat)

Kearney Hub, 13 E. 22nd; PO Box 1988, Kearney, NE 68848; tel (308) 237-2152; fax (308) 234-5736. Omaha World-Herald Co. group.
Circulation: 12,836(e); 12,836(m-sat); ABC Sept. 30, 1995.
Price: 50¢(d); $1.00(sat).
Advertising: Open inch rate $8.80(e); $8.80(m-sat). **Representative:** Newspaper Mktg Group.
News Service: AP. **Politics:** Independent. **Established:** 1888.
Not Published: Thanksgiving; Christmas.
Special Editions: University of Nebraska-Kearney; Prep Football; Winter Sports; Home Furnishing; Holiday Food and Fun; Christmas; Health and Medical Services; Business and Industry; Bridal; Spring Fashion; Agriculture; Mother's Day; Father's Day; Graduation; Tourism; Valentine/Romance; Automotive; Senior Citizens Magazine (quarterly).
Special Weekly Sections: 50 Plus, Best Food Day (mon); Lifestyles, University Report, Best Food Day (tues); Lifestyles, Farm and Ranch (wed); Entertainment (thur); Prep Sports, Health, Cooking, Lifestyles, Engagements/Weddings, Church, Business Week, Happenings, Entertainment, Home Improvement, Cover Story (sat).
Magazines: Midstater TMC (tues); Cover Story; TV Magazine.

CORPORATE OFFICERS
President Steve Chatelain
Vice Pres A William Kernen
Secretary Robert Moncrief
Treasurer George Wachtler

GENERAL MANAGEMENT
Publisher Steve Chatelain
Business Manager Robert Moncrief

ADVERTISING
Director Gina Mortimore
Manager-Sales Lori Guthard

MARKETING AND PROMOTION
Coordinator-Marketing/Promotion Crystal Glatter

TELECOMMUNICATIONS
Audiotex Manager Buck Mahoney

CIRCULATION
Manager Corey Mann

NEWS EXECUTIVES
Editor Steve Chatelain
Managing Editor Michael Konz

EDITORS AND MANAGERS
Editorial Page Editor Michael Konz
Education Editor Kim Schimdt-McKeon
Farm/Agriculture Editor Chrystal Peterson
Food/Women's Editor Kelley Gavin
News Editor Kelly Gold
Regional Editor Lori Potter
Religion Editor Kelley Gavin
Sports Editor Buck Mahoney

MANAGEMENT INFORMATION SERVICES
Data Processing Manager Robert Moncrief

PRODUCTION
Manager Dale A Sickler
Foreman-Composing Kim Covi
Foreman-Press Jerry Schmitz

Market Information: TMC; ADS; Operate audiotex.
Mechanical available: Offset; Black and 3 ROP colors; insert accepted — preprinted, minimum 5"x7"; maximum 11"x13½"; page cut-offs — 22".
Mechanical specifications: Type page 13" x 21"; E - 6 cols, 2¹⁄₁₆", ⅛" between; A - 6 cols, 2¹⁄₁₆", ⅛" between; C - 9 cols, 1⅜", ¹⁄₁₆" between.
Commodity consumption: Newsprint 700 short tons; widths 27½", 13¾"; black ink 17,000 pounds; color ink 2,900 pounds; single pages printed 8,263; average pages per issue 26(d); single plates used 9,250.
Equipment: EDITORIAL: Front-end hardware — Mk; Front-end software — Mk/1100 Plus. CLASSIFIED: Front-end hardware — Mk; Front-end software — Mk/1100 Plus; Printers — Clippers. AUDIOTEX: Hardware — Info-Connect; Supplier name — Info-Connect. DISPLAY: Adv layout systems — Ap/Mac; Front-end hardware — Ap/Mac Radius; Front-end software — Multi-Ad/Creator; Printers — Clippers; Other equipment — Ap/Mac Scanner. PRODUCTION: Typesetters — 2-XIT/Clipper; Plate exposures — 1-Nu/Flip Top FT40V3UPNS; Plate processors — 1-Nat/A-250; Electronic picture desk — Lf/AP Leaf Picture Desk; Scanners — Lf/Leafscan; Production cameras — 1-SCREEN/C 240; Automatic film processors — 1-LE/LD 18; Color separation equipment (conventional) — Lf/AP Leaf Picture Desk.
PRESSROOM: Line 1 — 13-G/SSC (formers); Press drives — Fin; Folders — 1-G/SSC; Press control system — Fin; Press registration system — Carlson/Ternis. MAILROOM: Counter stackers — 1-Id/440; Inserters and stuffers — 1-KAN/480 7-into-1; Bundle tyer — 1-MLN/MLN2, 1-MLN/Spirit; Addressing machine — 1-KAN/600PS labeler. WIRE SERVICES: News — AP, SHNS; Stock tables — AP; Syndicates — SHNS, NEA; Receiving dishes — size-9ft, AP. BUSINESS COMPUTERS: DEC/VAX II, Hyundai/PC; Applications: Microsoft/Excel, Cyborg: Payroll; PCs & micros networked; PCs & main system networked.

LINCOLN
Lancaster County
'90 U.S. Census- 191,972; E&P '96 Est. 203,604
ABC-CZ (90): 193,400 (HH 75,792)

Lincoln Journal Star
(m-mon to fri; m-sat; S)

Lincoln Journal Star, 926 P St.; PO Box 81609, Lincoln, NE 68501; tel (402) 475-4200; web site http://newsone.com/. Lee Enterprises Inc. group.
Circulation: 81,301(m); 82,060(m-sat); 83,833(S); ABC Sept. 30, 1995.
Price: 50¢(d); 50¢(sat); $1.75(S).
Advertising: Open inch rate $40.40(m); $40.40(m-sat); $42.40(S). **Representative:** Landon Associates Inc.
News Services: AP, NYT, NNS, LAT-WP. **Politics:** Independent. **Established:** 1867.
Note: Effective Aug. 7, 1995, the Lincoln Journal (e-mon to fri) merged with the Lincoln Star (m-mon to fri) to form the Lincoln Journal Star (m-mon to fri; m-sat; S).
Special Editions: Weddings, Year In Review (Jan); Health & Fitness (Feb); Girls Basketball, Design-An-Ad, Boys Basketball, Lincoln Living (Mar); Futurelinc (Progress), Lincoln Living (Apr); Spring Parade of Homes, Lincoln Living (May); Discover Lincoln, Lincoln Living, Baby Steps (June); Baby Steps, Annual Football, Ultimate Campus Guide, Nebraska State Fair Program, Lincoln Living (Aug); Living the Better Years, Inside Football (3 times), Lincoln Living (Sept); Fall Parade of Homes, Inside Football (2 times), Lincoln Living, College Fair (Oct); Inside Football (2 times), Gift Guide (Nov); Last Minute Gift Ideas (Dec).
Special Weekly Sections: Best Food Day (wed); Entertainment Pages (fri); Travel Pages, Garden/Home, Entertainment Pages, Financial Pages (S).
Magazines: TV Section (sat); Parade, Focus (S).

CORPORATE OFFICERS
Chairman Lloyd Schermer
President Richard D Gottlieb

GENERAL MANAGEMENT
Publisher Bill Roesgen
Controller Gary Powell
Manager-Operations Gene Retzlaff
Personnel Manager Barbara Jurgens

ADVERTISING
Manager-Retail Kevin Mowbray
Manager-Classified Todd Nelson

MARKETING AND PROMOTION
Manager-Marketing & Promotion Michael Carpenter

TELECOMMUNICATIONS
Audiotex Manager Michael Carpenter

CIRCULATION
Manager Jerry Genrich
Manager-Division Wes Farley

NEWS EXECUTIVES
Editor Tom White
Asst Editor W James Johnson

EDITORS AND MANAGERS
Book Review Editor Vicki Reynolds
Business Reporter Jim Joyce
Business Reporter Ed Russo
City Editor Kathleen Rutledge
Asst City Editor Bill Eddy
Asst City Editor Cathie Huddle
Asst City Editor JoAnne Young
City Hall Reporter Ann Harrell
Courts/Corrections Reporter Butch Mabin
Editorial Page Editor Nancy Hicks
Asst Editorial Page Editor Art Hovey
Education-Reporter Lower Martha Stoddard
Education-Reporter Higher Karen Griess
Entertainment Reporter L Kent Wolsamott
Entertainment/Features Reporter Dan Moser
Entertainment/Features Reporter Cindy Lange-Kubick
Environment Reporter Fred Knapp
Environment Reporter Donna Biddle
Farm/Agribusiness Reporter Jolene Daib
Features Editor Linda Olig
Asst Features Editor Marc Krasnowsky
Features Reporter JoAnne Young
Features/General Assignment Reporter Bob Reeves
Features Reporter Kathy Moore
Focus/TV Week Editor Connie Walter
General Assignment Reporter Mary Kay Roth
General Assignment Reporter Patty Beutler
Health/Fitness Reporter David Swartzlander
Kids/Features Reporter Mary Kay Roth
Librarian Pat Sloan
Neighbors/People Reporter JoAnne Young
News Editor Alexandra Egan
Asst News Editor George Wright
Outdoors/Recreation Reporter Joe Duggan
Photography Manager Randy Hampton
Police Reporter Margaret Reist
Police Reporter John Barrette
Police Reporter Betty VanDeventer
Politics/People Reporter Don Walton
Regional Reporter Larry Peirce
Regional Reporter Joe Duggan
Regional/Lancaster County Reporter Al Laukaitis
Religion/Values Reporter Bob Reeves
Special Sections Editor Steve Batie
Sports Editor Gordon Winters
State Government Reporter Fred Knapp
State Government Reporter Donna Biddle
TV Week Editor Connie Walter
Teens/Features Reporter Patty Beutler
Wire Editor Jeanne Mohatt

MANAGEMENT INFORMATION SERVICES
Data Processing Manager Jaelene Koll
Online Manager Michael Carpenter
Online Manager John Rood

PRODUCTION
Manager David Brolhorst
Manager-Composing Kristy Gerry
Manager-Plate/Press Frank Jordan
Manager-Mailroom Mike Cox

Market Information: Split Run; TMC; ADS; Operate database; Operate audiotex.
Mechanical available: Letterpress (direct); Black and 3 ROP colors; insert accepted — preprinted; page cut-offs — 22¾".
Mechanical specifications: Type page 13" x 21½"; E - 6 cols, 2¹⁄₁₆", ⅛" between; A - 6 cols, 2¹⁄₁₆", ⅛" between; C - 9 cols, 1⁵⁄₁₆", ¹⁄₁₆" between.
Commodity consumption: Newsprint 6,700 metric tons; widths 55", 41¼", 27½"; black ink 242,800 pounds; color ink 45,080 pounds; single pages printed 23,436; average pages per issue 21(d), 84(S); single plates used 64,000.
Equipment: EDITORIAL: Front-end hardware — 12-RSK/100ND, 12-PC/486, HI/Newsmaker; Front-end software — Microsoft/Excel, HI. CLASSIFIED: Front-end hardware — 1-HI/Cash, 80-Excel/486 PC; Front-end software — HI. AUDIOTEX: Hardware — Micro Voice, Brite. DISPLAY: Front-end hardware — 8-HI/2100; Front-end software — HI. PRODUCTION: Typesetters — 2-AU/APS-6; Plate exposures — 2-Na/Starlite; Plate processors — 2-Na/NP80; Scanners — 2-ECR/1000, Dest/213A; Production cameras — 2-C/Spartan II; Automatic film processors — 4-C, 2-LE/LD2600A; Film transporters — 2-C; Shrink lenses — 1-C; Color separation equipment (conventional) — 1-CD/646.
PRESSROOM: Line 1 — 8-G/Mark II; Folders — 2-G. MAILROOM: Counter stackers — 3-QWI; Inserters and stuffers — 1-MM/227, 1-AM/NP-630; Bundle tyer — 4-Dynaric/NP-2; Addressing machine — 3-MG/1530, 1-Avery/5209. LIBRARY: Electronic — 1-Data Times. WIRE SERVICES: News — AP, NYT; Photos — AP; Stock tables — TMS; Receiving dishes — size-3m, AP. BUSINESS COMPUTERS: 1-IBM/Sys 38; Applications: Circ, Adv, Payroll, Gen accounting; PCs & micros networked; PCs & main system networked.

McCOOK
Red Willow County
'90 U.S. Census- 8,112; E&P '96 Est. 8,180

McCook Daily Gazette
(e-mon to sat)

McCook Daily Gazette, W. 1st & E Sts.; PO Box 1268, McCook, NE 69001; tel (308) 345-4500; fax (308) 345-7881. USMedia Inc. group.
Circulation: 7,704(e); 7,704(e-sat); Sworn Sept. 28, 1995.
Price: 50¢(d); 50¢(sat); $5.65/mo.
Advertising: Open inch rate $7.35(e); $7.60(e-sat). **Representative:** Papert Companies.
News Service: AP. **Politics:** Independent. **Established:** 1911.
Not Published: New Year; Independence Day; Labor Day; Memorial Day; Thanksgiving; Christmas.
Special Editions: Spring Farm; Fall Farm; Progress; Half Day Clearance; Crazy Days; Car Care; Home Improvement; Mother's Day;

Father's Day; Physical Fitness; Heritage Days; Spring Garden; Beef; Pork; Boat Show; Bridal; Fall & Winter Sports; Hunting; Annual Cookbook; Tourism Guide.
Magazines: Senior, Grocery (tues); Farm (thur); Weekly TV (fri).

CORPORATE OFFICERS
President	Eugene A Mace
Vice Pres	Al Portner
Secretary/Treasurer	Bill Ruhlman

GENERAL MANAGEMENT
Publisher	Gene O Morris
Business Manager	Sharyn Skiles

ADVERTISING
Director	Butch Mires
Manager	LaVonne Clapp

CIRCULATION
Manager	Glenda Ellerton

NEWS EXECUTIVES
Editor	Bruce Crosby
Managing Editor	Brent Cobb

EDITORS AND MANAGERS
City Editor	Scott Hoffman
Entertainment Editor	Brent Cobb
Lifestyle Editor	Connie Brown
Sports Editor	Herb Teter

PRODUCTION
Manager	Roger Schmidt
Manager-Pressroom	Dave Mefford

Market Information: Split Run; TMC; ADS.
Mechanical available: Offset; Black and 3 ROP colors; insert accepted — preprinted; page cut-offs — 22¾".
Mechanical specifications: Type page 13" x 21½"; E - 6 cols, 2", ⅛" between; A - 6 cols, 2", ⅛" between; C - 6 cols, 2", ⅛" between.
Commodity consumption: Newsprint 350 short tons; widths 27", 13.5"; black ink 16,000 pounds; color ink 550 pounds; single pages printed 5,302; average pages per issue 17(d); single plates used 7,000.
Equipment: EDITORIAL: Front-end hardware — 2-HI, Mk; Front-end software — Mk; Printers — 2-Ap/Mac Laser typesetter; Other equipment — 2-HI/2221. CLASSIFIED: Front-end hardware — 1-HI, Mk; Other equipment — 2-IBM. DISPLAY: Adv layout systems — 3-Ap/Mac II AdWriter. PRODUCTION: Typesetters — 2-Ap/Mac Laser; Platemaking systems — 1-BKY; Plate exposures — 1-BKY/150-40; Plate processors — 1-Ic/25-1; Production cameras — 1-R/400; Automatic film processors — 1-P/24-1; Shrink lenses — 1-CK Optical. PRESSROOM: Line 1 — 6-G/Suburban (2 Stacked units). MAILROOM: Bundle tyer — 2-Bu; Wrapping singles — 8-Sa; Addressing machine — 1-LN/25 Auto Mecha. WIRE SERVICES: News — AP; Syndicates — NEA, United Features, Universal Press, LATS, Creators; Receiving dishes — AP. BUSINESS COMPUTERS: 3-IBM/PC, AT; Applications: Nomads: Circ.; Solomon: Gen ledger, Accts payable; Synoptic: Accts receivable.

NEBRASKA CITY
Otoe County
'90 U.S. Census- 6,547; **E&P '96 Est.** 6,484

Nebraska City News-Press
(e-tues to sat)

Nebraska City News-Press, 123 S. 8th St.; PO Box 757, Nebraska City, NE 68410; tel (402) 873-3334; fax (402) 873-5436. Hollinger International Inc. group.
Circulation: 2,685(e); 2,685(e-sat); Sworn Sept. 30, 1994.
Price: 35¢(d); 35¢(sat); $6.25/mo; $75.00/yr.
Advertising: Open inch rate $6.00(e); $6.00(e-sat).
Representative: Papert Companies.
News Services: AP, NEA. **Politics:** Independent.
Established: 1854.
Note: Effective July 3, 1995, this publication changed its publishing plan from (e-mon to fri; S) to (e-tues to sat).
Not Published: New Year; Memorial Day; Independence Day; Labor Day; Thanksgiving; Christmas.
Special Editions: Tourism (Mar); Arbor Day, Pulse, Bridal (Apr); Tourism (July); Football, County Fair (Aug); Applejack, Home Improvement (Sept); Pork Producers (Oct); Recipe, Winter Sports (Nov).

CORPORATE OFFICERS
Chairman	Craig McMillan
Comptroller	Janet Nason

GENERAL MANAGEMENT
Publisher	Doug Knight

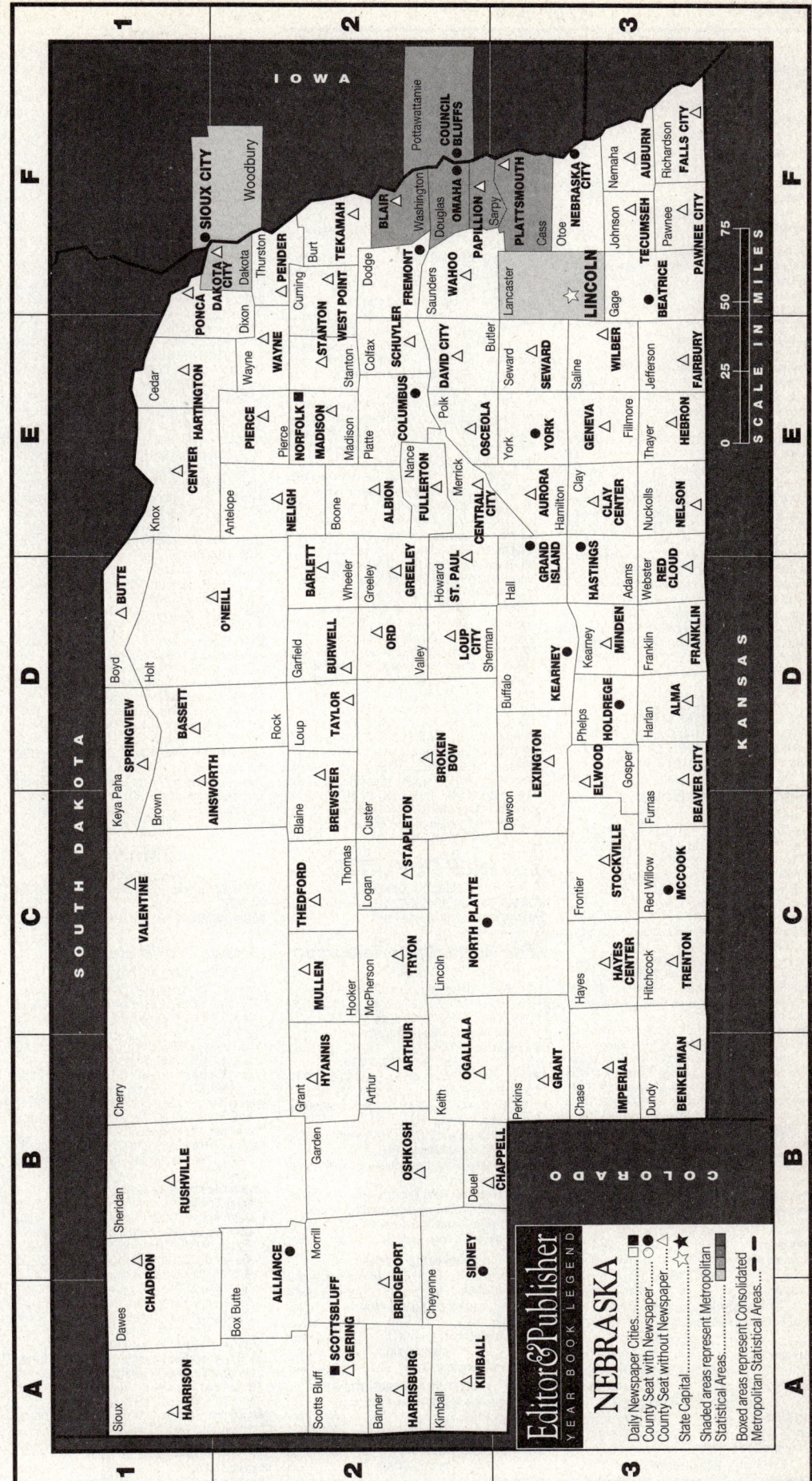

Copyright ©1996 by the Editor & Publisher Co.

I-242 Nebraska

Business Manager Theresa Bebout
Purchasing Agent Theresa Bebout

ADVERTISING

Director Kathy Caufman

CIRCULATION

Manager Susie Wilson

NEWS EXECUTIVES

Editor Dan Swanson
Managing Editor Dan Swanson

PRODUCTION

Superintendent Dan Swanson

Market Information: TMC.
Mechanical available: Offset; Black and 3 ROP colors; insert accepted — preprinted; page cut-offs — 22 3/4".
Mechanical specifications: Type page 13 1/4" x 21 1/2"; E - 6 cols, 2 1/16", 3/16" between; A - 6 cols, 2 1/16", 3/16" between; C - 6 cols, 2 1/16", 3/16" between.
Commodity consumption: Newsprint 149 short tons; widths 28", 14"; black ink 3,348 pounds; color ink 307 pounds; single pages printed 3,070; average pages per issue 10(d); single plates used 2,211.
Equipment: EDITORIAL: Front-end hardware — Ap/Mac Quadra 610; Printers — Ap/Mac LaserWriter Pro. CLASSIFIED: Front-end hardware — Ap/Mac Quadra 610; Printers — Ap/Mac LaserWriter Pro. DISPLAY: Front-end hardware — Ap/Mac 660 AU; Front-end software — Multi-Ad/Creator, QuarkXPress, Microsoft/Word 5.1; Printers — Ap/Mac LaserWriter Pro; Other equipment — XYQUEST, Microtek/ScanMaker II XG Scanner. PRODUCTION: OCR software — Caere/OmniPage 2.1; Plate exposures — 1-Nu; Production cameras — B/Vertical; Automatic film processors — P/261Q.
PRESSROOM: Line 1 — 4-HI; Folders — 1-HI. MAILROOM: Bundle tyer — 1-B; Addressing machine — Epson. WIRE SERVICES: News — AP; Receiving dishes — size-2ft, AP.

NORFOLK

Madison County

'90 U.S. Census- 21,476; E&P '96 Est. 22,798
ABC-CZ (90): 21,476 (HH 8,412)

Norfolk Daily News

(e-mon to sat)

Norfolk Daily News, 525 Norfolk Ave.; PO Box 977, Norfolk, NE 68701; tel (402) 371-1020; fax (402) 371-5802.
Circulation: 20,446(e); 20,446(e-sat); ABC Sept. 30, 1995.
Price: 35¢(d); 35¢(sat); $77.00/yr.
Advertising: Open inch rate $10.50(e); $10.50(e-sat). **Representative:** Papert Companies.
News Service: AP. **Politics:** Independent-Republican. **Established:** 1887.
Not Published: New Year; Memorial Day; Independence Day; Labor Day; Thanksgiving; Christmas.
Special Editions: Insight (Progress) (Feb); Bridal, Spring Car Care (Mar); Fashion, Agriculture (Apr); All About Norfolk (July); Back-to-School, Football (Aug); Restaurant (Oct); Car Care (Nov); Christmas Greetings (Dec).
Special Weekly Sections: Youth Pages (tues); Food Pages (wed); Farm Pages (thur); Church Pages, TV Tab (fri).
Magazine: TV Week (fri).
Broadcast Affiliates: Radio WJAG/KEXL.

CORPORATE OFFICERS

President Jerry Huse
Vice Pres W H Huse Jr

GENERAL MANAGEMENT

Publisher Jerry Huse
Business Manager W H Huse Jr

ADVERTISING

Director Larry Bartscher

MARKETING AND PROMOTION

Director-Marketing/Promotion Brad Olsen

CIRCULATION

Manager Cindy Barritt

NEWS EXECUTIVE

Editor Kent Warneke

EDITORS AND MANAGERS

City Editor Dorothy Fryer
Sports Editor Mike Fuehrer
Teen-Age/Youth Editor Jennifer Gerrietts

PRODUCTION

Manager Ken Morris
Foreman-Pressroom Larry Hansen
Foreman-Mailroom Gary Heppner

Market Information: Split Run; TMC.
Mechanical available: Offset; Black and 3 ROP colors; insert accepted — preprinted; page cut-offs — 22 3/4".
Mechanical specifications: Type page 13" x 21 1/2"; E - 6 cols, 2 1/16", 1/8" between; A - 6 cols, 2 1/16", 1/8" between; C - 9 cols, 1 1/2", 1/8" between.
Commodity consumption: average pages per issue 25(d).
Equipment: EDITORIAL: Front-end hardware — Dewar/System IV, Ap/Mac II C; Front-end software — Dewar, Novell 3.11; Printers — Printware/1217 LaserPrinter, Panasonic/1093, Ap/Mac LaserWriter NT, HI; Other equipment — Lf/AP Leaf Picture Desk. CLASSIFIED: Front-end hardware — 4-PC, Dewar/System IV; Front-end software — Dewar, Novell 3.11; Printers — Printware/LaserPrinter 1217, Okidata/320, Okidata/393; Other equipment — Novell/Network. DISPLAY: Adv layout systems — 3-Dewar/Discovery; Front-end hardware — PC, 2-Ap/Power Mac 7100, 2-Ap/Mac Quadra; Front-end software — Dewar, Adobe/Photoshop, Aldus/PageMaker, QuarkXPress, Multi-Ad; Printers — Printware/1217, Ap/Mac LaserWriter Pro 630; Other equipment — Microtek/MSII flatbed color scanner. PRODUCTION: Pagination software — Nu; OCR software — Caere/OmniPage; Typesetters — 2-Printware/1217 Laser; Plate exposures — 1-Nu; Plate processors — Nat; Electronic picture desk — Lf/AP Leaf Picture Desk; Scanners — Microtek/MSII; Production cameras — 1-DAI/Vertical, 1-DAI/Horizontal; Automatic film processors — AG; Color separation equipment (conventional) — Duc Systems.
PRESSROOM: Line 1 — 7-G/Urbanite; Press control system — Fin. MAILROOM: Counter stackers — 1-Id; Inserters and stuffers — KAN/5-into-1, MM/4-into-1; Bundle tyer — 2-Bu, 1-MLN/2A; Addressing machine — 2-KR, 1-KAN. COMMUNICATIONS: Facsimile — HP/Plain paper. WIRE SERVICES: News — AP, AP Datafeatures; Photos — AP; Syndicates — Creators, TMS, SHNS, LATS, Universal Press, King Features; Receiving dishes — size-3m, AP. BUSINESS COMPUTERS: IBM/Sys 36, Ap/Mac, Gateway/486; PCs & micros networked; PCs & main system networked.

NORTH PLATTE

Lincoln County

'90 U.S. Census- 22,605; E&P '96 Est. 22,108
ABC-CZ (90): 22,605 (HH 9,050)

The North Platte Telegraph

(m-tues to sat; S)

The North Platte Telegraph, 621 N. Chestnut (69101); PO Box 370, North Platte, NE 69103; tel (308) 532-6000; fax (308) 532-9268. Western Publishing Co. group.
Circulation: 14,401(m); 14,401(m-sat); 14,587(S); ABC Sept. 30, 1995.
Price: 50¢(d); 75¢(sat); 75¢(S); $135.00/yr.
Advertising: Open inch rate $9.40(m); $9.40(m-sat); $9.40(S). **Representative:** Newspaper Mktg Group.
News Services: AP, SHNS, NYT. **Politics:** Independent. **Established:** 1881.
Not Published: Day after Thanksgiving & Christmas.
Special Editions: Real Estate Guide (first thur); Farm/Ranch Exchange (monthly).
Special Weekly Section: TV Week (S).
Magazine: USA Weekend (S).

CORPORATE OFFICERS

President James C Seacrest
Exec Vice Pres Eric Seacrest

GENERAL MANAGEMENT

Publisher Larry Shearer
Business Manager Tami Larson

ADVERTISING

Manager-Newspaper Sales Dee Klein

MARKETING AND PROMOTION

Marketing Info Manager-New Business Development Joe Volcek

TELECOMMUNICATIONS

Audiotex Manager Joe Volcek

CIRCULATION

Manager Joe Volcek

NEWS EXECUTIVE

Editor Jill Claflin

PRODUCTION

Manager Glenn Taylor

Market Information: Zoned editions; Split Run; TMC; Operate audiotex.
Mechanical available: Offset; Black and 3 ROP colors; insert accepted — preprinted, others contact for specs; page cut-offs — 22 3/4".
Mechanical specifications: Type page 13" x 21 3/4"; E - 6 cols, 2 1/16", 1/8" between; A - 6 cols, 2 1/16", 1/8" between; C - 9 cols, 1 3/8", 1/16" between.
Commodity consumption: Newsprint 970 metric tons; widths 27", 27", 13 1/2"; black ink 18,000 pounds; color ink 7,950 pounds; single pages printed 7,830; average pages per issue 24(d), 34(S); single plates used 13,600.
Equipment: EDITORIAL: Front-end hardware — 2-Gateway/2000 PS-75, 1-Ap/Mac, 2-Gateway/2000 486-66, 2-Gateway/2000 486-66 clones; Front-end software — Dewar/DewarView 1.13f, Dewar, QuarkXPress 3.31; Other equipment — 1-Nat/News Event Picture Desk, 1-Kk/RFS 2035 Plus Film Scanner, HP/ScanJet IIcx. CLASSIFIED: Front-end hardware — 4-AST/PC 486-33; Front-end software — Graph-X. AUDIOTEX: Hardware — PC; Supplier name — Business Telecommunication Systems. DISPLAY: Adv layout systems — CNI/Ad Tracking Database; Front-end hardware — 5-Gateway/2000 PS-90 w/ 21" monitor; Front-end software — CNI/Ad Tracking Database, QuarkXPress 3.31; PRODUCTION: Typesetters — 2-Tegra/Varityper/Paper Typesetter, 2-Truetech/Typesetting, LaserMaster/Printers; Plate exposures — 1-Nu; Plate processors — Nat/A-250; Production cameras — Acti/225; Automatic film processors — P/1800 IS; Color separation equipment (conventional) — XIT/94HS Schooner, Graphic Enterprises/Full-page Negative Setter.
PRESSROOM: Line 1 — 9-HI/V-22; Line 2 — 1-Miller-Bevco/4100G; Folders — 1-Miller-Bevco/Quarter. MAILROOM: Counter stackers — HL; Inserters and stuffers — 24-HI/6; Bundle tyer — MLN/MLEE, MLN/Sprit; Addressing machine — KR. LIBRARY: Combination — 1-Microcopy/1000 Micro Fiche. COMMUNICATIONS: Facsimile — Sharp/FO-4900. WIRE SERVICES: News — AP, SHNS, NYT; Photos — AP; Receiving dishes — AP. BUSINESS COMPUTERS: 3-AST/486, 11-AST/386; Applications: Circ, Adv billing, Accts receivable, Gen ledger, Accts payable, Payroll; PCs & micros networked; PCs & main system networked.

OMAHA

Douglas County

'90 U.S. Census- 335,795; E&P '96 Est. 348,973
ABC-NDM (90): 519,027 (HH 195,073)

Omaha World-Herald

(all day-mon to fri; m-sat; S)

Omaha World-Herald, World-Herald Sq., Omaha, NE 68102; tel (402) 444-1000; fax (402) 444-1299. Omaha World-Herald Co. group.
Circulation: 232,360(a); 225,521(m-sat); 290,804(S); ABC Sept. 30, 1995.
Price: 35¢(d); 35¢(sat); $1.25(S); $2.25/wk (carrier); $117.00/yr (carrier).
Advertising: Open inch rate $96.92(a); $96.92(m-sat); $120.30(S). **Representative:** Cresmer, Woodward, O'Mara & Ormsbee.
News Services: AP, LAT-WP, KRT, NYT, TV DATA. **Politics:** Independent. **Established:** 1865.
Advertising not accepted: Anything unlawful.
Special Editions: Cruise Vacation, Weddings (Jan); Active Times, Higher Education (Feb); Lawn & Garden, Midlands Golf, Midlands Travel, Active Times (Apr); Small Business, Nurses (May); College World Series (June); Active Times (July); Football Preview (Aug); Fall Lawn & Garden, Healthy Living (Sept); Fall Energy/Home Improvement, Women at Work, Investing, College Fair (Oct); Active Times, Skiing, Christmas Guide (Nov); Auto Show of Midlands (Jan '97).
Special Weekly Sections: Health & Fitness (mon); Family & Friends, Teen Page (tues); Best Food Day (wed); Fashion (thur); Weekend (fri); Religion (sat).
Magazines: Parade; Entertainment/TV (local, newsprint); Color Comics.

CORPORATE OFFICERS

President/CEO John E Gottschalk
Vice Pres/Editor G Woodson Howe
Vice Pres-Sales William L Donaldson
Vice Pres/Chief Financial Officer A William Kernen

GENERAL MANAGEMENT

Controller/Director-Finance & Administration George Wachtler
Director-Administrative Services Joel Long
Coordinator-Public Affairs Deb Klanderud
Publisher-Affairs Charles A Wood
Personnel Manager Steve Hoff
Chief Purchasing Agent E Terry Ausenbaugh

ADVERTISING

Director Thomas R Golden
Manager-Classified Dale Harris
Manager-Advertising Development Robert Gerken
Manager-Retail Diana Condon
Manager-Creative Service Ron Larson
Coordinator-Sales/Promotion Service Rhonda Gray
Coordinator-Sales/Promotion Manager David Sanders
Manager-Research Richard Hunt

TELECOMMUNICATIONS

Director-Info Service Ken Kroeger

CIRCULATION

Director Richard R Seibert
Manager-Administration Ayman Sharif
Manager-MSA Pat Dennis
Manager-State Troy Niday
Manager-Sales/Marketing Joy Dunlap
Manager-Single Copy Pat Roll
Manager-Training Bob Thiesen
Manager-Transportation Dennis Cronin
Manager-Alternate Delivery Jim Ristow
Coordinator-Education Service Leslie Nicas

NEWS EXECUTIVES

Vice Pres/Editor G Woodson Howe
Exec Editor Michael Finney
Managing Editor Deanna Sands
Asst Managing Editor Larry King

EDITORS AND MANAGERS

Action Line Editor Gerald Wade
Art Director Mike Drummy
Automotive Editor Robert Maffitt
Book Editor Jim Bresette
Business/Finance Editor Steve Jordon
City Editor-Day Joanne Stewart
City Editor-Night Virgil Larson
Consumer Interest Editor Gerald Wade
Editorial Page Editor Frank Partsch
Editorial Writer Virginia Bensheimer
Editorial Writer Robert Niles
Education-Higher Rick Ruggles
Schools Editor Deborah Shanahan
Entertainment Editor Jim Bresette
Environment/Ecology Editor Fred Thomas
Fashion Editor Kathleen Brown
Farm Writer Ann Toner
Films/Theater Editor Jim Minge
Food Editor Jane Palmer
Features Editor Patricia Waters
Librarian Jeanne Hauser
Living Editor Patricia Waters
Medical/Science Editor Mary McGrath
Music Editor Kyle MacMillan
Exec News Editor Nelson Lampe
Outdoors Editor Larry Porter
Photo Department Director Jim Burnett
Radio/Television Editor Jim Delmont
Real Estate Editor Chris Olson
Sports Editor Steve Sinclair
Sunday Editor Don Summerside
Travel Editor Marilee Magiera
Youth Editor Julie Zelenka

PRODUCTION

Director Ed Babcock
Asst Director William W Blumel
Asst Director (Night) Bob D'Agosta
Manager-Research Lon Dunn
Manager-Systems Bill Davis
Manager-Quality Assurance Steve Jordan
Supervisor-Composing (Day) Bill Partusch
Supervisor-Composing (Night) Mike D'Agosta
Supervisor-Platemaking Kenneth McPherson
Superintendent-Pressroom Ron Hopkins
Superintendent-Mailroom Sam Nahriri
Superintendent-Electronic Maintenance Steven Gray
Superintendent-Mechanical Maintenance Marvin McManigal

Market Information: Zoned editions; Split Run; TMC; ADS; Electronic edition.
Mechanical available: Letterpress (direct); Black and 3 ROP colors; insert accepted — preprinted; page cut-offs — 22 3/4".
Mechanical specifications: Type page 13" x 21 1/2"; E - 6 cols, 2 1/16", 1/8" between; A - 6 cols, 2 1/16", 1/8" between; C - 9 cols, 1 3/8", 1/16" between.

Copyright ©1996 by the Editor & Publisher Co.

Commodity consumption: average pages per issue 50(d), 217(S); single plates used 195,000.

Equipment: EDITORIAL: Front-end hardware — 112-CD; Front-end software — CD; Printers — 7-Epson. CLASSIFIED: Front-end hardware — 40-AT; Front-end software — AT; Printers — 2-DEC/LA 120. DISPLAY: Adv layout systems — 5-HI/2100xP21; Front-end hardware — 6-PC, 3-Sun/Spare 20; Front-end software — HI/PLS; Printers — 2-MON/ExpressMaster. PRODUCTION: Typesetters — 2-HI/7500, 2-MON/1000; Plate exposures — 1-Na/Titan, 1-Na/Titan; Plate processors — 1-Na/120, 1-Na/120; Electronic picture desk — Lf/AP Leaf Picture Desk; Scanners — HP/ScanJet Plus, 2-ECR/Autokon 1000, Calera/Wordscan; Production cameras — 1-C/Spartan III, 1-C/Pager II; Automatic film processors — 2-DP/24-L, 1-DP/26-C; Film transporters — 2-C; Shrink lenses — 1-Alan/24" Variable; Color separation equipment (conventional) — 1-CD/636 E; Digital color separation equipment — 1-CD/636 E. PRESSROOM: Line 1 — 8-G/Mark I double width (4 half decks); Line 2 — 8-G/Mark I double width (4 half decks); Line 3 — 8-G/Mark I double width (4 half decks); Folders — 3-G/2:1; Pasters — 24-Automatic Pasters; Press control system — Hurletron. MAILROOM: Counter stackers — 2-G/5000, 3-QWI/SJ201, 1-QWI/SJ300; Inserters and stuffers — 2-S/48-P; Bundle tyer — 2-EAM/Mosca Cross-Tie, 1-Dynaric, 3-Dynaric, 2-Dynaric; Addressing machine — 2-Ch, 1-Ch. LIBRARY: Electronic — Battelle. WIRE SERVICES: News — AP, NYT, LAT-WP, KRT; Stock tables — AP Dataspeed, AP SelectStox; Syndicates — TV Data, LATS; Receiving dishes — AP.

SCOTTSBLUFF

Scotts Bluff County

'90 U.S. Census- 13,711; E&P '96 Est. 13,751
ABC-CZ (90): 24,036 (HH 9,484)

Star-Herald (m-tues to sat; S)

Star-Herald, 1405 Broadway (69361); PO Box 1709, Scottsbluff, NE 69363-1709; tel (308) 632-0670; fax (308) 635-1258. Western Publishing Co. group.

Circulation: 15,589(m); 15,589(m-sat); 16,424(S); ABC Sept. 30, 1995.

Price: 50¢(d); 75¢(sat); 75¢(S); $10.00/mo; $101.00/yr.

Advertising: Open inch rate $12.15(m); $12.15(m-sat); $12.15(S). **Representative:** Papert Companies.

News Services: AP, SHNS. **Politics:** Independent. **Established:** 1903.

Special Editions: Home Magazine (bi-monthly); Senior Lifestyles (Quarterly).

Magazines: Business News (tues); Best Food Day (wed); Youth Day, Health & Science (thur); Entertainment, Farm/Ranch (fri); Home, Church & Religious, TV Star (sat).

CORPORATE OFFICERS

President James C Seacrest
Vice Pres Eric Seacrest
Secretary/Treasurer Gary Seacrest
Business Manager Debbie Bohl

GENERAL MANAGEMENT

Publisher/Vice Pres Steven E Hungerford

ADVERTISING

Director Bernie Schutz

MARKETING AND PROMOTION

Manager-Marketing/Promotion Gary Gwin

CIRCULATION

Director Roger Tollefson

NEWS EXECUTIVE

Managing Editor John H Walker

EDITORS AND MANAGERS

Photography Rick Myers
Sports Editor Bob Schaller

MANAGEMENT INFORMATION SERVICES

Data Processing Manager Debbie Bohl

PRODUCTION

Director Roger Tollefson

Market Information: Zoned editions; Split Run; TMC; ADS.

Mechanical available: Offset; Black and 3 ROP colors; insert accepted — preprinted, quarter-fold, coupon books, alternate delivery; page cut-offs — 21¾".

Mechanical specifications: Type page 13" x 21½"; E - 6 cols, 2.07", .08" between; A - 6 cols, 2.07", .08" between; C - 9 cols, 1.36", .08" between.

Commodity consumption: Newsprint 985 metric tons; widths 23", 27½", 13⅝"; black ink 25,000 pounds; color ink 8,500 pounds; single pages printed 9,480; average pages per issue 20(d), 34(S); single plates used 29,024.

Equipment: EDITORIAL: Front-end hardware — Dewar/Disc Net, Nat; Front-end software — Dewar/Disc Net, Adobe/Photoshop; Printers — Okidata; Other equipment — Lf/AP Leaf Picture Desk. CLASSIFIED: Front-end hardware — Dewar/Disc Net; Printers — Okidata. DISPLAY: Adv layout systems — Dewar/Disc Net, Ap/Mac; Front-end hardware — PC, Dewar/Disc Net; Front-end software — Archetype/Corel Draw, Adobe/Photoshop; Printers — Okidata, HP/Laser Color. PRODUCTION: Typesetters — Tegra/Varityper Laser Typesetter, LaserMaster/Type, Nat; Plate exposures — 1-Nu; Plate processors — Nat/A-250; Electronic picture desk — Lf/AP Leaf Picture Desk, Nat, Adobe/Photoshop; Scanners — Nikon/Neg, Microtek/Flatbed; Production cameras — Kk/Image Maker, 1-Acti/SSII; Color separation equipment (conventional) — Nat. PRESSROOM: Line 1 — 6-HI/845; Press drives — Haley/Control PCL; Folders — HI/Cotrell; Press control system — MHI/PLC. MAILROOM: Counter stackers — 1-BG/107, 1-HL/Monitor, 1-BG/108; Inserters and stuffers — 1-HI/624P; Bundle tyer — 2-MLN/ML-2EES; Addressing machine — 1-KR/215. WIRE SERVICES: News — AP; Syndicates — Universal Press, TV Data, SHNS; Receiving dishes — size-3m, AP. BUSINESS COMPUTERS: 5-NEC/MultiSync 2A; Applications: Archetype/Corel Draw, Microsoft/Works, Microsoft/Windows: Gen ledger, Accts payable, Accts receivable; PCs & micros networked; PCs & main system networked.

SIDNEY

Cheyenne County

'90 U.S. Census- 5,959; E&P '96 Est. 5,875

The Sidney Telegraph (e-mon to fri)

The Sidney Telegraph, 809 Illinois St.; PO Box 219, Sidney, NE 69162-0219; tel (308) 254-5555; fax (308) 254-5607. Hollinger International Inc. group.

Circulation: 2,650(e); Sworn Oct. 6, 1995.

Price: 50¢(d).

Advertising: Open inch rate $7.32(e).

News Service: AP. **Politics:** Independent. **Established:** 1989.

Not Published: New Year; Memorial Day; Independence Day; Labor Day; Thanksgiving Day; Christmas.

Special Editions: We are Sidney (Jan); Progress, Valentine's Day (Feb); St. Pat's Day, Spring Ag, Easter Coloring Contest (Mar); Moonlight Madness, Home Improvement, Spring Car Care, National Secretaries Week, Easter Specials (Apr); Graduation, Mother's Day, Memorial Day, Beef Tab (May); Father's Day, Golf Guide (June); Honor Roll, Appreciation Days, Christmas in July, Salute to Seniors (July); Fair Edition, Football/Volleyball, Back-to-School (Aug); Car Care, After Fair Results, Fall Home Improvement, Rod and Roll Coupon, Oktoberfest Edition, Salute to Women, Fall Car Care (Sept); Fall Ag, Bosses' Day, Trick or Treat Trail, Moonlight (Oct); Gift Guide, Merchant Give-away, Fall Sports Round-up (Nov); Christmas Coloring Contest, Christmas Greetings, ABC's of Christmas, 1st Baby Contest, Gift Guide (Dec).

Special Weekly Section: TV Time.

GENERAL MANAGEMENT

Publisher Don Evans

ADVERTISING

Director Don Evans
Director Sue Mizell

CIRCULATION

Manager Margaret Evans

NEWS EXECUTIVE

Editor Gordon Tustin

PRODUCTION

Manager Warren Johnson

Market Information: Zoned editions; TMC.

Mechanical available: Offset; Black and 3 ROP colors; insert accepted — preprinted.

Mechanical specifications: Type page 13" x 21½"; E - 6 cols, 2 1/16", ⅛" between; A - 6 cols, 2 1/16", ⅛" between; C - 9 cols, 1⅜", ⅛" between.

Commodity consumption: average pages per issue 10(d).

Equipment: DISPLAY: Front-end hardware — Ap/Mac. PRESSROOM: Line 1 — 4-G/Community.

YORK

York County

'90 U.S. Census- 7,884; E&P '96 Est. 8,171

York News-Times (e-mon to sat)

York News-Times, 327 Platte Ave.; PO Box 279, York, NE 68467; tel (402) 362-4478; fax (402) 362-6748. Morris Communications Corp. group.

Circulation: 5,142(e); 5,142(e-sat); Sworn Sept. 30, 1995.

Price: 35¢(d); 35¢(sat); $6.25/mo; $67.50/yr.

Advertising: Open inch rate $6.95(e); $6.95(e-sat). **Representative:** Papert Companies.

News Service: AP. **Politics:** Independent. **Established:** 1887.

Not Published: New Year; Memorial Day; Independence Day; Labor Day; Thanksgiving; Christmas.

Special Editions: Back-to-School; Bridal Edition; Business Update; Guide to York County; Silver (Senior) Salute; Spring & Fall; Fall Car Care; Fall & Winter Sports Editions; Christmas Opening; Yorkfest; County Fair.

Special Weekly Sections: Regional News (mon); Best Food Day (tues); Farm and Agriculture Page, Prime Time TV Tab (thur); Church Directory/Religion Page, Professional Service Directory (fri).

Magazine: Prime Time (wkly Television Rolling Logs & Grids).

CORPORATE OFFICERS

Chairman of the Board W S Morris III
President Paul S Simon
Secretary/Treasurer William A Herman III

GENERAL MANAGEMENT

Publisher Dan D Collin

ADVERTISING

Manager David H Sjuts

TELECOMMUNICATIONS

Audiotex Manager Carol Faller

CIRCULATION

Manager Darren Hromadka
Manager Debra Klatt

NEWS EXECUTIVES

Editor Dan D Collin
Managing Editor J Mark Lile

PRODUCTION

Manager Donald J Rossiter

Market Information: TMC; Operate audiotex.

Mechanical available: Offset; Black and 3 ROP colors; insert accepted — preprinted, preprinted; page cut-offs — 22¾".

Mechanical specifications: Type page 13" x 21"; E - 6 cols, 2.08", ⅛" between; A - 6 cols, 2.08", ⅛" between; C - 6 cols, 2.08", ⅛" between.

Commodity consumption: Newsprint 220 short tons; widths 27", 13½"; black ink 7,510 pounds; color ink 825 pounds; single pages printed 4,200; average pages per issue 13(d); single plates used 2,108.

Equipment: EDITORIAL: Front-end hardware — Ap/Mac SE, Ap/Mac Server 60; Front-end software — QuarkXPress, Microsoft/Word; Printers — Ap/Mac II NTX, Ap/Mac LaserWriter Pro 600. CLASSIFIED: Front-end hardware — Ap/Mac Quadra 605, Ap/Mac IIsi; Front-end software — Baseview; Printers — Ap/Mac II NTX. AUDIOTEX: Hardware — Samsung; Supplier name — SMS. DISPLAY: Adv layout systems — Ap/Mac; Front-end hardware — Ap/Mac IIsi, Ap/Mac II NTX; Front-end software — Aldus/PageMaker 4.2; Other equipment — Ap/Mac One Scanner. PRODUCTION: OCR software — Caere/OmniPage; Typesetters — MON/1270; Plate exposures — 1-Nu/Flip Top FT40APRNS; Scanners — Nikon/LS-3510, Microtek/ScanMaker II, Ap/Mac One; Production cameras — DAI/Screen, C/240-LA; Automatic film processors — SCREEN/LD-220 QT; Color separation equipment (conventional) — Nikon/LS-3510 AF, MON/1270; Digital color separation equipment — Ca/Sharpshooter EC12DM. PRESSROOM: Line 1 — 6-KP/Newsking (w/upper former); Press drives — CH; Folders — 1-KP/KJ6; Reels and stands — 6-KP/Newsking; Press control system — CH. MAILROOM: Bundle tyer — Ty-Tech/Model 40 Tyer; Addressing machine — Ch/Mod IV Labeler, Ch/4-up Model 542090. LIBRARY: Electronic — SMS/Stauffer Gold. WIRE SERVICES: News — AP; Syndicates — King Features, NEA, Universal Press; Receiving dishes — size-2 1/2ft, AP. BUSINESS COMPUTERS: NCR/System 3230; Applications: SMS: Payroll, Accts payable, Adv, Circ, Gen ledger.

NEVADA

CARSON CITY

An Independent City

'90 U.S. Census- 40,443; E&P '96 Est. 45,428
ABC-NDM (90): 40,443 (HH 15,895)

Nevada Appeal (m-mon to fri; S)

Nevada Appeal, 200 Bath St.; PO Box 2288, Carson City, NV 89702-2288; tel (702) 882-2111; fax (702) 882-6664. Swift Newspapers group.

Circulation: 12,211(m); 13,157(S); ABC Sept. 30, 1995.

Price: 35¢(d); $1.00(S); $8.00/mo (carrier); $90.00/yr (carrier), $234.00/yr (mail).

Advertising: Open inch rate $14.40(m); $16.75(S). **Representative:** Papert Companies.

News Service: AP. **Politics:** Independent. **Established:** 1865.

Special Editions: Carson Country, Deadline President's Day Bonus (Mar); Deadline Easter Bonus, Deadline Home Improvement, Home Improvement Appeal (Apr); Home Improvement Chronicle, Deadline Mother's Day, Mother's Day Bonus Section (May); Deadline Father's Day Bonus (June); Deadline Customer Appreciation Appeal (July); Deadline Primary Election (Aug); Deadline Thanksgiving GG, Christmas Fair, Thanksgiving Gift (Nov); Deadline Song Book, Song Book Appeal, Last Minute Appeal Bonus (Dec).

Special Weekly Sections: Best Food Day, Business News (wed); Business News, Dining/Entertainment, Real Estate (fri); Business News, TV log (S).

Magazines: Real Estate, Entertainment (Jackpot) (fri); TV Mag (S).

CORPORATE OFFICERS

President Richard K Larson
Vice Pres Bradley F Henke
Vice Pres/Secretary/Treasurer Arne Hoel

GENERAL MANAGEMENT

Publisher Phil Neiswanger

ADVERTISING

Director Steve Reynolds

CIRCULATION

Director Thomas L Berner

NEWS EXECUTIVE

Editor Pat Quinn-Davis

EDITORS AND MANAGERS

City Editor Pat Quinn-Davis
Editorial Page Editor Pat Quinn-Davis
Entertainment/Amusements Editor Kevin Jenkins
News Editor Sandi Wright
Photo Editor Rick Gann
Religion Editor Kevin Jenkins
Sports Editor Lou Thomas
Television/Film Editor Kevin Jenkins
Theater/Music Editor Kevin Jenkins

PRODUCTION

Manager-Pressroom John A Silva
Supervisor-Composing Rosemary Woods

Market Information: Zoned editions; TMC.

Mechanical available: Offset; Black and 3 ROP colors; insert accepted — preprinted, single sheets; page cut-offs — 22¾".

Mechanical specifications: Type page 13" x 21½"; E - 6 cols, 2 1/16", ⅛" between; A - 6 cols, 2 1/16", ⅛" between; C - 9 cols, 1 5/16", ⅛" between.

Commodity consumption: Newsprint 670 metric tons; widths 27½", 13½"; single pages printed 8,625; average pages per issue 20(d), 54(S).

Equipment: EDITORIAL: Front-end hardware — SII/Sys 22; Other equipment — 12-SII/ET960, 1-Ap/Mac. CLASSIFIED: Front-end hardware — SII; Other equipment — 5-SII/ET960. DISPLAY: Adv layout systems — 2-Ap/Mac; Front-end hardware — 1-Ap/Mac cx, 1-Ap/Mac Centris 650, CD-Rom; Front-end software — Multi-Ad/Creator, Broderbund/TypeStyler, Claris/MacWrite, Aldus/PageMaker, Microsoft/ Excel; Printers — Ap/Mac LaserWriter II NTX, Ap/Mac Color Printer. PRODUCTION: Typesetters — 2-

I-244 Nevada

Ap/Mac, Microcraft/Translator II; Platemaking systems — 3M/Deadliner; Plate exposures — 1-Nu/Flip Top FT40UP; Scanners — 1-Hx/150B, 1-CK Optical; Production cameras — 1-Hx/150B.
PRESSROOM: Line 1 — 6-G/Urbanite; Folders — 1-G/2:1. MAILROOM: Inserters and stuffers — KAN/320; Bundle tyer — 1-MLN/ML2EE. COMMUNICATIONS: Systems used — satellite. WIRE SERVICES: News — AP; Syndicates — NEA, SHNS; Receiving dishes — AP. BUSINESS COMPUTERS: 2-IBM/PC, Link/MC5 Business ET960. Applications: Bus.

ELKO
Elko County
'90 U.S. Census- 14,736; E&P '96 Est. 19,154

Elko Daily Free Press (e-mon to sat)
Elko Daily Free Press, 3720 Idaho St., Elko, NV 89801; tel (702) 738-3119; fax (702) 738-2215.
Circulation: 7,097(e); 7,097(e-sat); Sworn Sept. 30, 1995.
Price: 35¢(d); 35¢(sat); $84.50/yr.
Advertising: Open inch rate $8.22(e); $8.22(e-sat).
News Service: AP. **Politics:** Independent. **Established:** 1883.
Not Published: New Year; Independence Day; Thanksgiving; Christmas.
Special Editions: Cowboy Poetry Gathering (Jan); Presidential Showcase (Feb); Bride's Guide, Celebrate You, Celebrate Children (Mar); Home Improvement Guide (Apr); Graduation Special, Recreation Guide (May); Mining Expo (June); Silver State Stampede, Customer Appreciation (July); Back-to-School, Fair Edition (Aug); Fall Sports Review, Hunting Edition (Sept); Home Makers' School, Castles & Carriages (Oct); Pre Holiday Show, Christmas Kick-off (Nov); Christmas Gift Guide, Cooking at Christmas, Christmas Countdown, Christmas Greetings Songbook, New Year's Baby (Dec).
Special Weekly Sections: Best Food Day, Extra (tues); Entertainment & TV Guide (fri); Comics, Society/Events/Business (sat).
Magazine: Free Press Extra (tues).

CORPORATE OFFICERS
President Kim Steninger
Treasurer Rex Steninger
Secretary Dan Steninger

GENERAL MANAGEMENT
Co-Publisher Rex Steninger
Co-Publisher Kim Steninger
Co-Publisher Dan Steninger

ADVERTISING
Manager Glenes J Bir

NEWS EXECUTIVE
Editor Rex Steninger

EDITORS AND MANAGERS
Business Editor Adella Harding
Opinion Editor Dan Steninger
Sports Editor Mark Lenz

PRODUCTION
Manager Rod Crouch

Market Information: TMC.
Mechanical available: Offset; Black and 3 ROP colors; insert accepted — preprinted; page cut-offs — 21½".
Mechanical specifications: Type page 13" x 21½"; E - 6 cols, 2 1/16", ⅛" between; A - 6 cols, 2 1/16", ⅛" between; C - 6 cols, 2 1/16", ⅛" between.
Commodity consumption: Newsprint 350 short tons; widths 71.1"; single pages printed 7,250; average pages per issue 18(d); single plates used 2,600.
Equipment: EDITORIAL: Front-end hardware — 1-Mk; Front-end software — Mk. CLASSIFIED: Front-end hardware — 1-Mk. DISPLAY: Other equipment — 3-M/MUP, 1-Mk. PRODUCTION: Typesetters — Linotype-Hell/Linotronic 101, Printware/720IQ; Plate exposures — 2-B; Scanners — Lf/Leafscan 35; Production cameras — 1-B/2000, 1-Acti; Automatic film processors — AG/Rapidline 43.
PRESSROOM: Line 1 — 7-KP/Newsking; Folders — 1-KP/2:1. WIRE SERVICES: News — AP; Photos — AP; Receiving dishes — size-3m, AP. BUSINESS COMPUTERS: 2-IBM/PC; Applications: Bus news; PCs & micros networked; PCs & main system networked.

ELY
White Pine County
'90 U.S. Census- 4,756; E&P '96 Est. 4,655

Ely Daily Times (e-mon to fri)
Ely Daily Times, 655 Aultman; PO Box 1139, Ely, NV 89301; tel (702) 289-4491; fax (702) 289-4566. Donrey Media group.
Circulation: 2,549(e); Sworn Sept. 29, 1995.
Price: 50¢(d); $9.00/mo; $108.00/yr.
Advertising: Open inch rate $8.87(e). **Representative:** Papert Companies.
News Service: AP. **Politics:** Independent. **Established:** 1920.
Not Published: New Year; Memorial Day; Independence Day; Labor Day; Thanksgiving; Christmas.
Special Editions: Graduation; Christmas; New Year.
Special Weekly Sections: Best Food Day (tues); TV Times (thur).
Magazine: "Weekender" TV Guide (thur).

CORPORATE OFFICERS
Founder Donald W Reynolds
President/Chief Operating Officer Emmett Jones
Exec Vice Pres/Chief Financial Officer Darrell W Loftin
Vice Pres-Western Newspaper Group David A Osborn
Vice Pres-Eastern Newspaper Group Don Schneider

GENERAL MANAGEMENT
Publisher George Carnes

ADVERTISING
Director Ken Kliewer

NEWS EXECUTIVE
Editor Kent Harper

EDITORS AND MANAGERS
Business/Finance Editor Kent Harper
City/Metro Editor Kent Harper
Editorial Page Editor Kent Harper
National Editor Kent Harper
News Editor Kent Harper
Sports Editor Kent Harper

Mechanical available: Offset; Black and 2 ROP colors; insert accepted — preprinted; page cut-offs — 22¾".
Mechanical specifications: Type page 13" x 21½"; E - 6 cols, 2", ⅙" between; A - 6 cols, 2", ⅙" between; C - 9 cols, 1⅓", ⅑" between.
Commodity consumption: Newsprint 60 metric tons; widths 27½", 13¾"; black ink 1,000 pounds; single pages printed 2,550; average pages per issue 8(d); single plates used 1,500.
Equipment: EDITORIAL: Front-end hardware — Ap/Mac, 2-Ap/Power Mac 6100-66; Front-end software — QuarkXPress, Baseview; Printers — Ap/Mac LaserWriter NTX. CLASSIFIED: Front-end hardware — Ap/Mac SE; Front-end software — QuarkXPress, Baseview; Printers — Ap/Mac LaserWriter NT, HP/LaserJet 4MV 11x17. DISPLAY: Front-end hardware — Ap/Power Mac 6100, Ap/Mac; Front-end software — QuarkXPress, Aldus/FreeHand, Multi-Ad; Printers — Ap/Mac LaserWriter NTX. PRODUCTION: Pagination software — Ap/Mac LC, Ap/Power Mac 7100, Multi-Ad, QuarkXPress 3.5; Plate exposures — 1-Nu; Production cameras — K/Vertical.
PRESSROOM: Line 1 — G/Community (12 pages). MAILROOM: Bundle tyer — 1-Bu/Strapper. WIRE SERVICES: News — AP; Syndicates — NEA; Receiving dishes — size-2ft, AP. BUSINESS COMPUTERS: Colorado 250MB, Brainworks.

FALLON
Churchill County
'90 U.S. Census- 4,643; E&P '96 Est. 5,303

Lahontan Valley News & Fallon Eagle Standard (m-mon to sat)
Lahontan Valley News & Fallon Eagle Standard, 562 N. Maine St.; PO Box 1297, Fallon, NV 89406; tel (702) 423-6041; fax (702) 423-0474.
Circulation: 4,863(m); 4,863(m-sat); Sworn Sept. 29, 1995.
Price: 35¢(d); 35¢(sat); $74.00/yr (local); $99.00/yr.
Advertising: Open inch rate $7.66(m); $7.66(m-sat).
News Service: AP. **Politics:** Independent. **Established:** 1903 (Standard), 1906 (Eagle), 1985 (daily).
Not Published: Federal Holidays.
Special Weekly Section: TV Section (fri).

CORPORATE OFFICER
Exec Vice Pres Anne Pershing

GENERAL MANAGEMENT
Co-Publisher David C Henley
Co-Publisher Ludie Henley

ADVERTISING
Manager Joyce Thompson

NEWS EXECUTIVE
Editor Anne Pershing

Mechanical available: Black and 3 ROP colors; insert accepted — preprinted.
Mechanical specifications: Type page 13" x 21½"; E - 6 cols, 2 1/16", ⅛" between; A - 6 cols, 2 1/16", ⅛" between; C - 8 cols, 1 5/16", ⅛" between.
Commodity consumption: Newsprint 80 metric tons; widths 28", 14"; black ink 3,450 pounds; color ink 200 pounds; average pages per issue 10(d).
Equipment: EDITORIAL: Front-end hardware — COM; Printers — Ap/Mac LaserPrinter. CLASSIFIED: Front-end hardware — Ap/Mac. DISPLAY: Adv layout systems — Ap/Mac. PRODUCTION: Typesetters — COM; Production cameras — Acti; Reproportion units — AG/5000.
PRESSROOM: Line 1 — 4-KP/Newsking Offset; Press control system — CH/Respondor Drive. MAILROOM: Counter stackers — PB; Inserters and stuffers — 4-KAN/620; Bundle tyer — PAK/Tyer, Felins/F-16. WIRE SERVICES: News — AP; Receiving dishes — AP. BUSINESS COMPUTERS: DA, NCR, IBM.

LAS VEGAS
Clark County
'90 U.S. Census- 258,295; E&P '96 Est. 322,046
ABC-NDM (90): 741,459 (HH 287,025)

Las Vegas Sun (e-mon to fri) *Las Vegas Review-Journal & Las Vegas Sun* (m-sat; S)
Las Vegas Sun, 800 S. Valley View (89107); PO Box 4275, Las Vegas, NV 89127; tel (702) 385-3111; fax (702) 383-7264; e-mail thompson@lvsun.com.
Circulation: 38,497(e); 173,968(m-sat); 211,361(S); ABC Sept. 30, 1995.
Price: 50¢(d); 50¢(sat); $2.50(S).
Advertising: Open inch rate $39.95(e); $101.20(m-sat); $114.00(S); comb with Las Vegas Review-Journal (m) $101.20. **Representative:** Papert Companies.
News Services: AP, NYT, SHNS. **Politics:** Independent. **Established:** 1950.
Note: Printed at the Las Vegas Review-Journal. For detailed mechanical information, see the Las Vegas Review-Journal listing.
Special Editions: Health and Fitness, Super Bowl (Jan); Seniors' Magazine, Dining Guide (Feb); Best of Las Vegas, Home and Garden (Mar); Guide to Pool & Patio, Senior Golf Classic, Home Furnishings, Wine and Dine (UNLVino) (Apr); Seniors' Magazine, Legal Handbook (May); Dining Guide (June); Guide to Las Vegas, Guide to Pool & Patio (July); Seniors' Magazine, Football Preview (Aug); Medical Handbook, Desert Living, Dining Guide (Sept); Las Vegas Invitational, Health & Fitness, Seniors' Magazine (Oct); Ski the West, Meet the Rebels, National Finals Rodeo (Nov); Holiday Entertainment and Dining Guide (Dec).
Special Weekly Sections: Monday Business Tab (mon); Food (wed); Religion, Entertainment (sat); Real Estate, Travel, Business, Entertainment, Focus (Opinions), Sun Opinions (S).
Magazine: TV Magazine (S).
Cable TV: Operate leased cable TV in circulation area; Own cable TV in circulation area.

CORPORATE OFFICERS
Chairman of the Board Mike O'Callaghan
President Brian Greenspun
Vice Pres Daniel Greenspun
Secretary Ruth Deskin
Treasurer Barbara Greenspun

GENERAL MANAGEMENT
Publisher Barbara Greenspun

ADVERTISING
Director Jack Harpster
Director-National Trudy Patterson
Manager-Classified Randa Todd
Manager-Retail Dave Siminatis

CIRCULATION
Manager Steve Coffeen

NEWS EXECUTIVES
Exec Editor Mike O'Callaghan
Editor Brian Greenspun
Managing Editor Sandra Thompson
Asst Managing Editor Ken Ward

EDITORS AND MANAGERS
Business Editor Rick Velotta
City Editor Geoff Schumacher
Editorial Page Editor Larry Wills
Features Editor Phil Hagen
Photo Editor Brad Talbutt
Sports Editor Ron Kantowski

MANAGEMENT INFORMATION SERVICES
Data Processing Manager Deena Caudle

Market Information: TMC.
Commodity consumption: widths 55", 41¼", 27½"; average pages per issue 52(d), 210(S).
Equipment: EDITORIAL: Front-end hardware — Sun/Micro Systems; Front-end software — Custom Developed. PRODUCTION: Typesetters — Hyphen/SpectraSet 2000, AG/Proset 9800; Electronic picture desk — HI/XP-21; Scanners — Sharp/JX-600, Nikon/LS-3510 AF. WIRE SERVICES: News — AP; Photos — AP; Syndicates — NYT; Receiving dishes — AP.

Las Vegas Review-Journal (m-mon to fri) *Las Vegas Review-Journal & Las Vegas Sun* (m-sat; S)
Las Vegas Review-Journal, 1111 W. Bonanza; PO Box 70, Las Vegas, NV 89125-0070; tel (702) 383-0211; fax (702) 383-4665. Donrey Media group.
Circulation: 142,149(m); 173,968(m-sat); 211,361(S); ABC Sept. 30, 1995.
Price: 50¢(d); 50¢(sat); $2.50(S); $3.00/wk; $156.00/yr.
Advertising: Open inch rate $77.90(m); $101.20(m-sat); $114.00(S); comb with Las Vegas Sun (e) $101.20. **Representative:** Papert Companies.
News Services: AP, LAT-WP, KRT. **Politics:** Independent. **Established:** 1905.
Special Editions: Health & Fitness, Super Bowl (Jan); Seniors Magazine, Dining Guide (Feb); Best of Las Vegas, Home and Garden (Mar); Guide to Pool & Patio, Senior Golf Classic, Home Furnishings, Wine and Dine (Apr); Seniors' Magazine, Legal Handbook (May); Dining Guide (June); Guide to Las Vegas, Guide to Pool & Patio (July); Seniors Magazine, Football Preview (Aug); Medical Handbook, Desert Living, Dining Guide (Sept); Las Vegas Invitational, Health and Fitness, Seniors' Magazine (Oct); Ski the West, Meet the Rebels, National Finals Rodeo (Nov); Holiday Entertainment and Dining Guide (Dec).
Special Weekly Sections: Your Money (mon); Food (wed); Weekend Living - Entertainment (fri); Religion (sat); Real Estate, Travel, Business, Entertainment, Focus, Sun Opinions (S).
Magazines: Parade (own, newsprint), TV Magazine (S).

CORPORATE OFFICERS
Founder Donald W Reynolds
President/Chief Operating Officer Emmett Jones
Exec Vice Pres/Chief Financial Officer Darrell W Loftin
Vice Pres-Western Newspaper Group David A Osborn
Vice Pres-Eastern Newspaper Group Don Schneider

GENERAL MANAGEMENT
Publisher Sherman Frederick
General Manager Lynn Mosier
Manager-Business Office Pat Johnson
Personnel Manager Jim Hannah
Manager-Credit Jim Wood

ADVERTISING
Director Jack Harpster
Manager-Retail Dave Siminatis
Manager-National Trudy Patterson
Manager-Classified Randa Todd
Manager-Sales Development Emily Billings

MARKETING AND PROMOTION
Director-Marketing/Promotion Allan Fleming
Asst Director-Promotion/Coordinator-Community Service Christian Kolberg

CIRCULATION
Director Steve Coffeen

NEWS EXECUTIVES
Editor Thomas Mitchell
Managing Editor Charles Zobell

Copyright ©1996 by the Editor & Publisher Co.

EDITORS AND MANAGERS

Business Editor	Rafael Tammariello
City Editor	Laura Wingard
Editorial Page Editor	John Kerr
Features Editor	Frank Fertado
Food Editor	Ken White
News Editor	Mary Greeley
Photo Editor	Jim Laurie
Real Estate Editor	Carmel Hopkins
Religion Editor	John Przybys
Television Editor	Chris Stanley
Weekend Editor	Christine Mason

PRODUCTION

Director-Operations	Terry Duck
Asst Manager	Dick Borghi

Market Information: Zoned editions; TMC; ADS.
Mechanical available: Offset; Black and 3 ROP colors; insert accepted — preprinted; page cut-offs — 22¾".
Mechanical specifications: Type page 13" x 21½"; E - 6 cols, 2¹⁄₁₆", ⅛" between; A - 6 cols, 2¹⁄₁₆", ⅛" between; C - 9 cols, 1³⁄₁₆", ³⁄₃₂" between.
Commodity consumption: Newsprint 35,000 metric tons; widths 55", 41¼", 27½"; black ink 672,000 pounds; color ink 120,000 pounds; single pages printed 56,000; average pages per issue 75(d), 80(sat), 180(S); single plates used 168,000.
Equipment: EDITORIAL: Front-end hardware — DTI; Front-end software — ESP/2, DTI; Printers — MON/3850 Express Masters; Other equipment — Ap/Mac, Lf. CLASSIFIED: Front-end hardware — AT; Front-end software — ESP/2; Printers — TI, XIT/Clipper, PageScan/III plus. DISPLAY: Adv layout systems — Ap/Mac; Front-end hardware — Ap/Mac, DTI; Front-end software — DTI/Ad Speed; Printers — XIT/Clippers, MON/3850 Express Masters. PRODUCTION: Pagination software — DTI/Page Speed; Typesetters — 3-XIT/Clipper, MON/3850 Express Masters; Platemaking systems — 2-WL/Lith-X-Pozer; Scanners — Lf/Leafscan 35, Microsoft/Excel 26, Kk/2035, ECR/Autokon 2045c, Sharp/JX-610, Lf/Leafscan 45; Production cameras — C/Marathon, B; Automatic film processors — 2-LE; Color separation equipment (conventional) — Ap/Mac, Adobe/Photoshop, Kk/2035, Sharp/Jx-610, Lf/Leafscan 45; Digital color separation equipment — DTI/Page Speed, DTI/Ad Speed.
PRESSROOM: Line 1 — 9-G/Metro; Line 2 — 9-G/Metro; Folders — 2-G; Pasters — MGD, G/Metro flying pasters; Reels and stands — MGD; Press control system — MGD.
MAILROOM: Counter stackers — 6-HL/Monitor, 1-MM; Inserters and stuffers — 2-HI/1472A, 1-MM; Bundle tyer — 8-Dynaric/NP-1; Addressing machine — Ch. LIBRARY: Electronic — Data Times. WIRE SERVICES: News — AP, LAT-WP; Stock tables — AP SelectStox I; Syndicates — AP; Receiving dishes — AP. BUSINESS COMPUTERS: HP/3000-932; Applications: CJ; Adv; PCs & micros networked; PCs & main system networked.

Nevada

I-245

RENO
Washoe County

'90 U.S. Census- 133,850; E&P '96 Est. 147,102
ABC-NDM (90): 306,190 (HH 121,926)

Reno Gazette-Journal
(m-mon to sat; S)

Reno Gazette-Journal, 955 Kuenzli; Box 22000, Reno, NV 89520; tel (702) 788-6200; e-mail rgj@libcom.dps.com. Gannett Co. Inc. group.
Circulation: 68,318(m); 68,318(m-sat); 86,492(S); ABC Sept. 30, 1995.
Price: 50¢(d); 50¢(sat); $1.50(S); $3.25/wk (carrier); $13.00/mo (carrier); $169.00/yr (carrier).

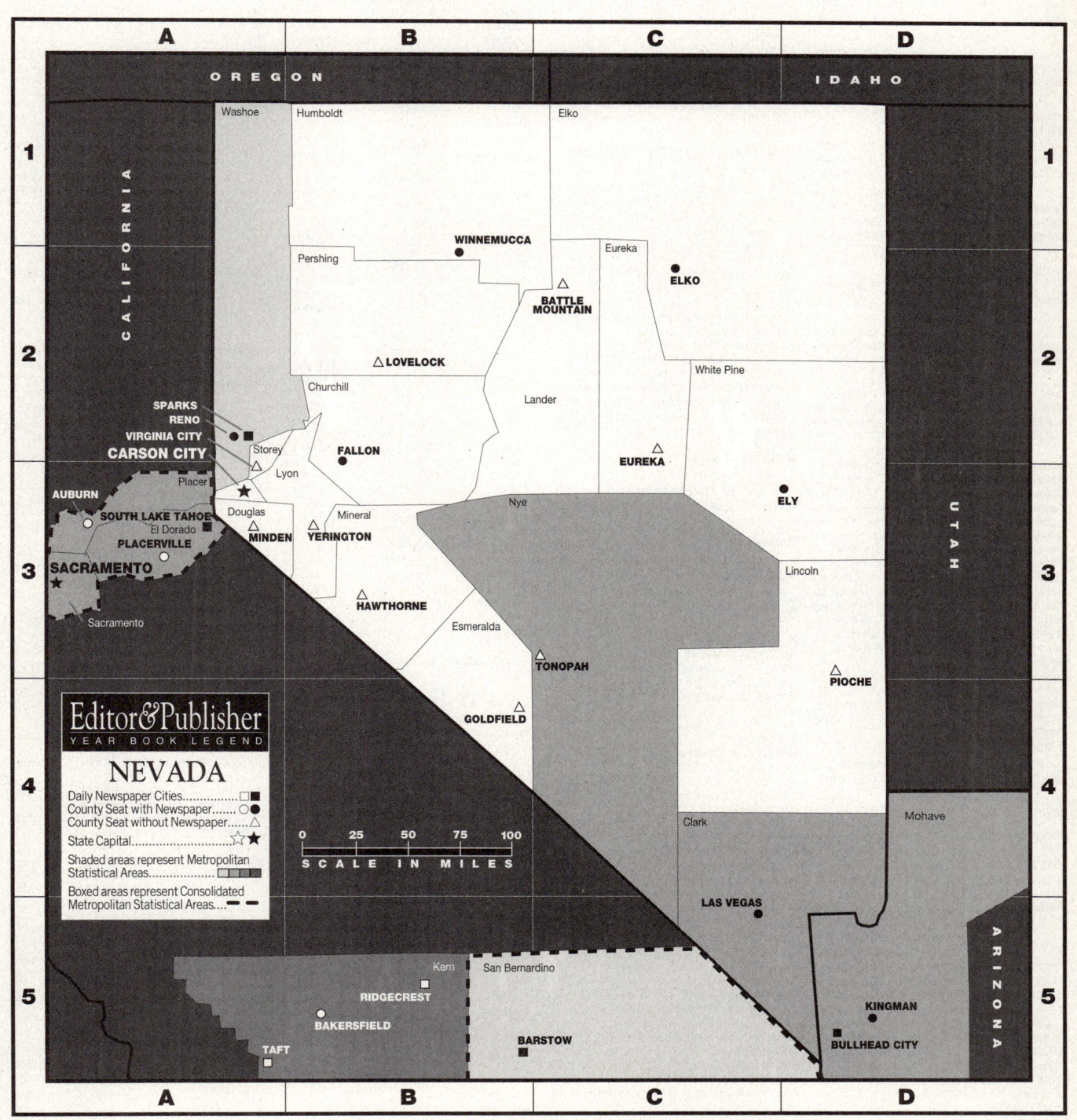

I-246 Nevada

Advertising: Open inch rate $63.41(m); $63.41(m-sat); $72.85(S). **Representative:** Gannett National Newspaper Sales.
News Services: AP, GNS, LAT-WP. **Established:** 1870 (Journal), 1876 (Gazette).
Special Editions: Super Bowl (Jan); Reno Rodeo (June); Hot August Nights (July); Football '96 (Aug); Balloon Races, National Air Races, HEALTH Source (Sept); Dining Guide, Women in Business (Oct); Gift Guide (Dec); Auto Catalog, Prime Time Plus, Silver State Clipper (monthly); The Coupon Book.
Special Weekly Sections: Business Monday (mon); Best Bets (thur); Sierra Living (fri); Homefinder (sat); TV Week, Business Outlook, Comics (S).

CORPORATE OFFICERS
President Susan Clark-Jackson
Secretary Thomas L Chapple
Treasurer Jimmy L Thomas

GENERAL MANAGEMENT
Publisher Susan Clark-Jackson
Controller Evan Ray
Asst Controller Becky Christiansen

ADVERTISING
Director John Zidich
Manager-Classified Carol Young
Manager-National John Murphy
Manager-Retail Dave Kennedy
Manager-Entertainment Cami Kaiser

MARKETING AND PROMOTION
Director-Marketing Karen Kokiko
Market Development Evan Mecah
Consumer Marketing Laura Smissaert

TELECOMMUNICATIONS
Director-Management Info Services Marlene Iacometti
Audiotex Manager Carol Young

CIRCULATION
Director Jerry K Hill
Manager-Sales/Marketing Dan Moriarty
Manager-Operations Scott Landers

NEWS EXECUTIVES
Exec Editor Ward Bushee
Managing Editor Tonia Cunning
Asst Managing Editor Kenn Altine
Asst Managing Editor Michael Limon

EDITORS AND MANAGERS
Business Editor Steve Falcone
City Editor Pat Harrison
Columnist Cory Farley
Columnist Rollan D Melton
Columnist Lenita Powers
Columnist Steve Sneddon
Courts Editor Steve Timko
Editorial Page Editor Bruce Bledsoe
Education Editor Mary Warejcka
Films/Theater Editor Jeannie Rasmussen
Food Editor Sandra Macias
Asst Librarian Katie MacDonald-Galli
Lifestyle Editor James Sloan
News Editor Mark Murphy
Director-Photography Tim Dunn
Police Editor Phil Barber
Radio/Television Editor Jeannie Rasmussen
Religion Editor Sharon Genung
Sports Editor Ray Hager
Sunday Editor Jody Murray
Water/Washoe County Editor Faith Bremner

MANAGEMENT INFORMATION SERVICES
Data Processing Manager Marlene Iacometti

PRODUCTION
Director Larry Urrutia

Market Information: Zoned editions; Split Run; TMC; Operate database; Operate audiotex.
Mechanical available: Offset; Black and 3 ROP colors; insert accepted — preprinted; page cutoffs — 22¾".
Mechanical specifications: Type page 13" x 21½"; E - 6 cols, 2.07", ⅛" between; A - 6 cols, 2.07", ⅛" between; C - 10 cols, 1.21", 1/12" between.
Commodity consumption: Newsprint 11,317 short tons; width 54¾"; black ink 230,800 pounds; color ink 48,600 pounds; single pages printed 23,596; average pages per issue 58(d), 102(S); single plates used 91,630.
Equipment: EDITORIAL: Front-end hardware — AT/J-11; Front-end software — AT; Printers — IBM. CLASSIFIED: Front-end hardware — AT; Front-end software — AT; Printers — IBM. DISPLAY: Front-end hardware — Ap/Mac; Front-end software — Multi-Ad; Printers — AU; Other equipment — PageScan/III. PRODUCTION: Typesetters — AU/APS 6; Plate exposures — 1-Nu; Plate processors — WL; Electronic picture desk — Lf/AP Leaf Picture Desk; Scanners — Truvell, RZ, AG/Horizon; Production cameras — C/Spartan III, Panasonic, ECR/Autokon 1000, ECR/Autokon 8400; Automatic film processors — 2-LE, 2-P; Film transporters — P; Color separation equipment (conventional) — RZ/200S.
PRESSROOM: Line 1 — 7-G/Metro (4 Half decks); Pasters — G/Automatic; Reels and stands — G/Automatic, 7-G/3-arm. MAILROOM: Counter stackers — 2-HL, 2-Id/440, 1-HI/25; Inserters and stuffers — HI/1372P; Bundle tyer — MLN; Addressing machine — Ch. WIRE SERVICES: News — AP Datastream, AP Datafeatures; Stock tables — AP Dataspeed; Syndicates — LAT-WP, GNS, NYT; Receiving dishes — size-3m, AP. BUSINESS COMPUTERS: IBM/Sys 38 model 700; PCs & micros networked; PCs & main system networked.

SPARKS
Washoe County
'90 U.S. Census- 53,367; E&P '96 Est. 59,679

The Daily Sparks Tribune
(e-mon to fri; S)

The Daily Sparks Tribune, 1002 C St. (89431); PO Box 887, Sparks, NV 89432; tel (702) 358-8061; fax (702) 359-3837. Kearns-Tribune Corp. group.
Circulation: 6,128(e); 6,128(S); Sworn Sept. 30, 1994.
Price: 35¢(d); 35¢(S); $78.00/yr.
Advertising: Open inch rate $10.75(e); $13.50(S).
News Service: AP. **Politics:** Independent. **Established:** 1910.
Not Published: New Year; Memorial Day; Independence Day; Labor Day; Thanksgiving; Christmas.
Special Edition: Hometown Christmas (Dec).
Special Weekly Sections: Senior Spotlight (mon); Business (tues); Food & Health (wed); Entertainment (thur); Religion (fri); Sports Tab (S).
Magazines: TV Week (S); Parade.

GENERAL MANAGEMENT
General Manager Linda Brown

CIRCULATION
Manager Blaine Dickman

NEWS EXECUTIVE
Managing Editor Bryan Jacobson

PRODUCTION
Foreman-Press/Camera Cheryl Bain

Market Information: TMC.
Mechanical available: Offset; Black and 3 ROP colors; insert accepted — preprinted; page cutoffs — 22¾".
Mechanical specifications: Type page 13½" x 21½"; E - 6 cols, 2 1/16", ⅛" between; A - 6 cols, 2 1/16", ⅛" between; C - 7 cols, 1 9/16", ⅛" between.
Commodity consumption: Newsprint 412 metric tons; widths 27½", 30"; black ink 7,200 pounds; color ink 1,200 pounds; single pages printed 8,312; average pages per issue 24(d); single plates used 9,200.
Equipment: EDITORIAL: Front-end hardware — Ap/Mac Plus; Front-end software — Ap/Mac II, Ap/Mac SE30; Printers — Ap/Mac LaserWriter. CLASSIFIED: Front-end hardware — CText; Front-end software — RSK/Tandy 3000; Printers — Ap/Mac LaserWriter. PRODUCTION: Typesetters — Ap/Mac LaserWriter; Plate exposures — 1-Nu; Plate processors — Nat/A-250; Production cameras — R; Automatic film processors — P.
PRESSROOM: Line 1 — 5-G/Community; Folders — 1-G/Community. MAILROOM: Inserters and stuffers — MM; Bundle tyer — Bu. WIRE SERVICES: News — AP; Syndicates — King Features, United Features, Chronicle, Crown, Universal Press. BUSINESS COMPUTERS: Tandy/486ei-33, Wyse/60 terminals; Applications: PBS/Media: Adv management, Circ, Payroll, Gen accounting; PCs & micros networked; PCs & main system networked.

WINNEMUCCA
Humboldt County
'90 U.S. Census- 6,134; E&P '96 Est. 7,034

The Humboldt Sun
(e-mon to fri)

The Humboldt Sun, 1022 S. Grass Valley Rd.; PO Box 3000, Winnemucca, NV 89446; tel (702) 623-5011; fax (702) 623-5243.
Circulation: 3,742(e); Sworn Sept. 26, 1995.
Price: 35¢(d); $22.50/3mo, $45.00/6mo, $67.50/9mo; $85.00/yr.
Advertising: Open inch rate $6.35(e).
News Service: AP. **Established:** 1972.
Special Editions: Progress (Feb); Bridal (Mar); Agri Business, HomeStyles (Apr); Cross Roads (Visitor's Guide) (June); Mining (July); Outdoor Recreation/Hunting (Oct); Gift Guide (Nov); Holiday Greetings (Dec).
Special Weekly Sections: TV Guide (thur); El Sol (Spanish language page) (fri).

CORPORATE OFFICERS
President Howard M McMahon
Secretary June M McMahon
Treasurer Susan M Brockus

GENERAL MANAGEMENT
Publisher Susan M Brockus
Office Manager Peggy Smith

ADVERTISING
Manager Elaine Heit

NEWS EXECUTIVE
Assoc Editor Jackie Kaczmarek

PRODUCTION
Manager Lewis Brockus

Mechanical available: Offset; Black and 3 ROP colors; insert accepted — preprinted, Some; page cut-offs — 21¼".
Mechanical specifications: Type page 13" x 21½"; E - 6 cols, 2", ⅙" between; A - 6 cols, 2", ⅙" between; C - 6 cols, 2", ⅙" between.
Equipment: EDITORIAL: Front-end hardware — 7-Zeos/486, Pentium; Front-end software — SunType/Editorial, Ventura/Publisher, QuarkXPress; Printers — LaserMaster/1800 PMR, LaserMaster/1000, 10-IBM/Laserprinter; Other equipment — LaserMaster/Pressmate. CLASSIFIED: Front-end hardware — Zeos/486; Front-end software — SunType/Classified, Ventura/Publisher. DISPLAY: Adv layout systems — 3-Zeos/486; Front-end hardware — 3-Zeos/486; Front-end software — Ventura/Publisher 4.2, QuarkXPress 3.31, Archetype/Corel Draw 5.0, Archetype/Corel Draw 4.0; PRODUCTION: Typesetters — LaserMaster/Pressmate; Plate exposures — Nu; Scanners — Nikon/Coolscan; Automatic film processors — Kk.
PRESSROOM: Line 1 — 6-G/Community; Folders — G. MAILROOM: Bundle tyer — Akebono/Strapper. LIBRARY: Electronic — Folio Views. WIRE SERVICES: News — AP; Receiving dishes — size-18", AP. BUSINESS COMPUTERS: Applications: Cyma, Synaptic: Accts receivable; PCs & micros networked.

NEW HAMPSHIRE

BERLIN
Coos County
'90 U.S. Census- 11,824; E&P '96 Est. 11,882

The Berlin Reporter
(m-mon to fri; m-sat)

The Berlin Reporter, 151 Main St.; PO Box 38, Berlin, NH 03570; tel (603) 752-1200; fax (603) 752-2339. James Newspapers Inc. group.
Circulation: 2,690(m); 4,848(m-wed); 9,073(m-sat); Sworn Sept. 29, 1994.
Price: 25¢(d); 40¢(wed); 25¢(sat); $1.00/wk; $4.00/mo; $48.00/yr; $13.00 (quarterly).
Advertising: Open inch rate $4.50(m); $7.30(m-wed); $7.30(m-sat).
News Service: AP. **Established:** 1883 (weekly), 1992 (daily).
Not Published: New Year; Memorial Day; Independence Day; Labor Day; Thanksgiving; Christmas.
Advertising not accepted: Tobacco; Alcohol.

CORPORATE OFFICERS
Chairman Judith V James
President/Publisher Howard A James
Treasurer Judith V James

GENERAL MANAGEMENT
General Manager Deborah Harwell

ADVERTISING
Manager Deborah Harwell

CIRCULATION
Manager Ken Burrows

NEWS EXECUTIVE
Managing Editor Ben Gagnon

Market Information: TMC; ADS.
Mechanical available: Offset; Black and 4 ROP colors; insert accepted — preprinted.
Mechanical specifications: Type page 10" x 15".
Commodity consumption: Newsprint 60 short tons; widths 33", 28"; black ink 5,000 pounds; color ink 1,000 pounds; average pages per issue 20(d), 24(sat); single plates used 2,200.
Equipment: EDITORIAL: Front-end hardware — Ap/Mac; Front-end software — QuarkXPress; Printers — Xante. CLASSIFIED: Front-end hardware — Ap/Mac. PRODUCTION: Pagination software — QuarkXPress; Typesetters — Xante/Lasersetter.
PRESSROOM: Line 1 — 4-G/Community. WIRE SERVICES: News — AP.

The Berlin Daily Sun
(m-mon to fri)

The Berlin Daily Sun, 177 Main St., Berlin, NH 03570; tel (603) 752-5858; fax (603) 752-4160; e-mail dailysun@mountwashingtonvalley.com; web site http://www.mountwashingtonvalley.com.
Circulation: 7,200(m); Sworn Nov. 27, 1995.
Price: Free.
Advertising: Open inch rate $3.00(m); comb with the Conway Daily Sun (m) $6.00.
News Service: AP. **Politics:** Independent. **Established:** 1992.
Note: For detailed production information, see The Conway Daily Sun.

CORPORATE OFFICER
President David N Danforth

GENERAL MANAGEMENT
Publisher Mark Guerringue

ADVERTISING
Manager-Sales Bob Waters
Manager-Classified Debbie Peck

CIRCULATION
Manager Babben West

NEWS EXECUTIVES
Editor Adam Hirshan
Managing Editor Rose Dodge

PRODUCTION
Manager Frank Haddy

CLAREMONT
Sullivan County
'90 U.S. Census- 16,592; E&P '96 Est. 17,783
ABC-CZ (90): 13,902 (HH 5,610)

Eagle Times (e-mon to fri; S)

Eagle Times, RFD 2; Box 301, Claremont, NH 03743; tel (603) 543-3100; fax (603) 542-9705; e-mail etimes@cyberportal.net.
Circulation: 8,750(e); 9,851(S); ABC Sept. 30, 1995.
Price: 50¢(d); $1.25(S); $3.30/wk; $13.20/mo; $171.60/yr.
Advertising: Open inch rate $9.95(e); $9.95(S). **Representative:** Landon Associates Inc.
News Service: AP. **Politics:** Independent. **Established:** 1835, 1914 (Daily Eagle), 1974 (Eagle Times).
Not Published: New Year; Christmas.
Special Editions: Industry; Car Care; Bridal; Grad 'n' Dad; Founder's Day; Back-to-School; Christmas Opening; Drug & Alcohol; Gift Guide; Progress.
Special Weekly Sections: Best Food Day (wed); Entertainment (thur); Religion Page (fri); Local, State and Regional, World & National, Sports, Business, Best of Times, Classified, Social (S).
Magazines: TV Update (offset), Color Comics (S).

CORPORATE OFFICERS
President William R Galloway Jr
Senior Vice Pres Gloria Galloway

GENERAL MANAGEMENT
Publisher William R Galloway Jr
General Manager Claire Piaggi

New Hampshire I-247

ADVERTISING
Director Robert M Shomphe
MARKETING AND PROMOTION
Director-Marketing Robert M Shomphe
CIRCULATION
Director Charisse Huot
NEWS EXECUTIVE
Editor Todd Driscoll
EDITOR AND MANAGER
Sports Editor Lawrence Walsh
PRODUCTION
Foreman-Composing Pru Russell
Foreman-Pressroom Richard Lobdell

Mechanical available: Offset; Black and 3 ROP colors; insert accepted — preprinted; page cut-offs — 22¾".
Mechanical specifications: Type page 12¾" x 21¼"; E - 6 cols, 2 1/16", ⅛" between; A - 6 cols, 2 1/16", ⅛" between; C - 8 cols, 1 9/16", 1/16" between.
Commodity consumption: Newsprint 388 short tons; widths 13¾", 27½"; black ink 15,034 pounds; color ink 762 pounds; single pages printed 6,932; average pages per issue 20(d), 44(S); single plates used 3,926.
Equipment: EDITORIAL: Front-end hardware — 12-lk. CLASSIFIED: Front-end hardware — 2-lk. DISPLAY: Adv layout systems — 2-lk. PRODUCTION: Typesetters — 2-Linotype-Hell/Linotronic 202N; Plate exposures — Nu/Flip Top FT40V3UP; Plate processors — Nat/A-250; Production cameras — N/SSTE2024S-19LT, N/VE-14-18; Automatic film processors — LE/1800A; Color separation equipment (conventional) — Lf/AP Leaf Picture Desk; Digital color separation equipment — Lf/AP Leaf Picture Desk.
PRESSROOM: Line 1 — G/Community (SC 468). MAILROOM: Counter stackers — Mid America Graphics/News stacker; Bundle tyer — 2-Sa, 1-Sterling. LIBRARY: Combination — Microfilm. WIRE SERVICES: News — AP; Receiving dishes — AP. BUSINESS COMPUTERS: IBM; Applications: INSI.

CONCORD

Merrimack County
'90 U.S. Census- 36,006; E&P '96 Est. 41,785
ABC-CZ (90): 36,006 (HH 14,222)

Concord Monitor

(m-mon to sat)

Sunday Monitor (S)

Concord Monitor, 1 Monitor Dr.; PO Box 1177, Concord, NH 03302-1177; tel (603) 224-5301; fax (603) 228-8238; e-mail news@cmonitor.com; web site http://www.cmonitor.com/primary. Newspapers of New England group.
Circulation: 21,985(m); 21,985(m-sat); 22,679(S); ABC Sept. 30, 1995.
Price: 50¢(d); 50¢(sat); $1.50(S); $3.15/wk; $163.00/yr, $75.00/yr (S only).
Advertising: Open inch rate $13.08(m); $13.08(m-sat); $13.61(S). **Representative:** Landon Associates Inc.
News Services: AP, LAT-WP. **Politics:** Independent. **Established:** 1808.
Not Published: Christmas.
Special Editions: Wedding Edition (Jan); Auto Edition (Feb); Town Meeting, Home Improvement (Mar); Speedway Parade (Apr); Summer Directory (June); Market Days (July); Back-to-School, Belknap County Fair (Aug); Business Profiles, Home Improvement (Sept); Fall Recreation (Oct); Gift Guide (Nov); Gift Guide (Dec).
Special Weekly Sections: Business Section (tues); Food (wed); Weekend, Real Estate, Auctions (thur); Real Estate, Auctions (sat); Entertainment, Business Section, Real Estate, Auctions, Society/Wedding Page, Viewpoints/Travel, Family (S).
Magazines: Monitor Extra (sat); Shopper (TMC).

CORPORATE OFFICER
President/Treasurer George W Wilson
GENERAL MANAGEMENT
Publisher Tom C Brown
General Manager Chuck Vincent
Controller Barry Lyons
Manager-Human Resources Laurie Murphy
ADVERTISING
Director Roger Proulx
Manager-Retail/Training Mike Corbett
Supervisor-Classified Telephone Charlotte Ingalls
CIRCULATION
Director Arthur R Dwight
NEWS EXECUTIVES
Editor Michael Pride
Managing Editor Mark Travis
EDITORS AND MANAGERS
Business Editor Scott Calvert
City Editor Geordie Wilson
Columnist Scott Hilyard
Editorial Page Editor John Fensterwald
News Editor Rick Tracewski
Regional Editor Beth Cote
Sports Editor Sandra Smith
Sunday Editor Hans Schulz
MANAGEMENT INFORMATION SERVICES
Data Processing Manager Duane Coventry
Online Manager Mark Travis

Market Information: Zoned editions; Split Run; TMC; ADS; Operate database.
Mechanical available: Flexo; Black and 3 ROP colors; insert accepted — preprinted; page cut-offs — 22".
Mechanical specifications: Type page 13" x 21"; E - 6 cols, 2 1/16", ⅛" between; A - 6 cols, 2 1/16", ⅛" between; C - 9 cols, 1⅜", 3/32" between.
Commodity consumption: Newsprint 2,300 metric tons; widths 27½", 41¼", 55"; black ink 55,000 pounds; color ink 19,000 pounds; single pages printed 13,900; average pages per issue 35(d), 58(S); single plates used 33,000.
Equipment: EDITORIAL: Front-end hardware — IBM/AT; Front-end software — MPS; Printers — Tegra/Varityper XP1000. CLASSIFIED: Front-end hardware — IBM; Front-end software — PPI; Printers — Tegra/Varityper XP1000. AUDIOTEX: Hardware — IBM/486. DISPLAY: Adv layout systems — SCS/Layout 8000; Front-end hardware — IBM; Printers — Tegra/Varityper XP1000. PRODUCTION: Typesetters — Tegra/Varityper XP1000; Plate exposures — BKY/Ascor; Plate processors — Na/FPI; Electronic picture desk — Lf/AP Leaf Picture Desk; Scanners — ECR/Autokon; Production cameras — C/Spartan II; Automatic film processors — LE/LD24; Shrink lenses — CK Optical/SQU-7; Color separation equipment (conventional) — RZ/4050; Digital color separation equipment — Howtek, Kk/RFS-2035, Pixelcraft.
PRESSROOM: Line 1 — 6-PEC/double width (17 printing couples); Folders — 2-H/3:2; Pasters — PEC; Reels and stands — H; Press control system — PEC. MAILROOM: Counter stackers — HL/Monitor HTII; Inserters and stuffers — GMA/SLS-1000; Bundle tyer — MVP; Wrapping singles — HL/Monarch; Addressing machine — KR/211. WIRE SERVICES: News — AP Datafeatures; Syndicates — LAT-WP, AP; Receiving dishes — size-10ft, AP. BUSINESS COMPUTERS: HP/Micro 3000XE; Applications: CJ; PCs & micros networked; PCs & main system networked.

CONWAY-NORTH CONWAY

Carroll County
'90 U.S. Census- 10,354 (Conway 8,250; North Conway 2,104); E&P '96 Est. 13,592 (Conway 10,981; North Conway 2,611)

The Conway Daily Sun

(m-mon to sat)

The Conway Daily Sun, Seavey St.; PO Box 1940, North Conway, NH 03860; tel (603) 356-3456; fax (603) 356-8774; e-mail dailysun@mountwashingtonvalley.com; web site http://www.mountwashingtonvalley.com.
Circulation: 13,800(m); 15,200(m-sat); Sworn Nov. 27, 1995.
Price: Free.
Advertising: Open inch rate $4.75(m); $4.75(m-sat); comb with The Berlin Daily Sun (m) $6.00.
News Service: AP. **Politics:** Independent. **Established:** 1989.

CORPORATE OFFICER
President David N Danforth
GENERAL MANAGEMENT
Publisher Mark Guerringue
ADVERTISING
Manager-Sales Bob Waters
Manager-Classified Debbie Peck
CIRCULATION
Manager Mark Guerringue
NEWS EXECUTIVE
Exec Editor Adam Hirshan
EDITOR AND MANAGER
City Editor Bart Bachman
PRODUCTION
Manager Frank Haddy

Mechanical available: Offset Web; Black and 1 ROP color; insert accepted — preprinted; page cut-offs — 15".
Mechanical specifications: Type page 10¼" x 13½"; E - 4 cols, 2.72", ⅓" between; A - 6 cols, 1.57", ⅙" between; C - 6 cols, 1.57", ⅙" between.
Commodity consumption: Newsprint 360 metric tons; width 30"; single pages printed 7,488; average pages per issue 24(d), 28(sat); single plates used 5,000.
Equipment: EDITORIAL: Front-end hardware — 10-Ap/Mac; Printers — 2-Ap/Mac LaserWriter, 2-HP/Fa Jet; Other equipment — Ap/Mac Scanner. CLASSIFIED: Front-end hardware — 2-Ap/Mac Quadra; Front-end software — Baseview. DISPLAY: Adv layout systems — Aldus/PageMaker, QPS, Adobe/Photoshop, Aldus/FreeHand. PRODUCTION: Typesetters — 1-Ap/Mac LaserWriter; Platemaking systems — Nu/30x40 Platemaker; Production cameras — Kk/Image Maker 5060B; Automatic film processors — Kk/42A.
PRESSROOM: Line 1 — 4-G/Community. WIRE SERVICES: News — AP; Receiving dishes — size-2ft, AP. BUSINESS COMPUTERS: Ap/Mac Plus; Applications: Accts receivable, Runsheets, Gen ledger; PCs & micros networked; PCs & main system networked.

DOVER

Strafford County
'90 U.S. Census- 25,042; E&P '96 Est. 27,727
ABC-NDM (90): 109,983 (HH 39,820)

Foster's Democrat

(e-mon to fri; m-sat)

Foster's Democrat, 333 Central Ave., Dover, NH 03820; tel (603) 742-4455; fax (603) 749-7079.
Circulation: 22,238(e); 22,238(m-sat); ABC Sept. 30, 1995.
Price: 50¢(d); 50¢(sat); $8.05/mo (carrier), $11.00/mo (mail); $114.00/yr (mail).
Advertising: Open inch rate $21.43(e); $21.43(m-sat). **Representative:** Landon Associates Inc.
News Services: AP, UPI, NYT. **Politics:** Independent. **Established:** 1873.
Not Published: New Year; President's Day; Memorial Day; Independence Day; Labor Day; Veteran's Day; Thanksgiving; Christmas.
Special Editions: Weddings (Jan); Valentine's Gift Guide, Vacation Package, Bridal Page, President's Day Auto Section (Feb); Vacation Package, St. Patrick's Auto Section, Bridal Page (Mar); Spring Home Improvement, Bridal Page (Apr); Mother's Day Gifts, Lawn & Garden, Mother's Day Promotion, Bridal Page, Dining Guide, Vacation Planner (May); Dover Chamber of Commerce, Bridal Page, Father's Day Promotion (June); Parenting, Bridal Page (July); Back-to-School, Bridal Page (Aug); Business & Industry, Rochester Fair, Bridal Page (Sept); Fall Home Improvement, National Business Women's Week, Bridal Page, New Car Section (Oct); Sports Play-off Preview, Bridal Page, Let It Snow, Christmas Gift Guide, Christmas Tree Promotion (Nov); Christmas Tree Promotion, Last Minute Gift Guide, Christmas Greetings (Dec).
Special Weekly Sections: Best Food Day (wed); TV Spotlight (fri); Best Food Day (sat); Financial/Business, Amusement/Entertainment (daily).

CORPORATE OFFICERS
President Robert H Foster
Vice Pres Therese D Foster
GENERAL MANAGEMENT
Publisher Robert H Foster
Assoc Publisher Therese D Foster
Asst to Publisher Patrice Foster
General Manager Robert H Foster
Personnel Manager Janet Rene
Purchasing Agent Joan Martel
Director-Sales/Marketing Frank J McSweegan
ADVERTISING
Manager-Classified Dave Kennedy
CIRCULATION
Director Jerry Perkins
NEWS EXECUTIVES
Exec Editor Rod Rodney
Managing Editor Mary Pat Rowland
EDITORS AND MANAGERS
Business Editor Beverly Welch
Family Page Editor Mary Ulinski
PRODUCTION
Manager Lois Mulcahy-Reed
Foreman-Mailroom William Norton

Mechanical available: Offset.
Mechanical specifications: Type page 13" x 21½"; E - 6 cols, 2 1/16", ⅛" between; A - 6 cols, 2 1/16", ⅛" between; C - 9 cols, 1⅜", 1/16" between.
Equipment: EDITORIAL: Front-end hardware — 6-AX. PRODUCTION: Typesetters — 7-P, 2-DEC/PDP; Production cameras — 1-R, 1-K. MAILROOM: Inserters and stuffers — 1-W; Bundle tyer — 1-Sa. COMMUNICATIONS: Facsimile — 4-X.

HANOVER

See LEBANON

KEENE

Cheshire County
'90 U.S. Census- 22,430; E&P '96 Est. 23,498
ABC-NDM (90): 70,121 (HH 25,856)

The Keene Sentinel

(e-mon to fri; m-sat)

The Keene Sentinel, 60 West St.; PO Box 546, Keene, NH 03431; tel (603) 352-1234; fax (603) 352-0437; e-mail tfk@keenesentinel.com; web site http://www.keenesentinel.com.
Circulation: 15,507(e); 15,507(m-sat); ABC Sept. 30, 1995.
Price: 50¢(d); 50¢(sat); $105.00/yr.
Advertising: Open inch rate $11.60(e); $11.60 (m-sat). **Representative:** Landon Associates Inc.
News Service: AP. **Politics:** Independent. **Established:** 1799.
Not Published: New Year; Memorial Day; Independence Day; Labor Day; Thanksgiving; Christmas.
Special Editions: Economic Outlook (Jan); Brides (Feb); Answerbook (Mar); Home & Garden (Apr); Senior Living (May); New England Summer (June); Mid-Summer (July); Back-to-School (Aug); Home & Hearth (Sept); Health (Oct); Holiday Ideas (Nov); Last Minute Gift Ideas (Dec).
Special Weekly Sections: Entertainment (fri); USA Weekend, Business, Religion (sat).
Magazine: The Keene Sentinel Magazine (fri).

CORPORATE OFFICERS
President James A Rousmaniere Jr
Vice Pres Cynthia R Ewing
GENERAL MANAGEMENT
Publisher Thomas M Ewing
Publisher Emeritus James Ewing
Editor James A Rousmaniere Jr
Controller Joseph D Antosiewicz
ADVERTISING
Director Colin R Lyle
Manager-Classified Lorraine Ellis
Manager-Co-op Harry Ahern
TELECOMMUNICATIONS
Audiotex Manager Colin R Lyle
CIRCULATION
Manager Patrick Trubiano
Asst Manager Kevin Lougee
NEWS EXECUTIVES
Exec Editor Thomas Kearney
Editor-Special Sections Diane Riley
EDITORS AND MANAGERS
Editorial Page Editor Guy MacMillin
Living Editor Marilou Blaine
Local News Editor Tom Auclair
News Editor Tom Auclair
Sports Editor Paul Miller
PRODUCTION
Manager David J Cleveland
Foreman-Pressroom Gregory Walker
Coordinator-Systems Michael Plotczyk

Market Information: Zoned editions; TMC; Operate audiotex.
Mechanical available: Offset; Black and 3 ROP colors; insert accepted — preprinted; page cut-offs — 21½".
Mechanical specifications: Type page 13" x 21½"; E - 6 cols, 2.04", ⅙" between; A - 6 cols, 2.04", ⅙" between; C - 9 cols, 1.36", ⅙" between.
Commodity consumption: Newsprint 800 short tons; width 27½"; black ink 20,000 pounds; color ink 2,300 pounds; single pages printed 8,564; average pages per issue 28(d), 36(sat); single plates used 7,000.

Equipment: EDITORIAL: Front-end hardware — IBM; Front-end software — CText, Novell/Network; Printers — 1-Ap/Mac Laser. CLASSIFIED: Front-end hardware — IBM; Front-end software — CText, Novell/Network. AUDIOTEX: Hardware — Northgate; Software — Info-Connect; Supplier name — VNN, TMS, AP. DISPLAY: Adv layout systems — SCS/Layout 8000; Front-end hardware — 4-Ap/Mac; Front-end software — Multi-Ad/Creator 3.63; Printers — LaserMaster/1200 XL-O, LaserMaster 1800 XL-O; Other equipment — 2-Ap/Mac CD-Rom. PRODUCTION: Pagination software — QuarkXPress 3.3; OCR software — Caere/OmniPage; Typesetters — 1-LaserMaster/1800 XL-O; Plate exposures — 1-Nu; Plate processors — Nat; Electronic picture desk — Lf/AP Leaf Picture Desk; Scanners — 2-Ap/Mac; Production cameras — R/24-580, ECR/Autokon; Automatic film processors — LE/18; Color separation equipment (conventional) — Lf/AP Leaf Picture Desk, IBM.

PRESSROOM: Line 1 — 8-G/Community; Folders — 1-G; Press control system — G. MAILROOM: Inserters and stuffers — MM/4-pocket; Bundle tyer — 2-Sa. WIRE SERVICES: News — AP, LAT-WP; Photos — AP; Receiving dishes — size-3m, AP. BUSINESS COMPUTERS: IBM; Applications: PBS/MediaPlus; PCs & micros networked; PCs & main system networked.

LACONIA

Belknap County

'90 U.S. Census- 15,743; E&P '96 Est. 16,046
ABC-NDM (90): 37,619 (HH 14,600)

Citizen (e-mon to fri; m-sat)

Citizen, 171 Fair St., Laconia, NH 03246; tel (603) 524-3800; fax (603) 524-6702.
Circulation: 12,095(e); 12,095(m-sat); ABC Sept. 30, 1995.
Price: 50¢(d); 50¢(sat).
Advertising: Open inch rate $11.08(e); $11.08(m-sat). **Representative:** Landon Associates Inc.
News Service: AP. **Politics:** Independent. **Established:** 1925.
Special Weekly Sections: Health Page, Senior Page (alternate mon); Money/Business Page (tues); BFD (wed); Weekender (thur); BFD (sat).

GENERAL MANAGEMENT

General Manager	Frank J McSweegan

ADVERTISING

Director	Donald Sprague

CIRCULATION

Director	Peter Fallon

NEWS EXECUTIVE

Exec Editor	John Howe

EDITORS AND MANAGERS

Regional Editor	Mike Mortensen
Sports Editor	Steve Ambroze

PRODUCTION

Manager	Ron DeDuca

Market Information: TMC; ADS.
Mechanical available: Offset; insert accepted — preprinted; page cut-offs — 23".
Mechanical specifications: Type page 13" x 21½"; E - 6 cols, 2.07", ⅛" between; A - 6 cols, 2.07", ⅛" between; C - 9 cols, 1.33", ⅛" between.
Commodity consumption: average pages per issue 30(d).
Equipment: EDITORIAL: Front-end hardware — Mk; Front-end software — Mk; Printers — TI. CLASSIFIED: Front-end hardware — Mk; Front-end software — Mk; Printers — TI. DISPLAY: Front-end hardware — Ap/Mac; Front-end software — Multi-Ad; Printers — Ap/Mac Laser. PRODUCTION: Typesetters — Mycro Craft/Laser; Electronic picture desk — Lf/AP Leaf Picture Desk; Production cameras — 1-Nu; Automatic film processors — Kk; Color separation equipment (conventional) — DigiColour.
PRESSROOM: Line 1 — 16-STD/Pgs Plus Quard; Line 2 — 16-STD/Pgs Plus Quard. MAILROOM: Counter stackers — BG; Inserters and stuffers — MM. WIRE SERVICES: News — AP; Receiving dishes — size-3m, AP. BUSINESS COMPUTERS: CJ/Compuserve; PCs & micros networked; PCs & main system networked.

LEBANON-HANOVER, NH-WHITE RIVER JUNCTION, VT

Grafton County, NH
Windsor County, VT

'90 U.S. Census- 28,125 (Lebanon, NH 12,183; Hanover, NH 6,538; Hartford, VT 9,404); E&P '96 Est. 29,334 (Lebanon, NH 13,243; Hanover, NH 5,920; Hartford, VT 10,171)
ABC-NDM (90): 33,892 (HH 12,514)

Valley News (m-mon to sat) *Sunday Valley News* (S)

Valley News, 7 Interchange Dr. (West Lebanon 03784); PO Box 877, White River Jct., VT 05001; tel (603) 298-8711; fax (603) 298-8711 ext. 695, (603) 298-0212. Newspapers of New England group.
Circulation: 17,988(m); 17,988(m-sat); 17,233(S); ABC Sept. 30, 1995.
Price: 50¢(d); 50¢(sat); $1.25(S); $2.75/wk (carrier); $13.75/mo (carrier); $138.80/yr (carrier).
Advertising: Open inch rate $14.40(m); $14.40(m-sat); $14.40(S). **Representative:** Landon Associates Inc.
News Services: AP, LAT-WP. **Established:** 1952.
Not Published: Christmas.
Special Editions: Bridal (Jan); Coupon Book, Recipes (Feb); Auto Show, Home & Trade Show (Mar); Homes (Apr); Summer Calendar (May); Summer Calendar (June); Summer Calander (July); Back-to-School, Summer Calendar (Aug); Fall Sports, Consumer Electronics (Sept); Fall Car Care, Snow (Oct); Christmas (Nov); Letters to Santa (Dec).
Special Weekly Sections: Science and Technology (mon); Education (tues); Food and Garden (wed); Arts, Automotive, Real Estate, Automotive (thur); Books (fri); Automotive, Movies, Real Estate (sat); Travel, Life & Leisure, Wedding, Business (S).
Magazines: ADvantage-TMC (sat); Valley Television (S).

CORPORATE OFFICERS

President	George W Wilson
Controller	Michael Kapusta

GENERAL MANAGEMENT

Publisher	John B Kuhns
Controller	Daniel D McClory

ADVERTISING

Manager	Richard Wallace
Asst Manager	Martina Rutkovsky
Supervisor-Classified	Susan Countiss

CIRCULATION

Director	Bruce Whitman
Manager	Randy Yanick

NEWS EXECUTIVE

Editor	Jim Fox

EDITORS AND MANAGERS

Arts/Entertainment Editor	Anne Adams
Editorial Page Editor	Martin Frank
Education/Books Editor	Anne Adams
Health/Science Editor	Bryan Marquard
Home/Food Editor	Anne Adams
Garden Editor	Anne Adams
News Editor	Ernie Kohlsaat
Sports Editor	Donald Mahler
Sunday Editor	Steve Gordon
Wire Editor	Jill Marquard

PRODUCTION

Manager-Operations	Bob Mathewson
Foreman-Pressroom	Lawrence H Leonard Jr
Manager-Pre Press	Glen Grote
Manager-Mailroom	Lawrence H Leonard Jr

Market Information: Split Run; TMC; ADS.
Mechanical available: Flexography; Black and 3 ROP colors; insert accepted — preprinted; page cut-offs — 22".
Mechanical specifications: Type page 13" x 21"; E - 6 cols, 2$\frac{1}{16}$", ⅛" between; A - 6 cols, 2$\frac{1}{16}$", ⅛" between; C - 9 cols, 1$\frac{5}{16}$", ⅛" between.
Commodity consumption: Newsprint 1,607 short tons; widths 55", 27⅜", 41⅛"; black ink 59,408 pounds; color ink 14,160 pounds; single pages printed 13,200; average pages per issue 30(d), 42(sat), 60(S); single plates used 34,620.
Equipment: EDITORIAL: Front-end hardware — 40-PC, Compaq/Fileserver, Novell/Network 3.12; Front-end software — Quark for Windows 3.31, Microsoft/Word 6.0, Azimuth Wire Capture; Printers — QMS/860, HP/LaserJet 4. CLASSIFIED: Front-end hardware — PC/Clones; Front-end software — Graph-X; Printers — QMS/860. DISPLAY: Adv layout systems — 1-Mk/Managing Editor; Front-end hardware — 2-Ap/Mac Quadra 650, 2-Ap/Mac II; Front-end software — Multi-Ad/Creator 4.X; Printers — QMS/860; Other equipment — Microtek/Flatbed Scanner. PRODUCTION: Typesetters — QMS/860 LaserPrinter, ECR/Autokon; Platemaking systems — Na; Plate exposures — 2-Burgess/Consolux; Plate processors — 2-Na/FP2; Electronic picture desk — 2-Lf/AP Leaf Picture Desk; Scanners — ECR/Autokon 1000DE, Lf/Leafscan 35; Production cameras — R; Automatic film processors — 1-Kk/Kodamatic 65A; Color separation equipment (conventional) — Lf/Leafscan 35.
PRESSROOM: Line 1 — 5-H/PEC (Colormatic Flexo Conversion); Press drives — PEC; Folders — 2-H/3:2; Pasters — PEC; Reels and stands — PEC; Press control system — PEC; Press registration system — Nu-Graphics, 4-PIN. MAILROOM: Counter stackers — 3-HL/Monitor HT; Inserters and stuffers — HI/848; Bundle tyer — 1-EAM/Mosca, 2-MVP; Mailroom control system — Ic. WIRE SERVICES: News — AP, LAT-WP; Syndicates — LAT-WP; Receiving dishes — size-3m, AP. BUSINESS COMPUTERS: 7-IBM/Sys 36; Applications: INSI: Circ, Accts payable, Gen ledger, Accts receivable; PCs & micros networked; PCs & main system networked.

MANCHESTER

Hillsborough County

'90 U.S. Census- 99,567; E&P '96 Est. 108,284
ABC-CZ (90): 159,141 (HH 59,939)

The Union Leader (all day-mon to fri; m-sat) *New Hampshire Sunday News* (S)

The Union Leader, 100 William Loeb Dr. (03109); PO Box 9555, Manchester, NH 03108-9555; tel (603) 668-4321; fax (603) 668-0040.
Circulation: 69,213(a); 67,074(m-sat); 98,165(S); ABC Sept. 30, 1995.
Price: 50¢(d); 50¢(sat); $1.50(S); $2.40/wk; $9.60/mo; $112.32/yr.
Advertising: Open inch rate $37.50(a); $37.50(m-sat); $41.00(S); $69.13(m & S). **Representative:** Sawyer-Ferguson-Walker Co.
News Services: SHNS, AP, LAT-WP. **Politics:** Independent. **Established:** 1863 (Union Leader), 1946 (Sunday News).
Not Published: Christmas.
Advertising not accepted: At publisher's option.
Special Editions: Truck & Van, Baby Review, Brides (Jan); Washington's Birthday Auto, NH Engineers Week, NH Farm and Forest, Your Money (Feb); Seniors, Made in NH (Mar); NH Home Show, Earth Day, Health & Fitness (Apr); Spring Home Improvement, Summer Vacation (May); Summer Sizzlers (June); NASCAR Winston Cup (July); League of Craftsman, Back-to-School, PPG Indy Car World Series (Aug); Fall House & Home, Fall Dining & Lodging (Sept); New Cars and Trucks Section, Homemakers School, Seniors, Crime Prevention (Oct); Home for Holidays (Nov); Christmas Crafts (Dec).
Special Weekly Sections: Monday's Business (mon); Senior Page (tues); Consumers, Best Food Day (wed); NH Weekend (thur); TGIF Friday (fri); Weekly Guide to Real Estate, Religion (sat); Travel, Business, Arts, Home, Real Estate (S).
Magazines: React (sat); Parade, New Hampshire TV Week (S).

CORPORATE OFFICER

President/Publisher	Nackey S Loeb

GENERAL MANAGEMENT

General Manager	Joseph W McQuaid
Vice Pres-Finance	John E MacKenzie
Vice Pres-Operations	Dirk F Ruemenapp
Manager-Credit	Robert Long
Director-Human Resources	Sharon Ciechon
Director-Accounting	Louis Luscher
Manager-Education/Youth Service	Jeanne Tancrede

ADVERTISING

Director	H Kenneth Clouse
Manager-National/Co-op	Sheila K Holland
Manager-Retail	David M Rousseau
Manager-Classified	George Stachokas
Manager-Ad Service	Barbara Giovinelli

MARKETING AND PROMOTION

Director-Community Relations	Donald C Anderson

CIRCULATION

Director	Michael C Rhodes
Manager	Lucien G Trahan

NEWS EXECUTIVES

Editor in Chief	Joseph W McQuaid
Exec Editor	Charles Perkins III
Managing Editor	James R Linehan

EDITORS AND MANAGERS

Automotive Editor	Jim Ferriter
Book Editor	Peter Swanson
Cooking School Director	Donald C Anderson
Editorial Page Editor	Greg Andruskevich
Entertainment Editor	Barry Palmer
Farm Editor	James Adams
Fashion/Food Editor	Ellie Ferriter
Features Editor	Robert Charest
Garden Editor	Ellie Ferriter
Health/Medical Editor	Ellie Ferriter
Home Furnishings Editor	Ellie Ferriter
Music Editor	James Adams
News Editor	Charles Perkins
Photo Editor	Len Stuart
Radio/Television Editor	James Adams
Real Estate Editor	Jim Ferriter
Religion Editor	Barry Palmer
Sunday Editor	Peter Swanson
Travel Editor	Jim Hodson
Union Leader	
Business/Finance Editor	Bill Regan
Cartoonist	Robert Dix
City Editor	Patrick C Sheeran
Columnist	Donn Tibbetts
Columnist	John DiStaso
Education Editor	Roger Talbot
Night Editor	Edward C Domaingue II
Sports Editor (Daily)	Maureen Milliken
Sports Editor (Sunday)	Dave Johnson
Women's Editor	Ellie Ferriter

MANAGEMENT INFORMATION SERVICES

Data Processing Manager	Robert T Dwyer

PRODUCTION

Vice Pres	Dirk F Ruemenapp
Manager	J Ronald Murdock
Foreman-Composing	Robert Godzyk
Foreman-Platemaking	Ira Cohen
Foreman-Pressroom	Richard R Bergeron

Market Information: Zoned editions; TMC.
Mechanical available: Flexographic; Black and 3 ROP colors; insert accepted — preprinted, samples; page cut-offs — 22".
Mechanical specifications: Type page 13" x 21¼"; E - 6 cols, 2$\frac{1}{16}$", ⅛" between; A - 6 cols, 2$\frac{1}{16}$", ⅛" between; C - 9 cols, 1⅜", ⅛" between.
Commodity consumption: Newsprint 9,600 metric tons; widths 54", 40.5", 27"; black ink 320,000 pounds; color ink 90,000 pounds; single pages printed 23,206; average pages per issue 53(d), 126(S); single plates used 50,211.
Equipment: EDITORIAL: Front-end hardware — 3-DEC/PDP 11-84, CD/2400; Front-end software — CSI/112-B. CLASSIFIED: Front-end hardware — 2-Dell/466-Mx, 21-Dell/433-NP; Front-end software — HI/CASH. DISPLAY: Adv layout systems — 5-Cx/Breeze; Front-end hardware — DEC/VT-102. PRODUCTION: Pagination software — HI/Pagination; Typesetters — 2-Bidco/80, 2-AU/Alpha RIP, 2-HI/XP-21, 8-HI/2100 Pagination Work Station; Platemaking systems — 2-LX/100; Scanners — 2-ECR/Autokon, CD/Sirius 250-E Color Scanner; Production cameras — 1-C/Spartan III, 1-SCREEN, C/474-DL; Automatic film processors — 2-LE/24, 3-SCREEN, LD/281-L, LD/281-Q; Film transporters — 1-C, 1-SCREEN; Shrink lenses — 1-Allen Bradley/variable squeeze; Digital color separation equipment — Lf/AP Leaf Picture Desk.
PRESSROOM: Line 1 — 9-MOT/FX-4; Folders — 2-MOT; Pasters — 9-MOT; Reels and stands — 9-MOT; Press control system — 1-Honeywell, 1-Cline. MAILROOM: Counter stackers — 2-Id/EDS 660, 1-Id/EDS 440, 1-QWI/SJ100A, 3-HL/Monitor HT; Inserters and stuffers — HI/2299; Bundle tyer — 3-OVL/JP-80, 2-EAM/Mosca, 3-OVL/JP-40. LIBRARY: Electronic — SCS/Personal Librarian. WIRE SERVICES: News — AP, SHNS, LAT-WP; Photos — AP; Stock tables — AP; Syndicates — King Features, AP; Receiving dishes — size-10ft, AP. BUSINESS COMPUTERS: 2-DEC/VAX 4106 clustered; Applications: CJ: Circ, Accts receivable, Payroll, Accts payable, Adv billing, Gen ledger; PCs & micros networked; PCs & main system networked.

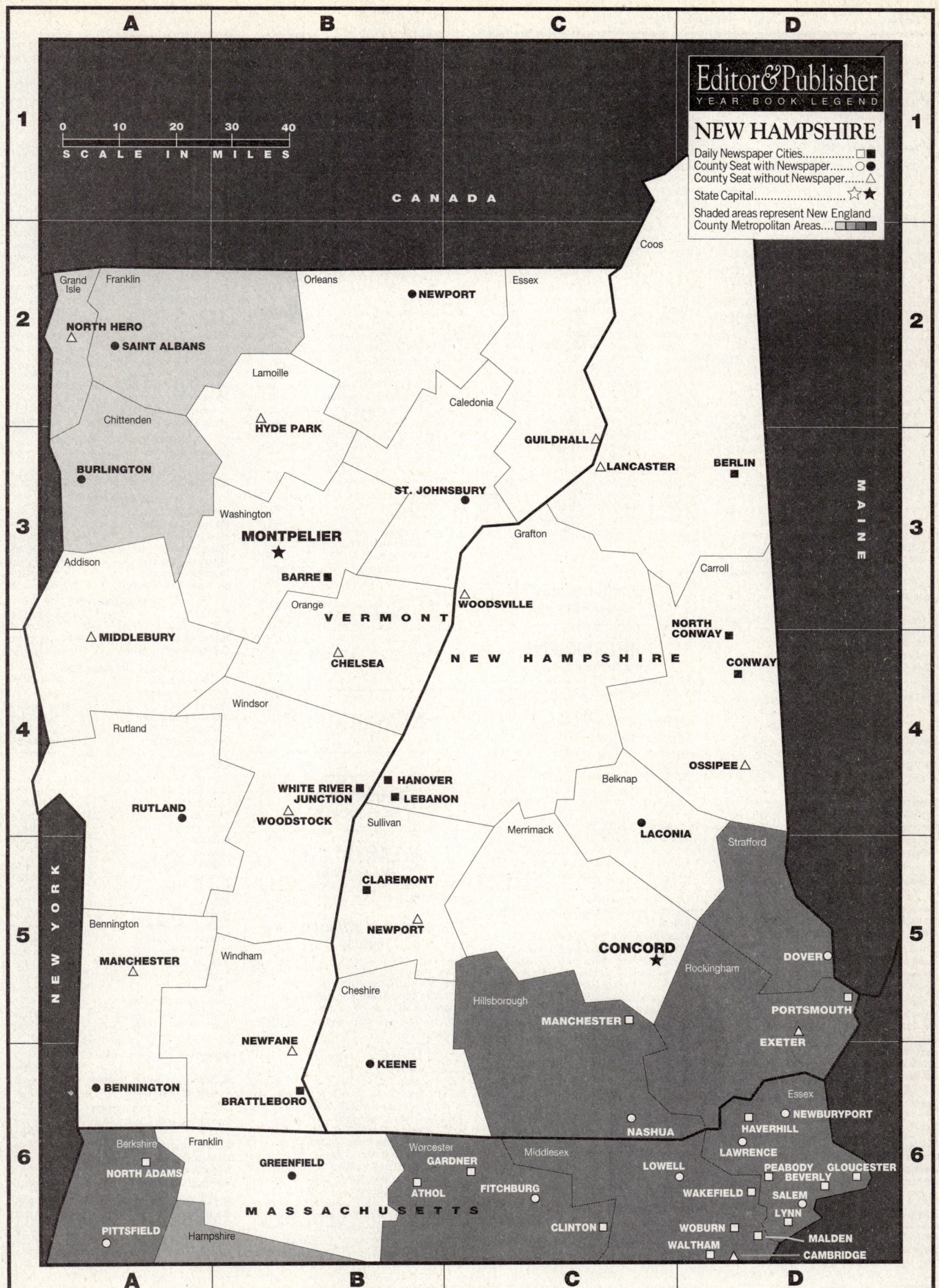

I-250 New Hampshire

NASHUA
Hillsborough County
'90 U.S. Census- 79,662; E&P '96 Est. 91,758
ABC-CZ (90): 116,788 (HH 43,203)

The Telegraph
(m-mon to sat; S)

The Telegraph, 17 Executive Dr. Hudson (03051); PO Box 1008, Nashua, NH 03061; tel (603) 882-2741; fax (603) 882-5138; e-mail news@telegraph-nh.com; web site http://www.cmonitor.com/primary. Independent Publications Inc. group.

Circulation: 29,362(m); 29,362(m-sat); 34,359(S); ABC Sept. 30, 1995.

Price: 50¢(d); 50¢(sat); $1.50(S); $3.25/wk; $156.00/yr (carrier).

Advertising: Open inch rate $22.58(m); $22.58(m-sat); $22.58(S). **Representative:** Landon Associates Inc.

News Service: AP. **Politics:** Independent. **Established:** 1832.

Not Published: New Year; Memorial Day; Independence Day; Labor Day; Christmas.

Special Editions: The Perfect Wedding (Jan); President's Day Auto Section, Coupon Book, Valentine's Day Dining (Feb); Progress Edition, Spring Car Care, Easter Dine Out (Mar); Colossal Classified, Spring Home & Garden, Kid's Stuff (Apr); Mother's Day Dine Out, Coupon Book, Shop Daniel Webster Highway (May); Summer Guide, Graduation (June); Coupon Book (July); Back-to-School, Senior Scene (Aug); Fall Home & Garden, Colossal Classified, Discover Souhegan Valley (Sept); 1997 Auto Preview, Dining Guide, Amherst Street Guide (Oct); Cookbook, Alphabet of Gifts, Coupon Book, Thanksgiving Dine Out, Christmas Downtown Nashua (Nov); Holiday Gift Guide, Last Minute Gift Guide, Celebrate New Year's Eve (Dec).

Special Weekly Sections: Best Food (wed); Community Spotlight, Entertainment Calendar (thur); Community Spotlight (fri); Religious Pages (sat); Community Spotlight (S); Business, Amusement/Entertainment, Lifestyle (daily).

Magazine: USA Weekend.

CORPORATE OFFICERS

President	William L McLean III
Vice Pres/Secretary	Andrew T Bickford

GENERAL MANAGEMENT

Publisher	Terrence L Williams
Controller	William Jaquith
Manager-Accounting	Donald Smith
Personnel Manager	Marge Soper

ADVERTISING

Manager	Mark Iacuessa
Asst Manager	John Armenio
Manager-Inside Sales	Paula Goodridge
Manager-Outside Sales	Steven Pare
Manager-Major Accounts	Ed Tausky

TELECOMMUNICATIONS

Audiotex Manager	John Armenio

CIRCULATION

Manager	David Rowe
Manager-Home Delivery	David Carlin
Manager-Database Marketing	Michael Brooks

NEWS EXECUTIVES

Managing Editor	George Geers
Managing Editor	David Solomon

EDITORS AND MANAGERS

Business Editor	John Iacoboni
Editorial Page Editor	Claudette Durocher
City Editor	Nick Pappas
News Editor	Thomas Grilli
Regional Editor	Marty Karlon
Sports Editor	Alan Greenwood
Sunday Editor	Margaret Walter

MANAGEMENT INFORMATION SERVICES

Data Processing Manager	Geoffrey Ziminsky

PRODUCTION

Manager-Technical Service	Donald Le Shane
Manager-Distribution	William Tyers
Foreman-Composing	Dianne Stangroom
Foreman-Press	Richard Talcott
Foreman-Mailroom	Tom Bishop

Market Information: TMC; ADS; Operate audiotex.

Mechanical available: Offset; Black and 3 ROP colors; insert accepted — preprinted; page cutoffs — 22".

Mechanical specifications: Type page 13" x 21"; E - 6 cols, 2.04", 1/8" between; A - 6 cols, 2.04", 1/8" between; C - 9 cols, 1.38", 1/12" between.

Commodity consumption: Newsprint 3,100 metric tons; widths 55", 41 1/4", 27 1/2"; single pages printed 16,800; average pages per issue 40(d), 86(S); single plates used 18,000.

Equipment: EDITORIAL: Front-end hardware — 38-CD/PC 1200E; Front-end software — CD/2400; Other equipment — DEC/PDP 1184. CLASSIFIED: Front-end hardware — 13-P5-75 on Novell 4.1 Server; Front-end software — PPI/Classified; Printers — HP/V. AUDIOTEX: Hardware — Computer Group/Ads-on-call. DISPLAY: Adv layout systems — SCS/Layout 8000, Informatel/Pagination; Front-end hardware — DEC/VAX 8350, P5-90. PRODUCTION: Pagination software — HI/8300, HI/8900; OCR software — PC/MS DOS-WIN 3.3, Caere/OmniPage Pro; Typesetters — 2-AG/Accuset 1500; Plate exposures — 2-P/33-43; Plate processors — 2-Nat/A-250; Scanners — ECR/Autokon 1200; Production cameras — 1-C/Spartan, 1-R/500, 1-C/Marathon; Automatic film processors — 2-LE/LD 1800, 1-LE/PC 1800, 1-Kk/660; Shrink lenses — 1-Alan/Variable 24; Color separation equipment (conventional) — 1-Howtek/4500 Drum Scanner; Digital color separation equipment — Lf/Leafscan 35. PRESSROOM: Line 1 — 5-MAN/Uniman 4x2; Pasters — 5-MEG; Press control system — GE. MAILROOM: Counter stackers — MM/228, 2-QWI/300B; Inserters and stuffers — 1-GMA/SLS-1000 (10:1); Bundle tyer — 2-PSN/6E; Addressing machine — 2-Ch/525-E. LIBRARY: Electronic — SMS/Stauffer Gold. WIRE SERVICES: News — AP Datastream, AP Datafeatures, AP Photostream; Stock tables — AP SelectStox; Receiving dishes — AP, AdSat (on AP). BUSINESS COMPUTERS: DEC/VAX 8350; Applications: Gen ledger, Circ, Subscriber/non-subscriber, Class, Display, Transient billing.

NORTH CONWAY
See CONWAY

PORTSMOUTH
Rockingham County
'90 U.S. Census- 25,925; E&P '96 Est. 25,980
ABC-NDM (90): 39,895 (HH 15,587)

Portsmouth Herald
(m-mon to sat; S)

Portsmouth Herald, 111 Maplewood Ave., Portsmouth, NH 03801; tel (603) 436-1800; fax (603) 427-0550; e-mail pherald@aol.com; web site http://www.nh-meseacoast.com. Thomson Newspapers group.

Circulation: 15,977(m); 15,977(m-sat); 17,893(S); ABC Sept. 30, 1995.

Price: 50¢(d); 50¢(sat); $1.25(S); $2.75/wk; $35.75/3mo; $143.00/yr.

Advertising: Open inch rate $15.38(m); $15.38(m-sat); $15.38(S). **Representative:** Landon Associates Inc.

News Service: AP. **Politics:** Independent. **Established:** 1886.

Not Published: New Year; Christmas.

Special Editions: Bridal, Coupon Mini Tab (Jan); Healthfile, Pres. Auto Section (Feb); Home Improvement, Coupon, St. Pat's Auto Section (Mar); Herald 100, Lawn/Garden (Apr); Coupon, Mother's Day (May); Tourist Mini (June); LPGA Mini, Summer Lifestyles (July); Coupon, Back-to-School (Aug); Tourist, Parenting (Sept); Coupon, Cookbook, Auto Preview '97, Healthfile, Home/Garden (Oct); Holly, Big Kids Toys (Nov); Last Minute Gift (Dec).

Special Weekly Sections: Best Food Day (wed); Spotlight Weekly Magazine (thur); Entertainment/TV Grid (S).

Magazines: Spotlight Magazine, Arts & Entertainment (thur); Cover Story (sat); TV Times, Color Comics (S); Parade of Homes, R.E. Guide, Auto Market (monthly).

GENERAL MANAGEMENT

General Manager	Ted Staszak
Accountant	Mary Beth Taylor

ADVERTISING

Director	Gloria Bonito

MARKETING AND PROMOTION

Director-Marketing/Promotion	Peter Johnson

CIRCULATION

Director	Dennis Thompson

NEWS EXECUTIVES

Editor (Acting)	Jane Murphy
Managing Editor	John Whiteman

EDITORS AND MANAGERS

Business Editor	Sharon Gaudin
City Editor	Michael McGrail
Librarian	Robin Silva
Lifestyle Editor	Tracy Rauh
Sports Editor	Ed Flaherty
Sunday Editor	Christine Gilette

MANAGEMENT INFORMATION SERVICES

Data Processing Manager	Mary Beth Taylor

PRODUCTION

Foreman-Composing Room	Brian Corkery
Foreman-Pressroom	Ted Staszak

Market Information: TMC; ADS; Electronic edition.

Mechanical available: Offset; Black and 3 ROP colors; insert accepted — preprinted; page cutoffs — 22 3/4".

Mechanical specifications: Type page 13" x 21 1/2"; E - 6 cols, 2 1/16", 1/8" between; A - 6 cols, 2 1/16", 1/8" between; C - 9 cols, 1 3/8", 1/16" between.

Commodity consumption: Newsprint 1,000 short tons; 909 metric tons; widths 27 1/2", 13 3/4"; black ink 30,000 pounds; color ink 800 pounds; single pages printed 13,375; average pages per issue 36(d), 40(S); single plates used 12,800.

Equipment: EDITORIAL: Front-end hardware — Mk/6000; Front-end software — RSK/Tandy 1000, Mk/NewsTouch. CLASSIFIED: Front-end hardware — Mk/Sys; Front-end software — Mk. DISPLAY: Adv layout systems — 1-Mk; Front-end hardware — Ap/Mac SE. PRODUCTION: Typesetters — 2-V/4000, 2-V/5100; Plate exposures — 1-Nu/Flip Top FT 40V6UPNS; Plate processors — 1-Nat/A250; Production cameras — 1-LE/121, 2-SCREEN/680C; Automatic film processors — 1-LE/18; Film transporters — 1-LE; Color separation equipment (conventional) — Digi-Colour, Lf/AP Leaf Picture Desk. PRESSROOM: Line 1 — 7-G/Urbanite. MAILROOM: Bundle tyer — 1-OVL/Constellation, 1-CYP; Addressing machine — KR/Labeler. LIBRARY: Electronic — 1-Micro-Photo. COMMUNICATIONS: Digital ad delivery system — AP AdSend. WIRE SERVICES: News — AP; Receiving dishes — AP. BUSINESS COMPUTERS: 1-ATT/3B2-500; Applications: Circ, Accts receivable, Accts payable, Payroll, Gen ledger.

NEW JERSEY

ASBURY PARK
See NEPTUNE

ATLANTIC CITY
Atlantic County
'90 U.S. Census- 37,986; E&P '96 Est. 36,307
ABC-NDM (90): 466,310 (HH 175,349)

The Press of Atlantic City
(m-mon to sat; S)

The Press of Atlantic City, 1000 W. Washington Ave., Pleasantville, NJ 08232-3806; tel (609) 272-7000; fax (609) 272-7059; e-mail acpress@acy.digex.net; web site http://www.acy.digex.net, http://www.acpress/acpress.html. Independent Newspaper group.

Circulation: 77,117(m); 77,117(m-sat); 98,872(S); ABC Sept. 30, 1995.

Price: 50¢(d); 50¢(sat); $1.50(S); $3.35/wk, $13.40/mo, $174.20/yr.

Advertising: Open inch rate $49.75(m); $49.75(m-sat); $61.86(S); $92.79(m & S). **Representative:** Landon Associates Inc.

News Services: AP, LAT-WP, SNS, SHNS. **Politics:** Independent. **Established:** 1895.

Special Editions: Business Review-Progress and Forecast Edition (Jan); The Wedding Preview (Feb); Home and Garden (Mar); Baseball Tab, Showcase of Homes, Create An Ad (NIE Section) (Apr); Women of Distinction (May); LPGA Tab, Fishing & Boating (June); Outdoor Living (July); Back-to-School, Pro/College Football Tab (Aug); Miss America, The Wedding Preview (Sept); Home Decor and Design, Medical Tab (Oct); Fall Auto Focus, Holiday Gift Guide (Nov); Holiday Catalog, Holiday Gift Guide 2, Holiday Gift Guide 3, Holiday Gift Guide 4, Holiday Greetings/Songbook (Dec).

Special Weekly Sections: Food Pages (wed); Auto Pages (thur); Real Estate Tab, At the Shore Tab (Weekly Entertainment Guide) (fri); Church Page (sat); Marketplace, Real Estate, Lifestyle, Food Pages, Auto Pages (S).

Magazines: TV Magazine, USA Weekend (S).

CORPORATE OFFICERS

President	John F Bitzer Jr
Exec Vice Pres	Robert M McCormick
Asst Treasurer	Charles A Bryant Jr

GENERAL MANAGEMENT

Publisher	Robert M McCormick
Director-Finance/Operations	Charles A Bryant Jr
Director-Sales/Marketing	Robert E Mawhinney
Director-Circulation	Vito T Cicero
Director-Personnel	Kathleen J Leonard
Exec Editor	Paul Merkoski

ADVERTISING

Director-Sales/Marketing	Robert E Mawhinney
Manager-Retail	Terri Traczyk-Thomas
Manager-Classified	Jayne Doherty
Manager-Telemarketing	Ron Pino
Manager-City Sales	Timothy Biringer
Manager-Major/National	Debra Hillman
Manager-Co-op	Darla Johnson
Manager-Phone Room	Kathy Waldron
Manager-Ad Production	Anthony Sakson
Manager-Ad Processing	Colleen Basile
Coordinator-National	Clifford Madsen
At the Shore Business Manager	Larry West

MARKETING AND PROMOTION

Director-Sales/Marketing	Robert E Mawhinney

TELECOMMUNICATIONS

Manager-Telecommunications	Gary McClintock

CIRCULATION

Director	Vito T Cicero
Manager-Marketing	Joel Kopke
Manager-Sales	William Muller
Manager-Single Copy Sales	Gary Ruble
Manager-Operations	Patrick Hathaway
Manager-Mailroom	James Martin
Manager-Transportation	David Sonnie

NEWS EXECUTIVES

Exec Editor	Paul A Merkoski
Asst to Editor	Mary Post
Managing Editor	Maryjane Briant
Deputy Managing Editor	Steven Warren

EDITORS AND MANAGERS

Action Line Editor	Kevin Post
Automotive Editor	Kevin Post
Books Editor	Alice Cranston
Business/Finance Editor	Kevin Post
City Editor	Charles Wray
Community Editor	Mona Moore
Consumer Editor	Kevin Post
Editorial Page Editor	Carla Linz
Assoc Editorial Page Editor	Jim Perskie
Entertainment Editor	Alice Cranston
Fashion Editor	Gail Wilson
Features Editor	Alice Cranston
Films/Theater Editor	Alice Cranston
Food Editor	Cindy Nevitt
Graphics Editor	Tim Faherty
Health/Medical Editor	Alice Cranston
Librarian	Linda Uhrmann
Lifestyle Editor	Alice Cranston
Music Editor	Kevin Post
News Editor	Peter Bropny
Photography Editor	Gary Shivers
Production Editor	David Benson
Real Estate Editor	Kevin Post
Religion Editor	Alice Cranston
Science/Technology Editor	Richard Degener
Sports Editor	Mike Shepherd
Teen-Age/Youth Editor	Gail Wilson
Television Editor	Alice Cranston
Travel Editor	Cindy Nevitt

MANAGEMENT INFORMATION SERVICES

Manager-Management Info Services	James Young
Manager-Applications Systems	William Bloom
Analyst-Info Systems	Timothy McGlynn

PRODUCTION

Director-Finance & Operations	Charles A Bryant Jr
Manager-Maintenance	Jack Steinhauer
Manager-Mechanical Operations	Harry Cottrill
Manager-Quality Control	Charles Giddings
Manager-Pressroom	Dick Whedbee

Market Information: Zoned editions; Split Run;

Mechanical available: Flexo; Black and 3 ROP colors; insert accepted — preprinted; page cutoffs — 22 3/4".

Mechanical specifications: Type page 13" x 21 1/2"; E - 6 cols, 2 1/16", 1/8" between; A - 6 cols, 2 1/16", 1/8" between; C - 10 cols, 1 1/4", 1/16" between.

Copyright ©1996 by the Editor & Publisher Co.

Commodity consumption: Newsprint 11,479 short tons; widths 55", $41\frac{1}{8}$", $27\frac{3}{8}$"; black ink 458,578 pounds; color ink 147,835 pounds; average pages per issue 44(d), 102(S); single plates used 101,239.

Equipment: EDITORIAL: Front-end hardware — DEC/PDP 11-84, DEC/Alpha server, DEC/PC; Front-end software — TMS/NSSE V6E, Dewar/View, QuarkXPress; Printers — DEC/LA 50, DEC/LA 75, DEC/LA 100, QMS/860; Other equipment — 2-AU/Softpip, Bidco/Imagesetters, AU/APS-100, AG/Accuset Imagesetter. CLASSIFIED: Front-end hardware — DEC/Alpha server, DEC/PC; Front-end software — Computext 4.4.0; Printers — DEC/LA 70, DEC/LQP02, QMS/860; Other equipment — 2-AU/Softpip, Bidco/Imagesetters. DISPLAY: Adv layout systems — CJ/AIM Layout; Front-end hardware — Ap/Mac, CNI/486Dx266 File-server; Front-end software — QuarkXPress 3.3.1, Novell/Netware 3.12; Printers — Ap/Mac LaserWriter, XIT/Clipper, QMS/860; Other equipment — X/Scanner, ScanView/ScanMate. PRODUCTION: Pagination software — QuarkXPress 3.2, Dewar/View 1.11, Computext 4.40; OCR software — Claera/M-Pro; Typesetters — 2-Bidco/Laser, AG/Accset; Platemaking systems — Na; Plate exposures — Na/FX4; Plate processors — Na/FP1; Electronic picture desk — Lf/AP Leaf Picture Desk; Scanners — 1-ECR/Autokon 1000, ScanView/ScanMate 5000; Production cameras — 1-C/Spartan, 1-C/Newspager; Automatic film processors — 3-LE/PC 24, 2-LE/PC 18, 1-C; Film transporters — 1-C; Color separation equipment (conventional) — ScanView/ScanMate 5000, TI/Phoenix Photo System; Digital color separation equipment — 1-ScanView/ScanMate 5000.

PRESSROOM: Line 1 — 8-H/Colormatic converted to Flexo; Line 2 — 8-H/Colormatic converted to Flexo; Folders — 3-H/3:2; Pasters — 16-H/RTP; Press control system — PEC. MAILROOM: Counter stackers — 9-HL/1; Inserters and stuffers — 2-HI/1472; Bundle tyer — 2-MLN/MLN2A, 4-Power Strap; Addressing machine — KR. LIBRARY: Electronic — Vu/Text, Alpha/Server. WIRE SERVICES: News — AP, AP Datafeatures; Stock tables — AP SelectStox; Receiving dishes — AP. BUSINESS COMPUTERS: 2-DEC/Microvax 3100-95, 1-Acerframe/486Dx66 Fileserver; Applications: CJ/AIM: Layout, Circ; Platinum/Premier: Gen ledger, Accts payable; ADP: Payroll; Excaliber/POS, Novell/Netware; PCs & micros networked; PCs & main system networked.

BERGEN COUNTY-HACKENSACK

Bergen County

'90 U.S. Census- 37,049; **E&P '96 Est.** 38,459
ABC-NDM (90): 1,278,440 (HH 464,149)

The Record (m-mon to sat; S)

The Record, 150 River St., Hackensack, NJ 07602; tel (201) 646-4000, (201) 646-4444 (product srv.); fax (201) 646-4405, (201) 646-4043 (product srv.); e-mail newsroom@bergen-record.com; web site http://www.bergen.com. Macromedia Inc. group.

Circulation: 156,726(m); 156,726(m-sat); 212,269(S); ABC Sept. 30, 1995.

Price: 50¢(d); 50¢(sat); $1.50(S); $42.25/13wk (d & S), $84.50/26wk (d & S), $161.20/52wk (d & S), $117.00/52wk (wknd).

Advertising: Open inch rate $72.71(m); $72.71(m-sat); $103.06(S). **Representatives:** Sawyer-Ferguson-Walker Co.; Publishers' Representatives of Florida; Metropolitan Publishers Reps. Inc.

News Services: AP, LAT-WP, Accu-Weather, KRT, Bloomberg, PR Newswire, States News Service, US Newswire, Business Wire. **Politics:** Independent. **Established:** 1895.

Advertising not accepted: Libel; Fraud; Indecent.

Special Editions: Books & Music, Super Bowl '96, Health Care Report Part I, Health Care Report Part II (Jan); North Jersey Business, Valentine's Day Dine-Out, Wedding Guide, Homescape, Spring Outlet Shopping Guide, Education, Books & Music (Feb); Homescape, Personal Finance/Taxes, St. Patrick's Day, NJ International Auto Show, Spring Fashions, Books & Music, Garden, North Jersey Health Care Guide, NCAA Final Four (Mar); Spring Auto, Health & Fitness, Easter Dine-Out, Homescape, Books & Music, Wheels '96/Greater NY Auto Show, Spring Home Improvement and Yard, NJ Golf/Golf Vacations, Education, Secretary's Day (Apr); Homescape, Mother's Day Dine-Out, Elderly Care, Health & Medical Careers, Books & Music (May); Homescape/Summer Living, Books & Music (June); Books & Music, Olympics, Bride's Book (July); Books & Music, Back-to-School (Aug); Pro Football, Catalog/Brochure, Homescape, Fall Fashions, Books & Music, Keeping Healthy, High School Football, Home and Yard, Bride's Guide (Sept); Autumn Outlet Shopping Guide, Homescape, Dining Out Guide, Personal Finance/Retirement Planning, Health & Fitness, Education, Automotive Buyer's Guide, Books & Music (Oct); East Coast International Auto Show, Homescape, Thanksgiving Dine-Out, Holiday Gift Guide, Books & Music (Nov); Homescape/Holidays, Holiday Entertainment, Holiday Dine-Out, Last Minute Gift Guide, New Year's Dine-Out, Books & Music (Dec).

Special Weekly Sections: Health and Exercise, Keeping Fit, Road Warrior, Small Business, Work Place/Job Mailbag (mon); Athlete of the Week, Education, Geo CLUB, The Mini Page, Computers (tues); Around N.J. Sports, Births, Children's Activities, Community Bulletin Boards, Dinner Express, FOOD, Hunting & Fishing, Military Notes, Real Estate Sales, Recreation, Small Business, Theatre, Volunteer of the Week, Weddings & Engagements, Wine Column, Warren Boronson/Investing, Regional Advertising (wed); Automotive, Antiques, Boating, Children, Fashion/Home Furnishings, Gardening, Home and Family, Senior Citizens, Singles, Skiing (Seasonal) (thur); Dine-Out, Film, Music, Comedy, Previews-Weekend Entertainment, Real Estate, Religion, Saltwater Fishing (Seasonal), Video, Books (fri); At the Malls, Day Trips, For Kids Only, Gardening, Home Clinic, Home Town Hero, Smart Dining, Smart Shopper, Sports Insider, Sports Odds On, Things to Do, Videos (sat); Baseball: Youth, High School, College, Pro, Basketball: Youth, High School, College, Pro, Bloomberg Personnel, Books, Bowling, Camp Directory, Color Comics, Food, Football: Youth, High School, College, Pro, Golf, High School Sports, Hockey: High School, College, Pro, Hunting & Fishing, Inside Trenton, Investment Mailbag, Lively Arts, Personal Finance/Stock Market, Real Estate, Regional Advertising, Relationships, Review & Outlook, Senior Citizens, Television Book, Travel, Washington File (S).

Magazines: Parade, TV Record (own, offset) (S).

Broadcast Affiliates: WBNG-TV Binghamton, NY; WTAJ-TV Altoona, PA; WLYH-TV Lancaster-Lebanon, PA; WOWK-TV Huntington, WV.

CORPORATE OFFICERS

Board Chairman/CEO/Publisher Malcolm A Borg
President Robert J Sapanara
Senior Vice Pres/Chief Financial Officer/Treasurer Charles W Gibney
Exec Vice Pres-Manufacturing/Sales Jonathan H Markey
Vice Pres-Human Resources Jennifer A Borg Esq
Vice Pres-Editor Glenn H Ritt
Vice Pres-Sales John E Kimball
Vice Pres-Product Service Donald J Sherlock
Secretary/Asst Treasurer Melissa Ludlum

GENERAL MANAGEMENT

Manager-Purchasing Gabe Mariniello
Manager-Credit Michael Nelson
Manager-Facilities Thomas Massey
Manager-Education Service Ellen Dolgin
Manager-Business Systems Jim Lawler

ADVERTISING

General Manager-Passaic/Morris Jonathan J Theophilakos
Manager-National Sales Rod Rodrigues
Manager-Display Lou Stancampiano
Manager-Consumer Sales John Aramini
Manager-Co-op John Ceraso

MARKETING AND PROMOTION

Director-Marketing Service Patricia Stone-D'Amico
Manager-Public Relations Nancy Sergeant

TELECOMMUNICATIONS

Computer Operations/Telecommunications Richard Rounds
Audiotex Manager Gary Kowal

CIRCULATION

Manager-Product Service/Systems/Administration Jane Maxcy
Manager-Product Service/Consumer Relations Dolores Hunt
Manager-Product Service/Delivery Systems Rich Klypka
Manager-Product Service/Distribution/Fleet Operations John Duca

NEWS EXECUTIVES

Editor Glenn H Ritt
Managing Editor Vivian Waixel

EDITORS AND MANAGERS

Art/Architecture Editor John Zeaman
Automotive Editor Aaron Elson
Bergen Editor Tim Nostrand
Books Editor Laurence Chollet
Business Editor Kathleen Sullivan
Columnist Kevin Demarrais
Columnist John Rowe
Columnist Jeff Page
Columnist Bill Pennington
Columnist Mike Celizic
Columnist Mike Kelly
Columnist Rod Allee
Columnist Miguel Perez
Columnist Kathleen O'Brien
Chief Copy Editor Theresa Forsman
Consumer Affairs Editor Sue Edelman
Consumer Interests Editor Lois DiTommaso
Director-Photography Rich Gigli
Editorial Page Editor Richard Benfield
Editorial Systems Manager Anna Fragetta
Education Editor Caroline Hendrie
Entertainment/Amusements Editor Steve Marsh
Environment Emily Laber
Fashion Editor Judy Jeannin
Family Editor Mary Amoroso
Features Editor Lois DiTommaso
Films Editor Lou Lumenick
Food Editor Patricia Mack
Gardening Editor Elizabeth Houlton
Director-Graphics Dennis McCulley
Graphics Editor Kevin O'Neil
Health Editor Kevin Granville
Investigative News Editor Bruce Locklin
Legal Affairs Editor Elliot Pinsley
Leisure Editor Jill Schensul
Living/Lifestyle Editor Lois DiTommaso
Music Editor-Popular Barbara Jaeger
Chief News Editor Robert Cunningham
News Room Administrator Laura Paino
Passaic Editor Mike Semel
Personal Finance Editor Warren Boroson
Real Estate Editor Warren Boroson
Religion Columnist David Gibson
Special Sections Editor Lois DiTommaso
Sports Editor Gabe Buonauro
State Assignment Editor Deirdre Sykes
Television Editor Virginia Mann
Theater/Broadway Editor Robert Feldberg
Transportation Editor Pat Gilbert
Travel Editor Jill Schensul
Trenton Bureau Editor Eugene Kiely
Women's Editor Lois DiTommaso

MANAGEMENT INFORMATION SERVICES

Data Processing Manager Rick Rounds
Manager-Editorial Info Services Paul Schulman

PRODUCTION

Director Ben Cannizzaro
Manager-Pressroom Tony Maglio
Manager-Mailroom Bob Meyer
Manager-Systems Support Charles Whitehead
Manager-Pre Press Charles Havel
Manager-Technology Support Chris Kapsalis

Market Information: Zoned editions; Split Run; TMC; ADS; Operate database; Operate audiotex; Electronic edition.

Mechanical available: Offset; Black and 3 ROP colors; insert accepted — preprinted; page cut-offs — 22".

Mechanical specifications: Type page 13" x 21"; E - 6 cols, $2\frac{1}{16}$", $\frac{1}{8}$" between; A - 6 cols, $2\frac{1}{16}$", $\frac{1}{8}$" between; C - 10 cols, $1\frac{3}{16}$", $\frac{1}{16}$" between.

Commodity consumption: Newsprint 54,000 metric tons; widths 55", $41\frac{1}{4}$", $27\frac{1}{2}$", 54"; black ink 1,200,000 pounds; color ink 300,000 pounds; single pages printed 49,000; average pages per issue 80(d), 230(S); single plates used 240,000.

Equipment: EDITORIAL: Front-end hardware — AT, DEC; Front-end software — AT 4.7.4; CLASSIFIED: Front-end hardware — DEC; Front-end software — CSI. AUDIOTEX: Supplier name — Micro Voice. DISPLAY: Adv layout systems — SCS/Layout 8000, Ap/Mac, Multi-Ad/Creator, QuarkXPress; Front-end hardware — III; Front-end software — AMS. PRODUCTION: Pagination software — AT/Press-To-Go; Typesetters — 4-III/3850; Platemaking systems — WL/Lith-X-Pozer; Plate processors — WL; Electronic picture desk — Lf/AP Leaf Picture Desk; Scanners — Ik, 2-Ik/350i; Production cameras — C; Automatic film processors — P; Film transporters — P; Digital color separation equipment — Ap/Mac. PRESSROOM: Line 1 — 8-TKS; Line 2 — 8-TKS; Line 3 — 9-MHI; Line 4 — 9-MHI; Line 5 — 12-MAN/Uniset; Press drives — Fin; Folders — 8-TKS, 9-MHI, 2-MAN; Pasters — TKS, MHI, MM. MAILROOM: Counter stackers — Id, HL, QWI; Inserters and stuffers — 2-Fg, MM, S; Bundle tyer — Dynaric, MLN, Power Strap; Addressing machine — 5-Barstrom, 2-KAN. LIBRARY: Electronic — Battelle/Basis Release K, 2-DEC/VAX 4000-600, Information Dimensions Inc. COMMUNICATIONS: Facsimile — 3-CD/PageFax reader, 4-CD/PageFax writer; Remote imagesetting — 2-III/3850 Imagesetter; Digital ad delivery system — AP AdSend; Systems used — satellite, fiber optic. WIRE SERVICES: News — AP; Photos — AP; Stock tables — AP Grand Central Stocks; Receiving dishes — size-5m, AP. BUSINESS COMPUTERS: 2-DEC/VAX-4000-6000V, 1-DEC/VAX II-730; Applications: Microsoft/Office: Manufacturing, Mktg research; Borland/Paradox: Manufacturing; Software Ventures/Microphone Pro: Manufacturing; Microsoft/Project: Manufacturing; EM320: Mktg, Circ; Microsoft/Word: Mktg; Microsoft/PowerPoint: Mktg; Claris/Claris Works: Mktg; Claris/Filemaker Pro: Mktg; Calender/Maker: Mktg; Microsoft/Excel: Mktg; Aldus/FreeHand: Mktg, Creative services, Editorial graphics; QuarkXPress: Mktg, Creative services, Editorial graphics; Aldus/PageMaker: Mktg, Creative services, Editorial graphics; Adobe/Illustrator: Mktg, Creative services, Editorial graphics; Adobe/Photoshop: Mktg, Creative services, Editorial graphics; Adobe/TypeStyler: Mktg, Creative services, Editorial graphics; Adobe/Streamline: Mktg, Creative services, Editorial graphics; WordPerfect: Corporate, Circ; Symphony: Corporate, Fin, Circ; Harvard Graphics: Fin, Circ; Multi-Ad/Creator: Creative services; Atlas/MapMaker: Creative services; Lotus 1-2-3: Circ; Freelance graphics: Circ; MS-DOS, Microsoft/Windows; PCs & micros networked; PCs & main system networked.

BRICK TOWNSHIP

See TOMS RIVER

BRIDGETON

Cumberland County

'90 U.S. Census- 18,942; **E&P '96 Est.** 19,379
ABC-NDM (90): 50,633 (HH 17,497)

Bridgeton Evening News

(e-mon to sat)

Bridgeton Evening News, 100 E. Commerce St.; Box 596, Bridgeton, NJ 08302; tel (609) 451-1000; fax (609) 451-7214. Hollinger International Inc. group.

Circulation: 9,144(e); 9,144(e-sat); ABC Sept. 30, 1995.

Price: 35¢(d); 35¢(sat); $1.85/wk.

Advertising: Open inch rate $12.50(e); $12.50(e-sat). **Representative:** Landon Associates Inc.

News Service: AP. **Politics:** Independent. **Established:** 1879.

Not Published: New Year; Memorial Day; Independence Day; Labor Day; Thanksgiving; Christmas.

Special Editions: Business Review (Jan); Bridal, Great Outdoors, Farm & Garden (Mar); Bridal, Great Outdoors, Farm & Gardens (Apr); Bridal, Great Outdoors, Farm & Gardens (May); Bridal, Great Outdoors, Farm & Gardens (June); Bridal, Great Outdoors, Farm & Gardens (July); Bridal, Great Outdoors, Farm & Gardens (Aug); Christmas Gift Guides (Dec); Agriculture Tab.

Special Weekly Sections: Bridal, Great Outdoors, Farm & Gardens (fri).

Magazines: Food (wed); Business Section (thur); Building Page (fri).

GENERAL MANAGEMENT

Publisher John M Ewing
Purchasing Agent John M Ewing

ADVERTISING

Director Bernie Heller
Manager-Classified Bernie Heller

CIRCULATION

Director Brenda Morriseau

NEWS EXECUTIVE

Editor Jack Hummel

EDITORS AND MANAGERS

Automotive/Aviation Editor Sheryl Chlele
Books Editor Sheryl Chlele

Columnist	Richard Beecroft
Editorial Page Editor	Eileen Bennett
Features/Food Editor	Sheryl Chlele
Films/Theater Editor	Sheryl Chlele
Food Editor	Sheryl Chlele
Librarian	Jody Musso
Music Editor	Sheryl Chlele
News/Political Editor	Chris Blake-Grant
Radio/Television Editor	Sheryl Chlele
Religion Editor	Jody Russo
Sports Editor	Eric Chlele
Wire Editor	Chris Grant
Women's Editor	Sheryl Chlele

Market Information: Zoned editions; TMC.
Mechanical available: Offset; Black and 3 ROP colors; insert accepted — preprinted; page cut-offs — 22¾".
Mechanical specifications: Type page 13" x 21½"; E - 6 cols, 2 1/6", 1/8" between; A - 6 cols, 2 1/6", 1/8" between; C - 9 cols, 1⅜", 1/8" between.
Commodity consumption: Newsprint 2,500 metric tons; widths 27¼", 13⅝"; black ink 96,000 pounds; color ink 4,229 pounds; single pages printed 7,288; average pages per issue 22(d); single plates used 9,900.
Equipment: EDITORIAL: Front-end hardware — 12-TC; Front-end software — RSK/Tandy Remote. CLASSIFIED: Front-end hardware — 2-OS, TC. PRODUCTION: Typesetters — 2-COM/8400, COM/MCS-10-2; Plate exposures — 2-Nu; Plate processors — 1-Nat/A-250; Production cameras — 1-C/Spartan III; Automatic film processors — 2-LE; Film transporters — 1-LE; Shrink lenses — 1-CK Optical/SQU-7. PRESSROOM: Line 1 — 6-G/Urbanite; Folders — 1-G. MAILROOM: Counter stackers — 1-BG/105; Bundle tyer — 1-Sa/S1100, 2-MLN. COMMUNICATIONS: Facsimile — BS/Express 2010. WIRE SERVICES: News — AP; Receiving dishes — AP. BUSINESS COMPUTERS: 1-Cado/Tiger; Applications: Circ, Adv billing, Accts receivable, Gen ledger, Payroll; PCs & micros networked; PCs & main sys. networked.

BRIDGEWATER

Somerset County

'90 U.S. Census- 32,509; E&P '96 Est. 35,803
ABC-NDM (90): 454,054 (HH 159,607)

The Courier-News

(m-mon to sat; S)

The Courier-News, 1201 Rt. 22; PO Box 6600, Bridgewater, NJ 08807; tel (908) 722-8800 (pub); fax (908) 707-3272 (pub). Gannett Co. Inc. group.
Circulation: 50,000(m); 50,000(m-sat); 52,208(S); ABC Sept. 30, 1995.
Price: 25¢(d); 25¢(sat); 75¢(S); $2.50/wk; $10.00/mo; $130.00/yr.
Advertising: Open inch rate $46.92(m); $46.92(m-sat); $49.88(S). **Representatives:** Gannett National Newspaper Sales; US Suburban Press.
News Services: AP, GNS, LAT-WP. **Politics:** Independent. **Established:** 1884.
Not Published: New Year; Christmas.
Special Editions: Super Bowl, Health & Fitness, Automarket, Bridal Section (Jan); Forecast (Feb); NJ Auto Show, Personal Finance, NY Auto Show (Mar); Spring Decor and Design, Health Tab (Apr); Tour of Somerville, Be Aware (May); Bridal Guide, Graduation Tab, Automarket (June); Dream Home (July); Balloon Festival Program (Aug); H.S. Football, College/Pro Football, Fall Home Improvement, USER's Guide, Super Summer Reader, Super Classified (Sept); Fall Home Improvement, Financial Update, Automarket (Oct); Wishbook, Holiday Essentials (Nov); What the Holidays Mean to Me, Holiday Section II, Holiday Section III (Dec); Homesource, Courier-Clips (monthly).
Special Weekly Sections: Weekend Sports Wrap-up (mon); Food, Health, Fitness (Lifestyle) (wed); Get Out! Weekend Preview (thur); Home Buyer's Guide (fri); Money, Lifestyle & Arts, Travel (S).

CORPORATE OFFICER

President	Henry M Freeman

GENERAL MANAGEMENT

Publisher	Henry M Freeman
Director-Finance	Jerome G Bammel

ADVERTISING

Director	Peter W Ricker
Manager-Inside Sales	Greta Lesh
Manager-Display	Laura Bader

MARKETING AND PROMOTION

Director-Marketing/Promotion	Robert G Roach

TELECOMMUNICATIONS

Audiotex Manager	Greta Lesh

CIRCULATION

Asst Director	Mark Wessner

NEWS EXECUTIVES

Editor	Carol Hunter
Managing Editor	Laura Harrigan
Asst Managing Editor	Linda Monroe
Asst Managing Editor	Marilyn Dillon

EDITORS AND MANAGERS

Business Editor	Marilyn Ostemiller
Columnist/Assoc Editor	Tom Perry
Editorial Page Editor	Philip Showell
Features Editor	Paul Grzella
Metro Editor	Lee McDonald
Asst Metro Editor	Tom Evans
Asst Metro Editor	Mike Daigle
Asst Metro Editor	Joe McDonald
News Editor	Mark Dobrow
Photo Editor	Ed Pagliarini
Real Estate Editor	Cynthia Hellerman
Sports Editor	Bill Price

MANAGEMENT INFORMATION SERVICES

Data Processing Manager	Todd Carmosino

PRODUCTION

Asst Director	Michael Grafe
Manager-Pressroom	Steven Haight
Manager-Pre Press	Judy Glowinski
Manager-Maintenance	Bob Bianci
Manager-Mailroom	Joe Loregio

Market Information: Zoned editions; TMC; Operate audiotex.
Mechanical available: Offset; Black and 3 ROP colors; insert accepted — preprinted, sampling; page cut-offs — 21½".
Mechanical specifications: Type page 13" x 21½"; E - 6 cols, 2 1/16", 1/8" between; A - 6 cols, 2 1/16", 1/8" between; C - 10 cols, 1¼", 1/16" between.
Commodity consumption: Newsprint 5,460 short tons; widths 54½", 40.88", 27¼"; black ink 127,200 pounds; color ink 34,000 pounds; single pages printed 14,418; average pages per issue 34(d), 82(S); single plates used 42,500.
Equipment: EDITORIAL: Front-end hardware — DEC; Front-end software — AT 4.6.4; Other equipment — 6-AT/CPU, 51-AT/ADT. CLASSIFIED: Front-end hardware — 17-AT, 3-Sun/Microsystems; Front-end software — AT; Other equipment — 3-AT/Display AD. AUDIOTEX: Hardware — PEP. PRODUCTION: Pagination software — QuarkXPress; Typesetters — 2-AU/Micro 570, 2-III/3850; Plate exposures — 2-Nu/Flip Top FT40V6UPNS; Plate processors — 2-WL; Electronic picture desk — Lf/AP Leaf Picture Desk; Scanners — RZ/200-S; Production cameras — 2-C/Marathon; Automatic film processors — 3-LE/LD-24; Film transporters — 2-LE; Shrink lenses — 2-CK Optical/Squeeze Lens.
PRESSROOM: Line 1 — 9-H/Lithomatic 60 (plus 6 color decks); Folders — 2-H/3:2; Pasters — 9-H/Lithomatic; Reels and stands — 9-H/Lithomatic 60; Press control system — Hurletron. MAILROOM: Counter stackers — 2-QWI; Inserters and stuffers — 1-HI/1472P; Bundle tyer — 2-Power Strap, 1-MLN; Wrapping singles — 2-QWI; Addressing machine — 1-Ch/539, 2-Spegram. COMMUNICATIONS: Digital ad delivery system — AdSat, AP AdSend. WIRE SERVICES: News — AP Datastream, AP Datafeatures, GNS, LAT-WP; Receiving dishes — AP. BUSINESS COMPUTERS: IBM/AS400, IBM/PC, IBM/PS2; Applications: Circ, Adv billing, Accts receivable, Payroll, Gen ledger, Accts payable, Spreadsheet; PCs & micros networked; PCs & main system networked.

BURLINGTON
See WILLINGBORO

CAMDEN-CHERRY HILL

Camden County

'90 U.S. Census- 156,840 (Camden 87,492; Cherry Hill 69,348); E&P '96 Est. 161,943 (Camden 90,975; Cherry Hill 70,968)
ABC-NDM (90): 811,077 (HH 289,182)

Courier-Post (m-mon to sat; S)

Courier-Post, 301 Cuthbert Blvd.; PO Box 5300, Cherry Hill, NJ 08002; tel (609) 663-6000; fax (609) 663-3190. Gannett Co. Inc. group.
Circulation: 89,110(m); 89,110(m-sat); 98,285(S); ABC Sept. 30, 1995.
Price: 35¢(d); 35¢(sat); $1.50(S); $3.25/wk; $13.00/mo; $169.00/yr.
Advertising: Open inch rate $81.95(m); $81.95(m-sat); $81.95(S). **Representative:** Gannett National Newspaper Sales.
News Services: AP, GNS. **Politics:** Independent. **Established:** 1875.
Special Editions: Pulse (Health & Medicine Magazine), Home Styles & Designs Magazine (monthly); Pic-A-Home Real Estate Magazine (bi-monthly).
Special Weekly Sections: Your Money, Family, Living (mon); Education Express, Living, Business & Financial, Prime Time (+50) (tues); Food, Singles, Business & Financial, Living (wed); Business & Financial, Living (thur); TGIF Dining & Entertainment Tab, Living It Up, Business & Financial, Real Estate (fri); Religion, At Home Decorating & Remodeling (sat); Travel, Health & Medicine, Real Estate, Dining & Entertainment, Food, Living, TV Book, Color Comics (S).
Magazines: South Jersey Business, First & Ten (Pro football) (mon); Seniors, Education Express (tues); Singles, Food (wed); Building & Real Estate, Dining, TGIF (Entertainment) (fri); Varsity High School Sports, Religion, "At Home" (Decorating & Remodeling) (sat); Building & Real Estate, Dining (S); "This Week" (TMC) (weekly); Pulse (health issue) (monthly).

CORPORATE OFFICERS

President	Robert T Collins
Treasurer	Jimmy L Thomas
Secretary	Thomas Chapple

GENERAL MANAGEMENT

Publisher	Robert T Collins
Controller	Lawrence Jock
Director-Human Resources	Lori Trasmondi

ADVERTISING

Director	John E Ziomek
Manager-National	Sophie Falkenstein
Manager-Retail	Roy Briggs
Manager-Classified	Domenic Zanghi
Manager-Promotion	Alaine Stanczyk

MARKETING AND PROMOTION

Director-Marketing	Carl Lovern

TELECOMMUNICATIONS

Audiotex Manager	Lee Morgan

CIRCULATION

Director	Gary DiSanto

NEWS EXECUTIVE

Exec Editor	Everett S Landers

EDITORS AND MANAGERS

Editorial Page Editor	Robert Ingle
Education Editor	David Hoh
Entertainment/Amusements Editor	Robbie Kenney
Environmental Editor	Larry Hajna
Farm/Agriculture Editor	Joe Busler
Fashion/Food Editor	Pam Lyons
Features Editor	Deidre Comegys
Graphics Editor/Art Director	Helen Driggs
Health/Medical Editor	Jim Koncos
Living/Lifestyle Editor	Deidre Comegys
Metro Editor	Rose McIver
News Editor	Paul Barone
Photography Editor	Curt Hudson
Political/Government Editor	Rose McIver
Science/Technology Editor	Jim Koncos
Sports Editor	Chuck Bausman
Television/Film Editor	Stewart Ettinger
Theater/Music Editor	Robert Baxter
Travel Editor	Deidre Comegys

MANAGEMENT INFORMATION SERVICES

Data Processing Manager	John Mead

PRODUCTION

Director	Mark Frisby
Asst Director	Duke Friedel
Manager-Mailroom	Phil Long
Manager-Technical Service	Steve Smith
Manager-Pre Press	Robert Kenney
Superintendent-Building	Steve Smith

Market Information: Zoned editions; Split Run; TMC; ADS; Operate audiotex.
Mechanical available: Offset; Black and 4 ROP colors; insert accepted — preprinted, quarter fold; page cut-offs — 22¾".
Mechanical specifications: Type page 13" x 21 7/16"; E - 6 cols, 2 1/16", 1/8" between; A - 6 cols, 2 1/16", 1/8" between; C - 10 cols, 1¼", 1/16" between.
Commodity consumption: Newsprint 13,000 short tons; widths 54½", 40 15/16", 27¼"; black ink 507,600 pounds; color ink 100,000 pounds; average pages per issue 72(d), 100(S); single plates used 100,000.
Equipment: EDITORIAL: Front-end hardware — SII/Mac 55; Front-end software — SII/Mac 55; Printers — HP, Ibon; Other equipment — 3-Ap/Mac Quadra 900, 4-Ap/Mac IIfx, 1-Lf/AP Leaf Picture Desk. CLASSIFIED: Front-end hardware — 1-SII/Sys 25; Front-end software — SII/Dakota, SII/Sequoia, SII, SII/Tahoe. DISPLAY: Adv layout systems — 4-HI/2222 (on-line), 6-Ap/Mac; Front-end hardware — Sigma Designs/L-View. PRODUCTION: Pagination software — SII; Typesetters — 2-AU/APS5, 1-Hyphen/RIP, 2-AU/APS 108C, AU/APS 5000; Platemaking systems — 2-KNF/lines; Plate processors — 2-KNF; Scanners — 1-ECR/Autokon; Production cameras — 2-C/Marathon; Automatic film processors — 1-LE/LD24A, 1-LE/LD 2600; Film transporters — 2-C; Digital color separation equipment — 1-Diadem/230S.
PRESSROOM: Line 1 — 24-G/Headliner (12 half decks); Folders — 2-G/160-page double delivery; Pasters — Automatic Pasters; Press control system — CH. MAILROOM: Counter stackers — 5-HL/Monitor; Inserters and stuffers — 2-AmGraphics, HI/NP 630; Bundle tyer — 1-MLN, 5-Power Strap/Model 5; Mailroom control system — Id. LIBRARY: Electronic — SII/Lasr. WIRE SERVICES: News — AP, GNS, Bloomberg; Photos — AP, GNS; Stock tables — AP; Syndicates — INA, Universal Press; Receiving dishes — size-12ft, AP. BUSINESS COMPUTERS: 1-IBM/AS-400; Applications: Lotus: Circ, Adv billing, Accts receivable, Gen ledger, Payroll, Accts payable; WordPerfect, Harvard Graphics; PCs & micros networked; PCs & main system networked.

CLIFTON
See PASSAIC

EAST BRUNSWICK
See MIDDLESEX COUNTY

HACKENSACK
See BERGEN COUNTY

JERSEY CITY

Hudson County

'90 U.S. Census- 228,537; E&P '96 Est. 236,281
ABC-CZ (90): 595,299 (HH 231,006)

The Jersey Journal

(m-mon to sat)

The Jersey Journal, 30 Journal Sq., Jersey City, NJ 07306; tel (201) 653-1000; fax (201) 217-2455. Advance Publications group.
Circulation: 53,693(m); 53,693(m-sat); ABC Sept. 30, 1995.
Price: 50¢(d); 50¢(sat); $1.85/wk; $9.40/mo; $70.00/yr.
Advertising: Open inch rate $39.70(m); $39.70(m-sat). **Representative:** Newhouse Newspapers/Metro Suburbia.
News Services: AP, KRT, NNS. **Politics:** Independent. **Established:** 1867.
Not Published: New Year; Memorial Day; Independence Day; Labor Day; Thanksgiving; Christmas.
Special Editions: School Guide Pages (3x), Winter Bridal Tab, Health Fitness Tab, Discount Tab, JOBS-JOBS-JOBS (Jan); Valentine's Day Dine Out (2x), President's Pages I & II, Spotlight I & II (Feb); Discount Tab, Women in Business, Doctor's Day Pages, Spring Fashion I (Mar); Home Sweet Homes Tab, Easter Dine Out I & II, Spring Fashion II, NY Auto Show Section, Home Improvement, Home Furnishings (Apr); Mother's Day Tab, Mother's Day Dine-Out I & II, Bayonne Home Town Fair Tab I & II, Health Tab, JOBS-JOBS-JOBS, Seniors Tab (May); Kids Tab, Father's Day Tab, Discount Tab, Valedictorian Tab (June); Clearance Tab, School Guide (3x), Women In Business, Retail Back-to-School (Aug); Newcomer's Guide, Local High School & College Football Tab, Fall Fashion Section, Fall Bridal Tab I, Home Furnishings Section, Jersey City Artist's Tour Tab, Women In Medicine Pages (Sept); Home Improvement Section, Hoboken Artist's Tour, Home Sweet Homes Tab, New Car Guide, Fall Bridal Tab II (Oct); Discount Tab, Thanksgiving Day Dine-Out I & II, Holiday Memories Tab (Nov); Holiday Gift Guide Tab (2x), Letters to Santa, Last Minute Gift Guide Tab (Dec).
Special Weekly Sections: Food, Health (wed); Senior (thur); Real Estate, Tempo Entertainment Guide, Travel, TV (fri).

CORPORATE OFFICER
President .... S I Newhouse III
GENERAL MANAGEMENT
Publisher .... Scott Ring
General Manager .... S I Newhouse III
Controller .... Ronald Organek
Manager-Credit .... James Trotta
ADVERTISING
Manager-Retail .... Ed Burns
MARKETING AND PROMOTION
Director-Marketing .... Elicia Greenberg
TELECOMMUNICATIONS
Audiotex Manager .... Paul Lanaris
CIRCULATION
Director .... Chris Chesar
NEWS EXECUTIVES
Editor in Chief .... Steven Newhouse
Editor .... Judith Locorriere
Managing Editor .... George Latanzio
EDITORS AND MANAGERS
City Editor .... John Oswald
Lifestyle Editor .... Margaret Schmidt
News Editor .... John Watson
Sports Editor .... Harvey Zucker
MANAGEMENT INFORMATION SERVICES
Data Processing Manager .... Denise Copeland

Market Information: Zoned editions; Split Run; TMC.
Mechanical available: Letterpress (direct); Black and 3 ROP colors; insert accepted — preprinted; page cut-offs — 23½".
Mechanical specifications: Type page 13¼" x 22½"; E - 6 cols, 2 1/16", 1/8" between; A - 6 cols, 2 1/16", 1/8" between; C - 10 cols, 1¼", ½" between.
Commodity consumption: width 27½"; black ink 14,000 pounds; color ink 200 pounds; single pages printed 74,000; average pages per issue 42(d).
Equipment: EDITORIAL: Front-end hardware — AT; Other equipment — 30-AT, 2-HI/8300, 9-HI/8900, 1-HI/2100. CLASSIFIED: Front-end hardware — 2-AT; Printers — 1-Ap/Mac Laser-Printer NTX; Other equipment — 18-AT/ADT, AX, Sharp, 2-Ap/Mac SE, 1-Ap/Mac IIx, 2-Wyse/2. DISPLAY: Adv layout systems — 3-HI/2100, 4-Ap/Mac. PRODUCTION: Typesetters — 1-AX/Ultra Count, 4-AX/PC-100, 4-AX/Pro Count, 2-AU/800; Platemaking systems — 1-Na; Plate exposures — Na; Plate processors — 2-Na; Direct-to-plate imaging — 1-Lf/AP Leaf Picture Desk; Scanners — 2-X/BxW-11x17, 2-Nikon/3510 color; Production cameras — 1-C/Marathon, 1-R/500; Automatic film processors — 1-LE/LB24Q, 1-LE/LB24; Film transporters — 2-LE; Shrink lenses — Alan; Digital color separation equipment — 4-HI/Images.
PRESSROOM: Line 1 — 2-H; Folders — H/2:1.
MAILROOM: Counter stackers — 1-St; Bundle tyer — 1-MLN. LIBRARY: Electronic — SMS. WIRE SERVICES: News — AP, KRT, NNS; Photos — AP, KRT, NNS; Syndicates — NNS. BUSINESS COMPUTERS: DEC/1173; Applications: Accts receivable; PCs & micros networked; PCs & main system networked.

MIDDLESEX COUNTY- EAST BRUNSWICK
Middlesex County
'90 U.S. Census- 43,548; E&P '96 Est. 44,569
ABC-NDM (90): 811,077 (HH 289,182)

The Home News & Tribune
(m-mon to sat; S)

The Home News & Tribune, 35 Kennedy Blvd., East Brunswick, NJ 08816; tel (908) 246-5500; fax (908) 246-3167; web site http://www.injersey.com. Asbury Park Press Inc. group.
Circulation: 41,881(m); 41,881(m-sat); 51,122(S); ABC Sept. 30, 1995.
Price: 35¢(d); 35¢(sat); 75¢(S); $2.85/wk.
Advertising: Open inch rate $31.47(m); $31.47(m-sat); $35.96(S).
News Services: AP, AP Telephotos. **Established:** 1786 (Sunday), 1879 (Daily).
Note: Effective Oct. 9, 1995 the Woodbridge (NJ) News Tribune (m-mon to fri; m-sat; S) merged with the Home News (m-mon to sat; S) to form the Home News & Tribune (m-mon to sat; S).
Not Published: New Year; Memorial, Independence Day; Labor Day; Christmas.
Special Editions: Martin Luther King, Health & Fitness, Super Bowl, Forecast (Jan); Camps, Classes & More, Bridal, NJ Flower & Garden Show, This New House (Feb); Auto Show, Salute to Family Business, Brunswick Square Mall (Mar); Dining Guide Day Tripper, Spring Home & Garden, NIE Create-An-Ad, Spring Home, Real Estate Showcase (Apr); Mother's Day, Golfing, Daisy Fair (May); The Guide to Central NJ, Dads and Grads (June); Baby Face, Pet Pics, Parenting, Middlesex Chamber (July); Middlesex County Fair, Back-to-School, Somerset 4-H Fair, College Football, Bridal (Aug); Literacy, High School Football, Home Energy, Out & About, Seniors, Just Kids, Home & Garden (Sept); Fall Real Estate, Halloween Coloring Contest, Holiday Entertainment (Oct); New Brunswick City Market (Nov); Comic Book, Gift Guide (Dec).
Magazines: USA Weekend, The Home News & Tribune TV Magazine, Sunday Comics (S).

CORPORATE OFFICERS
Board Chairman .... Jules L Plangere Jr
President .... E Donald Lass
Exec Vice Pres .... Jules L Plangere III
Vice Pres-Marketing/Sales .... Charles W Ritscher
GENERAL MANAGEMENT
Publisher .... E Donald Lass
General Manager .... David Thaler
Vice Pres-Corporate Service/Chief Financial
Officer .... Alfred D Colantoni
ADVERTISING
Manager-Display .... Bonnie Verriest
Manager-Major Accounts/Preprint ... Dan Curtis
MARKETING AND PROMOTION
Director-Marketing/Promotion
.... Ellen Mullins Bollinger
TELECOMMUNICATIONS
Audiotex Manager .... Richard Onloff
CIRCULATION
Director .... Michael Murray
Manager-Home Delivery .... Michael Murray
NEWS EXECUTIVES
Editor .... Richard A Hughes
Managing Editor .... Teresa Klink
Editor-Sunday .... Phil Hartman
EDITORS AND MANAGERS
Art Director .... Tom Kerr
Asst Business Editor .... Allison Salerno
Copy Desk Chief .... Charles H Johnson Jr
Database Manager for Newsroom
.... Paul D'Ambrosio
Director-Editorial Pages .... Barbara Frankel
Features Editor .... Theresa Klink
Metro Editor .... Suzanne J Pavkovic
Metro Editor .... Charles Paolino
Sports Editor .... Jack Genung
MANAGEMENT INFORMATION SERVICES
Director-Info Service .... Russ Nicolosi
PRODUCTION
Vice Pres-Operations .... Anthony J Ordino
Manager-Pressroom .... William Salemme

Market Information: Zoned editions; Split Run; TMC; Operate audiotex; Electronic edition.
Mechanical available: Offset; Black and 3 ROP colors; insert accepted — preprinted; page cut-offs — 22".
Mechanical specifications: Type page 13" x 21"; E - 6 cols, 2 1/16", 1/8" between; A - 6 cols, 2 1/16", 1/8" between; C - 9 cols, 1 3/8", 1/16" between.
Commodity consumption: Newsprint 5,000 short tons; width 54 7/8"; black ink 200,000 pounds; color ink 30,000 pounds; single pages printed 17,000; average pages per issue 44(d), 90(S); single plates used 25,000.
Equipment: EDITORIAL: Front-end hardware — SII; Front-end software — SII; Printers — QMS. CLASSIFIED: Front-end hardware — SII; Front-end software — SII. DISPLAY: Adv layout systems — SCS/Layout 8000; Front-end hardware — 1-PC/286, 1-PC; Front-end software — SCS; Printers — 1-C.Itoh/300. PRODUCTION: Pagination software — HI, Typesetters — 2-AU/APS6; Plate exposures — 1-Nu; Plate processors — 1-WL.
PRESSROOM: Line 1 — 12-G/Urbanite offset; Pasters — Enkel; Press control system — AB. MAILROOM: Counter stackers — 1-QWI/300, 2-QWI/S2100, 1-Id/NS550; Inserters and stuffers — 1-HI/1372; Bundle tyer — 3-MLN/MLN-2A. LIBRARY: Electronic — SMS/Stauffer(networked); Combination — Lektriever. COMMUNICATIONS: Facsimile — Scitex/Eskofot. WIRE SERVICES: News — AP, AP Datastream, AP Datafeatures; Syndicates — AP. BUSINESS COMPUTERS: PCs & micros networked; PCs & main system networked.

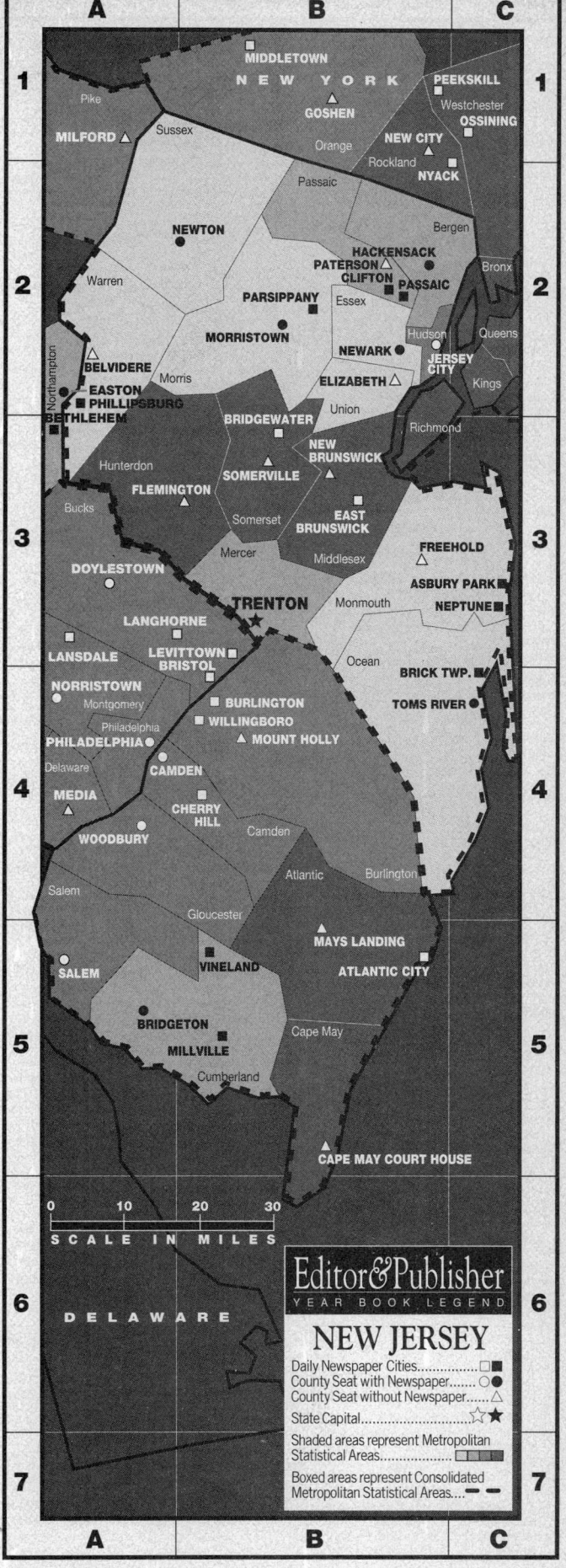

Copyright ©1996 by the Editor & Publisher Co.

MILLVILLE
Cumberland County

'90 U.S. Census- 25,992; E&P '96 Est. 27,353

Millville News (e-mon to sat)

Millville News, 100 E. Commerce St., Bridgeton, NJ 08302; tel (609) 451-1000; fax (609) 451-7214. Hollinger International Inc. group.

Circulation: 1,596(e); 1,596(e-sat); Sworn Sept. 30, 1994.

Price: 30¢(d); 30¢(sat); $1.40/wk.

Advertising: Open inch rate $4.65(e); $4.65(e-sat).

News Service: AP. **Politics:** Independent. **Established:** 1990.

Note: For detailed printing and production information, see Bridgeton Evening News listing.

Not Published: New Year; Memorial Day; Independence Day; Labor Day; Thanksgiving Day; Christmas.

Special Editions: Business Review (Jan); Bridal; Great Outdoors; Farm & Garden; Home Improvement; Agriculture; Christmas Gifts (2x).

Magazines: Food (wed); Business (thur); Farm & Garden (fri).

GENERAL MANAGEMENT

Publisher John M Ewing

ADVERTISING

Director Bernie Heller

CIRCULATION

Director Brenda Morriseau

NEWS EXECUTIVE

Editor Jack Hummel

EDITORS AND MANAGERS

Features Editor Sheryl Chlele
Sports Editor Eric Chlele

Market Information: TMC.

Mechanical available: Offset; Black and 3 ROP colors; insert accepted — preprinted; page cut-offs — 22¾".

Mechanical specifications: Type page 13" x 21½"; E - 6 cols, 2¹⁄₁₆", ⅛" between; A - 6 cols, 2¹⁄₁₆", ⅛" between; C - 9 cols, 1⅜", ⅛" between.

Commodity consumption: Newsprint 110 metric tons; widths 27¼", 13⅝"; black ink 4,000 pounds; single pages printed 6,120; average pages per issue 20(d); single plates used 3,800.

MORRISTOWN-PARSIPPANY
Morris County

'90 U.S. Census- 64,667 (Morristown 16,189; Parsippany 48,478); E&P '96 Est. 63,790 (Morristown 16,160; Parsippany 47,630)

ABC-NDM (90): 371,473 (HH 131,563)

Daily Record (m-mon to fri; m-sat; S)

Daily Record, 629 Parsippany Rd.; PO Box 217, Parsippany, NJ 07054-0217; tel (201) 428-6200; fax (201) 428-6666. Goodson Newspaper group.

Circulation: 54,840(m); 51,174(m-sat); 60,833(S); ABC Sept. 30, 1995.

Price: 25¢(d); 25¢(sat); $1.00(S); $2.25/wk; $9.00/mo; $117.00/yr.

Advertising: Open inch rate $50.45(m); $50.45(m-sat); $54.85(S). **Representative:** Landon Associates Inc.

News Services: AP, KRT. **Politics:** Independent. **Established:** 1900.

Special Editions: Winter, Coupon Clippers, Super Bowl, Forecast (Jan); Bridal, Personal Finance, Coupon Clippers (Feb); Fashion, Dining Guide, Homes, Gardens, Pools (Mar); Coupon Clippers, Creative Home, Tennis Classic, Health & Leisure (Apr); Home Improvement, Coupon Clippers, Summer Fun (May); Seniors, NJ Cardinals, Living, Coupon Clippers (June); Back-to-School, Bridal, Family, Coupon Clippers (Aug); Fall Fashion, High School Football, Home Improvement, Celebrate the Arts (Sept); Coupon Clippers, Morris City's Best, Creative Home, Health & Leisure, Dining Guide (Oct); Morris City's Best, Going Shopping, Holiday Gift Guide 1 (Nov); Holiday Gift Guide 2 & 3, Last Minute Gift Gifts, First Night (Dec).

Special Weekly Sections: Business (tues); Food (wed); Home (thur); Automotive, Real Estate, TGIF (fri); Automotive, Real Estate, Careers, TV (Prime Time), Arts Etc, Opinion, Your Money, Women, Log On, USExpress (mailed TMC) (S).

Magazines: Prime Time (S); Comics; USA Weekend.

GENERAL MANAGEMENT

Publisher Thomas P Geyer
General Manager Walt T Lafferty

ADVERTISING

Director Heidi Chiles-Wheeler
Manager-Classified Lois McEntee
Manager-Retail Bill Selwood

CIRCULATION

Director Ramona Rowe

NEWS EXECUTIVES

Editor William Donnellon
Managing Editor Jack Bowie

EDITORS AND MANAGERS

Business Editor Ron Stepenski
Graphics Editor Lesley Crozier
Metro Editor Jim McGarvey
News Editor Kathryn Adams
Chief Photographer Karen Fucito
Sports Editor Robert Decker

MANAGEMENT INFORMATION SERVICES

Data Processing Manager Jack Francis

PRODUCTION

Director Al Leu
Foreman-Pre Press Dawn Larson
Foreman-Press Loren Ortman

Market Information: Zoned editions; TMC; ADS.

Mechanical available: Offset; Black and 3 ROP colors; insert accepted — preprinted; page cut-offs — 22".

Mechanical specifications: Type page 13" x 21"; E - 6 cols, 2.07", ⅛" between; A - 6 cols, 2.07", ⅛" between; C - 9 cols, 1.38", .08" between.

Commodity consumption: Newsprint 6,353 short tons; widths 55", 41⅛", 27½"; black ink 108,832 pounds; color ink 39,148 pounds; single pages printed 18,130; average pages per issue 40(d), 28(sat), 104(S); single plates used 51,173.

Equipment: EDITORIAL: Front-end hardware — DEC/PDP 11-84; Front-end software — IAS/TMS; Printers — DEC/LA 120; Other equipment — Ap/Mac Workstation. CLASSIFIED: Front-end hardware — PC Network; Front-end software — Internet/Classified Rev II; Printers — Okidata/3410; Other equipment — Ap/Mac Workstation. DISPLAY: Adv layout systems — SCS/Layout 8000; Front-end hardware — PC; Front-end software — SCS; Printers — Printronix. PRODUCTION: Pagination software — QuarkXPress 3.3; Typesetters — ECR/1245 CS(Scripsetter 4); Plate exposures — Nu, Burgess, Nu/FT 40UPNS; Plate processors — WL/MAS; Electronic picture desk — Lf/AP Leaf Picture Desk; Scanners — Howtek/Flat Bed, Kk/RFS-2035, HP/3C; Production cameras — C/Marathon, C/Spartan III; Automatic film processors — 2-Glunz Jensen APS6-108, 2-LE/24D.
PRESSROOM: Line 1 — 9-MAN; Press drives — GE; Folders — 1-MAN; Pasters — MEG; Reels and stands — MEG; Press control system — GE; Press registration system — NuGraphics. MAILROOM: Counter stackers — HL/Monitors, 2-HL/ Dual Carrier; Inserters and stuffers — HI/1472; Bundle tyer — 2-EAM/Mosca; Addressing machine — Domino/Ink Jet Labeller. WIRE SERVICES: News — AP; Photos — AP; Stock tables — NYSE, AMEX, NASDAQ, Mutual Funds; Syndicates — KRT; Receiving dishes — size-10ft, AP. BUSINESS COMPUTERS: HP/3000; Applications: CJ; PCs & micros networked; PCs & main system networked.

NEPTUNE-ASBURY PARK
Monmouth County

'90 U.S. Census- 21,796 (Asbury Park 16,799; Neptune 4,997); E&P '96 Est. 21,731 (Asbury Park 16,491; Neptune 5,240)

ABC-NDM (90): 986,327 (HH 365,717)

Asbury Park Press (e-mon to sat; S)

Asbury Park Press, 3601 Hwy. 66; PO Box 1550, Neptune, NJ 07754-1550; tel (908) 922-6000; web site http://www.injersey.com/doc/pn/pnhome.html.

Circulation: 161,052(e); 161,052(e-sat); 232,275(S); ABC Sept. 30, 1995.

Price: 40¢(d); 40¢(sat); $1.25(S).

Advertising: Open inch rate $71.19(e); $71.19(e-sat); $103.29(S). **Representative:** Sawyer-Ferguson-Walker Co.

News Services: AP, LAT-WP, KRT, CSM. **Established:** 1879.

Not Published: New Year; Memorial Day; Independence Day; Labor Day; Christmas.

Special Editions: Forecast '96, Winter Day & Winter Nights (Jan); Weddings '96, This New House (Feb); American Cancer Society, Spring Fashion (Mar); Spring Garden, Spring Home, Real Estate Showcase, NIE Create-An-Ad (Apr); Summer Days I & Summer Nights I (May); Summer Days II & Summer Nights II (June); Summer Days III & Summer Nights III (July); College Football, Fall Fashion, Bridal '96 (Aug); Literacy, This New House, American Heart Association, High School Football, Fall Home & Garden (Sept); Real Estate Showcase, Personal Finance, Women Today (Oct).

Special Weekly Sections: Business Monday, Sports Weekend Wrap-up (mon); Health (tues); Food, Community, Family Matters (wed); Home (thur); Jersey Alive!, Wheels, Real Estate (fri); Sports Weekend (sat); Arts & Entertainment, Travel, Business, Food, Books, Real Estate & Home, Section X, Seniority, Sports Weekend, Essentials (S); Stock Listing (daily except mon).

Magazines: USA Weekend, TV Week, Color Comics (S).

Broadcast Affiliates: Radio WBUD-AM; WTKS-FM Orlando, FL; WKCF-TV Melbourne, Orlando, Daytona Beach, FL; WBSS-FM Pleasantville, NJ; WBSS-FM, Pleasantville; WKXW-FM Trenton, NJ.

CORPORATE OFFICERS

Board Chairman Jules L Plangere Jr
President E Donald Lass
Exec Vice Pres Jules L Plangere III
Vice Pres-Sales/Marketing Charles W Ritscher

GENERAL MANAGEMENT

Publisher E Donald Lass
Controller John DiMaiolo
Vice Pres-Human Resources Stephen D Rice
Vice Pres-Finance Richard T Morena
Vice Pres-Corporate Service/Chief Financial Officer Alfred D Colantoni
Manager-Accounting David Salmon
Manager-Credit Peter Rutledge
Manager-Facilities Thomas F Petersen

ADVERTISING

Manager-Regional Dan Curtis
Manager-Local Sam Siciliano
Manager-Direct Marketing Thomas Sferlazzo
Manager-Classified James Easley
Manager-TeleSales Lauren Calvosa
Manager-Classified Telephone Christine Burrough
Manager-Co-op Marie Tuohy
Manager-Preprint Gail Rible
Manager-National Diane Rogala
Manager-Presentation Donald Phillips

MARKETING AND PROMOTION

Director-Marketing Ellen Mullins Bollinger
Manager-Research Cheryl Christiansen
Manager-Public Relations Timothy P Zeiss
Manager-Education Service Gail Berger
Manager-Info Stategies Richard Orloff

TELECOMMUNICATIONS

Director-Info Service Charles D'Onofrio
Manager-Computer Service Murray Shannon
Manager-Network/Engineering Ted Hall
Manager-Systems Development Frank Lewis
Audiotex Manager Richard Orloff

CIRCULATION

Vice Pres Terry Whitney
Manager-Home Delivery Steve Todd
Manager-Marketing Melinda Heller
Manager-Operations Nancy Carter
Manager-Sales Agatha Pardo
Manager-Single Copy Sales Warren Fenimore
Manager-Transportation Ronald West

NEWS EXECUTIVES

Vice Pres-News W Raymond Ollwerther
Editor E Donald Lass
Assoc Editor-Administration Andrew Sharp
Senior Managing Editor Raymond J Tuers
Managing Editor-News Frederick J Kerr Jr
Asst Managing Editor-Metro Lawrence Benjamin
Asst Managing Editor-Legal Affairs Gary Deckelnick
Deputy Managing Editor Jody Calendar
Deputy Managing Editor Peter Donoghue
Asst Managing Editor-Design Harris Siegel

EDITORS AND MANAGERS

Art Director Andrew Robert Prendimano
Business Editor Robert Hordt
Community Editor Edward Marino
Entertainment Editor Jill Williams
Editorial Page Editor Richard Pretorius
Features Editor Harry Ziegler
Food Editor Andrea Clurfeld
Librarian Molly Graham
Monmouth County Editor John Hudzinski
Night Editor Robert Ware
Ocean County Editor Fred Simmonds
Photo Editor Dave May
Sunday Editor Gary Schoening
Asst Sunday Editor Arlene Schneider
Sports Editor John Quinn
Exec Sports Editor Joseph Adelizzi
Troubleshooter Editor George Brown
Systems Editor Robert Foxworth

PRODUCTION

Vice Pres-Operations Anthony J Ordino
Manager-Pressroom William Salemme
Manager-Pre Press Operations Robert J Schaad
Manager-Color Lab Bill Harned
Manager-Distribution Henry Kachelriess

Market Information: Zoned editions; Split Run; TMC; ADS; Operate audiotex.

Mechanical available: Offset; Black and 3 ROP colors; insert accepted — preprinted; page cut-offs — 22¾".

Mechanical specifications: Type page 13" x 21½"; E - 6 cols, 2¹⁄₁₆", ⅛" between; A - 6 cols, 2¹⁄₁₆", ⅛" between; C - 9 cols, 1⅜", ¹⁄₁₆" between.

Commodity consumption: Newsprint 45,000 short tons; widths 55", 41⅛"; black ink 630,000 pounds; color ink 160,000 pounds; single pages printed 33,000; average pages per issue 80(d), 172(S); single plates used 200,000.

Equipment: EDITORIAL: Front-end hardware — SII/55, 30-IBM, Ap/Mac; Other equipment — RSK/TRS-80, 7-RSK/TRS-200, 10-HI/8900, 2-HI/8300, 170-SII/Coyote. CLASSIFIED: Front-end hardware — SII/55; Other equipment — 54-SII/Coyote. DISPLAY: Adv layout systems — 10-DTI, Sun/Database; Front-end hardware — Ap/Mac; Other equipment — 5-EDT/III. PRODUCTION: Typesetters — 2-AU/800 SX PIPS, 2-AU/APS PIP IIs, 2-AU/AGI; Plate exposures — 1-BKY/1801, 1-Nu, 2-Nu/Flip Top, 2-WL/Lith-X-Pozer III; Plate processors — 1-WL/30D, 2-WL/38D, 2-Nugraphics/Plate Bender-02200; Scanners — CD/Scantext; Production cameras — 1-C/Newspager I, 1-C/Spartan III; Automatic film processors — 1-P/Pakoquick, 1-LE/2600; Reproportion units — 1-CK Optical; Film transporters — 1-C/Spartan III, 1-C/Newspager; Shrink lenses — ECR/Autokon 1000, C/Spartan, C/Pager; Digital color separation equipment — 1-CD/635, Scitex/Response Ceps, 2-Pixet, 1-ELP, 1-Raystar.
PRESSROOM: Line 1 — 9-G/Metro Offset; Line 2 — 9-G/Metro Offset; Folders — 4-G/3:2; Pasters — 18-G; Press control system — Fin/System, GE/motors. MAILROOM: Counter stackers — 6-St/257S, 3-QWI/SJ100, 2-MM/CN70, 2-QWI/SJ200A, 1-Boss Stacker; Inserters and stuffers — 2-S/NP-1472; Bundle tyer — 6-MLN/MLN-2, 1-Dynaric/NP-1, 4-Power Strap/PSN-5, 1-Power Strap/PSN-250; Wrapping singles — 2-MLN; Addressing machine — 1-MM/335 TV Saddle Stitcher, 4-Ch/539. LIBRARY: Electronic — SII. WIRE SERVICES: News — AP, LAT-WP, KRT, CSM, PR Newswire, Sports Agate; Stock tables — AP; Syndicates — AP; Receiving dishes — size-3m, AP, Perception Tech. BUSINESS COMPUTERS: 2-IBM/AS-400; Applications: IBM/AS-400: Adv billing, Accts receivable, Gen ledger, Payroll, Sales, Mktg, Accts payable, Broadcast; DISCUS: Circ; PCs & micros networked; PCs & main system networked.

NEWARK
Essex County

'90 U.S. Census- 275,221; E&P '96 Est. 251,994

ABC-NDM (90): 3,552,803 (HH 1,272,388)

The Star-Ledger (m-mon to fri; m-sat; S)

The Star-Ledger, One Star Ledger Plz., Newark, NJ 07102-1200; tel (201) 877-4141; fax (201) 565-0422; web site http://www.nj.com/weather/. Advance Publications group.

Circulation: 436,634(m); 403,441(m-sat); 645,767(S); ABC Sept. 30, 1995.

Price: 25¢(d); 25¢(sat); 75¢(S).

Advertising: Open inch rate $246.84(m); $246.84(m-sat); $307.30(S). **Representative:** Newhouse Newspapers/Metro Suburbia.

News Services: AP, NNS, LAT-WP, DJ, RN, PR Newswire. **Politics:** Independent. **Established:** 1832.
Note: Advertising for the Star-Ledger automatically includes advertising in the Trenton Times (mS).
Special Editions: Auto Expo, Executive Outlook, Corporate Outlook (Jan); The Money Book, Consumer Outlook, NJ Bride & Groom, Safety & Security (Feb); Ringling Bros. Circus, The Money Book, NJ Auto Show, Spring Fashion, Money Manager, Home & Garden (Mar).
Special Weekly Sections: Best Food Days (wed); Real Estate Marketplace, Weekend (fri); Best Food Days, Real Estate Marketplace, Accent, Leisure, Opinion/Business, TV Time of the Week, Employment, Travel (S).
Magazine: Parade (S).

CORPORATE OFFICER

President Donald E Newhouse

GENERAL MANAGEMENT

Publisher Martin Bartner
General Manager Mark Newhouse
Manager-Credit Jim Benedict
Controller Alex Miller
Director-Human Resources Cherran Evans

ADVERTISING

Director Mark Herrick
Manager-Retail James Hagaman
Manager-General Fred Marks
Manager-Classified Bud Haynes
Manager-Marketing Raymond Simon
Manager-Sales Development Jay Petrie

CIRCULATION

Director Al Gittrich

NEWS EXECUTIVES

Editor James Willse
Managing Editor Charles Harrison
Asst Managing Editor Leonard Fisher
Asst Managing Editor Rick Everett
Asst Managing Editor Art Lenehan
Asst Managing Editor Lilah Lahr
Asst Managing Editor Susan Olds

EDITORS AND MANAGERS

Art Critic Eileen Watkins
Art/Graphic Director George Frederick
Book Critic Roger Harris
Business Editor David Allen
City Editor Glenn Proctor
Columnist Robert Braun
Columnist Lawrence Hall
Columnist John Farmer
Columnist John McLaughlin
Columnist Matt Zoller Seitz
Dance Critic Valerie Sudol
Drama Critic (New Jersey) Peter Filichia
Drama Critic (New York) Michael Sommers
Editorial Page Editor Richard Aregood
Education Editor Nick Chiles
Entertainment Editor Linda Fowler
Entertainment Editor Emily Hathaway
Environment Editor Gordon Bishop
Fashion/Women's Editor Tere Greendorfer
Features/Entertainment Editor Art Martinez
Film Critic Allan Barra
Films Critic Robert Campbell
Food Critic Karla Cook
Garden Editor John VandeWater
Home Furnishings Editor Shirley Friedman
Labor Editor Donald Warshaw
Medical Editor Gail Scott
Metro Editor-Day Dee Murphy
Metro Editor-Night Scott Ladd
Asst Metro Editor Josh McMahon
Asst Metro Editor Jason Jett
Asst Metro Editor Anne Marie Cattone
Music Critic-Classical Michael Redmond
Music Critic-Pop/Rock Jay Lustig
Music Critic-Jazz George Kanzler
Picture Editor Sharon Russel
Political Editor David Wald
Religion Editor Monica Maske
Science Editor Kitta MacPherson
Special Sections Editor Dean Rowland
Sports Editor Pete Wevuski
Sunday Editor Tony Verga
Telegraph Editor Arnold Braeske
Television Critic Jerry Krupnick
Television Book (Scanner) Editor Steve Hedgpeth
Travel Editor Joel Sleed
Washington Bureau Robert Cohen
Washington Bureau J Scott Orr

MANAGEMENT INFORMATION SERVICES

Manager Norm Darvie

PRODUCTION

Director-Pre Press Thomas Cusack

Market Information: Zoned editions; Split Run.
Mechanical available: Offset; Black and 3 ROP colors; insert accepted — preprinted; page cutoffs — 22".
Mechanical specifications: Type page 13" x $21\frac{1}{4}$"; E - 6 cols, $2\frac{1}{16}$", $\frac{1}{8}$" between; A - 6 cols, $2\frac{1}{16}$", $\frac{1}{8}$" between; C - 10 cols, $1\frac{1}{4}$", $\frac{1}{8}$" between.
Commodity consumption: Newsprint 146,000 short tons; width $54\frac{3}{4}$"; black ink 3,635,000 pounds; color ink 255,000 pounds; single pages printed 41,676; average pages per issue 82(d), 274(S); single plates used 299,000.
Equipment: EDITORIAL: Front-end hardware — CSI; Front-end software — CSI; Printers — 2-Graphic Enterprises/Full Page; Other equipment — 10-HI/8900, 15-Ap/Mac. CLASSIFIED: Front-end hardware — CSI; Front-end software — CSI; Other equipment — 2-HI/8900. AUDIOTEX: Hardware — DTK/486-66; Software — Speech Soft. DISPLAY: Adv layout systems — SCS; Front-end hardware — 4-HI/8300, 18-HI/8900, 3-HI/2100; Front-end software — HI 8.0; Other equipment — Lf/Leaf Interface. PRODUCTION: Typesetters — 2-AU/APS-5, 2-AU/APS-6, 3-AU/APS-108; Plate exposures — 3-WL/Lith-X-Pozer 10, 1-WL/Lith-X-Pozer 3; Plate processors — 4-WL, 2-WL; Electronic picture desk — Lf/AP Leaf Picture Desk; Scanners — 1-ECR/Autokon, Esroscan; Automatic film processors — 2-C; Reproportion units — Scitex; Film transporters — 2-C; Shrink lenses — 2-Alan/Anamorphic; Color separation equipment (conventional) — Scitex; Digital color separation equipment — Scitex.
PRESSROOM: Line 1 — 9-TKS; Line 2 — 9-TKS; Line 3 — 10-TKS; Line 4 — 10-TKS; Line 5 — 10-TKS; Line 6 — 10-TKS; Press drives — 69-Toyo Dinki; Folders — 11-TKS; Pasters — TKS/Automatic; Reels and stands — TKS; Press control system — TKS. MAILROOM: Counter stackers — 28-HL, 14-HL; Inserters and stuffers — 1-S, 2-S; Bundle tyer — 22-Dynaric, 6-MLN. LIBRARY: Electronic — Vu/Text, Data Times. COMMUNICATIONS: Remote imagesetting — Scitex/Bit stars; Systems used — microwave. WIRE SERVICES: News — AP, RN, DJ, PR Newswire, NNS, Dorf Features; Stock tables — AP SelectStox II; Receiving dishes — AP. BUSINESS COMPUTERS: HP/Micro XE, HP/927, HP/937, HP/947; Applications: CJ: Circ, Billing, Payroll, Court; PCs & micros networked; PCs & main system networked.

NEWTON

Sussex County

'90 U.S. Census- 7,521; E&P '96 Est. 7,487
ABC-NDM (90): 142,772 (HH 48,694)

New Jersey Herald

(e-mon to fri; S)

New Jersey Herald, 2 Spring St.; PO Box 10, Newton, NJ 07860; tel (201) 383-1500; fax (201) 383-9284. Quincy Newspapers Inc. group.
Circulation: 17,304(e); 24,286(S); ABC Sept. 30, 1995.
Price: 35¢(d); $1.00(S).
Advertising: Open inch rate $23.44(e); $25.48 (S). **Representative:** Landon Associates Inc.
News Service: AP. **Politics:** Independent. **Established:** 1829.
Not Published: New Year; Memorial Day; Independence Day; Labor Day; Christmas.
Special Editions: President's Day, Progress '96, Wedding Guide (Feb); EXPO '96, Spring Auto Care (Apr); Spring Home Improvement, Home and Garden (May); Newton Sidewalk Sale (July); Sussex Co. Farm & Horse Show, Back-to-School (Aug); Fall Home Improvement (Oct); Winter Car Care, Human Resources (Nov); Christmas Gift Guides, Holiday Guide (Dec).
Special Weekly Sections: Business (mon); Best Food Day (wed); Entertainment (fri); Food, Business (S).

CORPORATE OFFICERS

President Thomas A Oakley
Vice Pres James W Collins

GENERAL MANAGEMENT

Publisher Kent Roeder
Chief Financial Officer David Oakley
Manager-Operations David E Green

ADVERTISING

Director Dianne Ryan
Manager Joan Driscoll

CIRCULATION

Manager Terry Sattely

NEWS EXECUTIVES

Editor Kent Roeder
Assoc Editor Kenneth Smith

EDITORS AND MANAGERS

Features Editor Beth Ambrose
Friday/Day Editor Tom Moore
Morning/Special Sections Editor Gail Pendelton
News Editor Joe Moszczynski
Sports Editor Tom Jacobs

MANAGEMENT INFORMATION SERVICES

Data Processing Manager Carol Romme

PRODUCTION

Superintendent Andy Porter
Foreman-Composing John Frey
Foreman-Pressroom Kurt Smith
Foreman-Mailroom Lorraine Freeborn

Market Information: TMC.
Mechanical available: Offset; Black and 3 ROP colors; insert accepted — preprinted; page cutoffs — $22\frac{3}{4}$".
Mechanical specifications: Type page 13" x $21\frac{1}{2}$"; E - 6 cols, $2\frac{1}{16}$", $\frac{1}{8}$" between; A - 6 cols, $2\frac{1}{16}$", $\frac{1}{8}$" between; C - 9 cols, $1\frac{3}{8}$", $\frac{1}{16}$" between.
Commodity consumption: Newsprint 1,200 metric tons; widths $27\frac{1}{2}$", $13\frac{5}{8}$"; black ink 30,000 pounds; color ink 7,000 pounds; single pages printed 9,500; average pages per issue 24(d), 68(S); single plates used 14,000.
Equipment: EDITORIAL: Front-end hardware — SIA/386 fileserver; Front-end software — Dewar/Disc Net; Printers — Okidata/320; Other equipment — 16-AST/286. CLASSIFIED: Front-end hardware — SIA/386 fileserver; Front-end software — Dewar/Disc Net; Printers — Okidata/320; Other equipment — 7-AST/286. AUDIOTEX: Software — SMS/Stauffer Gold; Supplier name — TMS. DISPLAY: Front-end hardware — SIA/386 fileserver; Front-end software — Dewar/Disc Net; Other equipment — 3-SIA/386, Dewar/Discovery, 2-AST/286. PRODUCTION: Typesetters — 2-Tegra/VarityperXP-1000; Plate exposures — 1-Nu; Plate processors — 1-Nat; Production cameras — 1-C/Spartan III; Automatic film processors — 1-LE; Film transporters — 1-C/Transporter; Color separation equipment (conventional) — WDS.
PRESSROOM: Line 1 — 4-G/Urbanite, 4-G/Urbanite; Reels and stands — 2-G/Stands; Press control system — 2-Fin; Press registration system — Duarte. MAILROOM: Counter stackers — 1-BG/Count-O-Veyor, 1-BG/Count-O-Veyor; Inserters and stuffers — 5-KAN/480, KAN/Twin Stacker; Bundle tyer — 1-MLN, 1-MLN/Spirit; Other mailroom equipment — MM/1509 MinuteMan Stitcher-Trimmer. LIBRARY: Electronic — SMS/Stauffer Gold. WIRE SERVICES: News — AP; Photos — AP; Receiving dishes — size-10ft, AP. BUSINESS COMPUTERS: IBM/Sys 36B25; Applications: INSI: Circ, Payroll, Accts payable, Gen ledger; PCs & micros networked.

PARSIPPANY

See MORRISTOWN

PASSAIC-CLIFTON

Passaic County

'90 U.S. Census- 129,783 (Passaic 58,041; Clifton 71,742); E&P '96 Est. 133,988 (Passaic 63,585; Clifton 70,403)
ABC-NDM (90): 1,194,266 (HH 432,409)

North Jersey Herald & News

(m-mon to sat; S)

North Jersey Herald & News, 988 Main Ave.; PO Box 1019, Passaic, NJ 07055; tel (201) 365-3000; fax (201) 365-5887. MediaNews Inc. (Garden State Newspapers) group.
Circulation: 53,757(m); 50,139(m-sat); 44,646(S); ABC Sept. 30, 1995.
Price: 35¢(d); 35¢(sat); 50¢(S); $2.10/wk; $54.60/6mo (carrier); $156.00/yr (mail).
Advertising: Open inch rate $67.04(m); $67.04(m-sat); $67.04(S).
News Services: AP, KRT, SHNS. **Politics:** Independent. **Established:** 1872.
Special Editions: Forecast Edition; Bridal Tab; Spring Fashion & Home Improvement; Back-to-School; Fall Fashion & Home Improvement; Dining Out Guide; Christmas Gift Tab; New Car Auto; President's Auto; Spring Real Estate; Fall Real Estate.
Special Weekly Sections: Food, Entertainment Primetime (wed); Automotive (thur); Entertainment Primetime (fri); Entertainment Primetime, Travel (S).
Magazines: TV Magazine (S); USA Weekend.

CORPORATE OFFICERS

Chairman of the Board Richard B Scudder
President Richard J Vezza
Exec Vice Pres Joseph Gioioso

GENERAL MANAGEMENT

Vice Pres-Finance Peter E Leddy
Publisher Richard J Vezza
Director-Operations Joseph Gioioso

ADVERTISING

Director Anthony Viggiano
Director-National Anthony Viggiano
Manager-Classified Jeannette Dowd

CIRCULATION

Director Tom Heck

NEWS EXECUTIVES

Vice Pres/Editor Ian Shearn
Managing Editor Kenneth Pringle

EDITORS AND MANAGERS

Business Editor Wes Pollard
City Editor Richard Zmijewski
Editorial Page Editor Kenneth G Pringle
Features Editor Michael Starr
News Editor Merry Firschein
Sports Editor Jim Brennan

PRODUCTION

Director John Nulholland

Mechanical available: Offset; Black and 3 ROP colors; insert accepted — preprinted, total and part run inserts; page cut-offs — 22".
Mechanical specifications: Type page 13" x 21"; E - 6 cols, $2\frac{1}{16}$", $\frac{1}{8}$" between; A - 6 cols, $2\frac{1}{16}$", $\frac{1}{8}$" between; C - 9 cols, $1\frac{1}{4}$", $\frac{1}{16}$" between.
Commodity consumption: Newsprint 7,000 short tons; widths 55", $41\frac{7}{8}$", $22\frac{7}{8}$"; black ink 193,000 pounds; color ink 8,200 pounds; single pages printed 15,750; average pages per issue 50(d), 169(S); single plates used 26,000.
Equipment: EDITORIAL: Front-end hardware — 2-DEC/PDP 11-70; Front-end software — Rainbow, DEC/72, DEC/61, AST. CLASSIFIED: Front-end hardware — 1-DEC/PDP 11-70; Front-end software — DEC/61. PRODUCTION: Typesetters — 2-Linotron/202; Plate exposures — Nu/Flip Top FT40UPNS; Plate processors — Nat/A-340; Production cameras — 2-C/Spartan II; Automatic film processors — 1-LE/24A, 1-LE/24BQ, 2-LE/13; Film transporters — 1-C; Shrink lenses — 1-CK Optical/SQU-7, 1-Alan/Anamorphic; Color separation equipment (conventional) — RZ/200S.
PRESSROOM: Line 1 — 6-MAN/4-2; Folders — 1-MAN/2:1 Double; Pasters — Automatic Pasters; Reels and stands — 6-MEG/RTP. MAILROOM: Counter stackers — 3-HL/HT Monitor; Inserters and stuffers — HI/1372 P; Bundle tyer — 2-MLN/2A. LIBRARY: Combination — 1-Lektriever/200. WIRE SERVICES: News — AP, KRT, SHNS; Stock tables — AP; Syndicates — AP Datafeatures; Receiving dishes — AP. BUSINESS COMPUTERS: 1-Unisys/80 Model 8; Applications: Circ, Adv billing, Accts receivable, Gen ledger, Payroll; PCs & micros networked; PCs & main system networked.

PHILLIPSBURG

See EASTON, PA

SALEM

Salem County

'90 U.S. Census- 6,883; E&P '96 Est. 6,946
ABC-NDM (90): 65,294 (HH 23,794)

Today's Sunbeam

(m-mon to fri; S)

Today's Sunbeam, 93 Fifth St., Salem, NJ 08079; tel (609) 935-1500; fax (609) 845-3139. MediaNews Inc. (Garden State Newspapers) group.
Circulation: 10,754(m); 10,680(S); ABC Sept. 30, 1995.
Price: 35¢(d); $1.00(S); $147.00/yr.
Advertising: Open inch rate $17.20(m); $17.20(S); $2.40(m & S). **Representatives:** Landon Associates Inc.; US Suburban Press.
News Service: AP. **Politics:** Independent. **Established:** 1819.
Note: For detailed production information, see the Woodbury Gloucester County Times listing.
Not Published: Christmas (except if it falls on Sunday).

I-256 New Jersey

Special Editions: Progress (Jan); Brides, Income Tax (Feb); Green Thumb, Home Improvement (Apr); Sidewalk Days, Graduation, Summer Recreation (June); Back-to-School, County Fair (Aug); Brides, Green Thumb, Home Improvement, Football (Sept); Christmas Gifts Catalog (Dec).
Special Weekly Section: Real Estate (wed).
Magazines: Parade; TV Times.

CORPORATE OFFICERS

Chairman Richard B Scudder
President William Dean Singleton

GENERAL MANAGEMENT

Publisher Wayne A Studer
Business Manager Frank Gargano

ADVERTISING

Manager Ceil Smith

CIRCULATION

Director Harold A Rittler

NEWS EXECUTIVE

Editor John Barna

EDITORS AND MANAGERS

Business/Finance Editor Karen Levinson
Columnist Ron Lehew
Columnist John Barna
Editorial Page Editor John Barna
Education Editor Reesa Marchetti
Entertainment/Amusements Editor Susan Coulby
Environmental Editor Matt Gray
Fashion/Food Editor Elizabeth Smith
Features Editor Susan Coulby
Health/Medical Editor Joy Davis
National Editor William J Gallo Jr
News Editor William J Gallo Jr
Photo Editor Stephan Harrison
Chief Photographer Stephan Harrison
Political/Government Editor William J Gallo Jr
Religion Editor Elizabeth Smith
Senior Reporter Susan Coulby
Science/Technology Editor Chris Bishop
Society Editor Elizabeth Smith
Sports Editor Erma Oliver
Television/Film Editor Susan Coulby
Theater/Music Editor Susan Coulby
Travel Editor John Barna
Women's Editor Elizabeth Smith

MANAGEMENT INFORMATION SERVICES

Data Processing Manager Edward J Murray

Market Information: TMC.
Mechanical available: Offset; Black and 3 ROP colors; insert accepted — preprinted; page cut-offs — 22 3/4".
Mechanical specifications: Type page 13" x 21 1/2"; E - 6 cols, 2 1/16", 1/8" between; A - 6 cols, 2 1/16", 1/8" between; C - 9 cols, 1 1/3", 1/8" between.
Commodity consumption: widths 13 3/4", 27 1/2"; average pages per issue 24(d), 36(S).
Equipment: EDITORIAL: Front-end hardware — IBM, PC; Front-end software — CText; Printers — Okidata. CLASSIFIED: Front-end hardware — IBM, PC; Front-end software — CText. WIRE SERVICES: News — AP; Photos — AP; Syndicates — AP. BUSINESS COMPUTERS: HP; Applications: CJ; PCs & micros networked; PCs & main system networked.

TOMS RIVER-BRICK TOWNSHIP

Ocean County

'90 U.S. Census- 70,342 (Brick Township 66,473; Toms River 3,869); E&P '96 Est. 83,003 (Brick Township 79,254; Toms River 3,749)
ABC-NDM (90): 375,135 (HH 145,901)

Ocean County Observer

(m-mon to fri; S)

Ocean County Observer, 8 Robbins St., Toms River, NJ 08753; tel (908) 349-3000; fax (908) 240-0545. Goodson Newspaper group.
Circulation: 17,849(m); 16,050(S); ABC Sept. 30, 1995.
Price: 25¢(d); 75¢(S); $2.25/wk; $9.00/mo, $117.00/yr.
Advertising: Open inch rate $20.85(m); $20.85(S). **Representatives:** Landon Associates Inc.; US Suburban Press; Robert Hitchings.
News Service: AP. **Politics:** Independent. **Established:** 1850.
Not Published: New Year; Christmas.
Special Editions: Motor News, Health & Fitness, Trends (monthly); Pride; Bridal; Newcomer's Guide; Home Improvement; Christmas Gift Guide; Football Tab.
Special Weekly Sections: Best Food Day (wed); Real Estate, Religion (fri); PrimeTime-TV (S); Business, Living (daily).
Magazines: TV Primetime; Full Color Comics.

CORPORATE OFFICERS

President David Carr
Treasurer Roy Cockburn

GENERAL MANAGEMENT

Publisher Robert J Juzwiak
Business Manager Michael J Balabon

ADVERTISING

Director Paul Haney

CIRCULATION

Director Scott Moreland

NEWS EXECUTIVE

Editor Chuck Triblehorn

EDITORS AND MANAGERS

Automotive Editor Ed Prince
Business/Finance Editor Ed Prince
City/Metro Editor Mark DiMartini
Editorial Page Editor Helen Fitzsimmons
Entertainment/Amusements Editor Helen Fitzsimmons
Environmental Editor Don Bennett
Fashion/Style Editor Barbara Seidel
Living/Lifestyle Editor Barbara Seidel
News Editor Mark DiMartini
Photo Editor Tom Spader
Religion Editor Barbara Seidel
Sports Editor Mike Lazorchak
Television/Film Editor Helen Fitzsimmons
Theater/Music Editor Helen Fitzsimmons
Women's Editor Barbara Seidel

MANAGEMENT INFORMATION SERVICES

Data Processing Manager Michael J Balabon

PRODUCTION

Director-Composing Jody Boyle
Manager Michelle Boyle

Market Information: Split Run; TMC; ADS.
Mechanical available: Offset; Black and 4 ROP colors; insert accepted — preprinted, any; page cut-offs — 22 3/4".
Mechanical specifications: Type page 12 5/16" x 21 1/2"; E - 6 cols, 2.03", 1/6" between; A - 6 cols, 2.03", 1/6" between; C - 9 cols, 1 1/3", 1/12" between.
Commodity consumption: Newsprint 1,995 short tons; width 13 3/4"; black ink 53,000 pounds; color ink 6,800 pounds; single pages printed 13,626; average pages per issue 32(d), 46(S); single plates used 13,200.
Equipment: EDITORIAL: Front-end hardware — IBM/PC; Front-end software — Cx; Printers — Okidata. CLASSIFIED: Front-end hardware — IBM/PC; Front-end software — Cx; Printers — Okidata. DISPLAY: Front-end hardware — Ap/Mac; Front-end software — QuarkXPress, Multi-Ad/Creator; Printers — Ap/Mac Laser-Writer, NewGen/Turbo Laser. PRODUCTION: Typesetters — Linotype-Hell/Linotronic 202, NewGen/Design Express 12; Plate exposures — Amerigraph, Nu; Plate processors — Graham; Scanners — LE/M-480, AG; Production cameras — C; Automatic film processors — P/RA-700; Film transporters — C; Shrink lenses — Ca; Color separation equipment (conventional) — SCREEN/606 II; Digital color separation equipment — SCREEN/606 II, AG. PRESSROOM: Line 2 — 8-G/Urbanite; Pasters — Manual. MAILROOM: Bundle tyer — MLN; Addressing machine — KR, AMS/211. COMMUNICATIONS: Systems used — satellite. WIRE SERVICES: News — AP; Photos — AP; Receiving dishes — AP. BUSINESS COMPUTERS: IBM/Sys 36; Applications: INSI; PCs & micros networked; PCs & main system networked.

TRENTON

Mercer County

'90 U.S. Census- 88,675; E&P '96 Est. 87,055
ABC-CZ (90): 267,160 (HH 96,583)

The Times (m-mon to sat; S)

The Times, 500 Perry St.; PO Box 847, Trenton, NJ 08605; tel (609) 989-5454; fax (609) 396-3633; e-mail 76666.1313@compuserve.com. Advance Publications group.
Circulation: 84,787(m); 84,787(m-sat); 96,761(S); ABC Sept. 30, 1995.
Price: 25¢(d); 25¢(sat); $1.00(S); $2.10/wk; $8.40/mo; $109.20/yr.
Advertising: Open inch rate $48.82(m); $48.82(m-sat); $61.79(S); $110.61(m & S). **Representative:** Newhouse Newspapers/Metro Suburbia.
News Services: AP, LAT-WP, NYT. **Politics:** Independent. **Established:** 1882.
Special Editions: Philadelphia Auto Show, January Clearance, QB Mall Auto Show, Review & Forecast (Jan); Engineering Week, Spring Wedding (Feb); Mercer Medical, Golf Tab, NJ Auto Show, Prom (Mar); Away for a Day, Parenting, Spring Dining Guide, Spring Auto, Women In Business, Spring Home Improvement, Spring Real Estate (Apr); Source Book, Nursing Week, Hospital Week, Mother's Day Gift Guide, Grads Pages (May); Core States Bike Race, Heritage Days, Father's Day & Grad, Shore/Resort, Class of 1996 (June); July Clearance, Senior Living, Family Business, MC Black Business Assn. (July); Back-to-School, Interior & Exteriors (Aug); Septemberfest, Fall Wedding, Fall Real Estate, Taste of Chambersburg, NJ Top 100, Atlantic City, Fall Home Improvement, Travel Brochures, Fall Automotive (Sept); Focus on Careers, Commercial/Industry, Hispanic Tab, Atlantic City Auto Show, Election Guide (Oct); Islands in the Sun, Holiday Guide I & II (Nov); Holiday Guide III, Last Minute Gift Guide (Dec).
Special Weekly Sections: Food and Home (wed); Entertainment Tab (fri); Style, Business News, Food and Home, Entertainment, Travel (S).
Magazines: Good Times (fri); TV Times, Parade (S).

CORPORATE OFFICERS

President/Publisher Richard Bilotti
Vice Pres/Secretary Michael Newhouse
Vice Pres/Treasurer Martin Stewart
Vice Pres-Production Robert Jarrach

GENERAL MANAGEMENT

General Manager Michael Newhouse
Controller Martin Stewart
Manager-Data Processing James Albanowski

ADVERTISING

Director Sandra Lohr
Manager-General Jonathan Kramer

MARKETING AND PROMOTION

Director-Marketing Service Frank Tyger

CIRCULATION

Director Ed Hippo
Asst Director Jerome Pollock

NEWS EXECUTIVE

Editor Brian S Malone

EDITORS AND MANAGERS

Features Editor Kristin Jesson
Director-Photography Martin Griff
Exec Sports Editor Jim Gauger

PRODUCTION

Director-Operations Robert Jarrach
Asst Manager James Bryant
Manager-Mailroom Charles Bouchelle
Manager-Pre Press Michael Lawson
Manager-Transportation Joseph Kustrup
Manager-Pressroom Bill Heider Jr

Market Information: Zoned editions; Split Run; TMC; ADS.
Mechanical available: Offset; Black and 3 ROP colors; insert accepted — preprinted; page cut-offs — 22 3/4".
Mechanical specifications: Type page 13" x 21 1/4"; E - 6 cols, 2 1/16", 1/8" between; A - 6 cols, 2 1/16", 1/8" between; C - 10 cols, 1 3/8", 1/16" between.
Commodity consumption: Newsprint 15,320 short tons; widths 54", 40 1/2", 27"; black ink 293,630 pounds; color ink 77,001 pounds; single pages printed 25,518; average pages per issue 60(d), 150(S).
Equipment: EDITORIAL: Front-end hardware — AT. CLASSIFIED: Front-end hardware — AT. DISPLAY: Front-end hardware — 1-HI/2200, AT. PRODUCTION: Pagination software — HI/XP-21; Typesetters — 1-AU/APS-5, 2-AU/APS-6; Plate exposures — 1-Nu/Flip Top FT40UPNS, 2-Nu, 1-WL/Lith III; Plate processors — 1-WL/38C, 1-WL/38G; Scanners — 1-ECR/Autokon; Production cameras — 1-C/1211, 1-C/1292, 1-C/Marathon, 1-C/Newspager; Automatic film processors — 1-LE/LD24A, 1-LE/LD24BQ; Film transporters — 1-C; Shrink lenses — 1-CK Optical/SQU-7. PRESSROOM: Line 1 — 10-G/Metro; Folders — 2-G/ 3:2. MAILROOM: Counter stackers — 3-HL/HT, 1-HL/HT II; Inserters and stuffers — 2-S/72P; Bundle tyer — 2-MLN, 3-Dynaric; Addressing machine — 3-Wm. LIBRARY: Electronic — 3-Sperry/Rem Lektriever 200. WIRE SERVICES: News — AP; Stock tables — AP; Syndicates — LAT-WP, UPI, AP. BUSINESS COMPUTERS: 1-TS/SII.

The Trentonian

(m-mon to fri; m-sat; S)

The Trentonian, 600 Perry St., Trenton, NJ 08618-3996; tel (609) 989-7800; fax (609) 394-1358. Journal Register Co. group.
Circulation: 72,460(m); 61,861(m-sat); 57,164(S); ABC Sept. 30, 1995.
Price: 35¢(d); 35¢(sat); 75¢(S); $2.30/wk.
Advertising: Open inch rate $50.39(m); $50.39(m-sat); $50.39(S); $80.61(m & S). **Representatives:** Landon Associates Inc.; Robert Hitchings.
News Services: AP, SNS, KRT. **Politics:** Independent. **Established:** 1946 (m), 1975 (S).
Special Editions: Progress, Super Bowl (Jan); Bridal, Business Profiles, Valentine (Feb); Spring Fashion, Today's Home (Mar); Guide to Greater Trenton/Trenton Thunder (Apr); Summer Dining Guide, Summertime (May); Heritage Days/Bridal, 4th of July (June); Family Living Dog Days of Summer, Down the Shore (July); Back-to-School, Bucks County, Car Care (Aug); Fall Dining, Women in Business, HS Sports Guide (Sept); Bridal, Today's Home (Oct); Election Tab, Holiday Fashion (Nov); Holiday Gift Guides, Winter HS Sports Guide (Dec).
Special Weekly Sections: Best Food Days (wed); Real Estate & Builders Page (fri); Reports, Best Food Days, Travel (S).
Magazines: Real Estate, Entertainment (fri); Auto (sat); Real Estate, Entertainment, Food, TV (S).

CORPORATE OFFICERS

President/CEO Robert M Jelenic
Exec Vice Pres/Chief Financial Officer/Treasurer Jean B Clifton

GENERAL MANAGEMENT

Publisher H L (Sandy) Schwartz III
Controller J Timothy Hogan

ADVERTISING

Director Edward Condra
Manager-Promotion Lori Phoenix
Manager-Art Department Lisa Penas
Manager-Retail Robert Geiger
Manager-Classified Chad Beatty

CIRCULATION

Director Michael Ihnatenko
Asst Director Michael G Rafter

NEWS EXECUTIVES

Editor Gale Baldwin
Managing Editor Mark Walgore

EDITORS AND MANAGERS

Automotive Editor Judi Mauro
Business/Finance Editor Jim Fitzsimmons
City/Metro Editor Mark Mueller
Editorial Page Editor Mark Stradling
Entertainment/Amusements Editor Jeffrey Price
Graphics Editor/Art Director Lisa Aaens-Penas
Health/Medical Editor Mary Mooney
Librarian Patricia Shanahan
News Editor Barbara Lempert
Photo Editor Craig Orosz
Sports Editor John Buonora
Television/Film Editor Jeffrey Price
Theater/Music Editor Jeffrey Price

PRODUCTION

Director Jim Hager
Foreman-Pressroom Rocco A Gallo Jr
Foreman-Mailroom John Basile

Mechanical available: Letterpress (direct)/Flexo; Black and 3 ROP colors; insert accepted — preprinted; page cut-offs — 23 9/16".
Mechanical specifications: Type page 10 11/16" x 14 1/4"; E - 5 cols, 2 1/16", 1/8" between; A - 5 cols, 2 1/16", 1/8" between; C - 7 cols, 1 3/8", 1/8" between.
Commodity consumption: Newsprint 5,500 short tons; widths 60", 60", 45", 30"; black ink 225,000 pounds; color ink 51,000 pounds; single pages printed 24,560; average pages per issue 72.45(d), 68(S); single plates used 27,698.
Equipment: EDITORIAL: Front-end hardware — Dewar/Information System, PC Network; Front-end software — Dewar/View. CLASSIFIED: Front-end hardware — PC Network; Front-end software — PPI; Other equipment — 4-IBM/PCXT, Lf/AP Leaf Picture Desk, HL/299 Color Scanner. DISPLAY: Adv layout systems — Ik/730, ZC/SI; Front-end hardware — Ap/Mac Network; Front-end software — Multi-Ad/Creator. PRODUCTION: Typesetters — 2-Hyphen/Bidco 108; Platemaking systems — 2-Na/NP40; Plate exposures — 1-Na/Starlite, 2-Nu/Exposure, Burgess; Plate processors — 2-NP/40, 1-Na/FP, 2-Na; Electronic picture desk — Lf/AP Leaf Picture Desk; Scanners — 2-ECR/Autokon, 1-Hel/299 Color Scanner, Lf/Leafscan 35; Production cameras — 1-C/SP III, 1-C/Newspager; Automatic film processors — 1-LE, 1-P/24, Kk/710, 1-C/R660, 1-P/26;

Reproportion units — 2-ECR/Autokon; Film transporters — 2-C; Shrink lenses — 1-Alan/Prime; Digital color separation equipment — 1-Hel/299.
PRESSROOM: Line 1 — 8-H/Colormatic-PEC Rebuilt (2 humps, 2 decks); Pasters — 8-H; Press control system — PEC/Supervisors. MAILROOM: Counter stackers — 1-HL/HT Monitor; Bundle tyer — 1-MSB, 1-MLN/2A HS, 2-MLN/IIEE. LIBRARY: Combination — Rem/Lektriever 110. WIRE SERVICES: News — AP; Stock tables — AP; Syndicates — SHNS, KRT; Receiving dishes — size-3m, AP. BUSINESS COMPUTERS: IBM/AS 400; Applications: INSI: Circ, Adv billing, Accts receivable, Gen ledger, Payroll, Inventories, Accts payable, Credit mgmt; PCs & micros networked; PCs & main system networked.

VINELAND
Cumberland County

'90 U.S. Census- 54,780; E&P '96 Est. 56,503
ABC-NDM (90): 143,319 (HH 48,517)

The Daily Journal
(e-mon to fri; m-sat)

The Daily Journal, 891 E. Oak Rd.; PO Box 1504, Vineland, NJ 08360; tel (609) 691-5000; fax (609) 691-2031. Gannett Co. Inc. group.
Circulation: 18,003(e); 18,003(m-sat); ABC Sept. 30, 1995.
Price: 35¢(d); 35¢(sat); $2.30/wk (carrier), $2.35/wk (motor route); $9.20/mo (carrier), $9.40/mo (motor route); $119.60/yr (carrier), $124.80/yr (motor route).
Advertising: Open inch rate $28.52(e); $28.52(m-sat). **Representative:** Gannett National Newspaper Sales.
News Services: AP, GNS. **Politics:** Independent. **Established:** 1875.
Special Editions: Progress; Home Improvement; Car Care; Football; Community Guide; Senior Citizens; Home Furnishings; Christmas; Best of the Best; Hispanic Festival.
Special Weekly Section: Travel (weekly).
Magazine: TV Magazine (sat).

CORPORATE OFFICER
President Sal DeVivo
GENERAL MANAGEMENT
Publisher Sal DeVivo
Manager-Credit Larry Rossello
Controller Edward Yucis
ADVERTISING
Director Al Frattura
Manager-Retail Joe Calchi
Manager-Classified Debbie LeFort-Clintron
MARKETING AND PROMOTION
Manager-Marketing Service H Elayne Sama
TELECOMMUNICATIONS
Audiotex Manager Debbie LeFort
CIRCULATION
Director Lou Thompson
NEWS EXECUTIVE
Exec Editor William Chanin
EDITORS AND MANAGERS
Editorial Page Editor Joe Smith
Living Editor Corrine Sheppard-Borton
News Editor Gerald Covella
Sports Editor Lincoln Wonham
MANAGEMENT INFORMATION SERVICES
Data Processing Manager Dave Dematte
PRODUCTION
Director Gary Herman
Manager-Composing Dottie Picconi
Manager-Pressroom Vince Berti
Manager-Litho Joe Carvalho
Manager-Mailroom Charles Hill

Market Information: Zoned editions; TMC; ADS; Operate database; Operate audiotex.
Mechanical available: Offset; Black; insert accepted — preprinted; page cut-offs — 22¾".
Mechanical specifications: Type page 13" x 21½"; E - 6 cols, 2¹⁄₁₆", ⅛" between; A - 6 cols, 2¹⁄₁₆", ⅛" between; C - 10 cols, 1¼", ⅛" between.
Commodity consumption: Newsprint 1,300 metric tons; width 55½"; black ink 25,000 pounds; color ink 10,000 pounds; single pages printed 8,736; average pages per issue 28(d), 28(sat); single plates used 7,176.
Equipment: EDITORIAL: Front-end hardware — 15-Dewar/Disc Net; Front-end software — Dewar/Disc Net; Printers — Okidata/320, HP/4MT; Other equipment — Lf/AP Leaf Picture Desk, 2-AG/Studio Scanner. CLASSIFIED: Front-end hardware — 5-Dewar/Disc Net; Front-end software — Dewar/Disc Net; Printers — Okidata/192. DISPLAY: Adv layout systems — 4-Dewar/Disc Net, 3-Ap/Power Mac 7100, 1-Ap/Mac Quadra 800; Front-end hardware — 4-Dewar/Disc Net, Ap/Mac Server; Front-end software — Dewar/Disc Net, QuarkXPress, Adobe/Photoshop, Aldus/FreeHand; Printers — 2-HP/4VM; Other equipment — 2-AG/Studio Scanner. PRODUCTION: Pagination software — Dewar; Typesetters — 2-V/5000 Controller, 2-V/5100, 1-V/550, 1-V/5300E; Plate exposures — 3-BKY, Nu, Douthitt; Plate processors — 2-WL; Scanners — ECR/Autokon 1000; Production cameras — C/Marathon, C/Spartan II; Automatic film processors — LE/LD24, LE/LD24AQ, LE/LD800A, LE/R660; Film transporters — C; Shrink lenses — CK Optical; Color separation equipment (conventional) — RZ/200S.
PRESSROOM: Line 1 — 4-G/Metro; Folders — G/2:1 double; Pasters — Automatic Pasters; Press control system — Fin. MAILROOM: Counter stackers — QWI/200, QWI/300; Inserters and stuffers — 2-MM/227 (5-into-1); Bundle tyer — 2-MLN, 2-Power Strap/Newstyer 2000; Addressing machine — 1-Domino/Ink Jet. WIRE SERVICES: News — AP Datastream, AP Datafeatures, AP GraphicsNet; Photos — AP, GNS; Receiving dishes — AP, GNS. BUSINESS COMPUTERS: 1-IBM/AS-400B30; Applications: Circ, Accts payable, Accts receivable, Adv, Payroll; PCs & micros networked; PCs & main system networked.

WILLINGBORO-BURLINGTON
Burlington County

'90 U.S. Census- 46,126 (Willingboro 36,291; Burlington 9,835); E&P '96 Est. 44,059 (Willingboro 34,442; Burlington 9,617)
ABC-CZ (90): 377,493 (HH 131,250)

Burlington County Times
(e-mon to fri; S)

Burlington County Times, 4284 Route 130 N., Willingboro, NJ 08046; tel (609) 871-8000; fax (609) 877-2706; e-mail bctimes@bctimes.com. Calkins Newspapers group.
Circulation: 39,646(e); 46,262(S); ABC Sept. 30, 1995.
Price: 35¢(d); $1.50(S); $2.75/wk; $11.00/mo; $128.70/yr.
Advertising: Open inch rate $96.75(e); $101.25(S). **Representative:** Sawyer-Ferguson-Walker Co.
News Services: AP, NEA. **Politics:** Independent. **Established:** 1958.
Not Published: New Year; Memorial Day; Independence Day; Christmas (unless on a Sunday).
Special Editions: Best of Burlington (Jan); Bridal (Feb); Home & Garden (Mar); NIE, Best of Burlington (Apr); Discover Burlington (May); Back-to-School (Aug); Pro & H.S. Sports (Sept); Fall Home Improvement, Car Care (Oct); Holiday Gifts (Dec); Mini Coupon Books (monthly).
Special Weekly Sections: Real Estate Tab, Wheels (wkly auto section) (fri).
Magazines: "What's Happening" (own, newsprint) (thur); Travel (newsprint), Parade; TV Time (S).

CORPORATE OFFICERS
President Grover J Friend
Exec Vice Pres Charles P Smith
Vice Pres/Secretary Shirley C Ellis
Vice Pres Stanley M Ellis
Vice Pres Carolyn C Smith
Vice Pres Sandra C Hardy
Treasurer Edward J Birch
GENERAL MANAGEMENT
Publisher Stanley M Ellis
Controller Joseph H Bright
Supervisor-Data Processing Steve Carpenter
ADVERTISING
Director David S Renne
Manager-Retail Jack Lough
Manager-Promotion Lori Smith
Manager-Classified Nancy Smith
Manager-Major Accounts Peggy Hollister
TELECOMMUNICATIONS
Audiotex Manager Steve Carpenter
CIRCULATION
Director Frank Leon
Manager-Distribution Doug Campbell
Manager-Sales Charles Whiting
NEWS EXECUTIVES
Exec Editor Jennie L Phipps
Senior Assoc Editor Gary Lindenmuth
EDITORS AND MANAGERS
Assoc Editor Kerry McKean
Assoc Editor Mario Constantino
Automotive Editor Jim Donnelly
Business Editor Mario Constantino
Editorial Editor Kevin Keane
Entertainment Editor Lou Gaul
Feature Editor Penny Sundstrom
News Editor Mike Ryan
Sports Editor Wayne Richardson
Travel Editor Penny Sundstrom
MANAGEMENT INFORMATION SERVICES
Data Processing Manager Bill Clark
PRODUCTION
Director John R Donnelly
Superintendent-Pressroom Joe Jaconia
Superintendent-Maintenance Joe Griffin

Market Information: Zoned editions; Split Run; TMC; Operate audiotex.
Mechanical available: Offset; Black and 3 ROP colors; insert accepted — preprinted, product samples; page cut-offs — 22¾".
Mechanical specifications: Type page 13¾" x 21½"; E - 6 cols, 2¹⁄₁₆", ⅕" between; A - 6 cols, 2¹⁄₁₆", ⅕" between; C - 9 cols, 1⅓", .11" between.
Commodity consumption: Newsprint 3,600 metric tons; widths 55", 55", 41¼"; black ink 94,000 pounds; color ink 21,500 pounds; single pages printed 15,600; average pages per issue 38(d), 70(S); single plates used 24,500.
Equipment: EDITORIAL: Front-end hardware — Compaq/Prolinea PC, IBM/3090; Front-end software — Calkins/Text Editing System (PC), QuarkXPress. CLASSIFIED: Front-end hardware — IBM/3090; Front-end software — Calkins/Adv & Acct System; Printers — IBM/4224. AUDIOTEX: Hardware — PEP; Software — PEP/Voice Print 19000 2.4; DISPLAY: Adv layout systems — SCS/Layout 8000; Front-end hardware — IBM/486 PC; Front-end software — Archetype; Printers — HP/II Laser-Printer, New Gen/11x17. PRODUCTION: Pagination software — QPS 3.3; Typesetters — AU/APS Micro 5, QMS/860-11x17, MON/1016 HS; Plate processors — W; Electronic picture desk — Lf/AP Leaf Picture Desk; Scanners — ECR/Autokon News Graphic System, Dest; Production cameras — C/Marathon, C/Spartan III; Automatic film processors — 4-LE, 1-C; Reproportion units — ECR/Autokon; Film transporters — 2-LE; Color separation equipment (conventional) — ECR/Autokon; Digital color separation equipment — ECR/Autokon.
PRESSROOM: Line 1 — 7-G/Metro; Folders — 1-G/2:1; Reels and stands — 7-G; Press control system — Fin. MAILROOM: Counter stackers — QWI; Bundle tyer — 1-Power Strap, 2-MLN; Addressing machine — Ch. WIRE SERVICES: News — AP; Receiving dishes — AP, BDR. BUSINESS COMPUTERS: IBM/3090; Applications: Admarc: Adv, Accounting; PCs & main system networked.

WOODBRIDGE
See MIDDLESEX COUNTY

WOODBURY
Gloucester County

'90 U.S. Census- 10,904; E&P '96 Est. 10,954
ABC-NDM (90): 230,082 (HH 78,845)

The Gloucester County Times (e-mon to fri; S)

The Gloucester County Times, 309 S. Broad St., Woodbury, NJ 08096; tel (609) 845-3300; fax (609) 845-4318. MediaNews Inc. (Garden State Newspapers) group.
Circulation: 27,286(e); 28,486(S); ABC Sept. 30, 1995.
Price: 35¢(d); $1.00(S); $2.60/wk (carrier), $2.70/wk (motor route); $190.00/yr.
Advertising: Open inch rate $41.22(e); $41.22(S). **Representatives:** Landon Associates Inc.; US Suburban Press.
News Services: AP, NEA. **Politics:** Independent. **Established:** 1897.
Not Published: Christmas (except on Sunday).
Special Editions: Pennsylvania Auto Show, Spring Bridal (Jan); Progress (Feb); Spring Lawn & Garden (Mar); Phillies '96, Spring Real Estate (Apr); Here Comes Summer (May); New Homes, Best Years (June); Guide to Gloucester County (July); Back-to-School (Aug); Eagles '96, High School Football, Fall Real Estate, Interiors/Exteriors (Sept); 1997 New Car (Oct); Holiday Gift Guide (Nov); Holiday Gift Guide II (Dec).
Magazines: TV Update; The Advertiser (TMC Product); Comics; Parade.

CORPORATE OFFICERS
Chairman of the Board Richard B Scudder
President W Dean Singleton
GENERAL MANAGEMENT
Publisher Wayne A Studer
Controller Frank Gargano
Manager-Credit Ellen Cummings
ADVERTISING
Manager-Classified/Marketing Service Marie Vito
CIRCULATION
Director Harold A Rittler
NEWS EXECUTIVE
Editor William B Long
EDITORS AND MANAGERS
Arts/Music Editor Jen Watson
Automotive Editor Jim Childs
Business Editor Tom Durso
City/Metro Editor Jen Watson
Editorial Page Editor John Schoonejongen
Education Editor Nancy Cambria
Entertainment/Amusements Editor Jen Watson
Environmental Editor Ron Southwick
Farm/Energy Editor Jeremy Kohler
Fashion/Style Editor Jim Childs
Features Editor Jim Childs
Films/Theater Editor Jen Watson
Food Editor Jim Childs
Health/Medical Editor Christi Milligan
Living/Lifestyle Editor Jim Childs
National Editor Elliot Goldberg
News Editor Susan Caulfield
Political/Government Editor Elliot Goldberg
Radio/Television Editor Jane Humes
Religion Editor Jane Humes
Science/Technology Editor Tom Durso
Sports Editor Tom Murray
Sunday Editor Jim Childs
Travel Editor Jim Six
Women's/Society Editor Jim Childs
MANAGEMENT INFORMATION SERVICES
Manager-Management Info Services Charles H MacDonald Jr
Data Processing Manager Edward J Murray
PRODUCTION
Superintendent Edwin Agren
Foreman-Composing Lena Newton
Foreman-Pressroom Michael Brown

Market Information: TMC.
Mechanical available: Offset; Black and 3 ROP colors; insert accepted — preprinted; page cut-offs — 22¾".
Mechanical specifications: Type page 13" x 21½"; E - 6 cols, 2¹⁄₁₆", ⅛" between; A - 6 cols, 2¹⁄₁₆", ⅛" between; C - 9 cols, 1⅓", ⅛" between.
Commodity consumption: Newsprint 2,535 metric tons; widths 13¾", 27½"; black ink 45,210 pounds; color ink 7,525 pounds; single pages printed 11,974; average pages per issue 36(d), 60(S).
Equipment: EDITORIAL: Front-end hardware — IBM, PC; Front-end software — CText; Printers — Okidata. CLASSIFIED: Front-end hardware — IBM, PC; Front-end software — CText; Printers — Epson. DISPLAY: Front-end hardware — IBM, PC, HI; Front-end software — CText, HI; Printers — Okidata, Epson. PRODUCTION: Typesetters — 2-Ap/Mac 7100-66, 1-Ap/Mac 8100-80, 1-Ap/Mac Scanner, 1-New-Gen/1200 2pi, 1-Ap/Mac Printer; Plate exposures — Nu, Magnum; Plate processors — Nat, MAS; Electronic picture desk — Lf/AP Leaf Picture Desk; Production cameras — C/Spartan III, SCREEN; Automatic film processors — P, AG; Color separation equipment (conventional) — RZ/4050E.
PRESSROOM: Line 1 — 9-G/Urbanite; Folders — 1-G; Reels and stands — 7-G/Roll stand; Press control system — Fin. MAILROOM: Counter stackers — Id, HL; Inserters and stuffers — Amerigraph/NP1372; Bundle tyer — MLN. WIRE SERVICES: News — AP; Photos — AP; Syndicates — AP; Receiving dishes — size-10ft, AP. BUSINESS COMPUTERS: HP; Applications: CJ; PCs & micros networked; PCs & main system networked.

NEW MEXICO

ALAMOGORDO

Otero County

'90 U.S. Census- 27,596; E&P '96 Est. 30,764
ABC-CZ (90): 29,744 (HH 11,217)

Alamogordo Daily News

(e-mon to fri; S)

Alamogordo Daily News, 518 24th (88310); PO Box 870, Alamogordo, NM 88311; tel (505) 437-7120; fax (505) 437-7795. Donrey Media group.

Circulation: 8,001(e); 9,186(S); ABC Sept. 30, 1995.
Price: 50¢(d); $1.00(S); $7.00/mo.
Advertising: Open inch rate $14.12(e); $14.12 (S). **Representative:** Papert Companies.
News Service: AP. **Politics:** Independent. **Established:** 1898.
Special Editions: Progress (Mar); Land of Enchantment (May); Back-to-School (July); Football (Aug); Holiday Gift Guide (Nov); Christmas Special (Dec).
Special Weekly Sections: Business Section (mon); Food Page (tues).
Magazine: Showtime (TV magazine) (S).

CORPORATE OFFICERS

Founder Donald W Reynolds
President/Chief Operating Officer Emmett Jones
Exec Vice Pres/Chief Financial Officer Darrell W Loftin
Vice Pres-Western Newspaper Group David A Osborn
Vice Pres-Eastern Newspaper Group Don Schneider

GENERAL MANAGEMENT

Publisher/Purchasing Agent Thomas W Reeves

ADVERTISING

Director Mildred C House

CIRCULATION

Director Sharon Rudisill

NEWS EXECUTIVE

Editor Richard Coltharp

EDITORS AND MANAGERS

Editorial Page Editor Thomas W Reeves
News Editor Dave Rogers
Photo Editor Ron Keller

PRODUCTION

Supervisor-Composing Sue Hisaw
Supervisor-Press Lupe Reyes

Market Information: TMC.
Mechanical available: Offset; Black and 3 ROP colors; insert accepted — preprinted; page cut-offs — 22¾".
Mechanical specifications: Type page 13" x 21½"; E - 6 cols, 2⅟₁₆", ⅛" between; A - 6 cols, 2⅟₁₆", ⅛" between; C - 8 cols, 1⅜", ⅟₁₆" between.
Commodity consumption: width 27½".
Equipment: EDITORIAL: Front-end hardware — Mk; Front-end software — Mk; Printers — Ap/Mac LaserWriter NTX. CLASSIFIED: Front-end hardware — Mk; Front-end software — Mk. DISPLAY: Adv layout systems — Ap/Macs; Front-end hardware — Ap/Macs; Front-end software — Multi-Ad/Creator; Printers — Ap/Mac LaserWriter NTX. PRODUCTION: Typesetters — Ap/Mac LaserWriter NTX; Plate exposures — 3M/Deadliner; Plate processors — 3M/Deadliner; Production cameras — 1-R. PRESSROOM: Line 1 — 6-G/Community. MAILROOM: Inserters and stuffers — 1-KAN. WIRE SERVICES: News — AP; Receiving dishes — AP. BUSINESS COMPUTERS: Unisys, HP; Applications: CJ, SSPS; PCs & micros networked; PCs & main system networked.

ALBUQUERQUE

Bernalillo County

'90 U.S. Census- 384,736; E&P '96 Est. 425,939
ABC-NDM (90): 1,042,540 (HH 377,691)

Albuquerque Publishing Co.

Albuquerque Publishing Co., 7777 Jefferson NE (87103); PO Drawer J, Albuquerque, NM 87109-4343; tel (505) 823-7777; fax (505) 823-3499.

Established: 1931.
Note: The Albuquerque Tribune and Albuquerque Journal are corporately and editorially separate but have merged their business, circulation and mechanical departments. The Albuquerque Publishing Co. was created to conduct publication of both papers.

CORPORATE OFFICERS

President/Treasurer Thompson H Lang
Vice Pres William Burleigh
Vice Pres-Finance Lowell A Hare
Secretary D J Castellini

GENERAL MANAGEMENT

General Manager Thompson H Lang
Asst General Manager/Business Director William P Lang
Controller Peggy Seis

ADVERTISING

Director Scott Haskins
Manager-General Paul Campbell
Manager-Classified Bill Tafoya

CIRCULATION

Director Michael Boody

MANAGEMENT INFORMATION SERVICES

Data Processing Manager Olin Haines

PRODUCTION

Director Fred Wyche
Manager Manuel Chavez

Mechanical available: Offset Lithography; Black and 3 ROP colors; insert accepted — preprinted, most; page cut-offs — 22¾".
Mechanical specifications: Type page 13" x 21½"; E - 6 cols, 2.07", ⅛" between; A - 6 cols, 2.07", ⅛" between; C - 9 cols, 1.40".
Commodity consumption: Newsprint 21,127 short tons; 19,166 metric tons; widths 55", 41¼", 27⅜"; black ink 424,866 pounds; color ink 115,437 pounds; single pages printed 44,124; average pages per issue 59(d), 80(sat), 102(S); single plates used 154,650.
Equipment: EDITORIAL: Front-end hardware — HP/Vectra 486, WS, Sun/Sparc 10 OPI; Front-end software — XYQUEST/XyWrite, Novell/LAN, QuarkXPress, Adobe/Photoshop; Printers — 3-AG/Select Set 5000; Other equipment — Ap/Mac Quadra 950, Ap/Mac Quadra 800-840. CLASSIFIED: Front-end hardware — M/5500; Front-end software — M/5500; Printers — M/606. DISPLAY: Adv layout systems — HP/2394A; Front-end hardware — HP/Vectra E5-12; Front-end software — SCS/Layout 8000 6.6; Printers — HP/2564B. PRODUCTION: Pagination software — QPS 3.31; OCR software — Caere/OmniPage 3.0; Typesetters — M/606, SCS/Select Set 5000; Plate exposures — BKY, Nu/Flip Top; Plate processors — Anacoil; Electronic picture desk — AG/Horizon, Lf/Leafscan 35; Scanners — CD/Scanners, AG, Lf; Production cameras — C/Spartan; Automatic film processors — LE; Color separation equipment (conventional) — Ap/Mac, Adobe/Photoshop; Digital color separation equipment — Adobe/Photoshop 2.5, QuarkXPress 3.1. PRESSROOM: Line 1 — 9-G/Metroliner(5 half decks); Line 2 — 9-G/Metroliner(5 half decks); Folders — G/DD. MAILROOM: Counter stackers — HL/Monitor; Inserters and stuffers — Fg/5-into-1 drums (on-line); Bundle tyer — OVL, Power Strap. WIRE SERVICES: News — AP; Stock tables — AP; Syndicates — KRT, NYT; Receiving dishes — size-10ft, AP. BUSINESS COMPUTERS: HP; Applications: HP, CJ; PCs & micros networked; PCs & main system networked.

Albuquerque Journal

(m-mon to sat; S)

Albuquerque Journal, 7777 Jefferson NE (87103); PO Drawer J, Albuquerque, NM 87109; tel (505) 823-7777; fax (505) 823-3499.

Circulation: 113,031(m); 113,031(m-sat); 166,472(S); ABC Sept. 30, 1995.
Price: 50¢(d); 50¢(sat); $1.25(S); $10.25/mo.
Advertising: Open inch rate $61.25(m); $61.25(m-sat); $77.75(S); comb with Albuquerque Tribune (e) $73.00.
News Services: AP, LAT-WP, CSM, KRT, RN. **Politics:** Independent. **Established:** 1880.
Note: For detailed production and printing information see Albuquerque Publishing Co.
Special Editions: Women's Trade Fair (Jan); Bridal, Business Outlook (Feb); Senior, Spring Coupon Book (Mar); Home and Garden, American Home Week (Apr); Auto Care (May); Summer Coupon Book (June); Home Furnishings, Back-to-School (July); Santa Fe Parade of Homes (Aug); State Fair, Fall Coupon Book, Balloon Fiesta (Sept); Parade of Homes, Restaurant Guide (Oct); Restaurant Guide, Holiday Gift Guide, Winter Guide (Nov); Winter Guide, Last Minute Gift Guide/Holiday Planner, Last Minute Gift Guide 2/Holiday Planner (Dec).
Special Weekly Sections: Business Outlook (mon); Venue, Cars and Trucks (fri); Wheels (sat).
Magazines: Rio Leisure & Nightlife Magazine (thur); Entertainer (TV & Entertainment Section) (fri); Parade (S); Sage Women's Magazine (S/monthly).

CORPORATE OFFICERS

President/Treasurer Thompson H Lang
Vice Pres William P Lang
Vice Pres-Finance Lowell A Hare

NEWS EXECUTIVES

Editor Gerald J Crawford
Senior Asst Editor Kent Walz
Managing Editor Rod Deckert
Asst Managing Editor-Features Karen Moses
Asst Managing Editor-Technology Carolyn Flynn

EDITORS AND MANAGERS

Arts Editor Dan Herrera
Automotive/Aviation Editor Ken Walston
Books Editor David Steinberg
Business/Finance Editor Steve McMillan
City Editor Judy Giannettino
Columnist Jim Belshaw
Columnist Larry Calloway
Copy Desk Chief/News Editor Mike Les
Editorial Page Editor Bill Hume
Editorial Cartoonist John Trever
Education (Higher) Steve Brewer
Farm Editor Fritz Thompson
Fashion/Style Editor Nancy Baca
Features Editor Tom Harmon
Films/Theater Editor Dan Herrera
Food/Garden Editor Nancy Baca
Graphics Editor/Art Director Carolyn Flynn
Health/Medical Editor Donna Olmstead
Librarian Judy Pence
Music Editor Rick Masongon
Deputy News Editor Ken Walston
Northern Bureau Editor Sharon Hendrix
Photo Department Paul Bearce
Photo Editor Paul Bearce
Political Editor John Robertson
Radio/Television Editor Rick Nathanson
Real Estate Editor David Staats
Religion Editor Bruce Daniels
Science/Technology Editor John Fleck
Sports Editor Mike Hall
State Editor Tim Coder
Travel Editor Tom Harmon
Wire Editor Ken Walston
Women's Magazine Editor Susan Stiger

Commodity consumption: average pages per issue 56(d), 110(S).
Equipment: EDITORIAL: Front-end hardware — HP/486-33; Front-end software — XYQUEST/XyWrite.

The Albuquerque Tribune

(e-mon to sat)

The Albuquerque Tribune, 7777 Jefferson NE (87103); PO Drawer J, Albuquerque, NM 87109-4343; tel (505) 823-7777; fax (505) 823-3689. Scripps Howard group.

Circulation: 30,012(e); 30,012(e-sat); ABC Sept. 30, 1995.
Price: 50¢(d); 50¢(sat); $5.25/mo.
Advertising: Open inch rate $45.75(e); $45.75(e-sat); comb with Albuquerque Journal (mS) $73.00.
News Services: AP, SHNS, NYT. **Politics:** Independent. **Established:** 1922.
Note: For detailed production and printing information, see Albuquerque Publishing Co.
Special Editions: Bridal, Business Outlook (Feb); Senior, Spring Coupon Book (Mar); Home and Garden, American Home Week (Apr); Auto Care (May); Summer Coupon Book (June); Home Furnishings, Back-to-School (July); Santa Fe Parade of Homes (Aug); State Fair, Fall Coupon Book, Balloon Fiesta (Sept); Parade of Homes, Restaurant Guide (Oct); Restaurant Guide, Winter Guide, Holiday Gift Guide (Nov); Winter Guide, Last Minute Gift Guide 1/Holiday Planner, Last Minute Gift Guide 2/Holiday Planner (Dec).
Special Weekly Sections: Business Outlook (mon); Venue (fri); Entertainer, Wheels (sat).
Magazines: Wild Life (entertainment) (thur); Cars and Trucks (classified) (fri); TV Week (sat); Sage's Women Magazine (S/monthly).

CORPORATE OFFICER

President Lawrence Leser

ADVERTISING

Director David Ohms

MARKETING AND PROMOTION

Manager-Marketing/Promotion Scott Haskins

NEWS EXECUTIVES

Editor Scott Ware
Managing Editor Neal Pattison
Coordinator-AME/Graphics Randall Roberts
Coordinator-AME/Features Kevin Hellyer
Coordinator-AME/News Kelly Brewer
Office Manager Louise Lefkovitz

EDITORS AND MANAGERS

Arts/Entertainment Editor Joline Glenn
Business Community Editor Dan Vukelich
Consumer News Joline Glenn
Columnist-Sports Richard Stevens
Columnist-News Harrison Fletcher
Columnist-Restaurant Joline Glenn
Editorial Page Editor Jack Ehn
Education Editor Kate Nelson
Education Editor Shari Bluto
Family/Neighbors Editor Kate Nelson
Health/Medicine Editor Shari Bluto
Librarian Pat Seligman
News Editor John Hill
Politics/Institutions Editor John Hill
Pop/Culture Ed Joline Glenn
Presentation (Design & Copydesk) David Carrillo
Presentation (Design & Copydesk) Kevin Reilly
Religion Editor Shari Bluto
Science/Technology Editor Shari Bluto
Sports Editor John O'Rourke
Visuals (Photo and Graphics) Joan Carlin

MANAGEMENT INFORMATION SERVICES

Manager-Systems Art Duran
Online Manager Roy Buergi

PRODUCTION

Director Fred Wyche

Market Information: Operate database; Electronic edition.
Mechanical available: Offset; Black and 3 ROP colors; insert accepted — preprinted.
Mechanical specifications: Type page 13" x 21.5"; E - 6 cols, 2¾", ⅛" between; A - 6 cols, 2¾", ⅛" between; C - 9 cols.
Commodity consumption: average pages per issue 56(d).
Equipment: EDITORIAL: Front-end hardware — HP/PCs, Ap/Mac Quadra; Front-end software — XYQUEST/XyWrite 4.0, QuarkXPress 3.3, Adobe/Photoshop 2.5; Printers — Hyphen/Dash 600. PRODUCTION: Pagination software — XYQUEST/XyWrite 4.0, QuarkXPress 3.3, Adobe/Photoshop 2.5; Typesetters — AG/SelectSet 5000; Plate exposures — KFM; Plate processors — Anacoil; Electronic picture desk — Lf, Ap/Mac Quadra; Scanners — AG/Horizon; Automatic film processors — LE; Digital color separation equipment — AG/Horizon. PRESSROOM: Line 1 — G/Metroliner; Line 2 — G/Metroliner. WIRE SERVICES: News — AP, SHNS, NYT; Photos — AP; Stock tables — AP; Receiving dishes — AP.

ARTESIA

Eddy County

'90 U.S. Census- 10,610; E&P '96 Est. 10,828

Artesia Daily Press

(e-tues to fri; S)

Artesia Daily Press, 503 W. Main (88210); PO Box 190, Artesia, NM 88211; tel (505) 746-3524.

Circulation: 3,540(e); 3,540(S); Sworn Sept 29, 1995.
Price: 50¢(d); 75¢(S); $5.75/mo (city), $6.50/mo (mail); $69.00/yr (city), $78.00/yr (mail).
Advertising: Open inch rate $6.65(e); $6.65(S).
News Service: AP. **Politics:** Independent. **Established:** 1954.
Not Published: New Year; Independence Day; Labor Day; Thanksgiving; Christmas.
Special Editions: Taxes (Jan); Home, Car Care Edition (May); Oil & Progress, Soil Conservation (Sept); Health Edition (Nov).

CORPORATE OFFICERS

President/Treasurer Walt Green
Vice Pres Ken Green

GENERAL MANAGEMENT

Publisher/Business Manager/Purchasing Agent Gary Scott

ADVERTISING

Manager Gary Scott
Manager-Classified Barbara Beans
Manager-Promotion Gary Scott

CIRCULATION	
Manager	Danny Scott
NEWS EXECUTIVE	
Editor	Darrell J Pehr
EDITORS AND MANAGERS	
Aviation/Travel Editor	Lynn Koenig
Books Editor	Lynn Koenig
Sports Editor	Rick Hassler
PRODUCTION	
Superintendent	Danny Scott
Foreman-Pressroom	Danny Scott

Market Information: TMC.
Mechanical available: Offset; Black and 2 ROP colors; insert accepted — preprinted; page cut-offs — 21½".
Mechanical specifications: Type page 13¼" x 21"; E - 6 cols, 2 1/16", 1/16" between; A - 6 cols, 2 1/16", 1/16" between; C - 6 cols, 2 1/16", 1/16" between.
Commodity consumption: Newsprint 10 short tons; widths 28", 14"; black ink 3,360 pounds; color ink 40 pounds.
Equipment: EDITORIAL: Front-end hardware — CText; Front-end software — CText; Printers — 2-Ap/Mac LaserWriter. CLASSIFIED: Front-end software — CText. PRODUCTION: Typesetters — 2-Ap/Mac LaserWriter; Plate exposures — 1-Nu/Flip Top FT40M; Plate processors — 1-Nu; Production cameras — 1-Acti/183; Shrink lenses — 1-CK Optical/SQU-7.
PRESSROOM: Line 1 — 4-G/Community; Folders — 1-G. MAILROOM: Addressing machine — RSK. WIRE SERVICES: News — AP; Receiving dishes — size-1-m, AP. BUSINESS COMPUTERS: PC-Compatible.

New Mexico

CARLSBAD
Eddy County
'90 U.S. Census- 24,952; E&P '96 Est. 24,616
ABC-CZ (90): 26,119 (HH 9,715)

Carlsbad Current-Argus
(m-tues to sat; S)
Current-Argus, 620 S. Main St.; PO Box 1629, Carlsbad, NM 88220; tel (505) 887-5501; fax (505) 885-1066. Omaha World-Herald Co. group.

Circulation: 8,297(m); 8,297(m-sat); 8,692(S); ABC Sept. 30, 1995.
Price: 50¢(d); $1.25(S); $9.25/mo; $111.00/yr.
Advertising: Open inch rate $9.09(m); $9.09(S).
News Service: AP. **Politics:** Independent. **Established:** 1889.
Not Published: Day after Thanksgiving & Christmas.
Special Editions: Chronology (Jan); Valentine's Love Photos (Feb); Our Town (Mar); The Spring Edition (Apr); Newspapers in Schools & Design-An-Ad, High School Graduation

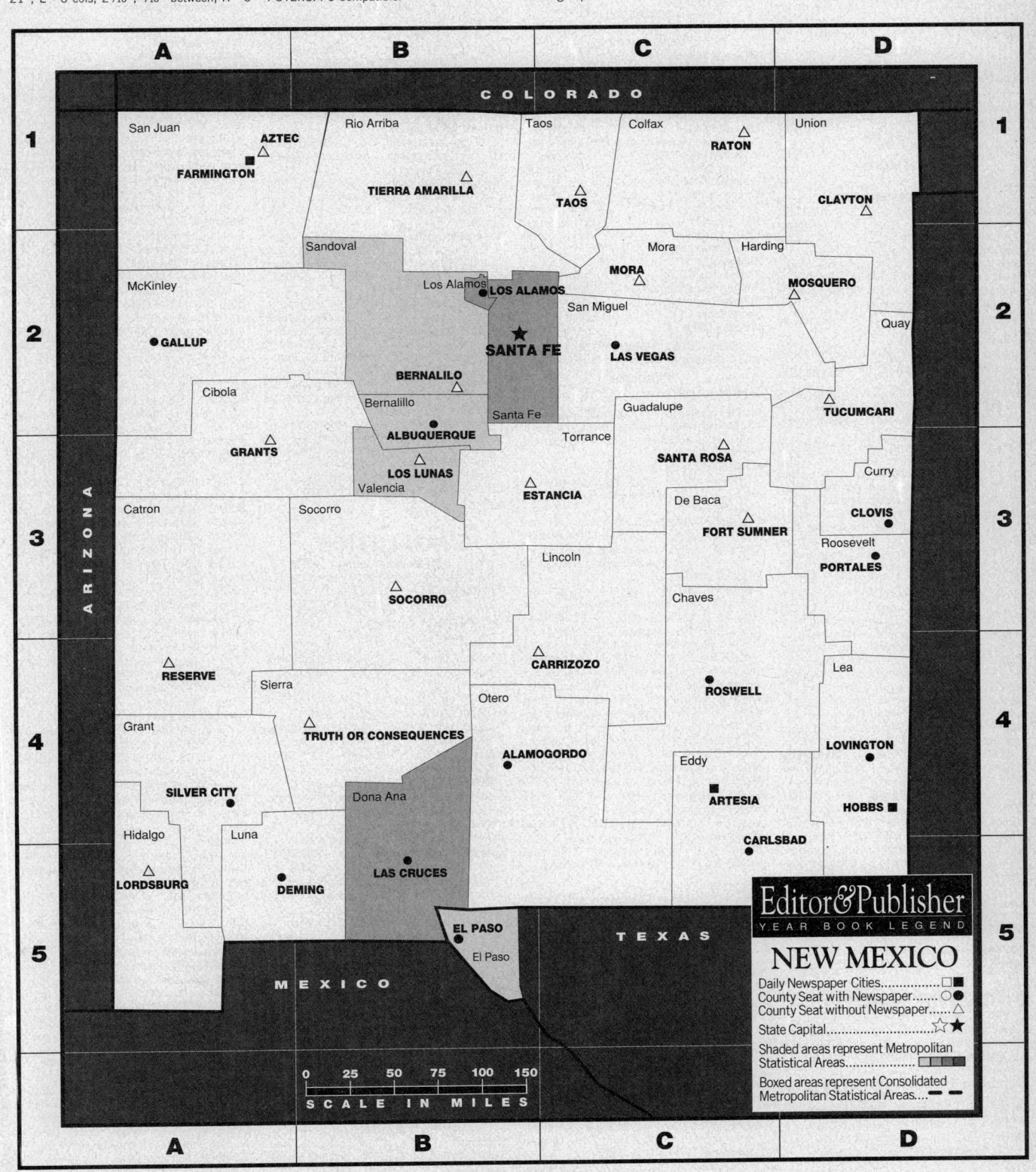

I-260 New Mexico

(May); Western Days (July); Back-to-School (Aug); Football (Sept); Salute To Local Business, Retirement (Oct); Thanksgiving Shopping Guide, Christmas Gift Guide (Nov); Christmas Greetings (Dec).
Special Weekly Sections: Best Food Day (wed); Best Automotive Days, Best Real Estate Days (fri); Business Page, Best Automotive, Best Real Estate Days (S).
Magazines: Pecos Valley Shopper (TMC) (thur); TV Spotlight (fri); Sunday Comics, USA Weekend (S).

CORPORATE OFFICERS

President Daryl Hall
Vice Pres Terry Kroeger
Treasurer A William Kernen

GENERAL MANAGEMENT

Publisher Daryl Hall
Manager-Business Amy McKay

ADVERTISING

Manager Will Parks
Manager-Classified Brad Treptow

CIRCULATION

Manager Joe Warren

NEWS EXECUTIVE

Managing Editor Hal Miller

EDITORS AND MANAGERS

Editorial Page Editor Hal Miller
Education Editor Teresa Lambright
Farm/Agriculture Editor Toni Walker Chiri
Food/Women's Editor Julyne Derrick
Government Editor Marle Martin
News Editor Eric Fisher
Religion Editor Julyne Derrick

PRODUCTION

Manager-Operations Shan Barenklau

Market Information: TMC.
Mechanical available: Offset; Black and 3 ROP colors; insert accepted — preprinted; page cut-offs — 22½".
Mechanical specifications: Type page 13" x 21½"; E - 6 cols, $2\frac{1}{16}$", ⅛" between; A - 6 cols, $2\frac{1}{16}$", ⅛" between; C - 6 cols, $2\frac{1}{16}$", ⅛" between.
Commodity consumption: Newsprint 381.00 short tons; width 27½"; black ink 7,200 pounds; color ink 560 pounds; single pages printed 6,182; average pages per issue 18(d), 20(sat), 30(S); single plates used 9,000.
Equipment: EDITORIAL: Front-end hardware — CText; Front-end software — XYQUEST/XyWrite, CText; Printers — Ap/Mac LaserPrinters; Other equipment — ECR/Image Setter. CLASSIFIED: Front-end hardware — CText; Front-end software — XYQUEST/XyWrite, CText; Printers — Ap/Mac LaserPrinters; Other equipment — ECR/Image Setter. DISPLAY: Adv layout systems — CText; Front-end hardware — CText/Adept; Front-end software — Microsoft/Windows; Printers — Ap/Mac LaserPrinters; Other equipment — ECR/Image Setter. PRODUCTION: Typesetters — ECR/Image Setter; Plate processors — Nu/FT40 V6 UP Ultra-Plus PlateMaker; Electronic picture desk — Lf/AP Leaf Picture Desk; Production cameras — Nu/2024 M2 Camera; Automatic film processors — P/26 RT Processor.
PRESSROOM: Line 1 — 6-G/Community; Press drives — Fin; Folders — G/Community Quarter. MAILROOM: Inserters and stuffers — KAN/5-into-1 4086; Bundle tyer — Bu/Tyer. WIRE SERVICES: News — AP; Photos — AP; Stock tables — AP; Receiving dishes — size-3m, AP. BUSINESS COMPUTERS: IBM/5363; Applications: In-house, Circ, Accts receivable; PCs & micros networked; PCs & main system networked.

CLOVIS

Curry County

'90 U.S. Census- 30,954; E&P '96 Est. 30,829
ABC-CZ (90): 30,954 (HH 11,676)

Clovis News Journal

(e-mon to fri; S)

Clovis News Journal, 521 Pile; PO Box 1689, Clovis, NM 88102-1689; tel (505) 763-3431; fax (505) 762-3879. Freedom Communications Inc. group.
Circulation: 9,928(e); 10,277(S); ABC Sept. 30, 1995.
Price: 50¢(d); $1.00(S); $7.00/mo (carrier); $84.00/yr (carrier).
Advertising: Open inch rate $8.75(e); $8.75 (S). **Representative:** Papert Companies.
News Service: AP. **Politics:** Independent. **Established:** 1938.
Special Editions: Football Preview; Back-to-School; County Fair; Home & Garden.
Special Weekly Section: Entertainer (fri).
Magazine: USA Weekend Tab.

GENERAL MANAGEMENT

Publisher Julie Moreno
Business Manager/Controller Charlene Harris
Purchasing Agent Paul Tiedemann

ADVERTISING

Director Wendell Jones
Manager-Classified Julie Mason

CIRCULATION

Manager Lynn Berry

NEWS EXECUTIVE

Managing Editor Mike Wheeler

EDITORS AND MANAGERS

Action Line Editor Mike Wheeler
City/Metro Editor Ronn Smith
Editorial Page Editor Tony Farkas
Education Editor Mike Wheeler
Entertainment/Amusements Editor Mike Wheeler
Fashion/Women's Editor Leticia Gomez
Features Editor Mike Wheeler
Food/Garden Editor Leticia Gomez
Graphics Editor/Art Director Mike Wheeler
Health/Medical Editor Mike Wheeler
Lifestyle Editor Leticia Gomez
National Editor Mike Wheeler
News Editor Tony Farkas
Picture Editor John Faught
Photo Editor Mike Wheeler
Political/Government Editor Mike Wheeler
Science/Technology Editor Mike Wheeler
Sports Editor Gary Mitchell
Women's Editor Mike Wheeler

MANAGEMENT INFORMATION SERVICES

Data Processing Manager Charlene Harris

PRODUCTION

Superintendent Paul Tiedemann

Market Information: TMC; Operate database.
Mechanical available: Offset; Black and 3 ROP colors; insert accepted — preprinted; page cut-offs — 22¾".
Mechanical specifications: Type page $13\frac{1}{8}$" x 21½"; E - 6 cols, $2\frac{1}{16}$", ⅛" between; A - 6 cols, $2\frac{1}{16}$", ⅛" between; C - 9 cols, $1\frac{5}{16}$", ⅛" between.
Commodity consumption: Newsprint 415 short tons; width 27½"; black ink 14,400 pounds; color ink 1,440 pounds; single pages printed 6,000; average pages per issue 16(d), 52(S); single plates used 5,000.
Equipment: EDITORIAL: Front-end hardware — Ap/Mac; Front-end software — Baseview; Printers — V; Other equipment — 4-PC. CLASSIFIED: Front-end hardware — Ap/Mac; Front-end software — Baseview; Printers — Okidata/Laser Printer. DISPLAY: Front-end hardware — Ap/Mac; Front-end software — AdForce 1.5; PRODUCTION: Typesetters — Ap/Mac LaserWriter II NTX, Accel-A-Writer/8100; Plate exposures — 1-Nu; Scanners — Ap/Mac Scanner; Production cameras — R/580; Automatic film processors — LE; Color separation equipment (conventional) — V/3990, Ap/Mac; Digital color separation equipment — V/3990.
PRESSROOM: Line 1 — 8-HI/V15A. MAILROOM: Inserters and stuffers — 6-KAN. WIRE SERVICES: News — AP; Receiving dishes — size-12ft, AP. BUSINESS COMPUTERS: 2-IBM/Model 80, 2-IBM/486; Applications: Southware, Vision Data, Arwoks; PCs & micros networked; PCs & main system networked.

DEMING

Luna County

'90 U.S. Census- 10,970; E&P '96 Est. 11,738

Deming Headlight

(m-mon to fri)

Deming Headlight, 219 E. Maple (88031); PO Box 881, Deming, NM 88030; tel (505) 546-2611; fax (505) 546-8116. WorldWest Limited Liability Co. group.
Circulation: 3,387(m); Sworn Oct. 2, 1995.
Price: 50¢(d); $54.00/yr (mail).
Advertising: Open inch rate $7.28(m).
News Service: AP. **Politics:** Independent. **Established:** 1881.
Not Published: New Year; Memorial Day; Independence Day; Labor Day; Thanksgiving; Christmas.
Special Editions: Horizons (Mar); Car Care (Apr); Graduation (May); Life Off the Land (July); Back-to-School, Duck Race (Aug); Southwestern Fair (Oct); Christmas (Nov); Christmas Greetings (Dec).
Magazine: Entertainment (TV weekly).

CORPORATE OFFICERS

Owner Dolph C Simons Jr
Owner Dan C Simons
Owner Dolph C Simons III
Owner Ralph D Gage Jr

GENERAL MANAGEMENT

Publisher Tamara M Montes
General Manager Patty Ciccotelli

ADVERTISING

Manager-Classified Merline Hensley
Representative Rachel Baldwin

CIRCULATION

Director Joey Prieto

NEWS EXECUTIVE

Editor John Brennan

EDITOR AND MANAGER

Sports Editor Billy Armendariz

PRODUCTION

Manager-Layout Margaret Borden

Market Information: TMC.
Mechanical available: Offset; Black and 3 ROP colors; insert accepted — preprinted; page cut-offs — 22½".
Mechanical specifications: Type page $12\frac{11}{16}$" x 21"; E - 6 cols, 2", ⅛" between; A - 6 cols, 2", ⅛" between; C - 8 cols, $1\frac{7}{16}$", ⅛" between.
Commodity consumption: Newsprint 115 metric tons; widths 13½", 27"; black ink 1,620 pounds; color ink 200 pounds; single pages printed 2,684; average pages per issue 10(d); single plates used 1,500.
Equipment: EDITORIAL: Front-end hardware — CText; Other equipment — 5-COM. CLASSIFIED: Front-end hardware — Graph X; Other equipment — 2-COM. DISPLAY: Front-end hardware — Ap/Mac; Other equipment — Ap/Mac LaserWriter. PRODUCTION: Typesetters — 1-COM/Hd, 2-COM/2-Laser; Plate exposures — Nu/Flip Top FT40M; Production cameras — R/Horizontal.
PRESSROOM: Line 1 — G/Community; Folders — 1-G/4:1. MAILROOM: Bundle tyer — Bu; Addressing machine — Dispensa-Matic. WIRE SERVICES: News — AP; Syndicates — AP; Receiving dishes — size-3m, AP. BUSINESS COMPUTERS: 3-IBM/PC; Applications: Bookkeeping, Circ.

FARMINGTON

San Juan County

'90 U.S. Census- 33,997; E&P '96 Est. 36,101
ABC-CZ (90): 33,997 (HH 11,979)

The Daily Times

(m-mon to sat; S)

The Daily Times, 201 N. Allen; PO Box 450, Farmington, NM 87401; tel (505) 325-4545.
Circulation: 17,297(m); 17,297(m-sat); 18,335(S); ABC Sept. 30, 1995.
Price: 50¢(d); 50¢(sat); $1.00(S); $8.00/mo; $88.00/yr.
Advertising: Open inch rate $13.50(m); $16.25(m-wed); $13.50(m-sat); $13.50(S). **Representative:** Papert Companies.
News Services: AP, NYT. **Politics:** Independent. **Established:** 1949.
Not Published: Christmas.
Advertising not accepted: Objectionable.
Special Editions: Health & Fitness (Jan); Bridal (Feb); Newspaper in Education, Oil & Gas (Mar); Travel Guide, Home and Garden (Apr); Hunting, Sports & Recreation (July); Back-to-School, Local Football (Aug); Literacy (Sept); Homemakers School (Oct); Christmas (Nov); Basketball (Dec).
Special Weekly Sections: Business (wed); Automobiles, Religion (fri); TV Update (sat); Off Hours Leisure Guide, Real Estate (S).
Magazines: Off Hours (fri); Parade (S).

CORPORATE OFFICERS

Board Chairman/President Eliot O'Brien
Vice Board Chairman Eliot O'Brien
Secretary Renee' Swickard

GENERAL MANAGEMENT

Publisher Eliot O'Brien
Business Manager Phillip Prier
Exec Editor Jack Swickard

ADVERTISING

Director Dennis Gross
Supervisor-Display Susanna Bayless
Coordinator-Design Carmen Shoquist
Manager-Classified Robert Lovett

TELECOMMUNICATIONS

Audiotex Manager Steve Bulloch

CIRCULATION

Manager Steve Mascarenas

NEWS EXECUTIVES

Editor Jack Swickard
Managing Editor Ralph Damiani

EDITORS AND MANAGERS

City Editor Christine Willmsen
News Editor Barry Heifner
Sports Editor Ed Thompson

MANAGEMENT INFORMATION SERVICES

Data Processing Manager Steve Bulloch
Online Manager Steve Bulloch

PRODUCTION

Superintendent-Pressroom Donna Tobin

Market Information: TMC; Operate database; Operate audiotex.
Mechanical available: Offset; Black and 3 ROP colors; insert accepted — preprinted, job shop; page cut-offs — 22¾".
Mechanical specifications: Type page 13" x 21½"; E - 6 cols, $2\frac{1}{16}$", ⅛" between; A - 6 cols, $2\frac{1}{16}$", ⅛" between; C - 9 cols, $7\frac{5}{16}$", ⅛" between.
Commodity consumption: Newsprint 1,078 short tons; widths 27", 13½"; black ink 23,187 pounds; color ink 2,700 pounds; single pages printed 8,115; average pages per issue 22(d), 30(S); single plates used 9,575.
Equipment: EDITORIAL: Front-end hardware — 1-Ap/Mac PowerBook 520c, 3-Ap/Mac PowerBook 145, 5-Ap/Mac Classic, 6-Ap/Mac LC, 2-Ap/Mac IIci, 1-Ap/Mac Centris 650, 1-Ap/Mac IIcx, 1-Ap/Mac Quadra 605, 4-Ap/Mac Quadra 610, 1-Ap/Mac Quadra 630, 3-Ap/Mac Quadra 700, 1-Ap/Mac Quadra 900, 1-CD-Rom Reader; Front-end software — Baseview/NewsEdit, Adobe/Photoshop, O-Photo, Caere/OmniPage, Microphone, Global Fax, First Class, Word Perfect; Printers — 1-Ap/Mac LaserWriter Pro; Other equipment — 1-Toshiba/Copier 003910, Lf/Leafscan 35, 1-Kk/DCS 200, 1-Ap/Mac One Scan. CLASSIFIED: Front-end hardware — 1-Ap/Mac LC, 1-Ap/Mac Power Mac 6100 CD, 1-Ap/Mac CPerForma 636 CD, 5-Ap/Mac Quadra 630, 5-CD-Rom Player, 1-Cannon/Video Floppy D-D, 1-Ap/Mac Quadra 900, 2-Ap/Mac Classic, 1-Ap/Mac LCIII, 1-Okidata/Pacemaker 3410, 3-Ap/Mac Quadra 610, 1-Ap/Mac Quadra 660AV, 1-Ap/Mac Quadra 800, 3-Ap/Mac Centris 650; Front-end software — QuarkXPress, Adobe/Photoshop, Adobe/FreeHand, Adobe/Illustrator, FirstClass; Printers — 1-HP/ScanJet Scanner, 1-Ap/Mac LaserWriter; Other equipment — 1-Toshiba/Copier, 1-Toshiba/Fax. AUDIOTEX: Hardware — IBM. DISPLAY: Adv layout systems — Ap/Mac network; Front-end hardware — 5-Ap/Mac LC, 1-Ap/Mac Centris 650, 1-Ap/Mac Centris 660, 2-Ap/Mac Centris 610, 1-Ap/Mac IIci; Front-end software — QuarkXPress, Adobe/Photoshop, Caere/OmniPage, Baseview; Printers — Ap/Mac LaserWriter II. PRODUCTION: Pagination software — QuarkXPress; Typesetters — 1-Sun/Sparc II, 2-Hyphen/Spectraset 2200, 2-Ap/Mac IIfx, 1-Ap/Power Mac 6100 w/CD, 1-Ap/Mac LaserMaster 1200XL, 1-Ap/Power Mac 7100 w/CD, 2-Ap/Mac Classic II, 3-Ap/Mac Quadra 650, 5-Ap/Mac LC, 1-Sun/Sparc 4; Plate exposures — 1-Nu/FT40V6 UPNS Plate Burner, 1-Nu/FT40 UPNS Plate Burner; Plate processors — 2-Nat; Electronic picture desk — Lf/AP Leaf Picture Desk; Scanners — 1-AG/Arcus, 1-AG/Horizon; Production cameras — 1-B, 1-K/530; Automatic film processors — 1-LE/LD-18, 1-AG, 1-Kk/400; Digital color separation equipment — Lf/Leafscan.
PRESSROOM: Line 1 — 6-G/Urbanite; Folders — 1-G. MAILROOM: Counter stackers — 1-HL/Monitor HT II; Inserters and stuffers — 2-MM/227; Bundle tyer — OVL/415; Other mailroom equipment — 1-Quarterfolder Cashline 552. LIBRARY: Electronic — Ap/Mac Classic, Optical Disk, IBM, SMS/Stauffer Gold; Combination — Minolta/RP407. COMMUNICATIONS: Facsimile — 1-Toshiba. WIRE SERVICES: News — AP Datastream, AP Photostream, AP; Stock tables — AP SelectStox; Syndicates — AP; Receiving dishes — size-12ft, AP. BUSINESS COMPUTERS: PC/Network, 2-AT, 1-Epson/LQ2550, 1-Ap/Mac IIsi, 2-Ap/Mac Quadra 610, 1-Ap/Mac PowerBook 520c, 1-Ap/Mac Quadra 900; Applications: Adv billing, Gen ledger; Lotus, WordPerfect, First Choice: Payroll; Baseview: Circ; Baseview: Accts receivable; PCs & micros networked; PCs & main system networked.

GALLUP

McKinley County

'90 U.S. Census- 19,154; **E&P '96 Est.** 19,895
ABC-CZ (90): 19,154 (HH 6,204)

Gallup Independent

(e-mon to sat)

Gallup Independent, 500 N. 9th; PO Box 1210, Gallup, NM 87305; tel (505) 863-6811; fax (505) 722-5750.

Circulation: 14,571(e); 14,571(e-sat); ABC Sept. 30, 1995.

Price: 35¢(d); 75¢(sat); $8.50/mo; $102.00/yr.

Advertising: Open inch rate $11.55(e); $11.55(e-sat).

News Services: AP, NYT. **Politics:** Independent. **Established:** 1889.

Not Published: New Year; Memorial Day; Independence Day; Labor Day; Thanksgiving; Christmas.

Advertising not accepted: Objectionable.

Special Edition: Native Sun (June to Sept).

Magazine: USA Weekend (S).

CORPORATE OFFICERS

Chairman John K Zollinger
Vice Pres Robert C Zollinger

GENERAL MANAGEMENT

Publisher Robert C Zollinger

ADVERTISING

Manager Tina Garcia

MARKETING AND PROMOTION

Manager-Marketing/Promotion Carol Gonzales

NEWS EXECUTIVE

Managing Editor Ted Ruston

EDITORS AND MANAGERS

Education Editor Toni Belleranti
Photo Editor Guy Jacobs
Sports Editor Allan Arthur

PRODUCTION

Superintendent Lawrence Castaneda

Market Information: Zoned editions; TMC.

Mechanical available: Offset; Black and 3 ROP colors; insert accepted — preprinted; page cut-offs — 22¾".

Mechanical specifications: Type page 13" x 21½"; E - 6 cols, 2 1/16", 1/8" between; A - 6 cols, 2 1/16", 1/8" between; C - 7 cols, 1¾", 1/8" between.

Commodity consumption: widths 31½", 27".

Equipment: EDITORIAL: Front-end hardware — HI; Front-end software — HI; Printers — MON. CLASSIFIED: Front-end hardware — HI; Front-end software — HI. DISPLAY: Front-end hardware — HI. PRODUCTION: Typesetters — 2-MON/2850; Plate exposures — 2-Nu; Plate processors — 2-Nat; Production cameras — R/Lens, OH, LE/500; Automatic film processors — 1-LE/PC-13, 1-LE/LD-18; Color separation equipment (conventional) — Lf/AP Leaf Picture Desk, 2-Nikon/Coolscan.
PRESSROOM: Line 1 — 9-G/Community; Folders — 1-G/SC, 1-G/Community. MAILROOM: Inserters and stuffers — 1-MM/227-E; Bundle tyer — 2-Wilton/Stra Pack. LIBRARY: Combination — 1-Kk/C. WIRE SERVICES: News — AP, NYT; Syndicates — AP; Receiving dishes — size-3m, AP. BUSINESS COMPUTERS: 2-IBM/34; Applications: Newsprint, Accts payable, Legal ads, Classified, Circ, Adv billing, Accts receivable, Gen ledger, Payroll, Financial.

HOBBS

Lea County

'90 U.S. Census- 29,115; **E&P '96 Est.** 29,126
ABC-CZ (90): 29,115 (HH 10,242)

Hobbs Daily News-Sun

(e-mon to fri; S)

Hobbs Daily News-Sun, 201 N. Thorp; PO Box 860, Hobbs, NM 88240; tel (505) 393-2123; fax (505) 393-5724. Shearman Newspapers group.

Circulation: 10,832(e); 11,465(S); ABC Sept. 30, 1995.

Price: 50¢(d); $1.00(S); $7.00/mo; $84.00/yr.

Advertising: Open inch rate $9.48(e); $10.43 (e-wed); $9.48(S).

News Services: AP, KRT. **Politics:** Independent. **Established:** 1929.

Advertising not accepted: X-rated movies.

Special Editions: Health & Fitness, Money & Finance (Jan); Progress Issue, Spring Fashion (Mar); Home & Garden (Apr); Recreation, Leisure & Summer, High School & College Graduation (May); Sidewalk Sale (July); Back-to-School (Aug); Football, Fall Fashion (Sept); Car Care (Oct); Christmas Gift Guide (Nov).

Special Weekly Sections: Business/Industry (mon); Best Food Edition (wed); Education (thur); Religion (fri); Entertainment (S).

Magazines: Parade, TV Week (S).

GENERAL MANAGEMENT

Publisher Maynard Woodhatch
General Manager Kathi Bearden
Controller Sandra Catlett

ADVERTISING

Director Linda Koenig

CIRCULATION

Director George Cotton

NEWS EXECUTIVE

Editor Manny Marquez

EDITORS AND MANAGERS

Business/Finance Writer Daniel Russell
Columnist Terry Sholin
Design Editor Scott Jones
Editorial Page Editor Manny Marquez
Entertainment/Amusements Editor Ruth Friedberg
Environmental Editor Daniel Russell
Farm/Agriculture Editor Daniel Russell
Fashion/Style Editor Ruth Friedberg
Features Editor Ruth Friedberg
Food/Lifestyles Editor Ruth Friedberg
Graphics Editor/Art Director Donita Evans
Living Editor Ruth Friedberg
News Editor Terry Sholin
News/Regional Editor Terry Sholin
Photo Department Manager Bill Ross
Photo Department Manager Tim Fischer
Political/Government Editor Scott Freeman
Radio/Television Editor Ruth Friedberg
Religion Editor Ruth Friedberg
Sports Editor Rick Ingebritson
Teen-age/Youth Editor Ruth Friedberg
Travel Editor Scott Jones
Women's Editor Evelyn Rising

PRODUCTION

Manager Bennie Gaddy

Market Information: TMC.

Mechanical available: Offset; Black and 3 ROP colors; insert accepted — preprinted; page cut-offs — 21½".

Mechanical specifications: Type page 13" x 21½"; E - 6 cols, 2 1/16", 1/8" between; A - 6 cols, 2 1/16", 1/8" between; C - 9 cols, 1 5/16", 1/8" between.

Commodity consumption: Newsprint 585 short tons; widths 27½", 13¾"; black ink 18,000 pounds; color ink 2,400 pounds; single pages printed 7,260; average pages per issue 20(d), 44(S); single plates used 9,600.

Equipment: EDITORIAL: Front-end hardware — Ap/Mac; Front-end software — Baseview; Printers — XIT/Clipper, V/5300B, Panther/Imagesetter, Ap/Mac Color LaserPrinter, Tektronic/Phaser 300. CLASSIFIED: Front-end hardware — Ap/Mac; Front-end software — Baseview; Printers — Okidata, Imagesetter/II, Ap/Mac LaserPrinter; Other equipment — 2-OS. DISPLAY: Front-end hardware — Ap/Mac; Front-end software — QuarkXPress, Multi-Ad, Aldus/FreeHand; Printers — Ap/Mac LaserPrinter; Other equipment — Microtek/Scanmaker, 3-CD-Rom, Umax/Color Scanner, Pinnacle/CD Recorder. PRODUCTION: Typesetters — XIT/Clipper, Ap/Mac LaserWriter, ImageSetter II, V/5300B, Ap/Mac Color LaserWriter, Panther, Tektronic/Phaser 300; Plate exposures — Nu/Flip Top FT40V6UP; Plate processors — Nat/250; Scanners — 1-Nikon/Coolscan, 1-Lf/Leafscan; Automatic film processors — 1-LE/BQ24, V/7210; Color separation equipment (conventional) — Ap/Mac, Lf/Leafscan 35, Nikon/Coolscan.
PRESSROOM: Line 1 — 6-G/Urbanite; Press control system — Console. MAILROOM: Inserters and stuffers — 1-MM; Bundle tyer — Wilton/Stra Pack. COMMUNICATIONS: Systems used — satellite. WIRE SERVICES: News — AP Datastream, AP Datafeatures, KRT; Photos — AP; Stock tables — AP; Syndicates — King Features, United Features, CNS, TMS, Universal Press, KRT; Receiving dishes — AP. BUSINESS COMPUTERS: BFR, GAT, Standard, IBM; Applications: Certiflex: Payroll, Gen ledger, Accts receivable; Lotus, Zen Write & Calc, WordPerfect, BMF: Accts receivable; PCs & micros networked.

LAS CRUCES

Dona Ana County

'90 U.S. Census- 62,126; **E&P '96 Est.** 74,928
ABC-CZ (90): 62,126 (HH 23,797)

Las Cruces Sun-News

(m-mon to fri; m-sat; S)

Las Cruces Sun-News, 256 W. Las Cruces Ave., Las Cruces, NM 88005; tel (505) 523-4581; fax (505) 523-7913. MediaNews Inc. group.

Circulation: 20,507(m); 19,176(m-sat); 21,438(S); ABC Sept. 30, 1995.

Price: 35¢(d); 35¢(sat); $1.00(S); $6.75/mo.

Advertising: Open inch rate $21.95(m); $21.95(m-sat); $21.95(S). **Representative:** Papert Companies.

News Services: NYT, AP. **Politics:** Independent. **Established:** 1937.

Advertising not accepted: Multi-sig inserts.

Special Editions: Annual Business Review (Feb); Bridal Tab (Mar); Car Care (July); Southern N.M. Fair (Sept); Whole Enchilada (Oct); Christmas Greetings, Cookbook, Gift Guide (Dec).

Magazines: TV Weekly (fri); Parade (S).

GENERAL MANAGEMENT

Publisher George Smith
Manager-Human Resources Judy Luna
Manager-Credit Verlaine Davies

ADVERTISING

Manager-Retail/Display Roy Granado
Manager-Classified Leigh Davis

CIRCULATION

Manager Robert A Duran

NEWS EXECUTIVE

Editor Harold Cousland

EDITORS AND MANAGERS

Amusements/Films Editor Michele Daniels
City Editor Charles Brunt
Education Editor Todd Dickson
Features Editor Michele Daniels
Librarian Gloria Araiza
Political Editor Debra Bordanaro
Sports Editor Craig Massey
Theater Editor Michele Daniels

MANAGEMENT INFORMATION SERVICES

Data Processing Manager Leigh Ruther

PRODUCTION

Superintendent-Composing Leigh Ruther
Superintendent-Pressroom Tommy Jaurigue

Market Information: TMC.

Mechanical available: Offset; Black and 3 ROP colors; insert accepted — preprinted, any; page cut-offs — 22¾".

Mechanical specifications: Type page 13" x 21½"; E - 6 cols, 2 1/16", 1/8" between; A - 6 cols, 2 1/16", 1/8" between; C - 9 cols, 1 3/8", 1/16" between.

Commodity consumption: Newsprint 1,400 metric tons; width 27½"; black ink 26,555 pounds; color ink 2,200 pounds; single pages printed 11,232; average pages per issue 28(d), 32(sat), 48(S); single plates used 1,059.

Equipment: EDITORIAL: Front-end hardware — PC/486, Ethernet; Printers — LaserMaster/1200XL, HP/LaserJet 4si; Other equipment — 7-IBM/Selectric. CLASSIFIED: Front-end hardware — 1-PC/486; Printers — LaserMaster/1200 XL. DISPLAY: Adv layout systems — 2-PC/486. PRODUCTION: Typesetters — 5-Ap/Mac LaserWriter, 1-Ap/Mac LaserWriter 1200 XL, 1-HP/LaserJet 4si; Plate exposures — 1-Nu/Flip Top FT40LSN, 1-Nu/Flip Top FT40; Plate processors — 1-Nat/A-250; Scanners — 2-Cp/Alpha; Production cameras — 3-C/Spartan; Automatic film processors — 1-LE/LD-24BQ; Film transporters — 1-C; Shrink lenses — 1-CK Optical, Alan/Prime Variable Squeeze 610mm; Color separation equipment (conventional) — C/E-Z Color.
PRESSROOM: Line 1 — 8-G/U1187; Folders — 1-G. MAILROOM: Bundle tyer — 1-Bu, 1-Ace/50; Addressing machine — 1-El/Communications. WIRE SERVICES: News — AP; Stock tables — AP; Syndicates — NYT; Receiving dishes — size-10ft, AP. BUSINESS COMPUTERS: PC/Network, PC/486; Applications: Real World (6.5): Accts payable, Payroll, Accts receivable, Gen ledger; PCs & micros networked; PCs & main system networked.

LAS VEGAS

San Miguel County

'90 U.S. Census- 14,753; **E&P '96 Est.** 15,076

Las Vegas Optic (e-mon to fri)

Las Vegas Optic, 612 Lincoln; PO Box 2607, Las Vegas, NM 87701; tel (505) 425-6796; fax (505) 425-1005.

Circulation: 6,103(e); Sworn Oct. 1, 1995.

Price: 25¢(d); $59.40/yr.

Advertising: Open inch rate $9.85(e).

News Service: AP. **Politics:** Independent. **Established:** 1879.

Not Published: New Year; Independence Day; Labor Day; Thanksgiving; Christmas.

Special Editions: Chambers of Commerce, George Washington (Feb); Fire Prevention, Graduation, Little League, Law Enforcement (May); Fiesta (July); Santa's Workshop (Dec).

CORPORATE OFFICERS

President Stuart R Beck
Vice Pres Robert H Beck
Secretary Charles Taylor
Treasurer Charles Taylor

GENERAL MANAGEMENT

Publisher Stuart R Beck
General Manager Charles Taylor

ADVERTISING

Manager Anna Hule
Manager-Classified Berna Trujillo

CIRCULATION

Manager Luis Martinez

NEWS EXECUTIVES

Editor Stuart R Beck
Managing Editor Sharon Vander Meer

EDITORS AND MANAGERS

Books Editor Stuart R Beck
Editorial Page Editor Stuart R Beck

Market Information: TMC; ADS.

Mechanical available: Offset; Black and 1 ROP color; insert accepted — preprinted; page cut-offs — 21½".

Mechanical specifications: Type page 15½" x 22½"; E - 6 cols, 2 1/16", 1/8" between; A - 6 cols, 2 1/6", 1/8" between; C - 6 cols, 2 1/6", 1/8" between.

Commodity consumption: Newsprint 120 metric tons; width 27½"; average pages per issue 12(d).

Equipment: EDITORIAL: Front-end hardware — Mk; Front-end software — Mk; Printers — Ap/Mac LaserPrinter. CLASSIFIED: Front-end hardware — Mk; Front-end software — Mk; Printers — Ap/Mac LaserPrinter. PRODUCTION: Typesetters — Ap/Mac Laser; Plate exposures — 1-Nu; Production cameras — AG; Automatic film processors — AG, Vastec.
PRESSROOM: Line 1 — G/Community; Line 2 — G/Community; Line 3 — G/Community; Line 4 — G/Community. WIRE SERVICES: News — AP; Receiving dishes — AP. BUSINESS COMPUTERS: 2-PC; Applications: AccPac: Payroll, Adv billing; Interlink: Circ.

LOS ALAMOS

Los Alamos County

'90 U.S. Census- 11,455; **E&P '96 Est.** 11,780

Los Alamos Monitor

(e-tues to fri; S)

Los Alamos Monitor, 256 D.P. Rd.; PO Box 1268, Los Alamos, NM 87544; tel (505) 662-4185; fax (505) 662-4334; e-mail lamonitr@rt66.com; web site http://www.rt66.com//amonitr. Landmark Communications Inc. group.

Circulation: 4,897(e); 4,897(S); Sworn Sept. 29, 1995.

Price: 50¢(d); 50¢(S); $59.95/yr.

Advertising: Open inch rate $9.00(e); $9.00(S). **Representative:** Landon Associates Inc.

News Services: AP, NYT. **Politics:** Independent. **Established:** 1963.

Not Published: Christmas.

Special Weekly Sections: Religion (fri); Business (S).

Magazine: "Calliope" (TV/Entertainment section) (thur).

GENERAL MANAGEMENT

Editor/Publisher Evelyn Vigil

ADVERTISING

Director Evelyn Vigil

CIRCULATION

Director Sally Moore

NEWS EXECUTIVE

Managing Editor Charmian Schaller

PRODUCTION

Foreman-Pressroom Dan Brown

Market Information: TMC.

Mechanical available: Offset; Black and 3 ROP colors; insert accepted — preprinted; page cut-offs — 22¾".

Mechanical specifications: Type page 13" x 21½"; E - 6 cols, 2.03", 1/6" between; A - 6 cols, 2.03", 1/6" between; C - 8 cols, 1.46", 1/6" between.

Commodity consumption: Newsprint 132 short tons; width 27½"; black ink 4,600 pounds; color ink 200 pounds; average pages per issue 10(d), 18(S).

Equipment: EDITORIAL: Front-end hardware — Ap/Mac; Printers — TI/OMNI 800; Other equipment — RSK/Tandy WP-2, 1-Mk/A-3420. CLASSIFIED: Front-end hardware — AST/Bravo 4-33; Printers — Okidata/Microline 591. DISPLAY: Adv layout systems — 1-Ap/Mac IIsi, 1-Ap/Mac SE, 2-Mk/Adcomp, 1-Mk/TouchWriter Plus; Front-end hardware — Ap/Mac; Printers — 3-Ap/Mac LaserPrinter. PRODUCTION: Typesetters — 3-Ap/Mac LaserPrinter; Plate exposures — 1-Nu/Flip Top; Production cameras — Nu/2024.
PRESSROOM: Line 1 — 4-G/Community; Folders — 1-G. MAILROOM: Counter stackers — BG/104A. COMMUNICATIONS: Facsimile — ATT/3520D. WIRE SERVICES: News — NYT, AP; Receiving dishes — size-10ft, AP. BUSINESS COMPUTERS: VGA/PC, Dell/Hard Disk 3165X; Applications: Dell/Hard Disc 3165X; PCs & micros networked; PCs & main system networked.

LOVINGTON

Lea County

'90 U.S. Census- 9,322; E&P '96 Est. 9,065

The Lovington Daily Leader

(e-tues to fri; S)

Lovington Daily Leader, 14 W. Ave. B; PO Box 1717, Lovington, NM 88260; tel (505) 396-2844; fax (505) 396-5775.

Circulation: 1,877(e); 1,877(S); Sworn Oct. 1, 1995.

Price: 50¢(d); 50¢(S); $5.50/mo; $66.00/yr.

Advertising: Open inch rate $5.00(e); $5.00(S).

News Service: AP. **Politics:** Independent. **Established:** 1909.

Not Published: New Year; Thanksgiving; Christmas.

Special Editions: Basketball State Sig Page (Mar); Car Special, Secretaries Week (Apr); Restaurant Edition, Wildcats Page, LHS Graduation, New Mexico Junior College Graduation, College of The Southwest Graduation (May); Father's Day Special (June); Lovington Business & Progress Edition, All-Stars Sports Edition, Home Edition (July); Fair & Rodeo Special, Buyer's Pages, Wildcat Special (Aug); Football Contest, Tatum Football (Sept); 4-H Sig Page, Oil Edition, Boss' Week, National Cosmetology Month (Oct); Christmas Wish Book, Wildcat Sig Pages, Electric Light Parades, Basketball Special (Nov); Christmas Edition (Dec).

CORPORATE OFFICERS

President	Ken Green
Vice Pres	Roy McQueen
Secretary/Treasurer	Walt Green

GENERAL MANAGEMENT

Publisher/General Manager	John Graham

ADVERTISING

Manager	Joyce Clemens

CIRCULATION

Manager	Wilma Palmer

NEWS EXECUTIVE

Editor	Jeanne Graham

EDITORS AND MANAGERS

Society Editor	Louise Killingsworth
Sports Editor	Mark Carter

Market Information: TMC.

Mechanical available: Offset; Black and 3 ROP colors; insert accepted — preprinted; page cut-offs — 22 1/2".

Mechanical specifications: Type page 13" x 21"; E - 6 cols, 2 1/16", 1/8" between; A - 6 cols, 2 1/16", 1/8" between; C - 6 cols, 2 1/16", 1/8" between.

Commodity consumption: Newsprint 80 short tons; 73 metric tons; width 28"; black ink 3,600 pounds; color ink 50 pounds; single pages printed 3,120; average pages per issue 8(d), 16(S); single plates used 2,600.

Equipment: EDITORIAL: Front-end hardware — Wyse/IBM Compatible. CLASSIFIED: Front-end hardware — Wyse. DISPLAY: Adv layout systems — Wyse. PRODUCTION: Typesetters — QMS/810 Turbo; Plate exposures — 2-Nu/30x40; Plate processors — Nat/250; Scanners — Microtek/MSF-300G; Production cameras — 1-Miller; Automatic film processors — Kk/42 RC.
PRESSROOM: Line 1 — HI/Offset. MAILROOM: Bundle tyer — 1-BU; Addressing machine — 1-Am. COMMUNICATIONS: Facsimile — Sharp/40215. WIRE SERVICES: News — AP; Receiving dishes — size-2 1/2ft, AP. BUSINESS COMPUTERS: 1-Epson/Equity I; Applications: Front office mgmt.

PORTALES

Roosevelt County

'90 U.S. Census- 10,690; E&P '96 Est. 11,254

Portales News-Tribune

(e-tues to fri; S)

Portales News-Tribune, 101 E. First St.; PO Box 848, Portales, NM 88130; tel (505) 356-4481; fax (505) 356-3630. Southern Newspapers Inc. group.

Circulation: 2,771(e); 2,771(S); Sworn Oct. 1, 1995.

Price: 50¢(d); $1.00(S); $5.90/mo; $86.00/yr.

Advertising: Open inch rate $6.24(e); $6.24(S). **Representative:** Papert Companies.

News Service: AP. **Politics:** Independent. **Established:** 1935 (News), 1955 (Tribune).

GENERAL MANAGEMENT

Publisher	Lone Beasley
Publisher Emeritus/Special Projects Coordinator	Lone Beasley
Bookkeeper	Milly Hillesheim

ADVERTISING

Director	Lone Beasley

CIRCULATION

Manager	John Harvey

NEWS EXECUTIVE

Editor	Daren Watkins

EDITOR AND MANAGER

Home Furnishings Editor	Anna Nixon

PRODUCTION

Foreman	Mark Morrison

Market Information: TMC.

Mechanical available: Offset; Black and 3 ROP colors; insert accepted — preprinted; page cut-offs — 22 3/4".

Mechanical specifications: Type page 13 1/16" x 21 1/2"; E - 6 cols, 2 1/16", 1/6" between; A - 6 cols, 2 1/16", 1/6" between; C - 8 cols, 1 1/2", 1/6" between.

Commodity consumption: average pages per issue 32(d), 60(S).

Equipment: EDITORIAL: Front-end hardware — Mk; Front-end software — Mk; Printers — 2-Ap/Mac LaserPrinter; Other equipment — Panther/Plus ImageSetter. CLASSIFIED: Front-end hardware — Mk; Front-end software — Mk; Printers — 1-Ap/Mac LaserPrinter. PRODUCTION: Typesetters — Mk, Ap/Mac LaserPrinters, Panther/Plus ImageSetter; Plate exposures — 1-Nu; Plate processors — 1-Nat; Electronic picture desk — Lf/AP Leaf Picture Desk; Scanners — 2-Ap/Mac Scanner; Production cameras — 1-C/Spartan II; Automatic film processors — 1-LE; Film transporters — C, LE; Color separation equipment (conventional) — C/E-Z Color.
PRESSROOM: Line 1 — 5-G/Community; Line 2 — 2-G/Community. MAILROOM: Counter stackers — 1-MM; Inserters and stuffers — MM; Bundle tyer — 1-Bu/TS-210; Addressing machine — 1-Mk/ACE 50. LIBRARY: Electronic — COM/Microfilm. WIRE SERVICES: News — AP; Stock tables — AP SelectStox; Receiving dishes — AP. BUSINESS COMPUTERS: 2-NCR/1 Tower, PC; Applications: BMF; PCs & micros networked; PCs & main system networked.

ROSWELL

Chaves County

'90 U.S. Census- 44,654; E&P '96 Est. 49,056

Roswell Daily Record

(m-mon to fri; S)

Roswell Daily Record, 2301 N. Main St.; Box 1897, Roswell, NM 88201; tel (505) 622-7710; fax (505) 625-0421.

Circulation: 14,303(m); 14,638(S); Sworn Sept. 30, 1995.

Price: 35¢(d); $1.00(S); $13.00/mo (mail); $156.00/yr (mail).

Advertising: Open inch rate $11.45(m); $11.45(S). **Representative:** Papert Companies.

News Service: AP. **Politics:** Independent. **Established:** 1891.

Not Published: Christmas.

Special Editions: Blue Tag Special (Jan); Income Tax Section, Valentine's Specials, Washington's Birthday (Feb); American Home Week, Roving Sands, Easter Specials (Apr); Graduation, Mother's Day (May); Dining Guide, Summer Specials (June); Pet Tab, Fiesta Days (July); Back-to-School and College, Sports Tab (Aug); Car Care Tab, Fall Values, Air Show (Sept); Fair Days, Adopt a Dog Page, Harvest Values (Oct); Pre-Christmas Coupon Book (Nov); Last Minute Gift Ideas, Christmas Time Page (Dec).

Special Weekly Section: TV/Lineup (fri).

Magazine: USA Weekend (S).

CORPORATE OFFICERS

President	Robert H Beck
Vice Pres	J W Jackson
Secretary	Jean M Pettit
Treasurer	W M Denny Jr

GENERAL MANAGEMENT

Publisher	Cory R Beck
Business Manager	Jean M Pettit
Purchasing Agent	Cory R Beck

ADVERTISING

Director	Marion Saint
Manager-Classified	Jim Richards

CIRCULATION

Manager	Alex Clark
Manager	Mark Raney

NEWS EXECUTIVES

Editor	Jerry McCormack
Managing Editor	Greg Peretti

EDITORS AND MANAGERS

Action Line Editor	Jerry McCormack
Area/Sunday Editor	Mike Bush
Automotive Editor	Jerry McCormack
Business/Finance Editor	Richard Olmsted
City/Metro Editor	Mike Bush
Editorial Page Editor	Jerry McCormack
Education Editor	Jerry McCormack
Entertainment/Amusements Editor	Jerry McCormack
Environmental Editor	Jerry McCormack
Farm/Agriculture Editor	Richard Olmsted
Fashion/Food Editor	Marifrank DaHarb
Features Editor	Jerry McCormack
Graphics Editor/Art Director	Jerry McCormack
Health/Medical Editor	Marifrank DaHarb
Home/Garden Editor	Marifrank DaHarb
National Editor	Jerry McCormack
News Editor	Mike Bush
Photo Editor	Mike Pettit
Political/Government Editor	Jerry McCormack
Religion Editor	Jerry McCormack
Science/Technology Editor	Jerry McCormack
Sports Editor	Harry Readel
Television/Film Editor	Jerry McCormack
Theater/Music Editor	Jerry McCormack
Travel Editor	Jerry McCormack
Women's/Society Editor	Marifrank DaHarb

MANAGEMENT INFORMATION SERVICES

Manager	Marion Saint

PRODUCTION

Director	Frank Castillo

Market Information: Operate database.

Mechanical available: Offset; Black and 3 ROP colors; insert accepted — preprinted; page cut-offs — 22 3/4".

Mechanical specifications: Type page 13 1/16" x 21 1/2"; E - 6 cols, 2 1/16", 1/6" between; A - 6 cols, 2 1/16", 1/6" between; C - 8 cols, 1 1/2", 1/6" between.

Commodity consumption: Newsprint 776 short tons; 69.8 metric tons; widths 13 3/4", 27 1/2", 34", 13 1/2", 17"; black ink 24,000 pounds; color ink 300 pounds; single pages printed 7,714; average pages per issue 24(d), 36(S); single plates used 8,000.

Equipment: EDITORIAL: Front-end hardware — Mk, Ap/Mac IIcx; Front-end software — Mk/NewsTouch, Mk/NewsTouch II; Other equipment — Lf/AP Leaf Picture Desk, Lf/Leafscan, Lf/AP Laserphoto. CLASSIFIED: Front-end hardware — 1-Mk/3000 System; Front-end software — Synaptic/Classified Program, Eye Computer Systems Hardware; Printers — 1-Panasonic/KX-P1624, 1-Ap/Mac LaserWriter Plus. PRODUCTION: Typesetters — 1-Mk/NewsTouch II, 1-Ap/Mac II, 4-Ap/Mac LaserPrinter; Plate exposures — 1-Nu; Plate processors — 1-Nat; Scanners — 2-Ap/Mac Scanner; Production cameras — 1-C/Spartan II, VG/II; Automatic film processors — 1-LE/24; Film transporters — 1-LE; Shrink lenses — 1-CK Optical; Color separation equipment (conventional) — 1-C/E-Z Color.
PRESSROOM: Line 1 — 6-G/Urbanite (1 balloon former); Folders — 1-G. MAILROOM: Counter stackers — 1-MM; Inserters and stuffers — 1-MM/5 Pocket, 1-MM/1509 Minuteman Saddle Stitcher; Bundle tyer — 1-EAM/Mosca Rom, 1-ACE/50; Addressing machine — 1-Tandy/4000LX. LIBRARY: Electronic — Comgraphix/microfilm. COMMUNICATIONS: Facsimile — Toshiba/TF-251 (8 1/2 x 11; 8 1/2 x 14). WIRE SERVICES: News — AP; Photos — AP; Stock tables — AP; Syndicates — TMS, United Features, Universal Press, King Features; Receiving dishes — AP. BUSINESS COMPUTERS: Mk/Acer-View, Epson/Printer, BMF/Newspaper System. Applications: Display billing, Payroll, Legals, Class, Gen ledger.

SANTA FE

Santa Fe County

'90 U.S. Census- 55,859; E&P '96 Est. 61,959

ABC-CZ (90): 66,007 (HH 26,707)

The Santa Fe New Mexican

(m-mon to sat; S)

The Santa Fe New Mexican, 202 E. Marcy St.; PO Box 2048, Santa Fe, NM 87504; tel (505) 983-3303; fax (505) 984-1785.

Circulation: 23,979(m); 23,979(m-sat); 26,328(S); ABC Sept. 30, 1995.

Price: 50¢(d); 50¢(sat); $1.00(S); $2.75/wk; $11.92/mo; $143.00/yr.

Advertising: Open inch rate $26.40(m); $26.40(m-sat); $28.30(S). **Representative:** Cresmer, Woodward, O'Mara & Ormsbee.

News Services: AP, NYT, LAT-WP. **Politics:** Independent. **Established:** 1849.

Special Editions: Brides & Grooms (Feb); The Student Press (Mar); The Business of Santa Fe, Homebuilders, KidSummer (Apr); Bienvenidos (May); Chefs de Santa Fe (June); Spanish Market (July); Indian Market (Aug); Fiesta (Sept); New Car Models (Oct); Winterlife (Nov); Feliz Navidad (Dec); Vista (monthly); Nest Egg (bi-monthly).

Special Weekly Sections: Neighbors, El Nuevo Mexicano (mon); Food Day/Taste (wed); Outdoors (thur); Automotive, Religion, Teen Page (sat); Outlook, Que Pasa, Travel, Real Estate Talk, Mutual Fund Wrap-up (S).

Magazines: Pasatiempo-Weekend Art & Entertainment Magazine (fri); TV Book, Vista (sat); USA Weekend, Comics (S).

CORPORATE OFFICERS

Board Chairman	Robert M McKinney
President	Stephen E Watkins
Secretary	Bruce Herr
Treasurer	William Simmons

GENERAL MANAGEMENT

Publisher	Robert M McKinney
Assoc Publisher	Billie Blair
Controller	Pamela Fernandez
Manager-Systems	Robert Taylor

ADVERTISING

Director	Virginia Sohn-Shahi
Manager-Retail	Joseph Vigil
Manager-Classified	Michael Grover
Manager-Credit	Caroline Cartwright

MARKETING AND PROMOTION

Manager-Marketing/Promotion	Linda Kiraly

TELECOMMUNICATIONS

Audiotex Manager	B G Meeks

CIRCULATION

Director	Chuck Peterson

NEWS EXECUTIVE

Managing Editor	Rob Dean

EDITORS AND MANAGERS

Arts Editor	Denise Kusel
Business/Finance Editor	Bob Quick
City Editor	Inez Russell
Asst City Editor	K C Compton
Asst City Editor	Howard Houghton
Editorial Page Editor	Bill Waters
Entertainment Editor	Denise Kusel
Features Editor	Nancy Plevin
Graphics Editor	Bill Reifsnyder
News Editor	Dagny Scott
Photo Editor	Clyde Mueller
Sports Editor	Pancho Morris

MANAGEMENT INFORMATION SERVICES

Data Processing Manager	Robert Taylor

PRODUCTION

Director	Edward R Booth

Market Information: TMC; ADS; Operate audiotex.

Mechanical available: Offset; Black and 9 ROP colors; insert accepted — preprinted, pre-scrted A/B; page cut-offs — 22 3/4".

Mechanical specifications: Type page 13" x 21 1/2"; E - 6 cols, 2 1/16", 1/8" between; A - 6 cols, 2 1/16", 1/8" between; C - 9 cols, 1 3/8", 1/16" between.

Commodity consumption: Newsprint 2,217 metric tons; width 27"; black ink 51,644 pounds; color ink 8,263 pounds; single pages printed 13,000; average pages per issue 32(d), 56(S); single plates used 76,346.

Equipment: EDITORIAL: Front-end hardware — CText; Front-end software — CText; Printers — Panasonic/KX-P4410 Laser; Other equipment — Lf/Leafscan 35. CLASSIFIED: Front-end hardware — CText; Front-end software — CText; Printers — C.Itoh/5000. AUDIOTEX: Hardware — PC/486 DX-2-66, Info-Connect; Software — Info-Connect. DISPLAY: Adv layout systems — 3-Ap/Mac Quadra 800, 3-Ap/Mac Quadra 950; Front-end hardware — Ap/Mac; Front-end software — QuarkXPress 3.3; Printers — 1-QMS/860, 2-Hyphen/SpectraSet 2000; Other equipment — 2-Umax, 2-LaCie, 2-Nikon/Coolscan. PRODUCTION: Typesetters — 2-Hyphen/SpectraSet 2000; Plate exposures — 1-Nu/Flip Top FT40V6UP; Plate processors — 1-Anitee/NP-B5; Scanners — 1-ECR/Autokon 1000DE; Production cameras — 1-C/Spartan II, 1-R/VWR440; Automatic film processors — 1-LE/LD-1800, 1-C, 2-P/1800 IS; Shrink lenses — 1-CK Optical/SQU-7; Color separation equipment (conventional) — 1-C/E-Z Color; Digital color separation equipment — 1-Lf/Leafscan 35. PRESSROOM: Line 1 — 7-G/U870=U870A; Press drives — 2-ABB, 2-HP/200 Baldor Motors; Folders — 1-G; Reels and stands — 7-G w/Jardis/Tension Control; Press control system — Ry/Spray Bar System; Press registration system — Carlson Pin System. MAILROOM: Counter stackers — 1-Id, 2-QWI/300, QWI/350; Inserters and stuffers — 1-GMA/SLS 1000 8-into-1; Bundle tyer — 1-MLN/Spirit, 2-Power Strap/PSN-6E. LIBRARY: Electronic — 1-NewsView. WIRE SERVICES: News — AP; Stock tables — AP SelectStox I; Syndicates — NYT, LATS, WP, RN, KRT; Receiving dishes — size-12ft, AP. BUSINESS COMPUTERS: 2-DEC/Micro VAX 3100 Model 90; Applications: CJ/AIM-CIS: Gen ledger, Payroll, Accts payable, Class billing; PCs & micros networked; PCs & main system networked.

SILVER CITY

Grant County

'90 U.S. Census- 10,683; E&P '96 Est. 11,408

Silver City Daily Press & Independent (e-mon to sat)

Silver City Daily Press & Independent, 300 W. Market; Box 740, Silver City, NM 88062; tel (505) 388-1576; fax (505) 388-1196.

Circulation: 7,075(e); 7,075(e-sat); Sworn Sept. 30, 1994.

Price: 45¢(d); 45¢(sat); $1.50/wk (carrier); $6.00/mo (carrier); $77.00/yr (mail in county), $94.00/yr (out of county).

Advertising: Open inch rate $6.90(e); $6.90(e-sat).

News Service: AP. **Politics:** Independent. **Established:** 1896 (weekly), 1935 (daily).

Not Published: New Year; Independence Day; Labor Day; Thanksgiving; Christmas.

Special Weekly Section: Arts & Entertainment (thur).

Magazine: TV Guide (fri).

GENERAL MANAGEMENT

Publisher Betty J Ely

ADVERTISING

Director Christina B Ely

CIRCULATION

Manager Billy Ogas

EDITOR AND MANAGER

News Editor Richard Correa

PRODUCTION

Manager Bill Archibald

Market Information: TMC.

Mechanical available: Offset; Black and 2 ROP colors; insert accepted — preprinted, all; page cut-offs — 21".

Mechanical specifications: Type page 14½" x 21"; E - 6 cols, 2¼", ⅛" between; A - 7 cols, 1⅝", ⅛" between; C - 7 cols, 1⅝", ⅛" between.

Commodity consumption: Newsprint 180 short tons; 200 metric tons; width 28"; average pages per issue 10(d).

Equipment: EDITORIAL: Front-end hardware — Ap/Mac; Front-end software — Baseview/Wire Manager; Printers — Ap/Mac Laser. CLASSIFIED: Front-end hardware — Ap/Mac; Printers — Ap/Mac Laser. DISPLAY: Front-end hardware — Ap/Mac LC II; Front-end software — Aldus/PageMaker, Claris/MacDraw; Printers — Ap/Mac Laser. PRODUCTION: Typesetters — Ap/Mac; Production cameras — B/4000; Automatic film processors — Kk. PRESSROOM: Line 1 — 4-KP/Newsking. LIBRARY: Electronic — Bound Volumes. WIRE SERVICES: News — AP; Receiving dishes — size-3ft, AP.

NEW YORK

ALBANY

Albany County

'90 U.S. Census- 101,082; E&P '96 Est. 100,548

ABC-CZ (90): 197,694 (HH 80,324)

Times Union (m-mon to sat; S)

Times Union, 645 Albany-Shaker Rd.; PO Box 15000, Albany, NY 12211; tel (518) 454-5694; fax (518) 489-5877; e-mail jdco@aol.com. Hearst Newspapers group.

Circulation: 100,705(m); 100,705(m-sat); 161,226(S); ABC Sept. 30, 1995.

Price: 50¢(d); 50¢(sat); $1.75(S); $3.60/wk (d/S); $187.20/yr.

Advertising: Open inch rate $126.00(m); $126.00(m-sat); $126.00(S). **Representative:** Sawyer-Ferguson-Walker Co.

News Services: AP, HN, HAS, LAT-WP, NYT, SHNS, KRT. **Politics:** Independent. **Established:** 1856.

Special Editions: Thanksgiving; Capitaland.

Special Weekly Sections: Preview, Automotive Weekly (thur).

Magazines: Parade, TV Magazine (S).

CORPORATE OFFICERS

President Frank A Bennack Jr
Vice Pres Robert J Danzig
Secretary Victor F Ganzi

GENERAL MANAGEMENT

Publisher Timothy O White
General Manager Robert S Wilson
Controller-Resident Thomas R Maginn
Director-Operations/Planning George R Hearst III
Manager-New Media Ventures Tricia Buhr

ADVERTISING

Director David White
Manager-Classified Michael C Danieli
Manager-Display Kathi Recore

MARKETING AND PROMOTION

Director-Marketing Robert Provost

TELECOMMUNICATIONS

Audiotex Manager Judith Vopelak

CIRCULATION

Director George Martin Jr

NEWS EXECUTIVES

Exec Editor Jeff Cohen
Editor Harry M Rosenfeld
Assoc Editor William M Dowd
Managing Editor-News Rex Smith
Managing Editor-Features Joann M Crupi
Asst Managing Editor-Systems Michael V Spain
Exec Editor-City Colleen Fitzpatrick
Exec Editor-Features Karen Potter
Exec Business Editor Alan D Abbey
Exec Editor-Sports Joe Layden
Exec Editor-Photo Katherine Friedrich

EDITORS AND MANAGERS

Art Director Thomas Palmer
City Editor Rob Brill
Columnist Daniel Lynch
Columnist Fred LeBrun
Editorial Page Editor Howard T Healy
Editorial Cartoonist Rex Babin
Librarian Richard Matturro
National Editor Paul Gibbons
Online Electronic News Editor Patricia Hart
State Editor Harvy Lipman
Television Writer Keith Marder
Travel Editor Michael Virtanen

MANAGEMENT INFORMATION SERVICES

Director-Technology Art Raymond

PRODUCTION

Manager Joseph Brunetto
Superintendent/General Foreman-Composing Room William Kelly
Superintendent-Press Angelo Serafino
Superintendent-Photoengraving Michael Mace
Superintendent-Mailroom John J Cipollo

Market Information: Zoned editions; Split Run; Operate database; Operate audiotex; Electronic edition.

Mechanical available: Letterpress (direct); Black and 3 ROP colors; insert accepted — preprinted; page cut-offs — 22¾".

Mechanical specifications: Type page 13" x 21½"; E - 6 cols, 2 1/16", ⅛" between; A - 6 cols, 2 1/16", ⅛" between; C - 10 cols, 1 3/16", ⅛" between.

Commodity consumption: Newsprint 16,400 metric tons; widths 54", 40½"; black ink 550,000 pounds; color ink 72,000 pounds; single pages printed 21,000; average pages per issue 50(d), 112(S); single plates used 85,000.

Equipment: EDITORIAL: Front-end hardware — SII/Synthesis 66; Front-end software — SII/Synthesis-INTL Road Runner, Ap/Mac; Printers — AG/SelectSet 2600; Other equipment — AG/Colorscape, Ap/Mac. CLASSIFIED: Front-end hardware — Tandem/Sun, PC; Front-end software — SII/Synthesis Roadrunner, Microsoft/Windows; Printers — HP/Deskjets, HP/LaserPrinters. AUDIOTEX: Hardware — PEP/Voice Print; Software — PEP/Voice Print; Supplier name — BDR. DISPLAY: Adv layout systems — SII/IAL, SII/ICP; Front-end hardware — Tandem, HP; Front-end software — SII/Synthesis 66 Roadrunner, CJ/AIM; Printers — HP/Deskjet, HP/Laser Printer. PRODUCTION: Typesetters — 2-AG/Selectset 5000; Platemaking systems — Na; Plate exposures — 1-III/Titan, 1-MAS; Plate processors — 2-Na/NP-80; Electronic picture desk — Lf/AP Leaf Picture Desk; Scanners — 2-ECR/Autokon 1080; Production cameras — 1-C/Spartan, 1-C/Newspager; Automatic film processors — 1-LE/26, 1-LE/2600A, 1-Kk/710, 3-LE/PC-13, 2-AG/Rapidline; Film transporters — 2-LE, 1-C; Color separation equipment (conventional) — AG/Colorscope; Digital color separation equipment — 2-ACS/100. PRESSROOM: Line 1 — 10-G/II, 4-G/V; Folders — 2-G. MAILROOM: Counter stackers — 8-QWI; Inserters and stuffers — 2-HI/2299 online; Bundle tyer — 6-Power Strap; Addressing machine — 1-Ch, LSI. LIBRARY: Electronic — Vu/Text, Vu/Text SAVE RS 6000, SII/Laser. WIRE SERVICES: News — AP Datastream, AP Datafeatures, NYT, KRT, LAT-WP, SHNS, HN; Photos — AP; Stock tables — AP Stock, AP SelectStox; Receiving dishes — AP. BUSINESS COMPUTERS: HP/3000-967, H/PE55, Tandem (SII); Applications: CJ: Circ, Adv, Financial; Database: Mktg; PCs & micros networked; PCs & main system networked.

AMSTERDAM

Montgomery County

'90 U.S. Census- 20,714; E&P '96 Est. 19,799

ABC-NDM (90): 126,989 (HH 48,359)

The Recorder (e-mon to fri; m-sat; S)

The Recorder, 1 Venner Rd.; PO Box 640, Amsterdam, NY 12010; tel (518) 843-1100; fax (518) 843-6580.

Circulation: 11,301(e); 11,301(m-sat); 11,373(S); ABC Sept. 30, 1995.

Price: 50¢(d); 50¢(sat); $1.00(S); $2.50/wk; $130.00/yr.

Advertising: Open inch rate $15.15(e); $15.15(m-sat); $15.15(S). **Representative:** Papert Companies.

News Services: LAT-WP, AP, KRT. **Politics:** Independent. **Established:** 1878.

Not Published: New Year; Memorial Day; Independence Day; Labor Day; Christmas.

Special Editions: Super Bowl, Health & Fitness, Bridal Book I (Jan); Year Outlook (Feb); Cooking Contest (Mar); Spring Car Care, Spring Home Improvement, Pro Baseball Preview (Apr); Dad & Grad, Family Business, Bridal Book II, Vacation Guide (June); Saratoga Horse Racing (July); Summer Projects, County Fair (Aug); Autumn Leaves (Sept); Fall Car Care, Fall Home Improvement (Oct); Christmas Gift Guide I (Nov); Christmas Gift Guide II, Holiday Memories (Dec).

Special Weekly Sections: Business (mon); Best Food Days (wed); Arts & Leisure, Lifestyle, TV Listing, Senior Citizens, Travel, Home & Garden, Outdoors, Horse Racing (S); Arts & Leisure, Education, Seasonal Sports (daily).

Magazines: TV Update, Currents-Arts (S); Golden Age Sentinel (1st S/mo).

CORPORATE OFFICER

Publisher/Corporate Secretary Richard Barker

GENERAL MANAGEMENT

General Manager Kevin McClary
Controller Charles Tobey
Business Manager Mary Stachnik

ADVERTISING

Director Kevin McClary

CIRCULATION

Director Doug Hill

NEWS EXECUTIVES

Exec Editor Tony Benjamin
Managing Editor Kevin Mattison

EDITORS AND MANAGERS

City Editor David Turner
Editorial Writer Tony Benjamin
Films/Theater Editor Kevin Mattison
Music Editor Kevin Mattison
News Editor Nancy Quick
Radio/Television Editor Kevin Mattison

PRODUCTION

Supervisor Robert Engle
Foreman-Pressroom Robert Wancewicz

Market Information: TMC.

Mechanical available: Offset; Black and 3 ROP colors; insert accepted — preprinted, samples, cards; page cut-offs — 22¾".

Mechanical specifications: Type page 13" x 21½"; E - 6 cols, 2 1/16", ⅛" between; A - 6 cols, 2 1/16", ⅛" between; C - 8 cols, 1 9/16", 1/16" between.

Commodity consumption: Newsprint 780 short tons; widths 27½", 30", 34"; black ink 20,000 pounds; color ink 1,000 pounds; single pages printed 10,000; average pages per issue 22(d), 54(S); single plates used 18,000.

Equipment: EDITORIAL: Front-end hardware — 1-AT/7000; Other equipment — 1-LE/PC13-Dry Film Processor. CLASSIFIED: Front-end hardware — 1-AT/7000. DISPLAY: Adv layout systems — 4-Ap/Mac II; Printers — 2-Compaq/Pagemarq 20 Tabloid. PRODUCTION: Pagination software — QuarkXPress 3.3; Typesetters — 2-AU/APS U5, Bidco; Plate exposures — 1-B/Ultra-Lite 1500, 1-B/MP2, 1-Amerigraph/437S-S; Plate processors — Nat/A250; Scanners — HP/Scanner; Production cameras — 1-B/24, 1-AG/2024; Automatic film processors — 1-Kk/710; Color separation equipment (conventional) — Howtek/Colorscan Sys. PRESSROOM: Line 1 — 6-G/Urbanite (3-N3 in Line); Folders — G/2:1; Press control system — 2-Fin/Console. MAILROOM: Inserters and stuffers — KAN/320 (4 heads); Bundle tyer — Bu/SA 505; Addressing machine — Ch/596. WIRE SERVICES: News — LAT-WP, KRT, AP; Photos — AP; Stock tables — AP; Syndicates — Universal Press, McNaught, King Features; Receiving dishes — size-8ft, AP. BUSINESS COMPUTERS: 1-TI/1505; Applications: Bus, Circ, Payroll, Adv; Papertrak: Circ, Adv, Accounting; PCs & micros networked; PCs & main system networked.

AUBURN

Cayuga County

'90 U.S. Census- 31,258; E&P '96 Est. 30,225

ABC-CZ (90): 31,258 (HH 11,936)

Citizen (e-mon to fri; S)

Citizen, 25 Dill St., Auburn, NY 13021; tel (315) 253-5311; fax (315) 253-6031; e-mail remlapkaj@aol.com. Howard Publications group.

Circulation: 15,411(e); 16,947(S); ABC Sept. 30, 1995.

Price: 35¢(d); $1.25(S); $2.35/wk (carrier); $10.18/mo; $122.20/yr (carrier).

Advertising: Open inch rate $13.85(e); $13.85(S).

News Service: AP. **Politics:** Independent. **Established:** 1905.

Not Published: New Year; Memorial Day; Independence Day; Labor Day; Christmas.

Special Editions: Health (Jan); Progress Edition, Brides (Feb); Home Improvement, Fashion (Mar); Home, Golden Citizen (Apr); Finger Lake Summer Guide (May); Tomato Fest (Sept).

Special Weekly Sections: Food (mon); Business/Agriculture, Price Busters Tab (tues); Home (wed); Arts & Entertainment (thur); Community and Family Features (S).

Magazines: Parade, Color Comics (S); TV Weekly.

CORPORATE OFFICER

President Robert S Howard

GENERAL MANAGEMENT

Publisher Jack Palmer

ADVERTISING

Director Doris G Rush
Manager-Classified Jennifer Griffin
Manager-Retail Stacy Davis
Director-Creative Lee Cunningham

CIRCULATION

Director George Alles

NEWS EXECUTIVE

Managing Editor Don Rogers

I-264 New York

EDITORS AND MANAGERS
Business/Finance Editor — Steve Fennesy
Editorial Page Editor — Don Rogers
Education Editor — Allan Vaugh
Fashion/Style Editor — Anita Messina
Graphics Editor/Art Director — Lee Cunningham
News Editor — John Allen
Newspapers in Education Community Projects Editor — George Alles
Photo Editor — Kevin Rivoli
Television/Music Editor — Jen Willard
Theater/Film Editor — Jen Willard
Wire Editor — John Allen

PRODUCTION
Manager — Slade Wentworth
Foreman-Pressroom — Carl Abate

Market Information: Zoned editions; Split Run; TMC; ADS.
Mechanical available: Offset; Black and 3 ROP colors; insert accepted — preprinted, spadea; page cut-offs — 22¾".
Mechanical specifications: Type page 13" x 21½"; E - 6 cols, 2¹/₁₆", ⅛" between; A - 6 cols, 2¹/₁₆", ⅛" between; C - 9 cols, 1⅜", ¹/₁₆" between.
Commodity consumption: Newsprint 900 metric tons; width 27½"; black ink 20,000 pounds; color ink 6,000 pounds; average pages per issue 28(d), 56(S); single plates used 14,000.
Equipment: EDITORIAL: Front-end hardware — 17-Sun/3-50, 2-Sun/Sparc, 6-Ap/Mac II, 2-Ap/Power Mac 7100-80 CD; Front-end software — Unix, Arbortext, Ap/Mac OS, Quark-XPress 3.3; Printers — 2-Ap/Mac NTX; Other equipment — 1-Telebit/Qblazer 9600 modem. CLASSIFIED: Front-end hardware — 7-Sun/Sparc IPC; Front-end software — Island Write 4.0; Printers — 1-HP/LaserJet 4ML. DISPLAY: Front-end hardware — 10-Ap/Mac II, 2-Ap/Mac SE, 2-Ap/Mac Quadra 605, 1-Ap/Mac LC III; Front-end software — QuarkXPress 3.3, Adobe/Illustrator 5.0, Adobe/Photoshop 3.0; Printers — Copal/Dash 600, Ap/Mac LaserWriter II NTX; Other equipment — 1-AG/Focus Color Plus Scanner. PRODUCTION: Pagination software — SCS/Layout 8000, Lynx 4.0; OCR software — Typereader 3.0, Caere/OmniPage Pro; Typesetters — 1-ECR/Pelbox 108, Copal/Dash 600, 1-Ap/Mac LaserWriter II NTX; Platemaking systems — 1-LE; Plate exposures — 2-Nu/Flip Top FT40UPNS; Plate processors — 1-Graham/M-28; Electronic picture desk — Lf/AP Leaf Picture Desk; Scanners — 1-Lf/Leafscan 35, 1-Nikon/LS 3500, AG/Horizon, 1-AG; Production cameras — 2-SCREEN/Companion 640C; Automatic film processors — 1-LE, 1-P; Film transporters — 1-C; Digital color separation equipment — 1-Lf/Leafscan 35, 1-Nikon/LS3500.
PRESSROOM: Line 1 — 5-G/Urbanite single width; Press drives — 1-Westinghouse/100 h.p. DC Motor; Folders — 1-G/2:1; Press control system — 1-Fin; Press registration system — Stoesser/Register Systems. MAILROOM: Counter stackers — 2-Id; Inserters and stuffers — 6-MM; Bundle tyer — 1-OVL, 1-MLN. LIBRARY: Electronic — Verity. WIRE SERVICES: News — AP; Photos — AP; Receiving dishes — size-3m, AP, NSN. BUSINESS COMPUTERS: 1-Sun/Sparc Station 2, 1-Compaq/386sx; Applications: Vision Data: Circ, Accts receivable; Ciridian; PCs & micros networked; PCs & main system networked.

BATAVIA
Genesee County
'90 U.S. Census: 16,310; E&P '96 Est. 15,990
ABC-NDM (90): 22,365 (HH 8,504)

The Daily News
(e-mon to fri; m-sat)
The Daily News, 2 Apollo Dr., PO Box 870, Batavia, NY 14021; tel (716) 343-8000; fax (716) 343-2623. Johnson Newspaper Corp. group.
Circulation: 15,764(e); 15,764(m-sat); ABC Sept. 30, 1995.
Price: 50¢(d); 50¢(sat); $2.10/wk (carrier).
Advertising: Open inch rate $19.82(e); $19.82 (m-sat). **Representative:** Landon Associates Inc.
News Service: AP. **Politics:** Independent. **Established:** 1878.
Not Published: New Year; Memorial Day; Independence Day; Labor Day; Thanksgiving; Christmas.
Special Editions: Bridal Guide, Business Cards (Jan).

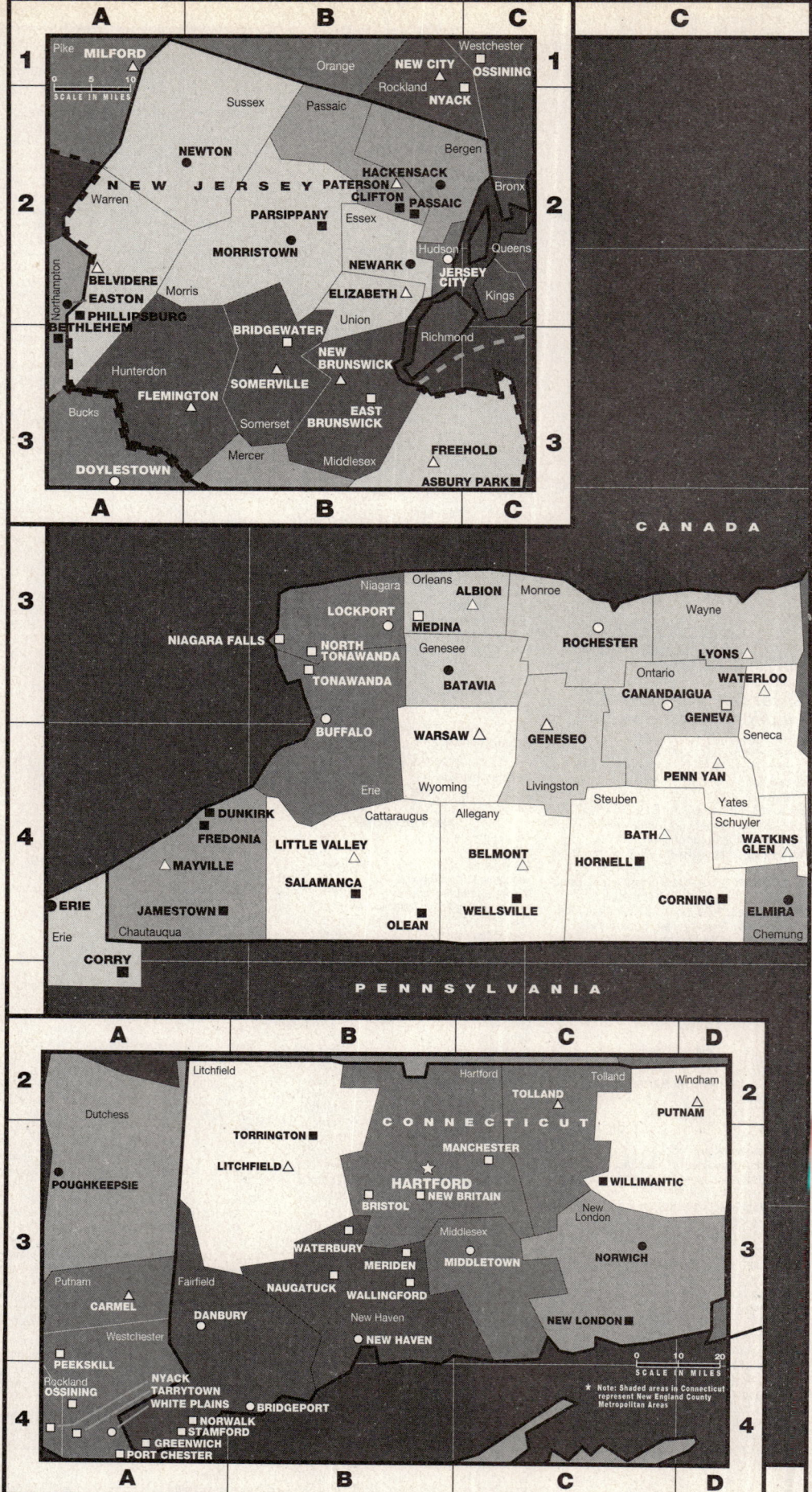

Copyright ©1996 by the Editor & Publisher Co.

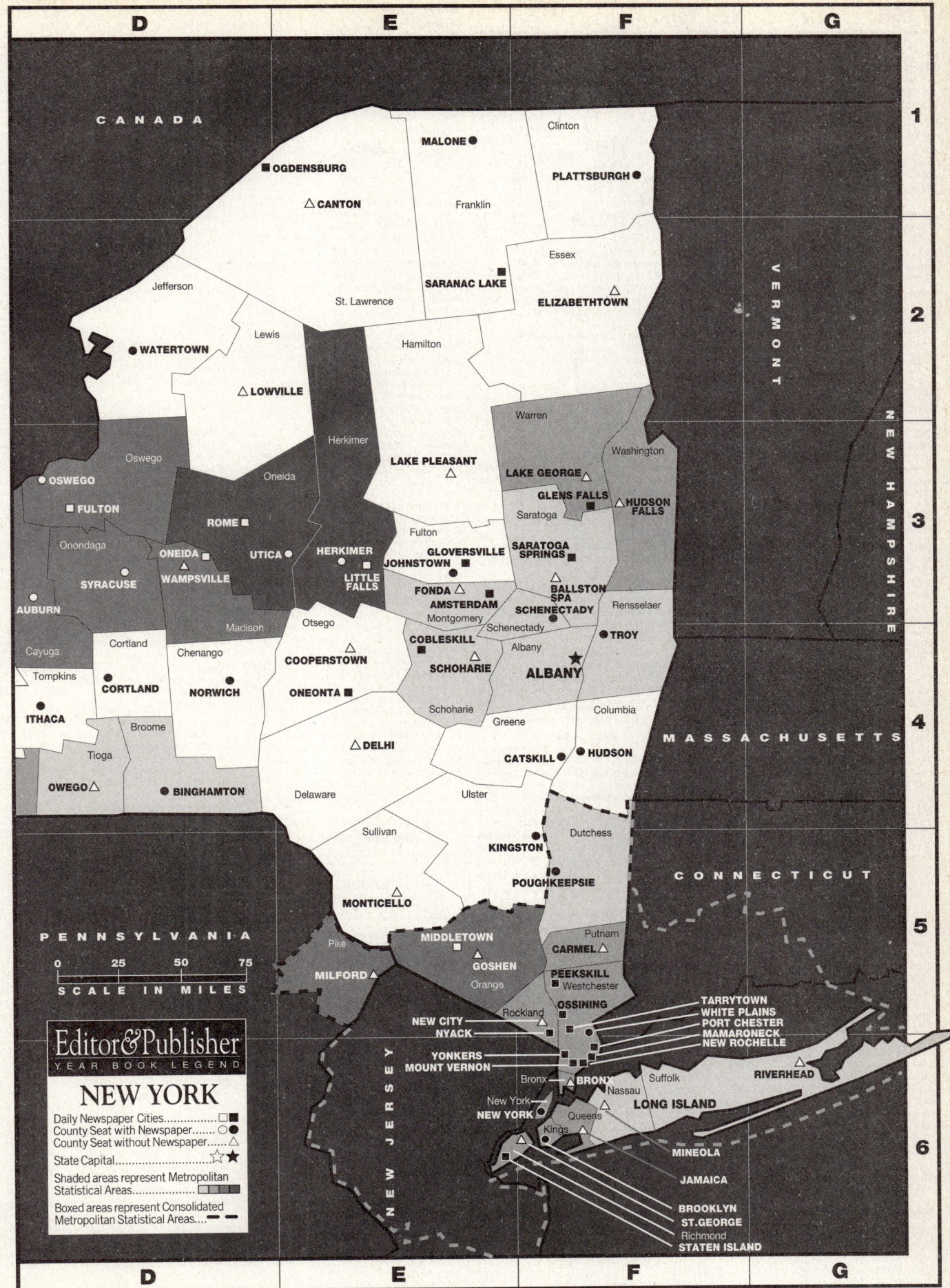

Special Weekly Sections: Business (mon); Agriculture (tues); Schools, Recreation (summer) (wed); Entertainment (thur, fri); Religion (sat).

CORPORATE OFFICER

President John B Johnson

GENERAL MANAGEMENT

Publisher Roger L Mosher
Asst Publisher Thomas Turnbull
Manager-Business Department Donna Elliott

ADVERTISING

Director Thomas Turnbull
Manager-Classified Joan Roschke
Coordinator-National Bridget Gass

MARKETING AND PROMOTION

Director-Marketing/Promotion Thomas Turnbull

CIRCULATION

Director Keith Witmer

NEWS EXECUTIVES

Editor Roger L Mosher
Managing Editor Mark Graczyk

EDITORS AND MANAGERS

Business/Finance Editor Jennifer Rowley
Columnist Scott De Smit
Editorial Page Editor Sharon Larsen
Farm/Agriculture Editor Jennifer Ficcaglia
Living/Lifestyle Editor Tessie Dubois
News Editor Dirk Hoffman
Regional News Editor Dirk Hoffman
Religion Editor Jennifer Ficcaglia
Sports Editor Bill Bruton
Teen-Age/Youth Editor Tessie Dubois
Women's Editor Tessie Dubois
Wire Editor Eric Morse

PRODUCTION

Manager Coley Webb
Foreman-Composing L Brian Clark

Market Information: Zoned editions.

Mechanical available: Offset; Black and 3 ROP colors; insert accepted — preprinted; page cutoffs — 22¾".

Mechanical specifications: Type page 12¾" x 21½"; E - 6 cols, 2¹⁄₁₆", ⅛" between; A - 6 cols, 2¹⁄₁₆", ⅛" between; C - 9 cols, 1⁵⁄₁₆", ¹⁄₁₆" between.

Commodity consumption: Newsprint 749 short tons; widths 27", 13½", 33½"; black ink 17,063 pounds; color ink 3,013 pounds; single pages printed 6,496; average pages per issue 21(d); single plates used 9,199.

Equipment: EDITORIAL: Front-end hardware — AT, 17-AT/A500, 3-Ap/Mac base File Server; Front-end software — Baseview; Printers — 1-Pro Setter; Other equipment — 2-HP/LaserJet 4MV. CLASSIFIED: Front-end hardware — 3-AT, 3-Ap/Mac; Front-end software — Baseview. DISPLAY: Adv layout systems — 5-Ap/Power Mac 8100; Front-end hardware — 5-AT; Front-end software — Multi-Ad/Creator 3.71, QuarkXPress 3.31; Printers — Compaq/Page Marq 15; Other equipment — HP/LaserJet 4MV. PRODUCTION: Pagination software — QuarkXPress 3.31; Typesetters — 2-Linotype-Hell/Linotron 202N Typesetter; Plate exposures — 2-Nu/FT140UP, Nu/Flip Top FT40APRNS 631, 1-Nu/FT40APRNS; Plate processors — 1-Nat/A-340, WL/30D; Electronic picture desk — Lf; Scanners — 2-Linotype-Hell/Linotron 202N, 1-AG/V20x24; Production cameras — 1-R/480, 1-Eskofot/6006; Automatic film processors — P-25RT; Shrink lenses — 1-Kamerak/Scandia I; Color separation equipment (conventional) — Lf/Leafscan 35. PRESSROOM: Line 1 — 15-G single width; Press drives — 3-GE, 1-Westinghouse; Folders — 1-G/V1102, 1-G/V1370; Press control system — Fin. MAILROOM: Counter stackers — 2-Fg, 1-BG; Inserters and stuffers — KAN/760 6 packets; Bundle tyer — 2-MLN, 1-Barstrom; Addressing machine — Ch. LIBRARY: Electronic — Baseview. WIRE SERVICES: News — AP; Photos — AP; Receiving dishes — AP. BUSINESS COMPUTERS: IBM; Applications: Gen ledger, Accts receivable, Payroll, Accts payable; PCs & main system networked.

BINGHAMTON

Broome County

'90 U.S. Census- 53,008; E&P '96 Est. 50,751
ABC-CZ (90): 178,198 (HH 69,987)

Press & Sun-Bulletin

(m-mon to sat; S)

Press & Sun Bulletin, 4421 Vestal Pkwy. E. (Vestal 13850); PO Box 1270, Binghamton, NY 13902; tel (607) 798-1234; fax (607) 798-0261. Gannett Co. Inc. group.

Circulation: 68,919(m); 68,919(m-sat); 88,679(S); ABC Sept. 30, 1995.

Price: 40¢(d); 40¢(sat); $1.50(S); $3.30/wk.

Advertising: Open inch rate $71.45(m); $71.45(m-sat); $83.00(S). **Representative:** Gannett National Newspaper Sales.

News Services: AP, GNS, LAT-WP. **Politics:** Independent. **Established:** 1822 (Sun-Bulletin), 1904 (Press).

Advertising not accepted: All copy subject to publisher's approval.

Special Editions: Bridal, Frontiers (Feb); Car Care (Mar); Health, Home & Garden (Apr); Summer of '96, Mother's Day (May); Graduation, Bridal, Life Underwriters, Health (June); July Fest (July); Guide to Southern Tier (Aug); Bridal, Home Furnishings, Health, H.S. Football (Sept); College Information (Oct); Thanksgiving Day Issue, Reader's Choice Awards, Holiday Almanac (Nov); Gift Guide, Health (Dec); 50 Something (monthly).

Special Weekly Sections: Business (mon); Sports (tues); Food (wed); Consumer (thur); Good Times (fri); Family & Friends (sat); Travel, TV Week (S).

Magazines: Real Estate Today (every other thur); Southern Tier Good Times, Tioga Community (fri); Chenango Community (sat); USA Weekend, TV Week (S); Home Builders & Remodelers (monthly).

CORPORATE OFFICERS

President Bernard M Griffin
Treasurer Jimmy L Thomas
Asst Secretary/Asst Treasurer J Bruce Klink

GENERAL MANAGEMENT

Publisher Bernard M Griffin
Controller J Bruce Klink
Director-Human Resources Dorothy Petrulis
Purchasing Agent Sarah J Dunphy

ADVERTISING

Director Lewis F Roberts
Manager-Display Vivian Toups
Manager-Account Development Jan Mott
Manager-Data/Co-op Phyllis Leuci
Manager-Classified Gail Boysick

MARKETING AND PROMOTION

Director-Market Development Enon Merhavy
Manager-Promotion Jennifer Boardman
Manager-Research Anthony Valenta

TELECOMMUNICATIONS

Manager-Talking Phonebook Irene Kingsley

CIRCULATION

Director Brian Donovan
Asst to Director Nadine Callaghan
Manager-Customer Service Joanne Crawford
Manager-Regional Thomas Canny
Manager-Sales/Marketing USA Today Kevin Foley
Manager-Fleet Steve Pavlovich
Manager-Metro East Frank Regulski
Manager-Metro West Rick Benko

NEWS EXECUTIVES

Exec Editor Barry Rothfeld
Exec Editor-Sports Charles Jaworski
Managing Editor Martha Steffens
Asst Managing Editor Bruce Estes
Asst Managing Editor Steve Spero

EDITORS AND MANAGERS

Amusements/Books Editor Gene Grey
Business/Finance Editor Jeffrey Platsky
Columnist-Outdoors Dave Rossie
Columnist-Sports John W Fox
Columnist Dave Rossie
Education Editor George Basler
Editorial Page Editor Frank Roessner
Fashion Editor Lee Shepherd
Features Editor Joy Crocker
Films/Theater Editor Gene Grey
Food Editor Cathy Lord
Garden Editor Barb Van Atta
Home Furnishings Editor Barb Van Atta
Library Coordinator Nancy George
Metro Editor Steve Morelli
Music Editor Gene Grey
Photo/Graphics Editor Dave Zeggert
Radio/Television Editor Laurie Miner
Real Estate Editor Jeffrey Platsky
Society Editor Lori Tripp
Sports Editor Dave Bohrer
Sunday Editor Steve Morelli

MANAGEMENT INFORMATION SERVICES

Data Processing Manager Rose Ward

PRODUCTION

Director Bernard A Szachara
Manager-Pressroom John Clark
Manager-Systems Rose Ward
Manager-Pre Press Jim Mitrowitz
Manager-Distribution Center Theodore G Huntley
Manager-T/S & Building Craig Clark
Purchasing Agent Sarah J Dunphy

Market Information: Zoned editions; Split Run; TMC; Operate audiotex.

Mechanical available: DiLitho; Black and 3 ROP colors; insert accepted — preprinted; page cutoffs — 22¾".

Mechanical specifications: Type page 13" x 21½"; E - 7 cols, 2¹⁄₁₆", ⅛" between; A - 6 cols, 2¹⁄₁₆", ⅛" between; C - 10 cols, 1³⁄₁₆", ¹⁄₁₆" between.

Commodity consumption: Newsprint 7,798 short tons; width 54½"; black ink 236,000 pounds; color ink 25,500 pounds; single pages printed 15,630; average pages per issue 36(d), 72(S); single plates used 62,400.

Equipment: EDITORIAL: Front-end hardware — SII/Sys 55SX; Front-end software — QPS 3.2, Microsoft/Windows 3.0; Printers — Okidata/600; Other equipment — Ap/Mac Quadra 800. CLASSIFIED: Front-end hardware — SII/Sys 55SX, 12-PC/486; Printers — Okidata/600; Other equipment — 2-Ap/Mac Quadra. DISPLAY: Adv layout systems — SCS/Layout 8000; Front-end hardware — IBM/PS2 80; Front-end software — SCI; Printers — Epson, HP/LaserJet. PRODUCTION: Pagination software — QPS 3.2, Pongrass; Typesetters — 2-Hyphen/Imaging Sys, Sun/Sparc Controller, 2-Harlequin/RIP, ECR/3850 Film; Plate exposures — 1-Nu/Flip Top FT40NS, 1-Amerigraph/437 DS; Plate processors — 2-Nat/A-340; Electronic picture desk — Adobe/Photoshop, Ap/Mac Quadra 800, Lf/AP Leaf Picture Desk; Scanners — 1-ECR/Autokon 1000, Lf/Leafscan 35; Production cameras — 1-C/Marathon, 1-C/Spartan; Automatic film processors — 1-LE/24-A, 1-LE/24AQ, AG/660, 1-C/66F; Shrink lenses — 1-Alan; Color separation equipment (conventional) — RZ/200S LED; Digital color separation equipment — Lf/AP Leaf Picture Desk, Adobe/Photoshop, Ap/Mac Quadra 800. PRESSROOM: Line 1 — 12-G/Headliner I; Press drives — Fin; Folders — 2-G; Pasters — G/Auto; Reels and stands — G/Mark I; Press control system — Fin. MAILROOM: Counter stackers — 2-QWI/Stacker, 2-HL/Monitor; Inserters and stuffers — 1-S/NP 1472, 13-M/5; Bundle tyer — 2-MLN/MLN2A, 2-Power Strap/PSN5; Addressing machine — Ch; Mailroom control system — Id; Parajust. WIRE SERVICES: News — AP, GNS, LAT-WP; Stock tables — AP; Syndicates — AP, GNS; Receiving dishes — size-3m, AP. BUSINESS COMPUTERS: 1-IBM/AS-400 Model 300; Applications: WordPerfect: Circ, Financial; Lotus, Gannett, AdServ; PCs & micros networked; PCs & main system networked.

BRONX

See NEW YORK CITY

BROOKLYN

See NEW YORK CITY

BUFFALO

Erie County

'90 U.S. Census- 328,123; E&P '96 Est. 307,470
ABC-NDM (90): 879,249 (HH 346,565)

The Buffalo News

(all day-mon to fri; m-sat; S)

The Buffalo News, 1 News Plz.; PO Box 100, Buffalo, NY 14240; tel (716) 849-3434.

Circulation: 274,614(a); 272,837(m-sat); 362,345(S); ABC Sept. 30, 1995.

Price: 50¢(d); 50¢(sat); $1.75(S); $3.80/wk; $197.60/yr.

Advertising: Open inch rate $167.28(a); $167.28(m-sat); $210.34(S). **Representatives:** American Publishers Reps.; Sawyer-Ferguson-Walker Co.

News Services: AP, UPI, KRT, LAT-WP, RN. **Politics:** Independent. **Established:** 1880.

Special Editions: Weddings '96, Prospectus '96, Junior Achievement, Play-off Preview, Conference Champions, Super Bowl (Jan); Spring Cruise, Auto Show, Your Taxes, Valentine's Day, Health, Pets & Vets, Black History Month, Salute to Black Professionals, Home Decor, Frozen Food (Feb); International Travel, Buffalo Home Show, Financial Opportunities, Ontario/Toronto Travel, Auto Leasing, Spring Fashion, Spring Travel Brochure (Mar); Florida Travel; Holiday Gift Guides; Summer Fun; Winter; Dining Out Restaurant Guide.

Special Weekly Sections: Your Health, Your Money (tues); Food (wed); Prime Time (fri); Careers, Pets, Know Your Antiques (sat).

Magazines: Monday Sports (tab) (mon); NEXT (children's tab) (tues); Gusto (entertainment tab) (fri); Home Finder (sat); Sunday Magazine Tab, TV Topics (newsprint), Metro Comics (S).

CORPORATE OFFICERS

Board Chairman Warren E Buffett
President Stanford Lipsey
Senior Vice Pres Murray B Light
Senior Vice Pres-Employee Relations Ralph L Wray
Senior Vice Pres Warren T Colville
Vice Pres David W Perona
Vice Pres Barry B Breig
Vice Pres Robert J Casell
Treasurer Rodney E Layton
Secretary Barbara A Urbanczyk

GENERAL MANAGEMENT

Publisher Stanford Lipsey
Controller Rodney E Layton
Manager-Office/Purchasing Agent Judith M Webster
Manager-Credit Frank Vollmer

ADVERTISING

Director Warren T Colville
Manager-Classified Scott H Brooks
Manager-Retail David A Alpher
Manager-Outside Classified Sales Maurice Materise
Manager-Sunday Magazine Sales Roy A Skoba
Manager-Marketing Research Nancy Starzynski
Manager-Marketing Services Philip N Maher
Manager-New Business Development Cheryl A Ludwig
Manager-National Matthew J Pronko

TELECOMMUNICATIONS

Audiotex Manager Barry B Breig

CIRCULATION

Director David W Perona
Asst Director Michael A Benevento
Asst Director Clyde B Barrow
Manager-Customer Service Peggy Pomana
Manager-Single Copy John Casey
Manager-Distribution Gerald Roach
Manager-Newspapers in Education Susan Levine

NEWS EXECUTIVES

Editor Murray B Light
Managing Editor Foster L Spencer
Deputy Managing Editor Edward L Cuddihy
Asst Managing Editor-Local News Stan Evans
Asst Managing Editor-Sunrise Gerald Goldberg
Asst Managing Editor-Features Margaret Sullivan
Asst Managing Editor-Graphics/Photo Joe Gibbs

EDITORS AND MANAGERS

Automotive Editor Donald O'Hara
Aviation Editor William Flynn
Books Editor Jeff Simon
Business/Finance Editor William Flynn
Cartoonist Tom Toles
City Editor Steve Bell
Columnist-Sports Larry Felser
Columnist-Sports Jerry Sullivan
Columnist-General Robert Curran
Columnist-Local Donn Ismonde
Editorial Page Editor Barbara Ireland
Deputy Editorial Page Editor Laurence Paul
Editorial Writer George Gates
Editorial Writer Rod Watson
Education Editor Karen Brady
Education Editor James Heaney
Entertainment Editor Terry Doran
Environmental Editor Michael Vogel
Farm Editor Robert Buyer
Fashion Editor Susan Martin
Features Editor Margaret Sullivan
Films/Theater Editor Jeff Simon
Food Editor Janice Okun
Garden Editor Joyce Ware
Graphics Editor John Davis
Graphics Editor Alan Dise
Health/Medical Editor Henry Davis
Home Furnishings Editor Paula Voell
Librarian Elliott Shapiro
Lifestyle Pages Editor Margaret Sullivan
Magazine Editor Melinda Miller
Music Editor Herman Trotter
News Editor John Neville
Photo Editor Roy Russell
Political Editor Robert McCarthy
Radio/Television Columnist Alan Pergament
Real Estate Editor David Robinson
Religion Editor Dave Condren

New York I-267

Science/Technology Editor Michael Vogel
Exec Sports Editor Howard Smith
Sports Editor Larry Felser
Travel Editor Joyce Ware
Television Topics Editor Jim Brennan
Wire Editor Velton Peabody

MANAGEMENT INFORMATION SERVICES

Director Barry B Breig

PRODUCTION

Director Robert J Casell
Manager Albert Wainwright
Manager-Facility Joseph Manno
Asst Manager Mel Walz
Foreman-Composing/Ad Operations Ronald Pajak
Foreman-Pressroom/Paper Handlers Bryan Carr
Foreman-Engraving Florian Pawlowski
Foreman-Mailroom Michael Gatherwright
Foreman-Machinist Gerald Burkley
Foreman-Electrician William Senchyne
Foreman-Engineering Terry Hausrath
Foreman-Plant Maintenance Joseph Manno

Market Information: Split Run; Operate audiotex.
Mechanical available: Letterpress (direct); Black and 3 ROP colors; insert accepted — preprinted, preprinted tabs, card stock; page cut-offs — $23\frac{9}{16}$".
Mechanical specifications: Type page 13" x 22"; E - 6 cols, $2\frac{1}{16}$", $\frac{1}{8}$" between; A - 6 cols, $2\frac{1}{16}$", $\frac{1}{8}$" between; C - 10 cols, $1\frac{1}{4}$", $\frac{1}{16}$" between.
Commodity consumption: Newsprint 41,400 metric tons; widths 54", 54", 40.5", 40.5", 27", 27"; black ink 1,352,398 pounds; color ink 144,620 pounds; single pages printed 23,168; average pages per issue 48(d), 124(S); single plates used 210,000.
Equipment: EDITORIAL: Front-end hardware — SII/Sys 55; Front-end software — SII/Sys 55 INL; Printers — Hyphen/Dash 600; Other equipment — Lf/AP Leaf Picture Desk. CLASSIFIED: Front-end hardware — SII/Sys 55; Front-end software — SII/Sys 55 ICP; Printers — Ap/Mac LaserWriter NTX. AUDIOTEX: Supplier name — Newspaper Voice Systems. DISPLAY: Adv layout systems — SII/Sys 55 IAL; Front-end hardware — Ap/Mac; Front-end software — DTI/AdSpeed; Printers — HP/LaserJet II. PRODUCTION: Pagination software — SII/Sys 55 INL; Typesetters — 2-ECR/PelBox 108, III/3850, 1-AU/APS 3850; Platemaking systems — KFM; Plate exposures — 1-MAS, 2-Titan; Plate processors — 1-Na/C120, 1-Na/C220; Electronic picture desk — Lf/AP Leaf Picture Desk; Scanners — 1-ECR/Autokon 1000, 1-AG/Horizon Plus; Production cameras — 2-C/Marathon, 2-C/Newspager II, 1-C/Spartan III; Automatic film processors — 3-LE/24AQ, 1-LE/24A, 1-LE/24; Reproportion units — 1-C/Spartan, 1-ECR/Autokon 1000; Film transporters — 3-C; Color separation equipment (conventional) — 1-R, 1-Ca; Digital color separation equipment — 1-ECR/Autokon 1000.
PRESSROOM: Line 1 — 6-Wd/Metropolitan (4-color deck); Line 2 — 6-Wd/Metropolitan (4-color deck); Line 3 — 6-Wd/Metropolitan (4-color deck); Line 4 — 6-Wd/Metropolitan (4-color deck); Line 5 — 6-Wd/Metropolitan (4-color deck); Folders — 5-Wd; Pasters — Wd/Semi-auto; Reels and stands — 30-Wd; Press control system — CH. MAILROOM: Counter stackers — 8-HPS/Dual Carrier, 3-HPS/Dual Carrier; Inserters and stuffers — 1-AM Graphics/25-head dual delivery inserter, 1-AM Graphics/30-head single delivery inserter; Bundle tyer — 9-Dynaric/NP-1, 8-Dynaric/NP-2; Wrapping singles — Manually; Addressing machine — 3-Dm/Hand, 1-Wm; Mailroom control system — 2-Ic/NP-630 Inserter. LIBRARY: Electronic — Vu/Text Save System. WIRE SERVICES: News — AP, RN, LAT-WP, KRT; Stock tables — AP SelectStox; Receiving dishes — AP. BUSINESS COMPUTERS: 1-HP/3000-70, 1-HP/3000-918LX, 1-HP/3000-928; Applications: CJ: Class, Payroll, Accts payable, Gen ledger, Circ, Personnel; PCs & micros networked; PCs & main system networked.

CANANDAIGUA

Ontario County

'90 U.S. Census- 10,725; **E&P '96 Est.** 10,987
ABC-CZ (90): 10,725 (HH 4,413)

The Daily Messenger (e-mon to fri)
The Sunday Messenger (S)

The Daily Messenger, 73 Buffalo St., Canandaigua, NY 14424-1085; tel (716) 394-0770; fax (716) 394-1675.
Circulation: 13,213(e); 13,836(S); ABC Sept. 30, 1995.
Price: 50¢(d); $1.00(S); $2.40/wk (carrier); $10.40/mo (carrier); $118.60/yr (carrier).
Advertising: Open inch rate $11.75(e); $15.50(S); $27.80(e & S). **Representative:** Papert Companies.
News Services: AP, SHNS, LAT-WP. **Politics:** Independent. **Established:** 1796.
Not Published: New Year; Memorial Day; Independence Day; Labor Day; Christmas (unless holiday falls on a Sunday).
Special Editions: Chamber of Commerce Annual Report (Jan); Wedding Tab (Feb); Western Finger Lakes Vacationer's Guide (May); Who's Who in Area Businesses (Sept); Christmas Opening (Nov).
Special Weekly Sections: Business/Consumer Page (mon); Weddings and Engagements, Business/Consumer Page (tues); Seniors Page, Business/Consumer Page (wed); At Ease, Religion, Business/Consumer Page (thur); Home and Garden, Farm Page, Real Estate, Business/Consumer Page (fri); Freestyle Section, Best Food Day (S).
Magazines: At Ease Tab (thur); Accent on Homes (fri); TV Viewer (S); Comics; Parade; Arts; Entertainment; Features Tab.

CORPORATE OFFICERS

Chairman of the Board/Treasurer George M Ewing Sr
President George M Ewing Jr
Vice Pres/Secretary M M Ewing

GENERAL MANAGEMENT

Publisher George M Ewing Jr
Vice Pres-Finance Andrew P Kavulich
Vice Pres-Marketing H Robert Schadewald
Vice Pres-News Robert Matson

ADVERTISING

Manager Cathy Mamoone
Manager-Classified Katherine M Nemecek

CIRCULATION

Director-Marketing Carl D Helbig

NEWS EXECUTIVES

Editor George M Ewing Sr
Vice Pres-News Robert Matson
Exec Managing Editor Robert Matson
Asst Managing Editor Mark Syverud

EDITORS AND MANAGERS

Automotive Editor Steve Circh
Business/Finance Editor Mark Syverud
City/Metro Editor Mark Syverud
Editorial Page Editor Kevin Frisch
Editorial Page Editor Richard Zitrin
Entertainment/Amusements Editor Kathie Meredith
Environmental Editor John Hatcher
Farm/Agriculture Editor Lenore Friend
Features Editor Kathie Meredith
Health/Medical Editor John Hatcher
News Editor Kathy Hovis-Younger
News Editor Steve Circh
Photo Editor Rikki Van Camp
Religion Editor Richard Zitria
Sports Editor Steve Bradley
Television/Music Editor Kathy Horvis-Younger
Theater/Film Editor Kathy Horvis-Younger
Travel Editor Mark Syverud

PRODUCTION

Director-Pre Press Joy Daggett
Superintendent-Press Howard Broderick

Market Information: TMC; ADS.
Mechanical available: Offset; Black and 3 ROP colors; insert accepted — preprinted, pocket book style, product samples with pre-approval; page cut-offs — 21.5".
Mechanical specifications: Type page 13" x 20.5"; E - 6 cols, $2\frac{1}{16}$", $\frac{1}{8}$" between; A - 6 cols, $2\frac{1}{16}$", $\frac{1}{8}$" between; C - 8 cols, $1\frac{1}{2}$", $\frac{1}{8}$" between.
Commodity consumption: Newsprint 1,350 short tons; widths 32", $27\frac{1}{2}$"; black ink 45,000 pounds; color ink 6,000 pounds; single pages printed 10,022; average pages per issue 26(d), 34(S); single plates used 9,000.
Equipment: EDITORIAL: Front-end hardware — 28-COM/Intrepid One System; Front-end software — COM/Intrepid; Other equipment — 2-COM/8600 Typesetter. CLASSIFIED: Front-end hardware — COM/Intrepid One system; Front-end software — COM/Intrepid; Other equipment — 2-COM/8600 Typesetters, 1-Accuset/1000. DISPLAY: Front-end hardware — 4-Ap/Mac IIci, 1-Ap/Power Mac 7100-66; Front-end software — QuarkXPress, Aldus/FreeHand; Printers — 1-QMS/860, 1-QMS/1660; Other equipment — 1-HP/Scanner. PRODUCTION: Pagination software — QPS 3.3; Typesetters — 2-COM/8600, Accuset/1000; Platemaking systems — Nu/Flip Top; Scanners — Umax/Power Look, Kk/Professional 2035; Production cameras — B; Automatic film processors — Kk/Rapiline 17, Multi-Ad, Wing-Lynch/Model 5; Shrink lenses — X; Color separation equipment (conventional) — AG/Accuset 1000.
PRESSROOM: Line 1 — 10-G/Community; Folders — 1-G/SSC-8384; Press control system — Allen Bradley. MAILROOM: Inserters and stuffers — KAN/480 5-into-1; Bundle tyer — MLN/Spirit Auto, Bu/Semi-Auto. COMMUNICATIONS: Digital ad delivery system — AP AdSend. Systems used — fiber optic. WIRE SERVICES: News — AP, SHNS, LAT-WP; Photos — AP; Stock tables — AP; Syndicates — Universal Press, King Features, Creators, NAS, United Media; Receiving dishes — AP. BUSINESS COMPUTERS: 1-Compaq/Deskpro 286, 2-Samsung/286, 3-Epson/286, 1-NEC/286, 1-AST/286, 4-PC/386; Applications: MSSI: Circ delivery, Circ subscriber, Adv, Manifest, Class, Accts payable, Gen ledger; PCs & micros networked; PCs & main system networked.

CATSKILL

Greene County

'90 U.S. Census- 4,690; **E&P '96 Est.** 4,667

Daily Mail (e-mon to fri; m-sat)

Daily Mail, 30 Church St.; PO Box 484, Catskill, NY 12414; tel (518) 943-2100; fax (518) 943-2063. Johnson Newspaper Corp. group.
Circulation: 4,971(e); 4,971(m-sat); Sworn Oct. 1, 1993.
Price: 50¢(d); 50¢(sat); $81.00/yr.
Advertising: Open inch rate $13.80(e); $13.80(m-sat). **Representative:** Landon Associates Inc.
News Service: AP. **Politics:** Independent. **Established:** 1879.
Special Editions: Progress Report; Bridal; Old Catskill Days; Home Improvement; Fun in the Sun; Energy Section; Ready for Winter; Vacationer; Christmas.
Special Weekly Section: TV (sat).

GENERAL MANAGEMENT

Publisher Anthony Panetta

ADVERTISING

Coordinator-Legal Barbara Craigie
Manager-Marketing/Promotion Pamela Farrell
Manager-Classified Arlene Gabrele

CIRCULATION

Manager Charles Yott

NEWS EXECUTIVE

Managing Editor Annibar Jensis

MANAGEMENT INFORMATION SERVICES

Data Processing Manager Julie Johnson

PRODUCTION

Foreman-Press Dale Schnare

Mechanical available: Offset; Black and 1 ROP color; insert accepted — preprinted; page cut-offs — $21\frac{1}{2}$".
Mechanical specifications: Type page $14\frac{3}{4}$" x 21"; E - 6 cols, $2\frac{1}{16}$", $\frac{1}{9}$" between; A - 6 cols, $2\frac{1}{16}$", $\frac{1}{9}$" between; C - 8 cols, $2\frac{1}{16}$", $\frac{1}{9}$" between.
Commodity consumption: Newsprint 30 short tons; average pages per issue 22(d), 124(sat).
Equipment: EDITORIAL: Front-end hardware — Ap/Mac; Front-end software — Baseview; Printers — 3-HP; Other equipment — 10-Ap/Power Mac 6100, 2-Ap/Power Mac 7100, 1-Ap/Mac IIci. CLASSIFIED: Front-end hardware — Ap/Mac, Ap/Power Mac 6100, Ap/Power Mac 7100; Front-end software — Baseview; Printers — HP. DISPLAY: Adv layout systems — Ap/Mac; Front-end hardware — 1-Ap/Mac Quadra 850, 1-Ap/Mac Centris 650; Front-end software — Multi-Ad/Creator; Printers — Ap/Mac LaserPrinter II NT, Compaq/ PageMarq 15. PRODUCTION: Typesetters — 3-Laser; Platemaking systems — Nu/Platemaker; Production cameras — Repromaster/2001.
PRESSROOM: Line 1 — 6-G/Community; Folders — G/SC. MAILROOM: Addressing machine — 1-Wm, 1-X. COMMUNICATIONS: Systems used — satellite. WIRE SERVICES: News — AP; Receiving dishes — size-10ft, AP. BUSINESS COMPUTERS: 1-Ap/Mac.

COBLESKILL

Schoharie County

'90 U.S. Census- 5,268; **E&P '96 Est.** 5,664

Daily Editor (e-mon to fri; S)

Daily Editor, 59 E. Main St.; PO Box 170, Cobleskill, NY 12043; tel (518) 234-4368; fax (518) 234-8849. Hollinger International Inc. group.
Circulation: 2,253(e); 2,253(S); Sworn Oct. 4, 1994.
Price: 35¢(d); 35¢(S); $1.40/wk.
Advertising: Open inch rate $6.33(e); $8.63(S).
News Service: AP. **Politics:** Independent. **Established:** 1990.
Not Published: Thanksgiving; Christmas.
Special Editions: Home Improvement; Summer Prices; Bridal Tab.

GENERAL MANAGEMENT

Publisher Frederick W Lee
General Manager John Snyder

ADVERTISING

Manager Kevin O'Connor

CIRCULATION

Manager Ron Tippet

NEWS EXECUTIVE

Editor Dana Cudmore

Market Information: TMC.
Mechanical available: Offset; black; insert accepted — preprinted.
Mechanical specifications: Type page 21" x $13\frac{1}{3}$"; E - 6 cols, $2\frac{1}{16}$", $\frac{1}{8}$" between; A - 6 cols, $2\frac{1}{16}$", $\frac{1}{8}$" between; C - 8 cols.
Commodity consumption: average pages per issue 18(d).
Equipment: EDITORIAL: Front-end hardware — Ap/Mac; Front-end software — Aldus/PageMaker; Printers — Ap/Mac LaserWriter II NT. CLASSIFIED: Front-end hardware — Ap/Mac; Front-end software — Claris/FileMaker; Printers — Ap/Mac LaserWriter Plus.
PRESSROOM: Line 1 — 6-KP; Line 2 — 4-KP. MAILROOM: Inserters and stuffers — KAN; Bundle tyer — EAM/Mosca; Addressing machine — Ch. WIRE SERVICES: Receiving dishes — AP. BUSINESS COMPUTERS: Unysis; PCs & micros networked.

CORNING

Steuben County

'90 U.S. Census- 11,938; **E&P '96 Est.** 11,157
ABC-CZ (90): 25,068 (HH 10,370)

The Leader (m-mon to sat; S)

The Leader, 34 W. Pulteney, Corning, NY 14830; tel (607) 936-4651; fax (607) 936-9939. Howard Publications group.
Circulation: 16,079(m); 16,079(m-sat); 15,410(S); ABC Sept. 30, 1995.
Price: 35¢(d); 35¢(sat); $1.25(S); $2.75/wk.
Advertising: Open inch rate $13.94(m); $13.94(m-sat); $13.94(S). **Representative:** Papert Companies.
News Service: AP. **Politics:** Independent. **Established:** 1846.
Not Published: Christmas.
Special Editions: Healthy Moms and Kids, Perspective, At Home (Jan); Valentine's Day Gifts, Tax Supplement, Bridal (Feb); People Who Make a Difference, Easter Gifts and Dining, No Foolin' (Mar); Home Improvement, Twin Tiers Golf Guide, Spring Car Care (Apr); Corning Classic Shopping Guide, Spring Home Improvement, LPGA Corning Classic, Mother's Day (May); Dads and Grads, Finger Lakes Dining Guide, July Finger Lakes Fun Book (June); August Finger Lakes Fun Book (July); Child Care, Sept Finger Lakes Fun Book, Watkins Glen NASCAR, Senior Services & Savings, Back-to-School (Aug); On the Town, Autumn, Fall Home Furnishings (Sept); Home Improvement, Fall Winter Car Care, Women in Business (Oct); Thanksgiving Dining, Shop Downtown, Holiday Gift Guide (Nov); Sparkle of Christmas, Eleventh Hour Santa, Gift Certificates, New Year '97 Celebration (Dec); Coupon Short Cuts (monthly).
Special Weekly Sections: Entertainment (thur); Health (S).
Magazines: Weekend (thur); Twin Tiers Television, Parade (S).

I-268 New York

CORPORATE OFFICER
President Robert S Howard
GENERAL MANAGEMENT
Publisher Neil C Hopp
Office Manager Wendy Rosenwinkle
ADVERTISING
Manager Michael Bartelli
CIRCULATION
Manager Steven Parsons
NEWS EXECUTIVE
Managing Editor Paul Guggina
EDITORS AND MANAGERS
News Editor John Kelleher
Photo Editor Jim Gill
Religion Editor Bonnie Albee
Sports Editor Bob Warburton
MANAGEMENT INFORMATION SERVICES
Data Processing Manager Wendy Rosenwinkle
PRODUCTION
Foreman-Pressroom James Jones

Market Information: Zoned editions; Split Run; TMC.
Mechanical available: Offset; Black and 3 ROP colors; insert accepted — preprinted, spadea; page cut-offs — 22¾".
Mechanical specifications: Type page 13¼" x 21¼"; E - 6 cols, 2¹⁄₁₆", ⅛" between; A - 6 cols, 2¹⁄₁₆", ⅛" between; C - 8 cols, 1⁹⁄₁₆", ¹⁄₁₆" between.
Commodity consumption: Newsprint 1,100 metric tons; widths 27½", 27½", 34", 34"; black ink 26,000 pounds; color ink 7,000 pounds; single pages printed 11,586; average pages per issue 24(d), 40(S); single plates used 14,000.
Equipment: EDITORIAL: Front-end hardware — Sun/Microsys 4-110, 14-Sun/Microsys 350, 5-Ap/Mac II, 3-Sun/Sparc II; Front-end software — Unix, Arbortext; Printers — 1-Hyphen/Dash 600, 1-ECR/PelBox 108; Other equipment — Nikon/Film Scanner, 2-Ap/Mac IIci, Lf/AP Leaf Picture Desk. CLASSIFIED: Front-end hardware — Sun/Microsys 4-110, 3-Sun/Microsys, Sun/Sparc; Front-end software — CText/Classified Sys; Printers — Ap/Mac LaserWriter II NTX. DISPLAY: Adv layout systems — SCS/Layout 8000; Front-end hardware — Sun/Microsys 4-110, 5-Ap/Mac II, 1-Ap/Mac SE30, 2-Ap/Mac IIci; Front-end software — QuarkXPress, Adobe/Illustrator; Printers — 1-Hyphen/Dash 600; Other equipment — AG/Arcus Horizon Scanner, Ap/Mac Scanner. PRODUCTION: Platemaking systems — Offset; Plate exposures — 1-Nu; Plate processors — 1-Nat; Production cameras — 1-K; Automatic film processors — 1-P/26EL, 1-LE. PRESSROOM: Line 1 — 1-G/Community. MAILROOM: Counter stackers — 1-BG/Count-O-Veyor, 1-Id; Inserters and stuffers — 1-MM/Tandem heads; Bundle tyer — 2-MLN/Plastic; Wrapping singles — 1-Id; Addressing machine — 1-Automecha/Accufast Labeler. LIBRARY: Electronic — Verity. WIRE SERVICES: News — AP, AP Photostream; Stock tables — AP; Syndicates — KRT, TV Data; Receiving dishes — size-3m, AP. BUSINESS COMPUTERS: Sun/Micro 4-110, 3-Sun/Sparc SLC; Applications: Vision Data: Accts receivable, Payroll, Circ; WordPerfect, Access Tech/20-20; PCs & micros networked; PCs & main system networked.

CORTLAND

Cortland County

'90 U.S. Census- 19,801; E&P '96 Est. 19,525

Cortland Standard

(e-mon to sat)

Cortland Standard, 110 Main St.; PO Box 5548, Cortland, NY 13045-5548; tel (607) 756-5665; fax (607) 756-5665 ext 27.
Circulation: 11,366(e); 11,366(e-sat); Sworn Oct. 1, 1995.
Price: 35¢(d); 35¢(sat); $2.10/wk (carrier); $109.20/yr (carrier), $133.10/yr (mail).
Advertising: Open inch rate $9.95(e); $9.95(e-sat). **Representative:** Landon Associates Inc.
News Service: AP. **Politics:** Independent. **Established:** 1867.
Not Published: New Year; Memorial Day; Independence Day; Labor Day; Thanksgiving; Christmas.
Special Editions: Year in Review (Jan); "People Who Make Area Business Run" (Feb); Bridal (Mar); Summer Sun & Fun (May); "Dairy", "High School Graduation" (June); College (Aug); The New Season, Car Care (Oct); Gift Guide (Nov); "Christmas Greetings", "First Baby of the Year" (Dec).
Special Weekly Sections: Best Food Day, Consumer News (mon); Best Food Day (sat); Business Pages (mon-fri).
Magazines: Intermission; TV Magazine.

CORPORATE OFFICERS
President/Treasurer Paul L Geibel
Vice Pres Ann G Howe
Secretary Kevin R Howe
GENERAL MANAGEMENT
Publisher Kevin R Howe
General Manager Edward J Rounds
Business Manager Wayne L Clark
ADVERTISING
Manager-General Edward J Rounds
Manager-Retail Edward J Rounds
Manager-Classified Mildred Briggs
MARKETING AND PROMOTION
Coordinator-Marketing/Promotion Guy C Ussery
CIRCULATION
Manager James Quattro
Coordinator Guy C Ussery
NEWS EXECUTIVE
Editor Kevin R Howe
EDITORS AND MANAGERS
News Editor Sherwood W Chapman
Society/Women's Editor Jennifer Conkling
Sports Editor Jere Dexter
PRODUCTION
Foreman-Composing Stanley Carruthers
Foreman-Pressroom Dennis Woodward

Market Information: TMC.
Mechanical available: Offset; Black and 2 ROP colors; insert accepted — preprinted; page cut-offs — 22¾".
Mechanical specifications: Type page 13¼" x 21½"; E - 6 cols, 2¹⁄₁₆", ⅛" between; A - 6 cols, 2¹⁄₁₆", ⅛" between; C - 9 cols, 1⅜", ¹⁄₁₆" between.
Commodity consumption: Newsprint 495 short tons; widths 28", 28", 14", 14"; black ink 11,400 pounds; color ink 230 pounds; single pages printed 6,964; average pages per issue 23.4(d); single plates used 3,800.
Equipment: EDITORIAL: Front-end hardware — Mk/Sys 3000; Front-end software — Mk/ACE 2.20; Printers — Epson/LQ1010. CLASSIFIED: Front-end hardware — Mk/Sys 3000; Front-end software — Mk/NewsTouch, AT/Classified; Printers — TI/810. DISPLAY: Adv layout systems — Ap/Mac Local Talk Network; Front-end hardware — Ap/Mac IIcx, Ap/Mac IIci; Front-end software — Claris/MacDraw Pro, Aldus/FreeHand 4.0, QuarkXPress 3.3; Printers — Ap/Mac LaserWriter II NT. PRODUCTION: OCR software — Read-it/Pro 3.0A; Typesetters — 2-NewGen/PS480; Plate exposures — 2-Nu/Flip Top FT40; Plate processors — 1-Nat/A250; Electronic picture desk — Lf/AP Leaf Picture Desk; Scanners — Applescan; Production cameras — 1-Eskofot/6006, 1-B/Commodore 24; Automatic film processors — DAI/LD-220-QT. PRESSROOM: Line 1 — 4-G/Urbanite; Folders — 1-G; Press control system — Fin. MAILROOM: Bundle tyer — 1-MLN. WIRE SERVICES: News — AP; Photos — AP; Receiving dishes — size-10ft, AP. BUSINESS COMPUTERS: Axil/311; Applications: Vision Data: Bus, Gen ledger, Accts receivable, Accts payable, Circ.

DUNKIRK-FREDONIA

Chautauqua County

'90 U.S. Census- 24,425 (Dunkirk 13,989; Fredonia 10,436); E&P '96 Est. 22,877 (Dunkirk 12,981; Fredonia 9,896)
ABC-CZ (90): 25,907 (HH 9,472)

Evening Observer

(e-mon to fri; m-sat; S)

Evening Observer, 8-10 E. 2nd St., Dunkirk, NY 14048-0391; tel (716) 366-3000; fax (716) 366-3005. Ogden Newspapers group.
Circulation: 14,512(e); 14,512(m-sat); 13,850(S); ABC Sept. 30, 1995.
Price: 35¢(d); 35¢(sat) 35¢(S); $1.80/wk (carrier); $90.00/yr.
Advertising: Open inch rate $35.66(e); $35.66(m-sat); $35.66(S). **Representative:** Landon Associates Inc.
News Service: AP. **Politics:** Independent. **Established:** 1882.
Note: Effective May 7, 1995, this publication added a Sunday edition.
Not Published: New Year; Memorial Day; Independence Day; Labor Day; Thanksgiving; Christmas.
Special Editions: Health & Fitness, New Year's Resolutions, Winter Blues Busters, Dream Vacations (Jan); Income Tax Pages, Bridal Edition, Valentine's Sweets & Treats, National Dental Health, Babies of '96 (Feb); Money Matters, Ag Week, Red Cross, E911 Reminder (Mar); Spring Car Care, International Earth Day, National Secretaries Week/March of Dimes, Home & Garden (Apr); Modular Homes, National Law, Memorial Day, Spring/Summer Tourism (May); High School Graduates, Vacation Edition, Flag Day, A Great Cup of Coffee (June); Welcome Back Bills, National Ice Cream Month, National Eye Exam Month, Chautauqua County Fair Tab (July); Fredonia Farm Festival, SUNY College Education, Back-to-School (Aug); High School Sports, Labor Day Edition, SC Festival of Grapes, Chamber/Progress, School Safety, Just Say "NO" (Sept); Is It Grapes?, Fall Car Care, Halloween Safety, Fire Prevention/Red Ribbon, Cooking/Recipes, Fall Tourism (Oct); Christmas Shop, Veteran's Day, Things We're Thankful For (Nov); Christmas Greetings, Shop Locally, New Year's Greetings (Dec).
Magazine: TV Showtime Tab (sat).

GENERAL MANAGEMENT
Publisher/General Manager Charles Jarvis
Business Manager Norma Eltringham
ADVERTISING
Director Karl T Davis
CIRCULATION
Manager Andy Gee
NEWS EXECUTIVES
Editor Charles Jarvis
Managing Editor Keith Sheldon
Asst Managing Editor Jon Swerens
EDITORS AND MANAGERS
City/Metro Editor Kyle Kubera
Editorial Page Editor Jon Swerens
Education Editor Keith Sheldon
Entertainment/Amusements Editor Bill Hammond
Features Editor Jen Osborne
Health/Medical Editor Jen Osborne
Living Editor Jen Osborne
National Editor Kyle Kubera
News Editor Kyle Kubera
Regional Editor Keith Sheldon
Religion Editor Kyle Kubera
Science/Technology Editor Keith Sheldon
Sports Editor Jerry Reily
Television/Music Editor Jen Osborne
Theater/Film Editor Jen Osborne
Travel Editor Keith Sheldon
PRODUCTION
Manager-Press John Konegni
Manager-Systems/Pre Press Wayne Carpenter

Market Information: ADS.
Mechanical available: Offset; Black and 3 ROP colors; insert accepted — preprinted, all; page cut-offs — 22½".
Mechanical specifications: Type page 13" x 21½"; E - 6 cols, 2.04", ⅛" between; A - 6 cols, 2.04", ⅛" between; C - 9 cols, 1⅓", .08" between.
Commodity consumption: Newsprint 590 metric tons; widths 28", 14"; black ink 14,800 pounds; color ink 400 pounds; single pages printed 7,376; average pages per issue 24(d); single plates used 5,320.
Equipment: EDITORIAL: Front-end hardware — 14-RSK/Tandy 3000; Front-end software — CText, Caere/OmniPage; Printers — NewGen/PS480 LaserPrinter. CLASSIFIED: Front-end hardware — 5-RSK/Tandy 3000; Front-end software — CText; Printers — NewGen/PS480, Ap/Mac LaserPrinter, Dataproducts/DMP Printer; Other equipment — Mountain/Tape Drive. DISPLAY: Front-end hardware — 3-Ap/Mac II, 1-Ap/Mac Quadra 950, CD-Rom; Front-end software — QuarkXPress, Multi-Ad/Creator, Aldus/FreeHand, Hyphen/Mac RIP; Printers — Graphic Enterprises/PS 3, Ap/Mac LaserWriter Plus w/Accel-a-Writer Plus. PRODUCTION: Typesetters — NewGen; Plate exposures — B, BKY/Ascor; Plate processors — Roconex; Electronic picture desk — Lf/AP Leaf Picture Desk; Scanners — ECR/Autokon 1000, Graphic Enterprises/PageScan 3, Nikon/3510 Scanner; Production cameras — B; Automatic film processors — LE/LD-18; Color separation equipment (conventional) — Adobe/Photo-Shop. PRESSROOM: Line 1 — 5-G/Urbanite; Folders — G. MAILROOM: Bundle tyer — 2-Bu, 1-Sa. LIBRARY: Combination — 2-Minolta/Microfishe readers. WIRE SERVICES: News — AP Datastream; Receiving dishes — size-10ft, AP. BUSINESS COMPUTERS: 5-Bs/25; Applications: Western Computer: Circ, Adv billing, Accts receivable, Gen ledger, Payroll, Adv scheduling; PCs & micros networked; PCs & main system networked.

ELMIRA

Chemung County

'90 U.S. Census- 33,724; E&P '96 Est. 32,448
ABC-NDM (90): 175,274 (HH 35,156)

Star-Gazette (m-mon to sat; S)

Star-Gazette, 201 Baldwin St.; PO Box 285, Elmira, NY 14902-9976; tel (607) 734-5151; fax (607) 733-4408. Gannett Co. Inc. group.
Circulation: 34,735(m); 34,735(m-sat); 48,191(S); ABC Sept. 30, 1995.
Price: 35¢(d); 35¢(sat); $1.50(S); $3.25/wk (carrier).
Advertising: Open inch rate $44.15(m); $44.15(m-sat); $57.27(S). **Representative:** Gannett National Newspaper Sales.
News Services: AP, GNS, Presslink. **Politics:** Independent. **Established:** 1829 (Gazette), 1879 (Telegram), 1888 (Star).
Special Editions: Economic Forecast Super Bowl, Auto Update (Jan); Brides, Valentine's Love Lines, Rotary Home Show (Feb); Around the House, Reader's Choice Awards (Mar); Auto Update, Around the House, Lake Country (Apr); Around the House, LPGA Preview, LPGA Sports Wraps, Lake Country (May); Around the House, Lake Country, Grads '96 (June); Around the House, Airfest, Auto Update, NASCAR-Bud at the Glen, Lake Country (July); Around the House, Lake Country, Back-to-School, Football (Aug); Around the House, Trade Show, Lake Country (Sept); Newcomer's Guide, Around the House, Auto Update, College Info Day (Oct); Around the House, Gift Guide 1 & 2 (Nov); Around the House, Gift Guide 3, Last Minute Gifts (Dec).
Special Weekly Sections: Food Inserts, Seniors (mon); Health, Doctor's (tues); Food (wed); Time Out (thur); Shopping, Going Out Calendar (fri); Religion Page, Going Out Calendar, Auto Racing (sat); TV Week, Going Out Calendar, Coupons, Engagements/Anniversaries, Wedding of the Week, Pet, Outdoor, Family Spotlight, Home (S); Money, Sports, Twin Tiers Life, Stock Pages (daily).
Magazines: Time Out (thur); USA Weekend, TV Week, Full-Color Comics (S).

CORPORATE OFFICER
President E Pat Thompson Frantz
GENERAL MANAGEMENT
Publisher E Pat Thompson Frantz
Controller Todd E Miller
Personnel Director Lois Haidvogel
ADVERTISING
Director Mark Logsdon
Manager-Classified Paula Van Kuren
Exec-Major Accounts Jan Gossie
MARKETING AND PROMOTION
Director-Market Development Sheila Coon
TELECOMMUNICATIONS
Manager-Telecommunications Jay Keller
CIRCULATION
Director Kevin O'Neil
NEWS EXECUTIVES
Editor Charles W Nutt Jr
Exec Editor David Kubissa
EDITORS AND MANAGERS
Editorial Page Editor Ray Finger
Features Editor Kathryn Frank
Films/Theater Editor Dan Aloi
Director-Graphics Peg Lyon
Librarian Margaret Ridosh
Metro Editor Ron Ostroff
News Editor Michael Gossie
Photo Editor Jeff Richards
Sports Editor Roger Neumann
MANAGEMENT INFORMATION SERVICES
Data Processing Manager Kate Rathbun
PRODUCTION
Director Andrew Swanton
Manager-Pressroom George Van Houten
Manager-Systems Jay Keller
Manager-Mailroom Ron Garrison

Market Information: Zoned editions; Split Run; TMC; ADS; Operate audiotex; Electronic edition.
Mechanical available: DiLitho; Black and 3 ROP colors; insert accepted — preprinted, card, standard & tab; page cut-offs — 22¾".

Copyright ©1996 by the Editor & Publisher Co.

New York   I-269

Mechanical specifications: Type page 12.5" x 21½"; E - 6 cols, 2", ⅛" between; A - 6 cols, 2", ⅛" between; C - 9 cols, 1 7/16", 1/16" between.
Commodity consumption: Newsprint 2,700 short tons; width 54"; black ink 67,000 pounds; color ink 11,000 pounds; single pages printed 11,600; average pages per issue 26(d), 60(S); single plates used 40,000.
Equipment: EDITORIAL: Front-end hardware — Ap/Mac, SII. CLASSIFIED: Front-end hardware — SII. DISPLAY: Adv layout systems — Multi-Ad/Creator; Front-end software — Multi-Ad/Creator; Printers — Clipper/3850. PRODUCTION: Pagination software — QuarkXPress; Typesetters — 2-III/3850; Platemaking systems — DiLitho; Plate exposures — 1-Nu/Flip Top 40L, 1-Nu/Flip Top FT40LNS; Plate processors — 1-Nat/A-340; Electronic picture desk — Lf/AP Leaf Picture Desk; Scanners — 1-ECR/Autokon 1000DE; Production cameras — 1-R/580, 1-R, C/Marathon; Automatic film processors — 2-LE, 2-LD/24; Color separation equipment (conventional) — Lf/AP Leaf Picture Desk, Adobe/Photoshop.
PRESSROOM: Line 1 — 7-G/Headliner double width; Folders — 2-G/2:1. MAILROOM: Counter stackers — QWI/300; Inserters and stuffers — 3-M/227-S; Bundle tyer — MLN/News 90. COMMUNICATIONS: Digital ad delivery system — AP AdSend, Imagetext. WIRE SERVICES: News — AP, GNS; Photos — AP; Stock tables — AP; Syndicates — AP, GNS, PR Newswire; Receiving dishes — size-10ft, AP. BUSINESS COMPUTERS: 1-IBM/AS-400; Applications: Accts payable, Accts receivable, Class, Gen ledger, Payroll; PCs & main system networked.

FREDONIA
See DUNKIRK

FULTON
See OSWEGO

GENEVA
Ontario County
'90 U.S. Census- 14,143; E&P '96 Est. 13,371
ABC-CZ (90): 14,143 (HH 5,284)

Finger Lakes Times
(e-mon to fri; S)
Finger Lakes Times, 218 Genessee St., Geneva, NY 14456; tel (315) 789-3333; fax (315) 789-4077. Independent Publications Inc. group.
Circulation: 18,986(e); 20,341(S); ABC Sept. 30, 1995.
Price: 50¢(d); $1.00(S); $2.25/wk; $10.00/mo; $138.00/yr.
Advertising: Open inch rate $11.88(e); $11.88(S). Representative: Papert Companies.
News Services: AP, LAT-WP. Politics: Independent. Established: 1895.
Not Published: New Year; Memorial Day; Independence Day; Labor Day; Thanksgiving; Christmas.
Special Edition: Vacation Guide (May).
Special Weekly Sections: Real Estate (thur); Best Food Day (S).
Magazines: Parade, TV Times (S).

CORPORATE OFFICER
President .... William L McLean III
GENERAL MANAGEMENT
Publisher .... George A Park Jr
Controller .... Mark Berkowitz
ADVERTISING
Director .... Thomas R Miller
CIRCULATION
Director .... Mark Berkowitz
NEWS EXECUTIVES
Editor .... Donald C Hadley
Managing Editor .... Philip Beckley
PRODUCTION
Manager .... John Duquette
Foreman-Composing ..... Grace Moore
Foreman-Pressroom ..... Gerald Lamphier

Market Information: TMC.
Mechanical available: Offset; Black and 3 ROP colors; insert accepted — preprinted; page cut-offs — 22¾".
Mechanical specifications: Type page 13" x 21"; E - 6 cols, 2 1/16", ⅛" between; A - 6 cols, 2 1/16", ⅛" between; C - 8 cols, 1 9/16", 1/16" between.

Commodity consumption: Newsprint 1,200 short tons; widths 27½", 13¾"; black ink 20,000 pounds; color ink 1,000 pounds; single pages printed 7,000; average pages per issue 24(d); single plates used 4,000.
Equipment: EDITORIAL: Front-end hardware — 24-III; Front-end software — III; Other equipment — 6-RSK/TRS-80-100. CLASSIFIED: Front-end hardware — 4-III; Front-end software — III. DISPLAY: Front-end hardware — 6-Ap/Mac si. PRODUCTION: Pagination software — QuarkXPress; Typesetters — 2-XIT/Clipper, 1-XIT/Schooner Imagesetter; Plate exposures — 1-Nu; Electronic picture desk — Lf/AP Leaf Picture Desk; Production cameras — 1-AG/RPS204 Vertical; Digital color separation equipment — Nikon/LS-3510AF.
PRESSROOM: Line 1 — 5-G/Urbanite; Folders — 1-G. MAILROOM: Counter stackers — 1-KAN; Inserters and stuffers — 1-KAN/480; Bundle tyer — 2-MLN; Addressing machine — 1-El. LIBRARY: Electronic — III. WIRE SERVICES: News — LAT-WP, AP; Receiving dishes — AP. BUSINESS COMPUTERS: 8-Everex/PC; Applications: MSSI: Accts receivable, Accts payable, Gen ledger, Circ; PCs & micros networked.

GLENS FALLS
Warren County
'90 U.S. Census- 15,023; E&P '96 Est. 14,334
ABC-CZ (90): 29,741 (HH 11,867)

The Post-Star (m-mon to sat; S)
The Post-Star, Lawrence and Cooper Sts.; PO Box 2157, Glens Falls, NY 12801; tel (518) 792-3131; fax (518) 761-1255; e-mail poststar@globalone.net; web site http://www.global1.net/poststar/. Howard Publications group.
Circulation: 35,061(m); 35,061(m-sat); 38,001(S); ABC Sept. 30, 1995.
Price: 50¢(d); 50¢(sat); $1.50(S); $3.15/wk (carrier); $23.50/mo; $250.00/yr.
Advertising: Open inch rate $36.00(m); $36.00(m-sat); $36.00(S). Representative: Landon Associates Inc.
News Services: AP, KRT. Politics: Independent. Established: 1897 (Times), 1904 (Post-Star).
Not Published: Christmas.
Magazines: Real Estate (sat); TV Book (S).

CORPORATE OFFICERS
President .... Robert S Howard
Vice Pres .... James G Marshall
GENERAL MANAGEMENT
Publisher .... James G Marshall
Office Manager .... Jeff Reynolds
ADVERTISING
Manager-Display .... Nick Caimano
CIRCULATION
Manager .... Bill Sara
Manager-Electronic Edition ... Sam Gayle
NEWS EXECUTIVE
Managing Editor .... Steve Bennett
EDITORS AND MANAGERS
City Editor .... Mark Mahoney
Features Editor .... Tamara Dietrich
News Editor .... Jim White
Director-Photography .. Monty Calvert
Regional Editor .... Bob Condon
Sports Editor .... Ken Tingley
PRODUCTION
Manager .... Sam Gayle
Foreman-Press .... Jeff Guay
Foreman-Distribution .. Matt Pidgeon
Foreman-Composing ... Bill Owens
Foreman-Shipping & Receiving ... Dale Trombley
Officer-Safety & Training ... Tom Augstein

Market Information: Zoned editions; Split Run; Electronic edition.
Mechanical available: Offset; Black and 3 ROP colors; insert accepted — preprinted; page cut-offs — 22¾".
Mechanical specifications: Type page 13" x 21½"; E - 6 cols, 2 1/16", ⅛" between; A - 6 cols, 2 1/16", ⅛" between; C - 9 cols, 1 1/16", ⅛" between.
Commodity consumption: Newsprint 3,800 metric tons; widths 27½", 13 5/8"; black ink 100,000 pounds; color ink 20,000 pounds; single pages printed 11,300; average pages per issue 45(d), 70(S); single plates used 72,000.
Equipment: EDITORIAL: Front-end hardware — 3-Sun/460II, 36-Sun/460, 4-Ap/Mac 7100-66, 9-Ap/Mac II, 3-Ap/Mac SE; Front-end software — CText/Publisher, QuarkXPress; Printers — HP/LaserJet 4M, Hyphen/Dash 600. CLASSIFIED: Front-end hardware — 1-Sun/670, 2-Sun/460II, 8-NCD; Front-end software — Vision Data/Island Write; Printers —

HP/LaserJet 3p. DISPLAY: Adv layout systems — SCS/Layout 8000; Front-end hardware — 6-Ap/Mac II, 2-Ap/Mac SE, 7-Ap/Mac 7100-66; Front-end software — QuarkXPress, Adobe/Illustrator; Printers — LaserMaster/1800, Hyphen/Dash-600, Ap/Mac LaserWriter 16-600 PS; Other equipment — Compaq/486. PRODUCTION: Pagination software — QuarkXPress 3.31; Typesetters — 2-ECR/PelBox 108-S, 1-Ap/Mac NTX; Plate exposures — 1-Nu/Flip Top FT40V6UPNS; Electronic picture desk — Lf/AP Leaf Picture Desk; Scanners — 2-Nikon/LS3500, 1-HP, 2-AG/Horizon, 1-Lf; Automatic film processors — 2-LE/LS2600; Film transporters — 2-LE; Digital color separation equipment — Adobe/Photoshop.
PRESSROOM: Line 1 — 10-G/Urbanite single width; Press drives — Fin; Folders — 1-G; Reels and stands — 8-G; Press control system — Fin. MAILROOM: Counter stackers — 1-MM/338, 1-Id/Marathon, 1-MM/310-20; Inserters and stuffers — 1-MM/308; Bundle tyer — 1-MLN/MLN2HS, 1-OVL; Wrapping singles — 1-HL/Monarch. LIBRARY: Electronic — Topic. WIRE SERVICES: News — AP, KRT; Photos — AP; Stock tables — AP; Receiving dishes — size-10ft, AP. BUSINESS COMPUTERS: 1-Sun/460, 10-DEC/VT 420; Applications: Vision Data; PCs & micros networked; PCs & main system networked.

GLOVERSVILLE-JOHNSTOWN
Fulton County
'90 U.S. Census- 25,714 (Gloversville 16,656; Johnstown 9,058); E&P '96 Est. 24,551 (Gloversville 15,737; Johnstown 8,814)
ABC-CZ (90): 29,444 (HH 11,950)

The Leader-Herald
(e-mon to fri; m-sat; S)
The Leader-Herald, 8 E. Fulton St.; PO Box 1280, Gloversville, NY 12078; tel (518) 725-8616; fax (518) 725-8616 ext 447. Ogden Newspapers group.
Circulation: 12,125(e); 12,125(m-sat); 12,553(S); ABC Sept. 30, 1995.
Price: 35¢(d); 35¢(sat); $1.00(S); $2.45/wk.
Advertising: Open inch rate $14.00(e); $14.00(m-sat); $14.00(S). Representative: Landon Associates Inc.
News Service: AP. Politics: Independent. Established: 1887.
Special Editions: Portraits (Feb); Spring Car Care, Bridal Tab (Mar); Spring Home Improvement & Garden Time (Apr); Spring & Summer Vacation Guide (May); Lake Country (June, July, Aug); Fall & Winter Vacation Guide (Sept); Fall Home Improvement, Fall Car Care (Oct); Fall & Winter Sports Guide, Cookbook, Christmas Gift Guide (Nov); Senior Scene, Real Estate (monthly).
Special Weekly Sections: Best Food (wed); Church News (sat); Business-Stocks, Best Food, TV Listings, Travel (S).
Magazines: Free Distribution Tab; Sunday Leader Mini-Pages.

CORPORATE OFFICERS
President .... G Ogden Nutting
Vice Pres .... William C Nutting
Vice Pres .... Robert M Nutting
Secretary .... William D Nutting
Treasurer .... Duane D Wittman
GENERAL MANAGEMENT
Publisher .... Joseph Bradley
Purchasing Agent ..... Gary Brothers
ADVERTISING
Director .... Pat Beck
Manager-Retail .... William A Roosa
CIRCULATION
Director/Promotion Manager ... Mark R Balzano
NEWS EXECUTIVE
Editor .... Tom Nevich
EDITORS AND MANAGERS
Automotive Editor .... Wally Truesdell
Books/Food Editor .... Tom Nevich
Business/Finance Editor ... Dianne Nevich
City Editor .... Jim Harris
Editorial Page Editor .. Tom Nevich
Fashion/Style Editor .. Kathy Smith
Home Furnishings Editor ... Kathy Smith
Living/Lifestyle Editor ... Kathy Smith
Photo Editor .... Harold Laird
Sports Editor .... Tammy Dorman
Women's Editor .... Kathy Smith

Market Information: TMC.
Mechanical available: Offset; Black and 3 ROP colors; insert accepted — preprinted, cards and booklets; page cut-offs — 22¾".
Mechanical specifications: Type page 13" x 21¼"; E - 6 cols, 2 1/16", ⅛" between; A - 6 cols, 2 1/16", ⅛" between; C - 8 cols, 1½", ⅛" between.
Commodity consumption: Newsprint 759 short tons; widths 27", 13½"; single pages printed 7,286; average pages per issue 20(d), 53(S); single plates used 7,832.
Equipment: EDITORIAL: Front-end hardware — COM/OS 140, 5-Ap/Mac; Front-end software — QuarkXPress, Aldus/FreeHand, Adobe/Photoshop; Printers — Ap/Mac LaserWriter, MON/ExpressMaster 1270 Imagesetter, ECR/URL 36; Other equipment — 18-COM. CLASSIFIED: Front-end hardware — 3-COM/OS 140. DISPLAY: Front-end hardware — 4-Ap/Mac; Front-end software — Multi-Ad/Creator, Adobe/Photoshop; Printers — New Gen/660B, ECR/VRL 36, MON/Expressmaster 1270. PRODUCTION: Pagination software — QuarkXPress 3.11; OCR software — Typereader 1.0.1; Typesetters — 1-MON/ExpressMaster 1270, 1-ECR/URL 36; Plate exposures — 1-Nu/Flip Top FT40UPNS, 1-Nu/Flip Top FT40M; Plate processors — 1-WL/30C, 1-Imperial/Top Coater; Electronic picture desk — 1-Lf/AP Leaf Picture Desk; Scanners — 2-HP/ScanJet IIcx, 1-Kk/RS-2035; Production cameras — 1-R/5000H, 1-A; Automatic film processors — 1-Polychrome/24PL; Shrink lenses — 1-CK Optical/SQU-7; Color separation equipment (conventional) — Kk/RS-2035 Scanner.
PRESSROOM: Line 1 — 6-G/Urbanite; Line 2 — 6-HI/V15A; Folders — 1-G/2, 1-HI/Combination; Pasters — 4-Martin. MAILROOM: Counter stackers — 2-BG/Count-O-Veyor; Bundle tyer — 2-MLN, 1-Sa; Addressing machine — Ch. WIRE SERVICES: News — AP; Photos — AP; Stock tables — TMS; Receiving dishes — AP. BUSINESS COMPUTERS: NCR/386, Unix/486 System; Applications: Accts payable, Accts receivable, Gen ledger, Payroll, Newsprint, Roll inventory.

HERKIMER
Herkimer County
'90 U.S. Census- 7,945; E&P '96 Est. 7,599
ABC-CZ (90): 19,819 (HH 7,884)

Evening Telegram
(e-mon to fri; m-sat)
Evening Telegram, 111-113 Green St.; PO Box 551, Herkimer, NY 13350; tel (315) 866-2220; fax (315) 866-5913. Hollinger International Inc. group.
Circulation: 6,733(e); 6,733(m-sat); ABC Sept. 30, 1995.
Price: 40¢(d); 40¢(sat); $2.00/wk (carrier); $8.80/mo (mail).
Advertising: Open inch rate $11.22(e); $11.22(m-sat).
News Service: AP. Politics: Independent. Established: 1898.
Not Published: New Year; Christmas.
Special Editions: Progress, Bridal (Feb); Spring Sports Preview (Apr); Back-to-School, Fall Sports Preview (Sept); Winter Sports Preview, Christmas (Nov).

GENERAL MANAGEMENT
Publisher .... Beth A Brewer
Controller .... Kim Knapp
ADVERTISING
Manager .... Wesley Williams
NEWS EXECUTIVE
Managing Editor ...... Dan Guezewich
EDITORS AND MANAGERS
Education Editor ..... Donna Thompson
Features Editor ...... Donna Thompson
PRODUCTION
Foreman-Composing ... Herm Harris

Market Information: Zoned editions; TMC.
Mechanical available: Offset; Black and 2 ROP colors; insert accepted — preprinted.
Mechanical specifications: Type page 13¼" x 21½"; E - 6 cols, 2 1/16", ⅛" between; A - 6 cols, 2 1/16", ⅛" between; C - 8 cols, 1¾", ⅛" between.
Commodity consumption: average pages per issue 12(d).
Equipment: EDITORIAL: Front-end hardware — Mk; Printers — Ap/Mac AdWriter. CLASSIFIED: Front-end hardware — Mk; Printers — TI. PRO-

Copyright ©1996 by the Editor & Publisher Co.

I-270 New York

DUCTION: Typesetters — 1-COM/4961, 1-COM/2961; Platemaking systems — Nu-, SCREEN; Production cameras — 1-B. PRESSROOM: Line 1 — G/Community. MAILROOM: Bundle tyer — 1-Sa; Addressing machine — 1-El. WIRE SERVICES: Receiving dishes — size-3ft, AP.

HORNELL

Steuben County

'90 U.S. Census- 9,877; E&P '96 Est. 9,590

The Evening Tribune

(e-mon to fri)

The Spectator (S)

The Evening Tribune, 85 Canisteo St., Hornell, NY 14843; tel (607) 324-1425; fax (607) 324-1462. Hollinger International Inc. group.

Circulation: 7,643(e); 11,783(S); Sworn Oct. 2, 1995.

Price: 50¢(d); $1.50(S); $8.25/mo (carrier), $8.50/mo (motor route).

Advertising: Open inch rate $7.25(e); $8.45(S). **Representative:** Landon Associates Inc.

News Service: AP. **Politics:** Independent. **Established:** 1851.

Note: The Hornell Evening Tribune (e) and the Wellsville Daily Reporter (e) share a Sunday edition.

Not Published: New Year; Memorial Day; Independence Day; Labor Day; Thanksgiving; Christmas.

Special Editions: Outdoor; Car Care (spring/fall); Christmas.

CORPORATE OFFICERS

President Larry J Perrotto
Comptroller Roland McBride

GENERAL MANAGEMENT

Publisher John Frungillo
Controller Robert Rowley

ADVERTISING

Director David Broderick

CIRCULATION

Manager Mark Newcomb

NEWS EXECUTIVE

Managing Editor Cindy Lorow

EDITORS AND MANAGERS

Society Editor Terry Clark
Sports Editor Steve Demartz
Sunday Editor Rob Price

PRODUCTION

Manager Don Howe

Market Information: TMC; ADS.

Mechanical available: Offset; Black and 3 ROP colors; insert accepted — preprinted; page cut-offs — 22¾".

Mechanical specifications: Type page 13" x 21½"; E - 6 cols, 2¹⁄₁₆", ⅛" between; A - 6 cols, 2¹⁄₁₆", ⅛" between; C - 6 cols, 2¹⁄₁₆", ⅛" between.

Commodity consumption: average pages per issue 16(d), 32(S).

Equipment: EDITORIAL: Front-end hardware — Mk, 1-Ap/Mac si. CLASSIFIED: Front-end hardware — Mk. DISPLAY: Front-end hardware — 2-Ap/Mac si. PRODUCTION: Typesetters — 2-COM/Comp 4, 1-COM/Comp 7200-7700, Ap/Mac Laser; Plate exposures — Nu/Flip Top FT40U2UP; Scanners — 1-Kk/5060A; Production cameras — 1-C/Spartan III; Automatic film processors — 1-LE/24BQ; Film transporters — 1-C.
PRESSROOM: Line 1 — 6-G/Suburban; Line 2 — 4-G/Suburban. MAILROOM: Inserters and stuffers — 1-MM/EM 10, 1-KAN/7 unit; Bundle tyer — 4-Bu/18, 1-Sa/1100, 1-Gd; Addressing machine — 1-Am/2605, 1-Am/2600, 1-S/5-E collator, 1-Ch. WIRE SERVICES: News — AP; Receiving dishes — size-10ft, AP. BUSINESS COMPUTERS: 3-IBM/Nomad; Applications: Adv billing, Accts receivable, Gen ledger, Payroll, Mail circ; PCs & micros networked.

HUDSON

Columbia County

'90 U.S. Census- 8,034; E&P '96 Est. 8,074

Register-Star (e-mon to fri; S)

Register-Star, 364 Warren St.; PO Box 635, Hudson, NY 12534; tel (518) 828-1616; fax (518) 828-9437. Park Communications Inc. group.

Circulation: 7,429(e); 7,860(S); Sworn Oct. 6, 1995.

Price: 35¢(d); 35¢(S); $93.60/yr.

Advertising: Open inch rate $13.40(e); $13.40(S). **Representative:** Landon Associates Inc.

News Service: AP. **Politics:** Independent. **Established:** 1785.

Not Published: Christmas.

Special Editions: Progress (Jan); Cupid's Corner, Expo, Taxes (Feb); Bridal, Spring (Mar); Auto (Apr); Woman to Woman (May, June); Back-to-School, Fair-Farm (Aug); Interior, Sports (Sept); Fall (Oct); Holidays (Nov); Season's Greetings, Year-End (Dec).

Special Weekly Sections: Best Food Days (mon); TV Tab, Best Food Days (S).

Magazine: Scene (fri).

CORPORATE OFFICERS

President Wright M Thomas
Vice Pres-Newspapers Ralph J Martin

GENERAL MANAGEMENT

Publisher/General Manager William C Lundquest
Manager-Business/Personnel Terry Drobner

ADVERTISING

Manager Steve Mortefolio

CIRCULATION

Manager John Vogt

NEWS EXECUTIVE

Managing Editor Jack Kehrer

EDITORS AND MANAGERS

City Editor Joseph Kilcoyne
Sunday Editor Linda Fenoff

PRODUCTION

Manager-Pressroom Richard Dellavechia

Market Information: TMC; ADS.

Mechanical available: Offset; Black and 3 ROP colors; insert accepted — preprinted, all; page cut-offs — 22¾".

Mechanical specifications: Type page 13" x 21½"; E - 6 cols, 2.03", ⅙" between; A - 6 cols, 2.03", ⅙" between; C - 10 cols, 1.22", ¹⁄₁₂" between.

Commodity consumption: Newsprint 600 metric tons; widths 27½", 34"; black ink 9,900 pounds; color ink 180 pounds; single pages printed 6,200; average pages per issue 16(d), 16(S).

Equipment: EDITORIAL: Front-end hardware — Mk; Front-end software — Mk; Printers — Ap/Mac LaserWriter II NTX. CLASSIFIED: Front-end hardware — Mk; Front-end software — Mk; Printers — Ap/Mac LaserWriter II NTX. DISPLAY: Adv layout systems — Mk, Ap/Mac; Front-end hardware — Ap/Mac IIcx; Front-end software — Mk/Mycro-Comp AdWriter; Printers — Ap/Mac LaserWriter II NTX. PRODUCTION: Typesetters — Ap/Mac LaserWriter II NTX; Plate exposures — Nu/Flip Top; Plate processors — Nu/A-250.
PRESSROOM: Line 1 — 7-G/Community. MAILROOM: Inserters and stuffers — KAN/320; Bundle tyer — Bu/Strapping machine. WIRE SERVICES: Receiving dishes — size-12ft, AP. BUSINESS COMPUTERS: 1-Convergent/5320; Applications: Vision Data: Accts receivable, Accts payable, Payroll, Gen ledger, Circ.

ITHACA

Tompkins County

'90 U.S. Census- 29,541; E&P '96 Est. 30,234
ABC-NDM (90): 94,097 (HH 33,338)

The Ithaca Journal

(e-mon to sat)

The Ithaca Journal, 123 W. State St., thaca, NY 14850; tel (607) 272-2321; fax (607) 275-9103; e-mail ithjournal@aol.com. Gannett Co. Inc. group.

Circulation: 19,012(e); 23,752(e-sat); ABC Sept. 30, 1995.

Price: 35¢(d); 50¢(sat); $2.50/wk (motor route); $10.00/mo (motor route); $113.00/yr (motor route).

Advertising: Open inch rate $31.75(e); $31.75(e-sat). **Representative:** Gannett National Newspaper Sales.

News Services: AP, GNS. **Politics:** Independent. **Established:** 1815.

Special Editions: Business Outlook (Jan); Brides, Interiors (Feb); Business Journal, Auto Journal (Mar); Home Improvement, Coupon Book (Apr); Interiors, Coupon Book, Travel Guide (May); Business Journal, Summer Fun (June); Coupon Book (July); Interiors, Newcomer's Guide (Aug); Home Improvement, Business Journal, Football, Coupon Book (Sept); Interiors, Auto Journal (Oct); Gift Guides, Voter's Guide (Nov); Gift Guides, Coupon Book (Dec); Health Watch (monthly).

Special Weekly Sections: Food, Education, Wine Column (mon); Relationships, Seniors, High School Sports, Weddings and Engagements (tues); Outdoor Column, Real Estate (wed); Entertainment (Arts & Leisure), Health and Science, Nature Highlight (thur); Running Column, Movie Review, Kids Page (fri); Travel, Religion, Book Review (sat).

Magazines: Arts & Leisure (local, newsprint) (thur); TV Book (fri).

CORPORATE OFFICERS

President Ellen Leifeld
Secretary Thomas Chapple
Treasurer Jimmy L Thomas

GENERAL MANAGEMENT

Publisher Ellen Leifeld

ADVERTISING

Director Carol Becker
Manager-Classified Sherri Deaton
Manager-Retail John Miller

MARKETING AND PROMOTION

Marketing Director-Market Development Michele Sardinia

CIRCULATION

Director Barbara Gallo

NEWS EXECUTIVES

Managing Editor Ted Haider
Asst Managing Editor Mike Beck

EDITORS AND MANAGERS

Business/Finance Editor David Hill
Columnist Franklin Crawford
Editorial Page Editor Gary Stewart
Features Editor Stephen Landesman
Films/Theater Editor Mathew Palm
News Editor Mathew Palm
News Editor Melinda Crowcroft
Photo Editor Eric Hegedus
Sports Editor Tom Fleischman

MANAGEMENT INFORMATION SERVICES

Manager-Info Service Ron Siemering

PRODUCTION

Director Howard Lawrence
Foreman-Composing Jeanette Bates
Manager-Technical Service Ron Havington

Market Information: TMC.

Mechanical available: Offset; Black and 3 ROP colors; insert accepted — preprinted, print and deliver; page cut-offs — 21½".

Mechanical specifications: Type page 13" x 21⅜"; E - 6 cols, 2¹⁄₁₆", ⅛" between; A - 6 cols, 2¹⁄₁₆", ⅛" between; C - 9 cols, 1⅜", ¹⁄₁₆" between.

Commodity consumption: Newsprint 2,500 short tons; widths 27½", 13¾"; black ink 42,016 pounds; color ink 3,526 pounds; single pages printed 9,296; average pages per issue 30(d), 32(sat); single plates used 21,167.

Equipment: EDITORIAL: Front-end hardware — DEC, SCS, 3-Dell/486; Front-end software — SCS/Editorial 8000; Other equipment — 17-Dell/Edit. CLASSIFIED: Front-end hardware — Dell; Front-end software — SCS/Classified. DISPLAY: Adv layout systems — SCS; Front-end hardware — 1-Dell/Edit, 2-Ap/Mac IIci, 1-Ap/Mac IIcx; Printers — Ap/Mac LaserWriter; Other equipment — CD-Rom, Ap/Mac Scanner. PRODUCTION: Pagination software — QuarkXPress; Typesetters — Tegra/Varityper 5500C; Platemaking systems — LE; Plate exposures — 2-Nu/Flip Top; Plate processors — Nat/A-340; Electronic picture desk — Lf/AP Leaf Picture Desk; Scanners — Microtek; Production cameras — 1-B/Commodore 24; Automatic film processors — 1-LE/LD 24AQ; Color separation equipment (conventional) — 1-C/E-Z Color, BKY.
PRESSROOM: Line 1 — 6-G/Urbanite; Folders — 1-G; Press control system — Fin. MAILROOM: Counter stackers — 1-MM/CS 70, 1-MM/310-20-350, 2-HL/Monitor; Inserters and stuffers — 1-MM/227, 1-Emio/5-into-1; Bundle tyer — 2-MLN/MLEE; Addressing machine — 1-Ch/596. WIRE SERVICES: News — AP Datastream, AP Datafeatures, GNS; Photos — GNS, AP; Receiving dishes — AP, GNS. BUSINESS COMPUTERS: DEC/1144, IBM/XT, IBM/AS400; Applications: Circ, Adv billing, Accts receivable, Gen ledger, Payroll, Human resources.

JAMESTOWN

Chautauqua County

'90 U.S. Census- 34,681; E&P '96 Est. 33,797
ABC-CZ (90): 44,763 (HH 18,445)

Post-Journal

(e-mon to fri; m-sat; S)

Post-Journal, 15 W. 2nd St.; PO Box 190, Jamestown, NY 14702-0190; tel (716) 487-1111; fax (716) 664-3119. Ogden Newspapers group.

Circulation: 24,663(e); 24,663(m-sat); 25,539(S); ABC Sept. 30, 1995.

Price: 35¢(d); 35¢(sat); 75¢(S).

Advertising: Open inch rate $22.82(e); $22.82(m-sat); $22.82(S). **Representative:** Landon Associates Inc.

News Service: AP. **Politics:** Independent-Republican. **Established:** 1826.

Special Editions: Super Bowl Tab, Spring Bridal Book (Jan); Frozen Food Tab, Income Tax Book (Feb); Women's World Book (Mar); Spring Car Care Tab, Golf Guide, Coupon Book (Apr); Home Improvement Tab, Lawn & Garden Tab, Vacation Guide Book (May); Chautauqua Institution Book (June); Dining Guide, Seniors Book (July); Coupon Book, Fall & Winter Bridal Book (Aug); Football Tab, Kitchen & Bath Tab (Sept); Home Furnishings Tab, Fall Car Care Tab (Oct); Cookbook, Hunting Tab, Winter/Spring Guide Book, Coupon Book, Thanksgiving Edition (Nov); Holiday Wishes Book, Calendar, 1st Baby Contest (Dec).

Special Weekly Section: Best Food Day (tues).

Magazines: Tempo Magazine, Television Guide (sat); USA Weekend (S).

CORPORATE OFFICERS

President G Ogden Nutting
Vice Pres William C Nutting
Vice Pres Robert M Nutting
Secretary William O Nutting
Treasurer Duane D Wittman

GENERAL MANAGEMENT

Publisher Donald L Meyer

ADVERTISING

Director Nancy K Phillips
Clerk-National Beverly Laurin

CIRCULATION

Director Christopher Doyle

NEWS EXECUTIVE

Editor Cristie L Herbst

EDITORS AND MANAGERS

Business/Finance Editor Manley Anderson
City Editor Tina Marsh
Editorial Page Editor Cristie L Herbst
Family Editor Bridgetta Overcash
Librarian Sandra Terry
Magazine Editor Bridgetta Overcash
News Editor Jack D'Agostino
Photo Department Manager Joe R Liuzzo
Region Editor David Hrinda
Sports Editor James H Riggs
Television Editor Michael Zabrodsky

PRODUCTION

Manager Kenneth Hampton
Foreman-Pressroom Steven Tedquest
Foreman-Composing Sid Sweeney
Foreman-Mailroom John Donnelly

Market Information: Zoned editions; Split Run; TMC; ADS.

Mechanical available: Offset; Black and 3 ROP colors; insert accepted — preprinted; page cut-offs — 22¾".

Mechanical specifications: Type page 13" x 21¾"; E - 6 cols, 2¹⁄₁₆", ⅛" between; A - 6 cols, 2¹⁄₁₆", ⅛" between; C - 8 cols, 1⅝", ¹⁄₁₆" between.

Commodity consumption: widths 34", 27", 26", 31"; average pages per issue 30(d), 48(S); single plates used 65,800.

Equipment: EDITORIAL: Front-end hardware — SII/Sys 22, 24-SII/ET-960, 3-CCI/XT Clone; Front-end software — SII/Sys 22, EPN; Printers — 2-Ap/Mac LaserWriter II, 1-Dataproducts/LZR 1560, 1-MON/EM 1270, 2-NewGen/360; Other equipment — 5-RSK/TRS-100, 2-RSK/TRS-102, 2-RSK/TRS-200, 1-RSK/TRS-4-P, 1-Lf/AP Leaf Picture Desk, Lf/Leafscan 35, HP/ScanJet C, 4-Ap/Mac Centris 610, 1-Ap/Mac si. CLASSIFIED: Front-end hardware — SII/Sys 22, 6-SII/ET-960; Front-end software — SII/Sys 22, EPN; Printers — 2-Ap/Mac LaserWriter II, 1-Dataproducts/LZR 1560, 1-MON/EM 1270, 2-NewGen/360; Other equipment — 3-Ap/Mac Plus, 5-Ap/Mac Centris 610. DISPLAY: Adv layout systems — 3-Ap/Mac IIsi, 3-Ap/Mac Radius Pivot, 2-Ap/Mac SE20, 5-Ap/Mac Centris 610; Printers — 2-Ap/Mac LaserWriter II, Dataproducts/LZR 1560, 1-MON/EM 1270, 2-NewGen/360;

Other equipment — Nikon/Coolscan, HP/Scan-Jet C. PRODUCTION: Pagination software — QuarkXPress 3.3; Typesetters — 3-Ap/Mac LaserWriter, 2-NewGen/360, 3-NEC/2-290, 1-Dataproducts/LZR 1560, 1-MON/EM 1270, 1-Ap/Mac LCIII Print Server, 1-Ap/Mac AWS-60 Server; Plate exposures — Nu/Flip Top FT40UPNS; Plate processors — 1-WL/30D; Electronic picture desk — Lf/AP Leaf Picture Desk; Scanners — 1-Lf/Leafscan 35, 1-Nikon/Coolscan, 2-HP/ScanJet C; Production cameras — 1-C/Spartan II, 1-C/Pager; Automatic film processors — 1-Trek/25; Film transporters — 1-C; Shrink lenses — 1-CK Optical/SQU-7; Digital color separation equipment — Ap/Mac.
PRESSROOM: Line 1 — 10-G/Urbanite; Press drives — 2-Fin/150 Hp; Folders — 1-G/Urbanite, 1-G/Suburban; Pasters — 6-Martin/Splicer; Press control system — Fin. MAILROOM: Counter stackers — 1-St/251, 1-RS/25, 2-HL/Monitor; Inserters and stuffers — HI/NP 1372; Bundle tyer — 1-MLN/ML2-EE, 2-OVL, 1-Ty-Tech; Wrapping singles — 1-Sa/SR-1A; Addressing machine — 1-KR/215. WIRE SERVICES: News — AP; Photos — AP; Stock tables — TMS; Receiving dishes — size-10ft, AP. BUSINESS COMPUTERS: NCR/Unix; Applications: Adv billing, Accts receivable, Payroll, Accts payable, Gen ledger, Personnel, Circ; PCs & micros networked.

JOHNSTOWN

See GLOVERSVILLE

KINGSTON

Ulster County

'90 U.S. Census- 23,095; E&P '96 Est. 22,004
ABC-CZ (90): 41,642 (HH 16,702)

Daily Freeman (m-mon to fri) *Sunday Freeman* (S)

Daily Freeman, 79-97 Hurley Ave., Kingston, NY 12401; tel (914) 331-5000; fax (914) 338-0672; e-mail dailyfree@aol.com; web site http://www.mhrcc.org/kingston/index.html. Goodson Newspaper group.
Circulation: 22,855(m); 30,821(S); ABC Sept. 30, 1995.
Price: 50¢(d); $1.25(S); $2.45/wk (carrier), $2.70/wk (motor route); $11.00/mo (carrier), $12.00/mo (motor route); $124.00/yr (carrier), $130.00/yr (motor route).
Advertising: Open inch rate $18.74(m); $22.40(S). **Representative:** Papert Companies.
News Service: AP. **Politics:** Independent. **Established:** 1871.
Advertising not accepted: All advertising copy accepted subject to publisher's approval.
Special Editions: YMCA, Business Review, Homebuyer's Guide (Jan); Brides, Meal Planner, Drug Abuse (Feb); Mature Years, Home & Garden, Lion's Expo, Spring Car Care, Dining Guide, UC Home Show, YMCA, Modular Homes (Mar); Kingston Classic, New Autos, Health & Fitness, Homebuyer's Guide (Apr); Women's View, Getting Around, Mindworks, YMCA, Homebuyer's Guide (May); Getting Around, Cars, Boats & Spokes, Youth Views, Summer Lifestyles (June); Summer Car Care, Newcomer's Guide, Parenting, Getting Around, Homebuyer's Guide (July); Ulster County Fair, Mature Years, Broadway, Back-to-School, Dutchess County Fair, YMCA (Aug); Football, Living Designs, Saugerties Festival, Fall Car Care, Pets, Focus on the Arts (Sept); Mindworks, Dining Guide, Home Improvement, New Cars, YMCA, Homebuyer's Guide (Oct); Education, Women's View, Winter Car Care, Winter Lifestyles, Holiday Gift Guide I (Nov); Holiday Gift Guide II, Holiday Gift Guide III, Uptown Kingston, Holiday Song Book (Dec); Doorways (2x/mo).
Special Weekly Sections: Best Food Edition (wed); Youth (thur); Entertainment (fri); Realtors (alternate fri); Auto, Best Food Edition, Financial, Hobbies, Real Estate, Travel, Youth (S).
Magazines: Preview Tab, USA Weekend (fri); People & Events Magazine, Channels (newsprint) (S).

CORPORATE OFFICERS

President	David N Hurwitz
Vice Pres	David B Carr
Secretary	Royal E Blakeman
Treasurer	Benjamin J Kowalczyk

GENERAL MANAGEMENT

Publisher	Ira Fusfeld
Controller	Robert McClintock
Manager-Operations	G T Cincotta

ADVERTISING

Director	John P Martin
Manager-Marketing	John M Greklek
Manager-Classified	Penny Ducker
Manager-Retail	Charles Walker

CIRCULATION

Director	George Markevicz

NEWS EXECUTIVE

Managing Editor	Sam A Daleo

EDITORS AND MANAGERS

Automotive Editor	Jeremy Schiffres
Business/Finance Editor	Jeremy Schiffres
City Editor	Jeremy Schiffres
Editorial Page Editor	Hugh Reynolds
Education Editor	Jeremy Schiffres
Entertainment/Amusements Editor	Edwina Henderson
Environmental Editor	Jeremy Schiffres
Farm/Agriculture Editor	Jeremy Schiffres
Fashion/Style Editor	Edwina Henderson
Features/Women's Editor	Edwina Henderson
Health/Medical Editor	Edwina Henderson
Living/Lifestyle Editor	Edwina Henderson
News Editor	Jeremy Schiffres
Northern Dutchess Editor	Tony Adamis
Photo Editor	Jeremy Schiffres
Political Editor	Hugh Reynolds
Religion Editor	Claude Dixon
Sports Editor	Edward A Palladino Jr
Television/Film Editor	Edwina Henderson

PRODUCTION

Manager	William E Studt
Manager-Systems	David Hyatt
Foreman-Pressroom	William E Studt
Foreman-Composing	Leonard Bovee

Market Information: Zoned editions.
Mechanical available: Offset; Black and 3 ROP colors; insert accepted — preprinted; page cut-offs — 22¾".
Mechanical specifications: Type page 13" x 21½"; E - 6 cols, 2 1/16", ⅛" between; A - 6 cols, 2 1/16", ⅛" between; C - 9 cols, 1⅜", 1/16" between.
Commodity consumption: Newsprint 2,200 short tons; widths 27½", 13¾", 30", 15"; black ink 48,700 pounds; color ink 3,300 pounds; single pages printed 11,250; average pages per issue 26(d), 72(S); single plates used 15,700.
Equipment: EDITORIAL: Front-end hardware — 2-Ik/17A20; Front-end software — Rev 5.4; Other equipment — 1-Ap/Mac SE, Lf/Leafscan 35. CLASSIFIED: Front-end hardware — Cx/2AST3-33, 7-IBM/XT; Front-end software — Rev/7D; Printers — Okidata/2410. DISPLAY: Adv layout systems — Ap/Mac; Front-end hardware — 3-Ap/Power Mac 7100; Front-end software — Multi-Ad/Creator 3.6; Printers — Hewgen/Imager Plus 12; Other equipment — HP/II Cx Scanner. PRODUCTION: Typesetters — 2-M/202; Plate exposures — 1-Nu/Ultra-Plus; Plate processors — 1-Nat/A-250; Production cameras — 1-R, 1-C/Spartan III, 1-AG/RPS-6100-S, 1-AG/3800; Automatic film processors — 1-LE/2600-A, 1-Litex/26, 1-LE/PC 13; Film transporters — 1-C; Shrink lenses — 1-SK; Color separation equipment (conventional) — 1-Newscolor/Sys.
PRESSROOM: Line 1 — 10-G/SCC Community; Folders — 2-G/2:1; Press control system — Fin. MAILROOM: Counter stackers — 1-HL, 1-RKW; Inserters and stuffers — HI/1372; Bundle tyer — OVL, MLN/Spirit; Addressing machine — Ch/Mailer. COMMUNICATIONS: Facsimile — 3-M/7118G. WIRE SERVICES: News — AP; Receiving dishes — size-8ft, AP. BUSINESS COMPUTERS: IBM/Sys 36; Applications: Payroll, Gen ledger, Accts receivable, Circ.

LITTLE FALLS

Herkimer County

'90 U.S. Census- 5,829; E&P '96 Est. 5,571

The Evening Times (e-mon to sat)

The Evening Times, 347 S. Second St.; PO Box 1007, Little Falls, NY 13365; tel (315) 823-3680, (315) 823-3690; fax (315) 823-4086. Alta Group Newspapers group.
Circulation: 7,152(e); Sworn Sept. 30, 1995.
Price: 40¢(d); $120.00/yr.
Advertising: Open inch rate $8.70(e). **Representative:** Landon Associates Inc.
News Services: NEA, AP. **Established:** 1886.
Not Published: New Year; Memorial Day; Independence Day; Labor Day; Thanksgiving; Christmas.
Special Edition: Business Card (monthly).
Special Weekly Sections: Bridal (tues); Doctors (wed); Seniors (sat).

GENERAL MANAGEMENT

Publisher	Donald A Paparella
Purchasing Agent	Lester Lemik

ADVERTISING

Manager-National	Kathy Kelly
Manager-Classified	Elaine McEvoy
Manager-Promotion	Peggy Vespi

CIRCULATION

Manager	Ernest Countryman

NEWS EXECUTIVE

Editor	Larry Neely

EDITORS AND MANAGERS

Science Editor	Eric Janecki
Society Editor	Hunter Marlo
Sports Editor	Jon Rathbun
Teen-Age/Youth Editor	Eric Janecki

PRODUCTION

Manager	Lester Lemik

Market Information: Zoned editions; TMC.
Mechanical available: Offset; Black and 2 ROP colors; insert accepted — preprinted; page cut-offs — 21½".
Mechanical specifications: Type page 13⅛" x 21½"; E - 6 cols, 2 1/16", ⅛" between; A - 6 cols, 2 1/16", ⅛" between; C - 8 cols, 1½", ⅛" between.
Commodity consumption: Newsprint 185 metric tons; width 28"; black ink 5,600 pounds; color ink 1,125 pounds; single pages printed 3,978; average pages per issue 12(d); single plates used 1,995.
Equipment: EDITORIAL: Front-end hardware — DTK/486-66; Front-end software — Microsoft/Word, Microsoft/Windows; Printers — HP/Laser, Ap/Mac Laser. CLASSIFIED: Front-end hardware — DTK/486-25; Front-end software — Merrimac/Publishing Manager, Microsoft/Word. PRODUCTION: Typesetters — HP/LaserPrinter; Plate exposures — Nu/Flip Top; Production cameras — 1-R.
PRESSROOM: Line 1 — 4-G/SC1085. MAILROOM: Addressing machine — 1-Wm. WIRE SERVICES: News — AP; Receiving dishes — size-2ft, AP. BUSINESS COMPUTERS: TI/Sys; Applications: Accts payable, Payroll, Circ, Adv billing; PCs & micros networked; PCs & main system networked.

LOCKPORT

Niagara County

'90 U.S. Census- 24,426; E&P '96 Est. 24,083
ABC-CZ (90): 24,426 (HH 9,865)

Union-Sun & Journal (e-mon to sat)

Union-Sun & Journal, 459-491 S. Transit St.; PO Box 503, Lockport, NY 14094; tel (716) 439-9222; fax (716) 439-9249. Park Communications Inc. group.
Circulation: 17,160(e); 17,160(e-sat); ABC Sept. 30, 1995.
Price: 50¢(d); 50¢(sat); $2.10/wk; $9.10/mo; $109.20/yr (home delivery).
Advertising: Open inch rate $19.04(e); $19.04(e-sat). **Representative:** Landon Associates Inc.
News Service: AP. **Politics:** Independent. **Established:** 1821.
Not Published: Christmas.
Special Editions: "Impact" (Mar); Home-Garden, Spring Fashion (Apr); Car Care (June); Back-to-School, Farm Home (Aug); Women's World (Sept); Better Homes (Oct); Gift Guide (Nov).

CORPORATE OFFICER

Treasurer	Randolph N Stair

GENERAL MANAGEMENT

General Manager	Thomas N Ceravolo

ADVERTISING

Manager	Daniel Caswell
Manager-Retail	Richard Conley

TELECOMMUNICATIONS

Audiotex Manager	Daniel Caswell

CIRCULATION

Manager	Philip Barancotta

NEWS EXECUTIVE

Managing Editor	Daniel V Kane

EDITORS AND MANAGERS

Editorial Page Editor	Daniel V Kane
Women's Editor	Ann Calos

PRODUCTION

Foreman-Composing	David Cushman
Foreman-Pressroom	K Hilwig

Market Information: TMC; Operate audiotex.
Mechanical available: Offset; Black and 3 ROP colors; insert accepted — preprinted, free standing inserts; page cut-offs — 21½".
Mechanical specifications: Type page 13½" x 21½"; E - 6 cols, 2.07", 1/10" between; A - 6 cols, 2.07", 1/10" between; C - 10 cols, 1.21", .07" between.
Commodity consumption: Newsprint 700 short tons; widths 27½", 13¾"; single pages printed 7,000; average pages per issue 18(d); single plates used 7,500.
Equipment: EDITORIAL: Front-end hardware — Ap/Mac; Front-end software — QuarkXPress, Baseview/NewsEdit; Printers — Ap/Mac Laser; Other equipment — 1-HP. CLASSIFIED: Front-end hardware — Ap/Mac; Front-end software — QuarkXPress; Printers — Ap/Mac Laser-Writer. AUDIOTEX: Supplier name — CT. DISPLAY: Adv layout systems — Ap/Mac; Front-end hardware — Ap/Mac; Front-end software — QuarkXPress; Printers — Ap/Mac Laser-Writer. PRODUCTION: Electronic picture desk — Lf/AP Leaf Picture Desk.
PRESSROOM: Line 1 — 10-G/Community; Press drives — 2-HP/60; Folders — 1-G; Press registration system — Duarte/Pin Registration. MAILROOM: Bundle tyer — 2-Bu. WIRE SERVICES: News — AP; Photos — AP; Receiving dishes — AP. BUSINESS COMPUTERS: Vision Data; Applications: Vision Data.

LONG ISLAND

Nassau & Suffolk Counties

'90 U.S. Census- 2,609,212 (Nassau 1,287,348; Suffolk 1,321,864); E&P '96 Est. 2,652,095 (Nassau 1,269,367; Suffolk 1,382,728)
ABC-NDM (90): 2,609,212 (HH 856,234)

Newsday (all day-mon to fri; m-sat; S)

Newsday, 235 Pinelawn Rd., Melville, NY 11747; tel (516) 843-2020; fax (516) 843-5424. Times Mirror Co. group.
Circulation: 634,627(a); 580,125(m-sat); 702,031(S); ABC Sept. 30, 1995.
Price: 50¢(d); 50¢(sat); $1.50(S); $4.50/wk (carrier); $28.00/mo (mail).
Advertising: Open inch rate $375.00(a); $375.00(m-sat); $458.75(S).
News Services: AP, LAT-WP, RN, SHNS, CSM, DJ, NNS. **Politics:** Independent. **Established:** 1940.
Note: Circulation is combined for Queens & Long Island editions. Effective July 16, 1995, New York Newsday ceased publishing.
Special Editions: After New Year Auto, Spring Learning, Bridal, Home Away from Home, Skiing Private Lessons, City Fitness (Jan); Gardening Magazine, Bridal, City Fitness, President's Forum (Feb); Spring Bridal, (LIBSO) Long Island Business Speaks Out, Tax Advice (Mar); Auto Show '96, Campus, Poconos, Bridal, Spring Home Magazine, College Directory, Home, Lawn & Garden, Auto Show '96, Restaurants Directory, After Auto Market Car Care (Apr); Designer Showcase, Mother's Day Gift Ideas, Home, Lawn & Garden II, College Fair, Summer Learning, Bridal (May); Summer '96, Dads & Grads, Caribbean Cultural Heritage Festival, Black Expo '96, US Open, Bridal (June); College Directory, Bridal (July); College for the Ages, Adult Living, Back-to-School, Fall Learning (Aug); 1996 Financial Planner, Home Improvement, NY Festival in Queens, Bridal, Fall Festival, Home Improvement & Energy Expo, Career Expo (Sept); Cars '97, Bridal, College Directory, College Choice Magazine, Personal Computer & Electronic Expo (Oct); Discover Queens, Holiday Almanac, Holiday Gift Guide, Festival of Trees, Bridal (Nov); After Christmas Auto, Last Minute Gift, The Last Semester, Bridal, After New Year's Auto (Dec).
Special Weekly Sections: Auto, Travel (S).
Magazines: Parade Magazine (Roto); TV Book.

GENERAL MANAGEMENT

Publisher/CEO/President	Raymond A Jansen
Editor/Exec Vice Pres	Anthony Marro
Senior Vice Pres-Finance/Chief Financial Officer	James D Shaw
Vice Pres-Distribution	Louis Sito

Copyright ©1996 by the Editor & Publisher Co.

Vice Pres-Advertising John McKeon
Vice Pres-Marketing Randy Charles
Vice Pres-Operations Jim Norris
Vice Pres-Info Systems & Engineering Services Frank Toner
Vice Pres-Employee, Labor & Public Affairs Elizabeth Drewry
Director-Operations Administration John Willis
Manager-Research Ed Farrell

ADVERTISING

Vice Pres John C McKeon
Director-Sales Planning Patricia A Burnagiel
Director-Display Raymond McCutcheon
Director-Classified Bruce Murray
Manager-Retail/Local Richard Viola
Manager-National/Retail Mike Perry
Manager-National Tom DiChiara

MARKETING AND PROMOTION

Vice Pres-Marketing/New Business Development Randolph R Charles
Director-Promotion Susan Fletcher
Director-Marketing Charlotte H Hall
Director-New Media & Products Frederick J Tuccillo

CIRCULATION

Vice Pres-Distribution Louis Sito
Distribution Director-Transportation George Brandenberger
Director Robert Brennan

NEWS EXECUTIVES

Editor/Senior Vice Pres Anthony Marro
Vice Pres/Queens Editor Don Forst
Managing Editor-Operations Robert Brandt
Managing Editor Howard Schneider
Asst Managing Editor-News Miriam Pawel
Asst Managing Editor-National/Foreign Les Payne
Asst Managing Editor-Administration Robert Keane
Asst Managing Editor-Features Phyllis Singer
Asst Managing Editor-Sports Steve Ruinsky
Assoc Managing Editor Richard Galant

EDITORS AND MANAGERS

Book Editor Laurie Muehnick
Business Editor Steve Sink
Cartoonist Doug Marlette
Criminal Justice Editor Gwen Young
Columnist Jonathan Schell
Design Director Robert Eisner
Editor-Investigations Joe Demma
Education Editor John Hildebrand
Editorial Page Editor Jim Klurfeld
Fashion/Lifestyle Editor Barbara Schuler
Food Editor Kari Granville
Home Living Editor Barbara Schuler
Kidsday Editor Rosemary Skapley
Library Director Mary Ann Skinner
Long Island Editor Alex Martin
Long Island Night Editor Bill Seddon
Long Island Lifestyle Adam Horvath
Mid East Correspondent Nick Goldberg
National Lonnie Isabel
Photography Director Jim Dooley
Political Editor Ken Fireman
Science/Health Editor Elizabeth Bass
Special Sections Editor Warren Berry
Sunday Editor Ben Weller
Travel Marjorie Kaplan Robins
Washington Bureau Chief Jim Toedtman
Weekend Editor Bob Heisler

MANAGEMENT INFORMATION SERVICES

Vice Pres-Info Systems & Engineering Services Frank Toner
Manager-Info Systems Art Schmidt
Manager-Business Systems Software John Koehler
Manager-Production Systems Software Dan Egan
Manager-Operations Business Data Center Pat Orsini
Manager-Publishing Data Center Tom Norris
Manager-Telecommunications Warren Kimball
Manager-Network Management Dick Stein

PRODUCTION

Senior Vice Pres/Operations Director Jim Norris
Director-Management John Wills
Director-Packaging Martin J Bartow
Director-Pre Press & Advertising Tom Pidgeon
Manager-Mechanical Bob Oswald
Manager-Composing/Platemaking George Montebello
Manager-Quality Assurance & Electric Pre Press Ron Chiavaro
Manager-Planning & Analysis Ron Hulsen
Manager-Nightside Operations Ron Clementelli
Manager-Electronic Pre Press Jack Calcado
Manager-Operations Wally Wenchell
Manager-Electronic Systems Ed Bushey
General Foreman-Mechanical Shop Bob Ryder
General Foreman-Platemaking Doug Dattoma
General Foreman-Pressroom Joe Ferrante
General Foreman-Electric Shop Blake Boucher
General Foreman-Daily Inserting Charlie Tighe
General Foreman-Newsprint Tom Reilly

Market Information: Zoned editions; TMC; Operate database; Operate audiotex; Electronic edition.

Mechanical available: Offset; Black and 3 ROP colors; insert accepted — preprinted, subscription blanks; page cut-offs — $21\frac{1}{2}$".

Mechanical specifications: Type page $9\frac{25}{64}$" x 13"; E - 6 cols, $1\frac{1}{2}$", $\frac{1}{16}$" between; A - 6 cols, $1\frac{1}{2}$", $\frac{5}{64}$" between; C - 8 cols, $1\frac{3}{16}$", $\frac{1}{16}$" between.

Commodity consumption: Newsprint 111,620 metric tons; widths 59", $44\frac{1}{4}$", $29\frac{1}{2}$"; black ink 2,750,000 pounds; color ink 500,000 pounds; single pages printed 55,000,000; average pages per issue 140(d), 300(S); single plates used 1,200,000.

Equipment: EDITORIAL: Front-end hardware — 22-AT/Series 6, 2-AT/Series 4, 2-AT/Series 30, 1-AT/9080, 14-AT/GT-68, 9-Sun/Microsys 360; Other equipment — 120-RSK/100, 2-IBM/PC, 1-ATT/6300, 1-Ap/Mac, 1-HP/Portable. CLASSIFIED: Front-end hardware — 68-PC. DISPLAY: Adv layout systems — Cx/Desktop; Front-end hardware — Sun/360, Ap/Macs; Front-end software — Cx/Breeze, QuarkXPress; Printers — Bitco, QMS; Other equipment — ECR/Scanners. PRODUCTION: Typesetters — 3-Bitco/108, 3-Sparccaster/RIPs, 5-Harlequin/RIP, 3-Cx/Bitcaster, 2-III/3850 Sierra, 2-Dolev/800, Scitex, 2-Opti, NEC; Plate exposures — 5-WL/Lith-X-Pozer III, 1-WL/Lith-X-Pozer 10; Plate processors — 5-WL/38D; Electronic picture desk — Lf; Scanners — 3-ECR/2000, 3-ECR/1000, 2-Smartscanner, HP/ScanJet Plus, 1-Eskofot; Production cameras — 2-C/Pager, 2-C/Spartan III, 2-C/Spartan II; Automatic film processors — 5-LE, 3-P; Film transporters — 2-Dolev, 1-Raystor, 5-P; Color separation equipment (conventional) — 2-Nikon, 2-Valax; Digital color separation equipment — Scitex, 3-Prisma, 1-Assemblec, 1-PS/Star.
PRESSROOM: Line 1 — 2-G/Metro 144 pg., 4-G/Metro half decks, 4-G/Metro, 2-TKS/M72; Line 2 — 1-G/Metro 144 pg., 4-G/Metro half decks, 4-G/Metro, 2-TKS/M72; Line 3 — 1-G/Metro 144 pg., 4-G/Metro half decks, 4-G/Metro, 2-TKS/M72; Line 4 — 1-G/Metro 144 pg., 4-G/Metro half decks, 4-G/Metro, 2-TKS/M72; Line 5 — 1-G/Metro 144 pg., 4-G/Metro half decks, 4-G/Metro, 2-TKS/M72; Line 6 — 1-G/Metro, 4-G/Metro half decks, 4-G/Metro, 2-TKS/M72; Line 7 — 1-TKS/Offset, 5-TKS/M72, 4-TKS/M72 half decks, 1-TKS/Satellite; Line 8 — 1-TKS/Offset, 3-TKS/M72 half decks, 6-TKS/M72, 1-TKS/Satellite, 1-TKS/Offset, 3-TKS/M72 half decks, 6-TKS/M72, 1-TKS/Satellite, 1-TKS/Offset, 3-TKS/M72 half decks, 6-TKS/M72, 1-TKS/Satellite, 1-TKS/Offset, 3-TKS/M72 half decks, 6-TKS/Satellite; Press drives — Fin; Folders — 6-G/3:2, 4-TKS/3:2 160pg.; Pasters — G; Reels and stands — 48-G/RTP, 32-TKS/ARL RIP; Press control system — Id/PMS Totalizer, TKS, G/PCS, G/PAR. MAILROOM: Counter stackers — 23-Id/2000, 5-Fg/Multicell complex (6 cell); Inserters and stuffers — 4-Fg/3:1, 2-Amerigraphic/NP 630, 3-HI/1472, 4-HI/2299; Bundle tyer — 40-Dynaric/NP1, Dynaric/NP2; Addressing machine — 5-AVY/Labeler; Mailroom control system — Id; B. LIBRARY: Electronic — Information Dimension/Basis. WIRE SERVICES: News — AP, LAT-WP, CSM, RN, NNS, DJ, PR Newswire; Stock tables — AP, NYSE, AMEX, OTC, Select Mutuals; Syndicates — AP Datafeatures; Receiving dishes — size-10ft, AP. BUSINESS COMPUTERS: 1-IBM/3090-400E; Applications: Gen ledger, Accts payable, Circ, Adv billing, Accts receivable, Fixed assets, Payroll, Human resources; PCs & micros networked; PCs & main system networked.

MALONE

Franklin County

'90 U.S. Census- 6,777; E&P '96 Est. 6,119

The Malone Telegram (e-mon to fri; m-sat)

The Malone Telegram, 387 E. Main St.; PO Box 69, Malone, NY 12953; tel (518) 483-4700; fax (518) 483-8579. Johnson Newspaper Corp. group.

Circulation: 5,661(e); 5,661(m-sat); Sworn Oct. 2, 1995.

Price: 50¢(d); 50¢(sat); \$1.65/wk (carrier); \$7.00/mo (carrier/motor route), \$8.75/mo (in county), \$10.00/mo (out of county); \$97.50/yr, \$112.50/yr (out of county).

Advertising: Open inch rate \$8.64(e); \$8.64(m-sat).

News Service: AP. **Established:** 1905.

Not Published: New Year; Memorial Day; Independence Day; Labor Day; Thanksgiving; Christmas.

Special Editions: Winter Carnival (Jan); Bridal Tab (Feb); Spring Tab (Mar); Summer Visitor (May); Meet the Merchants (June); Fair Tab (Aug); Christmas Gift Guide (Nov).

Special Weekly Sections: TV Tab (fri); Farm Page; Kids Page.

Magazine: TV Scene (fri).

CORPORATE OFFICER

President John B Johnson

GENERAL MANAGEMENT

Publisher Russell F Webster
Business Manager Betsy McGivney

ADVERTISING

Director Russell F Webster
Supervisor Karen Carre

CIRCULATION

Manager Maureen Holmes

NEWS EXECUTIVE

Managing Editor Thomas Graser

EDITOR AND MANAGER

Sports Editor John Gokey

PRODUCTION

Manager-Operations Paul Bissonette

Mechanical available: Offset; Black and 2 ROP colors; insert accepted — preprinted; page cut-offs — $22\frac{5}{8}$".

Mechanical specifications: Type page 13" x $21\frac{1}{2}$"; E - 6 cols, $2\frac{1}{16}$", $\frac{1}{8}$" between; A - 6 cols, $2\frac{1}{16}$", $\frac{1}{8}$" between; C - 8 cols, $1\frac{1}{2}$", $\frac{1}{8}$" between.

Commodity consumption: Newsprint 600 short tons; widths 27.5", 13.75", 30", 15"; black ink 5,200 pounds; color ink 200 pounds; single pages printed 4,302; average pages per issue 12(d); single plates used 7,000.

Equipment: EDITORIAL: Front-end hardware — CText. CLASSIFIED: Front-end hardware — CText. DISPLAY: Adv layout systems — 2-Adept/Advertising Workstation. PRODUCTION: Typesetters — 2-Ap/Mac Lasersetter; Platemaking systems — 1-Nu/Flip Top FT40VUP; Plate processors — 1-Nu; Production cameras — SCREEN/Auto Companica 690D; Automatic film processors — LE/17A.
PRESSROOM: Line 1 — 1-G/Community; Folders — 1-G/2:1. MAILROOM: Wrapping singles — 1-Bu; Addressing machine — 1-Wm. LIBRARY: Combination — Minolta/Microfilm Viewer, NIMI/2020. COMMUNICATIONS: Facsimile — Canon. WIRE SERVICES: News — AP; Receiving dishes — size-10ft, AP. BUSINESS COMPUTERS: 1-IBM/VDT Mid M; PCs & main system networked.

MAMARONECK

Westchester County

'90 U.S. Census- 17,325; E&P '96 Est. 17,086
ABC-NDM (90): 35,679 (HH 13,395)

The Mamaroneck Daily Times (e-mon to sat; S)

The Mamaroneck Daily Times, One Gannett Dr., White Plains, NY 10464; tel (914) 694-9300; web site http://www.nynews.com/nynews. Gannett Co. Inc. group.

Circulation: 5,202(e); 5,202(e-sat); 5,380(S); ABC Sept. 24, 1995.

Price: 40¢(d); 40¢(sat); \$1.50(S).

Representative: Gannett National Newspaper Sales.

News Services: AP, GNS, LAT-WP. **Politics:** Independent.

Note: White Plains is the headquarters for the Gannett Suburban Newspapers, Inc. The following newspapers are printed at the Harrison White Plains plant: Mt. Vernon Daily Argus, Mamaroneck Daily Times, New Rochelle Standard-Star, Port Chester Daily Item, White Plains Reporter-Dispatch, Tarrytown Daily News, Peekskill Star, Ossining Citizen Register and Yonkers Herald Statesman. The Rockland Journal-News is printed in Nyack, NY. All advertising is sold in combination fo: \$177.43 (d) and \$200.52 (S). For detailed mechanical equipment information, see the Gannett Suburban Newspapers, Inc. listing in White Plains. Individual newspaper rates not made available.

Special Editions: Spring Bridal (Feb); Spring Home Design (Mar); Spring Home & Garden, Suburban Golf, Greater New York Auto Show, Summer Education, Suburban Business Review (Apr); Suburban Golf, Builder's Showcase (May); Summer Dine Out Guide (June); Suburban Golf (July); Back-to-School, Fall Education, Suburban Golf (Aug); Suburban Golf, Pro Football Preview, Local Football Preview, Fall Bridal, Community Guide (Sept); Suburban Golf, Fall Home Design, New Autos '97, Fall Dine Out Guide (Oct); Holiday Gift Guide, Thanksgiving Day Special, Holiday Planner (Nov); Holiday Food, Hot Holiday Gifts, Last Minute Gift Guide (Dec).

Special Weekly Sections: Career Opportunities (mon); Best Food Day, Fashion (wed); Home Style, Weekend, Dining Out (thur); Garden & Home Improvement (fri); Travel & Resort, Real Estate, Career Opportunities, TV Week, Education (S).

CORPORATE OFFICERS

President/Publisher Gary F Sherlock
Vice Pres/Exec Editor Kenneth A Paulson
Vice Pres/President-Advertising John C Green
Vice Pres/Director-Circulation Mike Huot
Vice Pres-Finance Charles Schmitt
Vice Pres-Marketing Michael G Kane
Vice Pres-Operations Fal A Bolzner

ADVERTISING

Director-Classified Candida Canfield
Director-Display Robert Twesten
Manager-Display Jeanne Westby
Manager-Display Steve Havelka
Manager-Business Development Joan Perreault

TELECOMMUNICATIONS

Audiotex Manager Carl Iacona

CIRCULATION

Director Jonathan Alvord
Manager Paul Felicissimo

NEWS EXECUTIVES

Senior Managing Editor Janet McMillan
Operations Editor Rich Kleban
Managing Editor-Administration Bill Madden
Editor-Reader Services Gayle T Williams
Acting Asst Managing Editor-Lifestyles Tad Clarke
Asst Managing Editor-Business Mark Land
Asst Managing Editor-Sports David Georgette

EDITORS AND MANAGERS

Editorial Page Editor Ron Patafio
Entertainment Editor Kathy McClusky
Graphics Editor Chris Kiesler
Health/Medical Editor Barbara Durkin
Metro Editor Phil Reisman III
Asst Managing Editor Sandy Coyle
Asst Managing Editor-Nights Dan Murray
Photo Director Robert Rodriguez
Photo Editor-Day Danielle Perillat
Travel Editor Kathy McClusky

MANAGEMENT INFORMATION SERVICES

Director-Systems & Technology Sherman Bodner

PRODUCTION

Director Nat Hogan

Market Information: Operate audiotex; Electronic edition.

MANHATTAN

See NEW YORK CITY

MEDINA

Orleans County

'90 U.S. Census- 6,686; E&P '96 Est. 6,942
ABC-NDM (90): 17,223 (HH 6,280)

The Journal-Register (e-mon to fri)

The Journal-Register, 409-13 Main St., Medina, NY 14103; tel (716) 798-1400; fax (716) 798-0290. Park Communications Inc. group.

Circulation: 4,878(e); ABC Sept. 30, 1995.

Price: 50¢(d); \$99.00/yr (mail).

Advertising: Open inch rate \$8.55(e). **Representative:** Landon Associates Inc.

News Services: NEA, AP. **Politics:** Independent-Republican. **Established:** 1903.

Not Published: Christmas.

Advertising not accepted: 900 phone numbers.

Special Editions: Martin Luther King, Progress Edition (Jan); Crime Prevention, Boy Scout, Bridal Section, Valentine Pictures, President's Day Sale, Income Tax Tab (Feb); Girl Scout, AG Week, Spring Promotion, Spring Home Improvement (Mar); Bike Safety,

Downtown Easter, Health & Fitness, Spring Car Care (Apr); Downtown Mother's Day, In Memorial Section, Memorial Days (May); Flag Day, Downtown Dads & Grads (June); July 4th, Downtown Sidewalk Sale (July); 20-Hour Downtown Sale, Back-to-School, Labor Day Promo (Aug); Mustang Football, Labor Day, Moonlight Madness, Hunting & Fishing Promo, Fall Home Improvement (Sept); Fire Prevention, Columbus Day Promo, Fall Car Care, Halloween Promo (Oct); Veteran's Day, Recipe Tab, Downtown Christmas Promo (Nov); Downtown Christmas Promo, Don't Drink & Drive, Christmas Greetings (Dec).

Special Weekly Sections: Best Food Day (mon); Business Section (wed); Farm Section (thur); Church Page (fri).

GENERAL MANAGEMENT

General Manager Owen P Toale

ADVERTISING

Manager Gregory P Kerth

NEWS EXECUTIVE

Managing Editor Michael Wertman

EDITORS AND MANAGERS

Librarian Lynne Harling
Photo Editor Donald Cook
Society Editor Mary Jo Gill
Sports Editor Michael Wertman

MANAGEMENT INFORMATION SERVICES

Data Processing Manager Diana Stafford

Mechanical available: Offset; Black and 3 ROP colors; insert accepted — preprinted; page cutoffs — 21".

Mechanical specifications: Type page 13" x 21"; E - 6 cols, 2¹⁄₁₆", ⅛" between; A - 6 cols, 2¹⁄₁₆", ⅛" between; C - 10 cols, ⅛" between.

Commodity consumption: Newsprint 200 short tons; width 28"; black ink 4,380 pounds; color ink 62 pounds; average pages per issue 12(d); single plates used 4,460.

Equipment: EDITORIAL: Front-end hardware — Mk; Front-end software — Mk; Printers — Ap/Mac LaserWriter Plus. CLASSIFIED: Front-end hardware — Mk; Front-end software — Mk; Printers — Ap/Mac LaserWriter Plus. DISPLAY: Adv layout systems — Mk; Front-end hardware — Mk; Front-end software — Mk; Printers — Ap/Mac LaserWriter Plus. PRODUCTION: Typesetters — Ap/Mac LaserWriter Plus; Production cameras — B/Horizontal.
PRESSROOM: Line 1 — 4-G/Community. MAILROOM: Bundle tyer — Bu. WIRE SERVICES: News — AP; Receiving dishes — AP. BUSINESS COMPUTERS: IBM; Applications: Peachtree.

MIDDLETOWN

Orange County

'90 U.S. Census- 24,160; E&P '96 Est. 26,704
ABC-CZ (90): 52,694 (HH 18,252)

Times Herald-Record (m-mon to sat)
Sunday Record (S)

Times Herald-Record, 40 Mulberry St.; PO Box 2046, Middletown, NY 10940; tel (914) 341-1100; fax (914) 343-2050. Ottaway Newspapers Inc. group.

Circulation: 87,520(m); 87,520(m-sat); 103,023(S); ABC Sept. 30, 1995.

Price: 50¢(d); 50¢(sat); $1.50(S); $241.80/yr.

Advertising: Open inch rate $41.05(m); $41.05(m-sat); $44.23(S). **Representative:** Landon Associates Inc.

News Services: AP, NYT, ONS. **Politics:** Independent. **Established:** 1956.

Special Editions: Progress (Feb); Home & Garden (Apr); Summer Guide (May); Almanac (June); Summer Guide (July); Back-to-School (Aug); Home Design, Wedding Guide, Car Care (Oct); Gift Guide (Nov); Gift Guide (Dec).

Special Weekly Section: Best Food Day (wed).

Magazines: Tracks (tues); Neighbors (wed); Go (fri); Sunday Magazine, TV Week, Parade, Real Estate Guide (S).

GENERAL MANAGEMENT

Director-Human Resources Debra A Sherman
Director-Facilities James A Botti
Controller Edward J Hayes
Administrative Asst Linda Weyant

ADVERTISING

Manager-Classified Daniel R Pauley

MARKETING AND PROMOTION

Director-Marketing Susan Krafve-Brown

TELECOMMUNICATIONS

Audiotex Manager Pierre Johnson

CIRCULATION

Director Chet Valiante
Manager Jack Saunders
Manager-Marketing Steve Piersa

NEWS EXECUTIVES

Managing Editor Jeff Storey
Asst Managing Editor Lance Theroux

EDITORS AND MANAGERS

Action Line Editor Jean Kaufman
Arts/Entertainment Editor Dennis Sprick
Business Editor Robert Riemann
Columnist Mike Levine
Columnist Barbara Bedell
Economic Development Editor Judy Rife
Editorial Page Editor Robert Gaydos
Education Editor Tracy Williams
Entertainment/Amusements Editor Dennis Sprick
Family/Living Editor Brenda Gilhooly
Fashion/Style Editor Deborah Botti
Features Editor Brenda Gilhooly
Living/Lifestyle Editor Deborah Botti
Medical/Health Editor Beth Mullally
National Editor Mark Pittman
News Editor Allan Gaul
Photo Editor Mike Carey
Chief Photographer Mike Carey
Political/Government Editor Mark Pittman
Regional Editor David Figura
Religion Editor Deborah Botti
Science/Technology Editor Brenda Gilhooly
Sports Editor Bill Burr
Television/Film Editor Dennis Sprick
Theater/Music Editor Dennis Sprick
Travel Editor Emily Morrison
Wire Editor Carol Reif
Women's Editor Deborah Botti

PRODUCTION

Superintendent-Pressroom Allan Craven
Manager-Pre Press Duane Neverman

Market Information: Zoned editions; Split Run; TMC; Operate audiotex.

Mechanical available: Offset; Black and 3 ROP colors; insert accepted — preprinted; page cutoffs — 16".

Mechanical specifications: Type page 10¼" x 15"; E - 4 cols, 3.17", ⅙" between; A - 6 cols, 1.57", ⅙" between; C - 7 cols, 1.57", ⅙" between.

Commodity consumption: Newsprint 11,500 metric tons; widths 64", 48", 32"; black ink 278,438 pounds; color ink 60,000 pounds; single pages printed 52,842; ave. pages per issue 104(d), 280(S); single plates used 105,000.

Equipment: EDITORIAL: Front-end hardware — 3-DEC/PDP 11-84, 20-CSI/112B, 32-CSI/112, 16-CSI/90; Front-end software — CSI; Printers — 1-DEC/LA 120, 1-DEC/LA 75. CLASSIFIED: Front-end hardware — 3-DEC/PDP 11-84, 30-CSI/112B; Front-end software — CSI; Printers — 1-DEC/LA 120. DISPLAY: Adv layout systems — DJ; Front-end hardware — HI/8300, 2-Ap/Mac Centris 610, 1-Ap/Mac Quadra 950, Ap/Power Mac 7100; Front-end software — Multi-Ad/Creator, Ap/Mac OS, HI/8300, QuarkXPress, Adobe/Photoshop; Printers — Ap/Mac LaserWriter. PRODUCTION: Pagination software — QuarkXPress 3.3; Typesetters — 1-ECR/Script Setter I, 2-Copal/600 PostScript Imager, 1-ECR/Autokon 1000; Plate exposures — 2-NuGraphics; Plate processors — 2-NuGraphics; Electronic picture desk — 3-Lf/AP Leaf Picture Desk; Scanners — ECR/Autokon 1000, Ap/Mac Scanner, LaCie/Scanner, Kk/2035; Production cameras — C/Spartan II, AG/6200; Automatic film processors — LE, Kk, Konica; Reproportion units — ECR/Autokon 1000; Film transporters — ECR/UR-30; Color separation equipment (conventional) — Ap/Mac Quadra, Ap/Mac fx; Digital color separation equipment — LaCie, Lf/Leafscan 35, Kk/RFS2035, Kk/2035, Ap/Mac Quadra 950.
PRESSROOM: Line 1 — 7-G (w/TKS Satellites); Press control system — DJ. MAILROOM: Counter stackers — 5-QWI; Inserters and stuffers — 3-GMA/SLS-1000 (8-into-1), 1-GMA/SLS-1000 (20-into-1); Bundle tyer — 5-OVL; Addressing machine — 2-Ch. LIBRARY: Electronic — Vu/Text. COMMUNICATIONS: Facsimile — CD/PageFax; Systems used — microwave. WIRE SERVICES: News — AP Datastream, AP Datafeatures, NYT, ONS; Stock tables — AP; Syndicates — NYT, ONS, KRT; Receiving dishes — size-3m, AP. BUSINESS COMPUTERS: 29-IBM/Terminal, 3-IBM/Printer, IBM/AS-400; Applications: Microsoft/Word, Microsoft/Excel; PCs & micros networked; PCs & main system networked.

MOUNT VERNON

Westchester County

'90 U.S. Census- 67,153; E&P '96 Est. 67,522
ABC-NDM (90): 67,153 (HH 25,175)

The Mount Vernon Daily Argus (e-mon to sat; S)

The Mount Vernon Daily Argus, One Gannett Dr., White Plains, NY 10604; tel (914) 694-9300; web site http://www.nynews.com/nynews. Gannett Co. Inc. group.

Circulation: 6,147(e); 6,147(e-sat); 7,927(S); ABC Sept. 24, 1995.

Price: 40¢(d); 40¢(sat); $1.50(S).

News Services: AP, GNS, LAT-WP. **Politics:** Independent.

Note: White Plains is the headquarters for the Gannett Suburban Newspapers, Inc. The following newspapers are printed at the Harrison White Plains plant: Mt. Vernon Daily Argus, Mamaroneck Daily Times, New Rochelle Standard-Star, Port Chester Daily Item, White Plains Reporter-Dispatch, Tarrytown Daily News, Peekskill Star, Ossining Citizen Register and Yonkers Herald Statesman. The Rockland Journal-News is printed in Nyack, NY. All advertising is sold in combination for $177.43 (d) and $200.52 (S). For detailed mechanical equipment information, see the Gannett Suburban Newspapers, Inc. listing in White Plains. Individual newspaper rates not made available.

Special Editions: Spring Bridal (Feb); Spring Home Design (Mar); Spring Home & Garden, Suburban Golf, Greater New York Auto Show, Summer Education, Suburban Business Review (Apr); Suburban Golf, Builder's Showcase (May); Summer Dine Out Guide (June); Suburban Golf (July); Back-to-School, Fall Education, Suburban Golf (Aug); Suburban Golf, Pro Football Preview, Local Football Preview, Fall Bridal, Community Guide (Sept); Suburban Golf, Fall Home Design, New Autos '97, Fall Dine Out Guide (Oct); Holiday Gift Guide, Thanksgiving Day Special, Holiday Planner (Nov); Holiday Food, Hot Holiday Gifts, Last Minute Gift Guide (Dec).

Special Weekly Sections: Career Opportunities (mon); Best Food Day, Fashion (wed); Home Style, Weekend, Dining Out (thur); Garden & Home Improvement (fri); Travel & Resort, Real Estate, Career Opportunities, TV Week, Education (S).

CORPORATE OFFICERS

President/Publisher Gary F Sherlock
Vice Pres/Exec Editor Kenneth A Paulson
Vice Pres/President-Advertising John C Green
Vice Pres/Director-Circulation Mike Huot
Vice Pres-Finance Charles Schmitt
Vice Pres-Marketing Michael G Kane
Vice Pres-Operations Fal A Bolzner

ADVERTISING

Director-Classified Candida Canfield
Director-Display Robert Twesten
Manager-Display Jeanne Westby
Manager-Display Steve Havelka
Manager-Business Development Joan Perreault

TELECOMMUNICATIONS

Audiotex Manager Carl Iacona

CIRCULATION

Director Jonathan Alvord
Manager Paul Felicissimo

NEWS EXECUTIVES

Senior Managing Editor Janet McMillan
Operations Editor Rich Kleban
Managing Editor-Administration Bill Madden
Editor-Reader Services Gayle T Williams
Acting Asst Managing Editor-Lifestyles Tad Clarke
Asst Managing Editor-Business Mark Land
Asst Managing Editor-Sports David Georgette

EDITORS AND MANAGERS

Editorial Page Editor Ron Patafio
Entertainment Editor Kathy McClusky
Graphics Editor Chris Kiesler
Health/Medical Editor Barbara Durkin
Metro Editor Phil Reisman III
Asst Managing Editor Sandy Coyle
Asst Managing Editor-Nights Dan Murray
Photo Director Robert Rodriguez
Photo Editor-Day Danielle Perillat
Travel Editor Kathy McClusky

MANAGEMENT INFORMATION SERVICES

Director-Systems & Technology Sherman Bodner

PRODUCTION

Director Nat Hogan

Market Information: Operate audiotex; Electronic edition.

NEW ROCHELLE

Westchester County

'90 U.S. Census- 67,265; E&P '96 Est. 64,469
ABC-NDM (90): 79,121 (HH 29,532)

The New Rochelle Standard-Star (e-mon to sat; S)

The New Rochelle Standard-Star, One Gannett Dr., White Plains, NY 10604; tel (914) 694-9300; web site http://www.nynews.com/nynews. Gannett Co. Inc. group.

Circulation: 10,180(e); 10,180(e-sat); 11,115(S); ABC Sept. 24, 1995.

Price: 40¢(d); 40¢(sat); $1.50(S).

News Services: AP, GNS, LAT-WP. **Politics:** Independent.

Note: White Plains is the headquarters for the Gannett Suburban Newspapers, Inc. The following newspapers are printed at the Harrison White Plains plant: Mt. Vernon Daily Argus, Mamaroneck Daily Times, New Rochelle Standard-Star, Port Chester Daily Item, White Plains Reporter-Dispatch, Tarrytown Daily News, Peekskill Star, Ossining Citizen Register and Yonkers Herald Statesman. The Rockland Journal-News is printed in Nyack, NY. All advertising is sold in combination for $177.43 (d) and $200.52 (S). For detailed mechanical equipment information, see the Gannett Suburban Newspapers, Inc. listing in White Plains. Individual newspaper rates not made available.

Special Editions: Spring Bridal (Feb); Spring Home Design (Mar); Spring Home & Garden, Suburban Golf, Greater New York Auto Show, Summer Education, Suburban Business Review (Apr); Suburban Golf, Builder's Showcase (May); Summer Dine Out Guide (June); Suburban Golf (July); Back-to-School, Fall Education, Suburban Golf (Aug); Suburban Golf, Pro Football Preview, Local Football Preview, Fall Bridal, Community Guide (Sept); Suburban Golf, Fall Home Design, New Autos '97, Fall Dine Out Guide (Oct); Holiday Gift Guide, Thanksgiving Day Special, Holiday Planner (Nov); Holiday Food, Hot Holiday Gifts, Last Minute Gift Guide (Dec).

Special Weekly Sections: Career Opportunities (mon); Best Food Day, Fashion (wed); Home Style, Weekend, Dining Out (thur); Garden & Home Improvement (fri); Travel & Resort, Real Estate, Career Opportunities, TV Week, Education (S).

CORPORATE OFFICERS

President/Publisher Gary F Sherlock
Vice Pres/Exec Editor Kenneth A Paulson
Vice Pres/President-Advertising John C Green
Vice Pres/Director-Circulation Mike Huot
Vice Pres-Finance Charles Schmitt
Vice Pres-Marketing Michael G Kane
Vice Pres-Operations Fal A Bolzner

ADVERTISING

Director-Classified Candida Canfield
Director-Display Robert Twesten
Manager-Display Jeanne Westby
Manager-Display Steve Havelka
Manager-Business Development Joan Perreault

TELECOMMUNICATIONS

Audiotex Manager Carl Iacona

CIRCULATION

Director Jonathan Alvord
Manager Paul Felicissimo

NEWS EXECUTIVES

Senior Managing Editor Janet McMillan
Operations Editor Rich Kleban
Managing Editor-Administration Bill Madden
Editor-Reader Services Gayle T Williams
Acting Asst Managing Editor-Lifestyles Tad Clarke
Asst Managing Editor-Business Mark Land
Asst Managing Editor-Sports David Georgette

EDITORS AND MANAGERS

Editorial Page Editor Ron Patafio
Entertainment Editor Kathy McClusky
Graphics Editor Chris Kiesler
Health/Medical Editor Barbara Durkin
Metro Editor Phil Reisman III
Asst Managing Editor Sandy Coyle
Asst Managing Editor-Nights Dan Murray

Photo Director Robert Rodriguez
Photo Editor-Day Danielle Perillat
Travel Editor Kathy McClusky

MANAGEMENT INFORMATION SERVICES

Director-Systems & Technology Sherman Bodner

PRODUCTION

Director Nat Hogan

Market Information: Operate audiotex; Electronic edition.

NEW YORK CITY

Note: New York City is made up of five boroughs, and boundaries are the same as county lines. Newspapers are listed in the boroughs of their publication's offices. Population and statistics by boroughs follow:

BRONX Bronx County

'90 U.S. Census- 1,203,789; E&P '96 Est. 1,286,305

BROOKLYN Kings County

'90 U.S. Census- 2,300,664; E&P '96 Est. 2,445,790

MANHATTAN New York County

'90 U.S. Census- 1,487,536; E&P '96 Est. 1,610,755

QUEENS Queens County

'90 U.S. Census- 1,951,598; E&P '96 Est. 2,063,770

STATEN ISLAND Richmond County

'90 U.S. Census- 378,977; E&P '96 Est. 450,901

ABC-NDM (90): 19,697,031 (HH 7,212,029)

The Daily Challenge

(m-mon to fri; wknd)

The Daily Challenge, 1360 Fulton St., Brooklyn, NY 11216; tel (718) 636-9500; fax (718) 857-9115.

Circulation: 79,540(m); 79,540(m-sat); CPVS Sept. 30, 1992.

Price: 35¢(d); 35¢(sat); $22.50/6mo (d), $28.00/6mo (d, wknd); $48.00/yr.

Advertising: Open inch rate $45.90(m); $44.00(m-sat).

News Service: UPI. **Established:** 1972.

GENERAL MANAGEMENT

Publisher Thomas Watkins Jr
Assoc Publisher Kerri Watkins

ADVERTISING

Director Pat Stevenson

NEWS EXECUTIVE

Editor Dawad Philip

EDITOR AND MANAGER

Arts/Entertainment Editor Charles Lewis

The Journal of Commerce & Commercial (m-mon to fri)

The Journal of Commerce & Commercial, 2 World Trade Center, 27th Fl., New York, NY 10048; tel (212) 837-7000. Economist Group.

Circulation: 20,436(m); ABC Sept. 30, 1995.

Price: $1.50(d); $112.00/3mo, $209.00/6mo; $349.00/yr.

Advertising: Open inch rate $91.92(m).

News Services: RN, KRT Financial. **Politics:** Independent. **Established:** 1827.

Not Published: New Year; Martin Luther King Jr's Birthday; Washington's Birthday; Good Friday; Memorial Day; Independence Day; Labor Day; Columbus Day; Veteran's Day; Thanksgiving; Christmas.

Special Editions: The Journal of Commerce International Edition; The China Edition.

CORPORATE OFFICERS

President Don C Becker
Vice Pres/Chief Financial Officer Ken Manz

GENERAL MANAGEMENT

Publisher Don C Becker
Publisher-Emeritus Eric Ridder
Assoc Publisher Harold Gold
Senior Vice Pres-Advertising James Devine
Senior Vice Pres-Finance/Operations Kenneth W Manz
Senior Vice Pres-International Alan D Newborn
Vice Pres-Promotion & Research Marcia Holland
Vice Pres-Operations James R Steckel
Controller Mark Harabedian
General Manager Stanford Erickson

ADVERTISING

Senior Vice Pres James Devine

MARKETING AND PROMOTION

Vice Pres-Promotion & Research Marcia Holland

CIRCULATION

Director Roy Haddock Sr
Manager-Distribution Bradley L Stout

NEWS EXECUTIVES

Editor Donald Holt
Editor-Washington Thomas J Connors
Editor-West Coast Peter Tirschwell
Managing Editor-Transport Mark S Getzfred
Managing Editor-Trade Rosalind McLymont
Managing Editor Donald F Amerman
Chief European Correspondent (London) Janet Porter
Senior News Editor-Statistics Paul Schaffer
Editorial Systems Manager Joseph A Hummell

EDITORS AND MANAGERS

Commodities/Energy Editor Alan Gersten
Bureau Chief-Boston Michael Lelyveld
Bureau Chief-Chicago Paul Conley
Bureau Chief-Los Angeles Bill Mongelluzzo
Bureau Chief-Mexico City Kevin Hall
Bureau Chief-Miami Craig Dunlap
Bureau Chief-San Francisco Peter Tirschwell
Bureau Chief-Seattle Bill DiBenedetto
Bureau Chief-Washington Keith M Rockwell
Bureau Chief-Tokyo Mark Magnier
Editorial Director Leo Abruzzese
Deputy Editorial Director Aviva Freudmann
Energy Editor Arthur Gottschalk
Finance Editor Gordon Platt
Graphics Editor Joseph Yeninas
Insurance and Commodities Editor Alan Gersten
Library Manager Christine Karpevych
Manager-Transportation Ira Rosenfeld
Maritime Editor Allen Wastler
Trade Editor Robin Bulman
Senior Correspondent William Armbruster
Senior Correspondent Richard Lawrence
Senior Correspondent Michael S Lelyveld

MANAGEMENT INFORMATION SERVICES

Online Manager Ed Dear
Data Processing Manager Mike Heller

PRODUCTION

Vice Pres-Operations James Steckel
Foreman-Composing Michael Cavanaugh

Market Information: ADS; Operate database.

Mechanical available: Offset; Black and 4 ROP colors; insert accepted — preprinted; page cut-offs — 22$\frac{3}{4}$".

Mechanical specifications: Type page 13" x 21$\frac{7}{16}$"; E - 6 cols, 2$\frac{1}{16}$", $\frac{1}{8}$" between; A - 6 cols, 2$\frac{1}{16}$", $\frac{1}{8}$" between; C - 9 cols, 1$\frac{3}{8}$", .08" between.

Commodity consumption: widths 54$\frac{1}{2}$", 40$\frac{7}{8}$", 27$\frac{1}{4}$"; average pages per issue 44(d); single plates used 43,656.

Equipment: PRODUCTION: Typesetters — 2-AU/APS 5, 1-Hyphen/2200; Production cameras — 2-C; Automatic film processors — 2-P; Shrink lenses — Alan.
PRESSROOM: Pasters — 9-H; Reels and stands — 9-H; Press control system — 1-Hurletron. WIRE SERVICES: News — Stock tables — KRT; Receiving dishes — KRT. BUSINESS COMPUTERS: IBM/ES-9000-250, 3-Tandem/TXP, 2-Tandem/Non Stop II, HP/3000-947, 13-Novell; Applications: Circ, Adv billing, Accts receivable; PCs & micros networked; PCs & main system networked.

New York Daily News

(m-mon to sat; S)

New York Daily News, 450 W. 33rd St., New York, NY 10001; tel (212) 210-2100; fax (212) 949-2120.

Circulation: 738,091(m); 622,611(m-sat); 979,076(S); ABC Sept. 30, 1995.

Price: 40¢(d); 40¢(sat); $1.00(S); $3.95/wk (carrier); $35.50/mo (mail).

Advertising: Open inch rate $322.00(m); $322.00(m-sat); $400.38(S).

News Services: AP, KRT, TMS, UPI. **Politics:** Independent. **Established:** 1919.

Advertising not accepted: Objectionable.

Special Weekly Sections: Food (wed); Style (thur); City Lights, Travel (S); Business, New York Now (daily).

Magazines: Sunday Gravure, TV Week, Parade, Vista (S).

CORPORATE OFFICERS

Chairman/Co-Publisher Mortimer B Zuckerman
CEO/Co-Publisher Fred Drassner
Chief Financial Officer Thomas Peck
Exec Vice Pres/Chief Legal Officer Martin Krall
Exec Vice Pres/Assoc Publisher Delbert Spurlock
Exec Vice Pres/Assoc Publisher Les Goodstein
Senior Vice Pres-Advertising William D Holiber
Senior Vice Pres-Marketing Mike Presto
Vice Pres-National Sales Julian R Lowin
Vice Pres-Retail Sales Tina Hounigringer

GENERAL MANAGEMENT

Director-Communications & Media Relations C Adrienne Rhodes
Assoc General Counsel Marc Kramer

ADVERTISING

Vice Pres-Group Sales Andrea Dove
Vice Pres-Operations Edwin Costello
Vice Pres/Group Sales Director John Polizano

MARKETING AND PROMOTION

Vice Pres-Promotion/Public Relations John G Campi
Director/Vice Pres-Marketing Christine Curtin

TELECOMMUNICATIONS

Vice Pres-Technical Frank Schilero

CIRCULATION

Vice Pres/Director Jimmy Brill
Director/Vice Pres-Sales & Communications Ann Everhart
Manager-Home Delivery Dennis Carletta

NEWS EXECUTIVES

Editor in Chief Martin Dunn
Exec Editor Debby Krenek
Managing Editor Arthur Browne
Deputy Managing Editor Clem Richardson
Deputy Managing Editor Richard Rosen
Deputy Managing Editor-Features Fran Wood
Deputy Managing Editor-Graphics Tom Ruis
Deputy Managing Editor-News Bob Sapio
Asst Managing Editor James (Hap) Hairston

EDITORS AND MANAGERS

Arts/Entertainment Editor John Sullivan
Business Editor Alan Mirabella
Columnist Mike McAlary
Columnist Michael Daly
Columnist Linda Stasi
Gossip Columnist Joanna Molloy
Gossip Columnist George Lush
Gossip Columnist A J Benza
Gossip Columnist Michael Lewitts
Critic-At-Large David Hinckley
Chief Editorial Writer Robert Laird
Editorial Art Director Carl Walker
Editorial Page Editor Michael Goodwin
Deputy Editorial Page Editor Brian Kates
Editorial Cartoonist Paul Rigby
Editorial Writer Karen Zautyk
Features Editor Larry Hackett
Deputy Features Editor Jane Freiman
Food Editor Rosemary Black
Librarian Faigi Rosenthal
Lifestyle Editor-Daily Margaret Farley
National Editor Susan Jordan
Picture Assignment Editor Jo Barefoot
Director-Photography Eric Meskauskas
Deputy Director-Photography Mike Lipack
Assoc Sports Editor Bill Gallo
Sunday Editor Bill Boyle
Television Editor Jeff Weingrad
Travel Editor Guna Bite-Dickson

PRODUCTION

Vice Pres Gene Nussbaum
Vice Pres Andy Riggs
Director-Engineering Conrad Rausch
Manager-Press/Paper Handler Mike Maloney
Manager-Press (Brooklyn) Ray Walsh
Manager-Plant (Kearny) John Zucca
Manager-Building (Brooklyn) Don Paccione
Manager-Engineering (Kearny) Ron Wishart
Manager-Technical Training Rob Sabolowsky
Manager-Security Joseph Bussam
Manager-Mailroom William Mulham
Manager-Plateroom Joe Russo
General Foreman-Composing Sean Cox
Superintendent-Engraving James Minoque

Market Information: Zoned editions; Split Run.

Mechanical available: Letterpress; insert accepted — preprinted; page cut-offs — 21$\frac{1}{2}$".

Mechanical specifications: Type page 9$\frac{3}{8}$" x 14"; E - 5 cols, 1$\frac{3}{4}$", $\frac{3}{8}$" between; A - 6 cols, 1$\frac{1}{2}$", $\frac{1}{8}$" between; C - 7 cols, 1$\frac{1}{4}$", $\frac{1}{8}$" between.

Commodity consumption: Newsprint 153,841 metric tons; widths 58$\frac{1}{2}$", 43$\frac{3}{4}$", 29$\frac{1}{8}$"; black ink 3,453 pounds; single pages printed 120,162; average pages per issue 110(d), 216(S); single plates used 1,040,000.

Equipment: EDITORIAL: Front-end hardware — AT/Series 6; Other equipment — 4-Ap/Mac, 2-Ap/Mac Plus. CLASSIFIED: Front-end hardware — 5-AT/9000; Other equipment — 25-IBM/Selectric II, 25-TM/2277. DISPLAY: Adv layout systems — 4-Cx/135, 8-Cx/2351. PRODUCTION: Typesetters — 4-M/606, 3-Cx/Supersetter; Platemaking systems — Na; Plate exposures — 4-GSI/200T, 6-GSI/200RF, 9-DP/Cronaflow; Plate processors — 4-Na/220, 4-Na/120 (12-Titan Expose Units); Scanners — 2-ECR/Autokon 1000, 2-ECR/Autokon 5300; Production cameras — 1-K/187, 3-C/Marathon, 1-C/Spartan III, 2-C/Newspager; Automatic film processors — 4-LE/18, 1-LE/LD24AQ, 2-LE/LD24BQ, 2-LE/LD24, 1-LE/LD26-CH660; Film transporters — 3-C; Shrink lenses — 2-Alan/Anamorphic.
PRESSROOM: Line 1 — 37-G/4-Wide Headliner; Line 2 — 36-G/4-Wide Headliner; Line 3 — 18-G/4-Wide Headliner; Line 4 — 18-G/4-Wide Headliner; Folders — 9-G/3:2-2:1, 9-G/3:2; Pasters — PEC; Reels and stands — 76-Wd, 33-G; Press control system — 109-PEC. MAILROOM: Counter stackers — 30-Id/550, 12-HL/Monitor; Inserters and stuffers — 4-SH/72P, 1-ARS; Bundle tyer — 40-MLN/2A, 11-MLN/EE. LIBRARY: Combination — Vu/Text. COMMUNICATIONS: Facsimile — 36-X/400-1, 4-X/200, 4-Rapicom/R-100. WIRE SERVICES: News — AP, KRT, TMS, UPI. BUSINESS COMPUTERS: 2-DEC/Sys 2060, 1-IBM/MVS; Applications: Circ, Adv, Accts payable, Accts receivable, Financial; PCs & micros networked; PCs & main system networked.

The New York Times

(m-mon to fri; m-sat; S)

The New York Times, 229 W. 43rd St., New York, NY 10036; tel (212) 556-1234; e-mail letters@nytimes.com, bizday@nytimes.com, mainwall@ nytimes.com, onthejob@nytimes.com, viewpts@nytimes.com, mediabiz@ nytimes.com, jersey@nytimes.com, review@nytimes.com, scitimes @nytimes.com; web site http://www.nytimes. com/. New York Times Co. group.

Circulation: 1,081,541(m); 1,003,411(m-sat); 1,667,780(S); ABC Sept. 30, 1995.

Price: 60¢(d); 60¢(sat); $2.50(S); $6.70/wk.

Advertising: Open inch rate $481.00(m); $481.00(m-sat); $577.00(S).

News Services: AP, RN, PR Newswire, DJ, Tass. **Politics:** Independent. **Established:** 1851.

Note: Sunday single copy price is $2.50 outside of the Newspaper Designated Market in the northeast corridor, $4.00 nationally. The New York Times prints a national satellite edition at eight locations around the U.S.: Chicago; Warren, OH; Austin, TX; Torrance, CA; Walnut Creek, CA; Tacoma, WA; Atlanta; Ft. Lauderdale, FL. The national edition serves the entire country, including Alaska and Hawaii, as well as Mexico City, the Caribbean and parts of Canada.

Advertising not accepted: Determined by Times Standards of Acceptability.

Special Editions: Education Life, Spring Term Banner, Winter in the Sun (Jan); National College & University Directory, Spring/Summer Cruise Guide (Feb); Europe: Fetes and Festivals (Mar); Asia/Pacific, Education Life, Summer Team Banner (Apr); New England Vacations, Spas Sports (May); National College & University Directory, Weekend Getaways (June); Education Life, Fall Term Banner (Aug); American Cities including New York, Europe: Fall/Winter, National College & University Directory (Sept); Winter Cruise Guide, Winter in the Sun (Caribbean) (Oct); Education Life, Winter in the Snow, Winter Term Banner (Nov).

Special Weekly Sections: Sports Monday (mon); Science Times (tues); The Living Section (wed); The Home (thur); Weekend (fri); Arts & Leisure, Travel, Real Estate, Help Wanted Display, Business/Finance, Education, Health Care, Sports, Auto Zones (S).

Magazines: The New York Times Magazine (S); 4 Thematic Magazine Part 2's for 1996 on subjects like Fashion, Home Design and Sophisticated Traveler.

Broadcast Affiliates: WHNT-TV Huntsville, AL; KFSM-TV Fort Smith, AR; WQAD-TV Quad Cities, IA; WQAD-TV Quad Cities, IL; WQEW-AM/WQXR-FM New York; WNEP-TV Scranton, PA; WNEP-TV Wilkes-Barre, PA; WREG-TV Memphis, TN.

CORPORATE OFFICERS

Chairman/CEO Arthur Ochs Sulzberger
President/Chief Operating Officer Lance R Primis
Senior Vice Pres/Chief Operating Officer Diane P Baker

Senior Vice Pres/Deputy Chief Operating Officer David L Gorham
Senior Vice Pres/Chief Financial Officer Diane P Baker
Senior Vice Pres-Corporate Dev./Broadcasting Katharine P Darrow
Vice Pres/General Counsel Solomon B Watson IV
Vice Pres-Internal Audit Jack Hayon
Vice Pres-Corporate Communications Nancy Neilsen
Vice Pres-Corporate Controller Frank R Gatti
Vice Pres-Forest Products Stephen Golden
Vice Pres-Operations and Planning Gordon Medenica
Vice Pres-Taxation Thomas H Neid
Vice Pres-Human Resources Leslie Mardenborough
Secretary Laura Corwin
Treasurer Richard Thomas

OPERATING GROUPS

President/Chief Operating Officer-Regional Newspaper Group James C Weeks
President/CEO-Sports/Leisure Magazine James W Fitzgerald
President-Broadcasting C Frank Roberts
Exec Vice Pres Michael Golden
Exec Vice Pres-Operations Reginald Davenport

GENERAL MANAGEMENT

Publisher Arthur Sulzberger Jr
President/General Manager Russell T Lewis
Deputy General Manager/Exec Vice Pres John M O'Brien
Senior Vice Pres-Operations Richard H Gilman
Vice Pres-Human Resources Donna C Miele
Vice Pres/Chief Financial Officer Karen Messineo
Senior Vice Pres-Planning & Human Resources Penelope Muse Abernathy
Controller James Terrill
Asst Controller Phyllis Calvano
Group Director-Financial Service Liam Carlos

ADVERTISING

Senior Vice Pres Janet L Robinson
Vice Pres-Sales Jyll Holzman
Vice Pres-Sales Alexis Buryk
Vice Pres-Sales Daniel Cohen

MARKETING AND PROMOTION

Director-Marketing Research Kathleen Love
Director-Database Marketing Kerrie Gillis
Group Director-Promotion Alyse Myers
Group Director-Community Affairs Sharon Yakata
Art Director Amy Heit

TELECOMMUNICATIONS

Vice Pres-Systems/Technology Ray Douglas
Group Director-Administration Systems David Applebaum
Director-Sales Systems/Service Joe Flynn
Director-Management Systems Abha Kumar
Exec Director-Communications Service Gerry McGrath
Director-Publishing Systems Kris Tennent
Director-News Info Service Charles Robinson
Director-Color Service Scott Cornish
Director-Pre Press Lucy Chin

CIRCULATION

Exec Vice Pres William L Pollak
Vice Pres-Distribution Charles E Shelton
Vice Pres-Sales/Marketing Harold F Woldt Jr
Vice Pres-Home Delivery/Customer Service Lauretta Prestera
Director-Home Delivery Expansion Team John Daly
Director-Home Delivery Expansion Team Yasmin Namini
Director-Single Copy Expansion Team Raymond Pearce

NEWS EXECUTIVES

Exec Editor Joseph Lelyveld
Managing Editor Gene Roberts
Asst Managing Editor David R Jones
Asst Managing Editor Carolyn Lee
Asst Managing Editor Gerald Boyd
Asst Managing Editor Allan M Siegal
Asst Managing Editor Soma Golden
Asst Managing Editor/Magazine Editor Jack Rosenthal
Asst Managing Editor Warren M Hoge
Assoc Managing Editor-Art Tom Bodkin
Assoc Managing Editor-Personnel/Administration Dennis Lee Stern
Editorial Page Editor Howell Raines
Deputy Editorial Page Editor Phillip M Boffey
Op-Ed Editor Katherine J Roberts

EDITORS AND MANAGERS

Arts/Leisure Editor Connie Rosenblum
Book Review Editor Charles McGrath
Business Manager Pamela A Gubitosi
Business/Finance Editor John Geddes
Deputy Business/Finance Editor Glenn Kramon
Sunday Business Editor Alison Cowan
Education Editor Nancy Sharkey
Director-Fashion News Claudia Payne
Fashion Editor Bill Keller
Foreign Editor Bernard Gwertzman
Health/Science Editor Nicholas Wade
Home Section Editor Barbara Graustark
Living Section Editor Trish Hall
Metro Editor Michael Oreskes
National Edition Editor David R Jones
National Editor Dean Baquet
Senior Editor-News William Borders
News Surveys Editor Michael Kagay
Picture Editor Nancy Lee
Real Estate Editor Michael Leahy
Sports Editor Neil Amdur
Style Editor John Montorio
Technology Editor Judith Wilner
Travel Editor Nancy Newhouse
Washington Bureau Chief R W Apple Jr
Washington Editor Andrew Rosenthal
Week in Review Editor Jonathan Landman
Weekend Section Editor Myra Forsberg

MANAGEMENT INFORMATION SERVICES

Director-Operations Frank Januzzi
Managing Editor-Times Online James Patterson

PRODUCTION

Vice Pres David A Thurm
Asst to Vice Pres Roland Caputo
Group Director-Production James Fitzhenry
Group Director-Production Gerald McCauley
Manager-Edison Plant Tom Lombardo

Market Information: Zoned editions; Split Run; Operate database; Operate audiotex; Electronic edition.

Mechanical available: Offset; Black and 3 ROP colors; insert accepted — preprinted; page cut-offs — 22¼".

Mechanical specifications: Type page 13" x 21⅜"; E - 6 cols, 2", ⅛" between; A - 6 cols, 2", ⅛" between; C - 10 cols, 1³⁄₁₆", ¹⁄₁₆" between.

Commodity consumption: Newsprint 307,000 short tons; 278,000 metric tons; widths 54", 40½", 27"; black ink 4,200,000 pounds; color ink 252,000 pounds; single pages printed 44,100; average pages per issue 75(d), 400(S); single plates used 600,000.

Equipment: EDITORIAL: Front-end hardware — 42-AT/J-11, 950-PC, 20-AT/ADT, 150-Ap/Mac; Front-end software — AT 4.7; Printers — 55-HP/LaserJet, 25-Ap/Mac Laser-Writer; Other equipment — 250-RSK, 60-Zenith. CLASSIFIED: Front-end hardware — 300-IBM/3192; Front-end software — CICS; Printers — 1-HP/LaserJet, 3-C.Itoh. DISPLAY: Adv layout systems — 5-AT/Architect RS-600; Front-end hardware — IBM/3090 MF; Front-end software — NWI/Admarc 7.0; Printers — 2-Dataproducts, 2-HP/LaserJet. PRODUCTION: Pagination software — AT/Edpage 1.5; Typesetters — 2-Bidco/3120, 1-MON, 4-AU/APS-5, 2-Scitex/Raystart, 4-AU/PSPIP2, 3-AU/APS-6, 1-MON/Express Master; Plate-making systems — WL/10; Plate exposures — 6-WL/11; Plate processors — 6-WL/38E; Scanners — 3-ECR/Autokon 1000, 4-ECR/Autokon 2000, Scitex/Smartscanner; Production cameras — 2-C/Spartan III, 1-C/Marathon; Automatic film processors — 2-LE/2600 online, 3-LE/24-18-25A, AG/Rapidline, 2-Fuji/603; Film transporters — 2-LE; Color separation equipment (conventional) — 2-Scitex/Smart Scanner, 2-AG/Horizon Scanner; Digital color separation equipment — 3-Scitext/Workstation, Prisma, 3-Ap/Mac. PRESSROOM: Line 1 — 72-PEC/Converted offset (NY); Line 2 — 60-G/Colorliner (Edison NJ); Press drives — 7-GE, 7-Allen Bradley, 1-Siemens; Folders — 9-G, 6-G/Sovereign; Pasters — 1-G; Reels and stands — 168-G; Press control system — Allen Bradley. MAILROOM: Counter stackers — 20-QWI/1000, 20-Id/2000, 6-Id/3000; Inserters and stuffers — 8-HI/1472; Bundle tyer — MLN/MLN News 90, 12-Dynaric/Strap, 29-Metaverpa/Tyer; Addressing machine — KR, St. LIBRARY: Electronic — Mead Data Central/Nexis System. COMMUNICATIONS: Facsimile — 4-Datrax/Reader, 3-Datrax/Writer, 2-III/3750 Scanner, Scitex Network, Edison, 2-Datrax/Writers, 2-III/Recorders, 2-Scitex/Telepress Systems, 16-Datrax/Writers; Systems used — satellite, fiber optic. WIRE SERVICES: News — AP Datastream, AP Datafeatures, AP, PR Newswire, DJ, RN, Bloomberg; Photos — All Sports, AP Photostream, RN, AFP; Stock tables — TMS, Morningstar, Bloomberg; Syndicates — AP, RN; Receiving dishes — AP. BUSINESS COMPUTERS: 2-IBM/9121-621; Applications: Circ, Adv, Financial, Human resources; PCs & micros networked; PCs & main system networked.

The Wall Street Journal

(m-mon to fri)

The Wall Street Journal, 200 Liberty St., New York, NY 10281; tel (212) 416-2000; web site http://update.wsj.com, http://ptech.wsj.com, http://dowvision.wais.net/, http://www.adnet.wsj.com. Dow Jones & Co. Inc. group.

Circulation: 1,763,140(m); ABC Sept. 30, 1995.

Price: 75¢(d); $149.00/yr (carrier-U.S.).

Advertising: Open inch rate $974.26(m).

News Services: AP, DJ. **Politics:** Independent. **Established:** 1889.

Note: The Wall Street Journal is published in four regional editions: Eastern, Midwest, Southwest and Western. News content is the same in all editions but advertising can be purchased in one or all editions or a combination thereof. Eastern Edition printed in White Oak, MD, Chicopee, MA, South Brunswick, NJ and Orlando, FL, with plants in La Grange, GA and Charlotte, NC-Circ. 747,857. Midwest Edition printed in Naperville, IL, Highland, IL, Bowling Green, OH, Sharon, PA and Des Moines, IA-Circ. 478,028. Southwest Edition printed in Dallas, TX and Beaumont, TX-Circ. 163,434. Western Edition printed in Palo Alto and Riverside, CA, Seattle, WA and Denver, CO-Circ. 373,821. Figures are averages for 6 months ending 9/30/95. National (agate lines) rates: $73.70; Eastern Edition $33.54; Midwest $24.38; Western $18.10; Southwest $9.84.

Not Published: New Year; Washington's Birthday; Memorial Day; Independence Day; Labor Day; Thanksgiving; Christmas.

Special Editions: Year-End Review of Markets & Finance (Jan); Corporate Performance Review, Careers Report (Feb); Technology I Report: Entertainment (Mar); Capital Markets Underwriting Review, Stock Markets Winners & Losers Review, Mutual Funds Review, Executive Pay Report (Apr); Corporate Performance Review, Small Business Report, The European Economic Survey Report (Int'l only) (May); Technology II Report: Innovations, All-Star Analysts Review (June); Capital Markets Underwriting Review, Stock Market Winners & Losers Review (July); Corporate Performance Review (Aug); Technology III Report: Telecommunications, World Business Report (Sept); Capital Markets Underwriting Review, Stock Market Winners & Losers Review, Mutual Funds Review, Health, The Asian Economic Survey Report (Int'l only) (Oct); Corporate Performance Review, Technology IV Report (Nov); Personal Finance Report (Dec).

Special Weekly Sections: Travel, Sports, The Home Front (fri).

Magazine: Smart Money.

Cable TV: Own cable TV in circulation area.

GENERAL MANAGEMENT

Board Chairman/CEO/Publisher Peter R Kann
President/Chief Operating Officer Kenneth L Burenga
President/Publisher-Dow Jones Telerate Carl Valenti
President/Business Info Services Dorothea Coccoli Palsho
President-Television & Multimedia Peter Skinner
Senior Vice Pres-Dow Jones & Co. Carl Valenti
Exec Vice Pres-Dow Jones Telerate William Clabby
Exec Editor-Dow Jones News Services William Clabby
Vice Pres/Managing Editor-News Services Richard J Levine
Exec Vice Pres-Dow Jones Telerate Henry Becker
Exec Vice Pres-Dow Jones Telerate Julian Childs
Senior Vice Pres-Dow Jones Telerate Kenneth Herts
Senior Vice Pres James H Ottaway Jr
Senior Vice Pres-General Counsel & Secretary Peter Skinner
Vice Pres-Employee Relations James Scaduto
Vice Pres/Chief Financial Officer Kevin J Roche
Vice Pres-International Group Karen Elliot House
Director-Corporate Relations Roger B May

ADVERTISING

Vice Pres-Marketing (Dow Jones Co.) Bernard Flanagan
Vice Pres-Advertising (The Wall Street Journal) Paul Atkinson
Director-Classified Michael Wilson

CIRCULATION

Vice Pres Danforth W Austin

NEWS EXECUTIVES

Editor Robert L Bartley
General Manager Danforth W Austin
Managing Editor Paul Steiger
Deputy Managing Editor Byron Calame
Asst Managing Editor Daniel Hinson
Asst Managing Editor Carolyn Phillips
Asst Managing Editor Richard Tofel
Exec Editor-D.C. Albert R Hunt
Editor-Foreign John Bussey
Editor-Spot News (New York) Ann Podd
Bureau Chief-Atlanta Amanda Bennett
Bureau Chief-Boston Gary Putka
Bureau Chief-Chicago Tim Schellhardt
Bureau Chief-Dallas Kevin Helliker
Bureau Chief-Detroit Robert Simison
Bureau Chief-Houston Rick Wartzman
Bureau Chief-Los Angeles Steve Sansweet
Bureau Chief-Miami Jose de Cordoba
Bureau Chief-Pittsburgh Carol Hymowitz
Bureau Chief-San Francisco Greg Hill
Bureau Chief-Washington Alan Murray
Bureau Chief-Berlin Peter Gumbel
Bureau Chief-London Larry Ingrassia
Bureau Chief-Paris Thomas Kamm
Bureau Chief-Tokyo Steve Yoder
Bureau Chief-Montreal Christopher Chipello
Bureau Chief-Moscow Adi Ignatius
Bureau Manager-Ottawa John Urguhart
Bureau Manager-Toronto John Moritsugu
Bureau Manager-Calgary Tamsin Carlisle
Page One Editor John Brecher
Reporter-in-Charge (Kansas City) Dennis Farney
Reporter-in-Charge (Vienna) Clifford Stevens
Reporter-in-Charge (Tel Aviv) Amy Dockser Marcus
Reporter-in-Charge (Beijing) Kathy Chen
Reporter-in-Charge (Mexico) Paul Carroll
Reporter-in-Charge (Rio de Janeiro) Matt Moffeitt
Reporter-in-Charge (Seoul) Steven Glain
Reporter-in-Charge (Hong Kong) Marcus Brauchli
Reporter-in-Charge (Shangai) Joseph Kahn
Reporter-in-Charge (Buenos Aires) Jonathan Friedland

EDITORS AND MANAGERS

Editorial Page Editor Robert L Bartley
Entertainment/Amusements Editor Ray Sokolov
Features Editor David Asman
Sports Editor Fred Klein
Travel Editor Jonathan Dahl
Weekend Editor Lee Lescaze

PRODUCTION

Vice Pres-Operations F Thomas Kull Jr
Vice Pres-Technology Charles F Russell
Director-National William Harmer
Director-Communications Network Service Virgil Carden
Director-Operations Support Karen Kennedy
Director/Engineer Frank Lepelis
Director-Publishing Systems Alan Miner
Director-Corporate Data Processing Bernard Ostrowski
Senior Manager (Orlando FL) Ed Gareau
Senior Manager (Chicopee MA) Bill Reed
Senior Manager (South Brunswick NJ) Mike Clark
Senior Manager (Sharon Purchasing Agent) Richard Arnold
Senior Manager (Beaumont TX) Chris Galassini
Senior Manager (Dallas TX) James E Bland
Manager-Operations Nicholas Barbosa Jr
Manager-Construction & Facilities John Conboy
Manager (Palo Alto CA) Warren Reed
Manager (Riverside CA) Gary Ringo
Manager (Denver CO) Jeff Slack
Manager (La Grange GA) Darrell Foster
Manager (Highland IL) Timothy Goldsbury
Manager (Naperville IL) Steve Tomb
Manager (Des Moines IA) Keith Robbins
Manager (White Oak MD) Will Horner
Manager (Charlotte NC) Michele Bakarich
Manager (Bowling Green OH) Pam Broderick
Manager (Chickopee MA) Paul Cousineau
Manager (Seattle WA) Bruce Palkowetz

Market Information: Zoned editions; Split Run; TMC; ADS; Operate database; Operate audiotex; Electronic edition.

Mechanical available: Black and 3 ROP colors; page cut-offs — 22¾".

Mechanical specifications: Type page 14¼" x 21⅝".

Commodity consumption: average pages per issue 50(d).

Eastern Edition

Wall Street Journal-Eastern Edition, 200 Liberty St., New York, NY 10281; tel (212) 416-2000.
Special Edition: The Wall Street Journal Reports.

ADVERTISING
Director Paul Atkinson

Market Information: Zoned editions; Split Run.
Mechanical available: Offset; Black and 3 ROP colors; page cut-offs — $22\frac{3}{4}$".
Mechanical specifications: Type page $14\frac{1}{8}$" x $21\frac{5}{8}$"; E - 6 cols, 2.29", $\frac{1}{18}$" between; A - 6 cols, 2.29", $\frac{1}{18}$" between; C - 8 cols, 1.71", $\frac{1}{24}$" between.
Commodity consumption: average pages per issue 54(d).
Equipment: EDITORIAL: Front-end hardware — 2-CSI/1170, 2-DEC/PDP 11-84, 2-DEC/VAX 8250, 18-CSI/VT. CLASSIFIED: Front-end hardware — 2-CSI/1170, 4-Sun/360, 18-CSI/VT 112. DISPLAY: Adv layout systems — 2-CSI/1170, Cx/Sun 360; Other equipment — 4-ALS/Sun 360. PRODUCTION: Typesetters — 4-AU/APS Micro 5, 1-BKY/34x33 Vacuum printer; Plate exposures — 9-Nu/Flip Top FT, 2-WL, 5-Dow/scan IF, 21-Dow/Recorder; Plate processors — 2-Nat, 4-WL; Scanners — 2-ECR; Production cameras — 2-C/Newspager II, C/Spartan III; Automatic film processors — 19-LE, 3-C/R650; Film transporters — 4-C, 4-AU. PRESSROOM: Line 1 — 12-G/Metro; Line 2 — 12-G/Metro; Press drives — 5-G, 3-TKS; Folders — 5-G, 3-TKS; Pasters — 50-G, 30-TKS; Reels and stands — 50-G, 30-TKS; Press control system — 8-ABB. MAILROOM: Counter stackers — 14-QWI, 2-LD; Bundle tyer — 6-MLN/ML2EE, 22-OVL, 8-Power Strap; Addressing machine — 16-AVY/5209. WIRE SERVICES: Stock tables — AP, UPI; Receiving dishes — size-3m, AP, UPI. BUSINESS COMPUTERS: 9-IBM/3090, 1-HP/1000, 1-HP/9845; Applications: Word Processing: Adv lineage, Paper storage, Personnel, Accounting; PCs & micros networked; PCs & main system networked.

Midwest Edition

Wall Street Journal-Midwest Edition, 1 S. Wacker Dr., Ste. 2100, Chicago, IL 60606; tel (312) 750-4000.
Special Edition: The Wall Street Journal Reports.

ADVERTISING
Director Paul Atkinson
Manager Joseph Gurgone
Manager-Classified Michelle Bernstein

NEWS EXECUTIVES
News Bureau Chief Timothy D Schellhardt
Deputy News Bureau Chief Susan Carey

Mechanical available: Offset; Black and 3 ROP colors; page cut-offs — $22\frac{3}{4}$".
Mechanical specifications: Type page $14\frac{1}{8}$" x $21\frac{5}{8}$"; E - 6 cols, 2.29", $\frac{1}{18}$" between; A - 6 cols, 2.29", $\frac{1}{18}$" between; C - 8 cols, 1.71", $\frac{1}{24}$" between.
Commodity consumption: average pages per issue 54(d).
Equipment: PRODUCTION: Typesetters — 4-AU/APS Micro 5; Plate exposures — 4-Nu/Flip Top FT; Plate processors — 1-WL, 1-Nat, 4-C; Scanners — 2-ECR; Production cameras — 2-C/Spartan III, 1-C/Newspager; Automatic film processors — 3-LE, 1-C/F66; Film transporters — 3-C.
PRESSROOM: Line 1 — 12-G/Metro; Line 2 — 12-G/Metro; Press drives — 2-Fin, 3-TKS; Folders — 2-G/Metro, 3-TKS; Pasters — 20-G, 30-TKS; Reels and stands — 20-G, 30-TKS; Press control system — 5-ABB. MAILROOM: Counter stackers — 10-QWI; Bundle tyer — 8-OVL, 6-Power Strap; Addressing machine — 10-AVY. WIRE SERVICES: News — AP, UPI; Stock tables — AP SelectStox, UPI, AP Xeta; Receiving dishes — size-3m, AP. BUSINESS COMPUTERS: 3-IBM/3090; Applications: Bus; PCs & micros networked; PCs & main system networked.

Southwest Edition

Wall Street Journal-Southwest Edition, 1233 Regal Row, Dallas, TX 75247.

ADVERTISING
Director Paul Atkinson

Mechanical available: Offset; Black and 3 ROP colors; page cut-offs — $22\frac{3}{4}$".
Mechanical specifications: Type page $14\frac{1}{8}$" x $21\frac{5}{8}$"; E - 6 cols, 2.29", $\frac{1}{18}$" between; A - 6 cols, 2.29", $\frac{1}{18}$" between; C - 8 cols, 1.71", $\frac{1}{24}$" between.
Commodity consumption: average pages per issue 56(d).
Equipment: EDITORIAL: Front-end hardware — 2-DEC/PDP 11-84, 2-DEC/VAX 8250, 7-CSI. DISPLAY: Adv layout systems — Cx/Sun 360, 4-ALS/Sun 360. PRODUCTION: Typesetters — 4-AU/APS Micro 5; Plate exposures — 7-Nu/Flip Top FT, 1-BKY; Plate processors — 2-W, 1-Wd; Production cameras — 2-C/Spartan III, 1-C/Newspager; Automatic film processors — 3-LE, 1-C; Film transporters — 3-C.
PRESSROOM: Line 1 — 12-G/Metro, 12-TKS; Folders — 1-G/Metro, 1-TKS; Pasters — 10-G/Metro, 10-TKS; Reels and stands — 10-G/Metro, 10-TKS. MAILROOM: Counter stackers — 4-QWI; Bundle tyer — 8-Power Strap; Addressing machine — 4-AVY. WIRE SERVICES: Stock tables — AP Xeta; Receiving dishes — size-11m. BUSINESS COMPUTERS: 5-IBM/PC-XT, 3-ICL/8433 Disc Drive, Unisys/2200, Unisys/2200-400; Applications: Reports, Billing, Payroll, Newsprint inventory, Personnel, Ad services, Circ services, Office systems; Word processing; PCs & micros networked; PCs & main system networked.

Western Edition

Wall Street Journal-Western Edition, 1701 Page Mill Rd., Palo Alto, CA 94304.

ADVERTISING
Director Paul Atkinson

Mechanical available: Offset; Black and 3 ROP colors; page cut-offs — $22\frac{3}{4}$".
Mechanical specifications: Type page $14\frac{1}{8}$" x $21\frac{5}{8}$"; E - 6 cols, 2.29", $\frac{1}{18}$" between; A - 6 cols, 2.29", $\frac{1}{18}$" between; C - 8 cols, 1.71", $\frac{1}{24}$" between.
Commodity consumption: widths 60", 45", 30"; average pages per issue 52(d).
Equipment: PRODUCTION: Typesetters — 4-AU/APS Micro 5; Plate exposures — 6-Nu/Flip Top FT, 1-WL/Lith-X-Pozer III; Plate processors — 4-W; Scanners — 2-ECR; Production cameras — 2-C; Automatic film processors — 4-LE, 1-DAI/DS LD-360, 2-Fuji/FG 660F; Film transporters — 4-AU.
PRESSROOM: Line 1 — 12-G/Metro, 12-TKS; Press drives — 2-Fin, 2-TKS; Folders — 2-G, 2-TKS; Pasters — 20-G, 20-TKS; Reels and stands — 20-G, 20-TKS; Press control system — 4-ABB. MAILROOM: Counter stackers — 8-QWI; Bundle tyer — 6-MLN, 16-OVL, 10-Power Strap; Addressing machine — 8-AVY. WIRE SERVICES: Stock tables — AP Xeta. BUSINESS COMPUTERS: IBM/3090; Applications: Billing, Electronic mail; Word processing; PCs & micros networked; PCs & main system networked.

New York Post

(m-mon to fri; m-sat)

New York Post, 1211 6th Ave., New York, NY 10036; tel (212) 930-8000.
Circulation: 413,705(m); 330,306(m-sat); ABC Sept. 30, 1995.
Price: 50¢(d); 50¢(sat).
Advertising: Open inch rate $243.10(m); $243.10(m-sat). **Representatives:** James Elliott Co; Dynamedia.
News Services: AP, UPI, LAT-WP. **Politics:** Independent. **Established:** 1801.
Note: Effective April 14, 1996, this publication will add a Sunday edition.
Special Editions: Mid-winter Get-aways, Alaska (Jan); Spring & Summer Cruises, Western Europe, Mediterranean (Mar); Mexico, Mountain Retreats, Caribbean (Apr); Catskills, Eastern Europe, Day Tripping, Family Vacations (May); Asia, Summer Getaways (June); Autumn Travel (Sept); Fall/Winter Cruises, South Pacific, Follow the Sun, South America (Oct); Sun & Snow Holidays, Mexico, Caribbean (Nov); Ski Vacations (Dec).
Special Weekly Section: Travel (tues).

CORPORATE OFFICER
Chairman K Rupert Murdoch

GENERAL MANAGEMENT
Publisher Martin Singerman
Vice Pres/General Manager Richard R Hawkes
Vice Pres-Finance Michael Carvalhido
Controller Michael Lafemina
Business Manager Vito Catania

ADVERTISING
Vice Pres John Ancona
Director-Display Sales Patrick Judge
Director-Operations Lionel Saturn
Director-Classified Elaine Clisham
Manager-Retail Ralph D'Onofrio
Manager-Research Mike DiPreta

MARKETING AND PROMOTION
Vice Pres-Promotion Lou Perullo
Director-Promotion Lisa Barnett
Asst Director-Promotion Keelin Kavanagh

CIRCULATION
Vice Pres/Operations Manager John Amann
Director-Operations Joseph Steo
Manager Danny Carr
Manager-Customer Info Service Alida Rojas
Manager-Metro James Collins
Manager-Suburban/Country Mary Fennessey
Manager-Night Robert Roge
Superintendent-Delivery Gerard Bilbao
General Foreman-Mailroom Glenn Dellafacoma

NEWS EXECUTIVES
Editor Ken Chandler
Exec Editor Steve Cuozzo
Managing Editor Marc Kalech

EDITORS AND MANAGERS
Administrative Editor Anne Aquilina
Columnist Andrea Peyser
Columnist Jack Newfield
Columnist Ray Kerrison
Drama/Dance Editor Clive Barnes
Editorial Page Editor/Columnist Eric Breindel
Entertainment/Amusements Editor Vincent Musetto
Finance Editor David Yelland
Films Critic Editor Michael Medved
Graphics Editor/Art Director Dennis Wickman
Metro Editor Stuart Marques
Photo Editor Seth E Jones
Sports Editor Greg Gallo
Washington Bureau Deborah Orin
Women's Editor Kathy Bishop

MANAGEMENT INFORMATION SERVICES
Vice Pres-Technology Barry Mechanic
Manager-Editorial Systems Tom Greendyk
Manager-Info Systems Mike Lillis
Manager-Technical Support Rafael Quirindongo

PRODUCTION
Director Dan Schaible
Superintendent-Mechanical Robert Isakson
General Foreman-Composing Dennis Kiamie
Foreman-Pressroom Thomas Stephens
Foreman-Stereo Robert Henaghan
Foreman-Paperhandler Tom Scollan
Foreman-Machinist Guy Buonpane
Foreman-Electrical Bill Depuy

Market Information: Split Run.
Mechanical available: Letterpress (direct); Black and 1 ROP color; page cut-offs — $23\frac{9}{16}$".
Mechanical specifications: Type page $10\frac{13}{16}$" x 14"; E - 5 cols, $2\frac{1}{16}$", $\frac{1}{8}$" between; A - 5 cols, $2\frac{1}{16}$", $\frac{1}{8}$" between; C - 8 cols, $1\frac{1}{2}$", $\frac{1}{8}$" between.
Commodity consumption: Newsprint 44,863 metric tons; widths $58\frac{1}{2}$", $43\frac{7}{8}$", $29\frac{1}{4}$"; black ink 2,000,000 pounds; color ink 60,000 pounds; average pages per issue 76(d); single plates used 275,000.
Equipment: EDITORIAL: Front-end hardware — 4-HI, 36-HI/1720, 29-HI/1740, 36-HI/1780, 55-AST. DISPLAY: Adv layout systems — 6-HI/2200 (on-line). PRODUCTION: Typesetters — 2-AU/APS 5; Platemaking systems — 3-Na; Plate exposures — 3-Na; Plate processors — 3-Na/Titan; Scanners — 1-ECR/Autokon; Production cameras — 2-C, 3-SCREEN/240; Automatic film processors — 4-DP, 1-Kk; Shrink lenses — 1-Alan.
PRESSROOM: Line 1 — 8-G/Mk II; Line 2 — 8-G/Mk II; Line 3 — 8-G/Mk II; Line 4 — 8-G/Mk II; Folders — 4-G/3:2, 4-G/2:1; Press control system — Fin. MAILROOM: Counter stackers — 9-St, 1-HL; Bundle tyer — 9-MLN; Addressing machine — 1-Am. WIRE SERVICES: News — AP, UPI, LAT-WP, DFW, BQ, TP; Stock tables — AP; Syndicates — LAT-WP, DFW. BUSINESS COMPUTERS: 2-DEC/6210; Applications: Circ, Adv billing, Accts receivable, Gen ledger, Payroll, Class adv, Bus admin; PCs & main system networked.

NEW YORK CITY

See STATEN ISLAND

NIAGARA FALLS

Niagara County

'90 U.S. Census- 61,840; **E&P '96 Est.** 54,920
ABC-NDM (90): 115,948 (HH 45,267)

Niagara Gazette

(m-mon to sat; S)

Niagara Gazette, 310 Niagara St.; PO Box 549, Niagara Falls, NY 14302-0549; tel (716) 282-2311. Gannett Co. Inc. group.
Circulation: 26,499(m); 26,499(m-sat); 27,847(S); ABC Sept. 30, 1995.
Price: 35¢(d); 35¢(sat); $1.00(S); $3.00/wk (carrier); $156.00/yr.
Advertising: Open inch rate $33.12(m); $33.12(m-sat); $33.12(S). **Representative:** Gannett National Newspaper Sales.
News Services: AP, GNS. **Politics:** Independent. **Established:** 1854.
Special Editions: Brides, New Year-New Business, Martin Luther King (Jan); Boat Show, Valentine's Day, Strictly Business (Feb); March Madness, Outlook, New Car, Home Improvement, St. Patrick's Day (Mar); Home Furnishings, Choose Your School, Employment, Easter (Apr); Family Owned, Can-Am, In-Memoriam (May); Say No to Drugs, Graduates' Day, Baby Tab (June); Strictly Business, Porter Cup, Home Furnishings (July); Back-to-School, Restaurant Guide (Aug); Welcome Back, Peach Festival, Buffalo Bills, Grandparents Day, Salute to Labor (Sept); Little Italy, Can-Am, Fall Car Care, Fall Home Improvement, Bosses' Day, Strictly Business (Oct); Holly, Festival of Lights, Christmas Greetings, Giving Thanks (Nov); Here Come the Holidays, Wrapping Up the Holidays, Baby's First Christmas, Christmas Angels (Dec).
Special Weekly Sections: Food (mon); Night & Day, Home & Garden (fri); Religion (sat); Travel, Schools (S).
Magazines: TV Times, USA Weekend, Comics (S).

CORPORATE OFFICERS
President Mark Francis
Controller Martha DeShong

GENERAL MANAGEMENT
Publisher Mark Francis

ADVERTISING
Director Mike Kellogg

MARKETING AND PROMOTION
Director-Market Development Luann Labedz

CIRCULATION
Director Vincent Tropea

NEWS EXECUTIVES
Exec Editor Dennis M Lyons
Managing Editor Daniel Bowerman

EDITORS AND MANAGERS
Community News Editor Cathalena Burch
Features Editor Linda Noworyta
Graphics Editor Eric Craven
Sports Editor Mal Van Valkenburg

MANAGEMENT INFORMATION SERVICES
Data Processing Manager Catriena Thomas

PRODUCTION
Director Alvin Walker
Manager-Technical Service Harold Rinehart
Foreman-Pressroom Harold Bartel

Market Information: Zoned editions; TMC; ADS.
Mechanical available: Letterpress; Black and 3 ROP colors; insert accepted — preprinted; page cut-offs — $23\frac{5}{8}$".
Mechanical specifications: Type page 13" x 22"; E - 6 cols, $2\frac{1}{16}$", $\frac{1}{8}$" between; A - 6 cols, $2\frac{1}{16}$", $\frac{1}{8}$" between; C - 9 cols, $1\frac{7}{16}$", $\frac{1}{16}$" between.
Commodity consumption: Newsprint 1,500 metric tons; widths $54\frac{1}{2}$", $40\frac{7}{8}$", $27\frac{1}{4}$"; black ink 39,000 pounds; color ink 6,000 pounds; single pages printed 9,600; average pages per issue 24(d), 48(S); single plates used 25,000.
Equipment: EDITORIAL: Front-end hardware — 2-Sun/Sparc filesaver; Front-end software — DTI 3.0.21; Other equipment — 20-Ap/Mac Centris 610, 2-Ap/Mac IIci, 7-Ap/Mac Quadra 800 Graphics Server, 1-Ap/Mac IIfx. CLASSIFIED: Front-end hardware — 6-Ap/Mac Centris 610; Front-end software — DTI 3.0.14; Printers — Ap/Mac LaserWriter Pro. DISPLAY: Front-end hardware — 5-Ap/Mac Centris 610, 1-Ap/Mac Quadra 800; Front-end software — DTI/AdSpeed 3.0.16; Printers — 1-New Gen/Turbo P.S., 1-Ap/Mac LaserWriter. PRODUCTION: Pagination software — DTI/Speedwriter 3.0.16, DTI/Pagespeed 3.0.16, DTI/Speedplanner 3.0.16; Typesetters — 2-AU/APS-6-82 ACS, AU/APS SoftPip, 1-9gig harddrive, 1-3.5gig harddrive; Platemaking systems — 1-Na; Plate exposures — 1-Na/Starlite; Plate processors — 1-Na/NP40; Electronic picture desk — Lf/AP Leaf Picture Desk;

Scanners — 1-ECR/Autokon 1000; Production cameras — 1-C/Marathon; Film transporters — 1-C; Color separation equipment (conventional) — DTI; Digital color separation equipment — DTI.
PRESSROOM: Line 1 — 6-G/Headliner-Mark I; Folders — 1-G; Reels and stands — 6-Cline; Press control system — Cline. MAILROOM: Counter stackers — 2-Quipp/350; Inserters and stuffers — 1-Mc/660-20; Bundle tyer — 1-Bu, 2-Power Strap; Wrapping singles — 2-Quipp/Bottom Wrap. LIBRARY: Electronic — DTI. WIRE SERVICES: News — AP Datastream, AP Datafeatures, GNS; Photos — AP; Stock tables — AP; Syndicates — GNS, AP Datafeatures; Receiving dishes — size-3m, AP. BUSINESS COMPUTERS: IBM/AS-400; Applications: Payroll, Adv, Circ, Gen ledger, Accts payable, Budgeting; PCs & micros networked; PCs & main system networked.

NORTH TONAWANDA-TONAWANDA

Niagara and Erie Counties

'90 U.S. Census- 52,273 (Tonawanda 17,284; N. Tonawanda 34,989); E&P '96 Est. 50,557 (Tonawanda 16,197; N. Tonawanda 34,360)

Tonawanda News

(e-mon to fri; m-sat)

Tonawanda News, 435 River Rd.; PO Box 668, North Tonawanda, NY 14120; tel (716) 693-1000; fax (716) 693-8573. Hollinger International Inc. group.

Circulation: 12,036(e); 12,036(m-sat); CAC Sept. 30, 1995.

Price: 35¢(d); 35¢(sat); $1.70/wk; $22.10/3mo; $88.40/yr.

Advertising: Open inch rate $15.29(e); $15.29(m-sat). **Representatives:** Landon Associates Inc.; US Suburban Press.

News Service: AP. **Politics:** Independent. **Established:** 1880.

Special Weekly Sections: Best Food Day (mon); Best Amusement/Entertainment Day (thur); TV Section (sat).

CORPORATE OFFICERS

President Larry J Perrotto
Comptroller Roland McBride

GENERAL MANAGEMENT

Publisher Joseph P Armenia
Controller Wayne Tylec
General Manager Frank Skally

CIRCULATION

Manager Bruce Putnum

NEWS EXECUTIVE

Managing Editor Charles Hewitt

EDITORS AND MANAGERS

Editorial Page Editor Charles Hewitt
Fashion/Food Editor Joseph Amadio
Films/Theater Editor Joseph Amadio
Home Editor Joseph Amadio
Radio/Television Editor Joseph Amadio
Sports Editor Robert Salzman

PRODUCTION

Foreman-Composing Irving Myers

Market Information: Zoned editions; Split Run; TMC.

Mechanical available: Offset; Black and 3 ROP colors; insert accepted — preprinted, all; page cut-offs — 22¾".

Mechanical specifications: Type page 13" x 21½"; E - 6 cols, 2⅟₁₆", ⅛" between; A - 6 cols, 2⅟₁₆", ⅛" between; C - 8 cols, 1⁹⁄₁₆", ⅟₁₆" between.

Commodity consumption: Newsprint 560 short tons; widths 27½", 13¾"; black ink 16,435 pounds; color ink 350 pounds; single pages printed 4,963; average pages per issue 13(d); single plates used 7,504.

Equipment: EDITORIAL: Front-end hardware — Ap/Mac; Front-end software — Aldus/PageMaker; Printers — Ap/Mac Pro 630. CLASSIFIED: Front-end hardware — COM/PC; Front-end software — System Facilities; Printers — Ap/Mac Pro 630. DISPLAY: Adv layout systems — Ap/Mac; Front-end hardware — Ap/Mac; Front-end software — Aldus/PageMaker; Printers — Ap/Mac Pro 630. PRODUCTION: Plate exposures — 1-Nu/FT40V, 1-Nu/CN42; Plate processors — 1-Nat/A340; Production cameras — 1-Kl/Sum-A-Lum; Automatic film processors — 1-LE/LD24.
PRESSROOM: Line 1 — 8-G/SC-175; Line 2 — 8-G/SC-175; Folders — 2-G/2:1. MAILROOM: Counter stackers — 1-BG/106; Bundle tyer — 1-MLN/ML2EE; Addressing machine — 1-Am/1955P. COMMUNICATIONS: Facsimile — UPI/UF. WIRE SERVICES: News — AP; Receiving dishes — size-2ft, AP. BUSINESS COMPUTERS: PC/System; Applications: Circ, Adv billing, Accts receivable, Gen ledger, Accts payable.

NORWICH

Chenango County

'90 U.S. Census- 7,613; E&P '96 Est. 7,244

The Evening Sun (e-mon to fri)

The Evening Sun, 45-47 Hale St.; PO Box 151, Norwich, NY 13815; tel (607) 334-3276; fax (607) 334-8273. Hollinger International Inc. group.

Circulation: 5,460(e); Sworn Oct. 2, 1995.

Price: 40¢(d); $1.50/wk; $6.50/mo; $78.00/yr.

Advertising: Open inch rate $10.15(e). **Representative:** Landon Associates Inc.

News Service: AP. **Politics:** Independent. **Established:** 1891.

Not Published: Christmas.

Special Editions: Progress; Bridal; Home Improvement; Car Care; Dairy Section; Graduation Section; Fall Sports; Lucky Numbers; Christmas.

Special Weekly Sections: Business, Sports (mon); Senior Forum, Health (tues); Farm, Food (wed); Lifestyle (thur); The Weekend Sun (fri).

GENERAL MANAGEMENT

General Manager Richard Snyder

ADVERTISING

Manager Russ Foote

CIRCULATION

Manager Judy Cole

NEWS EXECUTIVE

Managing Editor Jeff Genung

Market Information: Zoned editions; Split Run; TMC.

Mechanical available: Offset; Black and 2 ROP colors; insert accepted — preprinted; page cut-offs — 22¾".

Mechanical specifications: Type page 13" x 21½"; E - 6 cols, 2⅟₁₆", ⅛" between; A - 6 cols, 2⅟₁₆", ⅛" between; C - 10 cols, 1⅟₁₆", ⅟₁₆" between.

Commodity consumption: Newsprint 110 short tons; widths 27½", 13¾"; black ink 4,400 pounds; color ink 170 pounds; single pages printed 3,536; average pages per issue 12(d); single plates used 2,360.

Equipment: EDITORIAL: Front-end hardware — Mk. CLASSIFIED: Front-end hardware — Mk. PRODUCTION: Typesetters — 1-COM/Unisetter, 1-COM/7200, 1-COM/2961HS; Platemaking systems — 1-Nu/AG Camera LE; Production cameras — 1-AG; Automatic film processors — 1-LE.
PRESSROOM: Line 1 — 5-G/Community; Folders — 1-G. MAILROOM: Bundle tyer — MA; Addressing machine — 1-Am. WIRE SERVICES: News — AP; Receiving dishes — AP.

NYACK

Rockland County

'90 U.S. Census- 6,558; E&P '96 Est. 6,669
ABC-NDM (90): 265,475 (HH 84,874)

The Rockland Journal-News (e-mon to fri; m-sat; S)

The Rockland Journal-News, 200 N. Rte. 303, West Nyack, NY 10994; tel (914) 358-2200; web site http://www.nynews.com/nynews. Gannett Co. Inc. group.

Circulation: 40,735(e); 40,735(m-sat); 51,191(S); ABC Sept. 24, 1995.

Price: 50¢(d); 50¢(sat); $1.25(S).

Advertising: Open inch rate $42.58(e); $42.58(m-sat); $47.18(S).

Note: White Plains is the headquarters for the Gannett Suburban Newspapers, Inc. The following newspapers are printed at Harrison White Plains plant: Mt. Vernon Daily Argus, Mamaroneck Daily Times, New Rochelle Standard-Star, Port Chester Daily Item, White Plains Reporter-Dispatch, Tarrytown Daily News, Peekskill Star, Ossining Citizen Register and Yonkers Herald Statesman. The Rockland Journal-News is printed in Nyack, NY. For detailed mechanical equipment information, see the Gannett Suburban Newspapers, Inc. listing in White Plains.

Special Editions: Spring Bridal (Feb); Spring Home Design (Mar); Spring Home & Garden, Suburban Golf, Greater New York Auto Show, Summer Education, Suburban Business Review (Apr); Suburban Golf, Builder's Showcase (May); Summer Dine Out Guide (June); Suburban Golf (July); Back-to-School, Fall Education, Suburban Golf (Aug); Suburban Golf, Pro Football Preview, Local Football Preview, Fall Bridal, Community Guide (Sept); Suburban Golf, Fall Home Design, New Autos '97, Fall Dine Out Guide (Oct); Holiday Gift Guide, Thanksgiving Day Special, Holiday Planner (Nov); Holiday Food, Hot Holiday Gifts, Last Minute Gift Guide (Dec).

CORPORATE OFFICERS

President/Publisher Gary F Sherlock
Vice Pres/Exec Editor Kenneth A Paulson
Vice Pres/President-Advertising John C Green
Vice Pres/Director-Circulation Mike Huot
Vice Pres-Finance Charles Schmitt
Vice Pres-Marketing Michael G Kane
Vice Pres-Operations Fal A Bolzner

ADVERTISING

Director Enedina Vega

TELECOMMUNICATIONS

Audiotex Manager Carl Iacona

CIRCULATION

Director Jonathan Alvord
Manager Paul Felicissimo

NEWS EXECUTIVES

Exec Editor Caesar Andrews
Managing Editor Steve Lambert

EDITORS AND MANAGERS

Art Director John Cornell
Copy Desk Chief Russell Rein
Editorial Page Editor Arthur Gunther III
Enterprise Editor Camille Cooper
Entertainment/Amusements Editor Greg Weber
Fashion/Style Editor Greg Weber
Features Editor Greg Weber
Local News Editor Tony Davenport
News Editor Jon Murray
Sports Editor John Humenn

MANAGEMENT INFORMATION SERVICES

Director-Systems & Technology Sherman Bodner

PRODUCTION

Manager Saul Doctor

Market Information: Operate audiotex; Electronic edition.

OGDENSBURG

St. Lawrence County

'90 U.S. Census- 13,521; E&P '96 Est. 14,565

Courier-Observer

(m-tues to sat)

The Journal (e-mon to fri)

Advance-News (S)

The Courier-Observer, The Journal & The Advance-News, 308-312 Isabella St.; PO Box 409, Ogdensburg, NY 13669; tel (315) 393-1000; fax (315) 393-5108. Park Communications Inc. group.

Circulation: 5,282(m); 4,873(e); 5,282(m-sat); 10,613(S); Sworn Sept. 29, 1995.

Price: 35¢(d); 35¢(sat); 75¢(S); $1.15/wk (e), 75¢/wk (S), $1.75/wk (m); $5.00/mo (e), $3.35/mo (S), $7.00/mo (m); $59.80/yr (e), $37.00/yr (S), $85.00/yr (m).

Advertising: Open inch rate $10.96(m); $10.96(e); $10.96(m-sat); $9.41(S). **Representative:** Landon Associates Inc.

News Service: AP. **Politics:** Journal-Republican, Advance-News-Democrat. **Established:** 1830 (Advance-News), 1855 (Journal).

Advertising not accepted: Adoption.

Special Editions: Progress (Jan); Dairy Month (June); Automotive (Aug); Sports Profiles (Sept); Chrismas Card (Nov); Back-to-School; Graduation; Income Tax Tips; Spring Home Improvement; Energy; Bridal; Vacation Guide; Holiday Recipe; Boys and Girls Club Expo Edition; Christmas Gift Guide.

Special Weekly Section: TV (S).

Magazines: At your Leisure; Sunday Television Supplement.

CORPORATE OFFICERS

President Wright M Thomas
Vice Pres-Newspapers Ralph J Martin

GENERAL MANAGEMENT

General Manager Charles W Kelly
Asst General Manager Patricia A Charlebois
Business Manager Brenda King
Manager-Credit Lisa Decker

ADVERTISING

Director Mary McGee

NEWS EXECUTIVES

Editor Charles W Kelly
Managing Editor (Journal/Advance News) James E Reagen
Managing Editor (The Courier-Observer) Ryne R Martin

EDITOR AND MANAGER

Sports Editor David Shea

PRODUCTION

Manager Shawn Cameron
Superintendent Barbara Burnett
Foreman-Pressroom Shawn Cameron
Foreman-Mailroom John Shea

Market Information: TMC.

Mechanical available: Offset; Black and 1 ROP color; insert accepted — preprinted, minimum 4-page tabloid; page cut-offs — 20".

Mechanical specifications: Type page 13" x 21½"; E - 6 cols, 2⅟₁₆", ⅛" between; A - 6 cols, 2⅟₁₆", ⅛" between; C - 9 cols, 1⅜", ⅟₁₆" between.

Commodity consumption: Newsprint 205 short tons; width 28"; black ink 8,700 pounds; color ink 1,025 pounds; single pages printed 5,064; average pages per issue 13(d), 33(S); single plates used 4,784.

Equipment: EDITORIAL: Front-end hardware — Mk. CLASSIFIED: Front-end hardware — 1-Mk/Mycro-Comp. PRODUCTION: Typesetters — 3-COM; Platemaking systems — 3M/Pyrofax; Plate processors — 3M/Pyrofax; Production cameras — 1-C; Automatic film processors — LE.
PRESSROOM: Line 1 — 5-G/Urbanite (40 broadsheet pages). MAILROOM: Bundle tyer — 1-Bu, 2-Gd; Addressing machine — 4-Am. WIRE SERVICES: News — Receiving dishes — AP. BUSINESS COMPUTERS: Vision Data; Applications: Bus, Circ; PCs & micros networked; PCs & main system networked.

OLEAN

Cattaraugus County

'90 U.S. Census- 16,946; E&P '96 Est. 15,967
ABC-CZ (90): 24,113 (HH 8,921)

Olean Times-Herald

(e-mon to fri; m-sat; S)

Olean Times-Herald, 639 Norton Dr., Olean, NY 14760; tel (716) 372-3121; fax (716) 372-0740. Hollinger International Inc. group.

Circulation: 20,410(e); 20,410(m-sat); 20,151(S); ABC Sept. 30, 1995.

Price: 50¢(d); 50¢(sat); $1.50(S); $2.50/wk (carrier); $11.00/mo (carrier); $132.00/yr (carrier).

Advertising: Open inch rate $18.90(e); $18.90(m-sat); $18.90(S). **Representative:** Landon Associates Inc.

News Services: AP, NEA, SHNS, CNS. **Politics:** Independent. **Established:** 1860.

Special Editions: Winter Sports, Bridal (Jan); Tax Tab (Feb); Progress, Health Tab, Frozen Food (Mar); Car Care, Golf Tab (Apr); Consumer Electronics (Sept); Car Care, Hunting (Oct); Christmas Edition (Nov); Christmas Stories (Dec); Spring Buyer Tab.

Special Weekly Sections: Best Food Day (mon); House and Garden (thur); Directory (fri); Church Pages (sat); Travel, Auto Page, TV Digest (S).

Magazines: Olean Review; Wellsville Review.

CORPORATE OFFICERS

President/CEO Larry J Perrotto
Comptroller Roland McBride

GENERAL MANAGEMENT

Publisher Charles M Ward
Business Manager William B Fitzpatrick

ADVERTISING

Director Larry Chiott
Manager-Classified Kristi Appleby
Manager-National Julie Keim

CIRCULATION

Manager Randy Lewis

NEWS EXECUTIVE

Managing Editor Thomas Donahue

EDITORS AND MANAGERS

Automotive Editor Pat Vecchio
Business Editor George Nianiatus
Films/Theater Editor Pat Vecchio
Librarian Judy Moyer

Lifestyle Editor Beth Danias
Religion Editor Joe Downey
School Editor Rick Miller
Sports Editor Chuck Pollock
Sports Editor Gary Maloney

PRODUCTION

Foreman-Composing John Pfeiffer
Foreman-Pressroom John Fitzpatrick

Market Information: TMC; ADS.
Mechanical available: Offset; Black and 3 ROP colors; insert accepted — preprinted; page cut-offs — 21½".
Mechanical specifications: Type page 13" x 21½"; E - 6 cols, 2¹⁄₁₆", ⅛" between; A - 6 cols, 2¹⁄₁₆", ⅛" between; C - 9 cols, 1⅜", ¹⁄₁₆" between.
Commodity consumption: Newsprint 1,360 metric tons; widths 27", 13½", 34", 19"; black ink 27,468 pounds; single pages printed 8,916; average pages per issue 23(d), 32(S); single plates used 5,900.
Equipment: EDITORIAL: Front-end hardware — 2-COM/1210, 16-IBM. CLASSIFIED: Front-end hardware — Dewar, 3-Dewar/Disc Net; Printers — Okidata/193 Line Printer. PRODUCTION: Typesetters — 1-COM/7200, 2-COM/ACM9000, 2-COM/8600, 2-Unified/Composer; Platemaking systems — 2-Nu/52; Scanners — 3-Dewar/Disc Net 55 Terminal, 3-Dewar/Discovery Display Ad Terminal; Production cameras — 1-B/Commodore, 1-K/187; Automatic film processors — 1-Kk, 1-LE/PC-13, LE/PC-17; Shrink lenses — 1-Rodenstock; Color separation equipment (conventional) — Digi-Colour.
PRESSROOM: Line 1 — 7-G/U791 (1 balloon former). MAILROOM: Bundle tyer — 2-MLN/ML2-EE. COMMUNICATIONS: Digital ad delivery system — AP AdSend. Systems used — satellite. WIRE SERVICES: News — AP; Receiving dishes — size-10ft, AP. BUSINESS COMPUTERS: ATT/Sys 332-500; Applications: Bus, Circ, Accts receivable, Payroll, Gen ledger.

ONEIDA

Madison County

'90 U.S. Census- 10,850; E&P '96 Est. 10,883

The Oneida Daily Dispatch (e-mon to fri; m-sat)

The Oneida Daily Dispatch, 130 Broad St.; PO Box 120, Oneida, NY 13421; tel (315) 363-5100; fax (315) 363-9832. Goodson Newspaper group.
Circulation: 9,023(e); 9,023(m-sat); Sworn Oct. 1, 1994.
Price: 35¢(d); 35¢(sat); $2.10/wk; $109.20/yr.
Advertising: Open inch rate $11.94(e); $11.94 (m-sat). **Representative:** Papert Companies.
News Service: AP. **Politics:** Independent. **Established:** 1851.
Not Published: New Year; Christmas.
Special Editions: Progress (Jan); Wedding, Agriculture (Feb); Health and Fitness (Mar); Business Edition (Apr); Car Care, Home Improvement (May); Summer Travel (June); Agriculture (Aug); Car Care (Oct).
Special Weekly Section: Best of Times (thur).

GENERAL MANAGEMENT

Publisher Ann Campanie
Business Manager Mary Anne Hawthorne

ADVERTISING

Director Frank McGivern

CIRCULATION

Director Debra Casciano

NEWS EXECUTIVES

Managing Editor Phyllis Montague Harris
Assoc Editor Andy Marino

EDITORS AND MANAGERS

Features Editor Kelly Homan
Sports Editor Ken Schimpf III

PRODUCTION

Director Robert Bennett

Mechanical available: Offset; Black and 2 ROP colors; insert accepted — preprinted; page cut-offs — 22¾".
Mechanical specifications: Type page 13" x 21.5"; E - 6 cols, 2.07", ⅛" between; A - 6 cols, 2.07", ⅛" between; C - 8 cols, 1.53", .11" between.
Commodity consumption: Newsprint 389 short tons; widths 27½", 34", 30"; black ink 9,267 pounds; color ink 266 pounds; single pages printed 4,486; average pages per issue 14(d); single plates used 5,802.
Equipment: EDITORIAL: Front-end hardware — IBM/PC-XT; Front-end software — Cx; Printers — New Gen/Turbo PS. CLASSIFIED: Front-end hardware — IBM/PC-XT; Front-end software — Cx; Printers — New Gen/Turbo PS. DISPLAY: Front-end hardware — Ap/Mac Quadra 605; Front-end software — Multi-Ad/Creator, Ofoto, QuarkXPress; Printers — NewGen/Turbo PS. PRODUCTION: OCR software — OFOTO 2; Plate exposures — B; Plate processors — Manual; Production cameras — B/Caravel, SCREEN/C-6500 D; Automatic film processors — LE/LD-1800A.
PRESSROOM: Line 1 — 5-G/Community; Press drives — Fin; Folders — 1-G/SC. MAILROOM: Bundle tyer — 1-Bu/TyPac. WIRE SERVICES: News — AP; Receiving dishes — AP. BUSINESS COMPUTERS: IBM/60 fileserver, 1-IBM/30-286, 5-IBM/25; Applications: Novell/MSSI: Accts receivable, Gen ledger, Payroll, Accts payable, Circ; PCs & main system networked.

ONEONTA

Otsego County

'90 U.S. Census- 4,963; E&P '96 Est. 1,687
ABC-CZ (90): 15,779 (HH 5,161)

The Daily Star (m-mon to sat)

The Daily Star, 102 Chestnut St.; PO Box 250, Oneonta, NY 13820-0250; tel (607) 432-1000; fax (607) 432-5847. Ottaway Newspapers Inc. group.
Circulation: 19,648(m); 19,648(m-sat); ABC Mar. 31, 1995.
Price: 50¢(d); 50¢(sat); $1.85/wk; $7.40/mo; $92.55/yr.
Advertising: Open inch rate $14.26(m); $14.26(m-sat). **Representative:** Papert Companies.
News Services: AP, DJ, ONS. **Politics:** Independent. **Established:** 1890.
Not Published: New Year; Memorial Day; Independence Day; Labor Day; Thanksgiving; Christmas.
Special Editions: Progress (Jan); Cookbook, Bridal (Feb); Home & Garden, NIE (Mar); Golden Years, Vacation Guide (Apr); Annual Canoe Regatta, The Infielder (May); Farmers' Yearbook, The Infielder (June); Otsego County Fair, Golden Years, Baseball Hall of Fame, The Infielder (July); Delaware County Fair, College Guide, The Infielder (Aug); The Infielder (Sept); Energy Tab (Oct); Hunting Tab, Gift Guide (Nov); Gift Guide (Dec); Car Care, Fashion, Home Improvements (Spring); Home Improvements (Summer); Car Care, Fashion, Home Improvements (Fall).
Special Weekly Sections: Health Page, Medical Directory (tues); Business Briefs, College Issues (wed); Farm Page, College Issues (thur); Neighbors (fri); Best Food Day (sat).
Magazine: TV Channels (fri).

GENERAL MANAGEMENT

President/Publisher Richard J Anthony

ADVERTISING

Manager William Reeves

CIRCULATION

Manager Thomas G Falk

NEWS EXECUTIVE

Editor R Kenneth Hall

EDITORS AND MANAGERS

City Editor Cary Brunswick
Editorial Page Editor R Kenneth Hall
Features Editor Cary Brunswick
Librarian Melody Morgan
Photo Department Manager Julie Lewis
Radio/Television Editor Cary Brunswick
Real Estate Editor Cary Brunswick
Regional Editor Terri Hallenbeck
Religion Editor Barbara Allison
Sports Editor Jim Wojtanik
Wire Editor Mark Hopkins

MANAGEMENT INFORMATION SERVICES

Data Processing Manager Bruce Endries

PRODUCTION

Foreman-Composing (Day) Olin Benedict
Foreman-Composing (Night) Doug Rose
Foreman-Pressroom John McCoy

Market Information: Zoned editions; TMC.
Mechanical available: Offset; Black and 3 ROP colors; insert accepted — preprinted; page cut-offs — 22¾".
Mechanical specifications: Type page 13" x 21½"; E - 6 cols, 2¹⁄₁₆", ⅛" between; A - 6 cols, 2¹⁄₁₆", ⅛" between; C - 9 cols, 1⅜", ¹⁄₁₆" between.
Commodity consumption: Newsprint 1,001 metric tons; widths 28", 14"; black ink 14,000 pounds; color ink 500 pounds; single pages printed 9,827; average pages per issue 28(d); single plates used 13,000.
Equipment: EDITORIAL: Front-end hardware — 4-Dewar; Front-end software — Dewar/System II, Dewar/System III Editorial Pagination. CLASSIFIED: Front-end hardware — 4-Dewar; Front-end software — Dewar/System II, Dewar/System III Classified Pagination. DISPLAY: Adv layout systems — 2-Dewar/Discovery; Front-end hardware — 1-PC, 1-Ap/Mac; Front-end software — Aldus/PageMaker, Archetype/Corel Draw. PRODUCTION: Typesetters — 2-Prosetter/1000 Plain Paper; Plate exposures — 2-BKY/1601-40; Plate processors — Nat; Production cameras — 1-C/Spartan III; Automatic film processors — 1-LE/18. PRESSROOM: Line 1 — 5-G/Urbanite; Folders — 1-G (w/balloon). MAILROOM: Counter stackers — QWI; Inserters and stuffers — MM/227E; Bundle tyer — 1-MLN/ML2EE, 2-Sa/SR1A; Addressing machine — Ch/Quarter folder Labeler. WIRE SERVICES: News — AP, DJ, ONS; Photos — AP; Stock tables — AP; Receiving dishes — size-3m, AP, UPI. BUSINESS COMPUTERS: IBM/AS-400; Applications: Circ, Gen ledger; Microsoft/Excel, Microsoft/Word; PCs & main system networked.

OSSINING

Westchester County

'90 U.S. Census- 22,582; E&P '96 Est. 24,809
ABC-NDM (90): 53,499 (HH 17,872)

The Ossining Citizen Register (e-mon to sat; S)

The Ossining Citizen Register, One Gannett Dr., White Plains, NY 10464; tel (914) 694-9300; web site http://www.nynews.com/nynews. Gannett Co. Inc. group.
Circulation: 5,828(e); 5,828(e-sat); 7,175(S); ABC Sept. 24, 1995.
Price: 40¢(d); 40¢(sat); $1.50(S).
Representative: Gannett National Newspaper Sales.
News Services: AP, GNS, LAT-WP. **Politics:** Independent.
Note: White Plains is the headquarters for the Gannett Suburban Newspapers, Inc. The following newspapers are printed at the Harrison White Plains plant: Mt. Vernon Daily Argus, Mamaroneck Daily Times, New Rochelle Standard-Star, Port Chester Daily Item, White Plains Reporter-Dispatch, Tarrytown Daily News, Peekskill Star, Ossining Citizen Register and Yonkers Herald Statesman. The Rockland Journal-News is printed in Nyack, NY. All advertising is sold in combination for $177.43 (d) and $200.52 (S). For detailed mechanical equipment information, see the Gannett Suburban Newspapers, Inc. listing in White Plains. Individual newspaper rates not made available.
Special Editions: Spring Bridal (Feb); Spring Home Design (Mar); Spring Home & Garden, Suburban Golf, Greater New York Auto Show, Summer Education, Suburban Business Review (Apr); Suburban Golf, Builder's Showcase (May); Summer Dine Out Guide (June); Suburban Golf (July); Back-to-School, Fall Education, Suburban Golf (Aug); Suburban Golf, Pro Football Preview, Local Football Preview, Fall Bridal, Community Guide (Sept); Suburban Golf, Fall Home Design, New Auto '97, Fall Dine Out Guide (Oct); Holiday Gift Guide, Thanksgiving Day Special, Holiday Planner (Nov); Holiday Food, Hot Holiday Gifts, Last Minute Gift Guide (Dec).
Special Weekly Sections: Career Opportunities (mon); Best Food Day, Fashion (wed); Home Style, Weekend, Dining Out (thur); Garden & Home Improvement (fri); Travel & Resort, Real Estate, Career Opportunities, TV Week, Education (S).

CORPORATE OFFICERS

President/Publisher Gary F Sherlock
Vice Pres/Exec Editor Kenneth A Paulson
Vice Pres/President-Advertising John C Green
Vice Pres/Director-Circulation Mike Huot
Vice Pres-Finance Charles Schmitt
Vice Pres-Marketing Michael G Kane
Vice Pres-Operations Fal A Bolzner

ADVERTISING

Director-Classified Candida Canfield
Director-Display Robert Twesten
Manager-Display Jeanne Westby
Manager-Display Steve Havelka
Manager-Business Development Joan Perreault

TELECOMMUNICATIONS

Audiotex Manager Carl Iacona

CIRCULATION

Director Jonathan Alvord
Manager Charles Farrell

NEWS EXECUTIVES

Senior Managing Editor Janet McMillan
Operations Editor Rich Kleban
Managing Editor-Administration Bill Madden
Editor-Reader Services Gayle T Williams
Acting Asst Managing Editor-Lifestyles Tad Clarke
Asst Managing Editor-Business Mark Land
Asst Managing Editor-Sports David Georgette

EDITORS AND MANAGERS

Editorial Page Editor Ron Patafio
Entertainment Editor Kathy McClusky
Graphics Editor Chris Kiesler
Health/Medical Editor Barbara Durkin
Metro Editor Phil Reisman III
Asst Managing Editor Sandy Coyle
Asst Managing Editor-Nights Dan Murray
Photo Director Robert Rodriguez
Photo Editor-Day Danielle Perillat
Travel Editor Kathy McClusky

MANAGEMENT INFORMATION SERVICES

Director Systems & Technology Sherman Bodner

PRODUCTION

Director Nat Hogan

Market Information: Operate audiotex; Electronic edition.

OSWEGO-FULTON

Oswego County

'90 U.S. Census- 32,124 (Oswego 19,195; Fulton 12,929); E&P '96 Est. 31,331 (Oswego 18,712; Fulton 12,619)
ABC-CZ (90): 19,195 (HH 7,416)

The Palladium-Times (e-mon to sat)

The Palladium-Times, 140 W. First St., Oswego, NY 13126; tel (315) 343-3800; fax (315) 343-0273; e-mail palltimes@aol.com. Hollinger International Inc. group.
Circulation: 10,932(e); 10,932(e-sat); ABC Sept. 30, 1995.
Price: 35¢(d); 35¢(sat); $1.90/wk (carrier); $9.75/mo (mail).
Advertising: Open inch rate $10.13(e); $10.13(e-sat). **Representative:** Landon Associates Inc.
News Services: AP, SHNS. **Politics:** Independent. **Established:** 1845.
Not Published: New Year; Independence Day; Thanksgiving; Christmas.
Advertising not accepted: Spurious mining; mail order; oil stock; bed & board.
Special Editions: Weather (Jan); Bridal, Welcome Back SUNY Tab, Home Improvement (Feb); Garden, Progress (Mar); Fishing, Mother's Day (May); Father's Day (June); Preview Weekly (Travel & Tourism), Harborfest, Auto Racing (July); Newcomer's Guide (Aug); Bridal (Sept); Fall Sports (Oct); Christmas Shopping, Winter Sports (Dec); Weather, Historic, Home Improvement, Health & Fitness, Home Interiors, Senior Scene (monthly).
Special Weekly Sections: Food (mon); Business Pages (tues); Entertainment, Dining Guide, Education (thur); Health (fri).

GENERAL MANAGEMENT

Publisher Bruce Frassinelli
Accountant Judy DeGroff

ADVERTISING

Manager Brad Sterling

CIRCULATION

Manager Don Bowman Jr

EDITORS AND MANAGERS

City Editor Steve Yablonski
Regional Editor Chris Brock

PRODUCTION

Manager-Composing Patricia Shatrau
Foreman-Press Raymond De Groff

Market Information: TMC.
Mechanical available: Offset; Black and 3 ROP colors; insert accepted — preprinted, free-standing cards; page cut-offs — 22½".
Mechanical specifications: Type page 13" x 21½"; E - 6 cols, 2¹⁄₁₆", ⅛" between; A - 6 cols, 2¹⁄₁₆", ⅛" between; C - 8 cols, 1⁹⁄₁₆", ¹⁄₁₆" between.
Commodity consumption: Newsprint 341 short tons; width 27½"; black ink 8,305 pounds; color ink 275 pounds; single pages printed 5,400; average pages per issue 18(d); single plates used 3,000.

Equipment: EDITORIAL: Front-end hardware — Mk; Printers — Ap/Mac LaserPrinters; Other equipment — Ap/Mac Classic II. CLASSIFIED: Front-end hardware — Mk; Printers — Ap/Mac LaserPrinter. PRODUCTION: Typesetters — Ap/Mac LaserPrinter; Platemaking systems — Nu; Production cameras — LE/Horizontal; Automatic film processors — 1-LD/220-QT; Color separation equipment (conventional) — V/4000.
PRESSROOM: Line 1 — 8-G/Community (2 Forms). MAILROOM: Bundle tyer — Aldebo/Bundler. WIRE SERVICES: News — AP Laserphoto; Syndicates — NEA, TMS, Media Link, SHNS; Receiving dishes — size-1m, AP. BUSINESS COMPUTERS: Ap/Mac, NEC/386; Applications: Multi-Ad/Creator, Claris/Mac-Draw, Microsoft/Works, Lotus; PCs & main system networked.

PEEKSKILL

Westchester County

'90 U.S. Census- 19,536; E&P '96 Est. 20,697
ABC-NDM (90): 46,662 (HH 17,116)

Peekskill Star (e-mon to sat; S)

Peekskill Star, One Gannett Dr., White Plains, NY 10464; tel (914) 694-9300; web site http://www.nynews.com/nynews. Gannett Co. Inc. group.

Circulation: 6,073(e); 6,073(e-sat); 8,530(S); ABC Sept. 24, 1995.
Price: 40¢(d); 40¢(sat); $1.50(S).
News Services: AP, GNS, LAT-WP. **Politics:** Independent.
Note: White Plains is the headquarters for the Gannett Suburban Newspapers, Inc. The following newspapers are printed at the Harrison White Plains plant: Mt. Vernon Daily Argus, Mamaroneck Daily Times, New Rochelle Standard-Star, Port Chester Daily Item, White Plains Reporter-Dispatch, Tarrytown Daily News, Peekskill Star, Ossining Citizen Register and Yonkers Herald Statesman. The Rockland Journal-News is printed in Nyack, NY. All advertising is sold in combination for $177.43 (d) and $200.52 (S). For detailed mechanical equipment information, see the Gannett Suburban Newspapers, Inc. listing in White Plains. Individual newspaper rates not made available.
Special Editions: Spring Bridal (Feb); Spring Home Design (Mar); Spring Home & Garden, Suburban Golf, Greater New York Auto Show, Summer Education, Suburban Business Review (Apr); Suburban Golf, Builder's Showcase (May); Summer Dine Out Guide (June); Suburban Golf (July); Back-to-School, Fall Education, Suburban Golf (Aug); Suburban Golf, Pro Football Preview, Local Football Preview, Fall Bridal, Community Guide (Sept); Suburban Golf, Fall Home Design, New Autos '97, Fall Dine Out Guide (Oct); Holiday Gift Guide, Thanksgiving Day Special, Holiday Planner (Nov); Holiday Food, Hot Holiday Gifts, Last Minute Gift Guide (Dec).
Special Weekly Sections: Career Opportunities (mon); Best Food Day, Fashion (wed); Home Style, Weekend, Dining Out (thur); Garden & Home Improvement (fri); Travel & Resort, Real Estate, Career Opportunities, TV Week, Education (S).

CORPORATE OFFICERS

President/Publisher Gary F Sherlock
Vice Pres/Exec Editor Kenneth A Paulson
Vice Pres/President-Advertising John C Green
Vice Pres/Director-Circulation Mike Huot
Vice Pres-Finance Charles Schmitt
Vice Pres-Marketing Michael G Kane
Vice Pres-Operations Fal A Bolzner

ADVERTISING

Director-Classified Candida Canfield
Director-Display Robert Twesten
Manager-Display Jeanne Westby
Manager-Display Steve Havelka
Manager-Business Development Joan Perreault

TELECOMMUNICATIONS

Audiotex Manager Carl Iacona

CIRCULATION

Director-Home Delivery John Czarnecki
Manager Charles Farrell

NEWS EXECUTIVES

Senior Managing Editor Janet McMillan
Operations Editor Rich Kleban
Managing Editor-Administration Bill Madden
Editor-Reader Services Gayle T Williams
Acting Asst Managing Editor-Lifestyles Tad Clarke
Asst Managing Editor-Business Mark Land
Asst Managing Editor-Sports David Georgette

EDITORS AND MANAGERS

Editorial Page Editor Ron Patafio
Entertainment Editor Kathy McClusky
Graphics Editor Chris Kiesler
Health/Medical Editor Barbara Durkin
Metro Editor Phil Reisman III
Asst Managing Editor Sandy Coyle
Asst Managing Editor-Nights Dan Murray
Photo Director Robert Rodriguez
Photo Editor-Day Danielle Perillat
Travel Editor Kathy McClusky

MANAGEMENT INFORMATION SERVICES

Director-Systems & Technology Sherman Bodner

PRODUCTION

Director Nat Hogan

Market Information: Operate audiotex; Electronic edition.

PLATTSBURGH

Clinton County

'90 U.S. Census- 21,255; E&P '96 Est. 21,422
ABC-CZ (90): 38,486 (HH 13,416)

Press-Republican (m-mon to sat; S)

Press-Republican, 170 Margaret St.; PO Box 459, Plattsburgh, NY 12901; tel (518) 561-2300; fax (518) 561-3362; e-mail prepub@aol.com. Ottaway Newspapers Inc. group.

Circulation: 23,570(m); 23,570(m-sat); 25,094(S); ABC Sept. 30, 1995.
Price: 50¢(d); 50¢(sat); $1.25(S); $2.55/wk (carrier), $3.15/wk (motor route), $3.95/wk (mail); $132.60/yr (carrier), $163.80/yr (motor route), $176.00/yr (mail).
Advertising: Open inch rate $17.30(m); $17.30(m-sat); $19.80(S). **Representative:** Papert Companies.
News Services: AP, DJ, ONS, SHNS. **Politics:** Independent. **Established:** 1811 (Republican), 1894 (Press), 1942 (merged).
Not Published: Thanksgiving; Christmas.
Advertising not accepted: Speculative investments; 900 number ads.
Special Editions: Pet Care, For Your Health, Deals & Wheels (Jan); Brides, Progress (Feb); North Country Business Directory, Business Connection (Mar); Car Care, Spring Sports, Adirondack Guidebook, Spring Home Improvement, Auto/Outdoor Show (May); North Country Business Directory, Deals & Wheels, Video Review (June); Mayor's Cup, Clinton Co. Review (July); City School, Welcome to Plattsburgh, Essex Co. Fair, Franklin Co. Fair, Almanac (Aug); P-R Home Show, Fall Sports, Deals & Wheels (Sept); North Country Business Directory, Home Improvement, Pet Photo, Car Care (Oct); Gift Guide, Winter Sports, Songbook, Video Review (Nov); Santa's Tour, Adirondack Guidebook, Last Minute Gifts (Dec); Home (monthly).
Special Weekly Section: Best Food Day (S).
Magazines: TV Spotlight, Color Comics, Parade (S).

GENERAL MANAGEMENT

Publisher Brenda J Tallman
General Manager Daniel B Swift
Controller Catherine A Duquette

ADVERTISING

Manager-Marketing Sean McNamara
Manager-Classified Lyman Bezio
Manager-Retail George Rock

TELECOMMUNICATIONS

Audiotex Manager Sean McNamara

CIRCULATION

Manager Chris Christian

NEWS EXECUTIVES

Editor James Dynko
Managing Editor Robert Grady

EDITORS AND MANAGERS

Design Editor John Downs
News Editor Lois Clermont
Photo Editor Dave Paczak
Regional Editor Bruce Rowland
Sports Editor Bob Goetz
Sunday Editor Damian Fanelli

PRODUCTION

Manager Daniel Thayer
Foreman-Press Virgil Cross
Supervisor-Distribution James Frenya

Market Information: Zoned editions; TMC; Operate audiotex.
Mechanical available: Offset; Black and 3 ROP colors; insert accepted — preprinted; page cutoffs — 22$\frac{5}{8}$".
Mechanical specifications: Type page 13" x 21$\frac{1}{2}$"; E - 6 cols, 2$\frac{1}{16}$", $\frac{1}{16}$" between; A - 6 cols, 2$\frac{1}{16}$", $\frac{1}{16}$" between; C - 9 cols, 1$\frac{3}{8}$", $\frac{1}{16}$" between.
Commodity consumption: Newsprint 1,572 metric tons; widths 28", 14"; black ink 9,600 pounds; single pages printed 11,470; average pages per issue 28(d), 54(S); single plates used 11,225.
Equipment: EDITORIAL: Front-end hardware — COM/ONE; Other equipment — 4-RSK/TRS-80, Lf/AP Leaf Picture Desk, Lf/Leafscan, Ap/Mac Quadra. CLASSIFIED: Front-end hardware — COM. DISPLAY: Front-end hardware — 2-PC/486; Front-end software — Archetype/Corel Draw; Printers — 2-NewGen/840, 1-NewGen/600T. PRODUCTION: Typesetters — NewGen/Plain paper; Plate exposures — 2-Nat/FT40; Plate processors — 1-KFM/XPS; Scanners — 1-ECR/Autokon; Production cameras — 1-C/Spartan; Automatic film processors — 1-LE/LD 1800; Film transporters — 1-LE; Shrink lenses — 1-C.
PRESSROOM: Line 1 — 6-G/Urbanite (2-Staked;DEV); Folders — 1-G; Press control system — Fin. MAILROOM: Counter stackers — 2-HL/Monitor, 1-HL/Monitor H-T; Inserters and stuffers — GMA/SLS-1000; Bundle tyer — 2-MLN/2EE, 1-Power Strap. WIRE SERVICES: News — AP, DJ, ONS, SHNS; Photos — AP; Stock tables — AP; Receiving dishes — size-10ft, AP, Newspaper Satellite Network. BUSINESS COMPUTERS: 1-IBM/AS-400; Applications: Payroll, Gen ledger, Accts payable, Analysis, Circ, Accts receivable, Adv; PCs & micros networked; PCs & main system networked.

PORT CHESTER

Westchester County

'90 U.S. Census- 24,728; E&P '96 Est. 25,745
ABC-NDM (90): 56,638 (HH 20,802)

The Port Chester Daily Item (e-mon to sat; S)

The Port Chester Daily Item, One Gannett Dr., White Plains, NY 10604; tel (914) 694-9300; web site http://www.nynews.com/nynews. Gannett Co. Inc. group.

Circulation: 8,707(e); 8,707(e-sat); 9,694(S); ABC Sept. 24, 1995.
Price: 40¢(d); 40¢(sat); $1.50(S).
Advertising: Open inch rate
News Services: AP, GNS, LAT-WP. **Politics:** Independent.
Note: White Plains is the headquarters for the Gannett Suburban Newspapers, Inc. The following newspapers are printed at the Harrison White Plains plant: Mt. Vernon Daily Argus, Mamaroneck Daily Times, New Rochelle Standard-Star, Port Chester Daily Item, White Plains Reporter-Dispatch, Tarrytown Daily News, Peekskill Star, Ossining Citizen Register and Yonkers Herald Statesman. The Rockland Journal-News is printed in Nyack, NY. All advertising is sold in combination for $177.43 (d) and $200.52 (S). For detailed mechanical equipment information, see the Gannett Suburban Newspapers, Inc. listing in White Plains. Individual newspaper rates not made available.
Special Editions: Spring Bridal (Feb); Spring Home Design (Mar); Spring Home & Garden, Suburban Golf, Greater New York Auto Show, Summer Education, Suburban Business Review (Apr); Suburban Golf, Builder's Showcase (May); Summer Dine Out Guide (June); Suburban Golf (July); Back-to-School, Fall Education, Suburban Golf (Aug); Suburban Golf, Pro Football Preview, Local Football Preview, Fall Bridal, Community Guide (Sept); Suburban Golf, Fall Home Design, New Autos '97, Fall Dine Out Guide (Oct); Holiday Gift Guide, Thanksgiving Day Special, Holiday Planner (Nov); Holiday Food, Hot Holiday Gifts, Last Minute Gift Guide (Dec).
Special Weekly Sections: Career Opportunities (mon); Best Food Day, Fashion (wed); Home Style, Weekend, Dining Out (thur); Garden & Home Improvement (fri); Travel & Resort, Career Opportunities, TV Week, Education, Real Estate (S).

CORPORATE OFFICERS

President/Publisher Gary F Sherlock
Vice Pres/Exec Editor Kenneth A Paulson
Vice Pres/President-Advertising John C Green
Vice Pres/Director-Circulation Mike Huot
Vice Pres-Finance Charles Schmitt
Vice Pres-Marketing Michael G Kane
Vice Pres-Operations Fal A Bolzner

ADVERTISING

Director-Classified Candida Canfield
Director-Display Robert Twesten
Manager-Display Jeanne Westby
Manager-Display Steve Havelka
Manager-Business Development Joan Perreault

TELECOMMUNICATIONS

Audiotex Manager Carl Iacona

CIRCULATION

Director Jonathan Alvord
Manager Paul Felicissimo

NEWS EXECUTIVES

Senior Managing Editor Janet McMillan
Operations Editor Rich Kleban
Managing Editor-Administration Bill Madden
Editor-Reader Services Gayle T Williams
Acting Asst Managing Editor-Lifestyles Tad Clarke
Asst Managing Editor-Business Jeffrey Mangum
Asst Managing Editor-Sports David Georgette

EDITORS AND MANAGERS

Editorial Page Editor Ron Patafio
Entertainment Editor Kathy McClusky
Graphics Editor Chris Kiesler
Health/Medical Editor Barbara Durkin
Metro Editor Phil Reisman III
Asst Managing Editor Sandy Coyle
Asst Managing Editor-Nights Dan Murray
Photo Director Robert Rodriguez
Photo Editor-Day Danielle Perillat
Travel Editor Kathy McClusky

MANAGEMENT INFORMATION SERVICES

Director-Systems & Technology Sherman Bodner

PRODUCTION

Director Nat Hogan

Market Information: Operate audiotex; Electronic edition.

POUGHKEEPSIE

Dutchess County

'90 U.S. Census- 28,844; E&P '96 Est. 28,106
ABC-NDM (90): 259,462 (HH 89,567)

Poughkeepsie Journal (m-mon to sat; S)

Poughkeepsie Journal, 85 Civic Center Plz. (12601); PO Box 1231, Poughkeepsie, NY 12602; tel (914) 454-2000. Gannett Co. Inc. group.

Circulation: 42,382(m); 42,382(m-sat); 59,284(S); ABC Sept. 30, 1995.
Price: 50¢(d); 50¢(sat); $1.50(S); $14.00/mo (carrier), $14.50/mo (motor route).
Advertising: Open inch rate $40.85(m); $41.60(m-fri); $40.85(m-sat); $49.95(S). **Representative:** Gannett National Newspaper Sales.
News Services: AP, GNS, LAT-WP. **Politics:** Independent. **Established:** 1785.
Special Edition: Topical Themes.
Magazines: USA Weekend, Comics, TV Log (S).

CORPORATE OFFICERS

Secretary Thomas Chapple
Treasurer James Thomas

GENERAL MANAGEMENT

Publisher Richard K Wager
Controller Randy Sutherland
Asst Controller Geneva Burris
Manager-Office Rita Lombardi
Director-Systems Jean (Mitzi) Bainbridge
Personnel Director Dolores Pinto

ADVERTISING

Director George Lawson
Manager-Retail Tom Claybaugh
Manager-Classified Jan Dewey

MARKETING AND PROMOTION

Director-Marketing Services Cynthia Andersen

TELECOMMUNICATIONS

Audiotex Manager Jean (Mitzi) Bainbridge

CIRCULATION

Director Ronald E Betros

NEWS EXECUTIVES

Exec Editor Derek Oseyenko
Managing Editor Diana Mitsuklos

I-280   New York

QUEENS
See NEW YORK CITY

ROCHESTER
Monroe County

'90 U.S. Census- 231,646; E&P '96 Est. 223,580
ABC-NDM (90): 850,289 (HH 320,971)

Rochester Democrat and Chronicle
(m-mon to fri; m-sat; S)

Rochester, New York Times-Union (e-mon to fri)

Rochester Democrat and Chronicle; Rochester, NY Times-Union, 55 Exchange Blvd., Rochester, NY 14614-2001; tel (716) 232-7100, (800) 767-7539; fax (716) 232-3027; web site http://www.rochesterdandc.com. Gannett Co. Inc. group.
Circulation: 141,204(m); 53,473(e); 207,191(m-sat); 251,873(S); ABC Sept. 30, 1995.
Price: 50¢(m), 35¢(e); 50¢(sat); $1.50(S); $3.05/wk (m), $1.50/wk (e); $12.20/4wk (m), $6.00/4wk (e), $39.65/13wk (m), $19.50/13wk (e), $79.30/26wk (m), $39.00/26wk (e); $158.60/yr (m), $78.00/yr (e).
Advertising: Open inch rate $222.13(m); $222.13(e); $201.97(m-sat); $254.55(S); $236.42(m & e); $324.91 (S/wknd mag).
Representatives: American Publishers Reps.; Gannett National Newspaper Sales.
News Services: AP, NYT, GNS, LAT-WP, KRT, SHNS, Bloomburg, National Weather Service. **Politics:** Independent. **Established:** 1826.
Not Published: Times-Union (e): New Year, Memorial Day, Labor Day, Thanksgiving; Christmas.
Special Weekly Sections: Rochester Inc. (mon); OUR TOWNS (wed); Home and Real Estate (sat); Travel, Sports, State/Nation, Business (S).
Magazines: Weekend Magazine (thur); TV Book, USA Weekend, Comics (S).

CORPORATE OFFICERS
President/CEO .... John J Curley
President/Publisher .... David J Mack

GENERAL MANAGEMENT
Vice Pres-Finance .... Theresa M McCoy
Controller .... James C Paul
Vice Pres-Communications .... Thomas P Flynn
Vice Pres-Human Resources .... Richard Greene

ADVERTISING
Vice Pres .... Patrick J Birmingham
Manager-Classified .... Ellie Cruze
Manager-National/Department Stores .... Michael Magee
Manager-Community Newspapers .... George Heissenberger
Exec Manager-Support .... Dean R Spencer
Manager-Retail .... Donald Parks

MARKETING AND PROMOTION
Vice Pres-Market Development .... Jeffrey A Kapuscinski
Manager-Marketing Projects .... Debbie DiNardo
Manager-Marketing Info .... Jay Peak

CIRCULATION
Vice Pres .... L Gayle Pryor
Manager-Sales/Marketing .... Sheldon E Lasda
Manager .... JoAnn F Reed

NEWS EXECUTIVES
Editor/Vice Pres .... Thomas E Callinan
Managing Editor .... Carolyn K Washburn
Asst Managing Editor-Business .... Doug Mandelaro
Asst Managing Editor-Features .... Sebby Jacobson
Asst Managing Editor-Sports .... John Gibson
Asst Managing Editor-Design & Photo .... Monica Moses
Asst Managing Editor-Outreach & Training .... Cynthia Benjamin
Asst Managing Editor-Metro .... Glenn Proctor
Asst Managing Editor-Administration .... Matt Dudek
Asst Managing Editor-News .... Peggy Bellows

EDITORS AND MANAGERS
Automotive Editor .... Bob Frick
Books/Arts Editor .... Elizabeth Forbes
Editorial Page Editor-Democrat and Chronicle .... James Lawrence
Deputy Editorial Page Editor-Democrat and Chronicle .... Arthur Coulson
Editorial Page Editor-Times-Union .... Mark Hare
Deputy Editorial Page Editor-Times-Union .... Sharon Dickman
Education Editor .... Robin Wilson-Glover
Entertainment Editor .... Patrick Farrell
Environment Editor .... Corydon Ireland
Farm/Agriculture Editor .... Bob Frick
Fashion Editor .... Lisa Gutierrez
Features Editor .... Patrick Farrell
Graphics Editor .... Dennis Floss
Health Editor .... Diana Carter
Library Manager .... Virginia Wheeler
Movies/Videos Editor .... Jack Garner
News Editor-Democrat and Chronicle .... Leonard LaClara
News Editor-Times-Union .... Frank Cardon
Photo Editor .... Don Marquis
Pop Music/Nite Scene Editor .... Jeff Spevak
Public Affairs Editor .... Blair Claflin
Religion Editor .... Sue McNamara
Sports Editor .... James Holleran
Television/Radio Editor .... Eugene Marino
Theater Editor .... Eugene Marino
Travel Editor .... Mike Johansson
Weekend Magazine Editor .... Steve Boerner

MANAGEMENT INFORMATION SERVICES
Director-Info Systems .... Roger R Forness
Manager-Telecommunications .... Virginia L Wenner
Data Processing Manager .... Richard Clark
Manager-Computer Publishing Systems .... Edward Cloos
Manager-Computer Digital Systems .... John Cumbo
Manager-Computer Electro Mechanical Service .... Robert Krueger

PRODUCTION
Vice Pres .... Michael J Monscour
Manager-Pre Press .... Jeremiah Clifford
Foreman-Composing (Democrat and Chronicle) .... Bernd Matties
Foreman-Composing (Times-Union) .... Paul Leuschner
Foreman-Camera/Platemaking (Democrat and Chronicle) .... Eric Gustavson
Foreman-Camera/Platemaking (Times-Union) .... Thomas Goethals
Manager-Press Production .... Terry Hamilton
Foreman-Pressroom (Democrat and Chronicle) .... John Sawyer
Foreman-Pressroom (Times-Union) .... Edward Hasman
Foreman-Paperhandler .... Leslie Howell
Manager-Distribution .... Richard Nicol
Foreman-Mailroom (Democrat and Chronicle) .... Charles Hawken
Foreman-Mailroom (Times-Union) .... Nick Harris
Superintendent-Building .... George Alden
Engineer-Plant .... Christopher Uhl

Market Information: Zoned editions; Split Run; TMC; ADS; Electronic edition.
Mechanical available: Letterpress; Black and 3 ROP colors; insert accepted — preprinted; page cut-offs — 22¾".
Mechanical specifications: Type page 13" x 21½"; E - 6 cols, 2¹/₁₆", ⅛" between; A - 6 cols, 2¹/₁₆", ⅛" between; C - 10 cols, 1¼", ¹/₃₂" between.
Commodity consumption: Newsprint 25,605 short tons; widths 54½", 41", 27¼"; black ink 782,579 pounds; color ink 129,200 pounds; single pages printed 31,048; average pages per issue 44(d), 66(sat), 88(S); single plates used 194,370.
Equipment: EDITORIAL: Front-end hardware — AT/114, 6-CPVS; Front-end software — AT, QuarkXPress, Digital Collections/Archive; Printers — 4-Okidata, 2-Epson, Pagescan, Chelgraph, QMS, NewGen, Ap/Mac, 4-HP, 3-TI/Laserprinter; Other equipment — 52-Ap/Mac, 5-Information Engineering/Editorial News Layout, Kk/2035 plus Negative Scanner, HP/Server. CLASSIFIED: Front-end hardware — SII/55-AMTX, 2-Tandem/K-1000 CPOs; Front-end software — SII; Printers — Lexmark/Optra LXI; Other equipment — HP/Netserver LM Pentium, Novell/Netware. DISPLAY: Adv layout systems — SCS/Layout 8000; Front-end hardware — 2-IBM/Model 80, 1-IBM/555X, 9-Falco, 20-Ap/Mac; Front-end software — Multi-Ad/Creator, QuarkXPress, Aldus/FreeHand; Printers — 3-Linotype-Hell/Printer 60. PRODUCTION: Typesetters — 2-AU/APS-5U, 1-AU/APS-6, 1-AU/APS-3850; Plate exposures — 2-Titan/III; Plate processors — 2-Na/NP 120; Electronic picture desk — Adobe/Photoshop; Scanners — ECR/Autokon 1000, ECR/News Recorder, RZ/210L Laser Scanner; Production cameras — C/Marathon, C/Newspager; Automatic film processors — 1-Glunz & Jensen/Model 667, P/Pakoquick, 1-AG/Rapidline 540, 1-Glunz & Jensen/0388; Film transporters — C, Konica. PRESSROOM: Line 1 — 8-H/Color Convertible; Line 2 — 16-H/Color Convertible; Press drives — 3-C/Line Drives; Folders — 3-H/3:2, 1-H/2:1; Pasters — 24-H/Semi-Auto; Reels and stands — 1-CH, 5-Cline. MAILROOM: Counter stackers — 5-QWI/300, 1-QWI/200, 2-Id/440; Inserters and stuffers — 9-Power Strap/PSN-6, 3-P/1372, 2-On-Line Doubleout, 1-Del/Single; Bundle tyer — 13-Power Strap, 4-Power Strap/PSN. LIBRARY: Electronic — Digital Collections/Gannet Archive Sys. WIRE SERVICES: News — AP, NYT, GNS, LAT-WP, KRT, SHNS, Bloomburg, National Weather Service, NYT; Photos — AP; Stock tables — AP Select Stocks, Grand Central Stocks; Receiving dishes — size-3m, AP. BUSINESS COMPUTERS: IBM/AS-400; Applications: Adv, Circ, Bus; PCs & micros networked; PCs & main system networked.

ROME
Oneida County

'90 U.S. Census- 44,350; E&P '96 Est. 44,792
ABC-CZ (90): 44,317 (HH 15,720)

Daily Sentinel (e-mon to sat)

Daily Sentinel, 333 W. Dominick St. (13440); PO Box 471, Rome, NY 13442-0471; tel (315) 337-4000; fax (315) 337-4704; e-mail 76304.3271@compuserve.com.
Circulation: 17,356(e); 17,356(e-sat); ABC Sept. 30, 1995.
Price: 50¢(e); 50¢(sat); $2.40/wk (carrier), $2.50/wk (motor route); $124.80/yr (carrier), $130.00/yr (motor route).
Advertising: Open inch rate $12.86(e); $12.86(e-sat).
News Service: AP. **Politics:** Independent-Democrat. **Established:** 1821.
Not Published: New Year; Memorial Day; Independence Day; Labor Day; Thanksgiving; Christmas.
Special Editions: Know Your Retailer (Jan); Bridal Planner, Business Review, Home Show (Feb); Spring Fashion (Easter); Outdoor World, Home Improvement/Energy, Bridal Planner (Apr); Graduation (June); Senior Citizens Tab (July); Back-to-School, Football (Aug); Recipe (Sept); Fall Fashion, Wheels (Oct); Christmas Wish Book, Famous Brands (Nov); Christmas Coupon, Last Minute Gift Guide, Famous Brands (Dec); Attractions (monthly).
Special Weekly Section: Best Food Day (mon).
Magazine: TV Guide (S).

CORPORATE OFFICERS
President .... George B Waters
Vice Pres .... Shirley B Waters
Vice Pres .... Stephen B Waters
Secretary .... Shirley B Waters
Treasurer .... Kenneth J Kakaty

GENERAL MANAGEMENT
Publisher .... Stephen B Waters
Controller .... Kenneth J Kakaty

ADVERTISING
Director .... Ronald O'Neil
Manager-Classified .... Linda Carlson

MARKETING AND PROMOTION
Manager-Promotion/Marketing .... Kathleen O'Mara Gratch

CIRCULATION
Director .... William A Kustyn

NEWS EXECUTIVES
Editor .... George B Waters
Managing Editor .... David C Swanson

EDITORS AND MANAGERS
Copy Editor .... Norm Landis
Living/Lifestyle Editor .... Virginia Herrmann
News Editor .... Thomas H Merz
Sports Editor .... Joseph Silkowski
Women's Editor .... Virginia Herrmann

MANAGEMENT INFORMATION SERVICES
Manager-Applications .... Daniel P Bronson

PRODUCTION
Manager .... Ronald Schultz
Foreman-Composing .... Larry Burch
Foreman-Composing .... Linda Karsten

Market Information: TMC.
Mechanical available: Offset; Black and 3 ROP colors; insert accepted — preprinted; page cut-offs — 21½".
Mechanical specifications: Type page 13" x 21½"; E - 6 cols, 2¹/₁₆", ⅛" between; A - 6 cols, 2¹/₁₆", ⅛" between; C - 9 cols, 1⅜", ⅛" between.
Commodity consumption: Newsprint 713 short tons; widths 28", 14"; black ink 26,200 pounds; color ink 300 pounds; single pages printed 6,321; average pages per issue 21(d); single plates used 6,321.
Equipment: EDITORIAL: Front-end hardware — IBM/PC; Front-end software — CText/Editorial System; Printers — NewGen/Turbo PS 840e. CLASSIFIED: Front-end hardware — IBM/PC; Front-end software — CText/Classified Management System; Printers — NewGen/Turbo PS 840e. DISPLAY: Adv layout systems —

Ap/Mac; Front-end hardware — Ap/Mac SE, Ap/Mac Plus, Ap/Mac II, Ap/Mac IIcx, Ap/Mac IIci, Ap/Mac IIfx, Ap/Mac SE30, Ap/Mac Centris 650, Ap/Mac Quadra 650, Ap/Mac Quadra 660 AV, Ap/Power Mac 6100, Ap/Power Mac 7100; Front-end software — Multi-Ad/Creator 3.7, QuarkXPress 3.3, Adobe/Illustrator 5.5, Aldus/FreeHand 3.1, Adobe/Photoshop 3.0; Printers — NewGen/Turbo PS 840e, Ap/Mac LaserWriter II NTX, Copal/Dash 600, Hyphen/Dash BX, Ap/Mac LaserWriter 16-600; Other equipment — LaCie/Silver scanner, Lf/Leafscan 35, Polaroid/SprintScan. PRODUCTION: Pagination software — Mk/Page Director, QuarkXPress 3.3; OCR software — Caere/OmniPage; Typesetters — AG/9800 ImageSetter; Plate exposures — Burgess/Consolux; Plate processors — MAS/WO26; Scanners — Lf/Leafscan 35, LaCie/Silver scanner, Polaroid/SprintScan 35; Production cameras — C/Spartan II; Automatic film processors — Konica/720; Digital color separation equipment — Lf/Leafscan 35, Adobe/Photoshop, Ap/Mac IIfx, Ap/Power Mac 7100.
PRESSROOM: Line 1 — 6-G/Urbanite (1-3 color); Folders — 1-G/Urbanite. MAILROOM: Bundle tyer — 1-Sa, 2-MLN/ML2EE, MLN. WIRE SERVICES: News — AP Datafeatures, AP Datastream; Photos — AP Photostream; Stock tables — TMS Stocks; Syndicates — AP, UPI, Creators, WP, LATS, King Features, TMS, United Features, TV Data; Receiving dishes — AP. BUSINESS COMPUTERS: 1-Sun/Microsystems, Sun/4110; Applications: Vision Data: Circ, Payroll, Accts payable, Gen ledger, Accts receivable; PCs & micros networked; PCs & main system networked.

SALAMANCA

Cattaraugus County

'90 U.S. Census- 6,566; E&P '96 Est. 6,309

Salamanca Press (e-mon to sat)

Salamanca Press, 36-42 River St.; PO Box 111, Salamanca, NY 14779; tel (716) 945-1644; fax (716) 945-4285. Hollinger International Inc. group.

Circulation: 2,445(e); 2,445(e-sat); Sworn Sept. 30, 1995.

Price: 35¢(d); 35¢(sat); $7.35/mo (carrier).

Advertising: Open inch rate $6.26(e); $6.26(e-sat). **Representative:** Landon Associates Inc.

News Service: AP. **Politics:** Independent. **Established:** 1867 (weekly), 1904 (daily).

Not Published: New Year; Memorial Day; Independence Day; Labor Day; Thanksgiving; Christmas.

Special Editions: Summer Vacation Guide; Christmas Shopping Guide; Festival; Christmas Gifts.

GENERAL MANAGEMENT

Publisher	Patrick Patterson

ADVERTISING

Manager	P J Hooker

NEWS EXECUTIVE

Editor	Kevin Burleson

EDITOR AND MANAGER

Sports Editor	Mike Sharbaugh

Market Information: TMC.

Mechanical available: Offset; Black and 3 ROP colors; insert accepted — preprinted; page cut-offs — 22¾".

Mechanical specifications: Type page 13" x 21½"; E - 6 cols, 2", ⅛" between; A - 6 cols, 2", ⅛" between; C - 6 cols, 2", ⅛" between.

Commodity consumption: average pages per issue 10(d).

Equipment: PRODUCTION: Typesetters — Ap/Mac Laser, Ap/Mac SE20; Plate exposures — 1-B; Plate processors — 1-Ic; Production cameras — 1-B/Caravel; Automatic film processors — 1-LE/LD-24.
PRESSROOM: Line 1 — 5-G/Community(1 folder). MAILROOM: Bundle tyer — 1-Akebono; Addressing machine — 1-Am. WIRE SERVICES: News — AP. BUSINESS COMPUTERS: Epson/Equity II; Applications: Accts receivable, Class ads.

SARANAC LAKE

Franklin and Essex Counties

'90 U.S. Census- 5,377; E&P '96 Est. 5,215

Adirondack Daily Enterprise (e-mon to fri; m-sat)

Adirondack Daily Enterprise, 61 Broadway; PO Box 318, Saranac Lake, NY 12983; tel (518) 891-2600; fax (518) 891-2756. Ogden Newspapers group.

Circulation: 5,126(e); Sworn Sept. 29, 1995.

Price: 35¢(d); $113.30/yr.

Advertising: Open inch rate $7.15(e). **Representative:** Landon Associates Inc.

News Service: AP. **Politics:** Independent-Democrat. **Established:** 1895.

Note: Effective Dec. 2, 1995, this publication started publishing a Saturday morning edition. Saturday circulation figure not made available by press time.

Not Published: New Year; Memorial Day; Independence Day; Labor Day; Thanksgiving; Christmas.

Advertising not accepted: Firearms.

Special Editions: Bridal (Feb); Human Services (Mar); Home Improvement (Apr); Adirondack Summer Guide (June); July 4th Blast (July); Back-to-School (Aug); Bridal (Sept); Home Improvement, Warming Up For Winter (Oct); Christmas Gift Guide (Nov); Adirondack Winter Guide, Seasons Greetings (Dec); Wheelin' & Dealin' Car (monthly); Business Profile.

Magazine: Weekender.

CORPORATE OFFICERS

President	G Ogden Nutting
Vice Pres	William C Nutting
Vice Pres	Robert M Nutting
Secretary	William O Nutting
Treasurer	Duane D Wittman

GENERAL MANAGEMENT

Publisher	Catherine Moore

ADVERTISING

Director	Catherine Moore

CIRCULATION

Director	James Bishop

NEWS EXECUTIVE

Editor	John Penney

EDITORS AND MANAGERS

Sports Editor	Jim Stowell
Television/Film Editor	Tom Henecker
Theater/Music Editor	Tom Henecker

MANAGEMENT INFORMATION SERVICES

Data Processing Manager	David Munn

PRODUCTION

Superintendent	David Munn

Market Information: Zoned editions; Split Run; TMC; ADS.

Mechanical available: Offset; Black and 3 ROP colors; insert accepted — preprinted, all; page cut-offs — 21".

Mechanical specifications: Type page 13" x 21"; E - 6 cols, $2\frac{1}{16}$", ⅛" between; A - 6 cols, $2\frac{1}{16}$", ⅛" between; C - 8 cols, 1½", ⅛" between.

Commodity consumption: widths 27", 30", 34"; average pages per issue 12(d).

Equipment: EDITORIAL: Front-end hardware — 8-OS, COM, Ap/Mac Classic; Front-end software — Write-now. CLASSIFIED: Front-end hardware — 2-OS. DISPLAY: Adv layout systems — Ap/Mac; Front-end hardware — Ap/Mac SE; Front-end software — QPS. PRODUCTION: Typesetters — 2-Laser; Platemaking systems — 1-Nu; Plate exposures — X; Plate processors — X; Electronic picture desk — 1-Nu; Direct-to-plate imaging — 1-Nu; Scanners — 4-Ap/Mac.
PRESSROOM: Line 1 — 4-G/Community. WIRE SERVICES: News — AP; Receiving dishes — AP. BUSINESS COMPUTERS: NCR.

SARATOGA SPRINGS

Saratoga County

'90 U.S. Census- 25,001; E&P '96 Est. 25,955

ABC-CZ (90): 35,624 (HH 13,198)

The Saratogian (m-mon to sat; S)

The Saratogian, 20 Lake Ave., Saratoga Springs, NY 12866; tel (518) 584-4242; fax (518) 587-7750. Gannett Co. Inc. group.

Circulation: 13,391(m); 13,391(m-sat); 14,900(S); ABC Sept. 30, 1995.

Price: 35¢(d); 35¢(sat); 75¢(S); $2.25/wk; $117.00/yr (carrier), $186.00/yr (mail).

Advertising: Open inch rate $20.70(m); $20.70(m-sat); $23.55(S). **Representative:** Gannett National Newspaper Sales.

News Services: AP, GNS. **Politics:** Independent. **Established:** 1855.

Special Editions: Business Review (Jan); Summer Magazines (June); Opening Saratoga Race Track, Summer Magazines (July); Summer Magazines, Thoroughbred Racing (daily) (Aug); New Car Preview (Oct).

Magazines: Preview (local, newsprint), USA Weekend (S).

CORPORATE OFFICERS

President/Chairman/CEO	John J Curley

New York I-281

Treasurer	Jimmy L Thomas
Secretary	Thomas L Chapple

GENERAL MANAGEMENT

Publisher	Monte I Trammer
Controller	Linda Feltman

ADVERTISING

Director	Nancy Meyer

MARKETING AND PROMOTION

Director-Marketing/Promotion	Mary H Miller

CIRCULATION

Director	Ellison Rhodes
Manager	David Maxam

NEWS EXECUTIVE

Managing Editor	Barbara Lombardo

EDITORS AND MANAGERS

Business Reporter	Roberta Nelson
Coordinator-Special Projects	Mary Caroline Powers
City Editor	Edward Fitzpatrick
Editorial Page Editor	Mary Caroline Powers
Education Editor	Michelle Falardeau
Features Editor	Beverly McKim
Librarian	Eleanor Brower
News Editor	Jenn Richardson
Chief Photographer	Clark Bell
Religion Editor	Beverly McKim
Sports Editor	Rik Stevens
Wire Editor	Jenn Richardson

PRODUCTION

Director	John Semo
Foreman-Composing	Christine Duguay
Foreman-Pressroom	Dale Sherman

Market Information: Zoned editions.

Mechanical available: Offset; Black and 4 ROP colors; insert accepted — preprinted; page cut-offs — 22¾".

Mechanical specifications: Type page $12\frac{3}{8}$" x 21½"; E - 6 cols, ⅞", $\frac{5}{16}$" between; A - 6 cols, ⅞", $\frac{5}{16}$" between; C - 9 cols, 1¼", $\frac{5}{16}$" between.

Commodity consumption: Newsprint 1,000 short tons; widths 27", 13½"; black ink 19,500 pounds; color ink 4,000 pounds; single pages printed 5,000; average pages per issue 24(d), 38(S).

Equipment: EDITORIAL: Front-end hardware — HAS; Front-end software — HAS. CLASSIFIED: Front-end hardware — HAS, HI/58; Front-end software — HAS. DISPLAY: Adv layout systems — HAS; Front-end hardware — HAS; Front-end software — HAS. PRODUCTION: Typesetters — 2-COM/8600; Plate exposures — Nu; Plate processors — Nat; Scanners — ECR/Autokon; Production cameras — C/Spartan; Color separation equipment (conventional) — Lf/Leafscan.
PRESSROOM: Line 1 — 6-G/Community. MAILROOM: Counter stackers — HL/Monitor; Inserters and stuffers — MM/227; Bundle tyer — OVL/415N. COMMUNICATIONS: Digital ad delivery system — AP AdSend. WIRE SERVICES: News — GNS, AP; Receiving dishes — AP. BUSINESS COMPUTERS: IBM/AS-400; PCs & micros networked; PCs & main system networked.

SCHENECTADY

Schenectady County

'90 U.S. Census- 65,566; E&P '96 Est. 63,631

ABC-CZ (90): 135,438 (HH 54,356)

The Daily Gazette (m-mon to sat)
The Sunday Gazette (S)

The Daily Gazette, 2345 Maxon Rd. (12308); PO Box 1090, Schenectady, NY 12301-1090; tel (518) 395-3025; fax (518) 372-5986.

Circulation: 59,158(m); 59,158(m-sat); 62,514(S); ABC Sept. 30, 1995.

Price: 50¢(d); 50¢(sat); $1.50(S).

Advertising: Open inch rate $33.00(m); $33.00(m-sat); $33.00(S); $56.10(m & S). **Representative:** Sawyer-Ferguson-Walker Co.

News Service: AP. **Politics:** Independent. **Established:** 1894.

Advertising not accepted: Gambling; X-rated movies.

Special Editions: Baptist Retirement Center (Feb); NCAA, Outdoor Living (Mar); Boating, Lawn & Garden, Trade Show, Spring Car Care, Stock Car Racing, Real Estate, Senior Lifestyles, Best of Travel (Apr); Spring Building, Health (May); Summer Lifestyles, Family Business (June); Saratoga Track, Senior Lifestyles, Tuesday in the Park (July); Car Show (Aug); Hunting & Fishing, Health, Fall, Fall Car Care (Sept); Fall Building, Bridal, Auto Leasing, Senior Lifestyles (Oct); Christmas Gift Guide (Nov).

Special Weekly Sections: Food Section (wed); Outdoors (thur); Building & Garden, Ski Page (Dec-Mar) (fri); Travel, Science & Technology (S).

Magazines: TV Tab (S); USA Weekend.

CORPORATE OFFICERS

President	John E N Hume III
Vice Pres	Elizabeth L Lind
Secretary	William S Hume
Treasurer	Ernest R Grandy

GENERAL MANAGEMENT

Publisher	John E N Hume III
General Manager	Denis Paquette
Manager-Credit	Mary Fitch
Manager-Education Service	John E N Hume III

ADVERTISING

Manager-Retail	Scott Osswald
Manager-Classified	Daniel Beck

CIRCULATION

Manager	Stephen Wilary

NEWS EXECUTIVES

Editor	John E N Hume III
Managing Editor	Denis Paquette

EDITORS AND MANAGERS

Business/Finance Editor	Eric Anderson
City Editor	Nicholas Cantiello
Editorial Page Editor	Arthur J Clayman
Entertainment/Amusements Editor	Peg Churchill Wright
Fashion Editor	Richard Bennett
Films/Theater Editor	Dan DiNicola
Food Editor	Richard Bennett
Librarian	Susan Whiteman
Life/Leisure Editor	Richard Bennett
Outdoors Editor	John E N Hume III
Manager-Photo Department	David Kraus
Sports Editor	Cecil Walker
Wire Editor	Louis Rappaport

MANAGEMENT INFORMATION SERVICES

Data Processing Manager	John Carbone

PRODUCTION

Manager	Bruce Donadio
Manager-Pre Press	Peter Garrison
Manager-Ad Services	Sheilah DiBlasio
Foreman-Pressroom	William Varno
Foreman-Camera/Platemaking	Peter Anson
Foreman-Mailroom	Marty Budnik

Market Information: Split Run.

Mechanical available: Letterpress; Black and 3 ROP colors; insert accepted — preprinted; page cut-offs — 22¾".

Mechanical specifications: Type page 13" x 21¼"; E - 6 cols, $2\frac{1}{16}$", ⅙" between; A - 6 cols, $2\frac{1}{16}$", ⅙" between; C - 9 cols, $1\frac{11}{32}$", ⅛" between.

Commodity consumption: Newsprint 7,500 metric tons; widths 55", 41¼", 27½"; black ink 251,670 pounds; color ink 4,882 pounds; single pages printed 14,376; average pages per issue 46(d), 104(S); single plates used 20,000.

Equipment: EDITORIAL: Front-end hardware — DEC/PDP 11-84, 33-CD/2400, 61-PC; Front-end software — CD/2400, HI/XP-21. CLASSIFIED: Front-end hardware — DEC/PDP 11-84, 15-PC, 14-MeD/112B; Front-end software — CD/2400, HI/CPAG; Other equipment — LaCie/Scanner. DISPLAY: Adv layout systems — 2-SCS/Layout 8000; Front-end hardware — 13-Ap/Mac, 1-XIT/Clipper, 1-AU/Black Writer; Front-end software — Multi-Ad/Creator 3.7. PRODUCTION: Pagination software — HI/XP-21 2.52; OCR software — ISSI/Scanning System; Typesetters — 2-AU/5U, 1-AU/6, 2-ECR/3850; Platemaking systems — Na; Plate exposures — 2-Va/Starlite; Plate processors — 2-NP/40; Electronic picture desk — Lf/AP Leaf Picture Desk; Scanners — 2-ECR; Production cameras — 1-C/Spartan III, 1-C/Newspager; Automatic film processors — 1-LE/LD2600, 2-LE/PC18, 1-LE/PC13, 1-LE/LD1800; Shrink lenses — 1-Alan, Nikon; Color separation equipment (conventional) — 2-Ap/Mac Quadra, Konsensus/2 Color Proofer; Digital color separation equipment — 1-Lf/Leafscan 45.
PRESSROOM: Line 1 — 4-G/PEC (1-color hump; 2-color decks); Folders — 4-G/PEC; Pasters — G/PEC Auto; Reels and stands — 8-G/PEC; Press control system — PEC. MAILROOM: Counter stackers — 5-QWI; Inserters and stuffers — 2-S/N630; Bundle tyer — 2-MLN, Power Strap; Wrapping singles — 1-QWI; Addressing machine — 1-Ch. COMMUNICA-

TIONS: Remote imagesetting — AP AdSend, AdSat, ImageNet; Systems used — satellite. WIRE SERVICES: News — AP; Stock tables — AP; Syndicates — AP, LAT-WP, CNS, Maturity News Service, CSM; Receiving dishes — size-3m, AP. BUSINESS COMPUTERS: 1-IBM/Sys 36, PC; PCs & micros networked; PCs & main system networked.

STATEN ISLAND
Richmond County, Borough of Staten Island

'90 U.S. Census- 378,977; E&P '96 Est. 450,901
ABC-CZ (90): 378,977 (HH 130,519)

Staten Island Advance
(e-mon to fri; m-sat; S)

Staten Island Advance, 950 Fingerboard Rd., Staten Island, NY 10305; tel (718) 981-1234; fax (718) 981-1456. Advance Publications group.

Circulation: 72,873(e); 72,873(m-sat); 91,658(S); ABC Sept. 30, 1995.

Price: 50¢(d); 50¢(sat); $1.25(S); $2.50/wk.

Advertising: Open inch rate $52.00(e); $52.00(m-sat); $58.00(S). **Representative:** Newhouse Newspapers/Metro Suburbia.

News Services: AP, NNS, LAT-WP, INS-BS. **Politics:** Independent. **Established:** 1886.

Not Published: New Year; Memorial Day; Independence Day; Labor Day; Thanksgiving; Christmas.

Special Editions: % Off Clearance Sale Tab, Health & Fitness, Coupon Tab, Parent & Child (Jan); Personal Finance, Bride & Groom Tab, Senior Lifestyles, Health & Fitness, Coupon Tab (Feb); Cookbook, NJ Auto Show, Health & Fitness, Spring Fashion Feature, Spring Real Estate (4 times), Your Home/Spring, Parent & Child, Coupon Tab, Baseball Preview (Mar); Lawn & Garden Guide, NY Auto Show Section, Easter Greetings, Guide '96, Coupon Tab, Health & Fitness (Apr); Pool & Patio Guide, Car Care Tab, Health & Fitness, Your Home/Summer, Coupon Tab, Memorial Section, Four-Mile Run Section (May); Wedding Planner '96, Senior Lifestyles, Health & Fitness, Coupon Tab (June); Parenting Section, Health & Fitness, Coupon Tab (July); % Off Clearance Sale Tab, Back-to-School, Fall Fashion Feature, Coupon Tab, Football Preview (Aug); Fall Real Estate (4 times), Health & Fitness, Coupon Tab, Your Home/Fall, Bride & Groom (Sept); Health & Fitness, Coupon Tab, New Car Preview, Car Care Tab (Oct); Holiday Gift Guide (3 times), Coupon Tab (Nov); Christmas Greetings (Dec).

Special Weekly Sections: Health & Fitness (mon); Parent & Child (tues); The Sexes-Men, Food (wed); Your Home, The Sexes-Women (thur); Friday (Weekend Guide) (fri); Punch, Travel (S).

Magazines: React (thur); Parade, Sunday TV (S).

GENERAL MANAGEMENT

Publisher	Richard E Diamond
Controller	Arthur Silverstein
Manager-Credit	William Tosonotti

ADVERTISING

Manager	Gary V Cognetta
Manager-Classified	George Fries
Manager-Shopping Center	Sal Cassati
Manager-Marketing	Jack Furnari
Manager-Co-op	Edward Rudiger
Manager-Ad Service	Vincent Cowhig

CIRCULATION

Manager	Richard Salerno

NEWS EXECUTIVES

Editor	Brian Laline
Managing Editor	William Huus

EDITORS AND MANAGERS

Automotive Editor	Sandra Zummo
Arts Editor	Michael Fressola
Business/Finance Editor	Todd Hill
City Editor	Tom Checchi
Editorial Page Editor/Books Editor	Mark Hanley
Education Editor	Laura D'Angelo
Entertainment/Amusements Editor	Richard Ryan
Environmental Editor	Carolyn Rushefsky
Fashion Editor	Elaine Boies
Features Editor	Tom Checchi
Food Editor	Jane Milza
Graphic Arts Editor	Susan McDermott
Health/Medical Editor	Carolyn Rushefsky
Home Furnishings Editor	Sandra Zummo
Librarian	Melinda Gottlieb
Lifestyle Editor	Ken Paulsen
News Editor	Edward Donnelly
Asst News Editor	Claire Regan
Asst News Editor	Rob Wolf
National News Editor	Stephannia Cleaton
Perspective Editor	Stevie Lacy-Pendleton
Photo Department Manager	Steve Zaffarano
Political Editor	Judy Randall
Production Editor	William Huus
Religion Editor	Julia Martin
School Editor	Laura D'Angelo
Sports Editor	Lou Bergonzi
Sunday Editor	Charles Schmidt
Television Editor	Dan Breen
Travel Editor	Sharon Silke
World News Editor	Stephannia Cleaton

MANAGEMENT INFORMATION SERVICES

Data Processing Manager	Nick Guido

PRODUCTION

Manager-Systems	Michael J Lapcevic
Foreman-Composing Room	John Bruno
Asst-Composing Room	Charles Eller
Foreman-Pressroom	Walter Tambini
Foreman-Mailroom	Vincent Matusiak
Foreman-Camera Department	Charles Dugan

Market Information: Zoned editions; Split Run.

Mechanical available: DiLitho; Black and 3 ROP colors; insert accepted — preprinted; page cut-offs — 21½".

Mechanical specifications: Type page 13" x 21½"; E - 6 cols, 2$\frac{1}{16}$", ⅛" between; A - 6 cols, 2$\frac{1}{16}$", ⅛" between; C - 10 cols, 1$\frac{3}{16}$", $\frac{1}{16}$" between.

Commodity consumption: Newsprint 12,500 short tons; average pages per issue 55(d), 120(S).

Equipment: EDITORIAL: Front-end hardware — 5-DEC/PDP 11-34, 6-HP, 3-IBM, 4-Sun/Sparc 20, 1-Laserplex/Flex, 1-Multiplexer 4x4; Front-end software — AT; Printers — 4-HP, 1-DP, 2-Florida Data, 1-Genicom, 2-MNT, 1-Ap/Mac Laser Pro 630, 2-MON/3850; Other equipment — Lf/AP Leaf Picture Desk, 5-Ap/Mac Quadra 850, 2-Ap/Mac Centris 650, 2-Imager Plus/1200. CLASSIFIED: Front-end hardware — 3-DEC/PDP 11-34; Front-end software — AT; Printers — 2-HP/Laser; Other equipment — 2-AT/GT-68. DISPLAY: Adv layout systems — 6-Ap/Mac cx, 2-Ap/Mac Quadra 700, Ap/Mac 950 fileserver; Front-end software — DTI/AdSpeed; Printers — 2-NewGen/600s; Other equipment — 2-Microtek/300. PRODUCTION: Typesetters — 2-LE, AU/APS Micro 5, 2-MON/3850; Plate exposures — 1-Nu/Flip Top FT2CV, 1-Nu/2VPNS, 2-Nu/Flip Top FT40UPNS; Plate processors — 2-WL/Lith-plate; Scanners — HP/ScanJet IIc, 1-HDF; Production cameras — 1-AG/RPS-2024, 1-C/Spartan III; Film transporters — 2-LE/APS-34; Shrink lenses — 1-Kamerak/Distorta; Digital color separation equipment — 1-ECR/Autokon 1000, News Graphic Sys. PRESSROOM: Line 1 — 7-MAN/Color Convertible; Folders — 1-MAN; Pasters — 7-MAN/Auto; Reels and stands — 7-MAN. MAILROOM: Counter stackers — 4-HL, 1-S/13728; Inserters and stuffers — 1-S/624, 1-S/1372; Bundle tyer — 2-MLN/2A, 1-MLN/2A Retrofit. LIBRARY: Electronic — Mead Data Central/Nexis NewsView Novell 2:3. COMMUNICATIONS: Facsimile — AdSat; Digital ad delivery system — AP AdSend. WIRE SERVICES: News — AP; Photos — AP; Syndicates — NNS, LAT-WP; Receiving dishes — size-3m, AP, BS. BUSINESS COMPUTERS: 1-HP/3000-68; Applications: CJ; PCs & micros networked; PCs & main system networked.

SYRACUSE
Onondaga County

'90 U.S. Census- 163,860; E&P '96 Est. 158,845
ABC-CZ (90): 385,437 (HH 148,956)

The Post-Standard
(m-mon to sat)

Syracuse Herald-Journal
(e-mon to sat)

Syracuse Herald American (S)

The Post-Standard/Syracuse Herald-Journal/American, Clinton Sq.; Box 4915, Syracuse, NY 13221-4915; tel (315) 470-0011; e-mail linhorst@syracuse.com; web site http://www.syracuse.com. Advance Publications group.

Circulation: 86,735(m); 74,745(e); 86,735 (m-sat); 74,745(e-sat); 208,262(S); ABC Sept. 30, 1995.

Price: 35¢(d); $1.75(S); $3.85/wk (m, e & S); $15.40/mo; $200.20/yr.

Advertising: Open inch rate $125.95(m & e); $145.15(S). **Representatives:** American Publishers Reps.; Newhouse Newspapers/Metro Suburbia.

News Services: NNS, NYT, LAT-WP, AP, KRT, CSM. **Politics:** Independent. **Established:** 1829 (The Post-Standard), 1877 (Herald-Journal).

Not Published: Herald on Christmas.

Special Editions: Syracuse Power Boat Show, Progress Edition & Bus Review, % Off Section (Jan); Bridal Section, Interiors/Kitchen & Bath, Tax Guide, CNY Boat Show, % Off Tab (Feb); Women's Spring Fashion, Men's Spring Fashions, Summer Camps, Refund '96, Prom Guide, Fishing Guide (Mar); Home Beautiful Show, Home & Garden, Career & Educational Opportunities, TV Cable Guide "Big Sweeps" Issue, Healthcare, Your New Home, Home Office & Computer, Spring Dining Guide (Apr); Summer Guide to New York State, Spring Car Care, Your New Home, Oswego Speedway Section, Summertime (May); Summer Travel, Yard 'n' Home, 50 Plus, Summer Auto Spectacular, Parade of Homes, Graduation, Bridal Section II, Insurance & Financial Planning (June); % Off Section (July); Back-to-School, State Fair, Madison-Bouckville Antique Show, Discover Syracuse (Aug); SU Football Preview, Women's Fall Fashion, Men's Fall Fashions, TV Cable Guide, Fall Preview I & II, Home Beautiful, Fall Car Care (Sept); Fall Dining Guide, 1997 Auto Preview, Homes Etc., College Prep, Insurance & Financial Planning (Oct); Ski Guide, Shop Early Gift Guide, SU Basketball Preview, TV Cable Guide, Christmas Show Round-up, Holiday Magic, Holiday Cookbook (Nov); Focus on Women, Holiday Magic, 11th Hour Santa, Stars Winter Guide (Dec).

Special Weekly Sections: Food, Business Extra, Sports Extra (mon); Relationships (tues); Fashion (wed); Weekend (Entertainment), Neighbors Accent (thur); Outdoors/Recreation, Health & Fitness (fri); Sports Extra, Driving, Religion, Home & Real Estate (sat); Employment (S).

Magazines: Sports (PS), Business (PS), Business (HJ) (mon); Accent (HJ), H J Zone (zoned editions) (HJ) (wed); Accent (PS), Neighbors (zoned editions) (PS) (thur); Sports (HJ) (fri); Sports (PS) (sat); Local Stars Magazine (Newsprint) (HA), Comics (HA), Parade (HA), Real Estate (HA), TV Cable Guide (HA) (S); CNY (PS & HJ) (daily).

CORPORATE OFFICER

President	Stephen A Rogers

GENERAL MANAGEMENT

Publisher	Stephen A Rogers
Manager-Production	Michael Stern
Controller	Alice Miranda
Manager-Credit	Jeffrey Pole
Purchasing Agent	Steve Dievendorf

ADVERTISING

Director	James F Kleinklaus
Manager-Retail	Ken Brill
Manager-Classified	Bill Allison

MARKETING AND PROMOTION

Manager-Promotion	Stephen Hogens

TELECOMMUNICATIONS

Director-Info Systems	Carol Sholes

CIRCULATION

Director	Jeffrey A Barber

NEWS EXECUTIVES

Post Standard	
Exec Editor	Mike Connor
Managing Editor	Rosemary Robinson
Deputy Managing Editor	Mark Libbon
Herald Journal/Herald American	
Exec Editor	Timothy D Bunn
Managing Editor	Timothy Atseff
Asst Managing Editor	Bob Lloyd
Managing Editor-Shared Departments	Bart Pollack
Asst Managing Editor-Shared Departments	Charles Hickey

EDITORS AND MANAGERS

Post Standard	
City Editor	Adrianne Montgomery
CNY Editor	Kathy Schneider
Editorial Page Editor	Fred Fiske
Librarian	Bonnie Ross
Projects Editor	Tom Foster
Regional Editor	Rich Sullivan
Herald Journal/Herald American	
Administrative Editor	William Robinson
Automotive Editor	Kenn Peters
Books Editor	William Robinson
Business/Finance Editor	Dan Padovano
Cartoonist	Frank Cammuso
City Editor	Janis Barth
Editorial Page Editor	L Peter Lyman
Librarian	Bonnie Ross
News Editor	Barry Katz
Real Estate Editor	Dan Padavano
Religion Editor	Steve Billmyer
Sports Editor	Steve Carlic
Travel Editor	Mike Hirsch

MANAGEMENT INFORMATION SERVICES

Director-Info Systems	Carol Sholes
Director-New Media	Stan Linhorst

PRODUCTION

Manager-Camera/Platemaking	Patrick Magdziuk
Manager-Mailroom	William Steinbacher
Manager-Pressroom	Roger Coulombe
Manager-Composing	Terry Lawson
Asst Manager	Arthur LaGraffe
Asst Manager (Night)	Charles Rogers

Market Information: Zoned editions; Split Run; Operate database; Operate audiotex; Electronic edition.

Mechanical available: Letterpress; Black and 3 ROP colors; insert accepted — preprinted; page cut-offs — 22¾".

Mechanical specifications: Type page 13" x 21½"; E - 6 cols, 2$\frac{1}{16}$", ⅛" between; A - 6 cols, 2$\frac{1}{16}$", ⅛" between; C - 10 cols, 1$\frac{5}{16}$", $\frac{1}{32}$" between.

Commodity consumption: Newsprint 26,000 short tons; widths 49⅞", 41", 27½"; black ink 800,000 pounds; color ink 200,000 pounds; single pages printed 60,000; average pages per issue 56(d), 158(S); single plates used 175,000.

Equipment: EDITORIAL: Front-end hardware — 4-DEC/PDP 11-84; Front-end software — CSI. CLASSIFIED: Front-end hardware — 1-Tandem/55; Front-end software — SII. AUDIOTEX: Hardware — 1-Brite Voice Systems. DISPLAY: Adv layout systems — CJ/Ad Layout; Front-end hardware — Ap/Mac, HI/2100; Front-end software — Aldus/FreeHand, Multi-Ad/Creator, QuarkXPress, Adobe/Photoshop, HI/Display Ad; Printers — Ap/Mac LaserWriters; Other equipment — AU/APS-6, AU/3850. PRODUCTION: Pagination software — HI/XP-21; Typesetters — III/3850, 2-AU/APS-6; Platemaking systems — Na; Plate exposures — 1-MAS, 1-Homemade; Plate processors — 2-Na/C120; Electronic picture desk — Lf/AP Leaf Picture Desk; Scanners — 2-ECR/Autokon; Production cameras — 2-C; Automatic film processors — 2-P; Film transporters — 2-P; Shrink lenses — 1-Alan/Prime; Color separation equipment (conventional) — 1-Scanmate, 6-Kk/2100. PRESSROOM: Line 1 — 18-G/MK II, 2-G/MK V (6 half decks), 9-Common I; Press drives — CH; Folders — 3-G/3:2; Pasters — G; Reels and stands — G; Press control system — CH; Press registration system — Mk. MAILROOM: Counter stackers — 3-Id, 3-SH; Inserters and stuffers — 2-Fg; Bundle tyer — 6-Dynaric, 4-MLN; Wrapping singles — 1-St; Addressing machine — 1-Image. LIBRARY: Electronic — Vu/Text. COMMUNICATIONS: Systems used — satellite. WIRE SERVICES: News — AP; Photos — AP, KRT; Stock tables — AP; Receiving dishes — size-3m, AP. BUSINESS COMPUTERS: 2-HP; Applications: CJ/AIM: Mitchell Humphrey-Gen ledger, Accts payable; PCs & micros networked; PCs & main system networked.

TARRYTOWN
Westchester County

'90 U.S. Census- 10,814; E&P '96 Est. 10,954
ABC-NDM (90): 28,083 (HH 10,571)

The Daily News
(e-mon to sat; S)

The Daily News, One Gannett Dr., White Plains, NY 10464; tel (914) 694-9300; web site http://www.nynews.com/nynews. Gannett Co. Inc. group.

Circulation: 3,249(e); 3,249(e-sat); 4,013(S); ABC Sept. 24, 1995.

Price: 40¢(d); 40¢(sat); $1.50(S).

News Services: AP, GNS, LAT-WP. **Politics:** Independent.

Note: White Plains is the headquarters for the Gannett Suburban Newspapers, Inc. The following newspapers are printed at the Harrison White Plains plant: Mt. Vernon Daily Argus, Mamaroneck Daily Times, New Rochelle Standard-Star, Port Chester Daily Item, White Plains Reporter-Dispatch, Tarrytown Daily News, Peekskill Star, Ossining Citizen Register and Yonkers Herald States-

man. The Rockland Journal-News is printed in Nyack, NY. All advertising is sold in combination for $177.43 (d) and $200.52 (S). For detailed mechanical equipment information, see the Gannett Suburban Newspapers, Inc. listing in White Plains. Individual newspaper rates not made available.

Special Editions: Spring Bridal (Feb); Spring Home Design (Mar); Spring Home & Garden, Suburban Golf, Greater New York Auto Show, Summer Education, Suburban Business Review (Apr); Suburban Golf, Builder's Showcase (May); Summer Dine Out Guide (June); Suburban Golf (July); Back-to-School, Fall Education, Suburban Golf (Aug); Suburban Golf, Pro Football Preview, Local Football Preview, Fall Bridal, Community Guide (Sept); Suburban Golf, Fall Home Design, New Autos '97, Fall Dine Out Guide (Oct); Holiday Gift Guide, Thanksgiving Day Special, Holiday Planner (Nov); Holiday Food, Hot Holiday Gifts, Last Minute Gift Guide (Dec).

Special Weekly Sections: Career Opportunities (mon); Best Food Day, Fashion (wed); Home Style, Weekend, Dining Out (thur); Garden & Home Improvement (fri); Travel & Resort, Real Estate, Career Opportunities, TV Week, Education (S).

CORPORATE OFFICERS

President/Publisher Gary F Sherlock
Vice Pres/Exec Editor Kenneth A Paulson
Vice Pres/President-Advertising John C Green
Vice Pres/Director-Circulation Mike Huot
Vice Pres-Finance Charles Schmitt
Vice Pres-Marketing Michael G Kane
Vice Pres-Operations Fal A Bolzner

ADVERTISING

Director-Classified Candida Canfield
Director-Display Robert Twesten
Manager-Display Jeanne Westby
Manager-Display Steve Havelka
Manager-Business Development Joan Perreault

CIRCULATION

Director Jonathan Alvord
Manager Paul Felicissimo

NEWS EXECUTIVES

Senior Managing Editor Janet McMillan
Operations Editor Rich Kleban
Managing Editor-Administration Bill Madden
Editor-Reader Services Gayle T Williams
Acting Asst Managing Editor-Lifestyles Tad Clarke
Asst Managing Editor-Business Mark Land
Asst Managing Editor-Sports David Georgette

EDITORS AND MANAGERS

Editorial Page Editor Ron Patafio
Entertainment Editor Kathy McClusky
Graphics Editor Chris Kiesler
Health/Medical Editor Barbara Durkin
Metro Editor Phil Reisman III
Asst Managing Editor Sandy Coyle
Asst Managing Editor-Nights Dan Murray
Photo Director Robert Rodriguez
Photo Editor-Day Danielle Perillat
Travel Editor Kathy McClusky

MANAGEMENT INFORMATION SERVICES

Director-Systems & Technology Sherman Bodner

PRODUCTION

Director Nat Hogan

Market Information: Operate audiotex; Electronic edition.

TONAWANDA

See NORTH TONAWANDA

TROY

Rensselaer County

'90 U.S. Census- 54,269; **E&P '96 Est.** 52,376
ABC-CZ (90): 110,104 (HH 43,556)

The Record (m-mon to sat)
The Sunday Record (S)

The Record, 501 Broadway, Troy, NY 12181; tel (518) 270-1200; fax (518) 270-1202; web site http://www.albany/glob-alone.net/record/. Journal Register Co. group.

Circulation: 30,012(m); 30,012(m-sat); 33,011(S); ABC Sept. 30, 1995.

Price: 50¢(d); 50¢(sat); $1.25(S); $2.85/wk; $148.20yr.

Advertising: Open inch rate $28.65(m); $28.65(m-sat); $28.65(S). **Representative:** Landon Associates Inc.

News Services: AP, KRT. **Politics:** Independent. **Established:** 1896 (Times Record), 1974 (Sunday Record).

Special Editions: Wedding Album, Health Watch, New Car Preview (Jan); 100th Anniversary Issue, Business Update '96, Baby Album (Feb); Medical Physicians Guide, Health File (Mar); Spring Home & Garden, Spring Car Care, Celebrating 100 Years (Apr); Summer Excitement, Nature Living (May); Father's Day, Health File, Graduation (June); Saratoga Life (July); Answer Book, Back-to-School, Truck Tab (Aug); Fall Home, Antiques & Fall Festing, Health File (Sept); Fall Car Care, Harvest Festival (Oct); Christmas Gift Guide, Health File (Nov); Holiday Recipes, Last Minute Gift Ideas, 50 Things to do After Christmas (Dec).

Magazines: USA Weekend, Steppin' Out (thur); Real Estate (3rd thur); Home Front (1st fri); Color Comics (Metro) 6 full pages, TV & Cable quarter-fold magazine (S); Getaway Magazine, HealthFile (quarterly).

CORPORATE OFFICERS

President/CEO Robert M Jelenic
Exec Vice Pres/Chief Financial Officer/Treasurer Jean B Clifton

GENERAL MANAGEMENT

Publisher J Stephen Buckley
Controller Thomas Conti

ADVERTISING

Director Michael O'Sullivan

CIRCULATION

Director Mike Fern

NEWS EXECUTIVES

Editor Charles Delafuente
Managing Editor Lisa Robert Lewis

EDITORS AND MANAGERS

Business/Finance Editor James Smith
City Editor Jan Shields
Entertainment Editor Doug DeLisle
Focus/Fashion Editor Doug DeLisle
Food Editor Heidi Legenbauer
Librarian Jill Parsons
News Editor Alex Rothenberg
Chief Photographer Mike McMahon
Sports Editor Kevin Moran

MANAGEMENT INFORMATION SERVICES

Systems Manager John Jones

PRODUCTION

Director Paul DiLauro
Foreman-Composing James Lewis
Superintendent-Pre Press/Press Edward Heffem

Market Information: Zoned editions; Split Run; TMC.

Mechanical available: Offset; Black and 3 ROP colors; insert accepted — preprinted; page cutoffs — 22.08".

Mechanical specifications: Type page 13" x 21"; E - 6 cols, 2$\frac{1}{16}$", $\frac{1}{8}$" between; A - 6 cols, 2$\frac{1}{16}$", $\frac{1}{8}$" between; C - 9 cols, 1$\frac{3}{8}$", $\frac{1}{16}$" between.

Commodity consumption: Newsprint 4,000 short tons; widths 55", 55", 41$\frac{1}{4}$", 41$\frac{1}{4}$", 27$\frac{1}{2}$", 27$\frac{1}{2}$"; black ink 110,000 pounds; color ink 11,600 pounds; single pages printed 14,800; average pages per issue 28(d), 68(S); single plates used 34,800.

Equipment: EDITORIAL: Front-end hardware — Dewar System; Front-end software — Dewar/View. CLASSIFIED: Front-end hardware — Dewar/Information System; Front-end software — Dewar System IV. DISPLAY: Adv layout systems — Dewar System; Front-end hardware — Ap/Mac Network; Front-end software — Multi-Ad/Creator. PRODUCTION: Typesetters — 2-MON/Image Setter 1000; Plate exposures — 2-Nu/Flip Top FTU64PNS; Plate processors — 2-Nat/A-240; Electronic picture desk — Lf/AP Leaf Picture Desk; Scanners — Lf/Leafscan 35, Kk/Negative Scanner; Production cameras — 2-C/Spartan III; Automatic film processors — 2-LE/24, 2-AG/Rap 66, 1-Kk/66S; Shrink lenses — 1-Alan/Image Reverse; Color separation equipment (conventional) — 1-RZ/4050E. PRESSROOM: Line 1 — 6-G/Headliner Offset w/gluer; Folders — 1-G/quarter 2:1; Pasters — 6-G/Digital; Press control system — Fin. MAILROOM: Counter stackers — 2-QWI; Inserters and stuffers — 3-MM/EM227; Bundle tyer — 4-MLN, MLN/II HS. WIRE SERVICES: News — AP, KRT; Stock tables — AP; Receiving dishes — AP. BUSINESS COMPUTERS: IBM/AS400; Applications: INSI: Circ, Ad mgmt, Transient mgmt, Accts payable, Gen ledger; PCs & main system networked.

UTICA

Oneida County

'90 U.S. Census- 68,637; **E&P '95 Est.** 63,864
ABC-NDM (90): 316,633 (HH 117,498)

Observer-Dispatch
(m-mon to sat; S)

Observer-Dispatch, 221 Oriskany Plz., Utica, NY 13501; tel (315) 792-5000; fax (315) 792-5138. Gannett Co. Inc. group.

Circulation: 50,745(m); 50,745(m-sat); 65,747(S); ABC Sept. 30, 1995.

Price: 50¢(d); 50¢(sat); $1.50(S); $3.30/wk (carrier), $3.65/wk (motor route); $13.20/mo (carrier), $14.60/mo (motor route); $171.60/yr (carrier), $189.80/yr (motor route).

Advertising: Open inch rate $62.31(m); $62.31(m-sat); $73.87(S). **Representative:** Gannett National Newspaper Sales.

News Services: AP, GNS, LAT-WP, PR Newswire, TMS, Warmer Weather. **Politics:** Independent. **Established:** 1922.

Special Editions: Bridal (Jan); Business Review (Feb); Best of the Best, Living Here, Good Times Upstate (May); Best of the Best Winners Tab, Blue Sox Season Kick-Off, Good Old Summertime, Teen All-Stars (June); Boilermaker Sections, Gambling Tab (July); Back-to-School (Aug); Chamber of Commerce Tab (Sept); Career Night Tab, Fall Home Improvement, Holiday Cook Book, Innovative Auto (Oct); Thanksgiving Day (Nov); Gift Guide, Christmas Memories (Dec); Motor Deals Tab (S); Home Showcase; Treasure Chest of Coupons (monthly).

Special Weekly Sections: Family (mon); Health (tues); Food/Nutrition (wed); Weekend Plus (thur); Home/Garden (fri); Religion, TV Book (sat).

Magazines: TV Observer (sat); USA Weekend (S).

CORPORATE OFFICERS

President Gary Watson
Treasurer Jimmy L Thomas
Secretary Thomas L Chapple

GENERAL MANAGEMENT

Publisher Donna M Donovan
Controller Mark Blum
Director-Human Resources Patrick Moran
Systems Manager James Wessing

ADVERTISING

Director Bob Parker
Manager-Classified David Parsons

CIRCULATION

Director Bob Scott
Manager Peter Barresi
Manager-Transportation Cheryle Platte

NEWS EXECUTIVES

Editor Richard Jensen
Managing Editor Bobbi Bowman
Asst Managing Editor Nick Assendelft

EDITORS AND MANAGERS

Business Editor Victor Andino
Editorial Page Editor Tim A Chavez
Features Editor Sandra Dimsdale
Graphics Editor/Art Director Nick Assendelft
Health/Medical Writer Bill Farrell
Metro Editor Mike Killian
Opinion Editor Tim Chavez
Photo Editor Nancy Ford
Sports Editor Mike Sherman
TV Book Editor Gary Harke

MANAGEMENT INFORMATION SERVICES

Data Processing Manager Sue Hughes

PRODUCTION

Director Mike O'Connor
Manager Elaine Lisle
Manager-Pressroom Philip Surace
Manager-Post Press Bill Blackshear
Manager-Post Press Aaron Fischer
Manager-Technical Service Robert Mundrick

Market Information: Zoned editions; Split Run; TMC.

Mechanical available: DiLitho; Black and 3 ROP colors; insert accepted — preprinted; page cutoffs — 22$\frac{3}{4}$".

Mechanical specifications: Type page 13" x 21$\frac{1}{2}$"; E - 6 cols, 2.08", .08" between; A - 6 cols, 2.08", .08" between; C - 10 cols, 1$\frac{1}{4}$", .06" between.

Commodity consumption: Newsprint 4,626 short tons; widths 55", 41$\frac{1}{4}$", 27$\frac{1}{2}$"; black ink 133,199 pounds; color ink 23,093 pounds; single pages printed 13,329; average pages per issue 32(d), 68(S); single plates used 45,538.

Equipment: EDITORIAL: Front-end hardware — SII/Sys 55 XR, Tandem/CLX-RISC, 50-PCs, 30-Ap/Mac; Front-end software — SII/LASR, Ap/Mac 55, QPS, Mk/Page Director, QuarkXPress; Printers — QMS/860, Okidata, 18-HT; Other equipment — 33-SII/Coyote, Ap/Macs for Pagination. CLASSIFIED: Front-end hardware — SII/Ad Sys 55, 11-SII/Coyote, Ap/Macs for Ad Director; Front-end software — SII/Ad Director, Pongrass/Classified Pagemaker; Printers — DEC/LA 120, Data Products/GP 1500, DEC/LA 310; Other equipment — 11-SII/Coyote. DISPLAY: Adv layout systems — SCS/Layout 8000, SII/Ad Director; Front-end hardware — IBM/PC, 4-Ap/Mac Centris 650, 2-Ap/Mac Centris 610, 3-Ap/Mac Quadra 950; Front-end software — Pongrass, Mk/Ad Director, Multi-Ad/Creator, QPS; Printers — QMS/860; Other equipment — ECR/Autokon 1000DE, Ap/Mac Interface. PRODUCTION: Pagination software — QuarkXPress 3.3; OCR software — Caere/OmniPage 2.1; Typesetters — 2-Scitex/Dolev 440 Drum Recorder; Platemaking systems — KFM; Plate exposures — 2-Nu/Flip Top FT40V3UPNS; Plate processors — 2-GraphCoat/DN85; Electronic picture desk — Ap/Mac Pac Interface, Lf/AP Leaf Picture Desk; Scanners — Ap/Mac Pac Interface, ECR/Autokon 1000DE, AG/Arcus Plus; Production cameras — C/Marathon; Automatic film processors — 2-LE/PC-18, 2-LE, LS/2800R; Digital color separation equipment — Adobe/Photoshop 2.5.1 on Ap/Mac Quadra 950. PRESSROOM: Line 1 — G/Mark I Headliner double width (3 humps); Press drives — Allen-Bradley; Folders — 2-G/2:1; Pasters — Manual; Reels and stands — G; Press control system — Allen-Bradley; Press registration system — Web Tech. MAILROOM: Counter stackers — 1-Id/440, Id/660, QWI; Inserters and stuffers — HI/1472; Bundle tyer — 2-MLN/MLN2A, 1-Power Strap/PSN5; Addressing machine — Ch. LIBRARY: Electronic — SII/Laser System. COMMUNICATIONS: Digital ad delivery system — AP AdSend, ImageNet. WIRE SERVICES: News — AP Datafeatures, AP Datastream, AP Datafeatures, TMS (TV), Warmer Weather; Photos — AP Photostream; Stock tables — CT, Tribune Stocks; Syndicates — AP; Receiving dishes — size-3m, AP. BUSINESS COMPUTERS: 1-IBM/AS400; Applications: Masterpiece: Accts payable, Gen ledger, Computer assoc, Public relations; PCs & micros networked; PCs & main system networked.

WATERTOWN

Jefferson County

'90 U.S. Census- 29,429; **E&P '96 Est.** 30,809
ABC-CZ (90): 41,617 (HH 15,628)

Watertown Daily Times
(e-mon to fri; m-sat; S)

Watertown Daily Times, 260 Washington St., Watertown, NY 13601; tel (315) 782-1000; fax (315) 782-2337. Johnson Newspaper Corp. group.

Circulation: 39,802(e); 39,802(m-sat); 44,973(S); ABC Sept. 30, 1995.

Price: 50¢(d); 50¢(sat); $1.75(S); $3.35/wk; $156.00/yr.

Advertising: Open inch rate $30.65(e); $30.65(m-sat); $30.65(S).

News Services: AP, UPI, NYT, LAT-WP, KRT. **Politics:** Independent-Republican. **Established:** 1861.

Not Published: New Year; Memorial Day; Independence Day; Labor Day; Thanksgiving; Christmas.

Special Weekly Section: Best Food Day (tues).

Magazines: Farm & Garden Tab (newsprint) (sat); Sunday Weekly Tab, TV Showcase Tab (S).

CORPORATE OFFICERS

President John B Johnson
Vice Pres Catherine C Johnson
Secretary Catherine C Johnson
Treasurer John B Johnson

GENERAL MANAGEMENT

General Manager Kenneth A Holloway
Controller Loren Walts

ADVERTISING

Director Robert C Cornell
Manager-Classified David Schaab
Manager-National/Co-op Robert Sholette

MARKETING AND PROMOTION

Manager-Marketing/Promotion Barb Peck

CIRCULATION

Director Stephen A Laird
Manager Robert R Ritchie
Manager-Office Stephen Gaines

NEWS EXECUTIVES

Editor John B Johnson
Managing Editor John B Johnson Jr

EDITORS AND MANAGERS

Books Editor Jan Thiessen
Business Editor Jan Thiessen
Farm Editor Judy Jacobs
Radio/Television Editor Jan Thiessen
Society Editor Jan Thiessen
Sports Editor Matt Dorney

MANAGEMENT INFORMATION SERVICES

Data Processing Manager Tom Kitto

PRODUCTION

Manager Richard Dietrich

Market Information: Zoned editions; Split Run; ADS.

Mechanical available: Offset; Black and 3 ROP colors; insert accepted — preprinted; page cut-offs — 22".

Mechanical specifications: Type page 13" x 21"; E - 6 cols, 2 1/16", 1/8" between; A - 6 cols, 2 1/16", 1/8" between; C - 9 cols, 1 3/8", 1/16" between.

Commodity consumption: Newsprint 3,844 metric tons; widths 55", 41 1/4", 27 1/2"; black ink 87,500 pounds; color ink 27,000 pounds; single pages printed 13,000; average pages per issue 30(d), 68(S); single plates used 65,000.

Equipment: EDITORIAL: Front-end hardware — Tandem/CLX-RISC, 55-SII/Coyote, Ap/Power Mac 8100, Sun/Sparc 20; Front-end software — SII/Editorial; Printers — AU/APS-6600 H, AU/APS Broadsheet. CLASSIFIED: Front-end hardware — Tandem/CLX-RISC, 7-SII/Coyote; Front-end software — SII; Printers — AU/APS. DISPLAY: Adv layout systems — Ap/Mac Ad System; Front-end hardware — Sun/Classic, Ap/Mac Quadras, Ap/Mac Centris; Front-end software — Multi-Ad; Printers — Compaq/Pagescan. PRODUCTION: Typesetters — 2-Linotype-Hell/Linotronic 202; Plate exposures — 2-DSA, 1-Nu; Plate processors — 2-Nat; Electronic picture desk — Lf/AP Leaf Picture Desk; Production cameras — 1-SCREEN/475, 1-Graphline/260D; Automatic film processors — 2-LE, 2-SCREEN; Film transporters — 1-SCREEN; Color separation equipment (conventional) — RZ/200S, Nikon/Coolscan; Digital color separation equipment — 1-RZ/200S.

PRESSROOM: Line 1 — 7-MAN/4-2; Press drives — Fin; Folders — 2-MAN; Pasters — 7-MEG; Reels and stands — 7-MEG. MAILROOM: Counter stackers — 3-HL, 1-KAN; Inserters and stuffers — 2-GMA/SLS-1000; Bundle tyer — 1-MLN/ML2EE, 2-Dynaric; Addressing machine — 1-Ch/582N. LIBRARY: Electronic — Vu/Text. COMMUNICATIONS: Systems used — satellite. WIRE SERVICES: News — AP; Stock tables — AP, TTS. BUSINESS COMPUTERS: IBM/AS400; Applications: Accts payable, Accts receivable, Gen ledger, Payroll, Newsprint inventory; PCs & micros networked; PCs & main system networked.

WELLSVILLE

Allegany County

'90 U.S. Census- 5,241; E&P '96 Est. 4,840

Wellsville Daily Reporter (e-mon to fri)
The Spectator (S)

Wellsville Daily Reporter, 159 N. Main St., Wellsville, NY 14895; tel (716) 593-5300; fax (716) 593-5303. Hollinger International Inc. group.

Circulation: 3,302(e); 11,783(S); Sworn Oct. 1, 1992.

Price: 35¢(d); $1.50(S); $7.50/mo (motor route); $87.00/yr.

Advertising: Open inch rate $6.15(e); $12.50 (S). **Representative:** Landon Associates Inc.

News Service: AP. **Established:** 1880.

Note: The Wellsville Daily Reporter (e) and the Hornell Evening Tribune (e) share a Sunday edition.

Not Published: New Year; Memorial Day; Independence Day; Labor Day; Thanksgiving; Christmas.

Special Editions: Bride's Guide (Jan); Basketball Edition, Spring Outdoor (Mar); Graduation (June); Balloon Rally Guide (July); Medical-Health Guide (Aug); Football Guide, Annual Fall Outdoor Guide (award winning) (Sept); Christmas (Nov).

CORPORATE OFFICERS

President Larry J Perrotto
Publisher Oak Duke

CIRCULATION

Manager Gary Shaver

NEWS EXECUTIVE

News Editor Neal Simon

EDITORS AND MANAGERS

Sports Editor Rodney Stebbins
Reporter Becky Sutton
Reporter Neal Simon

Market Information: TMC.

Mechanical available: Offset; Black and 3 ROP colors; insert accepted — preprinted; page cut-offs — 22 3/4".

Mechanical specifications: Type page 13" x 21 1/2"; E - 6 cols, 2 1/16", 1/8" between; A - 6 cols, 2 1/16", 1/8" between; C - 6 cols, 2 1/16", 1/8" between.

Commodity consumption: widths 27 1/2", 34"; average pages per issue 16(d), 56(S).

Equipment: EDITORIAL: Front-end hardware — Mk/1100; Other equipment — 2-IBM/Selectric II. CLASSIFIED: Front-end hardware — Mk/1100. BUSINESS COMPUTERS: 1-DEC/Rainbow 100; Applications: Billing, Accts receivable, Reports.

WHITE PLAINS

Westchester County

'90 U.S. Census- 48,718; E&P '96 Est. 50,203
ABC-NDM (90): 382,766 (HH 133,828)

Gannett Suburban Newspapers Inc.

Gannett Suburban Newspapers Inc., One Gannett Dr., White Plains, NY 10604; tel (914) 694-9300; web site http://www.nynews.com/nynews. Gannett Co. Inc. group.

Representative: Gannett National Newspaper Sales.

News Services: AP, GNS, LAT-WP. **Politics:** Independent.

Note: White Plains is the headquarters for Gannett Suburban Newspapers, Inc. The following newspapers are printed at the Harrison White Plains plant: Mt. Vernon Daily Argus, Mamaroneck Daily Times, New Rochelle Standard-Star, Port Chester Daily Item, White Plains Reporter Dispatch, Tarrytown Daily News, Peekskill Star, Ossining Citizen Register and Yonkers Herald Statesman. The Rockland Journal-News is printed in Nyack, NY. All advertising is sold in combination for $177.43 (d) and $200.52 (S). Combined circulation for the 26 weeks ending Sept. 30, 1995 is 153,638 (e) and 191,580 (S).

Special Editions: Spring Bridal (Feb); Spring Home Design (Mar); Spring Home & Garden, Suburban Golf, Greater New York Auto Show, Summer Education, Suburban Business Review (Apr); Suburban Golf, Builder's Showcase (May); Summer Dine Out Guide (June); Suburban Golf (July); Back-to-School, Fall Education, Suburban Golf (Aug); Suburban Golf, Pro Football Preview, Local Football Preview, Fall Bridal, Community Guide (Sept); Suburban Golf, Fall Home Design, New Autos '97, Fall Dine Out (Oct); Holiday Gift Guide, Thanksgiving Day Special, Holiday Planner (Nov); Holiday Food, Hot Holiday Gifts, Last Minute Gift Guide (Dec).

Magazines: Business Monday (mon); Health (tues); Food (wed); Suburban Weekend (thur); Real Estate, Home & Garden (fri); Lively Arts, Travel, Perspective, Real Estate, TV Book, USA Weekend, Comics (S).

CORPORATE OFFICERS

President/Publisher Gary F Sherlock
Vice Pres/Exec Editor Kenneth A Paulson
Vice Pres/President-Advertising John C Green
Vice Pres/Director-Circulation Mike Huot
Vice Pres-Finance Charles Schmitt
Vice Pres-Marketing Michael G Kane
Vice Pres-Operations Fal A Bolzner

ADVERTISING

Director-Classified Candida Canfield
Director-Display Robert Twesten
Manager-Display Jeanne Westby
Manager-Display Steve Havelka
Manager-Business Development Joan Perreault

MARKETING AND PROMOTION

Director- Sales/Marketing Elaine Huot
Manager-Consumer Market Laura Versau Nisbet

TELECOMMUNICATIONS

Audiotex Manager Carl Iacona

CIRCULATION

Director Jonathan Alvord
Manager-Single Copy Samuel (Sam) G Elliot

NEWS EXECUTIVES

Senior Managing Editor Janet McMillan
Operations Editor Rich Kleban
Managing Editor-Administration Bill Madden
Editor-Reader Services Gayle T Williams
Acting Asst Managing Editor-Lifestyles Tad Clarke
Asst Managing Editor-Business Mark Land
Asst Managing Editor-Sports David Georgette

EDITORS AND MANAGERS

Editorial Page Editor Ron Patafio
Entertainment Editor Kathy McClusky
Graphics Editor Chris Kiesler
Health/Medical Editor Barbara Durkin
Metro Editor Phil Reisman III
Asst Managing Editor Sandy Coyle
Asst Managing Editor-Nights Dan Murray
Photo Director Robert Rodriguez
Photo Editor-Day Danielle Perillat
Travel Editor Kathy McClusky

MANAGEMENT INFORMATION SERVICES

Director-Systems & Technology Sherman Bodner

PRODUCTION

Director Nat Hogan

Market Information: Zoned editions; Split Run; TMC; ADS; Operate audiotex; Electronic edition.

Mechanical available: Offset; Black and 4 ROP colors; insert accepted — preprinted; page cut-offs — 22 3/4".

Mechanical specifications: Type page 13" x 21 1/2"; E - 6 cols, 2.06", 1/8" between; A - 6 cols, 2.06", 1/8" between; C - 10 cols, 1 1/4", .08" between.

Commodity consumption: Newsprint 23,644 short tons; widths 54 1/2", 41 1/4"; black ink 427,946 pounds; color ink 88,435 pounds; single pages printed 21,163; average pages per issue 48(d), 116(S); single plates used 329,816.

Equipment: EDITORIAL: Front-end hardware — SII; Front-end software — Guardian/Operating System; Printers — HP/III, Okidata; Other equipment — HAS/Pagination, DEC/VAX Output Graphic Database. CLASSIFIED: Front-end hardware — AT; Front-end software — IAS; Printers — Genicom; Other equipment — Ad-Star. DISPLAY: Adv layout systems — SCS/Layout 8000; Front-end hardware — Dell/Sys 310; Printers — HP/LaserJet 11D. PRODUCTION: Typesetters — MON/Lasercomp; Plate exposures — WL, Nu; Plate processors — WL; Scanners — ImagiTex/300, ImagiTex/940; Production cameras — SCREEN, C/Spartan; Automatic film processors — LE; Film transporters — LE, C; Color separation equipment (conventional) — Diadem; Digital color separation equipment — Diadem.

PRESSROOM: Line 1 — 7-G/Metro (3 color decks); Line 2 — 8-G/Metro (4 color decks); Line 3 — 7-G/Metro (3 color decks); Line 4 — 7-G/Metro (3 color decks); Folders — 6-G/3:2, 2-G/2:1; Press control system — Fin. MAILROOM: Counter stackers — 12-QWI/200 SX; Inserters and stuffers — 2-HI/1372P, 1-HI/1472P; Bundle tyer — 15-Power Strap/PSN.5, 2-MLN/MLM 2EE; Wrapping singles — 12-QWI/bottom wraps; Addressing machine — 2-Ch, 4-Barstrom/Labelers. LIBRARY: Electronic — Data Times. WIRE SERVICES: News — AP Datastream, AP Datafeatures, AP Sports; Stock tables — AP Stocks; Receiving dishes — AP. BUSINESS COMPUTERS: 1-IBM/4381R92E, 1-IBM/AS-400 F60; Applications: Payroll, Accts payable, Circ, Promotion; Admarc, G/2; PCs & micros networked; PCs & main system networked.

White Plains Reporter Dispatch (e-mon to sat; S)

White Plains Reporter Dispatch, One Gannett Dr., White Plains, NY 10464; tel (914) 694-9300; web site http://www.nynews.com/nynews. Gannett Co. Inc. group.

Circulation: 45,524(e); 45,524(e-sat); 57,417(S); ABC Sept. 24, 1995.

Price: 40¢(d); 40¢(sat); $1.50(S).

News Services: AP, GNS, LAT-WP. **Politics:** Independent. **Established:** 1916.

Note: White Plains is the headquarters for Gannett Suburban Newspapers, Inc. The following newspapers are printed at the Harrison White Plains plant: Mt. Vernon Daily Argus, Mamaroneck Daily Times, New Rochelle Standard-Star, Port Chester Daily Item, White Plains Reporter Dispatch, Tarrytown Daily News, Peekskill Star, Ossining Citizen Register and Yonkers Herald Statesman. The Rockland Journal-News is printed in Nyack, NY. All advertising is sold in combination for $177.43 (d) and $200.50 (S). For detailed mechanical equipment information, see the Gannett Suburban Newspapers, Inc. listing in White Plains. Individual newspaper rates not made available.

Special Editions: Spring Bridal (Feb); Spring Home Design (Mar); Spring Home & Garden, Suburban Golf, Greater New York Auto Show, Summer Education, Suburban Business Review (Apr); Suburban Golf, Builder's Showcase (May); Summer Dine Out Guide (June); Suburban Golf (July); Back-to-School, Fall Education, Suburban Golf (Aug); Suburban Golf, Pro Football Preview, Local Football Preview, Fall Bridal, Community Guide (Sept); Suburban Golf, Fall Home Design, New Autos '97, Fall Dine Out Guide (Oct); Holiday Gift Guide, Thanksgiving Day Special, Holiday Planner (Nov); Holiday Food, Hot Holiday Gifts, Last Minute Gift Guide (Dec).

Special Weekly Sections: Career Opportunities (mon); Best Food Day, Fashion (wed); Home Style, Weekend, Dining Out (thur); Garden & Home Improvement (fri); Travel & Resort, Real Estate, Career Opportunities, TV Week, Education (S).

CORPORATE OFFICERS

President/Publisher Gary F Sherlock
Vice Pres/Exec Editor Kenneth A Paulson
Vice Pres/President-Advertising John C Green
Vice Pres/Director-Circulation Mike Huot
Vice Pres-Finance Charles Schmitt
Vice Pres-Marketing Michael G Kane
Vice Pres-Operations Fal A Bolzner

ADVERTISING

Director-Classified Candida Canfield
Director-Display Robert Twesten
Manager-Display Jeanne Westby
Manager-Display Steve Havelka
Manager-Business Development Joan Perreault

TELECOMMUNICATIONS

Audiotex Manager Carl Iacona

CIRCULATION

Director Jonathan Alvord
Manager Paul Felicissimo

NEWS EXECUTIVES

Senior Managing Editor Janet McMillan
Operations Editor Rich Kleban
Managing Editor-Administration Bill Madden
Editor-Reader Services Gayle T Williams
Acting Asst Managing Editor-Lifestyles Tad Clarke
Asst Managing Editor-Business Mark Land
Asst Managing Editor-Sports David Georgette

EDITORS AND MANAGERS

Editorial Page Editor Ron Patafio
Entertainment Editor Kathy McClusky
Graphics Editor Chris Kiesler
Health/Medical Editor Barbara Durkin
Asst Managing Editor Phil Reisman III
Metro Editor Mickey Hirten
Asst Managing Editor-Nights Dan Murray
Photo Director Robert Rodriguez
Photo Editor-Day Danielle Perillat
Travel Editor Kathy McClusky

MANAGEMENT INFORMATION SERVICES

Director-Systems & Technology Sherman Bodner

PRODUCTION

Director Nat Hogan

Market Information: Operate audiotex; Electronic edition.

YONKERS

Westchester County

'90 U.S. Census- 188,082; E&P '96 Est. 182,247
ABC-NDM (90): 206,022 (HH 78,800)

The Yonkers Herald Statesman (e-mon to sat; S)

The Yonkers Herald Statesman, One Gannett Dr., White Plains, NY 10604; tel (914) 694-9300; web site http://www.nynews.com/nynews. Gannett Co. Inc. group.

Circulation: 21,993(e); 21,993(e-sat); 29,148(S); ABC Sept. 24, 1995.

Price: 40¢(d); 40¢(sat); $1.50(S); $3.45/wk (carrier); $288.00/yr (mail).

News Services: AP, GNS, LAT-WP. **Politics:** Independent.

Note: White Plains is the headquarters for Gannett Suburban Newspapers, Inc. The following newspapers are printed at the Harrison

White Plains plant: Mt. Vernon Daily Argus, Mamaroneck Daily Times, New Rochelle Standard-Star, Port Chester Daily Item, White Plains Reporter Dispatch, Tarrytown Daily News, Peekskill Star, Ossining Citizen Register and Yonkers Herald Statesman. Rockland Journal- News is printed in Nyack, NY. All advertising is sold in combination for $177.43 (d) and $200.52 (S). For detailed mechanical equipment information, see the Gannett Suburban Newspapers, Inc. listing in White Plains. Individual newspaper rates not made available.

Special Editions: Spring Bridal (Feb); Spring Home Design (Mar); Spring Home & Garden, Suburban Golf, Greater New York Auto Show, Summer Education, Suburban Business Review (Apr); Suburban Golf, Builder's Showcase (May); Summer Dine Out Guide (June); Suburban Golf (July); Back-to-School, Fall Education, Suburban Golf (Aug); Suburban Golf, Pro Football Preview, Local Football Preview, Fall Bridal, Community Guide (Sept); Suburban Golf, Fall Home Design, New Autos '97, Fall Dine Out Guide (Oct); Holiday Gift Guide, Thanksgiving Day Special, Holiday Planner (Nov); Holiday Food, Hot Holiday Gifts, Last Minute Gift Guide (Dec).

Special Weekly Sections: Career Opportunities (mon); Best Food Day, Fashion (wed); Home Style, Weekend, Dining Out (thur); Garden & Home Improvement (fri); Travel & Resort, Real Estate, Career Opportunities, TV Week, Education (S).

CORPORATE OFFICERS

President/Publisher Gary F Sherlock
Vice Pres/Exec Editor Kenneth A Paulson
Vice Pres/President-Advertising John C Green
Vice Pres/Director-Circulation Mike Huot
Vice Pres-Finance Charles Schmitt
Vice Pres-Marketing Michael G Kane
Vice Pres-Operations Fal A Bolzner

ADVERTISING

Director-Classified Candida Canfield
Director-Display Robert Twesten
Manager-Display Jeanne Westby
Manager-Display Steve Havelka
Manager-Business Development Joan Perreault

TELECOMMUNICATIONS

Audiotex Manager Carl Iacona

CIRCULATION

Director Jonathan Alvord
Manager Paul Felicissimo

NEWS EXECUTIVES

Senior Managing Editor Janet McMillan
Operations Editor Rich Kleban
Managing Editor-Administration Bill Madden
Editor-Reader Services Gayle T Williams
Acting Asst Managing Editor-Lifestyles Tad Clarke
Asst Managing Editor-Business Mark Land
Asst Managing Editor-Sports David Georgette

EDITORS AND MANAGERS

Editorial Page Editor Milton Hoffman
Entertainment Editor Kathy McClusky
Graphics Editor Chris Kiesler
Health/Medical Editor Barbara Durkin
Metro Editor Phil Reisman III
Asst Managing Editor Sandy Coyle
Asst Managing Editor-Nights Dan Murray
Photo Director Robert Rodriguez
Photo Editor-Day Danielle Perillat
Travel Editor Kathy McClusky

MANAGEMENT INFORMATION SERVICES

Director Systems & Technology Sherman Bodner

PRODUCTION

Director Nat Hogan

Market Information: Operate audiotex; Electronic edition.

NORTH CAROLINA

ABERDEEN

Moore County

'90 U.S. Census- 2,700; **E&P '96 Est.** 2,216

Citizen News-Record

(m-mon to fri; S)

Citizen News-Record, 206 N. Sandhills Blvd.; PO Box 336, Aberdeen, NC 28315; tel (910) 944-2356; fax (910) 944-3586. Park Communications Inc. group.

Circulation: 1,818(m); 1,818(S); Sworn Sept. 29, 1994.

Price: 25¢(d); 50¢(S); $54.00/yr.

Advertising: Open inch rate $12.75(m); $12.75(S). **Representative:** Papert Companies.

News Service: AP. **Politics:** Independent. **Established:** 1917.

Not Published: Christmas.

Special Editions: Football; Basketball; Sandhills Golf Outlook (monthly); Profile Edition (May).

Special Weekly Section: Church Page (weekly).

Magazines: TV Section (weekly); Real Estate Magazine (monthly).

CORPORATE OFFICERS

President Wright M Thomas
Vice Pres Robert J Rossi

GENERAL MANAGEMENT

Publisher/General Manager Mary Ann Panek

ADVERTISING

Director Mary Ann Panek

CIRCULATION

Manager Kevin Gardner

NEWS EXECUTIVE

Managing Editor Randall Rigsbee

PRODUCTION

Supervisor Randall Rigsbee

Market Information: TMC.

Mechanical available: Offset; Black and 3 ROP colors; insert accepted — preprinted, any size-minimum 8"x10"; page cut-offs — $19\frac{1}{2}$".

Mechanical specifications: Type page 13" x 21"; E - 6 cols, 2", $\frac{1}{8}$" between; A - 6 cols, 2", $\frac{1}{8}$" between; C - 10" cols, $1\frac{5}{8}$", $\frac{1}{16}$" between.

Commodity consumption: Newsprint 150 short tons; width 27"; average pages per issue 12(d), 12(S); single plates used 3,000.

Equipment: CLASSIFIED: Front-end hardware — 1-COM/Unified. PRODUCTION: Typesetters — COM/Videosetter, COM/Trendsetter, 2-COM/Compuwriter IV; Platemaking systems — Nu/Flip Top; Production cameras — R/Vertical; Automatic film processors — LE. PRESSROOM: Line 1 — WPC/Leader Model 36; Reels and stands — 5-Roll/Stands; Press control system — WPC. MAILROOM: Bundle tyer — Bu; Addressing machine — 2-Am/1900. WIRE SERVICES: News — AP; Stock tables — AP; Syndicates — NEA, Universal Press, TV Data; Receiving dishes — AP.

ASHEBORO

Randolph County

'90 U.S. Census- 16,362; **E&P '96 Est.** 17,847
ABC-NDM (90): 85,206 (HH 33,057)

The Courier-Tribune

(e-mon to fri; S)

The Courier-Tribune, 500 Sunset Ave.; PO Box 340, Asheboro, NC 27204; tel (910) 625-2101; fax (910) 626-7074. Donrey Media Group group.

Circulation: 16,628(e); 17,994(S); ABC Sept. 30, 1995.

Price: 50¢(d); $1.00(S); $6.50/mo (carrier); $140.00/yr (mail).

Advertising: Open inch rate $15.85(e); $17.85(e-wed); $15.85(S). **Representative:** Papert Companies.

News Services: AP, KRT, SHNS. **Politics:** Independent. **Established:** 1876, 1978 (Sunday edition).

Special Editions: Progress (Jan); Lawn & Garden (Mar); Recreation, Graduation (May); Back-to-School, Football (Aug); Car Care, Home Improvement, Textile (Oct).

Special Weekly Sections: Food Section, Total Market Coverage, Business (wed); Church (fri); Business, Children's Page, Lifestyles (S).

Magazines: Food (wed); TV Focus, Color Comics (S); USA Weekend.

CORPORATE OFFICERS

Founder Donald W Reynolds
President/Chief Operating Officer Emmett Jones
Exec Vice Pres/Chief Financial Officer Darrell W Loftin
Vice Pres-Western Newspaper Group David A Osborn
Vice Pres-Eastern Newspaper Group Don Schneider

GENERAL MANAGEMENT

Publisher David Renfro
Office Manager Maria Payne

ADVERTISING

Senior Exec Chris Allen

CIRCULATION

Director Gary Lockhart

NEWS EXECUTIVE

Editor Ray Criscoe

EDITORS AND MANAGERS

News Editor Annette Jordan
Sports Editor Dennis Garcia

PRODUCTION

Manager-Composing Wendy Oliver
Manager-Press Ben Kane

Market Information: TMC.

Mechanical available: Offset; Black and 3 ROP colors; insert accepted — preprinted; page cut-offs — $22\frac{5}{8}$".

Mechanical specifications: Type page 13" x $21\frac{1}{2}$"; E - 6 cols, $2\frac{1}{16}$", $\frac{1}{8}$" between; A - 6 cols, $2\frac{1}{16}$", $\frac{1}{8}$" between; C - 9 cols, $1\frac{3}{8}$", $\frac{1}{16}$" between.

Commodity consumption: Newsprint 900 metric tons; widths $27\frac{1}{2}$", $13\frac{3}{4}$"; black ink 16,880 pounds; color ink 4,320 pounds; single pages printed 7,280; average pages per issue 20(d), 52(S); single plates used 9,000.

Equipment: EDITORIAL: Front-end hardware — 16-HAS; Front-end software — HAS; Printers — IBM; Other equipment — 2-Ap/Mac, Lf/Leafscan 35, Lf/AP Leaf Picture Desk. CLASSIFIED: Front-end hardware — 4-HAS; Front-end software — HAS; Printers — IBM. DISPLAY: Front-end hardware — 4-Ap/Mac; Front-end software — Multi-Ad/Creator; Printers — Ap/Mac LaserWriter. PRODUCTION: Typesetters — V/4990, XIT/Clipper; Plate exposures — 1-Nu; Plate processors — Graham; Production cameras — C/Spartan III; Automatic film processors — Polychrome/PL24; Color separation equipment (conventional) — Lf/AP Leaf Picture Desk. PRESSROOM: Line 1 — 9-G/Urbanite; Folders — 1-G. MAILROOM: Counter stackers — HL; Inserters and stuffers — MM/4-into-1; Bundle tyer — 1-MLN. WIRE SERVICES: News — AP; Receiving dishes — AP. BUSINESS COMPUTERS: 1-IBM/Sys 34, 1-HP/3000; Applications: CJ; PCs & micros networked.

ASHEVILLE

Buncombe County

'90 U.S. Census- 61,607; **E&P '96 Est.** 71,454
ABC-CZ (90): 85,114 (HH 36,467)

The Asheville Citizen-Times

(m-mon to sat; S)

The Asheville Citizen-Times, 14 O. Henry Ave. (28801); PO Box 2090, Asheville, NC 28802; tel (704) 252-5611; fax (704) 252-5887. Gannett Co. Inc. group.

Circulation: 66,432(m); 66,432(m-sat); 77,283(S); ABC Sept. 30, 1995.

Price: 50¢(d); 75¢(sat); $1.50(S); $3.50/wk; $15.17/mo; $182.00/yr.

Advertising: Open inch rate $54.76(m); $54.76(m-sat); $56.16(S). **Representative:** Landon Associates Inc.

News Services: AP, KRT. **Politics:** Independent. **Established:** 1870.

Not Published: If holidays fall on a weekday, 1 combined issue is published.

Special Editions: Industrial Review (Jan); Get-away (June); Get-away (July); Get-away (Aug); Building Page, Get-away (Sept); Schools & Colleges, Get-away (Oct); Western North Carolina Woman, Country Style, This Olde Home (monthly).

Special Weekly Sections: Health & Fitness (mon); Food Section (wed); Family (thur); TV Spotlight (sat); Travel, Business, Leisure, Book Page, House Plan Page (S).

Magazines: TV Spotlight (sat); Parade (S).

CORPORATE OFFICERS

President James B Banks
Senior Vice Pres/Director-Operations Wayne E Gay

GENERAL MANAGEMENT

Publisher James B Banks
Controller Joe Volrath

ADVERTISING

Director Jim Walther
Manager-Classified Michael Smith
Key Accounts Representative David Honeycutt

MARKETING AND PROMOTION

Manager-Database Marketing Jill Avett
Manager-Promotion Jerry Crouch

TELECOMMUNICATIONS

Coordinator-Database Systems Deb Baker
Audiotex Manager Jeff Howell

CIRCULATION

Coordinator-Newspapers in Education Ellie Franklin
Manager-Distribution Gary Breedlore

NEWS EXECUTIVES

Vice Pres/Exec Editor Larry Pope
Senior Editor John Parris
Managing Editor Ed Dawson

EDITORS AND MANAGERS

City Editor Charles Guthrie
Lifestyle Editor Nancy Marlowe
Photo Department Manager Gary Fields
Radio/Television Editor Tony Kiss
Religion Editor Henry Robinson
Sports Editor Doug Mead
Sports Editor Jim Hamer
Women's Editor Carole Currie

MANAGEMENT INFORMATION SERVICES

Online Manager Jill Clark
Data Processing Manager Mark Rogers

PRODUCTION

Manager Gary Christensen
Coordinator Cheryl Donnelly
Superintendent-Mailroom Dennis McCraven

Market Information: Zoned editions; Split Run; TMC; Operate database; Operate audiotex.

Mechanical available: Offset; Black and 3 ROP colors; insert accepted — preprinted; page cut-offs — 22".

Mechanical specifications: Type page 13" x 21"; E - 6 cols, 2.03", $\frac{1}{6}$" between; A - 6 cols, 2.03", $\frac{1}{6}$" between; C - 9 cols, 1.38", $\frac{1}{12}$" between.

Commodity consumption: Newsprint 7,200 short tons; widths 54", $40\frac{1}{2}$", $13\frac{1}{2}$"; black ink 155,000 pounds; color ink 55,800 pounds; single pages printed 18,580; average pages per issue 37(d), 48(sat), 94(S); single plates used 90,700.

Equipment: EDITORIAL: Front-end hardware — III; Front-end software — III/Tecs2; Printers — Okidata/Microline 393 Plus, IBM/Proprinta III XL; Other equipment — Ap/Mac Quadra 950, Ap/Mac IIcx, Lf/AP Leaf Picture Desk. CLASSIFIED: Front-end hardware — HI/Classified; Front-end software — HI/CASH; Printers — Fujitsu/5400. AUDIOTEX: Hardware — Wyse; Software — Master Menu System 1.00.02; Supplier name — Brite. DISPLAY: Adv layout systems — HI/PLS Ad Display System; Front-end hardware — 7-HI/8900, 5-Ap/Mac Quadra 950, 1-Ap/Mac IIsi; Front-end software — HI/PLS; Printers — 1-3M/Rainbow color proofer; Other equipment — X/Scanner, 2-XIT/PC interface. PRODUCTION: Pagination software — HI/CASH 3.0; Typesetters — 2-ECR/108 Pelbox, 2-Copal/Plain paper printer, 1-QMS/860 Laser Printer; Plate exposures — 1-BKY; Plate processors — 2-DP/36" Subtractive; Scanners — Scanmate/Plus, 5-Microtek/Scanmaker II XE, 3-HP/ScanJet IIcx; Production cameras — 1-C/Marathon, 1-C/Newspager; Automatic film processors — 3-Glunz Jensen/APS Dot 6, 2-Powermatic/66RA; Digital color separation equipment — ECR/Autokon 1430. PRESSROOM: Line 1 — Y/Unit double width; Line 2 — 8-MAN/Colorman 75 double width (4 half decks); Folders — MAN/double 3:2; Pasters — 8-Wd-H/RTP; Press control system — Fin. MAILROOM: Counter stackers — 4-HL; Inserters and stuffers — 3-MM; Bundle tyer — 4-MLN, 2-EAM/Mosca; Addressing machine — 2-Ch, 3-Wm. LIBRARY: Electronic — Nexis/NewsView, Nexis/PhotoView. WIRE SERVICES: News — AP Dataspeed; Stock tables — AP SelectStox II; Syndicates — KRT; Receiving dishes — size-10ft, AP. BUSINESS COMPUTERS: IBM/AS-400; Applications: Circ, Adv billing, Accts receivable, Gen ledger, Payroll.

BURLINGTON

Alamance County

'90 U.S. Census- 39,498; **E&P '96 Est.** 42,630
ABC-CZ (90): 61,306 (HH 24,807)

Times-News (m-mon to sat; S)

Times News Publishing Co., 707 S. Main; PO Box 481, Burlington, NC 27215; tel (910) 227-0131; fax (910) 229-2642. Freedom Communications Inc. group.

Circulation: 27,522(m); 27,522(m-sat); 28,867(S); ABC Sept. 30, 1995.

Price: 50¢(d); 50¢(sat); $1.00(S); $9.00/mo; $97.20/yr.

Advertising: Open inch rate $20.31(m); $20.31(m-sat); $20.31(S). **Representative:** Papert Companies.
News Service: AP. **Politics:** Independent. **Established:** 1887.
Special Editions: Tax Planner (Jan); Bridal (Feb); Progress, Summer Car Care (Apr); Balloon Fest, Parade of Homes, Graduation (May); Back-to-School, Football, National Hosiery Week, National Housing Week (Aug); Design-An-Ad, Fall Car Care, Women in Business (Oct); Holiday Lifestyles (Nov); Senior Sunshine Times (monthly).
Special Weekly Sections: Youth Page (mon); Health-Tech, Starwatch (tues); Food Day, Mini Page (wed); Accent on Family (thur); Accent on Entertainment (fri); Automotive, Real Estate (S).
Magazines: TV Times Friday (fri); Color Comics, Parade (S); Alamance Magazine (Historical).

CORPORATE OFFICERS

Chairman Robert C Hardie
President/CEO James Rosse
President-Community Newspapers East Jonathan Segal
President-Community Newspapers West Scott Fischer
Vice Pres-Finance/Chief Financial Officer David Kuykendall
Secretary Richard A Wallace

GENERAL MANAGEMENT

Publisher Robert M Lyons
General Manager Tim Timmons

ADVERTISING

Director James H (Trip) Hatley III
Manager-Sales Eddie Shatterly

MARKETING AND PROMOTION

Manager-Marketing/Promotion Michele Terry

CIRCULATION

Director Bill Woodrome

NEWS EXECUTIVES

Exec Editor Don Bolden
Managing Editor John Pea
Asst Managing Editor Frances Woody

EDITORS AND MANAGERS

Accent Editor Mike Pollard
City Editor Jim Lee
Copy Desk Chief Micah Boyd
Editorial Page Editor Don Bolden
Director-Photography Woody Marshall
Sports Editor Bob Sutton

PRODUCTION

Director Sam Jenkins
Manager-Systems Chuck Reavis
Foreman-Pressroom Allen Bennett
Asst Foreman-Pressroom Bill Strout
Foreman-Composing Debora Brower
Foreman-Mailroom Rodney Harris

Market Information: TMC; Operate audiotex.
Mechanical available: Offset; Black and 3 ROP colors; insert accepted — preprinted; page cut-offs — 22¾".
Mechanical specifications: Type page 13" x 21½"; E - 6 cols, 2 1/16", ⅛" between; A - 6 cols, 2.03", ⅛" between; C - 9 cols, 1.33", ⅛" between.
Commodity consumption: Newsprint 2,200 short tons; widths 55", 41½", 27¾", 13¾"; black ink 22,000 pounds; color ink 5,000 pounds; single pages printed 12,000; average pages per issue 28(d), 58(S); single plates used 25,000.
Equipment: EDITORIAL: Front-end hardware — Dewar/Sys IV; Front-end software — Dewar/Sys IV; Printers — Okidata/320; Other equipment — Dest/Scanner, Lf/Leafscan 35, Lf/AP Leaf Picture Desk, Dewar/Bridge. CLASSIFIED: Front-end hardware — Dewar/Sys IV; Printers — Okidata/320. DISPLAY: Adv layout systems — Dewar/Sys IV; Front-end hardware — PC, Ap/Mac; Front-end software — Dewar/Sys IV, Dewar/Ad Dummy, Dewar/Discovery, Archetype/Corel Draw; Printers — Okidata/2410, HP/LaserJet III; Other equipment — Dewar/Bridge. PRODUCTION: Pagination software — Dewar/Sys IV; Typesetters — V/5100, V/5510, 2-V/5300E; Plate exposures — Nu; Plate processors — Nat/Enco A-250, WL; Electronic picture desk — Lf/AP Leaf Picture Desk, Adobe/Photoshop; Scanners — X/7650, HP/ScanJet IIc; Production cameras — C/Spartan III; Automatic film processors — LE/HX 150B, Kk/710, LE/LogETEK 26; Color separation equipment (conventional) — CD/626; Digital color separation equipment — Lf/AP Leaf Picture Desk, Adobe/Photoshop.
PRESSROOM: Line 1 — 5-MAN/(half color deck) double width; Press drives — GE/Varitrol; Folders — 1-H/double 2:1; Pasters — 5-Wd; Reels and stands — 5-Wd; Press control system — GE. MAILROOM: Counter stackers — HL/1900, 2-Quip/351; Inserters and stuffers — 1-GMA/SLS-2000 8:2; Bundle tyer — 2-MLN/MLN 2. LIBRARY: Electronic — SMS/Stauffer Gold. WIRE SERVICES: News — AP Datastream, AP Datafeatures, KRT; Photos — AP; Stock tables — AP SelectStox; Receiving dishes — AP, Newspaper Satellite Network. BUSINESS COMPUTERS: Business/Office Southware, Lotus 1-2-3, AR/Works, PC/Netware; Applications: Circ; PCs & micros networked; PCs & main system networked.

CHARLOTTE

Mecklenburg County

'90 U.S. Census- 395,934; E&P '96 Est. 477,506
ABC-CZ (90): 511,433 (HH 200,219)

The Charlotte Observer

(m-mon to sat; S)

The Charlotte Observer, 600 S. Tryon St.; PO Box 32188, Charlotte, NC 28232; tel (704) 358-5000. Knight-Ridder Inc. group.
Circulation: 239,173(m); 239,173(m-sat); 305,021(S); ABC Sept. 30, 1995.
Price: 50¢(d); 50¢(sat); $1.25(S); $2.50/wk; $10.83/mo; $130.00/yr.
Advertising: Open inch rate $126.98(m); $126.98(m-sat); $136.79(S); $205.27(m & S). **Representative:** Newspapers First.
News Services: AP, KRT, LAT-WP, NYT. **Politics:** Independent. **Established:** 1886.
Special Editions: Marathon, Business Review/Stocks, Coupon, Chiropractic, Tax Preparation, Retirement Living (Jan); Weddings, Southern Spring Show (Feb); Spruce It Up, Frozen Foods, Spring Fashion, Car Care, Cruise, Retirement Living, Home & Garden (Mar); Parade of Homes, Insurance, Dogwood Festival, Family-owned Businesses, Spruce It Up, Tribute To Business, Coastal Carolina (Apr); Car Care, New Cars, Share Cabarrus, Boating, Virginia, Race Week (May); Florida-Bahamas, Father's Day (June); Back-to-School, Coupon, Georgia, Paine Webber Invitational Mountain Travel (July); Back-to-School, Fall Fashion, Summer Fest (Aug); Historic Morganton, Home Improvement, Fall Affair, Lawn & Garden, Murray's Mill Festival, Balloon Rally, Lincoln Apple (Sept); Southern Women's Show, Octoberfest, Fish Camp Jam, York Insurance, Ideal Home Show, New Car Preview, Design-An-Ad, Arts-A-Poppin, Art Fest, Race Week, Caribbean Travel, Home & Garden, Carolina Business Fair, Florida, Dining & Entertainment (Oct); Holiday Gift Guide, Hornets Opener, Holidays, Home for the Holidays, New Car Preview, Southern Christmas Show, Virginia (Nov); Last Minute Gifts, Home for the Holidays, Holiday Travel, Winter Travel (Dec).
Special Weekly Sections: Business Monday, Health (mon); Food, Break (wed); Extra, Family (fri); Travel (S).
Magazines: TV Week (S); Lake Norman Magazine; Parade; University City Magazine.

CORPORATE OFFICERS

Chairman Rolfe Neill
Vice Pres Jennie Buckner
Vice Pres Debbie Abels
Vice Pres William H McNey
Vice Pres Steve Stone
Vice Pres Mark Wilfley
Exec Vice Pres Gene Williams
Senior Vice Pres John Luby
Secretary Douglas C Harris
Treasurer/Asst Secretary Steve Stone

GENERAL MANAGEMENT

Publisher Rolfe Neill
General Manager John Luby
Director-Finance/Administration Steve Stone
Director-Human Resources Debbie Abels
Director-Administrative Service Dave Orbaugh
Manager-Education Service Ginny Swinson

ADVERTISING

Director William H McNey
Manager-Display Gordie Cherry
Manager-Classified Dennis West
Manager-Co-op Shirley Brown
Manager-Zone Greg Ward
Manager-Sales Development Dave Dodson
Manager-Production Service Patsy Stringer

MARKETING AND PROMOTION

Manager-Research Joe Denneny
Manager-Promotion Jim Banbury

CIRCULATION

Director Mark Wilfley
Director-Distribution Gus Howell
Director-Marketing Aleksei Reid
Manager-Office Tom Moore

NEWS EXECUTIVES

Editor Jennie Buckner
Managing Editor Frank Barrows
Asst Managing Editor-Local/Regional News Cheryl Carpenter
Asst Managing Editor-News Rick Thames
Asst Managing Editor-Administration Robert D DePiante
Asst Managing Editor-Weekends Tom Tozer
Asst Managing Editor-Graphics Todd Duncan
Asst Managing Editor-Projects Jim Walser

EDITORS AND MANAGERS

Books Editor Polly Paddock
Business/Finance Editor Brian Melton
Editorial Page Editor Ed Williams
Education Editor Neil Mara
Features Editor Mary Curtis
Films Editor Larry Toppman
Food Editor Kathi Purvis
Graphics Director Mike Fisher
Librarian Sara Klemmer
Music Editor-Classical Dean Smith
Radio/Television Editor Tim Funk
Exec Sports Editor Gary Schwab
Theater/Dance Editor Tony Brown
TV Week Editor David White

PRODUCTION

Director-Operations Bob Burns
Manager-Quality & Planning Sammy Helms
Manager-Composing Gary Hollifield
Manager-Camera/Platemaking Joe Galarneau
Manager-Pressroom Susan McRae
Manager-Mailroom Bob Gardner

Market Information: Zoned editions; Split Run; TMC; ADS; Operate database.
Mechanical available: Flexo, Letterpress; Black and 3 ROP colors; insert accepted — preprinted; page cut-offs — 23 9/16".
Mechanical specifications: Type page 13" x 22½"; E - 6 cols, 2 1/32", ⅙" between; A - 6 cols, 2 1/16", ⅛" between; C - 10 cols, 1 3/16", ⅛" between.
Commodity consumption: Newsprint 41,970 short tons; 38,075 metric tons; widths 55", 41¼", 27½"; black ink 1,312,340 pounds; color ink 390,645 pounds; single pages printed 48,254; average pages per issue 59(d), 92(S); single plates used 314,169.
Equipment: EDITORIAL: Front-end hardware — SII/Sys 55, SII/Tandem; Front-end software — SII/Sys 55; Printers — Okidata, HP/Laser. CLASSIFIED: Front-end hardware — SII/Sys 55, SII/Tandem-TXP; Front-end software — SII/Sys 55; Printers — Okidata, HP/Laser; Other equipment — Echo/terminals. DISPLAY: Adv layout systems — III, AMS, Ap/Mac; Front-end hardware — III, 10-Sun/3-60, 7-Ap/Mac; Front-end software — III, AMS, QuarkXPress, Multi-Ad/Creator, Aldus/FreeHand; Printers — 2-III/3850, Ultre, 1-Pagescan/Broadsheet, Plain Paper Clipper/11x17 1200 DPI; Other equipment — 6-Lacie/Silver Scanners, 1-Syquest/Removable Drive 44 88MB, 1-ECR, 6-NEC, Ap/Mac CD-Rom. PRODUCTION: Typesetters — 3-AU/APS-5U, 1-Ultre, 2-III/3850; Platemaking systems — Na, Na/Flexo; Plate exposures — Titan/LF2000; Plate processors — Na/NP120; Electronic picture desk — Lf/AP Leaf Picture Desk; Scanners — ECR/Autokon 1000, ECR/Autokon 1000DE, SCREEN/608 Drum Scanner; Production cameras — C/Spartan; Automatic film processors — C/66RA; Film transporters — C; Shrink lenses — Alan; Digital color separation equipment — Lf.
PRESSROOM: Line 1 — 2-MAN, 7-H; Line 2 — 2-MAN, 7-H; Line 3 — 2-MAN, 7-H; Line 4 — 9-MAN; Line 5 — 9-MAN; Folders — 7-H; Reels and stands — 45-H/Reelstand. MAILROOM: Counter stackers — 4-HL/Monitor, 5-HL/Monitor HT, 4-HL/Monitor HT-2; Inserters and stuffers — 1-MM/275, 2-MM/375; Bundle tyer — 13-Power Strap, 6-MLN/MLN 2A; Addressing machine — 1-Ch/543, 1-Ch/525E. LIBRARY: Electronic — Vu/Text SAVE. WIRE SERVICES: News — AP; Stock tables — AP SelectStox; Receiving dishes — AP. BUSINESS COMPUTERS: 2-IBM/4381, 1-HP/3000-947; Applications: CJ: Accts payable, Gen ledger, Adv, Circ, Payroll, HR; MSA, In-house; PCs & micros networked; PCs & main system networked.

CLINTON

Sampson County

'90 U.S. Census- 8,204; E&P '96 Est. 9,048
ABC-NDM (90): 47,297 (HH 17,526)

The Sampson Independent

(e-mon to fri; S)

The Sampson Independent, 303 Elizabeth St. (28328); PO Box 110, Clinton, NC 28329; tel (910) 592-8137; fax (910) 592-8756. Park Communications Inc. group.
Circulation: 7,832(e); 8,508(S); ABC Sept. 30, 1995.
Price: 35¢(d); 75¢(S).
Advertising: Open inch rate $8.78(e); $8.78(S). **Representative:** Landon Associates Inc.
News Service: AP. **Established:** 1924.
Not Published: Christmas.
Special Editions: Insight (Feb); Spring Fashion (Apr); Bridal (May); Tobacco (July); Back-to-School (Aug); Fall Fashion (Sept); Fall Car Care (Oct); Cookbook (Nov); X'mas Gift Guide (Dec); Realtors Guide (monthly).

GENERAL MANAGEMENT

General Manager Debby Chiarella

ADVERTISING

Manager Gary Pate

CIRCULATION

Manager Tony Jordan

NEWS EXECUTIVES

Editor Cherri Mathis
Managing Editor Debby Chiarella

EDITORS AND MANAGERS

Lifestyle/Religion Editor Kendra Gerlach
Sports Editor Andy Rackley
Sunday Editor Andy Rackley
Travel Editor Kendra Gerlach

PRODUCTION

Superintendent-Composing Wanda Buckner

Market Information: TMC.
Mechanical available: Offset; Black and 2 ROP colors; insert accepted — preprinted; page cut-offs — 22¾".
Mechanical specifications: Type page 13" x 21½"; E - 6 cols, 2 1/16", ⅛" between; A - 6 cols, 2 1/16", ⅛" between; C - 9 cols, 1⅜", 1/16" between.
Commodity consumption: Newsprint 335 short tons; width 27½"; black ink 11,352 pounds; color ink 649 pounds; single pages printed 5,050; average pages per issue 18(d), 26(S); single plates used 3,800.
Equipment: EDITORIAL: Front-end hardware — 1-Mk/1100, 12-Mk/4100. PRODUCTION: Typesetters — 1-COM/4961, 1-COM/7200, 2-COM/Videosetter; Plate exposures — 1-Nu; Production cameras — 1-CL/J-76CC; Automatic film processors — 1-LE/24.
PRESSROOM: Line 1 — 4-G/Community(1 folder); Line 2 — 5-KP. MAILROOM: Inserters and stuffers — 1-DG/320-3; Bundle tyer — 1-Malow. WIRE SERVICES: News — AP; Receiving dishes — AP.

CONCORD

Cabarrus County

'90 U.S. Census- 27,347; E&P '96 Est. 34,906
ABC-CZ (90): 31,219 (HH 12,221)

The Concord Tribune

(e-mon to fri; S)

The Concord Tribune, 125 Union St.; PO Box 608, Concord, NC 28026; tel (704) 333-1718; fax (704) 782-3155. Park Communications Inc. group.
Circulation: 12,698(e); 13,980(S); ABC Sept. 30, 1995.
Price: 25¢(d); 75¢(S); $6.50/wk; $78.00/yr.
Advertising: Open inch rate $10.75(e); $10.75 (S). **Representative:** Papert Companies.
News Service: AP. **Politics:** Independent. **Established:** 1900.
Note: All national advertising in the Concord Tribune is sold in conjunction with the Kannapolis Independent (eS). The combination rate is $21.00.
Special Editions: Chamber of Commerce Update (Jan); Progress, Pride Edition (Feb); Farm & Garden, Spring Fashion (Mar); Private Property, Outdoor, Car Care, FYI-Newcomers (Apr); World 600 Racing Edition (May); June Bride (June); Back-to-School, Football (Aug); National 500 Racing Edition, Women's Edition (Oct); Recipes, Family Business Focus, Gift Guide (Nov); Christmas Greetings (Dec).
Special Weekly Sections: Health News (mon); Racing Specials (tues); Best Food Day (wed);

School News (thur); Business News (Special), Religious Page (fri); Business News, Sports Coverage (daily).
Magazines: TV/Entertainment Magazine (fri); Weekly TV Section (S); USA Weekend; Color Comics.

GENERAL MANAGEMENT
General Manager .... John W Kennedy
ADVERTISING
Manager .... Sharon Eudy-Dixon
Manager-Classified .... Larry Norris
NEWS EXECUTIVE
Managing Editor .... Dale Kline
EDITOR AND MANAGER
Sports Editor .... Donnie Biggers

Market Information: Split Run; TMC.
Mechanical available: Offset; Black and 3 ROP colors; insert accepted — preprinted, all types & sizes; page cut-offs — 21½".
Mechanical specifications: Type page 13" x 21½"; E - 6 cols, 2¹/₁₆", ⅛" between; A - 6 cols, 2¹/₁₆", ⅛" between; C - 9 cols, 1³/₈", ¹/₁₆" between.
Commodity consumption: Newsprint 850 short tons; width 27½"; black ink 34,000 pounds; color ink 1,400 pounds; single pages printed 7,800; average pages per issue 24(d), 36(S); single plates used 6,000.
Equipment: EDITORIAL: Front-end hardware — Ap/Macs, Ethernet; Front-end software — QuarkXPress, Baseview; Printers — Ap/Mac LaserPrinter. CLASSIFIED: Front-end hardware — Ap/Macs; Front-end software — Fox; Printers — Ap/Mac LaserPrinters. DISPLAY: Front-end hardware — Ap/Macs; Front-end software — QPS/Ad Builder; Printers — Ap/Mac LaserWriters. PRODUCTION: Typesetters — 2-COM/8400S; Plate exposures — 1-Nu/Ultra Plus Flip Top; Plate processors — 1-Nat/A-340; Production cameras — C/Spartan III, AG/Repromaster 2100; Automatic film processors — LE/24; Color separation equipment (conventional) — 1-BKY/Direct Separation. PRESSROOM: Line 1 — 4-G/Urbanite; Folders — G. MAILROOM: Counter stackers — 1-BG; Inserters and stuffers — MM; Bundle tyer — 1-Bu; Addressing machine —Vista-Data. WIRE SERVICES: News — AP; Receiving dishes — size-10ft, AP. BUSINESS COMPUTERS: Convergent; Applications: Vision Data: Bus, Circ; PCs & micros networked; PCs & main system networked.

DUNN
Harnett County
'90 U.S. Census- 8,336; E&P '96 Est. 7,836

The Daily Record (e-mon to fri)
The Daily Record, 99 W. Broad St.; PO Box 1448, Dunn, NC 28335; tel (910) 891-1234; fax (910) 891-4445.
Circulation: 10,029(e); Sworn Sept. 29, 1995.
Price: 50¢(d).
Advertising: Open inch rate $9.55(e).
News Service: AP. **Politics:** Independent. **Established:** 1950.
Advertising not accepted: Liquor.
Special Editions: Bridal Section, Valentine's Day Gift Guide (Feb); Spring Lawn & Garden/Home Improvement, Spring Car Care (Mar); Hollerin' Tab, Gen. William E. Lee Edition (June); Best of Harnett County (July); Back-to-School, Football (Aug); Fall Lawn & Garden/Home Improvement Tab (Sept); Fall Car Care, Holiday Cookbook (Oct); Holiday Gift Guide (Nov); Christmas Greetings, New Year's Greetings (Dec).
Special Weekly Sections: Best Food Day (wed); Weekend (fri).
Magazine: Home Finder (monthly).

CORPORATE OFFICERS
President .... Bart Adams
Vice Pres .... Maere Kay Lashmit
Vice Pres .... Brent Adams
Vice Pres/Secretary/Treasurer ... Mellicent Adams
GENERAL MANAGEMENT
Publisher/General Manager .... Bart Adams
Business Manager .... Bart Adams
ADVERTISING
Director .... Maere Kay Lashmit
Manager-Classified .... Alice Whitley
MARKETING AND PROMOTION
Manager-Promotion .... Maere Kay Lashmit
TELECOMMUNICATIONS
Audiotex Manager .... Bart Adams
CIRCULATION
Director .... Melissa Dichiera
NEWS EXECUTIVE
Editor .... Bart Adams

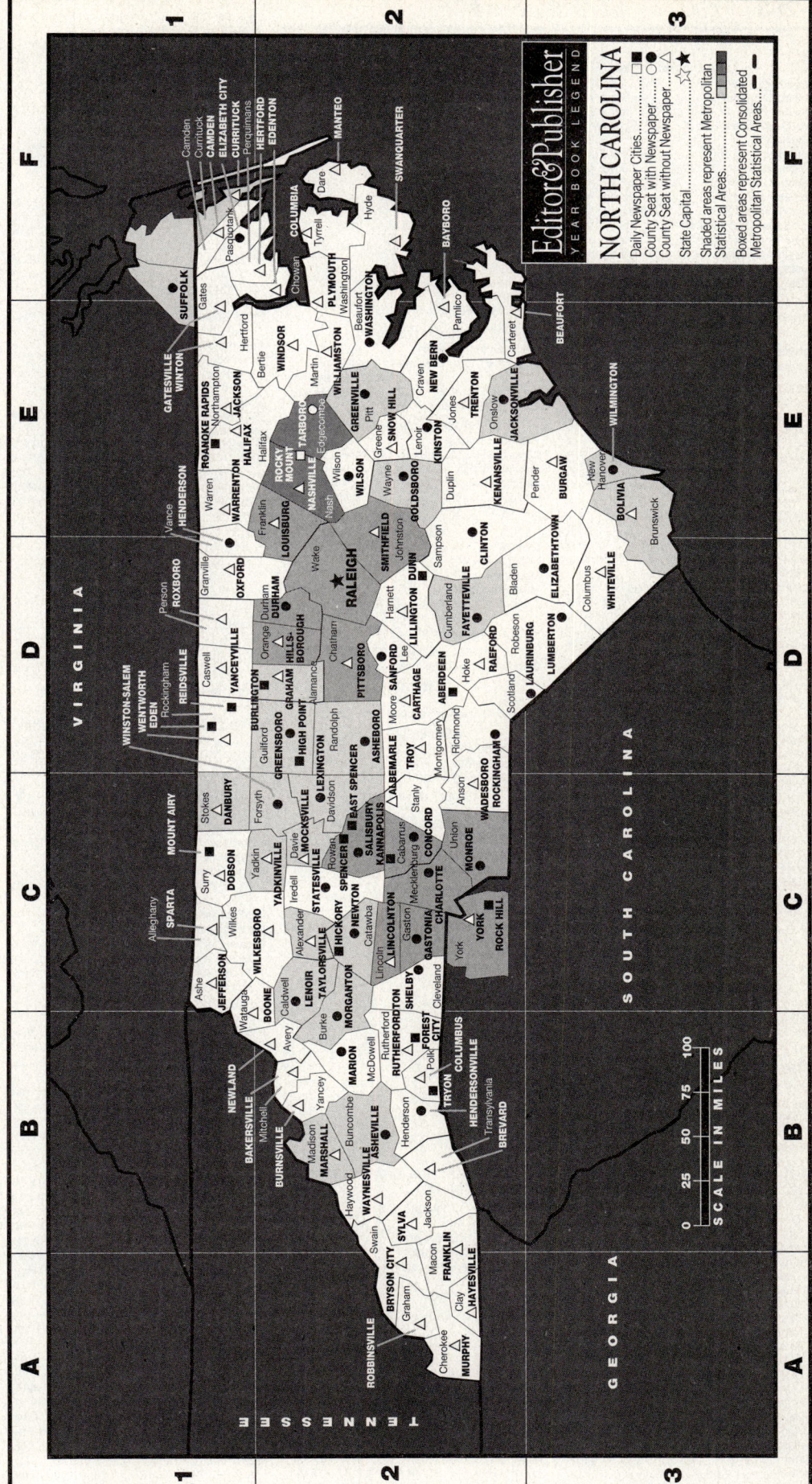

Copyright ©1996 by the Editor & Publisher Co.

EDITORS AND MANAGERS

Amusements Editor Mellicent Adams
Automotive Editor Mellicent Adams
Aviation Editor Merle Stalder
Business/Finance Editor Hoover Adams
Columnist Eric Brodin
Columnist Rev Tom Freeman
Columnist Hoover Adams
Editorial Page Editor Maere Kay Lashmit
Editorial Writer Hoover Adams
Films/Theater Editor Mellicent Adams
Home Furnishings Editor Regina Adams
Radio/Television Editor Hoover Adams
Real Estate Editor Maere Kay Lashmit
Society/Women's Editor Sandra Ashworth
Travel Editor Mellicent Adams

MANAGEMENT INFORMATION SERVICES

Data Processing Manager Sandra Bezgela

PRODUCTION

Foreman-Pressroom Ray Ellington
Foreman-Mailroom Ray Ellington

Market Information: Zoned editions; TMC; Operate audiotex.

Mechanical available: Offset; Black and 3 ROP colors; insert accepted — preprinted, any; page cut-offs — 22¾".

Mechanical specifications: Type page 13¼" x 22"; E - 6 cols, $2\frac{1}{16}$", ⅛" between; A - 6 cols, $2\frac{1}{16}$", ⅛" between; C - 6 cols, $2\frac{1}{16}$", ⅛" between.

Commodity consumption: Newsprint 600 short tons; width 27½"; black ink 2,000 pounds; color ink 500 pounds; single pages printed 4,680; average pages per issue 18(d); single plates used 2,340.

Equipment: EDITORIAL: Front-end hardware — Ap/Mac; Front-end software — Baseview/NewsEdit, QuarkXPress; Printers — Ap/Mac LaserWriter II NTX. CLASSIFIED: Front-end hardware — Mk; Front-end software — Mk. AUDIOTEX: Hardware — EduCom Services Inc.; Supplier name — Bob Howe. DISPLAY: Adv layout systems — Ap/Mac, Multi-Ad/Creator; Front-end hardware — Ap/Mac Centris 650, Ap/Mac Centris 610; Front-end software — Multi-Ad/Creator; Printers — Ap/Mac LaserWriter NTX. PRODUCTION: Pagination software — QuarkXPress; OCR software — Caere/OmniPage Pro; Typesetters — ECR/VRL 36; Plate exposures — 1-Nu; Plate processors — Nat/A-250; Electronic picture desk — Adobe/Photoshop on Ap/Mac; Production cameras — C/Spartan III; Automatic film processors — LE.
PRESSROOM: Line 1 — 6-G/Community; Folders — 1-G/SE. MAILROOM: Counter stackers — BG/Count-O-Veyor; Bundle tyer — 2-Bu; Addressing machine — X. WIRE SERVICES: News — AP. BUSINESS COMPUTERS: Vision Data.

DURHAM

Durham County

'90 U.S. Census- 136,611; E&P '96 Est. 159,227
ABC-CZ (90): 138,645 (HH 56,606)

The Herald-Sun (m-mon to sat; S)

The Herald-Sun, 2828 Pickett Rd.; PO Box 2092, Durham, NC 27702; tel (919) 419-6500; fax (919) 419-6892.

Circulation: 52,589(m); 52,589(m-sat); 64,143(S); ABC Sept. 30, 1995.

Price: 50¢(d); 50¢(sat); $1.50(S); $2.94/wk; $12.75/mo; $153.00/yr.

Advertising: Open inch rate $44.65(m); $44.65(m-sat); $47.40(S). **Representative:** Landon Associates Inc.

News Services: AP, NYT, SHNS, RN, KRT. **Politics:** Independent. **Established:** 1889 (Sun), 1894 (Herald).

Special Editions: Stock Car, Public Education Network, Medical Opportunities (Feb); ACC Tournament, Summer Activities, Home Improvement (Mar); Durham Bulls New Ball Park, Earth Day Celebration, Parenting (Apr); Duke Children's Classic, Car Care (May); Eno Festival (June); NFL Panthers Preview (July); Durham Public Schools Annual Report, Hunting & Fishing, Football (Aug); Literacy Day, Centerfest, Blues Festival, Parade of Homes, New Car Guide (Sept); Home Furnishings (Oct); Basketball Preview, Holiday Gift Guide (Nov); Action, Business Today, Choices in Leisure, Downtown Durham (monthly); Duke University & You; Fun Finder; Listen; Museum of Life and Science Adventures; North Carolina Museum of Art; Perspective Magazine; Senior Post; Senior Source; Senior Times; Spotlight; Think Again; Your Health.

Special Weekly Sections: School (mon); Business (tues); Best Food Day (wed); "Wheels" (Automotive) (thur); "Preview" (Entertainment Tab) (fri); Church Pages, Real Estate (sat); Color Comics, Book Pages, Business Pages, Travel Section "Get-aways", Gardening Page, Life, Body & Mind, Entertainment (S).

Magazines: USA Today, TV Herald (S); Listen Magazine (NPR), Museum Adventures, Downtown, Chamber of Commerce Newsletter (monthly).

Broadcast Affiliate: WDNC-AM.

CORPORATE OFFICERS

Chairman of the Board E T Rollins Jr
Vice Pres/Treasurer/Business Manager James G Alexander
Vice Pres/Secretary David Hughey
Vice Pres/Exec Editor William E N Hawkins

GENERAL MANAGEMENT

Publisher (acting) David Hughey
Director-Sales/Marketing W Toland Barfield
Director-Human Resources Henry Wood
Director-Finance Nancy Robertson
Personnel Director Sandra Gainey
Manager-New Media Bryan Burnett

ADVERTISING

Director Eugene S Bobbitt
Manager-Retail Clark Godfrey
Manager-Classified Robert Bryan
Manager-National Clark Godfrey
General Manager-Chapel Hill Herald Beth Deacon
General Manager-Raleigh Extra Melinda Phillips

MARKETING AND PROMOTION

Director-Corporate Relations Steed Rollins Jr

CIRCULATION

Director David Kirkman
Manager-Education Service Katheryne Corrigan

NEWS EXECUTIVES

Exec Editor William E N Hawkins
Managing Editor Jon C Ham
Assoc Managing Editor Carlton Harrell

EDITORS AND MANAGERS

Amusements Editor Kim Spurr
Body/Mind (Health) Editor Jeff Zimmer
Books Editor Mark Donovan
Business Editor Ward Best
Chapel Hill Herald Editor Mark Schultz
City Editor Bill Stagg
Columnist Carlton Harrell
Columnist Jon C Ham
Education Editor Betsy Hall
Entertainment Preview Editor Kim Spurr
Editorial Page Editor James R Wilson
Films/Theater Editor Kim Spurr
Food Editor Kim Spurr
Graphics Editor John Cole
Hometown Editor Julian Sereno
Librarian Janet Sammons
Life Editor Kim Spurr
Medical Reporter Jeff Zimmer
Music Editor Kim Spurr
News Editor Deborah Jackson
Photo Department Manager Harold Moore
Radio/Television Editor Kim Spurr
Religion Editor Florence Johnston
Sports Editor Jimmy Dupree
State Editor Ron Landfried

MANAGEMENT INFORMATION SERVICES

Director-Info Systems Mary Taylor

PRODUCTION

Director Lewis Kearney
Manager-Press Distribution Jerry Rich
Manager-Pre Press (Night) Jerry Kline
Manager-Camera/Platemaking (Day) Blair Parrott
Manager-Typesetting Jack Barrow

Market Information: Zoned editions; TMC; Electronic edition.

Mechanical available: Offset; Black and 3 ROP colors; insert accepted — preprinted, product sampling, plastic delivery bags; page cut-offs — 22".

Mechanical specifications: Type page 13" x 21¼"; E - 6 cols, 2.03", ⅙" between; A - 6 cols, 2.03", ⅙" between; C - 9 cols, 1.33", ⅛" between.

Commodity consumption: Newsprint 7,600 short tons; widths 54¾", 41¼", 27½", 13¾"; black ink 200,000 pounds; color ink 35,000 pounds; single pages printed 26,000; average pages per issue 36(d), 86(S); single plates used 86,000.

Equipment: EDITORIAL: Front-end hardware — 70-AST/386; Front-end software — Dewar; Other equipment — 1-HP/IIc scanner. CLASSIFIED: Front-end hardware — 10-AST/386; Front-end software — Dewar/Classified. DISPLAY: Adv layout systems — Dewar/Ad Dummy; Front-end hardware — 10-AST/386; Front-end software — Dewar/Ad Dummy; Other equipment — 1-X/7650 scanner. PRODUCTION: Typesetters — 2-AU/APS6; Plate exposures — 2-Nu; Plate processors — 2-Nat; Electronic picture desk — Lf/AP Leaf Picture Desk; Scanners — 1-ECR/Autokon, 1-Microtek; Production cameras — 1-C/Marathon, 1-C/Spartan III; Automatic film processors — 3-LE/LD 24, 1-DP/LC 250; Film transporters — 1-C/Spartan III; Shrink lenses — 1-CK Optical/SQU-7; Color separation equipment (conventional) — 1-CD/636.
PRESSROOM: Line 1 — 6-G/Headliner Offset (3-half decks); Folders — 1-G/3:2; Pasters — Automatic Pasters; Reels and stands — Cline; Press control system — MCPS. MAILROOM: Counter stackers — 1-HL, 3-QWI/300; Inserters and stuffers — 1-MM/227 5-into-1, 1-MM/375-16, 1-MM/335; Bundle tyer — 3-OVL; Addressing machine — 1-Ch. LIBRARY: Electronic — Vu/Text, 1-Meade; Combination — Microfilm & clippings. WIRE SERVICES: News — AP; Stock tables — AP SelectStox; Syndicates — AP, KRT, SHNS, NYT, RN; Receiving dishes — AP. BUSINESS COMPUTERS: HP/3000-925; Applications: CJ: Payroll, Personnel, Accts payable, Gen ledger, Circ, Adv; PCs & main system networked.

EAST SPENCER
See SALISBURY

EDEN

Rockingham County

'90 U.S. Census- 15,238; E&P '96 Est. 14,875

The Daily News (e-mon to fri)

The Daily News, 804 Washington St.; PO Box 308, Eden, NC 27289; tel (910) 623-2155; fax (910) 623-2228. Park Communications Inc. group.

Circulation: 5,925(e); Sworn Sept. 27, 1995.

Price: 35¢(d); $53.00/yr; $47.70/yr (senior citizens).

Advertising: Open inch rate $9.75(e). **Representative:** Landon Associates Inc.

News Services: AP, Universal Press Syndicate, NEA. **Politics:** Independent. **Established:** 1924 (weekly), 1980 (daily).

Not Published: Christmas.

Advertising not accepted: 900 numbers.

Special Editions: Basketball Tab, Kiwanis Week, Jaycee Week, Martin Luther King Page, Tax Time 1996, YMCA Family News Tab (Jan); Rotary Foundation Week, Heart Month, Love Lines, Boy Scout Tab, Bridal Tab (Feb); Girl Scout Camp Fire Week, St. Patrick's Day Sale, Red Cross Page, Progress and Pride Edition, Design-An-Ad Contest, Golden Opportunities, Easter (Mar); Secretaries Day Honor Roll, Spring Racing Tab, Home and Garden Section, RCC Folk Festival Tab, Bike Safety Week (Apr); Mother's Day Special, YMCA Family News Tab, The Great Outdoors, Memorial Signature Page (May); Father's Day Tab, Flag Day, Golden Opportunitites, Graduation Tab, July 4th Tab (June); Women in Progress, YMCA Family News Tab, Back-to-School Tab (July); Football Tab, Reader's Choice, Football Contest, Labor Day, Fall Home & Garden (Aug); Fall Fashion, Fall Racing Tab, Honor Roll of Businesses (Sept); YMCA Family News Tab, Automotive Section, Halloween (Oct); Election Day Edition, Holiday Cookbook, Thanksgiving Day, Holiday Gift Guide (Nov); Holiday Songbook, Basketball Contest, Shop Eden Page, Stocking Stuffer, Holiday Greetings, Chamber of Commerce, Golden Opportunities (Dec).

Special Weekly Sections: Business Directory (Display) (mon); Business Directory (Classified), Public Opinion Poll (tues); Food Pages, Book Review (wed); Church Information, School Lunch Menus, Real Estate Page (thur); Yard Sales, Calendar, Weekend Features, TV Highlights, Pages of Yesteryear (fri).

Magazines: Carolina-Virginia Beacon (sat); Golden Opportunities (quarterly); Real Estate Guide (monthly).

CORPORATE OFFICER

General Manager Eddie Dettmar

ADVERTISING

Manager Maureen Craig

CIRCULATION

Manager Carrie Hutchens

NEWS EXECUTIVES

Editor Eddie Dettmar
Managing Editor Ross Chandler

EDITORS AND MANAGERS

Agriculture Editor Angela Stadler
Automotive Editor Ross Chandler
Business/Finance Editor Angela Stadler
City/Metro Editor Ross Chandler
Editorial Page Editor Ross Chandler
Education Editor Angela Stadler
Entertainment Editor Bill Cresenzo
Farm Editor Angela Stadler
Fashion/Style Editor Bill Cresenzo
Features Editor Bill Cresenzo
Graphics Editor/Art Director Lisa Doss
Health/Medical Editor Angela Stadler
National Editor Ross Chandler
News Editor Ross Chandler
Photo Editor Ross Chandler
Political/Government Editor Ross Chandler
Religion Editor Mickey Powell
Sports Editor Travis Martin
Television/Film Editor Bill Cresenzo
Travel Editor Bill Cresenzo
Wire Editor Ross Chandler
Women's Editor Bill Cresenzo

PRODUCTION

Manager Charles Hopper

Market Information: TMC.

Mechanical available: Offset; Black and 3 ROP colors; insert accepted — preprinted; page cut-offs — 22¾".

Mechanical specifications: Type page 13" x 21½"; E - 6 cols, $2\frac{1}{16}$", ⅛" between; A - 6 cols, $2\frac{1}{16}$", ⅛" between; C - 10 cols, 1⅜", ⅛" between.

Commodity consumption: Newsprint 205 short tons; width 27½"; single pages printed 4,176; average pages per issue 16(d); single plates used 2,000.

Equipment: EDITORIAL: Front-end hardware — Ap/Mac, 10-Mk; Front-end software — QPS 3.3, Baseview/NewsEdit; Printers — Ap/Mac, HP, NewGen, Ap/Mac LaserPrinter NT; Other equipment — Smith-Corona/7000. CLASSIFIED: Front-end hardware — 10-Mk, Ap/Mac; Front-end software — Baseview; Printers — HP. DISPLAY: Adv layout systems — Ap/Mac, 1-COM. PRODUCTION: Pagination software — QPS 3.3; Plate exposures — 1-Mercury/Mark II; Plate processors — 1-WL; Scanners — 5-Ap/Mac; Production cameras — CL/19X24; Automatic film processors — P.
PRESSROOM: Line 1 — 6-G/Community. MAILROOM: Bundle tyer — 1-Bu; Addressing machine — 1-Ch. WIRE SERVICES: News — AP; Syndicates — NEA, King Features, LATS, Columbia, CT, Universal Press. BUSINESS COMPUTERS: IBM; Applications: Vision Data.

ELIZABETH CITY

Pasquotank County

'90 U.S. Census- 14,292; E&P '96 Est. 14,925
ABC-CZ (90): 14,263 (HH 5,324)

The Daily Advance (e-mon to fri; S)

The Daily Advance, 216 S. Poindexter St.; PO Box 588, Elizabeth City, NC 27907-0588; tel (919) 335-0841; fax (919) 335-4415. Thomson Newspapers group.

Circulation: 13,055(e); 13,111(S); ABC Sept. 30, 1995.

Price: 50¢(d); $1.25(S); $9.50/mo.

Advertising: Open inch rate $12.84(e); $12.84 (S). **Representatives:** Thomson Newspapers; Landon Associates Inc.

News Service: AP. **Politics:** Independent. **Established:** 1911.

Special Editions: Tax Guide, Farm Tab, Merchants Against Drugs, Real Estate Guide (Feb); Spring Fashion, Farm Tab, Home Improvement Tab, Real Estate Guide (Mar); Cooking School, Farm Tab, Home-owned Business, Real Estate Guide (Apr); Health Care Tab, Bridal Tab, Farm Tab, OBA/Spring Edition, Riverspree, Real Estate Guide (May); Little League Tab, Historic Albermarle Tab, Farm Tab, Real Estate Guide, Progress Edition (June); Southgate Mall (Standard), OBA Summer Edition, Farm Tab, Real Estate Guide, Coast Guard (July); Back-to-School, Farm Tab, Real Estate Guide, OBA/Summer II, Football Tab (Aug); Crafts

North Carolina I-289

Fair, Farm Tab, Hunting & Fishing, Real Estate Guide (Sept); 4-H Tab, Southgate Mall, Farm Tab, Real Estate Guide, Car Care (Oct); Cookbook, X'mas Gift Guide, Farm Tab, Real Estate Guide (Nov); Songs of Christmas, Basketball Tab, Banker's Guide (Dec); Super Bowl Tab, Farm Tab, Senior Citizens Guide, Real Estate Guide, Manufactured Home Speed (monthly); Health File, Outdoorsman (quarterly).

Special Weekly Sections: School Page (mon); Best Food Days, Newspaper in Education, Business Page (wed); Church Page, TV Section (fri); Best Food Days, Business Page, Buyer-Seller Connection (S).

Magazines: Cover Story-TMC (wed); Currituck Advance, Chowan Advance (fri); Buyer-Seller Connection Shopper (S); Outdoorsman (monthly); Advance Prime Time (Ent.-TV Guide); USA Weekend.

GENERAL MANAGEMENT

Publisher Richard D Brown

ADVERTISING

Director Gregg Ratliff

CIRCULATION

Manager Richard Evans III

NEWS EXECUTIVES

Exec Editor Mike Goodman
Managing Editor Julian Evre

EDITORS AND MANAGERS

Automotive Editor Mike Goodman
Editorial Page Editor Mike Goodman
Fashion/Women's Editor Jeff Hampton
Photo Department Manager Brian McGaughlin
Science Editor Jeff Hampton
Sports Editor Charles Schroeder

PRODUCTION

Manager Sarah Copely
Superintendent-Composing Sarah Copely
Superintendent-Pressroom Pete Gray

Market Information: Zoned editions; TMC.

Mechanical available: Offset; Black and 3 ROP colors; insert accepted — preprinted; page cut-offs — 22¾".

Mechanical specifications: Type page 13¼" x 21½"; E - 6 cols, $2\frac{1}{16}$", ⅛" between; A - 6 cols, $2\frac{1}{16}$", ⅛" between; C - 9 cols, $1\frac{5}{16}$", ⅛" between.

Commodity consumption: Newsprint 1,500 short tons; widths 27½", 32", 34"; black ink 42,000 pounds; color ink 4,000 pounds; single pages printed 7,800; average pages per issue 16(d), 40(S); single plates used 8,500.

Equipment: EDITORIAL: Front-end hardware — Mk/1100 Plus; Front-end software — QuarkXPress 3.3; Printers — V/5060; Other equipment — 4-Ap/Mac Quadra 650, 1-Ap/Power Mac 7100 Image Desk, Lf/AP Leaf Picture Desk. CLASSIFIED: Front-end hardware — 3-Ap/Mac Quadra 605; Front-end software — SII. DISPLAY: Adv layout systems — 2-Ap/Mac Quadra 650; Front-end software — Multi-Ad/Creator 3.70; Printers — V/5060. PRODUCTION: Pagination software — QuarkXPress 3.3; OCR software — Mk, Caere/OmniPage Pro 5.0; Typesetters — 2-V/4000, 2-V/5060; Plate exposures — 2-Nu; Plate processors — Nat; Electronic picture desk — Lf/AP Leaf Picture Desk; Scanners — AG/Plus; Production cameras — 1-R/500; Automatic film processors — 1-RA/20, K, Jobo/Processor; Color separation equipment (conventional) — V/5300. PRESSROOM: Line 1 — 1-G/Urbanite; Line 2 — 4-G/Urbanite; Folders — 1-G/2:1, 1-G/Half, 1-G/Quarter; Press registration system — Duarte/Pin Registration. MAILROOM: Counter stackers — 1-BG; Inserters and stuffers — 1-MM; Bundle tyer — 2-Bu; Addressing machine — Digital Label, KAN/Label; Other mailroom equipment — Mueller/3-Blade Trimmer. COMMUNICATIONS: Facsimile — Nu. WIRE SERVICES: News — AP; Photos — AP; Receiving dishes — size-2ft. BUSINESS COMPUTERS: ATT; Applications: WordPerfect: Accounting, Billing; Lotus 1-2-3; PCs & micros networked; PCs & main system networked.

ELIZABETHTOWN

Bladen County

'90 U.S. Census- 3,704; E&P '96 Est. 3,942

Bladen Daily Journal (m-mon to fri)

Bladen Daily Journal, 109 E. Broad St., Elizabethtown, NC 28337; tel (910) 862-4163; fax (910) 862-4136. Park Communications Inc. group.

Circulation: 3,785(m); Sworn Sept. 29, 1995.

Price: 35¢(d).

Advertising: Open inch rate $6.75(m).

News Service: AP. **Politics:** Independent. **Established:** 1988.

Not Published: Christmas.

Special Editions: Senior Citizen (Jan); Business (Feb); Spring Fashion (Mar); Progress (Apr); Bridal (June); Fitness (July); Back-to-School (Aug); Open House, Cook-off (Sept); Halloween (Oct); Holiday Shopping Guides (Nov); Holiday Shopping Guides (Dec).

Special Weekly Sections: Agriculture (mon); Business (tues); Society (wed); Education (thur); Religion (fri).

CORPORATE OFFICER

President Wright M Thomas

GENERAL MANAGEMENT

Publisher Lynn McLamb
General Manager Lynn McLamb

ADVERTISING

Manager Sharon Barnhill

CIRCULATION

Manager Tammy Perkins

NEWS EXECUTIVE

Managing Editor Michael Simmons

Mechanical available: Black and 3 ROP colors; insert accepted — preprinted; page cut-offs — 22".

Mechanical specifications: Type page 13" x 21½"; E - 6 cols, 2½", ⅛" between; A - 6 cols, 2½", ⅛" between; C - 9 cols, 1⅜", $\frac{1}{11}$" between.

Commodity consumption: single pages printed 2,758; average pages per issue 14(d).

Equipment: EDITORIAL: Front-end hardware — 9-Ap/Mac II. WIRE SERVICES: News — AP; Receiving dishes — AP. BUSINESS COMPUTERS: Ap/Mac; PCs & micros networked.

FAYETTEVILLE

Cumberland County

'90 U.S. Census- 75,695; E&P '96 Est. 94,635
ABC-CZ (90): 190,025 (HH 69,481)

Fayetteville Observer-Times (m-mon to fri; m-sat; S)

Fayetteville Observer-Times, 458 Whitfield St.; PO Box 849, Fayetteville, NC 28306; tel (910) 323-4848; fax (910) 486-3544; e-mail foto@norfolk.infi.net; web site http://www.infi.net/foto.

Circulation: 70,929(m); 86,005(m-sat); 84,479(S); ABC Sept. 30, 1995.

Price: 50¢(d); 50¢(sat); $1.50(S); $10.40/mo; $124.80/yr.

Advertising: Open inch rate $36.22(m); $36.22(m-sat); $42.02(S).

News Services: AP, LAT-WP. **Politics:** Independent. **Established:** 1816 (Observer).

Special Editions: Home & Garden (Feb); Spring Bride, Discover Fayetteville (Mar); Dogwood Festival (Apr); Armed Forces, Manufactured Housing (Classified) (May); Operation Appreciation (June); Discover Robeson (July); Back to School (Aug); ACC Basketball, Holly Day Fair (Nov).

Special Weekly Sections: Health (mon); Family (tues); Food, Youth (wed); Military (thur); Entertainment (fri); Business (S).

Magazines: TV Week (sat); Parade (S).

CORPORATE OFFICERS

President Ramon L Yarborough
Vice Pres Charlotte L Broadwell
Secretary/Treasurer Ashton L Fox
Asst Secretary Anthony G Chavonne

GENERAL MANAGEMENT

Publisher Ramon L Yarborough
General Manager Anthony G Chavonne
Controller Karen Hall
Manager-Credit Amy M Owens
Director-Personnel John Holmes

ADVERTISING

Director Ron Watts
Director-Marketing Ron Watts
Manager-Retail John Jones
Manager-Classified Craig Emerson
Manager-Regional Sales Alyson Cox

MARKETING AND PROMOTION

Manager-Marketing Service Renee Lane

CIRCULATION

Director Ronald G Watts
Manager Dean Richardson
Manager-Sales Christy Cole
Manager-Packaging Paul Rollins

NEWS EXECUTIVES

Editor Charles Broadwell
Managing Editor Michael Arnholt

EDITORS AND MANAGERS

Action Line Editor Bob Horne
Business Editor Catherine Pritchard
City Editor Mike Adams
Columnist Larry Cheek
Columnist Kim Hasty
Copy Desk Chief Charles Rondinelli
Editorial Page Editor Charles Reinken
Education Editor Scott Mooneyham
Features/Lifestyle Editor Chick Jacobs
Graphics Director Suzanne Schubert-Cox
Live Wire (Consumer) Editor Bob Horne
Metro Editor Jeff Couch
Military Affairs Editor Henry Cuningham
News Editor John Rains
Photo Editor Alan English
Religion Editor Earl Vaughan
Sports Editor Howard Ward
State Editor Greg Barnes
Travel Editor Chick Jacobs

MANAGEMENT INFORMATION SERVICES

Data Processing Manager William Steigerwald
Online Editor George Frink

PRODUCTION

Manager W H Owen
Manager-Pressroom Ervin White
Asst Manager Grisson Bain
Asst Manager Ronnie Criminger
Administration-Pressroom Archie Fields

Market Information: Zoned editions; Split Run; TMC.

Mechanical available: Letterpress (direct); Black and 3 ROP colors; insert accepted — preprinted, all; page cut-offs — 22¾".

Mechanical specifications: Type page 13" x 21½"; E - 6 cols, $2\frac{1}{16}$", ⅛" between; A - 6 cols, $2\frac{1}{16}$", ⅛" between; C - 10 cols, $1\frac{3}{16}$", $\frac{1}{16}$" between.

Commodity consumption: Newsprint 11,118 short tons; widths 54", 40½", 27", 13½"; black ink 319,647 pounds; color ink 107,344 pounds; single pages printed 21,786; average pages per issue 50(d), 80.2(sat), 88.8(S); single plates used 85,413.

Equipment: EDITORIAL: Front-end hardware — 63-SII, Tandem/PC CLX-840; Front-end software — SII/Sys 55; Printers — Ap/Mac LaserWriter; Other equipment — Ap/Mac Quadra 800, Ap/Mac II, Ap/Mac fx, HP/ScanJet IIcx, Kk/RFS-2035 Scanner, Nikon/Coolscan. CLASSIFIED: Front-end hardware — 15-SII/PC, Tandem/CLX 840; Front-end software — SII/Sys 55; Other equipment — IBM/PC. DISPLAY: Adv layout systems — SCS/Layout 8000; Front-end hardware — Ap/Mac; Front-end software — Multi-Ad/Creator; Printers — HP/LaserPrinter. PRODUCTION: Typesetters — 3-Au/3850, 3-AU/Soft Pips (Window NT); Platemaking systems — 2-LX/135A, 1-LX/135; Electronic picture desk — 2-Lf/AP Leaf Picture Desk, 10-Nat/Digital Work Station; Scanners — 2-ECR, 1-Pixel Craft; Production cameras — 2-C; Automatic film processors — 2-LE, 7-Konica; Film transporters — 1-Konica; Shrink lenses — 2-CK Optical; Color separation equipment (conventional) — Diadem/Color Scanner. PRESSROOM: Line 1 — 10-G/Mark I (5 Color half decks, 2 color humps); Press drives — 12-Fin; Folders — 1-G/3:2-2:1 Double, 1-G/2:1 Single; Pasters — G; Press control system — Fin/DC; Press registration system — Micro Trak. MAILROOM: Counter stackers — 3-Id/660, 1-Id/2200, 1-QWI/350, 1-S/2200-2; Inserters and stuffers — HI/1372; Bundle tyer — 3-MLN/MLN2A H.5., 2-Dynaric/NP2; Wrapping singles — 3-Id/Bottom Wrapper, 2-QWI/Cobra 3/4 Wrap w/inkjet; Addressing machine — Ch/596, 2-Ch/596; Other mailroom equipment — 1-MM/890 Trimmer & TV Head. 1-BH/A340 Stuffer. LIBRARY: Electronic — SII/Laser. WIRE SERVICES: News — AP Datastream, AP, LAT-WP, AP Datafeatures; Stock tables — AP SelectStox; Receiving dishes — size-10ft, AP. BUSINESS COMPUTERS: IBM/AS-400 F35; Applications: Lotus 1-2-3, INSI: Circ; AdMarc: Profit sharing trust services; PCs & micros networked; PCs & main system networked.

FOREST CITY

Rutherford County

'90 U.S. Census- 7,475; E&P '96 Est. 7,297

The Daily Courier (e-mon to fri)

The Daily Courier, 601 Oak St.; PO Box 1149, Forest City, NC 28043; tel (704) 245-6431; fax (704) 248-2790.

Circulation: 11,482(e); Sworn Sept. 7, 1995.

Price: 25¢(d); $4.00/mo; $60.00/yr.

Advertising: Open inch rate $8.10(e).

News Service: AP. **Established:** 1978.

Not Published: New Year; Thanksgiving; Christmas.

Special Editions: Income Tax (Jan); June Bride (Feb); Lawn & Garden (Mar); Home Improvement (Apr); Graduation (May); Vacation (June); Back-to-School (July); Fall Home Improvement (Sept); Textile (Oct); Christmas Gift Guide (Dec).

CORPORATE OFFICERS

President Ron Paris
Secretary/Treasurer Bill Blair

GENERAL MANAGEMENT

Publisher Ron Paris
Publisher/General Manager Bill Blair

ADVERTISING

Director Jim Deviney
Manager Douglas Flowe
Manager-Classified Deborah Oakes
Manager-Promotion Jim Deviney
Coordinator-Co-op Jim Deviney

CIRCULATION

Director Joyce Chandler

NEWS EXECUTIVES

Editor Ron Paris
Exec Editor Wister Jackson

EDITORS AND MANAGERS

Action Line/Hot Line Editor Ron Paris
Amusements Editor Danny Hirt
Art Director Amy Revis
Automotive/Aviation Editor Danny Hirt
Books Editor Virginia Rucker
Business/Finance Editor Ron Paris
City Editor Amy Revis
Columnist Wister Jackson
Editorial Page Editor Ron Paris
Editorial Writer Wister Jackson
Education Editor Ron Paris
Environment/Ecology Editor Amy Revis
Fashion/Food Editor Virginia Rucker
Features Editor Jean Gordon
Graphics Editor Amy Revis
Health/Medical Editor Amy Revis
Librarian Virginia Rucker
Living/Lifestyle Editor Abbe Byers
National Editor Wister Jackson
News Editor Amy Revis
Photo Department Manager Danny Hirt
Political/Government Editor Wister Jackson
Radio/Television Editor Danny Hirt
Real Estate Wister Jackson
Religion Editor Abbe Byers
Science Editor Ron Paris
Society/Women's Editor Abbe Byers
Sports Editor Tim Brown
State Editor Wister Jackson
Travel Editor Wister Jackson
Travel Editor Virginia Rucker
Women's Editor Abbe Byers

MANAGEMENT INFORMATION SERVICES

Data Processing Manager Lynn Watson

PRODUCTION

Manager/Foreman-Composing Pam Dixon
Foreman-Pressroom Randy Fish

Market Information: TMC.

Mechanical available: Offset; Black and 3 ROP colors; insert accepted — preprinted; page cut-offs — 21".

Mechanical specifications: Type page 13" x 21"; E - 6 cols, $2\frac{1}{16}$", ⅛" between; A - 6 cols, $2\frac{1}{16}$", ⅛" between; C - 9 cols, 1⅜", $\frac{1}{16}$" between.

Commodity consumption: Newsprint 280 short tons; width 27½"; black ink 7,200 pounds; color ink 960 pounds; single pages printed 4,680; average pages per issue 18(d); single plates used 2,500.

Equipment: EDITORIAL: Front-end hardware — Ap/Mac; Front-end software — Ap/Mac; Printers — 4-Ap/Mac. CLASSIFIED: Front-end hardware — Ap/Mac; Front-end software — Ap/Mac; Printers — Okidata. DISPLAY: Adv layout systems — Mk, 2-Ap/Mac; Front-end hardware — Mk; Front-end software — Ap/Mac; Printers — 2-Ap/Mac LaserPrinter, Umax. PRODUCTION: Pagination software — Ap/Mac; Typesetters — 4-Ap/Mac Laser; Plate exposures — Amerigraph; Plate processors — Nat; Production cameras — Acti; Automatic film processors — P. PRESSROOM: Line 1 — 6-G; Folders — G. MAILROOM: Inserters and stuffers — MM; Addressing machine — Versyss. LIBRARY: Electronic — Dukane/Microfilm reader. COMMUNICATIONS: Facsimile — HP. WIRE SERVICES: News — AP; Receiving dishes — size-2ft, AP. BUSINESS COMPUTERS: 3-Ap/Mac, Contel; PCs & micros networked; PCs & main system networked.

I-290 North Carolina

GASTONIA

Gaston County

'90 U.S. Census- 54,732; E&P '96 Est. 63,805
ABC-CZ (90): 101,239 (HH 38,386)

The Gaston Gazette

(m-mon to sat; S)

The Gaston Gazette, 2500 E. Franklin Blvd. (28054); PO Box 1538, Gastonia, NC 28053; tel (704) 864-3291; fax (704) 867-6988. Freedom Communications Inc. group.

Circulation: 38,075(m); 38,075(m-sat); 43,204(S); ABC Sept. 30, 1995.

Price: 50¢(d); 50¢(sat); $1.25(S); $8.50/mo; $102.00/yr.

Advertising: Open inch rate $29.24(m); $29.24(m-sat); $29.24(S). **Representatives:** Landon Associates Inc.; Papert Companies.

News Services: AP, SHNS, NYT. **Established:** 1880.

Special Editions: Tax (Jan); Boy/Girl Scouts, Design-An-Ad (Feb); Realtor, Spring Fashion, Expo Tab, Home & Garden, Business Card (Mar); Swimsuit, American Home Week (Apr); Vacation Tab (May); Graduation, Bride, Car Care (June); Answer Book (July); Football, Back-to-School (Aug); Fall Fashion, Home & Garden (Sept); Bride, Car Care, Textile, Pet Care, New Cars, Fish Camp Jam (Oct); NBA Preview (Nov); Christmas Gift Guide (Dec).

Magazines: Extra (TMC publication), Eastern Gazette (wed); Home (fri); Preview, USA Weekend, Lincoln Gazette (S).

GENERAL MANAGEMENT

Publisher Mike McMillan

ADVERTISING

Director Earl K Brackett

TELECOMMUNICATIONS

Audiotex Manager Jim Bretzius

CIRCULATION

Director Sam Ashe

NEWS EXECUTIVES

Editor Jennie Lambert
Managing Editor Skip Foster

EDITORS AND MANAGERS

Action Line Editor Dot Wallace
Amusements Editor Heather Hay
Art Director Hunter Bretzias
Automotive Editor Jeff Owens
Business Editor Nancy Moore
City Editor John Jimison
Editorial Page Editor Barry Smith
Editorial Writer Barry Smith
Education Editor Kristen Scheve
Environmental Editor Bo Peterson
Farm/Agriculture Editor Mike Carr
Features Editor Heather Hay
Films/Theater Editor Heather Hay
Graphics Editor Hunter Bretzias
Health/Medical Editor Heather Hay
Librarian Dot Wallace
Music Editor Heather Hay
National Editor Nancy Moore
News Editor Barry Bridges
Photo Editor Jamey Reynolds
Political/Government Editor Nancy Moore
Radio/Television Editor Heather Hay
Real Estate Editor Nancy Moore
Regional Editor Will MacDonald
Religion Editor Heather Hay
Science/Technology Editor Bo Peterson
Sports Editor Bo Peterson
Teen-Age/Youth Editor Heather Hay
Travel Editor Heather Hay
Wire Editor John Jimison
Women's Editor Heather Hay

PRODUCTION

Manager Ray Martin
Foreman-Pressroom James Cook

Market Information: TMC; ADS; Operate audiotex.

Mechanical available: Offset; Black and 3 ROP colors; insert accepted — preprinted; page cutoffs — 22¾".

Mechanical specifications: Type page 13" x 23"; E - 6 cols, 2 1/16", ⅛" between; A - 6 cols, 2 1/16", ⅛" between; C - 8 cols, 1 9/16", 1/16" between.

Commodity consumption: Newsprint 4,731 short tons; widths 55", 41¼", 27½"; black ink 89,500 pounds; color ink 31,700 pounds; single pages printed 16,000; average pages per issue 40(d), 68(S); single plates used 40,000.

Equipment: EDITORIAL: Front-end hardware — Dewar/Disc, 21-PC/286, 9-PC/386, 7-PC/386 file server. CLASSIFIED: Front-end hardware — Dewar. AUDIOTEX: Hardware — Brite Voice Systems; Software — Brite Voice Systems; Supplier name — Brite Voice Systems. DISPLAY: Adv layout systems — Dewar, 3-PC/286. PRODUCTION: Typesetters — 2-Tegra/XP-1000, Tegra/5510; Platemaking systems — 1-CD; Plate exposures — 2-Nu/Ultra-Plus; Plate processors — 1-Nat/A250; Production cameras — 1-B/Caravel, 1-C/Spartan III; Automatic film processors — 1-LE/18; Film transporters — 1-C; Digital color separation equipment — CD/626.
PRESSROOM: Line 1 — 5-HI/1650; Folders — 1-HI; Pasters — 5-MEG. MAILROOM: Counter stackers — 1-QWI, 1-HL; Inserters and stuffers — GMA; Bundle tyer — 2-MLN; Wrapping singles — 1-NJP; Addressing machine — 1-X/542-090. COMMUNICATIONS: Facsimile — 2-Sharp/5210. WIRE SERVICES: News — AP; Stock tables — AP; Syndicates — AP, NEA, AP Datafeatures, SHNS, NYT, CNS; Receiving dishes — AP. BUSINESS COMPUTERS: 1-IBM/Sys 36, 5-IBM/PS 2 Model 30; Applications: Circ, Adv billing, Accts receivable, Gen ledger, Accts payable, Payroll; PCs & micros networked; PCs & main system networked.

GOLDSBORO

Wayne County

'90 U.S. Census- 40,709; E&P '96 Est. 51,957
ABC-CZ (90): 40,216 (HH 13,723)

Goldsboro News-Argus

(e-mon to fri; S)

Goldsboro News-Argus, 310 N. Berkeley Blvd.; PO Box 10629 (27532), Goldsboro, NC 27530; tel (919) 778-2211; fax (919) 778-9891.

Circulation: 22,120(e); 24,794(S); ABC Sept. 30, 1995.

Price: 50¢(d); $1.00(S); $7.75/mo.

Advertising: Open inch rate $13.00(e); $13.00(S). **Representative:** Landon Associates Inc.

News Service: AP. **Politics:** Independent. **Established:** 1885.

Not Published: Independence Day; Christmas.

Advertising not accepted: Alcoholic beverages except beer and wine.

Special Editions: Bridal (Jan); Progress (Feb).

Special Weekly Sections: The Extra (TMC) (tues); Food (wed); Health Pages (thur); TV Showtime (fri); Real Estate Update, Military Page (S); Business Page (daily).

Magazine: USA Weekend (S).

CORPORATE OFFICERS

President Hal Tanner Jr
Vice Pres Eugene Price
Secretary/Treasurer Janet R Walston

GENERAL MANAGEMENT

Publisher Hal Tanner Jr
Business Manager Janet R Walston
Manager-Credit Janet R Walston
Purchasing Agent Janet R Walston

ADVERTISING

Director Nelson Mitchell
Manager-National Harold Caldwell
Manager-Classified Paul Worrell

CIRCULATION

Director Neal Tachney

NEWS EXECUTIVE

Editor Mike Rouse

EDITORS AND MANAGERS

Amusements Editor Winkie Lee
Automotive Editor James Meachen
Aviation/Books Editor Eugene Price
Book Editor Winkie Lee
Business Editor James Meachen
City Editor Robert Johnson
Editorial Page Editor Eugene Price
Education Editor Stan Alleyne
Environmental Editor Karinne Young
Fashion Editor Becky Barclay
Features Editor Winkie Lee
Films/Theater Editor Winkie Lee
Food/Home Furnishings Editor Becky Barclay
Graphics Editor James Meachen
Health/Medical Editor Stan Alleyne
Living/Lifestyle Editor Becky Barclay
News Editor James Meachen
Political/Government Editor Dennis Hill
Photo Department Manager Kaye Farmer
Religion Editor Linda Luck
Science Editor Robert Johnson
Society/Women's Editor Becky Barclay
Systems Editor David Rouse
Teen-Age/Youth Editor Winkie Lee
Travel Editor Winkie Lee

PRODUCTION

Manager Eugene Westbrook

Market Information: TMC.

Mechanical available: Offset; Black and 3 ROP colors; insert accepted — preprinted; page cutoffs — 22½".

Mechanical specifications: Type page 13" x 21½"; E - 6 cols, 2 1/16", ⅛" between; A - 6 cols, 2 1/16", ⅛" between; C - 9 cols, 1⅜", 1/16" between.

Commodity consumption: Newsprint 1,631 short tons; widths 27½", 13¾"; black ink 22,610 pounds; color ink 5,295 pounds; single pages printed 10,784; average pages per issue 32(d), 68(S); single plates used 18,500.

Equipment: EDITORIAL: Front-end hardware — 18-COM/Intrepid, 15-Ap/Mac; Front-end software — COM, Baseview; Printers — COM/KSR, Printronix, Ap/Mac LaserWriter II, HP/LaserJet; Other equipment — 1-Ap/Mac IIcx, Lf/AP Leaf Picture Desk, Lf/Leafscan 35. CLASSIFIED: Front-end hardware — 8-COM/Intrepid. DISPLAY: Adv layout systems — Baseview/Ad Director; Front-end hardware — 1-Ap/Mac Quadra 650, 1-Ap/Mac; Front-end software — Baseview; Printers — 1-LaserMaster/Unity 1000. PRODUCTION: Pagination software — Baseview 3.0; OCR software — Caere/Omni-Page; Typesetters — 2-COM/8600, 2-ECR/Autokon 1000, 5-Ap/Mac, 1-PC, 1-Laser-Master/Unity 1000, 1-LaserMaster/1200 XL-O, ECR/Scriptsetter VRL 36; Plate exposures — 2-Nu; Plate processors — Braham; Scanners — 4-Microtek/II; Production cameras — C/Spartan II; Automatic film processors — P/ML-26, 2-C/650; Shrink lenses — 1-Alan.
PRESSROOM: Line 1 — 6-G/Urbanite(w/Color deck). MAILROOM: Counter stackers — Fg/H-500; Inserters and stuffers — 2-MM/2275 (4-into-1); Bundle tyer — 2-MLN/ML2; Addressing machine — 1-Ch/569; Mailroom control system — 1-MM/1509 Minuteman Saddle Stitches; Other mailroom equipment — 1-Fg/Bottom Wrap. WIRE SERVICES: News — AP Datastream; Photos — AP; Stock tables — AP; Syndicates — NEA; Receiving dishes — AP. BUSINESS COMPUTERS: Sun/Sparc server 670 MP; Applications: Payroll, Accts payable, Accts receivable, Gen ledger, Adv billing, Circ.

GREENSBORO

Guilford County

'90 U.S. Census- 183,521; E&P '96 Est. 209,899
ABC-NDM (90): 278,438 (HH 110,381)

News & Record

(m-mon to fri; m-sat; S)

News & Record, 200 E. Market St.; PO Box 20848, Greensboro, NC 27420; tel (910) 373-7000; fax (910) 373-7183; e-mail edpage@nr.infi.net; web site http://www.infi.net/nr/triad.html. Landmark Communications Inc. group.

Circulation: 95,973(m); 117,006(m-sat); 124,031(S); ABC Sept. 30, 1995.

Price: 50¢(d); 50¢(sat); $1.25(S); $2.70/wk (carrier); $44.85/3mo (mail).

Advertising: Open inch rate $58.20(m); $65.20(m-sat); $65.20(S).

News Services: AP, NYT, LAT-WP, SHNS. **Politics:** Independent. **Established:** 1890 (Record), 1909 (News), 1986 (News & Record).

Advertising not accepted: Bingo; Surrogate mothers; Fortune telling; Spiritualism; Palm reading; Clairvoyance; Mail-order medical merchandise.

Special Editions: Economic Review & Forecast, The Business Weekly (TBW) (Jan); Bridal, Health Guide (Feb); Spring Fashion, Home & Garden, ACC Tournament (TBW), Housing Outlook (Mar); Auto Showcase, Vacation & Travel, Sports Extra-Greater Greenboro Open (Apr); Parade of Homes, Discover the Triad (May); Coupon Days (July); Sports Extra-Pro & College Football, Prep Football, Back-to-School (Aug); Fall Fashion, Showcase of Homes (Sept); Auto Show (Oct); Pro & College Basketball Preview, Holiday Focus I (Nov); Holiday Focus II (Dec); Newcomer's Guide, Visitor's Guide (Spring & Fall).

Special Weekly Sections: Health-Life (tues); US Express (TMC), Life, Food, Fashion (wed); Life (Health & Fitness) (fri); Garden-Life (sat); Real Estate, Travel, Book Review (S).

Magazines: Weekend (fri); "TV Week" Tab (own, newsprint) (sat); Parade (S).

CORPORATE OFFICERS

Board Chairman Frank Batten
President Van King
Editor Patrick A Yack

GENERAL MANAGEMENT

Publisher Van King
Manager-Human Resources Jane Sharp
Business Manager Sarah Baker

ADVERTISING

Director Kathy Lambeth
Manager-Classified Vivienne Mays

TELECOMMUNICATIONS

Audiotex Manager David Stroble

CIRCULATION

Director Mark Fentress
Manager David Berrier
Distribution Manager-Home Delivery Tim Howard
Manager-Distribution/Single Copy/TMC Byron Ritter

NEWS EXECUTIVE

Editor Patrick A Yack

EDITORS AND MANAGERS

Asst Manager-Technology Bob Pettit
Books Editor Ron Miller
Business/Finance Editor Mark Sutton
Editorial Page Editor David DuBuisson
Librarian Robert L Beall
Life Editor Ann Alexander
Metro Editor Tom Corrigan
Deputy Metro Editor Ed Williams
National Editor Frank Oathoudt
News Editor Cindy Loman
Director-Photography Al Spicer
Sports Editor Allen Johnson

MANAGEMENT INFORMATION SERVICES

Data Processing Manager Neil Rothrock
Online Manager Christopher Fields

PRODUCTION

Director David Reno
Manager-Pressroom Dennis Clark
Manager-Platemaking Dennis Clark
Manager-Mailroom Dennis Creamer

Market Information: Zoned editions; Split Run; TMC; ADS; Operate database; Operate audiotex; Electronic edition.

Mechanical available: Offset; Black and 3 ROP colors; insert accepted — preprinted, hi fi printed by newspaper; page cut-offs — 22¾".

Mechanical specifications: Type page 13" x 21½"; E - 6 cols, 2 1/16", ⅛" between; A - 6 cols, 2 1/16", ⅛" between; C - 10 cols, 1¼", 1/16" between.

Commodity consumption: Newsprint 17,000 short tons; widths 54.5", 40⅞", 27¼"; black ink 382,548 pounds; color ink 205,105 pounds; single pages printed 27,254; average pages per issue 45(d), 48(sat), 100(S); single plates used 148,130.

Equipment: EDITORIAL: Front-end hardware — SII/Sys 55, NEC/820 PC, 130-SII/Coyote QB, 17-SII/Coyote 22; Front-end software — SII/Sys 55; Printers — 2-Centronics, 1-HP/LaserJet. CLASSIFIED: Front-end hardware — SII/Sys 55, 22-SII/Coyote QB; Front-end software — SII/Sys 55; Printers — 1-TI/810. AUDIOTEX: Hardware — Intec/24 EX modem, ATT/NFX laptop; Supplier name — Voice News Network. DISPLAY: Adv layout systems — SII/Layout; Front-end hardware — 8-III/AMS 4500, 2-III/AMS 4500 (color); Front-end software — SII, III. PRODUCTION: Pagination software — SII/INL, SII/IAL, QuarkXPress; OCR software — Expervision, TypeReader; Typesetters — 2-III/Laser Imager 3810, III/3850; Plate exposures — 1-KFM/Exposure, 2-KFM/Plate Bender, 2-Nu/Flip Top UP; Plate processors — MAS/W03600, 1-COM; Electronic picture desk — Lf/AP Leaf Picture Desk; Scanners — 1-III/3700, 1-III/3650; Production cameras — 1-C/Marathon, 1-C/Newspager, 1-C/Spartan III; Automatic film processors — LE/AQ-1800, 1-LE/LD 1800, 1-Konica; Film transporters — 2-C; Shrink lenses — 1-Kamerak; Color separation equipment (conventional) — RZ/Diamdem 2205, Ap/Mac, Adobe/Photoshop, Polaroid/SprintScan; Digital color separation equipment — Ap/Mac, III.
PRESSROOM: Line 1 — 13-G/Metro; Folders — 2-G/Double; Pasters — 13-G/DTP; Reels and stands — 13-G/Reels. MAILROOM: Counter stackers — 5-HL/Monitor; Inserters and stuffers — 2-HI/1472; Bundle tyer — 9-Power Strap, 3-Strapex; Addressing machine — 1-Ch, MM/Quarterfolder; Mailroom control system — IBM/AS-400. In-house. LIBRARY: Electronic — 2-Diebold/7300 Series, Vu/Text; Combination — 2-Automatic/filing machines. WIRE SERVICES: News — AP, NYT, LAT-WP, TV Data, PR Newswire, KRT, Bloomberg; Photos — AP; Stock tables — AP SelectStox; Receiving dishes — size-3m, AP. BUSINESS COMPUTERS: 1-IBM/AS-400 B45; Applications: Lotus, Microsoft/Excel; PCs & main system networked.

GREENVILLE
Pitt County

'90 U.S. Census- 44,972; E&P '96 Est. 56,609
ABC-CZ (90): 44,972 (HH 17,017)

The Daily Reflector
(m-mon to sat; S)

The Daily Reflector, 209 Cotanche St.; PO Box 1967, Greenville, NC 27835; tel (919) 752-6166; fax (919) 752-9583.

Circulation: 18,527(m); 18,527(m-sat); 21,327(S); ABC Sept. 30, 1995.

Price: 50¢(d); 50¢(sat); $1.00(S); $9.00/mo; $104.00/yr.

Advertising: Open inch rate $12.25(m); $12.25(m-sat); $12.25(S). **Representative:** Papert Companies.

News Services: AP, KRT. **Politics:** Independent. **Established:** 1882.

Not Published: Christmas.

Special Editions: Bridal Planner (Jan); Money (Feb); Home & Garden, NASCAR (Mar); Parenting, Graduation (May); M. Jordan Golf Classic (June); Agri-Business (July); Fall Fashion, Pitt County Fact Book (Sept); Community Business (Oct); Holiday Gift Guide (Nov).

Special Weekly Sections: Best Food Day (wed); Church (sat); Building (S).

Magazines: Workweek (mon); East Magazine (thur); Pirate Gameday (during football season) (sat); Parade, Color Comics (S).

CORPORATE OFFICERS

Chairman David Jordan Whichard II
Vice Chairman/Secretary John S Whichard
President David Jordan Whichard III

GENERAL MANAGEMENT

Publisher David Jordan Whichard III
Director-Administration/Personnel Barbara Jarvis

ADVERTISING

Director J Tim Holt
Manager-National Janiece Joyner

MARKETING AND PROMOTION

Director-Marketing J Tim Holt
Manager-Promotion Lynn Sulliven

CIRCULATION

Director Richard L Bryant

NEWS EXECUTIVES

Exec Editor Al Clark
Senior Assoc Editor Alvin Taylor

EDITORS AND MANAGERS

Business Editor Stuart Savage
City Editor Kathy Harrelson
Community News Editor Tom Baines
Copy Desk Chief Greg Laudick
Editorial Page Editor Mary C Schulken
Features Editor Lori Goodson
Lifestyle Editor Rosalie Trotman
News Editor Melvin Lang
Photo Editor Cliff Hollis
Senior Sports Writer/Columnist Elwood Peele
Special Sections Editor Kim Jones Grizzard
Sports News Editor Mike Grizzard

PRODUCTION

Manager-Pre Press/Systems Tim Jones
Manager-Press/Post Press Brooks Best
Manager Tim Sabo
Manager-Press Daniel Coyne

Market Information: TMC.

Mechanical available: Offset; Black and 3 ROP colors; insert accepted — preprinted; page cut-offs — 22¾".

Mechanical specifications: Type page 13" x 21½"; E - 6 cols, 2.04", ⅙" between; A - 6 cols, 2.04", ⅙" between; C - 9 cols, 1.33", ⅛" between.

Commodity consumption: Newsprint 1,917 short tons; width 27½"; black ink 58,830 pounds; color ink 9,070 pounds; single pages printed 13,318; average pages per issue 30(d), 75(S); single plates used 27,200.

Equipment: EDITORIAL: Front-end hardware — Ap/Mac SunClassic; Front-end software — DTI/Sybase, DTI/Ushare, DTI/PageSpeed, DTI/Speedplanner; Printers — Ap/Mac LaserWriters. CLASSIFIED: Front-end hardware — Ap/Mac; Front-end software — DTI/ClassSpeed, DTI/ClassPagination; Printers — NewGen. DISPLAY: Adv layout systems — DTI/AdSpeed; Front-end hardware — 4-Ap/Mac; Front-end software — DTI; Printers — 2-Ap/Mac LaserWriter. PRODUCTION: Pagination software — DTI/PageSpeed; OCR software — Caere/OmniPage 5.0; Typesetters — 2-NewGen/LaserWriter, 2-ECR/VRL36 Imagesetter; Plate exposures — 1-Nu/Flip Top FT40L, 1-Nu/Flip Top; Plate processors — 1-Nat/Subtrac 26; Electronic picture desk — Lf/AP Leaf Picture Desk; Scanners — 1-ECR, 2-Umax/1260, Lf/Leafscan 35, 2-Polaroid/SprintScan 35; Production cameras — 1-C/Spartan III; Automatic film processors — LE; Shrink lenses — 1-Alan; Color separation equipment (conventional) — Lf; Digital color separation equipment — ECR/RIP.
PRESSROOM: Line 1 — 9-G/Urbanite; Folders — 1-G. MAILROOM: Counter stackers — 1-QWI; Inserters and stuffers — 2-MM/4-Station; Bundle tyer — 2-MLN; Other mailroom equipment — MM/Minuteman ¼ folder-stitcher-trimmer. LIBRARY: Electronic — DTI/Editorial Software. COMMUNICATIONS: Digital ad delivery system — AP AdSend. WIRE SERVICES: News — AP Datastream, AP Datafeatures; Stock tables — AP SelectStox; Receiving dishes — size-10ft, AP. BUSINESS COMPUTERS: Sun/Sparc server 670mp; Applications: PBS: Adv, Circ, Mgmt, Gen ledger.

HENDERSON
Vance County

'90 U.S. Census- 15,655; E&P '96 Est. 18,270
ABC-CZ (90): 17,029 (HH 6,526)

Henderson Daily Dispatch
(m-tues to sat; S)

Henderson Daily Dispatch, 304 S. Chestnut St.; PO Box 908, Henderson, NC 27536; tel (919) 492-4001; fax (919) 430-0125. Paxton Media group.

Circulation: 9,357(m); 9,357(m-sat); 9,234(S); ABC Sept. 30, 1995.

Price: 50¢(d); 50¢(sat); $1.00(S); $1.38/wk; $7.00/mo; $102.00/yr.

Advertising: Open inch rate $11.88(m); $11.88(m-sat); $11.88(S). **Representative:** Landon Associates Inc.

News Service: AP. **Politics:** Independent. **Established:** 1914.

Note: Effective April 2, 1995, this publication changed its publishing plan from (e-mon to fri; m-sat) to (m-tues to sat; S).

Not Published: Christmas.

Advertising not accepted: Liquor.

Special Editions: Tax Supplement, Bridal Section (Jan); Best of Vance County (Feb); Pillars, Spring Fashion (Mar); Recipe Section, Spring Home & Garden (Apr); Trade Show, Spring/Summer Car Care, Memorial Lake Edition (May); Graduation Section (June); July 4 Lake Edition, Health & Fitness, Funeral & Estate Planning (July); Back-to-School, Parade of Homes, Fall Sports (Aug); Colorfest, Fall Home Improvement, Football Contest (Sept); Christmas Gift Guide (Nov); Winter Sports, Christmas Greetings (Dec).

Special Weekly Section: Best Food Day (wed).

Magazine: TV Week (fri).

CORPORATE OFFICERS

President Fred Paxton
Vice Pres/Treasurer David M Paxton
Vice Pres/Secretary Jim Paxton
Vice Pres Richard Paxton

GENERAL MANAGEMENT

Publisher Rick Bean

ADVERTISING

Director Deborah Tuck

CIRCULATION

Manager Ken Pugh

NEWS EXECUTIVE

Managing Editor James Dutra

EDITORS AND MANAGERS

Editorial Page Editor James Dutra
Photo Department Manager Janet Blackmon Morgan
Regional Editor Katherine Joyce
Society Editor Laverne Jeffries
Sports Editor Gray Wilkerson

PRODUCTION

Foreman-Pressroom Jackie Peoples
Foreman-Composing Catherine Jefferson

Market Information: TMC.

Mechanical available: Offset; Black and 3 ROP colors; insert accepted — preprinted, any; page cut-offs — 22¾".

Mechanical specifications: Type page 13" x 21½"; E - 6 cols, 2.04", .15" between; A - 6 cols, 2.04", .15" between; C - 8 cols, 1½", .15" between.

Commodity consumption: Newsprint 550 short tons; width 27½"; black ink 39,000 pounds; color ink 4,000 pounds; single pages printed 7,500; average pages per issue 24(d); single plates used 9,000.

Equipment: EDITORIAL: Front-end hardware — Ap/Mac SE; Front-end software — DTI/NewsSpeed, DTI/PageSpeed; Printers — Ap/Mac LaserWriter II NTX, Ultra/94E; Other equipment — Sun/Sparc station. CLASSIFIED: Front-end hardware — Ap/Mac LC III; Front-end software — DTI/ClassSpeed; Printers — Ap/Mac LaserWriter II NTX, Ultra/94E. DISPLAY: Adv layout systems — Speedplanner; Front-end hardware — Ap/Mac II; Front-end software — DTI/AdSpeed; Printers — Ap/Mac LaserWriter II NTX. PRODUCTION: Plate exposures — 1-Nu; Plate processors — 1-Nat/A-250; Scanners — 1-Ap/Mac Scanner 300 dpi, Umax/1200 dpi flatbed scanner; Production cameras — 1-DAI/C-24-D-LA; Automatic film processors — 1-P/26RA; Shrink lenses — 1-CK Optical/(2½ - 7½% Squeeze); Digital color separation equipment — 1-Kk/2035 AF 2,000 dpi.
PRESSROOM: Line 1 — 7-G/Community; Folders — 1-G. MAILROOM: Counter stackers — 1-PPK; Inserters and stuffers — 1-MM/227-E; Bundle tyer — 1-Bu/Tyer; Wrapping singles — 1-MLN/Spirit; Addressing machine — 1-Ch/4-up. WIRE SERVICES: News — AP; Photos — AP Photostream; Receiving dishes — size-10ft, AP. BUSINESS COMPUTERS: 1-DEC/486 50 MHz fileserver; Applications: Vision Data; PCs & micros networked; PCs & main system networked.

HENDERSONVILLE
Henderson County

'90 U.S. Census- 7,284; E&P '96 Est. 7,872
ABC-CZ (90): 7,284 (HH 3,192)

The Times-News
(m-mon to sat; S)

The Times-News, 1717 Four Seasons Blvd.; PO Box 490, Hendersonville, NC 28793; tel (704) 692-0505; fax (704) 692-2319. New York Times Co. group.

Circulation: 21,526(m); 21,526(m-sat); 20,922(S); ABC Sept. 30, 1995.

Price: 25¢(d); 25¢(sat); 50¢(S); $8.25/mo; $99.00/yr.

Advertising: Open inch rate $16.95(m); $16.95(m-sat); $16.95(S). **Representative:** Landon Associates Inc.

News Service: AP. **Politics:** Independent-Democrat. **Established:** 1927.

Special Editions: January Jubilee (Jan); Almanac, Brides (Feb); Spring (Mar); Spring Tour of Homes (Apr); Cookbook (May); Retirement (June); Football (Aug); Health & Fitness (Sept); Home & Car Care, Motorama (Oct); Holiday Gift Guide (Nov); Last Minute Gift Guide (Dec).

Special Weekly Sections: Best Food Day (wed); Church Directory (sat); Travel Feature (S).

Magazines: TV Book (sat); Parade (S).

CORPORATE OFFICER

President James C Weeks

GENERAL MANAGEMENT

Publisher Paul Bairstow

ADVERTISING

Director Mike Sternberg

TELECOMMUNICATIONS

Audiotex Manager Mike Sternberg

CIRCULATION

Director Ned Cowan

NEWS EXECUTIVE

Editor Joy Franklin

EDITORS AND MANAGERS

City Editor Penny Leigh
Community Editor Sally Cook Anderson
Lifestyle Editor Sally Cook Anderson
News Editor Dan Sullivan
Sports Editor Bob Dalton

MANAGEMENT INFORMATION SERVICES

Data Processing Manager Sandra Prince

PRODUCTION

Foreman-Pressroom J R Blackwell
Manager-Systems/Data Processin Sandra Prince

Market Information: TMC; Operate audiotex.

Mechanical available: Offset; Black and 3 ROP colors; insert accepted — preprinted; page cut-offs — 22¾".

Mechanical specifications: Type page 13" x 21½"; E - 6 cols, 2¹⁄₁₆", ⅛" between; A - 6 cols, 2¹⁄₁₆", ⅛" between; C - 9 cols, 1⅜", ¹⁄₁₆" between.

Commodity consumption: Newsprint 2,000 short tons; width 27", 13½"; black ink 60,000 pounds; color ink 2,000 pounds; single pages printed 13,500; average pages per issue 34(d), 54(S); single plates used 29,300.

Equipment: EDITORIAL: Front-end hardware — 2-AT/7000, 15-AT/VDT, Ap/Mac IIsi; Printers — 2-MOD/40-line; Other equipment — Ap/Mac IIci, Lf/Leafscan 35, Lf/AP Leaf Picture Desk, Ap/Mac Quadra 650. CLASSIFIED: Front-end hardware — AT/7000, 4-AT/VDT. AUDIOTEX: Hardware — Brite Voice Systems. DISPLAY: Adv layout systems — AT/7000, 4-AT/VDT, 4-Ap/Mac 7100; Printers — Umax/1200 XL; Other equipment — Ap/Mac II. PRODUCTION: Typesetters — 2-V/5000, 1-V/5300E; Plate exposures — 2-Nu; Plate processors — 1-GNS/28; Production cameras — 1-C/Spartan II, 1-Ik/560; Automatic film processors — 1-P/26M, 1-AG/RAP 43.
PRESSROOM: Line 1 — 7-G/Urbanite (w/Color deck). MAILROOM: Counter stackers — Id/440; Inserters and stuffers — MM/EM 102; Bundle tyer — MLN; Wrapping singles — Id/Bottomwrap; Addressing machine — Am. WIRE SERVICES: News — AP, NYT; Stock tables — AP; Receiving dishes — AP. BUSINESS COMPUTERS: IBM/Sys 3600; Applications: Adv billing, Accts receivable, Accts payable, Gen ledger, Payroll.

HICKORY
Catawba County

'90 U.S. Census- 28,301; E&P '96 Est. 34,294
ABC-CZ (90): 49,346 (HH 19,943)

The Hickory Daily Record
(e-mon to fri; m-sat; S)

The Hickory Daily Record, 1100 Park Pl. 11th Ave. S.E.; PO Box 968, Hickory, NC 28603; tel (704) 322-4510; fax (704) 328-9378.

Circulation: 22,594(e); 22,594(m-sat); 20,663(S); ABC Sept. 30, 1995.

Price: 50¢(d); 50¢(sat); $1.00(S).

Advertising: Open inch rate $16.40(e); $16.40(m-sat); $16.40(S). **Representative:** Papert Companies.

News Service: AP. **Politics:** Independent. **Established:** 1915.

Not Published: Thanksgiving; Christmas.

Advertising not accepted: Liquor (hard); Vending machine; Work at home; Cash investment; Worm, Mink & Chinchilla.

Magazines: TV Record; USA Weekend.

CORPORATE OFFICERS

President Suzanne G Millholland
Vice Pres Kenneth Millholland
Secretary/Treasurer John G Millholland

GENERAL MANAGEMENT

General Manager John G Millholland

ADVERTISING

Director David K Millholland

CIRCULATION

Manager Lloyd R Hall

NEWS EXECUTIVE

Editor Larry D Clark

EDITORS AND MANAGERS

Business Editor Troy L Houser
Editorial Page Editor Larry D Dale
Lifestyle Editor John Dayberry
Sports Editor Bret Cornwright
Wire Editor Michelle L Thornewell

PRODUCTION

Manager Randy Hines
Foreman-Composing Jerry Rector
Foreman-Pressroom Gerald L Hines

Mechanical available: Offset; Black and 3 ROP colors; insert accepted — preprinted; page cut-offs — 22".

Mechanical specifications: Type page 13" x 21"; E - 6 cols, 2¹⁄₁₆", ⅛" between; A - 6 cols, 2¹⁄₁₆", ⅛" between; C - 8 cols, 1¾", ¹⁄₁₆" between.

Commodity consumption: Newsprint 2,315 short tons; width 27½"; black ink 40,070 pounds; color ink 6,330 pounds; average pages per issue 36(d), 54(S).

Equipment: EDITORIAL: Front-end hardware — 23-Cybergraphics. CLASSIFIED: Front-end hardware — 3-Cybergraphics. PRODUCTION: Typesetters — 2-AU/APS-6; Plate exposures — 1-Nu; Plate processors — 2-Nat; Electronic picture desk — Lf/AP Leaf Picture Desk; Scanners — 1-ECR/Autokon 1000, Laukotou; Production cameras — 1-C/Spartan III; Automatic film processors — 1-P; Digital color separation equipment — Nikon, Ap/Mac.
PRESSROOM: Line 1 — 7-MAN/Uniman; Pasters — MEG; Reels and stands — MEG. MAILROOM: Counter stackers — 1-MM; Inserters and stuffers — 2-MM; Bundle tyer — 2-OVL; Addressing machine — 1-Wm. WIRE SERVICES: News — AP; Receiving dishes — AP. BUSINESS COMPUTERS: IBM/Sys 36.

HIGH POINT
Guilford County

'90 U.S. Census- 69,496; E&P '96 Est. 76,823
ABC-CZ (90): 82,992 (HH 32,899)

High Point Enterprise
(m-mon to sat; S)

High Point Enterprise, 210 Church Ave.; PO Box 1009, High Point, NC 27261; tel (910) 888-3500; fax (910) 841-5165.

Circulation: 29,872(m); 29,872(m-sat); 32,106(S); ABC Sept. 30, 1995.

Price: 50¢(d); 50¢(sat); $1.00(S); $7.95/mo; $95.40/yr.

Advertising: Open inch rate $19.95(m); $19.95(m-sat); $20.45(S). **Representative:** Landon Associates Inc.

News Services: AP, KRT. **Politics:** Independent. **Established:** 1884.

Special Weekly Sections: Total Market Coverage, Food (wed); Entertainment (thur); TV (fri); Business, Travel, Real Estate (S).

Magazine: USA Weekend (S).

CORPORATE OFFICERS

President Randall B Terry Jr
Vice Pres David A Rawley Jr
Vice Pres/Secretary/Treasurer Joseph P Rawley

GENERAL MANAGEMENT

General Manager Gary B Moore
Controller David Bowman

ADVERTISING

Director Demi Foust
Manager-Retail David Sharp
Manager-General Lane Oldham
Manager-Classified Van Griffith

CIRCULATION

Director Donald Wilson

NEWS EXECUTIVES

Editor Thomas L Blount
Managing Editor Kenneth Irons
Assoc Editor Doug Clark

EDITORS AND MANAGERS

Amusements Editor Vicki Knopfler
Automotive Editor Dusty Donaldson
Book Editor Vicki Knopfler
Business/Finance Editor Thomas Russell
Columnist Thomas L Blount
Columnist Jimmy Tomlin
Editorial Page Editor Doug Clark
Education Editor Kathleen Keener
Fashion Editor Jane Ronalter
Films/Theater Editor Vicki Knopfler
Food Editor Jane Ronalter
Garden Editor Judy Phillips
Home Furnishing Editor Jimmy Carrol
Librarian Linda Peronto
News Editor Sherrie Dockery
Radio/Television Editor Vicki Knopfler
Society/Women's Editor Judy Phillips
Sports Editor Benny Phillips
Sunday Editor Vince Wheeler
Wire Editor Sherrie Dockery

MANAGEMENT INFORMATION SERVICES

Data Processing Manager David Bowman

PRODUCTION

Director Newman Wills
Manager-Technical Service Joe Bryant
Manager-Dispatch Terri Rabon
Superintendent-Pressroom Jack Armfield
Superintendent-Camera Buddy Cadle

Market Information: Split Run; TMC; ADS.

Mechanical available: Offset; Black and 3 ROP colors; insert accepted — preprinted; page cutoffs — 22".

Mechanical specifications: Type page 13" x 21"; E - 6 cols, 2 1/16", 1/8" between; A - 6 cols, 2 1/16", 1/8" between; C - 9 cols, 1 3/8", 1/16" between.

Commodity consumption: Newsprint 2,500 short tons; widths 55", 41½", 27½", 13¾"; black ink 68,000 pounds; color ink 3,600 pounds; single pages printed 13,460; average pages per issue 32(d), 74(S); single plates used 30,500.

Equipment: EDITORIAL: Front-end hardware — CD/2400, 34-Intel/386 PC. CLASSIFIED: Front-end hardware — CD/2400, 10-Intel/386 PC; Other equipment — 3-Digital Ad Wizard. DISPLAY: Adv layout systems — SCS/Layout 8000, Digital Ad Wizards, Ap/Mac; Front-end hardware — Ap/Mac; Printers — 1-Ap/Mac LaserPrinter. PRODUCTION: Typesetters — MON/Express 82; Plate exposures — 1-BKY/Astro, 1-Nu/FT36; Plate processors — 1-Nat/A-250; Electronic picture desk — Lf/AP Leaf Picture Desk; Scanners — 1-Lf/Leafscan 35, 1-Umax/6000, 1-C/Autokon, 1-Polaroid/SprintScan; Production cameras — 1-C/Marathon; Automatic film processors — 1-LE/LD24A; Reproportion units — 1-Typeflex; Color separation equipment (conventional) — 1-C. PRESSROOM: Line 1 — 5-G/Metroliner; Folders — 1-G/2:1; Pasters — 5-G. MAILROOM: Counter stackers — 1-SH/MON; Inserters and stuffers — 2-MM/227; Bundle tyer — 1-MLN/ML 2EE, 2-CCS; Other mailroom equipment — MM/Stitcher-Trimmer. LIBRARY: Electronic — SMS/Stauffer Gold. COMMUNICATIONS: Digital ad delivery system — AP AdSend. WIRE SERVICES: News — AP, KRT; Receiving dishes — size-10ft, AP. BUSINESS COMPUTERS: 1-IBM/Sys; Applications: Gen ledger, Payroll, Accts payable, Accts receivable, Circ billing, TMC, Sales reports.

JACKSONVILLE
Onslow County

'90 U.S. Census- 30,013; E&P '96 Est. 52,676
ABC-CZ (90): 76,461 (HH 15,446)

The Daily News
(m-mon to sat; S)

The Daily News, 724 Bell Fork Rd.; PO Box 0196, Jacksonville, NC 28541-0196; tel (910) 353-1171; fax (910) 353-7316; web site http://eastnc.coastalnet.com/cnmedia/jdnews/breaker1.htm. Freedom Communications Inc. group.

Circulation: 22,629(m); 22,629(m-sat); 25,147(S); ABC Sept. 30, 1995.

Price: 50¢(d); 50¢(sat); $1.25(S); $9.50/mo; $84.00/yr (mon to sat only), $108.00/yr.

Advertising: Open inch rate $18.57(m); $18.57(m-sat); $18.57(S). **Representative:** Papert Companies.

News Service: AP. **Politics:** Independent. **Established:** 1953.

Special Editions: Super Bowl (Jan); Valentine's Gift Guide, NASCAR Preview (Feb); Spring Fashion, NCAA Tab, Spring Gardening (Mar); Spring Car Care (Apr); Spring Home Improvement, Graduation (May); June Bride (June); Celebrate the Fourth (July); Answer Book, Football Preview, Shrimp Festival (Aug); Farmer's Festival, Fall Home Improvement, Coloring Book (Sept); Swansboros Mullet Festival, Winter Car Care (Oct); Cookbook (Nov); Christmas Color Book (Dec); 13th Month Sell-A-Bration, Coupon Book (monthly).

Special Weekly Sections: Business Page (mon); Business Spotlights (tues); Food Section (wed); Visions, Accent (S).

Magazines: Max Magazine (thur); TV Update (S).

GENERAL MANAGEMENT

Publisher Charles Fischer

ADVERTISING

Manager W R Taylor
Manager-Classified E H Huffman
Manager-Retail Harold Foster

TELECOMMUNICATIONS

Audiotex Manager Ken Lowe

CIRCULATION

Manager Bobby Williams

NEWS EXECUTIVES

Editor Elliott Potter
Managing Editor Madison Taylor

EDITORS AND MANAGERS

Automotive Editor Eileen Brady
Business/Finance Editor Eileen Brady
City Editor Aileen Streng
Editorial Page Editor Elliott Potter
Education Editor Carolyn Alford
Entertainment/Amusements Editor David Shelley
Environmental Editor Madison Taylor
Farm/Agriculture Editor Eileen Brady
Fashion/Style Editor Eileen Brady
Features Editor Madison Taylor
Home Furnishings Editor David Shelley
Food Editor Aileen Streng
Graphics Editor/Art Director Paul Woodward
Health/Medical Editor Eileen Brady
Living/Lifestyle Editor Eileen Brady
National Editor Elliott Potter
News Editor Madison Taylor
Photo Editor Don Bryan
Political/Government Editor Elliott Potter
Religion Editor Carolyn Alford
Science/Technology Editor J T Oliver
Sports Editor R Holland
Television Editor David Shelley
Travel Editor J T Oliver
Women's Editor Eileen Brady

MANAGEMENT INFORMATION SERVICES

Data Processing Manager Otis Gardner
Online Manager Ken Lowe

PRODUCTION

Manager Linda Walker
Foreman-Pressroom Wayne Parker

Market Information: Zoned editions; Split Run; TMC; Operate database; Operate audiotex.

Mechanical available: Offset; Black and 3 ROP colors; insert accepted — preprinted; page cutoffs — 22¾".

Mechanical specifications: Type page 13" x 21½"; E - 6 cols, 2 1/16", 1/8" between; A - 6 cols, 2 1/16", 1/8" between; C - 8 cols, 1½", 1/8" between.

Commodity consumption: Newsprint 22,009 metric tons; widths 55", 41", 27½"; black ink 50,000 pounds; color ink 2,000 pounds; single pages printed 15,292; average pages per issue 40(d), 40(sat), 64(S); single plates used 20,000.

Equipment: EDITORIAL: Front-end hardware — AST, Ap/Mac; Front-end software — Dewar; Printers — Okidata, V; Other equipment — Ap/Mac. CLASSIFIED: Front-end hardware — AST; Front-end software — Dewar; Printers — Okidata, V. DISPLAY: Adv layout systems — Dewar; Front-end hardware — AST; Front-end software — Dewar; Printers — Okidata. PRODUCTION: Pagination software — Dewar; OCR software — Caere/OmniPage; Typesetters — 4-V, V/Pre Press; Plate exposures — 2-Nu; Plate processors — 1-Nat; Electronic picture desk — Lf/AP Leaf Picture Desk; Scanners — X, AG, Umax; Production cameras — 2-C/Spartan III; Automatic film processors — LE, Konica; Color separation equipment (conventional) — RZ. PRESSROOM: Line 1 — 8-HI/1660; Line 2 — 6-G/Community; Folders — 2-HI; Pasters — Wd; Reels and stands — Wd; Press control system — HI; Press registration system — KFM. MAILROOM: Counter stackers — HL; Bundle tyer — 2-MLN. LIBRARY: Electronic — SMS/Stauffer Gold. COMMUNICATIONS: Facsimile — HP; Digital ad delivery system — AP AdSend. Systems used — satellite. WIRE SERVICES: News — AP; Photos — AP; Stock tables — AP; Syndicates — KRT, SHNS; Receiving dishes — size-12ft, AP. BUSINESS COMPUTERS: 10-IBM/KLH; Applications: Southware; PCs & micros networked; PCs & main system networked.

KANNAPOLIS
Cabarrus County

'90 U.S. Census- 29,696; E&P '96 Est. 30,529
ABC-CZ (90): 32,029 (HH 13,005)

The Daily Independent
(e-mon to fri; S)

The Daily Independent, 123 N. Main St.; PO Box 147, Kannapolis, NC 28082-0147; tel (704) 932-3131; fax (704) 933-4444. Park Communications Inc. group.

Circulation: 9,466(e); 10,246(S); ABC Sept. 30, 1995.

Price: 50¢(d); $1.00(S); $7.80/mo; $93.60/yr.

Advertising: Open inch rate $10.50(e); $10.50(S); comb with Concord Tribune (eS) $21.00. **Representative:** Papert Companies.

News Service: AP. **Politics:** Independent. **Established:** 1927.

Not Published: Christmas.

Advertising not accepted: X-rated movies; Abortion clinics; liquor.

Special Editions: Bridal Directory (Jan); Car Care (Apr); Insight (July); Football (Aug); Car Care (Oct); Holiday Cookbook (Nov).

Special Weekly Section: Entertainment Section (thur).

Magazine: USA Weekend (S).

CORPORATE OFFICERS

President Wright M Thomas
Vice Pres-Newspapers Ralph J Martin

GENERAL MANAGEMENT

General Manager Floyd S Alford Jr
Business Manager Marg Harbaugh
Asst Business Manager Toni Patterson

ADVERTISING

Director Beverly Basinger

CIRCULATION

Manager Homer Smith

NEWS EXECUTIVES

Editor Floyd S Alford Jr
Managing Editor Eric Millsaps

EDITORS AND MANAGERS

City Editor Jessie Burchette
Religion Editor Ethel Sechler
Society/Women's Editor G Jennie Stamy
Sports Editor Steve Winzenread

PRODUCTION

Foreman-Composing Steve Linebarrier
Foreman-Photo/Camera/Plate Steve Linebarrier
Foreman-Pressroom Robbie Lowe

Market Information: Split Run; TMC.

Mechanical available: Offset; Black and 3 ROP colors; insert accepted — preprinted; page cutoffs — 22¾".

Mechanical specifications: Type page 13" x 21½"; E - 6 cols, 2¼", 1/8" between; A - 6 cols, 2¼", 1/8" between; C - 10 cols, 1 3/8", 1/16" between.

Commodity consumption: Newsprint 464 short tons; width 27½"; black ink 17,188 pounds; color ink 1,608 pounds; single pages printed 8,993; average pages per issue 20(d), 70(S).

Equipment: EDITORIAL: Front-end hardware — Ap/Mac; Front-end software — Baseview; Printers — Compaq. CLASSIFIED: Front-end hardware — Ap/Mac; Front-end software — Baseview; Printers — Compaq. DISPLAY: Adv layout systems — QuarkXPress; Front-end hardware — Ap/Mac; Front-end software — QuarkXPress; Printers — Compaq. PRODUCTION: Platemaking systems — 1-W/31A; Plate exposures — 1-Nu/Flip Top; Production cameras — 1-C/Spartan II; Automatic film processors — 1-LE/LD 24. PRESSROOM: Line 1 — 5-G/Urbanite 678; Folders — 1-G. MAILROOM: Counter stackers — 1-BG/Count-O-Veyor; Inserters and stuffers — 1-KAN/4 station; Bundle tyer — 2-Sa; Wrapping singles — 2-Cr; Addressing machine — 1-Am, 1-Gr. COMMUNICATIONS: Systems used — satellite. WIRE SERVICES: News — AP; Receiving dishes — size-12ft, AP. BUSINESS COMPUTERS: Unix; Applications: Vision Data.

KINSTON
Lenoir County

'90 U.S. Census- 25,295; E&P '96 Est. 26,007
ABC-CZ (90): 25,295 (HH 9,987)

The Free Press (e-mon to fri; S)

The Free Press, 2103 N. Queen St. (28501); PO Box 129, Kinston, NC 28502-0129; tel (919) 527-3191; fax (919) 527-8838; e-mail porterwork@aol.com. Freedom Communications Inc. group.

Circulation: 12,303(e); 13,922(S); ABC Sept. 30, 1995.

Price: 50¢(d); $1.00(S); $7.25/mo; $72.00/yr (carrier), $168.00/yr (mail in state), $174.00/yr (mail out of state).

Advertising: Open inch rate $11.00(e); $11.00 (S). **Representative:** Papert Companies.

News Service: AP. **Established:** 1882.

Not Published: Christmas.

Special Edition: Health File (quarterly).

Magazine: Homes Magazine (6xyr).

CORPORATE OFFICERS

President James Rosse
Senior Vice Pres Jonathan Segal
Vice Pres Tom Porter

GENERAL MANAGEMENT

Publisher Tom Porter
Manager-Business Bill Kraus

ADVERTISING

Director Billy Moore

CIRCULATION

Manager Frances Jones

NEWS EXECUTIVE

Editor Rick Thomason

EDITORS AND MANAGERS

City Editor Caroline Waller
Community News Editor Mary Ellison Turner
Sports Editor Todd Murray

PRODUCTION

Manager Larry Powell

Market Information: Zoned editions; TMC.

Mechanical available: Offset; Black and 3 ROP colors; insert accepted — preprinted; page cutoffs — 22.80".

Mechanical specifications: Type page 13" x 21½"; E - 6 cols, 2 1/16", 1/8" between; A - 6 cols, 2 1/16", 1/8" between; C - 8 cols, 1 15/32", 5/32" between.

Commodity consumption: Newsprint 700 short tons; widths 27½", 13¾"; single pages printed 720; average pages per issue 20(d), 70(S).

Equipment: EDITORIAL: Front-end hardware — Ap/Mac; Front-end software — QuarkXPress, Baseview; Printers — Ap/Mac LaserWriter IIg, Xante/Accel-a-Writer 8200; Other equipment — Ap/Mac Scanner. CLASSIFIED: Front-end hardware — Ap/Mac; Front-end software — Baseview; Printers — Okidata/320. DISPLAY: Front-end hardware — Ap/Mac; Front-end soft-

North Carolina I-293

ware — Mk/Ad Director, Baseview; Printers — Ap/Mac LaserWriter II NTX; Other equipment — 3-IBM/8X. PRODUCTION: Pagination software — Baseview, QuarkXPress; OCR software — Caere/OmniPage; Typesetters — 2-Ap/Mac LaserWriter IIg, Xante/8200, Panther-Pro 36; Plate exposures — 2-Nu; Plate processors — 1-Nat/A-250; Electronic picture desk — Lf/AP Leaf Picture Desk; Scanners — HP/ScanJet, AG, Kk/2035 plus; Production cameras — C/Spartan III; Automatic film processors — LE/LD 2600; Film transporters — Konica; Color separation equipment (conventional) — Adobe/Photoshop; Digital color separation equipment — Kk/Scanners, AG/Scanners, Ap/Mac 8100.
PRESSROOM: Line 1 — 3-G/Urbanite (w/1-3 color unit); Press registration system — Duarte. MAILROOM: Bundle tyer — 1-MLN, 1-EAM/Mosca. LIBRARY: Electronic — Ap/Mac, SMS. WIRE SERVICES: News — AP; Photos — AP; Receiving dishes — AP. BUSINESS COMPUTERS: 2-Compaq/Pro Liner 486, 1-Generic/486 PC, 1-IBM/386 PC, 1-Epson/DFX 8000 Printer, 1-Epson/DFX 5000 Printer; Applications: Brainworks: Accts receivable; Southware, Lotus 1-2-3, WordPerfect; PCs & micros networked.

LAURINBURG

Scotland County

'90 U.S. Census- 11,643 **E&P '96 Est.** 13,740

The Exchange (e-mon to fri)

The Exchange, 211 Cronly St.; PO Box 459, Laurinburg, NC 28353; tel (910) 276-2311; fax (910) 276-3815. Mid-South Management Co. Inc. group.
Circulation: 9,400(e); Est Nov. 1, 1995.
Price: 50¢(d); $58.00/yr (home), $63.00/yr (mail in town), $65.00/yr (mail out of town); $15.75/3mo, $30.00/6mo.
Advertising: Open inch rate $6.25(e). **Established:** 1882 (weekly), 1995 (daily).
Note: Effective Nov. 1, 1995, this paper went from three days a week to five days a week. The circulation is an estimate of the new daily paper. Equipment information was not available at press time.

GENERAL MANAGEMENT
Publisher Michael Milligan
ADVERTISING
Director Chris Cray
NEWS EXECUTIVE
Editor Mark N Durham
EDITOR AND MANAGER
Lifetimes Editor Dot Cable

LENOIR

Caldwell County

'90 U.S. Census- 14,192; **E&P '96 Est.** 14,968
ABC-CZ (90): 17,011 (HH 7,081)

Lenoir News-Topic
(e-mon to fri; m-sat)

Lenoir News-Topic, 123 Pennton Ave.; PO Box 1110, Lenoir, NC 28645; tel (704) 758-7381. Paxton Media group.
Circulation: 12,252(e); 12,252(m-sat); ABC Sept. 30, 1995.
Price: 50¢(d); 50¢(sat); $7.50/mo; $90.00/yr.
Advertising: Open inch rate $13.45(e); $13.45(m-sat). **Representative:** Landon Associates Inc.
News Service: AP. **Politics:** Independent. **Established:** 1875.
Not Published: Christmas.
Special Editions: Progress Edition (Feb); Sports Tab (Aug); Sports Tab (Nov).
Special Weekly Sections: TMC/Food Day (wed); TV Section (fri); Church News (sat).
Magazines: TV/Leisure Guide (fri); USA Weekend (sat).

CORPORATE OFFICER
President Fred Paxton
GENERAL MANAGEMENT
Publisher Richard A Mitchell
Controller A Dent Sullivan
ADVERTISING
Director Richard Paiva
CIRCULATION
Manager Steve Minton
NEWS EXECUTIVE
Editor Richard Tuttell
EDITORS AND MANAGERS
Lifestyle Editor Eric Beam
News Editor Michael Johnson
Photo Department Manager Greg Floyd
Sports Editor Paul Teague
MANAGEMENT INFORMATION SERVICES
Info Technologies Brenda Penley
PRODUCTION
Manager-Pressroom Gary Young
Foreman-Composing Merry Cable

Market Information: Zoned editions; TMC; Operate audiotex.
Mechanical available: Offset; Black and 3 ROP colors; insert accepted — preprinted; page cutoffs — 21½".
Mechanical specifications: Type page 13" x 21½"; E - 6 cols, 2 1/16", ⅛" between; A - 6 cols, 2 1/16", ⅛" between; C - 9 cols, 1⅜", 1/16" between.
Commodity consumption: Newsprint 947 short tons; width 27½"; black ink 24,000 pounds; color ink 950 pounds; single pages printed 7,265; average pages per issue 23.3(d); single plates used 4,200.
Equipment: EDITORIAL: Front-end hardware — 2-AT/7000, 11-AT; Printers — 1-Ap/Mac LaserPrinter; Other equipment — 1-Ap/Mac II, 1-Microtek/Scanner, 2-Ap/Mac III. CLASSIFIED: Front-end hardware — 3-AT. AUDIOTEX: Hardware — Brite Voice Systems. DISPLAY: Adv layout systems — 3-AT. PRODUCTION: Typesetters — 2-COM; Platemaking systems — PRO; Plate exposures — 1-PRO/Nu; Plate processors — 1-PRO, MAS; Electronic picture desk — Lf/AP Leaf Picture Desk; Production cameras — 1-C; Automatic film processors — 2-LE. PRESSROOM: Line 1 — 8-HI/Cotrell V15; Folders — 1-HI. MAILROOM: Inserters and stuffers — KAN/480 5-into-1; Bundle tyer — 1-MLN. LIBRARY: Electronic — 1-Bell & Howell. COMMUNICATIONS: Systems used — fiber optic. WIRE SERVICES: News — AP; Photos — AP; Syndicates — NYT; Receiving dishes — AP. BUSINESS COMPUTERS: DPT/1800, IBM/Sys 36; Applications: Adv billing, Accts receivable, Payroll, Accts payable, Gen ledger, Circ; PCs & micros networked; PCs & main system networked.

LEXINGTON

Davidson County

'90 U.S. Census- 16,581; **E&P '96 Est.** 17,829
ABC-CZ (90): 16,581 (HH 6,985)

The Dispatch (e-mon to sat)

The Dispatch, 30 E. 1st Ave. (27292); PO Box 908, Lexington, NC 27293; tel (704) 249-3981. New York Times Co. group.
Circulation: 13,746(e); 13,746(e-sat); ABC Sept. 30, 1995.
Price: 50¢(d); 50¢(sat); $7.00/mo.
Advertising: Open inch rate $17.10(e); $17.10(e-sat). **Representative:** Landon Associates Inc.
News Services: AP, NYT. **Politics:** Independent. **Established:** 1882.
Not Published: Christmas.

GENERAL MANAGEMENT
Publisher Joe S Sink Jr
Purchasing Agent Joe S Sink Jr
Controller-Business Office Wayne L Bradby
ADVERTISING
Director Betty Barnes
CIRCULATION
Director Bill Walser
NEWS EXECUTIVE
Exec Editor Robert Stiff
EDITORS AND MANAGERS
Business Editor Vikki Hodges
Editorial Page Editor Chad Killebrew
Education Editor Divania Smith
Family Editor Joyce Weaver
Films/Theater Editor Joyce Weaver
Food Editor Joyce Weaver
Graphics Editor Chad Killebrew
Photo Department Manager Donnie Roberts
Political Editor Jill Doss
Special Sections Editor Chad Killebrew
Sports Editor Bruce Wehrle
Television Editor Joyce Weaver
Wire Editor Chad Killebrew
Youth Editor Divania Smith
PRODUCTION
Foreman-Composing Judith Stanford
Foreman-Pressroom Danny Koonts

Market Information: Split Run; TMC.
Mechanical available: Offset; Black and 3 ROP colors; insert accepted — preprinted.
Mechanical specifications: Type page 13" x 21½"; E - 6 cols, 2 1/16", ⅛" between; A - 6 cols, 2 1/16", ⅛" between; C - 9 cols, 1⅜", 1/16" between.
Commodity consumption: Newsprint 800 short tons; width 27½"; average pages per issue 22(d).
Equipment: EDITORIAL: Front-end hardware — AT. CLASSIFIED: Front-end hardware — AT. AUDIOTEX: Hardware — Brite Voice Systems. PRODUCTION: Typesetters — V. PRESSROOM: Line 1 — 4-HI/Cotrell 845; Folders — 1-HI. WIRE SERVICES: News — Receiving dishes — AP. BUSINESS COMPUTERS: 1-IBM/Sys 36; PCs & micros networked; PCs & main system networked.

LUMBERTON

Robeson County

'90 U.S. Census- 18,601; **E&P '96 Est.** 19,411
ABC-CZ (90): 18,601 (HH 7,093)

The Robesonian
(e-mon to fri; S)

The Robesonian, 121 W. 5th St.; PO Box 1028, Lumberton, NC 28359; tel (910) 739-4322; fax (910) 739-6553. Park Communications Inc. group.
Circulation: 13,771(e); 16,659(S); ABC Sept. 30, 1995.
Price: 35¢(d); 75¢(S).
Advertising: Open inch rate $15.68(e); $15.68(S).
News Service: AP. **Politics:** Independent. **Established:** 1870.
Not Published: Christmas.
Special Editions: Progress Edition; Gift Guide; Fall and Spring Fashions; Football; Hunting & Fishing; Car Care; Tobacco Market; Fun in the Sun; New Car; Brides.
Special Weekly Sections: Religious Page (tues); Food Page, Lifestyle (wed); Farm, Entertainment (thur); Religious Page (fri); Business Page, Lifestyle (S).
Magazines: USA Weekend; TV Spotlight; Mini Page.

GENERAL MANAGEMENT
General Manager Billy M Lewis
Manager-Accounting Worth Graham
ADVERTISING
Manager Ed Knight
Manager-Classified Pat Edwards
CIRCULATION
Manager Ed Knight
NEWS EXECUTIVES
Editor Billy M Lewis
Managing Editor John Culbreth
EDITORS AND MANAGERS
Business Editor Scott Witten
City Editor Ed Wilcox
Education Editor James Bass
Farm Editor Ellen Church
Lifestyle Editor Barbara Graham
Photo Department Manager Steve Humbert
Political Editor Norman L Morton
Sports Editor Bob Sloan
PRODUCTION
Manager-Composing Joe Druzak
Manager-Pressroom Mike Skipper

Market Information: Split Run; TMC.
Mechanical available: Offset; Black and 3 ROP colors; insert accepted — preprinted; page cutoffs — 21½".
Mechanical specifications: Type page 13" x 21½"; E - 6 cols, 2 1/16", ⅛" between; A - 6 cols, 2 1/16", ⅛" between; C - 9 cols, 1⅜", 1/16" between.
Commodity consumption: Newsprint 782 short tons; widths 28", 14"; black ink 19,100 pounds; color ink 3,100 pounds; single pages printed 6,630; average pages per issue 18(d), 30(S); single plates used 3,800.
Equipment: EDITORIAL: Front-end hardware — 4-Ap/Mac Centris 650; Front-end software — QuarkXPress, Baseview/Qtools, Ap/Mac LC III, Baseview/NewsEdit; Printers — 1-Ap/Mac LaserPrinter IIg. CLASSIFIED: Front-end hardware — Ap/Mac, Ap/Mac II, 3-Ap/Mac LC III; Front-end software — Baseview/Class Manager Plus; Printers — 1-Okidata/320 Billing Printer. DISPLAY: Adv layout systems — 3-Mk/Ad Setter; Front-end hardware — 3-Ap/Mac Centris 650; Front-end software — QuarkXPress, Caere/OmniPage, Baseview/NewsEdit; Printers — 2-Ap/Mac LaserWriter 11" x 17"; Other equipment — CD-Rom/Scanner. PRODUCTION: Typesetters — Ap/Mac; Plate processors — 3M/Deadliner; Scanners — CD-Rom/Scanner, Ap/Mac; Production cameras — AG. PRESSROOM: Line 1 — 9-HI/V15; Folders — 2-HI/2:1. MAILROOM: Bundle tyer — 1-Sa/1 Strapping Machine; Addressing machine — 1-Ch. WIRE SERVICES: News — AP; Receiving dishes — AP. BUSINESS COMPUTERS: Applications: Vision Data: Adv billing, Accts receivable, Payroll.

MARION

McDowell County

'90 U.S. Census- 4,765; **E&P '96 Est.** 6,153

The McDowell News
(e-mon to fri)

The McDowell News, 26 N. Logan St.; PO Box 610, Marion, NC 28752; tel (704) 652-3313. Park Communications Inc. group.
Circulation: 5,894(e); Sworn Oct. 1, 1994.
Price: 50¢(d); $78.00/yr.
Advertising: Open inch rate $9.00(e).
News Service: AP. **Established:** 1929.
Special Weekly Sections: Business Page (tues); Foothills Life (wed); Entertainment-Weekend (fri).

GENERAL MANAGEMENT
Publisher Scott Hollifield
General Manager David Setzer
ADVERTISING
Director Vangie Peek
CIRCULATION
Director Dal Nanney
NEWS EXECUTIVES
Editor David Setzer
Managing Editor Scott Hollifield
PRODUCTION
Manager-Composing Lynell Burnette

Market Information: TMC.
Mechanical available: Offset; Black and 4 ROP colors; insert accepted — preprinted; page cutoffs — 23".
Mechanical specifications: Type page 27½" x 21½"; E - 6 cols, 2 1/16", ⅛" between; A - 6 cols, 2 1/16", ⅛" between; C - 9 cols, 1½", ⅛" between.
Commodity consumption: width 27½"; single pages printed 7,250; average pages per issue 22(d).
Equipment: EDITORIAL: Front-end hardware — COM. CLASSIFIED: Front-end hardware — COM. WIRE SERVICES: News — AP; Receiving dishes — AP.

MONROE

Union County

'90 U.S. Census- 16,127; **E&P '96 Est.** 20,563
ABC-CZ (90): 16,127 (HH 5,935)

The Enquirer-Journal
(e-mon to fri; S)

The Enquirer-Journal, 500 W. Jefferson St.; PO Box 5040, Monroe, NC 28111-5040; tel (704) 289-1541; fax (704) 289-2929. Thomson Newspapers group.
Circulation: 13,273(e); 15,163(S); ABC Sept. 30, 1995.
Price: 50¢(d); 75¢(S); $1.85/wk; $7.40/mo; $96.20/yr.
Advertising: Open inch rate $13.10(e); $13.10 (S). **Representative:** Papert Companies.
News Service: AP. **Politics:** Independent. **Established:** 1873.
Special Editions: Bridal, Spring Fashion (Feb); Spring Lawn & Garden; Fall Lawn & Garden; Auto Care; Senior Citizens Section; Gift Guide; Progress; FYI; Racing Magazine, Regional Business (monthly); Home Improvement (Spring & Fall); Ag Appreciation (annual).
Special Weekly Sections: Food (wed); Entertainment (thur); Church, Auto Showcase (fri); Business, Weddings/Engagements (S).
Magazines: TV Scene (S); USA Weekend; Real Estate; Farm Focus; Health Quest; Senior Scene; Chamber of Commerce Directory.

GENERAL MANAGEMENT
Publisher/General Manager Ray West
Business Manager Jamie Green
ADVERTISING
Manager Olin Sikes
Manager-Classified Mary Ann Helms
CIRCULATION
Manager Van Rowell
Foreman-Mailroom Ed Vaughn
NEWS EXECUTIVE
Exec Editor Luanne Williams

North Carolina

MORGANTON
Burke County
'90 U.S. Census- 15,085; E&P '96 Est. 16,768
ABC-CZ (90): 15,085 (HH 6,048)

The News Herald
(e-mon to fri; S)

The News Herald, 301 Collett St.; PO Box 280, Morganton, NC 28680-0280; tel (704) 437-2161; fax (704) 437-5372. Park Communications Inc. group.
Circulation: 11,455(e); 11,699(S); ABC Sept. 30, 1995.
Price: 50¢(d); 50¢(S); $7.80/mo; $93.60/yr.
Advertising: Open inch rate $10.75(e); $10.75(S). **Representative:** Landon Associates Inc.
News Service: AP. **Politics:** Independent. **Established:** 1885.
Not Published: Christmas.
Special Editions: % Off Sale (Jan); Bride Guide, Valentine's Gift Ideas, President's Day Sale (Feb); NCAA Basketball Tournament, Review & Forecast (Mar); Spring Fashions, Home & Garden (Apr); Mother's Day Gift Guide, Graduation Edition (May); June Bride, Father's Day Gift Guide, Sunrise Sale (June); Coupon Book, % Off Sale (July); Back-to-School, Football (Aug); Downtown Festival Promotion (Sept); Fall Home Improvement, 1997 New Car Guide, Halloween Sale (Oct); Early Gift Ideas, Shop At Home, Christmas Around Burke (Nov); Christmas Wishbook, Drive Safely Page, Last Minute Gift Ideas, Holiday Greetings (Dec).
Special Weekly Sections: Food Day (wed); TV Entertainer (thur); Church News (fri); Business News (S).
Magazines: TV News (own, newsprint), USA Weekend (S).

GENERAL MANAGEMENT
General Manager — H Eugene Willard
ADVERTISING
Manager — Randy Hart
CIRCULATION
Manager — James Grady
NEWS EXECUTIVE
Managing Editor — Bill Poteat
EDITORS AND MANAGERS
Amusements Editor — Anna Wilson
Business/Finance Editor — Anna Wilson
Books Editor — H Eugene Willard
City/Metro Editor — Kim Duncan
Columnist — Bill Poteat
Columnist — H Eugene Willard
Editorial Page Editor — Bill Poteat
Education Editor — Charlanda Clay
Fashion Editor — Edna Mae Herman
Features Editor — Anna Wilson
Films/Theater Editor — Kim Duncan
Food/Garden Editor — Edna Mae Herman
Living/Lifestyle Editor — Edna Mae Herman
Music Editor — Kim Duncan
News Editor — Anna Wilson
Political Editor — Kevin Ellis
Radio/Television Editor — Anna Wilson
Real Estate Editor — Anna Wilson
Religion Editor — Paige Richardson
Society/Women's Editor — Edna Mae Herman
Sports Editor — Todd Runkle
Teen-Age/Youth Editor — Kim Duncan
Travel Editor — H Eugene Willard
Wire Editor — Anna Wilson
MANAGEMENT INFORMATION SERVICES
Data Processing Manager — Betty McCurry
PRODUCTION
Superintendent — Fred Robinson

Market Information: TMC; ADS.
Mechanical available: Offset; Black and 3 ROP colors; insert accepted — preprinted, all; page cut-offs — 22¾".
Mechanical specifications: Type page 13¼" x 21½"; E - 6 cols, 2", ⅛" between; A - 6 cols, 2", ⅛" between; C - 10 cols, 1³⁄₁₆", ¹⁄₁₆" between.
Commodity consumption: Newsprint 650 short tons; width 27½"; black ink 15,800 pounds; color ink 1,000 pounds; single pages printed 6,600; average pages per issue 19(d), 36(S); single plates used 4,200.
Equipment: EDITORIAL: Front-end hardware — Ap/Mac; Front-end software — Baseview. CLASSIFIED: Front-end hardware — 3-Ap/Mac; Front-end software — Baseview. DISPLAY: Front-end hardware — Ap/Mac; Front-end software — QuarkXPress; Printers — 2-Ap/Mac LaserPrinter. PRODUCTION: Typesetters — 2-Ap/Mac; Platemaking systems — 1-3M; Direct-to-plate imaging — 1-3M; Scanners — Ap/Mac; Production cameras — 1-B; Automatic film processors — 1-P; Digital color separation equipment — Ap/Power Mac, Adobe/Photoshop.
PRESSROOM: Line 1 — 9-G; Folders — 1-G. MAILROOM: Bundle tyer — 1-Bu; Addressing machine — 1-X/730. COMMUNICATIONS: Systems used — satellite. WIRE SERVICES: News — AP; Photos — AP; Receiving dishes — AP. BUSINESS COMPUTERS: 3-Data General/Vision Data; Applications: Accts receivable, Accts payable, Payroll, Gen ledger, Circ mgmt.

MOUNT AIRY
Surry County
'90 U.S. Census- 7,156; E&P '96 Est. 7,615

Mount Airy News
(e-mon to fri; S)

Mount Airy News, 319 N. Renfro St.; PO Box 808, Mount Airy, NC 27030; tel (910) 786-4141; fax (910) 789-2816. Mid-South Management Co. Inc. group.
Circulation: 8,879(e); 9,345(S); Sworn Sept. 30, 1995.
Price: 50¢(d); $1.00(S); $1.95/wk; $9.10/mo; $93.00/yr.
Advertising: Open inch rate $11.16(e); $11.16(S). **Representative:** Papert Companies.
News Service: AP. **Politics:** Independent. **Established:** 1880.
Not Published: Christmas (unless it falls on a Sunday).
Special Editions: Progress (Mar); Foothill Farmer (monthly); Simple Pleasures (Apr through Oct).
Special Weekly Sections: Farm Page (tues); Best Food Day (wed); Entertainment (fri).
Magazines: Farm Page (tues); Best Food Day (wed); Weekend Real Estate; TV Guide.

CORPORATE OFFICER
President/Chairman of the Board (Mid-South Management Co, SC) — Phyllis DeLapp
GENERAL MANAGEMENT
Publisher — George W Summerlin
ADVERTISING
Manager — Anthony Summerlin
TELECOMMUNICATIONS
Manager-Info Line — Wanda Dillard
CIRCULATION
Manager — Roger Jolly
NEWS EXECUTIVES
Editor — Peter Williams
Managing Editor — Tom Joyce
PRODUCTION
Foreman-Pressroom — Jerry Beasley

Market Information: Zoned editions; TMC; Operate audiotex.
Mechanical available: Offset; Black and 3 ROP colors; insert accepted — preprinted; page cut-offs — 21½".
Mechanical specifications: Type page 13" x 21½"; E - 6 cols, 2¹⁄₁₆", ⅛" between; A - 6 cols, 2¹⁄₁₆", ⅛" between; C - 9 cols, 1³⁄₈", ¹⁄₁₆" between.
Commodity consumption: Newsprint 510 short tons; widths 30"; single pages printed 6,000; average pages per issue 18(d), 32(S); single plates used 6,000.
Equipment: EDITORIAL: Front-end hardware — 7-Mk/Touchwriter Plus, 2-Mk/Touchwriter; Front-end software — Mk; Printers — Ap/Mac LaserWriter Plus, Okidata; Other equipment — Ap/Mac LC, Lf/AP Leaf Picture Desk. CLASSIFIED: Front-end hardware — 2-Mk/Touchwriter, 2-Ap/Mac; Front-end software — Mk. AUDIOTEX: Hardware — Edu Com. DISPLAY: Adv layout systems — Ap/Mac; Front-end hardware — Ap/Mac IIci, Ap/Mac IIcx; Front-end software — Multi-Ad/Creator, Mk/Touchwriter Plus, Mk/Ad Touch; Printers — Ap/Mac LaserWriter IIg. PRODUCTION: Typesetters — Ap/Mac LaserWriter Plus, Ap/Mac LaserWriter IIg; Plate exposures — Nu/Flip Top FTUP; Plate processors — Nat/A-250; Electronic picture desk — Lf/AP Leaf Picture Desk; Scanners — Polaroid/SprintScan; Production cameras — SCREEN/C-260-D; Automatic film processors — LE/2100 Rapid Access; Shrink lenses — 1-Kamerak/Squeeze Lens; Color separation equipment (conventional) — Ik/Scanitek 100, Ik/RC.
PRESSROOM: Line 1 — 6-G/Community. MAILROOM: Inserters and stuffers — MM/267 9722; Bundle tyer — 2-MLN/Spirit; Wrapping singles — KR/Quarterfolder 324; Addressing machine — KR. WIRE SERVICES: News — AP; Photos — AP; Receiving dishes — size-12ft, AP. BUSINESS COMPUTERS: Unisys/S-4040; Applications: Gen ledger, Accts payable, Payroll, Adv mgmt, Circ.

NEW BERN
Craven County
'90 U.S. Census- 17,363; E&P '96 Est. 20,814
ABC-NDM (90): 102,399 HH (37,557)

The Sun Journal
(m-mon to sat; S)

The Sun-Journal, 226 Pollock St.; PO Box 1149, New Bern, NC 28560-1149; tel (919) 638-8101; fax (919) 638-4664; e-mail ke907@pro-finders.c&s.com. Freedom Communications Inc. group.
Circulation: 16,353(m); 16,353(m-sat); 17,420(S); ABC Sept. 30, 1995.
Price: 50¢(d); 50¢(sat); $1.00(S); $6.50/mo.
Advertising: Open inch rate $10.80(m); $10.80(m-sat); $10.80(S). **Representative:** Papert Companies.
News Services: AP, NEA. **Politics:** Independent. **Established:** 1876.
Note: Effective Sept. 1, 1995, this publication changed its publishing plan from (e-mon to fri; S) to (m-mon to sat; S).
Special Editions: Shriners (Jan); Brides (Feb); Home and Garden (Mar); Hurricane Awareness (July); Back-to-School (Aug); Home and Garden (Sept); Christmas Catalog (Nov).
Special Weekly Sections: Food Section (wed); Farm Page (thur); Church News, Church Page (sat); Business Page, TV View (S).
Magazines: TV View (S); Real Estate (monthly); Vintage Times (bi-monthly).

GENERAL MANAGEMENT
Publisher — John R Graham
ADVERTISING
Director — Dennis A Frazier
MARKETING AND PROMOTION
Director-Marketing — Dennis A Frazier
CIRCULATION
Manager — Billie Heuser
NEWS EXECUTIVE
Editor — Patrick Holmes
EDITORS AND MANAGERS
Business Editor — Maureen Donald
City Editor — Steve Jones
Life Editor — Laurie Gengenbach
Sports Editor — Ken Buday
MANAGEMENT INFORMATION SERVICES
Data Processing Manager — Ken Edwards
PRODUCTION
Manager-Graphics — Dennis A Frazier
Foreman-Pressroom — James Mattocks

Market Information: Zoned editions; Split Run; TMC.
Mechanical available: Offset; Black and 3 ROP colors; insert accepted — preprinted, single sheet; page cut-offs — 22¾".
Mechanical specifications: Type page 13" x 21½"; E - 6 cols, 2¹⁄₁₆", ⅛" between; A - 6 cols, 2¹⁄₁₆", ⅛" between; C - 8 cols, 1½", ⅛" between.
Commodity consumption: Newsprint 960 metric tons; width 27½"; black ink 21,500 pounds; color ink 1,850 pounds; single pages printed 8,775; average pages per issue 24(d), 46(S); single plates used 12,285.
Equipment: EDITORIAL: Front-end hardware — Ap/Mac; Front-end software — Baseview 1.1.2; Printers — Ap/Mac LaserWriter, Xante/Accel-a-Writer. CLASSIFIED: Front-end hardware — Ap/Mac; Front-end software — Baseview 3.1.1; Printers — Ap/Mac LaserWriter II NTX, Xante/Accel-a-Writer. DISPLAY: Adv layout systems — Ap/Mac; Front-end hardware — Ap/Mac; Front-end software — QuarkXPress 3.3, Aldus/FreeHand 3.1.1; Printers — Ap/Mac LaserWriter II NTX, Xante/Accel-a-Writer. PRODUCTION: Pagination software — QuarkXPress 3.3, Baseview 1.1.2; OCR software — Caere/OmniPage 2.12; Typesetters — Ap/Mac LaserWriters, Xante/Accel-a-Writer, Panther/Plus; Platemaking systems — Nu/FT40; Plate processors — Nat; Electronic picture desk — Lf/AP Leaf Picture Desk; Scanners — Kk/RFS-2035, Polaroid/SpiritScan 35, Microtek/Scan-Maker, III, Ap/Mac; Production cameras — C/Spartan III; Automatic film processors — Wing Lynch/RS-41, Konica/PowerMatic 66F; Color separation equipment (conventional) — Ap/Power Mac, Adobe/Photoshop 3.0.
PRESSROOM: Line 1 — 6-G/Urbanite; Folders — 1-G; Press control system — Fin. MAILROOM: Bundle tyer — 1-M/Weldloc. LIBRARY: Electronic — SMS/Stauffer 3.2. WIRE SERVICES: News — AP; Stock tables — TMS (via ARA); Receiving dishes — size-10ft, AP. BUSINESS COMPUTERS: PC; Applications: Adv, Circ; Vision Data; PCs & micros networked; PCs & main system networked.

NEWTON
Catawba County
'90 U.S. Census- 9,304; E&P '96 Est. 11,388

The Observer-News-Enterprise
(e-mon to fri)

The Observer-News-Enterprise, 309 N. College Ave.; PO Box 48, Newton, NC 28658; tel (704) 464-0221; fax (704) 464-1267. Hollinger International Inc. group.
Circulation: 3,271(e); Sworn Nov. 16, 1995.
Price: 50¢(d); $51.22/yr.
Advertising: Open inch rate $7.57(e). **Representative:** Landon Associates Inc.
News Service: AP. **Politics:** Independent. **Established:** 1879.
Not Published: Christmas.
Advertising not accepted: Fortune tellers; Work at Home; Job List.
Special Editions: Friday Magazine (monthly); Outdoor Living; Back-to-School; Spring and Fall Fashion; Christmas Gift Guide; Brides; Football; Graduation; Home Improvement; Farming; Holiday Cookbook; Newcomers; Insight.
Special Weekly Sections: Mini Pages (tues); Food (wed); Business (thur); Religion (fri).

GENERAL MANAGEMENT
Publisher — Jerry Hodge
Business Manager — Sherly Taylor
General Manager — Jerry Hodge
ADVERTISING
Director — Sharon Rhymer
Manager-Classified — Norma McKinney
TELECOMMUNICATIONS
Audiotex Manager — Jerry Hodge
NEWS EXECUTIVE
Managing Editor — Jennifer Miller
EDITORS AND MANAGERS
Editorial Writer — Jennifer Miller
Photo Department Manager — Jennifer Miller
Sports Editor — Jeffery Waker

PRODUCTION

Manager Bobby Jolley
Foreman-Pressroom Frank Killian

Market Information: TMC.
Mechanical available: Offset; Black and 3 ROP colors; insert accepted — preprinted; page cut-offs — 21 1/4".
Mechanical specifications: Type page 13" x 21"; E - 6 cols, 2 1/16", 1/8" between; A - 6 cols, 2 1/16", 1/8" between; C - 10 cols, 1 3/16", 3/32" between.
Commodity consumption: Newsprint 406.29 short tons; widths 28", 14"; black ink 7,685 pounds; color ink 1,458 pounds; single pages printed 6,258; average pages per issue 14(d); single plates used 5,704.
Equipment: EDITORIAL: Front-end hardware — COM; Printers — COM. CLASSIFIED: Front-end hardware — COM. DISPLAY: Adv layout systems — COM; Printers — Ap/Mac Laser-Printer. PRODUCTION: Typesetters — COM; Plate exposures — Nu/Flip Top; Production cameras — LE; Automatic film processors — LE.
PRESSROOM: Line 1 — 7-KP/Offset web; Line 2 — 1-Stubbs/Stacker; Press control system — TF&E/Press Room Devices. MAILROOM: Addressing machine — Am. WIRE SERVICES: News — AP; Receiving dishes — AP. BUSINESS COMPUTERS: L/9000.

RALEIGH
Wake County

'90 U.S. Census- 207,951; E&P '96 Est. 254,622
ABC-CZ (90): 207,951 (HH 85,822)

The News & Observer
(m-mon to sat; S)

The News & Observer, 215 S. McDowell St.; PO Box 191, Raleigh, NC 27602; tel (919) 829-4500; fax (919) 829-4872; e-mail forum@rnope.nando.net; web site http://www.nando.net.
Circulation: 146,688(m); 169,028(m-sat); 196,434(S); ABC Sept. 30, 1995.
Price: 50¢(d); 50¢(sat); $1.50(S); $2.77/wk (carrier); $12.00/mo (carrier); $144.00/yr (carrier).
Advertising: Open inch rate $81.07(m); $84.98(m-sat); $90.23(S).
News Services: AP, Bloomberg, CT, KRT, LAT-WP, NYT. **Politics:** Independent-Democrat. **Established:** 1865.
Advertising not accepted: Massage parlors; Bingo; Fortune tellers; Discriminatory ads; Ads with 900 numbers.
Special Editions: Triangle Homes, Triangle Auto (monthly).
Special Weekly Sections: Mini Page (mon); Food Section (wed); Auto Section (thur); Weekend (fri); Channels, Home (sat); Arts & Entertainment, Travel, Sunday (Features), Color Comics (S).
Cable TV: Operate leased cable TV in circulation area.

CORPORATE OFFICERS

President Frank A Daniels Jr
Vice Pres Richard L Henderson
Vice Pres Jack Andrews
Vice Pres Fred Crisp
Secretary John S Barton Jr
Treasurer Bob Woronoff

GENERAL MANAGEMENT

Publisher Frank A Daniels Jr
Personnel Director Eddie Jackson
Controller John S Barton Jr
General Manager Fred Crisp

ADVERTISING

Director-Sales/Marketing Richard L Henderson
Director-Display Jim McClure
Director-Marketing/Research Bob Oney
Manager-Retail Tim Allen
Manager-National Boyd Spence
Manager-Regional Mack McCormick
Manager-Classified Durwood Canaday

TELECOMMUNICATIONS

Publisher-Online Service/Electronic Publishing Frank Daniels III

CIRCULATION

Director Jeff Burcham
Manager-Operations Ed Ketron
Manager-Marketing Maria Buckley
Manager-Home Delivery/Single Copy Curt Phipps
Manager-Distribution Joedie Spence
Manager-State Talmadge Ingram
Manager-Development Denise Hampton
Manager-Audiotex Pat Collins

NEWS EXECUTIVES

Senior Managing Editor Anders Gyllenhaal
Managing Editor/Enterprise Judy Bolch
Managing Editor/Daily Mike Yopp
Newsroom Administrator Patricia Hall
Newsroom Asst Trina Sydnor

EDITORS AND MANAGERS

Arts/Entertainment Editor Suzanne Brown
Books Editor David Perkins
Business Editor Dan Gearino
Cartoonist Dwane Powell
Columnist/Editorial Writer Dennis Rogers
Columnist/Editorial Writer Barry Saunders
Columnist Nicole Brodeur
Columnist A C Snow
Computer-aided Editor Pat Smith
Design/Features Kate Anthony
Design/News Damon Cain
Editorial Page Editor Steven B Ford
Editorial Writer James Jenkins
Editorial Writer Jane Ruffin
Editorial Writer Allen Torrey
Entertainment Editor-Day Mary Cornatzer
Features Editor Felicia Gressette
Food Editor Debbie Moose
Graphics Editor Ken Mowry
Home/Travel Editor Laurie Evan
Metro Editor Ned Barnett
Metro Editor-Day Paul Brown
Deputy Metro Editor/Durham Nancy Barnes
News Editor Thad Ogburn
News Editor-Day Pam Nelson
New Media Editor Bruce Siceloff
News/Research Director Teresa Leonard
Night Editor Eric Frederick
North Carolina Editor Rob Waters
Photography Editor John Hansen
Presentation Editor David Pickel
Specialties Editor Trish Wilson
Sports Editor George Lawrence
State Editor Sheon Ladson
Sunday Projects Editor Melanie Sill
Weekend/Entertainment Editor Joe Miller

MANAGEMENT INFORMATION SERVICES

Programming Manager Mary Anne Blue

PRODUCTION

Director-Operations Danny Collins
Manager Fleet Woodley
Manager-Electronic Service Larry Benson
Manager-Packaging Daniel Mattei
Manager-Programming Mary Anne Blue
Manager-Computer Operations Glenn Wilks
Manager-Operations Support Robert Pierce
Manager-Mechanical/Electrical Service Allen Sanders
Manager-Printed Quality Bruce Toy
Manager-Resource Development Sharon Vignali
Coordinator-Material Safety Frank Trainer
Coordinator (Night) Jan Brown
Press Trainer Jeff Magner

Market Information: Zoned editions; Split Run; TMC; ADS; Operate database; Operate audiotex; Electronic edition.
Mechanical available: Flexo (direct); Black and 3 ROP colors; insert accepted — preprinted; page cut-offs — 22".
Mechanical specifications: Type page 13" x 21"; E - 6 cols, 2 1/16", 1/8" between; A - 6 cols, 2 1/16", 1/8" between; C - 10 cols, 1 3/16", 1/8" between.
Commodity consumption: Newsprint 31,277 short tons; widths 54", 40 1/2", 27"; black ink 599,000 pounds; color ink 65,000 pounds; single pages printed 27,298; average pages per issue 100(d), 200(S); single plates used 141,733.
Equipment: EDITORIAL: Front-end hardware — 1-Sun/Sparc 1000, 1-Ap/Mac Quadra 950 file server, 160-Ap/Power Mac; Front-end software — Quark Copy Desk, QPS, Quick Wire; Printers — Laser. CLASSIFIED: Front-end hardware — SII/Sys 55-TXP, 105-SII/Coyote QB, 5-PC/CAT 30, 5-Ap/Mac IIfx, Ap/Mac IIci; Printers — Laser, 3-HP/Dot Matrix. AUDIOTEX: Hardware — Brite Voice Systems/City Line, Computalk, N&O/Property Line, Nio/AutoLine, N&O/Class News; Software — Brite Voice Systems, AP, Weatherwatch/City Line, Computalk; Supplier name — Micro Voice. DISPLAY: Adv layout systems — Mk/Managing Editor ALS, Multi-Ad/Creator; Printers — 1-HP/Laserwriter Pro RB 121 30-N, 1-HP/LaserJet, 4-HP/LaserJet 4, 3-HP/LaserJet 4L, 1-HP/Line Printer 2562C, 1-HP/Resolution Enhance, 2-LaserWriter 6/bb; Other equipment — 56-Ap/Mac, 27-PC. PRODUCTION: Pagination software — QPS; Typesetters — 4-MON/3850, 2-Graphic Enterprises/Pagescan 3, 2-Sun/1000S OPI, 6-Sun/10-51 RIP, MON/RIPs; Platemaking systems — 3-Na/Flex; Plate exposures — 3-FX/IVS; Plate processors — 3-FP/II CE; Electronic picture desk — Lf/AP Leaf Picture Desk, Adobe/Photoshop; Scanners — 1-ECR/Autokon 1000; Production cameras — 1-C/Marathon, 1-C/Spartan III; Automatic film processors — 2-P/26 ML, 1-L/LS2600; Film transporters — 1-C/1246; Shrink lenses — 2-CK Optical/SQU-7; Digital color separation equipment — 2-Sharp/JX6000, 5-Kk/20-3Plus, 5-Ap/Mac Quadra 950, 5-Kk/RFS-35, Adobe/Photoshop. PRESSROOM: Line 1 — 9-KBA-MOT (CIC Fullcolor); Line 2 — 9-KBA-MOT (CIC Fullcolor); Folders — 2-3:2 KBA-MOT/160 page capacity Folders, 1-3:2 KBA-MOT/160 page capacity Folders; Pasters — 18-G/w AGS upgrader; Press control system — Eurotherm; Press registration system — 4-pin no bend magnetic lock up, New Graphics. MAILROOM: Counter stackers — 6-HL/Monitor, 4-HL/Dual Carriers; Inserters and stuffers — 3-HI/1472 on-line; Bundle tyer — 5-OVL/JP80, 1-MLN/2A, 4-Power Strap/PS5, 1-MLN/MLIEE; Addressing machine — 1-Ch/525E, 2-AVY/on-line. LIBRARY: Electronic — WAIS/Archive Vended through Data Times. COMMUNICATIONS: Remote imagesetting — Hyphen/OPI, Sun/Sparc II; Digital ad delivery system — AP AdSend, AdSat, HEX. Systems used — fiber optic. WIRE SERVICES: News — AP, Bloomberg, CT, KRT, LAT-WP, NYT; Stock tables — AP SelectStox; Syndicates — North America Syndicate; Receiving dishes — size-10ft, AP. BUSINESS COMPUTERS: 2-HP/3000-960, Sun/Sparc 1000; Applications: Payroll, Human resource mgmt, Adv billing, Accts payable, Accts receivable, Gen ledger, 401K mgmt, Newsprint inventory tracking, Fixed assets, Resource mgmt, Electronic office; PCs & micros networked; PCs & main system networked.

REIDSVILLE
Rockingham County

'90 U.S. Census- 12,183; E&P '96 Est. 11,924

The Reidsville Review
(e-tues to fri; S)

The Reidsville Review, 1921 Vance St.; PO Box 2157, Reidsville, NC 27320; tel (910) 349-4331; fax (910) 342-2513. Southern Newspapers Inc. group.
Circulation: 6,590(e); 6,590(S); Sworn Oct. 1, 1995.
Price: 50¢(d); $1.00(S); $1.25/wk; $58.95/yr.
Advertising: Open inch rate $6.25(e); $7.00(e-wed); $6.25(S). **Representative:** Landon Associates Inc.
News Service: AP. **Politics:** Independent. **Established:** 1888.
Not Published: Christmas.
Special Editions: Tax Supplement (Jan); Progress Edition (Feb); Home Improvement (Mar); Car Care, Home Improvement (Apr); Folk Festival, Home Improvement, Car Care (May); Brides, Little League, Home Improvement, Car Care (June); Home Improvement, Car Care (July); Home Improvement, Car Care, Ag (Aug); Home Improvement, Car Care (Sept & Oct); All Major Sports; Back-to-School; Fashion Edition.

CORPORATE OFFICERS

President James M DeLapp
Vice Pres Lissa W Walls
Vice Pres Cooper Walls

GENERAL MANAGEMENT

Publisher James M DeLapp
Purchasing Agent James M DeLapp

CIRCULATION

Manager John O'Bryant

NEWS EXECUTIVES

Editor James M DeLapp
Managing Editor Glenn Cook

EDITORS AND MANAGERS

Action Line Editor/Public Eye Glenn Cook
Amusements/Books Editor Glenn Cook
Business/Finance Editor Glenn Cook
City/Metro Editor Glenn Cook
Education Editor Glenn Cook
Environmental Editor Glenn Cook
Editorial Page Editor James M DeLapp
Features Editor Glenn Cook
Graphics Editor/Art Director Glenn Cook
Health/Medical Editor Glenn Cook
National Editor Glenn Cook
News Editor Glenn Cook
Photo Editor Glenn Cook
Political/Government Editor Glenn Cook
Religion Editor Glenn Cook
Sports Editor Rick Papson
Women's Editor Glenn Cook

PRODUCTION

Superintendent Jimmy Delancy

Market Information: TMC.
Mechanical available: Offset; Black and 3 ROP colors; insert accepted — preprinted, up to 24 pages 8 1/2"x11"; page cut-offs — 21 1/2".
Mechanical specifications: Type page 13" x 21 1/2"; E - 6 cols, 2 1/16", 1/8" between; A - 6 cols, 2 1/16", 1/8" between; C - 9 cols, 1 5/16", 1/8" between.
Commodity consumption: Newsprint 280 short tons; width 27 1/2"; black ink 9,660 pounds; color ink 500 pounds; single pages printed 4,035; average pages per issue 16(d), 16(S); single plates used 2,017.
Equipment: EDITORIAL: Front-end hardware — Ap/Mac SE, Ap/Mac IIcx; Front-end software — QuarkXPress, Baseview/NewsEdit; Printers — Ap/Mac LaserWriter II; Other equipment — Ap/Mac Scanner. CLASSIFIED: Front-end hardware — Ap/Mac SE; Front-end software — Baseview/Class Manager; Printers — Ap/Mac LaserWriter II. DISPLAY: Adv layout systems — Ap/Mac IIcx; Front-end hardware — Ap/Mac IIcx; Front-end software — Multi-Ad/Creator; Printers — Ap/Mac LaserWriter II. PRODUCTION: Typesetters — Ap/Mac IIcx; Plate exposures — Nu/Flip Top FT4043UP; Scanners — Ap/Mac; Production cameras — C/Marathon.
PRESSROOM: Line 1 — G/Community; Line 2 — G/Community; Line 3 — G/Community; Line 4 — G/Community; Line 5 — G/Community; Line 6 — G/Community. WIRE SERVICES: News — AP; Receiving dishes — size-2ft, AP. BUSINESS COMPUTERS: IBM/Newsware, Smith Corona/PC 386SX HD; Applications: IBM/Newsware; PCs & micros networked; PCs & main system networked.

ROANOKE RAPIDS
Halifax County

'90 U.S. Census- 15,722; E&P '96 Est. 17,102
ABC-CZ (90): 15,722 (HH 6,321)

Daily Herald (e-mon to fri; S)

Daily Herald, 916 Roanoke Ave.; PO Box 520, Roanoke Rapids, NC 27870; tel (919) 537-2505; fax (919) 537-2314. Wick Communications group.
Circulation: 12,289(e); 13,027(S); ABC Sept. 30, 1995.
Price: 50¢(d); $1.25(S); $1.70/wk; $88.40/yr.
Advertising: Open inch rate $8.95(e); $8.95(S). **Representative:** Landon Associates Inc.
News Service: AP. **Politics:** Independent. **Established:** 1914.
Not Published: New Year; Memorial Day; Independence Day; Labor Day; Thanksgiving; Christmas.
Special Editions: Honor Roll of Business, Jaycee Week (Jan); Bride & Groom, Boy Scouts, Washington's Birthday (Feb); Girl Scouts, Spring Opening, Home & Garden (Mar); Auto Racing Edition (Apr); Progress Tab (May); July 4th Sales, Christmas in July (July); Back-to-School, Football Kick-off Tab (Aug); Fall Opening (Sept); Businesswomen's Week (Oct); Christmas Gift Guide (Nov); Basketball Tip-off, Christmas Shoppers Tab, Christmas Greetings (Dec).
Magazines: TV Showtime (tab), USA Weekend (S).

CORPORATE OFFICERS

President Walter M Wick
Vice Pres Lou Major Sr

GENERAL MANAGEMENT

Publisher Stephen Woody
Purchasing Agent Stephen Woody
Office Manager Linda Smith

ADVERTISING

Director Tim Frates
Manager-Classified Linda Foster

MARKETING AND PROMOTION

Director-Marketing/Promotion Tim Frates

CIRCULATION

Director Carol Moseley

NEWS EXECUTIVE

Editor Philip Vega

EDITORS AND MANAGERS

Business/Finance Editor Lance Martin
Editorial Page Editor Stephen Woody
Education Editor Philip Vega
Features Editor Philip Vega
Living/Lifestyle Editor Dot Benthall
National Editor Philip Vega

News Editor	Lance Martin
Political/Government Editor	Philip Vega
Society Editor	Dot Benthall
Sports Editor	Greg Jenkins
Photo Editor	Walt Petruska
Women's Editor	Dot Benthall

PRODUCTION

Foreman-Pressroom	David Hager

Market Information: Zoned editions; Split Run; TMC; ADS.
Mechanical available: Offset; Black and 3 ROP colors; insert accepted — preprinted, single sheets; page cut-offs — 22¾".
Mechanical specifications: Type page 13" x 21½"; E - 6 cols, 2 1/16", ⅛" between; A - 6 cols, 2 1/16", ⅛" between; C - 9 cols, 1 5/16", ⅛" between.
Commodity consumption: Newsprint 530 metric tons; widths 27½", 13¾"; black ink 11,500 pounds; color ink 700 pounds; single pages printed 6,550; average pages per issue 16(d), 38(S); single plates used 7,000.
Equipment: EDITORIAL: Front-end hardware — Mk/3000. CLASSIFIED: Front-end hardware — Mk/3000. DISPLAY: Adv layout systems — Ap/Mac; Front-end hardware — 1-Ap/Mac IIci, 2-Ap/Mac Centris 650, 1-Ap/Mac 7100 AV; Front-end software — Multi-Ad/Creator 3.8; Printers — 1-Xante/8200, 1-Ap/Mac IIf; Other equipment — Nikon/Coolscan. PRODUCTION: Typesetters — Mk/3000; Platemaking systems — Nat; Plate exposures — 1-Nu/FT40; Plate processors — 1-Ic; Scanners — Konica/Scanner; Production cameras — 1-B, Acti/Prod Camera; Digital color separation equipment — Adobe/Photoshop on Ap/Power Mac 7100. PRESSROOM: Line 1 — 7-Web Leader/Atlas. MAILROOM: Bundle tyer — 1-Bu; Addressing machine — Vision Data. WIRE SERVICES: News — AP; Receiving dishes — size-10ft, AP. BUSINESS COMPUTERS: Applications: Vision Data: Accounting, Circ.

ROCKINGHAM

Richmond County

'90 U.S. Census- 9,399; E&P '96 Est. 10,754
ABC-CZ (90): 13,557 (HH 5,371)

Richmond County Daily Journal (e-mon to fri; S)

Richmond County Daily Journal, 105 E. Washington St.; PO Box 1888, Rockingham, NC 28380; tel (910) 997-3111; fax (910) 997-4321. Park Communications Inc. group.
Circulation: 8,610(e); 8,852(S); ABC Sept. 30, 1995.
Price: 50¢(d); 75¢(S).
Advertising: Open inch rate $8.50(e); $8.50(S). **Representative:** Landon Associates Inc.
News Service: AP. **Politics:** Independent. **Established:** 1931.
Special Editions: Senior Citizens, Bridal Guide (Jan); Personal Finance, NASCAR Race Week (Feb); Spring Fashion, Home Improvement (Mar); Spring Car Care, Lawn and Garden (Apr); Small Business, Outdoor's Bridal Guide (May); Graduation, Health & Fitness (June); Progress Edition (July); Back to School, Football (Aug); Fall Home Improvement, Lay-away, Fall Fashions (Sept); NASCAR Race Week, Cosmetology, Women in Business (Oct); Holiday Recipes, Holiday Gift Guide (Nov); Christmas Carols, Last Minute Gift Guide, Christmas Greetings (Dec).
Special Weekly Sections: Food Section, Real Estate (wed); Local Life (S).
Magazines: Weekly TV Supplement; Real Estate Guide (monthly).

GENERAL MANAGEMENT

General Manager	Marvin Enderle

ADVERTISING

Manager-General	Terry Cooper

CIRCULATION

Manager	Molly Partin

NEWS EXECUTIVE

Editor	Glenn Sumpter

EDITORS AND MANAGERS

Editorial Writer	Glenn Sumpter
News Editor	Bert Unger
Society/Women's Editor	Catherine Monk
Sports Editor	Bill Lindau
Sunday Editor	Clark Cox

PRODUCTION

Foreman-Engraving	Randy Jarrell
Foreman-Pressroom	John Covington

Market Information: TMC.
Mechanical available: Offset; Black and 3 ROP colors; insert accepted — preprinted; page cut-offs — 21".
Mechanical specifications: Type page 13" x 21"; E - 6 cols, 2 1/16", ⅛" between; A - 6 cols, 2 1/16", ⅛" between; C - 10 cols, 1 7/32", ⅛" between.
Commodity consumption: Newsprint 400 short tons; width 27½"; average pages per issue 20(d), 38(S).
Equipment: EDITORIAL: Front-end hardware — Mk. CLASSIFIED: Front-end hardware — Mk. DISPLAY: Front-end hardware — Ap/Mac. PRODUCTION: Plate exposures — 1-Nu/FS114; Plate processors — 1-Nat/104; Production cameras — 1-B/Caravel; Automatic film processors — 1-P. PRESSROOM: Line 1 — 7-KP/Color King; Folders — 1-KP. MAILROOM: Inserters and stuffers — 4-MM; Bundle tyer — 2-Bu; Addressing machine — 2-El. LIBRARY: Electronic — 1-CS. WIRE SERVICES: News — AP; Syndicates — United Features; Receiving dishes — AP.

ROCKY MOUNT

Nash and Edgecombe Counties

'90 U.S. Census- 48,997; E&P '96 Est. 58,474
ABC-CZ (90): 48,997 (HH 18,871)

Rocky Mount Telegram (e-mon to sat; S)

Rocky Mount Telegram, 150 Howard St.; PO Box 1080, Rocky Mount, NC 27802; tel (919) 446-5161; fax (919) 446-4057. Thomson Newspapers group.
Circulation: 15,362(e); 15,362(e-sat); 17,045(S); ABC Sept. 30, 1995.
Price: 50¢(d); 75¢(wed); 50¢(sat); $1.25(S); $9.50/mo.
Advertising: Open inch rate $13.70(e); $13.70(e-sat); $13.70(S). **Representative:** Landon Associates Inc.
News Service: AP. **Politics:** Independent. **Established:** 1911 (Evening), 1949 (Sunday).
Advertising not accepted: Envelope stuffing.
Special Editions: Spring & Fall Fashion Section, Car Care (Spring & Fall); Bride & Groom, Chronology, Parade of Homes (Realtors) (Jan); To your Good Health (Feb); Perspective (Mar); Home & Garden, A Day in the Life (Apr); To Mom with Love, Mobile Home, Industry of the Year, Medical Health, Customer Appreciation (May); Foot Ball, Health & Fitness, Literacy, Downtown, Home Furnishing (Sept); Downeast Fest., Business Profile (Oct); New Car Preview (Nov); Jolly Holly X'mas, HO HO HO Holiday Bargains, Last Minute X'mas, X'mas Greetings, Christmas Gift Guide (Dec).
Special Weekly Sections: Best Food Day (wed); Seniors, Automotive, Outdoors (thur); TV Magazine, Church News (sat); Business, Automotive, Real Estate, Women's (S).
Magazines: TV Telegram, TV (sat); Thomson Newspapers Comic Group, Parade, Local Color Comics (S); Real Estate Guide, Tarboro Telegram (zoned-S).

GENERAL MANAGEMENT

Publisher/General Manager	Den Dickerson
Accountant	Nancy Duncan
Purchasing Agent	Jim Butt

ADVERTISING

Director	Mark Fortune
Manager-Classified	Paula Johnson
Manager-National	Terri Goda

CIRCULATION

Director	Dave Roe

NEWS EXECUTIVE

Managing Editor	Jeff Herrin

EDITORS AND MANAGERS

Action Line Editor/Open Line	Jeff Herrin
Automotive Editor	Erick Eckard
City Editor	Charlie Hall
Editorial Page Editor	Jeff Herrin
Farm Editor	Tom Murphy
Fashion/Food Editor	Shawn Lewis
Features Editor	Shawn Lewis
Photo Department Manager	Chuck Beckley
Sports Editor	Mark Aumann
Women's Editor	Shawn Lewis

MANAGEMENT INFORMATION SERVICES

Data Processing Manager	Nancy Duncan

PRODUCTION

Supervisor	Keith Abbott
Foreman-Composing	Russell Matthews
Foreman-Pressroom	Ray Walker

Market Information: Zoned editions; TMC.
Mechanical available: Offset; Black and 3 ROP colors; insert accepted — preprinted, single sheets, cards, coupons; page cut-offs — 21½".
Mechanical specifications: Type page 13" x 21½"; E - 6 cols, 2 1/16", ⅛" between; A - 6 cols, 2 1/16", ⅛" between; C - 9 cols, 1⅜", 1/16" between.
Commodity consumption: Newsprint 1,130 short tons; widths 27½", 13¾"; black ink 16,775 pounds; color ink 5,750 pounds; single pages printed 9,144; average pages per issue 24(d), 48(S); single plates used 1,025.
Equipment: EDITORIAL: Front-end hardware — Mk/1100 Plus; Front-end software — Mk; Printers — Ap/Mac LaserWriter II NT; Other equipment — Ap/Mac. CLASSIFIED: Front-end hardware — Mk/1100 Plus; Front-end software — Mk; Printers — 1-TI/810. DISPLAY: Front-end hardware — 3-Ap/Mac IIci. PRODUCTION: Typesetters — 2-V/5100A; Plate exposures — 1-Nu/Flip Top FT40LNS, 1-Nu/Flip Top FT40V6UPNS; Plate processors — 1-Nat/A-250; Production cameras — 1-DSA/680-C; Automatic film processors — 2-LE/LD-220-QT; Color separation equipment (conventional) — Lf/Leafscan 35. PRESSROOM: Line 1 — 6-G/Urbanite; Folders — G. MAILROOM: Bundle tyer — 2-OVL. WIRE SERVICES: News — AP, TNN; Photos — AP; Receiving dishes — size-3m, AP. BUSINESS COMPUTERS: ATT/3B2-500, ATT/477, ATT/444.

SALISBURY-SPENCER-EAST SPENCER

Rowan County

'90 U.S. Census- 28,361 (Salisbury 23,087; Spencer 3,219; East Spencer 2,055); E&P '96 Est. 36,750 (Salisbury 31,270; Spencer 3,484; East Spencer 1,996)
ABC-CZ (90): 32,545 (HH 12,902)

Salisbury Post (e-mon to sat; S)

Salisbury Post, 131 W. Inner St.; PO Box 4639, Salisbury, NC 28145; tel (704) 633-8950.
Circulation: 25,569(e); 25,569(e-sat); 26,388(S); ABC Sept. 30, 1995.
Price: 50¢(d); 50¢(sat); $1.00(S); $8.00/mo (carrier); $96.00/yr (carrier).
Advertising: Open inch rate $17.00(e); $17.00(e-sat); $18.00(S). **Representative:** Papert Companies.
News Service: AP. **Politics:** Independent. **Established:** 1905.
Not Published: Christmas.
Advertising not accepted: Hard liquor.
Special Editions: Tax Section, Spelling Bee (Jan); Bridal Section (Feb); Spring Home Improvement (Mar); Nat'l Sportscasters & Sportswriters Association (Apr); Drugs, Summer Fun Section (May); Graduation (June); A Day in the Life (July); Back-to-School, Football Section (Aug); Fall Fashion, Fall Home Improvement (Sept); OctoberTour (Oct); New Car Introduction, Holiday Recipe Favorites, Holiday Gift Guide, High School Basketball (Nov); Christmas Carol Book (Dec).
Special Weekly Sections: Farm Page (mon); Best Food Day (wed); The Scene (thur); Youth Page (fri); Outdoor, TV Section, Church/Religion (sat); Travel, Book Page, Insight, Business, Real Estate, Automotive Sections (S); Stock Page, Entertainment, TV, Business (daily).
Magazine: USA Weekend (S).

CORPORATE OFFICERS

Board Chairman	J F Hurley III
President	Gordon P Hurley
Secretary/Treasurer	J F Hurley III

GENERAL MANAGEMENT

Publisher	J F Hurley III
Assoc Publisher	Jason R Lesley
General Manager	John Rink
Business Manager/Purchasing Agent	John Rink

ADVERTISING

Manager-General	Steve Johnson

MARKETING AND PROMOTION

Manager-Marketing/Promotion	Don Stiller

CIRCULATION

Director	Ron Brooks

NEWS EXECUTIVES

Editor	Elizabeth G Cook
Managing Editor	Frank DeLoache

EDITORS AND MANAGERS

Area News Editor	Frank DeLoache
Books Editor	Deirdre Parker Smith
Editorial Page Editor	Geitner Simmons
Education Editor	Tracy Presson
Features Editor	Sylvia Wiseman
Films/Theater Editor	Jan Boone
Librarian	Nancy Fisher
Photo Department Manager	Wayne Hinshaw
Political Editor	Tim Ball
Radio/Television Editor	Carole Anne Hallyburton
Religion Editor	Debbie Miller
Sports Editor	Mark Wineka
Teen-Age/Youth Editor	Deirdre Parker Smith
Women's Editor	Sylvia Wiseman
Wire Editor	Gordon Peacock

MANAGEMENT INFORMATION SERVICES

Data Processing Manager	Charlie Frank Hendrix

PRODUCTION

Foreman-Composing	Charlie Frank Hendrix
Foreman-Pressroom	Wade W Fisher
Foreman-Mailroom	Allen Mabe

Market Information: TMC.
Mechanical available: Offset; Black and 3 ROP colors; insert accepted — preprinted, all; page cut-offs — 22".
Mechanical specifications: Type page 13" x 21"; E - 6 cols, 2 1/16", ⅛" between; A - 6 cols, 2 1/16", ⅛" between; C - 9 cols, 1⅜", 1/16" between.
Commodity consumption: Newsprint 2,266 short tons; widths 55", 41¼", 27½"; black ink 37,272 pounds; color ink 3,000 pounds; single pages printed 13,272; average pages per issue 30(d), 67(S); single plates used 30,300.
Equipment: EDITORIAL: Front-end hardware — Ik; Front-end software — ECS 4; Printers — 2-Epson, 2-C.Itoh, 1-Centronics, AU/APS 6600, Ap/Mac LaserWriter, Phases/440 Color; Other equipment — 1-Ap/Mac, DTI/PageSpeed, Kk/2035 Scanner. CLASSIFIED: Front-end hardware — Ik; Front-end software — ECS 4; Printers — 1-Centronics. DISPLAY: Front-end hardware — 6-Ap/Mac; Front-end software — DTI/AdSpeed. PRODUCTION: Pagination software — DTI/PageSpeed; OCR software — Caere/OmniPage 6.0; Typesetters — 2-AU/APS6-108 CHS, 1-Ap/Super Mac; Plate exposures — 2-Nu/Flip Top FT40UPNS; Plate processors — 1-Nat/A-250; Electronic picture desk — Lf/AP Leaf Picture Desk, Mac/Leaf-Leaf/Mac Transfer; Scanners — 1-ECR/Autokon 1000, 2-Umax 1200 dpi color scanner, 2-Epson/1200 DPI; Production cameras — 1-C/Spartan II, 1-C/Spartan III; Automatic film processors — 1-LE/LD-24-AQ, 1-LE/LD-2600A; Film transporters — 1-C/1247, 1-C/1271; Shrink lenses — 1-Alan/24 Variable; Color separation equipment (conventional) — Lf/AP Leaf Picture Desk, AU/108CHS; Digital color separation equipment — Lf/Leafscan 35, Ap/Mac, Adobe/Photoshop, Kk/Scanner. PRESSROOM: Line 1 — 5-G/Metro; Line 2 — 5-G/Metro; Folders — 4-G/2:1. MAILROOM: Counter stackers — 1-HL, 1-MM; Inserters and stuffers — 1-MM; Bundle tyer — 2-Power Strap; Addressing machine — 2-Dispensa-Matic/U-45. WIRE SERVICES: News — AP Datafeatures, AP Datastream; Stock tables — AP; Receiving dishes — AP. BUSINESS COMPUTERS: 2-Convergent/Mighty Frame, 8-Wyse; Applications: Vision Data; PCs & main system networked.

SANFORD

Lee County

'90 U.S. Census- 14,475; E&P '96 Est. 14,224
ABC-CZ (90): 14,475 (HH 5,735)

The Sanford Herald (e-mon to fri; m-sat)

The Sanford Herald, 208 St. Clair Ct.; PO Box 100, Sanford, NC 27331-0100; tel (919) 708-9000; fax (919) 708-9001.
Circulation: 14,056(e); 14,056(m-sat); ABC Sept. 30, 1995.
Price: 50¢(d); 50¢(sat); $6.00/mo; $72.00/yr.
Advertising: Open inch rate $11.25(e); $11.25(m-sat). **Representative:** Landon Associates Inc.
News Service: AP. **Politics:** Democrat-Independent. **Established:** 1930.
Not Published: Labor Day; Christmas.
Advertising not accepted: Envelope stuffing; Liquor; 900 numbers.
Special Editions: IRS Section (Feb); Car Care (Apr); Small Business Expo (May); Summer Lifestyle (June); Back-to-School, Football (Aug); Industrial Edition, Fair Edition (Sept); Christmas Gift Guide (Dec).
Special Weekly Sections: Food (wed); Business (thur); Church (fri).
Magazine: TV Preview (fri).

North Carolina I-297

CORPORATE OFFICERS
President W E Horner Jr
Vice Pres James C Banks
Secretary Bill Horner III
Treasurer Bill Horner III

GENERAL MANAGEMENT
Publisher W E Horner Jr
General Manager Bill Horner III
Purchasing Agent Bill Horner III

ADVERTISING
Director James C Banks
Asst Director Freddie Atkins

MARKETING AND PROMOTION
Manager-Marketing/Promotion Bill Horner III

CIRCULATION
Director Raymond McNeill

NEWS EXECUTIVE
Editor Cornelia Olive

EDITORS AND MANAGERS
Action Line Editor Bill Horner III
City Editor R V Hight
Columnist Bill Horner III
Editorial Page Editor Cornelia Olive
Editorial Writer R V Hight
Editorial Writer Cornelia Olive
Features Editor Bob Roule
Food Editor Marci Smith
Graphics Editor/Art Director Bill Horner III
Librarian Willie Butts
Lifestyle Editor Marci Smith
News Editor R V Hight
Political Editor Bill Horner III
Sports Editor Matt Martin
Television Editor Marci Smith

MANAGEMENT INFORMATION SERVICES
Data Processing Manager Don Bailey

PRODUCTION
Superintendent/Manager Don Bailey
Asst Foreman-Composing Robert O Stone
Foreman-Pressroom Claude Street
Foreman-Camera Don Bailey

Market Information: Zoned editions; Split Run; TMC.
Mechanical available: Offset; Black and 3 ROP colors; insert accepted — preprinted, up to 10 ¾"x13"; page cut-offs — 21½".
Mechanical specifications: Type page 13" x 21½"; E - 6 cols, 2.03", ⅙" between; A - 6 cols, 2.06", ⅛" between; C - 8 cols, 1.33", ⅛" between.
Commodity consumption: Newsprint 725 short tons; widths 27½", 13¾"; black ink 10,000 pounds; color ink 1,000 pounds; single pages printed 8,000; average pages per issue 24(d); single plates used 4,400.
Equipment: EDITORIAL: Front-end hardware — Grid; Front-end software — CText; Printers — COM/8400, Unity/1200XLO LaserWriter. CLASSIFIED: Front-end hardware — Grid; Front-end software — CText; Printers — COM/8400. DISPLAY: Front-end hardware — CText/Adept; Front-end software — CText/Adept; Printers — LaserMaster. PRODUCTION: Typesetters — CG/8400; Platemaking systems — 1-Nu; Plate exposures — 1-Nu; Plate processors — 1-Nat; Scanners — Auto Companica/6500C, Microtek/IIXE ScanMaker, Microtek/MSII; Automatic film processors — 1-AG/66, 1-SCREEN/LD-220-QT. PRESSROOM: Line 1 — 8-G/Community; Folders — 1-G/2:1. MAILROOM: Inserters and stuffers — KAN/480 5-1 inserter; Bundle tyer — 1-Bu, 1-MLN. COMMUNICATIONS: Facsimile — Canon/3030. WIRE SERVICES: News — AP; Photos — AP; Stock tables — AP; Syndicates — United Media, Creators, King Features, TMS, Universal Press, NAS; Receiving dishes — size-8ft, AP. BUSINESS COMPUTERS: DEC; Applications: Data Sciences; PCs & micros networked; PCs & main system networked.

SHELBY
Cleveland County
'90 U.S. Census- 14,669; **E&P '96 Est.** 14,141
ABC-CZ (90): 29,702 (HH 11,730)

The Shelby Star
(e-mon to fri; m-sat; S)

The Shelby Star, 315 E. Graham St.; PO Box 48, Shelby, NC 28150; tel (704) 484-7000; fax (704) 484-0805. Thomson Newspapers group.
Circulation: 16,600(e); 16,600(m-sat); 16,587(S); ABC Sept. 30, 1995.
Price: 50¢(d); 50¢(sat); 75¢(S); $9.50/mo.
Advertising: Open inch rate $15.32(e); $15.32(m-sat); $15.32(S). **Representative:** Papert Companies.
News Service: AP. **Politics:** Independent. **Established:** 1894.
Special Editions: Income Tax Tips; Brides; Home Improvements; Outdoors; Graduation; Vacation; Progress Edition; Back-to-School; Football; Auto Racing; Manufactured Homes; Textiles; Cookbook; Christmas Edition.
Special Weekly Sections: Food (wed); Church Page (sat).
Magazine: TV Time (local, offset) (S).

GENERAL MANAGEMENT
Publisher R Keith Walters

ADVERTISING
Director Charlie Price
Manager-Retail Scott MacRae

TELECOMMUNICATIONS
Audiotex Manager Holly Chatham

CIRCULATION
Manager Kay Stone

EDITORS AND MANAGERS
Business/Finance Editor Steve Doyle
Education Editor Jim Spanks
Entertainment Editor John Hoyle
Fashion/Style Editor Jackie Bridges
Features Editor Chris Horeth
Graphics Editor/Art Director Chris Horeth
Health/Medical Editor Jackie Bridges
Living/Lifestyle Editor Jackie Bridges
News Editor Chris Horeth
Photo Editor Gina Cox
Religion Editor Jim Spanks
Society Editor Jackie Bridges
Sports Editor Alan Ford
Television/Films Editor John Hoyle
Theater/Music Editor Jim Spanks
Travel Editor John Hoyle
Women's Editor Jackie Bridges

PRODUCTION
Superintendent-Composing Arlis Holmes
Superintendent-Press/Plate Arlis Holmes

Market Information: Zoned editions; TMC; Operate audiotex.
Mechanical available: Offset; Black and 3 ROP colors; insert accepted — preprinted; page cut-offs — 27½".
Mechanical specifications: Type page 13" x 21⅜"; E - 6 cols, 2", ⅛" between; A - 6 cols, 2", ⅛" between; C - 9 cols, 1 5/16", ⅛" between.
Commodity consumption: Newsprint 1,000 short tons; widths 13¾", 27½"; average pages per issue 20(d), 20(sat), 28(S).
Equipment: EDITORIAL: Front-end hardware — 16-Mk; Front-end software — Mk. CLASSIFIED: Front-end hardware — 2-Mk; Front-end software — Mk; Printers — Mk. DISPLAY: Front-end hardware — 3-Ap/Mac; Front-end software — Mk/Mycro-Comp AdWriter; Printers — 2-Tegra/Varityper, 1-Tegra/Varityper 5300 Film Recorder. PRODUCTION: Typesetters — 2-V, 1-V/5300; Plate exposures — 2-BKY/Ascor; Plate processors — 1-Nat; Production cameras — 1-B, 1-SCREEN; Automatic film processors — 1-P; Color separation equipment (conventional) — Lf/AP Leaf Picture Desk; Digital color separation equipment — 1-Digi-Colour. PRESSROOM: Line 1 — 6-G/Urbanite; Folders — G/2:1; Reels and stands — G; Press control system — G. MAILROOM: Counter stackers — 1-QWI; Bundle tyer — 2-Strapex; Wrapping singles — 1-QWI; Addressing machine — 1-KR. WIRE SERVICES: News — AP; Receiving dishes — size-10ft, AP. BUSINESS COMPUTERS: 1-IBM/Sys 36; Applications: Bus, Circ; PCs & main system networked.

SPENCER
See SALISBURY

STATESVILLE
Iredell County
'90 U.S. Census- 17,567; **E&P '96 Est.** 16,712
ABC-NDM (90): 68,989 (HH 26,257)

Statesville Record & Landmark (e-mon to fri; S)

Statesville Record & Landmark, 222 E. Broad St.; PO Box 1071, Statesville, NC 28677; tel (704) 873-1451; fax (704) 872-3150. Park Communications Inc. group.
Circulation: 16,047(e); 16,360(S); ABC Sept. 30, 1995.
Price: 50¢(d); $1.00(S); $1.80/wk (carrier); $15.00/mo (mail).
Advertising: Open inch rate $12.07(e); $12.07(S). **Representative:** Papert Companies.
News Service: AP. **Politics:** Independent. **Established:** 1874.
Not Published: Christmas.
Advertising not accepted: Ads suspected of being fraudulent.
Special Editions: Progress; Home Beautification; 4-H; Football; Dogwood Festival; Womens Tab; Holiday Tab; Balloon Rally; Spring Bride; Car Care; Gardening.
Magazines: TV Preview, USA Weekend, NEA Color Comics (S).

CORPORATE OFFICER
President Wright M Thomas

GENERAL MANAGEMENT
General Manager Tim Dearman
Business Manager Carol Rimmer
Purchasing Agent Tim Dearman

ADVERTISING
Director Dwaine Menscer
Manager-Classified Betty Morton

TELECOMMUNICATIONS
Audiotex Manager Sally Neely

CIRCULATION
Manager Scott Wheeler

NEWS EXECUTIVE
Managing Editor Jerry Josey

EDITORS AND MANAGERS
Editorial Page Editor Jerry Josey
Sports Editor Mike Owens

PRODUCTION
Manager Jeff Edwards
Foreman-Composing Don Webber

Market Information: Zoned editions; TMC; Operate audiotex.
Mechanical available: Offset; Black and 3 ROP colors; insert accepted — preprinted; page cut-offs — 22¾".
Mechanical specifications: Type page 13" x 21½"; E - 6 cols, 2 1/16", ⅛" between; A - 6 cols, 2 1/16", ⅛" between; C - 10 cols, 1 3/16", ⅛" between.
Commodity consumption: Newsprint 1,100 short tons; widths 27½", 13¾"; black ink 26,800 pounds; color ink 850 pounds; single pages printed 9,500; average pages per issue 28(d), 48(S); single plates used 7,000.
Equipment: EDITORIAL: Front-end hardware — 14-Ap/Mac; Front-end software — Baseview; Printers — ECR. CLASSIFIED: Front-end hardware — 3-Ap/Mac; Front-end software — Baseview. AUDIOTEX: Hardware — IBM/486 Clone; Software — Info Connect; Supplier name — TMS. DISPLAY: Front-end hardware — 3-Ap/Power Mac; Front-end software — QuarkXPress, Multi-Ad/Creator; Printers — NewGen. PRODUCTION: Typesetters — 3-Ap/Mac LaserWriter IIg; Direct-to-plate imaging — 3M/Deadliner; Production cameras — SCREEN/2024. PRESSROOM: Line 1 — 6-G/Urbanite; Folders — 1-G/2:1; Press registration system — Duarte. MAILROOM: Counter stackers — BG; Inserters and stuffers — MM; Bundle tyer — Alles. WIRE SERVICES: News — AP Datastream, AP Datafeatures; Photos — AP; Receiving dishes — size-10m, AP. BUSINESS COMPUTERS: Digital/560; Applications: Vision Data: Gen ledger, Accts receivable, Accts payable, Payroll.

TARBORO
Edgecombe County
'90 U.S. Census- 11,037; **E&P '96 Est.** 14,097

The Daily Southerner
(e-tues to fri)

The Daily Southerner, 504 W. Wilson St.; PO Box 1199, Tarboro, NC 27886; tel (919) 823-3106; fax (919) 823-4599. Hollinger International Inc. group.
Circulation: 6,117(e); 6,117(S); Sworn Sept. 29, 1995.
Price: $50(d); 50¢(S); $5.25/mo; $59.00/yr.
Advertising: Open inch rate $6.30(e); $6.30(S). **Representative:** Landon Associates Inc.
News Service: AP. **Politics:** Democrat. **Established:** 1889.
Not Published: Independence Day; Thanksgiving; Christmas.
Special Editions: Lawn-Garden & Home Improvement; Tobacco.
Special Weekly Sections: Lifestlyes (mon); Farm News (tues); Best Food Day, School News (wed); Business News (thur); Church Notes & News, Senior Citizens (fri); Entertainment (daily).

CORPORATE OFFICER
President Jerome Creech

GENERAL MANAGEMENT
Publisher Jerome Creech

ADVERTISING
Manager Ellis Hooks

CIRCULATION
Manager Alan Cale

NEWS EXECUTIVE
Editor Josh Boyer

EDITOR AND MANAGER
County Editor Robert Hughes

PRODUCTION
Manager Billy Harrell

Market Information: TMC.
Mechanical available: Offset; Black and 3 ROP colors; insert accepted — preprinted; page cut-offs — 22¾".
Mechanical specifications: Type page 13" x 21½"; E - 6 cols, 2 1/16", ⅛" between; A - 6 cols, 2 1/16", ⅛" between; C - 9 cols, 1⅜", 1/16" between.
Commodity consumption: average pages per issue 18(d).
Equipment: EDITORIAL: Front-end hardware — 1-COM/MDT. DISPLAY: Adv layout systems — 1-COM/7700, 1-COM/7200, 2-Trendsetter/812, 1-COM/4TG. PRODUCTION: Typesetters — 1-L, 4-COM; Plate exposures — 3-Nu; Plate processors — Nat/A-250; Production cameras — 1-BV. PRESSROOM: Line 1 — 4-KP/Color King, 1-KP/Newsking; Reels and stands — 4-KP. MAILROOM: Bundle tyer — 2-Sa; Addressing machine — 1-Am. WIRE SERVICES: News — COM, AP.

TRYON
Polk County
'90 U.S. Census- 1,680; **E&P '96 Est.** 1,587

The Tryon Daily Bulletin
(m-mon to fri)

The Tryon Daily Bulletin, 106 N. Trade St.; PO Box 790, Tryon, NC 28782; tel (704) 859-9151; fax (704) 859-5575.
Circulation: 4,109(m); Sworn Oct. 1, 1994.
Price: 25¢(d); $35.00/yr.
Advertising: Open inch rate $4.50(m). **Politics:** Independent. **Established:** 1928.
Not Published: New Year; Independence Day; Labor Day; Thanksgiving; Christmas; Postal holidays.
Special Editions: "Come See Us Almanac (Newcomer's Guide) (Mar); Christmas Catalogue.
Special Weekly Sections: The Hoof Beat (Equestrian); Arts & More.

GENERAL MANAGEMENT
Publisher Jeffrey A Byrd
General Manager Jeffrey A Byrd

ADVERTISING
Manager Mike Edwards

CIRCULATION
Director Wanda Cash

NEWS EXECUTIVE
Editor Jeffrey A Bryd

EDITOR AND MANAGER
Community Editor Judy Lanier

MANAGEMENT INFORMATION SERVICES
Data Processing Manager Barbara Briggs

PRODUCTION
Superintendent Barbara Briggs

Mechanical available: Offset; insert accepted — preprinted; page cut-offs — 11".
Mechanical specifications: Type page 22½" x 17"; E - 4 cols, 1⅞", ⅛" between; A - 4 cols, 1⅞", ⅛" between; C - 4 cols, 1⅞", ⅛" between.
Commodity consumption: Newsprint 50 metric tons; average pages per issue 24(d).
Equipment: EDITORIAL: Front-end hardware — PC; Front-end software — Aldus/PageMaker; Printers — Ap/Mac LaserPrinter, Canon/LBP4. CLASSIFIED: Front-end hardware — PC; Front-end software — Aldus/PageMaker, Alpha 4. DISPLAY: Adv layout systems — PC; Front-end hardware — Aldus/PageMaker. PRODUCTION: Pagination software — Aldus/PageMaker; Plate exposures — Nu/Plate Maker. PRESSROOM: Line 1 — 2-KP/Newsking. MAILROOM: Addressing machine — 1-Automecha/Accufast PL. BUSINESS COMPUTERS: Varsity/ATC; PCs & micros networked.

I-298 North Carolina

WASHINGTON

Beaufort County

'90 U.S. Census- 9,075; E&P '96 Est. 9,942
ABC-CZ (90): 9,478 (HH 3,762)

Washington Daily News

(m-mon to sat; S)

Washington Daily News, 217 N. Market St.; PO Box 1788, Washington, NC 27889; tel (919) 946-2144; fax (919) 946-9797.

Circulation: 10,121(m); 10,121(m-sat); 10,149(S); ABC Sept. 30, 1995.

Price: 50¢(d); 50¢(sat); 75¢(S); $7.00/mo; $84.00/yr.

Advertising: Open inch rate $10.70(m); $10.70(m-sat); $10.70(S). **Representative:** Papert Companies.

News Service: AP. **Politics:** Independent-Democrat. **Established:** 1909.

Not Published: Christmas.

Special Editions: Bridal Tab, Tax Tab (Jan); Lawn and Garden Tab (Mar); Visitor's Tourist Guide Tab (Apr); Graduation Tab (May); Summer Festival, Back-to-School Tab (July); Football Tab (Aug); Basketball Tab, Christmas Gift Guide Tab (Dec).

Special Weekly Sections: Food (wed); Farm (thur); Church, This Week (fri); Channel Marker, Food (S).

CORPORATE OFFICERS

President	Ashley B Futrell Jr
Vice Pres	Susan B Futrell
Treasurer	Rachel F Futrell

GENERAL MANAGEMENT

Publisher-Emeritus	Ashley B Futrell Sr
Publisher	Ashley B Futrell Jr
Controller	Addie B Laney

ADVERTISING

Director	Gene King
Manager-Classified	Brenda Foster
Manager-Promotion	Gene King

CIRCULATION

Director	Butch Weston

NEWS EXECUTIVE

Managing Editor	Mark Inabinett

EDITORS AND MANAGERS

City Editor	Mark Inabinett
Lifestyle Editor	Pam Nuckols
News Editor	Mark Inabinett
Photo Department Manager	Ric Carter
Picture Editor	Ric Carter
Sports Editor	Jason Jenkins

PRODUCTION

Foreman-Composing	John Alligood
Foreman-Pressroom	Vance Bell
Foreman-Mailroom	Vance Bell

Market Information: Zoned editions; TMC.

Mechanical available: Offset; Black and 3 ROP colors; insert accepted — preprinted; page cutoffs — $22\frac{3}{4}$".

Mechanical specifications: Type page 13" x $21\frac{1}{2}$"; E - 6 cols, $2\frac{1}{16}$", $\frac{1}{8}$" between; A - 6 cols, $2\frac{1}{16}$", $\frac{1}{8}$" between; C - 6 cols, $2\frac{1}{16}$", $\frac{1}{8}$" between.

Commodity consumption: Newsprint 532 short tons; width 27"; black ink 21,748 pounds; color ink 2,500 pounds; single pages printed 7,988; average pages per issue 20(d), 40(S); single plates used 4,200.

Equipment: EDITORIAL: Front-end hardware — 9-Mk. CLASSIFIED: Front-end hardware — Mk. DISPLAY: Adv layout systems — 1-Mk. PRODUCTION: Typesetters — 1-COM, 1-M; Platemaking systems — 1-Nu; Plate exposures — 1-Nu; Production cameras — 1-Nu, C; Automatic film processors — LE.
PRESSROOM: Line 1 — 1-Zenith/Jobber 22, G/Community W/SC; Line 2 — 5-G/SC 210; Folders — 1-Zenith, 1-G. MAILROOM: Inserters and stuffers — MM/2(3 Stations); Bundle tyer — 1-Strap Tyer; Addressing machine — 4-Wm. WIRE SERVICES: News — AP; Receiving dishes — AP. BUSINESS COMPUTERS: 1-Bs, 1-TI/300A, DSI/Papertrak; Applications: Business/Software: Circ.

WILMINGTON

New Hanover County

'90 U.S. Census- 55,530; E&P '96 Est. 70,091
ABC-CZ (90): 120,284 (HH 48,139)

Morning Star (m-mon to sat)
The Sunday Star-News (S)

Morning Star/Sunday Star-News, 1003 S. 17th St.; PO Box 840, Wilmington, NC 28401; tel (910) 343-2000; web site http://www.wilmington.net/starnews/. New York Times Co. group.

Circulation: 55,213(m); 55,213(m-sat); 66,760(S); ABC Sept. 30, 1995.

Price: 50¢(d); 50¢(sat); $1.50(S); $9.95/mo; $119.40/yr.

Advertising: Open inch rate $38.68(m); $38.68(m-sat); $38.68(S).

News Services: AP, NYT, KRT, LAT-WP. **Politics:** Independent. **Established:** 1867 (Star), 1928 (Star-News).

Advertising not accepted: Palmistry.

Special Editions: Brides (Jan); NASCAR, Update (Feb); Home & Garden, Fashion (Mar); Azalea, Earth Day (Apr); Brides (June); Back-to-School, Fact Book, Home Improvement (Aug); Fashion (Sept); Parade of Homes (Oct); Christmas Gift Guide (Nov).

Special Weekly Sections: Finances (tues); Finances, Best Food Day (wed); Finances (thur, fri); Church, Finances (sat); Travel, Finances (S).

Magazines: Parade, TV Week (S).

GENERAL MANAGEMENT

Publisher	John A Lynch
Controller	C Mendel Ham
Director-Human Resources	Beverly Jurgensen

ADVERTISING

Director	David Schuette
Manager-Classified	Julianne Jones

TELECOMMUNICATIONS

Director-Info Technical Service	Ed Willis

CIRCULATION

Director	Anthony Meinert

NEWS EXECUTIVES

Editor	Charles M Anderson
Managing Editor	John Meyer

EDITORS AND MANAGERS

Automotive Editor	Barbara Booth
Books Editor	Ben Steelman
Business Editor	Josiah Cantwell
City Editor	Dave Ennis
Columnist	Charles M Anderson
Columnist	Celia Rivenbark
Editorial Page Editor	Charles W Riesz Jr
Education	T Vance
Entertainment/Amusements Editor	Maile Carpenter
Environmental Editor	Jeff Selingo
Farm Editor	Scott Whisnant
Fashion/Food Editor	Pam Sander
Features Editor	Pam Sander
Films/Theater Editor	Maile Carpenter
Graphics Editor/Art Director	Carol Collier
Health/Medical Editor	Roger Friedman
Home Furnishings Editor	Pam Sander
Librarian	James Gill
Lifestyle Editor	Pam Sander
Music Editor	Maile Carpenter
News Editor	Donna Pipes
Chief Photographer	The' Pham
Radio/Television Editor	Maile Carpenter
Real Estate Editor	Barbara Booth
Religion Editor	Margaret Sullivan
Sports Editor	Mike Boaz
Travel Editor	Pam Sander

MANAGEMENT INFORMATION SERVICES

Data Processing Manager	Ed Willis

PRODUCTION

Director	Doug Beck
Foreman-Composing (Night)	Vivan Hardy
Foreman-Composing (Day)	Sherry Rich
Foreman-Distribution Center	Maurice Maisonville
Foreman-Pressroom	Robert Dodd

Market Information: Zoned editions; Split Run; TMC; Operate audiotex.

Mechanical available: Offset; Black and 3 ROP colors; insert accepted — preprinted; page cutoffs — $22\frac{3}{4}$".

Mechanical specifications: Type page 13" x $21\frac{1}{2}$"; E - 6 cols, $2\frac{1}{16}$", $\frac{1}{8}$" between; A - 6 cols, $2\frac{1}{16}$", $\frac{1}{8}$" between; C - 9 cols, $1\frac{3}{8}$", $\frac{1}{8}$" between.

Commodity consumption: Newsprint 6,200 short tons; widths 55", $41\frac{1}{4}$", $27\frac{1}{2}$"; black ink 120,000 pounds; color ink 36,000 pounds; single pages printed 16,902; average pages per issue 46(d), 88(S); single plates used 90,000.

Equipment: EDITORIAL: Front-end hardware — AT/7000, 25-PC/486, ATS/Osiris, XYQUEST/XyWrite, ATS/Quik Layout; Front-end software — AT/Editorial 3.4; Printers — Teletype/MOD 40; Other equipment — 3-AU/3850, 2-AU/100, On-Line Transport, 3-Window/NT RIP. CLASSIFIED: Front-end hardware — AT/IAS; Front-end software — AT/IAS 4.6; Printers — Florida Data. AUDIOTEX: Hardware — Brite Voice Systems. DISPLAY: Adv layout systems — AT/Editorial on IAS, 10-Ap/Mac 7500 w/Multi-Ad/Creator; Front-end hardware — AT; Front-end software — SCS/Ad-Tracking; Other equipment — 1-Window/Advanced Server for Ad Storage. PRODUCTION: Typesetters — 2-Linotype-Hell/Linotronic 202, 2-AU/3850; Platemaking systems — 3M/Deadliner; Plate exposures — 5-WL; Plate processors — W; Electronic picture desk — 2-Ap/Mac, Adobe/Photoshop; Scanners — ECR/Autokon; Production cameras — Kl; Automatic film processors — 2-C/OL Processor; Film transporters — 2-C/Transporter; Digital color separation equipment — CD/626.
PRESSROOM: Line 1 — 4-G/(1-half deck); Line 2 — 4-G/(2-half decks); Folders — 1-G/2:1, 1-G/3:2; Pasters — 8-G; Reels and stands — 8-G; Press control system — Fin. MAILROOM: Counter stackers — 3-QWI, 1-Id; Inserters and stuffers — HI/1372; Bundle tyer — 3-MLN; Addressing machine — 1-Ch. LIBRARY: Electronic — Newsview, Photoview; Combination — Clip Files. COMMUNICATIONS: Digital ad delivery system — AP AdSend. WIRE SERVICES: News — AP Datastream, AP Datafeatures, NYT, Weather Wire, LAT-WP, KRT; Photos — AP, Wieck; Stock tables — AP Datastream; Receiving dishes — AP, Audiotex. BUSINESS COMPUTERS: 1-IBM/Sys 38; Applications: Accts payable, Gen ledger, Payroll; CDC: Circ; PCs & micros networked; PCs & main system networked.

WILSON

Wilson County

'90 U.S. Census- 36,930; E&P '96 Est. 40,283
ABC-CZ (90): 36,930 (HH 14,461)

The Wilson Daily Times

(e-mon to fri; m-sat)

The Wilson Daily Times, 2001 Downing St. Ext.; PO Box 2447, Wilson, NC 27895-2447; tel (919) 243-5151; fax (919) 243-2999.

Circulation: 16,841(e); 16,841(m-sat); ABC Sept. 30, 1995.

Price: 50¢(d); $1.00(sat); $6.50/mo; $78.00/yr.

Advertising: Open inch rate $11.45(e); $11.45 (m-sat). **Representative:** Landon Associates Inc.

News Services: AP, CNS, NEA, United Media Service. **Politics:** Democrat. **Established:** 1896.

Not Published: Independence Day; Christmas.

Advertising not accepted: Liquor.

Special Editions: Spring Fashion; Spring Festival; Fall Fashion; Farm Show Edition; Race Tab; The Wilson Co. Fair Book; Christmas Gift Guide I & II; Last Minute Gift Suggestions.

Special Weekly Sections: Weddings, Farm Page, Community Service (mon); Seniors (tues); Family, Best Food Day (wed); Arts (thur); Health (fri); Church, TV (sat).

CORPORATE OFFICERS

President	Morgan Paul Dickerman III
Vice Pres	Margaret Dickerman
Secretary/Treasurer	Delores Evans

GENERAL MANAGEMENT

Publisher	Morgan Paul Dickerman III

ADVERTISING

Director	Ray McKeithan
Manager-Classified	Karen Boykin

CIRCULATION

Manager	Alan Evans

NEWS EXECUTIVE

Editor	Harold V Tarleton

EDITORS AND MANAGERS

Editorial Page Editor	Harold V Tarleton
Features Editor	Claude Starling
Lifestyle Editor	Lisa Batts
Sports Editor	Alan Wooten

PRODUCTION

Director	Royce Goff
Foreman-Pressroom	Jarvis Aycock
Foreman-Composing	Sandra Brantley

Market Information: Zoned editions; TMC.

Mechanical available: Offset; Black and 3 ROP colors; insert accepted — preprinted; page cutoffs — $22\frac{3}{4}$".

Mechanical specifications: Type page 13" x $21\frac{1}{2}$"; E - 6 cols, $2\frac{1}{16}$", $\frac{1}{8}$" between; A - 6 cols, $2\frac{1}{16}$", $\frac{1}{8}$" between; C - 9 cols, $1\frac{3}{8}$", $\frac{1}{16}$" between.

Commodity consumption: Newsprint 1,000 short tons; width $27\frac{1}{2}$"; black ink 18,010 pounds; color ink 1,120 pounds; average pages per issue 30(d); single plates used 10,000.

Equipment: EDITORIAL: Front-end hardware — 18-COM/One System; Front-end software — COM/One System; Printers — TI. CLASSIFIED: Front-end hardware — IBM/PC; Front-end software — QuarkXPress, Baseview/Class Act, Baseview/Class Ad; Printers — TI. DISPLAY: Adv layout systems — 6-Ap/Mac; Front-end software — Multi-Ad, QuarkXPress; Printers — Ap/Mac LaserWriter II, 1-HP. PRODUCTION: Typesetters — 2-NewGen; Plate exposures — 1-Nu; Plate processors — Nat; Production cameras — C; Reproportion units — 2-AU/Accuset; Color separation equipment (conventional) — Ap/Power Mac 7100, Ap/Mac Quadra 950; Digital color separation equipment — Nikon, AG/Arcus.
PRESSROOM: Line 1 — 5-G/Urbanite; Line 2 — 2-G/Urbanite. WIRE SERVICES: News — AP; Receiving dishes — AP. BUSINESS COMPUTERS: IBM/Sys 36; Applications: Custom; PCs & main system networked.

WINSTON-SALEM

Forsyth County

'90 U.S. Census- 143,485; E&P '96 Est. 158,457
ABC-NDM (90): 265,878 (HH 107,419)

Winston-Salem Journal

(m-mon to sat; S)

Winston-Salem Journal, 418 N. Marshall (27101); PO Box 3159, Winston-Salem, NC 27102; tel (910) 727-7211; fax (910) 727-7424. Media General Inc. group.

Circulation: 90,268(m); 90,268(m-sat); 103,058(S); ABC Sept. 30, 1995.

Price: 50¢(d); 50¢(sat); $1.25(S); $2.30/wk; $119.60/yr.

Advertising: Open inch rate $50.51(m); $50.51(m-sat); $56.50(S). **Representative:** Sawyer-Ferguson-Walker Co.

News Services: AP, NYT, LAT-WP. **Established:** 1887.

Special Edition: Senior Scene (monthly).

Special Weekly Sections: Family, Kid's SAM (mon); Consumer Review, Health & Fitness (tues); Best Food Day (wed); Trends (thur); Automotive Friday (Classified), "What's On" Calendar (fri); Home & Garden Section, TV Journal, People (sat); "Homeplace" Real Estate, Insight, Travel, Book Reviews, The Arts (S).

CORPORATE OFFICERS

President	J H Witherspoon
Treasurer	Raymond McDowell
Vice Pres/Business Manager	Jim Fowler

GENERAL MANAGEMENT

Publisher	J H Witherspoon
Controller	Raymond McDowell
Director-Human Resources	Randy Noftle
Purchasing Agent	Dennis Walsh

ADVERTISING

Director	Timothy Maby
Manager-Retail	Ken Warren
Manager-Classified	Pat Ranson

CIRCULATION

Manager	Jim Flick

NEWS EXECUTIVE

Managing Editor	Jim Laughrun

EDITORS AND MANAGERS

Arts Editor	Sara Fox
Book Editor	Linda Brinson
Business/Finance Editor	Frank Brill
City Editor	Ken Otterbourg
Editorial Page Editor	John Gates
Entertainment/Travel Editor	Sara Fox
Food Editor	Sara Fox
Garden Editor	Juliann Berckman
Librarian	Virginia Hauswald
Films/Theater Editor	Roger Moore
Music Editor	Gordon Sparber
News Editor	Charles Elkins
Asst News Editor	Jo Dawson
Sports Editor	Terry Oberle
State Editor	Guy Lucas
Sunday/Women's Editor	Sara Fox

MANAGEMENT INFORMATION SERVICES

Data Processing Manager	Doug Tucker

PRODUCTION

Manager	Richard Dickey
Manager-Pre Press	Larry Addington
Manager-Press	Mike Pfaff
Manager-Packaging	Kevin Garris

Market Information: Zoned editions; Split Run; TMC; ADS.

Mechanical available: Offset; Black and 3 ROP colors; insert accepted — preprinted; page cutoffs — 22".

Copyright ©1996 by the Editor & Publisher Co.

Mechanical specifications: Type page 13" x 21"; E - 6 cols, 2 1/16", 3/16" between; A - 6 cols, 2 1/16", 3/16" between; C - 9 cols, 1 3/8", 1/8" between.
Commodity consumption: Newsprint 15,500 short tons; widths 54 3/4", 41 1/16", 27 3/8"; black ink 300,000 pounds; color ink 80,000 pounds; single pages printed 30,000; average pages per issue 56(d), 76(S); single plates used 110,000.
Equipment: EDITORIAL: Front-end hardware — 6-AT/9000; Front-end software — AT/Editorial 4.7.7; Other equipment — AT/Ed Page, 9-IBM/RS6000. CLASSIFIED: Front-end hardware — HP/3000 918LX; Front-end software — Media General Classified. DISPLAY: Adv layout systems — SCS/Layout 8000; Front-end hardware — Dell/PC-1, HP/Vectra-2; Printers — 2-HP/LaserJet II, 1-HP/LaserJet IIP. PRODUCTION: Typesetters — 3-III/3810, 1-III/3850; Plate exposures — 2-Nu, 2-WL/Lith-X-Pozer III; Plate processors — 2-WL; Scanners — 2-ECR/Autokon 1000, 1-III/3750, 1-III/3725; Production cameras — 1-C/Spartan III; Automatic film processors — 4-LE, 2-Konica; Film transporters — 4-LE, 2-Konica; Shrink lenses — 1-Alan/24"; Color separation equipment (conventional) — 1-CD/636.
PRESSROOM: Line 1 — 1-MHI; Press drives — Allen Bradley; Folders — 2-MHI; Pasters — 10-MHI; Reels and stands — 10-MHI; Press control system — MHI; Press registration system — Quad Tech. MAILROOM: Counter stackers — 3-HL/Monitor, 6-QWI/300; Inserters and stuffers — 2-GMA/SLS-1000 (20-into-2), GMA/SG-1000 gripper; Bundle tyer — 3-OVL, 6-Dynaric; Addressing machine — 2-Ch. COMMUNICATIONS: Remote imagesetting — 2-III/3810. WIRE SERVICES: News — AP, NYT, LAT-WP, AP Datafeatures; Stock tables — AP; Receiving dishes — AP, RN. BUSINESS COMPUTERS: HP/3000 918LX; PCs & micros networked; PCs & main system networked.

NORTH DAKOTA

BISMARCK

Burleigh County

'90 U.S. Census- 49,256; E&P '96 Est. 53,140
ABC-CZ (90): 64,433 (HH 24,923)

The Bismarck Tribune

(m-mon to sat; S)

The Bismarck Tribune, 7th & Front Sts.; PO Box 1498, Bismarck, ND 58501; tel (701) 223-2500; fax (701) 223-4240; e-mail bis707@aol.com. Lee Enterprises Inc. group.
Circulation: 30,250(m); 30,250(m-sat); 32,439(S); ABC Sept. 30, 1995.
Price: 50¢(d); 75¢(m-wed); 50¢(sat); $1.75 (S); $3.75/wk; $16.25/mo; $185.00/yr.
Advertising: Open inch rate $25.85(m); $25.85(m-sat); $27.15(S). **Representative:** Landon Associates Inc.
News Services: AP, LAT-WP, NEA. **Politics:** Independent. **Established:** 1873.
Special Editions: Active Times, Bridal Preview, Brides Direct, Super Bowl, Taxes, Canadian Passport Books (Jan); Rodeo, Bismarck Tribune Sport Show (Feb); State Home & Garden, Class B Boys Basketball, Progress Edition, Career Fair (Mar); Active Times, Yard, Lawn & Garden, Homemaker's Show, Fishing Guide, Spring Car Care, Week of the Child, American Home Week (Apr); Graduation, Parade of Pets - "National Pet Week", Yard, Garden, Home Improvement (May); Summer Make Over, Mandan Rodeo Days, Yard, Garden, Home Improvement (June); Bismarck Trivia, Active Times, Governor Cup Fishing Tournament (July); Back-to-School, Fall Home Improvement, Football Kick-off, International Pow Wow (Aug); Arts Beat, Fall Home Improvement, Folkfest, Parade of Homes, Books/Business Directory (Sept); Badlands Circuit Finals Rodeo, Sale of the Century, Break-away/Get-away (Oct); Christmas Songbook, Christmas Kick-off, Holiday Gift Guide, Girls' Class B, New Car Auto Show (Nov); Holiday Gift Guide, Taste of Christmas, Basketball Tip-off, Last Minute Shopping, Christmas Greetings, Year-End Clearance (Dec); Your Home, Ag Extra (monthly).
Special Weekly Sections: Business Page (tues); Best Food Day (wed); Religion Page (fri); Best Food Day, Business Page (S).
Magazines: Now (Teen Page) (mon); Money (tues); Ag Day Cag (thur); Fanfare (fri); Money, TV Week (TV Listings) (S).

GENERAL MANAGEMENT
Publisher Margaret Wade
Controller Paul Patera
Manager-Human Resources Libby Simes

ADVERTISING
Director Lani Renneau

MARKETING AND PROMOTION
Manager-Marketing/Promotion Paula Redmann

TELECOMMUNICATIONS
Audiotex Manager Chad Kourajian

CIRCULATION
Director Phil Grider

NEWS EXECUTIVE
Editor Kevin Giles

EDITORS AND MANAGERS
Business/Finance Reporter Chris Steinbach
Education Reporter Rebecca Lentz
Librarian Barbara Herzberg-Bender
Living/Lifestyle Editor Troy Melhus
Metro Editor Ken Rogers
News Editor Steve Wallick
Photographer Tom Stromme
Religion Reporter Karen Herzog
Sports Editor Abe Winter
State Editor Peter Salter
Women's Editor Troy Melhus

MANAGEMENT INFORMATION SERVICES
Data Processing Manager Lowell E Hunke
Online Manager Kevin Giles

PRODUCTION
Manager Mike Tandy
Manager-Pressroom Steve Pfaff
Manager-Mailroom Pat Sitter
Manager-Systems/Computers Lowell E Hunke
Supervisor-Graphic Services Stace Gooding

Market Information: Zoned editions; Split Run; TMC; ADS; Operate database; Operate audiotex; Electronic edition.
Mechanical available: Offset; Black and 4 ROP colors; insert accepted — preprinted; page cutoffs — 22 3/4".
Mechanical specifications: Type page 13" x 21 1/2"; E - 6 cols, 2 1/16", 1/8" between; A - 6 cols, 2 1/16", 1/8" between; C - 9 cols, 1 3/8", 1/16" between.
Commodity consumption: Newsprint 2,500 short tons; widths 13 3/4", 27 1/2", 35"; black ink 56,000 pounds; color ink 16,000 pounds; single pages printed 11,500; average pages per issue 24(d), 24(sat), 48(S); single plates used 36,000.
Equipment: EDITORIAL: Front-end hardware — 1-HI/8306, 4-HI/8903; Front-end software — HI/PLS-PEN; Other equipment — ISYS/Library System. CLASSIFIED: Front-end hardware — HI/PC Sys, UNIX; Front-end software — HI/CASH. AUDIOTEX: Hardware — VRI; Supplier name — VRI, Lee Enterprises. DISPLAY: Front-end hardware — 1-HI/8306, 4-HI/8903, 4-HI/8863; Front-end software — HI/PLS. PRODUCTION: Pagination software — HI/PLS 6.5; Typesetters — 2-COM/8600, 1-Panther/Pro 36, 1-Panther/Pro 46; Plate exposures — 2-Nu/Flip Top FT40UPNS; Plate processors — 1-Nat; Scanners — 2-Nikon/Coolscan, 2-Polaroid/SprintScan 35, 10-Microtek/Flatbed ScanMakers; Production cameras — 1-C/Spartan III, 2-Ik/530; Automatic film processors — 1-LE/LD-24A; Shrink lenses — CK Optical; Color separation equipment (conventional) — Ap/Mac w/Photoshop; Digital color separation equipment — Ap/Mac, 2-Panther/Pro Imagesetter.
PRESSROOM: Line 1 — 10-G/Urbanite single width; Folders — 1-G/2:1, 1-G/1200 1/4Folder; Press control system — Fin; Press registration system — Duarte. MAILROOM: Inserters and stuffers — 2-MM/227-E; Bundle tyer — 1-MLN/MLN2A, 2-MLN/Spirit; Addressing machine — 1-Ch/528-010, 1-Ch/542-093, 1-Ch/542-090; Other mailroom equipment — Ch/552-01 1/4 Folder. LIBRARY: Electronic — ISYS; Combination — non-electronic. WIRE SERVICES: News — AP, LAT-WP; Photos — AP; Stock tables — AP; Receiving dishes — AP.

DEVILS LAKE

Ramsey County

'90 U.S. Census- 7,782; E&P '96 Est. 8,069

Devils Lake Daily Journal

(e-mon to fri)

Devils Lake Daily Journal, 516 4th St.; Box 1200, Devils Lake, ND 58301; tel (701) 662-2127; fax (701) 662-3115. Park Communications Inc. group.
Circulation: 4,510(e); Sworn Oct. 2, 1995.
Price: 50¢(d); $1.35/wk; $6.50/mo; $70.00/yr (carrier), $80.00/yr (state).
Advertising: Open inch rate $8.05(e). **Representative:** Papert Companies.
News Service: AP. **Politics:** Independent. **Established:** 1905.
Not Published: Christmas.
Magazines: Golden Opportunities (monthly-last wed); TV Preview (fri).

GENERAL MANAGEMENT
General Manager Kathy Svidal

ADVERTISING
Manager-Retail Kathy Svidal

CIRCULATION
Manager Brenda Bednarz

NEWS EXECUTIVE
Managing Editor Gordon Wexeil

EDITORS AND MANAGERS
Action Line Editor Annette Thompson
Action Line Editor Jerry Kram
Society Editor Kristi Mead

PRODUCTION
Superintendent Bev Bachmeier

Market Information: TMC.
Mechanical available: Offset; Black and 4 ROP colors; insert accepted — preprinted; page cutoffs — 21".
Mechanical specifications: Type page 13" x 21"; E - 6 cols, 2.01", 1/6" between; A - 6 cols, 2.01", 1/6" between; C - 10 cols, 1 1/4", 1/12" between.
Commodity consumption: Newsprint 225 short tons; widths 28", 14"; single pages printed 4,848; average pages per issue 12(d); single plates used 6,900.
Equipment: EDITORIAL: Front-end hardware — Mk/1100 Plus; Front-end software — Mk/NewsTouch; Printers — 2-Ap/Mac LaserPrinter II. CLASSIFIED: Front-end hardware — 2-Mk, AT; Printers — 2-Ap/Mac LaserPrinter II. DISPLAY: Adv layout systems — Ap/Mac IIci; Printers — Ap/Mac LaserWriter II NTX. PRODUCTION: Typesetters — Mk, AT; Plate exposures — 1-B/Mark II, 1-Amerigraph/457 SEDS; Production cameras — 1-B/Caravel; Automatic film processors — 1-P/Rapid Access 26; Shrink lenses — 1-CK Optical/SQU-7.
PRESSROOM: Line 1 — 4-HI/Cottrell V-15A; Folders — 1-HI. MAILROOM: Bundle tyer — 1-Felins/16; Addressing machine — 1-Am/2600. COMMUNICATIONS: Facsimile — Canon/20. WIRE SERVICES: News — AP; Receiving dishes — size-3ft, AP. BUSINESS COMPUTERS: IBM/Sys 34; Applications: Accts receivable, Billing, Payroll, Accts payable, Circ, Accounting; PCs & micros networked; PCs & main system networked.

DICKINSON

Stark County

'90 U.S. Census- 16,097; E&P '96 Est. 16,306

Dickinson Press

(m-tues to sat; S)

Dickinson Press, 127 1st St. W., Dickinson, ND 58601; tel (701) 225-8111; fax (701) 225-4205. Forum Communications group.
Circulation: 7,858(m); 7,858(m-sat); 7,858(S); Sworn Sept. 28, 1994.
Price: 50¢(d); 50¢(sat); $1.00(S); $9.00/mo; $101.00/yr.
Advertising: Open inch rate $10.48(m); $10.48(m-sat); $10.48(S). **Representative:** Landon Associates Inc.
News Service: AP. **Politics:** Independent. **Established:** 1883.
Special Editions: Spring & Winter Car Care; Basketball; Dickinson State College Homecoming; Income Tax Guide; Progress; Cookbook; Fire Prevention Tab; Football Preview; Weddings.
Special Weekly Sections: Food (wed); Business (thur); Farm (sat); Food, Youth, Senior Citizen (S).
Magazines: Home Improvement Guide; Farm & Ranch Rural Gravure; TV Guide; Entertainment.

GENERAL MANAGEMENT
Publisher Peter D Rogers
Office Manager Marilyn Wanner
Purchasing Agent Peter D Rogers

ADVERTISING
Manager Erv Barth
Manager-Classified Cathy Brinda-Praus

MARKETING AND PROMOTION
Manager-Promotion Peter D Rogers

CIRCULATION
Director Bob Dwyer

NEWS EXECUTIVE
Managing Editor Sharon Dietz

EDITORS AND MANAGERS
Books Editor Linda Sailer
Business/Finance Editor Cary Shimek
Editorial Page Editor Sharon Dietz
Entertainment Editor Linda Sailer
Family/Food Editor Linda Sailer
Farm Editor Sue Carter
Fashion/Women's Editor Linda Sailer
Films/Theater Editor Linda Sailer
Home Furnishings Editor Linda Sailer
Librarian Linda Sailer
Religion Editor Sharon Dietz
School Editor Sharon Dietz
Sports Editor Brian Alexander

PRODUCTION
Foreman-Composing Twila Benz
Foreman-Pressroom Nick Morel

Market Information: Zoned editions; Split Run; TMC; ADS; Operate database.
Mechanical available: Offset; Black and 3 ROP colors; insert accepted — preprinted; page cutoffs — 22 3/4".
Mechanical specifications: Type page 13" x 21 1/2"; E - 6 cols, 2 1/16", 1/8" between; A - 6 cols, 2 1/16", 1/8" between; C - 9 cols, 1 3/8", 1/8" between.
Commodity consumption: Newsprint 350 short tons; widths 27 1/4", 13 3/4"; black ink 9,000 pounds; color ink 329 pounds; average pages per issue 16(d), 30(S); single plates used 3,000.
Equipment: EDITORIAL: Front-end hardware — Mk. CLASSIFIED: Front-end hardware — Mk. PRODUCTION: Typesetters — 2-Ap/Mac LaserPrinter, 4-Ap/Mac; Plate exposures — 1-Nu/Flip Top; Plate processors — 1-Nat/A340; Production cameras — 1-R/500; Automatic film processors — P.
PRESSROOM: Line 1 — 7-G/Community; Folders — 1-G/SC. MAILROOM: Bundle tyer — 1-Bu; Addressing machine — Ch. WIRE SERVICES: News — AP; Receiving dishes — AP. BUSINESS COMPUTERS: IBM/PL, Lotus, CPPS.

FARGO, ND-MOORHEAD, MN

Cass County, ND
Clay County, MN

'90 U.S. Census- 106,406 (Fargo, ND 74,111; Moorhead, MN 32,295): E&P '96 Est. 119,286 (Fargo, ND 84,953; Moorhead, MN 34,333)
ABC-CZ (90): 121,255 (HH 46,595)

Forum (m-mon to sat; S)

Forum, 101 5th St.; PO Box 2020, Fargo, ND 58107; tel (701) 253-7311; fax (701) 241-5406. Forum Communications group.
Circulation: 55,051(m); 55,051(m-sat); 69,474(S); ABC Sept. 30, 1995.
Price: 50¢(d); 75¢(sat); $1.75(S); $15.00/mo.
Advertising: Open inch rate $36.00(m); $36.00(m-sat); $42.00(S). **Representative:** Cresmer, Woodward, O'Mara & Ormsbee.
News Services: AP, NYT. **Politics:** Independent-Republican. **Established:** 1878.
Special Editions: Brides; Car Care; Home Improvement; Fair; Student; Generations; Vacation; Health; Winter Survival; American Homeweek; Mothers; Fathers; Scandinavian Festival; Outdoor; Merry Prairie Christmas.
Special Weekly Sections: Sports Section (mon); Financial (tues); Food Section (wed); Religious Page (fri); Business Section, Financial (sat); Food Advertising, Home & Garden Pages, Business News, Travel Section, Entertainment (S).
Magazines: Farmer's Forum Tab (fri); TV Forum Tab (sat); Parade (S).
Broadcast Affiliates: KBMY Bismarck, ND; WDAZ Devils Lake, ND; WDAY-AM Fargo, ND; WDAYTV Fargo, ND; WDAZ Grand Forks, ND; KMCY Minot, ND.

CORPORATE OFFICERS
President William C Marcil
Vice Pres-Operations Charles Bohnet
Vice Pres-Finance Lloyd Case

GENERAL MANAGEMENT
Publisher William C Marcil
General Manager Chuck Bohnet

Copyright ©1996 by the Editor & Publisher Co.

I-300 North Dakota

Controller Lloyd Case
Manager-Education Service Linda Pearson
Human Resources Lois Erickson

ADVERTISING

Director James Boberg
Manager-National Wayne Diest

MARKETING AND PROMOTION

Manager-Marketing Bill Marcil Jr

TELECOMMUNICATIONS

Audiotex Manager James Boberg

CIRCULATION

Director Jeff Nyquist
Manager-Operations Jeff Nyquist

NEWS EXECUTIVES

Editor Joseph Dill
Assoc Editor John Lohman
Managing Editor Terry DeVine
Asst Managing Editor Dennis Doeden
Editor-Minnesota Craig McEwen

EDITORS AND MANAGERS

Business Editor David Jurgens
Copy Chief Jay Ulku
Editorial Page Editor Jack Zaleski
Entertainment Editor Cathy Zaiser
Farm Editor Mikkel Pates
Fashion Editor Cathy Zaiser
Food Editor Andrea Halgrimson
Graphics Editor Dennis Doeden
Librarian Andrea Halgrimson
Lifestyle Editor Catherine Zaiser
Photo Department Manager Colburn Hvidston III
Picture Editor Colburn Hvidston III
Political Editor (MN) John Sundvor
Political Editor (ND) William Nowling
Sports Editor Kevin Schnepf
Sunday Editor Terry DeVine

MANAGEMENT INFORMATION SERVICES

Manager-Management Info Services Brad Motschenbacher

PRODUCTION

Director Harold Schmunk
Superintendent-Pressroom Thomas Flynn

Market Information: Zoned editions; Split Run; TMC; Operate audiotex.

Mechanical available: Offset; Black and 3 ROP colors; insert accepted — preprinted; page cut-offs — 22".

Mechanical specifications: Type page 13" x 20¾"; E - 4 cols, 3.08", ⅛" between; A - 6 cols, 2.08", ⅛" between; C - 9 cols, 1⅓", ⅛" between.

Commodity consumption: Newsprint 5,000 metric tons; widths 27½", 27½", 41¼", 41¼", 55", 55"; black ink 194,500 pounds; color ink 29,650 pounds; single pages printed 14,026; average pages per issue 28(d), 75(S); single plates used 48,500.

Equipment: EDITORIAL: Front-end hardware — Novell/Network; Front-end software — Dewar/DewarView 1.2J; Other equipment — Ap/Mac Quadra 800, PC/486-33s. CLASSIFIED: Front-end hardware — SIA; Front-end software — Dewar; Printers — Okidata/320, Okidata/321, Okidata/393. AUDIOTEX: Supplier name — Micro Voice. DISPLAY: Adv layout systems — Multi-Ad; Front-end hardware — SIA, Ap/Power Mac 7100; Front-end software — Dewar/Ad Dummy, Ap/Mac Quadra 800; Other equipment — 1-Flatbed Scanner. PRODUCTION: Pagination software — Dewar/DewarView, QPS 3.3; Typesetters — 2-AU/APS 6-108C, 2-AU/APS 100; Platemaking systems — WL/Lithotech; Plate exposures — Amerigraph; Plate processors — Aqualith/32 Subtractive; Electronic picture desk — Lf/AP Leaf Picture Desk; Scanners — ECR/Autokon 1000 DE, Howtek/D-4000 Drum Scanner, Kk/Scanner, Nikon/Scanner; Production cameras — C/Spartan III; Automatic film processors — LE, Konica; Reproportion units — GAM/III; Film transporters — C; Digital color separation equipment — 3-Ap/Mac Quadra 950.
PRESSROOM: Line 1 — 10-MAN/Roland MediaMan (Offset double width); Press drives — Seamans; Folders — MAN; Pasters — MEG; Reels and stands — MEG/45 inch; Press control system — Allen Bradley. MAILROOM: Counter stackers — 2-Id/2100, 2-Id/550; Inserters and stuffers — HI/72P; Bundle tyer — OVL; Addressing machine — AVY. LIBRARY: Electronic — SMS/Stauffer Gold. WIRE SERVICES: News — AP; Stock tables — AP SelectStox; Syndicates — NYT; Receiving dishes — AP. BUSINESS COMPUTERS: 1-DEC/VAX 6000-410; Applications: Circ, Adv, Accts payable, Gen ledger, Payroll; PCs & micros networked; PCs & main system networked.

GRAND FORKS, ND-EAST GRAND FORKS, MN

Grand Forks County, ND
Polk County, MN

'90 U.S. Census- 58,083 (Grand Forks, ND 49,425; East Grand Forks, MN 8,658); **E&P '96 Est.** 62,820 (Grand Forks, ND 54,061; East Grand Forks, MN 8,759)
ABC-CZ (90): 58,083 (HH 21,690)

Grand Forks Herald

(m-mon to sat; S)

Grand Forks Herald, 303 Second Ave. N.; PO Box 6008, Grand Forks, ND 58206; tel (701) 780-1100; fax (701) 780-1189. Knight-Ridder Inc. group.

Circulation: 37,054(m); 37,054(m-sat); 38,409(S); ABC Sept. 30, 1995.

Price: 50¢(d); 75¢(sat); $1.75(S); $3.25/wk (carrier).

Advertising: Open inch rate $27.63(m); $27.63(m-sat); $28.58(S). **Representative:** Landon Associates Inc.

News Service: AP. **Politics:** Independent. **Established:** 1879.

Special Editions: Outlook, Bride & Groom (Jan); Personal Finance, Senior Lifestyles (Feb); City-wide Celebration, Ag Day, Forx Home Builders, Coupon Book (Mar); Spring Car Care, Home Improvement (Apr); Chamber of Commerce, Guide to GF, Regional Health Care (May); Buying a Home, Canadian Appreciation, Senior Lifestyles (June); East Grand Forks Pride, Canadian Holiday (July); Back-to-School, Crookston Section, Friends & Neighbors (Aug); Senior Lifestyles, Coupon Book, Business Profile (Sept); Fall Car Care, Fall Home Improvement, Salute to Harvest (Oct); Cookbook, Senior Lifestyles (Nov); Reflections of the Season, Babies of 1996 (Dec).

Special Weekly Sections: Expanded Sports (mon); Agriculture, Home Improvement (tues); Food Advertising (wed); Science, Outdoors (thur); Entertainment (fri); Business, TV Herald (sat); Expanded Editorial, Family (S).

Magazine: TV (sat).

CORPORATE OFFICERS

President Michael Maidenberg
Vice Pres Mike Jacobs
Vice Pres/Asst Treasurer Ross Jones
Secretary Douglas C Harris
Asst Secretary Ana Sejeck
Treasurer/Asst Secretary Eulalie A Geer
Asst Treasurer Stephen H Sheriff

GENERAL MANAGEMENT

Publisher Michael Maidenberg
Purchasing Agent Ken Curfman
Manager-Human Resources Anne Van Camp
Controller/Chief Financial Officer Eulalie A Geer

ADVERTISING

Director Tom Kuchera Jr
Director-Sales (Ag week) Noel Letexier
Manager-Display Dave Austin
Manager-National Sales Kirk Holcomb
Manager-Ad Service/Commercial Print Linda Jacobson
Supervisor-Classified Phone Room Peggy Brodeur
Coordinator-Marketing Research Marsha Gunderson

CIRCULATION

Director Bob Jacobson
Manager-City Zone Jared Thorson
Manager-Retail Zone Roger Larson

NEWS EXECUTIVES

Editor Mike Jacobs
Managing Editor-Content Jim Durkin
Managing Editor-Administration Greg Turosak

EDITORS AND MANAGERS

Agweek Editor Julie Copeland
Books Editor Carissa Green
Business Editor Matt Okerlund
Cultural Issues Editor Sally Thompson
Consumer Interest Editor Darrel Koehler
Editorial Page Editor Tim Fought
Education Editor Steve Schmidt
Entertainment Editor Sally Thompson
Entertainment Reporter Mike Brue
Environmental Reporter Sue Ellyn Scaletta
Family Editor Gail Stewart Hand
Farm Editor Julie Copeland
Fashion/Style Editor Sally Thompson
Food Editor Marilyn Hagerty
Health Editor Sue Ellyn Scaletta
Librarian Cynthia Valtierra
News Editor Kevin Grinde
Personal Issues Editor Gail Stewart Hand
Photo Editor John Stennes
Political Editor Randy Bradbury
Religion Editor Steve Lee
Exec Sports Editor Ryan Bakken
Television Reporter Mike Brue

MANAGEMENT INFORMATION SERVICES

Manager-Info Systems Dewey Kvidt

PRODUCTION

Director David Aarvig
Manager-Composing David Brodeur
Manager-Pressroom David McMenamy
Manager-Mailroom Jim Litzinger
Superintendent-Newsprint Ken Curfman

Market Information: Split Run; ADS.

Mechanical available: Offset; Black and 3 ROP colors; insert accepted — preprinted; page cut-offs — 22¾".

Mechanical specifications: Type page 13" x 21½"; E - 6 cols, 2 1/16", ⅛" between; A - 6 cols, 2 1/16", ⅛" between; C - 9 cols, 1⅜", 1/16" between.

Commodity consumption: Newsprint 3,200 metric tons; widths 13.50", 27.0"; black ink 43,000 pounds; color ink 15,000 pounds; single pages printed 16,253; average pages per issue 42(d), 60(S); single plates used 40,000.

Equipment: EDITORIAL: Front-end hardware — 4-AT/9000, 3-HI/8900; Front-end software — AT, HI; Printers — 2-Dataproducts. CLASSIFIED: Front-end hardware — HI/CASH; Front-end software — HI/CASH 5.0; Printers — 1-Dataproducts. DISPLAY: Adv layout systems — 2-HI/8300, Ap/Mac; Front-end hardware — HI, Ap/Mac 8500; Front-end software — HI, QuarkXPress 3.3; Other equipment — MON/Graphics System. PRODUCTION: Pagination software — HI/8900, HI/2100 CPAG 2.0; Typesetters — 2-AU/APS Micro 5, 2-MON/Express, 1-III/3850 Imagesetter; Plate exposures — 1-Nu/Flip Top FT40V6UP; Plate processors — 1-Nat/A-250; Electronic picture desk — Lf/AP Leaf Picture Desk; Scanners — 2-ECR/Autokon 1000 DE; Production cameras — C/Spartan III; Automatic film processors — 5-LE; Film transporters — 4-LE; Color separation equipment (conventional) — 1-Howtek/7500.
PRESSROOM: Line 1 — 8-G/Urbanite; Folders — G/2:1; Pasters — Manual; Reels and stands — 6-Kohler/Reels, 2-Roll/Stands; Press control system — Fin. MAILROOM: Counter stackers — 1-Id/2000, 1-Id/660, 1-Id/440, 1-BG/108; Inserters and stuffers — 2-MM/227E; Bundle tyer — 2-MLN/MLN2A; Wrapping singles — 1-Bu/BT16, 1-Bu/BT18; Addressing machine — 2-AVY. WIRE SERVICES: News — AP, TV Data, NYT, KRT; Stock tables — AP; Receiving dishes — size-10ft, AP, INS. BUSINESS COMPUTERS: 1-HP/Spectrum 922RX; Applications: Cyborg: Circ, Payroll, Adv, Gen ledger, Accts payable, Fixed assets, Human resources; PCs & main system networked.

JAMESTOWN

Stutsman County

'90 U.S. Census- 15,571; **E&P '96 Est.** 15,185

The Jamestown Sun

(m-mon to sat)

The Jamestown Sun, 122 2nd St. N.W.; PO Box 1760, Jamestown, ND 58401; tel (701) 252-3120; fax (701) 251-2873. Hollinger International Inc. group.

Circulation: 7,231(m); 7,231(m-sat); Sworn Sept. 29, 1995.

Price: 50¢(d); 50¢(sat); $7.75/mo; $87.00/yr.

Advertising: Open inch rate $8.50(m); $8.50 (m-sat). **Representative:** Landon Associates Inc.

News Service: AP. **Politics:** Independent. **Established:** 1925.

Not Published: New Year; Independence Day; Thanksgiving; Christmas.

Special Editions: Sport and Home (Feb); Auto Show (Apr); Fire Prevention (Oct); Entertainment; TV Section; Weddings.

Special Weekly Sections: Food (mon); Bridal (wed); TV & Entertainment, Children's Mini Page (thur); Outdoors, Religious Page (fri); Business News, Farm-Home, Garden Page (sat).

GENERAL MANAGEMENT

Publisher Bruce Henke
Business Manager Bruce Henke
Purchasing Agent Darrell Schelske

ADVERTISING

Manager Gene Keller

CIRCULATION

Manager Peter Colbenson

NEWS EXECUTIVE

Editor Kathy Wicks

EDITORS AND MANAGERS

Editorial Page Editor Kathy Wicks
Education Editor Kathy Wicks
Films/Theater Editor Scott Kraus
Food/Home Editor Gail Hogan
Picture Editor Scott Kraus
Political Editor Scott Kraus
Religion Editor Gail Hogan
Society/Women's Editor Gail Hogan
Sports Editor Kathy Wicks
Teen-Age/Youth Editor Gail Hogan

PRODUCTION

Foreman Darrell Schelske

Market Information: Zoned editions; Split Run; TMC.

Mechanical available: Offset; Black and 3 ROP colors; insert accepted — preprinted; page cut-offs — 22¾".

Mechanical specifications: Type page 12¾" x 21½"; E - 6 cols, 2", ⅛" between; A - 6 cols, 2", ⅛" between; C - 7 cols, 1⅝", ⅛" between.

Commodity consumption: Newsprint 480 metric tons; widths 27", 32"; black ink 10,050 pounds; color ink 1,408 pounds; average pages per issue 24(d); single plates used 6,000.

Equipment: EDITORIAL: Front-end hardware — 11-M/2800; Printers — 2-Ap/Mac LaserWriter; Other equipment — 1-RSK/TRS-80, 1-RSK/TRS-100. CLASSIFIED: Front-end hardware — IBM; Front-end software — Suntype; Printers — Ap/Mac LaserWriter II. PRODUCTION: OCR software — Aldus/PageMaker, Multi-Ad, Aldus/FreeHand; Typesetters — 3-Ap/Mac; Plate exposures — Nu/Flip Top FT40LNS; Plate processors — Ic; Production cameras — DAI/Screen G-24-D-LA; Automatic film processors — P/Super G.
PRESSROOM: Line 1 — 2-G/Community, 2-G/Community; Line 2 — 4-G/Community; Press drives — 75-HP; Folders — 1-G/Upper Former. MAILROOM: Bundle tyer — OVL/415, Bu; Addressing machine — 2-Dispensa-Matic/16. BUSINESS COMPUTERS: IBM/Mega 4000, IBM/LEAT; Applications: Nomads/Listmaster: Accts receivable, Circ.

MINOT

Ward County

'90 U.S. Census- 34,544; **E&P '96 Est.** 35,964
ABC-CZ (90): 34,544 (HH 13,965)

Minot Daily News

(m-mon to sat; S)

Minot Daily News, 301 4th St. S.E.; PO Box 1150, Minot, ND 58701; tel (701) 857-1900; fax (701) 857-1907. Ogden Newspapers group.

Circulation: 26,005(m); 26,005(m-sat); 27,165(S); ABC Sept. 30, 1995.

Price: 50¢(d); 50¢(sat); $1.50(S); $10.25/mo (carrier); $123.00/yr (carrier).

Advertising: Open inch rate $22.29(m); $22.29(m-sat); $22.29(S).

News Service: AP. **Politics:** Independent. **Established:** 1884.

Advertising not accepted: Clairvoyant; Fortune teller; Magnetic healer; Doubtful medical; Fake sale; Any other objectionable.

Special Editions: Tax Tab (Jan); Bridal Section (Feb); Progress Edition (Mar); Senior Lifestyles, Fishing Guide (Apr); Spring Section, Graduation Section (May); State Fair (June); Health & Fitness (Aug); Hunting Guide, Fall Sports, Home Town (Sept); Norsk Hostfest (Oct); Christmas Gift Guide, Winter Sports (Dec).

Special Weekly Sections: Agriculture (mon); Best Food Day, Best Real Estate (wed); Best Automotive Day (thur); Best Entertainment Day, Agriculture (fri); TV, Religion, Best Real Estate, Agriculture (sat); Outdoor, Military, Best Automotive Day, Agriculture (S).

Magazines: TV Week (S); Home Market Magazine, Dakota Business, Holiday Minot (monthly); Home Town (annually).

CORPORATE OFFICERS

President G Ogden Nutting
Vice Pres Dave Frame

GENERAL MANAGEMENT

General Manager David A Frisch

ADVERTISING

Director Steven Baker

CIRCULATION

Director Ken Bohl

NEWS EXECUTIVE

Editor Mark Hanson

Copyright ©1996 by the Editor & Publisher Co.

North Dakota I-301

EDITORS AND MANAGERS	
News Editor	Matthew Gerszewski
Sports Editor	Dave Dondoneau
PRODUCTION	
Foreman-Composing	Andrew Deck
Foreman-Pressroom	Barry Bruce
Foreman-Mailroom	Bob Berntson

Market Information: Split Run; TMC.
Mechanical available: Offset; Black and 3 ROP colors; insert accepted — preprinted; page cut-offs — 22¾".
Mechanical specifications: Type page 13" x 21½"; E - 5 cols, 2.36", ⅙" between; A - 6 cols, 2.03", ⅛" between; C - 9 cols, 1.36", .11" between.
Commodity consumption: Newsprint 1,900 short tons; widths 27", 35"; black ink 42,000 pounds; color ink 4,000 pounds; average pages per issue 26(d), 40(S); single plates used 16,000.
Equipment: EDITORIAL: Front-end hardware — AT; Front-end software — AT; Printers — Ap/Mac LaserWriter II, MON/Imagemaster 1270; Other equipment — Ap/Mac. CLASSIFIED: Front-end hardware — AT; Front-end software — AT; Printers — Ap/Mac LaserWriter II, MON/Imagemaster 1270. DISPLAY: Adv layout systems — Ap/Mac; Front-end hardware — Ap/Mac; Front-end software — NTI; Printers — Ap/Mac LaserWriter II, MON/Imagemaster 1270. PRODUCTION: Typesetters — MON/Imagemaster 1270; Plate exposures — Magnum; Plate processors — Nat; Scanners — VG; Production cameras — SCREEN; Automatic film processors — P; Color separation equipment (conventional) — Lf/AP Leaf Picture Desk.

PRESSROOM: Line 1 — 7-G/Urbanite. MAILROOM: Counter stackers — Id; Inserters and stuffers — HI; Bundle tyer — Bu, MLN; Addressing machine — Ch. LIBRARY: Electronic — AP. BUSINESS COMPUTERS: IBM/Sys 36; Applications: Circ, Accts receivable, Accts payable.

VALLEY CITY
Barnes County
'90 U.S. Census- 7,169; E&P '96 Est. 6,818

Valley City Times-Record
(e-mon to fri)
Valley City Times-Record, 146 Third St. N.E.; PO Box 697, Valley City, ND 58072; tel (701) 845-0463; fax (701) 845-0175. Hollinger International Inc. group.
Circulation: 3,414(e); Sworn Oct. 1, 1995.
Price: 50¢(d); $71.00/yr.
Advertising: Open inch rate $6.50(e). **Representative:** American Newspaper Representatives Inc.
News Services: AP, NEA. **Politics:** Independent. **Established:** 1879.
Not Published: New Year; Memorial Day; Independence Day; Labor Day; Thanksgiving; Christmas.
Magazine: T-R Shopper.

GENERAL MANAGEMENT
Publisher .... Dennis L Vernon
ADVERTISING
Manager .... Janice Olafson
Manager-Classified .... Bobbi Miller

CIRCULATION
Manager .... Keith Barta
NEWS EXECUTIVE
Editor .... R Duane Coates

Market Information: Zoned editions; TMC.
Mechanical available: Offset; Black and 1 ROP color; insert accepted — preprinted; page cut-offs — 22¾".
Mechanical specifications: Type page 13¼" x 21"; E - 6 cols, 2¹¹⁄₁₆", ⅛" between; A - 6 cols, 2¹⁄₁₆", ⅛" between; C - 6 cols, 2¹⁄₁₆", ⅛" between.
Commodity consumption: Newsprint 140 short tons; width 28"; average pages per issue 14(d); single plates used 2,000.
Equipment: EDITORIAL: Front-end hardware — 6-HI/Compuedit. CLASSIFIED: Front-end hardware — 1-HI/Compuedit, COM/Unisetter. PRODUCTION: Typesetters — 1-COM/2961, 1-COM/7200, 1-COM/4; Plate exposures — 1-B/Mercury; Plate processors — 1-Ic/25; Direct-to-plate imaging — 3M/Pyrofax Deadliner; Production cameras — 1-B/Commander.
PRESSROOM: Line 1 — 4-G/Community; Folders — 1-G. MAILROOM: Bundle tyer — 1-Bu; Addressing machine — 1-Am. WIRE SERVICES: News — AP; Syndicates — NEA; Receiving dishes — AP. BUSINESS COMPUTERS: Vector/4; Applications: Circ, Accts receivable, Accts payable, Payroll, Gen ledger.

WAHPETON, ND-BRECKENRIDGE, MN
Richland County, ND
Wilkin County, MN
'90 U.S. Census- 12,459 (Wahpeton, ND 8,751; Breckenridge, MN 3,708); E&P '96 Est. 12,139 (Wahpeton, ND 8,589; Breckenridge, MN 3,550)

The Daily News
(m-tues to fri; S)
The Daily News, 601 Dakota Ave.; PO Box 970, Wahpeton, ND 58074; tel (701) 642-8585; fax (701) 642-1501. Wick Communications group.
Circulation: 4,324(m); 4,324(S); Sworn Oct. 1, 1995.
Price: 50¢(d); 75¢(fri); $1.25(S); $8.25/mo; $89.00/yr; $24.00/3mo; $47.00/6mo.
Advertising: Open inch rate $5.95(m); $5.95(S). **Representative:** American Newspaper Representatives Inc.
News Service: AP. **Politics:** Independent. **Established:** 1880.
Not Published: New Year; Memorial Day; Independence Day; Labor Day; Thanksgiving; Christmas.
Special Editions: News in Review (Jan); School Activities Issue (Fall); Valley Voices (month-

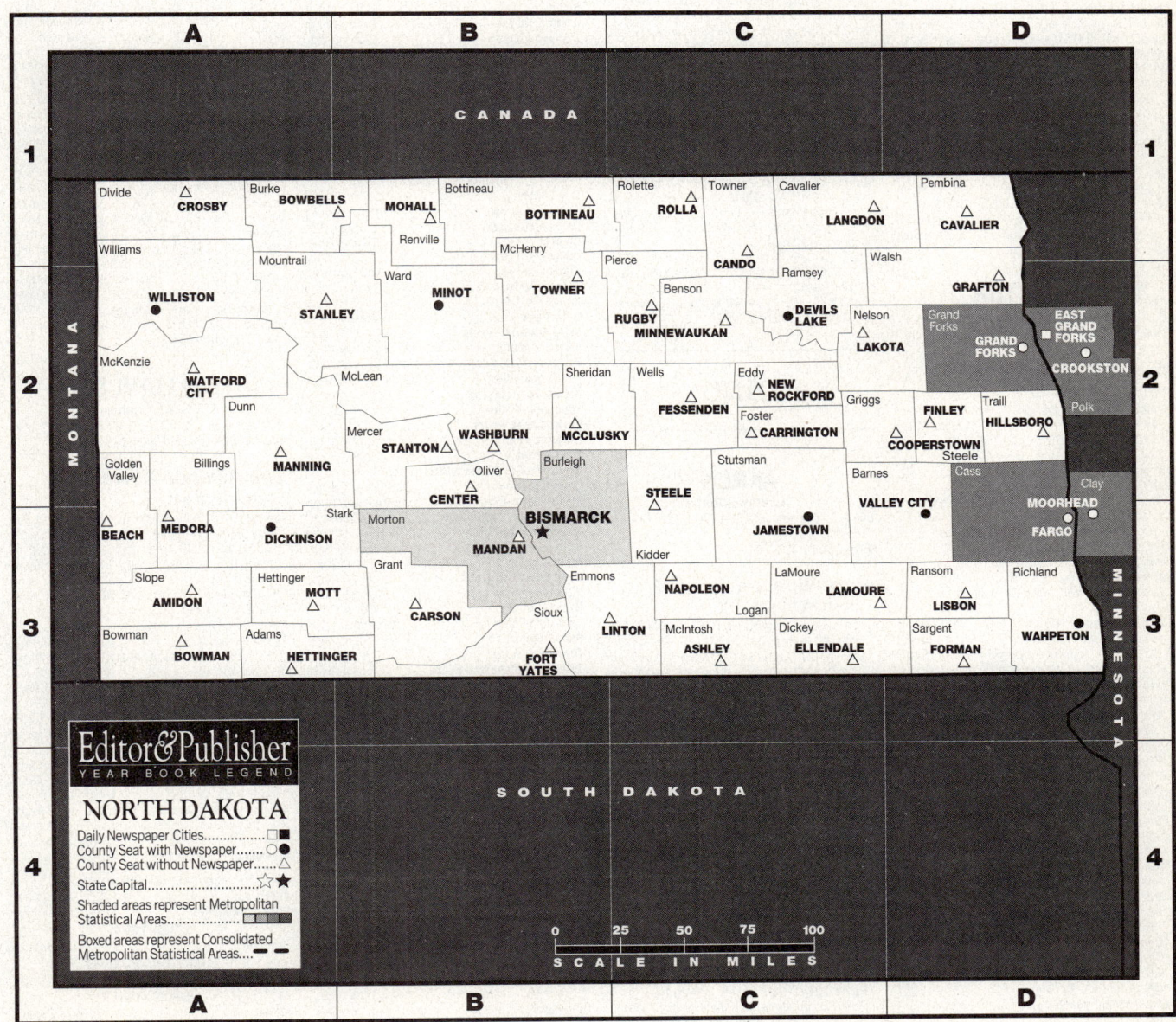

ly); Voters Guide (election years); Bridal Issue; Spring & Fall Car Care; Seasonal Sports Issue; Progress Issue.
Special Weekly Section: Channels.
Magazine: Channeling (TV Section).

CORPORATE OFFICERS
President Walter M Wick
Secretary/Treasurer Robert J Wick
Exec Vice Pres Lou Major

GENERAL MANAGEMENT
Publisher/Editor Newell C Grant
Asst Publisher Jim DeVries

ADVERTISING
Manager Roger Harty

CIRCULATION
Manager Jim DeVries

NEWS EXECUTIVE
Managing Editor Barbara Grant

EDITOR AND MANAGER
Sports Editor Scott Nulph

PRODUCTION
Foreman-Composing Mark Lahaise

Market Information: TMC.
Mechanical available: Offset; Black and 3 ROP colors; insert accepted — preprinted; page cut-offs — 21¾".
Mechanical specifications: Type page 13" x 21"; E - 6 cols, 2 1/16", ⅛" between; A - 6 cols, 2 1/16", ⅛" between; C - 8 cols, 1½", 1/16" between.
Commodity consumption: Newsprint 242 short tons; widths 27½", 33", 27½", 33"; black ink 8,680 pounds; color ink 250 pounds; single pages printed 4,739; average pages per issue 14(d), 24(S); single plates used 6,000.
Equipment: EDITORIAL: Front-end hardware — Mk/1100 Plus. PRODUCTION: Typesetters — Ap/Mac LaserWriter II; Platemaking systems — 1-B/Mercury; Plate exposures — Ic; Plate processors — Nat/250; Production cameras — 1-B; Automatic film processors — 1-P. PRESSROOM: Line 1 — 6-G/Community; Folders — 1-G/Community. MAILROOM: Bundle tyer — 2-Felin/Pak-Tyer; Addressing machine — 1-Am/R500. COMMUNICATIONS: Facsimile — Panafax/Uf-250. WIRE SERVICES: News — AP; Receiving dishes — AP. BUSINESS COMPUTERS: DEC; Applications: Accts receivable, Accts payable, Payroll.

WILLISTON
Williams County
'90 U.S. Census- 13,131; E&P '96 Est. 13,063

Williston Daily Herald
(e-mon to fri; S)

Williston Daily Herald, 14 W. 4th St.; PO Box 1447, Williston, ND 58802-1447; tel (701) 572-2165; fax (701) 572-1965. Wick Communications group.
Circulation: 5,731(e); 5,731(S); VAC June 30, 1995.
Price: 50¢(d); $1.00(S); $7.85/mo; $90.00/yr.
Advertising: Open inch rate $9.10(e); $9.10(S). **Representative:** Landon Associates Inc.
News Service: AP. **Established:** 1899.
Not Published: New Year; Memorial Day; Independence Day; Labor Day; Thanksgiving; Christmas.
Special Editions: National Hard Red Spring Wheat Show, Valentine's Day, Heart Month, Basketball Tournaments, FFA Week (Feb); Poison Control Week, National Girl Scout Week, National Agriculture Day, Spring Car Care, Sport & Recreation Show (Mar); Spring Home & Garden, Fishing & Recreation Guide (Apr); Law Day, National Hospital Week, National Nurses Day, Nursing Home Week, Senior Health Care Tab, Roughrider Art Show, Band Day, Graduation (May); Miss North Dakota Pageant, Fort Union Rendezvous, County Fair (June); Fourth of July, Crazee Days (July); Back-to-School, Healthstyles, Fall Sports Review (Aug); Comic Book, Labor Day, Football Contest, Fall Hunting, Moonlight Madness, National Farm Safety, Fall Home Improvement, Oktoberfest (Sept); Rodeo, Basketball Tournament, Fire Prevention Week, Fall Car Care, Halloween Safety (Oct); Deer Hunting & Ice Fishing, Holiday Cookbook, Christmas Kick-off (Nov); Winter Sports, Last Minute Gift Guide, Christmas Greetings, New Year's Party Guide, First Baby Contest (Dec).
Special Weekly Section: TV Guide (S).
Magazine: TV Guide (fri).

CORPORATE OFFICER
President Walter M Wick

GENERAL MANAGEMENT
Publisher Don Mrachek
Business Manager Beverly Forthun

ADVERTISING
Manager Brian Stanfield
Manager-Classified Rod Neer

CIRCULATION
Manager David Boeck

NEWS EXECUTIVE
Managing Editor Margo Ryan

EDITORS AND MANAGERS
Lifestyle Editor Sue Neft
News Editor Mike Weber
Sports Editor Chris Kirchmeier

PRODUCTION
Manager Dan Bundy
Supervisor-Composing Wanda Olaf

Market Information: Zoned editions; Split Run; TMC.
Mechanical available: Offset; Black and 3 ROP colors; insert accepted — preprinted; page cut-offs — 21½".
Mechanical specifications: Type page 13" x 21"; E - 6 cols, 2.07", ⅛" between; A - 6 cols, 2.07", ⅛" between; C - 9 cols, 1⅜", .08" between.
Commodity consumption: Newsprint 395 short tons; widths 27½", 13¾", 30", 28"; black ink 12,000 pounds; color ink 400 pounds; single pages printed 8,200; average pages per issue 10(d), 16(S); single plates used 6,000.
Equipment: EDITORIAL: Front-end hardware — Mk; Printers — Ap/Mac LaserWriter. CLASSIFIED: Front-end hardware — Mk; Printers — Ap/Mac LaserWriter. DISPLAY: Front-end hardware — Ap/Mac IIci; Front-end software — Multi-Ad/Creator, Caere/OmniPage, Caere/OmniPhoto; Printers — Ap/Mac LaserWriter II; Other equipment — Ap/Mac CD-Rom, Ap/Mac One Scanner. PRODUCTION: Typesetters — Ap/Mac LaserWriter II; Platemaking systems — Nu/FT40V6UPNS; Plate exposures — 1-Nu; Plate processors — 1-Hoechst/Economatic N323; Production cameras — B; Automatic film processors — P. PRESSROOM: Line 1 — 5-HI/V-15A; Folders — 2-HI/F-7 (w/1 balloon). MAILROOM: Inserters and stuffers — KR/512; Bundle tyer — EAM/Mosca RO-M. WIRE SERVICES: News — AP; Receiving dishes — AP.

OHIO

AKRON
Summit County
'90 U.S. Census- 223,019; E&P '96 Est. 211,582
ABC-CZ (90): 495,769 (HH 193,128)

Akron Beacon Journal
(m-mon to sat; S)

Akron Beacon Journal, 44 E. Exchange St.; PO Box 640, Akron, OH 44309-0640; tel (216) 996-3000; fax (216) 376-9235; web site http://www.beaconjournal.com/. Knight-Ridder Inc. group.
Circulation: 152,211(m); 152,211(m-sat); 219,137(S); ABC Sept. 30, 1995.
Price: 35¢(d); 35¢(sat); $1.25(S); $8.45/wk (mail); $33.80/mo (mail); $439.40/yr (mail).
Advertising: Open inch rate $81.02(m); $81.02(m-sat); $108.44(S); $158.60(m & S). **Representative:** Newspapers First.
News Services: AP, KRT, LAT-WP, NYT, RN. **Politics:** Independent. **Established:** 1839.
Special Editions: High Tech Recruitment, Excellence in Education (Jan); Winter Break (Travel), Family Health, Income Tax, Sale-A-Rama, Weddings, Cruises, Auto Show (Feb); Design-An-Ad, Health Care Careers, Exotic Travel (Mar); American Home Week, Golf Directory, Lawn & Garden, Spring Recruitment, Spring Car Care (Apr); National Nurses' Day, Baby's Coming, Family Travel (May); Canada Travel (June); Pro Football Hall of Fame (July); Fall Fashion, World Series of Golf (Aug); Fall Foliage, Fall Lawn & Garden, Health Care Careers (Sept); Fall Recruitment, Temporary Help, Auto, Truck & Van Preview-1997, Dinner on Us-Restaurant Month, Fall Car Care, Skiing Adventures (Oct); Medical Directory, Casinos and Gambling (Nov); Golf Get-aways (Dec).
Magazines: Parade, Channels (S).

CORPORATE OFFICERS
President John L Dotson Jr
Senior Vice Pres W Dale Allen
Vice Pres-Finance/Treasurer Glen L McCaulley
Vice Pres/Asst Treasurer/Asst Secretary Larry A Levine
Secretary Douglas C Harris
Asst Secretary Glen L McCaulley
Asst Treasurer Stephen H Sheriff

GENERAL MANAGEMENT
Publisher John L Dotson Jr
Asst to Publisher Joette Riehle
Vice Pres-Finance Glen L McCaulley
Vice Pres-Human Resources/General Counsel Jyrl James
Manager-Human Resources Robert Christoff

ADVERTISING
Vice Pres Mitch Allen
Manager-National Nancy Whitehead
Manager-Retail Jandell L W Herum
Manager-Classified Skip Knight

MARKETING AND PROMOTION
Director-Marketing Communications Kurt O Landefeld

TELECOMMUNICATIONS
Director-Info Systems Robert J Tigelman

CIRCULATION
Vice Pres Harry C Davis
Director Don Clark

NEWS EXECUTIVES
Editor Dale Allen
Assoc Editor David Cooper
Managing Editor Glenn Guzzo
Deputy Managing Editor-Operations Stuart Warner
Deputy Managing Editor-News Charles Stevens
Deputy Managing Editor-Administration Mike Needs
Asst Managing Editor-Business/Region Geoff Gevalt
Asst Managing Editor-Graphics Susan Curtis

EDITORS AND MANAGERS
City Editor Karen Chuparkoff
Columnist-Local Fran Murphey
Columnist-Local Carl Chancellor
Columnist-Local Regina Brett
Columnist-Local Bob Dyer
Columnist-Local Jewell Cardwell
Columnist-Business Diane Evans
Columnist-Sports Terry Pluto
Copy Desk Chief Kathleen Fraze
Chief Editorial Writer Michael Douglas
Editorial Writer Sarah Vrandenburg
Editorial Writer Laura Ofobike
Enterprise Editor Michelle Le Comte
Higher Education Writer Ron Kirksey
Education Writer Paula Scleis
Environment Writer Bob Downing
Features Editor Margaret Corvini
Food Writer Jane Snow
Governmental Affairs Editor Mitzell Stewart III
Chief Librarian Catherine Tierney
Music Editor-Classical Elaine Guregian
Music Editor-Pop/Culture Kevin Johnson
National Editor Olga Reswow
Exec News Editor-Daily Bruce Winges
Night City Editor Gloria Irwin
Night Suburban Editor Cristal Williams
Director-Photography Michael Good
Region Editor David Hertz
Suburban Editor Bonnie Bolden
Sports Editor Bill Eichenberger
Television Writer R D Heldenfels
Television Magazine Editor John Olesky
Travel Editor Betsy Lammerding
Weekend News Editor Val Pipps

MANAGEMENT INFORMATION SERVICES
Data Processing Manager Robert J Tigelman

PRODUCTION
Vice Pres Michael K Mayo
Director-Pre Press Richard M Coddington
Manager-Printing Ron MacAdam
Manager-Engraving Vicki Franklin
Manager-Mailroom Melvin Holmes
Manager-Building/Facilities Robert Lewis
Foreman-Composing Dick Latshaw

Market Information: Zoned editions; Split Run; Operate audiotex.
Mechanical available: Flexography, Letterpress; Black and 3 ROP colors; insert accepted — preprinted; page cut-offs — 23 9/16".
Mechanical specifications: Type page 12⅞" x 22"; E - 6 cols, 2 1/16", ⅛" between; A - 6 cols, 2 1/16", ⅛" between; C - 10 cols, 1 3/16", ⅛" between.
Commodity consumption: Newsprint 24,831 short tons; 22,527 metric tons; widths 54½", 40¾", 27⅛"; black ink 731,470 pounds; color ink 151,212 pounds; single pages printed 22,632; average pages per issue 55(d), 106(S); single plates used 163,071.
Equipment: EDITORIAL: Front-end hardware — 6-Tandem/TXP, 100-SII/Coyote QB, 5-PCAT; Front-end software — Adobe/Photoshop, QuarkXPress, SII/Sys 55; Printers — 2-DEC/Writers, 3-TI/810, 1-HP/LaserJet, 2-IBM/PPS II; Other equipment — 3-Lf/AP Leaf Picture Desk, 2-Lf/Leafscan 35, Lf/Leafax 35, III/D, Sharp/Flatbed, 4-Ap/Mac fx. CLASSIFIED: Front-end hardware — 6-Tandem/TXP, 44-SII/Coyote 4; Front-end software — SII/Sys 55; Printers — 1-TI/810, 2-HP/LaserJet. AUDIOTEX: Hardware — Micro Voice/Audiotext 2000; Software — Micro Voice/Audiotext 2000, AP Stock Quotes. DISPLAY: Adv layout systems — SCS/Layout 8000; Front-end hardware — III/2-3650 Scanners, 10-AMS; Front-end software — III; Printers — 1-HP/LaserJet; Other equipment — 6-SII/Coyote 4. PRODUCTION: Typesetters — 1-III/2-3810, 1-III/3850; Platemaking systems — 2-He/SR100-, 1-He/SRA; Plate exposures — He; Plate processors — He; Electronic picture desk — Lf/AP Leaf Picture Desk, III; Scanners — ECR/720, ECR/8400; Production cameras — C/Newspager, 1-C/Spartan III, C/F; Automatic film processors — Kk/710, AG/Litex 26, P/TQ26, 3-LE/Online; Film transporters — 2-C; Color separation equipment (conventional) — CD/635; Digital color separation equipment — 1-Howtek/Scanmaster D4000. PRESSROOM: Line 1 — 2-H/Color Convertables (14 units; 18 humps), 4-MAN/Flexoman (3 4-color units); Line 2 — 1-H/Colormatic (7 units), 2-MAN/Flexoman; Folders — 3-H/3:2, 1-H/2:1; Pasters — 18-H/CC Semi-automatic, 9-H/Colormatic automatic; Reels and stands — 18-H/CC Semi-automatic, 9-H/Colormatic automatic; Press control system — GE/DIT 6 plus, GE/SCR speed variator drive. MAILROOM: Counter stackers — 2-RKW, 4-QWI/100, 4-QWI/300; Inserters and stuffers — Fg/8-into-1, Amerigraph/NP630 21-into-1; Bundle tyer — 5-Power Strap/Nu-6, 5-Power Strap/Nu-5; Wrapping singles — 4-QWI, 3-Power Strap/Standard, 2-Power Strap/¾ wrap. LIBRARY: Electronic — Vu/Text SAVE. WIRE SERVICES: News — KRT, PR Newswire, Weather, DJ, RN, AP Datafeatures, AP Datastream, Bloomberg; Photos — AP, KRT; Stock tables — Ap/Mac Stocks; Receiving dishes — AP, RN, Weather. BUSINESS COMPUTERS: 1-HP/3000 Series 960; Applications: Adv billing, Accts receivable, Gen ledger, Truck manifests, Subscription, Carrier billing, Accts payable, Payroll, PBM; PCs & micros networked; PCs & main system networked.

ALLIANCE
Stark County
'90 U.S. Census- 23,376; E&P '96 Est. 22,600
ABC-CZ (90): 31,864 (HH 12,048)

The Alliance Review
(e-mon to sat)

The Alliance Review, 40 S. Linden Ave.; PO Box 2180, Alliance, OH 44601-0180; tel (216) 821-1200; fax (216) 821-8258; e-mail reviewedit@aol.com. Dix Communications group.
Circulation: 12,588(e); 12,588(e-sat); ABC Sept. 30, 1995.
Price: 50¢(d); 50¢(sat).
Advertising: Open inch rate $10.19(e); $10.19(e-sat). **Representative:** Landon Associates Inc.
News Service: AP. **Politics:** Republican. **Established:** 1888.
Not Published: New Year; Memorial Day; Independence Day; Labor Day; Thanksgiving; Christmas.
Special Editions: Year in Review (Jan); Outdoor Sports; Auto Tab; Home Improvement; Football; Baby Contest.
Special Weekly Sections: Business Page (wed); Entertainment-Let's Go (thur); Real Estate (fri); Church Page (sat); TV Page (daily).
Magazine: TV Magazine.

GENERAL MANAGEMENT
Publisher G Charles Dix II
General Manager Robert C Shaffer

ADVERTISING
Director Don Watson

TELECOMMUNICATIONS
Audiotex Manager Don Watson

CIRCULATION
Manager Ken Pagani

Ohio I-303

NEWS EXECUTIVE

Editor James Hastings

EDITORS AND MANAGERS

Editorial Page Editor James Hastings
Entertainment/Amusements Editor Tom Harper
Living/Lifestyle Editor Barbara Graf
News Editor Michael Patterson
Women's Editor Barbara Graf

PRODUCTION

Foreman-Composing Ray Gonzales
Foreman-Pressroom Robert Kiser

Market Information: Zoned editions; Split Run; TMC; ADS; Operate audiotex.
Mechanical available: Offset; Black and 3 ROP colors; insert accepted — preprinted; page cutoffs — 21½".
Mechanical specifications: Type page 13" x 21½"; E - 6 cols, 2 1/16", ⅛" between; A - 6 cols, 2 1/16", ⅛" between; C - 6 cols, 2 1/16", ⅛" between.
Commodity consumption: Newsprint 1,000 short tons; widths 27.5", 13.75"; black ink 4,000 pounds; color ink 350 pounds; average pages per issue 20(d), 20(sat).
Equipment: EDITORIAL: Front-end hardware — AST; Front-end software — Dewar; Printers — Okidata, Printware/720IQ. CLASSIFIED: Front-end hardware — AST; Front-end software — Dewar; Printers — Okidata. AUDIOTEX: Supplier name — Educom of Ohio. DISPLAY: Front-end hardware — Wyse/Terminal, Dec/Processor; Front-end software — Data Sciences 1993; Printers — Okidata, Tally. PRODUCTION: Typesetters — Printware/720IQ; Plate exposures — 1-Nu; Plate processors — 3M/Deadliner; Direct-to-plate imaging — 3M/Deadliner; Automatic film processors — 1-P/26. PRESSROOM: Line 1 — 6-G/Urbanite; Folders — 1-G. MAILROOM: Counter stackers — BG/Count-O-Veyor; Inserters and stuffers — MM; Bundle tyer — Bu. WIRE SERVICES: News — AP, SHNS; Syndicates — NYT, LATS, King Features, TMS, Media Link, CNS, UPS, United Media; Receiving dishes — AP. BUSINESS COMPUTERS: DSI; PCs & main system networked.

ASHLAND

Ashland County

'90 U.S. Census- 20,079; E&P '96 Est. 19,869
ABC-CZ (90): 24,369 (HH 9,117)

Ashland Times-Gazette

(e-mon to fri; m-sat)

Ashland Times-Gazette, 40 E. 2nd St., Ashland, OH 44805; tel (419) 281-0581; fax (419) 281-5591. Dix Communications group.
Circulation: 11,738(e); 11,738(m-sat); ABC Sept. 30, 1995.
Price: 50¢(d); 50¢(sat); $1.95/wk; $8.45/mo; $101.40/yr.
Advertising: Open inch rate $10.50(e); $10.50(m-sat). **Representative:** Landon Associates Inc.
News Service: AP. **Politics:** Independent. **Established:** 1850.
Not Published: New Year; Memorial Day; Independence Day; Labor Day; Thanksgiving; Christmas.
Special Editions: Finance 1996, January Clearance, Bridal Tab (Jan); Progress, Sr. Citizens (Feb); Health and Beauty, Spring Home Improvement, Agriculture (Mar); Earth Day, Auto Tab (Apr); Outdoor Tab, Graduation, Hospital Nursing (May); Sidewalk Days, Lawn & Garden, Balloon Fest (June); Small Business, Lawn & Garden Section, Senior Citizens, Christmas in July (July); Back-to-School, Football Preview, Old Fashion Days (Aug); Fall Home Improvement, Fair (Sept); Businesswomen, Fall Car Care, Health Focus (Oct); Lay Away, Basketball Preview, Holiday Cookbook, Holiday Gift Guide (Nov); Last Minute Gift Guide, Christmas Songbook, Christmas in Ashland (Dec).
Special Weekly Sections: Best Food Day, Education (wed); Health (thur); Church (fri); Farm (sat).
Magazine: TV Weekly.

CORPORATE OFFICER

President Raymond Victor Dix

GENERAL MANAGEMENT

General Manager William C McKinney

ADVERTISING

Director Rhonda J Geer

CIRCULATION

Manager Michael Igo

NEWS EXECUTIVES

Managing Editor Mel McKeachie
Asst Managing Editor Susan Lime

EDITORS AND MANAGERS

Education Editor LeAnn Grose
Fashion Editor Mary Ann Dull
Chief Photographer Chic Knight
Sports Editor Steve Eighinger
Teen-Age/Youth Editor LeAnn Grose

PRODUCTION

Manager-Systems Cheryl Leluika
Foreman-Composing Eric Spencer
Foreman-Press Doug Gillespie

Market Information: TMC.
Mechanical available: Offset; Black and 3 ROP colors; insert accepted — preprinted, single sheet; page cut-offs — 22¾".
Mechanical specifications: Type page 13" x 21½"; E - 6 cols, 2", ⅛" between; A - 6 cols, 2", ⅛" between; C - 9 cols, 1⅜", 1/16" between.
Commodity consumption: Newsprint 600 short tons; 545 metric tons; widths 13¾", 27½"; black ink 13,438 pounds; color ink 723 pounds; single pages printed 7,176; average pages per issue 24(d); single plates used 4,485.
Equipment: EDITORIAL: Front-end hardware — Ap/Mac Quadra 610, Ap/Mac Quadra 650, Ap/Mac Quadra 840 AU; Front-end software — Linotype-Hell/Linopress 3.0; Printers — ECR/UR 36 Imagesetter, NewGen/Systems. CLASSIFIED: Front-end hardware — Ap/Mac Quadra 610; Front-end software — Linotype-Hell/Linopress 3.0; Printers — Ap/Mac LaserWriter NTX. DISPLAY: Front-end hardware — 1-Ap/Mac, Ap/Mac Quadra 800, 3-Ap/Mac Quadra 840 AU, 1-Ap/Mac 7200; Front-end software — Multi-Ad; Printers — Ap/Mac LaserWriter NTX, 2-ECR/UR 36 Imagesetter. PRODUCTION: Pagination software — Linotype-Hell/Linopress 3.0; Typesetters — 2-ECR/UR36; Plate exposures — 1-Nu; Plate processors — 1-Anitec; Electronic picture desk — Ap/Mac Quadra 840 AU, Adobe/Photoshop, Lf/AP Leaf Picture Desk; Scanners — AG/Argus Plus; Production cameras — SCREEN/Auto Companica-670D; Automatic film processors — 2-Konica; Color separation equipment (conventional) — Ap/Mac Quadra 840 AU, Adobe/Photoshop; Digital color separation equipment — Lf/Leafscan 35. PRESSROOM: Line 1 — 8-G/Community, 1-G/Community. MAILROOM: Bundle tyer — Tri-Star/210; Addressing machine — Ch/563001. WIRE SERVICES: News — AP; Photos — AP; Receiving dishes — size-8ft, AP. BUSINESS COMPUTERS: DSI; Applications: Circ, Business office; PCs & micros networked; PCs & main system networked.

ASHTABULA

Ashtabula County

'90 U.S. Census- 21,633; E&P '96 Est. 20,193
ABC-CZ (90): 33,086 (HH 12,976)

The Star-Beacon

(m-mon to sat; S)

The Star-Beacon, 4626 Park Ave., Ashtabula, OH 44004; tel (216) 992-9655/(216) 998-5870 (adm). Thomson Newspapers group.
Circulation: 23,985(m); 23,985(m-sat); 23,808(S); ABC Sept. 30, 1995.
Price: 35¢(d); 35¢(sat); $1.00(S); $2.50/wk.
Advertising: Open inch rate $27.23(m); $27.23(m-sat); $27.23(S). **Representative:** Landon Associates Inc.
News Service: AP. **Politics:** Independent. **Established:** 1888.
Special Editions: Bridal (Jan); Washington's Birthday, Home & Flower Show (Mar); Health Care (May); Ashtabula County Almanac (June); Dog Days (July); Back-to-School, Football Features, Ashtabula County Fair (Aug); Progress (Sept); Covered Bridge (Oct); Women in Business (Nov); Christmas (Dec); Family Life (monthly).
Special Weekly Sections: Best Food Day (mon); Entertainment (fri); Church News (sat); TV Update, Best Food Day (S).
Magazines: TV Scene Magazine (S); USA Weekend-Inns and Outs; Summer Guide; Auto Express; Homeseeker.

GENERAL MANAGEMENT

Publisher Ed Looman
Accountant Marilyn Surkala

ADVERTISING

Manager-Display Vanessa Koper
Manager-Classified Vanessa Koper

CIRCULATION

Director Jared Spencer

NEWS EXECUTIVE

Editor Neil Freider

EDITORS AND MANAGERS

City Editor Bob Lebzelter
Lifestyle Editor Carl Feather
Sports Editor Craig Muder

PRODUCTION

Director Jim Hanson
Foreman-Pressroom Marvin Ralph

Market Information: Zoned editions; Split Run; TMC; ADS.
Mechanical available: Offset; Black and 3 ROP colors; insert accepted — preprinted, any; page cut-offs — 21¼".
Mechanical specifications: Type page 13" x 21½"; E - 6 cols, 2 1/16", ⅛" between; A - 6 cols, 2 1/16", ⅛" between; C - 9 cols, 1½", 1/16" between.
Commodity consumption: Newsprint 2,169 short tons; width 27½"; single pages printed 9,812; average pages per issue 24(d), 40(S).
Equipment: EDITORIAL: Front-end hardware — Mk, Ap/Mac, IBM, Lf; Front-end software — Mk; Printers — 1-II. CLASSIFIED: Front-end hardware — 1-Mk; Front-end software — Mk; Printers — 1-TI; Other equipment — IBM. DISPLAY: Adv layout systems — ATT; Front-end hardware — ATT; Front-end software — ATT. PRODUCTION: Typesetters — Tegra/Varityper 5300, 2-Tegra/Varityper 5100; Plate exposures — 1-Nu; Production cameras — 1-Nu; Automatic film processors — Tegra/Varityper 5300; Film transporters — AG/Rapidline, 17-AG/660; Color separation equipment (conventional) — Tegra/Varityper; Digital color separation equipment — Lf/AP Leaf Picture Desk. PRESSROOM: Line 1 — 6-G/Urbanite (1 color deck); Folders — 1-G. MAILROOM: Counter stackers — BG/108; Inserters and stuffers — MM/227; Bundle tyer — Sa/S1100. WIRE SERVICES: News — AP; Receiving dishes — AP. BUSINESS COMPUTERS: 6-ATT/3B2-500, 1-DEC/1173, 1-DEC; Applications: Adv billing, Accts receivable, Gen ledger, Payroll; PCs & micros networked; PCs & main system networked.

ATHENS

Athens County

'90 U.S. Census- 21,265; E&P '96 Est. 22,677
ABC-CZ (90): 27,428 (HH 8,098)

The Athens Messenger

(e-mon to fri; S)

The Athens Messenger, US Rte. 33 N. & Johnson Rd.; PO Box 4210, Athens, OH 45701; tel (614) 592-6612; fax (614) 592-4647; web site gopher://seorf.ohiou.edu:2001//11/seorf.stuff/med/xx005.
Circulation: 13,019(e); 15,823(S); ABC Sept. 30, 1995.
Price: 35¢(d); $1.00(S); $1.90/wk (carrier); $8.23/mo (carrier); $98.80/yr (carrier).
Advertising: Open inch rate $13.19(e); $13.19(S). **Representative:** Papert Companies.
News Services: AP, SHNS. **Established:** 1905 (daily), 1922 (Sunday).
Not Published: Memorial Day; Labor Day; Christmas.
Special Editions: Wedding Guide (Feb); Fashion (Mar); New Babies, Design-An-Ad, Yard and Garden Tab (Apr); Spring/Summer Car Care, Home and Garden, Vacation Tab, Home Improvement Guide (May); County Fair (July); College Edition, Football Tab (Aug); Fall Car Care (Oct); Basketball Tab (Nov).
Special Weekly Sections: Farm Page, Business Page, Best Food Day, TV Week (S); Church Page (fri).
Magazines: TV Week, TV Listings, USA Weekend, Color Comics (S).
Cable TV: Operate leased cable TV in circulation area.

CORPORATE OFFICERS

President G Kenner Bush
Secretary Jennie Ray Bush
Treasurer Fred Bush

GENERAL MANAGEMENT

Publisher G Kenner Bush
Asst Publisher Fred Bush
General Manager Fred W Weber II

ADVERTISING

Manager Chuck Douglas

CIRCULATION

Manager T Mark Shorts

NEWS EXECUTIVES

Editor G Kenner Bush
Managing Editor Karl Runser
Asst Managing Editor Herb Amey

EDITORS AND MANAGERS

Business/Finance Editor Herb Amey
City Editor Carol James
Editorial Page Editor Ann Kamody
Education Editor Carol James
Farm/Home Editor Carol James
Food/Fashion Editor Carol James
Radio/Television Editor Kathy Robb
Senior Writer Roy Cross
Women's Editor Carol James

PRODUCTION

Manager William Conrad
Foreman-Mailroom Tom King

Market Information: TMC; ADS.
Mechanical available: Offset; Black and 3 ROP colors; insert accepted — preprinted; page cutoffs — 22¾".
Mechanical specifications: Type page 13" x 21½"; E - 5 cols, 2⅜", ¼" between; A - 6 cols, 2 1/16", ⅛" between; C - 8 cols, 1⅜", 1/16" between.
Commodity consumption: Newsprint 976 metric tons; widths 27½", 13¾", 34"; black ink 18,000 pounds; color ink 3,000 pounds; single pages printed 7,066; average pages per issue 18(d), 40(S); single plates used 18,000.
Equipment: EDITORIAL: Front-end hardware — 19-SIA/386, 3-AST/386-33, 7-AST/286; Front-end software — Dewar/Sys IV; Printers — Okidata/393, Epson/LQ-570. CLASSIFIED: Front-end hardware — 2-SIA/386; Front-end software — Dewar/Sys IV. DISPLAY: Front-end hardware — 2-Ap/Mac Quadra 800, 2-Ap/Mac Quadra 650, 1-Ap/Mac IIci, 1-Global/Dos-486; Front-end software — QuarkXPress, Aldus/PageMaker, Multi-Ad/Creator; Other equipment — 1-Ap/Mac Quadra 800 fileserver, 1-Power/PC 6100 print server. PRODUCTION: OCR software — Caere/OmniPage 5.0; Typesetters — 2-Ap/Mac LaserWriter II, 2-NewGen/Turbo PS-660B, 2-NewGen/Design Express 1200 dpi; Plate exposures — 1-Nu/Flip Top FT40APRNS, 1-Nu/Ultra Plus; Plate processors — 1-Nat/Universal 26; Electronic picture desk — Lf/AP Leaf Picture Desk, Ap/Mac Quadra 800; Scanners — 1-ECR/Autokon 1030N, Umax/UC-1260; Production cameras — 1-C/Spartan III, 1-C/Vertical; Automatic film processors — 1-LE; Color separation equipment (conventional) — Lf/AP Leaf Picture Desk, 1-Ap/Mac Quadra 800; Digital color separation equipment — Lf/Leafscan 35. PRESSROOM: Line 1 — 5-G/Urbanite, 1-G/Urbanite, 1-G/Urbanite; Line 2 — 4-G/Community, 2-G/Community; Press drives — 3-Fin; Folders — 2-G; Press registration system — G/pin system. MAILROOM: Counter stackers — 1-HI/2510; Inserters and stuffers — 1-MM; Bundle tyer — 2-MLN/Spirit, 1-Bu/Akebone; Addressing machine — 1-Ch/596. WIRE SERVICES: News — AP; Photos — AP; Receiving dishes — size-6ft, AP. BUSINESS COMPUTERS: 1-Convergent/S80, 10-Wyse; Applications: Vision Data: Accts receivable, Accts payable, Gen ledger, Circ.

BEAVERCREEK

Greene County

'90 U.S. Census- 33,626; E&P '96 Est. 35,493

Beavercreek News-Current

(e-mon to fri; m-sat)

Beavercreek News-Current, 1350 N. Fairfield Rd., Beavercreek, OH 45432; tel (513) 426-5263; fax (513) 426-4548. Amos Press group.
Circulation: 4,233(e); 4,233(m-sat); Sworn Oct. 1, 1995.
Price: 35¢(d); 35¢(sat); $1.25/wk; $65.00/yr.
Advertising: Open inch rate $10.21(e); $10.21(m-sat).
News Service: AP. **Politics:** Independent. **Established:** 1961.
Not Published: New Year; Independence Day; Thanksgiving; Christmas.
Special Editions: Spring Bridal, Tax Preparation (Jan); Progress Edition (Feb); Spring/Summer Car Care (Mar); Home & Garden, Senior Life (Apr); Outdoor Living, Health & First Aid (May); County Fair, Summer Bridal, Living Here (July); School Bus Schedules (Aug); Home Improvement, Popcorn Festival Supplement (Sept); Fall/Winter Car Care, Senior Life, Health & First Aid (Oct); Holiday Ideas, Greene Co. Winterfest (Nov); Gift Guide (Dec).

Copyright ©1996 by the Editor & Publisher Co.

GENERAL MANAGEMENT

Publisher — Mark E Raymond

ADVERTISING

Manager — Ruth Mitsoff

CIRCULATION

Manager — Kelly Wods

NEWS EXECUTIVE

Editor — Tom Mitsoff

EDITORS AND MANAGERS

Business/Finance Editor — Tom Mitsoff
Editorial Page Editor — Tom Mitsoff
Education Editor — Steve Schelb
Entertainment/Amusements Editor — Chris Mitsoff
Sports Editor — Mike Ungard

Market Information: TMC.
Mechanical available: Offset; Black and 3 ROP colors; insert accepted — preprinted; page cut-offs — 22¾".
Mechanical specifications: Type page 13" x 21½"; E - 6 cols, ⅙" between; A - 6 cols, ⅙" between; C - 9 cols, ⅙" between.
Commodity consumption: average pages per issue 14(d).
Equipment: EDITORIAL: Front-end hardware — Ap/Mac; Front-end software — QuarkXPress, Microsoft/Word, Caere/OmniPage, Adobe/Illustrator; Printers — Ap/Mac LaserWriter II. DISPLAY: Adv layout systems — Ap/Mac; Front-end software — Aldus/PageMaker, QuarkXPress, Multi-Ad/Creator; Printers — Ap/Mac LaserWriter II. PRODUCTION: Plate processors — 1-Nu; Production cameras — 1-K/240; Automatic film processors — 1-Kk.
PRESSROOM: Line 1 — 3-G/Community; Line 2 — 3-G/Community; Folders — 1-G/2:1, 1-G/3:2. MAILROOM: Counter stackers — 1-BG; Bundle tyer — 2-Sa. WIRE SERVICES: News — UPI; Syndicates — UPI.

BELLAIRE

See MARTIN'S FERRY

BELLEFONTAINE

Logan County

'90 U.S. Census- 12,142; **E&P '96 Est.** 12,365
ABC-CZ (90): 12,142 (HH 4,759)

Bellefontaine Examiner

(e-mon to fri; m-sat)

Bellefontaine Examiner, 127 E. Chillicothe Ave., Bellefontaine, OH 43311; tel (513) 592-3060; fax (513) 592-4463.
Circulation: 10,562(e); 10,562(m-sat); ABC Sept. 30, 1995.
Price: 35¢(d); 35¢(sat); $1.45/wk (carrier), $1.60/wk (motor route); $5.80/mo (carrier), $6.40/mo (motor route); $75.40/yr (carrier), $83.20/yr (motor route).
Advertising: Open inch rate $8.35(e); $8.35(m-sat). **Representative:** Landon Associates Inc.
News Service: AP. **Politics:** Independent. **Established:** 1891.
Not Published: New Year; Memorial Day; Independence Day; Labor Day; Thanksgiving; Christmas.
Advertising not accepted: Hard liquor; mail order; vending machine.
Special Editions: Sale Days (Feb); Farm Tab, Real Estate Tab (Apr); Indian Lake Resort Tab, Real Estate Tab, Car Care Tab (May); Bridal, Real Estate Tab, Car Care Tab (June); Real Estate Tab, Car Care Tab (July); County Fair, Sale Days, Real Estate Tab, Car Care Tab (Aug); Real Estate Tab, Car Care Tab (Sept); Christmas Greetings (Dec 24); Home Maintenance (Spring & Fall).
Special Weekly Section: Coves Story (bi-weekly-fri).

CORPORATE OFFICERS

President — Thomas E Hubbard
Vice Pres — Janet K Hubbard
Treasurer — Thomas E Hubbard

GENERAL MANAGEMENT

General Manager — Jon B Hubbard

ADVERTISING

Manager-General — Cindy Titus

TELECOMMUNICATIONS

Audiotex Manager — Jim Mason

CIRCULATION

Manager — John L Sullivan

NEWS EXECUTIVE

Editor — David Wagner

EDITORS AND MANAGERS

City Editor — Ben McLaughlin
Editorial Page Editor — David Wagner
Features Editor — David Wagner
Librarian — Miriam Baier
News Editor — David Wagner
Political Editor — David Wagner
Radio/Television Editor — Miriam Baier
Religion Editor — Joel Mast
Society & Education Editor — Miriam Baier
Sports Editor — Don Hensley
Wire Editor — Ben McLaughlin

PRODUCTION

Manager — Jim Gilroy
Foreman-Composing — Perry Hodies Jr
Foreman-Pressroom — Dave Weikoff

Market Information: TMC; Operate audiotex.
Mechanical available: Offset; Black and 3 ROP colors; insert accepted — preprinted; page cut-offs — 22¾".
Mechanical specifications: Type page 13" x 21½"; E - 6 cols, 2 1/16", ⅛" between; A - 6 cols, 2 1/16", ⅛" between; C - 8 cols, 1⅜", 1/16" between.
Commodity consumption: Newsprint 562 short tons; widths 27½", 13¾", 6⅞"; black ink 16,800 pounds; color ink 6,200 pounds; single pages printed 5,720; average pages per issue 22(d); single plates used 8,850.
Equipment: EDITORIAL: Front-end hardware — Dewar/Disc Net IV, 16-AST/286, 5-SIA/386; Front-end software — Dewar/Disc Net IV; Printers — Okidata/320; Other equipment — dBase/IV, XYQUEST/XyWrite III, Novell/Netware. CLASSIFIED: Front-end hardware — Dewar/Disc Net IV, 1-AST/286; Front-end software — Dewar/Disc Net IV; Printers — Okidata/393. AUDIOTEX: Hardware — Northgate/486; Software — Info-Connect; Supplier name — Info-Connect. DISPLAY: Adv layout systems — Dewar, 2-SIA/386; Front-end hardware — Dewar/Discovery; Front-end software — Dewar/Discovery. PRODUCTION: Typesetters — 3-Ap/Mac LaserWriter NTX; Plate exposures — 1-Nu/Flip Top FT40APRNS; Plate processors — 1-Nat/250; Production cameras — 1-R/500; Automatic film processors — 1-DAI/Screen 220; Color separation equipment (conventional) — 1-Lf/Leafscan 35.
PRESSROOM: Line 1 — 8-G/SC; Folders — 1-G. MAILROOM: Counter stackers — 1-BG/106; Inserters and stuffers — 5-KAN; Bundle tyer — 1-Bu, 1-EAM/Mosca; Addressing machine — 1-Ch/515. LIBRARY: Combination — 1-BH/16.35. WIRE SERVICES: News — AP; Photos — AP; Receiving dishes — size-10ft, AP. BUSINESS COMPUTERS: 2-Laser/486; Applications: MSSI: Circ; Synaptic.

BELLEVUE

Huron and Sandusky Counties

'90 U.S. Census- 8,146; **E&P '96 Est.** 8,111

Bellevue Gazette

(e-mon to fri; m-sat)

Bellevue Gazette, 107 N. Sandusky St.; PO Box 269, Bellevue, OH 44811-0269; tel (419) 483-4190; fax (419) 483-3737.
Circulation: 3,066(e); 3,066(m-sat); Sworn Oct. 4, 1995.
Price: 50¢(d); 50¢(sat); $1.80/wk; $7.90/mo; $87.00/yr.
Advertising: Open inch rate $17.44(e); $17.44 (m-sat). **Representative:** Papert Companies.
News Service: AP. **Politics:** Independent. **Established:** 1867.
Not Published: New Year; Memorial Day; Independence Day; Labor Day; Thanksgiving; Christmas.
Special Editions: Football; Basketball; Progress; Car Care; Home Improvement; Energy; Holiday Cookbook; Money & Taxes; We Like It Here.

GENERAL MANAGEMENT

General Manager — Thomas R Smith
Asst General Manager — Rick Miller
Purchasing Agent — Thomas R Smith

ADVERTISING

Manager — Rick Miller

CIRCULATION

Manager — Rick Miller

NEWS EXECUTIVE

Managing Editor — Dennis Sabo

Market Information: TMC.
Mechanical available: Offset; Black and 3 ROP colors; insert accepted — preprinted, any; page cut-offs — 22¾".
Mechanical specifications: Type page 13¾" x 21½"; E - 6 cols, 2 1/16", ⅛" between; A - 6 cols, 2 1/16", ⅛" between; C - 9 cols, 1⅜", 1/16" between.
Commodity consumption: Newsprint 738 short tons; widths 27½", 34", 13¾"; black ink 15,660 pounds; color ink 1,172 pounds; single pages printed 3,518; average pages per issue 10(d); single plates used 3,780.
Equipment: EDITORIAL: Front-end hardware — Mk/3000; Other equipment — 10-AP Photostream. DISPLAY: Adv layout systems — 2-Ap/Mac, Mk/Mycro-Comp AdWriter. PRODUCTION: Typesetters — 2-Ap/Mac Plus Laser, 1-Ap/Mac LaserWriter NTX; Plate exposures — 1-Nu/FPT240; Plate processors — 1-Nat; Direct-to-plate imaging — 3M; Production cameras — R; Automatic film processors — 1-LE.
PRESSROOM: Line 1 — 5-G/Community; Folders — G. MAILROOM: Counter stackers — 1-BG/Count-O-Veyor; Inserters and stuffers — 1-KAN/401; Bundle tyer — 2-Bu/Quarter Poly Strapper, 2-Bu/String; Addressing machine — KR. WIRE SERVICES: News — AP; Receiving dishes — AP.

BOWLING GREEN

Wood County

'90 U.S. Census- 28,176; **E&P '96 Est.** 30,487
ABC-CZ (90): 28,176 (HH 8,502)

The Sentinel-Tribune

(e-mon to sat)

The Sentinel-Tribune, 300 E. Pope Rd.; PO Box 88, Bowling Green, OH 43402; tel (419) 352-4611; fax (419) 354-0314.
Circulation: 13,502(e); 13,502(e-sat); ABC Sept. 30, 1995.
Price: 35¢(d); 35¢(sat); $1.75/wk (carrier); $7.00/mo (carrier); $85.00/yr (carrier).
Advertising: Open inch rate $10.00(e); $10.00(e-sat). **Representative:** Landon Associates Inc.
News Service: AP. **Politics:** Independent. **Established:** 1867.
Not Published: New Year; Memorial Day; Independence Day; Labor Day; Thanksgiving; Christmas.
Special Editions: Baby Edition, Health & Fitness (Jan); Bride & Groom (Feb); Career Opportunities, Farm Forecast (Mar); Home & Garden, Private Property, Car Care (Apr); Graduation, Travel & Recreation (May); Fair (June); National Tractor Pullers Association Championships, Football Preview, Back-to-College, Fair (Aug); Farm Safety (Sept); Fall Home Improvement, Christmas Gifts (Nov).
Special Weekly Sections: Best Food Day (wed); Church Page (fri); School, Farm, Entertainment, Sports (daily).

CORPORATE OFFICERS

President — T M Haswell
Vice Pres — Richard Morris
Secretary/Treasurer — Kathryn A Haswell

GENERAL MANAGEMENT

Publisher — T M Haswell
General Manager — Richard Morris

ADVERTISING

Director — Vicky Graf

CIRCULATION

Director — Ivan Avery

NEWS EXECUTIVE

Editor — David C Miller

EDITORS AND MANAGERS

Automotive Editor — Chris Miller
City Editor — Harold Brown
County Editor — Jan Larson
Editorial Page Editor — David C Miller
Education Editor — Rita Sobol
Farm/Agriculture Editor — Julie Carle
Fashion/Food Editor — Karen Cota
Features Editor — David C Miller
Films/Theater Editor — Debbie Rogers
Home Furnishings Editor — Karen Cota
Manager-Photo Department — Mark Deckard
Radio/Television Editor — Debbie Rogers
Real Estate Editor — Harold Brown
Religion Editor — Carla Zanetos
Society/Women's Editor — Karen Cota
Sports Editor — Jack Carle

PRODUCTION

Manager-Computer Systems — James Instone
Foreman-Composing — Richard Drury
Foreman-Pressroom — Greg Loomis

Mechanical available: Offset; Black and 3 ROP colors; insert accepted — preprinted; page cut-offs — 22¾".
Mechanical specifications: Type page 13" x 21"; E - 6 cols, 2 1/16", ⅛" between; A - 6 cols, 2 1/16", ⅛" between; C - 8 cols, 1 9/16", 1/16" between.
Commodity consumption: Newsprint 740 short tons; widths 27½", 13¾"; black ink 14,700 pounds; color ink 1,200 pounds; single pages printed 10,185; average pages per issue 26(d); single plates used 9,850.
Equipment: EDITORIAL: Front-end hardware — CText; Other equipment — Lf/AP Leaf Picture Desk, Lf/Leafscan. CLASSIFIED: Front-end hardware — CText. DISPLAY: Front-end hardware — Ap/Mac Centris 610; Front-end software — Multi-Ad/Creator; Printers — Ap/Mac LaserWriter Pro. PRODUCTION: Typesetters — 2-Ap/Mac Plus, 1-Ap/Mac LaserWriter, 2-NEC/890 SilentWriter; Platemaking systems — Nat; Plate exposures — 1-Nu/Flip Top FT40L; Plate processors — 1-WL/30A; Production cameras — 1-B/Caravel-19; Automatic film processors — 1-LE/LD24A; Shrink lenses — 1-Ck Optical.
PRESSROOM: Line 1 — 5-G/Urbanite; Folders — 1-G. MAILROOM: Counter stackers — HL/Monitor; Bundle tyer — 1-Sa/SR2A; Addressing machine — 2-Wm/No 2. LIBRARY: Electronic — 1-Recordak/Film Reader MPE-1. WIRE SERVICES: News — AP, SHNS; Photos — AP; Receiving dishes — AP. BUSINESS COMPUTERS: 1-BF/2000, DSI/Papertrak, DEC/590XL, 1-HP/Veltra VL2, 1-DEC/433 SX; Applications: Lotus 1-2-3: Bookkeeping, Inventory; PCs & micros networked; PCs & main system networked.

BRYAN

Williams County

'90 U.S. Census- 8,348; **E&P '96 Est.** 8,776
ABC-CZ (90): 8,348 (HH 3,407)

The Bryan Times

(e-mon to fri; m-sat)

The Bryan Times, 127 S. Walnut St.; PO Box 471, Bryan, OH 43506; tel (419) 636-1111; fax (419) 636-8937.
Circulation: 11,125(e); 11,125(m-sat); ABC Sept. 30, 1995.
Price: 50¢(d); 50¢(sat); $8.00/mo (in county), $10.50/mo (in state), $11.50/mo (out of state); $86.00/yr (in county), $119.00/yr (in state), $132.00/yr (out of state).
Advertising: Open inch rate $8.50(e); $8.50(m-sat).
News Services: AP, CT. **Politics:** Independent. **Established:** 1949.
Not Published: Legal holidays.
Special Editions: Bridal Tab, Tax Tab (Jan); Baby Tab, Seniors (Feb); Home Improvement Tab, Cooking (Mar); Car Care Tab, Lawn & Garden Tab (Apr); Graduation Tab (May); Summer Guide to Fun (June); Seniors (July); Fair Tab, Football Tab, Back-to-School Tab (Aug); Fair Tab (Sept); Election Tab (Oct); Basketball Tab, Pre Christmas Tab (Nov); Gift Guide (Dec).
Special Weekly Sections: Business (tues); Farm (wed).
Magazines: Business (tues); Farm (wed); Daily TV Section (daily); Realty Northwest (Real Estate Magazine) (monthly).

CORPORATE OFFICER

President — Christopher Cullis

GENERAL MANAGEMENT

General Manager — Tom Voigt

ADVERTISING

Manager — Tom Voigt

MARKETING AND PROMOTION

Manager-Marketing/Promotion — Tom Voigt

TELECOMMUNICATIONS

Audiotex Manager — Nancy Hale

CIRCULATION

Manager — Mark J Keller

NEWS EXECUTIVE

Managing Editor — Linda Freed

EDITORS AND MANAGERS

County Editor — Don Allison
Home Furnishings Editor — Linda Freed
News Editor — Linda Freed
Radio/Television Editor — Mary Brodbeck
Sports Editor — Jim Wrinkle
Women's Editor — Sharon Patten

MANAGEMENT INFORMATION SERVICES

Online Manager — Tom Voigt
Data Processing Manager — Pam Miller

PRODUCTION

Manager — Christopher Cullis
Foreman-Pressroom — William Beagle

Market Information: TMC; ADS; Operate database; Operate audiotex.

Mechanical available: Offset; Black and 4 ROP colors; insert accepted — preprinted; page cut-offs — 22¾".
Mechanical specifications: Type page 13" x 21"; E - 6 cols, 2¹⁄₁₆", ⅛" between; A - 6 cols, 2¹⁄₁₆", ⅛" between; C - 9 cols, 1⁵⁄₁₆", ⅛" between.
Commodity consumption: Newsprint 1,000 metric tons; width 28"; average pages per issue 20(d).
Equipment: EDITORIAL: Front-end hardware — CText; Front-end software — CText; Printers — Ap/Mac LaserWriter Plus. CLASSIFIED: Front-end hardware — CText; Printers — C.Itoh. DISPLAY: Adv layout systems — Ap/Mac; Front-end hardware — 3-Ap/Mac Ilsi, 80-MB; Front-end software — Multi-Ad/Creator; Printers — 1-Ap/Mac LaserWriter II NTX. PRODUCTION: Plate exposures — 2-Nu; Plate processors — 1-Graham/Plate Processor; Direct-to-plate imaging — 2-3M/Pyrofax; Scanners — Ap/Mac; Production cameras — 1-B/Caravel, 1-DSA/Vertical Camera; Automatic film processors — 1-DSA/Film Processor; Color separation equipment (conventional) — Lf/leafscan. PRESSROOM: Line 1 — 6-G/Community; Line 2 — 3-G/Community. MAILROOM: Inserters and stuffers — 1-KAN/480 4:1; Bundle tyer — 1-EAM/Mosca Strapper, 1-Ty-Tech, 1-EAM/Mosca Strapper; Addressing machine — Epson/DF-5000, Epson/Equity 2. LIBRARY: Electronic — Northwest Microfilm/20-20; Combination — Northwest Microfilm/20-20 (Electronic). WIRE SERVICES: News — AP, AP Datafeatures, Receiving dishes — size-10ft, AP. BUSINESS COMPUTERS: 2-PC/80; Applications: Gen ledger, Payroll, Accts payable, Accts receivable.

BUCYRUS
Crawford County
'90 U.S. Census- 13,496; E&P '96 Est. 13,550
ABC-CZ (90): 13,496 (HH 5,426)

Telegraph-Forum
(e-mon to fri; m-sat)
Telegraph-Forum, 119 W. Rensselaer St., Bucyrus, OH 44820; tel (419) 562-3333; fax (419) 562-9162. Thomson Newspapers group.
Circulation: 7,404(e); 7,404(m-sat); ABC Sept. 30, 1995.
Price: 35¢(d); 50¢(sat); $1.75/wk; $92.60/yr.
Advertising: Open inch rate $7.90(e); $7.90(m-sat). **Representative:** Papert Companies.
News Service: AP. **Politics:** Libertarian. **Established:** 1927.
Not Published: New Year; Memorial Day; Independence Day; Labor Day; Thanksgiving; Christmas.
Advertising not accepted: Fortune tellers; Clairvoyants.
Magazines: County Week, TV Extra (TMC); TV Listings & Consumer Information.

CORPORATE OFFICERS
President..................Richard J Harrington
Vice Pres..................Jim Hopson
GENERAL MANAGEMENT
Publisher..................James F Croneis
Business Manager..........James F Croneis
Controller................Cheryl York
Purchasing Agent..........James F Croneis
ADVERTISING
Manager...................Jeanette Parker
CIRCULATION
Manager...................Rob Jenney
NEWS EXECUTIVE
Managing Editor...........Lisa Miller
EDITORS AND MANAGERS
News Editor...............Don Tudor
Society Editor............Janet Kohls
Sports Editor.............Dan Clutter
PRODUCTION
Foreman-Pre Press.........Richard Hyde
Foreman-Pressroom.........Joseph Weiler
Creative Service..........Judy Lust

Market Information: Zoned editions; Split Run; TMC.
Mechanical available: Offset; Black and 4 ROP colors; insert accepted — preprinted, anything mailable; page cut-offs — 21¼".
Mechanical specifications: Type page 13" x 21"; E - 6 cols, 2¹⁄₁₆", ⅛" between; A - 6 cols, 2¹⁄₁₆", ⅛" between; C - 6 cols, 2¹⁄₁₆", ⅛" between.
Commodity consumption: Newsprint 220 metric tons; widths 27½", 13¾"; single pages printed 5,000; average pages per issue 16(d); single plates used 5,000.
Equipment: EDITORIAL: Front-end hardware — 1-Mk/61, 9-Mk. CLASSIFIED: Front-end hardware — 1-Mk/61, TI, 1-DEC/I; Printers — 1-TI, 1-DEC/I. DISPLAY: Adv layout systems — COM/MCS22, 2-MCS. PRODUCTION: Typesetters — 2-COM/8400; Plate exposures — 1-Nu; Plate processors — C/Sink; Production cameras — 1-R/500; Automatic film processors — AG/N.
PRESSROOM: Line 1 — 6-G/Community; Folders — 1-G/SC. MAILROOM: Bundle tyer — 1-Bu; Addressing machine — 1-KAN/Labeler, Vision Data/Circ System, Unix, D.O.S. WIRE SERVICES: News — AP; Receiving dishes — size-9ft, AP. BUSINESS COMPUTERS: Bs/B25, ATT/3BI, DEC/321, IBM/Sys 80 Model 30, Epson; Applications: Adv billing, Accts receivable, Circ, Gen ledger, Payroll; PCs & micros networked; PCs & main system networked.

CAMBRIDGE
Guernsey County
'90 U.S. Census- 11,748; E&P '96 Est. 10,389
ABC-CZ (90): 21,424 (HH 8,545)

The Daily Jeffersonian
(e-mon to sat)
The Daily Jeffersonian, 831 Wheeling Ave.; PO Box 10, Cambridge, OH 43725; tel (614) 439-3531; fax (614) 432-6219. Dix Communications group.
Circulation: 13,125(e); 13,125(e-sat); ABC Sept. 30, 1995.

Ohio
I-305

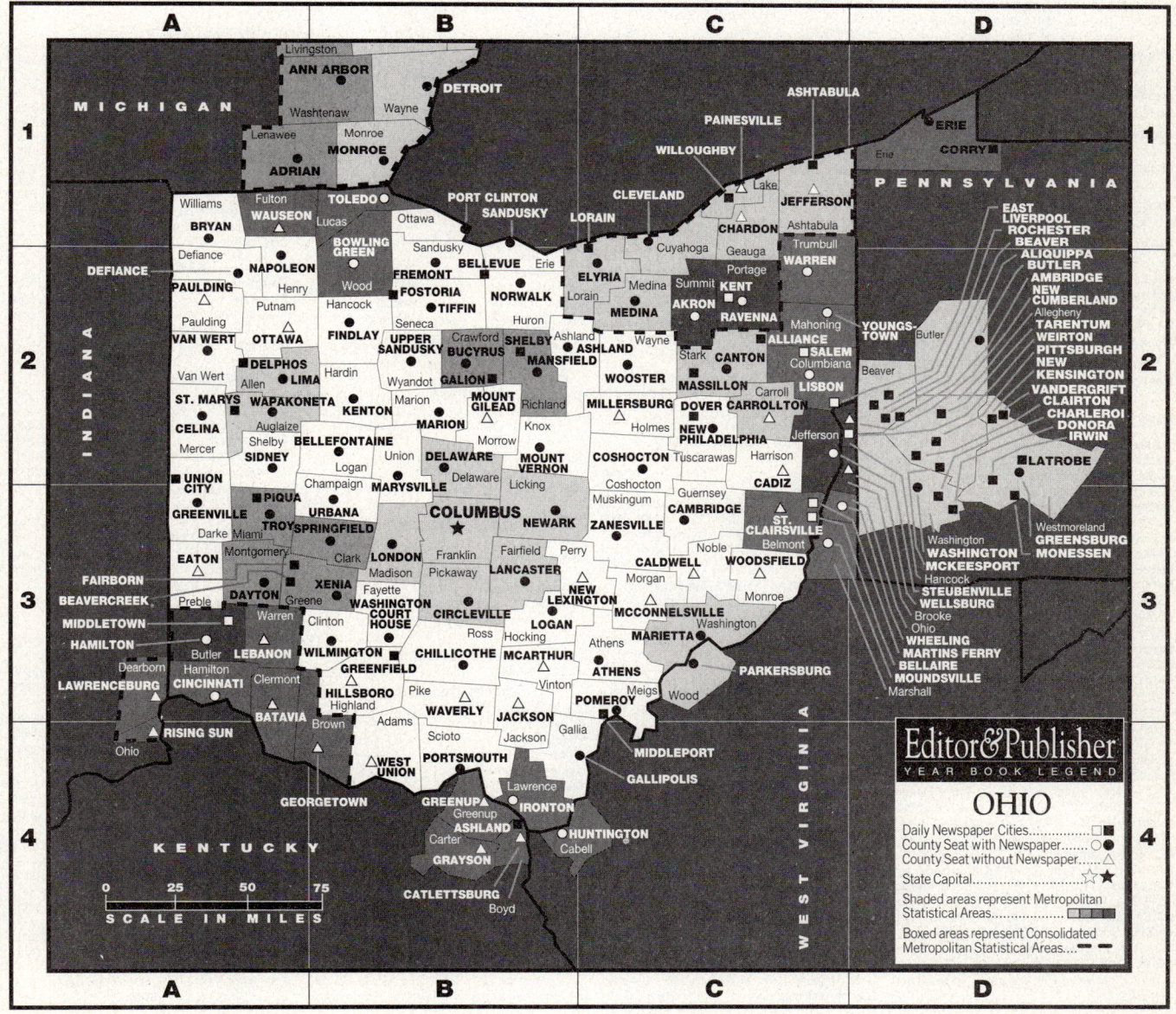

Price: 35¢(d); 35¢(sat); $1.85/wk; $8.00/mo; $96.20/yr.
Advertising: Open inch rate $11.90(e); $11.90(e-sat). **Representative:** Landon Associates Inc.
News Service: AP. **Politics:** Independent. **Established:** 1892.
Not Published: New Year; Memorial Day; Independence Day; Labor Day; Thanksgiving; Christmas.
Special Editions: Dollar Days, Tax Guide (Jan); Health & Fitness, Bride & Groom (Feb); NIE, Lawn & Garden, Spring Home & Garden Section, Swing into Spring, Spring Car Care, Easter Coloring Contest, Town Art Party (Mar); Babies, 4-H Salute, Hopalong Cassidy Festival, I Love My Pet Section Tab (Apr); Mother's Day, Vacationland Guide, In Memorian, Memories Guide (May); Father's Day (June); Ohio Hills Folk Fest, Sidewalk Sales, L.L. Baseball (July); Back-to-School, Salt Fork, Football Preview (Aug); Football Contest, Guernsey Co. Fair, United Way Cup Challenge, Oktoberfest & New Car Show (Sept); Home Improvement, Auto Care Section (Oct); Yuletide Gift Guide & Cash Giveaway, Deer Hunters Page, Christmas Opening, Winter Sports Preview (Nov); Christmas Coloring Contest, Last Minute Shoppers Guide, Elected Officials Greetings, Christmas Greetings, First Baby, New Year's Greetings (Dec).
Special Weekly Sections: Best Food Day (mon); Business Page, Engagement Announcements (wed); Farm Page (thur); Church Page, The Entertainer (fri); Wedding Announcements (sat); Entertainment (daily).
Magazine: Entertainer.

CORPORATE OFFICER
President Robert C Dix Jr
GENERAL MANAGEMENT
Publisher Robert C Dix Jr
ADVERTISING
Director Ed Archibold
CIRCULATION
Manager Randy Machan
NEWS EXECUTIVE
Editor Greg Parks
EDITORS AND MANAGERS
City Editor Ted Barnhart
Editorial Page Editor Greg Parks
Sports Editor Mike Fitzpatrick
Wire Editor John Lowe
Women's Editor Nicole Redd
MANAGEMENT INFORMATION SERVICES
Manager Merle Johnson
PRODUCTION
Manager R W Keith

Market Information: TMC.
Mechanical available: Offset; Black and 3 ROP colors; insert accepted — preprinted, min 6x9, max 11½x15; page cut-offs — 21½".
Mechanical specifications: Type page 13" x 21½"; E - 6 cols, 2 1/16", 1/8" between; A - 6 cols, 2 1/16", 1/8" between; C - 8 cols, 1 3/8", 1/16" between.
Commodity consumption: Newsprint 640 metric tons; widths 14", 28"; black ink 24,000 pounds; color ink 2,000 pounds; single pages printed 7,200; average pages per issue 22(d); single plates used 15,000.
Equipment: EDITORIAL: Front-end hardware — 2-Mk/4000; Front-end software — Mk/4000; Printers — 1-Ap/Mac LaserPrinter NTX; Other equipment — 4-Swintec. CLASSIFIED: Front-end hardware — 2-Mk/4000; Front-end software — Mk; Printers — 1-Ap/Mac LaserPrinter NTX; Other equipment — 1-Swintec. DISPLAY: Adv layout systems — Mk/4000, Ap/Mac II ci; Front-end hardware — Ap/Mac; Front-end software — Mk; Printers — Ap/Mac LaserPrinter NTX. PRODUCTION: Typesetters — 3-Ap/Mac LaserPrinter NTX; Platemaking systems — 2-3M/Pyrofax; Scanners — 2-Ap/Mac Scanner; Production cameras — DAI/Screen-6500C. PRESSROOM: Line 1 — 9-G/Community. MAILROOM: Bundle tyer — 1-EAM/Mosca 13992, 1-Ty-Tech/RO-M, CYP, 1-Ty-Tech/Rot 500m, Sa/13626; Addressing machine — Ch/995150-06. WIRE SERVICES: News — AP; Photos — AP; Receiving dishes — AP. BUSINESS COMPUTERS: Alpha/Micro 1000; PCs & micros networked; PCs & main system networked.

CANTON

Stark County

'90 U.S. Census- 84,161; E&P '96 Est. 76,087
ABC-CZ (90): 191,568 (HH 75,698)

The Repository

(e-mon to sat; S)

The Repository, 500 Market Ave. S. (44702); PO Box 9901, Canton, OH 44711-0901; tel (216) 454-5611; fax (216) 454-5610. Thomson Newspapers group.
Circulation: 61,210(e); 61,210(e-sat); 79,710(S); ABC Sept. 30, 1995.
Price: 25¢(d); 25¢(sat); $1.00(S); $2.70/wk (home delivery); $11.70/mo (home delivery), $22.00/mo (mail); $140.40/yr (home delivery), $198.00/yr (mail).
Advertising: Open inch rate $46.29(e); $46.29(e-sat); $50.55(S). **Representative:** Landon Associates Inc.
News Services: AP, NYT. **Politics:** Independent. **Established:** 1815.
Advertising not accepted: Vending machine.
Special Editions: Brides, Spring Car Care (Mar); Building and Garden (Apr); Outdoor Living, Building and Garden (May); Building and Garden (June); Professional Football Hall of Fame Tab, Building and Garden (July); Stark Co. Fair, Football (Aug); Fall Car Care (Sept); Christmas (Thanksgiving Day) (Nov).
Special Weekly Sections: Monday Business Tab (mon); Best Food Day, Fashion (wed); Garden, Weekend Entertainment (fri); Wheels, Television, Travel, Medicine/Science, Books, Agriculture, Education (S); Business/Financial (daily).
Magazines: Parade, Comics (S).

GENERAL MANAGEMENT
Publisher James C Smith
Director-Finance Roger Mumford
Manager-Retail/Credit Manager Mike Darnell
ADVERTISING
Director Michael J Miller
Manager-Retail Mark A Yocum
Manager-Classified Kim B Bergman
Manager-National/Co-op Patrick Barthel
Manager-Service Rose Soliday
MARKETING AND PROMOTION
Manager-Marketing Service Paula Mastroianni
TELECOMMUNICATIONS
Audiotex Manager Paula Mastroianni
CIRCULATION
Director Ronald N Astman
Manager-Home Delivery Timothy R Coles
NEWS EXECUTIVES
Editor Michael E Hanke
Managing Editor David Kaminski
Asst Managing Editor Will Kennedy
Bureau Chief Pat Kelley
EDITORS AND MANAGERS
City Editor Rick Senften
Design Editor Lewis Sagermann
Editor-at-Large James Weber
Editorial Page Editor William Hopper
Living Section Editor Gayle Beck
New Media Editor James Hillibish
Photo Editor Stan Myers
Sports Editor Robert Stewart
MANAGEMENT INFORMATION SERVICES
Data Processing Manager Cathy Schwab
PRODUCTION
Director Dan M Ferrier
Manager-Pressroom Steve Swenson
Manager-Computer Operations Bruce Brunner
Superintendent-Mailroom Andrew Mangini

Market Information: Zoned editions; Split Run; Operate audiotex.
Mechanical available: Offset; Black and 3 ROP colors; insert accepted — preprinted, envelopes, cards; page cut-offs — 22¾".
Mechanical specifications: Type page 13.5" x 21½"; E - 6 cols, 2.03", 1/6" between; A - 6 cols, 2 1/16", 1/16" between; C - 10 cols, 1¼", 1/16" between.
Commodity consumption: Newsprint 7,500 short tons; widths 55", 27½", 41¼"; black ink 150,000 pounds; color ink 40,000 pounds; single pages printed 20,000; average pages per issue 50(d), 88(S); single plates used 95,000.
Equipment: EDITORIAL: Front-end hardware — CD, 3-DEC/PDP 11-84, 10-MeD/112B, 45-Intel/386SX, 10-Ap/Mac Quadra; Front-end software — CSI, QuarkXPress 3.31R; Printers — 3-DEC/LA 120, 1-Okidata/393, Graphic Enterprises/PageScan 18"x24"; Other equipment — 1-Lf, 2-Ap/Power Mac PC 8100, 1-Ap/Mac Quadra 950. CLASSIFIED: Front-end hardware — CD, 9-MeD/112B, 1-Intel/386SX; Front-end software — CSI; Printers — 1-Okidata/393, 1-ATT/LR 4505; Other equipment — IBM/Selectric II. AUDIOTEX: Supplier name — Telepublishing. DISPLAY: Adv layout systems — CO/Ad Stack; Front-end hardware — Sun/3-380, 4-Ap/Mac Quadra; Front-end software — CD, Multi-Ad/Creator, QuarkXPress; Printers — NEC/2-70, DEC/VT-800 Plain Paper. PRODUCTION: Pagination software — QuarkXPress 3.31R; Typesetters — 2-Lind/L-350, 2-Panther/5500, Tegra/Varityper 4000-4300; Platemaking systems — WL/V; Plate exposures — W; Plate processors — W; Electronic picture desk — 1-Lf/AP Leaf Picture Desk, 2-Ap/Mac; Scanners — 1-ECR/Autokon 1000, 1-ECR; Production cameras — DAI/Screen 475; Automatic film processors — DAI, LE; Film transporters — DAI, LE; Shrink lenses — 1-Nu; Color separation equipment (conventional) — 2-Kk/M-2035 Scanners, Lf/AP Leaf Picture Desk; Digital color separation equipment — 1-Optronics/Drum Scanner. PRESSROOM: Line 1 — G/Colorliner(9 stands; 19 modules; 35 couples); Press drives — Allen Bradley; Folders — G/3:2 Sovereign; Pasters — G/RTP-50; Reels and stands — G/RTP-50; Press control system — AB/APCS; Press registration system — G/APCS. MAILROOM: Counter stackers — Id; Inserters and stuffers — GMA; Bundle tyer — Dynaric; Addressing machine — KAN/Labeler; Mailroom control system — PMS/7 Series. LIBRARY: Electronic — SMS/Stauffer Gold. WIRE SERVICES: News — AP Datastream, NYT; Photos — AP, NYT; Stock tables — AP SelectStox; Receiving dishes — size-12ft, AP. BUSINESS COMPUTERS: Pyramid/7040, ATT/21705, ATT/Sys 5, Unix; PCs & micros networked; PCs & main system networked.

CELINA

Mercer County

'90 U.S. Census- 9,650; E&P '96 Est. 10,116

The Daily Standard

(e-mon to sat)

The Daily Standard, 123 E. Market St.; PO Box 140, Celina, OH 45822; tel (419) 586-2371; fax (419) 586-6271; e-mail dailystad@bright.net.
Circulation: 5,528(e); 5,528(e-sat); Sworn Oct. 1, 1995.
Price: 50¢(d); 50¢(sat).
Advertising: Open inch rate $8.00(e); $8.00(e-sat). **Representative:** Papert Companies.
News Service: AP. **Politics:** Independent. **Established:** 1848.
Not Published: New Year; Memorial Day; Independence Day; Labor Day; Thanksgiving; Christmas.
Special Editions: Fall Sports, Back-to-School (Aug); Fall Opening (Sept); Christmas Opening (Nov); Christmas Greetings (Dec); Football; Basketball Preview.
Special Weekly Sections: State Line Farmer (tues); Weekender (fri).
Magazines: Entertainment Section, Weekender (sat).

GENERAL MANAGEMENT
Publisher Frank M Snyder
Business Manager Angie Topp
ADVERTISING
Director-National Pat Hartings
Manager John Lake
CIRCULATION
Manager Diane Buening
NEWS EXECUTIVE
Managing Editor Mike Buettner
EDITORS AND MANAGERS
City Editor/Wire Editor Richard Geist
Editorial Page Editor Mike Buettner
Farm Editor Chris Pierce
Films/Theater Editor Vivien Borger
Society/Women's Editor Betty Lawrence
Sports Editor Tom Bruns
PRODUCTION
Superintendent Larry Smelser

Market Information: Split Run; TMC.
Mechanical available: Web Offset; Black and 3 ROP colors; insert accepted — preprinted, free-standing; page cut-offs — 22¾".
Mechanical specifications: Type page 15" x 21"; E - 7 cols, 2.04", 1/8" between; A - 7 cols, 2.04", 1/8" between; C - 7 cols, 2.04", 1/8" between.
Commodity consumption: Newsprint 380 metric tons; widths 32", 16"; black ink 13,100 pounds; single pages printed 5,790; average pages per issue 20(d); single plates used 2,750.
Equipment: EDITORIAL: Front-end hardware — Ap/Mac; Front-end software — Ap/Mac; Printers — Ap/Mac NTX, Ap/Mac IIg, Ap/Mac 630, Ap/Mac 810. CLASSIFIED: Front-end hardware — Ap/Mac. DISPLAY: Front-end hardware — Ap/Mac; Front-end software — Ap/Mac. PRODUCTION: Pagination software — QPS, Baseview; OCR software — Caere/OmniPage; Typesetters — Ap/Mac 810; Plate exposures — 1-Nu; Plate processors — 1-Nu; Scanners — HP, AP; Automatic film processors — LE; Color separation equipment (conventional) — Nikon. PRESSROOM: Line 1 — G/Surburban. MAILROOM: Bundle tyer — Bu. WIRE SERVICES: News — AP; Photos — AP; Receiving dishes — size-3m, AP. BUSINESS COMPUTERS: PC.

CHILLICOTHE

Ross County

'90 U.S. Census- 21,923; E&P '96 Est. 20,719
ABC-NDM (90): 93,579 (HH 33,130)

Chillicothe Gazette

(e-mon to fri; m-sat)

Chillicothe Gazette, 50 W. Main St.; PO Box 4400, Chillicothe, OH 45601; tel (614) 773-2111; fax (614) 773-2160; e-mail gazpub@bright.net. Gannett Co. Inc. group.
Circulation: 16,472(e); 19,321(m-sat); ABC Sept. 30, 1995.
Price: 35¢(d); 75¢(sat); $2.28/wk (carrier); $9.75/mo (carrier); $117.00/yr (carrier).
Advertising: Open inch rate $21.00(e); $21.00(m-sat). **Representative:** Gannett National Newspaper Sales.
News Services: AP, GNS. **Politics:** Independent. **Established:** 1800.
Not Published: Christmas.
Special Editions: Weddings, Super Bowl (Jan); Progress Magazine (Feb); Downtown Open House, Spring Home & Garden, Life's a Beach (Apr); Play Ball!, Graduation (May); Baby Edition (June); Weddings, Back-to-School (July); Ross County Fair (Aug); Recipe Guide, Football Preview, Fall Home & Garden (Sept); Voter's Guide (Oct); Holiday Gift Guide, Downtown Open House, Basketball Preview (Nov); 1997 Calendar (Dec); Auto Monthly (monthly).
Special Weekly Sections: Religion, TV Times, Homes (sat); Entertainment (daily).
Magazines: USA Weekend, TV Times (sat).

CORPORATE OFFICERS
President Marvin E Jones
Secretary Thomas L Chapple
Treasurer/Asst Secretary Jimmy L Thomas
GENERAL MANAGEMENT
Publisher Marvin E Jones
Controller Erich J Walburn
Personnel/Administration Secretary Connie S Gaul
ADVERTISING
Director Ron Clausen
Manager-Sales Janet Littler
Manager-Major Accounts Jim Hilles
Manager-Creative Service Carol Thompson
MARKETING AND PROMOTION
Director-Market Development Mary Ann Cristiano
CIRCULATION
Director James Curry
Manager-Sales Deborah Rush
NEWS EXECUTIVE
Managing Editor Chaz Osburn
EDITORS AND MANAGERS
Lifestyle Editor Tyrone Johston
Local News Editor Gere McClellan
Opinion Editor Ruth Runyon
Photo Editor Tim Johnson
PRODUCTION
Director Tom Barcikowski
Manager-Pressroom Bill Bennett
Manager-Pre Press Gary Graves

Market Information: TMC.
Mechanical available: Offset; Black and 3 ROP colors; insert accepted — preprinted, data books, other inserts accepted (require special approval); page cut-offs — 22¾".
Mechanical specifications: Type page 13" x 21½"; E - 6 cols, 2 1/16", 1/8" between; A - 6 cols, 2 1/16", 1/8" between; C - 9 cols, 1 3/8", 1/16" between.
Commodity consumption: Newsprint 630 short tons; widths 27½", 13¾"; black ink 17,700 pounds; color ink 500 pounds; single pages printed 6,194; average pages per issue 20(d); single plates used 1,300.
Equipment: EDITORIAL: Front-end hardware — Dewar/DiscNet. CLASSIFIED: Front-end hard-

Ohio I-307

ware — Dewar/DiscNet. DISPLAY: Adv layout systems — Ap/Mac; Front-end software — Multi-Ad/Creator, QuarkXPress. PRODUCTION: Typesetters — 2-COM/8600, MON/1000; Plate exposures — 1-Nu; Plate processors — 1-Nat/A-250; Production cameras — 1-C/Spartan II, 1-AG/3500, ECR/Autokon 1000; Automatic film processors — 1-LE/24LD.
PRESSROOM: Line 1 — 10-G/Community SSC. MAILROOM: Counter stackers — 1-PPK, 1-HI; Inserters and stuffers — 1-MM; Bundle tyer — 1-MLN, 1-Bu; Addressing machine — 1-Am, 1-Wm. WIRE SERVICES: News — AP, GNS; Photos — AP, GNS; Receiving dishes — AP. BUSINESS COMPUTERS: IBM/AS-400.

CINCINNATI

Hamilton County

'90 U.S. Census- 364,040; E&P '96 Est. 346,663
ABC-NDM (90): 1,744,124 (HH 652,920)

The Cincinnati Enquirer
(m-mon to sat; S)

The Cincinnati Enquirer, 312 Elm St., Cincinnati, OH 45202; tel (513) 721-2700. Gannett Co. Inc. group.
Circulation: 203,158(m); 203,158(m-sat); 350,979(S); ABC Sept. 30, 1995.
Price: 35¢(d); 35¢(sat); $1.50(S); $15.25/mo (mS); $183.00/yr (mS).
Advertising: Open inch rate $139.86(m); $139.86(m-sat); $210.03(S); comb with Cincinnati Post (e) $209.37. **Representative:** Gannett National Newspaper Sales.
News Services: AP, NYT, LAT-WP, KRT, GNS. **Politics:** Independent. **Established:** 1841.
Note: The Cincinnati Enquirer, the Cincinnati Post and the Covington Kentucky Post are corporately and editorially separate. The Cincinnati Enquirer acts as agent for E W Scripps Co. in advertising, circulation, production and printing functions of the Cincinnati Post and the Kentucky Post.
Advertising not accepted: X-rated movies; Abortion advertising.
Special Editions: Adventure Travel (Jan); Auto Expo '96, National Cruise Month Celebration, The Carolinas-Travel (Feb); Flower & Garden Show, Reds Opening Day Edition, Beaches & Mountains-Travel (Apr); Summer Vacations-Travel (May); Family Vacations-Travel, Homearama '96 (June); Senior Golf Tournament, Travel Close to Home (July); Fall Vacations, ATP Tennis (Aug); Fall/Winter Cruises-Travel, Bengels Opener (Sept); Senior Travel (Oct); Holiday Travel (Nov); Winter Travel, Holiday Home Gift Guides (Dec); Tempo at Home, City Clips (6x/yr).
Special Weekly Sections: Business Monday (mon); Best Food Day (wed); Let's Go Weekend (fri); At Home (sat); Travel, Business, Real Estate (S).

CORPORATE OFFICERS

President/Publisher Harry M Whipple
Vice Pres/Editor Lawrence K Beaupre
Vice Pres-Advertising David L Hunke
Vice Pres-Circulation William W Hunsberger
Vice Pres-Production Mark S Mikolajczyk
Vice Pres-Finance H Theodore Bergh
Vice Pres-Community Affairs George R Blake
Vice Pres-Market Development Gerald T Silvers
Secretary Martha L Flanagan

GENERAL MANAGEMENT

Publisher Harry M Whipple
Controller Shannon Huber
Manager-Credit Steve Gerard
Director-Purchasing Patricia A Runge
Director-Human Resources James H Deavy
Personnel/Labor Relations Manager Maureen L Donohue

ADVERTISING

Vice Pres David L Hunke
Director-Operations Victoria Jonas
Director-Display Carol Hahn
Director-Classified Charles Cornelius
Manager-Classified/Automotive Tom Smith
Manager-Classified/Real Estate Patrick Peregrin
Manager-Sales Pam Stricker
Manager-Sales Brad Harmon
Manager-Sales Pam McFarland
Manager-Sales/Major Accounts George M McIveen
Manager-National Charles Hammond
Manager-Kentucky Connie Cooper
Manager-Make-Up Glen Johnston
Manager-Service Donald D Shepard
Manager-Sales Janice White
Coordinator-Co-op Jack Connolly
Coordinator-Preprint Shelby Smith

TELECOMMUNICATIONS

Director-Systems Bette M Kinder
Coordinator Charles Raya
Coordinator Kenneth Austin
Coordinator Jeffrey Roe

CIRCULATION

Vice Pres William W Hunsberger
Director-Sales Stephen Cooper
Director Bradley J Veldkamp
Manager-Single Copy Joseph S Roper

NEWS EXECUTIVES

Editor Lawrence K Beaupre
Editor-Training Michael Roberts
Managing Editor Janet C Leach
Managing Editor-Night Peter Johnson
Asst Managing Editor Everett J Mitchell
Assoc Editor Peter W Bronson

EDITORS AND MANAGERS

Art Editor Owen Findsen
Business Editor Jon Talton
Columnist Tony Lang
Columnist Allen Howard
Columnist Jim Knippenberg
Columnist Laura Pulfer
Columnist Cliff Radel
Editorial Page Editor Peter W Bronson
Editorial Writer Ramon Cooklis
Education Editor Mark Skertic
Features Editor Sara Pearce
Deputy Features Editor William Cieslewicz
Films/Theater Editor Margaret McGurk
Food Editor Chuck Martin
Garden News Kathy Doane
Kentucky Editor Andrew Oppman
Librarian Ray Zwick
Metro Editor James Smith
News Editor Jenny Barker Green
National Editor Bruce Holtgren
Director-Photography Liz Dufour
Production Manager Randy Allen
Radio/Television Editor John Kiesewetter
Readers Representative Betty Barnett
Real Estate Editor Denise Stockstill
Sports Editor Greg Noble
Deputy Sports Editor Susan Lancaster
Sports Columnist Tim Sullivan
Sports Columnist Paul Daugherty

MANAGEMENT INFORMATION SERVICES

Data Processing Manager Bette M Kinder

PRODUCTION

Director-Systems Bette M Kinder
Manager-Quality/Night Coordinator Dave Barker
Manager-Pre Press Larry Reynolds
Manager-Mailroom Steve Neiheisel
Manager-Pressroom Charles Robertson
Manager-Building Service/Newsprint Frank Woesman
Engineer-Plant Ed Magliano

Market Information: Zoned editions; Split Run; TMC; Operate database; Operate audiotex; Electronic edition.
Mechanical available: Offset; Black and 3 ROP colors; insert accepted — preprinted, based on sample submitted; page cut-offs — 21½".
Mechanical specifications: Type page 13" x 21½"; E - 6 cols, 2", 3⁄16" between; A - 6 cols, 2", 3⁄16" between; C - 10 cols, 1", 7⁄32" between.
Commodity consumption: Newsprint 48,746 short tons; widths 54½", 40⅞", 27¼"; black ink 850,340 pounds; color ink 331,631 pounds; single pages printed 42,012; average pages per issue 66(d), 162(S); single plates used 327,086.
Equipment: EDITORIAL: Front-end hardware — Tandem/CLX; Front-end software — SII/Sys 55; Printers — Centronics/351, Dataproducts/LZR-2600, Ap/Mac LaserWriter NTX, Xante/8200, Textronix/Phaser 300 I; Other equipment — SII/Coyote QB, SII/Dakota, 22-Ap/Mac, SII/CAT-ST, SII/Coyote 22. CLASSIFIED: Front-end hardware — Tandem/CLX; Front-end software — SII/Sys 55, SII/Coyote Pagination; Printers — Centronics/351, Dataproducts/LZR-2600; Other equipment — 22-SII/Coyote QB, SII/Coyote 22. DISPLAY: Adv layout systems — Multi-Ad; Front-end hardware — 10-Ap/Mac IIci, 1-Ap/Mac SE30, 1-Ap/Mac WGS 80, 1-Ap/Mac Quadra 60; Front-end software — Ap/Mac Appleshare 4.0, First class/BBS software; Printers — Ap/Mac Laser-Writer NTX, Textronix/Phaser 300 I; Other equipment — V/5510E Plain-Paper Imagesetter. PRODUCTION: Typesetters — 4-AU/APS-6-800S, 1-III/3850; Plate exposures — 2-WL/III, 2-Nu/Flip Top; Plate processors — 2-WL/38D; Electronic picture desk — Lf/AP Leaf Picture Desk; Scanners — 2-ECR/Autokon 1000; Production cameras — 2-C/Marathon, 2-C/Newspager; Automatic film processors — 4-LE/Film Processor, 1-C/Processor; Reproportion units — 1-Onyx/RIP, 2-AU/PC w/Harlequin RIP, 2-AU/DecAlpha w/Harlequin RIP; Film transporters — 2-LE/Transporter; Shrink lenses — 2-Alan/24; Color separation equipment (conventional) — AG/desktop, Ap/Mac desktop system; Digital color separation equipment — 1-RZ/Carat 500.
PRESSROOM: Line 1 — 10-G/Metro (6 half deck); Line 2 — 7-G/Metro (4 half deck); Line 3 — 10-G/Metro (6 half deck); Line 4 — 10-G/Metro (6 half deck); Folders — 4-G/double; Pasters — G; Reels and stands — G; Press control system — G. MAILROOM: Counter stackers — 8-QWI/200; Inserters and stuffers — 1-HI/1472, 2-HI/1372, Amerigraph/NP630; Bundle tyer — 8-Dynaric; Addressing machine — 1-Ch, X. LIBRARY: Electronic — SII/LASR (Text), Digicol/Archive System (Photo). COMMUNICATIONS: Digital ad delivery system — AP AdSend, AdSat, AdXpress, AdLink, Enquirer Ad BBS. WIRE SERVICES: News — AP Datastream, AP Datafeatures, TV Data; Photos — AP; Stock tables — AP Grand Central Stocks; Receiving dishes — size-3m, AP. BUSINESS COMPUTERS: IBM/AS 400-320, PC/Micro; Applications: AdServ: Accts payable, Payroll, Human resources, Gen ledger; PCs & micros networked; PCs & main system networked.

The Cincinnati Post
(e-mon to sat)

The Cincinnati Post, 125 E. Court St., Cincinnati, OH 45202; tel (513) 352-2000; fax (513) 621-3962. Scripps Howard group.
Circulation: 82,146(e); 113,670(e-sat); ABC Sept. 30, 1995.
Price: 35¢(d); 35¢(sat); $90.00/yr.
Advertising: Open inch rate $116.23(e); $116.23(e-sat); comb with Cincinnati Enquirer (mS) $209.37. **Representative:** Gannett National Newspaper Sales.
News Services: SHNS, AP. **Politics:** Independent. **Established:** 1881.
Note: The Cincinnati Enquirer, the Cincinnati Post and the Covington Kentucky Post are corporately and editorially separate. The Cincinnati Enquirer acts as agent for E W Scripps Co. in advertising, circulation, production and printing functions of the Cincinnati Post and the Kentucky Post. For personnel and all information on printing functions, see the Cincinnati Enquirer.
Special Weekly Sections: Neighbors; Moneywise.
Magazine: Timeout (thur).

GENERAL MANAGEMENT

Director-Community Service Gayle Harden-Renfro

ADVERTISING

Director David L Hunke

CIRCULATION

Vice Pres William W Hunsberger
Director-Sales Bradley J Veldkamp
Manager-Single Copy Sales Joseph S Roper
Manager-Kentucky Post Home Delivery Michael Knollman

NEWS EXECUTIVES

Editor Paul F Knue
Managing Editor Robert F Kraft

EDITORS AND MANAGERS

Business Editor Dan Andriacco
Columnist David Wecker
Courts/Law Editor Lisa Popyk
Crime Editor George Lecky
Editorial Page Editor Robert White
Education Editor Michael Clark
Features Editor Carule Philipps
Food Editor Joyce Rosencrans
Graphics Editor Rick Millians
Legislature Editor Randy Ludlow
Local Government Editor Sarah Sturmon-Dale
Librarian Robert Hahn
Metro Editor Michael Philipps
Deputy Metro Editor Kerry Duke
Asst Metro Editor Lisa Warren
Asst Metro Editor Becky Chambers
Neighbors Editor Mike Kaiser
News Editor Keith Herrell
Politics Editor Sharon Moloney
Radio/Television Editor Greg Paeth
Sports Editor Mark Tomasik

Market Information: Zoned editions.
Mechanical available: Black and 3 ROP colors; insert accepted — preprinted.
Mechanical specifications: E - 6 cols, 2¹⁄16", ⅛" between; A - 6 cols, 2¹⁄16", ⅛" between; C - 9 cols, 1⅜", ¹⁄16" between.
Commodity consumption: average pages per issue 66(d).
Equipment: LIBRARY: Electronic — Vu/Text. WIRE SERVICES: News — SHNS, AP; Photos — AP.

CIRCLEVILLE

Pickaway County

'90 U.S. Census- 11,666; E&P '96 Est. 11,637

Herald (e-mon to fri; m-sat)

Herald, 210 N. Court St.; PO Box 498, Circleville, OH 43113; tel (614) 474-3131; fax (614) 474-9525. Brown Publishing Co. group.
Circulation: 7,411(e); 7,411(m-sat); ABC Sept. 30, 1995.
Price: 50¢(d); 50¢(sat); $9.40/mo (mail); $85.80/yr (carrier).
Advertising: Open inch rate $7.85(e); $7.85(m-sat). **Representatives:** Papert Companies; US Suburban Press.
News Service: AP. **Politics:** Independent. **Established:** 1883.
Not Published: New Year; Memorial Day; Independence Day; Labor Day; Thanksgiving; Christmas.
Special Editions: Progress Edition (Feb); 4-H Edition, Car Care (Mar); Real Estate (Apr); Graduation, Pickaway County Fair (June); Football Review (Aug); Pumpkin Show, Car Care (Oct); Basketball Preview (Nov); Christmas Greetings (Dec).
Special Weekly Sections: Best Food Days (mon, wed); Farm Pages (sat).

CORPORATE OFFICERS

Chairman Clarence J Brown
President Mark R Policinski
Secretary Joyce E Brown
Treasurer John Aston

GENERAL MANAGEMENT

Publisher Timothy C Kay

ADVERTISING

Director Jerry Shasteen

CIRCULATION

Manager William Pontious

NEWS EXECUTIVE

Editor Willie Ehrlich

PRODUCTION

Manager Larry Herron
Supervisor-Composing Karen Snyder

Market Information: TMC.
Mechanical available: Offset; Black and 3 ROP colors; insert accepted — preprinted; page cut-offs — 22¾".
Mechanical specifications: Type page 13¾" x 21½"; E - 6 cols, 2¹⁄16", ⅛" between; A - 6 cols, 2¹⁄16", ⅛" between; C - 10 cols, 1⁵⁄16", ¹⁄16" between.
Commodity consumption: Newsprint 611 metric tons; widths 28", 30", 35"; black ink 22,000 pounds; color ink 2,100 pounds; single pages printed 5,600; average pages per issue 18(d); single plates used 3,875.
Equipment: EDITORIAL: Front-end hardware — Ap/Mac; Front-end software — QuarkXPress 3.3, Baseview/NewsEdit. CLASSIFIED: Front-end hardware — Ap/Mac; Front-end software — QuarkXPress 3.3, Baseview/Class Manager; Printers — AP. PRODUCTION: Pagination software — QuarkXPress 3.3; Typesetters — Ap/Mac; Plate exposures — 2-Nu; Plate processors — Nat; Scanners — HP; Production cameras — 1-B/Caravel; Automatic film processors — 1-LE.
PRESSROOM: Line 1 — 8-G/Community; Folders — 1-G/(w/upper former). MAILROOM: Bundle tyer — 1-Bu, 1-Akebono; Addressing machine — 1-KR. WIRE SERVICES: News — AP; Receiving dishes — size-10ft, AP. BUSINESS COMPUTERS: IBM; Applications: MSSI: Accts receivable; Manifest: Circ mgmt; PCs & micros networked.

CLEVELAND

Cuyahoga County

'90 U.S. Census- 505,616; E&P '96 Est. 453,929
ABC-CZ (90): 1,412,140 (HH 563,243)

The Plain Dealer
(m-mon to sat; S)

The Plain Dealer, 1801 Superior Ave., Cleveland, OH 44114; tel (216) 999-4500; web site http://www.rockhall.com/. Advance Publications group.
Circulation: 396,773(m); 396,773(m-sat); 533,615(S); ABC Sept. 30, 1995.

Price: 35¢(d); 35¢(sat); $1.50(S); $2.75/wk; $143.00/yr.
Advertising: Open inch rate $233.01(m); $233.01(m-sat); $279.00(S). **Representative:** Newhouse Newspapers/Metro Suburbia.
News Services: AP, NYT, LAT-WP, Advance News Services, UPI. **Politics:** Independent. **Established:** 1842.
Special Editions: Year in Review, Bridal Features, Annual Financial Review, C.O.S.E., Get-away Weekend, Home Modernization Expo (Jan); Black History Month, New Home Guide, Cleveland Flower Festival, National Home & Garden Show (Feb); Cleveland Auto Show, Apartment Living, Every woman Expo, New Home Guide (Mar); Indians Baseball, Spring Garden Section, Scholastic Excellence, Employment Opportunities, New Home Guide, Women's Spring Fashion, Spring Home Fix-up (Apr); See Ohio First, New Home Guide, Sports Excellence, Grilling Made Easy, Best of the Best Nurse's Section, Home Improvement (May); Buying into Cleveland Expo, New Home Guide, Apartment Living, Plain Dealer Top 100, Condoquest (June); New Home Guide, Answer Book, Trucks & Vans, Grand Prix (July); Women's Fall Fashion, Vintage Ohio Wineries, County Fair, NCB Triathlon, Homerama (Aug); Pro-Football, Lawn, Garden & Power Equipment, Women's Fall Fashion, New Home Guide (Sept); Employment Opportunties, New Home Guide, New Car Introduction, Fall Home Remodeling (Oct); Trucks & Vans, Get-away Weekend, Ski Fair, Holiday Shopping Guide, Financial & Estate Planning (Nov).
Special Weekly Sections: Sports Monday, Next (Teen Feature), Personal Finance/Personal Technology (mon); Business Tuesday, Everywoman, Health (tues); Food/Wine (wed); Style, Autos (thur); Friday Magazine (Entertainment) (fri); Your Home Magazine, Family (sat); Perspective, Sunday Homes, Travel, Arts & Books (S).
Magazines: Friday! Magazine (fri); Color Comics, Driving, Your Home Magazine (sat); Sunday Magazine, TV Week, Color Comics (S).

CORPORATE OFFICERS
President/Publisher Alex Machaskee
Exec Vice Pres Robert M Long
Treasurer Richard Morway

GENERAL MANAGEMENT
Director-Public Affairs William C Barnard
Director-Info Systems Joseph Cillo
Director-Operations William Moore
Director-Labor Relations/Personnel William Calaiacovo
Director-Building/Transportation Service Joseph DeAngelo
Manager-Living Textbook Program Michele Hill
Manager-Purchasing Luis Arce
Manager-Credit George Giannakos
Controller William Mickey

ADVERTISING
Director Terrell Hebert
Manager-General Charles Tarantino
Manager-Retail Stephen Casey
Manager-Classified Margaret Draper

MARKETING AND PROMOTION
Director-Promotion Jerry Hoegner
Manager-Marketing/Research Robert Thein

TELECOMMUNICATIONS
Manager-Voice Info Service Jacob Rosenheim
Audiotex Manager Jake Rosenheim

CIRCULATION
Director Richard Epstein

NEWS EXECUTIVES
Vice Pres/Senior Editor Thomas H Greer
Editor David Hall
Managing Editor Gary R Clark
Managing Editor-Personnel Maxine Lynch
Managing Editor-Production Rosemary Kovacs
Asst Managing Editor Ted Diadium
Asst Managing Editor Robert McAuley
Asst Managing Editor Tom Coscarelli
Asst Managing Editor-Features Christine Jindra
Deputy Managing Editor James A Fabris
Assoc Editor Robert Stock
Assoc Editor Sharon Broussard
Assoc Editor Jean Dubail
Assoc Editor John Clark
Assoc Editor Patricia McCubbin
Assoc Editor Gloria Millner
Assoc Editor Liz Auster
Assoc Editor Roger Brown
Assoc Editor Phillip Morris

EDITORS AND MANAGERS
Automotive Editor Christine Jensen
Book Editor Janice Harayda
Business/Finance Editor Mark Russell
Cartoonist Jeff Darcy
Chief Editorial Artist Vince Matteucci
Chief Photographer Jim Hatch
Chief Editorial Writer Kevin O'Brien
Editorial Director Brent Larkin
Education Editor Jane Kahoun
Entertainment Editor Cheryl Kushner
Editorial Page Editor Brent Larkin
Fashion Editor Janet McCue
Films Editor Joanna Connors
Food Editor Toni Tipton
Foreign/National Editor James Strang
Head Librarian Patti Graziano
Health/Medical Editor Joan Mazzolini
Homes Editor Karen Sandstrom
Living Editor Michael Bennett
Metro Editor Richard Urban
Deputy Metro Editor David Squires
Deputy Metro Editor Jim Darr
Deputy Metro Editor Clara Roberts
Music Editor-Classical Donald Rosenberg
News Systems Director Dennis Webb
Photo Editor Bob Dorksen
Political Editor Mary Anne Sharkey
Real Estate Editor William Lubinger
Religion Editor Darrell Holland
Special Projects Editor John Griffith
Sports Editor Roy Hewitt
State Editor Barbara Galbincea
Sunday Magazine Editor Anne Gordon
Travel Editor David Molyneaux
Washington Bureau Chief Tom Brazaitis

MANAGEMENT INFORMATION SERVICES
Director-Info Systems Joseph Cillo
Management Info Services Director Donald Stroud
Online Manager Patti Graziano
Info Systems Manager-Imaging Mark Holthaus
Info Systems Manager-Ad Service Millard England
Info Systems Manager-Publishing David Smith
Info Systems Manager-Telecommunication Kathy Luengo
Info Systems Superintendent-Composing Richard Burns

PRODUCTION
Director-Operations H William Moore
Manager David Ring
Manager-Printing Joseph Giles
Manager-Quality Assurance Tony Adeshina
Asst Manager William Collins
Asst Manager William Calaiacovo Jr
Superintendent-Pressroom Jerry O'Flannagan
Superintendent-Newsprint Handling Chuck Garven
Foreman-Mailroom Jack Morabito
Engineer-Project Systems Tom Rowe
Chief Engineer Michael Cast

Market Information: Zoned editions; Split Run; TMC; Operate database; Operate audiotex; Electronic edition.
Mechanical available: Offset; Black and 3 ROP colors; insert accepted — preprinted; page cutoffs — 22".
Mechanical specifications: Type page 13" x 21.250"; E - 6 cols, $2\frac{1}{16}$", $\frac{1}{8}$" between; A - 6 cols, $2\frac{1}{16}$", $\frac{1}{8}$" between; C - 10 cols, $1\frac{3}{8}$", $\frac{1}{16}$" between.
Commodity consumption: Newsprint 104,272 short tons; 94,595 metric tons; widths 55", $41\frac{1}{4}$", $27\frac{1}{2}$"; black ink 1,516,332 pounds; color ink 376,472 pounds; single pages printed 34,560; average pages per issue 80.40(d), 180.65(S); single plates used 815,575.
Equipment: EDITORIAL: Front-end hardware — 3-DEC/PDP 11-70, CSI; Printers — 1-Graphic Enterprises/PageScan Printer, 1-Dataprodocts/LZR; Other equipment — 150-CSI/Edit, 10-HI/8900, 2-Sun/Sparc 10, 3-HI/83C6, 11-HI/2100. CLASSIFIED: Front-end hardware — 3-DEC/PDP 11-70, CSI; Other equipment — 110-CSI/CT-112, 9-Cx/Sun Breeze. DISPLAY: Adv layout systems — 7-Cx/Sun Breeze. PRODUCTION: Pagination software — HI/XP21; Typesetters — 3-Cx/Supersetter, 2-AU/APS-6, XIT/Interface; Platemaking systems — 3-WL/Lith 10; Production cameras — 2-C/Newspager II, 1-C/Spartan III, 2-C/Marathon; Automatic film processors — 2-LE/AQ, 2-LE/LD24, 1-P/Pakiquick, 1-Polychrome/PQ26; Reproportion units — 3-ECR/Autokon, 2-Eskofot; Film transporters — 3-C; Shrink lenses — 3-Alan/Variable.
PRESSROOM: Line 1 — 4-G/Colorliner; Press drives — Allen Bradley/AC Drives; Folders — 4-G/Double; Press control system — G. MAILROOM: Counter stackers — 20-HL/Monitor, 22-HL; Inserters and stuffers — 7-GMA/SL51000, 1-AT/26:1, 6-AT/15:1; Bundle tyer — 22-OVL; Addressing machine — 2-Am; Mailroom control system — Ferag/Intek. COMMUNICATIONS: Facsimile — Scitex/Eskofot; Remote imagesetting — Scitex/Bitstars; Systems used — fiber optic. WIRE SERVICES: News — AP Datafeatures, AP Dataspeed, AP Datastream; Stock tables — AP Datastream; Syndicates — AP, LATS, Ohio News Wire, NNS, NYT, SHNS, WP; Receiving dishes — size-3m, AP. BUSINESS COMPUTERS: 1-HP/140: Advertising, Development, 1-HP/I-50: Circ, 1-Unisys/BS A6K, 1-Unisys/1BS A4F; Applications: Circ, Mktg statistics, Subscriber billing, Payroll, Personnel; PCs & micros networked; PCs & main system networked.

COLUMBUS
Franklin County

'90 U.S. Census- 632,910; E&P '96 Est. 698,700
ABC-CZ (90): 961,437 (HH 378,723)

The Columbus Dispatch
(m-mon to fri; m-sat; S)

The Columbus Dispatch, 34 S. Third St., Columbus, OH 43215; tel (614) 461-5000; e-mail crow@cd.columbus.oh.us; web site http://www.cd.columbus.oh.us/.
Circulation: 255,390(m); 275,890(m-sat); 400,016(S); ABC Sept. 30, 1995.
Price: 35¢(d); 35¢(sat); $1.75(S); $3.00/wk; $156.00/yr.
Advertising: Open inch rate $124.70(m); $124.70(m-sat); $179.95(S). **Representative:** Sawyer-Ferguson-Walker Co.
News Services: AP, KRT, LAT-WP, NYT, RN. **Politics:** Independent. **Established:** 1871.
Advertising not accepted: Tobacco.
Special Editions: Self Improvement, Weddings, Your Money, Black History Month, Bonus Package (Jan); Sports, Vacation & Boat Show, Business Outlook, Women's History Month, National Engineer's Week, Home & Garden Show (Feb); Frozen Foods, Auto Show, Travel Brochure Pages, Bonus Package, Habitat, Spring Fashion (Mar); Major League Baseball Preview, Baseball, Easter Dining, Spring Home Improvement, Central Ohio Golf Directory, A Guide to Affordable Homes, Employment '96, Volunteer Week, Earth Day 26th Anniversary, Bonus Package, Lawn & Garden (Apr); Senior Lifestyles, Mother's Day Dining, Nurse Appreciation, Ohio Summer Fun Guide, Bonus Package, Summer in the City (May); Muirfield Daily Features, Parade of Homes, Auto Leasing, Central Ohio Auto Racing, Father's Day Dining, Single Lifestyles, Bonus Package (June); Health Care Employment, Cookbook (July); Bonus Package, Fall Fashions, New Home Show, Legal Resource Guide (Aug); College Football, Arts/Entertainment, Travel Brochure Pages, Television Season Previews, Resources for Small Business, Bonus Package, Dining Guide, Employment '96, Habitat, Corporate Gift Guide, Frozen Foods, OSU/Notre Dame 61st Anniversary, Health Care Directory (Sept); Temporary Help Week, 1997 New Car Review, Fall Home & Garden, In Time of Need, Bonus Package, Senior Lifestyles (Oct); Home Entertainment, Holiday Dining, Bonus Package, Basketball '96/'97 (Nov); Holiday Idea Guide, Ring in the New (Dec).
Special Weekly Sections: Business Today (mon); Food, Now (wed); Weekender (thur); Wheels, Arts & Leisure (sat); Sports, The Arts, Accent (daily); Business (daily except mon).

CORPORATE OFFICERS
Board Chairman John F Wolfe
Publisher/President/CEO John F Wolfe
Vice Pres-Human Resources Mark A Evans
Vice Pres/Chief Financial Officer A Kenneth Pierce Jr
Vice Pres-Production Floyd V Jones
Vice Pres-Marketing Thomas B Sherrill
Vice Pres-Community Affairs William C Wolfe Jr
Editor Robert B Smith

GENERAL MANAGEMENT
Controller John C Witzel
Director-Information/Planning Ronald J Trubisky
Director-Maintenance/Engineering Daniel L Sickels
Asst Treasurer E D Goodyear

ADVERTISING
Director Gary D Merrell
Manager-Retail Timothy P Doty
Manager-National Peter J Kooiker
Manager-Classified William T Goddard
Manager-Customer Service Paul G Clouse
Coordinator-Co-op Ardith Holloway

MARKETING AND PROMOTION
Director-Marketing Services Darrell D Durham
Manager-Promotion/Asst Director-Marketing Services Wayne E Harshaw
Manager-Research Douglas J Cavanaugh

CIRCULATION
Director John R Brigham
Asst Director Terry L DeVassie
Asst Director James G Lawson
Manager-City William E Sanders
Manager-State Thomas P Meier
Manager-Marketing/Training Herbert H Baur
Manager-Single Copy Sales Richard F Leopard
Manager-Administration Gerald W Wisemiller

NEWS EXECUTIVES
Editor Robert B Smith
Exec Managing Editor Michael Curtin
Managing Editor-Features Gary Kiefer
Managing Editor-News Andrew J Murphy Jr
Managing Editor-Graphics Karl Kuntz

EDITORS AND MANAGERS
Accent Editor T R Fitchko
Director-Arts Scott Minister
Books Editor George Myers Jr
Business Editor Jerry Tebben
Cartoonist James Larrick
City Editor Mark Ellis
Editorial Page Editor Richard W Carson
Editorial Writer Mary Ann Edwards
Editorial Writer Doug McCormick
Editorial Writer Charles Stella
Editorial Writer Mark Fisher
Editorial Writer Phil Porter
Entertainment Editor Michele Toney
Fashion Editor Marshall Hood
Films Editor Frank Gabrenya
Food Editor Sue Dawson
Home/Real Estate Editor Joseph Blundo
Insight Editor Owen DeWolfe
Librarian James Hunter
News Editor Dennis Mahoney
Director-Photography Barth Falkenberg
Radio/Television Editor Julia Keller
Religion Editor Sylvia Brooks
School Editor Tim Doulin
Sports Editor George Strode
State Editor Frank Hinchey
Theater Editor Michael Grossberg
Travel Editor Lisa Reuter

MANAGEMENT INFORMATION SERVICES
Manager-Info Service James Hunter
Data Processing Manager Ronald J Trubisky

PRODUCTION
Director Robert L Tucker
Asst Director Robert J Brown
Manager Mike McGarity
Manager-Pre Press Art Vogel
Manager-Press Terry Betts
Manager-Packaging David Callahan
Manager-Newsprint Bruce Merriman
Manager-Quality Assurance Tim Bader
Manager-Color Al Shuler
Supervisor-Make-up Jeanneane Simon

Market Information: Zoned editions; Split Run; TMC; ADS; Operate database; Electronic edition.
Mechanical available: Offset; Black and 3 ROP colors; insert accepted — preprinted; page cutoffs — 22".
Mechanical specifications: Type page 13" x 21"; E - 6 cols, $2\frac{1}{16}$", $\frac{1}{8}$" between; A - 6 cols, $2\frac{1}{16}$", $\frac{1}{8}$" between; C - 10 cols, $1\frac{5}{16}$", $\frac{1}{16}$" between.
Commodity consumption: Newsprint 50,000 metric tons; widths $54\frac{3}{4}$", $41\frac{1}{16}$", $27\frac{3}{8}$"; black ink 700,000 pounds; color ink 250,000 pounds; average pages per issue 56(d), 160(S).
Equipment: EDITORIAL: Front-end hardware — AT, 12-AT/GT-68, 30-IBM/PS2, 25-Ap/Mac ci, Ap/Mac fx, Ap/Mac Quadra, 90-RSK/Tandy 100, Lf/AP Leaf Picture Desk, Kk, ECR/Autokon; Front-end software — QuarkXPress, AT, Cx, Sun/Unix; Printers — Florida Data, V, Ap/Mac LaserWriter, NEC, DEC, HP; Other equipment — Lf/AP Leaf Picture Desk, Kk, ECR/Autokon. CLASSIFIED: Front-end hardware — AT, 2-Sun; Front-end software — AT, Unix; Printers — Florida Data. PRODUCTION: Typesetters — 3-Cx/BitSetter, 3-Cx/Bitcaster L-500; Plate exposures — 2-WL/Lith III; Automatic film processors — 2-LE/24-3-C-24; Shrink lenses — 1-CK Optical; Digital color separation equipment — Scitex.
PRESSROOM: Line 1 — 10-TKS/M-72; Line 2 — 10-TKS/M-72; Line 3 — 10-TKS/M-72; Line 4 — 10-TKS/M-72; Folders — 4-TKS. MAILROOM: Counter stackers — 4-Id/660, 9-Id/2000; Inserters and stuffers — 4-Fg/Drums

Ohio I-309

($\frac{4}{10}$-into-1); Bundle tyer — 13-Power Strap. LIBRARY: Electronic — DEC/VAX 3400, Ap/Mac AXS. COMMUNICATIONS: Facsimile — AdSat, T-1/Fiber. WIRE SERVICES: News — AP Datafeatures, AP Photostream, AP Datastream, AP SelectStox, TV Data; Stock tables — AP Xeta, Bloomberg; Syndicates — AP SportStats, KRT, North America Syndicate; Receiving dishes — size-3m, AP. BUSINESS COMPUTERS: DEC/PDP 1183, 1-DEC/VAX 3400; PCs & micros networked; PCs & main system networked.

COSHOCTON

Coshocton County

'90 U.S. Census- 12,193; E&P '96 Est. 11,246
ABC-CZ (90): 12,193 (HH 5,155)

The Coshocton Tribune

(e-mon to fri; m-sat; S)

The Coshocton Tribune, 550 Main St.; PO Box 59, Coshocton, OH 43812; tel (614) 622-1122; fax (614) 622-7341. Thomson Newspapers group.

Circulation: 8,050(e); 8,050(m-sat); 8,450(S); ABC Sept. 30, 1995.

Price: 35¢(d); 35¢(sat); $1.00(S); $2.40/wk (carrier); $10.40/mo (motor route); $117.00/yr.

Advertising: Open inch rate $14.93(e); $14.93(m-sat); $14.93(S). **Representative:** Thomson Newspapers.

News Service: AP. **Politics:** Independent. **Established:** 1909.

Not Published: New Year; Memorial Day; Independence Day; Labor Day; Thanksgiving; Christmas.

Special Editions: Showcase of Homes; Wheels (Automotive Supplement) (monthly).

Special Weekly Sections: Best Food Days (mon); Health & Science (thur); Farm News (sat); Best Food Days, Entertainment, Color Comics, Lifestyles/Business (S); TV Today (weekly).

Magazine: USA Weekend (S).

GENERAL MANAGEMENT

Publisher Don Miller Jr
Business Manager Robert W Pell

ADVERTISING

Manager Paul Stubler
Classified Sales Beth Tackett
Classified Telemarketing Debra Phillabaum
Exec-Accounts Brad Knight
Exec-Accounts Michelle Thornsley
Exec-Accounts Kori Hardesty
Exec-Accounts Wendi Shook
Exec-Accounts Wendy Wilson

CIRCULATION

Manager-Distribution Brian Barker
Manager-District #1 Nicole Weaver
Manager-District #2 Kimberley Speaks
Head Clerk Heather Walker
Accounting Supervisor Melissa Schlupp

NEWS EXECUTIVE

Managing Editor Kenneth Smailes

EDITORS AND MANAGERS

Business/Finance Editor Kenneth Smailes
City Editor Patricia Wherley
Editorial Page Editor Kenneth Smailes
Farm Editor Sharienne Sweeney
News Editor Dean Fox
Sports Editor Perry Myers

PRODUCTION

Manager-Composing Beth Saylor

Market Information: TMC; ADS.

Mechanical available: Offset; Black and 3 ROP colors; insert accepted — preprinted, any; page cut-offs — $22\frac{3}{4}$".

Mechanical specifications: Type page $13\frac{5}{8}$" x $21\frac{1}{4}$"; E - 6 cols, $2\frac{1}{16}$", $\frac{1}{8}$" between; A - 6 cols, $2\frac{1}{16}$", $\frac{1}{8}$" between; C - 9 cols, $1\frac{3}{8}$", $\frac{1}{16}$" between.

Commodity consumption: Newsprint 216 short tons; widths $27\frac{1}{4}$", $13\frac{5}{8}$"; black ink 5,238 pounds; color ink 196 pounds; average pages per issue 56(d), 160(S); single plates used 2,370.

Equipment: EDITORIAL: Front-end hardware — Ap/Mac; Front-end software — QuarkXPress; Printers — V/5300R, Ap/Mac LaserWriters. CLASSIFIED: Front-end hardware — Ap/Mac; Front-end software — Baseview/Class Manager Plus; Printers — Ap/Mac LaserWriter NTX, Okidata/320. DISPLAY: Adv layout systems — Ap/Mac; Front-end hardware — Ap/Mac; Front-end software — QuarkXPress 3.31; Printers — V/UT 820, V/5300B. PRODUCTION: Pagination software — QuarkXPress 3.31, Baseview/Q-Tools; OCR software — Caere/Omni-Page; Typesetters — 2-COM/MCS 100, V/5300B, Ap/Mac LaserWriter; Plate exposures — Nu/FT40V6UPNS; Plate processors — Nat/A-250; Electronic picture desk — Lf/AP Leaf Picture Desk; Scanners — Lf/Leafscan 35, Ap/Mac Scanner, Umax/UL 1200 SE; Production cameras — SCREEN/Companica 660C; Automatic film processors — LE, Adobe/Photoshop; Color separation equipment (conventional) — Ap/Mac, Ap/Power Mac 8100-80, Adobe/Photoshop.
PRESSROOM: Press registration system — Duarte/Pin System. MAILROOM: Bundle tyer — 2-OVL/K101, EAM/Mosca ROM Strapper, EAM. Addressing machine — 1-Am/1957; WIRE SERVICES: News — AP, SHNS; Photos — AP; Syndicates — United Media; Receiving dishes — AP. BUSINESS COMPUTERS: IBM/PC Clones, HP; Applications: Quickbooks, Lotus 1-2-3, DAC/Easy, Ceridian System, Oracle G/L: Payroll; PCs & micros networked.

DAYTON

Montgomery and Greene Counties

'90 U.S. Census- 182,044; E&P '96 Est. 165,632
ABC-CZ (90): 436,052 (HH 172,714)

Dayton Daily News

(m-mon to sat; S)

Dayton Daily News, 45 S. Ludlow St.; PO Box 1287, Dayton, OH 45401; tel (513) 225-2000; fax (513) 225-2054. Cox Newspapers Inc. group.

Circulation: 163,187(m); 163,187(m-sat); 220,586(S); ABC Sept. 30, 1995.

Price: 50¢(d); 50¢(sat); $1.50(S); $3.40/wk (carrier); $176.80/yr (carrier).

Advertising: Open inch rate $146.88(m); $146.88(m-sat); $156.78(S). **Representative:** Gannett National Newspaper Sales.

News Services: AP, NYT, KRT, LAT-WP, TV Data. **Politics:** Independent. **Established:** 1898.

Special Edition: "Forecast" Progress Edition (Mar).

Special Weekly Sections: "Smart Money" (Personal Finance) (mon); Lifestyle, Food Features, Neighbors (zoned editions) (wed); "Go" (Entertainment) (fri); Music, Arts, Weekend Life (sat); Travel, Entertainment, Business, Sports, Lifestyle, Home, TV Week (S).

Magazine: TV Date Book (S).

CORPORATE OFFICERS

Publisher J Bradford Tillson
Exec Vice Pres/General Manager Douglas E Franklin

GENERAL MANAGEMENT

Controller James E Ripley
Vice Pres Austin L Smith
Director-Human Resources Madolyn Mumma
Director-Info/Technical Service Jack Gaines
Director-Purchasing Carol Self
Manager-Personnel Elvin Taylor

ADVERTISING

Vice Pres Patricia Keil
General Manager-ADS Darlene Lensch
Manager-National Joyce Hayden
Manager-Classified Mark Stange
Manager-Display Toni Richardson

MARKETING AND PROMOTION

Director-Readership Marketing Kelly Mikesell
Coordinator-Info Marketing Scott Bateman

TELECOMMUNICATIONS

Audiotex Manager Scott Bateman

CIRCULATION

Director Patrick Knickrehm
Manager-Customer Service Phonda Cartwright
Manager-North Chuck Friend
Manager-South Mark Tormeno
Manager-Single Copy John Williams
Manager-Telemarketing Jean Nugent

NEWS EXECUTIVES

Editor Max Jennings
Managing Editor Steve Sidlo
Asst Managing Editor John Thomson
Deputy Managing Editor Cheryl Bratz

EDITORS AND MANAGERS

Automotive Editor Greg Stricharchuk
Aviation Editor Keri Cohen
Books Editor Laura Dempsey
Business/Finance Editor Greg Stricharchuk
Cartoonist Mike Peters
Columnist D L Stewart
Columnist Ellen Belcher
Columnist Dale Huffman
Columnist Mickey Davis
Editorial Page Editor Hap Cawood
Editorial Writer/Columnist Martin Gottlieb
Editorial Writer Ellen Belcher
Environmental Editor Greg Stricharchuk
Fashion/Style Editor Keri Cohen
Food Editor Ann Heller
Garden Editor Doris Schuster
Graphics Editor/Art Director Lee Waigand
Health/Medical Editor Greg Stricharchuk
Living/Lifestyle Editor Keri Cohen
Music Editor Dave Larsen
News Editor Kevin Riley
Outdoor Editor Jim Morris
Political/Government Editor Vince McKelvey
Science/Technology Editor Greg Stricharchuk
Exec Sports Editor Ray Marcano
Sports Columnist Ritter Collett
Theater/Dance Editor Terry Morris
Television Editor Tom Hopkins

MANAGEMENT INFORMATION SERVICES

Director-Info/Technology Service Jack Gaines
Online Manager Scott Bateman

PRODUCTION

Director-Operations Stan Richmond
Manager Michael Joseph
Manager-Pressroom Bill Kohl
Manager-Pre Press Bill Kohl
Manager-Post Press David Wade
Foreman-Imaging Norm Keiser
Engineer-Building/Facilities Richard Hartle

Market Information: Zoned editions; Split Run; TMC; ADS; Operate database; Operate audiotex; Electronic edition.

Mechanical available: Offset; Black and 3 ROP colors; insert accepted — preprinted; page cut-offs — $23\frac{9}{16}$".

Mechanical specifications: Type page 13" x 22"; E - 6 cols, $2\frac{1}{16}$", $\frac{1}{8}$" between; A - 6 cols, $2\frac{1}{16}$", $\frac{1}{8}$" between; C - 10 cols, $1\frac{1}{4}$", $\frac{1}{16}$" between.

Commodity consumption: Newsprint 28,400 short tons; widths 54", $40\frac{1}{2}$", 27"; black ink 655,000 pounds; color ink 160,400 pounds; single pages printed 26,104; average pages per issue 54(d), 110(S); single plates used 200,000.

Equipment: EDITORIAL: Front-end hardware — AT, Synaptic, Unix, Ap/Mac; Front-end software — AT 4.4.2, DTI 3.66; Printers — Teletype/40, Teletype/43, HP/Laser MV; Other equipment — AU/APS-6. CLASSIFIED: Front-end hardware — AT; Front-end software — AT 4.2; Printers — Teletype/40. AUDIOTEX: Hardware — Brite Voice Systems; Software — PEP/Voice Print; Supplier name — Brite Voice Systems. DISPLAY: Adv layout systems — DTI; Front-end hardware — Sun/Work Station 3-50, Synaptic, Unix, Sun/Sparc 20, Ap/Macs; Front-end software — DTI 3.66; Printers — HP/Laser MV; Other equipment — AU/APS-6. PRODUCTION: Pagination software — DTI 3.66; OCR software — Caere/Omni Pro; Typesetters — Bidco, AU/APS-6; Plate exposures — 1-WL/Lith-X-Pozer III, 2-Nu/Flip Top, 1-Theimer; Plate processors — 2-Anacoil/Plate Processor; Scanners — 1-ECR/Autokon 1000, PixelC; Production cameras — 1-Aldus/PageMaker; Automatic film processors — 4-LE; Film transporters — 1-C; Digital color separation equipment — Kk, 1-Optronics/Color Getter II, Nikon/LS 3510.
PRESSROOM: Line 1 — 10-MAN/Lithomatic II (double delivery); Line 2 — 10-MAN/Lithomatic II (double delivery); Folders — 2-Wd-H; Reels and stands — MAN/Lithomatic II, H; Press control system — GE. MAILROOM: Counter stackers — 5-HL/Monitor, 6-HL/DC, 4-HL/Monitor HT; Inserters and stuffers — 3-SLS/1000A 12:2; Bundle tyer — 6-MLN/MLN 2A, 3-Dynaric/NP 2. LIBRARY: Electronic — Vu/Text, ATT/1000. WIRE SERVICES: News — AP, NYT, LAT-WP, LAT-WP, Cox News Service; Stock tables — AP Selectstox I; Receiving dishes — size-12ft, AP. BUSINESS COMPUTERS: IBM/4381-P13, HP/867, HP/670; Applications: CJ: Payroll, Human resources, Adv, Circ; PCs & micros networked; PCs & main system networked.

DEFIANCE

Defiance County

'90 U.S. Census- 16,768; E&P '96 Est. 16,732
ABC-CZ (90): 16,768 (HH 6,186)

The Crescent-News

(e-mon to fri; S)

The Crescent-News, 624 W. Second St.; PO Box 249, Defiance, OH 43512; tel (419) 784-5441; fax (419) 784-1492. Dix Communications group.

Circulation: 16,719(e); 16,572(S); ABC Sept. 30, 1995.

Price: 50¢(d); $1.00(S); $8.50/mo; $102.00/yr.

Advertising: Open inch rate $9.55(e); $9.55(S).

News Services: AP, SHNS. **Politics:** Independent. **Established:** 1888.

Not Published: New Year; Memorial Day; Independence Day; Labor Day; Thanksgiving; Christmas.

Advertising not accepted: Mail order; vending machine; 900 numbers.

Special Editions: Brag Books (Jan); Bridal Edition, Crime Prevention Page, Farm Review Forecast Tab, Cabin Fever (Feb); Kids Design-An-Ad, Step Into Spring, Home/Auto Show (Mar); Easter Page, Lawn & Garden Tab, Garage Sale (Apr); Senior Lifestyle, Spring Car Care Tab (May); Dairy Month, John Paulding Days ROP, Flowing Rivers Festival Tab, Defiance County Fair (June); Sidewalk Days (July); Football Tab, Antwerp Days, Back-to-School Tab (Aug); Johnny Appleseed Festival, Fall Home Improvement Tab (Sept); Restaurant Guide Tab, National Cosmetology Month Guide, Focus Issue, Fire Prevention Page (Oct); Cookbook Tab (Nov); Greetings Edition, Basketball Edition, Holiday Gift Guide (Dec).

Special Weekly Sections: Food (mon); Courthouse News, Bulletin Board (thur); Farm Outdoor, Church Page (fri); Home/Lawn, Health, Business Advice (S).

Magazine: The Marketeer (mon).

CORPORATE OFFICERS

President Albert E Dix
Vice Pres Robert Victor Dix

GENERAL MANAGEMENT

General Manager Steve VanDemark

ADVERTISING

Manager-Retail Amy J Dunbar
Manager-Classified Mark Ryan

CIRCULATION

Manager Keith Foutz

NEWS EXECUTIVE

Editor Robert M Cummins

EDITORS AND MANAGERS

Area Editor Teri Hageman
Automotive Editor Mike Cummins
Business/Finance Editor Dennis Van Scoder
City/Metro Editor Todd Helberg
Editorial Page Editor Todd Helberg
Education Editor Michelle Raike
Entertainment/Amusements Editor Mark Froelich
Farm/Agri-Business Editor Michele Raike
Fashion/Style Editor Wendy Scheurich
Features Editor Mark Froelich
Health/Medical Editor Mark Froelich
Lifestyle Editor Wendy Scheurich
National Editor Al Smith
News Editor Al Smith
Political/Government Editor Todd Helberg
Religion Editor Wendy Scheurich
Television/Film Editor Mark Froelich
Theater/Music Editor Mark Froelich
Sports Editor Bruce Hefflinger
Asst Sports Editor Tim McDonough
Wire Editor Al Smith

MANAGEMENT INFORMATION SERVICES

Data Processing Manager Linda Good

PRODUCTION

Manager Roy Chapman
Foreman-Engraving Donald Meyer
Foreman-Pressroom Gary Richey

Market Information: Zoned editions; TMC; Operate audiotex.

Mechanical available: Offset; Black and 3 ROP colors; insert accepted — preprinted, 11x14 max, 6x9 min; page cut-offs — $22\frac{5}{8}$".

Mechanical specifications: Type page $13\frac{1}{4}$" x 21"; E - 6 cols, $2\frac{1}{16}$", $\frac{1}{8}$" between; A - 6 cols, $2\frac{1}{16}$", $\frac{1}{8}$" between; C - 8 cols, $1\frac{5}{8}$", $\frac{1}{8}$" between.

Commodity consumption: Newsprint 1,265 short tons; widths 14", 28"; black ink 22,987 pounds; color ink 6,318 pounds; single pages printed 8,911; average pages per issue 28(d), 32(S); single plates used 12,933.

Equipment: EDITORIAL: Front-end hardware — AST, PC; Front-end software — Dewar, III; Printers — Printware, XIT. CLASSIFIED: Front-end hardware — AST, PC; Front-end software — Dewar, III; Printers — Printware, XIT. AUDIOTEX: Supplier name — Educom. DISPLAY: Adv layout systems — Dewar/Discovery; Front-end hardware — AST; Front-end software — Dewar; Printers — Okidata/321. PRODUCTION: Typesetters — XIT/Clipper, Print-

ware/1217; Platemaking systems — 1-Nu; Plate exposures — 1-Nu; Plate processors — 1-Ic; Electronic picture desk — 2-Ap/Mac 950; Scanners — 35-MM, Nikon, Howtek/Flatbed Scanner, Nikon/Coolscan; Production cameras — 2-B; Automatic film processors — Kk/Kodamatic 710 (w/Job Color Processor); Color separation equipment (conventional) — 2-Ap/Mac Quadra 950, Adobe/Photoshop, QuarkXPress.
PRESSROOM: Line 1 — 6-G/Urbanite; Press drives — 2-HP/100, 2-CH; Folders — 1-G/Urbanite, Quarter folder; Press control system — CH; Press registration system — Ca. MAILROOM: Inserters and stuffers — MM; Bundle tyer — 2-MLN; Addressing machine — Ch. COMMUNICATIONS: Systems used — satellite. WIRE SERVICES: News — AP; Syndicates — AP, SHNS; Receiving dishes — AP. BUSINESS COMPUTERS: DSI.

DELAWARE
Delaware County
'90 U.S. Census- 20,030; E&P '96 Est. 21,178

The Delaware Gazette
(e-mon to fri; m-sat)

The Delaware Gazette, 18 E. William St.; PO Box 100, Delaware, OH 43015-2332; tel (614) 363-1161; fax (614) 363-6262.
Circulation: 8,056(e); 8,056(m-sat); Sworn Sept. 26, 1995.
Price: 50¢(d); 50¢(sat); $2.28/wk; $110.00/yr.
Advertising: Open inch rate $9.00(e); $9.50(m-sat). **Representatives:** Landon Associates Inc.; US Suburban Press.
News Service: AP. **Politics:** Independent. **Established:** 1818.
Not Published: New Year; Memorial Day; Independence Day; Labor Day; Thanksgiving; Christmas.
Advertising not accepted: Personals.
Special Editions: Bride & Groom, Baby Bulletin (Jan); Bargain Days (Feb); Home Improvement, Spring Sports Tab (Mar); Graduation, Arts (May); Car Care (June); Bargain Days, Fall Sports Tab (Aug); Fair (Sept); Winter Sports Tab, Holiday Tab (Nov).
Special Weekly Sections: The Delaware Gazette Express, Food, Farm Page, Lifestyle Page (mon); Lifestyle Page (tues); Business Page, Lifestyle Page (wed); Lifestyle Page (thur); Entertainment Page, Church Page (fri); Extended Sports Coverage (sat).

CORPORATE OFFICERS
President/CEO W D Thomson II
Vice Pres Helen U Thomson
Secretary H C Thomson III
Treasurer Thomas T Thomson
GENERAL MANAGEMENT
Publisher W D Thomson II
Asst to Publisher Verne Edwards
General Manager Art Ruth
ADVERTISING
Manager Dierdre Warden
Manager-Classified Judy Kern
TELECOMMUNICATIONS
Audiotex Manager Paul Spiers
CIRCULATION
Manager H C Thomson III
NEWS EXECUTIVE
Managing Editor Tom Williams
EDITORS AND MANAGERS
Business Editor Paul Comstock
City/County Editor Paul Comstock
Editorial Page Editor Tom Williams
Entertainment Editor Gary Motz
Farm/Agriculture Editor Paul Comstock
Lifestyle/Religion Editor Barbara Hancock
Chief Photographer Dave Swisher
Sports Editor Gary Henery
Wire Editor Gary Motz
MANAGEMENT INFORMATION SERVICES
Data Processing Manager Lindsey Tope
PRODUCTION
Manager Thomas T Thomson
Foreman-Composing Susan Caudill

Market Information: TMC; Operate audiotex.
Mechanical available: Offset; Black and 3 ROP colors; insert accepted — preprinted; page cut-offs — 22¾".
Mechanical specifications: Type page 13" x 21½"; E - 6 cols, 2¹⁄₁₆", ⅛" between; A - 6 cols, 2¹⁄₁₆", ⅛" between; C - 8 cols, 1½", ⅛" between.
Commodity consumption: Newsprint 800 metric tons; widths 27½", 13¾"; black ink 21,000 pounds; color ink 7,100 pounds; single pages printed 4,992; average pages per issue 16(d); single plates used 4,600.
Equipment: EDITORIAL: Front-end hardware — 8-PC/6100, 2-Ap/Mac IIci, 2-Ap/Mac 610; Front-end software — QuarkXPress, Claris/MacDraw Pro, Aldus/FreeHand, Baseview/NewsEdit; Printers — Ap/Mac NT, Ap/Mac NTX. CLASSIFIED: Front-end hardware — 1-Quad/650-2-PPC-6100-60, WG/Server 8150; Front-end software — Baseview; Printers — Ap/Mac NTX, 2-Ap/Mac ImageWriter II. AUDIOTEX: Hardware — IBM/Infoconnect. DISPLAY: Adv layout systems — Synaptic; Front-end hardware — Synaptic, Ap/Mac 650, Ap/Mac 660, Ap/Mac NTX, Ap/Mac 650 (w/CD); Front-end software — Synaptic, Multi-Ad/Creator 3.7, Aldus/Freehand 3.1; Printers — New-Gen/Imager Plus 1200, HP/LaserJet 4MV.600DPI. PRODUCTION: OCR software — Caere/OmniPage Pro 4.1.0, Caere/OmniPage Direct; Typesetters — 4-Ap/Mac NTX, 1-New-Gen/Plus, 1-Linotype-Hell/190; Plate exposures — 1-Nu/Flip Top FT40U60PNS; Plate processors — Nat/A-250; Electronic picture desk — 1-Ap/Mac 950, 1-Lf/AP Leaf Picture Desk; Scanners — 1-HP, 1-AP, 1-AG; Production cameras — 1-Nikon/35mm, 2-Nikon/F-4, 4-Nikon/F-3; Automatic film processors — AG/Rapidline 43; Color separation equipment (conventional) — Ap/Mac Quadra 950, Adobe/Photoshop, Linotype-Hell/Lino-190 Imagesetter.
PRESSROOM: Line 1 — 8-G; Folders — 1-G/SC; Press control system — Fin. MAILROOM: Counter stackers — 1-BG; Bundle tyer — 1-MLN; Addressing machine — 1-KR. COMMUNICATIONS: Digital ad delivery system — AP AdSend. WIRE SERVICES: News — AP; Stock tables — AP Stock Quote, Hotline; Receiving dishes — size-10ft, AP. BUSINESS COMPUTERS: Applications: PCs & micros networked.

DELPHOS
Allen and Van Wert Counties
'90 U.S. Census- 7,093; E&P '96 Est. 6,909

Delphos Daily Herald
(e-mon to fri; m-sat)

Delphos Daily Herald, 405 N. Main St., Delphos, OH 45833; tel (419) 695-0015; fax (419) 692-7704.
Circulation: 3,834(e); 3,834(m-sat); Sworn Sept. 29, 1994.
Price: 35¢(d); 35¢(sat); $1.55/wk; $6.00/mo; $67.00/yr.
Advertising: Open inch rate $5.32(e); $5.32(m-sat). **Representative:** Papert Companies.
News Service: UPI. **Politics:** Independent. **Established:** 1869.
Not Published: New Year; Memorial Day; Independence Day; Labor Day; Thanksgiving; Christmas.
Special Editions: 2 Dollar Days (Jan); Cooking School (Feb); National Secretaries Week (Apr); 2 Dollar Days (July); Old Fashioned Heritage Days (Sept); Basketball, Christmas Opening (mon before Thanksgiving) (Nov); Christmas Greetings, New Year's Greetings, New Year Baby (Dec).
Magazines: Baby Times Tab (Feb); 4-H Tab (Mar); Bride Tab (May); Auto Show Tab, Tri-County Guide (July); Football Tab (Aug); Get Ready for Winter Tab (Oct); Christmas Carol Tab (Dec); Senior Scenes (last tues/each month).

CORPORATE OFFICERS
President Murray Cohen
Vice Pres-Finance John W Reiniger
Treasurer Murray Cohen
Asst Treasurer Ray Geary
Secretary John W Reiniger
Asst Secretary Ray Geary
GENERAL MANAGEMENT
Publisher Murray Cohen
Business Manager Ray Geary
Purchasing Agent Ruth Ann Wittler
ADVERTISING
Director Jane Ricker
CIRCULATION
Manager Debra Myers
NEWS EXECUTIVE
Managing Editor Esther Bielawski
EDITOR AND MANAGER
Sports Editor Frank Noonan
PRODUCTION
Manager-Graphic Arts Sandra Bohn

Market Information: Split Run; TMC.
Mechanical available: Offset; Black and 3 ROP colors; insert accepted — preprinted, cards, envelopes; page cut-offs — 22¾".
Mechanical specifications: Type page 13.11" x 21½"; E - 6 cols, 2¹⁄₁₆", ⅛" between; A - 6 cols, 2¹⁄₁₆", ⅛" between; C - 8 cols, 1⅝", ⅛" between.
Commodity consumption: Newsprint 2,677 metric tons; widths 27½", 30", 34"; black ink 76,536 pounds; color ink 45,325 pounds; single pages printed 4,912; average pages per issue 16(d); single plates used 25,854.
Equipment: EDITORIAL: Front-end hardware — 2-Mk/3000. CLASSIFIED: Other equipment — 2-Ap/Mac Plus Laser. PRODUCTION: Plate exposures — 2-Nu; Plate processors — 1-Ic, 1-Nat; Production cameras — 1-R, 1-Ik; Automatic film processors — 1-LE.
PRESSROOM: Line 1 — 8-HI; Line 2 — 4-HI; Folders — 2-HI/2:1, 1-HI/1:1; Pasters — 2-Enkel. MAILROOM: Counter stackers — 3-BG; Bundle tyer — 3-Bu, 4-MLN/Strapper; Addressing machine — 1-KR. WIRE SERVICES: News — UPI; Receiving dishes — size-10ft, UPI. BUSINESS COMPUTERS: 1-RSK/TRS 80 III, 1-IBM/PC; Applications: Commercial, Printing, Estimating.

DOVER-NEW PHILADELPHIA
Tuscarawas County
'90 U.S. Census- 27,027 (Dover 11,329; New Philadelphia 15,698); E&P '96 Est. 25,706 (Dover 10,955; New Philadelphia 14,751)
ABC-CZ (90): 39,093 (HH 15,509)

The Times Reporter
(m-mon to sat; S)

The Times Reporter, 629 Wabash Ave. N.W., New Philadelphia, OH 44663; tel (216) 364-5577; fax (216) 364-8449. Journal Register Co. group.
Circulation: 25,829(m); 25,829(m-sat); 28,412(S); ABC Sept. 30, 1995.
Price: 50¢(d); 50¢(sat); $1.25(S); $3.10/wk.
Advertising: Open inch rate $22.24(m); $22.24(m-sat); $22.70(S). **Representative:** Landon Associates Inc.
News Services: AP, KRT, SHNS. **Politics:** Independent. **Established:** 1903.
Special Editions: Progress, Religion, The Year in Review (Jan); Estate Planning, Bridal, Basketball (Feb); NCAA Basketball, Home & Garden (Mar); Home Builders, Senior/Active Times, Housing, Travel (Apr); Weeder's Digest, Graduation, Travel, Mother's Day (May); Dairy, Father's Day (June); Senior/Active Times, Summer Fun (July); Decadesin Business, Football Preview, Italian Festival, Back-to-School (Aug); Fair Guide, Swiss Festival, Wellness Guide, Home Improvement (Sept); Active Times, Interior Design, Cookbook (Oct); Holiday Cookbook, Home Furnishings, Basketball (Nov); Medical, Gift Guide (Dec); Religion (monthly).
Special Weekly Sections: Best Food Day (mon); Senior Citizen (tues); Family/Lifestyle (wed); Entertainment (fri); Religion, Engagements/Bridal (sat); Automotive Showcase (S).
Magazines: USA Weekend; Showcase (S).

CORPORATE OFFICERS
President/CEO Robert M Jelenic
Exec Vice Pres/Chief Financial Officer/Treasurer Jean B Clifton
GENERAL MANAGEMENT
President/Publisher James Shrader
Controller Bret Kettlewell
ADVERTISING
Director Mark Conrad
Manager-National Lynn Berger
Supervisor-Retail Karin Maldonado
CIRCULATION
Director Howard Marsh
NEWS EXECUTIVES
Editor Richard Farrell
Managing Editor Sandy Stewart
Asst Managing Editor Richard Craven
EDITORS AND MANAGERS
Action Line/Hot Line Editor Anna Lee Brendza
Business Editor Norm Singleton
City Editor Darrin Leutenschleger
Editorial Page Editor Steven Long
Entertainment/Amusements Editor Rex Huffman
Farm/Agriculture Editor Ed DeGraw
Photo Editor Jon Conklin
Radio/Television Editor Rex Huffman
Religion Editor Norm Singleton
Sports Editor Dave Whitmer
State Editor Linda Davis
Sunday Weekend Editor Jacqi Geggus
Wire Editor Joe Wright
MANAGEMENT INFORMATION SERVICES
Data Processing Manager Ed Berichon
PRODUCTION
Asst Manager Dan Miles
Foreman-Composing Joseph Conidi
Foreman-Pressroom Robert Thompson
Foreman-Distribution Carroll Elliott

Market Information: Zoned editions; TMC.
Mechanical available: Offset; Black and 3 ROP colors; insert accepted — preprinted, any; page cut-offs — 23½".
Mechanical specifications: Type page 13" x 22½"; E - 6 cols, 2¹⁄₁₆", ⅛" between; A - 6 cols, 2¹⁄₁₆", ⅛" between; C - 9 cols, 1⅜", ¹⁄₁₆" between.
Commodity consumption: Newsprint 1,850 short tons; widths 27½", 41¼", 55"; black ink 38,000 pounds; color ink 13,500 pounds; single pages printed 11,000; average pages per issue 28(d), 150(S); single plates used 12,500.
Equipment: EDITORIAL: Front-end hardware — HI/Composition System 8300; Front-end software — HI/Composition. CLASSIFIED: Front-end hardware — HI/Composition System 8300; Front-end software — HI/Composition. DISPLAY: Front-end hardware — Ap/Mac, HI/8300 Ad MakeUp; Front-end software — HI. PRODUCTION: Typesetters — 2-MON/Express; Plate exposures — 3-Nu; Plate processors — 1-Nat/A-340; Electronic picture desk — Lf/AP Leaf Picture Desk; Scanners — ECR; Production cameras — SCREEN/458; Automatic film processors — LE; Film transporters — LE; Color separation equipment (conventional) — 1-DSA/458.
PRESSROOM: Line 1 — 4-G/Metro (3 color decks); Line 2 — 8-G/H-V; Line 3 — 8-Ha/Mark 10; Folders — 4-G, 2-Ha; Pasters — 2-Cary/Auto, 2-Enkel/Auto (Heat Set; Commercial). MAILROOM: Counter stackers — HL/Monitor, BG/107, 4-HI; Inserters and stuffers — 2-Mc/4-Packet; Bundle tyer — 1-Bu, 1-EAM/Mosca, 3-MLN, 1-EAM/Mosca Wrapper. WIRE SERVICES: News — AP, KRT, SHNS; Stock tables — AP; Syndicates — AP; Receiving dishes — AP. BUSINESS COMPUTERS: IBM/Sys 38; Applications: Commercial printing bidding analysts, INSI: Accts payable, Gen ledger, Ad mgmt, Transient mgmt, Circ, Credit mgmt.

EAST LIVERPOOL
Columbiana County
'90 U.S. Census- 13,654; E&P '96 Est. 11,513
ABC-CZ (90): 33,542 (HH 13,265)

The Evening Review
(e-mon to fri; m-sat)

The Evening Review, 210 E. 4th St., East Liverpool, OH 43920; tel (216) 385-4545; fax (216) 385-7114. Thomson Newspapers group.
Circulation: 11,606(e); 11,060(m-sat); ABC Sept. 30, 1995.
Price: 35¢(d); 35¢(sat); $1.90/wk (carrier); $16.75/mo (mail).
Advertising: Open inch rate $14.11(e); $14.11(m-sat). **Representative:** Thomson Newspapers.
News Service: AP. **Politics:** Independent. **Established:** 1879.
Not Published: Christmas.
Special Editions: Bridal Edition (Jan); Progress (Mar); Car Care, Home Improvement (Apr); Area Festivals Tab (June); Bridal Edition (July); Football (Aug); Homemakers (Sept); Car Care, Home Improvement (Oct); Cookbook, Basketball, Thanksgiving Day (Nov); Senior Citizen (Monthly).
Special Weekly Sections: Best Food Day, Church (sat).
Magazine: PrimeLife (50 plus mkt) (last tues/mo).

GENERAL MANAGEMENT
Publisher Charles W Govey
ADVERTISING
Manager Tammie McIntosh
CIRCULATION
Manager John Hale
NEWS EXECUTIVE
Editor James C Smith
EDITOR AND MANAGER
City Editor Robin Webster
PRODUCTION
Manager Fred Henderson
Foreman-Pressroom Scott Gregory

Ohio I-311

Market Information: TMC.
Mechanical available: Offset; Black and 3 ROP colors; insert accepted — preprinted; page cut-offs — 22½".
Mechanical specifications: Type page 13" x 21½"; E - 6 cols, 2¹⁄₁₆", ⅛" between; A - 6 cols, 2¹⁄₁₆", ⅛" between; C - 9 cols, 1⅓", ⅛" between.
Commodity consumption: average pages per issue 18(d).
Equipment: EDITORIAL: Front-end hardware — CText; Front-end software — CText; Printers — V/5100; Other equipment — Lf/Leafscan 35, Ap/Mac, V/5300. CLASSIFIED: Front-end hardware — CText; Front-end software — CText; Printers — V/5100. PRODUCTION: Typesetters — V; Plate exposures — Nu; Plate processors — Nat; Production cameras — SCREEN/Companica 680E; Automatic film processors — DAI/Screen; Color separation equipment (conventional) — Lf/Leafscan 35. PRESSROOM: Line 1 — 8-G/Community. MAILROOM: Bundle tyer — OVL/Constellation; Addressing machine — 1-Am. COMMUNICATIONS: Facsimile — Cannon. WIRE SERVICES: News — AP; Photos — AP; Syndicates — United Media, NAS, TMS, TV Data, King Features, Universal Press, Creators, Compass; Receiving dishes — size-1m, AP. BUSINESS COMPUTERS: ATT; Applications: Adv billing, Circ billing, Gen ledger, Accts payable, Payroll.

ELYRIA

Lorain County

'90 U.S. Census- 56,746; **E&P '96 Est.** 56,075
ABC-NDM (90): 137,507 (HH 47,765)

Chronicle-Telegram

(e-mon to fri; m-sat; S)

Chronicle-Telegram, 225 East Ave.; PO Box 4010, Elyria, OH 44036; tel (216) 329-7000; fax (216) 329-7272/7282; e-mail macroncl@freenet.lorain.oberlin.edu. Loraine County Printing & Publishing Corp. group.
Circulation: 25,508(e); 25,508(m-sat); 28,549(S); ABC Sept. 30, 1995.
Price: 35¢(d); 35¢(sat); $1.00(S); $3.30/wk (mail), $2.25/wk (carrier); $171.60/yr (mail).
Advertising: Open inch rate $24.76(e); $24.76(m-sat); $24.76(S). **Representative:** Papert Companies.
News Services: AP, KRT, SHNS. **Politics:** Independent-Republican. **Established:** 1829.
Not Published: Christmas.
Special Editions: Midway Mall Bridal Show, Midway Mall Auto Show, DeLuca's Bridal Show (Jan); Romance/Valentine's Day, Health & Fitness, Craft & Hobby Map Page, Income Tax/Financial (Feb); Car Care, Travel Guide, BIA Home Show/JVS, Spring Home Improvement (Mar); Golf Guide, Garden Guide I, Earth Day, Design-An-Ad (Apr); Mother's Day/Why I Love Mom, Ohio Edison Parade of Homes, Home & Garden II, Academic Excellence, In Memory...., Election Section (May); Truck & Van Guide, International Festival Guide (June); Medical Society (July); Corn Festival, Melon Festival, Potato Festival, Lorain County Fair Tab, Football Section (Aug); Fall Bridal Guide, Apple Festival Guide (Sept); BIA Parade of Homes, Home Improvement Guide, Car Care Guide, Craft & Hobby Map Page, Election Guide (Oct); New Car Preview, Holiday Planning Guide, Farm/City Pages, Downtown Elyria Pages, Cleveland Street Map Page, Oberlin Pages, Grafton Pages, Sheffield Center Pages, Basketball Section (Nov); Gift Guide, Letters to Santa, Greetings Pages, Oberlin Pages, North Ridgeville Pages (Dec).
Special Weekly Sections: Accent on Seniors, Mini Pages (tues); Best Food Day (wed); Real Estate, Travel, Business (S).
Magazines: Encore (own, newsprint), TV Weekly Booklet (fri).
Broadcast Affiliates: WEDL-AM/WMWV-FM Elyria, OH.

CORPORATE OFFICERS

President Arthur D Hudnutt
Secretary/Treasurer Philip W Kelly

GENERAL MANAGEMENT

Publisher Arthur C Hudnutt
Controller Philip W Kelly
Manager-Credit William Posey
Manager-Education Service Barbara Stephens
Personnel Manager E H Murphy

ADVERTISING

Director William Posey
Manager-Display Tom Meecha
Manager-Service Kathy Whitmore

CIRCULATION

Manager Gary Cozart

NEWS EXECUTIVES

Editor Arthur D Hudnutt
Exec Editor Andrew R Young
Managing Editor Arnold Miller

EDITORS AND MANAGERS

Accent Exec Editor Amy Richards
Business/Finance Editor Bob Penick
Editorial Page Editor Andrew Ruckman
Education Editor Madelyn Dinnerstein
Entertainment/Amusements Editor Steve Brown
Environmental Editor Walter Topp
Graphics Editor Patti Ewald
Health/Medical Editor Jack Lucentini
Metro Editor Beth Thanes
News Editor Jos Gluvna Sr
Photo Editor Gene Krebs
Religion Editor Bonnie Santos
Sports Editor Jerry Rombach
Sunday Editor Joe Klinec
Television/Music Editor Steve Brown
Theater/Film Editor Steve Brown
Travel Editor Joe Klinec

MANAGEMENT INFORMATION SERVICES

Data Processing Manager Linda Jones

PRODUCTION

Superintendent Melvin K Shook
Superintendent-Pressroom Dean Shook
Asst Superintendent William McCartney

Market Information: Zoned editions; TMC.
Mechanical available: Offset; Black and 3 ROP colors; insert accepted — preprinted; page cut-offs — 23⁹⁄₁₆".
Mechanical specifications: Type page 13" x 22½"; E - 6 cols, 2", .17" between; A - 6 cols, 2", .17" between; C - 9 cols, 1.42", .04" between.
Commodity consumption: Newsprint 3,600 short tons; 3,500 metric tons; widths 55", 41¼", 27½"; black ink 76,000 pounds; color ink 22,000 pounds; single pages printed 15,500; average pages per issue 40(d), 67(S); single plates used 27,500.
Equipment: EDITORIAL: Front-end hardware — CText; Front-end software — CText; Printers — Panasonic. CLASSIFIED: Front-end hardware — CText; Front-end software — CText. DISPLAY: Adv layout systems — CJ/Layout; Front-end hardware — HP; Front-end software — CJ; Printers — HP/2564B. PRODUCTION: Typesetters — XIT/Clipper; Plate exposures — 1-Nu, Douthitt; Plate processors — Nat; Production cameras — 1-C, 1-B; Automatic film processors — SCREEN; Color separation equipment (conventional) — Ap/Mac Quadra 900, Ap/Mac Quadra 950; Digital color separation equipment — Mirror, Lf/Leafscan 35. PRESSROOM: Line 1 — 5-G/Metro; Folders — 1-G; Pasters — G; Reels and stands — G; Press control system — Fin. MAILROOM: Counter stackers — 2-HL; Bundle tyer — MLN. LIBRARY: Electronic — CText, Ap/Mac Archive. WIRE SERVICES: News — AP; Photos — AP; Stock tables — AP; Receiving dishes — AP. BUSINESS COMPUTERS: HP; Applications: CJ; PCs & micros networked; PCs & main system networked.

FAIRBORN

Greene County

'90 U.S. Census- 31,300; **E&P '96 Est.** 32,749

Fairborn Daily Herald

(e-mon to sat)

Fairborn Daily Herald, 1 Herald Sq., Fairborn, OH 45324-5170; tel (513) 878-3993; fax (513) 878-8314. Amos Press group.
Circulation: 5,028(e); 5,028(e-sat); Sworn Oct. 1, 1993.
Price: 25¢(d); 25¢(sat).
Advertising: Open inch rate $7.44(e); $7.44(e-sat). **Representatives:** Landon Associates Inc.; US Suburban Press.
News Service: AP. **Politics:** Independent. **Established:** 1867.
Not Published: New Year; Memorial Day; Independence Day; Labor Day; Thanksgiving; Christmas.
Special Editions: Business Directory (Mar); Lawn & Garden, Private Property (Apr); Home Improvement, Car Care (May); Sidewalk Days (July); Car Care, Home Improvement (Oct); Christmas Kick-off (Nov).

GENERAL MANAGEMENT

Publisher Mark E Raymond

ADVERTISING

Director John Carnahan

CIRCULATION

Director Tim Yostt

NEWS EXECUTIVE

Managing Editor William Flanagan Jr

EDITORS AND MANAGERS

Family Editor Kay Click
Reporter Thomas Gnau
Reporter Thomas Lucente
Sports Editor Keith Walther

Market Information: Split Run; TMC.
Mechanical available: Offset; Black and 3 ROP colors; insert accepted — preprinted; page cut-offs — 21¾".
Mechanical specifications: Type page 13" x 21½"; E - 6 cols, 2¹⁄₁₆", ⅛" between; A - 6 cols, 2¹⁄₁₆", ⅛" between; C - 9 cols, 2¹⁄₁₆", ⅛" between.
Commodity consumption: Newsprint 1,600 short tons; average pages per issue 20(d).
Equipment: EDITORIAL: Front-end hardware — Ap/Mac; Front-end software — Microsoft/Word, QPS. CLASSIFIED: Front-end hardware — Ap/Mac. DISPLAY: Adv layout systems — Ap/Mac. PRODUCTION: Typesetters — COM/MCS 8400, Linotype-Hell/Linotronic 101; Plate exposures — 2-Nu; Plate processors — 1-WL; Production cameras — 1-B, 1-K/Vertical; Automatic film processors — 1-LE. PRESSROOM: Line 1 — 9-G/Suburban; Line 2 — 9-G/Suburban; Folders — 4-G. MAILROOM: Inserters and stuffers — 1-MM/5 Station; Bundle tyer — 2-Bu. WIRE SERVICES: News — AP; Receiving dishes — AP. BUSINESS COMPUTERS: IBM/PC; Applications: Payroll, Billing, Accts payable, Circ.

FINDLAY

Hancock County

'90 U.S. Census- 35,703; **E&P '96 Est.** 35,797
ABC-CZ (90): 35,703 (HH 14,117)

The Courier (m-mon to sat)

The Courier, 701 W. Sandusky; PO Box 609, Findlay, OH 45840-0609; tel (419) 422-5151; fax (419) 422-2937.
Circulation: 25,114(m); 25,114(m-sat); ABC Sept. 30, 1995.
Price: 50¢(d); 50¢(sat); $104.00/yr (carrier); $4.00/bi-wkly (carrier), $26.00/3mo (carrier), $52.00/6mo (carrier).
Advertising: Open inch rate $10.90(m); $10.90(m-sat).
News Service: AP. **Politics:** Independent. **Established:** 1836.
Not Published: New Year; Memorial Day; Independence Day; Labor Day; Thanksgiving; Christmas.
Advertising not accepted: Mail order.
Special Editions: First Baby Contest, Wedding Showcase (Jan); Progress (Feb); Student Express, Women Today (Mar); Home Improvement (Apr); Senior Prom (May); Personal Finance, Investing & Retirement, Pet Parade (June); Wedding Showcase, Talent Showcase (July); Parenting, Fitness & Nutrition (Aug); Football, Fall Home Improvement (Sept); Funeral Planning, Design-An-Ad (Oct); Christmas (Nov); Basketball, Christmas (Dec).
Special Weekly Sections: Best Food Day (mon); Entertainment Plus (tues); Church (sat).
Magazine: USA Weekend (sat).
Broadcast Affiliates: WKKG/WCSI-AM Columbus, IN; WFIN/WKXA Findlay, OH; WMOH Hamilton, OH.

CORPORATE OFFICERS

Board Chairman Edwin L Heminger
President Kurt P Kah
Vice Pres Robert L Gordon
Vice Pres C George Shannon
Vice Pres Karl Heminger
Secretary Margaret H Gordon
Treasurer Kurt P Kah
Controller Robert L Gordon
Asst Secretary Joan L Nichols

GENERAL MANAGEMENT

Publisher Edwin L Heminger
Assoc Publisher Karl Heminger
General Manager Kurt P Kah
Business Manager Robert L Gordon
Manager-Education Service Roger Powell
Manager-Data Processing James R Ford

ADVERTISING

Director-Market Development Roger Powell
Manager-Sales Eugene T Weber
Manager-Office Sally Cramer
Manager-Market C George Shannon

MARKETING AND PROMOTION

Director-Marketing C George Shannon

TELECOMMUNICATIONS

Audiotex Manager Michael Quinlan

CIRCULATION

Manager John Cain
Manager-Sales Terry Kah

NEWS EXECUTIVES

Editor Robert Hesse
Managing Editor James Harrold
Assoc Editor Parker Sams

EDITORS AND MANAGERS

Business/Finance Reporter Mike Sobczyk
City Editor Kurt Leonard
Editorial Page Editor Parker Sams
Entertainment/Amusements Editor Cindy Moorhead
Farm/Agriculture Reporter Mike Sobczyk
Family Editor Laura Tucker
Living/Lifestyle Editor Cindy Moorhead
Photo Editor Nick Moore
Sports Editor Larry Alter
Television/Film Editor Cindy Moorhead
Theater/Music Editor Cindy Moorhead
Travel Editor Cindy Moorhead

MANAGEMENT INFORMATION SERVICES

Data Processing Manager James R Ford

PRODUCTION

Manager Karl Heminger
Manager-Pre Press Deborah Perkins
Manager-Systems Albert Flinn
Foreman-Pressroom Jerry Wertz
Foreman-Mailroom Tom Manley

Market Information: TMC; Operate audiotex.
Mechanical available: Offset; Black and 3 ROP colors; insert accepted — preprinted; page cut-offs — 22¾".
Mechanical specifications: Type page 13" x 21¾"; E - 6 cols, 2¹⁄₁₆", ⅛" between; A - 6 cols, 2¹⁄₁₆", ⅛" between; C - 8 cols, 1⅜", ¹⁄₁₆" between.
Commodity consumption: Newsprint 1,250 metric tons; widths 27½", 13¾"; black ink 20,000 pounds; single pages printed 7,700; average pages per issue 24(d); single plates used 12,000.
Equipment: EDITORIAL: Front-end hardware — 1-DEC/11-84; Front-end software — DEC/TMS; Printers — 2-DEC/LA-120, 1-DEC/LA-50; Other equipment — 16-DEC/PC, 8-IBM/PC, 1-PC/486, Gateway, 2-Ap/Power Mac. CLASSIFIED: Front-end hardware — 1-DEC/11-84, 6-DEC; Front-end software — CMS, DEC; Printers — 1-DEC/LA-120; Other equipment — 7-NS/100, 1-PC/286, 1-PC/486, Gateway. AUDIOTEX: Hardware — 1-PC/486-66 MHZ, TI/Micro DeskTop; Supplier name — New Horizons Group. DISPLAY: Adv layout systems — 3-Dewar/Discovery Workstation, 3-AST/PC Input Terminal; Front-end hardware — 1-AST/386; Front-end software — Dewar/System 3; Printers — 1-Okidata/320. PRODUCTION: Typesetters — 2-V/5060W, 1-V/5300; Platemaking systems — 2-3M/Pyrofax; Plate exposures — 2-Ultra-Lite/5000; Electronic picture desk — Lf/AP Leaf Picture Desk; Scanners — Wordscan/Plus; Production cameras — SCREEN/Companica 680C; Automatic film processors — 1-LE; Digital color separation equipment — Lf/Leafscan 35. PRESSROOM: Line 2 — 7-HI/845; Folders — 1-HI; Pasters — 6-MEG. MAILROOM: Counter stackers — 2-HL/Monitor, 1-HL/Dual Carrier; Inserters and stuffers — 1-AMgraphics/630; Bundle tyer — 1-Sa/SR1, 1-PPK, 1-Sterling/MR 40CH; Addressing machine — 1-Prism/Online Ink Jet. WIRE SERVICES: News — AP; Photos — AP; Stock tables — AP; Syndicates — CT, WP, LATS, TV Data; Receiving dishes — size-10ft, AP, CT. BUSINESS COMPUTERS: 1-DEC/11-84; Applications: Microsoft/Office: Radio station log & billing, Accts payable, Accts receivable; PCs & micros networked; PCs & main system networked.

FOSTORIA

Seneca, Hancock and Wood Counties

'90 U.S. Census- 14,983; **E&P '96 Est.** 14,362

The Review Times

(e-mon to sat)

The Review Times, 113 E. Center St.; PO Drawer C, Fostoria, OH 44830; tel (419) 435-6641; fax (419) 435-9073.
Circulation: 7,363(e); 7,363(e-sat); Sworn Oct. 10, 1995.
Price: 35¢(d); 35¢(sat).
Advertising: Open inch rate $14.71(e); $14.71 (e-sat). **Representative:** Papert Companies.

Copyright ©1996 by the Editor & Publisher Co.

I-312 Ohio

News Service: AP. **Politics:** Independent. **Established:** 1860.
Not Published: New Year; Memorial Day; Independence Day; Labor Day; Thanksgiving; Christmas.
Special Editions: Progress (Feb); Today's Woman (June); Football (Aug); Homemaker's School (Oct); Basketball, Christmas Opener (Nov).
Special Weekly Section: Tri-County This Week (wed).
Magazines: Food & Household (mon); Expanded Entertainment, Church Page (fri); Farm Page (daily).

CORPORATE OFFICERS
President Clarence Pennington
Vice Pres J C Pennington
Vice Pres C Dean Kieffer

GENERAL MANAGEMENT
Publisher Clarence Pennington
General Manager C Dean Kieffer

NEWS EXECUTIVE
Editor Clarence Pennington

EDITORS AND MANAGERS
Editorial Page Editor Clarence Pennington
Outdoor Editor Clarence Pennington
Sports Editor Scott Cottos

PRODUCTION
Manager Charlotte Yarbrough

Market Information: TMC.
Mechanical available: Offset; Black and 3 ROP colors; insert accepted — preprinted; page cutoffs — 21½".
Mechanical specifications: Type page 13 3/16" x 21½"; E - 6 cols, 2 1/16", 3/16" between; A - 8 cols, 1½", ⅛" between; C - 8 cols, 1½", ⅛" between.
Commodity consumption: width 28"; average pages per issue 16(d).
Equipment: EDITORIAL: Front-end hardware — 9-CText, Intel/PC; Front-end software — CText. CLASSIFIED: Front-end hardware — 2-CText, Intel/PC; Front-end software — CText; Printers — Tandy/2104; Other equipment — 2-IBM/Selectric II. PRODUCTION: Typesetters — 2-Ap/Mac LaserWriter II; Plate processors — 1-3M/Pyrofax; Production cameras — 1-Nu/AG RPS 6100S.
PRESSROOM: Line 1 — 6-G/Community; Folders — 1-G. MAILROOM: Bundle tyer — 1-Sa, 1-Bu; Addressing machine — 1-El. LIBRARY: Combination — Microfilm and bound copies. WIRE SERVICES: News — AP; Photos — AP; Receiving dishes — AP. BUSINESS COMPUTERS: Intel/486; PCs & micros networked.

FREMONT
Sandusky County
'90 U.S. Census- 17,648; **E&P '96 Est.** 17,490
ABC-NDM (90): 61,963 (HH 22,464)

The News-Messenger
(e-mon to fri; m-sat)

The News-Messenger, 1700 Cedar St.; PO Box 1230, Fremont, OH 43420; tel (419) 332-5511; fax (419) 332-9750. Gannett Co. Inc. group.
Circulation: 13,983(e); 13,983(m-sat); ABC Sept. 30, 1995.
Price: 35¢(d); 35¢(sat); $2.25/wk (carrier); $117.00/yr (carrier).
Advertising: Open inch rate $17.45(e); $17.45(m-sat); comb with Port Clinton News (e) $26.15. **Representative:** Gannett National Newspaper Sales.
News Services: AP, GNS. **Politics:** Independent. **Established:** 1856.
Special Editions: Wellness (Health), Baby Edition, Bridal Edition (Jan); Progress Edition (Feb); Accent on Agriculture, Car Care (Mar); Spring Home Improvement, Home Week (Apr); Car Care (Mar); Graduation (May); Wellness (June); Fair Edition (Aug); Wellness, Pigskin Preview, Sandusky County Showcase (Sept); Fall Home Improvement, Car Care (Oct); Winter Sports (Nov); Gift Guide, Holiday Greetings (Dec).
Special Weekly Sections: Food, Our Neighbor, Help Line (mon); Dollars & Sense (tues); Family, Outdoors (wed); Time Out (thur); Entertainment, Wheels (fri); Marketplace, Religion (sat); Wheels (fri).
Magazines: TV Week (fri); USA Weekend (sat).

CORPORATE OFFICERS
President James F Daubel
Secretary Thomas Chapple
Asst Treasurer Jimmy Thomas

GENERAL MANAGEMENT
Publisher James F Daubel
Controller Amy Schwartz

ADVERTISING
Director Genia Lovett
Manager-Sales Mary Alt

MARKETING AND PROMOTION
Director-Marketing/Promotion J Richard Harshbarger

CIRCULATION
Director Thomas Leite

NEWS EXECUTIVES
Editor James F Daubel
Exec Editor John Dye
Assoc Editor Roy Wilhelm

EDITOR AND MANAGER
Editorial Page Editor Joyce Huntley

MANAGEMENT INFORMATION SERVICES
Technical Support Stacy Floriana

PRODUCTION
Director Roger Gard
Manager-Pressroom Donald Roddy
Manager-Commercial Sales Henry Karcher
Manager-Systems/Imaging Diana Sanford
Manager-Mailroom Paul Benevento
Manager-Service Ken Burkett

Market Information: TMC.
Mechanical available: Offset; Black and 3 ROP colors; insert accepted — preprinted; page cutoffs — 22¾".
Mechanical specifications: Type page 13" x 21½"; E - 6 cols, 2 1/16", ⅛" between; A - 6 cols, 2 1/16", ⅛" between; C - 9 cols, 1⅜", 1/16" between.
Commodity consumption: Newsprint 564 short tons; 512 metric tons; widths 27¼", 26½", 34"; black ink 10,338 pounds; color ink 2,610 pounds; single pages printed 6,450; average pages per issue 20(d); single plates used 13,000.
Equipment: EDITORIAL: Front-end hardware — Ap/Mac; Front-end software — Baseview, QuarkXPress; Printers — NewGen/Turbo, AU/APS 6-82 ACS; Other equipment — Lf/AP Leaf Picture Desk. CLASSIFIED: Front-end hardware — Ap/Mac; Front-end software — QuarkXPress, Baseview; Printers — Okidata/3410, NewGen/Turbo, AU/APS 6-82 ACS, ImageWriter II. AUDIOTEX: Hardware — PC/IBM-compatible; Software — Ads-on-Call. DISPLAY: Adv layout systems — IBM/AS-400, SCS/Layout 8000; Front-end hardware — Ap/Mac; Front-end software — QuarkXPress, Multi-Ad/Creator; Printers — Ap/Mac LaserWriter, NewGen/Turbo PS66B, AU/APS 6-82 ACS. PRODUCTION: Pagination software — QuarkXPress; OCR software — Caere/OmniPage 2.1; Typesetters — AU/APS 6-82 ACS; Plate exposures — 1-BKY/Ascor 30 x 40, 1-Nu/Flip Top 40V6UPNS; Plate processors — 2-Nat/250; Electronic picture desk — Lf/AP Leaf Picture Desk; Scanners — Umax/UC-1260, Mikrotek 1600 ZS, AG/Arcus Plus, AG/Arcus II; Production cameras — 1-R/580, 1-I/530; Automatic film processors — 1-LE/LD-24A; Shrink lenses — 1-Alan; Color separation equipment (conventional) — Lf/Leafscan 35, AG/Arcus Plus, Umax; Digital color separation equipment — ECR/Microtek, AU-6-82-ACS.
PRESSROOM: Line 1 — 6-G/Urbanite; Folders — 1-G/Quarter, 1-G/2:1 Half; Pasters — 3-Enkel; Reels and stands — 3-G; Press control system — Fin. MAILROOM: Counter stackers — 1-BG/107, 1-BG/109; Inserters and stuffers — 1-MM/227-E; Bundle tyer — 2-MLN/ML2-EE, 1-Sa; Addressing machine — Ch/539. COMMUNICATIONS: Digital ad delivery system — AP AdSend. Systems used — satellite. WIRE SERVICES: News — AP Datastream, AP Datafeatures; Receiving dishes — size-7ft, AP. BUSINESS COMPUTERS: IBM/AS-400; Applications: Adv billing, Accts receivable, Gen ledger, Payroll, Accts payable; PCs & main system networked.

GALION
Crawford County
'90 U.S. Census- 11,859; **E&P '96 Est.** 11,422

The Galion Inquirer
(e-mon to fri; m-sat)

The Galion Inquirer, 378 N. Market St.; PO Box 648, Galion, OH 44833; tel (419) 468-1117; fax (419) 468-7255.
Circulation: 4,617(e); 4,617(m-sat); Sworn Oct. 1, 1995.
Price: 35¢(d); 35¢(sat); $1.55/wk; $20.15/3mo; $75.40/yr.
Advertising: Open inch rate $7.60(e); $7.60(m-sat). **Representative:** Papert Companies.
News Service: AP. **Politics:** Independent. **Established:** 1877.
Not Published: New Year; Memorial Day; Independence Day; Labor Day; Thanksgiving; Christmas.
Advertising not accepted: Vending Machines.
Special Editions: Bridal Tab (Jan); Galion Area Taking Pride (Feb); Spring Home Improvement Page (Apr); Recreation & Travel Guide (May); Graduation Tab (June); Football Preview Tab (Aug); Pickle Run Tab (Sept); Octoberfest Tab, Fall Fix-up, Car Care Tab (Oct); Winter Sports Tab, Christmas Gift Guide (Nov); Chirstmas Gift Guide, Year-In-Review (Dec).

CORPORATE OFFICERS
President Edgar Koehl III
Vice Pres Fred Koehl
Secretary Fred Koehl
Treasurer Edgar Koehl III

GENERAL MANAGEMENT
Publisher Edgar Koehl III
Business Manager Edgar Koehl III
Manager-Education Service Brenda Young

ADVERTISING
Administrator Connie Axline
Manager-National Iona Prosser
Manager-Classified Eileen Davis

CIRCULATION
Manager Ed Fortney

NEWS EXECUTIVE
Editor Craig Wagner

EDITORS AND MANAGERS
Business/Finance Editor Brenda Young
Editorial Writer Craig Wagner
Family Editor Theresa Haferd
Historical Editor Craig Wagner
News Editor Brenda Young
Manager-Photo Department Jodi Myers
School Editor Brenda Young
Sports Editor Rusty Kent
State Editor Jan Spraw
Women's Editor Theresa Haferd

PRODUCTION
Manager George Mathews
Foreman-Photocomp George Mathews
Foreman-Pressroom William Rausch

Market Information: TMC; ADS.
Mechanical available: Offset; Black and 3 ROP colors; insert accepted — preprinted; page cutoffs — 22¾".
Mechanical specifications: Type page 13" x 21½"; E - 6 cols, 2.07", ⅙" between; A - 6 cols, 2.07", ⅙" between; C - 8 cols, 1.53", .14" between.
Commodity consumption: Newsprint 400 short tons; width 27½"; black ink 7,600 pounds; color ink 1,800 pounds; single pages printed 4,014; average pages per issue 14(d); single plates used 5,600.
Equipment: EDITORIAL: Front-end hardware — Mk; Front-end software — Mk. CLASSIFIED: Front-end hardware — Mk; Front-end software — Mk. DISPLAY: Front-end hardware — Ap/Mac IIci, Ap/Mac II; Front-end software — Mk/Mycro-Comp AdWriter. PRODUCTION: Typesetters — 2-Ap/Mac LaserWriter II NTX; Plate exposures — 1-Nu; Production cameras — R/400; Automatic film processors — AG/43.
PRESSROOM: Line 1 — 6-G/Community(inline). MAILROOM: Bundle tyer — Tri-Star/210. WIRE SERVICES: News — AP; Receiving dishes — size-3m, AP. BUSINESS COMPUTERS: 4-Pony/386; Applications: Accts payable, Accts receivable, Payroll, Gen ledger, TMC.

GALLIPOLIS
Gallia County
'90 U.S. Census- 4,831; **E&P '96 Est.** 4,276

Gallipolis Daily Tribune
(e-mon to fri)
Sunday Times-Sentinel (S)

Gallipolis Daily Tribune/Sunday Times-Sentinel, 825 Third Ave.; PO Box 469, Gallipolis, OH 45631; tel (614) 446-2342; fax (614) 446-3008. Gannett Co. Inc. group.
Circulation: 5,817(e); 12,270(S); Sworn Sept. 29, 1995.
Price: 35¢(d); $1.00(S); $2.00/wk; $8.70/mo; $104.00/yr.
Advertising: Open inch rate $5.50(e); $7.55(S). **Representative:** Landon Associates Inc.
News Service: AP. **Politics:** Independent. **Established:** 1893.
Note: The Gallipolis Daily Tribune and the Pomeroy Daily Sentinel share their (S) edition, called the Sunday Times-Sentinel. The Gallipolis Daily Tribune (eS) has a combination rate of $11.80 with Pomeroy Daily Sentinel (eS) & Point Pleasant (WV) Register (e).
Not Published: New Year; Memorial Day; Labor Day; Thanksgiving; Christmas.
Special Editions: Running Edition; Football Kick-off; Christmas; Car Care; Fair; Health Care; Retirement Planning; Hunting; Holiday Cookbook.
Special Weekly Sections: Best Food Day (wed); Church Page, TV Times (fri); Business Page, Farm Page, Best Food Day (S).
Magazine: TV Guide.

GENERAL MANAGEMENT
Publisher Robert L Wingett
Controller Margaret Lehew
General Manager Larry L Boyer

ADVERTISING
Manager Larry L Boyer

CIRCULATION
Manager Paul Barker

NEWS EXECUTIVES
Editor Hobart Wilson Jr
Managing Editor Larry Ewing

PRODUCTION
Manager Fred Hoffman
Foreman-Press/Camera Don Coleman

Market Information: TMC.
Mechanical available: Offset; Black and 3 ROP colors; insert accepted — preprinted; page cutoffs — 21¼".
Mechanical specifications: Type page 13" x 21¼"; E - 6 cols, 2 1/16", ⅛" between; A - 6 cols, 2 1/16", ⅛" between; C - 8 cols, 1½", ⅛" between.
Commodity consumption: Newsprint 222 short tons; average pages per issue 16(d), 64(S).
Equipment: EDITORIAL: Front-end hardware — Ap/Mac; Front-end software — Baseview; Printers — Ap/Mac LaserWriter; Other equipment — HP/ScanJet Plus. CLASSIFIED: Front-end hardware — Ap/Mac; Front-end software — Baseview; Printers — Ap/Mac LaserWriter. PRODUCTION: OCR software — Caere/OmniPage; Typesetters — Ap/Mac LaserWriter IIg; Platemaking systems — 3M/Pyrofax; Plate exposures — B/Ultra-Lite 5000; Plate processors — Roconex; Scanners — HP/ScanJet Plus; Production cameras — B/Caravel, ECR/Autokon 8400.
PRESSROOM: Line 1 — 3-G/Urbanite; Line 2 — 1-G/Urbanite; Line 3 — 1-G/Urbanite; Line 4 — G/Upper Former; Folders — 1-G/Suburban, 1-G/Urbanite; Press control system — 1-Fin/Console. MAILROOM: Counter stackers — 1-BG; Inserters and stuffers — MM/1 Main Feeder, 4-MM/Insert feeder; Bundle tyer — 3-Bu, 1-MLN/Strapper; Addressing machine — 3-Wm. WIRE SERVICES: News — AP Datafeatures, AP, AP GraphicsNet; Syndicates — United Media, NAS; Receiving dishes — AP. BUSINESS COMPUTERS: 1-IBM/AS-400; Applications: Gen ledger, Accts payable, Payroll, Accts receivable, Circ; PCs & micros networked; PCs & main system networked.

GREENFIELD
Highland County
'90 U.S. Census- 5,172; **E&P '96 Est.** 5,294

Greenfield Daily Times
(e-mon to fri)

Greenfield Daily Times, 345 W. Jefferson St.; PO Box 118, Greenfield, OH 45123; tel (513) 981-2141; fax (513) 981-2880.
Circulation: 4,181(e); Sworn Sept. 30, 1994.
Price: 40¢(d); $65.00/yr.
Advertising: Open inch rate $5.96(e). **Representative:** Papert Companies.
News Service: AP. **Politics:** Independent. **Established:** 1932.
Not Published: New Year; Memorial Day; Independence Day; Labor Day; Thanksgiving; Christmas.
Special Editions: Christmas Tab; Basketball Tab; Football Tab; Fall Festival of Leaves Tab; Summer Tab; Spring Tab.
Special Weekly Sections: Best Food Page, Farm Page (mon); Church Page (fri).

CORPORATE OFFICER
President/Owner Jack Schluep

ADVERTISING
Manager Gary Schluep

CIRCULATION
Manager Peg Looney

NEWS EXECUTIVES
Editor Jeff Gilliland
Managing Editor Leona Bihl

Ohio I-313

EDITORS AND MANAGERS

Society Editor Mary Schluep
Sports Editor John Wend

Mechanical available: Offset; Black and 2 ROP colors; insert accepted — preprinted; page cut-offs — 21½".
Mechanical specifications: Type page 15¾" x 21½"; E - 8 cols, 1½", ⅙" between; A - 8 cols, 1½", ⅙" between; C - 8 cols, 1½", 1⁄16" between.
Commodity consumption: Newsprint 230 short tons; width 29½"; black ink 5,000 pounds; color ink 500 pounds; average pages per issue 16(d).
Equipment: EDITORIAL: Front-end hardware — COM. PRODUCTION: Typesetters — 3-COM; Production cameras — 1-B, 1-Nu. PRESSROOM: Line 1 — G. MAILROOM: Bundle tyer — Bu; Addressing machine — 1-Am, 1-El. WIRE SERVICES: News — AP; Receiving dishes — AP.

GREENVILLE

Darke County

'90 U.S. Census- 12,863; E&P '96 Est. 12,747
ABC-CZ (90): 12,863 (HH 5,253)

Daily Advocate

(e-mon to fri; m-sat)

Daily Advocate, 133 W. Main & Sycamore St.; PO Box 220, Greenville, OH 45331; tel (513) 548-3151; fax (513) 548-3913. Thomson Newspapers group.
Circulation: 8,447(e); 8,447(m-sat); ABC Sept. 30, 1995.
Price: 50¢(d); 50¢(sat).
Advertising: Open inch rate $13.50(e); $13.50(m-sat). **Representative:** Thomson Newspapers.
News Services: AP, NEA. **Politics:** Independent. **Established:** 1883.
Not Published: New Year; Memorial Day; Independence Day; Labor Day; Thanksgiving; Christmas.
Special Editions: Christmas; Spring Opening; Fall Opening; Dollar Day; Progress; Cookbook; Car Care; Back-to-School; Annie Oakley Days; Darke County Fair Edition.
Special Weekly Sections: CoverStory, Youth Page (mon); Her Space, Golden Years (wed); Teen Scene (thur); Religion Page (fri).
Magazines: Market Basket (mon); Darke County Farmer Page (tues); Ohio Week (fri); TV & Entertainment Tab (sat).

GENERAL MANAGEMENT

Publisher Vickey Rifenberg
Manager-Credit Karen D Lehman

MARKETING AND PROMOTION

Director-Marketing Operations Mary K Boyer

CIRCULATION

Manager Sheila Willett

NEWS EXECUTIVE

Managing Editor Richard Gillette

EDITORS AND MANAGERS

Lifestyle Editor Linda Moody
Sports Editor Don McDurmot

Market Information: Zoned editions; TMC.
Mechanical available: Offset; Black and 3 ROP colors; insert accepted — preprinted, catabook and mini-tab size; page cut-offs — 22¾".
Mechanical specifications: Type page 13¾" x 21½"; E - 6 cols, 2⅟16", ⅛" between; A - 6 cols, 2⅟16", ⅛" between; C - 9 cols, 1⁹⁄16", ⅛" between.
Commodity consumption: width 27½"; average pages per issue 16(d).
Equipment: EDITORIAL: Front-end hardware — 9-Mk/Touchwriter Plus, Toshiba/T-1000. CLASSIFIED: Front-end hardware — 2-Mk/Mycrocomp Plus. PRODUCTION: Typesetters — 2-COM/MCS 8400 HS, V/ImageSetter Plus; Plate processors — 1-Nu; Production cameras — R; Automatic film processors — LE. PRESSROOM: Line 1 — 6-G/Community. MAILROOM: Bundle tyer — 1-Bu; Addressing machine — 1-Am. WIRE SERVICES: News — AP; Stock tables — Local; Syndicates — NEA; Receiving dishes — AP.

HAMILTON

Butler County

'90 U.S. Census- 61,368; E&P '96 Est. 59,849
ABC-CZ (90): 96,992 (HH 36,538)

The Journal-News

(m-mon to sat; S)

The Journal-News, Court St. & Journal Sq.; PO Box 298, Hamilton, OH 45011; tel (513) 863-8200; fax (513) 863-7988. Thomson Newspapers group.
Circulation: 25,364(m); 25,364(m-sat); 27,241(S); ABC Sept. 30, 1995.
Price: 35¢(d); 35¢(sat); $1.25(S); $2.65/wk; $11.48/mo; $137.80/yr.
Representative: Landon Associates Inc.
News Service: AP. **Politics:** Independent. **Established:** 1886.
Note: The Journal-News (mS) has a combination rate of $36.32 with the Middletown Journal (eS). Individual newspaper rates not made available.
Special Weekly Sections: Journal News (mon); Best Food Day (tues).
Magazines: Parade, TV Update, Comics (S).

CORPORATE OFFICERS

Chairman Kenneth Thomson
President Richard J Harrington

GENERAL MANAGEMENT

Publisher Robert W Murphy
Controller Larry Ruehl
General Manager-Press Mark Cole

ADVERTISING

Director Mike Bennett

TELECOMMUNICATIONS

Audiotex Manager Mike Bennett

CIRCULATION

Director Robert Giambelluca
Manager-Sales Barry T Collins

NEWS EXECUTIVE

Managing Editor Tammy Ramsdell

EDITORS AND MANAGERS

Automotive Editor Deborah Turcotte
Business/Finance Editor Bette Pearce
City/Metro Editor David Heitfield
Education Editor Greg Flannery
Entertainment/Amusements Editor Rick Jones
Environmental Editor Joe Feirtag
Fashion/Style Editor Rick Jones
Graphics Editor/Art Director Bill Parrish
Health/Medical Editor Bette Pearce
Lifestyle Editor Rick Jones
National Editor David Heitfield
News Editor Bob Walker
Opinion Page Editor Dirk Allen
Picture Editor Jim Denney
Photo Editor Jim Denney
Political/Government Editor Mike Sheehy
Religion Editor Peggy McCracken
Science/Technology Editor Joe Feirtag
Sports Editor Pete Conrad
Television/Film Editor Rick Jones
Theater/Music Editor Rick Jones
Travel Editor Rick Jones

MANAGEMENT INFORMATION SERVICES

Data Processing Manager Jerry Leasure

PRODUCTION

Foreman-Composing Dave Sames

Market Information: TMC; Operate audiotex.
Mechanical available: Offset; Black and 3 ROP colors; insert accepted — preprinted, all; page cut-offs — 22.5".
Mechanical specifications: Type page 13" x 21.5"; E - 6 cols, 2⅟16", ⅛" between; A - 6 cols, 2⅟16", ⅛" between; C - 10 cols, 1⁵⁄16", 1⁄16" between.
Commodity consumption: widths 30", 27½", 13¾"; average pages per issue 30(d), 36(S).
Equipment: EDITORIAL: Front-end hardware — CText/486-66; Front-end software — CText/AFM V6X, Expressline Pagination; Printers — Tegra/5000-5100, Panther/Plus; Other equipment — Lf/AP Leaf Picture Desk, Ap/Mac Laserphoto, SMS/Stauffer Library. CLASSIFIED: Front-end hardware — CText, PC/486-66; Front-end software — CText/Standard Classified, CText/ALPS Pagination; Printers — Tegra/5000-5100, Panther/Plus; Other equipment — Ap/Mac LaserWriter II NTX, HP/ScanJet Plus. AUDIOTEX: Hardware — PC/386; Software — Ads-on-Call. DISPLAY: Adv layout systems — 3-Ap/Mac, 3-CText, CText/Adept on PC/486-66, 3-Ap/Mac Quadra 950, 1-Ap/Power Mac 8100-80AV; Front-end hardware — 3-CText/486-66, AP/WGS 8100-110; Front-end software — CText/Adept 3.2, QuarkXPress 3.31; Printers — 2-NewGen/Imager Plus 12, Tegra/5000-5100, Panther/Plus; Other equipment — 2-HP/ScanJet IIcx, Umax/1200 Color Scanner, 2-HP/ScanJet 3C. PRODUCTION: Pagination software — QuarkXPress 3.31; OCR software — Caere/OmniPage Pro, Tegra/Varityper; Typesetters — Panther/Plus, 2-NewGen/Imager Plus, 2-Tegra/5000-5100; Electronic picture desk — Ap/Power Mac 8100-110; Scanners — Polaroid/SprintScan; Production cameras — 1-C/Spartan III, 1-ECR/Autokon 8400; Automatic film processors — 1-LE/LD24AQ, 2-AG/Rapidline 17, Screen/LD-281-Q; Color separation equipment (conventional) — 1-WDS. LIBRARY: Electronic — SMS/Stauffer Library. COMMUNICATIONS: Digital ad delivery system — AP AdSend. Systems used — satellite. WIRE SERVICES: News — AP; Stock tables — NYSE, Amex, Mutual Funds; Receiving dishes — size-3m, AP. BUSINESS COMPUTERS: 1-HP/3000; Applications: Circ, Adv billing, Accts receivable, Gen ledger, Payroll, Spreadsheet; PCs & micros networked; PCs & main system networked.

IRONTON

Lawrence County

'90 U.S. Census- 12,751; E&P '96 Est. 11,570
ABC-CZ (90): 15,308 (HH 6,233)

The Ironton Tribune

(e-tues to fri; S)

The Ironton Tribune, 2903 S. 5th St.; PO Box 4647, Ironton, OH 45638; tel (614) 532-1441; fax (614) 532-1506. Boone Newspapers Inc. group.
Circulation: 7,403(e); 7,963(S); ABC Sept. 30, 1995.
Price: 50¢(d); $1.25(S); $9.75/mo.
Advertising: Open inch rate $10.05(e); $10.05(S). **Representative:** Papert Companies.
News Service: AP. **Politics:** Independent. **Established:** 1880.
Special Editions: Home-owned Business, Dollar Days (Jan); Progress (Feb); Bridal Section (Mar); Women's World (Apr); No to Drugs Tab (May); Newcomer's Guide, Dollar Days (July); Football Tab (Aug); Senior Citizen Guide (Sept); Thanksgiving Day (Nov); Christmas (Dec); Holiday Greetings (Dec 24).
Special Weekly Sections: Business Review, Largest Circulation Day (tues); Best Food Day (wed); Religion, TV Guide (fri); Best Food Day, Focus (S).
Magazine: Family Weekly (S).

CORPORATE OFFICER

President Jennifer Allen

GENERAL MANAGEMENT

Publisher Jennifer Allen

ADVERTISING

Representative Brenda Renfroe
Representative Mary James
Representative Keith Cordes
Representative Sandra Frazier

MARKETING AND PROMOTION

Director-Marketing Tony Morris

CIRCULATION

Manager Aaron Myers
Asst Manager Edsel Hignite

NEWS EXECUTIVE

Managing Editor Renee Carey

EDITORS AND MANAGERS

News Editor Lucia Moses
Sports Editor James Walker

PRODUCTION

Foreman-Press Henry Elliott
Foreman-Mailroom Gary Creger

Market Information: Zoned editions; TMC; ADS.
Mechanical available: Offset; Black and 3 ROP colors; insert accepted — preprinted; page cut-offs — 21¼".
Mechanical specifications: Type page 13" x 21½"; E - 6 cols, 2⅟16", ⅛" between; A - 6 cols, 2⅟16", ⅛" between; C - 9 cols, 1⅜", 1⁄16" between.
Commodity consumption: Newsprint 480 short tons; widths 27½", 16¼"; single pages printed 5,000; average pages per issue 18(d), 64(S); single plates used 5,000.
Equipment: EDITORIAL: Front-end hardware — Ap/Mac; Front-end software — Baseview/NewsEdit, Baseview/Classified. CLASSIFIED: Front-end hardware — Ap/Mac; Front-end software — Baseview/NewsEdit, Baseview/Classified. DISPLAY: Adv layout systems — Ap/Mac; Front-end software — QuarkXPress; Printers — 3-Ap/Mac LaserWriter. PRODUCTION: Plate exposures — 1-Nu; Plate processors — Milart; Production cameras — C; Automatic film processors — P; Digital color separation equipment — Ap/Mac, Adobe/Photoshop. PRESSROOM: Line 1 — 6-G/Suburban; Press control system — Fin. MAILROOM: Inserters and stuffers — 4-KAN/320; Bundle tyer — It. WIRE SERVICES: News — AP News, AP Sports; Receiving dishes — AP. BUSINESS COMPUTERS: Tandy, Tandy/3000; Applications: COM, Lotus, Quicken.

KENT-RAVENNA

Portage County

'90 U.S. Census- 40,904 (Kent 28,835; Ravenna 12,069); E&P '96 Est. 43,513 (Kent 31,373 Ravenna 12,140)
ABC-CZ (90): 56,833 (HH 19,934)

Record-Courier

(e-mon to sat; S)

Record-Courier, 124 N. Chestnut St., Kent-Ravenna, OH 44266; tel (216) 296-9657; fax (216) 296-2698. Dix Communications group.
Circulation: 21,167(e); 21,167(e-sat); 22,341(S); ABC Sept. 30, 1995.
Price: 35¢(d); 75¢(S); $9.00/mo; $99.00/yr.
Advertising: Open inch rate $14.15(e); $14.15(e-sat); $14.15(S). **Representative:** Landon Associates Inc.
News Service: AP. **Politics:** Independent. **Established:** 1833.
Not Published: New Year; Memorial Day; Independence Day; Labor Day; Christmas.
Special Editions: Bridal Tab (Jan); Car Care (Mar); Home Improvement, Lawn & Garden (Apr); Graduation Tab, Summer Lifestyles (May); County Fair Tab, Football & Fall Sports (Aug); Car Care, Home Improvement (Sept); Gift Guide (Dec).
Special Weekly Sections: Best Food Day (tues); Entertainment (thur).
Magazines: TV Magazine (S); USA Weekend; TV Update.
Broadcast Affiliates: WMMZ-FM, Ocala FL; WTBO/WKGO, Cumberland MD; TV-8, Billings MT; KFBB TV-5, Great Falls MT; WKVX/WQKT, Wooster OH; WRAD/WRIQ, Radford VA.

CORPORATE OFFICERS

President David E Dix
President Albert E Dix
Vice Pres Robert Victor Dix
Secretary Robert C Dix Jr
Treasurer G Charles Dix II

GENERAL MANAGEMENT

Publisher David E Dix
Manager-Education Service Roger DiPaolo
General Manager Richard M Sekella

ADVERTISING

Director Ron Waite

MARKETING AND PROMOTION

Director-Marketing Ron Waite

CIRCULATION

Director Harry Newman

NEWS EXECUTIVES

Exec Editor Roger DiPaolo
Managing Editor Steve Harbert

EDITORS AND MANAGERS

Automotive/Aviation Editor Steve Harbert
Books Editor Steve Harbert
Building Pages Editor Roger DiPaolo
Business/Finance Editor Steve Harbert
Editorial Page Editor Roger DiPaolo
Farm/Garden Editor Steve Harbert
Fashion/Food Editor Dottie Lane
Food Editor Peggy Hale
Home Furnishings Editor Dottie Lane
Military Editor Steve Harbert
News Editor Steve Harbert
Outdoors Editor Bill Gressard
Manager-Photo Department Richard Sweet
Radio/Television Editor Steve Harbert
Religion Editor Roger DiPaolo
State Editor Steve Harbert
Society Editor Dottie Lane
Society Editor Peggy Hale
Sports Editor (Pro-Scholastic) Tim Housen
Sports Editor (Collegiate-Scholastic) Harry DeVault
Wire Editor Mark Bednar

MANAGEMENT INFORMATION SERVICES

Data Processing Manager Linda Try

PRODUCTION

Superintendent Jeff Morton
Foreman-Composing Linda Trautman
Foreman-Pressroom Donald Leightner
Foreman-Engraving Harley Lannum
Foreman-Mailroom Harry Newman

Market Information: Zoned editions; Split Run; TMC.
Mechanical available: Offset; Black and 3 ROP colors; insert accepted — preprinted; page cut-offs — 22¾".

Mechanical specifications: Type page 12⅞" x 21½"; E - 6 cols, $2\frac{1}{16}$", ⅛" between; A - 6 cols, $2\frac{1}{16}$", ⅛" between; C - 6 cols, $2\frac{1}{16}$", ⅛" between.
Commodity consumption: Newsprint 2,000 short tons; width 27"; average pages per issue 24(d), 28(sat), 39(S).
Equipment: EDITORIAL: Front-end hardware — Dewar, XIT, Ap/Mac; Printers — XIT. CLASSIFIED: Front-end hardware — 3-Mk; Front-end software — Baseview. AUDIOTEX: Software — Educom. DISPLAY: Adv layout systems — 5-Ap/Mac; Front-end hardware — Ap/Mac; Front-end software — Multi-Ad/Creator; Printers — XIT. PRODUCTION: Pagination software — QPS; Typesetters — 1-Ap/Mac LaserWriter, 2-XIT/Clipper; Platemaking systems — 1-WL/Offset; Plate exposures — 3M/Deadliner; Production cameras — SCREEN; Automatic film processors — 1-LE/Lith-X-Pozer III; Color separation equipment (conventional) — Digi-Colour. PRESSROOM: Line 1 — 8-G/Urbanite; Line 2 — 10-G/Community; Folders — 1-G/1:1, 1-G/2:1. MAILROOM: Counter stackers — 1-BG; Inserters and stuffers — 1-MM; Bundle tyer — 1-MLN, 2-Sa; Wrapping singles — 1-Sa; Addressing machine — 1-Ch. COMMUNICATIONS: Remote imagesetting — XIT; Systems used — fiber optic. WIRE SERVICES: News — AP; Photos — AP; Receiving dishes — AP. BUSINESS COMPUTERS: 1-DSI; Applications: Circ, Adv billing, Accts receivable, Gen ledger, Payroll; PCs & micros networked.

KENTON

Hardin County

'90 U.S. Census- 8,356; **E&P '96 Est.** 8,148

Kenton Times (e-mon to sat)

Kenton Times, 201 E. Columbus St.; PO Box 230, Kenton, OH 43326; tel (419) 674-4066. Ray Barnes Newspapers Inc. group.
Circulation: 6,884(e); 6,884(e-sat); Sworn Sept. 30, 1995.
Price: 50¢(d); 50¢(sat); $88.20/yr (mail), $71.20/yr (carrier).
Advertising: Open inch rate $7.83(e); $7.83(e-sat). **Representative:** Papert Companies.
News Service: AP. **Politics:** Independent. **Established:** 1953.
Advertising not accepted: Vending machine.
Special Editions: Baby Times (Jan); President's Day Promotion, Boy Scouts (Feb); 4-H Section (Mar); Car Care, Home & Garden (Apr); Graduation (May); Moonlight Madness Promotion (June); Sidewalk Sale, Summer Sizzler, Fair Premium (July); Pre-Fair Section, Fall Sports, Back-to-School/Safety Pages (Aug); Post Fair Section, Farm Safety (Sept); Moonlight Madness Promotion, Fire Prevention (Oct); Winter Sports, Christmas Shopping Kick-off (Nov); Christmas Shopping Guide, Christmas Greetings, First Baby Sections (Dec).

CORPORATE OFFICERS

President Charles G Barnes
Secretary/Treasurer Jack L Barnes

GENERAL MANAGEMENT

Publisher Jeff Barnes
General Manager/Purchasing Agent Jeff Barnes

ADVERTISING

Director James Grauel
Manager-General/Promotion James Grauel
Manager-Retail James Grauel
Bookkeeper Lois Bowman

NEWS EXECUTIVE

Editor Timothy Thomas

EDITORS AND MANAGERS

Entertainment/Fashion Editor Jeff Barnes
Home Furnishings/Food Editor Jeff Barnes
Photo Department Manager Jeff Barnes
Radio/Television Editor Timothy Thomas
Society Editor Kar Craigo
Sports Editor Russell Goulet
Wire Editor Timothy Thomas

PRODUCTION

Superintendent James Taylor
Foreman-Composing James Taylor
Foreman-Pressroom Dan Robinson

Market Information: TMC.
Mechanical available: Offset; Black and 3 ROP colors; insert accepted — preprinted; page cut-offs — 21½".
Mechanical specifications: Type page 13" x 21½"; E - 6 cols, $2\frac{1}{16}$", ⅛" between; A - 6 cols, $2\frac{1}{16}$", ⅛" between; C - 6 cols, $2\frac{1}{16}$", ⅛" between.
Commodity consumption: Newsprint 422 short tons; widths 27½", 13¾"; black ink 9,000 pounds; color ink 300 pounds; average pages per issue 16(d).
Equipment: EDITORIAL: Front-end hardware — Mk. DISPLAY: Adv layout systems — 2-Ap/Mac SE. PRODUCTION: Typesetters — 2-Ap/Mac LaserWriter Plus, 1-Ap/Mac LaserWriter NTX; Plate exposures — 1-BKY/1600; Production cameras — 1-B; Automatic film processors — 1-LE.
PRESSROOM: Line 1 — 1-G/Community; Folders — 1-G/2:1. MAILROOM: Bundle tyer — 1-Bu; Addressing machine — 1-Kr, 1-St. COMMUNICATIONS: Facsimile — Sharp/550. WIRE SERVICES: News — AP; Receiving dishes — size-1m, AP. BUSINESS COMPUTERS: 3-B/25; Applications: Payroll, Display billing, Accts payable, GE; PCs & micros networked.

LAKE COUNTY-WILLOUGHBY

Lake County

'90 U.S. Census- 20,510; **E&P '96 Est.** 21,522
ABC-NDM (90): 215,499 (HH 80,421)

The News-Herald (m-mon to sat; S)

The News-Herald, 7085 Mentor Ave., Willoughby, OH 44094; tel (216) 951-0000; fax (216) 951-0917. Journal Register Co. group.
Circulation: 53,914(m); 53,914(m-sat); 65,912(S); ABC Sept. 30, 1995.
Price: 35¢(d); 35¢(sat); $1.25(S); $2.95/wk.
Advertising: Open inch rate $42.95(m); $42.95(m-sat); $47.25(S). **Representative:** Landon Associates Inc.
News Services: AP, LAT-WP, KRT. **Politics:** Independent. **Established:** 1878.
Special Editions: Chronology, Bridal, Super Bowl (Jan); Mid-Winter Car Care, Income Tax Guide, Mid-Winter Motoring, Answer Book, Leasing Cars & Trucks (Feb); Spring Lawn & Garden, Careers, Home Furnishings, Home Buyers Guide, Health Care (Mar); Investment Guide, Spring Car Care, Golf, Spring Fashions, Indians Home Opener, Spring Gardens (Apr); To Mom with Love, Builders Guide, Senior Citizens, Home Improvement (May); Graduation, Father's Day Gift Guide (June); Mid-summer Motoring, Progress Edition, Careers and Education (July); Fair Tabs, High School Football, Most Beautiful Babies, Back-to-School, New Home Development Guide (Aug); Pro Football, Fall Car Care, Fall Fashions, Home Builders, Business Directory, Death: An Experience of Life (Sept); Fall Car Care, Home Improvement, Home Winterization (Oct); Truck Tab, Elections, Hobby & Craft (Nov); Holiday Gift & Dining (Dec).
Special Weekly Sections: Chatter (TMC) (tues); TGIF (Entertainment Tab) (fri); Marketplace & Business (S).
Magazines: Coupon Books (monthly); Homes Almanac; USA Weekend; TV Channels; Collectable Comics.

CORPORATE OFFICERS

President/CEO Robert M Jelenic
Exec Vice Pres/Chief Financial Officer/Treasurer Jean B Clifton

GENERAL MANAGEMENT

Publisher Joseph A Cocozzo
Controller Ray Wolk

ADVERTISING

Director Scott Ruff
Manager-Classified Bert Knop
Manager-Co-op Margaret Lewis
Manager-National Melissa Billington
Manager-Retail Jeff Sudbrook

CIRCULATION

Director Duane Newnes
Manager Parke Votaw

NEWS EXECUTIVES

Editor James K Collins
Exec Editor Talmage A Campbell
Managing Editor Glenn Gilbert

EDITORS AND MANAGERS

Automotive Editor Bill DeBus
Business/Finance Editor Bill DeBus
City/Metro Editor Cole Hatcher
Columnist Bob August
Columnist Hal Lebowitz
Community Editor Ron Hollowell
Copy Desk Chief Alan Ashworth
Editorial Page Editor James K Collins
Education Writer Jennifer Owens
Environmental Writer Jeff Frischkorn
Features Editor Patricia Ambrose
Films/Theater Editor Michael Miller
Food Editor Janet Podolak
Home/Garden Editor Patricia Ambrose
Librarian Jane Strachan
Living/Lifestyle Editor Patricia Ambrose
News Editor Michael Miller
Photo Department Manager Duncan Scott
Political Editor David W Jones
Radio/Television Writer David S Glasier
Sports Editor Jim Murphy
Travel Editor Janet Podolak
Women's Editor Patricia Ambrose

MANAGEMENT INFORMATION SERVICES

Data Processing Manager Dave Wilson

PRODUCTION

Director-Systems Dave Wilson
Manager-Pre Press Lou Merlene
Manager-Press Operations Sam Kosinar
Manager-Mailroom George Szarka
Superintendent-Building Ron Penko

Market Information: Zoned editions; Split Run; TMC; Operate audiotex.
Mechanical available: Offset; Black and 3 ROP colors; insert accepted — preprinted; page cut-offs — 22¾".
Mechanical specifications: Type page 13" x 21"; E - 6 cols, $2\frac{1}{16}$", ⅛" between; A - 6 cols, $2\frac{1}{16}$", ⅛" between; C - 6 cols, $2\frac{1}{16}$", $\frac{1}{16}$" between.
Commodity consumption: Newsprint 7,179 short tons; widths 27½", 41¼", 55"; black ink 153,225 pounds; color ink 26,887 pounds; single pages printed 20,125; average pages per issue 46(d), 112(S); single plates used 72,708.
Equipment: EDITORIAL: Front-end hardware — SII/Sys 25. CLASSIFIED: Front-end hardware — SII/Sys 25. DISPLAY: Adv layout systems — DTI/Make-up Sys; Front-end hardware — Ap/Mac Network. PRODUCTION: Typesetters — 2-AU/APS Micro 5, 3-Hyphen/Dash 600 Imagesetter; Plate exposures — 3-Nu; Plate processors — 2-Nat/A340; Scanners — 1-ECR/Autokon; Production cameras — 1-C, 1-DAI; Automatic film processors — 1-LE, 1-P; Shrink lenses — 2-C; Color separation equipment (conventional) — Newscolor; Digital color separation equipment — 1-Hel/399.
PRESSROOM: Line 1 — 7-G/Metroliner (3 decks); Folders — 2-G/3:2; Pasters — 7-G; Press control system — Fin. MAILROOM: Counter stackers — 6-MM; Inserters and stuffers — 4-MM/inserter; Bundle tyer — 3-MLN, 3-Bu; Addressing machine — 1-KR, Ch/596-552 Quarter folder. WIRE SERVICES: News — AP, KRT, LAT-WP, National Weather Service; Stock tables — AP; Syndicates — AP; Receiving dishes — AP. BUSINESS COMPUTERS: 2-IBM/Sys 34; Applications: Circ, Adv billing, Accts receivable, Accts payable; PCs & micros networked; PCs & main system networked.

LANCASTER

Fairfield County

'90 U.S. Census- 34,507; **E&P '96 Est.** 34,129
ABC-CZ (90): 34,507 (HH 13,981)

Lancaster Eagle-Gazette (e-mon to fri; m-sat; S)

Lancaster Eagle-Gazette, 138 W. Chestnut St.; PO Box 848, Lancaster, OH 43130; tel (614) 654-1321; fax (614) 654-8271. Thomson Newspapers group.
Circulation: 16,363(e); 16,363(m-sat); 16,618(S); ABC Sept. 30, 1995.
Price: 35¢(d); 35¢(sat); $1.25(S); $11.27/mo (carrier), $12.35/mo (motor route); $127.00/yr (carrier), $135.20/yr (motor route).
Advertising: Open inch rate $16.57(e); $16.57(m-sat); $16.57(S). **Representative:** Landon Associates Inc.
News Service: AP. **Politics:** Independent. **Established:** 1807.
Special Editions: Health File, Chamber Tab (Jan); New Car Show, Valentine's Gifts, Progress (Feb); Home & Garden, Race Car Show (Mar); Bridal Tour, Spring Car Care, Ohio Power Tab (Apr); Mother's Day, Great American Outdoors, Graduation Tab, Memorial Day Tab (May); Father's Day, Pictorial Review, Career Planning (June); Health File, Christmas in July (July); Back-to-School, Fall Sports Preview (Aug); Hunting Guide, Home & Energy Guide, Fall/Winter Car Care (Sept); Say NO to Drugs, New Neighbors, County Fair Tab (Oct); Holiday Arts & Crafts, Cookbook, Gift Guide, New Car Preview (Nov); Christmas Carols Tab, Christmas Showcase, Last Minute Gifts, Year-In-Review (Dec).
Special Weekly Sections: Best Food Day, Real Estate Insight (wed); Entertainment (thur); Ohio Week, Farm News (fri); Senior Citizens, TV Week, Color Comics, Business, Real Estate (S).
Magazines: Real Estate Section (wed); TV & Entertainment Guide, USA Weekend (S).

GENERAL MANAGEMENT

Publisher/General Manager Gregory Ptacin
Business Manager Leslie Dunlap

ADVERTISING

Manager-Retail Janet Blair

CIRCULATION

Manager Frank Conidi

NEWS EXECUTIVE

Editor Roy Youst

EDITORS AND MANAGERS

Accent Society Editor Christine Hanna
Automotive Editor Roy Youst
Business/Finance Editor C J Cross
City/Metro Editor Vikki Michalski
Editorial Page Editor Roy Youst
Education Editor Molly O'Reilly
Features Editor Christine Hanna
Living/Lifestyle Editor Christine Hanna
National Editor Jason Maddux
News Editor Vikki Michalski
Photo Editor Dick Prochaska
Political/Government Editor Denise Dick
Religion Editor Denise Dick
Sports Editor Fred Main
Television/Film Editor Christine Hanna
Travel Editor Christine Hanna
Women's Editor Christine Hanna

PRODUCTION

Foreman-Composing C J Arnold-Hall

Market Information: TMC.
Mechanical available: Offset; Black and 3 ROP colors; insert accepted — preprinted, free-standing card; page cut-offs — 22¾".
Mechanical specifications: Type page 13¾" x 21½"; E - 6 cols, $2\frac{1}{16}$", ⅛" between; A - 6 cols, $2\frac{1}{16}$", ⅛" between; C - 9 cols, $1\frac{5}{16}$", ⅛" between.
Commodity consumption: Newsprint 1,000 short tons; width 37¼"; black ink 25,000 pounds; color ink 10,000 pounds; single pages printed 7,500; average pages per issue 20(d), 20(sat), 32(S); single plates used 12,000.
Equipment: EDITORIAL: Front-end hardware — Mk, Ap/Mac; Front-end software — Mk/Newstouch; Printers — V/5100. CLASSIFIED: Front-end hardware — Mk; Front-end software — Mk/Ace II; Printers — V. DISPLAY: Adv layout systems — Mk/MasterPlanner; Front-end hardware — Mk; Front-end software — Mk/Ace II; Printers — Ap/LaserWriter. PRODUCTION: Pagination software — Mk, QuarkXPress; OCR software — Wordlinx 20; Typesetters — V/4990; Platemaking systems — 1-Nu; Plate exposures — 1-Nu; Plate processors — 1-Nu; Electronic picture desk — Lf; Scanners — Umax/Powerlook; Production cameras — 1-Nu; Automatic film processors — 1-LE; Color separation equipment (conventional) — Digi-Colour. MAILROOM: Bundle tyer — 1-MLN/Strap, 1-Okibono. WIRE SERVICES: News — AP; Receiving dishes — AP. BUSINESS COMPUTERS: IBM; Applications: Bookkeeping; PCs & micros networked.

LIMA

Allen County

'90 U.S. Census- 45,549; **E&P '96 Est.** 44,036
ABC-CZ (90): 77,778 (HH 28,318)

The Lima News (m-mon to sat; S)

The Lima News, 3515 Elida Rd.; PO Box 690, Lima, OH 45802-0690; tel (419) 223-1010; fax (419) 229-0426. Freedom Communications Inc. group.
Circulation: 35,446(m); 35,446(m-sat); 46,125(S); ABC Sept. 30, 1995.
Price: 35¢(d); 35¢(sat); $1.25(S); $10.00/mo; $114.00/yr.
Advertising: Open inch rate $25.50(m); $25.50(m-sat); $30.72(S).
News Services: AP, CT, Freedom Wire, KRT. **Politics:** Independent. **Established:** 1884.
Note: Effective July 3, 1995, this publication changed its publishing plan from (e-mon to fri; m-sat; S) to (m-mon to sat; S).
Special Weekly Sections: Food Day (mon); Weekend Entertainment (thur); Business Section (S).
Magazines: Local TV Week (sat); USA Weekend, Color Comics (S).

GENERAL MANAGEMENT
Publisher Thomas J Mullen
Business Manager Marie Lawrence
ADVERTISING
Director James Shine
MARKETING AND PROMOTION
Director-Marketing Chuck Dell
CIRCULATION
Director Todd Russell
NEWS EXECUTIVES
Editor Ray Sullivan
Managing Editor Jim Krumel
EDITORS AND MANAGERS
City Editor Keith Helmlinger
News Editor Karen Jantzi
PRODUCTION
Manager Howard Morris

Market Information: TMC; ADS.
Mechanical available: Offset; Black and 3 ROP colors; insert accepted — preprinted; page cut-offs — 22¾".
Mechanical specifications: Type page 13" x 21½"; E - 6 cols, 2 1/16", ⅛" between; A - 6 cols, 2 1/16", ⅛" between; C - 9 cols, 1⅜", 1/16" between.
Commodity consumption: Newsprint 3,725 short tons; 3,326 metric tons; widths 55", 41¼", 27½"; black ink 78,550 pounds; color ink 10,400 pounds; single pages printed 13,302; average pages per issue 32(d), 54(sat), 160(S); single plates used 35,000.
Equipment: EDITORIAL: Front-end hardware — Dewar/Disc Sys IV; Front-end software — Dewar/Disc System IV; Printers — Tegra/5510; Other equipment — 26-Dewar/386. CLASSIFIED: Front-end hardware — Dewar/Disc Sys IV; Front-end software — Dewar/Disc System IV; Printers — Tegra/5510; Other equipment — 6-Dewar/386. DISPLAY: Adv layout systems — Dewar/Discovery; Front-end hardware — 1-PC/386; Front-end software — Dewar/Ad Dummy; Printers — Tegra/5510. PRODUCTION: Typesetters — V/5300E; Plate exposures — Nat, Nu/Flip Top FT40APRNS; Plate processors — Nat/A-340; Electronic picture desk — Lf/AP Leaf Picture Desk; Production cameras — Ik, LE; Automatic film processors — AG/Rapidline/17; Film transporters — LE/121; Color separation equipment (conventional) — Lf/LeafScan 35, Lf/AP Leaf Picture Desk, Ap/Mac Quadra 900; Digital color separation equipment — RZ/4050E.
PRESSROOM: Line 1 — 6-MAN/Lithoflex; Folders — 2-G; Pasters — 6-Wd; Press control system — Fin. MAILROOM: Inserters and stuffers — SLS/1000; Bundle tyer — 1-MLN/2A, 1-MLN, 1-Bu/Ribbon Tyer; Wrapping singles — 2-St/720; Addressing machine — MMS/Labeler quarterfolder. WIRE SERVICES: News — AP, Freedom Wire, KRT, Freedom Wire, PressLink; Photos — AP; Receiving dishes — AP. BUSINESS COMPUTERS: PC/386, Compaq; Applications: IBM/PS2, Southware, Vision Data.

LISBON
Columbiana County
'90 U.S. Census- 3,037; E&P '96 Est. 2,936
ABC-NDM (90): 108,276 (HH 40,775)

Morning Journal
(m-mon to sat; S)

The Morning Journal, 308 W. Maple; PO Box 249, Lisbon, OH 44432; tel (216) 424-9541; fax (216) 424-0048. Trinity Holdings Inc. group.
Circulation: 13,203(m); 13,203(m-sat); 11,965(S); ABC Sept. 30, 1995.
Price: 35¢(d); 35¢(sat); 50¢(S).
Advertising: Open inch rate $14.67(m); $14.67(m-sat); $14.67(S). **Representative:** Landon Associates Inc.
News Service: AP. **Politics:** Independent. **Established:** 1857.
Not Published: New Year; Christmas.
Special Editions: January Clearance (Jan); Bridal (Feb); Spring Home Improvement (Mar); Car Care (Apr); Fun in the Sun (May); Free Enterprise (June); "Christmas in July" (July); Columbiana County Fair, Canfield Fair, Fall Home Improvement, Football (Aug); Car Care (Oct); Christmas Gift Guide, Basketball (Nov); Factbook (Dec).
Special Weekly Sections: Education (mon); Roasts & Toasts (tues); Farm (wed); Entertainment (thur); Dining Guide (fri); Church, Football (sat); TV Journal, Business, Auto, Health, Food, Real Estate (S).
Magazines: TV Journal (own), USA Weekend (S).

CORPORATE OFFICERS
President K Aylmer
Vice Pres John C Blanchflower
GENERAL MANAGEMENT
Publisher John C Blanchflower
ADVERTISING
Manager-Retail Machen Pavelek
CIRCULATION
Director Ed Martin
NEWS EXECUTIVE
Editor Dorma Tolson
EDITORS AND MANAGERS
Amusements/Books Editor Dennis Spalvieri
Community Editor Nancy Johngrass
News Editor Robert Fusco
Sports Editor Tim Leonard
MANAGEMENT INFORMATION SERVICES
Data Processing Manager John Umbrazon
PRODUCTION
Manager-Press Mike Sweeney

Market Information: Zoned editions; TMC; ADS.
Mechanical available: Offset; Black and 3 ROP colors; insert accepted — preprinted; page cut-offs — 21".
Mechanical specifications: Type page 13" x 20"; E - 6 cols, 2 1/16", ⅛" between; A - 6 cols, 2 1/16", ⅛" between; C - 9 cols, 1 15/16", ⅛" between.
Commodity consumption: Newsprint 2,800 short tons; widths 27½", 26", 13"; black ink 125,000 pounds; color ink 52,000 pounds; single pages printed 13,500; average pages per issue 18(d), 20(S).
Equipment: EDITORIAL: Front-end hardware — 13-XIT, 7-XIT/fileserver, CText; Printers — V/600; Other equipment — 21-IBM/Selectric, 4-Ap/Mac, 3-PC/AT386. CLASSIFIED: Front-end hardware — IBM, 3-IBM/XT; Front-end software — CText; Printers — V/600. DISPLAY: Adv layout systems — 4-Ap/Mac; Front-end hardware — Ap/Mac; Front-end software — Multi-Ad/Creator, QPS; Printers — V/600, Ap/Mac LaserWriter, XIT/Imagesetter. PRODUCTION: Pagination software — QPS; Typesetters — V/600, XIT/Imagesetter; Plate exposures — 2-Nu; Plate processors — 1-Nat/250; Electronic picture desk — Lf/AP Leaf Picture Desk; Scanners — HP; Automatic film processors — 1-P; Digital color separation equipment — Multi-Ad/Creator, QPS.
PRESSROOM: Line 1 — 8-HI/NC 400; Folders — 2-HI. MAILROOM: Bundle tyer — 1-Bu, 1-Gs, 1-Sa; Addressing machine — 2-Am, 1-Ch. WIRE SERVICES: News — AP; Photos — AP; Syndicates — AP, Universal Press, King Features, United Features, Creators, TMS; Receiving dishes — size-10ft, AP. BUSINESS COMPUTERS: TI/1500, DSI; Applications: Circ, Adv billing, Accts receivable; PCs & micros networked.

LOGAN
Hocking County
'90 U.S. Census- 6,725; E&P '96 Est. 6,873

Logan Daily News
(e-mon to fri; m-sat)

Logan Daily News, 72 E. Main; PO Box 758, Logan, OH 43138; tel (614) 385-2107; fax (614) 355-4514. Brown Publishing Co. group.
Circulation: 5,028(e); 5,028(m-sat); Sworn Oct. 10, 1995.
Price: 35¢(d); 35¢(sat).
Advertising: Open inch rate $7.00(e); $7.00(m-sat). **Representative:** Papert Companies.
News Service: AP. **Politics:** Independent. **Established:** 1842.
Not Published: New Year; Memorial Day; Independence Day; Labor Day; Thanksgiving Day; Christmas.
Special Editions: Visitor's Guide, Tax Supplement (Jan); Baby, Valentine, Academic Salute (Feb); Bridal, Spring Car Care (Mar); Home Improvement, Academic Salute (Apr); Mother's Day, Graduation, Memorial Day (May); Nature Festival, Father's Day, Academic Salute (June); Sidewalk Sale, Fair Guide (July); Football Kick-off, Back-to-School (Aug); Fair Edition, Football, Moonlight Madness, Grandparents (Sept); Football, Fall Car Care, Fall Harvest, Pet Edition, Football (Oct); Holiday Shopper, Academic Salute, Holiday Open House (Nov); Holiday Entertainment Section, Holiday Wish List, Christmas Greetings, Christmas Songbook (Dec).

CORPORATE OFFICERS
Board Chairman Clarence J Brown
President Mark Policinski
Secretary Joyce E Brown

GENERAL MANAGEMENT
Publisher Dan Rodenfels
ADVERTISING
Manager Keith Conner
Manager-Classified Missy Woltz
CIRCULATION
Director Rich Burcham
NEWS EXECUTIVE
Editor Dwight Crum
EDITORS AND MANAGERS
Sports Editor Mark Hartman
Women's Editor Wendy Green
PRODUCTION
Manager Lucy Burcham

Market Information: Zoned editions; Split Run; ADS.
Mechanical available: Offset; Black and 3 ROP colors; insert accepted — preprinted; page cut-offs — 22¾".
Mechanical specifications: Type page 13¾" x 21½"; E - 6 cols, 2 3/16", 3/16" between; A - 6 cols, 2 3/16", 3/16" between; C - 8 cols, 1 1/16", ⅛" between.
Commodity consumption: Newsprint 125 metric tons; widths 27½", 13¾"; black ink 4,950 pounds; color ink 120 pounds; average pages per issue 12(d).
Equipment: EDITORIAL: Front-end hardware — Ap/Mac 7100; Front-end software — Baseview/NewsEdit, QuarkXPress. CLASSIFIED: Front-end hardware — Ap/Mac IIsi; Front-end software — Baseview, QuarkXPress; Printers — Okidata/Microline 320. PRODUCTION: Pagination software — Ap/Mac 7100 7.5; Typesetters — HP/LaserJet 4MV, HP/LaserJet 4M Plus; Plate exposures — 1-Nu; Scanners — HP/ScanJet IIcx; Production cameras — 1-R. MAILROOM: Bundle tyer — 1-Bu; Addressing machine — 2-Wm. WIRE SERVICES: News — AP; Receiving dishes — AP. BUSINESS COMPUTERS: AST/Bravo LC 4-660; Applications: MSSI: Budget, Circ, Accts receivable; PCs & micros networked.

LONDON
Madison County
'90 U.S. Census- 7,807; E&P '96 Est. 8,629

The Madison Press
(e-mon to fri)

The Madison Press, 30 S. Oak St.; PO Box 390, London, OH 43140; tel (614) 852-1616; fax (614) 852-1620. Cleveland Newspapers Inc. group.
Circulation: 6,500(e); Sworn Sept. 30, 1994.
Price: 50¢(d); $72.00/yr.
Advertising: Open inch rate $9.55(e). **Representative:** Papert Companies.
News Service: AP. **Politics:** Independent. **Established:** 1843.
Not Published: New Year; Independence Day; Memorial Day; Labor Day; Thanksgiving; Christmas.
Special Editions: Farm & Garden Tab (Mar); Bridal Tab, Antique Section (Apr); Home Improvement Tab (May); Summer Tab (June); Variety Edition (Sept); Car Tab (Oct).
Special Weekly Sections: Food Page (mon); Kids Page (wed); Outdoor Page (thur); Church Page, Farm Page (fri); TV Listings (daily).

CORPORATE OFFICER
President Donald L Hartley
GENERAL MANAGEMENT
Publisher Donald L Hartley
ADVERTISING
Manager William Armstrong
CIRCULATION
Manager Donald L Hartley
NEWS EXECUTIVE
Editor Bill McCullick
PRODUCTION
Manager Tony Stephens

Market Information: TMC.
Mechanical available: Offset; Black and 3 ROP colors; insert accepted — preprinted; page cut-offs — 22¾".
Mechanical specifications: Type page 13" x 21½"; E - 6 cols, 2 1/16", ⅛" between; A - 6 cols, 2 1/16", ⅛" between; C - 8 cols, 1½", ⅛" between.
Commodity consumption: Newsprint 150 short tons; widths 13¾", 27½"; average pages per issue 12(d).
Equipment: EDITORIAL: Front-end hardware — Mk; Front-end software — Mk; Printers — Ap/Mac. CLASSIFIED: Front-end hardware — Mk; Front-end software — Mk; Printers — Ap/Mac. DISPLAY: Adv layout systems — Ap/Mac; Front-end hardware — Ap/Mac; Front-end software — Multi-Ad w/CD-Rom; Printers — NewGen/1200 DPI. PRODUCTION: Typesetters — Ap/Mac; Plate exposures — Douthitt; Plate processors — WL; Scanners — Ap/Mac; Production cameras — Acti/204; Automatic film processors — SCREEN.
PRESSROOM: Line 1 — 6-G/S-1075. MAILROOM: Counter stackers — BG/104; Bundle tyer — Bu; Addressing machine — KR. WIRE SERVICES: News — AP; Receiving dishes — AP. BUSINESS COMPUTERS: 3-RSK; PCs & micros networked; PCs & main system networked.

LORAIN
Lorain County
'90 U.S. Census- 71,245; E&P '96 Est. 67,860
ABC-NDM (90): 143,737 (HH 51,960)

The Morning Journal
(m-mon to sat; S)

The Morning Journal, 1657 Broadway, Lorain, OH 44052; tel (216) 245-6901; fax (216) 245-6922; e-mail mamjornl@freenet.lorain.oberlin.edu. Journal Register Co. group.
Circulation: 43,560(m); 43,560(m-sat); 47,275(S); ABC Sept. 30, 1995.
Price: 35¢(d); 35¢(sat); $1.00(S); $2.50/wk.
Advertising: Open inch rate $36.70(m); $36.70(m-sat); $40.10(S). **Representative:** Landon Associates Inc.
News Services: AP, NYT, KRT. **Politics:** Independent. **Established:** 1879.
Special Editions: Midway Mall Auto Show, Bridal I & II (Honeymoon), Town Crier, Progress I & II, Home Modernization (Jan); Sandusky Mall Auto Show, Finance/Tax, Baby's Coming, Senior Lifestyles, Answer Book, Meet the Merchants, Bed & Breakfast, Valentine Tab (Feb); BIA Home Craft Show, Spring Car Care I & II, Weeder's Digest, Bed & Breakfast, Coupon Book, Living Here (Mar); Golf I, Home Improvement, Earth Day, Weeder's Digest II, Great Outdoors, Tour of Homes, Coupon Book (Apr); Golf II, Lawn & Garden I & II, Lorain Pride, Norwalk Merchants, Cleveland Entertainment, Graduation, Living with Loss (May); Job Digest Tab, Summer Activities, International Festival, Father's Day, Mature Lifestyles, Business to Business, Home-O-Rama (June); BIA Home-O-Rama II, Truck I Tab, Huron Riverfest, Medical Society, Best of Lorain County, Meeting the Challenge, Cleveland Indians Update (July); Truck II Tab, Tour of Homes, Sidewalk Sales, Lorain County Fair, Back-to-School I & II, Clean Sweep, Too Hot to Cook (Aug); Football, Country Living, Crime Awareness, BIA Parade of Homes, Fall Home Furnishings I & II, Fall Home Improvement, "Best of" Section (Sept); BIA Home Tab, Fall Car Care I & II, '97 Car Preview, Health & Fitness, Academic Achievement, Sweetest Day Wedding Guide, Women of Achievement, Walk through History, Buy Now-We'll Show You How, Heroes (Oct); X'mas in Your Community, Early Holiday Gift Guide (Nov); Truck I & II Tab, Cutest Baby Tab, Holiday I & II, Last Minute Gift, Basketball, Holiday Shopping in Your Neighborhood (Dec).
Special Weekly Sections: Food (wed); Sports (thur); Real Estate (sat); Sports, Business, Arcade/Entertainment, Travel, Real Estate (S).
Magazines: The Edge (sports edition), Today's Woman (mon); Arcade/Entertainment (fri); USA Weekend, Color Comics (8 pages), Sports Extra, Real Estate (sat); TV Journal (local) (S); Job Digest (monthly).

CORPORATE OFFICERS
President/CEO Robert M Jelenic
Exec Vice Pres/Chief Financial Officer Jean B Clifton
GENERAL MANAGEMENT
Publisher Kevin F Walsh
Controller Ken Phillips
ADVERTISING
Director William Cyran
Director-National Gary Oliver
Coordinator-Co-op Deb Janscure

I-316 Ohio

MARKETING AND PROMOTION

Manager-Promotion Denise Bailey

CIRCULATION

Director Fred Presler

NEWS EXECUTIVES

Editor John G Cole
Managing Editor Tom Skoch

EDITORS AND MANAGERS

Business Editor Ken Stammen
City Editor David Price
Editorial Page Editor Richard Hendrickson
Entertainment/Amusements Editor Howard Gollop
Home Furnishings Editor Carol Zientarski
Living Editor Carol Zientarski
News Editor Sue Sowa
Chief Photographer Tom Whittington
Sports Editor Kermit Rowe
Sunday Editor Dan Smith
Television Editor Dan Smith

PRODUCTION

Director Tom Muessel
Director-Data Processing Troy Werner

Market Information: Zoned editions; TMC.
Mechanical available: Offset; Black and 3 ROP colors; insert accepted — preprinted; page cut-offs — 22¾".
Mechanical specifications: Type page 13" x 21⅝"; E - 6 cols, 2 1/16", ⅛" between; A - 6 cols, 2 1/16", ⅛" between; C - 9 cols, 1⅜", 1/16" between.
Commodity consumption: Newsprint 4,100 short tons; widths 27½", 13¾"; black ink 125,000 pounds; color ink 26,500 pounds; single pages printed 20,000; average pages per issue 38(d), 60(S); single plates used 30,000.
Equipment: EDITORIAL: Front-end hardware — SII/System 25 w/32 workstation; Front-end software — SII. CLASSIFIED: Front-end hardware — SII/System 25 w/11 workstation; Front-end software — SII; Printers — 1-Printronix/300, 1-Star/10. DISPLAY: Front-end hardware — Dewar/Discovery; Front-end software — Dewar; Printers — 2-CG/8600. PRODUCTION: Typesetters — CG/8600, 2-Linotype-Hell/L-500 Imagesetter; Plate exposures — 2-Nu/Flip Top FT40V6UPNS; Plate processors — 1-Nat/A-340, 1-American Litho/M-28; Electronic picture desk — Lf/AP Leaf Picture Desk; Scanners — Lf/Leafscan 35; Production cameras — ECR/Spartan II, C/Newspager; Automatic film processors — 1-Kk/520, 1-C/T45, 1-P/26EL, 1-P/24ML; Color separation equipment (conventional) — Hel/399c, Umax/1200 Flatbed.
PRESSROOM: Line 2 — 12-G/Urbanite; Folders — 2-G/2:1; Pasters — 9-Cary. MAILROOM: Counter stackers — 3-HL/Monitor, 1-HL/Monitor HT; Inserters and stuffers — 3-MM/227 7:1; Bundle tyer — 2-Power Strap, 1-MLN; Addressing machine — 1-BH. WIRE SERVICES: News — AP Datastream, AP Datafeatures; Stock tables — AP SelectStox; Receiving dishes — size-12ft, AP. BUSINESS COMPUTERS: 1-IBM/AS400; Applications: Adv, Circ, Transient adv, Gen ledger, Accts payable, Payroll; PCs & micros networked; PCs & main system networked.

MANSFIELD

Richland County

'90 U.S. Census- 50,627; E&P '96 Est. 47,965
ABC-CZ (90): 82,392 (HH 31,909)

News Journal

(e-mon to fri; m-sat; S)

News Journal, 70 W. Fourth St.; PO Box 25, Mansfield, OH 44901; tel (419) 522-3311; fax (419) 522-5877. Thomson Newspapers group.
Circulation: 37,523(e); 37,523(m-sat); 48,676(S); ABC Sept. 30, 1995.
Price: 50¢(d); 50¢(sat); $1.50(S); $3.00/wk; $156.00/yr.
Advertising: Open inch rate $29.50(e); $29.50(m-sat); $33.50(S). **Representative:** Landon Associates Inc.
News Services: AP, LAT-WP, KRT. **Politics:** Independent. **Established:** 1930.
Special Editions: Bridal Guide, Tax Guide (Jan); Valentine's Day, Progress Edition (Feb); Home Improvement, Home Show, Car Care (Mar); Home & Garden, Home Buyers Guide (Apr); Mother's Day, Backyard Vacation, Graduation (May); Father's Day, Miss Ohio (June); Living Here, Monster Trucks, Shop Locally (July); Back-to-School, Football (Aug); Home Improvement, Autumn in Ohio (Sept); Car Care, Women in Business, Share the Faith, Gift Guide (Nov); Basketball Preview, Last Minute Gift Guide (Dec).
Special Weekly Sections: Mind & Body (mon); Living (tues); Food (wed); Weekend (thur); TV Book (fri); Religion (sat); Generations (S).
Magazine: USA Weekend (sat).

CORPORATE OFFICER

President Nickolas Monico

GENERAL MANAGEMENT

Publisher Nickolas Monico
Controller Jay Hollon
Manager-Credit Larry Gilliam

ADVERTISING

Director Beth Richey
Coordinator-National Ann Danuloff

CIRCULATION

Director Brian Bumpus
Manager-Operations/Home Delivery Charles Fleming
Manager-Customer Service Laura Adams
Manager-Motor Route Abby Schlereth
Manager-Distribution Dennie Miller
Manager-Single Copy Sales Rhonda Ray

NEWS EXECUTIVES

Exec Editor Tom Brennan
Managing Editor Randy Dunham

EDITORS AND MANAGERS

Business Writer Dan Kopp
City/Metro Editor Rick Armon
Editorial Page Editor Tom Brennan
Education Editor Heather Smith
Features Editor Alisa Nass
Librarian Ellen Smith
News Editor Paul Corbitt
Photo Editor Alex Horvath
Religion Writer Karen Palmer
Sports Editor Scot Fagerstorm
Wire Editor Jeanne Gorgas

MANAGEMENT INFORMATION SERVICES

Data Processing Manager Mark Carr

PRODUCTION

Director David Austin
Manager-Pre Press Robert Lykins
Manager-Plate Composing Bill Remy
Manager-Distribution Center Dennie Miller
Foreman-Pressroom Jim Ferguson

Market Information: Split Run; TMC; ADS.
Mechanical available: Offset; Black and 3 ROP colors; insert accepted — preprinted, free standing cards; page cut-offs — 22".
Mechanical specifications: Type page 13" x 20½"; E - 6 cols, 2 1/16", ⅛" between; A - 6 cols, 2 1/16", ⅛" between; C - 9 cols, 1⅜", 1/16" between.
Commodity consumption: Newsprint 4,272 short tons; widths 54½", 40⅞", 27¼"; black ink 107,000 pounds; color ink 17,000 pounds; single pages printed 17,850; average pages per issue 38(d), 90(S); single plates used 40,000.
Equipment: EDITORIAL: Front-end hardware — Tandem; Front-end software — CText/Dateline; Printers — Genicom/3810S Single Tractor. CLASSIFIED: Front-end hardware — RSK/6000; Front-end software — CText/Advision; Printers — Printronix/8260L, IBM/Laser 10L; Other equipment — CText/ALPS Classified Pagination. DISPLAY: Adv layout systems — 3-CText/Adept; Front-end hardware — DEC/433 ST; Front-end software — CText; Printers — 2-Tegra/Varityper 5000. PRODUCTION: Typesetters — 2-Tegra/Varityper 5100 Imagesetters, Tegra/Varityper 5300E, Veri-Color/2000; Plate exposures — 1-Nu/Flip Top Mercury Vapor, 1-Nu/Flip Top Mercury Vapor; Plate processors — 2-Nat/Super A-250; Electronic picture desk — Lf/AP Leaf Picture Desk; Production cameras — 1-C/Spartan I, 1-C/Spartan II, 1-DAI/260D, ECR/Autokon 1000; Automatic film processors — P/ML 24, LE/2600A, Powermatic/T45; Shrink lenses — Kamesak/Hi-directional (3½%); Color separation equipment (conventional) — Newscolor/Sys 3000C; Digital color separation equipment — Lf/AP Leaf Picture Desk, Veri-Color/2000.
PRESSROOM: Line 1 — 6-G/Metroliner (3 decks); Folders — 1-G/double; Reels and stands — 6-G; Press control system — Fin. MAILROOM: Counter stackers — 4-HL/Monitor; Inserters and stuffers — 2-Mc/660 6 pocket; Bundle tyer — 2-MLN/on-line; Addressing machine — KR/512 labeler & quarterfolder. WIRE SERVICES: News — AP; Syndicates — KRT; Receiving dishes — AP. BUSINESS COMPUTERS: 1-IBM/Sys 36, 1-IBM/AS400; PCs & micros networked; PCs & main system networked.

MARIETTA

Washington County

'90 U.S. Census- 15,026; E&P '96 Est. 13,896
ABC-NDM (90): 51,963 (HH 19,577)

The Marietta Times

(e-mon to fri; m-sat)

The Marietta Times, 700 Channel Ln., Marietta, OH 45750; tel (614) 373-2121; fax (614) 373-7819; web site gopher://seorf.ohiou.edu:2001/11/seorf.stuff/med/xx031. Gannett Co. Inc. group.
Circulation: 13,062(e); 13,062(m-sat); ABC Sept. 30, 1995.
Price: 35¢(d); 75¢(sat); $2.50/wk; $130.00/yr.
Advertising: Open inch rate $15.40(e); $15.40(m-sat). **Representative:** Gannett National Newspaper Sales.
News Services: AP, GNS. **Politics:** Independent. **Established:** 1864.
Special Editions: Back-to-School; Cookbook; Football; Car Care; Basketball; Auto Racing; Bridal Editions; Sternwheel Festival; County Fair Edition; Progress; Hunting & Fishing; Graduation; Monthly Tourism Section; New Car Intro; Monthly Senior Citizen; Scary Stories; Home Sections.
Special Weekly Sections: Best Food Day (mon); Education (tues); Health & Fitness (wed); Entertainment (thur); Religion Page (fri); Times Weekend Edition (sat).
Magazines: Valley View; TV Magazine; USA Weekend; Comics.

CORPORATE OFFICERS

President David A Whitehead
Secretary Thomas L Chapple
Treasurer Jimmy L Thomas

GENERAL MANAGEMENT

Publisher David A Whitehead

ADVERTISING

Director Lori Klinger Smith
Supervisor-Retail Peg Bailey
Supervisor-Classified Christine McIlyar

MARKETING AND PROMOTION

Director-Market Development Robert P Johnson

CIRCULATION

Director Nick Lewis

NEWS EXECUTIVE

Managing Editor Juli Metzger

EDITORS AND MANAGERS

City Editor Jennifer Houtman
Community Editor Karen Bates
Copy Desk Chief Mary Alice Casey
Presentation Editor Art Smith

PRODUCTION

Director Sharon Dennis
Manager-Pressroom Mark Boylard
Manager-Mailroom Frosty Schneider

Market Information: Zoned editions; TMC; ADS.
Mechanical available: Offset; Black and 3 ROP colors; insert accepted — preprinted; page cut-offs — 22¾".
Mechanical specifications: Type page 13" x 21½"; E - 6 cols, 2 1/16", ⅛" between; A - 6 cols, 2 1/16", ⅛" between; C - 9 cols, 1⅜", 1/16" between.
Commodity consumption: Newsprint 637 short tons; widths 27", 14½", 33", 25", 16½"; black ink 12,800 pounds; color ink 1,400 pounds; single pages printed 7,121; average pages per issue 24(d); single plates used 10,967.
Equipment: EDITORIAL: Front-end hardware — Dewar/Disc Net. CLASSIFIED: Front-end hardware — Dewar/Disc Net VDT 55. DISPLAY: Front-end hardware — 2-Dewar/Discovery. PRODUCTION: Typesetters — 2-MON/Imagesetter 1000; Plate exposures — 2-Nu; Plate processors — 2-Nat/A-250; Electronic picture desk — Lf/AP Leaf Picture Desk; Scanners — ECR/Autokon, Lf/Leafscan 35; Production cameras — 1-B/Commodore, 1-N/VT1418; Automatic film processors — 1-LE/LD 1800.
PRESSROOM: Line 1 — 8-G/Urbanite; Folders — 1-G; Reels and stands — G; Press control system — Fin. MAILROOM: Counter stackers — HI/Rima RS-2517; Inserters and stuffers — 5-MM/227E (5 inserts); Bundle tyer — 1-MLN, 1-Ty-Tech; Addressing machine — 1-Ch; Mailroom control system — MM/Saddle Stitcher. WIRE SERVICES: News — AP, GNS; Receiving dishes — AP. BUSINESS COMPUTERS: IBM/PC, IBM/AS-400; Applications: Payroll, Gen ledger, Circ distribution and PIA, Accts receivable; PCs & micros networked; PCs & main system networked.

MARION

Marion County

'90 U.S. Census- 34,075; E&P '96 Est. 31,731
ABC-CZ (90): 43,564 (HH 16,126)

The Star (e-mon to fri; m-sat; S)

The Star, 150 Court St., Marion, OH 43302; tel (614) 387-0400; fax (614) 382-2210. Thomson Newspapers group.
Circulation: 17,472(e); 17,472(m-sat); 17,474(S); ABC Mar. 31, 1995.
Price: 35¢(d); 35¢(sat); $1.25(S); $2.25/wk; $9.75/mo; $117.00/yr.
Advertising: Open inch rate $15.71(e); $15.71(m-sat); $15.71(S). **Representative:** Thomson Newspapers.
News Service: AP. **Politics:** Independent. **Established:** 1877.
Special Editions: Bride (Jan); Progress (Mar); Drum Corps Championships (Aug); Popcorn Festival (Sept); Cookbook Tab, Christmas Gifts (Nov); Christmas Greetings (Dec).
Special Weekly Sections: Feminine Trends (mon); Young Minds (tues); Closer Look (wed); Community Focus (thur); Church (fri); High School Sports, Real Estate (sat); Senior Citizen, Education, Business, School News, Food, Farm, Entertainment, Area News (S).
Magazines: Reflections (wed); TV Update Tab (S); Golden Opportunities (Senior Citizen), Doing Business (Business) (monthly).

GENERAL MANAGEMENT

Publisher Tim Powel
Controller Dave Motes

ADVERTISING

Director Donna Huffman
Manager-National Bev Sisler
Manager-Classified Cheryl Wilcox

NEWS EXECUTIVES

Managing Editor Mary Lawrence
Asst Managing Editor Laura Ustaszewski

EDITORS AND MANAGERS

Business Editor Karen Lillis
City Editor Laura Ustaszewski
District Editor John Jarvis
Editorial Page Editor Mary Lawrence
Education Editor Karen Lillis
Food Editor Brenda Donigan
Political Editor Ahmed Bundick
Religion Editor Brenda Donegan
Sports Editor Eric Davis

MANAGEMENT INFORMATION SERVICES

Data Processing Manager Al Kahrel

PRODUCTION

Supervisor-Composing Al Kahrel

Market Information: Zoned editions; Split Run; TMC; ADS.
Mechanical available: Offset; Black and 3 ROP colors; insert accepted — preprinted; page cut-offs — 22¾".
Mechanical specifications: Type page 13" x 21½"; E - 6 cols, 2 1/16", ⅛" between; A - 6 cols, 2 1/16", ⅛" between; C - 9 cols, 1⅜", 1/16" between.
Commodity consumption: Newsprint 910 short tons; widths 27½", 13¾"; black ink 37,000 pounds; color ink 10,000 pounds; single pages printed 8,350; average pages per issue 24(d), 44(S); single plates used 7,765.
Equipment: EDITORIAL: Front-end hardware — CText, 20-RSK/Tandy, CText. CLASSIFIED: Front-end hardware — 4-RSK/Tandy, CText. DISPLAY: Adv layout systems — CText/Adept. PRODUCTION: Typesetters — 2-Ap/Mac Laser, 2-Tegra/Varityper/5100A, 3-Ap/Mac Laser 486 SX; Plate exposures — Nu/Flip Top; Plate processors — Nat/A-250; Electronic picture desk — Lf/AP Leaf Picture Desk; Scanners — Nu; Production cameras — 1-R/500-LB, SCREEN/C-680; Automatic film processors — SCREEN/LD-220-QT.
PRESSROOM: Line 1 — 8-G/Community (w/2 half decks); Folders — 1-G/SSC. MAILROOM: Bundle tyer — 1-Bu/Straping; Addressing machine — 2-Am/2000. LIBRARY: Electronic — Minolta/Microfilm. WIRE SERVICES: News — AP; Receiving dishes — size-10ft, AP. BUSINESS COMPUTERS: ATT; Applications: Payroll, Adv, Billings, Accts payable.

Ohio I-317

MARTINS FERRY-BELLAIRE
Belmont County

'90 U.S. Census- 14,018 (Martins Ferry 7,990; Bellaire 6,028); E&P '96 Est. 11,623 (Martins Ferry 7,002; Bellaire 4,621)
ABC-NDM (90): 78,038 (HH 31,039)

The Times Leader
(e-mon to fri; S)

The Times Leader, 200 S. Fourth St., Martins Ferry, OH 43935; tel (614) 633-1131; fax (614) 633-1122. Ogden Newspapers group.
Circulation: 20,353(e); 22,687(S); ABC Sept. 30, 1995.
Price: 35¢(d); 75¢(S).
Advertising: Open inch rate $19.21(e); $19.21 (S). **Representative:** Landon Associates Inc.
News Service: AP. **Politics:** Independent. **Established:** 1891 (Times), 1913 (Leader).
Not Published: New Year; Memorial Day; Independence Day; Labor Day; Christmas (except on a Sunday).
Advertising not accepted: Palm reading; Blind mail in investment schemes seeking local capital; Personals.
Special Editions: Investment and Tax Guide (Jan); Bridal (Feb); Home/Garden/Farm, Spring Car Care, March Dining and Entertaining Guide (Mar); Summer Outdoor Living (May); Health and Fitness (June); Back-to-School (Aug); Football, Home Improvements, Fall Car Care (Sept); Golden Years, Health Care (Oct); Winter Sports (Nov); Class Real Estate Tab (monthly).
Special Weekly Section: "Drive" (Auto Section) (thur).
Magazines: USA Weekend, Color Comics, TV Times/TV Magazine (S).

CORPORATE OFFICERS

President G Ogden Nutting
Vice Pres William C Nutting
Vice Pres Robert M Nutting
Secretary William O Nutting
Treasurer Duane D Wittman

GENERAL MANAGEMENT

Publisher Alexander F Marshall III
Manager-Credit Nancy McSwords

ADVERTISING

Director Jeff Herr

CIRCULATION

Director E J Miller

NEWS EXECUTIVE

Editor Kathy Showalter

EDITORS AND MANAGERS

Amusements Editor Phyllis Sigal
Business Editor Kelly Klubert
Editorial Page Editor Kathy Showalter
Education Editor Betty Pokas
Fashion/Food Editor Phyllis Sigal
Home Furnishings/Women's Editor Phyllis Sigal
Librarian Jean Thomas
Music Editor Betty Pokas
Photo Department Manager Michael McNell
Radio/Television Editor Jean Thomas
Religion Editor Jean Thomas
Society Editor Phyllis Sigal
Sports Editor Jeff Harrison
Telegraph Editor Stan Pawlowski

MANAGEMENT INFORMATION SERVICES

Data Processing Manager Bruce Harkness

PRODUCTION

Coordinator-Systems Stan Pawlowski

Market Information: Zoned editions; TMC; ADS.
Mechanical available: Offset; Black and 3 ROP colors; insert accepted — preprinted; page cut-offs — 23 9/16".
Mechanical specifications: Type page 13" x 22"; E - 6 cols, 2 1/16", ⅛" between; A - 6 cols, 2 1/16", ⅛" between; C - 8 cols, 1 9/16", 1/16" between.
Commodity consumption: average pages per issue 19(d), 40(S).
Equipment: EDITORIAL: Front-end hardware — COM/OS; Other equipment — 18-COM. CLASSIFIED: Front-end hardware — COM/OS; Other equipment — 3-COM. DISPLAY: Adv layout systems — Ap/Mac; Front-end hardware — Ap/Mac Quadra 700, 2-Ap/Mac Centris; Front-end software — QuarkXPress, Adobe/Photoshop, Aldus/FreeHand, Multi-Ad/Creator; Printers — Dataproducts/LZR 1560, NewGen/Turbo 360; Other equipment — 2-Microtek/Scanmaker II. PRODUCTION: Typesetters — 1-Ap/Mac LaserWriter NTX, MON/1270 Imagesetter; Platemaking systems — 1-C/News-Plater; Plate exposures — Magnum; Plate processors — Nat/A-250; Scanners — RZ/Scanner, HP/IIC Nikon/35, 2-Microtek; Production cameras — 1-AG/2024; Automatic film processors — LE; Film transporters — LE; Color separation equipment (conventional) — 1-BKY/Enlarger, Ap/Power Mac 7100. PRESSROOM: Line 1 — 4-G/Mark (Offset); Line 2 — 2-PEC/Eagle (3 Color Ink); Press drives — PEC/Bond; Pasters — PEC/Bond. MAILROOM: Counter stackers — 2-HL/Monitor, 1-HL/H12; Inserters and stuffers — 5-HI/1372; Bundle tyer — MLN/2EE, MLN/2, MLN/2A. COMMUNICATIONS: Facsimile — Canon. WIRE SERVICES: News — AP; Stock tables — CT; Receiving dishes — AP. BUSINESS COMPUTERS: NCR; Applications: Adv billing, Accts receivable, Payroll, Circ, Gen ledger.

MARYSVILLE
Union County

'90 U.S. Census- 9,656; E&P '96 Est. 12,210

Marysville Journal-Tribune
(e-mon to fri; m-sat)

Marysville Journal-Tribune, 207 N. Main St.; PO Box 226, Marysville, OH 43040; tel (513) 644-9111; fax (513) 644-9211. Ohio League of Home Dailies group.
Circulation: 9,603(e); 9,603(m-sat); Sworn Sept. 27, 1995.
Price: 35¢(d); 35¢(sat); $84.00/yr.
Advertising: Open inch rate $6.80(e); $6.80(m-sat). **Representatives:** Papert Companies; US Suburban Press.
News Service: AP. **Politics:** Independent. **Established:** 1848.
Not Published: New Year; Memorial Day; Independence Day; Labor Day; Thanksgiving; Christmas.
Special Editions: 4-H Clubs (Mar); Football Opener, Back-to-School (Aug); Automative (Oct); Christmas Shopping Guide (Nov); Christmas Greetings (Dec); Honda Homecoming (Summer); Home Improvement (Spring).
Magazine: Countywide TV Guide.

CORPORATE OFFICERS

President Daniel E Behrens
Vice Pres Julie Behrens-LeRoy
Vice Pres Mary Behrens-Miller
Secretary D G Behrens

GENERAL MANAGEMENT

Publisher D G Behrens
Business Manager D E Behrens
Purchasing Agent D E Behrens

ADVERTISING

Manager Marie Woodford
Manager-Classified Janice Levan

CIRCULATION

Manager Terri Holloway

NEWS EXECUTIVES

Editor D E Behrens
Managing Editor Holly Zacharian

EDITORS AND MANAGERS

Editorial Page Editor Daniel E Behrens
Photo Editor Thomas Powell
Society Editor Judy Boehler
Sports Editor Tim Miller

PRODUCTION

Manager Donald Streng
Foreman-Composing Nancy Clark

Market Information: TMC.
Mechanical available: Offset; Black and 3 ROP colors; insert accepted — preprinted; page cut-offs — 22¾".
Mechanical specifications: Type page 13¼" x 21½"; E - 6 cols, 2 1/16", ⅛" between; A - 6 cols, 2 1/16", ⅛" between; C - 8 cols, 1½", ⅛" between.
Commodity consumption: Newsprint 240 short tons; widths 27½", 13¾"; black ink 6,300 pounds; color ink 60 pounds; average pages per issue 14(d).
Equipment: EDITORIAL: Front-end hardware — Mk; Front-end software — Mk. CLASSIFIED: Front-end hardware — Mk; Front-end software — Mk. DISPLAY: Front-end hardware — Ap/Mac Radius; Front-end software — Ap/Mac Radius. PRODUCTION: Production cameras — 1-B; Automatic film processors — 1-LE. PRESSROOM: Line 1 — 6-G, 1-G/Stacked; Folders — 1-G/Community; Press registration system — Duarte. MAILROOM: Bundle tyer — 1-Bu; Addressing machine — Add-Tac. LIBRARY: Electronic — BH. WIRE SERVICES: News — AP; Receiving dishes — AP. BUSINESS COMPUTERS: Burroughs; PCs & micros networked.

MASSILLON
Stark County

'90 U.S. Census- 31,007; E&P '96 Est. 31,400
ABC-CZ (90): 31,007 (HH 12,110)

The Independent
(e-mon to fri; m-sat)

The Independent, 50 North Ave. N.W.; PO Box 809, Massillon, OH 44648-0809; tel (216) 833-2631; fax (216) 833-2635. Goodson Newspaper group.
Circulation: 15,260(e); 15,942(m-sat); ABC Sept. 30, 1995.
Price: 35¢(d); 75¢(sat); $2.00/wk (carrier); $8.67/mo (carrier); $104.00/yr (carrier).
Advertising: Open inch rate $17.05(e); $17.05(m-sat). **Representative:** Landon Associates Inc.
News Service: AP. **Politics:** Independent. **Established:** 1863.
Not Published: New Year; Christmas.
Advertising not accepted: Publisher reserves the right to reject or revise any advertisement we deem objectionable.
Special Editions: January Clearance, Tax Tab (Jan); Valentine, President's Day (Feb); Progress Edition (Mar); Holy Week & Easter Church Guide (Apr); Mother's Day, Health & Fitness, Great Outdoors (May); Father's Day, Half Price Sale (June); North-South, Hall of Fame (July); Football Contest, The Football Preview (Aug); Football Contest, Strike Up the Bands (Sept); Golden Years, Football Contest (Oct); Letters to Santa, Election, Christmas Countdown (Nov); Letters to Santa, Gift Ideas, Christmas Greetings, Christmas Church Guide, Basketball (Dec).
Special Weekly Sections: Best Food Days, Best Automotive Day (mon); Business & Industry (tues); Bridal Directory (wed); Best Automotive Day (thur); Church News, Total Market Coverage (sat).
Magazine: TV Times (entertainment tab) (sat).

CORPORATE OFFICER

Vice Pres David Carr

GENERAL MANAGEMENT

Publisher Jack D Shores
Business Manager Mark Schott

ADVERTISING

Director Richard M Duncovich
Manager-National Elaine M Johnson
Manager-Co-op Elaine M Johnson
Manager-Classified William Hamilton

CIRCULATION

Director Mike Gorsich

NEWS EXECUTIVES

Editor James E Davis
Managing Editor Kevin D Coffey

EDITORS AND MANAGERS

Editorial Page Editor Kevin D Coffey
Living/Society Editor Peggy Dottavio
Radio/Television Editor David Crookston
Religion Editor Chris Beers
Sports Editor Joe Shaheen
Suburban Editor Teresa Melcher

PRODUCTION

Superintendent William Matthews
Superintendent-Photo Comp Mark Judy
Foreman-Pressroom Rick Wineman

Market Information: Zoned editions; Split Run; TMC.
Mechanical available: Offset; Black and 3 ROP colors; insert accepted — preprinted, broadsheet preprints less than 13x21¼; tabloids less than 9¼x13; page cut-offs — 22¾".
Mechanical specifications: Type page 13" x 21½"; E - 6 cols, 2 1/16", ⅛" between; A - 6 cols, 2 1/16", ⅛" between; C - 9 cols, 1 5/16", ⅛" between.
Commodity consumption: Newsprint 1,543 short tons; widths 27", 13½"; black ink 38,960 pounds; color ink 5,714 pounds; single pages printed 7,700; average pages per issue 28(d), 40(sat); single plates used 10,160.
Equipment: EDITORIAL: Front-end hardware — Mk, 15-Mk/4003; Printers — HP/LaserJet III; Other equipment — Ap/Mac II fx, Radius/Color Display 121. CLASSIFIED: Front-end hardware — Mk, 3-Mk/4010; Printers — TI; Other equipment — 1-Mk/88LP, 1-Mk/150LP. DISPLAY: Adv layout systems — Multi-Ad/Creator, QuarkXPress, AP AdSend; Printers — 2-Design Express/6, 2-Ap/Power Mac 7500, 2-Ap/Multi Scan 20. PRODUCTION: OCR software — Wordscan 3.0; Typesetters — 2-M/202, 2-AD, COM, 2-Mk, Mk/4003; Plate exposures — 1-BKY/1601-40, 2-Nu/631; Plate processors — 1-C/A250; Scanners — 1-HP/ScanJet 3C; Production cameras — 1-R/500, 1-Co; Automatic film processors — 1-P/SQ; Color separation equipment (conventional) — Lf/AP Leaf Picture Desk. PRESSROOM: Line 1 — 10-G/Community single width; Folders — 2-G. MAILROOM: Counter stackers — 2-Id/2000; Bundle tyer — 1-Bu, 1-Polychem/PC500, 2-MLN/MLN-24; Addressing machine — Ch. WIRE SERVICES: News — AP, SHNS; Photos — AP, SHNS; Stock tables — AP; Syndicates — United Media, Creators, SHNS, Universal Press, King Features, TMS, LATS, Business Wire, PR Newswire, NAS, WPW; Receiving dishes — size-10ft, AP, SHNS. BUSINESS COMPUTERS: 3-IBM/Aptivas, IBM/RS6000; Applications: Circ, Billing, Accts receivable, Adv, Payroll, Accts payable, Gen ledger; PCs & main system networked.

MEDINA
Medina County

'90 U.S. Census- 19,231; E&P '96 Est. 23,580
ABC-CZ (90): 56,653 (HH 19,146)

The Medina County Gazette
(m-mon to sat)

The Medina County Gazette, 885 W. Liberty, Medina, OH 44256; tel (216) 725-4166; fax (216) 725-4299; e-mail ghundnutt@ohio.net; web site http://www.ohio.net/gazette.html. Loraine County Printing & Publishing Corp. group.
Circulation: 16,263(m); 16,263(m-sat); ABC Sept. 30, 1995.
Price: 35¢(d); 35¢(sat).
Advertising: Open inch rate $15.18(m); $15.18(m-sat). **Representative:** Papert Companies.
News Service: AP. **Politics:** Independent. **Established:** 1832.
Not Published: Christmas.
Special Editions: Year in Pictures, Brides Tab (Jan); Your Heart's Desire (Feb); Fitness Tab (Mar); Welcome Spring, Golf (Apr); "Wheels" Tab (May); Your Lucky Day (June); Sizzlin' Summer Bargain Days (July); H.S. Football (Aug); International Literacy Bay Tab (Sept); Car Care (Oct); H.S. Basketball, Christmas Kick-off (Nov); Christmas Gift Tab (Dec).
Special Weekly Sections: Best Food (mon); Best Food (tues); Cover Story (wed); Accents, TV Magazine (fri); Accents, Church/Religious Pages (sat); Stock Market (daily).
Magazines: Gazette TV Week (complete local & cable listing); Accent-featuring, Photo Page (mon); Food (tues); Pastimes, Cover Story (wed); Entertainment (thur); Travel (fri); Miscellaneous (sat).

CORPORATE OFFICER

President Arthur D Hudnutt

GENERAL MANAGEMENT

Publisher George D Hudnutt

ADVERTISING

Director-Sales Dennis Holsinger
Director-Sales Kristina High

CIRCULATION

Manager Wayne Workman

NEWS EXECUTIVES

Editor-City M K Blakely
Managing Editor Liz Sheaffer
Assoc Editor Betty Szudlo

MANAGEMENT INFORMATION SERVICES

Data Processing Manager Russel Kunkler
Online Manager Larry Norton

PRODUCTION

Superintendent Shirley Wellman

Market Information: Zoned editions; Split Run; TMC; ADS; Operate database; Electronic edition.
Mechanical available: Offset; Black and 3 ROP colors; insert accepted — preprinted, any; page cut-offs — 22¾".
Mechanical specifications: Type page 13" x 21½"; E - 6 cols, 2 1/16", ⅛" between; A - 6 cols, 2 1/16", ⅛" between; C - 9 cols, 1⅜", 1/16" between.
Commodity consumption: Newsprint 1,075 short tons; 998 metric tons; widths 27½", 13¾"; black ink 12,350 pounds; color ink 6,175 pounds; single pages printed 9,180; average pages per issue 30(d).

Equipment: EDITORIAL: Front-end hardware — IBM/Compatibles; Front-end software — CText; Other equipment — IBM/Compatibles. CLASSIFIED: Front-end hardware — IBM/Compatibles. DISPLAY: Adv layout systems — 2-CText/Adept. PRODUCTION: Typesetters — XIT/Clipper, XIT/Page Scan; Plate exposures — 2-Nu; Scanners — 1-Microtek/MS-300A Image Scanner; Production cameras — 1-LE/R500; Automatic film processors — 1-LE/LD-18; Color separation equipment (conventional) — Nikon/Scanner.
PRESSROOM: Line 1 — 8-G/Community; Folders — 1-G. MAILROOM: Counter stackers — HL/Stackpack, HL/Monitor; Inserters and stuffers — HI/NP-848; Bundle tyer — 1-Bu, 1-Sa, MLN; Addressing machine — 1-Am/6341, 1-Ch. WIRE SERVICES: News — Stock tables — AP; Receiving dishes — size-6ft, AP. BUSINESS COMPUTERS: 1-HP; Applications: Adv billing, Accts receivable, Gen ledger, Payroll; PCs & micros networked.

MIDDLEPORT

See POMEROY

MIDDLETOWN

Butler County

'90 U.S. Census- 46,022; E&P '96 Est. 48,108
ABC-CZ (90): 62,043 (HH 24,088)

Middletown Journal

(e-mon to fri; m-sat; S)

Middletown Journal, 52 S. Broad St.; PO Box 490, Middletown, OH 45044; tel (513) 422-3611; fax (513) 422-8698. Thomson Newspapers group.
Circulation: 22,550(e); 22,550(m-sat); 23,880(S); ABC Sept. 30, 1995.
Price: 50¢(d); 50¢(sat); $1.25(S); $2.50/wk; $130.00/yr.
Advertising: Open inch rate $37.02(e); $37.02(m-sat); $37.02(S). **Representatives:** Thomson Newspapers; Landon Associates Inc.
News Service: AP. **Politics:** Independent. **Established:** 1857.
Note: Now printed and mailed by Butler County Printing Company. The Middletown Journal (eS) has a combination rate of $36.32 with the Hamilton Journal News (eS).
Not Published: Independence Day.
Special Editions: Bridal (Jan); Progress (Feb); Tax Guide, Spring Car Tab, Builders (Mar); Health, Home Improvement (Apr); Graduation, Outdoor Living (May); Health & Fitness (July); Football, Back-to-School (Aug); Home Improvement (Sept); Fall Car Care, Election Guide (Oct); Christmas Gift Guide, Holiday Entertaining (Nov).
Special Weekly Sections: Food Day (mon); Seniors Page (tues); Youth Page (wed); Entertainment Pages (thur); Workplace Page, Garden Page (fri); Religion Page (sat).
Magazines: Parade, TV Journal (S).

GENERAL MANAGEMENT
Publisher/General Manager Carl E Esposito
Group Controller Pamela Keller

ADVERTISING
Director Barbara Staples
Manager-Classified Rita Bowman
Manager-Retail Terri Dearth

CIRCULATION
Manager Bill Stutler

NEWS EXECUTIVES
Managing Editor Jim Mills
Asst Managing Editor Mike Williams

EDITORS AND MANAGERS
Business Editor John Carter
City Editor Mike Shearer
News Editor Frank Schaeffer
Sports Editor Mark Berry

PRODUCTION
Foreman-Composing Max Bernard

Market Information: TMC.
Mechanical available: Offset; Black and 3 ROP colors; insert accepted — preprinted; page cut-offs — 22¾".
Mechanical specifications: Type page 13" x 21½"; E - 6 cols, 2¹⁄₁₆", ⅛" between; A - 6 cols, 2¹⁄₁₆", ⅛" between; C - 10 cols, 1³⁄₁₆", ⅛" between.
Commodity consumption: average pages per issue 28(d), 44(S).
Equipment: EDITORIAL: Front-end hardware — 24-CText, 3-Ventura, Ap/Mac IIci; Front-end software — XYQUEST/XyWrite, QuarkXPress; Printers — Tegra/Varityper 6990. CLASSIFIED: Front-end hardware — 6-CText; Front-end software — XYQUEST/XyWrite. DISPLAY: Other equipment — Ap/Mac Quadra 660AV. PRODUCTION: Typesetters — 2-Tegra/Varityper; Production cameras — 1-B/500LB; Automatic film processors — 1-DP/24L. COMMUNICATIONS: Digital ad delivery system — Ap AdSend. WIRE SERVICES: News — AP; Syndicates — AP Datafeatures; Receiving dishes — size-3m, AP. BUSINESS COMPUTERS: HP/9000 Model G30; Applications: Oracle: Financial; PBS: Adv, Circ; PCs & main system networked.

MOUNT VERNON

Knox County

'90 U.S. Census- 14,550; E&P '96 Est. 14,748
ABC-CZ (90): 14,550 (HH 5,942)

Mount Vernon News

(e-mon to fri; m-sat)

Mount Vernon News, 18 E. Vine St.; PO Box 791, Mount Vernon, OH 43050; tel (614) 397-5333; fax (614) 397-1321.
Circulation: 10,517(e); 10,517(m-sat); ABC Sept. 30, 1995.
Price: 50¢(d); 50¢(sat); $5.65/mo; $58.70/yr.
Advertising: Open inch rate $8.77(e); $8.77(m-sat).
News Service: AP. **Politics:** Independent. **Established:** 1838.
Not Published: Christmas.
Advertising not accepted: Vending machine; Mail order; Fortune telling; Adult entertainment.
Special Editions: Spring & Fall Auto Care; Looking Glass-Reflections of Knox County; Fredricktown Tomato Show; Tax Planning Guide; Ohio Jr Miss; Home; Lawn & Garden; Real Estate Tab; Wedding Tab; Fall Sports; Travel/Tourism; Health & Fitness; County Fair; Christmas Parade Tab; Dan Emmett Festival.
Magazine: TV tab.

CORPORATE OFFICERS
Vice Pres Andrew G Weber
Vice Pres Michele L Weber

GENERAL MANAGEMENT
Publisher Kay H Culbertson
Asst Publisher Elizabeth Lutwick

ADVERTISING
Director John Nesbit
Manager-Classified Cathy Doup

CIRCULATION
Manager Dennis Meekins

NEWS EXECUTIVE
Managing Editor Bob Nitzel

EDITORS AND MANAGERS
City Editor Samantha Scoles
Editorial Page Editor Bob Nitzel
Lifestyle Editor Shelly Becker
Sports Editor Tom Wilson

MANAGEMENT INFORMATION SERVICES
Data Processing Manager John Nesbit

PRODUCTION
Manager Thomas N Knouff

Market Information: TMC; ADS; Operate audiotex.
Mechanical available: Offset; Black and 3 ROP colors; insert accepted — preprinted; page cut-offs — 22¾".
Mechanical specifications: Type page 13" x 21½"; E - 6 cols, 2¹⁄₁₆", ⅛" between; A - 6 cols, 2¹⁄₁₆", ⅛" between; C - 8 cols, 1⁹⁄₁₆", ¹⁄₁₆" between.
Commodity consumption: Newsprint 490 short tons; width 27½"; black ink 19,925 pounds; color ink 2,300 pounds; single pages printed 5,598; average pages per issue 18(d); single plates used 6,220.
Equipment: EDITORIAL: Front-end hardware — 11-Ap/Mac Quadra 605; Front-end software — QuarkXPress 3.3; Printers — 1-XIT/Clipper. CLASSIFIED: Front-end hardware — 4-Ap/Mac Quadra 605; Printers — 1-Ap/Mac LaserWriter. AUDIOTEX: Supplier name — Sprint/United. DISPLAY: Adv layout systems — 7-Ap/Mac; Printers — 3-Ap/Mac LaserWriter. PRODUCTION: OCR software — Caere/OmniPage Direct; Plate exposures — 1-BKY/Ascor Adalux, 1-Nu/Flip Top FT40LNS; Plate processors — 2-Nat/A-250; Electronic picture desk — Lf/AP Leaf Picture Desk; Scanners — Umax/UC 1200 SE, Nikon/Coolscan; Production cameras — 1-B, 1-R; Automatic film processors — 1-LE, 2-COM/1416-1417; Color separation equipment (conventional) — Adobe/Photoshop 2.0.1, Ap/Mac Quadra AV.
PRESSROOM: Line 1 — 5-G/Urbanite; Folders — 1-G. MAILROOM: Counter stackers — 1-HI/RS-25; Inserters and stuffers — 4-KAN/480; Bundle tyer — 2-Bu, 1-Ca; Addressing machine — 1-Ch, 2-Am. COMMUNICATIONS: Facsimile — Toshiba. WIRE SERVICES: News — AP; Photos — AP Photostream; Receiving dishes — size-2½ft, AP. BUSINESS COMPUTERS: Basic IV/MHI; Applications: Circ, Payroll, Inventory, Accts payable, Accts receivable; PCs & micros networked; PCs & main system networked.

NAPOLEON

Henry County

'90 U.S. Census- 8,884; E&P '96 Est. 9,123

Northwest Signal

(e-mon to fri)

Northwest Signal, 595 E. Riverview Ave.; PO Box 567, Napoleon, OH 43545; tel (419) 592-5055; fax (419) 592-9778.
Circulation: 5,658(e); Sworn Sept. 30, 1995.
Price: 40¢(d); $6.50/mo.
Advertising: Open inch rate $9.00(e). **Representative:** Papert Companies.
News Service: AP. **Politics:** Independent. **Established:** 1852.
Not Published: New Year; Memorial Day; Independence Day; Labor Day; Thanksgiving; Christmas.
Special Editions: First Baby (Jan); Bride/Groom (Feb); Automotive, Home Improvement (Mar); Community Salute (July); Pigskin Preview (Aug); Christmas (Nov); Greetings (Dec).
Special Weekly Sections: Health & Medicine (tues); Business (wed); Farm, Education (thur); Church Weekender (fri).

CORPORATE OFFICERS
President James K Kuser
Vice Pres Jamie K Kuser
Secretary/Treasurer Helen L Kuser

GENERAL MANAGEMENT
Publisher James K Kuser
General Manager Jamie K Kuser
Manager-Credit Irma Follett

ADVERTISING
Director Jim Hull
Manager-Classified Cecilia Vicars
Manager-National Jim Hull
Manager-Legal Peg Woods

MARKETING AND PROMOTION
Manager-Promotion Shonda Okuley

CIRCULATION
Manager John L Kuser

NEWS EXECUTIVES
Editor Jamie K Kuser
Asst Editor Paul A Miller

EDITORS AND MANAGERS
Amusements Editor Brian Koeller
City Editor James K Kuser Jr
Farm Editor Paul Miller
Librarian Irma Follett
Photo Department Manager Melanie Garza
Sports Editor Moe Brubaker

PRODUCTION
Superintendent Jamie K Kuser
Foreman-Mailroom John L Kuser

Market Information: TMC.
Mechanical available: Offset; Black and 3 ROP colors; insert accepted — preprinted, card; page cut-offs — 21½".
Mechanical specifications: Type page 13" x 21½"; E - 6 cols, 2¹⁄₁₆", ⅛" between; A - 6 cols, 2¹⁄₁₆", ⅛" between; C - 6 cols, 2¹⁄₁₆", ⅛" between.
Commodity consumption: Newsprint 150 metric tons; width 28"; single pages printed 3,500; average pages per issue 12(d); single plates used 3,500.
Equipment: EDITORIAL: Front-end hardware — Ap/Mac; Front-end software — Microsoft/Word, Baseview/NewsEdit; Printers — Ap/Mac IIg; Other equipment — 1-Ap/Mac LaserWriter. CLASSIFIED: Front-end hardware — Ap/Mac; Front-end software — Baseview/Class Manager, QuarkXPress. DISPLAY: Adv layout systems — Mk. PRODUCTION: Pagination software — Aldus/PageMaker 5.0; OCR software — Caere/OmniPage; Typesetters — Xante/8200; Scanners — Epson/800; Production cameras — 1-Nu. MAILROOM: Bundle tyer — 1-MLN, 1-Brainard; Addressing machine — 1-Am. LIBRARY: Electronic — 1-Am/2480, 1-DM/340, 1-Am/AL-10. COMMUNICATIONS: Facsimile — RSK/Tandy fax. WIRE SERVICES: News — AP; Receiving dishes — size-1m, AP. BUSINESS COMPUTERS: 1-CDS/PC-XT.

NEW PHILADELPHIA

See DOVER

NEWARK

Licking County

'90 U.S. Census- 44,389; E&P '96 Est. 47,348
ABC-NDM (90): 55,973 (HH 21,636)

The Advocate

(e-mon to fri; m-sat; S)

The Advocate, 22 N. First St., Newark, OH 43055; tel (614) 345-4053; fax (614) 345-1634; e-mail 573.2418@mcimail.com. Thomson Newspapers group.
Circulation: 22,245(e); 22,245(m-sat); 22,559(S); ABC Sept. 30, 1995.
Price: 35¢(d); 35¢(sat); $1.00(S); $2.40/wk; $124.00/yr.
Advertising: Open inch rate $18.38(e); $18.38(m-sat); $18.38(S). **Representative:** Landon Associates Inc.
News Services: AP, THO. **Politics:** Independent. **Established:** 1820.
Special Editions: Tax Guide, Bridal Guide (Jan); Annual Progress (Mar); Car Care, Lawn & Garden (Apr); Summer Recipe Contest (May); Medical, Mature Years (July); Football (Aug); Fall Home Improvement (Sept); Fall Car Care (Oct); Basketball, Various Christmas Sections (Nov); Various Christmas Sections (Dec); Crossroads, Auto, Business, Maturity, Health & Fitness (monthly).
Special Weekly Sections: Best Food Days (mon,wed); Agriculture, Entertainment (thur); Church News (sat); Stocks, Outdoors, Food (S).
Magazines: Real Estate Magazine (sat); USA Weekend, Color Comics, TV Update (S).

GENERAL MANAGEMENT
Publisher/General Manager Mark D Richmond
Manager-Credit Gail Betz

ADVERTISING
Director Ronald L Frailly
Manager-Classified Rami Piar
Manager-Retail Steve Bash

CIRCULATION
Director Gina Miller

NEWS EXECUTIVE
Editor Jeri Kornegay

EDITORS AND MANAGERS
Automotive Editor Randy Gammage
Business Editor Mark Shaw
Editor Jeri Kornegay
Entertainment/Amusements Editor Joe Williams
Food Editor Amy Halblaub
News Editor Brian Goth
Photo Editor Flint Carlton
Sports Editor John Barns

PRODUCTION
Manager Ken Shelby

Market Information: TMC.
Mechanical available: Offset; Black and 3 ROP colors; insert accepted — preprinted; page cut-offs — 22¾".
Mechanical specifications: Type page 13" x 21½"; E - 6 cols, 2¹⁄₁₆", ⅛" between; A - 6 cols, 2¹⁄₁₆", ⅛" between; C - 9 cols, 1⅜", ¹⁄₁₆" between.
Commodity consumption: Newsprint 4,510 short tons; widths 27¼", 13⅝"; black ink 165,000 pounds; color ink 44,800 pounds; single pages printed 38,690; average pages per issue 24(d), 36(S); single plates used 73,500.
Equipment: EDITORIAL: Front-end hardware — 17-Cx. CLASSIFIED: Front-end hardware — 4-Cx. DISPLAY: Front-end hardware — HP; Front-end software — PBS. PRODUCTION: Typesetters — 2-Tegra/XP-1000, 2-Tegra/Varityper/XP 1000; Plate exposures — 3-Nu/Flip Top 404611PNS; Plate processors — 3-Nat/A-250; Electronic picture desk — Lf/AP Leaf Picture Desk; Scanners — Lf/Leafscan 35; Production cameras — SCREEN/260 Horizontal; Automatic film processors — 1-LE/LD-24, SCREEN/281Q; Color separation equipment (conventional) — ECR/Autokon.
PRESSROOM: Line 1 — 10-G/Urbanite (2-stacked units); Line 2 — 16-G/Urbanite (8-stacked units); Press drives — Fin, Allen Bradley; Folders — G/2:1; Pasters — Jardis;

Reels and stands — 8-G/Urbanite; Press control system — Fin, Allen Bradley; Press registration system — Carlson. MAILROOM: Counter stackers — 3-Id/2000; Inserters and stuffers — 2-GMA/SLS 1000; Bundle tyer — 2-Dynaric, 2-Bu; Addressing machine — 2-Ch/596; Mailroom control system — 1-Id. 2-GMA/PMS1; Other mailroom equipment — MM. COMMUNICATIONS: Facsimile — 1-Konica; Systems used — fiber optic. WIRE SERVICES: News — AP, THO; Photos — AP; Stock tables — AP; Receiving dishes — size-3m, AP. BUSINESS COMPUTERS: PBS, Oracale; Applications: Oracle: Finance; PBS: Circ, Adv.

NORWALK

Huron County

'90 U.S. Census- 14,731; E&P '96 Est. 15,060
ABC-CZ (90): 14,731 (HH 5,663)

Norwalk Reflector

(e-mon to sat)

Norwalk Reflector, 61 E. Monroe St., Norwalk, OH 44857; tel (419) 668-3771; fax (419) 668-2424; e-mail JRBPUB@aol.com. Sandusky-Norwalk Newspapers group.
Circulation: 9,172(e); 9,172(e-sat); ABC Sept. 30, 1995.
Price: 35¢(d); 35¢(sat); $1.75/wk; $91.00/yr.
Advertising: Open inch rate $9.84(e); $12.49(e-mon); $9.84(e-sat). **Representatives:** Landon Associates Inc.; The Newspaper National Network.
News Service: AP. **Politics:** Independent. **Established:** 1830.
Not Published: New Year; Memorial Day; Independence Day; Labor Day; Thanksgiving; Christmas.
Advertising not accepted: Fortune telling.
Special Editions: Car Care, Home and Garden (Apr); Firelands Factbook (June); Car Care (Oct); Christmas Gift Guide (Nov).
Magazine: TV Week (fri).

CORPORATE OFFICERS

President/Chairman of the Board	David A Rau
Secretary/Treasurer	Alice W Rau

GENERAL MANAGEMENT

Publisher	James R Brown

ADVERTISING

Manager	John Ringenberg
Manager-Classified	Anne Roderick

CIRCULATION

Manager	Steven Bovia

NEWS EXECUTIVES

Editor	James R Brown
Managing Editor	Jay Thwaite

EDITORS AND MANAGERS

News Editor	Jeff Merritt
Sports Editor	Joe Centers

MANAGEMENT INFORMATION SERVICES

Data Processing Manager	Carol McLaughlin

PRODUCTION

Manager-Systems	John Eiden
Manager-Systems	Carol McLaughlin
Foreman-Pressroom	Ken LaRoche

Market Information: TMC.
Mechanical available: Offset; Black and 2 ROP colors; insert accepted — preprinted; page cut-offs — 21 3/4".
Mechanical specifications: Type page 13" x 21 1/2"; E - 6 cols, 2 1/16", 1/8" between; A - 6 cols, 2 1/16", 1/8" between; C - 9 cols, 1 9/16", 1/16" between.
Commodity consumption: Newsprint 435 short tons; widths 27 1/2", 13 3/4", 17", 34"; black ink 9,000 pounds; single pages printed 4,262; average pages per issue 13.8(d); single plates used 3,000.
Equipment: EDITORIAL: Front-end hardware — Ap/Mac; Front-end software — Baseview/NewsEdit, QuarkXPress 3.3; Printers — Ap/Mac LaserWriter II NTX, Xante/8200; Other equipment — Lf/AP Leaf Picture Desk, Lf/Leafscan 35, Kk/2035 Negative Scanner. CLASSIFIED: Front-end hardware — Ap/Mac SE 30; Front-end software — Baseview/Class Manager; Printers — Ap/Mac PowerWriter II NTX, Xante/8200. DISPLAY: Front-end hardware — Ap/Power Mac PC 8100, CD, Ap/Mac IIfx; Front-end software — Multi-Ad/Creator; Printers — Ap/Mac LaserWriter II NTX, Xante/8200; Other equipment — Microtek/Scanner. PRODUCTION: Pagination software — QuarkXPress 3.3; OCR software — Caere/OmniPage 2; Typesetters — Ap/Mac, 2-Xante/8200, 2-Ap/Mac LaserWriter IINTX; Plate exposures — 1-Nu/Flip Top FT40; Plate processors — 1-Nat/A-250; Scanners — Microtek/Scanner; Production cameras — 1-DAI; Automatic film processors — P/26RT.
PRESSROOM: Line 1 — 4-G/Community single width; Line 2 — 1-G/Community single width; Press drives — Emerson/DC; Folders — 1-G/941 Community; Press control system — Fin. MAILROOM: Inserters and stuffers — 8-MM; Bundle tyer — Bu/TS-21, Akebono/TS 250 APP. WIRE SERVICES: News — AP; Photos — AP Photostream; Receiving dishes — AP. BUSINESS COMPUTERS: Unisys/S280; Applications: Vision Data: Circ, Adv, Payroll, Accts payable, Gen ledger; PCs & main system networked.

PIQUA

Miami County

'90 U.S. Census- 20,612; E&P '96 Est. 20,726
ABC-CZ (90): 22,595 (HH 8,426)

Piqua Daily Call

(e-mon to fri; m-sat)

Piqua Daily Call, 310 Spring St.; PO Box 921, Piqua, OH 45356; tel (513) 773-2721; fax (513) 773-2782. Thomson Newspapers group.
Circulation: 8,961(e); 8,961(m-sat); ABC Sept. 30, 1995.
Price: 50¢(d); 75¢(sat); $2.10/wk; $8.40/mo; $109.20/yr (mail), $135.00/yr (out of county), $118.00/yr (in county).
Advertising: Open inch rate $11.11(e); $11.11(m-sat). **Representatives:** Thomson Newspapers; Landon Associates Inc.
News Service: AP. **Politics:** Independent. **Established:** 1883.
Not Published: Independence Day; Christmas.
Special Editions: Bridal; Tax; Spring; Home Improvement; Car Care; Progress; Newcomers; Back-to-School; Heritage Festival; Football; County Fair; Cookbook; Basketball; Christmas.
Special Weekly Sections: Best Food Day (mon); Farm Page, Senior Page (tues); Health Page (wed); TV Week, Business Page (sat).
Magazine: Television (weekly).

GENERAL MANAGEMENT

General Manager/Publisher	Vicky Rifenberg
Accountant	Carol Devers

ADVERTISING

Director	Sandy Klipsteine

CIRCULATION

Manager	Brian Szwajkos

NEWS EXECUTIVE

Managing Editor	Greg Floyd

EDITORS AND MANAGERS

City Editor	Gloria McCoy
News Editor	Gloria McCoy
Sports Editor	John Barton

PRODUCTION

Manager	Tom Brown

Market Information: TMC.
Mechanical available: Web Offset; Black and 3 ROP colors; insert accepted — preprinted; page cut-offs — 22 3/4".
Mechanical specifications: Type page 13" x 21 1/2"; E - 6 cols, 2 1/16", 1/8" between; A - 6 cols, 2 1/16", 1/8" between; C - 9 cols, 1 3/8", 1/16" between.
Commodity consumption: widths 27", 13 1/2", 34"; average pages per issue 16(d).
Equipment: EDITORIAL: Front-end hardware — 11-Mk; Other equipment — Ap/Mac, Ap/Super Mac, Lf/Color Photo. CLASSIFIED: Front-end hardware — 2-Mk; Printers — 1-TI/Omni 800. DISPLAY: Adv layout systems — Ap/Mac; Front-end hardware — 2-Ap/Mac IIfx, 1-Ap/Mac IIsi, 1-Ap/Mac IIci; Front-end software — QuarkXPress, Aldus, Adobe/Photoshop, Aldus/Freehand; Printers — Ap/Mac Laser-Writer II; Other equipment — Ap/Mac One Scanner, CD/SC Plus. PRODUCTION: Typesetters — 2-V/5100, 1-V/4900; Plate exposures — 1-Nu/Flip Top FT40UP; Plate processors — 1-Nat/A-250; Production cameras — 1-DAI/Screen C/680-C; Automatic film processors — 1-AG, 1-LE/LD 220; Digital color separation equipment — 1-Lf/Leafscan 35. PRESSROOM: Line 1 — 5-G/Urbanite; Folders — 1-G. MAILROOM: Bundle tyer — OVL/415A; Addressing machine — SC/100. WIRE SERVICES: News — AP, THO; Syndicates — NYT, CNS, THO, Universal Press, United Media, King Features, Creators; Receiving dishes — size-8ft, AP. BUSINESS COMPUTERS: 1-ATT/3B2; Applications: Unix.

Ohio I-319

POMEROY-MIDDLEPORT

Meigs County

'90 U.S. Census- 4,984 (Pomeroy 2,259; Middleport 2,725); E&P '96 Est. 4,455 (Pomeroy 1,924; Middleport 2,531)

The Daily Sentinel

(e-mon to fri)

Sunday Times-Sentinel (S)

The Daily Sentinel/Sunday Times-Sentinel, 111 Court St.; PO Box 729, Pomeroy, OH 45769; tel (614) 992-2155; fax (614) 992-2157. Gannett Co. Inc. group.
Circulation: 5,050(e); 12,270(S); Sworn Sept. 29, 1995.
Price: 35¢(d); $1.00(S); $2.00/wk; $8.70/mo; $104.00/yr.
Advertising: Open inch rate $5.00(e); $7.55(S). **Representative:** Landon Associates Inc.
News Service: AP. **Politics:** Independent. **Established:** 1948.
Note: The Gallipolis Daily Tribune and Pomeroy Daily Sentinel share their Sunday edition called Sunday Times-Sentinel. The Daily Sentinel has a combination rate of $11.80 with Gallipolis Daily Tribune (eS) & Point Pleasant (WV) Register (e).
Not Published: New Year; Memorial Day; Labor Day; Thanksgiving; Christmas.
Special Editions: Fair; Progress; Hospital; Car Care; Football; Hunting; Health Care; Retirement Planning; Christmas Greetings.
Special Weekly Sections: Best Food Day (wed); Church Page, TV Times (fri); Best Food Day, Business Page, Farm Page (S).
Magazine: TV Guide.

GENERAL MANAGEMENT

Publisher	Robert L Wingett
Controller	Margaret Lehew
General Manager	Charlene Hoeflich
Purchasing Agent	Robert L Wingett

ADVERTISING

Manager	Larry L Boyer
Manager-Classified	Margaret Lehew

CIRCULATION

Manager	Paul Barker

NEWS EXECUTIVE

News Editor	Charlene Hoeflich

PRODUCTION

Foreman-Composing	Fred Hoffman
Foreman-Pressroom	Don Coleman

Market Information: TMC.
Mechanical available: Offset; Black and 3 ROP colors; insert accepted — preprinted; page cut-offs — 21 1/4".
Mechanical specifications: Type page 13" x 21 1/4"; E - 6 cols, 2 1/16", 1/8" between; A - 6 cols, 2 1/16", 1/8" between; C - 8 cols, 1 1/2", 1/8" between.
Commodity consumption: Newsprint 185 short tons; average pages per issue 14(d), 36(S).
Equipment: EDITORIAL: Front-end hardware — Ap/Mac; Front-end software — Baseview; Printers — Ap/Mac LaserWriter. CLASSIFIED: Front-end hardware — Ap/Mac; Front-end software — Baseview. PRODUCTION: Typesetters — Mk/Ad Typesetting. WIRE SERVICES: News — AP; Syndicates — TMS, NAS.

PORT CLINTON

Ottawa County

'90 U.S. Census- 7,106; E&P '96 Est. 7,007
ABC-NDM (90): 28,820 (HH 11,215)

News-Herald (e-mon to sat)

News-Herald, 115 W. Second St.; PO Box 550, Port Clinton, OH 43452; tel (419) 734-3141; fax (419) 734-4662. Gannett Co. Inc. group.
Circulation: 6,203(e); 6,203(e-sat); ABC Sept. 30, 1995.
Price: 35¢(d); 35¢(sat); $2.00/wk; $8.00/mo; $104.00/yr.
Advertising: Open inch rate $11.60(e); $11.60(e-sat); comb with Fremont News-Messenger (e) $26.15. **Representative:** Gannett National Newspaper Sales.
News Service: AP. **Established:** 1865 (News), 1887 (Herald).
Note: Printed under contract by the Fremont News-Messenger. For production information, see Fremont listing.
Special Editions: Showcase (Jan); County Fair (July); Football (Aug).
Special Weekly Sections: Best Food Day (mon); Outdoor (wed); Entertainment (thur); Religion (sat).
Magazines: USA Weekend; TV Weekly.

CORPORATE OFFICERS

President	James F Daubel
Secretary	Thomas L Chapple
Treasurer	Jimmy L Thomas

GENERAL MANAGEMENT

General Manager	David Barth
Manager-Office	Darleen Rohde

ADVERTISING

Director	David Barth

CIRCULATION

Manager	Dave Overmyer

NEWS EXECUTIVE

Exec Editor	John Dye

EDITOR AND MANAGER

News Editor	Julie Holman

Market Information: Split Run; TMC.
Mechanical available: Offset; Black and 3 ROP colors; insert accepted — preprinted; page cut-offs — 22 3/4".
Mechanical specifications: Type page 13" x 21 1/2"; E - 6 cols, 2 1/16", 1/8" between; A - 6 cols, 2 1/16", 1/8" between; C - 9 cols, 1 3/8", 1/16" between.
Commodity consumption: average pages per issue 12(d).
Equipment: EDITORIAL: Front-end hardware — Ap/Mac; Front-end software — Baseview, QuarkXPress. CLASSIFIED: Front-end hardware — Ap/Mac; Front-end software — Baseview/Class Manager. WIRE SERVICES: News — AP, GNS. BUSINESS COMPUTERS: IBM/PC II.

PORTSMOUTH

Scioto County

'90 U.S. Census- 22,676; E&P '96 Est. 20,220
ABC-CZ (90): 37,805 (HH 15,555)

The Portsmouth Daily Times (e-mon to fri; m-sat; S)

The Portsmouth Daily Times, 637 Sixth St.; PO Box 581, Portsmouth, OH 45662; tel (614) 353-3101; fax (614) 353-7280. Hollinger International Inc. group.
Circulation: 16,924(e); 16,924(m-sat); 16,374(S); ABC Sept. 30, 1995.
Price: 35¢(d); 35¢(sat); $1.00(S); $2.40/wk (motor route); $9.60/mo (motor route); $124.80/yr (motor route).
Advertising: Open inch rate $17.03(e); $17.03(m-sat); $17.03(S).
News Service: AP. **Politics:** Independent. **Established:** 1852.
Not Published: Christmas.
Special Editions: Bridal (Jan); Car Care, Progress (Mar); Bridal, Home & Garden (June); Back-to-School, River Days, Football (Aug); Car Care (Oct); Basketball, Christmas Preview (Nov).
Special Weekly Sections: Education (mon); Entertainment (thur); Religion (sat); Business, Agriculture, Viewer's Digest (S).
Magazine: TV Supplement (S).

GENERAL MANAGEMENT

Publisher	William J Riley

ADVERTISING

Manager	Sandy Belli
Manager-National	Sandy Belli

CIRCULATION

Manager	Sandra Creitz

NEWS EXECUTIVE

Editor	Gary Abernathy

MANAGEMENT INFORMATION SERVICES

Data Processing Manager	Jeff Middleton

PRODUCTION

Foreman-Press Stereo	Wendell E Skinner
Manager	Tammy Wheeler

Market Information: Zoned editions; TMC; ADS.
Mechanical available: Offset; Black and 3 ROP colors; insert accepted — preprinted, single sheet; page cut-offs — 23 9/16".
Mechanical specifications: Type page 13" x 21 1/2"; E - 6 cols, 2 1/16", 1/8" between; A - 6 cols, 2 1/16", 1/8" between; C - 9 cols, 1 3/8", 1/16" between.

Commodity consumption: Newsprint 783 short tons; 816 metric tons; widths 55", 41¼", 27½"; black ink 33,485 pounds; color ink 708 pounds; single pages printed 7,075; average pages per issue 20(d).
Equipment: EDITORIAL: Front-end hardware — CText. CLASSIFIED: Front-end hardware — CText. DISPLAY: Adv layout systems — Ap/Mac, 2-PE/10; Printers — Ap/Mac Laser-Printer. PRODUCTION: Production cameras — 1-R/500; Automatic film processors — 1-LE/LD-24B.
PRESSROOM: Line 1 — 10-G/Community; Pasters — Web/Cement; Press control system — CH. MAILROOM: Bundle tyer — 1-MLN/ML-2-EE; Addressing machine — 1-Am/1900, FBM/90 Labeler. LIBRARY: Electronic — 1-Dukane. WIRE SERVICES: News — AP Data-features, AP; Syndicates — NEA, LATS, NAS, CNS, King Features; Receiving dishes — size-10ft, AP. BUSINESS COMPUTERS: 1-NCR.

RAVENNA

See KENT

ST. MARYS

Auglaize County

'90 U.S. Census- 8,441; E&P '96 Est. 8,464

The Evening Leader

(e-mon to fri; m-sat)

The Evening Leader, 102 E. Spring St., St. Marys, OH 45885; tel (419) 394-7414; fax (419) 394-7202. Hollinger International Inc. group.
Circulation: 6,077(e); 6,077(m-sat); Sworn Oct. 1, 1995.
Price: 50¢(d); 50¢(sat); $2.70/wk; $11.70/mo; $135.20/yr.
Advertising: Open inch rate $8.30(e); $9.32(m-sat). **Representative:** Papert Companies.
News Service: AP. **Politics:** Independent. **Established:** 1902.
Not Published: Independence Day; Thanksgiving; Christmas.
Special Weekly Sections: Best Food Day, Business Page (mon); Second Food Day, Farm Page (wed); Entertainment (thur); Business Page, Farm Page (fri); Lifestyle (daily).

GENERAL MANAGEMENT

Publisher David Creech
Business Manager/Purchasing Agent Cindy Sawmiller

ADVERTISING

Manager David Creech
Manager-Commercial Sales David Creech

MARKETING AND PROMOTION

Manager-Promotion David Creech

NEWS EXECUTIVE

Managing Editor Jose Noguerus

PRODUCTION

Superintendent/Manager Herb Bruns Jr

Market Information: TMC.
Mechanical available: Offset; Black and 4 ROP colors; insert accepted — preprinted, all; page cut-offs — 21".
Mechanical specifications: Type page 13" x 21½"; E - 6 cols, 2$\frac{1}{16}$", .17" between; A - 9 cols, 1⅜", .17" between; C - 9 cols, 1⅜", .17" between.
Commodity consumption: Newsprint 1,100 short tons; widths 27½", 35", 32"; average pages per issue 18(d).
Equipment: EDITORIAL: Front-end hardware — Ap/Mac; Front-end software — Baseview, QPS, Adobe/Photoshop; Printers — 3-Ap/Mac Laser. DISPLAY: Adv layout systems — Ap/Mac; Front-end hardware — 7-Ap/Mac; Front-end software — Aldus/FreeHand, Aldus/PageMaker, QuarkXPress, Caere/OmniPage, Multi-Ad; Printers — 3-Ap/Mac LaserPrinter. PRODUCTION: Typesetters — 2-IBM; Plate processors — Nu/Flip Top; Scanners — 1-Nu, DEC; Production cameras — Nikon; Automatic film processors — Adobe/Photoshop.
PRESSROOM: Line 1 — 6-G/Community. MAILROOM: Addressing machine — 1-MLN. WIRE SERVICES: News — AP, AP GraphicsNet; Stock tables — AP; Syndicates — King Features; Receiving dishes — AP. BUSINESS COMPUTERS: 2-IBM; Applications: Great Plains; PCs & micros networked; PCs & main system networked.

SALEM

Columbiana County

'90 U.S. Census- 12,233; E&P '96 Est. 11,714
ABC-CZ (90): 17,215 (HH 6,836)

Salem News (e-mon to sat)

Salem News, 161 N. Lincoln Ave., Salem, OH 44460; tel (216) 332-4601; fax (216) 332-1441. Thomson Newspapers group.
Circulation: 9,063(e); 9,063(e-sat); ABC Sept. 30, 1995.
Price: 35¢(d); 35¢(sat).
Advertising: Open inch rate $13.25(e); $13.25(e-sat). **Representative:** Thomson Newspapers.
News Service: AP. **Politics:** Independent. **Established:** 1889.
Special Editions: Bridal (Jan); Progress (Feb); Car Care (Mar); Spring Home Improvement (Apr); Health & Fitness (May); Family Business (June); Jubilee (July); Fair (Aug); Home Improvement, Football (Sept); Health & Fitness, Cookbook (Oct); Thanksgiving Edition (Nov); Christmas Gift Savings (Dec).
Special Weekly Sections: Mini Page, Society Pages, Yesteryears (tues); Food Page (wed); Business (thur); TV Edition, 50 Plus (fri); Food, Church (sat).
Magazine: Leisure Time/TV (fri).

GENERAL MANAGEMENT

Publisher/General Manager Thomas E Spargur

ADVERTISING

Director Jim Williams Jr

CIRCULATION

Director Frank Baldwin

NEWS EXECUTIVE

Editor Catherine M DeFazio

PRODUCTION

Foreman-Composing Cindy Wright
Foreman-Pressroom Glen Shonce

Market Information: TMC.
Mechanical available: Offset; Black and 3 ROP colors; insert accepted — preprinted, envelopes, standing cards, catabooks; page cut-offs — 22½".
Mechanical specifications: Type page 13¾" x 21½"; E - 6 cols, 2$\frac{1}{16}$", ⅛" between; A - 6 cols, 2$\frac{1}{16}$", ⅛" between; C - 9 cols, 1⅜", $\frac{1}{16}$" between.
Commodity consumption: Newsprint 419 metric tons; width 27½"; black ink 9,396 pounds; color ink 1,000 pounds; single pages printed 6,200; average pages per issue 20(d).
Equipment: EDITORIAL: Front-end hardware — Mk. CLASSIFIED: Front-end hardware — Mk. PRODUCTION: Typesetters — Ap/Mac Laser-Writers; Plate exposures — 1-Nu; Plate processors — 1-Nu; Production cameras — 1-R/500, 1-LE; Automatic film processors — 1-LE/LD18; Color separation equipment (conventional) — Digi-Colour.
PRESSROOM: Line 1 — 8-G/Community; Folders — 1-G/SC. MAILROOM: Bundle tyer — Ty-Tech/Strapper; Addressing machine — KR, Toshiba, Okidata, Am. COMMUNICATIONS: Facsimile — Savin. WIRE SERVICES: News — AP; Receiving dishes — AP. BUSINESS COMPUTERS: 1-ATT/3B2 500.

SANDUSKY

Erie County

'90 U.S. Census- 29,764; E&P '96 Est. 28,463
ABC-CZ (90): 49,854 (HH 19,399)

Sandusky Register

(e-mon to sat; S)

Sandusky Register, 314 W. Market St.; PO Box CN 5071, Sandusky, OH 44870; tel (419) 625-5500; fax (419) 625-7211 (bus office); e-mail regforum@ad.com. Sandusky-Norwalk Newspapers group.
Circulation: 24,842(e); 24,842(e-sat); 28,820(S); ABC Sept. 30, 1995.
Price: 35¢(d); 35¢(sat); $1.00(S); $2.10/wk (carrier); $2.20/mo (motor route); $109.20/yr (carrier), $114.40/yr (motor route).
Advertising: Open inch rate $21.00(e); $21.00(e-sat); $21.98(S). **Representative:** Landon Associates Inc.
News Service: AP. **Politics:** Independent. **Established:** 1822.
Not Published: New Year; Memorial Day; Independence Day; Labor Day; Christmas.
Special Editions: Home Improvement (Mar); Progress, Private Property Week (Apr); Back-to-School, Football (Aug); Fall Car Care (Oct); Thanksgiving Day Gift Guide (Nov).
Special Weekly Sections: Spectrum, TV Magazine (wed).

CORPORATE OFFICERS

Board Chairman David A Rau
Chief Financial Officer Peter Vogt
President David A Rau
Vice Pres/Treasurer Alice W Bott
Vice Pres Jim Hofmann
Secretary Susan E White
General Counsel Peter Vogt

GENERAL MANAGEMENT

Publisher Jim Hofmann
Manager-Credit Jane Righi

ADVERTISING

Director Walling E Gray
Manager-Retail William Berry
Manager-Classified James Rusincovitch

CIRCULATION

Director Lee Carter
Asst Manager Ken Metzdorf

NEWS EXECUTIVES

Managing Editor Rex Rhoades
Asst Managing Editor Eilene Guy

EDITORS AND MANAGERS

Area Editor Eilene Guy
Automotive Editor Don Lee
Boating Editor Bob Russ
Church Editor Karen Mork
City Editor Bob Russ
Farm Editor Bob Russ
Industry/Labor Editor Kris Weiss
Librarian Deborah Vonthron
News Editor Robert Derby
Outdoors/Sports Editor Bob Russ
Photo Editor Tim Fleck
Radio/Television Editor John Bruno
School Editor Karen Mork
Sports Editor Charles Wagner

PRODUCTION

Supervisor-Electronics Leo L Hartman
Foreman-Composing Leo L Hartman
Foreman-Pressroom Howard Scroggins
Foreman-Mailroom Mike Lippus
Engineer-Maintenance William Burch

Market Information: TMC.
Mechanical available: Offset; Black and 3 ROP colors; insert accepted — preprinted; page cut-offs — 22¾".
Mechanical specifications: Type page 13" x 21½"; E - 6 cols, 2", ⅙" between; A - 6 cols, 2", ⅙" between; C - 9 cols, 1$\frac{5}{16}$", ⅙" between.
Commodity consumption: Newsprint 1,514 short tons; widths 27½", 13¾"; black ink 31,000 pounds; color ink 2,500 pounds; single pages printed 9,700; average pages per issue 24(d), 42(S); single plates used 29,214.
Equipment: EDITORIAL: Front-end hardware — DEC; Front-end software — CD; Printers — 2-Facit, 1-DEC/LA 75, 3-Okidata. CLASSIFIED: Front-end hardware — DEC; Front-end software — CD; Printers — 1-Facit. DISPLAY: Front-end hardware — 2-Ap/Mac 700; Front-end software — Multi-Ad; Printers — Seikosha/BP5780, 2-XIT/Clipper. PRODUCTION: Typesetters — 2-XIT/Clipper; Plate exposures — 1-Nu/Flip Top FT46U6UPNS-KH; Plate processors — 1-Nat/A-340; Electronic picture desk — Lf/AP Leaf Picture Desk; Scanners — Microtek/600ZS, Microtek/Scanmaker II HR; Production cameras — SCREEN/Liberator; Automatic film processors — Litex/25; Film transporters — SCREEN; Color separation equipment (conventional) — Ap/Mac, XIT/Clipper-Schooner.
PRESSROOM: Line 1 — 8-G/Urbanite; Folders — 1-G/Urbanite; Reels and stands — G; Press control system — Fin; Press registration system — Duarte. MAILROOM: Counter stackers — 3-MM/231, 1-QWI; Inserters and stuffers — 3-MM/227-S 6 units; Bundle tyer — 1-MLN/ML2EE, 1-Bu/1230, 1-MLN/MAG 330; Addressing machine — MMS/Pressure Sensitive. WIRE SERVICES: News — AP; Photos — AP; Stock tables — AP SelectStox I; Syndicates — KRT; Receiving dishes — size-8ft, AP. BUSINESS COMPUTERS: 9-TI; Applications: Gen ledger, Accts payable, Accts receivable, Adv billing; PCs & main system networked.

SHELBY

Richland County

'90 U.S. Census- 9,564; E&P '96 Est. 9,494

Daily Globe (e-mon to sat)

Daily Globe, 37 W. Main St., Shelby, OH 44875; tel (419) 342-4276.
Circulation: 4,037(e); 4,037(e-sat); Sworn Sept. 29, 1995.
Price: 30¢(d); 30¢(sat); $1.40/wk; $6.10/mo; $71.00/yr.
Advertising: Open inch rate $7.07(e); $7.07(e-sat). **Representative:** Papert Companies.
News Service: AP. **Politics:** Independent. **Established:** 1900.
Not Published: New Year; Memorial Day; Independence Day; Labor Day; Thanksgiving; Christmas.
Special Editions: Progress (Feb); Home Improvement (Apr); City Directory, Car Care (Oct); Christmas Gift Guide (Nov).
Special Weekly Sections: Best Food Day (mon); Farm Page (thur).

GENERAL MANAGEMENT

President Ken C Gove
Publisher Scott M Gove

ADVERTISING

Director Barbara Sponseller

CIRCULATION

Director Sally Howerton

NEWS EXECUTIVES

Editor Scott M Gove
News Editor Isabel Hurley

EDITOR AND MANAGER

Sports Editor Chuck Ridenour

PRODUCTION

Manager Jim Arnoczky

Market Information: TMC; ADS.
Mechanical available: Offset; Black and 3 ROP colors; insert accepted — preprinted; page cut-offs — 22¾".
Mechanical specifications: Type page 13" x 21½"; E - 6 cols, 2$\frac{1}{16}$", ⅛" between; A - 6 cols, 2$\frac{1}{16}$", ⅛" between; C - 6 cols, 2$\frac{1}{16}$", ⅛" between.
Commodity consumption: width 27½"; average pages per issue 10(d).
Equipment: EDITORIAL: Front-end hardware — Mk. CLASSIFIED: Front-end hardware — Mk. DISPLAY: Adv layout systems — Mk. PRODUCTION: Typesetters — COM/8400; Plate exposures — 1-B; Production cameras — 1-SCREEN/Companica.
PRESSROOM: Line 1 — 4-G/Community. MAILROOM: Bundle tyer — 1-Kogyo, 1-Ty-Tech; Addressing machine — 1-SC. WIRE SERVICES: News — AP; Receiving dishes — AP. BUSINESS COMPUTERS: 1-RSK/Tandy 3100, 1-Club; Applications: Accts receivable, Payroll.

SIDNEY

Shelby County

'90 U.S. Census- 18,710; E&P '96 Est. 19,670
ABC-CZ (90): 19,755 (HH 7,376)

The Sidney Daily News

(e-mon to sat)

The Sidney Daily News, 911 S. Vandemark Rd.; PO Box 4099, Sidney, OH 45365; tel (513) 498-2111; fax (513) 498-0806. Amos Press group.
Circulation: 13,356(e); 13,356(e-sat); ABC Sept. 30, 1995.
Price: 50¢(d); 50¢(sat).
Advertising: Open inch rate $10.50(e); $10.50(e-sat). **Representative:** Papert Companies.
News Service: AP. **Politics:** Independent. **Established:** 1891.
Not Published: New Year; Memorial Day; Independence Day; Labor Day; Thanksgiving; Christmas.
Advertising not accepted: Tobacco.
Special Editions: Progress (Jan); Bride (Feb); Home Improvement, Spring Sports (Mar); Baby (Apr); Graduation (May); Fair (July); Back-to-School, Fall Sports (Aug); Cruise News (Automotive Section) (Oct); Winter Sports, Cookbook (Nov); Kids Christmas Greetings (Dec).
Special Weekly Sections: Best Food Day (mon); Second Food Day (tues); Business, Farm News, Second Food Day (sat).
Magazine: Kaleidoscope (entertainment guide that includes TV listings).

GENERAL MANAGEMENT

Publisher Linda K Coffman
Controller Richard Guenther
Purchasing Agent Bob Bryan

ADVERTISING

Director Mark Kaufman

CIRCULATION

Manager Tina Waterman

NEWS EXECUTIVE

Managing Editor Jeffrey Billiel

EDITORS AND MANAGERS

Automotive Editor Christine Henderson

Ohio I-321

Business/Finance Editor Christine Henderson
City/Metro Editor Judy Owen
Editorial Page Editor Jeffrey Billiel
Education Editor Mike Seffrin
Entertainment/Amusements Editor Helen Taylor
Environmental Editor Glenn Daniels
Farm/Agriculture Editor Mike Seffrin
Fashion/Style Editor Margie Wuebker
Features Editor Margie Wuebker
Graphics Editor/Art Director Jeffrey Billiel
Health/Medical Editor Tom Millhouse
Home Furnishings Editor Mike Seffrin
Living/Lifestyle Editor Margie Wuebker
National Editor Tom Millhouse
News Editor Beckie King
Photo Editor Todd Acker
Political/Government Editor Tom Millhouse
Real Estate Editor Christine Henderson
Religion Editor Beckie King
Science/Technology Editor Christine Henderson
Sports Editor Kenneth Barhorst
Television/Film Editor Jeffrey Billiel
Theater/Music Editor Jeffrey Billiel
Travel Editor Judy Owen
Society/Women's Editor Margie Wuebker

MANAGEMENT INFORMATION SERVICES

Data Processing Manager Tim Bodenhorn

PRODUCTION

Manager Bill Wise
Foreman-Pressroom Leroy Baker
Foreman-Mailroom Pete Arnold

Market Information: Zoned editions.
Mechanical available: Offset; Black and 3 ROP colors; insert accepted — preprinted; page cut-offs — 22¾".
Mechanical specifications: Type page 13" x 21½"; E - 6 cols, 2 1/16", ⅛" between; A - 6 cols, 2 1/16", ⅛" between; C - 9 cols, 1⅜", 1/16" between.
Commodity consumption: Newsprint 500 short tons; widths 27½", 13¾"; black ink 11,280 pounds; color ink 1,440 pounds; single pages printed 7,000; average pages per issue 19(d); single plates used 4,200.
Equipment: EDITORIAL: Front-end hardware — Dewar, 11-PC; Other equipment — 40-IBM/Selectric. CLASSIFIED: Front-end hardware — Dewar, 5-PC; Other equipment — 3-IBM/Selectric. DISPLAY: Front-end hardware — Ap/Mac, 5-PC. PRODUCTION: Typesetters — 2-AU/Micro 5, 2-Hyphen/Dash 600; Plate exposures — 2-Nu; Plate processors — 1-WL; Scanners — ECR/Autokon, Lf/Leafscan, 1-Cp/Super-Alpha; Production cameras — 1-C/Spartan III; Automatic film processors — 2-LE; Film transporters — 1-C.
PRESSROOM: Line 1 — 8-HI/845; Folders — 2-HI; Pasters — 6-Butler. MAILROOM: Counter stackers — 1-HI; Inserters and stuffers — 2-MM/5-pocket; Bundle tyer — 2-MLN. WIRE SERVICES: News — AP; Receiving dishes — AP.

SPRINGFIELD

Clark County

'90 U.S. Census- 70,487; **E&P '96 Est.** 68,755
ABC-CZ (90): 94,015 (HH 36,330)

Springfield News-Sun

(m-mon to sat; S)

Springfield News-Sun, 202 N. Limestone St.; PO Box 660, Springfield, OH 45501-0660; tel (513) 328-0300; fax (513) 328-0227. Cox Newspapers Inc. group.
Circulation: 35,660(m); 35,660(m-sat); 43,150(S); ABC Sept. 30, 1995.
Price: 50¢(d); 50¢(sat); $1.25(S); $3.40/wk.
Advertising: Open inch rate $34.91(m); $34.91(m-sat); $39.11(S). **Representative:** Gannett National Newspaper Sales.
News Service: AP. **Established:** 1817.
Special Editions: Home-Garden; Spring Car Care; Football Section; Fall Home Improvement; Finance/Taxes; Earth Day; New Car Section; Fall Car Care; Christmas Section.
Special Weekly Sections: Health, Finances (tues); Best Food Day (wed); Entertainment (thur); Sports (fri); Hobbies, Sports, Entertainment (sat); Travel, Business, Financial, Agri-Business (S).
Magazines: Parade, Channels-TV Book (S).

GENERAL MANAGEMENT

Publisher Charles H Rinehart
Controller Mary Mendelhallo
Vice Pres/General Manager William R Swaim

ADVERTISING

Director Robert Mercer

CIRCULATION

Manager Richard Fuller

NEWS EXECUTIVES

Editor Karla Garrett Harshaw
Managing Editor Jack Bianchi

EDITORS AND MANAGERS

Action Line Editor Carl Hunnell
Automotive Editor Ron Ware
Business Editor Carl Hunnell
City Editor Carl Hunnell
Asst City Editor Rod Lockwood
Editorial Page Editor Karla Garrett Harshaw
Education Editor Mike Wagner
Environmental Editor Bill Monaghan
Features/Travel Editor Carl Hunnell
Films/Theater Editor Steve Cooper
Food Editor Tom Stafford
Graphics Editor/Art Director Tom Hawkins
Health/Medical Editor Lawrence Calder
Librarian Anita Beaver
Music Editor Belinda Paschal
News Editor Richard Minning
Photo Editor Chuck Matthews
Political Editor Carl Hunnell
Science/Technology Editor Carl Hunnell
Sports Editor Dave Shedloski
Wire Editor Tom McCatherine
Women's Editor Tom Stafford

PRODUCTION

Manager Myron Nicewaner
Manager-Mailroom Barbara Parker
Manager-Electronic Systems Robert Walters
Manager-Composing Jerry Day
Supervisor-Building/Post Press James Gruber
Superintendent-Pressroom Paul Thompson
Superintendent-Platemaking Keith Blauvett

Market Information: Split Run; TMC; ADS.
Mechanical available: Offset; Black and 3 ROP colors; insert accepted — preprinted, preprints only; page cut-offs — 22¾".
Mechanical specifications: Type page 13" x 21½"; E - 6 cols, 2 1/16", ⅛" between; A - 6 cols, 2 1/16", ⅛" between; C - 9 cols, 1⅜", 1/16" between.
Commodity consumption: Newsprint 4,000 short tons; widths 54", 27", 40½"; black ink 80,000 pounds; color ink 17,000 pounds; single pages printed 10,000; average pages per issue 24(d), 46(S); single plates used 38,000.
Equipment: EDITORIAL: Front-end hardware — AT/7000; Front-end software — AT/7000; Printers — Ap/Mac LaserWriter Plus, 1-TI/800. CLASSIFIED: Front-end hardware — 1-AT/7000; Front-end software — AT/7000; Printers — 1-TI/800. DISPLAY: Adv layout systems — 3-Dewar; Front-end hardware — Dewar; Front-end software — Dewar, XIT, AT; Printers — 1-TI/810. PRODUCTION: Typesetters — 2-AU/APS Micro 5; Plate exposures — 3-Nu; Plate processors —2-Nat; Production cameras — 1-C/Marathon, 1-C/Spartan; Automatic film processors — 4-LE; Film transporters — 1-C, 2-AU/APS 35; Shrink lenses — 1-Alan; Color separation equipment (conventional) — 1-C/E-Z Color.
PRESSROOM: Line 1 — 5-G/Metro; Pasters — 5-G/RTP; Reels and stands — 5-G/Reel. MAILROOM: Counter stackers — 4-QWI; Inserters and stuffers — 1-HI/6-24, 1-SLS/1000; Bundle tyer — 2-MLN, 1-MLN/News-90, Ty-Tech; Addressing machine — 2-KR. LIBRARY: Electronic — Mead Data Central/Nexis NewsView. WIRE SERVICES: News — AP, KRT, ONS, Cox News Service, LAT-WP; Stock tables — AP SelectStox; Receiving dishes — size-10ft, AP. BUSINESS COMPUTERS: 1-HP/9000-817S; Applications: HP/UX, CJ: Adv; PCs & micros networked; PCs & main system networked.

STEUBENVILLE, OH-WEIRTON, WV

Jefferson County, OH
Hancock and Brooke Counties, WV

'90 U.S. Census- 44,249 (Steubenville, OH 22,125; Weirton, WV 22,124); **E&P '96 Est.** 39,487 (Steubenville 19,038; Weirton 20,449)
ABC-CZ (90): 53,864 (HH 21,957)

Herald-Star

(e-mon to fri; m-sat; S)

Herald-Star, 401 Herald Sq., Steubenville, OH 43952; tel (614) 283-4711; fax (614) 282-4261. Thomson Newspapers group.
Circulation: 28,826(e); 28,826(m-sat); 28,403(S); ABC Sept. 30, 1995.
Price: 35¢(d); 35¢(sat); $1.00(S); $2.20/wk (carrier); $20.00/mo (mail).
Advertising: Open inch rate $22.10(e); $22.10(m-sat); $22.10(S). **Representative:** Landon Associates Inc.
News Service: AP. **Politics:** Independent. **Established:** 1806.
Note: The Weirton (WV) Daily Times (e) is a zoned edition of the Steubenville Herald-Star.
Special Editions: Progress (Feb); Home & Garden (Mar); Bridal (Apr); Car Care (May); Vacation, City, Fort Festival (June); Back-to-School, Football (Aug); Home Improvements, Cadiz Mining Festival (Sept); Cookbook, Car Care, College & Career (Oct); Early Gift Guide, Christmas Opening and Gift Guide (Nov); Basketball (Dec).
Special Weekly Sections: Food (wed); Entertainment (thur); Senior Page (fri); Religion, Food (sat); Business (S); Business, Lifestyles (daily).
Magazines: Comics, TV Times (S); Parade.

GENERAL MANAGEMENT

Publisher Robert J Dunn
Director-Finance Tom Purcell

ADVERTISING

Director Stacie Boering

CIRCULATION

Director Amy Mason

NEWS EXECUTIVES

Exec Editor Dan Shaw
Managing Editor Judy McGovern

EDITORS AND MANAGERS

City Editor Chuck Massaro
Editorial Page Editor Paul Giannamore
Features Editor Marian Houser
News Editor Ross Galabrese
Sports Editor John Enrietto

MANAGEMENT INFORMATION SERVICES

Data Processing Manager Robert J Dunn

PRODUCTION

Director Tony Ruble
Foreman-Pressroom Glenn Moore

Market Information: Zoned editions; TMC; ADS; Operate audiotex.
Mechanical available: Offset; Black and 3 ROP colors; insert accepted — preprinted, catabook, card, envelope; page cut-offs — 22".
Mechanical specifications: Type page 13" x 21½"; E - 6 cols, 2 1/16", ⅛" between; A - 6 cols, 2 1/16", ⅛" between; C - 9 cols, 1⅜", 1/16" between.
Commodity consumption: Newsprint 1,851 short tons; widths 13¾", 27½"; single pages printed 9,859; average pages per issue 24(d), 42(S).
Equipment: EDITORIAL: Front-end hardware — Mk/6000, Ap/Mac; Front-end software — Mk/Ace 2, QuarkXPress 3.3; Printers — Tegra/Varityper 5000, 2-Tegra/Varityper 5300, Tegra/Varityper 5300 E. CLASSIFIED: Front-end hardware — Mk; Front-end software — Mk/Ace 2; Printers — Tegra/Varityper 5000, Tegra/Varityper 5300. DISPLAY: Adv layout systems — Ap/Mac; Front-end hardware — Ap/Mac; Front-end software — Multi-Ad/Creator 3.54; Printers — Tegra/Varityper 5000, Tegra/Varityper 5300. PRODUCTION: Typesetters — 2-V, 3-Mk/VDT; Platemaking systems — Offset; Plate exposures — 2-Nu; Plate processors — 2-Nat/A-250; Electronic picture desk — Ap/Mac Quadra, Adobe Photostop, Nikon/Color Access; Scanners — Mirror/1200, Imax; Production cameras — 2-DSA/680C, LE/121; Automatic film processors — DSA/220; Color separation equipment (conventional) — Adobe/Photoshop, Nikon/Color Access.
PRESSROOM: Line 1 — 7-G/Urbanite; Press drives — Fin; Folders — G/Urbanite; Press control system — Fin; Press registration system — Duarte. MAILROOM: Counter stackers — 1-Id; Bundle tyer — 1-MLN/Strapper, 1-Dynaric; Addressing machine — Packard Bell. LIBRARY: Electronic — Newsview, Intel/PC; Combination — Minolta/Microfilm. WIRE SERVICES: News — AP; Photos — AP; Stock tables — AP; Syndicates — NEA; Receiving dishes — size-3m, AP. BUSINESS COMPUTERS: NCR, Packard Bell, HP; Applications: Lotus 4.0: Accounting.

TIFFIN

Seneca County

'90 U.S. Census- 18,604; **E&P '96 Est.** 17,831
ABC-CZ (90): 25,635 (HH 9,446)

The Advertiser-Tribune

(m-mon to sat; S)

The Advertiser-Tribune, 320 N. Nelson St.; PO Box 778, Tiffin, OH 44883; tel (419) 448-3200; fax (419) 447-3274. Ogden Newspapers group.
Circulation: 11,015(m); 11,015(m-sat); 11,577(S); ABC Sept. 30, 1995.
Price: 50¢(d); 50¢(sat); $1.00(S); $10.00/mo (carrier), $11.00/mo (motor route), $13.75/mo (mail); $120.00/yr (carrier), $132.00/yr (motor route), $165.00/yr (mail).
Advertising: Open inch rate $12.08(m); $12.08(m-sat); $12.08(S).
News Service: AP. **Politics:** Independent. **Established:** 1832.
Not Published: New Year; Memorial Day; Independence Day; Labor Day; Christmas.
Special Editions: Our Town (Feb); Home Improvement, Spring Sports (Mar); Spring Car Care Tab (May); Fair Tab (July); Fall Sports Tab (Aug); Heritage Festival Tab (Sept); Home Improvement, Women, Winter Car Care Tab (Oct); Auto, Holiday Gift Ideas, Cooking Show (Nov); Winter Sports Tab, Holiday Gift Ideas, Last Minute Christmas Guide, Chronology Pages (Dec).
Special Weekly Sections: Best Auto Days, Best Food Day (mon); Home Front Page (wed); Best Real Estate Day, Best Auto Days (thur); Best Auto Days (sat); Best Food Days, Best Real Estate Day (S).
Magazine: USA Weekend.

CORPORATE OFFICERS

President G Ogden Nutting
Vice Pres Robert M Nutting
Secretary/Treasurer William O Nutting

GENERAL MANAGEMENT

Publisher John T Elchert
Business Manager Sharon Lee

ADVERTISING

Director Peter Lynch

TELECOMMUNICATIONS

Audiotex Manager Peter Lynch

CIRCULATION

Manager Chris Dixon

NEWS EXECUTIVE

Managing Editor John Kauffman

EDITORS AND MANAGERS

Action Line Editor John Kauffman
City Editor Rob Weaver
Editorial Page Editor John Kauffman
Education Editor Christina Wise
Entertainment/Amusements Editor Nancy Kleinhenz
Farm/Agriculture Editor Melinda Ruble
Fashion/Style Editor Nancy Kleinhenz
Features Editor Nancy Kleinhenz
Graphics Editor/Art Director Rob Weaver
Living/Lifestyle Editor Nancy Kleinhenz
National Editor Beth Church
News Editor Rob Weaver
Photo Editor Randy Roberts
Political/Government Editor Beth Church
Sports Editor Pat Magers
Women's Editor Nancy Kleinhenz

MANAGEMENT INFORMATION SERVICES

Data Processing Manager Sharon Lee

PRODUCTION

Superintendent Janet Vallery

Market Information: TMC; ADS; Operate audiotex.
Mechanical available: Offset; Black and 3 ROP colors; insert accepted — preprinted, all; page cut-offs — 22¾".
Mechanical specifications: Type page 13" x 21½"; E - 6 cols, 2 1/16", ⅛" between; A - 6 cols, 2 1/16", ⅛" between; C - 6 cols, 2 1/16", ⅛" between.
Commodity consumption: Newsprint 839 short tons; widths 27½", 13¾", 27", 34"; black ink 12,000 pounds; color ink 1,200 pounds; single pages printed 8,530; average pages per issue 20(d), 46(S); single plates used 14,000.
Equipment: EDITORIAL: Front-end hardware — AT/Series 4, 12-AT; Front-end software — AT; Printers — 2-Ap/Mac LaserWriter II NTX, 3-HP/LaserJet 4MV, 1-ECRM/Scriptsetter VRL

36. CLASSIFIED: Front-end hardware — AT/Series 4, 2-AT. AUDIOTEX: Hardware — PEP; Software — PEP; Supplier name — PEP, BDR. PRODUCTION: Pagination software — QuarkXPress; Typesetters — 2-Ap/Mac LaserWriter II NTX, 3-HP/LaserJet 4MV, 1-ECRM/Scriptsetter VRL 36; Plate exposures — 1-Nu; Plate processors — 1-Nat; Scanners — Lf/AP Leaf Picture Desk 35, Polaroid/Sprintscan 35, Umax/Vista-S6; Color separation equipment (conventional) — AP. PRESSROOM: Line 1 — 7-G/Community; Folders — 1-G; Reels and stands — 7-G; Press control system — Fin. MAILROOM: Counter stackers — 1-BG/Count-O-Veyor; Bundle tyer — 2-MLN/Strapper. WIRE SERVICES: News — AP; Photos — AP; Receiving dishes — AP. BUSINESS COMPUTERS: IBM/Sys 36, PBS, NCR; Applications: INSI: Accts receivable, Payroll, Circ, Accts payable, Gen ledger; PCs & micros networked; PCs & main system networked.

TOLEDO

Lucas County

'90 U.S. Census- 332,943; E&P '96 Est. 315,447
ABC-CZ (90): 495,576 (HH 190,555)

The Blade (m-mon to sat; S)

The Blade, 541 N. Superior St., Toledo, OH 43660; tel (419) 245-6000; fax (419) 245-6471. Blade Communications Inc. group.

Circulation: 147,526(m); 147,526(m-sat); 201,098(S); ABC Sept. 30, 1995.

Price: 50¢(d); 50¢(sat); $1.50(S); $2.60/wk (carrier); $135.20/yr (carrier).

Advertising: Open inch rate $72.55(m); $72.55(m-sat); $96.35(S). **Representatives:** Sawyer-Ferguson-Walker Co.; American Publishers Reps.

News Services: AP, RN, LAT-WP, KRT, CSM, NYT. **Politics:** Independent. **Established:** 1835.

Special Editions: Wedding Plans, Feeling Good (Health) (Jan); Focus '96, Community Assets (Feb); Destinations Vacation Brochures, Toledo Auto Show, Financial Future, Easter Super Coupons, Spring Homes, The Vacationer Area Tourist Guide (Mar); Employment Connection, Golf, Boating/Water Sports/Recreation, Lawn & Garden (Apr); Feeling Good (Health), Mature Lifestyles, Spring Parade of Homes (May); Fourth of July Super Coupons, Jamie Farr LPGA Toledo Classic (June); Feeling Good (Health), Destinations Vacations Brochures, Football (Aug); Home Design, Fall Parade of Homes, Funeral/Bereavement (Sept); Employment Connection, After 5 (Oct); Thanksgiving Super Coupons, Feeling Good (Health), Holiday Potpourri Gift Ideas (Nov); Christmas Super Coupons (Dec).

Special Weekly Sections: Living (Health) (mon); Food (tues); Living (Fashion) (wed); High Tops (Children) (thur); Living (Weekend) (fri); Living (sat); Business, Arts & Entertainment, Travel (S).

Magazines: TV Week, Comics (S); Parade.

Cable TV: Operate leased cable TV in circulation area; Own cable TV in circulation area.

CORPORATE OFFICERS

Board Chairman William Block Sr
Vice Chairman Allan Block
President William Block Jr
Exec Vice Pres John Robinson Block
Vice Pres/Treasurer Gary Blair
Secretary Fritz Byers
Asst Secretary/Treasurer Joseph F Restivo

GENERAL MANAGEMENT

President & Co-Publisher William Block Jr
Co-Publisher & Editor in Chief John Robinson Block
Vice Pres-Administration Gary Blair
Vice Pres/General Manager David Beihoff
Treasurer Joseph F Restivo
Director-Finance Linda Hoyt
Director-Human Resources Jo Kerns
Director-Systems Lee Gagle
Manager-Human Resources Janelle Authur
Manager-Human Resources John R Husman

ADVERTISING

Director Jerry Grabowski
Manager-Retail Sales Kevin O'Connell
Manager-General Sales Hank Baker
Manager-Ad Service Department Dave Georgia
Manager-Classified Jay Kowalski
Asst Manager-Classified Roxanne Bailey

MARKETING AND PROMOTION

Director-Marketing Joseph H Frederickson
Coordinator-Newspapers in Education Debby Geyer

CIRCULATION

Director Michael McCaffrey
Asst Director Cheryl Lutz
Manager-Home Delivery Lyle Endsley
Manager-State Bill Herzig
Manager-Distribution Stan Secord
Manager-Database Bob Gall
Manager-Customer Service Deb Grimes

NEWS EXECUTIVES

Editor in Chief John Robinson Block
Senior Editor Patrick O'Gara
Editor Thomas Walton
Managing Editor Ron Royhab
Asst Managing Editor Tom Bendycki
Asst Managing Editor Eileen Foley
Asst Managing Editor Frank Craig
Asst Managing Editor Rick Maas
Editorial Director Ralph Johnson
Assoc Editor William Brower
Assoc Editor Richard Paton
Assoc Editor Thomas Wellman
Assoc Editor Rose Russell Stewart

EDITORS AND MANAGERS

Art Director Rick Nease
Business/Real Estate Editor Greg Braknis
City Editor David Murray
Editorial Page Editor Thomas Walton
Editorial Cartoonist Kirk Walters
Fashion Editor Rhonda B Sewell
Farm/Agriculture Editor Ned Bell
Features/Entertainment Editor Tom Gearhart
Food Editor Joe Crea
Health/Medical Editor Michael Woods
Librarian Mary Mackzum
Outdoors Editor Steve Pollick
Science Editor Michael Woods
Sports Editor Bob Kinney
Travel Editor William Ferguson
Washington Bureau Chief Patricia Griffith
Columbus Bureau Chief Joe Hallett

MANAGEMENT INFORMATION SERVICES

Data Processing Manager Malcolm Edge

PRODUCTION

Director-Operations Charles K Stroh
Manager Jim Frederick
Manager-Facilities & Engineering Jeff Latcheran
Coordinator (Night) John Pellek
Superintendent-Pre Press Bob Campbell
Superintendent-Pressroom John Buczkowski
Superintendent-Maintenance Larry Geis
Superintendent-Mailroom Ron Hojnacki
Foreman-Paperhandlers Larry Carter

Market Information: Zoned editions; Split Run.

Mechanical available: Flexography; Black and 3 ROP colors; insert accepted — preprinted; page cut-offs — 22".

Mechanical specifications: Type page 13" x $21\frac{1}{8}$"; E - 6 cols, $2\frac{1}{16}$", $\frac{1}{8}$" between; A - 6 cols, $2\frac{1}{16}$", $\frac{1}{8}$" between; C - 10 cols, $1\frac{3}{16}$", $\frac{1}{8}$" between.

Commodity consumption: Newsprint 16,453 metric tons; widths 55", $41\frac{1}{4}$", $27\frac{1}{2}$"; black ink 528,786 pounds; color ink 91,077 pounds; single pages printed 18,050; average pages per issue 44(d), 102(S); single plates used 120,804.

Equipment: EDITORIAL: Front-end hardware — AT/7000, PC; Front-end software — AT/7000, ATS/Osiris; Printers — Okidata/300. CLASSIFIED: Front-end hardware — AT/7000, PC; Front-end software — AT/7000, CText; Printers — Okidata/300. DISPLAY: Adv layout systems — SCS/Layout 8000; Front-end hardware — Ap/Mac, AT/7000, PCs, Ap/Mac; Front-end software — Aldus/PageMaker, AT/7000, QuarkXPress, Multi-Ad/Creator, Adobe/Photoshop; Printers — Ap/Mac Laser, AU/APS Broadsheet; Other equipment — Microtek/Scanner. PRODUCTION: Pagination software — SCS/Layout 8000; Typesetters — 3-AU/APS-5, 1-III/3850, 2-AU/3850; Platemaking systems — 2-LX/LF-100 (Flexo); Plate exposures — 1-Nu/631; Electronic picture desk — 2-Lf/AP Leaf Picture Desk; Scanners — 2-ECR/Autokon 1000DE; Production cameras — 1-C/Newspager, 1-SCREEN/690D; Automatic film processors — 2-DP/HT-26, 2-LE/PC 1800, 1-LE/PC 18, 3-Konica/3850 OL; Film transporters — 1-C; Digital color separation equipment — 1-RZ/210L, 2-RZ/Carat 500, 1-SCREEN/1030 AI. PRESSROOM: Line 1 — 9-G/Flexoliner double width; Line 2 — 9-G/Flexoliner double width; Line 3 — 9-G/Flexoliner double width; Press drives — Allen Bradley; Folders — 3-G/3:2; Pasters — 18-PEC, 9-G; Press control system — Allen Bradley. MAILROOM: Counter stackers — 2-HL/Monitor Programmable Laser, 6-HL/Monitor HT2; Inserters and stuffers — 1-S/1372P, 1-S/1472P; Bundle tyer — 7-Power Strap; Wrapping singles — 4-Dynaric/SM 65. WIRE SERVICES: News — AP Datafeatures, AP Datastream; Photos — AP, RN; Stock tables — AP SelectStox I; Syndicates — NYT, KRT, LAT-WP, SHNS, CSM, RN; Receiving dishes — size-10ft, AP, RN. BUSINESS COMPUTERS: HP/3000 Series 935; Applications: CJ: Circ, Adv, Class; PCs & micros networked; PCs & main system networked.

TROY

Miami County

'90 U.S. Census- 19,478; E&P '96 Est. 19,822
ABC-CZ (90): 21,851 (HH 8,425)

Troy Daily News (e-mon to sat) *Miami Valley Sunday News* (S)

Troy Daily News/Miami Valley Sunday News, 224 S. Market St., Troy, OH 45373; tel (513) 335-5634; fax (513) 335-3552.

Circulation: 11,129(e); 11,129(e-sat); 12,898(S); ABC Sept. 30, 1995.

Price: 50¢(d); 50¢(sat); $1.25(S); $12.50/mo.

Advertising: Open inch rate $11.77(e); $11.77(e-sat); $11.77(S). **Representatives:** US Suburban Press; Landon Associates Inc.

News Service: AP. **Politics:** Independent. **Established:** 1909.

Not Published: Christmas.

Special Editions: Bridal (Feb); Miami Community Guide, Thanksgiving (Nov); Football, Progress, Spring Lawn & Garden, Car Care, Home Fix Up (Spring & Fall).

Special Weekly Sections: Best Food Day, Health (mon); Business (wed); Farm & Agricultural News (thur); Arts Page (fri); Church News and Listings (sat); TV Week (S).

Magazines: Parade; Color Comics; React.

CORPORATE OFFICERS

President/CEO Joel H Walker
Exec Vice Pres Thomas E Thokey
Treasurer Joel H Walker
Secretary Thomas E Thokey

GENERAL MANAGEMENT

Publisher Joel H Walker
General Manager Thomas E Thokey
Vice Pres-Operations Charles E Elliott
Vice Pres-News David R Lindeman
Chief Financial Officer Charles T Lobaugh

ADVERTISING

Director Vicki Yetter

MARKETING AND PROMOTION

Director-Community Relations Michael W Walker

TELECOMMUNICATIONS

Director-Systems/Technology Charles T Lobaugh

CIRCULATION

Director Samuel R Ronicker

NEWS EXECUTIVES

Editor Joel H Walker
Exec Editor David Lindeman
Managing Editor Nancy Bowman
News Editor Scott Elliot

EDITORS AND MANAGERS

Arts Editor Kevin Tucker
Business Editor Nancy Bowman
Columnist Kermit Vandivier
Columnist David Lindeman
Columnist Bill Begley
Editorial Page Editor David Lindeman
Entertainment/Amusements Editor Kevin Tucker
Environmental Editor Nancy Bowman
National Editor Nancy Bowman
Photo Department Manager J D Pooley
Political/Government Editor Nancy Bowman
Sports Editor Bill Begley
Television Editor Stacey Burns

PRODUCTION

Director Gary Niswonger
Manager-Pressroom Bill Pummill
Manager-Composing Rosemary Saunders
Manager-Mailroom Carlon Vanchure

Market Information: TMC; ADS.

Mechanical available: Offset; Black and 3 ROP colors; insert accepted — preprinted, all; page cut-offs — $22\frac{3}{4}$".

Mechanical specifications: Type page 13" x $21\frac{1}{2}$"; E - 6 cols, $2\frac{1}{16}$", $\frac{1}{8}$" between; A - 6 cols, $2\frac{1}{16}$", $\frac{1}{8}$" between; C - 9 cols, $1\frac{3}{8}$", $\frac{1}{16}$" between.

Commodity consumption: Newsprint 2,150 short tons; widths 34", $27\frac{1}{2}$", 35", 30", 27"; black ink 50,000 pounds; color ink 9,000 pounds; single pages printed 19,500; average pages per issue 16(d), 44(S); single plates used 25,000.

Equipment: EDITORIAL: Front-end hardware — 1-Mk/1100 Plus; Front-end software — Mk/1100 Plus, QuarkXPress/Pagination, Mk/Managing Editor; Printers — 2-Ap/Mac LaserWriter II NTX, 2-Xante/Accel-a-Writer 8200, 1-NewGen/660B; Other equipment — 1-Ap/Power Mac 7200, 1-Ap/Mac Quadra 950, 1-Lf/AP Leaf Picture Desk, 3-Ap/Power Mac 8100, 4-CD-Rom. CLASSIFIED: Front-end hardware — 1-Mk/1100 Plus; Printers — 1-Ap/Mac LaserWriter II NTX, TI/Dot Matrix. DISPLAY: Front-end hardware — 1-Ap/Mac Quadra 900, 2-Ap/Mac Quadra 800, 1-Ap/Power Mac 8100, Ap/Power Mac 7100, 2-Ap/Power Mac 7200; Front-end software — Multi-Ad/Creator, QuarkXPress, Mk/Managing Editor; Printers — 2-Ap/Mac LaserWriter II NTX, 2-Xante/Accel-a-Writer 8200, 1-NewGen/660B; Other equipment — CD-Rom, HP/ScanJet IIc, Ap/Mac Work Group Server 80, Ap/Mac Quadra 605 Print Server. PRODUCTION: Pagination software — QuarkXPress 3.31, Mk/Managing Editor; OCR software — Caere/OmniPage Pro 5.0; Typesetters — Xante/Accel-a-Writer 8200 Laserprinter, Pre-Press/System, Panther/Pro 36 w/Ap/Power Mac RIP; Plate exposures — 2-Roconex/V-44; Plate processors — 1-Graham; Electronic picture desk — Lf/AP Leaf Picture Desk; Scanners — HP/ScanJet IIc, Ofoto, Caere/OmniPage Pro, Adobe/Photoshop, AG/Arcus II, Kk/2035 Plus; Production cameras — 3-SCREEN; Automatic film processors — 2-SCREEN; Color separation equipment (conventional) — 1-Digi-Colour; Digital color separation equipment — Lf/AP Leaf Picture Desk. PRESSROOM: Line 1 — 10-G/Urbanite; Folders — 2-G; Pasters — 2-Butler/Splicer; Press control system — G. MAILROOM: Counter stackers — 2-H/RS 2512; Inserters and stuffers — 1-KAN/320; Bundle tyer — 2-EAM/Mosca 4044; Addressing machine — IBM/Sys 36, 1-KR. LIBRARY: Electronic — Baseview. COMMUNICATIONS: Digital ad delivery system — AP AdSend. WIRE SERVICES: News — AP; Photos — AP Photostream; Receiving dishes — size-10ft, AP, NSN. BUSINESS COMPUTERS: IBM/Sys 36, Ap/Mac; Applications: Microsoft/Excel, Claris/Works, INSI: Payroll, Accts payable, Accts receivable; PCs & micros networked; PCs & main system networked.

UNION CITY

See WINCHESTER, IN

UPPER SANDUSKY

Wyandot County

'90 U.S. Census- 5,906; E&P '96 Est. 5,854

The Daily Chief-Union (e-mon to sat)

The Daily Chief-Union, 111 W. Wyandot Ave.; PO Box 180, Upper Sandusky, OH 43351-0180; tel (419) 294-2332; fax (419) 294-5608. Ray Barnes Newspapers Inc. group.

Circulation: 4,207(e); 4,207(e-sat); Sworn Oct. 1, 1995.

Price: 35¢(d); 35¢(sat); $83.16/yr.

Advertising: Open inch rate $5.50(e); $5.50(e-sat). **Representative:** Papert Companies.

News Service: AP. **Politics:** Independent. **Established:** 1936.

Note: Printed by Kenton (OH) Times.

Not Published: New Year; Memorial Day; Independence Day; Labor Day; Thanksgiving; Christmas.

Special Editions: Baby Times; Fair Tab; Sidewalk Days; Graduation; Christmas Kick-off; Christmas Greetings; Moonlight Madness; Football; January Sale; President's Sale; Welcome Section; Boy and Girl Scouts; 4-H; June Dairy; Memorial Day; Basketball.

Magazines: Fair Premiun Book; Business Cards.

CORPORATE OFFICERS

President Jack L Barnes
Vice Pres Charles G Barnes
Secretary/Treasurer Jack L Barnes

GENERAL MANAGEMENT

Publisher Thomas E Martin
General Manager/Purchasing Agent Thomas E Martin
Manager-Education Service Bette Snyder

Ohio I-323

ADVERTISING

Manager Thomas E Martin

MARKETING AND PROMOTION

Manager-Marketing/Promotion Thomas E Martin

CIRCULATION

Director Francis Haner

NEWS EXECUTIVE

Editor Bette Snyder

EDITORS AND MANAGERS

Action Line Editor Jim Petsche
Automotive/Aviation Editor Chris Richman
Business/Finance Editor Al Sray
City Editor Jim Petsche
Editorial Page Editor Bette Snyder
Education Editor Bette Snyder
Entertainment Editor Bette Snyder
Fashion/Style Editor Dolores Moore
Features Editor Al Sray
Features Editor Bette Snyder
Films/Theater Editor Jim Petsche
Food/Home Editor Dolores Moore
Graphics Editor/Art Director Al Sray
Health/Medical Editor Bette Snyder
Librarian Dolores Moore
National Editor Bette Snyder
News Editor Bette Snyder
Photo Editor Bette Snyder
Political/Government Editor Bette Snyder
Radio/Television Editor Dolores Moore
Religion Editor Dolores Moore
Science/Technology Editor Bette Snyder
Sports Editor Chris Richman
Travel Editor Jim Petsche
Women's Editor Dolores Moore

PRODUCTION

Manager Ronald Pool

Market Information: TMC.
Mechanical available: Offset; Black and 3 ROP colors; insert accepted — preprinted; page cut-offs — 21½".
Mechanical specifications: Type page $12\frac{15}{16}$" x 21½"; E - 6 cols, 2", $\frac{1}{8}$" between; A - 6 cols, 2", $\frac{1}{8}$" between; C - 6 cols, 2", $\frac{1}{8}$" between.
Commodity consumption: width 28"; average pages per issue 12(d).
Equipment: EDITORIAL: Front-end hardware — Ap/Mac; Front-end software — Ap/Mac; Printers — TI; Other equipment — Ap/Mac. CLASSIFIED: Front-end hardware — Ap/Mac; Front-end software — Ap/Mac; Printers — TI; Other equipment — Ap/Mac. DISPLAY: Front-end hardware — Ap/Mac IIsi; Front-end software — Multi-Ad/Creator; Printers — Ap/Mac LaserWriter Plus. PRODUCTION: Pagination software — Ap/Mac; Typesetters — 2-Ap/Mac LaserWriter Plus; Production cameras — Nu/UV-1418; Automatic film processors — Kk. MAILROOM: Bundle tyer — Ty-Tech; Addressing machine — Am. WIRE SERVICES: News — AP; Receiving dishes — size-1¼ft, AP.

URBANA

Champaign County

'90 U.S. Census- 11,353; **E&P '96 Est.** 11,890

Urbana Daily Citizen

(e-mon to sat)

Urbana Daily Citizen, 220 E. Court St.; PO Box 191, Urbana, OH 43078; tel (513) 652-1331; fax (513) 652-1336. Brown Publishing Co. group.
Circulation: 6,651(e); 6,651(e-sat); Sworn Sept. 30, 1995.
Price: 50¢(d); 50¢(sat).
Advertising: Open inch rate $8.00(e); $8.00(e-sat). **Representative:** Papert Companies.
News Service: AP. **Politics:** Independent. **Established:** 1838.
Not Published: New Year; Memorial Day; Independence Day; Labor Day; Thanksgiving; Christmas.
Special Editions: Real Estate Quarterly (Jan); 4-H, Bride (Feb); Agri News, House and Home (Mar); Real Estate Quarterly (Apr); Progress (May); Health & Fitness (June); County Fair (July); Real Estate Quarterly, Football Preview (Aug); Crafts, Real Estate Quarterly (Oct); Winter Sports, Christmas (Nov); Christmas, Christmas Greetings, New Year's Baby (Dec).
Special Weekly Sections: Education (tues); Business (wed); Home Improvement, Health & Fitness, Farm/Agriculture, Environment, Travel, Food (S).

CORPORATE OFFICERS

Board Chairman Clarence J Brown
Controller John Aston
President Mark R Policinski
Secretary Joyce E Brown

GENERAL MANAGEMENT

Publisher Linda Anderson
Manager-Commercial William Cromwell

ADVERTISING

Director Deborah Madison

CIRCULATION

Manager Gina Riefstall

NEWS EXECUTIVE

Managing Editor Art Kahn

EDITOR AND MANAGER

Sports Editor Steve Stout

PRODUCTION

Foreman-Pressroom Don King
Foreman-Composing Wendy Cromer
Foreman-Distribution Debbie Fields

Market Information: TMC; ADS.
Mechanical available: Offset; Black and 3 ROP colors; insert accepted — preprinted; page cut-offs — 22¾".
Mechanical specifications: Type page 13" x 21"; E - 6 cols, $2\frac{1}{16}$", $\frac{1}{8}$" between; A - 6 cols, $2\frac{1}{16}$", $\frac{1}{8}$" between; C - 9 cols, $1\frac{3}{8}$", $\frac{1}{16}$" between.
Commodity consumption: Newsprint 500 short tons; width 27½"; average pages per issue 12(d).
Equipment: EDITORIAL: Front-end hardware — 7-Mk. CLASSIFIED: Front-end hardware — 1-Mk. DISPLAY: Adv layout systems — Ap/Mac IIsi; Front-end software — QuarkXPress; Printers — Ap/Mac LaserWriter. PRODUCTION: Typesetters — 2-COM; Plate exposures — 1-Douthitt; Plate processors — 1-Nat/A-340; Production cameras — 1-R/400, 1-B/Caravel; Automatic film processors — LE/LD 18. PRESSROOM: Line 1 — 5-KP/Color King; Line 2 — 4-KP/Newsking. MAILROOM: Inserters and stuffers — 3-KAN; Bundle tyer — 1-Bu, 1-Strap Tyer, 1-Strapex; Addressing machine — Ch/525. WIRE SERVICES: News — AP; Receiving dishes — size-10ft, AP. BUSINESS COMPUTERS: Applications: Whalen: Adv, Circ, Bus; PCs & micros networked; PCs & main system networked.

VAN WERT

Van Wert County

'90 U.S. Census- 10,891; **E&P '96 Est.** 10,769

Times-Bulletin

(e-mon to fri; m-sat)

Times-Bulletin, 700 Fox Rd.; PO Box 271, Van Wert, OH 45891; tel (419) 238-2285. Brown Publishing Co. group.
Circulation: 6,552(e); 6,552(m-sat); Sworn Oct. 5, 1994.
Price: 50¢(d); 50¢(sat); $1.75/wk; $7.58/mo; $91.00/yr.
Advertising: Open inch rate $10.25(e); $10.25 (m-sat). **Representative:** Papert Companies.
News Service: AP. **Politics:** Independent. **Established:** 1846.
Not Published: New Year; Memorial Day; Independence Day; Labor Day; Thanksgiving; Christmas.
Special Editions: Financial Guide to '96, Progress Edition (Jan); Bridal Planner, Valentine's Day, Home Furnishings (Feb); Age & Youth, Home Improvement, Spring Fashion, St. Patrick's Day (Mar); Spring Sports Magazine, Business Card Directory, Spring Car Care, Senior Lifestyle, Golf Guide (Apr); Mother's Day, Baby Album, Graduation 1996 (May); Father's Day, 150th Anniversary (June); Van Wert Answer Book (July); Farm Focus, Bridal Book, Hot Air Fair, Van Wert County Fair, Fall Sports Magazine (Aug); Home Improvement, Business Card Directory, College Guide (Sept); Senior Lifestyle, Fall Car Care, Restaurant Directory (Oct); Gift Guide, Winter Sports Magazine (Nov); Gift Guide, Gift Guide/Santa Letters, Christmas Greetings (Dec); Real Estate Resource (monthly).
Special Weekly Sections: Farm & Agribusiness (mon); Business Review (tues); Arts & Culture (wed); Business, Youth of Today (thur); Church & Religion, TV & Leisure (fri); Real Estate (sat); Best Food Day (S).
Magazine: Real Estate Resource (monthly).

CORPORATE OFFICERS

President Mark R Policinski
Treasurer Robert Townsley
Board Chairman Clarence J Brown
Secretary Joyce E Brown

GENERAL MANAGEMENT

Publisher Larry R Joseph
Asst Publisher/General Manager Donald R Hemple
Office Manager Vickie Trisel
Manager-Credit Donald R Hemple

ADVERTISING

Manager-Retail Tracy Hoghe
Manager-Classified Tracy Hoghe
Manager-National Donald R Hemple

MARKETING AND PROMOTION

Director-Marketing Donald R Hemple

TELECOMMUNICATIONS

Audiotex Director-Sales/Operations Donald R Hemple
Audiotex Manager Tracy Hoghe

CIRCULATION

Manager Rob Wagner
Supervisor-Mailroom Louise Huelsman

NEWS EXECUTIVE

Editor David L Mosier

EDITORS AND MANAGERS

Business/Finance Editor David L Mosier
City Editor Babita Sharma
Editorial Page Editor David L Mosier
Education Editor Sherry Missler
Entertainment/Amusements Editor Sherry Missler
Farm/Agriculture Editor Sherry Missler
Fashion/Style Editor Norma Sommers
Living/Lifestyle Editor Norma Sommers
News Editor Babita Sharma
Religion Editor Norma Sommers
Society Editor Norma Sommers
Sports Editor Tim Cox
Youth/Culture Editor Sherry Missler

PRODUCTION

Director Eugene Byrne
Foreman-Pressroom Greg Smith

Market Information: TMC; Operate audiotex.
Mechanical available: Offset; Black and 3 ROP colors; insert accepted — preprinted; page cut-offs — 22¾".
Mechanical specifications: Type page 13¾" x 21½"; E - 6 cols, $2\frac{1}{16}$", $\frac{1}{8}$" between; A - 6 cols, $2\frac{1}{16}$", $\frac{1}{8}$" between; C - 8 cols, $1\frac{9}{16}$", $\frac{1}{16}$" between.
Commodity consumption: Newsprint 280 metric tons; widths 28", 14"; black ink 9,400 pounds; color ink 1,200 pounds; single pages printed 4,784; average pages per issue 16(d); single plates used 5,200.
Equipment: EDITORIAL: Front-end hardware — Mk. CLASSIFIED: Front-end hardware — Mk. PRODUCTION: Typesetters — 2-COM/Unisetter, 1-COM/7200; Plate exposures — 1-Nu; Production cameras — 1-R/500; Automatic film processors — 1-LE. PRESSROOM: Line 1 — 7-G/Community; Folders — 1-G/2:1. MAILROOM: Bundle tyer — 1-Bu; Addressing machine — 1-MMS. WIRE SERVICES: News — AP; Receiving dishes — AP. BUSINESS COMPUTERS: Bs/3611, IBM/Sys 23; Applications: Adv billing, Accts receivable, Circ, Accounting.

WAPAKONETA

Auglaize County

'90 U.S. Census- 9,214; **E&P '96 Est.** 9,982

Wapakoneta Daily News

(e-mon to fri; m-sat)

Wapakoneta Daily News, 8 Willipie St.; PO Box 389, Wapakoneta, OH 45895; tel (419) 738-2128; fax (419) 738-5352. Hollinger International Inc. group.
Circulation: 4,729(e); 4,729(m-sat); Sworn Sept. 30, 1995.
Price: 50¢(d); 50¢(sat); $11.00/mo (carrier); $126.00/yr (carrier), $165.00/yr (mail).
Advertising: Open inch rate $9.66(e); $9.66(m-sat). **Representative:** Papert Companies.
News Service: AP. **Politics:** Independent. **Established:** 1904.
Not Published: New Year; Independence Day; Thanksgiving; Christmas.
Special Editions: Bridal, Baby (Jan); Progress Edition (Feb); Newspapers in Education, Farming in the Heartland (Mar); Spring Sports, Home Improvement (Apr); Graduation, Memorial Day Edition (May); Citizen's Defense (safety tab), Who, What, Where Guide (June); Fair (July); Personal Image, Fall Sports (Aug); Labor Day Edition, Home Improvement, Indian Summerfest (Sept); Car Care, Hobbies and Past Times (Oct); Songbook, Cookbook, Winter Sports, Christmas Kick-off (Nov); Holiday Greetings, Gift Guide (Dec).
Special Weekly Sections: Best Food Day, Business (mon); Farm News, Second Food Day (wed); Entertainment (thur); Business (fri); Farm News (sat); Lifestyle Pages (daily).
Magazine: Monthly TV Guide (last day of each month).

GENERAL MANAGEMENT

Publisher Dianna Epperly
Manager-Business Office Lea Knepper

ADVERTISING

Manager Karen Brown

TELECOMMUNICATIONS

Audiotex Manager Dianna Epperly

CIRCULATION

Manager Thomas Bault

NEWS EXECUTIVE

Managing Editor Deborah Bauman

EDITORS AND MANAGERS

Agriculture Business Editor Timothy Presar
Local News Editor J Swygart
News Editor Deborah Bauman
Sports Editor Joseph Menden
Women's/Society Editor Melanie Speicher

PRODUCTION

Manager-Composing Nina Lee
Manager-Printing Nina Lee

Market Information: Zoned editions; TMC; Operate audiotex.
Mechanical available: Offset; Black and 3 ROP colors; insert accepted — preprinted; page cut-offs — 22¾".
Mechanical specifications: Type page 13" x 21½"; E - 6 cols, $2\frac{1}{16}$", $\frac{1}{8}$" between; A - 6 cols, $2\frac{1}{16}$", $\frac{1}{8}$" between; C - 9 cols, $1\frac{5}{16}$", $\frac{1}{8}$" between.
Commodity consumption: widths 28", 32", 14"; average pages per issue 18(d); single plates used 12,000.
Equipment: EDITORIAL: Front-end hardware — Ap/Mac Quadra 630; Printers — Laser-Writer/16/600 PS, Ap/Mac. CLASSIFIED: Front-end hardware — Ap/Mac Quadra 630; Front-end software — Adobe/PageMaker 5.0; Printers — LaserWriter/16/600 PS. AUDIOTEX: Supplier name — Premiere Audiotex. DISPLAY: Front-end hardware — Ap/Mac Quadra 630; Front-end software — Adobe/PageMaker 5.0, Multi-Ad/Creator 3.63; Printers — Laser-Writer/16/600 PS. PRODUCTION: Typesetters — Ap/Mac; Plate exposures — Nu; Plate processors — Nat; Production cameras — 1-Nu, 1-LE; Automatic film processors — 1-SCREEN; Color separation equipment (conventional) — Mk. MAILROOM: Bundle tyer — 1-Sa; Addressing machine — 3-Wm. WIRE SERVICES: News — AP; Receiving dishes — AP. BUSINESS COMPUTERS: 1-Samsung/S550; Applications: Circ, Mailing, Gen office, Accts receivable; PCs & micros networked; PCs & main system networked.

WARREN

Trumbull County

'90 U.S. Census- 50,793; **E&P '96 Est.** 46,293
ABC-CZ (90): 57,040 (HH 22,577)

The Tribune Chronicle

(e-mon to sat)

The Sunday Tribune (S)

The Tribune Chronicle, 240 Franklin St. S.E., Warren, OH 44782; tel (216) 841-1600; fax (216) 841-1721. Thomson Newspapers group.
Circulation: 39,596(e); 39,596(e-sat); 44,939(S); ABC Sept. 30, 1995.
Price: 25¢(d); 25¢(sat); $1.00(S); $2.25/wk; $11.25/mo; $117.45/yr.
Advertising: Open inch rate $41.69(e); $41.69(e-sat); $41.69(S). **Representative:** Landon Associates Inc.
News Services: AP, KRT. **Politics:** Independent. **Established:** 1812 (Chronicle), 1876 (Tribune).
Advertising not accepted: Mail order copy.
Special Weekly Sections: Health (tues); Food (wed); Entertainment (thur).

CORPORATE OFFICERS

President Richard J Harrington
Senior Vice Pres/Chief Financial Officer Robert Daleo
Senior Vice Pres Gerald Flake Sr

GENERAL MANAGEMENT

Publisher Stephen Roszczyk
General Manager John Perfette
Business Manager/Controller Fred J Schomer

Copyright ©1996 by the Editor & Publisher Co.

I-324 Ohio

ADVERTISING

Director-Marketing Tim LaRose
Manager-Classified Ronald Davis

CIRCULATION

Director Thomas Stith
Manager-Single Copy Andy Karafa
Manager-Home Delivery Mark Jeffery
Manager-Home Delivery James McElrath

NEWS EXECUTIVES

Exec Editor Susan Jessup Svihlik
Managing Editor Lee C Gordon

EDITORS AND MANAGERS

Business Editor Larry Ringler
Design Editor Joe Giampietro
Editorial Page Editor Steve Oravecz
Education Reporter Ed Simpson
Entertainment/Amusements Reporter Andy Gray
Features Editor Ellen Kleinerman
Health/Medical Reporter Ellen Kleinerman
Lifestyle Editor Ellen Kleinerman
Metro Editor Ed Simpson
News Editor Joe Giampietro
Photo Editor Rob Engelhardt
Religion Editor Marilyn Anobile
Sports Editor David Burcham

PRODUCTION

Manager John Perfette
Manager-Technical Service Jack Cottrill
Foreman-Pressroom George Furry
Foreman-Composing Nancy Warren
Foreman-Mailroom James Marko

Market Information: Zoned editions; TMC.
Mechanical available: Offset; Black and 3 ROP colors; insert accepted — preprinted; page cut-offs — 22.75".
Mechanical specifications: Type page 13" x $21\frac{1}{2}$"; E - 6 cols, $2\frac{1}{16}$", $\frac{1}{8}$" between; A - 6 cols, $2\frac{1}{16}$", $\frac{1}{8}$" between; C - 9 cols, $1\frac{3}{8}$", $\frac{1}{16}$" between.
Commodity consumption: Newsprint 3,900 short tons; widths 55", $41\frac{1}{4}$", $27\frac{1}{2}$"; black ink 59,475 pounds; color ink 19,560 pounds; single pages printed 14,692; average pages per issue 32(d), 44(sat), 80(S); single plates used 42,490.
Equipment: EDITORIAL: Front-end hardware — RSK/Tandem Data Base, PC/386; Front-end software — SQL/OS2-Dateline; Printers — Genicom. CLASSIFIED: Front-end hardware — RSK/6000, IBM, Unix; Front-end software — SQL/Sybase-OS2; Printers — Printronix, TI/Postscript. DISPLAY: Adv layout systems — Adept; Front-end hardware — 4-Intel/486; Front-end software — Novell/Network (MS-DOS). PRODUCTION: Typesetters — 2-V/5000, 1-V, 1-Panther/Pro 46; Plate exposures — 2-Nu; Plate processors — 2-Nat; Electronic picture desk — Lf/AP Leaf Picture Desk; Production cameras — 2-C; Automatic film processors — 2-SCREEN; Color separation equipment (conventional) — 1-Panther/Pro 46. PRESSROOM: Line 1 — 8-H/mono double width (6 half decks); Folders — 2-H; Pasters — 8-Allen Bradley; Reels and stands — 8-Allen Bradley; Press control system — Fin. MAILROOM: Counter stackers — 3-HL/Monitor, 1-Id; Inserters and stuffers — HI/848, HI/1148; Bundle tyer — 2-MLN, 2-Dynamic; Addressing machine — 1-Ohio mailing machine. LIBRARY: Electronic — SMS/Stauffer. WIRE SERVICES: News — AP; Stock tables — AP; Syndicates — KRT, THO; Receiving dishes — AP. BUSINESS COMPUTERS: 1-IBM/AS-4000; Applications: IBM: Bus.

WASHINGTON COURT HOUSE

Fayette County

'90 U.S. Census- 12,983; E&P '96 Est. 13,248

Record Herald

(e-mon to fri; m-sat)

Record Herald, 138 S. Fayette St., Washington Court House, OH 43160; tel (614) 335-3611; fax (614) 335-5728. Brown Publishing Co. group.
Circulation: 5,743(e); 5,743(m-sat); Sworn Sept. 30, 1994.
Price: 50¢(d); 50¢(sat); \$7.60/mo; \$91.20/yr.
Advertising: Open inch rate \$13.38(e); \$13.38 (m-sat). **Representative:** Papert Companies.
News Service: AP. **Politics:** Independent. **Established:** 1883.
Not Published: New Year; Memorial Day; Independence Day; Labor Day; Thanksgiving; Christmas.
Advertising not accepted: 900 numbers.

CORPORATE OFFICERS

Board Chairman/CEO Clarence J Brown
President Mark R Policinski
Vice Pres Dave Tyo
Treasurer John Aston
Secretary Joyce E Brown

GENERAL MANAGEMENT

Publisher Jeff Pollard

CIRCULATION

Manager Ailiene Saunders

EDITOR AND MANAGER

Editor Anthony Conchel

PRODUCTION

Manager Steve Sword

Market Information: TMC; ADS.
Mechanical available: Offset; Black and 3 ROP colors; insert accepted — preprinted; page cut-offs — $22\frac{3}{4}$".
Mechanical specifications: Type page 13" x $21\frac{1}{2}$"; E - 6 cols, $2\frac{1}{16}$", $\frac{1}{8}$" between; A - 6 cols, $2\frac{1}{16}$", $\frac{1}{8}$" between; C - 8 cols, $1\frac{3}{4}$", $\frac{1}{16}$" between.
Commodity consumption: Newsprint 221 metric tons; widths 28", 14"; single pages printed 3,786; average pages per issue 14(d), 12(sat); single plates used 1,893.
Equipment: EDITORIAL: Front-end hardware — 6-Ap/Mac; Front-end software — QuarkXPress 7.11; Printers — 1-Ap/Mac; Other equipment — 2-Ap/Mac Scanner. CLASSIFIED: Front-end hardware — 1-Ap/Mac. DISPLAY: Front-end software — QuarkXPress, Multi-Ad/Creator, Mk/Ad Builder; Printers — 1-Ap/Mac; Other equipment — CD-Rom. PRODUCTION: Production cameras — 1-B/Caravel. MAILROOM: Bundle tyer — 1-Bu. WIRE SERVICES: News — AP; Receiving dishes — size-10ft, AP. BUSINESS COMPUTERS: 1-IBM/AT, 4-AST/Bravo LC 4-33; Applications: MSSI/Ad Manager: Circ, Mgmt files; PCs & micros networked; PCs & main system networked.

WILLOUGHBY

See LAKE COUNTY

WILMINGTON

Clinton County

'90 U.S. Census- 11,199; E&P '96 Est. 11,909

Wilmington News Journal

(e-mon to sat)

Wilmington News Journal, 47 S. South St., Wilmington, OH 45177; tel (513) 382-2574; fax (513) 382-4392. Brown Publishing Co. group.
Circulation: 6,478(e); 6,478(e-sat); Sworn Oct. 10, 1995.
Price: 50¢(d); 50¢(sat); \$1.85/wk (carrier), \$1.95/wk (motor route); \$96.20/yr (carrier), \$101.40/yr (motor route).
Advertising: Open inch rate \$8.54(e); \$8.54(e-sat). **Representative:** Papert Companies.
News Service: AP. **Politics:** Republican. **Established:** 1838.
Not Published: New Year; Memorial Day; Independence Day; Labor Day; Thanksgiving; Christmas.
Special Editions: New Year's Baby Edition; Farm; June Bride; Car Care; Moonlight Madness; County Fair; Welcome to Clinton; Basketball Preview; Football Preview; County Booklet; Christmas Progress Edition.

CORPORATE OFFICERS

Board Chairman Clarence J Brown
President Mark R Policinski
Treasurer John Aston
Secretary Joyce E Brown

GENERAL MANAGEMENT

Publisher Clarence Graham

ADVERTISING

Director Rick Irvin

CIRCULATION

Director Thomas Martin

NEWS EXECUTIVE

Editor Jay Carey

EDITORS AND MANAGERS

Food/Society Editor Vickie Patton
Music Editor Vickie Patton
Sports Editor Mark Huber

PRODUCTION

Manager Terry Henderson

Market Information: TMC.
Mechanical available: Offset; Black and 3 ROP colors; insert accepted — preprinted; page cut-offs — $22\frac{3}{4}$".
Mechanical specifications: Type page 13" x $21\frac{1}{2}$"; E - 6 cols, $2\frac{1}{16}$", $\frac{1}{8}$" between; A - 6 cols, $2\frac{1}{16}$", $\frac{1}{8}$" between; C - 10 cols, $1\frac{3}{16}$", $\frac{1}{16}$" between.
Commodity consumption: widths 28", 33"; average pages per issue 16(d).
Equipment: EDITORIAL: Front-end hardware — Ap/Mac IIsi. CLASSIFIED: Front-end hardware — Ap/Macs. DISPLAY: Front-end hardware — Ap/Mac IIsi. PRODUCTION: Plate exposures — 1-Nu; Production cameras — 1-B. PRESSROOM: Line 1 — 7-G/SC; Folders — 1-G. MAILROOM: Bundle tyer — 1-Bu. LIBRARY: Electronic — 1-Kodagraph. WIRE SERVICES: News — AP; Receiving dishes — size-22ft, AP. BUSINESS COMPUTERS: 1-Bs, 1-IBM/PC; Applications: Adv billing, Accts receivable.

WOOSTER

Wayne County

'90 U.S. Census- 22,191; E&P '96 Est. 25,077
ABC-CZ (90): 27,109 (HH 10,504)

The Daily Record

(e-mon to fri; m-sat; S)

The Daily Record, 210-212 E. Liberty St.; PO Box 918, Wooster, OH 44691; tel (216) 264-1125; fax (216) 264-3756. Dix Communications group.
Circulation: 24,722(e); 24,722(m-sat); 24,158(S); ABC Sept. 30, 1995.
Price: 35¢(d); 35¢(sat); 35¢(S); \$7.45/mo (carrier), \$7.80/mo (motor route); \$81.20/yr (carrier), \$85.65/yr (motor route), \$90.50/yr (mail).
Advertising: Open inch rate \$18.00(e); \$18.00(m-sat); \$18.00(S). **Representative:** Landon Associates Inc.
News Services: AP, NYT. **Politics:** Independent. **Established:** 1889.
Note: Effective Apr. 2, 1995, this publication added a Sunday edition.
Not Published: New Year; Memorial Day; Independence Day; Labor Day; Thanksgiving; Christmas.
Special Editions: Progress Edition, Bridal Showcase (Jan); Financial Journal, Valentine Special Pages - Happy Ads (Feb); Builders Edition (Mar); Home & Garden (Apr); Summer Lifestyles, Senior Memories (May); Farm Focus (June); Wayne County Fair (Aug); Football Preview, Literacy Day, Wayne County Fair Week, Woosterfest (Sept); Restaurant Guide, At Home (Oct); Christmas Kick-off (Nov); Basketball Preview, Holiday Greetings (Dec).
Special Weekly Sections: Coupon Page (tues); Business Page (fri); Farm Page (weekly).
Magazine: TV News (printed in plant) (sat).
Broadcast Affiliates: Radio WKVX-AM; WQKT-FM.

CORPORATE OFFICERS

President Albert E Dix
Vice Pres Raymond Victor Dix
Controller Dale E Gerber

GENERAL MANAGEMENT

Publisher Raymond Victor Dix
General Manager Frank Beeson

ADVERTISING

Director Bob Anderson
Manager-Classified Bruce Polen
Manager-National Randy Wilson

CIRCULATION

Manager Merv Conn
Asst Manager-Mailroom Don Daniels

NEWS EXECUTIVE

Managing Editor Melody L Snure

EDITORS AND MANAGERS

Agriculture Editor Laurie Sidle
Business Editor June Bablak
City Editor Tami Lange
Education Editor Denise Scott
Editorial Page Editor Melody L Snure
Entertainment Editor Mike Dewey
Family/Fashion Editor Ann Gasbarre
Food Editor Betsy Bower
Mechanical Superintendent Bob Rodi
News Editor Charles Cicconetti
Region Editor Judy Wasson
Specialty Publications Manager Jan Conrad
Special Edition Editor Melody L Snure
Sports Editor Brian Questel
Weekly Division Manager Ken Blum
Women's Editor Ann Gasbarre
Wire Editor Charles Cicconetti

MANAGEMENT INFORMATION SERVICES

Manager-Systems Bud Bender

PRODUCTION

Manager-Typesetting/Ad Composition Brian Zerrer
Superintendent-Mechanical Bob Rodi
Foreman-Pressroom Bill Hackett
Foreman-Plate Room Larry Wetz

Market Information: Zoned editions; Split Run; TMC.
Mechanical available: Offset; Black and 3 ROP colors; insert accepted — preprinted, slip sheets; page cut-offs — $22\frac{3}{4}$".
Mechanical specifications: Type page 13" x $21\frac{1}{2}$"; E - 6 cols, $2\frac{1}{16}$", $\frac{1}{8}$" between; A - 6 cols, $2\frac{1}{16}$", $\frac{1}{8}$" between; C - 9 cols, $1\frac{5}{16}$", $\frac{1}{8}$" between.
Commodity consumption: Newsprint 1,605 short tons; widths $27\frac{1}{2}$", $13\frac{3}{4}$"; black ink 31,305 pounds; color ink 8,000 pounds; single pages printed 11,396; average pages per issue 37(d); single plates used 10,685.
Equipment: EDITORIAL: Front-end hardware — 35-Ap/Mac Quadra (610s, 840s); Front-end software — Linotype-Hell/Linotype; Printers — Linotype-Hell/L-190, Linotype-Hell/L-560. CLASSIFIED: Front-end hardware — Ap/Mac Quadra 610; Front-end software — Linotype-Hell/LinoPress. DISPLAY: Adv layout systems — Multi-Ad/Creator; Front-end hardware — 5-Ap/Mac Quadra 840; Front-end software — Multi-Ad/Creator. PRODUCTION: Pagination software — Linotype-Hell/Linopress, Mk/Managing Editor, Mk/Page Director; Typesetters — 2-XIT/Laser Image Processor, Linotype-Hell/L-190, Linotype-Hell/L-560; Platemaking systems — 3M/Pyrofax Deadliner; Plate exposures — 3M/Pyrofax Deadliner; Plate processors — 1-W; Scanners — 1-Nikon/Coolscan, 4-Microtek/Flatbed; Production cameras — 1-W, SCREEN/Auto Companica 670B; Automatic film processors — LE; Color separation equipment (conventional) — CA, Ap/Mac Electronic Darkroom-PowerBook; Digital color separation equipment — CA, Ap/Mac Electronic Darkroom-PowerBook. PRESSROOM: Line 1 — 12-G/Urbanite 724; Line 2 — 6-G/Community; Folders — 1-G/Half, 1-G/Quarter. MAILROOM: Inserters and stuffers — 1-S/P24, 1-HI, 1-MM/Inserter 6-into-1; Bundle tyer — 2-Bu, 1-MLN; Addressing machine — 1-Ch, COMMUNICATIONS: Facsimile — 1-AP. Systems used — satellite. WIRE SERVICES: News — AP, NYT, NEA; Photos — AP; Stock tables — AP; Syndicates — AP; Receiving dishes — size-8ft, AP. BUSINESS COMPUTERS: DSI; Applications: Linotype-Hell/Linopress Link: Circ, Adv billing, Accts receivable, Gen ledger, Payroll; PCs & main system networked.

XENIA

Greene County

'90 U.S. Census- 24,664; E&P '96 Est. 24,673
ABC-CZ (90): 32,297 (HH 10,917)

The Xenia Daily Gazette

(e-mon to fri; m-sat)

The Xenia Daily Gazette, 37 S. Detroit St.; PO Box 400, Xenia, OH 45385; tel (513) 372-4444; fax (513) 372-3385. Thomson Newspapers group.
Circulation: 10,765(e); 10,765(m-sat); ABC Sept. 30, 1995.
Price: 50¢(d); 50¢(sat); \$1.90/wk; \$98.80/yr, \$114.00/yr (mail).
Advertising: Open inch rate \$13.50(e); \$13.50(m-sat). **Representative:** Landon Associates Inc.
News Service: AP. **Politics:** Independent. **Established:** 1869.
Not Published: New Year; Memorial Day; Independence Day; Labor Day; Thanksgiving; Christmas.
Special Editions: Bridal, Income Tax Pages (Jan); Valentine's Day Pages (Feb); Progress (Mar); Spring Sports Pages, Spring Home Improvement (Apr); Mother's Day Pages (May); Greene County Fair Book (June); Sidewalk Sale Tab, Success in Greene County Edition, Greene County Fair Preview (July); Back-to-School Safe, Fall Sports Pages (Aug); Old Fashioned Days Special Edition, Fall Home Improvement (Sept); Fall Car Care Pages (Oct); Winter Sports Pages, Christmas Kick-off Tab (Nov); Last Minute Gift Tab, Greeting Ads, First Baby of Greene County (Dec).
Special Weekly Sections: Best Food Day, Essentials (mon); Education (tues); Business, Farm & Garden (wed); Entertainment (thur); Outdoors (fri); Religion (sat).

GENERAL MANAGEMENT

Publisher Stanton L Miller

Copyright ©1996 by the Editor & Publisher Co.

ADVERTISING

Manager Dan Emerich

CIRCULATION

Manager Jason Hodson

NEWS EXECUTIVE

Managing Editor Gary Brock

EDITORS AND MANAGERS

Editorial Page Editor Dennis Hoerig
Lifestyle Editor Connie Hart
News Editor Jacquelyn Masar
Sports Editor Bill Duffield

PRODUCTION

Foreman-Composing John Long
Foreman-Pressroom Donald C Tucker

Market Information: TMC.
Mechanical available: Offset; Black and 3 ROP colors; insert accepted — preprinted, all; page cut-offs — $23\frac{9}{16}$".
Mechanical specifications: Type page 13" x 21½"; E - 6 cols, $2\frac{1}{16}$", ⅛" between; A - 6 cols, $2\frac{1}{16}$", ⅛" between; C - 9 cols, $1\frac{3}{8}$", $\frac{1}{16}$" between.
Commodity consumption: Newsprint 324 short tons; width 27½"; single pages printed 5,150; average pages per issue 14(d), 18(sat); single plates used 7,600.
Equipment: EDITORIAL: Front-end hardware — 2-Mk/3000, 8-Mk/Newstouch, 3-Ap/Mac. CLASSIFIED: Front-end hardware — 2-Mk/Newstouch II; Printers — 1-TI. PRODUCTION: OCR software — Mk/Newstouch II; Typesetters — 3-Ap/Mac LaserWriter II; Platemaking systems — Nu; Plate processors — 1-Nu/Flip Top FT40; Electronic picture desk — Lf/AP Leaf Picture Desk; Production cameras — DSA; Automatic film processors — 1-LE; Color separation equipment (conventional) — Lf/Leafscan 35.
PRESSROOM: Line 1 — 6-G/Community; Folders — 1-G, G/SC Quarterfolder; Press registration system — Duarte. MAILROOM: Bundle tyer — 2-Bu. LIBRARY: Electronic — 1-Recordak. WIRE SERVICES: News — AP; Photos — AP; Syndicates — TNN; Receiving dishes — size-3m, AP. BUSINESS COMPUTERS: 2-HP/486; Applications: Bus office use.

YOUNGSTOWN

Mahoning County

'90 U.S. Census- 95,732; **E&P '96 Est.** 81,647
ABC-CZ (90): 203,277 (HH 79,695)

Vindicator (e-mon to sat; S)

Vindicator, Vindicator Sq.; PO Box 780, Youngstown, OH 44501-0780; tel (216) 747-1471; fax (216) 747-0399.
Circulation: 84,666(e); 84,666(e-sat); 126,031(S); ABC Sept. 30, 1995.
Price: 25¢(d); 25¢(sat); 75¢(S); $2.00/wk.
Advertising: Open inch rate $37.13(e); $37.13(e-sat); $52.49(S). **Representative:** Sawyer-Ferguson-Walker Co.
News Services: AP, CT, LAT-WP, KRT, NYT, SHNS. **Politics:** Independent. **Established:** 1869.
Special Editions: Bridal Section (Jan); Business Review (Feb); Health & Fitness, Spring Fashion, Spring New Car, Spring Home Improvement (Mar); Spring Lawn & Garden, Golf Season, American Home, Spring Home Improvement (Home Builder's Show), Mother's Day Gift Guide (Apr); Senior Citizens, Spring Car Care, Graduates/Career, Hot Rod Super Nationals (May); Personal Finance & Banking H.B.A., Bridal (June); Youngstown-Warren LPGA Classic (July); Fall Fashion, Back-to-School, Canfield Fair, Football '96/High School (Aug); Community Cup (YMCA), American Heart Association, H.B.A. Showcase of Homes, Fall Home Improvement (Sept); Dining Guide, New Car Section '97, Fall Car Care (Oct); Holiday Gift Guide (Nov); Late Gift Guide (Dec).
Special Weekly Sections: Consumer (mon); Health/Fitness (tues); Food (wed); Entertainment (thur); Fashion/Trends (fri); Education, Religion (sat); Travel, Family, Home/Garden, Best Food Day (S).
Magazine: TV Week Magazine (fri).
Broadcast Affiliate: WFMJ (NBC).

CORPORATE OFFICERS

President/Treasurer Betty H Brown Jagnow
Vice Pres/Secretary/Asst Treasurer Mark A Brown

GENERAL MANAGEMENT

Publisher Betty H Brown Jagnow
General Manager Mark A Brown
Asst General Manager Ted E Suffolk
Controller James J Meehan
Personnel Manager/Labor Relations Robert Wiseman

ADVERTISING

Director-Community Affairs Helen Paes
Manager-General/Co-op Nena Perkins
Manager-Classified John W Sovik
Manager-Retail David S Burns

CIRCULATION

Manager C Edward Powell

NEWS EXECUTIVE

Managing Editor Paul C Jagnow

EDITORS AND MANAGERS

Books/Science Editor Paul C Jagnow
Editorial Page Editor Dennis Mangan
Editorial Writer Patricia R Klevin
Editorial Writer Bertram deSouza
Education Editor Ronald Cole
Farm/Agriculture Editor Jeff Sheban
Fashion/Food Editor Mike McGowan
Features Editor Mike McGowan
Films/Theater Editor Debra Shaulis
Garden Editor Michael A Braun
Graphics Editor/Art Director Robert McFerren
Health/Medical Editor Mike McGowan
Living/Lifestyle Editor Mike McGowan
Music Editor Debra Shaulis
News Editor Richard Logan
Outdoors Editor Michael A Braun
Photo Editor Bob Yosay
Political Editor Mark Niquette
Radio/Television Editor Debra Shaulis
Science/Technology Editor Mike McGowan
Senior Regional Editor Tony Paglia
Regional Editor-Trumbull Edition Carl Basic
Regional Editor-City Edition Rea Taiclet
Regional Editor-Mahoning & Pennsylvania Cindy Rickard
Religion Editor Marie Shellock
School Editor Ronald Cole
Society/Women's Editor Barbara Shaffer
Sports Editor Matthew Arnold
Sunday Editor Michael A Braun
Travel Editor Michael A Braun

PRODUCTION

Manager DeWayne Gray
Manager-Properties/Facilities William Lafferre
Foreman-Composing Ralph Camp
Foreman-Pressroom John Dee Davis
Foreman-Mailroom Russell J Golden

Market Information: Zoned editions; Split Run.
Mechanical available: LetterPress (Direct); Black and 3 ROP colors; insert accepted — preprinted; page cut-offs — $23\frac{9}{16}$".
Mechanical specifications: Type page 13" x 22½"; E - 6 cols, 2", $\frac{3}{16}$" between; A - 6 cols, $2\frac{1}{16}$", ⅛" between; C - 9 cols, $1\frac{3}{8}$", $\frac{1}{16}$" between.
Commodity consumption: average pages per issue 32(d), 100(S).
Equipment: EDITORIAL: Front-end hardware — SII/Sys 25; Front-end software — SII/Sys 25; Printers — 1-Ap/Mac NT, 3-Ap/Mac NTX, 1-Centronics/351; Other equipment — 9-Ap/Mac, 1-Dell/450DE, 9-Dell/486P16, 10-HI/Composition. CLASSIFIED: Front-end hardware — SII/Sys 25; Printers — Centronics/351, HP/Rugged Writer; Other equipment — X/7017 automatic fax, 14-IBM/Selectric. DISPLAY: Adv layout systems — SCS/Layout 8000; Front-end hardware — Dell/320 LX PC, 2-Ap/Mac; Front-end software — SCS/Layout 8000, Microsoft/Windows, CJ; Printers — HP/LaserJet II, HP/LaserJet III; Other equipment — X/5042 copier. PRODUCTION: Pagination software — HI/8900, XP 21; Typesetters — 2-MON/1016, 3-MON/Image Master 1200; Platemaking systems — Na; Plate exposures — 2-Na/Starlite; Plate processors — 2-Na/80; Electronic picture desk — 2-Lf/AP Leaf Picture Desk; Scanners — 2-ECR; Production cameras — 1-C/Spartan III, 1-C/Newspager II; Automatic film processors — 2-C, 1-LE; Film transporters — 2-C, 1-LE; Digital color separation equipment — Adobe/Photoshop.
PRESSROOM: Line 1 — 9-G/Mk-2; Line 2 — 9-G/Mk-2; Pasters — 18-G; Reels and stands — 18-G. MAILROOM: Counter stackers — HL/3; Inserters and stuffers — 1-S/72P; Bundle tyer — 4-MLN/2, 5-Power Strap; Addressing machine — 2-Am. WIRE SERVICES: News — Stock tables — TMS; Receiving dishes — size-10ft. BUSINESS COMPUTERS: 1-HP/3000 925LX; Applications: Cort: Payroll; CJ/Geac; PCs & main system networked.

ZANESVILLE

Muskingum County

'90 U.S. Census- 26,778; **E&P '96 Est.** 25,402
ABC-CZ (90): 32,167 (HH 13,016)

The Times Recorder (m-mon to sat; S)

The Times Recorder, 34 S. Fourth St., Zanesville, OH 43701; tel (614) 452-4561; fax (614) 452-5390; e-mail 5639078@mcimail.com. Thomson Newspapers group.
Circulation: 21,969(m); 21,969(m-sat); 21,841(S); ABC Sept. 30, 1995.
Price: 35¢(d); 35¢(sat); $1.00(S); $2.40/wk; $10.40/mo (motor route); $124.80/yr.
Advertising: Open inch rate $19.05(m); $19.05(m-sat); $19.05(S). **Representative:** Landon Associates Inc.
News Services: AP, SHNS, THO. **Politics:** Independent. **Established:** 1852.
Special Editions: Progress (Feb); Spring Home Improvement (Mar); Spring Home Improvement (Apr); Car Care (May); Zane's Trace Commemoration, Car Care (June); Car Care (July); County Fair, Football Edition (Aug); Car Care (Sept, Oct); Basketball, Cookbook (Nov).
Magazines: Color Comics, TV Booklet (S).

GENERAL MANAGEMENT

Publisher John B Raytis

ADVERTISING

Director John Bunn
Manager-Retail Greg Bauryer
Manager-Classified Ron Boering

CIRCULATION

Manager Russ Easter

NEWS EXECUTIVE

Managing Editor Richard Stubbe

EDITORS AND MANAGERS

Business/Finance Editor David Ball
City/News Editor Jim Rudloff
Editorial Page Editor Chuck Martin
Education Editor David Ball
Entertainment/Amusements Editor Pam Swingle
Fashion/Style Editor Pam Swingle
Features Editor Pam Swingle
Lifestyle Editor Pam Swingle
National Editor Patrick Jackson
News Editor Tricia Davis
Photo Editor Rick Harrison
Political/Government Editor Patrick Jackson
Sports Editor David Weidig

PRODUCTION

Manager-Composing Barb Starbuck

Market Information: TMC.
Mechanical available: Offset; Black and 3 ROP colors; insert accepted — preprinted, catabooks, coupon envelopes; page cut-offs — 22¾".
Mechanical specifications: Type page 13" x 21½"; E - 6 cols, $2\frac{1}{16}$", ⅛" between; A - 6 cols, $2\frac{1}{16}$", ⅛" between; C - 9 cols, $1\frac{5}{16}$", ⅛" between.
Commodity consumption: Newsprint 1,439 short tons; widths 27¼", 41¼", 55"; black ink 45,200 pounds; color ink 3,700 pounds; single pages printed 8,951; average pages per issue 23(d), 32(S); single plates used 6,770.
Equipment: EDITORIAL: Front-end hardware — Mk; Front-end software — Mk; Printers — COM, V; Other equipment — ECR/Autokon, V/5300B. CLASSIFIED: Front-end hardware — Mk; Front-end software — Mk. DISPLAY: Adv layout systems — Ap/Mac; Front-end hardware — Ap/Mac; Front-end software — Multi-Ad/Creator, QuarkXPress; Printers — V. PRODUCTION: Typesetters — V/5160; Electronic picture desk — Lf/AP Leaf Picture Desk; Scanners — Polaroid/Sprint Scan 35; Automatic film processors — Wing-Lynch/Pro 6; Color separation equipment (conventional) — Lf/AP Leaf Picture Desk.
PRESSROOM: Line 1 — 4-G/Urbanite. MAILROOM: Counter stackers — EDS. COMMUNICATIONS: Facsimile — News-Scan 1000. WIRE SERVICES: News — AP, THO; Photos — AP; Stock tables — AP; Syndicates — Creators, Universal Press, NAS, TMS, King Features, CNS; Receiving dishes — size-12ft, AP. BUSINESS COMPUTERS: NCR; Applications: Payroll, Circ, Adv billing, Accts receivable, Inventory.

OKLAHOMA

ADA

Pontotoc County

'90 U.S. Census- 15,820; **E&P '96 Est.** 15,816
ABC-CZ (90): 15,820 (HH 6,671)

The Ada Evening News (e-mon to fri)
The Ada Sunday News (S)

The Ada Evening News, 116 N. Broadway; PO Box 489, Ada, OK 74820; tel (405) 332-4433; fax (405) 332-8734. Hollinger International Inc. group.
Circulation: 10,190(e); 9,790(S); ABC Sept. 30, 1995.
Price: 25¢(d); $1.25(S); $7.80/mo (city), $7.95/mo (RTZ).
Advertising: Open inch rate $11.47(e); $11.47(S). **Representative:** Papert Companies.
News Service: AP. **Politics:** Independent. **Established:** 1904.
Not Published: Memorial Day; Independence Day; Labor Day; Thanksgiving; Christmas.
Special Editions: Progress; Cookbook; Football; Christmas; Basketball; Newcomer's Guide.
Special Weekly Sections: Business (mon); Education (tues); Best Food Day (wed); Religion (fri); Real Estate (S).
Magazine: Sunday Comics.

GENERAL MANAGEMENT

Publisher/General Manager Roy D Biondi
Accountant Patty Allen

ADVERTISING

Manager Rick Cash

CIRCULATION

Manager Jim Pebworth

NEWS EXECUTIVE

Managing Editor Steve Boggs

EDITORS AND MANAGERS

Business/Finance Editor Tony Pippen
City/Metro Editor Roy Deering
Editorial Page Editor Steve Boggs
Education Editor Jim Miller
Entertainment/Amusements Editor Hank Foster
Farm/Agriculture Editor Hank Foster
Fashion/Style Editor Brenda Tollett
Living/Lifestyle Editor Brenda Tollett
National Editor Christi Holman
News Editor Roy Deering
Photo Editor Richard R Baaron
Political/Government Editor Roy Deering
Sports Editor Mike Wingo
Travel Editor Brenda Tollett
Women's Editor Brenda Tollett

PRODUCTION

Manager James Mouser

Market Information: Zoned editions; TMC.
Mechanical available: Offset; Black and 3 ROP colors; insert accepted — preprinted; page cut-offs — 22⅞".
Mechanical specifications: Type page 13" x 21½"; E - 6 cols, $2\frac{1}{16}$", ⅛" between; A - 6 cols, $2\frac{1}{16}$", ⅛" between; C - 9 cols, $1\frac{3}{8}$", $\frac{1}{16}$" between.
Commodity consumption: Newsprint 300 short tons; width 27½"; black ink 1,000 pounds; color ink 50 pounds; average pages per issue 16(d), 78(S).
Equipment: EDITORIAL: Front-end hardware — Ap/Mac OneScan, Ofoto, Ap/Mac Quadra 600 Avs, Ethernet; Front-end software — QuarkXPress 3.3, Aldus/PageMaker 4.0, Multi-Ad/Creator, Adobe/Illustrator, Aldus/FreeHand 4.0; Printers — Ap/Mac LaserWriter IIG. CLASSIFIED: Front-end hardware — Mk/1100 Plus; Printers — Ap/Mac LaserWriter NTX. DISPLAY: Adv layout systems — Ap/Mac; Front-end software — Multi-Ad/Creator, QPS 3.3; PRODUCTION: Pagination software — QPS 3.3; Typesetters — 2-Ap/Mac LaserWriter NTX, Ap/Mac LaserWriter IIg; Plate exposures — BKY/Ascor; Plate processors — Nat/A-250; Scanners — Ap/Mac OneScan; Production cameras — Acti; Automatic film processors — DAI/Screen; Color separation equipment (conventional) — Digi-Colour/DC-4000.
PRESSROOM: Line 1 — 6-KP/Newsking; Press control system — CH. MAILROOM: Bundle tyer — Akebono. WIRE SERVICES: News — AP, THO, NEA; Photos — AP Photostream; Syndicates — NEA; Receiving dishes — size-1m, AP.

ALTUS

Jackson County

'90 U.S. Census- 21,910; **E&P '96 Est.** 21,219

The Altus Times (e-mon to fri; S)

Altus Times, 218 W. Commerce; PO Box 578, Altus, OK 73521-0578; tel (405) 482-1221; fax (405) 482-5709. Donrey Media group.
Circulation: 5,161(e); 5,161(S); Sworn Oct. 1, 1995.
Price: 50¢(d); $1.00(S); $6.00/mo; $72.00/yr.
Advertising: Open inch rate $7.67(e); $7.67(S). **Representative:** Papert Companies.

I-326 Oklahoma

News Service: AP. **Politics:** Independent. **Established:** 1927.
Not Published: Christmas.
Special Editions: Back-to-School; Progress Review; Football; Cookbook; Graduation; Christmas Shopping; Christmas Greetings; Spring Fashion; Basketball; Brides; Farm & Ranch; Fair; Women's Club; Winter Sports.
Special Weekly Sections: Best Food Day (wed); TV Listings (S).

CORPORATE OFFICER
President/Chief Operating Officer Emmett Jones

GENERAL MANAGEMENT
Chairman of the Board Jack Stephens
Publisher Lyle Exstrom
Purchasing Agent Lyle Exstrom

ADVERTISING
Director Renee Carpenter

CIRCULATION
Manager-Subscriber Service Sandy Graham

NEWS EXECUTIVE
Editor Rick Lomenick

PRODUCTION
Superintendent Sue Bryant

Market Information: Zoned editions; TMC.
Mechanical available: Offset; Black and 3 ROP colors; insert accepted — preprinted; page cut-offs — 22¾".
Mechanical specifications: Type page 13" x 21½"; E - 6 cols, 2.07", ⅙" between; A - 6 cols, 2.07", ⅙" between; C - 8 cols, 1.67", ⅙" between.
Commodity consumption: width 27"; average pages per issue 16(d), 78(S).
Equipment: EDITORIAL: Front-end hardware — Ap/Mac; Front-end software — Aldus/PageMaker 4.2; Printers — Ap/Mac. CLASSIFIED: Front-end hardware — Ap/Mac; Printers — Ap/Mac. DISPLAY: Adv layout systems — Ap/Mac; Front-end software — Aldus/PageMaker 4.2, Multi-Ad/Creator; Printers — Ap/Mac NTX. PRODUCTION: Plate exposures — 1-Nu; Plate processors — Ic; Production cameras — R; Automatic film processors — LE. PRESSROOM: Line 1 — 5-G/Community. MAILROOM: Bundle tyer — MLN/MCD-700; Addressing machine — Label/4 Across. WIRE SERVICES: Receiving dishes — AP. BUSINESS COMPUTERS: Ap/Mac; PCs & micros networked; PCs & main system networked.

ALVA
Woods County
'90 U.S. Census- 5,495; E&P '96 Est. 5,100

Alva Review-Courier
(m-mon, tues, thur, fri; S)

Alva Review-Courier, 620 Choctaw, Alva, OK 73717; tel (405) 327-2200; fax (405) 327-2454.
Circulation: 1,580(m); 1,580(S); Sworn Sept. 29, 1994.
Price: 25¢(d); 50¢(S); $59.00/yr (in county).
Advertising: Open inch rate $3.50(m); $3.50(S).
News Service: AP. **Politics:** Independent. **Established:** 1893.
Special Editions: Basketball (Jan); Graduation (May); Back-to-School, Football (Aug); Christmas (Dec).
Special Weekly Section: Church News (S).

CORPORATE OFFICER
Publisher Lynn L Martin

GENERAL MANAGEMENT
General Manager Lynn L Martin

ADVERTISING
Manager Maxine Bebermeyer

NEWS EXECUTIVE
Editor Marione Martin

PRODUCTION
Manager Tom Derrickson

Market Information: TMC.
Mechanical available: Offset; Black and 2 ROP colors; insert accepted — preprinted.
Mechanical specifications: Type page 11" x 17"; E - 5 cols, 2 1/16", ⅛" between; A - 5 cols, 2 1/16", ⅛" between; C - 5 cols, 2 1/16", ⅛" between.
Commodity consumption: widths 27½", 35"; average pages per issue 12(d), 16(S).
Equipment: EDITORIAL: Front-end hardware — 3-PC; Front-end software — Symantec/Q & A Write. CLASSIFIED: Front-end hardware — 1-PC. DISPLAY: Front-end hardware — 3-PC; Front-end software — Ventura/Publisher, Archetype/Corel Draw; Printers — HP/LaserJet 4. PRESSROOM: Line 1 — 4-HI/U-15A. MAILROOM: Addressing machine — 1-Am. WIRE SERVICES: News — AP; Receiving dishes — AP. BUSINESS COMPUTERS: 3-PC; PCs & micros networked; PCs & main system networked.

ANADARKO
Caddo County
'90 U.S. Census- 6,586; E&P '96 Est. 6,765

The Anadarko Daily News
(e-mon to fri; m-sat)

The Anadarko Daily News, 117-119 E. Broadway; PO Box 548, Anadarko, OK 73005-0548; tel (405) 247-3331; fax (405) 247-5571.
Circulation: 5,128(e); 5,128(m-sat); Sworn Sept. 30, 1995.
Price: 50¢(d); 50¢(sat); $72.00/yr (in county, carrier & mail), $75.00/yr (in county, mail).
Advertising: Open inch rate $6.00(e); $6.00(m-sat). **Representatives:** Papert Companies; The Newspaper National Network.
News Services: AP, NEA. **Politics:** Independent. **Established:** 1901.
Not Published: January 2; Memorial Day; Independence Day; Labor Day; December 26.
Special Editions: Vacation/Visitor's Guide (May-for distribution all year); American Indian Exposition Edition (Aug).
Magazines: TV Tab (fri); Extra (TMC) (weekly).

CORPORATE OFFICERS
President Carolyn N McBride
Secretary/Treasurer Joe W McBride Jr

GENERAL MANAGEMENT
Publisher Joe W McBride Jr
Publisher Carolyn N McBride

ADVERTISING
Manager Cindy J Fletcher

CIRCULATION
Manager Philip Gomez

NEWS EXECUTIVES
Editor Jack Stone
Asst Editor Paula L McBride-Savage

EDITORS AND MANAGERS
Entertainment/Amusements Editor Carla McBride-Alexander
Features Editor Jack Stone
News Editor Paula L McBride-Savage
Television/Music Editor Carla McBride-Alexander
Theater/Films Editor Carla McBride-Alexander
Travel Editor Carolyn N McBride
Weekender Editor Paula L McBride-Savage

PRODUCTION
Superintendent JoNell McBride-Thomas

Market Information: TMC.
Mechanical available: Offset; Black and 7 ROP colors; insert accepted — preprinted; page cut-offs — 22¾".
Mechanical specifications: Type page 13 5/16" x 21"; E - 6 cols, 2.17", ⅙" between; A - 6 cols, 2.17", ⅙" between; C - 8 cols, 1.67", ⅙" between.
Commodity consumption: Newsprint 161 short tons; widths 30", 15"; black ink 4,000 pounds; color ink 200 pounds; single pages printed 3,608; average pages per issue 11.5(d); single plates used 4,400.
Equipment: EDITORIAL: Front-end hardware — Ap/Mac Preforma 575; Front-end software — QPS, SNews-Wire; Printers — Ap/Mac Laser-Printers. CLASSIFIED: Front-end hardware — Ap/Mac IIsi, Ap/Mac Quadra 605; Front-end software — QPS, SNews-Wire; Printers — Ap/Mac LaserWriter II, Ap/Mac LaserWriter 630. PRODUCTION: Typesetters — 2-Mk/Laserprinter, Ap/Mac Pro, 600 DPI, 1-Ap/Power Mac w/LaserPrinter 630, Ap/Mac Performa 575; Platemaking systems — 1-Nu; Plate exposures — 1-Nu; Plate processors — Ic; Electronic picture desk — Nikon/Coolscan, Quick Take Cameras; Scanners — Ap/Mac Scanner, Abaton/300 DPI, Ap/Mac One Scanner 600 DPI; Production cameras — AG/2202 Repromaster; Automatic film processors — Devotech. PRESSROOM: Line 1 — 3-G/Community, 1-G/Community; Folders — KAN, G/Community. MAILROOM: Bundle tyer — Miller-Bauco/Bun Strapper; Addressing machine — KAN. WIRE SERVICES: News — AP; Syndicates — AP, United Features; Receiving dishes — AP. BUSINESS COMPUTERS: 3-Wa, DEC; Applications: Accts receivable, Gen ledger, Payroll; DEC, Real World Acct (in-house program): WA/Acct Payable, WA/Circ; PCs & micros networked.

ARDMORE
Carter County
'90 U.S. Census- 23,079; E&P '96 Est. 23,392

The Daily Ardmoreite
(e-mon to fri; S)

The Daily Ardmoreite, 117 W. Broadway; PO Box 1328, Ardmore, OK 73402; tel (405) 223-2200; fax (405) 226-2363. Morris Communications Corp. group.
Circulation: 11,495(e); 14,043(S); VAC June 30, 1995.
Price: 50¢(d); 75¢(S); $7.50/mo; $90.00/yr.
Advertising: Open inch rate $9.95(e); $9.95(S). **Representative:** Landon Associates Inc.
News Service: AP. **Politics:** Independent. **Established:** 1893.
Special Editions: Fashion (Spring & Fall); Vacation; Bride; Cooking; Sports; Back-to-School; Home Improvement.
Special Weekly Sections: Senior Lifestyles (tues); Food Section, Business (wed); Kids Page, Education Page (thur); Restaurant (fri); Weddings/Engagements, Business, Education (S).
Magazine: "Carousel" (local, newsprint) (S).

GENERAL MANAGEMENT
Publisher Bill Stauffer
General Manager/Purchasing Agent Bill Stauffer
Business Manager Kathy Worley
Controller/Credit Manager Kathy Worley
Personnel Manager Kathy Worley

ADVERTISING
Manager Barbara Winkler
Manager-Sales Jerry Winton

MARKETING AND PROMOTION
Manager-Promotion Barbara Winkler

CIRCULATION
Manager Jim Hefley
Manager-Promotion Stan Middleton

NEWS EXECUTIVE
Managing Editor John Bridwell

EDITORS AND MANAGERS
Amusements/Books Editor Leah Allen
Automotive Editor Tim Parks
Business/Finance Editor Bud Chambers
City Editor Michael Strand
Editorial Page Editor John Bridwell
Editorial Writer/Sunday Editor John Bridwell
Education Editor Karen Treat
Environmental Editor Michael Strand
Features Editor Leah Allen
Films/Theater Editor Leah Allen
Health/Medical Editor Leah Allen
Living/Lifestyle Editor Leah Allen
Music/Society Editor Leah Allen
National Editor Tim Parks
Photo Department Manager Steve Biehn
Police Marsha Miller
Political/Government Editor Bud Chambers
Religion Editor Sue Newman
Sports Editor Clay Horning
Women's Editor Leah Allen

MANAGEMENT INFORMATION SERVICES
Data Processing Manager Kathy Worley

PRODUCTION
Manager Ortrey Hawley
Foreman-Mailroom Stan Middleton

Market Information: TMC; ADS; Operate database.
Mechanical available: Offset; Black and 3 ROP colors; insert accepted — preprinted, post cards, placards, etc.; page cut-offs — 22¾".
Mechanical specifications: Type page 13 1/16" x 21½"; E - 6 cols, 2 1/16", ⅛" between; A - 6 cols, 2 1/16", ⅛" between; C - 8 cols, 1½", 1/16" between.
Commodity consumption: Newsprint 800 short tons; widths 27½", 13¾", 27"; black ink 20,000 pounds; color ink 400 pounds; single pages printed 9,000; average pages per issue 24(d), 48(S); single plates used 20,000.
Equipment: EDITORIAL: Front-end hardware — Ap/Mac; Front-end software — Baseview; Printers — 2-Tl/Lineprinter; Other equipment — 1-Ap/Mac Plus. CLASSIFIED: Front-end hardware — Ap/Mac; Front-end software — Baseview; Printers — Ap/Mac LaserWriter NTX. DISPLAY: Front-end hardware — Ap/Mac Quadra 800, CD, Ap/Power Mac, Mk/Scan-Maker II, Ap/Mac IIci; Front-end software — Multi-Ad/Creator 3.6.2, Multi-Ad/Creator 3.6.3, Adobe/Photoshop 3.0, Aldus/PageMaker 4.0; Printers — MON/Express Master 1270; Other equipment — Ap/Mac LaserWriter IIg. PRODUCTION: Typesetters — MON/Express Master 1270; Plate exposures — 1-Nu/FT41; Plate processors — Nat/250; Electronic picture desk — Lf/AP Leaf Picture Desk, Ap/Mac Quadra 800; Scanners — Ap/Mac Scanner Flat Top; Production cameras — 1-LE/500, R; Automatic film processors — 1-P/531, 1-Richmond, P/26ML; Color separation equipment (conventional) — Ap/Mac Quadra 800. PRESSROOM: Line 1 — 9-G; Line 2 — G/Community; Folders — 1-G; Press control system — Duarte/Pin Register Sys. MAILROOM: Inserters and stuffers — 1-MM; Bundle tyer — 1-Sa, 1-Stra-Pack; Addressing machine — Ch. LIBRARY: Electronic — SMS/Stauffer Gold. WIRE SERVICES: News — AP; Photos — AP; Receiving dishes — AP. BUSINESS COMPUTERS: ATT; Applications: Accts receivable, Payroll, Circ, Payables, Gen ledger.

BARTLESVILLE
Washington County
'90 U.S. Census- 34,526; E&P '96 Est. 34,608
ABC-CZ (90): 41,443 (HH 16,779)

Examiner-Enterprise
(e-mon to fri; S)

Examiner-Enterprise, 4125 Nowata Rd.; PO Box 1278, Bartlesville, OK 74006; tel (918) 335-8200; fax (918) 335-3111. Donrey Media group.
Circulation: 11,903(e); 14,548(S); ABC Sept. 30, 1995.
Price: 50¢(d); 75¢(S); $1.75/wk; $7.00/mo; $84.00/yr.
Advertising: Open inch rate $13.50(e); $13.50(S). **Representative:** Papert Companies.
News Service: AP. **Politics:** Independent. **Established:** 1895.
Note: Effective July 30, 1995, this publication changed its publishing plan from (e-mon to fri; m-sat; S) to (e-mon to fri; S).
Special Editions: Bridal Tab (Jan); Vacation Tab (Feb); Spring Fashion (Mar); Summer Lifestyles Tab (May); OK Mozart (June); How-to-Section (Aug); Fall Fashion, Hunting & Fishing Guide (Sept); Back-to-School, Christmas, Home Improvement, Real Estate Guide, Ideas for Kids (Oct).
Special Weekly Sections: Business, Lifestyle, Best Food (wed); Arts & Entertainment, Health (thur); Garden, Church, Travel Page, Business, Lifestyle (S); Real Estate Guide (every other S).
Magazines: Parade, TV Spotlight (S).
Cable TV: Operate leased cable TV in circulation area.

CORPORATE OFFICERS
Founder Donald W Reynolds
President/Chief Operating Officer Emmett Jones
Exec Vice Pres/Chief Financial Officer Darrell W Loftin
Vice Pres-Western Newspaper Group David A Osborn
Vice Pres-Eastern Newspaper Group Don Schneider

GENERAL MANAGEMENT
Publisher Joseph H Edwards

ADVERTISING
Director Phil Evans
Manager-Retail Donna Silver

TELECOMMUNICATIONS
Contact Susan D Savage

CIRCULATION
Director Pam Yandle
District Manager Quinn Street
District Manager Kim Powers
Distribution Clerk Joseph Severns
Distribution Clerk Adam Phillips
Distribution Clerk Earnest Adams
Distribution Clerk James Jones
Distribution Clerk Larry Evans
Distribution Clerk Brian Schultz

NEWS EXECUTIVES
Managing Editor Susan D Savage
Cable Newspaper Exec Phil Evans

EDITORS AND MANAGERS
Business/Finance Editor Jim Butcher
Cablevision Editor Derrick Harris
Editorial Page Editor Susan D Savage
Education Editor Susan D Savage
Entertainment/Amusements Editor Ian Danziger
Features Editor Ian Danziger
Living/Lifestyle Editor Ian Danziger

News Editor	Susan D Savage
Photo Editor	Becky Burch
Radio/Television Editor	Derrick Harris
Religion Editor	Krystal Carmen
Society/Women's Editor	Ian Danziger
Sports Editor	Mike Skinner
Women's Editor	Ian Danziger
PRODUCTION	
Superintendent	J Hughey
Foreman-Mark-up/Dispatch	Bill Beavers
Foreman-Pressroom	Tom Guffey
Foreman-Camera/Platemaking	Pete Gray

Market Information: Split Run; TMC.
Mechanical available: Offset; Black and 4 ROP colors; insert accepted — preprinted; page cut-offs — 22¾".
Mechanical specifications: Type page 13" x 21½"; E - 6 cols, 2¹⁄₁₆", ⅛" between; A - 6 cols, 2¹⁄₁₆", ⅛" between; C - 9 cols, 1³⁄₈", ⅛" between.
Commodity consumption: Newsprint 720 metric tons; widths 27½", 13¾"; black ink 36,000 pounds; color ink 2,500 pounds; average pages per issue 24(d), 40(S); single plates used 10,000.
Equipment: EDITORIAL: Front-end hardware — AST; Front-end software — Dewar/Disc Net; Printers — Ap/Mac LaserWriter II NT; Other equipment — Ap/Mac IIcx, AP Photostream, Lf/Leafscan 35, HP/ScanJet Flatbed. CLASSIFIED: Front-end hardware — AST; Front-end software — Dewar/Disc Net; Printers — Ap/Mac LaserWriter II NT. DISPLAY: Front-end hardware — Ap/Mac; Printers — Ap/Mac LaserWriter II. PRODUCTION: Typesetters — Ap/Mac LaserWriter II; Platemaking systems — 3M/Deadliner (Pyrofax); Plate exposures — Nu/Plate Maker; Plate processors — 1-Nu; Electronic picture desk — AP/Photostream, Lf/AP Leaf Picture Desk; Scanners — HP/ScanJet; Production cameras — C/Spartan III; Automatic film processors — Vastech/VT-22; Color separation equipment (conventional) — C/Spartan III.
PRESSROOM: Line 1 — 8-G/Urbanite; Press drives — 2-Fin/75 h.p.; Folders — 1-U599; Press registration system — Duarte. MAILROOM: Counter stackers — HL/Monitor; Inserters and stuffers — KAN; Bundle tyer — MLN; Mailroom control system — BG/Count-O-Veyor. 2-MLN/Strapping Machines. COMMUNICATIONS: Systems used — satellite. WIRE SERVICES: News — AP, NYT; Photos — AP; Receiving dishes — size-8ft, AP. BUSINESS COMPUTERS: SCS; Applications: Lotus 1-2-3, Orchestrator: Adv & subscriber service records, Payroll.

BLACKWELL
Kay County
'90 U.S. Census- 7,538; **E&P '96 Est.** 7,409

Blackwell Journal-Tribune
(e-tues to fri; S)
Blackwell Journal-Tribune, 113 E. Blackwell Ave.; Box 760, Blackwell, OK 74631; tel (405) 363-3370; fax (405) 363-4451. Donrey Media group.
Circulation: 3,025(e); 3,025(S); Sworn Oct. 2, 1995.
Price: 50¢(d); 50¢(S); $5.50/mo; $66.00/yr.
Advertising: Open inch rate $6.30(e); $6.30(S). **Representative:** Papert Companies.
News Service: AP. **Established:** 1893.
Not Published: Thanksgiving, Christmas.
Special Editions: Spring Fashion; Graduation; Kay County Fair; Back-to-School; Christmas Gifts; Christmas Greetings.
Special Weekly Sections: Food Pages (wed); Church Pages (fri).

CORPORATE OFFICERS	
Founder	Donald W Reynolds
President/Chief Operating Officer	Emmett Jones
Exec Vice Pres/Chief Financial Officer	Darrell W Loftin
Vice Pres-Western Newspaper Group	David A Osborn
Vice Pres-Eastern Newspaper Group	Don Schneider
GENERAL MANAGEMENT	
Publisher	Dayle E McGaha
General/Personnel Manager	Dayle E McGaha
Manager-Credit	Mary R Cormack
Purchasing Agent	Dayle E McGaha
ADVERTISING	
Director	Lamar Allen
Manager-Classified	Mary R Cormack
CIRCULATION	
Manager	Dean Smith

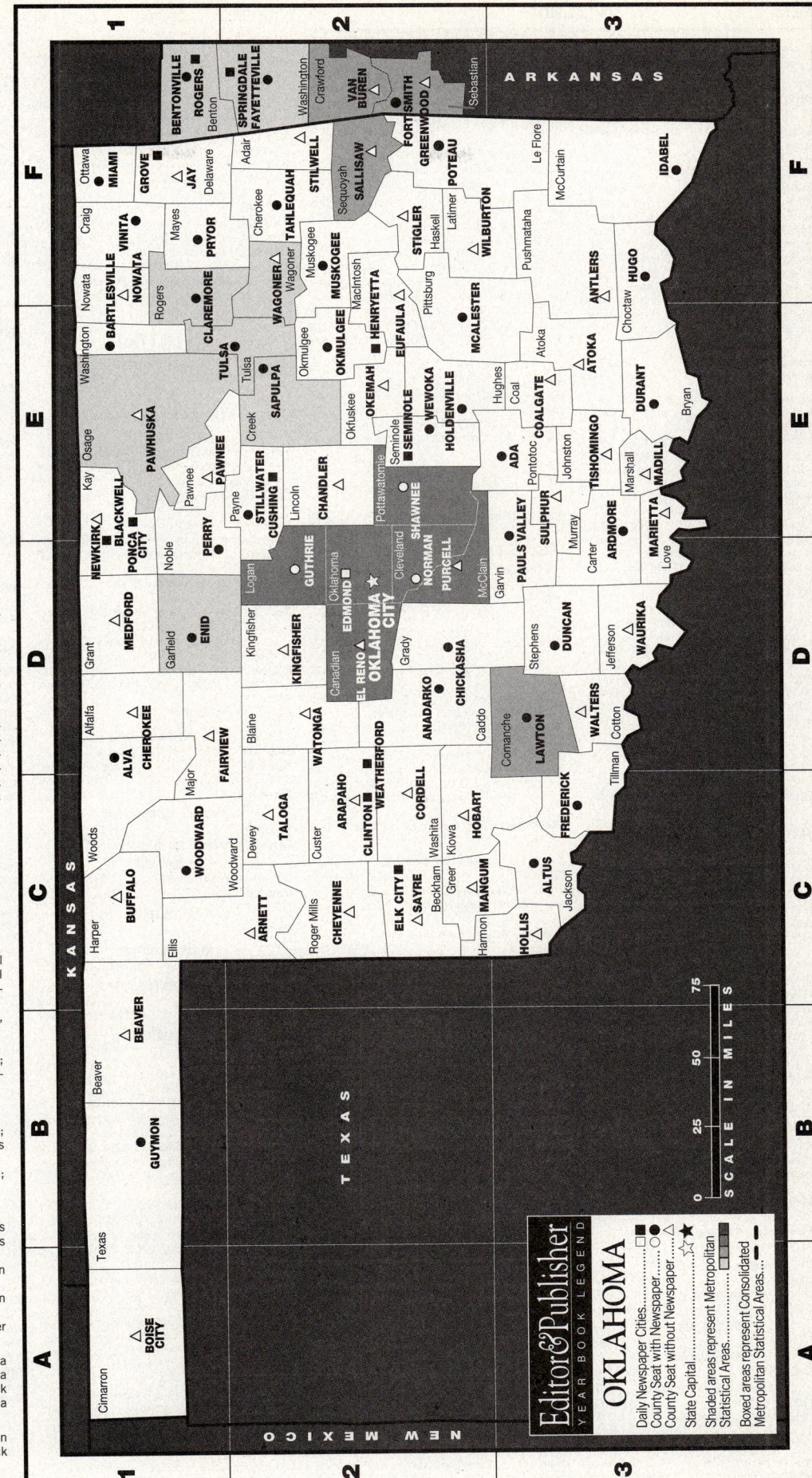

Copyright ©1996 by the Editor & Publisher Co.

I-328 Oklahoma

NEWS EXECUTIVES

Editor Dayle E McGaha
Managing Editor Terry Groover

EDITORS AND MANAGERS

Amusements Editor Helen Seubert
Aviation/Farm Editor Charles Abbott
Books/Films Editor Dayle E McGaha
Business Editor/Columnist Dayle E McGaha
Cartoonist Charles Abbott
City Editor Helen Seubert
Consumer Interest/Food Editor Helen Seubert
Editorial Page Editor Dayle E McGaha
Education/Religion Editor Helen Seubert
Garden Editor Dayle E McGaha
Home Furnishings Editor Helen Seubert
Photo Department Manager Charles Abbott
Director-Photography Charles Abbott
Society Editor Helen Seubert
Sports Editor Charles Abbott

PRODUCTION

Foreman-Composing Celia Balli
Superintendent-Pressroom John Franz

Mechanical available: Offset; Black and 1 ROP color; insert accepted — preprinted, standing cards; page cut-offs — 22¾".
Mechanical specifications: Type page 13" x 21½"; E - 6 cols, 2 1/16", ⅛" between; A - 6 cols, 2 1/16", ⅛" between; C - 8 cols, 1½", 1/16" between.
Commodity consumption: Newsprint 72 metric tons; widths 27", 13½"; black ink 2,250 pounds; color ink 50 pounds; single pages printed 2,678; average pages per issue 8(d), 12(S); single plates used 2,000.
Equipment: EDITORIAL: Front-end hardware — Mk/Mycro-Comp 1100; Printers — 2-Ap/Mac LaserWriter. DISPLAY: Front-end hardware — Ap/Mac IIsi, Ap/Mac IIci; Front-end software — QuarkXPress, Adobe/Illustrator, Microsoft/Word, Adobe/Photoshop, Microtek/Scanmaker 600ZS; Printers — NewGen/400dpi; Other equipment — Microtek/Scanmaker 600ZS. PRODUCTION: Typesetters — Ap/Mac Laser-Writer; Production cameras — 1-R/Centurion. PRESSROOM: Line 1 — 5-G/Community. WIRE SERVICES: News — AP.

CHICKASHA

Grady County

'90 U.S. Census- 14,988; E&P '96 Est. 14,863

Chickasha Daily Express

(e-mon to fri; S)

Chickasha Daily Express, 302 N. 3rd St. (73018); PO Drawer E, Chickasha, OK 73023; tel (405) 224-2600; fax (405) 224-7087. Donrey Media group.
Circulation: 4,646(e); 5,328(S); VAC June 30, 1995.
Price: 50¢(d); $1.00(S); $6.50/mo; $78.00/yr.
Advertising: Open inch rate $7.25(e); $7.25(S). **Representative:** Papert Companies.
News Service: AP. **Politics:** Democrat. **Established:** 1892.
Not Published: Christmas.
Special Editions: Progress (Feb); Cookbook (Apr); Spring Fashion, Fall Fashion, Gift Guide, Super Value (Aug).
Special Weekly Sections: Best Food Day, Farm Page (wed); Farm Page (S).
Magazine: TV Marquee (S).

CORPORATE OFFICERS

Founder Donald W Reynolds
President/Chief Operating Officer Emmett Jones
Exec Vice Pres/Chief Financial Officer Darrell W Loftin
Vice Pres-Western Newspaper Group David A Osborn
Vice Pres-Eastern Newspaper Group Don Schneider

GENERAL MANAGEMENT

Publisher Reg Freemyer

ADVERTISING

Manager Elaine Johnson

CIRCULATION

Director Mike Gallaway

NEWS EXECUTIVE

Managing Editor Kent Bush

EDITORS AND MANAGERS

Fashion/Food Editor Ronda Huffines
Home Furnishings/Society Editor Ronda Huffines

PRODUCTION

Foreman-Composing Room Jim Ward
Foreman-Pressroom Kevin Bogdan

Mechanical available: Offset; Black and 3 ROP colors; insert accepted — preprinted; page cut-offs — 22¾".
Mechanical specifications: Type page 13" x 21½"; E - 6 cols, 2 1/16", ⅛" between; A - 6 cols, 2 1/16", ⅛" between; C - 8 cols, 1⅝", ⅛" between.
Commodity consumption: Newsprint 220 metric tons; widths 27½", 13¾"; black ink 8,000 pounds; color ink 250 pounds; single pages printed 6,000; average pages per issue 10(d), 30(S); single plates used 3,000.
Equipment: EDITORIAL: Front-end hardware — 6-Ap/Mac SE30; Printers — Ap/Mac Laser-Writer IIcx. CLASSIFIED: Front-end hardware — 1-Ap/Mac SE30; Printers — 1-Ap/Mac ImageWriter; Other equipment — Ap/Mac SE20. DISPLAY: Adv layout systems — 2-Ap/Mac SE20. PRODUCTION: Platemaking systems — 1-B/2500-, Nu; Production cameras — 1-R, C.
PRESSROOM: Line 1 — 5-G/Community; Folders — 1-G. MAILROOM: Bundle tyer — Ca; Addressing machine — Wm. WIRE SERVICES: Syndicates — AP; Receiving dishes — AP. BUSINESS COMPUTERS: PCs & micros networked; PCs & main system networked.

CLAREMORE

Rogers County

'90 U.S. Census- 13,280; E&P '96 Est. 14,276

The Claremore Daily Progress (e-tues to fri; S)

The Claremore Daily Progress, 315 W. Will Rogers Blvd.; PO Box 248, Claremore, OK 74017; tel (918) 341-1101; fax (918) 341-1131. Donrey Media group.
Circulation: 6,112(e); 6,112(S); Sworn Oct. 3, 1995.
Price: 50¢(d); 50¢(S); $6.50/mo; $39.00/6mo; $78.00/yr.
Advertising: Open inch rate $8.67(e); $8.67(S). **Representative:** Papert Companies.
News Service: AP. **Politics:** Independent. **Established:** 1893.
Not Published: Thanksgiving; Christmas.
Special Editions: Graduation; Rodeo; Fair; Will Rogers Day; Most Progressive Citizen; Christmas; Medical Services; Football; Spring Sports.
Special Weekly Sections: Best Food Day (wed); Church (fri); Health (S).

CORPORATE OFFICERS

Founder Donald W Reynolds
President/Chief Operating Officer Emmett Jones
Exec Vice Pres/Chief Financial Officer Darrell W Loftin
Vice Pres-Western Newspaper Group David A Osborn
Vice Pres-Eastern Newspaper Group Don Schneider

GENERAL MANAGEMENT

Publisher/Purchasing Agent Dave Story

ADVERTISING

Manager Dave Kucifer

CIRCULATION

Director Terry Ladd

NEWS EXECUTIVE

Editor Dave Story

EDITORS AND MANAGERS

Action Line Editor (U-Ask-It) Pat Reeder
City Editor Lisa Willhoit
City Editor Pat Reeder
Editorial Page Editor Dave Story
Education Editor Lisa Willhoit
Environmental Editor Dorothy Willman
Farm/Agriculture Editor Dorothy Willman
Features Editor Dorothy Willman
Lifestyle Editor Dorothy Willman
Political/Government Editor Dave Story
Religion Editor Dorothy Willman
Sports Editor Jim Perry

PRODUCTION

Superintendent Chris Hughey

Market Information: TMC.
Mechanical available: Offset; Black and 3 ROP colors; insert accepted — preprinted, hi-fi, spectacolor, speed 12; page cut-offs — 22½".
Mechanical specifications: Type page 13" x 21½"; E - 6 cols, 2 1/16", ⅛" between; A - 6 cols, 2 1/16", ⅛" between; C - 6 cols, 2 1/16", ⅛" between.
Commodity consumption: Newsprint 240 short tons; widths 28", 14"; black ink 25,000 pounds; color ink 1,250 pounds; single pages printed 8,100; average pages per issue 20(d), 36(S); single plates used 5,000.
Equipment: EDITORIAL: Front-end hardware — Mk; Front-end software — Mk. CLASSIFIED: Front-end hardware — Mk; Other equipment — 1-DEC/LA 80. DISPLAY: Adv layout systems — Ap/Mac II; Front-end hardware — Mk/Ad Builder. PRODUCTION: Typesetters — 1-Mk/AdWriter; Plate exposures — 1-Nu; Plate processors — 1-Ic; Scanners — 2-COM; Production cameras — 1-R; Automatic film processors — 1-LE.
PRESSROOM: Line 1 — 7-HI; Folders — 1-HI. MAILROOM: Inserters and stuffers — 1-KAN/320; Bundle tyer — 1-Bu; Addressing machine — 1-Am. WIRE SERVICES: News — AP; Receiving dishes — size-2ft, AP, Donrey Satellite Network. BUSINESS COMPUTERS: 1-DPT/8200; Applications: Billing records, Customer data.

CLINTON

Custer County

'90 U.S. Census- 9,298; E&P '96 Est. 9,715

The Clinton Daily News

(e-mon to fri; S)

The Clinton Daily News, 522 Avant Ave., Clinton, OK 73601; tel (405) 323-5151; fax (405) 323-5154.
Circulation: 5,091(e); 5,091(S); Sworn Sept. 29, 1995.
Price: 50¢(d); 50¢(S); $64.00/yr.
Advertising: Open inch rate $5.58(e); $5.58(S). **Representative:** Papert Companies.
News Service: AP. **Politics:** Independent. **Established:** 1927.
Not Published: New Year; Memorial Day; Independence Day; Labor Day; Thanksgiving; Christmas (except when holidays other than Thanksgiving fall on Thursday).
Special Weekly Sections: Food (wed); Entertainment, Farm, Legal (thur); Real Estate, Business (S).
Magazine: TV Guide (fri & S).

CORPORATE OFFICERS

President Chas E Engleman
Vice Pres Steve Engleman
Vice Pres Carol Sander
Secretary Jean Engleman

GENERAL MANAGEMENT

Publisher Chas E Engleman
General Manager/Assoc Publisher Rod Serfoss

ADVERTISING

Manager-National Reba Donley
Manager-Classified Gaylene Roulet

CIRCULATION

Manager Ronda Scott

NEWS EXECUTIVE

Editor Chas E Engleman

EDITORS AND MANAGERS

News Editor Steve Belcher
Sports Editor Steve McGaughey

PRODUCTION

Superintendent Pete Sawatzky
Foreman-Composing Irene Williams

Market Information: TMC.
Mechanical available: Offset; Black and 2 ROP colors; insert accepted — preprinted; page cut-offs — 22¾".
Mechanical specifications: Type page 13" x 21½"; E - 6 cols, 2 1/16", ⅛" between; A - 6 cols, 2 1/16", ⅛" between; C - 8 cols, 1½", ⅛" between.
Commodity consumption: Newsprint 324 short tons; width 30"; black ink 7,000 pounds; color ink 400 pounds; single pages printed 4,590; average pages per issue 18(d), 30(S); single plates used 5,000.
Equipment: EDITORIAL: Front-end hardware — 4-COM/MDT, COM/Mk; Front-end software — Mk. CLASSIFIED: Front-end hardware — COM/MDT. PRODUCTION: Typesetters — 1-COM/Unisetter, 1-COM/Trendsetter; Plate processors — 1-Nu; Production cameras — 1-Carey; Automatic film processors — 1-LE.
PRESSROOM: Line 1 — 4-G/Community; Folders — 1-G. MAILROOM: Inserters and stuffers — 1-KAN/Inserter (3 station); Bundle tyer — 1-Felins; Addressing machine — 1-Am. WIRE SERVICES: AP. BUSINESS COMPUTERS: 1-Wa/Professional; Applications: Accts receivable.

CUSHING

Payne County

'90 U.S. Census- 7,218; E&P '96 Est. 7,071

Cushing Daily Citizen

(e-mon to fri)

Cushing Daily Citizen, 115 S. Cleveland, Cushing, OK 74023; tel (918) 225-3333; fax (918) 225-1050.
Circulation: 3,110(e); Sworn Sept. 30, 1995.
Price: 50¢(d); $6.00/mo (carrier); $60.00/yr (mail).
Advertising: Open inch rate $5.93(e). **Representative:** Papert Companies.
News Service: AP. **Politics:** Republican. **Established:** 1895.
Note: Effective Feb. 26, 1995, this publication changed its publishing plan from (e-tues to fri; S) to (e-mon to fri).
Not Published: Independence Day; Thanksgiving; Christmas.
Special Editions: Spring Style; Fall Style Show; Christmas Opening; Christmas Greetings; Dollar Day; Graduation; School Opening; Progress; Pride.
Magazine: Young at Heart/Senior Citizen (semi-monthly).

CORPORATE OFFICER

Secretary Myra Reid

GENERAL MANAGEMENT

Publisher David W Reid

ADVERTISING

Manager Brian Hammock

MARKETING AND PROMOTION

Manager-Marketing & Promotion Brian Hammock

CIRCULATION

Manager Cito Trujillo

NEWS EXECUTIVE

Managing Editor Terry Hoggatt

PRODUCTION

Manager Shon Treat

Market Information: Zoned editions; Split Run; TMC.
Mechanical available: Offset; Black and 2 ROP colors; insert accepted — preprinted, all; page cut-offs — 21".
Mechanical specifications: Type page 13" x 21"; E - 6 cols, 2.07", 1/12" between; A - 6 cols, 2.07", 1/12" between; C - 8 cols, 1.58", 1/12" between.
Commodity consumption: Newsprint 132 short tons; widths 27½", 13¾"; black ink 4,000 pounds; color ink 250 pounds; single pages printed 3,750; average pages per issue 10(d); single plates used 1,320.
Equipment: EDITORIAL: Front-end hardware — 4-Ap/Mac; Front-end software — Aldus/Page-Maker; Printers — NewGen/600 dpi Laser. CLASSIFIED: Front-end hardware — 1-Ap/Mac; Front-end software — Hypercard; Printers — NewGen/600 dpi. DISPLAY: Adv layout systems — Ap/Mac; Front-end software — Multi-Ad/Creator; Printers — NewGen/600 dpi, Ap/Mac Laser Pro 630; Other equipment — Scan-CD. PRODUCTION: Pagination software — Caere/OmniPage; Typesetters — Ap/Mac LP 630; Scanners — Umax.
PRESSROOM: Line 1 — 4-G/Community. MAILROOM: Inserters and stuffers — KAN/780. WIRE SERVICES: News — AP Pony Service; Syndicates — NEA. BUSINESS COMPUTERS: IBM/Hard; Applications: Peachtree.

DUNCAN

Stephens County

'90 U.S. Census- 21,732; E&P '96 Est. 21,864

The Duncan Banner

(e-mon to fri; S)

The Duncan Banner, 10th & Elm; PO Box 1268, Duncan, OK 73534; tel (405) 255-5354; fax (405) 255-8889; e-mail bannernews@ad.com.
Circulation: 9,552(e); 10,849(S); Sworn June 30, 1995.
Price: 50¢(d); $1.00(S); $6.75/mo; $73.00/yr.
Advertising: Open inch rate $8.10(e); $8.10(S). **Representative:** Papert Companies.
News Services: AP, NEA. **Politics:** Independent. **Established:** 1892.
Special Editions: Christmas Gift Guide; Football; Bridal; Junior Livestock Show; County Fair; Customer Appreciation; Home Improvement; Car Care; Graduation; Horizons; World's Largest Garage Sale; Heritage Day Festival; Back-to-School.
Special Weekly Section: TV Magazine (S).

CORPORATE OFFICERS

President Alexander J Hruby
Vice Pres M M Wheeler

GENERAL MANAGEMENT

Publisher Alexander J Hruby
General Manager Carl Bowers

ADVERTISING

Manager Jill Hunt
Manager-Classified Paula Blair

MARKETING AND PROMOTION

Director-Marketing/Promotion Jill Hunt

CIRCULATION

Manager John A Hruby

NEWS EXECUTIVES

Editor Alexander J Hruby
Exec Editor Carl Bowers
Managing Editor Larry Gittings

EDITORS AND MANAGERS

Books Editor Mary Louise Buckley
Business Editor Glen Seeber
Editorial Page Editor Al Hruby
Editorial Writer Larry Gittings
Education Editor Heidi Brandes
Librarian Joanne Templeton
Political Editor Glen Seeber
Sports Editor Jeff Kaley
Women's Editor Donna Van Treese

PRODUCTION

Manager Alvin Oliver
Manager-Systems Karen Kaley

Market Information: Zoned editions; Split Run; TMC; ADS.
Mechanical available: Offset; Black and 3 ROP colors; insert accepted — preprinted; page cutoffs — 22¾".
Mechanical specifications: Type page 13" x 21"; E - 6 cols, 2$^{1}/_{16}$", ⅛" between; A - 6 cols, 2$^{1}/_{16}$", ⅛" between; C - 8 cols, 1⅜", $^{1}/_{16}$" between.
Commodity consumption: Newsprint 462 short tons; width 27"; black ink 6,260 pounds; color ink 1,050 pounds; single pages printed 6,268; average pages per issue 16(d), 36(S); single plates used 5,625.
Equipment: EDITORIAL: Front-end hardware — 11-Epson, Mk/4000; Front-end software — Mk/Newstouch AT; Printers — Ap/Mac LaserWriter II NTX; Other equipment — 2-PC Notebook, 2-RSK/TRS 80 model 100. CLASSIFIED: Front-end hardware — 3-Epson, Mk/4000; Printers — TI/OMNI 800, Ap/Mac LaserWriter Plus. DISPLAY: Front-end hardware — Ap/Mac IIcx, 1-Mk, Ap/Power Mac 7100; Front-end software — Aldus/PageMaker, Claris/MacWrite, Aldus/FreeHand, Multi-Ad/Creator 3.7; Printers — NewGen/Imager Plus 12; Other equipment — 2-Ap/Mac Scanner, CD-Rom Drive. PRODUCTION: OCR software — Caere/OmniPage; Typesetters — Ap/Mac LaserWriters, NewGen/ImagerPlus 12; Plate exposures — 1-Nu; Electronic picture desk — Lf/AP Leaf Picture Desk, Ap/Power Mac 8100; Scanners — Ap/Mac Scanner, Nikon/Coolscan; Production cameras — C/Spartan III; Automatic film processors — LE/LD-18; Color separation equipment (conventional) — C.
PRESSROOM: Line 1 — 6-HI/Cotrell V25; Folders — 1-HI; Reels and stands — HI/Cotrell; Press control system — HI/Cotrell. MAILROOM: Inserters and stuffers — 5-KAN/480; Bundle tyer — 1-MLN/ML2-EE; Addressing machine — 2-Wm; Other mailroom equipment — Kohner/Quick Stitcher. WIRE SERVICES: News — AP; Photos — AP; Receiving dishes — size-14ft, AP. BUSINESS COMPUTERS: 7-Sun/Sparc 10; Applications: PBS: Acct, Circ, Adv, Mgmt; PCs & main system networked.

DURANT

Bryan County

'90 U.S. Census- 12,823; E&P '96 Est. 13,553

Durant Daily Democrat

(e-mon to fri; S)

Durant Daily Democrat, 200 W. Beech St. (74701); PO Box 250, Durant, OK 74702-0250; tel (405) 924-4388; fax (405) 924-6026. Donrey Media group.
Circulation: 6,291(e); 6,291(S); Sworn Sept. 29, 1995.
Price: 50¢(d); $1.00(S); $7.00/mo; $84.00/yr.
Advertising: Open inch rate $8.36(e); $8.36(S). **Representative:** Papert Companies.
News Services: AP, NEA. **Politics:** Democrat. **Established:** 1900.
Not Published: New Year; Memorial Day; Independence Day; Labor Day; Thanksgiving; Christmas.
Special Editions: Space Clearance (Jan); Chamber of Commerce (Feb); Home Improvement (Apr); Bridal Tab, Car Care, Graduation (May); Football Opening, County Fair (Sept); Basketball Opening, Car Care, Home Improvement (Oct); Holiday Cooking Guide, Christmas Promotion (Nov); Last Minute Gift Guide, Christmas Greetings (Dec).
Special Weekly Sections: Texoma Valve Pac (wed); Texoma Wheels (S).
Magazine: Entertainment Showcase (local entertainment & TV listings) (S).

CORPORATE OFFICERS

Founder Donald W Reynolds
President/Chief Operating Officer Emmett Jones
Exec Vice Pres/Chief Financial Officer Darrell W Loftin
Vice Pres-Eastern Newspaper Group Don Schneider
Vice Pres-Western Newspaper Group David Osborn

GENERAL MANAGEMENT

Publisher David L Crouch

ADVERTISING

Director Paula Howell
Manager-Classified Dianne Harp
Manager-Retail Frankie Foster

CIRCULATION

Manager-Sales Joe Potts

NEWS EXECUTIVE

News Editor John A Small

EDITORS AND MANAGERS

Amusements Editor Patrick Barrett
Editorial Page Editor David L Crouch

PRODUCTION

Superintendent-Press Dan Ballew
Superintendent-Composing Betty Argo

Market Information: TMC.
Mechanical available: Offset; Black and 3 ROP colors; insert accepted — preprinted; page cutoffs — 22¾".
Mechanical specifications: Type page 13" x 21½"; E - 6 cols, 2$^{1}/_{16}$", ⅛" between; A - 6 cols, 2$^{1}/_{16}$", ⅛" between; C - 8 cols, 1½", $^{1}/_{16}$" between.
Commodity consumption: Newsprint 240 metric tons; widths 13.50", 27"; black ink 10,000 pounds; color ink 1,200 pounds; single pages printed 5,000; average pages per issue 12(d), 22(S); single plates used 10,000.
Equipment: EDITORIAL: Front-end hardware — 6-Ap/Mac SE; Front-end software — Microsoft/Word, Aldus/PageMaker, SNews-Wire 1.0; CLASSIFIED: Front-end hardware — 1-Ap/Mac SE; Front-end software — Computers Associates/Classified. DISPLAY: Front-end software — Aldus/PageMaker, Microsoft/Word, Deneba/Canvas, Adobe/Illustrator, Caere/OmniPage. PRODUCTION: OCR software — Caere/OmniPage 3.0; Typesetters — 2-Ap/Mac NTX, 1-Ap/Mac SE, 3-Ap/Mac cx; Plate exposures — 1-Nu/FT 40V6VPNS; Scanners — 1-Ap/Mac Scanner; Production cameras — 1-Walzberg/26-10; Automatic film processors — LE/17.
PRESSROOM: Line 1 — 5-KP/Newsking; Folders — 1-KP. MAILROOM: Bundle tyer — MLN; Wrapping singles — 4-Sa. WIRE SERVICES: News — AP; Receiving dishes — size-2ft, AP. BUSINESS COMPUTERS: Starlit/386-DX-40, CTX/Monitor, 3-Acer/Open, 3-Acer/View 34T Monitor, Scout Classic 144C Modem; Applications: Progress/4GC Base System, Smart/One modem, Brainworks, Window; PCs & main system networked.

EDMOND

Oklahoma County

'90 U.S. Census- 52,315; E&P '96 Est. 70,483

Edmond Evening Sun

(e-tues to fri; S)

Edmond Evening Sun, 123 S. Broadway; PO Box 2470, Edmond, OK 73083; tel (405) 341-2121; fax (405) 340-7363; e-mail edmond.sun@icon.net; web site http://www.edmondsun.com/. Livermore Newspapers group.
Circulation: 9,532(e); 10,383(S); VAC Dec. 30, 1994.
Price: 50¢(d); 75¢(S); $7.00/mo; $78.00/yr.
Advertising: Open inch rate $9.30(e); $9.30(S). **Representative:** US Suburban Press.
News Service: AP. **Politics:** Independent. **Established:** 1889.
Not Published: New Year; Independence Day; Thanksgiving; Christmas.
Special Editions: Wedding Planner, Chamber Plan of Action (Jan); Lawn & Garden/Home Improvement, Vacation Give-away (Feb); Services & Celebrations (Mar); Here's to the Good Life, Spring & Summer Arts Alive (Apr); Edmond's Critical 18 (Golf), Salute to Seniors (May); Community Review, Family Owned Businesses, Parade of Homes (June); IPRA Rodeo, EASP Little League Review, Krazy Daze, Back-to-School (July); Computer Friendly, Fall & Winter Arts Alive, Cheers, Fall Sports Preview (Aug); College Bound (Sept); Christmas Gift Guide, Christmas Kick-off (Nov); Christmas Greetings (Dec).
Special Weekly Sections: Pet Page, Health Page (tues); Education Pages, Food, Lifestyle Pages (wed); Business Pages (thur); Education Pages, Home/Garden, Religion, Entertainment (fri); Travel, Sports, Women's, Lifestyle Pages, Education Pages (S).
Magazine: Ruff Draft (teen).

CORPORATE OFFICERS

President Ed Livermore Jr
Vice Pres Melba H Livermore
Secretary Sarah Spencer
Treasurer Marcia H Livermore

GENERAL MANAGEMENT

Publisher Ed Livermore Jr
Controller Marcia H Livermore

ADVERTISING

Director Tammy Clare

CIRCULATION

Director Jay Holman

NEWS EXECUTIVES

Editor Ed Livermore Jr
Managing Editor Carol Hartzog

EDITORS AND MANAGERS

City Editor Steve Gust
Editorial Page Editor Carol Hartzog
Films/Theater Editor Clif Warren
Food Editor Carol Smaglinski
Photo Department Manager James Coburn
Sports Editor Terry Tush

PRODUCTION

Foreman-Press Wade Davidson
Foreman-Composing Michael Wehrenberg

Market Information: TMC.
Mechanical available: Offset; Black and 3 ROP colors; insert accepted — preprinted; page cutoffs — 22¾".
Mechanical specifications: Type page 13" x 21½"; E - 6 cols, 2", ⅛" between; A - 6 cols, 2", ⅛" between; C - 9 cols, 2", ⅛" between.
Commodity consumption: Newsprint 600 short tons; widths 27½", 13¾"; black ink 10,000 pounds; color ink 500 pounds; single pages printed 7,500; average pages per issue 24(d), 40(S); single plates used 3,500.
Equipment: EDITORIAL: Front-end hardware — Mk; Front-end software — Mk/MC2000. CLASSIFIED: Front-end hardware — 4-Ap/Mac; Front-end software — Baseview. DISPLAY: Adv layout systems — 2-Ap/Mac AdWriter; Front-end software — Multi-Ad/Creator. PRODUCTION: Pagination software — SII; Typesetters — 3-Ap/Mac LaserWriter, 2-ECR/Imagesetter; Plate processors — 1-Ic; Electronic picture desk — Lf/AP Leaf Picture Desk; Production cameras — 1-C/Spartan III; Automatic film processors — 1-B; Film transporters — 1-LE; Color separation equipment (conventional) — Adobe/Photoshop.
PRESSROOM: Line 1 — 6-HI/V15-A (W/Color hump). MAILROOM: Counter stackers — 1-BG; Inserters and stuffers — 1-DG; Bundle tyer — 2-Bu. WIRE SERVICES: News — AP; Syndicates — NYT; Receiving dishes — size-10ft, AP. BUSINESS COMPUTERS: IBM/Personal Sys II; Applications: Circ, Payroll, Gen ledger, Accts receivable, Accts payable; PCs & micros networked; PCs & main system networked.

ELK CITY

Beckham County

'90 U.S. Census- 10,428; E&P '96 Est. 11,163

Elk City Daily News

(e-mon to fri; S)

Elk City Daily News, 200-206 W. Broadway; PO Box 1009, Elk City, OK 73648; tel (405) 225-3000; fax (405) 243-2414.
Circulation: 4,931(e); 4,931(S); Sworn Sept. 15, 1994.
Price: 50¢(d); 50¢(S); $6.00/mo; $60.00/yr (mail), $63.00/yr (carrier).
Advertising: Open inch rate $5.73(e); $5.73(S). **Representative:** Papert Companies.
News Service: AP. **Politics:** Independent-Democrat. **Established:** 1901.
Not Published: New Year; Monday after Easter; Memorial Day; Independence Day; Labor Day; Thanksgiving; Christmas.
Special Editions: Rodeo; Christmas; Oil & Gas Industry; Recipe; Downtown Tab; Progress Tab; Bridal; Chamber Tab; Jaycee Tab; Home Improvement Tab; Community Theater Tab.
Special Weekly Section: TV Tab (S).
Magazine: Television.

CORPORATE OFFICERS

President Larry R Wade
Secretary/Treasurer Mary Jane Wade

GENERAL MANAGEMENT

Publisher Larry R Wade

ADVERTISING

Director Sharon Denney

CIRCULATION

Manager Calvin Stone

NEWS EXECUTIVE

Managing Editor Robert Fisher

EDITORS AND MANAGERS

Automotive Editor Sharon Denney
Business/Finance Editor Larry R Wade
City/Metro Editor John Lyon
Editorial Page Editor Larry R Wade
Education Editor Jo Ann Meddrens
Environmental Editor John Lyon
Farm/Agriculture Editor Bob Fisher
Graphics Editor/Art Director Bob Fisher
Health/Medical Editor John Lyon
National Editor Larry R Wade
News Editor Bob Fisher
Photo Editor Bob Fisher
Political/Government Editor Larry R Wade
Religion Editor Bob Fisher
Sports Editor Danny Fletcher
Television/Film Editor Owene Scott
Travel Editor Helen Burnett

PRODUCTION

Manager Calvin Stone

Market Information: Zoned editions; TMC.
Mechanical available: Offset; Black and 2 ROP colors; insert accepted — preprinted; page cutoffs — 21".
Mechanical specifications: Type page 13" x 20½"; E - 6 cols, 2$^{1}/_{16}$", ⅛" between; A - 6 cols, 2$^{1}/_{16}$", ⅛" between; C - 6 cols, 2$^{1}/_{16}$", ⅛" between.
Commodity consumption: Newsprint 320 short tons; widths 30", 15"; black ink 7,650 pounds; color ink 500 pounds; single pages printed 4,822; average pages per issue 18(d), 36(S); single plates used 6,596.
Equipment: EDITORIAL: Front-end hardware — Innovative Technology, 5-PC; Printers — 3-Ap/Mac LaserPrinter. CLASSIFIED: Front-end hardware — Innovative Technology; Printers — 3-Ap/Mac LaserPrinter, 3-Dot Matrix. DISPLAY: Front-end hardware — 3-Innovative Technology. PRODUCTION: Platemaking systems — 1-WL, 1-Nat/A-250; Plate exposures — 1-Nu/FT40LNS; Plate processors — 1-Nat/A-250; Production cameras — 1-B, 1-Acti/125; Automatic film processors — LE/LD24AQ.
PRESSROOM: Line 1 — 4-G/Community; Folders — 1-G/2:1. MAILROOM: Inserters and stuffers — 1-Cr, KAN; Bundle tyer — 1-Cr; Addressing machine — Am/Farrington, Innovative Technology/IBM-Compatible. WIRE SERVICES: News — AP; Receiving dishes — size-4ft, AP. BUSINESS COMPUTERS: Innovative Technology/IBM-compatible; Applications: WordPerfect/Editorial; PCs & micros networked.

ENID

Garfield County

'90 U.S. Census- 45,309; E&P '96 Est. 43,360
ABC-CZ (90): 49,152 (HH 19,615)

Enid News & Eagle

(m-mon to sat; S)

Enid News & Eagle, 227 W. Broadway; PO Box 1192, Enid, OK 73702; tel (405) 233-6600; fax (405) 233-7645. Thomson Newspapers group.
Circulation: 22,281(m); 22,281(m-sat); 24,373(S); ABC Sept. 30, 1995.
Price: 35¢(d); 35¢(sat); $1.25(S); $9.65/mo (carrier); $115.80/yr.
Advertising: Open inch rate $17.26(m); $17.26(m-sat); $17.26(S). **Representative:** Landon Associates Inc.
News Services: AP, NEA, THO. **Politics:** Republican. **Established:** 1893.

Copyright ©1996 by the Editor & Publisher Co.

Special Editions: Neighbor; Lawn & Garden; Recreation; Home Improvement; Bridal; Graduation; Car Care; Garfield County Fair; Dining Guide; Fall Car Care; Christmas Gift Guide; Football Tab; Senior Citizen; Real Estate; Travel & Recreation.
Special Weekly Sections: Best Food Day (wed); CoverSTORY (fri).
Magazine: USA Weekend.

GENERAL MANAGEMENT
Publisher Ed J Hauck
Accountant Glenda Hicks

ADVERTISING
Director Nancy Walton

NEWS EXECUTIVE
Managing Editor Jerry Pittman

EDITORS AND MANAGERS
City Editor Jeff Mullin
News Editor Kevin Hassler
Sports Editor Mark Rountree

MANAGEMENT INFORMATION SERVICES
Data Processing Manager Glenda Hicks

PRODUCTION
Superintendent-Composing David Allred
Superintendent-Pressroom Vance Trammell

Market Information: TMC.
Mechanical available: Offset; Black and 3 ROP colors; insert accepted — preprinted, cards; page cut-offs — 21½".
Mechanical specifications: Type page 13" x 21½"; E - 6 cols, 2", ⅛" between; A - 6 cols, 2", ⅛" between; C - 9 cols, 1⅜", 1/16" between.
Commodity consumption: Newsprint 1,357 short tons; width 27½"; black ink 31,500 pounds; color ink 4,000 pounds; single pages printed 10,876; average pages per issue 22(d), 56(S); single plates used 17,430.
Equipment: EDITORIAL: Front-end hardware — 2-CD/12300, 10-CD/Magician Plus, 4-CD/Page Magician; Front-end software — CD, DP. CLASSIFIED: Front-end hardware — 5-CD/Magician Plus; Printers — Okidata/393. DISPLAY: Front-end hardware — 3-Ap/Mac, 2-CD/Magician Plus; Front-end software — Multi-Ad/Creator; Printers — 2-Ap/Mac LaserWriter II. PRODUCTION: Typesetters — 2-V/5100E; Plate processors — Nat/A-250; Production cameras — C/Spartan II 1244; Automatic film processors — LE/LD-2600A; Film transporters — C/Spartan II 1247; Color separation equipment (conventional) — Lf/Leafscan 35.
PRESSROOM: Line 1 — 8-G/Urbanite; Press drives — 2-75 h.p. motor; Press control system — 2-Fin/Consoles; Press registration system — Pin System. MAILROOM: Inserters and stuffers — MM/227; Bundle tyer — 2-MLN, 1-OVL; Addressing machine — Ch. WIRE SERVICES: News — AP, THO; Photos — AP; Stock tables — AP; Receiving dishes — size-10ft, AP. BUSINESS COMPUTERS: ATT/3B2-500; Applications: Payroll, Accts receivable, Gen ledger, Circ, Accts.

FREDERICK
Tillman County
'90 U.S. Census- 5,221; E&P '96 Est. 4,694

Frederick Leader
(e-tues to fri; S)

Frederick Leader, 304 W. Grand; PO Box 190, Frederick, OK 73542; tel (405) 335-2188; fax (405) 335-2047. Donrey Media group.
Circulation: 2,340(e); 2,340(S); Sworn Oct. 1, 1995.
Price: 50¢(d); 50¢(S).
Advertising: Open inch rate $4.88(e); $4.88(S). **Representative:** Papert Companies.
News Services: NEA, CNS, Compulog. **Politics:** Independent. **Established:** 1904.
Not Published: New Year; Independence Day; Thanksgiving; Christmas.
Special Editions: Ag Week (Apr); Graduation (May); Back-to-School (Aug); Christmas (Dec).
Special Weekly Sections: Best Food Day (wed); TV listings (fri).
Magazine: Food (wed).

CORPORATE OFFICERS
Founder Donald W Reynolds
President/Chief Operating Officer Emmett Jones
Exec Vice Pres/Chief Financial Officer Darrell W Loftin
Vice Pres-Western Newspaper Group David A Osborn
Vice Pres-Eastern Newspaper Group Don Schneider

GENERAL MANAGEMENT
Publisher/General Manager Barbara Tucker

ADVERTISING
Manager-Local/National Robin Coronado

MARKETING AND PROMOTION
Manager-Promotion Barbara Tucker

CIRCULATION
Manager Kimi Strickland

NEWS EXECUTIVES
Co-Editor John Banks
Co-Editor Terri Erickson

EDITORS AND MANAGERS
Amusements Editor Terri Erickson
Military/Religion Editor John Banks
Society Editor Terri Erickson
Sports Editor John Banks
Women's Interests Editor Terri Erickson

Mechanical available: Offset; Black; insert accepted — preprinted.
Mechanical specifications: Type page 13" x 21½"; E - 6 cols, 2 1/16", ⅛" between; A - 6 cols, 2 1/16", ⅛" between; C - 6 cols, 2 1/16", ⅛" between.
Equipment: EDITORIAL: Front-end hardware — 3-Ap/Mac II. PRODUCTION: Typesetters — 2-Ap/Mac LaserWriter II, 2-Ap/Mac.

GROVE
Delaware County
'90 U.S. Census- 4,020; E&P '96 Est. 5,425

The Source (m-tues to sat)

The Source, 103A 1st St., Grove, OK 74344; tel (918) 786-9002; fax (918) 786-6048. Pryor Publishing Co. group.
Circulation: 5,000(m); 5,000(m-sat). Estimate Sept. 30, 1995.
Price: 25¢(d); 25¢(sat); $5.00/mo; $39.95/yr.
Advertising: Open inch rate $3.75(m); $3.75(m-sat). **Established:** 1995.

GENERAL MANAGEMENT
Publisher Greg Hardin

ADVERTISING
Director Pam Weeks
Sales Linda On-The-Hill

CIRCULATION
Manager Rick Jordan

NEWS EXECUTIVE
Editor Sherrie Langston

EDITORS AND MANAGERS
Education Writer Janet Perry
News Reporter Jim Weeks
Sports Editor Jack Perkins

Mechanical available: Black and 4 ROP colors; page cut-offs — 21".
Mechanical specifications: Type page 13" x 21"; E - 6 cols, 2 1/18", ⅙" between; A - 6 cols, 2⅛", ⅙" between.
Commodity consumption: average pages per issue 12(d).

GUTHRIE
Logan County
'90 U.S. Census- 10,518; E&P '96 Est. 10,707

Guthrie Daily Leader
(e-tues to fri; S)

Guthrie Daily Leader, 107 W. Harrison; PO Box 879, Guthrie, OK 73044; tel (405) 282-2222. Donrey Media group.
Circulation: 2,196(e); 2,439(S); VAC June 30, 1995.
Price: 50¢(d); 50¢(S); $5.50/mo; $66.00/yr.
Advertising: Open inch rate $5.85(e); $5.85(S). **Representatives:** Papert Companies; Oklahoma Press Service. **Politics:** Independent. **Established:** 1889.
Not Published: New Year; Labor Day; Day before Thanksgiving; Christmas.
Special Editions: Restoration; FFA; Chamber Tab; Home & Garden; Graduation; Back-to-School; Football; Christmas Gifts; Newcomers; Folk Festival; Krazy Daze; Visitor's Guide; Arts & Crafts; Statehood.
Special Weekly Sections: Best Food Day (wed); Best Church News (thur); TV Schedule (daily).
Magazine: Entertainment Guide (television listings) (fri).

CORPORATE OFFICERS
Founder Donald W Reynolds
President/Chief Operating Officer Emmett Jones
Exec Vice Pres/Chief Financial Officer Darrell W Loftin
Vice Pres-Eastern Newspaper Group Don Schneider
Vice Pres-Western Newspaper Group David A Osborn

GENERAL MANAGEMENT
Publisher Robert Hager

ADVERTISING
Manager Lynn McMahan

CIRCULATION
Manager Brian Brock

NEWS EXECUTIVE
Editor Bob Williams

EDITORS AND MANAGERS
Food Editor Robert Hager
Sports Editor Jeff Halpern

PRODUCTION
Superintendent-Composing Linda Powell

Market Information: TMC.
Mechanical available: Offset; Black and 1 ROP color; insert accepted — preprinted; page cut-offs — 22¾".
Mechanical specifications: Type page 13" x 21½"; E - 6 cols, 2⅛", ⅙" between; A - 6 cols, 2⅛", ⅙" between; C - 8 cols, 1½", ⅙" between.
Commodity consumption: Newsprint 39 short tons; widths 27.5", 13.74"; black ink 4,900 pounds; color ink 150 pounds; single pages printed 2,900; average pages per issue 10(d), 16(S); single plates used 1,800.
Equipment: EDITORIAL: Front-end hardware — Mk; Front-end software — Mk. CLASSIFIED: Front-end hardware — Mk; Front-end software — Mk. DISPLAY: Adv layout systems — Ap/Mac; Front-end hardware — Ap/Mac IIsi; Front-end software — QuarkXPress; Printers — 1-Ap/Mac LaserWriter. PRODUCTION: Typesetters — Ap/Mac LaserWriter; Plate exposures — 1-Nu; Production cameras — Acti/204.
PRESSROOM: Line 1 — 4-G/Community. MAILROOM: Bundle tyer — Strapex. WIRE SERVICES: Syndicates — NEA.

GUYMON
Texas County
'90 U.S. Census- 7,803; E&P '96 Est. 7,399

Guymon Daily Herald
(e-mon to sat)

Guymon Daily Herald, 515 N. Ellison St.; PO Box 19, Guymon, OK 73942; tel (405) 338-3355; fax (405) 338-5000. Donrey Media group.
Circulation: 3,578(e); 3,578(e-sat); Sworn Sept. 29, 1995.
Price: 50¢(d); 50¢(sat); $6.00/mo; $72.00/yr.
Advertising: Open inch rate $5.95(e); $5.95(e-sat). **Representative:** Papert Companies.
News Service: AP. **Politics:** Independent. **Established:** 1891 (weekly), 1945 (daily).
Not Published: New Year; Independence Day; Thanksgiving; Christmas.
Special Editions: Progress (Feb); Pioneer Days (Apr); Graduation (May); Texas County Fair (Sept); Cookbook, Christmas Gift Guide (Nov); Christmas Greetings (Dec).
Magazine: TV Guide Tab (fri).
Cable TV: Own cable TV in circulation area.

CORPORATE OFFICERS
Founder Donald W Reynolds
President/Chief Operating Officer Emmett Jones
Exec Vice Pres/Chief Financial Officer Darrell W Loftin
Vice Pres-Western Newspaper Group David A Osborn
Vice Pres-Eastern Newspaper Group Don Schneider

GENERAL MANAGEMENT
Publisher Bill Murphy

ADVERTISING
Manager Donna Stephens
Manager-Classified Myrna Campbell

CIRCULATION
Manager Sherril Wicker

NEWS EXECUTIVES
Editor Bill Murphy
Managing Editor Linda Holbert

EDITORS AND MANAGERS
Society Editor Linda O'Leary
Sports Editor William (Bill) Garrett

Market Information: TMC.
Mechanical available: Offset; Black and 3 ROP colors; insert accepted — preprinted, card; page cut-offs — 21½".
Mechanical specifications: Type page 13" x 21½"; E - 6 cols, 2 1/16", ⅛" between; A - 6 cols, 2 1/16", ⅛" between; C - 8 cols, 1⅜", 1/16" between.
Commodity consumption: Newsprint 120 metric tons; width 27½"; black ink 300 pounds; color ink 100 pounds; average pages per issue 12(d).
Equipment: EDITORIAL: Front-end hardware — Mk/4003; Front-end software — Mk; Printers — 2-Ap/Mac LaserWriter. CLASSIFIED: Front-end hardware — Mk/4003; Printers — Ap/Mac LaserWriter. DISPLAY: Adv layout systems — Ap/Mac; Printers — Ap/Mac LaserWriter. PRODUCTION: Production cameras — Acti/214; Automatic film processors — C/T-45; Shrink lenses — 1-CK Optical/SQU-7.
PRESSROOM: Line 1 — 4-G/Community; Folders — 1-G/2:1. MAILROOM: Bundle tyer — 1-Malow/Mc Heavy Duty. LIBRARY: Electronic — Recordak/Magnaprint Reader. WIRE SERVICES: News — AP; Receiving dishes — AP.

HENRYETTA
Okmulgee County
'90 U.S. Census- 5,872; E&P '96 Est. 5,544

Henryetta Daily Free-Lance
(e-tues to fri; S)

Henryetta Daily Free-Lance, 812-16 W. Main St.; PO Box 848, Henryetta, OK 74437; tel (918) 652-3311; fax (918) 652-7347. Donrey Media group.
Circulation: 1,967(e); 1,967(S); Sworn Oct. 4, 1995.
Price: 50¢(d); 50¢(S); $6.00/mo; $72.00/yr.
Advertising: Open inch rate $6.00(e); $6.00(S). **Representative:** Papert Companies.
News Services: AP, NEA. **Politics:** Independent. **Established:** 1902.
Note: Printing and production are done at Okmulgee Daily Times.
Advertising not accepted: Porno numbers.
Special Editions: Fashion Section (Mar); Garden Tab (Apr); Do it Yourself Tab (May); Labor Day Celebration (Sept); Football Tab (Oct); Christmas Guide (Dec); Health & Beauty Section.
Special Weekly Sections: Best Food Day (wed); Religion (fri); TV Guide (daily).
Magazines: School Tab; X'mas Gift Supplement.

CORPORATE OFFICERS
Founder Donald W Reynolds
President/Chief Operating Officer Emmett Jones
Exec Vice Pres/Chief Financial Officer Darrell W Loftin
Vice Pres-Western Newspaper Group David A Osborn
Vice Pres-Eastern Newspaper Group Don Schneider

GENERAL MANAGEMENT
Publisher Nancy Miller

ADVERTISING
Manager-Retail Charlotte Klutts

MARKETING AND PROMOTION
Director-Marketing/Promotion Charlotte Klutts

CIRCULATION
Manager Charlene Pemberton

NEWS EXECUTIVE
News Editor Chelsea C Cook

EDITORS AND MANAGERS
Feature Editor Cy Selfridge
Sports Editor Jeff Sparks

PRODUCTION
Manager Gina Bates

Market Information: TMC.
Mechanical available: Offset; Black and 2 ROP colors; insert accepted — preprinted, cards, envelopes; page cut-offs — 21½".
Mechanical specifications: Type page 13" x 21½"; E - 6 cols, 2 1/16", ⅙" between; A - 6 cols, 2 1/16", ⅙" between; C - 8 cols, 1½", ⅙" between.
Commodity consumption: single pages printed 2,300; average pages per issue 10(d), 14(S).
Equipment: EDITORIAL: Front-end hardware — Ap/Mac SE; Front-end software — Microsoft/Word, Aldus/PageMaker; Printers — Ap/Mac LaserWriter II NT, Ap/Mac LaserWriter Pro 630. CLASSIFIED: Front-end hardware — Ap/Mac SE; Front-end software — Microsoft/Word, Aldus/PageMaker; Printers — Ap/Mac ImageWriter. DISPLAY: Adv layout systems — Ap/Mac SE, 2-Ap/Mac Centris 610; Front-end

Copyright ©1996 by the Editor & Publisher Co.

Oklahoma I-331

software — Microsoft/Word, Aldus/PageMaker; Printers — Ap/Mac LaserWriter II NT, Ap/Mac LaserWriter Pro 630. MAILROOM: Addressing machine — 1-Wm. WIRE SERVICES: News — AP; Receiving dishes — AP.

HOLDENVILLE
Hughes County

'90 U.S. Census- 4,792; E&P '96 Est. 4,402

Holdenville Daily News
(e-tues to fri; S)

Holdenville Daily News, 112 S. Creek St.; PO Box 751, Holdenville, OK 74848; tel (405) 379-5411; fax (405) 379-5413. Robinson-Pettis Publishing group.

Circulation: 2,800(e); 2,800(S); Sworn Sept. 30, 1992.

Price: 25¢(d); 25¢(S); $4.00/mo.

Advertising: Open inch rate $4.15(e); $4.15(S). **Representative:** Papert Companies. **Politics:** Democrat. **Established:** 1898 (weekly), 1927 (daily).

Special Editions: Western Week, Fall Festival (Aug); Christmas Greetings (Dec).

GENERAL MANAGEMENT

Publisher — Bill Robinson
Publisher — Dayna Robinson

ADVERTISING

Manager — Debbie Carter

NEWS EXECUTIVE

Editor — Gertrude Robinson

Market Information: Split Run; TMC.

Mechanical available: Offset; Black and 1 ROP color; insert accepted — preprinted; page cut-offs — 21½".

Mechanical specifications: Type page 13" x 21½"; E - 6 cols, 2 1/16", 1/8" between; A - 6 cols, 2 1/16", 1/8" between; C - 6 cols, 2 1/16", 1/8" between.

Commodity consumption: average pages per issue 8(d), 8(S).

Equipment: EDITORIAL: Other equipment — 4-Ap/Mac SE, 1-Ap/Mac LaserWriter. CLASSIFIED: Other equipment — SCM/250. PRODUCTION: Typesetters — 1-Ap/Mac SE, Ap/Mac LaserWriter.
PRESSROOM: Line 1 — 1-KP/3 unit; Folders — 1-KP/2:1. MAILROOM: Addressing machine — Wm.

HUGO
Choctaw County

'90 U.S. Census- 5,978; E&P '96 Est. 5,311

Hugo Daily News (e-mon to fri)

Hugo Daily News, 128 E. Jackson St., Hugo, OK 74743; tel (405) 326-3311; fax (405) 326-6397.

Circulation: 2,454(e); Sworn Oct. 4, 1995.

Price: 35¢(d); $5.00/mo.

Advertising: Open inch rate $4.30(e).

News Service: AP. **Politics:** Independent. **Established:** 1915.

Not Published: Thanksgiving; Christmas; Monday holidays.

Special Weekly Sections: Business (mon); Best Food Day (wed); Agriculture (thur); TV Guide, Real Estate (fri).

CORPORATE OFFICERS

President — Stan Stamper
Vice Pres/Secretary/Treasurer — Judy Stamper

GENERAL MANAGEMENT

Publisher/General Manager — Stan Stamper

ADVERTISING

Director — Linda Packard

CIRCULATION

Director — Christy Todd

NEWS EXECUTIVE

Editor — Pam Proctor

Market Information: TMC.

Mechanical available: Offset; Black and 1 ROP color; insert accepted — preprinted.

Mechanical specifications: Type page 13" x 21"; E - 6 cols, 2 1/16", 1/8" between; A - 6 cols, 2 1/16", 1/8" between; C - 6 cols, 2 1/16", 1/8" between.

Commodity consumption: average pages per issue 10(d).

Equipment: EDITORIAL: Front-end hardware — Ap/Mac; Front-end software — Ap/Mac. CLASSIFIED: Front-end hardware — 1-Ap/Mac. DISPLAY: Printers — Ap/Mac LaserPrinter. PRODUCTION: Typesetters — 2-Ap/Mac LaserWriter; Plate exposures — 1-B/3000, 1-Nu/Flip Top; Scanners — Ap/Mac Scanner; Production cameras — 1-B.
PRESSROOM: Line 1 — 3-Color King (offset). MAILROOM: Bundle tyer — 1-Bu. LIBRARY: Electronic — 1-AP. WIRE SERVICES: News — AP; Receiving dishes — size-1m, AP. BUSINESS COMPUTERS: Applications: Bookkeeping, Circ, Adv.

IDABEL
McCurtain County

'90 U.S. Census- 6,957; E&P '96 Est. 6,568

McCurtain Daily Gazette
(e-tues to fri; S)

McCurtain Daily Gazette, 107 S. Central; PO Box 179, Idabel, OK 74745; tel (405) 286-3321; fax (405) 286-2208.

Circulation: 6,200(e); 7,900(S); Sworn Sept. 29, 1995.

Price: 25¢(d); 50¢(S); $3.60/mo (carrier).

Advertising: Open inch rate $5.35(e); $5.65(S). **Representative:** Papert Companies.

News Service: AP. **Politics:** Independent. **Established:** 1969.

Special Editions: Lawn & Garden (Feb); Owa-Chito Celebration (June); Football (Aug); Community Builders Annual (Oct); Hunters Edition (Nov); Christmas Kick-off (Dec); Seasonal Tab Sections; Annual Festival Tab.

Special Weekly Sections: Food (wed); TV Section, Farm Page (S).

Magazine: Sunday Showcase Entertainment Tab (S).

CORPORATE OFFICERS

President — Bruce Willingham
Vice Pres — Gwen Willingham
Secretary/Treasurer — Haskell Willingham

GENERAL MANAGEMENT

Publisher — Bruce Willingham

ADVERTISING

Manager — Marge Jones

CIRCULATION

Manager — Donna Barber

EDITORS AND MANAGERS

News Editor — Jeff Holliday
Sports Editor — Brad Reesing

Market Information: TMC.

Mechanical available: Offset; Black and 2 ROP colors; insert accepted — preprinted; page cut-offs — 22¾".

Mechanical specifications: Type page 13" x 21"; E - 6 cols, 2 1/16", 1/8" between; A - 6 cols, 2 1/16", 1/8" between; C - 8 cols, 1 3/8", 1/16" between.

Commodity consumption: width 28"; average pages per issue 12(d), 32(S).

Equipment: EDITORIAL: Front-end hardware — TC; Front-end software — TC. CLASSIFIED: Front-end hardware — Ap/Mac. DISPLAY: Adv layout systems — 3-Ap/Mac; Printers — Ap/Mac LaserWriter. PRODUCTION: Typesetters — TC/Laserwriter; Plate exposures — 1-Nu; Production cameras — 1-B.
PRESSROOM: Line 1 — 3-HI/V15. MAILROOM: Bundle tyer — 2-WT; Addressing machine — 1-RSK/TRS 80 Computer Printer. WIRE SERVICES: News — AP; Syndicates — NEA; Receiving dishes — AP. BUSINESS COMPUTERS: 2-RSK/TRS 80 II; Applications: Circ, Adv billing, Bookkeeping; PCs & micros networked; PCs & main system networked.

LAWTON
Comanche County

'90 U.S. Census- 80,561; E&P '96 Est. 81,160
ABC-CZ (90): 80,802 (HH 29,616)

The Lawton Constitution
(m-mon to sat)
The Sunday Constitution (S)

The Lawton Constitution, 102 S. 3rd St.; PO Box 2069, Lawton, OK 73502; tel (405) 353-0620; fax (405) 353-6020; e-mail paper@ionet.net.

Circulation: 24,713(m); 24,713(m-sat); 30,505(S); ABC Sept. 30, 1995.

Price: 50¢(d); 50¢(sat); $1.00(S); $9.50/mo, $108.00/yr.

Advertising: Open inch rate $11.75(m); $11.75(m-sat); $12.35(S). **Representative:** Landon Associates Inc.

News Services: AP, NYT. **Politics:** Democrat. **Established:** 1901.

Special Weekly Sections: Business Review Page, Neighbors, Markets/Financial (tues); Best Food Day, Markets/Financial (wed); Home & Garden, Markets/Financial (thur); Markets/Financial (fri); Neighbors, Markets/Financial (sat).

Magazine: Tele Tab (S).

GENERAL MANAGEMENT

Co-Publisher — Don Bentley
Co-Publisher — Steve Bentley
Business Manager — James Cottingham

ADVERTISING

Manager-Classified — Edna Stanley
Manager-Retail — Mike Owensby

TELECOMMUNICATIONS

Audiotex Manager — Teresa Jensen

CIRCULATION

Director — J David Cleland

NEWS EXECUTIVES

Co-Editor — Don Bentley
Co-Editor — Steve Bentley
Managing Editor — Dennis Lang
Asst Managing Editor — Steve Robertson

EDITORS AND MANAGERS

Amusements/Books Editor — Charles Clark
Business/Finance Editor — Steve Robertson
City Editor — Dee Ann Patterson
City Editor — Bob Hudson
Columnist — Eve Sandstrom
Editorial Page Editor — David Hale
Education Editor — Sue Sprenkle
Farm Editor — Jeanne Grimes
Fashion/Style Editor — Charles Clark
Films/Theater Editor — Charles Clark
Food Editor — Dee Ann Patterson
Librarian — Phyllis Sleet
Librarian — Joan Mello
Living/Lifestyle Editor — Charles Clark
Music Editor — Charles Clark
Political Editor — Tom Jackson
Radio/Television Editor — Dee Ann Patterson
Religion Editor — Rini Knitter
Sports Editor — Joey Goodman
Wire Editor — Eve Sandstrom
Wire Editor — Mitch Mattek
Wire Editor — Jayne Boykin
Women's Editor — Charles Clark

MANAGEMENT INFORMATION SERVICES

Data Processing Manager — James Cottingham

PRODUCTION

Superintendent-Composing — Glen Dunn
Superintendent-Pressroom — Michael Cross
Foreman-Mailroom — Greg Hines
Foreman-Pressroom (Night) — James Tweedy

Market Information: Operate audiotex.

Mechanical available: Offset; Black and 3 ROP colors; insert accepted — preprinted.

Mechanical specifications: Type page 13" x 21½"; E - 6 cols, 2 1/16", 1/8" between; A - 6 cols, 2 1/16", 1/8" between; C - 9 cols, 1 5/16", 1/8" between.

Commodity consumption: Newsprint 2,261 short tons; widths 27½", 41¼", 55", 13¾"; black ink 39,241 pounds; color ink 14,998 pounds; single pages printed 12,946; average pages per issue 28.68(d), 31.50(sat), 73.50(S); single plates used 35,400.

Equipment: EDITORIAL: Front-end hardware — PC/386, Ap/Mac; Front-end software — Mk, QuarkXPress; Printers — TI/8920. CLASSIFIED: Front-end hardware — PC/386SX; Front-end software — Mk; Printers — TI/8920. AUDIOTEX: Supplier name — Brite Voice Systems. DISPLAY: Adv layout systems — Mk; Front-end hardware — Ap/Mac; Front-end software — Multi-Ad/Creator. PRODUCTION: Pagination software — QuarkXPress 3.2; OCR software — Caere/OmniPage; Typesetters — 2-ECR/3850; Plate exposures — 1-Nu; Plate processors — 1-Graham/S-3A-27; Electronic picture desk — Lf/AP Leaf Picture Desk; Scanners — Hel; Production cameras — 2-C; Color separation equipment (conventional) — Hel; Digital color separation equipment — Hel.
PRESSROOM: Line 1 — 6-HI/1650 offset double width; Press drives — HI; Folders — HI/2:1 RBF; Pasters — 5-MEG. MAILROOM: Counter stackers — Id/440, Id/550, 2-MM/310; Inserters and stuffers — 2-MM/2275 0-6; Bundle tyer — 2-Dynaric; Addressing machine — KR. LIBRARY: Electronic — News View. WIRE SERVICES: News — AP, NYT, CNS; Photos — AP; Stock tables — AP; Syndicates — AP, NYT, CNS. BUSINESS COMPUTERS: TI/1500; Applications: Payroll, Accts payable, Accts receivable, Gen ledger; PCs & micros networked; PCs & main system networked.

McALESTER
Pittsburg County

'90 U.S. Census- 16,370; E&P '96 Est. 15,856
ABC-CZ (90): 18,325 (HH 7,267)

McAlester News-Capital & Democrat (e-mon to fri; S)

McAlester News-Capital & Democrat, 500 S. 2nd; PO Box 987, McAlester, OK 74501; tel (918) 423-1700. Park Communications Inc. group.

Circulation: 11,979(e); 11,951(S); ABC Sept. 30, 1995.

Price: 50¢(d); $1.00(S); $7.50/mo (carrier); $90.00/yr (carrier).

Advertising: Open inch rate $13.78(e); $13.78(S). **Representative:** Landon Associates Inc.

News Services: AP, NEA. **Established:** 1896.

Not Published: Christmas.

Special Editions: Winter Madness, January Clearance, Reader's Choice (Jan); Heart Smart, Total Living Show (Feb); Livestock Show, Spring Fix-up Guide, Lake Eufaula/Crappiethon (Mar); Drug Tab, Arrowhead Mall, Progress Edition, Armed Forces Tab (Apr); Mother's Day, Graduation, Nursing Home Week, Italian Festival (May); Father's Day, Family Owned Business (June); Arrowhead Mall, 4th of July, Crazy Days (July); Pittsburg County Free Fair, Football Section, Back-to-School (Aug); All Around the House, OSP Rodeo, Gold Years, Fall Fashion (Sept); Early Holiday Shopping, Nat'l. Businesswomen, Newcomer's Guide, Fall Home Page (Oct); Shop Early, Lay-away, Thanksgiving Food, Holiday Cookbook, Holly Edition (Nov); Open Sunday, Christmas Countdown, Santa's Elves, Last Minute Shopping, Christmas Cards, Don't Open until after Christmas (Dec).

Special Weekly Sections: Business and Industry Page (mon); Children's Mini Page (tues); Grocery Day (TMC) (wed); Church (thur); Sports, Society (daily).

Magazines: TV Magazine (fri); USA Weekend, Color Comics (S).

CORPORATE OFFICER

President — Wright M Thomas

GENERAL MANAGEMENT

Publisher/General Manager — Owen Jones

ADVERTISING

Manager — Jeanette Griden

CIRCULATION

Manager — Charley Staton

NEWS EXECUTIVE

Managing Editor — Shawn Ashley

EDITORS AND MANAGERS

Area Editor — James Beaty
City Editor — Shawn Ashley
Editorial Page Editor — Owen Jones
Entertainment/Amusements Editor — Teresa Atkerson
Living/Lifestyle Editor — Teresa Atkerson
Society Editor — Teresa Atkerson
Sports Editor — Bill Scott
Women's Editor — Teresa Atkerson

PRODUCTION

Supervisor — Debra Durbin

Market Information: TMC.

Mechanical available: Offset; Black and 4 ROP colors; insert accepted — preprinted, standing cards; page cut-offs — 21½".

Mechanical specifications: Type page 13" x 21½"; E - 6 cols, 2.07", 1/8" between; A - 6 cols, 2.07", 1/8" between; C - 10 cols, 1.22", 1/12" between.

Commodity consumption: Newsprint 550 short tons; widths 27½", 13¾"; black ink 8,000 pounds; color ink 400 pounds; single pages printed 7,198; average pages per issue 22(d), 28(S).

Equipment: EDITORIAL: Front-end hardware — 9-Ap/Mac; Front-end software — Mk/Mycro-Comp Freedom-Pagination; Printers — Ap/Mac LaserWriter II; Other equipment — Ap/Mac One Scanner. CLASSIFIED: Front-end hardware — 2-Ap/Mac; Front-end software — Mk; Printers — Ap/Mac LaserWriter II. DISPLAY: Adv layout systems — CD-Rom/Electronic Art; Front-end hardware — Mk, Ap/Mac; Front-end software — Multi-Ad; Printers — Ap/Mac LaserWriter II; Other equipment — Recas/Electronic Co-Op Service. PRODUCTION: Pagination software — Mk/Mycro-Comp Freedom; Typesetters — 2-Ap/Mac LaserWriter II; Plate processors — 1-Nu; Production cameras — 1-C; Automatic film processors — 1-C.
PRESSROOM: Line 1 — 8-G/Community; Folders — 1-G/SC; Press registration system —

Duarte. MAILROOM: Bundle tyer — 1-Dynaric/SM-50, 1-Malow/Mc Heavy Duty Tyer. WIRE SERVICES: News — AP; Syndicates — NEA; UPI. BUSINESS COMPUTERS: Applications: Vision Data: Accts payable, Accts receivable, Gen ledger, Circ; PCs & micros networked.

MIAMI
Ottawa County
'90 U.S. Census- 13,142; E&P '96 Est. 12,500

Miami News-Record
(e-mon to fri; S)

Miami News-Record, 14 First Ave.; PO Box 940, Miami, OK 74355; tel (918) 542-5533; fax (918) 542-1903. Boone Newspapers Inc. group.
Circulation: 7,226(e); 7,226(S); Sworn Sept. 29, 1995.
Price: 50¢(d); $1.25(S); $7.50/mo; $90.00/yr.
Advertising: Open inch rate $8.15(e); $8.15(S). **Representative:** Papert Companies.
News Service: AP. **Politics:** Independent. **Established:** 1890.
Special Editions: Progress, Washington's Birthday, Tax Tips (Feb); Spring Living, Oklahoma Springtime (Mar); Rodeo Days, Sidewalk (July); Football (Aug); Pre Christmas Value Days, Basketball, Car Care, Christmas Gift Guide (Nov); Christmas Greetings (Dec).
Magazine: TV Record (S).

CORPORATE OFFICERS
Chairman of the Board James B Boone Jr
President John Mathew
GENERAL MANAGEMENT
Publisher Jerry Turner
Bookkeeper Jalene Chambers
ADVERTISING
Manager-Display Chris Rush
CIRCULATION
Manager Mike Norris
NEWS EXECUTIVES
Exec Editor Jerry Turner
Editor John Fox
EDITOR AND MANAGER
Sports Editor Jim Ellis
PRODUCTION
Foreman-Pressroom Robert Cook

Market Information: Zoned editions; Split Run; TMC.
Mechanical available: Offset; Black and 3 ROP colors; insert accepted — preprinted, standing cards; page cut-offs — 22¾".
Mechanical specifications: Type page 13" x 21"; E - 6 cols, 2 1/16", 1/8" between; A - 6 cols, 2 1/16", 1/8" between; C - 9 cols, 1 7/16", 1/16" between.
Commodity consumption: Newsprint 336 short tons; width 27"; black ink 6,000 pounds; color ink 200 pounds; single pages printed 6,600; average pages per issue 14(d), 40(S); single plates used 4,000.
Equipment: EDITORIAL: Front-end hardware — 7-Ap/Mac. CLASSIFIED: Front-end hardware — Ap/Mac. PRODUCTION: Typesetters — 2-Ap/Mac II, 2-Ap/Mac LaserWriter II; Platemaking systems — 1-Nu; Production cameras — 1-C/1244; Automatic film processors — 1-LE; Shrink lenses — 1-CK Optical. PRESSROOM: Line 1 — G/Offset. MAILROOM: Inserters and stuffers — KAN/320; Bundle tyer — MLN; Wrapping singles — Sa/E; Addressing machine — 1-Am/1957E. WIRE SERVICES: News — AP; Receiving dishes — size-3ft, AP. BUSINESS COMPUTERS: 1-Compaq/286; Applications: Accts receivable, Statistics economic.

MUSKOGEE
Muskogee County
'90 U.S. Census- 37,708; E&P '96 Est. 36,364
ABC-NDM (90): 118,042 (HH 44,663)

Muskogee Daily Phoenix & Times-Democrat
(m-mon to sat; S)

Muskogee Daily Phoenix & Times Democrat, 214 Wall St. (74401); PO Box 1968, Muskogee, OK 74402-1968; tel (918) 684-2828; fax (918) 684-2878. Gannett Co. Inc. group.
Circulation: 19,189(m); 19,189(m-sat); 20,522(S); ABC Sept. 30, 1995.
Price: 35¢(d); 35¢(sat); $1.00(S); $10.75/mo, $8.50/mo (daily only), $5.50/mo (S/holiday).
Advertising: Open inch rate $20.69(m); $20.69(m-sat); $21.69(S). **Representative:** Gannett National Newspaper Sales.
News Services: AP, GNS. **Politics:** Independent. **Established:** 1904.
Advertising not accepted: Brokered space.
Special Editions: Progress Edition (Feb); The Newcomer's Guide (June); The Football Preview, The Air Show Preview Program (Sept); Basketball Preview (Oct); Garden of Lights (Dec).
Special Weekly Sections: Health and Fitness, Business Monday (mon); 55 Plus (tues); Food Day (wed); Education, Outdoor (thur); On the Go (Entertainment) (fri); Wheels, Recreation & Travel (sat); TV Book, Agri-business, Books, Fashions, Weddings, Consumer Affairs (S).
Magazines: Azalea Festival; TV Extra; Visitor's Guide.

CORPORATE OFFICERS
President Lawrence Corvi
Secretary Thomas L Chapple
Treasurer Jimmy L Thomas
GENERAL MANAGEMENT
Publisher Lawrence Corvi
ADVERTISING
Director Kathryn A Powell
MARKETING AND PROMOTION
Director-Marketing/Promotion Becky Lucht
CIRCULATION
Director Ed Kutz
NEWS EXECUTIVES
Exec Editor Dan Elliot
Asst Managing Editor Kristi Fry
EDITORS AND MANAGERS
Asst City Editor Marketta Gregory
Editorial Page Editor Derek Melot
Education Writer BJ Brown
Farm/Agriculture Reporter Joan Morrison
Health/Medical Editor Barbara Schwartz
Librarian Pauline Foster
News Editor Vicky Holland
Photo Department Manager Jerry Willis
Sports Editor Mike Jones
MANAGEMENT INFORMATION SERVICES
Manager-Technical Service Keith Stewart
PRODUCTION
Director John McCarthy

Market Information: TMC.
Mechanical available: Offset; Black and 3 ROP colors; insert accepted — preprinted; page cut-offs — 22¾".
Mechanical specifications: Type page 13" x 21½"; E - 6 cols, 2 1/16", 1/8" between; A - 6 cols, 2 1/16", 1/8" between; C - 9 cols, 1 3/8", 1/16" between.
Commodity consumption: Newsprint 1,496 short tons; 1,357 metric tons; widths 27", 13½", 33", 11"; black ink 31,000 pounds; color ink 8,100 pounds; single pages printed 10,523; average pages per issue 25(d), 50(S).
Equipment: EDITORIAL: Front-end hardware — Ap/Mac; Front-end software — Baseview/NewsEdit Pro, Baseview/IQUE 1.0; Printers — MON/1500; Other equipment — Ap/Mac, AP Photos. CLASSIFIED: Front-end hardware — Ap/Mac; Front-end software — Baseview; Printers — Okidata. DISPLAY: Adv layout systems — Ap/Mac, Cascade/OPI Server; Front-end hardware — Ap/Mac IIci, Ap/Mac fx; Front-end software — Aldus/PageMaker, Aldus/FreeHand, Multi-Ad/Creator; Printers — Ap/Mac LaserWriter, Hammerhead/600 DPI 11" x 17", Ultre/94E Imagesetter, Phaser/300i Color Proofer, MON/1500; Other equipment — CD-Rom, Nikon/Coolscan. PRODUCTION: Pagination software — QuarkXPress 3.31; Typesetters — MON/1500, Konica, ECR, Ultre/94E Imagesetter; Plate exposures — Amerigraph/Magnum; Plate processors — Nat/A-250; Electronic picture desk — Lf/AP Leaf Picture Desk, Ap/Mac fx, Nikon/Coolscan; Scanners — Lf/Leafscan 35, Nikon/Coolscan; Production cameras — C/Spartan; Automatic film processors — LE, Konica; Color separation equipment (conventional) — Lf/AP Leaf Picture Desk, ECR/Autokon. PRESSROOM: Line 1 — 7-G/Urbanite; Pasters — 2-Enkel; Reels and stands — 4 stands. MAILROOM: Counter stackers — HI/RS 2510, MM/310; Inserters and stuffers — MM/227; Bundle tyer — MLN/ML-2EE; Addressing machine — Ch; Other mailroom equipment — Mueller/Stitcher & Trimmer. COMMUNICATIONS: Digital ad delivery system — AP AdSend. WIRE SERVICES: News — AP Photo, AP, GNS; Photos — AP; Syndicates — AP, GNS, TV Data; Receiving dishes — size-3m, AP. BUSINESS COMPUTERS: AS-400; Applications: Lotus 1-2-3, Word Perfect.

NORMAN
Cleveland County
'90 U.S. Census- 80,071; E&P '96 Est. 90,603
ABC-CZ (90): 73,706 (HH 29,745)

The Norman Transcript
(e-mon to fri; m-sat; S)

The Norman Transcript, 215 E. Comanche St.; PO Drawer 1058, Norman, OK 73070-1058; tel (405) 321-1800; fax (405) 366-3520. Donrey Media group.
Circulation: 13,772(e); 13,772(m-sat); 14,830(S); ABC Sept. 30, 1995.
Price: 50¢(d); 50¢(sat); $1.00(S); $7.00/mo.
Advertising: Open inch rate $13.25(e); $13.25(m-sat); $13.25(S). **Representative:** Papert Companies.
News Service: AP. **Politics:** Independent. **Established:** 1889.
Advertising not accepted: Fortune tellers; Palmists; Massage parlors; Singles.
Special Editions: Tax Guide (Jan); Brides, Spring Fashion (Feb); Garden Guide (Mar); Football (Aug); Fall Fashion (Sept); Gift Guide (Nov); Gift Guide, Greetings (Dec).
Special Weekly Sections: Food (wed); TV Guide (fri); Real Estate (S).
Magazine: USA Weekend.

CORPORATE OFFICERS
Founder Donald W Reynolds
President/Chief Operating Officer Emmett Jones
Exec Vice Pres/Chief Financial Officer Darrell W Loftin
Vice Pres-Western Newspaper Group David A Osborn
Vice Pres-Eastern Newspaper Group Don Schneider
GENERAL MANAGEMENT
Publisher Jim Miller
ADVERTISING
Director Walt Disney
CIRCULATION
Manager Don Helms
NEWS EXECUTIVE
Managing Editor Jane Bryant
EDITORS AND MANAGERS
Editorial Page Editor Ed Montgomery
News Editor Karen Dorrell
Sports Editor David Lanier
PRODUCTION
Manager James Sparks

Market Information: TMC.
Mechanical available: Offset; Black and 3 ROP colors; insert accepted — preprinted.
Mechanical specifications: Type page 13" x 21½"; E - 5 cols, 2½", 1/8" between; A - 6 cols, 2 1/16", 1/8" between; C - 6 cols, 2 1/16", 1/8" between.
Commodity consumption: Newsprint 1,300 metric tons; widths 27¼", 13¾"; black ink 35,000 pounds; color ink 2,500 pounds; single pages printed 8,700; average pages per issue 28(d), 24(sat), 60(S); single plates used 28,800.
Equipment: EDITORIAL: Front-end hardware — Mk. CLASSIFIED: Front-end hardware — Mk. PRODUCTION: Typesetters — III; Platemaking systems — 3M; Plate exposures — 1-Nu; Plate processors — 1-Nat/A-250; Electronic picture desk — Lf/AP Leaf Picture Desk; Production cameras — 1-C/Spartan III; Automatic film processors — 1-Kk/66S Rapid-Access; Film transporters — C/Conveyor; Shrink lenses — CK Optical/SQU-7; Color separation equipment (conventional) — 1-Ca; Digital color separation equipment — Lf/Leafscan 35. PRESSROOM: Line 1 — 8-G; Folders — 1-G; Press control system — Fin. MAILROOM: Inserters and stuffers — HI. WIRE SERVICES: News — AP; Syndicates — AP; Receiving dishes — size-10ft, AP.

OKLAHOMA CITY
Oklahoma County
'90 U.S. Census- 444,719; E&P '96 Est. 479,254
ABC-CZ (90): 729,101 (HH 282,658)

The Daily Oklahoman
(m-mon to fri)
Saturday Oklahoman and Times (m-sat)
The Sunday Oklahoman (S)

The Daily Oklahoman, 9000 N. Broadway; PO Box 25125, Oklahoma City, OK 73125; tel (405) 475-3311.
Circulation: 212,382(m); 209,735(m-sat); 315,118(S); ABC Sept. 30, 1995.
Price: 50¢(d); 50¢(sat); $1.50(S); $12.85/mo; $138.75/yr.
Advertising: Open inch rate $144.34(m); $144.34(m-sat); $167.30(S); $233.80(m & S). **Representative:** Sawyer-Ferguson-Walker Co.
News Services: AP, CNS, CT, DJ, LAT-WP, RN. **Politics:** Independent. **Established:** 1889 (Times), 1894 (Oklahoman).
Special Editions: Business; Sports; Accent on Today's Woman; Travel.
Special Weekly Sections: Health (tues); Best Food Day (wed); Weekend (fri); Travel & Entertainment (S); Business (daily).
Magazines: Network Comics, Parade (S).
Broadcast Affiliates: Radio WKY, Gaylord Broadcasting Co.

CORPORATE OFFICERS
Chairman of the Board/Publisher Edward L Gaylord
President Edward K Gaylord II
Vice Pres Thelma F Gaylord
Vice Pres Edmund O Martin
Secretary Christine Gaylord Everest
Vice Pres/Treasurer David Story
Secretary-Emerita Edith Gaylord-Harper
GENERAL MANAGEMENT
Publisher Edward L Gaylord
General Manager Edmund O Martin
Controller Kirk Jewell
Manager-Credit Bill Wallace
Personnel Manager Elizabeth Payne
Purchasing Administrator Janet Tucker
ADVERTISING
Director David L Thompson
Manager-Display Larry Skoch
Manager-Classified Roger Hoffman
Manager-Creative Service Ron Clarke
Manager-Market Research Clydette Womack
Coordinator-Co-op Gary Shaffer
MARKETING AND PROMOTION
Director-Marketing Clydette Womack
Manager-Promotion Dick Dugan
TELECOMMUNICATIONS
Audiotex Manager Matt Jones
CIRCULATION
Director Gerald Beattie
Manager John E Norlin
Manager-Marketing Tom Brower
Manager-Education Hal Young
NEWS EXECUTIVES
Editor Edward L Gaylord
Managing Editor Ed Kelley
Senior Asst Managing Editor Mike Shannon
Asst Managing Editor Sue Hale
EDITORS AND MANAGERS
Art Director Bill Sandlin
Automotive Editor Dan Bush
Books Editor Ann DeFrange
Business Editor Dan Bush
Cartoonist James J Lange
City Editor Gene Triplett
Community Editor Joe Hight
Editorial Writer Pat McGuigan
Education Editor Jim Killackey
Entertainment/Amusements Editor Kelly Hochenauer
Farm Editor Don Gammill
Fashion Editor Linda Miller
Features Editor Kelly Hochenauer
Films/Theater Editor Sandi Davis
Food Editor Sharon Dowell
Health/Medical Reporter Karen Klinka
Home Furnishings Editor Kelly Hochenauer
Librarian Carol Campbell
Living/Lifestyle Editor Kelly Hochenauer
Music Editor Rick Rogers
News Editor Ed Sargent
Photo Chief George Wilson
Television Editor Maxine Cole
Religion Editor Pat Gilliland
Society Editor Peggy Gandy
Sports Editor Bob Colon
Sunday Editor Kelly Hochenauer
Travel Editor Kelly Hochenauer
Women's Editor Kelly Hochenauer
MANAGEMENT INFORMATION SERVICES
Data Processing Manager Dick Clark
PRODUCTION
Director Louis A Messina
Manager-Pre Press Service Bart Williams
Manager-Building Service Bob Mackey
Manager-Packaging/Distribution Glenn James
Manager-Publishing Systems Hank Foos
Manager-Mechanical Service Dee Harmon
Coordinator A B Alexander
Superintendent-Pressroom James Crabtree

Market Information: Zoned editions; Split Run; TMC; ADS; Operate audiotex.
Mechanical available: Offset; Black and 3 ROP colors; insert accepted — preprinted; page cut-offs — 22¾".

Mechanical specifications: Type page 13¼" x 21½"; E - 9 cols, 1⅜", 3/32" between; A - 9 cols, 1⅜", 3/32" between; C - 10 cols, 1¼", 3/32" between.
Commodity consumption: Newsprint 36,000 short tons; widths 55", 41¼", 27½"; black ink 647,000 pounds; color ink 257,000 pounds; single pages printed 22,000; average pages per issue 45(d), 120(S); single plates used 281,000.
Equipment: EDITORIAL: Front-end hardware — 4-SII/Tandem TXP, 110-Oli/P-500, 18-Compaq/INL; Front-end software — SII/Editorial, SII/INL Pagination. CLASSIFIED: Front-end hardware — 4-SII/Tandem TXP, 80-Oli/P-500, 2-Compaq/ICP; Front-end software — SII/Classified, ICP/Pagination. AUDIOTEX: Hardware — Brite Voice Systems. DISPLAY: Adv layout systems — 2-SII, Compaq/386 IAL; Front-end hardware — 10-SII, DTI/AdSpeed, Ap/Mac; Front-end software — SII, DTI; Other equipment — 2-X/7650 scanner, 2-X/8000 Color Scanner. PRODUCTION: Typesetters — 2-MON/MK2i, 3-Hyphen/RIP, 3-III/3850 Color Image Setter, 3-Harleguin/RIP; Plate exposures — 1-WL/III, WL V; Plate processors — 2-WL/38-D; Electronic picture desk — Lf/AP Leaf Picture Desk; Scanners — 3-ECR/Autokon D-1000; Production cameras — 1-SCREEN, 1-C/Newspager; Automatic film processors — 3-LE/LD2400, 2-AG/660; Film transporters — 2-C; Digital color separation equipment — X/Pixel Craft 7650C, X/Pixel Craft 4520.
PRESSROOM: Line 1 — 10-G/Metroliner; Line 2 — 10-G/Metroliner; Line 3 — 10-G/Metroliner; Pasters — G; Reels and stands — 30-G; Press control system — G/PCS. MAILROOM: Counter stackers — 10-Id/440, 1-HL, 15-HL; Inserters and stuffers — 1-HI/1372P, 3-HI/1472P; Bundle tyer — 10-MLN/3, 1-JP/80, 16-Power Strap; Addressing machine — 1-BH. LIBRARY: Electronic — 1-DEC/VAX 4000, Battelle/software. WIRE SERVICES: News — AP, DJ, LAT-WP, DJ; Stock tables — AP; Receiving dishes — size-10ft, AP. BUSINESS COMPUTERS: Hitachi/EX-27; Applications: Adv; Admarc, DB: Gen ledger, HR, Payroll; In-house: Circ; PCs & micros networked; PCs & main system networked.

OKMULGEE

Okmulgee County

'90 U.S. Census- 13,441; E&P '96 Est. 11,874

Okmulgee Daily Times

(m-tues to sat; S)

Okmulgee Daily Times, 114 E. 7th St.; PO Box 1218, Okmulgee, OK 74447; tel (918) 756-3600; fax (918) 756-8197. Donrey Media group.
Circulation: 5,142(m); 5,142(m-sat); 5,142(S); Sworn Oct. 1, 1995.
Price: 50¢(d); 50¢(sat); 75¢(S).
Advertising: Open inch rate $7.90(m); $7.90(m-sat); $7.90(S). **Representative:** Papert Companies.
News Service: AP. **Politics:** Democrat. **Established:** 1910.
Advertising not accepted: Condom.
Special Editions: Pecan Festival; Okmulgee County Fair; Oklahoma India Art Mart; Progress Edition; Okmulgee Trade Show.
Special Weekly Sections: Food Page (wed); Religion, TV Guide, Real Estate (sat).
Magazine: Entertainment Times (television section) (S).

CORPORATE OFFICERS

Founder Donald W Reynolds
President/Chief Operating Officer Emmett Jones
Exec Vice Pres/Chief Financial Officer Darrell W Loftin
Vice Pres-Western Newspaper Group David A Osborn
Vice Pres-Eastern Newspaper Group Don Schneider

GENERAL MANAGEMENT

Publisher Jerry Quinn
Office Manager Gwen Shandy

ADVERTISING

Director Larry Lucas

MARKETING AND PROMOTION

Manager-Marketing/Promotion Larry Lucas

TELECOMMUNICATIONS

Telecommunications Manager Kathryn Andrews

CIRCULATION

Manager-Subscriber Service Robert Wilson

NEWS EXECUTIVE

News Editor Herman Brown

EDITORS AND MANAGERS

Mainstream Editor Fran Collaway
Society Editor Marti Blackwood
Sports Editor Troy Brown

PRODUCTION

Foreman-Composing Kathryn Andrews
Foreman-Pressroom Mike Rhodes

Market Information: Zoned editions; TMC.
Mechanical available: Offset; Black and 3 ROP colors; insert accepted — preprinted; page cutoffs — 23".
Mechanical specifications: Type page 13" x 21½"; E - 6 cols, 2¹⁄₁₆", ⅛" between; A - 6 cols, 2¹⁄₁₆", ⅛" between; C - 8 cols, 1½", ⅛" between.
Commodity consumption: Newsprint 302 short tons; 280 metric tons; widths 27½", 13¾"; black ink 2,000 pounds; color ink 200 pounds; single pages printed 26,000; average pages per issue 14(d), 40(S); single plates used 13,000.
Equipment: EDITORIAL: Front-end hardware — Ap/Power Mac 8100; Front-end software — Baseview/NewsEdit Pro, QuarkXPress 2.1; Printers — Ap/Mac LaserWriter II NTX; Other equipment — Ap/Mac Classic. CLASSIFIED: Front-end hardware — Ap/Mac 630; Front-end software — Baseview; Printers — Ap/Mac LaserWriter NTX. DISPLAY: Adv layout systems — Ap/Mac; Front-end hardware — Ap/Mac; Front-end software — QuarkXPress 2.1, Baseview; Printers — Ap/Mac LaserWriter NTX. PRODUCTION: Pagination software — Baseview/NewsEdit Pro, QuarkXPress 2.1; Typesetters — NewGen/Design Xpress 12; Platemaking systems — 3M; Production cameras — 1-Acti/225; Automatic film processors — 1-C/Powermatic T-45; Shrink lenses — CK Optical/SQU-7.
PRESSROOM: Line 1 — 6-G/Community. MAILROOM: Bundle tyer — Ca/Bond Tyer; Addressing machine — Wm. WIRE SERVICES: News — AP; Receiving dishes — AP.

PAULS VALLEY

Garvin County

'90 U.S. Census- 6,150; E&P '96 Est. 6,543

Pauls Valley Daily Democrat

(e-tues to fri; S)

Pauls Valley Daily Democrat, 108 S. Willow; PO Box 790, Pauls Valley, OK 73075; tel (405) 238-6464; fax (405) 238-3042. Donrey Media group.
Circulation: 3,965(e); 3,965(S); Sworn Sept. 30, 1995.
Price: 50¢(d); 50¢(S); $66.00/yr.
Advertising: Open inch rate $6.35(e); $6.35(S). **Representative:** Papert Companies.
News Services: NEA, AP. **Politics:** Independent. **Established:** 1904 (weekly), 1935 (daily).
Not Published: Christmas.
Special Editions: After Christmas Clearance (Jan); Progress (Mar); Graduation, Vacation (May); Back-to-School, Football (Aug); Moonlight Madness, Christmas Opening (Nov); Christmas Greetings (Dec).
Special Weekly Sections: Best Food Day (wed); Farm (fri); TV (S).
Magazine: Oklahoma TV (local, newsprint) (S).

CORPORATE OFFICERS

Founder Donald W Reynolds
President/Chief Operating Officer Emmett Jones
Exec Vice Pres/Chief Financial Officer Darrell W Loftin
Vice Pres-Western Newspaper Group David A Osborn
Vice Pres-Eastern Newspaper Group Don Schneider

GENERAL MANAGEMENT

Publisher Mary Anne Lynn
Manager-Accounting/Office Sheila Murray

ADVERTISING

Manager Jerry Crenshaw
Manager-Classified Sheila Murray

CIRCULATION

Director Connie White

NEWS EXECUTIVE

Editor Mark Finley

EDITORS AND MANAGERS

Editorial Page Editor Mark Finley
News Editor Mark Finley
Sports Editor Mike Aire

PRODUCTION

Foreman-Press Patrick Bolan
Supervisor-Composing Jimmy Dobbins

Market Information: TMC.
Mechanical available: Offset; Black and 3 ROP colors; insert accepted — preprinted; page cutoffs — 21½".
Mechanical specifications: Type page 13½" x 21½"; E - 6 cols, 2¹⁄₁₆", ⅛" between; A - 6 cols, 2¹⁄₁₆", ⅛" between; C - 8 cols, 1½", ⅛" between.
Commodity consumption: Newsprint 140 metric tons; widths 27½", 13¾"; single pages printed 4,200; average pages per issue 10(d), 30(S); single plates used 3,000.
Equipment: EDITORIAL: Front-end hardware — 4-Mk/4003; Front-end software — Ap/Mac. CLASSIFIED: Front-end hardware — Ap/Mac. DISPLAY: Adv layout systems — Ap/Mac. PRODUCTION: Production cameras — 1-Acti; Automatic film processors — C/T-45; Shrink lenses — 1-CK Optical.
PRESSROOM: Line 1 — 4-KP. COMMUNICATIONS: Facsimile — Canon. WIRE SERVICES: News — AP; Syndicates — NEA; Receiving dishes — size-1⅝ ft, AP. BUSINESS COMPUTERS: Ap/Mac; PCs & micros networked; PCs & main system networked.

PERRY

Noble County

'90 U.S. Census- 4,978; E&P '96 Est. 4,512

Perry Daily Journal

(e-mon to sat)

The Perry Daily Journal, 714 Delaware; PO Box 311, Perry, OK 73077; tel (405) 336-2222; fax (405) 336-3222.
Circulation: 3,140(e); 3,140(e-sat); Sworn Sept. 25, 1992.
Price: 25¢(d); 25¢(sat); $5.00/mo; $54.00/yr.
Advertising: Open inch rate $3.50(e); $3.50(e-sat).
News Service: AP. **Politics:** Independent. **Established:** 1893.
Not Published: New Year; Independence Day; Thanksgiving; Christmas.
Special Editions: High School Graduation; Christmas Greetings; Anniversary of Opening of Cherokee Strip.

CORPORATE OFFICERS

President Milo W Watson
Secretary/Treasurer Mary Lee Streller

GENERAL MANAGEMENT

Publisher/General Manager Milo W Watson

ADVERTISING

Director Mabel Miller

CIRCULATION

Manager Marilyn Alley

NEWS EXECUTIVES

Editor Milo W Watson
Managing Editor Gene Taylor

EDITORS AND MANAGERS

Books/Music Editor Milo W Watson
City Editor Sharon Courtright
Society Editor Gloria Brown

MANAGEMENT INFORMATION SERVICES

Data Processing Manager Mark Washington

PRODUCTION

Manager Mark Washington

Market Information: ADS.
Mechanical available: Offset; insert accepted — preprinted; page cut-offs — 21½".
Mechanical specifications: Type page 13⅛" x 21"; E - 8 cols, 1.57", ⅙" between; A - 8 cols, 1.57", ⅙" between; C - 8 cols, 1.57", ⅙" between.
Commodity consumption: Newsprint 80 short tons; widths 32", 16"; black ink 3,250 pounds; single pages printed 3,640; average pages per issue 12(d); single plates used 1,900.
Equipment: EDITORIAL: Front-end hardware — Tandy/1000 RL, Tandy/VGM-220, Dell/System 200; Front-end software — Deskmate, Symantec/Q&A; Printers — Tandy/DMP 134, Tandy/DMP 136, Panasonic/KX-P1624. DISPLAY: Adv layout systems — QuarkXPress; Front-end hardware — 4-Ap/Mac Centris 650; Front-end software — Ap/Mac System 7.1; Printers — 2-NewGen/Turbo PS 660B; Other equipment — 1-Syquest/88MR. PRODUCTION: Pagination software — QuarkXPress 3.11; OCR software — Caere/OmniPage Direct 2.0; Typesetters — 2-NewGen/Turbo PS 660B LaserPrinter; Platemaking systems — Nu; Plate exposures — 1-Nu; Plate processors — 1-Nu; Scanners — Umax/VC840; Production cameras — 1-lk, SCREEN/DS; Automatic film processors — Devotec/20.
PRESSROOM: Line 1 — 3-HI/Cotrell V-15A; Folders — 1-HI, JF/7. MAILROOM: Bundle tyer — 1-Malow; Addressing machine — 1-Am. COMMUNICATIONS: Systems used — satellite. WIRE SERVICES: News — AP; Receiving dishes — size-15ft, AP. BUSINESS COMPUTERS: 1-RSK/TRS 80; Applications: Circ, Adv billing.

PONCA CITY

Kay County

'90 U.S. Census- 26,359; E&P '96 Est. 26,525
ABC-CZ (90): 26,359 (HH 10,733)

The Ponca City News

(e-mon to fri; S)

The Ponca City News, 300 N. Third; PO Box 191, Ponca City, OK 74602; tel (405) 765-3311; fax (405) 762-6397.
Circulation: 11,730(e); 13,484(S); ABC Sept. 30, 1995.
Price: 35¢(d); $1.00(S); $2.75/wk; $6.25/mo, $71.00/yr.
Advertising: Open inch rate $9.00(e); $9.00(S). **Representative:** Landon Associates Inc.
News Service: AP. **Politics:** Independent. **Established:** 1918.
Special Editions: Everybody Loves A Baby; Brides; Up Date; Lawn & Garden; Father's Day; Mother's Day; Oklahoma Football; Christmas Gift Guide; Your Social Security; Your Money; Spring Fashion; Car Care; Travel; Senior Citizens.
Magazine: TV Week (S).
Broadcast Affiliate: Radio WBBZ.

GENERAL MANAGEMENT

Publisher Allan W Muchmore
Asst to Publisher Ellsworth Rains Jr
Business Manager Tom Muchmore
Purchasing Agent Tom Muchmore

ADVERTISING

Director Ellsworth Rains Jr
Manager Everett Lockwood

CIRCULATION

Manager Kevin Kreger

NEWS EXECUTIVES

Editor Allan W Muchmore
Managing Editor Foster Johnson

Market Information: TMC.
Mechanical available: Offset; Black and 3 ROP colors; insert accepted — preprinted, oddsizes upon approval; page cut-offs — 22¾".
Mechanical specifications: Type page 13" x 21½"; E - 6 cols, 2¹⁄₁₆", ⅛" between; A - 6 cols, 2¹⁄₁₆", ⅛" between; C - 9 cols, 1⅜", ¹⁄₁₆" between.
Commodity consumption: Newsprint 660 short tons; width 28"; black ink 16,500 pounds; color ink 2,347 pounds; single pages printed 7,995; average pages per issue 25(d), 52(S); single plates used 7,900.
Equipment: EDITORIAL: Front-end hardware — Ap/Mac; Front-end software — Baseview; Printers — Ap/Mac LaserWriter 630, NewGen/1200B, ECR/VR 36; Other equipment — Lf/AP Leaf Picture Desk, Lf/Leafscan 35, Umax/Flatbed Scanner. CLASSIFIED: Front-end hardware — Ap/Mac; Front-end software — Baseview. DISPLAY: Front-end hardware — Ap/Mac Quadra, Ap/Mac Centris, DLI/CD-Roms, Sony, Ap/Super Mac Monitors; Front-end software — QuarkXPress 3.3, Aldus/FreeHand 4.0, Adobe/Illustrator 5.5, Microsoft/Word 5.1a, Aldus/Fetch; Printers — LW/Pro 630, NewGen/1200B, ECR/VR 36 Imagesetter. PRODUCTION: OCR software — Caere/OmniScan Pro; Typesetters — ECR/VR 36; Plate exposures — 1-Nu; Plate processors — Nat; Electronic picture desk — Lf/AP Leaf Picture Desk; Production cameras — C; Automatic film processors — LE; Color separation equipment (conventional) — C.
PRESSROOM: Line 1 — 8-G/Community, 2-Stacked Units; Press control system — Fin. MAILROOM: Inserters and stuffers — KAN. LIBRARY: Electronic — Baseview. WIRE SERVICES: News — AP; Photos — AP; Receiving dishes — size-3m, AP. BUSINESS COMPUTERS: PCs.

POTEAU

LeFlore County

'90 U.S. Census- 7,210; E&P '96 Est. 7,315

Poteau News & Sun

(m-tues to fri; S)

Poteau News & Sun, 804 N. Broadway; PO Box 1237, Poteau, OK 74953; tel (918) 647-3188; fax (918) 647-8198. McGinnis Communications group.
Circulation: 4,323(m); 4,323(S); Sworn Sept. 30, 1995.
Price: 35¢(d); $1.00(S); $60.00/yr (in county), $96.00/yr (outside county).

Advertising: Open inch rate $6.05(m); $6.05(S). **Representative:** Papert Companies.
News Service: AP. **Established:** 1895.
Special Editions: Progress (Feb); Fact Book (July).
Special Weekly Sections: Shopper's Guide (wed); TV, Bubble Gum Rapper, Church (S).

GENERAL MANAGEMENT
Publisher Wally Burchett
ADVERTISING
Director Janie Fox
CIRCULATION
Manager Janice Rogers
NEWS EXECUTIVE
Editor Laura Young
PRODUCTION
Manager Wally Burchett

Mechanical available: Offset; Black and 3 ROP colors.
Mechanical specifications: Type page 21½" x E - 6 cols, 2 1/16", 1/8" between; A - 6 cols, 2 1/16", 1/8" between; C - 6 cols, 2 1/16", 1/8" between.
Commodity consumption: Newsprint 250 short tons; width 27½"; average pages per issue 14(d), 24(S).
Equipment: EDITORIAL: Front-end hardware — Ap/Mac. DISPLAY: Adv layout systems — Ap/Mac, Ap/Mac SE30. PRODUCTION: Automatic film processors — LE.

PRYOR
Mayes County
'90 U.S. Census- 8,327; E&P '96 Est. 8,251

The Daily Times
(e-tues to fri; S)

The Daily Times, 105 S. Adair; Box 308, Pryor, OK 74361; tel (918) 825-3292; fax (918) 825-1965. Pryor Publishing Co. group.
Circulation: 7,504(e); 7,504(S); Sworn Sept. 24, 1993.
Price: 50¢(d); $1.00(S); $4.50/mo.
Advertising: Open inch rate $7.26(e); $7.26(S). **Representative:** Papert Companies.
News Service: AP. **Politics:** Independent. **Established:** 1938.
Special Editions: Mayes County Free Fair; Christmas; Back-to-School; Vacation & Boating; Wedding; Real Estate; Fall and Spring Fashions.
Magazine: TV Times Magazine (local).

GENERAL MANAGEMENT
General Manager Henry L Goodman
ADVERTISING
Director Anna Morgan
CIRCULATION
Manager Marc Goodman
NEWS EXECUTIVE
Editor Terry Aylward

Market Information: TMC.
Mechanical available: Offset; Black and 2 ROP colors; insert accepted — preprinted.
Mechanical specifications: Type page 16½" x 21"; E - 6 cols, 2 1/16", 1/8" between; A - 6 cols, 2 1/16", 1/8" between; C - 8 cols, 2 1/16", 1/8" between.
Commodity consumption: Newsprint 14 short tons; 40 metric tons; average pages per issue 10(d), 30(S).
Equipment: EDITORIAL: Front-end hardware — HI/Computype. CLASSIFIED: Front-end hardware — HI/Computype. PRODUCTION: Typesetters — 1-COM, 2-F; Plate exposures — B; Production cameras — 1-B, 1-K.
PRESSROOM: Line 1 — 4-HI/Cotrell; Line 2 — 4-HI/Cotrell; Line 3 — 4-HI/Cotrell. MAILROOM: Addressing machine — 1-Am. WIRE SERVICES: News — UPI.

SAPULPA
Creek County
'90 U.S. Census- 18,074; E&P '96 Est. 19,944

Sapulpa Daily Herald
(e-mon to fri; S)

Sapulpa Daily Herald, 16 S. Park (74066); PO Box 1370, Sapulpa, OK 74067; tel (918) 224-5185; fax (918) 224-5196. Park Communications Inc. group.
Circulation: 7,020(e); 7,020(S); Sworn Sept. 27, 1994.
Price: 50¢(d); $1.00(S); $6.00/mo.
Advertising: Open inch rate $9.14(e); $9.14(S). **Representative:** Landon Associates Inc.
News Service: AP. **Politics:** Independent-Democrat. **Established:** 1914.
Not Published: Christmas.
Advertising not accepted: X-rated movies.
Special Weekly Sections: Business (mon); Grocery Day (wed); Expanded Society (S).
Magazine: TV Today (entertainment tab) (S).

CORPORATE OFFICER
President Wright M Thomas
GENERAL MANAGEMENT
General Manager Charles S Lake
Business Manager Darrel Hardy
ADVERTISING
Manager Juanita Brewer
CIRCULATION
Director Roy Roop
NEWS EXECUTIVE
Managing Editor Don Diehl
EDITOR AND MANAGER
News Editor Lorie Quinelly
PRODUCTION
Manager Bill Armstrong

Market Information: Split Run; TMC.
Mechanical available: Offset; Black and 3 ROP colors; insert accepted — preprinted; page cutoffs — 22¾".
Mechanical specifications: Type page 13" x 21½"; E - 6 cols, 2.07", 1/8" between; A - 6 cols, 2.07", 1/8" between; C - 10 cols, 1.22", 1/12" between.
Commodity consumption: Newsprint 350 short tons; widths 13¾", 27½"; black ink 7,825 pounds; color ink 840 pounds; single pages printed 4,240; average pages per issue 8(d), 14(S); single plates used 10,000.
Equipment: EDITORIAL: Front-end hardware — Ap/Mac; Front-end software — Ap/Mac; Printers — Ap/Mac Laser. CLASSIFIED: Front-end hardware — Ap/Mac; Front-end software — Ap/Mac. PRODUCTION: Pagination software — QuarkXPress; Typesetters — 2-Ap/Mac Laser-Printer; Plate exposures — Nu; Plate processors — Ic; Production cameras — Uves/2024 MZ; Automatic film processors — SCREEN/LD-280-Q4; Digital color separation equipment — Radius/Precision Color Display 17, Image Plus/12.
PRESSROOM: Line 1 — 5-G/Community double width Folders — 1-G/Suburban. MAILROOM: Counter stackers — BG/Count-O-Veyor; Bundle tyer — Marlow. WIRE SERVICES: News — AP. BUSINESS COMPUTERS: Applications: Vision Data; PCs & main system networked.

SEMINOLE
Seminole County
'90 U.S. Census- 7,071; E&P '96 Est. 6,230

The Seminole Producer
(e-tues to fri; S)

The Seminole Producer, 121 N. Main St.; Box 431, Seminole, OK 74868; tel (405) 382-1100; fax (405) 382-1104.
Circulation: 5,156(e); 5,156(S); Sworn Oct. 1, 1994.
Price: 35¢(d); 75¢(S); $6.00/mo; $68.00/yr.
Advertising: Open inch rate $5.46(e); $5.46(S). **Representatives:** Papert Companies; Oklahoma Press Service.
News Services: CNS, NEA, Capitol Press Report. **Politics:** Independent. **Established:** 1927.
Not Published: Thanksgiving; Christmas.

CORPORATE OFFICERS
President Ted M Phillips
Secretary/Treasurer Nancy Phillips
GENERAL MANAGEMENT
Co-Publisher Ted M Phillips
General Manager Stu Phillips
Business Manager Jim Keisman
Personnel Manager Ted M Phillips
Purchasing Agent Gary Ogle
ADVERTISING
Director Jim Keisman
Manager-Retail Mike Gifford
MARKETING AND PROMOTION
Director-Marketing/Promotion Jim Keisman
TELECOMMUNICATIONS
Director-Telecommunications Stu Phillips
CIRCULATION
Director Stu Phillips
NEWS EXECUTIVE
Editor Ken Milam
EDITORS AND MANAGERS
Action Line Editor Ted M Phillips
Automotive Editor Stu Phillips
Books Editor Nancy Phillips
Business/Finance Editor Ken Milam
City/Metro Editor Ken Milam
Editorial Page Editor Ted M Phillips
Education Editor Karen Anson
Entertainment/Amusements Editor Nancy Phillips
Environmental Editor Ted M Phillips
Farm Editor Ken Milam
Food/Home Editor Karen Anson
Graphics Editor/Art Director Stu Phillips
Librarian Karen Anson
National Editor Ted M Phillips
News Editor Ken Milam
Political/Government Editor Ted M Phillips
Photo Department Manager Stu Phillips
Religion Editor Karen Anson
Science/Technology Editor Stu Phillips
Science Editor Ken Milam
Sports Editor Darren Heusel
Teen-Age/Youth Editor Karen Anson
Travel Editor Nancy Phillips
Women's/Society Editor Karen Anson
MANAGEMENT INFORMATION SERVICES
Data Processing Manager Stu Phillips
PRODUCTION
Manager/Foreman-Composing Gary Ogle
Foreman-Pressroom/Engraving John Lewis
Foreman-Mailroom Stu Phillips

Market Information: TMC; Operate audiotex.
Mechanical available: Offset; Black and 2 ROP colors; insert accepted — preprinted; page cutoffs — 22¾".
Mechanical specifications: Type page 13" x 21"; E - 6 cols, 2 1/16", 1/8" between; A - 6 cols, 2 1/16", 1/8" between; C - 9 cols, 1 3/8", 1/16" between.
Commodity consumption: Newsprint 88 short tons; width 30"; black ink 2,180 pounds; single pages printed 2,888; average pages per issue 10(d), 18(S); single plates used 2,900.
Equipment: EDITORIAL: Front-end hardware — PC; Front-end software — Microsoft/Windows; Printers — HP/IV; Other equipment — Microtek/ScanMaker IIsp. CLASSIFIED: Front-end hardware — PC; Front-end software — ListMaster; Printers — HP/LaserWriter 4. AUDIOTEX: Hardware — PC; Software — Community Information Systems 3.9; DISPLAY: Adv layout systems — PC/486-50; Front-end hardware — PC; Front-end software — Microsoft/Windows; Printers — HP/LaserWriter 4. PRODUCTION: Typesetters — Ap/Mac NT; Plate exposures — 1-Nu/Flip Top FT40; Production cameras — 1-CL/24".
PRESSROOM: Line 1 — 3-G/Community; Folders — 1-G. MAILROOM: Addressing machine — RSK/Model II-LP V, Wm. WIRE SERVICES: Syndicates — NEA, CNS; Receiving dishes — size-8ft. BUSINESS COMPUTERS: 2-RAM/486, 1-HP/386; Applications: Gen ledger, Payroll, Adv billing, Adv scheduling, Accts payable; PCs & micros networked; PCs & main system networked.

SHAWNEE
Pottawatomie County
'90 U.S. Census- 26,017; E&P '96 Est. 25,778

The Shawnee News-Star
(m-tues to sat; S)

Shawnee News-Star, 215 N. Bell; PO Box 1688, Shawnee, OK 74802-1688; tel (405) 273-4200; fax (405) 273-4207. Morris Communications Corp. group.
Circulation: 11,590(m); 11,590(m-sat); 12,692(S); VAC June 30, 1995.
Price: 50¢(d); 50¢(sat); $1.00(S); $8.25/mo (city); $90.00/yr (city).
Advertising: Open inch rate $8.90(m); $8.90(m-sat); $8.90(S). **Representative:** Landon Associates Inc.
News Service: AP. **Politics:** Independent. **Established:** 1929.
Special Editions: Bridal (Jan); Lawn and Garden (Mar); School (Aug); Home Improvement (Sept); Gift Guide (Nov); Christmas (Dec).
Magazines: Escort Magazines (S); Color Comics.

CORPORATE OFFICER
President W S Morris III
GENERAL MANAGEMENT
Publisher John L Tucker
ADVERTISING
Director Sherry J Wilkins
CIRCULATION
Manager M L (Jess) James
NEWS EXECUTIVES
Editor John L Tucker
Managing Editor Mike McCormick
EDITORS AND MANAGERS
City Editor Beverly Bostick
Editorial Page Editor John L Tucker
Religion Editor Betty Lam
Society/Women's Editor Karen Green
Sports Editor Fred Fehr
Sunday Escort Magazine Editor April Wilkerson
PRODUCTION
Manager David Watson
Foreman-Pressroom Robby Parsons

Market Information: TMC.
Mechanical available: Offset; Black and 3 ROP colors; insert accepted — preprinted; page cutoffs — 21½".
Mechanical specifications: Type page 13" x 21½"; E - 6 cols, 2 1/16", 1/8" between; A - 6 cols, 2 1/16", 1/8" between; C - 8 cols, 1½", 1/16" between.
Commodity consumption: Newsprint 1,300 short tons; widths 27½", 13¾"; black ink 35,000 pounds; color ink 9,000 pounds; single pages printed 10,500; average pages per issue 28(d), 66(S); single plates used 15,000.
Equipment: EDITORIAL: Front-end hardware — Ap/Mac, 6-Ap/Mac IIci; Front-end software — Baseview; Printers — Ap/Mac LaserWriter IIg, MON/1270. CLASSIFIED: Front-end hardware — Ap/Mac, 4-Ap/Mac IIsi; Front-end software — Baseview; Printers — Ap/Mac LaserWriter NTX. DISPLAY: Adv layout systems — Ap/Mac II, Ap/Mac IIcx, Ap/Mac SE30; Front-end software — Multi-Ad, Aldus/PageMaker, QuarkXPress; Printers — 2-Ap/Mac LaserWriter NTX. PRODUCTION: OCR software — Mk, Caere/OmniPage Pro 2.1; Typesetters — Ap/Mac LaserWriter, MON/1270; Plate exposures — 1-Nu; Plate processors — Nat/A-340; Scanners — Ap/Mac, Dest, Microtek/IIx, Microtek, Ap/Mac One Scanner; Production cameras — 1-R/500; Automatic film processors — B, LE/24; Color separation equipment (conventional) — Ap/Mac Quadra 800, Microtek/IIxe, Adobe/Photoshop.
PRESSROOM: Line 1 — 7-G/U-1083; Folders — 1-G; Press registration system — Duarte. MAILROOM: Counter stackers — 1-BG/Count-O-Veyor; Inserters and stuffers — 1-MM/227; Bundle tyer — 1-MLN/ML2EE; Addressing machine — 1-Ch/559, 1-Ch/539-Quarter Folder. WIRE SERVICES: News — AP; Stock tables — AP; Syndicates — AP; Receiving dishes — AP. BUSINESS COMPUTERS: ATT/Unix PC; Applications: Circ, Adv billing, Accts receivable, Gen ledger, Payroll; PCs & micros networked; PCs & main system networked.

STILLWATER
Payne County
'90 U.S. Census- 36,676; E&P '96 Est. 35,766
ABC-CZ (90): 36,676 (HH 14,172)

News Press (e-mon to fri; S)

The News Press, 211 W. 9th (74074); PO Box 2288, Stillwater, OK 74076; tel (405) 372-5000; fax (405) 372-3112.
Circulation: 9,882(e); 10,780(S); ABC Sept. 30, 1995.
Price: 50¢(d); $1.00(S); $6.75/mo; $73.00/yr.
Advertising: Open inch rate $8.92(e); $8.92(S). **Representative:** Landon Associates Inc.
News Services: AP, KRT. **Politics:** Independent. **Established:** 1909.
Special Editions: Bridal Section (Jan); Restaurant Guide (Feb); Home Improvement (Mar); Krazy Days, Payne County Fair (July); Back-to-School, Football Preview (Aug); Fall Fashion (Sept); Home Improvement, Early Bird/Christmas Layaway (Oct); Basketball Preview, Christmas Gift Guide (Nov); Last Minute Gift Guide (Dec).
Special Weekly Sections: TV Guide (fri); Sr. Citizens, Business, Agriculture, School (S).
Magazines: Hospital; Chamber of Commerce.
Broadcast Affiliate: KSPI-AM/KSPI-FM Stillwater, OK.

GENERAL MANAGEMENT
Publisher L F Bellatti
Publisher James R Bellatti
Purchasing Agent/Assoc Publisher Rick Bellatti
ADVERTISING
Director Rhesa Funk
Manager-National Jacqueline Lightcap
CIRCULATION
Manager-Promotion Jerry Pace

NEWS EXECUTIVES

Editor James R Bellatti
Managing Editor Lawrence Gibbs

EDITORS AND MANAGERS

Agriculture Editor Paul Newlin
Business Editor Laura Wilson
Editorial Page Editor Dale Himes
Education Editor Craig Fuqua
Fashion/Style Editor Lisa Miller
Features Editor Lisa Miller
Housing/Home Furnishings Editor Max Rodgers
Living Editor Lisa Miller
Photo Editor Steve Holman
Real Estate Editor Max Rodgers
Sports Editor Ron Holt

MANAGEMENT INFORMATION SERVICES

Data Processing Manager Chuck Turman

PRODUCTION

Superintendent Dale Van Deventer

Market Information: Zoned editions; TMC; ADS.
Mechanical available: Offset; Black and 3 ROP colors; insert accepted — preprinted; page cut-offs — 22¾".
Mechanical specifications: Type page 13¾" x 21½"; E - 6 cols, 2¹⁄₁₆", ⅛" between; A - 6 cols, 2¹⁄₁₆", ⅛" between; C - 8 cols, 1⅞", ⅛" between.
Commodity consumption: Newsprint 836 short tons; widths 27½", 13¾"; black ink 24,000 pounds; color ink 780 pounds; single pages printed 10,920; average pages per issue 30(d), 60(S); single plates used 5,460.
Equipment: EDITORIAL: Front-end software — FSI. CLASSIFIED: Front-end hardware — 3-Ap/Mac; Front-end software — FSI. DISPLAY: Adv layout systems — 5-Ap/Super Mac; Front-end hardware — 2-Ap/Super Mac IIci; Front-end software — Multi-Ad/Creator. PRODUCTION: Pagination software — FSI; OCR software — Deskscan II 2.1; Typesetters — Laser-Writer/Pro 810, ECR/Scriptsetter VRL-36; Platemaking systems — C/Power Plater 7; Plate exposures — 1-B; Plate processors — 1-Nat; Electronic picture desk — Lf/AP Leaf Picture Desk; Scanners — ECR/Autokon; Production cameras — 1-L; Automatic film processors — 1-C/Powermatic R-650, 1-Konica/720; Shrink lenses — 1-CK Optical/SQU-7; Digital color separation equipment — Lf/AP Leaf Picture Desk w/Adobe Photoshop 3.0.
PRESSROOM: Line 1 — 7-G/Community; Press drives — 50 h.p.; Folders — 1-G/Suburban. MAILROOM: Counter stackers — 1-BG; Inserters and stuffers — 1-KAN/480; Bundle tyer — 3-Bu; Addressing machine — St. WIRE SERVICES: News — AP, KRT; Photos — AP; Receiving dishes — size-10ft, AP. BUSINESS COMPUTERS: 1-IBM/370-168; Applications: Adv billing, Accts receivable, Gen ledger, Payroll; PCs & micros networked; PCs & main system networked.

TAHLEQUAH

Cherokee County

'90 U.S. Census- 10,398; E&P '96 Est. 11,035

Tahlequah Daily Press

(e-tues to fri; S)

Tahlequah Daily Press, 106 W. Second St.; PO Box 888, Tahlequah, OK 74465; tel (918) 456-8833; fax (918) 456-2019. Indian Nations Communications group.
Circulation: 5,913(e); 5,913(S); Sworn Sept. 27, 1993.
Price: 35¢(d); 75¢(S); $60.00/yr.
Advertising: Open inch rate $7.43(e); $7.43(S). **Representative:** Papert Companies.
News Service: AP. **Politics:** Independent. **Established:** 1828.
Special Editions: Progress Edition (Apr); Vacation (May); Retirement (July); Football (Aug); Gift-A-Rama (Nov).
Special Weekly Sections: Food Day (wed); That's Entertainment (thur); Dining, Church (fri); Car Page (S).
Magazines: TV Spotlight; Realtors Tab.

CORPORATE OFFICER

President Francis Stipe

GENERAL MANAGEMENT

Publisher Brad Sugg

ADVERTISING

Director Pam Hudson

CIRCULATION

Manager Tom Dunavan

NEWS EXECUTIVE

Managing Editor Kim Poindexter

EDITORS AND MANAGERS

City Editor Brad Sugg
Columnist/Features Kim Poindexter
Editorial Page Editor Kim Poindexter
Features Editor Kim Poindexter
Food Editor Kim Deerhammer
Photographer Eddie Glen
Real Estate Editor Laura Johnsen
Sports Editor Doyle Barlow
Wire/Women's Editor Kim Poindexter

PRODUCTION

Manager Debbie Sugg

Market Information: TMC.
Mechanical available: Offset; Black and 3 ROP colors; insert accepted — preprinted; page cut-offs — 21½".
Mechanical specifications: Type page 13¼" x 21½"; E - 6 cols, 2¹⁄₁₆", ⅛" between; A - 6 cols, 2¹⁄₁₆", ⅛" between; C - 9 cols, 1½", ⅛" between.
Commodity consumption: average pages per issue 20(d), 50(S).
Equipment: EDITORIAL: Front-end hardware — 9-Ap/Mac; Other equipment — 2-COM/II, 2-COM/7200. CLASSIFIED: Other equipment — 2-COM/Junior. PRODUCTION: Typesetters — 1-COM/2961; Plate exposures — 1-Nu; Production cameras — 1-K/Vertical 240.
PRESSROOM: Line 1 — 5-KWG. MAILROOM: Bundle tyer — 1-Bu; Addressing machine — 2-Am/1900. WIRE SERVICES: News — AP; Receiving dishes — AP.

TULSA

Tulsa and Osage Counties

'90 U.S. Census- 367,302; E&P '96 Est. 373,328
ABC-CZ (90): 518,741 (HH 207,763)

Tulsa World (m-mon to sat; S)

Tulsa World, 315 S. Boulder; PO Box 1770, Tulsa, OK 74102; tel (918) 581-8300; fax (918) 581-8514.
Circulation: 168,529(m); 168,529(m-sat); 230,186(S); ABC Sept. 30, 1995.
Price: 50¢(d); 50¢(sat); $1.50(S); $12.10/mo; $145.20/yr.
Advertising: Open inch rate $81.40(m); $81.40(m-sat); $93.50(S).
News Services: AP, LAT-WP, KRT, NYT, GNS. **Politics:** Independent. **Established:** 1905.
Not Published: New Year; Christmas.
Special Editions: Football Preview (Aug); Christmas Gift Guide (Dec).
Special Weekly Sections: Best Food Day (wed); Fashion (thur); "Wheels" (Auto Section), Entertainment (fri); Travel, Entertainment (S).
Magazines: Sunday Magazine, TV World (S); Real Estate Guide; Spot (entertainment).

CORPORATE OFFICERS

Chairman of the Board Robert E Lorton
President/Chief Operating Officer Kenneth S Fleming
Secretary/Treasurer Frank Hawkins
Vice Pres-Administration/Operations Robert E Lorton III

GENERAL MANAGEMENT

Publisher Robert E Lorton III
Vice Pres Robert E Lorton III
Manager-Credit Sam Smith
Chief Accountant Marlene Hall

ADVERTISING

Director Lynnette Scott
Manager-Sales Development Steve Bright
Manager-National Roy Berry
Manager-Classified Dave Fairlie
Manager-Retail Tom Morris

MARKETING AND PROMOTION

Manager-Creative Service John Rhodes

CIRCULATION

Manager-Metro Area Robert Walker

NEWS EXECUTIVES

Exec Editor Joe Worley
Managing Editor Susan Ellerbach

EDITORS AND MANAGERS

Action Line Editor Phil Mulkins
Books Editor Judy Randle
Business/Finance Editor Gene Seabolt
Senior Editor Alex Adwan
Editorial Page Editor Ken Neal
Editorial Writer Mike Jones
Editorial Writer Ken Neal
Editorial Writer David Averill
Editorial Writer Janet Pearson
Education Editor Melaine Busch
Entertainment Editor Cathy Logan
Farm Editor Mark Lee
Fashion/Style Editor Rusty Lang
Features Editor David Housh
Health/Medical Editor Mary Ellen Matava
Librarian Austin Farley
Living/Lifestyle Editor Rusty Lang
Metro Editor Wayne Green
Oil Editor Ray Tuttle
Photo Department Manager Rabbit Hare
Radio/Television Editor Rita Sherrow
Real Estate Editor Ellen Averill
Religion Editor Carolyn Jenkins
Sports Editor Phil Parrish
Assoc Sports Editor John Klein
State Editor Dana Sterling
Sunday Editor Debbie Jackson
Women's Editor Rusty Lang

MANAGEMENT INFORMATION SERVICES

Data Processing Manager-Business/Circulation Richard Major
Data Processing Manager-Production Systems Randy Rutledge

PRODUCTION

Vice Pres-Operations Robert E Lorton III
Operations Manager Bill Harper
Superintendent-Composing Marion Wood
Superintendent-Camera/Plate David Horn
Superintendent-Pressroom Roy Neighbors
Superintendent-Mailroom Don Clements
Superintendent-Mechanical Maintenance Richard Reinart
Supervisor-Electrical Maintenance Jeff Callahan

Market Information: Zoned editions; Split Run; TMC; ADS; Operate database; Operate audiotex.
Mechanical available: Letterpress; Black and 3 ROP colors; insert accepted — preprinted; page cut-offs — 22¾".
Mechanical specifications: Type page 13" x 21¹¹⁄₁₆"; E - 6 cols, 2¹⁄₁₆", ⅛" between; A - 6 cols, 2¹⁄₁₆", ⅛" between; C - 9 cols, 1⅜", ¹⁄₁₆" between.
Equipment: EDITORIAL: Front-end hardware — 2-Tandem/CLX RISC-File Server; Front-end software — SII; Printers — DEC, Tandem. CLASSIFIED: Front-end hardware — 2-Tandem/CLX RISC-File Server; Front-end software — SII; Printers — Dataproducts, DEC, Tandem. PRODUCTION: Pagination software — SII/ICP (Classified); Typesetters — 2-AU/APS-5, 2-AU/3850; Platemaking systems — Na/Letterpress; Plate exposures — 1-MAS, 1-Na/Titan III; Plate processors — Na/Satellite, Na/NP-120; Scanners — 1-ECR/Autokon 1030C; Production cameras — 3-C/Marathon, C/Spartan III, C/Newspager II; Automatic film processors — 6-LE; Color separation equipment (conventional) — 2-RZ/200S; Digital color separation equipment — 2-RZ/Z00S.
PRESSROOM: Line 1 — 8-Wd/Colormatic (3-half decks; 8-Color humps); Line 2 — 8-Wd/Colormatic (3-half decks; 8-Color humps); Line 3 — 5-H/Color Convertible; Press drives — GE; Folders — Wd-H; Pasters — Wd, Automatic, Wd; Reels and stands — Wd-H, Wd; Press control system — GE; Press registration system — Pin. MAILROOM: Counter stackers — 6-QWI/350, 2-HL/HT; Inserters and stuffers — 2-S/72P; Bundle tyer — 5-MLN/MLN2, 7-Power Strap; Wrapping singles — 4-Power Strap (¾); Addressing machine — 1-BH. LIBRARY: Electronic — Data Times/software, DEC/Micro VAX II. WIRE SERVICES: News — AP Datastream, AP Datafeatures; Photos — AP; Syndicates — TMS, KRT, LATS, NYT, King Features, Universal Press; Receiving dishes — size-6ft, AP. BUSINESS COMPUTERS: 2-DEC/VAX 4000-100; Applications: In-house, VMS, Cobol, RDB, Nomads; PCs & micros networked; PCs & main system networked.

VINITA

Craig County

'90 U.S. Census- 5,804; E&P '96 Est. 5,270

Vinita Daily Journal

(e-mon to fri)

Vinita Daily Journal, 140 S. Wilson St.; PO Box 328, Vinita, OK 74301-0328; tel (918) 256-6422; fax (918) 256-7100.
Circulation: 3,946(e); Sworn Sept. 30, 1992.
Price: 25¢(d); $48.00/yr.
Advertising: Open inch rate $5.85(e). **Representative:** Papert Companies.
News Services: NEA, UPI. **Politics:** Independent. **Established:** 1907.
Not Published: New Year; Memorial Day; Independence Day; Labor Day; Thanksgiving; Christmas.
Special Editions: Home Improvement (Apr); Business Profiles (July); Back-to-School, Rodeo Pioneer, Football Preview (Aug); Calf Fry (Sept); Alamanac, Working Women, Car Care (Oct); Christmas (Nov); Christmas (Dec).
Magazines: Television Guide, Vinita Viewer (fri).

CORPORATE OFFICERS

President Ken Reid
Vice Pres Phillip R Reid
Secretary Noreen Harrison
Treasurer Jeanne Ann Reid

GENERAL MANAGEMENT

Publisher John Link

ADVERTISING

Manager Helen Walker
Manager-Classified Pat Yarder

CIRCULATION

Manager Freddy Montana

EDITOR AND MANAGER

Lifestyle Editor Rita Sims

PRODUCTION

Superintendent Robert Jones

Market Information: Split Run; TMC.
Mechanical available: Offset; Black and 2 ROP colors; insert accepted — preprinted, cards; page cut-offs — 22¾".
Mechanical specifications: Type page 13" x 21½"; E - 6 cols, 2¹⁄₁₆", ⅛" between; A - 6 cols, 2¹⁄₁₆", ⅛" between; C - 8 cols, 1½", ¹⁄₁₆" between.
Commodity consumption: Newsprint 66 short tons; widths 27½", 13¾"; black ink 3,600 pounds; color ink 150 pounds; single pages printed 2,600; average pages per issue 8(d); single plates used 3,600.
Equipment: EDITORIAL: Front-end hardware — Ap/Mac; Front-end software — Ap/Mac. DISPLAY: Adv layout systems — Ap/Mac; Front-end hardware — Ap/Mac; Front-end software — Aldus/PageMaker 3.0; PRODUCTION: Typesetters — Ap/Mac LaserPrinter; Platemaking systems — 1-Nu; Plate exposures — 1-Nu; Production cameras — 1-R/HOR12; Automatic film processors — 1-C.
PRESSROOM: Line 1 — 3-KP/Newsking; Folders — 1-KP. MAILROOM: Inserters and stuffers — 1-DG/320, KAN; Addressing machine — 1-St. COMMUNICATIONS: Facsimile — Panasonic/150. WIRE SERVICES: News — UPI; Receiving dishes — size-2ft, UPI. BUSINESS COMPUTERS: PC; Applications: Bookkeeping, Circ.

WEATHERFORD

Custer County

'90 U.S. Census- 10,124; E&P '96 Est. 10,509

Weatherford Daily News

(e-tues to fri; S)

Weatherford Daily News, 118 S. Broadway; PO Box 191, Weatherford, OK 73096; tel (405) 772-3301; fax (405) 772-7329.
Circulation: 5,004(e); 5,004(S); Sworn Sept. 14, 1995.
Price: 50¢(d); 50¢(S); $6.50/mo; $58.00/yr.
Advertising: Open inch rate $5.85(e); $5.85(S). **Representative:** Oklahoma Press Service.
News Service: AP. **Established:** 1900.
Special Editions: January Clearance, Health Quarterly, Koupon Kraze, Chamber Tab, SWOSU Pageant Page, Tax Tab (Jan); ET Car Care, Valentine Promo, Spring Break Promo, FFA Page, Space Clearance Section, Hog Wild - Hog Calling, Bridal Tab (Feb); Spring Fling Begins, Spring Home Improvement Tab, St. Patrick's Promo, Easter Coloring Contest, Business Honor Roll (Mar); Just Us Kids, Health Quarterly, Parade of Homes, Mother's Day Promo (Apr); Law Enforcement Promo, Sidewalk Sales, Grad Section, Vacation & Travel Section (May); Father's Day Gift Guide, Little League Tab (June); Car Care Show, Summer Clearance Section, Health Quarterly, Back to School (July); Koupon Kraze, Summer Sidewalk Sale, Weatherford Magazine, Football Contest (Aug); Arts Tab, Arts Festival, Farm Safety Week, Fall Fashion Section, SWOSU Homecoming Tab (Sept); 4-H Week, Fire Prevention Week, Health Quarterly, Fall Home Improvement Tab, Halloween Coloring Contest, Red Ribbon Week, Nite Owl Sale (Oct); Thanksgiving Coloring Contest, Christmas Openers,

Gift Guide (Nov); Gift Guide, Last Minute Gift Guide, Christmas Greetings, After Christmas Sale Edition, First Baby Contest (Dec).
Magazine: TV Entertainment Tab (S).

CORPORATE OFFICERS

President Phillip R Reid
Secretary/Treasurer Jeanne Ann Reid

GENERAL MANAGEMENT

Publisher/General Manager Phillip R Reid
Manager-Credit/Purchasing Agent Phillip R Reid
Bookkeeper Teresa Wardell

ADVERTISING

Manager-Display Kristi Regier
Manager-Classified Karen Nowlin

CIRCULATION

Manager Mike Auge

NEWS EXECUTIVE

Editor Larry Adler

EDITORS AND MANAGERS

City Editor Ann Marcy
Columnist Ken Reid
Columnist Phillip R Reid
Editorial Page Editor Larry Adler
Education/Lifestyle Editor Kristi Hill
News/Religion Editor Larry Adler
Sports Editor Thomas Lee
Women's Editor Kristi Hill

PRODUCTION

Manager John Raleigh
Foreman-Composing John Raleigh

Market Information: TMC; ADS.
Mechanical available: Offset; Black and 3 ROP colors; insert accepted — preprinted, any; page cut-offs — 18½".
Mechanical specifications: Type page 13½" x 21½"; E - 6 cols, 2¹⁄₁₆", ⅛" between; A - 6 cols, 2¹⁄₁₆", ⅛" between; C - 6 cols, 2¹⁄₁₆", ⅛" between.
Commodity consumption: Newsprint 11 short tons; width 28"; black ink 46 pounds; color ink 12 pounds; single pages printed 3,864; average pages per issue 10(d), 34(S); single plates used 2,600.
Equipment: EDITORIAL: Front-end hardware — IBM/PC; Front-end software — IBM; Printers — HP/LaserWriters. CLASSIFIED: Front-end hardware — IBM/PC; Front-end software — IBM, Microsoft/Word; Printers — HP/Laser-Printer. DISPLAY: Adv layout systems — IBM/PC; Front-end software — Aldus/Page-Maker, Adobe/Typestyler, Ap/Mac Scan. PRODUCTION: Typesetters — 2-COM, Ap/Mac LaserWriter, IBM/PC; Plate exposures — 1-B/1500, Nu; Scanners — HP/Scan; Production cameras — 1-Nu/SST 1822x2024; Automatic film processors — P/24SQ; Color separation equipment (conventional) — Ap/Mac Scan. PRESSROOM: Line 1 — 4-G/0-1047; Folders — 1-G. MAILROOM: Inserters and stuffers — KAN/320; Bundle tyer — 1-Ca; Addressing machine — 1-RSK/TRS-80, St/Miller Labeler. COMMUNICATIONS: Facsimile — Panasonic-IBM/PC; Systems used — satellite. WIRE SERVICES: News — AP; Receiving dishes — size-10ft, AP. BUSINESS COMPUTERS: 2-RSK, IBM; Applications: All bookkeeping, Circ; PCs & micros networked; PCs & main system networked.

WEWOKA

Seminole County

'90 U.S. Census- 4,050; E&P '96 Est. 3,317

Wewoka Daily Times

(e-tues to fri; S)

Wewoka Daily Times, 210 S. Wewoka Ave.; PO Box 61, Wewoka, OK 74884; tel (405) 257-3341. Robinson-Pettis Publishing group.
Circulation: 1,120(e); 1,120(S); Sworn Sept. 30, 1992.
Price: 25¢(d); 25¢(S); $36.00/yr.
Advertising: Open inch rate $4.15(e); $4.15(S). **Representative:** Papert Companies.
News Services: UPI, NEA. **Politics:** Democrat. **Established:** 1920.
Note: Printed by the Holdenville (OK) News.
Special Editions: Hospital Tab; Sorghum Day Edition; Heritage Day; Alumni Edition; Chamber of Commerce Progress Tab.
Magazine: Food (wed).

GENERAL MANAGEMENT

Publisher Bill Robinson
General Manager Kelly Robinson
Bookkeeper Tammy Giles

ADVERTISING

Director-Classified Tammy Giles

CIRCULATION

Director Joe Holley

EDITOR AND MANAGER

News Editor Vicky Pettis

PRODUCTION

Foreman-Mailroom James Easley

Market Information: TMC.
Mechanical available: Offset; Black and 3 ROP colors; insert accepted — preprinted; page cut-offs — 22⅝".
Mechanical specifications: Type page 13½" x 21½"; E - 6 cols, 2⅛", ¹⁄₁₆" between; A - 6 cols, 2⅛", ¹⁄₁₆" between; C - 8 cols, 1⅜", ¹⁄₁₆" between.
Commodity consumption: average pages per issue 34(d), 72(S).
Equipment: EDITORIAL: Front-end hardware — COM; Other equipment — 1-BM. CLASSIFIED: Front-end hardware — COM; Printers — Ap/Mac LaserWriter; Other equipment — 1-BM. PRODUCTION: Typesetters — 1-COM, 3-Ap/Mac Plus, 3-Ap/Mac LaserWriter; Plate processors — Ic/1cm25; Production cameras — B/1822; Automatic film processors — P/24; Color separation equipment (conventional) — Ca. PRESSROOM: Line 1 — 7-HI/V15-A. MAILROOM: Inserters and stuffers — KR/Inserter; Addressing machine — 1-Wm. COMMUNICATIONS: Facsimile — Sharp/Fu-5000. WIRE SERVICES: News — AP; Receiving dishes — AP. BUSINESS COMPUTERS: 1-BM/3600.

WOODWARD

Woodward County

'90 U.S. Census- 12,340; E&P '96 Est. 11,598

Woodward News

(m-tues to sat; S)

Woodward News, 904 Oklahoma; PO Box 928, Woodward, OK 73802-0928; tel (405) 256-2200; fax (405) 254-2159. Hollinger International Inc. group.
Circulation: 6,145(m); 6,145(m-sat); 6,145(S); Sworn Sept. 29, 1995.
Price: 35¢(d); 35¢(sat); 35¢(S); $72.20/yr.
Advertising: Open inch rate $6.69(m); $9.81(m-wed); $6.69(m-sat); $6.69(S). **Representative:** Papert Companies.
News Service: AP. **Established:** 1984.
Not Published: Thanksgiving; Christmas.
Special Weekly Sections: Best Food Day (wed); Church (fri); Church (sat); TV Magazine (S).

GENERAL MANAGEMENT

Publisher Gloria Fletcher

ADVERTISING

Director Amy Pulson

CIRCULATION

Director JoAnn Barker

NEWS EXECUTIVE

Editor Johnny McMahan

Market Information: Zoned editions; TMC.
Mechanical available: Offset; Black and 3 ROP colors; insert accepted — preprinted; page cut-offs — 16½".
Mechanical specifications: Type page 10.75" x 16.5"; E - 5 cols, 2¹⁄₁₆", ⅛" between; A - 5 cols, 2¹⁄₁₆", ⅛" between; C - 5 cols, 2¹⁄₁₆", ⅛" between.
Commodity consumption: widths 35", 27½"; average pages per issue 20(d), 18(S).
Equipment: EDITORIAL: Front-end hardware — Ap/Mac; Front-end software — Baseview/NewsEdit, QuarkXPress; Printers — Ap/Mac LaserWriter IIf. CLASSIFIED: Front-end hardware — Ap/Mac; Front-end software — Baseview; Printers — Ap/Mac LaserWriter IIg. DISPLAY: Front-end hardware — Ap/Mac; Front-end software — QuarkXPress, Claris/MacWrite, Microsoft/Excel; Printers — Ap/Mac Laser-Writer IIg. PRODUCTION: Typesetters — 2-Ap/Mac LaserWriter; Automatic film processors — P; Color separation equipment (conventional) — Digi-Colour. PRESSROOM: Line 1 — 4-G/(1 Universal Color deck). WIRE SERVICES: Receiving dishes — AP. BUSINESS COMPUTERS: 2-Mitsubishi; Applications: Nomads/Listmaster: Accts receivable.

OREGON

ALBANY

Linn County

'90 U.S. Census- 29,462; E&P '96 Est. 32,714
ABC-NDM (90): 90,869 (HH 34,503)

Albany Democrat-Herald

(e-mon to sat)

Albany Democrat-Herald, 600 Lyon St. S.W.; PO Box 130, Albany, OR 97321-0041; tel (503) 926-2211; fax (503) 926-7209. Capital Cities/ABC Inc. group.
Circulation: 21,563(e); 21,563(e-sat); ABC Sept. 30, 1995.
Price: 50¢(d); 75¢(sat); $8.50/mo (carrier), $11.50/mo (mail), $13.50/mo (out-of-county); $102.00/yr (carrier), $138.00/yr (mail), $162.00/yr (out-of-county).
Advertising: Open inch rate $15.39(e); $15.39(e-sat). **Representative:** Landon Associates Inc.
News Service: AP. **Politics:** Independent. **Established:** 1865.
Special Editions: Half-off Extravaganza (Jan); Progress (Mar); Home Improvement/Lawn & Garden (Apr); Summer Activities (May); Timber Carnival (June); Crazy Days (July); Back-to-School (Aug); Fall Sports, Hunting, Home-scapes (Sept); Holiday Bazaar (Oct); Christmas Opening (Nov); Gift Guides (Dec); Brides' Guide (1st sat), Car Care (2nd sat), Senior Page (last sat) (monthly); People & Places (bi-monthly).
Special Weekly Sections: Business News (mon); Best Food Day, People (tues); The Mid-Valley Neighbor (TMC Shopper), People (wed); People (thur); Entertainment Calendar, Religion Page, Home & Garden Advice (fri); People (sat); Theater/Restaurant Directory, Sports (daily).
Magazine: Fan Fare (fri).

CORPORATE OFFICER

President Pacific-Northwest Group Richard F Anderson

GENERAL MANAGEMENT

Publisher John E Buchner
General Manager/Sales W Clark Gallagher
Controller John Irwin
Asst Controller Kathy Hannahs
Director-Management Info Services Daniel L Roddy
Administrator-Employee Benefits Sandi Yingling

ADVERTISING

Manager-Retail Judie Weissert
Manager-Classified John Hauck
Supervisor-Service Tina Leonard
Coordinator-National Glenna Slenning

TELECOMMUNICATIONS

Audiotex Coordinator John E Buchner

CIRCULATION

Manager Michael D Miller
Coordinator-TMC Jason Smith
Supervisor-Office Jeannettia Mickler

NEWS EXECUTIVES

Editor Hasso Hering
Managing Editor Graham Kislingbury

EDITORS AND MANAGERS

Business Editor James A Magruder II
Editorial Page Hasso Hering
Food Editor Mary Parkinson
Librarian Glenda Suklis
Assoc Editor James Magruder II
News Editor Kim Jackson
Asst News Editor Steve Collier
People Editor Mary Parkinson
Photo Editor Stanford Smith
Regional Editor Carolyn Spanier
Sports Editor Steve Lundeberg
Asst Sports Editor Aaron Yost

PRODUCTION

Manager-Operations Robert F Phillips
Foreman-Pressroom/Safety Coordinator Rodney Hyde
Asst Foreman-Pressroom Greg McDaniel
Supervisor-Mailroom Rae Utley

Market Information: Split Run; TMC; ADS; Operate audiotex.
Mechanical available: Offset; Black and 3 ROP colors; insert accepted — preprinted, FSI; page cut-offs — 22¾".
Mechanical specifications: Type page 13" x 21½"; E - 6 cols, 2¹⁄₁₆", ³⁄₁₆" between; A - 6 cols, 2¹⁄₁₆", ³⁄₁₆" between; C - 9 cols, 1⅜", ⅛" between.
Commodity consumption: Newsprint 1,334 short tons; 1,210 metric tons; widths 27½", 13¾"; black ink 28,568 pounds; color ink 3,485 pounds; single pages printed 9,462; average pages per issue 28(d); single plates used 14,402.
Equipment: EDITORIAL: Front-end hardware — 1-Ap/Mac II, 1-Ap/Mac si, 2-Ap/Mac Quadra 950 fileserver; Front-end software — Quark-XPress, Baseview/NewsEdit Pro 2.0; Printers — 1-Ap/Mac LaserPrinter NT, ECR/Scriptsetter IV. CLASSIFIED: Front-end hardware — Ap/Mac Centris 650 fileserver; Front-end software — Baseview/Class Manager Plus; Printers — Ap/Mac LaserPro 630; Other equipment — Ap/Mac III LC. AUDIOTEX: Hardware — U.S. Telecom; Software — Phonemaster/2000 12-line #1590. DISPLAY: Adv layout systems — 3-Ap/Mac ci, 1-Ap/Mac LC II, 1-Ap/Mac Centris 650 fileserver; Front-end hardware — 4-Ap/Mac; Front-end software — Multi-Ad/Creator 3.7, AP AdSend; Printers — Compaq/Page Mark 20, Dataproducts/LZR 2080. PRODUCTION: Pagination software — QPS 3.3; Typesetters — 2-ECR/Scriptsetter IV; Plate exposures — 1-Nu; Plate processors — 1-Nu; Electronic picture desk — Lf/AP Leaf Picture Desk; Scanners — ECR/Autokon 1030C; Production cameras — 1-C/Spartan II; Automatic film processors — 1-P, 1-Konica/K-400, 1-Konica/K-550; Film transporters — 1-LE; Shrink lenses — 1-CK Optical; Color separation equipment (conventional) — Wing-Lynch/processor; Digital color separation equipment — Ap/Mac Quadra 950, Ap/Mac Quadra 700, ECR/Autokon. PRESSROOM: Line 1 — 6-G/Urbanite; Folders — 1-G; Press control system — 2-Fin; Press registration system — Duarte/Pin Registration System. MAILROOM: Counter stackers — 1-BG; Inserters and stuffers — 2-KAN/480 6-into-1; Bundle tyer — 1-MLN, 1-Strapex, 1-EAM/Mosca; Addressing machine — 1-KAN/650, KR/label head. LIBRARY: Electronic — SMS/Stauffer. COMMUNICATIONS: Facsimile — Panafax/UF-640, Panafax/UF-300; Remote imagesetting — AP AdSend. WIRE SERVICES: News — AP, AP Newsfeatures; Photos — AP; Stock tables — AP Stock; Receiving dishes — size-12ft, AP, Newspaper Satellite Network. BUSINESS COMPUTERS: NCR/10000-55; Applications: Gen ledger, Payroll, Accts payable, Circ, Adv billing; PCs & micros networked; PCs & main system networked.

ASHLAND

Jackson County

'90 U.S. Census- 16,234; E&P '96 Est. 17,701
ABC-CZ (90): 16,234 (HH 6,853)

The Daily Tidings

(e-mon to sat)

The Daily Tidings, 1661 Siskiyou Blvd.; PO Box 7, Ashland, OR 97520; tel (541) 482-3456; fax (541) 482-3688. Capital Cities/ABC Inc. group.
Circulation: 5,527(e); 5,527(e-sat); ABC Sept. 30, 1995.
Price: 50¢(d); 50¢(sat); $6.00/mo; $72.00/yr.
Advertising: Open inch rate $8.10(e); $8.10(e-sat).
News Service: AP. **Politics:** Independent. **Established:** 1876.
Not Published: New Year; Memorial Day; Independence Day; Labor Day; Thanksgiving; Christmas.
Special Editions: Health and Fitness (Jan); Scene (Feb); Home and Garden, Who's Who (Mar); Home (Apr); Shakespeare (May); Fourth of July (June); Football, Back-to-School (Aug); Southern Oregon State College (Sept); Women in Business (Oct); Winter Sports (Nov); Christmas Songbook, Christmas Gift Guides (Dec).
Special Weekly Sections: Business (mon); Best Food Day (tues); Revels (thur); Restaurant Page (fri); Service Directory (daily).
Magazine: Revels/On Television (Entertainment) (thur).

GENERAL MANAGEMENT

Publisher Mike O'Brien

ADVERTISING

Director Susan Howard

CIRCULATION

Manager Chuck Colosant

NEWS EXECUTIVE

Managing Editor Ted Taylor

EDITORS AND MANAGERS

Business/Finance Editor Jeff Keating
City/Metro Editor Ted Taylor
Editorial Page Editor Ted Taylor

Entertainment/Amusements Editor Amy Richard
News Editor Jeff Keating
Picture Editor Randy Wrighthouse
Television/Film Editor Amy Richard
Theater/Music Editor Amy Richard

Market Information: TMC; ADS.
Mechanical available: Offset; Black and 3 ROP colors; insert accepted — preprinted, any; page cut-offs — 22¾".
Mechanical specifications: Type page 13" x 21½"; E - 6 cols, 2 1/16", 1/8" between; A - 6 cols, 2 1/16", 1/8" between; C - 9 cols, 1 3/8", 1/16" between.
Commodity consumption: Newsprint 480 short tons; 450 metric tons; widths 28", 30", 35"; single pages printed 5,200; average pages per issue 18(d).
Equipment: EDITORIAL: Front-end hardware — 10-Mk. CLASSIFIED: Front-end hardware — 3-Mk. PRODUCTION: Typesetters — 4-Ap/Mac, 2-Ap/Mac LaserPrinter; Plate exposures — 1-Nu/FT40; Plate processors — 1-LE/LP32; Production cameras — 1-SCREEN/650-D; Automatic film processors — 1-LE/LD24.
PRESSROOM: Line 1 — 7-G/Community; Folders — 1-G/2:1. MAILROOM: Bundle tyer — 1-Bu, MLN; Addressing machine — Pressure Sensitive/Labeling. WIRE SERVICES: News — AP; Receiving dishes — AP. BUSINESS COMPUTERS: NCR; Applications: Circ, Bookkeeping.

ASTORIA
Clatsop County
'90 U.S. Census- 10,069; E&P '96 Est. 10,299
ABC-CZ (90): 10,069 (HH 4,216)

The Daily Astorian
(e-mon to fri)

The Daily Astorian, 949 Exchange; PO Box 210, Astoria, OR 97103-0210; tel (541) 325-3211; fax (541) 325-6573.
Circulation: 9,413(e); ABC Sept. 30, 1995.
Price: 50¢(d); $6.00/mo (carrier), $9.00/mo (mail).
Advertising: Open inch rate $12.35(e). **Representative:** Papert Companies.
News Service: AP. **Politics:** Independent. **Established:** 1873.
Not Published: Christmas.
Special Editions: Who's Who in Clatsop (Feb); Car Care (Mar); Midsummer Scandinavian Festival, Vacation (June); Regatta (July); Car Care (Oct).
Special Weekly Sections: Food Day (tues); Business, TV (thur); Religion Page (fri).
Magazine: Panache! (fri).

CORPORATE OFFICERS
President Michael A Forrester
Vice Pres Steve Forrester
Vice Pres Jacqueline Bedford Brown
Secretary Amy Bedford
Treasurer Eleanor A Forrester

GENERAL MANAGEMENT
General Manager George Potter

ADVERTISING
Director Jennifer Rees

CIRCULATION
Manager Linda Long

NEWS EXECUTIVES
Editor Stephen A Forrester
Managing Editor Laura Sellers-Earl

EDITORS AND MANAGERS
Amusements Editor Laura Sellers-Earl
Editorial Page Editor Stephen A Forrester
Education Editor Catherine Hawley
Food Editor Brian McNeill
Photo Department Manager Karl Maasdam
Radio/Television Editor Allen Messick
Sports Editor Paul Danzer
Wire Editor Laura Sellers-Earl

PRODUCTION
Manager-Systems Carl Earl

Market Information: TMC.
Mechanical available: Web Offset; Black and 3 ROP colors; insert accepted — preprinted; page cut-offs — 22¾".
Mechanical specifications: Type page 12¾" x 21"; E - 6 cols, 2", 1/6" between; A - 6 cols, 2", 1/6" between; C - 8 cols, 1½", 1/8" between.
Commodity consumption: Newsprint 420 metric tons; width 27"; black ink 12,000 pounds; color ink 1,800 pounds; single pages printed 5,120; average pages per issue 20(d); single plates used 2,700.
Equipment: EDITORIAL: Front-end hardware — Ap/Mac; Front-end software — QuarkXPress, Baseview, Mutli-Ad; Printers — Ap/Mac LaserWriter NTX, Ap/Mac LaserWriter IIg, Ap/Mac LaserWriter Pro 630. CLASSIFIED: Front-end hardware — Ap/Mac; Front-end software — QuarkXPress, Baseview, Multi-Ad. DISPLAY: Front-end hardware — Ap/Mac; Front-end software — Multi-Ad/Creator; Printers — Ap/Mac LaserWriter NTX, Ap/Mac LaserWriter IIg, Ap/Mac LaserWriter Pro 630. PRODUCTION: OCR software — Caere/OmniPage; Scanners — HP/JetScan, La Cie/Silver Scan II; Production cameras — K/V-241; Automatic film processors — P/Pakonolith 524.
PRESSROOM: Line 1 — 7-G/Community; Folders — 1-G/SC. MAILROOM: Inserters and stuffers — 1-KAN/420. LIBRARY: Electronic — SMS/Stauffer. COMMUNICATIONS: Facsimile — Sharp. WIRE SERVICES: News — AP; Receiving dishes — size-12ft, AP.

BAKER CITY
Baker County
'90 U.S. Census- 9,500; E&P '96 Est. 9,684
ABC-CZ (90): 9,140 (HH 3,706)

Baker City Herald
(e-mon to fri)

Baker City Herald, 1915 First St.; PO Box 807, Baker City, OR 97814; tel (541) 523-3673; fax (541) 523-6426. Western Communications Inc. group.
Circulation: 3,256(e); 3,760 (e-fri); ABC Sept. 30, 1995.
Price: 35¢(d); $6.75/mo; $81.00/yr.
Advertising: Open inch rate $5.60(e).
News Service: AP. **Politics:** Independent. **Established:** 1870.
Not Published: Christmas.
Special Editions: Trends (Jan); Sports-District Basketball Tournament (Feb); Home Show (Mar); Fishing (Apr); Recreation on the Oregon Trail (May); Restaurant Guide (June); Miners' Jubilee (July); Shrine Football Game (Aug); Fall Sports (Sept); Who's Who (Oct); Christmas Song Book, Christmas Parade, 1997 Date Book (Dec).
Special Weekly Sections: Business & Industry (mon); Schools (tues); Living (wed); Recreation-Outdoor (thur); Religion, Arts & Leisure (fri).
Magazines: Show and Tel (TV); Entertainment (Arts & Leisure) (fri).

CORPORATE OFFICERS
Board Chairman Elizabeth C McCool
President/CEO Gordon Black
Vice Pres Janet Stevens
Vice Pres John Shaver
Vice Pres Robert K Moody
Treasurer Elizabeth C McCool
Secretary Margaret C Cushman
Chief Editorial Officer Robert W Chandler

GENERAL MANAGEMENT
Publisher Jack Turner
Bookkeeper Janice Monaco

ADVERTISING
Manager Lynette Perry

MARKETING AND PROMOTION
Manager-Marketing/Promotion Lynette Perry

CIRCULATION
Manager Jim Sherman

NEWS EXECUTIVE
Editor Dean Brickey

EDITORS AND MANAGERS
Business/Finance Editor Gerry Steele
Columnist Dean Brickey
Editorial Page Editor Dean Brickey
Education Editor Christine Collins
Entertainment/Amusements Editor Christina Wood
Environmental Editor Jayson Jacoby
Farm/Agriculture Editor Gerry Steele
Fashion/Style Editor Christina Wood
Health/Medical Editor Christine Collins
Photo Editor S John Collins
Political Editor Dean Brickey
Religion Editor Christina Wood
Sports Editor Gerry Steele
Women's Editor Christina Wood

PRODUCTION
Manager Frank Everidge

Market Information: Split Run.
Mechanical available: Offset; Black and 3 ROP colors; insert accepted — preprinted; page cut-offs — 22¾".
Mechanical specifications: Type page 13" x 21"; E - 6 cols, 2 1/16", 1/8" between; A - 6 cols, 2 1/16", 1/8" between; C - 8 cols, 1 9/16", 1/8" between.
Commodity consumption: Newsprint 120 short tons; widths 78", 14"; black ink 5,400 pounds; color ink 600 pounds; single pages printed 3,442; average pages per issue 14(d); single plates used 3,000.

Equipment: EDITORIAL: Front-end hardware — Ap/Mac; Printers — Ap/Mac LaserWriter II NTX. CLASSIFIED: Front-end hardware — Ap/Mac; Front-end software — Mk/Ad Manager. DISPLAY: Adv layout systems — Ap/Mac; Front-end hardware — Ap/Mac; Front-end software — Aldus/DeskPaint, Aldus/SuperPaint, QuarkXPress, Adobe/Illustrator; Printers — Ap/Mac LaserWriter II NTX, AG/P-3400-PS; Other equipment — HP/ScanJet Plus Scanner. PRODUCTION: Typesetters — Ap/Mac LaserWriter II NTX; Scanners — SCREEN/670C, HP/ScanJet Plus; Reproportion units — SCREEN/Companica 5161.
PRESSROOM: Line 1 — 6-G/Community; Folders — 1-G/SSC. MAILROOM: Inserters and stuffers — KAN/320; Bundle tyer — MLN/Single strap; Addressing machine — Wm. COMMUNICATIONS: Facsimile — Sharp/FO-700. WIRE SERVICES: News — AP; Syndicates — Universal Press, TMS, Creators, King Features. BUSINESS COMPUTERS: Packard Bell.

BEND
Deschutes County
'90 U.S. Census- 20,469; E&P '96 Est. 24,061
ABC-CZ (90): 26,861 (HH 10,893)

The Bulletin (e-mon to fri; S)

The Bulletin, 1526 N.W. Hill St., Bend, OR 97701; tel (541) 382-1811; fax (541) 385-5802; e-mail bulletin@bendnet.com. Western Communications Inc. group.
Circulation: 25,817(e); 27,205(S); ABC Sept. 30, 1995.
Price: 35¢(d); 50¢(fri); $1.25(S); $9.00/mo (carrier), $13.50/mo (mail); $108.00/yr (carrier), $162.00/yr (mail).
Advertising: Open inch rate $14.25(e); $14.25(S). **Representative:** Landon Associates Inc.
News Services: AP, LAT-WP. **Politics:** Independent. **Established:** 1903.
Special Editions: Captain Coupon (½flexie), Baby Book Tab (Jan); Spring Fashion and Bridal Section (Std.), Home and Outdoor Section Tab, Progress Tab (Mar); Spring Recreation (Std.) (Apr); Mother's Day, Pole-Pedal-Paddle Tab, Results Pole-Pedal Tab (May); Graduation (Std.) (June); Central Oregon Highlights Tab, Cascade Cycling Classic (flexie), Tour of Homes (flexie), Fair Edition Tab (July); Football Preview Tab, Public School Directory Mini-tab (Aug); Fall Fashion (Std.), Autumn Home (Std.), Hunting (Std.), Jazz Festival (Sept); Women in Business Tab, Wheels/Car Care (Std.), Autumn Home Interiors & Consumer & Electronics (Oct); Winter Recreation (Std.) (Nov); Christmas Greetings (flexie) (Dec).
Special Weekly Sections: Horizons (senior citizens) (mon); Foods (tues); Travel, Real Estate (S).
Magazines: TV/Entertainment book `Scene' (fri); Parade, Color Comics (S).

CORPORATE OFFICERS
Chairman of the Board Elizabeth C McCool
President Gordon Black
Vice Pres Janet Stevens
Vice Pres John Shaver
Vice Pres Robert K Moody
Treasurer Robert W Chandler Jr
Secretary Mary Jean Chandler
Chief Editorial Officer Robert W Chandler

GENERAL MANAGEMENT
Publisher Gordon Black
Controller John Shaver

ADVERTISING
Director-Marketing Mike Thorpe
Manager-Classified Martha Tiller
Manager-Retail Cathy Spencer

TELECOMMUNICATIONS
Audiotex Manager Martha Tiller

CIRCULATION
Director Bob Barth

NEWS EXECUTIVES
Editor Robert W Chandler
Exec Editor Rick Attig
Deputy Editor Janet Stevens
Managing Editor Steven K Bagwell

EDITORS AND MANAGERS
Business Editor Mike Freeman
City Editor Frank Fiedler
Education Editor Mike Van Meter
Entertainment Editor Andy Whipple
Environmental Editor Steve Lundgren
Features Editor Andy Whipple
Food Editor Faith Leith
Graphics Editor Greg Cross
Health/Medical Editor Keith Fredrickson
News Editor Bob Buxton
Asst News Editor Dave Pinkerton
Photo Editor Diane Kulpinski
Religion Editor Barney Lerten
Sports Editor Bill Bigelow
Television/Film Editor Andy Whipple
Theater Editor Andy Whipple
Travel Editor Keith Fredrickson

MANAGEMENT INFORMATION SERVICES
Data Processing Manager Corey Book

PRODUCTION
Manager-Operations Mike Greening
Manager-Systems Harry Mastrud
Supervisor-Pressroom Alan Nelson
Supervisor-Composing Jeanne Krewson
Supervisor-Mailroom Kevin Eldred

Market Information: TMC; Operate audiotex.
Mechanical available: Offset; Black and 3 ROP colors; insert accepted — preprinted; page cut-offs — 22¾".
Mechanical specifications: Type page 13" x 21½"; E - 6 cols, 2.06", 1/6" between; A - 6 cols, 2.06", 1/6" between; C - 9 cols, 1.36", 1/16" between.
Commodity consumption: Newsprint 2,025 short tons; widths 27½", 32"; black ink 52,000 pounds; color ink 12,800 pounds; single pages printed 12,896; average pages per issue 44(d), 42(S); single plates used 21,000.
Equipment: EDITORIAL: Front-end hardware — SII/66XR; Front-end software — SII/66XR; Printers — 1-Genicom/3410; Other equipment — 32-SII. CLASSIFIED: Front-end hardware — SII/66 XR; Front-end software — SII/66 XR; Printers — 1-Genicom/3410; Other equipment — 10-SII. DISPLAY: Adv layout systems — 10-Ap/Mac; Front-end software — QuarkXPress, Adobe/Illustrator 3.2, Aldus/FreeHand; Other equipment — 3-HP/ScanJet Scanner. PRODUCTION: Pagination software — QuarkXPress 3.31; OCR software — Caere/OmniPage; Typesetters — 2-V/Imagesetter; Plate exposures — 3-Nu; Plate processors — Nat/A-250; Electronic picture desk — Lf/AP Leaf Picture Desk; Scanners — ECR/Autokon 1000DE, HP/ScanJet scanner; Production cameras — C/Marathon; Automatic film processors — P, P/26-RA, 2-LE/LS 2800R; Film transporters — 1-C, 2-LE; Digital color separation equipment — Lf/Leafscan 35, V/Color Getter.
PRESSROOM: Line 1 — 2-G/Urbanite, 7-G/Urbanite. MAILROOM: Counter stackers — 1-MM/388, 1-BG/105, 1-MM; Inserters and stuffers — 16-MM/375; Bundle tyer — 1-MLN, 1-Dynaric/NPI; Other mailroom equipment — 1-MM. LIBRARY: Electronic — PC/386 Indexing system, SII/LASR; Combination — Minolta/RP 407E, Microfilm Reader/Printer. WIRE SERVICES: News — AP, LAT-WP; Photos — AP; Stock tables — AP SelectStox; Receiving dishes — size-3m, AP. BUSINESS COMPUTERS: AT, Novell/Network; Applications: Accts payable, Accts receivable, Payroll, Gen ledger, Circ; PCs & micros networked; PCs & main system networked.

COOS BAY-NORTH BEND
Coos County
'90 U.S. Census- 24,926 (Coos Bay 15,076; North Bend 9,850); E&P '96 Est. 25,985 (Coos Bay 15,909; North Bend 10,076)
ABC-CZ (90): 25,932 (HH 10,513)

The World (e-mon to fri; m-sat)

The World, 350 Commercial Ave; PO Box 1840, Coos Bay, OR 97420; tel (541) 269-1222; fax (541) 267-0294. Scripps League Newspapers Inc. group.
Circulation: 16,695(e); 16,695(m-sat); ABC Sept. 30, 1995.
Price: 35¢(d); 50¢(sat); $9.25/mo (mail); $111.00/yr (mail).
Advertising: Open inch rate $15.79(e); $15.79(m-sat).
News Service: AP. **Politics:** Independent. **Established:** 1878.
Not Published: New Year; Independence Day; Labor Day; Christmas.
Advertising not accepted: Vending machine.
Special Editions: Horizon (Feb); Home Improvement (May); Salute to Old Glory (June); Let's Go Vacation Guide, Salute to Old Glory (July); Let's Go Vacation Guide (Aug); Home Improvement, Horizon (Sept); Women In

Business (Oct); Christmas Opening (Nov); Year in Review (Dec); Spring and Fall Car Care; Milestones.

Special Weekly Sections: Best Food Day (tues); Real Estate (sat).

Magazines: USA Weekend, TV Times (local), Color Comics (sat).

CORPORATE OFFICERS

Board Chairman/Treasurer E W Scripps
Vice Chairman/Corporate Secretary Betty Knight Scripps
President Barry H Scripps
Exec Vice Pres Roger N Warkins
Vice Pres-Finance Thomas E Wendel

GENERAL MANAGEMENT

Publisher Don Brown
Manager-Office Teresa Britton

ADVERTISING

Director Juan Mejia
Manager-Classified Susie Allsop
Manager-South Coast Week Juan Mejia

TELECOMMUNICATIONS

Audiotex Manager Juan Mejia

CIRCULATION

Manager Mary Ann Mason

NEWS EXECUTIVES

Editor Don Brown
Managing Editor Veronica Combs

EDITORS AND MANAGERS

Assoc Editor Susan Chambers
City Editor Kate Tave
Fashion/Food Editor Linda Meierjurgen
Milestones Veronica Combs

PRODUCTION

Manager Walter Johnson
Foreman-Pressroom Ronald Breedlove

Market Information: TMC; ADS; Operate audiotex.

Mechanical available: Offset; Black and 3 ROP colors; insert accepted — preprinted; page cut-offs — 21½".

Mechanical specifications: Type page 13" x 21½"; E - 6 cols, 2 1/16", 1/8" between; A - 6 cols, 2 1/16", 1/8" between; C - 9 cols, 1 5/16", 1/8" between.

Commodity consumption: Newsprint 747 short tons; widths 27½", 13¾"; black ink 14,500 pounds; color ink 2,850 pounds; single pages printed 6,982; average pages per issue 20(d), 30(sat); single plates used 7,250.

Equipment: EDITORIAL: Front-end hardware — 11-ScrippSat/PC; Front-end software — ScrippSat, Suntype, QPS, Adobe/Photoshop, QuarkXPress. CLASSIFIED: Front-end hardware — 3-ScrippSat/PC; Front-end software — Synaptic; Printers — Okidata/393 LaserMaster. DISPLAY: Adv layout systems — 3-ScrippSat; Front-end hardware — PC, ScrippSat; Front-end software — Archetype/Corel Draw-Trace, Aldus/PhotoStyles, QuarkXPress, Ethernet; Printers — 2-Unity/1200 Laser, QMS, LaserMaster/1800x60. PRODUCTION: Pagination software — QuarkXPress; OCR software — HP; Typesetters — 2-LaserMaster/Unity; Plate exposures — Nu; Plate processors — Nat/A-250; Electronic picture desk — Lf/AP Leaf Picture Desk, Adobe/Photoshop, ECR/Imagesetter; Scanners — HP/ScanJet; Production cameras — K; Automatic film processors — C; Digital color separation equipment — ECR/Scriptsetter IV, Ap/Mac Quadra 950, Ap/Power Mac.
PRESSROOM: Line 1 — 9-G/Community, 1-G/Community; Folders — 1-G. MAILROOM: Inserters and stuffers — 1-MM, 1-MM/EM-10; Bundle tyer — 2-MLN; Addressing machine — 2-Ch. COMMUNICATIONS: Digital ad delivery system — AP AdSend. WIRE SERVICES: News — AP; Syndicates — NEA; Receiving dishes — size-3m, AP. BUSINESS COMPUTERS: 3-Acer/1100SX, 3-Acer/710, Suntype/Classified System, ScrippSat; Applications: Lotus 1-2-3; PCs & main system networked.

CORVALLIS

Benton County

'90 U.S. Census- 44,757; E&P '96 Est. 49,041
ABC-CZ (90): 44,757 (HH 16,743)

Corvallis Gazette-Times

(m-mon to sat; S)

Corvallis Gazette-Times, 600 S.W. Jefferson Ave. (97333); PO Box 368, Corvallis, OR 97339-0368; tel (541) 753-2641; fax (541) 758-9505; e-mail 74250.2373@compuserve.com, gt@peak.org. Lee Enterprises Inc. group.

Circulation: 13,775(m); 13,775(m-sat); 15,693(S); ABC Sept. 30, 1995.

Price: 35¢(d); 35¢(sat); $1.50(S); $11.45/mo (city), $11.95/mo (motor route); $136.95/yr.

Advertising: Open inch rate $15.70(m); $17.70(m-sat); $17.27(S). **Representative:** Landon Associates Inc.

News Services: AP, KRT. **Politics:** Independent. **Established:** 1862.

Special Editions: Bridal (Jan); Baby Book (Feb); Visitor's Guide, Home & Garden (Mar); Community (May); da Vinci Days (July); Our Town, Visitor's Guide (Sept); Home Improvement (Oct); X'mas Gift Guide (Nov); X'mas Gift Guide (Dec); Fashion (Spring & Fall); Connection, Real State Extra (monthly).

Special Weekly Sections: Senior Page (mon); Students Page (tues); Best Food Day, TMC (wed); Venture/Outdoor (thur); Entertainment & Arts Tab (fri); Church Page (sat); Accent/Weddings, Home and Garden, Travel (S); Business and Stock (daily except mon).

Magazines: Entertainment & Arts Guide Tab (fri); Sunday Comics, Parade, TV This Week Tab (S).

Broadcast Affiliates: KGUN, AZ; KREZ, CO; KEMB,HI; KSNC, KSNG, KSDK, KSNT, KSNW, KS; KMTV, KE; KBIM, KRQE, NM; KOIN, OR; KZIA, TX; WSAZ,WV.

CORPORATE OFFICERS

President Richard D Gottlieb
Vice Pres Ron L Rickman
Vice Pres Floyd Whellan
Vice Pres Larry L Bloom

GENERAL MANAGEMENT

Publisher Beth Clark
Controller Sharon Emenegger
Personnel Coordinator Lisa Yahnke
Manager-Credit Rosa Hill

ADVERTISING

Manager-Retail Kevin Haezebroeck
Manager-Classified Brad Erlandson

MARKETING AND PROMOTION

Manager-Marketing Carol Blodgett

TELECOMMUNICATIONS

Audiotex Manager Brad Erlandson

CIRCULATION

Manager Jim Thompson

NEWS EXECUTIVE

Editor Dan Shryock

EDITORS AND MANAGERS

City Editor-Day Barbara Curtin
City Editor-Night Rob Priewe
News Editor Tim Leslie
Chief Photographer Tony Overman
Sports Editor Jeff Welsch

MANAGEMENT INFORMATION SERVICES

Online Manager Tim Leslie
Data Processing Manager Sharon Emenegger

PRODUCTION

Manager Rod Hayden
Supervisor-Distribution Mike Edwards

Market Information: TMC; Operate database; Operate audiotex; Electronic edition.

Mechanical available: Offset; Black and 3 ROP colors; insert accepted — preprinted, standing card stock; page cut-offs — 22¾".

Mechanical specifications: Type page 13" x 21"; E - 6 cols, 2 1/16", 1/8" between; A - 6 cols, 2 1/16", 1/8" between; C - 9 cols, 1 5/16", 1/16" between.

Commodity consumption: Newsprint 943 metric tons; widths 27½", 35", 13¾", 17½"; black ink 25,500 pounds; color ink 3,100 pounds; single pages printed 10,062; average pages per issue 20(d), 20(sat), 40(S); single plates used 22,000.

Equipment: EDITORIAL: Front-end hardware — DEC/PDP 11-24, 21-DEC/VT-220; Front-end software — LNS; Printers — DEC/LA 100. CLASSIFIED: Front-end hardware — DEC/PDP 11-24, 6-DEC/VT-220; Front-end software — LNS; Printers — DEC/LA 120. AUDIOTEX: Hardware — Auto Agent; Software — Talking Yellow Pages/proprietary. DISPLAY: Adv layout systems — 2-HI/2221, 1-Ap/Mac IIfx, 3-Ap/Mac IIci, 3-DEC/VT220. PRODUCTION: Typesetters — 2-COM/8400, 3-Laser, Pre-Press/Panther Plus; Plate exposures — 1-Nu/Flip Top FT40UP, 1-Nu/Flip Top FT40V6; Plate processors — Nat/A-250; Production cameras — 1-C/Spartan II, 1-Nu/2024; Automatic film processors — 1-P/G, AG/Lith 26; Shrink lenses — 2-CK Optical.
PRESSROOM: Line 1 — 5-G/Urbanite; Folders — 2-G; Press control system — 2-Fin/Console. MAILROOM: Inserters and stuffers — 1-MM; Bundle tyer — 2-MLN. LIBRARY: Electronic — SMS/Stauffer Gold. WIRE SERVICES: News — AP, KRT; Photos — AP; Stock tables — AP; Receiving dishes — AP. BUSINESS COMPUTERS: IBM/AS400; Applications: Circ, Subscriber info, Accounting, Class, Display adv; PCs & micros networked.

EUGENE

Lane County

'90 U.S. Census- 112,669; E&P '96 Est. 120,955
ABC-CZ (90): 199,009 (HH 79,200)

The Register-Guard

(m-mon to fri; m-sat; S)

The Register-Guard, 975 High St.; PO Box 10188, Eugene, OR 97440; tel (541) 485-1234.

Circulation: 75,140(m); 84,844(m-sat); 78,358(S); ABC Sept. 30, 1995.

Price: 35¢(d); 50¢(sat); $1.25(S); $9.00/mo (carrier); $108.00/yr (mail).

Advertising: Open inch rate $36.33(m); $36.33(m-sat); $39.05(S). **Representative:** Landon Associates Inc.

News Services: AP, NYT, LAT-WP. **Politics:** Independent. **Established:** 1867.

Special Weekly Sections: HomeFront (Lifestyle) (mon); Business, Complete Stock Listings (tues); Best Food Day, Complete Stock Listings (wed); Business, Complete Stock Listings (thur); Arts & Entertainment, Complete Stock Listings (fri); TV Tab, Complete Stock Listings, Auto Market (sat); Resort, Travel, Business Section, Oregon Life (S).

Magazines: TV Week (sat); Oregon Life (local), Parade (S).

CORPORATE OFFICERS

Chairman of the Board Edwin M Baker
President Alton F Baker III
Vice Pres R Fletcher Little
Secretary Bridget D Baker
Asst Secretary Richard A Baker Jr
Treasurer Ann Baker Mack

GENERAL MANAGEMENT

Publisher Alton F Baker III
General Manager R Fletcher Little
Controller Scott Diehl
Personnel/Human Resources Manager Cynthia Walden

ADVERTISING

Director Michael Raz
Manager-Classified Kelly Redfeam

MARKETING AND PROMOTION

Manager-Promotion Jim Hinton

TELECOMMUNICATIONS

Audiotex Manager Kevin Miller

CIRCULATION

Director Charles Downing
Manager-Operations Frank Bertrand

NEWS EXECUTIVES

Editor Alton F Baker III
Managing Editor James Godbold
Asst Managing Editor David Baker

EDITORS AND MANAGERS

Automotive Editor Christian Wihtol
Business/Finance Editor Christian Wihtol
Acting City Editor Dave Baker
Editorial Page Editor Don W Robinson
Editorial Writer Jackman Wilson
Editorial Writer Henny Willis
Entertainment/Amusements Editor Robt Welch
Features Editor Robt Welch
Graphics Editor/Art Director Carl Davaz
Health/Medical Editor Joe Rojas-Burke
Librarian Sue Boyd
Living/Lifestyle Editor Robt Welch
News Editor James Holman
Outdoors Editor Mike Stahlberg
Photography Director Carl Davaz
Sports Editor John Conrad
Television/Film Editor Neil Cawood
Theater/Music Editor Robt Welch
Travel Editor Robt Welch
Women's Editor Robt Welch

MANAGEMENT INFORMATION SERVICES

Data Processing Manager Richard A Baker Jr

PRODUCTION

Manager Jerry LaCamp
Manager-Facilities James Dougher
Foreman-Composing Bill Miller
Foreman-Pressroom Marion Frydendall
Foreman-Plate/Camera Brad Bennett

Market Information: Split Run; TMC; Operate audiotex.

Mechanical available: Offset; Black and 3 ROP colors; insert accepted — preprinted; page cut-offs — 22".

Mechanical specifications: Type page 13" x 21"; E - 6 cols, 2 1/16", 1/8" between; A - 6 cols, 2 1/16", 1/8" between; C - 9 cols, 1 3/8", 1/16" between.

Commodity consumption: Newsprint 8,400 metric tons; widths 55", 41.25", 27.5"; black ink 164,500 pounds; color ink 35,275 pounds; single pages printed 20,800; average pages per issue 53(d), 78(S); single plates used 54,000.

Equipment: EDITORIAL: Front-end hardware — DEC/PDP 11-84; Front-end software — DEC/TMS. CLASSIFIED: Front-end hardware — DEC/PDP 11-84; Front-end software — DEC/CMS. DISPLAY: Adv layout systems — SCS/Layout 8000; Front-end hardware — DEC/4000-300; Printers — DEC/LG01. PRODUCTION: Typesetters — 1-AU/5U, 1-AU/5, 2-Cx/Bitsetter; Plate exposures — WL/Lith-X-Pozer 3; Plate processors — 1-WL/38D, 1-WL/38G; Production cameras — LE/242; Automatic film processors — LE/2600; Color separation equipment (conventional) — RZ/200S; Digital color separation equipment — Ap/Macs w/QuarkXPress.
PRESSROOM: Line 1 — 10-Mitsubishi/Lithopia; Press drives — Fin; Folders — 1-Mitsubishi/Double 3:2; Reels and stands — 8-Mitsubishi. MAILROOM: Counter stackers — 5-QWI; Inserters and stuffers — 3-AM Graphics/NP 630; Bundle tyer — 5-Dynaric; Mailroom control system — AM/Graphics/AMCS. COMMUNICATIONS: Remote imagesetting — CD/Pagefax. WIRE SERVICES: News — AP, NYT, LAT-WP; Stock tables — AP; Syndicates — AP; Receiving dishes — AP. BUSINESS COMPUTERS: 2-DEC/4000-300, 1-DEC/3100; Applications: Circ, TMC, Adv billing, Accts receivable, Payroll; PCs & micros networked; PCs & main system networked.

GRANTS PASS

Josephine County

'90 U.S. Census- 17,488; E&P '96 Est. 20,221
ABC-CZ (90): 17,488 (HH 7,145)

Grants Pass Daily Courier

(e-mon to fri; m-sat)

Grants Pass Daily Courier, 409 S.E. 7th St.; PO Box 1468, Grants Pass, OR 97526; tel (541) 474-3700; fax (541) 474-3814.

Circulation: 18,470(e); 18,470(m-sat); ABC Sept. 30, 1995.

Price: 50¢(d); 50¢(sat); $8.00/mo; $96.00/yr.

Advertising: Open inch rate $8.50(e); $8.50(m-sat).

News Service: AP. **Politics:** Independent. **Established:** 1885.

Not Published: New Year; Thanksgiving; Christmas.

Special Editions: Facts and Faces, Super Bowl Preview, Tax Guide (Jan); Brides, Grooms, Honeymoons, Couples in Business, Spring Coupon Book (Feb); People of the Valley, Wheels (Mar); Home & Garden (Apr); Summer Recreation Guide, Horse Racing (May); Summer Coupon, Summer Sizzlers (June); Prime Time (July); Josephine County Fair Program, Football (Aug); Fall Coupon Book, Fall Home Improvement, Historical Souvenir Scrapbook (Sept); Winter Recreation Guide, Community Christmas Catalog (Oct); Christmas Opener, Christmas Songbook (Nov); Holiday Gift Guide (Dec).

Special Weekly Sections: Local Business (mon); Best Food Day (tues); Under 21 Youth Page (wed); Entertainment, Gardening (thur); Churches, Weeksworth, TV Magazine (fri); Color Comics, Dimensions, Stocks, Mutual Funds (sat).

Magazine: TV and Entertainment (local, newsprint, signature) (fri).

CORPORATE OFFICER

President John E Voorhies

GENERAL MANAGEMENT

Publisher Dennis Mack
Purchasing Agent Bill Parker

ADVERTISING

Director Michele Thomas

CIRCULATION

Manager Ted Elworthy

NEWS EXECUTIVE

Editor Dennis Roler

EDITORS AND MANAGERS

Amusements/Books Editor Kathleen Alaks
Business Editor Greg Smiley
City Editor David Haerle
Editorial Page Editor Dennis Roler
Education Editor Howard Buck

Films/Theater Editor	Edith Decker
Food Editor	Edith Decker
Librarian	Mary Bradford
Music Editor	Kathleen Alaks
News Editor	Jim Mitchell
Real Estate Editor	Greg Smiley
Religion Editor	Kathleen Alaks
Sports Editor	Greg Hanberg
Teen-Age/Youth Editor	Edith Decker
Wire Editor	Jim Mitchell
Women's Editor	Edith Decker

MANAGEMENT INFORMATION SERVICES
Data Processing Manager — Danny Lawrence

PRODUCTION
Superintendent — Randy Omdahl
Foreman-Composing — Merle Grineager
Foreman-Pressroom — Darrell Shoemaker

Market Information: Zoned editions; TMC; ADS.
Mechanical available: Offset; Black and 3 ROP colors; insert accepted — preprinted; page cut-offs — 22¾".
Mechanical specifications: Type page 13" x 21½"; E - 6 cols, 2 1/16", ⅛" between; A - 6 cols, 2 1/16", ⅛" between; C - 6 cols, 2 1/16", ⅛" between.
Commodity consumption: Newsprint 1,200 metric tons; widths 13¾"; black ink 27,020 pounds; color ink 1,100 pounds; single pages printed 10,481; average pages per issue 34(d); single plates used 19,200.
Equipment: EDITORIAL: Front-end hardware — 27-AT/Series 4; Front-end software — AT; Other equipment — 6-Ap/Mac, 1-Lf/AP Leaf Picture Desk. CLASSIFIED: Front-end hardware — 5-AT/Dual Series 4; Front-end software — AT. DISPLAY: Front-end hardware — 16-Ap/Mac; Front-end software — Multi-Ad/Creator, Adobe/Illustrator, QuarkXPress; Printers — Ap/Mac LaserWriter II, Dataproducts/LZR-2600; Other equipment — Ap/Mac Scanner. PRODUCTION: Pagination software — QPS; Typesetters — 2-CG/8600, 2-AU/APS-6-108, 6-Ap/Mac, 2-AU/APS-100; Plate exposures — Nu/631; Plate processors — Nat/24; Scanners — 2-Nikon/LS-3500; Production cameras — R, AG/6100; Automatic film processors — 1-LE/AQ24, 2-C/66F. PRESSROOM: Line 1 — 5-G/Urbanite 1240; Line 2 — 6-G/Community; Folders — 2-G, 1-G/Quarter; Press control system — Fin; Press registration system — Duarte. MAILROOM: Counter stackers — 2-BG/Count-O-Veyor 108; Inserters and stuffers — 2-MM/227E; Bundle tyer — 2-MLN/Strapper, 2-Bu/Tyer; Addressing machine — 3-Wm/Dick Gum labeler. LIBRARY: Combination — 1-BH/16-35. COMMUNICATIONS: Digital ad delivery system — AP AdSend. WIRE SERVICES: News — AP; Stock tables — AP; Receiving dishes — size-10ft, AP. BUSINESS COMPUTERS: Alpha/Micro, 4-Ap/Mac, 2-Dell/Unix; Applications: Payroll, Circ, Inventory, Adv scheduling, Dummying, Gen ledger; PCs & micros networked; PCs & main system networked.

KLAMATH FALLS
Klamath County
'90 U.S. Census- 17,737; E&P '96 Est. 19,009
ABC-CZ (90): 36,328 (HH 14,461)

Oregon

Herald and News
(e-mon to fri; S)
Herald and News, 1301 Esplanade; PO Box 788, Klamath Falls, OR 97601; tel (541) 885-4410; fax (541) 885-4456. Pioneer Newspapers group.
Circulation: 17,363(e); 17,779(S); ABC Sept. 30, 1995.
Price: 50¢(d); $1.00(S); $8.50/mo; $102.00/yr (carrier).
Advertising: Open inch rate $12.90(e); $12.90(S). **Representative:** Papert Companies.
News Service: AP. **Politics:** Independent. **Established:** 1906.
Special Editions: Progress (Feb); Today's Seniors; Cascade Horseman; Cascade Cattleman; Dollar Saver; Business; Photo Shopper; Real Estate Review.
Special Weekly Sections: Kids Page (mon); Agri-Business, Farm (tues); Food (wed); Outdoors, Home and Garden, Teen Scene (thur); Automotive, Religious, TV (fri); Financial, Fashion, Outdoor (S); Sports (daily).
Magazines: TV Section, Dollar Saver (wed); Limelighter (fri); USA Weekend (S).

CORPORATE OFFICER
President — Dwight Tracy

GENERAL MANAGEMENT
Publisher/Editor — Dwight Tracy

I-339

ADVERTISING
Director — Mike Waltman
TELECOMMUNICATIONS
Audiotex Manager — Mike Waltman
CIRCULATION
Manager — Steve Tippin
NEWS EXECUTIVE
Managing Editor — Pat Bushey
EDITORS AND MANAGERS
Sports Editor — Mike Quigley
Women's Editor — Mary Nobel
PRODUCTION
Supervisor — S Lynn Arnold
Supervisor-Printing — Ray DeLonge

Market Information: TMC; Operate audiotex.
Mechanical available: Offset; Black and 3 ROP colors; insert accepted — preprinted, envelopes, cards; page cut-offs — 22¾".
Mechanical specifications: Type page 13" x 21½"; E - 6 cols, 2 1/16", ⅛" between; A - 6 cols, 2 1/16", ⅛" between; C - 9 cols, 1⅜", ⅛" between.
Commodity consumption: Newsprint 1,311 metric tons; width 27¼"; single pages printed 10,386; average pages per issue 31(d), 42(S).
Equipment: EDITORIAL: Front-end hardware — Ap/Mac; Front-end software — QuarkXPress, Adobe/Photoshop, Baseview/NewsEdit; Printers — 2-AG, COM/Accuset. CLASSIFIED: Front-end hardware — Ap/Mac; Front-end soft-

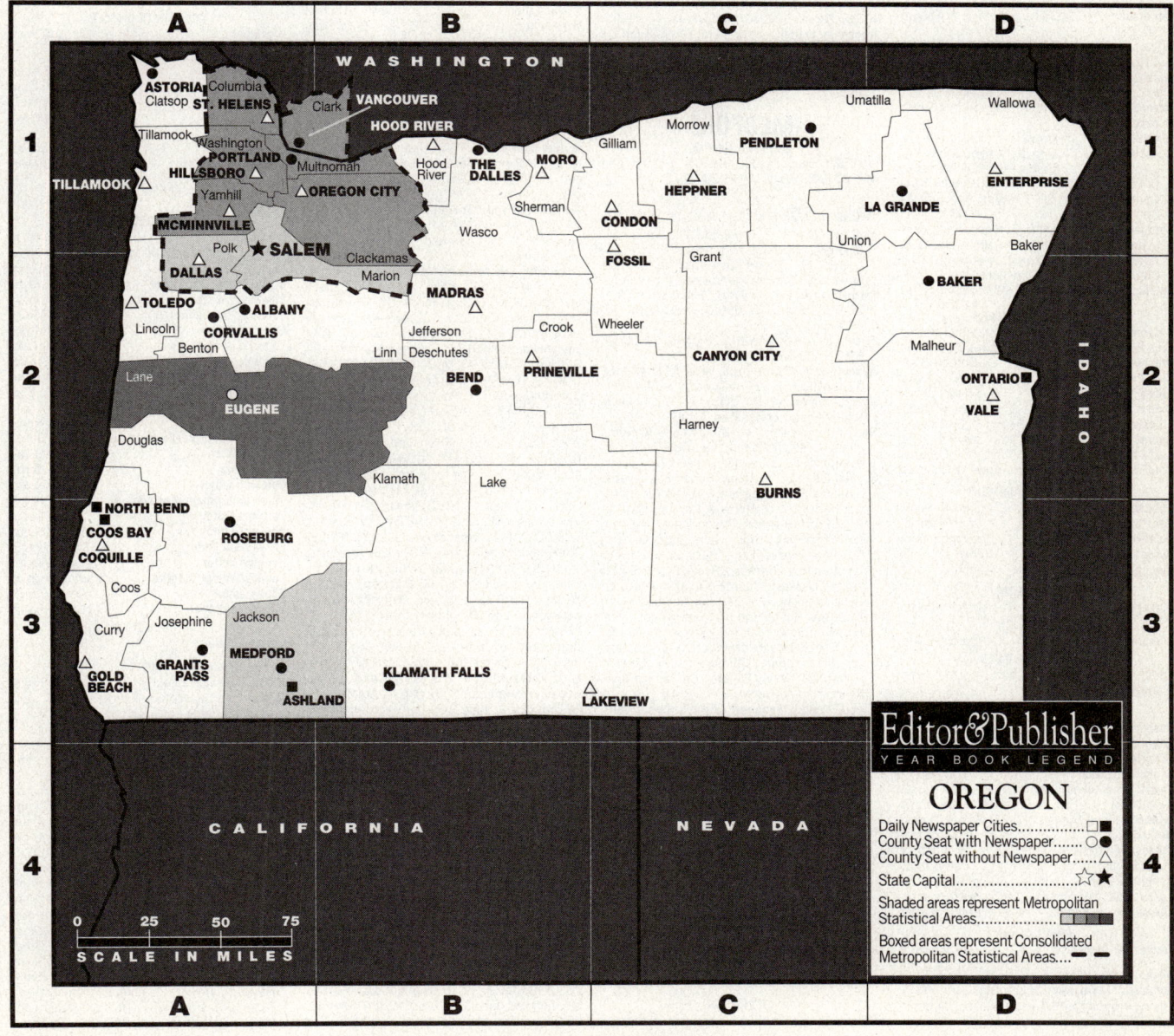

ware — Baseview/Class Manager. AUDIOTEX: Hardware — IBM/386; Software — Vicki. DISPLAY: Adv layout systems — QuarkXPress, ALS; Front-end hardware — Ap/Mac. PRODUCTION: Plate exposures — 1-Nu/Flip Top; Plate processors — 1-Nat/250; Electronic picture desk — Lf/AP Leaf Picture Desk; Scanners — 4-HP/ScanJet Plus, 2-Nikon; Production cameras — 1-MG/Photomaster; Automatic film processors — 1-P; Digital color separation equipment — Ap/Mac Quadra, Adobe/Photoshop, Nikon/Scanner.
PRESSROOM: Line 1 — 7-G/U-650; Folders — 1-G; Press registration system — Duarte. MAILROOM: Counter stackers — 1-BG/Count-O-Veyor; Inserters and stuffers — 2-MM/Stitcher-Trimmer; Bundle tyer — MLN; Wrapping singles — 1-Typak/#40. WIRE SERVICES: News — AP; Receiving dishes — UPI. BUSINESS COMPUTERS: PC; Applications: Bus office; PCs & main system networked.

LA GRANDE
Union County

'90 U.S. Census- 11,766; E&P '96 Est. 12,327
ABC-CZ (90): 12,462 (HH 4,898)

The Observer (e-mon to sat)

The Observer, 1406 5th St.; PO Box 3170, La Grande, OR 97850; tel (541) 963-3161; fax (541) 963-7804. Western Communications Inc. group.
Circulation: 7,650(e); 7,650(e-sat); ABC Sept. 30, 1995.
Price: 35¢(d); 35¢(sat); $7.50/mo (carrier), $12.00/mo (mail).
Advertising: Open inch rate $7.00(e); $7.00(e-sat). **Representative:** Papert Companies.
News Service: AP. **Politics:** Independent. **Established:** 1896.
Not Published: Christmas.
Special Editions: Fishing (Apr); Agriculture, Progress (May); Fair Edition (July); Oregon Trail Days (Aug); Football, Eastern Oregon State College (Sept); Elk Hunting (Oct); Snow Sports (Nov).
Special Weekly Sections: Outdoors Page, Best Food Day (tues); Portraits Page (wed); Business-Agriculture (thur); Weddings (fri); Church News, Mini Page (sat).
Magazine: Own Show and Tell (newsprint) (fri).

CORPORATE OFFICERS
Chairman of the Board Elizabeth C McCool
Vice Board Chairman Margaret C Cushman
President/CEO Gordon Black
Vice Pres Janet Stevens
Vice Pres John Shaver
Vice Pres Robert K Moody
Treasurer Robert W Chandler Jr
Secretary Mary Jean Chandler
Asst Secretary Judith L Coleman
Chief Editorial Officer Robert W Chandler

GENERAL MANAGEMENT
Publisher Robert K Moody
General Manager Donald Powell
Manager-Office LaWanda Laing
Purchasing Agent Robert K Moody
Manager-Education Service Robert K Moody

ADVERTISING
Manager Donald Powell

CIRCULATION
Manager Darold Dayley

NEWS EXECUTIVES
Editor Dave Stave
Managing Editor Ted Kramer

EDITORS AND MANAGERS
Business/Finance Editor Rebecca Merritt
Editorial Writer Dave Stave
Editorial Writer Ted Kramel
Education Editor Dick Mason
Entertainment/Amusements Editor Jeff Petersen
Farm Editor Rebecca Merritt
Health/Medical Editor Greg Van Tighem
News Editor Jeff Petersen
Outdoors Editor Dick Mason
Photo Editor Phil Bullock
Religion Editor Greg Van Tighem
Television/Film Editor Jeff Petersen
Theater/Music Editor Jeff Petersen

PRODUCTION
Foreman-Pressroom Frank Everidge

Market Information: ADS.
Mechanical available: Offset; Black and 3 ROP colors; insert accepted — preprinted; page cut-offs — 21½".
Mechanical specifications: Type page 13" x 21½"; E - 6 cols, 2 1/16", ⅛" between; A - 6 cols, 2 1/16", ⅛" between; C - 8 cols, 1 9/16", 1/16" between.
Commodity consumption: Newsprint 560 metric tons; widths 27", 13½", 30", 15"; black ink 15,000 pounds; color ink 3,800 pounds; single pages printed 4,600; average pages per issue 15(d); single plates used 12,000.
Equipment: EDITORIAL: Front-end hardware — 14-Ap/Mac, 2-Ap/Mac Quadra 800, 1-HP/Storage Drive; Front-end software — QuarkXPress 3.2, Baseview/Wire Manager, Ap/Mac System 7.1; Printers — 2-LaserMaster/Unity 1200 XL-T; Other equipment — 1-IBM/Selectric. CLASSIFIED: Front-end hardware — 2-Ap/Mac LC III; Front-end software — Baseview/Class Manager, Ap/Mac System 7.1, QuarkXPress 3.2; Printers — 2-Okidata/Microline 590; Other equipment — 1-IBM/Selectric. DISPLAY: Front-end hardware — 1-Ap/Mac LC III; Front-end software — QuarkXPress 3.2, Adobe/Illustrator; Printers — 2-LaserMaster/Unity 1200 XL-T; Other equipment — HP/Desk Top Scanner, 1-Ap/Mac CD 300. PRODUCTION: Typesetters — 2-LaserMaster/Unity 1200 XL; Plate exposures — Nu/Flip Top FT40V3UPNS; Plate processors — Nat/Super A-250; Production cameras — SCREEN/670 D Auto; Automatic film processors — AG/Lith 26.
PRESSROOM: Line 1 — 6-G/Community; Folders — 1-G/SSC. MAILROOM: Inserters and stuffers — KAN/320 D; Bundle tyer — MLN/MS-B; Addressing machine — 4-Wm, 1-Dispensa-Matic/16 label picker. WIRE SERVICES: News — AP; Syndicates — Media; Receiving dishes — size-10m, AP. BUSINESS COMPUTERS: 2-Packard Bell/Microsphere; Applications: Circ, Accts receivable; M/FOX-PLUS (MSDOS); PCs & micros networked.

MEDFORD
Jackson County

'90 U.S. Census- 46,951; E&P '96 Est. 55,184
ABC-CZ (90): 62,655 (HH 24,721)

Mail Tribune (m-mon to sat; S)

Mail Tribune, 111 N. Fir St.; PO Box 1108, Medford, OR 97501; tel (541) 776-4411; fax (541) 776-4415; e-mail mail-trib@mind.net. Ottaway Newspapers Inc. group.
Circulation: 26,950(m); 34,884(m-fri); 26,950(m-sat); 31,838(S); ABC Sept. 30, 1995.
Price: 50¢(d); 50¢(m-fri); 50¢(sat); $1.00(S); $9.75/mo; $114.50/yr.
Advertising: Open inch rate $18.44(m); $18.44(m-fri); $18.44(m-sat); $18.44(S).
News Services: AP, DJ, ONS, LAT-WP. **Politics:** Independent. **Established:** 1906.
Note: Effective Apr. 3, 1995, this publication changed its publishing plan from (e-mon to fri; m-sat; S) to (m-mon to sat; S).
Special Editions: Wedding, Super Bowl, Tax & Financial Planning (Jan); Travel & Vacations, Our Valley (Mar); Home & Garden, Fishing, Real Estate Review, Rogue Valley, Agriculture/Progressive (Apr); Home Improvement, Summer Recreation, Pets Plus, Manufactured Housing (May); Pools, Spas & Patios (June); Jackson County Fair, Home (July); Back-to-School, Fall Fashion, Football (Aug); Hunting, Home Energy Guide (Sept); Fall Home Improvement, Wild Rogue Pro Rodeo, Fall Real Estate Review (Oct); Southern Oregon Menu Guide, Christmas Gift, Ashland Christmas (Nov); Holiday Cooking, Classroom Tribune (Dec).
Special Weekly Sections: Prime Times, Health and Science Page (mon); Leisure Features, Teen X-Press (tues); Best Food Day (wed); Home and Family Life (thur); Religion Pages, Automotive Feature, Arts & Entertainment (fri); Expanded Stock Market Report, Day Trips and Saturday Spectator (sat); Business Section, Music and Arts, Senior Calendar, Color Comics, Expanded Sports Coverage, Real Estate Feature, Family Page (S).
Magazines: Prime Time (Senior tab) (every other mon); Tempo (movies, radio, TV, entertainment) (fri); Parade (S).

GENERAL MANAGEMENT
Publisher Gregory H Taylor
General Manager James J Osborn
Controller Roy Atkins
Manager-Human Resources Gina Meyer

ADVERTISING
Manager Teresa Keplinger
Coordinator-Classified Phone Sales Susie Wenaus

CIRCULATION
Manager Steve Whipple

NEWS EXECUTIVES
Editor Robert Hunter
Exec Editor John Reid

EDITORS AND MANAGERS
Automotive Editor Paul Macomber
Books Editor Cleve Twitchell
Business Editor Paul Macomber
City Editor Robert Sterling
Asst City Editor Gary Nelson
Columnist Paul Fattig
Columnist Randy Hammericksen
Columnist Al Reiss
Columnist Cleve Twitchell
Editorial Page Editor Bill Manny
Education Editor Alberto Enriquez
Fashion Editor JoNel Aleccia
Features Editor Cleve Twitchell
Films/Theater Editor Al Reiss
Food/Garden Editor Cleve Twitchell
Librarian Pam Sieg
Life/Tempo Editor Cleve Twitchell
Music Editor Bill Varble
News Editor Jim Peak
Asst News Editor Ellen Wakefield
Outdoors Editor Mark Freeman
Photo Editor Steve Johnson
Political Editor Peter Wong
Radio/Television Editor Cleve Twitchell
Religion Editor Gary Nelson
Special Section Graphics Editor Steve Dieffenbacher
Sports Editor Randy Hammericksen
Sunday Editor Julie Wurth
Travel Editor Cleve Twitchell
Wire Editor Bill Powell

MANAGEMENT INFORMATION SERVICES
Data Processing Manager Bill Greenstein

PRODUCTION
Manager-Composing Jerry Spielbusch
Supervisor Larry Lindeman

Market Information: TMC; Operate audiotex.
Mechanical available: Offset; Black and 3 ROP colors; insert accepted — preprinted, cards; page cut-offs — 22¾".
Mechanical specifications: Type page 13" x 21½"; E - 6 cols, 2 1/16", ⅛" between; A - 6 cols, 2 1/16", ⅛" between; C - 9 cols, 1⅜", 1/16" between.
Commodity consumption: Newsprint 2,650 metric tons; widths 54", 40½", 27", 13½"; black ink 58,200 pounds; color ink 8,500 pounds; single pages printed 17,522; average pages per issue 44(d), 70(S); single plates used 32,400.
Equipment: EDITORIAL: Front-end hardware — DEC/VAX 4000-200, DEC/VAX 4000-300, 33-IBM/70, IBM/PS2 PC; Front-end software — Cybergraphics 7.5; Printers — DEC/LA 210, LA/75, LPM/600 Band Printer; Other equipment — 2-RSK/TRS-80-100, 4-RSK/TRS-80-200. CLASSIFIED: Front-end hardware — IBM/PS2 PC, DEC/VAX 4000-200, DEC/VAX 4000-300; Front-end software — Cybergraphics 7.5; Printers — DEC/LA 210, DEC/LA 75; Other equipment — 12-IBM/Sys 70. DISPLAY: Adv layout systems — 4-HI/8300, 6-Ap/Mac. PRODUCTION: Typesetters — 2-MON/82E; Platemaking systems — Nu; Plate exposures — 1-BKY/5KW-160145, 1-Nu/Flip Top 631; Plate processors — 1-Nat; Electronic picture desk — Lf/AP Leaf Picture Desk; Production cameras — 1-B/18X24 horizontal, 1-LE/17, 1-AP; Automatic film processors — 1-LE/24LA; Reproportion units — 2-ECR/Autokon 12" max; Film transporters — Konica/OL66C transport, Konica/OL66C Processor; Color separation equipment (conventional) — Ap/Mac.
PRESSROOM: Line 1 — 6-B/Metroliner-two half decks, double width; Press drives — Fin; Folders — 1-G/2:1, 2-G/3:2; Pasters — 6-G/Reel-Tension Paster; Reels and stands — 6-G/Triple Reels; Press control system — Fin; Press registration system — G/Pin Register. MAILROOM: Counter stackers — 2-HL/Monitor, 1-QWI/300; Inserters and stuffers — GMA/SLS-1000 16-pocket; Bundle tyer — 2-MLN, 1-Power Strap/PSN-6, 1-Power Strap/PSN-6E; Wrapping singles — 2-QWI/2x44½"; Addressing machine — KR. LIBRARY: Electronic — Data Times; Combination — 1-Kk/Microfilm. WIRE SERVICES: News — AP; Stock tables — AP Datastream; Syndicates — DJ, Ottaway News Service, LAT-WP; Receiving dishes — size-6ft, AP. BUSINESS COMPUTERS: 15-IBM/3179, 3-Acer PC, 2-IBM/5262 PTR; Applications: All bus functions except circ; PCs & micros networked; PCs & main system networked.

NORTH BEND
See COOS BAY

ONTARIO
Malheur County

'90 U.S. Census- 8,900; E&P '96 Est. 9,123

Argus Observer
(e-mon to fri; S)

Argus Observer, 1160 S.W. 4th St.; PO Box 130, Ontario, OR 97914; tel (541) 889-5387; fax (541) 889-3347. Wick Communications group.
Circulation: 7,465(e); 8,061(S); VAC June 30, 1995.
Price: 50¢(d); $1.25(S); $8.00/mo; $96.00/yr.
Advertising: Open inch rate $8.26(e); $8.26(S). **Representative:** Landon Associates Inc.
News Service: AP. **Politics:** Independent. **Established:** 1897.
Not Published: New Year; Memorial Day; Independence Day; Labor Day; Thanksgiving; Christmas.
Special Editions: Annual Farm Festival (Aug); Farm Tab (monthly).
Special Weekly Sections: Best Food Day (tues); Business, Amusements, TV Guide (wed); Church Page (thur); Amusements, TV Guide, Church Page, Weddings/Engagements, Farm Page, Outdoor Page, Business (S).
Magazines: TV Guide Tab, Comics and Entertainment (S).

CORPORATE OFFICER
President Bob Wick

GENERAL MANAGEMENT
Publisher Francis R McLean
General Manager Francis R McLean
Manager-Credit Judy West
Asst Publisher Gene Rhinehart

ADVERTISING
Director Linda Warren
Manager-Classified Kari Sleight

CIRCULATION
Manager Gaylen Curry

NEWS EXECUTIVE
Editor Larry Hurrle

EDITORS AND MANAGERS
Books Editor Francis R McLean
Business/Finance Editor Scot Crosby
City/Metro Editor Scot Crosby
Editorial Page Editor Chris Moore
Editorial Writer Chris Moore
Editorial Writer Francis R McLean
Education Editor Ann Crosby
Environment/Ecology Editor Francis R McLean
Farm/Garden Editor Eric Ellis
Fashion/Home Improvement Editor Shanna Wiggins
Graphics Editor/Art Director Larry Hurrle
Music Editor Joy McLean
News Editor Larry Hurrle
Outdoors Editor Scot Crosby
Photo Department Manager Larry Hoffman
Political Editor Chris Moore
Political Editor Francis R McLean
Real Estate Editor Kari Sleight
Religion Editor Shanna Wiggins
Society/Women's Editor Shanna Wiggins
Sports Editor Annie Fowler
State/Wire Editor Larry Meyers

PRODUCTION
Manager/Foreman Gene Rhinehart

Market Information: TMC; ADS.
Mechanical available: Offset; Black and 3 ROP colors; insert accepted — preprinted, all sizes from 3 x 5 cards up; page cut-offs — 22¾".
Mechanical specifications: Type page 13" x 21½"; E - 6 cols, 2 1/16", ⅛" between; A - 6 cols, 2 1/16", ⅛" between; C - 9 cols, 1¼", ⅛" between.
Commodity consumption: Newsprint 460 metric tons; widths 27", 13½", 22¾"; black ink 13,006 pounds; color ink 1,800 pounds; single pages printed 8,200; average pages per issue 20(d), 58(S); single plates used 4,980.
Equipment: EDITORIAL: Front-end hardware — Ap/Mac; Front-end software — Baseview; Printers — HP/LaserJet; Other equipment — Panther/Imagesetter. CLASSIFIED: Front-end hardware — Ap/Mac; Front-end software — Baseview; Printers — 2-HP/LaserJet; Other equipment — Panther/Imagesetter. DISPLAY: Adv layout systems — Ap/Mac w/Baseview; Front-end hardware — Ap/Mac; Printers — 2-HP/LaserJet. PRODUCTION: Pagination software — Baseview; Typesetters — Panther;

Plate exposures — Nu/Ultra Plus; Scanners — Umax, Polaroid/SprintScan; Production cameras — SCREEN; Automatic film processors — P/Pakonolith Processor.
PRESSROOM: Line 1 — 6-G; Folders — 1-G. MAILROOM: Inserters and stuffers — KAN. WIRE SERVICES: News — AP; Photos — AP; Receiving dishes — AP. BUSINESS COMPUTERS: DEC/Micro-VAX/3100; Applications: Vision Data.

PENDLETON

Umatilla County

'90 U.S. Census- 15,126; E&P '96 Est. 15,916
ABC-CZ (90): 15,126 (HH 5,715)

East Oregonian

(e-mon to fri; m-sat)

East Oregonian, 211 S.E. Byers St.; PO Box 1089, Pendleton, OR 97801; tel (541) 276-2211; fax (541) 276-8314; e-mail eoonline@aol.com.
Circulation: 12,300(e); 12,300(m-sat); ABC Sept. 30, 1995.
Price: 50¢(d); 50¢(sat); $8.00/mo (carrier), $9.00/mo (motor route).
Advertising: Open inch rate $13.00(e); $13.00(m-sat). **Representative:** Landon Associates Inc.
News Service: AP. **Politics:** Independent. **Established:** 1875.
Not Published: Christmas.
Special Editions: Agriculture (Feb); Vacation (May); County Fair (Aug); Hunting (Sept); Hunting (Oct).
Special Weekly Sections: Food Day (tues); Entertainment (Time Out) (thur); Religion Page (fri); Business Page, TV Week Tab (sat); Sports, Society/Community (daily).
Magazine: TV Update (sat).

CORPORATE OFFICERS
Chairman of the Board J W Forrester
President Michael A Forrester
Vice Pres Jacqueline Bedford Brown
Vice Pres Stephen A Forrester
Secretary Amy Aldrich Bedford
Treasurer Eleanor A Forrester
Corporate General Manager C K Patterson

GENERAL MANAGEMENT
General Manager Clyde Bentley
Controller Diana Porter
Manager-Education Service Amy Aldrich Bedford
Manager-Human Resources Jacqueline Bedford Brown

ADVERTISING
Manager-Sales Christine Moore
Manager-Retail Christine Moore
Manager-National Janet Parks
Manager-Classified Bob Pokovny

MARKETING AND PROMOTION
Manager-Promotion Amy Aldrich Bedford

CIRCULATION
Director Janet K Jones

NEWS EXECUTIVE
Editor David Cash

EDITORS AND MANAGERS
Business/Finance Editor Marina Parr
Editorial Page Editor David Cash
Farm Editor Steve Brown
Food Editor Gaylee Baker
News Editor Hal McCune
Teen-Age/Youth Editor Jeri Lessard
Women's/Community Editor Jeri Lessard

Mechanical available: Offset; Black and 3 ROP colors; insert accepted — preprinted; page cutoffs — 22¾".
Mechanical specifications: Type page 13" x 21½"; E - 6 cols, 2 1/16", ⅛" between; A - 6 cols, 2", 5/32" between; C - 8 cols, 1⅜", 1/16" between.
Commodity consumption: Newsprint 700 metric tons; widths 27", 30"; black ink 20,000 pounds; color ink 1,800 pounds; single pages printed 7,200; average pages per issue 18(d); single plates used 700.
Equipment: EDITORIAL: Front-end hardware — Ap/Mac, Dewar, AST/286, 16-Dewar; Other equipment — RSK/TRS-200. CLASSIFIED: Front-end hardware — 3-Baseview, Ap/Mac 610; Front-end software — Baseview. DISPLAY: Adv layout systems — 9-Ap/Mac; Front-end hardware — Ap/Super Mac, Ap/Mac Radius. PRODUCTION: Pagination software — QPS; Typesetters — 4-Ap/Mac LaserWriter PS (w/drive); Plate exposures — 2-Nu/Flip Top FT40LHS; Plate processors — 1-Nat/A-340; Scanners — Ap/Mac Scanner w/OCR software; Production cameras — 1-R/Comet, 1-R; Automatic film processors — 1-P/Pakorol; Shrink lenses — 1-CK Optical.
PRESSROOM: Line 1 — 9-G/SC-1017 Community; Folders — 1-G. MAILROOM: Inserters and stuffers — KAN/320; Bundle tyer — 1-Bu, 1-Gd/OVL; Addressing machine — Vision Data, Ch/labeler. LIBRARY: Electronic — SMS; Combination — Kk. WIRE SERVICES: News — AP, AP Phone, AP GraphicsNet; Photos — AP; Receiving dishes — AP. BUSINESS COMPUTERS: LSI/1173; Applications: Vision Data: Circ, TMC, Gen ledger, Payroll, Accts payable, Accts receivable; PCs & micros networked; PCs & main system networked.

PORTLAND

Multnomah, Clackamas and Washington Counties

'90 U.S. Census- 437,319; E&P '96 Est. 517,052
ABC-NDM (90): 1,174,291 (HH 464,667)

Daily Journal of Commerce

(m-mon to fri)

Daily Journal of Commerce, 2840 N.W. Guam; PO Box 10127, Portland, OR 97210-0127; tel (503) 226-1311; fax (503) 224-7140.
Circulation: 3,497(m); Sworn Oct. 1, 1995.
Price: $1.00(d); $92.00/6mo; $158.00/yr.
Advertising: Open inch rate $20.00(m).
News Services: Business Wire, PR Newswire, RN. **Politics:** Independent. **Established:** 1872.
Special Editions: The Annual (Jan); Building Materials/Equipment (Feb); Engineering (Mar); Environmental (Apr); Real Estate/Development (May); Top 25 Projects (June); Infrastructure (July); Healthcare (Aug); Business Management (Sept); Construction (Oct); Architectural Review (Nov); Regions Top 20 Companies to work for (Dec).
Magazines: Law/Courts, Technology, Real Estate, Finance, Design & Construction (mon); Finance, Design & Construction (wed); Health, Small Business, Finance, Design & Construction (fri).

CORPORATE OFFICERS
President Lawrence M Smith
Vice Pres Peter Smith
Publisher/Secretary/Treasurer Dorothy Haugsten Smith

GENERAL MANAGEMENT
Manager-Accounting Chrystine Ostgard

ADVERTISING
Manager-Bid Calls/Public Notices Irwin J Caplan
Manager-Display Steve Smith

CIRCULATION
Manager Sharon Peterson
Manager-Commercial Sales Peter Smith

NEWS EXECUTIVE
Editor Kevin Harden

EDITOR AND MANAGER
Assoc Editor Theresa Lamb

PRODUCTION
Superintendent Diane Bullas
Foreman-Composing Ali Hassania
Foreman-Pressroom Jay Thompson

Mechanical available: Offset; Black and 3 ROP colors; insert accepted — preprinted; page cutoffs — 22¾".
Mechanical specifications: Type page 10 3/16" x 13¾"; E - 5 cols, 2 1/16", ⅛" between; A - 5 cols, 2 1/16", ⅛" between; C - 5 cols, 2 1/16", ⅛" between.
Commodity consumption: Newsprint 175 short tons; width 29"; single pages printed 8,975; average pages per issue 34(d).
Equipment: EDITORIAL: Front-end hardware — Mk, Ap/Mac, Ap/Power Mac 9500-120, Ap/MacPower Book S20; Front-end software — Mk, QuarkXPress 3.31, Aldus/PageMaker 5.0, Multi-Ad/Creator 3.7, Word Perfect 3.0; Printers — 1-Ap/Mac LaserPrinter. CLASSIFIED: Front-end hardware — Mk, Ap/Mac; Front-end software — Mk, QuarkXPress 3.31; DISPLAY: Front-end hardware — Mk, Ap/Mac; Front-end software — Mk, QuarkXPress 3.31; PRODUCTION: Pagination software — QuarkXPress 3.31, Adobe/Photoshop 3.0.1, Aldus/PageMaker 5.0, Multi-Ad/Creator 3.7, Word Perfect 3.0; OCR software — Ap/Mac Scanner, Caere/OmniPage 2.1, AG/Arcus II w/FotoLook, FotoTunele, FotoSnap; Typesetters — V/5100, V/5000, AG/Accuset 1500, AG/Viper 1.5 w/APS/Level 2 Software RIP; Platemaking systems — Douthitt, Millington, Misomex/500 step & repeat system; Plate exposures — Duolith, BKY; Plate processors — Kk/N85, Cookson Graphics; Scanners — Ap/Mac; Production cameras — 1-AG/RPS 2226 Vertical Camera; Automatic film processors — LE/LD 281-Q.
PRESSROOM: Line 1 — 1-G/Community (4 units w/half; quarter; double parallel); Line 2 — 1-G/Community (4 units w/half; quarter; double parallel); Line 3 — 1-Ha/HeatSet (2 webs; 5 units); Line 4 — 1-HI/110 (Heat Set 2 webs; 5 units); Line 5 — 1-KP/(22 3/4-36-Heat Set; 2 webs; 6 units); Folders — 2-G/SSC, 1-HA, 1-HI, 1-KP. MAILROOM: Inserters and stuffers — S. COMMUNICATIONS: Remote imagesetting — Toshiba/Lap-Tops, W/Bitcoms; Systems used — satellite. WIRE SERVICES: News — RN, PR Newswire, Business Wire; Receiving dishes — size-18", RN, PR News, Business Wire. BUSINESS COMPUTERS: Mk, Vs, Ap/Mac cis, Ap/Power Mac 9500; Applications: QuarkXPress, Mk, Multi-Ad/Creator; PCs & micros networked; PCs & main system networked.

The Oregonian

(all day-mon to fri; m-sat; S)

The Oregonian, 1320 S.W. Broadway, Portland, OR 97201; tel (503) 221-8327; fax (503) 227-5306; e-mail oreeditors@aol.com. Advance Publications group.
Circulation: 333,654(a); 323,478(m-sat); 441,086(S); ABC Sept. 30, 1995.
Price: 35¢(d); 35¢(sat); $1.50(S); $12.00/4wk.
Advertising: Open inch rate $126.90(a); $126.90(m-sat); $131.69(S). **Representative:** Newhouse Newspapers/Metro Suburbia.
News Services: AP, LAT-WP, NYT, NNS, KRT. **Politics:** Independent. **Established:** 1850.
Special Weekly Sections: Business Features, Accent on Health & Fitness (mon); Food Day, Accent on Consumer News (tues); Accent on Family Life (wed); Northwest Outdoors, Accent on Home Technology, Science (thur); A & E, Accent on Gardening (fri); Drive Time, Accent on Religion and Ethics (sat); Lively Arts, Travel, TV Click, Real Estate, Business (S).
Magazine: Parade (S).

CORPORATE OFFICERS
President Fred A Stickel
Vice Pres Theodore Newhouse
Treasurer S I Newhouse III
Asst Treasurer D W Palmer
Asst Treasurer Richard E Diamond

GENERAL MANAGEMENT
Publisher Fred A Stickel
President Patrick F Stickel
Controller D W Palmer
Manager-Credit Betty Kirk
Manager-Human Resources Tom Whitehouse
Director-Public Affairs Stephanie Oliver
Purchasing Agent James Brown

ADVERTISING
Director Dennis Atkin
Manager-Retail John Mannex
Manager-General Debi Walery
Manager-Classified Gayle Timmerman

MARKETING AND PROMOTION
Director-Marketing Service Steve Hubbard

TELECOMMUNICATIONS
Audiotex Manager Marsha Davis

CIRCULATION
Director Patrick L Marlton

NEWS EXECUTIVES
Editor Sandra Mims Rowe
Asst Editor Richard C Johnston
Managing Editor Peter Bhatia
Recruiting Director George Rede

EDITORS AND MANAGERS
Audiotex Editor Jeff Wohler
Books Editor Ellen Heltzel
Business Editor Patrick Chu
Columnist Steve Duin
Columnist Jonathan Nicholas
Columnist Margie Boule
Copy Desk Chief Jerry Sass
Editorial Cartoonist Jack Ohman
Entertainment Editor Karen Brooks
Editorial Writer Nanine Alexander
Editorial Writer Phil Cogswell
Editorial Writer Larry Hilderbrand
Editorial Writer David Reinhard
Editorial Writer David Sarasohn
Editorial Writer Wayne Thompson
Editorial Page Editor Robert J Caldwell
Food Editor Virginia Johnston
Graphics Editor Michelle Wise
Librarian Sandy Macomber
Photo Director Serge McCabe
Public Editor Bob Caldwell
Senior Editor-Enterprise Jacqui Banaszynski
Senior Editor-Features Mark Wigginton
Senior Editor-Production John Harvey
Senior Editor-Spot News Dennis Peck
Senior Editor-Training Jack Hart
Suburban Editor Quinton Smith
Sports Columnist Dwight Jaynes
Sports Columnist Julie Vader
Sports Editor Dennis Peck
Systems Director John Hamlin
Team Leader-City Life John Killen
Team Leader-Crime David Austin
Team Leader-East Kathleen Glanville
Team Leader-Environment Jacqui Banaszynski
Team Leader-Family/Education Sally Cheriel
Team Leader-Government Michele McLellan
Team Leader-Health Therese Bottomly
Team Leader-Living Michael Rollins
Team Leader-Nation/World John Harvey
Team Leader-North Beth Erickson
Team Leader-Presentation Galen Barnett
Team Leader-South Michael Arrieta-Walden
Team Leader-West Wilda Wahpepah
Travel Editor Sue Hobart
Television Editor Stan Horton

MANAGEMENT INFORMATION SERVICES
Director-Computer Service Carol Howard
Manager-Production Systems Dick Rickman
Manager-Communications Arthur Dummor

PRODUCTION
Manager Ed Hagstrom
Manager-Ad Service Larry Wilson
Asst Manager-Ad Service John Bailey
Superintendent-Plant Joe Crawford
Superintendent-Composing Richard Dorr
Superintendent-Mailroom James Holman
Superintendent-Platemaking Dan Tucker
Superintendent-Pressroom Dennis Russell
Asst Superintendent-Mailroom Ed Spencer
Asst Superintendent-Mailroom Will Sousley
Asst Superintendent-Pressroom Herman Etzel
Coordinator-Quality John McKinney

Market Information: Zoned editions; Split Run; TMC; Operate audiotex.
Mechanical available: Offset; Black and 3 ROP colors; insert accepted — preprinted; page cutoffs — 22¾".
Mechanical specifications: Type page 13" x 21½"; E - 6 cols, 2 1/16", ⅛" between; A - 6 cols, 2 1/16", ⅛" between; C - 10 cols, 1¼", .07" between.
Commodity consumption: Newsprint 90,470 short tons; widths 55", 41¼", 27½"; black ink 1,774,000 pounds; color ink 451,200 pounds; average pages per issue 84(a), 164(S); single plates used 470,000.
Equipment: EDITORIAL: Front-end hardware — 4-CCSI/CPU, DEC/PDP 11-70, 2-HI/Pagination; Other equipment — 213-CCSI/112 BS, 22-HI/2100. CLASSIFIED: Front-end hardware — 4-CCSI/CPU, 3-DEC/PDP 11-70, 1-DEC/PDP 11-84; Other equipment — 100-CCSI/CT97. AUDIOTEX: Hardware — Brite Voice Systems. DISPLAY: Adv layout systems — In-house; Front-end hardware — Cx; Other equipment — 14-Cx/Sun Breeze. PRODUCTION: Typesetters — 1-MON/MK IIi, 4-MON/Express, 4-III/3850; Plate exposures — 2-WL/III; Plate processors — 2-WL/38-D; Electronic picture desk — Lf/AP Leaf Picture Desk; Scanners — 2-ECR/Autokon; Production cameras — 1-C/Marathon; Automatic film processors — P; Film transporters — LE; Digital color separation equipment — CD/646, Lf/Leafscan 45, Nikon/3510.
PRESSROOM: Line 1 — 10-G/Metro double; Line 2 — 10-G/Metro; Line 3 — 10-G/Metro double; Line 4 — 10-G/Metro double; Line 5 — 10-G/Metroliner; Press drives — Fin; Folders — G; Pasters — 50-G; Press control system — 1-G/PCS. MAILROOM: Counter stackers — 14-QWI; Inserters and stuffers — 3-S/72P; Bundle tyer — 3-MLN/2, 5-MLN/MLE, 4-MLN/MLNCC, 9-OVL/JP40; Addressing machine — 6-Dm, 1-Am/2300-P, 1-Gp/6283; Mailroom control system — Machine Design belt distribution. LIBRARY: Electronic — Vu/Text. COMMUNICATIONS: Facsimile — Pagefax; Systems used — microwave. WIRE SERVICES: News — AP, KRT, NNS, NYT, LAT-WP, CSM, CNS, Cox News Service, McClatchy; Photos — AP, NYT, AFP, KRT; Stock tables — AP; Receiving dishes — AP, AFP. BUSINESS COMPUTERS: Unisys/2200; Applications: Cyborg: Payroll; PCs & micros networked; PCs & main system networked.

Copyright ©1996 by the Editor & Publisher Co.

ROSEBURG
Douglas County

'90 U.S. Census- 17,032; E&P '96 Est. 17,655
ABC-NDM (90): 94,649 (HH 35,872)

The News-Review
(e-mon to fri; S)

The News-Review, 345 N.E. Winchester St.; PO Box 1248, Roseburg, OR 97470; tel (541) 672-3321; fax (541)673-5994; web site http://www.oregonnews.com. Swift Newspapers group.
Circulation: 19,308(e); 19,964(S); ABC Sept. 30, 1995.
Price: 35¢(d); 75¢(S); $7.75/mo; $88.75/yr.
Advertising: Open inch rate $14.10(e); $14.10(S).
News Service: AP. **Politics:** Independent. **Established:** 1867.
Not Published: Christmas.
Special Editions: UMPQUA (Feb); Recreation Tab (Apr); Visitor's Guide (May); Recreation Tab, Rodeo (June); Fair, Back-to-School (Aug); Football, Hunting (Sept); Basketball (Nov); Christmas (Mid-Nov); Senior Times (monthly).
Special Weekly Sections: Food Day (tues); Business (wed); People Page (thur); TV, Entertainment, Church Page (fri); People Page (S).
Magazines: Own Valley Viewer (fri); Parade (S).

CORPORATE OFFICERS	
Board Chairman	Philip E Swift
President	Richard K Larson
GENERAL MANAGEMENT	
Publisher	Ronald J Stewart
Manager-Office	Jeannie Peeler
ADVERTISING	
Director	Kelly Gant
CIRCULATION	
Director	Earl Hand
NEWS EXECUTIVE	
Editor	Bart Smith
EDITORS AND MANAGERS	
Business Editor	James Sinks
Editorial Writer	Bart Smith
Editorial Writer	Shawn Vestal
Food Editor	Vicki Menard
Librarian	Capri Moore
Radio/Television Editor	Tricia Jones
Society Editor	Elaine Smith
Sports Editor	Craig Reed
PRODUCTION	
Manager-Composing	Ron Gander
Foreman-Pressroom	Ernest Crane

Market Information: Zoned editions; Split Run; TMC; Electronic edition.
Mechanical available: Offset; Black and 3 ROP colors; insert accepted — preprinted; page cut-offs — 21½".
Mechanical specifications: Type page 13" x 21½"; E - 6 cols, 2 1/16", ⅛" between; A - 6 cols, 2 1/16", ⅛" between; C - 9 cols, 1⅜", 1/16" between.
Commodity consumption: Newsprint 1,175 metric tons; widths 27½", 13¾"; single pages printed 9,708; average pages per issue 32(d), 44(S).
Equipment: EDITORIAL: Front-end hardware — Ap/Mac, 26-Ap/Mac SE30, 2-TM, 1-Ap/Mac Plus, 5-Ap/Mac SE, 2-Ap/Mac Power PC 7100; Front-end software — QuarkXPress; Other equipment — 16-Ap/Mac SE30, 3-Ap/Mac Plus. CLASSIFIED: Front-end hardware — 4-Ap/Mac SE30. DISPLAY: Front-end hardware — 5-Ap/Mac IIci, 4-Ap/Mac Power PC 8100; Front-end software — QuarkXPress. PRODUCTION: Pagination software — QuarkXPress; Typesetters — 1-Ap/Mac II, SE, Ap/Mac LaserWriter, 1-COM/Universal, 2-QMS/800II, 2-Panther/Imager 11.0; Plate exposures — 1-Nu; Plate processors — GRAHAM/M-28; Production cameras — 1-SCREEN; Automatic film processors — 1-P; Color separation equipment (conventional) — Adobe/Photoshop, Ap/Power Mac PC 8100, Kk/35mm scanner, AG/Arcus Scanner.
PRESSROOM: Line 1 — 6-G/Urbanite; Folders — 1-G/quarter folder. MAILROOM: Counter stackers — 1-BG/Count-O-Veyor; Inserters and stuffers — 1-MM/227E, 1-KAN/480; Bundle tyer — 2-MLN/ML2EE. LIBRARY: Electronic — Ap/Mac IIci. WIRE SERVICES: News — AP; Receiving dishes — AP. BUSINESS COMPUTERS: 1-PBS/Convergent; Applications: Gen ledger, Payroll, Circ, Adv; PCs & micros networked.

SALEM
Marion County

'90 U.S. Census- 107,786; E&P '96 Est. 128,771
ABC-CZ (90): 157,836 (HH 59,887)

Statesman Journal
(m-mon to sat; S)

Statesman Journal, 280 Church St. N.E. (97301); PO Box 13009, Salem, OR 97309; tel (503) 399-6611; fax (503) 399-6808. Gannett Co. Inc. group.
Circulation: 59,625(m); 70,376(m-sat); 70,530(S); ABC Sept. 30, 1995.
Price: 50¢(d); 50¢(sat); $1.50(S); $11.50/mo, $12.25/mo (motor route).
Advertising: Open inch rate $47.00(m); $47.00(m-sat); $52.68(S). **Representative:** Gannett National Newspaper Sales.
News Services: AP, GNS, LAT-WP. **Politics:** Independent. **Established:** 1851.
Special Editions: Home Show, People, Brides (Feb); Spring Fashion (Mar); Lawn & Garden (Apr); Graduation, Tourism (May); Tour of Homes, Newcomers (July); State Fair (Aug); Home Improvement (Oct); Gift Guides (Dec).
Special Weekly Sections: Weekend Entertainment Guide (fri); CAR Talk (sat).
Magazines: USA Weekend, TV This Week, Comics (S).

CORPORATE OFFICERS	
President	Sara Bentley
Secretary	Thomas Chapple
Treasurer	Jimmy L Thomas
GENERAL MANAGEMENT	
Publisher	Sara Bentley
Controller	John Swanson
Manager-Credit	Connie Johnson
ADVERTISING	
Director	Frank Bauer
Manager-Classified	Karen Schultz
MARKETING AND PROMOTION	
Director-Marketing	Barbara Adams
CIRCULATION	
Director	J Timothy Stone
NEWS EXECUTIVES	
Exec Editor	Mike Whitehead
Managing Editor	Kristin Gilger
EDITORS AND MANAGERS	
Business/Finance Editor	Joan Drake
City Editor	Richard Aguirre
Editorial Page Editor	Don Scarborough
Education Editor	Jillyn McCullough
Entertainment/Amusements Editor	Grant Butler
Environmental Editor	Theresa Novak
Farm/Agriculture Editor	Joan Drake
Fashion/Style Editor	Grant Butler
Features Editor	Grant Butler
Food Editor	Tommy Forstrom
Garden Editor	Grant Butler
Graphics Editor/Art Director	Kay Worthington
Health/Medical Editor	Diane Dietz
Librarian	Keri Horn
Living/Lifestyle Editor	Grant Butler
Metro Editor	Richard Aguirre
National Editor	Kathy Sheldon
News Editor	Kathy Sheldon
Photo Editor	Jay Reiter
Political/Government Editor	Richard Aguirre
Regional Editor	Larry Roby
Religion Editor	Lewis Arends
Sports Editor	Roy Gault
Television/Film Editor	Ron Cowan
Theater/Music Editor	Ron Cowan
Travel Editor	Grant Butler
Women's Editor	Grant Butler
MANAGEMENT INFORMATION SERVICES	
Director-Management Info Services	Allen Hammond
Data Processing Manager	Vicky Clarksmith
Asst Manager-Technical Service	Terry Kirkpatrick
PRODUCTION	
Director	Jerry Quinn
Manager-Production Service	Patty Littleton
Manager-Pressroom	Bill Walker

Market Information: Zoned editions; Split Run; TMC; ADS.
Mechanical available: Offset; Black and 4 ROP colors; insert accepted — preprinted; page cut-offs — 22¾".
Mechanical specifications: Type page 13" x 21½"; E - 6 cols, 2.03", ⅙" between; A - 6 cols, 2.03", ⅙" between; C - 10 cols, 1.21", 1/12" between.
Commodity consumption: Newsprint 6,897 metric tons; widths 54", 40¼", 27"; black ink 141,000 pounds; color ink 18,000 pounds; single pages printed 12,688; average pages per issue 32(d), 52(S); single plates used 52,000.
Equipment: EDITORIAL: Front-end hardware — SIA/386, SIA/386 SX; Front-end software — Dewar System IV; Printers — V/5100, V/5500, V/5300 B, Tectronix/Phaser III, QMS. CLASSIFIED: Front-end hardware — PC/386; Front-end software — Dewar System IV; Printers — V/5100, V/5300 B, V/5500, Tectronix/Phaser III, QMS; Other equipment — 2-Harlequin/Software RIP (for V/5500), 1-V/5300 Pixelburst Software RIP. DISPLAY: Adv layout systems — Dewar/Discovery, Dewar System IV; Front-end hardware — SIA/386 25 DX, 1-Ap/Mac Quadra 700, 1-Ap/Mac Quadra 950, 1-Ap/Mac Quadra 840 Av; Front-end software — Dewar/Discovery, Multi-Ad/Creator, QPS, Archetype/Corel Draw; Printers — V/5100-5500, Tectronix/Phaser III, V/5300 B, QMS; Other equipment — X/Scanner, Pixelcraft/7650C flatbed scanner. PRODUCTION: Typesetters — V/5100, V/5500, V/5300 B, QMS; Plate exposures — Nu/Flip Top FT40V6UPN, KFM/Twin-Line & Auto Bender; Plate processors — WL; Scanners — CD, Lf/Leafscan 35, Sharp/Flatbed, Lf/Leafscan 45; Production cameras — Spartan/II Page; Automatic film processors — LE, P; Film transporters — C; Shrink lenses — CK Optical; Color separation equipment (conventional) — CD, Lf/Leafscan 35, Ap/Mac, Lf/Leafscan 45; Digital color separation equipment — CD, Lf/Leafscan 35, Sharp/Flatbed, Pixelcraft/7650C flatbed scanner.
PRESSROOM: Line 1 — 7-G/Metro double width; Pasters — G/Digital Pilot and surface sensing; Reels and stands — Spyder/arms; Press control system — Fin. MAILROOM: Counter stackers — 3-HL/Monitor; Inserters and stuffers — 1-HI/1372; Bundle tyer — 2-MLN/MLN 2AHS; Addressing machine — Ch. WIRE SERVICES: News — AP Datastream, AP Datafeatures, GNS, TV Data, AP AdSend; Stock tables — AP SelectStox, AP Grand Central Stocks; Receiving dishes — size-10ft, AP. BUSINESS COMPUTERS: 1-IBM/AS400; PCs & micros networked; PCs & main system networked.

THE DALLES
Wasco County

'90 U.S. Census- 11,060; E&P '96 Est. 11,454

The Dalles Daily Chronicle
(e-mon to fri; S)

The Dalles Daily Chronicle, 414 Federal St.; PO Box 902, The Dalles, OR 97058; tel (541) 296-2141; fax (541) 298-1365. Scripps League Newspapers Inc. group.
Circulation: 5,253(e); 5,253(S); Sworn Oct. 2, 1995.
Price: 35¢(d); 35¢(S); $6.50/mo (carrier), $7.50/mo (mail); $78.00/yr (carrier), $90.00/yr (mail).
Advertising: Open inch rate $9.30(e); $11.88 (e-tues); $9.30(S).
News Services: ScrippSat, AP. **Politics:** Independent. **Established:** 1890.
Not Published: New Year; Memorial Day; Independence Day; Labor Day; Thanksgiving; Christmas.
Special Editions: Progress (Feb); Gorge East (May, Aug).
Special Weekly Section: Food (tues).

CORPORATE OFFICERS	
Board Chairman/Treasurer	E W Scripps
Vice Chairman/Corporate Secretary	Betty Knight Scripps
President	Barry H Scripps
Exec Vice Pres	Roger N Warkins
Vice Pres-Finance	Thomas E Wendel
GENERAL MANAGEMENT	
Publisher	Harold Steininger
Manager-Credit	Virginia Delco
Purchasing Agent	Harold Steininger
ADVERTISING	
Director	Skip Tschanz
Manager-Classified	Skip Tschanz
CIRCULATION	
Manager	Harold Steininger
NEWS EXECUTIVES	
Editor	Tom Stevenson
Managing Editor	Tom Stevenson
EDITOR AND MANAGER	
Assoc Editor	Kathy Gray
PRODUCTION	
Superintendent	Nancy Morinville

Market Information: Zoned editions; TMC.
Mechanical available: Offset; Black and 3 ROP colors; insert accepted — preprinted, zoned pre-prints available; page cut-offs — 21".
Mechanical specifications: Type page 13" x 21"; E - 6 cols, 2", ⅛" between; A - 6 cols, 2", ⅛" between; C - 6 cols, 2", ⅛" between.
Commodity consumption: Newsprint 133 metric tons; widths 27", 13¾"; black ink 7,530 pounds; color ink 1,000 pounds; single pages printed 4,260; average pages per issue 14(d), 14(S); single plates used 5,000.
Equipment: EDITORIAL: Front-end hardware — 5-ScrippSat/PC; Front-end software — ScrippSat/PC; Printers — QMS/810 Turbo, 2-PS. CLASSIFIED: Front-end hardware — 2-ScrippSat/PC; Front-end software — Synaptic; Printers — QMS/810 Turbo, Okidata/Microline 393 P14S. DISPLAY: Adv layout systems — ScrippSat; Front-end hardware — ScrippSat; Front-end software — Archetype/Designer; Printers — QMS/810 Turbo, 2-PS. PRODUCTION: Typesetters — 2-QMS/810 Turbo, Post-Script/Printer; Plate exposures — 1-Nu; Direct-to-plate imaging — 1-Nu; Production cameras — 1-K; Automatic film processors — 1-K/65A.
PRESSROOM: Line 1 — 4-G; Folders — 1-G; Press control system — Fin. MAILROOM: Inserters and stuffers — KAN/3-into-1; Bundle tyer — Bu, MLN, MLM/Spirit Strapper; Addressing machine — 1-Wm. WIRE SERVICES: News — AP; Syndicates — AP. BUSINESS COMPUTERS: Mk/Acers.

PENNSYLVANIA

ALIQUIPPA
See BEAVER

ALLENTOWN
Lehigh County

'90 U.S. Census- 105,090; E&P '96 Est. 106,214
ABC-CZ (90): 194,444 (HH 77,548)

The Morning Call
(m-mon to sat; S)

The Morning Call, 101 N. 6th St.; PO Box 1260, Allentown, PA 18105; tel (610) 820-6500; fax (610) 770-3780; e-mail mnews@mcall.com. Times Mirror Co. group.
Circulation: 133,140(m); 133,140(m-sat); 185,914(S); ABC Sept. 30, 1995.
Price: 50¢(d); 50¢(sat); $1.50(S); $3.65/wk; $189.80/yr.
Advertising: Open inch rate $62.30(m); $64.20(m-sat); $73.60(S).
News Services: AP, NYT, LAT-WP, CT. **Established:** 1883 (Call), 1921 (Sunday).
Special Editions: Valley Guide, Winter Focus, Auto Focus, Super Bowl XXX (Jan); Bride & Groom, DMD Super Saver, Auto Focus, Outlook '96 (Feb); Mature Visions, Home Mechanix, DMD Super Saver, Real Estate, SME Week, Auto Focus/Car Care (Mar); Valley Guide, Real Estate, Lawn & Garden, Outdoor Living & Travel, Triple Travel Challenge I (Apr); Real Estate, Lehigh Valley Woman, Auto Focus/Trucks & RVs, Spring Coupons (May); Real Estate, Mature Visions, DMD Super Saver, Auto Focus (June); Valley Guide, Lehigh Valley Woman, Real Estate, Summer Coupons, Bride & Groom, Triple Travel Challenge II (July); Real Estate, Musikfest, DMD Super Saver, Auto Focus (Aug); Football Preview, Real Estate, Mature Visions, Fall Coupons, Lehigh Valley Woman, Auto Focus (Sept); Valley Guide, Auto Trends '96, DMD Super Saver, Real Estate, Home Mechanix, Triple Travel Challenge III (Oct); Personal Finance, Lehigh Valley Woman, Real Estate, Auto Focus, Holiday Traditions (Nov); Auto Focus, Mature Visions (Dec).
Special Weekly Sections: Food Features (wed); Neighbours Tab (thur); Celebrity Insider (fri); Food Features, Entertainment, Art, Travel, Real Estate, Home Section (S).
Magazines: Parade (S); Own TV Channel Choices (newsprint); Zoned Neighbors Tabs.

CORPORATE OFFICERS	
Publisher/CEO	Gary K Shorts
Editor/Vice Pres	Roger D Oglesby
Controller	Thomas F Brown
Vice Pres-Marketing	Vincent Adone

Copyright ©1996 by the Editor & Publisher Co.

Pennsylvania I-343

GENERAL MANAGEMENT

Publisher/CEO Gary K Shorts
Director-Management Service Robert Schuchart
Director-Operations Kevin Lindgren
Director-Finance/Administration Jonathan Best
Manager-Credit Glenn W Adams
Manager-Human Resources Stephen Budihas

ADVERTISING

Director Howard F Renner
Manager-Administrative Service Richard Subber
Manager-Retail Rocky DeLeo
Manager-Classified Elaine Hall
Manager-National Robert Richelderfer
Manager-Marketing Service Mary Klunk

TELECOMMUNICATIONS

Audiotex Manager Elaine Hall

CIRCULATION

Director Donald J Belasco
Manager-Single Copy Sales Gary L Nowlin
Manager-Home Delivery Keith Lenhart
Manager-Marketing Richard Forgay

NEWS EXECUTIVES

Editor/Vice Pres Roger D Oglesby
Managing Editor Raymond B Holton
Deputy Managing Editor Alfred G Roberts
Asst Managing Editor-News (Night) John Gum

EDITORS AND MANAGERS

Bethlehem Editor Robert Orenstein
Business Editor Eloise De Haan
City Editor David Erdman
Comment Page Editor Van Cavett
Easton Editor Jack Tobias
Features Editor Paul Willistein
Graphics Director Jeff Lindenmuth
Home/Food Editor Diane Stoneback
Lehighton Editor Tyra Braden
Library Director Lois Doncevic
National Editor Dave Dawson
Neighbors Coordinator Janice B Shellenberger
Outdoors Editor Tom Fegley
Photo Editor Naomi Halperin
Sports Editor Paul Reinhard
Television Editor Sylvia Lawler
Exec Women's Editor Polly Rayner
Quakertown Editor Mary Gagnier

MANAGEMENT INFORMATION SERVICES

Data Processing Manager John Burns

PRODUCTION

Director-Operations Kevin Lindgren
Director-Management Info Services John Burns
Manager-Facilities James M Calafati
Manager-Pre Press Beth Sholar
Manager-Packaging/Distribution Richard Molchany
Superintendent-Pressroom Ron Elsasser
Foreman-Trucking Paul Lynch

Market Information: Zoned editions; Split Run; TMC; ADS; Operate audiotex.
Mechanical available: Offset; Black and 3 ROP colors; insert accepted — preprinted; page cut-offs — 22".
Mechanical specifications: Type page 13" x 21"; E - 6 cols, 2 1/16", 1/8" between; A - 6 cols, 2 1/16", 1/8" between; C - 10 cols, 1 3/16", 1/8" between.
Commodity consumption: Newsprint 22,314 metric tons; widths 54½", 41⅓", 27¼"; black ink 550,000 pounds; color ink 55,635 pounds; single pages printed 54,000; average pages per issue 60(d), 80(sat), 120(S); single plates used 140,000.
Equipment: EDITORIAL: Front-end hardware — SII/Sys 55, RSK/Tandem TXP; Front-end software — SII; Printers — Dataproducts/B1000, TI/TI-810. CLASSIFIED: Front-end hardware — SII/Sys 55, RSK/Tandem TXP; Front-end software — SII; Printers — Dataproducts/B1000, TI/TI-810. AUDIOTEX: Hardware — Brite Voice Systems. DISPLAY: Adv layout systems — SCS; Front-end hardware — Dell/286; Front-end software — SCS/Layout 8000; Printers — C.Itoh. PRODUCTION: Pagination software — QuarkXPress 3.3, Cascade/ImageFlow, Cascade/DataFlow; Typesetters — MON/Series III, AG, 2-AG/Accuset w/Harlequin RIP, 1-UHrel/Imagesetter w/Hyphen RIP; Platemaking systems — 2-KFM, Hyphen; Plate exposures — 2-KFM/ Twinline Exposure Unit; Plate processors — 2-KFM/XPH Subtractive Processor Unit; Electronic picture desk — Lf; Scanners — 1-ECR/Autokon, 5-AG/Arcus Plus Desktop, 3-Microtek/Desktop, 1-R2/Drum Scanner; Production cameras — 1-C/Spartan, 1-C/Newspager; Automatic film processors — 1-Kk/520, 2-LE/LD 281 SCREEN, 1-F/66; Color separation equipment (conventional) — RZ/210L; Digital color separation equipment — Ap/Mac w/Adobe/Photoshop.
PRESSROOM: Line 1 — 9-G/Metroliner; Line 2 — 9-G/Metroliner; Press drives — Fin; Folders — 3-G/3:2; Pasters — G; Reels and stands — G; Press control system — G/PCS II; Press registration system — KFM/Lock-ups. MAILROOM: Counter stackers — 5-Id/2100, 5-Id/2000, 2-HL/Monitor; Inserters and stuffers — 6-GMA/SLS 1000; Bundle tyer — 4-Dynaric/NP2, 4-Dynaric/NP1, 1-MLN, 1-EAM/Mosca, 3-Dynaric/N2; Addressing machine — 1-Ch; Mailroom control system — Id/Odd Count System 4340; Other mailroom equipment — MM/Stacker 335. LIBRARY: Electronic — Vu/Text SAVE. WIRE SERVICES: News — AP Dataspeed, AP Datafeatures; Photos — AP Photostream; Stock tables — AP SelectStox; Syndicates — AP, KRT, PressLink; Receiving dishes — size-3m, AP. BUSINESS COMPUTERS: 1-Unisys/V380; Applications: Financial, Circ; PCs & micros networked; PCs & main system networked.

ALTOONA

Blair County

'90 U.S. Census- 51,881; E&P '96 Est. 47,936
ABC-CZ (90): 78,218 (HH 30,611)

Altoona Mirror

(e-mon to fri; m-sat; S)

Altoona Mirror, 301 Cayuga Ave.; PO Box 2008, Altoona, PA 16602; tel (814) 946-7411; fax (814) 946-7539; e-mail altmirror@aol.com. Thomson Newspapers group.
Circulation: 34,128(e); 34,128(m-sat); 41,501(S); ABC Sept. 30, 1995.
Price: 50¢(d); 50¢(sat); $1.50(S); $2.65/wk, $1.75/wk (sat & S only); $11.50/mo; $138.00/yr.
Advertising: Open inch rate $25.65(e); $25.65(m-sat); $27.65(S). **Representative:** Landon Associates Inc.
News Service: AP. **Politics:** Independent. **Established:** 1874.
Special Editions: Healthy Living, Bridal (Jan); Outlook (Feb); Spring Home Improvement (Mar); Spring Car Care (May); Earth Day, Gas Tab (Apr); Lawn & Garden-package, N.I.E. Design-an-Ad (May); Mature Lifestyles (June); Olympic Preview, Answer Book (July); Tour de Toona, Back-to-School, High School-Pro/College Football (Aug); Gas Tab, Home Improvement & Home Decorating, Fall/Winter Car Care (Oct); Holiday Magazine (Nov); Christmas Recipe Book, Winter Sports, Last Minute Gift Guide, Holiday Greetings (Dec).
Magazines: Cover Story (thur); Classified Extra (TMC), TV Mirror (sat); USA Weekend (S); Real Estate Advantage (last fri/mo).

GENERAL MANAGEMENT

Publisher Steven A Braver
Director-Finance Michael White
Director-Human Resources/Community Service Denise D Dishman

ADVERTISING

Director Ed Gaydos
Manager-Creative Services Anne Pfautz
Manager-Commercial Printing Doug Fetzer
Manager-Outside Sales Chuck Boteler
Manager-Inside/Classified Sales Jodi Lynch

MARKETING AND PROMOTION

Manager-Marketing/Promotion Ann Singer

CIRCULATION

Director Richard Hite
Manager-Sales Daniel Slep

NEWS EXECUTIVE

Exec Editor Linda White

EDITORS AND MANAGERS

City Editor Michael Bieger
Editorial Page Editor Steve Carpenter
Features/Women's Editor Linda T Gracey
Librarian Tim Doyle
Living/Lifestyle Editor Linda T Gracey
News Editor Ray Eckenrode
Photo Department Manager J D Cavrich
Picture Editor Paul Singer
Political Editor Mary Haley
Sports Editor James Lane
Wire Editor Ed Frank

MANAGEMENT INFORMATION SERVICES

Data Processing Manager Dan Vicars

PRODUCTION

Director David M Mentzer Sr
Foreman-Composing James Rudy
Foreman-Pressroom Nelson Stephens

Market Information: TMC.
Mechanical available: Offset; Black and 3 ROP colors; insert accepted — preprinted, others upon request-with publisher's approval; page cut-offs — 22¾".
Mechanical specifications: Type page 13" x 21"; E - 6 cols, 2 1/16", 1/8" between; A - 6 cols, 2 1/16", 1/8" between; C - 6 cols, 2 1/16", 1/8" between.
Commodity consumption: Newsprint 3,300 short tons; widths 55", 41½", 27¾"; black ink 12,405 pounds; color ink 1,500 pounds; single pages printed 12,056; average pages per issue 40(d), 56(S); single plates used 19,582.
Equipment: EDITORIAL: Front-end hardware — CText; Front-end software — QuarkXPress, CText. CLASSIFIED: Front-end hardware — IBM/RISC 6000; Front-end software — Unix, CText; Printers — Panther/Pro 46 Imagesetter, IBM. DISPLAY: Adv layout systems — SCS/Layout 8000, Ap/Mac Quadra 650, Ap/Mac Quadra 800, QuarkXPress, Multi-Ad/Creator; Front-end hardware — HP, Ap/Mac; Front-end software — Ap/Mac NLM 3.12, Novell/Netware 386 3.12, Microsoft/Windows, PBS; Printers — Panther/Pro 46 Imagesetter; Other equipment — Microtek/Scanners, Sharp/High Resolution Flatbed Scanner. PRODUCTION: Pagination software — Ap/Mac NLM 3.12, Novell/Netware 386 3.12, Microsoft/Windows, Cheyenne/Arcserve; Typesetters — 2-Tegra/Varityper 5500, Panther/Pro 46s; Platemaking systems — KFM; Plate exposures — KFM/AR-6000; Plate processors — SCREEN; Electronic picture desk — Lf/AP Leaf Picture Desk; Scanners — ECR/Autokon, Sharp/35mm; Production cameras — SCREEN, LD/281-Q; Automatic film processors — Panther/Pro 46; Color separation equipment (conventional) — Lf/AP Leaf Picture Desk.
PRESSROOM: Line 1 — 6-G/Headliner offset, double width, 4-G/half decks double width; Press drives — Allen Bradley; Folders — 2-G; Pasters — Automatic; Reels and stands — 5-G/Stands, 5-G/3-Arm Reels; Press control system — Fin. MAILROOM: Counter stackers — 2-PPK, 2-Id/2200; Inserters and stuffers — 6-KAN, MC/660-20, GMA/SLS-1000; Bundle tyer — 5-Sa, 2-MLN, Id; Addressing machine — PBS/CIS; Mailroom control system — GMA; Other mailroom equipment — MM. LIBRARY: Electronic — SMS/Stauffer Media Systems. WIRE SERVICES: News — AP, LAT-WP, CNS; Photos — AP; Stock tables — AP; Receiving dishes — size-10ft, AP. BUSINESS COMPUTERS: PBS/Oracle on HP hardware; Applications: Fleet maintenance, Accts payable, Accts receivable (adv), Payroll, Carrier data, Subscription/dealer data, Billing.

AMBRIDGE
See BEAVER

ASHLAND
See SHENANDOAH

ATHENS
See SAYRE

BEAVER-ROCHESTER-AMBRIDGE-ALIQUIPPA

Beaver County

'90 U.S. Census- 30,691 (Aliquippa 13,374; Ambridge 8,133; Beaver 5,028; Rochester 4,156); E&P '96 Est. 26,452 (Aliquippa 10,921; Ambridge 7,107; Beaver 4,709; Rochester 3,715)
ABC-NDM (90): 186,903 (HH 71,939)

Beaver County Times

(e-mon to fri; S)

Beaver County Times, 400 Fair Ave.; PO Box 400, Beaver, PA 15009; tel (412) 775-3200; fax (412) 775-7212; web site http://www.pgh.net/beaver/. Calkins Newspapers group.
Circulation: 44,785(e); 53,610(S); ABC Sept. 30, 1995.
Price: 50¢(d); $1.25(S); $2.60/wk (carrier), $2.80/wk (motor route); $121.68/yr (carrier), $131.04/yr (motor route).
Advertising: Open inch rate $35.85(e); $35.85(S). **Representative:** Landon Associates Inc.
News Service: AP. **Politics:** Independent. **Established:** 1874.
Not Published: New Year; Memorial Day; Independence Day; Labor Day; Christmas.
Advertising not accepted: Mail order.
Special Editions: Economy (Jan); Tax Corner, Bridal (Feb); Community Guide, Home, Farm & Garden (Mar); Car Care (Apr); Hookstown Fair (May); Big Knob Fair (July); Air Show, Hookstown Fair, Football, Coupon Book, RiverFest (Aug); Bridal, Car Care (Sept); People's Gas (Oct); Cookbook, Gift Guide (Nov); Basketball, Coupon Book (Dec).
Special Weekly Section: Garden (thur).
Magazines: Times Weekend (fri); Sunday Times Magazine, TV Times (S).

CORPORATE OFFICERS

President Grover J Friend
Exec Vice Pres Charles P Smith
Senior Vice Pres Edward J Birch
Vice Pres F Wallace Gordon
Vice Pres Sandra C Hardy
Vice Pres Stanley M Ellis
Vice Pres Carolyn C Smith
Vice Pres/Secretary Shirley C Ellis
Treasurer Edward J Birch

GENERAL MANAGEMENT

Publisher F Wallace Gordon
Controller E S Metzger
Manager-Credit Debbie Hays
Manager-Education Service Connie Fields

ADVERTISING

Director Terry L Tolson
Manager-Sales Robert W Woelfel
Manager-Service William A O'Dell

TELECOMMUNICATIONS

Audiotex Manager Patrick A Bingle

CIRCULATION

Director Louis E Ottey
Manager Richard Pietro
Manager William Budris
Manager-Distribution William Hannan
Manager-Marketing Vaughn Vacar
Manager-Single Copy Sales James Hupp

NEWS EXECUTIVES

Exec Editor Dennis D Dible
Editor-Local News Greg Brown
Editor-Allegheny Times Sandra Fischione-Donovan
Managing Editor Richard Wasko
Assoc Editor Tom Bickert

EDITORS AND MANAGERS

Amusements Editor Marsha Keefer
Business Editor Stephanie Waite
Editorial Page Editor Robert Uhriniak
Education Editor Adam Boone
Environmental Editor Cathy O'Donnell
Fashion/Style Editor Marsha Keefer
Features Editor Marsha Keefer
Food Editor Patti Conley
Graphics Editor/Art Director Clif Page
Health/Medical Editor Cathy O'Donnell
Leisure Editor Marsha Keefer
Librarian Linda Disante
Living/Lifestyle Editor Marsha Keefer
Photo Department Manager Clif Page
Radio/Television Editor Marsha Keefer
Real Estate Editor Stephanie Waite
Religion Editor Denyse Yourse
Sports Editor Ed Rose
Women's Editor Marsha Keefer

PRODUCTION

Director Gerald A Spielvogel
Manager-Control John N George
Manager-Maintenance Gerald B McCowin
Manager-Mailroom/Insert James L Jenkins
Supervisor-Composing Thomas M Auld
Supervisor-Composing Gary R Barley
Supervisor-Composing Marvin K Neidergall
Supervisor-Night/Weekend Monica Wozniak
Supervisor-Press Dave Mengel
Supervisor-Plate William Wachsmuth
Supervisor-Insert Jeffrey L Shea
Supervisor-Systems R Wesley Werner

Market Information: Zoned editions; TMC; ADS; Operate audiotex.
Mechanical available: Other; Black and 3 ROP colors; insert accepted — preprinted, any size insert accepted; page cut-offs — 22¾".
Mechanical specifications: Type page 13" x 21½"; E - 6 cols, 2 1/16", 1/8" between; A - 6 cols, 2 1/16", 1/8" between; C - 9 cols, 1 3/8", 1/16" between.
Commodity consumption: Newsprint 3,585 metric tons; widths 55", 41¼", 27½", 13¾"; black ink 96,000 pounds; color ink 11,000 pounds; single pages printed 13,882; average pages per issue 45(d), 52(S); single plates used 27,800.
Equipment: EDITORIAL: Front-end hardware — 45-IBM/486; Other equipment — 1-IBM/Series I, 7-IBM/PC, 3-IBM/PC-25, 3-

I-344 Pennsylvania

RSK/TRS-80. CLASSIFIED: Front-end hardware — 6-IBM/3179. AUDIOTEX: Supplier name — Accu-Weather. DISPLAY: Adv layout systems — 6-PC/486, 2-PC/386, 1-Novell/Scanner, SCS/Layout 800; Front-end hardware — IBM/Value-Point 486; Printers — Ap/Mac LaserPrinter; Other equipment — Hyphen/Dash 600. PRODUCTION: Pagination software — QuarkXPress; OCR software — OCR, Caere/OmniPage; Typesetters — 2-AU/Micro 5, 2-MON/1016 H.S.; Platemaking systems — 2-Na/40; Plate exposures — Na/Starlite; Scanners — 2-IBM/3278, 1-IBM/3178, 1-IBM/3179, 3-PC/286, Dest/650; Production cameras — 1-K/Vertical 241, 1-C/Spartan III; Automatic film processors — 1-LE/LD24A, 2-LE/APS35; Film transporters — 1-C, 2-LE, 2 Gluntz & Jensen/HS; Color separation equipment (conventional) — Lf/AP Leaf Picture Desk.
PRESSROOM: Line 1 — 6-G/Mark I Headliner (Model 2362); Folders — 1-G/2:1; Pasters — G/RTP; Press control system — Ch/SCR. MAILROOM: Counter stackers — 1-St/257; Inserters and stuffers — 11-KAN/DG-320; Bundle tyer — 1-MLN/2, 1-OVL; Addressing machine — 1-IBM/3031. WIRE SERVICES: News — AP, KRT; Photos — AP, KRT; Stock tables — AP; Syndicates — KRT; Receiving dishes — AP. BUSINESS COMPUTERS: 1-Univac/Sys 80; Applications: Circ, Adv billing, Accts receivable, Gen ledger, Payroll; PCs & main system networked.

BEDFORD

Bedford County

'90 U.S. Census- 3,137; E&P '96 Est. 2,988

Bedford Gazette

(m-mon to sat)

Bedford Gazette, 424 W. Penn St.; PO Box 671; Bedford, PA 15522; tel (814) 623-1151; fax (814) 623-5055.

Circulation: 9,915(m); 9,915(m-sat); Sworn Sept. 30, 1995.

Price: 35¢(d); 35¢(sat); $9.00/mo; $75.00/yr.

Advertising: Open inch rate $9.15(m); $9.15 (m-sat). **Representative:** Landon Associates Inc.

News Service: AP. **Politics:** Independent. **Established:** 1805.

Not Published: New Year; Memorial Day; Independence Day; Labor Day; Christmas.

Special Editions: Interiors, Jaycee Week Pages (Jan); Boy Scout Week Pages, Business and Industry, Bedford County Farming, Tax and Finances (Feb); Girl Scout Week Pages, Spring Home & Garden, Bridal & Spring Fashion (Mar); Home & Garden Edition (Apr); Vacation Bedford County, Graduation and Careers (May); Dairy Farm Edition (June); Just for Her, Bedford County Fair (July); Back-to-School Edition (Aug); Football Edition, Homemakers Edition, Fall Foliage #1 Edition (Sept); 4-H Week Pages, Fall Foliage #2 Edition, Farm Safety, Hunting Editon #1, New Car Care Guide (Oct); Christmas Edition #1, Christmas Edition #2, Winter Sports Edition (Nov); Christmas Edition #3, Christmas Songbook, Christmas Edition #4 (Dec); Golden Years (monthly).

Special Weekly Sections: Lifestyles (mon, tues); Food Page (wed); Lifestyles (thur); Village Crier, Farm Page (fri); Church Page (sat); Television, Village Crier, Business Page, Outdoors Page, Food Page (S); UpDate Listing, TV Listing, Comics (daily).

CORPORATE OFFICERS

President	Edward K Frear
Secretary	M L Frear

GENERAL MANAGEMENT

Publisher	Edward K Frear
General Manager	Don Hopf

ADVERTISING

Director	Keith Landis

CIRCULATION

Manager	Bill Lally

NEWS EXECUTIVES

Editor	Edward K Frear
Managing Editor	Rich Ralston

PRODUCTION

Foreman-Composing	Keith Landis
Foreman-Pressroom	Phil Langham

Market Information: TMC; Operate audiotex.

Mechanical available: Offset; Black and 4 ROP colors; insert accepted — preprinted; page cut-offs — 22¾".

Mechanical specifications: Type page 13" x 21½"; E - 6 cols, 2 1/16", ⅛" between; A - 6 cols, 2 1/16", ⅛" between; C - 6 cols, 2 1/16", ⅛" between.

Commodity consumption: average pages per issue 18(d).

Equipment: EDITORIAL: Front-end hardware — Ap/Mac; Front-end software — Baseview/NewsEdit; Printers — Ap/Mac Laser. CLASSIFIED: Front-end hardware — Ap/Mac; Front-end software — Baseview; Printers — Ap/Mac Laser. AUDIOTEX: Hardware — Gateway/2000. PRODUCTION: Typesetters — Ap/Mac Laser; Plate exposures — Nu/Flip Top; Production cameras — K; Automatic film processors — Kk.
PRESSROOM: Line 1 — 5-G/Community; Folders — 1-G/S-C. MAILROOM: Bundle tyer — Nichiro Kogyo; Addressing machine — Ch/515. LIBRARY: Combination — Dukzare. WIRE SERVICES: News — AP; Photos — AP; Syndicates — AP Laserphoto, AP GraphicsNet; Receiving dishes — AP. BUSINESS COMPUTERS: IBM/Sys 36.

BERWICK

See BLOOMSBURG

BETHLEHEM

See EASTON

BLOOMSBURG-BERWICK

Columbia County

'90 U.S. Census- 23,415 (Bloomsburg 12,439; Berwick 10,976); E&P '96 Est. 23,378 (Bloomsburg 13,078; Berwick 10,300)

Press-Enterprise

(m-mon to sat; S)

Press Enterprise, 3185 Lackawanna Ave., Bloomsburg, PA 17815; tel (717) 784-2121; fax (717) 784-9226.

Circulation: 22,020(m); 22,020(m-sat); 22,020(S); CAC June 30, 1995.

Price: 50¢(d); 75¢(sat); 75¢(S); $2.40/wk; $11.20/mo; $110.00/yr.

Advertising: Open inch rate $14.50(m); $14.50(m-sat); $14.50(S). **Representative:** Papert Companies.

News Service: AP. **Politics:** Independent. **Established:** 1902.

Note: Effective Oct. 1, 1995, this publication added a Sunday edition. Sunday circulation figure is an estimate.

Advertising not accepted: Liquor (excluding beer and wine).

Special Editions: Newlywed (Jan); Progress (Feb); Health & Fitness (Mar); Your Home (Apr); Newlywed, Senior Citizen (May); Recreation (June); Newcomers (July); Back-to-School, Football (Aug); Fair (Sept); New Autos, Your Home, Recreation (Oct); Gift Guide, Thanksgiving (Nov); Gift Guide (Dec).

Special Weekly Sections: Best Food Day (wed); Business and Service Directory (thur).

Magazines: TV Preview, USA Weekend, Comics (sat).

CORPORATE OFFICERS

President	Paul R Eyerly III
Treasurer	James T Micklow
Vice Pres	James A Wells

GENERAL MANAGEMENT

Publisher	Paul R Eyerly III
General Manager	James A Wells

ADVERTISING

Manager-Retail	Sandy Bower
Manager-Inside Sales	Mary Sue Woolcock

TELECOMMUNICATIONS

Audiotex Manager	Kathleen Baylor

CIRCULATION

Manager	James Haas

NEWS EXECUTIVES

Editor	James Sachetti
Managing Editor-News	Tim Konski
Managing Editor-Sports/Features	Mike Stewart

EDITORS AND MANAGERS

Editorial Page Editor	James Sachetti
Entertainment/Amusements Editor	James Stewart
Fashion/Style Editor	Judy Hill
Graphics Editor/Art Director	Lori Getty
Living Editor	Judy Hill
Photo Editor	Bill Hughes
Television/Film Editor	James Stewart
Theater/Music Editor	James Stewart

MANAGEMENT INFORMATION SERVICES

Data Processing Manager	Dennis Ashenfelder

PRODUCTION

Manager-Operations	Tom Sitler
Manager-Color Division	Bob Braun
Superintendent-Press	Ervin Rough

Market Information: Zoned editions; TMC; ADS; Operate audiotex.

Mechanical available: Offset; Black and 3 ROP colors; insert accepted — preprinted; page cut-offs — 22¾".

Mechanical specifications: Type page 13" x 21½"; E - 6 cols, 2 1/16", ⅛" between; A - 6 cols, 2 1/16", ⅛" between; C - 9 cols, 1 5/16", 1/16" between.

Commodity consumption: Newsprint 2,000 short tons; width 27"; black ink 44,000 pounds; color ink 14,000 pounds; single pages printed 11,648; average pages per issue 32(d).

Equipment: EDITORIAL: Front-end hardware — 27-Ap/Mac; Front-end software — Baseview. CLASSIFIED: Front-end hardware — 6-Pentium/PC; Front-end software — PPI; Printers — Data Product/500. AUDIOTEX: Hardware — Brite Voice Systems/AudioText. DISPLAY: Adv layout systems — Ap/Mac; Front-end software — Multi-Ad/Creator 3.7; Printers — Ap/Mac LaserWriter 810 Pro. PRODUCTION: Pagination software — Baseview; Typesetters — 2-ECR/PelBox; Platemaking systems — KFM/Stretch Twin Line Exposure; Plate exposures — 3-Nu/Flip Top FT; Plate processors — 2-Anitec; Scanners — 1-ECR/Autokon, Graphic Enterprises/PageScan 18x24; Production cameras — 1-C/Spartan III 1270, Canon/11x17; Automatic film processors — 2-Kk/710; Film transporters — 1-C/1274; Color separation equipment (conventional) — AG/Horizon Plus Flatbed.
PRESSROOM: Line 1 — 7-G/Urbanite (w/3 color unit); Line 2 — 8-HI/NC 400; Line 3 — Tensor/1400; Folders — 2-G; Pasters — Cary, Butler. MAILROOM: Counter stackers — 1-BG/108, 1-BG/107, 1-PPK, 2-HI/RS25; Inserters and stuffers — 1-SH; Bundle tyer — 2-MLN/ML2EE, 1-Sa, 3-BU; Addressing machine — 1-KR/Communications, 1-KAN. LIBRARY: Electronic — SMS. COMMUNICATIONS: Digital ad delivery system — AP AdSend. WIRE SERVICES: News — AP, KRT; Receiving dishes — AP. BUSINESS COMPUTERS: 1-IBM/Sys 36; Applications: Unix/PC w/DSI Software: Circ, Gen ledger, Payroll, Accts receivable, Inventory, Job costing; PCs & micros networked.

BRADFORD

McKean County

'90 U.S. Census- 9,625; E&P '96 Est. 8,485

The Bradford Era

(m-mon to sat)

Bradford Era, 43 Main St.; PO Box 365, Bradford, PA 16701; tel (814) 368-3173; fax (814) 368-3173. Hollinger International Inc. group.

Circulation: 11,165(m); 11,165(m-sat); VAC June 30, 1995.

Price: 50¢(d); 50¢(sat); $2.35/wk; $10.50/mo; $117.50/yr, $138.00/yr (mail).

Advertising: Open inch rate $11.93(m); $11.93(m-sat). **Representative:** Landon Associates Inc.

News Service: AP. **Politics:** Republican. **Established:** 1877.

Not Published: July 5; Dec 26.

Special Editions: Progress Edition (Jan); Spring Fashion, Brides (Mar); Design An Ad (May); Car Care, Sun 'n Fun (June); Univ. of Pittsburgh at Bradford (Sept); Hunting Guide (Oct); Christmas Guide (Nov).

Magazines: Daily TV Guide; USA Weekend.

GENERAL MANAGEMENT

Publisher	John H Satterwhite
General Manager	H L Woodruff
Manager-Credit	Richard Kautz
Personnel Manager	Nelson Russell
Purchasing Agent	Nelson Russell

ADVERTISING

Manager	H L Woodruff
Manager-Classified	H L Woodruff
Manager-National	Patricia Woodruff

TELECOMMUNICATIONS

Audiotex Manager	Richard Kautz

CIRCULATION

Director	Richard Kautz

NEWS EXECUTIVES

Editor	John H Satterwhite
Managing Editor	Paul Reichart

EDITORS AND MANAGERS

City Editor	Marty Robacker Wilder
Sports Editor	Ron Kloss

PRODUCTION

Manager	Joseph F Errera

Market Information: TMC; Operate audiotex.

Mechanical available: Offset; Black and 3 ROP colors; insert accepted — preprinted, all; page cut-offs — 22¾".

Mechanical specifications: Type page 13" x 21½"; E - 6 cols, 2.03", .17" between; A - 6 cols, 2.06", .14" between; C - 9 cols, 1.36", .08" between.

Commodity consumption: Newsprint 1,200 short tons; widths 27½", 13⅝"; black ink 33,000 pounds; color ink 17,000 pounds; single pages printed 6,531; average pages per issue 21(d); single plates used 7,100.

Equipment: EDITORIAL: Front-end hardware — 20-RSK/Tandy; Front-end software — CText; Printers — 1-Dataproducts; Other equipment — 1-Ap/Mac IIsi, AP GraphicsNet, 1-Lf/AP Leaf Picture Desk (w/Laser Photo). CLASSIFIED: Front-end hardware — 4-RSK/Tandy; Front-end software — CText; Printers — 1-Dataproducts. AUDIOTEX: Hardware — 1-PC/486. DISPLAY: Adv layout systems — SCS/Layout 8000, Cumulas/PC, Unix/ADS; Front-end hardware — 1-Ap/Mac IIci, 2-Ap/Mac Quadra; Front-end software — Multi-Ad/Creator; Printers — 1-Ap/Mac LaserWriter; Other equipment — Microtek/Scanner, NEC/CD-Rom, 2-Ap/Mac CD-Rom. PRODUCTION: Typesetters — 1-Ap/Mac LaserWriter, 1-Ap/Mac LaserWriter Pro 630, 1-V/Imagesetter 6990 (Full Page); Plate exposures — 1-Nu; Plate processors — Ic; Electronic picture desk — Lf/AP Leaf Picture Desk; Scanners — 1-Lf/Leafscan 45, 1-Mk/ScanMaker 11XE; Production cameras — R/500 Overhead; Automatic film processors — LE/Excel 26"; Shrink lenses — CK Optical/7 ¼%; Color separation equipment (conventional) — Adobe/Photoshop, Ap/Mac Quadra 650.
PRESSROOM: Line 1 — 8-HI/V15-D; Folders — 2-HI; Reels and stands — 8-HI; Press control system — 1-CH/Responder 210. MAILROOM: Counter stackers — 1-BG; Bundle tyer — 2-MLN, 1-EAM/Mosca, 1-Akebono; Addressing machine — 1-St, 1-Am. LIBRARY: Combination — 1-Dukane. COMMUNICATIONS: Facsimile — 1-X, 1-Ricoh. WIRE SERVICES: News — AP Newswire, AP Featurewire; Syndicates — King Features, Universal Press, LAT-WP, NAS; Receiving dishes — size-3m, AP. BUSINESS COMPUTERS: 1-Continental/Unix Box, 5-PC; Applications: Vision Data: Circ, Accts receivable, TMC; PCs & micros networked; PCs & main system networked.

BRISTOL

See LEVITTOWN

BUTLER

Butler County

'90 U.S. Census- 15,714; E&P '96 Est. 14,703
ABC-CZ (90): 53,267 (HH 20,895)

Butler Eagle (e-mon to fri; S)

Butler Eagle, 114 W. Diamond St., Butler, PA 16001; tel (412) 282-8000; fax (412) 282-1280.

Circulation: 30,165(e); 31,173(S); ABC Sept. 30, 1995.

Price: 35¢(d); 50¢(S); $2.10/wk; $9.10/mo; $109.20/yr.

Advertising: Open inch rate $19.07(e); $19.07(S). **Representative:** Landon Associates Inc.

News Service: AP. **Politics:** Independent-Republican. **Established:** 1869.

Not Published: Memorial Day; Independence Day; Labor Day; Thanksgiving; Christmas.

Advertising not accepted: Beer; Liquor; 900 numbers.

Special Editions: Progress; Football; Bridal; Father's Day; Christmas; Health & Fitness; Ethnic; Homecoming.

Special Weekly Section: TV Focus (fri).

Magazine: TV Focus (fri).

CORPORATE OFFICERS

President/Publisher	Vernon L Wise Jr
Vice Pres/Secretary	John Laing Wise III
Vice Pres/Treasurer	Vernon L Wise III

GENERAL MANAGEMENT
General Manager ..... Ronald A Vodenichar
Controller ..... Ronald Knauf

ADVERTISING
Director-Retail ..... Art Kephart
Manager-Classified ..... Jon McKain

MARKETING AND PROMOTION
Director-Marketing/Promotion ..... Ronald A Vodenichar

CIRCULATION
Director ..... Joseph Kreutzer

NEWS EXECUTIVES
Editor ..... John Laing Wise III
Managing Editor ..... Mark Mann

EDITORS AND MANAGERS
Photo Editor ..... Jack Neely
Sports Editor ..... Rick Davis

PRODUCTION
Foreman-Composing ..... John Galbreth
Foreman-Pressroom ..... David Wogan
Foreman-Electronics/Computers ..... Russ Dunlap

Market Information: Split Run; TMC; ADS.
Mechanical available: Black and 4 ROP colors; insert accepted — preprinted, any; page cut-offs — 21½".
Mechanical specifications: Type page 13½" x 21½"; E - 6 cols, 2³⁄₃₀", ⅛" between; A - 6 cols, 2¹⁄₃₀", ⅛" between; C - 9 cols, 1¹⁄₃", ¹⁄₁₀" between.
Commodity consumption: Newsprint 2,000 short tons; width 27½"; black ink 47,000 pounds; color ink 5,000 pounds; average pages per issue 24(d), 36(S); single plates used 8,000.
Equipment: EDITORIAL: Front-end hardware — Novell/Network, PC; Front-end software — Dewar, QPS, Microsoft/Word; Printers — 1-Okidata/80, 1-Ap/Mac LaserWriter Plus, XIT/Clipper, AG/9800, AG/Avantra 25; Other equipment — 3-Ap/Mac IIci, 1-Ap/Mac LC. CLASSIFIED: Front-end hardware — 1-Ap/Mac Quadra 950, 7-Ap/Mac IIci; Front-end software — Mk/Freedom, QuarkXPress; Printers — 1-XIT/Clipper, 1-Ap/Mac ImageWriter; Other equipment — 1-Microtek/Scanner. DISPLAY: Front-end hardware — 2-Ap/Mac Quadra 700, 4-Ap/Mac IIci, 1-Ap/Mac fx, 2-Ap/Mac Quadra 950; Front-end software — Multi-Ad, Adobe/Photoshop, QuarkXPress; Other equipment — 3-Microtek/Scanmaker IIXE, AG/9800, AG/Accuset 1000. PRODUCTION: Typesetters — 1-AG/9800 Imagesetter, 1-XIT/Clipper, 1-AG/Avantra; Plate exposures — Douthitt; Scanners — Graphic Enterprises/PageScan 800, AG/Arcus, CD/Scanner 645 IM, CD/Scanview 600; Production cameras — 1-C, 1-B; Automatic film processors — 1-P; Film transporters — 1-C; Shrink lenses — CK Optical; Digital color separation equipment — CD/870.
PRESSROOM: Line 1 — 7-G/Cosmo; Folders — 1-G. MAILROOM: Inserters and stuffers — MM; Bundle tyer — MLN. LIBRARY: Electronic — SMS/Stauffer Gold. COMMUNICATIONS: Digital ad delivery system — AP AdSend. Systems used — satellite. WIRE SERVICES: News — AP; Photos — AP; Syndicates — NYT; Receiving dishes — AP. BUSINESS COMPUTERS: Vision Data on Pentium/100; Applications: Circ, Adv billing, Accts receivable, Gen ledger, Payroll.

CARLISLE
Cumberland County
'90 U.S. Census- 18,419; E&P '96 Est. 18,507
ABC-CZ (90): 28,252 (HH 10,849)

The Sentinel
(e-mon to fri; m-sat)
The Sentinel, PO Box 130, Carlisle, PA 17013-0130; tel (717) 243-2611; fax (717) 243-3754; e-mail sentinel@epix.net; web site http://www1.trib.com/CUMBERLINK/. Howard Publications group.
Circulation: 16,638(e); 16,638(m-sat); ABC Sept. 30, 1995.
Price: 50¢(d); 50¢(sat); $2.20/wk; $114.40/yr.
Advertising: Open inch rate $17.68(e); $17.68(m-sat). **Representative:** Landon Associates Inc.
News Service: AP. **Politics:** Independent. **Established:** 1881.
Special Editions: Brides (Jan); Annual (Feb); Home Improvement (Mar); Car Care, Graduation (May); Fall Sports, Welcome (Aug); Car Care (Oct); Holiday Gift Guide (Nov).
Special Weekly Sections: Food (wed); Alive (Entertainment) (thur); People, TV Week (sat).
Magazine: Sentinel TV (local).

CORPORATE OFFICER
President ..... Robert S Howard

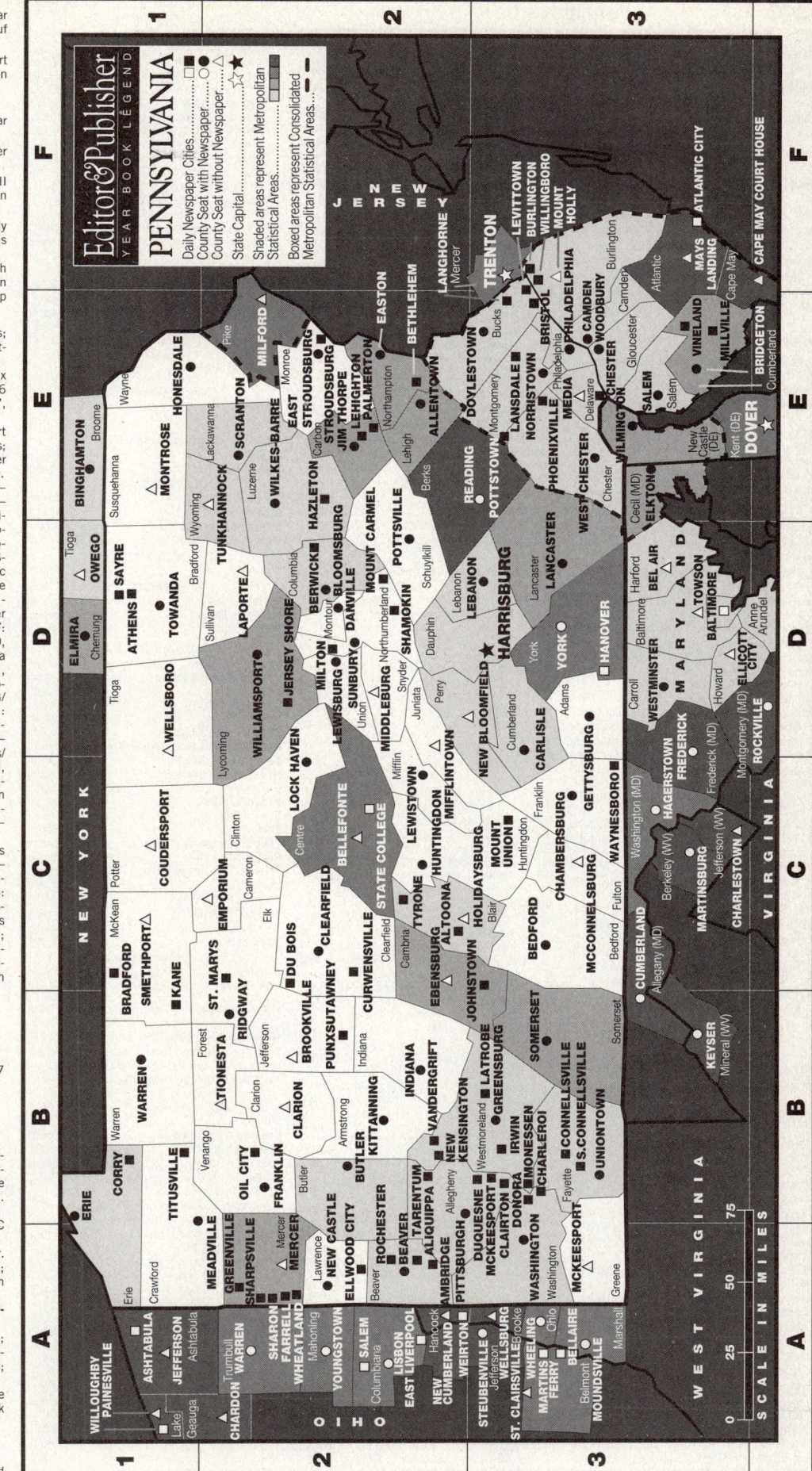

Copyright ©1996 by the Editor & Publisher Co.

I-346 Pennsylvania

GENERAL MANAGEMENT
Publisher Wayne Powell
ADVERTISING
Director Stephen Crowley
TELECOMMUNICATIONS
Audiotex Manager Sharon De Venney
CIRCULATION
Director Ben Vinson
NEWS EXECUTIVES
Editor Carol Talley
Managing Editor Kurt Wanfried
EDITOR AND MANAGER
City Editor Fred Burgess
MANAGEMENT INFORMATION SERVICES
Data Processing Manager Jerry Harvill
Online Manager Kurt Wanfried
PRODUCTION
Manager-Operations Jerry Harvill

Market Information: Zoned editions; Split Run; TMC; Operate database; Operate audiotex.
Mechanical available: Offset; Black and 3 ROP colors; insert accepted — preprinted; page cut-offs — 22¾".
Mechanical specifications: Type page 13" x 21½"; E - 6 cols, 2 1/16", 1/8" between; A - 6 cols, 2 1/16", 1/8" between; C - 6 cols, 2 1/16", 1/8" between.
Commodity consumption: Newsprint 1,399 short tons; 1,240 metric tons; widths 27½", 13¾", 34", 17"; black ink 33,174 pounds; color ink 10,164 pounds; single pages printed 10,914; average pages per issue 35(d); single plates used 13,467.
Equipment: EDITORIAL: Front-end hardware — 15-Sun/Sparc; Front-end software — Arbor-Text/UShare; Printers — Ap/Mac LaserWriter; Other equipment — 8-Ap/Mac II. CLASSIFIED: Front-end hardware — 2-Sun/Sparc 2, 3-X/Window; Front-end software — Vision Data/Classified. AUDIOTEX: Hardware — Info-Connect. DISPLAY: Adv layout systems — QuarkXPress 3.2; Front-end hardware — 3-Ap/Mac II, 2-Ap/Mac ci, 1-Ap/Mac II VX; Front-end software — QuarkXPress, Adobe/Illustrator, Streamline. PRODUCTION: OCR software — Caere/OmniPage, QuarkXPress; Typesetters — 1-Hyphen/Copal, 1-Hyphen/Pelbox; Plate exposures — 1-Nu; Plate processors — Nat; Scanners — Ap/Mac SE; Production cameras — 1-SCREEN; Automatic film processors — 1-P, 1-LE; Film transporters — 1-LE; Color separation equipment (conventional) — 1-Ap/Mac IIfx, Adobe/Photoshop; Digital color separation equipment — Nikon/35mm, AG/Flatbed.
PRESSROOM: Line 1 — 10-G/Community single width; Folders — 1-G/SSC. MAILROOM: Inserters and stuffers — 4-MM; Bundle tyer — 1-MLN; Addressing machine — 1-Ch. LIBRARY: Electronic — Verity, Sun/Sparc. WIRE SERVICES: News — AP; Photos — AP; Receiving dishes — size-6ft, AP. BUSINESS COMPUTERS: Sun/Sparc 1; Applications: Vision Data; PCs & micros networked; PCs & main system networked.

CHAMBERSBURG
Franklin County

'90 U.S. Census- 16,647; E&P '96 Est. 17,053
ABC-NDM (90): 104,713 (HH 39,158)

Public Opinion
(e-mon to fri; m-sat)

Public Opinion, 77 N. Third St.; PO Box 499, Chambersburg, PA 17201; tel (717) 264-6161; fax (717) 264-2009. Gannett Co. Inc. group.
Circulation: 21,808(e); 21,808(m-sat); ABC Sept. 30, 1995.
Price: 35¢(d); 75¢(sat).
Advertising: Open inch rate $22.70(e); $22.70(m-sat). **Representative:** Gannett National Newspaper Sales.
News Services: AP, GNS. **Politics:** Independent. **Established:** 1869.
Special Editions: Bridal, Baby Yearbook, Chronologies (Jan); Business and Industry (Feb); Builder's Show, Car Care, NIE (Mar); Great Outdoors, Golf Card, Swing into Spring (Apr); Draw Mom, Reader's Choice Ballot, Flag Insert (May); Living in the Valley, Farm/Dairy, Reader's Choice Tab (June); Shippensburg Fair (July); Back-to-School, Franklin County Fair, Manufactured Housing, Pigskin Preview (Aug); Home Improvement, College Night (Sept); Chamber Pages (Oct); Gift Guide I, Auto Fest 3, Big Game, Gift Guide II (Nov); Gift Guide III, Songbook (Dec).
Special Weekly Sections: Your Money, Sports Extra (mon); Education, Business (tues); Food, Business, Home (wed); Business/Real Estate, Weekender (thur); Deeds/Permits, Religion, Health, Real Estate (fri); TV Book, Engagement/Brides, USA Weekend (sat).
Magazine: USA Weekend (sat).

GENERAL MANAGEMENT
Publisher Nancy Monaghan
Controller Christine Brew
ADVERTISING
Director Rob Paz
Manager-Sales Andy Faust
CIRCULATION
Director Thomas R Iacona
Asst Director Ronald Sisto III
Director-Customer Service Nancy Ramer
Manager-Home Delivery Mike Snyder
NEWS EXECUTIVES
Exec Editor Steve Davis
Managing Editor Lorrie DeFrank
EDITORS AND MANAGERS
Lifestyle Editor Ann Marie Sradromski
Sports Editor Tom Coccagna
Wire Editor Katy Hamilton
PRODUCTION
Director Ronda Jacobs
Asst Director Ronald John
Manager-Composing/Camera Patty Clugston

Market Information: Zoned editions; Split Run; TMC; ADS.
Mechanical available: Letterpress (direct); Black and 3 ROP colors; insert accepted — preprinted; page cut-offs — 22¾".
Mechanical specifications: Type page 13" x 21½"; E - 6 cols, 2 1/16", 1/8" between; A - 6 cols, 2 1/16", 1/8" between; C - 9 cols, 1 3/8", 1/16" between.
Commodity consumption: Newsprint 985 short tons; 1,055.1 metric tons; widths 27", 13½"; black ink 32,000 pounds; color ink 4,200 pounds; single pages printed 9,145; average pages per issue 24(d); single plates used 16,300.
Equipment: EDITORIAL: Front-end hardware — AT/5000; Front-end software — AT/5000; Printers — Teletype/40. CLASSIFIED: Front-end hardware — AT/5000; Front-end software — AT/5000; Printers — Teletype/40. DISPLAY: Adv layout systems — 6-Ap/Mac; Front-end hardware — 1-Ap/Mac IIci, 2-Ap/Mac fx, 2-Ap/Mac Quadra 700; Front-end software — Multi-Ad, QuarkXPress; Printers — MON/1200, Ap/Mac LaserWriter II; Other equipment — SCS. PRODUCTION: Typesetters — 2-COM/8645; Electronic picture desk — Lf/AP Leaf Picture Desk; Scanners — SCREEN/Scanner; Automatic film processors — SCREEN; Color separation equipment (conventional) — Ap/Mac, Adobe/Photoshop, 1-Ap/Power Mac 8100.
PRESSROOM: Line 1 — 6-G/Universal; Reels and stands — G; Press control system — CH. MAILROOM: Counter stackers — 2-QWI, 1-SH; Inserters and stuffers — MM/227 5-into-1; Bundle tyer — MLN; Addressing machine — Ch. WIRE SERVICES: News — AP, GNS; Receiving dishes — size-10ft, AP. BUSINESS COMPUTERS: IBM/AS-400; Applications: Gannett/Custom; PCs & main system networked.

CHARLEROI
See MONESSEN

CHESTER
Delaware

'90 U.S. Census- 41,856; E&P '96 Est. 38,851
ABC-NDM (90): 316,532 (HH 114,725)

Delaware County Daily Times (m-mon to fri; S)

Delaware County Daily Times, 500 Mildred Ave., Primos, PA 19018; tel (610) 622-8800. Goodson Newspaper group.
Circulation: 53,635(m); 51,164(S); ABC Sept. 30, 1995.
Price: 50¢(d); $1.00(S); $3.30/wk; $14.30/mo; $171.60/yr.
Advertising: Open inch rate $41.00(m); $41.00(S). **Representatives:** Landon Associates Inc.; Robert Hitchings & Co.
News Services: AP, States News Service. **Politics:** Independent. **Established:** 1876.
Not Published: Independence Day; Christmas (unless Sunday).
Special Editions: Education Guide, Super Bowl Auto Section (Jan); President's Day Auto Section, Bridal Guide, Swimsuit Guide (Feb); Progress, Celebrate St. Pat's, Prom Guide (Mar); Spring Home & Garden, Prom Guide, Easter Dine Out, Health Care, Truck & Van Special (Apr); Mother's Day Gift Guide, Spring Car Care Section, Restaurant Guide (May); Father's Day Gift Pages, Grad Tab (June); 55 & Up (July); Back-to-School, Softball (Aug); Football Issue, Fall Bridal (Sept); Fall Car Care, Energy & Home Improvement Section (Oct); Where to Dine Thanksgiving, Thanksgiving Day Edition (Nov); Christmas Greetings, Great Gifting, Celebrate New Year's Eve (Dec).
Special Weekly Sections: Best Food Day, Birth Announcements (wed); Weddings & Engagements (thur); Best Food Day, Weddings & Engagements, Real Estate Transfers, Travel (S); TV/Cable, Business, Entertainment (daily).
Magazines: USA Weekend; Sunday Comics; TV Times; Cover Story.

CORPORATE OFFICERS
President David N Hurwitz
Senior Vice Pres David Carr
GENERAL MANAGEMENT
Publisher Frank Gothie
Controller John Tashjian
ADVERTISING
Manager-Retail Elaine D'Arienzo
Asst Manager-Retail William Breingan
Manager-Classified Thomas Abbott
Manager-Classified Display Al Holcombe
CIRCULATION
Director Wayne Ziegler
NEWS EXECUTIVES
Editor Andy Reynolds
Managing Editor Linda DeMeglio
Assoc Editor Phil Heron
EDITORS AND MANAGERS
Automotive Editor Len Casterline
Business/Finance Editor Joe Monchecourt
City Editor Bonnie Healy
City Editor (Night) Len Labarth
Columnist Gil Spencer
Editorial Page Editor Andy Reynolds
Entertainment/Amusements Editor Tricia Cofiel
Fashion/Style Editor Tricia Cofiel
Harrisburg Bureau Editor Harold D Ellis
Librarian Barbara Budgick
National Editor Andy Reynolds
News Editor Phil Heron
Photo Editor Phil Heron
Political/Government Editor Andy Reynolds
Real Estate Editor Len Labarth
Science/Technology Editor Andy Reynolds
Sports Editor Bob Tennant
Television/Film Editor Andy Reynolds
Theater/Music Editor Andy Reynolds
Wire Editor Jim Atkins
Youth Editor Tricia Cofiel
PRODUCTION
Director Michael D'Arienzo
Foreman-Pressroom Tom Egolf

Market Information: Zoned editions; Split Run; TMC.
Mechanical available: Offset; insert accepted — preprinted, flexi's product samples (flat)card-stock; page cut-offs — 22¾".
Mechanical specifications: Type page 10¼" x 14.25"; E - 5 cols, 2", .03" between; A - 5 cols, 2", .03" between; C - 7 cols, 1 5/8", .03" between.
Commodity consumption: Newsprint 5,000 short tons; widths 30", 45", 60"; black ink 127,000 pounds; color ink 1,490 pounds; single pages printed 24,000; average pages per issue 72(d), 80(S); single plates used 6,100.
Equipment: EDITORIAL: Front-end hardware — PC; Front-end software — Dewar; Other equipment — Lf/AP Leaf Picture Desk. CLASSIFIED: Front-end hardware — PC, Raycet; Front-end software — Cx, Intertext. DISPLAY: Front-end hardware — Ap/Mac Quadra 840 AU; Front-end software — Multi-Ad 3.6.3; Printers — HP. PRODUCTION: Pagination software — MESI/ALS 1.7, MESI/CLS 1.6, MESI/ELS 1.6; Typesetters — New Gen/660 B Imager Plus 12; Plate exposures — 1-Nu; Plate processors — 4-LE; Electronic picture desk — Lf/AP Leaf Picture Desk; Scanners — 2-ECR/Autokon; Production cameras — C/Spartan Vertical, C/Spartan III; Color separation equipment (conventional) — Ap/Macs, Lf, HP/IIIC, Sharp.
PRESSROOM: Line 1 — 5-HI/1650; Line 2 — 1-HI/1650; Press drives — 300-HP/DC SCR (460-Volt; 3 phase); Folders — HI/1650; Pasters — 4-MEG; Reels and stands — 1-Rewinder/Reel Stand. MAILROOM: Counter stackers — 4-HL; Inserters and stuffers — 2-GMA/SLS 1000 6-into-1; Bundle tyer — 2-Dynaric, 1-MLN; Wrapping singles — 1-Na; Addressing machine — 1-Na; Mailroom control system — GMA. LIBRARY: Electronic — SMS/Stauffer; Combination — electronic. WIRE SERVICES: News — AP, RN; Stock tables — AP; Syndicates — United Media, Chronicle, LATS, Universal Press, NAS, Creators, WP; Receiving dishes — AP. BUSINESS COMPUTERS: IBM/Sys 36; PCs & micros networked.

CLAIRTON
See McKEESPORT

CLEARFIELD-CURWENSVILLE
Clearfield County

'90 U.S. Census- 9,557 (Clearfield 6,633; Curwensville 2,924); E&P '96 Est. 8,714 (Clearfield 5,940; Curwensville 2,774)
ABC-NDM (90): 64,931 (HH 24,799)

The Progress (e-mon to sat)

The Progress, 206 E. Locust St.; PO Box 291, Clearfield, PA 16830-0291; tel (814) 765-5581; fax (814) 765-5165.
Circulation: 14,972(e); 14,972(e-sat); ABC Sept. 30, 1995.
Price: 35¢(d); 35¢(sat); $2.00/wk (carrier); $8.00/mo (carrier), $11.50/mo (out-of-state); $93.00/yr (carrier), $128.00/yr (out-of-state).
Advertising: Open inch rate $15.70(e); $15.70(e-sat). **Representative:** Landon Associates Inc.
News Service: AP. **Politics:** Independent. **Established:** 1913.
Not Published: New Year; Memorial Day; Independence Day; Labor Day; Thanksgiving; Christmas.
Special Editions: Yearly Senior Lifestyles, Teen, Business (monthly); Bridal; County Fair; Football Tab; Hunting; Christmas.
Special Weekly Sections: Food (mon); Outdoors (wed); Postscript TV (fri); USA Weekend (sat).
Broadcast Affiliates: Clearfield Broadcasters, Licensee of WCPA-AM & WQYX-FM, Clearfield, PA.

CORPORATE OFFICERS
Board Chairman William K Ulerich
President Margaret E Krebs
Vice Pres Alethea M Ulerich
Secretary Ann K Law
Treasurer/Controller F Clair Thompson
GENERAL MANAGEMENT
Publisher William K Ulerich
Assoc Publisher Margaret E Krebs
Asst Publisher/Business Manager Ann K Law
Manager-Credit Margaret E Krebs
Purchasing Agent Margaret E Krebs
ADVERTISING
Exec-Marketing Patrick P Domico
Manager-Display Jeannine Selfridge
Manager-Classified Martha Lynch
CIRCULATION
Manager Cindy Aughenbaugh
NEWS EXECUTIVES
Exec Editor L B Mather
Editor Michelle Moyer
EDITORS AND MANAGERS
Photo Department Manager Clair M Law
Sports Editor Todd Irwin
PRODUCTION
Foreman-Pressroom Larry Ruffner
Superintendent-Plant Charles N Natoli

Market Information: TMC.
Mechanical available: Offset; Black and 3 ROP colors; insert accepted — preprinted; page cut-offs — 22¾".
Mechanical specifications: Type page 13" x 21½"; E - 6 cols, 2 1/16", 1/8" between; A - 6 cols, 2 1/16", 1/8" between; C - 8 cols, 1 5/8", 1/16" between.
Commodity consumption: Newsprint 877 short tons; widths 28", 14"; black ink 10,600 pounds; color ink 300 pounds; average pages per issue 23(d); single plates used 10,000.
Equipment: EDITORIAL: Front-end hardware — COM/One System; Printers — 4-NewGen. CLASSIFIED: Front-end hardware — COM/One System; Front-end software — COM/One Sys-

Pennsylvania I-347

tem; Printers — NewGen. PRODUCTION: Typesetters — NewGen; Plate exposures — 1-Nu; Plate processors — 1-Nat/250.
PRESSROOM: Line 1 — 9-G/Community; Folders — 1-G; Press control system — Fin. MAILROOM: Counter stackers — 1-BG/Count-O-Veyor; Inserters and stuffers — KAN/320; Bundle tyer — Sa. WIRE SERVICES: News — AP; Receiving dishes — size-10m, AP. BUSINESS COMPUTERS: IBM; PCs & main system networked.

CONNELLSVILLE-SOUTH CONNELLSVILLE
Fayette County

'90 U.S. Census- 11,433 (Connellsville 9,229; South Connellsville 2,204); E&P '96 Est. 10,547 (Connellsville 8,414; South Connellsville 2,133)
ABC-CZ (90): 11,433 (HH 4,681)

The Daily Courier
(e-mon to fri; m-sat)

The Daily Courier, 127 W. Apple St.; PO Box 864, Connellsville, PA 15425; tel (412) 628-2000; fax (412) 628-4496. Thomson Newspapers group.
Circulation: 11,196(e); 11,196(m-sat); ABC Sept. 30, 1995.
Price: 35¢(d); 35¢(sat); $1.80/wk (carrier), $2.00/wk (motor route); $9.40/mo (mail), $38.50/3mo; $92.10/yr (carrier), $130.05/yr (mail), $104.00/yr (motor route).
Advertising: Open inch rate $15.46(e); $15.46(m-sat). **Representative:** Thomson Newspapers.
News Service: AP. **Politics:** Independent. **Established:** 1902.
Not Published: New Year; Memorial Day; Independence Day; Labor Day; Thanksgiving; Christmas.
Special Editions: Bridal Edition (Jan); Progress (Mar); Visitor's Guide (Apr, May); Bridal Edition, Visitor's Guide (June); Fayette County Fair, Visitor's Guide (July); Football Preview, Visitor's Guide (Aug); Visitor's Guide (Sept, Oct); Christmas Tab, Visitor's Guide (Nov); Year in Review (Dec); Celebrate-Getting the Most Out of your Senior Years (Monthly).
Special Weekly Sections: Best Food Day (mon); Business & Finance (tues); Education (wed); Entertainment (thur); Restaurant Page, Seniors, TV Week (fri); TV Grid (daily).

GENERAL MANAGEMENT
Publisher/General Manager Andrew B Kniceley
ADVERTISING
Director Nancy Henry
CIRCULATION
Manager-Sales Kim Adamo
Manager-Distribution Roger Rhodes
NEWS EXECUTIVE
Managing Editor Shawnee Lee Culbertson
EDITORS AND MANAGERS
City Editor Rose Snyder
Features Editor Roxanne Abramowitz
Sports Editor Jim Damp
PRODUCTION
Manager Harry M Fox
Foreman-Pressroom David Hatter

Market Information: TMC.
Mechanical available: Offset; Black and 2 ROP colors; insert accepted — preprinted; page cutoffs — 22¾".
Mechanical specifications: Type page 13" x 21½"; E - 6 cols, 2¹⁄₁₆", ⅛" between; A - 6 cols, 2¹⁄₁₆", ⅛" between; C - 9 cols, 1⅜", ¹⁄₁₆" between.
Commodity consumption: Newsprint 372 short tons; widths 27½", 13¾"; black ink 8,736 pounds; color ink 1,148 pounds; single pages printed 4,932; average pages per issue 16(d); single plates used 5,500.
Equipment: EDITORIAL: Front-end hardware — 10-Mk, Ap/Mac; Front-end software — QuarkXPress. CLASSIFIED: Front-end hardware — 3-Mk. DISPLAY: Adv layout systems — 3-Ap/Mac w/File Server; Front-end software — QuarkXPress, Multi-Ad/Creator; Printers — 1-Ap/Mac LaserPrinter, 2-LaserPrinter/11x17. PRODUCTION: Typesetters — 2-XIT/Clipper; Plate exposures — 2-Nu; Plate processors — 1-Nat/A250; Production cameras — 1-B, 2-Nu, 1-SCREEN; Automatic film processors — 1-LE.
PRESSROOM: Line 1 — 6-KP; Folders — 1-KP. MAILROOM: Bundle tyer — OVL. WIRE SERVICES: News — AP; Photos — AP; Receiving dishes — size-3m. BUSINESS COMPUTERS: Applications: NCR/Software.

CORRY
Erie County

'90 U.S. Census- 7,216; E&P '96 Est. 7,272

Corry Evening Journal
(e-mon to sat)

Corry Evening Journal, 28 W. South St., Corry, PA 16407; tel (814) 665-8291; fax (814) 664-2288. Hollinger International Inc. group.
Circulation: 4,106(e); 4,106(e-sat); Sworn Sept. 28, 1995.
Price: 35¢(d); 35¢(sat); $72.00/yr (mail), $78.00/yr (carrier).
Advertising: Open inch rate $6.30(e); $6.30(e-sat). **Representative:** Landon Associates Inc.
News Service: AP. **Politics:** Independent. **Established:** 1898.
Not Published: New York; Memorial Day; Independence Day; Labor Day; Thanksgiving; Christmas.

GENERAL MANAGEMENT
Publisher George R Sample
General Manager Kevin Downey
ADVERTISING
Manager Linnell Ashby
CIRCULATION
Manager Terri Malek
NEWS EXECUTIVE
Managing Editor Steve Bishop
EDITORS AND MANAGERS
Sports Editor Doug Kates
Women's Editor Michelle Sporer
PRODUCTION
Foreman Carl Wascak

Mechanical available: Offset; Black and 3 ROP colors; insert accepted — preprinted; page cutoffs — 22¼".
Mechanical specifications: Type page 13¾" x 21½"; E - 6 cols, 2¹⁄₁₆", ⅛" between; A - 6 cols, 2¹⁄₁₆", ⅛" between; C - 6 cols, 2¹⁄₁₆", ⅛" between.
Commodity consumption: Newsprint 300 short tons; widths 34", 27½"; average pages per issue 14(d).
Equipment: EDITORIAL: Front-end hardware — 1-HI, 1-TC. PRODUCTION: Typesetters — Ap/Mac Laser; Scanners — 1-L/32; Production cameras — SCREEN; Automatic film processors — 1-C; Film transporters — 1-LE.
PRESSROOM: Line 1 — 5-G; Press control system — Fin. MAILROOM: Bundle tyer — 1-Sa; Addressing machine — 1-Am. WIRE SERVICES: News — AP; Receiving dishes — size-9ft, AP.

CURWENSVILLE
See CLEARFIELD

DANVILLE
Montour County

'90 U.S. Census- 5,165; E&P '96 Est. 5,104

The Danville News
(e-mon to fri; m-sat)

The Danville News, 14 E. Mahoning St.; PO Box 200, Danville, PA 17821-0020; tel (717) 275-3235; fax (717) 275-7624. Stauffer Media Inc. group.
Circulation: 3,563(e); 3,563(m-sat); Sworn Sept. 29, 1994.
Price: 50¢(d); 50¢(sat); $2.00/wk; $6.50/mo; $83.20/yr.
Advertising: Open inch rate $6.00(e); $6.00(m-sat). **Representative:** Landon Associates Inc.
News Service: AP. **Politics:** Independent. **Established:** 1897.
Not Published: New Year; Memorial Day; Independence Day; Labor Day; Thanksgiving; Christmas.
Advertising not accepted: Vending machine.
Special Editions: Progress (Mar); Real Estate/Home Improvement (Apr, May, June); Back-to-School (Aug); Real Estate/Home Improvement (Sept); Guidebook (Oct); Christmas (Dec).
Magazine: TV Guide (fri).

CORPORATE OFFICER
President L W Stauffer
GENERAL MANAGEMENT
General Manager D F Jeffrey
Manager-Business Ed Christine
ADVERTISING
Director Donna Keefer
Manager-Classified Michelle Dunn
CIRCULATION
Manager-Distribution Maureen Tinsman
Manager Ed Christine
NEWS EXECUTIVES
Editor Pam Christine
Managing Editor Holly Brandon
PRODUCTION
Superintendent Larry Kauffman

Mechanical available: Offset; Black and 3 ROP colors; insert accepted — preprinted; page cutoffs — 22¾".
Mechanical specifications: Type page 13" x 21½"; E - 6 cols, 2¹⁄₁₆", ⅛" between; A - 6 cols, 2¹⁄₁₆", ⅛" between; C - 9 cols, 1⁵⁄₁₆", ⅛" between.
Commodity consumption: Newsprint 654 short tons; widths 28", 14"; black ink 3,750 pounds; color ink 200 pounds; single pages printed 5,000; average pages per issue 16(d); single plates used 2,750.
Equipment: EDITORIAL: Front-end hardware — Mk/1100 Plus; Front-end software — Mk/1100 Plus; Printers — Ap/Mac Laser NTX. CLASSIFIED: Front-end hardware — IBM; Front-end software — Suntype/Classad; Printers — Ap/Mac Laser NTX. DISPLAY: Front-end hardware — 2-Ap/Mac II, Ap/Mac NTX; Front-end software — Multi-Ad/Creator; Other equipment — Ap/Mac Scanner, Ap/Mac CD Reader. PRODUCTION: Platemaking systems — P/Pakolith; Plate exposures — 1-Nu; Plate processors — Roconex; Production cameras — DAI/Screen; Automatic film processors — P.
PRESSROOM: Line 1 — 6-G/Community; Folders — 1-G/SC, 1-G/Community. MAILROOM: Counter stackers — BG/Count-O-Veyor; Bundle tyer — OVL/Constellation. WIRE SERVICES: News — AP. BUSINESS COMPUTERS: 4-IBM; Applications: Synaptic: Accts receivable, Circ; CYMA: Gen ledger.

DONORA
See MONESSEN

DOYLESTOWN
Bucks County

'90 U.S. Census- 8,575; E&P '96 Est. 8,459
ABC-NDM (90): 309,483 (HH 113,709)

The Intelligencer/Record
(m-mon to fri; S)

The Intelligencer/Record, 333 N. Broad St.; PO Box 858, Doylestown, PA 18901; tel (215) 345-3000; fax (215) 345-3150. Calkins Newspapers group.
Circulation: 45,478(m); 51,712(S); ABC Sept. 30, 1995.
Price: 35¢(d); $1.25(S); $3.20/wk; $197.00/yr.
Advertising: Open inch rate $96.75(m); $101.25(S). **Representative:** Sawyer-Ferguson-Walker Co.
News Service: AP. **Politics:** Independent. **Established:** 1804.
Special Editions: Your Money, Savings (Jan); Health, Fitness, Brides (Feb); Home (Mar); Real Estate, Garden, NIE, Gardening (Apr); Restaurant Guide (May); Brides, Summer Savings (June); Coupon Book (July); Fall, School Guide (Aug); Sports Guide (Sept); Cookbook, Auto '97 (Oct); Shopping Guide (Nov); Holiday Gifts, Caroling Book (Dec).
Magazines: Parade; Local Entertainment Guide; TV Book, TV Time (S).

CORPORATE OFFICERS
President Grover Friend
Vice Pres Charles P Smith
Secretary Carolyn C Smith
Treasurer Edward J Birch
GENERAL MANAGEMENT
Publisher Charles P Smith
General Manager Charles P Smith
Asst General Manager Bob Mayer
Controller Timothy J Weaver
ADVERTISING
Director Rosemary Rocconi
Manager-Retail Judy Isely
Manager-Classified Karen Wohl
TELECOMMUNICATIONS
Audiotex Manager Ken Kress
CIRCULATION
Director William B Lobecker
NEWS EXECUTIVES
Exec Editor Lanny Morgnanesi
Managing Editor Joan Bastel
EDITORS AND MANAGERS
Business Editor Stacy Briggs
Editorial Page Editor Alan Kerr
Entertainment/Amusements Editor Trilla Ramage
Outdoor Editor Bob Mayer
MANAGEMENT INFORMATION SERVICES
Data Processing Manager Bill Clark
PRODUCTION
Director Bob Mayer
Foreman-Composing Bob Williams
Foreman-Pressroom Tom Newman

Market Information: Zoned editions; Split Run; TMC; Operate audiotex.
Mechanical available: Offset; Black and 3 ROP colors; insert accepted — preprinted, odd size accepted; page cut-offs — 22½".
Mechanical specifications: Type page 13" x 21½"; E - 6 cols, 2¹⁄₁₆", ⅛" between; A - 6 cols, 2¹⁄₁₆", ⅛" between; C - 9 cols, 1⅜", ¹⁄₁₆" between.
Commodity consumption: Newsprint 4,200 short tons; widths 27", 13½"; single pages printed 15,000; average pages per issue 38(d), 64(S).
Equipment: EDITORIAL: Front-end hardware — 14-IBM/3278, 6-IBM/3179; Front-end software — IBM/PrinText; Printers — 1-IBM/3287. CLASSIFIED: Front-end hardware — 10-IBM/3279; Front-end software — Cras; Printers — 1-IBM/3287. AUDIOTEX: Hardware — PEP. DISPLAY: Adv layout systems — IBM/PC, SCS/Layout 8000; Front-end hardware — 3-Ap/Mac, 3-PC/486; Front-end software — Archetype; Printers — IBM/3287. PRODUCTION: Typesetters — 2-AU/Micro 5, 1-New-Gen/Laser; Plate exposures — 2-Nu/Flip Top FT40L; Plate processors — Nat/A-250; Scanners — 2-Dest/Scanner; Production cameras — 1-C/Spartan II, 1-AG/6000; Automatic film processors — 1-LE/LD24, 1-C/66T; Film transporters — 1-LE; Shrink lenses — 1-CK Optical/SQU-7; Color separation equipment (conventional) — RZ/4050, Lf/AP Leaf Picture Desk; Digital color separation equipment — Lf/Leafscan 35.
PRESSROOM: Line 1 — 10-G/Urbanite; Press control system — Fin. MAILROOM: Counter stackers — 1-QWI; Bundle tyer — 1-Power Strap, 1-MLN; Wrapping singles — 1-Sa; Addressing machine — 1-KR. WIRE SERVICES: News — AP; Stock tables — AP; Receiving dishes — AP. BUSINESS COMPUTERS: IBM/4381, IBM/3090; PCs & micros networked; PCs & main system networked.

DU BOIS
Clearfield County

'90 U.S. Census- 8,286; E&P '96 Est. 7,538
ABC-CZ (90): 10,081 (HH 4,231)

The Courier-Express
(e-mon to fri)
Tri-County Sunday (S)

The Courier-Express/Tri-County Sunday, 500 Jeffers St.; PO Box 407, Du Bois, PA 15081; tel (814) 371-4200; fax (814) 371-3241. Independent Publications Inc. group.
Circulation: 10,572(e); 13,775(S); ABC Sept. 30, 1995.
Price: 50¢(d); $1.00(S); $9.00/mo; $103.00/yr.
Advertising: Open inch rate $15.60(e); $15.60 (S). **Representative:** Landon Associates Inc.
News Service: AP. **Politics:** Independent. **Established:** 1879.
Not Published: New Year; Memorial Day; Independence Day; Labor Day; Thanksgiving; Christmas.
Special Editions: Home Improvement Month; Graduation; Spring Bridal; Mother's Day; Father's Day; Back-to-School; Hunters; Fall Sports; Fall Fashion; Fall Bridal; Christmas Kick-off; Christmas Countdown Edition; Christmas Greetings; Home & Garden; Fall Car Care; Cook Book; Spring Car Care; Summer.
Special Weekly Sections: Business & Finance; Farm & Grange; Outdoors; Church Page.
Magazine: CE TV (TV Section Tab).

CORPORATE OFFICERS
Board Chairman/President William L McLean III
Vice Pres/Publisher W Dock Lias

I-348 Pennsylvania

Secretary Joseph A Grecco
Treasurer Charles E Catherwood

GENERAL MANAGEMENT

Purchasing Agent W Dock Lias

ADVERTISING

Director Linda L Smith
Manager-Classified Dory Ferra

TELECOMMUNICATIONS

Audiotex Manager Joseph A Grecco

CIRCULATION

Manager James Norwood

NEWS EXECUTIVE

Managing Editor Dennis Bonavita

EDITORS AND MANAGERS

Business/Finance Editor Nick Hoffman
Editorial Page Editor Dennis Bonavita
Farm/Agriculture Editor Alice Sylvis
Living/Lifestyle Editor Barbara Azzato
Metro Editor Nick Hoffman
Sports Editor Rich Rhoades
Sunday Editor Joy Norwood
Women's Editor Barbara Azzato

PRODUCTION

Foreman-Composing Jake Caylor
Foreman-Press Fred Leech Jr

Market Information: TMC; Operate audiotex.
Mechanical available: Offset; Black and 3 ROP colors; insert accepted — preprinted; page cut-offs — 22¾".
Mechanical specifications: Type page 13" x 21½"; E - 6 cols, $2\frac{1}{16}$", .14" between; A - 6 cols, $2\frac{1}{16}$", .14" between; C - 8 cols, 1½", .14" between.
Commodity consumption: Newsprint 658 short tons; widths 27½", 13¾"; black ink 11,500 pounds; color ink 520 pounds; single pages printed 7,808; average pages per issue 22(d), 44(S); single plates used 7,120.
Equipment: EDITORIAL: Front-end hardware — Mk, 3-Ap/Mac fx. CLASSIFIED: Front-end hardware — Mk; Printers — 1-TI/810 Line Printer, 1-OTC/Line Printer. AUDIOTEX: Hardware — Northgate/386, Info/Direct. DISPLAY: Adv layout systems — 5-Mk, Ap/Mac IIcx, 2-Ap/Mac Quadra 650. PRODUCTION: Pagination software — QPS 3.3, Mk; Typesetters — 2-Ap/Mac LaserWriter NTX, XIT/Clipper, MON/Express 1270; Plate exposures — 1-Nu/Flip Top; Plate processors — Nat/A-340; Production cameras — SCREEN/20 x 24 Horizontal Low Bed; Automatic film processors — Kk/65A Kodakmatic, LE, PC/1800; Digital color separation equipment — Imapro, Lf/AP Leaf Picture Desk.
PRESSROOM: Line 1 — 8-WPC/Atlas (w/2-Quadra-Color Unit); Line 2 — 8-KP/Newsking. MAILROOM: Counter stackers — 2-BG/Count-O-Veyor; Inserters and stuffers — 1-MM/227E; Bundle tyer — 2-Sa, Power Strap/250; Other mailroom equipment — MM/1509 TV Stitcher-Trimmer. WIRE SERVICES: News — AP; Receiving dishes — size-10ft, AP. BUSINESS COMPUTERS: IBM/RISC 6000; Applications: Bookkeeping, Circ.

DUQUESNE

See McKEESPORT

EAST STROUDSBURG

See STROUDSBURG

EASTON-BETHLEHEM, PA-PHILLIPSBURG, NJ

Northampton County, PA
Warren County, NJ

'90 U.S. Census- 113,461 (Easton, PA 26,276; Bethlehem, PA 71,428; Phillipsburg, NJ 15,757); E&P '96 Est. 114,304 (Easton, PA 26,485; Bethlehem, PA 72,420; Phillipsburg, NJ 15,399)
ABC-NDM (90): 329,800 (HH 120,856)

The Express-Times

(m-mon to sat; S)

The Express-Times, 30 N. Fourth St.; PO Box 391, Easton, PA 18044-0391; tel (610) 258-7171; fax (610) 258-6794 (Pub). MediaNews Inc. group.

Circulation: 47,835(m); 47,835(m-sat); 47,671(S); ABC Sept. 30, 1995.
Price: 35¢(d); 35¢(sat); $1.00(S); $3.10/wk (carrier); $12.40/mo (carrier); $148.30/yr (carrier).
Advertising: Open inch rate $32.75(m); $32.75(m-sat); $32.75(S). **Representative:** Papert Companies.
News Services: AP, KRT, LAT-WP. **Politics:** Independent. **Established:** 1855.
Special Editions: Bridal Tab, Health Tab (Jan); Progress (Feb); Health Tab, Home & Garden I (Mar); Home & Garden II & III, Mother's Day (Apr); Bridal Tab, Senior Citizens (May); Car Care, Newcomers, Health Tab (June); Warren County Fair, Musikfest Preview (July); Back-to-School, Musikfest Guide (Aug); Football, Home Improvement (Sept); New Car Review, Energy Guide, Health Tab (Oct); Shop Early, Thanksgiving Gift Guide (Nov); Basketball & Wrestling Tab, Holiday Spirit, Letters to Santa & Last Minute Gift Guide, Year in Review (Dec).
Special Weekly Sections: Sports Plus (mon); Best Food Day (wed); Enjoy, Entertainment Guide (fri); At Home, Building & Real Estate Guide (sat); TV Book TV Magazine (S).
Magazines: Enjoy/Entertainment (fri); At Home (sat); TV Update Quarterfold, USA Weekend (S).

GENERAL MANAGEMENT

Publisher Timothy M Sowecke
General Manager David McCollum
Controller Gary A Snow
Manager-Credit Kenneth C Snyder
Purchasing Agent Diane Cremer
Manager-Accounting Donald Roseberry

ADVERTISING

Director Ernest S Reed
Manager-Retail David Yanoshik
Manager-Retail Jane Pierce
Manager-Major Accounts/National Donald Lewars
Manager-Promotion Richard A King
Supervisor-Special Sections K J Galati
Supervisor-Service Pam James
Inside Supervisor-Classified Christine Evans

TELECOMMUNICATIONS

Audiotex Supervisor Sherry Kober
Manager-Communications Walter Benack

CIRCULATION

Director Robert Schwenk
Manager-Home Delivery Frank Wehinger

NEWS EXECUTIVES

Editor Frank Keegan
Editorial Page Editor James Flagg

EDITORS AND MANAGERS

Action Line Editor (Action Express) Anthony Salamone
Amusements Editor Robert Hays
Area Editor (PA) Will Scheihing
Area Editor (NJ) Gregory Karp
Area Editor (Bethlehem) Joe Lyons
Automotive Editor K J Galati
Books Editor Robert Hays
Business/Finance Editor Jeff Ward
City Editor Terry Anderson
Copy Desk Chief Scott Toole
Editorial Page Editor James Flagg
Fashion/Food Editor Robert Hays
Features Editor Robert Hays
Films/Theater Editor Robert Hays
Graphics Design Editor Tony Rhodin
Home/Garden Editor Robert Hays
Librarian Carol King
Living/Lifestyle Editor Robert Hays
Music Editor Robert Hays
National Editor Scott Toole
News Editor Scott Toole
Photo Department Manager Midic Castelletti
Political/Government Editor Scott Toole
Real Estate Editor K J Galati
Religion Editor Robert Hays
Sports Editor Edward Laubach
Wire Editor Scott Toole

MANAGEMENT INFORMATION SERVICES

Data Processing Manager Walter Benack

PRODUCTION

Manager-Plant Operations Barry L Miers
Manager-Composing Jack Moser
Manager-Mailroom James Enea
Manager-Pressroom Charles Smith

Market Information: Zoned editions; Split Run; TMC; Operate audiotex.
Mechanical available: Letterpress (direct); Black and 3 ROP colors; insert accepted — preprinted; page cut-offs — 22¾".
Mechanical specifications: Type page 13" x 21¼"; E - 6 cols, $2\frac{1}{16}$", ⅛" between; A - 6 cols, $2\frac{1}{16}$", ⅛" between; C - 10 cols, $1\frac{3}{16}$", $\frac{1}{16}$" between.
Commodity consumption: Newsprint 5,136 short tons; 4,660 metric tons; widths 55", 41¼", 27½"; black ink 168,700 pounds; color ink 21,450 pounds; single pages printed 15,198; average pages per issue 39(d), 56(S); single plates used 26,739.
Equipment: EDITORIAL: Front-end hardware — 51-CText; Front-end software — CText; Printers — 1-C.Itoh/5000, 1-C.Itoh/800. CLASSIFIED: Front-end hardware — 9-CText; Front-end software — CText; Printers — 1-C.Itoh/5000. AUDIOTEX: Hardware — Brite Voice Systems/Bus-2000; Supplier name — Brite Voice Systems, Comstock. DISPLAY: Adv layout systems — SCS/Layout 8000; Front-end hardware — Dell/310 fileserver; Front-end software — SCS/Layout 8000; Printers — Lips/Plus. PRODUCTION: Typesetters — 3-V/5100; Platemaking systems — Na; Plate exposures — Na/Starlite, Mini Star; Plate processors — Na/NP-40, Twin Star; Electronic picture desk — 2-Lf/AP Leaf Picture Desk; Scanners — ECR/Autokon 1000; Production cameras — 1-C/Spartan II; Automatic film processors — 2-LE/LD-24; Reproportion units — 1-Pro-Flex; Film transporters — C; Shrink lenses — 1-CK Optical.
PRESSROOM: Line 1 — 6-Sc/Letterpress, 2-Sc/Cl deck; Folders — 2-Sc; Press control system — HES. MAILROOM: Counter stackers — 3-HL/Monitor, 1-MM; Inserters and stuffers — HI/1372; Bundle tyer — 2-OVL, 1-Mg; Addressing machine — 1-BH, 1-MG. WIRE SERVICES: News — AP Datastream, AP Datafeatures, THO; Photos — AP; Stock tables — AP SelectStox; Syndicates — KRT, WP, LATS; Receiving dishes — AP. BUSINESS COMPUTERS: DEC/VAX 4000-300, 4-PC/286-386, 3-PC/486 LapTop Notebook; Applications: CJ/AIM: Accts payable, Gen ledger, Payroll; CIS, Lotus 1-2-3, WordPerfect: Gen ledger, Payroll, Accts payable; CJ; PCs & main system networked.

ELLWOOD CITY

Lawrence and Beaver Counties

'90 U.S. Census- 8,894; E&P '96 Est. 8,073

Ellwood City Ledger

(e-mon to sat)

Ellwood City Ledger, 835 Lawrence Ave., Ellwood City, PA 16117; tel (412) 758-5573; fax (412) 758-2410.

Circulation: 6,671(e); 6,671(e-sat); Sworn Sept. 30, 1994.
Price: 35¢(d); 35¢(sat); $1.70/wk (carrier); $7.35/mo; $81.25/yr.
Advertising: Open inch rate $9.69(e); $9.69(e-sat). **Representatives:** Landon Associates Inc.; US Suburban Press.
News Service: AP. **Established:** 1920.
Not Published: New Year; Memorial Day; Independence Day; Labor Day; Thanksgiving; Christmas.
Special Editions: Lawn and Garden (Mar); Annual Progress Edition, Bridal Edition (Apr); Car Care (May); Visitor's Guide (June); Arts, Crafts and Food Festival (July); Fall Bridal Edition (Aug); Home Improvement (Sept); Health Care (Oct).
Special Weekly Sections: Food Day (mon); Food Day (wed & sat).

CORPORATE OFFICER

President W C Kegel

GENERAL MANAGEMENT

Publisher W Ryan Kegel
General Manager Scott R Kegel

ADVERTISING

Director Dom A Viccari

CIRCULATION

Manager E Crawford
Asst Manager B Prestopine

NEWS EXECUTIVE

Editor K Kastner

EDITOR AND MANAGER

Action Line Editor K Kastner

PRODUCTION

Foreman-Pressroom Tony Woloszyn

Market Information: Zoned editions; TMC.
Mechanical available: Offset; black; insert accepted — preprinted, single sheet; page cut-offs — 22¾".
Mechanical specifications: Type page 13" x 21"; E - 6 cols, 2.07", ⅛" between; A - 6 cols, 2.07", ⅛" between; C - 6 cols, 2.07", ⅛" between.
Commodity consumption: Newsprint 816 short tons; widths 27½", 13¾"; black ink 18,400 pounds; color ink 1,400 pounds; single pages printed 8,304; average pages per issue 16(d); single plates used 8,600.
Equipment: EDITORIAL: Front-end hardware — 14-PC; Front-end software — Newscraft; Printers — Dataproducts/1560; Other equipment — Lf/AP Leaf Picture Desk. CLASSIFIED: Front-end hardware — 4-PC; Front-end software — System Facilities/Classcraft; Printers — QMS/860+. DISPLAY: Adv layout systems — 3-Ap/Power Mac, 1-Ap/Mac fx, 1-Ap/Mac LC; Front-end hardware — 2-Ap/Mac Cx, Ap/Mac; Front-end software — DTI/Adspeed, Aldus/PageMaker, QuarkXPress; Printers — QMS/860+; Other equipment — Epson/Scanner. PRODUCTION: Typesetters — QMS/860+ 1200dpi plain paper; Plate exposures — 1-Nu; Plate processors — 1-K; Production cameras — 1-B; Automatic film processors — 1-LE. PRESSROOM: Line 1 — 5-G/Community; Folders — 1-G/SSC. MAILROOM: Inserters and stuffers — 1-KAN (w/5 stations); Bundle tyer — 2-EAM/Mosca; Addressing machine — 2-Ch. WIRE SERVICES: News — AP; Receiving dishes — AP. BUSINESS COMPUTERS: 1-ATT/Unix, Wyse; Applications: Vision Data; PCs & micros networked.

ERIE

Erie County

'90 U.S. Census- 108,718; E&P '96 Est. 100,789
ABC-CZ (90): 191,734 (HH 72,913)

Morning News (m-mon to fri)
Erie Daily Times (e-mon to fri)
Weekender (m-sat)
Times-News (S)

Morning News/Erie Daily Times, Times Sq. W. 12th & Sassafras Sts., Erie, PA 16534; tel (814) 870-1600; fax (814) 870-1615; e-mail retail@timesnews.com; web site http://www.timesnews.com. Times Publishing Inc. group.

Circulation: 32,307(m); 37,404(e); 61,534 (m-sat); 99,491(S); ABC Sept. 30, 1995.
Price: 35¢(d); 35¢(sat); $1.50(S); $3.00/wk (m & S), $4.25/wk (m,e & S), $2.75/wk (m, e).
Advertising: Open inch rate $40.85(m); $40.85(e); $40.85(m-sat); $58.60(S). **Representative:** Landon Associates Inc.
News Services: AP, LAT-WP, KRT. **Politics:** Independent. **Established:** 1888 (Times), 1949 (Times-News), 1957 (News).
Not Published: Christmas.
Advertising not accepted: Some mail order.
Special Editions: Bridal, Taxes (Jan); Annual Progress Edition, Builders Awards, Valentines, Tax Guide, Home Remodeling, Auto Show, Financial & Estate Planning (Feb); Senior Lifestyle, Education, Easter, Easter Dining, Baseball (Mar); Fishing Season, Spring Car Care, Realtors Week, Home & Garden, Insurance (Apr); Mother's Day Dining Guide, Golf (May); Festival of Arts, Graduation (June); Bridal, Golf Classic, Senior Lifestyle (July); Olympics, We Love Erie, Football (Aug); Soccer, Erie Excellence, Home Improvement (Sept); Today's Home, Hunting, Fall Car Care (Oct); Thanksgiving Dining Guide (Nov); Basketball, Christmas Gift Guide, Last Minute Holiday Planning, New Year's Dining Guide, Winter Storm, First Night at Erie (Dec); Sunday Travel Page (monthly).
Special Weekly Sections: Sports Week (mon); Your Money (tues); Best Food Day (wed); Showcase (thur); Pulse (fri); Religion (sat); House to Home, Travel Pages, Home Improvement, Business, Bridal Directory (S).
Magazines: Movie, Restaurant & Entertainment Guide (thur); Pulse-Health & Fitness & Nutrition (fri); Times-News TV Week (local newsprint quarter-fold TV schedule), Parade, Color Comics (S).
Cable TV: Own cable TV in circulation area.

CORPORATE OFFICERS

President/Treasurer Edward M Mead
Exec Vice Pres/Secretary Michael Mead
Vice Pres/Asst Treasurer Kevin Mead

GENERAL MANAGEMENT

Co-Publisher Edward M Mead
Co-Publisher Michael Mead
Controller Thomas Diefenbach
Asst Controller Henry Bujalski
Human Resources Herb Gilroy
Manager-Credit Bill Bollman

ADVERTISING

Director John O Andersen
Manager-Retail Alan J Haskins
Manager-Classified A Ted Benson Jr
Manager-National Gerald Szorek
Manager-Research Gerald Szorek
Manager-Telesales Geri Cicchetti
Manager-Creative Service Joe Wojcik
Coordinator-Co-op Sandra Hartel

MARKETING AND PROMOTION

Manager-Marketing Service/Promotion Christopher Mead

TELECOMMUNICATIONS

Audiotex Manager Ted Benson
Asst Audiotex Manager Christopher Mead

CIRCULATION

Director Chuck Jenkins
Manager Frank Lamanna

NEWS EXECUTIVES

Editor Edward M Mead
Managing Editor (Times) Tony Pasquale
Managing Editor (News) Jeff Pinski
Managing Editor-Supplements/Sports Kevin Cuneo
Managing Editor-Bureaus Fran Fry Jr

EDITORS AND MANAGERS

Morning News
Amusements Editor Liz Allen
Books Editor Bob Guerrein
Business Editor Dale Shidemantle
City Editor Bill Welch
Editorial Page Editor Bob Guerrein
Education Editor Liz Allen
Harrisburg Bureau Al Neri
Films/Theater Editor Kevin Cuneo
News Editor Paul Groucutt
Political Editor Bill McKinney
Sports Editor Jim Camp

Daily Times
Amusements Editor Kevin Cuneo
Books Editor Pat Howard
Business Editor Marnie Mead Oberle
City Editor Paul Corbran
Columnist-Business & Politics Pat Howard
Columnist Edward M Mead
Editorial Page Editor Pat Howard
Education Editor Dana Massing
Films/Theater Editor Kevin Cuneo
Harrisburg Bureau Al Neri
Librarian Penny Joint
Music Editor Dave Richards
News Editor Dick Deckert
Political Editor Jim Thompson
Science/Technology Editor Jack Grazier

Times-News
Amusements Editor William Rogosky
Automotive Editor Jerry Trambley
Books Editor Pat Howard
Business Editor Marnie Mead Oberle
City Editor Ron Wasielewski
Columnist Edward M Mead
Columnist Bill McKinney
Columnist Fran Fry Jr
Columnist Al Neri
Editorial Page Editor Pat Howard
Education Editor Paul Corbran
Librarian Penny Joint
Music Editor William Rogosky
News Editor William Rogosky
Political Editor Pat Howard
Radio/Television Editor Brenda Martin
Religion Editor Jerry Trambley
Science/Technology Editor Jerry Trambley
Sunday Editor William Rogosky
Travel Editor William Rogosky
Wire Editor Jack Martin

MANAGEMENT INFORMATION SERVICES

Data Processing Manager Charles Evans

PRODUCTION

Manager Harry D Rhodes
Manager-Systems Bill Dietz Sr
Manager-Technical Service Larry Showronski
General Foreman-Composing Bob Sharples
General Foreman-Press Rodger Parsons
General Foreman-Distribution Fred Schuerger

Market Information: Zoned editions; Split Run; TMC; ADS; Operate audiotex.
Mechanical available: Offset; Black and 3 ROP colors; insert accepted — preprinted; page cut-offs — 22¾".
Mechanical specifications: Type page 13" x 21½"; E - 6 cols, 2.07", .13" between; A - 6 cols, 2.07", .13" between; C - 10 cols, 1¼", .04" between.
Commodity consumption: Newsprint 7,727 short tons; widths 55", 41¼", 27½"; black ink 139,750 pounds; color ink 39,230 pounds; single pages printed 27,800; average pages per issue 46(d), 84(S); single plates used 82,000.
Equipment: EDITORIAL: Front-end hardware — DEC/PDP 11-84; Front-end software — DEC/TMS; Other equipment — 30-NSSE/400, 4-Ap/Mac Quadra. CLASSIFIED: Front-end hardware — DEC/PDP 11-84; Front-end software — DEC/CMS, NNSE/CAPS; Other equipment — 12-NSSE/400, 2-Sun/Sparc II. AUDIOTEX: Hardware — Info-Connect/Pottsville; Supplier name — New Horizons Group, VNN, AP Stockline. DISPLAY: Adv layout systems — SCS/Layout 8000, Cx, 2-Sun/Sparc II; Front-end hardware — 2-Cx/380, Sun/Breeze, 2-Cx, Ap/Mac Quadras, 3-Cx, Sun/Sparc 5 Breeze, Ap/Power Mac 8100-80; Front-end software — Cx/Release 8, Multi-Ad/Creator 3.6.1; PRODUCTION: Typesetters — 1-Bidco/80c, Cx, 1-Bidco/105C; Plate exposures — 2-Douthitt/Gemini Twins; Plate processors — 2-Nat/A340; Electronic picture desk — 4-Lf/AP Leaf Picture Desk; Scanners — 1-ECR/Autokon 1000DE, 1-ECR/Autokon 2030; Production cameras — 1-B/Commodore, 1-C/Spartan; Automatic film processors — 1-P/26ML, 1-P/26TQ, 1-P/26RA; Film transporters — 1-C; Color separation equipment (conventional) — 1-Ap/Mac Quadra 700, Adobe/Photoshop, 1-Pm/6100; Digital color separation equipment — Lf/Leafscan 35, Nikon/35mm, Sharp.
PRESSROOM: Line 1 — 7-G/Metro (3 half decks); Press drives — GE; Folders — 1-G/double 2:1; Pasters — G; Reels and stands — G; Press control system — GE. MAILROOM: Counter stackers — 1-Id/NS550, 2-Id/NS2000, 1-Id/2100; Inserters and stuffers — 1-SLS/1000 (17-Head), 1-SLS/1000 (9-Head); Bundle tyer — 3-MLN/2A, 2-Sa, 3-Power Strap. LIBRARY: Electronic — Datatek. WIRE SERVICES: News — AP, KRT, LAT-WP; Photos — AP; Stock tables — AP; Receiving dishes — size-10ft, AP. BUSINESS COMPUTERS: 2-DEC/VAX 6510; Applications: Compushare: Accts payable, Payroll, Newsprint inventory, HR, Adv entry, Billing, Accts payable, Circ; In-house; PCs & micros networked; PCs & main system networked.

FARRELL

See SHARON

FRANKLIN-OIL CITY

Venango County

'90 U.S. Census- 19,278 (Franklin 7,329; Oil City 11,949); E&P '96 Est. 17,272 (Franklin 6,715; Oil City 10,557)

The Derrick (m-mon to sat)

The Derrick, 1510 W. 1st St.; PO Box 928, Oil City, PA 16301; tel (814) 676-7444.
Circulation: 18,042(m); 18,042(m-sat); Sworn Sept. 30, 1995.
Price: 35¢(d); 35¢(sat); $9.00/mo; $108.00/yr.
Advertising: Open inch rate $25.18(m); $25.18(m-sat). **Representative:** Landon Associates Inc.
News Service: AP. **Politics:** Independent. **Established:** 1871.
Note: The Oil City Derrick and the Franklin News-Herald are editorially separate. All business and production are handled by Venango Newspapers Inc.
Not Published: New Year; Memorial Day; Independence Day; Labor Day; Thanksgiving; Christmas.
Special Editions: Senior Citizen, Today's Bride (Feb); Your Home, Fashion & Fitness (Mar); Car Care (Apr); Summer Lifestyles (May); Graduation (June); Clarion County Today (July); Back-to-School (Aug); Home Improvement, Football (Sept); Care for Your Car, Football Contest, Autumn Leaf Festival (Oct); Football Contest, Holiday Recipes, Hunting (Nov); Last Minute Gift Guide (Dec).
Special Weekly Sections: Best Food Days; Entertainment (wed & thur).

CORPORATE OFFICERS

Board Chairman E P Boyle
President P C Boyle
Exec Vice Pres E Michael Boyle
Vice Pres W R Lutz
Secretary Peter T Boyle
Treasurer E Michael Boyle

GENERAL MANAGEMENT

Publisher E P Boyle
Controller W R Lutz

ADVERTISING

Director Edward B Cowart

CIRCULATION

Manager Melvin J Basham

NEWS EXECUTIVES

Exec Editor Lou Ziegler
Editor P C Boyle

EDITOR AND MANAGER

Sports Editor Edward Brannon

Market Information: TMC; ADS.
Mechanical available: DiLitho; Black and 3 ROP colors; insert accepted — preprinted; page cut-offs — 22¾".
Mechanical specifications: Type page 13" x 21¼"; E - 6 cols, 2¹⁄₁₆", ⅛" between; A - 6 cols, 2¹⁄₁₆", ⅛" between; C - 9 cols, 1⅜", ¹⁄₁₆" between.
Commodity consumption: widths 27", 13½"; average pages per issue 24(d).
Equipment: EDITORIAL: Front-end hardware — 2-SII/22. CLASSIFIED: Front-end hardware — 4-SII/22. AUDIOTEX: Hardware — Gateway; Software — Info-Connect; Supplier name — Info-Connect/Pottsville Republican. DISPLAY: Adv layout systems — 1-SCS/Layout 8000. PRODUCTION: Typesetters — 2-COM/8600; Platemaking systems — 1-3M/Pyrofax.
PRESSROOM: Line 1 — 5-G/Offset Community. MAILROOM: Inserters and stuffers — 14-MM/227; Bundle tyer — 2-Ty-Tech/45, 2-MLN/SP 330; Addressing machine — 2-KR/211. WIRE SERVICES: News — AP Datastream; Syndicates — AP Datafeatures; Receiving dishes — AP. BUSINESS COMPUTERS: PCs & main system networked.

The News-Herald

(m-mon to sat)

The News-Herald, 1510 W. 1st St.; PO Box 928, Oil City, PA 16301; tel (814) 676-7444.
Circulation: 7,383(m); 7,383(m-sat); Sworn Sept. 10, 1995.
Price: 35¢(d); 35¢(sat); $9.00/mo; $108.00/yr.
Advertising: Open inch rate $25.18(m); $25.18(m-sat). **Representative:** Landon Associates Inc.
News Service: AP. **Politics:** Independent. **Established:** 1876.
Note: The Franklin News-Herald and the Oil City Derrick are editorially separate. All business and production are handled by Venango Newspapers Inc.
Not Published: New Year; Memorial Day; Independence Day; Labor Day; Thanksgiving; Christmas.
Special Editions: Senior Citizen (Jan); Bridal (Feb); Home Improvement, Fashion & Fitness (Mar); Car Care (Apr); Summer Lifestyle (May); Graduation (June); Clarion County Today (July); Back-to-School (Aug); Fall Home Improvement, Football Contest, Autumn Leaf Festival (Sept); Car Care, Football Contest (Oct); Hunting, Holiday Recipes, Football Contest (Nov); Last Minute Gift Guide (Dec).
Special Weekly Sections: Best Food Days, Entertainment (wed & thur).

CORPORATE OFFICERS

Board Chairman E P Boyle
President P C Boyle
Exec Vice Pres E Michael Boyle
Vice Pres W R Lutz
Secretary Peter T Boyle
Treasurer E Michael Boyle

GENERAL MANAGEMENT

Publisher E P Boyle
Controller W R Lutz

ADVERTISING

Director Edward B Cowart

CIRCULATION

Manager Melvin J Basham

NEWS EXECUTIVES

Exec Editor Lou Ziegler
Editor P C Boyle

EDITORS AND MANAGERS

News Editor Robert Venturella
Sports Editor Edward Brannon

Market Information: TMC.
Mechanical available: Black and 3 ROP colors; insert accepted — preprinted; page cut-offs — 22¾".
Mechanical specifications: E - 6 cols, 2¹⁄₁₆", ⅛" between; A - 6 cols, 2¹⁄₁₆", ⅛" between; C - 9 cols, 1⅜", ¹⁄₁₆" between.
Commodity consumption: widths 27", 13½"; average pages per issue 24(d).
Equipment: EDITORIAL: Front-end hardware — 2-SII/22. CLASSIFIED: Front-end hardware — 4-SII/22. AUDIOTEX: Hardware — Gateway; Software — Info-Connect; Supplier name — Info-Connect/Pottsville Republican. DISPLAY: Adv layout systems — 1-SCS/Layout 8000. PRODUCTION: Typesetters — 2-COM/8600; Platemaking systems — 1-3M/Pyrofax.
PRESSROOM: Line 1 — 5-G/Universal DiLitho. MAILROOM: Inserters and stuffers — 14-MM/227; Bundle tyer — 2-Ty-Tech/45, 2-MLN/SP 330; Addressing machine — 2-KR/211. WIRE SERVICES: News — AP Datastream; Syndicates — AP Datafeatures; Receiving dishes — AP. BUSINESS COMPUTERS: PCs & main system networked.

GETTYSBURG

Adams County

'90 U.S. Census- 7,025; E&P '96 Est. 6,887
ABC-CZ (90): 10,574 (HH 3,910)

The Gettysburg Times

(m-mon to sat)

The Gettysburg Times, 1570 Fairfield Rd.; PO Box 3669, Gettysburg, PA 17325; tel (717) 334-1131; fax (717) 334-4243.
Circulation: 9,216(m); 9,216(m-sat); ABC Sept. 30, 1995.
Price: 35¢(d); 35¢(sat); $8.75/mo; $75.00/yr.
Advertising: Open inch rate $11.55(m); $11.55(m-sat). **Representative:** Landon Associates Inc.
News Service: AP. **Politics:** Independent. **Established:** 1902.
Not Published: New Year; Thanksgiving Day; Christmas Day.
Special Editions: Mid-Winter Coupon Book, Progress/Business Outlook, Spring/Summer Wedding Planner (Jan); Spring Home & Building, Design-An-Ad (Mar); Farm & Garden, Springtime Coupon Book (Apr); Business Profile, Summer/Fall Wedding Planner (May); Community Fact Book, Salute to Our Graduates (June); Housing, Homes & Building (July); "Summer Sizzlers" Coupon Book, Fall/Winter Wedding Planner, Back-to-School, Fall Sports Preview (Aug); Dining/Entertainment, Fall Home Improvement (Sept); "Harvest of Values" Coupon Book, Winter/Spring Wedding Planner, New Car/Car Care (Oct); Holiday Gift Guide-Vol. I, Holiday Songbook (Nov); Basketball Preview, Holiday Gift Guide-Vol. II (Dec).
Special Weekly Sections: Health (tues); Best Food Days, Church (wed); Entertainment (thur); Housing & Real Estate (fri); Church (sat); Business (daily).
Magazines: The Item-TV/entertainment supplement (fri); Senior Living (monthly); Tourism Magazine (Apr to Oct).
Broadcast Affiliates: WGET-AM/WGTY-FM Gettysburg, PA.

CORPORATE OFFICERS

Chairman of the Board Philip M Jones
President Cynthia A Ford

GENERAL MANAGEMENT

Director-News Operations Larry Rhoten

ADVERTISING

Director Donald Bixel

MARKETING AND PROMOTION

Director-Marketing/Promotion Robert J Small

CIRCULATION

Director Belinda Walde

NEWS EXECUTIVE

Editor Bill Pukmel

PRODUCTION

Manager Loretta Plitt

Market Information: Zoned editions; Operate audiotex.
Mechanical available: Offset; Black and 3 ROP colors; insert accepted — preprinted; page cut-offs — 22¾".
Mechanical specifications: Type page 13" x 21"; E - 6 cols, 2¹⁄₁₆", ⅛" between; A - 6 cols, 2¹⁄₁₆", ⅛" between; C - 9 cols, 1⅜", ¹⁄₁₆" between.
Commodity consumption: Newsprint 525 short tons; widths 28", 14"; black ink 12,854 pounds; color ink 1,286 pounds; single pages printed 7,587; average pages per issue 20(d); single plates used 6,891.
Equipment: EDITORIAL: Front-end hardware — Ap/Mac; Front-end software — FSI. CLASSIFIED: Front-end hardware — Ap/Mac; Front-end software — FSI. AUDIOTEX: Software — Info-Connect/Pottsville Republican. DISPLAY: Adv layout systems — Ap/Mac IIci, Ap/Mac Quadra; Front-end software — Multi-Ad/Creator, Adobe/Illustrator, QuarkXPress. PRODUCTION: Pagination software — SII; Type-

I-350 Pennsylvania

setters — Mk/Laser, Xante/Accel-a-Writer 8100, HP, Graphic Enterprise/Negsetter, Panther; Plate exposures — 1-B/Ultra-Lite 2500; Plate processors — Nat/A-250; Scanners — Ap, AG/Arcus; Production cameras — 1-R/432; Automatic film processors — Kk/66S. PRESSROOM: Line 1 — 8-G/Community Offset; Line 2 — 4-G; Folders — 1-G, 2-G/2:1. MAILROOM: Inserters and stuffers — 4-Kk; Bundle tyer — 2-Sa. LIBRARY: Electronic — 1-BH/Mk II. WIRE SERVICES: News — AP; Photos — AP AdSend; Receiving dishes — size-3m, AP. BUSINESS COMPUTERS: 1-NCR/9300, 2-Zenith/Z386, Zenith/Z157, 2-ALR/FlexCache 33-386, Zenith/Z-125, 5-Dell/486; Applications: Circ, Adv billing, Adv scheduling, Accts receivable, Gen ledger; PCs & micros networked; PCs & main system networked.

GREENSBURG

Westmoreland County

'90 U.S. Census- 16,318; E&P '96 Est. 15,356
ABC-NDM (90): 266,136 (HH 102,094)

Tribune-Review
(m-mon to sat; S)

Tribune-Review, Cabin Hill Dr., Greensburg, PA 15601; tel (412) 834-1151; fax (412) 838-5170; web site http://tribune-review.com/trib/. Tribune-Review Publishing Co. group.

Circulation: 73,805(m); 73,805(m-sat); 129,748(S); ABC Sept. 30, 1995.

Price: 35¢(d); 35¢(sat); $1.00(S); $2.50/wk (carrier).

Advertising: Open inch rate $46.20(m); $46.20(m-sat); $60.50(S). **Representative:** Landon Associates Inc.

News Services: AP, CNS, LAT-WP. **Politics:** Independent-Republican. **Established:** 1886 (Tribune), 1903 (Review).

Note: Advertising in the Greensburg Tribune Review automatically includes advertising in the Irwin Standard Observer.

Not Published: New Year; Memorial Day; Independence Day; Labor Day.

Special Editions: Bridal Tab (Jan); Senior Citizen, Enterprise (Feb); Car Care, Health and Fitness (Apr); Fun in the Sun (May); Football Tab, Bridal Tab (Aug); Literacy (Sept).

Special Weekly Sections: Business Review Pages (mon, tues); Dining Page (fri); Business Review Pages (sat); Best Food, Travel (S).

Magazines: Leisure Magazine (fri); Focus Magazine, TV Magazine (S).

CORPORATE OFFICERS

Board Chairman Richard M Scaife
President Edward H Harrell
Vice Pres George A Beidler
Secretary Arthur McMullen

GENERAL MANAGEMENT

Publisher Richard M Scaife
President Edward H Harrell
Vice Pres George A Beidler
Director-Employee Relations Arthur McMullen
Treasurer/Controller Robert J Acri

ADVERTISING

Director Kraig Cawley
Manager-National Fred McMullen
Manager-Classified Andrea Mroz
Manager-Key Accounts Fred McMullen
Manager-Retail Karen McElhatten
Manager-Telemarketing Judy Rohrbaugh

MARKETING AND PROMOTION

Manager-Promotion Nancy Deemer

TELECOMMUNICATIONS

Audiotex Manager Earl Schisles

CIRCULATION

Director-Pittsburgh Carroll Quinn

NEWS EXECUTIVE

Exec Editor George A Beidler

EDITORS AND MANAGERS

Action Editor Popsy Sadock
Business Editor Jack Markowitz
City Editor Frank Myers
Editorial Page Editor Paul Koloski
Focus Editor Robin Stahl
News Editor Tom Stewart
News Editor Dave Miller
Radio/Television Editor Laura Dell
Scholastic Sports Editor Rich Emert
Sports Editor David Ailes
Style Editor Val Glenz
Asst Sunday Editor Robert Broderick

MANAGEMENT INFORMATION SERVICES

Online Manager Greg Gendrom
Data Processing Manager Fran Liberty

PRODUCTION

Manager Thomas Trauth
Manager-Pre Press Joe Blansett
Asst Manager Dick Webb
Superintendent-Press Frank Mento

Market Information: Zoned editions; Split Run; TMC; ADS; Operate database; Operate audiotex.

Mechanical available: Offset; Black and 3 ROP colors; insert accepted — preprinted; page cut-offs — 22¾".

Mechanical specifications: Type page 13" x 21½"; E - 6 cols, $2\frac{1}{16}$", ⅛" between; A - 6 cols, $2\frac{1}{16}$", ⅛" between; C - 9 cols, 1⅜", $\frac{1}{16}$" between.

Commodity consumption: Newsprint 10,016 short tons; widths 55", 41¾", 27½"; black ink 138,000 pounds; color ink 27,000 pounds; single pages printed 20,000; average pages per issue 40(d), 84(S); single plates used 72,000.

Equipment: EDITORIAL: Front-end hardware — CText; Front-end software — CText/AFM; Other equipment — Ap/Mac Pagination. CLASSIFIED: Front-end hardware — Intel/PJ PCs; Front-end software — Compuclass; Other equipment — 14-PC, Computext/Pagination. AUDIOTEX: Hardware — Micro Voice. DISPLAY: Adv layout systems — Ap/Mac; Front-end hardware — Ap/Mac; Front-end software — Multi-Ad/Creator; Printers — MON. PRODUCTION: Pagination software — Computext 4.4, QPS; Typesetters — 3-MON/Express Master, 3-MON/Paper Express; Plate exposures — 1-Nu; Plate processors — W; Electronic picture desk — Lf/AP Leaf Picture Desk; Production cameras — C; Automatic film processors — LE, Glunz & Jensen; Film transporters — C, Glunz & Jensen; Color separation equipment (conventional) — CD; Digital color separation equipment — Ap/Mac, Nikon.
PRESSROOM: Line 1 — 5-G/Metro(2 color); Line 2 — 1-G/Metro (Color Tower); Press drives — Fin; Folders — G/double 2:1; Pasters — 2-G; Reels and stands — 7-G. MAILROOM: Counter stackers — 2-HL, 2-QWI; Inserters and stuffers — HI, GMA, 72-P/Double Out; Bundle tyer — 2-MLN; Addressing machine — KR. LIBRARY: Electronic — SMS. COMMUNICATIONS: Remote imagesetting — 3-Lf/Leafscan; Systems used — satellite. WIRE SERVICES: News — AP News; Stock tables — AP SelectStox; Syndicates — LAT-WP, CNS, RN; Receiving dishes — size-3m, AP, RN. BUSINESS COMPUTERS: DEC/VAX 6310, DEC/VAX 750; Applications: CJ: Circ, Adv billing, Accts receivable, Payroll, Accts payable, TMC, Gen ledger; PCs & micros networked; PCs & main system networked.

GREENVILLE

Mercer County

'90 U.S. Census- 6,734; E&P '96 Est. 6,008
ABC-CZ (90): 6,734 (HH 2,628)

The Record-Argus
(m-mon to sat)

The Record-Argus, 10 Penn Ave.; Box 711, Greenville, PA 16125; tel (412) 588-5000; fax (412) 588-4691.

Circulation: 5,490(m); 5,490(m-sat); ABC Sept. 30, 1995.

Price: 35¢(d); 35¢(sat); $1.70/wk; $7.35/mo; $88.20/yr.

Advertising: Open inch rate $9.00(m); $9.00(m-sat).

News Service: AP. **Politics:** Independent. **Established:** 1848.

Not Published: New Year; Memorial Day; Independence Day; Labor Day; Thanksgiving; Christmas.

Special Editions: Bridal (Jan); Progress (Feb); Easter (Mar); Fishing (Apr); Camping (May, June); Lakeland Festival (July); Back-to-School, Fall Sports (Aug); Cook Book, Thiel College (Oct); Christmas (Dec).

Special Weekly Sections: Best Food Day (mon, wed).

Magazine: TV & Entertainment (thur).

CORPORATE OFFICERS

President/CEO Robert N Bracey
Vice Pres Harvey Childs
Vice Pres Cheryl Burns

GENERAL MANAGEMENT

Publisher/General Manager Robert N Bracey

ADVERTISING

Director Steve Gargasz

MARKETING AND PROMOTION

Director-Marketing Steve Gargasz

CIRCULATION

Manager Rob Ruszkiewicz

NEWS EXECUTIVE

Editor Ron Woughter

EDITORS AND MANAGERS

City Editor Shaun Ryan
Society Editor Yvonne Raymond
Sports Editor Ralph Gammon

PRODUCTION

Manager Terry Soult

Market Information: ADS.

Mechanical available: Offset; Black and 3 ROP colors; insert accepted — preprinted, standing card; page cut-offs — 21½".

Mechanical specifications: Type page 13" x 21½"; E - 6 cols, $2\frac{1}{16}$", ⅛" between; A - 6 cols, $2\frac{1}{16}$", ⅛" between; C - 9 cols, 1⅜", ⅛" between.

Commodity consumption: widths 13¾"; single pages printed 5,156; average pages per issue 14(d), 16(sat).

Equipment: EDITORIAL: Front-end hardware — CText. CLASSIFIED: Front-end hardware — CText. PRODUCTION: Typesetters — 1-CText/Adept; Platemaking systems — 1-Nu; Production cameras — 1-Nu. MAILROOM: Bundle tyer — 1-MLN, 1-S/Plastic Strap; Addressing machine — 1-Am. LIBRARY: Electronic — BH. WIRE SERVICES: News — AP; Photos — AP; Syndicates — AP Datastream; Receiving dishes — size-3m, AP. BUSINESS COMPUTERS: PCs & main system networked.

HANOVER

York County

'90 U.S. Census- 14,399; E&P '96 Est. 14,003
ABC-CZ (90): 26,995 (HH 11,200)

The Evening Sun
(e-mon to fri; m-sat; S)

The Evening Sun, 135 Baltimore St.; PO Box 514, Hanover, PA 17331; tel (717) 637-3736; fax (717) 637-7730; e-mail esunl@netrax.net; web site http://www.sunlink.com/. Thomson Newspapers group.

Circulation: 21,371(e); 21,371(m-sat); 21,198(S); ABC Sept. 30, 1995.

Price: 35¢(d); 35¢(sat); $1.00(S); $2.50/wk; $10.00/mo; $117.00/yr.

Advertising: Open inch rate $19.08(e); $19.08(m-sat); $19.08(S). **Representative:** Thomson Newspapers.

News Service: AP. **Politics:** Independent. **Established:** 1915.

Not Published: New Year; Christmas.

Special Editions: Progress, Spring Car Care, Bridal (Feb); Spring Home (Apr); Outdoor (May); 4-H Fair (Aug); Fall Home Improvement, Football (Sept); Auto Review, Fall Car Care (Oct); Cookbook, Christmas Gifts, Winter Sports (Nov); Christmas Gifts, Holly (Dec).

Special Weekly Sections: Kitchen Cabinet, Out & About-Entertainment & Travel (wed); TV Views (S).

GENERAL MANAGEMENT

Publisher Edward R Moss
Chief Financial Officer Stephen Arthur

ADVERTISING

Manager William Shufflebarger

MARKETING AND PROMOTION

Director-Marketing/Promotion Amy Lynn Warner

CIRCULATION

Manager Tammy Yoder

NEWS EXECUTIVE

Editor Wayne K Lowman

EDITORS AND MANAGERS

City Editor Mark Franklin
Editorial Page Editor Jack LeFevre
Features Editor Maria Mauro
Graphics Editor Wanda Murren
News Editor Bob Marchio
Sports Editor Phil Glatfelter

MANAGEMENT INFORMATION SERVICES

Online Manager Brenda Cable
Data Processing Manager Stephen Arthur

PRODUCTION

Manager Gene Plowman
Manager-Commercial Print Sales David Auchey
Supervisor-Pre Press Sharon Crouse
Supervisor-Post Press Duane Morgan
Foreman-Press Dave Myers

Market Information: Zoned editions; TMC; ADS; Operate database; Electronic edition.

Mechanical available: Offset; Black and 3 ROP colors; insert accepted — preprinted; page cut-offs — 22¾".

Mechanical specifications: Type page 13" x 21½"; E - 6 cols, $2\frac{1}{16}$", ⅛" between; A - 6 cols, $2\frac{1}{16}$", ⅛" between; C - 6 cols, $2\frac{1}{16}$", ⅛" between.

Commodity consumption: Newsprint 1,400 short tons; widths 27", 13½"; single pages printed 10,034; average pages per issue 26(d), 40(S).

Equipment: EDITORIAL: Front-end hardware — Mk. CLASSIFIED: Front-end hardware — Mk. DISPLAY: Adv layout systems — Ap/Mac; Front-end hardware — Ap/Mac; Front-end software — Adobe/PageMaker 5.0, QuarkXPress 3.2; Printers — V/5100 (600 dpi); Other equipment — Panther/Pro Imagesetter. PRODUCTION: OCR software — Caere/OmniPage; Typesetters — Ap/Mac LaserPrinter, V/5100, Panther Pro, V/5300E; Platemaking systems — Offset; Plate exposures — 1-Nu; Electronic picture desk — Lf/AP Leaf Picture Desk, Lf/Leafscan 35; Automatic film processors — 1-LE; Film transporters — 1-LE.
PRESSROOM: Line 1 — 8-G/Unitubular; Folders — 1-G/2:1; Press registration system — Duarte/Pin Register. MAILROOM: Bundle tyer — 1-MLN; Addressing machine — 2-Am. WIRE SERVICES: News — AP; Photos — AP; Receiving dishes — size-3m, AP. BUSINESS COMPUTERS: HP; Applications: Newzware; PCs & main system networked.

HARRISBURG

Dauphin County

'90 U.S. Census- 52,376; E&P '96 Est. 51,648
ABC-CZ (90): 323,687 (HH 129,264)

The Patriot (m-mon to fri)
The Evening News (e-mon to fri)
The Patriot-News (m-sat)
Sunday Patriot-News (S)

The Patriot-News, 812 Market St.; PO Box 2265, Harrisburg, PA 17105; tel (717) 255-8100; fax (717) 232-9307, (717) 232-8450. Advance Publications group.

Circulation: 63,340(m); 38,756(e); 95,960(m-sat); 175,230(S); ABC Sept. 30, 1995.

Price: 50¢(d); 50¢(sat); $1.50(S); $1.50/wk (S), $1.80/wk (d); $78.00/yr (S), $93.60/yr (d).

Advertising: Open inch rate $44.50(m); $44.50(e); $44.50(m-sat); $50.80(S). **Representative:** Newhouse Newspapers/Metro Suburbia.

News Services: AP, KRT, LAT-WP, NNS, NYT. **Politics:** Independent. **Established:** 1854 (Patriot), 1917 (News).

Special Editions: Auto Show, Healthy Living, Active Times, Hawaii and Cruise (Jan); Islands, National Engineers' Week, Wedding Guide, Home Builders (Feb); Lawn & Garden, Spring & Summer Fashions, Spring Home Improvement, Newspaper in Education, Mature Traveler (Mar); Harrisburg Senators, Kids Travel & Beach Bound, Active Times (Apr); Mother's Day Gifts, Summer Travel, Outdoor Living, Day Tripping, NY State, Memorial Day (May); Life After School/Graduation, Virginia (June); Pre School & Day Care, Active Times, Canada, Neighbors I (July); Day Tripping, Football 1996 (Aug); Lawn & Garden, Fall Foliage & Heading South, Fall & Winter Fashions (Sept); Designs for Living, New Car Section, Car Care Pages, Active Times (Seniors), Europe (Oct); Holiday Vacation (Nov); Skiing, Holiday Gift Guides (Dec).

Special Weekly Sections: Arts and Leisure, Travel, Sports, Living, Business/Financial (S); Sports (daily).

CORPORATE OFFICERS

President Edwin F Russell
Vice Pres Raymond L Gover
Asst Treasurer Frank J Epler

GENERAL MANAGEMENT

Publisher Raymond L Gover
General Manager Caroline D Harrison
Controller Frank J Epler
Purchasing Agent Geraldine Wiest
Director-Community Service Susan Anthony
Personnel Manager Tina Clark
Manager-Education Service Susan Anthony

Copyright ©1996 by the Editor & Publisher Co.

ADVERTISING

Director Larry R Dodge
Manager-National Robert E Cobaugh
Manager-Classified Timothy D Ruhl
Manager-Retail James J Stephanak

MARKETING AND PROMOTION

Manager-Marketing/Promotion Karen T Golin

TELECOMMUNICATIONS

Audiotex Manager Alan Hayakawa

CIRCULATION

Director Betty Way
Asst Director-Distribution/Service Thomas J McGeehan
Asst Director-Sales & Marketing Kurt Hower

NEWS EXECUTIVES

Editor John A Kirkpatrick
Managing Editor Thomas Baden

EDITORS AND MANAGERS

Business Editor Allen Mayers
City Editor (Night) Robert Heisse
City Editor (Day) John Troutman
Editorial Page Editor Dale Davenport
Entertainment Editor John McGinley
Features Editor Cate Barron
Graphics Editor Jon Williams
Librarian Deanna Mills
Living Editor Nance Woodward
Exec News Editor Bob Vucic
Photo Editor Maureen Hughs
Religion Editor Tony Perry
Sports Editor Nick Horvath
Systems Editor David Browne
Travel Editor Connie McNamara

MANAGEMENT INFORMATION SERVICES

Data Processing Manager Gregory E Woods

PRODUCTION

Manager Fred Stickel Jr

Market Information: Zoned editions; Split Run; TMC; ADS; Operate audiotex.
Mechanical available: Letterpress; Black and 3 ROP colors; insert accepted — preprinted, spadeas; page cut-offs — 22¾".
Mechanical specifications: Type page 13" x 21½"; E - 6 cols, 2", ⅙" between; A - 6 cols, 2.04", ⅙" between; C - 10 cols, 1.17", ⅛" between.
Commodity consumption: Newsprint 20,250 short tons; 18,370 metric tons; widths 55", 41¼", 27½"; black ink 459,109 pounds; color ink 55,228 pounds; single pages printed 41,552; average pages per issue 63(d), 45(sat), 139(S); single plates used 103,665.
Equipment: EDITORIAL: Front-end hardware — Tandem; Front-end software — SII/Sys 55; Other equipment — 13-Echo/Pagination Workstation, 8-SII/Coyote-22, 100-SII/Coyote-QB, 5-Toshiba/1000SE. CLASSIFIED: Front-end hardware — Tandem; Front-end software — SII/Sys 55; Other equipment — 18-SII/Coyote QB, 3-SII/Coyote-15, 2-SII/Sequoia. AUDIOTEX: Hardware — PC/486; Software — Info-Connect, U.S. Telecom Voice Application Language 4.30; Supplier name — Tribune Voice News Network. DISPLAY: Adv layout systems — IAL; Front-end hardware — Tandem, 13-Ap/Mac; Front-end software — SII/Sys 55, Multi-Ad/Creator; Printers — HP/LaserJet III, MON/PaperMaster 1200, Hyphen/Copol printer, QMS/860; Other equipment — DTI/AdSpeed 81. PRODUCTION: Typesetters — 2-AU/APS-6; Platemaking systems — Na; Plate exposures — 2-Na/Titan III; Plate processors — 2-Na/C220; Scanners — 2-ECR/Autokon; Production cameras — 1-C/Newspager, 1-C/Spartan III; Automatic film processors — LE, AG; Film transporters — C; Color separation equipment (conventional) — Lf/Leafscan 35; Digital color separation equipment — Sharp/1650.
PRESSROOM: Line 1 — 10-H/Colormatic double width; Folders — 1-H/3:2; Pasters — H/Automatic; Reels and stands — H; Press control system — GE; Press registration system — 3-WebTech. MAILROOM: Counter stackers — 4-QWI/350; Inserters and stuffers — 2-Fg/10-into-1, 2-Fg/Rotadisc; Bundle tyer — 5-Dynaric/NP2; Wrapping singles — 1-OVL; Addressing machine — 1-Ch. LIBRARY: Electronic — Data Times, Battelle/Basis. COMMUNICATIONS: Digital ad delivery system — AP AdSend, Ad Express. WIRE SERVICES: News — AP Datanews, AP Datastream; Photos — AP Photostream; Stock tables — AP SelectStox I; Syndicates — NNS, North America Syndicate, NYT; Receiving dishes — size-3m, AP. BUSINESS COMPUTERS: 2-DEC/VAX 8530 Cluster; Applications: CJ: Circ, Adv, Accts payable; DEC; PCs & micros networked; PCs & main system networked.

HAZLETON

Luzerne County

'90 U.S. Census- 24,730; E&P '96 Est. 22,773
ABC-CZ (90): 43,118 (HH 18,110)

Standard-Speaker

(m-mon to sat; S)

Standard-Speaker, 21 N. Wyoming St.; PO Box 578, Hazleton, PA 18201-0578; tel (717) 455-3636; fax (717) 455-4244.
Circulation: 23,470(m); 23,470(m-sat); 12,947(S); ABC Sept. 30, 1995.
Price: 35¢(d); 35¢(sat); 75¢(S); $2.10/wk (home delivery), $3.00/wk (mail); $12.00/mo (mail); $106.20/yr (home delivery), $114.00/yr (mail).
Advertising: Open inch rate $16.50(m); $16.50(m-sat); $16.50(S). **Representative:** Papert Companies.
News Service: AP. **Politics:** Independent. **Established:** 1866.
Note: Effective June 30, 1995 this publication changed its publishing plan from (all day-mon to sat) to (m-mon to sat; S).
Special Editions: Progress (Jan); Bridal (Feb); Car Care (Mar); Home Improvement, Chamber of Commerce (Apr); Senior Citizen (May); Back-to-School, Football Preview (Aug); Car Care (Oct); Holiday Gift Guide (Nov); Winter Sports/Basketball, Christmas Greetings (Dec).
Special Weekly Sections: Outdoors (mon); Health, Science, School News (tues); Business (thur); Homes, Arts (fri); Food, Consumer, Travel (S).
Magazines: Best Food Days (wed, sat); USA Weekend (S).

CORPORATE OFFICERS

President Jane N Walser
Vice Pres Paul N Walser

GENERAL MANAGEMENT

Publisher Jane N Walser
Publisher Paul N Walser
Director-Operations Jack Williams
Controller John Patton

ADVERTISING

Director Jack Williams
Asst Director Gary Yacubeck

MARKETING AND PROMOTION

Director-Marketing/Promotion Jack Williams

CIRCULATION

Director Gary Klinger
Manager-Credit Steven Walser
Manager-Distribution Paul Witcofski

NEWS EXECUTIVES

Managing Editor Ray Saul
Editor-Day Chas Gloman
Editor-Night Edward Socha
Editor-Sunday Carl Christopher

EDITORS AND MANAGERS

Business Editor Carl Christopher
Lifestyle Editor Margaret Lloyd
Sports Editor Bill Crooks

PRODUCTION

Foreman-Composing (Day) Donald Johnson
Foreman-Composing (Night) Lester Stanton
Superintendent-Pressroom Joseph Clatch

Market Information: Zoned editions; Split Run; TMC.
Mechanical available: Offset; Black and 3 ROP colors; insert accepted — preprinted; page cut-offs — 21½".
Mechanical specifications: Type page 13" x 21½"; E - 6 cols, 2¹⁄₁₆", ⅛" between; A - 6 cols, 2¹⁄₁₆", ⅛" between; C - 9 cols, 1⅜", ⁵⁄₆₄" between.
Commodity consumption: Newsprint 1,741.1 short tons; 1,579.5 metric tons; widths 55", 41¼", 27½"; black ink 43,000 pounds; color ink 7,000 pounds; single pages printed 11,560; average pages per issue 37.5(d); single plates used 26,180.
Equipment: EDITORIAL: Front-end hardware — COM/One 140, 6-COM/Intrepid, Ap/Mac Classic II, 11-PC, Ap/Mac Centris 650; Front-end software — COM; Printers — 2-NewGen/Turbo PS 400, 2-Microcraft/Translator II, HP/LaserJet 4, HP/LaserJet 3, Printronix; Other equipment — ECR/Imagesetter. CLASSIFIED: Front-end hardware — QED, 6-IBM, Ap/Mac Quadra 605; Front-end software — QED/Soft Page; Printers — NewGen/Turbo PS 400, Microcraft/Translator II, 2-HP/LaserJet; Other equipment — Ap/Mac Quadra 605, Ap/Super Mac. DISPLAY: Front-end hardware — 6-IBM, 4-Ap/Mac 605-610, 1-Ap/Power Mac 6100; Front-end software — Archetype/Corel Draw, Microsoft/Windows, Claris/Professional Write, QuarkXPress; Printers — NewGen/Turbo PS 600T, Ap/Mac LaserWriter II; Other equipment — Image Scanner. PRODUCTION: Typesetters — ECR; Plate exposures — Nu/Flip Top; Plate processors — Wd; Scanners — HP/Scan Jet IIC; Production cameras — C/Spartan III; Automatic film processors — LE/Maxim 26; Shrink lenses — CK Optical/SQU-7; Color separation equipment (conventional) — 2-Lf/AP Leaf Picture Desk; Digital color separation equipment — Lf/Leafscan.
PRESSROOM: Line 1 — 5-G/Cosmo; Press control system — Fin/Cabinet 2. MAILROOM: Bundle tyer — 1-MLN/ML2EE, 1-WeldLoc. COMMUNICATIONS: Digital ad delivery system — AP AdSend. Systems used — satellite. WIRE SERVICES: News — AP; Photos — AP; Receiving dishes — size-12ft, AP, CNS. BUSINESS COMPUTERS: Data General/AV 3200; Applications: Vision Data: Accts receivable, Accts payable, Circ, Gen ledger, Class, Newsprint inventory.

HONESDALE

Wayne County

'90 U.S. Census- 4,972; E&P '96 Est. 4,846

The Wayne Independent

(e-mon to fri)

The Wayne Independent, 220 8th St.; PO Box 122, Honesdale, PA 18431; tel (717) 253-3055; fax (717) 253-5387. Hollinger International Inc. group.
Circulation: 4,785(e); Sworn Sept. 29, 1995.
Price: 50¢(d).
Advertising: Open inch rate $8.51(e).
News Service: AP. **Politics:** Independent. **Established:** 1878.
Not Published: Christmas.
Advertising not accepted: 900 numbers.
Special Editions: Early Filers Directory, Independent Plus Page, Volunteer Blood Donor Page (Jan); Bridal Guide, Valentine's Day, President's Day, Heart Month Page (Feb); Spring Car Care, Progress Report, Mature Lifestyles, St. Patrick's Day (Mar); Railways, Design-An-Ad, Cancer Month, Volunteer Month (Apr); Memorial Day, Mother's Day, Antique Page (May); Railways, Graduation, Dairy Month, Father's Day, Mature Lifestyles (June); 4th of July, Railways, Sidewalk Sales (July); GDS Fair, Wayne Co. Fair, Football, Railways, Back-to-School (Aug); Railways, Labor Day, School Safety, Fall Home Improvement, Mature Lifestyles (Sept); 4-H Page, Harvest Days, Fall Car Care, Anti-Drug Coloring Book, Fire Prevention, Christmas Layaway Page, BPW Section (Oct); Christmas Song Book, Christmas Gift Guide, Fall Bridal Guide, Thanksgiving Page, Christmas Gift Page, Hunting Page (Nov); Christmas Greetings, New Year's Page, Christmas Recipes, Railways, Last Minute Gift Page, Mature Lifestyles, Basketball Preview (Dec).
Special Weekly Sections: Social (mon); Auto, Business (tues); Health, Entertainment, Food (wed); Business (thur); Home, Real Estate, Entertainment, Auto, Church (fri).

GENERAL MANAGEMENT

Publisher Donald Doyle

ADVERTISING

Manager-Sales Michelle Hessling

CIRCULATION

Manager Lee Weekely

NEWS EXECUTIVE

Managing Editor Paul Quigley

PRODUCTION

Supervisor Brian Hernawoez

Market Information: TMC.
Mechanical available: Offset; Black and 1 ROP color; insert accepted — preprinted, all; page cut-offs — 22½".
Mechanical specifications: Type page 13" x 21"; E - 6 cols, 2⅛", ¼" between; A - 6 cols, 2¹⁄₁₆", ¼" between; C - 10 cols, 1⁵⁄₁₆", .13" between.
Commodity consumption: Newsprint 421 short tons; width 27½"; single pages printed 4,250; average pages per issue 12(d); single plates used 4,420.
Equipment: EDITORIAL: Front-end hardware — Mk; Front-end software — Mk/NewsTouch; Printers — Ap/Mac LaserWriter II. CLASSIFIED: Front-end hardware — Mk; Front-end software — Mk/Newstouch; Printers — Ap/Mac LaserWriter II. DISPLAY: Front-end hardware — Mk; Front-end software — Aldus/PageMaker; Printers — Ap/Mac LaserWriter. PRODUCTION: Typesetters — Ap/Mac II LaserWriter; Plate exposures — Nu; Plate processors — Nat/A-250; Production cameras — SCREEN/Companica 680C; Automatic film processors — LE/LD220T.
PRESSROOM: Line 1 — 4-G/Suburban; Folders — 1-G/SC; Press control system — Fin. WIRE SERVICES: News — AP; Receiving dishes — AP.

HUNTINGDON-MOUNT UNION

Huntingdon County

'90 U.S. Census- 9,721 (Huntingdon 6,843; Mount Union 2,878); E&P '96 Est. 9,387 (Huntingdon 6,682; Mount Union 2,705)

The Daily News

(e-mon to fri; m-sat)

The Daily News, 325 Penn St., Huntingdon, PA 16652; tel (814) 643-4040.
Circulation: 10,053(e); 10,053(m-sat); Sworn Sept. 30, 1995.
Price: 50¢(d); 50¢(sat); $132.00/yr.
Advertising: Open inch rate $15.35(e); $15.35(m-sat). **Representative:** Landon Associates Inc.
News Service: AP. **Politics:** Independent. **Established:** 1874.
Not Published: New Year; Memorial Day; Independence Day; Labor Day; Thanksgiving; Christmas.
Special Editions: Bridal; Home & Garden; Spring Car Care; Leisure/Travel (2); Back-to-School; Football; Fall Home Improvement; United Way; Fall Car Care; Christmas Eve.
Special Weekly Section: TV (Fri).
Magazines: TV Section (fri); Real Estate (monthly).

CORPORATE OFFICER

President George R Sample

GENERAL MANAGEMENT

Publisher George Sample III
Business Manager Jean Hetrick
Purchasing Agent Kenneth J Smith
Director-Operations Kenneth J Smith

ADVERTISING

Director Carol A Cutshall
Manager-Classified Ada Miller

CIRCULATION

Manager Lori L Stevens

NEWS EXECUTIVE

Editor James D Hunt

EDITORS AND MANAGERS

Business/Finance Editor Sue McElwee
Columnist Sue McElwee
Columnist Polly McMullen
Columnist Lori Centi
Editorial Page Editor James D Hunt
Features/Films Editor Sue McElwee
News Editor Polly McMullen
Political Editor James D Hunt
Sports Editor Terry Bowser
Wire Editor James D Hunt
Women's Editor Amy Christopher

PRODUCTION

Manager Robert Dietz

Market Information: Split Run; TMC.
Mechanical available: Offset; Black and 3 ROP colors; insert accepted — preprinted; page cut-offs — 22½".
Mechanical specifications: Type page 13" x 21½"; E - 6 cols, 2¹⁄₁₆", ⅛" between; A - 6 cols, 2¹⁄₁₆", ⅛" between; C - 9 cols, 1⅜", ¹⁄₁₆" between.
Commodity consumption: average pages per issue 18(d), 18(sat); single plates used 5,600.
Equipment: EDITORIAL: Front-end hardware — Mk, Ro, IBM; Front-end software — Mk. CLASSIFIED: Front-end hardware — Mk; Front-end software — Mk; Other equipment — IBM. PRODUCTION: Typesetters — Ap/Mac LaserWriter; Plate exposures — 1-Nu; Plate processors — Nat; Scanners — Ap/Mac Scanner, AG/Scanner; Production cameras — C. MAILROOM: Bundle tyer — Sa, WeldLoc; Addressing machine — Wm, KR. WIRE SERVICES: News — AP; Photos — AP; Receiving dishes — size-10ft, AP. BUSINESS COMPUTERS: DEC/486, 6-DEC; Applications: Circ, Accts receivable, Accts payable, Gen ledger; PCs & main system networked.

I-352 Pennsylvania

INDIANA
Indiana County

'90 U.S. Census- 15,174; **E&P '96 Est.** 14,482
ABC-CZ (90): 28,962 (HH 9,800)

The Indiana Gazette
(e-mon to sat; S)

The Indiana Gazette, 899 Water St.; PO Box 10, Indiana, PA 15701; tel (412) 465-5555; fax (412) 349-4550.
Circulation: 17,727(e); 17,727(e-sat); 8,173(S); ABC Sept. 30, 1995.
Price: 50¢(d); 50¢(sat); $1.00(S); $12.00/mo; $132.95/yr (carrier).
Advertising: Open inch rate $17.69(e); $17.69(e-sat); $17.69(S). **Representative:** Landon Associates Inc.
News Services: AP, NEA, NYT. **Politics:** Independent-Republican. **Established:** 1890.
Not Published: New Year; Memorial Day; Independence Day; Labor Day; Thanksgiving; Christmas.
Advertising not accepted: Objectionable.
Special Editions: Bridal (Jan); Financial Fitness (Feb); Financial Fitness, Homemaker School, Newspaper in Education, Real Estate (Mar); Financial Fitness, Lawn & Garden (Apr); Summer Recreation (May); Car Care, Family Business (June); Arts Festival, Car Care (July); Football Contest, Senior Style, Football Edition, Car Care (Aug); Car Care, Football Contest, Energy Section (Sept); Car Care, Football Contest, Business Indiana (Oct); Holiday Gift Guide (Nov); Winter Sports (Dec).
Special Weekly Sections: Best Food Day (wed); TV, Business, Best Food Day, Family Leisure (local) (S).
Magazine: USA Weekend (S).

CORPORATE OFFICERS

Chairman	Joseph L Donnelly
President	Michael J Donnelly
Secretary	Hastie D Kinter
Treasurer	Stacie D Gottfredson

GENERAL MANAGEMENT

Co-Publisher	Joseph L Donnelly
Co-Publisher	Michael J Donnelly
Controller	Robert W Kanick Jr
General Manager	Joseph L Geary

ADVERTISING

Director-Marketing	Carol B Fletcher

CIRCULATION

Manager	David L Dickie

NEWS EXECUTIVES

Exec Editor	Samuel J Bechtel
Asst Exec Editor	Lynn Scott
Editor-Sunday	Frank B Hood
Managing Editor	Carl A Kologie
Asst Editor	William Graff
Asst Editor	John Phillips

EDITORS AND MANAGERS

Family/Fashion Editor	Lynn Scott
Photo Department Manager	W D Bechtel
Religion Editor	Pat Rich

PRODUCTION

Manager-Operations	Donna Rethi
Manager-Systems	Ed Yasick
Foreman-Pressroom	Joseph Naman
Superintendent-Mechanical	Ed Yasick

Market Information: TMC; Operate database.
Mechanical available: Offset; Black and 3 ROP colors; insert accepted — preprinted, odd sizes accepted, zoned; page cut-offs — 22¾".
Mechanical specifications: Type page 13" x 21½"; E - 6 cols, 2¹⁄₁₆", ⅛" between; A - 6 cols, 2¹⁄₁₆", ⅛" between; C - 8 cols, 1½", ⅛" between.
Commodity consumption: Newsprint 3,500 short tons; widths 27½", 13¾"; black ink 43,600 pounds; color ink 1,700 pounds; single pages printed 11,194; average pages per issue 26(d), 24(sat), 52(S).
Equipment: EDITORIAL: Front-end hardware — Tandem/Non-Stop, SII/CLX, SII/System 55; Front-end software — Tandem/Non-Stop, SII/CLX, SII/System 55; Printers — LaserMaster/Unity, AU/APS-6-82 ACS; Other equipment — 4-RSK/100. CLASSIFIED: Front-end hardware — Tandem/Non-Stop, SII/CLX, SII/System 55; Front-end software — Tandem/Non-Stop, SII/CLX, SII/System 55; Printers — LaserMaster/Unity, AU/APS-6-82 ACS. DISPLAY: Adv layout systems — SII; Front-end hardware — Anpa/RI, SII, IAL, Ap/Power Mac 7100; Front-end software — Multi-Ad/Creator, SII. PRODUCTION: Pagination software — SII/INL; Typesetters — Hyphen/Ultra, Hyphen/L202, LaserMaster/Unity, AU/APS-6-82 ACS; Plate exposures — 1-Nu/FT4OLNS, 1-Nu/FT40UPNS; Plate processors — 1-WL/25 inch; Electronic picture desk — Lf/AP Leaf Picture Desk; Scanners — ECR/Autokon, AG/Horizon Scanner; Production cameras — 1-C/Marathon; Automatic film processors — 1-LE/LD-24, LE/LD-2600 A; Film transporters — CH; Color separation equipment (conventional) — AG/Horizon Scanner, Ap/Mac Quadra.
PRESSROOM: Line 1 — 6-G/Urbanite (1 color unit), 1-U/788; Line 2 — 10-HI/V-15-D; Press drives — Fin; Folders — G/2:1; Reels and stands — 2-G/Rollstands, 4-Martin/Splicer; Press registration system — Carlson. MAILROOM: Counter stackers — MM; Inserters and stuffers — MM; Bundle tyer — MM; Addressing machine — 2-Ch; Other mailroom equipment — UniTrim (Rock Built). COMMUNICATIONS: Facsimile — Sharp. WIRE SERVICES: News — AP Dataspeed, AP Datafeatures; Stock tables — AP; Syndicates — AP Datafeatures; Receiving dishes — size-10ft, AP. BUSINESS COMPUTERS: SII/Tandem CLX 25; Applications: Accts payable, Gen ledger, Adv, Accts receivable, Circ, TMC, Newsprint, Inventory; PCs & micros networked.

IRWIN
Westmoreland County

'90 U.S. Census- 4,604; **E&P '96 Est.** 4,303
ABC-NDM (90): 117,775 (HH 44,740)

Standard Observer
(e-mon to fri; m-sat)

Standard Observer, RD #1, Route 136, Greensburg, PA 15601; tel (412) 523-6588; fax (412) 523-6805; e-mail stdobsv@aol.com. Tribune-Review Publishing Co. group.
Circulation: 8,528(e); 8,528(m-sat); ABC Sept. 30, 1995.
Price: 35¢(d); 35¢(sat); $1.50/wk; $78.00/yr (carrier), $99.00/yr (mail).
Advertising: Open inch rate $11.60(e); $11.60(m-sat). **Representative:** Landon Associates Inc.
News Service: AP. **Politics:** Independent-Republican. **Established:** 1901.
Not Published: Christmas.
Special Editions: Christmas; Home; Furniture; New Automobile; Progress Edition; Bridal.
Special Weekly Sections: Wheels (mon); Best Food Days, Business Directory (wed); Best Food Days (thur); Business Directory, Dining Guide (fri).
Magazine: TV/Entertainment Tab (sat).

CORPORATE OFFICERS

Publisher	Richard M Scaife
President	Edward H Harrell
General Manager	Richard T Rae

GENERAL MANAGEMENT

General Manager	Richard T Rae
Exec Editor	Craig J Smith
Manager-Business Office	Teresa Svec
Accountant	Mark Livingston

ADVERTISING

Manager	Don Iezzi
Manager-Classified	Sidra DeRose

CIRCULATION

Manager	John DeAugustine

NEWS EXECUTIVES

Exec Editor	Craig J Smith
Asst Editor	Linda Metz

EDITORS AND MANAGERS

Features Editor	Linda Metz
Lifestyle Editor	Debbie Kondel
Chief Photographer	Phil Wilson
Sports Editor	Jim Wexell

PRODUCTION

Manager-Press	Gary Moore
Mailroom/Distribution	Pat Lewis

Mechanical available: Offset; and 3 ROP colors; insert accepted — preprinted; page cut-offs — 21".
Mechanical specifications: Type page 13" x 21"; E - 6 cols, 2¹⁄₁₆", ⅛" between; A - 6 cols, 2¹⁄₁₆", ⅛" between; C - 9 cols, 1½", ⅛" between.
Commodity consumption: Newsprint 1,400 short tons; widths 27.5", 13.75"; average pages per issue 24(d).
Equipment: EDITORIAL: Front-end hardware — 16-CText/286 MFP; Other equipment — Lf/AP Leaf Picture Desk. CLASSIFIED: Front-end hardware — Ik, 3-Ap/Mac IIsi; Front-end software — Baseview; Printers — Ap/Mac. DISPLAY: Front-end hardware — 2-Ap/Mac 6100, 2-Ap/Mac Quadra 630; Front-end software — QuarkXPress 3.2, Adobe/Photoshop 3.3, Adobe/PageMaker 5.0; Printers — Ap/Mac; Other equipment — ECR/Imagesetter VRL-36. PRODUCTION: Typesetters — 2-Dataproducts/LZR1580, Ap/Mac LaserWriter; Platemaking systems — 1-LE; Plate processors — 1-Nat, 1-BKY; Electronic picture desk — Lf/AP Leaf Picture Desk; Scanners — Nikon; Production cameras — 1-B; Automatic film processors — 1-LE.
PRESSROOM: Line 1 — 10-G/Community; Folders — 2-G/SSC; Pasters — 4-Jardis; Press registration system — Duarte. MAILROOM: Counter stackers — 2-BG; Inserters and stuffers — 1-KAN/320; Bundle tyer — 3-Bu. WIRE SERVICES: News — AP; Receiving dishes — size-3m. BUSINESS COMPUTERS: DEC/VAX 750; Applications: Circ, Accts receivable, Accts payable, Payroll, Gen ledger; PCs & micros networked.

JERSEY SHORE
See LOCK HAVEN

JIM THORPE
See LEHIGHTON

JOHNSTOWN
Cambria County

'90 U.S. Census- 28,134; **E&P '96 Est.** 23,221
ABC-CZ (90): 86,302 (HH 35,415)

The Tribune-Democrat
(m-mon to sat; S)

The Tribune-Democrat, 425 Locust St.; PO Box 340, Johnstown, PA 15907; tel (814) 532-5199; fax (814) 539-1409. MediaNews Inc. group.
Circulation: 46,328(m); 46,328(m-sat); 53,427(S); ABC Sept. 30, 1995.
Price: 50¢(d); 50¢(sat); $1.25(S); $126.00/yr (carrier).
Advertising: Open inch rate $36.25(m); $36.25(m-sat); $36.25(S).
News Services: AP, KRT. **Politics:** Independent. **Established:** 1853.
Not Published: New Year; Memorial Day; Independence Day; Labor Day; Christmas.
Advertising not accepted: Brokerage Space.
Special Editions: Active Times, Bridal Guide (Jan); Progress, Auto Show, Engineering Week (Feb); Home Improvement, Fashion (Mar); Active Times, Auto Racing, Car Care, Fashion (Apr); Home Improvement, Active Times, Bridal Guide (July); Simply the Best, Folk Fest (Aug); Home Improvement, Football Round-up, Fashion, Simply the Best (Sept); Restaurant Dining, Active Times, Car Care, Football Round-up, Kitchen & Bath, Fashion (Oct); Football Round-up, Holiday Gift Guides (Nov); Holiday Gift Guides (Dec).
Special Weekly Sections: Best Food Days, Automotive, Outdoors, Neighbors (wed); Weekend (Entertainment/Leisure) (fri); Religion (sat); Best Food Day, Travel, Home (S).
Magazines: Weekend (fri); React (sat); Parade, TV (S).

CORPORATE OFFICERS

President	William Dean Singleton
Vice Pres	Anthony F Tierno

GENERAL MANAGEMENT

Publisher	Pamela J Mayer
Controller	Victor W Bilak
Personnel Manager	Joan Hunter

ADVERTISING

Director	Brian L Long
Manager-Classified	Barbara Mangus

CIRCULATION

Director	Thomas M McCarty

NEWS EXECUTIVES

Editor	Howard Saltz
Managing Editor	Larry Hudson

EDITORS AND MANAGERS

Art Director	Clifford Kepple
Editorial Page Editor	Bruce Wissinger
Regional Editor	Steve Liebman
Sports Editor	Chip Minemyer
Travel Editor	Art Heinz

MANAGEMENT INFORMATION SERVICES

Data Processing Manager	Thomas Shaffer

PRODUCTION

Director-Operations	Richard Wyckoff

Market Information: Zoned editions; Split Run; TMC.
Mechanical available: Offset; Black and 3 ROP colors; insert accepted — preprinted; page cut-offs — 22¾".
Mechanical specifications: Type page 13" x 21½"; E - 6 cols, 2¹⁄₁₆", .13" between; A - 6 cols, 2¹⁄₁₆", .13" between; C - 9 cols, 1⁵⁄₁₆", .13" between.
Commodity consumption: Newsprint 3,794 metric tons; widths 55", 41¼", 27½"; black ink 109,225 pounds; color ink 18,000 pounds; single pages printed 13,318; average pages per issue 32(d), 76(S); single plates used 32,043.
Equipment: EDITORIAL: Front-end hardware — DEC/PDP 11-84; Front-end software — TMS; Printers — 2-DEC/LA 120, DEC/LPO5, DEC/LP14; Other equipment — 27-NS. CLASSIFIED: Front-end hardware — DEC/PDP 11-84; Front-end software — CMS; Printers — 2-DEC/LA 120, DEC/LPO5, DEC/LP14; Other equipment — 11-NS. DISPLAY: Adv layout systems — SCS/Layout 8000. PRODUCTION: Pagination software — HI 6.6; OCR software — Dest/Workless Station; Typesetters — AU/APS Micro 5, 2-ECR/VRL 36; Plate exposures — Nu/WT40, Nu/Flip Top FT40; Electronic picture desk — Ap/Power Mac 7100 w/Adobe/Photoshop Ver. 3.0; Scanners — Microtec/2SPX; Production cameras — 1-K/Vertical 18, C/Marathon; Automatic film processors — P/36ML, DP/Chronaflow; Reproportion units — ECR/Autokon; Film transporters — 2-LE/APS 350; Color separation equipment (conventional) — Digi-Colour/4000, LE/Bessler enlarger; Digital color separation equipment — ECR/Autokon, Ap/Power Mac 7100 w/Adobe/Photoshop, Microtec/2SPX.
PRESSROOM: Line 1 — 5-G/Metro (2 decks); Press control system — Fin. MAILROOM: Counter stackers — 2-QWI/SJ100A, CH/Mk II; Inserters and stuffers — 1-HI/624; Bundle tyer — 2-MVP/P-53; Addressing machine — 1-MG/50. WIRE SERVICES: News — AP; Photos — AP; Stock tables — AP SelectList; Syndicates — KRT; Receiving dishes — AP. BUSINESS COMPUTERS: 2-DEC/PDP 11-84; Applications: Accts payable, Gen ledger, Accts receivable, Circ, Subscriber-non-subscriber, Newsprint inventory, Payroll, Class adv billing.

KANE
McKean County

'90 U.S. Census- 4,590; **E&P '96 Est.** 4,336

The Kane Republican
(e-mon to fri; m-sat)

The Kane Republican, 200 N. Fraley St.; PO Box 838, Kane, PA 16735; tel (814) 837-6060. Hollinger International Inc. group.
Circulation: 2,361(e); 2,361(m-sat); Sworn Oct. 2, 1995.
Price: 50¢(d); 50¢(sat).
Advertising: Open inch rate $6.25(e); $6.25(m-sat). **Representative:** Landon Associates Inc.
News Service: AP. **Politics:** Independent. **Established:** 1894.
Special Editions: Racing (May); Design-An-Ad (June); Football Preview (Aug); Timber/Progress (Oct); Christmas (Dec); Spring.
Magazine: TV Section (sat).

GENERAL MANAGEMENT

Publisher/General Manager	Kay Pearson

ADVERTISING

Director	Kay Pearson

CIRCULATION

Director	Peggy Kepler

EDITORS AND MANAGERS

News Editor	John Knapp
Sports Editor	Tony Battaglia

Mechanical available: Offset; Black and 1 ROP color; insert accepted — preprinted; page cut-offs — 22¾".
Mechanical specifications: Type page 13" x 21½"; E - 6 cols, 2¹⁄₁₆", ⅛" between; A - 6 cols, 2¹⁄₁₆", ⅛" between; C - 8 cols, 1½", ⅛" between.
Commodity consumption: average pages per issue 10(d).
Equipment: EDITORIAL: Front-end hardware — Mk/550 Sys; Front-end software — Mk/Newswriter. MAILROOM: Bundle tyer — 1-Sa; Addressing machine — 1-Am. WIRE SERVICES: News — AP.

KITTANNING
Armstrong County

'90 U.S. Census- 5,120; **E&P '96 Est.** 4,875
ABC-CZ (90): 17,346 (HH 7,205)

Leader Times (e-mon to sat)

Leader Times, 115-121 N. Grant Ave., Kittanning, PA 16201; tel (412) 543-1303; fax (412) 545-6768. Thomson Newspapers group.

Pennsylvania   I-353

Circulation: 11,672(e); 11,672(e-sat); ABC Sept. 30, 1995.
Price: 35¢(d); 35¢(sat); $1.75/wk (carrier); $1.90/wk (motor route); $91.00/yr (carrier); $99.00/yr (motor route).
Advertising: Open inch rate $14.42(e); $14.42(e-sat). **Representative:** Thomson Newspapers.
News Services: AP, THO. **Politics:** Independent. **Established:** 1872.
Not Published: New Year; Memorial Day; Independence Day; Labor Day; Thanksgiving; Christmas.
Special Weekly Sections: Food (wed); Cover Story (TMC), TV Magazine (fri); Religion, Home, Entertainment, School, Food (sat); Business, Lifestyles, TV, Comics (daily).

CORPORATE OFFICER
CEO-Pittsburg Tri-State Group .... Karen Wiltmer

GENERAL MANAGEMENT
Publisher/General Manager .... Kristy L Green

ADVERTISING
Director .... Barbara J Sheasly

CIRCULATION
Manager-Sales .... Larry Shuster

NEWS EXECUTIVE
Managing Editor .... Michael O'Hare

EDITORS AND MANAGERS
City Editor .... Janice Heller
Lifestyle Editor .... Jim Heasley

PRODUCTION
Foreman-Composing .... Richard Morgan
Foreman-Pressroom .... Thomas Hawley

Market Information: TMC.
Mechanical available: Offset; Black and 3 ROP colors; insert accepted — preprinted; page cut-offs — 21½".
Mechanical specifications: Type page 13" x 21½"; E - 6 cols, 2¹⁄₁₆", ⅛" between; A - 6 cols, 2¹⁄₁₆", ⅛" between; C - 9 cols, 1³⁄₈", ⅛" between.
Commodity consumption: average pages per issue 14(d).
Equipment: EDITORIAL: Front-end hardware — Mk/Mycrocomp 1100 Plus. CLASSIFIED: Front-end hardware — Mk/Mycrocomp 1100 Plus. PRODUCTION: Typesetters — 2-COM/Trendsetter, 2-Mk, Ap/Mac, 3-Laser; Platemaking systems — 1-B/Commodore II; Plate exposures — 1-Nu; Production cameras — 1-B/Commodore; Automatic film processors — 1-LE/LD-24-BQ, SCREEN/LD-220QT. PRESSROOM: Line 1 — 6-KP/Newsking; Folders — 1-KP. MAILROOM: Bundle tyer — 1-Bu; Addressing machine — 1-Am/1700. WIRE SERVICES: News — THO, AP; Syndicates — NEA; Receiving dishes — size-1m, AP.

LANCASTER
Lancaster County
'90 U.S. Census- 55,551; E&P '96 Est. 56,250
ABC-NDM (90): 422,822 (HH 150,956)

Intelligencer Journal
(m-mon to sat)
Lancaster New Era
(e-mon to sat)
Sunday News (S)

Lancaster Newspapers Inc., 8 W. King St.; PO Box 1328, Lancaster, PA 17608-1328; tel (717) 291-8811; fax (717) 291-8728; e-mail intell@news.cpcnet.com; web site http://www.adone.com/lancaster.
Circulation: 43,371(m); 48,986(e); 43,371(m-sat); 48,986(e,sat); 105,198(S); ABC Sept. 30, 1995.
Price: 50¢(d); 50¢(sat); $1.50(S); $3.00(wk (mail), $2.40/wk (carrier); $10.40/mo (mail); $104.20/yr (mail); $120.20/yr (carrier).
Advertising: Open inch rate $51.60(m); $51.60(e); $51.60(m-sat); $51.60(e-sat); $57.50(S); $53.00(m & e).
News Services: AP, NYT, KRT, LAT-WP, States News Service, NEA. **Politics:** Independent. **Established:** 1794 (Intelligencer Journal), 1877 (New Era), 1923 (Sunday News).
Special Editions: Business Review, 1996 Home Plans, Weddings (Jan); Financial Planner, Spring Home Improvement, New & Used Trucks (Feb); NIE Week/Design-An-Ad, Auto Leasing, Spring Outlet Guide, Economic Update, Spring Home, Lawn & Garden (Mar); Guide to Parenting, Fix Up Your Home, Resort & Travel, Manufacturing Housing (Apr); Dining-Restaurant Guide, Father's Day, Retirement Home Directory (June); Weddings, Opportunities in Education, Active Life (July); Family-owned Business Album, Fall Home, Lawn & Garden (Aug); Keystone National Races, Homemakers School, Manufactured Housing (Sept); Fall Home Improvement, Fall Outlet Guide, New Car Guide (Oct); Holiday Showcase (Nov); 1996 Gift Guide, In the Nick of Time (Dec).
Special Weekly Sections: Business Monday (mon-m & e); Food (wed-m & e); Neighbors (wed-m & e, zoned); Entertainment (thur-e, fri-m, S); Church (fri-e, sat-m).
Magazine: Local TV Week (S).

CORPORATE OFFICERS
Board Chairman .... Willis W Shenk
President/CEO .... John M Buckwalter
Vice Pres/Secretary .... Dennis A Getz
Vice Pres-Marketing .... Harold E Miller Jr
Treasurer .... Jay H Wenrich
Controller .... Jane L Nauman
Asst Treasurer .... David A Olsen

GENERAL MANAGEMENT
Business Manager .... Jay H Wenrich
Personnel Manager .... M Steven Weaver
Manager-Credit .... James D Hess
Coordinator-Newspapers in Education
.... Sherrye D Garrett

ADVERTISING
Manager-Retail .... Darwin R Hartsfeld
Manager-Classified .... Russell C Gillespie
Manager-National .... Melvin W Williams

MARKETING AND PROMOTION
Manager-Promotion .... James B McGrew
Manager-Marketing/Advertising
.... Annette F Strothers
Manager-Marketing/Circulation .. David B Lincoln

TELECOMMUNICATIONS
Audiotex Coordinator .... Allison E Miller

CIRCULATION
Director .... Keith S Kirchner

NEWS EXECUTIVES
Editor (Intelligencer Journal) ...... William H Cody
Editor (Lancaster New Era) .... Robert J Kozak
Editor (Sunday News) .... David M Hennigan

EDITORS AND MANAGERS
Librarian .... Edward G Wilson Jr
Intelligencer Journal
Business Editor .... Edward R Kamen
Lifestyle Editor .... Lynn Schmidt
News Editor .... Charles R Shaw
Sports Editor .... James P Hersh
Lancaster New Era
Business Editor .... James Loose
Magazine Editor .... Jean Korten
News Editor .... Peter C Mekeel
Sports Editor .... Dennis A Fisher
Sunday News
Business Editor .... Mary Ellen Wright
Entertainment Editor .... James R Ruth
News Editor .... Marvin I Adams
Style Editor .... Linda A Collingwood
Sports Editor .... William G Fisher

MANAGEMENT INFORMATION SERVICES
Data Processing Manager .... Douglas R Glouner

PRODUCTION
Coordinator-Quality .... Michael D Krayer

Market Information: Zoned editions; Split Run; TMC; Operate audiotex.
Mechanical available: Flexographic; Black and 3 ROP colors; insert accepted — preprinted; page cut-offs — 22".
Mechanical specifications: Type page 13" x 21"; E - 6 cols, 2¹⁄₁₆", ⅛" between; A - 6 cols, 2¹⁄₁₆", ⅛" between; C - 10 cols, 1³⁄₈", ¹⁄₁₆" between.
Commodity consumption: Newsprint 13,300 short tons; widths 55", 27½", 41¼", 48⅘", 13¾"; black ink 400,000 pounds; color ink 125,000 pounds; single pages printed 42,900; average pages per issue 45(d), 131(S); single plates used 130,000.
Equipment: EDITORIAL: Front-end hardware — 1-DEC/PDP 11-84; Front-end software — DEC/TMS; Printers — 2-DEC/LP25, 3-DEC/LA 180, 3-DEC/LA 124; Other equipment — 5-Lf/AP Leaf Picture Desk. CLASSIFIED: Front-end hardware — 1-HI/Cash; Front-end software — HI/Cash 5.0; Printers — Epson/OFX-8000. AUDIOTEX: Hardware — Brite Voice Systems, VRU; Software — Brite Voice Systems 3.21; DISPLAY: Adv layout systems — SCS/Layout 8000, SCS/Lynx; Front-end hardware — 17-HI/2100, Ap/Mac IIci; Front-end software — HI/PLS System, Multi-Ad/Creator; Printers — Dataproducts/LZR2600, Ap/Mac LaserWriter NTX. PRODUCTION: Pagination software — HI/PLS 2.1, QPS 3.3; OCR software — Caere/OmniPage 3.0; Typesetters — 2-AU/Laser, 1-AU/3850T; Platemaking systems — 2-LX/LF100; Plate processors — 2-NuGraphics/PTB; Electronic picture desk — Lf/AP Leaf Picture Desk, HI/Images; Scanners — ECR/Autokon 1000, 1-X/7650, 1-X/7650C, Newsrecorder; Production cameras — 1-C/Newspaper, 1-C/Marathon; Automatic film processors — 2-LE/2600, 1-LE/PC24BQ, 1-LE/LogE Teck 26, 1-LE/MAX 26; Film transporters — 1-C; Digital color separation equipment — Diadem/220, Diadem/410R, 1-Carat/Onyx System. PRESSROOM: Line 1 — 7-MAN/Flexoman; Line 2 — 7-MAN/Flexoman; Folders — 3-MAN/3:2; Pasters — 14-MAN/Automatic; Reels and stands — 14-MAN; Press control system — Fin. MAILROOM: Counter stackers — 4-QWI, 1-Id; Inserters and stuffers — 2-HI/72; Bundle tyer — 2-MLN, 2-MLN/2A, 4-Power Strap; Addressing machine — 1-Ch, 1-Buskro; Other mailroom equipment — AMGraphics/650 Stitcher-Trimmer. LIBRARY: Electronic — Data Times. COMMUNICATIONS: Digital ad delivery system — AP AdSend. Systems used — satellite. WIRE SERVICES: News — AP, NYT, KRT, LAT-WP, Photos — AP, NYT; Stock tables — AP; Receiving dishes — AP. BUSINESS COMPUTERS: 2-DEC/VAX 7610; Applications: CJ; Circ, Adv, Accts payable, Gen ledger; Best Programs: Fixed asset system; Armor: Purchasing system; PCs & micros networked; PCs & main system networked.

LANGHORNE
See LEVITTOWN

LANSDALE
Montgomery County
'90 U.S. Census- 16,362; E&P '96 Est. 16,227
ABC-NDM (90): 130,499 (HH 48,174)

The Reporter
(e-mon to fri; m-sat)

The Reporter, 307 Derstine Ave., Lansdale, PA 19446; tel (215) 855-8440; fax (215) 361-2142. Gannett Co. Inc. group.
Circulation: 19,474(e); 19,474(m-sat); ABC Sept. 30, 1995.
Price: 35¢(d); 35¢(sat); $2.25/wk (carrier); $117.00/yr (carrier), $164.00/yr (mail).
Advertising: Open inch rate $21.95(e); $21.95(m-sat). **Representatives:** Gannett National Newspaper Sales; US Suburban Press; Landon Associates Inc.; Robert Hitchings & Co.
News Services: AP, GNS. **Politics:** Independent. **Established:** 1870.
Special Editions: Business Outlook (Feb); Home Improvement, Health & Fitness (Mar); Garden, Car Care, Pool & Spa Garden (Apr); Mother's Day (May); Community Guide Book (July); Back-to-School, Fall Sports (Aug); Fall Fix-up, New Cars (Oct); Gift Guide (Nov); Christmas Greetings, Merchant Promotions, Gift Guide (Dec); Bridal (monthly).
Special Weekly Sections: Sports, Family (mon); Health, Business Calendar (tues); Food, Weddings & Engagements (wed); Garden, Encore (thur); Home Report (fri); Business Saturday, Real Estate Open House Directory, Church (sat).
Magazines: USA Weekend; Weekly TV Book; Weekly Entertainment Tab.

CORPORATE OFFICERS
President .... Suzanne L Bush
Treasurer .... Bernard DeAngelis

GENERAL MANAGEMENT
Publisher .... Suzanne L Bush
Director-Personnel .... Denette Holmes
Purchasing Agent .... Bernard DeAngelis
Controller .... Bernard DeAngelis

ADVERTISING
Director .... Tom Geonnotti
Manager-Retail .... Michelle Vernon
Manager-Classified .... Diana Augustine

CIRCULATION
Director .... Andy LeNoir

NEWS EXECUTIVES
Exec Editor .... John X Miller
Managing Editor .... Barb Delp

EDITORS AND MANAGERS
Business/Finance Editor .... Scott Kraws
City Editor .... Nona Breaux
Editorial Page Editor .... Richard Shearer
Education Editor .... Jamie Reese
Fashion/Women's Editor .... Mary Rowe
Films/Theater Editor .... Mary Rowe
Graphics Editor/Art Director .... Mark Locher
News Editor .... Phil Freedman

PRODUCTION
Photo Department Manager .... Ken Zepp
Sports Editor .... Vince Carey

MANAGEMENT INFORMATION SERVICES
Data Processing Manager .... Sally Verghese

PRODUCTION
Director .... A J Generotti
Asst Director .... John Weisberg

Market Information: TMC, ADS.
Mechanical available: Offset; Black and 3 ROP colors; insert accepted — preprinted; page cut-offs — 22¾".
Mechanical specifications: Type page 13" x 21½"; E - 6 cols, 2.03", ⅛" between; A - 6 cols, 2.06", ⅛" between; C - 10 cols, 1³⁄₁₆", ⅛" between.
Commodity consumption: Newsprint 1,200 short tons; widths 27¼", 13⅝"; black ink 15,120 pounds; color ink 9,500 pounds; single pages printed 11,193; average pages per issue 34(d); single plates used 15,600.
Equipment: EDITORIAL: Front-end hardware — HAS/H-555, 19-HAS; Printers — Facit/5000C; Other equipment — Ap/Mac Quadra. CLASSIFIED: Front-end hardware — HAS; Printers — Facit/5000C. DISPLAY: Adv layout systems — HAS; Front-end hardware — 3-AdPro, 2-HAS/Edit VIII; Other equipment — SCS/Layout 8000. PRODUCTION: Typesetters — 2-COM/8600; Plate exposures — Nu/Flip Top FT52LNS, Nu/Flip Top FT50UPNS; Plate processors — Nat/A-340, D; Electronic picture desk — Lf/AP Leaf Picture Desk; Scanners — ECR/Autokon; Production cameras — C/Spartan II; Automatic film processors — LE/LD 2600, LE/Line 27; Film transporters — LE; Shrink lenses — Kamerak/Scandia I; Digital color separation equipment — Howtek/Scanmaster, Lf/Leafscan 35. PRESSROOM: Line 1 — 15-G/Urbanite; Press drives — Fin; Folders — 2/G; Pasters — 8-Cary/Automatic; Press control system — G/PA. MAILROOM: Counter stackers — HL/Monitor, HL/HT, 2-PPK, HI/RS 25; Inserters and stuffers — GMA/SLS 1000; Bundle tyer — 3-MLN, Power Strap; Addressing machine — Ch. COMMUNICATIONS: Facsimile — X/5028; Systems used — satellite. WIRE SERVICES: News — AP Photostream, AP Datastream, AP Datafeatures, GNS; Syndicates — AP, GNS; Receiving dishes — size-4m, AP. BUSINESS COMPUTERS: 1-IBM/AS400; Applications: Circ, Adv billing, Accts receivable, Gen ledger, Payroll, Accts payable, Subscriber; PCs & micros networked; PCs & main system networked.

LATROBE
Westmoreland County
'90 U.S. Census- 9,265; E&P '96 Est. 8,163

The Latrobe Bulletin
(e-mon to fri; m-sat)

The Latrobe Bulletin, PO Box 111, Latrobe, PA 15650; tel (412) 537-3351.
Circulation: 8,867(e); 8,867(m-sat); Sworn Oct. 1, 1994.
Price: 25¢(d); 25¢(sat); $1.50/wk (in-county); $5.75/mo (in-county); $68.00/yr (in-county).
Advertising: Open inch rate $8.65(e); $8.65(m-sat). **Representative:** Landon Associates Inc.
News Service: AP. **Politics:** Independent. **Established:** 1902.
Not Published: New Year; Memorial Day; Independence Day; Labor Day; Thanksgiving; Christmas.
Special Editions: Spring Bridal (Jan); Spring Home Improvement (Mar); Spring Car Care, Mother's Day (Apr); Summer Fun (May); Fall Bridal (Aug); Fall Home Improvement (Sept); Senior Citizen (Nov).

CORPORATE OFFICERS
CEO .... Thomas M Whiteman
President .... Carl A De Pasqua
Vice Pres .... Hazel D Whiteman

GENERAL MANAGEMENT
President .... Carl A De Pasqua
Manager-Office .... Edward C Bodner

ADVERTISING
Manager .... Ken Seremet
Manager-Classified .... Connie Sabella

CIRCULATION
Manager .... Richard Pochet

NEWS EXECUTIVE
Editor .... Marie MacCamdless

EDITORS AND MANAGERS
Religion Editor .... Louise F Fritz

Copyright ©1996 by the Editor & Publisher Co.

I-354 Pennsylvania

Sports Editor Randy Skubek
Women's Editor Louise F Fritz

PRODUCTION

Superintendent Al Krinock
Foreman-Composing Al Krinock

Mechanical available: Letterpress (direct); Black and 3 ROP colors; insert accepted — preprinted; page cut-offs — 22¾".
Mechanical specifications: Type page 13⅛" x 21"; E - 6 cols, 2 1/16", ⅛" between; A - 6 cols, 2 1/16", ⅛" between; C - 8 cols, 1¼", 3/16" between.
Commodity consumption: Newsprint 500 metric tons; widths 25", 37.5", 50"; black ink 2,500 pounds; average pages per issue 20(d).
Equipment: EDITORIAL: Front-end hardware — Mk/Mycro-Comp Editorial Program. PRODUCTION: Typesetters — 2-COM/8600; Platemaking systems — LX; Scanners — 4-MES/100; Production cameras — 24-B/Commodore, B; Automatic film processors — LE/LD-24-AQ.
PRESSROOM: Line 1 — 4-S; Folders — 1-S/3:2; Pasters — 4-Cline; Reels and stands — 4-Cline. MAILROOM: Inserters and stuffers — KAN/301-124; Bundle tyer — 1-Sa/SRIA 2460, 1-Sa/S-1000 4991; Addressing machine — Am/Class 1900 852321. COMMUNICATIONS: Facsimile — Sharp/F334. WIRE SERVICES: News — AP, Extel/Monitor, Reperf Puncher. BUSINESS COMPUTERS: IBM/XT2; Applications: Payroll, Gen ledger; PCs & micros networked; PCs & main system networked.

LEBANON

Lebanon County

'90 U.S. Census- 24,800; E&P '96 Est. 24,067
ABC-CZ (90): 24,800 (HH 10,468)

The Daily News

(e-mon to fri; m-sat; S)

The Daily News, 718 Poplar St.; PO Box 600, Lebanon, PA 17042; tel (717) 272-5611; fax (717) 274-1608; web site http://www.leba.net/lebnews. Thomson Newspapers group.
Circulation: 21,406(e); 21,406(m-sat); 21,011(S); ABC Sept. 30, 1995.
Price: 50¢(d); 50¢(sat); $1.50(S); $3.25/wk; $14.08/mo; $169.00/yr.
Advertising: Open inch rate $25.70(e); $25.70(m-sat); $25.70(S). **Representative:** Landon Associates Inc.
News Service: AP. **Politics:** Independent. **Established:** 1872.
Special Weekly Sections: Builders Page (mon); Senior Citizen Page (wed); Farm Page, Church Pages (sat); Business Page (daily).
Magazines: TV Tab, USA Weekend Tab (S).

GENERAL MANAGEMENT

Publisher Blake L Sanderson
General Manager Blake L Sanderson

ADVERTISING

Manager-Retail Karen Williams
Manager-Classified Laura Baker Stocker

TELECOMMUNICATIONS

Audiotex Manager Kate Quick

CIRCULATION

Manager Mike Sheehan

NEWS EXECUTIVE

Managing Editor James Burchik

EDITORS AND MANAGERS

Art Director Gene Sholly
Business/Finance Editor Todd Meyers
City Editor Paul Baker
Editorial Page Editor James Burchik
Entertainment/Amusements Editor Laura Ritter
Fashion/Style Editor Patricia Seaman
Government Editor Paul Baker
Graphics Editor Gene Sholly
National Editor Karol Gress
News Editor Paul Baker
Photo Editor Earl Brightbill
Political Editor James Burchik
Sports Editor Bill Warner
Women's Editor Patricia Seaman

MANAGEMENT INFORMATION SERVICES

Data Processing Manager Karen Williams

PRODUCTION

Foreman-Composing Tom Carpenter
Foreman-Press Mike Novak Jr

Market Information: Zoned editions; TMC; Operate audiotex.
Mechanical available: Offset; Black and 3 ROP colors; insert accepted — preprinted; page cut-offs — 22¾".
Mechanical specifications: Type page 13" x 21½"; E - 6 cols, 2 1/16", ⅛" between; A - 6 cols, 2 1/16", ⅛" between; C - 9 cols, 1⅜", 1/16" between.
Commodity consumption: widths 55", 27½"; average pages per issue 24(d), 140(S).
Equipment: EDITORIAL: Front-end hardware — Mk/6000 System; Front-end software — Mk/ACE II; Printers — 1-TI. CLASSIFIED: Front-end hardware — Mk/6000; Front-end software — Mk/ACE II; Printers — 1-TI. AUDIOTEX: Hardware — Relisys; Software — Info-Connect/Pottsville Republican; Supplier name — TMS, AP. DISPLAY: Adv layout systems — Mk, Ap/Mac; Front-end hardware — Ap/Mac IIci; Front-end software — Multi-Ad/Creator; Printers — XIT/Clipper; Other equipment — Ap/Mac fileserver. PRODUCTION: Typesetters — 2-V/4000; Plate exposures — Nu/Double Flip Top; Plate processors — Nat/A-250; Scanners — V/4000, V/5300; Production cameras — 2-C/Marathon; Automatic film processors — SCREEN/LD 281Q, SCREEN/LD 220 QT; Shrink lenses — 1-CK Optical; Color separation equipment (conventional) — Lf/Leafscan 35; Digital color separation equipment — Lf/Leafscan 35.
PRESSROOM: Line 1 — 5-HI/Cotrell 1650; Folders — 2-HI; Reels and stands — 6-HI; Press control system — HI. MAILROOM: Counter stackers — 2-HL; Inserters and stuffers — 2-MM; Bundle tyer — 2-MLN; Wrapping singles — 1-MLN; Addressing machine — PBS. COMMUNICATIONS: Facsimile — III/Savin. WIRE SERVICES: News — AP; Photos — AP; Stock tables — AP SelectStox; Receiving dishes — size-10ft, AP. BUSINESS COMPUTERS: Oracle, PBS; PCs & micros networked; PCs & main system networked.

LEHIGHTON-JIM THORPE-PALMERTON

Carbon County

'90 U.S. Census- 16,356 (Lehighton 5,914; Palmerton 5,394; Jim Thorpe 5,048); E&P '95 Est. 16,208 (Lehighton 5,988; Palmerton 5,344; Jim Thorpe 4,876)
ABC-NDM (90): 121,183 (HH 45,562)

The Times News (e-mon to sat)

The Times News, First & Iron Sts.; PO Box 239, Lehighton, PA 18235; tel (610) 377-2051; fax (610) 377-5800; web site http://www.tnonline.com/sports.net/index.html. Pencor Services group.
Circulation: 15,968(e); 15,968(e-sat); ABC Sept. 30, 1995.
Price: 50¢(d); 50¢(sat); $8.75/mo; $105.00/yr.
Advertising: Open inch rate $22.70(e); $22.70 (e-sat). **Representatives:** Landon Associates Inc.; Papert Companies.
News Service: AP. **Politics:** Independent. **Established:** 1883.
Not Published: New Year; Memorial Day; Independence Day; Labor Day; Thanksgiving; Christmas.
Special Editions: Spring Bridal (Jan); Home Improvement (Apr); Spring Car Care (May); Pocono 500 (June); Football, Fall House Plans & Home Improvement (Sept); Fall Car Care (Oct); Christmas Shopping (Nov).
Special Weekly Sections: Best Food Day (mon); Business Page (tues, fri); Feature Section (sat).
Magazines: TV News 'n' Views, Saturday (sat).
Cable TV: Operate leased cable TV in circulation area; Own cable TV in circulation area.

GENERAL MANAGEMENT

General Manager Fred L Masenheimer
Asst General Manager Conrad Sthare

ADVERTISING

Director-Marketing Donald Reese
Director-National Donna Hall
Manager-Promotion Scott Masenheimer

CIRCULATION

Manager Sharon Wentz

NEWS EXECUTIVES

Editor Robert Parfitt
Managing Editor Robert Urban
Assoc Editor Jim Zbick

EDITORS AND MANAGERS

Action Line Editor Marigrace Heyer
Automotive Editor Al Sword
Business/Finance Editor Robert Urban
City/Metro Editor Robert Parfitt
Editorial Page Editor Robert Urban
Education Editor George Taylor
Fashion/Style Editor Marigrace Heyer
Features Editor Pattie Mihalik
Graphics Editor/Art Director George Taylor
National Editor Jim Zbick
Political/Government Editor Jim Zbick
Science/Technology Editor Ron Gower
Sports Editor Ed Hedes
Theater/Music Editor Ron Gower
Wire Editor Jim Zbick

MANAGEMENT INFORMATION SERVICES

Data Processing Manager Mike Reeder

PRODUCTION

Director David Helmer

Market Information: Zoned editions; Split Run; Operate audiotex.
Mechanical available: Offset; Black and 3 ROP colors; insert accepted — preprinted, all; page cut-offs — 22¾".
Mechanical specifications: Type page 13" x 21"; E - 6 cols, 2 1/16", ⅛" between; A - 6 cols, 2 1/16", ⅛" between; C - 9 cols, 1⅜", 1/16" between.
Commodity consumption: Newsprint 1,700 short tons; widths 34", 30", 27½"; black ink 31,300 pounds; color ink 4,025 pounds; single pages printed 7,800; average pages per issue 26(d); single plates used 3,900.
Equipment: EDITORIAL: Front-end hardware — Mk, 3-COM/MDT 350, 22-Mk/Mc 4003. Other equipment — 10-Ap/Mac; CLASSIFIED: Front-end hardware — Mk/Mc 1100, 2-Mk/Mc 4010. DISPLAY: Adv layout systems — 1-COM/AdVantage, Mk/Mc Ad Touch, 1-COM/Dawn. PRODUCTION: Typesetters — 1-COM/Unisetter, 1-COM/Videosetter, 1-COM/7200, 1-COM/8600; Plate exposures — 3-Nu/Flip Top; Plate processors — 2-Nat/250; Production cameras — 1-R/20x24, 1-AG/Repromaster, 1-Eskofot, 2-Kk; Automatic film processors — 2-LE/LD 18; Shrink lenses — 1-CK Optical/SQU-7.
PRESSROOM: Line 1 — W/Colorflex; Line 2 — MAN/Uni Man. MAILROOM: Counter stackers — 1-BG/108, 1-HL/Monitor; Inserters and stuffers — 1-MM/227E; Bundle tyer — 2-MLN/MLOAE. COMMUNICATIONS: Facsimile — BS. WIRE SERVICES: News — AP; Receiving dishes — size-3m, AP. BUSINESS COMPUTERS: 2-IBM/AS400; Applications: Circ, Adv billing, Accts receivable, Gen ledger, Payroll; PCs & micros networked; PCs & main system networked.

LEVITTOWN-BRISTOL-LANGHORNE

Bucks County

'90 U.S. Census- 62,690 (Bristol 10,405; Levittown 50,924; Langhorne 1,361); E&P '96 Est. 60,303 (Bristol 10,036; Levittown 49,133; Langhorne 1,134)
ABC-NDM (90): 343,611 (HH 120,576)

Bucks County Courier Times (m-mon to fri; S)

Bucks County Courier Times, 8400 Rte. 13, Levittown, PA 19057; tel (215) 949-4000; fax (215) 949-4114. Calkins Newspapers group.
Circulation: 69,243(m); 75,956(S); ABC Sept. 30, 1995.
Price: 35¢(d); $1.50(S); $3.00/wk; $25.00/mo (mail); $175.00/yr (mail).
Advertising: Open inch rate $62.15(m); $66.00(S). **Representatives:** Sawyer-Ferguson-Walker Co.; Robert Hitchings & Co.
News Service: AP. **Politics:** Independent. **Established:** 1910.
Not Published: Christmas.
Special Editions: Winter Clearance (Jan); Wedding Planner (Feb); Home Improvements, Spring Sports Guide, Education Guide, Homefinder (Mar); NIE Section (Apr); Summer Fun Guide (May); Fall Education Guide, Grange Fair, Back-to-School (Aug); Pro Sports Tab, Fall Sports Tab, Discover Bucks County (Sept); Brides Book, New Car Guide (Oct); Holiday Gift Guide (Nov); Winter Sports Guide, Last Minute Gift Guide (Dec); Coupon Booklets (monthly).
Magazines: Re-act (thur); 'Enjoy' (entertainment magazine) (fri); TV Time, Parade (S).

CORPORATE OFFICERS

President Grover J Friend
Vice Pres Arthur E Mayhew
Vice Pres Carolyn C Smith
Vice Pres Sandra C Hardy
Vice Pres/Secretary Shirley C Ellis
Vice Pres Stanley M Ellis
Director-Promotion Bernard (Bud) Umbaugh
Secretary Sandra C Hardy
Treasurer Edward J Birch

GENERAL MANAGEMENT

Publisher Arthur E Mayhew
Controller Robert M White
Purchasing Agent Lucy Lynch

ADVERTISING

Director Timothy J Birch

MARKETING AND PROMOTION

Manager-Promotion Carol Shapcott

TELECOMMUNICATIONS

Audiotex Manager Carol Shapcott

CIRCULATION

Director George W Stevenson

NEWS EXECUTIVES

Exec Editor Bill Steinauer
Assoc Editor Charles McCurdy
Assoc Editor Guy Petroziello
Assoc Editor Milt Krugman
Assoc Editor Mary Ellen Bornak

EDITORS AND MANAGERS

Amusements Editor Tom Haines
Business/Health Editor Mary Ellen Bornak
Editorial Page Editor Bruce Henderson
Education Writer Susan Lonkevich
Enterprise Editor Mary McInerney
Environmental Writer Rick Martinez
Features Editor Carl La VO
Graphics Editor/Art Director Jim Pitrone
Head Librarian Sue Ditterline
Health/Medical Writer Amy Neff
Night Editor Pat Walker
Photo Department Manager Jim Pitrone
Political/Government Editor Guy Petroziello
Exec Sports Editor Gary Silvers
Sports Editor Dick Dougherty
Theater/Music Editor Tom Haines

MANAGEMENT INFORMATION SERVICES

Director-Info Services Bill Clark

PRODUCTION

Director Gene Rosenberger
Foreman-Mailroom Al Farrell
Foreman-Press/Plate Al Farrell

Market Information: Zoned editions; Split Run; TMC; ADS; Operate audiotex.
Mechanical available: Letterpress; Black and 3 ROP colors; insert accepted — preprinted, all; page cut-offs — 22¾".
Mechanical specifications: Type page 13" x 21½"; E - 6 cols, 2", ⅛" between; A - 6 cols, 2", ⅛" between; C - 9 cols, 1.39", 1/12" between.
Commodity consumption: Newsprint 7,081 metric tons; widths 55", 41¼", 27½"; black ink 259,500 pounds; color ink 30,660 pounds; single pages printed 31,580; average pages per issue 52(d), 94(S); single plates used 35,745.
Equipment: EDITORIAL: Front-end hardware — IBM; Front-end software — Calkins/Text Editing System; Printers — 1-IBM/3287; Other equipment — 36-IBM/3278, 2-IBM/3178, 11-IBM/3179. CLASSIFIED: Front-end hardware — IBM/3090; Front-end software — Calkins/Adv & Acct System; Printers — 1-IBM/3287; Other equipment — 17-IBM/3179. AUDIOTEX: Hardware — PC/486; Software — Microvoice/MVA200; Supplier name — Tribune Media Services, VNN. DISPLAY: Adv layout systems — SCS/Layout 8000; Front-end hardware — 2-PC/486, 15-PC/486; Front-end software — SCS/Layout 8000, Archetype/Designer 3.2, CNI/Display Ad Tracking; Printers — 1-Okidata/OL830 LaserPrinter, 1-QMS/860 Laserprinter, 1-HP/4MV; Other equipment — 1-PixelCraft/8000, 1-MON/ProofXPress. PRODUCTION: Typesetters — 2-AU/APS Micro 5, 2-MON/ExpressMaster 3850; Platemaking systems — Na; Plate exposures — 2-Na/Starlite; Plate processors — 2-Na/40; Production cameras — C; Automatic film processors — LE; Film transporters — C.
PRESSROOM: Line 1 — 6-G, 2-G; Pasters — 8-G. MAILROOM: Counter stackers — QWI; Bundle tyer — 2-Power Strap. COMMUNICATIONS: Facsimile — Sharp/FO-6000. WIRE SERVICES: News — AP, SHNS; Photos — AP; Stock tables — Grand Central Stocks; Syndicates — NEA, CNS; Receiving dishes — AP. BUSINESS COMPUTERS: IBM/3090; Applications: Calkins: Accounting system; PCs & micros networked; PCs & main system networked.

Pennsylvania I-355

LEWISBURG
Union County
'90 U.S. Census- 5,785; E&P '96 Est. 6,122

Lewisburg Daily Journal
(e-mon to fri; m-sat)

Lewisburg Daily Journal, 19 Arch St.; PO Box 259, Milton, PA 17847; tel (717) 742-9671; fax (717) 742-9876. Hollinger International Inc. group.
Circulation: 1,910(e); 1,910(m-sat); Sworn Sept. 30, 1993.
Price: 35¢(d); 35¢(sat); $1.50/wk; $6.00/mo; $78.00/yr (carrier).
Advertising: Open inch rate $8.80(e); $8.80(m-sat).
News Service: AP. **Politics:** Independent.
Note: For production and printing information, please see the Milton Standard listing. Ad rates include a forced combination with the Milton Standard (e).
Not Published: New Year; Christmas.

CORPORATE OFFICER
Publisher Dorothy Park
GENERAL MANAGEMENT
General Manager David Barton
Accountant Eileen Kuhns
ADVERTISING
Manager Amy Moyer
CIRCULATION
Manager Michael Meckley Jr
EDITOR AND MANAGER
Managing Editor Eileen Winter
PRODUCTION
Director Gary Mitchell

Market Information: TMC.
Mechanical available: Offset; Black and 3 ROP colors; insert accepted — preprinted, post card up to SAU size; page cut-offs — 22¾".
Mechanical specifications: Type page 13" x 21½"; E - 6 cols, 2.07", ⅛" between; A - 6 cols, 2.07", ⅛" between; C - 10 cols, 1.22", 1/12" between.
Commodity consumption: Newsprint 52 short tons; width 28"; black ink 1,800 pounds; color ink 60 pounds; single pages printed 3,644; average pages per issue 24(d); single plates used 2,400.
Equipment: EDITORIAL: Front-end hardware — Mk/550, 3-Mk/NewsTouch; Front-end software — Mk; Printers — Ap/Mac LaserWriter Plus. CLASSIFIED: Front-end hardware — Mk/3000, 1-Mk/NewsTouch II; Front-end software — Mk; Printers — Ap/Mac LaserWriter Plus, Okidata/Microline 293 line printer. DISPLAY: Front-end hardware — Mk; Front-end software — Mk/NewsTouch II, Mk/Ad Touch; Printers — Ap/Mac LaserWriter Plus. PRODUCTION: Typesetters — 2-Ap/Mac LaserWriter Plus; Plate exposures — 3M/Deadliner; Plate processors — 3M/Deadliner; Production cameras — LE/Horizontal; Shrink lenses — CK Optical/5%. PRESSROOM: Line 1 — 6-G/Community; Folders — 1-G/SC. MAILROOM: Counter stackers — 1-BG/Count-O-Veyor; Inserters and stuffers — DG/320 2-into-1; Bundle tyer — 1-Bu/SP 505, 1-MLN/MS-T; Addressing machine — Dispensa-Matic/U 45. LIBRARY: Combination — Kk/Micro-Film viewer. COMMUNICATIONS: Facsimile — Canon/23. WIRE SERVICES: News — AP Datastream; Stock tables — NYSE, DJ; Syndicates — King Features, NEA, Universal Press, United Features; Receiving dishes — size-10ft, AP. BUSINESS COMPUTERS: 4-ATT/Unix PC 7300-3B1; Applications: Vision Data; PCs & micros networked; PCs & main system networked.

LEWISTOWN
Mifflin County
'90 U.S. Census- 9,341; E&P '96 Est. 8,953
ABC-CZ (90): 14,271 (HH 6,207)

The Sentinel (m-mon to sat)

The Sentinel, 375 Sixth St.; PO Box 588, Lewistown, PA 17044; tel (717) 248-6741; fax (717) 248-8317. Ogden Newspapers group.
Circulation: 12,820(m); 12,820(m-sat); ABC Sept. 30, 1995.
Price: 50¢(d); 50¢(sat); $8.25/mo (carrier), $9.25/mo (motor route).
Advertising: Open inch rate $14.01(m); $14.01(m-sat). **Representative:** Landon Associates Inc.
News Service: AP. **Politics:** Independent. **Established:** 1903.
Not Published: New Year; Memorial Day; Independence Day; Labor Day; Thanksgiving; Christmas.
Special Editions: Brides (Jan); Juniata Valley (Feb); Agriculture, Spring Sports (Mar); Fishing, Home & Garden, Spring Car Care (Apr); Grads, Low-fat Cookbook (May); Brides (June); Get to Know Us (July); Hall of Fame (Aug); Falls Sports, Juniata County Fair, Goose Day, Hunting (Sept); Winter Car Care (Oct); Holiday Gift Guide, Cook's Book, Dear Lonely Ladies (Nov); Happy Holidays, Last Minute Gift Guide (Dec).
Special Weekly Sections: Community/Life, Auto Racing, Agriculture (mon); Senior Citizens, Snapshots (tues); Food (wed); Pastimes, Outdoors, Region (thur); TV Today, Health, Schools (fri); Religion, People (sat); Business, Sports, Comics (daily).

CORPORATE OFFICER
President G Ogden Nutting
GENERAL MANAGEMENT
Publisher Bart Leath
Business Manager Ruth Eddy
ADVERTISING
Director Diane Brown
CIRCULATION
Manager Ed Williams
NEWS EXECUTIVE
Managing Editor Brad Siddons
EDITORS AND MANAGERS
Editorial Page Editor Brad Siddons
Features/Food Editor Jane Mort
Films/Theater Editor Scott Franco
Government Editor Anthony Demangone
Lifestyles/Education Brenda Ritter
News Editor Tom Knarr
Obituaries Editor Chris Gahagan
Photo Department Editor Dan Gleiter
Radio/Television Editor Scott Franco
Religion/Women's Editor Mary Margaret Pecht
Sports Editor Scott Franco
PRODUCTION
Foreman-Composing Jay McCaulley
Foreman-Pressroom Jay McCaulley

Market Information: TMC; Operate audiotex.
Mechanical available: Offset; Black and 3 ROP colors; insert accepted — preprinted.
Mechanical specifications: Type page 13" x 21½"; E - 6 cols, 2 1/16", ⅛" between; A - 6 cols, 2 1/16", ⅛" between; C - 6 cols, 2 1/16", ⅛" between.
Commodity consumption: Newsprint 1,416 short tons; widths 27", 13½", 30", 15", 27½", 13¾"; black ink 14,000 pounds; color ink 1,500 pounds; single pages printed 7,800; average pages per issue 25(d); single plates used 3,800.
Equipment: EDITORIAL: Front-end hardware — Ap/Mac; Front-end software — Inhouse. CLASSIFIED: Front-end hardware — Ap/Mac; Front-end software — Baseview; Printers — Okidata/210. AUDIOTEX: Hardware — PEP; Supplier name — Brite Voice Systems. DISPLAY: Adv layout systems — NCR; Front-end hardware — NCR; Printers — Talley. PRODUCTION: Typesetters — Ap/Mac Laser; Plate exposures — Nu/Flip Top; Plate processors — Nat; Electronic picture desk — Lf/AP Leaf Picture Desk; Scanners — Nikon; Production cameras — K/Vertical; Automatic film processors — LE; Color separation equipment (conventional) — Nikon.
PRESSROOM: Line 1 — 9-G/Community. MAILROOM: Inserters and stuffers — 4-MM; Bundle tyer — Bu/Strapper; Addressing machine — KAN. WIRE SERVICES: News — AP; Photos — AP; Receiving dishes — AP. BUSINESS COMPUTERS: NCR; Applications: Lotus: Circ, Payroll, Adv, Accts receivable; Microsoft/Windows; PCs & micros networked; PCs & main system networked.

LOCK HAVEN-JERSEY SHORE
Clinton and Lycoming Counties
'90 U.S. Census- 13,583 (Lock Haven 9,230; Jersey Shore 4,353); E&P '96 Est. 13,055 (Lock Haven 8,920; Jersey Shore 4,135)
ABC-CZ (90): 14,927 (HH 5,438)

The Express (e-mon to sat)

The Express, 9-11 W. Main St.; PO Box 208, Lock Haven, PA 17745; tel (717) 748-6791; fax (717) 748-1544. Thomson Newspapers group.
Circulation: 10,203(e); 10,203(e-sat); ABC Sept. 30, 1995.
Price: 35¢(d); 35¢(sat); $1.95/wk; $101.40/yr, $105.00/yr (outside PA).
Advertising: Open inch rate $13.95(e); $13.95 (e-sat). **Representative:** Thomson Newspapers.
News Service: AP. **Politics:** Independent. **Established:** 1882.
Not Published: New Year; Memorial Day; Independence Day; Labor Day; Thanksgiving; Christmas.
Special Editions: Friday the 13th (Jan); Tax Tab, Outlook Edition (Feb); Bridal Edition, Class of 2001 (Mar); Fishing Edition, Car Care Edition, Better Homes (Apr); Club Directory, Expo '96 (May); Vacation Edition (June); Careers Edition, Energy Edition (July); Social Security, Football Tab, Back-to-College (Aug); Boat Regatta, Fall Furniture, Fall Home Improvement (Sept); Hunting Edition, Car Care, Cookbook, Election Guide, Home-owned Businesses (Oct); Christmas Edition (Nov); Song Book (Dec).
Special Weekly Section: Susquehanna Sunrise (sat).
Magazine: TV All Week (sat).

GENERAL MANAGEMENT
Publisher Charles R Ryan
General Manager Charles R Ryan
ADVERTISING
Manager Richard Noll
CIRCULATION
Director Larry Rupert
NEWS EXECUTIVE
Managing Editor Chuck Yorks
EDITORS AND MANAGERS
Editorial Page Editor Chuck Yorks
Lifestyle Editor Wendy Stiver
Sports Editor Bob Sealy
PRODUCTION
Manager Chuck Smith

Mechanical available: Offset; Black and 4 ROP colors; insert accepted — preprinted; page cut-offs — 21½".
Mechanical specifications: Type page 13¾" x 27½"; E - 6 cols, 2.04", ⅛" between; A - 6 cols, 2.04", ⅛" between; C - 9 cols, 1⅓", 1/12" between.
Commodity consumption: Newsprint 300 short tons; width 55"; black ink 7,100 pounds; color ink 87 pounds; single pages printed 5,178; average pages per issue 16(d), 24(sat); single plates used 2,498.
Equipment: EDITORIAL: Front-end hardware — Mk; Front-end software — Mk; Printers — COM/8400. CLASSIFIED: Front-end hardware — Mk; Front-end software — Mk; Printers — COM/8400. PRODUCTION: Typesetters — COM/8400; Plate exposures — 1-Nu; Production cameras — R; Automatic film processors — DAI/LD-220-QT.
PRESSROOM: Line 1 — 8-G/Community. WIRE SERVICES: News — AP; Photos — AP; Receiving dishes — AP. BUSINESS COMPUTERS: 500-ATT/3B2; PCs & micros networked; PCs & main system networked.

MAHANOY CITY
See SHENANDOAH

McKEESPORT-DUQUESNE-CLAIRTON
Allegheny County
'90 U.S. Census- 44,197 (McKeesport 26,016; Duquesne 8,525; Clairton 9,656); E&P '96 Est. 37,883 (McKeesport 22,502; Duquesne 7,414; Clairton 7,967)
ABC-CZ (90): 88,909 (HH 37,047)

The Daily News
(e-mon to fri; m-sat)

The Daily News, 409 Walnut St.; PO Box 128, McKeesport, PA 15134; tel (412) 664-9161; fax (412) 664-3972.
Circulation: 25,038(e); 25,038(m-sat); ABC Sept. 30, 1995.
Price: 35¢(d); 35¢(sat); $3.10/wk; $10.90/mo; $98.10/yr.
Advertising: Open inch rate $22.80(e); $22.80(m-sat). **Representative:** Landon Associates Inc.
News Service: AP. **Politics:** Independent. **Established:** 1884.
Not Published: New Year; Memorial Day; Independence Day; Labor Day; Thanksgiving; Christmas.
Special Editions: Spring Bridal (Feb); Baseball (Mar); Graduation (May); International Village Anniversary Special, Football (Aug); Health & Senior Living (Oct); Gift Guide (Nov).
Special Weekly Sections: Travel (tues); Best Food Day (wed).

CORPORATE OFFICERS
President William J Cox
Vice Pres Mary H Mansfield
Secretary/Treasurer Patricia J Mansfield
GENERAL MANAGEMENT
Publisher Patricia K Mansfield
Chief Financial Officer Chris Miles
Business Manager Ramona W Burns
ADVERTISING
Director Mark Caruso
CIRCULATION
Director Larry Hilsen
NEWS EXECUTIVE
Assoc Editor Donald T Dulac
EDITORS AND MANAGERS
Business Editor Pam Reinsel Cotter
City Editor Bonniejean Adams
Editorial Page Editor Donald T Dulac
Education Editor John Cindrich
Entertainment/Amusements Editor David Sallinger
Society Editor Eleanor Kratzer
Sports Editor Norman Vargo
PRODUCTION
Manager Ernest Harkless
Foreman-Composing Richard Andrews
Foreman-Pressroom Patrick Burns
Foreman-Mailroom Larry Hilsen

Mechanical available: Offset; Black and 3 ROP colors; insert accepted — preprinted, card size inserts booklets; page cut-offs — 22¾".
Mechanical specifications: Type page 13" x 21½"; E - 6 cols, 2 1/16", ⅛" between; A - 6 cols, 2 1/16", ⅛" between; C - 9 cols, 1⅜", 1/16" between.
Commodity consumption: Newsprint 1,200 short tons; width 27.52"; black ink 65,600 pounds; color ink 820 pounds; single pages printed 7,500; average pages per issue 24(d); single plates used 7,650.
Equipment: EDITORIAL: Front-end hardware — SII/Sys 22, 23-SII/ET 960. CLASSIFIED: Front-end hardware — SII/ET 960. DISPLAY: Adv layout systems — 8-SII/ET 96 (on line). PRODUCTION: Typesetters — 2-M/202; Platemaking systems — 2-3M/Pyrofax; Production cameras — 1-Bo.
PRESSROOM: Line 1 — 6-G; Folders — 1-G/3:2. MAILROOM: Counter stackers — 1-Ch; Bundle tyer — 1-MLN. WIRE SERVICES: News — AP; Stock tables — AP; Syndicates — AP; Receiving dishes — size-3m, AP. BUSINESS COMPUTERS: 2-PC/386-25 MHE Model Keen-2530; Applications: Accts receivable; PCs & micros networked; PCs & main system networked.

MEADVILLE
Crawford County
'90 U.S. Census- 14,318; E&P '96 Est. 13,375
ABC-CZ (90): 20,988 (HH 8,297)

The Meadville Tribune
(m-mon to sat; S)

The Meadville Tribune, 947 Federal Ct., Meadville, PA 16335; tel (814) 724-6370; fax (814) 724-8755. Thomson Newspapers group.
Circulation: 16,502(m); 16,502(m-sat); 15,356(S); ABC Sept. 30, 1995.
Price: 35¢(d); 35¢(sat); 75¢(S); $2.15/wk (carrier); $9.32/mo (carrier); $111.80/yr (carrier).
Advertising: Open inch rate $17.96(m); $17.96(m-sat); $17.96(S). **Representative:** Thomson Newspapers.
News Service: AP. **Politics:** Independent. **Established:** 1884.
Not Published: Christmas.
Special Editions: Tax Guide, Bridal (Jan); Report to People (Feb); NIE Design-An-Ad, AG Day, Car Care, NASCAR (Mar); Health/Fitness, Home Improvement (Apr); Hot Air Balloons (June); Heritage Days, NASCAR (July); Back-to-School, Fair (Aug); Fall Sports, Outdoor, Car Care, Home Improvement (Sept); Cookbook (Oct); Christmas Opening (Nov); Winter Sports, NASCAR (Dec); Country Living (monthly).

I-356 Pennsylvania

Special Weekly Sections: Bravo! (entertainment) (fri); Crawford County West (zoned) (sat).
Magazine: On TV (S).

GENERAL MANAGEMENT
Publisher/General Manager Jeanne Moore-Yount
ADVERTISING
Director Marcia Martsolf-Miller
CIRCULATION
Director Rodney J Tirey
NEWS EXECUTIVE
Editor Hope Stephan
EDITORS AND MANAGERS
Business Editor Keith Gushard
Community Editor Jean Shanley
Editorial Page Editor Jack Yoset
Lifestyle Editor Sandy Pickup
News Editor Kevin M Hart
Photo Editor Jim Stefanucci
Special Sections Editor Ed Mailliard
Sports Editor Robert Heist
MANAGEMENT INFORMATION SERVICES
Data Processing Manager Glen A Ikirt
PRODUCTION
Director Glen A Ikirt

Market Information: Zoned editions; TMC; ADS; Operate database; Electronic edition.
Mechanical available: Offset; Black and 3 ROP colors; insert accepted — preprinted; page cut-offs — 22¾".
Mechanical specifications: Type page 13" x 21½"; E - 6 cols, 2¹⁄₁₆", ⅛" between; A - 6 cols, 2¹⁄₁₆", ⅛" between; C - 9 cols, 1⁵⁄₁₆", ⅛" between.
Commodity consumption: Newsprint 1,034 short tons; widths 27½", 13¾"; black ink 35,000 pounds; color ink 1,000 pounds; single pages printed 8,549; average pages per issue 23(d), 36(S); single plates used 15,442.
Equipment: EDITORIAL: Front-end hardware — 2-CText, 21-Compaq; Front-end software — CText; Printers — Ap/Mac LaserWriter IIg; Other equipment — Ap/Mac. CLASSIFIED: Front-end hardware — CText, 3-Compaq; Front-end software — CText. DISPLAY: Adv layout systems — SCS/Layout 8000; Printers — Ap/Mac LaserWriter; Other equipment — Risograph/Duplicator, AP AdSend. PRODUCTION: Typesetters — V/5300; Plate exposures — 2-Nu; Plate processors — 1-Nat/Super A250; Electronic picture desk — Lf/AP Leaf Picture Desk; Production cameras — 1-C/Spartan, 1-SCREEN/680C; Automatic film processors — 1-SCREEN/220, 1-SCREEN/LD281Q; Digital color separation equipment — V/4000, Lf/Leafscan 35, Ap/Mac 8500 w/Polaroid/Sprint Scan.
PRESSROOM: Line 1 — 10-G/Community w/color deck; Folders — 1-G; Press registration system — Duarte/Pin System. MAILROOM: Bundle tyer — EAM/Mosca, ROM, Constellation. WIRE SERVICES: News — AP; Stock tables — NYSE; Receiving dishes — AP. BUSINESS COMPUTERS: PC.

MILTON
Northumberland County
'90 U.S. Census- 6,746; E&P '96 Est. 6,759

The Milton Daily Standard
(e-mon to fri; m-sat)

The Milton Daily Standard, 19 Arch St.; PO Box 259, Milton, PA 17847-0259; tel (717) 742-9671; fax (717) 742-9876. Hollinger International Inc. group.
Circulation: 2,958(e); 2,958(m-sat); Sworn Sept. 30, 1992.
Price: 35¢(d); 35¢(sat); $1.50/wk; $78.00/yr (carrier), $94.00/yr (mail).
Advertising: Open inch rate $8.80(e); $8.80(m-sat).
News Service: AP. **Politics:** Independent. **Established:** 1890.
Note: Ad rates include a forced combination with the Lewisburg Journal (e).
Not Published: New Year; Memorial Day; Independence Day; Labor Day; Christmas.
Special Edition: Progress (Feb).

GENERAL MANAGEMENT
General Manager David Barton
Accountant Eileen Kuhns
ADVERTISING
Manager Amy Moyer
CIRCULATION
Manager Gary Mitchell
EDITOR AND MANAGER
Managing Editor Bill Kohler
PRODUCTION
Director Gary Mitchell

Market Information: TMC.
Mechanical available: Offset; Black and 3 ROP colors; insert accepted — preprinted, post card up to SAU size; page cut-offs — 22¾".
Mechanical specifications: Type page 13" x 21½"; E - 6 cols, 2.07", ⅙" between; A - 6 cols, 2.07", ⅙" between; C - 9 cols, 1.22", ¹⁄₁₂" between.
Commodity consumption: Newsprint 470 short tons; width 27½"; black ink 13,480 pounds; color ink 250 pounds; single pages printed 4,992; average pages per issue 16(d); single plates used 14,210.
Equipment: EDITORIAL: Front-end hardware — Mk/3000, 6-Mk; Front-end software — Mk/NewsTouch; Printers — Ap/Mac LaserWriter Plus. CLASSIFIED: Front-end hardware — Mk/3000, Mk; Front-end software — Mk/NewsTouch II; Printers — Ap/Mac LaserWriter Plus, Okidata/Microline 293 line printer. DISPLAY: Front-end hardware — Mk/3000, Ap/Mac Power Macs; Front-end software — Mk/NewsTouch II; Printers — Ap/Mac LaserWriter Plus. PRODUCTION: Typesetters — 2-Ap/Mac LaserWriter Plus; Plate exposures — 3M/Deadliner; Plate processors — 3M/Deadliner; Scanners — HP/ScanJet IIcx; Production cameras — LE/Horizontal; Shrink lenses — CK Optical/5%.
PRESSROOM: Line 1 — 6-G/Community; Folders — 1-G/SC. MAILROOM: Counter stackers — 1-BG/Count-O-Veyor; Inserters and stuffers — DG/320 2-into-1; Bundle tyer — 1-Bu, 1-MLN; Addressing machine — 1-Dispensa-Matic. LIBRARY: Combination — Kk/Micro Film viewer. COMMUNICATIONS: Facsimile — Canon/23. WIRE SERVICES: News — AP Datastream; Syndicates — King Features, NEA, Universal Press, United Features; Receiving dishes — size-10ft, AP. BUSINESS COMPUTERS: 4-ATT/Unix PC 7300-381; Applications: Vision Data; PCs & micros networked; PCs & main system networked.

MONESSEN-CHARLEROI-DONORA
Westmoreland and Washington Counties
'90 U.S. Census- 20,843 (Monessen 9,901; Charleroi 5,014; Donora 5,928); E&P '96 Est. 17,856 (Monessen 8,489 Charleroi 4,498; Donora 4,869)
ABC-CZ (90): 22,405 (HH 9,983)

The Valley Independent
(e-mon to sat)

The Valley Independent, Eastgate 19, Monessen, PA 15062; tel (412) 684-5200; fax (412) 684-8104. Thomson Newspapers group.
Circulation: 17,891(e); 17,891(e-sat); ABC Sept. 30, 1995.
Price: 50¢(d); 50¢(sat); $115.00/yr.
Advertising: Open inch rate $18.66(e); $18.66(e-sat). **Representative:** Landon Associates Inc.
News Service: AP. **Politics:** Independent. **Established:** 1902.
Not Published: New Year; Memorial Day; Independence Day; Labor Day; Thanksgiving; Christmas.
Special Editions: Bridal (Jan); Progress (Apr); Home Improvement, Car Care (May); Bridal (July); Football Preview (Aug); Social Security (Sept); Home Improvement, Car Care (Oct); Christmas Preview (Nov); Christmas Wrap-Up (Dec).
Special Weekly Sections: Best Food Day (mon); Best Food Day (wed).
Magazines: TMC 'Bonus' (wed); TV Section (fri).

GENERAL MANAGEMENT
Publisher Barbara Raitano
Accountant Vi Minjock
ADVERTISING
Manager John Bennati
CIRCULATION
Manager Kevin Hickey
NEWS EXECUTIVE
Managing Editor J Frank Jaworowski
EDITORS AND MANAGERS
City Editor Rebecca Miller
News Editor Rebecca Miller
Sports Editor Brian Herman
PRODUCTION
Superintendent John Crea
Foreman-Pressroom Philip Goin
Coordinator-Commercial Printing John Eckert III

Market Information: TMC.
Mechanical available: Offset; Black and 3 ROP colors; insert accepted — preprinted; page cut-offs — 22¾".
Mechanical specifications: Type page 13" x 21½"; E - 6 cols, 2¹⁄₁₆", ⅛" between; A - 6 cols, 2¹⁄₁₆", ⅛" between; C - 9 cols, 1⅜", ¹⁄₁₆" between.
Commodity consumption: Newsprint 1,000 short tons; widths 27½", 13¾", 34"; black ink 20,860 pounds; color ink 672 pounds; average pages per issue 18(d).
Equipment: EDITORIAL: Front-end software — Mk/TouchWriter; Printers — NewGen/Laser-Printer. CLASSIFIED: Front-end hardware — Mk/TouchWriter; Printers — NewGen/Laser-Printer. DISPLAY: Front-end hardware — Intel/GX Workstation, Hitachi/20" monitor; Front-end software — Archetype/Corel Draw; Printers — NewGen/Laser Printer. PRODUCTION: Typesetters — NewGen/Laser Printers; Plate exposures — Nu/Ultra Plus Flip Top; Plate processors — Nat/A-250; Electronic picture desk — Ap/Mac Quadra 800, Lf/LeafScan 35, Lf/AP Leaf Picture Desk; Scanners — Umax/UC-1200-SE, AVR/8000 GSX; Production cameras — 2-SCREEN/Companica 680C; Automatic film processors — LE/121, DAI/Screen LD-220-QT; Color separation equipment (conventional) — Digi-Colour/DC-5000.
PRESSROOM: Line 1 — 8-G/Community; Folders — G/SSC (w/balloon), G/SC Quarterfolder; Press registration system — Duarte. MAILROOM: Bundle tyer — Bu/210, TS/210H; Addressing machine — Wm. WIRE SERVICES: News — AP; Syndicates — THO; Receiving dishes — size-3m, AP. BUSINESS COMPUTERS: 2-PC, 2-HP/9000, HP/200 terminals, HP/60 terminals, HP/2300 Line Printer, HP/840 L Line Printer, HP/Laser Jet 4si; Applications: Lotus 1-2-3, Oracle, PRS; PCs & micros networked.

MOUNT CARMEL
See SHAMOKIN

MOUNT UNION
See HUNTINGDON

NEW CASTLE
Lawrence County
'90 U.S. Census- 28,334; E&P '96 Est. 24,599
ABC-CZ (90): 33,446 (HH 13,330)

New Castle News (e-mon to fri)
Weekend (m-sat)

New Castle News, 27 N. Mercer St.; PO Box 60, New Castle, PA 16103; tel (412) 654-6651; fax (412) 654-9593. Thomson Newspapers group.
Circulation: 20,161(e); 20,161(m-sat); ABC Sept. 30, 1995.
Price: 35¢(d); 35¢(sat); $2.20/wk; $9.53/mo; $108.40/yr.
Advertising: Open inch rate $17.90(e); $17.90(m-sat). **Representative:** Landon Associates Inc.
News Service: AP. **Politics:** Independent. **Established:** 1880.
Not Published: Christmas.
Special Editions: Brides, First Baby (Jan); Business-Industrial Review (Feb); Home Improvement (Mar); Car Care (Apr); Mother's Day (May); Summer Fun (June); Senior Citizens (July); Style, Football (Aug); Home Improvement (Sept); Car Care (Oct); First Baby, Christmas Greetings (Dec).
Magazines: TV Program, Children's Mini Page (fri).

GENERAL MANAGEMENT
Publisher/General Manager Max Thomson
Director-Business James P Hubenthal
Manager-Computer Service Tom Covert
Manager-Education Service Ray Keffer
ADVERTISING
Director Chris D'Angelo
Director-Creative Service Scott Fracul
Manager-Retail Daryl Neve
Manager-Classified Joelynne Koury
CIRCULATION
Manager F Len Blose
NEWS EXECUTIVES
Editor Max Thomson
Managing Editor Tim Kolodziej
EDITORS AND MANAGERS
Editorial Page Editor Mitchel Olszak
Education Editor Kathy Quimby
Entertainment/Amusements Editor Lisa Micco
Environmental Editor Debbie Bonnie
Layout Editor Dan Irwin
Librarian Jill McConnell
Lifestyle Editor Lisa Micco
News Editor Dan Irwin
Political Editor John Manna
Religion Editor Lisa Micco
Sports Editor Kayleen Cubbal
Television/Film Editor Tim Kolodziej
Theater/Music Editor Mary Alice Meli
MANAGEMENT INFORMATION SERVICES
Data Processing Manager James P Hubenthal
PRODUCTION
Manager-Composing James Burkholder
Manager-Press Scott Bair

Market Information: Split Run; TMC.
Mechanical available: Offset; Black and 3 ROP colors; insert accepted — preprinted; page cut-offs — 22¾".
Mechanical specifications: Type page 13" x 21½"; E - 6 cols, 2¹⁄₁₆", ⅛" between; A - 6 cols, 2¹⁄₁₆", ⅛" between; C - 9 cols, 1⅜", ⅛" between.
Commodity consumption: Newsprint 1,200 short tons; widths 55", 41¼", 27⅜"; black ink 21,400 pounds; color ink 500 pounds; single pages printed 8,850; average pages per issue 28(d); single plates used 12,064.
Equipment: EDITORIAL: Front-end hardware — 21-PC; Front-end software — III/Tecs 2; Printers — 2-Panasonic/KXP180. CLASSIFIED: Front-end hardware — 4-PC; Front-end software — III/Tecs 2; Printers — Panasonic/KXP180. DISPLAY: Adv layout systems — SCS/Layout 8000; Front-end hardware — 7-Ap/Mac; Front-end software — Multi-Ad/Creator. PRODUCTION: Typesetters — 2-XIT/Clipper; Plate exposures — Nu/Flip Top; Plate processors — 1-WL/30C Lithoplates; Production cameras — 1-C/Marathon, 1-B/2000, 1-K/240 Vertical; Automatic film processors — 1-LE/24AQ, 1-LE/PC13; Color separation equipment (conventional) — Lf/AP Leaf Picture Desk; Digital color separation equipment — ECR/Autokon 1000DE.
PRESSROOM: Line 1 — 4-G/Metro (color deck); Folders — 1-G; Pasters — G/Metro Automatic; Reels and stands — G/Reels; Press control system — Fin. MAILROOM: Bundle tyer — 1-Sa/59SR1A, 1-MLN/ML2EE; Addressing machine — IBM/Sys 34. LIBRARY: Electronic — MPS/TecsII. WIRE SERVICES: News — AP; Photos — AP; Stock tables — AP; Syndicates — SHNS; Receiving dishes — size-3m, AP. BUSINESS COMPUTERS: IBM/Sys 36; Applications: Lotus; PCs & micros networked.

NEW KENSINGTON-TARENTUM-VANDERGRIFT
Westmoreland and Allegheny Counties
'90 U.S. Census- 27,472 (New Kensington 15,894; Tarentum 5,674; Vandergrift 5,904); E&P '96 Est. 25,572 (New Kensington 14,566; Tarentum 5,123; Vandergrift 5,883)
ABC-NDM (90): 153,328 (HH 61,081)

Valley News Dispatch
(e-mon to fri; m-sat; S)

Valley News Dispatch, 210 Fourth Ave.; PO Box 311, Tarentum, PA 15084; tel (412) 224-4321; fax (412) 226-7787. Gannett Co. Inc. group.
Circulation: 34,284(e); 34,284(m-sat); 33,636(S); ABC Sept. 30, 1995.
Price: 35¢(d); 35¢(sat); $1.00(S); $2.75/wk (carrier), $3.00/wk (motor route); $143.00/yr (carrier), $156.00/yr (motor route).
Advertising: Open inch rate $43.63(e); $43.63(m-sat); $43.63(S). **Representative:** Gannett National Newspaper Sales.
News Services: AP, GNS. **Politics:** Independent. **Established:** 1891 (Daily Dispatch), 1904 (Valley Daily News).
Special Edition: Progress (Feb).
Special Weekly Section: Home Section (fri).
Magazines: Go! Entertainment Guide (thur); TV Magazine (S).

Pennsylvania I-357

CORPORATE OFFICER

President/Publisher Scott M Brown

GENERAL MANAGEMENT

Director-Human Resources Michele Shaw
Controller Linda Huet

ADVERTISING

Director Randy Mooney

MARKETING AND PROMOTION

Director-Marketing Marian Wait

CIRCULATION

Director Garth Groshans

NEWS EXECUTIVES

Exec Editor Richard Leonard
Managing Editor Richard Monti

EDITORS AND MANAGERS

City Editor Bob Fryer
Editorial Page Editor Debra Duncan
Librarian Louise McCleary
Lifestyle Editor Sally Webb
Asst Lifestyles Editor Lisa Clark
News Editor Mark Gruetze
Photo Department Manager William Larkin
Local Sports Editor Kevin Smith
Sunday Editor Cara Bonnett

PRODUCTION

Director Darrell Sandlin
Asst Director Jim Slater
Manager-Pressroom Raymond Drane
Manager-Distribution Center Bill Diller
Manager-Systems Tech Bob Walters
Manager-Pre Press Greg Killian
Manager-Service Lisa Baxter

Market Information: Split Run; TMC.
Mechanical available: Offset; Black and 3 ROP colors; insert accepted — preprinted; page cut-offs — 22¾".
Mechanical specifications: Type page 13⅛" x 21½"; E - 6 cols, 2.04", ⅛" between; A - 6 cols, 2.04", ⅛" between; C - 9 cols, 1.38", ⅛" between.
Commodity consumption: Newsprint 1,570 short tons; 1,424 metric tons; widths 54½", 40⅞", 27¼"; black ink 30,317 pounds; color ink 8,400 pounds; single pages printed 7,569; average pages per issue 29(d), 36(S); single plates used 15,000.
Equipment: EDITORIAL: Front-end hardware — SII; Front-end software — SII, QuarkXPress; Printers — Epson, Facit. CLASSIFIED: Front-end hardware — SII; Front-end software — SII; Printers — Epson. DISPLAY: Adv layout systems — SII; Front-end hardware — Ap/Mac; Front-end software — Multi-Ad, QuarkXPress; Printers — Ap/Mac LaserPrinters. PRODUCTION: Pagination software — QuarkXPress; Typesetters — 2-Hyphen/Spark Station, Hyphen/RIPs, 1-Hyphen/OPI, 2-AU/APS-108-6C Imager; Plate exposures — 3-Nu/Flip Top FT40UPNS; Plate processors — 2-W/300; Electronic picture desk — 2-Lf/AP Leaf Picture Desk; Scanners — RZ/4050, 1-ECR/Autokon 1000DC, Umax/Flatbed Scanner; Production cameras — C/Spartan III; Automatic film processors — LE/LD 2600A; Color separation equipment (conventional) — RZ/4050; Digital color separation equipment — ECR/Autokon 1000DE, Adobe/Photoshop.
PRESSROOM: Line 1 — G/Metro(2 half decks); Line 2 — G/RTP; Press drives — Fin; Folders — G/2:1; Reels and stands — 6-G/RTP; Press control system — Fin. MAILROOM: Counter stackers — 2-QWI/350B, QWI/1000, , QWI/5J20X, BG; Inserters and stuffers — HI/1372-P; Bundle tyer — 2-MLN/M62NA, 2-Power Strap/PSN 25, 2-Power Strap/PSN-6E; Addressing machine — Ch, Barstrom/Labeler; Mailroom control system — Id/On-line; Other mailroom equipment — Mc. WIRE SERVICES: News — AP, GNS; Photos — AP; Stock tables — AP; Syndicates — AP SelectStox; Receiving dishes — AP. BUSINESS COMPUTERS: IBM/S-38; PCs & micros networked; PCs & main system networked.

NORRISTOWN

Montgomery County

'90 U.S. Census- 30,749; E&P '96 Est. 27,833
ABC-NDM (90): 198,525 (HH 73,909)

The Times Herald

(m-mon to sat; S)

The Times Herald, 410 Markley St.; PO Box 591, Norristown, PA 19404-0591; tel (610) 272-2500; fax (610) 272-4003. Journal Register Co. group.
Circulation: 26,041(m); 26,041(m-sat); 22,512(S); ABC Sept. 30, 1995.
Price: 35¢(d); 35¢(sat); $1.00(S); $2.10/wk; $109.20/yr.
Advertising: Open inch rate $18.92(m); $18.92(m-sat); $18.92(S). **Representatives:** Landon Associates Inc.; Robert Hitchings & Co.
News Service: AP. **Established:** 1799.
Advertising not accepted: Obscene, etc.
Special Editions: Ed. Guide, Super Sale I & II (Jan); Spring Bridal, Progress Edition, Coupon Book (Feb); Coupon Book, Home & Garden I, Today's Woman (Mar); Home & Garden II & III, Education, Real Estate, Senior Lifestyles (Apr); Home & Garden IV (June); Summertime Fun, Coupon Book (May); Living Here, Coupon Book (June); Coupon Book, Fall Education, Business Profiles, A Day in the Life (July); Back-to-School, Football, History & Archive (Aug); Fall Lawn & Garden, Fall Bridal, Fall Real Estate (Sept); Home Improvement, Dining Out, Car Care, Coupon Book (Oct); Cookbook, Educational Guide, Holiday Season Preview (Nov); Holiday Shopper/Letter to Santa (Dec).
Special Weekly Sections: Best Food Day (wed); Automotive News (thur); Real Estate Focus, Weekend Entertainment (fri); Church News, Business Directory (sat); Automotive, Real Estate, Travel (S).
Magazines: USA Weekend; TV Time, Comics (S).

CORPORATE OFFICERS

President/CEO Robert M Jelenic
Exec Vice Pres/Chief Financial Officer/Treasurer Jean B Clifton

GENERAL MANAGEMENT

Publisher Geoffrey L Moser
Controller Kathy Morris

ADVERTISING

Director Keith Dawn

CIRCULATION

Director Robert Rothacker

NEWS EXECUTIVES

Editor Charles Pukanecz
Editor-Sunday Gregg Lawson
Managing Editor David Gilmartin

EDITORS AND MANAGERS

Business Editor Gregg Lawson
City Editor Johanna Church
Editorial Page Editor David Gilmartin
Lifestyle Editor Philomena Roberto
Sports Editor Mark Schiele

PRODUCTION

Director John Barlow
Foreman-Composing Richard Renninger
Foreman-Pressroom Art Golomboski

Market Information: Zoned editions; Split Run; TMC.
Mechanical available: Offset; black; insert accepted — preprinted; page cut-offs — 23$\frac{9}{16}$".
Mechanical specifications: Type page 13" x 22"; E - 6 cols, 2.07", ⅛" between; A - 6 cols, 2.07", ⅛" between; C - 10 cols, 1¼", $\frac{1}{12}$" between.
Commodity consumption: Newsprint 2,500 short tons; widths 55", 41¼", 27½"; black ink 62,500 pounds; color ink 10,775 pounds; single pages printed 12,812; average pages per issue 38(d); single plates used 27,670.
Equipment: EDITORIAL: Front-end hardware — Dewar/Disc Net; Front-end software — Dewar; Printers — Okidata. CLASSIFIED: Front-end hardware — Dewar; Front-end software — Dewar Sys VI; Printers — Dataproducts/LB 325. DISPLAY: Front-end hardware — Dewar/Discovery; Front-end software — Dewar. PRODUCTION: Typesetters — 2-Tegra/Varityper XP-1000, 1-Tegra/Varityper XM-108; Platemaking systems — Amerigraph; Scanners — ECR/Autokon; Production cameras — C/Spartan III, R/Vertical; Automatic film processors — LE; Film transporters — LE; Digital color separation equipment — Lf/AP Leaf Picture Desk.
PRESSROOM: Line 1 — HI/1650; Press drives — GE/200 h.p. Twin; Folders — 1-HI/double 2:1; Reels and stands — 5-G/Manual Reel. MAILROOM: Counter stackers — KAN, QWI/SJ 101; Inserters and stuffers — 2-KAN/480; Bundle tyer — MLN/ML2CC, 1-MLN/ML2EE; Wrapping singles — 1-HL/Monarch. COMMUNICATIONS: Systems used — satellite. WIRE SERVICES: News — AP; Stock tables — AP Datastream, AP SelectStox; Syndicates — Accu-Weather; Receiving dishes — AP. BUSINESS COMPUTERS: IBM/AS 400; Applications: INSI: Circ, Ad mgmt, Accts payable/Gen ledger, Payroll; PCs & micros networked; PCs & main system networked.

NORTH HILLS

See PITTSBURGH

OIL CITY

See FRANKLIN

PALMERTON

See LEHIGHTON

PHILADELPHIA

Philadelphia County

'90 U.S. Census- 1,585,577; E&P '96 Est. 1,534,451
ABC-NDM (90): 4,856,881 (HH 1,777,365)

The Philadelphia Inquirer

(m-mon to fri; m-sat; S)

The Philadelphia Inquirer, 400 N. Broad St.; PO Box 8263, Philadelphia, PA 19101; tel (215) 854-2000; e-mail editpage@aol.com; web site http://www.phillynews.com/. Knight-Ridder Inc. group.
Circulation: 469,398(m); 411,795(m-sat); 906,747(S); ABC Sept. 30, 1995.
Price: 50¢(d); 50¢(sat); $1.50(S); $3.60/wk.
Advertising: Open inch rate $350.00(m); $350.00(m-sat); $489.00(S); $678.75 (m & S); comb with Philadelphia Daily News (m) $392.00. **Representative:** Newspapers First.
News Services: AP, DJ, KRT, LAT-WP, RN, UPI. **Politics:** Independent. **Established:** 1829.
Note: Commodity consumption statistics are combined for the Philadelphia Inquirer and the Philadelphia Daily News.
Special Weekly Sections: Sports Special, Philadelphia Business, South Jersey Section, Suburban West Section, Suburban North Section, Health & Fitness (mon); Suburban West Section, Suburban North Section, South Jersey Section (tues); South Jersey Section, Suburban West Section, Suburban North Section, Food (wed); South Jersey Section, Home & Design, Weekend, Suburban North Section, Suburban West Section (fri); Travel, Food, Lifestyle, Bucks, Arts & Entertainment, Mainline/Delco Neighbors, Chester County Neighbors, Bucks, Montgomery County Neighbors, Gloucester County Neighbors, Cherry Hill Neighbors, Burlington County Neighbors (S).
Magazines: Local Gravure Magazine, Local TV, Color Comics (S).

CORPORATE OFFICERS

Publisher/Chairman of the Board Robert J Hall
Exec Vice Pres/Editor (Daily News) Zachary (Zack) Stalberg
Exec Vice Pres/Editor (Inquirer) Maxwell E P King

GENERAL MANAGEMENT

Exec Vice Pres/General Manager Steve Rossi
Senior Vice Pres-Employee Relations Louis W Sabatino
Senior Vice Pres-Marketing Charles Champion
Senior Vice Pres-Circulation (Inquirer & Daily News) Charles Champion
Vice Pres-Transportation Joseph Chandler
Vice Pres-Communications/Public Affairs Charles B Fancher
Deputy Editor/Vice Pres Gene Foreman
Vice Pres-Circulation Tim Ryan
Vice Pres-Finance Bob Mies
Vice Pres-Advertising Robert McCray
Vice Pres/General Counsel Katherine Hatton
Director-Production Patrick McHugh
Director-Labor Relations Thomas Duffin
Director-Project/Customer Info Service Walter Evans
Director-Augmentation Joan Praiss
Vice Pres-Systems/Technology Tom Sims
Director-Publishing Systems William Stroud

ADVERTISING

Director-Retail Todd Brownrout
Director-National Harvey Hill
Director-Classified Jeanie Enyart

MARKETING AND PROMOTION

Director-Promotion Gari Brindle
Director-Marketing John Friedman

TELECOMMUNICATIONS

Manager-Telecommunications Linda Paris

NEWS EXECUTIVES

Editor/Exec Vice Pres Maxwell E P King
Deputy Editor/Vice Pres Gene Foreman
Exec Editor Jim Naughton
Senior Editor-Systems Rick Scwwein
Managing Editor Steve Lovelady
Asst Managing Editor Jeffrey Price
Asst Managing Editor Lois Wark
Asst Managing Editor Sandra Long
Asst Managing Editor David Milne
Asst Managing Editor Paula Moore
Asst Managing Editor Arlane Morgan
Asst to Editor John V R Bull
Asst to Editor David Taylor
Assoc Managing Editor Sandy Wood
Assoc Managing Editor Lorraine Branham
Assoc Managing Editor Robert Rosenthal
Assoc Managing Editor Fran Dauth
Assoc Editor Acel Moore
News Editor Steve Glynn
News Editor Charles Krittle
News Editor Bill Sniffen
Sunday Editor Ron Patel

EDITORS AND MANAGERS

Architectural Writer Tom Hine
Art Critic Ed Sozanski
Automotive Writer Al Haas
Books Editor Mike Schaffer
Book Critic Carlin Romano
Beijing Bureau Jennifer Lin
London Bureau Fawn Vrazo
Moscow Bureau Inga Saffron
Berlin Bureau Barbara Demick
Johannesburg Bureau Glenn Burkins
Cairo Bureau Alan Sipress
Washington Bureau Steve Goldstein
Washington Bureau Jodi Enda
New York Bureau Terrence Samuel
New Jersey Editor Matt Golas
Pittsburgh Bureau Jeff Fleischman
Chicago Bureau Dan Le Duc
Boston Bureau Michael Matza
Business Editor Linda Austin
City Editor David Tucker
Columnist David Baldt
Columnist Melissa Dribben
Columnist Richard Jones
Columnist Steve Lopez
Columnist Claude Lewis
Columnist-Business Jeff Brown
Columnist-Business B J Phillips
Columnist-Lifestyle Lucia Herndon
Columnist-Society David Iams
Columnist-Sports Bill Lyon
Columnist-Sports Diane Pucin
Columnist-Sports Tim Dwyer
Design Director Bill March
Editor-Philadelphia Business Section Leslie Allen
Editorial Page Editor Jane R Eisner
Deputy Editorial Page Editor Chris Satullo
Assoc Editorial Page Editor Mike Leary
Editorial Cartoonist Tony Auth
Editorial Writer Russell Cooke
Editorial Writer Rick Nichols
Editorial Writer Trudy Rubin
Editorial Writer Henry Bryan
Editorial Writer Alexis Moore
Editorial Writer Doug Pike
Education Writer Dale Mezzacappa
Education Writer Martha Woodall
Education Writer Laura Bruch
Features Editor Beth Gillin
Films Critic Desmond Ryan
Films Critic Steven Rea
Films Critic Carrie Rickey
Fine Arts Editor Howie Shapiro
Food Columnist Marilynn Marter
Food Columnist Elaine Tait
Food Editor Gerald Etter
Foreign Editor Donald Kimelman
Health/Science Editor Dotty Brown
Higher Education Writer Howard Goodman
Higher Education Writer Lily Eng
Inquirer Magazine Editor Avery Rome
Labor Writer Marc Duvoisin
Librarian M J Crowley
Lifestyle Editor Beth Gillin
Lifestyle Editor Julie Busby
Media Editor Peter Kaufman
Medicine Writer Susan FitzGerald
Music Critic-Classical Daniel Webster
Music Critic-Classical Lesley Valdes
Music Critic-Popular Tom Moon
Music Critic-Popular Don De Luca
National Editor Ashley Halsey
Outdoors Writer Fen Montaigne
Photography Director Clem Murray
Popular Arts Editor Linda Hasert
Religion Writer David O'Reilly
Real Estate Writer Lisa Tracy

I-358 Pennsylvania

Residential Real Estate Writer Gene Austin
Residential Real Estate Writer Al Heavens
Science Writer Faye Flam
Sports Editor Nancy Cooney
State Editor Doug Robinson
Suburban Editor Larry Eichel
Exec Travel Editor Jack Severson
Travel Editor Michael Shoup
Theater Critic Doug Keating
Theater Critic Cliff Ridley
Television Magazine Editor Karl Schaeffer
Weekend Section Editor Don Sapatkin

MANAGEMENT INFORMATION SERVICES

Data Processing Manager Tom Sims

PRODUCTION

Director-Planning & Facilities Thomas Roth
Director-Printing Richard Danze
Director-Packaging & Distribution Lynn Steely
Director-Mechanical & Technical Services Ed Poletti
Asst Director-Printing Jim Brown
Asst Director-Packaging & Distribution Marion Todd

Market Information: Zoned editions; Split Run; TMC; ADS; Electronic edition.
Mechanical available: Offset; black; insert accepted — preprinted, all; page cut-offs — 22".
Mechanical specifications: Type page 13" x 21"; E - 6 cols, $2\frac{1}{16}$", $\frac{1}{8}$" between; A - 6 cols, $2\frac{1}{16}$", $\frac{1}{8}$" between; C - 10 cols, $1\frac{3}{16}$", $\frac{1}{16}$" between.
Commodity consumption: Newsprint 140,000 metric tons; widths 54", $40\frac{15}{16}$", $27\frac{1}{4}$"; black ink 2,304,000 pounds; color ink 364,800 pounds; single pages printed 47,114.88; average pages per issue 72.14(d), 200.54(S); single plates used 950,000.
Equipment: EDITORIAL: Front-end hardware — AT/30, 14-AT/J-11; Front-end software — AT 4.7.4; Other equipment — AT, 27-Ap/Mac. CLASSIFIED: Front-end hardware — AT/IAS, 150-AT, Sun; Front-end software — AT 4.7.2, AT/ClassPage; Other equipment — 2-Konica, 2-Bs/DEX. DISPLAY: Adv layout systems — AT/Architect; Front-end hardware — 13-Sun, 10-Ap/Mac; Front-end software — QuarkXPress 3.1, Camex; Printers — 4-Graphics Enterprises, 3-Artologic/108CS; Other equipment — 2-AU/APS 200, 2-DEC/Alpha RIP, 2-Eskofot/Scanners. PRODUCTION: Typesetters — 2-AU/APS-5, 4-AU/APS-6; Platemaking systems — WL/Lith, 5-WL/Lith 10; Plate exposures — 5-WL/Lith 10; Plate processors — 5-38G/Plate Processor; Electronic picture desk — Lf/AP Leaf Picture Desk; Scanners — 3-ECR/Autokon, 1-Newsrecorder, Phoenix, Lf/Leafscan, AG, Nikon, X; Production cameras — 1-C/Marathon, 2-C/Newspager II; Automatic film processors — 4-LE/2600; Film transporters — 7-LE; Color separation equipment (conventional) — 1-C/Color Computer, 1-BKY/Enlarger; Digital color separation equipment — Scitex.
PRESSROOM: Line 2 — 9-G/Color Liners (10 units); Press drives — 99-Allen Bradley; Folders — 9-Sovereign/160 Page 3:2; Pasters — 90-G/CT-50; Reels and stands — 90-G/CT-50; Press control system — G/APCS. MAILROOM: Counter stackers — 16-HT, 12-HT/2; Inserters and stuffers — 7-GMA/SLS 1000 8:1, 3-GMA/SLS 1000 24:1; Bundle tyer — 10-Dynaric/NR2, 15-Dynaric/SSB79, 12-MLN/2A, 3-Dynaric/NP2; Wrapping singles — 27-QWI; Addressing machine — 27-Ink Jet Printers; Mailroom control system — 9-Video Jet. LIBRARY: Electronic — Save Central, Vu/Text, PressLine Explorer on Ap/Mac, Digital Photo Archiving. COMMUNICATIONS: Facsimile — III/Rich Telepress; Remote imagesetting — III/Recorder, 3-III/3810, 1-III/3850; Digital ad delivery system — AP AdSend, AdFax, AdExpress, DigiFlex. Systems used — fiber optic. WIRE SERVICES: News — LAT-WP, AP, AFP, RN; Photos — AP; Stock tables — AP Selectstocks; Receiving dishes — AP. BUSINESS COMPUTERS: 1-IBM/3090 170E, 1-IBM/4381 GRPIZ, 2-HP/937, 2-HP/957 Processor; PCs & micros networked; PCs & main system networked.

The Philadelphia Daily News (m-mon to fri; m-sat)

The Philadelphia Daily News, 400 N. Broad St.; PO Box 8263, Philadelphia, PA 19101; tel (215) 854-2000; web site http://www.phillynews.com/. Knight-Ridder Inc. group.
Circulation: 195,447(m); 103,549(m-sat); ABC Sept. 30, 1995.
Price: 60¢(d); 60¢(sat); $3.00/wk.
Advertising: Open inch rate $175.00(m); $175.00(m-sat); comb with Philadelphia Inquirer (mS) $392.00. **Representative:** Newspapers First.
News Services: AP, KRT, SHNS, RN. **Politics:** Independent. **Established:** 1925.
Note: Commodity consumption statistics are combined for the Philadelphia News and the Philadelphia Inquirer. For corporate and general management officers, refer to the Philadelphia Inquirer listing.
Not Published: New Year; Memorial Day; Independence Day; Labor Day; Thanksgiving; Christmas.
Special Editions: M.L.K. Tribute; Philadelphia Women's Show; Shore Guide; United Way; Education Guide (6x); Back-to-School Fashion; Christmas Gift Guide; Eagles Playbook.
Special Weekly Sections: Food (wed); Travel & Resort, Sportsweek (thur); YO! Friday (fri); Fresh Ink (tues/month).
Magazines: Food & Home (wed); Entertainment Package (fri); Resort and Travel (monthly).

CORPORATE OFFICERS

Publisher/Chairman of the Board Robert J Hall
Exec Vice Pres/Editor (Daily News) Zachary (Zack) Stalberg
Exec Vice Pres/Editor (Inquirer) Maxwell E P King

GENERAL MANAGEMENT

Senior Vice Pres-Circulation (Inquirer & Daily News) Charles Champion
Vice Pres-Marketing Charles Champion
Vice Pres/General Counsel Katherine Hatton
Vice Pres-Circulation (Daily News) Charles J Tramo

ADVERTISING

Senior Vice Pres Robert McCray

MARKETING AND PROMOTION

Director-Promotion Gari Brindle
Director-Marketing John Friedman

TELECOMMUNICATIONS

Manager-Telecommunications Linda Paris

CIRCULATION

Vice Pres Charles J Tramo

NEWS EXECUTIVES

Editor Zachary (Zack) Stalberg
Managing Editor Brian Toolan
Asst Managing Editor Michael Days
Asst Managing Editor-Nights Michael Schefer
Asst Managing Editor Sandra Shea
Assoc Editor Gene Castellano

EDITORS AND MANAGERS

Automotive Editor Scott Heimer
Business Columnist Harriet Lessy
Cartoonist Signe Wilkinson
City Editor David Tucker
Deputy City Editor Dave Warner
Asst City Editor Al Hunter
Asst City Editor Gar Joseph
Asst City Editor Robin Palley
Asst City Editor Joanne Sills
Columnist-Features Stuart D Bykofsky
Columnist-Op-Ed Linda Moore
Columnist-News Elmer Smith
Columnist-News Jill Porter
Columnist-News Dan Geringer
Columnist-News Russell Byers
Columnist-Sports Bill Conlin
Columnist-Sports Stan Hochman
Columnist-Sports Rich Hofmann
Columnist-Washington Sandy Grady
Courts Dave Racher
Courts Jim Smith
Editorial Page Editor Morris Thompson
Education Editor Al Hunter
Entertainment/Amusements Editor Jill Williams
Environment Editor Robin Palley
Features Editor Deborah Licklider
Fresh Ink Editor Tonya Pendelton
Graphics Editor John Sherlock
Harrisburg Bureau John Baer
Health Editor Deborah Licklider
Library Manager M J Crowley
Music Editor Sandra Shea
News Editor-Day Jonathan Takiff
News Editor-Night Jerry Carrier
Obit Writer Don Hawkins
Personal Finance Editor Randolph Smith
Photography Editor Michael Mercanti
Politics Editor Gar Joseph
Exec Sports Editor Mike Rathet
Sports Editor Pat McLoone
Deputy Sports Editor Caesar Alsop
Sportsweek Editor Jeff Samuels
Systems Editor Frank Heick
Television Editor Jill Williams

MANAGEMENT INFORMATION SERVICES

Data Processing Manager Tom Sims

Market Information: Electronic edition.
Mechanical available: Letterpress (direct); Black and 3 ROP colors; insert accepted — preprinted, all; page cut-offs — 22".
Mechanical specifications: Type page $10\frac{1}{8}$" x 13"; E - 5 cols, $1\frac{29}{32}$", $\frac{1}{8}$" between; A - 5 cols, $1\frac{29}{32}$", $\frac{1}{8}$" between; C - 8 cols, $1\frac{13}{64}$" between.
Commodity consumption: Newsprint 134,000 metric tons; widths 54", 40.5", 27"; black ink 2,304,000 pounds; color ink 364,800 pounds; single pages printed 47,114.88; average pages per issue 47.28(d); single plates used 771,981.
Equipment: EDITORIAL: Front-end hardware — 8-AT/CPU, 6-AT/J-11, 128-AT; Front-end software — AT 4.7.2; CLASSIFIED: Front-end hardware — AT/IAS, 12-AT/CPU, 150-AT, 8-Sun; Other equipment — Fax Machines, 2-Konica, 2-BS/DEX. DISPLAY: Adv layout systems — AT/Architect; Front-end hardware — 6-Sun/3-80. PRODUCTION: Typesetters — 2-AU/APS-5, 4-AU/APS-6; Platemaking systems — WL/Lith-, 5-WL/Lith 10; Plate exposures — 5-WL/Lith 10; Plate processors — 5-38G/Plate Processor, 6-Bender; Electronic picture desk — Lf/AP Leaf Picture Desk; Scanners — 3-ECR/Autokon, Phoenix, Lf, AG, Nikon, X; Production cameras — 2-C/PagerII, 1-C/Marathon; Automatic film processors — 4-DP/24L, 3-LE/2600; Film transporters — 2-C/Pager II, 7-LE/Transport; Color separation equipment (conventional) — 1-C/Color Computer, 1-BKY/Enlarger; Digital color separation equipment — Scitex.
PRESSROOM: Line 1 — 9-G/Color Liner (10 units); Press drives — 99-Allen Bradley; Folders — 9-Sovereign/160 Page 3:2; Pasters — 90-G/CT-50; Reels and stands — 90-G/CT-50; Press control system — G/APCS. MAILROOM: Counter stackers — 15-HT/2, 16-HT; Inserters and stuffers — 7-GMA/SLS 1000 8:1, 3-GMA/SLS 1000 24:1; Bundle tyer — 3-Dynaric/NP2, 10-Dynaric/NR2, 12-MLN/2A, 17-Dynaric/SSB79; Wrapping singles — 27-QWI; Addressing machine — 27-InkJet Printers; Mailroom control system — 9-Video Jets. LIBRARY: Electronic — Vu/Text, Save Central, Ap/Mac AXX Digital Photo Archiving, Pressline Explorer. COMMUNICATIONS: Facsimile — III/Rick Telepress; Remote imagesetting — 3-III/3810, 1-III/3850; Digital ad delivery system — AdFax, AdExpress, AP AdSend, DigiFlex Image Net. Systems used — fiber optic. WIRE SERVICES: News — AP, KRT, UPI, RN, DJ, LAT-WP; Receiving dishes — size-10ft, AP, UPI, RN. BUSINESS COMPUTERS: 1-IBM/3090 170E, 1-IBM/4381 GRPIZ, 2-HP/937 Processor, 2-HP/957 Processor; Applications: Circ, Adv billing, Accts receivable, Gen ledger, Payroll, Prod, Mfg; PCs & micros networked; PCs & main system networked.

PHOENIXVILLE

Chester County

'90 U.S. Census- 15,066; E&P '96 Est. 15,865
ABC-CZ (90): 15,066 (HH 6,270)

The Phoenix (m-mon to sat)

The Phoenix, 225 Bridge St., Phoenixville, PA 19460; tel (610) 933-8926; fax (610) 933-1187. Journal Register Co. group.
Circulation: 4,841(m); 4,841(m-sat); ABC Sept. 30, 1995.
Price: 35¢(d); 35¢(sat); $1.75/wk (carrier), $2.00/wk (motor route).
Advertising: Open inch rate $11.23(m); $11.23(m-sat). **Representatives:** Landon Associates Inc.; Robert Hitchings & Co.
News Service: AP. **Politics:** Independent. **Established:** 1888.
Note: The Phoenix is printed by the Daily Local News, West Chester PA, a Journal Register Company Newspaper.
Special Editions: Progress Report (Jan); Bridal (Feb); House & Garden (Mar); Sr. Citizens, Car Care (May); Education Guide, Football (Sept); Home & Garden (Oct); Holiday Gift Guide (Nov); Christmas Mini Guide, Drink and Drive Pages (Dec).
Special Weekly Sections: Health (mon); Business (tues); Food, Education (wed); Entertainment, Dining, Business (thur); Home and Garden (fri); Education, TV Section (sat).

CORPORATE OFFICERS

President/CEO Robert M Jelenic
Exec Vice Pres/Chief Financial Officer/Treasurer Jean B Clifton

GENERAL MANAGEMENT

Publisher Daniel I Goodrich
Business Manager Scott Armstrong

ADVERTISING

Director Michael Joyce

CIRCULATION

Director Brian Vaughan

NEWS EXECUTIVE

Editor Rita Cellucci

EDITOR AND MANAGER

Editor Rita Cellucci

PRODUCTION

Foreman-Composing Room Bobbi Hamler
Foreman-Composing Room Laurin Seaman

Mechanical available: Offset; Black and 3 ROP colors; insert accepted — preprinted, up to $\frac{1}{8}$" thickness; page cut-offs — $22\frac{3}{4}$".
Mechanical specifications: Type page 13" x $21\frac{1}{2}$"; E - 6 cols, $2\frac{1}{16}$", $\frac{1}{8}$" between; A - 6 cols, $2\frac{1}{16}$", $\frac{1}{8}$" between; C - 8 cols, $1\frac{1}{2}$", $\frac{1}{8}$" between.
Commodity consumption: Newsprint 275 short tons; widths $27\frac{1}{2}$", $13\frac{3}{4}$"; black ink 6,000 pounds; color ink 800 pounds; single pages printed 5,900; average pages per issue 20(d); single plates used 10,000.
Equipment: EDITORIAL: Front-end hardware — Intertext; Front-end software — Intertext. CLASSIFIED: Front-end hardware — Intertext; Front-end software — Intertext; Other equipment — 1-FAX/Telecopier. DISPLAY: Front-end hardware — Ap/Mac Network; Front-end software — Multi-Ad/Creator Network. PRODUCTION: Typesetters — 2-M/202, V/600; Plate exposures — 1-Nu/Flip Top FT40L; Production cameras — 1-LE/5000H, 1-Spartan III; Automatic film processors — 1-P/Pakorol, 1-LE. LIBRARY: Combination — 1-BH/Microfilm reader. COMMUNICATIONS: Facsimile — FAX/230. WIRE SERVICES: News — AP; Receiving dishes — AP. BUSINESS COMPUTERS: PC/Network; Applications: MSSI: Adv billing, Accts receivable, Circ, Accts payable, Gen ledger, Payroll; PCs & micros networked; PCs & main system networked.

PITTSBURGH

Allegheny County

'90 U.S. Census- 369,879; E&P '96 Est. 330,420
ABC-CZ (90): 1,019,387 (HH 418,142)

North Hills News Record (e-mon to fri; m-sat; S)

North Hills News Record, 137 Commonwealth Dr., Warrendale, PA 15086; tel (412) 772-3900; fax (412) 772-7379; e-mail nhnr@gannett.nauticom.net; web site http://www.nauticom.net/www/nhnr/top.htm l. Gannett Co. Inc. group.
Circulation: 22,178(e); 22,178(m-sat); 22,178(S); Sworn Sept. 28, 1995.
Price: 35¢(d); 35¢(sat); 75¢(S); $2.25/wk; $117.00/yr.
Advertising: Open inch rate $35.65(e); $35.65(m-sat); $39.25(S). **Representative:** Gannett National Newspaper Sales.
News Services: AP, GNS. **Politics:** Independent. **Established:** 1962, 1992 (daily).
Special Editions: Progress Edition (Mar); Community Guide (Aug).
Special Weekly Sections: Food (wed); Go! (entertainment guide) (thur); Home (fri); High School Sports Section (sat); Real Estate, Travel (S).
Magazine: TV Magazine (fri).

CORPORATE OFFICER

President/Publisher/CEO Kathy M Kozdemba

GENERAL MANAGEMENT

Director-Finance Ketan N Gandhi
Director-Human Resources Debbie Alexander

ADVERTISING

Director Jack Robb

MARKETING AND PROMOTION

Director-Marketing Service Suzette Cook

CIRCULATION

Director Garth Groshans

NEWS EXECUTIVES

Exec Editor Richard Leonard
Managing Editor David C Fritz

EDITORS AND MANAGERS

Business/Finance Editor Mark Whittaker
City/Metro Editor Tom Krisher
Editorial Page Editor Lou Ransom
Editor Richard Leonard
Entertainment/Amusements Editor Sally Webb
Features/Travel Editor Sally Webb
Health/Medical Editor Sally Webb

Pennsylvania I-359

News Editor Mark Gruetze
Photo Editor Chuck Kimmerle
Political/Government Editor Tom Krisher
Religion Editor Sally Webb
Sports Editor Tom Hayden
Women's Editor Sally Webb

MANAGEMENT INFORMATION SERVICES
Data Processing Manager Patty Burdett

PRODUCTION
Director Darrell Sandlin
Manager-Ad Service Caroll Stacklin

Market Information: TMC.
Mechanical available: Offset; Black and 3 ROP colors; insert accepted — preprinted; page cut-offs — 22¾".
Mechanical specifications: Type page 13⅛" x 21½"; E - 6 cols, 2.04", ⅛" between; A - 6 cols, 2.04", ⅛" between; C - 9 cols, 1.38", ⅛" between.
Commodity consumption: Newsprint 2,045 short tons; widths 54½", 40⅞", 27¼"; black ink 58,811 pounds; color ink 9,393 pounds; single pages printed 12,727; average pages per issue 31(d), 57(S); single plates used 14,124.
Equipment: EDITORIAL: Front-end hardware — SII, Ap/Mac; Front-end software — SII, QuarkXPress; Printers — Ap/Mac LaserWriter. CLASSIFIED: Front-end hardware — SII; Front-end software — SII; Printers — Ap/Mac Laser-Writer. DISPLAY: Adv layout systems — SII; Front-end hardware — Ap/Mac; Front-end software — Multi-Ad, QuarkXPress; Printers — Ap/Mac LaserPrinters. PRODUCTION: Pagination software — QuarkXPress; Typesetters — 2-Hyphen/Spark Station RIP, 1-Hyphen/OPI, 2-AU/APS-108-6C Imager; Plate exposures — 3-Nu/Flip Top FT40UPNS; Plate processors — 2-W/300; Electronic picture desk — 2-Lf/AP Leaf Picture Desk; Scanners — RZ/4050, 1-ECR/Autokon 1000DC, Umax/Flatbed Scanner; Production cameras — C/Spartan III; Automatic film processors — LE/LD 2600A; Color separation equipment (conventional) — RZ/4050; Digital color separation equipment — ECR/Autokon 1000DE, Adobe/Photoshop. PRESSROOM: Line 1 — 6-G/Metro (2 half decks); Line 2 — G/RTP; Press drives — Fin; Folders — G/2:1; Reels and stands — 6-G/RTP; Press control system — Fin. MAILROOM: Counter stackers — 2-QWI/350B, QWI/1000, QWI/5J20X, BG; Inserters and stuffers — HI/1372-P; Bundle tyer — 2-MLN/M62NA, 2-Power Strap/PSN 25, 2-Power Strap/PSN-6E; Addressing machine — Ch, Barstrom/Labeler; Mailroom control system — Id/On-line. LIBRARY: Electronic — Archivist Image Cataloging System. WIRE SERVICES: News — AP, GNS; Photos — AP, GNS; Stock tables — AP Grand Central Stocks; Receiving dishes — AP. BUSINESS COMPUTERS: IBM/S-38; PCs & micros networked; PCs & main system networked.

Pittsburgh Post-Gazette
(m-mon to sat; S)

Pittsburgh Post-Gazette, 34 Blvd. of the Allies, Pittsburgh, PA 15222; tel (412) 263-1100. Blade Communications Inc. group.
Circulation: 242,723(m); 239,152(m-sat); 442,471(S); ABC Sept. 30, 1995.
Price: 50¢(d); 50¢(sat); $1.50(S); $3.00/wk; $156.00/yr.
Advertising: Open inch rate $163.84(m); $163.84(m-sat); $277.50(S); $386.65(m & S). **Representative:** Newspapers First.
News Services: AP, NYT, DJ, RN. **Politics:** Independent. **Established:** 1786 (Gazette), 1842 (Post).
Advertising not accepted: Fortune tellers; Speculative investments.
Special Editions: Bridal, Careers (Jan); Home Design, Auto Show (Feb); Home & Garden Show, Top 50, Fashion, Careers/Health/Medical, Baseball (Mar); Real Estate, Golf (Apr); Spring Gas Tab, Summer Stuff, Summer in the City, Careers, Weekend of Wheels (May); Fitness/Recreation, Senior Citizens Expo (June); Olympics (July); Regatta, Fall Fashion/Bridal, Football, Weekend of Wheels (Aug); Fall Arts Preview, Careers/Engineering/Computers, Fall Gas Tab (Sept); Hockey, Baby Faire, Real Estate, Small Business (Oct); Election '96, Light-Up Weekend/Gift Guide, Weekend of Wheels (Nov); Gift Guide (Dec).
Special Weekly Sections: Business/Economics (tues); Best Food Day (wed); Weekend Magazine, Travel & Resorts (fri); Best Food Day, Travel & Resorts (S).
Magazine: TV Week (S).

CORPORATE OFFICERS
Chairman William Block Sr
President William Block Jr
Vice Pres John Robinson Block
Vice Pres Robert B Higdon
Vice Pres John G Craig Jr

GENERAL MANAGEMENT
Co-Publisher William Block Jr
Co-Publisher John Robinson Block
General Manager Robert B Higdon
Director-Labor Relations Raymond N Burnett
Director-Human Resources Wayne J Bjerregaard
Director-Finance Edward B Lasak

ADVERTISING
Manager-Display Barbara Chodos
Manager-Retail Sue Ellen Olsen
Manager-Classified Jack E Heyl
Manager-Sales National Harry Molchen
Manager-Sales Development Janice S Crile

MARKETING AND PROMOTION
Director-Marketing Debra Alward

TELECOMMUNICATIONS
Audiotex Manager Janice S Crile

CIRCULATION
Director Thomas G Herrmann
Manager-Transportation James M Gorman
Manager-Sales Peter Pfluger
Manager-Home Delivery Randy K Waugaman
Manager-Single Copy David M Stolar

NEWS EXECUTIVES
Editor in Chief John Robinson Block
Editor John G Craig Jr
Senior Editor William Deibler
Editor-Sunday Magazine Mark Murphy
Editor-Weekend Scott Mervis
Asst to Editor Woodene Merriman
Asst to Editor Matthew Kennedy
Assoc Editor-News Carl Remensky
Assoc Editor-Graphics Tracy Collins
Assoc Editor-Features Allan Walton
Assoc Editor Don Hammonds
Assoc Editor Tom Waseleski
Assoc Editor Jane Blotzer
Managing Editor Madelyn Ross
Asst Managing Editor-Graphics Christopher Pett-Ridge
Asst Managing Editor-Projects Mark Roth
Asst Managing Editor-News Barbara Griffin
Asst Managing Editor-News Production Ced Kurtz
Asst Managing Editor-Sports Frederick Huysman
Asst Managing Editor-Features Susan Puskar

EDITORS AND MANAGERS
Art Critic Donald Miller
Books Editor Robert Hoover
Cartoonist Tim Menees
Cartoonist Rob Rogers
Columnist Brian O'Neill
Columnist Thomas Hritz
Columnist Peter Leo
Editorial Page Editor Michael McGough
Environment/Ecology Editor Don Hopey
Fashion Editor Georgia Sauer
Films/Theater Editor Christopher Rawson
Food Editor Suzanne Martinson
Harrisburg Bureau Frank Reeves
Harrisburg Bureau Peter Shelly
Director-Info Service Timothy Rozgonyi
Librarian Angelika Kane
Metro Editor Edwina Kaikai
Music Editor Robert Croan
Picture Editor Andy Starnes
Chief Photographer John Beale
Director-Public Service Richard Macino
Radio/Television Editor Robert Bianco
Science Editor Sharon Voas
Science Editor Byron Spice
Sports Columnist Bruce Keidan
Sports Columnist Ron Cook
Sports Columnist Robert Smizik
Sports Columnist Gene Collier
Technology Systems Editor Tim Dunham
Travel Editor Jayne Clark
Washington Bureau Patricia Griffith
Washington Bureau Jack Torey

MANAGEMENT INFORMATION SERVICES
Director-Systems & Technology Michael L Pearson
Technology Systems Editor Tim Dunham

PRODUCTION
Director Joseph E Horner
Manager-Operations Timothy Mahaney
Manager-North Plant Alfred H Serafini
Manager-Systems Nicholas Mares
Manager-Post Press Fred Francis
Manager-Pre Press Anthony Sebastian
Manager-Press/Paper Thomas R Hans

Market Information: Zoned editions; Split Run; TMC; Operate audiotex; Electronic edition.
Mechanical available: Letterpress; Black and 3 ROP colors; insert accepted — preprinted; page cut-offs — 23$\frac{9}{16}$".
Mechanical specifications: Type page 13" x 22½"; E - 6 cols, 2$\frac{1}{16}$", ⅛" between; A - 6 cols, 2$\frac{1}{16}$", ⅛" between; C - 10 cols, 1$\frac{3}{16}$", $\frac{1}{16}$" between.
Commodity consumption: Newsprint 41,192 metric tons; widths 55", 41¼", 27½"; black ink 1,440,748 pounds; color ink 77,627 pounds; single pages printed 27,760; average pages per issue 60(d), 151(S); single plates used 216,909.
Equipment: EDITORIAL: Front-end hardware — AT/9000, 10-AT/J-11; Front-end software — AT/Rel 4.6.7; Printers — Toshiba, HP/LaserJet; Other equipment — 217-AT/SDT. CLASSIFIED: Front-end hardware — AT/9000, 4-AT/J-11CAK; Front-end software — AT/IAS 4.7.6; Printers — Dataproducts/2290, Toshiba; Other equipment — 69-AT/SDT. AUDIOTEX: Hardware — Brite Voice Systems/Unix, VSM/VDN; Supplier name — Brite Voice Systems, AP. DISPLAY: Adv layout systems — SCS/Layout 8000; Front-end hardware — 2-DEC/VAX 8600, 18-Sun/380; Front-end software — VMS, Cx/Rel. 8.76, Sun 4.1.1; Printers — Dataproducts; Other equipment — 3-ECR/Autokon. PRODUCTION: Typesetters — 2-Cx/Supersetter, 2-Bidco, III/3850 Color imager; Platemaking systems — Na; Plate exposures — 3-Na/Titan III, 1-Na/Starlite; Plate processors — 3-Na/120, 1-Na/40, 1-DT/Processor; Electronic picture desk — Lf/AP Leaf Picture Desk; Scanners — 2-ECR/Autokon 1000-DE; Production cameras — 1-C/Marathon, 1-C/F, 2-C/Newspager II; Automatic film processors — 1-LE/PC 18, 2-LE/LD 24 AQ, 1-DP/Processor; Film transporters — 2-Cx, 2-C; Digital color separation equipment — Ik/3501. PRESSROOM: Line 1 — 16-H/Colormatic; Line 2 — 21-H/Color Convertible, 3-H/Colormatic; Line 3 — 8-H/Colormatic; Press drives — 3-GE, 4-Powertronic; Folders — 7-H/3:2, 4-H/2:1; Reels and stands — 27-H/Fully Automatic, 21-H/Manual; Press control system — In-house design. MAILROOM: Counter stackers — 14-HL/Monitor, 3-HL/Monitor HT, 3-HL/Monitor HT II; Inserters and stuffers — 49-Head/SLS1000; Bundle tyer — 2-MLN/MLN2A, 6-Power Strap/PS5, 8-Dynaric/NP1500; Wrapping singles — 2-Bu. LIBRARY: Electronic — Dialog; Combination — Photo. WIRE SERVICES: News — AP, AP Datafeatures, SHNS, NYT, RN, KRT, LAT-WP; Stock tables — AP; Syndicates — WP, LATS, KRT, RN, AP Datafeatures. BUSINESS COMPUTERS: 2-DEC/VAX 7610; Applications: Microsoft/Office; PCs & micros networked; PCs & main system networked.

POTTSTOWN
Montgomery County

'90 U.S. Census- 21,831; E&P '96 Est. 21,112
ABC-NDM (90): 151,194 (HH 55,378)

The Mercury (m-mon to sat; S)

The Mercury, 24 N. Hanover St.; PO Box 599, Pottstown, PA 19464; tel (610) 323-3000; fax (610) 323-0682. Goodson Newspaper group.
Circulation: 28,820(m); 28,820(m-sat); 29,385(S); ABC Sept. 30, 1995.
Price: 50¢(d); 50¢(sat); $1.25(S); $3.00/wk (carrier); $13.00/mo (carrier); $156.00/yr (carrier).
Advertising: Open inch rate $18.30(m); $18.30 (m-sat); $18.30(S). **Representatives:** Landon Associates Inc.; Robert Hitchings & Co.
News Service: AP. **Politics:** Independent. **Established:** 1931.
Not Published: New Year; Memorial Day; Independence Day; Labor Day; Christmas.
Special Editions: Financial Issue, Health & Fitness, Super Bowl Preview, Heating & Energy (Jan); Progress, Washington's Birthday Auto Section, Bridal Edition (Feb); Spring Fashion, Spring Gardening, Home Improvement, Home Show, Coupon Pages (Mar); Outdoors, Lawn & Garden, Earth Day, Careers, Car Care (Apr); House Blue Prints, Travel, Senior Citizen, Racer's Edge, Summer Fun, Mother's Day Gift Guide, Senior Lifestyles (May); Graduation Scene, Fall Bridal (June); Made in America, Consumer Information Guide, Education Guide, Financial (July); Modern Living, Back-to-School (Aug); Football, Coupons, Community Guide, Home Improvement, Fall Fashion, Energy (Sept); Fire Prevention, Car Care, Auto Show, Careers, Home Winterizing, Kitchen & Bath (Oct); Holiday Cookbook, Pre-Holiday Gift Guide (Nov); Gift Guide, Last Minute Gift Guide (Dec); Automotive Today (monthly).
Special Weekly Sections: Pet Care Page (mon); Stock Listings (tues); Food (wed); Weekend Guide, Auctions (fri); Church, Engagements (sat); TV Book, Travel, Arts and Entertainment, Stock Listings, Church, Real Estate, Food, Weddings (S); Health (daily).
Magazines: Market Place (wed); US Express (sat); Channels (S); Real Estate Today Magazine (monthly).

GENERAL MANAGEMENT
Publisher Barry Hopwood
Controller Robin L Myers
Personnel Director Tracy Reinholt

ADVERTISING
Director Denis Pfeiffer
Manager-Classified Mary Ann Edleman
Asst Manager-Retail John Zatratz

CIRCULATION
Manager Richard H DeHaven

NEWS EXECUTIVES
Editor Walter L Herring
Managing Editor Andrew Hachadorian

EDITORS AND MANAGERS
City Editor James Kerr
Photo Department Manager John W Strickler

PRODUCTION
Manager-Pre Press Donald Gunzelmann
Manager-Pressroom Daniel Matalavage
Manager-Distribution Charles Pierce

Market Information: Zoned editions; TMC.
Mechanical available: Letterpress (direct); Black and 3 ROP colors; insert accepted — preprinted; page cut-offs — 23$\frac{9}{16}$".
Mechanical specifications: Type page 13" x 22"; E - 6 cols, 2$\frac{1}{16}$", ⅛" between; A - 6 cols, 2$\frac{1}{16}$", ⅛" between; C - 9 cols, 1⅜", $\frac{1}{16}$" between.
Commodity consumption: Newsprint 2,800 short tons; widths 28", 42", 56"; black ink 81,645 pounds; color ink 12,909 pounds; single pages printed 16,676; average pages per issue 36(d), 56(sat), 64(S); single plates used 23,484.
Equipment: EDITORIAL: Front-end hardware — 1-Ik/1020-80, 21-Ik/40, Ap/Mac Quadra 950; Front-end software — Ik; Printers — 2-NewGen/660B. CLASSIFIED: Front-end hardware — Cx/Classified Sys, 11-IBM/PC 5150; Front-end software — Intertext/REV 7D PS; Printers — NewGen/660B. DISPLAY: Front-end hardware — Ap/Mac. PRODUCTION: Typesetters — 1-News Printer/II; Platemaking systems — 6-Na/System-1; Plate exposures — 2-Starlite, Na; Plate processors — 1-Na/NP80, 1-Na/NP40; Scanners — ECR/Autokon 1030, Nikon/Scanner; Production cameras — 1-C/Spartan III, 1-R/Vertical; Automatic film processors — 1-LE/LD-24AW, 1-C/Spartan III, 1-R/Vertical; Film transporters — C. PRESSROOM: Line 1 — 6-G/1913; Press drives — 5-W, 30-HP/A-C, 100-HP/D-C; Folders — 2-G/2:1; Pasters — CW; Reels and stands — CW; Press control system — CW/AC, Amicon/TPY3; Press registration system — Beach. MAILROOM: Counter stackers — 2-HL; Inserters and stuffers — 1-KAN; Bundle tyer — 1-Sa/Auto, 1-Sa/Man, 1-Stark/Auto; Wrapping singles — 1-Sa/810; Addressing machine — 2-Am/1900, 1-Am/5000. WIRE SERVICES: News — AP; Stock tables — AP; Syndicates — NEA, CNS, King Features, United Media, LATS, NNS; Receiving dishes — AP. BUSINESS COMPUTERS: IBM/Sys 36; Applications: Adv billing, Accts payable, Gen ledger, Payroll, Budgets, Class receivables, Circ, Accts receivable; PCs & micros networked; PCs & main system networked.

POTTSVILLE
See SCHUYLKILL COUNTY

PUNXSUTAWNEY
Jefferson County

'90 U.S. Census- 6,782; E&P '96 Est. 6,254

The Spirit (m-mon to sat)

The Spirit, 111 N. Findley; PO Box 444, Punxsutawney, PA 15767; tel (814) 938-8740; fax (814) 938-3794. Hollinger International Inc. group.

I-360 Pennsylvania

Circulation: 5,554(m); 5,554(m-sat); Sworn Oct. 3, 1995.
Price: 35¢(d); 35¢(sat); $8.00/mo; $89.00/yr.
Advertising: Open inch rate $6.75(m); $6.75(m-sat). **Representative:** Landon Associates Inc.
News Service: AP. **Established:** 1872.
Not Published: New Year; Memorial Day; Independence Day; Labor Day; Thanksgiving; Christmas.
Special Editions: Bridal Editions (Feb); Spring Home Improvement, Outdoors Edition (Mar); Outdoors Edition (Apr); Outdoors Edition (May); Fall Sports, Outdoors Edition (Aug); Outdoors Edition (Sept, Nov).
Magazine: USA Weekend (fri).

GENERAL MANAGEMENT
Publisher William C Anderson
General Manager William C Anderson
Editor David R Divelbiss

ADVERTISING
Manager William C Anderson

CIRCULATION
Manager Sandy Payne

EDITORS AND MANAGERS
City Editor David R Divelbiss
Editorial Page Editor David R Divelbiss
Fashion/Food Editor Polly Barilar
Photo Department Manager David R Divelbiss
Radio/Television Editor Heidi Giavedoni
Sports Editor Kelly Shaffer

PRODUCTION
Foreman-Composing Heidi Giavedoni
Foreman-Pressroom Ken Foster

Market Information: Zoned editions; TMC.
Mechanical available: Offset; Black and 3 ROP colors; insert accepted — preprinted; page cut-offs — 23".
Mechanical specifications: Type page 12.75" x 21"; E - 6 cols, $2\frac{1}{16}$", $\frac{1}{8}$" between; A - 6 cols, $2\frac{1}{16}$", $\frac{1}{8}$" between; C - 8 cols, $1\frac{9}{16}$", $\frac{1}{16}$" between.
Commodity consumption: widths 27", 13.5"; single pages printed 6,500; average pages per issue 16(d).
Equipment: EDITORIAL: Front-end hardware — 2-IBM/PC. DISPLAY: Adv layout systems — Ap/Mac SE. PRODUCTION: Plate processors — 1-Ic/ICM-25; Automatic film processors — C/T-65.
PRESSROOM: Line 1 — 5-G/Community; Folders — 1-G/Community. MAILROOM: Bundle tyer — Sa/S1100; Addressing machine — Ch. WIRE SERVICES: News — AP.

READING
Berks County
'90 U.S. Census- 78,380; E&P '96 Est. 78,126
ABC-NDM (90): 338,429 (HH 128,393)

Reading Times (m-mon to fri)
Reading Eagle (e-mon to fri; S)
Reading Times/Reading Eagle (m-sat)

Reading Times/Eagle, 345 Penn St.; PO Box 582, Reading, PA 19603-0582; tel (610) 371-5000; fax (610) 371-5194.
Circulation: 48,032(m); 22,806(e); 67,811 (m-sat); 105,993(S); ABC Sept. 30, 1995.
Price: 50¢(d); 50¢(sat); $1.50(S); $3.90/wk; $15.60/4wk, $202.80/52wk.
Advertising: Open inch rate $33.72(m); $33.72(e); $33.72(m-sat); $36.28(S). **Representative:** Cresmer, Woodward, O'Mara & Ormsbee.
News Services: AP, RN, LAT-WP, SHNS. **Politics:** Independent. **Established:** 1858 (Times), 1868 (Eagle).
Special Editions: Spring/Summer Bridal Showcase; Progress Edition; Jazz Fest Tab; Spring Home Improvement; Today's Woman; Spring Lawn & Garden; Golden Years: Sr. Citizens; Mother's Day; Fall Sports Guide; Fall Home Improvement; Pioneer Keystone Nat'l Drag Racing Tab; Fall in for Planting; Home Building Show; Winter Scholastic Sports Guide; Last Minute Christmas Gift Guide; Plus numerous community-related sections.
Special Weekly Sections: Best Food Day (wed); Restaurant & Entertainment (fri); Church (sat); Best Food Day, Travel/Resort, Home & Building/Real Estate, Amusement, Lifestyles (S); Business (daily).
Magazines: "Voices" (Teen Section) (thur); TV Times (local, newsprint) (S); Parade.
Broadcast Affiliates: Radio WEEU.

CORPORATE OFFICERS
Board Chairman Myrtle B Quier
Vice Pres/President William S Flippin
Vice Pres/Secretary James C Flippin
Treasurer Thomas A Gannon

GENERAL MANAGEMENT
Publisher William S Flippin
Assoc Publisher Larry R Orkus
Treasurer Thomas A Gannon
Manager-Accounting/Credit Benjamin J Coco

ADVERTISING
Director Walter W Woolwine
Asst Director Terry L Beilhart
Manager-Retail Sales Anne T Chubb
Manager-National/Co-op Thurman R Bartman
Manager-Classified Lori E Gerhart
Manager-Electronic Media Services Keith A Fritz

MARKETING AND PROMOTION
Director-Marketing/Promotion John M Ernesto
Special Sections Editor Suzanne G Bowers
Newspapers in Education Connie Andrews

TELECOMMUNICATIONS
Audiotex Manager Keith Fritz

CIRCULATION
Director Richard D Auman
Manager-Home Delivery Joseph Pelchar
Manager-Single Copy Edmond G Floto
Manager-Database/Marketing Beth S Quickel
Supervisor-Mailroom Charles P Tornielli

NEWS EXECUTIVES
Managing Editor Charles M Gallagher
Asst Managing Editor-Graphics Harry J Deitz
News Editor Nicholas S Yost
Assign Editor Deborah M Martin
Administration Editor Donald P Davis

EDITORS AND MANAGERS
Business/Finance Editor Gregory A Kreitz
City Editor Dennis V Deysher
Design Editor Albert W Walentis
Editorial Gary Trollinger
Entertainment Editor George L Hatza Jr
Info Systems Manager Mark P Lukens
Lifestyle Editor Christine A Burger
Metro Editor Michael C Zielinski
Photo Manager J Charles Gardner
Sports Editor Michael M Miorelli

MANAGEMENT INFORMATION SERVICES
Data Processing Manager John J Rockowicz

PRODUCTION
Director-Electronic Systems John J Rockowicz
Superintendent-Composing David H Huyett
Superintendent-Pressroom J Michael Engle
Superintendent-Engraving Patrick S Amtosy

Market Information: Operate audiotex.
Mechanical available: Letterpress (direct); 3 Flexo Units; Black and 3 ROP colors; insert accepted — preprinted; page cut-offs — 23".
Mechanical specifications: Type page 13" x $21\frac{1}{2}$"; E - 6 cols, $2\frac{1}{16}$", $\frac{1}{8}$" between; A - 6 cols, $2\frac{1}{16}$", $\frac{1}{8}$" between; C - 9 cols, $1\frac{3}{8}$", $\frac{1}{12}$" between.
Commodity consumption: Newsprint 22,238 short tons; 10,087 metric tons; widths 55", $41\frac{1}{4}$", $27\frac{3}{8}$"; black ink 325,147 pounds; color ink 42,000 pounds; single pages printed 37,446; average pages per issue 45(d), 132(S); single plates used 40,000.
Equipment: EDITORIAL: Front-end hardware — 3-DEC/PDP 11-84, DEC/Rainbow NS200; Front-end software — DEC/NSSE-EMS; Printers — 2-Panasonic, HP/LaserJet, Ap/Mac LaserWriter; Other equipment — 12-Ap/Mac, Nikon/3510 scanners. CLASSIFIED: Front-end hardware — DEC/PDP 11-84, DEC/NS400, DEC/NS100; Front-end software — DEC/NSSE-CMS; Printers — DEC/LA 180, DEC/LA 120. AUDIOTEX: Hardware — Brite Voice Systems, Audio Lab. DISPLAY: Adv layout systems — CJ/Layout; Front-end hardware — Ap/Mac; Front-end software — Multi-Ad/Creator; Printers — DEC/LC01. PRODUCTION: Pagination software — QuarkXPress 3.3; OCR software — Caere/OmniPage 1.0; Typesetters — 2-MON/Xpress 3, 2-AG/7000; Platemaking systems — 2-Na/NP80; Plate exposures — 2-Burgess/Consolux; Plate processors — 2-Na/FPII; Electronic picture desk — Lf/AP Leaf Picture Desk; Scanners — ECR/Autokon 1000, Nikon/3500 Scanner; Production cameras — 1-C/Marathon, 1-C/Newspager; Automatic film processors — LE/24AQ, LE/24BQ, C/Powermat, AG/Rapidline 28; Film transporters — 1-C/Powermat; Digital color separation equipment — Howtek/D 4000, Nikon/3510 AF, Adobe/Photoshop, PixelCraft/Scanner.
PRESSROOM: Line 1 — 10-G/Mark II (w/2 half decks), 3-KBA/Motter, Flexographic/Color Max; Line 2 — 3-KBA/Colormax Flexographic; Press drives — Hurletron; Folders — 2-G/3:2; Pasters — 11-G, 2-PEC; Reels and stands — 11-G, 2-PEC; Press control system — Hurletron. MAILROOM: Counter stackers — 3-QWI/SJ10X; Inserters and stuffers — 1-HI/1472P; Bundle tyer — 5-OVL/JP80; Wrapping singles — 2-OVL/EX311, 2-OVL/415; Addressing machine — Ch/VideoJet System 7000. LIBRARY: Electronic — Data Times. COMMUNICATIONS: Facsimile — 8-Fujitsu/DEX; Digital ad delivery system — AP AdSend. Systems used — satellite. WIRE SERVICES: News — AP Datastream; Photos — AP; Stock tables — AP Dataspeed; Syndicates — RN, WP, LATS, KRT, SHNS; Receiving dishes — size-3m, AP. BUSINESS COMPUTERS: 2-DEC/VAX 4000-200; Applications: CJ, CIS, CJ/AIM-CIS: Class; PCs & micros networked; PCs & main system networked.

RIDGWAY
Elk County
'90 U.S. Census- 4,793; E&P '96 Est. 4,212

The Ridgway Record
(e-mon to fri; m-sat)

The Ridgway Record, 20 Main St.; PO Box T, Ridgway, PA 15853; tel (814) 773-3161; fax (814) 776-1086. Hollinger International Inc. group.
Circulation: 3,288(e); 3,288(m-sat); Sworn Oct. 1, 1995.
Price: 50¢(d); 50¢(sat); $11.00/mo.
Advertising: Open inch rate $5.50(e); $5.50(m-sat). **Representative:** Landon Associates Inc.
News Service: AP. **Politics:** Independent. **Established:** 1892.
Not Published: New Year; Memorial Day; Independence Day; Labor Day; Thanksgiving; Christmas.
Special Weekly Section: American Weekend (includes TV schedules).
Magazine: TV Section (sat).

GENERAL MANAGEMENT
General Manager/Publisher Joseph C Piccirillo

ADVERTISING
Manager Todd Stenta

CIRCULATION
Director Barb Viglione

EDITORS AND MANAGERS
Editor Bekki Guilyard
Sports Editor Charles Ferra

PRODUCTION
Foreman Richard Nelson

Market Information: TMC.
Mechanical available: Offset; Black and 2 ROP colors; insert accepted — preprinted, any; page cut-offs — $22\frac{1}{2}$".
Mechanical specifications: Type page 13" x $21\frac{1}{2}$"; E - 6 cols, $2\frac{1}{16}$", $\frac{1}{8}$" between; A - 6 cols, $2\frac{1}{16}$", $\frac{1}{8}$" between; C - 8 cols, $1\frac{1}{2}$", $\frac{1}{8}$" between.
Commodity consumption: Newsprint 550 short tons; widths $27\frac{1}{2}$", $13\frac{3}{4}$"; average pages per issue 12(d).
Equipment: EDITORIAL: Front-end hardware — Ap/Mac; Front-end software — Baseview; Printers — Ap/Mac LaserWriter. CLASSIFIED: Front-end hardware — Ap/Mac SE; Front-end software — Baseview; Printers — Ap/Mac LaserWriter. DISPLAY: Front-end hardware — Ap/Mac. PRODUCTION: Pagination software — Baseview; Production cameras — Kk; Automatic film processors — Kk/65A.
PRESSROOM: Line 1 — 7-G/Community; Folders — 1-G/SE, 1-G/Community. MAILROOM: Bundle tyer — 2-Sa, 2-Gd/808. WIRE SERVICES: News — AP.

ROCHESTER
See BEAVER

ST. MARYS
Elk County
'90 U.S. Census- 5,511; E&P '96 Est. 5,435

The Daily Press
(e-mon to fri; m-sat)

The Daily Press, 245 Brussells St.; PO Box 353, St. Marys, PA 15857; tel (814) 781-1596, (814) 781-1539; fax (814) 834-7473. Hollinger International Inc. group.
Circulation: 5,139(e); 5,139(m-sat); Sworn Oct. 6, 1995.
Price: 50¢(d); 50¢(sat); $11.00/mo; $128.00/yr.
Advertising: Open inch rate $6.30(e); $6.30(m-sat). **Representative:** Landon Associates Inc.
News Service: AP. **Politics:** Non-partisan. **Established:** 1910.
Not Published: New Year; Memorial Day; Independence Day; Labor Day; Thanksgiving; Christmas.
Special Editions: Boy Scouts (Feb); Bridal, Progress (Apr); Spring Home Improvement, Memorial Day (May); Pet Parade (July); Football (Aug); Hometown Festival, Boy Scouts, Football Contest (Sept); Octoberfest, Fire Protection, Halloween (Oct); Holiday Gift Guide, Hunting, Veteran's Day (Nov); Elk Haven Greetings, Football Contest (Dec).
Special Weekly Section: Weekender TV Section (sat).

ADVERTISING
Manager-National Thomas E Miller
Manager-Retail Robin Salberg

CIRCULATION
Manager James R Bauer

NEWS EXECUTIVES
Editor Jill Golden
Managing Editor Wayne Bauer

EDITORS AND MANAGERS
City Editor Mike Herzing
City Sports Editor James Mulcahy
Home Furnishings Editor Robin Salberg

MANAGEMENT INFORMATION SERVICES
Data Processing Manager James R Bauer

Market Information: Split Run; TMC.
Mechanical available: Offset; Black and 3 ROP colors; insert accepted — preprinted; page cut-offs — $21\frac{1}{2}$".
Mechanical specifications: Type page 13" x $21\frac{1}{2}$"; E - 6 cols, 2", $\frac{1}{6}$" between; A - 6 cols, 2", $\frac{1}{6}$" between; C - 8 cols, $1\frac{1}{2}$", $\frac{1}{8}$" between.
Commodity consumption: Newsprint 180 short tons; widths $27\frac{1}{2}$", $13\frac{3}{4}$"; black ink 5,200 pounds; color ink 56 pounds; single pages printed 5,650; average pages per issue 18(d); single plates used 2,204.
Equipment: EDITORIAL: Front-end hardware — Ap/Mac; Front-end software — Baseview; Printers — Ap/Mac Laser. CLASSIFIED: Front-end hardware — Ap/Mac; Front-end software — Mk, Baseview; Printers — Okidata/320. DISPLAY: Adv layout systems — Ap/Mac; Front-end hardware — Ap/Mac; Front-end software — Aldus/PageMaker; Printers — Ap/Mac Laser. PRODUCTION: Production cameras — Kk/Image Maker; Automatic film processors — Kk/Kodamatic 65A. MAILROOM: Bundle tyer — 1-JIA-IN/Industries Brand. COMMUNICATIONS: Facsimile — Sharp. WIRE SERVICES: News — AP; Syndicates — King Features; Receiving dishes — size-2ft, AP. BUSINESS COMPUTERS: Apache Rival; Applications: Tallgrass; PCs & micros networked.

SAYRE-ATHENS
Bradford County
'90 U.S. Census- 9,259 (Sayre 5,791; Athens 3,468); E&P '96 Est. 8,325 (Sayre 4,980; Athens 3,345)

The Evening Times
(e-mon to sat)

The Evening Times, 201 N. Lehigh Ave., Sayre, PA 18840; tel (717) 888-9643; fax (717) 888-6463. Hollinger International Inc. group.
Circulation: 7,218(e); 7,218(e-sat); Sworn Sept. 30, 1995.
Price: 50¢(d); 50¢(sat); $126.00/yr.
Advertising: Open inch rate $8.25(e); $8.25(e-sat). **Representative:** Landon Associates Inc.
News Service: AP. **Politics:** Independent. **Established:** 1890.
Not Published: New Year; Memorial Day; Independence Day; Labor Day; Thanksgiving; Christmas.
Special Editions: Bridal; Spring Home Improvement; Real Estate; Football; Cooking; Christmas; Progress.

GENERAL MANAGEMENT
Publisher Ted Mike
Purchasing Agent Ted Mike

ADVERTISING
Manager Vickee Mike
Manager-Classified Phoebe Marshall

CIRCULATION
Manager Brenda Benjamin

NEWS EXECUTIVE
Managing Editor Steve Piatt

Pennsylvania I-361

EDITORS AND MANAGERS

City Editor Steve Piatt
Editorial Page Editor L D Glover
Features Editor Nellie Brewster
Sports Editor Glenn Rolfe

PRODUCTION

Manager Nick Witmar

Market Information: TMC.
Mechanical available: Offset; black; insert accepted — preprinted; page cut-offs — 22¾".
Mechanical specifications: Type page 13" x 21½"; E - 6 cols, 2", 1/8" between; A - 9 cols, 1⅓", 1/16" between; C - 9 cols, 1⅓", 1/16" between.
Commodity consumption: Newsprint 335 short tons; widths 27½", 13¾"; black ink 6,300 pounds; color ink 500 pounds; single pages printed 6,140; average pages per issue 20(d); single plates used 3,500.
Equipment: EDITORIAL: Front-end hardware — IBM; Front-end software — Titus; Printers — Ap/Mac. DISPLAY: Front-end hardware — Ap/Mac; Front-end software — Aldus/PageMaker; Printers — Ap/Mac LaserPrinter. PRODUCTION: Plate processors — Roconex; Production cameras — B; Automatic film processors — LE.
PRESSROOM: Line 1 — 6-G/Community. MAILROOM: Counter stackers — BG/Count-O-Veyor; Bundle tyer — Bu. BUSINESS COMPUTERS: IBM; Applications: Nomads, MSSI.

SCHUYLKILL COUNTY-POTTSVILLE

Schuylkill County

'90 U.S. Census- 152,585 (Pottsville 16,603); E&P '96 Est. 146,195 (15,390)
ABC-NDM (90): 93,762 (HH 36,901)

Pottsville Republican

(e-mon to fri; m-sat)

Pottsville Republican, 111-113 Mahantongo St.; PO Box 209, Pottsville, PA 17901; tel (717) 622-3456; fax (717) 628-6092; e-mail republican@pottsville.infi.net; web site http://www.pottsville.com/pottsville.
Circulation: 29,580(e); 29,580(m-sat); ABC Sept. 30, 1995.
Price: 50¢(d); 75¢(sat); $2.50/wk; $11.00/mo; $121.00/yr.
Advertising: Open inch rate $23.75(e); $23.75(m-sat). **Representatives:** Landon Associates Inc.; The Newspaper National Network.
News Services: AP, SHNS. **Politics:** Independent. **Established:** 1884.
Note: Effective July 31, 1995, the Shenandoah Evening Star (e) became a zoned edition of the Pottsville Republican (e).
Not Published: New Year; Memorial Day; Independence Day; Labor Day; Thanksgiving; Christmas.
Special Editions: Brides '96, Health & Fitness (Jan); Annual Business Review (Feb); Design-An-Ad, Spring Fashion, Spring Home Improvement, Pottsville School Sections, Home & Garden (Mar); Brides '96, Spring Car Care, Home & Garden, Pets (Apr); Graduation '96, Health & Fitness II, Parenting (May); Brides '96, Summer '96 (June); Summer Home Improvement, Home Buyers Guide (July); Schuylkill County Fair, Back-to-College, Back-to-School, Football 1996 (Aug); Fall Fashion, Fall Home Improvement, Hunting Section, Health & Fitness III, Home Buyers Guide (Sept); Christmas Club, Fall Car Care, Senior Citizens, Chamber of Commerce (Oct); Holiday Gift Guide, Recipe Contest (Nov); Christmas Greetings (Dec).
Magazines: Mini-Page (tues); Perspective Youth, USA Weekend, TV Today (sat); USA Weekend, TV Today (S).
Broadcast Affiliate: WMBT-AM Shenandoah, PA.

CORPORATE OFFICERS

President Uzal H Martz Jr
Secretary Margaretta L Paduch
Asst Secretary/Treasurer JoHanne Zerbey Martz
Treasurer Uzal H Martz Jr

GENERAL MANAGEMENT

Publisher Uzal H Martz Jr
Director-Human Resources Nadine F Oswald
Controller Edgar Kleffman
Purchasing Agent James McDonald

ADVERTISING

Director Henry H Nyce
Manager-Retail James M Vitale
Manager-Classified James Riotto

MARKETING AND PROMOTION

Director-Marketing/Community Service Henry H Nyce

TELECOMMUNICATIONS

Director-New Horizons Group James E Dible

CIRCULATION

Director Joseph Dries

NEWS EXECUTIVES

Editor James C Kevlin III
Managing Editor James B Kane
News Editor Terry Rang

EDITORS AND MANAGERS

Business/Finance Editor James C Stoner
Education Editor Kathleen Roberts
Fashion/Society Editor Cindy D'Alio
Librarian Joanne Gretsky
Chief Photographer Tim Leedy
Real Estate Editor James C Stoner
Science Editor James B Kane
Special Sections Editor James B Kane
Sports Editor Brian Rippey

PRODUCTION

Director-Corporate Services James McDonald
Supervisor-Ad-Tech Department James Rosenberger
Foreman-Pressroom Edward Grieff
Coordinator-Pre Press Dennis Melnick
Manager-Electronic Systems Harold Workman

Market Information: Zoned editions; Split Run; ADS; Operate audiotex; Electronic edition.
Mechanical available: Offset; Black and 3 ROP colors; insert accepted — preprinted, product sample inserts; page cut-offs — 22¾".
Mechanical specifications: Type page 13" x 21"; E - 6 cols, 2 1/16", 1/8" between; A - 6 cols, 2 1/16", 1/8" between; C - 8 cols, 1½", 1/8" between.
Commodity consumption: widths 27½", 13¾".
Equipment: EDITORIAL: Front-end hardware — Sun/Sparc 10s; Front-end software — HI/XP21, HI/Newsmaker; Printers — AU/APS Broadsheeter, 2-AU/APS-6-84ACS 14" Imager. CLASSIFIED: Front-end hardware — HI/Cash, PC/486s; Front-end software — HI/Cash; Printers — 2-Panasonic/Dot Matrix. AUDIOTEX: Hardware — Info-Connect/Voice Info System; Software — Info-Connect 4.2; Supplier name — TMS/AP. DISPLAY: Adv layout systems — Ap/Macs, HI/2100; Front-end hardware — HI/2100, PC/486s, Ap/Mac Quadras; Front-end software — HI/21000 PLS, Multi-Ad/Creator; Printers — AU/APS Broadsheeter, Ap/Mac LaserWriters. PRODUCTION: Pagination software — HI/2100 2.5; OCR software — Calera/WordScan Plus; Typesetters — 2-AU/APS-6/84-ACS 14"; Plate exposures — 2-Nu/VP27P; Plate processors — 1-Nat/A-250; Electronic picture desk — Lf/AP Leaf Picture Desk, HI/Images; Scanners — HP/Text Scanner, 1-ECR/Autokon 1000D, 1-ECR/Autokon 2045, 2-Umax/2400; Production cameras — 1-C/Spartan II, 1-DAI/C-690-C; Automatic film processors — 1-LE/LD-24, 2-Glunz-Jenson/Multi-Line 400; Film transporters — 1-C, 2-Bray/Film Transport; Shrink lenses — 2-CK Optical; Color separation equipment (conventional) — Lf/Leafscan 35; Digital color separation equipment — ECR/Autokon 1000, Umax/1200.
PRESSROOM: Line 1 — 6-G/Urbanite, 1-G/Urbanite; Reels and stands — 7-G; Press control system — 2-G, Fin. MAILROOM: Inserters and stuffers — 2-MM/227E; Bundle tyer — 1-MLN/ML2-EE, 1-Bu/TP-452, Sterling/MR40CH; Wrapping singles — 1-PM/160LS. LIBRARY: Combination — 1-Minolta/RP407E. COMMUNICATIONS: Facsimile — Dell/286. WIRE SERVICES: News — AP, AP Datafeatures, AP Photostream, AP GraphicsNet, AP AdSend; Receiving dishes — AP. BUSINESS COMPUTERS: 1-Sun/Sparc Classic, 1-Sun/Sparc 2; Applications: Circ, Adv billing, Accts receivable, Accts payable, Gen ledger, Financial mgmt reports, Budgets; PCs & micros networked; PCs & main system networked.

SCRANTON

Lackawanna County

'90 U.S. Census- 81,805; E&P '96 Est. 76,915
ABC-NDM (90): 219,039 (HH 84,528)

The Tribune

(m-mon to fri; m-sat)

The Scranton Times

(e-mon to fri)

The Sunday Times (S)

The Tribune & The Scranton Times, 149 Penn. Ave.; PO Box 3311, Scranton, PA 18505-3311; tel (717) 348-9100; fax (717) 348-9145. Times Newspapers group.
Circulation: 31,688(m); 40,802(e); 63,774 (m-sat); 83,279(S); ABC Sept. 30, 1995.
Price: 35¢(d); 35¢(sat); $1.25(S); $3.05/wk (d); $158.60/yr (d) (carrier).
Advertising: Open inch rate $58.13(m); $58.13(e); $52.32(m-sat); $55.36(S); $76.12(m & S). **Representative:** Sawyer-Ferguson-Walker Co.
News Services: AP, NYT, KRT. **Politics:** Independent. **Established:** 1870.
Note: Advertising for the Scranton Times (e) automatically includes advertising in the Tribune (m). There is no separate advertising rate per se for the Tribune.
Special Editions: Good Times, Governor Casey Salute (Jan); Home Builders Expo '96, Speed Sports Showcase Tab, Bridal Tab (Feb); Good Times (Mar); Progress Edition, Easter Dining Guide, Red Barons Tab, Spring Home & Garden (Apr); Good Times, Cancer Society Tab, Mother's Day Dining Guide, Voter's Guide, Mother's Day Edition, Chamber of Commerce Business Show (May); Pocono Raceway Feature, Bridal Tab (June); Good Times, All Star Baseball, 125th Anniversary Edition (July); Football Tab, Race for the Cure, Back-to-School Section (Aug); Good Times, Fall Home Improvement Tab, Bridal Tab (Sept); United Way Tab, Walt Disney Promotion, '97 New Car Showcase (Oct); Good Times, Estate Planning Tab, Thanksgiving Edition (Nov); Holiday Shopping Guide, Christmas Song Book, Scranton School District Tab (Dec).
Special Weekly Sections: Business (tues); Best Food Day (ROP) (wed); Real Estate Buy of Week, Weekend Entertainment (thur); Travel, Entertainment, Business/Finance, Color Comics, Real Estate, Stocks, TV Times, Today's Living, Food Section, Lively Arts, Real Estate Buy of Week, Best Food Day (inserts) (S); Amusements, Comics, Financial/Stocks, Neighbors, TV Listings (daily).
Magazines: TV Times; Parade Magazine.
Broadcast Affiliates: Radio WEJL-AM, WEZX-FM.

GENERAL MANAGEMENT

Publisher Edward J Lynett Jr
Publisher George V Lynett
Publisher William R Lynett
General Manager Harold F Marion Jr
Controller Daniel Houlihan
Manager-Office Barry T Bowen
Manager-Credit Romayne Washner
Manager-Education Service R Gary Kruger
Purchasing Agent Barry T Bowen

ADVERTISING

Manager Steven Sauder
Manager-Display Robert Magdelinic
Manager-National Renee Puchalski

MARKETING AND PROMOTION

Director-Marketing/Promotion R Vincent Puchalski
Community Relations Director Joseph E Cummings

TELECOMMUNICATIONS

Systems Manager Frank O'Hearn

CIRCULATION

Director Gary Kruger

NEWS EXECUTIVES

Managing Editor Robert L Burke
Asst Managing Editor Joe Dowd

EDITORS AND MANAGERS

Automotive Editor John Hambrose
Aviation Editor John Hambrose
Business/Finance Editor Vince Covaleskie
Cartoonist Dennis Draughon
City Editor Doug Haddix
City Editor Robert Gelik
Editorial Page Editor Joseph X Flannery
Editorial Page Editor Patrick J McKenna
Ecology/Environment Editor John Murphy
Farm Editor Frank Scholz
Features Editor Karen Kelley Mears
Garden Editor Joe Dowd
Graphics Editor Ron Cioffi
Librarian William Hines
Picture Editor Mike Mullen
Real Estate Editor Vince Covaleskie
Religion Editor John Hambrose
Science/Travel Editor Robert L Burke
Sports Editor Tom Robinson
Sunday Editor Bill Wagner

MANAGEMENT INFORMATION SERVICES

Data Processing Manager Barry T Bowen

PRODUCTION

Manager Thomas E Braunschweig
Foreman-Composing John Novak
Foreman-Mailroom Frank Biagioli

Market Information: Zoned editions; Split Run; TMC; ADS.
Mechanical available: Offset; Black and 3 ROP colors; insert accepted — preprinted, cards, envelopes; page cut-offs — 21½".
Mechanical specifications: Type page 13" x 21½"; E - 6 cols, 2 1/16", 1/8" between; A - 6 cols, 2 1/16", 1/8" between; C - 9 cols, 1⅜", 1/8" between.
Commodity consumption: Newsprint 10,366 metric tons; widths 55", 52", 41¼", 27½"; black ink 303,655 pounds; color ink 32,500 pounds; single pages printed 32,380; average pages per issue 37(d), 39(sat), 124(S); single plates used 52,730.
Equipment: EDITORIAL: Front-end hardware — 48-PC, 2-Sun/Server; Front-end software — HI/Newsmaker; Printers — HP. CLASSIFIED: Front-end hardware — PPI, 14-PC; Front-end software — PPI; Printers — HP. DISPLAY: Adv layout systems — SCS/Layout 8000; Front-end hardware — 20-Ap/Mac; Front-end software — Multi-Ad/Creator 3.7; Printers — NewGen/600 DPI. PRODUCTION: Pagination software — HI/Newsmaker Pagination; Typesetters — 1-AU/APS-108C, MON/3850, Adobe/RIPs; Platemaking systems — 2-W/Automatic Platemaking Sys; Plate exposures — 2-W; Plate processors — 2-W; Scanners — 5-SII/ET960; Production cameras — 1-C/Newspager, 1-C/Spartan III; Automatic film processors — 2-LE/24AQ, 1-LE/PC-18; Film transporters — 3-LE, 2-SCREEN/Rapid Access; Color separation equipment (conventional) — 1-Hel/Studio System; Digital color separation equipment — Kk/2035, Lf/Leafscan 35.
PRESSROOM: Line 1 — 6-G/HO (3 half decks); Press drives — Fin; Folders — 1-G/3:2, 1-G/Page Jaw Folder; Pasters — 6-Automatic Pasters/50-Inch Reels; Press control system — 1-G/MPCS. MAILROOM: Counter stackers — 3-Id/2000, 2-Sa/25/75; Inserters and stuffers — 1-SLS/1000, 10-Pocket, 2-Main Feeders; Bundle tyer — 3-Dynaric; Addressing machine — 1-Dm. LIBRARY: Electronic — Mead Data Central/Newsview. COMMUNICATIONS: Facsimile — 1-X/410. WIRE SERVICES: News — AP, KRT, NYT; Photos — AP; Stock tables — AP; Syndicates — LATS, United Features, Universal Press, Sun Features; Receiving dishes — size-3m, AP. BUSINESS COMPUTERS: IBM/AS-400; Applications: Circ, Adv billing, Accts receivable, Gen ledger, Newsprint inventory, Adv, Accts payable, Payroll, Carrier labels, TMC; PCs & micros networked; PCs & main system networked.

SHAMOKIN-MOUNT CARMEL

Northumberland County

'90 U.S. Census- 16,380 (Shamokin 9,184; Mount Carmel 7,196); E&P '96 Est. 14,780 (Shamokin 8,314; Mount Carmel 6,466)

The News-Item

(e-mon to fri; m-sat)

The News-Item, 707 N. Rock; PO Box 587, Shamokin, PA 17872-0587; tel (717) 648-4641; fax (717) 644-0892. Thomson Newspapers group.
Circulation: 13,051(e); 13,051(m-sat); Sworn Sept. 30, 1995.
Price: 50¢(d); 50¢(sat); $96.00/yr.
Advertising: Open inch rate $13.50(e); $13.50(m-sat). **Representative:** Landon Associates Inc.
News Service: AP. **Politics:** Independent. **Established:** 1893.
Not Published: New Year; Independence Day; Christmas.
Special Editions: Bridal (Jan); Progress/Economic Review (Feb); Home Improvement, Car Care (Apr); Back-to-School (Aug); Home Improvement, Car Care, Fall Football Preview (Sept); Christmas Lay-away (Oct); Christmas Gift Guide (Nov).
Special Weekly Sections: Best Food Day, Wedding and Engagement Pages (tues); Business World Page (wed); Outdoors Sports Page (thur); The Golden Years Page, Area Schools Page (fri); Church Pages (sat); Entertainment/TV Guide (fri); Living Today (daily).
Magazine: Television Today.

GENERAL MANAGEMENT

Publisher/General Manager M Philip Yucha
Purchasing Agent M Philip Yucha

ADVERTISING

Director John Kaminski
Manager-Classified Barbara Freeman

I-362 Pennsylvania

CIRCULATION
Director Robert McPherson
NEWS EXECUTIVE
Managing Editor Jacob P Betz
EDITORS AND MANAGERS
Editor Paul McTrocavage
Graphics Editor Glenn A Knarr Jr
Sports Editor Charlie Roth
PRODUCTION
Foreman-Pressroom Gary Sheriff
Foreman-Composing Glenn A Knarr Jr

Market Information: TMC.
Mechanical available: Offset; Black and 3 ROP colors; insert accepted — preprinted; page cut-offs — 22¾".
Mechanical specifications: Type page 13" x 21½"; E - 6 cols, 2¹⁄₁₆", ⅛" between; A - 6 cols, 2¹⁄₁₆", ⅛" between; C - 9 cols, 1⅜", ¹⁄₁₆" between.
Commodity consumption: Newsprint 400 short tons; widths 27", 13.75"; black ink 9,000 pounds; color ink 310 pounds; single pages printed 7,000; average pages per issue 20(d); single plates used 4,500.
Equipment: EDITORIAL: Front-end hardware — Mk, 10-DTK/386, 2-RSK/Model 100 Portable; Front-end software — DTK/DOS 5.0, Mk/Editorial; Printers — V/5100; Other equipment — SW, AP. CLASSIFIED: Front-end hardware — Mk, DTK/386; Front-end software — DTK/DOS 5.0, Mk; Printers — TI, V/5100, 1-T/Line Printer. DISPLAY: Front-end hardware — 2-Ap/Mac IIci, 1-Ap/Mac LC II, Ap/Mac Quadra 800; Front-end software — Multi-Ad/Creator, Aldus/FreeHand, Adobe/Photoshop; Printers — V/5100; Other equipment — CD-Rom, AUR/8000 Scanner, Nikon, Lf/Leafscan 35, Micronet/180mb SCSI Drive. PRODUCTION: Typesetters — 2-V/4000-5100A Laserprinter; Platemaking systems — 1-Nu; Plate exposures — 1-Nu; Electronic picture desk — Lf/AP Leaf Picture Desk; Scanners — AUR/8000 CLX, Nu, Lf/Leafscan 35; Production cameras — 1-C; Automatic film processors — 1-LE; Shrink lenses — 1-C; Color separation equipment (conventional) — Lf/AP Leaf Picture Desk, Nikon, Lf/Leafscan; Digital color separation equipment — 1-Ap/Mac Portable Transmission System. PRESSROOM: Line 1 — 6-KP; Folders — 1-KP. MAILROOM: Inserters and stuffers — 3-MM; Bundle tyer — 1-Sa; Addressing machine — 1-RSK/Printer. LIBRARY: Electronic — RSK. WIRE SERVICES: News — AP, SW; Photos — AP; Syndicates — United Features; Receiving dishes — size-3m, AP. BUSINESS COMPUTERS: 2-Bios, 1-HP/486 DX-33; Applications: Circ, Carrier, Air mail, Gen ledger, Accts payable, Accts receivable, Reports, Payroll; PCs & micros networked.

SHARON-FARRELL-SHARPSVILLE-WHEATLAND

Mercer County

'90 U.S. Census- 29,823 (Sharon 17,493; Farrell 6,841; Sharpsville 4,729; Wheatland 760); E&P '96 Est. 26,734 (Sharon 16,295; Farrell 5,639; Sharpsville 4,254; Wheatland 546)
ABC-CZ (90): 45,123 (HH 18,412)

The Herald

(e-mon to fri; m-sat; S)

The Herald, S. Dock & E. State Sts.; PO Box 51, Sharon, PA 16146; tel (412) 981-6100; fax (412) 981-5116; e-mail heraldmail@aol.com. Ottaway Newspapers Inc. group.
Circulation: 25,123(e); 25,123(m-sat); 24,964(S); ABC Sept. 30, 1995.
Price: 40¢(d); 40¢(sat); 75¢(S); $2.15/wk.
Advertising: Open inch rate $20.35(e); $20.35(m-sat); $20.35(S). **Representative:** Landon Associates Inc.
News Services: AP, ONS. **Politics:** Independent. **Established:** 1864.
Note: The Herald is printed by Dow Jones Co. at their West Middlesex, PA plant.
Not Published: New Year; Memorial Day; Independence Day; Labor Day; Thanksgiving; Christmas.
Special Editions: Review (Feb); Car Care (Mar); Design-An-Ad, Estate Guide, Home Improvement, Penn Power, Lawn & Garden (Apr); Golden Years (May); Summer Fun (June); Football Magazine (Aug); Back-to-School, Home Improvement, Banking & Investment (Sept); Car Care, Women's World, Cookbook (Oct); Christmas Gift Guide (Nov).
Magazine: Spectrum Weekend Magazine.

GENERAL MANAGEMENT
Publisher John Lima
Controller Thomas Onestak
Manager-Business Office Betty J Schultz
Coordinator-Education Service Mary Beth LoScalzo
ADVERTISING
Director-Marketing Dave Armstrong
Manager-Classified Doug Homer
CIRCULATION
Director Michael Linden
NEWS EXECUTIVES
Editor James A Raykie
Managing Editor Peggy Dunder
EDITORS AND MANAGERS
Automotive Editor Larry Sanata
Business Editor Michael Roknick
City Editor Joseph Kapusta
Editorial Page Editor Noel G Carroll
Education Editor Joe Wiercinski
Environmental Editor Gwen Albers-Freson
Farm/Agriculture Ed Jim Martin
Features Editor Linda Linonis
Graphics Editor/Art Director John Zavinski
Health/Medical Editor Larry Sanata
National Editor Dennis Jennings
News Editor Sarah Adams
Photo Editor David Dale
Political/Government Editor Joe Wiercinski
Religion Editor Shawn Starkey
Science/Technology Editor Larry Sanata
Society/Home Furnishings Editor Linda Linonis
Sports Editor Lynn Saternow
Television/Film Editor Joe Pinchot
Theater/Music Editor Joe Pinchot
Travel Editor Richard Young
PRODUCTION
Manager-Systems & Composing Barry Winger

Market Information: TMC.
Mechanical available: Offset; Black and 3 ROP colors; insert accepted — preprinted; page cut-offs — 22¾".
Mechanical specifications: Type page 13" x 21½"; E - 6 cols, 2¹⁄₁₆", ⅛" between; A - 6 cols, 2¹⁄₁₆", ⅛" between; C - 9 cols, 1⅜", ¹⁄₁₆" between.
Commodity consumption: Newsprint 1,725 metric tons; width 60"; black ink 34,512 pounds; color ink 5,760 pounds; single pages printed 10,787; average pages per issue 30(d), 48(S); single plates used 36,811.
Equipment: EDITORIAL: Front-end hardware — 2-AT/Series 4, Dewar/Disc Sys, 1-AT/Remote Series 3, 31-AT, 8-Dewar, AT/Remote Series 3. CLASSIFIED: Front-end hardware — 7-AT. DISPLAY: Adv layout systems — 6-Dewar/Disc, 2-Ap/Mac IIcx. PRODUCTION: Typesetters — L/M Linotronic 500, 1-M/Linotronic 300, Cora/Imagesetter w/RIP 40; Platemaking systems — 2-Nu; Plate exposures — 2-Nu; Plate processors — 1-WL; Scanners — ECR/Autokon 1000DE, RZ/Linoscan 3040; Production cameras — 1-C/Spartan I, 1-C/Spartan III, 1-RZ; Automatic film processors — 3-P/SQ 24, Kodamatic/520 Processor; Color separation equipment (conventional) — Lf/AP Leaf Picture Desk.
PRESSROOM: Line 1 — 10-TKS/Offset; Folders — 2-TKS/3:2; Pasters — TKS; Reels and stands — TKS/30 Reels on 10 Stands; Press control system — DJ. MAILROOM: Counter stackers — 2-SH; Inserters and stuffers — 1-Mc/4 Jacket; Bundle tyer — 4-OVL/J80; Wrapping singles — 2-AR/DAC; Addressing machine — 2-AVY. COMMUNICATIONS: Facsimile — Ricoh/60E. WIRE SERVICES: News — AP, ONS, SHNS; Stock tables — AP; Syndicates — ONS, NEA; Receiving dishes — size-12ft, AP. BUSINESS COMPUTERS: 2-IBM/Sys 38, IBM/AS-400; Applications: Circ, Payroll, Adv, Gen ledger, Accts payable, Human resources; PCs & micros networked; PCs & main system networked.

SOMERSET

Somerset County

'90 U.S. Census- 6,454; E&P '96 Est. 6,437
ABC-CZ (90): 6,454 (HH 2,861)

Daily American (m-mon to sat)

Daily American, 334 W. Main St; PO Box 638, Somerset, PA 15501-0638; tel (814) 445-9621; fax (814) 445-2935.
Circulation: 13,558(m); 13,558(m-sat); ABC Sept. 30, 1995.
Price: 35¢(d); 50¢(sat); $84.00/yr.
Advertising: Open inch rate $12.25(m); $12.25(m-sat). **Representative:** Landon Associates Inc.
News Service: AP. **Politics:** Republican. **Established:** 1929.
Not Published: New Year; Memorial Day; Independence Day; Labor Day; Thanksgiving; Christmas.
Advertising not accepted: Beer; Wine; Liquor; Cigarette.
Special Editions: Cooking; Bridal; Maple Princess; Dairy Princess; Progress; Home Improvement; Outdoor; Car Care; Somerfest; Somerset County Fair; Craft Days; Fireman; Threshermen; New Car; Primary Election; General Election; Christmas.
Special Weekly Section: Best Food Day (wed & sat).

CORPORATE OFFICERS
President Betty Homes Reiley
Vice Pres Ronnie G Reiley
Treasurer David H Reiley
Secretary James Courtney
GENERAL MANAGEMENT
Publisher David H Reiley
General Manager Jon G Starn
Purchasing Agent Jon G Starn
ADVERTISING
Manager Tom Koppenhofer
Manager-Classified Pat Foley
MARKETING AND PROMOTION
Manager-Promotion Jon G Starn
TELECOMMUNICATIONS
Audiotex Manager James Oliver
CIRCULATION
Manager Sam Foglesong
NEWS EXECUTIVES
Editor James Oliver
Editor-City Wade Thomas
EDITORS AND MANAGERS
Editorial Page Editor James Oliver
Editorial Writer James Oliver
Farm/Food Editor Roberta Black
Society Editor Roberta Black
Sports Editor Ronald Pritts
Travel Editor Ronie G Reiley
MANAGEMENT INFORMATION SERVICES
Data Processing Manager Darl Bason
PRODUCTION
Foreman-News Department James Oliver
Foreman-Pressroom Sam Foglesong

Market Information: Zoned editions; Split Run; TMC; ADS; Operate audiotex.
Mechanical available: Offset; Black and 3 ROP colors; insert accepted — preprinted; page cut-offs — 21½".
Mechanical specifications: Type page 13" x 21½"; E - 6 cols, 2¹⁄₁₆", ⅛" between; A - 6 cols, 2¹⁄₁₆", ⅛" between; C - 9 cols, 1⅜", ¹⁄₁₆" between.
Commodity consumption: Newsprint 590 short tons; widths 27", 34"; black ink 5,800 pounds; single pages printed 5,400; average pages per issue 18(d).
Equipment: EDITORIAL: Front-end hardware — RSK/Tandy-TL 1000; Front-end software — Synaptic; Printers — Ap/Mac LaserWriter II; Other equipment — Ap/Mac II. CLASSIFIED: Front-end hardware — 2-RSK/Tandy-TL 1000; Front-end software — Synaptic; Printers — Ap/Mac LaserWriter II. AUDIOTEX: Hardware — Info-Connect. DISPLAY: Adv layout systems — Ap/Mac II; Front-end hardware — 1-Ap/Mac II, 2-Ap/Mac Quadra 950; Front-end software — QuarkXPress; Printers — Ap/Mac LaserWriter II. PRODUCTION: Plate exposures — 1-B/1601-45-M, 1-Nu/Flip Top FT40L; Plate processors — 1-Ic/ICM 25-1; Scanners — Microtek/Scanmaker IIXC; Production cameras — 1-Ik/430, 1-Nu/Horizontal SST2024; Automatic film processors — 1-LE.
PRESSROOM: Line 1 — 6-G/Community, 2-G/Community single width; Folders — 1-G. MAILROOM: Counter stackers — 1-BG/105; Bundle tyer — 2-Sa/SR1A, 1-MLN, 2-Mosca/Rom 50-55; Addressing machine — 1-Ch/544010, 1-KR w/Accufast. WIRE SERVICES: News — AP; Receiving dishes — size-10ft, AP.

SOUTH CONNELLSVILLE
See CONNELLSVILLE

STATE COLLEGE

Centre County

'90 U.S. Census- 38,923; E&P '96 Est. 41,432
ABC-NDM (90): 123,786 (HH 42,683)

Centre Daily Times

(m-mon to sat; S)

Centre Daily Times, 3400 E. College Ave.; PO Box 89, State College, PA 16804; tel (814) 238-5000; fax (814) 237-5966. Knight-Ridder Inc. group.
Circulation: 25,428(m); 25,428(m-sat); 34,126(S); ABC Sept. 30, 1995.
Price: 50¢(d); 50¢(sat); $1.25(S); $3.10/wk (carrier); $154.44/yr.
Advertising: Open inch rate $20.70(m); $20.70(m-sat); $26.00(S). **Representative:** Landon Associates Inc.
News Services: AP, KRT. **Politics:** Independent. **Established:** 1898, 1934.
Special Editions: Welcome Students/Weekender, Apartment Living, Business Outlook (Jan); The Wedding Album, Home Builders Show Guide, Apartment Living (Feb); Spring Car Care, Apartment Living, NIE (Mar); Spring Gardening, Apartment Living, Blue/White Football Magazine, Senior Outlook (Apr); Home Improvement (May); Bride & Groom (June); Art Festival Magazine, Apartment Living (July); Bellefonte Arts & Crafts Fair, Apartment Living, This is Penn State, Grange Fair Magazine, Football Preview (Aug); PSU Gameday Magazine, Apartment Living, Home Furnishings (Sept); PSU Gameday Magazines, Fall Car Care, Apartment Living (Oct); PSU Gameday Magazines, Apartment Living, Gift Guide One (Nov); Victorian Christmas, Gift Guide Two (Dec); Real Estate Buyers Guide (monthly).
Special Weekly Sections: Food (wed); Weekender, Travel (fri); TV (quarterfold) (S); Business (daily).
Magazine: Parade (S).

GENERAL MANAGEMENT
Publisher/President James A Moss
Chief Financial Officer Bevan Noack
ADVERTISING
Director Gene Kneller
Manager Mark Mateer
Manager-National/Major Accounts Carol Young Foley
MARKETING AND PROMOTION
Manager-Promotion Joan Koester
CIRCULATION
Director Randy Deason
Manager-Home Delivery Shirley Rupert
Manager-Customer Service Shirley Rupert
NEWS EXECUTIVE
Exec Editor/Vice Pres Cecil Bentley
EDITORS AND MANAGERS
Editorial Page Editor Paul Carty
Features Editor Russell Frank
News Editor Rebecca Bennett
Sports Editor Dwight Kier
MANAGEMENT INFORMATION SERVICES
Data Processing Manager Jim Guthrie
PRODUCTION
Manager Bill Lieb

Market Information: TMC; ADS.
Mechanical available: Offset; Black and 3 ROP colors; insert accepted — preprinted; page cut-offs — 22¾".
Mechanical specifications: Type page 12¾" x 21½"; E - 6 cols, 2¹⁄₁₆", ⅛" between; A - 6 cols, 2¹⁄₁₆", ⅛" between; C - 10 cols, 1¼", ¹⁄₁₆" between.
Commodity consumption: Newsprint 3,025 short tons; 2,700 metric tons; widths 27", 13½", 13¾", 28", 27½", 14"; black ink 50,000 pounds; color ink 7,000 pounds; single pages printed 18,000; average pages per issue 36(d), 28(sat), 65(S); single plates used 22,500.
Equipment: EDITORIAL: Front-end hardware — HI/PEN 8900s, HI/PLS 8900s, PCs, Ap/Power Mac 7100-66S; Front-end software — Baseview, QPS, Baseview/NewsEdit, Adobe/Photoshop; Printers — LaserMaster/Unity 1800-XLO; Other equipment — Lf/AP Leaf Picture Desk. CLASSIFIED: Front-end hardware — HI/Cash, Zenith/PC. DISPLAY: Front-end hardware — Ap/Power Mac 7100-66S; Front-end software — QPS 3.3, Adobe/Illustrator, Adobe/Photoshop; Other equipment — AP AdSend. PRODUCTION: Typesetters — MON/ImageMaster 1000, MON/ImageMaster 1200, ECR/Pelbox 108, MON/ImageMaster 1016; Plate exposures — 2-Nu; Plate processors — 1-Graham/Subtractive Plate Processor; Electronic picture desk — Lf/AP Leaf Picture

Desk; Scanners — Kk/RFS-2035+, Sharp/JX-610, AG/Arcus+, RZ/4050; Production cameras — 1-SCREEN/260D, 1-R/432 Mk II; Automatic film processors — 1-LE/LD-24; Film transporters — 1-C; Digital color separation equipment — Phoenix.
PRESSROOM: Line 1 — G/Urbanite; Folders — 7-G/2:1. MAILROOM: Counter stackers — 1-PPK/Mini Stack, 1-BG/106; Inserters and stuffers — 2-MM; Bundle tyer — 3-MLN/M1255; Addressing machine — 1-Ch. LIBRARY: Electronic — Vu/Text. COMMUNICATIONS: Facsimile — 2-Toshiba, 1-PB. WIRE SERVICES: News — AP, KRT; Stock tables — AP; Receiving dishes — AP. BUSINESS COMPUTERS: 1-HP/3000, 8-ATT/6300, 10-PCs, 5-HP/Vectra 386; Applications: Accts, Adv, Circ, Ledger, Accts payable, Payroll, Cash accts receivable, Legals;, Lotus 1-2-3, Claris/MacWrite, Aldus/PageMaker, Adobe, XYQUEST/XyWrite, WordPerfect; PCs & micros networked; PCs & main system networked.

STROUDSBURG-EAST STROUDSBURG

Monroe County

'90 U.S. Census- 14,093 (Stroudsburg 5,312; East Stroudsburg 8,781); E&P '96 Est. 14,093 (Stroudsburg 5,453; East Stroudsburg 9,457)
ABC-CZ (90): 24,693 (HH 9,068)

Pocono Record

(m-mon to sat; S)

Pocono Record, 511 Lenox St., Stroudsburg, PA 18360; tel (717) 421-3000; fax (717) 424-2625. Ottaway Newspapers Inc. group.
Circulation: 21,873(m); 21,873(m-sat); 26,341(S); ABC Sept. 30, 1995.
Price: 50¢(d); 50¢(sat); $1.50(S); $3.15/wk (carrier); $151.55/yr (carrier), $215.30/yr (mail).
Advertising: Open inch rate $12.93(m); $12.93(m-sat); $14.87(S). **Representative:** Landon Associates Inc.
News Services: AP, ONS. **Politics:** Independent. **Established:** 1894.
Not Published: New Year; Christmas.
Special Editions: Bridal (Jan); Progress, Furniture (Feb); N.I.E. (Mar); Today's Woman, Funeral & Estate Planning (Apr); Pocono Summer (May); Bridal (June); Pocono Summer (July); W E Fair, Pocono Summer (Aug); Fall Sports (Sept); Fall Planting (Oct); Gift Guide, Cookbook (Nov); Car Care, Home Improvement, Spring Lawn & Garden (Spring); Home Improvement (Summer, Fall); Car Care (Winter).
Special Weekly Section: Weekend (Entertainment) (fri).
Magazines: TV World (S); Real Estate Review; Dignity (a senior publication) (monthly); Northeastern Pennsylvania Factory Outlet & Off Price Guide (May, annually); Pocono Summer (May, July, Aug).

GENERAL MANAGEMENT
President/Publisher Carolynn Allen-Evans

ADVERTISING
Director Peter L Berry
Manager-Sales Teri F Bryant
Telephone Sales (Classified) Barbara S Schoebel
New Media Ventures Jinx M Perszyk

TELECOMMUNICATIONS
Audiotex Manager Jinx M Perszyk

CIRCULATION
Manager Bernard Kozen

NEWS EXECUTIVES
Editor Ronald Bouchard
Managing Editor William Kline

EDITORS AND MANAGERS
Action Line Editor Gail Nevins
City Editor Dan Burnett
Editorial Page Editor Kevin McCaney
Features Editor Robert Groff
Food Editor Marta Lindenmoyer
Photo Department Manager David Coulter
Radio/Television Editor Sonja Meyer
Real Estate Editor Robert Groff
Sports Editor Tom DeSchriver
Sunday Editor Sonja Meyer
Women's Editor Marta Lindenmoyer

PRODUCTION
Director Vaughn Gravel
Foreman-Composing Tom Hinton
Foreman-Pressroom Bob Lebar
Foreman-Mailroom Joe Gilroy
Technician-Systems Warren Loney

Market Information: TMC; Operate audiotex.
Mechanical available: Offset; Black and 4 ROP colors; insert accepted — preprinted; page cut-offs — $22\frac{3}{4}$".
Mechanical specifications: Type page 13" x $21\frac{1}{2}$"; E - 6 cols, $2\frac{1}{16}$", $\frac{1}{8}$" between; A - 6 cols, $2\frac{1}{16}$", $\frac{1}{8}$" between; C - 8 cols, $1\frac{7}{16}$", $\frac{3}{16}$" between.
Commodity consumption: Newsprint 2,270 metric tons; widths $13\frac{1}{4}$", $27\frac{1}{2}$", 30"; black ink 30,603 pounds; color ink 2,500 pounds; single pages printed 16,600; average pages per issue 36(d), 70(S); single plates used 18,000.
Equipment: EDITORIAL: Front-end hardware — SII, PC; Front-end software — SII; Other equipment — Lf/AP Leaf Picture Desk. CLASSIFIED: Front-end hardware — PC, Novell/Network, Ap/Mac Quadra 800, Ap/Mac II; Front-end software — Dewar/Sys IV. AUDIOTEX: Hardware — Info-Connect; Software — Info-Connect; Supplier name — TMS. DISPLAY: Front-end hardware — PC; Front-end software — Dewar/Ad Dummy. PRODUCTION: Pagination software — Dewar/Sys IV Classified; OCR software — Caere/OmniPage Pro; Typesetters — Tegra/Varityper/Imagesetter, Linotype-Hell/Linotronic 202; Plate exposures — 1-Nu/Flip Top FT40; Plate processors — MAS/W026, Anocoil/Subtractive; Scanners — ECR/Autokon, HP/Scanner, Epson/ES-600C; Production cameras — C/Spartan III; Automatic film processors — P/Quik; Shrink lenses — Allen Bradley; Color separation equipment (conventional) — Lf/AP Leaf Picture Desk.
PRESSROOM: Line 1 — 6-G/Urbanite; Line 2 — 8-G/Urbanite; Press drives — Fin; Folders — G. MAILROOM: Counter stackers — QWI; Inserters and stuffers — Amerigraph/NP630; Bundle tyer — Power Strap; Addressing machine — KR. COMMUNICATIONS: Digital ad delivery system — AP AdSend. WIRE SERVICES: News — AP, ONS; Stock tables — AP; Receiving dishes — AP. BUSINESS COMPUTERS: IBM/AS-400; Applications: Accts receivable, Accts payable, Gen ledger, Payroll, Adv billing; PCs & micros networked.

SUNBURY

Northumberland County

'90 U.S. Census- 11,591; E&P '95 Est. 11,040
ABC-NDM (90): 147,158 (HH 52,788)

The Daily Item

(m-mon to sat; S)

The Daily Item, 200 Market St.; PO Box 607, Sunbury, PA 17801; tel (717) 286-5671; fax (717) 286-2570. Ottaway Newspapers Inc. group.
Circulation: 25,529(m); 25,529(m-sat); 28,968(S); ABC Sept. 30, 1995.
Price: 50¢(d); 50¢(sat); $1.50(S); $2.50/wk; $10.00/mo; $117.00/yr.
Advertising: Open inch rate $19.58(m); $19.58(m-sat); $20.48(S). **Representative:** Landon Associates Inc.
News Services: AP, ONS, KRT. **Politics:** Independent. **Established:** 1872.
Note: Effective July 4, 1995, this publication changed its publishing plan from (e-mon to fri; m-sat; S) to (m-mon to sat; S).
Not Published: Thanksgiving; Christmas.
Special Edition: Bridal (monthly).
Special Weekly Sections: Food, Business (wed); Lawn & Garden (fri); Religion (sat); Travel, TV Update, Best Food Day, Business, Farm Page (S).
Magazines: Daily Item/TV Update, Parade (S).

CORPORATE OFFICER
President Donald P Micozzi

GENERAL MANAGEMENT
Publisher Donald P Micozzi
General Manager Janet Mittelstadt Tippett

ADVERTISING
Director Martin J Hughes
Manager-Classified John Leeser

TELECOMMUNICATIONS
Audiotex Manager Martin J Hughes

CIRCULATION
Manager Richard Richter

NEWS EXECUTIVES
Editor Leonard M Ingrassia
Editorial Page Editor John L Moore

EDITOR AND MANAGER
Sunday Editor Judy Casimir

PRODUCTION
Director Edward R Thomas
Foreman-Pressroom Thomas Hosey
Supervisor-Pre Press Jerry Beaver
Supervisor-Mailroom Brett Neidig

Market Information: Split Run; TMC; ADS; Operate audiotex.
Mechanical available: Offset; Black and 4 ROP colors; insert accepted — preprinted; page cut-offs — $22\frac{3}{4}$".
Mechanical specifications: Type page $13\frac{1}{4}$" x 21"; E - 6 cols, $2\frac{1}{16}$", $\frac{1}{8}$" between; A - 6 cols, $2\frac{1}{16}$", $\frac{1}{8}$" between; C - 9 cols, $1\frac{5}{16}$", $\frac{1}{8}$" between.
Commodity consumption: Newsprint 1,837 metric tons; widths 56", 42", 28"; black ink 38,000 pounds; color ink 5,250 pounds; single pages printed 12,972; average pages per issue 29(d), 64(S); single plates used 16,000.
Equipment: EDITORIAL: Front-end hardware — 2-IBM/RS-6000; Front-end software — Microsoft/DOS, Microsoft/Windows, QuarkXPress, Microsoft/Word, Dewar/View, Adobe/Photoshop, Adobe/Illustrator; Printers — HP/LaserJet; Other equipment — Kk, Polaroid/35mm Scanner. CLASSIFIED: Front-end hardware — HAS; Front-end software — CD/TOPS; Printers — Printronix. AUDIOTEX: Software — New Horizons; Supplier name — TMS, Voice News Network. DISPLAY: Adv layout systems — Mk/Managing Editor; Front-end hardware — IBM/RS 6000 w/Raid Drive; Front-end software — Archetype Designer; Printers — HP/LaserJet; Other equipment — 2-Flatbed Scanner. PRODUCTION: Pagination software — QuarkXPress, Dewar/View; Typesetters — 2-AU/APS-684ACS; Plate exposures — 2-Nu/Flip Top; Plate processors — Nat/A-340; Scanners — Kk, Polaroid; Production cameras — 2-Konica/Spartan; Automatic film processors — LE; Film transporters — Konica; Digital color separation equipment — Adobe/Photoshop on PC.
PRESSROOM: Line 1 — TKS/double width offset (1-half deck); Folders — 2-TKS/2:1; Pasters — 3-TKS/Core Tension; Press control system — TKS. MAILROOM: Counter stackers — 2-Id, 2-PPC; Inserters and stuffers — AM/Sheridan 630; Bundle tyer — Power Strap/PSN5; Wrapping singles — Power Strap/SP-555; Addressing machine — Machtronic, Wm; Other mailroom equipment — Mc/Stitcher-Trimmer, Q-Folder, Mac-tronic Mailer. COMMUNICATIONS: Digital ad delivery system — AP AdSend. WIRE SERVICES: News — AP, DJ, ONS; Photos — AP; Receiving dishes — AP, Voice News Network. BUSINESS COMPUTERS: IBM/AS 400; PCs & micros networked; PCs & main system networked.

TARENTUM
See NEW KENSINGTON

TITUSVILLE

Crawford County

'90 U.S. Census- 6,434; E&P '96 Est. 6,083

The Titusville Herald

(m-mon to fri)

The Titusville Herald, 209 W. Spring St.; PO Box 328, Titusville, PA 16354; tel (814) 827-3634; fax (814) 827-2512. Hollinger International Inc. group.
Circulation: 4,720(m); Sworn Oct. 10, 1995.
Price: 35¢(d); $9.00/mo; $108.00/yr.
Advertising: Open inch rate $6.90(m). **Representative:** Landon Associates Inc.
News Service: AP. **Politics:** Independent-Republican. **Established:** 1865.
Note: Printing contracted with Corry Journal, Corry PA.
Not Published: New Year; Memorial Day; Independence Day; Labor Day; Thanksgiving; Christmas.
Special Editions: Coupons (Jan); Growth & Progress (Feb); Spring Preview & Bridal (Mar); Trophy Trout Contest, The Golden Years (Apr); Discover, Mother's Day (May); Graduation, Father's Day, Drugs, Signing of the Declaration (June); Tionesta Indian Festival, Oil Heritage Week, Pleasantville Festival, Sidewalk Sales (July); Historic Titusville, Football, All Sports, Back-to-School, Venango Fair (Aug); Auto Promo, Spartansburg Fair (Sept); Christmas Cash Giveaway, Home Improvement (Oct); Thanksgiving, Joy of Giving (Nov); Wrapping It Up, Holiday Songbook, Titusville Yearbook (Dec).

GENERAL MANAGEMENT
Publisher Michael D Sample

ADVERTISING
Director Michael D Sample
Manager-National Michael D Sample

CIRCULATION
Manager Karol Carlin

EDITOR AND MANAGER
City Editor John Yates

MANAGEMENT INFORMATION SERVICES
Data Processing Manager Karol Carlin

PRODUCTION
Manager John Toriski

Market Information: TMC.
Mechanical available: Offset; black; insert accepted — preprinted; page cut-offs — $21\frac{3}{4}$".
Mechanical specifications: Type page 13" x $21\frac{1}{2}$"; E - 6 cols, $2\frac{1}{16}$", $\frac{1}{8}$" between; A - 6 cols, $2\frac{1}{16}$", $\frac{1}{8}$" between; C - 9 cols, $1\frac{3}{8}$", $\frac{1}{16}$" between.
Commodity consumption: widths 27", $13\frac{1}{2}$"; single pages printed 4,112; average pages per issue 14(d).
Equipment: EDITORIAL: Front-end hardware — 4-Ap/Mac Centris 650; Front-end software — Aldus/PageMaker 5.0, QuarkXPress 3.2, Microsoft/Word 5.0; Printers — Ap/Mac LaserWriter Pro 630. CLASSIFIED: Front-end hardware — Mk, 2-Ap/Mac Centris 650; Printers — Ap/Mac LaserWriter Plus. DISPLAY: Front-end hardware — 1-Ap/Mac Quadra 610; Front-end software — Multi-Ad/Creator 3.5.4, Ofoto; Printers — 1-Ap/Mac LaserWriter Pro 630; Other equipment — Ap/Mac Scanner. PRODUCTION: OCR software — Caere/OmniPage Direct; Typesetters — 2-COM/Unisetter, 2-Ap/Mac Laser; Platemaking systems — Ultra-Lite/1500; Plate exposures — B; Plate processors — Ic; Production cameras — 1-Acti/204; Shrink lenses — 1-Kamerak/119. MAILROOM: Addressing machine — 1-Automecha/Accufast PL Labeller, 1-Wm. WIRE SERVICES: News — AP; Receiving dishes — size-3m, AP. BUSINESS COMPUTERS: Bs/20; Applications: Accts receivable; PCs & main system networked.

TOWANDA

Bradford County

'90 U.S. Census- 3,242; E&P '96 Est. 3,024

The Daily Review

(m-mon to sat)

The Sunday Review (S)

The Daily Review, 116 Main St.; PO Box 503, Towanda, PA 18848-0503; tel (717) 265-2151; fax (717) 265-4200. Times Newspapers group.
Circulation: 8,822(m); 8,822(m-sat); 9,276(S); CAC Mar. 31, 1995.
Price: 40¢(d); 40¢(sat); $1.25(S); $2.75/wk; $13.75/5wk; $125.00/yr.
Advertising: Open inch rate $13.10(m); $13.10(m-sat); $13.10(S). **Representative:** Landon Associates Inc.
News Service: AP. **Established:** 1879.
Not Published: New Year; Memorial Day; Independence Day; Labor Day; Thanksgiving; Christmas (unless they fall on a Sunday).
Special Editions: Year in Review (Jan); Bridal, Northeast Woman (Feb); Walt Disney World, Spring Home Improvement I (Mar); Dining & Entertainment I, Spring Home Improvement II, Chamber Directory, Northeast Outdoors Spring Edition (Apr); Bridal, Human Services (May); Vacation Guide I, Graduation (June); Vacation Guide II, Valley Directory, Senior's Scene (July); Football (Aug); Fall Home Improvement I (Sept); Fall Home Improvement II, Northeast Outdoors Fall Edition, School News, Dining & Entertainment II (Oct); Christmas Gift Guide (Nov); Community Directory, 1997 Calendar (Dec).
Special Weekly Sections: Senior's Column (mon); Color Comics (S).
Magazine: Parade Magazine.

CORPORATE OFFICERS
President George V Lynett
Vice Pres William R Lynett
Vice Pres James E Towner
Vice Pres James J Haggerty Esq
Secretary/Treasurer Edward J Lynett Jr

GENERAL MANAGEMENT
Publisher James E Towner
Purchasing Agent James E Towner

ADVERTISING

Director	Laura Sylvester
Manager-Classified	Donna Winski
Manager-Retail	Melinda Raub

TELECOMMUNICATIONS

Manager-Customer Service	Barbara Davis

CIRCULATION

Manager	Debbie Fero

EDITORS AND MANAGERS

Editorial Page Editor	Dennis Irvine
Features Editor	Nancy Coleman
Graphics Editor/Art Director	Dave Colton
Managing Editor	Dennis Irvine
News Editor	Irma Henson
Photo Editor	Rick Jennings
Society Editor	Sue Corie
Sports Editor	Robert Baker
Travel Editor	Dennis Irvine

PRODUCTION

Manager	Dave Colton
Superintendent (Day)	Martin Frey
Superintendent (Night)	Michelle Lamphere
Foreman-Pressroom (Day)	John Hatch
Foreman-Pressroom (Night)	Brian Schlosser

Market Information: Split Run; TMC.
Mechanical available: Offset; black; insert accepted — preprinted; page cut-offs — 22".
Mechanical specifications: Type page 13" x 21½"; E - 6 cols, 2", 1/6" between; A - 6 cols, 2", 1/6" between; C - 8 cols, 1½", 1/8" between.
Commodity consumption: Newsprint 2,000 metric tons; widths 27½", 16¾", 13¾", 34"; black ink 48,600 pounds; color ink 2,000 pounds; average pages per issue 18(d), 16(sat), 40(S); single plates used 24,000.
Equipment: EDITORIAL: Front-end hardware — CText; Front-end software — XYQUEST/XyWrite III; Printers — Epson/LX-800. CLASSIFIED: Front-end hardware — CText; Front-end software — CText; Printers — HP/LaserJet 4. DISPLAY: Front-end hardware — 3-Ap/Power Mac 6100-66, 2-Ap/Mac SE, 2-Ap/Mac Plus; Front-end software — QuarkXPress 3.3, Multi-Ad/Creator 3.7, Aldus/FreeHand, Adobe/PageMaker 5.0, Adobe/Photoshop 3.0, Adobe/Streamline 3.1; Printers — Ap/Mac LaserWriter Plus MODIA, NewGen/Turbo PS 880, HP/LaserJet 4, NewGen/Design Xpress 6; Other equipment — 1-Prodigy/2400 Modem. PRODUCTION: Plate exposures — 1-Nu/Flip Top FT40UPNS, 1-Nu/Flip Top 40UP; Plate processors — 1-Nat/A-250; Scanners — Microtek/MS-II, Polaroid/SprintScan 35, Umax/Vista S-8; Production cameras — 1-R/24-580; Film transporters — 1-DAI/Screen LD-260-Q.
PRESSROOM: Line 1 — 6-HI/Cottrell V-22. MAILROOM: Counter stackers — 1-BG/Count-O-Veyor; Inserters and stuffers — 6-MM/227, 3-MM/227; Bundle tyer — 4-Dynaric/Strapping Machines; Addressing machine — 1-Ch/538-525. COMMUNICATIONS: Facsimile — 1-dex Express/2500. WIRE SERVICES: News — AP; Receiving dishes — AP. BUSINESS COMPUTERS: IBM; PCs & micros networked; PCs & main system networked.

TYRONE

Blair County

'90 U.S. Census- 5,743; E&P '96 Est. 5,287

The Daily Herald

(e-mon to fri; m-sat)

The Daily Herald, 1018 Pennsylvania Ave., Tyrone, PA 16686; tel (814) 684-4000; fax (814) 684-4238.
Circulation: 2,024(e); 2,024(m-sat); Sworn Sept. 30, 1994.
Price: 35¢(d); 35¢(sat); $100.00/yr.
Advertising: Open inch rate $4.50(e); $4.50(m-sat). **Representative:** Landon Associates Inc.
News Service: AP. **Politics:** Independent. **Established:** 1867.
Note: The Tyrone Daily Herald is owned by the Joseph F Biddle Publishing Co.
Not Published: New Year; Memorial Day; Independence Day; Labor Day; Thanksgiving; Christmas.
Special Editions: Back-to-School (Aug); Football (Sept); Christmas Opening (Dec); Basketball/Wrestling; First Baby of the Year; Graduation.
Special Weekly Sections: Food (wed); TV Week (fri); Food (sat).

CORPORATE OFFICER

President	George Sample III

GENERAL MANAGEMENT

General Manager	Harry Hartman

ADVERTISING

Manager-Retail	Deb Garner

CIRCULATION

Manager	Lori L Stevens

NEWS EXECUTIVE

Editor	Matt Swayne

EDITOR AND MANAGER

Sports Editor	Len Slother

PRODUCTION

Manager	Harry Hartman

Market Information: TMC; ADS.
Mechanical available: Offset; black and 3 ROP colors; insert accepted — preprinted; page cut-offs — 22½".
Mechanical specifications: Type page 13" x 21½"; E - 6 cols, 2 1/16", 1/8" between; A - 6 cols, 2 1/16", 1/8" between; C - 9 cols, 1⅜", 1/16" between.
Commodity consumption: Newsprint 190 short tons; widths 27½", 13¾"; black ink 6,000 pounds; color ink 750 pounds; average pages per issue 10(d); single plates used 3,700.
Equipment: EDITORIAL: Front-end hardware — Mk/550; Front-end software — Mk/550. CLASSIFIED: Front-end hardware — Mk/1100 Plus; Front-end software — Mk/1100 Plus. DISPLAY: Front-end hardware — Mk, Ap/Mac; Front-end software — Mk/Mycro-Comp AdWriter; Printers — Ap/Mac LaserWriter. PRODUCTION: Typesetters — Ap/Mac LaserWriter; Scanners — Ap/Mac Scanner, AG/Scanner. COMMUNICATIONS: Facsimile — Ricoh. WIRE SERVICES: News — AP; Receiving dishes — size-10ft, AP.

UNIONTOWN

Fayette County

'90 U.S. Census- 12,034; E&P '96 Est. 10,311
ABC-CZ (90): 36,167 (HH 14,712)

Herald-Standard

(m-mon to fri; S)

Herald-Standard, 8-18 E. Church St.; PO Box 848, Uniontown, PA 15401; tel (412) 439-7500; fax (412) 439-7528. Calkins Newspapers group.
Circulation: 31,077(m); 33,302(S); ABC Sept. 30, 1995.
Price: 40¢(d); $1.25(S); $2.80/wk (carrier); $3.05/wk (motor route), $3.00/wk (mail); $131.04/yr (carrier), $142.74/yr (motor route), $156.00 (mail).
Advertising: Open inch rate $24.12(m); $24.12(S). **Representative:** Landon Associates Inc.
News Services: AP, SHNS. **Politics:** Independent. **Established:** 1888 (Standard), 1907 (Herald).
Not Published: New Year; Memorial Day; Independence Day; Labor Day; Christmas.
Special Editions: Mature Years (monthly); Bride & Groom; Personal Finance; NIE Design An Ad; Estate Planning; Cooking Tab; Car Care Tab; Neighborhood; Spring Fashion Tab; Play Ball Tab; Home Tab; Super Sunday Section; Kids Tab; Vacation & Travel Tab; Class of '96 Section 1; Summer Bride Tab; Back-to-School Tab; Brownsville Community Days Section; Football Tab; Fall/Winter Home Tab; Gas Tab; Fall Car Care; Culinary Collection Tab; Thanksgiving Section; Basketball Tab; Christmas Greeting Section; New Year's Greeting Section.
Special Weekly Sections: Health (mon); Religion (fri); Food, Business (S).
Magazines: Enjoy (fri); Color Comics, Parade, TV & E (S).
Cable TV: Operate leased cable TV in circulation area.

CORPORATE OFFICERS

President	Grover J Friend
Publisher	Thomas J Spurgeon
Senior Vice Pres/Treasurer	Edward J Birch
Exec Vice Pres	Charles P Smith
Vice Pres	Sandra C Hardy
Vice Pres	Carolyn C Smith
Vice Pres	Shirley C Ellis
Vice Pres	Stanley M Ellis
Secretary	Sandra C Hardy

GENERAL MANAGEMENT

Business Manager	Kenneth J Long

ADVERTISING

Director	Maureen M Zorichak
Manager-Retail	Lin Cappellini
Manager-Classified	Freeda Walls
Manager-Design	Eugene Koffler
Coordinator-National	Gloria Ryland

MARKETING AND PROMOTION

Director-Marketing	Maureen M Zorichak

CIRCULATION

Director	Val J Laub
Manager-Distribution	Samuel Calabro

NEWS EXECUTIVES

Editor (Herald)	Michael C Ellis
Assoc Editor	Mark O'Keefe
Assoc Editor	Phillip Brown
Assoc Editor	James Smith
Managing Editor	Gloria Czuchan-Pasinski

EDITORS AND MANAGERS

Business Editor	James Pletcher
Editorial Page Editor	James Pletcher
Living Section Editor	Gloria Czuchan-Pasinski
Chief Photographer	Charles Rosendale
Sports Editor	Michael Ciarochi
Sunday Editor	Gloria Czuchan-Pasinski

MANAGEMENT INFORMATION SERVICES

Data Processing Manager	William Palya

PRODUCTION

Director	Jon M Noel
Manager-Mailroom	Patty Thomas
Manager-Pressroom	Tadd Kezmarsky
Supervisor-Page Makeup	Harry McClelland

Market Information: Zoned editions; Split Run; TMC.
Mechanical available: Offset; Black and 3 ROP colors; insert accepted — preprinted; page cut-offs — 22¾".
Mechanical specifications: Type page 13" x 21½"; E - 6 cols, 2 1/16", 1/8" between; A - 6 cols, 2 1/16", 1/8" between; C - 9 cols, 1 5/16", 1/8" between.
Commodity consumption: Newsprint 1,904 short tons; widths 27½", 13¾"; black ink 36,720 pounds; color ink 10,000 pounds; single pages printed 9,000; average pages per issue 24(d), 52(S); single plates used 12,000.
Equipment: EDITORIAL: Front-end hardware — 2-DEC/PDP 11-70, 8-Ap/Mac IIcx. CLASSIFIED: Front-end hardware — 1-DEC/PDP 11-70. DISPLAY: Adv layout systems — SCS/Layout 8000, UT/100-AA; Front-end hardware — Ap/Mac II. PRODUCTION: Typesetters — 2-COM/8600, 2-MON/1016 HS; Plate exposures — 2-BKY; Plate processors — 1-AT/S26; Production cameras — 1-Bo, 1-K/V241; Automatic film processors — 1-Kk/317, 1-Kk/214-K, 1-LE; Digital color separation equipment — 1-Lf/Leafscan, 1-Ap/Mac IIfx, Lf/AP Leaf Picture Desk.
PRESSROOM: Line 1 — 8-HI/845; Folders — 2-HI; Press registration system — Duarte. MAILROOM: Counter stackers — 1-HPS /Dual Carrier; Inserters and stuffers — KAN/320-6 station; Bundle tyer — 1-MLN/Sure Tyer. WIRE SERVICES: News — AP; Photos — AP; Stock tables — AP, NYSE Mutual Funds; Syndicates — NEA, SHNS; Receiving dishes — size-10ft, AP. BUSINESS COMPUTERS: 2-DEC/PDP 11-70, SCS/Layout 8000; Applications: Adv billing, Accts receivable, Payroll, Accts payable, Gen ledger, Circ billing, Subscription list; PCs & micros networked.

VANDERGRIFT

See NEW KENSINGTON

WARREN

Warren County

'90 U.S. Census- 11,122; E&P '96 Est. 10,339
ABC-CZ (90): 14,824 (HH 6,221)

Warren Times-Observer

(m-mon to sat)

Warren Times-Observer, 205 Pennsylvania Ave. W.; PO Box 188, Warren, PA 16365; tel (814) 723-8200; fax (814) 723-6922. Times Publishing Inc. group.
Circulation: 12,150(m); 12,150(m-sat); ABC Sept. 30, 1995.
Price: 50¢(d); 50¢(sat); $8.50/mo (carrier/motor route), $9.00/mo (mail); $85.00/yr (carrier/motor route), $90.00/yr (mail).
Advertising: Open inch rate $12.69(m); $12.69(m-sat). **Representative:** Landon Associates Inc.
News Services: AP, NYT. **Politics:** Independent. **Established:** 1966.
Not Published: Christmas.
Advertising not accepted: Some mail order.
Special Editions: Progress, Coupon Books (quarterly); Football; Hunting; Bridal; Christmas; Car Care; Vacation (quarterfold) (all tabloid size); Holiday Cookbook (quarterfold); Spring Home Improvement; Lawn & Garden.
Special Weekly Sections: Spotlite (thur); TV Times (fri); Best Food Day (sat); TMC.
Magazine: TV Week (local, newsprint, quarterfold) (sat).

GENERAL MANAGEMENT

Publisher	Kevin Mead
Business Manager/Purchasing Agent	Lee J Ericson

ADVERTISING

Director	Matt Mead
Manager-Classified	Jack Albaugh
Manager-Retail	Don Burger

CIRCULATION

Manager	Dennis M Nosel
Manager-Office	Cindy Hollabaugh

NEWS EXECUTIVE

Managing Editor	Jude Dippold

EDITORS AND MANAGERS

Business/Finance Editor	Jude Dippold
City Editor	Eric Paddock
Editorial Page Editor	Jude Dippold
Editorial Writer	Eric Paddock
Education Editor	Eric Paddock
Environment Editor	C Hayes
Family/Fashion Editor	Diana Anderson
Food Editor	Diana Anderson
Night Editor	Tom Schultz
Radio/Television Editor	Tom Schultz
Sports Editor	John White
Women's Editor	Diana Anderson

PRODUCTION

Foreman-Composing	Chuck Strandburg
Foreman-Pre Press	Rose McCanna
Foreman-Pressroom	Kenneth Sheldon

Market Information: Zoned editions; TMC.
Mechanical available: Offset; Black and 3 ROP colors; insert accepted — preprinted; page cut-offs — 21½".
Mechanical specifications: Type page 13" x 21½"; E - 6 cols, 2 1/16", 1/8" between; A - 6 cols, 2 1/16", 1/8" between; C - 9 cols, 1⅜", 1/16" between.
Commodity consumption: Newsprint 1,200 short tons; widths 27½", 23¼", 31", 15½", 13¾"; black ink 5,000 pounds; color ink 500 pounds; single pages printed 4,800; average pages per issue 18(d); single plates used 5,000.
Equipment: EDITORIAL: Front-end hardware — Ap/Mac Quadra; Front-end software — DTI/Page Speed, DTI/Speedwriter, DTI, Adobe/Photoshop 3.0, Caere/OmniPage 2.1; Printers — Ap/Mac LaserWriter, ECR/Imagesetter. CLASSIFIED: Front-end hardware — Ap/Mac Quadra; Front-end software — DTI/ClassSpeed, DTI/AdSpeed, DTI, Adobe/Photoshop 2.5; Printers — ECR/Imagesetter. DISPLAY: Adv layout systems — DTI/SpeedPlanner, DTI; Front-end hardware — Ap/Mac Quadra 650; Front-end software — DTI/AdSpeed, DTI, Adobe/Photoshop; Printers — Ap/Mac LaserWriter; Other equipment — AP AdSend. PRODUCTION: Pagination software — DTI/SpeedPlanner, DTI; OCR software — Caere/OmniPage 2.1; Typesetters — ECR/Imagesetter; Plate exposures — Mercury/Mark II; Plate processors — Nat; Scanners — 1-EC; Production cameras — 1-B/Commodore 24, 1-R/432MK II; Automatic film processors — 1-LE/24BQ; Shrink lenses — 1-CK Optical/SQU-7.
PRESSROOM: Line 1 — 5-G/Urbanite; Press drives — Fin/100 h.p.; Folders — G/½; Reels and stands — G; Press control system — Fin; Press registration system — KFM. MAILROOM: Counter stackers — 1-BG/Count-O-Veyor; Bundle tyer — 2-Sa, Gd, 1-Nichiro Kogyo/Strapper; Wrapping singles — Olson/Bostitcher; Addressing machine — St. WIRE SERVICES: News — AP, NYT; Stock tables — AP; Receiving dishes — AP. BUSINESS COMPUTERS: 1-RSK/TRS-80 Model II, 3-DEC/VT102 & Printer; Applications: Circ, Bus office.

WASHINGTON

Washington County

'90 U.S. Census- 15,864; E&P '96 Est. 14,057
ABC-CZ (90): 17,990 (HH 7,595)

Observer-Reporter

(m-mon to sat; S)

Observer-Reporter, 122 S. Main St., Washington, PA 15301; tel (412) 222-2200; fax (412) 229-2754.
Circulation: 38,503(m); 38,503(m-sat); 39,641(S); ABC Sept. 30, 1995.
Price: 40¢(d); 40¢(sat); $1.00(S); $2.70/wk; $36.00/3mo; $127.50/yr.

Copyright ©1996 by the Editor & Publisher Co.

Advertising: Open inch rate $28.59(m); $28.59(m-sat); $28.59(S). **Representatives:** Landon Associates Inc.; US Suburban Press.
News Services: AP, NYT. **Politics:** Independent-Republican. **Established:** 1808 (Reporter), 1871 (Observer).
Not Published: New Year; Memorial Day; Independence Day; Labor Day; Thanksgiving; Christmas.
Advertising not accepted: Mail order; X-rated movies.
Special Editions: Progress; Spring & Fall Bridal Tab; Car Care; Furniture; Vacation/Recreation Guide; Lawn & Garden; Auto Show; Football; Country Living; Gift Guide; Spring & Fall Home Improvement; Health & Fitness; Recipe; Family Business; County Fair.
Special Weekly Sections: Seniors (mon); Business, Automotive (tues); Best Food Day, Business (wed); Automotive, Youth Beat, Business (thur); Weekend Entertainment, Business, Religion (fri); Business (sat); Automotive, Coupons, Home & Garden, TV Observer, Rural News, Sunday Plus, Home Section (S).
Magazine: USA Weekend (S).

CORPORATE OFFICERS

President John L S Northrop
Vice Pres William B Northrop
Vice Pres/Secretary Patti J Lacock
Vice Pres Edward R DeVoge
Asst Vice Pres Thomas P Northrop
Asst Vice Pres William B Northrop Jr
Chief Financial Officer/Treasurer R Allen Schatz

GENERAL MANAGEMENT

Co-Publisher John L S Northrop
Co-Publisher William B Northrop
General Manager Edward R DeVoge
Director-Human Resources Patti J Lacock
Purchasing Agent E R DeVoge

ADVERTISING

Director Barry Martin
Manager-Retail Matt Chisler
Manager-Special Sections Mary Paul Reese

MARKETING AND PROMOTION

Director-Marketing William B Northrop Jr
Director-Community Relations Robert W McFeely

TELECOMMUNICATIONS

Audiotex Manager Richard A McCullough

CIRCULATION

Director Richard A McCullough
Asst Director Jennifer Fischer
Manager-Distribution Gerald Hickman

NEWS EXECUTIVES

Managing Editor Park Burroughs
Asst Managing Editor Terry P Hazlett
Asst Managing Editor-Graphics/Production Maureen Stead

EDITORS AND MANAGERS

City/Metro Editor Elizabeth Rogers
Editorial Page Editor Louis F Florian
Education Editor Pat Ponticel
Entertainment/Amusements Editor Dave Molter
Farm/Agriculture Editor Don Herschell
Features Editor Terry P Hazlett
Graphics Editor/Art Director Maureen Stead
Health/Medical Editor Terri Johnson
Living/Lifestyle Editor Terry P Hazlett
News Editor Elizabeth Rogers
Asst News Editor Linda Ritzer
Night Editor Brant Newman
Photo Editor Maureen Stead
Chief Photographer James McNutt
Religion Editor Don Herschell
Sports Editor Thomas Rose
Television/Film Editor Dave Molter
Travel Editor Terry P Hazlett
Women's Editor Terry P Hazlett

MANAGEMENT INFORMATION SERVICES

Data Processing Manager Robert G Bradford

PRODUCTION

Director-Operations Thomas P Northrop
General Foreman Howard Pattison
Foreman-Night Ernest R Donaldson
Foreman-Pressroom James Helicke
Foreman-Plate Prep John Johnson
Supervisor-Mailroom Gerald Hickman
Supervisor-Systems Robert G Bradford
Asst Supervisor-Systems Reese Dugan

Market Information: Zoned editions; Operate audiotex.
Mechanical available: MAN/Roland Offset, Mediaman; Black and 3 ROP colors; insert accepted — preprinted; page cut-offs — 22".
Mechanical specifications: Type page 13" x 21"; E - 6 cols, 2$\frac{1}{16}$", ⅛" between; A - 6 cols, 2$\frac{1}{16}$", ⅛" between; C - 9 cols, 1⅜", $\frac{1}{16}$" between.
Commodity consumption: Newsprint 3,500 short tons; widths 27½", 41¼", 55"; black ink 120,000 pounds; color ink 8,600 pounds; single pages printed 13,459; average pages per issue 30(d), 56(S); single plates used 48,000.
Equipment: EDITORIAL: Front-end hardware — Cybergraphics, DEC, 41-Cybergraphics/CGS 250, 3-Cybergraphics/CGS 300; Other equipment — 2-Ap/Mac Quadra 950, Ap/Mac SE, 1-Ap/Mac si, 2-Ap/Mac Quadra 650. CLASSIFIED: Front-end hardware — Cybergraphics/CGS, 6-Cybergraphics/CGS 250; Printers — Facit/Printer #4528. AUDIOTEX: Hardware — TI; Software — Info Connect; Supplier name — Tribune News Services, AP. DISPLAY: Adv layout systems — SCS/Layout 8000, 2-Cybergraphics/CGS 250; Front-end hardware — 3-Ap/Mac Quadra 650, 1-Ap/Mac Centris 610, 2-Ap/Power Mac PC; Front-end software — Multi-Ad/Creator, QuarkXPress 7.1; PRODUCTION: Typesetters — 2-MON/Lasercomp, Mk/21, 1-X/P26 LaserPrinter, XIT/Schooner-Imagesetter, ECR/Pelbox 1045; Plate exposures — 2-BKY/Ascor 30 x 40; Plate processors — 1-WL/30d; Electronic picture desk — Lf/AP Leaf Picture Desk; Scanners — 1-ECR/Autokon News Graphics; Production cameras — 1-C/Spartan III; Automatic film processors — 1-LE/2600A, 1-Glunz-Jensen, AU/APS-6-108; Film transporters — LE; Shrink lenses — 1-CK Optical/SQU-7; Digital color separation equipment — Lf/Leafscan 35, 2-Lf/AP Leaf Picture Desk, 1-Kk/RFS-2035. PRESSROOM: Line 1 — MAN/Roland Mediaman (3 half decks); Line 2 — 4-G/Community; Press drives — Allen Bradley; Folders — 2-MAN/2:1; Pasters — MEG/2-45; Reels and stands — 5-G/Reel; Press control system — Allen Bradley. MAILROOM: Counter stackers — 3-QWI/SJ 2X4; Inserters and stuffers — 1-S/1148P; Bundle tyer — 2-EAM/Mosca, 1-Dynaric; Addressing machine — 1-KR, 5-Wm. COMMUNICATIONS: Facsimile — 2-Panafax/OF 250, 1-Murata/F-37, 1-Toshiba/TF 211. WIRE SERVICES: News — AP, NYT; Photos — AP; Syndicates — AP; Receiving dishes — AP. BUSINESS COMPUTERS: 2-DEC/MicroVAX II, 12-DEC/LXY Printers, Data Products/B-600; Applications: Lotus, Microsoft/Excel, Adv billing, Accts receivable, Gen ledger, Payroll, Circ, Subscriber/Non-Subscriber, Spreadsheets; Database, Word Processing.

WAYNESBORO

Franklin County

'90 U.S. Census- 9,578; E&P '96 Est. 9,457

The Record Herald

(e-mon to fri; m-sat)

The Record Herald, 30 Walnut St.; PO Box 271, Waynesboro, PA 17268; tel (717) 762-2151; fax (717) 762-3824. Hollinger International Inc. group.
Circulation: 10,109(e); 10,109(m-sat); Sworn Oct. 9, 1995.
Price: 50¢(d); 50¢(sat); $8.25/mo; $99.00/yr.
Advertising: Open inch rate $9.20(e); $9.20(m-sat). **Representative:** Landon Associates Inc.
News Service: AP. **Politics:** Independent. **Established:** 1847.
Not Published: New Year; Memorial Day; Independence Day; Labor Day; Thanksgiving; Christmas.
Special Editions: Bridal (Jan); Progress (Feb); Golden Years (Mar); Home Improvement (Apr); Bridal No. 2 (May); Spotlight Newcomers (July); Back-to-School, Progress No. 2 (Aug); Home Improvement No. 2 (Sept); Financial (Oct); Gift Guides (3) (Nov); Gift Guides (3) (Dec).
Special Weekly Section: Accent (TV Guide) (sat).

GENERAL MANAGEMENT

Publisher Kelly Luvison
Business Manager George McKee
Manager-Education Service Dennis Shockey

ADVERTISING

Manager Dennis Shockey
Manager-Classified Shirley Gossert

CIRCULATION

Manager Linda Aldridge

NEWS EXECUTIVE

Editor Sue Ernde

EDITORS AND MANAGERS

Business/Finance Editor Sue Ernde
City/Metro Editor Sue Ernde
Editorial Page Editor Sue Ernde
Fashion/Style Editor Jill Ercolino
National Editor Sue Ernde
News Editor Sue Ernde
Photo Editor Sue Ernde
Political/Government Editor Sue Ernde
Religion Editor Shawn Hardy
Sports Editor Scott Weaver
Theater/Music Editor Jill Ercolino
Women's Editor Jill Ercolino

MANAGEMENT INFORMATION SERVICES

Data Processing Manager George McKee

PRODUCTION

Superintendent Jeffery Wishmyer
Foreman-Pressroom Darious Walter

Mechanical available: Offset; Black and 3 ROP colors; insert accepted — preprinted; page cut-offs — 22¾".
Mechanical specifications: Type page 13" x 21½"; E - 6 cols, 2.07", ⅛" between; A - 6 cols, 2.07", ⅛" between; C - 8 cols, 1½", ⅛" between.
Commodity consumption: Newsprint 600 short tons; widths 13¾", 27½", 32", 34"; single pages printed 6,800(approx.); average pages per issue 21(d); single plates used 15,000(approx.).
Equipment: EDITORIAL: Front-end hardware — Mk/1100 Plus; Front-end software — Mk/1100 Plus; Printers — Ap/Mac LaserWriter; Other equipment — Lf/AP Leaf Picture Desk. CLASSIFIED: Front-end hardware — Mk/1100 Plus; Front-end software — Mk/1100 Plus; Printers — Ap/Mac LaserWriter. DISPLAY: Adv layout systems — Ap/Mac; Front-end hardware — Ap/Mac IIsi, Ap/Mac IIci; Front-end software — Aldus/PageMaker; Printers — Ap/Mac Laser-Writer IIf. PRODUCTION: Typesetters — Ap/Mac IIf, Ap/Mac LaserWriter Pro 630; Plate exposures — Nu/Flip Top FT40V3UPNS; Plate processors — Nat/5000; Electronic picture desk — Lf/AP Leaf Picture Desk; Scanners — HP/LaserJet Plus; Production cameras — C, VG/Graphline 760, K/Vertical 24"; Automatic film processors — LE.
PRESSROOM: Line 1 — 4-G/Urbanite; Folders — 1-G/500. MAILROOM: Bundle tyer — 2-OVL; Addressing machine — 1-Ch. COMMUNICATIONS: Facsimile — Ricoh/therma. WIRE SERVICES: News — AP; Photos — AP; Receiving dishes — size-8ft, AP. BUSINESS COMPUTERS: IBM/Sys 36; PCs & micros networked.

WEST CHESTER

Chester County

'90 U.S. Census- 18,041; E&P '96 Est. 18,564
ABC-CZ (90): 36,123 (HH 12,593)

Daily Local News

(m-mon to fri; m-sat; S)

Daily Local News, 250 N. Bradford Ave., West Chester, PA 19382; tel (610) 696-1775; fax (610) 430-1180. Journal Register Co. group.
Circulation: 35,201(m); 33,042(m-sat); 33,298(S); ABC Sept. 30, 1995.
Price: 50¢(d); 50¢(sat); $1.25(S); $3.30/wk; $171.60/yr.
Advertising: Open inch rate $30.00(m); $30.00(m-sat); $30.00(S). **Representative:** Landon Associates Inc.
News Service: AP. **Politics:** Independent. **Established:** 1872.
Note: The Daily Local News also prints the Phoenixville (PA) Phoenix (m), a Journal Register Newspaper.
Special Editions: Education Guide, Business & Industry (Jan); Valentine's Day, Cutest Baby, Cabin Fever, Medical Directory, Bridal Guide, Leap Year Sales (Feb); Design An Ad, Women in History, Chester Co. Business Expo, Spring Car Care, Fashion, Healthly Living (Mar); Education Guide, Baseball, Fitness/Summer Fun, Real Estate, Garden Section, Funeral Director's Guide, Home Decorating (Apr); Mother's Day, Radnor Hunt, MADD Poster Contest, Auto Leasing Tab, BEN Awards, Charlestown Nature Ctr., 101 Things to do in Del. Valley (May); Graduation Tab, Father's Day, Tourist Book, Good Neighbor's Day, The Answer Book (June); All in the Family, Chester County Guide, Newcomers, Eagles Preview, Women in Business (July); Education Guide, Back-to-School, Chester Co. Intermediate, Bridal Guide, Home Maintenance Dir., One Day in Chester County (Aug); Home Buyers Guide, Ludwig's Corner, Mushroom Festival, Youth Education Literacy & Learning (YELL), Timeless Treasures, Ideas for Kids, Best of Chester Co., Dining Guide & Restaurant Fest, PA Nurserymen's (Sept); Your Home, Car Care, New Car Guide, Radnor Hunt Races, Breast Cancer Awareness, Pet Care, Home Builders, Readers Choice (Oct); Education Guide, Holiday Cookbook, Gift Guide, Mature Lifestyles, Savor the Flavor of Mushrooms (Nov); Song Book, Holiday Catalog, Last Minute Gift Guide, What Christmas Means to Me (Dec); Employment Monthly, Business Update, The Coupon Book (monthly).
Special Weekly Sections: Food Section (wed); Church News, Weekender (fri); Travel, Chester County Living Tab (S).
Magazines: USA Weekend; TV Magazine; Color Comics.

CORPORATE OFFICERS

President/CEO Robert M Jelenic
Exec Vice Pres/Chief Financial Officer/Treasurer Jean B Clifton

GENERAL MANAGEMENT

Publisher Richard T Stenger
Controller Craig Graves

ADVERTISING

Director Regina B Burkhart
Manager-Classified Kimberly Simmins

MARKETING AND PROMOTION

Director-Promotion D J Metcalf

CIRCULATION

Director Michael B Starn

NEWS EXECUTIVES

Editor William M Caufield
Managing Editor Bruce Mowday

EDITORS AND MANAGERS

City Editor Bill Lowe
Editorial Page Editor Michael Lefkowitz
Entertainment Editor John Chambless
Features Editor Kristen Frasch
News Editor Bill Mooney
Photo Editor Larry McDevitt
Special Sections Editor Dave Lanute
Sports Editor John De Santo
Television/Film Editor John Chambless
Theater/Music Editor John Chambless

PRODUCTION

Director Jim McMahon
Manager-Composing Karl Sickafus
Superintendent-Pressroom Ralph Diorio

Market Information: Zoned editions; TMC.
Mechanical available: Offset; Black and 3 ROP colors; insert accepted — preprinted; page cut-offs — 22¾".
Mechanical specifications: Type page 13" x 21½"; E - 6 cols, 2$\frac{1}{16}$", ⅛" between; A - 6 cols, 2$\frac{1}{16}$", ⅛" between; C - 8 cols, 1½", ⅛" between.
Commodity consumption: Newsprint 3,743 short tons; widths 27½", 31"; black ink 89,832 pounds; color ink 15,346 pounds; single pages printed 20,822; average pages per issue 48(d), 95(S); single plates used 35,818.
Equipment: EDITORIAL: Front-end hardware — Intertext; Front-end software — Intertext; Printers — Okidata. CLASSIFIED: Front-end hardware — Intertext; Front-end software — Intertext; Printers — Okidata. DISPLAY: Adv layout systems — Ap/Mac Network w/4-Workstations. PRODUCTION: Typesetters — 2-Ap/Mac Network, Linotype-Hell/Linotronic; Plate exposures — 1-Nu/Flip Top FT40L, 1-Nu/Flip Top FT40APNS; Plate processors — 2-Nat/340; Direct-to-plate imaging — M/28 Additive; Scanners — Digi-Colour/Sys 3000, Lf/Leafscan 35; Production cameras — C/Spartan II; Automatic film processors — 1-LE/24 BQ; Shrink lenses — 7-CK Optical/500; Color separation equipment (conventional) — Digi-Colour/Sys 3000; Digital color separation equipment — Digi-Colour/Sys 3000.
PRESSROOM: Line 1 — 10-G/Urbanite; Pasters — 7-Enkel/Autoweb; Press control system — Fin. MAILROOM: Counter stackers — 2-HL/Monitor; Inserters and stuffers — 1-GMA/SLS 1000 10:1; Bundle tyer — 2-Power Strap/PSN-6; Addressing machine — Ch. COMMUNICATIONS: Facsimile — Fujitsu/Bu. WIRE SERVICES: News — AP; Stock tables — AP; Receiving dishes — AP. BUSINESS COMPUTERS: 2-IBM/Sys 36; Applications: INSI: Adv, Billing, Payroll, Accts payable, Gen ledger, Circ; PCs & micros networked; PCs & main system networked.

WHEATLAND
See SHARON

I-366 Pennsylvania

WILKES-BARRE

Luzerne County

'90 U.S. Census- 47,523; E&P '96 Est. 44,424
ABC-CZ (90): 115,568 (HH 47,414)

The Citizens' Voice
(m-mon to sat)
The Sunday Voice (S)

The Citizens' Voice, 75 N. Washington St., Wilkes-Barre, PA 18711-0502; tel (717) 821-2091; fax (717) 821-2249.

Circulation: 40,635(m); 40,635(m-sat); 30,215(S); ABC Sept. 30, 1995.

Price: 35¢(d); 35¢(sat); 75¢(S); $2.00/wk; $8.00/mo; $104.00/yr (carrier).

Advertising: Open inch rate $27.00(m); $27.00(m-sat); $27.00(S). **Representatives:** US Suburban Press; Papert Companies.

News Service: AP. **Politics:** Independent. **Established:** 1978.

Special Editions: Health & Wellness, Super Bowl Preview (Jan); Bridal (Feb); Spring Car Care, Voices (Mar); Home & Garden, Cherry Blossom (Apr); Who's Who In Wyoming Valley, Fun in the Sun (June); Miller 500 (July); Senior Lifestyles (Aug); Pigskin Preview (Sept); Automotive Showcase, Fall Car Care (Oct); Great Outdoors, Thanksgiving Holiday Shopping Guide (Nov); Christmas Shopping Guide (Dec).

Special Weekly Sections: Best Food Day (tues); Weekend (fri); Travel, Real Estate, Entertainment, Suburban, Social (S); Business, Entertainment, Television, Sports (daily).

Magazine: Weekend.

CORPORATE OFFICERS

President Edward A Nichols Jr
Secretary Paul L Golias
Treasurer Frank M Cunis Jr

GENERAL MANAGEMENT

Publisher Edward A Nichols Jr
General Manager Robert Manganiello
Controller/Chief Financial Officer Frank M Cunis Jr

ADVERTISING

Director Mark Altavilla
Manager-National Esther Cohen Mager

CIRCULATION

Director Bradley D Sterling
Asst Director Suzanna Slator

NEWS EXECUTIVES

Managing Editor Paul L Golias
Asst Managing Editor Justin O'Donnell

EDITORS AND MANAGERS

Business/Finance Editor Howard Biederman
City Editor-Day William DeRemer
City Editor-Night Janine Dubik
Editorial Page Editor James Gittens
Education Editor Stanley Kieszek
Features/Food Editor Geri Anne Kaikowski
Librarian Ann Cadden
Music Editor Jerry Kishbaugh
Political Editor Michael McGlynn
Radio/Television Editor Geri Anne Kaikowski
Religion Editor Thomas Carten, Fr
Sports Editor Neil Corbett
Weekend Editor Jerry Kishbaugh
Wire Editor Howard Biederman
Women's Editor Pat Trosky

MANAGEMENT INFORMATION SERVICES

Data Processing Manager Barbara Pelak

PRODUCTION

Manager Roger Slator
Foreman-Composing Charles Sailus
Foreman-Pressroom Robert Stankiewicz

Market Information: TMC.

Mechanical available: Offset; Black and 3 ROP colors; insert accepted — preprinted; page cut-offs — 22.75".

Mechanical specifications: Type page 10.5" x 13"; E - 5 cols, 1.98", ⅛" between; A - 5 cols, 1.98", ⅛" between; C - 7 cols, 1.38", ⅛" between.

Commodity consumption: Newsprint 3,300 short tons; widths 27½", 13¾"; black ink 49,000 pounds; color ink 3,300 pounds; single pages printed 27,680; average pages per issue 70(d), 128(S); single plates used 13,000.

Equipment: EDITORIAL: Front-end hardware — COM/OS; Front-end software — COM/OS; Other equipment — 1-Ap/Mac Classic, 1-RSK/100, 1-RSK/200, 2-Everex/Notebook. CLASSIFIED: Front-end hardware — COM/OS; Front-end software — COM/OS. DISPLAY: Front-end hardware — 1-Ap/Mac IIcx, 2-Ap/Mac IIci, 1-Ap/Mac 7100, 1-PC, 2-Ap/Mac Centris 650, 1-Ap/Mac Centris 610, CD-Rom; Front-end software — Multi-Ad/Creator, Aldus/FreeHand, Adobe/Illustrator, Caere/OmniPage, Microsoft/Word, Adobe/Photoshop, Adobe/Streamline, Adobe/Dimensions, QuarkXPress; Printers — 1-Printronix/300, 1-TI/OMNI 300. PRODUCTION: Typesetters — 2-NewGen/Bx660, 1-NewGen/1200T, 1-LaserMaster/Unity 1200 XLO; Platemaking systems — 2-3M/Pyrofax Imager; Plate exposures — Amerigraph/Magnum 457SE; Electronic picture desk — 1-Lf/AP Leaf Picture Desk; Scanners — HP/ScanJet Plus, 2-Microtek/IIxe Scanmaker, 1-Microtek/Scanmaker 600Z; Production cameras — 1-Nu/Vertical VV1418, 1-DAI/670C. PRESSROOM: Line 1 — 7-G/Urbanite; Press drives — Reliance; Folders — G/1000; Press control system — Fin. MAILROOM: Counter stackers — 1-Id; Bundle tyer — 4-MLN/Spirits. WIRE SERVICES: News — AP; Photos — AP; Stock tables — AP; Syndicates — LAT-WP, SHNS; Receiving dishes — AP. BUSINESS COMPUTERS: 1-IBM/6000; Applications: Vision Data: Business, Circ, Adv.

The Times Leader
(m-mon to sat; S)

The Times Leader, 15 N. Main St.; PO Box 730, Wilkes-Barre, PA 18711; tel (717) 829-7100; fax (717) 829-2002; e-mail bobk@ccabc.com; web site http://www.microserve.net/weekender/. Capital Cities/ABC Inc. group.

Circulation: 47,537(m); 47,537(m-sat); 75,214(S); ABC Sept. 30, 1995.

Price: 35¢(d); 35¢(sat); $1.25(S); $2.65/wk (carrier); $10.60/mo (carrier); $137.80/yr (carrier).

Advertising: Open inch rate $32.76(m); $32.76(m-sat); $53.81(S); $69.43(m & S). **Representative:** Landon Associates Inc.

News Services: AP, KRT. **Politics:** Independent. **Established:** 1872.

Special Editions: Bridal; Spring Fashion; Car Care; Business & Industry Profile; Home Improvement; Mother's Day; Father's Day; Back-to-School; Fall Fashion; Health & Fitness; Football; Fall Bridal; Fall Home Improvement; Holiday Gift Guide; Holiday Carols.

Special Weekly Sections: Health (mon); Food, Fashion (thur); Travel, Food (S).

Magazines: Lifestyle (wed); Entertainment (fri); Travel & Business, TV Magazine (S).

GENERAL MANAGEMENT

Publisher/President Mark Contreras
Vice Pres/Director-Marketing Robert Kellagher
Personnel Director David W Daris
Controller Stephen Peterson

ADVERTISING

Vice Pres/Director Dennis Sheely
Manager-Retail Lesa Butera
Manager-National Charles Gibson
Manager-Classified Dawn Bobeck

MARKETING AND PROMOTION

Director-Marketing Service Jerry Konder

CIRCULATION

Vice Pres/Director-Operations Albert Manzi
Asst Director Karl Wurzbach

NEWS EXECUTIVE

Editor Allison Walzer

EDITORS AND MANAGERS

Business Editor Jim Mullay
Columnist Steve Corbett
Editorial Writer Tom Dennis
Features Editor Chris Ritchie
Librarian Katherine Krier
Sports Editor Scott Wasser

MANAGEMENT INFORMATION SERVICES

Data Processing Manager Prashant B Shitut

Market Information: Zoned editions; TMC.

Mechanical available: Letterpress; Black and 3 ROP colors; insert accepted — preprinted, minimum 7¾"x 5½"; page cut-offs — 22¾".

Mechanical specifications: Type page 13" x 21¼"; E - 6 cols, $2\frac{1}{16}$", ⅛" between; A - 6 cols, $2\frac{1}{16}$", ⅛" between; C - 9 cols, 1⅜", $\frac{1}{16}$" between.

Commodity consumption: Newsprint 6,930 short tons; widths 27⅜", $41\frac{1}{16}$", 54¾"; black ink 230,400 pounds; color ink 38,250 pounds; single pages printed 20,116; average pages per issue 50(d), 110(S); single plates used 40,980.

Equipment: EDITORIAL: Front-end hardware — 2-PC/486-66MHZ fileserver, 39-PC/286, 15-PC/386; Front-end software — CText 3.0, Novell/386 Netware 3.12; Printers — 3-Birmy/PowerPrint 11x17, 1-HP/III, 1-Panasonic, ECR/Pelbox 1045CS, 2-Data Products/Typhoon. CLASSIFIED: Front-end hardware — 2-PC/386 fileserver, 19-PC/386 SX; Front-end software — CText, Novell/386 Netware 3.11; Printers — 1-HP/III, 1-C.Itoh, Birmy/PowerPrint 11x17. DISPLAY: Adv layout systems — 1-Novell/Fileserver; Front-end hardware — 1-Ap/Mac NZM 486 DX66 w/Novell/Fileserver; Front-end software — Multi-Ad/Creator, QuarkXPress, Adobe/Illustrator, Adobe/Photoshop, Aldus/FreeHand, Data Products/Typhoon; Printers — 3-HP/III, 1-Birmy/Powerprint 11x17, ECR/1045 CS, 2-PrePress/Panther Pro Imagesetter; Other equipment — 2-AG/Arcus Scanner, Lf/Leafscan 35. PRODUCTION: Pagination software — QuarkXPress 3.3; Typesetters — Birmy/Powerprint 11x17, ECR/Pelbox 1045 CS, 1-PrePress/Panther Pro 46; Platemaking systems — Na; Plate exposures — Na/Starlite; Plate processors — Na/NP20, Na/NP40; Electronic picture desk — Lf/AP Leaf Picture Desk, 4-Ap/Mac, Lf/Leafnet; Scanners — ECR/Autokon 1000DE, 2-AG/1200 dpi, 2-Lf/Leafscan 35, 4-HP/ScanJet; Production cameras — C/Spartan III, C/PageMaker; Automatic film processors — C/Powermatic 66F, LE/LD 24A, LE/LD24BQ; Color separation equipment (conventional) — Ap/Mac. PRESSROOM: Line 1 — 8-H/3091-3092; Folders — 3-H. MAILROOM: Counter stackers — 2-QWI/300; Inserters and stuffers — 2-GMA/1000 SLS; Bundle tyer — 2-Dynaric; Wrapping singles — 2-QWI; Addressing machine — 1-Wm, 1-Ch, 1-Mc/2000 PB Folder. LIBRARY: Electronic — SMS/Stauffer Gold Star Library System, Novell/386 Netware. COMMUNICATIONS: Digital ad delivery system — AP AdSend. Systems used — fiber optic. WIRE SERVICES: News — AP Datastream, AP Datafeatures; Photos — AP; Stock tables — AP; Receiving dishes — size-3m, AP. BUSINESS COMPUTERS: 1-DEC/MV3100, 1-DEC/MV3100; Applications: Microsoft/Office: Circ, Adv billing, Transient, Accts payable, Gen ledger, Payroll, TMC; Boreland/Parabox; PCs & micros networked; PCs & main system networked.

WILLIAMSPORT

Lycoming County

'90 U.S. Census- 31,933; E&P '96 Est. 30,763
ABC-CZ (90): 55,257 (HH 22,002)

Williamsport Sun-Gazette
(e-mon to fri; m-sat; S)

Williamsport Sun-Gazette, 252 W. 4th St.; PO Box 728, Williamsport, PA 17701; tel (717) 326-1551; fax (717) 323-0948. Ogden Newspapers group.

Circulation: 33,077(e); 33,077(m-sat); 41,913(S); ABC Sept. 30, 1995.

Price: 35¢(d); 35¢(sat); $1.00(S); $2.00/wk (carrier); $104.00/yr (carrier).

Advertising: Open inch rate $29.51(e); $29.51(m-sat); $31.01(S). **Representative:** Landon Associates Inc.

News Service: AP. **Politics:** Independent. **Established:** 1801.

Not Published: New Year; Memorial Day; Independence Day; Labor Day; Thanksgiving; Christmas.

Special Editions: Money Matters, Winter Furniture (Jan); Winter Bridal (Feb); Spring Home Improvement, Car Care (Apr); Outdoors (May); Summer Furniture (July); Football Preview, Back-to-School, Visitors, Little League Section (Aug); Health & Fitness, Fall Home Improvement (Sept); Fall Bridal, Fall Car Care (Oct); Basketball and Wrestling, Christmas Opener (Nov); Year in Review (Dec).

Special Weekly Sections: Best Food Day (wed); Entertainment (thur); Home Improvement, Religion (sat); Business, Outdoors, TV Magazine (S).

Magazines: Parade, TV Week (S).

CORPORATE OFFICER

President G Ogden Nutting

GENERAL MANAGEMENT

Publisher Thomas C Briley
Controller Steven L Smith

ADVERTISING

Director John Yahner
Manager-Classified John D Miller
Manager-National James K Gates II

NEWS EXECUTIVES

Editor David F Troisi
News Editor Jeffrey Durham

EDITORS AND MANAGERS

Business Editor Bob Rolley
City Editor Tom Wilson
Entertainment Editor Tom Wilson
Environmental Editor Jim Barr
Farm Editor Wendy Corson
Lifestyle Editor Jan Ogurcak
Sports Editor James D Carpenter

PRODUCTION

Superintendent-Composing Albert E Lambert
Superintendent-Pressroom Richard Smith

Mechanical available: Offset; Black and 3 ROP colors; insert accepted — preprinted; page cut-offs — 22¾".

Mechanical specifications: Type page 13" x 21¼"; E - 6 cols, $2\frac{1}{16}$", ⅛" between; A - 6 cols, $2\frac{1}{16}$", ⅛" between; C - 8 cols, $1\frac{9}{16}$", ⅛" between.

Commodity consumption: Newsprint 3,500 short tons; widths 27", 40.5", 54"; black ink 8,050 pounds; color ink 2,250 pounds; single pages printed 14,556; average pages per issue 35(d), 74(S); single plates used 32,110.

Equipment: EDITORIAL: Front-end hardware — AT; Printers — Florida Data. CLASSIFIED: Front-end hardware — AT; Printers — Florida Data. PRODUCTION: Plate exposures — Nu/Flip Top FT40UP; Plate processors — WL/38; Production cameras — C/Spartan III; Automatic film processors — LE/24. PRESSROOM: Line 1 — 6-G/Metro-3007; Folders — 2-G; Pasters — G; Reels and stands — G; Press control system — Fin. MAILROOM: Counter stackers — HL/Monitor; Inserters and stuffers — HI/P48. WIRE SERVICES: News — AP; Photos — AP; Stock tables — TMS; Receiving dishes — AP. BUSINESS COMPUTERS: Motorola.

YORK

York County

'90 U.S. Census- 42,192; E&P '96 Est. 40,778
ABC-CZ (90): 133,103 (HH 52,801)

York Newspaper Company

York Newspaper Company, 1891 Loucks Rd.; PO Box 14401, York, PA 17404; tel (717) 767-6397; fax (717) 764-6233. MediaNews Inc. (Garden State Newspapers) group; Buckner News Alliance group.

Representative: Landon Associates Inc.

Note: The York Daily Record and the York Dispatch entered into a joint operating agreement. Both papers are corporately and editorially separate, but advertising, circulation, production and printing are handled jointly by the York Newspaper Company.

Special Editions: Brides Guide Tab (Jan); NIE Week Tab (Mar); Home Improvement, Lawn & Garden (Apr); Newcomer's Guide Tab (May); Bridal (June); High School Football Tab, Back-to-School Tab (Aug); Fall Home Improvement, Fall Fashion (ROP) (Sept); Holiday Gift Guide Tab (Nov); Holiday Gift Guide (ROP) (Dec).

Special Weekly Sections: York Weekend Tab (pm) (thur); York Magazine Tab (am) (fri).

Magazines: TV Week, Parade (S).

GENERAL MANAGEMENT

President Joseph H Zerbey IV
Vice Pres-Finance Edward J MaGee

ADVERTISING

Manager-Classified Nancy Nelson
Manager-Display Classified Bryan Kelly
Manager-Retail Fred Uffelman

CIRCULATION

Vice Pres Philip M Ferrara
Director Nello C Stover

MANAGEMENT INFORMATION SERVICES

Data Processing Manager Charles Burkhardt

PRODUCTION

Vice Pres-Operations Thomas R Norton
Manager-Pre Press Wayne Spangler
Manager-Pressroom Jim Englert
Manager-Mailroom Nick Ferro
Manager-Transportation Terry Zellers
Manager-Plant Gene Young

Market Information: Zoned editions; Split Run; TMC; ADS.

Mechanical available: Offset; Black and 3 ROP colors; insert accepted — preprinted, all; page cut-offs — 22¾".

Mechanical specifications: Type page 13" x 21½"; E - 6 cols, $2\frac{1}{16}$", ⅛" between; A - 6 cols, $2\frac{1}{16}$", ⅛" between; C - 10 cols, 1⅛", ⅛" between.

Commodity consumption: Newsprint 8,500 metric tons; widths 55", 41¼", 27½"; black ink 160,000 pounds; color ink 50,000 pounds; single pages printed 27,000; average pages per issue 40(d), 96(S); single plates used 84,500.
Equipment: EDITORIAL: Front-end hardware — AT; Front-end software — AT; Printers — Okidata/40; Other equipment — HI/Pagination. CLASSIFIED: Front-end hardware — HI; Front-end software — HI, HI/Pagination; Printers — Fujitsu. DISPLAY: Adv layout systems — SCS/Layout 8000; Front-end hardware — Ap/Power Mac 7100, Ap/Mac Quadra 900 fileserver, 4-Ap/Mac Centris 650; Front-end software — DTI/Adspeed, QuarkXPress; Printers — 1-Ap/Mac LaserWriter Pro, HP/LaserJet 4MV; Other equipment — AP AdSend. PRODUCTION: Typesetters — 2-MON/3850; Plate exposures — 2-WL/Light; Plate processors — 2-WL/Lithoplater 30D; Electronic picture desk — Lf/AP Leaf Picture Desk; Scanners — ECR/1000; Production cameras — 2-C/Spartan III; Automatic film processors — 2-LE/24A, 2-C/R660; Film transporters — 2-C. PRESSROOM: Line 1 — 8-G/Metro (w/2 CIC); Pasters — 8-G/RTP; Press control system — Fin. MAILROOM: Counter stackers — 4-HL/Monitor HTII; Inserters and stuffers — 1-S/11-48, 1-HL/14-72; Bundle tyer — 4-MLN. COMMUNICATIONS: Remote imagesetting — T-1/line; Digital ad delivery system — AP AdSend, ImageNet. Systems used — satellite. BUSINESS COMPUTERS: HP/918RX-3000; Applications: CJ, Vesoft, DB General, Cognos; PCs & main system networked.

York Daily Record
(m-mon to sat)

York Daily Record, 1750 Industrial Hwy.; PO Box 12015, York, PA 17402; tel (717) 840-4000; fax (717) 840-2009; e-mail dennisydr@aol.com, 73312.2632@compuserve.com; web site http://www.yrd.com. Buckner News Alliance group.
Circulation: 42,423(m); 72,203(m-sat); ABC Sept. 30, 1995.
Price: 35¢(d); 35¢(sat); $10.00/mo (carrier); $120.00/yr (carrier).
Advertising: Open inch rate $46.00(m); $46.00(m-sat). **Representative:** Landon Associates Inc.
News Services: AP, KRT. **Politics:** Independent. **Established:** 1796.
Note: For detailed printing and production information, see listing under York Newspaper Company. Advertising for the York Daily Record automatically includes advertising in the York Dispatch (eS) for $46.00.
Advertising not accepted: Hate groups.
Special Editions: Brides Guide Tab (Jan); NIE Week Tab (Mar); Home Improvement, Lawn & Garden (Apr); Newcomer's Guide Tab (May); Bridal (June); High School Football Tab, Back-to-School Tab (Aug); Fall Home Improvement, Fall Fashion (ROP) (Sept); Holiday Gift Guide Tab (Nov); Holiday Gift Guide (ROP) (Dec).
Special Weekly Sections: Weekly Zone Section (2) (tues); Food (wed); Entertainment (fri); Entertainment, Travel (S).
Magazines: Sunday Comment; York Magazine; Home Magazine (sat); TV Magazine (S).

CORPORATE OFFICERS
Chairman of the Board Philip F Buckner
President David B Martens
Treasurer Gail B Brown

GENERAL MANAGEMENT
Publisher Dennis Hetzel
Controller Michael Newsome

ADVERTISING
Manager-Classified Nancy Nelson
Manager-Display Classified Bryan Kelly
Manager-Retail Fred Uffelman

CIRCULATION
Vice Pres Philip M Ferrara
Director Nello C Stover

NEWS EXECUTIVES
Editor Dennis Hetzel
Managing Editor James McClure

EDITORS AND MANAGERS
Automotive Editor Earl McDaniel
Business/Finance Editor Earl McDaniel
Editorial Page Editor Linda Seligson
Entertainment Editor Kim Strong
Features Editor Kim Strong
Graphics Editor/Art Director Pam Panchak
Living Editor Kim Strong
Metro Editor Erin Esmont
News Editor Randy Parker
Photo Editor Pam Panchak
Religion Editor Rebecca Fishkin
Sports Editor Paul Vigna

MANAGEMENT INFORMATION SERVICES
Data Processing Manager Charles Burkhardt

PRODUCTION
Vice Pres-Operations Thomas R Norton
Manager-Pre Press Wayne Spangler
Manager-Pressroom Jim Englert
Manager-Mailroom Nick Ferro
Manager-Transportation Terry Zellers
Manager-Plant Gene Young

Market Information: Zoned editions; TMC.
Mechanical available: Offset; Black and 3 ROP colors; insert accepted — preprinted, all; page cut-offs — 22¾".
Mechanical specifications: Type page 13" x 21½"; E - 6 cols, 2¹⁄₁₆", ⅛" between; A - 6 cols, 2¹⁄₁₆", ⅛" between; C - 10 cols, 1⅛", ⅛" between.
Commodity consumption: Newsprint 8,500 metric tons; widths 55", 41¼", 27½"; black ink 160,000 pounds; color ink 30,000 pounds; single pages printed 27,000; average pages per issue 40(d), 96(S); single plates used 84,500.
Equipment: EDITORIAL: Front-end hardware — AT, HI; Front-end software — AT, HI; Printers — Okidata/40; Other equipment — HI/Pagination. CLASSIFIED: Front-end hardware — HI; Front-end software — HI, HI/Pagination; Printers — Fujitsu. DISPLAY: Adv layout systems — SCS/Layout 8000; Front-end hardware — 1-Ap/Power Mac 7100, Ap/Mac II NTX, Ap/Mac Quadra 900 fileserver, 4-Ap/Mac Centris; Front-end software — DTI/Adspeed, QuarkXPress; Printers — 1-Ap/Mac LaserWriter. PRODUCTION: Typesetters — 2-MON/3850; Plate exposures — 2-WL/Light; Plate processors — 2-WL/Lithoplater 30D; Scanners — ECR/1000; Production cameras — 2-C/Spartan III; Film transporters — 2-C. PRESSROOM: Line 1 — 8-G/Metro (w/2 CIC); Pasters — 8-G/RTP; Press control system — Fin. MAILROOM: Counter stackers — 4-HL/Monitor HTII; Inserters and stuffers — 1-S/11-48, 1-HL/14-72; Bundle tyer — 4-MLN. LIBRARY: Electronic — Data Times. COMMUNICATIONS: Remote imagesetting — T-1/line. WIRE SERVICES: News — AP, KRT, Religious News Service; Photos — AP; Stock tables — AP; Syndicates — KRT; Receiving dishes — size-3m, AP. BUSINESS COMPUTERS: 11-HP/925-3000; Applications: CJ, DB, Vesoft; PCs & micros networked; PCs & main system networked.

The York Dispatch
(e-mon to fri)

York Sunday News (S)

The York Dispatch/York Sunday News, 205 N. George St.; PO Box 2807, York, PA 17405; tel (717) 854-1575; fax (717) 843-2958; e-mail 75141.463@compuserve.com. MediaNews Inc. group.
Circulation: 40,286(e); 91,682(S); ABC Sept. 30, 1995.
Price: 35¢(d); $1.25(S); $10.00/mo (carrier); $120.00/yr (carrier).
Advertising: Open inch rate $46.00(e); $46.00(S).
News Services: NYT, LAT-WP, AP, MNS, NEA, SHNS. **Politics:** Independent. **Established:** 1876.
Note: For detailed printing and production information, see York Newspaper Company listing. Advertising for the York Dispatch automatically includes advertising for the York Daily Record (m) for $46.00.
Advertising not accepted: Hate groups.
Special Editions: Brides Guide Tab (Jan); NIE Week Tab (Mar); Home Improvement, Lawn & Garden (Apr); Newcomer's Guide Tab (May); Bridal (June); High School Football Tab, Back-to-School Tab (Aug); Fall Home Improvement, Fall Fashion (ROP) (Sept); Holiday Gift Guide Tab (Nov); Holiday Gift Guide (ROP) (Dec).
Special Weekly Section: Weekend (thur).
Magazines: TV Week, Parade (S).

CORPORATE OFFICERS
Chairman of the Board Richard Scudder
Vice Chairman William Dean Singleton
President/CEO William Dean Singleton
Exec Vice Pres/Chief Operating Officer Anthony F Tierno
Exec Vice Pres/Chief Financial Officer Joseph Lodovic

GENERAL MANAGEMENT
Publisher James D Sneddon
Business Manager Randy Ruck

ADVERTISING
Manager-Classified Nancy Nelson
Manager-Display Classified Bryan Kelly
Manager-Retail Fred Uffelman

CIRCULATION
Vice Pres Philip M Ferrara
Director Nello C Stover

NEWS EXECUTIVES
Editor James D Sneddon
Managing Editor Deena Gross

EDITORS AND MANAGERS
Business Editor Judy Hollingsworth
Editorial Page Editor Scott Fisher
Entertainment Editor Dara Dixon
Environmental Editor Pam Saylor
Features Editor Stan Hough
News Editor Bob Orr
Photo Editor Bob Orr
Chief Photographer Chris Edwards

MANAGEMENT INFORMATION SERVICES
Data Processing Manager Charles Burkhardt

PRODUCTION
Vice Pres-Operations Thomas R Norton
Manager-Pre Press Wayne Spangler
Manager-Pressroom Jim Englert
Manager-Mailroom Nick Ferro
Manager-Transportation Terry Zellers
Manager-Plant Gene Young

Market Information: Zoned editions; Split Run; TMC.
Mechanical available: Offset; Black and 3 ROP colors; insert accepted — preprinted, all; page cut-offs — 22¾".
Mechanical specifications: Type page 13" x 21½"; E - 6 cols, 2¹⁄₁₆", ⅛" between; A - 6 cols, 2⅛", ⅛" between; C - 10 cols, 1⅛", ⅛" between.
Commodity consumption: Newsprint 8,500 metric tons; widths 55", 41¼", 27½"; black ink 160,000 pounds; color ink 30,000 pounds; single pages printed 27,000; average pages per issue 40(d), 96(S); single plates used 84,500.
Equipment: EDITORIAL: Front-end hardware — AT, HI; Front-end software — AT, HI; Printers — Okidata/40; Other equipment — HI/Pagination. CLASSIFIED: Front-end hardware — HI; Front-end software — HI, HI/Pagination; Printers — Fujitsu. DISPLAY: Adv layout systems — SCS/Layout 8000; Front-end hardware — 1-Ap/Power Mac 7100, Ap/Mac II NTX, Ap/Mac Quadra 900 fileserver, 4-Ap/Mac Centris; Front-end software — DTI/Adspeed, QuarkXPress; Printers — 1-Ap/Mac LaserWriter. PRODUCTION: Typesetters — 2-MON/3850; Plate exposures — 2-WL/Light; Plate processors — 2-WL/Lithoplater 30D; Scanners — ECR/1000; Production cameras — 2-C/Spartan III; Automatic film processors — 2-LE/24a, 2-C/R660; Film transporters — 2-C. PRESSROOM: Line 1 — 8-G/Metro (w/2 CIC); Pasters — 8-G/RTP; Press control system — Fin. MAILROOM: Counter stackers — 4-HL/Monitor HTII; Inserters and stuffers — 1-S/11-48, 1-HL/14-72; Bundle tyer — 4-MLN. COMMUNICATIONS: Remote imagesetting — T-1/line. WIRE SERVICES: News — AP, LAT-WP, NYT, MNS, NEA, SHNS; Stock tables — AP; Syndicates — TMS, United Features, Universal Press, NAS, King Features, Crown, Creators, LAT-WP, NYT; Receiving dishes — size-3m, AP. BUSINESS COMPUTERS: 11-HP/925-3000; Applications: CJ, DB, Vesoft; PCs & micros networked; PCs & main system networked.

RHODE ISLAND

CENTRAL FALLS
See PAWTUCKET

NEWPORT
Newport County

'90 U.S. Census- 28,227; **E&P '96 Est.** 27,624
ABC-CZ (90): 47,687 (HH 17,783)

The Newport Daily News
(e-mon to fri; m-sat)

The Newport Daily News, 101 Malbone Rd.; PO Box 420, Newport, RI 02840; tel (401) 849-3300; fax (401) 849-3306.
Circulation: 14,415(e); 14,415(m-sat); ABC Sept. 30, 1995.
Price: 50¢(d); 50¢(sat); $8.50/mo; $93.50/yr.
Advertising: Open inch rate $14.02(e); $14.02(m-sat). **Representative:** Landon Associates Inc.
News Services: AP, KRT. **Politics:** Independent. **Established:** 1846.
Not Published: New Year; Thanksgiving; Christmas.
Special Editions: Winter Festival (Jan); Bridal Section (Feb); Senior Living Section (Mar); Home/Garden (Apr); Tour Guide (May); Summertime/Guide, Tour Guide (June); Black Ships, Tour Guide (July); Back-to-School, Tour Guide (Aug); Newport Yachting Center, Tour Guide (Sept); Car Care (Oct); Christmas Gift Guide (Nov); Last Minute Gift Guide (Dec).
Magazine: TV Tab.

CORPORATE OFFICERS
President Albert K Sherman Jr
Vice Pres William A Sherman
Secretary Bruce H Sherman

GENERAL MANAGEMENT
Publisher Albert K Sherman Jr
Purchasing Agent William F Lucey III
Business Manager William F Lucey III
Manager-Credit Lillian Blais

ADVERTISING
Director-Marketing Gary D Lawrence
Manager-Sales Mary Jane Mann
Manager-Classified Linda Anderson
Manager-National Louis P Mureddu

CIRCULATION
Manager Jerald Devine

NEWS EXECUTIVE
Editor David B Offer

EDITORS AND MANAGERS
City Editor Mary T Harrington
News Editor Harvey B Peters
Sports Editor Walter T Moody

PRODUCTION
Foreman-Composing Cesare P Berluti
Foreman-Pressroom George A Bradley
Manager-Mail/Distribution Kevin F Schoen

Market Information: Zoned editions; Split Run; TMC; ADS.
Mechanical available: Offset; Black and 3 ROP colors; insert accepted — preprinted, certain card stock and single sheets not accepted; page cut-offs — 22¾".
Mechanical specifications: Type page 13" x 21½"; E - 6 cols, 2¹⁄₁₆", ⅛" between; A - 6 cols, 2¹⁄₁₆", ⅛" between; C - 8 cols, 1⁹⁄₁₆", ¹⁄₁₆" between.
Commodity consumption: Newsprint 890 metric tons; widths 27½", 13¾"; black ink 25,000 pounds; color ink 1,150 pounds; single pages printed 10,500; average pages per issue 30(d), 44(sat); single plates used 11,000.
Equipment: EDITORIAL: Front-end hardware — 7-AST/386, Dewar/Disc Net, 16-AST/286; Other equipment — 10-RSK/Model 100. CLASSIFIED: Front-end hardware — Dewar/Disc, 6-AST/286. DISPLAY: Adv layout systems — 8-AST/286, Dewar, 2-AST/386; Printers — 1-Ap/Mac LaserWriter. PRODUCTION: Pagination software — Dewar; OCR software — Calera; Typesetters — 2-Tegra/Varityper/XP1000; Plate exposures — 1-Nu/Flip Top FT40LNS, 1-Nu/Flip Top FT40V6UPNS; Plate processors — 1-Roconex; Scanners — HP/ScanJet, Calera; Production cameras — 1-C/Spartan II, 1-R/1824; Automatic film processors — 1-LE/18; Film transporters — 1-C; Digital color separation equipment — Lf/Leafscan 35, Lf/AP Leaf Picture Desk. PRESSROOM: Line 1 — 5-G/Urbanite, DEV; Folders — 1-G; Press control system — Fin. MAILROOM: Counter stackers — 1-HL/Monitor HT; Inserters and stuffers — 1-S/624P; Bundle tyer — 1-MLN/ML-2, 1-Sa; Addressing machine — 1-KR. COMMUNICATIONS: Facsimile — 1-Panafax/F250. WIRE SERVICES: News — AP, KRT; Photos — AP; Stock tables — AP; Syndicates — AP; Receiving dishes — size-10ft, AP. BUSINESS COMPUTERS: 1-IBM/RS6000; Applications: Vision Data: Circ, Adv billing, Accts receivable, Gen ledger, Payroll, Accts payable, TMC, P & L; PCs & micros networked; PCs & main system networked.

PAWTUCKET-CENTRAL FALLS

Providence County

'90 U.S. Census- 90,281 (Pawtucket 72,644; Central Falls 17,637); E&P '96 Est. 91,192 (Pawtucket 73,003; Central Falls 18,189)
ABC-CZ (90): 90,281 (HH 36,354)

The Times (m-mon to sat)

The Times, 23 Exchange St., Pawtucket, RI 02862; tel (401) 722-4000; fax (401) 727-9290. Journal Register Co. group.

Circulation: 20,690(m); 21,717(m-sat); ABC Sept. 30, 1995.

Price: 50¢(d); 50¢(sat); $2.25/wk; $14.75/mo (mail); $175.50/yr (mail).

Advertising: Open inch rate $19.93(m); $19.93(m-sat). **Representative:** Landon Associates Inc.

News Service: AP. **Politics:** Independent. **Established:** 1885.

Special Editions: Super Bowl Preview, Bridal Showcase, Coupon Book, Chamber Report (Jan); President's Day Auto, Newcomer's Guide, Coupon Book, Business Profile (Feb); Profile: Massachusetts, Spring Bridal, Profile: Mineral Spring, Health & Fitness (Mar); Baseball Review, Spring Home & Garden, Spring Car Care, Coupon Book (Apr); Business Profiles, Momentum, Design an Ad (May); Chamber Report, Wedding Guide, Star Spangled Weekend, Summer Recreation (June); Home Improvement, BBB, Coupon Book (July); Business Profiles, Back-to-School, Bus Schedule (Aug); Fall Football, Reader's Choice, Octoberfest (Sept); Home Improvement, Car Care, Fall Bridal Tab, Coupon Book, Chamber Report (Oct); Profile: Cumberland, Winterize, Economize (Nov); Last Minute Gift Guide, Holiday Gift Guide I & II, Scrapbook (Dec).

Special Weekly Sections: Health (tues); Food (wed); Fashion (thur); The Entertainer Tab (fri); Real Estate, Religion (sat).

Magazines: USA Weekend, The Entertainer (sat).

CORPORATE OFFICERS

President/CEO Robert M Jelenic
Exec Vice Pres/Chief Financial Officer/Treasurer Jean B Clifton

GENERAL MANAGEMENT

Publisher T Paul Mahony
Controller Michael Kwolek
Manager-Business Office Michelle Spinella

ADVERTISING

Director Steven Pitocchelli
Manager-Classified Denise Tudino

CIRCULATION

Director Steven P Dolce

NEWS EXECUTIVE

Managing Editor Karen Hupp

EDITORS AND MANAGERS

News Editor John Cullen
Night Editor Rebecca Matuszek
City Editor Marcia Green

PRODUCTION

Manager Robert T Hughes
Superintendent Michael Brady

Market Information: Zoned editions; TMC.

Mechanical available: Offset; Black and 4 ROP colors; insert accepted — preprinted; page cut-offs — 22¾".

Mechanical specifications: Type page 13" x 21½"; E - 6 cols, $2\frac{1}{16}$", ⅛" between; A - 6 cols, $2\frac{1}{16}$", ⅛" between; C - 9 cols, 1⅜", $\frac{1}{16}$" between.

Commodity consumption: Newsprint 1,020 short tons; widths 27½", 13¾"; single pages printed 8,202; average pages per issue 26(d).

Equipment: EDITORIAL: Front-end hardware — Ik/CPS; Front-end software — Ik/CPS; Printers — Okidata. CLASSIFIED: Front-end hardware — Intertext; Front-end software — Intertext. DISPLAY: Adv layout systems — Ik/GDT; Front-end hardware — Ap/Mac IIcx, Ap/Mac SE, Ap/Mac Plus; Front-end software — Quark-XPress, Adobe/Illustrator. PRODUCTION: Typesetters — 2-Linotype-Hell/Linotron 202-N 202/N, Hyphen/Dash 72E; Electronic picture desk — Lf/AP Leaf Picture Desk; Production cameras — 1-C/Spartan III, 1-R/Mark II; Automatic film processors — 1-LE/LD18, 1-LE/LD 1800 A; Film transporters — 1-LE; Shrink lenses — 1-Alan; Digital color separation equipment — Lf/AP Leaf Picture Desk. MAILROOM: Bundle tyer — 1-MLN/ML2-EE. WIRE SERVICES: News — AP; Photos — AP; Stock tables — AP Stocks; Syndicates — AP; Receiving dishes — AP. BUSINESS COMPUTERS: IBM/Sys 36; Applications: INSI: Adv mgmt, Payroll, Accts payable, Gen ledger; PCs & main system networked.

PROVIDENCE

Providence County

'90 U.S. Census- 160,728; E&P '96 Est. 164,288
ABC-CZ (90): 1,214,356 (HH 457,709)

The Providence Journal-Bulletin (m-mon to sat)
The Providence Sunday Journal (S)

The Providence Journal-Bulletin, 75 Fountain St., Providence, RI 02902; tel (401) 277-7000; e-mail letters@projo.com.

Circulation: 185,014(m); 178,311(m-sat); 260,004(S); ABC Sept. 30, 1995.

Price: 50¢(d); 50¢(sat); $1.75(S); $3.60/wk; $15.60/mo; $187.20/yr.

Advertising: Open inch rate $129.28(m); $129.28(m-sat); $155.34(S). **Representative:** Cresmer, Woodward, O'Mara & Ormsbee.

News Services: AP, UPI, NYT, LAT-WP, KRT, SHNS, RN. **Politics:** Independent. **Established:** 1829.

Note: Effective June 5, 1995, this publication changed its publishing plan from (all day-mon to fri; m-sat; S) to (m-mon to sat; S).

Special Editions: Providence Boat Show, Year End Stock Tables Review/Outlook, Economic Outlook, Mid-Winter Vacations, Auto Show (Jan); Your Wedding, Snow & Sun Vacations, Flower Show (Feb); Rimta Boat Show, Spring Auto Section, Business Expo, Summer Cruises, Rhode Island Home Show (Mar); Golf, Spring Real Estate, Red Sox Section, Summer Travel Preview, Health Care, Continuing Education, Canadian Destinations (Apr); Summer Travel Showcase, Spring Home Improvement, Vacation Guide, New England Vacations (May); Nearby Regions (June); Continuing Education, Auto Closeouts (Aug); Fall Real Estate, Health Care, Fall Home Improvement, Winter Cruises, Autumn Vacations (Sept); New York City, Fall Travel Showcase, Career Guide, Auto Introductions (Oct); College Basketball, Survival Guide, Florida, Holiday Gifts (Nov).

Special Weekly Sections: Sports Monday (mon); Business Tuesday (tues); Food (wed); Style, Your Home, HERS (thur); Weekend (fri); Sports Weekend, Weekend Real Estate Preview (sat); Business, Real Estate/Your Home, Sports, Sunday Brunch, Society, Travel, Weddings (S); Lifebeat (mon-sat).

Magazine: Parade (S).

CORPORATE OFFICERS

Chairman/Publisher/CEO Stephen Hamblett
President/Chief Operating Officer Trygve Myhren
Vice Pres/Human Resources John Bowers
Vice Pres-Finance Thomas Matlack
Vice Pres-Legal Jack L Hammond
Vice Pres-Corporate Controller Joanne Yestamski
Treasurer/Secretary Harry Dyson

GENERAL MANAGEMENT

Vice Pres/General Manager Howard Sutton
Vice Pres/Exec Editor James V Wyman
Vice Pres-Publishing Business Development & Marketing Joel N Stark
Director-Systems Donald Almeida
Director-Financial Operations Ronald Barstis
Director-Operations Robert Shadrick
Director-Research Steven DeAngelis
Director-Circulation Michael Dooley
Director-Publishing Business Development John Granatino
Director-Quality Improvement John Hazard
Director-Human Resources R Barrie Schmitt
Director-Purchasing Michael A Parker
Distribution Director-Operations Nicholas J Kayata
Distribution Asst Director-Operations James V DeSimone
Distribution Manager-Packaging Operations Thomas F Lauro
Manager-Distribution Center Lawrence O'Brien
Distribution Sunday Inserting Manager Charles Mouradjian

ADVERTISING

Director Donald J Ross
Creative Director Christopher Lucock
Manager-Administration Robert F Pyper
Manager-Plans/Statistics Ronald J Treanor
Manager-Retail Sales Robert R Cardosa
Manager-Sales Development Richard J Murray
Asst Manager-Classified Maura Brodeur

MARKETING AND PROMOTION

Director-Marketing Communications John J Palumbo
Manager-Promotion Maria A Cassaday
Manager-Community Affairs Barbara J Nauman

TELECOMMUNICATIONS

Audiotex Manager Maggie Esposito

CIRCULATION

Director Michael J Dooley
Asst Director John F Peffer
Manager-Newspapers in Education Mary Ellen Ahern
Manager-Single Copy Sales Bob Zanfagna
Manager-Operations Mike Rahme
Administration Manager Patrick A Kennedy
Manager-Research Stephen P Volpe
Manager-Systems David Keaney
Manager-Telemarketing John Conaty
Manager-Marketing Services Rita G Casady

NEWS EXECUTIVES

Deputy Exec Editor Joel P Rawson
Deputy Exec Editor-Systems James K Sunshine
Director-Photography Thea Breite
Assoc Exec Editor Carol Young
Managing Editor-Administration John J Monaghan
Managing Editor (Journal-Bulletin) James Rosenthal
Managing Editor-Investigations Tom Heslin
Managing Editor-Metro Tom Heslin
Managing Editor-Graphics William Ostendorf
Managing Editor-Features Jack Major
Managing Editor-Technology David B Grey
Asst Managing Editor (Journal-Bulletin) Dave Reid

EDITORS AND MANAGERS

Art Director Mick Cochran
Automotive Editor Alan Kerr
Business/Finance Editor Peter Phipps
City Editor-Day Andrew Burkhardt
City Editor-Night John Khorey
Columnist Philip Terzian
Editorial Page Editor Robert Whitcomb
Editorial Columnist Brian Dickinson
Editorial Writer M J Andersen
Editorial Writer Froma Harrop
Editorial Writer Francis Mancini
Editorial Writer David Brussat
Education Writer D Morgan McVicar
Entertainment/Amusements Editor Alan Rosenberg
Environmental Writer Peter Lord
Fashion/Style Editor Gail Ciampa
Asst Features Editor Alan Rosenberg
Films Writer Michael Janusonis
Food Editor Donna Lee
Health/Medical Writer Felice Freyer
Librarian Linda Henderson
Music Writer-Classical Channing Gray
Music Writer-Pop Andy Smith
National Editor M Charles Bakst
Chief Photographer Michael Delaney
Political/Government Columnist M Charles Bakst
Radio/Television Writer John Martin
Religion Writer Richard C Dujardin
Science/Technical Writer C Eugene Emery
Sports Editor David Bloss
State Editor Philip Kukielski
State Editor-Night Leonard I Levin
Theater Writer William K Gale

MANAGEMENT INFORMATION SERVICES

Data Processing Manager Susan Edgar
Online Manager Edward M Huff

PRODUCTION

Director-Operations Robert A Shadrick
Asst Director Wayne Pelland
Superintendent-Composing Paul Pietrantonio
Superintendent-Facilities Douglas Fredericks
Manager-Pressroom Alvin F Mann
Manager-Properties Joseph Short
Manager-Advertising Robert A Gauvin

Market Information: Zoned editions; Split Run; TMC; Operate database; Operate audiotex; Electronic edition.

Mechanical available: Flexographic; Black and 3 ROP colors; insert accepted — preprinted; page cut-offs — 22".

Mechanical specifications: Type page 13" x 21"; E - 6 cols, $2\frac{1}{16}$", ⅛" between; A - 6 cols, $2\frac{1}{16}$", ⅛" between; C - 9 cols, 1⅜", $\frac{1}{16}$" between.

Commodity consumption: Newsprint 34,000 metric tons; widths 54", 41¼", 27½"; black ink 850,000 pounds; color ink 227,000 pounds; single pages printed 49,000; average pages per issue 68(d), 160(S); single plates used 178,000.

Equipment: EDITORIAL: Front-end hardware — 112-AT, 204-PC, 20-Ap/Mac, HP; Front-end software — AT, XYQUEST/XyWrite, Quark-XPress; Printers — HP, Teletype, Data Printers, QMS. CLASSIFIED: Front-end hardware — AT/IAS, 80-AT, 2-AT/CLSPAG; Front-end software — AT; Printers — HP, Teletype, Data Printers, Epson. AUDIOTEX: Hardware — PEP; Software — PEP/Voice Print. DISPLAY: Adv layout systems — IBM, HI; Front-end hardware — 6-HI, 13-Sun/Oracle, 10-Ap/Mac; Printers — Dataproducts, HP/LaserJet III; Other equipment — 3-X/Scanner. PRODUCTION: Pagination software — HI, QuarkXPress; Typesetters — 2-AU/APS-5, 2-AU/APS-6, ECR/3850; Platemaking systems — 2-Letterflex/LX100; Electronic picture desk — 3-Lf/AP Leaf Picture Desk, 2-Ap/Mac Workstation; Scanners — 3-ECR/Autokon, 2-Lf/Leafscan 45, 2-Microtek/II, CD/Magnascan, 3-X; Production cameras — 1-Nu/Horizontal; Automatic film processors — 2-Fuji/Mini lab, 1-Noritsu, 1-Wing Lynch; Film transporters — 5-C; Digital color separation equipment — Scitex/Visionary, 2-Kk/2035-646, 2-Visionary/Gateway, 1-Iris/Color Printer. PRESSROOM: Line 1 — 6-W&H/Flexo, 2-MOT/Flexo Tower; Line 2 — 6-W&H/Flexo, 2-MOT/Flexo Tower; Line 3 — 6-W&H/Flexo, 2-MOT/Flexo Tower; Pasters — 18-KB, 6-MOT; Reels and stands — 18-KB, 6-MOT; Press control system — PEC. MAILROOM: Counter stackers — 9-HL/HT; Inserters and stuffers — 3-Fg, 1-GMA; Bundle tyer — 7-EAM/Mosca, 4-Dynaric; Wrapping singles — 1-St. LIBRARY: Electronic — IBM, QLS/Systems software. COMMUNICATIONS: Facsimile — 2-Hellfax/scanner, 3-Hellfax/receiver; Systems used — fiber optic. WIRE SERVICES: News — AP; Stock tables — AP Digital Stocks; Syndicates — NYT, LAT-WP, KRT, SHNS, AP GraphicsNet, Bloomberg; Receiving dishes — size-12ft, AP. BUSINESS COMPUTERS: IBM/4381, IBM/4831, 690-Sun/4; Applications: Oracle: Circ, Distribution; PCs & micros networked; PCs & main system networked.

WEST WARWICK

Kent County

'90 U.S. Census- 29,268; E&P '96 Est. 31,124

The Kent County Daily Times (e-mon to sat)

The Kent County Daily Times, 1353 Main St., West Warwick, RI 02893; tel (401) 821-7400; fax (401) 828-0810.

Circulation: 7,656(e); 7,656(e-sat); Sworn Sept. 1, 1995.

Price: 35¢(d); 50¢(sat); $156.00/yr.

Advertising: Open inch rate $11.20(e); $11.20 (e-sat). **Representative:** Landon Associates Inc.

News Services: NEA, AP. **Politics:** Independent. **Established:** 1892.

Not Published: New Year; Memorial Day; Independence Day; Second Monday in Aug; Labor Day; Second Monday in Oct; Veteran's Day; Thanksgiving; Christmas.

Special Editions: Business; Car Care; Bridal; St. Patrick's Day; Health; Dining Guide; Holiday Cooking; Gift Guide; Education; Portuguese Fiesta; Home & Garden; Seniors; Business & Industry; Football.

Magazine: Good Times.

CORPORATE OFFICER

President Theodore Holmberg

GENERAL MANAGEMENT

Publisher Theodore Holmberg
General Manager Ed Vadnais

ADVERTISING

Manager Kelly Quinn

MARKETING AND PROMOTION

Exec Sales Director Robert D'Uva

CIRCULATION

Manager Thomas J Ames

NEWS EXECUTIVES

Editor Theodore Holmberg
Managing Editor Joseph Motta

EDITOR AND MANAGER

Sports Editor Pete Fontaine

MANAGEMENT INFORMATION SERVICES

Data Processing Manager Bruce Goodnow

PRODUCTION

Foreman-Pressroom Bruno Sonnenschein

Market Information: TMC; ADS.

Mechanical available: Offset; Black and 3 ROP colors; insert accepted — preprinted, any that will fit a standard size paper; page cut-offs — 22¾".

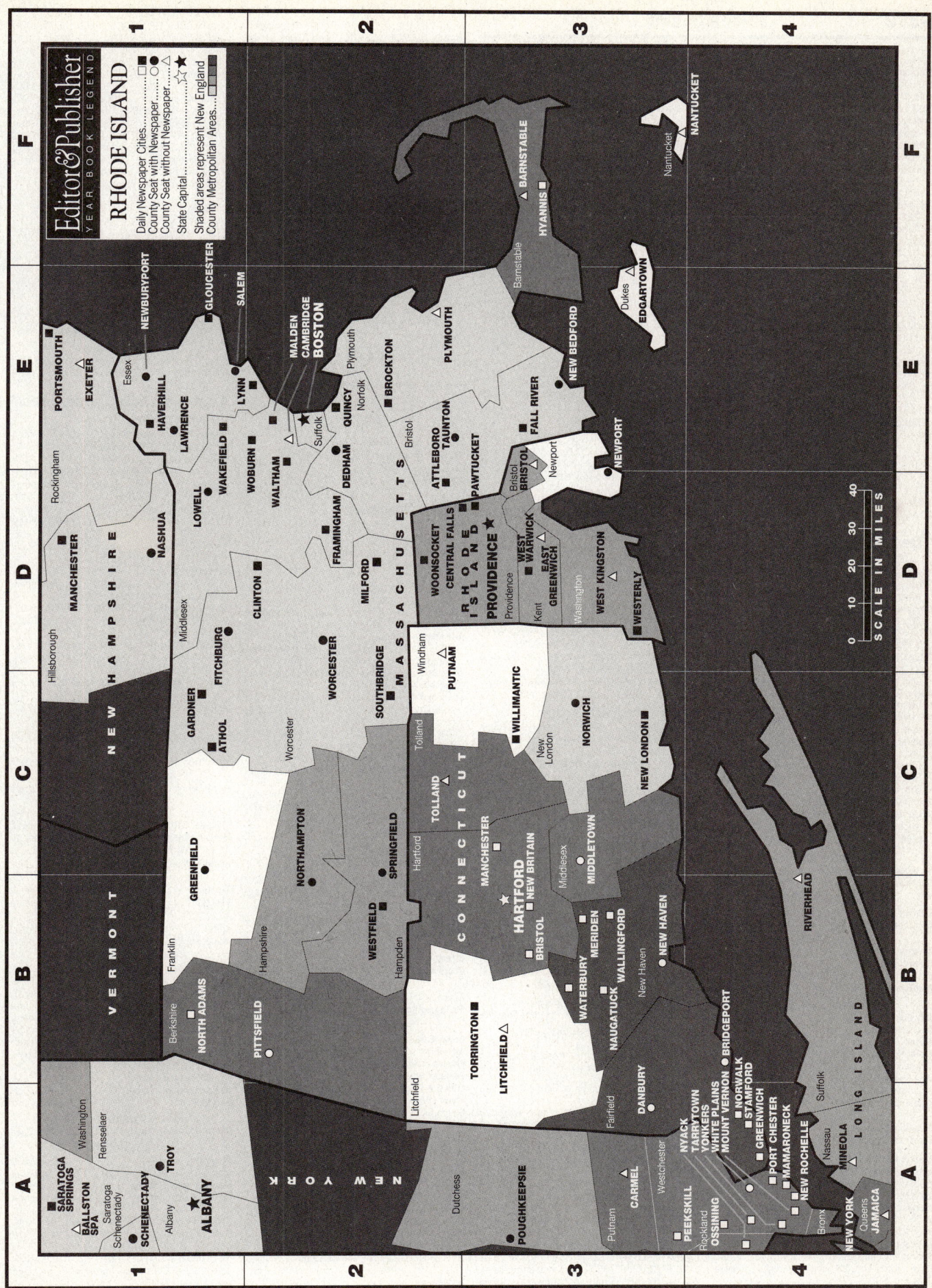

I-370 Rhode Island

Mechanical specifications: Type page 13" x 21¼"; E - 6 cols, 2 1/16", ⅛" between; A - 6 cols, 2 1/16", ⅛" between; C - 7 cols, 1⅝", 5/16" between.

Commodity consumption: Newsprint 520 short tons; widths 14", 28", 34"; black ink 22,000 pounds; color ink 840 pounds; average pages per issue 16(d).

Equipment: EDITORIAL: Front-end hardware — Mk/M Comp, 5-Mk/TouchWriter, 4-Mk/TouchWriter Plus, 5-IBM, Ap/Mac System; Other equipment — Sprint/III, RC/Processor. CLASSIFIED: Front-end hardware — 1-Ap/Mac II, 3-Ap/Mac IIse, 3-Mk/TouchWriter Plus; Other equipment — Linotronic/100, 1-IBM/Selectric II. DISPLAY: Adv layout systems — Ap/Mac II, 3-Ap/Mac IIse. PRODUCTION: Typesetters — L/100, QMS/2200PS, Ap/Mac NTX, Ap/Mac NT; Plate exposures — 1-Nu/Flip Top; Plate processors — Nat/A250; Scanners — HP/ScanJet Plus; Production cameras — 1-LE/500, R; Reproportion units — 1-LE/2 500. PRESSROOM: Line 1 — 5-HI/Cotrell 15, 4-HI/V15A; Folders — 2-HI. MAILROOM: Bundle tyer — 2-Bu. COMMUNICATIONS: Facsimile — ATT. WIRE SERVICES: News — UPI; Syndicates — NEA; Receiving dishes — size-4⅔ft, UPI. BUSINESS COMPUTERS: RSK/TRS 80 Model 16; Applications: Accts payable, Accts receivable, Payroll, Circ, Gen ledger.

WESTERLY

Washington County

'90 U.S. Census- 21,605; **E&P '96 Est.** 24,192
ABC-CZ (90): 29,476 (HH 11,605)

The Westerly Sun

(e-mon to fri; S)

The Westerly Sun, 56 Main St., Westerly, RI 02891; tel (401) 596-7791; fax (401) 348-5080.

Circulation: 11,666(e); 12,371(S); ABC Sept. 30, 1995.

Price: 50¢(d); 75¢(S); $2.10/wk (carrier); $39.00/13wk (mail); $86.40/yr (carrier).

Advertising: Open inch rate $12.00(e); $12.00(S). **Representative:** Landon Associates Inc.

News Service: AP. **Politics:** Republican. **Established:** 1893.

Not Published: New Year; Thanksgiving; Christmas.

Special Editions: Year in Review (Jan); Automobile Section (Feb); Brides, Home Improvement (Sept); Automobile Section (Oct); Schoolboy Football (Nov); Christmas Gift Guide (Dec).

Special Weekly Sections: Food, Business, The Guide (thur); Places in the Sun, Religion (fri); Business, Social (S); Entertainment, Sports (daily).

CORPORATE OFFICERS

Treasurer Nicholas C Utter
Secretary Robert D Utter

GENERAL MANAGEMENT

Publisher William E Sherman
Controller Priscilla Flynn

ADVERTISING

Manager Arthur B Morin Jr
Manager-Classified Susan Cline

CIRCULATION

Manager Robert D Utter

EDITORS AND MANAGERS

City Editor David D Smith
Asst City Editor Angela J Algier
Editor Donald P Lewis
Entertainment Editor Marilyn J Comrie
Sports Editor Robert L Marr
Asst Sports Editor Keith E Kimberlini
Suburban Editor David F Husband
Asst Suburban Editor Marilyn J Comrie

PRODUCTION

Foreman-Composing Renee Fortune
Foreman-Pressroom Tony Lionetti

Market Information: Split Run.

Mechanical available: Offset; Black and 3 ROP colors; insert accepted — preprinted, all; page cut-offs — 22¾".

Mechanical specifications: Type page 13" x 21½"; E - 6 cols, 2 1/16", ⅛" between; A - 6 cols, 2 1/16", ⅛" between; C - 8 cols, 1½", ⅛" between.

Commodity consumption: Newsprint 480 metric tons; widths 14", 28"; average pages per issue 28(d), 40(S).

Equipment: EDITORIAL: Front-end hardware — Mk. CLASSIFIED: Front-end hardware — Mk. DISPLAY: Adv layout systems — 3-Ap/Mac Quadra 800; Front-end software — Aldus/FreeHand 3.1, Adobe/Photoshop 2.5, Microsoft/Word 5.1a, Multi-Ad/Creator 3.5; Printers — 2-HP/LaserJet IV; Other equipment — 1-HP/ScanJet IIcx. PRODUCTION: Typesetters — 2-COM/Unisetter; Plate exposures — 1-B/14P2; Production cameras — 1-Nu/18X24; Automatic film processors — Polychrome/Poly-Quick 24; Shrink lenses — 1-CK Optical. PRESSROOM: Line 1 — 6-HI/V-15A single; Folders — HI. MAILROOM: Bundle tyer — 1-Chandler/Tyemaster. COMMUNICATIONS: Facsimile — 1-QWI/1200. WIRE SERVICES: News — AP; Photos — AP; Syndicates — AP; Receiving dishes — size-3m, AP. BUSINESS COMPUTERS: 1-DEC/BL 2; Applications: Accts payable, Accts receivable, Gen ledger, Circ; PCs & micros networked; PCs & main system networked.

WOONSOCKET

Providence County

'90 U.S. Census- 43,877; **E&P '96 Est.** 42,649
ABC-CZ (90): 78,639 (HH 30,405)

The Call (m-mon to sat; S)

The Call, 75 Main St.; PO Box A, Woonsocket, RI 02895; tel (401) 762-3000; fax (401) 765-0303. Journal Register Co. group.

Circulation: 22,877(m); 22,877(m-sat); 22,334(S); ABC Sept. 30, 1995.

Price: 50¢(d); 50¢(sat); $1.25(S); $2.95/wk; $11.80/mo.

Advertising: Open inch rate $21.26(m); $21.26(m-sat); $21.26(S). **Representative:** Landon Associates Inc.

News Service: AP. **Politics:** Independent. **Established:** 1892.

Special Edition: Chamber of Commerce Annual Report (Jan).

Special Weekly Sections: Focus Health (mon); Business (tues); Best Food Day (wed); Business (thur); Arcade, Cover Story (TMC) (fri); Business (sat); Best Food Day, Travel, Real Estate Today, Callamotive (S).

Magazines: USA Weekend; TV Channels Magazine.

CORPORATE OFFICERS

President/CEO Robert M Jelenic
Exec Vice Pres/Chief Financial Officer/Treasurer Jean B Clifton

GENERAL MANAGEMENT

Controller Loretta Zoglio

ADVERTISING

Director-Marketing James Sobiloff

CIRCULATION

Director Dean M Tortora

NEWS EXECUTIVE

Managing Editor Susan R Hawryluk

EDITORS AND MANAGERS

City Editor Paul R Dubois
Editorial Page Editor Susan R Hawryluk
Fashion/Women's Editor Kathie Raleigh
Finance Editor Susan R Hawryluk
Garden Editor Kathie Raleigh
Librarian Marie Cote
Photo Department Manager Lynda Read
Sports Editor Rich Pedroli
Sunday Editor Anna Chinappi

MANAGEMENT INFORMATION SERVICES

Data Processing Manager Everett Fargnoli

PRODUCTION

Foreman-Composing Walter Pristawa
Foreman-Pressroom Peter F Chambers
Superintendent-Mailroom Richard Tetreault

Market Information: Zoned editions; Split Run; TMC.

Mechanical available: Letterpress (direct); Black and 3 ROP colors; insert accepted — preprinted; page cut-offs — 22¾".

Mechanical specifications: Type page 13" x 21½"; E - 6 cols, 2 1/16", ⅛" between; A - 6 cols, 2 1/16", ⅛" between; C - 9 cols, 1⅜", 1/16" between.

Commodity consumption: Newsprint 1,800 short tons; widths 55", 41¼", 27½"; black ink 55,000 pounds; color ink 7,000 pounds; single pages printed 11,000; average pages per issue 28(d), 48(S); single plates used 18,200.

Equipment: EDITORIAL: Front-end hardware — SII/Sys 22, 25-ET/960; Front-end software — SII. CLASSIFIED: Front-end hardware — Intertext, 10-IBM/XT. DISPLAY: Adv layout systems — 2-COM/ADV, 2-ET/960; Front-end hardware — COM. PRODUCTION: Typesetters — 2-COM/8600, News Printer/II; Plate exposures — 2-Nu/FT40U; Plate processors — 1-Graham/53A subtractive; Electronic picture desk — Lf/AP Leaf Picture Desk; Production cameras — 1-C/Spartan III, 1-Nu/2024V; Automatic film processors — 1-LE, AG/Rapidline 66, K/720; Film transporters — 1-C; Color separation equipment (conventional) — 1-RZ/40-50 Direct Screen. PRESSROOM: Line 1 — 7-G/Urbanite U-615 (mono; 1-3 color unit); Press drives — C.E.S./200Hp-PLC; Folders — 2-Sc; Pasters — 5-Enkel/Autoweb; Press registration system — Stoesse/center pin. MAILROOM: Counter stackers — 1-HL/Monitor; Inserters and stuffers — 2-MM/227E; Bundle tyer — 1-Tri-Star/Weld-loc 210, 1-MLN. WIRE SERVICES: News — AP; Syndicates — AP; Receiving dishes — AP. BUSINESS COMPUTERS: IBM/Sys 36; Applications: INSI: Circ, Ad Mgmt, Accts payable, Gen ledger, Payroll.

SOUTH CAROLINA

AIKEN

Aiken County

'90 U.S. Census- 19,872; **E&P '96 Est.** 24,625
ABC-NDM (90): 63,306 (HH 24,291)

Aiken Standard

(e-mon to fri; m-sat; S)

Aiken Standard, 124 Rutland Dr.; PO Box 456, Aiken, SC 29802; tel (803) 648-2311; fax (803) 648-6052. Evening Post Publishing Co. group.

Circulation: 14,275(e); 14,275(m-sat); 14,924(S); ABC Sept. 30, 1995.

Price: 25¢(d); 25¢(sat); 75¢(S); $8.50/mo (carrier); $102.00/yr (carrier).

Advertising: Open inch rate $14.39(e); $14.39(m-sat); $15.10(S). **Representative:** Landon Associates Inc.

News Services: AP, KRT. **Politics:** Independent. **Established:** 1867.

Special Editions: Brides Book (Jan); Horse Industry (Mar); Masters Golf Tournament, Realtors (Apr); Graduation (May); Father's Day (June); Back-to-School, Football (Aug); Fall Fashion, Home Improvement (Sept); Car Care (Oct); Christmas Greetings (Dec).

Special Weekly Sections: Best Food Days, Health (wed); Entertainment (thur); Real Estate, Religious Page (fri); TV Update, Engagements (sat); Weddings, Business (S).

Magazines: USA Weekend Magazine; TV Update.

CORPORATE OFFICER

President/Publisher Scott B Hunter

GENERAL MANAGEMENT

Business Manager Ellen C Priest

ADVERTISING

Director Charles O Grice
Manager-National/Retail/Co-op Charles O Grice

CIRCULATION

Director Otto C Lee
Coordinator Phyllis Carpenter

NEWS EXECUTIVES

Editor Scott B Hunter
Managing Editor Jeffrey B Wallace

EDITORS AND MANAGERS

Books Editor Lynne Katonak
City Editor Gregory C Tyler
Entertainment/Society Editor John Boyette III
Features Editor John Boyette III
Lifestyle Editor John Boyette III
Photo Editor Ginny Southworth
Sports Editor Larry Taylor
Sunday Morning Editor John Boyette III

PRODUCTION

Manager Sue S Brown
Head James R Bennett
Head-Composing Margie Bennett

Market Information: TMC.

Mechanical available: Offset; Black and 3 ROP colors; insert accepted — preprinted; page cut-offs — 22".

Mechanical specifications: Type page 13⅛" x 21"; E - 6 cols, 2.08", ⅙" between; A - 6 cols, 2.08", ⅙" between; C - 8 cols, 1.58", 1/12" between.

Commodity consumption: Newsprint 950 short tons; widths 28", 14"; black ink 28,400 pounds; color ink 2,750 pounds; single pages printed 6,876; average pages per issue 28(d), 44(S); single plates used 4,990.

Equipment: EDITORIAL: Front-end hardware — AT/5000; Printers — TI/43. CLASSIFIED: Front-end software — Dewar 5.0, SIA/386; Printers — Okidata/Microline 393. DISPLAY: Front-end hardware — SIA/386; Front-end software — Dewar. PRODUCTION: Typesetters — V/5100, 2-V/5100; Plate exposures — Nu; Plate processors — Nat/250; Scanners — ECR/Autokon 1030N; Production cameras — SCREEN/C-240; Automatic film processors — Kk. PRESSROOM: Line 2 — 8-G/Community (1-full color unit) single width. MAILROOM: Inserters and stuffers — 6-KAN/480. WIRE SERVICES: News — AP, KRT; Photos — AP; Syndicates — KRT; Receiving dishes — AP. BUSINESS COMPUTERS: DEC/Micro VAX 3100, 6-DEC/VT220, 3-DEC/VT 420; Applications: Vision Data.

ANDERSON

Anderson County

'90 U.S. Census- 26,184; **E&P '96 Est.** 25,553
ABC-CZ (90): 47,723 (HH 18,849)

Anderson Independent-Mail

(m-mon to sat; S)

Anderson Independent-Mail, 1000 Williamston Rd. (29621); PO Box 2507, Anderson, SC 29622; tel (864) 224-4321; fax (864) 260-1276; e-mail anderson@globalvision.net; web site http://www.globalvision.net/anderson/index.html. Harte-Hanks Communications Inc. group.

Circulation: 42,366(m); 42,366(m-sat); 48,479(S); ABC Sept. 30, 1995.

Price: 50¢(d); 50¢(sat); $1.50(S); $12.95/mo; $155.40/yr.

Advertising: Open inch rate $39.01(m); $39.01(m-sat); $40.18(S). **Representative:** Landon Associates Inc.

News Services: AP, KRT, NYT. **Politics:** Independent. **Established:** 1924 (Independent), 1899 (Mail).

Special Editions: Progress Edition (Jan); Fact Book (June); Football (Aug); Cookbook (Nov); Carol Book (Dec).

Special Weekly Sections: Food (wed); Weekend (thur).

Magazines: TV Magazine, USA Weekend (S).

CORPORATE OFFICERS

President Fred L Foster
Vice Pres T Wayne Mitchell
Vice Pres David Gossett

GENERAL MANAGEMENT

Publisher Fred L Foster

ADVERTISING

Director Tony Marroni
Manager-Display Al Groves
Manager-Display Kevin McCoy

TELECOMMUNICATIONS

Audiotex Manager T Wayne Mitchell

CIRCULATION

Director David Gossett
Manager Steve Takacs

NEWS EXECUTIVES

Editor T Wayne Mitchell
Managing Editor John Gouch

EDITORS AND MANAGERS

Books Editor Amy Etmans
City Editor Lisa Ross
Editorial Page Editor Kathryn Smith
Fashion/Travel Editor Amy Etmans
Features Editor Amy Etmans
Librarian Willie McIntosh
Music Editor Amy Etmans
News Editor Leah Daniels
Director-Photography George Reynolds
Radio/Television Editor Amy Etmans
Religion/Society Editor Dale Emch
Sports Editor Randy Beard

MANAGEMENT INFORMATION SERVICES

Data Processing Manager Melissa Bellinger

PRODUCTION

Director David Leard
Manager-Pressroom Keith Dobbins
Manager-Info Systems Bill Bussey
Manager-Distribution Herb Chabek

Market Information: Zoned editions; Split Run; TMC; ADS; Operate audiotex; Electronic edition.

Mechanical available: Offset; Black and 3 ROP colors; insert accepted — preprinted, all; page cut-offs — 22¾".

Copyright ©1996 by the Editor & Publisher Co.

Mechanical specifications: Type page 13" x 21½"; E - 6 cols, 2 1/16", 1/8" between; A - 6 cols, 2 1/16", 1/8" between; C - 9 cols, 1 7/16", 1/8" between.
Commodity consumption: Newsprint 4,300 short tons; widths 27", 30", 34"; black ink 75,000 pounds; color ink 54,249 pounds; single pages printed 14,500; average pages per issue 32(d), 32(sat), 56(S); single plates used 66,000.
Equipment: EDITORIAL: Front-end hardware — III/Tecs-2; Printers — LaserMaster/1200, LaserMaster/1800, 2-Panther/Pro 46 Imagesetter; Other equipment — Ap/Mac, Lf/AP Leaf Picture Desk, AG/Horizon Plus Scanner, Kk/35 Scanner. CLASSIFIED: Front-end hardware — III/Tecs-2. AUDIOTEX: Hardware — Brite Voice Systems; Software — Brite Voice Systems. DISPLAY: Adv layout systems — 1-Ap/Mac; Front-end hardware — Ap/Power Mac; Front-end software — Multi-Ad, QuarkXPress, Adobe/Photoshop; Printers — Unity/1800, Panther/Pro 46 Imagesetter; Other equipment — AG/Arcus Scanner. PRODUCTION: Pagination software — QuarkXPress 3.3; Typesetters — 2-V/5000, ECR/Autokon, 2-M/202N; Plate exposures — 2-Nu; Plate processors — 2-DP; Electronic picture desk — Lf/AP Leaf Picture Desk; Scanners — AG/Horizon Plus, 2-AG/Arcus II; Production cameras — 2-C/Spartan III; Automatic film processors — 1-LE/2416, 1-LE/2600A; Reproportion units — 1-BKY/Graphic Master; Shrink lenses — 1-Alan; Digital color separation equipment — CD/6253.
PRESSROOM: Line 1 — 10-G/Urbanite; Line 2 — 6-Didde/Minicom; Folders — 2-G/2:1. MAILROOM: Counter stackers — 1-MM/388, 2-MM/310; Inserters and stuffers — 1-MM/Byliner 308; Bundle tyer — 1-MLN/280, 1-OVL, 2-MLN/2CC; Wrapping singles — 2-QWI/00300; Addressing machine — 1-Ch/525E. LIBRARY: Electronic — III/Tecs-2. COMMUNICATIONS: Facsimile — Canon, Panasonic. WIRE SERVICES: News — KRT, NYT, AP; Photos — AP; Stock tables — AP SelectStox; Receiving dishes — size-10ft, AP. BUSINESS COMPUTERS: HP/3000, 16-IBM/PC, 17-Ap/Mac, RSK, Epson; Applications: Circ, Adv billing, Financial; PCs & micros networked; PCs & main system networked.

BEAUFORT
Beaufort County
'90 U.S. Census- 9,576; E&P '96 Est. 10,370
ABC-CZ (90): 26,509 (HH 10,069)

The Beaufort Gazette
(m-mon to sat; S)

The Beaufort Gazette, 1556 Salem Rd.; PO Box 399, Beaufort, SC 29901; tel (803) 524-3183; fax (803) 524-8728. McClatchy Newspapers group.
Circulation: 10,558(m); 10,558(m-sat); 10,734(S); ABC Sept. 30, 1995.
Price: 25¢(d); 25¢(sat); $1.00(S).
Advertising: Open inch rate $14.10(m); $17.61(m-tues); $14.10(m-sat); $14.10(S). **Representative:** Papert Companies.
News Service: AP. **Politics:** Independent. **Established:** 1897.
Note: Effective Sept. 2, 1995, this publication changed its publishing plan from (m-mon to fri; S) to (m-mon to sat; S).
Special Editions: Bridal (Jan); Black History Month, Income Tax (Feb); '96 Almanac, Spring Tour of Homes (Mar); Garden & Home Improvement (Apr); Gullah Festival (May); Hurricane (June); Water Festival (July); Football (Aug); Coupon Pages (Sept); Fall Tour of Homes (Oct); Marine Corps, Cookbook/Gift Guide (Nov); Coupon Pages (Dec).
Special Weekly Sections: Best Food Days (tues & wed); Church Page, TV (sat); Books, Wedding, Travel (S).

GENERAL MANAGEMENT
Publisher John Heath
ADVERTISING
Director Ann Robb
CIRCULATION
Manager Roy Danford
NEWS EXECUTIVE
Editor James Cato
EDITORS AND MANAGERS
Action Line Editor Cathy Carter
Editorial Page Editor James Cato
Editorial Writer James Cato
Neighbors Editor Debbie Radford
Sports Editor Jeff Shrewsbury
PRODUCTION
Manager Steve Baldwin

Market Information: TMC; Operate audiotex.
Mechanical available: Offset; Black and 3 ROP colors; insert accepted — preprinted; page cut-offs — 22¾".
Mechanical specifications: Type page 13" x 21"; E - 6 cols, 2 1/16", 1/8" between; A - 6 cols, 2 1/16", 1/8" between; C - 8 cols, 1 3/8", 1/16" between.
Commodity consumption: Newsprint 2,300 metric tons; widths 27", 13½"; single pages printed 11,400; average pages per issue 30(d), 30(sat), 38(S).
Equipment: EDITORIAL: Front-end hardware — 22-Ap/Mac; Front-end software — Baseview; Printers — 2-Ap/Mac; Other equipment — Ap/Mac Scanner. CLASSIFIED: Front-end hardware — Cx, 4-Ap/Mac; Front-end software — Cx, Baseview; Printers — 2-Data Royal. AUDIOTEX: Hardware — PEP. DISPLAY: Adv layout systems — 4-Ap/Mac; Front-end hardware — 4-Ap/Mac; Front-end software — Baseview; Printers — 2-Ap/Mac. PRODUCTION: Pagination software — Baseview, QuarkXPress; OCR software — Ap/Mac; Typesetters — 2-Graphic Enterprises/Pro Setter; Plate exposures — 2-Nu; Plate processors — MAS; Production cameras — SCREEN; Automatic film processors — P; Color separation equipment (conventional) — Lf/AP Leaf Picture Desk, Ap/Mac.
PRESSROOM: Line 1 — 6-G/Urbanite; Folders — 1-G/Urbanite; Press registration system — Burgess. MAILROOM: Counter stackers — KAN; Inserters and stuffers — 2-KAN; Bundle tyer — 2-MLN. LIBRARY: Electronic — Baseview. WIRE SERVICES: News — AP; Stock tables — AP SelectStox; Syndicates — McClatchy, NYT, SHNS; Receiving dishes — AP. BUSINESS COMPUTERS: HP; Applications: CJ: Circ, Classified, Adv, Accts payable, Accts receivable; PCs & micros networked; PCs & main system networked.

CHARLESTON
Charleston County
'90 U.S. Census- 80,414; E&P '96 Est. 89,720
ABC-NDM (90): 506,875 (HH 177,668)

The Post and Courier
(m-mon to sat; S)

The Post and Courier, 134 Columbus St., Charleston, SC 29403-4800; tel (803) 577-7111; web site http://www.charleston.net/. Evening Post Publishing Co. group.
Circulation: 109,520(m); 109,520(m-sat); 123,821(S); ABC Sept. 30, 1995.
Price: 50¢(d); 50¢(sat); $1.25(S); $10.75/mo; $129.00/yr.
Advertising: Open inch rate $63.00(m); $63.00(m-sat); $73.83(S). **Representative:** Landon Associates Inc.
News Services: AP, KRT, NYT. **Politics:** Independent. **Established:** 1803 (News & Courier).
Special Editions: Economic Update; Brides; S.E. Wildlife; Home Show; Spring Fashion; Small Business; Living Well; Spoleto; SoCon Baseball; Parade of Homes; Prime Time; Fall Fashion; High School Football; College & Pro Football; Home Furnishings; Southern Living Cooking School; West Ashley Christmas; East Cooper Christmas; Lowcountry Holidays.
Special Weekly Sections: Business Review, Life (mon); INK (tues); Best Food Day (wed); Science/Health (thur); Fashion (fri); Automotive, High Profile (sat); Travel, Book Page, Real Estate, Homes, Style (S).
Magazines: Entertainment/Preview (thur); Television (TV Book) (fri); Parade (S).
Broadcast Affiliates: Sangre de Cristo Communications Inc, KOAA-TV Pueblo/Colorado Springs, CO; Sawtooth Communications Inc, KIVI-TV Nampa/Boise, ID; KXLF Communications Inc, KXLF-TV Butte, MT; KRTV Communications Inc, KRTV-TV Great Falls, MT; KCTZ Communications Inc, KCTZ-TV Bozeman, MT; KVOA Communications Inc, KVOA-TV Tucson, AZ; KPAX Communications Inc; KPAX-TV Missoula, MT; KATC Communications Inc, KATC-TV Laffayette, LA; KTVQ Communications Inc, KTVQ-TV Billings, MT.

CORPORATE OFFICERS
Board Chairman Peter Manigault
President Ivan V Anderson Jr
Vice Pres Travis O Rockey
Secretary A M Wilcox
Asst Secretary Mary M Gilbreth
Treasurer James W Martin
GENERAL MANAGEMENT
Publisher Ivan V Anderson Jr
Controller James W Martin
Manager-Credit Cal Purvis
Personnel Manager Paul M Sharry
Purchasing Agent Pam Wier Gill
ADVERTISING
Director-Sales Lucy C Talley
Manager-National/Major Accounts Kimberly Carter
Manager-Local/Retail Melanie L Arney
Manager-Classified Van Wilkerson
MARKETING AND PROMOTION
Manager-Promotion Susan Sanders
Manager-Market Research Jane Comfort
TELECOMMUNICATIONS
Audiotex Manager Kerry Huggins
CIRCULATION
Director James T Eddins
NEWS EXECUTIVES
Exec Editor Larry W Tarleton
Asst to Exec Editor Evan Z Bussey
Editor Barbara S Williams
Asst Managing Editor-Projects Steve Mullins
Asst Managing Editor-News Grace Kutkus
Asst Managing Editor-Features Elizabeth G Cantler
Asst Editor Robert J Cox
Asst Editor Charles Rowe
EDITORS AND MANAGERS
Amusements Editor Christine Randall
Automotive Editor David Munday
Books Editor Bill Thompson
Exec Business Editor Teresa Taylor
Business Editor Charles deV Williams
Editorial Page Editor Barbara S Williams
Education Editor Angela Rucker
Films/Theater Editor Bill Thompson
Graphics Editor/Art Director Gill Guerry
Librarian Mary Crockett
Medical Editor Lynne Langley
Metro Editor John Burbage
Asst Metro Editor Shirley Greene
News Editor John Hopkins
Director-Photography Tom Spain
Radio/Television Editor Frank Wooten
Sports Editor Malcolm Dewitt
State Editor Dan Conover
State Government Sid Gaulden
State Government John Heilprin
Travel Editor Elizabeth G Cantler
MANAGEMENT INFORMATION SERVICES
Data Processing Manager Ray Ruth
PRODUCTION
Director-Operations B K Clay
Manager-Pre Press Raymond A Minnis
Manager-Press Processing John D Nix

Market Information: Zoned editions; Split Run; TMC; ADS; Operate audiotex.
Mechanical available: Offset; Black and 3 ROP colors; insert accepted — preprinted, card stock; page cut-offs — 22".
Mechanical specifications: Type page 13" x 21"; E - 6 cols, 2 1/16", 1/8" between; A - 6 cols, 2 1/16", 1/8" between; C - 9 cols, 1 3/8", 1/16" between.
Commodity consumption: Newsprint 15,184 short tons; 15,000 metric tons; widths 55", 41¼", 27½"; black ink 320,700 pounds; color ink 110,000 pounds; single pages printed 12,500; average pages per issue 52(d), 105(S); single plates used 143,450.
Equipment: EDITORIAL: Front-end hardware — SII/Sys 55; Front-end software — SII; Other equipment — SII/INL Pagination. CLASSIFIED: Front-end hardware — SII/Sys 55; Front-end software — SII; Other equipment — SII/ICP Pagination. DISPLAY: Adv layout systems — 9-DTI/AdSpeed, 15-Ap/Mac fx, 2-Ap/Power Mac 8100, 3-DEC/Alpha Soft RIP, CJ/Page Layout Sys3; Front-end hardware — SII/IAL Page Layout, 1-Ap/Mac IIci, 2-Ap/Mac IIcx, 6-Ap/Mac Quadra 950, 2-Ap/Mac Quadra 800; Front-end software — DTI/AdSpeed, Adobe/Photoshop, Adobe/Illustrator, QuarkXPress, Multi-Ad/Creator; Printers — 3-AU/APS-6-108C, 1-AU/L2 2600, 1-AU/Broadsheet, 2-Ap/Mac LaserWriter NTX. PRODUCTION: Typesetters — 3-AU/APS6-108C, Autoprinter/10; Platemaking systems — 1-WL/Lith 7 38-D OPB; Plate exposures — 2-Nu/Flip Top FT40UPNS, 1-Nu/Flip Top FT40APNS, 1-WL/Lith 7; Plate processors — 1-Tas/Participator II model HP720, 1-WL/38-D; Scanners — 1-Howtek/Scanmaster 3, 1-ECR/Autokon DE, 1-ECR/Autokon 2045-C; Production cameras — 1-C/1270; Automatic film processors — 1-P/26ML, 1-C/T-45, 2-LE/LD, 19-R/A; Film transporters — 1-C/1274, 3-C/OL Conveyor Systems; Color separation equipment (conventional) — 1-C, 1-Color Commander; Digital color separation equipment — 1-Nikon/LS3500, 1-CD/636 IM, 1-Lf/Leafscan 35, 1-Lf/Leafscan 45.
PRESSROOM: Line 1 — 10-G/Metroliner (7 half decks); Line 2 — 10-G/Metroliner; Folders — 2-G/3:2 Double; Pasters — 20-G; Reels and stands — 20-G. MAILROOM: Counter stackers — 8-QWI/SJ 100; Inserters and stuffers — 1-HI/22-99, 1-HI/14-72; Bundle tyer — 4-MLN/2A, 6-Bu, Power Strap; Addressing machine — 2-Ch/528. LIBRARY: Electronic — SII; Combination — IBM/Microfiche. COMMUNICATIONS: Facsimile — 3M. WIRE SERVICES: News — AP Dataspeed, AP Datafeatures, KRT, NYT; Photos — AP; Stock tables — AP SelectStox; Syndicates — NYT, KRT; Receiving dishes — size-10ft, AP. BUSINESS COMPUTERS: 2-DEC/VAX 11-750, 1-DEC/VAX 8500; Applications: Microsoft/Windows: Gen ledger, Accts payable, Payroll, Newsprint; Lotus, WordPerfect, Pathworks; PCs & micros networked; PCs & main system networked.

COLUMBIA
Richland County
'90 U.S. Census- 98,052; E&P '96 Est. 96,362
ABC-MSA Area (90): 453,331 (HH 163,223)

The State (m-mon to sat; S)

The State, 1401 Shop Rd.; PO Box 1333, Columbia, SC 29202; tel (803) 771-6161; web site http://www.infi.net/thestate/. Knight-Ridder Inc. group.
Circulation: 126,074(m); 126,074(m-sat); 165,172(S); ABC Sept. 30, 1995.
Price: 50¢(d); 50¢(sat); $1.50(S); $3.40/wk, $27.20/8wk, $44.20/13wk, $85.13/26wk; $14.73/mo; $166.65/yr.
Advertising: Open inch rate $84.87(m); $84.87(m-sat); $88.62(S). **Representative:** Newspapers First.
News Services: AP, LAT-WP, NYT, KRT. **Politics:** Independent. **Established:** 1891.
Special Editions: WHEELS (Jan); Boat Show (Feb); Midlands Healthcare, Exploring the Midlands, Lawn & Garden & Home Improvement (Mar); Home Buyers Fair, Design-An-Ad, Attorney's Guide (Apr); Mayfest, Parenting (May); Best of '96 Reader's Choice (June); Olympics (July); College Guide for High School Students Tab, High School Football, Professional Football, College Football Preview Tab (Aug); Seniors, Okra Strut Tab (Sept); At Home '96, Pet Pageant, At Home Tab (Oct); 'Tis the Season, College Basketball (Nov); Season's Greetings (Dec).
Special Weekly Sections: Celebrations (mon); Home, Travel (S).
Magazines: Weekend (fri); TV Weekly, Parade Magazine, Sunday Comics (S).

CORPORATE OFFICER
President/Publisher Frederick Mott Jr
GENERAL MANAGEMENT
Publisher Frederick Mott Jr
Asst to Publisher Paula Ellis
Vice Pres-Operations Glen E Nardi
Business Manager Jerry C Whitley
Manager-Credit Dru Wright
Director-Human Resources Holly Rogers
Director-Newspapers in Education Ginny Lopiccolo
ADVERTISING
Director Edward Fierstos
Director-Display Mort Goldstrom
Manager-Coop Kirk Bennett
Manager-National George Shennan
Manager-Augmentation Linda Waltz
MARKETING AND PROMOTION
Manager-Promotion Jerry Chapman
CIRCULATION
Director Mickey Shull
Technology Service Administration Tim Bostick
Consumer Service Administration Eddie Parker
NEWS EXECUTIVES
Exec Editor Gil Thelen
Managing Editor Joe Oglesby
Deputy Managing Editor Harry Logan
Asst to Managing Editor Beverly Dominick
Asst to Managing Editor Eric Pearson
Assoc Editor Katherine W Gray
Assoc Editor G Kent Krell
EDITORS AND MANAGERS
Amusements/Arts Editor Bill Starr
Books Editor Bill Starr
Business/Finance Editor Claudia Raby
Editorial Cartoonist Robert Ariail
City/Metro Editor Charles Crumbo
Editorial Page Editor Thomas N McLean
Assoc Editorial Page Editor Katherine W Gray
Assoc Editorial Page Editor G Kent Krell
Education Editor Patty Hannon

Fashion/Food Editor Megan Sexton
Graphics Editor Scott Farrand
Home Furnishings Editor Pat McGovern
Librarian Dargan Richards
Living/Lifestyle Editor Megan Sexton
National Editor Scott Johnson
News Editor Steve Brook
News Editor-Advance Sections Megan Sexton
News Editor-Presentation Diane Frea
Political/Government Editor Carolyn Click
Photo Editor Bill Gugliotta
Religion Editor Jennifer Graham
Sports Editor Richard Bush
Travel Editor Dawn Kujawa
Women's Editor Megan Sexton

MANAGEMENT INFORMATION SERVICES

Data Processing Manager Charlie McCaskill

PRODUCTION

Vice Pres-Operations Glen E Nardi
Manager David Boozer
Manager-Maintenance Jim Welborn
Manager-Distribution Charlie Brunson
Manager-Pre Press Willie Munn
Manager-Operations Mikel Smith
Manager-ACS Brenda Baughman

Market Information: Zoned editions; Split Run; TMC; Electronic edition.

Mechanical available: Offset; Black and 3 ROP colors; insert accepted — preprinted; page cutoffs — 22".

Mechanical specifications: Type page 13" x 21"; E - 6 cols, $2\frac{1}{16}$", $\frac{1}{8}$" between; A - 6 cols, $2\frac{1}{16}$", $\frac{1}{8}$" between; C - 10 cols, $1\frac{3}{16}$", $\frac{1}{16}$" between.

Commodity consumption: Newsprint 22,364 metric tons; widths 55", $41\frac{1}{4}$", $27\frac{1}{2}$"; black ink 777,339 pounds; color ink 149,044 pounds; single pages printed 45,851; average pages per issue 55(d), 114(S); single plates used 215,000.

Equipment: EDITORIAL: Front-end hardware — 7-AT, 110-AT/SDT; Front-end software — AT 4.4.1; Printers — AU/APS-5; Other equipment — 3-AT/GT68. CLASSIFIED: Front-end hardware — 4-AT, 26-AT/SDT; Front-end software — AT 4.5.2; Printers — AU/APS-5. DISPLAY: Adv layout systems — 3-Compaq/386-25, 7-Compaq/386-25 Workstation; Front-end software — Dewar/Software; Printers — V/5000, V/5300E. PRODUCTION: Pagination software — QuarkXPress; Typesetters — 2-AU/100, 1-AU/5u, AU/APS-6, III/3850; Platemaking systems — WL/Anocoil Processor; Plate exposures — 2-WL; Plate processors — 2-WL, Anacoil; Electronic picture desk — Lf/AP Leaf Picture Desk; Scanners — CD/6451E; Production cameras — 1-C/Marathon, 1-C/Spartan III, 1-AG/PRS 6000; Automatic film processors — 1-LE/LO24, 1-LE/LO24AQ, 2-LE/1824, 1-P/ML24, 1-P/ML26, 1-LE/TEK26; Reproportion units — Typeflex/Senior; Film transporters — 2-C; Shrink lenses — CK Optical; Color separation equipment (conventional) — 1-Durst/Laborator 184, 1-EP01/Color Repo Control; Digital color separation equipment — 1-CD/6451.
PRESSROOM: Line 1 — 14-G/HO (10-Decks); Line 2 — 9-G/HO (6-Decks); Press drives — Allen Bradley; Folders — 3-G; Pasters — 23-G; Reels and stands — 23-G/CT-50; Press control system — DEC/11-84, G/MPCS; Press registration system — Pin Register (Head & Tail). MAILROOM: Counter stackers — 4-HL/Systems, 6-HL/HT Stacker; Inserters and stuffers — 2-HI, 1-MM; Bundle tyer — 8-MLN, 2-Power Strap; Addressing machine — 1-Ch/N-3000, 3-Wm, 2-Ch/539. LIBRARY: Electronic — Vu/Text. COMMUNICATIONS: Facsimile — 1-AP Laserphoto, 1-UPI/Unifax II. WIRE SERVICES: News — AP, NYT, KRT, LAT-WP; Stock tables — AP; Syndicates — WP, AP Datafeatures; Receiving dishes — size-10ft, AP, Bus Wire 6ft. BUSINESS COMPUTERS: HP/3000-937, 1-IBM/4361-LO5; Applications: Bus, Circ, Inventory, Payroll, Adv, Billing; PCs & micros networked; PCs & main system networked.

FLORENCE

Florence County

'90 U.S. Census- 29,813; E&P '96 Est. 29,759
ABC-CZ (90): 58,092 (HH 21,114)

Florence Morning News

(m-mon to sat; S)

Florence Morning News, 141 S. Irby; PO Box 100528, Florence, SC 29501-0528; tel (803) 669-1771; fax (803) 661-6558. Thomson Newspapers group.

Circulation: 31,639(m); 31,639(m-sat); 33,191(S); ABC Sept. 30, 1995.

Price: 50¢(d); 50¢(sat); $1.25(S); $2.17/wk; $9.50/mo; $114.00/yr.

Advertising: Open inch rate $23.19(m); $23.19(m-sat); $23.19(S). **Representative:** Thomson Newspapers.

News Service: AP. **Politics:** Independent. **Established:** 1922.

Advertising not accepted: Adoption; Abortion.

Special Editions: Customer Appreciation, YMCA Tab, Super Bowl Preview (Jan); Business Profiles, Senior Citizens (Feb); Progress Edition, Home Builders Section, Transouth 500 (Mar); Men on the Move, Home Improvement, Brides & Spring Fashion, Total Fashion Look, Friday 13th (Apr); Graduation, Working Women, To your Health (May); Father's Day; Southern Living Cooking School; Retailer Photo Highlights; Family Fling (June); Customer Appreciation Day, Business Profiles, Friday 13th (July); Back-to-School and College, YMCA Tab, Southern 500 (Aug); Hurricane Hugo Ann. Sale, Total Fashion Look, Pee Dee Guide, Fall Family Fashions, Hunting/Fishing Page (Sept); National Family Health Month, Home Fall Fashion, Hunting & Fishing, Home Interiors, Car Care (Oct); Fall/Winter Home Improvement, Cookbook, Expo '96, Consumer Electronics (Nov); Holiday Ideas, Last Minute Gifts (Dec).

Special Weekly Sections: Seniors, Agriculture (mon); Health and Fitness (tues); Best Food Day (wed); Family (thur); Best Auto Days, Leisure, Motor World (fri); Learning, Mini Page, Best Real Estate Day, TV Week (sat); Money, Editorial, Best Food Day, Best Real Estate Day Tab, Best Auto Day (S); Sports, Business, TV and Entertainment (daily).

Magazines: TV Week (sat); Real Estate, Parade, Color Comics (S); Manufactured Housing Tab (monthly).

GENERAL MANAGEMENT

Publisher C Thomas Marschel
Accountant Kevin Kenyon

ADVERTISING

Manager Dan Sutton
Manager-Classified Joseph Grice

TELECOMMUNICATIONS

Audiotex Manager Joseph Grice

CIRCULATION

Manager Thomas Clements

NEWS EXECUTIVE

Managing Editor Frank Sayles Jr

EDITORS AND MANAGERS

Amusements Editor Mike Morris
Business/Finance Editor Brian Hickey
City Editor Bob Pepalis
Editorial Page Editor Richard Whiting
Education Editor Denise Pridgen
Fashion/Style Editor Mike Morris
Graphics Editor/Art Director Jeff Chatlosh
Health/Medical Editor Bob Pepalis
Librarian Dana Sellers
Lifestyle Editor Mike Morris
National Editor Shawn Akers
News Editor Shawn Akers
Photo Department Manager/Picture Editor Jeff Chatlosh
Political/Government Editor Bob Pepalis
Sports Editor Henry Miller
Theater Editor Mike Morris
Travel Editor Bob Pepalis

PRODUCTION

Director Richard Johnson
Foreman-Mailroom Ray Reynolds
Foreman-Pressroom M J Gaymon

Market Information: TMC; Operate audiotex.

Mechanical available: Offset; Black insert accepted — preprinted, card stock; page cutoffs — $22\frac{3}{4}$".

Mechanical specifications: Type page 13" x $21\frac{1}{2}$"; E - 6 cols, $2\frac{1}{16}$", $\frac{1}{8}$" between; A - 6 cols, $2\frac{1}{16}$", $\frac{1}{8}$" between; C - 9 cols, $1\frac{5}{16}$", $\frac{1}{8}$" between.

Commodity consumption: Newsprint 2,100 short tons; widths $27\frac{1}{2}$", $13\frac{3}{4}$"; average pages per issue 55(d), 114(S).

Equipment: EDITORIAL: Front-end hardware — 23-CD, 1-Ap/Mac; Front-end software — Adobe/Photoshop, QuarkXPress, Aldus/FreeHand; Printers — 1-Ap/Mac LaserWriter II NTX; Other equipment — Umax/Scanner, 1-Ap/Mac II. CLASSIFIED: Front-end hardware — 4-CD; Front-end software — CD; Printers — Okidata/Microline 393. DISPLAY: Front-end hardware — 3-Ap/Mac IIci, Ap/Mac si; Front-end software — Multi-Ad, Adobe/Illustrator, Aldus/FreeHand, Search; Printers — 2-V/5100, 1-V/5300E; Other equipment — Microtek/CD-Rom. PRODUCTION: Pagination software — Multi-Ad 3.6; Typesetters — 2-V/5100; Platemaking systems — 1-Nu; Plate exposures — Nu/7200; Plate processors — Nat/250; Scanners — COM/C680C; Production cameras — COM/C618C, COM/C660C, COM/C680C; Automatic film processors — COM/220QC; Color separation equipment (conventional) — VPS/2000, Lf/Leafscan 35, Umax/1200.
PRESSROOM: Line 1 — 7-G/Urbanite (2 Stacks; Tri-Color); Press drives — 2-GE/150h.p.; Folders — 1-G; Reels and stands — Fin. MAILROOM: Counter stackers — MSI/220, Id, C/Marathon; Inserters and stuffers — MM/308 Byliner; Bundle tyer — MLN/Spirit; Wrapping singles — Id/Bottom wrap. COMMUNICATIONS: Facsimile — Brother/Instafax 300. WIRE SERVICES: Receiving dishes — size-8ft. BUSINESS COMPUTERS: 7-ATT/3B2; Applications: Unix/Informix: Gen ledger, Adv accts, Circ, Payroll, Accts payable.

GREENVILLE

Greenville County

'90 U.S. Census- 58,282; E&P '96 Est. 58,526
ABC-CZ (90): 223,004 (HH 87,812)

The Greenville News

(m-mon to fri; m-sat; S)

The Greenville News, 305 S. Main St.; PO Box 1688, Greenville, SC 29602; tel (864) 298-4100; fax (864) 298-4805. Gannett Co. Inc. group.

Circulation: 98,523(m); 118,683(m-sat); 140,822(S); ABC Sept. 30, 1995.

Price: 50¢(d); 50¢(sat); $1.25(S); $3.41/wk; $14.75/mo, $9.00/mo (sat & S only); $171.00/yr.

Advertising: Open inch rate $98.55(m); $98.55(m-sat); $103.50(S). **Representative:** Landon Associates Inc.

News Services: AP, LAT-WP, KRT, NYT. **Politics:** Independent. **Established:** 1874.

Note: On Sept. 29, 1995, the Greenville News (m-mon to fri) & the Greenville Piedmont (e-mon to fri) ceased publishing their evening edition and will now be known as the Greenville News (m-mon to fri; m-sat; S).

Advertising not accepted: Fortune tellers; Others may require information before acceptance.

Special Editions: Spring Bride, Home Show, NASCAR Preview (Feb); Southern Home & Garden, MSA Factbook, Careers, Spring Fashion (Mar); Spring Car Care (Apr); Mother's Day (May); Freedom Aloft Weekend, Best of the Upstate (June); Outdoors, Senior Citizens Month, Summer Fun, Auto Leasing, Home Furnishings & Appliances (July); Back-to-School, Fall Fashion, High School Football, College Football (Aug); The Arts (Sept); Bumper to Bumper (New Car/Car Care), Fall Home & Garden (Oct); Christmas Gift Guide, Progress (Nov).

Special Weekly Sections: Family and Parenting, Mini Page, Children (tues); Food (wed); Automotive, Health & Medicine (thur); Time Out (Entertainment) (fri); It's Saturday (sat); TV Spotlight, Upstate Business, Outdoors (S); Business, Sports, Recreation (daily).

Magazine: Parade (S).

CORPORATE OFFICER

President William deB Mebane

GENERAL MANAGEMENT

Publisher Steven R Brandt
Vice Pres/Business Manager Hal Tanner III
Director-Operations Bud Turner
Asst Director-Operations Drake Curry
Manager-Research Murray M Howard
Controller John P King

ADVERTISING

Vice Pres-Marketing Mark Johnston
Director-Classified/Sales/Special Publications William Boone
Manager-Retail Beth Batson

MARKETING AND PROMOTION

Manager-Promotion Elizabeth Cline

TELECOMMUNICATIONS

Audiotex Manager Jim Spencer

CIRCULATION

Director Drake Curry

NEWS EXECUTIVES

Exec Editor John S Pittman
Managing Editor-News/Sports Tom Hutchison
Managing Editor-Features/Administration Ann L Clark
Managing Editor-Local News Chris Weston

EDITORS AND MANAGERS

Amusements/Books Editor Jan Phillips
Automotive Editor Cheryl Street
Books/Women's Editor Prescilla Walker
Business/Finance Editor Robert Scott
City Editor Marian Elliott
Columnist Reese Fant
Columnist Jimmy Cornelison
Deputy Editorial Page Editor Beth Padgett
Editorial Page Editor Tom Inman
Editorial Writer Susan Simmons
Education Editor Steve Belli
Education Editor Bernadette Adams
Environmental Editor Marian Elliott
Farm/Agriculture Editor Robert Scott
Fashion/Style Editor Jan Phillips
Features/Food Editor Prescilla Walker
Films Editor Jan Phillips
Food Editor Frances Evans
Gardening Editor Frances Worthington
Health/Medical Editor Sheila Carnett
Librarian Amy Dickerson
Living/Lifestyle Editor Jan Phillips
Music Editor Prescilla Walker
News Editor Terry Cregar
News Editor Ralph Jeffrey
Photo Editor Fred Rollison
Political Editor Wayne Roper
Radio/Television Editor Jan Phillips
Regional Editor Ron Dekett
Religion Editor Ron Barnett
Sports Editor Ed McGranahan
Sports Columnist Dan Foster
State Editor Wayne Roper
Teen-Age/Youth Editor Prescilla Walker
Theater Editor Staci Sturrock
Travel Editor Jan Phillips
Wire Editor Cheryl Street
Women's Editor Jan Phillips

MANAGEMENT INFORMATION SERVICES

Online Manager Jim Spencer
Data Processing Manager John Armstrong

PRODUCTION

Manager George Gardner
Manager-Consumer Distribution Macon Rich
Foreman-Composing (Night) Charles Hendrix
Foreman-Composing (Day) Tom Rust
Superintendent-Pressroom Max Myers

Market Information: Zoned editions; Split Run; TMC; ADS; Operate database; Operate audiotex.

Mechanical available: Offset; Black and 3 ROP colors; insert accepted — preprinted, as requested; page cut-offs — 22".

Mechanical specifications: Type page 13" x 21"; E - 6 cols, $2\frac{1}{16}$", $\frac{1}{8}$" between; A - 6 cols, $2\frac{1}{16}$", $\frac{1}{8}$" between; C - 10 cols, $1\frac{7}{32}$", $\frac{5}{64}$" between.

Commodity consumption: Newsprint 17,950 short tons; widths 54", $40\frac{1}{2}$", 27"; black ink 400,000 pounds; color ink 80,000 pounds; single pages printed 51,225; average pages per issue 108(d), 136(S); single plates used 135,000.

Equipment: EDITORIAL: Front-end hardware — HI/XP-21; Front-end software — HI/8300, HI/8900, HI/XP-21-2100; Printers — Printronix/300, Data South; Other equipment — Lf/AP Leaf Picture Desk, HI/Imagers, 70-Novell/Network. CLASSIFIED: Front-end hardware — HI/486; Front-end software — HI/Cash 5.0; Printers — Epson/DFX 5000; Other equipment — HI/CPAG. AUDIOTEX: Hardware — Brite Voice Systems; Software — QNX, Brite Voice Systems/Proprietary; Supplier name — Brite Voice Systems. DISPLAY: Adv layout systems — SCS/Layout 8000; Front-end hardware — 2-Dell/286 (200); Front-end software — SCS/Layout 8000 6.0; Printers — DEC/LA 120; Other equipment — HI/2-Pixel Color PLS, HI/Autocopy SIPC, HI/Dual 8300 Graphic System, 4-HI/8000 PLS, Ap/Mac Quadra 950s, Ap/Super Macs. PRODUCTION: Pagination software — HI 8.4, HI 2.4; Typesetters — AU/APS-3850, 2-AU/APS-6-108SZ; Platemaking systems — KFM/Plate Express II; Plate exposures — 2-Nu/Flip Top FT40V6UPNS; Plate processors — WL/Lithoplater; Electronic picture desk — HI/Images, Lf/AP Leaf Picture Desk; Scanners — ECR/Autokon 1030, ECR/Autokon 2034, 2-X/7650, Scitex; Production cameras — C/Marathon, C/Spartan III; Automatic film processors — Konica/OC-6, LE; Reproportion units — ECR/Autokon 1030, ECR/Autokon 2030, X/7650, Scitex; Film transporters — C; Shrink lenses — Alan/Anamorhill; Color separation equipment (conventional) — Scitex; Digital color separation equipment — Scitex.
PRESSROOM: Line 1 — 8-G/Metroliner; Line 2 — 8-G/Headliner (offset); Press drives — Fin;

Folders — 4-G; Pasters — G/Hall Effect; Reels and stands — 16-G; Press control system — G/PCS II. **MAILROOM:** Counter stackers — 1-QWI/100, 2-QWI/200, 4-QWI/300, 2-QWI/1500; Inserters and stuffers — 2-HI/13-72, 1-AM Graphics/630; Bundle tyer — 4-MLN/MLNS, 4-Dynaric, 6-EAM/Mosca; Addressing machine — 3-Wm/hand labelers, 2-KR/Labeler; Mailroom control system — Ic/Insert System, ARS/Insert System; Other mailroom equipment — MM/335. **LIBRARY:** Electronic — Vu/Text SAVE. **COMMUNICATIONS:** Digital ad delivery system — AP AdSend. Systems used — fiber optic. **WIRE SERVICES:** News — AP, KRT, NYT, LAT-WP, AP Datastream; Stock tables — AP; Receiving dishes — size-10ft/3ft, AP, UPI. **BUSINESS COMPUTERS:** IBM/AS-400; Applications: CJ/AIM-CIS: Adv billing, Accts receivable, Gen ledger, Payroll; PCs & micros networked; PCs & main system networked.

GREENWOOD
Greenwood County

'90 U.S. Census- 20,807; E&P '96 Est. 20,362
ABC-CZ (90): 20,807 (HH 8,095)

The Index-Journal
(e-mon to fri; S)

The Index-Journal, 610 Phoenix & Fair; PO Box 1018, Greenwood, SC 29646; tel (864) 223-1411; fax (864) 223-7331.
Circulation: 15,590(e); 16,856(S); ABC Sept. 30, 1995.
Price: 50¢(d); $1.25(S); $2.25/wk; $9.75/mo; $105.30/yr.
Advertising: Open inch rate $15.00(e); $15.00(S). **Representative:** Papert Companies.
News Services: AP, NYT, NEA. **Politics:** Independent. **Established:** 1919.
Magazine: TV Index (S).

CORPORATE OFFICERS
CEO	Robert Bentley
President/Treasurer	Eleanor M Mundy
Vice Pres/Secretary	Judith M Burns

GENERAL MANAGEMENT
Controller	Richard Jackson

ADVERTISING
Director	Harry L Garrett
Manager	Ron Lucas

MARKETING AND PROMOTION
Manager-Sales/Promotion	Harry Garrett

CIRCULATION
Manager-City	Albert Ashley

NEWS EXECUTIVES
Exec Editor	William A Collins
Managing Editor	Jim Joyce

EDITORS AND MANAGERS
Amusements/Automotive Editor	William A Collins
Automotive/Travel Editor	Jim Joyce
Books/Music Editor	William A Collins
Business/Finance Editor	Joe Sitarz
City/Metro Editor	Jim Joyce
Editorial Page Editor	William A Collins
Education Editor	Bill Bengtsen
Features Editor	Jim Joyce
Films/Theater Editor	Jim Joyce
Food/Garden Editor	Alice Hite
Graphics Editor/Art Director	Joe Sitarz
Health/Medical Editor	Alice Hite
Living/Lifestyle Editor	Alice Hite
National Editor	William A Collins
News Editor	Dean Lollis
Photographer	Jim Joyce
Political/Government Editor	William A Collins
Real Estate Editor	William A Collins
Religion/School Editor	Jim Joyce
Science Editor	Jim Joyce
Sports Editor	Jim Joyce
Today's Living Editor	Alice Hite
Women's/Fashion Editor	Alice Hite

MANAGEMENT INFORMATION SERVICES
Data Processing Manager	Richard Jackson

PRODUCTION
Manager	Roger Burton
Foreman-Composing	Lorie Hough
Foreman-Pressroom	Ronnie Brown
Foreman-Mailroom	Kevin Coleman

Market Information: Split Run; TMC.
Mechanical available: Offset; Black and 3 ROP colors; insert accepted — preprinted; page cutoffs — 22¾".

South Carolina

Mechanical specifications: Type page 13" x 21½"; E - 6 cols, 2.07", ⅛" between; A - 6 cols, 2.07", ⅛" between; C - 6 cols, 2.07", ⅛" between.
Commodity consumption: Newsprint 800 short tons; widths 27½", 13¾"; black ink 2,500 pounds; color ink 1,000 pounds; single pages printed 8,400; average pages per issue 108(d), 136(S); single plates used 6,200.
Equipment: EDITORIAL: Front-end hardware — Mk; Front-end software — Mk. CLASSIFIED: Front-end hardware — Mk; Front-end software — Mk. DISPLAY: Front-end hardware — Ap/Mac; Front-end software — Multi-Ad/Creator; Printers — LaserMaster/1200, Ap/Mac LaserWriter NTX; Other equipment — Ap/Mac CD-Rom, Ap/Mac Scanner. PRODUCTION: Plate exposures — 2-Nu/Flip Top; Plate processors — 1-Nat; Production cameras — 1-VG/Daylighter, 1-C/Spartan III; Automatic film processors — 1-P; Film transporters — 1-C; Color separation equipment (conventional) — C. PRESSROOM: Line 1 — HI/Cotrell 845; Line 2 — 5-HI/Cotrell 845; Line 3 — 1-HI/Cotrell 845; Folders — 1-HI; Reels and stands — 5-G; Press control system — 1-G. MAILROOM: Counter stackers — BG/109; Inserters and stuffers — 2-MM; Bundle tyer — MLN. COMMUNICATIONS: Facsimile — Canon. WIRE SERVICES: News — AP; Stock tables — AP; Receiving dishes — AP. BUSINESS COMPUTERS: Applications: Circ, Adv billing, Accts receivable, Gen ledger, Payroll.

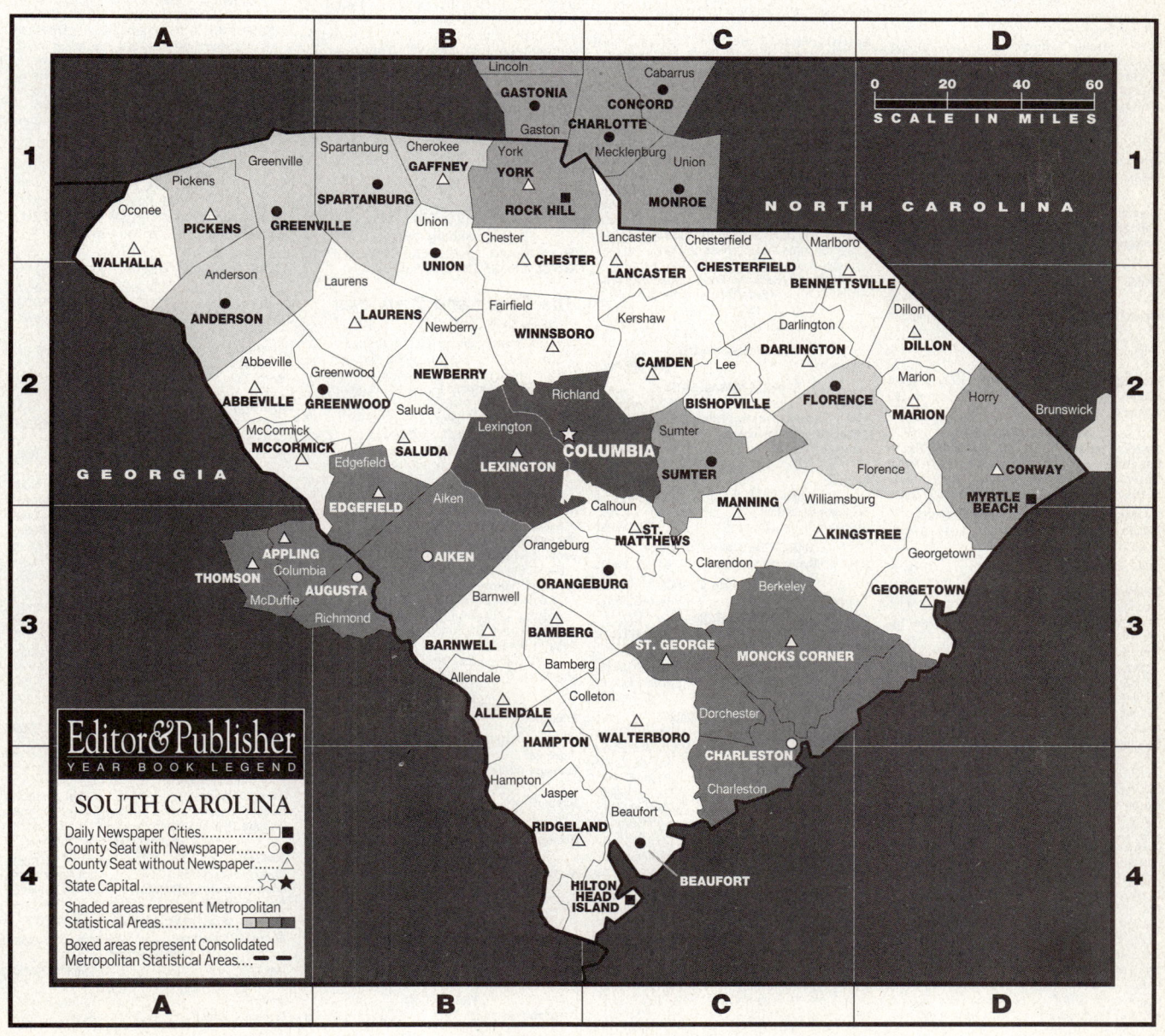

HILTON HEAD ISLAND
Beaufort County
'90 U.S. Census- 23,694; E&P '96 Est. 33,304
ABC-CZ (90): 23,694 (HH 10,344)

The Island Packet
(m-mon to thur; m-fri; m-sat; S)

The Island Packet, One Pope Avenue Mall; PO Box 5727, Hilton Head, SC 29938; tel (803) 785-4293; fax (803) 686-3407. McClatchy Newspapers group.
Circulation: 12,474(m); 14,356(m-fri); 12,474(m-sat); 15,214(S); ABC Sept. 30, 1995.
Price: 25¢(d); 25¢(fri); 25¢(sat); 75¢(S); $7.50/mo; $74.00/yr.
Advertising: Open inch rate $20.30(m); $20.30(m-fri); $20.30(m-sat); $21.85(S). **Representative:** Papert Companies.
News Services: AP, KRT, NYT, Pony Wire. **Politics:** Independent. **Established:** 1971.
Note: Effective Sept. 2, 1995, this publication started publishing a Saturday morning edition.
Special Editions: Tax Pages, Business Expo (Jan); Spring Fest, Wedding Showcase, Tax Pages (Feb); Family Circle, Home & Garden (Mar); Heritage Week Special (Apr); Mother's Day, Graduation, Summertime (May); Father's Day (June); Coupon Clipper (July); Back-to-School, Football (Aug); Hurricane, Fall Fashion (Sept); Automotive (Car Care), Home Interiors (Oct); Christmas (Nov); Christmas (Dec).
Special Weekly Sections: Health (tues); Food (wed); People (thur); Business, Arts & Entertainment (fri); TV, Family (sat); Travel, Book Pages, Homes & Real Estate, Brides (S).
Magazines: Best Food Day (wed); TV Week (sat); USA Weekend (S).

GENERAL MANAGEMENT
Publisher Sara Johnson Borton
Business Manager Susan Shreeves

ADVERTISING
Director Philip Porter
Manager-Retail Sales Sandy Gillis
Manager-Classified Gene Fowler Jr

MARKETING AND PROMOTION
Manager-Marketing/Promotion Beth Patton

TELECOMMUNICATIONS
Audiotex Manager Dave Martin

CIRCULATION
Manager Carolyn Davis

NEWS EXECUTIVES
Exec Editor Owen (Fitz) McAden
Editor Fran Smith
Managing Editor David Lauderdale

EDITORS AND MANAGERS
Business Editor Janet Smith
City Editor Tony Tharp
Leisure Editor Lynn Felder
Sports Editor Kevin Adams

MANAGEMENT INFORMATION SERVICES
Data Processing Manager Dave Martin

PRODUCTION
Director-Graphics John Bowen

Market Information: Operate audiotex.
Mechanical available: Offset; Black and 3 ROP colors; insert accepted — preprinted; page cut-offs — 21".
Mechanical specifications: Type page 13" x 21"; E - 6 cols, 2 1/16", 1/8" between; A - 6 cols, 2 1/16", 1/8" between; C - 8 cols, 1 1/2", 1/8" between.
Commodity consumption: average pages per issue 26(d), 75(S).
Equipment: EDITORIAL: Front-end hardware — CD, Ap/Mac; Front-end software — Baseview/IQ. CLASSIFIED: Front-end hardware — CD, Ap/Mac, Baseview/Classified. AUDIOTEX: Hardware — Brite Voice Systems; Supplier name — PEP, Brite Voice Systems. DISPLAY: Adv layout systems — Ap/Mac; Front-end hardware — 7-Ap/Mac IIci, 2-Ap/Power Mac; Front-end software — Multi-Ad/Creator 3.6.3, QuarkXPress 3.3, Aldus/FreeHand 4.0, Adobe/Photoshop 3.0; Printers — Graphic Enterprises/Pagescan 3, Birmy/11x17. PRODUCTION: Pagination software — QuarkXPress 3.31; OCR software — Caere/OmniPage 3.0; Typesetters — AG/Accuset 1000; Electronic picture desk — Lf/AP Leaf Picture Desk; Scanners — Polaroid/SprintScan 35, Microtek/Scanmaker III, Microtek/Scanmaker 6002S; Production cameras — 1-Nu; Automatic film processors — 1-DP/RAII, AG/Accuset Rapidline 20-OLP. LIBRARY: Electronic — Ap/Mac, Baseview. WIRE SERVICES: News — AP Graphics; Syndicates — AP; Receiving dishes — size-10ft, AP. BUSINESS COMPUTERS: 1-HP/3000 Series 58; Applications: Adv, Circ, Payroll, Gen ledger, Office productivity, Packages; PCs & micros networked; PCs & main system networked.

MYRTLE BEACH
Horry County
'90 U.S. Census- 24,848; E&P '96 Est. 31,120
ABC-CZ (90): 67,542 (HH 27,858)

The Sun News
(m-mon to sat; S)

The Sun News, 914 Frontage Rd. E.; PO Box 406, Myrtle Beach, SC 29577; tel (803) 626-8555 (Customer src.); fax (803) 626-0208 (Customer srv.). Knight-Ridder Inc. group.
Circulation: 40,403(m); 40,403(m-sat); 50,484(S); ABC Sept. 24, 1995.
Price: 50¢(d); 50¢(sat); $1.25(S); $70.00/6mo; $120.00/yr.
Advertising: Open inch rate $21.15(m); $21.15(m-sat); $24.35(S). **Representative:** Newspapers First.
News Services: AP, NYT, KRT. **Politics:** Independent. **Established:** 1936.
Advertising not accepted: Bingo; Lottery; Video Poker.
Special Editions: Brides (Jan); Outlook, Home Show, Great Winter Sale (Feb); Canadian-American, New Homes Parade, St. Patrick's Day, TranSouth 500 Race (Mar); Spring/Summer Fashions, Home Buyers Guide, Deals on Wheels (Apr); Menus and Maps, Sun Fun (May); Busch Grand Nat'l. Race (June); Celebration of Homes (July); Great Summer Sales, Southern 500 Race, World Amateur Golf Tournament (Aug); Auto Sell-Out, Menus and Maps, Parenting (Sept); Retirement Living, Businesswomen's Pages, Fashions and Furnishings, Automotive Preview (Oct); Holiday Gift Guide, Golf Magazine, Senior Tour Championship (Nov); Holiday Songs & Traditions (Dec).
Special Weekly Sections: Food (wed); Neighbors (thur); Kicks (Entertainment Section) (fri); Real Estate, TV (S).
Magazine: Parade (S).

CORPORATE OFFICER
President J Michael Pate

GENERAL MANAGEMENT
Publisher J Michael Pate
Vice Pres-Administration/Finance Laura Hensley
Director-Human Resources Jackie Olivetti
Manager-Finance Jean Young

ADVERTISING
Director Phil LaPorte
Manager-Retail Leslie Infield
Manager-Classified Ken Gilstrap
Manager-General/Co-op Carl Miller

MARKETING AND PROMOTION
Director-Marketing Services Milton Miles

TELECOMMUNICATIONS
Audiotex Manager Ken Gilstrap

CIRCULATION
Director Steve Davis

NEWS EXECUTIVES
Editor Susan C Deans
Managing Editor-Days Gwen Fowler
Managing Editor-Nights Bob Bestler

EDITORS AND MANAGERS
Business Editor Andrew Shain
Design/Graphics Editor Scott McCaffrey
Editorial Page Editor Jerry Ausband
Features Editor Mona Prufer
News Editor David Wilson
Photo Editor Charles Slate
Sports Editor John Brasier

PRODUCTION
Director-Operations Wendy Morrissey
Manager-Operations Clyde Owens

Market Information: Zoned editions; Split Run; TMC; ADS; Operate audiotex.
Mechanical available: Offset; Black and 3 ROP colors; insert accepted — preprinted, spadea; page cut-offs — 21".
Mechanical specifications: Type page 13" x 21"; E - 6 cols, 2 1/16", 1/8" between; A - 6 cols, 2 1/16", 1/8" between; C - 10 cols, 1 1/8", .14" between.
Commodity consumption: Newsprint 4,317 metric tons; widths 27 1/2", 55"; black ink 90,000 pounds; color ink 23,746 pounds; single pages printed 20,598; average pages per issue 45(d), 114(S); single plates used 68,391.
Equipment: EDITORIAL: Front-end hardware — 5-AT; Front-end software — AT 4.5.3; Printers — 1-QMS/860; Other equipment — 8-Ap/Mac. CLASSIFIED: Front-end hardware — AT; Front-end software — AT 4.5.3; Other equipment — AT/GT-68 Classified Pagination. AUDIOTEX: Supplier name — Micro Voice. DISPLAY: Adv layout systems — CJ/Layout 80; Front-end hardware — 11-Ap/Mac; Front-end software — QuarkXPress 3.3; Printers — QMS/860; Other equipment — 3-Flatbed Scanners. PRODUCTION: Pagination software — QuarkXPress 3.3; OCR software — Caere/OmniPage 3.0; Typesetters — 1-AU/APS 1000, 2-AU/108C, 1-AU/APS-100, 2-AU/APS Alpha Pip; Plate exposures — 2-Nu/Flip Top FT40LNS, 1-Nu/Flip Top FT40APRNS63; Plate processors — 2-Anatec/Subtractive; Electronic picture desk — Lf/AP Leaf Picture Desk; Scanners — 1-ECR/Autokon 1000; Production cameras — 1-R/500, 1-C/Spartan II 1244; Automatic film processors — Konica, 1-LE/24-AQ, 1-LE/142, C/66F; Color separation equipment (conventional) — CD/Scanner; Digital color separation equipment — 2-Kk/Rs-2035, 3-HP/ScanJet IIcx, 1-Microtek/600, 1-CD/636E, 1-Lf/Leafscan 35.
PRESSROOM: Line 1 — 6-G/Headliner offset (4 half decks); Folders — 1-G/3:2, 1-KAN/Quarterfolder Labeler; Pasters — 6-G/CT50; Press control system — 1-G/MPCS. MAILROOM: Counter stackers — HL/Monitors, HL/HT, HL/HT II; Inserters and stuffers — 1-MM/275, 1-HI/848; Bundle tyer — 1-MLN, 3-Power Strap, 1-Dynaric, Selco/Stitcher-Trimmer-Baler; Addressing machine — 1-Quarter-folder Labeler. LIBRARY: Electronic — Vu/Text. WIRE SERVICES: News — AP, KRT, NYT, LAT-WP; Photos — AP; Stock tables — AP SelectStox I; Receiving dishes — AP. BUSINESS COMPUTERS: HP/3000 model 947, HP/9000 model E55; Applications: CJ: Adv, Layout, Gen ledger, Accts payable, Circ, Cognos; PCs & micros networked; PCs & main system networked.

ORANGEBURG
Orangeburg County
'90 U.S. Census- 13,739; E&P '96 Est. 13,046
ABC-CZ (90): 25,287 (HH 8,470)

The Times and Democrat
(m-mon to sat; S)

The Times and Democrat, 211 Broughton St. S.W. (29115); PO Box 1766, Orangeburg, SC 29116; tel (803) 533-5500; fax (803) 533-5595. Howard Publications group.
Circulation: 17,586(m); 17,586(m-sat); 17,310(S); ABC Sept. 30, 1995.
Price: 35¢(d); 35¢(sat); $1.00(S); $11.00/mo; $125.00/yr.
Advertising: Open inch rate $13.75(m); $13.75(m-sat); $13.75(S). **Representative:** Papert Companies.
News Service: AP. **Politics:** Independent. **Established:** 1881.
Not Published: Dec 26.
Special Editions: Progress (Jan); Tax, Bridal (Feb); Spring Fashion, Lawn & Garden (Mar); Home Improvement (Apr); Health & Fitness (May); Car Care (June); Back-to-School, Football (Aug); Car Care (Oct); Farm, Gift Guide (Nov); Greetings (Dec).
Special Weekly Sections: Farm (mon); Food (wed); Garden City (lifestyles) (thur, S).
Magazine: TV Times Tab (S).

CORPORATE OFFICER
President Robert S Howard

GENERAL MANAGEMENT
Publisher Dean B Livingston
Manager-Office Georgianne Walton

ADVERTISING
Director Cathy Hughes

TELECOMMUNICATIONS
Audiotex Manager Cathy Hughes

CIRCULATION
Manager John Stewart

NEWS EXECUTIVE
Editor Lee Harter

EDITOR AND MANAGER
Photographer Ken Tyler

MANAGEMENT INFORMATION SERVICES
Data Processing Manager Georgianne Walton

PRODUCTION
Foreman-Pressroom Charles Garrick

Market Information: Zoned editions; TMC; Operate audiotex.
Mechanical available: Offset; Black and 3 ROP colors; insert accepted — preprinted; page cut-offs — 21".
Mechanical specifications: Type page 13" x 21"; E - 6 cols, 2 1/16", 1/8" between; A - 6 cols, 2 1/16", 1/8" between; C - 8 cols, 1 3/8", 1/16" between.
Commodity consumption: Newsprint 1,245 short tons; widths 27 1/2", 13 3/4"; black ink 20,000 pounds; color ink 2,750 pounds; single pages printed 11,281; average pages per issue 28(d), 20(sat), 50(S); single plates used 10,000.
Equipment: EDITORIAL: Front-end hardware — Sun/Microsys 4-110, 16-Sun/Sparc Station; Other equipment — 1-Ap/Mac Scanner, 1-Tru-Val/Scanner, 1-Nikon/Scanner. CLASSIFIED: Front-end hardware — 4-Sun/Microsystems 4-110, 3-Sun/Sparc Station. AUDIOTEX: Supplier name — Edu Com. DISPLAY: Adv layout systems — Amdek/Layout 8000, 6-Ap/Mac II, Ap/Mac IIci; Front-end hardware — Ap/Mac; Front-end software — QuarkXPress, Adobe/Illustrator; Printers — Copal, Ap/Mac Laser-writer II NTX; Other equipment — 1-Travel/Scanner, 1-Nikon/Scanner, 1-Ap/Mac Scanner. PRODUCTION: Typesetters — 4-Ap/Mac LaserWriter, 1-Hyphen/Pelbox; Plate exposures — 2-Nu; Plate processors — 1-Nat; Production cameras — 1-C; Automatic film processors — 2-LE; Film transporters — 1-C, 1-LE; Shrink lenses — 1-C.
PRESSROOM: Line 1 — 7-G/Urbanite; Folders — 1-G/Urbanite w/Balloon Former; Press control system — GE; Press registration system — Stoesser/Register Systems. MAILROOM: Counter stackers — 2-Id/Marathon; Inserters and stuffers — 1-MM; Bundle tyer — 2-Si, 1-OVL. LIBRARY: Electronic — Verity/Topic. COMMUNICATIONS: Digital ad delivery system — AP AdSend. Systems used — satellite. WIRE SERVICES: News — AP; Receiving dishes — AP. BUSINESS COMPUTERS: Sun/Microsys 410; Applications: Adv billing, Accts receivable, Circ, Subscriber-non subscriber; PCs & micros networked; PCs & main system networked.

ROCK HILL
York County
'90 U.S. Census- 41,643; E&P '96 Est. 47,049
ABC-NDM (90): 109,715 (HH 38,923)

The Herald (m-mon to sat; S)

The Herald, 132-136 W. Main; PO Box 11707, Rock Hill, SC 29730; tel (803) 329-4000; fax (803) 329-4021. McClatchy Newspapers group.
Circulation: 30,603(m); 30,603(m-sat); 31,683(S); ABC Sept. 30, 1995.
Price: 35¢(d); 35¢(sat); 75¢(S); $8.00/mo; $91.00/yr.
Advertising: Open inch rate $21.41(m); $21.41(m-sat); $21.41(S). **Representative:** Papert Companies.
News Services: AP, LAT-WP, McClatchy. **Politics:** Independent. **Established:** 1871.
Special Editions: Health Horizons (Jan); York County Magazine (Feb); NIE Student Stories, Spring Fashion, Home & Garden (Mar); Come See Me, Earth Day (Apr); Racing to Read, Emergency Medical Services (May); You Can Find it in York County, Health Horizons (June); York Summerfest, Back-to-School, Football (Aug); Carolina Panthers Magazine (Sept); Christmas Opening, Hornets, Wrap-up Christmas Early (Nov); Last Minute Gift Guide, Cel River Classic (Dec).
Special Weekly Sections: Food (wed); Good Times-Entertainment Section (thur); Automotive, Time Off (a guide to travel & leisure) (fri); Weddings & Engagements, Automotive (S); Business (daily).
Magazines: STAR Watch (wed); Home & Real Estate (sat); TV Herald (S).

GENERAL MANAGEMENT
Publisher/President Orage Quarles III
General Manager Roger L Sovde
Director-Finance George M McCanless
Director-Human Resources Helen van Ryswyck

ADVERTISING
Director William J Edinger
Manager-Classified J Andy Bass
Manager-National/Preprint Eva Jenkins
Manager-Retail Art Goddard

MARKETING AND PROMOTION
Director-Promotion Waldene C Edinger

CIRCULATION
Director Shanti Marie

NEWS EXECUTIVES
Editor Terry C Plumb
Managing Editor Betsy Lumbye

Copyright ©1996 by the Editor & Publisher Co.

EDITORS AND MANAGERS

Automotive Editor Will Parrish
Business Editor Ken Elkins
City Editor Rich Rassmann
Editorial Page Editor James Werrell
News Editor Fred Horlbeck
Photo Editor Andy Burriss
Sports Editor Stephen Vest
Women's Editor Jennifer Becknell

PRODUCTION

Director Patricia Simons
Manager-Camera/Plate/Press Tony Couto
Manager-Mailroom Hal Palmer

Market Information: Zoned editions; Split Run; TMC; Operate audiotex.
Mechanical available: Offset; Black and 3 ROP colors; insert accepted — preprinted, books, envelopes; page cut-offs — 21½".
Mechanical specifications: Type page 13" x 21½"; E - 6 cols, 2 1/16", ⅛" between; A - 6 cols, 2 1/16", ⅛" between; C - 9 cols, 1⅜", 1/16" between.
Commodity consumption: Newsprint 2,443 short tons; widths 27", 13"; black ink 65,000 pounds; color ink 9,000 pounds; single pages printed 15,000; average pages per issue 28(d), 50(S); single plates used 30,000.
Equipment: EDITORIAL: Front-end hardware — 20-Ap/Mac Quadra 605, 6-Ap/Mac LC, 2-Ap/Mac IIfx, 1-Ap/Mac II, 5-Ap/Mac Quadra 700, 3-Ap/Mac Quadra 650, 3-Ap/Power Mac 7500; Front-end software — Baseview/NewsEdit IQ 1.12; Printers — Ap/Mac ImageWriter, HP/LaserJet IIIsi; Other equipment — Nikon/LS-3510AF, Kk/RFS-2035 Plus. CLASSIFIED: Front-end hardware — Ap/Mac Quadra 630; Front-end software — Baseview/Class Manager Plus; Printers — Ap/Mac ImageWriter. AUDIOTEX: Hardware — Brite Voice Systems; Software — PEP/Voice Print 900 24.2; Supplier name — Brite Voice Systems. DISPLAY: Front-end hardware — 4-Ap/Mac Quadra; Printers — Compaq/Laser Printer. PRODUCTION: Pagination software — QuarkXPress 3.3; OCR software — Caere/Omni-Page Pro 2.12; Typesetters — Linotype-Hell/Linotronic 530, Compaq, Pagescan/3 Plus; Plate exposures — Nu/Flip Top FT40APR-NUS; Plate processors — GNS/28; Electronic picture desk — Lf/AP Leaf Picture Desk; Scanners — ECR/Autokon 1000, Umax/UC-630; Production cameras — SCREEN/260; Automatic film processors — SCREEN/DS, LE/Excel 26; Shrink lenses — CK Optical.
PRESSROOM: Line 2 — 10-G/Urbanite, 1-DEV; Press drives — GE/150h.p. DC; Folders — G/Urbanite 1000 Series 2:1; Press control system — Fin; Press registration system — Manual. MAILROOM: Counter stackers — Id, HL; Inserters and stuffers — MM/227, HI/848; Bundle tyer — Power Strap; Addressing machine — KR/Labeler. LIBRARY: Electronic — Data Times. WIRE SERVICES: News — AP Datastream, AP Datafeatures, LAT-WP, McClatchy; Photos — AP; Stock tables — AP SelectStox I; Receiving dishes — size-10m, AP. BUSINESS COMPUTERS: HP/3000-918 RX; Applications: CJ; PCs & micros networked; PCs & main system networked.

SPARTANBURG

Spartanburg County

'90 U.S. Census- 43,467; **E&P '96 Est.** 43,297
ABC-CZ (90): 117,759 (HH 44,731)

Herald-Journal

(m-mon to sat; S)

Herald-Journal, 189 W. Main St.; PO Box 1657, Spartanburg, SC 29304; tel (864) 582-4511; fax (864) 582-7413; e-mail 73511.522@compuserve.com; web site http://www.teleplex.net/shj/smith/. New York Times Co. group.
Circulation: 62,095(m); 62,095(m-sat); 69,171(S); ABC Sept. 30, 1995.
Price: 50¢(d); 50¢(sat); $1.00(S); $10.75/mo; $123.00/yr (carrier), $240.00/yr (mail).
Advertising: Open inch rate $45.00(m); $45.00(m-sat); $48.30(S). **Representative:** Landon Associates Inc.
News Services: AP, NYT, KRT. **Politics:** Independent. **Established:** 1844.
Special Editions: Brides (Jan); Autoracing (Feb); AnswerBook (Mar); Earth Day (Apr); Summer Fun (June); Cookbook, County Golf (July); Football (Aug); Auto Showcase, Textile (Oct); Gift Guide (Nov); Gift Guide (Dec); Today's Seniors, Real Estate Guide (monthly).
Special Weekly Sections: Best Food Day (wed); Entertainment (fri); Church News (sat); TV Week, Travel, Real Estate (S); Financial (daily except mon); Lifestyle (daily except sat).
Magazines: Parade, TV Magazine (S).

GENERAL MANAGEMENT

Publisher David O Roberts
Administrative Asst Tracie Foster
Controller Alan Green
Director-Finance Service Fred Klapper
Director-Human Resources Sheri Yoder

ADVERTISING

Director Bill Cranford
Manager-General Bill Cranford
Manager-Retail Read Neath
Manager-Classified Kathy Shepard

TELECOMMUNICATIONS

Manager-Telemarketing Thomas Doucet
Audiotex Manager Babette Cubitt

CIRCULATION

Director Ken Smith

NEWS EXECUTIVES

Exec Editor Carl E Beck Jr
Managing Editor Scott Kearns

EDITORS AND MANAGERS

Business Editor Kathy Nelson
City Editor Benjy Hamm
Columnist Lou Parris
Editorial Page Editor Mike Smith
Fashion/Society Editor Annie R Burress
Features Editor Jose Franco
Food Editor Jose Franco
Graphics Editor Jeff Zehr
Librarian Carolyn Edds
News Editor Gloria Fair
Photo Editor Bryan Stiles
Radio/Television Editor Ann Patterson-Rabon
Sports Editor Jim Fair
Women's Editor Annie R Burress

MANAGEMENT INFORMATION SERVICES

Director Joe Bagwell

PRODUCTION

Director-Operations James Fuller
Manager-Pressroom Mike Towery
Manager-Mailroom Don West
Manager-Electronical/Mechanical Ralph Widmyer
Manager-PrePress Douglas Pye

Market Information: TMC; Operate audiotex.
Mechanical available: Offset; Black and 3 ROP colors; insert accepted — preprinted; page cut-offs — 22".
Mechanical specifications: Type page 13" x 21¼"; E - 6 cols, 2 1/16", ⅛" between; A - 6 cols, 2 1/16", ⅛" between; C - 9 cols, 1⅜", 1/16" between.
Commodity consumption: Newsprint 7,000 short tons; widths 55", 41¼", 27½"; black ink 210,000 pounds; color ink 21,000 pounds; single pages printed 18,500; average pages per issue 48(d), 90(S); single plates used 32,000.
Equipment: EDITORIAL: Front-end hardware — AT/Series 4; Front-end software — AT; Printers — Ap/Mac LaserWriter NTX; Other equipment — Ap/Mac II fx, Ap/Mac IIci, AG/Argus Scanners, 2-Ap/Power Mac 8100-80. CLASSIFIED: Front-end hardware — AT/Series 4; Front-end software — AT/IAS; Printers — Dataproducts/8500. AUDIOTEX: Hardware — Brite Voice Systems/Bus-2000; Software — Brite Voice Systems. DISPLAY: Front-end hardware — 9-Ap/Mac Quadra Graphics Workstation; Front-end software — QuarkXPress 3.3.1, Multi-Ad, Adobe/Photoshop 3.0.4; Printers — Ap/Mac LaserWriter II NTX, Ap/Mac Select 360F, LaserMaster/1200; Other equipment — 1-Hayes/Accura 144, Fox/144 Data Modem. PRODUCTION: OCR software — Type Reader 1.1; Typesetters — 2-V/5500, 2-Panther/Pro; Plate exposures — 3-Nu/Flip Top FT40V6UPNS; Plate processors — WL; Electronic picture desk — Lf/AP Leaf Picture Desk, Ap/Mac Quadra; Scanners — 2-ECR/Autokon 1000DE, 3-AG/Argus, 2-Umax/2400x, 1-Ap/Mac Scan; Production cameras — 1-C/Spartan; Automatic film processors — 1-Konica/750, 1-LE/2600A, 2-LE/Excel 26; Film transporters — 2-LE/Transport Unit; Shrink lenses — C/Anamorphic Lens; Color separation equipment (conventional) — CD/645IE, 3-AG/Argus, 2-Umax 2400x, 1-Ap/Mac Scanner.
PRESSROOM: Line 1 — 8-G/Headliner (4-color decks); Press drives — Allen Bradley/PLC 5; Folders — RKW, 1-G/3:2; Pasters — G/CT 45; Press control system — Allen Bradley/PLC. MAILROOM: Counter stackers — 3-Id/2000; Inserters and stuffers — 1-HI/1472; Bundle tyer — 3-Power Strap/PSN5; Addressing machine — 1-KR. LIBRARY: Electronic — AT, In-house. COMMUNICATIONS: Facsimile — 2-Hel/Graphic Pressfax; Digital ad delivery system — AP AdSend; Systems used — fiber optic. WIRE SERVICES: News — AP, AFP, NYT, KRT, TV Data; Photos — AP; Stock tables — AP SelectStox II; Syndicates — CNS; Receiving dishes — AP. BUSINESS COMPUTERS: IBM/AS 400/36; Applications: INSI: Payroll, Circ, Accts payable, Adv, Gen ledger; Microsoft/Excel; PCs & main system networked.

SUMTER

Sumter County

'90 U.S. Census- 41,943; **E&P '96 Est.** 49,033
ABC-CZ (90): 63,831 (HH 20,402)

The Item (e-mon to fri; m-sat; S)

The Item, 20 N. Magnolia St. (29150); PO Box 1677, Sumter, SC 29151; tel (803) 775-6331; fax (803) 775-1024.
Circulation: 20,380(e); 20,380(m-sat); 20,283(S); ABC Sept. 30, 1995.
Price: 35¢(d); 35¢(sat); $1.00(S); $8.50/mo; $91.80/yr.
Advertising: Open inch rate $13.25(e); $13.25(m-sat); $13.25(S). **Representative:** Papert Companies.
News Services: AP, NEA. **Politics:** Independent. **Established:** 1894.
Not Published: Thanksgiving; Christmas.
Special Editions: Bride & Groom (Jan); Home & Gardens, Home Product Tab (Mar); Shaw AFB Retrospective, What's a Kid to Do Tab (May); Auto (June); Careers & Education, Football (Aug); Fall Fix Up (Sept); Business Expo Tab (Nov); Gift Guide (Dec).
Special Weekly Sections: Health/Science (mon); Arts/Culture (tues); Aging, Recipes and Ideas, Letters from Readers (wed); History/Community, Letters from Readers (thur); Local Events & Activities (fri); Family, The Mini Page, Religion (sat); Education & Opinion, Weddings & Engagements, Local Features, Business, Outdoors, Agriculture, Public Records (S).
Magazines: Star Watch (wed); Parade, TV Week (S).

CORPORATE OFFICERS

Board Chairman Margaret W Osteen
President Hubert D Osteen Jr
Vice Pres Hubert Graham Osteen II
Vice Pres Kyle Brown Osteen
Secretary Hubert Graham Osteen II

GENERAL MANAGEMENT

Publisher Hubert D Osteen Jr
General Manager Edward L Wazney
Business Manager Edward L Wazney
Manager-Credit Barbara Privette
Personnel Manager Edward L Wazney
Purchasing Agent Jeanette Gentele
Coordinator-Newspapers in Education Beverley Franz

ADVERTISING

Director Kyle Brown Osteen
Manager-Retail/Display Debora Sigmon
Manager-Classified Bobby Touchberry

MARKETING AND PROMOTION

Director-Marketing Caroline Sigmon

CIRCULATION

Director Earle Woodward
Manager-Distribution David Spencer

NEWS EXECUTIVES

Editor Hubert D Osteen Jr
Exec Editor Hubert Graham Osteen II

EDITORS AND MANAGERS

Action Line Editor Marilyn Anglea
Amusements Editor Rhonda Barrick
Automotive/Aviation Editor Robbie Evans
Business Editor Billy Quarles
City/Metro Editor Eileen Waddell
Editorial Page Editor Hubert Graham Osteen II
Education Editor Rhonda Barrick
Farm Editor Rhonda Barrick
Fashion/Society Editor Rhonda Barrick
Food Editor Rhonda Barrick
Graphics Editor/Art Director Jack Cooksey
Living/Lifestyle Editor Traci Duffy
National Editor Cleve O'Quinn
News Editor Billy Quarles
Photo Department Manager Bruz Crowson
Political/Government Editor Eileen Waddell
Sports Editor Robbie Evans
Teen-Age/Youth Editor Traci Duffy
Women's Editor Traci Duffy

MANAGEMENT INFORMATION SERVICES

Data Processing Manager Edward L Wazney

PRODUCTION

Superintendent Edward L Wazney
Foreman-Pressroom Wayne Geddings

Market Information: Zoned editions; TMC.
Mechanical available: Offset; Black and 3 ROP colors; insert accepted — preprinted, minimum 4" x 6"; page cut-offs — 21½".
Mechanical specifications: Type page 13" x 21½"; E - 6 cols, 2 1/16", ⅛" between; A - 6 cols, 2 1/16", ⅛" between; C - 8 cols, 1½", 1/12" between.
Commodity consumption: Newsprint 1,600 short tons; widths 27", 13"; black ink 18,000 pounds; color ink 1,200 pounds; average pages per issue 36(d), 90(S).
Equipment: EDITORIAL: Front-end hardware — 27-III/Tecs-2; Front-end software — III; Printers — 1-Toshiba/3-into-1 P3515X. CLASSIFIED: Front-end hardware — 8-III/Tecs-2; Front-end software — III; Printers — 1-Toshiba/3-into-1 P3515X. DISPLAY: Adv layout systems — 6-Ap/Mac; Front-end hardware — Ap/Mac; Front-end software — QuarkXPress, Multi-Ad/Creator, Aldus/FreeHand, Adobe/Illustrator, Broderbund/TypeStyler, Microsoft/Word, Microsoft/Excel 4.0, Claris/MacDraw II; Printers — HP/LaserJet IV, HP/DeskWriter C, Ap/Mac Personal LaserWriter; Other equipment — 1-Ap/Mac CD-Rom, 2-NEC/CD-Rom, 2-Ap/Mac Scanner, 1-Ap/Mac Modem. PRODUCTION: Typesetters — 2-V; Plate exposures — 1-Nu; Plate processors — 1-Nat; Scanners — 1-ECR; Production cameras — 1-Nu; Automatic film processors — 1-Konica/Nice print, 1-Konica/660, 1-Konica/4000; Color separation equipment (conventional) — 2-MHI, Lf/AP Leaf Picture Desk, 1-Lf/Leafscan 35, 1-Digi-Colour.
PRESSROOM: Line 1 — 7-G/Urbanite 772; Folders — G; Pasters — 6-Cary; Reels and stands — 2-G/Black Units (stacked); Press control system — 3-Fin. MAILROOM: Counter stackers — 1-BG/Count-O-Veyor, 2-QWI; Inserters and stuffers — 1-MM/6-into-1; Bundle tyer — 1-Dynaric; Wrapping singles — 1-QWI; Addressing machine — 1-KAN. LIBRARY: Electronic — III; Combination — Minolta/Microfilm. COMMUNICATIONS: Facsimile — 1-Canon. WIRE SERVICES: News — AP, AP GraphicsNet; Syndicates — NAS, TMS, WP, United Media, Creators, LATS; Receiving dishes — size-10ft, AP. BUSINESS COMPUTERS: 1-ATT/6386EW65; Applications: SMS: Circ, Accts receivable, Accts payable, Gen ledger, Payroll, Adv; PCs & micros networked; PCs & main system networked.

UNION

Union County

'90 U.S. Census- 9,836; **E&P '96 Est.** 9,439

Union Daily Times

(e-mon to sat)

Union Daily Times, 100 Times Blvd.; PO Box 749, Union, SC 29379; tel (864) 427-1234; fax (864) 427-1237. Mid-South Management Co. Inc. group.
Circulation: 6,601(e); 6,601(e-sat); Sworn Sept. 30, 1994.
Price: 35¢(d); 35¢(sat); $4.50/mo.
Advertising: Open inch rate $9.00(e); $9.00(e-sat).
News Services: NEA, AP. **Politics:** Independent. **Established:** 1850.
Not Published: Independence Day; Thanksgiving; Christmas.
Special Editions: Progress Edition; Christmas; Gardening; Spring Sports; Kudzu Festival; Graduation; Football.

CORPORATE OFFICER

President Phyllis DeLapp

GENERAL MANAGEMENT

Publisher David M (Mike) Pippen

ADVERTISING

Director Steve Blackwell

CIRCULATION

Manager Don Cody

NEWS EXECUTIVE

Editor Graham Williams

EDITORS AND MANAGERS

Editorial Page Editor Graham Williams
Food/Society Editor Anna Brown
Sports Editor Tracy Theo
Women's Editor Anna Brown

Market Information: Split Run; TMC.
Mechanical available: Offset; Black and 3 ROP colors; insert accepted — preprinted; page cut-offs — 21½".
Mechanical specifications: Type page 13" x 21½"; E - 6 cols, 2", ⅛" between; A - 6 cols, 2", ⅛" between; C - 9 cols, 1⅓", ⅛" between.
Commodity consumption: Newsprint 600 short tons; widths 28", 30", 34"; black ink 21,000 pounds; color ink 3,000 pounds; average pages per issue 12(d); single plates used 11,000.
Equipment: EDITORIAL: Front-end hardware — Wyse/PC, NEC/PC; Front-end software —

I-376 South Carolina

COM/Intrepid; Printers — Ap/Mac LaserWriter II NTX; Other equipment — Accuset/1200. CLASSIFIED: Front-end hardware — Wyse/PC, NEC/PC; Front-end software — COM/Intrepid; Printers — Ap/Mac LaserWriter II NTX; Other equipment — Accuset/1200. DISPLAY: Adv layout systems — Ap/Mac Classic, Ap/Mac SE, Ap/Mac Quadra; Front-end software — Quark-XPress, Aldus/PageMaker, Aldus/FreeHand, Adobe/Photoshop; Printers — Ap/Mac Laser-Writer II NTX, Accuset/1200. PRODUCTION: Typesetters — Accuset; Plate exposures — BKY/Ascor; Scanners — AG/Arcus, Abaton, Nikon; Production cameras — SCREEN; Automatic film processors — LE; Color separation equipment (conventional) — Ap/Mac Quadra. PRESSROOM: Line 1 — 9-KP/Newsking (w/KJ-8 balloon former); Press drives — GE/100 hp; Press control system — 8-ATR/Tensioning System; Press registration system — Carlson. MAILROOM: Counter stackers — 1-BG/Count-O-Veyor; Inserters and stuffers — 3-MM/227E; Bundle tyer — 2-MLN. WIRE SERVICES: News — AP; Receiving dishes — AP. BUSINESS COMPUTERS: PC; Applications: BMF; PCs & micros networked; PCs & main system networked.

SOUTH DAKOTA

ABERDEEN

Brown County

'90 U.S. Census- 24,927; E&P '96 Est. 24,487
ABC-CZ (90): 26,596 (HH 10,579)

Aberdeen American News

(m-mon to sat; S)

Aberdeen American News, 124 S. 2nd St.; PO Box 4430, Aberdeen, SD 57402-4430; tel (605) 225-4100; fax (605) 229-7532. Knight-Ridder Inc. group.

Circulation: 17,966(m); 17,966(m-sat); 20,099(S); ABC Sept. 30, 1995.

Price: 50¢(d); 50¢(sat); $1.25(S); $3.00/wk; $13.00/mo; $156.00/yr.

Advertising: Open inch rate $21.77(m); $21.77(m-sat); $23.65(S). **Representative:** Newspapers First.

News Services: AP, KRT. **Politics:** Independent. **Established:** 1885.

Special Editions: Perspective '96; Fair Days; Home Improvement; Dream Homes; Income Tax Guide; Back-to-School; Spring Farm Forum; Christmas Gift Guide; Hunter's Guide; Senior Lifestyles; Spring Home & Garden; Wedding Book; To Your Health; Football Preview; Basketball Preview; Fall Car Care; Spring Car Care; Personal Finance; Harvest.

Special Weekly Sections: Saver (mon); Best Food Day (wed); Out & About (Entertainment) (thur); Farm Forum (fri); Church Page (sat); Style Page (S).

Magazines: Sunday TV Preview, Comics, USA Weekend (S).

CORPORATE OFFICERS

President	Craig Wells
Vice Pres	Cindy Eikamp
Secretary	Douglas C Harris

GENERAL MANAGEMENT

Publisher	Craig Wells
Controller	Rita Johnsen
Manager-Human Resources	Susan Rozell

ADVERTISING

Director	Roger Brokke

TELECOMMUNICATIONS

Director-Info Systems	Dale Zalewski

CIRCULATION

Director	David Burgard
Manager-Office	Doug Schinkel

NEWS EXECUTIVES

Exec Editor	Cindy Eikamp
Managing Editor-City	Anita Meyer
Managing Editor-News	John Papendick

EDITORS AND MANAGERS

Amusements Editor	Don Hall
Editorial Page Editor	Betsy Rice
Farm/Agriculture Editor	Russ Keen
Features Editor	Marilyn Weishaar
Food/Garden Editor	Marilyn Weishaar
Music Editor	Don Hall
Sports Editor	Ronald Feickert
Sunday Editor	John Papendick
Teen-Age/Youth Editor	John Papendick
Women's Editor	Marilyn Weishaar

MANAGEMENT INFORMATION SERVICES

Data Processing Manager	Dale Zalewski

PRODUCTION

Director	Bob Herre
Manager-Camera/Plate	Joseph Burckhard
Manager-Press	Terry Salfrank
Manager-Mailroom	Paul Hanna
Manager-Composing	John Burckhard
Coordinator	Janie Patton

Market Information: TMC.

Mechanical available: Offset; Black and 3 ROP colors; insert accepted — preprinted; page cut-offs — 22¾".

Mechanical specifications: Type page $12\frac{13}{16}$" x 21½"; E - 6 cols, 2", ⅛" between; A - 6 cols, 2", ⅛" between; C - 8 cols, $1\frac{5}{8}$", ⅛" between.

Commodity consumption: Newsprint 1,565 short tons; 1,420 metric tons; widths 36", 13½", 27"; black ink 56,700 pounds; color ink 7,700 pounds; single pages printed 10,820; average pages per issue 26(d), 52(S); single plates used 24,000.

Equipment: EDITORIAL: Front-end hardware — Dewar/Disc Net IV; Front-end software — Dewar/Disc Net IV; Printers — Epson/LQ2550. CLASSIFIED: Front-end hardware — Dewar/Disc Net IV; Front-end software — Dewar/Disc Net IV; Printers — Okidata/182, Okidata/393. AUDIOTEX: Supplier name — Micro Voice. DISPLAY: Front-end hardware — Ap/Mac, Ap/Power Mac 8100; Front-end software — Multi-Ad/Creator 3.7; PRODUCTION: Pagination software — QuarkXPress 3.3; Typesetters — 2-AU/APS-6600, 1-AU/APS-6-82-ACS, AU/APS6-84ACS; Plate exposures — 1-Nu/Flip Top FTV6UPNS; Plate processors — 1-Nat/A-250; Electronic picture desk — Lf/AP Leaf Picture Desk, Adobe/Photoshop; Scanners — Lf/Leafscan 35, Howtek/Scanmaster 3+, AG/Arcus II; Production cameras — 1-B/4000, 1-C/Spartan II; Automatic film processors — 1-P/Litex 25, 1-SCREEN/LD-220-QT; Shrink lenses — CK Optical/SQU-7; Color separation equipment (conventional) — Lf/Leafscan 35, Howteck/Scanmaster 3+, Ap/Mac, AU/APS-6-82 ACS.
PRESSROOM: Line 1 — 7-G/Urbanite; Folders — 1-G; Pasters — Handmade; Press control system — Fin. MAILROOM: Counter stackers — 1-Id/NS440, 1-QWI/350; Inserters and stuffers — 1-MM/2275 (10 Station); Bundle tyer — 1-PSN/6E; Addressing machine — 1-Ch/528-010; Other mailroom equipment — MM/321 Fox. LIBRARY: Electronic — Vu/Text SAVE. WIRE SERVICES: News — AP Datafeatures, AP Datastream, KRT; Photos — AP; Receiving dishes — size-3m, AP. BUSINESS COMPUTERS: 1-HP/3000-5Y 937 RX; Applications: CJ: Gen ledger; PCs & micros networked; PCs & main system networked.

BROOKINGS

Brookings County

'90 U.S. Census- 16,270; E&P '96 Est. 16,940
ABC-CZ (90): 16,270 (HH 5,685)

Brookings Register

(e-mon to fri; m-sat)

Brookings Register, 312 5th St.; Box 177, Brookings, SD 57006; tel (605) 692-6271; fax (605) 692-2979. Omaha World-Herald Co. group.

Circulation: 5,847(e); 5,847(m-sat); ABC Sept. 30, 1994.

Price: 35¢(d); 35¢(sat); $1.57/wk; $78.00/yr (carrier).

Advertising: Open inch rate $7.93(e); $7.93(m-sat). **Representative:** Papert Companies.

News Service: AP. **Politics:** Independent. **Established:** 1879.

Note: On Mar. 4, 1995, the Brookings Register started publishing on Saturday.

Not Published: New Year; Memorial Day; Independence Day; Labor Day; Christmas.

Special Editions: Progress Edition (Mar); Business People (June); SDSU (University) Edition, Our Town (Aug).

Special Weekly Sections: Best Food Day (mon); Weddings, Business (tues); Agri-Business, Youth Features (wed); Arts, Outdoors, Religion (thur); Club & Community News (fri).

CORPORATE OFFICER

President	Terry Kroeger

GENERAL MANAGEMENT

Publisher	Joseph Karius

ADVERTISING

Manager	Phil Dahlmeier

CIRCULATION

Manager	Beverly Jensen

NEWS EXECUTIVE

Managing Editor	Amy Dunkle

EDITORS AND MANAGERS

News Editor	Dave Graves
Sports Editor	Billy McMacKen

PRODUCTION

Manager	Randall J Palli

Market Information: TMC.

Mechanical available: Offset; Black and 3 ROP colors; insert accepted — preprinted; page cut-offs — 22¾".

Mechanical specifications: Type page 13" x 21½"; E - 6 cols, 2", .19" between; A - 6 cols, 2", .19" between; C - 6 cols, 2", .19" between.

Commodity consumption: Newsprint 248 short tons; widths 32", 27"; black ink 9,500 pounds; color ink 1,400 pounds; average pages per issue 16(d), 16(sat); single plates used 6,000.

Equipment: EDITORIAL: Front-end hardware — Ap/Mac; Front-end software — QuarkXPress, WriteNow; Printers — Ap/Mac Laserwriter II, Ap/Mac LaserWriter Plus, Xante/1200; Other equipment — Dest/PC Scan 2000, Polaroid/SprintScan, Ap/Power Mac w/Adobe/Photoshop. CLASSIFIED: Front-end hardware — Ap/Power Mac 6100; Front-end software — SMS, Baseview/Class Ad; Printers — Ap/Mac LaserWriter Plus, Xante/1200; Other equipment — Dest/PC Scan 2000. DISPLAY: Adv layout systems — QuarkXPress; Front-end hardware — Ap/Mac SE, Ap/Mac w/Radius monitors, Ap/Power Mac 7100; Front-end software — Claris/MacDraw, Aldus/FreeHand, Multi-Ad/Creator; Printers — Ap/Mac Laser-Writer Plus, Xante/1200. PRODUCTION: Pagination software — QuarkXPress; Typesetters — Ap/Mac LaserWriter Plus NTX, Xante/1200; Plate exposures — Nu/UP platemaker; Plate processors — 1-Nat/A250; Electronic picture desk — Ap/Mac w/Adobe/Photoshop, Lf/AP Leaf Picture Desk; Production cameras — B/Horizontal; Automatic film processors — 1-LE/LD 1800A.
PRESSROOM: Line 1 — 5-G/Community; Folders — 1-G/SC (w/Upper former). MAILROOM: Inserters and stuffers — KAN/320 (5-into-1); Bundle tyer — 3-Bu; Addressing machine — Ch. WIRE SERVICES: News — AP; Photos — AP; Receiving dishes — size-2½ft, AP. BUSINESS COMPUTERS: 4-DEC; Applications: DSI/Paper Trak 2000; PCs & micros networked.

DEADWOOD

See SPEARFISH

HURON

Beadle County

'90 U.S. Census- 12,448; E&P '96 Est. 12,186
ABC-CZ (90): 12,845 (HH 5,392)

Huron Plainsman

(m-tues to sat; S)

Huron Plainsman, 49 3rd St. S.E.; PO Box 1278, Huron, SD 57350-1278; tel (605) 352-6401; fax (605) 352-7754. Omaha World-Herald Co. group.

Circulation: 9,387(m); 9,387(m-sat); 9,946(S); ABC Sept. 30, 1995.

Price: 50¢(d); 50¢(sat); $1.00(S); $8.00/mo; $96.00/yr.

Advertising: Open inch rate $9.65(m); $9.65(m-sat); $9.65(S); $8.00(m & S). **Representative:** Papert Companies.

News Service: AP. **Politics:** Independent. **Established:** 1885.

Note: Effective May 2, 1995, this publication changed its publishing plan from (e-mon to fri; S) to (m-tues to sat; S).

Not Published: New Year; Memorial Day; Independence Day; Labor Day; Thanksgiving; Christmas.

Advertising not accepted: Mail order.

Special Editions: Business & Agri-News, Senior Living (monthly).

Special Weekly Sections: Around Town (tues); Best Food Day, Food and Nutrition, Outdoors (wed); Extension (thur); Farm News, Church, Extension (fri); Society, Comics, Heartland Happening, Business (S); Sports, Public Record, Opinion, Comics, Markets, Heartland News, Community (daily).

Magazine: TV Guide (thur).

CORPORATE OFFICERS

President	Daryl Beall
Vice Pres/Secretary/Treasurer	A William Kernen

GENERAL MANAGEMENT

Publisher	Daryl Beall
Business Manager	Mary Walz

MARKETING AND PROMOTION

Manager-Marketing/Promotion	Susan Dietz

CIRCULATION

Director	Harvey Brock

NEWS EXECUTIVES

Exec Editor	Kurt Johnson
Managing Editor	Bette Pore
Assoc Editor	Dave Harles

EDITORS AND MANAGERS

Agriculture Editor	Robert Pore
Community Editor	Gloria Hanson
Political Editor	Roger Larsen
Region Editor	Crystal Pugsley
Sports Editor	Steve Merritt

PRODUCTION

Foreman-Pressroom	Gary Markesen
Manager-Pre Press	Gary Fenski
Manager-Mailroom	Robyn Worrall

Market Information: Zoned editions; Split Run; TMC.

Mechanical available: Offset; Black and 3 ROP colors; insert accepted — preprinted, card, envelope, single sheet; page cut-offs — 13".

Mechanical specifications: Type page 13" x 21½"; E - 6 cols, $2\frac{1}{16}$", ⅛" between; A - 6 cols, $2\frac{1}{16}$", ⅛" between; C - 8 cols, $1\frac{9}{16}$", $\frac{1}{16}$" between.

Commodity consumption: Newsprint 485 short tons; widths 27½", 13¾"; black ink 15,120 pounds; color ink 1,175 pounds; single pages printed 6,120; average pages per issue 16(d), 28(S); single plates used 12,650.

Equipment: EDITORIAL: Front-end hardware — 10-PC, 3-Ap/Power Mac; Front-end software — CText, QuarkXPress 3.3, Adobe/Photoshop 3.0; Printers — 1-Ap/Mac Laser, 1-LaserMaster/XLO; Other equipment — Polaroid/SprintScan 35. CLASSIFIED: Front-end hardware — 4-PC; Front-end software — CText; Printers — 1-Ap/Mac Laser. DISPLAY: Front-end hardware — 4-Ap/Mac; Front-end software — Multi-Ad/Creator, QuarkXPress, Adobe/Illustrator; Printers — 1-Ap/Mac Laser, 1-Xante/1200 DPI 11 x 17 Laser; Other equipment — 1-Flatbed Scanner. PRODUCTION: Typesetters — 3-Ap/Mac Laser; Platemaking systems — Nu/FT40 APNNS; Plate exposures — 1-Nu; Plate processors — 1-Nat/250; Production cameras — 1-Nikon, 1-SCREEN/Horizontal; Automatic film processors — P; Shrink lenses — 1-CK Optical.
PRESSROOM: Line 1 — 7-G/Community; Press drives — 1-Fin, 50 h.p.; Folders — 1-G/SC. MAILROOM: Inserters and stuffers — 5-DG; Bundle tyer — 1-Bu; Addressing machine — 1-Ch. COMMUNICATIONS: Facsimile — Sharp/Plain Paper. WIRE SERVICES: Receiving dishes — size-10m, AP. BUSINESS COMPUTERS: 3-IBM; Applications: Proprietary, Accts payable, Gen ledger, Accts receivable.

LEAD

See SPEARFISH

MADISON

Lake County

'90 U.S. Census- 6,257; E&P '96 Est. 6,280

The Madison Daily Leader

(e-mon to fri)

The Madison Daily Leader, 214 S. Egan Ave.; PO Box 348, Madison, SD 57042; tel (605) 256-4555; fax (605) 256-6190; e-mail hunterj@dsuvax.dsu.edu.

Circulation: 3,344(e); Sworn Oct. 1, 1995.

Price: 40¢(d); $6.50/mo; $73.00/yr (carrier).

Advertising: Open inch rate $4.70(e). **Representative:** American Newspaper Representatives Inc.

News Service: AP. **Politics:** Independent. **Established:** 1890.

Not Published: New Year; Independence Day; Labor Day; Thanksgiving; Christmas.

Special Editions: Business Review & Forecast (Feb); Prairie Village Jamboree (Aug).

Special Weekly Sections: Grocery (tues); Agri-News (wed); TV Guide (fri).

Magazine: TV Magazine (fri).

CORPORATE OFFICERS

President/Treasurer	Jon M Hunter
Vice Pres/Secretary	Beverly Hunter

Copyright ©1996 by the Editor & Publisher Co.

GENERAL MANAGEMENT
Publisher/Purchasing Agent .... Jon M Hunter
General Manager .... Jon M Hunter
ADVERTISING
Manager-Retail .... Glennys McCool
CIRCULATION
Manager .... Cheryl Wiseman
NEWS EXECUTIVE
Managing Editor .... Marcia Schoeberl
EDITORS AND MANAGERS
City Editor .... Alan Van Ormer
Editorial Writer .... Jon M Hunter
Sports Editor .... Dan Holsworth
Wire Editor .... Marcia Schoeberl
Women's Editor .... Rachel Miller
MANAGEMENT INFORMATION SERVICES
Data Processing Manager .... Nancy Jacobson
PRODUCTION
Foreman-Pressroom .... Keith Hakeman

Market Information: Split Run; TMC.
Mechanical available: Offset; Black and 3 ROP colors; insert accepted — preprinted; page cutoffs — 22¾".
Mechanical specifications: Type page 13.3" x 21"; E - 6 cols, 2.07', ⅛" between; A - 6 cols, 2.07", ⅛" between; C - 6 cols, 2.07", ⅛" between.
Commodity consumption: Newsprint 100 short tons; widths 28", 14"; single pages printed 2,800; average pages per issue 11(d); single plates used 1,400.
Equipment: EDITORIAL: Front-end hardware — PC/486 DX-2-50; Front-end software — Suntype/Editorial, Adobe/Photoshop 3.0; Printers — QMS/860 600 dpi. CLASSIFIED: Front-end hardware — PC/486 DX-2-66; Front-end software — QuarkXPress, Archetype/Corel Draw; Printers — QMS/860 600dpi. DISPLAY: Adv layout systems — PC/486 DX-2-66, Nikon/Coolscan, HP/ScanJet; Front-end software — QuarkXPress, Archetype/Corel Draw, Adobe/Photoshop; Printers — QMS/860. PRODUCTION: Pagination software — QuarkXPress; Typesetters — QMS/860+; Plate exposures — 2-Nu, Amerigraph; Scanners — HP/ScanJet, Nikon/Coolscan; Production cameras — B, SCREEN; Automatic film processors — Polychrome; Digital color separation equipment — PC486/DX2-66.
PRESSROOM: Line 1 — 5-G/Community single width; Folders — G/Community. MAILROOM: Counter stackers — 1-BG; Bundle tyer — 2-Bu; Wrapping singles — 1-Bu; Addressing machine — 2-Ch; Other mailroom equipment — Rosback/Stitcher-Trimmer. LIBRARY: Electronic — FolioViews; Combination — SunType/Editorial. COMMUNICATIONS: Facsimile — RSK/Tandy Fax; Systems used — satellite. WIRE SERVICES: News — AP; Syndicates — NAS, Universal Press; Receiving dishes — size-2ft, AP. BUSINESS COMPUTERS: 4-PC; Applications: Synaptic/Advanced: Accts payable; WordPerfect, Lotus 1-2-3, Javelin; PCs & micros networked.

MITCHELL
Davison County
'90 U.S. Census- 13,798; E&P '96 Est. 13,741

The Daily Republic
(m-mon to sat)

The Daily Republic, 120 S. Lawler St.; PO Box 1288, Mitchell, SD 57301; tel (605) 996-5514; fax (605) 996-7793. Forum Communications group.
Circulation: 12,075(m); 12,075(m-sat); Sworn Sept. 27, 1995.
Price: 50¢(d); 50¢(sat); $1.90/wk (carrier); $8.25/mo; $94.00/yr (carrier).
Advertising: Open inch rate $11.00(m); $13.00 (m-tues); $11.00(m-sat).
News Service: AP. **Politics:** Independent. **Established:** 1883.
Not Published: New Year; Memorial Day; Independence Day; Labor Day; Thanksgiving; Christmas.
Advertising not accepted: Morally offensive.
Special Editions: Bridal Edition (Jan); Farm & Ranch Edition (Feb); Home Improvement Series (Mar); Car Care Series (Apr); Lawn & Garden (May); Bridal Edition (June); Rodeo Edition (July); Progress Edition (Aug); Fall Home Improvement Series (Sept); Hunting Guide, Fall Car Care (Oct); Christmas Preview Edition (Nov).
Special Weekly Section: Best Food Day (tues).

GENERAL MANAGEMENT
Publisher/General Manager .... Steven K McLister
ADVERTISING
Director .... Linda Klein
CIRCULATION
Manager .... Don Fitzler
NEWS EXECUTIVE
Editor .... Noel L Hamiel
EDITORS AND MANAGERS
Sports Editor .... Korrie Wenzel
State Editor .... Kim Dohrer
PRODUCTION
Foreman-Composing .... Kevin Marx
Foreman-Pressroom .... Terry Abeln

Market Information: TMC.
Mechanical available: Offset; Black and 3 ROP colors; insert accepted — preprinted; page cutoffs — 22¾".
Mechanical specifications: Type page 13" x 21½"; E - 6 cols, 2¹⁄₁₆", ⅛" between; A - 6 cols, 2¹⁄₁₆", ⅛" between; C - 9 cols, 1½", ¹⁄₁₆" between.
Commodity consumption: Newsprint 388 short tons; widths 27½", 13¾"; black ink 10,800 pounds; color ink 900 pounds; single pages printed 5,526; average pages per issue 18(d); single plates used 6,448.
Equipment: EDITORIAL: Front-end hardware — HAS; Printers — V/5100 E; Other equipment — Ap/Mac. CLASSIFIED: Front-end hardware — Ap/Mac; Printers — V/5100 E. DISPLAY: Adv layout systems — 2-HAS, Ap/Mac; Front-end hardware — Ap/Mac; Front-end software — Multi-Ad, QuarkXPress, Adobe/Illustrator, Aldus/FreeHand; Printers — V/5100 E; Other equipment — Color Flatbed Scanner, Lf/Leafscan 35. PRODUCTION: Pagination software — CD; Typesetters — 3-V, V/5100 E, V/4990; Plate exposures — Nu/Ulta-Plus Flip Top; Plate processors — Nat/A-250; Scanners — Lf; Production cameras — 1-R/Press 500, 1-DSA/C-680-C; Automatic film processors — Jobo, AG/Rapidline 43, DTI/Devotec 20. PRESSROOM: Line 1 — 6-G/Community; Press registration system — Duarte/Pin System. MAILROOM: Bundle tyer — 2-Carlson; Addressing machine — 1-KR. WIRE SERVICES: News — AP; Photos — AP; Receiving dishes — size-1½m, AP. BUSINESS COMPUTERS: ATT; PCs & micros networked; PCs & main system networked.

PIERRE
Hughes County
'90 U.S. Census- 12,906; E&P '96 Est. 13,378

Capital Journal (e-mon to fri)

Capital Journal, 333 W. Dakota Ave.; PO Box 878, Pierre, SD 57501; tel (605) 224-7301; fax (605) 224-9210; e-mail 73613.3456@compuserve.com.
Circulation: 4,788(e); Sworn Sept. 30, 1994.
Price: 50¢(d); $2.00/wk; $7.50/mo; $70.00/yr.
Advertising: Open inch rate $6.00(e). **Representative:** American Newspaper Representatives Inc.
News Service: AP. **Politics:** Independent. **Established:** 1881.
Not Published: New Year; Memorial Day; Independence Day; Labor Day; Thanksgiving; Christmas.
Special Weekly Section: TV Preview (fri).
Magazine: Reminder Plus (wed).

CORPORATE OFFICER
President .... Terry J Hipple
GENERAL MANAGEMENT
Publisher .... Terry J Hipple

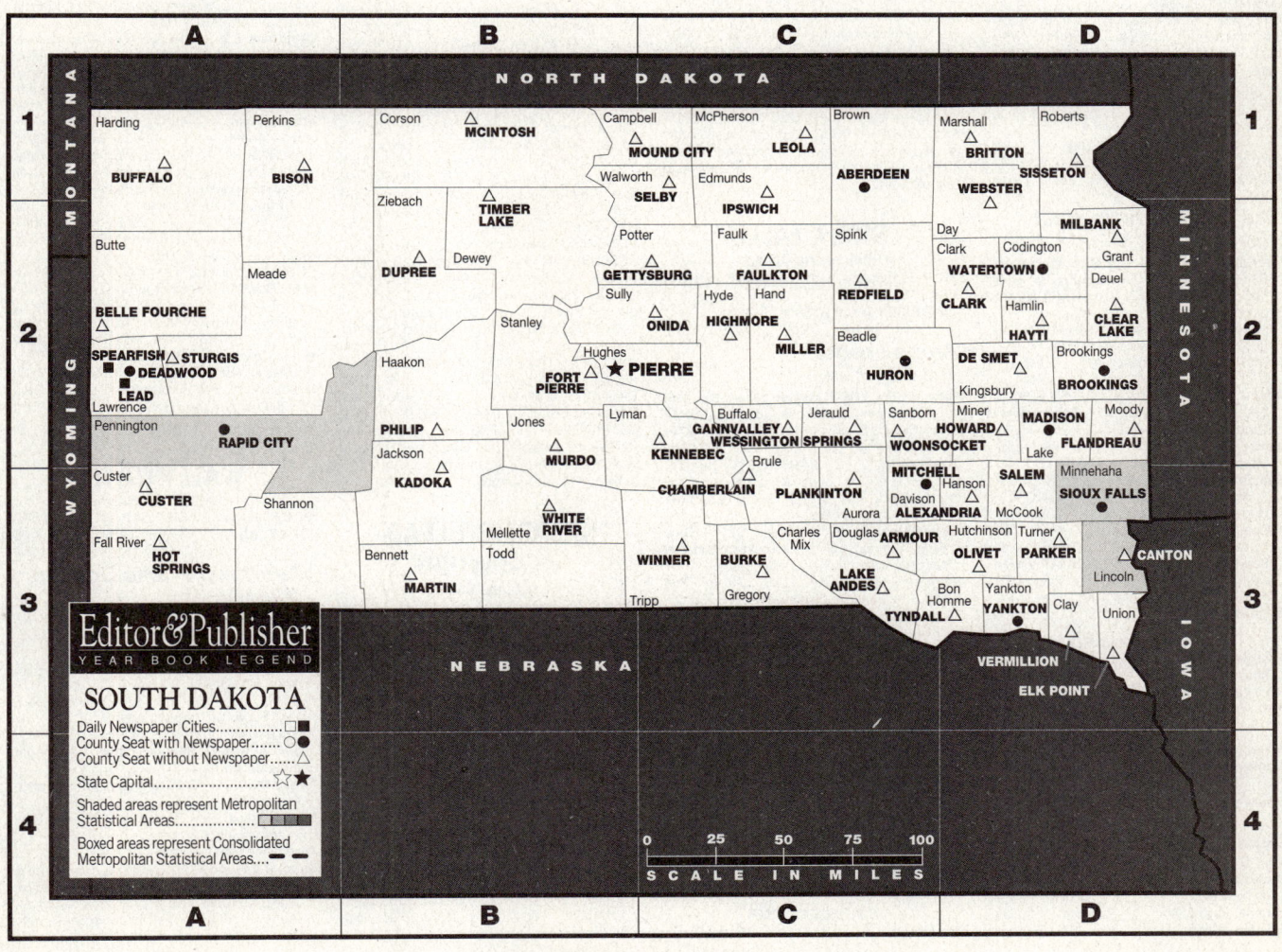

South Dakota I-377

Copyright ©1996 by the Editor & Publisher Co.

Vice Pres/Business Manager Brad Hipple
Business Manager Kevin Hipple

ADVERTISING

Manager Terry J Hipple

TELECOMMUNICATIONS

Audiotex Manager Terry J Hipple

CIRCULATION

Manager Terry J Hipple

NEWS EXECUTIVE

Editor Dana Hess

PRODUCTION

Superintendent Brad Hipple

Market Information: TMC; ADS; Operate audiotex.
Mechanical available: Offset; Black and 3 ROP colors; insert accepted — preprinted; page cut-offs — 22¾".
Mechanical specifications: Type page 13" x 21½"; E - 6 cols, 2 1/16", ⅛" between; A - 6 cols, 2 1/16", ⅛" between; C - 8 cols, 1 9/16", ⅛" between.
Commodity consumption: Newsprint 380 short tons; widths 28", 14"; black ink 6,000 pounds; color ink 120 pounds; single pages printed 4,550; average pages per issue 14(d); single plates used 8,500.
Equipment: EDITORIAL: Front-end hardware — Ap/Mac; Printers — Ap/Mac LaserWriter, Xante/8200. CLASSIFIED: Front-end hardware — Ap/Mac, IBM; Front-end software — Sun/Type 4.0; Printers — Ap/Mac LaserWriter. AUDIOTEX: Hardware — IBM; Software — Computer Group/Ads-on-call. DISPLAY: Adv layout systems — Ap/Mac; Printers — Ap/Mac LaserWriter, Xante. PRODUCTION: OCR software — TextBridge; Typesetters — Ap/Mac; Plate exposures — Nu/Flip Top FT40; Production cameras — Cl; Automatic film processors — P.
PRESSROOM: Line 1 — 4-G/Community. MAILROOM: Inserters and stuffers — 5-MM; Bundle tyer — 2-Bu/String Tyer, OVL; Addressing machine — 1-Ch/Model E base, 1-Wm. COMMUNICATIONS: Facsimile — Canon/8.5 x 11. WIRE SERVICES: News — AP; Receiving dishes — AP. BUSINESS COMPUTERS: 6-IBM/AT; Applications: Acct, Class, Spread sheet.

RAPID CITY

Pennington County

'90 U.S. Census- 54,523; E&P '96 Est. 60,576
ABC-CZ (90): 54,523 (HH 21,152)

The Rapid City Journal

(m-mon to sat; S)

The Rapid City Journal, 507 Main; PO Box 450, Rapid City, SD 57709; tel (605) 394-8300; fax (605) 394-8463; e-mail journ@rapidnet.com. Lee Enterprises Inc. group.
Circulation: 34,024(m); 34,024(m-sat); 36,061(S); ABC Sept. 30, 1995.
Price: 50¢(d); 50¢(sat); $1.50(S); $12.50/mo; $150.00/yr.
Advertising: Open inch rate $31.80(m); $31.80(m-sat); $31.80(S). **Representative:** Landon Associates Inc.
News Services: AP, NYT. **Politics:** Independent. **Established:** 1878.
Special Weekly Sections: Home & Garden, Sports (mon); Health & Fitness, Outdoor Update, Hometowns, Sports (tues); Food, Community Notes, Sports, Farm & Ranch Update (wed); Living, Outdoor Update, Sports, Hometowns (thur); Black Hills Weekend (fri); Outdoors, Hometowns, Forum, Religion, Sports, TV Journal (sat).
Magazine: Parade.

GENERAL MANAGEMENT

Publisher John VanStrydonck
Controller Judy Olson
Manager-Human Resources Linda J Harrington
Manager-Education Service Naomi Dempey

ADVERTISING

Manager-Classified Brad Slater
Manager-Retail Brenda Speth

CIRCULATION

Manager James P Christensen

NEWS EXECUTIVE

Editor-City Steve Miller

EDITORS AND MANAGERS

Business Editor Dan Daly
Copy Desk Chief Phyllis Pearson
Editorial Page Editor Theodore J Brockish
Education Editor Erin Andersen
Farm Editor Dick Rebbeck
Fashion/Garden Editor Robin McMacken
Features Editor Robin McMacken
Librarian Sheri Sponder
Outdoors Editor Dick Rebbeck
Special Sections Editor Laura Tonkyn
Sports Editor Don Lindner

MANAGEMENT INFORMATION SERVICES

Data Processing Manager Michael Doyle

PRODUCTION

Foreman-Composing Bruce Uhrig
Foreman-Mailroom Mark Gibbens

Market Information: Split Run; TMC.
Mechanical available: Offset; Black and 3 ROP colors; insert accepted — preprinted; page cut-offs — 22".
Mechanical specifications: Type page 13" x 21"; E - 6 cols, 2 1/16", ⅛" between; A - 6 cols, 2 1/16", ⅛" between; C - 9 cols, 1⅜", ⅛" between.
Commodity consumption: Newsprint 2,637 metric tons; widths 55", 41¼", 27½"; black ink 55,000 pounds; color ink 21,000 pounds; single pages printed 13,000; average pages per issue 28(d), 56(S); single plates used 24,000.
Equipment: EDITORIAL: Front-end hardware — 25-Dewar/Discribe, AST/286; Other equipment — 14-IBM/Selectric. CLASSIFIED: Front-end hardware — 6-Dewar/Discribe, SIA/386; Front-end software — Dewar; Other equipment — 6-IBM/Selectric. DISPLAY: Adv layout systems — 3-Dewar, SIA/386, AST/286; Front-end software — Dewar. PRODUCTION: Typesetters — Tegra/Varityper XP1000; Platemaking systems — WL, Nu/Flip Top; Plate exposures — WL; Plate processors — WL; Scanners — 2-ECR/Autokon 8400; Production cameras — C/Spartan III; Automatic film processors — LE/24; Color separation equipment (conventional) — Lf/Leafscan 35.
PRESSROOM: Line 1 — 5-G/Headliner(4 Color Decks); Folders — 2-G; Pasters — G; Reels and stands — 5-G. MAILROOM: Counter stackers — 2-Id/550; Inserters and stuffers — 1-MM/227E, 1-HI/1372; Bundle tyer — 3-MLN; Addressing machine — 1-Ch. COMMUNICATIONS: Facsimile — 1-Ricoh/Fax 20, 2-Ricoh/Fax 25. WIRE SERVICES: News — AP Datastream, AP Datafeatures, TV Data; Stock tables — AP; Syndicates — NYT; Receiving dishes — size-10ft, AP. BUSINESS COMPUTERS: 1-IBM/RS-6000; Applications: Gen ledger, Payroll, Accts payable, Circ, Accts receivable; PCs & micros networked; PCs & main system networked.

SIOUX FALLS

Minnehaha County

'90 U.S. Census- 100,814; E&P '96 Est. 115,148
ABC-CZ (90): 100,814 (HH 39,790)

Argus Leader

(m-mon to sat; S)

Argus Leader, 200 S. Minnesota Ave. (57102); PO Box 5034, Sioux Falls, SD 57117-5034; tel (605) 331-2200; fax (605) 331-2260 (Pub). Gannett Co. Inc. group.
Circulation: 51,303(m); 51,303(m-sat); 72,948(S); ABC Sept. 30, 1995.
Price: 50¢(d); 50¢(sat); $1.50(S); $3.25/wk; $169.00/yr (carrier).
Advertising: Open inch rate $38.48(m); $38.48(m-sat); $50.60(S). **Representative:** Gannett National Newspaper Sales.
News Services: AP, BPI, GNS, LAT-WP. **Politics:** Independent. **Established:** 1881.
Special Editions: Women (May); Welcome (Aug); Holiday Guide (Nov, Dec); Drive Time (monthly); Ninety-Eight Point Six (Health) (quarterly).
Special Weekly Sections: Young Life, Mutual Funds, Personal Finance, Business (mon); Outdoor/Recreation, Gardening (tues); Food, Life, Weddings, Shopping Leader (wed); Over the Fence, Venture (Entertainment) (thur); Movie Reviews, Entertainment, Weekend Calendar (fri); Religion News, Dakota Winds (sat); Lifestyles (sat once a month); Channels, Comics, Outdoor News (S); Dakota Dateline, Business (daily); Chamber News (monthly).
Magazines: Homes Mag (sat); USA Weekend, TV (S).

CORPORATE OFFICER

President Mary J Devish

GENERAL MANAGEMENT

Publisher Mary J Devish
Director-Human Resources Pat Curtis
Controller Jackie Stenseth

ADVERTISING

Director Martin Till
Manager-Retail Mark Gallaher
Manager-Classified Sales Lori Baye
Manager-Sales Denise Hoffman

MARKETING AND PROMOTION

Director-Marketing Brian Priester

CIRCULATION

Director John Vizzini
Asst Director Mary Bott

NEWS EXECUTIVES

Exec Editor John S Marsh Jr
Managing Editor Peter Ellis

EDITORS AND MANAGERS

Business Editor Brenda Wade Schmidt
City Editor Maricarrol Kueter
Editorial Page Editor Rob Swenson
Features Editor Jon Walker
News Editor Patrick Butler
Photo Chief Lloyd Cunningham
Sports Editor James Cheesman

PRODUCTION

Director Tom Boe
Manager-Pressroom Phil Mauk
Manager-Distribution Richard Thompson
Manager-Pre Press Joe Ziegler
Manager-Technical Service Adrien Miller

Market Information: TMC.
Mechanical available: Offset; Black and 3 ROP colors; insert accepted — preprinted, inquire; page cut-offs — 22¾".
Mechanical specifications: Type page 13" x 21½"; E - 6 cols, 2 1/16", ⅛" between; A - 6 cols, 2 1/16", ⅛" between; C - 9 cols, 1⅜", 1/16" between.
Commodity consumption: Newsprint 4,259 short tons; widths 54¾", 41⅛", 27⅜"; black ink 73,000 pounds; color ink 13,989 pounds; single pages printed 14,064; average pages per issue 30(d), 60(S); single plates used 32,000.
Equipment: EDITORIAL: Front-end hardware — SII/News Sys, 27-SII/EWS, 3-SII/XWS; Other equipment — 5-RSK/100, 3-RSK/200. CLASSIFIED: Front-end hardware — SII/Class Sys, 10-SII/Dakota EWS. DISPLAY: Adv layout systems — 7-Ap/Mac, 2-SII/XWS, 2-SII/EWS; Front-end hardware — 1-Ap/Mac 950, 5-Ap/Mac 850, Hyphen/File Sensor; Front-end software — Adobe/Photoshop, Multi-Ad/Creator, Aldus/PageMaker, Aldus/FreeHand, QuarkXPress; Printers — 2-Xante/Accel-a-Writer 8100. PRODUCTION: Typesetters — 2-COM/8668, 2-Hyphen/Image Setter; Plate exposures — 1-Amerigraph/437; Plate processors — 2-Nat; Electronic picture desk — Lf/AP Leaf Picture Desk; Production cameras — 1-C/Spartan III; Automatic film processors — 1-LE/LD24A; Film transporters — 1-C.
PRESSROOM: Line 1 — 6-HI/1650; Folders — 2-HI; Pasters — 6-HI/Auto. MAILROOM: Counter stackers — 2-Id/660, Id/2100; Inserters and stuffers — 1-HI/848; Bundle tyer — 1-MLN/2A, 1-MLN/2EE, MLN/News 90; Wrapping singles — Id/Plastic Wrap; Addressing machine — 1-Ch. WIRE SERVICES: News — AP, BPI, GNS, LAT-WP; Photos — AP, GNS, LAT-WP; Stock tables — AP SelectStox; Receiving dishes — size-3m, AP. BUSINESS COMPUTERS: 1-IBM/AS 400; Applications: Circ, Accts payable, Adv billing, Accts receivable, Payroll; PCs & micros networked; PCs & main system networked.

SPEARFISH-LEAD-DEADWOOD

Lawrence County

'90 U.S. Census- 12,428 (Lead 3,632; Deadwood 1,830; Spearfish 6,966) E&P '96 Est. 12,915 (Lead 3,323; Deadwood 1,736; Spearfish 7,856)

Black Hills Pioneer

(e-mon to fri; m-sat)

Black Hills Pioneer, 132 E. Grant; PO Box 7, Spearfish, SD 57783; tel (605) 642-2761; fax (605) 642-8179. Seaton group.
Circulation: 4,388(e); 4,388(m-sat); Sworn Sept. 27, 1994.
Price: 50¢(d); 50¢(sat); $6.00/mo; $72.00/yr.
Advertising: Open inch rate $8.00(e); $8.00(m-sat). **Representative:** Landon Associates Inc.
News Service: AP. **Politics:** Independent. **Established:** 1876 (Pioneer-Times), 1889 (Queen City Mail), 1894 (Call), 1993 (Black Hills Pioneer).
Not Published: New Year; Memorial Day; Independence Day; Labor Day; Thanksgiving; Christmas.
Special Editions: Black Hills Stock Show, Tax Tab, New Year's Eve (Jan); Valentine's Day, Health & Fitness (Feb); Progress, St. Patrick's Day (Mar); Home Improvement, Spearfish Optimist Home Show, Easter (Apr); Mother's Day, Graduation, Matthews Opera House (May); Belle Fourche "All Car Rally", Father's Day (June); Black Hills Roundup, 4th of July (July); Central States Fair, BHSU Edition, Deadwood Rodeo, Hills Alive (Music Festival) (Aug); Spearfish "Harvest Festival", Fall Sports, Football Contest (Sept); Swarm Day, Business & Profession, Halloween (Oct); Christmas Shopping, Thanksgiving, Christmas Greetings (Nov).
Special Weekly Section: Sports.

CORPORATE OFFICERS

Board Chairman R M Seaton
President Donald R Seaton
Exec Vice Pres Bill Masterson Jr
Vice Pres Edward Seaton

GENERAL MANAGEMENT

Publisher Bill Masterson Jr

ADVERTISING

Manager Letitia Lister

CIRCULATION

Manager Janet Asheim

NEWS EXECUTIVE

Exec Editor Larry Weiers

EDITORS AND MANAGERS

City Editor Todd Williams
City Editor Bill Cissell

PRODUCTION

Manager Scott Lister

Market Information: TMC; ADS.
Mechanical available: Offset; Black and 3 ROP colors; insert accepted — preprinted, all sizes; page cut-offs — 22¾".
Mechanical specifications: Type page 10¼" x 13½"; E - 5 cols, 1", ½" between; A - 5 cols, 1", ½" between; C - 5 cols, 1", ½" between.
Commodity consumption: Newsprint 300 metric tons; widths 34", 28"; black ink 12,000 pounds; color ink 2,000 pounds; single pages printed 7,200; average pages per issue 36(d); single plates used 4,000.
Equipment: EDITORIAL: Front-end hardware — 7-Ap/Mac, 7-HI/Compuedit format, 1-Ap/Mac; Printers — 3-Ap/Mac LaserWriter, 1-NewGen/Laserwriter 1200 DPI, 2-HP; Other equipment — Ap/Mac Scanners. CLASSIFIED: Front-end hardware — 1-Ap/Mac. DISPLAY: Adv layout systems — 2-Ap/Mac. PRODUCTION: Typesetters — Ap/Mac LaserWriter II, Ap/Mac LaserWriter Plus, Ap/Mac NT, Ap/Mac NTX; Platemaking systems — B; Plate exposures — 1-B/1500; Plate processors — Nu/Flip Top FT52; Scanners — 2-Ap/Mac Scanner; Production cameras — 1-B/4000; Automatic film processors — 1-P/4700.
PRESSROOM: Line 1 — 4-G; Folders — 1-G. MAILROOM: Inserters and stuffers — 1-KAN/4-station; Bundle tyer — 3-Bu; Wrapping singles — 1-Bu; Addressing machine — 1-Wm. WIRE SERVICES: News — AP; Receiving dishes — size-3ft, AP. BUSINESS COMPUTERS: Ap/Mac II, IBM/XT, Ap/Mac, RSK/Tandy 100; Applications: Bus, Typesetting, Layout, Circ; PCs & micros networked; PCs & main system networked.

WATERTOWN

Codington County

'90 U.S. Census- 17,592; E&P '96 Est. 18,597
ABC-CZ (90): 18,282 (HH 7,253)

Watertown Public Opinion

(e-mon to sat)

Watertown Public Opinion, 120 3rd Ave. N.W.; PO Box 10, Watertown, SD 57201; tel (605) 886-6901; fax (605) 886-4280.
Circulation: 15,062(e); 15,062(e-sat); ABC Sept. 30, 1995.
Price: 50¢(d); 50¢(sat); $7.90/mo (carrier); $91.80/yr, $81.00/yr (mail).
Advertising: Open inch rate $13.57(e); $13.57(e-sat). **Representative:** Newspaper Mktg Group.
News Service: AP. **Politics:** Independent. **Established:** 1887.
Not Published: New Year; Independence Day; Thanksgiving; Christmas.
Advertising not accepted: Mail order.
Special Editions: Agriculture, Building & Remodeling (Feb); Spring Fashion, Auto Care (Mar); Outdoor Tab (Apr); Back-to-School (Aug); Hunting Tab, Fall Fashion (Sept); Auto Care (Oct).

Special Weekly Sections: Green Farm Tab (fri); Builders Page (sat).
Magazines: Green Farm Tab, TV Week (fri).

CORPORATE OFFICERS
President Kenneth B Way
Vice Pres John R Lowrie
Secretary/Treasurer Steven W Lowrie

GENERAL MANAGEMENT
Publisher Steven W Lowrie
General Manager Steven W Lowrie
Manager-Systems/Office Steven W Lowrie

ADVERTISING
Manager A W (Windy) Johnson

MARKETING AND PROMOTION
Director-Marketing Christine Carter

CIRCULATION
Manager Paul C Reinschmidt

NEWS EXECUTIVE
Editor Gordon R Garnos

EDITORS AND MANAGERS
Action Line Editor John R Lowrie
Amusements Editor Gordon R Garnos
City Editor Robert P Mooney
Editorial Page Editor Gordon R Garnos
Farm Editor Jason Nordmark
Fashion/Neighbors Editor Carol Andring
Sports Editor J T Fey
Wire Editor Jo Ann Goette
Women's Editor Carol Andring

PRODUCTION
Manager-Press Dean Borns
Manager-Pre Press Pete Mack

Market Information: Split Run; TMC.
Mechanical available: Offset; Black and 3 ROP colors; insert accepted — preprinted; page cut-offs — 21½".
Mechanical specifications: Type page 13" x 21½"; E - 6 cols, 2 1/16", ⅛" between; A - 6 cols, 2 1/16", ⅛" between; C - 8 cols, 1½", ⅛" between.
Commodity consumption: Newsprint 750 short tons; widths 27½", 13¾"; black ink 18,700 pounds; color ink 3,000 pounds; single pages printed 7,702; average pages per issue 26(d); single plates used 7,000.
Equipment: EDITORIAL: Front-end hardware — Ap/Mac; Front-end software — QuarkXPress, Baseview/NewsEdit; Printers — Ap/Mac. CLASSIFIED: Front-end hardware — Ap/Mac, Baseview/Class Manager Plus; Front-end software — QuarkXPress, Baseview/NewsEdit; Printers — Ap/Mac LaserPrinter. DISPLAY: Front-end hardware — Ap/Mac; Front-end software — Aldus/PageMaker, QuarkXPress; Printers — NewGen/Turbo, Ap/Mac. PRODUCTION: Pagination software — QuarkXPress; Typesetters — Ap/Mac; Plate exposures — 1-Nu; Plate processors — 1-Nat/A-250; Production cameras — 1-B/1822, 1-DAI/0-24-D; Automatic film processors — SCREEN/LD-281-Q; Color separation equipment (conventional) — 1-Digi-Colour.
PRESSROOM: Line 1 — 5-HI/Cotrell 845; Folders — 1-G. MAILROOM: Inserters and stuffers — 1-KAN/480; Bundle tyer — 1-Bu/20, 1-Bu/18; Addressing machine — 1-Ch/528-041. WIRE SERVICES: News — AP; Receiving dishes — size-3m, AP. BUSINESS COMPUTERS: 1-IBM/Sys 36; Applications: Aldus/PageMaker, QuarkXPress; PCs & micros networked.

YANKTON
Yankton County
'90 U.S. Census- 12,703; E&P '96 Est. 13,049

Yankton Daily Press & Dakotan (m-mon to sat)
Yankton Daily Press & Dakotan, 319 Walnut St.; PO Box 56, Yankton, SD 57078; tel (605) 665-7811; fax (605) 665-1721. Morris Communications Corp. group.
Circulation: 9,243(m); 9,243(m-sat); Sworn Sept. 29, 1995.
Price: 50¢(d); 50¢(sat); $7.95/mo; $95.40/yr.
Advertising: Open inch rate $9.10(m); $9.10(m-sat). **Representative:** Papert Companies.
News Service: AP. **Politics:** Independent. **Established:** 1861.
Not Published: New Year; Memorial Day; Independence Day; Labor Day; Thanksgiving; Christmas.
Special Editions: Yankton Health, Tax Tab, Annual Chamber Report, Yankton Directory, Farm Show Tab, Salute to Police Dept. (Feb); Weeder's Digest (Mar); Spring Fashion Tab (Apr); Lake Tab, Graduation Tab (May); Treasure Hunt, Trivia Contest (June); Riverboat Days Tab, Back-to-School Tab (Aug); Christmas Lay Away, Fall Football Section (Sept); Fall Fashion Tab, Dining Guide, Fall Car Showing (Oct); Turkey Give-Away, Silver Salute, Early Shoppers Edition, Basketball Section (Nov); Holiday Cookbook, Late Shoppers Edition, Christmas Gift Ideas (Dec).
Special Weekly Sections: Best Food Day, Dining & Entertainment (tues); Dining & Entertainment (thur); Church Listings (fri); P & D Weekender, Auto Buyer's Guide (sat).
Magazines: TV Section, "River City Currents" (sat).

CORPORATE OFFICERS
Chairman of the Board W S Morris III
President Paul S Simon
Vice Pres for Newspapers Edward B Skinner

GENERAL MANAGEMENT
Publisher Don Smith
Business Manager Larry Benson

ADVERTISING
Manager Christy Orwig

NEWS EXECUTIVE
Editor Don Smith

EDITORS AND MANAGERS
Education Editor Lilah Gillis
Sports Editor Kelly Hertz

MANAGEMENT INFORMATION SERVICES
Data Processing Manager Larry Benson

PRODUCTION
Supervisor Bob Miles

Market Information: TMC.
Mechanical available: Offset; Black and 3 ROP colors; insert accepted — preprinted, packaged material, samples ¼' thick & under; page cut-offs — 22¾".
Mechanical specifications: Type page 13" x 21½"; E - 6 cols, 2 1/16", ⅛" between; A - 6 cols, 2 1/16", ⅛" between; C - 6 cols, 2 1/16", ⅛" between.
Commodity consumption: Newsprint 500 short tons; widths 27½", 27", 33"; single pages printed 5,500; average pages per issue 16(d), 20(sat); single plates used 3,750.
Equipment: EDITORIAL: Front-end hardware — Ap/Mac; Front-end software — QuarkXPress, Baseview/Extensions; Printers — Ap/Mac LaserWriter, MON/Express Master 1270. CLASSIFIED: Front-end hardware — Ap/Mac; Front-end software — Baseview; Printers — Ap/Mac ImageWriter, Ap/Mac LaserWriter. DISPLAY: Front-end hardware — Ap/Mac, Ap/Mac IIcx, Ap/Mac IIsi, Ap/Mac SE, Ap/Mac w/ Radius Monitor, 2-Ap/Mac Quadra 800, 3-Ap/Power Mac 6100, 1-Ap/Power Mac 9500-132; Front-end software — Multi-Ad/Creator; Printers — Ap/Mac LaserWriter IIg, MON/Express Master 1270. PRODUCTION: Pagination software — QuarkXPress 3.3; OCR software — Caere/OmniPage 2.0; Typesetters — Ap/Mac LaserWriter; Plate exposures — 1-Nu; Plate processors — Nat/A-250; Electronic picture desk — Adobe/Photoshop, Ap/Mac; Scanners — Ap/Mac, Nikon, Ap/Mac Scanner; Production cameras — B/Caravel; Automatic film processors — Jobo; Color separation equipment (conventional) — Nikon, Ap/Mac; Digital color separation equipment — Ap/Mac, MON.
PRESSROOM: Line 1 — 7-HI/V15A single width (w/upper former); Press registration system — Circumferetial. MAILROOM: Inserters and stuffers — 4-KAN/DG-320; Bundle tyer — 2-Bu/1900, 1-Malow/40; Addressing machine — 1-X, Ch/515. LIBRARY: Electronic — SMS/Stauffer Gold. WIRE SERVICES: News — AP; Receiving dishes — size-18", AP. BUSINESS COMPUTERS: Unix/80486; Applications: Proprietary; PCs & micros networked; PCs & main system networked.

TENNESSEE

ALCOA
See MARYVILLE

ATHENS
McMinn County
'90 U.S. Census- 12,054; E&P '96 Est. 12,033
ABC-CZ (90): 12,054 (HH 4,844)

The Daily Post-Athenian
(e-mon to fri)
The Daily Post-Athenian, 320 S. Jackson St.; PO Box 340, Athens, TN 37303; tel (423) 745-5664. Media Services group.
Circulation: 10,633(e); ABC Sept. 30, 1995.
Price: 50¢(d); $5.75/mo; $67.00/yr.
Advertising: Open inch rate $10.25(e). **Representative:** Landon Associates Inc.
News Service: AP. **Politics:** Independent. **Established:** 1848.
Not Published: Christmas.
Special Editions: January Clearance, Income Tax Guide, Senior Scene, Blood Donor Month (Jan); Boy Scout Salute, FFA Salute, Valentine's Gift Ideas, Progress, National Heart Month, Children Dental Month, Junior Achievement, Bridal Gift Guide (Feb); Girl Scout Salute, Farming Salute, Spring Fashion Issue, Spring Home Improvement (Mar); Health & Fitness, Recycle/Earth Day, American Home Week, Easter Sunday, Secretaries Week (Apr); Industry Salute, Keepsake, Mother's Day, Memorial Day, In Memory Page, National Nursing Home Week, Graduation/Prom Drunk Driving (May); Dairy Salute, Graduation, Father's Day, Summer Living (June); County Fair, 4th of July, Crime Prevention (July); Back-to-School Schedules, FYI, Football Contest Pages, Senior Scene, Parenting (Aug); Football Edition, Hunting & Fishing Specials, Fall Home Improvement, Labor Day Salute, Literary Salute (Sept); Car Care Guide, Working Women, National Bosses' Day, 4-H Salute, Halloween Safety Tips, Fire Prevention (Oct); Holiday Extravaganza, Holiday Cookbook, Veteran's Salute (Nov); Holiday Gift Ideas, Friendly Fellow Greetings, Drunk Driving (Dec).
Special Weekly Sections: Farm Page, Education (wed); Business (thur).
Magazines: TV Weekly Listings, Entertainment (fri).

GENERAL MANAGEMENT
Publisher/General Manager Ralph C Baldwin
Business Manager Rhonda Whaley

ADVERTISING
Director Sara Jane Locke

CIRCULATION
Manager Tom Cogdell

NEWS EXECUTIVE
Editor Doug Headrick

EDITORS AND MANAGERS
Editorial Writer Doug Headrick
Home Furnishings Editor Durrell Linton
Sports Editor Jack Slayton

MANAGEMENT INFORMATION SERVICES
Data Processing Manager Rhonda Whaley

PRODUCTION
Superintendent-Pressroom James King

Market Information: TMC.
Mechanical available: Offset; Black and 3 ROP colors; insert accepted — preprinted, in-house printed; page cut-offs — 22¾".
Mechanical specifications: Type page 13¼" x 21½"; E - 6 cols, 2 1/16", ⅛" between; A - 6 cols, 2 1/16", ⅛" between; C - 9 cols, 1 5/16", ⅛" between.
Commodity consumption: Newsprint 700 short tons; width 27½"; black ink 24,000 pounds; color ink 2,300 pounds; single pages printed 6,240; average pages per issue 24(d); single plates used 6,000.
Equipment: EDITORIAL: Front-end hardware — 1-Mk. CLASSIFIED: Front-end hardware — Hyundai/Synaptic Software. DISPLAY: Adv layout systems — Ap/Mac II. PRODUCTION: Typesetters — 2-Ap/Mac Laser; Platemaking systems — 1-Nu; Plate exposures — 1-Nu; Plate processors — 1-WL, Nat; Production cameras — 1-C, 1-Argyle, 1-C/Spartan II; Automatic film processors — 1-LE; Color separation equipment (conventional) — 1-Colortran.
PRESSROOM: Line 1 — 8-G; Folders — 1-G. MAILROOM: Inserters and stuffers — 3-MM; Bundle tyer — 2-Ca, 1-MLN; Addressing machine — 1-KR/Single Head. WIRE SERVICES: News — AP; Receiving dishes — AP. BUSINESS COMPUTERS: 1-Flex Cache/20386 DT; Applications: Accounting, Circ, TMC packages.

BRISTOL
See BRISTOL, VA

CHATTANOOGA
Hamilton County
'90 U.S. Census- 152,466; E&P '96 Est. 140,106
ABC-CZ (90): 241,099 (HH 97,830)

Chattanooga Free Press
(e-mon to sat; S)
Chattanooga Free Press, 400 E. 11th St.; PO Box 1447, Chattanooga, TN 37401-1447; tel (423) 756-6900; fax (423) 757-6337; web site http://www.chatfreepress.com/.
Circulation: 40,801(e); 40,801(e-sat); 111,224(S); ABC Sept. 30, 1995.
Price: 50¢(d); 50¢(sat); $1.50(S); $2.80/wk (eS); $12.14/mo.
Advertising: Open inch rate $22.38(e); $22.38(e-sat); $39.00(S); comb with Chattanooga Times (m) $31.20. **Representative:** Landon Associates Inc.
News Service: AP. **Politics:** Independent. **Established:** 1888.
Note: The Free Press and the Chattanooga Times are corporately and editorially separate but operate otherwise under a joint agreement with the Chattanooga Publishing Co., which acts as an agent for the two papers.
Advertising not accepted: Alcoholic beverages.
Special Editions: Progress (Feb); Home Improvements (Apr); Products & Services (July); Back-to-School, Football (Aug); Home Improvements (Sept); Health Trends, Dining Out (Oct); Gift Guide (Nov).
Special Weekly Sections: Lifestyle (mon); Health and Fitness (tues); Food, Lifestyle (wed); Lifestyle (thur); Kids Page, Lifestyle, Dining Out & Entertainment (fri); Church News, Lifestyle (sat); Arts & Travel, TV Magazine, Real Estate (S); Business, Sports, Entertainment (daily).
Magazine: Parade (S).

CORPORATE OFFICERS
Board Chairman Frank McDonald
President Frank McDonald
Exec Vice Pres Helen Exum
Vice Pres Roy Exum
Secretary Jeanne Johnston
Treasurer Clifford Welch

GENERAL MANAGEMENT
Publisher Lee S Anderson
Business Manager Russell Lively
Manager-Credit Peggy Blaylock
Purchasing Agent Jeanne Johnston

ADVERTISING
Director Dan Nausley
Manager-Retail Dan Card
Manager-Classified James McNelly
Manager-National Michelle Wagner

MARKETING AND PROMOTION
Director-Marketing/Promotion Dan Nausley

TELECOMMUNICATIONS
Audiotex Manager Charles Coulter

CIRCULATION
Director Gerry Gifford
Manager-Single Copy Sales Larry Sanders

NEWS EXECUTIVE
Editor Lee S Anderson

EDITORS AND MANAGERS
Art Editor Pete Hunter
Automobile Editor Judy Kimbro
Book Editor Helen Exum
Business Editor John Vass
City Editor Julius Parker
Editorial Art Director Pete Hunter
Editorial Page Editor Lee S Anderson
Fashion Editor Diane Siskin
Films/Theater Editor June Hatcher
Food/Garden Editor Helen Exum
Librarian Jackie Punneo
News Editor Stanton Palmer
Photo Department Manager John Penalver
Religion Editor Jim Ashley
Society Editor Susan Pierce
Exec Sports Editor Roy Exum
Asst Sports Editor Sam Woolwine
Travel Editor Diane Siskin
Urban Affairs Editor J B Collins

MANAGEMENT INFORMATION SERVICES
Data Processing Manager Glen Crawford

PRODUCTION
Director-Operations Frank Anthony
Manager-Pressroom Paul Campbell
Manager-Engraving Michael Miller
Manager-Mailroom Steve Richardson
Manager-Composing Cathy Lewis
Asst Manager Gary Webb

Copyright ©1996 by the Editor & Publisher Co.

Market Information: Zoned editions; Split Run; TMC; ADS; Operate audiotex.
Mechanical available: Letterpress (direct); Black and 3 ROP colors; insert accepted — preprinted; page cut-offs — 22¾".
Mechanical specifications: Type page 13" x 21¾"; E - 6 cols, 2", ⅙" between; A - 6 cols, 2", ⅙" between; C - 9 cols, 1⅓", 1/12" between.
Commodity consumption: Newsprint 15,791 short tons; widths 27½", 41¼", 55"; black ink 490,674 pounds; color ink 134,849 pounds; single pages printed 38,718; average pages per issue 38(d), 178(S); single plates used 83,678.
Equipment: EDITORIAL: Front-end hardware — 4-DEC/PDP 11-93, 2-Ap/Mac Quadra, 7-HI/2100, 2-HI/XP-21; Front-end software — Phoenix/EMS; Printers — DEC, HP, Ap/Mac, NewGen; Other equipment — 1-Sharp/JX-610 scanner. CLASSIFIED: Front-end hardware — 4-DEC/PDP 11-93, HI/2100, HI/XP-21, Ap/Mac Quadra; Front-end software — Phoenix/CMS, HI/Classified; Printers — DEC; Other equipment — 1-Sharp/JX-610 scanner. AUDIOTEX: Hardware — PC/486; Software — Info-Connect; Supplier name — TMS, AP. DISPLAY: Adv layout systems — Mk/Managing Editor, Mk/Ad Director; Front-end hardware — Sun/Sparc 2, Dell/486; Front-end software — HI/Advertising. PRODUCTION: Pagination software — QuarkXPress 3.5; Typesetters — 3-Unity, 2-ECR/1054C, 1-Graphic Enterprises/PageScan III Plus; Plate exposures — MAS; Plate processors — Na/Np-80; Electronic picture desk — Lf/AP Leaf Picture Desk, Ap/Mac Network, Adobe/Photoshop; Scanners — Nikon, 1-Sharp/JX-610, Kk, 2-ECR/Autokon, 2-Kk; Production cameras — 2-C; Automatic film processors — 2-Kk/520, 2-Kk/710; Color separation equipment (conventional) — Ap/Mac.
PRESSROOM: Line 1 — 8-G/Mark II; Folders — 2-G/3:2; Pasters — 8-G/Automatic; Reels and stands — 8-G; Press control system — Hurletron. MAILROOM: Counter stackers — 4-Id/2100, 1-Id/440, 1-QWI; Inserters and stuffers — 1-MM/375, 2-MM/227; Bundle tyer — 4-Power Strap; Addressing machine — 2-Ch; Other mailroom equipment — MM/221. LIBRARY: Electronic — Mead Data Central/Newsview, Mead Data Central/Photoview. WIRE SERVICES: News — AP, AP Datafeatures, TV Data; Photos — AP; Stock tables — AP; Syndicates — LATS, TMS; Receiving dishes — size-3m, AP. BUSINESS COMPUTERS: IBM/AS-400; Applications: Circ, Adv billing, Accts receivable, Payroll, Class; PCs & main system networked.

The Chattanooga Times

(m-mon to sat)

The Chattanooga Times, 100 E. 10th St.; PO Box 951, Chattanooga, TN 37401; tel (423) 756-1234; fax (423) 752-3388; web site http://www.chattimes.com/.
Circulation: 40,337(m); 40,337(m-sat); ABC Sept. 30, 1995.
Price: 50¢(d); 50¢(sat); $1.30/wk; $5.64/mo; $61.60/yr.
Advertising: Open inch rate $22.38(m); $22.38(m-sat); comb with Chattanooga Free Press (eS) $31.20. **Representative:** Landon Associates Inc.
News Services: AP, NYT. **Politics:** Independent. **Established:** 1869.
Note: For detailed information on production & printing, see Chattanooga Free Press listing.
Special Weekly Sections: Lifestyle (mon); Health and Fitness (tues); Food, Lifestyle (wed); Lifestyle (thur); Kids Page, Lifestyle, Dining Out & Entertainment (fri); Church News (sat); Arts & Travel, TV Magazine, Real Estate (S); Business, Sports, Entertainment (daily).

CORPORATE OFFICERS

President — A William Holmberg
Chairman of the Board — Ruth S Holmberg
Vice Pres/Treasurer — Stephen S Ingham
Secretary — J Guy Beatty Jr

GENERAL MANAGEMENT

Publisher — Paul Neely
General Manager — Stephen S Ingham

ADVERTISING

Director — Dan Nausley
Director-Classified — James McNelly
Director-Retail — Dan Card

NEWS EXECUTIVES

Managing Editor — Ronald C Smith
Asst Managing Editor — Mary Clarke Guenther

EDITORS AND MANAGERS

Books Editor — Wes Hasden
Business Editor — David Flessner
City Life Editor — John Gerome
Crime & Courts Editor — Mark Curridan
Editorial Page Editor — Michael Loftin
Entertainment Editor — Judy Walton
Food Editor — Suzanne Hall
Graphics Director — Walt Strizkland
Garden Editor — Patricia Lea
Leisure Editor — Noble Sprayberry
News Editor — Keith Vallier
Personal Life Editor — Mark Kennedy
Regional Editor — Judy Walton
Religion Editor — Michelle Baum
Sports Editor — Andy Daffron

Market Information: Zoned editions; TMC; ADS.
Mechanical available: Letterpress; Black and 3 ROP colors; insert accepted — preprinted; page cut-offs — 22¾".
Mechanical specifications: Type page 13" x 21¾"; E - 6 cols, 2", ⅙" between; A - 6 cols, 2", ⅙" between.
Commodity consumption: average pages per issue 28(d).
Equipment: WIRE SERVICES: News — AP, NYT; Photos — AP, NYT; Stock tables — AP; Receiving dishes — AP.

CLARKSVILLE

Montgomery County

'90 U.S. Census- 75,494; E&P '96 Est. 98,536
ABC-NDM (90): 100,498 (HH 34,345)

The Leaf-Chronicle

(m-mon to sat; S)

The Leaf-Chronicle, 200 Commerce St.; PO Box 829, Clarksville, TN 37041-0829; tel (615) 552-1808; fax (615) 648-8001. Gannett Co. Inc. group.
Circulation: 20,887(m); 20,887(m-sat); 23,565(S); ABC Sept. 30, 1995.
Price: 50¢(d); 50¢(sat); $1.25(S); $2.15/wk; $111.80/yr.
Advertising: Open inch rate $22.08(m); $22.08(m-sat); $22.94(S). **Representative:** Landon Associates Inc.
News Service: AP. **Politics:** Independent. **Established:** 1808.
Special Weekly Sections: Food Days (mon, wed, S); TV Page, Business Page (daily).
Magazines: TV Week; Parade.

CORPORATE OFFICERS

Vice Pres — F Gene Washer
Secretary — B N Smith
Treasurer — William DeB Mebane
Asst Treasurer — B N Smith

GENERAL MANAGEMENT

Publisher — F Gene Washer
Human Resources — Pat Goodwin
Manager-Credit — Michael Winn
Controller — B N Smith
Assoc Publisher — Don Connor

ADVERTISING

Manager-Classified/Consumer — Carrie Profit
Manager — Lee Ireland
Manager-National/Co-Op — Ray Roby

MARKETING AND PROMOTION

Director-Marketing — Don Connor

CIRCULATION

Director — Susan Miles
Manager-Mail — Reiner Davis

NEWS EXECUTIVE

Editor — Doug Ray

EDITORS AND MANAGERS

Business/Finance Editor — Jimmy Settle
City Editor — Patricia Ferrier
Asst City Editor — Terry Hollahan
Copy Desk Chief — Dewayne Wilson
Editorial Page Editor — Alane Megna
Fashion/Features Editor — Christine Kroeger
Food/Home Furnishings Editor — Christine Kroeger
Librarian — Julie Bartoch
Photo/Graphics Coordinator — Isolde Ray
Religion Editor — Jim Monday
Sports Editor — Larry Schmidt

PRODUCTION

Manager-Operations — Don Connor
Superintendent-Composing — Ronald Kendrick
Superintendent-Graphic Arts — Ronald Kendrick

Market Information: Zoned editions; Split Run; TMC.
Mechanical available: Offset; Black and 3 ROP colors; insert accepted — preprinted, all; page cut-offs — 21½".
Mechanical specifications: Type page 12⅞" x 21½"; E - 6 cols, 2", ⅙" between; A - 6 cols, 2", ⅙" between; C - 10 cols, 1¼", 1/12" between.
Commodity consumption: Newsprint 2,377 short tons; widths 27½", 13¾"; black ink 49,000 pounds; color ink 4,900 pounds; single pages printed 11,142; average pages per issue 30(d), 100(S); single plates used 8,000.
Equipment: EDITORIAL: Front-end hardware — Mk. CLASSIFIED: Front-end hardware — Mk; Other equipment — 3-IBM/Selectric II. DISPLAY: Adv layout systems — Mk. PRODUCTION: Typesetters — 2-ECR/Autokon Pel box 108; Platemaking systems — 3M/Pyrofax; Plate exposures — 1-Nu/Ultraplus; Plate processors — 1-WL/24; Scanners — 1-Graphic Enterprises/PageScan III; Production cameras — 1-B/24, 1-ECR/Autokon; Automatic film processors — 2-DP/24L, 1-LE/PC13; Shrink lenses — 1-Pyroflex/2430; Color separation equipment (conventional) — C/7080.
PRESSROOM: Line 1 — 10-G/Urbanite; Line 2 — 6-KP/Newsking; Folders — 1-G, 1-KP. MAILROOM: Counter stackers — 1-Id/2000; Inserters and stuffers — 1-HI/624, 1-MM/227; Bundle tyer — 2-MLN/ML2EE; Addressing machine — 1-MG/602, 1-Am/8000, 1-AVY/5209. COMMUNICATIONS: Facsimile — 2-X/400, AP Laserphoto; Systems used — satellite. WIRE SERVICES: News — AP Dataspeed, AP Datafeatures; Stock tables — NYSE, Amex, Mutual Funds; Syndicates — LAT-WP; Receiving dishes — size-8ft, AP. BUSINESS COMPUTERS: 1-IBM/AS400; Applications: Circ, Adv billing, Accts receivable, Gen ledger, Payroll, Accts payable, Lineage, Subscriber/Non-subscriber, Adv manifest; PCs & main system networked.

CLEVELAND

Bradley County

'90 U.S. Census- 30,354; E&P '96 Est. 33,972
ABC-CZ (90): 36,975 (HH 14,389)

Cleveland Daily Banner

(e-mon to fri; S)

Cleveland Daily Banner, 1505 25th St. N.W.; PO Box 3600, Cleveland, TN 37320; tel (423) 472-5041; fax (423) 476-1046. Cleveland Newspapers Inc. group.
Circulation: 16,159(e); 18,015(S); ABC Sept. 30, 1995.
Price: 25¢(d); 75¢(S); $6.00/mo (carrier).
Advertising: Open inch rate $7.70(e); $7.70(S). **Representative:** Papert Companies.
News Service: AP. **Politics:** Independent. **Established:** 1854.
Not Published: Christmas.
Advertising not accepted: Fortune telling.
Special Editions: Progress; Shopping Centers; Outdoors; Fashion; Baby; Bride; Christmas; School; Home Improvement; Monthly Shopping; Automotive.
Magazines: USA Weekend; Comics.

CORPORATE OFFICERS

Board Chairman — C Lee Walls
President — C Lee Walls

GENERAL MANAGEMENT

Publisher — Pledger L Wattenbarger
Controller — Joyce Taylor
Manager-Credit — Joyce Taylor
Personnel Manager — Pledger L Wattenbarger
General Manager — Jim Bryant

ADVERTISING

Director — Jack Bennett
Manager-Retail — Ron Kosemund
Manager-Classified — Debbie Arthur

MARKETING AND PROMOTION

Manager-Promotion — Jack Bennett

CIRCULATION

Manager — Todd Cunningham

NEWS EXECUTIVES

Exec Editor — George Starr
Editor — Pledger L Wattenbarger

EDITORS AND MANAGERS

Editorial Page Editor — Pledger L Wattenbarger
Education Editor — Angela Brown
Farm Editor — Betty Marlowe
Fashion/Food Editor — Tammie Goins
Films/Theater Editor — Byron Clarke
Garden Editor — Tammie Goins
Librarian — Mary Matthews
Living/Lifestyle Editor — Betty Marlowe
News Editor — George Starr
Society Editor — Betty Marlowe
Sports Editor — Chuck Thurmond
Women's Editor — Betty Marlowe

MANAGEMENT INFORMATION SERVICES

Data Processing Manager — Susan Carter

PRODUCTION

Foreman-Composing — Susan Carter
Foreman-Pressroom — Richard Anderson

Market Information: TMC.
Mechanical available: Offset; Black and 3 ROP colors; insert accepted — preprinted; page cut-offs — 21½".
Mechanical specifications: Type page 13" x 21½"; E - 6 cols, 2 1/16", ⅛" between; A - 6 cols, 2 1/16", ⅛" between; C - 6 cols, 2 1/16", ⅛" between.
Commodity consumption: Newsprint 784 short tons; widths 27½", 13¾"; black ink 25,000 pounds; color ink 2,500 pounds; single pages printed 8,652; average pages per issue 22(d), 46(S); single plates used 11,720.
Equipment: EDITORIAL: Front-end hardware — 12-Ap/Mac 15" color terminal; Front-end software — Baseview/News Edit Pro 1.0.4; Printers — 1-Xante/Accel-a-Writer 8200, 1-QMS/810. CLASSIFIED: Front-end hardware — 3-Ap/Mac 15" color terminal; Front-end software — Baseview/Classflow; Other equipment — IPC/HSPTR. DISPLAY: Adv layout systems — 4-Ap/Mac 7100; Front-end software — QuarkXPress 3.31, Multi-Ad/Creator 3.7; Printers — 2-Panther/Plus Imagesetter, 1-Xante/Accel-a-Writer 8200, 1-QMS/810. PRODUCTION: Pagination software — QuarkXPress 3.31; Typesetters — 2-Panther/Plus Imagesetter; Plate exposures — 1-Nu; Plate processors — 1-Nat; Electronic picture desk — Lf/AP Leaf Picture Desk, Ap/Mac 8100; Scanners — 1-Sharp/JX-450 Flatbed, 1-Lf/Leafscan 35; Production cameras — 1-C/Spartan III; Automatic film processors — 1-P, LE/Line 17, 1-K/550C; Reproportion units — Lf/AP Leaf Picture Desk; Film transporters — Konica/K-550C; Digital color separation equipment — Sharp/JX-450, Lf/Leafscan 35, AG/Arcus II Flatbed Scanner, Ap/Mac 8100 w/Photoshop 3.0.4.
PRESSROOM: Line 1 — 1-WPC/Quadra-Color single width, 9-WPC/Perfector single width; Line 2 — 9-WPC/Perfector single width; Press drives — 2-Marathon/200 AMP Drives; Folders — 2-Web Leader/Marc-25; Reels and stands — 9-Web Leader/Marc-25 roll stand; Press control system — Marathon. MAILROOM: Inserters and stuffers — 6-MM; Bundle tyer — Strapex. WIRE SERVICES: News — AP; Photos — AP; Receiving dishes — AP. BUSINESS COMPUTERS: 2-RSK/Tandy, 2-Mitsuba; Applications: Adv billing, Accts receivable, Gen ledger, Payroll, Circ; PCs & micros networked.

COLUMBIA

Maury County

'90 U.S. Census- 28,583; E&P '96 Est. 30,498
ABC-CZ (90): 28,583 (HH 11,267)

The Daily Herald

(e-mon to fri; S)

The Daily Herald, 1115 S. Main St. (38401); PO Box 1425, Columbia, TN 38402-1425; tel (423) 388-6464; fax (423) 388-1003. Donrey Media group.
Circulation: 11,567(e); 13,344(S); ABC Sept. 30, 1995.
Price: 50¢(d); $1.00(S); $6.25/mo (carrier); $75.00/yr (mail).
Advertising: Open inch rate $11.10(e); $11.10(S). **Representative:** Papert Companies.
News Services: AP, NEA. **Politics:** Independent. **Established:** 1899.
Not Published: New Year; Memorial Day; Independence Day; Labor Day; Thanksgiving; Christmas.
Advertising not accepted: Fortune teller; Adoptions.
Special Editions: Spring Fashion (Apr); Graduation (May); Bridal (June); Football (Aug); Fall Fashion (Sept); Christmas Gift Guide (Nov); Christmas Greetings (Dec).
Special Weekly Sections: Best Food Day (wed); Church Page (fri); Lifestyles, Showtime TV Guide, Business Section, Sports Section (S).
Magazine: Parade (S).

CORPORATE OFFICERS

Founder — Donald W Reynolds
President/Chief Operating Officer — Emmett Jones
Exec Vice Pres/Chief Financial Officer — Darrell W Loftin
Vice Pres-Eastern Newspaper Group — Don Schneider
Vice Pres-Western Newspaper Group — David Osborn

GENERAL MANAGEMENT
Publisher .... S D Beel
Manager-Credit .... Betty Stewart
ADVERTISING
Manager .... Charles Martin
CIRCULATION
Manager .... Fred Chappell
NEWS EXECUTIVE
Editor .... Don Hinkle
EDITORS AND MANAGERS
Farm Editor .... Keith Talley
News Editor .... Keith Talley
Outdoors Editor .... Marion Wilhoite
Photo Department Manager .... Susan Thurman
Picture Editor .... Fay Delk
Religion Editor .... Marvine Sugg
Society Editor .... Marvine Sugg
Sports Editor .... Marion Wilhoite
PRODUCTION
Manager .... Wendell Boyd

Market Information: Zoned editions; TMC.
Mechanical available: Offset; Black and 3 ROP colors; insert accepted — preprinted; page cut-offs — 21½".
Mechanical specifications: Type page 13" x 21½"; E - 6 cols, 2 1/16", 1/8" between; A - 6 cols, 2 1/16", 1/8" between; C - 8 cols, 1 3/8", 1/16" between.
Commodity consumption: Newsprint 600 short tons; width 27"; black ink 18,500 pounds; color ink 5,400 pounds; single pages printed 7,838; average pages per issue 24(d), 40(S); single plates used 5,600.
Equipment: EDITORIAL: Front-end hardware — Mk/1100 Plus, Ap/Mac; Printers — 4-Ap/Mac LaserWriter II, 3-Ap/Mac LaserWriter Plus. CLASSIFIED: Front-end hardware — Mk; Front-end software — Mk/1100 Plus; Printers — 2-Ap/Mac Laser. PRODUCTION: Typesetters — 2-Mk/Ad Touch, 2-Mk/TouchWriter Plus; Plate exposures — 1-Nu/Flip Top FT40; Plate processors — 1-Nat/A-250; Direct-to-plate imaging — 3M/Deadliner; Scanners — 1-Ap/Mac; Production cameras — 1-C/Spartan II; Automatic film processors — 1-P; Shrink lenses — lk.
PRESSROOM: Line 1 — 8-G/Community; Folders — 6-G. MAILROOM: Counter stackers — MSI; Inserters and stuffers — HI/NP624; Bundle tyer — 2-Bu, Akebond/Strapper; Addressing machine — Ch/Labeler. WIRE SERVICES: News — AP; Photos — AP; Receiving dishes — AP. BUSINESS COMPUTERS: Unisys, HP; Applications: CJ; Adv billing, Circ; PCs & micros networked; PCs & main system networked.

COOKEVILLE
Putnam County
'90 U.S. Census- 21,744; **E&P '96 Est.** 22,767
ABC-CZ (90); 25,210 (HH 9,941)

Herald-Citizen
(e-mon to fri; S)
Herald-Citizen, 124 S. Dixie Ave.; PO Box 2729, Cookeville, TN 38502; tel (615) 526-9715; fax (615) 526-1209. Cleveland Newspapers Inc. group.
Circulation: 10,974(e); 13,276(S); ABC Sept. 30, 1995.
Price: 35¢(d); 75¢(S) $5.50/mo (carrier); $16.50/3 mo (mail); $63.00/yr (carrier).
Advertising: Open inch rate $8.38(e); $8.38(S).
Representative: Papert Companies.
News Service: AP. **Politics:** Independent. **Established:** 1903.
Not Published: New Year; Independence Day; Labor Day; Thanksgiving; Christmas.
Special Editions: Progress (Jan); Home Show, Lawn & Garden (Feb); Venture Tourist Magazine (with 100,000 overprint for Tourist Development Agency)(May); Cookeville Cookoff Community Festival, Local Church Directory (Aug); Holidays in Upper Cumberland (Nov).
Special Weekly Sections: Best Food Day (mon); Business (wed); School News (thur); Auto Dealers, Church News (fri); Business, Auto Dealers, Real Estate (S).
Magazines: Parade, Focus TV Tab (S).

GENERAL MANAGEMENT
Publisher .... Bill Shuster
ADVERTISING
Manager .... Albert Thompson
MARKETING AND PROMOTION
Director-Marketing .... Albert Thompson
CIRCULATION
Manager .... Keith McCormick
NEWS EXECUTIVE
Exec Editor .... Charles Denning

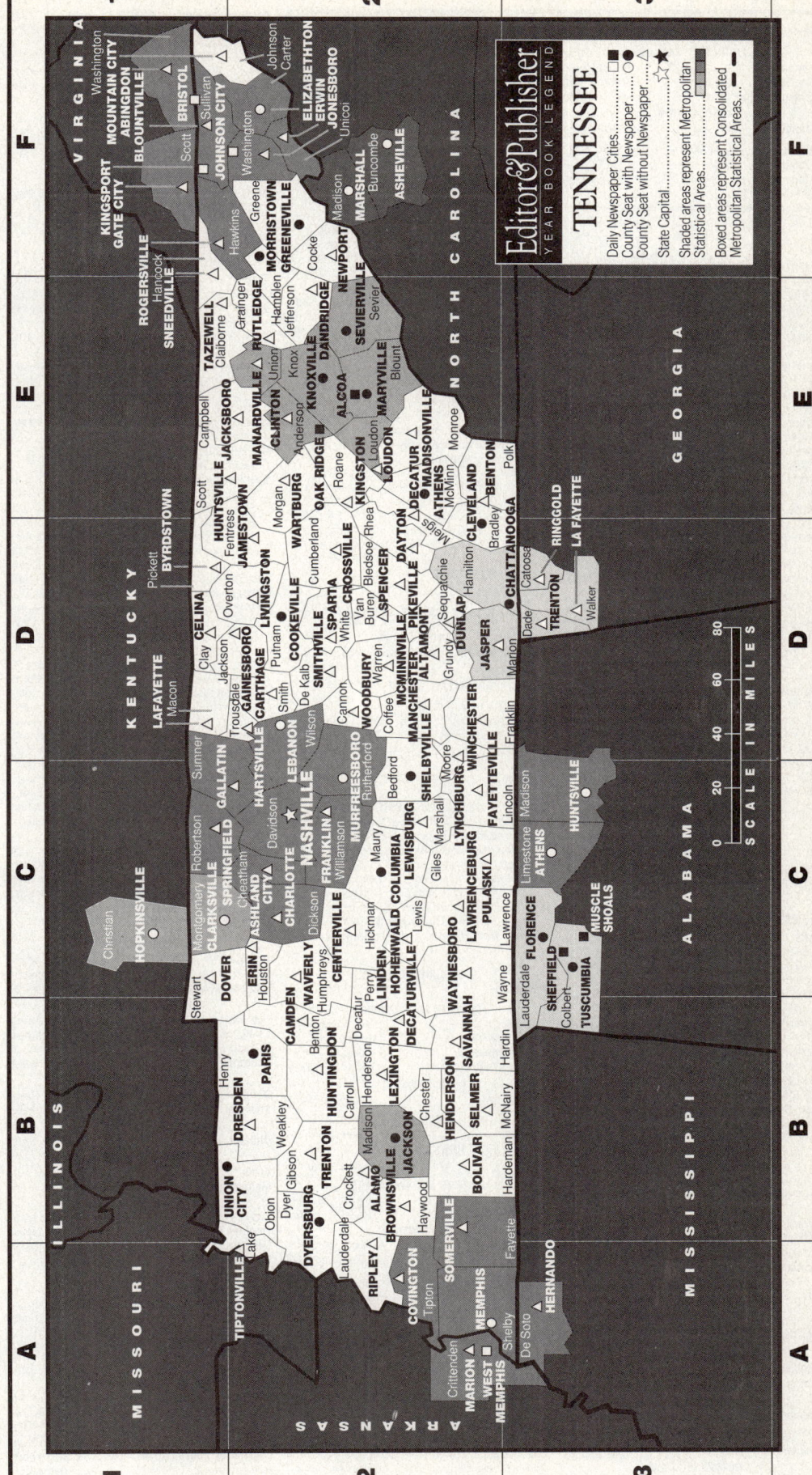

Copyright ©1996 by the Editor & Publisher Co.

EDITORS AND MANAGERS

Sports Editor Frank Layne
Wire Editor Bob McMillan
Women's Editor Debra Rami

PRODUCTION

Manager Stan Bullington

Market Information: Zoned editions; TMC; ADS.
Mechanical available: Offset; Black and 3 ROP colors; insert accepted — preprinted; page cut-offs — 22¾".
Mechanical specifications: Type page 13" x 21½"; E - 6 cols, 2 1/16", ⅛" between; A - 6 cols, 2 1/16", ⅛" between; C - 6 cols, 2 1/16", ⅛" between.
Commodity consumption: Newsprint 638 short tons; widths 14", 28"; black ink 11,635 pounds; color ink 1,424 pounds; single pages printed 6,578; average pages per issue 16(d), 40(S); single plates used 6,715.
Equipment: EDITORIAL: Front-end hardware — Mk; Front-end software — Mk; Printers — Ap/Mac LaserPrinter, Epson/Epl 7500. CLASSIFIED: Front-end hardware — IBM, RSK/Tandy; Front-end software — CText; Printers — Panasonic/KX-P1624, Ap/Mac LaserWriter Plus; Other equipment — PB/phone modem. DISPLAY: Front-end hardware — 2-Ap/Mac Quadra 700, Ap/Mac Quadra; Front-end software — Multi-Ad/Creator, Adobe/Illustrator; Printers — Ap/Mac LaserPrinter, HP/LaserJet. PRODUCTION: Pagination software — QuarkXPress 3.3; Typesetters — HP, Epson, V/3990; Plate exposures — Nu; Plate processors — Roconex; Electronic picture desk — Ap/Mac Quadra 800, AG/Arcus Plus Scanner; Scanners — Umax/UC 840; Production cameras — SCREEN; Automatic film processors — Glunz & Jenson, Konica/550; Color separation equipment (conventional) — Hel/299. PRESSROOM: Line 1 — WPC/Leader (4 b/w units; 1 Quadra color); Line 2 — WPC/Leader (3 b/w units); Folders — 2-WPC; Reels and stands — 7-WPC/Leader; Press control system — WPC/Leader. MAILROOM: Inserters and stuffers — MM/227 (5-into-1); Bundle tyer — MLN/Spirit, Strapex, Minimatic/351; Addressing machine — 3-Dispensa-Matic/16. COMMUNICATIONS: Facsimile — Canon/Fax L-700. WIRE SERVICES: News — AP; Receiving dishes — AP. BUSINESS COMPUTERS: RSK/4000LX, DEC/XL-466; Applications: PBS/MediaPlus.

DYERSBURG

Dyer County

'90 U.S. Census- 16,317; E&P '96 Est. 16,696
ABC-CZ (90): 16,317 (HH 6,696)

State Gazette (m-tues to sat; S)

State Gazette, 294 Hwy. 51-Bypass; PO Box 808, Dyersburg, TN 38024; tel (901) 285-4091; fax (901) 285-9747. Paxton Media group.
Circulation: 8,409(m); 8,409(m-sat); 8,409 (S); ABC Sept. 30, 1995.
Price: 50¢(d); 50¢(sat); 50¢(S); $6.50/mo (carrier), $8.35/mo (mail); $100.20/yr (mail).
Advertising: Open inch rate $11.25(m); $11.25(m-sat); $11.25(S). **Representative:** Papert Companies.
News Service: AP. **Politics:** Independent. **Established:** 1865.
Note: Effective Oct. 1, 1995, this publication changed its publishing plan from (e-mon to fri) to (m-tues to sat; S). Sunday circulation figure is an estimate.
Not Published: Independence Day; Thanksgiving; Christmas.
Advertising not accepted: Massage parlor, etc.
Special Editions: Progress; Brides; Home for the Holidays.
Special Weekly Sections: Food Section (wed); TV Entertainer (fri); Business (daily).
Magazine: Weekly TV Section (local).

CORPORATE OFFICER

President/CEO Fred Paxton

GENERAL MANAGEMENT

Publisher Billy R Smith
Controller Jeff King

ADVERTISING

Director Johnny McConnell

CIRCULATION

Director Doug Cook

NEWS EXECUTIVE

Exec Editor Dannye Crouch

EDITORS AND MANAGERS

City Editor Donna Whittle
Editorial Page Editor Dannye Crouch
Sports Coordinator Gayle Cavness

MANAGEMENT INFORMATION SERVICES

Data Processing Manager Jeff King

PRODUCTION

Manager-Press David Stom

Market Information: TMC.
Mechanical available: Offset; Black and 3 ROP colors; insert accepted — preprinted, single cards or sheets; page cut-offs — 22¾".
Mechanical specifications: Type page 13" x 21½"; E - 6 cols, 2 1/16", ⅛" between; A - 6 cols, 2 1/16", ⅛" between; C - 8 cols, 1 9/16", 1/16" between.
Commodity consumption: Newsprint 445 short tons; widths 27½", 13¾"; single pages printed 4,539; average pages per issue 18(d); single plates used 2,610.
Equipment: EDITORIAL: Front-end hardware — Dewar, 9-ZC/1060. CLASSIFIED: Front-end hardware — 2-ZC/1060. DISPLAY: Adv layout systems — 1-Dewar/Discovery. PRODUCTION: Typesetters — 2-COM/8400; Plate exposures — 1-Nu/Flip Top; Plate processors — 1-Nat/A-250; Production cameras — 1-R/401; Automatic film processors — 1-P. PRESSROOM: Line 1 — 6-KP; Folders — 1-KP/2:1. MAILROOM: Inserters and stuffers — KAN/480; Bundle tyer — 1-Yamada Tom; Addressing machine — 1-El. WIRE SERVICES: News — AP; Syndicates — Universal Press, NEA, King Features; Receiving dishes — AP. BUSINESS COMPUTERS: IBM/Sys 36; Applications: Accounting, Circ.

ELIZABETHTON

Carter County

'90 U.S. Census- 11,931; E&P '96 Est. 11,547

Elizabethton Star (e-mon to fri; S)

Elizabethton Star, 300 Sycamore St.; PO Box 1960, Elizabethton, TN 37643; tel (423) 928-4151, (423) 542-4151; fax (423) 542-2004.
Circulation: 9,021(e); 9,021(S); Sworn Sept. 29, 1995.
Price: 35¢(d); $1.00(S); $90.00/yr.
Advertising: Open inch rate $9.50(e); $9.50(S). **Representative:** Papert Companies.
News Service: AP. **Politics:** Independent. **Established:** 1914.
Not Published: New Year; Memorial Day; Independence Day; Labor Day; Christmas.
Special Editions: Progress; June Bride; Profitable Farming; Christmas Gift Guide.
Special Weekly Section: Entertainment Spotlight (fri).

CORPORATE OFFICER

President Charles I Robinson

GENERAL MANAGEMENT

Publisher Charles I Robinson
Assoc Publisher Harvey Prichard
General Manager Delaney Scalf
Business Manager Nathan O'Dell

ADVERTISING

Director Harvey Prichard

CIRCULATION

Manager Gene Helmick

NEWS EXECUTIVE

Editor Rozella Hardin

EDITORS AND MANAGERS

Home Furnishings Editor Rozella Hardin
Teen-Age/Youth Editor Rozella Hardin

PRODUCTION

Superintendent Delaney Scalf
Foreman-Pressroom Thomas Jung

Market Information: Zoned editions; TMC.
Mechanical available: Offset; Black and 3 ROP colors; insert accepted — preprinted; page cut-offs — 22⅝".
Mechanical specifications: Type page 13" x 21½"; E - 6 cols, 2 1/16", ⅛" between; A - 6 cols, 2 1/16", ⅛" between; C - 9 cols, 1½", ⅛" between.
Commodity consumption: average pages per issue 18(d), 38(S).
Equipment: EDITORIAL: Front-end hardware — COM; Other equipment — 1-BM. CLASSIFIED: Front-end hardware — COM; Printers — Ap/Mac LaserWriter; Other equipment — 1-BM. PRODUCTION: Typesetters — 1-COM/8400, 3-Ap/Mac Plus, 2-Ap/Mac LaserWriter, ECR; Plate processors — 1-Ic/Icm25-1; Production cameras — III/Sparta; Automatic film processors — P/24; Color separation equipment (conventional) — Ca. PRESSROOM: Line 1 — 7-HI/V-15-A. MAILROOM: Addressing machine — KR/Inserter. WIRE SERVICES: News — AP; Receiving dishes — AP. BUSINESS COMPUTERS: 1-IBM/3600; PCs & main system networked.

GREENEVILLE

Greene County

'90 U.S. Census- 13,532; E&P '96 Est. 13,097
ABC-CZ (90): 13,532 (HH 5,581)

The Greeneville Sun (e-mon to fri; m-sat)

The Greeneville Sun, 121 W. Summer; PO Box 1630, Greeneville, TN 37743; tel (423) 638-4181; fax (423) 638-3645. Media Services group.
Circulation: 14,992(e); 14,992(m-sat); ABC Sept. 30, 1995.
Price: 50¢(d); 50¢(sat); $182.00/yr (carrier).
Advertising: Open inch rate $13.25(e); $13.25(m-sat). **Representative:** Landon Associates Inc.
News Service: AP. **Politics:** Independent. **Established:** 1879.
Not Published: Christmas.
Advertising not accepted: Liquor.
Special Editions: Calender Girls, % Off Section (Jan); Boy Scouts, Basketball Tournament, FFA, Income Tax Edition, Valentine's Gift Pages, Benchmarks (Feb); Girl Scouts, Poison Prevention Day, Profitable Farming, Soil Conservation, National Teachers Day (Mar); Cooking School, Home Improvement, Secretaries Week (Apr); High School Seniors, Nat'l Pet Week, Salute to Industry, Memorial Day, Mother's Day, Law Day, Nursing Home Week (May); June Dairy Edition, Farm City Day, Father's Day, June Bride Edition (June); DUI Page (July); Back-to-School, Football Edition, Football Contest, Greene Co. Guidebook (Aug); Farm Safety, Grandparents Day, Hunting and Fishing, United Way, American Businesswomen, Financial Services Week, Cheerleaders and Band (Sept); National Newspaper Week, 4-H Club, National Restaurant Month, Cosmetology Month, Fire Prevention Week, Car Care, Spinal Health, Bosses' Day, Spay/Neuter Page (Oct); Basketball, Recipe Contest, Shoplifting, Veteran's Day, Design-an-Ad, Holiday Directory (Nov); Christmas Greetings, DUI Pages, Christmas Gift Guide (Dec).
Special Weekly Sections: Health (mon); Seniors ("Maturity") (tues); Education, Agriculture, Best Food Day (wed); Business, Calendar (thur); Religion (fri); Best Food Day, Comics, Mini Pages (sat).
Magazine: TV Week (sat).

CORPORATE OFFICERS

President John M Jones
Vice Pres Gregg K Jones
Secretary/Treasurer John M Jones Jr

GENERAL MANAGEMENT

Publisher John M Jones
Co-Publisher Gregg K Jones
General Manager Ken Hood Jr
Controller Robert J Wagler

ADVERTISING

Director John E Cash
Manager Arthur D Wehenkel

CIRCULATION

Director C Duane Uhls

NEWS EXECUTIVES

Editor John M Jones Jr
Managing Editor Douglas Watson

EDITORS AND MANAGERS

Copy Editor Valdean R Dobson
Features Editor Helena Z Jones
Lifestyle Editor Velma Presley
Sports Editor Wayne Phillips

PRODUCTION

Manager-Quality Phil Gentry
Manager-Creative Service Floyd Melton
Foreman-Pressroom Jerry Ottinger

Market Information: TMC.
Mechanical available: Offset; Black and 3 ROP colors; insert accepted — preprinted; page cut-offs — 22¾".
Mechanical specifications: Type page 13" x 21½"; E - 6 cols, 2 1/16", ⅛" between; A - 6 cols, 2 1/16", ⅛" between; C - 9 cols, 1⅜", 1/16" between.
Commodity consumption: Newsprint 900 short tons; widths 27½", 13¾"; average pages per issue 24(d).
Equipment: EDITORIAL: Front-end hardware — 1-Mk/4001, Mk/Mycro-Comp 1100 plus; Printers — 1-Ap/Mac LaserWriter Plus. CLASSIFIED: Front-end hardware — 3-Synaptic. DISPLAY: Printers — 3-Ap/Mac LaserWriter. PRODUCTION: Typesetters — 3-Ap/Mac LaserWriter, 2-Ultre, Hyphen/RIP; Plate exposures — 1-Nu, 1-B; Plate processors — 1-Nat/A-250; Scanners — Lf/Leafscan 45, Lf/Leafscan 35, Sharp/J600 Flatbed; Production cameras — 1-C/Spartan II; Automatic film processors — 1-LE/LD24, Wing-Lynch. PRESSROOM: Line 1 — 8-G/Urbanite; Folders — 1-G. MAILROOM: Counter stackers — 1-HI/Graphics, RS/25; Inserters and stuffers — 1-MM/227-E; Bundle tyer — 1-Nichiro Kogyo/Semi-Ace; Addressing machine — 1-DEC/LA 180, Ch/525E Stamping machine. LIBRARY: Electronic — SMS/Stauffer Gold. WIRE SERVICES: News — AP; Syndicates — King Features, LAT-WP, CSM; Receiving dishes — size-10ft, AP. BUSINESS COMPUTERS: ALR; Applications: Vision Data; PCs & micros networked; PCs & main system networked.

JACKSON

Madison County

'90 U.S. Census- 48,949; E&P '96 Est. 48,804
ABC-NDM (90): 245,651 (HH 94,075)

The Jackson Sun (m-mon to sat; S)

The Jackson Sun, 245 W. Lafayette (38301); PO Box 1059, Jackson, TN 38302-1059; tel (901) 427-3333; fax (901) 425-9604. Gannett Co. Inc. group.
Circulation: 40,112(m); 40,112(m-sat); 44,947(S); ABC Sept. 30, 1995.
Price: 35¢(d); 35¢(sat); $1.50(S); $10.50/mo (carrier); $141.00/yr (mail).
Advertising: Open inch rate $37.05(m); $37.05(m-sat); $42.25(S). **Representative:** Gannett National Newspaper Sales.
News Services: AP, GNS. **Politics:** Independent. **Established:** 1848.
Advertising not accepted: Publisher reserves right/all copy subject to publisher's approval.
Special Editions: Progress (Jan); Bridal, Fashion, Auto Car Care, Home Improvement, No-till Farming (Mar); Home & Lawn, YMCA, Home Builders, Chamber of Commerce (Apr); Mother's Day, Strawberry Festival, Teapot Festival, Newcomers (May); Miss Tennessee (June); Car Care (July); Back-to-School, Football (Aug); Fall Fashion (Sept); Lay-Away for Christmas, Auto, Home, Holiday Fashion (Oct); Thanksgiving (Nov); Christmas Gift Guide (Dec).
Special Weekly Sections: Best Food Day (wed); Preview Magazine (thur); Expanded Sports (sat); Color Comics (S).
Magazines: Preview (thur); USA Weekend, TV Week (own, newsprint) (S).

GENERAL MANAGEMENT

Publisher/President Michael Craft
Director-Operations Ron DeLoach
Controller Terry McCarrick
Manager-Credit Betty Allen

ADVERTISING

Director Robert Blake
Manager-Retail Teresa Ide
Manager-Classified Nancy Baird

MARKETING AND PROMOTION

Director-Marketing/Promotion Cathy Garrett

CIRCULATION

Director Bailey Dabney
Manager-Marketing/Sales Jeff Hartley

NEWS EXECUTIVES

Exec Editor Richard A Schneider
Managing Editor Pat Rice

EDITORS AND MANAGERS

Action Line Editor Renell Wynn
Books Editor Jacque Hillman
Business Editor Gregg Parker
City Editor Chris Rook
Editorial Page Editor Alan Bauer
Education Editor Chris Poynter
Features Editor Jacque Hillman
Graphics Editor/Art Director Steve Manning
Librarian Renell Wynn
News Editor Gwenda Anthony
Director-Photography Mike Silva
Religion Editor Jim Rainey
Sports Editor Steve Locklin

PRODUCTION

Director-Operations Ron DeLoach
Asst Director-Operations Randy Hammonds
Director-Building/Safety Bill Blurton
Manager-Data Processing Danny Walker
Manager-Pre Press Dorothy Layton

Tennessee I-383

Manager-Camera/Plate/Press Ellis Wood Jr
Manager-Post Press Gene Jones
Manager-Technical Service Randy Hammonds
Manager-Commercial Print Shop Susan Connell

Market Information: Zoned editions; Split Run; TMC; Operate audiotex.
Mechanical available: Letterpress (direct); Black and 3 ROP colors; insert accepted — preprinted, all; page cut-offs — 22¾".
Mechanical specifications: Type page 13" x 21½"; E - 6 cols, 2", ⅙" between; A - 6 cols, 2", ⅙" between; C - 9 cols, 1.53", ⅛" between.
Commodity consumption: Newsprint 3,097 short tons; 2,810 metric tons; widths 27", 13½"; black ink 80,200 pounds; color ink 14,700 pounds; single pages printed 12,691; average pages per issue 28(d), 64(S); single plates used 42,864.
Equipment: EDITORIAL: Front-end hardware — Dewar/Sys IV; Front-end software — Dewar/Sys IV; Printers — Okidata/393; Other equipment — 6-Toshiba/1100 portable. CLASSIFIED: Front-end hardware — Dewar/Sys IV; Front-end software — Dewar/Sys IV; Printers — Okidata/393; Other equipment — 6-Toshiba/1100 portable. DISPLAY: Adv layout systems — Dewar/Ad Dummy; Front-end hardware — SIA/386-33; Front-end software — Dewar/Sys IV; Printers — Okidata/393. PRODUCTION: Typesetters — Tegra/Varityper 5100, 1-Tegra/Varityper 5500; Platemaking systems — Na/Satellite; Plate exposures — 2-Na/Satellite; Plate processors — 1-Na/Satellite, 1-Na/NP80; Scanners — Lf/Leafscan 35; Production cameras — C/Spartan III, 1-SCREEN/C-220-E; Automatic film processors — 1-P/26ML, 2-C/PM R660; Film transporters — 1-C/1274; Digital color separation equipment — Lf/Leafscan 35.
PRESSROOM: Line 1 — 8-G/156 (4 color humps); Press drives — 2-Fin; Folders — 1-G; Press control system — Fin. MAILROOM: Counter stackers — 2-QWI/SJ-100, 1-QWI/SJ-200; Inserters and stuffers — GMA/10-48; Bundle tyer — 2-MLN/ML2EE, 1-MLN/MAG-330; Addressing machine — 1-MMS. WIRE SERVICES: News — AP Datastream, AP Datafeatures; Stock tables — AP SelectStox; Syndicates — AP, GNS; Receiving dishes — size-3m, AP. BUSINESS COMPUTERS: IBM/AS-400 B35; Applications: Gannett Corporate; PCs & micros networked; PCs & main system networked.

JOHNSON CITY

Washington County

'90 U.S. Census- 49,381; E&P '96 Est. 54,505
ABC-CZ (90): 65,016 (HH 25,709)

Johnson City Press

(m-mon to sat; S)

Johnson City Press, 204 W. Main St.; PO Box 1717, Johnson City, TN 37605-1717; tel (423) 929-3111; fax (423) 461-9546. Carl A Jones Newspapers group.
Circulation: 31,697(m); 31,697(m-sat); 35,914(S); ABC Sept. 30, 1995.
Price: 35¢(d); 35¢(sat); $1.25(S); $2.32/wk; $10.00/mo; $110.00/yr.
Advertising: Open inch rate $16.50(m); $16.50(m-sat); $16.50(S). **Representative:** Landon Associates Inc.
News Services: AP, NYT. **Politics:** Independent-Democrat. **Established:** 1934.
Not Published: Christmas.
Advertising not accepted: "Wife Wanted" copy; Objectionable medical copy.
Special Editions: Wedding Guide (Jan); Children's Valentines (Feb); Progress (Mar); Car Care Tab (May); Football Tab (Aug); School (Sept); Car Care (Oct); Basketball, Thanksgiving (Nov); Christmas Gift (Dec); Christmas Greetings (Dec 24).
Special Weekly Sections: Best Food Day (wed); Church News & Directory (sat); Best Food Day, Lifestyles, Business, Sports, Travel (S).
Magazines: Teen Pages (mon); TV Press (fri); Church Page (sat); Southeastern Color Comics, Business and Entertainment Pages, Parade (S); Senior Lifestyles (every other mo); The Arts Line (monthly).

CORPORATE OFFICERS

President Carleton A Jones
Treasurer Tim P Jones
Vice Pres John A Jones
Secretary Alice J Torbett

GENERAL MANAGEMENT

General Manager Tim P Jones
Editor in Chief John A Jones
Manager-Facilities John Castle
Manager-Education Service Lynn Richardson

ADVERTISING

Director Bill Breeden
Manager-Retail Frank Hawkins
Manager-Classified Lynda Widener

CIRCULATION

Director Phil Hensley

NEWS EXECUTIVES

Editorial Director Tom Hodge
Editor in Chief John A Jones
Managing Editor Henry Samples

EDITORS AND MANAGERS

Amusements Editor Lesia Paine-Brooks
Automotive Editor Henry Samples
Business/Finance Editor Phyllis Johnson
City Editor Brad Jolly
Editorial Page Editor Tom Hodge
Education/School Editor Sam Watson
Fashion/Women's Editor Mark Stevens
Films/Theater Editor Lesia Paine-Brooks
Food/Garden Editor Mark Stevens
Home Furnishings Editor Mark Stevens
Librarian Phyllis Brown
Lifestyle Editor Mark Stevens
News Editor Henry Samples
Photo Department Manager Lee Talbert
Radio/Television Editor Lesia Paine-Brooks
Real Estate Editor Phyllis Johnson
Religion Editor Henry Samples
Ski Editor Mark Stevens
Sports Editor Kelly Hodge
Teen-Age/Youth Editor Mark Stevens
Travel Editor Mark Stevens

PRODUCTION

Foreman-Composing Dan Dickson
Foreman-Pressroom Sidney Nave

Market Information: TMC.
Mechanical available: Letterpress; Black and 3 ROP colors; insert accepted — preprinted, samples up to 13" x 11" x ⅛"; page cut-offs — 22¾".
Mechanical specifications: Type page 13" x 21½"; E - 6 cols, 21⁄16", ⅛" between; A - 6 cols, 21⁄16", ⅛" between; C - 9 cols, 1⅜", 1⁄16" between.
Commodity consumption: Newsprint 2,500 short tons; widths 27½", 41¼", 55"; black ink 75,000 pounds; color ink 1,980 pounds; single pages printed 12,303; average pages per issue 31(d), 68(S); single plates used 21,000.
Equipment: EDITORIAL: Front-end hardware — 30-ECR; Front-end software — ECR; Printers — 1-Centronics. CLASSIFIED: Front-end hardware — ECR; Front-end software — ECR; Printers — 1-Centronics. DISPLAY: Front-end hardware — 1-Ap/Mac Quadra 950, 3-Ap/Mac IIfx; Front-end software — Multi-Ad/Creator; Printers — 2-QMS/860. PRODUCTION: OCR software — Typereader; Typesetters — 2-QMS/860; Platemaking systems — LX; Scanners — Microtek; Production cameras — 1-C/Spagton II, 1-Robinson/480; Automatic film processors — LE/24"; Film transporters — C; Color separation equipment (conventional) — Lf; Digital color separation equipment — Lf/Leafscan 35.
PRESSROOM: Line 1 — 6-SC; Reels and stands — 6-SC; Press control system — GE. MAILROOM: Inserters and stuffers — 2-MM; Bundle tyer — 1-MLN; Addressing machine — 1-KAN. LIBRARY: Combination — Indexing, Microfilming. WIRE SERVICES: News — AP; Photos — AP; Receiving dishes — size-12ft. BUSINESS COMPUTERS: IBM/RISC-6000, IBM/AS-400; Applications: Vision Data: Bus, Transient billing, Accts receivable, Circ.

KINGSPORT

Sullivan and Hawkins Counties

'90 U.S. Census- 36,365; E&P '96 Est. 40,302
ABC-CZ (90): 92,539 (HH 37,144)

Daily News

(m-tues to fri; wknd)

Daily News, 310 E. Sullivan St., Kingsport, TN 37660; tel (423) 246-4800; fax (423) 247-2502.
Circulation: 2,230(m); 2,230(wknd); Sworn Oct. 1, 1995.
Price: 25¢(d); 25¢(wknd); $36.00/yr.
Advertising: Open inch rate $8.10(m); $8.10(wknd).
News Service: RN. **Politics:** Independent. **Established:** 1963.
Not Published: Postal holidays; Christmas.
Special Editions: What's New (Jan); Home Fix-Up, Progress (Mar); Vacation Guide (Apr, May); Back-to-School, Football (Aug); Christmas Cook Book, Christmas Greetings (Dec).
Magazines: Seniority (Senior Citizens magazine) (monthly); School Daze (School Edition) (monthly, Oct-May).

CORPORATE OFFICERS

President Pete Dykes
Vice Pres J Steven Dykes
Secretary/Treasurer D R Dykes

GENERAL MANAGEMENT

Publisher J Steven Dykes
Purchasing Agent D R Dykes

ADVERTISING

Manager J Steven Dykes

CIRCULATION

Manager D R Dykes

NEWS EXECUTIVE

Editor Pete Dykes

EDITORS AND MANAGERS

City Editor Jean Fletcher
Features Editor Jean Fletcher

PRODUCTION

Foreman Jean Fletcher

Market Information: Zoned editions; Split Run; TMC.
Mechanical available: Offset; Black and 1 ROP color; insert accepted — preprinted; page cut-offs — 22½".
Mechanical specifications: Type page 10¾" x 16½"; E - 5 cols, 2", ⅛" between; A - 5 cols, 2", ⅛" between; C - 5 cols, 2", ⅛" between.
Equipment: PRODUCTION: Typesetters — 1-COM; Production cameras — 1-K.

Kingsport Times-News

(m-mon to fri; m-sat; S)

Kingsport Times-News, 701 Lynn Garden Dr.; PO Box 479, Kingsport, TN 37662; tel (423) 246-8121. Sandusky-Norwalk Newspapers group.
Circulation: 45,795(m); 44,498(m-sat); 49,359(S); ABC Sept. 30, 1995.
Price: 35¢(d); 50¢(sat); $1.00(S); $7.15/mo (d), $10.95/mo (d&S); $216.00/yr (d&S).
Advertising: Open inch rate $27.20(m); $27.20(m-sat); $28.60(S). **Representative:** Landon Associates Inc.
News Services: AP, KRT, CQ. **Politics:** Independent. **Established:** 1916.
Special Editions: Bridal (Jan); Progress (Mar); American Homes (Apr); Fun Fest (July); Football (Aug); Fashion (Sept); New Car (Oct); Basketball (Nov).
Special Weekly Sections: Food Day (wed); Religion, Entertainment (fri); Food Day, Business, Travel (S).
Magazines: TV Week (sat); Parade (S).

CORPORATE OFFICERS

Board Chairman Dudley A White
President David A Rau
Vice Pres/Treasurer Alice W Rau
Secretary Susan White Smith

GENERAL MANAGEMENT

Publisher Keith D Wilson
Manager-Office Debbie Salyers

ADVERTISING

Director George Coleman
Manager-Classified Pat Donaldson
Manager-National Cindy Bellamy

CIRCULATION

Director Dan Holland

NEWS EXECUTIVES

Managing Editor Edward (Ted) Como
Asst Managing Editor-News Stanley W Whitlock
Asst Managing Editor-Editorial/Features Don Fenley

EDITORS AND MANAGERS

Amusements/Arts Editor Allison Mechem
Books/Films Editor Edward (Ted) Como
Business Editor Sharon Hayes
Business/Finance Editor Sharon Caskey
Editorial Page Editor Don Fenley
Education Editor Lisa Eldreth
Fashion/Features Editor Leigh Ann Loube
Features Editor Becky Whitlock
Food Editor Carmen Archer
Librarian Kim Absher
News Editor Roger Davis
Senior News Editor Frank Cannon
Photo Department Manager Earl Carter
Political Editor Matt Franck
Radio/Television Editor Becky Whitlock
Real Estate Editor Amy Stevens
Religion Editor Brad Lifford
Science/Technology Editor Edward (Ted) Como
Exec Sports Editor Ron Bliss
Sports Editor Bill Lane
Teen-Age/Youth Editor Barbara Simms
Theater/Music Editor Becky Whitlock
Wire Editor Roger Davis
Women's Editor Becky Whitlock

MANAGEMENT INFORMATION SERVICES

Data Processing Manager Dan Strickler

PRODUCTION

Director-Operations Doug Hinson
Foreman-Composing Bernie Bewkey

Market Information: Zoned editions; Split Run; TMC.
Mechanical available: Offset; Black and 3 ROP colors; insert accepted — preprinted, tab or standard pre-print; page cut-offs — 23⁹⁄₁₆".
Mechanical specifications: Type page 13" x 22½"; E - 6 cols, 2.03", .22" between; A - 6 cols, 2.03", .22" between; C - 9 cols, 1⅜", .19" between.
Commodity consumption: Newsprint 3,918 short tons; widths 55", 41¼", 27½"; black ink 64,600 pounds; color ink 18,000 pounds; single pages printed 13,738; average pages per issue 33(d), 70(S); single plates used 36,600.
Equipment: EDITORIAL: Front-end hardware — HI/8000, 32-Hx/HS 46, 17-Hx/III, 6-MGD/Image III, 6-HI/8300; Front-end software — HI/8000 8.0; Printers — X; Other equipment — Lf/AP Leaf Picture Desk, Ap/Mac, HAS, HI/Imagers, Sun/Workstation, Sharp/JX-610 Scanner. CLASSIFIED: Front-end hardware — HI/8000; Front-end software — HI/8000; Other equipment — Lind/500, Imagitex/scanner. DISPLAY: Adv layout systems — HI/8000, 3-HI/8300; Front-end hardware — HI/8000, Ap/Mac; Front-end software — HI/8000. PRODUCTION: Pagination software — HI; OCR software — Solaris 2.1, Images 2.0; Typesetters — Linotype-Hell/Linotype 500; Plate exposures — 1-Nu; Plate processors — Nat; Scanners — Imagitex/1800, Sharp/JX-610, Nikon/3510 AF; Production cameras — C/Marathon; Automatic film processors — LE; Film transporters — LE; Color separation equipment (conventional) — C; Digital color separation equipment — HI/Imagitex.
PRESSROOM: Line 1 — 4-G/Metro 3077(2-half decks); Folders — 1-G/2:1; Pasters — G; Press control system — Fin. MAILROOM: Counter stackers — 2-MM, 2-QWI/300; Inserters and stuffers — Amerigraph/630 NP; Bundle tyer — 2-Power Strap, 2-MLN; Addressing machine — Wm; Mailroom control system — Ic. LIBRARY: Electronic — SMS/Stauffer Gold. COMMUNICATIONS: Digital ad delivery system — AP AdSend. WIRE SERVICES: News — AP; Stock tables — AP SelectStox; Receiving dishes — size-9ft, AP, KRT, Bizwire. BUSINESS COMPUTERS: DEC; Applications: CJ: Bus, Circ; PCs & micros networked; PCs & main system networked.

KNOXVILLE

Knox County

'90 U.S. Census- 165,121; E&P '96 Est. 157,626
ABC-CZ (90): 271,121 (HH 109,764)

The Knoxville News-Sentinel

(m-mon to sat; S)

The Knoxville News-Sentinel, 208 W. Church Ave.; PO Box 59038, Knoxville, TN 37950-9038; tel (423) 523-3131; fax (423) 673-3480; e-mail kns@knoxnews.com; web site http://www.scripps.com/knoxnews/. Scripps Howard group.
Circulation: 116,429(m); 141,503(m-fri); 142,322(m-sat); 174,759(S); ABC Sept. 30, 1995.
Price: 50¢(d); 50¢(fri); 50¢(sat); $1.75(S); $16.25/mo (d&S) (carrier), $20.40/mo (mail).
Advertising: Open inch rate $59.75(m); $59.75(m-fri); $59.75(m-sat); $67.65(S). **Representative:** Sawyer-Ferguson-Walker Co.
News Services: AP, SHNS, NEA, NYT, INS Bizwire, PR Newswire. **Politics:** Independent. **Established:** 1886.
Special Editions: Travel Pages, Progress Edition, Brides (Jan); Cruise Pages, Valentine's Day, Brides (Zoned), Auto Section, House & Garden, What's New (Feb); East TN Spring Guide, Travel Pages, Spring House & Garden, Spring Fashion, Prom Pages, Home Show, Townsend Visitor (Mar); Careers, Dogwood Festival, Spring Car Care, Spring Fling, Furniture Showcase (Apr); Women's Show,

Health & Fitness, Mother's Day Pages, Knox Nike Open, East TN Business Expo, First & Future 50, Auto Section (May); Father's Day Pages (June); Travel Pages, July 4th Holiday Pages (July); Children's Directory, Fall Fashion, Prep Football, Football Preview (Aug); Auto Section, Travel Pages, Townsend Visitor, Parade of Homes, Home Improvement, Fall Home & Garden (Sept); East TN Autumn Guide, Fall Car Care, Furniture Showcase, 1997 Auto Show (Oct); Holiday Hi-lites, Holiday Gift Guide, Christmas Gift Guide (Nov); Christmas Greeting, Holiday Hi-lites, Last Minute Gift (Dec).

Special Weekly Sections: Health & Science (mon); Food, Youth (wed); Entertainment (fri); Family, Religion (sat); Food, Entertainment, Fashion, Fifty-Plus (S); TV/Cable Listings, Business & Financial (daily).

Magazines: Parade, TV Week (S).

Cable TV: Own cable TV in circulation area.

GENERAL MANAGEMENT

General Manager Bruce R Hartmann
Director-Finance Janice Earheart
Director-Human Resources William R Redding
Manager-Credit Vickie Bolinger

ADVERTISING

Director Debbie Smiddy
Manager Richard McMillan
Manager-Sales Steve Bowman
Manager-Sales LaDonna Daugherty

MARKETING AND PROMOTION

Director-Marketing Shelba Murphy
Director-Public Service Susan Alexander
Editor-Special Publications Wade Saye

TELECOMMUNICATIONS

Manager-Online Publishing Jack Lail
Audiotex Manager Adrian Pearce

CIRCULATION

Director-Alternate Direct Delivery Dan Mashburn

NEWS EXECUTIVES

Editor Harry Moskos
Managing Editor Vince Vawter
Asst Managing Editor-Community News Georgiana Vines
Asst Managing Editor-News Frank Cagle
Asst Managing Editor-Graphics Robert L Wilson

EDITORS AND MANAGERS

Arts Editor Barbara Asbury
Aviation Editor Vince Vawter
Books Editor Jan Avent
Business/Finance Editor Michael Silence
Columnist Sam Venable
Editorial Page Editor Hoyt Canady
Lower Education Editor Jesse Mayshark
Higher Education Editor Amy Smith
Fashion/Features Editor Linda Fields
Films Editor Betsy Pickle
Food Editor Louise G Durman
Garden Editor Homer Clonts
Health Editor Amy Smith
Home Furnishings Editor Barbara Aston Wash
Librarian Shirley Carter
Music Editor Wayne Bledsoe
Photo Department Manager Jack Kirkland
Picture Editor Jack Kirkland
Radio/Television Editor Edwina Ralston
Real Estate Editor Michael Silence
Religion Editor Bob Barrett
Society/Women's Editor Linda Fields
Sports Editor Steve Ahillen
Travel Editor Linda Fields
Theater Editor Barbara Asbury

MANAGEMENT INFORMATION SERVICES

Manager-Info Systems Art Ridgway

PRODUCTION

Director Ted Milligan
Director-Quality Frank Wolfe
Manager-Systems Mike Corum
Manager-Night Coordination Mark Beaty
Superintendent-Pressroom Harold Wells
Superintendent-Pre Press Rick Wolfenbarger
Superintendent-Mailroom William Llewellyn

Market Information: Zoned editions; Split Run; TMC; ADS; Operate database; Operate audiotex; Electronic edition.

Mechanical available: Flexo; Black and 3 ROP colors; insert accepted — preprinted; page cutoffs — 23 9/16".

Mechanical specifications: Type page 13" x 22 1/2"; E - 6 cols, 2 1/16", 1/8" between; A - 6 cols, 2 1/16", 1/8" between; C - 10 cols, 1 1/4", 1/16" between.

Commodity consumption: Newsprint 21,772 metric tons; widths 53 7/8", 40 3/8", 26 7/8"; black ink 769,500 pounds; color ink 286,092 pounds; single pages printed 25,160; average pages per issue 54(d), 52(sat), 160(S); single plates used 112,286.

Equipment: EDITORIAL: Front-end hardware — 6-AT/9000; Other equipment — 3-ATS/WSII, 4-ATS/WS III. CLASSIFIED: Front-end hardware — 4-AT/9000; Other equipment — 4-ATS/WS III. AUDIOTEX: Hardware — Pony/120Mb, Pony/700Mb. DISPLAY: Adv layout systems — AT/Architect; Front-end hardware — 8-Sun/Sparc Workstation; Front-end software — AT/III AMS; Printers — 2-III/3810, AU/APS5. PRODUCTION: Pagination software — ATS; Typesetters — 2-III/3810, 1-III/3850; Platemaking systems — Na; Plate exposures — 2-Fx/4, 1-Burgess/Consolux; Plate processors — 2-Na/FP II; Electronic picture desk — Lf/AP Leaf Picture Desk, AP AdSend; Scanners — 2-Infoscan/III 3700; Production cameras — 1-C/Marathon, 1-C, 1-C/Newspager, 1-ECR/Autokon II; Automatic film processors — 1-LE/LD24AQ, 1-LE/PC-13, 2-Multiline/66RA Processor, 3-LE/LS-2600; Film transporters — C/3; Color separation equipment (conventional) — 2-Scitex/342 Scanner; Digital color separation equipment — 2-Scitex/342 Scanner. PRESSROOM: Line 1 — 16-PEC/Flexo Conv; Press drives — PEC; Folders — 1-H/2:1, 2-H/3:2; Pasters — 16-H/RTP; Reels and stands — 16-H/RTP; Press control system — PEC. MAILROOM: Counter stackers — 2-HL/Dual Carrier, 3-HT/II; Inserters and stuffers — 2-S/72P; Bundle tyer — 5-Power Strap; Wrapping singles — 1-Ca/Band Tyer; Addressing machine — 1-KR. LIBRARY: Electronic — Vu/Text. COMMUNICATIONS: Facsimile — Ricoh/FAX10E. WIRE SERVICES: News — AP Datastream, AP Datafeatures, NYT, SHNS, AP Photostream; Stock tables — AP SelectStox II; Syndicates — NYT, SHNS; Receiving dishes — size-3m, AP. BUSINESS COMPUTERS: 1-IBM/4381 P23; Applications: SQL: Group 1, Payroll, Adv billing, Accts receivable; Cobol; PCs & micros networked; PCs & main system networked.

LEBANON

Wilson County

'90 U.S. Census- 15,208; E&P '96 Est. 18,638

The Lebanon Democrat

(e-mon to fri)

The Lebanon Democrat, 402 N. Cumberland St.; PO Box 430, Lebanon, TN 37087; tel (615) 444-3952; fax (615) 444-1358. Carl A Jones Newspapers group.

Circulation: 8,566(e); Sworn Oct. 1, 1995.

Price: 35¢(d); $11.25/3mo (in county), $15.00/3mo (outside county), $22.50/6mo (in county), $30.00/6mo (outside county); $41.00/yr (in county), $55.00/yr (outside county).

Advertising: Open inch rate $6.80(e). **Representative:** Papert Companies.

News Services: NEA, AP. **Established:** 1888.

Not Published: New Year; Independence Day; Labor Day; Thanksgiving; Christmas.

Special Editions: Profitable Farming; Auto; Bride's Section; Fashion Section; Back-to-School; Horse Show; Industrial.

Magazines: Headliner, TV & Entertainment Section (thur).

CORPORATE OFFICER

CEO Yvonne Wallace

GENERAL MANAGEMENT

Director-Finance Yvonne Wallace
General Manager Yvonne Wallace
Purchasing Agent Wanda Candela

ADVERTISING

Manager David Beasley
Manager-Classified Patsy Wynns

CIRCULATION

Director Norma Bixler

NEWS EXECUTIVE

Editor Sam Hatcher

EDITORS AND MANAGERS

Books/Features Editor Marcia Poley
Food/Women's Editor Marcia Poley
News Editor Lounita Howard
Sports Editor Andy Reid

PRODUCTION

Superintendent Billy Carr
Foreman-Pressroom Alvin Collins

Market Information: Zoned editions; TMC.

Mechanical available: Offset; Black and 3 ROP colors; insert accepted — preprinted; page cutoffs — 22 1/2".

Mechanical specifications: Type page 13" x 21 1/2"; E - 6 cols, 2 1/16", 1/8" between; A - 6 cols, 2 1/16", 1/8" between; C - 6 cols, 2 1/16", 1/8" between.

Commodity consumption: Newsprint 405 short tons; width 27 3/4"; black ink 7,200 pounds; color ink 1,890 pounds; single pages printed 5,380; average pages per issue 24(d).

Equipment: EDITORIAL: Front-end hardware — Microtek; Front-end software — Microtek. CLASSIFIED: Front-end hardware — Ap/Mac, Baseview, 1-Centurion. DISPLAY: Adv layout systems — Ap/Mac, Mk/Ad Touch, Ap/Mac IIcx. PRODUCTION: Typesetters — Mk/Laserwriter, Mk/Ad Touch-Comp IV, Ap/Mac NTX, P; Platemaking systems — 1-Nu/Flip Top FT40L; Production cameras — 1-R/400, SCREEN/Companica; Automatic film processors — P. PRESSROOM: Line 1 — 8-G/Community (w/color stock unit); Folders — 1-G. MAILROOM: Bundle tyer — Bu; Addressing machine — 1-Ch. COMMUNICATIONS: Systems used — satellite. WIRE SERVICES: News — AP; Syndicates — King Features; Receiving dishes — size-2ft, AP. BUSINESS COMPUTERS: 3-Centurion; Applications: Circ, Accts receivable, Accts payable, Payroll, Job estimating; PCs & micros networked; PCs & main system networked.

MARYVILLE-ALCOA

Blount County

'90 U.S. Census- 25,608 (Maryville 19,208; Alcoa 6,400); E&P '96 Est. 26,774 (Maryville 20,725; Alcoa 6,049)

ABC-NDM (90): 89,192 (HH 34,872)

The Daily Times

(m-mon to fri)

The Daily Times, 307 E. Harper Ave.; PO Box 9740, Maryville, TN 37802-9740; tel (423) 981-1100; fax (423) 981-1175. Horvitz Newspapers Inc. group.

Circulation: 21,224(m); ABC Sept. 30, 1995.

Price: 35¢(d); $1.40/wk; $72.80/yr (carrier), $132.00/yr (mail).

Advertising: Open inch rate $13.00(m). **Representative:** Papert Companies.

News Service: AP. **Politics:** Independent. **Established:** 1883.

Special Editions: NASCAR, Progress (Feb); Home Improvement (Mar); Townsend Traveler (Apr); Brides (May); Father's Day (June); Football Round Up (Aug); Fall Home Improvement (Sept); Newcomer's Guide, Car Care (Oct).

Special Weekly Sections: Moneysaver (tues); Food (wed); Religious News, TV Times, Real Estate, Weekend Lifetimes (fri).

Magazine: USA Weekend (fri).

CORPORATE OFFICER

Chairman of the Board/President/Chief Financial Officer Peter A Horvitz

GENERAL MANAGEMENT

Publisher F Max Crotser

ADVERTISING

Director Raymond K Tuck

CIRCULATION

Director Steven A Learn

NEWS EXECUTIVES

Editor Dean Stone
Managing Editor Frank Trexler

EDITORS AND MANAGERS

City/Metro Editor Phyllis Cable
Editorial Page Editor Dean Stone
Entertainment/Amusements Editor Melanie Tucker
Features Editor Melanie Tucker
Home Furnishings/Society Editor Melanie Tucker
News Editor Phyllis Cable
Photo Editor Anna Irwin
Sports Editor Paul McAfee
Women's Editor Melanie Tucker

PRODUCTION

Manager Fred Tipton
Foreman-Composing Mark White

Market Information: TMC.

Mechanical available: Offset; Black and 3 ROP colors; insert accepted — preprinted, accept all; page cut-offs — 22 3/4".

Mechanical specifications: Type page 13" x 21 1/2"; E - 6 cols, 2 1/16", 1/8" between; A - 6 cols, 2 1/16", 1/8" between; C - 9 cols, 1 3/8", 1/6" between.

Commodity consumption: Newsprint 934 metric tons; width 27"; black ink 21,680 pounds; color ink 4,270 pounds; single pages printed 8,607; average pages per issue 32(d); single plates used 12,920.

Equipment: EDITORIAL: Front-end hardware — 2-IBM/RISC 6000; Front-end software — Dewarview 1.12; Printers — HP/4MV. CLASSIFIED: Front-end hardware — CText; Front-end software — CText. DISPLAY: Front-end hardware — NCR/System 3300; Front-end software — Unix/Stauffer; Printers — Printonix. PRODUCTION: Pagination software — QuarkXPress 3.3; OCR software — Caere/OmniPage; Typesetters — 2-AG/Accuset 1000; Plate exposures — 1-B, 1-Nu; Plate processors — 2-B, Nat/A250s; Electronic picture desk — Lf/AP Leaf Picture Desk; Scanners — Kk/RFS 2035 Plus, Microtek/ScanMaker 3; Production cameras — 1-C/Spartan II; Automatic film processors — 1-LE. PRESSROOM: Line 1 — 11-G/Urbanite (10 Black; 1-Tri Color); Folders — 1-G; Pasters — 6-Cary. MAILROOM: Counter stackers — 1-HI; Inserters and stuffers — 2-HI; Bundle tyer — 2-MLN/Spirit; Addressing machine — 1-El; Mailroom control system — HI. COMMUNICATIONS: Systems used — satellite. WIRE SERVICES: News — AP, AP Datafeatures; Photos — AP; Syndicates — AP; Receiving dishes — AP. BUSINESS COMPUTERS: NCR; Applications: Circ, Adv billing, Accts receivable, Payroll, Accts payable; PCs & micros networked; PCs & main system networked.

MEMPHIS

Shelby County

'90 U.S. Census- 610,337; E&P '96 Est. 633,420

ABC-NDM (90): 1,007,306 (HH 365,450)

The Commercial Appeal

(m-mon to sat; S)

The Commercial Appeal, 495 Union Ave. (38103); PO Box 364, Memphis, TN 38101; tel (901) 529-2211; fax (901) 529-5833. Scripps Howard group.

Circulation: 178,415(m); 184,174(m-wed); 213,409(m-fri); 208,362(m-sat); 269,406 (S); ABC Sept. 30, 1995.

Price: 50¢(d); 50¢(sat); $2.00(S); $15.50/mo (carrier), $11.00/mo (d); $186.00/yr, $132.00/yr (d).

Advertising: Open inch rate $191.31(m); $191.31(m-sat); $215.34(S). **Representative:** Sawyer-Ferguson-Walker Co.

News Services: AP, NYT, SHNS, LAT-WP, RN. **Politics:** Independent. **Established:** 1841.

Advertising not accepted: All advertising subject to approval.

Special Editions: Computer/Office Systems Show, Travel/Follow the Sun, Forecast '96, All About Collierville (Jan); Dining Guide, Travel/Cruise, Bridal Section, American Heart Association, Home Expo (Feb); Kidzine, Spring Garden/Home Improvement, Spring Fashion, Southern Women's Show, Travel/St. Louis, NCAA Men's Basketball Tournament, Spring Travel Brochure Pages (Mar); Collierville Home Show, Travel/Florida, Travel/Thailand, Summertime/Funtime, All About Bartlett, Parade of Homes (Apr); Nurses Day, Dining Guide, Spring Car Care, Senior Citizens, Weekend of Wheels, VESTA (TBA) (May); Adventure/Exotic Vacations, FedEx/St. Jude Golf Classic (June); Weekend of Wheels, Travel/Canada, All About Memphis (July); Elvis Presley, Travel/Great Smokies, Favorite Brands, Hunting/Fishing Guide, Football Preview, Keys to the City (Aug); Weekend of Wheels, Fall Travel Brochure Pages, Southern Heritage Classic, Fall Car Care, Travel/Skiing, Fall Fashion (Sept); Home Furnishing, Teens, Travel/United Kingdom, Mid-South Fair, Home/Office Technology, Directions '96, New Car Buyer's Guide, Financial Planning, All About Germantown (Oct); Travel/Atlanta, Medical Directory, Basketball (Nov); Liberty Bowl, Travel/Hawaii, Weekend of Wheels (Dec).

Special Weekly Sections: Mid-South Medicine (mon); Best Food Day, Non-subscriber Star Watch (wed); Neighbors (thur); Church and Religious Pages, Lawn and Garden Pages (sat); Fanfare Arts Section, Image (lifestyle), Real Estate (S); Appeal/Travel, Business, Metro (regional news), Sports (daily).

Magazines: Playbook (entertainment tab) (fri); Parade, Fanfare (local arts), TV This Week (quarterfold) (S); TV Listings, Comics (daily).

CORPORATE OFFICERS

President Angus McEachran
Vice Pres Richard H Remmert

GENERAL MANAGEMENT
General Manager Richard H Remmert
Controller Kenneth W McNamee
Manager-Credit Linda Huffman
Personnel Director Warren C Funk
Manager-Purchasing Robbie Jones
Manager-Office Ralph Austin

ADVERTISING
Manager-National Sales Rebecca L Alexander
Manager-Retail/Sales Robert Stewart
Manager-Classified Michael G Stanley

MARKETING AND PROMOTION
Director-Marketing David H Swearingen
Manager-Marketing Service John N Anderson

TELECOMMUNICATIONS
Audiotex Manager Terri Mayo

CIRCULATION
Director Thomas A Harrison
Manager Jeff Kimbro

NEWS EXECUTIVES
Editor/President Angus McEachran
Managing Editor Henry A Stokes
Deputy Managing Editor Otis Sanford
Asst Managing Editor-Graphics Mike Kerr
Asst Managing Editor-National/Business Jack Bradley
Asst Managing Editor-Community Affairs Mary Alice Quinn

EDITORS AND MANAGERS
Amusements/Arts Editor Jon Sparks
Books Editor Fredric Koeppel
Business/Finance Editor Bob Hetherington
Bureaus Editor Scott Hill
Design Editor Suzanne Myrick Kerr
Director-Editorial Promotion Mary Lou Brown
Editorial Page Editor David Vincent
Editorial Cartoonist Michael Ramirez
Director-Education Service Irene Crist-Flanagan
Education Reporter Cornell Christion
Entertainment Editor Jon Sparks
Environmental Editor Tom Charlier
Farm/Agriculture Reporter Charles Conner
Fashion Reporter Barbara Bradley
Features Editor Peggy Reisser Winburne
Films/Theater Reporter Donald La Badie
Food Reporter Christine Arpe Gang
Graphics Editor Rick Alley
Librarian Rosemary Nelms
Living/Lifestyle Editor Peggy Reisser Winburne
Medical Reporter Mary Powers
Exec Metro Editor Jesse Bunn
Sunday Metro Editor Sonny Albarado
Music Reporter Larry Nager
National Editor Kathy Brooks
Outdoors Reporter Larry Rea
Director-Photography Larry Coyne
Political Columnist Susan Adler Thorpe
Radio/Television Editor Tom Walter
Real Estate Reporter Jerry Obermark
Real Estate Reporter Cindy Wolff
Religion Reporter David Waters
Society Reporter Mary George Beggs
Society Reporter Michael Donahue
Exec Sports Editor John Stamm
Sports Columnist David Williams
Theater Reporter Whit Smith
Transportation Reporter David Hirschman
Travel Editor Amanda McGee Robbins
Women's Editor Peggy Reisser Winburne

MANAGEMENT INFORMATION SERVICES
Data Processing Manager Tom Bartlett

PRODUCTION
Director-Operations Jimmy V Hamilton
Manager Adrian (Stretch) Bolin
Manager-Pressroom Charley Duncan
Manager-Composing Carrol Rhodes
Manager-Engraving Marshall Durham
Manager-Mailroom Wiley Arnold

Market Information: Zoned editions; Split Run; TMC; Operate audiotex.
Mechanical available: Offset; Black and 3 ROP colors; insert accepted — preprinted; page cut-offs — $23\frac{9}{16}$".
Mechanical specifications: Type page 13" x $22\frac{1}{2}$"; E - 6 cols, $2\frac{1}{16}$", $\frac{1}{8}$" between; A - 6 cols, $2\frac{1}{16}$", $\frac{1}{8}$" between; C - 10 cols, $1\frac{3}{8}$", $\frac{1}{16}$" between.
Commodity consumption: Newsprint 34,649 metric tons; widths 55", $41\frac{1}{4}$", $27\frac{1}{2}$"; black ink 625,000 pounds; color ink 210,000 pounds; single pages printed 35,919; average pages per issue 60(d), 130(S); single plates used 220,612.
Equipment: EDITORIAL: Front-end hardware — 72-AT, 72-ATS; Front-end software — AT, ATS/Osiris; Other equipment — 24-ATS/New Pagination. CLASSIFIED: Front-end hardware — AT; Front-end software — AT, HI/Pagination. AUDIOTEX: Hardware — Micro Voice; Software — Audiotext/2000; Supplier name — TMS/VNN, AP Press Stock Quotes. DISPLAY: Adv layout systems — AT/Architect, III/Display Ad composition; Front-end hardware — 12-III/AMS; Front-end software — III. PRODUCTION: Pagination software — ATS; Typesetters — 3-III/3810 Pagesetter; Plate exposures — 2-WL; Plate processors — 2-WL; Scanners — 3-ECR/Autokon; Production cameras — 1-C/Newspager; Automatic film processors — 4-LE/PC18; Film transporters — 3-C; Color separation equipment (conventional) — 2-CD/645; Digital color separation equipment — 1-Scitex.
PRESSROOM: Line 1 — 32-G/Metro; Folders — 4-G/Double; Pasters — 32-G; Reels and stands — 32-G; Press control system — 4-PCS-PAR, 1-G. MAILROOM: Counter stackers — 12-HL/Monitor; Inserters and stuffers — GMA/SLS 1000, 3-28:2 machines, 3-20:2 machines; Bundle tyer — 13-Dynaric; Addressing machine — 1-MG/851, 1-Ch/NR. LIBRARY: Electronic — Vu/Text, Dialog. WIRE SERVICES: News — AP, SHNS, RN, LAT-WP; Photos — AP; Stock tables — AP; Receiving dishes — AP. BUSINESS COMPUTERS: IBM/9121M311; Applications: Circ; Admarc: Adv, Payroll; PCs & micros networked; PCs & main system networked.

MORRISTOWN
Hamblen County
'90 U.S. Census- 21,385; E&P '96 Est. 22,862
ABC-CZ (90): 38,172 (HH 14,967)

Citizen Tribune
(e-mon to fri; S)

Citizen Tribune, 1609 W. 1st N. St.; PO Box 625, Morristown, TN 37814; tel (423) 581-5630; fax (423) 581-3061.
Circulation: 18,941(e); 24,718(S); ABC Sept. 30, 1995.
Price: 50¢(d); $1.25(S); $8.25/mo (carrier); $75.00/yr (mail).
Advertising: Open inch rate $13.42(e); $13.42(S). **Representatives:** Landon Associates Inc.; US Suburban Press.
News Service: AP. **Politics:** Independent. **Established:** 1966.
Not Published: Labor Day; Christmas.
Special Weekly Sections: Best Food Day (wed); Church Page (fri); Lakeway Living, Entertainment/TV, Business, Sports Section (S).
Magazines: TV Entertainment (own, newsprint); Parade; Sunday Comics.

CORPORATE OFFICERS
Board Chairman R H Bible Sr
President R Jack Fishman
Vice Pres John Wallace
Secretary/Treasurer Jack Strate

GENERAL MANAGEMENT
Publisher R Jack Fishman

ADVERTISING
Director C Reece Sexton

TELECOMMUNICATIONS
Audiotex Manager Mike Walker

CIRCULATION
Director Don Cunningham

NEWS EXECUTIVE
Editor R Jack Fishman

EDITORS AND MANAGERS
Amusements Editor Jamia Blazer
Automotive Editor Teresa Ayers
Books Editor Carolyn Walter
Business Editor Teresa Ayers
City Editor Teresa Ayers
Conservation Editor Bob Moore
Editorial Page Editor Jamia Blazer
Education Editor Jim Hollifield
Entertainment Editor Jamia Blazer
Farm Editor Bob Moore
Fashion/Food Editor Carolyn Walter
Features Editor Vickie Seal
Health/Medical Editor Bob Moore
Lifestyle Editor Carolyn Walter
Chief Photographer Gary Smith
Photo Editor Gary Smith
Political/County Government Editor Jim Hollifield
Religion Editor Lillie Moore
Sports Editor Fred Williams
State Editor Alethia Belcher
Television/Film Editor Jamia Blazer
Theater/Music Editor Jamia Blazer
Travel Editor Teresa Ayers
Women's Editor Carolyn Walter

PRODUCTION
Manager Dallas Rose

Market Information: Zoned editions; Split Run; TMC; Operate audiotex.
Mechanical available: Offset; Black and 3 ROP colors; insert accepted — preprinted; page cut-offs — $22\frac{3}{4}$".
Mechanical specifications: Type page 13" x $21\frac{1}{2}$"; E - 6 cols, $2\frac{1}{16}$", $\frac{1}{8}$" between; A - 6 cols, $2\frac{1}{16}$", $\frac{1}{8}$" between; C - 8 cols, $1\frac{1}{2}$", $\frac{1}{8}$" between.
Commodity consumption: average pages per issue 70(d), 136(S).
Equipment: EDITORIAL: Front-end hardware — 1-Ik/Minitek II (CPS 1020). PRODUCTION: Platemaking systems — 1-Nat; Plate exposures — 1-Nu; Plate processors — 1-Nat; Production cameras — 1-C, 1-Cl; Automatic film processors — 1-P; Film transporters — 1-C; Shrink lenses — 1-C.
PRESSROOM: Line 1 — 5-G/U; Folders — 1-G. MAILROOM: Counter stackers — 1-BG; Inserters and stuffers — 4-MM; Bundle tyer — 1-MLN. WIRE SERVICES: News — AP; Syndicates — AP; Receiving dishes — AP. BUSINESS COMPUTERS: 1-DEC/11-70; Applications: Circ, Adv billing, Accts receivable, Gen ledger, Payroll.

MURFREESBORO
Rutherford County
'90 U.S. Census- 44,922; E&P '96 Est. 58,243
ABC-CZ (90): 44,922 (HH 17,110)

The Daily News Journal
(e-mon to fri; m-sat; S)

The Daily News Journal, 224 N. Walnut St., Murfreesboro, TN 37130; tel (423) 893-5860; fax (423) 896-8702. Morris Newspaper Corp. group.
Circulation: 16,063(e); 16,063(m-sat); 19,171(S); ABC Sept. 30, 1995.
Price: 35¢(d); 35¢(sat); $1.25(S); $10.50/mo; $120.00/yr.
Advertising: Open inch rate $18.10(e); $18.10(m-sat); $18.10(S). **Representatives:** Papert Companies; US Suburban Press.
News Service: AP. **Politics:** Independent. **Established:** 1849.
Special Editions: Income Tax Guide; Bridal; Community Pride; Secretaries' Tab; Day Care Page; Older American's Month; Mother's Day Gift Guide; Father's Day Gift Guide; 4th of July Savings Spectacular; Walkin' Horse Show; Back-to-College; Home Furnishings; Back-to-School; Car Care; Football; Cosmetology; Christmas Gift Guide; Holiday Journey; Christmas Greetings; Letters to Santa; Dining Out; Newcomers Guide; Lawn & Garden; Home Improvement; Fall Car Care; Health Care Tab; Tourism Guide (monthly).
Special Weekly Sections: Homes (mon); Seniors (tues); Educational Page, Best Food Day (wed); Health & Fitness (thur); Church Page, Movie Review (fri); Public Record (sat); Lifestyle Section, Business News, Sports (S); TV/Entertainment (daily).
Magazines: Cover Story (thur); TV Journal, Comics, Parade (S).

GENERAL MANAGEMENT
Publisher Ron Fryar

ADVERTISING
Manager-National Al Werner
Manager-Classified Judy Scartland

CIRCULATION
Manager Paul Mauney

NEWS EXECUTIVES
Editor Mike Pirtle
Managing Editor Tom Spigolon

EDITORS AND MANAGERS
Arts/Books Editor Suzanne Ghianni
Business/Finance Editor Mike Pirtle
Columnist Mike Pirtle
County Government Editor John Callow
Editorial Writer Mike Pirtle
Education Editor Angela Cannon
Entertainment/Music Editor Suzanne Ghianni
Features Editor Suzanne Ghianni
Home Furnishings Editor Suzanne Ghianni
Photo Department Manager Jim Davis
Photographer Jim Davis
Sports Editor Monte Hale
Wire Editor Ken Becker

PRODUCTION
Supervisor Charles Smotherman

Market Information: Zoned editions; TMC.
Mechanical available: Offset; Black and 3 ROP colors; insert accepted — preprinted; page cut-offs — $22\frac{3}{4}$".
Mechanical specifications: Type page 13" x $21\frac{1}{2}$"; E - 6 cols, $2\frac{1}{16}$", $\frac{1}{8}$" between; A - 6 cols, $2\frac{1}{16}$", $\frac{1}{8}$" between; C - 9 cols, $1\frac{1}{4}$", $\frac{1}{8}$" between.
Commodity consumption: Newsprint 2,171 short tons; widths $27\frac{1}{2}$", 32", 30"; black ink 41,530 pounds; color ink 8,391 pounds; single pages printed 10,620; average pages per issue 20(d), 60(S); single plates used 28,091.
Equipment: EDITORIAL: Front-end hardware — AG/One System, 14-COM/Intrepid; Front-end software — QPS; Printers — 1-Ap/Mac Laser-Writer 810; Other equipment — 1-Ap/Mac Quadra 650, 1-Ap/Mac SE-30, AP Wire, 1-Scanmaker/II Scanner. CLASSIFIED: Front-end hardware — 1-Ap/Mac fileserver 95, 5-Ap/Mac LC III; Front-end software — Ap/Mac Appleshare 4.0, Baseview/Classified Manager; Printers — 1-Ap/Mac 630 Pro Printer. AUDIOTEX: Hardware — 8-PC/486-8x, 33-CPU/16-250; Software — Baseview. DISPLAY: Front-end hardware — 2-Ap/Mac Quadra 800, 1-Ap/Mac 51, 4-Ap/Mac Quadra 650; Front-end software — QuarkXPress 3.3, Multi-Ad/Creator, Typeset; Printers — 2-Ap/Mac LaserWriter NTX, 2-Ap/Mac LaserWriter IIf, Ap/Mac Laser-Writer 630 Pro; Other equipment — CD-Rom, 2-XYQUEST/44-88 MB, 1-X/7650C Scanner, 1-Ap/Mac One Scanner. PRODUCTION: OCR software — Caere/OmniPage; Typesetters — MCS/100, Ap/Mac LaserWriter NTX; Plate processors — Nat/A-250; Scanners — Ap/Mac One Scanner; Production cameras — C/Spartan II; Automatic film processors — Polychrome; Shrink lenses — 1-C/squeeze lens; Color separation equipment (conventional) — Ap/Mac, Lf/AP Leaf Picture Desk.
PRESSROOM: Line 1 — 5-G/Urbanite, 4-DEV/Horizon; Press control system — Fin. MAILROOM: Counter stackers — 1-HI/RS-2517; Inserters and stuffers — 6-MM; Bundle tyer — 6-MLN; Addressing machine — 2-KR. WIRE SERVICES: News — AP; Syndicates — NEA, Creators, Universal Press, Crown; Receiving dishes — size-3ft, AP. BUSINESS COMPUTERS: 6-IBM/PC XT; Applications: Foxbase, Acctmate; PCs & micros networked.

NASHVILLE
Davidson County
'90 U.S. Census- 487,973; E&P '96 Est. 546,682
ABC-NDM (90): 826,066 (HH 318,806)

The Tennessean
(m-mon to fri; m-sat; S)

The Tennessean, 1100 Broadway, Nashville, TN 37203; tel (615) 259-8000; fax (615) 259-8875. Gannett Co. Inc. group.
Circulation: 146,466(m); 230,471(m-sat); 282,821(S); ABC Sept. 30, 1995.
Price: 35¢(d); 35¢(sat); $1.50(S); $14.00/mo (carrier); $182.00/yr (carrier).
Advertising: Open inch rate $153.35(m); $153.35(m-sat); $222.63(S); comb with Nashville Banner (e) $156.63. **Representative:** Gannett National Newspaper Sales.
News Services: AP, UPI, NYT, LAT-WP. **Established:** 1812.
Note: The Nashville Banner and the Tennessean are corporately and editorially separate. The Tennessean is agent for advertising, circulation, production and printing functions of the Nashville Banner.
Advertising not accepted: Fortune tellers; palmists; crystal gazers.
Special Editions: Taking Stock (Feb); Cruise & International Travel (Mar); Carolina and Georgia Coastal Travel, Florida Travel, Sara Lee Golf Classic (Apr); FYI (Sept); Reader's Choice (Oct); Christmas Books (Nov).
Special Weekly Sections: School News and Classroom (mon); Close-up, Food (wed); Weekend (fri); Perspective, Home, Travel (S); Living, Business, Sports (daily).
Magazines: USA Weekend, Showcase Magazine (S).

CORPORATE OFFICERS
President/Publisher Craig Moon
Secretary Thomas Chapple
Treasurer Jimmy L Thomas

GENERAL MANAGEMENT
Vice Pres/Asst to President Donald Stinson
Director-Finance Larry St Cyr
Controller Terry Walker
Director-Human Resources Sharon Lewis
Director-Systems W E Koelz
Director-Special Projects/Planning Michael Ciarimboli
Director-Customer Info Program Patti C Gibbons

ADVERTISING
Director Leslie Giallombardo

Manager-Display Gary Wortel
Manager-National Wendell Pedigo
Manager-Classified Anna Bartkowski

MARKETING AND PROMOTION

Director-Marketing & Development Edward L Cassidy

TELECOMMUNICATIONS

Audiotex Manager Michael Ciarimboli

CIRCULATION

Director Guy Gilmore

NEWS EXECUTIVES

Vice Pres-News/Editor Frank Sutherland
Managing Editor-Opinion Sandra Roberts
Managing Editor-Days David Green
Managing Editor-Nights Ted Power
Asst Managing Editor-News Catherine Mayhew
Asst Managing Editor-Planning Cindy Smith
Asst Managing Editor-Sports Neal Scarbrough
Deputy Managing Editor-Features Patrick Connolly

EDITORS AND MANAGERS

Art Director D'Anna Sharon
Arts/Fashion Director Alan Bostick
Books Editor Linda Quigley
Business News Editor Candy Preston
Cartoonist Herman Campbell
Cartoonist Chas O Bissell
City Editor Thomas Goldsmith
Close-Up Editor Jerry Manley
Copy Desk Chief Mike Tate
Database Editor Lisa Green
Editorial Writer Ellen Dahnke
Editorial Writer Mike Morrow
Food Editor Ann Byrn
Librarian Annette Morrison
News Editor Ted Rayburn
Newspapers in Education Manager Melissa Spradlin
Night/Weekend Editor Dwight Lewis
Night/Weekend Editor George Zepp
Night/Weekend Editor John Richards
Night/Weekend Editor Richard Stevens
Op-Editor Terry Quillen
Picture Editor Randy Piland
Regional Editor/Business Editor Emme Baxter
Regional Editor-Day Denise Williams
Regional Editor-Day Frank Gibson
Regional Editor-Day Bill Choyke
Regional Editor-Day Robert Sherborne
Religion Editor Ray Waddle
Special Projects Editor Cathy Straight
Senior Writer-Sports Jimmy Davy
Senior Writer-Sports David Climer
Asst Sports Editor-Planning Carol Stuart
Weekend Editor-Features Gloria Ballard
Wire Editor Susan Fink-Frazier
World News Extra Editor Karen Small

PRODUCTION

Director Ron Krengel

Market Information: Zoned editions; Split Run; TMC; ADS; Operate audiotex.
Mechanical available: Offset; Black and 3 ROP colors; insert accepted — preprinted; page cut-offs — 22".
Mechanical specifications: Type page 12⅞" x 21¼"; E - 6 cols, 2¹⁄₁₆", ⅛" between; A - 6 cols, 2¹⁄₁₆", ⅛" between; C - 10 cols, 1¼", ¹⁄₁₆" between.
Commodity consumption: Newsprint 33,095 short tons; widths 54½", 40⅞", 27¼"; black ink 958,530 pounds; color ink 128,393 pounds; single pages printed 41,600; average pages per issue 56(d), 133(S); single plates used 190,961.
Equipment: EDITORIAL: Front-end hardware — SII/CLX-RISC; Printers — 5-DEC/LA 120; Other equipment — 205-Intel/PC. CLASSIFIED: Front-end hardware — SII/CLX-RISC; Printers — 1-DEC/LA 120; Other equipment — 57-IBM/PS-2-50. DISPLAY: Adv layout systems — 8-Ap/Power Mac 8100; Front-end hardware — 2-SII/Tahoe, Ap/Mac Pac; Front-end software — SII/AdSpeed; Printers — 1-HP/LaserJet III, 1-Ap/Mac LaserWriter II, 2-AU/APS-6, 1-AU/APS-3850; Other equipment — Microtek/Scanner (RGB), Dovefax/modem, ECR/Autokon 1000 DE. PRODUCTION: Typesetters — 2-AU/APS-5, 2-AU/APS-6, AU/LZR 2600, 1-SII/Bar code printer, 1-SII/Bar code reader, 1-AU/3850; Plate exposures — 2-WL/Lith-X-Pozer 10; Plate processors — 2-WL/380D; Electronic picture desk — Lf/AP Leaf Picture Desk; Scanners — 2-ECR/Autokon 1000 w/DE upgrade; Production cameras — 1-C/Spartan III, 1-C/Pager; Automatic film processors — 4-LE/2600, 2-LE/PC 1800, 2-AU/APS 36, 1-LE/LS 2600; Film transporters — 2-C, 2-AU/APS 36; Shrink lenses — 1-Alan; Digital color separation equipment — 1-Scitex/340, 1-Scitex/340L, 2-Resolut. PRESSROOM: Line 1 — 10-G/Colorliner; Line 2 — 10-G/Colorliner; Pasters — 20-G/CT50; Reels and stands — 20-G/CT50; Press control system — G/APCS. MAILROOM: Counter stackers — Id/2000; Inserters and stuffers — 2-HI/2299, 1-HL/1372; Bundle tyer — Power Strap; Addressing machine — 2-Ch/596; Mailroom control system — Id. LIBRARY: Electronic — SII/LASR, Digital Collections/Photo Archive. WIRE SERVICES: News — AP, NYT, GNS; Photos — AP; Stock tables — AP SelectStox; Receiving dishes — AP. BUSINESS COMPUTERS: 2-IBM/AS 400, Lotus 1-2-3; PCs & micros networked.

Nashville Banner (e-mon to fri)

Nashville Banner, 1100 Broadway, Nashville, TN 37203; tel (615) 259-8800; fax (615) 259-8890; e-mail nashville.banner@nashville.com.
Circulation: 51,987(e); ABC Sept. 30, 1995.
Price: 35¢(d); $1.75/wk; $5.80/mo; $75.40/yr.
Advertising: Open inch rate $127.27(e); comb with Nashville Tennessean (mS) $156.63. **Representative:** Gannett National Newspaper Sales.
News Services: AP, LAT-WP. **Politics:** Independent. **Established:** 1876.
Note: The Nashville Banner and the Tennessean are corporately and editorially separate. The Tennessean is agent for advertising, circulation, production and printing functions of the Nashville Banner.
Special Editions: Lawn & Garden Fair (Mar); Import Cars (May); Car Care (Oct).
Special Weekly Sections: The Ledger (mon); Food (wed); Weekender (thur); Business; Lifestyles; Sports.

CORPORATE OFFICERS

President Brownlee Currey
Publisher Irby C Simpkins

ADVERTISING

Vice Pres Leslie Giallombardo
Manager-Display Gary Watel
Manager-National Wendell Pedigo
Manager-Classified Anna Bartkowski

NEWS EXECUTIVES

Editor Eddie Jones
Managing Editor Pat Embry

EDITORS AND MANAGERS

Auto Racing Editor Joe Caldwell
Books Editor Sue McClure
Business Editor Tim Tanton
Editorial Page Editor Dan Coleman
Education Editor Dana Pride
Food Editor Nicki Pendleton
Graphics Editor Mike McGeehee
Librarian Sally Moran
Lifestyle Editor Tim Ghianni
Medical Editor Bill Snyder
Music Editor Jay Orr
National Editor Kristin Whittlesey
Chief Photographer Turner Hutchinson
Political Editor Lyle Graves
Radio/Television Editor Jim Molpus
Region Editor Gina Fann
Religion Editor Frances Meeker
Sports Editor Joe Biddle
Youth Banner Editor Fronda Throckmorton

Equipment: WIRE SERVICES: News — AP, LAT-WP; Syndicates — North America Syndicate.

OAK RIDGE

Anderson County

'90 U.S. Census- 27,310; E&P '96 Est. 27,032

The Oak Ridger (e-mon to fri)

The Oak Ridger, 785 Oak Ridge Tpk.; PO Box 3446, Oak Ridge, TN 37831; tel (423) 482-1021; fax (423) 482-7834. Morris Communications Corp. group.
Circulation: 9,784(e); Sworn Oct. 3, 1994.
Price: 50¢(d); 75¢(fri); $10.25/mo (carrier), $13.25/mo (mail).
Advertising: Open inch rate $12.15(e); $13.65(e-fri).
News Service: AP. **Politics:** Independent. **Established:** 1949.
Special Editions: Bride (Jan); Gardening (Mar); Outdoor (May); Bride (June); Back-to-School, Football (Aug); Cooking (Oct); Christmas Gift Guide, Greetings (Dec).
Special Weekly Sections: Business, Science, Weekend Sports (mon); Lifestyle, Community News (tues); Best Food Day, Health News (wed); Focus on Community Issues (thur); Weekend Entertainment, TV Section, Real Estate, Automotive, Weddings/Engagements, Religion, Kid's Mini-Page (fri).
Magazines: Intermission (local entertainment), Real Estate Marketplace, USA Weekend (fri).

GENERAL MANAGEMENT

Publisher Pete Esser
Business Manager Carol Skyberg

ADVERTISING

Director David L McCoy

TELECOMMUNICATIONS

Audiotex Manager Miriam McFadden

CIRCULATION

Manager Miriam McFadden

NEWS EXECUTIVE

Editor Ron Bridgeman

EDITORS AND MANAGERS

Business Editor Beverly Nageotte
Entertainment Editor Bernadine Andrew
Films Editor Bernadine Andrew
Food Editor Bernadine Andrew
News Editor Donna Smith
Religion Editor Bernadine Andrew
Sports Editor Mike Blackerby

PRODUCTION

Manager Tom Watson
Foreman-Composing Charlotte Patterson

Market Information: TMC; Operate audiotex.
Mechanical available: Offset; Black and 3 ROP colors; insert accepted — preprinted, any; page cut-offs — 22¾".
Mechanical specifications: Type page 13" x 21½"; E - 6 cols, 2¹⁄₁₆", ⅛" between; A - 6 cols, 2¹⁄₁₆", ⅛" between; C - 9 cols, 1⅝", ⅛" between.
Commodity consumption: Newsprint 680 short tons; widths 27", 13½"; single pages printed 7,614; average pages per issue 22(d).
Equipment: EDITORIAL: Front-end hardware — Ap/Mac; Front-end software — Baseview/NewsEdit Pro; Printers — MON/1270 Imager, 2-Ap/Mac LaserWriter. CLASSIFIED: Front-end hardware — Ap/Mac, 2-PEC; Front-end software — Baseview; Printers — Ap/Mac Laser-Writer. AUDIOTEX: Hardware — Sanyo/486; Software — SMS; Supplier name — SMS. DISPLAY: Front-end hardware — 4-Ap/Mac II VX; Printers — 1-Ap/Mac LaserWriter 630 Pro. PRODUCTION: Plate exposures — 1-Nu/Flip Top FT40PNS; Plate processors — 1-Nat/A-250; Production cameras — 1-C; Automatic film processors — 1-LE; Shrink lenses — 1-Kamerak; Digital color separation equipment — 1-RZ/40-50. PRESSROOM: Line 1 — TKS; Reels and stands — 2-DEV/4-high, 1-DEV/3-high; Press control system — TKS. MAILROOM: Counter stackers — BG/Count-O-Veyor; Inserters and stuffers — KAN/480; Bundle tyer — 1-MLN/Spirit, 1-MLN. WIRE SERVICES: News — AP Datastream; Receiving dishes — size-6ft, AP. BUSINESS COMPUTERS: NCR/Unix; Applications: NCR/SMS Business Applications.

PARIS

Henry County

'90 U.S. Census- 9,332; E&P '96 Est. 8,354

The Paris Post-Intelligencer (e-mon to fri)

The Paris Post-Intelligencer, 208 E. Wood; PO Box 310, Paris, TN 38242; tel (901) 642-1162; fax (901) 642-1165.
Circulation: 8,403(e); Sworn Oct. 4, 1995.
Price: 30¢(d); $40.00/yr (in county).
Advertising: Open inch rate $6.11(e). **Representative:** Papert Companies.
News Service: AP. **Politics:** Independent. **Established:** 1866.
Not Published: New Year; Independence Day; Labor Day; Thanksgiving; Christmas.
Advertising not accepted: Liquor, wine.
Special Editions: Brides (Jan); Boy Scout/Girl Scout, Future Farmers (Feb); Business Anniversary, Farm, Lawn and Garden (Mar); Fish Fry, Paris in Spring, Tourism Guide (Apr); Mother's Day, Graduation, Home Improvement (May); Local Softball (June); Industry Recognition, Health and Fitness (July); Back-to-School (Aug); Football, Working Women (Sept); Soccer, 4-H, Winterizing (Oct); Basketball, Christmas Shopping (Nov).
Special Weekly Section: TV Schedules (every other fri).
Magazine: P-1 Plus (local, newsprint) (wed).

CORPORATE OFFICERS

President/Treasurer Bill Williams
Vice Pres Julia S Williams
Secretary Anne C Williams

GENERAL MANAGEMENT

Publisher Bill Williams
Purchasing Agent Jimmy Williams
Business Manager Bill Davis

ADVERTISING

Manager Brenda Stubblefield
Manager-Classified Rhonda Green

CIRCULATION

Manager Tim Forrest

NEWS EXECUTIVE

Editor Michael Williams

EDITORS AND MANAGERS

News Editor Gene McCutcheon
Outdoors Editor Steve McCadams
Society Editor Ann Broach
Sports Editor Tommy Priddy

MANAGEMENT INFORMATION SERVICES

Data Processing Manager Bill Davis

PRODUCTION

Superintendent Jimmy Williams

Market Information: Split Run; TMC.
Mechanical available: Offset; Black and 3 ROP colors; insert accepted — preprinted, does not accept mini catalogs; page cut-offs — 22¾".
Mechanical specifications: Type page 13" x 21½"; E - 6 cols, 2¹⁄₁₆", ⅛" between; A - 6 cols, 2¹⁄₁₆", ⅛" between; C - 9 cols, 1½", ¹⁄₁₆" between.
Commodity consumption: Newsprint 250 short tons; widths 27½", 13¾"; black ink 14,000 pounds; color ink 2,000 pounds; single pages printed 4,664; average pages per issue 18(d); single plates used 3,500.
Equipment: EDITORIAL: Front-end hardware — 8-Mk/MC4001, Ap/Mac IIcx; Front-end software — Mk; Printers — 1-Ap/Mac Laser Pro 630; Other equipment — 2-RSK/M100 lap top. CLASSIFIED: Front-end hardware — 1-Mk/MC4001; Front-end software — Mk; Printers — 1-DEC/Decprinter I. DISPLAY: Front-end hardware — 1-Ap/Mac IIci, 1-Ap/Mac Quadra 7100 AU; Front-end software — Multi-Ad/Creator; Printers — 1-Ap/Mac LaserWriter NTX. PRODUCTION: OCR software — Caere/Omni-Page Pro; Typesetters — 1-Ap/Mac Laser-Writer; Plate exposures — 1-Nu/Flip Top FT40 V6UPNS; Plate processors — 1-Nat; Electronic picture desk — 1-Ap/Mac Quadra 800, Adobe/Photoshop; Scanners — 1-Lf/Leafscan 35, 1-Microtek/IIXE, 1-Microtek/MSF-300GS; Production cameras — 1-DAI/2400; Automatic film processors — 1-LE/LD1800 A. PRESSROOM: Line 1 — 7-G/Community; Folders — 1-G/SC. MAILROOM: Bundle tyer — 2-Bu/18. LIBRARY: Electronic — SMS/Stauffer Gold, Ap/Mac Plus, Ap/Mac Classic II. WIRE SERVICES: News — AP; Receiving dishes — size-3ft, AP. BUSINESS COMPUTERS: 2-IBM, 1-Okidata/129; Applications: Circ, Payroll, Accts receivable, Gen ledger, Accts payable; PCs & micros networked.

SEVIERVILLE

Sevier County

'90 U.S. Census- 7,178; E&P '96 Est. 10,563

The Mountain Press (m-mon to sat; S)

The Mountain Press, 119 Riverbend Dr.; PO Box 4810, Sevierville, TN 37862; tel (423) 428-0746; fax (423) 453-4913. Paxton Media group.
Circulation: 9,189(m); 9,189(m-sat); 9,189 (S); Sworn Sept. 30, 1995.
Price: 50¢(d); 50¢(sat); $1.00(S); $8.33/mo; $100.00/yr.
Advertising: Open inch rate $11.00(m); $11.00(m-sat); $11.00(S). **Representative:** Papert Companies.
News Service: AP. **Politics:** Independent. **Established:** 1882.
Not Published: Christmas.
Special Editions: Bridal (Jan); Progress (Feb); Spring Fashion, Sevierville's Bicentennial, Home Show (Mar); Coupon Booklet (Apr); Car Guide, Today's Woman (May); Graduation (June); Newcomer's Guide (July); Back-to-School, Football (Aug); Apple Fest, Blue Book (Sept); New Car Guide (Oct); Winterfest, Gift Guide I, Christmas Carol Book (Nov); Gift Guide II, Christmas Greetings (Dec).
Magazines: Best Food Day (mon); Real Estate (fri); Business, Showcase, Lifestyles/Classified Section (S).

GENERAL MANAGEMENT

Publisher Robert L Childress

ADVERTISING

Director-Marketing Don Swartz

CIRCULATION

Manager Ed Trenholn

NEWS EXECUTIVE

Editor Anna Garber

EDITORS AND MANAGERS

Editorial Page Editor Anna Garber
Entertainment/Amusements Editor Terry Morrow
News Editor Robert McCarty
Sports Editor Jim Davis
Television/Film Editor Terry Morrow
Theater/Music Editor Terry Morrow

PRODUCTION

Director R Thomas McCarter

Market Information: Zoned editions; TMC.
Mechanical available: Offset; Black and 3 ROP colors; insert accepted — preprinted; page cut-offs — 22¾".
Mechanical specifications: Type page 13" x 21"; E - 6 cols, 2 1/16", ⅛" between; A - 6 cols, 2 1/16", ⅛" between; C - 8 cols, 1 9/16", ⅛" between.
Commodity consumption: Newsprint 600 short tons; width 27"; black ink 15,000 pounds; color ink 7,200 pounds; single pages printed 5,200; average pages per issue 20(d), 32(S); single plates used 8,000.
Equipment: EDITORIAL: Front-end hardware — EKI/Editorial System. CLASSIFIED: Front-end hardware — 3-EKI/Televideo. DISPLAY: Adv layout systems — Ap/Mac IIcx; Printers — 2-Ap/Mac LaserWriter, 1-NewGen/Imager Plus 12. PRODUCTION: Typesetters — 2-Ap/Mac LaserWriter, 1-NewGen/Printer, 1-NewGen/Imager Plus 12; Platemaking systems — R; Plate exposures — R, Nu/Flip Top FT40UPNS; Plate processors — R, Nat/A-250; Production cameras — LE/R 500; Automatic film processors — C, LE/LD 24A0; Color separation equipment (conventional) — Nikon/Coolscan, Mikrotek/Scanmaker II; Digital color separation equipment — Digi-Colour. PRESSROOM: Line 1 — 6-WPC/Leader. MAILROOM: Inserters and stuffers — KR/512; Bundle tyer — 2-Malow/50; Addressing machine — KR/211. WIRE SERVICES: News — AP; Receiving dishes — size-1ft, AP. BUSINESS COMPUTERS: IBM/PC-AT; Applications: Payroll, Accts receivable, Accts payable, Circ, Gen ledger; PCs & micros networked; PCs & main system networked.

SHELBYVILLE

Bedford County

'90 U.S. Census- 14,049; **E&P '96 Est.** 14,480

Shelbyville Times-Gazette

(e-mon to fri)

Shelbyville Times-Gazette, 323 E. Depot St.; PO Box 380, Shelbyville, TN 37160-0380; tel (615) 684-1200; fax (615) 684-3228.
Circulation: 8,699(e); Sworn Oct. 2, 1995.
Price: 35¢(d); $34.00/yr (mail), $44.20/yr (carrier).
Advertising: Open inch rate $6.00(e). **Representative:** Papert Companies.
News Services: AP, NEA. **Politics:** Independent. **Established:** 1874.
Not Published: New Year; Memorial Day; Independence Day; Labor Day; Thanksgiving; Christmas.
Advertising not accepted: Alcoholic beverages; Fortune tellers; Speculative non-local corp.
Special Editions: Jaycees (Jan); Farm (Mar); Private Property (Apr); Bride (May); Dairy (June); Back-to-School, Tennessee Walking Horse National Celebration (Aug); Gift Guide (Nov); Fashion (Fall); Sports (monthly).
Special Weekly Sections: Best Food Days, Mini-Youth, Senior Citizen (mon); Farm (tues); Best Food Day (wed); Farm (thur); TV Log, Church (fri).
Magazine: Business (tues).

CORPORATE OFFICERS

President Franklin Yates
Vice Pres Mrs Franklin Yates
Treasurer Mrs Johnaie Yates
Secretary Mrs Nina Gay Segroves

GENERAL MANAGEMENT

Publisher David Segroves
Assoc Publisher Wilene M Sandres
Manager-Office Wilene M Sanders

ADVERTISING

Manager Ruth Coop
Manager-Classified Blondell Fisher
Manager-Classified Sue Pylant

CIRCULATION

Manager Tommy Vaughn

NEWS EXECUTIVE

Editor Mark McGee

EDITORS AND MANAGERS

Editorial Page Editor Mark McGee
Photo Department Manager David Segroves
Society Editor Kay Rose

PRODUCTION

Manager David Segroves

Market Information: TMC.
Mechanical available: Offset; Black and 3 ROP colors; insert accepted — preprinted; page cut-offs — 22¾".
Mechanical specifications: Type page 13" x 21½"; E - 7 cols, 2⅙", ⅛" between; A - 7 cols, 2⅙", ⅛" between; C - 9 cols, 1 9/16", ⅛" between.
Commodity consumption: Newsprint 245 short tons; widths 32", 16"; black ink 7,200 pounds; single pages printed 4,274; average pages per issue 16(d); single plates used 2,000.
Equipment: EDITORIAL: Front-end hardware — PC; Front-end software — CText; Printers — Ap/Mac LaserWriter. CLASSIFIED: Front-end hardware — PC; Printers — Ap/Mac LaserWriter. DISPLAY: Front-end hardware — Ap/Mac; Printers — Ap/Mac LaserWriter. PRODUCTION: Production cameras — B; Automatic film processors — Konica. PRESSROOM: Line 1 — 6-KP/Colorking Web (Non heat O.S.). MAILROOM: Bundle tyer — 2-Bu. WIRE SERVICES: News — AP; Receiving dishes — AP. BUSINESS COMPUTERS: Centurion/7000; PCs & micros networked;

UNION CITY

Obion County

'90 U.S. Census- 10,513; **E&P '96 Est.** 10,575

Union City Daily Messenger

(e-mon to fri)

Union City Daily Messenger, 613 Jackson St., Union City, TN 38261; tel (901) 885-0744; fax (901) 885-0782.
Circulation: 8,384(e); Sworn Oct. 10, 1995.
Price: 50¢(d); $7.00/mo; $80.00/yr.
Advertising: Open inch rate $7.75(e). **Representative:** Papert Companies.
News Service: AP. **Politics:** Independent-Democrat. **Established:** 1926.
Not Published: Independence Day; Thanksgiving; Christmas.
Special Weekly Sections: Business (mon); Farm, Medical (tues); Food (wed); Church (thur).

GENERAL MANAGEMENT

Publisher/General Manager Dave Critchlow Sr
Business Manager Sherry Shanklin

ADVERTISING

Manager-Retail Gloria Chesteen
Manager-Classified Linda Hudson

CIRCULATION

Manager Troy Arnold

NEWS EXECUTIVE

Editor David Critchlow Jr

EDITORS AND MANAGERS

Editorial Page Editor David Bartholomew
Farm Editor Chris Menees
Fashion/Society Editor Darlene Hayes
Living/Lifestyle Editor Darlene Hayes
News Editor David Critchlow Jr
Photo Manager Dave Critchlow Sr
Sports Editor Mike Hutchens
Women's Editor Darlene Hayes

Market Information: TMC.
Mechanical available: Offset; Black and 3 ROP colors; insert accepted — preprinted; page cut-offs — 22¾".
Mechanical specifications: Type page 13" x 21½"; E - 6 cols, 2 1/16", ⅛" between; A - 6 cols, 2 1/16", ⅛" between; C - 9 cols, 1 5/16", ⅛" between.
Commodity consumption: average pages per issue 16(d).
Equipment: EDITORIAL: Front-end hardware — 12-Ap/Mac SE; Front-end software — Jus-Text; Printers — Ap/Mac LaserWriter. CLASSIFIED: Front-end hardware — 2-Ap/Mac SE; Printers — Ap/Mac LaserWriter. DISPLAY: Front-end hardware — 2-Ap/Mac; Front-end software — DTI; Printers — Ap/Mac LaserWriter. PRODUCTION: Plate exposures — 2-Nu; Plate processors — 1-WL; Electronic picture desk — Lf/AP Leaf Picture Desk; Production cameras — 1-C/Spartan; Automatic film processors — 1-P; Film transporters — 1-P; Color separation equipment (conventional) — Lf/Leafscan 35. PRESSROOM: Line 1 — 10-SLN; Folders — 2-SLN/2:1. MAILROOM: Bundle tyer — 2-Bu; Addressing machine — 1-Dispensa-Matic. WIRE SERVICES: News — AP; Photos — AP; Receiving dishes — AP. BUSINESS COMPUTERS: 1-IBM/Sys 36; Applications: Circ, Payroll, Accts payable, Accts receivable.

TEXAS

ABILENE

Taylor County

'90 U.S. Census- 106,654; **E&P '96 Est.** 111,110
ABC-CZ (90): 107,733 (HH 38,788)

Abilene Reporter-News

(m-mon to sat; S)

Abilene Reporter-News, 100 Block Cypress St., Abilene, TX 79604; tel (915) 673-4271; fax (915) 672-8754; web site http://www.abilene.com/arn/arnhome.html. Harte-Hanks Communications Inc. group.
Circulation: 42,704(m); 42,704(m-sat); 52,803(S); ABC Sept. 30, 1995.
Price: 50¢(d); 50¢(sat); $1.50(S); $14.50/mo; $162.00/yr.
Advertising: Open inch rate $34.90(m); $35.60(m-fri); $35.60(m-sat); $36.00(S). **Representative:** Papert Companies.
News Service: AP. **Politics:** Independent. **Established:** 1881.
Special Editions: Opportunities, Bundles of Joy (Jan); Spring Bridal, Oil and Gas (Feb); Auto Show, Rattlesnake Round-up, Lawn and Garden, Farm and Ranch, Home Improvement (Mar); Great Outdoors (Apr); West Texas Fair Catalog, Graduation Tab (May); Ft. Griffin Fandangle (June); Abilene Almanac, Best of the Big Country, Stamford Rodeo (July); Hunting and Fishing, Back-to-School, Kick-off '96 (Aug); West Texas Fair and Rodeo, Fall Bridal (Sept); Home Enhancement, Health Care '96, Today's Woman (Oct); Holiday Planner, Christmas Song Book (Nov); Holiday Greetings (Dec).
Special Weekly Sections: Oil, Farm, Business Pages (tues); Best Food Day, TMC delivered to non-subscribers (wed); Business Pages (thur); Travel Pages, Oil, Farm, Business Pages, Book Review, Farm (S); Entertainment (daily); Entertainment (Weekend).
Magazines: TV Week (S); Insider (TMC).

CORPORATE OFFICER

President Larry Franklin

GENERAL MANAGEMENT

Chairman of the Board A B Shelton
President/Publisher Frank Puckett Jr
Director-Finance Jesus A Vasquez

ADVERTISING

Director Mike Winter
Manager-Retail Sales John Bair
Manager-Classified John Bair
Manager-Marketing Service Bredgit Sommer

MARKETING AND PROMOTION

Manager-Marketing/Promotion Bredgit Sommer

TELECOMMUNICATIONS

Audiotex Manager Candy Holcombe

CIRCULATION

Director Steve Jordan

NEWS EXECUTIVES

Editor Glenn Dromgoole
Managing Editor-News Danny Reagon

EDITORS AND MANAGERS

Books Editor Larry Lawrence
Business Editor Doug Williamson
Cartoonist Jim Quinnett
Education Editor (Lower) Leslie Strader
Education Editor (Higher) Dean Williamson
Editorial Page Editor Jeff Wolf
Entertainment/Amusements Editor Greg Jaklewiez
Farm Editor J T Smith
Fashion Editor Carol Lackey
Features Editor Carol Lackey
Films/Theater Editor Bob Lapham
Food Editor Pam Percival
Graphics Editor/Art Director Layne Smith
Health/Medical Editor Carol Lackey
Life Editor Carol Lackey
Librarian Anne Holland
Living/Lifestyle Editor Carol Lackey
Military Editor Roy Jones
Music Editor Greg Jaklewicz
News Editor Kerry Cole
Photo Editor David Kent
Oil Editor Bob Bruce
Political/Government Editor Richard Horn
Religion Editor Roy Jones
Sports Editor Al Pickett
Teen-Age/Youth Editor Carl Kieke
Travel Editor Bob Bruce
Television Editor Bob Lapham
Weekend Editor Greg Jaklewiez
Women's Editor Carol Lackey

MANAGEMENT INFORMATION SERVICES

Data Processing Manager Tom McCusker

PRODUCTION

Director Steve Jordan
Foreman-Pressroom Ron Shannon
Foreman-Computers Tom McCusker

Market Information: Split Run; TMC; ADS; Operate audiotex.
Mechanical available: Black and 3 ROP colors; insert accepted — preprinted; page cut-offs — 22".
Mechanical specifications: Type page 13" x 21¼"; E - 6 cols, 2 1/16", ⅛" between; A - 6 cols, 2 1/16", ⅛" between; C - 9 cols, 1 5/16", ⅛" between.
Commodity consumption: Newsprint 4,664 short tons; widths 54", 40½", 27"; black ink 96,713 pounds; color ink 26,730 pounds; single pages printed 15,584; average pages per issue 36(d), 86(S); single plates used 40,428.
Equipment: EDITORIAL: Front-end hardware — SII/Sys 25 Tandem; Front-end software — SII/Sys 25; Printers — 1-Centronics/351. CLASSIFIED: Front-end hardware — SII/Sys Tandem; Front-end software — SII/Sys 25; Printers — 1-Centronics/351. AUDIOTEX: Hardware — Brite Voice Systems; Supplier name — Brite Voice Systems. DISPLAY: Adv layout systems — CJ; Front-end hardware — HP/3000; Front-end software — CJ; Printers — HP/LaserJet II. PRODUCTION: Pagination software — QuarkXPress 3.1; Typesetters — 2-COM/CG8600, Ap/Mac, Ap/Mac LaserWriter NTX, Ap/Mac Digi-Colour, 1-Panther/Pro 46 Imagesetter, 1-Panther/Pro Imagesetter 5300W; Platemaking systems — 1-Nu; Plate exposures — 2-Nu/Flip Top; Plate processors — 1-Nat; Direct-to-plate imaging — 3M/Pyrofax; Scanners — Digi-Colour, Ap/Mac, PixelCraft/ProImager 8000; Production cameras — 2-C; Automatic film processors — 2-Kk; Color separation equipment (conventional) — Digi-Colour, PixelCraft/ProImager 8000; Digital color separation equipment — Adobe/Photoshop w/PixelCraft/ProImager. PRESSROOM: Line 1 — 3-G/Community single width; Line 2 — 7-G/Headliner double width (Offset, Open Fountain, 4½ deck); Press drives — 4-GE/150LP motor; Folders — 2-Regent/2:1, 1-G/506, 1-G/Jaws; Pasters — G/Auto; Press control system — Fin; Press registration system — G. MAILROOM: Counter stackers — 2-Id/660, 1-Id/440, 1-KAN; Inserters and stuffers — HI/48P; Bundle tyer — 3-OVL, 1-Id; Addressing machine — 1-KR. LIBRARY: Combination — non-electronic. COMMUNICATIONS: Digital ad delivery system — AP AdSend. Systems used — satellite. WIRE SERVICES: News — AP; Stock tables — AP; Syndicates — AP; Receiving dishes — AP. BUSINESS COMPUTERS: HP/3000 937LX; Applications: Circ, Adv, Layout, Class; PCs & micros networked; PCs & main system networked.

ALICE

Jim Wells County

'90 U.S. Census- 19,788; **E&P '96 Est.** 19,211

Alice Echo-News

(e-mon to fri; S)

Alice Echo-News, 405 E. Main (78333); PO Box 1610, Alice, TX 78332; tel (512) 664-6588; fax (512) 668-1030. Boone Newspapers Inc. group.
Circulation: 4,483(e); 4,483(S); Sworn Sept. 22, 1993.
Price: 50¢(d); $1.25(S); $78.00/yr.
Advertising: Open inch rate $7.55(e); $8.30(S). **Representative:** Papert Companies.
News Service: AP. **Established:** 1894.
Special Editions: Horizons, Senior Life (Feb); Senior Life (Apr, June); Visitor's Guide (July); Football Preview, Senior Life (Aug); Senior Life (Oct); Winter Texans (Nov); Senior Life (Dec).
Special Weekly Sections: Color Comics, TV Listings (S).

I-388 Texas

GENERAL MANAGEMENT	
Publisher	Bruce Wallace
ADVERTISING	
Director	Linda Fowler-Nash
Manager-Classified	Deepa Subramanian
CIRCULATION	
Manager	Cynthia Gonzalez
NEWS EXECUTIVE	
Editor	Jim Terrell
EDITOR AND MANAGER	
News Editor	Jim Terrell

Market Information: TMC; ADS.
Mechanical available: Offset; Black and 3 ROP colors; insert accepted — preprinted; page cut-offs — 22½".
Mechanical specifications: Type page 13" x 21½"; E - 6 cols, 2 1/16", 1/8" between; A - 6 cols, 2 1/16", 1/8" between; C - 8 cols, 1½", 1/8" between.
Commodity consumption: black ink 10,000 pounds; color ink 2,000 pounds; average pages per issue 10(d), 36(S).
Equipment: EDITORIAL: Front-end hardware — Ap/Mac; Front-end software — Claris/MacWrite Pro, QuarkXPress; Printers — Ap/Mac Laser-Writers; Other equipment — Microtek/Scanner. CLASSIFIED: Front-end hardware — Ap/Mac; Front-end software — Baseview. DISPLAY: Adv layout systems — Ap/Mac; Front-end software — QuarkXPress. PRODUCTION: Typesetters — Ap/Mac; Production cameras — R. MAILROOM: Inserters and stuffers — 4-KAN; Bundle tyer — Ca; Addressing machine — Am. WIRE SERVICES: News — AP; Receiving dishes — AP. BUSINESS COMPUTERS: Onyx; Applications: Accts receivable; PCs & main system networked.

AMARILLO
Potter and Randall Counties
'90 U.S. Census- 157,615; E&P '96 Est. 162,023
ABC-CZ (90): 157,615 (HH 61,137)

Amarillo Daily News
(m-mon to sat)
Amarillo Globe Times
(e-mon to fri)
Amarillo Sunday News-Globe (S)

Amarillo Daily News/Globe Times, 900 Harrison St.; PO Box 2091, Amarillo, TX 79166; tel (806) 376-4488; fax (806) 376-9217. Morris Communications Corp. group.
Circulation: 42,175(m); 18,859(e); 42,175 (m-sat); 74,495(S); ABC Sept. 30, 1995.
Price: 50¢(d); 50¢(sat); $1.25(S); $8.60/mo, $9.85/mo (m & S); $9.50/mo (e & S), $8.25/mo (e only); $8.85/mo (sat & S), $7.60/mo (S only).
Advertising: Open inch rate $40.32(m); $40.32(e); $40.32(m-sat); $43.68(S); $36.26(m & e). **Representative:** Papert Companies.
News Services: AP, KRT, LAT-WP. **Politics:** Independent. **Established:** 1909 (News), 1924 (Globe).
Special Edition: Goodlife (over 50's) (monthly).
Special Weekly Sections: Business Review (mon); Business & Financial, Energy (tues); Food Section (wed); Arts & Entertainment (thur); Teen Section (fri); Business & Financial, TV Section, Arts & Entertainment, Farm Page, Energy, Real Estate (S).

CORPORATE OFFICER	
COB	W S Morris III
GENERAL MANAGEMENT	
Publisher	Garet von Netzer
Controller-Division	Larry Smith
Personnel Director	Jeane Bartlett
ADVERTISING	
Director	Steve Beasley
Manager-Retail	Joanne Gosselin
Manager-Classified	Gayle Hilpert
MARKETING AND PROMOTION	
Manager-Marketing/Promotion	Heather Sells
TELECOMMUNICATIONS	
Audiotex Manager	Gayle Hilpert
CIRCULATION	
Director	Paul R Haygood

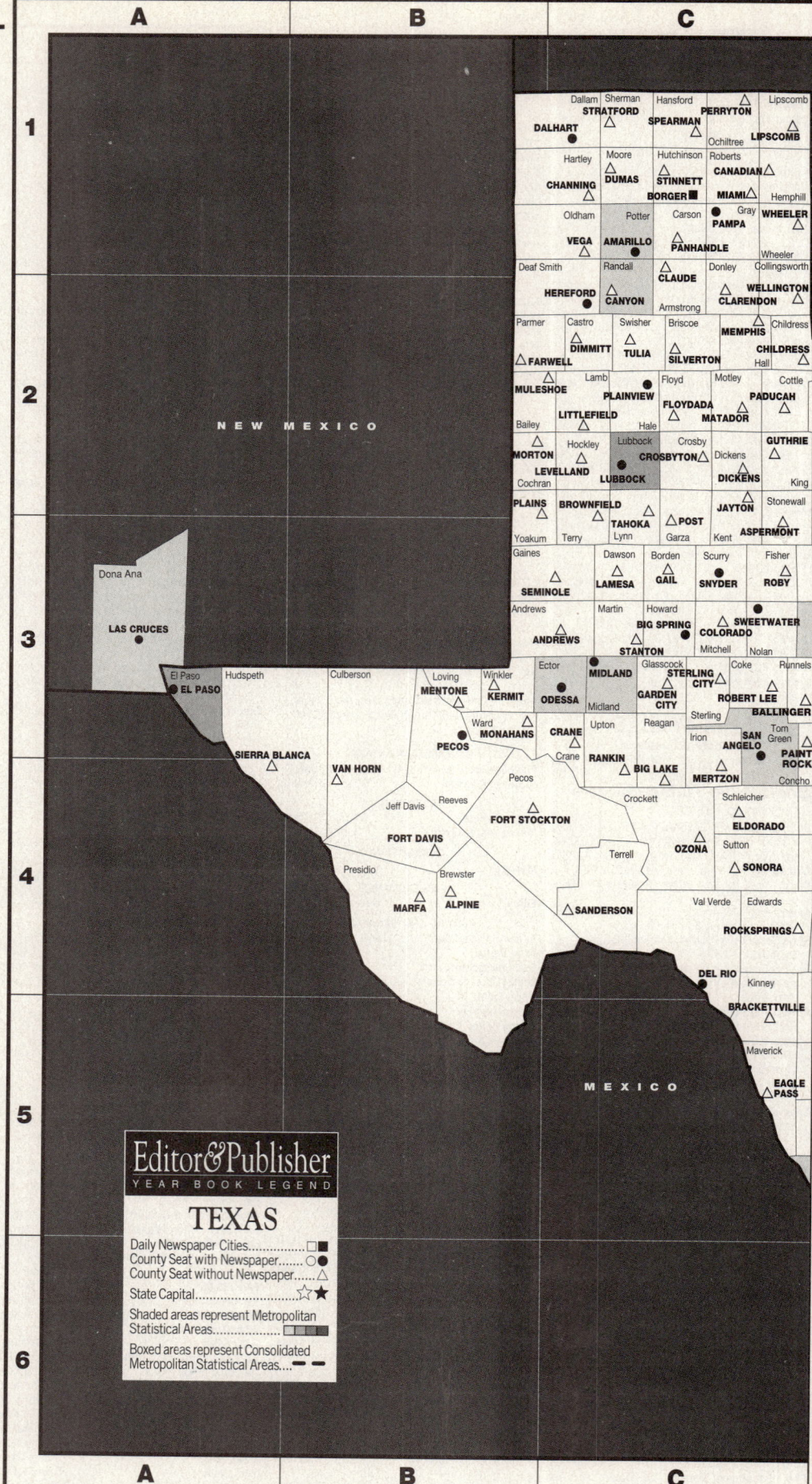

Copyright ©1996 by the Editor & Publisher Co.

Texas   I-389

Manager-Country	Wendell Smith
Manager-City	Janis Camfield

NEWS EXECUTIVES

Exec Editor	Cathy A Martindale
Managing Editor	Dennis Spies

EDITORS AND MANAGERS

Amusements/Music Editor	Jeff Rhodes
Artist	Pat McCarthy
Automotive Editor	Tom Allston
Books Editor	Mary K Tripp
Business/Finance Editor	Mike Rupe
City Editor (Globe-Times & News)	Matt Curry
Education Editor	Melanie Yeager
Editorial Page Editor	John Kanelis
Farm Editor	Kay Ledbetter
Fashion/Style Editor	Beth Duke
Features Editor	Beth Duke
Films/Theater Editor	Jeff Rhodes
Food/Home Furnishings Editor	Beth Duke
Health/Medical Editor	Mike Hughes
National Editor	Jim McBride
News Editor-Day	Bill Knox
News Editor-Night	Bill Knox
Oil Editor	Danny Boyd
Photo Department Manager	Ron Marlow
Political/Government Editor	Jim McBride
Radio/Television Editor	Greg Rohloff
Real Estate Editor	Mike Rupe
Religion Editor	Kerry Curry
Science/Technology Editor	Jim McBride
Sports Editor	Jon Mark Beilue
Travel Editor	Jeff Rhodes
Women's Editor (Globe-Times & News)	Beth Duke

MANAGEMENT INFORMATION SERVICES

Data Processing Manager	Larry Smith

PRODUCTION

Director	Robert Todd
Superintendent-Composing	Mike Kemp
Superintendent-Press	Rick Carstens
Superintendent-Mailroom	B E Lenerose

Market Information: Zoned editions; Split Run; TMC; Operate audiotex.
Mechanical available: Offset; Black and 3 ROP colors; insert accepted — preprinted; page cut-offs — 22¾".
Mechanical specifications: Type page 13" x 21½"; E - 6 cols, 2 1/16", 1/8" between; A - 6 cols, 2 1/16", 1/8" between; C - 10 cols, 1 3/16", 1/8" between.
Commodity consumption: Newsprint 7,952 short tons; widths 54", 40½", 27"; black ink 119,310 pounds; color ink 41,122 pounds; single pages printed 25,990; average pages per issue 35(d), 74(S); single plates used 76,610.
Equipment: EDITORIAL: Front-end hardware — IBM/PC-AT, 6-Gateway/2000; Front-end software — MPS; Printers — Okidata/Microline 320. CLASSIFIED: Front-end hardware — IBM/PC-AT PS-2; Front-end software — MPS; Printers — Okidata/Microline 320. AUDIOTEX: Hardware — Wyse/WY2214. DISPLAY: Front-end hardware — 4-Ap/Mac IIfx, 2-Ap/Mac Quadra 950, 2-Ap/Power Mac; Front-end software — Multi-Ad/Creator, Adobe/Illustrator; Printers — Ap/Mac LaserWriter II; Other equipment — Ap/Mac Scanner, Procom/Tape Backup, NEC/CD-Rom, AP AdSend, Micronet/Optical Drive. PRODUCTION: Pagination software — QuarkXPress 3.1; Typesetters — AG/Accuset 1000, 2-XIT/Clipper; Platemaking systems — 3M/Pyrofax; Plate exposures — 1-B, 1-Nu/Flip Top; Plate processors — WL/Aqualith 32A, Nat; Electronic picture desk — Lf/AP Leaf Picture Desk; Production cameras — 2-C/Spartan III; Automatic film processors — P/RA-26, Kk/Kodamatic 410 42S; Film transporters — C, Konica; Shrink lenses — 1-3M/Pyrofax, 1-C; Color separation equipment (conventional) — HP/Deskscan, Kk/Slide Scanner.
PRESSROOM: Line 1 — 6-G/Metro (w/3 half decks); Press drives — Fin; Folders — G/2:1; Pasters — 6-G; Reels and stands — 6-G; Press control system — Fin. MAILROOM: Counter stackers — 4-QWI/300; Inserters and stuffers — 2-GMA/SLS-1000 18-1; Bundle tyer — 4-Dynaric/NP-2, 2-Dynaric/Turntable; Wrapping singles — 2-QWI/Cobra wraps; Addressing machine — Wm; Mailroom control system — PMS. WIRE SERVICES: News — AP; Stock tables — AP; Syndicates — NYT; Receiving dishes — size-12ft, AP. BUSINESS COMPUTERS: 4-IBM/Sys II, 10-Memorex/Telex 11918; Applications: Lotus 1-2-3, WordPerfect; PCs & micros networked; PCs & main system networked.

I-390 Texas

ATHENS

Henderson County

'90 U.S. Census- 10,967; E&P '96 Est. 11,376

Athens Daily Review

(e-mon to fri; S)

Athens Daily Review, 201 S. Prairieville St.; PO Box 32, Athens, TX 75751; tel (903) 675-5626; fax (903) 675-9450. Donrey Media group.

Circulation: 6,730(e); 6,730(S); Sworn Sept. 24, 1995.

Price: 50¢(d); 50¢(S); $6.50/mo; $75.00/yr (carrier), $80.00/yr (mail).

Advertising: Open inch rate $8.24(e); $8.24(S). **Representative:** Papert Companies.

News Service: AP. **Politics:** Independent. **Established:** 1901.

Special Editions: Progress (Mar); Graduation, Trinity Valley Community College (May).

Special Weekly Sections: Best Food Days (tues); The Advertiser (TMC) (wed); Best Food Days (S).

Magazine: "Active Times Magazine" (quarterly).

CORPORATE OFFICERS

Founder Donald W Reynolds
President/Chief Operating Officer Emmett Jones
Exec Vice Pres/Chief Financial Officer Darrell W Loftin
Vice Pres-Western Newspaper Group David A Osborn
Vice Pres-Eastern Newspaper Group Don Schneider

GENERAL MANAGEMENT

Publisher Dan Dwelle

ADVERTISING

Manager-Classified Dan Youngman
Coordinator-Retail Sales Dan Youngman

CIRCULATION

Manager Nelta Jolliff

NEWS EXECUTIVE

Editor Gene Lehmann

EDITORS AND MANAGERS

Amusements Editor Sylvia Waters
Books Editor Sylvia Waters
Editorial Writer R E Dwelle
News Editor Charles Dukes
Religion/Science Editor Gene Lehmann
Sports Editor Benny Rogers

PRODUCTION

Superintendent Tommy Miers
Foreman-Mailroom Nelta Jolliff

Market Information: TMC.

Mechanical available: Offset; Black and 3 ROP colors; insert accepted — preprinted; page cutoffs — 22¾".

Mechanical specifications: Type page 13" x 21½"; E - 6 cols, 2¹⁄₁₆", ⅛" between; A - 6 cols, 2¹⁄₁₆", ⅛" between; C - 8 cols, 1½", ¹⁄₁₆" between.

Commodity consumption: Newsprint 360 short tons; width 27"; black ink 9,340 pounds; single pages printed 4,910; average pages per issue 15(d), 18(S); single plates used 2,470.

Equipment: EDITORIAL: Front-end hardware — TC/ZX-1, 7-TC/Sword-HD, 1-Ap/Mac Classic; Printers — Ap/Mac LaserWriter II NTX; Other equipment — Toshiba/portable terminal. CLASSIFIED: Front-end hardware — TC/ZX-1, 3-TC/Sword-HD; Printers — Ap/Mac LaserWriter II NTX. DISPLAY: Adv layout systems — 1-Ap/Mac SE30, 3-TC/Sword-HD, 1-Ap/Power Mac 6100-66; Printers — Ap/Mac LaserWriter 16-600PS. PRODUCTION: Plate exposures — 1-Nu/Flip Top FT40UP; Plate processors — 1-Ic/25; Scanners — 1-Ap/Mac Scanner; Production cameras — 1-Acti/183; Automatic film processors — 1-P/24-ML; Shrink lenses — 1-Kamerak/8% Shrink.
PRESSROOM: Line 1 — 6-HI/V-15A (upper former); Folders — 1-HI. MAILROOM: Inserters and stuffers — 4-KAN/320; Bundle tyer — 2-Bu; Addressing machine — 1-KR/215 (w/211). WIRE SERVICES: News — AP; Receiving dishes — size-1m, AP. BUSINESS COMPUTERS: Applications: Brainworks: Bookkeeping, Adv billing system; PCs & micros networked; PCs & main system networked.

AUSTIN

Travis County

'90 U.S. Census- 465,622; E&P '96 Est. 516,511
ABC-CZ (90): 531,991 (HH 216,794)

Austin American-Statesman

(m-mon to sat; S)

Austin American-Statesman, 305 S. Congress; PO Box 670-78767, Austin, TX 78704; tel (512) 445-3500; fax (512) 445-3557; e-mail news@statesman.com; web site http://hookem.com/. Cox Newspapers Inc. group.

Circulation: 177,704(m); 177,704(m-sat); 237,771(S); ABC Sept. 30, 1995.

Price: 50¢(d); 50¢(sat); $1.50(S); $12.49/mo; $135.69/yr.

Advertising: Open inch rate $101.95(m); $112.08(m-sat); $131.15(S).

News Services: AP, LAT-WP, NYT, KRT, Cox News Service. **Politics:** Independent. **Established:** 1871 (Statesman), 1914 (American).

Special Editions: Forecast (Feb); Summer in Austin (May); This is Austin (July); Football (Aug); Christmas Gift Guides (Dec).

Special Weekly Sections: Food (wed); Auto, Onward to the Weekend (thur); Friday Weekend (fri); Saturday Time Out, Auto (sat); Homes, Travel (S).

Magazines: Parade, Show World-TV Guide (local, newsprint) (S).

GENERAL MANAGEMENT

Publisher Michael Laosa
Vice Pres/Business Manager Harold Cline
Vice Pres-Operations Sam Hightower
Director-Human Resources Susan Davidson
Controller Robert Stewart
Manager-Credit Frank Warfield

ADVERTISING

Director George Gutierrez
Manager-Retail Teri Maxwell
Manager-Classified Erin Coats
Manager-National Jack Puryar

MARKETING AND PROMOTION

Director-Marketing Donya Ginest
Asst Director-Marketing Renet Presas

TELECOMMUNICATIONS

Director-Info Service John Triplett

CIRCULATION

Director Toby Pearson
Manager Ernie Silva
Manager-Operations Ralph Howard
Manager-Marketing Malcomb Gardner

NEWS EXECUTIVES

Editor Rich Oppel
Asst Managing Editor Drew Marcks

EDITORS AND MANAGERS

Art Director Larry Babb
Business Editor Jerry Mahoney
Editorial Page Editor Arnold Garcia
Entertainment/Amusements Editor Ed Crowell
Fashion/Style Editor Linda Wienandt
Features Editor Linda Wienandt
Living/Lifestyle Editor Linda Wienandt
Metro Editor Ricardo Gandara
News Editor Michelle Rice
Photography Director Zach Ryall
Political Editor Dave McNeely
Radio/Television Editor Diane Holloway
Sports Editor Tracy Dodds
State Editor Laylan Copelin
Travel Editor Janet Wilson
Women's Editor Linda Wienandt

MANAGEMENT INFORMATION SERVICES

Director Richard E Apperley
Asst Manager Steve Kendrick

PRODUCTION

Director-Operations Sam Hightower
Director-Transportation Sammy Powell
Manager-Composing Eloy Gonzales
Manager-Pressroom Operations Steve Howell
Manager-Mailroom James Mikulenka
Manager-Pre Press Ken Bennight
Manager-Commercial/Printing Projects Don Green

Market Information: Zoned editions; Split Run; TMC; Operate database; Operate audiotex.

Mechanical available: Offset; Black and 3 ROP colors; insert accepted — preprinted; page cutoffs — 22.08".

Mechanical specifications: Type page 13" x 21"; E - 6 cols, 2¹⁄₁₆", ⅛" between; A - 6 cols, 2¹⁄₁₆", ⅛" between; C - 10 cols, 1.21", ⅓" between.

Commodity consumption: Newsprint 44,000 short tons; widths 54", 40½", 27"; black ink 660,000 pounds; color ink 203,000 pounds; single pages printed 40,632; average pages per issue 72(d), 176(S); single plates used 218,000.

Equipment: EDITORIAL: Front-end hardware — AT; Front-end software — AT; Printers — TI/800. CLASSIFIED: Front-end hardware — AT; Front-end software — AT; Printers — TI/800. AUDIOTEX: Hardware — Brite Voice Systems. DISPLAY: Adv layout systems — DTI/AdSpeed; Front-end hardware — Ap/Mac II; Front-end software — DTI/AdSpeed 3.0; Printers — QMS/860. PRODUCTION: Typesetters — 2-AU/APS-6, 2-AU/APS-5; Plate exposures — 2-BKY, 1-WL/Lith-X-Pozer III; Plate processors — 1-WL/30D, 1-WL/38D; Scanners — 2-ECR/Autokon 8400, 1-Lf/Leafscan 45, 1-HP/Jetscan II, 1-AG/Focus II; Production cameras — 2-C/Marathon, 1-C/Newspager I; Automatic film processors — 1-C/66RA, 1-C/66F, 1-LE/tec26; Film transporters — 1-C/Newspager I; Shrink lenses — 1-CK Optical/9.2%, 1-Alan/Variable; Color separation equipment (conventional) — 1-Hel/DG-350 Analog Scanner.
PRESSROOM: Line 1 — 9-G/Metroliner (5 half decks); Line 2 — 9-G/Metroliner (5 half decks); Line 3 — 9-G/Metroliner (5 Half decks); Folders — 3-G/3:2; Pasters — 27-G/RTP; Press control system — Fin. MAILROOM: Counter stackers — 4-St/251, 5-St/2575, 4-GMS/5000, 3-HL/Monitor; Inserters and stuffers — 2-S/48P, 1-S/1472, 1-S/1372, 2-KR; Bundle tyer — 3-Power Strap, 2-MLN/Spirit, 8-MLN/2A; Addressing machine — 2-KR. LIBRARY: Electronic — Data Times. WIRE SERVICES: News — AP Datastream, AP Datafeatures; Stock tables — AP Dataspeed; Syndicates — NYT, KRT, LAT-WP; Receiving dishes — AP. BUSINESS COMPUTERS: 1-IBM/3081-K32, 6-Austin/486-33; Applications: Circ, Payroll, Accts payable, Gen ledger, Adv, Accts receivable (retail, class, national); PCs & micros networked; PCs & main system networked.

BAY CITY

Matagorda County

'90 U.S. Census- 18,170; E&P '96 Est. 18,341

The Daily Tribune & Matagorda County Tribune

(e-tues to fri; S)

The Daily Tribune & Matagorda County Tribune, Carrey Smith Blvd. (77404); PO Box 2450, Bay City, TX 77414; tel (409) 245-5555, (409) 245-3282 (audiotex); fax (409) 244-5908. Southern Newspapers Inc. group.

Circulation: 6,273(e); 6,273(S); Sworn Oct. 2, 1995.

Price: 50¢(d); 50¢(S); $4.75/mo; $57.00/yr (carrier), $84.00/yr (mail).

Advertising: Open inch rate $6.25(e); $6.25(S).

News Service: AP. **Politics:** Independent. **Established:** 1845.

Special Editions: Seasonal; Rice Festival; Rodeo; Fair & Livestock Show; Outdoorsman Tab; Fire Prevention; June Bride; C. of C. Progress.

Magazine: Farm & Ranch Tab (monthly).

CORPORATE OFFICERS

President Eric Bauer
Vice Pres Martha Ann Walls
Secretary/Treasurer Cooper Walls

GENERAL MANAGEMENT

Publisher Eric Bauer
Business Manager Mary Solis

ADVERTISING

Manager-Promotion Buzz Crainer

TELECOMMUNICATIONS

Audiotex Manager Marty Andrews

CIRCULATION

Manager Marty Andrews

NEWS EXECUTIVE

Managing Editor Curt Vincent

EDITORS AND MANAGERS

Society/Women's Editor Alicia Collier
Sports Editor Ed VanderStucken

PRODUCTION

Superintendent Aaron Tilton

Market Information: TMC; Operate audiotex.

Mechanical available: Offset; Black and 3 ROP colors; insert accepted — preprinted; page cutoffs — 23".

Mechanical specifications: Type page 13" x 21½"; E - 6 cols, 2¹⁄₁₆", ⅛" between; A - 6 cols, 2¹⁄₁₆", ⅛" between; C - 9 cols, 1⁷⁄₁₆", ¹⁄₁₆" between.

Commodity consumption: Newsprint 360 metric tons; width 27"; black ink 22,830 pounds; color ink 4,500 pounds; single pages printed 6,104; average pages per issue 18(d), 22(S).

Equipment: EDITORIAL: Front-end hardware — Mk; Front-end software — Baseview. CLASSIFIED: Front-end hardware — Mk; Front-end software — Mk, Baseview. AUDIOTEX: Hardware — IBM/PC 486; Software — BigMouth 4.15; DISPLAY: Front-end hardware — 1-Ap/Mac IIsi, 2-Ap/Mac SE30; Front-end software — Aldus/PageMaker; Printers — 1-Ap/Mac LaserWriter, 1-Microtek/Laserprinter. PRODUCTION: Typesetters — Mk/Laserprinter; Plate exposures — LE; Plate processors — LE; Scanners — 1-Ap/Mac One Scanner; Production cameras — C; Automatic film processors — C.
PRESSROOM: Line 1 — 6-HI/V15; Press control system — HI. MAILROOM: Inserters and stuffers — KAN; Bundle tyer — 2-Bu; Addressing machine — Am/1680. COMMUNICATIONS: Facsimile — 1-X. WIRE SERVICES: News — AP; Receiving dishes — AP. BUSINESS COMPUTERS: 2-IBM/PC; Applications: Newsware; PCs & main system networked.

BAYTOWN

Harris County

'90 U.S. Census- 63,850; E&P '96 Est. 67,629

The Baytown Sun

(e-mon to fri; S)

The Baytown Sun, 1301 Memorial Dr. (77520); PO Box 90, Baytown, TX 77522; tel (713) 422-8302; fax (713) 427-6283. Southern Newspapers Inc. group.

Circulation: 12,884(e); 13,390(S); VAC Dec. 30, 1994.

Price: 50¢(d); $1.00(S); $8.75/mo; $105.00/yr.

Advertising: Open inch rate $9.95(e); $9.95(S). **Representative:** US Suburban Press.

News Services: AP, NEA, CNS. **Established:** 1931.

Special Editions: Spring Chamber of Commerce Progress, Fashion (Mar); Outdoorsman (Fishing, Hunting) (Apr); Summer Fun, Outdoor Living (July); Back-to-School (Aug); Football (Sept); Outdoorsman (Fishing, Hunting) (Oct); Christmas (Dec).

Special Weekly Sections: Business, Best Food Days (tues); Religious, Arts & Entertainment (S).

Magazines: Food, TMC Publications (tues); Entertainment (Accent), TV Guide Listings (S).

GENERAL MANAGEMENT

Publisher Gary M Dobbs

ADVERTISING

Manager-Display Eric Bauer
Manager-Class Debbie Kimmey

NEWS EXECUTIVES

Editor Gary M Dobbs
Managing Editor David Eldridge

EDITORS AND MANAGERS

Editorial Page Editor David Eldridge
Editorial Writer David Eldridge
Home Furnishings Editor Jane Howard
Society/Women's Editor Rebecca McPhail
Sports Editor Kelly Kirkpatrick

PRODUCTION

Foreman-Composing Carol Avalos
Foreman-Pressroom Sam McWhirter

Market Information: TMC.

Mechanical available: Offset; Black and 3 ROP colors; insert accepted — preprinted; page cutoffs — 21".

Mechanical specifications: Type page 13" x 21"; E - 6 cols, 2¹⁄₁₆", ⅛" between; A - 6 cols, 2¹⁄₁₆", ⅛" between; C - 9 cols, 1⁵⁄₁₆", ⅛" between.

Commodity consumption: Newsprint 800 short tons; width 27½"; average pages per issue 21(d), 36(S).

Equipment: EDITORIAL: Front-end hardware — Mk/4000, 13-Mk/AT; Front-end software — Mk/Proprietary; Printers — Ap/Mac LaserWriter II NTX; Other equipment — Ap/Mac Quadra 700. CLASSIFIED: Front-end hardware — Mk/4000, 5-Mk/AT; Front-end software — Mk/Proprietary; Printers — Ap/Mac LaserWriter II NTX. DISPLAY: Adv layout systems — Mk/4000; Front-end hardware — 2-Ap/Mac IIcx, 2-Ap/Mac IIsi; Front-end software — Mk/Proprietary; Printers — Ap/Mac LaserWriter

Copyright ©1996 by the Editor & Publisher Co.

II NTX. PRODUCTION: Typesetters — Ap/Mac LaserWriter II NTX; Platemaking systems — 1-LE/LD-18; Plate exposures — 2-Nu/Flip Top FT40L; Plate processors — 1-WL; Production cameras — 1-C/Spartan III; Automatic film processors — 1-LE; Film transporters — 1-LE; Shrink lenses — 1-CK Optical/SQU-7; Color separation equipment (conventional) — RZ/4050.
PRESSROOM: Line 1 — 7-G/U 1220; Folders — 1-G. MAILROOM: Inserters and stuffers — 1-HI/P-24; Bundle tyer — 1-MLN; Addressing machine — 1-Ch/528N. WIRE SERVICES: News — AP; Receiving dishes — size-1ft, AP. BUSINESS COMPUTERS: 2-DG/Nova, HP/Vectra; PCs & micros networked.

BEAUMONT
Jefferson County
'90 U.S. Census- 114,323; E&P '96 Est. 112,438
ABC-CZ (90): 134,147 (HH 50,410)

Beaumont Enterprise
(m-mon to sat; S)
Beaumont Enterprise, 380 Main St. (77701); PO Box 3071, Beaumont, TX 77704; tel (409) 833-3311; fax (409) 838-2857. Hearst Newspapers group.
Circulation: 63,172(m); 63,172(m-sat); 77,200(S); ABC Sept. 30, 1995.
Price: 50¢(d); 50¢(sat); $1.50(S); $8.00/mo; $90.00/yr.
Advertising: Open inch rate $45.09(m); $46.45(m-sat); $55.13(S). **Representative:** Cresmer, Woodward, O'Mara & Ormsbee.
News Services: AP, KRT. **Politics:** Independent. **Established:** 1880.
Special Editions: Outlook (Jan); Bridal Guide, Health Care (Feb); Design-an-Ad, Today's Woman, Progress (Mar); Home Improvement (Apr); Reader's Choice, Vacations (May); Pre-Fourth Sale (June); Summer Sale (July); Football (Aug); Hunting, Fall Fashion (Sept); Shop S.E. Texas (Oct); Southern Living Cooking School, Auto Preview (Nov); Christmas Essay Contest (Dec).
Special Weekly Sections: Food, TMC-Exclusive (wed); Church (sat); Travel (S).
Magazines: TV Week, Parade (S).

GENERAL MANAGEMENT
Publisher Aubrey L Webb
Personnel Manager Marajane Lewis
Controller Alva Ellison
ADVERTISING
Director Mike Tieman
TELECOMMUNICATIONS
Audiotex Manager Dave Pero
CIRCULATION
Director Jeffrey Reedy
Manager-City Don Taylor
NEWS EXECUTIVES
Editor Ben Hansen
Managing Editor William Mock
EDITORS AND MANAGERS
Books/TV Scope Editor Shari Fey
Business Editor Kurt Gaston
City Editor David Long
Editorial Page Editor Tom Taschinger
Feature Editor Sheila Friedeck
Assoc Features Editor Melissa Galloway
Food Editor Elaine Wikstrom
Librarian Jeanne Walls
News Editor Sean McCrory
Chief Photographer Ron Japp
Records Editor Shari Fey
Sports Editor Joe Heiling
PRODUCTION
Director Don Sikes
Superintendent-Pressroom Frank Aiena
Superintendent-Mailroom Ken Middleton

Market Information: Zoned editions; Split Run; TMC; Operate audiotex.
Mechanical available: Offset; Black and 3 ROP colors; insert accepted — preprinted, card, tab, standard; page cut-offs — 22¾".
Mechanical specifications: Type page 13" x 21½"; E - 6 cols, 2¹⁄₁₆", ⅛" between; A - 6 cols, 2¹⁄₁₆", ⅛" between; C - 8 cols, 1⅜", ⅛" between.
Commodity consumption: Newsprint 5,874 short tons; widths 55¾", 41", 27"; black ink 106,138 pounds; color ink 25,304 pounds; single pages printed 16,466; average pages per issue 32(d), 62(S); single plates used 48,915.
Equipment: EDITORIAL: Front-end hardware — SII/Sys 55; Front-end software — SII; Other equipment — 27-SII/QB, 12-SII/Coyote, 7-SII/Echo. CLASSIFIED: Front-end hardware — SII/Sys 55; Front-end software — SII; Other equipment — 13-SII/QB, 2-SII/Coyote, 1-SII/Echo. AUDIOTEX: Hardware — Brite Voice Systems, Optel. DISPLAY: Adv layout systems — CD/Ad Wizard; Front-end hardware — CD/Ad Wizard, 6-DEC/VAX 3100 Work Station; Front-end software — CD/Ad Wizard. PRODUCTION: Typesetters — 2-MON/Express 100; Plate exposures — 1-WL/Lith-X-Pozer, 1-Nu/Flip Top FT40UPNS; Plate processors — 1-WL/Lithoplater 38D, 1-Nat/A-340; Production cameras — 1-C/Spartan III, 1-C/Marathon; Automatic film processors — 2-LE/LD-24, 2-CP, 2-C/OL Conveyor System; Film transporters — 2-C/Automatic, 2-LE/MTP, 2-CT; Shrink lenses — 1-C; Color separation equipment (conventional) — RZ/4050-E.
PRESSROOM: Line 1 — 9-G/Cosmo/3502 (double balloon); Press drives — G; Folders — 2-G; Pasters — 7-G/Automatic; Reels and stands — G. MAILROOM: Counter stackers — 1-Id/NS440, 2-Id/NS660, 1-QWI/300; Inserters and stuffers — 1-S/72P, HI/12 Hopper; Bundle tyer — 2-Dynaric/NPI; Wrapping singles — 2-Id; Addressing machine — 1-Ch/Labeler. WIRE SERVICES: News — AP; Stock tables — AP; Receiving dishes — AP. BUSINESS COMPUTERS: 1-HP/3000-52, 27-HP/700-64; Applications: CJ: Adv billing, Accts receivable, Gen ledger, Payroll, Personnel, Layout, Circ; PCs & micros networked; PCs & main system networked.

BIG SPRING
Howard County
'90 U.S. Census- 23,093; E&P '96 Est. 22,259
ABC-CZ (90): 23,093 (HH 8,256)

Big Spring Herald
(e-mon to fri; S)
Big Spring Herald, 710 Scurry; PO Box 1431, Big Spring, TX 79720; tel (915) 263-7331; fax (915) 264-7205. Hollinger International Inc. group.
Circulation: 7,088(e); 8,067(S); ABC Sept. 30, 1995.
Price: 50¢(d); $1.25(S); $8.65/mo (carrier), $12.00/mo (out-state).
Advertising: Open inch rate $11.50(e); $11.50(S). **Representative:** Papert Companies.
News Service: AP. **Politics:** Independent. **Established:** 1904 (weekly), 1923 (daily).
Not Published: Christmas.
Special Editions: Progress Edition (Mar); Rodeo (June); Football, Community Guide (Aug); Christmas Shopping Guide (Nov).
Magazine: TV-Leisure (newsprint).

GENERAL MANAGEMENT
Publisher Charles C Williams
Manager-Accounting Harry Morris
ADVERTISING
Director Ken Dulaney
Manager-Classified Elizabeth Flores
CIRCULATION
Manager Carlos Gonzales
NEWS EXECUTIVE
Editor Dan D Turner
EDITORS AND MANAGERS
Editorial Page Editor Dan D Turner
Food/Women's Editor Janet Ausbury
Lifestyle Editor Janet Ausbury
Sports Editor Steve Ragan
PRODUCTION
Manager-Composing Cindy Hepner
Foreman-Press Tony Hernandez

Market Information: TMC.
Mechanical available: Offset; Black and 3 ROP colors; insert accepted — preprinted; page cut-offs — 22¾".
Mechanical specifications: Type page 13" x 21½"; E - 6 cols, 2¹⁄₁₆", ⅛" between; A - 6 cols, 2¹⁄₁₆", ⅛" between; C - 6 cols, 2¹⁄₁₆", ⅛" between.
Commodity consumption: Newsprint 615 short tons; widths 27½", 34"; black ink 12,900 pounds; color ink 1,500 pounds; single pages printed 5,850; average pages per issue 12(d), 30(S); single plates used 6,250.
Equipment: EDITORIAL: Front-end hardware — Ap/Mac, 10-Mk/4003, 12-Ap/Mac Classic II; Front-end software — QuarkXPress, Adobe/Illustrator, Aldus/FreeHand, Baseview/NewsEdit. CLASSIFIED: Printers — Ap/Mac LaserWriter IIg. DISPLAY: Front-end hardware — 3-Ap/Mac IIsi; Front-end software — QuarkXPress, Adobe/Illustrator, Aldus/FreeHand, Baseview/NewsEdit; Printers — 2-Ap/Mac LaserWriter IIg. PRODUCTION: Plate exposures — 1-Nu/Flip Top FT40UP; Plate processors — 1-Nat/A-250; Production cameras — 1-R/500; Automatic film processors — 1-LE/LD 2600; Shrink lenses — 1-CK Optical/Variable; Color separation equipment (conventional) — WDS.
PRESSROOM: Line 1 — 8-G/Community; Folders — 1-G. MAILROOM: Bundle tyer — 1-MLN/ML2-EE, OVL; Addressing machine — 1-Am/5000, 1-St/73QFL. WIRE SERVICES: News — AP; Receiving dishes — size-10ft, AP. BUSINESS COMPUTERS: 1-IBM/PC-XT, IBM/PC-AT, 1-IBM/PC; PCs & micros networked; PCs & main system networked.

BONHAM
Fannin County
'90 U.S. Census- 6,686; E&P '96 Est. 6,372

Favorite (e-tues to fri; S)
Favorite, 314 N. Center; PO Box 550, Bonham, TX 75418; tel (903) 583-2124; fax (903) 583-8321.
Circulation: 2,613(e); 2,613(S); Sworn Oct. 29, 1995.
Price: 50¢(d); 75¢(S); $5.10/mo; $61.20/yr.
Advertising: Open inch rate $4.75(e); $4.75(S). **Representative:** Papert Companies.
News Service: AP. **Politics:** Democrat. **Established:** 1892.
Advertising not accepted: 900 numbers.
Special Editions: Christmas; High School Graduation; Industrial Week Progress; Cookbook; Football; Basketball; Home Improvement; Chamber.
Magazine: Screen Scene (TV Guide) (weekly).

CORPORATE OFFICERS
President Francis Stipe
Secretary/Treasurer Jim Monroe
GENERAL MANAGEMENT
Publisher John Frair
ADVERTISING
Manager Elaine Ashlock
NEWS EXECUTIVE
Editor John Frair
PRODUCTION
Manager Pat Robinson

Market Information: Zoned editions; Split Run; TMC.
Mechanical available: Offset; Black and 2 ROP colors; insert accepted — preprinted, cards; page cut-offs — 22¾".
Mechanical specifications: Type page 21½" x 21½"; E - 6 cols, 2¹⁄₁₆", ⅛" between; A - 6 cols, 2¹⁄₁₆", ⅛" between; C - 8 cols, 1⁹⁄₁₆", ¹⁄₁₆" between.
Commodity consumption: Newsprint 92 short tons; 1,600 metric tons; widths 13½", 27", 42"; black ink 1,963 pounds; color ink 286 pounds; average pages per issue 12(d), 16(S).
Equipment: EDITORIAL: Front-end hardware — Ap/Mac; Front-end software — QPS, QuarkXPress, Microsoft/Word; Printers — NewGen. CLASSIFIED: Front-end hardware — DOS; Front-end software — BMF; Printers — NewGen. DISPLAY: Adv layout systems — QuarkXPress; Front-end hardware — Ap/Mac; Front-end software — QPS; Printers — NewGen. PRODUCTION: OCR software — Mk; Typesetters — NewGen/Turbo 360; Plate exposures — B; Production cameras — 1-B.
PRESSROOM: Line 1 — 1-HI/Cotrell; Folders — 3-HI/3:2. MAILROOM: Addressing machine — 1-El. WIRE SERVICES: News — AP; Receiving dishes — size-10ft, AP. BUSINESS COMPUTERS: 3-Hyundai; PCs & micros networked; PCs & main system networked.

BORGER
Hutchinson County
'90 U.S. Census- 15,675; E&P '96 Est. 15,593

Borger News-Herald
(e-mon to fri; S)
Borger News-Herald, 207-209 N. Main; PO Box 5130, Borger, TX 79008-5130; tel (806) 273-5611; fax (806) 273-2552. Donrey Media group.
Circulation: 5,993(e); 6,833(S); Sworn Sept. 30, 1993.
Price: 25¢(d); 50¢(S); $6.00/mo; $72.00/yr.
Advertising: Open inch rate $8.92(e); $8.92(S). **Representative:** Papert Companies.
News Service: AP. **Politics:** Independent. **Established:** 1926.
Not Published: Christmas.
Special Editions: Birthday-City of Borger, Business and Industrial Review (Mar); Christmas Card (Dec); Seasonal merchant's promotions.
Special Weekly Sections: Food (wed, thur); Church News (fri); Food, Business (S).
Magazine: TV tab (S).

CORPORATE OFFICERS
Founder Donald W Reynolds
President/Chief Operating Officer Emmett Jones
Exec Vice Pres/Chief Financial Officer Darrell W Loftin
Vice Pres-Western Newspaper Group David A Osborn
Vice Pres-Eastern Newspaper Group Don Schneider
GENERAL MANAGEMENT
Publisher Tom Quinn
Manager-Office C Cole
ADVERTISING
Director Perry Lynch
CIRCULATION
Director Margaret Graham
NEWS EXECUTIVE
Editor Laura Frye
EDITORS AND MANAGERS
Business/Finance Editor Laura Frye
Home Furnishings/Lifestyles Editor Kim Mizar
News Editor Lois Ferguson
Photo Department Manager Don Rice
Picture Editor Don Rice
Sports Editor Stu Duncan

Market Information: TMC.
Mechanical available: Offset; Black and 3 ROP colors; insert accepted — preprinted, cards-catalog; page cut-offs — 22¾".
Mechanical specifications: Type page 13" x 21½"; E - 6 cols, 2¹⁄₁₆", ⅛" between; A - 6 cols, 2¹⁄₁₆", ⅛" between; C - 8 cols, 1½", ⅛" between.
Commodity consumption: Newsprint 300 metric tons; widths 27", 13"; average pages per issue 12(d), 26(S).
Equipment: EDITORIAL: Front-end hardware — 1-Mk/1100, 6-Mk/MC4003. CLASSIFIED: Front-end hardware — 1-Mk/MC4003. DISPLAY: Front-end hardware — Ap/Mac SE30; Front-end software — Multi-Ad/Creator; Other equipment — Raster/Ops. PRODUCTION: Typesetters — 3-Ap/Mac LaserWriter II NTX; Plate exposures — 1-Nu; Scanners — Ap/Mac Scanner; Production cameras — Acti; Automatic film processors — 1-LE; Shrink lenses — 1-CK Optical.
PRESSROOM: Line 1 — 6-G; Folders — 1-G. MAILROOM: Bundle tyer — 1-Bu/77011. WIRE SERVICES: News — AP; Receiving dishes — Newspaper Satellite Network. BUSINESS COMPUTERS: 1-IBM/PS2 MODEL 30, 1-Unisys/5000-50; Applications: Mail label files, Circ PIA records; PCs & main system networked.

BRENHAM
Washington County
'90 U.S. Census- 11,952; E&P '96 Est. 12,480

Brenham Banner-Press
(e-mon to fri; S)
Brenham Banner-Press, 2000 Stringer; PO Box 585, Brenham, TX 77834; tel (409) 836-7956; fax (409) 830-8577. Hartman Newspapers Inc. group.
Circulation: 6,340(e); 6,340(S); Sworn Oct. 5, 1995.
Price: 50¢(d); 50¢(S); $5.25/mo; $63.00/yr.
Advertising: Open inch rate $6.50(e); $6.50(S). **Representative:** US Suburban Press.
News Services: AP, NEA. **Politics:** Independent. **Established:** 1866.
Not Published: Christmas.
Special Editions: Progress (Jan); Graduation (May); Back-to-School, Football (Aug); Businesswomen (Oct); Cookbook (Nov); Gift Guide (Dec).
Special Weekly Sections: Food (tues); Church (fri).

CORPORATE OFFICER
President Charles Moser
GENERAL MANAGEMENT
Publisher Charles Moser
ADVERTISING
Manager-Retail Cindy Kissel
Manager-Classified Carol Kruger

CIRCULATION

Manager — Don Chandler

NEWS EXECUTIVES

Editor — Charles Moser
Managing Editor — Arthur Hahn

EDITORS AND MANAGERS

Editorial Page Editor — Charles Moser
Editorial Writer — Arthur Hahn
Editorial Writer-Political — Charles Moser
Sports Editor — Bruce White
Teen-Age/Youth Editor — Beverly Roehling
Women's Editor — Beverly Roehling

PRODUCTION

Foreman-Pressroom — Clem Krolczyk

Market Information: TMC.
Mechanical available: Offset; Black and 3 ROP colors; insert accepted — preprinted; page cut-offs — 22¾".
Mechanical specifications: Type page 13" x 21"; E - 6 cols, 2", ⅓" between; A - 6 cols, 2", ⅓" between; C - 9 cols, 1⅜", ⅙" between.
Commodity consumption: Newsprint 700 short tons; width 27½"; black ink 13,100 pounds; color ink 2,500 pounds; single pages printed 4,725; average pages per issue 10(d), 12(S); single plates used 11,650.
Equipment: EDITORIAL: Front-end hardware — Ap/Mac; Front-end software — Baseview/Qirk; Printers — Ap/Mac LaserWriter II NTX. CLASSIFIED: Front-end hardware — Ap/Mac; Front-end software — Baseview/Qirk; Printers — Ap/Mac LaserWriter II NTX, Okidata/Microline 320. DISPLAY: Adv layout systems — Aldus/PageMaker; Front-end hardware — Ap/Mac; Front-end software — Aldus/PageMaker; Printers — Ap/Mac LaserWriter II NTX. PRODUCTION: Plate processors — B; Production cameras — C/Spartan II; Automatic film processors — LE.
PRESSROOM: Line 1 — 6-WPC/Leader. MAILROOM: Counter stackers — BG; Inserters and stuffers — 3-KAN; Bundle tyer — 2-MLN. WIRE SERVICES: News — AP; Syndicates — NEA; Receiving dishes — AP. BUSINESS COMPUTERS: PCs & micros networked.

BROWNSVILLE

Cameron County

'90 U.S. Census- 98,962; E&P '96 Est. 106,762
ABC-CZ (90): 98,962 (HH 26,322)

The Brownsville Herald

(m-mon to sat; S)

The Brownsville Herald, 1135 E. Van Buren; PO Box 351, Brownsville, TX 78520; tel (210) 542-4301; fax (210) 982-4201. Freedom Communications Inc. group.
Circulation: 17,020(m); 17,020(m-sat); 19,146(S); ABC Sept. 30, 1995.
Price: 35¢(d); 35¢(sat); $1.00(S); $6.00/mo (carrier); $72.00/yr (carrier).
Advertising: Open inch rate $48.92(m); $48.92(m-sat); $52.09(S). **Representative:** Papert Companies.
News Services: AP, KRT. **Politics:** Independent. **Established:** 1892.
Note: Advertising for the Brownsville Herald automatically includes advertising in El Heraldo de Brownsville (eS), Harlingen Valley Morning Star (mS) & McAllen Monitor (mS).
Special Editions: Health & Fitness (Jan); Golden Years (Feb); Spring Fashion, Home & Garden (Mar); Bridal Guide, Mother's Day (Apr); Spring Car Care, Graduation (May); Today's Women (July); Back-to-School, Valley Football Preview (Aug); Fall Fashion (Sept); National Car Care (Oct); Welcome Winter Texans (Nov); Christmas Gift Guide (Dec).
Special Weekly Sections: Best Food Day (wed); Business (S); TV Listing, Entertainment (daily).
Magazines: Front Row, USA Weekend, Vista (S).

GENERAL MANAGEMENT

Publisher — Douglas Hardie
Manager-Credit — Olga Saldivar

ADVERTISING

Director — Julie Moreno
Director-National — Marcia Bleier
Manager-Classified — Mary Lou Davis

MARKETING AND PROMOTION

Manager-Marketing/Promotion — Julie Moreno

CIRCULATION

Manager — Julie Moreno

NEWS EXECUTIVES

Editor — Douglas Hardie
Managing Editor — Lavice Laney

EDITORS AND MANAGERS

City Editor — Rey Guevara Vazquez
Editorial Page Editor — Rey Guevara Vazquez
Photo Department Manager — Lavice Laney

PRODUCTION

Manager-Systems — Roberta J Saldivar
Superintendent — Roberta J Saldivar

Market Information: Zoned editions; Split Run; TMC.
Mechanical available: Offset; Black and 3 ROP colors; insert accepted — preprinted; page cut-offs — 22¾".
Mechanical specifications: Type page 13" x 21"; E - 6 cols, 2 1/16", ⅛" between; A - 6 cols, 2 1/16", ⅛" between; C - 10 cols, 1¼", 1/16" between.
Commodity consumption: Newsprint 1,166 metric tons; widths 27½", 13¾"; black ink 36,800 pounds; color ink 3,622 pounds; single pages printed 8,742; average pages per issue 20(d), 48(S); single plates used 12,729.
Equipment: EDITORIAL: Front-end hardware — Dewar. CLASSIFIED: Front-end hardware — Dewar. DISPLAY: Adv layout systems — Dewar, 2-Dewar/Discovery. PRODUCTION: Typesetters — 2-Tegra/Varityper; Plate exposures — 3M; Plate processors — 3M, Nu/Lithoplate; Production cameras — 1-C; Automatic film processors — 1-LE; Shrink lenses — 1-CK Optical; Digital color separation equipment — CD/626 Laser.
PRESSROOM: Line 1 — 6-HI/Cotrell 845; Line 2 — 4-HI/Cotrell 845; Folders — 2-HI/2:1. MAILROOM: Bundle tyer — 2-Si; Addressing machine — 1-Ch. WIRE SERVICES: News — KRT, AP; Photos — AP; Receiving dishes — AP. BUSINESS COMPUTERS: 1-IBM; Applications: Display billing, Payroll; PCs & micros networked; PCs & main system networked.

El Heraldo de Brownsville (Spanish Edition)

(e-mon to sat; S)

El Heraldo de Brownsville, 1135 E. Van Buren, Brownsville, TX 78520; tel (210) 542-4301. Freedom Communications Inc. group.
Circulation: 5,522(e); 5,522(e-sat); 6,105(S); Sworn Sept. 30, 1992.
Price: 35¢(d); 35¢(sat); $1.00(S); $6.00/mo.
Advertising: Open inch rate $4.75(e); $4.75(e-sat); $4.75(S). **Representative:** Papert Companies.
News Service: AP.

GENERAL MANAGEMENT

Publisher — Douglas Hardie

ADVERTISING

Director — Julie Moreno

CIRCULATION

Manager — Betty Miller

NEWS EXECUTIVES

Managing Editor — Lavice Laney
Editor-El Heraldo — Marcelino Gonzales

EDITORS AND MANAGERS

City Editor — Rey Guevara Vazquez
News Editor — Basilie Hernandez
Photo Editor — Brad Doherty
Sports Editor — James Irish

PRODUCTION

Manager — Roberta J Saldivar

Market Information: Zoned editions; TMC.
Mechanical available: Front end system; Black and 3 ROP colors; insert accepted — preprinted; page cut-offs — 21¼".
Mechanical specifications: Type page 13" x 21¼"; E - 6 cols, 2¼", ⅛" between; A - 6 cols, 2 1/16", ⅛" between; C - 10 cols, 1¼", ⅜" between.
Commodity consumption: Newsprint 109.71 short tons; 1,000 metric tons; widths 27½", 13¾"; black ink 20,339 pounds; color ink 900 pounds; single pages printed 31,200; average pages per issue 16(d), 56(S); single plates used 10,000.
Equipment: EDITORIAL: Front-end hardware — Dewar. CLASSIFIED: Front-end hardware — Dewar. DISPLAY: Adv layout systems — Dewar, 2-Dewar/Discovery. PRODUCTION: Typesetters — 2-Tegra/Varityper; Plate exposures — 3M; Plate processors — 3M, Nu/Lithoplate; Scanners — CD/Scanner; Production cameras — C; Automatic film processors — LE; Shrink lenses — C/Rodenstock; Digital color separation equipment — CD/626 Laser.
PRESSROOM: Line 1 — 6-HI/Cotrell 845. MAILROOM: Bundle tyer — Ca/TM36 Bank Tyer, Yamada/TOM 45; Addressing machine — Ch/525E. WIRE SERVICES: News — KRT, AP; Syndicates — KRT; Receiving dishes — AP, UPI. BUSINESS COMPUTERS: IBM; Applications: Display billing, Payroll; PCs & micros networked; PCs & main system networked.

BROWNWOOD

Brown County

'90 U.S. Census- 18,387; E&P '96 Est. 17,890

Brownwood Bulletin

(e-mon to fri; S)

Brownwood Bulletin, 700 Carnegie; PO Box 1189, Brownwood, TX 76804; tel (915) 646-2541; fax (915) 646-6835. Boone Newspapers Inc. group.
Circulation: 8,261(e); 8,261(S); Sworn Oct. 1, 1995.
Price: 50¢(d); $1.25(S); $9.00/mo (in RTZ), $11.00/mo (outside RTZ), $13.00/mo (outside Texas); $108.00/yr (in RTZ), $132.00/yr (outside RTZ), $156.00/yr (outside Texas).
Advertising: Open inch rate $11.50(e); $12.55(S). **Representative:** Papert Companies.
News Service: AP. **Politics:** Independent. **Established:** 1900.
Advertising not accepted: Advertising that is not in good taste.
Special Editions: Youth Fair, Parade of Progress (Jan); Horizons (Feb); Home & Garden, Brides, Love Star Rodeo, Health & Fitness (Mar); Farm & Ranch (Apr); Salute to Nursing (May); Family Business, Youth Baseball (June); Visitor's Guide, Brown County Rodeo (July); Football Kick-off (Aug); Pecan Valley Arts Festival, Homemaker's School (Sept); Women in Business (Oct); Christmas Catalog (Nov); Christmas Greetings (Dec); Senior Citizens; Central Texas Outdoors; Sunday's Homes.
Special Weekly Sections: Business (mon); Best Food Days (tues); Church, Dining Guide (fri); Best Food Days, Agriculture, Education, Outdoors (S).
Magazine: TV Week (S).

GENERAL MANAGEMENT

Publisher — H Shelton Prince Jr
Manager-Business — Jim Barnes

ADVERTISING

Director-Marketing — Jeff Little John

CIRCULATION

Manager — Chris Bradford

NEWS EXECUTIVE

Managing Editor — Gene Deason

EDITORS AND MANAGERS

Features Editor — Harriette Graves
Sports Editor — Bill Stovall

PRODUCTION

Manager — Rich Macke

Market Information: TMC.
Mechanical available: Offset; Black and 3 ROP colors; insert accepted — preprinted, all considered; page cut-offs — 22¾".
Mechanical specifications: Type page 13" x 21½"; E - 6 cols, 2 1/16", ⅛" between; A - 6 cols, 2 1/16", ⅛" between; C - 9 cols, 1 5/16", ⅛" between.
Commodity consumption: Newsprint 800 short tons; widths 27½", 13¾"; black ink 22,000 pounds; color ink 3,600 pounds; single pages printed 5,610; average pages per issue 14(d), 40(S); single plates used 15,200.
Equipment: EDITORIAL: Front-end hardware — 1-Ap/Power Mac; Front-end software — Baseview. CLASSIFIED: Front-end hardware — Ap/Power Mac; Front-end software — Baseview. DISPLAY: Adv layout systems — 2-Ap/Mac II, 1-Ap/Mac Plus; Front-end hardware — DTI/Adbuilders. PRODUCTION: Typesetters — 2-Ap/Mac LaserWriter II; Plate exposures — 1-Nu; Plate processors — Roconex; Electronic picture desk — Adobe/Photoshop; Scanners — La Cie/Silverscanner II; Production cameras — 1-C/Spartan II Automatic; Automatic film processors — 1-AG/Rapidline 66.
PRESSROOM: Line 1 — 7-G/Community; Folders — 1-G/SC 240. MAILROOM: Inserters and stuffers — 6-KAN/402; Bundle tyer — 1-MLN/7CD 700; Addressing machine — 1-El. WIRE SERVICES: News — AP; Syndicates — AP Datafeatures; Receiving dishes — AP. BUSINESS COMPUTERS: Compaq/486, Dell/486, 2-ALR/386; Applications: Circ, Adv billing, Accts receivable, Gen ledger, Mktg, Payroll; PCs & micros networked.

BRYAN-COLLEGE STATION

Brazos County

'90 U.S. Census- 107,458 (Bryan 55,002; College Station 52,456); E&P '96 Est. 123,275 (Bryan 61,207; College Station 62,068)
ABC-NDM (90): 121,862 (HH 43,725)

Bryan-College Station Eagle

(m-mon to sat; S)

Bryan-College Station Eagle, 1729 Briarcrest Dr. (77802); PO Box 3000, Bryan, TX 77805; tel (409) 776-4444; fax (409) 774-0496. A H Belo Corp. group.
Circulation: 20,381(m); 20,381(m-sat); 26,326(S); ABC Sept. 30, 1995.
Price: 50¢(d); 50¢(sat); $1.25(S); $10.50/mo; $116.64/yr.
Advertising: Open inch rate $25.65(m); $25.65(m-sat); $26.40(S). **Representative:** Papert Companies.
News Services: AP, KRT. **Politics:** Independent. **Established:** 1876.
Special Editions: Progress (Aug); Football (Sept); Fall Style, Early Christmas Shopping (Nov); Christmas Greetings, Wish Book, Last Minute Gift Guide (Dec); Bridal; Health & Fitness; Progress; Mother's Day; Father's Day; Design-an-Ad; Medical Directory; Women in Business; Spring Style; Newcomer; Back-to-School; Welcome Back Aggies.
Special Weekly Sections: Food, Business & Industrial Review (wed); Variety, Entertainment (thur); Garden (fri); Religion Pages (sat); Business, TV Week, Best Food Days, Lifestyle Section, Outdoors Features (S); Daily Page.
Magazines: TV Magazine (own) (S); TMC Product; Senior Citizen Newsletter; Direct Mail Coupon Book; Business Journal; Good News Eagle.

GENERAL MANAGEMENT

Publisher — Dennis E Thomas
Director-Finance — Roger F Armstrong

ADVERTISING

Director — Jean Wolff

TELECOMMUNICATIONS

Audiotex Manager-Sales — Phyllis Davis

CIRCULATION

Director — Bud Grubbs

NEWS EXECUTIVE

Editor — Bernard Hunt

EDITORS AND MANAGERS

City Editor — Kelli Levey
Editorial Page Editor — Robert C Borden
Education Editor — Stephanie Cherry
Entertainment/Amusements Editor — Jim Butler
Features Editor — Anton Riecher
Photo Department Manager — David McDermond
Radio/Television Editor — Jim Butler
Sports Editor — Robert Cessna

Market Information: TMC; Operate audiotex.
Mechanical available: Offset; Black and 3 ROP colors; insert accepted — preprinted, any; page cut-offs — 22¾".
Mechanical specifications: Type page 13" x 21½"; E - 6 cols, 2 1/16", ⅛" between; A - 6 cols, 2 1/16", ⅛" between; C - 9 cols, 1⅜", 1/16" between.
Commodity consumption: Newsprint 2,400 short tons; widths 27½", 13¾", 34"; black ink 71,064 pounds; color ink 11,421 pounds; single pages printed 17,554; average pages per issue 24(d), 60(S); single plates used 19,665.
Equipment: EDITORIAL: Front-end hardware — EKI/LAN Custom; Other equipment — 2-Lf/AP Leaf Picture Desk, Lf/Leafscan, ECR/Autokon. CLASSIFIED: Front-end hardware — 7-Mk/MC4001; Other equipment — Lf/AP Leaf Picture Desk. AUDIOTEX: Hardware — Micro Voice; Software — Micro Voice; Supplier name — TMS, VNN. PRODUCTION: Pagination software — QuarkXPress 3.2; OCR software — Mk/MC4001, Mk/MC500J Ad Comp Jr, Mk/MC500J Ad Comp; Plate exposures — 1-Nu, 3M/Pyrofax; Plate processors — 1-WL, 3M/Pyrofax; Production cameras — 1-C/Spartan II; Automatic film processors — 1-LE/24; Film transporters — 1-C; Color separation equipment (conventional) — Digi-Colour.
PRESSROOM: Line 1 — 9-G/Urbanite; Pasters — Cary. MAILROOM: Counter stackers — 1-Id, 1-HL/Monitor; Inserters and stuffers — 1-NJP/1372; Bundle tyer — 1-MLN/ML 2EE, MLN/SP 330; Addressing machine — 1-KR/12. WIRE SERVICES: News — AP, A&M University; Stock tables — AP SelectStox; Receiving dishes — AP. BUSINESS COMPUTERS: HP/3000, PC/Network; Applications: Circ, Adv billing, Accts receivable, Gen ledger, Accts payable.

CLEBURNE

Johnson County

'90 U.S. Census- 22,205; E&P '96 Est. 23,865

Cleburne Times-Review

(e-mon to fri; S)

Cleburne Times-Review, 108 S. Anglin; PO Box 1569, Cleburne, TX 76031; tel (817) 645-2441; fax (817) 645-4020. Donrey Media group.

Circulation: 8,027(e); 8,027(S); Sworn Sept. 29, 1995.

Price: 50¢(d); $1.00(S); $6.00/mo; $73.00/yr (in county).

Advertising: Open inch rate $10.20(e); $10.20(S). **Representative:** Papert Companies.

News Service: AP. **Politics:** Independent. **Established:** 1904.

Not Published: New Year; Memorial Day; Independence Day; Labor Day; Thanksgiving; Christmas.

Special Editions: Chamber of Commerce (Jan); Active Times (Feb); Active Times & Springfest (Apr); Graduation (May); Active Times (July); Football (Aug); Just Say NO to Drugs Coloring Book (Oct); Month Before X'mas (Nov); Wrap it Up & Greetings (Dec).

Special Weekly Sections: Best Food Day (tues); Business, Agriculture, Health, Best Food Days (S); Lifestyle, Sports (daily).

Magazine: Active Times (quarterly).

CORPORATE OFFICERS

Founder	Donald W Reynolds
President/Chief Operating Officer	Emmett Jones
Exec Vice Pres/Chief Financial Officer	Darrell W Loftin
Vice Pres-Western Newspaper Group	David A Osborn
Vice Pres-Eastern Newspaper Group	Don Schneider

GENERAL MANAGEMENT

Publisher	Bill Rice

ADVERTISING

Manager	Kay Pace
Manager-Classified	Kay Holly

CIRCULATION

Director	Art Davenport

NEWS EXECUTIVES

Managing Editor	Rob Fraser
Assoc Editor	Susann Wright

EDITORS AND MANAGERS

Amusements Editor	Lori Elmore
Business/Finance Editor	Rob Fraser
City/Metro Editor	Susann Wright
Education Editor	Don Peoples
Environmental/Farm Editor	Rob Fraser
Editorial Page Editor	Rob Fraser
Fashion/Style Editor	Lori Elmore
Features Editor	Rob Fraser
Food/Fashion Editor	Lori Elmore
Garden Editor	Lori Elmore
Graphics Editor/Art Director	Rob Fraser
Health/Medical Editor	Rob Fraser
Living/Lifestyle Editor	Lori Elmore
Photo Lab	Don Peoples
Radio/Television Editor	Rob Fraser
Religion/Society Editor	Lori Elmore
Sports Editor	Pete Kendall
Travel/Women's Editor	Lori Elmore

PRODUCTION

Manager	Alvin Liefeste

Market Information: TMC.

Mechanical available: Offset; Black and 3 ROP colors; insert accepted — preprinted; page cut-offs — 22¾".

Mechanical specifications: Type page 13" x 21¼"; E - 6 cols, 2⅟₁₆", ⅛" between; A - 6 cols, 2⅟₁₆", ⅛" between; C - 9 cols, 1⅜", ⅟₁₆" between.

Commodity consumption: Newsprint 420 metric tons; widths 27½", 13½"; black ink 12,860 pounds; color ink 100 pounds; single pages printed 8,244; average pages per issue 20(d), 40(S); single plates used 6,000.

Equipment: EDITORIAL: Front-end hardware — 7-Mk/1100; Front-end software — Mk. CLASSIFIED: Front-end hardware — 2-Mk/1100; Front-end software — Mk. DISPLAY: Adv layout systems — Ap/Mac; Front-end hardware — 2-Ap/Mac IIci; Printers — 1-Ap/Mac LaserWriter. PRODUCTION: Plate processors — 3M; Scanners — Ap/Mac Scanner; Production cameras — AG.

PRESSROOM: Line 1 — 6-G/Community; Folders — 1-G. MAILROOM: Bundle tyer — 1-MLN; Addressing machine — Wm. WIRE SERVICES: News — AP; Receiving dishes — AP.

CLUTE-FREEPORT-LAKE JACKSON

Brazoria County

'90 U.S. Census- 43,075 (Clute 8,910; Freeport 11,389; Lake Jackson 22,776); E&P '96 Est. 43,883 (Clute 8,585; Freeport 10,439; Lake Jackson 24,859)

ABC-CZ (90): 45,807 (HH 16,149)

The Brazosport Facts

(m-mon to sat; S)

The Brazosport Facts, 720 S. Main St.; PO Box 549, Clute, TX 77531; tel (409) 265-7411; fax (409) 265-2213. Southern Newspapers Inc. group.

Circulation: 17,650(m); 17,650(m-sat); 19,243(S); ABC Sept. 30, 1995.

Price: 50¢(d); 50¢(sat); $1.00(S); $7.75/mo (carrier), $8.75/mo; $105.00/yr.

Advertising: Open inch rate $10.80(m); $10.80(m-sat); $10.80(S). **Representative:** Landon Associates Inc.

News Services: AP, NEA. **Politics:** Independent. **Established:** 1913.

Advertising not accepted: All advertising subject to publisher's approval.

Special Editions: Bridal (Jan); Chamber of Commerce (Feb); Spring Fashion (Mar); Fishing (Apr); Fishing Fiesta (June); Profile/Progress (July); Fashion (Aug); Football, Safety (Sept); Hunting, Brazoria County Fair, Women in Business, Quality Control (Oct).

Special Weekly Sections: Focus & Forecast (mon); Food, Lifestyle (wed); Business (thur); Travel, Gardening (fri); Church (sat); Food, Lifestyle, Business (S).

Magazines: TV & Entertainment (fri); Color Comics (S); USA Weekend.

GENERAL MANAGEMENT

Publisher	Bill Cornwall
General Manager	Gilbert C Vetters

ADVERTISING

Director	Anita Bynun
Manager-Retail	Deana Lesco
Manager-Classified	Dena Mathews

CIRCULATION

Manager	Julie Fox

NEWS EXECUTIVES

Editor	Bill Cornwall
Managing Editor	Wanda Garner Cash

EDITORS AND MANAGERS

Business/Finance Editor	Rhonda Moran
Entertainment/Amusements Editor	Glenn Krampota
Editorial Page Editor	Greg Bar
Fashion/Style Editor	Leslie Burleson
Features Editor	Leslie Burleson
Graphics Editor/Art Director	Wayland Smart
Health/Medical Editor	Susan Avera-Roth
Living/Lifestyle Editor	Leslie Burleson
News Editor	Wanda Garner Cash
Photo Editor	Dwight Andrews
Political/Government Editor	Taylor Camp
Religion/Society Editor	Susan Avera-Roth
Science/Technology Editor	Joe Dodson
Sports Editor	Wanda Garner Cash
Television/Film Editor	Glenn Krampota
Theater/Music Editor	Glenn Krampota
Travel Editor	Susan Avera-Roth
Women's Editor	Leslie Burleson

PRODUCTION

Press	Steve Martin
Camera	Pat Quisenberry

Market Information: Zoned editions; TMC.

Mechanical available: Offset; Black and 3 ROP colors; insert accepted — preprinted; page cut-offs — 22¾".

Mechanical specifications: Type page 13" x 21"; E - 6 cols, 2⅟₁₆", ⅛" between; A - 6 cols, 2⅟₁₆", ⅛" between; C - 9 cols, 1⅜", ⅟₁₆" between.

Commodity consumption: Newsprint 1,835 short tons; widths 27½", 13¾"; black ink 38,140 pounds; color ink 1,730 pounds; single pages printed 11,700; average pages per issue 30(d), 52(S); single plates used 11,653.

Equipment: EDITORIAL: Front-end hardware — 19-PC, 6-Ap/Mac Centris 650; Front-end software — Ap/Mac, QuarkXPress, Microsoft/Word; Printers — Ap/Mac LaserWriter IIg, Panasonic/KXP1180, Ap/Mac LaserWriter Pro 630. CLASSIFIED: Front-end hardware — 7-PC, 2-Ap/Mac IIci; Front-end software — Computext/CompuClass, QuarkXPress; Printers — Ap/Mac LaserWriter IIq, TI/Omni 800; Other equipment — Panasonic/KX-E4000. DISPLAY: Front-end hardware — 4-Ap/Mac IIci; Front-end software — Aldus/PageMaker, QuarkXPress, Multi-Ad/Creator, Adobe/Illustrator; Printers — Ap/Mac LaserWriter IIq. PRODUCTION: Typesetters — Ap/Mac LaserWriter IIq, Ap/Mac LaserWriter Pro 630; Plate exposures — Nu; Plate processors — Nat/Universal 26; Electronic picture desk — Lf/AP Leaf Picture Desk; Scanners — ECR/Autokon 1000; Production cameras — C/Spartan III w/Transport; Automatic film processors — LE/LD 2600A, C/660; Film transporters — ECR/Autokon.

PRESSROOM: Line 1 — 10-G/Suburban; Press control system — Fin. MAILROOM: Counter stackers — HL/Monitor; Inserters and stuffers — HI; Bundle tyer — MLN; Addressing machine — Miller, Bevgo. LIBRARY: Electronic — SMS/Stauffer Gold, FileMaker/Pro. COMMUNICATIONS: Facsimile — Canon/50. WIRE SERVICES: News — AP; Receiving dishes — AP. BUSINESS COMPUTERS: Applications: Quattro/Pro, FileMaker/Pro.

COLLEGE STATION

See BRYAN

CONROE

Montgomery County

'90 U.S. Census- 27,610; E&P '96 Est. 32,206

ABC-CZ (90): 27,610 (HH 10,016)

Conroe Courier

(m-mon to sat; S)

Conroe Courier, 100 Ave. A; PO Box 609, Conroe, TX 77305; tel (409) 756-6671; fax (409) 756-6676. Westward Communications Inc. group.

Circulation: 12,800(m); 12,800(m-sat); 13,924(S); ABC Sept. 30, 1995.

Price: 50¢(d); 50¢(sat); $1.00(S); $9.00/mo; $108.00/yr (carrier), $132.00/yr (in county), $162.00/yr (out of county).

Advertising: Open inch rate $13.34(m); $13.34(m-sat); $13.34(S). **Representative:** US Suburban Press.

News Services: NEA, AP. **Politics:** Independent. **Established:** 1892.

Special Editions: Bridal (Jan); Progress Edition (Feb); Montgomery County Fair (Mar); Mother's Day, Graduation (May); Montgomery County Magazine (July); Back-to-School (Aug); High School Football (Sept); Answer Book (Oct); Holiday Cookbook, Holiday Shopping (Nov); Last Minute Gifts (Dec).

Special Weekly Sections: Medical (thur); Business, Entertainment (daily).

Magazines: TV Week (S); Montgomery County Magazine; The Answer Book (annually).

CORPORATE OFFICERS

Chairman	Kenneth Johnson
Vice Pres-Gulf Coast Newspaper	Christopher A Eddings

GENERAL MANAGEMENT

Publisher	Christopher A Eddings
Business Manager	Ann Toppel

ADVERTISING

Director	Brenda Roy
Director-Creative	Ron Rieke

CIRCULATION

Director	Sam McQueen

NEWS EXECUTIVE

Editor	Dan Turner

EDITORS AND MANAGERS

Films/Theater Editor	Jason Hargraves
Food Editor	Jason Hargraves
News Editor	Nancy Darnell
Religion Editor	Jason Hargraves
Sports Editor	Mike Jones
Trends Editor	Jason Hargraves

MANAGEMENT INFORMATION SERVICES

Data Processing Manager	Ann Toppel

PRODUCTION

Manager	Joe Munoz

Market Information: ADS.

Mechanical available: Offset; Black and 3 ROP colors; insert accepted — preprinted, all; page cut-offs — 22¾".

Mechanical specifications: Type page 13" x 21½"; E - 6 cols, 2⅟₁₆", ⅛" between; A - 6 cols, 2⅟₁₆", ⅛" between; C - 9 cols, 1¹¹⁄₃₂", ⅟₁₆" between.

Commodity consumption: Newsprint 1,600 short tons; width 27"; black ink 44,800 pounds; color ink 4,000 pounds; single pages printed 17,646; average pages per issue 16(d), 42(S); single plates used 18,000.

Equipment: EDITORIAL: Front-end hardware — IBM/MS-DOS. CLASSIFIED: Front-end hardware — IBM/MS-DOS. DISPLAY: Front-end hardware — IBM/MS-DOS, Ap/Mac II. PRODUCTION: Plate exposures — 1-Nu, 1-BKY; Plate processors — 1-Ic; Production cameras — 1-C/Spartan III; Automatic film processors — 1-P; Shrink lenses — 1-CK Optical/SQU-7; Color separation equipment (conventional) — Digi-Colour.

PRESSROOM: Line 1 — 10-G/C; Folders — 1-G. MAILROOM: Counter stackers — 1-BG; Bundle tyer — 2-Malow. WIRE SERVICES: News — AP; Syndicates — NEA; Receiving dishes — AP. BUSINESS COMPUTERS: IBM/MS-DOS; Applications: Adv billing, Accts receivable, Gen ledger, Payroll, Circ; PCs & micros networked.

CORPUS CHRISTI

Nueces County

'90 U.S. Census- 257,453; E&P '96 Est. 271,248

ABC-CZ (90): 259,506 (HH 90,136)

Corpus Christi Caller-Times

(m-mon to sat; S)

Corpus Christi Caller-Times, 820 Lower N. Broadway (78401); PO Box 9136, Corpus Christi, TX 78469; tel (512) 884-2011; fax (512) 886-3670, (512) 886-3732; web site http://www.wtr.com/cchome/. Harte-Hanks Communications Inc. group.

Circulation: 66,410(m); 66,410(m-sat); 96,142(S); ABC Sept. 30, 1995.

Price: 50¢(d); 50¢(sat); $2.00(S); $14.50/mo; $159.50/yr.

Advertising: Open inch rate $53.50(m); $53.50(m-sat); $55.00(S). **Representative:** Papert Companies.

News Services: AP, NYT, KRT. **Politics:** Independent. **Established:** 1883.

Advertising not accepted: Untrue and obscene material.

Special Editions: Horizons (Jan); South Texas Life (May); South Texas Football (Aug); Prime Time (last mon/month).

Special Weekly Sections: Medical (mon); Best Food Day (wed); Weekend Tab (fri); Garden, Church Page (sat); Oil & Gas, Travel, Business, Channels, Sunday Homes (S).

Magazines: People, Foc'sle, Weekend (fri); TV Channels, Parade, Pennysaver, Sunday Home (S).

CORPORATE OFFICER

President	Stephen W Sullivan

GENERAL MANAGEMENT

Publisher	Stephen W Sullivan
Exec Vice Pres/General Manager	Larry L Rose
Vice Pres/Exec Editor	David A House
Vice Pres-Human Resources	Kristin Millet
Chief Financial Officer	Darrell G Coleman
Manager-Credit	Genie Cortez

ADVERTISING

Vice Pres	Barry E Box
Manager-Classified	Leslie Wendlard
Manager-Territory Sales	Georgette Lampton
Manager-Territory Sales	Gary Cruse
Manager-Specialty Products/Direct Marketing	Benita Mendell

MARKETING AND PROMOTION

Director-Marketing/Promotion	Beverly Barnum

TELECOMMUNICATIONS

Audiotex Manager	Nick Jimenez

CIRCULATION

Vice Pres-Operations/Distribution	Chuck Venetian
Manager	Betty Albright
Manager-Subscriber Service/Single Copy	Sonia Merino
Manager-Sales/Promotion/Transportation	Ed Rehfeld

NEWS EXECUTIVES

Exec Editor	David A House
Editorial Page Editor	Nick Jimenez

EDITORS AND MANAGERS

Business Editor	Jim Steinberg
City Editor-Day	Deborah Wilkins
City Editor-Night	Scott Rothschild
Editorial Writer	Murphy Givens
Editorial Writer	Sylvia Reyes
Editorial Writer	Brooks Peterson
Editorial Page Editor	Nick Jimenez
Librarian	Margaret Neu
Metro Editor	Vaughn Hagerty
Metro Editor-Weekends	Tom Whitehurst

News Editor Mike Alexieff
People Editor Gretchen Ray
Photo Editor Paul Iverson
Sports Editor Richard Oliver
Sunday Editor Sarah Yoest
Television Editor Tina Vasquez
Weekend Magazine Editor Julie Palm

PRODUCTION

Manager-Creative Resources (Ad Production) Trina Haley
Manager-Pressroom Ron Febriby
Manager-Distribution Center Robert Soto

Market Information: Zoned editions; Split Run; TMC; Operate audiotex; Electronic edition.
Mechanical available: Offset; Black and 3 ROP colors; insert accepted — preprinted, small product samples with prior approval; page cut-offs — 22".
Mechanical specifications: Type page 13" x 20 5/8"; E - 6 cols, 2 1/16", 1/8" between; A - 6 cols, 2 1/16", 1/8" between; C - 9 cols, 1 3/8", 1/16" between.
Commodity consumption: Newsprint 10,000 short tons; widths 27", 54"; black ink 490,000 pounds; color ink 46,000 pounds; single pages printed 17,200; average pages per issue 48(d), 60(sat), 80(S); single plates used 46,200.
Equipment: EDITORIAL: Front-end hardware — Premio/486 DX-66 Server; Front-end software — CText, Novell 4.0; Printers — Epson/FX850, HP/DeskJet 500; Other equipment — PC/386sx, PC/386-33, PC/486-50, Ap/Mac Quadra 947, Ap/Mac IIcx. CLASSIFIED: Front-end hardware — Tandem, SII/Sys 55; Front-end software — Guardian Operating System; Printers — Dataproducts; Other equipment — SII/Coyote. AUDIOTEX: Hardware — PC/486; Software — Unix, Brite Voice Systems; Supplier name — Brite Voice Systems. DISPLAY: Adv layout systems — Ap/Mac, Novell/Network 4.0; Front-end hardware — Ap/Power Mac, Ap/Mac Quadra 700, Ap/Mac Quadra 947, Ap/Mac Centris; Front-end software — Multi-Ad/Creator, QPS 3.1, Adobe/Illustrator, Adobe/Photoshop; Printers — Lasermaster/Unity 1200, Panther/Pro, Panther/Pro 46, ECR/Scriptsetter II; Other equipment — CD-Rom, Syquest, ScanView/ScanMate 5000. PRODUCTION: Pagination software — CText/Advision; Typesetters — Panther/Pro 46, ECR/ScriptSetter II, Panther/5300H; Plate exposures — 1-B/5000, 1-Nu/Flip Top FT40V6UPNS; Plate processors — 2-Nat/A340; Electronic picture desk — Lf/AP Leaf Picture Desk; Scanners — ScanView/ScanMate 5000; Production cameras — 1-ECR/8400, 1-B/2000, 2-C/Spartan III; Automatic film processors — 2-Konica/Powermatic 66f; Film transporters — 1-C; Shrink lenses — 1-CK Optical/259; Color separation equipment (conventional) — Digi-Colour/DC-4000. PRESSROOM: Line 1 — 9-G/Metroliner double width (Offset; 5-half decks); Line 2 — 8-Tandemer/Narrow Web; Folders — 1-G/3:2; Pasters — G/Auto; Press control system — G/PCS. MAILROOM: Counter stackers — 3-HL/Monitor, 2-HL/Monitor; Inserters and stuffers — 1-GMA/SLS-1000 10-Z, 1-KAN/7:1; Bundle tyer — 2-MLN, 2-Dynaric; Addressing machine — 3-Wm/III, 2-BH. COMMUNICATIONS: Digital ad delivery system — AP AdSend. WIRE SERVICES: News — AP Datastream, AP Datafeatures; Syndicates — NYT, KRT; Receiving dishes — AP. BUSINESS COMPUTERS: HP/3000-947; Applications: CJ/AIM-CIS: Accts receivable, Adv billing, Layout; PCs & micros networked; PCs & main system networked.

CORSICANA

Navarro County

'90 U.S. Census- 22,911; E&P '96 Est. 23,541

Corsicana Daily Sun

(e-mon to fri; m-sat; S)

Corsicana Daily Sun, 405 E. Collin; PO Box 622, Corsicana, TX 75110; tel (903) 872-3931; fax (903) 872-6878. Hollinger International Inc. group.
Circulation: 7,020(e); 7,020(m-sat); 7,020(S); Sworn Oct. 4, 1995.
Price: 50¢(d); 50¢(sat); $1.00(S); $8.25/mo; $99.00/yr.
Advertising: Open inch rate $10.96(e); $10.96(m-sat); $10.96(S). **Representative:** Papert Companies.
News Service: AP. **Politics:** Independent. **Established:** 1895.
Not Published: Christmas.
Special Editions: Progress (Mar); Football (Aug); Newcomers (Sept).
Special Weekly Sections: Best Food Day (wed); Mini Page (S).
Magazines: Sunday TEMPO (local), Prime Time (local) (S).

CORPORATE OFFICERS

President Larry J Perrotto
Exec Vice Pres Ken Cope

GENERAL MANAGEMENT

Publisher Gary Connor

ADVERTISING

Director T C Hurst
Supervisor-Classified Betty Atkeisson

CIRCULATION

Manager Sharon Mertz

NEWS EXECUTIVE

Managing Editor Rob Ludwig

EDITORS AND MANAGERS

News Editor Judy Green
Photo Editor Kevin Painter
Sports Editor Todd Wills

MANAGEMENT INFORMATION SERVICES

Data Processing Manager Becky Lester

PRODUCTION

Foreman-Pressroom Billy Parnell
Manager-Composition Sue Stone

Market Information: Zoned editions; Split Run; TMC.
Mechanical available: Offset; Black and 3 ROP colors; insert accepted — preprinted; page cut-offs — 22 3/4".
Mechanical specifications: Type page 13 3/4" x 21 1/2"; E - 6 cols, 2 1/16", 1/8" between; A - 6 cols, 2 1/16", 1/8" between; C - 9 cols, 1 3/8", 1/16" between.
Commodity consumption: Newsprint 650 short tons; widths 27 1/2", 13 3/4"; black ink 51,000 pounds; color ink 3,000 pounds; single pages printed 5,824; average pages per issue 16(d), 36(S); single plates used 3,000.
Equipment: EDITORIAL: Front-end hardware — 7-Ap/Mac; Front-end software — Baseview/NewsEdit, QuarkXPress; Printers — 1-Ap/Mac LaserWriter IIg, 1-Ap/Mac LaserWriter IIf. CLASSIFIED: Front-end hardware — Ap/Mac. PRODUCTION: Typesetters — 4-Ap/Mac; Plate exposures — 1-W; Plate processors — 1-Nat/225; Production cameras — SCREEN, 1-C; Automatic film processors — 1-P. PRESSROOM: Line 1 — 5-G/Urbanite. MAILROOM: Counter stackers — 1-BG; Bundle tyer — 2-MLN; Addressing machine — 1-KR. WIRE SERVICES: News — AP; Receiving dishes — AP. BUSINESS COMPUTERS: 1-MDS, 1-HP, 3-IBM/AT; Applications: Circ, Adv billing, Accts receivable, Gen ledger, Payroll; PCs & main system networked.

DALHART

Dallam and Hartley Counties

'90 U.S. Census- 6,246; E&P '96 Est. 5,953

Dalhart Daily Texan

(e-tues to fri; S)

Dalhart Daily Texan, 410 Denrock St., Dalhart, TX 79022-0511; tel (806) 249-4511; fax (806) 249-2395.
Circulation: 2,389(e); 2,389(S); Sworn Sept. 30, 1994.
Price: 25¢(d); 25¢(S); $48.00/yr.
Advertising: Open inch rate $4.71(e); $4.71(S). **Representative:** Papert Companies.
News Service: AP. **Politics:** Independent. **Established:** 1901.
Not Published: Independence Day; Labor Day; Thanksgiving; Christmas.
Advertising not accepted: Cigarettes and tobacco.
Special Editions: XIT Ranch Celebration (Aug); Fair (Sept); Fair (Oct); Christmas (Nov); Christmas (Dec).

GENERAL MANAGEMENT

Publisher Robert S Clay
Business Manager Robert S Clay
Purchasing Agent (Shop) Robert S Clay

ADVERTISING

Manager Patrick Warden
Manager-Classified Eulene Phelps

CIRCULATION

Manager Eulene Phelps

NEWS EXECUTIVE

Editor Zelda Lang

EDITORS AND MANAGERS

Columnist Robert S Clay
Science Editor Warren Slaughrer
Society Editor Faye Plank

Mechanical available: Offset; insert accepted — preprinted; page cut-offs — 21".
Mechanical specifications: Type page 15" x 21"; E - 6 cols, 2 1/16", 1/8" between; A - 6 cols, 2 1/16", 1/8" between; C - 6 cols, 2 1/16", 1/8" between.
Commodity consumption: Newsprint 200 metric tons; widths 28", 14"; black ink 450 pounds; average pages per issue 16(d), 20(S).
Equipment: EDITORIAL: Front-end hardware — 4-IBM/386DX workstation, 1-IBM/486DX file-server; Front-end software — Novell/Netware; Printers — HP/LaserJet III, Panasonic/KX P1180. PRODUCTION: Plate processors — 1-BKY/Ultralite 1500; Production cameras — 1-B/3000. PRESSROOM: Line 1 — 3-KP/Newsking; Folders — 1-KP. MAILROOM: Addressing machine — 1-Am/1800. WIRE SERVICES: News — AP; Receiving dishes — AP.

DALLAS

Dallas and four other counties

'90 U.S. Census- 1,006,877; E&P '96 Est. 1,170,323
ABC-CZ (90): 1,893,473 (HH 724,255)

The Dallas Morning News

(m-mon to sat; S)

The Dallas Morning News, Communications Center; PO Box 655237, Dallas, TX 75265; tel (214) 977-8222; fax (214) 977-8168; e-mail 74774.2236@compuserve.com, tdmned@pic.net; web site http://www.pic.net/tdmn/tdmn.html. A H Belo Corp. group.
Circulation: 500,358(m); 621,769(m-fri); 581,979(m-sat); 800,147(S); ABC Sept. 30, 1995.
Price: 50¢(d); 50¢(sat); $1.50(S); $10.50/mo; $126.00/yr (carrier).
Advertising: Open inch rate $280.33(m); $292.84(m-fri); $292.84(m-sat); $321.36(S). **Representative:** Cresmer, Woodward, O'Mara & Ormsbee.
News Services: AP, NYT, RN, KRT. **Politics:** Independent-Democrat. **Established:** 1885.
Special Weekly Sections: Business, Discoveries, Health & Fitness (mon); Business, Education Extra, Today (tues); Fashion! Dallas, Food, Today (wed); Business, Today (thur); Guide, House and Garden, Metro Real Estate (fri); Religion, Today, Automotive, Homes (sat); High Profile, The Arts, Travel, Sunday Reader, Homes, Automotive (S).
Magazines: TV Magazine, Parade (S).
Broadcast Affiliates: KXTV (CBS) Sacramento, CA; KOTV (CBS) Tulsa, OK; WFAA-TV (ABC) Dallas; KHOU-TV (CBS) Houston; WVEC-TV (ABC) Hampton, VA; WVEC-TV (ABC) Norfolk, VA.

CORPORATE OFFICERS

Publisher/Editor Burl Osborne
President/General Manager Jeremy L Halbreich
Senior Vice Pres/Exec Editor Ralph Langer
Senior Vice Pres-Administration/Operations J William Cox
Senior Vice Pres-Sales/Marketing Richard Starks
Senior Vice Pres-Circulation Barry T Peckham
Vice Pres-Advertising Sergio H Sallinas
Vice Pres-Production James Correu
Vice Pres/Editorial Page Editor Rena Pederson
Vice Pres-Info Management Grover D Livingston
Vice Pres-Human Resources Ellen Silva Wilson
Vice Pres-Finance Reginald K Brown
Vice Pres-Community Service Nancy Barry
Vice Pres-Marketing Barbara van Pelt
Director-Business Development James Galli

GENERAL MANAGEMENT

Director-Research Barbara Wells
Director-Human Resources Joe Daume
Director-Plant & Purchasing Mel Kinch

ADVERTISING

Director Charles J Gerardi
Director-Retail Jerry Coley
Director-Classified Eileen Dyer
Manager-Dallas Life Lynn Britton
Manager-Retail Doug Burke

MARKETING AND PROMOTION

Manager-Promotion Bob Wasinger

TELECOMMUNICATIONS

Manager-Communications Doug Tracy

CIRCULATION

Director Darrell Martin
Manager-Single Copy Eric Wynn

NEWS EXECUTIVES

Senior Vice Pres/Exec Editor Ralph Langer
Managing Editor Bob Mong
Deputy Managing Editor/Exec Sports Editor Dave Smith
Deputy Managing Editor-Hard News Stuart Wilk
Asst Managing Editor-Washington Bureau Chief Carl Leubsdorf
Asst Managing Editor-National/International Lennox Samuels
Asst Managing Editor-Sunday Donnis Baggett
Asst Managing Editor-Lifestyles Mark Weinberg
Asst Managing Editor-Lifestyles Sue Smith
Asst Managing Editor-Personnel/Training Paula LaRocque
Asst Managing Editor-Universal Desk Walt Stallings
Asst Managing Editor-Projects Howard Swindle
Asst Managing Editor-Recruiting Vernon Smith
Asst Managing Editor-Metro Gilbert Bailon
Asst Managing Editor-Visuals John Davidson
Asst Managing Editor Don Smith
Special Asst to Managing Editor John Davenport

EDITORS AND MANAGERS

Architecture Critic David Dillon
Art Director-News Kathleen Vincent
Art Critic Janet Kutner
Arts/Entertainment Editor Tom Kessler
Books Editor Bob Compton
Exec Business Editor Gary Jacobson
Business Editor Mindy Fetterman
Columnist-Business News Scott Burns
Columnist-Business News Bob Miller
Columnist-Editorial Page Jim Wright
Columnist-Editorial Page Bill Murchison
Columnist-Metro Steve Blow
Columnist-Metro Bob St John
Columnist-Metro Larry Powell
Columnist-SportsDay Blackie Sherrod
Columnist-SportsDay Randy Galloway
Columnist-SportsDay Kevin Sherrington
Columnist-SportsDay Kevin Blackstone
Columnist-SportsDay Cathy Harasta
Columnist-SportsDay Frank Luksa
Columnist-Today John Anders
Columnist-Today Marilyn Schwartz
Editor-Texas Almanac Mary Ramos
Editorial Page Editor Rena Pederson
Assoc Editor-Editorial Page Richard Estrada
Editorial Cartoonist Bill DeOre
Editorial Writer Jesse James
Editorial Writer Jennifer Nagorka
Editorial Writer William McKenzie
Editorial Writer Timothy O'Leary
ELS Illustrator Randy Bishop
Education Editor David Sediño
Environmental Writer Randy Loftis
Fashion! Dallas Editor Tracy Hayes
Films Critic Philip Wuntch
Films Critic Jane Summer
Finance Editor Cheryl Hall
Food Editor Dotty Griffith
Foreign Editor Ricardo Chavira
Guide Editor Mike Maza
Health/Fitness Editor John Bayne
High Profile Editor Harriet Blake
House/Garden Editor Martha Sheridan
Metro Editor Gilbert Bailon
Music Critic John Ardoin
National Editor Edward Dufner
News Editor Rick Barrick
Outdoors Writer Ray Sasser
Radio/Television Editor Ed Bark
Real Estate Editor Steve Brown
Reference Editor Judy Sall
Science Editor Tom Siegfried
Sports Editor Bob Yates
State Editor Rodger Jones
TODAY Editor Ira J Hadnot
Travel Editor Karen Jordan
Viewpoints Page Editor Bob Moos

PRODUCTION

Director Frank Tyler
Director-Pre Press Terry Brown
Art Director-Pre Press Jim Norris
Director-Imaging Charlie Wideman
Director-Publishing Technology John Cranfill
Director-Systems Bonnie Rogers
Manager-Pre Press Phil Ashley
Manager-Quality Assurance Ken Goodson
Manager-Operations Paul Webb
Manager-Technical Services Paul Platt
Asst Manager Dean Jacoby
Asst Manager Tom Stamper
Senior Superintendent-Pressroom Don Dykema
Superintendent-Platemaking Ronnie Lewis
Superintendent-Pressroom Gary Gregg
Superintendent-Distribution Joe Stockrahm
Superintendent-Maintenance Dave Brantley
General Foreman-Paperhandle Billy Elliot

Market Information: Zoned editions; Split Run; TMC.
Mechanical available: Offset; Black and 3 ROP colors; insert accepted — preprinted; page cut-offs — 22".
Mechanical specifications: Type page 13" x 21"; E - 6 cols, 2 1/16", 1/8" between; A - 6 cols, 2 1/16", 1/8" between; C - 9 cols, 1 7/32", 1/16" between.
Commodity consumption: Newsprint 151,781 short tons; widths 54", 40 1/2", 27"; black ink 2,729,210 pounds; color ink 722,499 pounds; single pages printed 63,661; average pages per issue 136(d), 422(S); single plates used 819,338.
Equipment: EDITORIAL: Front-end hardware — DEC/TMS; Front-end software — SII/Tandem, IAS, DEC/TMS, DEC/Guardian; Printers — Dataproducts; Other equipment — Ap/Mac, Sun/Eternet network, 149-SII/Coyote-QB Terminals. CLASSIFIED: Front-end hardware — AT/(Rel. 4B); Other equipment — Oli, IBM/Selectric. DISPLAY: Adv layout systems — SCS/Layout 8000; Front-end hardware — Compaq/386-25; Front-end software — SCS/Layout 8000; Printers — C.Itoh/CI800 Q; Other equipment — 2-AST/286, Memorex. PRODUCTION: Pagination software — DTI; Typesetters — 2-AU/APS L-108 FC, 4-AU/APS-5, 4-AU/APS 6-800, 1-AU/APS 6-108C; Platemaking systems — 5-WL/Lith-X-Pozer; Plate exposures — 5-WL, 2-Nu; Plate processors — 6-W/38 D; Electronic picture desk — Lf/AP Leaf Picture Desk; Scanners — 1-ECR/Autokon 2045, 1-ECR/Autokon 2045C, 1-Scitex/Smart Scanner, 12-Desktop/Scanner, 2-Scitex/Smart Scanner 540L; Production cameras — 1-C/Spartan III, Newspaper; Automatic film processors — 1-DP, 1-P; Film transporters — 3-C, 1-P/Raystar; Shrink lenses — 1-Alan/Anamorphic; Color separation equipment (conventional) — 1-Hel/399, 1-Scitex; Digital color separation equipment — 1-Scitex.
PRESSROOM: Line 1 — 1-TKS/Offset; Line 2 — 1-TKS/Offset; Line 3 — 1-TKS/Offset; Line 4 — 1-TKS/Offset; Line 5 — 1-TKS/Offset; Line 6 — 1-TKS/Offset; Line 7 — 1-G/HO; Line 8 — 1-G/Offset; Press drives — 90-TKS, 28-G; Folders — 12-TKS/3:2, 3-G/3:2; Pasters — 64-TKS, 24-G; Reels and stands — 64-TKS, 24-G; Press control system — TKS. MAILROOM: Counter stackers — 27-Id/660, 4-QWI/350B; Inserters and stuffers — 1-HI/1372, 6-HI/1472, 1-GMA/1000A 28:2, 1-GMA/1000A 8:2; Bundle tyer — 7-HL/Monitor, 10-MLN/Minza, 23-Dynaric/NP-2, 2-Sterling/SSM 40; Addressing machine — 32-Willet/Ink Jet Printer; Mailroom control system — 1-Id. Carnegie Mellon; Other mailroom equipment — 23-QWI/Cobra 3/4 underwrap. 5-Power Strap/Ring Turners. 2-MLN/Shrink Wrap. 14-Caterpillar/Ride-on Pallet Jacks. 2-Caterpillar/4OSD Forklift Trucks. LIBRARY: Electronic — Data Times, Basis. COMMUNICATIONS: Facsimile — 3-Hel/Pressfax (Scanners & Recorders), 2-III/3850, 2-Eskofot/Scanners; Systems used — fiber optic. BUSINESS COMPUTERS: IBM/4381-P2, IBM/9121-210; Applications: Adv, Circ, Payroll, Fixed asset, Accts payable, Gen ledger; PCs & main system networked.

DEL RIO
Val Verde County
'90 U.S. Census- 30,705; E&P '96 Est. 31,051
ABC-CZ (90): 30,705 (HH 9,465)

Del Rio News-Herald
(e-mon to sat; S)

Del Rio News-Herald, 321 S. Main St.; PO Box 4020, Del Rio, TX 78841; tel (210) 775-1551; fax (210) 774-2610. Hollinger International Inc. group.
Circulation: 6,023(e); 6,023(e-sat); 6,492(S); ABC Sept. 30, 1995.
Price: 50¢(d); 50¢(sat); $1.25(S); $7.25/mo; $87.00/yr (carrier).
Advertising: Open inch rate $10.52(e); $10.52(e-sat); $10.52(S). **Representative:** Papert Companies.
News Services: AP, NEA. **Politics:** Independent. **Established:** 1924.
Special Weekly Section: View (S).

GENERAL MANAGEMENT
Publisher Joe San Miguel
Business Manager Amanda Aguirre

ADVERTISING
Manager Janie Sharp

CIRCULATION
Manager Rosie Garcia

NEWS EXECUTIVE
Editor Cleve O'Quinn

PRODUCTION
Supervisor-Composing Room Brigido Cardenas
Supervisor-Pressroom Reynaldo Nieto

Market Information: TMC; ADS.
Mechanical available: Offset; Black and 3 ROP colors; insert accepted — preprinted; page cut-offs — 22 3/4".
Mechanical specifications: Type page 13" x 21 1/2"; E - 6 cols, 2 1/16", 1/8" between; A - 6 cols, 2 1/16", 1/8" between; C - 9 cols, 1 3/8", 1/16" between.
Commodity consumption: Newsprint 407 short tons; width 27 1/2"; single pages printed 3,242; average pages per issue 20(d), 56(S).
Equipment: EDITORIAL: Front-end hardware — Mk/1100 System. CLASSIFIED: Front-end hardware — Mk. DISPLAY: Adv layout systems — Mk/Ad Touch. PRODUCTION: Typesetters — 1-COM/Computype II, 1-COM/4961, 2-COM/8400; Plate exposures — 1-Nu; Plate processors — 1-Nu; Production cameras — 1-C/Spartan III; Automatic film processors — LE; Shrink lenses — 1-Alan/19.
PRESSROOM: Line 1 — 7-G/Community; Folders — 1-G/Community. MAILROOM: Bundle tyer — MLN; Addressing machine — 1-KR. WIRE SERVICES: News — AP; Syndicates — NEA, LATS, CT; Receiving dishes — AP. BUSINESS COMPUTERS: IBM, AT, XT, PC; Applications: Accts receivable, Payroll, Gen ledger, Circ-router, Carrier billing, TMC; PCs & micros networked; PCs & main system networked.

DENISON
Grayson County
'90 U.S. Census- 21,505; E&P '96 Est. 20,367
ABC-CZ (90): 21,505 (HH 8,710)

The Denison Herald
(e-mon to fri; S)

The Denison Herald, 331 W. Woodward St.; PO Box 329, Denison, TX 75020; tel (903) 465-7171; fax (903) 465-7188; e-mail wpalmer@texoma.com; web site http://home.texoma.com/donrey. Donrey Media group.
Circulation: 9,287(e); 10,567(S); ABC Sept. 30, 1995.
Price: 50¢(d); $1.00(S); $7.50/mo; $90.00/yr (S-carrier).
Advertising: Open inch rate $11.20(e); $11.20(S). **Representative:** Papert Companies.
News Service: AP. **Politics:** Independent. **Established:** 1889.
Advertising not accepted: X-rated movies.
Special Editions: Industrial (Mar); Answer Book (July); Football (Aug).
Special Weekly Sections: Business & Industrial Picture Pages (mon); Best Food Day (wed); Lawn & Garden (thur); Church (fri); Business News, TV Magazine w/daily listings (S); Amusement & Entertainment, Auto (daily).
Magazine: Focus on Texoma (S).

CORPORATE OFFICERS
Founder Donald W Reynolds
President/Chief Operating Officer Emmett Jones
Exec Vice Pres/Chief Financial Officer Darrell W Loftin
Vice Pres-Eastern Newspaper Group Don Schneider
Vice Pres-Western Newspaper Group David A Osborn

GENERAL MANAGEMENT
Publisher Mark Palmer
Manager-Office Patsy Zachary
Manager-Education Service Steve Martaindale

ADVERTISING
Director Wes King

MARKETING AND PROMOTION
Manager-Marketing/Promotion Doug Simpson

CIRCULATION
Director Chris Howell

NEWS EXECUTIVE
Managing Editor Steve Martaindale

EDITORS AND MANAGERS
Fashion/Food Editor Pat Welch
Garden Editor Michelle Dooner
Home Furnishings/Women's Editor Pat Welch
Special Edition Editor Steve Martaindale
Sports Editor Ty Benz
Teen-Age/Youth Editor Don Munsch

MANAGEMENT INFORMATION SERVICES
Data Processing Manager Patsy Zachary

PRODUCTION
Foreman-Composing Jimmy Raney
Foreman-Pressroom Leslie Wines

Market Information: TMC.
Mechanical available: Offset; Black and 3 ROP colors; insert accepted — preprinted; page cut-offs — 22 3/4".
Mechanical specifications: Type page 13" x 21 1/2"; E - 6 cols, 2", 1/6" between; A - 6 cols, 2", 1/6" between; C - 9 cols, 1 1/3", 1/12" between.
Commodity consumption: Newsprint 400 metric tons; widths 27 1/2", 13 3/4"; black ink 26,000 pounds; color ink 2,000 pounds; single pages printed 8,300; average pages per issue 26(d), 46(S); single plates used 8,700.
Equipment: EDITORIAL: Front-end hardware — Mk; Front-end software — Mk; Printers — NewGen. CLASSIFIED: Front-end hardware — Mk; Front-end software — Mk; Printers — NewGen. DISPLAY: Adv layout systems — Ap/Mac; Front-end hardware — Ap/Mac; Front-end software — Multi-Ad/Creator; Printers — NewGen; Other equipment — CD-Rom, Scanners. PRODUCTION: Typesetters — NewGen, CD-Rom; Plate exposures — Nu; Plate processors — Nat; Electronic picture desk — Lf/AP Leaf Picture Desk; Scanners — Lf; Production cameras — C/Spartan I; Automatic film processors — LE; Shrink lenses — C; Color separation equipment (conventional) — Lf/AP Leaf Picture Desk, Digi-Colour; Digital color separation equipment — Ap/Mac.
PRESSROOM: Line 1 — 2-G/Urbanite; Line 2 — 2-G/Urbanite; Press drives — Fin; Press control system — Fin. MAILROOM: Inserters and stuffers — S; Bundle tyer — MLN. WIRE SERVICES: News — AP; Photos — AP; Receiving dishes — size-8ft, AP. BUSINESS COMPUTERS: IBM, HP; Applications: CJ, MSSI; PCs & micros networked; PCs & main system networked.

DENTON
Denton County
'90 U.S. Census- 66,270; E&P '96 Est. 77,635

Denton Record-Chronicle
(e-mon to fri; m-sat; S)

Denton Record-Chronicle, 314 E. Hickory, Denton, TX 76201; tel (817) 387-3811; fax (214) 434-2400.
Circulation: 15,907(e); 15,907(m-sat); 18,809(S); CAC Dec. 31, 1994.
Price: 25¢(d); 25¢(sat); $1.00(S); $96.00/yr.
Advertising: Open inch rate $13.00(e); $13.00(m-sat); $13.00(S).
News Service: AP. **Politics:** Independent. **Established:** 1903.
Special Editions: Progress (Jan); Back-to-School (Aug); Christmas (Dec).
Special Weekly Section: Steppin' Out (Entertainment) (thur).
Magazines: USA Weekend, TV Update (S).

CORPORATE OFFICERS
President Fred Patterson
Vice Pres Bill Patterson
Secretary/Treasurer Patsy Patterson

GENERAL MANAGEMENT
Publisher Fred Patterson
General Manager Bill Patterson

ADVERTISING
Director Sandra Kelly
Manager Shirley Cagle

MARKETING AND PROMOTION
Director-Marketing/Promotion Andrea Wagoner

CIRCULATION
Director Don Wroblewski
Asst Director Steve Latham

NEWS EXECUTIVE
Managing Editor Chris Cobler

EDITORS AND MANAGERS
Automotive Editor Kaycee Key
Business Editor Tony Cantu
City/Metro Editor Jim Fredericks
Entertainment/Amusements Editor Paula Felps
Environmental Editor Holly Becka
Editorial Page Editor Stella Winsett
Education Editor April Washington
Farm/Agriculture Editor Holly Becka
Fashion/Style Editor Cheri Johnson
Features Editor Cheri Johnson
Graphics Editor/Art Director Carolyn Martin
Health/Medical Editor Holly Becka
Librarian Julie Lehman
Music Editor Paula Felps
News Editor Terry Welbro
Chief Photographer Barron Ludlum
Photo Editor Barron Ludlum
Political Editor Kelly Harrison
Radio/Television Editor Paula Felps
Real Estate Editor Kaycee Key
Religion Editor Cheri Johnson
Science/Technology Editor Holly Becka
Sports Editor David Boclair
Wire Editor Terry Welbro
Women's Editor Cheri Johnson

PRODUCTION
Manager Lafayette Newland
Foreman-Composing Les Sheets
Foreman-Pressroom Carl Gary

Market Information: TMC.
Mechanical available: Flexography/Letterpress; Black and 3 ROP colors; insert accepted — preprinted, card, single sheet; page cut-offs — 22 3/4".
Mechanical specifications: Type page 13" x 21 1/2"; E - 6 cols, 2 1/16", 1/6" between; A - 6 cols, 2 1/16", 1/6" between; C - 9 cols, 1 3/8", 1/8" between.
Commodity consumption: Newsprint 1,640 metric tons; widths 55", 27 1/2", 41 1/4"; black ink 106,500 pounds; color ink 35,000 pounds; single pages printed 12,170; average pages per issue 36(d), 64(S); single plates used 22,570.
Equipment: EDITORIAL: Front-end hardware — Compudyne/386; Front-end software — SII/Sys 55XR; Printers — Okidata. CLASSIFIED: Front-end hardware — Compudyne/386; Front-end software — SII/Sys 55XR; Printers — Okidata. DISPLAY: Adv layout systems — SCS/Layout 8000; Front-end hardware — IBM/PC-AT; Front-end software — SCS/Layout 8000; Printers — CI/300 Plus. PRODUCTION: Typesetters — AG/3400, HP/LaserJet III, ECR/Scriptsetter VRL 36; Plate exposures — 2-Na/II, 1-Burgess; Plate processors — 1-Na/FP-1, 2-Na/NP20; Scanners — ECR/Autokon 1000; Production cameras — 2-C/Spartan III; Color separation equipment (conventional) — Hel/DC-350 Laser scanner.
PRESSROOM: Line 1 — 2-FOL/4-LP; Line 2 — 2-KBA/Conversion; Pasters — 6-H; Press control system — GE. MAILROOM: Counter stackers — 3-SH; Inserters and stuffers — 2-MM; Bundle tyer — 1-EAM/Mosca; Addressing machine — 1-KR. LIBRARY: Electronic — SII/SSXR. COMMUNICATIONS: Facsimile — 4-Omni/9-S; Digital ad delivery system — AP AdSend. WIRE SERVICES: News — AP Datastream, AP; Syndicates — NYT; Receiving dishes — size-3m, AP. BUSINESS COMPUTERS: ATT; Applications: Circ, Accts receivable, Accts payable, Payroll, Gen ledger; PCs & micros networked; PCs & main system networked.

EDINBURG
Hidalgo County
'90 U.S. Census- 29,885; E&P '96 Est. 33,267

Edinburg Daily Review
(e-tues to fri; S)

Edinburg Daily Review, 215 E. University; PO Box 148, Edinburg, TX 78539; tel (210) 383-2705; fax (210) 383-3172.
Circulation: 5,000(e); 5,000(S); Sworn Sept. 30, 1992.
Price: 25¢(d); 25¢(S); $60.00/yr.
Advertising: Open inch rate $4.80(e); $4.80(S).
News Service: AP. **Politics:** Independent. **Established:** 1914.
Not Published: Independence Day; Labor Day; Christmas.
Special Editions: Christmas Opening; Christmas Greetings; Texas Public Schools Week; Graduation; School Opening; Tourist; Winter Visitors.
Special Weekly Sections: Business & Industrial Page (tues); Best Food Day (wed); Church Page (fri).

CORPORATE OFFICER
President Pearl V Mathis

GENERAL MANAGEMENT
Publisher Pearl V Mathis
Asst Publisher-Business Rosie Briseno

ADVERTISING
Manager Debbie Moczygemba
Manager-Classified Lisa Tamez

CIRCULATION
Manager Rick Abrego

NEWS EXECUTIVES
Editor Gilbert Tagle
Managing Editor Gilbert Tagle

EDITOR AND MANAGER
Society Editor Brad Nibert

I-396 Texas

PRODUCTION

Supervisor Brad Nibert
Superintendent-Pressroom Jesse Palomo

Mechanical available: Offset; Black and 3 ROP colors; insert accepted — preprinted. **Mechanical specifications:** Type page 13" x 21½"; E - 6 cols, 2 1/16", ⅛" between; A - 6 cols, 2 1/16", ⅛" between; C - 9 cols, 1⅜", 1/16" between.
Commodity consumption: widths 27½", 13"; average pages per issue 24(d), 56(S).
Equipment: EDITORIAL: Front-end hardware — Ap/Mac. CLASSIFIED: Front-end hardware — Ap/Mac. PRODUCTION: Plate processors — Nu; Production cameras — R. PRESSROOM: Line 1 — 4-G/Suburban. MAILROOM: Addressing machine — 1-Am. LIBRARY: Electronic — Minolta/Microfilm. WIRE SERVICES: News — AP; Photos — AP; Syndicates — King Features, NYT; Receiving dishes — AP. BUSINESS COMPUTERS: Tandy/3000, IBM; Applications: Accts receivable, Payroll, Circ, Gen ledger.

EL PASO

El Paso County

'90 U.S. Census- 515,342; E&P '96 Est. 557,451
ABC-NDM (90): 559,898 (HH 170,951)

El Paso Times

(m-mon to sat; S)

El Paso Times, 300 N. Campbell (79901-1470); PO Box 20, El Paso, TX 79999-0020; tel (915) 546-6100. Gannett Co. Inc. group.
Circulation: 65,970(m); 64,721(m-sat); 99,006(S); ABC Sept. 30, 1995.
Price: 35¢(d); 35¢(sat); $1.25(S); $5.50/mo (d), $5.50/mo (S), $10.50/mo (dS).
Advertising: Open inch rate $62.45(m); $70.90(m-sat); $70.90(S); $66.25(m & S); $68.15(e & S); $57.75(m, e & S); comb with El Paso Herald-Post (e) $56.15. **Representative:** Gannett National Newspaper Sales.
News Services: AP, GNS, LAT-WP. **Politics:** Independent. **Established:** 1881.
Advertising not accepted: Objectionable.
Special Editions: Rodeo (Feb); Back-to-School (Aug); Home Fix-up (Sept); Christmas Guide (Nov); Last Minute (Dec).
Special Weekly Sections: Jobs (mon); Vecinos (Spanish TMC) (thur); Auto Showcase (fri); Homes of El Paso (S); Hot Ticket (TMC).
Magazines: TV Times, USA Weekend, Vista (S); Border Business (monthly).

CORPORATE OFFICER

President Chris Jensen

GENERAL MANAGEMENT

Publisher Dionicio (Don) Flores
Director-Finance Richard Beas
Manager-Data Processing Dave Nance
Manager-Credit Grace Arciero

ADVERTISING

Director J Michael Price
Manager-Classified Ken Drahan

MARKETING AND PROMOTION

Director-Marketing Marti Buscaglia

CIRCULATION

Exec Director Thomas Bibs
Manager-Marketing/Credit Yolanda McDonald
Manager-Single Copy Sales Joseph A Braunschweig
Manager-Transportation Vitterbo Gomez
Manager-Country Bruce Dotson

NEWS EXECUTIVES

Editor Dionicio (Don) Flores
Managing Editor Paula Moore

EDITORS AND MANAGERS

Action Line Editor Laurie Paternoster
Automotive Editor Laurie Paternoster
Business Editor Laurie Paternoster
City/Metro Editor Ramon Bracamontes
Design Editor Jeff Carr
Education Editor Ramon Renteria
Entertainment/Amusements Editor Leticia Zamarripa
Environmental Editor David Sheppard
Editorial Page Editor Elaine Ayala
Farm/Agriculture Editor Ramon Bracamontes
Fashion/Style Editor Leticia Zamarripa
Features Editor Leticia Zamarripa
Graphics Editor/Art Director Jeff Carr
Health/Medical Editor Jim Conley
Librarian Leslie Trich Humble
Living/Lifestyle Editor Leticia Zamarripa
National Editor Gary Scharrer
Chief Photographer Rudy Gutierrez
Photo Editor Rudy Gutierrez
Political/Government Editor Gary Scharrer
Religion Editor Coco Ballew
Science/Technology Editor David Sheppard
Sports Editor Lee Williams
Television/Film Editor Leticia Zamarripa
Theater/Music Editor Leticia Zamarripa
Travel/Women's Editor Leticia Zamarripa

MANAGEMENT INFORMATION SERVICES

Data Processing Manager Dave Nance

PRODUCTION

Director Gary Hughes
Manager-Systems Raymond Flores
Asst Manager Ernesto Reyes
Asst Manager Pat Luedke
Manager-Mailroom Larry Glasson
Manager-Building Maintenance Jesus Reza
Manager-Composing Jerry Stroud

Market Information: Zoned editions; Split Run; TMC; ADS.
Mechanical available: Black and 7 ROP colors; insert accepted — preprinted; page cut-offs — 23 9/16".
Mechanical specifications: Type page 13" x 22¼"; E - 6 cols, 2 1/16", ⅛" between; A - 6 cols, 2 1/16", ⅛" between; C - 10 cols, 1¼", 1/16" between.
Commodity consumption: Newsprint 11,113 short tons; widths 54½", 40⅞", 27¼"; black ink 384,000 pounds; color ink 96,300 pounds; single pages printed 28,570; average pages per issue 42(d), 100(S); single plates used 84,000.
Equipment: EDITORIAL: Front-end hardware — SII, 40-SII/Coyote 15, 26-SII/Coyote 22, 15-SII/Cat 30; Other equipment — 5-Ap/Mac. CLASSIFIED: Front-end hardware — SII, 22-SII/Coyote 15, 2-SII/Coyote 22, 2-SII/Cat 30; Other equipment — 2-SII, ICP. DISPLAY: Adv layout systems — SII/AdSpeed, QPS; Front-end hardware — 1-Ultra/Imagesetter, 2-X/Scanner, 5-Ap/Mac Quadra 700; Printers — 2-Ap/Mac LaserWriter. PRODUCTION: Pagination software — 1-Nu; Typesetters — 2-MON/Imagesetter; Platemaking systems — 2-Na; Plate exposures — 2-Na/Satellite; Plate processors — 2-Na/NP-80; Electronic picture desk — Lf/AP Leaf Picture Desk; Scanners — ECR/Autokon 1000 DE, HP/Flatbed Color, Lf/Leafscan 35; Production cameras — 2-C/Spartan; Automatic film processors — 3-LD/18, 2-LE/PC-13; Film transporters — 2-C; Shrink lenses — 2-CK Optical; Color separation equipment (conventional) — Adobe/Photoshop 2.5; Digital color separation equipment — 1-RZ/200S, QPS. PRESSROOM: Line 1 — 12-H/Colormatic; Press drives — GE; Folders — 2-H; Press registration system — KFM. MAILROOM: Counter stackers — 6-HL; Inserters and stuffers — 1-MM, 1-HI/48-P, 2-AM Graphics/1372-P; Bundle tyer — 4-MLN/2, 1-Mc, Stitcher-Trimmer; Addressing machine — KR/Labeler, Ch. COMMUNICATIONS: Remote imagesetting — AdSat, AP Adsend. WIRE SERVICES: News — AP, NYT, SHNS, GNS; Stock tables — AP; Syndicates — LATS, United Features; Receiving dishes — AP, LATS. BUSINESS COMPUTERS: 1-IBM/AS-400; Applications: Circ, Adv billing, Accts receivable, Gen ledger, Payroll; PCs & main system networked.

El Paso Herald-Post

(e-mon to fri; m-sat)

El Paso Herald-Post, 300 N. Campbell (79901-1470); PO Box 20, El Paso, TX 79999-0020; tel (915) 546-6340; fax (915) 546-6349; e-mail post@rgfn.epcc.edu; web site http://www.heraldpost.com. Scripps Howard group.
Circulation: 22,266(e); 64,721(m-sat); ABC Sept. 30, 1995.
Price: 35¢(d); 35¢(sat); $5.50/mo; $66.00/yr (carrier).
Advertising: Open inch rate $65.40(e); $66.90(m-sat); comb with El Paso Times (mS) $56.15. **Representative:** Gannett National Newspaper Sales.
News Services: AP, SHNS, NYT. **Politics:** Independent. **Established:** 1881.
Note: Printed by the El Paso Times. For detailed mechanical equipment information, see the El Paso Times listing.
Advertising not accepted: Objectionable.
Special Weekly Section: Family (wed).
Magazines: Accent (entertainment) (thur); Sports/Plus, TV Week (sat).

CORPORATE OFFICERS

President J Thomas King
Secretary/Treasurer E John Wolfzorn

ADVERTISING

Director J Michael Price

CIRCULATION

Director Thomas Bibs
Manager-City Craig Pogorzelski

NEWS EXECUTIVES

Editor Tom King
Asst Managing Editor Nan Keck

EDITORS AND MANAGERS

Amusement/Films Editor Deborah Martin
Books Editor Charles Edgren
Business Editor Ken Baake
City Editor Judy G Wiley
Columnist Charles Edgren
Education Editor Sonny Lopez
Editorial Page Editor Robbie Farley-Villalobos
Features Editor Karen A Brehm
Graphics Editor/Art Director Nan E Keck
Living/Lifestyle Editor Karen A Brehm
Music Editor-Classical Deborah Martin
Music Editor-Rock/Country Deborah Martin
News Editor Paul Maldonado
Photo Editor Ruben R Ramirez
Politics Editor Peter Brock
Director-Public Service Michelle Martin
Radio/Television Editor Deborah Martin
Real Estate Editor Ken Baake
Religion Editor Karen A Brehm
Sports Editor Joe Muench
Theater Editor Deborah Martin
Wire Editor Paul Maldonado
Women's Editor Karen A Brehm

Commodity consumption: average pages per issue 42(d).
Equipment: WIRE SERVICES: News — AP, NYT, SHNS.

ENNIS

Ellis County

'90 U.S. Census- 13,883; E&P '96 Est. 14,864

The Ennis Daily News

(e-mon to fri; S)

The Ennis Daily News, 213 N. Dallas St., Ennis, TX 75119; tel (214) 875-3801; fax (214) 875-9747.
Circulation: 3,175(e); 3,175(S); Sworn Oct. 1, 1993.
Price: 25¢(d); 25¢(S); $42.00/yr.
Advertising: Open inch rate $4.00(e); $4.00(S). **Representative:** Papert Companies.
News Service: AP. **Established:** 1891.

CORPORATE OFFICERS

President Charles E Gentry
Vice Pres Lester Jordan
Vice Pres Charles E Gentry II
Secretary/Treasurer Mary Helen Gentry

GENERAL MANAGEMENT

Publisher/General Manager Charles E Gentry

ADVERTISING

Director Roger N Gentry

CIRCULATION

Director Roger N Gentry

NEWS EXECUTIVE

Editor Charles E Gentry

Market Information: Zoned editions; Split Run; TMC.
Mechanical available: Offset; Black and 3 ROP colors; insert accepted — preprinted; page cut-offs — 22¾".
Mechanical specifications: Type page 13" x 21"; E - 6 cols, 2 1/16", ⅛" between; A - 6 cols, 2 1/16", ⅛" between; C - 6 cols, 2 1/16", ⅛" between.
Commodity consumption: Newsprint 200 short tons; width 27"; black ink 2,500 pounds; color ink 150 pounds; single pages printed 16; average pages per issue 42(d), 100(S).
Equipment: PRODUCTION: Typesetters — 1-COM/Trendsetter, 1-COM/7200; Plate exposures — 1-Nu; Production cameras — 1-B; Automatic film processors — 1-P. PRESSROOM: Line 1 — 4-G/Community; Folders — 1-G/2:1. MAILROOM: Addressing machine — Am. WIRE SERVICES: News — AP; Receiving dishes — AP.

FORT WORTH

Tarrant County

'90 U.S. Census- 447,619; E&P '96 Est. 504,510
ABC-NDM (90): 1,132,548 (HH 424,910)

Fort Worth Star-Telegram

(m-mon to sat; S)

Fort Worth Star-Telegram, 400 W. 7th St.; PO Box 1870, Fort Worth, TX 76101; tel (817) 390-7400; fax (817) 390-7831. Capital Cities/ABC Inc. group.
Circulation: 225,080(m); 276,354 (m-fri); 267,281(m-sat); 341,623(S); ABC Sept. 30, 1995.
Price: 50¢(d); 50¢(sat); $1.50(S); $10.95/mo (m & S); $131.40/yr.
Advertising: Open inch rate $172.08(m); $172.08(m-sat); $186.98(S). **Representative:** Sawyer-Ferguson-Walker Co.
News Services: AP, KRT, LAT-WP, SHNS. **Politics:** Independent. **Established:** 1895 (m), 1906 (e & S).
Note: Effective Apr. 3, 1995, this publication changed its publishing plan from (all day-mon to sat; S) to (m-mon to sat; S).
Advertising not accepted: X-rated movies.
Special Editions: JR Achievement, Book Show, Education, Stock Show I & II, Tax Guide (Jan); Auto Show, Cruise Show, Insurance, Engineers (Feb); Spring Bridal, Spring Home/Garden, Garden VIP, Golf Supplement, Smart Shopper (Mar); Baseball '96, Main Street, Volunteers, Earthday, Top 25, Summer Days, Southern Living Cooking School (Apr); Together, Healthsmart, Colonial Golf, Home Impressions, Visions NE, Outlook FW, Almanac ARL (May); Prime Time (June); Weatherford, Baseball All Star Game, Christmas in July, Education, Fall Bridal, Back-to-School (July); Long Term Health, TCU/UTA Campus Guide, Football '96 (Aug); Fall Garden, Prime Time, Heartwalk, Club Directory (Sept); Breast Cancer, Buy H-E-B, So. Women Show, Dining Restaurant Guide, Heartsmart, FW Beautiful, Camp Bowie (Oct); Smart Shopper, NE Christmas Pageant, Prime Time, Wishbook (Nov); Weatherford Christmas, Gift Guide II, Medical Directory, Cleburne Christmas, Christmas Song Book, SWC Revisited (Dec).
Special Weekly Section: Travel (S).
Magazines: Tarrant Business (mon); Class Acts (special section for kids) (tues); StarTime (fri); Parade, TV Star (weekly TV Guide) (S).

CORPORATE OFFICER

President Richard L Connor

GENERAL MANAGEMENT

President/Publisher Richard L Connor
Publisher (Arlington Star-Telegram) Mac Tully
Publisher NE Tarrant Jim Witt
Senior Vice Pres-Advertising Mac Tully
Vice Pres/Treasurer Dick Bibb
Vice Pres-Special Projects/New Media Maureen Hathaway
Vice Pres-Circulation Weldon Whiteman
Vice Pres/Chief Financial Officer Denise Spitler
Vice Pres/Chief Info Systems Officer Michael D Price
Vice Pres-Operations Gerald Zenick
Vice Pres/Editorial Chairman Jack B Tinsley
Editorial Director Paul Harral
Manager-Education Service Susan Wallace
Ombudsman Phil J Record

ADVERTISING

Director Craig Diebel
Manager-National Larry Bien
Manager-Retail Ann Caukins
Manager-Operations Richard Greene

MARKETING AND PROMOTION

Director-Marketing Jerry Scott

CIRCULATION

Director Weldon Whiteman
Director-Sales/Training Lonna Hoffman
Manager Dolan Stidom
Manager-Administration Ricky Tripp
Manager-Single Copy Jim Christinidis

NEWS EXECUTIVES

Senior Vice Pres/Editor-Arlington Star-Telegram Mac Tully
Vice Pres/Exec Editor Debbie M Price
Deputy Exec Editor Gary M Hardee
Senior Editor-News Dave Montgomery
Senior Editor-Design/Graphics Broc Sears
Senior Editor Metro Mike Norman
Assoc Editor-Photography/Graphics/Design Larry C Price
Editor/Northeast-Tarrant Joan Krauter
Editor-Arlington Michael Blackman
Editor-PM Ernie Makovy
Editor-Sports Kevin Dale
Editor-Business Rex Seline
Editor-La Estrella Lizabeth Zavala

EDITORS AND MANAGERS

Arts/Entertainment Editor Lisa Kestler
Book Editor Larry Swindell
Business Editor-Tarrant Phyllis Stone
Bureau Chief-Washington Ron Hutcheson
Bureau Chief-Austin John Gonzalez
Cartoonist Etta Hulme
City Editor D J Hill
City Editor-Night Libby Afflerbach
Asst City Editor Ann Thompson
Class Acts Sharon Cox
Columnist Sheila Taylor-Wells
Columnist Jon McConal
Columnist-Star Bud Kennedy
Columnist-Star Bill Thompson
Columnist-Political Molly Ivins
Copy Desk Chief Gene Zipperlen
Design Desk Chief Sarah Huffstetler
Editorial Director-StarText News Paul Harral
Editorial Director-Arlington Jill (JR) Labbe
Manager-Editorial Operations Lance Murray
Senior Editorial Writer Tommy Denton
Editorial Writer Cecil Johnson
Editorial Writer Pat Truly
Editorial Page Editor Paul K Harral
Films Editor Michael H Price
Food Editor Beverly Bundy
Foreign/National Editor Jim Peipert
Government Affairs Editor John Gravois
Asst Government Affairs Editor Kaye Northcott
Graphics Director Frank Pontari
Librarian Jan Fennell
Life Editor Holly Hanson
Asst National Editor Lou Hudson
Asst National Editor Tom Uhler
Asst News Editor Tom Leferink
Neighborhood Editor Jay Lewis
Obit Editor Roger Summers
Ombudsman/Special Asst to Publisher Phil J Record
Director of Photography Max Faulkner
Religion Editor Jim Jones
Radio/Television Editor Steven Cole Smith
Society Editor Mary Rogers
Sunday Editor Kathy Vetter
Star Time Editor Robert Camuto
Texas & Southwest Editor Roland Lindsey
Theater Editor Perry Stewart
Travel Editor Jerry Flemmons
TV Star Editor Jim Davis

MANAGEMENT INFORMATION SERVICES

Vice Pres-Info Service Michael D Price
Director-Info Systems Ken Clark
Director Technical Services Harry Smith
Online Manager Marla Hammond

PRODUCTION

Director-Operations (Administrative & Newsprint) Catherine Carter
Director-Operations David Whitaker
Manager-Pre Press Albert Adams
Manager-Packaging/Distribution John (Trey) Roberts III
Manager-Warehouse Richard Hooper
Manager-Press Operations Edwin Lane

Market Information: Zoned editions; Split Run; TMC; ADS; Operate database; Electronic edition.
Mechanical available: Offset; Black and 3 ROP colors; insert accepted — preprinted; page cutoffs — 22".
Mechanical specifications: Type page 13½" x 21¼"; E - 6 cols, 2.07", ⅙" between; A - 6 cols, 2.07", ⅙" between; C - 10 cols, 1.18", ⅙" between.
Commodity consumption: Newsprint 66,487 short tons; widths 54⅞", 27", 41"; black ink 1,178,881 pounds; color ink 431,555 pounds; single pages printed 64,447; average pages per issue 173(d), 195(S); single plates used 409,431.
Equipment: EDITORIAL: Front-end hardware — NEC/486; Front-end software — Dewar; Printers — Epson. CLASSIFIED: Front-end hardware — IBM/RS 6000-380; Front-end software — CText; Printers — Lexmark. DISPLAY: Front-end hardware — Ap/Mac II VX; Front-end software — Mk/Page Director, Mk/Ad Director; Printers — Ap/Mac LaserWriter III. PRODUCTION: Typesetters — 3-AU/APS-5, 2-Hyphen/Image Setter; Plate exposures — 2-WL/Lith-X-Pozer III, 1-KFM/Exposer; Plate processors — 3-W; Scanners — Scanmate/Scanview; Production cameras — 1-Acti, 2-C/Marathon, 1-C/New; Automatic film processors — 6-LE, 2-Konica; Film transporters — 1-Konica; Shrink lenses — 1-Alan, 1-CK Optical; Color separation equipment (conventional) — 4-SCREEN/818, Lf/Leafscan, Nikon; Digital color separation equipment — Lf/Leafscan, Nikon.
PRESSROOM: Line 1 — 10-G/Headliner(w/8 half decks); Line 2 — 10-G/Headliner(w/8 half decks); Line 3 — 10-G/Headliner(w/8 half decks); Line 4 — 12-G/Headliner(w/9 half decks); Press drives — Fin; Folders — G; Pasters — G; Reels and stands — G; Press control system — G/MPCS. MAILROOM: Counter stackers — 17-HL/Monitor; Inserters and stuffers — 4-HI/P-72; Bundle tyer — 16-MLN, 8-Dynaric/NP2; Wrapping singles — 2-MLN, 3-Bu, 3-Dynaric/AM-9000; Addressing machine — 2-Ch, 2-AVY, 1-MM. LIBRARY: Electronic — Data Times. COMMUNICATIONS: Systems used — fiber optic. WIRE SERVICES: News — AP; Syndicates — North America Syndicate; Receiving dishes — size-12ft, AP. BUSINESS COMPUTERS: DEC/6410, DEC/8350, DEC/3100; Applications: Circ, Accts payable, Payroll, Human resources, Adv; PCs & micros networked; PCs & main system networked.

FREEPORT

See CLUTE

GAINESVILLE

Cooke County

'90 U.S. Census- 14,256; E&P '96 Est. 14,346

Gainesville Daily Register (e-mon to fri; S)

Gainesville Daily Register, 306 E. California (76240); PO Box 309, Gainesville, TX 76241; tel (817) 665-5511; fax (817) 665-0920. Donrey Media group.
Circulation: 6,795(e); 6,795(S); Sworn Sept. 25, 1995.
Price: 50¢(d); 75¢(S); $6.50/mo; $78.00/yr.
Advertising: Open inch rate $8.84(e); $8.84(S). **Representative:** Papert Companies.
News Service: AP. **Politics:** Independent. **Established:** 1890.
Not Published: New Year; Independence Day; Labor Day; Christmas.
Advertising not accepted: 900 numbers.
Special Weekly Sections: Best Food Day (wed); Church News (fri); Best Food Day (S).

CORPORATE OFFICERS

Founder Donald W Reynolds
President/Chief Operating Officer Emmett Jones
Exec Vice Pres/Chief Financial Officer Darrell W Loftin
Vice Pres-Western Newspaper Group David A Osborn
Vice Pres-Eastern Newspaper Group Don Schneider

GENERAL MANAGEMENT

Publisher David Scott

ADVERTISING

Manager Sandy Jones

CIRCULATION

Manager Carol Richardson

NEWS EXECUTIVE

Managing Editor Jerry Prickett

EDITORS AND MANAGERS

Living/Lifestyle Editor Jodelle Greiner
Sports Editor George Watson
Women's Editor Jodelle Greiner

PRODUCTION

Superintendent-Composing Joe Grotte
Superintendent-Pressroom Tom Baker

Mechanical available: Offset; Black and 3 ROP colors; insert accepted — preprinted; page cutoffs — 19".
Mechanical specifications: Type page 13" x 21½"; E - 6 cols, $2\frac{1}{16}$", ⅛" between; A - 6 cols, $2\frac{1}{16}$", ⅛" between; C - 8 cols, 1½", ⅛" between.
Commodity consumption: Newsprint 300,000 short tons; width 27"; average pages per issue 10(d), 16(S).
Equipment: EDITORIAL: Front-end hardware — Mk; Printers — Ap/Mac LaserWriter II. CLASSIFIED: Front-end hardware — Mk; Printers — Ap/Mac LaserWriter II. DISPLAY: Adv layout systems — Raster/Ops; Front-end hardware — Ap/Mac IIci; Front-end software — Multi-Ad/Creator; Printers — Ap/Mac LaserWriter II NTX. PRODUCTION: OCR software — Mk; Typesetters — 2-Ap/Mac LaserWriter II NTX; Production cameras — 1-Nu; Automatic film processors — 1-P/26RT.
PRESSROOM: Line 1 — 24-G/Community. MAILROOM: Bundle tyer — MLN. LIBRARY: Electronic — Dukane/Microfilm reader. WIRE SERVICES: News — AP; Receiving dishes — AP.

GALVESTON

Galveston County

'90 U.S. Census- 59,070; E&P '96 Est. 57,669

The Galveston County Daily News (m-mon to sat; S)

The Galveston County Daily News, 8522 Teichman Rd.; PO Box 628, Galveston, TX 77553; tel (409) 744-3611; fax (409) 744-6268; e-mail Galvnews@aol.com; web site http://www.galvnews.com. Walls Investment Co. group.
Circulation: 25,667(m); 25,667(m-sat); 26,796(S); CAC June 30, 1995.
Price: 50¢(d); 50¢(sat); $1.50(S); $12.00/mo; $144.00/yr.
Advertising: Open inch rate $28.50(m); $28.50(m-sat); $28.50(S). **Representative:** Papert Companies.
News Service: AP. **Politics:** Independent. **Established:** 1842.
Advertising not accepted: Self improvement hypnosis ads.
Special Editions: Horizons; Back-to-School; Spring & Fall Fashion; Hurricane Guide; Design-an-Ad; Dickens Festival; Mardi Gras; Bridal Guide; Summer Visitor's Guide; Home Improvement Guide; Holiday Give Away Gift Guide; Super Turkey Day.
Special Weekly Sections: Food, Lifestyle (wed); Lifestyle, Travel (S).
Magazines: USA Weekend; Galveston Co. TV & Entertainment Guide.

CORPORATE OFFICER

President Leslie P Daughtry Sr

GENERAL MANAGEMENT

Publisher Dolph Tillotson
Business Manager Rosetta Bonnin
Manager-Education Service Clara Smith

ADVERTISING

Manager-Classified Cliff Clements
Director Ilana Cowan

CIRCULATION

Manager Jim Ellis

NEWS EXECUTIVES

Editor Dolph Tillotson
Managing Editor Doug Toney
Asst Managing Editor Heber Taylor
Asst Managing Editor Ken Lanterman

EDITORS AND MANAGERS

County News Editor Ken Lanterman
Editorial Page Editor Heber Taylor
Food Editor Linda Fradkin
Librarian Calvin Whitner
News Editor Greg Mefford
Travel Editor Frances K Harris

PRODUCTION

Superintendent Bill Cochrane
Foreman-Composing Karen Saunders
Foreman-Pressroom Cecil Dill

Market Information: TMC.
Mechanical available: Offset; Black and 3 ROP colors; insert accepted — preprinted, all; page cutoffs — 22¾".
Mechanical specifications: Type page 13" x 21½"; E - 6 cols, $2\frac{1}{16}$", ⅛" between; A - 6 cols, $2\frac{1}{16}$", ⅛" between; C - 9 cols, 1⅜", $\frac{1}{16}$" between.
Commodity consumption: Newsprint 2,420 short tons; widths 27½", 13¾"; black ink 3,500 pounds; single pages printed 12,702; average pages per issue 24(d), 48(S); single plates used 18,000.
Equipment: EDITORIAL: Front-end hardware — Ap/Mac; Front-end software — Microsoft/Word, QuarkXPress, Custom Developed; Printers — Ap/Mac LaserWriter IIg, AG/Imagesetters. CLASSIFIED: Front-end hardware — Ap/Mac, DEC; Front-end software — DEC; Printers — Unified/Laser. DISPLAY: Adv layout systems — Mk/Ad Director, Mk/Managing Editor; Front-end hardware — Ap/Mac, 2-Ap/Mac IIg; Front-end software — Multi-Ad/Director; Printers — LaserMaster. PRODUCTION: Typesetters — 6-Ap/Mac LaserWriter IIg, AG/Star 400, 2-AG/1000 Imagesetter; Plate exposures — 1-Nu; Plate processors — Nat; Scanners — ECR, RZ/Diadem; Production cameras — C/Spartan III; Automatic film processors — P; Shrink lenses — CK Optical; Color separation equipment (conventional) — Diadem, Lf/Leafscan; Digital color separation equipment — Ap/Mac One, HP.
PRESSROOM: Line 1 — 8-HI/Cotrell 845; Folders — 1-HI/2:1, G/Urbanite. MAILROOM: Counter stackers — 1-S; Inserters and stuffers — 1-S; Bundle tyer — 1-MLN; Addressing machine — 1-KAN. COMMUNICATIONS: Systems used — satellite, fiber optic. WIRE SERVICES: News — AP; Photos — AP; Receiving dishes — size-10ft, AP. BUSINESS COMPUTERS: Data General.

GREENVILLE

Hunt County

'90 U.S. Census- 23,071; E&P '96 Est. 23,545

Greenville Herald-Banner (m-mon to sat; S)

Greenville Herald-Banner, 2305 King St.; PO Box 6000, Greenville, TX 75403-3299; tel (903) 455-4220; fax (903) 455-6281. Hollinger International Inc. group.
Circulation: 11,235(m); 11,235(m-sat); 11,235(S); Sworn Sept. 25, 1994.
Price: 50¢(d); 50¢(sat); 75¢(S); $8.00/mo; $96.00/yr (carrier).
Advertising: Open inch rate $13.53(m); $13.53(m-sat); $13.53(S). **Representative:** Papert Companies.
News Service: AP. **Politics:** Independent. **Established:** 1865.
Not Published: Christmas.
Advertising not accepted: Fortune tellers.
Special Editions: Progress; Fall & Spring Fashions; Outdoor; Back-to-School; Homemakers School; Greenville Tourism Sampler (Spring); Cotton Jubilee; Almanac; Fall & Spring Fix-It-Up; Christmas Season Opener (at Thanksgiving); Pre-Christmas Gift Guide; Holiday Cookbook; Hunt County Fair; Football.
Special Weekly Section: TV Tabloid (S).

CORPORATE OFFICER

President Larry J Perrotto

GENERAL MANAGEMENT

Publisher Albert Vaughn
Business Manager Bernadine Ewing

ADVERTISING

Director Terri McCreary

NEWS EXECUTIVE

Editor Melva Geyer

EDITORS AND MANAGERS

Editorial Page Editor Melva Geyer
Fashion/Society Editor Carol Ferguson
Sports Editor David Claybourn

PRODUCTION

Foreman-Composing Brian Ruth
Foreman-Pressroom Robin Pavlicek

Market Information: TMC.
Mechanical available: Offset; Black and 3 ROP colors; insert accepted — preprinted; page cutoffs — 22¾".
Mechanical specifications: Type page 13" x 21½"; E - 6 cols, $2\frac{1}{16}$", ⅛" between; A - 6 cols, $2\frac{1}{16}$", ⅛" between; C - 6 cols, $2\frac{1}{16}$", $\frac{1}{16}$" between.
Commodity consumption: Newsprint 794 short tons; width 27½"; black ink 19,298 pounds; color ink 5,120 pounds; single pages printed 9,804; average pages per issue 16(d), 28(S); single plates used 16,326.
Equipment: EDITORIAL: Front-end hardware — Ap/Mac Classic, Ap/Mac LC, Ap/Mac IIsi; Front-end software — QuarkXPress 3.1, Baseview/NewsEdit, Aldus/FreeHand, Claris/Works 3.0, TI/Omni 450-Battery Backup; Printers — Ap/Mac LaserWriter IIg; Other equipment — Hayes/Smart modem 9600. CLASSIFIED: Front-end hardware — 3-Ap/Mac LC; Front-end software — QuarkXPress 3.1; Printers — Okidata/Microline 320. DISPLAY: Adv layout systems — Ap/Mac; Front-end hardware — Ap/Mac Quadra 700; Front-end software — QuarkXPress, Adobe/Illustrator; Printers — Ap/Mac LaserWriter IIg; Other equipment — Ap/Mac CD-Rom Driver CDSC Plus. PRODUCTION: Typesetters — Ap/Mac II, Ap/Mac Quadra 700; Plate exposures — Nu/Flip Top FT40LNS (double & single); Plate processors — Nat/A-250; Scanners — Ap/Mac One Scanner, Mita/DC-1656 Copier; Production cameras — SCREEN/Rollmatic C-475-D, SCREEN/Companica 680C; Automatic film processors — LE/24AQ; Color separation equipment (conventional) — Prentice/Color Process.
PRESSROOM: Line 1 — 8-G/Community; Folders — 1-G/SC; Press control system — VEE ARC/PWM 7000. MAILROOM: Counter stackers — BG/108; Inserters and stuffers — KAN; Bundle tyer — 1-MLN/ML2EE, Dynaric/5580.

WIRE SERVICES: News — AP; Receiving dishes — AP. BUSINESS COMPUTERS: IBM, EKI/Televideo; Applications: Accts receivable, Accts payable, Payroll, Gen ledger, Finance.

HARLINGEN

Cameron County

'90 U.S. Census- 48,735; E&P '96 Est. 51,564
ABC-CZ (90): 74,131 (HH 22,826)

Valley Morning Star

(m-mon to sat; S)

Valley Morning Star, 1310 S. Commerce; PO Box 511, Harlingen, TX 78550; tel (210) 423-5511; fax (210) 430-6202. Freedom Communications Inc. group.

Circulation: 25,703(m); 25,703(m-sat); 28,395(S); ABC Sept. 30, 1995.

Price: 35¢(d); 35¢(sat); $1.25(S); $8.25/mo; $99.00/yr (mS-carrier).

Advertising: Open inch rate $48.92(m); $48.92(m-sat); $52.09(S). **Representative:** Papert Companies.

News Service: AP. **Politics:** Independent. **Established:** 1911.

Note: Advertising for the Valley Morning Star automatically includes advertising in Brownsville Herald (mS), El Heraldo de Brownsville (eS) & McAllen Monitor (eS).

Special Edition: Winter Visitors Tourist Guide (Dec).

Special Weekly Sections: Best Food Day (wed); Garden, Agriculture (sat); Business Page (S); TV Listing, Entertainment (daily).

Magazines: Food Pages (wed); Vista, Parade (S); The Island Times (published 14x/yr).

GENERAL MANAGEMENT

Publisher — Vernon Lyle DeBolt Sr
Business Manager — Jill Stout
Manager-Credit — Cheryl M O'Mara
Purchasing Agent — Cheryl M O'Mara
Consultant — R M Juillard

ADVERTISING

Manager-Local — E G Gutierrez Jr
Manager-Classified — Robert Adams
Manager-National (Rio Grande Valley) — Marcia Bleier

MARKETING AND PROMOTION

Director-Marketing — Melanie Ortiz

CIRCULATION

Manager — Cynthia Maldonado

NEWS EXECUTIVES

Editor — Patrick Conty
Managing Editor — Jerry Deal

EDITORS AND MANAGERS

Amusements Editor — Bruce Lee Smith
Books Editor — Vernon Lyle DeBolt Sr
City Editor — Bill Hethcock
Columnist — Dan Henderson
Editorial Page Editor — Randy Davidson
Fashion/Food Editor — Joy Ault
Graphics Editor/Art Director — Matt Crocker
Golf Editor — Vernon Lyle DeBolt Sr
Outdoor Editor — Gary Ware
Photo Department Manager — Julian Mendoza
Society/Women's Editor — Joy Ault
Sports Editor — Lucio Castillo
Television/Film Editor — Bruce Lee Smith
Theater/Music Editor — Bruce Lee Smith

PRODUCTION

Director-Quality Control — Bob Dease
Superintendent — Bob Dease
Asst Superintendent — Gary Maley
Foreman-Composing — David Gladstone
Foreman-Pressroom — Ramiro Rincones
Foreman-Mailroom — Eleazar Garza

Mechanical available: Offset; Black and 3 ROP colors; insert accepted — preprinted, all; page cut-offs — 22¾".

Mechanical specifications: Type page 13" x 21¼"; E - 6 cols, 2⅟₁₆", ⅛" between; A - 6 cols, 2⅟₁₆", ⅛" between; C - 10 cols, 1¼", ⅟₁₆" between.

Commodity consumption: Newsprint 2,750 metric tons; widths 27½", 13¾"; black ink 83,600 pounds; color ink 32,150 pounds; single pages printed 14,178; average pages per issue 36(d), 70(S); single plates used 14,400.

Equipment: EDITORIAL: Front-end hardware — 29-Compaq, 3-Ap/Mac; Front-end software — Dewar; Printers — Okidata/320; Other equipment — Lf/AP Leaf Picture Desk. CLASSIFIED: Front-end hardware — 6-Compaq; Front-end software — Dewar; Printers — Okidata/320. DISPLAY: Adv layout systems — 1-Compaq, Dewar; Front-end hardware — 1-Compaq; Front-end software — Dewar; Printers — Okidata/320. PRODUCTION: Pagination software — Dewar 6.46; OCR software — Dest 2.0; Typesetters — V/5100, V/5300E, V/5510, ECR/3850; Platemaking systems — KFM/Printing Systems; Plate exposures — 2-Nu; Plate processors — Anitec; Scanners — 1-X/Scanner, 1-HP/Scanner; Production cameras — 1-C/Spartan III; Automatic film processors — 1-LE, 1-Konica/K-550; Color separation equipment (conventional) — RZ, Lf/AP Leaf Picture Desk.
PRESSROOM: Line 1 — 6-HI/Cotrell 845; Line 2 — 6-HI/Cotrell 845; Folders — 2-H/2:1. MAILROOM: Counter stackers — Id; Bundle tyer — 1-MLN/MLIEE, 2-MLN/MLN2. LIBRARY: Electronic — SMS. WIRE SERVICES: News — AP Datastream, AP Datafeatures; Stock tables — AP SelectStox; Syndicates — KRT, CNS; Receiving dishes — size-6m, AP. BUSINESS COMPUTERS: Prosig, 4-PC/4DX2-66, SCSI, 7-Compaq/486; Applications: Brainworks: Accts receivable; Southware: Financial; PCs & micros networked; PCs & main system networked.

HENDERSON

Rusk County

'90 U.S. Census- 11,139; E&P '96 Est. 10,972

Henderson Daily News

(e-mon to fri; S)

Henderson Daily News, 1711 S. Hwy. 79; PO Box 30, Henderson, TX 75653; tel (903) 657-2501; fax (903) 657-2452. Hartman Newspapers Inc. group.

Circulation: 6,205(e); 6,205(S); Sworn Sept. 25, 1995.

Price: 25¢(d); 50¢(S); $5.00/mo; $60.00/yr.

Advertising: Open inch rate $5.60(e); $5.60(S).

News Services: AP, NEA. **Politics:** Independent. **Established:** 1930.

Not Published: Independence Day; Labor Day; Christmas.

Advertising not accepted: Liquor.

Special Editions: Christmas; Newcomer's Guide; Fall Sports Preview; Summer/Winter Car Care; Holiday Cooking; Home Improvement; Oil and Progress.

Magazine: TV Magazine (S).

CORPORATE OFFICER

President — Noble Welch

GENERAL MANAGEMENT

Publisher — Noble Welch
Accountant — Elizabeth Kelly

ADVERTISING

Manager — William Ashby

CIRCULATION

Manager — Olga Reed

NEWS EXECUTIVES

Editor — Noble Welch
Managing Editor — Randy Chote

EDITOR AND MANAGER

Sports Editor — Joey Richards

PRODUCTION

Superintendent/Foreman-Composing — Joy Slaimaker
Superintendent/Foreman-Pressroom — Robert Cyphers

Market Information: TMC.

Mechanical available: Offset; Black and 3 ROP colors; insert accepted — preprinted; page cut-offs — 21½".

Mechanical specifications: Type page 13" x 21½"; E - 6 cols, 2⅟₁₆", ⅛" between; A - 6 cols, 2⅟₁₆", ⅛" between; C - 8 cols, 1⅜", ⅟₁₆" between.

Commodity consumption: Newsprint 210 short tons; width 27½"; black ink 5,400 pounds; color ink 380 pounds; single pages printed 4,780; average pages per issue 10(d), 34(S); single plates used 2,500.

Equipment: EDITORIAL: Front-end hardware — Ap/Mac; Other equipment — 4-Ap/Mac. CLASSIFIED: Front-end software — Baseview/Class Manager. DISPLAY: Front-end hardware — Ap/Mac. PRODUCTION: Typesetters — 3-Ap/Mac LaserWriter Plus; Plate exposures — Nu/Flip Top FT40UP; Plate processors — Nat; Scanners — 2-COM/MDR; Production cameras — R/500; Automatic film processors — LE/24 ADQ; Shrink lenses — 1-Kamerak/152.
PRESSROOM: Line 1 — 6-HI/V15A w/Upper former. MAILROOM: Bundle tyer — 1-Bu/64808. WIRE SERVICES: News — AP; Receiving dishes — AP.

HEREFORD

Deaf Smith County

'90 U.S. Census- 14,745; E&P '96 Est. 14,205

Hereford Brand

(e-tues to fri; S)

The Hereford Brand, 313 N. Lee; PO Box 673, Hereford, TX 79045; tel (806) 364-2030; fax (806) 364-8364.

Circulation: 3,350(e); 3,350(S); Sworn Sept. 29, 1995.

Price: 50¢(d); 50¢(S); $4.20/mo; $45.70/yr.

Advertising: Open inch rate $5.50(e); $5.50(S).

News Service: AP. **Politics:** Independent. **Established:** 1901.

Not Published: New Year; Thanksgiving; Christmas.

Special Edition: Farm (monthly).

Special Weekly Section: Television (S).

CORPORATE OFFICERS

President — O G Nieman
Vice Pres — Robert F Brown
Treasurer — Walter Buckel

GENERAL MANAGEMENT

Publisher — O G Nieman

ADVERTISING

Manager — Mauri Montgomery

CIRCULATION

Manager — Craig Nieman

NEWS EXECUTIVE

Managing Editor — Garry Wesner

EDITOR AND MANAGER

Amusements Editor — Becky Camp

Market Information: Split Run; TMC.

Mechanical available: Offset; Black and 3 ROP colors; insert accepted — preprinted; page cut-offs — 21".

Mechanical specifications: Type page 13" x 21"; E - 6 cols, 2⅟₁₆", ⅛" between; A - 6 cols, 2⅟₁₆", ⅛" between; C - 6 cols, 2⅟₁₆", ⅛" between.

Commodity consumption: Newsprint 300 short tons; width 28"; average pages per issue 12(d), 36(S).

Equipment: EDITORIAL: Front-end hardware — 1-Wyse/3225, 6-VGA/Monitor; Front-end software — WordPerfect; Printers — QMS/PS-810. CLASSIFIED: Front-end hardware — 1-Wyse/3225, VGA/Monitor; Front-end software — WordPerfect; Printers — QMS/PS-810. DISPLAY: Adv layout systems — Aldus/PageMaker, Archetype/Corel Draw; Front-end hardware — 1-Archetype/386 SX, 1-Wyse/3225, 2-VGA/Monitor; Front-end software — Microsoft/Windows; Printers — 1-QMS/PS-810. PRODUCTION: Typesetters — 1-QMS/PS-810; Plate exposures — 2-Nu/Flip Top FT40APRNS-631; Plate processors — 1-Nat/A-340; Scanners — CK Optical/SQU-7; Production cameras — 1-R, 1-Argyle/18-Process G18; Automatic film processors — 1-HOPE/GA2024V; Shrink lenses — 1-R/93%.
PRESSROOM: Line 1 — 4-HI/V-15. MAILROOM: Counter stackers — 1-BG/Count-O-Veyor; Bundle tyer — 2-Bu; Addressing machine — 1-Elliot Dynamic/3101. WIRE SERVICES: News — AP; Receiving dishes — size-3ft, AP. BUSINESS COMPUTERS: 1-Wyse/386; Applications: SBT: Payroll, Accts receivable, Gen ledger.

HOUSTON

Harris County

'90 U.S. Census- 1,630,553; E&P '96 Est. 1,895,807
ABC-CZ (90): 2,845,228 (HH 1,034,329)

Houston Chronicle

(m-mon to sat; S)

Houston Chronicle, 801 Texas St. (77002); PO Box 4260, Houston, TX 77210; tel (713) 220-7171; fax (713) 220-6677; web site http://www.chron.com. Hearst Newspapers group.

Circulation: 541,478(m); 541,478(m-sat); 743,689(S); ABC Sept. 30, 1995.

Price: 50¢(d); 50¢(sat); $1.50(S); $12.00/mo; $144.00/yr.

Advertising: Open inch rate $409.00(m); $409.00(m-sat); $477.28(S). **Representative:** Newspapers First.

News Services: AP, KRT, LAT-WP, NNS, UPI. **Politics:** Independent. **Established:** 1901.

Special Editions: Bridal Extravaganza, Auto Show, Super Bowl XXX, Boat Show (Jan); Livestock & Rodeo (Feb); Spring Gardening, Home Furnishings, Home Improvement/Home Show, Golf & Resort Show (Mar); Baseball '96, Houston Open, Kids Expo, Earth Day (Apr); 1996 Super Show, Better Sleep Month, Discover Diving-Seaspace, Chronicle Top 100, Hunting Show (May); Summer Bridal Extravaganza (July); Fall Gardening, Fine Arts Calendar, Fall Fashion, Football '96, Back-to-School, Astro World Series of Dog Show (Aug); House Beautiful, Texas Magazine ASID, Home Improvement (Home Show) (Sept); Rockets '96, Holiday Dining & Entertainment (Oct); Gift Guides, Holiday Fashion & Entertainment (Nov); Gift Guides, Letters to Santa (Dec).

Special Weekly Sections: Sports Section Weekend Highlight (mon); Food (wed); Fashion, Outdoors, Yo! Houston (thur); Weekend, Dining Out (fri); Religion, Mini Page, Food-Health-Beauty, This Weekend, Homeline (sat); Travel, Dining Out, Sports 2, Homeline, Real Estate & Rental Property (S).

Magazines: "Zest" (ROP) (fri); This Weekend (sat); "Texas Magazine" (local roto); TV Chronilog, Color Comics, Travel, Parade (S).

CORPORATE OFFICERS

Chairman/Publisher — Richard J V Johnson
President — G E McDavid
Vice Pres/General Manager — John Sweeney
Vice Pres-Operations — Jack Stanley
Exec Vice Pres/Editor — Jack Loftis
Vice Pres-Sales/Marketing — John Laird
Vice Pres-Sales — Gary Randazzo
Vice Pres-Administration/Human Resources — Robert E Carlquist
Vice Pres-Human Resources — Ann Turnbach
Vice Pres-Marketing and New Media — Joycelyn Marek
Treasurer — R W Youngblood

GENERAL MANAGEMENT

Controller — Richard Winegarden
Director-Administration Service — Bill Ralls
Director-Human Resources — Ann Turnbach
Director-Finance Accounting — Gary Randazzo
Director-Packaging and Distribution — Doyle H Evans
Manager-Purchasing — Tommy Miller

ADVERTISING

Vice Pres — Dwight Brown
Director — Jim Pollard
Director-Operations — Ron Sellars
Director-Display — Ralph Harrington
Director-Display — Jim Mitchell
Manager-Classified — Paula Biddy
Manager — Bob Conway
Manager — Shelley Lamb
Manager — Bill Offil
Manager — Joyce Waddel

MARKETING AND PROMOTION

Vice Pres-Marketing and New Media — Joycelyn Marek
Director-Advertising Service/New Business — Lynne Cook
Manager-Public Affairs — Laine Gordon
Manager-New Business Development — Donna Summer
Manager-Research — Nate Nelson

TELECOMMUNICATIONS

Director-Info/Technology Resources — Susan Shows
Audiotex Manager — Don Templett

CIRCULATION

Director — Hollis Price
Manager-Sales/Marketing — Noel Bolander

NEWS EXECUTIVES

Editor — Jack Loftis
Assoc Editor — Frank Michel
Deputy Managing Editor — Tommy Miller
Asst Managing Editor — Tony Pederson
Asst Managing Editor — Fernando Dovalina
Asst Managing Editor — Don Cunningham
Asst Managing Editor — Susan Bischoff
Asst Managing Editor — Walter Johns

EDITORS AND MANAGERS

Books Editor — Fritz Lanham
Business Editor — Scott Clark
Business Columnist — Jim Barlow
City Editor-Day — Mike Snyder
City Editor-Night — John C Henry
City Editor-Sunday — John Kling
Asst City Editor — Linda Gilchriest
Asst City Editor — Jim Newkirk
Asst City Editor — Lee Cearnal
Columnist — Leon Hale
Columnist — Thom Marshall
Columnist — Lori Rodriguez
Copy Desk Chief — David Eskridge
Editorial Writer — James Campbell
Editorial Writer — Andrea Greene
Editorial Writer — Frank Michel
Editorial Writer — James Gibbons
Editorial Writer — Larry Gage
Entertainment Editor — Melissa Aguilar
Fashion Editor — Linda Gillan Griffin
Features Editor — Jane P Marshall
Films Editor — Jeff Millar

Fine Arts Editor Lindsay Heinsen
Food Editor Ann Criswell
Garden Editor Kathy Huber
Graphics Director Court Smith
Home Furnishings Editor Madeleine McDermott Hamm
International Editor Chris Shively
Librarian Sherry Adams
Lifestyle Editor Renee Kientz
Medical Editor Ruth SoRelle
Music Critic Rick Mitchell
Metro Editor Steve Jetton
National Editor David R Gerraughty
News Editor Pat Terry
News Editor Paul McGrath
News Editor John Rice
News Editor Bruce Spinks
News Editor Jimmy James
News Service Editor Darlene Stinson
Chief Photographer George Honeycutt
Picture Editor Catherine McIntosh
Picture Editor Fred Bunch
Political Editor Wendy Benjaminson
Projects Editor Don Mason
Radio/Video Editor Bruce Westbrook
Religion Editor Cecile Holmes White
Science Editor Carlos Byars
Society Editor Shelby Hodge
Sports Editor Dan Cunningham
State Editor Kit Frieden
Suburban Editor Mary Moody
Television Editor Mike McDaniel
Texas Magazine Editor Ken Hammond
TV Book Editor Lana Berkowitz
Travel Editor Harry Shattuck
Weekend Editor Rich Quackenbush

MANAGEMENT INFORMATION SERVICES

Data Processing Manager Clayton Wiseman
Online Manager Amy Rabinoultz

PRODUCTION

Director-Operations/Technical Service Dale Nissen
Director-Info/Technology Resources Susan Shows
Asst Director Jerald Underwood
Manager-Technical Service Russell Cureton
Manager-Pressroom Dan West
Manager-Night Calvin Hilton
Asst Manager (Night) Barbara Paterson
Manager/Coordinator (Night) Pete Bryson
Manager-Mailroom Jim Davis
Manager-Paperhandling/Newsprint Charles Miller
Manager-Ads John Mercer
Manager-Page Assembly/Platemaking John Rankin
Engineer-Safety Bob Knight

Market Information: Zoned editions; Split Run; TMC; ADS; Operate database; Operate audiotex.
Mechanical available: Letterpress, offset, heat-set offset; Black and 3 ROP colors; insert accepted — preprinted; page cut-offs — 22 3/4".
Mechanical specifications: Type page 13 1/16" x 21 1/4"; E - 6 cols, 13 1/16", 1/6" between; A - 6 cols, 13 1/16", 1/6" between; C - 10 cols, 13 1/4", 1/24" between.
Commodity consumption: Newsprint 155,000 short tons; widths 53 3/4", 40.3125", 26.875"; black ink 4,300,000 pounds; color ink 988,000 pounds; single pages printed 69,436; average pages per issue 100(d), 226(S); single plates used 684,809.
Equipment: EDITORIAL: Front-end hardware — SII, Sun/Microsystem; Front-end software — SII, DP/Whirlwind; Printers — Qume/Laser Jet, Qume/Line; Other equipment — AU/APS-5, Lf/AP Leaf Picture Desk, Ap/Mac, Sun/Phoenix T-1. CLASSIFIED: Front-end hardware — SII; Front-end software — SII; Printers — Qume/Laser Jet, Qume/Line; Other equipment — DP/CD Merge System. AUDIOTEX: Supplier name — Celebration Computer Systems. DISPLAY: Adv layout systems — Cx, Magichron System; Front-end hardware — Sun; Front-end software — Sun/Breeze; Other equipment — AdSat, AP. PRODUCTION: Typesetters — AU/APS, Bidco; Plate exposures — 4-Titan/Exposure; Plate processors — 2-Na/NP120, 2-Satellite; Scanners — 1-APUMX, 4-ECR; Production cameras — C/Newspager, C/Spartan; Automatic film processors — 3-LE; Film transporters — 3-LE; Shrink lenses — Alan/Anamorphic; Color separation equipment (conventional) — AG/Colorscope; Digital color separation equipment — 2-SCREEN/737, Kk, Nikon.
PRESSROOM: Line 1 — 18-G/Mark IV; Line 2 — 18-G/Mark IV; Line 3 — 9-G/Mark V; Line 4 — 10-G/Mark V; Line 5 — 9-G/Metroliner; Press drives — Hurltron, Fin; Folders — G/3:2; Pasters — G; Press registration system — Web/Tech. MAILROOM: Counter stackers — 13-St/251, 2-St/257, 8-HL/Monitor, 12-QWI/301B; Inserters and stuffers — 4-HI/1372P, 3-HI/Model 6130; Bundle tyer — 36-MLN/MNL2-A, 3-Boss; Addressing machine — 2-KAN/Labeler. LIBRARY: Electronic — Data Times, Battelle/Basis software. COMMUNICATIONS: Systems used — fiber optic. WIRE SERVICES: News — Sun, Equities; Stock tables — AP Digital Stocks, AP SelectStox I; Syndicates — North America Syndicate; Receiving dishes — size-10ft, AP, RN, INS. BUSINESS COMPUTERS: PCs & micros networked; PCs & main system networked.

HUNTSVILLE

Walker County

'90 U.S. Census- 27,925; E&P '96 Est. 30,156
ABC-CZ (90): 27,925 (HH 7,853)

The Huntsville Item

(e-tues to fri; m-sat; S)

The Huntsville Item, 1409 Tenth St.; PO Box 539, Huntsville, TX 77340; tel (409) 295-5407; fax (409) 293-3909. Hollinger International Inc. group.
Circulation: 6,321(e); 6,321(m-sat); 7,129(S); ABC Mar 1995.
Price: 50¢(d); 50¢(sat); $1.00(S); $9.00/mo (home delivery), $10.00/mo (mail); $108.00/yr.
Advertising: Open inch rate $15.36(e); $15.36(m-sat); $15.36(S). **Representative:** Papert Companies.
News Services: AP, NEA. **Politics:** Independent. **Established:** 1850.
Special Editions: Progress (Jan); Brides (Feb); Home Improvement, Graduation (May); Newcomers (June); Back-to-School (Aug); Car Care, Women's (Oct); Christmas Gift Guides (Nov); Christmas Gift Guides (Dec); Health, Tourism (monthly).
Magazines: TeleView (local newsprint) (S); Texas Dept. Corrections Coupon Booklet (monthly).

GENERAL MANAGEMENT

Publisher Arlena McLaughlin
Accountant Paula P Johnson

ADVERTISING

Manager Karen Altom

CIRCULATION

Manager Kent Carpenter

NEWS EXECUTIVE

Editor Lisa Trow

EDITOR AND MANAGER

News Editor Kooter Roberson

PRODUCTION

Manager Kelly Lawson

Market Information: TMC.
Mechanical available: Offset; Black and 3 ROP colors; insert accepted — preprinted, all; page cut-offs — 22 3/4".
Mechanical specifications: Type page 13" x 21 1/2"; E - 6 cols, 2 1/16", 1/8" between; A - 6 cols, 2 1/16", 1/8" between; C - 9 cols, 1 3/8", 1/16" between.
Commodity consumption: Newsprint 654 short tons; widths 27 1/2", 13 3/4"; black ink 26,000 pounds; color ink 2,400 pounds; single pages printed 12,000; average pages per issue 16(d), 28(S); single plates used 22,256.
Equipment: EDITORIAL: Front-end hardware — Mk, Ap/Mac; Front-end software — Baseview/NewsEdit, QuarkXPress 3.3; CLASSIFIED: Front-end hardware — Mk. PRODUCTION: Typesetters — V, Panther/Pro 46; Platemaking systems — 1-P; Plate exposures — 1-Nu/FT40; Plate processors — 1-Nat/A340; Electronic picture desk — AP Graphics; Scanners — Unimax; Production cameras — 1-SCREEN/C-260; Automatic film processors — 1-LE/LD-24 AQ; Color separation equipment (conventional) — 1-Digi-Colour/4000; Digital color separation equipment — Polaroid, Silver Scan.
PRESSROOM: Line 1 — 4-WPC/Leader; Line 2 — 4-WPC/Leader; Reels and stands — 8-WPC/Leader; Press control system — Avtek. MAILROOM: Counter stackers — 1-BG/Count-O-Veyor 105; Bundle tyer — 1-MLN/MLI-EE-ML-MS. WIRE SERVICES: News — AP; Receiving dishes — AP. BUSINESS COMPUTERS: 3-IBM/AT; Applications: Gen ledger, Payroll, Circ billing; PCs & micros networked; PCs & main system networked.

JACKSONVILLE

Cherokee County

'90 U.S. Census- 12,765; E&P '96 Est. 13,026

Jacksonville Daily Progress

(e-mon to fri; S)

Jacksonville Daily Progress, 525 E. Commerce; PO Box 711, Jacksonville, TX 75766-0711; tel (903) 586-2236; fax (903) 586-0987. Donrey Media group.
Circulation: 4,953(e); 4,953(S); Sworn Sept. 29, 1995.
Price: 50¢(d); 75¢(S); $6.00/mo; $72.00/yr.
Advertising: Open inch rate $8.40(e); $8.40(S). **Representative:** Papert Companies.
News Service: AP. **Politics:** Independent. **Established:** 1910.
Not Published: New Year; Christmas.
Special Editions: Chamber of Commerce (Jan); Industrial Progress (Apr); Graduation, Nursing Home, Soil Conservation (May); Tops in Texas Rodeo (July); Football Preview (Sept); Fire Prevention (Oct); Christmas Gift Guide (Nov); Christmas Gift Guide (Dec).
Special Weekly Sections: Best Food Day (tues); Business (wed); Church, Schools (fri); Lifestyle (S).
Magazines: Television (fri); Active Times (quarterly).

CORPORATE OFFICERS

Founder Donald W Reynolds
President/Chief Operating Officer Emmett Jones
Exec Vice Pres/Chief Financial Officer Darrell W Loftin
Vice Pres-Western Newspaper Group David A Osborn
Vice Pres-Eastern Newspaper Group Don Schneider

GENERAL MANAGEMENT

Publisher Robb Grindstaff
Manager-Office Kathy Johnson

ADVERTISING

Manager James Hutchison

CIRCULATION

Manager Charles Roof

NEWS EXECUTIVE

Editor Maris Fletcher

EDITORS AND MANAGERS

Lifestyle Editor Pat Jackson
Sports Editor Don Wallace

PRODUCTION

Manager Chris Johnson

Mechanical available: Offset; Black and 3 ROP colors; insert accepted — preprinted; page cut-offs — 23".
Mechanical specifications: Type page 13" x 21 1/2"; E - 6 cols, 2 1/8", 1/8" between; A - 6 cols, 2 1/8", 1/8" between; C - 8 cols, 1 1/2", 1/8" between.
Commodity consumption: Newsprint 160 metric tons; widths 27", 13 1/2"; black ink 4,000 pounds; color ink 300 pounds; single pages printed 4,200; average pages per issue 12(d), 24(S); single plates used 2100.
Equipment: EDITORIAL: Front-end hardware — 7-Mk/MC4003; Printers — 1-Ap/Mac LaserWriter. CLASSIFIED: Front-end hardware — Ap/Mac Classic II; Front-end software — Snews; Printers — Ap/Mac LaserWriter, Ap/Mac ImageWriter. PRODUCTION: Typesetters — 2-Ap/Mac LaserWriter II; Plate exposures — 1-Nu/Flip Top FT400P; Plate processors — 1-Nat/A-250; Scanners — Ap/Mac Scanner; Production cameras — 1-Acti/CL240; Automatic film processors — 1-P/26-RA; Reproportion units — AG/CP-530 PMT processor.
PRESSROOM: Line 1 — 6-HI/V 15A. MAILROOM: Bundle tyer — 1-MLN. WIRE SERVICES: News — AP; Receiving dishes — AP. BUSINESS COMPUTERS: Unisys; Applications: Brainworks: Adv; PCs & micros networked; PCs & main system networked.

KERRVILLE

Kerr County

'90 U.S. Census- 17,384; E&P '96 Est. 18,545
ABC-CZ (90): 27,603 (HH 11,066)

Kerrville Daily Times

(e-mon to fri; S)

Kerrville Daily Times, 429 Jefferson; PO Box 1428, Kerrville, TX 78028; tel (210) 896-7000; fax (210) 896-1150. Southern Newspapers Inc. group.
Circulation: 9,434(e); 10,874(S); ABC Sept. 30, 1995.
Price: 50¢(d); $1.00(S); $6.95/mo (carrier), $8.65/mo (mail).
Advertising: Open inch rate $8.68(e); $8.68(S). **Representative:** Papert Companies.
News Service: AP. **Politics:** Independent. **Established:** 1908.
Not Published: New Year; Independence Day; Labor Day; Christmas (except when holiday falls on Sunday, then an official Monday holiday may be observed).
Special Editions: Brides (Mar); Progress, Home Improvement, Car Care (Apr); Graduation (May); Football (Aug); Hunting & Wild Game Guide (Nov); Christmas (Dec).
Special Weekly Sections: Food, Business (wed); Entertainment, Religion (fri); Business (S).
Magazines: Seniority (monthly); Texas Traveler (every other month); Healthfile (quarterly).

GENERAL MANAGEMENT

Editor/Publisher Greg Shrader
Controller Jan A Beltrone

ADVERTISING

Director Linda Robinson

CIRCULATION

Manager Hector Cueva

NEWS EXECUTIVE

Managing Editor Larry Hunter

EDITORS AND MANAGERS

Magazine Editor Bill Retit
Sports Editor Mike Previte

MANAGEMENT INFORMATION SERVICES

Data Processing Manager Larry Hunter

PRODUCTION

Superintendent Jimmie Rios

Market Information: TMC.
Mechanical available: Offset; Black and 3 ROP colors; insert accepted — preprinted, 8"x10" minimum size on pre-print inserts; page cut-offs — 22 3/4".
Mechanical specifications: Type page 13" x 21 1/2"; E - 6 cols, 2 1/16", 1/8" between; A - 6 cols, 2 1/16", 1/8" between; C - 9 cols, 1 1/4", 1/8" between.
Commodity consumption: Newsprint 515 short tons; widths 27 1/2", 13 7/8"; black ink 15,000 pounds; color ink 300 pounds; single pages printed 66,000,000; average pages per issue 14(d), 32(S); single plates used 66,000,000.
Equipment: EDITORIAL: Front-end hardware — Ap/Mac 7100; Printers — NewGen, HP/4M; Other equipment — 2-Ap/Power Mac PC, Nikon/Coolscan. CLASSIFIED: Front-end hardware — Ap/Mac 7100. DISPLAY: Adv layout systems — Baseview. PRODUCTION: Typesetters — 2-Ap/Mac LaserWriter; Platemaking systems — Nat/A-250; Plate exposures — 1-B/Ultra-Lite 2500; Plate processors — Nat/A-250; Production cameras — 1-SCREEN/Companica 680C; Automatic film processors — 1-SCREEN/LD-22-OT; Color separation equipment (conventional) — Digi-Colour/System DC4000.
PRESSROOM: Line 1 — 6-G/Community; Line 3 — Multi-Lith; Folders — 1-G/SC. MAILROOM: Bundle tyer — 1-Us/Q, 1-Us/TE, 1-Md. COMMUNICATIONS: Facsimile — RSK/Tandy. WIRE SERVICES: News — AP; Receiving dishes — size-3ft, AP. BUSINESS COMPUTERS: Applications: Payroll, Accts receivable, Gen ledger, Gen circ; PCs & micros networked; PCs & main system networked.

KILGORE

Gregg and Rusk Counties

'90 U.S. Census- 11,066; E&P '96 Est. 11,116

Kilgore News Herald

(e-mon to fri; S)

Kilgore News Herald, 610 E. Main St.; PO Box 1210, Kilgore, TX 75662; tel (903) 984-2593; fax (903) 984-7462. Donrey Media group.
Circulation: 4,294(e); 4,294(S); Sworn Sept. 29, 1995.
Price: 50¢(d); 75¢(S); $5.50/mo; $66.00/yr.
Advertising: Open inch rate $6.95(e); $6.95(S). **Representative:** Papert Companies.
News Service: AP. **Politics:** Independent. **Established:** 1931.
Not Published: New Year; Memorial Day; Independence Day; Labor Day; Thanksgiving; Christmas.

Special Editions: Chamber of Commerce (Feb); Spring Savings Spree (Apr); Brides, Graduation (May); Oil & Progress (June); Football Guide, Back-to-School (Aug); Christmas Gift Guide (Nov); Christmas Greetings (Dec).
Special Weekly Sections: Best Food Day (tues); Oil Page, Business (S).
Magazines: Parade, TV Week (S).

CORPORATE OFFICERS
Founder Donald W Reynolds
President/Chief Operating Officer Emmett Jones
Exec Vice Pres/Chief Financial Officer Darrel W Loftin
Vice Pres-Western Newspaper Group David A Osborn
Vice Pres-Eastern Newspaper Group Don Schneider

GENERAL MANAGEMENT
Publisher Frank Rowe

ADVERTISING
Director Don V Alexander

CIRCULATION
Manager Ron Hall

NEWS EXECUTIVE
Managing Editor Greg A Collins

EDITORS AND MANAGERS
Editorial Page Editor Frank Rowe
Education Editor Annelle Dugan
Sports Editor John Ringgold
Travel Editor Greg A Collins
Women's Editor Greg A Collins

PRODUCTION
Foreman-Composing Kay Owens
Foreman-Camera/Press Royce Baxley

Market Information: TMC.
Mechanical available: Offset; Black and 3 ROP colors; insert accepted — preprinted; page cutoffs — 22¾".
Mechanical specifications: Type page 13" x 21½"; E - 6 cols, $2\frac{1}{16}$", ⅛" between; A - 6 cols, $2\frac{1}{16}$", ⅛" between; C - 8 cols, 1½", ⅛" between.
Commodity consumption: Newsprint 140 metric tons; width 27"; single pages printed 4,880; average pages per issue 12(d), 36(S); single plates used 2,600.
Equipment: EDITORIAL: Front-end hardware — Ap/Mac SE. CLASSIFIED: Front-end hardware — Ap/Mac SE. DISPLAY: Adv layout systems — Ap/Mac IIcx. PRODUCTION: Typesetters — 2-Ap/Mac LaserWriter II NTX; Plate exposures — 1-B/UL 1500; Production cameras — Kk/Model 5060 vertical camera.
PRESSROOM: Line 1 — 5-G/Community; Folders — 1-G. WIRE SERVICES: News — AP. BUSINESS COMPUTERS: PCs & micros networked.

KILLEEN
Bell County
'90 U.S. Census- 63,535; E&P '96 Est. 74,262
ABC-CZ (90): 111,956 (HH 33,400)

Killeen Daily Herald
(m-mon to sat; S)

Killeen Daily Herald, PO Box 1300, Killeen, TX 76540; tel (817) 634-2125; fax (817) 634-3293. Frank Mayborn Enterprises Inc. group.
Circulation: 18,524(m); 18,524(m-sat); 22,625(S); ABC Sept. 30, 1995.
Price: 50¢(d); 50¢(sat); $1.00(S); $9.00/mo (home delivery); $99.00/yr (home delivery).
Advertising: Open inch rate $12.90(m); $12.90(m-sat); $12.90(S). **Representative:** Papert Companies.
News Service: AP. **Politics:** Independent-Democrat. **Established:** 1890.
Special Editions: Super Bowl XXX, Honor Roll (Jan); Bridal Tab, Central Texas Progress Edition (Feb); Design-An-Ad, Spring Home & Garden (Mar); Customers Count!, Senior Showcase (Apr); Festival of Flags Edition, Graduation (May); Better Business Bureau, The Lazy Guide (June); Central Texas' 100 Best, Locally-owned Business (July); Back-to-School, Football Edition (Aug); Medical Directory, Chamber of Commerce (Sept); AUSA Report, Newcomer's Guide (Oct); Auto Spectacular, Shopping with Santa (Nov); Last Minute Gift Ideas, Christmas Song Book (Dec).
Magazines: "Round Up" TV Tab (S); "Plus" Tab (monthly).

CORPORATE OFFICERS
President/Editor/Publisher Anyse Sue Mayborn
Secretary Jerry L Arnold

GENERAL MANAGEMENT
General Manager Richard Sloan
Accountant Rodney Sparks
Personnel Manager Michele Crabill

ADVERTISING
Director Thad Byars

TELECOMMUNICATIONS
Coordinator-Telecommunications Jeff Malmgren

CIRCULATION
Supervisor Vanessa VanWinkle

NEWS EXECUTIVES
Exec Editor G D Skidmore
News Director Phil Smith

EDITORS AND MANAGERS
Sports Editor Bill Rutkin
Sports Editor Robert Hester

PRODUCTION
Foreman-Composing Lloyd Boales
Foreman-Press/Stereo Robert Bargas

Market Information: Split Run; TMC.
Mechanical available: Offset; Black and 3 ROP colors; insert accepted — preprinted, all (subject to publisher's approval); page cut-offs — 22¾".
Mechanical specifications: Type page 13" x 21½"; E - 6 cols, $2\frac{1}{16}$", ⅛" between; A - 6 cols, $2\frac{1}{16}$", ⅛" between; C - 9 cols, 1⅜", $\frac{1}{16}$" between.
Commodity consumption: Newsprint 1,422 short tons; widths 27½", 13¾"; black ink 30,760 pounds; color ink 8,602 pounds; single pages printed 10,101; average pages per issue 22(d), 25(sat), 60(S); single plates used 35,200.
Equipment: EDITORIAL: Front-end hardware — IBM; Front-end software — Dewar; Other equipment — Lf/AP Leaf Picture Desk, Lf/Leafscan 35, Linotype-Hell/L-190, 2-AU/APS-840-AV. CLASSIFIED: Front-end hardware — IBM; Front-end software — Dewar. DISPLAY: Adv layout systems — Dewar; Front-end hardware — AP; Front-end software — Multi-Ad/Creator; Printers — 1-Ap/Mac LaserPrinter, 2-SelectPress/600, 1-LaserMaster/1200XL. PRODUCTION: Pagination software — QuarkXPress; OCR software — Caere/OmniPage Pro; Typesetters — 1-M/L-190; Plate exposures — 1-Nu/Flip Top FT40LNS; Plate processors — 1-Nat/A-250; Scanners — 1-Lf; Production cameras — 1-C/Spartan III; Automatic film processors — 1-LE/LD18, 1-LE/2100D; Shrink lenses — 1-Alan/Imaging; Color separation equipment (conventional) — Digi-Colour; Digital color separation equipment — Lf/AP Leaf Picture Desk, 2-Ap/Mac, 2-UMAX.
PRESSROOM: Line 1 — 7-G/Urbanite, 3-G/Urbanite. MAILROOM: Counter stackers — 1-HL; Inserters and stuffers — 1-S; Bundle tyer — 1-MLN, 1-EC; Addressing machine — 2-St. WIRE SERVICES: News — AP; Photos — AP; Syndicates — United Features, SHNS; Receiving dishes — size-3m, AP. BUSINESS COMPUTERS: NCR; Applications: SMS.

LAKE JACKSON
See CLUTE

LAREDO
Webb County
'90 U.S. Census- 122,899; E&P '96 Est. 136,892
ABC-CZ (90): 122,899 (HH 32,029)

Laredo Morning Times
(m-mon to sat; S)

Laredo Morning Times, 111 Esperanza Dr. (78041); PO Box 2129, Laredo, TX 78044; tel (210) 728-2500; fax (210) 723-1227. Hearst Newspapers group.
Circulation: 22,355(m); 22,355(m-sat); 24,692(S); ABC Sept. 30, 1995.
Price: 50¢(d); 50¢(sat); $1.25(S); $6.00/mo; $72.00/yr (home delivery).
Advertising: Open inch rate $17.91(m); $17.91(m-sat); $18.46(S). **Representative:** Papert Companies.
News Services: AP, LAT-WP, NYT, KRT, HN, CNS. **Politics:** Independent. **Established:** 1881.
Special Editions: Washington's Birthday (Feb); Fall Fashion (Aug); Border Olympics (Summer); Border Olympics (Spring); Follow the Sun; Viva Laredo; Christmas.
Special Weekly Sections: Food Day (wed); Business (S).

CORPORATE OFFICER
Vice Pres William B Green

GENERAL MANAGEMENT
Publisher William B Green
Manager-Office Norma Garcia
Controller Mark Lymm
Asst General Manager Odie Arambulo

ADVERTISING
Director-National Frank Escobedo
Manager-Retail Joe Martinez

CIRCULATION
Director Ernie Elizondo

NEWS EXECUTIVE
Editor Odie Arambulo

EDITORS AND MANAGERS
City Editor Talib Amir
Lifestyle Editor Ramiro Montoya
News Editor Estella Rodriguez
Photo Department Manager Craute Santos
Sports Editor Salo Otero
Sunday Editor Odie Arambulo
Teen-Age/Youth Editor Ramiro Montoya

PRODUCTION
Director Frank Escobedo
Manager-Systems Marco Gonzales
Foreman-Pressroom Julian Rodriguez

Market Information: Zoned editions; Split Run; TMC.
Mechanical available: Offset; Black and 3 ROP colors; insert accepted — preprinted, pocket book size (5"x 7").
Mechanical specifications: Type page 13⅞" x 21"; E - 6 cols, $2\frac{1}{16}$", ⅛" between; A - 6 cols, $2\frac{1}{16}$", ⅛" between; C - 6 cols, $2\frac{1}{16}$", ⅛" between.
Equipment: EDITORIAL: Front-end hardware — AT, 14-IBM/71. CLASSIFIED: Front-end hardware — M, 3-CRT/terminal; Printers — 1-NCR/Lineprinter; Other equipment — 4-IBM/71, 1-NCR/memory unit, Dewar. PRODUCTION: Typesetters — 1-Am/450, 2-Am/430, 1-Comp/Set 4510; Platemaking systems — 1-Nu/Flip Top FT40LNS; Plate exposures — 1-Nu/Flip Top FT40LNS; Plate processors — 1-Nat/A-250; Scanners — ECR/Autokon 5200; Production cameras — 1-C/Spartan II, 1-VG/320; Automatic film processors — 1-LE/LD-18.
PRESSROOM: Line 1 — 10-KP; Line 2 — 1-Multi-Lith/1250; Folders — 1-KP, 1-Multi-Lith. MAILROOM: Inserters and stuffers — 1-KAN/501, 1-DG/DG320; Bundle tyer — 2-Bu/PAT 27,744; Addressing machine — 1-Am/Class 640, 1-Am/4000. WIRE SERVICES: News — AP; Stock tables — AP; Syndicates — King Features, UPI, NAS, Universal Press, Register & Tribune; Receiving dishes — AP. BUSINESS COMPUTERS: 1-NCR/8200; Applications: Circ, Adv billing, Accts receivable, Payroll, Accts payable.

LONGVIEW
Gregg County
'90 U.S. Census- 70,311; E&P '96 Est. 74,426
ABC-CZ (90): 78,445 (HH 30,052)

Longview News-Journal
(m-mon to sat; S)

Longview News-Journal, 320 E. Methvin (75601); PO Box 1792, Longview, TX 75606; tel (903) 757-3311; fax (903) 236-3874. Cox Newspapers Inc. group.
Circulation: 28,807(m); 28,807(m-sat); 40,444(S); ABC Sept. 30, 1995.
Price: 50¢(d); 50¢(sat); $1.00(S); $8.75/mo (home delivery), $12.50/mo (mail); $105.00/yr (home delivery, dS), $150.00/yr (mail, dS).
Advertising: Open inch rate $20.20(m); $20.20(m-sat); $23.84(S). **Representative:** Papert Companies.
News Services: AP, Cox News Service, NYT, LAT-WP. **Politics:** Independent. **Established:** 1923.
Special Editions: Food; Real Estate; Industrial Edition.
Special Weekly Sections: Best Food Day (wed); Today's Family (thur); Entertainment (fri); Sports (sat); Business, Sports, Coupon Clipper, Leisure, Lifestyle (S).
Magazines: USA Weekend; TV Week (local).

GENERAL MANAGEMENT
Publisher Bill Martin

ADVERTISING
Director Tim Hobbs
Manager-Retail Marti Barnes
Supervisor-Classified Lainey Godsey

MARKETING AND PROMOTION
Manager-Marketing/Promotion Sheri O'Neal

CIRCULATION
Director Rick Deaver

NEWS EXECUTIVES
Editor Pete Litterski
Managing Editor Ana Pecina Walker

EDITORS AND MANAGERS
Action Line Editor Mike Hvezdos
Business Editor Rich Lundgren
Editorial Page Editor Mike Hvezdos
Editorial Writer Mike Hvezdos
Education Editor Ana Pecina Walker
Fashion/Style Editor Belinda McCoy
Films/Theater Editor Belinda McCoy
Food/Garden Editor Belinda McCoy
Graphics Editor Stephanie Richard
Home Furnishings/Music Editor Belinda McCoy
Night/News Editor Michael Ramey
Photo Department Manager Darlene Chapman
Sports Editor Temple Pomcey
Travel Editor Martha Griffin
Women's/Clubs Editor Belinda McCoy

PRODUCTION
Director James C (Kit) Yearty
Asst Director Pete Barnes
Foreman-Composing Debbie Williams
Foreman-Pressroom Larry Pope

Market Information: Zoned editions; TMC.
Mechanical available: Offset; Black and 3 ROP colors; insert accepted — preprinted, single cards; page cut-offs — 22¾".
Mechanical specifications: Type page 13" x 21½"; E - 6 cols, $2\frac{1}{16}$", ⅛" between; A - 6 cols, $2\frac{1}{16}$", ⅛" between; C - 9 cols, 1⅜", $\frac{1}{16}$" between.
Commodity consumption: Newsprint 2,765 short tons; widths 27", 13.5"; black ink 56,118 pounds; color ink 10,404 pounds; single pages printed 17,250; average pages per issue 32(d), 72(S); single plates used 30,280.
Equipment: EDITORIAL: Front-end hardware — SII/25, Ap/Mac; Front-end software — DTI 4.1; CLASSIFIED: Front-end hardware — 1-TS, SII. DISPLAY: Adv layout systems — DTI/AdSpeed. PRODUCTION: Pagination software — DTI 4.1; Typesetters — 2-AU/APS-Micro 5, 3-Hyphen/Ultra, AU/APS 8400; Plate exposures — 1-Nu/Flip Top Vitra Plus FT40, 1-Nu/Flip Top FT40; Plate processors — 2-Nat/A-250, WL; Scanners — 1-Nikon/Slide Scanner, 1-Howtek/Print Scanner, 1-Pixelcraft 11x17 Scanner; Production cameras — 2-C/Spartan III, 1-R/MK 432V; Automatic film processors — 1-LE/LD2600A, 1-LE/PC18, 1-LD/24AQ; Color separation equipment (conventional) — Adobe/Photostop; Digital color separation equipment — DTI.
PRESSROOM: Line 1 — 11-G/Urbanite; Folders — 2-G/2:1. MAILROOM: Counter stackers — 1-HL/PacePack; Inserters and stuffers — 3-MM/227; Bundle tyer — 3-MLN/ML2EE; Addressing machine — 1-Wm, 1-KR. COMMUNICATIONS: Digital ad delivery system — AP AdSend. WIRE SERVICES: News — AP, NYT, TV Data, LAT-WP, Cox News Service; Photos — AP; Stock tables — AP; Receiving dishes — AP. BUSINESS COMPUTERS: HP/9000; Applications: Adv, Accts receivable, Ad order, Circ, Sub/non-subscriber; PCs & main system networked.

LUBBOCK
Lubbock County
'90 U.S. Census- 186,206; E&P '96 Est. 192,686
ABC-CZ (90): 187,469 (HH 69,410)

Lubbock Avalanche-Journal
(m-mon to sat; S)

Lubbock Avalanche-Journal, 710 Ave. J (79401); PO Box 491, Lubbock, TX 79408; tel (806) 762-8844; fax (806) 765-8770. Morris Communications Corp. group.
Circulation: 64,943(m); 64,943(m-sat); 77,460(S); ABC Sept. 30, 1995.
Price: 50¢(d); 50¢(sat); $1.25(S); $10.95/mo; $131.40/yr.
Advertising: Open inch rate $42.65(m); $42.65(m-sat); $45.40(S). **Representative:** Papert Companies.
News Services: AP, KRT, LAT-WP. **Politics:** Independent. **Established:** 1922 (Avalanche), 1925 (Journal).
Special Weekly Sections: Business & Industry (mon); Food Section (wed); Zoned Edition (thur); Special Entertainment Tab (fri); Special Entertainment Pages, Business and Finance, Oil Pages, Travel (S); Home (bi-monthly).
Magazines: TV Magazine (S); Parade.

CORPORATE OFFICERS

Chairman of the Board W S Morris III
President Paul S Simon
Secretary/Treasurer William A Herman III

GENERAL MANAGEMENT

Publisher David C Sharp
Controller-Division Twila Aufill
Manager-Accounting Beverly Wilke
Manager-Personnel Glenda Mills
Manager-Credit Denise Green

ADVERTISING

Director Randy Hambrick
Manager-Classified Telemarketing Barbara Gee
Manager-Display Charles (Chuck) H Evers

MARKETING AND PROMOTION

Manager-Marketing Carol McWhorter

TELECOMMUNICATIONS

Audiotex Manager Renell McDaniel

CIRCULATION

Director Jack Whitaker
Asst Director Gordon Essary
Manager-State Larry Roberts
Manager-City Eliseo Torres

NEWS EXECUTIVES

Editor Burle Pettit
Exec Editor Randy Sanders
Asst Managing Editor-News Mel Tittle
Asst Managing Editor-Sports/Features Norval Pollard

EDITORS AND MANAGERS

Amusements/Books Editor Bill Kerns
Business/Finance Editor Chris Van Wagenen
City Editor Hank Murphy
Editorial Page Editor Joe Hughes
Editorial Writer/Columnist Bob Horton
Editorial Writer/Columnist Joe Gulick
Farm Editor Duane Howell
Features Editor Mel Tittle
Librarian Bobbie Morrelle
Music Bill Kerns
News Editor John Childress
Oil/Real Estate Editor Chris Van Wagenen
Photo Department Manager Joe Don Buckner
Radio/Television Editor Randy Sanders
Religion Editor Beth Pratt
Sports Editor Doug Hensley

PRODUCTION

Manager-Operations Dominic Caranfa
Manager-Dispatch Vickie Peterson
Superintendent-Pressroom Rodney Shaw
Superintendent-Composing Quincy Lamb
Superintendent-Mailroom Leon Lindley

Market Information: Zoned editions; TMC; Operate audiotex.
Mechanical available: Offset; Black and 3 ROP colors; insert accepted — preprinted; page cutoffs — 22⅞".
Mechanical specifications: Type page 13" x 21½"; E - 5 cols, 2.44", ⅙" between; A - 6 cols, 2.06", ⅙" between; C - 9 cols, 1⅓", ⅛" between.
Commodity consumption: Newsprint 7,300 short tons; widths 54", 40½", 27"; black ink 301,780 pounds; color ink 54,000 pounds; single pages printed 18,348; average pages per issue 44(d), 88(S).
Equipment: EDITORIAL: Front-end hardware — IBM/PC-AC, 55-AT/PC, Gateway/2000 P5-60, 1-Ap/Mac SE, 1-Ap/Power Mac 8100-80, 1-Ap/Mac IIfx; Front-end software — MPS, Adobe/Photoshop 3.0, Aldus/FreeHand 3.1, QuarkXPress 3.3, Macdraw 1.2, Microphone LT, Adobe/Illustrator 5.5; Printers — Toshiba/P351, Ap/Mac LaserWriter II; Other equipment — Ap/Mac IIfx, Proteon/LAN. CLASSIFIED: Front-end hardware — IBM/PC-AT; Front-end software — MPS; Printers — Toshiba/P351; Other equipment — Proteon/LAN. AUDIOTEX: Hardware — Packard Bell/Monitor, BDR/9000 Voice Gate, 2-Zephyrus, IBM, ATT, Packard Bell/2400 Plus, Wyse/WY2114. DISPLAY: Front-end hardware — Ap/Mac IIfx; Front-end software — Ap/Mac, Adobe/Photoshop, Multi-Ad/Creator 3.0.1; Printers — Ap/Mac LaserWriter II; Other equipment — CD-Rom. PRODUCTION: Typesetters — Accuset/1100, AG; Platemaking systems — KFM; Plate exposures — KFM/Twin Line; Plate processors — KFM/Subtractive; Production cameras — 2-C/Spartan III; Automatic film processors — Kk/710, Kk/662, Kk/42, Kk/65; Reproportion units — C/b&w Exposure Unit; Film transporters — C; Shrink lenses — 2-CK Optical; Digital color separation equipment — RZ/210L.
PRESSROOM: Line 1 — 12-G/Metro; Folders — 2-G; Pasters — G/Automatic; Reels and stands — G; Press control system — Fin. MAILROOM: Counter stackers — 6-HL, 2-Id; Inserters and stuffers — 2-GMA/1000 14-into-2; Bundle tyer — 4-MLN, 2-Power Strap; Wrapping singles — 2-SHT; Addressing machine — 1-Ch. WIRE SERVICES: News — AP, KRT, LATWP, AP Datastream; Stock tables — AP Dataspeed; Syndicates — NYT, SHNS, LATS, NAS, King Features, Crown, Creators; Receiving dishes — size-3m, AP. BUSINESS COMPUTERS: 56-IBM/PC-AT, 1-Ap/Mac SE, 1-Ap/Mac IIfx; Applications: MPS; PCs & micros networked; PCs & main system networked.

LUFKIN

Angelina County

'90 U.S. Census- 30,206; E&P '96 Est. 31,071
ABC-CZ (90): 30,206 (HH 11,222)

The Lufkin Daily News

(e-mon to fri; m-sat; S)

The Lufkin Daily News, 300 Ellis (75904); PO Box 1089, Lufkin, TX 75902-1089; tel (409) 632-6631; fax (409) 632-6655. Cox Newspapers Inc. group.
Circulation: 14,403(e); 14,140(m-sat); 16,659(S); ABC Sept. 30, 1995.
Price: 50¢(d); 50¢(sat); $1.25(S); $7.65/mo; $91.80/yr (carrier).
Advertising: Open inch rate $15.52(e); $15.52(m-sat); $15.95(S).
News Service: AP. **Politics:** Independent. **Established:** 1905.
Special Editions: Christmas Shopping Guide; Christmas Greetings; Back-to-School; Progress; Apartment Living; Football; Senior Living; Newcomers' Guide; Hunting Guide; Home Improvement; Graduation; Medical Guide; National Forest Product Weeks; Parade of Homes.
Special Weekly Sections: TV Spotlight, Business & Financial, Lifestyle, This Week (S).
Magazine: Parade (S).

GENERAL MANAGEMENT

Publisher Glenn McCutchen
Controller Greg Wagner

ADVERTISING

Director Jane Perry
Manager Jeannie Hensly

CIRCULATION

Director Bobby Tingle

NEWS EXECUTIVE

Editor Phil Latham

EDITORS AND MANAGERS

City Editor Jackie Zimmerman
News Editor Jeff Pownall
Photo Editor John Conrad
Society Editor Beverly Johnson
Sports Editor Jack Stallard

MANAGEMENT INFORMATION SERVICES

Data Processing Manager Greg Wagner

PRODUCTION

Director Ferris H Fain
Foreman-Pressroom Greg Griffith

Market Information: TMC; ADS.
Mechanical available: Offset; Black and 3 ROP colors; insert accepted — preprinted; page cutoffs — 22¾".
Mechanical specifications: Type page 13" x 21"; E - 6 cols, 2 1/16", ⅛" between; A - 6 cols, 2 1/16", ⅛" between; C - 9 cols, 1 5/16", ⅛" between.
Commodity consumption: Newsprint 902 short tons; widths 27", 13½"; single pages printed 7,560; average pages per issue 17(d), 45(S).
Equipment: EDITORIAL: Front-end hardware — Ap/Mac; Front-end software — DTI/Page Speed; Printers — Ap/Mac LaserWriter; Other equipment — 1-Nikon/RS-3500, Howtek/ScanMaster II. CLASSIFIED: Front-end hardware — PC; Front-end software — DTI/Class Speed. DISPLAY: Adv layout systems — DTI/Speedplanner; Front-end hardware — Ap/Mac IIg, Ap/Mac; Front-end software — DTI/AdSpeed. PRODUCTION: Typesetters — 2-Ultre/94; Plate exposures — 2-Nu/Flip Top 240; Plate processors — Nat/A250; Electronic picture desk — Lf/AP Leaf Picture Desk; Scanners — Microtek/60025, 1-Nikon/LS-3510; Automatic film processors — LE/AQ14; Color separation equipment (conventional) — DTP.
PRESSROOM: Line 1 — 7-G/Urbanite (1-tricolor); Folders — 1-G. MAILROOM: Counter stackers — QWI/200; Inserters and stuffers — 2-MM/227-S 6-into-1; Bundle tyer — 2-MLN/MLI-EE. WIRE SERVICES: News — AP; Photos — AP; Receiving dishes — size-10ft, AP. BUSINESS COMPUTERS: 1-HP/6000; Applications: CJ; PCs & micros networked; PCs & main system networked.

MARSHALL

Harrison County

'90 U.S. Census- 23,682; E&P '96 Est. 23,071
ABC-CZ (90): 23,682 (HH 8,622)

Marshall News Messenger

(e-mon to fri; S)

Marshall News Messenger, 309 E. Austin; PO Box 730, Marshall, TX 75670; tel (903) 935-7914; fax (903) 935-6242. Hollinger International Inc. group.
Circulation: 9,310(e); 9,933(S); ABC Sept. 30, 1995.
Price: 50¢(d); $1.00(S); $7.00/mo; $84.00/yr (carrier), $96.00/yr (mail).
Advertising: Open inch rate $10.10(e); $10.10(S). **Representative:** Papert Companies.
News Service: AP. **Politics:** Independent. **Established:** 1877.
Advertising not accepted: 900 numbers; Dating services.
Special Editions: Newcomers; Church; Progress; Spring Fashions; Health; Farm-City; Football; Back-to-School; Fall Fashions; Car Care Tab; Jefferson Pilgrimage; Stagecoach Festival; Fire Ant Festival; Our Kids Tab; Unique Gift Guide; Wonderland of Lights Tab; Salute to Family Business; Texas Traveler (Tourist) (bi-monthly).
Magazine: Faces & Places (TMC) (wed).

GENERAL MANAGEMENT

Publisher Reg Durant
Business Manager Dana Morton

ADVERTISING

Director Joe Rainwater

CIRCULATION

Manager Aimee Elwood

NEWS EXECUTIVE

Managing Editor Mike McNeill

EDITORS AND MANAGERS

Editorial Writer Reg Durant
Fashion/Food Editor Mike McNeill
Sports Editor Chris Roselius
Women's Editor Mike McNeill

PRODUCTION

Manager David Ledbetter

Market Information: Split Run; TMC.
Mechanical available: Offset; Black and 4 ROP colors; insert accepted — preprinted, single sheet; page cut-offs — 22¾".
Mechanical specifications: Type page 13¾" x 21¼"; E - 6 cols, 2 1/16", ⅛" between; A - 6 cols, 2 1/16", ⅛" between; C - 9 cols, 1⅜", ⅛" between.
Equipment: EDITORIAL: Front-end hardware — Mk/4000, Ap/Mac IIcx, Ap/Mac Quadra 610; Front-end software — Mk/Ace 1.3.2, Mk/NewsTouch AT, QuarkXPress 3.2, Mk/Page 3.1.3, Caere/OmniPage 3.0, Aldus/FreeHand 3.1; Printers — TI/Omni 800 line printer, 2-Xante/8200, Ap/Mac Plus, V/4990; Other equipment — Ap/Mac Scanner, Lf/LeafScan 35, Lf/AP Leaf Picture Desk. CLASSIFIED: Front-end hardware — Mk/4000; Front-end software — Mk/Ace 1.3.2; Printers — TI/Omni 800 line printer. DISPLAY: Front-end hardware — Ap/Mac IIcx; Front-end software — Mk/AdWriter 2.3.1, Aldus/PageMaker 5.0, Adobe/Illustrator 5.5; Printers — 2-Xante/8200, Ap/Mac Plus. PRODUCTION: Typesetters — 2-Ap/Mac Radius, 2-Ap/Mac IIcx; Plate exposures — 1-Nu; Plate processors — Milart; Production cameras — C/Spartan II; Automatic film processors — SCREEN; Shrink lenses — CK Optical.
PRESSROOM: Line 1 — 4-G/Urbanite; Press control system — G. MAILROOM: Inserters and stuffers — Manual. WIRE SERVICES: News — AP; Photos — AP; Receiving dishes — AP. BUSINESS COMPUTERS: IBM/PC-AT; Applications: Circ, Gen ledger, Payroll, Adv; PCs & micros networked; PCs & main system networked.

McALLEN

Hidalgo County

'90 U.S. Census- 84,021; E&P '96 Est. 94,489
ABC-CZ (90): 186,295 (HH 53,137)

The Monitor (m-mon to sat; S)

The Monitor, 1101 Ash St.; PO Box 760, McAllen, TX 78501; tel (210) 686-4343; fax (210) 686-4370. Freedom Communications Inc. group.
Circulation: 36,411(m); 36,411(m-sat); 43,508(S); ABC Sept. 30, 1995.
Price: 50¢(d); 50¢(sat); $1.25(S); $8.25/mo; $99.00/yr (carrier), $180.00/yr (mail).
Advertising: Open inch rate $48.92(m); $48.92(m-sat); $52.09(S). **Representative:** Papert Companies.
News Service: AP. **Politics:** Independent. **Established:** 1909.
Note: Advertising for the Monitor automatically includes advertising in the Brownsville Herald (mS), El Heraldo de Brownsville (eS) and the Harlingen Valley Star (mS).
Special Editions: Golden Texan (Jan, Feb); Medical Section, Golden Texan (Mar); Cinco de Mayo (May); Bride's Guide (June); B-T-S (Aug); Football Dieciseis (Sept); Golden Texan (Oct); El Turista, Golden Texan, New Auto Showcase, Gift Guide, Recipe Book (Nov); X'mas, Golden Texan, Gift Guide (Dec).
Special Weekly Sections: Let's Talk Business (mon); Food, Lifestyle (wed); Religious Directory, Real Estate & Showcase, Travel (fri); Festiva Entertainment Guide, Classified Home Guide, Automotive Showcase (S); Stock Market, Scene, Sports (daily).
Magazines: Festiva (weekend entertainment) (fri); TV Week Magazine; Vista.

GENERAL MANAGEMENT

Publisher Ray Stafford
Business Manager Jenise Diaz

ADVERTISING

Director Abel Fernandez
Manager-Classified Linda Gonzalez
Manager-Retail Betty Tamez
Manager-Retail Chris Hollister

CIRCULATION

Director Israel Jimenez
Manager-Single Copy Donald Fox
Manager-Customer Service Christina Perales

NEWS EXECUTIVES

Editor R Daniel Cavazos
Managing Editor Paul Binz
Asst Managing Editor Marcia Caltabiano

EDITORS AND MANAGERS

Arts/Entertainment Editor Tanzy Wilson
Asst Metro Editor Pam Coleman
Asst Metro Editor Sara Kessinger
News Editor Dan Murray
Photo Editor Patrick Hamilton
Sports Editor Roy Hess

MANAGEMENT INFORMATION SERVICES

Data Processing Manager Steven Muller

PRODUCTION

Director Stephen Wingert
Manager-Composing/Ad Service Ernie Cortez
Manager-Mailroom Craig Bricker
Manager-Press Baldemar Romero

Market Information: TMC; ADS.
Mechanical available: Offset; Black and 3 ROP colors; insert accepted — preprinted, all; page cut-offs — 22¾".
Mechanical specifications: Type page 13" x 21½"; E - 6 cols, 2⅛", ⅙" between; A - 6 cols, 2⅛", ⅙" between; C - 10 cols, 1.17", ⅙" between.
Commodity consumption: Newsprint 4,440.7 metric tons; widths 27½", 13¾"; black ink 91,000 pounds; color ink 24,288 pounds; single pages printed 17,000; average pages per issue 40(d), 40(sat), 100(S); single plates used 18,000.
Equipment: EDITORIAL: Front-end hardware — Compaq; Front-end software — Dewar System 4; Printers — Okidata/320, X/4220. CLASSIFIED: Front-end hardware — Compaq; Front-end software — Dewar System 4; Printers — Okidata/320, X/4213. DISPLAY: Front-end hardware — Compaq; Front-end software — Dewar System 4, Brainworks; Printers — Tegra/Varityper. PRODUCTION: Pagination software — Dewar System 4; Typesetters — Tegra/Varityper Laser; Plate exposures — 1-Nu; Plate processors — Nat; Electronic picture desk — Lf/AP Leaf Picture Desk; Production cameras — C/Spartan III; Automatic film processors — C; Film transporters — C; Color separation equipment (conventional) — Tegra/Varityper; Digital color separation equipment — Lf/Leafscan, Adobe/Photoshop on Ap/Mac.
PRESSROOM: Line 1 — 7-HI/845 single width; Line 2 — 7-HI/845 single width; Folders — 2-HI/2:1; Pasters — 8-Enkel; Press control system — Amicon; Press registration system — KFM. MAILROOM: Counter stackers — 1-HL; Bundle tyer — 2-MLN. LIBRARY: Electronic — SMS/Stauffer Gold. COMMUNICA-

TIONS: Digital ad delivery system — AP AdSend. WIRE SERVICES: News — AP, CNS, KRT; Photos — AP; Stock tables — AP; Receiving dishes — AP. BUSINESS COMPUTERS: Brainworks A/R Package; Applications: Vision Data: Circ; PCs & micros networked; PCs & main system networked.

McKINNEY

Collin County

'90 U.S. Census- 21,283; E&P '96 Est. 24,313

McKinney Courier-Gazette

(e-mon to fri; S)

McKinney Courier-Gazette, 4005 W. University; PO Box 400, McKinney, TX 75070; tel (214) 542-2631; fax (214) 548-7527. Hartman Newspapers Inc. group.

Circulation: 6,419(e); 6,954(S); VAC June 31, 1995.

Price: 50¢(d); 50¢(S); $15.00/mo; $60.00/yr.

Advertising: Open inch rate $7.40(e); $7.40(S). **Representative:** US Suburban Press.

News Services: AP, NEA. **Politics:** Independent. **Established:** 1897.

Not Published: Christmas.

Special Editions: Drug Awareness (Jan); Progress (Feb); Spring Fashion (Mar); Newcomers (July); Football (Aug); Cookbook, Fall Fashion (Sept); Health/Fitness (Oct); Wonderful World of Women, Thanksgiving (Nov); Christmas (Dec).

Magazine: Tel Aire (TV Log) (S).

GENERAL MANAGEMENT

Publisher Jim Robertson

ADVERTISING

Manager Pete Mulkey

CIRCULATION

Manager Dick O'Brien

NEWS EXECUTIVES

Editor Jim Robertson
Managing Editor Jean Ann Collins

EDITORS AND MANAGERS

Sports Editor Scott Caldwell
Women's Editor Ginny Beverly

MANAGEMENT INFORMATION SERVICES

Data Processing Manager Delores Hargett

PRODUCTION

Superintendent Phillip Cassell

Market Information: TMC.

Mechanical available: Offset; Black and 3 ROP colors; insert accepted — preprinted; page cutoffs — 22¾".

Mechanical specifications: Type page 13" x 21½"; E - 6 cols, 2 1/16", ⅛" between; A - 6 cols, 2 1/16", ⅛" between; C - 8 cols, 1½", ⅛" between.

Commodity consumption: Newsprint 360 short tons; width 27½"; black ink 34,000 pounds; color ink 6,000 pounds; single pages printed 5,490; average pages per issue 18(d), 32(S); single plates used 8,500.

Equipment: EDITORIAL: Front-end hardware — Mk; Front-end software — Mk; Printers — Ap/Mac. CLASSIFIED: Front-end hardware — 1-HI/Computype; Front-end software — Baseview/Class Manager. DISPLAY: Front-end hardware — Ap/Mac; Printers — Ap/Mac Laser-Printer. PRODUCTION: Typesetters — 6-COM, 3-Ap/Mac; Platemaking systems — 1-LE/24 Q; Plate exposures — 1-Nu; Plate processors — 1-Nat; Scanners — B; Production cameras — 1-Acti; Automatic film processors — 1-LE/24 Q; Shrink lenses — 1-CK Optical.
PRESSROOM: Line 1 — 6-HI/V-15A; Folders — 1-HI. MAILROOM: Counter stackers — 1-BG; Bundle tyer — 1-Bu. WIRE SERVICES: News — AP; Syndicates — NYT, NEA, CT; Receiving dishes — AP. BUSINESS COMPUTERS: IBM; Applications: Accts receivable, Payroll, Gen ledger, Balance sheet; PCs & micros networked.

MEXIA

Limestone County

'90 U.S. Census- 6,933; E&P '96 Est. 6,852

The Mexia Daily News

(e-tues to sat)

The Mexia Daily News, 214 N. Railroad St.; PO Box 431, Mexia, TX 76667; tel (817) 562-2868; fax (817) 562-3121. Hollinger International Inc. group.

Circulation: 2,825(e); 2,825(e-sat); Sworn Sept. 28, 1995.

Price: 50¢(d); 50¢(sat); $5.00/mo.

Advertising: Open inch rate $5.40(e); $5.40(e-sat).

News Services: AP, NEA. **Politics:** Independent. **Established:** 1872.

Not Published: New Year; Memorial Day; Independence Day; Labor Day; Thanksgiving; Christmas.

Special Weekly Sections: Best Food Day, Farm Page (tues); Freestone News (thur); TV (sat).

GENERAL MANAGEMENT

Publisher Dick Canaday
Bookkeeper Gail Thornton

ADVERTISING

Director-Retail Lynnette Copley
Manager-Classified Gail Thorton

CIRCULATION

Manager Doris Miller

NEWS EXECUTIVE

Editor Robert E Wright

PRODUCTION

Superintendent Jim Kirgan

Market Information: Split Run; TMC.

Mechanical available: Offset; Black and 3 ROP colors; insert accepted — preprinted; page cutoffs — 21½".

Mechanical specifications: Type page 13" x 21½"; E - 6 cols, 2 1/16", ⅛" between; A - 6 cols, 2 1/16", ⅛" between; C - 8 cols, 1½", ⅛" between.

Commodity consumption: widths 27.5"; average pages per issue 10(d).

Equipment: EDITORIAL: Front-end hardware — Ap/Mac; Front-end software — Baseview/NewsEdit, QuarkXPress; Printers — Ap/Mac LaserWriter; Other equipment — HP/Scanner IIp. CLASSIFIED: Front-end hardware — Ap/Mac; Front-end software — Baseview; Printers — Ap/Mac LaserWriter. DISPLAY: Front-end hardware — Ap/Mac; Front-end software — QuarkXPress; Printers — Ap/Mac LaserWriter. PRODUCTION: Typesetters — Ap/Mac LaserWriter; Plate exposures — 1-Nu; Plate processors — Nat; Production cameras — SCREEN/Companica Screen.
PRESSROOM: Line 1 — 4-HI/V-15A. MAILROOM: Bundle tyer — Bu; Addressing machine — Wm. WIRE SERVICES: News — AP; Syndicates — Creators, United Features; Receiving dishes — AP.

MIDLAND

Midland County

'90 U.S. Census- 89,443; E&P '96 Est. 100,610

ABC-CZ (90): 89,712 (HH 33,240)

Midland Reporter-Telegram

(m-mon to sat; S)

Midland Reporter-Telegram, 201 E. Illinois St. (79701); PO Box 1650, Midland, TX 79702; tel (915) 682-5311; fax (915) 682-6173; e-mail chip@basinlink; web site http://www.basinlink.com. Hearst Newspapers group.

Circulation: 23,029(m); 23,029(m-sat); 27,624(S); ABC Sept. 30, 1995.

Price: 50¢(d); 50¢(sat); $1.50(S); $11.00/mo (home delivery); $132.00/yr (home delivery).

Advertising: Open inch rate $22.55(m); $22.55(m-sat); $26.05(S). **Representative:** Papert Companies.

News Services: AP, CNS, HN, NYT. **Politics:** Independent. **Established:** 1929.

Special Editions: Money Show (Jan); Permorama (Feb); Spring Fashion, Spring Home & Garden (Mar); Design-an-Ad (Apr); Vacation & Travel (May); Best of Midland, Newcomers (July); Fall Fashion, Back-to-School (Aug); Football, Fall Home & Garden (Sept); Fall Car Care, Oil Edition (Oct); Christmas Gift Guide, Auto Showcase (Nov); Christmas Gift Guides, Spirit of Christmas (Dec).

Special Weekly Sections: Consumer Finance (mon); Business & Industry (tues); Food, Living Well (wed); Homes/Gardens, Nueva Vista, Fashion, Travel (thur); Lifestyle, Prime Time (Seniors) (fri); Church/Religion (sat); Oil Report, Brides/Engagements (S).

Magazines: USA Weekend, TV Week (S).

Broadcast Affiliates: ABC (KMID); CBS (KOSA); FOX (KPEJ); NBC (KTPX).

CORPORATE OFFICERS

Vice Pres Robert J Danzig
Controller David T Wedel

GENERAL MANAGEMENT

Publisher Charles A Spence

ADVERTISING

Director Sam E Bakke

MARKETING AND PROMOTION

Director-Marketing Sam E Bakke

TELECOMMUNICATIONS

Director-Telecommunications Gene Mills
Audiotex Manager Paige Moon

CIRCULATION

Director J R Ruiz

NEWS EXECUTIVES

Editor Jim Servatius
Managing Editor Gary Ott

EDITORS AND MANAGERS

Oil Editor John P Pitts
Business Editor John P Pitts
City/Metro Editor Gary Ott
Editorial Page Editor Bill Modisett
Education Editor Myra Salcedo
Entertainment/Amusements Editor Georgia Temple
Farm/Agriculture Editor Ed Todd
Fashion/Style Editor Elizabeth Edwin
Features Editor Elizabeth Edwin
Health/Medical Editor Ed Todd
Living/Lifestyle Editor Elizabeth Edwin
National Editor Gary Ott
News Editor Dallas Merrick
Oil & Gas Editor John P Pitts
Photo Editor Curt Wilcott
Political/Government Editor Gary Ott
Religion Editor Georgia Temple
Sports Editor Terry Williamson
Women's Editor Elizabeth Edwin

MANAGEMENT INFORMATION SERVICES

Online Manager Dee McClellan

PRODUCTION

Manager John Maddox
Manager-Info Systems Gene Mills

Market Information: TMC; Operate database; Operate audiotex; Electronic edition.

Mechanical available: Offset; Black and 3 ROP colors; insert accepted — preprinted, free standing stock cards, envelope inserts; page cut-offs — 22¾".

Mechanical specifications: Type page 13" x 21½"; E - 6 cols, 2", ⅛" between; A - 6 cols, 2", ⅛" between; C - 9 cols, 1⅜", 1/16" between.

Commodity consumption: Newsprint 2,322 short tons; widths 55", 41¼", 27½"; black ink 76,000 pounds; color ink 10,000 pounds; single pages printed 13,922; average pages per issue 32.3(d), 73.8(S); single plates used 35,620.

Equipment: EDITORIAL: Front-end hardware — Ap/Power Mac; Front-end software — Baseview/News Edit; Printers — Ap/Mac LaserWriter NT, QMS/860, ECR/1045, ECR/1245. CLASSIFIED: Front-end hardware — Baseview; Front-end software — Baseview/Class Manager; Printers — Ap/Mac LaserWriter IIg. AUDIOTEX: Hardware — Brite Voice Systems/City Line. DISPLAY: Adv layout systems — 4-Ap/Mac 6100; Front-end hardware — Ap/Mac; Front-end software — QuarkXPress, Multi-Ad/Creator; Printers — Ap/Mac LaserPrinter, QMS, V; Other equipment — IBM. PRODUCTION: Pagination software — QuarkXPress; Typesetters — V/600W, 1-Ap/Mac LaserWriter NTX, 2-QMS/860, ECR/1245-C's, ECR/1045; Plate exposures — 2-Nu/Flip Top; Plate processors — 2-Nat/A-250, 3M/Deadliner; Electronic picture desk — Lf/AP Leaf Picture Desk; Production cameras — 1-C/Spartan III, 3M/Deadliner; Automatic film processors — 1-P/2024I, 1-LE/LD 2600 A; Film transporters — 2-MGD, 1-C; Digital color separation equipment — Ap/Mac, Adobe/Photoshop, Lf/AP Leaf Picture Desk, Lf/Leafscan 45.
PRESSROOM: Line 1 — 6-HI/1650; Line 2 — 6-G/Community, 2-G/Community Universal Color; Line 3 — 2-G/SSC; Folders — 2-HI/2:1, 1-G (w/quarterfold); Pasters — Automatic Pasters; Reels and stands — 6-HI; Press control system — CH/Drive, HI, G, Fin. MAILROOM: Counter stackers — 3-Id/NS440; Inserters and stuffers — S/48-P (9-Head); Bundle tyer — Power Strap/PSM-4, 2-MLN/ML-2EE, 1-MLN/2A; Addressing machine — 1-KR/Model 211. LIBRARY: Electronic — Baseview. COMMUNICATIONS: Digital ad delivery system — AP AdSend. WIRE SERVICES: News — AP, AP Datastream, AP Dataspeed, AP Datafeatures; Photos — AP Photostream; Stock tables — AP, AP Custom Stocks; Syndicates — AP Datafeatures; Receiving dishes — size-10ft, AP. BUSINESS COMPUTERS: HP/3000 48, 5-IBM, IBM/AS 400; Applications: CJ: Graphics, Accts receivable, Payroll, Circ, Accts payable, Gen ledger, Class, Spread sheets, Software 2000; PCs & micros networked; PCs & main system networked.

MINERAL WELLS

Palo Pinto County

'90 U.S. Census- 14,870; E&P '96 Est. 15,078

Mineral Wells Index

(e-tues to fri; S)

Mineral Wells Index, 300 S.E. First St. (76067); PO Box 370, Mineral Wells, TX 76068; tel (817) 325-4465; fax (817) 325-2020. Livermore Newspapers group.

Circulation: 4,940(e); 5,140(S); Sworn Oct. 3, 1995.

Price: 25¢(d); 75¢(S); $6.50/mo; $60.00/yr.

Advertising: Open inch rate $7.40(e); $7.40(S). **Representative:** Papert Companies. **Politics:** Independent. **Established:** 1900.

Not Published: New Year; Independence Day; Thanksgiving; Christmas.

Advertising not accepted: Adoption; 900 numbers.

Special Editions: Chamber of Commerce (Feb); Rodeo (May); Crazy Water Festival (June); Back-to-School, Airfair (Aug); Best of Mineral Wells (Sept); Economic Development (Oct); Christmas Gift Guide (Dec).

Special Weekly Sections: Hunting & Fishing, Religion, Farm & Ranch (daily).

Magazine: TV Book (S).

CORPORATE OFFICER

President Ed Livermore Jr

GENERAL MANAGEMENT

Publisher/General Manager Gary D Adkisson

ADVERTISING

Manager-Promotion Bill Moore

NEWS EXECUTIVE

Editor Mel Rhodes

EDITORS AND MANAGERS

Lifestyle Editor Christy Moore
Sports Editor Theresa Finley

PRODUCTION

Manager-Composing Leah Park
Manager-Pressroom John Armstrong

Market Information: TMC; ADS.

Mechanical available: Offset; Black and 3 ROP colors; insert accepted — preprinted, all; page cut-offs — 22¾".

Mechanical specifications: Type page 13¾" x 21½"; E - 6 cols, 2", ⅛" between; A - 6 cols, 2", ⅛" between; C - 8 cols, 1½", ⅛" between.

Commodity consumption: Newsprint 130 short tons; widths 27½", 13¾"; black ink 3,200 pounds; color ink 150 pounds; single pages printed 3,776; average pages per issue 12(d), 20(S); single plates used 6,000.

Equipment: EDITORIAL: Front-end hardware — Ap/Mac; Front-end software — Multi-Ad/Creator, QuarkXPress, Claris/MacWrite II, QuarkXPress; Printers — Ap/Mac LaserWriter II NT, Ap/Mac LaserWriter NTR. CLASSIFIED: Front-end hardware — Ap/Mac; Front-end software — QuarkXPress, Claris/MacWrite. DISPLAY: Adv layout systems — Ap/Mac, Ap/Mac Centris 610; Front-end hardware — Ap/Mac Performa 405; Front-end software — Multi-Ad/Creator, QuarkXPress; Printers — Ap/Mac LaserWriter NTR. PRODUCTION: Typesetters — Ap/Mac LaserWriter II; Plate exposures — 1-Nu; Production cameras — LE/500, R.
PRESSROOM: Line 1 — 5-WPC/Leader; Folders — 1-WPC. MAILROOM: Bundle tyer — Bu; Addressing machine — Am, El/3101. BUSINESS COMPUTERS: 2-RSK/Tandy 3000, Panasonic/Printer; Applications: Victoria/advocate: Payable, Accts receivable, Circ; PCs & micros networked.

MOUNT PLEASANT

Titus County

'90 U.S. Census- 12,291; E&P '96 Est. 12,992

Mount Pleasant Daily Tribune

(e-mon to fri; S)

Mount Pleasant Daily Tribune, 1705 Industrial; PO Drawer 1177, Mount Pleasant, TX 75455; tel (903) 572-1705.

Circulation: 4,927(e); 4,927(S); Sworn Oct. 13, 1994.

Price: 50¢(d); $1.00(S); $6.00/mo; $66.00/yr.

Advertising: Open inch rate $9.00(e); $9.00(S). **Representative:** Landon Associates Inc.

News Services: AP, NEA. **Politics:** Independent. **Established:** 1872.

Not Published: Christmas.

Advertising not accepted: Fortune tellers.

Special Editions: Progress (Jan); Graduation (May); Baseball, Rodeo (June); Football, County Fair (Sept); Women in Business (Oct); Modern Living (quarterly).

Magazines: Tribune Magazine (own), TV Viewing (fri); Color Comics (S).
Broadcast Affiliates: K 54 (CBN) Mount Pleasant, TX.

CORPORATE OFFICERS

President Robert B Palmer
Secretary Mrs Robert B Palmer
Treasurer R L Palmer

GENERAL MANAGEMENT

Publisher R L Palmer

ADVERTISING

Manager Martha McGregor

CIRCULATION

Manager James McGregor

NEWS EXECUTIVES

Editor R L Palmer
Asst Managing Editor John Moody

EDITOR AND MANAGER

Sports Editor John Whitten

MANAGEMENT INFORMATION SERVICES

Data Processing Manager Tami Saldano

PRODUCTION

Manager Robert McKinney

Market Information: TMC; ADS.
Mechanical available: Offset; Black and 3 ROP colors; insert accepted — preprinted; page cutoffs — 22¾".
Mechanical specifications: Type page 13" x 21"; E - 6 cols, 2 1/16", ⅛" between; A - 6 cols, 2 1/16", ⅛" between; C - 8 cols, 1 9/16", 1/16" between.
Commodity consumption: Newsprint 400 short tons; widths 28", 14"; single pages printed 6,560; average pages per issue 20(d), 40(S); single plates used 4,000.
Equipment: EDITORIAL: Front-end hardware — PC; Front-end software — WordPerfect; Printers — Ap/Mac LaserWriter. CLASSIFIED: Front-end hardware — PC; Front-end software — BMF; Printers — Ap/Mac LaserWriter. DISPLAY: Adv layout systems — Ap/Mac; Front-end software — Aldus/PageMaker; Printers — Ap/Mac LaserWriter. PRODUCTION: Typesetters — Ap/Mac LaserWriter.
PRESSROOM: Line 1 — 5-HI/V-15A; Line 2 — 2-HI/V-15A. MAILROOM: Bundle tyer — 2-Bu; Addressing machine — 1-KAN. COMMUNICATIONS: Facsimile — Ricoh. WIRE SERVICES: News — AP; Receiving dishes — AP. BUSINESS COMPUTERS: PC; Applications: BMF; PCs & micros networked; PCs & main system networked.

NACOGDOCHES

Nacogdoches County

'90 U.S. Census- 30,872; E&P '96 Est. 32,921

The Daily Sentinel

(e-mon to fri; m-sat; S)

The Daily Sentinel, 4920 Colonial Dr.; Box 630068, Nacogdoches, TX 75963-0068; tel (409) 564-8361; fax (409) 560-4267. Cox Newspapers Inc. group.
Circulation: 8,398(e); 8,398(m-sat); 10,938(S); Sworn Oct. 1, 1994.
Price: 35¢(d); 35¢(sat); $1.00(S); $96.00/yr (mail), $83.40/yr (home delivery).
Advertising: Open inch rate $9.08(e); $9.08(m-sat); $9.88(S). **Representative:** Papert Companies.
News Service: AP. **Politics:** Independent-Democrat. **Established:** 1896.
Special Editions: Garden; Almanac; Bridal; Christmas Shopping Guide; Hunting/Fishing; Home Improvement; Car Care; Cookbook; Progress; Apartment Living; SFA Guide.
Special Weekly Sections: Best Food Day (tues); TV Spotlight, Business & Financial Pages, Lifestyle (S).
Magazines: TV Week, Parade (S).

GENERAL MANAGEMENT

Publisher Gary Borders
General Manager/President Ferris H Fain
Business Manager Greg Wagner

ADVERTISING

Director Jane Perry
Manager Jeannie Hensley

CIRCULATION

Director Rick Deaver
Manager Rick Easley

NEWS EXECUTIVES

Editor Gary Borders
Managing Editor Kristi Dempsey

EDITORS AND MANAGERS

Columnist Victor B Fain
Columnist Gary Borders

MANAGEMENT INFORMATION SERVICES

Data Processing Manager Delia Harris

Market Information: TMC.
Mechanical available: Offset; Black and 3 ROP colors; insert accepted — preprinted; page cutoffs — 22¾".
Mechanical specifications: Type page 13" x 21¼"; E - 6 cols, 2 1/16", ⅛" between; A - 6 cols, 2 1/16", ⅛" between; C - 9 cols, 1 5/16", ⅛" between.
Commodity consumption: Newsprint 459 short tons; widths 27", 13½"; single pages printed 7,764; average pages per issue 17(d), 51(S).
Equipment: EDITORIAL: Front-end hardware — Ap/Mac; Front-end software — DTI/PageSpeed; Printers — Ap/Mac NTX. CLASSIFIED: Front-end hardware — Wyse/150ES; Front-end software — DTI/ClassSpeed; Printers — TI/880. DISPLAY: Adv layout systems — DTI/AdSpeed; Front-end hardware — Ap/Mac, Ap/Mac NTX; Front-end software — DTI/AdSpeed; Other equipment — Ap/Mac Scanner. PRODUCTION: Typesetters — Ap/Mac NTX; Electronic picture desk — Lf/AP Leaf Picture Desk; Scanners — Lf/Leafscan. WIRE SERVICES: News — AP, Cox News Service, SHNS; Photos — AP, Cox; Receiving dishes — size-10ft, AP.

NEW BRAUNFELS

Comal County

'90 U.S. Census- 27,334; E&P '96 Est. 30,173

New Braunfels Herald-Zeitung

(e-tues to fri; S)

New Braunfels Herald-Zeitung, 707 Landa St. (78130); PO Box 311328, New Braunfels, TX 78131-1328; tel (210) 625-9144; fax (210) 625-1224. Southern Newspapers Inc. group.
Circulation: 7,382(e); 7,382(S); Sworn Sept. 28, 1994.
Price: 50¢(d); 75¢(S); $49.00/yr.
Advertising: Open inch rate $12.43(e); $12.75(S).
News Service: AP. **Politics:** Independent. **Established:** 1891.
Special Editions: Brides, Chamber Tab (Jan); Babies on Parade, Spring Fashion (Feb); Horizons '96, Visitors' Guide (Mar); Visitors' Guide, Spring Fix Up, Medical Tab (Apr); Visitors' Guide, Graduation Tab, Small Business (May); Vistors' Guide (June, July); Visitors' Guide, Football Tab, Fair Tab (Aug); Wurstfest Guide (Oct).
Special Weekly Sections: Best Food Day (wed); Scrapbook (Photo page), Outdoors (thur); Church Page (fri); Wedding, Engagements (S).
Magazines: Sunday Comics (S); TV Listings (daily); Montage; Entertainment Guide.

GENERAL MANAGEMENT

Publisher/Editor David J Sullens

ADVERTISING

Director Paul Davis

CIRCULATION

Manager Carol Ann Avery

NEWS EXECUTIVE

Managing Editor Mark Lyon

EDITORS AND MANAGERS

City/Metro Editor Roger Croteau
Editorial Page Editor Mark Lyon
News Editor Roger Croteau
Photo Editor John Huseth
Religion Editor David J Sullens
Sports Editor Richard Tijerina

PRODUCTION

Foreman-Composing Carol Ann Avery
Foreman-Press Douglas Brandt

Market Information: TMC.
Mechanical available: Offset; Black and 3 ROP colors; insert accepted — preprinted; page cutoffs — 21".
Mechanical specifications: Type page 13" x 21"; E - 6 cols, 2 1/16", ⅛" between; A - 6 cols, 2 1/16", ⅛" between; C - 9 cols, 1 5/16", ⅛" between.
Commodity consumption: Newsprint 550 short tons; width 13¾"; single pages printed 7,004; average pages per issue 16(d), 28(S); single plates used 3,502.
Equipment: EDITORIAL: Front-end hardware — 2-Ap/Mac Classic, 3-Mk, 1-Ap/Mac Quadra, 4-Ap/Mac IIci; Front-end software — Microsoft/Word, QuarkXPress; Printers — Ap/Mac LaserWriter; Other equipment — Ap/Mac Scanner. CLASSIFIED: Front-end hardware — Mk; Front-end software — Mk; Printers — TI. DISPLAY: Front-end hardware — 2-Ap/Mac IIci; Front-end software — Microsoft/Word, QuarkXPress; Printers — 1-Ap/Mac LaserPrinter. PRODUCTION: Typesetters — Ap/Mac LaserPrinter; Plate exposures — 1-Nu; Production cameras — R; Automatic film processors — P. PRESSROOM: Line 1 — 5-WPC/Leader. MAILROOM: Counter stackers — BG/Count-O-Veyor; Inserters and stuffers — KAN/780; Bundle tyer — Dynaric. WIRE SERVICES: News — AP; Receiving dishes — AP. BUSINESS COMPUTERS: 2-IBM; Applications: Quattro, Microsoft/Word.

ODESSA

Ector County

'90 U.S. Census- 89,699; E&P '96 Est. 89,533
ABC-CZ (90): 114,743 (HH 41,021)

Odessa American

(m-mon to sat; S)

Odessa American, 222 E. 4th (79761); PO Box 2952, Odessa, TX 79760; tel (915) 337-4661; fax (915) 334-8671. Freedom Communications Inc. group.
Circulation: 25,692(m); 25,692(m-sat); 31,856(S); ABC Sept. 30, 1995.
Price: 50¢(d); 50¢(sat); $1.50(S); $10.00/mo; $120.00/yr.
Advertising: Open inch rate $24.00(m); $24.00(m-sat); $26.50(S). **Representative:** Papert Companies.
News Services: AP, KRT. **Politics:** Independent. **Established:** 1948.
Special Editions: Progress (Feb); Mother's Day (May); Father's Day (June); Football (Aug); Auto Preview (Oct); Oil Show; Christmas West Texas; Seniors; Graduation.
Special Weekly Sections: Business & Industrial Review (mon); CHAMPS (Kid sports) (tues); Best Food Day (wed); Sports Extra (thur); Business Weekly (fri); Automotive Review, Religion (sat); Real Estate & Home Showcase, Travel, Lifestyle (S).
Magazines: Preview (TV News & Entertainment), Parade (S).

GENERAL MANAGEMENT

Publisher Bill Salter
Business Manager Frances Irvine

ADVERTISING

Director Tony Cooper
Manager-Promotion Dana Taylor
Manager-National Janice Graham

TELECOMMUNICATIONS

Audiotex Manager June Baumann

CIRCULATION

Director Tony Traven

NEWS EXECUTIVE

Editor Gary Newsom

EDITORS AND MANAGERS

Amusements Editor Laura Dennis
City Editor Patricia Gordon
Columnist Ken Brodnax
Editorial Page Editor Ken Brodnax
Education Editor Sarah Westbrook
Fashion/Food Editor Sonja Merrick
Graphics Editor/Art Director Janet Terry
Living/Lifestyle Editor Laura Dennis
News Editor Kim Kirkham
Photo Department Manager Larry Beckner
Religion Editor Sonja Merrick
Sports Editor Cameron Hollway
Television/Film Editor Laura Dennis
Theater/Music Editor Laura Dennis
Travel Editor Laura Dennis

MANAGEMENT INFORMATION SERVICES

Data Processing Manager Robert Braswell

PRODUCTION

Director Operations Robert Braswell
Foreman-Mailroom Gary Hesson

Market Information: Split Run; TMC; ADS; Operate audiotex.
Mechanical available: Offset; Black and 3 ROP colors; insert accepted — preprinted; page cutoffs — 22¾".
Mechanical specifications: Type page 13" x 21½"; E - 6 cols, 2 1/16", 1/12" between; A - 6 cols, 2 1/16", 1/12" between; C - 9 cols, 1 5/16", 1/12" between.
Commodity consumption: Newsprint 2,497 metric tons; widths 55", 27½", 13¾", 41¼"; black ink 56,269 pounds; color ink 15,270 pounds; single pages printed 14,820; average pages per issue 32(d), 42(sat), 80(S); single plates used 43,669.
Equipment: EDITORIAL: Front-end hardware — AST/PC-386; Front-end software — XYQUEST/XyWrite, dBase IV, Dewar; Printers — Panasonic/KX-P2123. CLASSIFIED: Front-end hardware — PC/AST 386; Front-end software — XYQUEST/XyWrite, dBase IV, Dewar; Printers — Okidata/393 Plus, Okidata/320. AUDIOTEX: Hardware — DTK/386; Software — Unix; Supplier name — Microvoice/VNN. DISPLAY: Adv layout systems — Dewar/Discovery; Front-end hardware — PC/AST 386, Ap/Power Mac 8100, Ap/Mac Quadra 950, Ap/Power Mac 7100; Front-end software — Multi-Ad/Creator, Dewar, QuarkXPress; Printers — HP/4M, Tegra/Varityper 5510, Tegra/Varityper 5100, ECR/VR 36; Other equipment — CD-Rom, Microtek/Scanner, Topaz, Lf/Leafscan 45, Umax/Powerlook, AG/Arcus Plus. PRODUCTION: Pagination software — Dewar System 4 6.30; OCR software — Caere/OmniPage Direct 5.02; Typesetters — V/5100, V/5510, V/5300E, ECR/VR 36, ECR/VR 36; Platemaking systems — 3M/Pyrofax; Plate exposures — Nu/Flip Top; Plate processors — Nat/A-250; Electronic picture desk — Lf/AP Leaf Picture Desk; Scanners — X, 2-Hand Held; Production cameras — C/Spartan II; Automatic film processors — LE/LD 1800-A, LE; Shrink lenses — CK Optical; Color separation equipment (conventional) — RZ/210-L, Ap/Mac Quadra 950, Topaz on Ap/Power Mac 8100.
PRESSROOM: Line 1 — 6-HI/1650; Line 2 — 1-Hamada/700; Press drives — 2-CH/150 HP; Folders — 2-HI/2:1; Pasters — MEG/Flying; Press control system — CH; Press registration system — KFM. MAILROOM: Counter stackers — 1-HL/HT, 1-HL/HT II; Inserters and stuffers — 1-MM/227, GMA/SLS 1000A; Bundle tyer — 1-EAM/Mosca, 1-MLN/ML-2; Other mailroom equipment — MM/Minuteman Saddle Stitcher. LIBRARY: Electronic — SMS/Stauffer Gold. COMMUNICATIONS: Digital ad delivery system — AP AdSend. WIRE SERVICES: News — AP, NYT, KRT, TMS; Photos — AP; Stock tables — AP Grand Central; Syndicates — TMS, KRT, Creators; Receiving dishes — AP. BUSINESS COMPUTERS: 1-AST/486 fileserver; Applications: Southware: Payroll, Accts payable, Gen ledger; Vision Data: Accts receivable; PCs & micros networked.

ORANGE

Orange County

'90 U.S. Census- 19,381; E&P '96 Est. 17,454

The Orange Leader

(e-mon to fri; m-sat; S)

The Orange Leader, 200 Front Ave.; PO Box 1028, Orange, TX 77630; tel (409) 883-3571; fax (409) 883-6342. Hollinger International Inc. group.
Circulation: 8,913(e); 8,913(m-sat); 11,000(S); VAC June 30, 1995.
Price: 35¢(d); 35¢(sat); $1.00(S); $8.50/mo; $102.00/yr.
Advertising: Open inch rate $11.19(e); $11.19(m-sat); $11.19(S). **Representative:** Papert Companies.
News Service: AP. **Politics:** Independent. **Established:** 1875.
Special Editions: Chamber of Commerce Report, Super Bowl, Best of Orange (Jan); Tax Tab, Bridal Tab, Progress & Development, Lawn & Garden (Mar); Churches, Just Say No, Home Improvement (Apr); Gumbo Cookoff, Graduates '96 (May); Car Care, Health Care (June); Meet your Neighbor (July); Back-to-School, Football Section (Aug); Hunting & Fishing Guide, Orange & Proud of It, Yesteryear's Brides (Sept); Truck, Rodeo (Oct); Shop Orange, Holiday Cookbook, Gift Guide (Nov); Shop Orange, Last Minute Gifts, Letters to Santa, Car (Dec); Homes Section, Golden Orange Seniors Section (monthly).
Magazines: TV Channels (local, newsprint); Comics; USA Weekend.

GENERAL MANAGEMENT

General Manager Jan Bromley

ADVERTISING

Director Jan Bromley
Manager-Classified Becky Hatfield

CIRCULATION

Director Paul Brown

NEWS EXECUTIVE

Exec Editor Ken Sury

EDITORS AND MANAGERS

Editorial Page Editor Ken Sury
Sports Editor Mike Rogers

MANAGEMENT INFORMATION SERVICES

Data Processing Manager Mrs Jeree Powell

Texas

I-404

PRODUCTION
Manager — Tom Wessel

Market Information: TMC.
Mechanical available: Offset; Black and 3 ROP colors; insert accepted — preprinted, all; page cut-offs — 22¾".
Mechanical specifications: Type page 13" x 21½"; E - 6 cols, 2.07", ⅛" between; A - 6 cols, 2.07", ⅛" between; C - 9 cols, 1⅓", ⅙" between.
Commodity consumption: Newsprint 440 short tons; widths 27", 13½"; black ink 13,716 pounds; color ink 3,904 pounds; single pages printed 6,900; average pages per issue 16(d), 36(S).
Equipment: EDITORIAL: Front-end hardware — Mk; Front-end software — Mk; Printers — Ap/Mac Laser. CLASSIFIED: Front-end hardware — Mk; Front-end software — Mk. DISPLAY: Adv layout systems — Ap/Mac; Front-end hardware — Ap/Mac; Front-end software — Multi-Ad, QuarkXPress, Ofoto, Caere/OmniPage; Other equipment — Ap/Mac Scanner. PRODUCTION: Typesetters — Ap/Mac II NTX; Plate exposures — Nu/FT4OUPNS Flip Top; Plate processors — Nat/A-250; Production cameras — C/500; Automatic film processors — LE/2100; Color separation equipment (conventional) — Lf/Leafscan, Lf/AP Leaf Picture Desk. PRESSROOM: Line 1 — G/32 page Suburban; Folders — 1-G (w/balloon); Pasters — 2-Martin; Reels and stands — 2-HI; Press control system — Fin. MAILROOM: Counter stackers — BG/Count-O-Veyor, BG/105; Inserters and stuffers — 4-MM/227E; Bundle tyer — MLN/L-2. COMMUNICATIONS: Facsimile — Canon/230 (8½" x 14"). WIRE SERVICES: News — AP; Receiving dishes — size-3m, AP. BUSINESS COMPUTERS: ATT; Applications: SMS/Stauffer; Accts receivable, Circ, Adv.

PALESTINE
Anderson County
'90 U.S. Census- 18,042; E&P '96 Est. 19,191
ABC-CZ (90): 18,042 (HH 6,611)

Palestine Herald-Press
(e-mon to fri; m-sat; S)
Palestine Herald-Press, 519 Elm St. (75801); PO Box 379, Palestine, TX 75802; tel (903) 729-0281; fax (903) 729-3380.
Circulation: 9,271(e); 9,271(m-sat); 9,595(S); ABC Sept. 30, 1995.
Price: 25¢(d); 25¢(sat); 75¢(S); $6.60/mo.
Advertising: Open inch rate $9.00(e); $9.00(m-sat); $9.00(S). **Representative:** Papert Companies.
News Service: AP. **Politics:** Independent. **Established:** 1898.
Not Published: Christmas.
Special Editions: Cooking School (Feb); Fashion Show, Dogwood Trails, Home and Auto Show (Mar); Hot Pepper Festival (Oct); Gift Guide (Nov).
Special Weekly Sections: Best Food Day (tues); Community (wed); Religious, Entertainment (fri); TV Guide, Weekend (sat); Community (S).
Magazine: TV Extra.

CORPORATE OFFICERS
President — Larry Mayo
Vice Pres — Wayne T Patrick
Secretary/Treasurer — William LeGrand
GENERAL MANAGEMENT
Publisher — Larry Mayo
Manager-Credit — Billy Foley
Purchasing Agent — Larry Mayo
ADVERTISING
Director — Mike Whitworth
Manager-Classified — Linda Legg
Manager-National — Alex Kobar
CIRCULATION
Manager — Ron Fulton
NEWS EXECUTIVE
Editor — Bonnie Lassiter
EDITOR AND MANAGER
Community Editor — Sheril Sweet
PRODUCTION
Manager — Clifton Henry
Supervisor-Composing — Carol Garner

Market Information: TMC.
Mechanical available: Offset; Black and 3 ROP colors; insert accepted — preprinted; page cut-offs — 21½".
Mechanical specifications: Type page 13" x 21½"; E - 6 cols, 2 1/16", ⅛" between; A - 6 cols, 2 1/16", ⅛" between; C - 8 cols, 1 9/16", 1/16" between.
Commodity consumption: Newsprint 214 metric tons; widths 14", 28"; black ink 5,400 pounds; color ink 174 pounds; single pages printed 5,500; single plates used 7,200.
Equipment: EDITORIAL: Front-end hardware — Ap/Mac Radius, Ap/Mac SE Radius; Other equipment — Lf/AP Leaf Picture Desk. CLASSIFIED: Front-end hardware — 2-Ap/Mac ci, 1-Ap/Mac ImageWriter II. PRODUCTION: Typesetters — Ap/Mac; Production cameras — 1-R; Shrink lenses — 1-CK Optical.
PRESSROOM: Line 1 — 6-G/Suburban; Press control system — Fin. MAILROOM: Bundle tyer — 1-Bu; Addressing machine — 1-Dispensa-Matic (computer labels). WIRE SERVICES: News — AP; Receiving dishes — AP. BUSINESS COMPUTERS: NCR/I9020, IBM/30 286, Compaq/Proline A 3-255; Applications: Southware: Bus; Vision Data: Circ; Brainworks: Acct receivable; PCs & micros networked.

PARIS
Lamar County
'90 U.S. Census- 24,699; E&P '96 Est. 24,300

The Paris News
(e-mon to fri; S)
The Paris News, 5050 S.E. Loop 286; PO Box 1078, Paris, TX 75460; tel (903) 785-8744; fax (903) 785-1263. Southern Newspapers Inc. group.
Circulation: 11,858(e); 11,858(S); Sworn Oct. 1, 1995.
Price: 50¢(d); $1.25(S); $8.75/mo; $105.00/yr (carrier), $117.00/yr (mail).
Advertising: Open inch rate $11.25(e); $11.25(S). **Representative:** Papert Companies.
News Service: AP. **Politics:** Independent. **Established:** 1869.
Advertising not accepted: X-rated movies.
Special Editions: Home Furnishings, Woman's World (Feb); Car Care, Quarterly Farm & Ranch Review, Home Improvement (Mar); Brides (Apr); Progress Edition (May); Quarterly Farm & Ranch Review (June); Newcomer's Guide (Aug); Football, Homemaker's Cooking School, Quarterly Farm & Ranch Review (Sept); New Car Edition (Oct); Last Minute Gift Guide, Car Care (Nov); Greetings Section, Quarterly Farm & Ranch Review (Dec).
Special Weekly Sections: Farm Page (wed); Outdoor Page, Business Review (thur); Religion Pages (fri); Business News, Lifestyle Section (S).
Magazine: TV & Entertainment Guide (S).

GENERAL MANAGEMENT
Publisher — Michael D Graxiola
Purchasing Agent — Relan Walker
ADVERTISING
Director — Michael D Graxiola
Manager-National — Evie Taber
Manager-Co-op — Relan Walker
CIRCULATION
Manager — Ricky Dority
NEWS EXECUTIVE
Managing Editor — Bill Hankins
EDITORS AND MANAGERS
Society Editor — Dorothy Vaughan
Sports Editor — Van Hilburn

Market Information: TMC.
Mechanical available: Offset; Black and 3 ROP colors; insert accepted — preprinted, standard; page cut-offs — 21½".
Mechanical specifications: Type page 13" x 21½"; E - 6 cols, 2.04", ⅛" between; A - 6 cols, 2.04", ⅛" between; C - 9 cols, 1⅓", ⅛" between.
Commodity consumption: Newsprint 800 short tons; widths 27½", 27"; black ink 15,000 pounds; color ink 4,000 pounds; single pages printed 7,790; average pages per issue 22(d), 40(S); single plates used 9,120.
Equipment: EDITORIAL: Front-end hardware — Ap/Mac; Front-end software — Ap/Mac, Baseview; Printers — Ap/Mac LaserWriter; Other equipment — AG/Accuset 1000, Microtek/ScanMaker III. CLASSIFIED: Front-end hardware — Ap/Mac; Front-end software — Baseview; Printers — Ap/Mac LaserWriter II NTX. DISPLAY: Adv layout systems — Ap/Mac; Front-end hardware — Ap/Mac; Front-end software — Multi-Ad/Creator; Printers — Ap/Mac LaserWriter II NTX; Other equipment — Ap/Mac Scanner. PRODUCTION: Pagination software — QuarkXPress 3.11; OCR software — Caere/OmniPage Pro; Typesetters — Ap/Mac LaserWriter Pro 630, AG/Accuset 1000; Platemaking systems — 1-Nu; Plate processors — Nat; Electronic picture desk — Lf/AP Leaf Picture Desk; Scanners — Microtek/ScanMaker III, Microtek/ScanMaker II; Production cameras — LE, R/500; Automatic film processors — P/26-RA; Shrink lenses — 1-CK Optical; Digital color separation equipment — Adobe/Photoshop, QuarkXPress, Viper RIP. PRESSROOM: Line 1 — 8-G/Community; Press control system — Fin. MAILROOM: Inserters and stuffers — 5-KAN/320; Bundle tyer —
MLN/ML II Et; Addressing machine — Uarco/4930. WIRE SERVICES: News — AP; Photos — AP; Syndicates — Creators, TMS, United Features; Receiving dishes — AP. BUSINESS COMPUTERS: 1-Dell; Applications: Netware; PCs & main system networked.

PASADENA
Harris County
'90 U.S. Census- 119,363; E&P '96 Est. 122,948

Pasadena Citizen
(m-tues to sat; S)
Pasadena Citizen, 102 Shaver; PO Box 6192, Pasadena, TX 77506; tel (713) 477-0221; fax (713) 477-9090. Westward Communications Inc. group.
Circulation: 7,251(m); 7,251(m-sat); 7,939(S); VAC Mar. 31, 1995.
Price: 50¢(d); 50¢(sat); 50¢(S); $7.00/mo; $72.00/yr.
Advertising: Open inch rate $11.03(m); $15.77(m-wed); $11.03(m-sat); $14.64(S).
Representative: US Suburban Press.
News Services: NEA, AP. **Politics:** Independent. **Established:** 1947.
Special Editions: Progress (Feb); Baseball, Newcomer's Guide (July); Football, Rodeo (Sept); Automotive, Drug Awareness (Oct); Christmas (Dec).
Magazine: Food.

CORPORATE OFFICER
President — Kenneth Johnson
GENERAL MANAGEMENT
Publisher — Mike Singletary
Business Manager — Gloria Boike
ADVERTISING
Director — Frank Graham
CIRCULATION
Director — Kent Carpenter
NEWS EXECUTIVE
Managing Editor — Michael Simmons
EDITOR AND MANAGER
Sports Editor — Scott Cory
MANAGEMENT INFORMATION SERVICES
Data Processing Manager — David Moran
PRODUCTION
Director — Gene Janski

Market Information: Zoned editions; Split Run; TMC.
Mechanical available: Offset; Black and 3 ROP colors; insert accepted — preprinted; page cut-offs — 22¾".
Mechanical specifications: Type page 13" x 21½"; E - 6 cols, 2", ⅛" between; A - 6 cols, 2", ⅛" between; C - 9 cols, 1⅛", ⅙" between.
Commodity consumption: Newsprint 3,400 short tons; widths 27", 30", 32"; black ink 48,000 pounds; color ink 20,000 pounds; single pages printed 30,000; average pages per issue 14(d), 24(S); single plates used 32,000.
Equipment: EDITORIAL: Front-end hardware — Ap/Mac; Front-end software — Microsoft/Word, QuarkXPress; Printers — Ap/Mac, HP/LaserJet. CLASSIFIED: Printers — HP/LaserJet. DISPLAY: Adv layout systems — Ap/Mac; Front-end hardware — Ap/Mac; Front-end software — QuarkXPress; Printers — HP/LaserJet. PRODUCTION: Typesetters — TI/Laser; Plate exposures — 2-Nu/Flip Top FT40UPNS; Plate processors — 2-Nat/A-250; Scanners — 1-Microtek/MS II; Production cameras — 1-Argyle/24, 1-Opti/30; Automatic film processors — 1-LE; Shrink lenses — 1-CK Optical/Squeeze; Digital color separation equipment — Digi-Colour/DC 4000. PRESSROOM: Line 1 — 15-G/Urbanite; Folders — 1-G. MAILROOM: Counter stackers — 1-BG/105, 1-Id; Bundle tyer — 2-MLN, 1-Stra Pack; Addressing machine — 1-C. WIRE SERVICES: News — AP; Receiving dishes — AP. BUSINESS COMPUTERS: PC; Applications: BMF; PCs & micros networked.

PECOS
Reeves County
'90 U.S. Census- 12,069; E&P '96 Est. 11,684

Pecos Enterprise
(e-mon to fri; S)
Pecos Enterprise, 324 S. Cedar St.; Box 2057, Pecos, TX 79772; tel (915) 445-5475; fax (915) 445-4321. Buckner News Alliance group.
Circulation: 2,210(e); 2,210(S); Sworn Oct. 1,

Copyright ©1996 by the Editor & Publisher Co.

1993.
Price: 35¢(d); 35¢(S); $6.00/mo; $72.00/yr.
Advertising: Open inch rate $7.84(e); $7.84(S).
News Service: AP. **Politics:** Independent. **Established:** 1887.
Not Published: New Year; Memorial Day; Independence Day; Labor Day; Thanksgiving; Christmas.
Special Editions: Youth Livestock Show, Chamber of Commerce (Jan); Progress Edition (Feb); Bridal Section, Health Fair Tab, Secretaries Week (Apr); Visitor's Guide, Graduation (May); Rodeo Edition (June); Cantaloupe Festival Tab, Back-to-School (Aug); Football Tab, Diez Y Seis Celebration, Homecoming Tab (Sept); Oil and Gas Edition, Volunteer Firemen, Women in Business (Oct); Holiday Recipes, Christmas Gift Guide (Nov); Christmas Gift Guide, Christmas Greetings (Dec).
Special Weekly Sections: Best Food Days (tues); Best Automotive Day (thur); Best Real Estate Day, Weekly Television Listings (fri).

CORPORATE OFFICERS

President Philip F Buckner
Vice Pres David Martens

GENERAL MANAGEMENT

Publisher Mac B McKinnon
Business Manager Ruth Wells

ADVERTISING

Director Christina Bitolas

CIRCULATION

Manager Jerry Palmer

NEWS EXECUTIVE

Managing Editor Jon Fulbright

EDITORS AND MANAGERS

Editorial Page Editor Mac B McKinnon
Education Editor Peggy McCracken
Food Editor Rosie Flores
Lifestyle Editor Rosie Flores
Political Editor Mac B McKinnon
Sports Editor Jon Fulbright

PRODUCTION

Foreman-Pressroom Carlos Nichols Jr

Market Information: TMC.
Mechanical available: Offset; Black and 3 ROP colors; insert accepted — preprinted; page cut-offs — 22¾".
Mechanical specifications: Type page 13" x 21½"; E - 6 cols, 2 1/16", 1/8" between; A - 6 cols, 2 1/16", 1/8" between; C - 6 cols, 2 1/16", 1/8" between.
Commodity consumption: Newsprint 130 short tons; widths 27½", 13¾"; black ink 5,000 pounds; color ink 250 pounds; single pages printed 3,318; average pages per issue 10(d); single plates used 5,000.
Equipment: EDITORIAL: Front-end hardware — CText. CLASSIFIED: Front-end hardware — CText. DISPLAY: Adv layout systems — CText. PRODUCTION: Plate exposures — Nu; Production cameras — 1-K.
PRESSROOM: Line 1 — 4-G/Community. MAILROOM: Bundle tyer — 1-Ace/Kiko; Addressing machine — RSK/TRS-80. WIRE SERVICES: News — AP; Syndicates — United Media, King Features, CNS, Universal Press, LAT-WP; Receiving dishes — AP. BUSINESS COMPUTERS: TRS/80; Applications: Circ.

PLAINVIEW

Hale County

'90 U.S. Census- 21,700; E&P '96 Est. 21,456

Plainview Daily Herald

(e-mon to fri; S)

Plainview Daily Herald, 820 Broadway; PO Box 1240, Plainview, TX 79072-1240; tel (806) 296-1300; fax (806) 296-1315; e-mail lonestarbbs.com. Hearst Newspapers group.
Circulation: 7,213(e); 7,213(S); Sworn Sept. 29, 1995.
Price: 50¢(d); $1.25(S); $8.25/mo; $99.00/yr.
Advertising: Open inch rate $11.21(e); $11.21(S). **Representative:** Papert Companies.
News Service: AP. **Politics:** Independent. **Established:** 1889.
Not Published: Christmas.
Advertising not accepted: Liquor.
Special Editions: Stock Show, Honor Roll (Mar); Back-to-School, Football (Aug); Wedding; Home Improvement; Christmas; Auto; Year Book; Clubs.
Special Weekly Sections: Business & Industrial Review (mon); Best Food Day (tues); Agriculture (wed); Church (fri); TV, Business, Agriculture (S).
Magazines: USA Weekend, Comics (S); TV Guide Tab.

CORPORATE OFFICER

Vice Pres Robert J Danzig

GENERAL MANAGEMENT

Publisher Rollie Hyde

ADVERTISING

Director-Retail Jeff Noble

CIRCULATION

Director Frank Silvas

NEWS EXECUTIVE

Editor Danny Andrews

EDITORS AND MANAGERS

Editorial Page Editor Danny Andrews
Lifestyle Editor Nicki Logan
News Editor/Wire Editor Doug McDonough
Sports Editor Kevin Lewis

MANAGEMENT INFORMATION SERVICES

Online Manager Gordon Zeiglex

PRODUCTION

Manager Ben Thompson
Asst Manager Bill Rushing
Foreman-Pressroom Bill Rushing

Market Information: TMC; Operate database; Electronic edition.
Mechanical available: Offset; Black and 3 ROP colors; insert accepted — preprinted; page cut-offs — 22¾".
Mechanical specifications: Type page 13" x 21½"; E - 6 cols, 2 1/16", 1/8" between; A - 6 cols, 2 1/16", 1/8" between; C - 8 cols, 1½", 1/8" between.
Commodity consumption: Newsprint 599 short tons; width 27½"; single pages printed 4,516; average pages per issue 11(d), 34(S).
Equipment: EDITORIAL: Front-end hardware — Mk, Ap/Mac; Front-end software — Mk, FSI. CLASSIFIED: Front-end hardware — Mk, Ap/Mac; Front-end software — Mk, FSI. DISPLAY: Adv layout systems — FSI; Front-end hardware — Ap/Mac; Front-end software — Aldus/PageMaker, QuarkXPress, Multi-Ad/Creator; Printers — 1-Ap/Mac LaserPrinter, 1-HP/DeskWriter. PRODUCTION: Pagination software — FSI; Typesetters — Ap/Mac Laser, 1-Ap/Mac NTX, Hyphen/94E; Plate exposures — 2-Nu; Plate processors — 1-Nat/A250; Scanners — Abaton/Scan 300 S, Umax, Microtek, Lf/Leafscan; Production cameras — 1-LE/500; Automatic film processors — 1-LE/TEK26; Shrink lenses — 1-CK Optical.
PRESSROOM: Line 1 — 7-HI/V15A; Folders — 1-HI. MAILROOM: Inserters and stuffers — 1-KAN/48 Inserter; Bundle tyer — Md/1862. WIRE SERVICES: News — AP; Receiving dishes — size-12ft, AP. BUSINESS COMPUTERS: 3-HP, 2-IBM, 2-Hyundai; Applications: CJ; PCs & main system networked.

PLANO

Collin County

'90 U.S. Census- 128,713; E&P '96 Est. 171,000
ABC-CZ (90): 117,572 (HH 40,605)

Plano Star Courier

(m-wed to sat; S)

Plano Star Courier, 801 E. Plano Pkwy. (75074); PO Box 860248, Plano, TX 75086-0248; tel (214) 424-6565; fax (214) 881-9495. Harte-Hanks Communications Inc. group.
Circulation: 12,296(m); 12,296(m-sat); 13,914(S); ABC Sept. 30, 1995.
Price: 25¢(d); 25¢(sat); $1.00(S); $7.00/mo; $84.00/yr.
Advertising: Open inch rate $11.76(m); $14.11(m-wed); $11.76(m-sat); $12.94(S). **Representatives:** US Suburban Press; Papert Companies.
News Service: AP. **Politics:** Independent. **Established:** 1888.
Advertising not accepted: Pornography; Topless bars.
Special Weekly Sections: Plano, Housing (fri); Viewing (S).
Magazine: USA Weekend.

CORPORATE OFFICER

President Lynn Dickerson

ADVERTISING

Director-Marketing Beth Roddy

MARKETING AND PROMOTION

Director-Marketing Leslie Mascari

CIRCULATION

Director Linda Frank

NEWS EXECUTIVE

Editor Tim Watterson

EDITORS AND MANAGERS

Business/Finance Editor Steve O'Brian
City/Metro Editor David May
Editorial Page Editor Tim Watterson

Texas I-405

Education Editor Cindy Ingram
Graphics Editor/Art Director Dollie Turpin
News Editor Tim Watterson
Photo Editor Doug Layton
Sports Editor Kevin Farr

MANAGEMENT INFORMATION SERVICES

Data Processing Manager Larry McWilliams

PRODUCTION

Director Bill Baldwin
Manager-Data Processing Bill Lindemenn

Market Information: TMC.
Mechanical available: Offset; Black and 3 ROP colors; insert accepted — preprinted, prepacked; page cut-offs — 22½".
Mechanical specifications: Type page 13.5" x 21"; E - 6 cols, 2 1/16", 1/8" between; A - 6 cols, 2 1/16", 1/8" between; C - 6 cols, 2 1/16", 1/8" between.
Commodity consumption: Newsprint 2,253 short tons; widths 27", 13½"; black ink 45,000 pounds; color ink 9,000 pounds; single pages printed 13,200; average pages per issue 32(d), 56(S); single plates used 80,000.
Equipment: EDITORIAL: Front-end hardware — Mk/4000; Front-end software — Mk; Printers — 3-Linotype-Hell/Linotronic 202; Other equipment — 1-Ap/Mac IIci. CLASSIFIED: Front-end hardware — Mk; Front-end software — Mk; Printers — Linotype-Hell/Linotronic 202; Other equipment — 1-Ap/Mac IIci. DISPLAY: Adv layout systems — CJ; Front-end hardware — HP/3000 series 58; Front-end software — CJ; Printers — HP/2566, 3-HP/2563, 1-HP/2564, 1-Dataproducts/B1000. PRODUCTION: Typesetters — 3-Linotype-Hell/Linotronic 202; Plate exposures — 1-Nu; Plate processors — 1-Nat; Automatic film processors — AG; Color separation equipment (conventional) — Prentice.
PRESSROOM: Line 1 — 5-G/Urbanite w/1-3 Color unit. MAILROOM: Counter stackers — HL; Inserters and stuffers — KAN; Bundle tyer — Miller-Bevco. WIRE SERVICES: News — AP, Southwest Newswire. BUSINESS COMPUTERS: 2-HP/Vectra; Applications: CJ/AIM: Layout, Class, Circ; IDEAS: Gen ledger, Fixed assets; PCs & micros networked; PCs & main system networked.

PORT ARTHUR

Jefferson County

'90 U.S. Census- 58,724; E&P '96 Est. 57,470

Port Arthur News

(m-mon to sat; S)

Port Arthur News, 549 4th St.; PO Box 789, Port Arthur, TX 77640; tel (409) 985-5541; fax (409) 983-7135. Hollinger International Inc. group.
Circulation: 21,374(m); 21,374(m-sat); 21,374(S); Sworn Sept. 26, 1995.
Price: 50¢(d); 50¢(sat); $1.00(S); $8.00/mo (carrier); $96.00/yr.
Advertising: Open inch rate $22.46(m); $22.46(m-sat); $22.46(S). **Representative:** Papert Companies.
News Service: AP. **Politics:** Independent. **Established:** 1897.
Special Editions: Family-owned Business (Jan); Visitor's Guide (May); Cav-oil-cade (Oct).
Special Weekly Section: Life & TV Guide.
Magazines: Parade, TV Channels (S).

CORPORATE OFFICER

President Larry J Perrotto

GENERAL MANAGEMENT

Publisher Ken Cope

ADVERTISING

Director Horace Fontenot Jr
Manager-Classified Ed Kestler

CIRCULATION

Corporate Director/Manager Ken Davis

NEWS EXECUTIVE

Editor Roger Cowles

EDITORS AND MANAGERS

Books Editor Darragh Castillo
City Editor Susan Walker
Columnist Bob West
Editorial Writer Roger Cowles
Education Editor Maxsane Mitchell
Features Editor Susan Flowers
Films/Theater Editor Darragh Castillo
Fashion/Food Editor Susan Walker
Librarian Voletta Collins
Music Editor Darragh Castillo
Political Editor Susan Walker
Radio/Television Editor Darragh Castillo
Sports Editor Bob West
Teen-Age/Youth Editor Susan Flowers
Wire Editor Diana Gonzales
Women's Editor Susan Flowers

PRODUCTION

Manager-Commercial Printing Eddie Blakeley
Manager-Layout/Design/Commercial Printing/Composing David Lowe
Manager-Pressroom Eddie Blakeley

Mechanical available: Offset; Black and 3 ROP colors; insert accepted — preprinted, news color; page cut-offs — 22¾".
Mechanical specifications: Type page 13" x 21½"; E - 6 cols, 2 1/16", 1/8" between; A - 6 cols, 2 1/16", 1/8" between; C - 9 cols, 1 3/8", 1/16" between.
Commodity consumption: Newsprint 3,100 short tons; widths 27", 13½"; black ink 60,200 pounds; color ink 45,570 pounds; single pages printed 9,767; average pages per issue 22(d), 48(S); single plates used 27,160.
Equipment: EDITORIAL: Front-end hardware — Ap/Mac, 1-Ap/Mac PC; Front-end software — Baseview; Printers — 1-Ap/Mac LaserPrinter, Image Setters/1016 Resolution. CLASSIFIED: Front-end hardware — Ap/Mac; Front-end software — Baseview; Printers — Ap/Mac LaserWriter. DISPLAY: Adv layout systems — 4-Ap/Mac ci, 3-Ap/Mac fx color monitor; Front-end hardware — Ap/Mac; Front-end software — Multi-Ad; Printers — Image Setters. PRODUCTION: Pagination software — QuarkXPress; Typesetters — V/4000 image setters; Plate exposures — 1-Nu/Flip Top F140, 1-Nu/Flip Top FT40V4UPNS, 2-Douthitt; Plate processors — 1-Nat/A-250; Electronic picture desk — Lf/AP Leaf Picture Desk; Scanners — Microteks; Production cameras — 1-C/Spartan II, 1-C/Spartan III; Automatic film processors — 2-RT/26; Shrink lenses — 2-CK Optical; Color separation equipment (conventional) — Digi-Colour, Nikon, Ap/Mac, Adobe/Photoshop flatbed.
PRESSROOM: Line 1 — 4-G/Urbanite (w/3-color unit); Line 2 — 4-G/Urbanite (w/balloon former); Folders — 2-G/2:1; Pasters — 5-QWI/Web Paster. MAILROOM: Counter stackers — 1-RKW, 2-BG; Inserters and stuffers — 2-MM/227; Bundle tyer — 2-MLN/ML2EE; Addressing machine — 1-KR, 1-CH. COMMUNICATIONS: Facsimile — QWI, Canon/Fax 230, Panafax/UF-130. WIRE SERVICES: News — AP; Stock tables — AP; Receiving dishes — size-10ft, AP. BUSINESS COMPUTERS: IBM/Sys 36; Applications: Accts receivable, Adv, Circ, TMC; PCs & main system networked.

ROSENBERG

Fort Bend County

'90 U.S. Census- 20,183; E&P '96 Est. 21,377

The Herald-Coaster

(e-mon to fri; S)

The Herald-Coaster, 1902 S. Fourth St.; PO Box 1088, Rosenberg, TX 77471; tel (713) 232-3737; fax (713) 342-3219. Hartman Newspapers Inc. group.
Circulation: 8,093(e); 7,612(S); VAC June 30, 1995.
Price: 50¢(d); 50¢(S); $7.00/mo; $72.00/yr (home delivery).
Advertising: Open inch rate $9.60(e); $9.60(S). **Representative:** US Suburban Press.
News Service: AP. **Politics:** Independent. **Established:** 1892.
Not Published: Christmas.
Special Editions: Progress; Bride; Homemakers' School; Chamber of Commerce; New Car; Home Improvement; Lawn & Garden; Czech Fest; Outdoor; Graduation; Clean Up; Fix Up; Harvest.

CORPORATE OFFICERS

President Bill Hartman
Vice Pres Clyde C King Jr

GENERAL MANAGEMENT

Editor/Publisher Clyde C King Jr

ADVERTISING

Director-Retail/Classified Jim Mosen

CIRCULATION

Manager Betty Hartfiel

NEWS EXECUTIVES

Editor Clyde C King Jr
Managing Editor Bob Haenel

EDITORS AND MANAGERS

City Editor Richard Zagrzecki
Fashion/Style Editor Betty Humphrey
Living/Lifestyle Editor Betty Humphrey
News Editor Bob Haenel
Religion Editor Denise Adams
Sports Editor Dave Mundy
Travel Editor Betty Humphrey
Women's Editor Betty Humphrey

PRODUCTION

Manager Peggy Scholl

Market Information: TMC.
Mechanical available: Offset; Black and 3 ROP colors; insert accepted — preprinted; page cut-offs — 22¾".
Mechanical specifications: Type page 13" x 21"; E - 6 cols, 2", ⅛" between; A - 6 cols, 2", ⅛" between; C - 9 cols, 1.17", $\frac{1}{12}$" between.
Commodity consumption: Newsprint 1,100 short tons; width 27½"; average pages per issue 16(d), 22(S).
Equipment: EDITORIAL: Front-end hardware — Ap/Mac; Front-end software — Baseview; Printers — ECR/Scriptsetter; Other equipment — HP/Flatbed Scanner, Radius/100 Photo Station, Polaroid/Film Scanner. CLASSIFIED: Front-end hardware — Ap/Mac LC; Front-end software — Baseview; Printers — QMS/860. DISPLAY: Front-end hardware — 4-Ap/Mac Quadra 650; Front-end software — QuarkXPress; Printers — QMS/860; Other equipment — HP/Scanner. PRODUCTION: Pagination software — QuarkXPress 3.31; OCR software — Caere/OmniPage Pro 5.0; Typesetters — HP/LaserJet 4MV, ECR/Scriptsetter; Plate exposures — Nu/Flip Top FT40U6UP; Plate processors — Nat/A-250; Electronic picture desk — Radius/100, Polaroid/Film Scanner; Scanners — HP; Production cameras — Konica, C; Automatic film processors — P/26HL; Shrink lenses — CK Optical.
PRESSROOM: Line 1 — WPC/Leader-Atlas; Line 2 — WPC/Leader-Atlas. MAILROOM: Counter stackers — KAN; Inserters and stuffers — KAN/320; Bundle tyer — Wilton/Stra Pack SS-80. COMMUNICATIONS: Digital ad delivery system — AP AdSend. WIRE SERVICES: News — AP; Receiving dishes — AP. BUSINESS COMPUTERS: IBM/AS-4000; PCs & micros networked; PCs & main system networked.

SAN ANGELO

Tom Green County

'90 U.S. Census- 84,474; **E&P '96 Est.** 90,711
ABC-CZ (90): 84,474 (HH 30,661)

Standard-Times

(m-mon to sat; S)

Standard-Times, 34 W. Harris (76903); PO Box 5111, San Angelo, TX 76902; tel (915) 653-1221; fax (915) 658-6752. Harte-Hanks Communications Inc. group.
Circulation: 32,659(m); 32,659(m-sat); 39,367(S); ABC Sept. 30, 1995.
Price: 50¢(d); 50¢(sat); $1.50(S); $12.00/mo; $144.00/yr.
Advertising: Open inch rate $25.30(m); $25.30(m-sat); $27.30(S). **Representative:** Papert Companies.
News Services: AP, SHNS, Harte-Hanks. **Politics:** Independent. **Established:** 1884.
Special Editions: Oil & Agriculture; Progress; Football; Auto Show; Car Care; Design-an-Ad; Fiesta del Concho; Stock Show & Rodeo; Hunting & Fishing; Bridal; Mature Lifestyles; Fashion; Newcomer's Guide; Back-to-School; Christmas Gift Guide; Locally-owned Business; Wool, Mohair and Cotton; Graduation; Homes.
Special Weekly Sections: Best Food Day (wed); Entertainment (fri); TV Book (S).
Magazines: Scene (local news weekly, zoned locally, broadsheet); TV Book (TV & entertainment guide, full circulation tab).

CORPORATE OFFICER

Vice Pres Kevin J Barry

GENERAL MANAGEMENT

Publisher/President Kevin J Barry
Director-Finance Jim Neary

ADVERTISING

Director Cheryl Ebright
Manager-Retail Richard Guerrero
Supervisor-Inside Sales Rita Carranco
Supervisor-Outside Sales/Classified Laura Sosa

MARKETING AND PROMOTION

Coordinator-Marketing Sheridan Mallory

TELECOMMUNICATIONS

Audiotex Manager Jack Gober

CIRCULATION

Manager Joe Solley

NEWS EXECUTIVE

Editor Dennis Ellsworth

EDITORS AND MANAGERS

Agriculture/Farm Editor Royce Jones
Amusements/Books Editor Diane Murray
Business/Finance Writer Todd Martin
Columnist Rick Smith
Editorial Page Editor Jack Cowan
Education Writer Ron Durham
Features Editor Diane Murray
Films/Theater Editor Diane Murray
Food Editor Joyce Piland
Health/Medicine Editor Jenny Strasburg
Librarian Edna Sedeno
Oil Editor Jane Stracener
Photo Department Manager Rick Choate
Religion Editor Diane Murray
Society/Women's Editor Diane Murray
Sports Editor Mike Lee
Teen-Age/Youth Editor Diane Murray

MANAGEMENT INFORMATION SERVICES

Data Processing Manager Joe Semanski

PRODUCTION

Manager-Pre Press Sheila Yoder
Superintendent-Pressroom Neal Chavez
Superintendent-Engraving Neal Chavez
Superintendent-Mailroom David Russell
Superintendent-Data Processing Joe Semanski

Market Information: Zoned editions; Split Run; TMC; Operate audiotex.
Mechanical available: Offset; Black and 3 ROP colors; insert accepted — preprinted; page cut-offs — 22¼".
Mechanical specifications: Type page 13" x 21½"; E - 6 cols, 2$\frac{1}{16}$", ⅛" between; A - 6 cols, 2$\frac{1}{16}$", ⅛" between; C - 9 cols, 1$\frac{5}{16}$", $\frac{1}{16}$" between.
Commodity consumption: Newsprint 2,400 short tons; widths 54", 40½", 27", 13½"; black ink 51,000 pounds; color ink 15,000 pounds; single pages printed 14,986; average pages per issue 28(d), 52(S); single plates used 42,900.
Equipment: EDITORIAL: Front-end hardware — Austin; Front-end software — III 2.39; Printers — 1-Panasonic/KX-P2411I; Other equipment — Ap/Power Mac 8100-80, Ap/Power Mac 6100. CLASSIFIED: Front-end hardware — Austin; Front-end software — III 2.39; Printers — 1-Okidata/2410, 1-Panasonic/KX-P2411I. AUDIOTEX: Hardware — Brite; Software — Brite 1.01; Supplier name — Brite. DISPLAY: Adv layout systems — Ap/Mac; Front-end hardware — 4-Ap/Mac 840AV, 1-Ap/Power Mac 8100, 3-Ap/Mac IIfx, CNI/860 File Server; Front-end software — Multi-Ad/Creator 3.7, Adobe/Photoshop 3.01, Adobe/Illustrator 5.5; Printers — Dataproducts/LZR1560, Ap/Mac LaserWriter II NTX, GCC Technology, HP/DeskJet 1200 c-ps; Other equipment — Nikon/Coolscan XP, Nikon/ScanTouch, HP/ScanJet IIc, CD-Rom, NEC, Pioneer, MicroNet/Techoptical, HP/ScanJet IIcx, SyQuest/200 MB. PRODUCTION: Pagination software — QuarkXPress 3.3; Typesetters — 2-COM/8600, Tegra/5400, Panther/Pro 46; Plate exposures — Nu/Flip Top FT40LNS, Nu/Flip Top FT40APRNS; Plate processors — Nat/A-250; Electronic picture desk — Lf/AP Leaf Picture Desk; Scanners — Kk/2035, AG/Arcus Flatbed, Nikon/Coolscan; Production cameras — C/Spartan II, 3M/Pyrofax Imager; Automatic film processors — AG/Litex 26, LE/LD 24 AR, Konica/K-550; Shrink lenses — Alan/Anamorphic 24"; Color separation equipment (conventional) — SCREEN, Digi-Colour.
PRESSROOM: Line 1 — 7-G/Cosmo double width; Press drives — Fin; Folders — 2-G; Pasters — 6-RIP, 2-Arm; Press control system — Fin. MAILROOM: Counter stackers — 3-KAN; Inserters and stuffers — 2-KAN/480; Bundle tyer — 5-MLN; Addressing machine — KR; Other mailroom equipment — MM/Minuteman Saddle Stitcher. LIBRARY: Electronic — III/TECS 2 Archiving System, MPS/TECS-2 Archiving System. COMMUNICATIONS: Digital ad delivery system — AP AdSend. WIRE SERVICES: News — AP; Photos — AP; Stock tables — AP SelectStox; Receiving dishes — size-3m, AP. BUSINESS COMPUTERS: HP/3000-927 LX; Applications: Cogent: Gen ledger, Fixed assets, Human resources; PCs & micros networked.

SAN ANTONIO

Bexar County

'90 U.S. Census- 935,933; **E&P '96 Est.** 1,038,635
ABC-NDM (90): 1,407,745 (HH 487,073)

San Antonio Express-News

(m-mon to thur; m-fri; m-sat; S)

San Antonio Express-News, Ave. E & 3rd St.; PO Box 2171, San Antonio, TX 78205; tel (210) 225-7411; fax (210) 225-8351. Hearst Newspapers group.
Circulation: 221,556(m); 285,852(m-fri); 284,151(m-sat); 389,638(S); ABC Sept. 30, 1995.
Price: 50¢(d); 50¢(fri); 50¢(sat); $1.25(S); $9.75/mo; $117.00/yr (carrier), $170.00/yr (mail).
Advertising: Open inch rate $167.62(m); $167.62(m-fri); $167.62(m-sat); $196.64(S). **Representative:** Sawyer-Ferguson-Walker Co.
News Services: AP, NYT, LAT-WP, SHNS. **Politics:** Independent. **Established:** 1865.
Note: Effective Apr. 28, 1993, this publication changed its publishing plan from (all day-mon to thur; all day-fri; m-sat; S) to (m-mon to thur; m-fri; m-sat; S).
Special Editions: Wedding (Jan); Livestock Show (Feb); Spring Garden (Mar); Retirement Living (Apr); Kid's Summertime Guide (May); Wedding (June); Guide to San Antonio (Aug); Fashion (Sept); Fall Garden (Oct); Auto, Retirement Living (Nov); Travel (monthly).
Special Weekly Sections: Stock Listings (tues); Food Section (wed); Stock Listings (thur); Stock Listings, Weekender, Drive (fri); Stock Listings, Drive, Designs for Better Living (sat); Travel/Leisure Section, Lively Arts, Designs for Better Living (S).
Magazines: Weekender (fri); San Antonio Star, Vista, TV Now, Images Magazine (S); Daily Star Magazine (daily); Fiesta Magazine (monthly).

CORPORATE OFFICERS

President/CEO W Lawrence Walker Jr
Vice Pres-Finance Fred Mergele
Vice Pres-Advertising/Marketing Edward K Prisco

GENERAL MANAGEMENT

Publisher W Lawrence Walker Jr
Controller Steve Jones
Vice Pres-Operations Louis J Franconeri
Vice Pres-Corporate Relations Veronica Salazar
Vice Pres-Human Resources Susan Ehrman
Purchasing Agent Wiley Galloway

ADVERTISING

Manager-Marketing Sylvia Chavez-Sitters
Manager-Retail Rosa Carnot
Manager-Classified Charlotte Aaron
Asst Manager-National Bruce Ford

MARKETING AND PROMOTION

Vice Pres-Marketing Edward K Prisco

CIRCULATION

Vice Pres-Distribution Vince Fusco
Manager-Operations Joe Ramon
Manager-Promotion George Ramos
Asst Manager-Operations Ralph Gauna

NEWS EXECUTIVES

Exec Editor/Vice Pres-News Jim Moss
Managing Editor Bob Rivard
Asst Managing Editor Terry Scott-Bertling
Asst Managing Editor Raul Reyes

EDITORS AND MANAGERS

Amusements Editor Kristina Paledes
Arts Editor Kristina Paledes
Austin Bureau Chief Laura Tolley
Books Editor Judyth Rigler
Business Editor Paul Hill
Business Writer Charlotte-Anne Lucas
Cartoonist John Branch
Cartoonist Leo Garza
City Editor Craig Thomason
Columnist Roddy Stinson
Columnist David Hendricks
Editorial Director Lynnell Burkett
Editorial Writer Veronica Flores
Entertainment Kristina Paledes
Fashion Editor Rose Mary Budge
Films/Theater Editor Bob Polunsky
Food Editor Karen Haram
Images Editor Beverly Purcell-Guerra
Info Services Editor Kathy Foley
Librarian Judith Zipp
Lifestyle Editor Marsha Harlow
Medical Writer Don Finley
Metro Editor-Day Kym Fox
News Editor Claude Simpson
Director of Photography Fred Wilson
Political Editor Bruce Davidson
Radio/Television Editor Jeanne Jakle
Religion Writer J Michael Parker
Sports Editor Barry Robinson
Sunday Editor Roger Downing
Travel Editor Julie Cooper
Weekender Editor Kristina Paledes

PRODUCTION

Vice Pres-Operations Louis J Franconeri
Manager-Facilities Paul Allison
Asst Manager David O'Neill
Superintendent-Composing Lee Roy Lawrence
Superintendent-Engraving Wayne Barker
Superintendent-Pressroom/Asst Manager Matthew Oliver
Foreman-Composing Pete Bode
Foreman-Composing Johnny Hohnstein

Market Information: Zoned editions; Split Run; TMC; ADS; Operate audiotex.
Mechanical available: Offset; Black and 3 ROP colors; insert accepted — preprinted; page cut-offs — 22".
Mechanical specifications: Type page 13" x 21"; E - 6 cols, 2$\frac{1}{16}$", ⅛" between; A - 6 cols, 2$\frac{1}{16}$", ⅛" between; C - 10 cols, 1$\frac{5}{16}$", $\frac{1}{16}$" between.
Commodity consumption: Newsprint 61,500 metric tons; widths 54", 40½", 27"; black ink 1,817,324 pounds; color ink 452,968 pounds; single pages printed 34,805; average pages per issue 80(d), 109(sat), 160(S); single plates used 163,000.
Equipment: EDITORIAL: Front-end hardware — USSI, 150-DC Terminals; Front-end software — USSI; Other equipment — HI/1100. CLASSIFIED: Front-end hardware — SII; Other equipment — 100-PC/Terminals. AUDIOTEX: Hardware — Brite. DISPLAY: Adv layout systems — SCS/Layout 8000; Front-end hardware — HI, Ap/Macs. PRODUCTION: Pagination software — HI; Typesetters — 2-MON/Express-Master 3850, 2-MON/Lasercomp Express; Platemaking systems — 2-WL; Plate exposures — 2-WL/Expose 10; Plate processors — 2-WL/Lithotech 38G; Electronic picture desk — Lf/AP Leaf Picture Desk; Scanners — 3-ECR/Autokon 1000; Production cameras — 2-Newspagers, 1-C/Spartan III, 1-Nu/SSI 1418, SCREEN/670c; Automatic film processors — 4-LE/24-AQ, 1-DP, LE/24 AQ, 3-Fuji/Rapid Access; Film transporters — 2-C; Shrink lenses — 1-Alan/Variable; Color separation equipment (conventional) — 1-Ca/PX51, 1-Hel/300L, 1-CD/635.
PRESSROOM: Line 1 — 3-G/Colorline (8 units); Press drives — Allen Bradley/1395 Drives; Folders — 4-G, 2-G/Sovereign 3:2 Single, 1-G/Sovereign 3:2 Double; Pasters — 10-G/CT50; Reels and stands — G/CT50; Press control system — G/APCS; Press registration system — G/APCS. MAILROOM: Counter stackers — 9-QWI/300, 4-QWI/SJ201A, 3-HS/257, 1-HS/1251, 1-HT, 3-Durant; Inserters and stuffers — 3-HI/72P, 1-HI/48P, 1-SLS/1000; Bundle tyer — 9-MLN/MLN2, 8-Power Strap. LIBRARY: Electronic — USSI/BS. COMMUNICATIONS: Facsimile — X/410 (classified adv), LD. WIRE SERVICES: News — AP; Stock tables — AP; Syndicates — AP; Receiving dishes — AP. BUSINESS COMPUTERS: 1-B/4955, 1-V/340, Bs, IBM/ES9000-150; Applications: Circ, Adv billing, Accts receivable, Gen ledger, Payroll, Accts payable, Depreciation; PCs & micros networked; PCs & main system networked.

SAN MARCOS

Hays County

'90 U.S. Census- 28,743; **E&P '96 Est.** 31,818

San Marcos Daily Record

(e-tues to fri; S)

San Marcos Daily Record, 1910 I.H. 35 S. (78666); PO Box 1109, San Marcos, TX 78667; tel (512) 392-2458; fax (512) 392-1514. Hollinger International Inc. group.
Circulation: 6,325(e); 6,325(S); Sworn July 25, 1994.
Price: 25¢(d); 75¢(S); $5.00/mo; $57.00/yr (in town), $90.00/yr (outside town).
Advertising: Open inch rate $9.55(e); $9.55(S).
News Service: AP. **Politics:** Independent. **Established:** 1912.
Special Editions: Progress (Feb); Back-to-School (Aug); Annual Salute to SW Texas State Univ. in San Marcos.
Special Weekly Sections: Food Page (wed); Entertainment Page (thur); TV Magazine (S).

GENERAL MANAGEMENT

Publisher Guy Trimble

Texas I-407

ADVERTISING
Director Janice Eaton
CIRCULATION
Manager Janie York
NEWS EXECUTIVE
Managing Editor Rowe Ray
EDITORS AND MANAGERS
Action/Hot Line Editor Rowe Ray
Editorial Page Editor Rowe Ray
Sports Editor Jimmy Stevenson
Women's Editor Diana Finnley
PRODUCTION
Manager Karen Ray
Foreman-Pressroom Clarence Johnson

Market Information: TMC.
Mechanical available: Offset; Black and 3 ROP colors; insert accepted — preprinted; page cutoffs — 22¾".
Mechanical specifications: Type page 13" x 21½"; E - 6 cols, 2 1/16", ⅛" between; A - 6 cols, 2 1/16", ⅛" between; C - 9 cols, 1⅜", 1/16" between.
Commodity consumption: average pages per issue 24(d), 56(S).
Equipment: EDITORIAL: Front-end hardware — EKI/Televideo. PRODUCTION: Typesetters — 1-COM/4961, 1-COM/2961, 1-COM/Unisetter; Plate exposures — 1-Nu/Flip Top; Scanners — EKI/Televideo; Production cameras — 1-C/J75CC.
PRESSROOM: Line 1 — 7-G/Community; Folders — 1-G. MAILROOM: Bundle tyer — 1-Bu; Addressing machine — 1-El. WIRE SERVICES: News — UPI. BUSINESS COMPUTERS: DPT/1100, IBM; Applications: Payroll, Accts receivable, Accts payable, Gen ledger.

SEGUIN
Guadalupe County
'90 U.S. Census- 18,853; E&P '96 Est. 19,378

The Seguin Gazette-Enterprise (e-tues to fri; S)

The Seguin Gazette-Enterprise, 1012 Schriewer Rd. (78155); PO Box 1200, Seguin, TX 78156-1200; tel (210) 379-5402; fax (210) 379-8328. Southern Newspapers Inc. group.
Circulation: 5,554(e); 5,554(S); Sworn Sept. 30, 1995.
Price: 50¢(d); $1.00(S); $55.00/yr.
Advertising: Open inch rate $10.40(e); $10.40(S). **Representative:** Papert Companies.
News Service: AP. **Politics:** Independent. **Established:** 1888.
Special Weekly Sections: Best Food Day (tues); Weddings, Engagements, Business (wed); Entertainment (thur); Church Page (fri); Weddings, Engagements, Business (S); TV Listings (daily).
Magazine: Weekly TV Guide/Comics.

GENERAL MANAGEMENT
Publisher Larry Reynolds
Business Manager Maggie Clarkson
ADVERTISING
Director Debbie Banta-Scott
CIRCULATION
Director Randy Fischer
NEWS EXECUTIVE
Managing Editor Kathie Ninneman
EDITORS AND MANAGERS
News Editor Jill Dickinson-Rader
Photo Editor Steve Boehm
Sports Editor Barry Halvorson
PRODUCTION
Superintendent Doug Plummer

Market Information: Zoned editions; TMC.
Mechanical available: Offset; Black and 3 ROP colors; insert accepted — preprinted; page cutoffs — 21".
Mechanical specifications: Type page 13" x 21"; E - 6 cols, 2 1/16", ⅛" between; A - 6 cols, 2 1/16", ⅛" between; C - 9 cols, 1⅜", 1/16" between.
Commodity consumption: Newsprint 250 short tons; widths 27½", 13¾", 22½"; black ink 8,500 pounds; color ink 1,500 pounds; single pages printed 4,400; average pages per issue 14(d), 24(S); single plates used 3,600.
Equipment: EDITORIAL: Front-end hardware — 6-Ap/Mac Quadra 610,650; Front-end software — Ap/Mac System 7.1, QuarkXPress 3.3, Baseview/NewsEdit; Printers — 1-Ap/Mac LaserWriter Pro 810, 1-Ap/Mac II NTX. CLASSIFIED: Front-end hardware — 3-Ap/Mac Quadra 610; Front-end software — QuarkXPress 3.3, Baseview; Printers — 1-Ap/Mac LaserWriter Pro 810, 1-Ap/Mac II NTX. DISPLAY: Adv layout systems — 3-Ap/Mac, Ap/Power Mac 6100, 2-Ap/Mac Quadra; Front-end hardware — 3-Ap/Mac, Ap/Power Mac 6100, 2-Ap/Mac Quadra; Front-end software — Ap/Mac System 7.5, QuarkXPress 3.3, Aldus/PageMaker, Baseview/NewsEdit; Printers — Ap/Mac LaserWriter 810, 1-Ap/Mac II NTX. PRODUCTION: Pagination software — QuarkXPress 3.3; OCR software — Caere/OmniPage; Plate processors — 1-lc; Production cameras — Acti/125.
PRESSROOM: Line 1 — 7-G/Suburban. MAILROOM: Counter stackers — 1-BG/Count-O-Veyor; Inserters and stuffers — 1-KAN/320; Addressing machine — 1-AM. WIRE SERVICES: News — AP. BUSINESS COMPUTERS: 3-IBM.

SHERMAN
Grayson County
'90 U.S. Census- 31,601; E&P '96 Est. 32,219
ABC-CZ (90): 31,601 (HH 12,454)

Sherman Democrat (m-mon to fri; S)

Sherman Democrat, 603 S. Sam Rayburn Expwy., Sherman, TX 75090; tel (903) 893-8181; fax (903) 868-1930. Donrey Media group.
Circulation: 17,569(m); 20,127(S); ABC Sept. 30, 1995.
Price: 25¢(d); 75¢(S); $6.00/mo.
Advertising: Open inch rate $14.50(m); $14.50(S). **Representative:** Papert Companies.
News Service: AP. **Politics:** Independent. **Established:** 1879.
Special Editions: Chamber of Commerce Industrial Review, Spring Garden, Car Care (Mar); Home Improvement, Car Care (Apr); Outdoor, Brides, Car Care, Home Improvement (May); Car Care, Home Improvement (June, July, Aug); Football, Car Care, Home Improvement (Sept); Car Care (Oct); Christmas Gift Guide (Nov); Christmas Greetings (Dec).
Special Weekly Sections: Best Food Day (wed); Church (fri); Business News (S).
Magazines: TV Magazine; Parade; Color Comics (S).

CORPORATE OFFICERS
President/Chief Operating Officer Emmett Jones
Exec Vice Pres/Chief Financial Officer Darrell W Loftin
Vice Pres-Western Newspaper Group David A Osborn
Vice Pres-Eastern Newspaper Group Don Schneider
GENERAL MANAGEMENT
Publisher John P Wright III
Manager-Credit Ann Miller
Purchasing Agent John P Wright III
ADVERTISING
Director James Tracy
Manager-Classified Ken Langford
CIRCULATION
Manager Sam Fowler
NEWS EXECUTIVE
Editor Donny Eldredge
EDITORS AND MANAGERS
City Editor Kathy Williams
News/Wire Editor Darrell McCorstin
Sports Editor Rusty Hall
PRODUCTION
Foreman-Composing Bruce Virgin
Foreman-Pressroom Roger DeYoung

Mechanical available: Offset; Black and 3 ROP colors; insert accepted — preprinted; page cutoffs — 22¾".
Mechanical specifications: Type page 13" x 21½"; E - 6 cols, 2 1/16", ⅛" between; A - 6 cols, 2 1/16", ⅛" between; C - 9 cols, 1 5/16", ⅛" between.
Commodity consumption: Newsprint 1,600 metric tons; widths 27½", 13¾"; black ink 45,000 pounds; color ink 5,200 pounds; single pages printed 10,601; average pages per issue 28(d), 64(S); single plates used 6,500.
Equipment: EDITORIAL: Front-end hardware — SII/Sys 22, 14-ET/960; Front-end software — SII/Sys 22. CLASSIFIED: Front-end hardware — SII/Sys 22, 4-ET/960; Front-end software — SII/Sys 22; Printers — 1-Ap/Mac LaserPrinter; Other equipment — 1-Ap/Mac SE. DISPLAY: Other equipment — Ap/Mac Raster OPS. PRODUCTION: Typesetters — 1-NewGen/Laserprinter, 2-Microcraft/Translator II, 1-Ap/Mac LaserPrinter; Plate exposures — 1-Nu/Flip Top; Plate processors — 1-Nat/A-250; Production cameras — C/Spartan III; Automatic film processors — LD/18; Color separation equipment (conventional) — 1-Digi-Colour/DC-4000, 1-Lf/AP Leaf Picture Desk.
PRESSROOM: Line 1 — 7-G/Urbanite, 1-G/Urbanite; Folders — 1-G; Press control system — G. MAILROOM: Counter stackers — 1-MRS/1220; Inserters and stuffers — 1-S/24-P; Bundle tyer — 2-MLN/ML2EE. WIRE SERVICES: News — AP; Stock tables — AP; Syndicates — AP; Receiving dishes — size-10ft, AP. BUSINESS COMPUTERS: 1-Unisys/5000, 1-HP/3000 927LX; Applications: CJ.

SNYDER
Scurry County
'90 U.S. Census- 12,195; E&P '96 Est. 11,942

Snyder Daily News (e-mon to fri; S)

Snyder Daily News, 3600 College Ave.; PO Box 949, Snyder, TX 79550; tel (915) 573-5486.
Circulation: 4,619(e); 4,619(S); Sworn Sept. 25, 1995.
Price: 50¢(d); 50¢(S); $85.00/yr.
Advertising: Open inch rate $5.04(e); $5.04(S).
News Service: AP. **Politics:** Independent. **Established:** 1950.
Not Published: Independence Day; Christmas.
Advertising not accepted: Alcoholic beverages.
Special Editions: Progress (Jan); Back-to-School, Progress (Sept); Christmas Greetings (Dec).
Special Weekly Section: TV Section.

CORPORATE OFFICERS
President Roy McQueen
Vice Pres Beecher McCormick
Secretary/Treasurer Walter Buckel
GENERAL MANAGEMENT
Publisher Roy McQueen
General Manager Roy McQueen
ADVERTISING
Director Wayne Burney
NEWS EXECUTIVE
Editor Bill McClellan
EDITORS AND MANAGERS
News Editor Shirley Gorman
Sports Editor Brent Taylor
PRODUCTION
Foreman-Pressroom James Evans

Market Information: TMC; Operate audiotex.
Mechanical available: Offset; Black and 2 ROP colors; insert accepted — preprinted; page cutoffs — 21".
Mechanical specifications: Type page 14½" x 21"; E - 6 cols, 2 1/16", ⅛" between; A - 6 cols, 2 1/16", ⅛" between; C - 6 cols, 2 1/16", ⅛" between.
Commodity consumption: Newsprint 276 short tons; width 27½"; average pages per issue 14(d), 56(S).
Equipment: EDITORIAL: Front-end hardware — Mk.
PRESSROOM: Line 1 — 6-G/Community; Folders — 1-G/SC. WIRE SERVICES: News — AP; Receiving dishes — AP. BUSINESS COMPUTERS: TI.

STEPHENVILLE
Erath County
'90 U.S. Census- 13,502; E&P '96 Est. 14,394

Stephenville Empire-Tribune (e-mon to fri; S)

Stephenville Empire-Tribune, 590 S. Loop; PO Box 958, Stephenville, TX 76401; tel (817) 965-3124; fax (817) 965-4269. Boone Newspapers Inc. group.
Circulation: 5,231(e); 5,231(S); Sworn Sept. 30, 1995.
Price: 50¢(d); $1.00(S); $7.75/mo; $93.00/yr.
Advertising: Open inch rate $9.00(e); $10.00(S). **Representative:** Papert Companies.
News Service: AP. **Politics:** Independent. **Established:** 1870.
Special Editions: Horizons; Back-to-School; Tarleton State University; FYI; Football.
Special Weekly Sections: Best Food Day (tues); School Page/NIE (wed); Restaurant Dining, Churches, Automotive (fri); Agriculture, Automotive, Outdoors, Lifestyle, Weddings/Engagements (S).
Magazines: TV Magazine, Comics (S).

CORPORATE OFFICER
Vice Pres Lee Leschper
GENERAL MANAGEMENT
Publisher Lee Leschper
ADVERTISING
Manager-Classified Penny Howell
CIRCULATION
Director Jim Roma
NEWS EXECUTIVE
Managing Editor Jeff Osborne

Market Information: Zoned editions; TMC.
Mechanical available: Offset; Black and 3 ROP colors; insert accepted — preprinted; page cutoffs — 23".
Mechanical specifications: Type page 13" x 21½"; E - 6 cols, 2 1/16", ⅛" between; A - 6 cols, 2 1/16", ⅛" between; C - 9 cols, 1.38", ⅛" between.
Commodity consumption: average pages per issue 28(d), 64(S).
Equipment: EDITORIAL: Front-end hardware — Ap/Mac; Front-end software — QuarkXPress; Printers — Ap/Mac Laser. CLASSIFIED: Front-end hardware — Ap/Mac; Front-end software — Baseview; Printers — Ap/Mac. DISPLAY: Front-end hardware — Ap/Mac; Front-end software — DTI/AdSpeed; Printers — Ap/Mac Laser. PRODUCTION: Typesetters — Ap/Mac Laser; Platemaking systems — Nu/Double Flip Top; Plate processors — Nat/A-250; Production cameras — C/Spartan II Roll Camera; Automatic film processors — LE/Rapid Access 22".
PRESSROOM: Line 1 — 7-G/Community Offset; Folders — 1-G/SC (w/upper former). MAILROOM: Inserters and stuffers — KAN/320 6 station; Bundle tyer — MLN/Strapper (plastic). WIRE SERVICES: News — AP; Receiving dishes — AP. BUSINESS COMPUTERS: IBM.

SULPHUR SPRINGS
Hopkins County
'90 U.S. Census- 14,062; E&P '96 Est. 14,739

Sulphur Springs News-Telegram (e-mon to fri; S)

Sulphur Springs News-Telegram, 401 Church St., Sulphur Springs, TX 75482; tel (903) 885-8663; fax (903) 885-8768.
Circulation: 6,538(e); 6,538(S); Sworn Sept. 19, 1994.
Price: 50¢(d); 75¢(S); $76.00/yr (mail).
Advertising: Open inch rate $8.44(e); $8.44(S). **Representative:** Landon Associates Inc.
News Service: AP. **Politics:** Independent. **Established:** 1915.
Not Published: New Year; Independence Day; Labor Day; Thanksgiving; Christmas.
Special Editions: Spring Fashion; Back-to-School; Fall Fashion; Christmas; Newcomers.
Special Weekly Sections: Best Food Days (tues); Business Pages (thur); T-Viewing (fri); Real Estate, Variety, Best Food Days (S).

CORPORATE OFFICERS
Chairman Ken Kraft
President Scott Keys
Exec Vice Pres Fred Frailey
Secretary/Treasurer Carolyn Keys
GENERAL MANAGEMENT
Publisher Scott Keys
Controller Jim Butler
General Manager Jim Butler
ADVERTISING
Director Johnie Hardgrave
TELECOMMUNICATIONS
Audiotex Manager Jim Butler
CIRCULATION
Manager Rob Kinsey
NEWS EXECUTIVES
Editor Scott Keys
Managing Editor Bill Lamb
EDITORS AND MANAGERS
News Editor Bruce Alsobrook
Sports Editor Charles Durrenberger
PRODUCTION
Superintendent David Hooper

Market Information: TMC; Operate audiotex.
Mechanical available: Offset; Black and 3 ROP colors; insert accepted — preprinted; page cutoffs — 22½".

I-408 Texas

Mechanical specifications: Type page 13" x 21"; E - 6 cols, 2 1/16", 1/8" between; A - 6 cols, 2 1/16", 1/8" between; C - 6 cols, 2 1/16", 1/8" between.
Commodity consumption: Newsprint 301 short tons; width 27 1/2"; black ink 7,895 pounds; color ink 500 pounds; single pages printed 6,130; average pages per issue 14(d), 38(S); single plates used 3,065.
Equipment: EDITORIAL: Front-end hardware — Ap/Mac SE, Ap/Mac SE30, Ap/Mac Classic, Ap/Mac fx, Ap/Mac si, 2-Ap/Power Mac 8100. CLASSIFIED: Front-end hardware — 2-Ap/Mac SE. PRODUCTION: Pagination software — QuarkXPress; Typesetters — 3-Ap/Mac Laser-Writer Plus, 1-LaserMaster/1200 Laser Printer, ECR; Plate exposures — 1-Nu; Plate processors — 1-Nat; Scanners — 4-Ap/Mac SE; Production cameras — 1-Acti; Automatic film processors — 1-KP; Film transporters — 1-P. PRESSROOM: Line 1 — 7-HI/Cotrell V-15A; Line 2 — 8-KP/ColorKing; Folders — 1-HI. MAILROOM: Counter stackers — 1-BG; Inserters and stuffers — 1-KR; Bundle tyer — 1-Bu, 1-Cn; Addressing machine — 1-KR. LIBRARY: Electronic — 1-Minolta/RP407E Microfilm Viewer. WIRE SERVICES: News — AP; Receiving dishes — AP. BUSINESS COMPUTERS: 2-Northstar/Horizon, 2-IBM/PC; Applications: Billing, Payroll, Mgmt, Gen ledger.

SWEETWATER
Nolan County
'90 U.S. Census- 11,967; E&P '96 Est. 11,829

Sweetwater Reporter
(e-mon to fri; S)

Sweetwater Reporter, 112 W. 3rd; PO Box 750, Sweetwater, TX 79556; tel (915) 236-6677; fax (915) 235-4967. Donrey Media group.
Circulation: 3,626(e); 3,626(S); Sworn Sept. 30, 1994.
Price: 50¢(d); 75¢(S); $6.00/mo; $72.00/yr.
Advertising: Open inch rate $7.00(e); $7.00(S). **Representative:** Papert Companies.
News Service: AP. **Politics:** Independent. **Established:** 1897.
Not Published: New Year; Memorial Day; Independence Day; Labor Day; Thanksgiving; Christmas.
Special Weekly Sections: Business (mon); Grocery Inserts, Business (tues); Church News (fri); Weekly TV Guide (S).

CORPORATE OFFICERS
Founder Donald W Reynolds
President/Chief Operating Officer Emmett Jones
Exec Vice Pres/Chief Financial Officer Darrel W Loftin
Vice Pres-Western Newspaper Group David A Osborn
Vice Pres-Eastern Newspaper Group Don Schneider

GENERAL MANAGEMENT
Publisher Mike Davis

ADVERTISING
Manager-Classified Janice Briscoe

CIRCULATION
Director JoAnn Henson

NEWS EXECUTIVE
Managing Editor Don Rogers

EDITORS AND MANAGERS
Fashion/Women's Editor Leigh Ann Whidden
Home Furnishings Editor Leigh Ann Whidden
Sports Editor Ron Howell

PRODUCTION
Superintendent Monica Vera
Foreman-Pressroom Bleu Reyes

Market Information: TMC; ADS.
Mechanical available: Offset; Black and 3 ROP colors; insert accepted — preprinted, all; page cut-offs — 22".
Mechanical specifications: Type page 13" x 21 1/2"; E - 6 cols, 2 1/16", 1/8" between; A - 6 cols, 2 1/16", 1/8" between; C - 8 cols, 1 1/2", 1/8" between.
Commodity consumption: Newsprint 110 short tons; width 27 1/2"; average pages per issue 12(d), 20(S); single plates used 2,500.
Equipment: EDITORIAL: Front-end hardware — Mk/1100, 4-Mk/4003, Mk/6000 Hyphenation; Printers — Ap/Mac LaserWriter II NTX. CLASSIFIED: Front-end hardware — 1-Mk/Cas. DISPLAY: Printers — 2-Ap/Mac LaserWriter II NTX. PRODUCTION: Typesetters — 2-Ap/Mac Laser-Writer II NTX; Plate exposures — 1-Nu/Flip Top F140; Production cameras — 1-R/500. PRESSROOM: Line 1 — 5-G, 1-G. MAILROOM: Bundle tyer — 1-Bu; Addressing machine — 1-Wm. WIRE SERVICES: News — AP; Syndicates — King Features, Creators. BUSINESS COMPUTERS: Ap/Mac Classic II; Applications: Microsoft.

TAYLOR
Williamson County
'90 U.S. Census- 11,472; E&P '96 Est. 11,927

Taylor Daily Press
(e-mon to fri)

Taylor Daily Press, 211 W. 3rd St.; PO Box 1040, Taylor, TX 76574; tel (512) 352-8535; fax (512) 352-2227. Dixie Newspapers group.
Circulation: 4,869(e); Sworn Sept. 29, 1995.
Price: 50¢(d); $62.00/yr.
Advertising: Open inch rate $7.70(e). **Representative:** Papert Companies.
News Service: AP. **Politics:** Independent. **Established:** 1913.
Special Editions: Customer Appreciation, Chamber Tab (Jan); Tax Facts Tab, Brides Tab (Feb); Lawn & Garden/Home Improvement Tab (Mar); Health & Fitness Tab (Apr); Mother's Day, Graduation Tab (May); Summer Baseball Leagues Tab, Father's Day, T.I.F. Tab (June); Business in Taylor, Customer Appreciation (July); Back-to-School Tab (Aug); Football Tab, Just Say No Coloring Book, Blackland Expo Tab (Sept); Healthfest Tab, Senior Citizen Tab (Oct); Holiday Head Start, Basketball Tab, Christmas Gift Guide (Nov); Christmas Coloring Contest, Christmas Greetings (Dec).
Special Weekly Sections: TV Listings (mon); Best Food Day (wed); Church Page (fri).

CORPORATE OFFICERS
President Jim Chionsini
Vice Pres Robert Swonke

GENERAL MANAGEMENT
Publisher Robert Swonke

ADVERTISING
Director Mark Henry
Manager-Retail David Ariola
Manager-Classified Rosalie Kohutek

CIRCULATION
Director Andrea Cuba

NEWS EXECUTIVE
Editor Don McAlister

PRODUCTION
Manager-Pressroom Robert Swonke

Mechanical available: Offset; Black and 3 ROP colors; insert accepted — preprinted; page cut-offs — 22 3/4".
Mechanical specifications: Type page 13" x 21"; E - 6 cols, 2 1/16", 1/8" between; A - 6 cols, 2 1/16", 1/8" between; C - 9 cols, 1 3/8", 1/16" between.
Commodity consumption: Newsprint 470 short tons; width 28"; average pages per issue 10(d); single plates used 8,400.
Equipment: EDITORIAL: Front-end hardware — Ap/Mac. CLASSIFIED: Front-end hardware — Ap/Mac si, 1-IBM/PC. DISPLAY: Front-end hardware — Ap/Mac. PRODUCTION: Typesetters — 2-NEC/Laserprinter; Plate exposures — 1-Nu/Flip Top; Plate processors — 1-Nat/A-250; Scanners — 1-GAM; Production cameras — 1-C/Spartan III; Automatic film processors — AG/Rapidline 66.
PRESSROOM: Line 1 — 7-G/Community; Folders — 1-G. MAILROOM: Counter stackers — 1-BG/Count-O-Veyor; Inserters and stuffers — 1-KAN/320 with quarterfold; Bundle tyer — 1-Malow; Addressing machine — 1-KR. WIRE SERVICES: News — Receiving dishes — size-1m, AP. BUSINESS COMPUTERS: 1-IBM/System 34; Applications: Payroll, Display, Accts receivable, Adv billing, Subscription lists, Mail & PIA circ billing, Gen ledger; PCs & micros networked.

TEMPLE
Bell County
'90 U.S. Census- 46,109; E&P '96 Est. 48,047
ABC-CZ (90): 58,584 (HH 22,367)

Temple Daily Telegram
(m-mon to sat; S)

Temple Daily Telegram, 10 S. 3rd St. (76501); PO Box 6114, Temple, TX 76503-6114; tel (817) 778-4444; fax (817) 778-4444 ext. 271. Frank Mayborn Enterprises Inc. group.
Circulation: 23,836(m); 23,836(m-sat); 26,129(S); ABC Sept. 30, 1995.
Price: 25¢(d); 25¢(sat); $1.00(S); $8.45/mo; $92.95/yr.
Advertising: Open inch rate $18.00(m); $18.00(m-sat); $18.00(S). **Representative:** Papert Companies.
News Service: AP. **Politics:** Independent-Democrat. **Established:** 1907.
Advertising not accepted: Liquor.
Special Editions: Coupon Tab, Bridal Tab, Activetimes (Jan); Junior Fair & Livestock, Income Tax Tab, Home & Garden EXPO, Progress Development Edition (Feb); Design-an-Ad, Cooking School, Home & Garden Tab (Mar); Activetimes (Apr); Graduation, Mother's Day, Memorial Day, Car Care, Community Guide (May); Belton Rodeo (June); Sidewalk Sale, Coupon Tab, Activetimes (July); Area Football Tab, Back-to-School (Aug); Car Care, Hunting Tab, Activetimes (Oct); Area Basketball Tab, Gift Guide (Nov); Christmas Greetings, Last Minute Gift Guide (Dec); Chamber Business Focus (monthly).
Special Weekly Sections: Farm Page (mon); Best Food Day (wed); Leisure (entertainment), Business, Best Food Day (S).
Magazines: Chamber of Commerce Update Tab (first fri/month); Leisure-TV & Entertainment Guide (S).

CORPORATE OFFICERS
President/Treasurer Mrs Frank W Mayborn
Secretary Jerry L Arnold
Vice Pres Charles R Harrell

GENERAL MANAGEMENT
Publisher Mrs Frank W Mayborn
General Manager Charles R Harrell

ADVERTISING
Director-Marketing C F McClughan
Director Gary Garner

CIRCULATION
Manager Pat Graham

NEWS EXECUTIVES
Editor Mrs Frank W Mayborn
Managing Editor Steve Walters

EDITORS AND MANAGERS
City Editor Tim Orwig
News Editor Dave Stevens
Sports Editor Larry Hauk
Women's Editor Tanya Cunningham

PRODUCTION
Director-Technical/Pre Press Vince Brown
Foreman-Composing Frank May
Foreman-Pressroom Bill Meadows

Mechanical available: Offset; Black and 3 ROP colors; insert accepted — preprinted; page cut-offs — 22 3/4".
Mechanical specifications: Type page 27 1/2" x 13 3/4"; E - 6 cols, 2 1/16", 1/8" between; A - 6 cols, 2 1/16", 1/8" between; C - 9 cols, 1 3/8", 1/16" between.
Commodity consumption: Newsprint 1,426 short tons; widths 27 1/2", 13 3/4"; black ink 30,075 pounds; color ink 5,766 pounds; single pages printed 8,941; average pages per issue 20(d), 52(S); single plates used 11,176.
Equipment: EDITORIAL: Front-end hardware — 3-Dewar/386, 7-SBC/486, 2-SBC/386, 22-Dewar/Bravo 45; Front-end software — Dewar System 4; Printers — Okidata/320, 1-Okidata/591, 1-Okidata/321. CLASSIFIED: Front-end hardware — 1-Dewar/Bravo 45, 7-SBC/486; Printers — Okidata/320; Other equipment — 1-Microtek/b&w Scanner w/OCR, 1-Kk/40 Digital Camera, 1-QuickTake/150 Digital Camera. DISPLAY: Adv layout systems — 2-Ap/Mac Quadra 950, 2-Ap/Power Mac 6100, 1-Ap/Mac Quadra 840 AU; Front-end hardware — 1-Ap/Mac 7100 Image Workstation, 1-Ap/Mac 6100, 3-PC/386, 2-SCS/Layout, Ap/Mac SE, Ap/Mac 7100 fileserver; Front-end software — Appleshare 4.0; Printers — Ap/Mac LaserWriter Plus, 3-LaserMaster/XLO Postscript Typesetter; Other equipment — Umax/Scanner 600 dpi color, Umax/Scanner 1200 dpi color, Microtek/300 dpi b&w. PRODUCTION: OCR software — Caere/OmniPage Direct 2.02; Typesetters — 1-Ap/Mac Laser-Writer Plus, 4-LaserMaster/XLO Postscript Typesetter, 1-L/190 Postscript Imagesetter Full Page; Plate exposures — 1-W, BKY/30A, 1-Nu; Plate processors — Graham/Substractive; Production cameras — 1-C/Spartan II; Automatic film processors — LE/23; Shrink lenses — Alan/Prime 610 NM variable; Digital color separation equipment — Lf/Leafscan 35. PRESSROOM: Line 1 — 10-G/Urbanite; Folders — 1-G/2:1. MAILROOM: Counter stackers — 2-HL/Monitor; Inserters and stuffers — 1-SLS/1000 8:1; Bundle tyer — 2-MLN/Plastic; Addressing machine — 1-St/Quarter fold. WIRE SERVICES: News — AP; Syndicates — AP; Receiving dishes — size-10ft, AP. BUSINESS COMPUTERS: 7-PC/286, 2-PC/386, 2-IBM/805; Applications: Circ, Adv billing, Accts receivable, Gen ledger, Payroll; PCs & main system networked.

TERRELL
Kaufman County
'90 U.S. Census- 12,490; E&P '96 Est. 12,129

The Terrell Tribune
(e-mon to fri; S)

The Terrell Tribune, 1125 S. Virginia; PO Box 669, Terrell, TX 75160; tel (214) 563-6476; fax (214) 563-6479. Hartman Newspapers Inc. group.
Circulation: 3,060(e); 3,060(S); VAC Dec. 31, 1994.
Price: 50¢(d); 50¢(S); $6.50/mo.
Advertising: Open inch rate $7.64(e); $7.64(S). **Representative:** US Suburban Press.
News Services: AP, NEA. **Politics:** Independent. **Established:** 1916.

CORPORATE OFFICER
President Bill Hartman

GENERAL MANAGEMENT
Publisher William Jordan

ADVERTISING
Manager William Jordan

CIRCULATION
Director Marvin Love

EDITORS AND MANAGERS
Aviation/Books Editor Jim T Raynes
City Editor Jim T Raynes
Columnist Jim T Raynes
Editorial Writer Jim T Raynes
Farm/Food Editor Jim T Raynes
Lifestyle Editor Jim T Raynes
Sports Editor Jeff Phillips

PRODUCTION
Manager-Composing Andrea Pickens

Market Information: TMC.
Mechanical available: Offset; Black and 2 ROP colors; insert accepted — preprinted, card; page cut-offs — 22 1/2".
Mechanical specifications: Type page 13" x 21 1/2"; E - 6 cols, 2 1/16", 1/8" between; A - 6 cols, 2 1/16", 1/8" between; C - 8 cols, 1 1/2", 1/8" between.
Commodity consumption: Newsprint 264 short tons; width 27 1/2"; black ink 3,000 pounds; color ink 600 pounds; single pages printed 2,700; average pages per issue 8(d), 16(S); single plates used 1,400.
Equipment: EDITORIAL: Front-end hardware — Ap/Mac; Front-end software — Baseview/NewsEdit, Baseview/QXEdit. CLASSIFIED: Front-end hardware — Ap/Mac; Front-end software — Baseview/Class Manager. PRODUCTION: Typesetters — 2-COM/Laserprinter; Platemaking systems — 2-Nu; Plate exposures — 2-Nu; Plate processors — 1-Nat/A-250; Production cameras — 1-C; Automatic film processors — 1-P.
PRESSROOM: Line 1 — 5-HI/Cotrell V-15A; Folders — 1-HI. MAILROOM: Counter stackers — 1-BG/Count-O-Veyor; Bundle tyer — 1-Akebond/Semi-Ace, 1-Bu; Addressing machine — 2-Am. WIRE SERVICES: News — AP.

TEXARKANA, TX-AR
Bowie County, TX/Miller County, AR
'90 U.S. Census- 54,287 (Texarkana, TX 31,656; Texarkana, AR 22,631); E&P '96 Est. 55,096 (Texarkana, TX 31,656; Texarkana, AR 23,440)
ABC-CZ (90): 74,042 (HH 27,950)

Texarkana Gazette
(m-mon to sat; S)

Texarkana Gazette, 315 Pine St.; PO Box 621, Texarkana, TX 75501; tel (903) 794-3311; fax (903) 792-7183. Wehco Media Inc. group.
Circulation: 32,280(m); 32,280(m-sat); 36,008(S); ABC Sept. 30, 1995.
Price: 35¢(d); 35¢(sat); $1.00(S); $9.50/mo; $114.00/yr.
Advertising: Open inch rate $22.86(m); $22.86(m-sat); $23.30(S). **Representative:** Papert Companies.

News Services: AP, TMS, SHNS. **Politics:** Independent. **Established:** 1875.
Advertising not accepted: Subject to review.
Special Editions: Brides Section (Jan); Tax Section, Drug Tab (Feb); Spring Fashion, Seniors Section (Mar); Travel Promotion (Apr); Progress Editions (May); Father's Day (June); Newcomers (July); Football Section, Nike Open Golf Section (Aug); Four States Fair, Fall Fashion (Sept); Working Women (Oct); Holiday Cookbook, Wrap it up Early, Thanksgiving Edition (Nov); Holidazzle (Fashion), Holiday Gift Guide, Kids' Letters to Santa (Dec).
Special Weekly Sections: Best Food Day (wed); Religion (sat).
Magazine: USA Weekend (S).
Broadcast Affiliate: Radio KCMC.

CORPORATE OFFICERS

President	Walter Hussman Jr
Secretary/Treasurer	Marilyn Augur

GENERAL MANAGEMENT

Publisher	Walter Hussman Jr
General Manager	Buddy King

ADVERTISING

Director-Marketing	Kirk Blair
Manager-Retail	Rick Meredith

CIRCULATION

Director	Bobby Perry

NEWS EXECUTIVE

Managing Editor	Les Minor

EDITORS AND MANAGERS

City Editor	Jim Harris
Editorial Page Editor	Ethel Channon
Education Editor	Tisha Gilbert
Farm Editor	Greg Bischof
Features/Films Editor	Lyn Blackmon
Graphics Editor/Art Director	Guy Wheatley
Radio/Television Editor	Lyn Blackmon
Photo Editor	Robert Coleman
Religion Editor	Fran Presley
Society Editor	Judy Morgan
Sports Editor	Johnny Green
Theater/Music Editor	Lyn Blackmon

PRODUCTION

Manager-Press	Jimmy Cooper
Manager-Mailroom	Betty Clements

Market Information: Zoned editions; Split Run; TMC; ADS.
Mechanical available: Headliner Offset; Black and 3 ROP colors; insert accepted — preprinted; page cut-offs — 22¾".
Mechanical specifications: Type page 13" x 21½"; E - 6 cols, 2¹⁄₁₆", ⅛" between; A - 6 cols, 2¹⁄₁₆", ⅛" between; C - 9 cols, 1⁵⁄₁₆", ⅛" between.
Commodity consumption: Newsprint 2,127 short tons; widths 55", 41¼", 27½", 13¾"; black ink 48,263 pounds; color ink 16,071 pounds; single pages printed 9,708; average pages per issue 24(d), 40(S); single plates used 27,504.
Equipment: EDITORIAL: Front-end hardware — 33-PC, 7-Ap/Mac fx, 2-Ap/Mac SE30, Compaq/386 fileserver; Front-end software — XYQUEST/XyWrite, QuarkXPress, Adobe/Photoshop, Novell 3.11; Printers — 2-AG/9800 w/Hyphen Software RIP. CLASSIFIED: Front-end hardware — 9-IBM/PC; Front-end software — Novell, CText. DISPLAY: Front-end hardware — 3-Ap/Mac SE, 3-Ap/Mac Quadra 800; Front-end software — DMS/410, Multi-Ad/Creator, QuarkXPress; Printers — 1-Ap/Mac LaserWriter, 1-V/600w, Graphic Enterprise/18x24 Plain Paper Printer. PRODUCTION: Pagination software — QuarkXPress 3.2; OCR software — Calera/Word Scan 1.01; Typesetters — 2-AG/Proset 9800 w/Hyphen RIP; Plate exposures — 1-Nu/404; Plate processors — 1-Nat/A250, 1-Nu/A340; Scanners — Microtek/ScanMaker IIXE flatbed color, Ap/Mac IIfx, Microtek/FB scanner, Calera/Wordscan, HP/ScanJet (plus flatbed b&w); Production cameras — 1-C/Spartan III, 1-C/Marathon; Automatic film processors — 1-LE/Maxim-26, 1-LE/Excel-26; Film transporters — 1-C/1274; Shrink lenses — 1-Alan/Anamorphic, 1-CK Optical/SQU-7; Digital color separation equipment — Lf/Leafscan 35, 2-HP.
PRESSROOM: Line 1 — 5-G/Headliner Offset 5044; Press drives — Fin; Folders — 2-G/2:1. MAILROOM: Counter stackers — 4-HL/Monitor (w/Ranger laser); Inserters and stuffers — S/848P 8-into-1, 1-MM/Three Knife Sticher; Bundle tyer — 1-MLN/ML-2-EE, 2-MLN/2A; Addressing machine — 1-Ch/515 (w/quarter folder), 1-WM. WIRE SERVICES: News — AP GraphicsNet, AP; Photos — AP; Stock tables — AP; Syndicates — KRT, SHNS; Receiving dishes — AP. BUSINESS COMPUTERS: Wyse, IBM/Sys 36; Applications: Wyse: Retail, Class; IBM/Sys 36: Circ, Payroll, Accts receivable; PCs & main system networked.

TEXAS CITY

Galveston County

'90 U.S. Census- 40,822; **E&P '96 Est.** 40,529

Texas City Sun

(m-mon to fri; S)

Texas City Sun, 7800 Emmett Lowry Expwy.; PO Box 2249, Texas City, TX 77592; tel (409) 945-3441; fax (409) 935-0428. Walls Investment Co. group.
Circulation: 7,600(m); 7,600(S); CAC Sept. 30, 1995.
Price: 50¢(d); $1.00(S); $8.95/mo; $107.40/yr.
Advertising: Open inch rate $11.50(m); $11.50(S). **Representative:** Papert Companies.
News Services: AP, CSM. **Politics:** Independent. **Established:** 1912.
Special Editions: Cook Book; Progress; Home Improvement.
Special Weekly Sections: Business Section (mon); Best Food Day, Lifestyle (wed); Church Page (sat); Lifestyle, Outdoors (S).
Magazines: TV Log (local) (S); USA Weekend.

CORPORATE OFFICERS

Board Chairman	Carmage Walls
President	Leslie P Daughtry Jr
Secretary/Treasurer	Debbie Urbanek

GENERAL MANAGEMENT

Publisher	Leslie P Daughtry Jr
Controller	Debbie Urbanek

ADVERTISING

Director	Larry Cocke
Manager-Classified	Linda Morton

CIRCULATION

Manager	Gurney King

NEWS EXECUTIVES

Editor	Leslie P Daughtry Jr
Managing Editor	John Simsen

EDITORS AND MANAGERS

Amusements Editor	Cathy Gillentine
City Editor	Stephen Hadley
Editorial Page Editor	John Simsen
Editorial Writer	John Simsen
Education/Fashion Editor	Cathy Gillentine
Food/Garden Editor	Cathy Gillentine
News Editor	John Simsen
School/Sunday Editor	John Simsen
Society/Women's Editor	Cathy Gillentine
Sports Editor	Rick Gilliam
Teen-Age/Youth Editor	Cathy Gillentine

PRODUCTION

Manager	Floyd Sims
Foreman-Pressroom	Lige B Ford

Market Information: Zoned editions; Split Run.
Mechanical available: Offset; Black and 3 ROP colors; insert accepted — preprinted; page cut-offs — 22¾".
Mechanical specifications: Type page 13" x 21½"; E - 6 cols, 2¹⁄₁₆", ⅛" between; A - 6 cols, 2¹⁄₁₆", ⅛" between; C - 9 cols, 1⅜", ¹⁄₁₆" between.
Commodity consumption: Newsprint 540 short tons; widths 13¾", 27½"; black ink 24,000 pounds; single pages printed 8,200; average pages per issue 28(d), 72(S).
Equipment: EDITORIAL: Front-end hardware — Ap/Mac; Front-end software — QuarkXPress 3.31; Printers — Ap/Mac LaserWriter II, HP/InkJet 4. CLASSIFIED: Front-end hardware — Ap/Mac; Front-end software — QuarkXPress 3.31, Baseview 3.3.1; Printers — Ap/Mac LaserWriter II. DISPLAY: Adv layout systems — Ap/Mac; Front-end software — QuarkXPress 3.31; Printers — Ap/Mac LaserWriter II. PRODUCTION: Pagination software — QuarkXPress 3.31; OCR software — Caere/OmniPage 5.0; Typesetters — ECR; Platemaking systems — Nu; Plate exposures — 1-Nu; Plate processors — 1-Nat; Production cameras — 1-C/Spartan II; Automatic film processors — P; Film transporters — 1-LE; Shrink lenses — CK Optical.
PRESSROOM: Line 1 — 7-G/Suburban Offset; Folders — 1-G/quarter. MAILROOM: Counter stackers — HL; Inserters and stuffers — 1-S/24P; Bundle tyer — Sivaron. LIBRARY: Electronic — BH/6300 Microfilm. COMMUNICATIONS: Digital ad delivery system — AP AdSend. WIRE SERVICES: News — AP; Photos — AP; Syndicates — CSM; Receiving dishes — size-8ft, AP. BUSINESS COMPUTERS: Ap/Mac, IBM/PC; Applications: Baseview/Fox: Payroll, Accts payable, Gen ledger; Micro Associated/Mica; PCs & micros networked.

TYLER

Smith County

'90 U.S. Census- 75,450; **E&P '96 Est.** 78,069
ABC-CZ (90): 77,061 (HH 29,995)

Tyler Morning Telegraph

(m-mon to sat; S)

Tyler Morning Telegraph, 410 W. Erwin St.; PO Box 2030, Tyler, TX 75710; tel (903) 597-8111.
Circulation: 39,241(m); 39,241(m-sat); 51,315(S); ABC Sept. 30, 1995.
Price: 25¢(d); 25¢(sat); $1.00(S); $7.50/mo (carrier), $11.00/mo (mail).
Advertising: Open inch rate $16.15(m); $16.15(m-sat); $18.65(S).
News Service: AP. **Politics:** Independent. **Established:** 1929.
Note: On Oct. 31, 1995, the Tyler Morning Telegraph (m-mon to sat), Tyler Courier-Times (e-mon to fri) and Tyler Courier, Times-Telegraph (S) ceased publishing the evening edition. The paper will now be known as the Tyler Morning Telegraph (m-mon to sat; S).
Not Published: Christmas.
Advertising not accepted: Beer; Wine; Liquor.
Special Editions: Brides, Pillars of Progress (Jan); Black History, Engineer's Week, Chamber Annual Report, Texas Forestry Assoc. (Feb); TALC, Political, Spring Fashions, Insurance Week (Mar); Worship Section, Business & Industry, Spring Car Care (Apr); Discover Summer, Eisenhower Tournament, End of School (May); Senior Citizens (June); Parade of Homes, Baby Contest (July); Back-to-School, Dog Days of Summer Sale, Football 1996 (Aug); Health Care, Fall Fashions, Clubs & Organizations (Sept); Rose Festival Section, Fall Car Care, Hunting (Oct); Mistletoe & Magic (Nov); Christmas Song Book, Last Minute Gift Guide, Christmas Greetings (Dec).
Magazines: Food (wed); Entertainment Showcase (fri); Color Comics (S).

CORPORATE OFFICER

President	Nelson Clyde

GENERAL MANAGEMENT

General Manager	J D Osborn
Business Manager	W E Hendley
Chief Financial Officer	Thomas Clyde

ADVERTISING

Director	Nelson Clyde IV
Manager-Retail	Art McClelland
Manager-Ad Production	Donna Turzer
Manager-Classified	Jasper Curtis
Manager-National	Jo Anne Smith

TELECOMMUNICATIONS

Audiotex Manager	Jim Bothwell

CIRCULATION

Director	Jerry Rives

NEWS EXECUTIVES

Exec Editor	Jim Giametta
Editor in Chief	Everett Taylor
Managing Editor	Dave Berry

EDITORS AND MANAGERS

Amusements Editor	Dan Mogle
Books Editor	Everett Taylor
Business Editor	Tony Floyd
City Editor	Gene Strickland
Columnist	Everett Taylor
Editorial Writer	Everett Taylor
Fashion Editor	Dan Mogle
Films/Theater	Dan Mogle
Food Editor	Shelly Roark
Home Furnishings Editor	Dan Mogle
Librarian	Diane May
Living/Lifestyle Editor	Dan Mogle
National Editor	Tom Pratt
Photo Department Manager	David Branch
Political/Government Editor	Tom Pratt
Religion Editor	Tom Pratt
School Editor	Betty Waters
Sports Editor	Phil Hicks
Travel Editor	Shelly Roark
Women's Editor	Joyce Turner
Youth Editor	Emily Battle

PRODUCTION

Foreman-Composing	Jim Pape
Foreman-Pressroom	Andrew Clyde
Foreman-Mailroom (Day)	John Comer
Foreman-Mailroom (Night)	Daryl Hendrix

Market Information: Operate audiotex.
Mechanical available: Offset; Black and 3 ROP colors; insert accepted — preprinted, hi fi, spadea; page cut-offs — 22¾".
Mechanical specifications: Type page 13" x 21½"; E - 6 cols, 2¹⁄₁₆", ⅛" between; A - 6 cols, 2¹⁄₁₆", ⅛" between; C - 9 cols, 1⅜", ⅛" between.
Commodity consumption: Newsprint 5,000 short tons; widths 27", 13½", 20.25"; black ink 72,000 pounds; color ink 27,000 pounds; average pages per issue 44(d), 36(sat), 96(S); single plates used 88,800.
Equipment: EDITORIAL: Front-end hardware — DEC/PDP 11-70; Front-end software — DEC/TMS; Printers — NewGen/PS-480; Other equipment — 1-Abaton/color scanner. CLASSIFIED: Front-end hardware — DEC/PDP 11-70; Front-end software — DEC/CMS; Printers — NewGen/PS-480. DISPLAY: Front-end hardware — 5-Ap/Mac; Front-end software — QuarkXPress, Adobe/Illustrator, Adobe/Photoshop; Printers — NewGen/Imager+, ECR/VRL36, 1-QMS/colorscript; Other equipment — Umax/color scanner, Nikon/LF3510AF, Lf/Leafscan 35, AP AdSend, XYQUEST/88 mg. removable, Micronet 1650 (1.3 removable optical drive). PRODUCTION: OCR software — Caere/OmniPage Pro; Typesetters — 2-ECR/VRL-36 Scriptsetter II; Plate exposures — 1-Nu, 1-B; Plate processors — WL; Electronic picture desk — Lf/ AP Leaf Picture Desk; Scanners — Umax/630, Lf/Leafscan 35; Production cameras — 1-B; Automatic film processors — 2-SCREEN/Rapid access LD-220.
PRESSROOM: Line 1 — 9-HI/845N single width; Line 2 — 1-ABD/360; Press drives — SECO/Warner Baldor; Folders — 1-HI; Pasters — Enkel; Press control system — Entertron/PLC; Press registration system — KFM. MAILROOM: Counter stackers — 1-HL; Inserters and stuffers — 2-MM; Bundle tyer — 3-MLN, 2-OVL; Addressing machine — 2-Wm. COMMUNICATIONS: Digital ad delivery system — AP AdSend. Systems used — satellite. WIRE SERVICES: News — AP, SHNS; Syndicates — SHNS; Receiving dishes — size-2ft, AP. BUSINESS COMPUTERS: 1-DEC/PDP 11-70; Applications: RSTS; PCs & micros networked; PCs & main system networked.

VERNON

Wilbarger County

'90 U.S. Census- 12,001; **E&P '96 Est.** 11,660

The Vernon Daily Record

(e-mon to fri; S)

The Vernon Daily Record, 3214 Wilbarger, Vernon, TX 76384; tel (817) 552-5454; fax (817) 553-4823.
Circulation: 4,991(e); 4,991(S); Sworn Sept. 26, 1995.
Price: 50¢(d); 50¢(S); $6.80/mo; $56.75/yr.
Advertising: Open inch rate $4.75(e); $4.75(S).
News Service: AP. **Politics:** Independent. **Established:** 1925.
Not Published: Independence Day; Christmas.
Special Editions: Rodeo; Christmas Shopping Guide; Progress; Basketball Preview; Football Preview; Christmas Opening; Christmas Greetings.
Special Weekly Section: Weekly TMC Shoppers Extra.

CORPORATE OFFICERS

President	Larry L Crabtree
Vice Pres	James Roberts
Secretary	Walter Buckel
Treasurer	Keith McCormick

GENERAL MANAGEMENT

Publisher/General Manager	Larry L Crabtree

ADVERTISING

Director	Jim Surber

NEWS EXECUTIVE

Editor	Jim Carr

EDITORS AND MANAGERS

Editorial Page Editor	Jim Carr
Fashion/Food Editor	Joyce Ashley
News Editor	Jim Carr
Society Editor	Joyce Ashley
Teen-Age/Youth Editor	Jim Carr

PRODUCTION

Manager	Charles Ashley

Market Information: TMC.
Mechanical available: Offset; Black and 3 ROP colors; insert accepted — preprinted; page cut-offs — 22¾".
Mechanical specifications: Type page 13" x 21"; E - 6 cols, 2¹⁄₁₆", ⅛" between; A - 6 cols, 2¹⁄₁₆", ⅛" between; C - 6 cols, 2¹⁄₁₆", ⅛" between.

I-410 Texas

Commodity consumption: Newsprint 110 short tons; width 27½"; average pages per issue 14(d), 26(S).
Equipment: EDITORIAL: Front-end hardware — Mk/1100 Plus; Front-end software — Mk/1100 Plus; Printers — QMS/Laser Printer. CLASSIFIED: Front-end hardware — Mk/1100 Plus; Front-end software — Mk/1100 Plus; Printers — QMS/Laser Printer. DISPLAY: Adv layout systems — Mk/1100 Plus; Front-end hardware — Mk/1100 Plus; Front-end software — Mk/1100 Plus; Printers — QMS/Laser Printer. PRODUCTION: Typesetters — QMS/Laser; Plate exposures — 1-Nu; Plate processors — 1-Nu; Production cameras — C; Automatic film processors — LE.
PRESSROOM: Line 1 — 6-G/Community. MAILROOM: Inserters and stuffers — KAN/340; Bundle tyer — Bu. WIRE SERVICES: News — AP; Receiving dishes — size-3ft, AP. BUSINESS COMPUTERS: IBM/Compatible.

VICTORIA

Victoria County

'90 U.S. Census- 55,076; E&P '96 Est. 57,419
ABC-CZ (90): 54,629 (HH 19,629)

The Victoria Advocate

(m-mon to sat; S)

The Victoria Advocate, 311 E. Constitution (77901); PO Box 1518, Victoria, TX 77902; tel (512) 575-1451; fax (512) 574-1202 (Pub).
Circulation: 40,853(m); 40,853(m-sat); 43,309(S); ABC Sept. 30, 1995.
Price: 50¢(d); 50¢(sat); $1.00(S); $9.00/mo; $108.00/yr.
Advertising: Open inch rate $24.15(m); $24.15(m-sat); $25.55(S). **Representative:** Papert Companies.
News Services: AP, LAT-WP. **Politics:** Independent. **Established:** 1846.
Advertising not accepted: Out of town mail order.
Special Editions: Brides, Super Bowl (Jan); Home & Garden, Livestock (Mar); Medical Directory, Football (Aug); Car Care (Oct); Cookbook (Nov); Christmas Traditions (Dec).
Special Weekly Section: TV Week (S).
Magazine: USA Weekend.

CORPORATE OFFICERS

President John M Roberts
Vice Pres Mrs Morris Roberts
Vice Pres/Chief Financial Officer Warren J Weed
Secretary/Treasurer Catherine McHaney

GENERAL MANAGEMENT

Publisher John M Roberts
Manager-Business Office Pat Strauss
Asst Manager-Business Office Rose Koenig

ADVERTISING

Director-Marketing Fred Hornberger
Manager-Retail Rene Schaefer
Manager-Classified Sue Gopffarth
Manager-National Tracy Heimbach
Manager-Voice Line Tracy Heimbach

TELECOMMUNICATIONS

Audiotex Manager Tracy Heimbach

CIRCULATION

Manager Al H Johnston

NEWS EXECUTIVES

Assoc Editor Vincent Reedy
Managing Editor James Bishop

EDITORS AND MANAGERS

City Editor Greg Brown
Editorial Page Editor Daniel Cobb
Editorial Writer Daniel Cobb
Graphics Editor Paco Rodriguez
Lifestyle Editor Lana Sweeten-Schults
News Editor Scott Walker
Chief Photographer Roger Curtner
Sports Editor Richard Croome

MANAGEMENT INFORMATION SERVICES

Data Processing Manager Galen Gerdes

PRODUCTION

Manager Charles Kulow
Asst Manager Preston Salziger
Foreman-Composing Melvin Janecka
Foreman-Pressroom Preston Salziger
Supervisor-Mailroom Earl Tibbets

Market Information: Zoned editions; Split Run; TMC; Operate audiotex.
Mechanical available: Offset; Black and 3 ROP colors; insert accepted — preprinted; page cutoffs — 22¾".
Mechanical specifications: Type page 13" x 21½"; E - 6 cols, 2 1/16", ⅛" between; A - 6 cols, 2 1/16", ⅛" between; C - 9 cols, 1⅜", 1/16" between.
Commodity consumption: Newsprint 3,918 short tons; widths 54", 40½", 27"; black ink 68,000 pounds; color ink 1,800 pounds; single pages printed 14,390; average pages per issue 36(d), 80(S); single plates used 42,000.
Equipment: EDITORIAL: Front-end hardware — IBM/PC-AT; Front-end software — MPS. CLASSIFIED: Front-end hardware — PC/386-40, PC/486-33; Front-end software — Newsware. AUDIOTEX: Hardware — PC/486-66. DISPLAY: Front-end hardware — PC/486-66, PC/PS-60; Front-end software — QuarkXPress. PRODUCTION: Typesetters — 2-COM/8600, 1-AU/APG-108C, Graphic Enterprises/Negsetter; Plate exposures — 1-Nu/Flip Top FT40UPNS; Plate processors — 2-MAS/WO-36, 1-W; Electronic picture desk — 1-Dell/OmniPlex, 2-IBM/486 90-P, Lf/AP Leaf Picture Desk; Scanners — Nikon/35AF, Kk/2055 Plus, 2-AG/Arcus; Production cameras — 1-C/Spartan II, 1-C/Newspager II; Automatic film processors — 2-LE/LD1800 Lith, 1-Konica/550, Wing-Lynch; Film transporters — 1-C; Shrink lenses — 1-CK Optical; Color separation equipment (conventional) — Adobe/Photostop, AU/APS-6 Imagesetter; Digital color separation equipment — Kk/XL-7700 Printer, QPS.
PRESSROOM: Line 1 — 6-HI/N1650 (5 Registron reels); Press drives — Haley/Controls; Reels and stands — 5-HI/Registron; Press control system — Haley; Press registration system — KFM. MAILROOM: Counter stackers — 2-Id/550, 2-Id/2100; Inserters and stuffers — 2-AM Graphics/848, 1-S/48P; Bundle tyer — 1-MLN/ML2-EE, 1-OVL/JP80, 1-OVL/JP40, 1-OVL/415-A; Addressing machine — 1-KR/KR-215. COMMUNICATIONS: Digital ad delivery system — AP AdSend. WIRE SERVICES: News — AP; Photos — AP, NYT, Wieck; Stock tables — AP SelectStox; Receiving dishes — AP. BUSINESS COMPUTERS: PC/486-33, PC/586-75; Applications: Macola Business Software, Newsware Advertising Software; PCs & micros networked.

WACO

McLennan County

'90 U.S. Census- 103,590; E&P '96 Est. 104,791
ABC-CZ (90): 149,997 (HH 56,222)

Waco Tribune-Herald

(m-mon to sat; S)

Waco Tribune-Herald, 900 Franklin Ave. (76701); PO Box 2588, Waco, TX 76702-2588; tel (817) 757-5757; fax (817) 756-6906. Cox Newspapers Inc. group.
Circulation: 43,023(m); 43,023(m-sat); 56,110(S); ABC Sept. 30, 1995.
Price: 50¢(d); 50¢(sat); $1.25(S); $11.80/mo; $130.27/yr.
Advertising: Open inch rate $44.21(m); $44.21(m-sat); $50.95(S). **Representative:** Papert Companies.
News Services: AP, NYT, Cox News Service. **Politics:** Independent. **Established:** 1891 (Times-Herald), 1895 (News-Tribune).
Advertising not accepted: Mail order.
Special Editions: Spring Fashion (Feb); Garden & Landscape (Apr); Back-to-School, Fall Football (Aug); Home Furnishings (Sept); Christmas Gift Guide (Dec).
Special Weekly Sections: Senior Citizens (mon); Health/Fitness, Business (tues); Food, Best Food Day, Business (wed); Family, Business (thur); Weekender, Gardening, Entertainment, Business (fri); Religion (sat); Farm, Business (S).
Magazines: Parade; Startime (local TV supplement) (S).

GENERAL MANAGEMENT

Publisher Raymond R Preddy
Controller David Hester
Director-Employee Relations Louise Jeffcoat
Director-Human Resources Lura Hancock

ADVERTISING

Manager-Classified Ed Gambardella
Manager-National Joey Dingrando

MARKETING AND PROMOTION

Director-Marketing Ann Roznovsky

TELECOMMUNICATIONS

Audiotex Manager Rowland Nethaway

CIRCULATION

Manager-Home Delivery Steve Sanders
Manager-Single Copy Frankie Koen

NEWS EXECUTIVES

Senior Editor Rowland Nethaway
Editor Bob Lott
Managing Editor Barbara Elmore
Asst Managing Editor Bruce Kabat

EDITORS AND MANAGERS

Amusements Editor Carl Hoover
Books Editor Carl Hoover
Brazos Living Editor Teresa Johnson
Business/Finance Editor Mike Copeland
City Editor Brian Blansett
Education Editor Mike Wallace
Farm Editor Brian Blansett
Fashion/Food Editor Teresa Johnson
Features Editor Teresa Johnson
Films/Theater Editor Carl Hoover
Graphics Editor/Art Director Jay Jeffers
Health/Medical Editor Lynn Bulmahn
News Editor Paula Blesener
Opinion Page Editor John Young
Chief Photographer Rod Aydelotte
Radio/Television Editor Susan Stevens
Sports Editor Kim Gorum
Systems Editor Freida Jackson
Travel Editor Teresa Johnson

PRODUCTION

Director Lyle Parker Jr
Manager-Pre Press Jim Burch
Manager-Systems Ron Richardson
Manager-Pressroom Steve Crum
Manager-Commercial Norman Huddleston
Superintendent-Mailroom Edward Lee
Asst Supervisor-Mail Rick Denney

Market Information: Zoned editions; Split Run; Operate audiotex.
Mechanical available: Offset; Black and 3 ROP colors; insert accepted — preprinted; page cutoffs — 21".
Mechanical specifications: Type page 13" x 21½"; E - 6 cols, 2.03", ⅛" between; A - 6 cols, 2.03", ⅛" between; C - 9 cols, 1.38", 1/12" between.
Commodity consumption: Newsprint 5,428 short tons; widths 54", 40½", 27"; black ink 109,807 pounds; color ink 41,310 pounds; single pages printed 14,937; average pages per issue 34(d), 80(S); single plates used 40,000.
Equipment: EDITORIAL: Front-end hardware — AT; Front-end software — AT; Printers — DEC/LA180; Other equipment — HI/XP21 Pagination. CLASSIFIED: Front-end hardware — AT; Front-end software — AT; Printers — Florida Data; Other equipment — HI/XP21 CPAG. DISPLAY: Adv layout systems — SCS/Layout 8000; Front-end hardware — Compaq/286; Front-end software — SCS/Layout 8000; Printers — Okidata. PRODUCTION: Pagination software — HI/XP21 2.0; Typesetters — AU/APS-6; Plate exposures — Tas; Plate processors — Tas; Scanners — 2-AG/Horizon Plus; Production cameras — C; Automatic film processors — LE, C; Film transporters — LE; Color separation equipment (conventional) — DTI, Ap/Mac Quadra 950, Ap/Power Mac 8100; Digital color separation equipment — Umax, 2-AG/Horizon Plus.
PRESSROOM: Line 1 — 6-TKS/72 double width (w/4 color decks); Folders — 2-TKS/3:2; Pasters — Automatic Pasters; Reels and stands — 4-G, 2-TKS; Press control system — Fin, TKS. MAILROOM: Counter stackers — 3-HL/Monitor; Inserters and stuffers — 1-Phillipburg, 2-MM/5-into-1 w/addressing heads, 3-MM/5-into-1; Bundle tyer — 3-MLN/MLN-2A, 1-MLN/MA, 1-Wilton/Stra Pack; Wrapping singles — 3-HL/Monarch; Addressing machine — 1-Ch/5251E; Other mailroom equipment — MM/Trimmer & Stitcher. COMMUNICATIONS: Digital ad delivery system — AP AdSend. Systems used — satellite. WIRE SERVICES: News — AP Datastream, AP Datafeatures; Photos — AP Photostream; Stock tables — AP SelectStox I; Syndicates — Cox; Receiving dishes — size-3m, AP. BUSINESS COMPUTERS: ATT; PCs & micros networked; PCs & main system networked.

WAXAHACHIE

Ellis County

'90 U.S. Census- 18,168; E&P '96 Est. 20,232

Waxahachie Daily Light

(e-mon to fri; S)

Waxahachie Daily Light, 200 W. Marvin; PO Box 877, Waxahachie, TX 75165; tel (214) 937-3310; fax (214) 937-1139. Boone Newspapers Inc. group.
Circulation: 5,039(e); 5,039(S); Sworn Oct. 2, 1995.
Price: 50¢(d); $1.25(S); $8.50/mo; $102.00/yr.
Advertising: Open inch rate $8.10(e); $8.91(S). **Representative:** Papert Companies.
News Service: AP. **Politics:** Independent. **Established:** 1867.
Special Editions: Progress (Feb); Gingerbread Trail (June); Newcomers (July); Football (Sept); A Day in the Life (Oct).

GENERAL MANAGEMENT

Publisher Jeff Stumb

ADVERTISING

Manager Don Wilson
Manager-Classified Cindy Crowder

CIRCULATION

Manager Roger Palmer

NEWS EXECUTIVE

Editor Allan Taylor

EDITOR AND MANAGER

Sports Editor John Cox

PRODUCTION

Foreman-Pressroom Johnny Bird

Market Information: TMC.
Mechanical available: Offset; Black and 4 ROP colors; insert accepted — preprinted; page cutoffs — 22¾".
Mechanical specifications: Type page 13" x 21.5"; E - 6 cols, 2 1/16", ⅛" between; A - 6 cols, 2 1/16", ⅛" between; C - 6 cols, 2 1/16", ⅛" between.
Commodity consumption: Newsprint 409 short tons; widths 27½", 13¾"; black ink 12,000 pounds; color ink 300 pounds; single pages printed 6,310; average pages per issue 16(d), 42(S); single plates used 5,000.
Equipment: EDITORIAL: Front-end hardware — Ap/Mac SE30. CLASSIFIED: Front-end hardware — Ap/Mac SE30. DISPLAY: Adv layout systems — Ap/Mac, Ap/Mac II. PRODUCTION: Plate exposures — 1-Nu; Plate processors — 1-Nat/A-250; Production cameras — 1-C/Spartan III; Automatic film processors — LE; Shrink lenses — 1-CK Optical/SQU-7-12 Variable.
PRESSROOM: Line 1 — 6-G/Community (upper former); Folders — 1-G/Community SC. MAILROOM: Inserters and stuffers — 4-KAN/Inserter; Bundle tyer — 4-Sa, 1-MLN; Addressing machine — 1-Am/1900. LIBRARY: Electronic — 1-MED. WIRE SERVICES: News — AP; Receiving dishes — AP. BUSINESS COMPUTERS: 2-COM; Applications: Accts receivable; PCs & micros networked; PCs & main system networked.

WEATHERFORD

Parker County

'90 U.S. Census- 14,804; E&P '96 Est. 16,397

The Weatherford Democrat

(e-mon to fri; S)

The Weatherford Democrat, 512 Palo Pinto, Weatherford, TX 76086; tel (817) 594-7447; fax (817) 594-9734. Donrey Media group.
Circulation: 6,083(e); 6,083(S); Sworn Sept. 30, 1994.
Price: 50¢(d); 75¢(S); $5.75/mo; $69.00/yr.
Advertising: Open inch rate $7.92(e); $7.92(S). **Representative:** Papert Companies.
News Service: AP. **Politics:** Independent. **Established:** 1895.
Not Published: New Year; Memorial Day; Independence Day; Labor Day; Thanksgiving; Christmas.
Special Editions: Chamber of Commerce (Feb); Peach Festival, Frontier Days (July); Football (Sept); Christmas Gift Guides (Nov, Dec).
Magazine: Active Times (quarterly).

CORPORATE OFFICERS

Founder Donald W Reynolds
President/Chief Operating Officer Emmett Jones
Exec Vice Pres/Chief Financial Officer Darrell W Loftin
Vice Pres-Western Newspaper Group David A Osborn
Vice Pres-Eastern Newspaper Group Don Schneider

GENERAL MANAGEMENT

Publisher Jane Ramos Trimble

ADVERTISING

Manager Frankie Tyler

CIRCULATION

Manager Bill Davis
Asst Manager Duane Sanders

NEWS EXECUTIVE

Managing Editor Tim Wood

Utah I-411

EDITORS AND MANAGERS

City Editor Bill Hodgson
Sports Editor Kelly Flanagan

Market Information: TMC.
Mechanical available: Offset; Black and 3 ROP colors; insert accepted — preprinted, card; page cut-offs — 23".
Mechanical specifications: Type page 13" x 21½"; E - 6 cols, 2 1/16", ⅛" between; A - 6 cols, 2 1/16", ⅛" between; C - 8 cols, 1½", ⅛" between.
Commodity consumption: Newsprint 320 metric tons; widths 27½", 13¾"; black ink 20,250 pounds; color ink 1,590 pounds; single pages printed 5,950; average pages per issue 21(d), 39(S); single plates used 9,984.
Equipment: EDITORIAL: Front-end hardware — Mk; Front-end software — Mk; Other equipment — Ap/Mac Centris, Ap/Mac LC III. CLASSIFIED: Front-end hardware — Mk; Front-end software — Mk. PRODUCTION: Typesetters — 2-Ap/Mac IIci, 1-Ap/Mac LaserWriter II, 2-Ap/Mac LaserWriter II NTX; Plate exposures — 1-Nu/Flip Top U4; Plate processors — City Plate; Scanners — Ap/Mac; Production cameras — Acti; Automatic film processors — Polyquik.
PRESSROOM: Line 1 — G/Community; Folders — 6-G/2:1; Press control system — Fin. MAILROOM: Bundle tyer — 1-Mk/ACE 420, 1-MLN. WIRE SERVICES: News — AP. BUSINESS COMPUTERS: Unisys/3105-00.

WICHITA FALLS
Wichita County
'90 U.S. Census- 96,259; E&P '96 Est. 97,319
ABC-CZ (90): 96,259 (HH 35,470)

Wichita Falls Times Record News (m-mon to sat; S)

Wichita Falls Times Record News, 1301 Lamar St.; PO Box 120, Wichita Falls, TX 76307; tel (817) 767-8341; fax (817) 767-5201; web site http://www.wtr.com. Harte-Hanks Communications Inc. group.
Circulation: 38,400(m); 38,400(m-sat); 46,789(S); ABC Sept. 30, 1995.
Price: 50¢(d); 50¢(sat); $1.00(S); $10.50/mo; $126.00/yr.
Advertising: Open inch rate $25.70(m); $25.70(m-sat); $28.28(S). **Representative:** Papert Companies.
News Service: AP. **Politics:** Independent-Democrat. **Established:** 1907.
Special Weekly Sections: Business Page, Financial Markets (tues); Best Food Day, Financial Markets (wed); Financial Markets (thur); Expanded Entertainment, Our Times Entertainment Tab, Financial Markets (fri); Garden Page, Church Page, Special Women's Page, Financial Markets (sat); Oil Page, Travel Pages, Book Reviews, TV Magazine, Business Page, Farm/Agriculture/Business, Expanded Entertainment (S).
Magazine: Our own local newsprint (S).

CORPORATE OFFICER

President Bill R Gulledge

GENERAL MANAGEMENT

Publisher Bill R Gulledge
Business Manager Gordon C Walker Jr

ADVERTISING

Director Lori Ellington
Manager-Retail Mark Terry
Manager-Classified Julie Ferguson
Coordinator-National Carla Dowlen

CIRCULATION

Manager Lynn Pace

NEWS EXECUTIVE

Editor Carroll Wilson

EDITORS AND MANAGERS

Arts/Amusements Editor Bridget Knight
Books Editor Dana Moffatt
Business/Oil Editor Ted Buss
Farm Editor Richard Mize
Fashion/Garden Editor Susan O'Bryan
Food Editor Judith McGinnis
Librarian Edith Busche
Lifestyle Editor Susan O'Bryan
Photo Department Manager Becky Chaney
Radio/Television Editor Jim Mannion
Regional Editor Richard Mize
Religion Editor Aldon Brown
Society/Women's Editor Susan O'Bryan
Sports Editor Nick Gholson

MANAGEMENT INFORMATION SERVICES

Data Processing Manager Roy Reaves

PRODUCTION

Manager Toby O'Bryan
Manager-Distribution Center Royce Coats
Foreman-Composing Glen Coats
Foreman-Pressroom Don Young
Foreman-Platemaking Buddy Grace

Market Information: Zoned editions; TMC.
Mechanical available: Offset; Black and 3 ROP colors; insert accepted — preprinted, all; page cut-offs — 22¾".
Mechanical specifications: Type page 13" x 21½"; E - 6 cols, 2 1/16", ⅛" between; A - 6 cols, 2 1/16", ⅛" between; C - 9 cols, 1⅜", 1/16" between.
Commodity consumption: Newsprint 4,300 short tons; widths 54¾", 41 1/16", 27⅜", 13 11/16"; black ink 70,000 pounds; color ink 16,000 pounds; single pages printed 16,306; average pages per issue 32(d), 48(S); single plates used 50,000.
Equipment: EDITORIAL: Front-end hardware — Ik; Printers — NewGen; Other equipment — Ap/Mac. CLASSIFIED: Front-end hardware — Ik; Front-end software — Ik; Printers — NewGen. DISPLAY: Adv layout systems — CJ/Layout 80; Front-end hardware — 2-Ap/Mac; Front-end software — Multi-Ad/Creator 3.6.3; Printers — NewGen, Tegra. PRODUCTION: Pagination software — QuarkXPress 3.3.1; Typesetters — NewGen, Tegra; Plate exposures — Amerigraph; Plate processors — Nat; Electronic picture desk — Lf/AP Leaf Picture Desk, Lf/Leafscan 35; Scanners — ECR, Umax; Production cameras — C; Automatic film processors — LE/LD2600, LE/LD24BQ; Film transporters — C; Shrink lenses — C; Color separation equipment (conventional) — Digi-Colour, Lf/Leafscan 35; Digital color separation equipment — Lf/AP Leaf Picture Desk.
PRESSROOM: Line 1 — 7-G/Cosmo; Press control system — Fin. MAILROOM: Counter stackers — 3-Id, HL; Inserters and stuffers — 3-MM; Bundle tyer — 4-MLN; Addressing machine — 1-KR. WIRE SERVICES: News — AP Datafeatures; Stock tables — AP; Syndicates — AP, KRT; Receiving dishes — AP. BUSINESS COMPUTERS: HP/3000; PCs & micros networked; PCs & main system networked.

UTAH

LOGAN
Cache County
'90 U.S. Census- 36,762; E&P '96 Est. 42,625

The Herald Journal (e-mon to fri; S)

The Herald Journal, 75 W. 3rd N. St.; PO Box 487, Logan, UT 84321; tel (801) 752-2121; fax (801) 753-6642. Pioneer Newspapers group.
Circulation: 15,383(e); 15,849(S); ABC Sept. 30, 1995.
Price: 50¢(d); $1.00(S); $8.00/mo (UT), $8.40/mo (ID).
Advertising: Open inch rate $10.00(e); $10.00(S).
News Service: AP. **Politics:** Independent. **Established:** 1931.
Special Editions: Tax Guide (Feb); Progress (Mar); Home & Garden (Apr); Tourist (May); Customer Appreciation Days (June); Summerfest, Sidewalk Days (July); Festival Days, Football Section (Aug); Hunter's Guide (Sept); Holiday Cookbook, Basketball Section (Nov).
Special Weekly Sections: Homefront (mon); Health & Fitness (tues); Food (wed); Discover (thur); Outdoor (fri); Focus (S).
Magazine: Parade (S).

GENERAL MANAGEMENT

President/Publisher Bruce K Smith

ADVERTISING

Director Wayne T Ashcroft

MARKETING AND PROMOTION

Manager-Marketing/Promotion Steven Woods

TELECOMMUNICATIONS

Audiotex Manager Rick Wallace

CIRCULATION

Manager Steven Woods

NEWS EXECUTIVE

Managing Editor Charles McCollum

EDITORS AND MANAGERS

City Editor Jennifer Hines
Features Editor Jared Thayne
Photo Editor Mitch Mascaro
Sports Editor Mike Ingraham

MANAGEMENT INFORMATION SERVICES

Data Processing Manager Steve Hess

PRODUCTION

Superintendent Steve Hess

Market Information: TMC; ADS; Operate audiotex.
Mechanical available: Offset; Black and 3 ROP colors; insert accepted — preprinted; page cut-offs — 22¾".
Mechanical specifications: Type page 13" x 21½"; E - 6 cols, 2", ⅛" between; A - 6 cols, 2", ⅛" between; C - 9 cols, 1⅜", 1/16" between.
Commodity consumption: Newsprint 680 metric tons; widths 27", 13"; single pages printed 8,505; average pages per issue 20(d), 42(S); single plates used 9,000.
Equipment: EDITORIAL: Front-end hardware — Ap/Mac Centris 660AU, Ap/Mac Quadra 840AU, Ap/Mac Centris 650, Ap/Mac IIfx, Ap/Mac III LC; Front-end software — QuarkXPress, Adobe/Photoshop, Baseview; Printers — 2-AG/Accuset 1000, Dataproducts/LZR 1560, Dataproducts/LZR 1580. CLASSIFIED: Front-end hardware — Ap/Mac III LC; Front-end software — Baseview; Printers — 2-AG/Accuset 1000, Dataproducts/LZR 1560, Dataproducts/LZR 1580. AUDIOTEX: Hardware — 1-IBM/PC 286. DISPLAY: Adv layout systems — 5-Ap/Mac Centris 660AU; Front-end hardware — 3-Ap/Mac fx; Front-end software — QuarkXPress, Ethernet, Adobe/Photoshop; Printers — 2-AG/Accuset 1000, Dataproducts/LZR 1560; Other equipment — 3-Burnelli/90. PRODUCTION: Pagination software — QuarkXPress; Typesetters — 2-AG/Accuset 1000; Platemaking systems — Offset; Plate exposures — 1-Nu; Plate processors — 1-Nat; Electronic picture desk — Lf/AP Leaf Picture Desk, Ap/Mac Centris 650; Scanners — COM, 2-Microtek/ScanMaker IIxe, Nikon/Coolscan, Nikon/LS3510AF; Production cameras — 1-SCREEN/Vertical; Automatic film processors — 1-Wing Lynch; Color separation equipment (conventional) — Adobe/Photoshop, Ap/Power Mac 8100; Digital color separation equipment — Ap/Power Mac 8100, Adobe/Photoshop.
PRESSROOM: Line 1 — 5-G/Community, 1-G/Community, 2-G/Community; Folders — 1-G/SC. MAILROOM: Counter stackers — 1-BG/Count-O-Veyor; Inserters and stuffers — 1-MM/4-station; Bundle tyer — 1-MLN; Addressing machine — Olympic/386. COMMUNICATIONS: Systems used — satellite. WIRE SERVICES: News — AP; Photos — AP; Stock tables — AP; Syndicates — SHNS; Receiving dishes — size-8ft, AP. BUSINESS COMPUTERS: Sun/Sparc workstation; Applications: WordPerfect, Quattro/Pro, Lotus 1-2-3, Fax/Pro, Turbo C, Genifer, Lap Link; PCs & micros networked.

OGDEN
Weber County
'90 U.S. Census- 63,909; E&P '96 Est. 63,661
ABC-NDM (90): 302,761 (HH 94,894)

Standard-Examiner (e-mon to fri; m-sat; S)

Standard-Examiner, 455 23rd St.; PO Box 951, Ogden, UT 84401; tel (801) 625-4200; fax (801) 625-4508; e-mail news@standard.net, sports@standard.net, advertising@standard.net, publisher@standard.net, circulation@standard.net; web site http://www.standard.net. Sandusky-Norwalk Newspapers group.
Circulation: 62,233(e); 62,233(m-sat); 65,541(S); ABC Sept. 30, 1995.
Price: 50¢(d); 50¢(sat); $1.50(S); $9.85/mo; $118.00/yr.
Advertising: Open inch rate $37.55(e); $37.55(m-sat); $38.75(S).
News Services: AP, KRT, SHNS, States News Service. **Politics:** Independent. **Established:** 1888.
Advertising not accepted: Offensive, misleading or detrimental to the public or to this publication.
Special Editions: Utah Centennial, Bride & Groom (Jan); Tax Guide (Feb); Home & Garden (Mar); Spring Car Care, Health, Medical & Fitness Guide (Apr); Graduation, Spring Home & Garden (May); Home Interiors, Life Insurance Underwriters (June); Progress Edition (July); Weber County Fair, Football Preview, Parade of Homes (Aug); Car Care, Weber State Homecoming (Oct); Celebration of the Auto, Basketball Preview, Ski Preview, Homemakers School (Nov); Answer Book (Dec).
Special Weekly Sections: Best Food Day (tues); Entertainment, Classified Auto (fri); Religion (sat); Outdoors, Travel, Real Estate (S); Life Styles, Sports, Business (daily).
Magazines: TV Preview (sat); Parade (S); Coupon Book (monthly).

CORPORATE OFFICERS

President/Chairman of the Board David A Rau
Vice Pres W Scott Trundle
Vice Pres/Treasurer Alice W Rau
Secretary Susan White Smith

GENERAL MANAGEMENT

Publisher W Scott Trundle
Director-Marketing Terry E Gandy
Manager-Accounting Rachael Crary

ADVERTISING

Manager Bradley N Roghaar
Manager-Major/National James L Barclay
Manager-Retail Randee Nielsen
Manager-Classified Tamara Krebs
Supervisor-Classified Telephone Sales Linda Shafter

MARKETING AND PROMOTION

Director-Marketing Terry E Gandy
Manager-Research Patti Woolman
Manager-Creative Craig Bielik

CIRCULATION

Manager Bud Neslin

NEWS EXECUTIVES

Editor-Design/Copy Mike Marino
Managing Editor Ron Thornburg
Asst Managing Editor Mark Shenefelt

EDITORS AND MANAGERS

Art Director Larry Stephens
Automotive Editor Steve Green
Business/Finance Editor Steve Green
Editorial Page Editor Flora Ogan
Education Editor Cheryl Buchta
Entertainment/Amusements Editor Vanessa Zimmer
Environmental Editor Pat Bean
Farm/Agriculture Editor Steve Green
Fashion/Style Editor Vanessa Zimmer
Health/Medical Editor Lori Bona Hunt
Librarian Donna Bingham
Living/Lifestyle Editor Vanessa Zimmer
Metro Editor Lisa Carricaburu
Military Editor Ralph Wakley
Outdoors Editor Jim Wright
Chief Photographer August Miller
Radio/Television Editor Vanessa Zimmer
Religion Editor Lisa Carricaburu
Sports Editor Ron Matthews
Systems Manager Marilyn Bennett
Travel Editor Vanessa Zimmer

MANAGEMENT INFORMATION SERVICES

Director-Management Info Services David J Wood

PRODUCTION

Director-Operations Alan Waldron
Manager-Pressroom Rick Oram
Manager-Mailroom Thomas L Jensen
Manager-Technical Service Larry White
Foreman-Plate/Camera Lance Wardle
Foreman-Letterpress Brent Wade
Foreman-Offset Jim Clark

Market Information: Zoned editions; TMC; ADS; Operate database; Electronic edition.
Mechanical available: Letterpress, Offset (TV & Special Sections); Black and 3 ROP colors; insert accepted — preprinted, product samples; page cut-offs — 22¾".
Mechanical specifications: Type page 13" x 21½"; E - 6 cols, 2.03", ⅙" between; A - 6 cols, 2.03", ⅙" between; C - 9 cols, 1⅓", ⅙" between.
Commodity consumption: Newsprint 8,000 short tons; widths 54", 40½", 27"; black ink 250,000 pounds; color ink 35,000 pounds; single pages printed 18,000; average pages per issue 40(d), 28(sat), 64(S); single plates used 28,000.
Equipment: EDITORIAL: Front-end hardware — 45-SII/MTX, SII/Synthesis 66, Tandem/CLX, Sun/Sparc 10, 6-SII/Techo Page Terms; Front-end software — SII/MTX Layout; Printers — Dataproducts, 3-TI/810, Ap/Mac Pro 600, AU/1560, QMS/860; Other equipment — Ap/Mac IIfx, AP GraphicsNet, Ap/Mac One Scanner, HP/ScanJet IIc. CLASSIFIED: Front-end hardware — SII/Sys 66, 15-SII/Roadrunner, 1-SII/Techo; Front-end software — SII/Classified, SII/ICP; Printers — 1-TI/810. DISPLAY: Adv layout systems — SII/IAL; Front-

end hardware — SII/Sys 55, 5-SII/Coyote I, Ap/Mac IIfx, Ap/Mac SE30, Ap/Mac IIci, SII/Synthesis 66, 4-SII/Roadrunner, 7-Ap/Mac Quadra 800; Front-end software — SII/Classified; Printers — Ap/Mac LaserWriter II, LaserMaster/1200 dpi 11" x 17". PRODUCTION: Pagination software — SII/System 66; OCR software — Caere/OmniPage; Typesetters — 2-AU/APSU5, 1-ECR/Autokon, 2-AU/3890, AU/PIPS, AU/MUX; Plate exposures — 2-DP; Plate processors — Na/40, Na/20; Electronic picture desk — Lf/AP Leaf Picture Desk; Scanners — Lf/Leafscan 35, Ap/Mac One Scanner; Production cameras — AG/2024, LE, R, SCREEN; Automatic film processors — Kk/665, 2-AG/Litex 26; Film transporters — C; Digital color separation equipment — Lf/Leafscan 35, Lf/AP Leaf Picture Desk, Ap/Mac Quadra 950, GPIB/Link to Leaf Desk, HP/Laser Jet Series II.
PRESSROOM: Line 1 — 6-G/MarkII double width; Line 2 — 8-G/Suburban single width; Folders — 1-G, 2-G/2:1. MAILROOM: Counter stackers — 2-Id, 2-Id/2100; Inserters and stuffers — 2-GMA/SLS-1000; Bundle tyer — 2-Power Strap; Mailroom control system — Ferag/Single Gripper. LIBRARY: Electronic — SII/LSR; Combination — Minolta/Microfilm, Novell/Network. COMMUNICATIONS: Facsimile — AP AdSend. WIRE SERVICES: News — AP, AP Datafeatures, AP GraphicsNet, PR Newswire, AP PhotoStream, SHNS, KRT; Stock tables — AP SelectStox; Receiving dishes — size-9ft, AP, PRN. BUSINESS COMPUTERS: 12-PC, Unix/A4-FX; Applications: Circ, Adv billing, Accts receivable, Accts payable, Gen ledger, Benefits; Lotus, WordPerfect, Harvard Graphics, ADP: Payroll; PCs & micros networked; PCs & main system networked.

PROVO

Utah County

'90 U.S. Census- 86,835; E&P '96 Est. 93,681
ABC-CZ (90): 189,906 (HH 51,006)

The Daily Herald

(e-mon to fri; m-sat; S)

The Daily Herald, 1555 N. 200 W.; PO Box 717, Provo, UT 84604; tel (801) 373-5050; fax (801) 373-5489; e-mail edit1@ itr-net.com. Scripps League Newspapers Inc. group.
Circulation: 31,855(e); 31,855(m-sat); 32,801(S); ABC Sept. 30, 1995.
Price: 50¢(d); $1.25(S); $9.00/mo (carrier), $9.25/mo (motor route).
Advertising: Open inch rate $17.36(e); $17.36(m-sat); $17.36(S).
News Service: AP. **Politics:** Independent. **Established:** 1873.
Advertising not accepted: X-rated and NC-17 movies; Alcohol ads on Sunday.
Special Editions: Tax Guide (Jan); Wedding Guide (Feb); Progress (Mar); Home & Garden (Apr); Fishing & Camping, Car Care and Vacation (May); Home Show (July); Football Edition (Aug); Hunting Edition (Sept); Basketball Edition (Nov); Gift Guide (Dec).
Special Weekly Sections: Best Food Day, Total Market Distribution (tues); Total Market Distribution (sat); Religion (S).
Magazines: TV Magazine (sat); USA Weekend (S).

CORPORATE OFFICERS

Board Chairman/President/Treasurer E W Scripps
Vice Chairman/Corporate Secretary Betty Knight Scripps
Exec Vice Pres Roger N Warkins
Vice Pres Jack C Morgan
Vice Pres-Finance Thomas E Wendel

GENERAL MANAGEMENT

Publisher Kirk Parkinson
Manager-Business Office Clark Linford

ADVERTISING

Manager-General Mike Stansfield
Manager-Retail Doug Christensen
Manager-Classified L Scott Murray

CIRCULATION

Director Larry Hatch
Asst Director Cory Lamb

NEWS EXECUTIVE

Editor Paul Richards

EDITORS AND MANAGERS

Business Editor Travis Jocobsen
City Editor Tom Norman
Editorial Page Editor Grayton Garbett
Education Editor Laura Golden
Entertainment/Amusements Editor Ann Niendorf
Farm/Garden Editor Josephine Zimmerman
Fashion/Style Editor Janet Hart
Features Editor Janet Hart
Health/Medical Editor Janet Hart
Lifestyle Editor Janet Hart
Photo Department Manager Jason Olson
Religion Editor Grayton Garbett
Society Editor Janet Hart
Sports Editor Doug Fox
Television Editor Ann Niendorf
Wire Editor Lara Banqerter

PRODUCTION

Foreman-Composing Brian Tregaskis
Foreman-Pressroom Steve Steele

Market Information: TMC.
Mechanical available: Offset; Black and 3 ROP colors; insert accepted — preprinted; page cutoffs — 22¾".
Mechanical specifications: Type page 13" x 21½"; E - 6 cols, 2 1/16", ⅛" between; A - 6 cols, 2 1/16", ⅛" between; C - 9 cols, 1 3/16", ⅛" between.
Commodity consumption: Newsprint 3,125 metric tons; widths 27½", 27"; black ink 63,000 pounds; color ink 31,000 pounds; single pages printed 14,375; average pages per issue 40(d), 40(sat), 72(S); single plates used 14,900.
Equipment: EDITORIAL: Front-end hardware — 30-Ap/Mac; Front-end software — Baseview/NewsEdit Ique 2.0; Printers — TI/dot matrix. CLASSIFIED: Front-end hardware — SII, Ap/Mac; Front-end software — SII, Baseview/Class Manager Pro; Printers — AG/Imagesetter. DISPLAY: Adv layout systems — SCS/Layout 8000; Front-end hardware — Dell/PC, Ap/Mac 7200; Front-end software — SCS, QuarkXPress 3.3.1; Printers — HP, C.Itoh/dot matrix, 1-Ap/Mac LaserWriter IIg, LaserMaster/1800 pmr. PRODUCTION: Pagination software — QuarkXPress 3.3.1, Baseview/Extension; Typesetters — 2-COM/8600, 1-AG/13" Imagesetter, 1-AG/14" Imagesetter, AG/19" Imagesetter; Plate exposures — 1-Nu; Plate processors — 1-Graham; Electronic picture desk — Lf/AP Leaf Picture Desk, Ap/Mac w/Adobe/Photoshop; Scanners — AG/Focus Color Scanner, Nikon/3500 Slide Scanner, Nikon/CoverScan; Production cameras — COM/680C, AG/Repromaster 2200; Automatic film processors — AG/Super 260, 2-AG/Rapidline 43; Color separation equipment (conventional) — Ap/Mac Quadra 900, Ap/Power Mac 7100; Digital color separation equipment — Adobe/Photoshop, Ap/Mac Quadra 900, Ap/Power Mac 7100.
PRESSROOM: Line 1 — 9-G/Urbanite; Folders — 1-G; Press control system — G/767. MAILROOM: Counter stackers — 1-BG/106, 2-Id/660, 1-MM/310; Inserters and stuffers — 2-MM/227E, 1-MM/308 Byliner; Bundle tyer — 2-MLN/ML2EE, 2-MLN/2A. COMMUNICATIONS: Facsimile — 1-Toshiba/TF-581, 1-Toshiba/TF-511. WIRE SERVICES: News — AP, KRT, TMS, NYSE, Mutuals, OTC, NASDAQ; Syndicates — Universal Press, King Features, TMS, SHNS; Receiving dishes — size-10ft, AP. BUSINESS COMPUTERS: ScrippSat, IBM/PC Novell/Network 198, SCS; Applications: SCS: Accts receivable; WordPerfect, Lotus, ScrippSat, PBS/MediaPlus: Circ; PCs & micros networked; PCs & main system networked.

ST. GEORGE

Washington County

'90 U.S. Census- 28,502; E&P '96 Est. 44,054

The Spectrum

(e-mon to fri; m-sat; S)

The Spectrum, 275 E. St. George Blvd., St. George, UT 84770; tel (801) 674-6200; fax (801) 674-6265; e-mail jsfont@aol.com (editorial). Thomson Newspapers group.
Circulation: 19,855(e); 19,855(m-sat); 20,392(S); Sworn Sept. 30, 1995.
Price: 50¢(d); 50¢(sat); $1.50(S); $13.00/mo (mail).
Advertising: Open inch rate $13.90(e); $13.90(m-sat); $13.90(S).
News Service: AP. **Established:** 1962.
Advertising not accepted: X-rated movies.
Special Editions: Brides (Jan); Parade of Homes (Feb); Home & Garden, Total Health (Mar); Spring Car Care, Progress (May); Shakespeare Festival Tab, Summer Games (June); Business & Industry Profile (July); Fall Sports (Aug); Marathon (Sept); Fall Home & Garden, Huntsman Senior Games, Fall Car Care (Oct); Color County Traditions (Cookbook), Season Opener (Nov); Entertainment Guide, Season Opener (Dec).
Special Weekly Sections: Discover (NIE Page) (mon); Health/Food (tues); Arts/Entertainment (thur); Religion & Beliefs (fri); Spotlights (S).
Magazines: TV Spotlight; Automotive; Southern Homes (weekly).

GENERAL MANAGEMENT

Publisher Roger Plothow
Director-Finance/Operations Brent Low

ADVERTISING

Director Jennie Johns

CIRCULATION

Director-Newspaper Sales & Promotion Skip Schneider
Manager-Creative Services Diana Niesen

NEWS EXECUTIVE

Managing Editor-Composing Services Janet Fontenot

EDITORS AND MANAGERS

Business/Finance Editor Shaun Stahle
Cedar City Bureau Editor Ray Sewell
City Editor-Night Jon Ferguson
Editorial Page Editor Janet Fontenot
Education Editor Shaun Stahle
Entertainment/Amusements Editor Amanda Baliff
Farm/Agriculture Editor Damon Cline
Features Editor Amanda Baliff
Food/Women's Editor Amanda Baliff
Living/Lifestyle Editor Amanda Baliff
National Editor Jon Ferguson
News Editor Jon Ferguson
News Editor-Local Jon Ferguson
Political/Government Editor Jon Ferguson
Religion Editor Shaun Stahle
Sports Editor Dean Rock

Market Information: Zoned editions; Split Run; TMC; ADS.
Mechanical available: Offset; Black and 3 ROP colors; insert accepted — preprinted; page cutoffs — 22¾".
Mechanical specifications: Type page 13" x 21½"; E - 6 cols, 2 1/16", ⅛" between; A - 6 cols, 2 1/16", ⅛" between; C - 9 cols, 1 3/16", ⅛" between.
Commodity consumption: Newsprint 1,080 metric tons; widths 27.5", 30"; black ink 31,951 pounds; color ink 8,200 pounds; single pages printed 9,279; average pages per issue 44(d), 96(S).
Equipment: EDITORIAL: Front-end hardware — Mk/PC 4000; Front-end software — Mk/4000 Page 1.1; Printers — V/4000-5100; Other equipment — Ap/Mac LC III, AP GraphicsNet, Ap/Mac Quadra, Ap/Mac Performas w/CD drives, Ap/Power Mac. CLASSIFIED: Front-end hardware — PC, Mk/1100+; Front-end software — Mk/1100+; Printers — V/4000, V/5100. DISPLAY: Adv layout systems — Mk/Page 1.1; Front-end hardware — Ap/Mac; Front-end software — QPS 3.3, Multi-Ad/Creator; Printers — V/4100, V/5100, V/Imagesetter 6990, Tektronix PX1; Other equipment — AUR/B-W Scanner. PRODUCTION: Pagination software — QuarkXPress 3.3; Typesetters — V/Imagesetter 6990, Panther/Pro; Platemaking systems — Nat/A-250; Plate exposures — Nu/FT40U6UPNS Ultra Plus; Plate processors — 1-Nu; Electronic picture desk — Ap/Mac fx, Lf/AP Leaf Picture Desk, Adobe/Photoshop, Caere/OmniPage; Scanners — AUR/B-W Flatbed, Umax/680 Color Flatbed, Lf/Leafscan 35; Production cameras — SCREEN/660 C; Automatic film processors — Vobo; Digital color separation equipment — QuarkXPress 3.3.
PRESSROOM: Line 1 — 9-G/Community; Folders — 1-G/2:1; Press registration system — Duarte. MAILROOM: Counter stackers — BG-Count-O-Veyor; Inserters and stuffers — 5-MM/227; Bundle tyer — 2-OVL. LIBRARY: Electronic — CD. WIRE SERVICES: News — AP; Photos — AP; Syndicates — King Features, Creators, United, CNS, Universal; Receiving dishes — size-3m, AP. BUSINESS COMPUTERS: ATT; PCs & micros networked; PCs & main system networked.

SALT LAKE CITY

Salt Lake County

'90 U.S. Census- 159,936; E&P '96 Est. 158,425
ABC-NDM (90): 855,997 (HH 279,955)

Newspaper Agency Corp.

Newspaper Agency Corp., 143 S. Main St.; PO Box 45838, Salt Lake City, UT 84145; tel (801) 237-2800; fax (801) 237-2856.
Established: 1952.
Note: Newspaper Agency Corp. performs business, advertising, circulation, production and printing functions for the Deseret News and the Tribune, which are corporately and editorially separate.
Special Editions: At Home in Utah, Career Section (Jan); Utah Auto Show (Mar); At Home in Utah (May); Salt Lake Tribune Home & Garden Show (Aug); Football Review, Parade of Homes, At Home In Utah (Oct); Utah Jazz Section & Deseret News Home Show.

CORPORATE OFFICERS

President Dominic Welch
Vice Pres/Secretary William James Mortimer

GENERAL MANAGEMENT

Administration Director-Human Resources Margaret A Hayes
Manager-Credit Julie Cooke
General Counsel Sharon E Sonnenreich

ADVERTISING

Director Ed McCaffrey
Manager-Retail Sales/National Michael J Fox
Manager-Major Accounts Jeannine Antus-Koncar
Manager-Classified/Display Diana Butcher
Manager-Classified/Inside Sales Linda Moon
Manager-Marketing/Promotion Cynthia Cook

CIRCULATION

Director Stephen W Kelsey

MANAGEMENT INFORMATION SERVICES

Director-Management Info Services Jerry Jennings
Data Processing Manager Jerry Jennings

PRODUCTION

Manager Terry Northrup
Foreman-Composing Gerald Norman
General Foreman-Pressroom John Littlefair
Foreman-Mailroom Robert Percival

Market Information: Zoned editions; Split Run; TMC; Electronic edition.
Mechanical available: Offset; Black and 3 ROP colors; insert accepted — preprinted, most inserts allocated; page cut-offs — 21½".
Mechanical specifications: Type page 13⅞" x 22⅞"; E - 6 cols, 2 1/16", ⅛" between; A - 6 cols, 2 1/16", ⅛" between; C - 10 cols, 1 7/32", 1/16" between.
Commodity consumption: Newsprint 25,902 metric tons; widths 55", 41¼", 27½", 13¾"; black ink 525,000 pounds; color ink 175,000 pounds; single pages printed 48,525; average pages per issue 58(d), 84(sat), 120(S); single plates used 220,000.
Equipment: EDITORIAL: Front-end hardware — AT; Front-end software — III/Makeup, PMS; Printers — III/3850; Other equipment — Lf/AP Leaf Picture Desk, Ap/Mac. CLASSIFIED: Front-end hardware — AT; Front-end software — IAS/Classified Pagination; Printers — III/3850; Other equipment — AT. DISPLAY: Adv layout systems — SCS; Front-end hardware — IBM, HP/957s; Front-end software — SCS/Layout 8000, CJ: AIM; Printers — HP/Laserprinter; Other equipment — III/AMS, Ap/Mac. PRODUCTION: Pagination software — III/PMS; Typesetters — 3-III/3850 Laser; Plate exposures — 2-WL; Plate processors — 2-Anacoil; Electronic picture desk — Lf/AP Leaf Picture Desk; Scanners — ECR/Autokon, 2-III/3750 Laser; Production cameras — 1-DSA; Automatic film processors — 8-LE, 1-SCREEN; Film transporters — 2-C, 1-SCREEN; Shrink lenses — ECR/Autokon; Color separation equipment (conventional) — Desktop, Ap/Mac; Digital color separation equipment — Desktop, Ap/Mac.
PRESSROOM: Line 1 — 10-G/Metro (5 decks, stacked mono unit); Line 2 — 10-G/HO (5 decks, stacked mono unit); Line 3 — 10-G/HO (5 decks, stacked mono unit); Line 4 — 20-G/Urbanite; Press drives — 3-Fin; Folders — 3-G/3:2, 1-G/2:1; Pasters — 27-G, 10-Enkel; Reels and stands — 27-G, 10-Enkel; Press control system — G/3-Par, G/4-Par; Press registration system — 1-G/5086, 1-G/5091, 1-U/1197, 1-G/3249A. MAILROOM: Counter stackers — 6-QWI, 2-Id, 2-HL; Inserters and stuffers — 1-HI/1372P, 1-HI/1372S, 1-HI/2299; Bundle tyer — 4-MLN, 9-Power Strap; Wrapping singles — Foster; Addressing machine — Barstrom/In-Line; Mailroom control system — 1-ARS. LIBRARY: Electronic — 3-Vu/Text, 1-ATT/Unix. WIRE SERVICES: News — AP Datafeatures, AP News, UPI, TV Data; Photos — AP; Stock tables — AP; Syndicates — AP, UPI; Receiving dishes — size-8ft, AP. BUSINESS COMPUTERS: 2-HP/957; Applications: CJ: Circ, Class, Adv, Newsprint inventory, Accounting, Gen ledger, Accts payable, Payroll, Personnel; Quattro/Pro-Win, WP/60-Win, Lotus; PCs & micros networked; PCs & main system networked.

The Salt Lake Tribune
(m-mon to sat; S)

The Salt Lake Tribune, 400 Tribune Bldg., Salt Lake City, UT 84111; tel (801) 237-2031; fax (801) 237-2022; e-mail the.editors@sltrib.com; web site http://www.sltrib.com/. Kearns-Tribune Corp. group.
Circulation: 126,076(m); 126,076(m-sat); 159,790(S); ABC Sept. 30, 1995.
Price: 50¢(d); 50¢(sat); $1.50(S); $4.12/wk (carrier); $214.24/yr (carrier).
Advertising: Open inch rate $40.10(m); $40.10(m-sat); $45.97(S).
News Services: AP, GNS, KRT, LAT-WP, RN.
Politics: Independent. **Established:** 1871.
Note: For advertising, circulation, production personnel and information on production and printing, see Salt Lake City Newspaper Agency Corp. The Tribune (mS) and the Deseret News (eS) have a combination rate of $56.14 (d) and $64.35 (S).

Special Editions: Careers (Jan); Boat, Sports & Travel (Feb); Home & Garden, Car Care, Family (Mar); Home Improvement, Earth Day (Apr); Summer Fun (May); Football (Aug); Hunting (Sept); Fall Car Care, Fall Home, Skiing (Oct).
Special Weekly Sections: Recreation Pages (mon); Business Pages (tues); Best Food Day, Business Pages (wed); Business Pages (thur, fri, sat); Business Pages, Lifestyle, Society, Arts, Travel (S).
Magazines: Parade, TV Book (S).
Cable TV: Operate leased cable TV in circulation area.

CORPORATE OFFICERS
Chairman of the Board	J W Gallivan
President	Dominic Welch
Controller	Tony Magann

GENERAL MANAGEMENT
General Counsel	Sharon E Sonnenreich

ADVERTISING
Director	Ed McCaffrey

TELECOMMUNICATIONS
Online Manager	John J Jordan

CIRCULATION
Director	Stephen W Kelsey

NEWS EXECUTIVES
Editor	James E Shelledy
Deputy Editor-Features	Judy B Rollins
Deputy Editor-Administration	Thomas K McCarthey
Deputy Editor-News	David Ledford
Administration Asst	Shirley Jones

EDITORS AND MANAGERS
Art Department Manager	Dennis Green
Auto Editor	John Cummins
Ballet/Dance Editor	Helen Forsberg
Books Editor	Terry Orme
Business/Finance Editor	Cherrill Crosby
Cartoonist	Pat Bagley
Data Center	Terri Ellefsen
Drama Editor	Nancy Melich
Editorial Promotion Manager	Carol Van Wagoner
Editorial Page Editor	Harry Fuller
Editorial Writer	Diane Cole
Editorial Writer	Lex Hemphill
Editorial Writer	Paul Wetzel
Entertainment Editor	Terry Orme
Environment Editor	Tim Fitzpatrick
Education Editor	Tim Fitzpatrick
Fashion Editor	Terry Orme
Features Editor	Terry Orme
Food Editor	Judith Selby
Garden Editor	Judith Selby
Health/Medical Editor	Tim Fitzpatrick

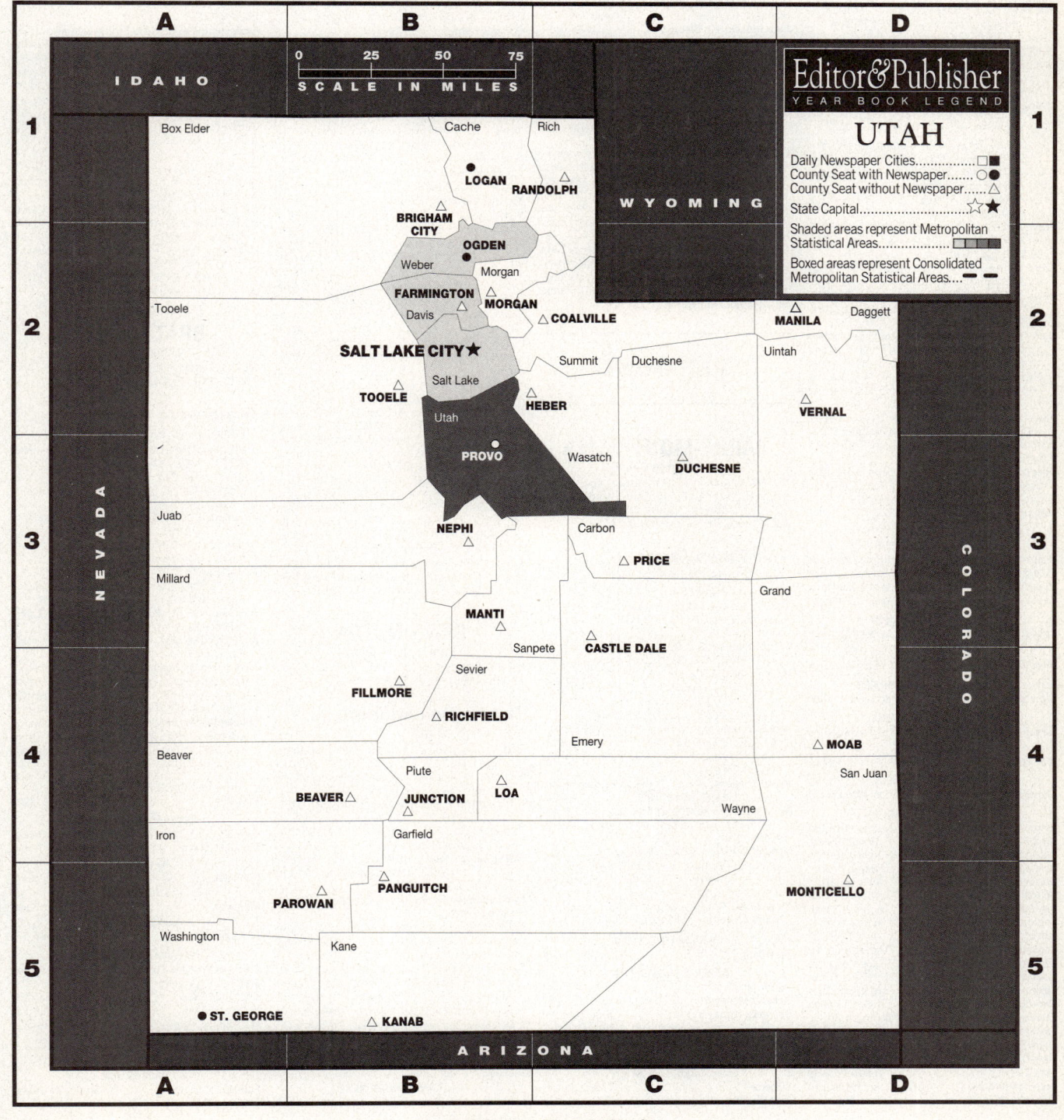

I-414 Utah

Home Furnishings Editor	Terry Orme
Medicine Editor	Tim Fitzpatrick
Music Editor-Classical	Lance Gudmundsen
Music Editor-Pop	Lori Buttars
Exec News Editor	Mark Trahant
Photo Department Manager	Jim Fisher
Ombudsman	John Cummins
Political Editor	Dawn House
Radio/Television Editor	Terry Orme
Real Estate Editor	John Cummins
Religion Editor	Peg McEntee
School Editor	Peg McEntee
Science Editor	Tim Fitzpatrick
Sports Editor	Kurt Kragthorpe
Travel Editor	Thomas K McCarthey

MANAGEMENT INFORMATION SERVICES
Data Processing Manager — Jerry Jennings

Market Information: TMC; Operate database; Electronic edition.
Equipment: EDITORIAL: Front-end hardware — AT; Front-end software — XYQUEST/XyWrite. PRODUCTION: Pagination software — III. WIRE SERVICES: News — AP; Syndicates — North America Syndicate.

The Deseret News
(e-mon to fri; m-sat; S)

The Deseret News, 135 Regent St.; PO Box 1257, Salt Lake City, UT 84110; tel (801) 237-2188; fax (801) 237-2121; web site http://www.desnews.com/.
Circulation: 61,635(e); 61,635(m-sat); 66,679(S); ABC Sept. 30, 1995.
Price: 50¢(d); 50¢(sat); $1.50(S); $5.76/4wk (d), $9.24/4wk (d & S); $7.00/4wk (S), $144.00/yr (mail).
Advertising: Open inch rate $40.10(e); $40.10(m-sat); $45.97(S).
News Services: AP, CSM, CT, LAT-WP, NNS, NYT, UPI. **Politics:** Independent. **Established:** 1850.
Note: For advertising, circulation, production personnel and information on production and printing, see Salt Lake City Newspaper Agency Corp. The Deseret News (eS) and the Tribune (mS) have a combination rate of $56.14 (d) and $64.35 (S).
Advertising not accepted: Liquor, beer, tobacco, coffee, tea; X-rated movies; Massage parlors.
Special Editions: LDS Church News; Travel Section.
Special Weekly Sections: Best Food Day (tues); Business Pages (tues to sat); Arts, Lifestyle, Society, Travel, Business Pages (S).
Magazines: Parade, TV Book (S).

CORPORATE OFFICERS
Chairman of the Board	Thomas S Monson
Vice Board Chairman	James E Faust
President	William James Mortimer
Secretary/Treasurer	Russell J Gallegos

GENERAL MANAGEMENT
Publisher/Editor — William James Mortimer

ADVERTISING
Director — Ed McCaffrey

MARKETING AND PROMOTION
Director-Marketing — Stephen G Handy

TELECOMMUNICATIONS
Director-Info Service — Stewart Shelline

CIRCULATION
Manager — Stephen W Kelsey

NEWS EXECUTIVE
Managing Editor — Don Woodward

EDITORS AND MANAGERS
Action Line Editor	Kathryn Clayton
Art Editor	David Gagon
Automotive Editor	Max Knudson
Books Editor	Jerry Johnston
Business/Finance Editor	Max Knudson
Church News	Dell Van Orden
City Editor	Richard D Hall
Editorial Page Editor	Richard Laney
Editorial Writer	Jay Evensen
Education Writer	Marjorie Cortez
Education Writer	Joe Costanzo
Entertainment Editor	Chris Hicks
Environmental Writer	Brent Israelsen
Farm/Agriculture Writer	Linda Thomson
Fashion Editor	Dennis Lythgoe
Feature Editor	Carma Wadley
Films/Theater Editor	Chris Hicks
Films/Theater Editor	Ivan Lincoln
Food Editor	Jean Williams
Graphics Director	Robert Noyce
Health/Medical Writer	Joseph Bauman
Librarian	Colleen Randall
Living/Lifestyle Editor	Carma Wadley
Music Editor-Vocal	Jerry Johnston
Music Editor-Classical	William Goodfellow
Music Editor-Pop	Scott Iwasaki
News Editor	Jon L Ringwood
Newspapers in Education Editor	Carolyn Dickson
Photo Editor	Tom Smart
Political Editor	Bob Bernick Jr
Religion Editor	Carrie Moore
Science Editor	Joseph Bauman
Society Editor	Carma Wadley
Sports Editor	Lee Benson
Sports Editor	John Robinson
Systems Manager	David Croft
Television Editor	Scott Pierce
Travel Editor	Kathryn Clayton
Women's Editor	Carma Wadley

MANAGEMENT INFORMATION SERVICES
| Manager | Stewart Shelline |
| Data Processing Manager | David Croft |

PRODUCTION
Director-Pagination — David Gagon

Market Information: Zoned editions; Split Run; TMC; ADS; Operate database; Electronic edition.
Commodity consumption: average pages per issue 64(d), 120(S).
Equipment: EDITORIAL: Front-end hardware — AT. LIBRARY: Electronic — 9-Vu/Text Info Sys. COMMUNICATIONS: Facsimile — 1-Ricoh. WIRE SERVICES: News — AP, UPI, RN, NYT, LAT-WP, KRT, SHNS; Photos — AP, RN, Syndicates — AP, LATS; Receiving dishes — size-8 ft., AP. BUSINESS COMPUTERS: 18-DEC/PCSA, 3-Ap/Mac, Word Processing, Data Base, PC Network: Accounting; Applications: Gen ledger, Fixed assets, Payroll, Accts payable, Financial statements, reports, Budgets; PCs & micros networked.

VERMONT

BARRE-MONTPELIER
Washington County
'90 U.S. Census- 17,729 (Barre 9,482; Montpelier 8,247); E&P '96 Est. 17,569 (Barre 9,319; Montpelier 8,250)
ABC-CZ (90): 18,949 (HH 8,019)

The Times Argus
(e-mon to fri; m-sat; S)

The Times Argus, 540 N. Main St.; PO Box 707, Barre, VT 05641; tel (802) 479-0191; fax (802) 479-4032; e-mail timesargus@aol.com.
Circulation: 12,147(e); 12,147(m-sat); 13,229(S); ABC Sept. 30, 1995.
Price: 50¢(d); 50¢(sat); $1.25(S); $2.65/wk; $13.25/mo (carrier), $15.50/mo (motor route), $19.28/mo (mail, VT); $127.60/yr (carrier), $148.00/yr (motor route).
Advertising: Open inch rate $10.80(e); $10.80(m-sat); $10.80(S); comb with Rutland Herald(mS) $25.12. **Representative:** Papert Companies.
News Services: AP, NYT, KRT. **Politics:** Independent. **Established:** 1897.
Not Published: New Year; Memorial Day; Independence Day; Labor Day; Thanksgiving; Christmas.
Special Editions: Bridal, Car Care, Home, Legislative (Spring & Fall); Fall Sports (Fall); Auto; Coupon; Christmas Gift Guide; Recipes.
Magazines: Country Courier (TMC) (fri); Vermont Magazine, TV Update (S).

CORPORATE OFFICER
President — R John Mitchell

GENERAL MANAGEMENT
Publisher	R John Mitchell
General Manager	Alan S Grigsby
Business Manager	Roy Somaini

ADVERTISING
| Director | Glenn Dunning |
| Manager-Classified | Nancy Fitzgerald |

CIRCULATION
| Director | Lana Potter |
| Asst Director | Greg Guyette |

NEWS EXECUTIVE
Managing Editor — Ann Gibbons

EDITORS AND MANAGERS
City Editor	Steve Costello
Courier Editor	James Lowe
Editorial Page Editor	Jim Falzarano
News Editor	Tom Sivret
News Systems Manager	Chris Gee
Sports Editor	Michael Helsabeck
Sunday Editor	Dirk Van Susteren

MANAGEMENT INFORMATION SERVICES
Data Processing Manager — Roy Somaini

PRODUCTION
| Coordinator | Brendan Fitzpatrick |
| Foreman-Pressroom/Mailroom | Donald Bazluke |

Market Information: Zoned editions; Split Run; TMC.
Mechanical available: Offset; Black and 3 ROP colors; insert accepted — preprinted, contact Adv. Director for specifications; page cut-offs — 22¾".
Mechanical specifications: Type page 13" x 21¼"; E - 6 cols, 2 1/16", 1/8" between; A - 6 cols, 2 1/16", 1/8" between; C - 9 cols, 1 3/8", 1/8" between.
Commodity consumption: Newsprint 1,060 metric tons; widths 27½", 34"; black ink 38,000 pounds; color ink 4,600 pounds; average pages per issue 20(d), 62(S); single plates used 56,000.
Equipment: EDITORIAL: Front-end hardware — Dewar. CLASSIFIED: Front-end hardware — Dewar. DISPLAY: Adv layout systems — ALS; Front-end hardware — 1-Ap/Mac SE, 4-Ap/Mac 7100, 1-Ap/Mac 6100, 4-CD-Rom, 1-Ap/Mac Classic II, Ap/Mac 650; Front-end software — Multi-Ad/Creator; Printers — Ap/Mac LaserWriter, Asante/8200, Asante/812; Other equipment — Ethernet. PRODUCTION: Typesetters — Tegra/Varityper Panther; Plate exposures — 2-Nu/Flip Top FT40UPNS; Plate processors — 1-Nat/A-250; Electronic picture desk — Ap/Mac Quadra 950, Ap/Mac 7100; Scanners — Kk/2035, Nikon/Coolscan, 2-Umax, Ap/Mac Scanner; Production cameras — 1-C/Spartan III; Automatic film processors — LE; Shrink lenses — 1-CK Optical; Color separation equipment (conventional) — Digi-Colour. PRESSROOM: Line 1 — 4-G/Urbanite; Folders — 1-G; Press registration system — Duarte. MAILROOM: Counter stackers — BG/Count-O-Veyor 108, 1-MM/231, 1-MM/310-14; Inserters and stuffers — 2-KAN/480; Bundle tyer — 2-OVL/Constellation, MLN/2A; Addressing machine — 2-Ch. LIBRARY: Electronic — Minolta/Microfilm, Reader/Printer, SMS/Stauffer Gold. COMMUNICATIONS: Systems used — satellite. WIRE SERVICES: News — AP, NYT, KRT; Stock tables — AP; Receiving dishes — AP. BUSINESS COMPUTERS: Data General/Avion 4100 Processor, Ap/Mac LC II; Applications: Vision Data: Financial statement, Payroll, Circ, Accts receivable, Accts payable, Class billing; PCs & main system networked.

BENNINGTON
Bennington County
'90 U.S. Census- 16,451; E&P '96 Est. 16,766
ABC-NDM (90): 22,276 (HH 8,193)

Bennington Banner
(m-mon to sat)

Bennington Banner, 425 Main St., Bennington, VT 05201; tel (802) 447-7567; fax (802) 442-3413. MediaNews Inc. (New England Newspapers) group.
Circulation: 7,595(m); 7,595(m-sat); ABC Sept. 30, 1995.
Price: 50¢(d); 50¢(sat); $9.00 (in county); $12.00 (out of county).
Advertising: Open inch rate $11.62(m); $11.62(m-sat). **Representative:** Landon Associates Inc.
News Service: AP. **Politics:** Independent. **Established:** 1903.
Not Published: New Year; Memorial Day; Independence Day; Labor Day; Thanksgiving; Christmas.
Special Editions: Business & Industry (Feb); Spring Home & Garden (Apr); Bennington Antique Car Show, Fall Home Improvement (Sept); In Vermont (monthly); Christmas Gift Guide.
Special Weekly Sections: Food Day, Sports, Bridal Page, Business Page (mon); Food Day (wed); Entertainment (thur to sat).

GENERAL MANAGEMENT
Publisher — Mark Nesbitt

| Manager-Office | Catherine Vosburgh |
| Manager-Systems | Cher Sharkey |

ADVERTISING
Director — Brian Hewitt

CIRCULATION
Manager — Vanessa Haverkoch

NEWS EXECUTIVE
Managing Editor — James Rogalski

EDITORS AND MANAGERS
Fashion/Food Editor	Maureen Burke
Sports Editor	Jon Potter
Wire Editor	Robin Smith

Market Information: Split Run.
Mechanical available: Offset; Black and 3 ROP colors; insert accepted — preprinted, any; page cut-offs — 22¾".
Mechanical specifications: Type page 13" x 21¼"; E - 6 cols, 2 1/16", 1/8" between; A - 6 cols, 2 1/16", 1/8" between; C - 9 cols, 1 3/8", 1/16" between.
Commodity consumption: Newsprint 395 short tons; width 28"; single pages printed 4,719; average pages per issue 16(d); single plates used 4,719.
Equipment: EDITORIAL: Front-end hardware — Dewar; Other equipment — 2-PC/AST 286 Premium, 1-Leading Edge/286, 2-PC/386SX. CLASSIFIED: Front-end hardware — Dewar; Printers — 1-TI/810 Printer. PRODUCTION: Typesetters — 2-COM/8400; Platemaking systems — 1-Nat; Plate exposures — 2-Nu; Production cameras — 1-Ik/530, 1-AG/RPS 6100; Automatic film processors — Vastech/EZ-14 V-22. PRESSROOM: Line 1 — 6-G/S1500; Line 2 — 4-G/Community; Folders — 1-G, 1-G/Community. MAILROOM: Counter stackers — 1-BG/Count-O-Veyor; Bundle tyer — 2-Sa/SR-1A, MLN; Addressing machine — 1-Am/CL-1900, 1-Ap/Mac II. WIRE SERVICES: News — AP; Receiving dishes — size-3ft, AP. BUSINESS COMPUTERS: DEC/PDP 11-73; Applications: Vision Data; PCs & micros networked; PCs & main system networked.

BRATTLEBORO
Windham County
'90 U.S. Census- 12,241; E&P '96 Est. 12,416
ABC-CZ (90): 12,241 (HH 5,092)

Brattleboro Reformer
(m-mon to sat)

Brattleboro Reformer, Black Mountain Rd.; PO Box 802, Brattleboro, VT 05302; tel (802) 254-2311; fax (802) 257-1305. MediaNews Inc. (New England Newspapers) group.
Circulation: 10,805(m); 10,805(m-sat); ABC Sept. 30, 1995.
Price: 50¢(d); 50¢(sat); $11.00/mo (carrier); $105.00/yr (carrier).
Advertising: Open inch rate $12.65(m); $12.65(m-sat). **Representative:** Landon Associates Inc.
News Service: AP. **Politics:** Independent. **Established:** 1913.
Not Published: New Year; Thanksgiving; Christmas.
Advertising not accepted: Adoption.
Special Editions: Business & Industry; Bridal Supplement; Home & Garden; Graduation Tab; Back-to-School; Christmas Gift Guide.
Special Weekly Sections: Best Food Days (mon); Education Page (tues); Living (wed); Entertainment (thur); Best Food Days, Religion Page, TV Tab (sat).

CORPORATE OFFICER
President — James Wall

GENERAL MANAGEMENT
| Publisher | Richard Macko |
| Manager-Office | Julie A Brooks |

ADVERTISING
Manager — Mark Elliot

CIRCULATION
Manager — Dean Shover

NEWS EXECUTIVE
Managing Editor — Stephen Fay

EDITORS AND MANAGERS
Cuisine/Lifestyles Editor	Marianne Ogden
Editorial Page Editor	Stephen Fay
Education Editor	James Pentland
Religion Editor	Stephen Fay
Wire Editor	Mark Tarnacki

MANAGEMENT INFORMATION SERVICES
Data Processing Manager — Sandra M Atkins

PRODUCTION
| Foreman-Composing | Sandra M Atkins |
| Manager-Pressroom (Night) | Chad Ketchum |

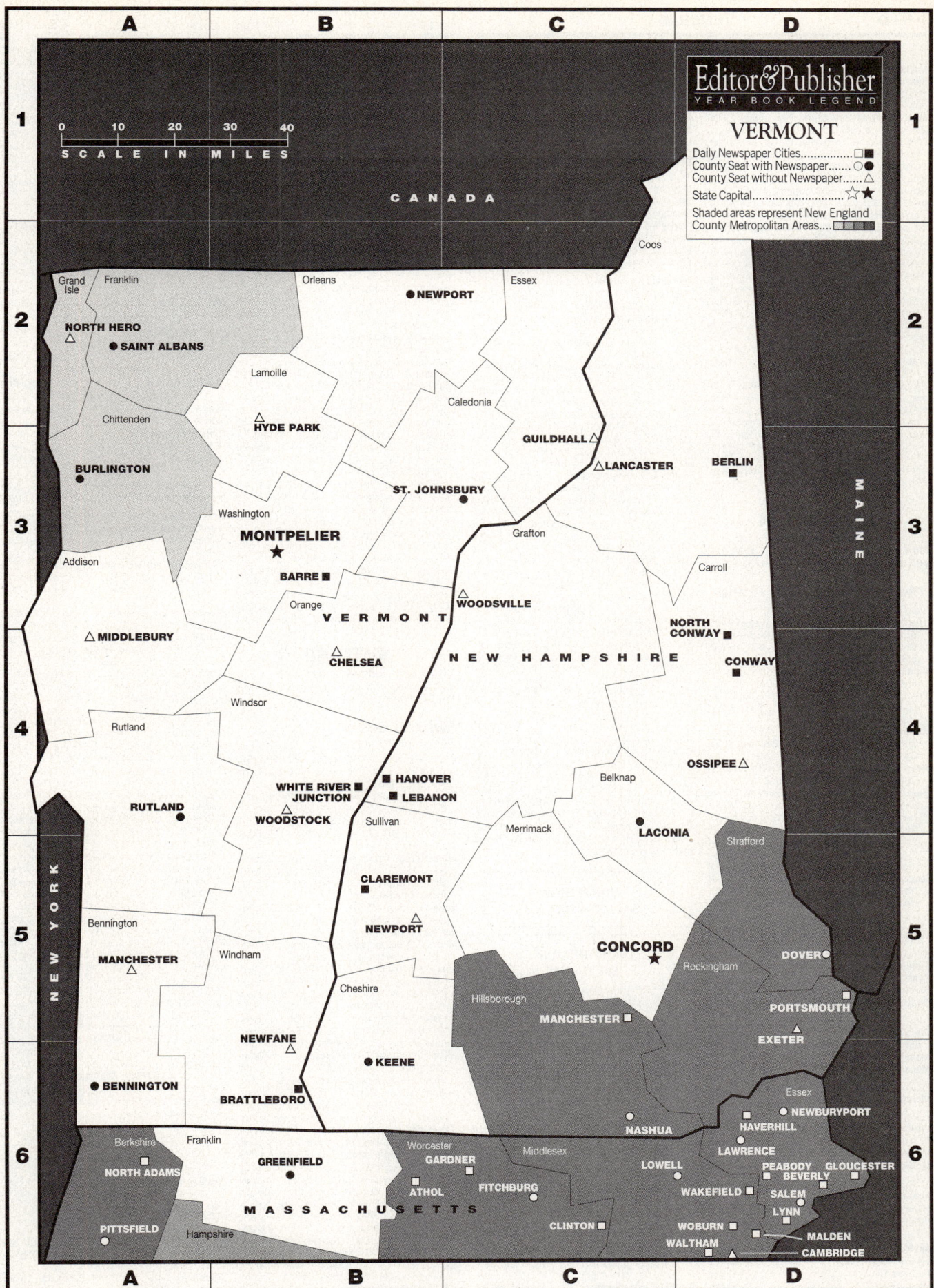

Market Information: TMC.
Mechanical available: Offset; Black and 3 ROP colors; insert accepted — preprinted; page cut-offs — 22¾".
Mechanical specifications: Type page 13" x 21¼"; E - 6 cols, 2 1/16", ⅛" between; A - 6 cols, 2 1/16", ⅛" between; C - 9 cols, 1⅜", 1/16" between.
Commodity consumption: Newsprint 483 short tons; widths 27", 13½"; black ink 13,500 pounds; color ink 800 pounds; single pages printed 7,500; average pages per issue 22(d); single plates used 7,500.
Equipment: EDITORIAL: Front-end hardware — 2-Dewar/Sys II; Front-end software — Dewar. CLASSIFIED: Front-end hardware — 2-Dewar/Sys II; Front-end software — Dewar. DISPLAY: Adv layout systems — Dewar/Discovery; Front-end hardware — 3-Dewar/Discovery, PC/386; Front-end software — Dewar, Aldus/PageMaker, Archetype/Corel Draw. PRODUCTION: Typesetters — 2-COM/8400; Plate exposures — 1-Nu; Plate processors — Nat; Scanners — Panasonic/505; Production cameras — C/Marathon; Automatic film processors — LE; Film transporters — C.
PRESSROOM: Line 1 — 8-G/Community; Folders — 2-G/SSC; Press control system — Fin. MAILROOM: Counter stackers — 1-Fg; Bundle tyer — 1-MLN, 1-OVL; Addressing machine — Wm. WIRE SERVICES: News — AP; Receiving dishes — AP. BUSINESS COMPUTERS: DEC/PDP 11-73; Applications: Vision Data: Accts receivable, Circ; PCs & micros networked; PCs & main system networked.

BURLINGTON

Chittenden County

'90 U.S. Census- 39,127; **E&P '96 Est.** 39,827
ABC-NDM (90): 247,258 (HH 89,873)

The Burlington Free Press

(m-mon to sat; S)

The Burlington Free Press, 191 College St.; PO Box 10, Burlington, VT 05401; tel (802) 863-3441; fax (802) 862-5622; e-mail bfreepress@aol.com. Gannett Co. Inc. group.
Circulation: 54,566(m); 54,566(m-sat); 69,048(S); ABC Sept. 24, 1995.
Price: 50¢(d); 50¢(sat); $1.50(S); $3.25/wk (carrier); $13.00/mo (carrier); $156.00/yr (carrier).
Advertising: Open inch rate $38.95(m); $38.95(m-sat); $42.50(S). **Representative:** Gannett National Newspaper Sales.
News Services: AP, GNS, LAT-WP. **Politics:** Independent. **Established:** 1827.
Special Editions: Stowe Winter Carnival, Spring Fashion, Bridal (Jan); Vermonters (Feb); Home Show (Apr); Vacation Vermont (May); Balloon Festival (June); Fall Fashion, College Edition (Aug); Fall Foliage, Marketfest (Sept); Car Care, Ski Vermont (Oct); Ski Vermont (Nov); Gift Guide, First Night (Dec).
Magazines: Business Monday (mon); Weekend (thur); Home in Vermont (sat); TV Week (S); Health in Vermont (quarterly).

CORPORATE OFFICER

President James M Carey

GENERAL MANAGEMENT

Publisher James M Carey
Controller Edward Bartholomew
Purchasing Agent Edward Bartholomew
Director-Human Resources Sharon Muellers

ADVERTISING

Director Mike Ricken
Sales Exec-Regional/National Teresa Lunsford
Manager-Classified Pam Sicard
Manager-Local/Retail Mike Tockey

MARKETING AND PROMOTION

Director-Marketing Service Linda Marabell

CIRCULATION

Director Jacalyn Malaguerra
Asst Director Reg Hayes
Manager-Single Copy Paul Bourassa
Manager-Promotion Rachel Edwards

NEWS EXECUTIVES

Exec Editor Jennifer Carroll
Managing Editor Mickey Hirten
Asst Managing Editor Candy Page

EDITORS AND MANAGERS

Business Editor Julie Warwick
Editorial Page Editor Nick Monsarrat
Features Editor Joe Cutts
Living Editor Joe Cutts
Metro Editor Rob Eley
Asst Metro Editor Helen Simon
Asst Metro Editor Jill Jemison
News Editor Joe Henry
Photo Editor Karen Pike Riesner
Sports Editor Steve Laughlin

MANAGEMENT INFORMATION SERVICES

Data Processing Manager Brian Hayes

PRODUCTION

Director Larry Stasulis
Manager-Composing (Days) Lyz Cover
Manager-Composing (Nights) Joe Bedard
Manager-Pressroom Dennis Latulippe
Manager-Mailroom Cleon Douglas
Manager-Technical Services Trevor Chase
Chief Systems Technician Philip Patnaude

Mechanical available: Offset; Black and 3 ROP colors; insert accepted — preprinted, free-standing; page cut-offs — 22¾".
Mechanical specifications: Type page 13" x 21½"; E - 6 cols, 2 1/16", ⅛" between; A - 6 cols, 2 1/16", ⅛" between; C - 10 cols, 1¼", 1/16" between.
Commodity consumption: Newsprint 4,997 short tons; widths 54½", 40⅞", 27¼"; black ink 113,973 pounds; color ink 28,325 pounds; single pages printed 14,255; average pages per issue 35(d), 63(S); single plates used 53,362.
Equipment: EDITORIAL: Front-end hardware — HAS/HS-58, 10-HAS/Magician, 34-HAS/Edit VIII, 7-HAS/PLT. CLASSIFIED: Front-end hardware — HAS/HS-58, 10-HAS/Magician. DISPLAY: Adv layout systems — 5-Ap/Mac 660 AU, 1-Ap/Mac ci, 1-Ap/Mac Quadra 610, 1-Ap/Power Mac 8100-100; Front-end software — QuarkXPress 3.31; Printers — 3-QMS/860, 1-Ap/Mac LaserWriter 600; Other equipment — 2-Microtek/Scanner, 1-Epson/1200C. PRODUCTION: Typesetters — 2-AU/Micro 5-57; Plate exposures — 1-Nu/Flip Top FT40V6UPNS; Plate processors — Cookson Graphics/S32; Electronic picture desk — 3-Lf/AP Leaf Picture Desk; Scanners — 1-ECR/Autokon 1000DE; Production cameras — 1-C/Spartan III; Automatic film processors — 1-LE/24AQ, RPD/18, 1-LE/24, 1-AU/APS 35; Film transporters — 1-AU/APS 35; Color separation equipment (conventional) — 1-RZ/450E.
PRESSROOM: Line 1 — 5-G/Metro (2-Color decks); Press drives — 6-Fin/3260; Folders — 2-G; Pasters — G/Automatic; Reels and stands — G. MAILROOM: Counter stackers — 2-QWI/SJ 20X, 2-HL/Monitor, 1-Fg, 1-HI/Rima RS-30; Inserters and stuffers — 1-HI/1472A; Bundle tyer — 1-MLN/2A, 1-MLN/2EE, 2-Power Strap. LIBRARY: Electronic — Mead Data Central/Nexis NewsView. WIRE SERVICES: News — AP, GNS, LAT-WP; Stock tables — AP; Receiving dishes — AP. BUSINESS COMPUTERS: 1-IBM/AS-400; Applications: Payroll, Circ draw, Gen ledger, Profit and loss statements; PCs & micros networked; PCs & main system networked.

HARTFORD

See LEBANON, NH

MONTPELIER

See BARRE

NEWPORT

Orleans County

'90 U.S. Census- 4,434; **E&P '96 Est.** 4,283

The Newport Daily Express

(e-mon to fri)

The Newport Daily Express, Hill St.; PO Box 347, Newport, VT 05855; tel (802) 334-6568; fax (802) 334-6891. Scripps League Newspapers Inc. group.
Circulation: 4,670(e); Sworn Sept. 29, 1995.
Price: 35¢(d); $6.75/mo; $81.00/yr.
Advertising: Open inch rate $8.53(e).
News Service: AP. **Politics:** Independent. **Established:** 1863.
Not Published: New Year; Memorial Day; Independence Day; Labor Day; Veteran's Day; Thanksgiving; Christmas.
Special Editions: Bridal (Feb); Gardening (Apr); Progress (June); National Kitchen & Bath Week, Car Care (Oct).
Special Weekly Section: TV Weekender (fri).

CORPORATE OFFICERS

Board Chairman/Treasurer E W Scripps
Vice Chairman/Corporate Secretary Betty Knight Scripps
President/Exec Vice Pres Roger N Warkins
Vice Pres-Finance Thomas E Wendel

GENERAL MANAGEMENT

Publisher Richard Rivard

ADVERTISING

Director Carolyn Blake

CIRCULATION

Manager Sadie Watters

NEWS EXECUTIVE

Managing Editor Terry Albee

EDITOR AND MANAGER

Sports Editor Maurice Jacobs

Market Information: TMC.
Mechanical available: Offset; Black and 3 ROP colors; insert accepted — preprinted; page cut-offs — 22¾".
Mechanical specifications: Type page 13⅛" x 21½"; E - 6 cols, 2⅕", 1/12" between; A - 6 cols, 2⅛", 1/12" between; C - 6 cols, 2⅛", 1/12" between.
Commodity consumption: Newsprint 160 metric tons; widths 27", 13½"; black ink 4,600 pounds; color ink 500 pounds; average pages per issue 14(d); single plates used 4,136.
Equipment: EDITORIAL: Front-end hardware — 6-ScrippSat/PC; Front-end software — Synaptic; Printers — 2-QMS/820. CLASSIFIED: Front-end hardware — ScrippSat; Front-end software — Synaptic, ScrippSat; Printers — QMS/Laser, Okidata/393. DISPLAY: Adv layout systems — ScrippSat; Front-end hardware — 2-ScrippSat/PC; Front-end software — Archetype/Corel Draw; Printers — 2-QMS/820. PRODUCTION: Typesetters — QMS/820; Plate exposures — 1-B; Scanners — HP/ScanJet; Production cameras — 1-K/241; Automatic film processors — LE.
PRESSROOM: Line 1 — 4-G/Community; Folders — 1-G. MAILROOM: Bundle tyer — 1-Saxmyer; Addressing machine — Wm. WIRE SERVICES: News — AP; Syndicates — SHNS; Receiving dishes — size-10ft, AP. BUSINESS COMPUTERS: Synaptic/Micro Solutions, Acct/100, Okidata/393 Plus, SunType.

RUTLAND

Rutland County

'90 U.S. Census- 18,230; **E&P '96 Est.** 18,131
ABC-CZ (90): 29,273 (HH 11,689)

Rutland Herald

(m-mon to sat; S)

Rutland Herald, 27 Wales St.; PO Box 668, Rutland, VT 05702-0668; tel (802) 747-6121; fax (802) 775-2423.
Circulation: 22,494(m); 22,494(m-sat); 23,826(S); ABC Sept. 30, 1995.
Price: 50¢(d); 50¢(sat); $1.50(S); $3.05/wk (carrier); $12.20/mo (carrier); $152.50/yr (carrier).
Advertising: Open inch rate $18.75(m); $18.75(m-sat); $18.75(S); comb with Barre-Montpelier Times Argus(eS) $25.12. **Representative:** Papert Companies.
News Services: AP, NYT, KRT. **Politics:** Independent. **Established:** 1794.
Not Published: Christmas.
Advertising not accepted: Mail order requiring cash in advance; some medical.
Special Editions: 1st Big Deal, Business Chronology, National Pizza Week, Rutland Bridal Show, Health Care Reform, Killington-Pico-Rutland Winter Carnival, Super Bowl (Jan); Sweetheart Promotion, Winter Sports, Valentine Love Lines, George Washington's Auto, Properties in your Price Range, Brides, President's Day Sales, Heart Month Signature Page (Feb); St. Patrick's Day, Spring Showcase of Homes, Downtown Cabin Fever, Who's Who in Business, Easter Egg Scramble, Easter Splash, Easter Worship (Mar); National Library Week, World Health Day, April Showers, Auto, American Home Week, Spring Car Care, Spring Fashion Preview, Earth Day, Spectacular Tour of Homes, Lions Club Home Show (Apr); Mother's Day Gifts, Mother's Day Greetings, National Nursing Home Week, Vermont Home, If it's on the Road, Vermont Green Up Day, Drive Safely, Memorial Day (May); Congratulations Grads, Father's Day Gifts, Father's Day Greetings, Wheels Promo, Your Search is Over, Summer Fun (June); Drive Safely, Beat the Heat, The Deals are Hot-Auto, Rutland Profiles, Downtown Sidewalk Sales (July); Back-to-School, End of Summer Clearance, Auto Leasing (Aug); Drive Safely, Vermont State Fair, Fall Fashion Preview, Grandparents, Spectacular Tour of Homes, Auto Year End-Closeouts (Sept); Fall Car Care, Vermont Home, Harvest Days, Just Say No Coloring Book, Halloween Safety Pages (Oct); Successful Hunter, Turkey Scramble, Christmas Coupons, Holiday Gift Guide (Nov); Santa Savers, Biggest Bucks Contest, Last Minute Gift Selections, Drive Safely, Christmas Angels, Holiday Greetings, First Night (Dec).
Special Weekly Sections: Best Food Day (mon); Business (wed); Business (fri); Worship Page (sat); Living, Business (S).
Magazines: TV Entertainment Weekly; Vermont Sunday Magazine; Parade.

CORPORATE OFFICER

President R John Mitchell

GENERAL MANAGEMENT

Publisher R John Mitchell
General Manager/Vice Pres Robert G Miller

ADVERTISING

Director Grace E Johnston
Manager-Telemarketing Service Glenda Hawley

TELECOMMUNICATIONS

Audiotex Manager Robert G Miller

CIRCULATION

Manager S K Wilson

NEWS EXECUTIVE

Managing Editor John VanHoesen

EDITORS AND MANAGERS

Business Editor Bruce Edwards
City Editor Jo-Anne MacKenzie
Editorial Page Editor David Moats
Editorial Writer David Moats
Sports Editor Tom Haley

PRODUCTION

Foreman-Pressroom/Pre Press Craig Snow
Foreman- Design Services Bernadette Robin

Market Information: TMC; Operate audiotex.
Mechanical available: Offset; Black and 3 ROP colors; insert accepted — preprinted; page cut-offs — 22¾".
Mechanical specifications: Type page 13½" x 21¼"; E - 6 cols, 2 1/16", ⅛" between; A - 6 cols, 2 1/16", ⅛" between; C - 9 cols, 1⅜", 1/16" between.
Commodity consumption: Newsprint 1,189 short tons; widths 27", 13½"; black ink 44,500 pounds; color ink 3,100 pounds; single pages printed 8,420; average pages per issue 27(d), 73(S); single plates used 7,500.
Equipment: EDITORIAL: Front-end hardware — PC; Front-end software — Dewar; Printers — Okidata/393. CLASSIFIED: Front-end hardware — PC; Front-end software — Dewar; Printers — Okidata/393. AUDIOTEX: Hardware — PC; Software — U.S.Telecom Val 4.20; DISPLAY: Adv layout systems — Mk/Managing Editor; Front-end hardware — Ap/Mac 6100; Front-end software — Multi-Ad/Creator; Printers — LaserMaster/1200 PDI. PRODUCTION: Pagination software — QuarkXPress; OCR software — Caere/OmniPage Pro; Typesetters — 2-Unity/1200 XL, 2-XIT; Platemaking systems — Nu/FT 40V6OP; Plate exposures — 1-Colight/Scanner 40, Nu/Flip Top FT40UPNS; Plate processors — 1-Nat/A-250; Electronic picture desk — Lf/AP Leaf Picture Desk, Adobe/Photoshop; Scanners — ECR/Scanner, Umax/840, Ap/Mac 610, Ofoto; Production cameras — C; Automatic film processors — Vastech/DT14; Digital color separation equipment — Digi-Colour/IDC-4000.
PRESSROOM: Line 1 — 6-G/Urbanite; Press drives — Hurletron; Press control system — Hurletron. MAILROOM: Counter stackers — H/Stack Pack; Inserters and stuffers — 1-KAN/480; Bundle tyer — 1-MLN/MLWZA, 2-MLN/ML1EE. LIBRARY: Electronic — SMS/Stauffer Gold. COMMUNICATIONS: Digital ad delivery system — AP AdSend. WIRE SERVICES: News — AP Datastream, AP Datafeatures, NYT; Photos — AP; Stock tables — AP; Receiving dishes — size-12ft, AP. BUSINESS COMPUTERS: DG/Aviion 4100; Applications: Vision Data: Payroll, Accts payable, Circ, Gen ledger; PCs & micros networked; PCs & main system networked.

ST. ALBANS

Franklin County

'90 U.S. Census- 7,339; **E&P '96 Est.** 7,354

St. Albans Messenger

(e-mon to fri; m-sat)

St. Albans Messenger, 281 N. Main St.; PO Box 1250, St. Albans, VT 05478; tel (802) 524-9771; fax (802) 527-1948.
Circulation: 4,850(e); 4,850(m-sat); Sworn Oct. 4, 1994.

Price: 35¢(d); 35¢(sat); $104.00/yr.
Advertising: Open inch rate $10.20(e); $10.20(m-sat).
News Service: AP. **Politics:** Independent. **Established:** 1861.
Not Published: New Year; Independence Day; Labor Day; Thanksgiving; Christmas.
Special Editions: Graduation, Dairy (June); Christmas (Nov); Fashion, Car Care, Home Improvements (Spring); Fashion, Car Care, Energy (Fall); Recipes, Sports (Winter); Meet Your Merchants; Meet Your Pros.
Magazine: Monthly supplements.

GENERAL MANAGEMENT

Co-Publisher Emerson Lynn
Co-Publisher Cynthia Lynn
General Manager Gary Rutkowski
Business Manager/Controller Cynthia Lynn

ADVERTISING

Director Jeremy Reed

CIRCULATION

Manager Thea J Whitcomb

NEWS EXECUTIVES

Editor Emerson Lynn
Managing Editor Gary Rutkowski

Market Information: Zoned editions; TMC.
Mechanical available: Offset; Black and 3 ROP colors; insert accepted — preprinted, any; page cut-offs — 22¾".
Mechanical specifications: Type page 13½" x 21"; E - 6 cols, $2\frac{1}{16}$", 1/8" between; A - 6 cols, $2\frac{1}{16}$", 1/8" between; C - 6 cols, $2\frac{1}{16}$", 1/8" between.
Commodity consumption: Newsprint 550 metric tons; widths 27", 32"; average pages per issue 20(d).
Equipment: EDITORIAL: Front-end hardware — 17-Ap/Mac Plus PC; Printers — 4-Ap/Mac LaserWriter Plus. CLASSIFIED: Front-end hardware — Ap/Mac Plus PC. PRODUCTION: Typesetters — Ap/Mac Plus PC, Ap/Mac Laser-Writer Plus; Plate exposures — 1-B/3200, 1-Nu/240V; Plate processors — 1-Nat/340, 1-Nat/250; Scanners — AG/FJF74/2200, Densitometer, Entre/Scanner; Production cameras — 1-Nu/20-24, 1-K/18-20 V241; Automatic film processors — LE.
PRESSROOM: Line 1 — 6-Wd/240; Folders — 1-Wd/2:1. MAILROOM: Counter stackers — 1-BG; Wrapping singles — 2-Us; Addressing machine — 1-Am. WIRE SERVICES: News — AP; Syndicates — UPI, TMS, King Features, Universal Press, TV Data; Receiving dishes — AP. BUSINESS COMPUTERS: RSK/TRS 80; Applications: Bills, Accts payable, Accts receivable, Profit & loss statements, Payroll, Mail lists.

ST. JOHNSBURY

Caledonia County

'90 U.S. Census- 7,608; E&P '96 Est. 7,451
ABC-CZ (90): 7,608 (HH 3,118)

The Caledonian-Record

(e-mon to sat)

The Caledonian-Record, 25 Federal St.; PO Box 8, St. Johnsbury, VT 05819; tel (802) 748-8121; fax (802) 748-1613.
Circulation: 11,423(e); 11,423(e-sat); ABC Sept. 30, 1995.
Price: 35¢(d); 35¢(sat); $2.10/wk (carrier); $10.50/mo (VT & NH), $12.00/mo (all other states); $110.00/yr (VT & NH), $128.00/yr (all other states).
Advertising: Open inch rate $8.00(e); $8.00(e-sat). **Representative:** Landon Associates Inc.
News Service: AP. **Politics:** Republican. **Established:** 1837.
Not Published: New Year; Memorial Day; Independence Day; Labor Day; Thanksgiving; Christmas.
Special Editions: Progress Edition (Jan); Bridal (Mar); Home Show (Apr); High School Graduation (June 15); Travel Guide (June); Back-to-School (Aug); Car Care (Oct); Christmas Gift Guide (Nov 22); Christmas Greeting Cards (Dec 24).
Special Weekly Sections: Fun, Food & Fashion (tues); Health Beat (thur); Religion (fri); Weddings, Business (sat); Entertainment (daily).

CORPORATE OFFICERS

President H G Smith
Vice Pres Mark Smith
Treasurer Barbara Smith
Clerk John Primmer

GENERAL MANAGEMENT

Publisher Mark Smith
Purchasing Agent Mark Smith
General Manager Arnold Munkittrick

ADVERTISING

Manager Mike Gonyaw

CIRCULATION

Manager Arnold Munkittrick
Asst Manager Judy Burke

NEWS EXECUTIVE

Managing Editor Ellie Dixon

EDITORS AND MANAGERS

Books/Food Editor Barbara Smith
City/Metro Editor Jan Newpher
Education Editor Karen Smith
Entertainment/Amusements Editor Roxi Jones
Picture Editor Wayland Sinclair
Sports Editor Dan Snapp
Women's Editor Barbara Smith

PRODUCTION

Manager Reed Garfield

Market Information: TMC.
Mechanical available: Offset; Black and 3 ROP colors; insert accepted — preprinted, all; page cut-offs — 22¾".
Mechanical specifications: Type page 13½" x 21½"; E - 6 cols, 2.06", .13" between; A - 6 cols, 2.06", .13" between; C - 8 cols, 1.56", .13" between.
Commodity consumption: Newsprint 445 short tons; widths 29", 14½"; black ink 13,200 pounds; color ink 745 pounds; single pages printed 6,792; average pages per issue 21.9(d); single plates used 3,396.
Equipment: EDITORIAL: Front-end hardware — Mk; Front-end software — Mk. CLASSIFIED: Front-end hardware — Mk; Front-end software — Mk; Printers — TI/OMNI 800. DISPLAY: Adv layout systems — Ap/Mac; Front-end hardware — 3-Ap/Mac Quadra 950, 6-Ap/Mac IIci; Front-end software — Aldus/FreeHand. PRODUCTION: Typesetters — 3-NewGen, Imager Plus 12; Plate exposures — 2-Nu/Flip Top FT40V6; Plate processors — Nat/250; Scanners — Ap/Mac; Production cameras — 1-R/500, 1-Kk/Image Maker 800; Automatic film processors — 2-Vostech/DT-22.
PRESSROOM: Line 1 — 5-G/Community; Folders — 1-G. MAILROOM: Bundle tyer — 1-Bu/PTM. WIRE SERVICES: News — AP; Receiving dishes — size-8m, AP. BUSINESS COMPUTERS: 2-ATT/3B1; Applications: Vision Data: Circ, Payroll, Accts receivable, Accts payable, Gen ledger; PCs & micros networked.

VIRGINIA

ALEXANDRIA

Independent City

'90 U.S. Census- 111,183; E&P '96 Est. 116,965
ABC-NDM (90): 111,183 (HH 53,280)

The Alexandria Journal

(m-mon to fri)

The Alexandria Journal, 2720 Prosperity Ave., Fairfax, VA 22034-1000; tel (703) 560-4000; e-mail journalexp@aol.com, journal@infi.net; web site http://www.infi.net/journal. Journal Newspapers Inc. group.
Circulation: 5,024(m); ABC Sept. 30, 1995.
Price: 25¢(d); $65.00/yr.
Advertising: Open inch rate $14.50(m). **Representative:** Cresmer, Woodward, O'Mara & Ormsbee.
News Services: AP, SHNS. **Established:** 1972 (weekly), 1981 (daily).
Not Published: Postal holidays.
Advertising not accepted: X-rated movies.
Special Weekly Sections: Home PC (mon); Food, Home (wed); Fashion (thur); Cover Story, Home Report, Auto Report (fri).
Magazine: USA Weekend (fri).

CORPORATE OFFICERS

Chairman Rupert Phillips
President Karl Spain

GENERAL MANAGEMENT

Publisher Ryan E Phillips

ADVERTISING

Director Kenneth Courter

TELECOMMUNICATIONS

Director-Telecommunications Jim Reeves

CIRCULATION

Director Michael Wynn

NEWS EXECUTIVE

Managing Editor Jane Touzalin

EDITORS AND MANAGERS

Bureau Editor Colin Clark
City/Metro Editor Bill Hollyer
Editorial Page Editor Alan Fogg
Entertainment/Amusements Editor Mary Ellen Webb
News Editor Will Scheltema
Chief Photographer Parker Daniell
Real Estate Editor James McCormick
Sports Editor Paul Bergeron
Tempo Editor Linda Schubert

MANAGEMENT INFORMATION SERVICES

Data Processing Manager Jim Reeves

PRODUCTION

Director Kim Council
Director-Operations Jim Reeves

Market Information: Zoned editions; Split Run; TMC; ADS; Electronic edition.
Mechanical available: Offset; Black and 3 ROP colors; insert accepted — preprinted; page cut-offs — 22¾".
Mechanical specifications: Type page 13" x 21½"; E - 6 cols, $2\frac{1}{16}$", 1/8" between; A - 6 cols, $2\frac{1}{16}$", 1/8" between; C - 10 cols, 1¼", 1/16" between.
Commodity consumption: Newsprint 11,000 short tons; widths 27½", 41¼", 55"; black ink 198,000 pounds; color ink 70,000 pounds; average pages per issue 40(d); single plates used 140,000.
Equipment: EDITORIAL: Front-end hardware — AT, Euromax; Front-end software — AT, Euromax. CLASSIFIED: Front-end hardware — AT; Front-end software — AT; Printers — Teletype. DISPLAY: Adv layout systems — SCS/Layout 8000; Front-end hardware — Dell/310; Front-end software — SCS/Layout 8000; Printers — HP/LaserJet II; Other equipment — Falco/terminals, Penril/modem 400 Watt UPS mouse. PRODUCTION: Typesetters — 2-Cx, 1-Linotype-Hell/Linotronic 100; Plate exposures — 1-WL/IV, 3-Nu/Flip Top; Plate processors — 1-W/38C, 1-W/3-D, 1-Kk/30", 1-3M; Scanners — 2-ECR/Autokon 1000; Production cameras — 1-C/Spartan III, 1-C/Spartan II; Automatic film processors — 2-LE/PC18, 2-LE/24L, 1-P/24, 1-P/48"; Color separation equipment (conventional) — Kl; Digital color separation equipment — CD/645 IE.
PRESSROOM: Line 1 — 8-G/Metro (w/4 half decks); Line 2 — 8-G/Metro (w/4 half decks); Line 3 — 8-G/Metro (w/4 half decks); Line 4 — G/Colorliner (4 Stacks/1 Mono); Folders — 2-G/double 3:2, 1-G/3:2, 1-G/Jaw, 2-G/double 2:1. MAILROOM: Counter stackers — 2-Fg/H500, 1-MM/259, 3-MM/288, 2-MM/1231, 5-HL/Monitor; Inserters and stuffers — 1-S/48P Double Delivery, 2-S/72P Double, 1-MM/308; Bundle tyer — 2-MLN/2A, 1-MLN/2, 1-MLN/2EE, 1-MLN/MA, 5-J/80; Wrapping singles — 5-Ideal/505-30N; Addressing machine — 4-ABD/9400 Ink Jet, 2-CH/525E, 1-CH/528, 2-BH/1530. LIBRARY: Electronic — QLS. WIRE SERVICES: News — SHNS, AP; Receiving dishes — AP. BUSINESS COMPUTERS: Applications: Accts receivable, Accts payable, Circ; AT: Editorial, Class, Legal; Vision Data, Lotus, Word-Perfect.

ARLINGTON

Arlington County

'90 U.S. Census- 152,875; E&P '96 Est. 153,222
ABC-NDM (90): 170,936 (HH 78,520)

The Arlington Journal

(m-mon to fri)

The Arlington Journal, 2720 Prosperity Ave., Fairfax, VA 22034-1000; tel (703) 560-4000; fax (703) 846-8301; e-mail journalexp@aol.com, journal@infi.net; web site http://www.infi.net/journal. Journal Newspapers Inc. group.
Circulation: 7,521(m); ABC Sept. 30, 1995.
Price: 25¢(d); $65.00/yr.
Advertising: Open inch rate $15.25(m). **Representative:** Cresmer, Woodward, O'Mara & Ormsbee.
News Services: AP, SHNS. **Established:** 1972 (weekly), 1981 (daily).
Note: For detailed production and printing information, see Alexandria (VA) Journal listing.
Not Published: Postal holidays.
Advertising not accepted: X-rated movies.
Special Weekly Sections: Home PC (mon); Food, Home (wed); Fashion (thur); Cover Story (Arts, Travel, Entertainment), Home Report, Auto Report (fri).
Magazine: USA Weekend.

CORPORATE OFFICERS

Chairman Rupert Phillips
President Karl Spain

GENERAL MANAGEMENT

Publisher Ryan E Phillips

ADVERTISING

Director Kenneth Courter

TELECOMMUNICATIONS

Director-Telecommunications Jim Reeves

CIRCULATION

Director Michael Wynn

NEWS EXECUTIVE

Managing Editor Jane Touzalin

EDITORS AND MANAGERS

Bureau Editor Colin Clark
City/Metro Editor Bill Hollyer
Editorial Page Editor Alan Fogg
Entertainment/Amusements Editor Mary Ellen Webb
News Editor Will Scheltema
Chief Photographer Parker Daniell
Real Estate Editor James McCormick
Sports Editor Paul Bergeron
Tempo Editor Linda Schubert

MANAGEMENT INFORMATION SERVICES

Data Processing Manager Jim Reeves

PRODUCTION

Director Kim Council
Director-Operations Jim Reeves

Market Information: TMC; ADS; Electronic edition.
Mechanical available: Offset; Black and 3 ROP colors; insert accepted — preprinted; page cut-offs — 22¾".
Mechanical specifications: Type page 13" x 21½"; E - 6 cols, $2\frac{1}{16}$", 1/8" between; A - 6 cols, $2\frac{1}{16}$", 1/8" between; C - 10 cols, 1¼", 1/16" between.
Commodity consumption: average pages per issue 15(d).
Equipment: EDITORIAL: Front-end hardware — AT, Euromax; Front-end software — AT, Euromax. CLASSIFIED: Front-end hardware — AT; Front-end software — AT; Printers — Teletype. DISPLAY: Adv layout systems — SCS/Layout 8000; Front-end hardware — Dell/310; Front-end software — SCS/Layout 8000; Printers — HP/LaserJet II; Other equipment — Falco, Penril. WIRE SERVICES: News — SHNS, AP; Receiving dishes — AP. BUSINESS COMPUTERS: NCR/3447; Applications: Accts payable, Accts receivable, Circ; Vision Data, Lotus, WordPerfect.

USA TODAY (m-mon to fri)

USA Today, 1000 Wilson Blvd., Arlington, VA 22229; tel (703) 276-3400; e-mail usatoday@clark.net; web site http://www.usatoday.com. Gannett Co. Inc. group.
Circulation: 1,523,610(m); 1,936,250(m-fri); ABC Sept. 30, 1995.
Price: 50¢(d); 50¢(fri); $156.00/yr (carrier).
Advertising: Open inch rate $707.69(m); $849.23 (m-fri).
News Services: Crain Communications, AP, UPI, GNS. **Politics:** Independent. **Established:** 1982.
Note: USA Today does not sell advertising on an inch rate basis: advertiser can purchase the specific sizes offered by the newspaper. Classified advertising is sold at a line rate. USA Today is published daily except Saturday, Sunday and legal holidays in Rosslyn, Virginia and pages are transmitted via satellite to printing facilities throughout the United States. USA Today is printed at Gannett plants in Harrison, NY; Lansdale, PA; Tarentum, PA; Port Huron, MI; Gainesville, GA; Fort Myers, FL; St. Cloud, MN; Fort Collins, CO; San Bernardino, CA; Marin County, CA; Olympia, WA; Hattiesburg, MS; Richmond, IN; Phoenix, AZ; Miramar, FL; Nashville, TN; Cocoa, FL; Atlanta, GA; St. Louis, MO and at contract printers in Springfield, VA; Chicago, IL; Kankakee, IL; Pasadena, TX; Greensboro, NC; Lawrence, KS; Batavia, NY; Rockaway, NJ; Columbia, SC; Boston, MA; Mansfield, OH; Arlington, TX; St. Louis, MO; Salt Lake City, UT. Printing facilities for the international edition of USA Today are located in Switzerland, Hong Kong and England.
Not Published: New Year; Memorial Day; Independence Day; Labor Day; Thanksgiving; Christmas.

Special Editions: Super Bowl '96 (Jan); Autos '96 (Feb); Leisure Travel, NCAA Playoffs (Mar); Business Travel, NBA Playoffs (Apr); Leisure Travel, Motor Racing (May); Business Travel, Technology: PC Expo (June); NFL Preview, Wheels (Sept); Leisure Travel, Technology: Fall Comdex (Nov).

GENERAL MANAGEMENT

Publisher Thomas Curley
Assoc Publisher Carolyn Vesper
President Thomas Curley
Vice Pres-Info Systems John Palmisano
Vice Pres-Business Operations Antoinette Miller
Vice Pres-Human Resources Terry T Sullivan

ADVERTISING

Senior Vice Pres Carolyn Vesper
Vice Pres/Assoc Director Jack Dickman
Vice Pres-Travel/Related Sales Janet Smith
Vice Pres-Midwest Sales Johanna DeBonte
Vice Pres-Atlantic Sales Ben Laureno
Director-Classified Susan Rannochio

MARKETING AND PROMOTION

Vice Pres-Marketing/Promotion Melissa Snyder

TELECOMMUNICATIONS

Vice Pres-Info Systems John Palmisano
Online Manager Lorraine Cichiowski

CIRCULATION

Senior Vice Pres Larry G Lindquist
Vice Pres-National Circulation Sales Denise Restauri
Vice Pres Jeff Webber
Vice Pres Russell Ford
Vice Pres Doris Kasold
Vice Pres-Marketing Melissa Snyder
General Manager-North Jersey Don Malone
General Manager-Atlanta Carol Alka
General Manager-Boston Bill Windsor
General Manager-Carolinas Jim Stephens
General Manager-Chicago Dave Fiedelman
General Manager-Cincinnati Ron Jackson
General Manager-Cleveland/Columbus Rick Gebensleben
General Manager-Dallas Charles Boles
General Manager-Denver Dan Creacy
General Manager-Detroit Bob Hamlin
General Manager-Houston Ed Wood
General Manager-Kansas City Rick Sass
General Manager-Los Angeles Fritz Stellrecht
General Manager-Minneapolis Ben Sahr
General Manager-Nashville Linda Boggs
General Manager-New York Peter Donohue
General Manager-N Central Florida Fran Cianciola
General Manager-Philadelphia Stephen Reynolds
General Manager-Phoenix Jean Downs
General Manager-Pittsburgh Lee Caylor
General Manager-San Francisco Angela Carmen
General Manager-Seattle Mike Donohue
General Manager-South Florida Kevin Cooper
General Manager-St Louis Newell Jensen
General Manager-Washington/Baltimore Jeff Scharfeld
General Manager-Western New York Debra Swift

NEWS EXECUTIVES

Editor Dave Mazzarella
Editor-USA Weekend Marcia Bullard
Editorial Page Editor Karen Jurgensen
Exec Editor Robert Dubill
Senior Editor Wanda Lloyd
Senior Editor Ray Gniewek
Assoc Editor Tom McNamara
Managing Editor-Life Susan Weiss
Managing Editor-News Hal Ritter
Managing Editor-Graphics/Photography Richard Curtis
Managing Editor-Sports Gene Policinski
Managing Editor-International Edition John Simpson
Managing Editor-Money John Hillkirk
Managing Editor-Page One Monte Lorell

EDITORS AND MANAGERS

Art Director Dash Parham
Automotive Editor James R Healey
Business/Travel Editor Doug Carroll
Education Editor Dennis Kelly
Entertainment Editor Kitty Yancey
Environmental Editor Rae Tyson
Fashion/Style Reporter Elizabeth Snead
Foreign Editor Johanna Neuman
Health/Medical Editor Anita Sama
Leisure/Travel Editor Ron Schoolmeester
National Editor Lee Ann Taylor
Photo Editor Richard Curtis
Political/Government Editor Lee Ann Taylor
Religion Reporter Cathy Grossman
Sports Editor Gene Policinski
Television Editor Dennis Moore
Trends Editor Kitty Yancey

PRODUCTION

Vice Pres Ken Kirkhart

Market Information: Operate database; Electronic edition.
Mechanical available: Offset; Black and 3 ROP colors; page cut-offs — $22\frac{3}{4}$".
Mechanical specifications: Type page 13" x 21"; E - 6 cols, $2\frac{1}{16}$", $\frac{1}{8}$" between; A - 6 cols, $2\frac{1}{16}$", $\frac{1}{8}$" between; C - 9 cols, $1\frac{3}{8}$", $\frac{1}{16}$" between.
Commodity consumption: Newsprint 150,000 metric tons; widths 55", $41\frac{1}{4}$", $27\frac{1}{2}$"; black ink 3,590,000 pounds; color ink 2,058,000 pounds; single pages printed 10,947; average pages per issue 42(d); single plates used 828,356.
Equipment: EDITORIAL: Front-end hardware — AT/9000, 1-AT/9080, 40-AT/A500, 60-TM, IBM. CLASSIFIED: Front-end hardware — 2-AT/5000. PRODUCTION: Typesetters — 2-AU/Micro 5; Plate exposures — 2-Nu/Flip Top; Plate processors — 2-Nu/Flip Top; Scanners — 6-Laps/Transport & Processor; Production cameras — 2-C/Spartan III; Automatic film processors — 4-LE/24AQ, 1-LE/24BQ, 1-DP/24L; Film transporters — 1-C; Color separation equipment (conventional) — 1-RZ/2005, 1-CD/645IE, 1-CD/635ES. COMMUNICATIONS: Facsimile — Ricoh. WIRE SERVICES: News — AP, UPI, GNS, PR Newswire, Sports Stat Wire; Stock tables — AP Digital Stocks; Receiving dishes — size-3m, AP, UPI, TVRO Uplink. BUSINESS COMPUTERS: 3-IBM/4381, 1-IBM/4361, S/38, S/36; Applications: Circ processing, Financial acct, Adv processing; PCs & micros networked; PCs & main system networked.

BLUEFIELD

See BLUEFIELD, WV

BRISTOL, VA-TN

An Independent City, VA
Sullivan County, TN

'90 U.S. Census- 41,847 (Bristol, VA 18,426; Bristol, TN 23,421); E&P '96 Est. 41,111 (Bristol, VA 18,132; Bristol, TN 22,979)
ABC-CZ (90): 48,575 (HH 19,782)

Herald-Courier Virginia Tennessean

(all day-mon to fri; m-sat; S)

Herald-Courier Virginia Tennessean, 320 Morrison Blvd.; PO Box 609, Bristol, VA 24201; tel (540) 669-2181; fax (540) 669-3696.
Circulation: 42,438(a); 42,764(m-sat); 45,997(S); ABC Sept. 30, 1995.
Price: 50¢(d); 50¢(sat); $1.00(S); $10.95/mo.
Advertising: Open inch rate $28.95(a); $28.95(m-sat); $28.95(S). **Representative:** Landon Associates Inc.
News Services: AP, SHNS. **Politics:** Independent. **Established:** 1870 (Herald Courier), 1949 (Virginia Tennessean).
Not Published: Christmas.
Advertising not accepted: Contraceptives.
Special Editions: Wedding Planner (Jan); June Bride (June); Business Showcase (July); Southern Living Cooking School, New Car Guide (Oct); Progress; Spring; Spring Home & Garden; Spring NASCAR Race; Fall NASCAR Race; Football; Graduation; Basketball.
Magazines: TV Week (fri); Parade (S); A! Arts Magazine (mailed monthly).

CORPORATE OFFICERS

Board Chairman Thomas Eugene Worrell
President Anne Worrell
Vice Pres Arthur S Powers

GENERAL MANAGEMENT

Publisher Arthur S Powers
Manager-Credit Jo Ann Cahill
Purchasing Agent Jo Ann Cahill

ADVERTISING

Manager-Retail Quentin Lewis
Manager-Classified David M Millsap

MARKETING AND PROMOTION

Director-Marketing J Wallace Coffey
Director-Sales Joseph H Adams
Asst Director-Marketing Kathy Graybeal

CIRCULATION

Manager Bill Hicks
Manager-Distribution John Arnold

NEWS EXECUTIVES

Exec Editor John Molley
Managing Editor Brian Reese

EDITORS AND MANAGERS

City Editor Susan Bolling
Community Editor Carla Twyman
Editor-Opinion Rebecca Masters
Fashion Editor Anne Worrell
Chief Photographer Bill Mckee
Radio/Television Editor Jan Patrick
Teen-Age/Youth Editor Carla Twyman

MANAGEMENT INFORMATION SERVICES

Data Processing Manager Belinda Whitaker

PRODUCTION

Manager-Computer Service Robert Horne
Superintendent-Pressroom Don Anderson

Market Information: Zoned editions; TMC.
Mechanical available: Offset; Black and 3 ROP colors; insert accepted — preprinted, all; page cut-offs — $21\frac{1}{2}$".
Mechanical specifications: Type page 13" x $21\frac{1}{2}$"; E - 6 cols, $2\frac{1}{16}$", $\frac{1}{8}$" between; A - 6 cols, $2\frac{1}{16}$", $\frac{1}{8}$" between; C - 9 cols, $1\frac{3}{8}$", $\frac{1}{16}$" between.
Commodity consumption: Newsprint 3,329 short tons; widths $27\frac{1}{2}$", $13\frac{3}{4}$"; black ink 100,000 pounds; color ink 6,000 pounds; single pages printed 11,700; average pages per issue 30(d), 64(S); single plates used 13,000.
Equipment: EDITORIAL: Front-end hardware — SIA; Front-end software — Dewar/Disc IV; Printers — 2-LaserMaster/1200; Other equipment — Okidata/393, HP/ScanJet II P, Ap/Mac Quadra 650. CLASSIFIED: Front-end hardware — SIA; Front-end software — Dewar/Disc IV; Printers — 2-LaserMaster/1200; Other equipment — Polaroid/SprintScan 35. DISPLAY: Adv layout systems — Ap/Mac; Front-end hardware — Ap/Mac, 5-Ap/Mac IIci, Ap/Mac Quadra 650; Front-end software — QuarkXPress; Printers — LaserMaster/1200, AG/3400, LaserMaster/Unity 1800; Other equipment — HP/ScanJet IIP. PRODUCTION: Pagination software — Dewar/Disk IV; Typesetters — COM/3400, LaserMaster/Unity 1800; Plate exposures — 2-Nu/Flip Top 40U6VPNS; Plate processors — 1-WL/Lithoplater 25; Scanners — 1-RZ/4050; Production cameras — 1-C/1244, 1-C/1270; Automatic film processors — 2-LE/LD-24 AQ; Film transporters — 1-C/1247; Shrink lenses — 1-CK Optical/SQU-7; Color separation equipment (conventional) — 1-RZ/4050; Digital color separation equipment — 1-RZ/4050.
PRESSROOM: Line 1 — 6-G/Urbanite single width, 4-G/Urbanite single width; Folders — 1-G; Pasters — 8-Cary/Flying Pasters; Press control system — Fin. MAILROOM: Counter stackers — 2-MM/CV70; Inserters and stuffers — 1-GMA/8 head SLS 1000; Bundle tyer — 1-MLN/2, 1-MLN/2A; Addressing machine — 6-Wm. LIBRARY: Electronic — Mead Data Central/Nexis NewsView; Combination — Fuji/Microfilm. WIRE SERVICES: News — AP; Photos — AP; Stock tables — AP; Syndicates — SHNS, King Features; Receiving dishes — size-10ft, AP. BUSINESS COMPUTERS: IBM/Sys 36-5360; Applications: Depreciation: Circ, Adv billing, Accts receivable, Gen ledger, Payroll, Accts payable; PCs & micros networked; PCs & main system networked.

CHARLOTTESVILLE

An Independent City

'90 U.S. Census- 40,341; E&P '96 Est. 41,097
ABC-NDM (90): 155,927 (HH 57,731)

The Daily Progress

(m-mon to sat; S)

The Daily Progress, 685 W. Rio Rd.; PO Box 9030, Charlottesville, VA 22906; tel (804) 978-7200; fax (804) 978-2985. Media General (Virginia Newspapers Inc.) group.
Circulation: 30,096(m); 30,096(m-sat); 33,500(S); ABC Sept. 30, 1995.
Price: 50¢(d); 50¢(sat); $1.50(S); $2.55/wk.
Advertising: Open inch rate $33.25(m); $33.25(m-sat); $33.25(S).
News Services: AP, LAT-WP. **Politics:** Independent. **Established:** 1892.
Special Weekly Sections: Best Food Day (wed, S).
Magazine: USA Weekend (S).

GENERAL MANAGEMENT

Publisher Lawrence McConnell
Business Manager Ford Bonardi

ADVERTISING

Director Wanda J Birckhead
Manager-Sales Joy P Monopoli
Manager-Sales Tina Hancock

TELECOMMUNICATIONS

Audiotex Manager Susan Wagner

CIRCULATION

Director Tony O Stophel

NEWS EXECUTIVES

Editor Wayne Mogielnicki
Editorial Page Editor Anita Shelburne

EDITORS AND MANAGERS

City Editor Andrea Shaw
News Editor Robert Knapp
Sports Editor Jerry Ratcliffe

PRODUCTION

Manager-Operations Warren Pitts

Market Information: Zoned editions; TMC; Operate audiotex.
Mechanical available: Offset; Black and 3 ROP colors; insert accepted — preprinted; page cut-offs — 22".
Mechanical specifications: Type page 13" x 21"; E - 6 cols, $2\frac{1}{16}$", $\frac{1}{8}$" between; A - 6 cols, $2\frac{1}{16}$", $\frac{1}{8}$" between; C - 9 cols, $1\frac{1}{8}$", $\frac{1}{16}$" between.
Commodity consumption: Newsprint 3,100 short tons; widths 56", 42", 14"; black ink 75,697 pounds; color ink 13,000 pounds; single pages printed 13,500; average pages per issue 36(d), 72(S); single plates used 21,250.
Equipment: EDITORIAL: Front-end hardware — 2-EKI/Televideo, Lf/Leafscan for Color Seperation, EKI/Televideo-Earth Station; Printers — 4-Ap/Mac Laser II NTX; Other equipment — 2-NewGen. CLASSIFIED: Front-end hardware — 5-Compaq; Other equipment — 7-Ap/Mac Laser, NewGen, Imager Plus/12. AUDIOTEX: Hardware — Unix; Software — Micro Voice; Supplier name — Micro Voice, VNN. DISPLAY: Adv layout systems — DTI/AD Makeup II, Adobe/Photoshop. PRODUCTION: Typesetters — 1-Ap/Mac Laser, 1-NewGen, Image Plus 12; Plate exposures — Nu/Flip Top FT40V2UPNS; Plate processors — WL/Plater, DP; Scanners — RZ; Production cameras — 1-C/Spartan III L270, SCREEN; Automatic film processors — 1-LE/EX 26, DP/24L; Reproportion units — C/BW; Film transporters — 1-C.
PRESSROOM: Line 1 — 5-MAN/Uniman 4-12 double width; Pasters — 5-MEG; Press control system — 3-GE/100 h.p. motor drive. MAILROOM: Counter stackers — 3-Id; Inserters and stuffers — HI/NR 1372 S, Ic; Bundle tyer — 2-MLN/ML2EE; Addressing machine — 5-Wm. LIBRARY: Electronic — Cannon/PC Printer. COMMUNICATIONS: Facsimile — 2-Sharp/FO-200, 1-Murata/M900; Systems used — satellite. WIRE SERVICES: News — AP; Photos — AP; Stock tables — AP; Syndicates — NYT; Receiving dishes — size-10ft, AP. BUSINESS COMPUTERS: 2-DPT/6600, 8-EKI/Televideo; Applications: Circ, Adv billing, Accts receivable, Gen ledger, Payroll; PCs & main system networked.

CHESAPEAKE

See NORFOLK

COVINGTON

An Independent City

'90 U.S. Census- 6,991; E&P '96 Est. 6,088
ABC-CZ (90): 6,991 (HH 2,998)

Virginian Review

(e-mon to sat)

Virginian Review, 128 N. Maple Ave.; PO Box 271, Covington, VA 24426-0271; tel (540) 962-2121; fax (540) 962-5072.
Circulation: 8,643(e); 8,643(e-sat); ABC Sept. 30, 1995.
Price: 50¢(d); 50¢(sat); $1.22/wk (carrier); $5.25/mo (carrier); $63.00/yr (carrier).
Advertising: Open inch rate $8.70(e); $8.70(e-sat). **Representative:** Landon Associates Inc.
News Service: AP. **Politics:** Independent. **Established:** 1914.
Not Published: New Year; Independence Day; Labor Day; Thanksgiving; Christmas.
Advertising not accepted: Erroneous medical cures.
Special Editions: Bridal (Feb); Home Improvement (Apr); Custom Antique Cars (Aug); Football (Sept); Hunting, Christmas Shopping (Nov); Basketball, Christmas Greetings (Dec).
Magazines: Leisure Times (sat); TV Listings Tab.

CORPORATE OFFICERS
President — Horton P Beirne
Vice Pres — Rose S Beirne
Secretary/Treasurer — Mary Lamb

GENERAL MANAGEMENT
General Manager — Horton P Beirne

ADVERTISING
Director — Robert Tucker

MARKETING AND PROMOTION
Director-Marketing/Promotion — Robert Tucker

CIRCULATION
Director — Ernie Lynn

NEWS EXECUTIVE
Editor — Horton P Beirne

EDITORS AND MANAGERS
Action Line Editor — Horton P Beirne
Automotive Editor — Coite Charles Beirne
Books Editor — Elizabeth Beirne
Business/Finance Editor — Horton P Beirne
City/Metro Editor — Horton P Beirne
Editorial Page Editor — Horton P Beirne
Education Editor — Horton P Beirne
Entertainment/Amusements Editor — Horton P Beirne
Features Editor — Horton P Beirne
Films/Theater Editor — Elizabeth Beirne
Graphics Editor/Art Director — Horton P Beirne
Librarian — Mary Lamb
Living/Lifestyle Editor — Horton P Beirne
Music Editor — Elizabeth Beirne
National Editor — Horton P Beirne
News Editor — Horton P Beirne
Photo Editor — Horton P Beirne
Political/Government Editor — Horton P Beirne
Radio/Television Editor — Elizabeth Beirne
Society Editor — Mary Bennett
Sports Editor — Emory Brackman
Teen-Age/Youth Editor — Elizabeth Beirne

Market Information: TMC; ADS.
Mechanical available: Offset; Black and 3 ROP colors; insert accepted — preprinted; page cut-offs — 21½".
Mechanical specifications: Type page 13" x 21½"; E - 6 cols, 2¹⁄₁₆", ⅛" between; A - 6 cols, 2¹⁄₁₆", ⅛" between; C - 8 cols, 1½", ⅛" between.
Commodity consumption: Newsprint 425 short tons; widths 27½", 13¾"; black ink 12,000 pounds; color ink 400 pounds; single pages printed 4,000; average pages per issue 14(d); single plates used 3,000.
Equipment: EDITORIAL: Front-end hardware — IBM/PC; Front-end software — NewsCraft/Edit; Printers — NewGen/PS1200T, NewGen/PS-630. CLASSIFIED: Front-end hardware — IBM/PC; Front-end software — NewsCraft/Classified; Printers — NewGen/PS1200T, NewGen/PS-630. DISPLAY: Front-end hardware — IBM, Ap/Mac; Front-end software — Newscraft, Aldus/PageMaker, Multi-Ad, Ap/Mac; Printers — NewGen. PRODUCTION: Plate exposures — Nu/Flip Top Ultra Plus; Plate processors — Nat; Production cameras — B; Automatic film processors — SCREEN/LD-281-Q.
PRESSROOM: Line 1 — 5-G/Community.
MAILROOM: Inserters and stuffers — KAN/320; Addressing machine — Ch/515.
COMMUNICATIONS: Facsimile — ATT/3500D. WIRE SERVICES: News — AP; Photos — AP; Syndicates — King Features, Universal Press, Chicago Tribune, LATS; Receiving dishes — size-14ft, AP. BUSINESS COMPUTERS: IBM; Applications: Novell, dBase.

CULPEPER
Culpeper County
'90 U.S. Census- 8,581; E&P '96 Est. 9,720

Culpeper Star-Exponent
(m-mon to sat; S)
Culpeper Star-Exponent, 122 W. Spencer St.; PO Box 111, Culpeper, VA 22701; tel (540) 825-0771; fax (540) 825-0778. Media General (Virginia Newspapers Inc.) group.
Circulation: 7,394(m); 7,394(m-sat); 7,394(S); Sworn Oct. 1, 1995.
Price: 35¢(d); 35¢(sat); $1.00(S); $1.90/wk.
Advertising: Open inch rate $13.90(m); $13.90(m-sat); $13.90(S).
News Service: AP. **Politics:** Independent. **Established:** 1881.
Not Published: New Year; Independence Day; Labor Day; Thanksgiving; Christmas.
Special Editions: Progress Edition; Football; Christmas.
Special Weekly Sections: Best Food Days (wed); Best Food Days, Church Pages (sat); Comics (daily).

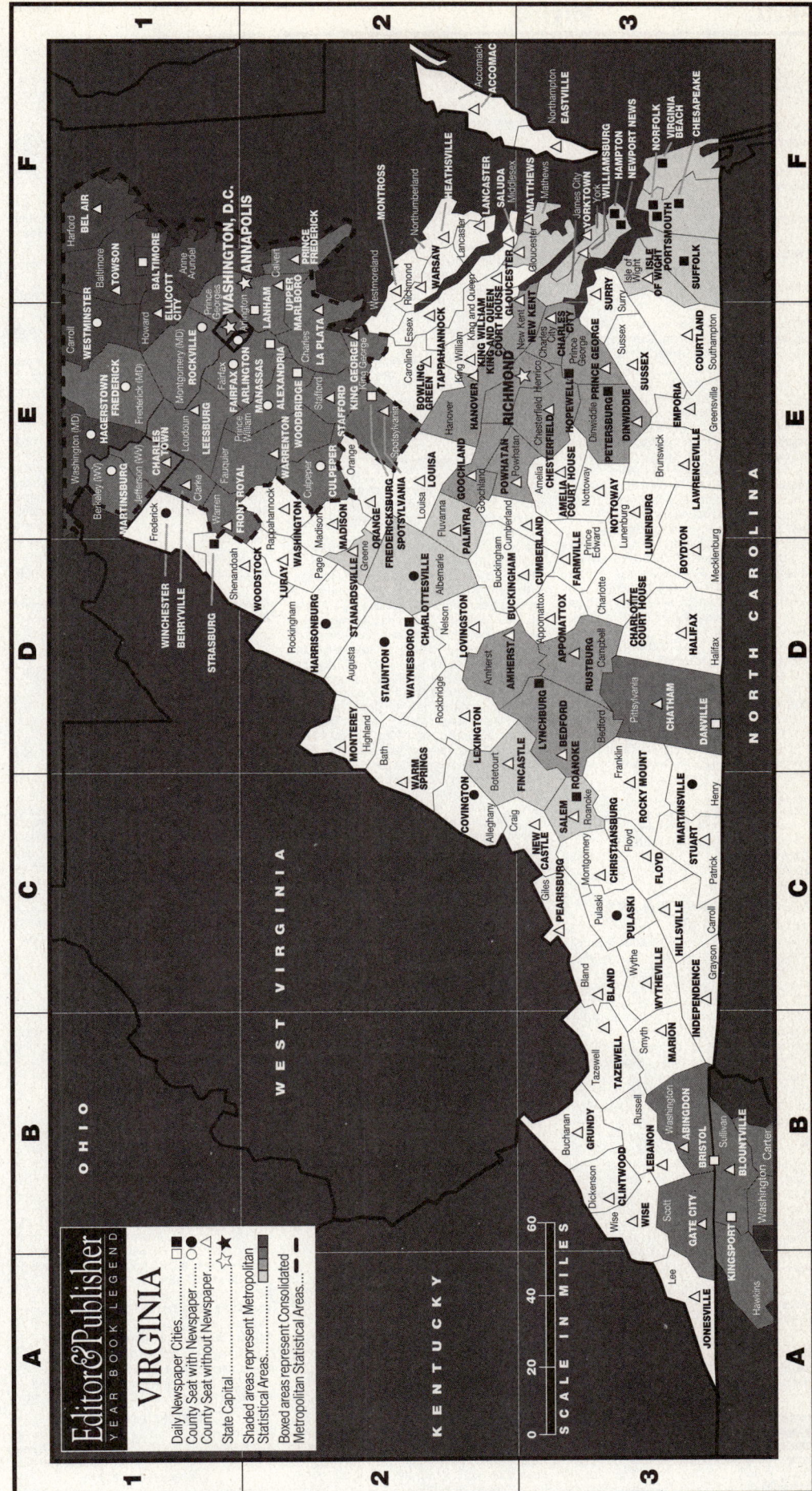

Copyright ©1996 by the Editor & Publisher Co.

I-420 Virginia

Magazines: Community Life (wed); TV Entertainer (sat).

GENERAL MANAGEMENT
Publisher Peter S Yates
Purchasing Agent Peter S Yates
ADVERTISING
Director Dyanne Holt
Classified Phone Person Kathy Mills
CIRCULATION
Manager Frances Smith
NEWS EXECUTIVE
Managing Editor Jeff Dute
PRODUCTION
Foreman-Composing Jack Griffin
Foreman-Pressroom Jack Griffin

Market Information: Zoned editions; TMC.
Mechanical available: Offset; Black and 3 ROP colors; insert accepted — preprinted; page cutoffs — 22 3/4".
Mechanical specifications: Type page 13" x 21 1/2"; E - 6 cols, 2 1/16", 1/8" between; A - 6 cols, 2 1/16", 1/8" between; C - 9 cols, 1 3/8", 1/16" between.
Commodity consumption: Newsprint 400 short tons; widths 28", 14"; single pages printed 6,200; average pages per issue 20(d).
Equipment: EDITORIAL: Front-end hardware — 4-EKI/Televideo, 9-EKI/Earth Station. CLASSIFIED: Front-end hardware — 1-EKI/Televideo. DISPLAY: Adv layout systems — 1-EKI/Televideo, 1-Ap/Mac II; Front-end software — Aldus/PageMaker. PRODUCTION: Typesetters — 2-Laser; Plate exposures — 2-Nu; Plate processors — 1-Nat; Scanners — 1-LE/MD-480; Production cameras — 1-C/Spartan III, 1-B/Caravelle; Automatic film processors — 1-LE.
PRESSROOM: Line 1 — 6-G/Urbanite; Folders — 1-G. MAILROOM: Counter stackers — 1-BG/Count-O-Veyor; Inserters and stuffers — 1-MM/4-into-1; Bundle tyer — 1-Bu, 1-MLN. COMMUNICATIONS: Facsimile — Sharp/FO-330. WIRE SERVICES: News — AP; Receiving dishes — AP. BUSINESS COMPUTERS: 2-EKI/Televideo; Applications: Adv billing, Accts receivable, Gen ledger, Payroll, Accts payable; PCs & micros networked.

DANVILLE

An Independent City
'90 U.S. Census- 53,056; E&P '96 Est. 57,833
ABC-NDM (90): 57,702 (HH 23,378)

Danville Register & Bee

(m-mon to sat; S)

Danville Register & Bee, 700 Monument St.; PO Box 131, Danville, VA 24541; tel (804) 793-2311; fax (804) 797-2299.
Circulation: 24,268(m); 24,268(m-sat); 27,723(S); ABC Sept. 30, 1995.
Price: 25¢(d); 25¢(sat); 75¢(S); $7.50/mo (carrier); $90.00/yr.
Advertising: Open inch rate $14.50(m); $14.50(m-sat); $16.00(S). **Representative:** Landon Associates Inc.
News Services: AP, NYT. **Politics:** Independent. **Established:** 1848.
Special Editions: Bridal; Progress; Harvest Jubilee; Festival in Park; Outdoor Living; Travel; Golden Years; Back-to-School; IRS; Home Improvement; Lawn & Garden; New Cars; Fashions; Food/Fitness; Car Care; Football Tab; Basketball Tab; Dining/Entertainment; Investments; Danville Braves Tab; NASCAR; Chamber of Commerce Tab (monthly); Extra Card Directory (quarterly).
Special Weekly Section: Church Page (weekly).
Magazines: TV Week, USA Weekend (S).

CORPORATE OFFICERS
President Lawson Grant
Secretary/Treasurer Carey Wilkes
GENERAL MANAGEMENT
Publisher Lawson Grant
General Manager Lawson Grant
Business Manager Carey Wilkes
ADVERTISING
Director George L Robinette
Manager-Co-op/Insert George L Robinette
Manager-Promotion Matt Dishman
Manager-Management Info Services Tony Canody
Manager-Retail Ann Browning
MARKETING AND PROMOTION
Director-Promotion Matt Dishman
TELECOMMUNICATIONS
Audiotex Manager Don Webb
CIRCULATION
Director R Morris Burnett
NEWS EXECUTIVE
Exec Editor Bonnie Cooper
EDITOR AND MANAGER
Sports Editor Allan C Milley
MANAGEMENT INFORMATION SERVICES
Manager-Info Service Tony Canody
PRODUCTION
Director-Audiotex Don Webb
Manager Michael Browning

Market Information: Zoned editions; TMC; ADS; Operate audiotex.
Mechanical available: Offset; Black and 3 ROP colors; insert accepted — preprinted, all; page cut-offs — 22 3/4".
Mechanical specifications: Type page 13" x 21 1/2"; E - 6 cols, 2 1/16", 1/8" between; A - 6 cols, 2 1/16", 1/8" between; C - 9 cols, 1 3/8", 1/16" between.
Commodity consumption: Newsprint 1,740 short tons; widths 27 1/2", 13 3/4", 28 1/2", 14 1/4"; black ink 37,000 pounds; color ink 7,900 pounds; single pages printed 11,884; average pages per issue 30(d), 62(S); single plates used 27,700.
Equipment: EDITORIAL: Front-end hardware — 1-SII/Synthesis 66 XR, 20-Roadrunner/PC 486, 4-Ap/Mac, 1-Ap/Mac fileserver; Front-end software — SII/Synthesis 66 XR; Printers — 3-Ap/Mac LaserPrinter, 2-Ap/Mac Pro, 1-Ap/Mac IIG. CLASSIFIED: Front-end hardware — 4-SII/Synthesis 66, Roadrunner/PC 486; Front-end software — Pongrass/Page Integrator. AUDIOTEX: Hardware — PEP/Voice System, BDR/Audio Package. DISPLAY: Adv layout systems — 1-Ap/Mac Quadra 950 fileserver; Front-end hardware — 6-Ap/Mac Quadra 950, 6-Mk/Flatbed Scanner; Front-end software — Adobe/Photoshop, Multi-Ad/Creator; Other equipment — 6-Ap/Mac Flatbed scanner. PRODUCTION: Pagination software — QuarkXPress 3.1; Typesetters — 2-Accuset/Laser Imager, 1-AU/APS 6600 (Hitachi Engine); Plate exposures — Nu/Flip Top FT40V6UPNS, Nu/Flip Top FT40LNS; Plate processors — 1-Nat/A-380; Electronic picture desk — Lf/Ap Leaf Picture Desk, Ap/Mac Quadra 950, Ap/Mac Quadra 840 AV, Microtek/Flatbed Scanner; Production cameras — 1-C/Pager, 1-C/Spartan III; Automatic film processors — 1-LE/LD 1800A, 1-Glunz & Jensen/MultiLine 400, 1-LE/LS 2100 RL On-line; Film transporters — 2-C; Shrink lenses — 1-CK Optical; Digital color separation equipment — 1-Lf/Leafscan 35, 1-Lf/Leafscan 45, Adobe/Photoshop.
PRESSROOM: Line 1 — 9-G/Urbanite 1215-1244, 2-G/Urbanite 1214-1244; Press drives — 2-Fin; Folders — 2-G; Press registration system — Duarte/Pin Registration. MAILROOM: Counter stackers — 1-Fg, 1-HL/Monitor, 1-Id/2000, 1-Id/2100; Inserters and stuffers — HI/48P; Bundle tyer — 1-MLN/ML, 1-MLN/Spirit, 1-MLN/SP-330; Addressing machine — 1-MM/Minuteman quarter folder. LIBRARY: Electronic — SII. WIRE SERVICES: News — AP SelectStox, AP Datastream, AP Datafeatures, AP GraphicsNet, NYT, AP Photostream; Photos — AP; Stock tables — AP SelectStox; Receiving dishes — size-3m, AP. BUSINESS COMPUTERS: DEC/XL-590, Data Sciences; Applications: Accts receivable, Accts payable, Gen ledger, Circ; PCs & micros networked; PCs & main system networked.

FAIRFAX

Fairfax County
'90 U.S. Census- 19,622; E&P '96 Est. 19,136
ABC-NDM (90): 979,479 (HH 364,148)

The Fairfax Journal

(m-mon to fri)

The Fairfax Journal, 2720 Prosperity Ave., Fairfax, VA 22034-1000; tel (703) 560-4000; fax (703) 846-8301; e-mail journalexp @aol.com, journal@infi.net; web site http://www.infi.net/journal. Journal Newspapers Inc. group.
Circulation: 54,636(m); ABC Sept. 30, 1995.
Price: 25¢(d); $65.00/yr.
Advertising: Open inch rate $39.50(m). **Representative:** Cresmer, Woodward, O'Mara & Ormsbee.
News Services: AP, SHNS. **Established:** 1972 (weekly), 1981 (daily).
Note: For detailed printing and production information, see Alexandria Journal listing.
Not Published: Postal holidays.
Advertising not accepted: X-rated movies.
Special Weekly Sections: Home PC (mon); Food, Home (wed); Fashion (thur); Cover Story, Home Report, Auto Report (fri).
Magazine: USA Weekend.

CORPORATE OFFICERS
Chairman Rupert E Phillips
President Karl Spain
GENERAL MANAGEMENT
Publisher Ryan E Phillips
ADVERTISING
Director Kenneth Courter
TELECOMMUNICATIONS
Director-Telecommunications Jim Reeves
CIRCULATION
Director Michael Wynn
NEWS EXECUTIVE
Managing Editor Jane Touzalin
EDITORS AND MANAGERS
City/Metro Editor Bill Hollyer
Editorial Page Editor Alan Fogg
Entertainment/Amusements Editor Mary Ellen Webb
News Editor Will Scheltema
Chief Photographer Parker Daniel
Real Estate Editor James McCormick
Sports Editor Paul Bergeron
Tempo Editor Linda Schubert
MANAGEMENT INFORMATION SERVICES
Data Processing Manager Jim Reeves
PRODUCTION
Director-Operations Jim Reeves
Director Kim Council

Market Information: TMC; ADS; Electronic edition.
Mechanical available: Offset; Black and 3 ROP colors; insert accepted — preprinted; page cutoffs — 22 3/4".
Mechanical specifications: Type page 13" x 21 1/2"; E - 6 cols, 2 1/16", 1/8" between; A - 6 cols, 2 1/16", 1/8" between; C - 10 cols, 1 1/4", 1/16" between.
Commodity consumption: average pages per issue 27(d).
Equipment: EDITORIAL: Front-end hardware — AT, Euromax; Front-end software — AT, Euromax; Printers — Centronics. CLASSIFIED: Front-end hardware — AT; Front-end software — AT; Printers — Teletype. DISPLAY: Adv layout systems — SCS/Layout 8000; Front-end hardware — Dell/310; Front-end software — SCS/Layout 8000; Printers — HP/LaserJet II; Other equipment — Falco, Penril. WIRE SERVICES: News — SHNS, AP; Receiving dishes — AP. BUSINESS COMPUTERS: NCR/3447; Applications: Accts receivable, Circ, Accts payable; Vision Data, Lotus, WordPerfect.

FREDERICKSBURG

An Independent City
'90 U.S. Census- 19,027; E&P '96 Est. 21,469
ABC-NDM (90): 170,410 (HH 57,177)

The Free Lance-Star

(e-mon to sat)

The Free Lance-Star, 616 Amelia St., Fredericksburg, VA 22401; tel (540) 374-5000; fax (540) 374-5449.
Circulation: 44,675(e); 48,702(e-sat); ABC Sept. 30, 1995.
Price: 35¢(d); $1.00(sat); $2.00; $2.00/wk.
Advertising: Open inch rate $18.00(e); $18.00(e-sat). **Representatives:** Landon Associates Inc.; US Suburban Press.
News Services: AP, KRT. **Politics:** Independent. **Established:** 1885.
Not Published: Christmas.
Advertising not accepted: Patent medicine, mail order.
Special Weekly Sections: Best Food (wed); Building, Real Estate (fri, sat).
Magazines: Town & County (local, newsprint); TV Star (local, newsprint); USA Weekend.
Broadcast Affiliates: WFLS-AM/FM; WYSK-FM.

CORPORATE OFFICERS
President Josiah P Rowe III
Secretary Charles S Rowe
Treasurer Charles S Rowe
GENERAL MANAGEMENT
Co-Publisher Charles S Rowe
Co-Publisher Josiah P Rowe III
General Manager Josiah P Rowe III
Director Human Resources Florence R Barnick
Director Technical Services Gary W Harrison
ADVERTISING
Director C Murphy Street
Manager-Classified Gene R Damoth
Manager-Retail John F Davenport Jr
CIRCULATION
Manager Thomas L Snellings
NEWS EXECUTIVES
Editor Charles S Rowe
Managing Editor Edward W Jones
Asst Managing Editor James A Mann
EDITORS AND MANAGERS
Automotive Editor Jeff Schulz
Books Editor Gwen Woolf
Business Editor Rusty Dennen
City Editor Nancy A Moore
Consumer Editor Marty Morrison
Editorial Page Editor Larry R Evans
Fashion Editor Cathy Jett
Food Editor Carol Anderson
Home Furnishings Editor Nancy Moore
Lifestyle Editor Susan Wallace
Photo Department Manager Thomas I Price
Sports Editor R Lee Woolf
Teen-Age/Youth Editor Susan Wallace
Wire Editor David Lyne
PRODUCTION
Manager Jack Helms
Foreman-Pressroom S William Beatty
Foreman-Pre Press Waynard Zimmerman
Foreman-Packaging Brenda J Cooper

Mechanical available: Offset; Black and 3 ROP colors; insert accepted — preprinted; page cutoffs — 22 3/4".
Mechanical specifications: Type page 13" x 21 1/2"; E - 6 cols, 2 1/16", 1/8" between; A - 6 cols, 2 1/16", 1/8" between; C - 9 cols, 1 3/8", 1/16" between.
Commodity consumption: Newsprint 3,600 metric tons; widths 14", 28"; black ink 75,600 pounds; color ink 26,300 pounds; single pages printed 14,310; average pages per issue 46(d); single plates used 20,000.
Equipment: EDITORIAL: Front-end hardware — 3-Sun/Sparc-20, 1-Sun/Sparc-2; Front-end software — Good News; Printers — 1-Copal, 1-Compaq-20; Other equipment — 50-Digital/Pentium. CLASSIFIED: Front-end hardware — 2-Sun/Sparc-20; Front-end software — Vision Data; Printers — Digital, Compaq. DISPLAY: Adv layout systems — SCS/Layout-8000; Front-end hardware — 10-Ap/Mac 8500; Front-end software — Multi-Ad/Creator 3.8; Printers — 2-Copal, 1-Tektronix/Phaser 300. PRODUCTION: Pagination software — Good News; Typesetters — 2-AG/Accuset 1000; Plate exposures — 1-Amergraph, 1-LE/Cobes; Plate processors — 2-Nat/A-340; Electronic picture desk — Lf/AP Leaf Picture Desk; Scanners — 1-RZ/Linoscan 4050, 2-ECR/Autokon, Lf/Leafscan 35, Microtek; Production cameras — 1-R/480, 1-C/Spartan 2; Automatic film processors — 1-LE/PC-13, 1-LE/24AQ, 1-LE/24, 2-AG/OLP-20; Color separation equipment (conventional) — S, RZ/200.
PRESSROOM: Line 1 — 10-G/Urbanite; Line 2 — 7-G/Urbanite; Press drives — 3-Allen Bradley/150 h.p. motor; Folders — 2-G; Pasters — Enkel/10. MAILROOM: Counter stackers — 2-Id/NS440, 2-QWI/300; Inserters and stuffers — 1-HI/848 (8-station), 1-Am-Sheridan/630 (14-Station, on-line to press conveyor); Bundle tyer — 1-MLN/ML2EE, 2-Power Strap/NP60; Addressing machine — 1-Ch. WIRE SERVICES: News — AP, KRT; Photos — AP, KRT; Stock tables — AP; Syndicates — AP Datafeatures, AP Graphics; Receiving dishes — size-10ft, AP. BUSINESS COMPUTERS: 2-Data General; Applications: Vision Data: Accts payable, Accts receivable, Gen ledger, Payroll, Circ; PCs & micros networked; PCs & main system networked.

HAMPTON

See NEWPORT NEWS

HARRISONBURG

An Independent City
'90 U.S. Census- 30,707; E&P '96 Est. 38,370
ABC-CZ (90): 30,707 (HH 10,310)

Daily News-Record

(m-mon to sat)

Daily News-Record, 231 S. Liberty; PO Box 193, Harrisonburg, VA 22801; tel (540) 574-6200; fax (540) 433-9112. Byrd Newspapers group.

Circulation: 32,830(m); 32,830(m-sat); ABC Sept. 30, 1995.
Price: 35¢(d); 35¢(sat); $5.60/wk; $11.50/mo; $58.00/yr.
Advertising: Open inch rate $18.35(m); $18.35(m-sat). **Representative:** Landon Associates Inc.
News Service: AP. **Politics:** Independent. **Established:** 1913.
Not Published: New Year; Memorial Day; Independence Day; Labor Day; Thanksgiving; Christmas.
Advertising not accepted: Alcoholic beverage exclusive of beer.
Special Editions: Bride; Garden; Graduation; Football; Car Care; Christmas Gift Guide; Our Valley; Cooking Tab; R'Ham County Fair; Little League; First Night Harrisonburg.
Magazine: Valley TV Week.

CORPORATE OFFICER
President H F Byrd Jr
GENERAL MANAGEMENT
Publisher H F Byrd Jr
General Manager Richard R J Morin
Purchasing Agent Richard R J Morin
ADVERTISING
Manager Linda Swecker
CIRCULATION
Manager K Gary Anderson
NEWS EXECUTIVES
Editor Richard R J Morin
Managing Editor Kenneth P Mink
EDITORS AND MANAGERS
Business Editor Bettina Tilson
City Editor Ray Lamont
Editorial Page Editor Dale McConnaughay
Education Editor Richard Prior
Farm Editor Randolph C Murphey III
Fashion Editor Joseph Emerson
Films/Theater Editor Joseph Emerson
Food/Fashion Editor Joseph Emerson
Graphics Editor/Art Director John Rose
Photo/Graphics Department Manager Allen Litten
Political Editor Jeff Mellott
Religion Editor Julie Collins-Clark
Sports Editor Chris Simmons
Travel Editor Richard R J Morin
Wire Editor Lewis Sword
Women's Editor Joseph Emerson
PRODUCTION
Supervisor-Composing David H Shiplett Jr
Supervisor-Mailroom Ron Dearing
Supervisor-Pressroom Dale Sherman

Market Information: TMC.
Mechanical available: Offset; Black and 3 ROP colors; insert accepted — preprinted; page cut-offs — 21¾".
Mechanical specifications: Type page 13" x 21½"; E - 6 cols, 2 1/16", ⅛" between; A - 6 cols, 2 1/16", ⅛" between; C - 9 cols, 1⅜", ⅛" between.
Commodity consumption: Newsprint 1,957 short tons; widths 27½", 13¾"; black ink 71,800 pounds; color ink 4,651 pounds; single pages printed 9,476; average pages per issue 30(d); single plates used 7,560.
Equipment: EDITORIAL: Front-end hardware — IBM; Front-end software — Dewar; Printers — NewGen, LaserMaster. CLASSIFIED: Front-end hardware — IBM; Front-end software — Dewar; Printers — NewGen. DISPLAY: Adv layout systems — Ap/Mac; Front-end hardware — IBM; Front-end software — Dewar, Multi-Ad; Printers — NewGen, Ap/Mac LaserWriter Plus, Ap/Mac LaserWriter II NT. PRODUCTION: Plate exposures — 1-Nu; Plate processors — Nat; Production cameras — C/Spartan II; Automatic film processors — LE; Color separation equipment (conventional) — Lf/AP Leaf Picture Desk; Digital color separation equipment — Lf/Leafscan.
PRESSROOM: Line 1 — 6-G/Urbanite; Press control system — Fin. MAILROOM: Counter stackers — 2-HL/Monitor, 1-BG/Count-O-Veyor; Inserters and stuffers — 2-MM/227S; Bundle tyer — 1-Power Strap, 3-Bu; Addressing machine — 1-Ch, 1-BH. LIBRARY: Electronic — Dewar. COMMUNICATIONS: Facsimile — Sharp/FO210. WIRE SERVICES: News — AP; Syndicates — CNS, NYT; Receiving dishes — size-10ft, AP. BUSINESS COMPUTERS: 8-IBM/Sys 36, 3-IBM/PC, 1-IBM/PS-2; Applications: Bus, Circ; PCs & main system networked.

HOPEWELL
An Independent City
'90 U.S. Census- 23,101; E&P '96 Est. 22,985
ABC-CZ (90): 23,101 (HH 9,014)

News (e-mon to fri)
News, 516 E. Randolph Rd.; PO Box 481, Hopewell, VA 23860; tel (804) 458-8511; fax (804) 458-7556. Lancaster Management Inc. group.

Circulation: 6,986(e); ABC Oct. 1, 1994.
Price: 50¢(d); $6.50/mo (carrier), $11.00/mo (mail); $66.00/yr (carrier), $108.00/yr (mail).
Advertising: Open inch rate $6.75(e). **Representative:** Landon Associates Inc.
News Service: AP. **Politics:** Independent. **Established:** 1949.
Not Published: Labor Day; Christmas.
Special Editions: Income Tax Planning, Richmond 400 Racing Tab, Reflections (Progress Edition) (Feb); Bridal, Home Improvement Section (Mar); Virginia Journey (May); Social Security Supplement (July); Football Edition (Aug); Miller 400 Racing Tab (Sept); Christmas is a Family Affair, Santa Greeting (Dec); Auto Care (Spring & Fall).
Special Weekly Sections: Best Food Day (wed); Church Page (fri).
Magazines: TV Channels, Own Magazine, Tri-cities Outdoors Weekly (fri); The Homebook Real Estate Magazine (monthly); Hunting & Fishing.

CORPORATE OFFICER
Secretary/Treasurer James D Lancaster
GENERAL MANAGEMENT
Publisher Andy Prutsok
ADVERTISING
Director Dixie Hawkins
CIRCULATION
Manager Donna Brenizer
NEWS EXECUTIVE
Editor Don Dibley
EDITORS AND MANAGERS
News Editor Hank Bilyeu
Religion Editor Rebecca Ison
Society Editor Rebecca Ison
Sports Editor Hank Bilyeu
PRODUCTION
Superintendent Don Baum
Superintendent-Pressroom Layman Cook

Market Information: TMC.
Mechanical available: Offset; Black and 3 ROP colors; insert accepted — preprinted, negotiable; page cut-offs — 22¾".
Mechanical specifications: Type page 13" x 21½"; E - 6 cols, 2 1/16", ⅛" between; A - 6 cols, 2 1/16", ⅛" between; C - 9 cols, 1⅜", ⅛" between.
Commodity consumption: Newsprint 1,100 short tons; widths 27½, 34½"; black ink 30,000 pounds; color ink 7,000 pounds; single pages printed 4,100; average pages per issue 16(d); single plates used 8,500.
Equipment: EDITORIAL: Front-end hardware — Ap/Mac; Front-end software — QuarkXPress, Baseview/NewsEdit IQ; Printers — NewGen/Turbo PS-630, AG/Select Set 5000; Other equipment — Ap/Mac One Scanner, Kk/RSF 3500 Transparency Scanner, AG/Arcus Plus Reflective Scanner. CLASSIFIED: Front-end hardware — Ap/Mac; Front-end software — Baseview; Printers — AG/Select Set 5000. DISPLAY: Adv layout systems — Ap/Mac; Front-end software — Multi-Ad/Creator, QuarkXPress, Adobe/PageMaker, Adobe/Illustrator, Adobe/Photoshop. PRODUCTION: Pagination software — QuarkXPress 3.3, Adobe/PageMaker 5.0; Typesetters — AG/Select Set 5000; Platemaking systems — 1-Nat/18; Plate exposures — Nu/Flip Top FT40APNS; Plate processors — 1-Nat; Production cameras — C/Spartan II; Automatic film processors — 1-LE/24.
PRESSROOM: Line 1 — 9-G/Community; Folders — G/Community; Pasters — Jardis; Press registration system — Stoesser. MAILROOM: Counter stackers — 2-Bu, PPK; Inserters and stuffers — 4-DG; Bundle tyer — 2-Bu; Addressing machine — KR; Other mailroom equipment — Mc/Speed Binder. LIBRARY: Electronic — Dukane/MPD. COMMUNICATIONS: Facsimile — ATT/FAX, AP. WIRE SERVICES: News — AP; Syndicates — King Features, United Media, Universal Press; Receiving dishes — AP. BUSINESS COMPUTERS: IBM; PCs & micros networked.

LYNCHBURG
An Independent City
'90 U.S. Census- 66,049; E&P '96 Est. 65,691
ABC-CZ (90): 97,362 (HH 36,670)

The News & Advance
(all day-mon to fri; m-sat; S)
The News & Advance, 101 Wyndale Dr.; PO Box 10129, Lynchburg, VA 24501; tel (804) 385-5400; fax (804) 385-5538. Media General (Virginia Newspapers Inc.) group.
Circulation: 38,733(a); 38,557(m-sat); 43,713(S); ABC Sept. 30, 1995.
Price: 50¢(d); 50¢(sat); $1.25(S).
Advertising: Open inch rate $31.90(a); $31.90(m-sat); $33.25(S).
News Services: AP, NYT. **Politics:** Independent. **Established:** 1866 (News), 1880 (Advance).
Not Published: Christmas.
Special Editions: Wedding March (Jan); Progress (Feb); Health & Fitness (Mar); Auto Extra, Smith Mt. Lake, Spring Fashion, Garden Week (Apr); Better Living Expo, Auto Extra (May); Southern Living Cooking School, James River Festival (June); Business Showcase (July); Discover Central VA, Back-to-School (Aug); Football, Kaleidoscope Festival, Fall Fashion, Virginia's Finest, Women's Resource Center (Sept); Auto Extra (Oct); Holiday Cook Book, Christmas Gift Guide, Basketball (Nov); Last Minute Gifts (Dec); Greater Lynchburg Chamber of Commerce Report (bi-monthly); 50 Plus (quarterly).
Special Weekly Sections: Community (tues); Food (wed); Television, Community (thur); Automotive, Entertainment (fri); Religion, Entertainment (sat); Business, Travel, Real Estate, Food (S).
Magazines: On the Tube (thur); Sunday Comics, Parade (S); Monthly Coupon Specials (Spadea) (2nd S); Business (quarterly).

CORPORATE OFFICERS
Board Chairman Thomas Eugene Worrell Jr
Vice Pres Terry L Hall
President Ed Freakley
GENERAL MANAGEMENT
Publisher Terry L Hall
Business Manager E Garland Key
ADVERTISING
Director Jo Pearse
TELECOMMUNICATIONS
Audiotex Manager Kelly Burton
CIRCULATION
Director Tony Stophel
Manager Deborah Maupin
NEWS EXECUTIVES
Exec Editor William C Cline
Managing Editor Joe Stinnett
EDITORS AND MANAGERS
Business Editor Tom Harrison
City Editor Bob Morgan
Editorial Page Editor Robert C Wimer
Education Editor Bob Morgan
Entertainment/Amusements Editor Sheryl Martin
Fashion/Style Editor Cecil Mullan
Feature Editor Cecil Mullan
Graphics/Art Director Donna Keesee
Librarian Gloria Staples
Lifestyle Editor Cecil Mullan
Medicine/Science Editor Cynthia Pegram
Politics Editor Steve Vaughan
Radio/Television Editor Sheryl Martin
Sports Editor Jeff Motley

Market Information: Split Run; TMC; Operate audiotex.
Mechanical available: Offset; Black and 3 ROP colors; insert accepted — preprinted; page cut-offs — 22¾".
Mechanical specifications: Type page 13" x 21½"; E - 5 cols, 2½", .13" between; A - 6 cols, 2.04", ⅙" between; C - 9 cols, 1⅜", .05" between.
Commodity consumption: Newsprint 3,029 short tons; widths 56", 42", 28"; black ink 8,100 pounds; single pages printed 12,738; average pages per issue 32(d), 54(S); single plates used 47,650.
Equipment: EDITORIAL: Front-end hardware — 35-EKI/Televideo, EKI/Earth Station; Front-end software — EKI; Printers — 1-Ap/Mac LaserWriter NTX, 1-NewGen/1200T; Other equipment — 2-Ap/Mac, 1-Lf/AP Leaf Picture Desk, 1-Lf/Leafscan 35. CLASSIFIED: Front-end hardware — 10-EKI/Televideo; Front-end software — EKI; Printers — 1-Ap/Mac LaserWriter NTX, 1-NewGen/480. AUDIOTEX: Software — Info-Connect/Pottsville Republican, TMS. DISPLAY: Front-end hardware — 6-Ap/Mac, 1-PC/386 fileserver; Front-end software — DTI, QuarkXPress, Adobe/Photoshop, Adobe/Illustrator; Printers — 1-NewGen/1200T, 1-NewGen/480, 1-NewGen/Turbo Plus 1200B; Other equipment — 2-Microtek/600 scanner, 1-HP/ScanJet IIC. PRODUCTION: Plate exposures — 1-Nu, 1-BKY/5000; Plate processors — 1-MAS/30; Production cameras — 1-C/Spartan III, 1-C/Spartan II; Automatic film processors — 1-P, 1-LE; Film transporters — 2-C; Color separation equipment (conventional) — Lf/AP Leaf Picture Desk, Ap/Mac, NewGen/1200T.
PRESSROOM: Line 1 — 5-HI/1650; Press drives — 2-Fin/250 h.p.; Folders — HI/2:1; Reels and stands — HI; Press control system — HI. MAILROOM: Counter stackers — 1-QWI, 1-QWI; Inserters and stuffers — 1-HI/1372; Bundle tyer — 1-OVR, 1-OVL; Addressing machine — 1-KR. WIRE SERVICES: News — AP; Photos — AP; Stock tables — AP; Syndicates — TMS; Receiving dishes — AP. BUSINESS COMPUTERS: EKI; Applications: Adv billing, Accts receivable, Gen ledger, Payroll, Circ, Class transient, Commercial; PCs & micros networked; PCs & main system networked.

MANASSAS
An Independent City
'90 U.S. Census- 27,957; E&P '96 Est. 37,530

Journal Messenger
(e-mon to fri; m-sat)
Journal Messenger, 9009 Church St.; PO Drawer 431, Manassas, VA 22110; tel (703) 368-3101; fax (703) 368-9017. Park Communications Inc. group.
Circulation: 7,727(e); 7,727(m-sat); Sworn Oct. 7, 1995.
Price: 30¢(d); 30¢(sat); $1.00/wk; $4.35/mo; $52.00/yr; $26.10/6mo.
Advertising: Open inch rate $12.26(e); $12.26(m-sat). **Representative:** Landon Associates Inc.
News Service: AP. **Politics:** Independent. **Established:** 1869.
Not Published: Christmas.
Advertising not accepted: Brokered preprints.
Special Editions: Progress Edition (Jan); Washington's Birthday (Feb); Automotive (Mar); Graduation, Mother's Day, June Brides (May); Newcomer's Guide (July); Back-to-School (Aug); Automotive, Restaurant Guide (Oct); Santa Welcome (Nov, Dec).
Special Weekly Sections: Family Focus (mon); Health & Fitness (tues); Food (wed); Auto & Leisure (thur); Real Estate (fri); Business & Religion (sat).
Broadcast Affiliate: Park Radio & TV.

CORPORATE OFFICERS
President Wright M Thomas
Vice Pres-Newspaper Division Ralph J Martin
GENERAL MANAGEMENT
General Manager Dennis E Bradshaw
Business Manager Iris McCandless
ADVERTISING
Director Craig Bender
CIRCULATION
Director Richard R Woolbright
NEWS EXECUTIVES
Editor Dennis E Bradshaw
Managing Editor Kathryn McQuaid
EDITOR AND MANAGER
Sports Editor Spencer Patterson
PRODUCTION
Manager-Pressroom Billy Outlaw

Market Information: Split Run; TMC.
Mechanical available: Offset; Black and 3 ROP colors; insert accepted — preprinted, flyer to 64 pgs; page cut-offs — 22¾".
Mechanical specifications: Type page 13" x 21¼"; E - 6 cols, 2 1/16", ⅛" between; A - 6 cols, 2 1/16", ⅛" between; C - 9 cols, 1⅜", ⅛" between.
Commodity consumption: Newsprint 547 short tons; 673 metric tons; widths 14½", 29"; single pages printed 8,300; average pages per issue 24(d), 18(sat); single plates used 8,500.
Equipment: EDITORIAL: Front-end hardware — Ap/Mac; Front-end software — Baseview; Printers — NewGen/Laser, HP/LaserJet; Other equipment — Lf/AP Leaf Picture Desk. CLASSIFIED: Front-end hardware — Ap/Mac; Front-end software — Baseview; Printers — HP/LaserJet. DISPLAY: Adv layout systems — Ap/Mac; Front-end hardware — Ap/Mac; Front-end software — QuarkXPress, Adobe/Photoshop; Printers — HP/Laserprinter; Other equipment — ECR/36 Imagesetter. PRODUCTION: Typesetters — ECR, Ap/Mac; Plate exposures — Spektra/Theimer; Production cameras — B/Caravel Horizontal; Automatic film processors — Kk/710 Kodimatic; Color separation equipment (conventional) — Lf/Leafscan 35.
PRESSROOM: Line 1 — 3-HI/Cotrell 845; Line 2 — 2-HI/845, 1-HI/800; Press registration system — Duarte. MAILROOM: Counter stack-

ers — HL/Monitor; Inserters and stuffers — 6-MM; Bundle tyer — MLN; Addressing machine — KR. LIBRARY: Electronic — BH/Microfilm. WIRE SERVICES: News — AP; Syndicates — NEA; Receiving dishes — size-3m, AP. BUSINESS COMPUTERS: Wyse; Applications: Vision Data.

Prince William Journal

(m-mon to fri)

Prince William Journal, 9275 Corporate Cir., Manassas, VA 22110; tel (703) 257-4600; fax (703) 257-4960; web site http://www.infi.net/journal. Journal Newspapers Inc. group.

Circulation: 10,000(m); Estimate Jan. 30, 1996.

Price: 25¢(d); $17.00/3mo; $39.00/6mo, $72.00/yr.

Advertising: Open inch rate $35.60(m). **Established:** 1988 (weekly), 1995 (daily).

Note: Effective Sept. 5, 1995, this newspaper started publishing daily (m-mon to fri). The circulation number is an estimate. An audit statement was not available at press time.

Not Published: Postal holidays.

Advertising not accepted: X-rated movies.

CORPORATE OFFICERS

Chairman Rupert Phillips
President Karl Spain

GENERAL MANAGEMENT

Publisher Ryan E Phillips

ADVERTISING

Director Kenneth Courter

MARKETING AND PROMOTION

Director-Marketing/Promotion David Melmer

CIRCULATION

Director Michael Wynn

NEWS EXECUTIVE

Managing Editor Mark Tapscott

EDITORS AND MANAGERS

News Editor Ester Venouziou
Sports Editor Marc Dovi

PRODUCTION

Director Kim Council

Market Information: Electronic edition.

Mechanical available: Offset; Black and 3 ROP colors; insert accepted — preprinted; page cut-offs — 22¾".

Mechanical specifications: Type page 13" x 21½"; E - 6 cols, 2 1/16", 1/8" between; A - 6 cols, 2 1/16", 1/8" between; C - 10 cols, 1¼", 1/16" between.

MARTINSVILLE

An Independent City

'90 U.S. Census- 16,162; E&P '96 Est. 15,260
ABC-CZ (90): 17,575 (HH 7,227)

Martinsville Bulletin

(e-mon to fri; S)

Martinsville Bulletin, 204 Broad St.; PO Box 3711, Martinsville, VA 24115; tel (540) 638-8801; fax (540) 638-4153. Haskell Newspapers group.

Circulation: 18,677(e); 20,382(S); ABC Sept. 30, 1995.

Price: 35¢(d); $1.00(S); $7.80/mo; $93.00/yr.

Advertising: Open inch rate $12.31(e); $12.90(S). **Representative:** Landon Associates Inc.

News Services: NEA, AP. **Politics:** Independent. **Established:** 1889.

Advertising not accepted: Vending machines.

Special Editions: Health & Fitness (Jan); Brides (Feb); Spring (Mar); Race (Apr); Real Estate (May); Graduation (June); Coupon (July); Football, Back-to-School (Aug); Women (Oct); Christmas Shopping (Nov); Christmas Greetings (Dec).

Magazine: Parade (S).

CORPORATE OFFICERS

Chairman of the Board Antoinette M Haskell
President/Treasurer Robert H Haskell
Vice Pres George H Harris
Vice Pres Elizabeth H Haskell
Secretary Ann B Winn

GENERAL MANAGEMENT

Publisher Robert H Haskell
General Manager George H Harris
Controller Ann B Winn

ADVERTISING

Manager Robert G Cox
Manager-General Betty Truman

CIRCULATION

Manager Al Novell

NEWS EXECUTIVES

Editor Ginny Wray
Managing Editor Richard Hammerstrom

EDITORS AND MANAGERS

Editorial Page Editor Mark Davis
Editorial Writer Ginny Wray
Features Editor Pat Koger
Food/Women's Editor Donna Brim
Librarian Sue Carter
Religion Editor Donna Brim
Sports Editor Mike Smith
Wire Editor Mark Davis

PRODUCTION

Asst Manager Matt Hall
Foreman-Pressroom Jimmy Flint

Market Information: TMC.

Mechanical available: Offset; Black and 3 ROP colors; insert accepted — preprinted; page cut-offs — 22¾".

Mechanical specifications: Type page 13" x 21½"; E - 6 cols, 2 1/16", 1/8" between; A - 6 cols, 2 1/16", 1/8" between; C - 9 cols, 1½", 1/8" between.

Commodity consumption: Newsprint 1,192 short tons; widths 27½", 13¾"; single pages printed 7,726; average pages per issue 22(d), 42(S); single plates used 5,200.

Equipment: EDITORIAL: Front-end hardware — COM/One 65, 14-COM/PE-12, Ap/Mac; Front-end software — Baseview; Printers — 2-AU/Laser Film Imager, 3-Okidata; Other equipment — Lf/Leafscan 35, Lecia/Flatbed Scanner. CLASSIFIED: Front-end hardware — Ap/Mac; Front-end software — Baseview; Printers — 2-AU/Laser Film Imager, 3-Okidata. PRODUCTION: Pagination software — Baseview; Typesetters — AU; Platemaking systems — WL-, Nu; Plate exposures — WL, Nu; Plate processors — Nu, W; Electronic picture desk — Lf/AP Leaf Picture Desk; Direct-to-plate imaging — 1-Nu; Scanners — Lf/Leafscan 35, Leica/Flatbed, AU/ Drum Scanner; Automatic film processors — LE, Konica; Film transporters — LE; Color separation equipment (conventional) — BKY, AU. PRESSROOM: Line 1 — 5-G/Urbanite U-920; Line 2 — 5-DEV/2400; Pasters — Enkel. MAILROOM: Counter stackers — HI/Rima RS255; Inserters and stuffers — S; Bundle tyer — MLN, Dynaric. WIRE SERVICES: News — AP; Photos — AP; Syndicates — NEA, WP Writers Group, United Features, Universal Press, Creators, NAS, King Features, United Media; Receiving dishes — AP. BUSINESS COMPUTERS: IBM/36; Applications: Gen ledger, Payroll, Accts payable, Accts receivable, Adv billing, Circ.

NEWPORT NEWS-HAMPTON

Independent Cities

'90 U.S. Census- 303,838 (Newport News 170,045, Hampton 133,793); E&P '96 Est. 328,209 (Newport News 186,529, Hampton 141,680)
ABC-NDM (90): 481,984 (HH 177,645)

Daily Press (m-mon to sat; S)

Daily Press, 7505 Warwick Blvd.; PO Box 746, Newport News, VA 23607; tel (804) 247-4600; fax (804) 247-7899; e-mail dpnews @aol.com; web site http://www.xso.com/viva. Tribune Co. group.

Circulation: 103,648(m); 103,648(m-sat); 125,758(S); ABC Sept. 30, 1995.

Price: 35¢(d); 35¢(sat); $1.50(S); $3.05/wk; $146.40/yr.

Advertising: Open inch rate $54.25(m); $60.60(m-sat); $60.60(S); $84.88(m & S). **Representative:** Tribune Newspaper Network.

News Services: AP, NYT, KRT, LAT-WP. **Politics:** Independent.

Advertising not accepted: Objectionable.

Special Editions: Progress (Jan); Auto Racing, Home Expo (Feb); Spring La Femme, Home Improvement, Oyster Point, New Cars, Trucks & Vans (Mar); Lawn & Garden, New Home Showcase (Apr); 50 Something, Spring Car Care, Summer La Femme (May); Your Health (June); Anheuser Busch Golf Classic (July); Welcome Neighbors, Parade of Homes, Football (Aug); Fall Lawn & Garden, Virginia's Finest (Sept); Remodeled Homes, La Femme (Oct); Holiday Gift Guide (Nov).

Special Weekly Sections: Food (thur); In-Roads, Wheels (fri); Real Estate (sat); Home, Travel, Art & Leisure (S); Business, Lifestyles (daily).

Magazines: Parade, TV Magazine (S).

CORPORATE OFFICERS

President/Publisher Jack W Davis Jr
Vice Pres George A McDaniel

GENERAL MANAGEMENT

Chief Financial Officer Eugene Park
Director-Human Resources LaDonna J Wade
Manager-Business Development Lisa Bohnaker

ADVERTISING

Vice Pres/Director George A McDaniel
Manager-Commercial Printing Charles E Giles Jr
Manager-Display Fred Penfield
Manager-General Edward Hicks
Manager-Classified Aubrey Johnson
Manager-Production Walt Russell
Manager-Systems/Pre Press Mike Asher

MARKETING AND PROMOTION

Manager-Public Relations Melissa T Hespenhide

TELECOMMUNICATIONS

Manager-New Media Digby Solomon

CIRCULATION

Director Philip A Valenti
Manager-Operations Tony Farley Jr
Manager-Sales Thomas V Cherry
Manager-Administrative Service Psyche R Page
Manager-Transportation Clarence Pearson
Manager-Alternate Delivery Service Robert D Matera
Manager-Production Michael L Bany

NEWS EXECUTIVES

Editor Will Corbin
Reader Editor Myrtle Barnes

EDITORS AND MANAGERS

Answer Editor Jeanne Peck
Amusement Editor Steve Arnold
Art Director Michael Dabrowa
Automotive Editor Mike Toole
Books Editor Will Molineux
Business Editor Mike Toole
City/Metro Editor Ernest Gates
Editorial Page Editor Will Molineux
Education Editor Cheryl Segal
Environmental Editor Richard Stradling
Farm/Agriculture Editor Mike Toole
Fashion/Style Editor Philana Patterson
Librarian Melissa Oakley
Newsgathering Editor Ernest Gates
Opportunities Editor Robin McCormick
Presentation Editor Maryann Hakowski
Radio/Television Editor Chris Tarantola
Reader Editor Myrtle Barnes
Religion Editor Cheryl Segal
Science/Technology Editor Dennis Elder
Special Projects Editor Jerry Micco
Staff Development Editor Felicia Mason
State Editor Dan Montgomery
Travel Editor Joan Johnston

Market Information: Zoned editions; Split Run; TMC; ADS; Operate database; Operate audiotex.

Mechanical available: Offset; Black and 3 ROP colors; insert accepted — preprinted, product samples; page cut-offs — 22".

Mechanical specifications: Type page 13" x 21"; E - 6 cols, 2 1/16", 1/8" between; A - 6 cols, 2 1/16", 1/8" between; C - 10 cols, 1⅜", 1/16" between.

Equipment: EDITORIAL: Front-end hardware — 120-IBM/PS2, 25-Ap/Mac IIfx; Front-end software — CText, QuarkXPress; Printers — HP, Okidata. CLASSIFIED: Front-end hardware — Austin/486-30; Front-end software — CText/Advision; Printers — HP. AUDIOTEX: Hardware — IBM; Software — Micro Voice; Supplier name — VNN. DISPLAY: Adv layout systems — SCS/Layout 8000; Front-end hardware — IBM; Front-end software — Multi-Ad. PRODUCTION: Pagination software — QuarkXPress 3.2; Typesetters — 3-Ultre/Hyphen Typesetters, Bidco/Supersetter, 2-ECR/3850; Platemaking systems — WL/Lith-X-Pozer III; Plate processors — 2-WL/38D; Electronic picture desk — Lf/AP Leaf Picture Desk, Ap/Mac, Adobe/Photoshop, Ap/Mac Preserver Archive; Scanners — 1-ECR/Autokon, 4-Kk/LS-3520 Plus, 1-Scitex, 2-Sharp/J-600, 2-PixelCraft/Flatbed; Production cameras — 1-R/400, 1-C/Pager, 1-C/Spartan III; Automatic film processors — 1-LE/LO24A, 1-P/Quick, LE/32 Exel, 4-C/66, 2-LE/CMX 24; Reproportion units — FLS; Film transporters — 5-C; Color separation equipment (conventional) — 1-C/E-Z Color, 1-CD/635; Digital color separation equipment — 1-ECR/1000. PRESSROOM: Line 1 — 16-G/3346-3347 (8 color half decks); Folders — 2-G. MAILROOM: Counter stackers — RKW/Stack Master, 3-QWI/SJ201, MM/Apollo, 2-QWI/52300; Inserters and stuffers — 2-HI/1472; Bundle tyer — 2-MLN, 7-Dynaric/Tyers; Addressing machine — 2-KR. LIBRARY: Electronic — Vu/Text SAVE; Combination — Clippings on File (Microfiche). COMMUNICATIONS: Facsimile — 12-X/401; Systems used — satellite. WIRE SERVICES: News — AP, NYT, KRT, LAT-WP; Photos — AP, KRT; Stock tables — TMS; Receiving dishes — size-10m, AP, KRT. BUSINESS COMPUTERS: Admarc, CICS; Applications: PCs & micros networked; PCs & main system networked.

NORFOLK-PORTSMOUTH-VIRGINIA BEACH-CHESAPEAKE

Independent Cities

'90 U.S. Census- 910,181 (Norfolk 261,229, Portsmouth 103,907, Virginia Beach 393,069, Chesapeake 151,976); E&P '96 Est. 1,012,810 (Norfolk 259,802, Portsmouth 103,623, Virginia Beach 472,903, Chesapeake 176,482)
ABC-CZ (90): 962,322 (HH 334,266)

The Virginian-Pilot

(m-mon to fri; m-sat; S)

The Virginian-Pilot, 150 W. Brambleton Ave., Norfolk, VA 23510; tel (804) 446-2000; fax (804) 446-2983; web site http://www.infi.net/pilot/. Landmark Communications Inc. group.

Circulation: 188,678(m); 236,018(m-sat); 239,274(S); ABC Sept. 30, 1995.

Price: 50¢(d); 50¢(sat); $1.25(S); $119.49/yr.

Advertising: Open inch rate $88.80(m); $123.00(m-sat); $123.00(S); $131.84(m & S).

News Services: AP, KRT, LAT-WP, NYT, Landmark News Service. **Politics:** Independent. **Established:** 1865.

Note: Effective Aug. 25, 1995, the Ledger-Star (e-mon to fri) ceased publication.

Advertising not accepted: Libelous, false claims.

Special Editions: Forecast (Jan); Taxes (Feb); Home Improvement, Weeders Digest, Commercial Real Estate (Mar); Vacation Guide, Affordable Housing, Shipping, Earth Day, Pet Care (Apr); Executive Salaries (May); Almanac '96, Scholastic Achievement (June); Finance, Discover Hampton Roads (July); Electronics, Football (Aug); Vacation Guide, Virginia's Finest, Insurance, Biz Expo '96 (Sept); Sunrise-Sunset, Homearama, Personal Finance (Oct); Auto Preview, Christmas Gift Guides (Nov); Best in Business (Dec).

Special Weekly Sections: Hampton Roads Business Weekly (mon); Flavor (thur); Auto Weekly, Preview (Entertainment) (fri); TV Week, Real Estate (sat); Flavor, Woman, Arts and Travel (S); Daily Break (Leisure) (daily).

Magazines: Hampton Roads Business Weekly (mon); Flavor, Venture (thur); Auto Weekly, Preview (fri); Hampton Roads Real Estate Weekly, TV Week (sat); Flavor (S).

CORPORATE OFFICERS

Board Chairman Frank Batten
Vice Board Chairman Richard F Barry III
CEO John D Wynne
Chief Operating Officer Doug Fox
Exec Vice Pres Donald H Patterson Jr
Exec Vice Pres Frank Batten Jr
Exec Vice Pres/General Counsel Louis F Ryan
Vice Pres/Treasurer James D Wagner
Vice Pres-Administration/Finance John F Estes III
Vice Pres-Human Resources Charlie Hill
Vice Pres Richard F Spears
Corporate Counsel Becky Powhatan
Controller Colleen Pittman
Secretary Louis F Spears

GENERAL MANAGEMENT

President/Publisher R Bruce Bradley
Manager-Credit Carol Lewis
Director-Human Resources Kay McGraw

ADVERTISING

Director Joe Antle
Manager-Marketing Tina Gill
Manager-Operations Tom Duke
Manager-Sales Development/Training Mike Herron
Manager-Display Robert Morgan Jr
Manager-Classified/General Dale Bowen
Manager-Business Development/General Sales Tommy Drew

Manager-Regional Sales Robert Morgan Jr
Manager-Co-op Randolph U Hargrave

MARKETING AND PROMOTION

Director-Marketing Joe DeLatte

TELECOMMUNICATIONS

General Manager-Voice Info Systems Allison Askew-Hahn

CIRCULATION

Director D R Carpenter
Manager-State Joseph Brown
Manager-Single Copy Nancy Lewis
Manager-Promotion Laura Howard
Manager-Marketing Lee Ann Dickson

NEWS EXECUTIVES

Editor Cole C Campbell
Deputy Managing Editor-Local News Dennis Hartig
Deputy Managing Editor-Presentation Nelson Brown
Deputy Managing Editor-Military/Virginia Business Edward Power
Deputy Managing Editor-Sports/Features Rosemary Goudreau
Deputy Managing Editor-Administration/ Community/Metro Joyce Ingram
Asst Managing Editor-Photo Robert Lynn
General Manager-North Carolina Ronald L Speer
Director-Recruiting Marvin Leon Lake
Editor-Virginia Sue Robinson Sain
Asst to Exec Administrator George Bryant
Director-Systems Randy Jessee
Director-Newsroom Staff Development Dave Word

EDITORS AND MANAGERS

Business/Finance Editor Joe Coccaro
Television Columnist Larry Bonko
Columnist Lawrence Maddry
Columnist Guy Friddell
Creative Director Eric Seidman
Entertainment Editor Roberta Vowell
Features Editor Denis Finley
Films/Theater Editor Mal Vincent
Food/Home Furnishings Editor Pat Dooley
Librarian Ann Johnson
Medicine Editor Tom Holden
Military Editor Edward Power
Music Editor Roberta Vowell
Political Editor Sue Robinson Sain
Chief Photo Editor Bob Lynn
Public Editor Lynn Feigenbaum
Radio/Television Editor Mal Vincent
Real Estate Editor Joe Coccaro
Religion Editor Mark O'Keefe
Sports Editor Chic Riebel
Women's/Fashion Editor Cammy Sessa

MANAGEMENT INFORMATION SERVICES

Data Processing Manager Jan Osborne
Online Manager Allison Askew-Hahn

PRODUCTION

Director-Engineering John Saltisiak
Manager-Press Operations Donnie Baines
Manager-Distribution Allen Byrd
Manager-Quality Assurance George Karangelen

Market Information: Zoned editions; Split Run; TMC; ADS; Operate database; Operate audiotex; Electronic edition.
Mechanical available: Offset; Black and 3 ROP colors; insert accepted — preprinted; page cut-offs — $22\frac{3}{4}$".
Mechanical specifications: Type page 13" x 20"; E - 6 cols, $2\frac{1}{16}$", $\frac{1}{8}$" between; A - 6 cols, $2\frac{1}{16}$", $\frac{1}{8}$" between; C - 9 cols, $1\frac{3}{8}$", $\frac{1}{16}$" between.
Commodity consumption: Newsprint 40,000 short tons; widths 55", $41\frac{1}{4}$", $27\frac{3}{8}$"; black ink 770,000 pounds; color ink 345,000 pounds; single pages printed 69,600; average pages per issue 52(d), 120(S); single plates used 350,000.
Equipment: EDITORIAL: Front-end hardware — 200-AT, 60-AT/Portable, 40-IBM/Compatibles, 12-AT/News Layout; Front-end software — QuarkXPress, AT/Atan Express, AT/Geode Express; Other equipment — 6-Canon/Fax, 3-Fu. CLASSIFIED: Front-end hardware — 35-AT. DISPLAY: Adv layout systems — 3-Sun, AT/R2, 28-AT. PRODUCTION: Typesetters — 3-Cx/Bitsetters; Plate exposures — 2-Nu/Flip Top, 1-WL/Lith-X-Pozer I, 1-WL/Lith-X-Pozer II; Plate processors — 2-WL; Production cameras — SCREEN/175, C/Marathon; Automatic film processors — 2-LE, 2-LE/LD-24-AQ, 2-Cronaflow, 1-LE/Excel 26; Reproportion units — 2-ECR/Autokon 1000, 1-ECR/Autokon 8400; Film transporters — SCREEN; Shrink lenses — 4-CK Optical; Digital color separation equipment — 1-CD/646IE.
PRESSROOM: Line 1 — 30-G/Metro; Folders — 5-G/Metro (w/double delivery); Pasters — 30-G; Reels and stands — 30-G; Press control system — G/PCSI. MAILROOM: Counter stackers — 12-HL/Monitor, 2-GPS/5000; Inserters and stuffers — 3-HI/72P, 1-HI/1472P; Bundle tyer — 9-MLN/MLN-2A, 2-Dynaric/SSB79. LIBRARY: Electronic — Vu/Text; Combination — Vu/Text Plus Clip Files. COMMUNICATIONS: Facsimile — 2-EA/Page Fax II Readers, 2-EA/Page Fax II Writers; Systems used — microwave. WIRE SERVICES: News — AP, TV Data, LAT-WP, NYT, KRT, PR Newswire, Bizwire; Stock tables — AP; Receiving dishes — size-3m, AP, INS. BUSINESS COMPUTERS: 13-IBM/4381, 1-IBM/AS400-B60 (midrange); Applications: Circ, Adv billing, Accts receivable, Gen ledger, Payroll, Accts payable, Joy fund system, TMC system; PCs & micros networked; PCs & main system networked.

PETERSBURG

An Independent City

'90 U.S. Census- 38,386; E&P '96 Est. 37,214
ABC-CZ (90): 74,943 (HH 26,738)

The Progress-Index

(e-mon to fri; m-sat; S)

The Progress-Index, 15 Franklin St.; PO Box 71, Petersburg, VA 23803; tel (804) 732-3456; fax (804) 861-9452. Thomson Newspapers group.
Circulation: 18,826(e); 18,826(m-sat); 19,156(S); ABC Sept. 30, 1995.
Price: 35¢(d); 35¢(sat); $1.00(S); $9.95/mo (carrier); $145.00/yr (mail).
Advertising: Open inch rate $17.50(e); $17.50(m-sat); $17.50(S). **Representative:** Thomson Newspapers.
News Service: AP. **Politics:** Independent. **Established:** 1865.
Not Published: Independence Day; Christmas.
Advertising not accepted: Vending machines.
Special Editions: First Aid, Business Card Page, Business Builder Promotion, Business in News (Jan); Valentine Rip-a-Strip, NASCAR Preview, Life Underwriters (Feb); Racin' in Richmond, Progress (Mar); Spring Fix-up, YMCA (Apr); Parade of Homes, Dining Guide, Tourism Guide, Business Builder (May); School's Out-Summer Fun Guide, Business Profile (June); Cruisin', Customer Appreciation, Business Builder (July); Back-to-School, Cruisin', End of Summer Savings, YMCA (Aug); Literacy Tab, Under the Lights, Greater Crater Day, Hooray for Hopewell, Cooking School (Sept); '97 Auto Preview, Fall Fix-up, Spooky Savings (Oct); Hometown Holiday, Holiday Happenings, Tourism Guide (Nov); Holiday Fashion, Dear Santa, Christmas Tradition, YMCA (Dec).
Special Weekly Sections: Entertainment (tues); Best Auto Day, Food (wed); Women (second wed); Young Life (first thur); Prime Times (third thur); Health, Best Auto Day (thur); Best Auto Day (fri); Church Schedules, Best Auto Day (sat); Agriculture (S); Lifestyle, Best Real Estate Day, Business (daily).
Magazine: Parade.

GENERAL MANAGEMENT

Publisher George R Fain
Manager-Accounting Jeanette Busby

ADVERTISING

Manager Monte Bracy

CIRCULATION

Director Lyle Stone

NEWS EXECUTIVE

Managing Editor Elizabeth Hedgepeth

EDITORS AND MANAGERS

Books/School Editor Cathy Ballou
Business/Finance Editor Samantha Gowen
City Editor Samantha Gowen
Columnist/Editorial Writer Elizabeth Hedgepeth
Editor Pat Sharpf
Photo Department Manager Brian Soule
Sports Editor Jim McConnell
Sunday Editor Elizabeth Hedgepeth
Wire Editor Cathy Ballou

PRODUCTION

Manager-Pre Press John Proper
Manager-Pressroom David N Hutchins

Market Information: TMC.
Mechanical available: Offset; Black and 3 ROP colors; insert accepted — preprinted; page cut-offs — $23\frac{1}{4}$".
Mechanical specifications: Type page 13" x $21\frac{1}{2}$"; E - 6 cols, $2\frac{1}{16}$", $\frac{1}{8}$" between; A - 6 cols, $2\frac{1}{16}$", $\frac{1}{8}$" between; C - 9 cols, $1\frac{5}{16}$", $\frac{1}{8}$" between.
Commodity consumption: Newsprint 1,195 short tons; width $27\frac{1}{2}$"; black ink 19,400 pounds; color ink 4,550 pounds; single pages printed 7,574; average pages per issue 18.3(d), 36(S); single plates used 5,320.
Equipment: EDITORIAL: Front-end hardware — Ap/Mac; Front-end software — QuarkXPress 3.11; Printers — TI. CLASSIFIED: Front-end hardware — Mk, Ap/Mac; Front-end software — Mk/4000, Multi-Ad/Creator, QuarkXPress; Printers — TI. DISPLAY: Adv layout systems — Ap/Mac; Front-end hardware — 2-Ap/Mac; Front-end software — Multi-Ad/Creator, QuarkXPress, Aldus/FreeHand; Printers — V/5100. PRODUCTION: Pagination software — QuarkXpress 3.1.1; Typesetters — 2-V/5100, 1-V/5300, 1-V/Panther Plus; Plate processors — Nu/Flip Top FT40V6UPNS; Direct-to-plate imaging — Nat/A-250; Production cameras — SCREEN/C-690-C; Automatic film processors — SCREEN/LD-220-QT; Color separation equipment (conventional) — Lf/AP Leaf Picture Desk, Adobe/Photoshop on Ap/Mac.
PRESSROOM: Line 1 — 8-G/Community; Folders — 1-G/SSC. MAILROOM: Bundle tyer — 1-MLN, 1-MLN. WIRE SERVICES: News — AP; Syndicates — THO, AP; Receiving dishes — AP. BUSINESS COMPUTERS: ATT; Applications: Gen ledger, Accts receivable, Accts payable, Payroll, Circ.

PORTSMOUTH

See NORFOLK

PULASKI

Pulaski County

'90 U.S. Census- 9,985; E&P '96 Est. 9,925

The Southwest Times

(e-mon to fri; S)

The Southwest Times, 34 Fifth St. Shopping Center; PO Box 391, Pulaski, VA 24301; tel (540) 980-5220; fax (540) 980-3618. New River Newspapers LLC group.
Circulation: 6,287(e); 6,460(S); Sworn Sept. 30, 1993.
Price: 25¢(d); 75¢(S); $1.70/wk.
Advertising: Open inch rate $10.01(e); $10.01 (S). **Representative:** Landon Associates Inc.
News Service: AP. **Politics:** Independent. **Established:** 1906.
Note: Effective June 1994, this publication ceased publishing the Saturday edition.
Not Published: New Year; Independence Day; Labor Day; Christmas.
Special Editions: Senior Years, Bridal (Jan); Progress Edition (Feb); Home Improvement (Apr); Graduation (May); Guide to Pulaski County (June); Fair Tab (July); Football Tab (Aug); Christmas Guide (Nov).
Special Weekly Sections: Best Food Day (wed); Religion (fri); Best Food Day (S).

GENERAL MANAGEMENT

Publisher Billy R Smith
Manager-Office Helen Stark

ADVERTISING

Manager Dan Callahan

CIRCULATION

Director Vanessa Anderson

NEWS EXECUTIVE

Editor Mike Williams

EDITORS AND MANAGERS

Editorial Writer Mike Williams
Sports Editor Kim Nelson

PRODUCTION

Superintendent Paul W Hines
Superintendent-Composing Joy Thornton

Market Information: TMC.
Mechanical available: Offset; Black and 3 ROP colors; insert accepted — preprinted, single sheets $8\frac{1}{2}$"x 11"; page cut-offs — $22\frac{3}{4}$".
Mechanical specifications: Type page $13\frac{1}{16}$" x $21\frac{1}{2}$"; E - 6 cols, $2\frac{3}{34}$", $\frac{1}{6}$" between; A - 6 cols, $2\frac{3}{64}$", $\frac{1}{6}$" between; C - 9 cols, $1\frac{5}{16}$", $\frac{1}{8}$" between.
Commodity consumption: Newsprint 400 short tons; width 28"; black ink 7,500 pounds; color ink 400 pounds; single pages printed 5,000; average pages per issue 12(d), 20(S); single plates used 6,800.
Equipment: EDITORIAL: Front-end hardware — Samtron; Front-end software — Microsoft/DOS TSS; Printers — NewGen/Turbos-400; Other equipment — Lf/AP Leaf Picture Desk. CLASSIFIED: Front-end hardware — Amdek/AM432N; Front-end software — Systems Facilities/Newscraft; Printers — Epson/DFX-8000. DISPLAY: Adv layout systems — ATT, Ap/Mac. PRODUCTION: Plate processors — Nu, Roconex; Production cameras — DAI/Screen; Automatic film processors — LE; Color separation equipment (conventional) — Lf/AP Leaf Picture Desk; Digital color separation equipment — HP.
PRESSROOM: Line 1 — 6-HI/V-15A (w/upper former). MAILROOM: Bundle tyer — 2-MLN/Strapper. WIRE SERVICES: News — AP; Receiving dishes — AP. BUSINESS COMPUTERS: EKI/Televideo; Applications: Lotus; PCs & main system networked.

RICHMOND

An Independent City

'90 U.S. Census- 203,056; E&P '96 Est. 198,166
ABC-NDM (90): 693,517 (HH 270,544)

Richmond Times-Dispatch

(m-mon to sat; S)

Richmond Times-Dispatch, 333 E. Grace St.; PO Box 85333, Richmond, VA 23293; tel (804) 649-6000; fax (804) 775-8059. Media General Inc. group.
Circulation: 211,859(m); 211,859(m-sat); 258,089(S); ABC Sept. 30, 1995.
Price: 50¢(d); 75¢(sat); $1.75(S); $3.25/wk; $24.10/mo (mail); $251.20/yr.
Advertising: Open inch rate $118.00(m); $118.00(m-sat); $146.00(S); $204.00(m & S). **Representative:** Sawyer-Ferguson-Walker Co.
News Services: AP, Business Wire, LAT-WP, Media General News, NYT, SHNS. **Politics:** Independent. **Established:** 1850.
Special Editions: Special Stock Report, Weddings (Jan); Planning for Retirement, Home Comfort, Crafted in Virginia, Tax Guide (Feb); Auto '400' Race, Careers, Top 50 Richmond Businesses, Working Parents Guide, Gardener's Guide, New Homes, The Richmond Look, Antiquing in Virginia, Interior Designs (Mar); Baseball, Car Care, Springtime in Virginia, Richmond Recycling, American Home Week (Apr); Week of the Nurse, Fur & Feathers (May); Tri-Cities Today (June); Retirement Lifestyles (July); Discover Richmond, The Richmond Look, Hunting & Fishing, Football (Aug); Miller 400 Auto Race, Fine Arts/Richmond After Dark, New Homes, Yard & Home, Fall Job Market, Interior Designs (Sept); Parade of Homes, Marathon, School & College Guide, Dining Out in Richmond, Fall Car Care, Home Energy (Oct); Happy Holidays, Holiday Cheers, Basketball (Nov); Holiday Book (Dec).
Special Weekly Sections: Metro Business, Prime Living, Sports (mon); Business, Sports (tues); Business, Sports, Food (wed); Weekend, Health and Science, Business, Sports (thur); Business, Sports (fri); InSync (teen section), Home, Green Section (sat); Travel, Entertainment, Real Estate, Sports, Business (S).

CORPORATE OFFICERS

Chairman-Exec Committee D Tennant Bryan
Chairman/CEO/President J Stewart Bryan III
Vice Chairman James S Evans
Senior Vice Pres/Chief Financial Officer Marshall N Morton
Vice Pres-Newspaper Operations H Graham Woodlief
Vice Pres Basil Snider Jr
General Counsel/Secretary George L Mahoney

GENERAL MANAGEMENT

Publisher J Stewart Bryan III
President/General Manager Albert T August III
Vice Pres/Business Manager O Scott Leath
Vice Pres/Exec Editor William H Millsaps Jr
Controller George Boatright
Vice Pres/Director-Human Relations Frank McDonald
Manager-Credit Clifton H Neal
Director-Research Steve Shaw
Manager-Special Events/Community Relations O DeWayne Davis
Manager-Education Service Betty White
Asst Controller James F Woodward

ADVERTISING

Director-Sales/Marketing Roger C Kain
Manager-Display Gary D Conner
Manager-Creative Service Haward Baar
Manager-Marketing Service T Floyd Spencer
Manager-Ad Service Linda Bricker

MARKETING AND PROMOTION

Director-Sales/Marketing Roger C Kain
Director-Promotion Robert A Beasley

TELECOMMUNICATIONS

Director-Info Service Walter L Waleski
Audiotex Marketing Paula Pulley

CIRCULATION

Director/Vice Pres Allen Walton
Manager-Metro Thomas C Smith
Manager-Metro Richard A Neely Jr
Manager-State W M White
Manager-Subscriber Relations John Beirne
Manager-Single Copy Gerry Spicer
Manager-Transportation Bill Groves

NEWS EXECUTIVES

Vice Pres/Exec Editor William H Millsaps Jr
Managing Editor Louise Seals
Asst Managing Editor-Night Operations Danny Finnegan
Deputy Managing Editor-City/State/Suburban News David L Burton
Deputy Managing Editor-Flair/Sports Howard Owen
Deputy Managing Editor-Administration/Photo/Copy Desk John A Dillon
Deputy Managing Editor-Weekend Operations Tom Silvestri

EDITORS AND MANAGERS

Aviation Editor Peter Bacque
Books Editor Ann Merriman
Business/Finance Editor Andrew Taylor
Cartoonist Gary Brookins
Cartoonist Bob Gorrell
City Editor Paul Gregory
Columnist Charles McDowell
Columnist Ray McAllister
Columnist Steve Clark
Columnist Jann Malone
Commentary Editor Ann Merriman
Chief Editorial Writer Todd Culbertson
Copy Desk Chief Robert Diehl
Editorial Page Editor Ross Mackenzie
Fashion Writer Jessica Ronky
Films Writer Dan Neman
Flair (Features) Editor Robert A Walsh
Food Writer Louis Mahoney
Garden Writer Jerry Williams
Graphics Editor Tom Bond
Librarian Charles Saunders
Music Writer Clarke Bustard III
Op-Editor Robert Holland
Op-Editor/Columnist Edward Grimsley
Photo Department Manager P A Gormus Jr
Radio/Television Writer Douglas Durden
Science/Medicine Writer Beverly Orndorff
Sports Editor Jack Berninger
State Editor Mary Anne Pikrone
Suburban Editor Tom Kapsidelis
Systems Editor Bob Knight
Teen-Age/Youth Writer Mary Louise Taylor

MANAGEMENT INFORMATION SERVICES

Director-Electronic Publishing Michael Steele

PRODUCTION

Vice Pres/Operations Robert W Rogers
Director William Barker
Director-Engineering Robert Cross
Manager-Pressroom Cliff Brown
Manager-Engraving Al Lane
Manager-Mailroom Douglas Parker
Manager-Advertising/News Herbert White
Manager-Commercial Ventures Judy Cheadle
Manager-Commercial Print Shop Joe Martin
Coordinator-Quality Joel Cox

Market Information: Zoned editions; Split Run; TMC; ADS; Operate database; Operate audiotex.

Mechanical available: Offset; Black and 3 ROP colors; insert accepted — preprinted; page cutoffs — 22".

Mechanical specifications: Type page 13" x 21"; E - 6 cols, 2 1/16", 1/8" between; A - 6 cols, 2 1/16", 1/8" between; C - 10 cols, 1 1/4", 1/18" between.

Commodity consumption: Newsprint 41,650 short tons; widths 55", 41 1/4", 27 1/2"; black ink 890,000 pounds; color ink 152,000 pounds; single pages printed 28,132; average pages per issue 68(d), 124(S); single plates used 300,000.

Equipment: EDITORIAL: Front-end hardware — Ap/Mac 950, Ap/Mac 900, Ap/Mac ci, Ap/Mac cx, Ap/Mac SE, 214-AT, 8-DEC/PDP 11-34, 2-AT/30; Front-end software — Aldus/FreeHand, QuarkXPress, AT/ESP II 4.64; Printers — 4-Okidata/320, 1-Okidata/400, 1-Okidata/2410, 4-Ap/Mac LaserWriter; Other equipment — 38-RSK/100, 5-RSK/1400, 1-Toshiba/1100. CLASSIFIED: Front-end hardware — HP/950; Printers — Okidata/2410, HP/2564, HP/2567. DISPLAY: Adv layout systems — SCS/Layout 8000; Front-end hardware — Dell/22, IBM/80286; Front-end software — SCS/Layout 800; Printers — HP/LaserJet III. PRODUCTION: Typesetters — 3-III/3810; Plate exposures — 2-WL/3; Plate processors — 2-WL/Lithoplater 380; Scanners — 2-Lf/Leafscan 35; Production cameras — 1-C/Spartan III; Automatic film processors — 1-LE/LD24A, 1-LE/LD24, LE/Excel 32, 6-L; Reproportion units — ECR/Autokon 1030, ECR/Autokon 1000; Film transporters — 1-C/Spartan; Color separation equipment (conventional) — 2-Scitex/PS-2, Scitex/Softproof; Digital color separation equipment — CD/645 IE, Scitex/Smart 2.
PRESSROOM: Line 1 — 36-MHI/Print couples (4 reversible half decks; 2 mono units); Line 2 — 36-MHI/Print couples (4 reversible half decks; 2 mono units); Line 3 — 36-MHI/Print Couples (4 reversible half decks; 2 mono units); Folders — 2-MHI/180-page; Reels and stands — 10-MHI; Press control system — 6-E. MAILROOM: Counter stackers — 14-Id/2100, 5-QWI, 9-HL/SH; Inserters and stuffers — S/b-72P, S/22-99, Amerigraph; Bundle tyer — 14-Dynaric; Addressing machine — Ch/539, Ch/537, 2-MS/110N, 2-AVY. LIBRARY: Electronic — Vu/Text SAVE System. COMMUNICATIONS: Facsimile — 3-III/3800-F, 2-III/3750-F, 1-III/3750-FC. WIRE SERVICES: News — AP Datafeatures, NYT, CSM, LAT-WP, TMS, KRT, AP; Stock tables — AP SelectStox, AP Datastream; Syndicates — TV Data, PR Newswire; Receiving dishes — size-10ft, AP, INS. BUSINESS COMPUTERS: HP/917, HP/935, HP/950, HP/949, HP/947; Applications: CJ: Accts receivable, Payroll, Bad debt, Report writer, Financial, Circ, Carrier, Billing, Mail subscriptions, Prepaid, Single copy sales; Visimage, Omnidex; PCs & micros networked; PCs & main system networked.

ROANOKE

An Independent City

'90 U.S. Census- 96,397; E&P '96 Est. 94,551
ABC-NDM (90): 738,676 (HH 284,885)

The Roanoke Times

(m-mon to sat; S)

The Roanoke Times, 201-209 W. Campbell Ave.; PO Box 2491, Roanoke, VA 24010-2491; tel (540) 981-3100; web site http://www.infi.net/roatimes/index.html. Landmark Communications Inc. group.

Circulation: 110,195(m); 110,195(m-sat); 124,196(S); ABC Sept. 30, 1995.

Price: 35¢(d); 50¢(sat); $1.50(S); $2.60/wk (carrier home-delivered).

Advertising: Open inch rate $55.69(m); $55.69(m-sat); $58.38(S).

News Services: AP, LAT-WP, NYT. **Politics:** Independent. **Established:** 1886 (Times), 1889 (World-News).

Advertising not accepted: Reserve right to revise or reject any advertisement.

Special Editions: Economy '96, Black History (Jan); Auto Racing Tab, Your Wedding Tab, Boat Show Tab (Feb); Lawn & Garden Tab, Trout Pages, Today's Home Tab, New Cars, Travel Pages, American Women's Show, Spring Fashion (Mar); Baseball Preview, Nurses Tab, Report on Small Business (Apr); American Home Week (May); Graduates Tab, Senior Style Tab (June); Salem Fair, Parent's Guide Tab, Discover Tab (July); Football (Aug); Arts '96, Fall Home and Landscape Tab, Fall Fashion (Sept); Travel Pages, Hunting Pages (Oct); NBA Previews, College Basketball, Holiday Gift Guide Tab (Nov); Ski Pages (Dec).

Special Weekly Sections: Food (wed); Dine & Dance (Entertainment) (thur).

Magazine: Parade (S).

CORPORATE OFFICERS

President/Publisher Walter Rugaber
Secretary Louis F Ryan
Treasurer Carl L Wright

GENERAL MANAGEMENT

Publisher Walter Rugaber
Controller Marilyn Yoder
Manager-Credit Joyce Argabright
Director-Human Resources Debra Meade
Purchasing Agent Carl L Wright

ADVERTISING

Director/Vice Pres Judith Perfater
Manager-Classified C Lee Clark
Manager-General Patricia Blackstock
Manager-Retail Don Porterfield

MARKETING AND PROMOTION

Director-Marketing Catherine Greenberg

TELECOMMUNICATIONS

Audiotex Manager Chuck Almarez

CIRCULATION

Director Helen A Burnett

NEWS EXECUTIVES

Editor Wendy Zomparelli
Managing Editor William K Warren
Deputy Managing Editor-Reporting & Writing L Richmond Martin III
Deputy Managing Editor-Editing & Design Roger Holtman

EDITORS AND MANAGERS

Amusements Editor Jeff DeBell
Automotive/Aviation Editor John Levin
Books Editor Mike Mayo
Business/Finance Editor John Levin
Columnist Ben Beagle
Editorial Page Editor Alan Sorensen
Environmental Editor Cathryn McCue
Coordinator-Features Section Jeff DeBell
Food Editor Almena Hughes
Garden/Home Furnishings Editor Sandra Kelly
Graphics/Design Manager Steve Stinson
Dayside Metro Editor John Levin
Dayside Metro Editor Sue Lindsey
Night Metro Editor Mark Layman
Medicine Editor Sandra Kelly
Music Editor Mark Morrison
Outdoors Editor Bill Cochran
Director-Photography John Cook
Real Estate Editor John Levin
Religion Editor Cody Lowe
Science Editor Sandra Kelly
Sports Editor Bill Bern
Travel Editor Carolyn Daugherty

PRODUCTION

Manager R Vincent Reynolds
Manager-Quality Control Gary Craddock
Manager-Pressroom Dennis Woodford
Manager-Maintenance/Support Service Dennis (Chip) Harris
Manager-Mailroom Art Carter

Market Information: Zoned editions; Split Run; TMC; Operate audiotex; Electronic edition.

Mechanical available: Offset; Black and 3 ROP colors; insert accepted — preprinted; page cutoffs — 23".

Mechanical specifications: Type page 13" x 21 1/2"; E - 6 cols, 2.03", 1/8" between; A - 6 cols, 2.07", 1/8" between; C - 10 cols, 1.18", 1/8" between.

Commodity consumption: Newsprint 13,685 short tons; widths 55", 41 1/8", 27 3/8"; black ink 236,860 pounds; color ink 85,960 pounds; single pages printed 29,058; average pages per issue 48(d), 79(S); single plates used 120,000.

Equipment: EDITORIAL: Front-end hardware — DTI; Front-end software — DTI; Other equipment — 50-Ap/Mac, 2-Sun/Sparcstation. CLASSIFIED: Front-end hardware — DTI; Front-end software — DTI. AUDIOTEX: Hardware — PEP, 1-VSM, 2-VDN; Software — VoicePrint/9000 2.4.2; Supplier name — Brite. DISPLAY: Adv layout systems — DTI; Front-end hardware — DTI. PRODUCTION: Typesetters — 2-AU/APS 108; Plate exposures — 1-WL/Lith-X-Pozer III; Plate processors — 1-WL, Lf, 1-Anacoil/Subtractive; Scanners — 1-CD/636 scanner & scanview; Production cameras — 1-C/Marathon, 1-C/Pager I; Automatic film processors — 1-LE/LD-24A, 2-LE/LD-24AQ, 1-DP; Film transporters — 1-C; Shrink lenses — 2-Alan/Variable squeeze. PRESSROOM: Line 1 — 6-PEC/3CIC; Line 2 — 6-PEC/3CIC; Folders — 1-PEC/Double 3:2-3:2, 1-PEC/Double 2:1-2:1; Pasters — 12-Enkel; Reels and stands — 12-Enkel; Press control system — PEC/James Bond. MAILROOM: Counter stackers — 5-HL/Monitor, 2-HL/Monitor HT; Inserters and stuffers — 2-HL/1472; Bundle tyer — 4-Dynaric/NP2; Addressing machine — Ch. LIBRARY: Electronic — Vu/Text SAVE system, Data Times; Combination — Vu/Text SAVE System. WIRE SERVICES: News — AP Datastream, AP Datafeatures, TV Data; Stock tables — AP SelectStox I; Syndicates — KRT, NYT, LAT-WP; Receiving dishes — AP. BUSINESS COMPUTERS: IBM/9370, HP/3000; Applications: Cobol, CA-ADR-DB, Cobol/II, CJ/AIM-CIS, NPS, RPG/II, MPEXL, RPG/3000; PCs & micros networked; PCs & main system networked.

STAUNTON

An Independent city

'90 U.S. Census- 24,461; E&P '96 Est. 26,209
ABC-CZ (90): 26,548 (HH 10,372)

The Daily News Leader

(m-mon to sat)

The Sunday News Leader (S)

The Daily News Leader, 11 N. Central Ave. (24401); PO Box 59, Staunton, VA 24402; tel (540) 885-7281; fax (540) 885-1904. Gannett Co. Inc. group.

Circulation: 18,803(m); 18,803(m-sat); 22,996(S); ABC Sept. 30, 1995.

Price: 50¢(d); 50¢(sat); $1.25(S); $1.60/wk (carrier); $109.20/yr (mail).

Advertising: Open inch rate $25.85(m); $25.85(m-sat); $27.50(S). **Representative:** Landon Associates Inc.

News Service: AP. **Politics:** Independent. **Established:** 1904.

Special Weekly Sections: Best Food Day (wed); Spotlight (TMC).

Magazines: Parade; TV Week; Color Comics (S).

GENERAL MANAGEMENT

Publisher Wesley B Wampler
Controller Andy Royer

ADVERTISING

Director Marty White

CIRCULATION

Director Danny L Allen

NEWS EXECUTIVE

Exec Editor Rick Gunter

PRODUCTION

Manager Billy A Robertson
Manager-Operations Ken Hilton

Market Information: Zoned editions; TMC.

Mechanical available: Offset; Black and 3 ROP colors; insert accepted — preprinted; page cutoffs — 21 1/2".

Mechanical specifications: Type page 13" x 21 1/4"; E - 6 cols, 2 1/16", 1/8" between; A - 6 cols, 2 1/16", 1/8" between; C - 9 cols, 1 3/8", 1/16" between.

Commodity consumption: Newsprint 1,180 short tons; widths 27 1/2", 13 3/4"; black ink 21,500 pounds; color ink 1,380 pounds; single pages printed 10,861; average pages per issue 20(d), 44(S); single plates used 10,000.

Equipment: EDITORIAL: Front-end hardware — 1-CText/80386 fileserver. CLASSIFIED: Front-end hardware — 1-CText/80386 fileserver; Other equipment — X/7650 Scanner. DISPLAY: Adv layout systems — 1-Adept/80286, 3-Adept/80386. PRODUCTION: Typesetters — 2-Hyphen/PC RIP/Ultre 94 Recorders; Plate exposures — 1-Nu; Plate processors — 1-Nat; Scanners — 1-ECR/Autokon 1000; Production cameras — 1-C/Spartan II, 1-R/432, ECR; Automatic film processors — 1-LE/LD-2600A; Film transporters — 1-C/1244; Color separation equipment (conventional) — Digi-Colour. PRESSROOM: Line 1 — 6-G/Urbanite; Line 2 — 1-AM/1650 MC Offset; Folders — 1-G/Urbanite. MAILROOM: Counter stackers — 1-Id/2000, 1-Id/440; Inserters and stuffers — 1-MM; Bundle tyer — 1-Bu, 1-MLN/MA, 1-MLN/Spirit, 1-Power Strap; Addressing machine — 1-KR/Mailer, 1-KR/Quarter Folder. LIBRARY: Electronic — 1-BH/Mark II. WIRE SERVICES: News — AP. BUSINESS COMPUTERS: 1-AT/386, 1-IBM/AS-400, 1-AST/286 Premium, 1-AT/286; Applications: Adv billing, Accts receivable, Payroll, Circ billing, Gen ledger, Accts payable; PCs & micros networked; PCs & main system networked.

STRASBURG

Shenandoah County

'90 U.S. Census- 3,762; E&P '96 Est. 4,627
ABC-NDM (90): 141,600 (HH 53,685)

Northern Virginia Daily

(m-mon to sat)

Northern Virginia Daily, 120 N. Holliday St.; PO Box 69, Strasburg, VA 22657; tel (540) 465-5137; fax (540) 465-9388.

Circulation: 15,550(m); 15,550(m-sat); ABC Sept. 30, 1995.

Price: 35¢(d); 35¢(sat); $6.60/mo; $56.00/yr.

Advertising: Open inch rate $10.45(m); $10.45(m-sat). **Representative:** Landon Associates Inc.

News Service: AP. **Politics:** Independent. **Established:** 1932.

Not Published: New Year; Memorial Day; Independence Day; Labor Day; Thanksgiving; Christmas.

Advertising not accepted: Horoscopes; Fortune Tellers; Palm Readers.
Special Editions: Bridal (Feb); Farm & Garden (Mar); Home Improvement (Apr); Shenandoah County Guide, Shenandoah Valley Seniors (May); Warren County Guide (June); Frederick County Guide (July); Shenandoah County Fair (Aug); Recipes, Car Care (Oct); Christmas, Holiday Gift Guide (Nov).
Special Weekly Sections: Best Food Day (wed); Real Estate-Shenadoah Valley (fri).

CORPORATE OFFICERS
President William Keister
Vice Pres/Secretary John D Keister

GENERAL MANAGEMENT
Publisher William Keister
Purchasing Agent Doug Walker
General Manager John F Horan Jr

ADVERTISING
Director William Miller

CIRCULATION
Manager Beverly George

NEWS EXECUTIVES
Editor John F Horan Jr
Managing Editor Joseph E Strohmeyer

MANAGEMENT INFORMATION SERVICES
Consultant Hank Zimmerman

PRODUCTION
Foreman-Pressroom Douglas Walker

Market Information: TMC.
Mechanical available: Offset; Black and 3 ROP colors; insert accepted — preprinted; page cutoffs — 22¾".
Mechanical specifications: Type page 13" x 21¼"; E - 6 cols, 2 1/16", ⅛" between; A - 6 cols, 2 1/16", ⅛" between; C - 9 cols, 1⅜", 1/16" between.
Commodity consumption: Newsprint 1,100 short tons; widths 28", 14"; single pages printed 8,300; average pages per issue 29(d), 36(sat).
Equipment: EDITORIAL: Front-end hardware — COM/OS; Front-end software — COM/OS; Other equipment — III/Translator. CLASSIFIED: Front-end hardware — COM/OS, COM/Intrepid; Front-end software — COM/OS; Other equipment — III/Translator. DISPLAY: Front-end hardware — PC/386, COM/MCS-20; Front-end software — Archetype/Corel Draw. PRODUCTION: Typesetters — NewGen; Plate exposures — Nu/Flip Top FT40NS; Plate processors — Nat/A-250; Electronic picture desk — Lf/AP Leaf Picture Desk; Scanners — Panasonic; Production cameras — 1-B/18x24; Automatic film processors — 1-LE/LD24AQ.
PRESSROOM: Line 1 — 6-G/Urbanite; Line 2 — 2-Dev/Horizon; Press drives — G; Press control system — Fin; Press registration system — Duarte. MAILROOM: Counter stackers — BG/Count-O-Veyor; Bundle tyer — Bu/Strapper; Addressing machine — 2-St. LIBRARY: Electronic — RSK/Tandy 3000. COMMUNICATIONS: Facsimile — Sharp/FO700. WIRE SERVICES: News — AP; Receiving dishes — size-3m, AP. BUSINESS COMPUTERS: DEC/V70; Applications: Vision Data; PCs & main system networked.

SUFFOLK
An Independent City
'90 U.S. Census- 52,141; E&P '96 Est. 55,524

Suffolk News-Herald
(m-tues to sat; S)

Suffolk News-Herald, 130 S. Saratoga St.; PO Box 1220, Suffolk, VA 23434; tel (804) 539-3437; fax (804) 539-8804. Media General (Virginia Newspapers Inc.) group.
Circulation: 4,373(m); 4,373(m-sat); 4,373(S); Sworn Sept. 29, 1994.
Price: 25¢(d); 25¢(sat); 75¢(S); $6.05/mo; $72.60/yr.
Advertising: Open inch rate $10.15(m); $10.15(m-sat); $10.15(S). **Representative:** Landon Associates Inc.
News Service: AP. **Politics:** Independent. **Established:** 1873.
Not Published: Christmas.
Special Editions: Year in Review (Jan); Progress Edition (Feb); Home Improvement, Farm Edition (Mar); The Great Outdoors (Apr); Senior Citizens, Car Care, Health & Fitness (May); June Bride, Historic Suffolk, Vacation Tab (June); Summer Lifestyles (July); Sketchbook, Football (Aug); Home Improvement (Sept); Peanut Festival Edition (Oct); Buckle Up for Safety Coloring Book (Nov); Christmas Greetings Edition (Dec).
Special Weekly Sections: Farm Page (tues); Best Food Days (wed); Schools (thur); Church News (fri); Best Food Days (S).
Magazine: USA Weekend (S).

CORPORATE OFFICER
President Gaither Perry

GENERAL MANAGEMENT
Publisher Gaither Perry
Business Manager Cathy Leonard

CIRCULATION
Manager Turk Bard

NEWS EXECUTIVE
Editor Tim Copeland

PRODUCTION
Foreman-Pressroom Len Cox
Supervisor Len Cox

Market Information: Split Run; TMC.
Mechanical available: Offset; Black and 3 ROP colors; insert accepted — preprinted; page cutoffs — 22¾".
Mechanical specifications: Type page 13" x 21½"; E - 5 cols, 2⅜", ⅛" between; A - 6 cols, 2 1/16", ⅛" between; C - 9 cols, 1⅜", 1/16" between.
Commodity consumption: Newsprint 600 short tons; widths 28", 30", 32"; black ink 30,000 pounds; color ink 2,500 pounds; single pages printed 5,036; average pages per issue 10(d), 20(S); single plates used 5,000.
Equipment: DISPLAY: Adv layout systems — Ap/Mac II. PRODUCTION: Typesetters — Ap/Mac LaserPrinter; Plate exposures — 1-Nu; Plate processors — 1-Nat/250; Production cameras — 1-C/Spartan II; Automatic film processors — 1-LE/BQ12.
PRESSROOM: Line 1 — 6-G/Community (24 pg b/w capacity). MAILROOM: Bundle tyer — 1-Bu/Wire, 1-Ty-Tech/4, 1-Us. COMMUNICATIONS: Facsimile — Sharp. WIRE SERVICES: News — AP; Syndicates — NEA. BUSINESS COMPUTERS: 2-EKI/Televideo 950.

VIRGINIA BEACH
See NORFOLK

WAYNESBORO
An Independent City
'90 U.S. Census- 18,549; E&P '96 Est. 20,688
ABC-CZ (90): 25,299 (HH 9,993)

The News-Virginian
(e-mon to fri; m-sat)

The News-Virginian, 544 W. Main St.; PO Box 1027, Waynesboro, VA 22980; tel (540) 949-8213. Park Communications Inc. group.
Circulation: 9,476(e); 9,476(m-sat); ABC Sept. 30, 1995.
Price: 50¢(d); 50¢(sat); $7.80/mo (carrier), $10.40/mo (mail); $93.60/yr.
Advertising: Open inch rate $12.28(e); $12.28(m-sat). **Representative:** Landon Associates Inc.
News Service: AP. **Politics:** Independent. **Established:** 1892.
Not Published: Christmas.
Special Editions: Weekly Stuarts Draft; Fall Foliage; Tourist Guide (Spring, Summer, Fall); Christmas Greetings; Fall & Spring Car Care; Progress Edition Update.
Special Weekly Sections: Business (mon); Health & Fitness (tues); Valley Flavor (wed); Leisure Time (thur); Church News (fri); Trends (sat).
Magazine: Weekend (local, newsprint) (sat).

GENERAL MANAGEMENT
Publisher/General Manager Harlan H Phillips

ADVERTISING
Director Harlan H Phillips
Manager-Classified Mildred K Trent

CIRCULATION
Director Bruce Kelso

NEWS EXECUTIVES
Editor Harlan H Phillips
Managing Editor Terry Smith

EDITORS AND MANAGERS
Amusements/Travel Editor Terry Smith
Business/Finance Editor Harlan H Phillips
Columnist E P Berlin Jr
Education Editor Michelle Lincoln
Farm Editor Michelle Lincoln
Fashion/Food Editor Ginger Wood
Features Editor Michelle Lincoln
Garden Editor Ginger Wood
Health/Medical Editor Ginger Wood
Home Furnishings Editor Ginger Wood
Living/Lifestyle Editor Ginger Wood
Music Editor Ginger Wood
Photo Department Manager Ginger Wood
Police Beat Editor Dan McCauley
Radio/Television Editor Terry Smith
Religion/School Editor Terry Smith
Society/Women's Editor Terry Smith
Sports Editor James Gordon
Women's Editor Ginger Wood

PRODUCTION
Manager John Prye

Market Information: TMC.
Mechanical available: Offset; Black and 3 ROP colors; insert accepted — preprinted; page cutoffs — 22¾".
Mechanical specifications: Type page 13" x 21½"; E - 6 cols, 2 1/16", ⅛" between; A - 6 cols, 2 1/16", ⅛" between; C - 10 cols, 1¼", ⅛" between.
Commodity consumption: Newsprint 400 short tons; width 27½"; single pages printed 6,500; average pages per issue 16(d).
Equipment: EDITORIAL: Front-end hardware — Mk/3000. CLASSIFIED: Front-end hardware — Mk/3000. PRODUCTION: Typesetters — Ap/Mac LaserPrinter; Plate exposures — 1-Nu/Flip Top FT40; Plate processors — 1-Nu/Flip Top FT40; Production cameras — 1-B/24x24, COM/M, 1-LE/R 20x24; Automatic film processors — 1-LE/18; Shrink lenses — 1-CK Optical.
PRESSROOM: Line 1 — 4-G/Urbanite; Folders — 1-G. MAILROOM: Bundle tyer — 1-Bu/42409, 1-MLN. WIRE SERVICES: News — AP; Receiving dishes — AP. BUSINESS COMPUTERS: Applications: Vision Data: Bus, Circ.

WINCHESTER
An Independent City
'90 U.S. Census- 21,947; E&P '96 Est. 23,202
ABC-CZ (90): 21,947 (HH 9,084)

The Winchester Star
(e-mon to fri; m-sat)

The Winchester Star, 2 N. Kent St., Winchester, VA 22601; tel (540) 667-3200; fax (540) 667-0012. Byrd Newspapers group.
Circulation: 22,456(e); 27,967(m-sat); ABC Sept. 30, 1995.
Price: 25¢(d); 25¢(sat); $68.00/yr; $24.00/3mo.
Advertising: Open inch rate $11.50(e); $11.50(m-sat). **Representative:** Landon Associates Inc.
News Service: AP. **Politics:** Independent. **Established:** 1896.
Not Published: New Year; Independence Day; Labor Day; Christmas.
Special Edition: Apple Blossom Festival (May).

GENERAL MANAGEMENT
Publisher Thomas T Byrd

ADVERTISING
Manager Jerry Howard
Manager-Classified Ann Whitacre
Manager-Outside Sales John Parkinson

CIRCULATION
Director Al Lowdermilk

NEWS EXECUTIVES
Managing Editor Ron Morris
Asst Managing Editor Wayde Byard

EDITOR AND MANAGER
Sports Editor Ben Brooks

PRODUCTION
Manager-Composing Joyce Williams
Foreman-Pressroom Mitchell O Heironimus

Market Information: Zoned editions; Split Run.
Mechanical available: Offset; Black and 3 ROP colors; insert accepted — preprinted; page cutoffs — 21½".
Mechanical specifications: Type page 13" x 21½"; E - 6 cols, 2 1/16", ⅛" between; A - 6 cols, 2 1/16", ⅛" between; C - 9 cols, 1 5/16", ⅛" between.
Commodity consumption: Newsprint 2,000 short tons; widths 27½", 13¾"; black ink 40,000 pounds; color ink 2,100 pounds; average pages per issue 36(d).
Equipment: EDITORIAL: Front-end hardware — COM; Front-end software — OS; Printers — Ap/Mac LaserWriter II; Other equipment — 2-Ap/Mac Quadra 700. CLASSIFIED: Printers — CText/ALPS ALQ324E, NewGen/Turbo PS-400; Other equipment — COM/Intrepid. PRODUCTION: Plate exposures — 2-BKY/2KW; Plate processors — Nat/Super A-250; Production cameras — C/Spartan III, SCREEN/Companica 5161; Automatic film processors — LE/LD24AQ; Film transporters — C; Color separation equipment (conventional) — Digi-Colour, Lf/AP Leaf Picture Desk.
PRESSROOM: Line 1 — 8-G/Urbanite U-1327; Folders — 1-G/Double former; Press control system — Fin, 1-Ebway/SU 300. MAILROOM: Counter stackers — 2-HL; Inserters and stuffers — MM/6 Head; Bundle tyer — 2-EAM/Mosca; Addressing machine — 1-Am/1900. LIBRARY: Electronic — Folio, Dewar. WIRE SERVICES: News — AP, LAT-WP; Photos — AP; Receiving dishes — AP. BUSINESS COMPUTERS: IBM/Sys 3600.

WOODBRIDGE
Prince William County
'90 U.S. Census- 19,750; E&P '96 Est. 22,631
ABC-NDM (90): 205,998 (HH 63,410)

Potomac News
(e-mon to fri; m-sat)
Sunday News (S)

Potomac News, 14010 Smoketown Rd.; PO Box 2470, Woodbridge, VA 22192; tel (703) 878-8000; fax (703) 878-3993. MediaNews Inc. group.
Circulation: 30,277(e); 30,277(m-sat); 31,306(S); ABC Sept. 30, 1995.
Price: 35¢(d); 35¢(sat); 90¢(S); $2.50/wk; $8.00/mo; $93.60/yr.
Advertising: Open inch rate $23.75(e); $23.75(m-sat); $28.03(S). **Representatives:** US Suburban Press; Landon Associates Inc.; Papert Companies.
News Services: AP, NYT, GNN. **Politics:** Independent. **Established:** 1959.
Note: Effective July 29, 1995, this publication started publishing a Saturday edition.
Magazines: Business (mon); Health, Federal Employees (tues); Food, Young Life, Lifestyle (wed); Lifestyle, Entertainment (thur); Real Estate, Religion (fri); Transportation, TV Week, USA Weekend, Comics (S).

GENERAL MANAGEMENT
Publisher Andy Mick
Business Manager Carole Bell

ADVERTISING
Director Sandra Peirce
Manager-Classified Bettye Butler

CIRCULATION
Director Richard Gathen

NEWS EXECUTIVE
Editor Luke West

EDITORS AND MANAGERS
Editorial Writer Clint Schemmer
News Editor Ellen Mitchell
Sports Editor Tom Clark

MANAGEMENT INFORMATION SERVICES
Data Processing Manager Edward Murray

PRODUCTION
Manager Renita Pryor
Manager-Operations Glenn Jessee

Market Information: Zoned editions; TMC.
Mechanical available: Offset; Black and 3 ROP colors; insert accepted — preprinted; page cutoffs — 22".
Mechanical specifications: Type page 13" x 21"; E - 6 cols, 2 1/16", ⅛" between; A - 6 cols, 2 1/16", ⅛" between; C - 9 cols, 1⅜", 1/16" between.
Commodity consumption: Newsprint 2,600 short tons; widths 28", 42", 56"; black ink 54,000 pounds; color ink 10,800 pounds; single pages printed 12,876; average pages per issue 35(d), 71(S); single plates used 36,000.
Equipment: EDITORIAL: Front-end hardware — 32-EKI/Televideo; Front-end software — TSS; Printers — 3-Ap/Mac LaserWriter. CLASSIFIED: Front-end hardware — 5-EKI/Televideo; Printers — 1-Ap/Mac LaserPrinter, 1-Dataproducts/DS-400. DISPLAY: Front-end hardware — 7-Ap/Mac II; Front-end software — DTI/AdSpeed; Printers — 1-Ap/Mac Laserview, 1-HP/LaserJet 4; Other equipment — ECR/Autokon, Microtek. PRODUCTION: Plate exposures — 2-Nu; Plate processors — 1-Cookson Graphics; Scanners — 1-ECR; Production cameras — 1-C; Automatic film processors — 1-LE; Digital color separation equipment — Ap/Mac Quadra 950, Lf/AP Leaf Picture Desk.
PRESSROOM: Line 1 — 4-MAN/Uniman 4x2; Press drives — GE; Folders — MAN/Jaw 2-3-2; Pasters — 2-MEG; Reels and stands — 2-MAN; Press control system — GE. MAILROOM: Counter stackers — 4-Id/440; Inserters and stuffers — 48-HI/8; Bundle tyer — 3-MLN/MLEE. WIRE SERVICES: News — AP; Photos — AP; Stock tables — AP; Receiving dishes — size-10ft, AP. BUSINESS COMPUTERS: HP/3000, 3-EKI/Televideo, 2-EKI/Earthstation, 1-IBM/PS2; Applications: CJ: Payroll, Circ, Accounting, Gen ledger, Accts payable; Lotus 1-2-3: Adv, Class; PCs & micros networked; PCs & main system networked.

Copyright ©1996 by the Editor & Publisher Co.

WASHINGTON

ABERDEEN

Grays Harbor County

'90 U.S. Census- 16,565; E&P '96 Est. 15,497
ABC-CZ (90): 26,909 (HH 11,149)

The Daily World

(e-mon to sat; S)

The Daily World, 315 S. Michigan; PO Box 269, Aberdeen, WA 98520; tel (360) 532-4000; fax (360) 533-1328. Donrey Media group.
Circulation: 16,860(e); 16,860(e-sat); 16,927(S); ABC Sept. 30, 1995.
Price: 50¢(d); 50¢(sat); $1.00(S); $8.75/mo.
Advertising: Open inch rate $25.70(e); $25.70(e-sat); $25.70(S). **Representative:** Papert Companies.
News Service: AP. **Politics:** Independent. **Established:** 1901.
Special Edition: Auto (monthly).
Special Weekly Sections: Best Food Day (wed); TV Section, Entertainment (fri); Seniors, Teens, Church Page, Business (sat).
Magazines: Preview; Parade.

CORPORATE OFFICERS

Founder Donald W Reynolds
President/Chief Operating Officer Emmett Jones
Exec Vice Pres/Chief Financial Officer Darrell W Loftin
Vice Pres-Western Newspaper Group David A Osborn
Vice Pres-Eastern Newspaper Group Don Schneider

GENERAL MANAGEMENT

Publisher Ted E Dixon

ADVERTISING

Director Theresa Company

MARKETING AND PROMOTION

Manager-Marketing/Promotion Dan Vines

CIRCULATION

Manager Gerry Atkinson

NEWS EXECUTIVE

Editor John C Hughes

EDITORS AND MANAGERS

Books Editor John C Hughes
Business/Finance Editor Bill Lindstrom
City Editor Bill Lindstrom
Editorial Writer John C Hughes
Editorial Writer Doug Barker
Farm Editor Bryn Beorse
Fashion/Food Editor Tommi Gatlin
Garden Editor Tommi Gatlin
Photo Department Manager Kathy Ewen
Picture Editor Kathy Ewen
Radio/Television Editor Doug Barker
Religion Editor Tommi Gatlin
Sports Editor Rick Anderson
Wire Editor Neil Pascale

PRODUCTION

Foreman-Composing Gene Kuhn
Foreman-Pressroom Tom Pentt

Market Information: TMC.
Mechanical available: Offset; Black and 3 ROP colors; insert accepted — preprinted, any; page cut-offs — 22¾".
Mechanical specifications: Type page 13" x 21½"; E - 6 cols, 2 1/16", ⅛" between; A - 6 cols, 2 1/16", ⅛" between; C - 9 cols, 1⅜", 1/16" between.
Commodity consumption: Newsprint 900 metric tons; widths 13½", 27"; black ink 36,000 pounds; color ink 2,200 pounds; single pages printed 8,200; average pages per issue 18(d), 24(S); single plates used 10,000.
Equipment: EDITORIAL: Front-end hardware — 1-SII/22; Front-end software — SII; Printers — Gencom. CLASSIFIED: Front-end hardware — 1-SII/22; Front-end software — SII; Printers — Gencom. DISPLAY: Adv layout systems — Ap/Mac IIcx, Ap/Mac w/Radius monitor; Printers — Ap/Mac LaserPrinter II NTX. PRODUCTION: Typesetters — 2-NewGen/Turbo P/S480; Plate exposures — 1-BKY/1601-40, 1-Nu/Flip Top FT40APNS; Plate processors — 1-Nat/A-240; Production cameras — 1-C/Spartan III; Automatic film processors — 1-LE/LD24A; Reproportion units — 1-C; Film transporters — 1-C; Shrink lenses — 1-CK Optical. PRESSROOM: Line 1 — 6-G/Urbanite. MAILROOM: Inserters and stuffers — MM/4 Station; Bundle tyer — 1-MLN. COMMUNICATIONS: Facsimile — Canon/630. WIRE SERVICES: News — AP; Syndicates — AP Datafeatures; Receiving dishes — AP. BUSINESS COMPUTERS: Applications: Word Processing; PCs & micros networked.

AUBURN

See KENT

BELLEVUE

King County

'90 U.S. Census- 86,874; E&P '96 Est. 94,450
ABC-NDM (90): 395,326 (HH 149,596)

Journal American

(m-mon to sat; S)

Journal American, 1705 132nd Ave. N.E. (98005); PO Box 90130, Bellevue, WA 98009-9230; tel (206) 455-2222; fax (206) 455-4989; e-mail jaedit@aol.com. Horvitz Newspapers Inc. (Northwest Media) group.
Circulation: 34,224(m); 34,224(m-sat); 33,945(S); ABC Sept. 30, 1995.
Price: 35¢(d); 35¢(sat); $1.00(S); $2.50/wk; $10.83/mo; $114.00/yr.
Advertising: Open inch rate $41.35(m); $41.35(m-sat); $41.35(S). **Representative:** Papert Companies.
News Services: AP, McClatchy, NYT. **Politics:** Independent. **Established:** 1976.
Special Editions: Seniors, Energy Guide (Jan); Brides, New Home Guide (Feb); Home & Garden (Mar, Apr); Mother's Day, New Home Guide (May); Eastside Summer, Father's Day (June); Pets, Street of Dreams (July); Back-to-School, Football, Cookbook (Aug); Dining & Entertainment (Sept); The Home, New Cars & Trucks (Oct); Automotive, Gift Guide (Nov); Holiday Gift Guide (Dec).
Special Weekly Sections: Food (wed); Weekend (fri); Religion (sat); Home (S); Business (daily).
Magazines: USA Weekend, TV Book (S).

CORPORATE OFFICER

Chairman of the Board/CEO/President Peter A Horvitz

GENERAL MANAGEMENT

Publisher Peter A Horvitz
Vice Pres-Finance Jeff Kok
Vice Pres-Human Resources Nick Chernock
Controller Brian Broucek

ADVERTISING

Exec Vice Pres Howard L Mullenary
Director-Retail Hallie Olson
Director-Classified Nicola A Myers
Manager-National Bill Walz

MARKETING AND PROMOTION

Vice Pres-Marketing/Interactive Technologies Gary Murfin

CIRCULATION

Vice Pres/Director Helmut Adler

NEWS EXECUTIVES

Editor/Vice Pres-News Barbara Morgan
Managing Editor Tom Wolfe

EDITORS AND MANAGERS

Business/Finance Editor Karl Thunemann
City/Metro Editor JoAnne Plank
Editorial Page Editor Craig Groshart
Entertainment/Editor Marilyn Bailey
Features Editor Marilyn Bailey
Librarian Renee Valois
News Editor Karl Kunkel
Photo Director Chuck Hallas
Special Sections Editor Lori Varosh
Sports Editor Greg Johns
Travel Editor Marilyn Bailey

MANAGEMENT INFORMATION SERVICES

Data Processing Manager James Beatty

PRODUCTION

Director Frank J Hoenig

Mechanical available: Offset; Black and 3 ROP colors; insert accepted — preprinted; page cut-offs — 22¾".
Mechanical specifications: Type page 13" x 21"; E - 6 cols, 2 1/16", ⅛" between; A - 6 cols, 2 1/16", ⅛" between; C - 9 cols, 1 3/16", 1/16" between.
Commodity consumption: Newsprint 3,700 metric tons; widths 27½", 27", 28"; black ink 71,000 pounds; color ink 15,750 pounds; single pages printed 15,664; average pages per issue 40(d), 72(S); single plates used 30,300.
Equipment: EDITORIAL: Front-end hardware — Dewar, Victor/486, Victor/386, Ap/Mac IIci, Ap/Power Mac 7100-8100; Front-end software — Dewar/Sys IV, XYQUEST/XyWrite, QuarkXPress; Printers — Ap/Mac LaserWriter IIg, AU/APS broadsheet; Other equipment — Ap/Mac One Scanner. CLASSIFIED: Front-end hardware — AT, 2-IBM/RISC 6000; Printers — HP/4M Plus; Other equipment — 1-IBM/RISC 6000 Pagination Station. DISPLAY: Adv layout systems — SCS/Layout 8000; Front-end hardware — Ap/Power Mac 7100-8100; Front-end software — Multi-Ad/Creator; Printers — Ap/Mac LaserWriter IIg; Other equipment — Tektronix/Phase Color. PRODUCTION: Typesetters — AU/APS broadsheet, 2-AG/Acuset 1000, Diadem/220S; Platemaking systems — Nu/Flip Top FT APRNS 30; Plate exposures — 2-Nu; Plate processors — 1-Nat/A-340, 1-Stark; Scanners — Diadem/220S; Production cameras — Carlson/Super Sharpshooter; Automatic film processors — SCREEN/LD 281Q. PRESSROOM: Line 1 — 10-G/Urbanite, 8-Cary, 4-WPE; Folders — 2-G. MAILROOM: Counter stackers — 1-BG/Count-O-Veyor, 2-MM/310, 1-MM/259; Inserters and stuffers — 1-MM/275 (12 station); Bundle tyer — 2-OVL/UP80, 1-OVL/Constellation; Addressing machine — 1-CH/525 E. LIBRARY: Electronic — Dewar/Folioview. WIRE SERVICES: News — NYT, AP, Cox News Service, McClatchy; Photos — AP; Stock tables — AP; Receiving dishes — AP. BUSINESS COMPUTERS: 2-IBM/RISC 6000; Applications: SBS: Financials; PBS: Circ, Adv; PCs & micros networked; PCs & main system networked.

BELLINGHAM

Whatcom County

'90 U.S. Census- 52,179; E&P '96 Est. 55,835
ABC-NDM (90): 127,780 (HH 48,543)

The Bellingham Herald

(e-mon to fri; m-sat; S)

The Bellingham Herald, 1155 State St.; PO Box 1277, Bellingham, WA 98227; tel (360) 676-2600; fax (360) 676-7672. Gannett Co. Inc. group.
Circulation: 26,854(e); 26,854(m-sat); 34,297(S); ABC Sept. 30, 1995.
Price: 35¢(d); 35¢(sat); $1.25(S).
Advertising: Open inch rate $27.69(e); $27.69(m-sat); $32.80(S). **Representative:** Gannett National Newspaper Sales.
News Services: AP, GNS. **Politics:** Independent. **Established:** 1890.
Advertising not accepted: Subject to publisher's review.
Special Editions: Annual Report; Outdoors Northwest; Visitor's Guide; Business Directory; Lawn & Garden; Holiday Cookbook; Logging Tab; Northwest Washington.
Special Weekly Sections: Food Day (wed); Major Dept. Store Advertising (thur); Major Dept. Store Advertising, Business (S).
Magazines: USA Weekend, Color Comics (6 pages), TV Book (Channels) (S).

GENERAL MANAGEMENT

Publisher J C Hickman
Personnel Director Heather Richendrfer

ADVERTISING

Director Gerald Rhea Jr
Manager-Retail Debbie Kaufman
Manager-Classified Linda Pressley

MARKETING AND PROMOTION

Director-Marketing Development Lisa Barkley Miller

CIRCULATION

Director Larry Lucas
Asst Director Brian Reed

NEWS EXECUTIVE

Managing Editor Jack Keith

EDITORS AND MANAGERS

City Editor Margaret Haberman
Editorial Page Editor Dick Beardsley
Living/Lifestyle Editor Ben Santarris
Photo Editor Martin Waidelich
Sports Editor Jim Carberry

MANAGEMENT INFORMATION SERVICES

Data Processing Manager David Thomsen

PRODUCTION

Director J L (Skip) Gibson
Manager-Composing Steve Carr
Manager-Pressroom Russ Gibbins
Manager-Mailroom Joe Taylor

Market Information: TMC.
Mechanical available: Offset; Black and 3 ROP colors; insert accepted — preprinted, single sheet card stock; page cut-offs — 22¾".
Mechanical specifications: Type page 13" x 21½"; E - 6 cols, 2 1/16", ⅛" between; A - 6 cols, 2 1/16", ⅛" between; C - 10 cols, 1¼", 1/16" between.
Commodity consumption: Newsprint 1,826 short tons; widths 27¼", 13⅝"; black ink 24,476 pounds; color ink 6,606 pounds; single pages printed 10,732; average pages per issue 25(d), 55(S); single plates used 13,784.
Equipment: EDITORIAL: Front-end hardware — Dewar, Ap/Mac; Front-end software — Dewar, QuarkXPress; Printers — Okidata/dot matrix. CLASSIFIED: Front-end hardware — Dewar; Front-end software — Dewar; Printers — Okidata. DISPLAY: Adv layout systems — Dewar, Ap/Macs; Front-end hardware — Dewar, Ap/Macs; Front-end software — Dewar, QuarkXPress; Printers — Okidata. PRODUCTION: Pagination software — Dewar, QuarkXPress; Typesetters — 1-V/5300E, 2-V/5100, 1-V/5500; Plate exposures — 2-BKY; Plate processors — 2-Nat/A-250; Scanners — ECR/Autokon; Production cameras — C/Spartan III; Automatic film processors — LE/24, LE/18, K/550; Color separation equipment (conventional) — Ap/Mac w/QuarkXPress; Digital color separation equipment — Ap/Mac w/QuarkXPress. PRESSROOM: Line 1 — 8-G/Urbanite; Reels and stands — G; Press control system — Fin. MAILROOM: Counter stackers — 2-MM/310-20; Inserters and stuffers — 2-MM/227 Jet-108-3TDF; Bundle tyer — 3-OVL/JP40; Mailroom control system — Id; Other mailroom equipment — 1-MM/1259. COMMUNICATIONS: Digital ad delivery system — AP AdSend. WIRE SERVICES: News — AP, GNS; Photos — AP; Stock tables — AP SelectStox; Receiving dishes — AP. BUSINESS COMPUTERS: 1-IBM/AS400; Applications: Circ, Adv billing, Accts receivable, Gen ledger, Payroll; PCs & micros networked; PCs & main system networked.

BREMERTON

Kitsap County

'90 U.S. Census- 38,142; E&P '96 Est. 39,196
ABC-NDM (90): 173,885 (HH 63,133)

The Sun (m-mon to fri; m-sat; S)

The Sun, 545 5th St.; PO Box 259, Bremerton, WA 98337; tel (360) 377-3711; fax (360) 377-9237; e-mail sunnews@aol.com. Scripps Howard group.
Circulation: 35,909(m); 35,909(m-sat); 39,609(S); ABC Sept. 30, 1995.
Price: 50¢(d); 50¢(sat); $1.25(S); $10.00/mo, $6.75/mo (S only); $108.00/yr (carrier), $216.00/yr (mail).
Advertising: Open inch rate $23.95(m); $23.95(m-sat); $24.58(S). **Representative:** Papert Companies.
News Services: AP, NYT, SHNS, States News Service. **Politics:** Independent. **Established:** 1935.
Note: Effective May 1, 1995 this publication changed its publishing plan from (e-mon to fri; m-sat; S) to (m-mon to fri; m-sat; S).
Special Editions: Spring Car Care (Mar); Visitor's Guide (Apr); Home Furnishing (May); Football (Sept); Home Furnishings (Oct); Auto Show, Christmas Opening (Nov).
Special Weekly Sections: Food (wed); At Home, Drive (fri); Your Money (sat).
Magazines: Bravo (arts & entertainment) (thur); TV Tab, R & R (for active individuals), West Sound Real Estate Weekly (S).

CORPORATE OFFICERS

Board Chairman (John P Scripps Newspapers) Paul K Scripps
Senior Vice Pres-Newspaper Division, Scripps Howard Alan M Horton

GENERAL MANAGEMENT

President/CEO Ron Muhleman
Director-Finance Tim Lavin
Director-Human Resources Marie LaMarche
Manager-Credit Robin Alexander

ADVERTISING

Director Earl Rush
Manager-Classified Cheryl Bolin
Manager-Sales Rick Herrell
Manager-Sales Steve Perry

MARKETING AND PROMOTION

Director-Marketing Gussie Schaeffer

CIRCULATION

Director Curtis Huber

Copyright ©1996 by the Editor & Publisher Co.

Washington

I-427

NEWS EXECUTIVES
Editor	Mike Phillips
Managing Editor	Brian Stallcop

EDITORS AND MANAGERS
Automotive Writer	Jim Campbell
Business/Finance Writer	Dawn Dressier
Books Editor	Seabury Blair
Community Editor	Ann Strosnider
Asst Community Editor	Michael Foley
Asst Community Editor	Jeff Brody
Columnist	Jim Rothgeb
Editorial Page Editor	Mike Phillips
Education Writer	Elena Castaneda
Entertainment/Amusements Writer	Deborah Woolston
Environmental Writer	Christopher Dunagan
Health/Medical Writer	Christopher Dunagan
Librarian	Beth Dyess
Living/Lifestyle Editor	Jeff Brody
Military Writer	Lloyd Pritchett
Presentation Editor	Suzette Moyer
Asst Presentation Editor	Denise Clifton
Religion Writer	Jim Campbell
Sports Editor	Chuck Stark
Travel/Outdoors Writer	Seabury Blair

MANAGEMENT INFORMATION SERVICES
Manager-Systems	Mike Bonomo
Manager-Systems	Steve Miller

PRODUCTION
Director	Geoff Gravett

Market Information: TMC; ADS.
Mechanical available: Web Offset; Black and 3 ROP colors; insert accepted — preprinted; page cut-offs — 22¾".
Mechanical specifications: Type page 13" x 21½"; E - 6 cols, 2", ⅛" between; A - 6 cols, 2", ⅛" between; C - 10 cols, 1¼", ⅛" between.
Commodity consumption: Newsprint 3,000 metric tons; black ink 75,000 pounds; color ink 7,000 pounds; single pages printed 12,500; average pages per issue 40(d), 64(S); single plates used 2,400.
Equipment: EDITORIAL: Front-end hardware — Ap/Mac; Front-end software — QuarkXPress, Adobe/Photoshop, Adobe/Illustrator, P.INK; Printers — Hyphen/Typesetters, TI; Other equipment — Microtek/Scanner, Nikon/Film-Scanner, Kk/Film Scanner, Lf/AP Leaf Picture Desk. CLASSIFIED: Front-end hardware — PC/Network; Front-end software — Dewar/Information Systems, XYQUEST/XyWrite; Printers — Epson. DISPLAY: Adv layout systems — ME; Front-end hardware — Ap/Mac; Front-end software — Multi-Ad/Creator, Mk/Ad Director; Printers — Ap/Mac LaserWriter; Other equipment — Microtek/Scanner. PRODUCTION: Pagination software — QuarkXPress; Typesetters — 1-AG, 2-Tegra/Varityper, 1-Ultre, Spectraset/3100; Platemaking systems — Offset; Plate exposures — 1-BKY/Ascor, 1-Burgess; Plate processors — 2-WL/38; Scanners — Microtek; Production cameras — 1-Acti/24V, 1-R/432 Mark II; Automatic film processors — Konica; Film transporters — Konica.
PRESSROOM: Line 1 — 5-HI/1650. MAILROOM: Counter stackers — 2-HL/Monitor, 1-HL/HT II; Inserters and stuffers — SLS/1000(8:1); Bundle tyer — 1-MLN/ML-2, 1-MLN/ML-EE, 1-Power Strap/PSNG; Addressing machine — 1-KR/quarter folder labeler, Ch. LIBRARY: Electronic — SMS/Stauffer Gold, Ap/Mac. WIRE SERVICES: News — SHNS, LAT-WP, NYT; Photos — AP; Stock tables — AP; Syndicates — AP; Receiving dishes — AP. BUSINESS COMPUTERS: IBM/AS-400; Applications: Circ, Adv billing, Accts receivable, Gen ledger, Payroll, Ad mgmt (Commercial).

CENTRALIA-CHEHALIS
Lewis County
'90 U.S. Census- 18,628 (Centralia 12,101, Chehalis 6,527); E&P '96 Est. 19,160 (Centralia 12,398, Chehalis 6,762)
ABC-CZ (90): 21,108 (HH 8,403)

The Chronicle
(e-mon to fri; m-sat)

The Chronicle, 321 N. Pearl; PO Box 580, Centralia, WA 98531-4323; tel (360) 736-3311; fax (360) 736-3623. Lafromboise Newspapers Inc. group.
Circulation: 15,949(e); 15,949(m-sat); ABC Sept. 30, 1995.
Price: 50¢(d); 50¢(sat); $7.60/mo (carrier); $91.20/yr (carrier).
Advertising: Open inch rate $12.25(e); $12.25(m-sat). **Representative:** Papert Companies.
News Service: AP. **Politics:** Independent. **Established:** 1889.
Not Published: New Year; Memorial Day; Independence Day; Labor Day; Christmas.
Special Editions: Newcomer's Guide (Jan); Lawn & Garden, Progress Edition (Mar); American Home Week, Spring Coupon, Little League, Mother's Day Section, Visitor's Guide (May); Southwest Washington Fair, Seahawks '96 (Aug); Prep Football (Sept); Fall Home & Garden, Women in Business (Oct); Christmas Gift Guide (Nov); Winter Sports (Dec).
Special Weekly Sections: Best Food Day (wed); Business, Garden & Farming (thur); Home and Building (fri); Religion, Business (sat); Entertainment (daily).
Magazine: Viewer's Choice (sat).

CORPORATE OFFICERS
President	Mrs J R Lafromboise
Vice Pres	Dennis R Waller
Treasurer	Steve Walker

GENERAL MANAGEMENT
Publisher	Dennis R Waller
Controller	Steve Walker

ADVERTISING
Director	Thomas E May

CIRCULATION
Director	William F Shannon

NEWS EXECUTIVE
Editor	Sarah Jenkins

EDITORS AND MANAGERS
Editorial Page Editor	Larry Zander
Librarian	Linda Stewart
News Editor	Gordon MacCracken
Photo Manager	Gary Cichowski
Sports Editor	Sam Bakotich
Women's Editor (Living)	Judy Panteleeff

PRODUCTION
Director	Jeff Anderson

Market Information: TMC; ADS.
Mechanical available: Offset; Black and 3 ROP colors; insert accepted — preprinted, any; page cut-offs — 22¾".
Mechanical specifications: Type page 13" x 21½"; E - 6 cols, 2", ⅛" between; A - 6 cols, 2", ⅛" between; C - 8 cols, 1½", ⅛" between.
Commodity consumption: Newsprint 1,200 metric tons; widths 29", 34"; black ink 30,000 pounds; color ink 10,000 pounds; single pages printed 7,988; average pages per issue 26(d); single plates used 5,078.
Equipment: EDITORIAL: Front-end hardware — Ap/Mac Quadra 700 fileserver, 13-Ap/Mac Classic II, 6-RSK/TRS 80-100, 2-Ap/Mac Quadra 700, 2-Ap/Mac IIci, 1-Ap/Mac Centris 650, 2-Ap/SuperMac, 3-Radius/TPD; Front-end software — QuarkXPress, Baseview/Comm Link; Printers — 2-COM/8868, Ap/Mac LaserWriter IIg, Dataproducts/LZR 1560, Ap/Mac ImageWriter; Other equipment — 5-RSK/TRS-80. CLASSIFIED: Front-end hardware — Ap/Mac Quadra 630, Ap/Mac fileserver, 2-Ap/Mac IIsi, 1-Ap/Mac Classic II; Front-end software — Baseview/Class Manager Plus;

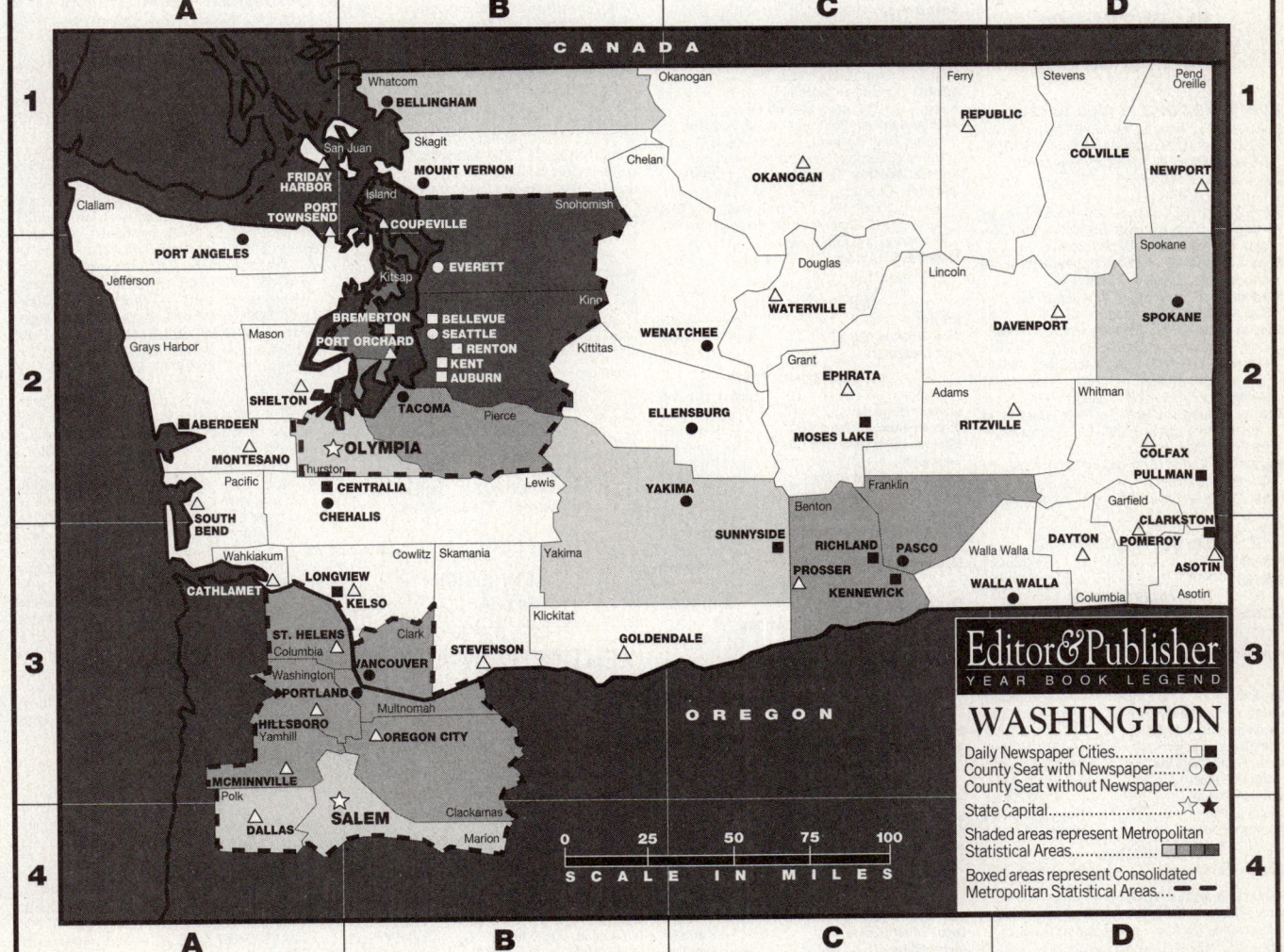

Printers — Ap/Mac LaserWriter II NT, Ap/Mac ImageWriter II; Other equipment — Okidata/320. DISPLAY: Adv layout systems — Ap/Mac; Front-end hardware — 3-Ap/Mac Quadra, 2-Ap/Super Mac, 1-Ap/Mac Quadra 630 fileserver, 2-Ap/Mac w/Radius TPD, 1-Ap/Mac Quadra 950, 1-Ap/Mac Centris 650; Front-end software — Multi-Ad/Creator 3.6, Adobe/Photoshop, Scanman 2.2; Printers — Ap/Mac LaserWriter IIg, Dataproducts/LZR 1560; Other equipment — 2-Umax/UC 630. PRODUCTION: Pagination software — Multi-Ad/Creator 3.6.3; Typesetters — 2-COM/8868; Plate exposures — 2-Nu/Flip Top FT40VPNS; Plate processors — 1-Nat/A-250; Scanners — 2-Umax/UC 630; Production cameras — 1-C/Spartan III; Automatic film processors — 1-C/Powermatic R650; Digital color separation equipment — 2-Umax/UC 630. PRESSROOM: Line 1 — 8-G/SC; Folders — 1-G/SC 2:1 (w/balloon former); Press control system — Fin. MAILROOM: Counter stackers — 2-MM/Counter Stacker 288; Inserters and stuffers — 2-MM/275; Bundle tyer — 2-MLN/2A, 2-MLN/ML2EE; Addressing machine — 215-KR/211; Mailroom control system — 1-Consolidated, 4-Station Jetstream/230 Auto saddle stitching, Trimmer System, 1-New Jersey/Stitcher. WIRE SERVICES: News — AP Datafeatures, AP Datastream; Photos — AP Photostream; Stock tables — AP; Syndicates — AP Datafeatures; Receiving dishes — size-10ft, AP. BUSINESS COMPUTERS: IBM/RS 6000, PCs; Applications: PBS: Circ, Adv, Gen Acctg; Lotus 1-2-3, WordPerfect; PCs & main system networked.

CLARKSTON

See LEWISTON, ID

ELLENSBURG

Kittitas County

'90 U.S. Census- 12,361; E&P '96 Est. 12,693

Daily Record (e-mon to sat)

Daily Record, 401 N. Main, Ellensburg, WA 98926; tel (509) 925-1414; fax (509) 925-5696. McClatchy Newspapers group.

Circulation: 5,329(e); 5,329(e-sat); Sworn Sept. 28, 1994.

Price: 35¢(d); 35¢(sat); $7.50/mo; $87.00/yr.

Advertising: Open inch rate $5.73(e); $5.73(e-sat). **Representative:** Papert Companies.

News Services: AP, McClatchy. **Politics:** Independent. **Established:** 1909.

Not Published: New Year; Independence Day; Thanksgiving; Christmas.

Special Editions: Vintage View (Seniors) (Mar); Conservation/Agriculture (Apr); Vintage View (Seniors) (July); Central Wash. State University Welcome (Sept); Holiday Food (Nov); Winter Sports (outdoor) (Dec).

Special Weekly Sections: Ag Page, Best Food (tues); Mini Page (fri); Religion, School Page, Business Page (sat).

Magazines: Rodeo (thur before Labor Day); TV Guide Clue (fri).

Cable TV: Operate leased cable TV in circulation area.

GENERAL MANAGEMENT

Publisher Keith Love
Manager-Credit Judi Harrison

ADVERTISING

Director David Martin

NEWS EXECUTIVE

Managing Editor Peggy Steward

EDITORS AND MANAGERS

City Editor Mike Johnston
Editorial Page Editor Keith Love
Education/Features Editor Dori O'Neal
Films/Theater Editor Hiedi Rose
Home Furnishings Editor Peggy Steward
Political Editor Keith Love
Religion Editor Cory Fisher
Sports Editor George Hansen
Women's Editor Peggy Steward

PRODUCTION

Director-Pressroom Mike Blackwood

Market Information: TMC.

Mechanical available: Offset; Black and 3 ROP colors; insert accepted — preprinted; page cut-offs — 22¾".

Mechanical specifications: Type page 12 15/16" x 21"; E - 6 cols, 2", 1/6" between; A - 6 cols, 2", 1/6" between; C - 8 cols, 1½", 1/12" between.

Commodity consumption: Newsprint 210 metric tons; widths 28", 14"; black ink 4,500 pounds; color ink 150 pounds; single pages printed 6,220; average pages per issue 18(d); single plates used 3,600.

Equipment: EDITORIAL: Front-end hardware — Ap/Mac; Front-end software — Baseview, QPS; Printers — NewGen; Other equipment — Ap/Mac. CLASSIFIED: Front-end hardware — Ap/Mac; Front-end software — Baseview, QPS; Printers — NewGen. PRODUCTION: Typesetters — NewGen/Laser Printer; Plate exposures — 1-Nu; Plate processors — Ic; Automatic film processors — P/26EL. PRESSROOM: Line 1 — 2-G/Community, 2-G/Community, 2-G/Community. MAILROOM: Inserters and stuffers — KAN/3-gate. WIRE SERVICES: News — AP, McClatchy; Stock tables — NYSE; Receiving dishes — AP, McClatchy. BUSINESS COMPUTERS: RSK; Applications: Synaptic: Circ; Cigma: Gen ledger.

EVERETT

Snohomish County

'90 U.S. Census- 69,961; E&P '96 Est. 79,590

ABC-CZ (90): 104,424 (HH 41,454)

The Herald (m-mon to sat; S)

The Herald, 1213 California St. (98201); PO Box 930, Everett, WA 98206-0930; tel (206) 339-3000; fax (206) 339-3049; e-mail e.herald@plink.geis.com. Washington Post Co. group.

Circulation: 51,306(m); 51,306(m-sat); 61,879(S); ABC Sept. 30, 1995.

Price: 35¢(d); 35¢(sat); $1.50(S).

Advertising: Open inch rate $35.20(m); $35.20(m-sat); $40.37(S). **Representative:** Sawyer-Ferguson-Walker Co.

News Services: AP, LAT-WP, NYT. **Politics:** Independent. **Established:** 1891.

Advertising not accepted: Sales or services requiring advance payment by mail.

Special Editions: Football; Home Furnishings; Home Improvement; Employment; Travel; Home & Garden; Health & Fitness.

Special Weekly Sections: Sports, Working (mon); Changes (tues); Food (wed); Outbound (thur); The Key (fri); Saturday Live (sat); Travel, Color Comics, Real Estate (S); Economy, NW Life (daily).

Magazines: Sunday Comic Spadea, TV Week Tab (S).

CORPORATE OFFICERS

President Larry L Hanson
Vice Pres/Secretary Alan R Finberg
Asst Treasurer Alan G Spoon

GENERAL MANAGEMENT

Publisher Larry L Hanson
General Manager Allen Funk
Director-Human Resources Ann Reed
Director-Labor Relations Jerry Knoblich
Controller Jerry Knoblich
Purchasing Agent (Office) Leanne McLeod

ADVERTISING

Director Steve Hawes
Manager-Retail John Hill
Manager-National Terry Bergren
Manager-Classified Sally Kortekaas

MARKETING AND PROMOTION

Manager-Marketing Kelly Hulin

TELECOMMUNICATIONS

Director-Systems/Technology Don Hendrix
Audiotex Manager Sally Kortekaas

CIRCULATION

Director Sandra Hollenbeck

NEWS EXECUTIVES

Exec Editor Stan Strick
Asst Managing Editor-Editing & Production Bob Bolerjack

EDITORS AND MANAGERS

Books Editor Diane Wright
Communities Editor Kristi O'Harran
Economy Editor Jeff Standaert
Editorial Page Editor Joe Copeland
Entertainment/Film Editor Mike Murray
Features Editor Julie Muhlstein
Food Editor Julie Muhlstein
Librarian Jonetta Coffin
Local Editor (Zoned) Mike Benbow
Metro Editor Mike Benbow
Photo Editor Rich Shulman
Real Estate Editor Jeff Standaert
Religion Editor Kathy Tussing
Sports Editor Kirby Arnold
Television Editor Mike Murray
Travel Editor Mike Murray

MANAGEMENT INFORMATION SERVICES

Data Processing Manager Don Hendrix

PRODUCTION

Director-Operations Robin Larson
Manager-Pre Press Kathy Lillquist
Manager-Ad Dennis Hanscom
Manager-Packaging/Distribution Janet Dean
Manager-Pagination/Special Projects Bill Scofield
Manager-Press Larry Earlywine
Manager-Color Separations Janet Orso
Manager-Pre Press Technical Service Michael Lapham

Market Information: Zoned editions; TMC; ADS; Operate audiotex.

Mechanical available: Offset; Black and 3 ROP colors; insert accepted — preprinted; page cut-offs — 22".

Mechanical specifications: Type page 13" x 21"; E - 6 cols, 2 1/16", 1/8" between; A - 6 cols, 2 1/16", 1/8" between; C - 10 cols, 1 3/16", 1/8" between.

Commodity consumption: Newsprint 5,355 metric tons; widths 55", 41¼", 27½"; black ink 220,000 pounds; color ink 42,600 pounds; single pages printed 18,209; average pages per issue 40(d), 60(S); single plates used 37,000.

Equipment: EDITORIAL: Front-end hardware — 68-Zenith/PC 486, 2-Ap/Mac IIci, 2-Ap/Power Mac, 2-Compaq/Novell fileserver; Front-end software — QuarkXPress 3.3, Microsoft/Word 2.0, Dewar/View 1.11; CLASSIFIED: Front-end hardware — 1-DEC/Micro VAX 4000-200, 19-NEC/386, 1-Sun/Sparc; Front-end software — Cybergraphics/Classified. DISPLAY: Front-end hardware — 6-Ap/Mac IIci, 4-Ap/Mac Centris, 4-Ap/Mac Quadra, 4-Ap/Power Mac 7100; Front-end software — Multi-Ad/Creator 3.5; PRODUCTION: Typesetters — Hyphen/Ultresetter, 1-AG/Selectset 5000, 1-III/3850, 1-Scriptwriter; Platemaking systems — KFM/Vision Bender; Plate exposures — KFM; Plate processors — KFM; Electronic picture desk — Lf/AP Leaf Picture Desk, 2-Ap/Mac (w/MacLeaf Card), Adobe/Photoshop; Scanners — X/7650, ECR/Autokon 1000 DE, 1-SCREEN/1030; Production cameras — 1-C/Marathon, 1-R/400, 1-R/475; Automatic film processors — 1-LE/LD-24AQ, 2-LE/APS35, 1-P/1800A; Film transporters — 1-C; Shrink lenses — 1-CK Optical/SQU-7; Digital color separation equipment — 2-Ap/Mac Quadra 900, Ap/Mac Quadra 840, Nikon/LS3510, 2-Ap/Power Mac. PRESSROOM: Line 1 — 9-G/MetroColor; Press drives — Allen Bradley; Folders — 3-G, G/3:2; Reels and stands — 3-G/Ct-50 RIP; Press control system — G/MPCS II. MAILROOM: Counter stackers — 4-QWI; Inserters and stuffers — 1-MM/227E, 1-Amerigraph/NP-630; Bundle tyer — 4-Dynaric; Wrapping singles — 1-St/510W; Addressing machine — Ch/Videojet II; Other mailroom equipment — S/SP705 Stitcher-Trimmer. RIMA/Stacker. LIBRARY: Electronic — Mead Data Central/Nexis NewsView. COMMUNICATIONS: Digital ad delivery system — AP AdSend. Systems used — satellite. WIRE SERVICES: News — AP; Stock tables — AP; Syndicates — LAT-WP, NYT, McClatchy; Receiving dishes — AP. BUSINESS COMPUTERS: 1-DEC/VAX 4200, 2-DEC/Micro VAX; PCs & micros networked; PCs & main system networked.

KENNEWICK

See PASCO

KENT-RENTON-AUBURN

King County

'90 U.S. Census- 112,750 (Kent 37,960; Renton 41,688; Auburn 33,102); E&P '96 Est. 134,824 (Kent 48,834; Renton 48,818; Auburn 37,172)

ABC-NDM (90): 354,968 (HH 134,243)

Valley Daily News (m-mon to fri; S)

Valley Daily News, 600 S. Washington (98032-5707); PO Box 130, Kent, WA 98035-0130; tel (206) 872-6600; fax (206) 854-1006. Horvitz Newspapers Inc. (Northwest Media) group.

Circulation: 31,233(m); 32,112(S); ABC Sept. 30, 1995.

Price: 35¢(d); $1.00(S); $9.00/4wks; $99.00/yr.

Advertising: Open inch rate $36.82(m); $36.82 (S). **Representative:** Papert Companies.

News Services: AP, NYT. **Politics:** Independent. **Established:** 1890.

Special Editions: Progress (Jan); Restaurant Review (Feb); Coupons (Mar); Home & Garden, Car Care (Apr); Mother's Day (May); Summer Fun (June); Fall Fashion, Fall Sports (Aug); Coupons, Home & Hearth (Oct); Christmas Gifts (Nov, Dec).

Special Weekly Sections: Food (wed); Weekend (fri); Business (daily).

Magazines: TViewfinders, USA Weekend, Home (S).

CORPORATE OFFICER

Chairman of the Board/CEO/President Peter A Horvitz

GENERAL MANAGEMENT

Publisher John S Perry

ADVERTISING

Exec Vice Pres Howard L Mullenary
Vice Pres-Sales Mike Stevens
Director Rick Riegle

CIRCULATION

Director Shirley Jacobs
Director-Classified Nicola A Myers

NEWS EXECUTIVE

Editor/Vice Pres-News Catherine Shen

EDITORS AND MANAGERS

Business/Finance Editor Chris Genna
Editorial Page Editor Robert Jones
Entertainment/Television Editor Dean Radford
Features Editor Peggy Ziebarth
Food Editor Peggy Ziebarth
Sports Editor Mark Klaas

PRODUCTION

Manager Jim Rasmussen
Manager-Commercial Printing Dan Keefe
Manager-Pre Press Stephanie Haase
Manager-Mailroom Forrest LeBlanc

Market Information: TMC.

Mechanical available: Offset; Black and 3 ROP colors; insert accepted — preprinted; page cut-offs — 21½".

Mechanical specifications: Type page 13" x 21½"; E - 6 cols, 2 1/16", 1/8" between; A - 6 cols, 2 1/16", 1/8" between; C - 9 cols, 1 5/8", 1/8" between.

Commodity consumption: Newsprint 2,500 metric tons; widths 27", 13½"; black ink 78,000 pounds; color ink 2,876 pounds; single pages printed 11,210; average pages per issue 32(d), 40(S); single plates used 15,900.

Equipment: EDITORIAL: Front-end hardware — 34-SII/Dakota; Front-end software — SII/Sys 25; Printers — 2-Centronics/351. CLASSIFIED: Front-end hardware — 3-IBM/PC; Front-end software — III; Printers — 1-Toshiba/321 SL. DISPLAY: Front-end hardware — Ap/Power Mac 7500; Front-end software — Multi-Ad/Creator; Printers — Ap/Mac LaserWriter IIf, NewGen/1200B, X/8½" x 11" Color Printer; Other equipment — Microtek/300QS, NEC/CDR25 (CD-Rom). PRODUCTION: Typesetters — 2-COM/8668, Panther/Pro 46; Plate exposures — 2-Nu/Flip Top FT40APNS, Nu/Flip Top FT40UPNS; Plate processors — Nat/A-340, W; Electronic picture desk — Lf/AP Leaf Picture Desk; Scanners — ECR/Autokon 8400, 1-CD/Magnascan, Nikon/Coolscan; Production cameras — SCREEN/C473-DST; Automatic film processors — 2-P/RA26, 1-P/24. PRESSROOM: Line 1 — 9-G/Urbanite single width; Line 2 — 5-G/Community single width, 1-DEV; Folders — 2-G/Urbanite, 1-G/Community; Press control system — Fin. MAILROOM: Counter stackers — 4-BG; Inserters and stuffers — 2-S/848, 1-MM/3-into-1; Bundle tyer — 2-MLN/2EE, 1-Spirit, 1-MLN/MLE; Addressing machine — 2-Wm. LIBRARY: Electronic — In-house. WIRE SERVICES: News — AP, Business Wire, PR Newswire, SHNS, Bloomberg; Photos — AP; Stock tables — AP; Syndicates — Universal Press, Creators, King Features, United Media, TMS, CNS; Receiving dishes — size-12ft, AP. BUSINESS COMPUTERS: IBM/System 38, PC; Applications: CDS: Trade billing; NGS: Business system; Lotus 1-2-3, Microsoft/Excel; PCs & main system networked.

LONGVIEW

Cowlitz County

'90 U.S. Census- 31,499; E&P '96 Est. 31,737

ABC-CZ (90): 53,433 (HH 21,243)

The Daily News (e-mon to sat)

The Daily News, 770 11th Ave.; PO Box 189, Longview, WA 98632; tel (360) 577-2500; fax (360) 577-7834; e-mail newslvkel@aol.com.

Circulation: 24,813(e); 24,813(e-sat); ABC Sept. 30, 1995.
Price: 50¢(d); 50¢(sat); $8.75/mo (carrier); $105.00/yr (carrier).
Advertising: Open inch rate $16.72(e); $16.72(e-sat).
News Services: AP, LAT-WP. **Politics:** Independent. **Established:** 1923.
Not Published: Christmas.
Special Editions: Spring Home Show/Home Improvement; Welcome Edition; Fall Fix Up; Kelso Hilander Festival; Thanksgiving; Christmas.
Special Weekly Section: TV Times-Flexi (fri).
Magazines: Real Estate Magazine; Business Focus (monthly).

CORPORATE OFFICERS

President Ted M Natt
Vice Pres John J Natt
Secretary Robert B Gaston
Treasurer Bonnie Snyder

GENERAL MANAGEMENT

Publisher Ted M Natt
Business Manager Bonnie Snyder
Manager-Human Resources Stephen A Lafady
Manager-Education Service Linda Manning

ADVERTISING

Director William Marcum
Manager-National Harold Luhn
Manager-Retail Harold Luhn
Supervisor-Classified Rhonda Madison

CIRCULATION

Manager Stephen A Lafady

NEWS EXECUTIVES

Editor Ted M Natt
Managing Editor Robert B Gaston

EDITORS AND MANAGERS

Business/Finance Editor Paula Stepankowsky
City Editor Dell Burner
Editorial Page Editor James Bross
Editorial Writer James Bross
Education Editor Pauline Bains
Entertainment/Amusements Editor Linda Wilson
Environmental Editor Andre Stepankowsky
Food/Women's Editor Cathy Zimmerman
Garden Editor Melissa Wallace
Librarian Donna Yardley
Lifestyle Editor Cathy Zimmerman
News Editor Alan Brettman
Outdoors Editor Chuck Downer
Photo Editor Roger Werth
Real Estate Editor Paula Stepankowsky
Religion Editor Nancy Edwards
Sports Editor John Pisapia

MANAGEMENT INFORMATION SERVICES

Data Processing Manager Brian Eckland

PRODUCTION

Director Bruce Myers

Market Information: TMC; ADS; Operate database; Electronic edition.
Mechanical available: Offset; Black and 3 ROP colors; insert accepted — preprinted; page cutoffs — 22¾".
Mechanical specifications: Type page 13" x 21½"; E - 6 cols, 2¹⁄₁₆", ⅛" between; A - 6 cols, 2¹⁄₁₆", ⅛" between; C - 9 cols, 1⅜", ¹⁄₁₆" between.
Commodity consumption: Newsprint 1,803 short tons; width 27¾"; black ink 36,000 pounds; color ink 5,000 pounds; single pages printed 9,782; average pages per issue 32(d); single plates used 17,000.
Equipment: EDITORIAL: Front-end hardware — 1-Ap/Mac WGS 8150 Server, 33-Ap/Mac Workstation; Front-end software — Baseview/IQUE D.B., Baseview/QXEDIT, Baseview/QUE TOOLS, Baseview/IQUEX, Baseview/IQUE Editorial Software, SCS, Linx, QuarkXPress, Aldus/FreeHand; Printers — Ap/Mac NTX LaserPrinter, Xante/Accel-a-Writer 8200; Other equipment — Kk/RFS 2035 Scanner, HP/ScanJet IIcx. CLASSIFIED: Front-end hardware — Dell/SP590, 1-Ap/Mac II, 1-Ap/Mac IIci; Front-end software — SCS/Class 8000 3.87; Printers — 1-HP/LaserJet III, 1-C.Itoh/Ci-5000. DISPLAY: Adv layout systems — SCS/Layout 8000; Front-end hardware — Ap/Mac WG Server 8150, 1-Ap/Mac II, 5-Ap/Mac 6100-60 AV, 2-Ap/Mac IIfx, Dell/SP590 Server, Dell/386; Front-end software — Multi-Ad/Creator, Aldus/FreeHand, Microsoft/Word; Printers — Xante/Accel-a-Writer 8200, XIT/Clipper, 1-C.Itoh/Ci-5000, 1-HP/LaserJet III; Other equipment — Sharp/JX-600 Scanner, HP/ScanJet, HP/ScanJet CX. PRODUCTION: Pagination software — QuarkXPress 3.31; OCR software — Caere/OmniPage Professional 5.0; Typesetters — 2-Ap/Mac Quadra 8100-80, 2-Hyphen/Mac RIP; Plate exposures — 2-Nu/Flip Top FT40UPNS; Plate processors — 1-Wd; Scanners — Nikon/LS-3510AF; Production cameras — 1-C/Spartan II; Automatic film processors — 1-Litex/26; Film transporters — 1-LE; Shrink lenses — CK Optical.
PRESSROOM: Line 1 — 4-G/Urbanite; Line 2 — 3-G/Urbanite; Press drives — 2-75 h.p.; Folders — 1-G/Urbanite, 1-G/Suburbanite; Press control system — Fin; Press registration system — Duarte. MAILROOM: Counter stackers — 3-Id/Marathoner; Inserters and stuffers — 2-MM/227(5-into-1); Bundle tyer — 1-MLN/2EE, 2-MLN/2A, 1-MLN/2; Addressing machine — KR/215 Mailing System; Other mailroom equipment — MM/1509 Stitcher-Trimmer. LIBRARY: Electronic — Mead Data Central/Nexis NewsView. COMMUNICATIONS: Digital ad delivery system — AP AdSend. Systems used — satellite. WIRE SERVICES: News — AP, LAT-WP; Photos — AP; Syndicates — AP, LAT-WP; Receiving dishes — size-6ft, AP. BUSINESS COMPUTERS: IBM/AS-400; Applications: Microsoft Word: Circ, Accts receivable, Gen ledger, Accts payable, Fixed assets; Microsoft/Excel, Lotus 1-2-3; PCs & micros networked; PCs & main system networked.

MOSES LAKE

Grant County

'90 U.S. Census- 11,235; E&P '96 Est. 11,566

Columbia Basin Herald

(e-mon to fri)

Columbia Basin Herald, 813 W. 3rd Ave.; PO Box 910, Moses Lake, WA 98837; tel (509) 765-4561; fax (509) 765-8659. Hagadone Corp. group.
Circulation: 8,741(e); Sworn Oct. 2, 1995.
Price: 50¢(d).
Advertising: Open inch rate $9.40(e).
News Service: AP. **Politics:** Independent. **Established:** 1941.
Not Published: New Year; Memorial Day; Labor Day; Thanksgiving; Christmas.
Special Edition: Basin Business Journal (monthly).
Special Weekly Section: TV & Entertainment (fri).
Magazines: Table Talk (weekly); Basin Business Journal (monthly).

CORPORATE OFFICER

President Duane B Hagadone

GENERAL MANAGEMENT

Publisher Steve Hill
Business Manager Judith Cerenzia

ADVERTISING

Director Steve Hill

CIRCULATION

Manager Ron Pufahl

PRODUCTION

Superintendent Curt Weaver
Manager-Pressroom Rick Horton

Market Information: TMC; ADS; Operate database.
Mechanical available: Offset; Black and 3 ROP colors; insert accepted — preprinted, others accepted.
Mechanical specifications: Type page 13" x 21½"; E - 6 cols, 2¹⁄₁₆", ⅛" between; A - 6 cols, 2¹⁄₁₆", ⅛" between; C - 8 cols, 1½", ⅛" between.
Commodity consumption: single pages printed 4,300; average pages per issue 18(d).
Equipment: PRODUCTION: Typesetters — 2-Fr, 1-P, 1-Ma, 1-Fi; Production cameras — 1-K. MAILROOM: Inserters and stuffers — MM/4 head; Bundle tyer — 1-Bu, 1-El; Addressing machine — Ch/730S. WIRE SERVICES: News — Receiving dishes — AP. BUSINESS COMPUTERS: PCs & micros networked; PCs & main system networked.

MOUNT VERNON

Skagit County

'90 U.S. Census- 17,647; E&P '96 Est. 20,625
ABC-NDM (90): 79,555 (HH 30,573)

Skagit Valley Herald

(e-mon to fri; m-sat)

Skagit Valley Herald, 1000 E. College Way; PO Box 578, Mount Vernon, WA 98273-0578; tel (360) 424-3251; fax (360) 424-5300. Pioneer Newspapers group.
Circulation: 20,638(e); 20,638(m-sat); ABC Sept. 30, 1995.
Price: 50¢(d); 50¢(sat); $7.75/mo (carrier); $93.00/yr (carrier).
Advertising: Open inch rate $17.90(e); $17.90(m-sat). **Representative:** Papert Companies.
News Service: AP. **Politics:** Independent. **Established:** 1884.
Special Editions: Baby Photo Tab, Bridal, Our Town (Feb); Newspaper in Education, Spring Home & Garden (Mar); Tulip Festival (Apr); Mom's Day, Spring Car Care (May); Berry Dairy Days, Dad's Day, Fields of Plenty, Loggerodeo, Skagit/Island County Builders Tab (June); Skagit Co. Fair, Zip up your Home (Aug); Sideliner (Football), Zip up your Home (Sept); Election Tab, Home Sweet Home, Swan (Woman of the Year) (Oct); New Car Showcase, Northwest Holiday (Nov); Christmas Gift Guide (Dec).
Special Weekly Sections: Best Food Day (wed); Applause (Art & Entertainment) (thur); Dining Guide (fri); Real Estate Open House (sat); Catalog of Homes (tues, bi-weekly).
Magazines: TV Week Magazine (TV Guide) (weekly); Ag Northwest (monthly).

CORPORATE OFFICERS

Board Chairman Leighton P Wood
President/Owner Leighton P Wood
Controller David P Sonnichsen

GENERAL MANAGEMENT

Publisher L Stedem Wood
Director-Human Resources Kimberly Somers
Manager-Office Tammy Force

ADVERTISING

Director Paul A Wood

TELECOMMUNICATIONS

Audiotex Manager Lisa Brown

CIRCULATION

Director Dale T Irvine

NEWS EXECUTIVE

Exec Editor Nancy G Erickson

EDITORS AND MANAGERS

Books/Films Editor Laura Dietz
City Editor Greg Lamm
Farm/Agriculture Editor Kari Ranten
Features/Travel Editor Laura Dietz
Food/Women's Editor Laura Dietz
Living/Lifestyle Editor Laura Dietz
News Editor Dan Abshier
Opinion Page Editor Nancy G Erickson
Photo Department Manager Scott Terrell
Religion Editor Gerald Erichsen
Sports Editor Kevin Brown
Television/Film Editor Laura Dietz
Wire Editor Dan Abshier

MANAGEMENT INFORMATION SERVICES

Manager-Info Systems Shamria Kirk

PRODUCTION

Foreman-Pressroom Richard E Buchanan

Market Information: TMC; ADS; Operate audiotex.
Mechanical available: Offset; Black and 3 ROP colors; insert accepted — preprinted, cards; page cut-offs — 22¾".
Mechanical specifications: Type page 13" x 21½"; E - 6 cols, 2¹⁄₁₆", ⅛" between; A - 6 cols, 2¹⁄₁₆", ⅛" between; C - 9 cols, 1⅜", ¹⁄₁₆" between.
Commodity consumption: Newsprint 1,192 metric tons; widths 27"; single pages printed 10,411; average pages per issue 24(d); single plates used 12,164.
Equipment: EDITORIAL: Front-end hardware — Ap/Mac Quadra 700, Ap/Mac LC; Front-end software — Baseview/NewsEdit, QuarkXPress; Printers — Ap/Mac LaserWriter IIg; Other equipment — Nikon/LS-3510 Negative Scanner, HP/ScanJet IIcx. CLASSIFIED: Front-end hardware — Ap/Mac Quadra 630; Front-end software — Baseview/Class Manager Plus 3.21; Printers — Ap/Mac ImageWriter, Ap/Mac LaserWriter NTX; Other equipment — Ap/Mac Scanner for OCR. AUDIOTEX: Hardware — PC w/Unix; Software — Marketlink; Supplier name — Marketlink, VNN. DISPLAY: Adv layout systems — ALS, Ap/Mac; Front-end hardware — Ap/Mac 8-Quadra 700, Ap/Power Mac 7100, Ap/Mac Quadra 605; Front-end software — QuarkXPress 3.31, Adobe/Photoshop 3.01; Printers — Ap/Mac LaserWriter 600/630, Ap/Mac LaserWriter 16-600, Hyphen/RIP 10.0; Other equipment — Canon/Xapshot, HP/ScanJet IIcx, Canon/Disk Scanner, SyQuest/drives. PRODUCTION: Pagination software — QuarkXPress 3.31; OCR software — Caere/OmniPage; Typesetters — 2-Hyphen/2200; Platemaking systems — Nu/FT40APRNS-631; Plate exposures — 3M/Pyrofax News 30; Plate processors — Anitec/S-26; Electronic picture desk — Lf/AP Leaf Picture Desk; Scanners — Nikon/3510 scanner, HP/ScanJet IIcx; Production cameras — SCREEN/Auto Companica 690D, Canon/Xapshot; Automatic film processors — Wing Lynch/5; Color separation equipment (conventional) — Adobe/Photoshop, Ap/Power Mac 8100; Digital color separation equipment — Adobe/Photoshop, Ap/Power Mac 8100.
PRESSROOM: Line 1 — 14-G/Community; Press drives — Fin; Folders — 2-SC, G/Community; Press registration system — Stroesser/Register System. MAILROOM: Counter stackers — 2-MM/310-20; Inserters and stuffers — 2-MM/5-pocket; Bundle tyer — 2-Gd, 1-MLN/ML2EE, 2-MLN/2A; Addressing machine — Ch/525; Other mailroom equipment — MM/235. COMMUNICATIONS: Digital ad delivery system — AP AdSend. WIRE SERVICES: News — AP, LAT-WP; Photos — AP; Syndicates — NEA, Unite Media; Receiving dishes — AP. BUSINESS COMPUTERS: IBM, Unix; Applications: MSSI: Accts receivable; PBS: Circ.

OLYMPIA

Thurston County

'90 U.S. Census- 33,840; E&P '96 Est. 37,691
ABC-CZ (90): 63,095 (HH 26,953)

The Olympian

(m-mon to sat; S)

The Olympian, 1268 4th Ave. E.; PO Box 407, Olympia, WA 98507; tel (360) 754-5400; fax (360) 754-5408; e-mail olympian@halcyon.com; web site http://www.halcyon.com/olympian/. Gannett Co. Inc. group.
Circulation: 37,236(m); 37,236(m-sat); 46,638(S); ABC Sept. 30, 1995.
Price: 35¢(d); 35¢(sat); $1.50(S); $12.25/mo (carrier), $12.75/mo (motor route); $147.00/yr (carrier), $153.00/yr (motor route).
Advertising: Open inch rate $28.62(m); $28.62(m-sat); $33.66(S). **Representative:** Gannett National Newspaper Sales.
News Services: AP, GNS, LAT. **Politics:** Independent. **Established:** 1891.
Special Editions: Progress (Mar); Home & Garden, Discover Western Washington (Apr); Newcomers (June); Street of Dreams (July); New Cars, Discover Western Washington (Oct).
Special Weekly Sections: Food (wed); Wheels, ETO (Entertainment-Travel-Outdoors) (fri); Religion, Home and Garden, Real Estate, Dining Guide (sat); Sports, Entertainment, TV, Business (daily).
Magazine: USA Weekend (S).

CORPORATE OFFICERS

Exec Board Chairman John J Curley
President John J Curley
Senior Vice Pres-Finance Service/Treasurer Jimmy L Thomas

GENERAL MANAGEMENT

Publisher Fred Hamilton
Director-Human Resources Carol Achatz
Controller Bruce Theis

ADVERTISING

Director Dan Walker
Manager-Classified Michael Leonard
Manager-Retail Laura Birmingham

MARKETING AND PROMOTION

Director-Marketing Service Bob Reitz

CIRCULATION

Director Rick Bell
Manager-Sales Marty Faulk
Manager-Home Delivery Joe Cassone

NEWS EXECUTIVES

Exec Editor Vikki Porter
Managing Editor Len Bruzzese

EDITORS AND MANAGERS

Amusements Editor Virginia Painter
Business Editor Jeff Smith
City Editor Linda Green
Editorial Page Editor Mike Oakland
Education Reporter Frieda Bush
ETO (Entertainment) Editor Virginia Painter
Environment Reporter John Dodge
Features Editor Jerre Redecker
Films/Theater Editor Virginia Painter
Librarian Lori Buker
Music Editor Virginia Painter
News Editor Karen Kurtz
Photo Editor Dick Milligan
Radio/Television Editor Virginia Painter

I-430 Washington

Real Estate Editor	Philip Watness
Sports Editor	Mike Burgess
Teen-Age/Youth Editor	Jerre Redecker
Women's/Food Editor	Jerre Redecker

MANAGEMENT INFORMATION SERVICES

Manager-Info Systems	David Olson

PRODUCTION

Director	John Wartinger
Manager-Pre Press	Darlene Kemery
Manager-Pressroom	Rick Alexander

Market Information: Zoned editions; TMC.
Mechanical available: Offset; Black and 3 ROP colors; insert accepted — preprinted, with prior approval; page cut-offs — 22¾".
Mechanical specifications: Type page 13" x 21½"; E - 6 cols, 2¹⁄₁₆", ⅛" between; A - 6 cols, 2¹⁄₁₆", ⅛" between; C - 9 cols, 1⅜", ¹⁄₁₆" between.
Commodity consumption: Newsprint 3,856 short tons; widths 27½", 13⅝"; black ink 66,951 pounds; color ink 27,152 pounds; single pages printed 16,524; average pages per issue 40(d), 76(S); single plates used 25,667.
Equipment: EDITORIAL: Front-end hardware — 2-PC; Front-end software — Dewarview; Printers — PrePress/Panther. CLASSIFIED: Front-end hardware — 2-PC; Front-end software — Dewar/Adv System. DISPLAY: Adv layout systems — Dewar; Front-end hardware — PC; Front-end software — QuarkXPress, MTS AdTracker. PRODUCTION: Pagination software — Dewarview, QuarkXPress 3.31 RS; Typesetters — 1-Tegra/Varityper 5500, 1-Tegra/Varityper 5300, 2-PrePress/Panther RIP; Plate exposures — 2-BKY; Plate processors — 3-Nu/Flip Top; Scanners — Polaroid/Sprintscan, 2-Microtek/II XE; Production cameras — 1-C/Spartan III; Automatic film processors — 3-LE; Film transporters — 1-LE; Shrink lenses — 1-CK Optical.
PRESSROOM: Line 1 — 15-G/Urbanite; Folders — 2-G/2:1. MAILROOM: Counter stackers — 2-HL/Monitor, 1-PPK, 1-Stackpack; Inserters and stuffers — 1-MM/Biliner(6-into-1), 1-MM/227(6-into-1); Bundle tyer — 2-MLN/2A, 1-MLN/EE, 1-Dynaric; Wrapping singles — 1-MM/Quarter fold Stitcher-Trimer; Addressing machine — 1-KAN/Labeler, 1-Barstrom/on-line. COMMUNICATIONS: Digital ad delivery system — AP AdSend. Systems used — satellite. WIRE SERVICES: News — AP, GNS; Stock tables — AP; Syndicates — GNS, LAT-WP; Receiving dishes — AP. BUSINESS COMPUTERS: 1-IBM/AS-400; Applications: Circ, Adv billing, Accts receivable, Gen ledger, Payroll, Accts payable; PCs & micros networked; PCs & main system networked.

PASCO-KENNEWICK-RICHLAND

Franklin and Benton Counties

'90 U.S. Census- 94,807 (Pasco 20,337; Kennewick 42,155; Richland 32,315); E&P '96 Est. 100,176 (Pasco 21,703; Kennewick 46,810; Richland 31,663);
ABC-CZ (90): 106,081 (HH 39,958)

Tri-City Herald
(m-mon to sat; S)

Tri-City Herald, 107 N. Cascade (Kennewick, 99336); PO Box 2608, Tri-Cities, WA 99302; tel (509) 582-1500. McClatchy Newspapers group.
Circulation: 40,349(m); 40,349(m-sat); 43,866(S); ABC Sept. 30, 1995.
Price: 50¢(d); 50¢(sat); $1.25(S); $10.75/mo; $129.00/yr.
Advertising: Open inch rate $27.00(m); $27.00(m-sat); $27.00(S). **Representative:** Landon Associates Inc.
News Services: AP, LAT-WP, KRT, NYT, McClatchy. **Politics:** Independent. **Established:** 1888.
Special Edition: Annual Progress (Feb-Mar).
Special Weekly Sections: Food (wed); Business (thur); Calendar (fri); Auto, Church (sat); Desert Living, Home, TV Log (S).
Magazines: Parade, Color Comics (S).

GENERAL MANAGEMENT

Publisher	Jack Briggs
General Manager	Ian Lamont
Director-Computer Service	Clay Myers
Director-Finance	Tina McCollum
Manager-Human Resources	Cyndy Miles

ADVERTISING

Director	Ellen Evans
Manager-Sales	Dixon Shoemaker
Manager-National	Dora Johns

MARKETING AND PROMOTION

Director-Marketing	Ellen Evans
Coordinator-Marketing	Leslie Culley

TELECOMMUNICATIONS

Audiotex Manager	Leslie Culley

CIRCULATION

Director	Chris Blaser

NEWS EXECUTIVES

Managing Editor	Ken Robertson
Asst Managing Editor	Rick Larson

EDITORS AND MANAGERS

Arts/Entertainment Editor	Annette Cary
Aviation Editor	Matt Taylor
Books Editor	Matt Taylor
City Editor	Laurie Williams
Columnist	Bill Bequette
Editorial Page Editor	Matt Taylor
Education Editor	Melissa O'Neil
Features Editor	Cal Fitz Simmons
Films/Theater Editor	Joshua Beach
Food Editor	Loretto Hulse
Graphics Editor	Sherry Emery
Librarian	Donna Ball
News Editor	Andy Perdue
Chief Photographer	Bob Baker
Political Editor	Erik Smith
Radio/Television Editor	Ken Hoopengauner
Real Estate Editor	Carrie Schafer
Religion Editor	Laurie Williams
Science/Technology Editor	John Stang
Sports Editor	Jim Riley
Sunday Editor	Cal Fitz Simmons
Wine Columnist	Bob Woehler
Wire Editor	Bill Ward

MANAGEMENT INFORMATION SERVICES

Data Processing Manager	Clay Myers

PRODUCTION

Director	Terry Robinson
Manager-Printing Operations	Le Roy Modine

Market Information: TMC; ADS; Operate audiotex.
Mechanical available: Offset; Black and 3 ROP colors; insert accepted — preprinted, all; page cut-offs — 21".
Mechanical specifications: Type page 13" x 21"; E - 6 cols, 2¹⁄₁₆", ⅛" between; A - 6 cols, 2¹⁄₁₆", ⅛" between; C - 9 cols, ¹⁵⁄₁₆", ¹⁄₁₆" between.
Commodity consumption: Newsprint 3,093 short tons; 2,806 metric tons; widths 54", 40½", 27", 13½"; black ink 50,580 pounds; color ink 18,676 pounds; single pages printed 11,672; average pages per issue 32(d), 44(S); single plates used 17,508.
Equipment: EDITORIAL: Front-end hardware — 2-SCS, Dell/SP590, 6-Ap/Mac 8100-110, Kk/2035+; Front-end software — SCS/8000 3.89, QuarkXPress 3.31; CLASSIFIED: Front-end hardware — SCS, Dell/466SE, 8-Falco/Termina; Front-end software — SCS/Classified 8000. AUDIOTEX: Hardware — Brite Voice Systems; Software — Brite Voice Systems. DISPLAY: Front-end hardware — 3-Ap/Mac 8100-100, 3-Ap/Mac 9500-120; Front-end software — Multi-Ad/Creator 3.7, Aldus/FreeHand 5.0; Other equipment — Sharp/JX600 Scanner, Umax/1260, Microtek/ScanMaster III, Relisys/9624 Scanner. PRODUCTION: Typesetters — 2-Panther/Pro 46; Plate exposures — Nu/631; Plate processors — Nat/A-340; Electronic picture desk — 2-Ap/Mac Quadra 800, Kk/2035+ 35mm Scanner, 1-Ap/Mac 8100-100; Scanners — 1-CD/626E; Production cameras — 1-C/1211, DAI/C-690-AX; Automatic film processors — 1-LE/24; Film transporters — 1-C.
PRESSROOM: Line 1 — 6-MAN/MediaMan; Line 2 — 7-G/Community; Reels and stands — 4-MEG; Press control system — Allen Bradley. MAILROOM: Counter stackers — 4-Id/2000; Inserters and stuffers — GMA/SLS-1000, HI/1372; Bundle tyer — 4-Power Strap; Addressing machine — 1-Ch/520-E. LIBRARY: Electronic — SCS. COMMUNICATIONS: Digital ad delivery system — AP AdSend. Systems used — fiber optic. WIRE SERVICES: News — Receiving dishes — AP. BUSINESS COMPUTERS: DEC/Micro VAX 3600, SCS, Dell/466SE; Applications: SCS: Adv, Class, Accts; CJ: Circ (TMC); PCs & micros networked.

PORT ANGELES

Clallam County

'90 U.S. Census- 17,710; E&P '96 Est. 17,924
ABC-CZ (90): 17,710 (HH 7,360)

Peninsula Daily News
(e-mon to fri; S)

Peninsula Daily News, 305 W. First; PO Box 1330, Port Angeles, WA 98362; tel (360) 452-2345; fax (360) 417-3521; e-mail pdn@olympus.net. Horvitz Newspapers Inc. (Northwest Media) group.
Circulation: 15,232(e); 17,329(S); ABC Sept. 30, 1995.
Price: 35¢(d); $1.25(S); $8.25/mo (junior dealer), $9.25/mo (motor route), $12.05/mo (mail).
Advertising: Open inch rate $16.94(e); $16.94 (S). **Representative:** Papert Companies.
News Services: AP, Maturity News Service. **Politics:** Independent. **Established:** 1916.
Special Editions: Home (Mar); Visitor's Guide (Apr); Fair (June, Aug); Visitor's Guide (Sept).
Special Weekly Sections: Food (wed); Entertainment (thur); The Viewbook (S).

CORPORATE OFFICER

Chairman of the Board/CEO/President Peter A Horvitz

GENERAL MANAGEMENT

Publisher	Frank D Ducceschi
Business Manager	Kathy Wahto

ADVERTISING

Director	John Huston
Supervisor-Inside Sales	Susan Stoneman
Supervisor-Ad Production	Marilyn Parrish

CIRCULATION

Manager	David Jacobsen
Asst Manager	Shelli Lynn

NEWS EXECUTIVE

Managing Editor	John McCartney

EDITORS AND MANAGERS

Business/Finance Writer	David Noonan
Editorial Page Editor	John McCartney
Education Writer	Dean Mosiman
Entertainment/Amusements Editor	Jim Guthrie
Librarian	Geri Zanon
News Editor	Steve Powell
Asst News Editor	Jeff Chew
Photo Chief	Tom Thompson
Sports Editor	John Heldt

PRODUCTION

Manager	Jeff Stalcup
Supervisor-Pressroom	Ron Rogers
Supervisor-Mailroom	Jerry White
Supervisor-Composing	Jay R Cline

Market Information: Zoned editions; Split Run; TMC.
Mechanical available: Offset; Black and 3 ROP colors; insert accepted — preprinted, cards; page cut-offs — 22¾".
Mechanical specifications: Type page 13" x 21"; E - 6 cols, 2¹⁄₁₆", ⅛" between; A - 6 cols, 2¹⁄₁₆", ⅛" between; C - 9 cols, 1⅜", ¹⁄₁₆" between.
Commodity consumption: Newsprint 771 metric tons; widths 27", 13½"; black ink 20,000 pounds; color ink 3,500 pounds; single pages printed 7,130; average pages per issue 21(d), 44(S); single plates used 8,100.
Equipment: EDITORIAL: Front-end hardware — 16-ECR/Autokon 7600; Front-end software — ECR; Printers — 1-Canon/K10070, 1-Centronics/6300, 1-HP/LaserJet IV; Other equipment — Lf/AP Leaf Picture Desk, Lf/Leafscan 35, Ap/Mac Centris, Ap/Mac IIci. CLASSIFIED: Front-end hardware — 4-ECR/Autokon 7600; Front-end software — ECR; Printers — 1-DEC/LA 36. DISPLAY: Front-end hardware — Ap/Mac IIci, 1-Ap/Mac II, 1-Ap/Mac Plus, 2-Ap/Mac Quadra 800; Front-end software — Multi-Ad/Creator. PRODUCTION: Typesetters — 1-LaserMaster/1000, 1-GCC/SelectPress 600, 2-AG/Accuset 1000; Plate exposures — 1-Nu/Flip Top FT40APRNS; Plate processors — WL/Lithoplater 38D, Lf/AP Leaf Picture Desk, 2-Ap/Mac 8100; Scanners — 2-Umax/UC630, 1-Umax/UC 1260; Production cameras — 1-SCREEN/C-6500-D; Automatic film processors — 1-Konica/K-550; Digital color separation equipment — Lf/Leafscan 35.
PRESSROOM: Line 1 — 6-G/Community; Press drives — 1-Fin/40 h.p. motor; Folders — G/Suburban (w/upper former). MAILROOM: Counter stackers — 1-BG/Count-O-Veyor 105; Inserters and stuffers — 1-MM/5-station 4:1; Bundle tyer — 2-MLN/Powerstrapper; Addressing machine — 1-KR. WIRE SERVICES: News — AP, Maturity News Service; Receiving dishes — size-10ft, AP. BUSINESS COMPUTERS: IBM/Sys 38, 1-IBM/5294, 5-Decision Data/3776; Applications: INSI: Circ; NGS: Bus; Lotus, Microsoft/Windows.

PULLMAN

See MOSCOW, ID

RENTON

See KENT

RICHLAND

See PASCO

SEATTLE

King County

'90 U.S. Census- 516,259; E&P '96 Est. 528,421
ABC-NDM (90): 1,725,586 (HH 700,509)

Seattle Daily Journal of Commerce (m-mon to sat)

Seattle Daily Journal of Commerce, 83 Columbia St. (98104); PO Box 11050, Seattle, WA 98111; tel (206) 622-8272; fax (206) 622-8416; e-mail djc.com.
Circulation: 5,288(m); 5,288(m-sat); Sworn Sept. 30, 1994.
Price: $1.25(d); $1.25(sat); $95.00/6mo; $160.00/yr.
Advertising: Open inch rate $20.00(m); $20.00(m-sat).
News Services: AP, Business Wire, NYT. **Politics:** Independent. **Established:** 1893.
Special Editions: Architecture; Environment; Machinery; Real Estate; Business; Law & Courts.
Special Weekly Sections: Heavy Equipment (mon); Auctions, Environment (tues); Architecture & Engineering (wed); Law & Courts (thur); Real Estate (fri); Plan Bulletin (sat).

CORPORATE OFFICERS

President	Denis Brown
Vice Pres	M E Brown

GENERAL MANAGEMENT

Publisher	Phil Brown
General Manager	John Mihalyo

ADVERTISING

Director	John Mihalyo
Manager-Legal	Valerie Gallagher

CIRCULATION

Manager	Owen O'Neil

NEWS EXECUTIVE

Editor	Maude Scott

EDITORS AND MANAGERS

Architectural/Engineering Editor	Clair Enlow
City Editor	Jerry Craig
Construction Editor	Ben Minnick
Environmental Editor	Tinku Saini
Graphics Editor/Art Director	Stan Eichwald
Real Estate Editor	Jon Savelle

MANAGEMENT INFORMATION SERVICES

Online Manager	John Elliott

PRODUCTION

Manager	Maryann Swingler
Foreman-Pressroom	David Elleby

Market Information: TMC; Operate database.
Mechanical available: Offset; Black and 3 ROP colors; insert accepted — preprinted; page cut-offs — 22¾".
Mechanical specifications: Type page 15" x 21½"; E - 7 cols, 2", ⅛" between; A - 7 cols, 2", ⅛" between; C - 8 cols, 1.67", ¼" between.
Commodity consumption: Newsprint 220 metric tons; width 32"; black ink 2,500 pounds; single pages printed 5,400; average pages per issue 18(d), 64(sat); single plates used 10.
Equipment: EDITORIAL: Front-end hardware — PCs; Front-end software — CText; Printers — 1-Ap/Mac LaserWriter II NT. CLASSIFIED: Front-end hardware — AST; Front-end software — PBS; Printers — Panasonic/KX-P1624, HP/LaserJet 4M. DISPLAY: Adv layout systems — CyberText; Front-end hardware — PC, Ap/Mac; Front-end software — CyberText, XYQUEST/XyWrite III, XYQUEST/XyWrite 4.0; Printers — Ap/Mac LaserWriter NT; Other equipment — Courier/HST Modems. PRODUCTION: Typesetters — 2-Ap/Mac LaserWriter NT; Plate exposures — Nu/Flip Top FT40V3UPNS; Scanners — Umax/840 MaxVision (color); Production cameras — 2-SCREEN/Auto Companica LE, R; Automatic film processors — LD/220-QT, LE/Line 17; Digital color separation equipment — Adobe/Photoshop.
PRESSROOM: Line 1 — 5-Econ/Web; Press

Copyright ©1996 by the Editor & Publisher Co.

control system — Manual. MAILROOM: Counter stackers — KR/3-Station Inserter; Bundle tyer — Bu, EAM/Mosca; Wrapping singles — Manual; Addressing machine — KR/Label Head. WIRE SERVICES: News — AP, BW, PR Newswire. BUSINESS COMPUTERS: AST/286, AST/386, PBS, Wyse, IBM/386s, IBM/486s; Applications: PBS: Ad mgmt, Circ; PCs & micros networked; PCs & main system networked.

Seattle Post-Intelligencer

(m-mon fri; m-sat)

Seattle Times/Seattle Post Intelligencer (S)

Seattle Post-Intelligencer, 101 Elliot Ave. W.; PO Box 1909, Seattle, WA 98111-1909; tel (206) 448-8000; fax (206) 448-8166 (News room). Hearst Newspapers group.

Circulation: 204,544(m); 181,372(m-sat); 505,604(S); ABC Sept. 30, 1995.

Price: 35¢(d); 35¢(sat); $1.50(S); $10.00/mo (carrier); $102.00/yr (in county).

Advertising: Open inch rate $149.56(m); $149.56(m-sat); $232.87(S). **Representative:** Newspapers First.

News Services: AP, NYT, HN, RN. **Politics:** Independent. **Established:** 1863.

Note: The Seattle Post-Intelligencer and the Seattle Times are corporately and editorially separate. Under a joint operating agreement, all circulation, advertising and production functions are being performed by the Seattle Times. The Sunday edition is a joint production with all news content produced by the Seattle Times. Both newspapers have a separate Saturday/holiday edition. There is a combined advertising rate of $199.64.

Advertising not accepted: Non-rated or X-rated movies; Handguns.

Special Editions: Boat Show; Home Show; Spring Fashion; Home & Garden; Northwest Women's Show; Summer Home Design; Summer Guide; Bite of Seattle; Fall Fashion; Football Preview; Buy New Homes; Fall Home Design; Auto Show; Gourmet; Health Care Job Fair; Christmas Gift Guide.

Special Weekly Sections: Travel (thur); Arts & Entertainment, What's Happening, Classified/Autos (fri); Weekend (sat); Travel (S); Living (daily).

Magazine: Parade (S).

CORPORATE OFFICERS

President/CEO (Hearst Corp) Frank A Bennack Jr
Exec Vice Pres/Chief Operating Officer (Hearst Corp) Gilbert C Maurer
Vice Pres/General Manager (Hearst Corp/Newspaper Division) Robert J Danzig

GENERAL MANAGEMENT

Publisher/Editor J D Alexander
Business Manager John E Currie
Director-Public Affairs John Joly
Manager-Technology Bill Stults
Managing Editor Ken Buntiag

CIRCULATION

Vice Pres Stephen R Sparks
Manager-Home Delivery Tim Carothers

NEWS EXECUTIVES

Editor J D Alexander
Assoc Editor Thomas A Read
Managing Editor Kenneth F Bunting
Asst Managing Editor Lee Rozen
Asst Managing Editor Don Smith

EDITORS AND MANAGERS

Arts/Entertainment Editor Duston Harvey
Business Editor John Leuesque
Night City Editor Mike Merritt
Night Asst City Editor Pete McConnell
Classical Music/Dance Editor R M Campbell
Columnist-City Susan Paynter
Columnist-Sports Laura Velsey
Columnist-Sports Art Theil
Columnist-Features Jon Hahn
Editorial Cartoonist David Horsey
Editorial Cartoonist Steven Greenberg
Editorial Page Editor Charles J Dunsire
Fashion/Beauty Editor Susan Phinney
Features Editor Janet Grimley
Films Editor William Arnold
Fine Arts Editor Regina Hackett
Food Editor Tom Sietsema
Government Affairs Editor Warren Wilson
Librarian Lytton Smith
Lifestyle Editor John Engstrom
Music Editor-Popular/Jazz Gene Stont
National Correspondent Joel Connelly
National/Foreign Editor Bob Schenet
Photo/Graphics Editor Laura Vecsey
Projects Editor Richard Clever
Regional Editor Gina Mills
Sports Editor Tim Kelly
Television Editor John Engstrom
Theater Editor Joe Adcock
Washington, DC Correspondent Christopher Hanson

Equipment: EDITORIAL: Front-end hardware — AT; Front-end software — AT/News Layout; Other equipment — Lf/AP Leaf Picture Desk. LIBRARY: Electronic — Vu/Text SAVE. WIRE SERVICES: News — AP, NYT, RN; Photos — AP, NYT; Stock tables — AP; Syndicates — WP Writers Group, Universal Press, United Features, Television Data, TMS, NYT, LATS, King Features, Crown, Creators, CNS, Chronicle, Cartoonists & Writers Syndicate, BPI, Asterisk; Receiving dishes — AP. BUSINESS COMPUTERS: DEC/11-23; Applications: Lotus 1-2-3; PCs & micros networked; PCs & main system networked.

The Seattle Times

(e-mon to fri; m-sat)

The Seattle Times/Seattle Post-Intelligencer (S)

The Seattle Times, Fairview Ave. N. & John; PO Box 70, Seattle, WA 98111; tel (206) 464-2111; e-mail ptech@seatimes.com; web site http://www.seatimes.com. Seattle Times Co. group.

Circulation: 232,616(e); 226,439(m-sat); 505,604(S); ABC Sept. 30, 1995.

Price: 35¢(d); 35¢(sat); $1.50(S); $2.50/wk; $10.83/mo; $111.80/yr.

Advertising: Open inch rate $149.56(e); $149.56(m-sat); $232.87(S). **Representative:** Newspapers First.

News Services: AP, LAT-WP, KRT, RN. **Politics:** Independent. **Established:** 1896.

Note: The Seattle Times and the Seattle Post-Intelligencer are corporately and editorially separate. Under a joint operating agreement, all circulation, advertising and production functions for both papers are being performed by the Seattle Times. The Sunday edition is a joint production with all news contents produced by the Seattle Times. Both newspapers have a separate Saturday/holiday edition. There is a combined advertising rate of $199.64.

Advertising not accepted: Handgun; X-rated movies; Escort services; Tobacco.

Special Editions: Home Show, Flower & Garden (Feb); Spring Fashion, Spring Mountains West (Mar); Summer Home Design, Summer Guide, Film Festival Guide (May); Seafair (July); Fall Fashion (Aug); Football Previews, Fall Arts, Fall Mountains West (Sept); Fall Home Design, Book Fair (Oct); Seattle Auto Show, M.A.M.E., Holiday Foods, Gourmet (Nov).

Special Weekly Sections: Travel (tues); Arts & Entertainment, Tempo (fri); Classified/Autos, Weekend (sat); Travel (S).

Magazines: Pacific (heatset, offset), TV Times (newsprint) (S); Parade.

CORPORATE OFFICERS

Board Chairman F A Blethen
Publisher/CEO F A Blethen
President/Chief Operating Officer H Mason Sizemore
Senior Vice Pres-Employee Resources Group James H Schafer
Senior Vice Pres/Chief Financial Officer Carolyn S Kelly
Senior Vice Pres-Exec Editor M R Fancher
Vice Pres-Circulation Stephen R Sparks
Vice Pres-Operations Frank Paiva
Vice Pres-Advertising Marji Ruiz
Vice Pres-Info Technology Kurt Dahl
Treasurer W K Blethen

GENERAL MANAGEMENT

Publisher F A Blethen
President H Mason Sizemore
Purchasing Agent Chuck Sender
Director-Labor Relations Duane Johnson
Director-Human Resources and Diversity Phyllis Mayo

ADVERTISING

Vice Pres Marji Ruiz
Manager-Display Greg Bennett
Manager-Classified Michael Lemke
Manager-Marketing Joanne Nelson
Manager-National Roy Schaefer

MARKETING AND PROMOTION

Manager-Marketing Robert C Blethen

TELECOMMUNICATIONS

Vice Pres-Info Technology Kurt Dahl
Audiotex Manager Linda Stelzner

CIRCULATION

Vice Pres Stephen R Sparks

NEWS EXECUTIVES

Vice Pres/Exec Editor Michael R Fancher
Managing Editor Alex MacLeod
Assoc Editor-Columnist Blaine Newnham
Assoc Managing Editor Cyndi Nash
Asst Managing Editor-Administration Millie A Quan
Asst Managing Editor-Graphics Stanley Farrar
Asst Managing Editor-News Carole Carmichael
Asst Managing Editor-Features Pat Foote
Photo Coach Gary Settle

EDITORS AND MANAGERS

Action Line/Troubleshooter Editor Shelby Gilje
Aerospace Reporter Polly Lane
Aerospace Reporter Byron Acohido
Art Critic Robin Updike
Arts/Entertainment Editor Jan Even
Books Editor Donn Fry
Business Editor Robert Weisman
Asst Business Editor Carol Pucci
Business News Editor Suzanne La Violette
Columnist John Hinterberger
Columnist Erik Lacitis
Columnist Jean Godden
Columnist Steve Kelly
Columnist Terry McDermott
Copy Desk Chief Karen Cater
Diversity Reporter/Coach Aly Colon
Editorial Page Editor Mindy Cameron
Assoc Editorial Page Editor Jim Vesely
Editorial Writer Don Hannula
Editorial Writer Terry Tang
Education Writer Ross Anderson
Education Writer Joni Balter
Education Editor Janet Horne
Environmental Editor Tom Brown
Fashion Writer Mary Cronin
Films Critic John Hartl
Food Editor Sharon Lane
Lifestyle/Scene Editor Terry Tazioli
Local/Suburban Editor Arlene Bryant
Asst Local Editor Mike Wyne
Asst Local Editor Nick Provenza
Asst Local Editor Janet Horne
Asst Suburban Editor Mary Rothschild
Asst Suburban Editor Steve Pierce
Asst Suburban Editor John DeLeon
Media Reporter Chuck Taylor
Medical Reporter Warren King
Music Critic-Rock/Popular C Patrick MacDonald
News Editor Mike Stanton
Deputy News Editor John Saul
Night News Editor Leon Espinoza
Pacific Magazine Editor Kathy Andrisevic
Political Editor Tom Brown
Regional Editor Dave Boardman
Asst Regional Editor Bill Ristow
Religion Reporter Lee Moriwaki
Science Reporter Bill Dietrich
Science/High Tech Editor Mark Watanabe
Sports Editor Cathy Henkel
Asst Sports Editor Don Shelton
Asst Sports Editor Paul Palazzo
Theater Critic Misha Bersen
Travel Editor John MacDonald
Wire News Editor Jim Mallery

MANAGEMENT INFORMATION SERVICES

Data Processing Manager Kurt Dahl

PRODUCTION

Manager-Plant (Fairview) Doug Ranes
Manager-Electrical (Fairview) Everett Olson
Manager-Night Operations (Fairview) Al Orwiler
Manager-Plant (North Creek) Fred Dal Broi
Manager-Electrical (North Creek) Dana Reed
Manager-Day Operations (North Creek) Larry Berg
Manager-Mechanical (North Creek) Eric Rosebrock
Manager-Facilities (North Creek) Dan Finn
Manager-Composing Donna Tuggle
Manager-Pressroom Al Sherrington
Manager-Color/Camera Dan Booker
Manager-Packaging Stan Gregory
Manager-Receiving Dave Clemens
Manager-Pagination Dave Wagner
Manager-Platemaking Larry Berg
Asst Plant Manager-Packaging Alan Sharrah
Asst Plant Manager-Maintenance Tom Hatcher

Market Information: Zoned editions; Split Run; TMC; ADS; Operate audiotex.

Mechanical available: Offset; Black and 3 ROP colors; insert accepted — preprinted; page cutoffs — 23$\frac{9}{16}$".

Mechanical specifications: Type page 13" x 22½"; E - 6 cols, 2$\frac{1}{16}$", ⅛" between; A - 6 cols, 2$\frac{1}{16}$", ⅛" between; C - 10 cols, 1¼", $\frac{1}{16}$" between.

Commodity consumption: Newsprint 70,000 metric tons; widths 55", 41¼", 27½"; black ink 1,300,000 pounds; color ink 200,000 pounds; single pages printed 44,000; average pages per issue 60(d), 150(S); single plates used 480,000.

Equipment: EDITORIAL: Front-end hardware — 14-Everex/486, 168-AT, 10-Ap/Mac Power-Book+, 28-Ap/Mac; Front-end software — AT/PC news layout, AT/Editorial 4.7; Printers — Epson, Okidata, HP, Cx; Other equipment — Lf/AP Leaf Picture Desk. CLASSIFIED: Front-end hardware — 96-AT/VDT, 2-IBM/RS 6000; Front-end software — AT/IAS 4.7, AT/Pagination V4; Printers — HP, Fujitsu. AUDIOTEX: Hardware — CTL/Comm. Vscript IVR system (24 lines), Brite Voice Systems/BVS 96 V, Micro Voice/Personal System. DISPLAY: Adv layout systems — Cx, AT/Architect, 12-Sun/3-80, 9-Ap/Mac, 1-Sun/Sparc Server; Front-end hardware — AT/Architect, 4-IBM/RS 6000; Front-end software — Cs, AT/Architect; Printers — HP, Graphic Enterprises, QMS; Other equipment — 7-Compaq/386 workstation. PRODUCTION: Typesetters — 1-Linotype-Hell/L-500, 3-Cx/Supersetter I, 3-Mon/Mark IV, 2-AG/SS-7000, 1-ITT/3850; Platemaking systems — 2-Na/NP 120; Plate exposures — 2-Titan, 2-WL/10, 1-Nu/Flip top, 1-WL/Lith-5; Plate processors — 2-WL/38G, 2-WL/38D; Electronic picture desk — 2-Lf/AP Leaf File Server, 2-Ap/Mac Workstation; Scanners — Microtek/300G, 2-ECR/Autokon, 2-ECR/Autokon 1000, ECR/Autokon 2045C; Production cameras — 1-SCREEN/C-260, 2-C/Newspager; Automatic film processors — 3-P/26RA, 1-SCREEN, 1-C/T65, 4-C/OL66C, 2-AG/OLP28, 2-DP/ECP72; Film transporters — 2-C; Shrink lenses — 1-C; Digital color separation equipment — 2-CD/656 EA, 2-CD/Studio 9600.
PRESSROOM: Line 1 — 8-G/Colorliner; Line 2 — 8-G/Colorliner; Line 3 — 8-G/Colorliner; Line 4 — 9-G/Metroliner; Line 5 — 9-G/Mark I Letterpress; Line 6 — 9-G/Mark I Letterpress; Press drives — 3-Allen Bradley, 2-CH, 1-Fin; Folders — 8-G/3:2; Pasters — 66-G; Reels and stands — 57-G; Press control system — 1-G/PAR, 1-G/PCS. MAILROOM: Counter stackers — 15-QWI, 8-QWI; Inserters and stuffers — 3-Amerigraph/2299, 2-HI/1372P; Bundle tyer — 16-Dynaric/NP-2, 6-Dynaric; Wrapping singles — 15-QWI/Cobra, 8-J. LIBRARY: Electronic — In-house, Microvax/3000, Battelle/Basis Software for text, T-one/Merlin for photos. COMMUNICATIONS: Facsimile — Linotype-Hell/PZ10K, Linotype-Hell/Pressfax (2 sets); Digital ad delivery system — AP AdSend, First Class/BBS. Systems used — microwave, fiber optic, satellite. WIRE SERVICES: News — RN, AP Datastream, AP Datafeatures, AP Weather Wire, AP SportStats; Stock tables — TMS, XETA Data; Receiving dishes — AP, RN, INS. BUSINESS COMPUTERS: 1-HP/3000-958, 1-IBM/9121-440, 5-IBM/RS-6000; Applications: Gen ledger, Accts payable, Fixed assets, Payroll, HR project tracking, TMC, Project scheduling, Single copy billing; IBM/MVS, Clark Lambert: Circ, Subscriber billing; Admarc, Discus CIS: Subscriber billing; PCs & micros networked; PCs & main system networked.

SPOKANE

Spokane County

'90 U.S. Census- 177,196; **E&P '96 Est.** 180,375
ABC-CZ (90): 288,392 (HH 117,379)

The Spokesman-Review

(m-mon to fri; m-sat; S)

The Spokesman-Review, W. 999 Riverside Ave.; PO Box 2160, Spokane, WA 99210; tel (509) 459-5000; fax (509) 459-5234.

Circulation: 122,961(m); 136,019(m-sat); 149,497(S); ABC Sept. 30, 1995.

Price: 50¢(d); 50¢(sat); $1.50(S); $13.00/mo (in county).

Advertising: Open inch rate $64.76(m); $64.76(m-sat); $78.52(S). **Representative:** Cresmer, Woodward, O'Mara & Ormsbee.

News Services: AP, NYT, McClatchy. **Politics:** Independent-Republican. **Established:** 1883.

Advertising not accepted: Tobacco.

Special Editions: New Car Auto Show, Bloomsday Training Guide (Feb); State B Basketball (Mar); Home & Gardening, Spring Travel (March); Fishing (Apr); Bloomsday (May); Football (Aug); Interstate Fair, Hunting Guide (Sept); Winter Travel (Nov).

Special Weekly Sections: Best Food, Our Generation (wed); Health (thur); Gardening, Weekend (Entertainment) (fri); Religion, Automotive (sat); Real Estate, Travel, Business, TV Week (S); Business, TV Log (daily).

Magazines: React (mon); Parade, TV Week (S).

CORPORATE OFFICERS

President — James P Cowles
Vice Pres/Publisher — William Stacey Cowles
Secretary/Treasurer — M K Nielsen

GENERAL MANAGEMENT

Director-Marketing/Sales — Shaun O'L Higgins
Director-Operations — Douglas W Osborn
Manager-Human Resources — Charles J Rehberg
Manager-Computer Service — Robert Davis

ADVERTISING

Director — C Daniel Grady
Manager-Display — Steve Westphal
Manager-Classified — Marlene Anderson
Manager-Retail Sales — Robert Boehme

MARKETING AND PROMOTION

Manager-Community Affairs — Jennifer Byrne
Manager-New Media Ventures — Shaun O'L Higgins

TELECOMMUNICATIONS

Audiotex Manager — Colleen Striegel

CIRCULATION

Director — Maurice Twomey
Manager-Marketing — Janet Hasson
Manager-Home Delivery — Robert Thomas
Coordinator-Newspapers in Education — Nancy Skog

NEWS EXECUTIVES

Editor — Christopher Peck
Managing Editor-Content — Peggy Kuhr
Managing Editor-Presentation & Opinion — Scott Sines
Assoc Editor — Frank Bartel

EDITORS AND MANAGERS

Business Editor — Mark Hester
Assoc Business Editor — Frank Bartel
City Editor — Joe Fenton
Entertainment Editor — Susan English
Features Editor — Kathryn DeLong
Food Editor — Graham Vink
Graphics Editor — Vince Grippi
News Editor — Kevin Graman
Opinion Editor — John Webster
Outdoors Editor — Rich Landers
Photography Editor — John Sale
Sports Editor — Jeff Jordan
Youth Page Editor — Anne Windishar

MANAGEMENT INFORMATION SERVICES

Prodigy Manager — David Bender
Data Processing Manager — Robert Davis

PRODUCTION

Manager — Larry L Lyon

Market Information: Zoned editions; Split Run; TMC; ADS; Operate audiotex; Electronic edition.
Mechanical available: Offset; Black and 3 ROP colors; insert accepted — preprinted, some product samples; page cut-offs — 22¾".
Mechanical specifications: Type page 13" x 21½"; E - 6 cols, 2¹⁄₁₆", ⅛" between; A - 6 cols, 2¹⁄₁₆", ⅛" between; C - 10 cols, 1¼", .04" between.
Commodity consumption: average pages per issue 80(d), 152(S).
Equipment: EDITORIAL: Front-end hardware — IBM/PS2 70, IBM/PS2 90; Front-end software — Cybergraphics; Other equipment — Ap/Mac. CLASSIFIED: Front-end hardware — IBM/PS2 70; Front-end software — Cybergraphics. AUDIOTEX: Hardware — Brite Voice Systems; Supplier name — Brite Voice Systems. DISPLAY: Adv layout systems — SCS/Layout 8000; Front-end hardware — III; Front-end software — SCS/Layout 8000. PRODUCTION: Typesetters — 2-III/3810; Plate exposures — 2-WL; Plate processors — 2-WL/38; Scanners — 1-III/3750, 1-III; Production cameras — 2-C/Pager, 2-C/Marathon; Automatic film processors — 4-P; Shrink lenses — 2-Nikon; Color separation equipment (conventional) — Hel/299, Howtek/Colorscan.
PRESSROOM: Line 1 — 6-G/Metro (4 decks); Line 2 — 6-G/Metro (4 decks); Line 3 — 8-G/Urbanite (Stacked); Pasters — 6-G/Metro, 3-G/Urbanite; Reels and stands — 3-G/Urbanite; Press control system — Fin, G/Metro, G/Urbanite. MAILROOM: Counter stackers — 4-Id/440, 2-Id/2000, 2-QWI/300; Inserters and stuffers — 1-S/11-72, 2-S/8-48; Bundle tyer — 4-MLN; Wrapping singles — 2-Bu; Addressing machine — 2-Ch. LIBRARY: Electronic — Vu/Text. WIRE SERVICES: News — AP; Photos — AP; Stock tables — AP; Receiving dishes — AP. BUSINESS COMPUTERS: 1-IBM/Sys 38 700, 1-IBM/AS-400-D45; Applications: INSI: Circ, Adv, Accts receivable, Transient adv; PCs & micros networked; PCs & main system networked.

SUNNYSIDE

Yakima County

'90 U.S. Census- 11,238; E&P '96 Est. 12,441

Daily Sun News (e-mon to fri)

Daily Sun News, 600 S. 6th St.; PO Box 878, Sunnyside, WA 98944; tel (509) 837-4500; fax (509) 837-6397. Eagle Newspapers Inc. group.
Circulation: 3,777(e); Sworn Oct. 2, 1995.
Price: 35¢(d); $3.50/mo; $42.00/yr (in county).
Advertising: Open inch rate $6.60(e). **Established:** 1962.
Special Editions: "Reflections"-Year in Review, Annual Baby Section (Jan); Valentine's Day, President's Day (Feb); St. Patrick's Day, Farm Edition, Easter (Mar); Auto Car Care Section, Home & Garden Section (Apr); Mother's Day, Memorial Day, Graduation, Senior Citizen Special Edition (May); Father's Day, Farm Edition, Vacation Getaway (June); Summer Car Care, Vacation Getaway (July); Sports Review Section, Back-to-School Edition (Aug); Sunshine Days Special Edition, Fall Harvest Section, Pride of Yakima Valley (Sept); Women in Business, Fire Prevention Week Section (Oct); Holiday Gift Guide, Thanksgiving Kickoff, Christmas Shopping Kickoff, "Cash for Christmas" (Nov); Letters to Santa, Special Holiday Edition (Dec).
Special Weekly Section: Sunshine Days (weekly).

CORPORATE OFFICERS

Board Chairman — Dennis Smith
President — Richard A Nafsinger

GENERAL MANAGEMENT

Publisher — Tom Lanctot
General Manager — Tim Graff

ADVERTISING

Director — Bob Dedolf

CIRCULATION

Director — Marsha Murphey

EDITOR AND MANAGER

Opinion Editor — Olaf Elze

PRODUCTION

Manager — Tim Graff

Market Information: TMC.
Mechanical available: Offset; Black and 1 ROP color; insert accepted — preprinted; page cut-offs — 22¾".
Mechanical specifications: Type page 10¼" x 16½"; E - 5 cols, 1.96", ⅛" between; A - 5 cols, 1.96", ⅛" between; C - 5 cols, 1.96", ⅛" between.
Commodity consumption: Newsprint 56 metric tons; width 35"; black ink 1,500 pounds; single pages printed 3,788; average pages per issue 15(d); single plates used 1,100.
Equipment: EDITORIAL: Front-end hardware — 1-Ap/Mac SE, 3-Ap/Mac Classic, Ap/Mac Quadra 610; Front-end software — Microsoft/Word 5.1; Printers — Ap/Mac LaserPrinter NTX. CLASSIFIED: Front-end hardware — Ma/386-SX20; Front-end software — Synaptic; Printers — Ap/Mac LaserWriter II. DISPLAY: Adv layout systems — 2-Ap/Mac SE 20, Ap/Mac; Front-end software — Ap/Mac Draw, Aldus/PageMaker, Broderbund/Typestyler, Microsoft/Word 5.1; Printers — Ap/Mac SE 30 LaserPrinter, NewGen/Turbo PS-1200 T. PRODUCTION: Typesetters — Ap/Mac LaserWriter; Plate exposures — Nu/30x40 plate burner; Production cameras — Nu/SST 20x24.
PRESSROOM: Line 1 — 4-G/Community; Folders — 1-G/Community. MAILROOM: Bundle tyer — Bu, Cypack; Addressing machine — Sperry Computer, Newsware. BUSINESS COMPUTERS: Tandy/3000; Applications: Synaptic.

TACOMA

Pierce County

'90 U.S. Census- 176,664; E&P '96 Est. 186,920
ABC-CZ (90): 359,703 (HH 139,884)

The News Tribune (m-mon to sat; S)

The News Tribune, 1950 S. State St.; PO Box 11000, Tacoma, WA 98411; tel (206) 597-8742; fax (206) 597-8263; web site http://www.tribnet.com/. McClatchy Newspapers group.
Circulation: 128,659(m); 128,659(m-sat); 146,512(S); ABC Sept. 30, 1995.
Price: 35¢(d); 35¢(sat); $1.50(S); $10.50/mo; $126.00/yr.
Advertising: Open inch rate $69.10(m); $77.15(m-sat); $77.15(S). **Representative:** Cresmer, Woodward, O'Mara & Ormsbee.
News Services: AP, NYT, LAT-WP, KRT, McClatchy, GNS. **Politics:** Independent. **Established:** 1883.
Special Weekly Sections: Employment, Your Money (mon); Family, Food, Communities, Venture (wed); 50+, Prep Page (thur); TGIF, Automotive (fri); Habitat, Religion (sat); Travel, Marketplace and New Homes, Video Week (S); Soundlife, Sports, Business (daily).
Magazines: 50+ (1st thur); TGIF (fri); Habitat (sat); Video Week (S); SoundLife (daily).

GENERAL MANAGEMENT

Publisher/President — Kelso Gillenwater
Director-Finance — Mike McKeller
Administrative Director — Steve Robinson
Administrative Services Manager — Harry Thacker
Exec Secretary — Laura Ficke

ADVERTISING

Director — Cathy J Brewis
Manager-Classified — Jacqueline Swant
Manager-Retail — Mike Klobuchar
Manager-National — Bob Shuckhart

MARKETING AND PROMOTION

Director-Marketing — Sara Long
Manager-Marketing/Promotion — Caroline McKee
Electronic Marketing Manager — Gary Smith

CIRCULATION

Director — Ronald Mladenich
Asst Director — Tara M Cady
Manager-Direct Delivery — Tanyalee Erwin

NEWS EXECUTIVES

Exec Editor — David A Zeeck
Editorial Page Editor — John D Komen
Senior Editor — Suki Dardarian
Senior Editor — Tom Osborne
Senior Editor-Sports — Glen Crevier

EDITORS AND MANAGERS

Business Editor — Christine Carson
Books Editor — Don Ruiz
Central/Tacoma Editor — Sandy Dunham
Chief Editorial Writer — David Seago
Education Reporter (Higher) — Cindy Brown
Education Reporter (Education K-12) — Susan Gordon
Entertainment Editor — Don Ruiz
Environmental Reporter — Sandi Doughton
Fashion/Style Editor — Don Ruiz
Films Critic — Soren Andersen
Food Editor — Gary Jasinek
Health/Medical Reporter — Caroline Ullmann
Chief Librarian — Toi Britton
Living/Lifestyle Editor — Gary Jasinek
Maritime Reporter — Al Gibbs
Director-Photography — Casey Madison
Political Editor — Michael Gilbert
Radio/Television Reporter — Don Ruiz
Real Estate Reporter — Jim Szymanski
Religion Reporter — Steve Maynard
Sports Editor — Glen Crevier
Suburban Editor — Lyn Watts
Travel Editor — Don Ruiz
Washington DC Reporter — Les Blumenthal

MANAGEMENT INFORMATION SERVICES

Data Processing Manager — John Dammeier

PRODUCTION

Director-Operations — Jeff Stalcup
Asst Director-Operations — Bob Evans
Manager-Composing Room — Jim Witter
Manager-Pressroom/Plateroom — Jerry Miller
Manager-Packaging — Joe Jovanovich

Market Information: Zoned editions; Split Run; TMC; ADS; Operate database; Operate audiotex; Electronic edition.
Mechanical available: Offset; Black and 3 ROP colors; insert accepted — preprinted, up to 22" x 13½"; single; page cut-offs — 22¾".
Mechanical specifications: Type page 13" x 21½"; E - 6 cols, 2¹⁄₁₆", ⅛" between; A - 6 cols, 2¹⁄₁₆", ⅛" between; C - 10 cols, 1¼", ¹⁄₁₆" between.
Commodity consumption: Newsprint 14,000 metric tons; widths 54", 40½", 27"; black ink 375,000 pounds; color ink 141,000 pounds; single pages printed 26,380; average pages per issue 58(d), 152(S); single plates used 132,000.
Equipment: EDITORIAL: Front-end hardware — 4-PC/386-33 server, 6-PC/486 server, 100-PC/386-16 workstation, 8-Ap/Mac Quadra, 16-Ap/Mac Centris; Front-end software — Dewar, QPS; Printers — Okidata/393, HP/LaserJet IV, Ap/Mac LaserWriters. CLASSIFIED: Front-end hardware — 1-SII/CLX-840; Front-end software — SII/Sys 55, Czar Costing, Decade/Coyote Emulator; Printers — 7-DEC/LA 75, 1-Printronix/600 LPM, 2-Printronix/300 LPM; Other equipment — 35-SII/Coyote, 15-CAT/30, 4-Echo, Compaq/DeskPro 386. AUDIOTEX: Hardware — 1-DEC/VAX 4705A, 128-MB/RAM, 2-RF/72, 1-RF/31, 1-B40/X, 1-DTC/N5, 11-DTC/05; Software — DEC/Voice, DEC/VAX C, AudioKit, DLB, I/D Express, GoldFax; Supplier name — TMS/VNN. DISPLAY: Adv layout systems — Cx/Ad Makeup, VP System, Ap/Mac System; Front-end hardware — Sun/IPC, Ap/Mac Quadra 700, Ap/Mac Quadra 800; Front-end software — Cx/Breeze, QuarkXPress; Printers — Cx. PRODUCTION: Typesetters — 5-Linotype-Hell/Linotronic 530; Plate exposures — 1-Theimer, 2-WL, 1-BTC/Ascor, 1-Nu/Flip Top FTUP; Plate processors — 2-WL/38; Scanners — Imagitex/500, ECR/Autokon 1000; Production cameras — 1-C/Marathon, 1-SCREEN/Vertical; Automatic film processors — 2-SCREEN, 5-LE; Film transporters — 1-C; Color separation equipment (conventional) — Diadem/220-420.
PRESSROOM: Line 1 — 20-G/Metro (10 half decks); Folders — 4-G/Metro 3:2; Pasters — 18-G; Reels and stands — 18-G. MAILROOM: Counter stackers — 6-HL, 6-QWI/301; Inserters and stuffers — 2-GMA/15-72, 2-GMA/SLS-1000A 24:2; Bundle tyer — 7-OVL/JP40, 3-OVL/JP80, 4-OVL/K101, 10-OVL/JP-40; Addressing machine — 10-OVL/JP-40; Mailroom control system — GMA/IPCS, GMA/GMS. LIBRARY: Electronic — Mead Data Central/Nexis NewsView. COMMUNICATIONS: Facsimile — AdSat. WIRE SERVICES: News — AP, NYT, LAT-WP, KRT, SHNS, McClatchy, GNS; Photos — AP, KRT, McClatchy; Stock tables — AP Stocks; Receiving dishes — AP, NYT. BUSINESS COMPUTERS: 1-DEC/VAX 8550, 1-DEC/VAX 6420, 1-DEC/VAX 3100, 1-DEC/VAX 3180; Applications: Microsoft/Word, Microsoft/Excel, Mail, Claris/File Maker Pro, CJ: Adv, Circ, Accts payable, Personnel, Ad layout, Transient, Class adv; PCs & micros networked; PCs & main system networked.

VANCOUVER

Clark County

'90 U.S. Census- 46,380; E&P '96 Est. 48,346
ABC-NDM (90): 238,053 (HH 88,440)

The Columbian (e-mon to fri; S)

The Columbian, 701 W. 8th St.; PO Box 180, Vancouver, WA 98666-0180; tel (360) 694-3391; fax (360) 737-4005; e-mail editors@columbian.com; web site http://www.columbian.com.
Circulation: 55,744(e); 65,799(S); ABC Sept. 30, 1995.
Price: 50¢(d); $1.50(S); $10.00/mo; $120.00/yr.
Advertising: Open inch rate $34.69(e); $40.48(S).
News Services: AP, LAT-WP. **Politics:** Independent. **Established:** 1890.
Advertising not accepted: Vending machines.
Special Editions: Health & Fitness (Jan); Auto Show, Portrait I, Portrait II, Portrait III (Feb); Cooking School, Home & Garden (Mar); Advertorial-Tour of Homes, Vacation (Apr); Home & Garden Idea Fair, Pet Section (May); Ft. Vancouver Days (June); Seniors (July); Clark County Fair, Parade of Homes, Back-to-School (Aug); Bridal, Clubs & Organizations, Wild West (Sept); Your Home, Restaurant Guide (Oct); Home for the Holidays (Nov, Dec).
Special Weekly Sections: Best Food Edition, Life, General (tues); Life/Discovery (Science) (wed); Life/Leisure/Neighbors (thur); Best Automotive Day, Entertainment & Movie Reviews (fri); Travel, Home (S); Business (daily).
Magazines: Entertainment Week (fri); USA Weekend, TV Times (own) (S).

CORPORATE OFFICERS

Chairman — Don Campbell
President — Scott Campbell
Secretary — Mason Nolan

GENERAL MANAGEMENT

Publisher — Scott Campbell
Vice Pres-Finance — Douglas Ness
Vice Pres-Marketing/Advertising — John McDonagh
Asst to Publisher — Shelley Arrington
Manager-Credit — Celeste Brower
Manager-Info Systems — Bill Peifer
Manager-Purchasing — Bill Case
Controller — Jerry Scobie

ADVERTISING

Vice Pres-Marketing — John McDonagh
Manager — Susan Hirtzel
Manager-Display — Mary Mitich
Manager-Classified — Rick Taylor
Manager-Marketing Service — Gary Dixon
Manager-Customer Service — David Sandvig

Copyright ©1996 by the Editor & Publisher Co.

Washington I-433

TELECOMMUNICATIONS

New Media Manager Ken Bilderback

CIRCULATION

Vice Pres/Director Marc Dailey
Manager-Dispatch Duane Buell
Manager-Customer Service/Office Manager Darlene Engstrom
Manager-Sales/Home Delivery Jim Cox
Manager-Promotion/Telemarketing Linda Braddock
Manager-Single Copy Sales/Motor Route Steve Schurkey
Manager-Zone Pam Hymas
Manager-Zone Jeff Lines
Manager-TMC/Alternate Delivery Joe Rehbein

NEWS EXECUTIVE

Vice Pres/Editor Tom Koenninger

EDITORS AND MANAGERS

Agriculture Editor Susan Farmer
Amusements Editor Dave Jewett
Automotive/Aviation Editor Tom Ryll
Books Editor Dave Jewett
Business Editor Julia Anderson
Community Editor Julia Anderson
Editorial Page Editor D Michael Heywood
Editorial Writer Mike Zuzel
Education Editor Tom Vogt
Environmental Editor Loretta Callahan
Fashion/Style Editor Angela Allen
Features Editor Dave Kern
Films/Theater Editor Dave Jewett
Food Editor Angela Allen
Graphics Editor Janet Cleaveland
Health/Medical Editor Bob Sisson
Living/Lifestyle Editor Dave Kern
Music/Drama Editor Lynn Matthews
News Editor Janet Cleaveland
Photo Editor Kevin Clark
Political Editor Sherri Nee
Radio/Television Editor Joanne Harris
Radio/Television Editor Dave Jewett
Real Estate Editor Susan Farmer
Religion Editor Brian Willoughby
Science/Technology Editor Loretta Callahan
Sports/Leisure Editor Don Chandler
Travel Editor R Mike Bailey
Wire Editor Pam Geisinger
Women's Editor Dave Kern

MANAGEMENT INFORMATION SERVICES

Data Processing Manager Bill Peifer

PRODUCTION

Manager-Distribution Center Ed Bell
Manager-Camera Room John Roberts
Manager-Pressroom Dale Lancaster

Market Information: Zoned editions; TMC; Operate audiotex; Electronic edition.

Mechanical available: Offset; Black and 3 ROP colors; insert accepted — preprinted; page cutoffs — 22¾".

Mechanical specifications: Type page 12.58" x 22¾"; E - 5 cols, 2½", ⅙" between; A - 6 cols, 2.04", ⅙" between; C - 9 cols, 1.4", 1/18" between.

Commodity consumption: Newsprint 5,464 short tons; 4,957 metric tons; widths 55", 41¼", 27½"; black ink 149,394 pounds; color ink 27,274 pounds; single pages printed 20,475; average pages per issue 40(d), 74(S); single plates used 39,880.

Equipment: EDITORIAL: Front-end hardware — AST/486, 24-AST/PC workstation, Ap/Power Mac, Ap/Mac workstations; Front-end software — QuarkXPress 3.31, Quick Wire 2.2; Printers — QMS/410 Laser Printer, AU/APS-108 Imager, HP/Laser; Other equipment — Sharp/600 scanner, Lf/AP Leaf Picture Desk. CLASSIFIED: Front-end hardware — AST/486, AST/PC workstations, Ap/Mac workstations, Sun, Cybergraphics/Genesis II; Front-end software — Cybergraphics; Printers — DEC/LA 180, Brother/HLIOVPS. AUDIOTEX: Hardware — Micro Voice, U.S. Telecom. DISPLAY: Adv layout systems — SCS/Layout 8000; Front-end hardware — Ap/Power Mac; Front-end software — Ap/Mac System 7.1, Multi-Ad/Creator 3.7; Printers — 2-AU/APS6 108C, 1-AU/APS BroadSheeter; Other equipment — X/7650 scanner, CD-Rom. PRODUCTION: Pagination software — QuarkXPress, Cybergraphic; Typesetters — 2-AU/APS-6-108C; Plate exposures — Nu/Flip Top FTNOAPRNS; Plate processors — WL/38D, 3M/1133; Electronic picture desk — Lf/AP Leaf Picture Desk, Ap/Mac Archive; Scanners — ECR/Autokon 2030, Sharp/600, DTS/1030 AI, X/7650, Nikon/LS-3510 AF; Production cameras — C/Marathon, 1-C/Spartan; Automatic film processors — Kk/24", Kk/710, P/26"; Film transporters — C; Shrink lenses — Alan; Color separation equipment (conventional) — Ap/Mac System, Adobe/Photoshop; Digital color separation equipment — 1-X/7650, DS/America, Nikon. PRESSROOM: Line 1 — 6-G/Metro; Line 2 — 11-G/SSC; Folders — 2-G/Metro 2:1, 1-G/SSC; Pasters — 2-MEG, 6-G; Reels and stands — 4-G/SSC; Press control system — Fin. MAILROOM: Counter stackers — 2-MM/259, 2-BG/105; Inserters and stuffers — 4-MM/227-E; Bundle tyer — 4-MLN/2-A, 2-MCD/700-L, 1-MLN/ML2EE, 2-Ca/TM-36; Addressing machine — 1-MG/602-50. LIBRARY: Electronic — NewsView. WIRE SERVICES: News — AP Datastream, AP Datafeatures; Stock tables — AP SelectStox; Syndicates — LATS; Receiving dishes — AP. BUSINESS COMPUTERS: 2-DEC/1170, PBS; Applications: Gen ledger, Accts payable, Accts receivable, Payroll, Billing, Inventory, Class bus, Adv Bus; PCs & micros networked; PCs & main system networked.

WALLA WALLA

Walla Walla County

'90 U.S. Census- 26,478; E&P '96 Est. 26,941
ABC-CZ (90): 36,749 (HH 13,649)

Walla Walla Union-Bulletin

(e-mon to fri; S)

Walla Walla Union-Bulletin, 1st & Poplar Sts., Walla Walla, WA 99362; tel (509) 525-3300. Seattle Times Co. group.

Circulation: 15,614(e); 16,511(S); ABC Sept. 30, 1995.

Price: 50¢(d); $1.00(S); $8.50/mo; $102.00/yr (carrier), $162.00/yr (mail).

Advertising: Open inch rate $15.08(e); $15.08(S).

News Service: AP. **Politics:** Independent. **Established:** 1869.

Not Published: Christmas.

Advertising not accepted: Tobacco.

Special Editions: Feature (Feb); On the Grow (Sept).

Special Weekly Sections: Best Food Day (tues); Your Time (thur); Panorama, Religion, Prospective (S).

Magazines: Your Time-TV/Entertainment Magazine (fri); USA Weekend (S).

CORPORATE OFFICER

Board Chairman F A Blethen

GENERAL MANAGEMENT

Publisher Charles C Cochrane Jr
Personnel Manager Norma Austin

ADVERTISING

Manager Carl Tyler

TELECOMMUNICATIONS

Audiotex Manager John Czarnecki

CIRCULATION

Manager Ken Hatch

NEWS EXECUTIVE

Managing Editor Rick Doyle

EDITORS AND MANAGERS

Editorial Page Editor Rick Eskil
Education Editor Richard Clayton
Food Editor Lana Brown
Librarian Janet Collins
News Editor Bob Crider
Political Editor Becky Kramer
Radio/Television Editor Lana Brown
Real Estate Editor Bryan Corliss
Sports Editor Jim Buchan

MANAGEMENT INFORMATION SERVICES

Data Processing Manager Ken Hatch

PRODUCTION

Manager-Pressroom John Partlow

Market Information: TMC; ADS; Operate audiotex.

Mechanical available: Offset; Black and 3 ROP colors; insert accepted — preprinted; page cutoffs — 22¾".

Mechanical specifications: Type page 13⅛" x 21½"; E - 6 cols, 2 1/16", ⅛" between; A - 6 cols, 2 1/16", ⅛" between; C - 9 cols, 1⅜", 1/16" between.

Commodity consumption: Newsprint 843 short tons; widths 28", 14"; black ink 22,500 pounds; color ink 3,400 pounds; single pages printed 8,968; average pages per issue 26(d), 42(S); single plates used 13,680.

Equipment: EDITORIAL: Front-end hardware — PC; Front-end software — Dewar. CLASSIFIED: Front-end hardware — PC; Front-end software — Dewar. AUDIOTEX: Hardware — PC; Software — Repartee. DISPLAY: Adv layout systems — Dewar/Ad Dummy; Front-end hardware — PC; Front-end software — Dewar/Discovery; Other equipment — X/Scanner. PRODUCTION: Typesetters — 1-V/5100, 1-V/5500; Plate exposures — 1-Nu; Plate processors — Nat; Scanners — CD/626; Production cameras — 1-C/Marathon, SCREEN; Automatic film processors — 1-LE; Color separation equipment (conventional) — CD/626; Digital color separation equipment — CD/626. PRESSROOM: Line 1 — 5-G/Urbanite; Folders — 1-G. MAILROOM: Inserters and stuffers — 1-MM (4 heads); Bundle tyer — 1-MLN. LIBRARY: Electronic — NewsView. WIRE SERVICES: News — AP Datastream, AP Datafeatures, AP Photo; Receiving dishes — size-3m, AP. BUSINESS COMPUTERS: 1-HP/3000; Applications: CJ: Adv, Circ, Payroll, Accts payable, Gen ledger; PCs & micros networked; PCs & main system networked.

WENATCHEE

Chelan County

'90 U.S. Census- 21,756; E&P '96 Est. 24,506
ABC-CZ (90): 39,216 (HH 15,506)

The Wenatchee World

(e-mon to fri; S)

The Wenatchee World, 14 N. Mission St.; PO Box 1511, Wenatchee, WA 98807-1511; tel (509) 663-5161; fax (509) 662-5413.

Circulation: 28,670(e); 31,827(S); ABC Sept. 30, 1995.

Price: 50¢(d); $1.25(S).

Advertising: Open inch rate $20.65(e); $20.65(S).

News Service: AP. **Politics:** Independent. **Established:** 1905.

Not Published: Christmas.

Advertising not accepted: Alcoholic beverages.

Special Editions: Brides (Jan); Home Improvement (Feb); Annual Report, Spring Fashions (Mar); Fishing (Apr); Car Care, Visitor's Guide (May); Summer Recipe Guide (July); Fairtime (Sept); Car Care, Home Furnishings (Oct); Winter Sports (Nov); Horticulture Convention, Gift Guide (Dec); Seasons 'For Senior Citizens', Ag World (monthly).

Special Weekly Sections: Food Section (tues); People Pages, Arts/Entertainment (thur); Religion (fri); People Section, Brides (S).

Magazines: Kiosk Entertainment Tab (thur); TV World, USA Weekend (S).

CORPORATE OFFICERS

President Wilfred R Woods
Vice Pres Katherine T Woods
Secretary Kathleen K Woods
Treasurer Robert W Woods

GENERAL MANAGEMENT

Publisher Wilfred R Woods
Assoc Publisher Robert W Woods
General Manager Ken Hunnicutt
Controller James Beam
Purchasing Agent/Credit Manager Nancy Dahlen

ADVERTISING

Director Jay White
Manager-Classified Gary Montague
Manager-Display Gary Phippen
Manager-Display Matt Kearny

MARKETING AND PROMOTION

Manager-Promotion/Education Service Linda Murphy

TELECOMMUNICATIONS

Audiotex Manager Matt Kearny

CIRCULATION

Director Linda Murphy

NEWS EXECUTIVE

Editor Rufus Woods

EDITORS AND MANAGERS

Business Editor Steve Maher
City Editor Steve Lachowicz
Consumer Interest Editor Dee Riggs
Editorial Page Editor Cromwell Warner
Education Editor Dan Wheat
Entertainment Editor Dave Kraft
Farm Editor Rick Steigmeyer
Fashion Editor Sheila Trimble
Films/Theater Editor Dave Kraft
Food Editor Kathleen Gilstras
Librarian Linda Barta
Photographer Don Seabrook
Political Editor Dan Wheat
Radio/Television Editor Mari Lindgreen
Real Estate Editor Steve Maher
Regional Editor Mary Barham
Religion Editor Kathleen Gilstras
Science/Technology Editor Rick Steigmeyer
Society/Women's Editor Dee Riggs
Sports Editor Nick Babcock
Travel Editor Rufus Woods
Wire Editor John Moffat

PRODUCTION

Foreman-Composing William McGaughey
Foreman-Pressroom Bob Koenig
Foreman-Packaging David Graybill

Market Information: Zoned editions; ADS; Operate database; Operate audiotex.

Mechanical available: Offset; Black and 3 ROP colors; insert accepted — preprinted; page cutoffs — 22¾".

Mechanical specifications: Type page 13" x 21½"; E - 6 cols, 2 1/16", ⅛" between; A - 6 cols, 2 1/16", ⅛" between; C - 8 cols, 1 9/16", 1/16" between.

Commodity consumption: Newsprint 1,600 metric tons; widths 30", 27", 13½"; black ink 52,500 pounds; color ink 8,200 pounds; single pages printed 13,000; average pages per issue 30(d), 40(S); single plates used 24,000.

Equipment: EDITORIAL: Front-end hardware — Dewar/Sys IV, 43-Pagination workstation, 1-Ap/Mac, 1-Compaq/Proliant fileserver; Front-end software — Dewar/Sys IV, XYQUEST/XyWrite 6.50; Printers — 4-Okidata/Line Printer, 2-HP/LaserJet; Other equipment — Telecopier. CLASSIFIED: Front-end hardware — 1-Dewar/Sys IV, 1-Compaq/Proliant Fileserver; Front-end software — Dewar/Sys IV 6.94; Printers — 1-Image Writer, 1-Okidata/Line Printer; Other equipment — 1-Ap/Mac II. AUDIOTEX: Software — Info-Connect/Pottsville Republican, Info-Connect, V.I.S. DISPLAY: Adv layout systems — 1-Dewar/Sys IV, 3-Dewar/286, 1-Dewar/386, 3-Ap/Mac; Front-end software — Dewar/Sys IV, QuarkXPress; Printers — 1-Okidata/Printer, 1-Dataproducts/Line Printer. PRODUCTION: Pagination software — Dewar/Sys IV; OCR software — Caere/Omni-Page OCR; Typesetters — 3-Xante/Accel-a-Writer 8100; Plate exposures — 1-Nu/Flip Top 40UPN, 1-Nu/Flip Top FT40APRNS; Plate processors — WL/Plater 30D; Electronic picture desk — Lf/AP Leaf Picture Desk; Scanners — Microtek/300Z Scanner, ECR/Autokon 1000N, Ap/Mac Interface, 1-Microtek/600Z Scanner, 2-Ap/Mac, 1-Nikon/Slide Scanner; Production cameras — 1-C/Spartan II, 1-K/V-241, ECR/Autokon 8400, AG/Autokon Newgraphic 1000; Automatic film processors — 1-LE/LD-24, AG/Rapidline 66; Film transporters — 1-C; Color separation equipment (conventional) — RZ/4050E. PRESSROOM: Line 1 — 7-G/848 single width; Folders — 1-G; Pasters — 4-Webeq/Webquip. MAILROOM: Counter stackers — 1-BG/Count-O-Veyor 106, 1-BG/Count-O-Veyor 108; Inserters and stuffers — 1-MM/227S, 2-MM/227E; Bundle tyer — 3-MLN/2EE; Wrapping singles — 1-MM/1509; Other mailroom equipment — 1-MM/1509 Stitcher-Trimmer, 2-CH/Bottom Wrap. LIBRARY: Electronic — 1-Mead Data Central/Nexis NewsView. WIRE SERVICES: News — AP; Receiving dishes — size-10m, AP. BUSINESS COMPUTERS: 1-IBM/AS-400; Applications: Transient class, Circ, Adv billing, Accts receivable, Gen ledger, Payroll; PCs & main system networked.

YAKIMA

Yakima County

'90 U.S. Census- 54,827; E&P '96 Est. 57,628
ABC-CZ (90): 87,662 (HH 34,187)

Yakima Herald-Republic

(m-mon to sat; S)

Yakima Herald-Republic, 114 N. 4th St.; PO Box 9668, Yakima, WA 98909; tel (509) 248-1251. Seattle Times Co. group.

Circulation: 41,108(m); 41,108(m-sat); 43,464(S); ABC Sept. 30, 1995.

Price: 50¢(d); 50¢(sat); $1.25(S); $9.50/mo; $144.00/yr (carrier), $129.00/yr (mail).

Advertising: Open inch rate $29.00(m); $29.00(m-sat); $29.00(S). **Representative:** Landon Associates Inc.

News Services: AP, KRT. **Politics:** Independent. **Established:** 1903.

Advertising not accepted: Accepted by advance approval only.

Special Editions: Baby Album (Jan); Bridal Fair, Annual (Feb); Home Show, Spring Home/Garden, Ag Today (Mar); Car Care (Apr); Seniors, CW Visitors, Ag Today, Air Fair (May); Antiques, Ag Today (July); Ag Today, CW Fair (Sept); Fall Home (Oct); Holiday Gift Guide (Nov, Dec).

Special Weekly Sections: Business News, Extra! (Community News) (tues); Best Food Section, Valley Shopper (wed); Venture/Outdoor (thur); Agriculture, Farm & Garden, Entertainment (fri); Religious News, Wheels, Home (sat); Business News, Travel (S); TV Page (daily).

Magazine: Parade (S).

I-434 Washington

GENERAL MANAGEMENT

Publisher James E Barnhill
Director-Operations Jack McAfee
Director-Human Resources Kay Gause

ADVERTISING

Director Brian Vaillancourt
Manager-Sales Rob Bickler

TELECOMMUNICATIONS

Audiotex Manager Beth Wilbanks

CIRCULATION

Director Jim Thomas

NEWS EXECUTIVES

Editor L Dan Coleman
Managing Editor-Production/Administration Tom Fluharty
Managing Editor-News/Features Kathleen Gilligan

EDITORS AND MANAGERS

Business/Finance Editor Brier Dudley
City Editor Spencer Hatton
Editorial Page Editor Bill Lee
Features Editor Joye Redfield
Entertainment/Amusements Editor Terry Campbell
Farm/Agriculture Editor Dave Lester
Fashion/Style Editor Karen Troianello
Films/Theater Editor Terry Campbell
Food Editor Terry Campbell
Librarian Donean Sinsel
Living/Lifestyle Editor Karen Troianello
News Editor Bill Epperheimer
Political/Real Estate Editor Spencer Hatton
Radio/Television Editor Liggett Taylor
Sports Editor Jim Scoggins
Women's Editor Joye Redfield
Women's Editor Karen Troianello

MANAGEMENT INFORMATION SERVICES

Data Processing Manager Mike Beach

PRODUCTION

Foreman-Pressroom Billy Wolfe
Foreman-Mailroom Donn Hinkle

Market Information: TMC; Operate audiotex.

Mechanical available: Offset; Black and 3 ROP colors; insert accepted — preprinted; page cut-offs — 22¾".

Mechanical specifications: Type page 13" x 21½"; E - 6 cols, $2\frac{1}{16}$", ⅛" between; A - 6 cols, $2\frac{1}{16}$", ⅛" between; C - 9 cols, ⅜", $\frac{3}{32}$" between.

Commodity consumption: Newsprint 3,637 short tons; 3,300 metric tons; widths 27½", 13¾"; black ink 102,000 pounds; color ink 18,500 pounds; single pages printed 14,400; average pages per issue 36(d), 48(S); single plates used 21,200.

Equipment: EDITORIAL: Front-end hardware — Dewar, V; Front-end software — Dewar, V; Other equipment — Ap/Mac. CLASSIFIED: Front-end hardware — Dewar, V; Front-end software — Dewar, V. DISPLAY: Adv layout systems — 3-Dewar/Discovery; Front-end hardware — 3-Dewar/Discovery; Front-end software — Dewar. PRODUCTION: Pagination software — Dewar/V; Typesetters — 2-V/Imagesetter; Plate exposures — 1-BKY/SKW; Plate processors — 1-Nat/A-340; Production cameras — 1-C/Marathon, 1-R/Vertical, 1-ATF/Horizontal; Automatic film processors — 1-LE/24BQ. PRESSROOM: Line 1 — 14-G/Urbanite; Folders — 2-G/2:1; Press control system — Fin; Press registration system — Duarte. MAILROOM: Counter stackers — QWI/300; Inserters and stuffers — 2-MM/227; Bundle tyer — 1-MLN/ML2EE, 1-MLN/2A; Addressing machine — 1-KR/215. WIRE SERVICES: News — AP, KRT; Stock tables — AP; Receiving dishes — AP. BUSINESS COMPUTERS: HP/937 XL; Applications: Circ, Adv, Accts receivable, Accts payable, Gen ledger; PCs & micros networked.

WEST VIRGINIA

BECKLEY

Raleigh County

'90 U.S. Census- 18,296; **E&P '96 Est.** 16,912
ABC-NDM (90): 215,064 (HH 82,013)

The Register-Herald

(m-mon to sat; S)

The Register Herald, 801 N. Kanawha St. (25801); PO Box P or R, Beckley, WV 25802; tel (304) 255-4400; fax (304) 255-4427; e-mail bnpaper@aol.com. Thomson Newspapers group.

Circulation: 31,948(m); 31,948(m-sat); 33,727(S); ABC Sept. 30, 1995.

Price: 50¢(d); 50¢(sat); $1.25(S); $11.95/mo; $143.40/yr.

Advertising: Open inch rate $22.81(m); $22.81(m-sat); $22.81(S). **Representative:** Landon Associates Inc.

News Service: AP. **Politics:** Independent. **Established:** 1880 (Raleigh Register), 1900 (Post Herald).

Special Editions: Tax Guide; Social Security; Spring Fashion; Spring Home Improvement; Spring New Car Care; Brides; Vacation Guide; Super Bowl; Black History; Graduation; Beauty & Fitness; Back-to-School; Football; Fall Fashion; Fall Home Improvement; Progress; Hunting; Fall Car Care; Cookbook; Christmas; Fall New Car; Ski West Virginia; Basketball; On Track; Health & Medical.

Special Weekly Sections: Mini Page, School (mon); Best Food Day (wed); Teen, TV Guide (fri); Church Page (sat); Lifestyles (S).

Magazine: USA Weekend Comics (S).

GENERAL MANAGEMENT

Publisher Robert R Hammond
Business Manager Drema Radford
Director-Operations R E (Bob) Zutaut

ADVERTISING

Director-Operations Jack L Scott
Manager-Classified Diana Slone

TELECOMMUNICATIONS

Systems Manager Jeff Stover

CIRCULATION

Director Robert J Binkley
Asst Director Eddie Bragg

NEWS EXECUTIVE

Exec Editor Dan Page

EDITORS AND MANAGERS

City Editor Pat Hanna
Editorial Page Editor Dan Page
Entertainment/Amusements Editor Judy Karbonit
Features Editor Bev Davis
Health/Medical Editor Dawn Keys
News Editor Mike Friel
Photo Editor Rick Barbero
Radio/Television Editor Judy Karbonit
Sports Editor David Morrison
Women's Editor Bev Davis

MANAGEMENT INFORMATION SERVICES

Data Processing Manager Drema Radford

PRODUCTION

Manager R E (Bob) Zutaut
Manager-Pressroom George Johnson

Market Information: Zoned editions; Split Run; TMC.

Mechanical available: Offset; Black and 3 ROP colors; insert accepted — preprinted; page cut-offs — 22¾".

Mechanical specifications: Type page 13" x 21¾"; E - 6 cols, $2\frac{1}{16}$", ⅛" between; A - 6 cols, $2\frac{1}{16}$", ⅛" between; C - 9 cols, $1\frac{11}{32}$", $\frac{1}{16}$" between.

Commodity consumption: average pages per issue 24(d), 44(S).

Equipment: EDITORIAL: Front-end hardware — CText, DEC, Ap/Power Mac 8100-00; Front-end software — CText, QuarkXPress 3.31r5; Printers — 2-Tegra/Varityper 5100e; Other equipment — 1-Tegra/Varityper 6990, 2-Panther/Pro 36. CLASSIFIED: Front-end hardware — CText, DEC/486; Front-end software — CText, CText/ALPS Pagination; Printers — 2-Tegra/Varityper 5100e, 1-Tegra/Varityper 6990, 2-Panther/Pro 36. DISPLAY: Adv layout systems — 5-Ap/Mac Centris 650; Front-end hardware — 1-Ap/Mac LC III; Front-end software — Microsoft/Word, Multi-Ad/Creator, QuarkXPress, Adobe/Photoshop, Aldus/Free-Hand; Printers — Tegra/Varityper 5100e, 1-Tegra/Varityper 6990, 2-Panther/Pro 36. PRODUCTION: Pagination software — CText, QuarkXPress 3.31r5; OCR software — OmniScan 2.1; Typesetters — 2-Tegra/Varityper 5100e Laserprinter, 1-Tegra/Varityper 6990 Laser; Plate exposures — 1-BKY, 1-Nu; Plate processors — W; Electronic picture desk — 2-Lf/AP Leaf Picture Desk; Scanners — 2-Lf/Leafscan 35, 2-AG/Arcus Plus Flatbed; Production cameras — C/Spartan III, C/Newspager; Automatic film processors — 2-LE/Screen 220 QT; Film transporters — LE; Digital color separation equipment — Ap/Mac Quadra 950, Ap/Power Mac 6100, Ap/Power Mac 8100-100. PRESSROOM: Line 1 — 10-G/Urbanite; Folders — 1-G; Press control system — Fin; Press registration system — Duarte. MAILROOM: Counter stackers — 1-Id; Inserters and stuffers — GMA/9 pockets, MM/7 pockets; Wrapping singles — St; Addressing machine — Chegier. COMMUNICATIONS: Digital ad delivery system — AP AdSend. WIRE SERVICES: News — AP, THO; Photos — AP; Stock tables — AP SelectStox; Receiving dishes — size-14ft, AP. BUSINESS COMPUTERS: IBM/AS 400; PCs & micros networked; PCs & main system networked.

BLUEFIELD, WV-VA

Mercer County, WV/Tazewell, VA

'90 U.S. Census- 18,119 (Bluefield, WV 12,756; Bluefield, VA 5,363); **E&P '96 Est.** 15,907 (Bluefield, WV 10,820; Bluefield, VA 5,087)
ABC-NDM (90): 191,672 (HH 72,533)

Bluefield Daily Telegraph

(m-mon to sat; S)

Bluefield Daily Telegraph, 928 Bluefield Ave.; PO Box 1599, Bluefield, WV 24701; tel (304) 327-2811. Thomson Newspapers group.

Circulation: 22,856(m); 22,856(m-sat); 25,417(S); ABC Sept. 30, 1995.

Price: 50¢(d); 50¢(sat); $1.25(S); $10.75/mo; $129.00/yr.

Advertising: Open inch rate $22.83(m); $22.83(m-sat); $22.95(S). **Representative:** Landon Associates Inc.

News Services: AP, Scripps Howard News Digest. **Politics:** Independent. **Established:** 1896.

Special Editions: Tax Guide, Super Bowl, Health & Fitness, Employee of the Year, Baby of the Year (Jan); Discount Book, Brides, Senior Citizens, Chamber of Commerce, Valentine Love (Feb); Progress, Spring Fashions, April Fools, Lawn & Garden, St. Patrick's Day, First Day of Spring (Mar); Indoor/Outdoor, Better Living, Spring Car Care, April Sales Catalog, Easter Bargain, Bluefield Chamber, Drug Tab (Apr); Mother's Day, Graduation, Mt. Festival, Swimsuit Issue, Nat'l Hospital, Fish Tales (May); Father's Day, Summerfest, Bridal, NASCAR, Summer Fun (June); Furniture & Fixin's, Vacation Specials, Business Profiles, Customer Appreciation, Super Shopper Sale (July); Mall Back-to-School, Golf Tab, Football, Women's Health Week, School Preview (Aug); Coal, Home Improvement, Fall Fashion, Cooking School, Drug Tab, Tazewell Co. Fair (Sept); Women in the Area, Car Care, Cosmetology, Early X'mas Guide, Substance & Child Abuse (Oct); Mall Anniversary, Electronics, Winter Sports, Holiday Lifestyles, Holiday Recipes (Nov); Holiday Cookbook, Dear Santa, Shopping Spree, Last Minute Gifts, Bowl Section, X'mas with Us (Dec).

Special Weekly Sections: Medley (fri); Sports (sat).

Magazines: TV Weekly (in-house) (fri); Sports Day (sat); USA Weekend (S).

GENERAL MANAGEMENT

Publisher Steve Smith

ADVERTISING

Director Terri Hale

CIRCULATION

Director Bobby English

NEWS EXECUTIVE

Exec Editor Tom Colley

EDITORS AND MANAGERS

Business Editor Teresa Cutlip
City Editor Barbara Hawkins
Columnist Barbara Hawkins
Education Editor Barbara Hawkins
Entertainment/Amusements Editor Samantha Perry
Fashion/Style Editor Samantha Perry
Living/Lifestyle Editor Samantha Perry
News Editor Melody Kinser
Photo Editor Melody Kinser
Real Estate Editor Teresa Cutlip
Special Projects Editor Jim Terry
Sports Editor Teddy Paynter
WV Desk Editor Barbara Hawkins
Women's Editor Samantha Perry

MANAGEMENT INFORMATION SERVICES

Data Processing Manager Leigh McVey

PRODUCTION

Manager-Operations Henry Meade
Foreman-Composing Michelle Williams
Foreman-Camera Henry Meade
Foreman-Mailroom Ray Sutphin

Market Information: TMC.

Mechanical available: Offset; Black and 3 ROP colors; insert accepted — preprinted, spadea wrap; page cut-offs — 22¾".

Mechanical specifications: Type page 13" x 21½"; E - 6 cols, $2\frac{1}{16}$", ⅛" between; A - 6 cols, $2\frac{1}{16}$", ⅛" between; C - 9 cols, ⅜", $\frac{1}{11}$" between.

Commodity consumption: Newsprint 1,400 short tons; widths 55", 41¼", 27½"; black ink 69,000 pounds; color ink 6,000 pounds; single pages printed 10,663; average pages per issue 24(d), 44(S); single plates used 32,988.

Equipment: EDITORIAL: Front-end hardware — 1-CText/ASFM, 25-EKI/Televideo; Front-end software — CText 6.08B; Printers — V/5100E, V/5300E. CLASSIFIED: Front-end hardware — 3-EKI/Televideo; Front-end software — CText. DISPLAY: Adv layout systems — Ap/Mac; Front-end hardware — 3-Ap/Mac IIci, 2-Ap/Mac Quadra 950; Front-end software — Multi-Ad/Creator; Printers — 2-V/5100, 1-V/5300E. PRODUCTION: Typesetters — 2-V/5100, 1-V/5300E; Plate exposures — 1-Nu/Flip Top FT40V3PNS, 1-Nu/Flip Top FT40VPNS; Plate processors — 1-Nat/250; Scanners — AG/Arcus, Lf/Leafscan 35, 1-Epson/GT-6500; Production cameras — C/Spartan III, SCREEN/C-680C; Automatic film processors — LE/LD-24, SCREEN/LD-220; Digital color separation equipment — AG/Arcus, Lf/Leafscan 35. PRESSROOM: Line 1 — 5-G/Cosmo; Folders — 2-G. MAILROOM: Counter stackers — HL/2; Inserters and stuffers — MM/2; Bundle tyer — 2-Power Strap. COMMUNICATIONS: Facsimile — 2-Fujitsu/DEX-170. WIRE SERVICES: News — AP Dataspeed, AP Datafeatures, SHNS, THO; Photos — AP; Syndicates — Universal Press, King Features, NAT, LATS, United Features; Receiving dishes — size-12ft, AP. BUSINESS COMPUTERS: 7-ATT/3B25100; Applications: PCs & micros networked; PCs & main system networked.

CHARLESTON

Kanawha County

'90 U.S. Census- 57,287; **E&P '96 Est.** 53,534
ABC-CZ (90): 88,240 (HH 38,589)

Charleston Newspapers

Charleston Newspapers, 1001 Virginia St. E., Charleston, WV 25301; tel (304) 348-5140; fax (304) 348-5133.

Representative: Cresmer, Woodward, O'Mara & Ormsbee.

Note: Charleston Newspapers is a joint operating agency for the Charleston Gazette and Charleston Daily Mail and performs business, advertising, circulation, production and printing functions for the two papers, which are corporately and editorially separate. The Sunday Gazette-Mail is published jointly by the two corporations through the joint operating agency.

Special Editions: Bridal (Jan); Forecast (Feb); Parenting (Mar); Home & Garden, Earth Day, Spring Car Care, Spring Super Styles (Apr); Graduation (May); So. Living Cooking School (June); Health & Fitness, Financial Planning (July); Regatta, Dance, Football (Aug); Hunting (Sept); Fall Car Care (Nov).

Special Weekly Sections: Business (tues); Food (wed); Weekend Entertainment (thur); Travel (S).

Magazines: NASCAR Race Magazine (Feb-Nov); FlipSide (teen publication) (monthly); Heritage (Senior citizens magazine) (1st tues, bi-monthly); Health File (Health magazine); Accent on Women (Women's magazine) (quarterly).

CORPORATE OFFICERS

President/General Manager Jack A Findley
Vice Pres/Treasurer David W Zinn
Vice Pres-Advertising Larry Levak

GENERAL MANAGEMENT

Director-Human Resources John F Bowyer

ADVERTISING

Manager-National Mike Morris
Manager-Retail Mac Bibbee
Manager-Classified Renae Roberts
Manager-Co-op Mike Morris

MARKETING AND PROMOTION

Director-Marketing Carolyn Perry

TELECOMMUNICATIONS

Audiotex Manager Sally R Snyder

CIRCULATION

Director Jeff Jobe
Manager-Home Delivery Bill Williams

MANAGEMENT INFORMATION SERVICES

Director Diana Morris
Online Manager Carolyn Perry

PRODUCTION

Director Richard Meek
Manager-Composing Paul Kelly
Manager-Camera/Platemaking Bill Plaster
Manager-Mailroom Kenneth Adkins

Copyright ©1996 by the Editor & Publisher Co.

West Virginia I-435

Manager-Ad Service — Maurice G Trail
Manager-Pressroom — Paul Ennis

Market Information: Zoned editions; Split Run; TMC; Operate database; Operate audiotex.
Mechanical available: Offset; Black and 3 ROP colors; insert accepted — preprinted, photo processor envelopes; page cut-offs — 22¾".
Mechanical specifications: Type page 13" x 21¾"; E - 6 cols, 2 1/16", 1/8" between; A - 6 cols, 2 1/16", 1/8" between; C - 9 cols, 1 3/8", 1/16" between.
Commodity consumption: Newsprint 9,950 short tons; widths 55", 41⅛", 27⅜"; black ink 220,000 pounds; color ink 100,000 pounds; single pages printed 29,300; average pages per issue 30(d), 84(S); single plates used 96,000.
Equipment: EDITORIAL: Front-end hardware — IBM/4341, 100-IBM/VP 486SX-25, 20-IBM/VP 486DX2-66, 4-IBM/PS-2 Model 95, Novell/Netware; Front-end software — IBM/Printext, ESE/TBase; Printers — Epson/DFX5000, HP/LaserJet IIIsi; Other equipment — Ap/Mac Quadra 700, Ap/Power Mac 7100. CLASSIFIED: Front-end hardware — 2-CompuAdd/486 File Server, 10-CompuAdd/386 PC; Front-end software — PPI/Tecs 2 Classified. AUDIOTEX: Hardware — Brite Voice Systems/2000; Software — Brite Voice Systems 3.12E; DISPLAY: Adv layout systems — SCS/Layout 8000, IBM/PS-2 Model 56; Front-end hardware — IBM/AS-400 300; Front-end software — Admarc 6.4; Printers — Decision Data/6714, Decision Data/6010. PRODUCTION: Pagination software — QuarkXPress 3.3; Typesetters — 2-III/3810 Image Setters, 3-Panther/Pro 46; Platemaking systems — 2-AU/APS-5 Typesetter-, 1-MAS/Plate Processor, 2-Nu; Plate processors — 2-Enco/Enomatic; Electronic picture desk — Lf/AP Leaf Picture Desk; Scanners — 2-III/3650-3750, Nikon/3510 AF, HP/ScanJet 3P, Nikon/ScanTouch; Production cameras — 3-K, 1-KI, 1-C; Automatic film processors — 2-LE; Color separation equipment (conventional) — Diadem/220S.
PRESSROOM: Line 1 — 11-G/Metro; Line 2 — 4-Didde/Apollo MCP; Press drives — Fin; Folders — 3-G/3:2; Pasters — 11-G; Reels and stands — 11-G. MAILROOM: Counter stackers — 7-QWI, Inserters and stuffers — 1-Sh/1372, 1-HI/1472, 1-KR/6 pos. w/Labeler; Bundle tyer — 3-MLN, 2-Bu; Wrapping singles — 2-St. LIBRARY: Electronic — 2-IBM/PS-2 Model 95 File Servers; Combination — NewsView. COMMUNICATIONS: Facsimile — Ricoh/Fax 60. WIRE SERVICES: News — AP; Photos — AP; Stock tables — AP; Syndicates — AP, NYT, LAT-WP; Receiving dishes — AP. BUSINESS COMPUTERS: 2-IBM/4341, 1-IBM/AS-400, IBM/RISC 6000; Applications: PBS 2.5: Circ; JD Edwards: Gen ledger, Accts payable, Payroll; PCs & micros networked; PCs & main sys tem networked.

Charleston Gazette
(m-mon to sat)
Sunday Gazette-Mail (S)

The Charleston Gazette, Sunday Gazette-Mail, 1001 Virginia St. E., Charleston, WV 25301; tel (304) 348-5140; fax (304) 348-5133.
Circulation: 53,686(m); 53,686(m-sat); 107,045(S); ABC Sept. 30, 1995.
Price: 50¢(d); 50¢(sat); $1.50(S); $14.30/mo; $117.00/yr.
Advertising: Open inch rate $58.70(m); $58.70(m-sat); $65.25(S); comb with Charleston Daily Mail (eS) $64.00.
News Services: NYT, AP. **Politics:** Independent-Democrat. **Established:** 1873.
Note: For detailed general management, business personnel & production information, see Charleston Newspapers listing. The Sunday Gazette-Mail is published jointly by the Daily Mail Publishing Co. and the Daily Gazette Co. The (S) circulation is the same for the Mail.
Special Editions: Bridal (Jan); Forecast I, Forecast II (Feb); Parenting, WV Home Show, Health File (Mar); Home & Garden, Spring Car Care, Swimsuit (Apr); NIE Great Adventure, In Step with Women (May); Southern Living Cooking School, Health File (June); In Step with Women, Health & Fitness, Insurance & Finance (July); Dance, Regatta, Football (Aug); In Step with Women, Health File, Hunting (Sept); Fall Home Improvement, Women of the 90's (Oct); In Step with Women, Fall Car Care, Made in West Virginia (Nov); Health File (Dec); Flipside, Builders Plus, Heritage (monthly).
Special Weekly Sections: Food Day (wed); Restaurants & Theaters (thur); Travel, Building Page (S).
Magazines: Parade, "Show-Time" (own, offset), Entertainment & TV Log (S).

CORPORATE OFFICERS
President — Elizabeth E Chilton
Vice Pres — Elizabeth Richman
Secretary — P T Smith

GENERAL MANAGEMENT
Publisher — Craig Selby

NEWS EXECUTIVES
Editor — James A Haught
Managing Editor — Rosalie Earle

EDITORS AND MANAGERS
Amusements Editor — Doug Imbrogno
Business/Finance Editor — Jim Balow
City Editor — Patty Vandergrift
Columnist — Danny Wells
Columnist — Rick Steelhammer
Columnist — Robert Baker
Columnist — Fanny Seiler
Editorial Page Editor — Dan Radmacher
Education Editor — Linda Blackford
Fashion Editor — Connie Shearer
Films/Theater Editor — Doug Imbrogno
Food Editor — Delmer Robinson
Garden Editor — Lynn Schwartz-Barker
Health/Medical Editor — Greg Stone
Home Furnishings Editor — Connie Shearer
Living/Lifestyle Editor — Doug Imbrogno
News Editor — Victor Burkhammer
Photo Editor — Kenny Kemp
Radio/Television Editor — Kathy Mobley
Real Estate Editor — Jim Balow
Religion Editor — Bob Schwartz
Sports Editor — Mitch Vingle
Travel Editor — Doug Imbrogno
Women's Editor — Doug Imbrogno

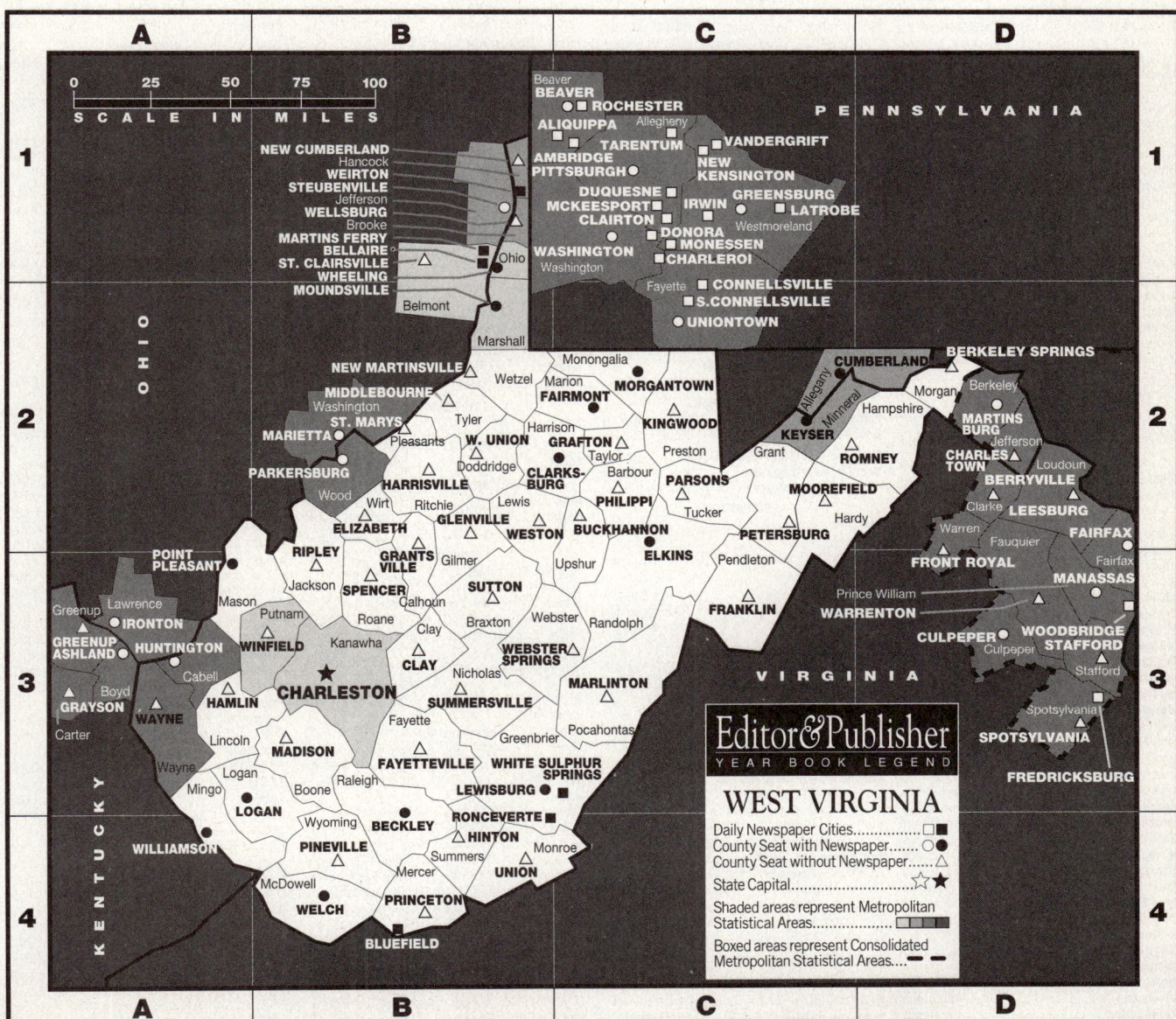

Copyright ©1996 by the Editor & Publisher Co.

Market Information: Zoned editions; Split Run; TMC; Operate audiotex.
Mechanical available: Offset; Black and 3 ROP colors; insert accepted — preprinted, all; page cut-offs — 22¾".
Mechanical specifications: Type page 13" x 21¾"; E - 6 cols, 2", ⅓" between; A - 6 cols, 2", ⅓" between; C - 9 cols.
Equipment: PRODUCTION: Typesetters — III/3810.
PRESSROOM: Line 1 — 11-G/Metro offset; Folders — 3-G.

Charleston Daily Mail
(e-mon to sat)
Sunday Gazette-Mail (S)

Charleston Daily Mail, 1001 Virginia St. E., Charleston, WV 25301; tel (304) 348-5140; fax (304) 348-5133. Thomson Newspapers group.
Circulation: 45,178(e); 45,178(e-sat); 107,045(S); ABC Sept. 30, 1995.
Price: 50¢(d); 50¢(sat); $1.50(S); $14.30/mo; $166.00/yr.
Advertising: Open inch rate $58.70(e); $58.70(e-sat); $65.25(S); $64.54(e & S); comb with Charleston Gazette (mS) $64.00.
News Service: AP. **Politics:** Independent-Republican. **Established:** 1881.
Note: For detailed general management, business personnel & production information see Charleston Newspapers listing. The Sunday Gazette-Mail is published jointly by the Daily Mail Publishing Co. and the Daily Gazette Co. The (S) circulation is the same for the Gazette.
Special Editions: In Step with Women, Bridal (Jan); Forecast I, Forecast II (Feb); In Step with Women, Parenting, WV Home Show, Health File (Mar); Home & Garden, Spring Car Care, Swimsuit (Apr); NIE Great Adventure, In Step with Women (May); Southern Living Cooking School, Health File (June); In Step with Women, Health & Fitness, Insurance & Finance (July); Dance, Regatta, Football (Aug); In Step with Women, Health File, Hunting (Sept); Fall Home Improvement, Women of the 90's (Oct); In Step with Women, Fall Car Care, Made in West Virginia (Nov); Health File (Dec); Flipside, Builders Plus, Heritage (monthly).
Special Weekly Sections: Business (tues); Best Food Day (wed); Entertainment/Weekend (thur); Travel (S).
Magazines: Food, "Show Time" (own, offset), Entertainment & TV Log (S); Flipside (monthly youth publication).

CORPORATE OFFICER

Publisher	David Greenfield

NEWS EXECUTIVES

Editor	David Greenfield
Managing Editor	Larry Aldridge

EDITORS AND MANAGERS

Action Line/Hotline Editor	Monica Orosz
Amusements Editor	Julianne Kemp
Automotive Editor	Chris Stadelman
Book Editor	Susan Jones
Business/Finance Editor	Chris Stadelman
City/Metro Editor	Nanya Friend
Columnist	Richard Grimes
Columnist	Don Hager
Columnist	Ron Hutchison
Columnist	Chuck Landon
Editorial Page Editor	Johanna Maurice
Education Editor	Amanda Crowell
Environment/Ecology Editor	Becky Fleming
Farm/Agriculture Editor	Chris Stadelman
Fashion Editor	Charlotte Cavender
Features Editor	Julianne Kemp
Films Editor	Steven Keith
Food/Home Furnishings Editor	Julianne Kemp
Garden Editor	Zeb Wright
Graphics Editor	Susan Jones
Health/Medical Editor	Therese Cox
Lifestyle Editor	Julianne Kemp
Music Editor	Brad Diller
News Editor	Greg Wood
Photo Department Manager	Chip Ellis
Political Editor	Richard Grimes
Religion Editor	Martha Jackson
Science Editor	Chris Stadelman
Sports Editor	Don Hager
Television	Ron Hutchison
Travel Editor	Julianne Kemp

Market Information: Zoned editions; Split Run; TMC; Operate audiotex.
Mechanical available: Offset; Black and 3 ROP colors; insert accepted — preprinted, all; page cut-offs — 22¾".
Mechanical specifications: Type page 13" x 21¾"; E - 6 cols, 2", ⅓" between; A - 6 cols, 2", ⅓" between; C - 9 cols.
Commodity consumption: average pages per issue 30(d), 84(S).

CLARKSBURG
Harrison County
'90 U.S. Census- 18,059; E&P '96 Est. 15,444
ABC-CZ (90): 37,760 (HH 15,482)

The Clarksburg Exponent
(m-tues to sat)
Clarksburg Telegram
(e-mon to sat)
Sunday Exponent-Telegram
(S)

The Clarksburg Exponent/Telegram, 324-326 Hewes Ave.; PO Box 2000, Clarksburg, WV 26301; tel (304) 624-6411; fax (304) 622-3629.
Circulation: 6,057(m); 13,103(e); 6,057(m-sat); 13,103(e-sat); 22,308(S); ABC Sept. 30, 1995.
Price: 35¢(d); 35¢(sat); $1.00(S); $15.35/mo; $184.18/yr.
Advertising: Open inch rate $10.94(m); $10.94(e); $10.94(m-sat); $10.94(e-sat); $14.59(S); $14.59(m & e). **Representative:** Landon Associates Inc.
News Service: AP. **Established:** 1861 (Telegram), 1909 (Exponent).
Not Published: New Year; Memorial Day; Independence Day; Labor Day; Thanksgiving; Christmas.
Magazines: Images TV/Magazine; Parade.

CORPORATE OFFICER

President/Treasurer	Cecil B Highland Jr

GENERAL MANAGEMENT

Publisher/General Manager	Cecil B Highland Jr
Business Manager/Asst Treasurer	Thomas C Kennedy

ADVERTISING

Manager	Jack L Smith
Office Manager-Classified	Debbie Veltri

CIRCULATION

Manager	Steven N Cross

NEWS EXECUTIVES

Editor-Exponent	Edwin Sweeney
Editor-Telegraph	Robert Stealey

EDITORS AND MANAGERS

Society Editor-Exponent	Darlene Taylor
Society Editor-Telegraph	Rose Ann Hurst

PRODUCTION

Director	Joe S Elam
Exponent	
Foreman-Composing	Tom Shaw
Telegram	
Foreman-Composing	Charles Stewart
Foreman-Mailroom	Denzil Sexton
Foreman-Pressroom	Frank J Bolyard

Market Information: TMC.
Mechanical available: Letterpress; Black and 2 ROP colors; insert accepted — preprinted; page cut-offs — 21¾".
Mechanical specifications: Type page 16" x 20"; E - 7 cols, 2", .14" between; A - 7 cols, 2", .14" between; C - 11 cols, 1.36", .1" between.
Commodity consumption: Newsprint 1,000 metric tons; widths 34", 51", 68"; black ink 40,000 pounds; color ink 3,000 pounds; single pages printed 12,241; average pages per issue 34(d), 45(S); single plates used 16,000.
Equipment: EDITORIAL: Front-end hardware — CD/2330; Front-end software — CD/TOPS; Other equipment — 5-Leading Edge/D-2. CLASSIFIED: Front-end hardware — CD/2330; Front-end software — CD/TOPS; Printers — Okidata. DISPLAY: Adv layout systems — SCS/Layout 8000; Front-end hardware — Dell/PC; Front-end software — SCS/Layout 8000; Printers — C.Itoh/5000, HP/Laser. PRODUCTION: Pagination software — CD, Magician Plus, Ap/Mac Quadra 950, Ap/Mac Quadra 800, Ap/Mac Sys 7; Typesetters — 1-AG/8668, 1-XIT/1200 DPI Laser, 1-New Gen/600 DPI Laser; Platemaking systems — 2-LX/135A; Plate exposures — LX/135; Plate processors — LX; Electronic picture desk — Lf/AP Leaf Picture Desk; Scanners — Microtek/Flatbed, Microtek/35mm, Adobe/Photoshop; Production cameras — 1-C/Spartan III; Automatic film processors — Multiline/66F; Film transporters — 1-LE/Verter; Shrink lenses — 1-Alan/24 Anamorphic.
PRESSROOM: Line 1 — 1-G/High Speed Straight Line; Line 2 — H/Right Angle; Folders — 1-G, 1-H. MAILROOM: Counter stackers — KAN/MSI; Inserters and stuffers — MM; Bundle tyer — 1-Bu, 1-Power Strap. WIRE SERVICES: News — AP; Stock tables — AP; Receiving dishes — AP. BUSINESS COMPUTERS: IBM/Sys 36, PC-Accts payable; Applications: IBM/Sys 36: Circ, Adv billing, Accts receivable, Payroll, Gen ledger; PCs & main system networked.

ELKINS
Randolph County
'90 U.S. Census- 7,420; E&P '96 Est. 6,808
ABC-CZ (90): 7,420 (HH 2,998)

The Inter-Mountain
(e-mon to fri; m-sat)

The Inter-Mountain, 520 Railroad Ave.; PO Box 1339, Elkins, WV 26241; tel (304) 636-2121; fax (304) 636-8252. Ogden Newspapers group.
Circulation: 10,934(e); 10,934(m-sat); ABC Sept. 30, 1995.
Price: 35¢(d); 50¢(sat).
Advertising: Open inch rate $12.62(e); $12.62(m-sat). **Representative:** Landon Associates Inc.
News Service: AP. **Politics:** Independent-Republican. **Established:** 1892.
Not Published: New Year; Memorial Day; Independence Day; Labor Day; Thanksgiving; Christmas.
Special Weekly Section: USA Weekend (sat).

CORPORATE OFFICERS

President	G Ogden Nutting
Vice Pres	William C Nutting
Vice Pres	Robert M Nutting
Secretary	William O Nutting
Treasurer	Duane D Wittman

GENERAL MANAGEMENT

General Manager/Publisher	Jim Hoffman

ADVERTISING

Director	Michael Duplaga
Manager-Production	Jennie Raines

CIRCULATION

Manager	Jeane Cowgill

NEWS EXECUTIVE

Editor	Frank Robinson

EDITORS AND MANAGERS

News Editor	Frank Robinson
Regional Editor	Nancy A Moore
Sports Editor	Joe Kittle

PRODUCTION

Foreman-Pressroom	Dave Ickes

Market Information: Zoned editions.
Mechanical available: Offset; Black and 3 ROP colors; insert accepted — preprinted; page cut-offs — 22¾".
Mechanical specifications: Type page 13" x 22"; E - 6 cols, 2¹⁄₁₆", ⅛" between; A - 6 cols, 2¹⁄₁₆", ⅛" between; C - 6 cols, 2¹⁄₁₆", ⅛" between.
Commodity consumption: Newsprint 420 short tons; width 27"; black ink 11,239 pounds; single pages printed 6,240; average pages per issue 24(d); single plates used 5,650.
Equipment: EDITORIAL: Front-end hardware — 8-COM/350. CLASSIFIED: Front-end hardware — 1-COM/350. DISPLAY: Front-end hardware — 1-COM/Display IV. PRODUCTION: Typesetters — 1-COM/2961, 1-COM/Trendsetter; Plate exposures — 1-Nu; Plate processors — 1-WL; Production cameras — 1-Nu; Automatic film processors — 1-P.
PRESSROOM: Line 1 — 8-HI/Cotrell V-15A; Folders — 1-HI. MAILROOM: Counter stackers — 1-BG/108. WIRE SERVICES: News — AP; Receiving dishes — size-10ft, AP. BUSINESS COMPUTERS: 1-NCR; Applications: Billing, Payroll, Circ.

FAIRMONT
Marion County
'90 U.S. Census- 20,210; E&P '96 Est. 17,861
ABC-CZ (90): 29,852 (HH 12,590)

Times-West Virginian
(m-mon to sat; S)

Times-West Virginian, 300 Quincy; PO Box 2530, Fairmont, WV 26555-2530; tel (304) 367-2500; fax (304) 367-2569. Thomson Newspapers group.
Circulation: 14,445(m); 14,445(m-sat); 15,242(S); ABC Sept. 30, 1995.
Price: 50¢(d); 50¢(sat); $1.25(S); $2.80/wk; $12.13/mo; $145.60/yr.
Advertising: Open inch rate $19.96(m); $19.96(m-sat); $19.96(S). **Representative:** Papert Companies.
News Service: AP. **Politics:** Independent. **Established:** 1900.
Special Editions: Income Tax Guide, Business Quarterly (Jan); Bridal (Feb); Fall & Spring Home Improvement, Progress Edition (Mar); Business Quarterly (Apr); Coal Festival Edition (May); Senior Citizens Tab, Tourism & Outdoor Living (June); Business Quarterly (July); Fall & Spring Car Care, Football Edition (Aug); Hunting Edition, Chamber of Commerce Tab, Holiday Food & Entertainment, Business Quarterly (Oct); Say No to Drugs, Gift Guide Edition (Nov); Real Country Magazine, Healthfile (end of the month) (monthly).
Special Weekly Sections: Entertainment TV, Weekend Section (fri); Lifestyles (S).
Magazines: Parade; Color Comics.

GENERAL MANAGEMENT

Publisher	Frank D Wood

ADVERTISING

Director	Carolyn S Hatting

MARKETING AND PROMOTION

Director-Marketing/Promotion	Carolyn S Hatting

NEWS EXECUTIVES

Exec Editor	Valerie Nieman
Editor	John Veasey

EDITORS AND MANAGERS

Sports Editor	Cliff Nichols
Women's Editor	Alice Bell

PRODUCTION

Manager-Systems	Jon Hart
Foreman-Pressroom	Robert Ison

Market Information: Zoned editions; TMC.
Mechanical available: Offset; Black and 3 ROP colors; insert accepted — preprinted; page cut-offs — 22¾".
Mechanical specifications: Type page 13" x 21½"; E - 6 cols, 2¹⁄₁₆", ⅛" between; A - 6 cols, 2¹⁄₁₆", ⅛" between; C - 9 cols, 1⅜", ¹⁄₁₆" between.
Commodity consumption: Newsprint 840 short tons; width 27½"; average pages per issue 16(d), 32(S).
Equipment: EDITORIAL: Front-end hardware — Mk/4000, Ap/Mac Pagination System; Front-end software — Mk/Mycro-Comp Standard Editorial, QuarkXPress, Mk/Mycro-Comp Page, Adobe/Photoshop; Printers — TI/Lineprinter; Other equipment — Ap/Mac Quadra 950, Lf/AP Leaf Picture Desk, Lf/Leafscan 35. CLASSIFIED: Front-end hardware — Mk/4000, Ap/Mac Pagination System; Front-end software — Mk/Mycro-Comp Standard Classified, QuarkXPress, Mk/Mycro-Comp Page; Printers — TI/Lineprinter. PRODUCTION: Pagination software — QuarkXPress 3.31; Typesetters — 1-COM/IV, 2-COM/MCS10, 2-COM/MCS 8400, 2-V/4000, 2-V/5100A, 1-V/5300E, Pre-Press/Panther Pro 36; Plate processors — 1-Amerigraph/P-18; Electronic picture desk — Ap/Mac Quadra 950, Lf/AP Leaf Picture Desk; Scanners — Lf/Leafscan 35, AG/Flatbed Scanner; Production cameras — 1-R/500, C, SCREEN/Companica 680; Automatic film processors — 1-LE/LD18, SCREEN/America LD220 QT; Color separation equipment (conventional) — Telectronic/Darkroom.
PRESSROOM: Line 1 — 6-G/Urbanite; Folders — 1-G; Press registration system — Duarte. MAILROOM: Counter stackers — 1-BG/Count-O-Veyor 109; Inserters and stuffers — 1-KAN/480 Inserter; Bundle tyer — 1-SP/330, 1-Gd. COMMUNICATIONS: Digital ad delivery system — AP AdSend, West Virginia PRESS-net. Systems used — satellite. WIRE SERVICES: News — AP; Photos — AP; Receiving dishes — size-3m, AP. BUSINESS COMPUTERS: PC/386; Applications: Lotus, WordPerfect; PCs & main system networked.

HUNTINGTON

Cabell and Wayne Counties

'90 U.S. Census- 58,844; E&P '96 Est. 55,515
ABC-NDM (90): 157,794 (HH 62,034)

The Herald-Dispatch

(m-mon to sat; S)

The Herald-Dispatch, 946 5th Ave. (25701); PO Box 2017, Huntington, WV 25720; tel (304) 526-4000; fax (304) 526-2858. Gannett Co. Inc. group.

Circulation: 38,644(m); 38,644(m-sat); 47,250(S); ABC Sept. 30, 1995.

Price: 35¢(d); 35¢(sat); $1.25(S); $3.25/wk (carrier), $3.45/wk (motor route); $14.08/mo (carrier), $14.95/mo (motor route); $169.00/yr (carrier), $179.40/yr (motor route).

Advertising: Open inch rate $41.84(m); $41.84(m-sat); $48.72(S). **Representative:** Gannett National Newspaper Sales.

News Services: AP, GNS. **Politics:** Independent. **Established:** 1927.

Advertising not accepted: Ads asking cash in advance.

Special Editions: Progress (Mar); Swimsuit Edition (May).

Magazines: USA Weekend; Television.

CORPORATE OFFICERS

President	Thomas A Bookstaver
Secretary	Thomas L Chapple
Treasurer	Jimmy L Thomas

GENERAL MANAGEMENT

Publisher	Thomas A Bookstaver
Controller	Leigh Thacker

ADVERTISING

Director	Cindy George
Manager-Retail	Kim Wilson
Manager-Classified	John Null
Manager-National	Cindy George

MARKETING AND PROMOTION

Director-Marketing/Promotion	Thomas R Cooper
Manager-Marketing/Promotion	Amy Kerr

CIRCULATION

Director	Alan Martin
Manager-Home Delivery	Jim Heady
Manager-Single Copy/Transportation	Tom Myers
Manager-Sales/Marketing	T Mark McFann
Manager-Customer Service	Terri Toth

NEWS EXECUTIVES

Exec Editor	Robert Gabordi
Managing Editor	Michael Johnson

EDITORS AND MANAGERS

City Editor	Fran Allred
Editorial Page Editor	James E Casto
Features Editor	Arlinda Smith
Librarian	Patty Clay
News Editor	Rick Nolte
Sports Editor	Dave Wellman

MANAGEMENT INFORMATION SERVICES

Data Processing Manager	Kevin Crane

PRODUCTION

Director	Jerry Epling
Manager-Pre Press	Roger Edwards
Manager-Systems	Kevin Crane
Manager-Pressroom	Aubrey Webb
Manager-Distribution Center	Danny Watson

Market Information: Zoned editions; Split Run; TMC.

Mechanical available: Letterpress; Black and 3 ROP colors; insert accepted — preprinted, any through a HI/1372 hopper; page cut-offs — 21½".

Mechanical specifications: Type page 13" x 21½"; E - 6 cols, 2", ⅙" between; A - 6 cols, 2", ⅙" between; C - 10 cols, 1.22", .10" between.

Commodity consumption: Newsprint 3,146 short tons; 2,854 metric tons; widths 54", 40½", 27", 13½"; black ink 118,811 pounds; color ink 11,000 pounds; single pages printed 12,094; average pages per issue 32(d), 72(S); single plates used 31,000.

Equipment: EDITORIAL: Front-end hardware — SIA/fileserver, SIA/386; Front-end software — Dewar/Sys 4; Printers — 2-Okidata/393. CLASSIFIED: Front-end hardware — SIA/fileserver, SIA/386; Front-end software — Dewar; Printers — 2-Accuset/1000 Imagesetter. DISPLAY: Adv layout systems — Dewar/Layout; Front-end hardware — Dewar/Server, PC/386, AST/25; Front-end software — Dewar/Layout System; Printers — IBM/Printer. PRODUCTION: Typesetters — 2-Accuset/1000, 1-SLS/11x17, V/Plain Paper Imager; Plate exposures — 2-Na/Starlite; Plate processors — 2-Na/NP40; Electronic picture desk — Lf/AP Leaf Picture Desk; Scanners — ECR/Autokon 1000, X/11x17-765 ProImager Scanner, Nikon/Coolscan; Production cameras — C/Marathon III, C/Marathon; Automatic film processors — 2-LE/LD24AQ, Kk/65A, C/R660; Film transporters — 2-C/Spartan III, C/Marathon; Shrink lenses — 1-CK Optical/SQU-7. PRESSROOM: Line 1 — 6-Wd/Metropolitan (3 half decks); Press drives — Allen Bradley, 5-GE/Motors; Reels and stands — Wd; Press control system — CH; Press registration system — Web Tech. MAILROOM: Counter stackers — HL/HT, HL/Monitor; Inserters and stuffers — HI/1372 (12 Heads); Bundle tyer — 2-Power Strap/PSD 5; Addressing machine — Ch/592. WIRE SERVICES: News — AP Dataspeed, AP Datafeatures, AP SelectStox; Stock tables — Mutuals; Receiving dishes — AP. BUSINESS COMPUTERS: IBM/AS400; PCs & main system networked.

KEYSER

Mineral County

'90 U.S. Census- 5,870; E&P '96 Est. 5,528

Mineral Daily News Tribune

(e-mon to fri; m-sat)

Mineral Daily News-Tribune, 24 Armstrong St.; PO Box 879, Keyser, WV 26726; tel (304) 788-3333; fax (304) 788-3398.

Circulation: 4,986(e); 4,986(m-sat); Sworn Oct. 2, 1995.

Price: 30¢(d); 30¢(sat); $90.95/yr (mail), $70.62/yr (carrier).

Advertising: Open inch rate $6.00(e); $6.00(m-sat). **Representative:** American Newspaper Representatives Inc.

News Service: UPI. **Politics:** Independent. **Established:** 1912.

Not Published: New Year; Memorial Day; Independence Day; Labor Day; Thanksgiving; Christmas.

Special Editions: Graduation; Greetings.

Special Weekly Sections: Food & Recipes (mon, tues, wed); Entertainment, Senior Citizens (thur, fri); TV Guide, Real Estate, Food Section, Recipes, Weddings, Engagements, Church News, Church Directory, Total Market Coverage (sat).

CORPORATE OFFICERS

President	James L Tetrick
Vice Pres	Robert G Tetrick
Secretary	Judy Tetrick Layman
Treasurer	Judy Tetrick Layman

GENERAL MANAGEMENT

Business Manager	James L Tetrick

ADVERTISING

Manager	Robert G Tetrick

CIRCULATION

Director	Peggy McNeil

EDITORS AND MANAGERS

City Editor	Elizabeth Stewart
Home Furnishings Editor	Judy Tetrick Layman
News Editor	Sam Sawyver
Society Editor	Elizabeth Stewart
Sports Editor	Scott Allen
Teen-Age/Youth Editor	Jennifer Westfall
Wire Editor	Sam Sawyver

PRODUCTION

Manager-Pressroom	DeSales Morgan
Superintendent	James L Tetrick

Market Information: Zoned editions; Split Run; TMC.

Mechanical available: Offset; Black and 2 ROP colors; insert accepted — preprinted; page cut-offs — 21½".

Mechanical specifications: Type page 13" x 21½"; E - 6 cols, 2 1/16", ⅛" between; A - 6 cols, 2 1/16", ⅛" between; C - 6 cols, 2 1/16", ⅛" between.

Commodity consumption: Newsprint 379 short tons; widths 27½", 13¾"; black ink 11,000 pounds; color ink 1,000 pounds; single pages printed 5,900; average pages per issue 18(d); single plates used 12,000.

Equipment: EDITORIAL: Front-end hardware — 7-IBM/PC. CLASSIFIED: Front-end hardware — 1-ATT/PC. DISPLAY: Adv layout systems — 1-Ap/Mac. PRODUCTION: Typesetters — 2-Ap/Mac, 3-MDT; Platemaking systems — 1-Nu-, 1-Nat/A-250; Production cameras — 1-K/241, 1-LE/480; Automatic film processors — 1-P/Pakorol. PRESSROOM: Line 1 — 8-G/Community; Folders — 1-G. MAILROOM: Counter stackers — 1-St; Inserters and stuffers — 1-KAN; Bundle tyer — 2-Bu; Addressing machine — 1-KR. LIBRARY: Electronic — 1-Dukane/Explorer 14. WIRE SERVICES: News — UPI; Receiving dishes — size-12ft, UPI.

LEWISBURG-RONCEVERTE-WHITE SULPHUR SPRINGS

Greenbrier County

'90 U.S. Census- 8,131 (Lewisburg 3,598; Ronceverte 1,754; White Sulphur Springs 2,779); E&P '96 Est. 8,371 (Lewisburg 4,291; Ronceverte 1,544; White Sulphur Springs 2,536)

West Virginia Daily News

(e-mon to fri)

West Virginia Daily News, 200 S. Court St.; PO Box 471, Lewisburg, WV 24901; tel (304) 645-1206; fax (304) 645-7104. Moffitt Newspapers group.

Circulation: 3,724(e); Sworn Oct. 4, 1994.

Price: 25¢(d); $4.10/mo; $72.08/yr (in-state).

Advertising: Open inch rate $5.00(e). **Politics:** Republican. **Established:** 1892.

Not Published: New Year; Memorial Day; Independence Day; Labor Day; Thanksgiving; Christmas.

Special Editions: Bridal (Jan); State Fair (Aug); Christmas Gift Guide (Nov).

CORPORATE OFFICERS

President	John F Moffitt
Vice Pres	Margret W Moffitt
Secretary/Treasurer	John F Moffitt

GENERAL MANAGEMENT

Publisher	Frank L Spicer

ADVERTISING

Manager	Judy Dowdy

CIRCULATION

Manager	Joan Lewis

NEWS EXECUTIVE

Managing Editor	Tina A Alvey

EDITOR AND MANAGER

Society Editor	Tina A Alvey

PRODUCTION

Manager-Press	Lea Ballard
Manager-Camera	Joyce Arbaugh

Market Information: TMC; ADS.

Mechanical available: Offset; Black and 1 ROP color; insert accepted — preprinted; page cut-offs — 21½".

Mechanical specifications: Type page 13" x 21½"; E - 6 cols, 2 1/16", ⅛" between; A - 6 cols, 2 1/16", ⅛" between; C - 6 cols, 2 1/16", ⅛" between.

Commodity consumption: Newsprint 250 short tons; width 27"; black ink 5,400 pounds; color ink 525 pounds; single pages printed 46; average pages per issue 8(d).

Equipment: EDITORIAL: Front-end hardware — 2-Ap/Mac; Front-end software — Aldus/PageMaker 5.0; Printers — 1-LaserMaster/1200. DISPLAY: Adv layout systems — 3-Ap/Mac; Front-end hardware — 3-Ap/Mac; Front-end software — Multi-Ad/Creator 3.6, Aldus/PageMaker 5.0; Printers — 1-LaserMaster/1200. PRODUCTION: Production cameras — 1-R. PRESSROOM: Line 1 — 5-G/Community; Press drives — Fin. MAILROOM: Inserters and stuffers — 1-St. BUSINESS COMPUTERS: 2-Leading Edge/MOD 2; Applications: Circ, Promotion, Billing.

LOGAN

Logan County

'90 U.S. Census- 2,206; E&P '96 Est. 1,791
ABC-CZ (90): 2,206 (HH 953)

The Logan Banner

(e-mon to fri; S)

The Logan Banner, 435 Stratton St.; PO Box 720, Logan, WV 25601; tel (304) 752-6950; fax (304) 752-1239. Smith Newspapers Inc. group.

Circulation: 9,673(e); 9,924(S); ABC Sept. 30, 1995.

Price: 35¢(d); 75¢(S); $6.00/mo.

Advertising: Open inch rate $8.95(e); $8.95(S). **Representative:** Landon Associates Inc.

News Service: UPI. **Politics:** Independent-Democrat. **Established:** 1888.

Not Published: Thanksgiving; Christmas.

Special Editions: Entertainment, Basketball Pages, Dollar Days, Valentine Photo Promo, Vacation Getaway, Medical Directory (Feb); Basketball Pages, Girl Scout Page, Say No to Drugs Essay Contest, Say No to Drugs Section, Medical Directory (Mar); Easter Services, Spring Car Care, Home Improvement, 606 Promotion, Photo Contest, Medical Directory (Apr); Memorial Day Signature Page, Graduation Section, Mother's Day Photos, Medical Directory, Mother's Day Section (May); Father's Day Photos, Father's Day Section, Summer Cookbook, Summer Celebration (June); July 4th Safety Page, Working Women, A to Z (July); Back-to-School Section, Back-to-School Safety Page, Football Signature Pages, Football Tab Section (Aug); Pride Edition, Football Pages, Harmon Football Forecast (Sept); Pride Repeats, Hunting Section, Halloween Safety Pages, Fall Home Improvement, Fall Car Care, Football Pages, Harmon Forecast, United Way Section (Oct); 606 Promotions, Harmon Football Forecast, Veteran's Day Page, Holiday Cookbook, Christmas Openings, Thanksgiving Page (Nov); Basketball Pages, 606 Promos, Christmas Songbook, Christmas Coloring Book, Christmas Greetings, Man Merchants Christmas Sale, Logan Merchants Christmas Sale, LBA Christmas Parade, First Baby of the Year, Christmas in the Park, New Year's Greeting (Dec).

Special Weekly Sections: Business Page (tues); Church Page (fri); Comic Pages, Shop at Home, TV Times, Here's My Card, Professional Page (weekly).

CORPORATE OFFICERS

President	Richard Osborne
Vice Pres	Ben M Smith

GENERAL MANAGEMENT

Publisher	Richard Osborne
Purchasing Agent	Richard Osborne

ADVERTISING

Manager	Kathy Chafin

CIRCULATION

Manager	Keith Rebar

NEWS EXECUTIVE

Managing Editor	Jack McNeely

EDITORS AND MANAGERS

Editorial Page Editor	Jack McNeely
Sports Editor	Dan Scott

PRODUCTION

Foreman-Composing	Gaynell Hughes
Foreman-Pressroom	Kevin Maynard

Market Information: TMC.

Mechanical available: Offset; Black and 3 ROP colors; insert accepted — preprinted, all; page cut-offs — 22¾".

Mechanical specifications: Type page 13¾" x 21½"; E - 6 cols, 2 1/16", ⅛" between; A - 6 cols, 2 1/16", ⅛" between; C - 9 cols, 1⅜", 1/16" between.

Commodity consumption: average pages per issue 24(d), 54(S).

Equipment: EDITORIAL: Front-end hardware — CText; Other equipment — 2-Ap/Mac Plus. CLASSIFIED: Front-end hardware — CText. PRODUCTION: Typesetters — 2-Ap/Mac Laser Plus Printers; Platemaking systems — 1-Nu; Plate exposures — 1-Nu; Production cameras — R/500; Automatic film processors — 1-LE. PRESSROOM: Line 1 — 8-F; Folders — 2-F. MAILROOM: Counter stackers — 1-Fg; Inserters and stuffers — 3-DG; Bundle tyer — 1-Ty-Tech/Tyer; Addressing machine — 2-Am. WIRE SERVICES: News — UPI; Stock tables — UPI; Receiving dishes — UPI. BUSINESS COMPUTERS: PCs & micros networked; PCs & main system networked.

MARTINSBURG

Berkeley County

'90 U.S. Census- 14,073; E&P '96 Est. 15,162
ABC-CZ (90): 14,073 (HH 6,040)

The Journal (m-mon to sat)
The Sunday Journal (S)

The Journal, 207 W. King St.; PO Box 807, Martinsburg, WV 25401; tel (304) 263-8931; fax (304) 263-8058. Ogden Newspapers group.

Circulation: 17,650(m); 17,650(m-sat); 19,361(S); ABC Sept. 30, 1995.

Price: 50¢(d); 50¢(sat); $1.00(S); $1.85/7days, $1.00/wk (S only); $24.00/3mo (7-day carrier), $13.00/3mo (S only paid in advance & carrier collect), $25.48/3mo (7-days); $101.92/yr (7-day carrier), $96.00/yr (7-day paid in advance).

Advertising: Open inch rate $19.86(m); $19.86(m-sat); $19.86(S). **Representative:** Landon Associates Inc.

News Service: AP. **Politics:** Independent. **Established:** 1907.

Special Editions: Bridal Section, Coupon Book, Welcome Home, Jump Start (Jan); Panhandle Progress, President's Day Automotive, Welcome Home, Valentine Kids' Page, NASCAR Tab (Feb); Home Improvement, Welcome Home, Health Care Handbook, Shamrock Theme Pages, Red Cross Month, Easter Directory (Mar); Coupon Book, Super Saver, Rain Drop Theme Pages, Menu Book, Welcome Home/American Home Week, Secretaries Day, Turn up Time (Apr); Discover the Tri-State (Tourism), Mother's Day Tab, Graduation Salute, Camp Frame BBQ, Memorial Day Tribute, Helping Hands, NASCAR Tab, Gifts for Grads, Spring Car Care, Welcome Home (May); Father's Day Tab, Welcome Home, All Around Town, Tri-State Spotlight, Salute to Graduates, Youth Fair BBQ (June); Welcome Home, Coupon Book, Youth Fair, All Around Town, NASCAR Tab, Independence Day, Summer Sizzler (July); Jefferson County Fair, Back-to-School, Football Kickoff, All Around Town, Home Care & Remodeling (Aug); Welcome Home, Discover the Tri-State, Football Picks, Football Forecast, Mountaineer Madness Weekly, Labor Day Sponsor Page, National Grandparents Day, Fall Home Improvement, Ask-A-Professional, Home Care & Remodeling, Camp Frame BBQ (Sept); Apple Harvest, Welcome Home, Apple Butter, Fall Coupon, Halloween Safety, All Around Town, Pumpkin Theme Pages, Mountaineer Madness Weekly, Ask-A-Professional, Turn up Time (Oct); Welcome Home, Veteran's Day, Christmas Ad Packages, Turkey Theme Pages, Holiday Gift Guide, Design-An-Ad, All Around Town, Mountaineer Madness, Football Forecast, Hunting Guide, NASCAR Tab, Ask-A-Professional (Nov); Last Minute Gift Guide, Christmas Songbook, Welcome Home, All Around Town, 1997 Business Calendar, Christmas Greetings, New Year's Eve Drunk Driving, Holiday Shopping Hours (Dec).

Special Weekly Sections: Expanded Market Coverage (tues); Food (wed); Auto Pages (thur); Church Pages, Dining Guide, Weekender (Entertainment) (fri); Real Estate, Auto Pages, Journal Plus (sat); Business/Stocks (S).

Magazines: TV Week (local), A.M. Magazine (local), Color Comics (S); Parade; Welcome Home (Real Estate); Discover (Tourism); All Around Town (Shopping, Tourism).

CORPORATE OFFICERS

President	G Ogden Nutting
Exec Vice Pres/General Manager	Robert M Nutting
Treasurer	Duane Wittman
Controller	Charles Deremer

GENERAL MANAGEMENT

Publisher	Jack Glarrow

ADVERTISING

Director	James Connors

CIRCULATION

Manager	Chris Fagiano

NEWS EXECUTIVE

Editor	Bill Doolittle

EDITORS AND MANAGERS

City Editor	Mark Moore
Editorial Page Editor	Bill Doolittle
Family Editor	Peggy Swisher
Farm/Food Editor	Peggy Swisher
Living/Lifestyle Editor	Peggy Swisher
Local Magazine Editor	Meg Partington
Sports Editor	Richard Kozlowski
Travel/Television	Deborah Silver
Photo Department Manager	Todd Harless
Women's Editor	Peggy Swisher

PRODUCTION

Manager	Craig Bohrer
Foreman-Composing	Nicholas Werder
Foreman-Pressroom	Art Taylor

Market Information: Zoned editions; Split Run; TMC.

Mechanical available: Offset; Black and 3 ROP colors; insert accepted — preprinted, all; page cut-offs — $22\frac{3}{4}$".

Mechanical specifications: Type page 13" x $21\frac{1}{2}$"; E - 6 cols, $2\frac{1}{16}$", $\frac{1}{8}$" between; A - 6 cols, $2\frac{1}{16}$", $\frac{1}{8}$" between; C - 8 cols, $1\frac{9}{16}$", $\frac{1}{16}$" between.

Commodity consumption: Newsprint 3,830 short tons; widths 27", $27\frac{1}{2}$", 32"; black ink 73,352 pounds; color ink 17,784 pounds; single pages printed 10,561; average pages per issue 24(d), 58(S); single plates used 43,703.

Equipment: EDITORIAL: Front-end hardware — SII; Front-end software — SII; Printers — TI/810; Other equipment — Ap/Mac Centris 610, Ap/Mac Centris 650, Ap/Mac Plus. CLASSIFIED: Front-end hardware — SII; Front-end software — SII; Other equipment — NCR. DISPLAY: Adv layout systems — QuarkXPress, Multi-Ad; Printers — Ap/Mac LaserWriter NTX, Ap/Mac Turbo 660B, ECR/VRL 36, MON/ExpressMaster 2000; Other equipment — Ap/Mac Centris 610, Ap/Mac Centris 660, Ap/Mac Centris 650, Ap/Power Mac 6100-66, Ap/Mac Quadra 610, Ap/Power Mac 7100-66. PRODUCTION: Pagination software — QuarkXPress, Adobe/Photoshop, Multi-Ad, Ethernet; Typesetters — 5-Ap/Mac SE, 4-Ap/LaserWriter II, Ap/Mac Centris 610, Ap/Mac Centris 660, MON/XPRESS Master 2000; Plate exposures — 1-Nu/Flip Top FT40UPNS, 1-Nu/Flip Top FT40V2OUPNS; Plate processors — Nu, WL/30D Lithoplater; Scanners — Microtek/ScanMaker, HP/ScanJet IIcx, Nikon/35mm LS-3510 AF, Umax/Vista 56; Production cameras — P, C/Spartan II; Automatic film processors — P/24.

PRESSROOM: Line 1 — 10-G/Urbanite; Line 2 — 6-HI/Cotrell 845; Press drives — G, 3-Fin, HI, CH; Folders — 1-G/2:1 (w/balloon), 2-HI/2:1 (w/balloon); Pasters — Martin. MAILROOM: Counter stackers — Id, HL/Monitors, HT; Inserters and stuffers — HI/1372, MM4-hopper in line; Bundle tyer — MLN; Addressing machine — KR. WIRE SERVICES: News — AP; Photos — AP; Stock tables — TMS; Receiving dishes — AP. BUSINESS COMPUTERS: NCR, Unix; Applications: Accounting; PCs & micros networked.

MORGANTOWN

Monongalia County

'90 U.S. Census- 25,879; E&P '96 Est. 24,739
ABC-CZ (90): 41,769 (HH 16,532)

Dominion Post

(m-mon to sat; S)

Dominion Post, 1251 Earl L Core Rd., Morgantown, WV 26505; tel (304) 292-6301; fax (304) 291-2326.

Circulation: 19,299(m); 19,299(m-sat); 26,803(S); ABC Sept. 30, 1995.

Price: 50¢(d); 50¢(sat); $1.25(S); $3.10/wk; $13.43/mo; $161.20/yr.

Advertising: Open inch rate $17.16(m); $17.16(m-sat); $20.03(S). **Representative:** Landon Associates Inc.

News Services: AP, LAT-WP, NEA. **Politics:** Independent. **Established:** 1864 (Post), 1876 (Dominion News).

Special Editions: Chamber of Commerce Tab (Jan); Wedding Planner Tab, Health Fair Tab (Feb); Spring Home & Garden (Std), Progress (Std) (Mar); Auto Care Tab, Coupon Book (Apr); Summer Fun (Std) (May); Seniors Today Tab, West Virgina's Birthday Party Tab (June); Futures Golf Mini-tab, Monongalra County Fair Mini-tab, Football (Std) (Aug); Buckwheat Festival Tab, Fall Home & Garden (Sept); Balloon Festival Tab, Active Years Tab (Oct); Winter Time, Basketball (Std) (Nov); X'mas Gift Guide #1 (Std), X'mas Gift Guide #2 (Std), X'mas Gift Guide #3 (Std), Songbook Mini-tab, First Night Tab (Dec).

Special Weekly Sections: TV Time (S); Restaurant Page; Stock Page; Marquee; Goal Post; Weather Page.

Magazines: Parade; TV Week (S).

Broadcast Affiliates: Radio WAJR/WVAQ.

CORPORATE OFFICERS

President	David A Raese
Vice Pres	John R Raese
Vice Pres-Secretary/Treasurer	James M Troy
Controller	Brian D Cole

GENERAL MANAGEMENT

Publisher	David A Raese
Assoc Publisher	Kathleen A Raese
Controller	Brian D Cole

ADVERTISING

Director	Titus Workman
Manager-Retail	Larry Tennant
Manager-Retail	Adrienne Davis
Manager-Classified	Brad Parker

MARKETING AND PROMOTION

Coordinator-Public Service	Renee D Matteo

TELECOMMUNICATIONS

Audiotex Manager	Cindy Barrish

CIRCULATION

Director	Phillip Miller
Manager-Operations	Joseph Duley
Manager-Promotion	Michelle Sicola

NEWS EXECUTIVE

Editor	Ralph Brem

EDITORS AND MANAGERS

Business/Special Sections Editor	John Samsell
Graphic Arts/Design Editor	Michael Fisher
Lifestyle Editor	Mya Koch
Marquee Editor	Mya Koch
News Editor-Day	John Pastor
News Editor-Night	Mark Stacy
Sports Editor	Robert Pastin
Sunday Editor	Kristin Connolly
Wire Editor	Randy Vealey

PRODUCTION

Director	Ernest West
Manager-Pre Press/Systems	Wendy West
Manager-Post Press	Mike Furnari
Foreman-Building & Maintenance	Terry Rankin

Market Information: TMC; Operate audiotex.

Mechanical available: Offset; Black and 3 ROP colors; insert accepted — preprinted; page cut-offs — $22\frac{3}{4}$".

Mechanical specifications: Type page $13\frac{1}{4}$" x $21\frac{1}{2}$"; E - 6 cols, $2\frac{1}{16}$", $\frac{1}{8}$" between; A - 6 cols, $2\frac{1}{16}$", $\frac{1}{8}$" between; C - 9 cols, $1\frac{3}{8}$", $\frac{1}{16}$" between.

Commodity consumption: Newsprint 2,013 short tons; widths 28", 14"; black ink 39,546 pounds; color ink 7,065 pounds; single pages printed 11,710; average pages per issue 25(d), 68(S); single plates used 12,523.

Equipment: EDITORIAL: Front-end hardware — SII/Tandem 31 PC, 10-Ap/Mac; Front-end software — SII; Printers — QMS/860 Laser. CLASSIFIED: Front-end hardware — SII; Front-end software — SII; Printers — QMS/860 Laser. AUDIOTEX: Hardware — Texas Micro/PC; Software — New Horizons Voice Information System. DISPLAY: Adv layout systems — SII; Front-end hardware — Ap/Mac. PRODUCTION: Typesetters — 2-Spectraset/2400; Plate exposures — 1-Nu/Flip Top; Plate processors — 1-WL; Scanners — AG/Arcus Plus, Ag/Horizon Plus; Production cameras — 1-Bo; Automatic film processors — 2-LE.

PRESSROOM: Line 1 — 7-G/Urbanite; Folders — 1-G. MAILROOM: Counter stackers — 1-QWI; Inserters and stuffers — MM/8-into-1; Bundle tyer — 1-MLN; Addressing machine — KAN. LIBRARY: Electronic — SII. WIRE SERVICES: News — AP; Stock tables — AP; Syndicates — AP, LAT-WP; Receiving dishes — size-10ft, AP. BUSINESS COMPUTERS: 5-DEC; Applications: Vision Data: Adv, Billing, Circ Billing; DSI: Gen ledger, Accts payable, Newsprint; PCs & main system networked.

MOUNDSVILLE

Marshall County

'90 U.S. Census- 10,753; E&P '96 Est. 9,781

Moundsville Daily Echo

(e-mon to sat)

Moundsville Daily Echo, 715 Lafayette Ave.; PO Box 369, Moundsville, WV 26041; tel (304) 845-2660; fax (304) 845-2661.

Circulation: 4,585(e); 4,585(e-sat); Sworn Sept. 28, 1994.

Price: 15¢(d); 15¢(sat); $46.00/yr.

Advertising: Open inch rate $4.17(e); $4.17(e-sat).

News Service: AP. **Politics:** Independent-Democrat. **Established:** 1891.

Advertising not accepted: Alcoholic beverage.

GENERAL MANAGEMENT

Publisher	Samuel Shaw
Purchasing Agent	Charlie Walton

ADVERTISING

Manager-Retail/National	Marian Walton

CIRCULATION

Manager	Linda Massie

NEWS EXECUTIVE

Editor	Samuel Shaw

EDITOR AND MANAGER

Sports Editor	Charlie Walton

Mechanical available: Offset; black; insert accepted — preprinted; page cut-offs — $22\frac{3}{4}$".

Mechanical specifications: Type page $15\frac{1}{8}$" x $21\frac{5}{8}$"; E - 7 cols, 2", $\frac{1}{8}$" between; A - 7 cols, 2", $\frac{1}{8}$" between; C - 7 cols, 2", $\frac{1}{8}$" between.

Commodity consumption: Newsprint 42 short tons; width 32"; black ink 1,389 pounds; average pages per issue 4(d), 4(sat); single plates used 600.

Equipment: EDITORIAL: Front-end hardware — PC; Front-end software — Aldus/PageMaker 3.01, Microsoft/Windows 3.1; Printers — Ap/Mac LaserWriter. DISPLAY: Front-end hardware — PC; Front-end software — Aldus/PageMaker 3.01, Microsoft/Windows 3.1, Archtype/Corel Draw 3.0; Printers — Ap/Mac LaserWriter. PRODUCTION: Typesetters — Ap/Mac Laser Plus; Plate exposures — 1-Nu; Plate processors — Manual; Production cameras — R.

PRESSROOM: Line 1 — 2-KP; Press control system — GE/SCR. MAILROOM: Addressing machine — 2-Am/Dispensa-Matic. COMMUNICATIONS: Facsimile — Murata. WIRE SERVICES: News — AP; Receiving dishes — size-3ft, AP. BUSINESS COMPUTERS: 1-PC/386.

PARKERSBURG

Wood County

'90 U.S. Census- 33,862; E&P '96 Est. 29,850
ABC-CZ (90): 56,996 (HH 24,045)

The Parkersburg News

(m-mon to sat; S)

The Parkersburg Sentinel

(e-mon to sat)

Parkersburg News & Sentinel, 519 Juliana St.; PO Box 1788, Parkersburg, WV 26102; tel (304) 485-1891; fax (304) 422-7134. Ogden Newspapers group.

Circulation: 23,066(m); 10,270(e); 23,066 (m-sat); 10,270(e-sat); 42,090(S); ABC Sept. 30, 1995.

Price: 50¢(d); 50¢(sat); $1.00(S); $25.88/mo; $225.66/yr.

Advertising: Open inch rate $27.66(m); $27.66(e); $27.66(m-sat); $27.66(e-sat); $30.91(S). **Representative:** Landon Associates Inc. **Established:** 1852 (News), 1875 (Sentinel).

Special Editions: Seniors, Speedway, Video News, Real Estate, M.O.V. Today (monthly).

Special Weekly Section: Best Food Day (wed, thur & S).

Magazines: Religion Tab (sat); Show Time Tab (S).

CORPORATE OFFICER

President	G Ogden Nutting

GENERAL MANAGEMENT

Publisher	Edward Kruger

ADVERTISING

Director	Ed Hofmann
Manager-National/Classified	Ed Hofmann

CIRCULATION

Director	Randy J Slabaugh

NEWS EXECUTIVES

News

Editor	Ben Sheroan
Managing Editor	Annetta Richardson

Sentinel

Editor	Dave Owen
Asst Managing Editor	Paul LaPann

EDITORS AND MANAGERS

News

City Editor	Annetta Richardson
Columnist	Jesse Mancini
Films/Theater Editor	Annetta Richardson
Society Editor	Janel Willis
Sports Editor	David Poe

Sentinel

Editorial Page Editor	Dave Owen
Editorial Writer	Dave Owen
Music/Religion Editor	Jeff Baughan
Photo Department Manager	Jeff Baughan
Society Editor	Pam Brust
Sports Editor	Nick Scala

PRODUCTION

News

Manager	Jim Freeland
Foreman-Composing	Donald Riel
Superintendent-Pressroom	Chuck Charlton

Market Information: TMC.

Mechanical available: Offset; Black and 3 ROP colors; insert accepted — preprinted; page cut-offs — $21\frac{3}{4}$".

Mechanical specifications: Type page 13" x $21\frac{3}{4}$"; E - 6 cols, $2\frac{1}{16}$", $\frac{1}{8}$" between; A - 6 cols, $2\frac{1}{16}$", $\frac{1}{8}$" between; C - 8 cols, $1\frac{9}{16}$", $\frac{1}{16}$" between.

Commodity consumption: average pages per issue 28(d), 54(S).

Equipment: EDITORIAL: Front-end hardware — 2-SII; Front-end software — SII; Printers — PSI/100. CLASSIFIED: Front-end hardware — 2-SII; Front-end software — SII. DISPLAY: Front-end hardware — 2-Ap/Mac SE; Front-end software — QuarkXPress, Multi-Ad/Creator; Printers — 4-Ap/LaserWriter II. PRO-

DUCTION: Typesetters — 2-Ap/Mac SE, 4-Ap/LaserWriter II; Plate exposures — 1-Nu/Flip Top FT40UPNS, 1-Nu/Flip Top FT40L; Plate processors — 1-WL/30B; Production cameras — 1-K/N243, 1-C/Newspager; Automatic film processors — 1-LE; Film transporters — 1-C/Newspager.
PRESSROOM: Line 1 — 5-HI/1650; Folders — 2-HI. MAILROOM: Counter stackers — 1-SH/251, 1-HL/Monitor; Inserters and stuffers — 1-HI/NP1372; Bundle tyer — MLN/ML-2EE, 1-Power Strap/TS2504. WIRE SERVICES: News — AP.

POINT PLEASANT
Mason County
'90 U.S. Census- 4,996; E&P '96 Est. 4,671

Point Pleasant Register
(e-mon to sat)

Point Pleasant Register, 200 Main St.; PO Box 237, Point Pleasant, WV 25550; tel (304) 675-1333; fax (304) 675-5234. Gannett Co. Inc. group.
Circulation: 5,575(e); 5,575(e-sat); Sworn Oct. 2, 1995.
Price: 35¢(d); 35¢(sat); $1.60/wk, $6.50/mo, $78.00/yr.
Advertising: Open inch rate $5.30(e); $5.30(e-sat). **Representative:** Landon Associates Inc.
News Service: AP. **Politics:** Independent. **Established:** 1938.
Note: Printed at the Gallipolis (OH) Daily Tribune. For pressroom information, see the Gallipolis Daily Tribune listing. The Point Pleasant Register has a combination rate of $11.80 with the Gallipolis (OH) Daily Tribune (eS) & Pomeroy (OH) Daily Sentinel (eS).
Not Published: New Year; Memorial Day; Labor Day; Thanksgiving; Christmas.
Special Editions: Battle Days; Side-Walk Days; Car Care; Football; Back-to-School; Christmas; Christmas Greetings; Christmas Gift Guide.
Special Weekly Sections: Church Page, TV Times (fri); Business Page, Farm Page (S).
Magazine: TV Guide.

GENERAL MANAGEMENT

Publisher	Robert L Wingett
General Manager	Robert L Wingett
Purchasing Agent	Robert L Wingett

ADVERTISING

Manager	Brian Billings

CIRCULATION

Manager	Paul Barker

NEWS EXECUTIVE

Editor	Mindy L Kearns

EDITOR AND MANAGER

Editorial Page Editor	Mindy L Kearns

Market Information: TMC.
Mechanical available: Offset; Black and 3 ROP colors; insert accepted — preprinted; page cut-offs — 21¼".
Mechanical specifications: Type page 13" x 21¼"; E - 6 cols, 2 1/16", 1/8" between; A - 6 cols, 2 1/16", 1/8" between; C - 8 cols, 1½", 1/8" between.
Commodity consumption: Newsprint 202 short tons; widths 27½", 13¾"; average pages per issue 14(d).
Equipment: EDITORIAL: Front-end hardware — Ap/Mac Quadra 650, Ap/Mac Quadra 610; Front-end software — Baseview; Printers — Ap/Mac LaserWriter Pro. CLASSIFIED: Front-end hardware — Ap/Mac; Front-end software — Baseview. PRODUCTION: OCR software — Caere/OmniPage; Typesetters — Ap/Mac LaserWriter II NTX; Scanners — HP/ScanJet Plus. WIRE SERVICES: News — AP; Syndicates — United Media, NAS, Universal Press, King Features; Receiving dishes — AP. BUSINESS COMPUTERS: IBM/PC, IBM/AS-400; PCs & micros networked; PCs & main system networked.

RONCEVERTE
See LEWISBURG

WEIRTON
See STEUBENVILLE, OH

WELCH
McDowell County
'90 U.S. Census- 3,028; E&P '96 Est. 2,627

The Welch Daily News
(e-mon to fri)

The Welch Daily News, 125 Wyoming St.; PO Box 569, Welch, WV 24801; tel (304) 436-3144; fax (304) 436-3146. Moffitt Newspapers group.
Circulation: 6,005(e); Sworn Sept. 30, 1994.
Price: 30¢(d); $5.20/mo; $75.00/yr (mail).
Advertising: Open inch rate $7.98(e). **Representative:** Landon Associates Inc.
News Service: UPI. **Politics:** Republican. **Established:** 1923.
Not Published: New Year; Memorial Day; Independence Day; Labor Day; Thanksgiving; Christmas.
Special Editions: Back-to-School (Aug); Christmas Shopping Guide; Annual Coal; Football; Basketball Local History.

CORPORATE OFFICERS

President	John F Moffitt
Secretary	Fred D Moffitt
Treasurer	Annie Laurie Moffitt

GENERAL MANAGEMENT

Publisher	W A Johnson
Purchasing Agent	Irene Wooten

ADVERTISING

Director	Vance Hayes
Manager-Classified	Tammy Hopkins

CIRCULATION

Manager	Kay Prevento

NEWS EXECUTIVE

Managing Editor	Mary Stillwell

EDITORS AND MANAGERS

Action Line/Ridge Runner	News Staff
Editorial Page Editor	W A Johnson
Food/Home Furnishings Editor	Betsy Osborne
Society Editor	Betsy Osborne
Sports Editor	Dan Stillwell

Market Information: TMC.
Mechanical available: Offset; Black and 3 ROP colors; insert accepted — preprinted; page cut-offs — 21½".
Mechanical specifications: Type page 13" x 21½"; E - 6 cols, 2 1/16", 1/8" between; A - 6 cols, 2 1/16", 1/8" between; C - 9 cols, 1 3/8", 1/16" between.
Commodity consumption: average pages per issue 12(d).
Equipment: EDITORIAL: Front-end hardware — COM/350, Ap/Mac; Other equipment — COM.
PRESSROOM: Line 1 — 5-G/Community; Folders — 1-G. MAILROOM: Addressing machine — 2-Am. WIRE SERVICES: News — UPI; Receiving dishes — UPI. BUSINESS COMPUTERS: Bs/L-9000, Hyundai/Computer, Ap/Mac; PCs & micros networked.

WHEELING
Ohio County
'90 U.S. Census- 34,882; E&P '96 Est. 30,892
ABC-CZ (90): 77,700 (HH 23,794)

The Intelligencer
(m-mon to sat)

Wheeling News-Register
(e-mon to fri; S)

The Intelligencer/Wheeling News-Register, 1500 Main St., Wheeling, WV 26003; tel (304) 233-0100; fax (304) 233-0327. Ogden Newspapers group.
Circulation: 22,997(m); 20,988(e); 42,163 (m-sat); 52,843(S); ABC Sept. 30, 1995.
Price: 35¢(d); 35¢(sat); $1.00(S); $2.00/wk; $8.00/mo; $104.00/yr.
Advertising: Open inch rate $54.20(m); $54.20(e); $54.20(m-sat); $56.88(S). **Representative:** Landon Associates Inc.
News Service: AP. **Established:** 1852 (Intelligencer), 1890 (News Register).
Not Published: New Year; Memorial Day; Independence Day; Labor Day; Thanksgiving; Christmas.
Special Editions: Progress Edition, Bride (Feb); Car Care (Mar); Home Improvement (Apr); Football (Aug); Physical Fitness, Car Care (Sept); Recipe Cookbook (Nov).
Special Weekly Section: Entertainment (TGIF) (fri).
Magazines: Parade, TV Book (own, local, newsprint) (S).

CORPORATE OFFICERS

President/Publisher	G Ogden Nutting
Vice Pres	William C Nutting
Vice Pres	Robert M Nutting
Treasurer	Duane D Wittman
Secretary	William O Nutting

GENERAL MANAGEMENT

General Manager	Robert DeFrancis
Controller	Duane D Wittman

ADVERTISING

Director	Robert Diehl
Manager-Classified	John Ford
Manager-Retail	Perry Nardo

CIRCULATION

Director	Allan W Bowlby

NEWS EXECUTIVES

Intelligencer	
Exec Editor	Robert A Kelly
Editor-City	Theadiane Gompers
Regional Editor	Joseph C Lampert
News-Register	
Exec Editor	J Michael Myer
Editor-City	Margaret Beltz
Regional Editor	Joseph C Lampert

EDITORS AND MANAGERS

Intelligencer	
Editorial Page Editor	Robert A Kelly
Food/Women's Editor	Cheryl Danehart
News Editor	Charles Creamer
Religion Editor	Charles Creamer
Sports Editor	Doug Huff
News-Register	
Business/Finance Editor	Al Molnar
Editorial Page Editor	J Michael Myer
Entertainment Editor	Theadiane Gompers
Fashion/Women's Editor	Gladys Van Horne
News Editor	Al Molnar
Sports Editor	Nick Bedway

MANAGEMENT INFORMATION SERVICES

Data Processing Manager	John Chaykowsky

PRODUCTION

Manager	Douglas J Hartlieb
Foreman-Pressroom	Danny Zelkowski

Market Information: Zoned editions; Split Run; TMC.
Mechanical available: Offset; Black and 3 ROP colors; insert accepted — preprinted; page cut-offs — 23 9/16".
Mechanical specifications: Type page 13" x 22"; E - 6 cols, 2 1/16", 1/8" between; A - 6 cols, 2 1/16", 1/8" between; C - 8 cols, 1 9/16", 1/16" between.
Commodity consumption: Newsprint 6,000 short tons; widths 54", 40½", 27"; black ink 130,500 pounds; color ink 27,000 pounds; average pages per issue 24(d), 54(S); single plates used 67,500.
Equipment: EDITORIAL: Front-end hardware — 1-SII/ET960, 34-SII/Terminal. CLASSIFIED: Front-end hardware — 1-SII, 5-SII/VDT. DISPLAY: Adv layout systems — Ap/Mac, QuarkXPress, Multi-Ad/Creator; Front-end hardware — 4-Ap/Power Mac 6100, New-Gen/Turbo PS-660B; Front-end software — QuarkXPress, Adobe/Photoshop, Multi-Ad/Creator, AP AdSend; Printers — NewGen/Turbo PS-660B, 2-MON/1270 Imagesetter; Other equipment — HP/ScanJet IIc. PRODUCTION: Pagination software — QuarkXPress 3.31; Typesetters — 2-Ap/LaserWriter NTX, 2-MON/1270 Imagesetter; Plate exposures — Magnum; Plate processors — Nat/A-250; Scanners — HP IIci, Kk/RFS-2035, Nikon/Coolscan; Production cameras — 1-C/Pager, 1-AG/2024; Automatic film processors — LE; Film transporters — LE; Color separation equipment (conventional) — Ap/Power Mac 7100.
PRESSROOM: Line 1 — 4-G/Mark I (offset); Line 2 — 2-PEC/Eagle (3 color ink); Press drives — PEC/Bond; Pasters — PEC. MAILROOM: Counter stackers — 2-HL/Monitor, 1-HL/HI2; Inserters and stuffers — S/1372; Bundle tyer — 2-MLN/2EE, 1-MLN/2, 1-MLN/2A; Wrapping singles — Sa; Addressing machine — Ch. COMMUNICATIONS: Facsimile — Canon. WIRE SERVICES: News — AP; Photos — AP; Stock tables — AP SelectStox, TMS; Receiving dishes — size-7ft, AP. BUSINESS COMPUTERS: Applications: Circ, Accts receivable, Gen ledger, Payroll, Newsprint inventory, NCR.

WHITE SULPHUR SPRINGS
See LEWISBURG

WILLIAMSON
Mingo County
'90 U.S. Census- 4,154; E&P '96 Est. 3,502
ABC-NDM (90): 126,719 (HH 45,001)

Williamson Daily News
(e-mon to sat)

Williamson Daily News, 100 E. 3rd Ave.; PO Box 1660, Williamson, WV 25661; tel (304) 235-4242; fax (304) 235-0730; e-mail theinnkeep@aol.com. Mid-South Management Co. Inc. group.
Circulation: 10,254(e); 10,254(e-sat); ABC Sept. 30, 1995.
Price: 50¢(d); 50¢(sat); $131.04/yr (mail); $37.44/3mo, $68.64/6mo.
Advertising: Open inch rate $9.48(e); $9.48(e-sat).
News Service: AP. **Politics:** Independent. **Established:** 1912.
Not Published: New Year; Memorial Day; Independence Day; Labor Day; Thanksgiving; Christmas.
Special Editions: West Virginia Football; Kentucky Football; Car Care; King Coal; Christmas; New Year.
Special Weekly Section: Sports Preview (6/8 pages broadsheet) (published for 12 wks beginning 1st sat in Sept).
Magazine: Golden News (last fri/mo).
Broadcast Affiliate: WXCC 96.5 FM.

CORPORATE OFFICERS

President	Donald E Wilder
Secretary/Treasurer	Sandy Criddle

GENERAL MANAGEMENT

Publisher	Donald E Wilder
Business Manager	Sandy Criddle

ADVERTISING

Manager-Retail	Lisa A Marcum
Manager-Classified	Michelle Allen

MARKETING AND PROMOTION

Manager-Marketing/Promotion	Lisa A Marcum

TELECOMMUNICATIONS

Systems Administrator/Operator	Steve May

CIRCULATION

Manager	John Ball

NEWS EXECUTIVE

Bureau Chief-Pikeville	Rosiland Stanley

EDITORS AND MANAGERS

Editorial Page Editor	Terri Richardson
Electronic Editor	Steve May
Science Editor	Terri Richardson
Sports Editor	Tom Bogar

PRODUCTION

Foreman-Composing	Lisa A Marcum
Foreman-Pressroom	Roger Lloyd

Market Information: TMC; Operate database; Electronic edition.
Mechanical available: Offset; Black and 2 ROP colors; insert accepted — preprinted; page cut-offs — 21½".
Mechanical specifications: Type page 13" x 21¾"; E - 6 cols, 2 1/16", 1/8" between; A - 6 cols, 2 1/16", 1/8" between; C - 9 cols.
Commodity consumption: widths 27½", 13¾"; average pages per issue 24(d).
Equipment: EDITORIAL: Front-end hardware — Server; Front-end software — Novell/Netware 2.0; Printers — Ap/Mac LaserWriter 16-600 PS. CLASSIFIED: Front-end hardware — Server; Front-end software — Novell/Netware 2.0.; Printers — Ap/Mac LaserWriter 16-600PS. DISPLAY: Adv layout systems — Ap/Power Mac 7100; Front-end software — QuarkXPress 3.11, Adobe/FreeHand 5.0, Adobe/Photoshop 3.0; Printers — AG/Accuset, Star/400 RIP, Ap/Mac LaserWriter 16-600 PS. PRODUCTION: Pagination software — QuarkXPress 3.11; OCR software — Caere/OmniPro; Typesetters — 2-COM/Unisetters, AG/Accuset, Star/400 RIP; Plate exposures — 2-Nu/Flip Top FT40; Electronic picture desk — Ap/Power Mac 8100 w/Adobe/Photoshop; Scanners — Nikon/Coolscan, AG/Arcus Flatbed; Production cameras — 1-B/24x24,

I-440 West Virginia

1-DAI/24x24; Automatic film processors — 1-LE/18; Shrink lenses — 1-CK Optical; Color separation equipment (conventional) — 1-Omega/30, 1-Vivitar/206; Digital color separation equipment — AG/Accuset, Star/400 RIP.
PRESSROOM: Line 1 — 6-KP/Daily King. MAILROOM: Counter stackers — 1-BG; Inserters and stuffers — 4-DG/320; Bundle tyer — 1-Bu/42409; Addressing machine — 1-Am, 1-KR. COMMUNICATIONS: Facsimile — Panasonic; Systems used — satellite. WIRE SERVICES: News — AP; Receiving dishes — size-5m, AP. BUSINESS COMPUTERS: IBM/Compat; Applications: Bookkeeping functions, TMC mailing list, Editorial, Paginate.

WISCONSIN

ANTIGO
Langlade County
'90 U.S. Census- 8,276; E&P '96 Est. 8,076

Antigo Daily Journal
(e-mon to fri; m-sat)

Antigo Daily Journal, 612 Superior St., Antigo, WI 54409; tel (715) 623-4191.
Circulation: 6,788(e); 6,788(m-sat); Sworn Oct. 2, 1995.
Price: 35¢(d); 35¢(sat); $50.00/yr.
Advertising: Open inch rate $5.70(e); $5.70(m-sat).
News Service: AP. **Politics:** Independent. **Established:** 1903.
Not Published: New Year; Memorial Day; Independence Day; Labor Day; Thanksgiving; Christmas.
Special Editions: Dollars & Sense (Tax Guide), Bridal Guide (Jan); USSA Snowmobile Series (Feb); Spring Home Improvement, Chamber Guide (Mar); Spring Home & Garden, Sports & Fishing Guide (Apr); Graduation '96 (May); June Dairy Month (June); Market Street Day, 4-H Youth Fair Days (July); Back-to-School (Aug); Fall Home Improvement (Sept); New Cars Intro '97 (Oct); Holiday Recipes, Holiday Gift Guide (Nov); Holiday Moonlight Madness (Dec); Primetimes (monthly).
Special Weekly Sections: Food (mon); Weekender (thur); TV Highlights (sat).

GENERAL MANAGEMENT
Publisher M F Berner
General Manager Fred A Berner

ADVERTISING
Director Jon Croce

NEWS EXECUTIVES
Editor Fred A Berner
Managing Editor Fred A Berner

EDITORS AND MANAGERS
Home Furnishings/Society Editor Lisa Erickson
Sports Editor Vernon Cahak
Teen-Age/Youth Editor Fred A Berner

Market Information: TMC.
Mechanical available: Offset; Black and 3 ROP colors; insert accepted — preprinted; page cutoffs — 22¾".
Mechanical specifications: Type page 13" x 21"; E - 6 cols, 2¹⁄₁₆", ⅛" between; A - 6 cols, 2¹⁄₁₆", ⅛" between; C - 8 cols, 1⅜", ¹⁄₁₆" between.
Commodity consumption: Newsprint 240 short tons; widths 29", 14½"; black ink 6,328 pounds; color ink 40 pounds; single pages printed 5,896; average pages per issue 16(d); single plates used 3,300.
Equipment:
PRESSROOM: Line 1 — 5-G/Community. MAILROOM: Counter stackers — St; Inserters and stuffers — KAN; Bundle tyer — 1-Bu; Addressing machine — RSK/Tandy printer. WIRE SERVICES: News — AP. BUSINESS COMPUTERS: IBM/PC-AT, RSK/Tandy 4000; Applications: Accts receivable, Mail, Circ notices, Payroll.

APPLETON-NEENAH-MENASHA
Outagamie and Winnebago Counties
'90 U.S. Census- 94,034 (Appleton 56,177; Neenah 23,219; Menasha 14,638); E&P '96 Est. 93,538 (Appleton 54,595; Neenah 24,190; Menasha 14,753)
ABC-CZ (90): 140,086 (HH 53,294)

The Post-Crescent
(e-mon to fri; m-sat; S)

The Post-Crescent, 306 W. Washington St.; PO Box 59, Appleton, WI 54912; tel (414) 733-4411; fax (414) 954-1945. Thomson Newspapers group.
Circulation: 60,230(e); 60,230(m-sat); 76,151(S); ABC Sept. 30, 1995.
Price: 50¢(d); 50¢(sat); $1.50(S); $3.25/wk; $169.00/yr (carrier), $182.00/yr (mail).
Advertising: Open inch rate $32.85(e); $32.85(m-sat); $40.39(S). **Representative:** Cresmer, Woodward, O'Mara & Ormsbee.
News Services: AP, SHNS. **Politics:** Independent. **Established:** 1853 (Crescent), 1883 (Post).
Advertising not accepted: Mail order, vending machines.
Special Editions: Spring Brides, Winter Wonderland of Homes (Jan); Health File, Appreciation Discount, Annual Report, American Dream Home Show (Feb); Design-An-Ad, Dollars & Sense, Area Visitors Guide, Paper Arts, Home & Garden (PC Home Show) (Mar); Baseball, Spring Fashion, Seniors, Foxes, Home & Garden II, Vacation & Travel, Healthfile II (Apr); Graduation, Mother's Day, Home & Garden III, Home Buying Helper, Recycling & Environment (May); Parade of Homes, Father's Day, Fall Brides, Street Gazette (June); Seniors, EAA, Healthfile III, Appreciation Discount, Health File (July); Fall Fashion, Football, Fall Home Improvement I (Aug); Packer/Badger, Home Furnishings, United Way, Fall Home Improvement II, Answer Book, Healthfile IV (Sept); Deer Hunting, Fox Cities Marathon, Credit Union, Seniors (Oct); Gift Guide I, Christmas Opening (Thanksgiving Edition), Gift Guide II, Basketball (Nov); Gift Guide III, Gift Guide IV (Dec).
Special Weekly Sections: Best Food Day, Farms (mon); Business (tues); Wine & Dine (thur); Church, Kids', Weekend/Home Tab (sat); Business, Travel (S).
Magazines: Weekend (sat); Parade, TV Today, Color Comics (S).

GENERAL MANAGEMENT
Publisher/General Manager James C Gleim
Manager-Credit Patrick Boeselager
Controller Dick Shikoski
Purchasing Agent Donald H Frank

ADVERTISING
Director Joel Morse
Manager-Retail Mary Buege
Manager-National/Regional Sales James Ultang

MARKETING AND PROMOTION
Manager-Promotion Judy Fischer

CIRCULATION
Director David Schwebs
Manager-Home Delivery David Gill

NEWS EXECUTIVES
Editor Kevin Doyle
Managing Editor William Knutson

EDITORS AND MANAGERS
Action Line Editor William Knutson
Automotive Editor Jolene Westerman
Business/Labor Editor Arlen Boardman
City Editor Bernie Petersen
Copy Desk Chief Dan Roherty
Editorial Page Editor Michael Walter
Editorial Writer Michael Walter
Editorial Writer Clifford Miller
Entertainment/Amusements Editor Ed Berthiaume
Farm Editor Roger Pitt
Features Editor Ed Berthiaume
Films/Theater Editor Ed Berthiaume
Food Editor Ed Berthiaume
Garden Editor Jolene Westerman
Graphics Editor/Art Director Steve Massie
Health/Medical Editor Maija Penikis
Home Furnishings Editor Jolene Westerman
Librarian Nancy Wetak
Lifestyle Editor Ed Berthiaume
Music Editor Ed Berthiaume
News Editor Dan Flannery
Outdoors Editor Ed Culhane
Photo Editor Dwight Nale
Picture Editor Dwight Nale
Political Columnist Judy Williams
Radio/Television Editor Tom Richards
Religion Editor Maija Penikis
School Editor Kathy Nufer
Sports Editor Larry Gallup
Travel Editor Ed Berthiaume
Weekend Editor Amy Pelishek

PRODUCTION
Manager Donald H Frank
Foreman-Mailroom Gene Mueller
Foreman-Composing (Day) Marion Holschuh-Van Zeeland
Foreman-Composing (Night) Rob T Flater
Foreman-Pressroom Everett Bornemann

Market Information: TMC.
Mechanical available: Offset; Black and 3 ROP colors; insert accepted — preprinted; page cutoffs — 23⁹⁄₁₆".
Mechanical specifications: Type page 13" x 22"; E - 6 cols, 2.07", ¹⁄₁₂" between; A - 6 cols, 2.07", ¹⁄₁₂" between; C - 9 cols, 1.36", ¹⁄₁₂" between.
Commodity consumption: Newsprint 5,000 short tons; widths 55", 41¼", 27½"; black ink 100,000 pounds; color ink 12,000 pounds; average pages per issue 32(d), 74(S); single plates used 15,000.
Equipment: EDITORIAL: Front-end hardware — CD/2300; Front-end software — CD; Printers — 2-LBF/20. CLASSIFIED: Front-end hardware — CD; Front-end software — CD; Other equipment — CD/CAP. DISPLAY: Adv layout systems — Cx/Breeze; Front-end hardware — 6-Sun/380; Front-end software — Cx. PRODUCTION: Typesetters — 2-Linotype-Hell/Linotronic 530; Plate exposures — 2-Nu; Plate processors — 2-WL; Scanners — 1-ECR/Autokon 8400; Production cameras — 1-C/Marathon, 1-R, 1-SCREEN; Automatic film processors — 1-LE/24, 1-LE/LD24AQ, 1-LE/18; Digital color separation equipment — 1-Veri-Color.
PRESSROOM: Line 1 — 7-G/Metro Offset (3 half decks); Folders — 2-G/3:2; Press control system — Fin. MAILROOM: Counter stackers — 2-Id/550, 2-Id/2000; Inserters and stuffers — 2-GMA/PTP 12-into-1; Bundle tyer — 3-Dynaric; Wrapping singles — 1-CYP, 1-Akebono; Addressing machine — 1-BH, 1-CH. WIRE SERVICES: News — Syndicates — AP, THO, SHNS; Receiving dishes — size-3m, AP. BUSINESS COMPUTERS: 2-IBM/Sys 34; Applications: Circ, Newsprint, Private party billing; PCs & main system networked.

ASHLAND
Ashland County
'90 U.S. Census- 8,695; E&P '96 Est. 8,476

The Daily Press (m-mon to sat)

The Daily Press, 122 W. 3rd St., Ashland, WI 54806; tel (715) 682-2313; fax (715) 682-4699. Murphy Newspaper group.
Circulation: 7,860(m); 7,860(m-sat); Sworn Sept. 29, 1995.
Price: 50¢(d); 50¢(sat); $6.00/mo (carrier).
Advertising: Open inch rate $7.30(m); $7.30(m-sat). **Representative:** Papert Companies.
News Service: AP. **Politics:** Independent. **Established:** 1888.
Not Published: New Year; Memorial Day; Independence Day; Labor Day; Thanksgiving; Christmas.

CORPORATE OFFICER
President John B Murphy

GENERAL MANAGEMENT
General Manager Marlin J Hofmeyer

ADVERTISING
Director Jeff Swiston

CIRCULATION
Manager Rebecca Karis

NEWS EXECUTIVE
Managing Editor Evan Sasman

EDITOR AND MANAGER
Area News Editor Clair S Duquette

PRODUCTION
Superintendent David Fisher

Market Information: Split Run; TMC.
Mechanical available: Offset; Black and 3 ROP colors; insert accepted — preprinted; page cutoffs — 22¾".
Mechanical specifications: Type page 13" x 21½"; E - 6 cols, 2¹⁄₁₆", ⅛" between; A - 6 cols, 2¹⁄₁₆", ⅛" between; C - 6 cols, 2¹⁄₁₆", ⅛" between.
Commodity consumption: Newsprint 291 metric tons; width 27½"; average pages per issue 16(d).
Equipment: PRODUCTION: Plate exposures — 1-Nu/Flip Top; Production cameras — 1-B; Automatic film processors — 1-LE.
PRESSROOM: Line 1 — 4-G/Community. MAILROOM: Inserters and stuffers — 1-KAN; Bundle tyer — 2-Bu. WIRE SERVICES: News — AP; Receiving dishes — size-10ft, AP. BUSINESS COMPUTERS: 2-RSK/12, 2-RSK/3000 HD; Applications: Accts receivable, Circ.

BARABOO
Sauk County
'90 U.S. Census- 9,203; E&P '96 Est. 10,386

News-Republic/South Central Wisconsin News
(m-mon to sat)

News-Republic/South Central Wisconsin News, 219 First St.; PO Box 9, Baraboo, WI 53913; tel (608) 356-4808; fax (608) 356-0344. Independent Media Group Inc. group.
Circulation: 4,062(m); VAC June 30, 1995.
Price: 50¢(d); 75¢(sat); $84.00/yr (carrier).
Advertising: Open inch rate $8.10(m); comb with Portage Daily Register (mS) $22.25. **Representative:** Landon Associates Inc.
News Service: AP. **Politics:** Independent. **Established:** 1855.
Note: Effective Oct. 14, 1995, this publication changed its publishing plan from (m-mon to fri; S) to (m-mon to sat).
Not Published: New Year; Memorial Day; Independence Day; Labor Day; Christmas.
Special Editions: Car Care; Summer Fun Guide; Progress; Home Improvement; June Dairy; Fall Sports.
Magazine: Prime Time.

GENERAL MANAGEMENT
Publisher David Gentry
Controller Cheryl Troost

ADVERTISING
Manager Tom Dugan

CIRCULATION
Director Michael Jeffery

NEWS EXECUTIVE
Editor Richard Pratt

EDITORS AND MANAGERS
Lifestyle Editor Kristin Gilpatrick
Sports Editor Paul Krueger

PRODUCTION
Manager-Composing Jason Sloaf
Manager-Press John Barber
Asst Manager-Press Al Zajda

Market Information: TMC.
Mechanical available: Offset; Black and 3 ROP colors; insert accepted — preprinted; page cutoffs — 21½".
Mechanical specifications: Type page 13" x 21½"; E - 6 cols, 2¹⁄₁₆", ⅛" between; A - 6 cols, 2¹⁄₁₆", ⅛" between; C - 9 cols, 1⁵⁄₁₆", ⅛" between.
Commodity consumption: Newsprint 200 short tons; widths 27", 34"; black ink 800 pounds; average pages per issue 14(d); single plates used 14.
Equipment: EDITORIAL: Front-end hardware — Mk. CLASSIFIED: Front-end hardware — Mk. DISPLAY: Printers — Ap/Mac LaserPrinter. PRODUCTION: Typesetters — Ap/Mac LaserPrinter; Plate exposures — 1-Nu; Scanners — 3-COM/2961HS, 1-COM/7200, 1-COM/4; Production cameras — B/Vertical.
PRESSROOM: Line 1 — 5-G/Community; Press control system — Fin. MAILROOM: Inserters and stuffers — 5-MM; Bundle tyer — 1-Bu. WIRE SERVICES: News — AP.

BEAVER DAM
Dodge County
'90 U.S. Census- 14,196; E&P '96 Est. 14,418

Daily Citizen
(e-mon to fri; m-sat)

Daily Citizen, 805 Park Ave.; PO Box 558, Beaver Dam, WI 53916; tel (414) 887-0321; fax (414) 887-8790.
Circulation: 11,255(e); 11,255(m-sat); Sworn Oct. 2, 1995.
Price: 50¢(d); 50¢(sat); $86.24/yr.
Advertising: Open inch rate $7.65(e); $7.65(m-sat).
News Services: AP, NYT. **Politics:** Independent. **Established:** 1911.

Copyright ©1996 by the Editor & Publisher Co.

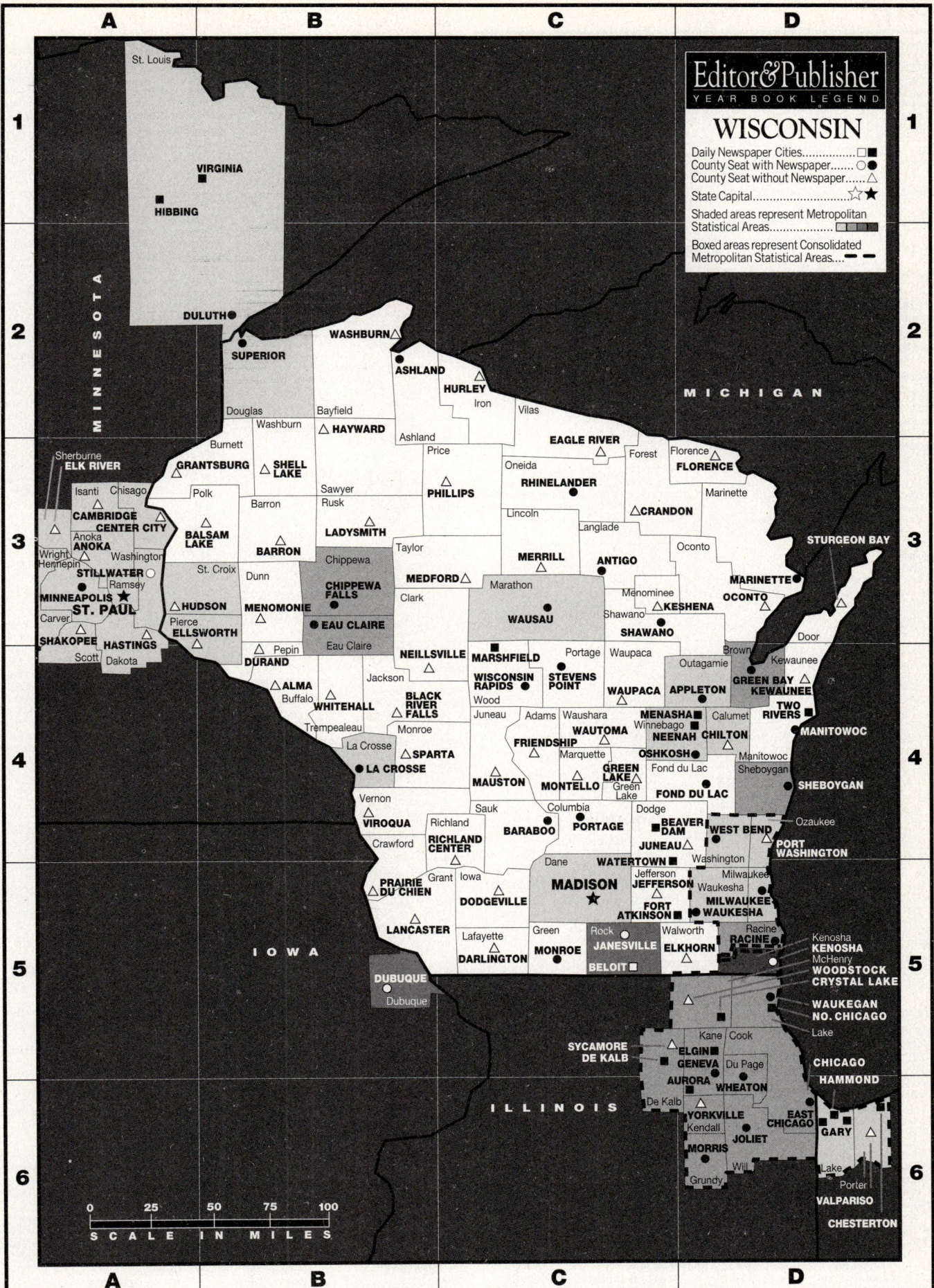

I-442 Wisconsin

Not Published: New Year; Memorial Day; Independence Day; Labor Day; Thanksgiving; Christmas.
Special Editions: Fashion; Seasonal Promotions.
Magazines: Monday-Mini; Tri-County.

CORPORATE OFFICER
President James E Conley Jr
GENERAL MANAGEMENT
Publisher James E Conley Jr
ADVERTISING
Director Steve Ciccantelli
CIRCULATION
Director Curtis Lenius
NEWS EXECUTIVE
Exec Editor Jeff Hovind
EDITORS AND MANAGERS
City Editor Jame Kelsh
Editorial Page Editor Jeff Hovind
MANAGEMENT INFORMATION SERVICES
Data Processing Manager Joy Nieman
PRODUCTION
Manager James Dittmann

Market Information: Zoned editions; TMC.
Mechanical available: Offset; Black and 3 ROP colors; insert accepted — preprinted; page cut-offs — 22¾".
Mechanical specifications: Type page 15¼" x 21⅜"; E - 6 cols, 2 1/16", ⅛" between; A - 6 cols, 2 1/16", ⅛" between; C - 9 cols, 1⅜", 1/16" between.
Commodity consumption: Newsprint 379 short tons; widths 32½", 16¼"; black ink 5,116 pounds; color ink 1,010 pounds; single pages printed 4,944; average pages per issue 16(d); single plates used 2,626.
Equipment: EDITORIAL: Front-end hardware — 2-Ap/Mac Plus, 8-Ap/Mac II. CLASSIFIED: Front-end hardware — 3-Ap/Mac II. DISPLAY: Adv layout systems — 5-Ap/Mac II. PRODUCTION: Plate exposures — 1-Nu/Flip Top FT40LNS, 1-Nu/Flip Top FT40UPNS; Plate processors — 2-WL/Lithoplater 380, 1-Nat/A-250; Production cameras — 1-B/Commodore; Automatic film processors — 1-P/Super G 24"; Reproportion units — 1-FLS.
PRESSROOM: Line 1 — 12-G/Community; Line 2 — 20-G/Community; Folders — 5-G/Community; Pasters — 7-MEG. MAILROOM: Counter stackers — 5-BG/Count-O-Veyor 104-108; Inserters and stuffers — 4-MM/227E, 6-MM/227; Bundle tyer — 4-Bu, 1-CYP; Addressing machine — 2-Am, 1-Kk. WIRE SERVICES: News — AP; Syndicates — NYT; Receiving dishes — AP, NYT. BUSINESS COMPUTERS: 10-IBM/PS2, 6-Ap/Mac II; Applications: Circ, Adv billing, Accts receivable, Payroll, Inventory, Purchasing; PCs & micros networked.

BELOIT, WI-SOUTH BELOIT-ROCKTON, IL

Rock County, WI
Winnebago County, IL

'90 U.S. Census- 42,573 (Beloit, WI 35,573; South Beloit, IL 4,072; Rockton, IL 2,928); E&P '96 Est. 43,571 (Beloit, WI 36,376; South Beloit, IL 4,190; Rockton, IL 3,005)

Beloit Daily News

(e-mon to sat)

Beloit Daily News, 149 State St., Beloit, WI 53511; tel (608) 365-8811; fax (608) 365-1420; web site http://www.bossnt.com/bdn.html. Hagadone Corp. group.
Circulation: 15,672(e); 15,672(e-sat); Sworn Oct. 1, 1995.
Price: 50¢(d); 50¢(sat); $9.75/mo (carrier), $10.00/mo (motor route); $108.00/yr (mail); $111.00/yr (in-county mail), $123.00/yr (out-county mail).
Advertising: Open inch rate $19.75(e); $19.75(e-sat). **Representative:** Landon Associates Inc.
News Services: AP, United Media Service. **Politics:** Independent. **Established:** 1848.
Not Published: New Year; Memorial Day; Independence Day; Labor Day; Thanksgiving; Christmas.
Advertising not accepted: At publisher's discretion.
Special Editions: Progress Edition (Mar); Map/Guide (May).
Special Weekly Sections: Showcase/Real Estate; Wheels/Automotive.
Magazine: TV Listing (fri).

CORPORATE OFFICERS
President Roy Wellman
Secretary/Treasurer Arthur S Flagan
GENERAL MANAGEMENT
Publisher Kent D Eymann
Manager-Office Debra J Arn
ADVERTISING
Director John Wingate
CIRCULATION
Manager Robert S Simonoff
NEWS EXECUTIVE
Editor Bill Barth
EDITORS AND MANAGERS
Society Editor Sue Kurth
Sports Editor James Franz
PRODUCTION
Manager Donald Behling

Market Information: Split Run; TMC.
Mechanical available: Offset; Black and 3 ROP colors; insert accepted — preprinted, all; page cut-offs — 22¾".
Mechanical specifications: Type page 13" x 21½"; E - 6 cols, 2 1/16", ⅛" between; A - 6 cols, 2 1/16", ⅛" between; C - 8 cols, 1½", ⅛" between.
Commodity consumption: Newsprint 650 short tons; widths 27½", 13¾"; black ink 9,800 pounds; color ink 3,000 pounds; single pages printed 7,444; average pages per issue 24(d); single plates used 12,000.
Equipment: EDITORIAL: Front-end hardware — 16-AST/Bravo; Front-end software — Dewar; Printers — Okidata/Microline 320. CLASSIFIED: Front-end hardware — 3-AST/Bravo 286; Front-end software — Dewar; Printers — OTC/850X2. DISPLAY: Front-end hardware — 2-Ap/Mac IIcx; Front-end software — Multi-Ad/Creator. PRODUCTION: OCR software — Caere/OmniPage; Typesetters — 2-Ap/Mac LaserWriter II NTX; Plate exposures — 1-Nu/Flip Top; Plate processors — 1-Nat/A-250; Electronic picture desk — Lf/AP Leaf Picture Desk; Scanners — Ap/Mac Scanner; Production cameras — 1-SCREEN/650D; Automatic film processors — CARNFELD/Rali Speed 28; Color separation equipment (conventional) — Lf/Leafscan 35.
PRESSROOM: Line 1 — 6-G/Urbanite; Folders — 1-G/2:1; Press control system — Fin. MAILROOM: Inserters and stuffers — MM/227 5-into-1; Bundle tyer — 1-MLN/Plastic strapper. WIRE SERVICES: News — AP; Photos — AP; Receiving dishes — size-10m, AP. BUSINESS COMPUTERS: 1-DEC/TC 3800; Applications: Micro/VMS.

CHIPPEWA FALLS

Chippewa County

'90 U.S. Census- 12,727; E&P '96 Est. 13,282

Chippewa Herald Telegram

(e-mon to thur; m-sat; S)

Chippewa Herald Telegram, 321 Frenette Dr.; PO Box 69, Chippewa Falls, WI 54729; tel (715) 723-5515; fax (715) 723-9644. Independent Media Group Inc. group.
Circulation: 7,391(e); 7,391(m-sat); 7,391(S); VAC Mar. 31, 1995.
Price: 50¢(d); 50¢(sat); $1.00(S); $8.95/mo; $101.00/yr.
Advertising: Open inch rate $12.90(e); $12.90(m-sat); $12.90(S).
News Service: AP. **Politics:** Independent. **Established:** 1867.
Not Published: New Year; Memorial Day; Labor Day; Christmas.
Magazines: TV Guide; Color Comics; Lifestyles (S); Golden Age Section (end of each month).

GENERAL MANAGEMENT
Publisher Mark Baker
ADVERTISING
Manager Andrew S Bruns
CIRCULATION
Manager Sam Arnold
NEWS EXECUTIVE
Editor Ross Evavold
EDITORS AND MANAGERS
Books Editor Ross Evavold
Music Critic Ross Evavold
Sports Editor Fred Maki
Women's Editor Cathy Hamlin
MANAGEMENT INFORMATION SERVICES
Data Processing Manager Lu Ann Oldenberg

Market Information: TMC; ADS.
Mechanical available: Offset; Black and 3 ROP colors; insert accepted — preprinted, any; page cut-offs — 21½".
Mechanical specifications: Type page 13" x 21½"; E - 6 cols, 2 1/16", ⅛" between; A - 6 cols, 2 1/16", ⅛" between; C - 10 cols, 1 3/16", 1/16" between.
Commodity consumption: Newsprint 420 short tons; widths 27", 30", 33"; black ink 15,300 pounds; color ink 2,000 pounds; single pages printed 6,500; average pages per issue 16(d), 24(S); single plates used 4,000.
Equipment: EDITORIAL: Front-end hardware — Mk. CLASSIFIED: Front-end hardware — Mk. DISPLAY: Adv layout systems — 2-Ap/Mac. PRODUCTION: Typesetters — 2-COM/Laserwriter; Platemaking systems — DiLitho; Plate exposures — 1-Nu/Flip Top FT40L, 1-Nu/Flip Top FT40x30 (two sided); Plate processors — 1-Nu; Scanners — HP/ScanJet Plus; Production cameras — SCREEN; Automatic film processors — P; Color separation equipment (conventional) — Hel; Digital color separation equipment — Lf/Leafscan 35.
PRESSROOM: Line 1 — 11-G, 2-DEV/Flexicolor; Line 2 — 10-G; Folders — 4-G/2:1. MAILROOM: Counter stackers — 2-BG; Inserters and stuffers — 2-KAN; Bundle tyer — 2-Bu, 1-It; Addressing machine — KR. COMMUNICATIONS: Systems used — satellite. WIRE SERVICES: News — AP; Photos — AP; Receiving dishes — AP. BUSINESS COMPUTERS: Sperry, Unisys; Applications: Bus, Circ, Adv; PCs & micros networked; PCs & main system networked.

EAU CLAIRE

Eau Claire and Chippewa Counties

'90 U.S. Census- 55,180; E&P '96 Est. 59,067
ABC-CZ (90): 66,975 (HH 24,993)

Leader-Telegram

(e-mon to fri; m-sat; S)

Leader-Telegram, 701 S. Farwell St.; Box 570, Eau Claire, WI 54702; tel (715) 833-9200; fax (715) 833-9244.
Circulation: 31,216(e); 36,667(m-sat); 41,367(S); ABC Sept. 30, 1995.
Price: 50¢(d); 50¢(sat); $1.50(S); $2.40/wk; $10.40/mo (carrier); $80.00/yr (mail).
Advertising: Open inch rate $21.44(e); $21.44(m-sat); $22.51(S). **Representative:** Landon Associates Inc.
News Services: AP, NYT, SHNS. **Politics:** Independent. **Established:** 1881 (Leader), 1894 (Telegram).
Not Published: New Year; Memorial Day; Independence Day; Labor Day; Christmas.
Special Weekly Sections: Best Food Day (tues); Automotive, Expanded Entertainment (thur); Outdoors (fri); Sports, Lifestyle, Arts/Entertainment, Business, Travel (S).
Magazines: TV Update, Color Comics (S).

CORPORATE OFFICERS
President Charles Graaskamp
Vice Pres Mark Atkinson
Secretary/Treasurer John Graaskamp
GENERAL MANAGEMENT
General Manager Charles Graaskamp
Controller John Graaskamp
ADVERTISING
Director Jerry Merryfield
MARKETING AND PROMOTION
Manager-Marketing/Promotion Tim Abraham
TELECOMMUNICATIONS
Audiotex Manager Jerry Merryfield
CIRCULATION
Manager Steve Svihovec
Coordinator-Country Jackie Giles
Coordinator-City Sue Pratt
Coordinator-Newspapers in Education Jackie Giles
NEWS EXECUTIVES
Editor Eugene Ringhand
Managing Editor Don Huebscher
EDITORS AND MANAGERS
Amusements/Books Editor Bill Foy
Business Editor Mike Klein
City Editor Doug Mell
Editorial Page Editor Eugene Ringhand
Editorial Writer Eugene Ringhand
Films/Theater Editor Bill Foy
Food Editor Blythe Wachter
Librarian Ann Erickson
Music Editor Bill Foy
Radio/Television Editor Bill Foy
Real Estate Editor Mike Klein
Religion Editor Blythe Wachter
Science/Technology Editor Bob Brown
Sports Editor Tad Reeves
Wire Editor Jerry Poling
MANAGEMENT INFORMATION SERVICES
Data Processing Manager Val Fisher
PRODUCTION
Manager Daryl Lorberter
Manager-Systems Roshan Sharif
Foreman-Pressroom Dan Anderson
Foreman-Composing Wayne Hamler

Market Information: Zoned editions; Split Run; TMC; ADS; Operate audiotex.
Mechanical available: Offset; black; insert accepted — preprinted, all; page cut-offs — 22 13/16".
Mechanical specifications: Type page 13" x 21½"; E - 6 cols, 2", ¼" between; A - 6 cols, 2", ¼" between; C - 9 cols, 1⅜", ⅛" between.
Commodity consumption: Newsprint 2,862 short tons; widths 28", 14"; black ink 33,525 pounds; color ink 13,732 pounds; single pages printed 14,324; average pages per issue 28(d), 56(S); single plates used 15,879.
Equipment: EDITORIAL: Front-end hardware — Ap/Mac PC Network, IBM, Mag, 1-Ap/Mac; Front-end software — Microsoft/Word, QuarkXPress; Printers — 1-Copal. CLASSIFIED: Front-end hardware — 10-PC, Novell/Network; Front-end software — Graph-X; Printers — Copal. AUDIOTEX: Hardware — PC; Software — Info-Connect/2000. DISPLAY: Adv layout systems — Ap/Mac fx, Ap/Mac Quadra, Novell/Network, Ap/Mac Appleshare; Front-end hardware — 15-Ap/Mac fx, 1-Ap/Mac NTX, Ap/Mac Quadra; Front-end software — Adobe/Illustrator, QuarkXPress; Printers — 1-Copal. PRODUCTION: Pagination software — QuarkXPress 3.3, Adobe/Illustrator; OCR software — Caere/OmniPage; Typesetters — 2-Hyphen/3100 Recorder, Novell, 2-OPI, Hyphen/RIPs; Plate exposures — 3-Nu; Plate processors — 1-American Litho; Electronic picture desk — Lf/AP Leaf Picture Desk; Scanners — 2-Nikon, 2-AG/Horizon; Production cameras — 1-Liberator; Automatic film processors — 2-AG; Reproportion units — 2-Ap/Mac Quadra; Color separation equipment (conventional) — 2-Ap/Mac Quadra; Digital color separation equipment — Ap/Mac Quadra.
PRESSROOM: Line 1 — 10-G; Folders — 1-G/Half, 1-G/Quarter; Pasters — 3-Cary; Reels and stands — 7-Stands. MAILROOM: Counter stackers — 2-QWI; Inserters and stuffers — 12-Mc, 2-Mc/660; Bundle tyer — 2-MLN; Addressing machine — 2-KR. LIBRARY: Electronic — SMS/Stauffer Gold. WIRE SERVICES: News — AP, SHNS; Stock tables — AP Select-Stox; Syndicates — NYT; Receiving dishes — size-7ft, AP. BUSINESS COMPUTERS: HP; Applications: Circ, Adv billing, Accts receivable, Gen ledger, Dummying; PCs & micros networked; PCs & main system networked.

FOND DU LAC

Fond du Lac County

'90 U.S. Census- 37,757; E&P '96 Est. 39,887
ABC-CZ (90): 42,049 (HH 16,252)

The Reporter (e-mon to fri; S)

The Reporter, 33 W. 2nd St.; PO Box 630, Fond du Lac, WI 54936-0630; tel (414) 922-4600; fax (414) 922-5388. Thomson Newspapers group.
Circulation: 19,489(e); 20,718(S); ABC Sept. 30, 1995.
Price: 50¢(d); $1.25(S); $3.00/wk (carrier), $1.25/wk (S only); $12.00/4wk, $13.00/mo, $5.42/mo (S only); $156.00/yr (mail), $65.00/yr (S only).
Advertising: Open inch rate $17.54(e); $17.54(S). **Representative:** Landon Associates Inc.
News Service: AP. **Politics:** Independent. **Established:** 1870.
Not Published: New Year; Memorial Day; Independence Day; Labor Day; Thanksgiving; Christmas.
Special Weekly Sections: Food (mon); Automotive, Go!/Entertainment (thur); Farm (S).
Magazine: TV (S).

GENERAL MANAGEMENT
Publisher/General Manager Larry Antony
Manager-Special Products Michael Haessly
Controller P James Lange
ADVERTISING
Manager Doug Rankin
Manager-Classified Kathy Schneider
Coordinator-National Tania Cota
TELECOMMUNICATIONS
Audiotex Manager Lori Ditter
CIRCULATION
Manager Dan Gerred

Copyright ©1996 by the Editor & Publisher Co.

NEWS EXECUTIVES

Managing Editor	Richard Roesgen
Assoc Editor	Harley Buchholz

EDITORS AND MANAGERS

Action Line Editor	Harley Buchholz
Automotive Editor	Wayne Noller
Business Editor	Thomas Guenther
City Editor	Michael Mentzer
Editorial Page Editor	Harley Buchholz
Education Editor	Paulette Kilmer
Entertainment/Amusements Editor	Polly Wilson
Environmental Editor	Michael Mentzer
Family Editor	Renee Russell
Farm Editor	Fran O'Leary
Fashion/Style Editor	Renee Russell
Features Editor	Michael Mentzer
Graphics Editor/Art Director	Richard Roesgen
Health/Medical Editor	Michael Mentzer
Living/Lifestyle Editor	Renee Russel
National Editor	Harley Buchholz
News Editor	Michael Mentzer
Photo Department Manager	Don Carson
Political/Government Editor	Harley Buchholz
Religion Editor	Polly Wilson
Science/Technology Editor	Michael Mentzer
Sports Editor	Greg Shriver
State Editor	Wayne Noller
Television/Film Editor	Polly Wilson
Theater/Music Editor	Polly Wilson
Travel Editor	Todd Jensen
Women's Editor	Renee Russell

PRODUCTION

Superintendent-Pressroom	Thomas Wehner

Market Information: Zoned editions; TMC; ADS; Operate audiotex.

Mechanical available: Offset; Black and 3 ROP colors; insert accepted — preprinted; page cut-offs — 22¾".

Mechanical specifications: Type page 13" x 21½"; E - 6 cols, 2 1/16", ⅛" between; A - 6 cols, 2 1/16", ⅛" between; C - 9 cols, 1⅜", 1/16" between.

Equipment: EDITORIAL: Front-end hardware — 15-CText/Grid 80286, CText/Grid, CText/fileserver; Front-end software — Novell 2.15, Postscript; Printers — Panasonic/Kk-P1180. CLASSIFIED: Front-end hardware — 1-CText/fileserver, 4-CText/Grid 80286; Front-end software — Novell 2.15; Printers — C.Itoh/C-15000; Other equipment — Mountain/Tape Drive 150 MB. AUDIOTEX: Hardware — 486 DX2 50/66 MHz CPU 16MB (both systems); Software — Audiotext 2000 2.2; Supplier name — Micro Voice. DISPLAY: Adv layout systems — Ap/Mac, Appletalk/Network, Ethernet; Front-end hardware — Ap/Mac II, Ap/Mac IIcx, Ap/Mac IIci, 5-Ap/Power Mac; Front-end software — Multi-Ad/Creator, Adobe/Illustrator, Aldus/FreeHand, QuarkXPress; Printers — Ap/Mac LaserWriter II, V/5060W, Tegra/Varityper Rm.3; Other equipment — CD-Rom. PRODUCTION: Pagination software — CText, Ventura Viking; Typesetters — Tegra/Varityper 200, Tegra/Varityper 4000, Tegra/Varityper 20, V/5060 W Laser Printers; Platemaking systems — Nu/Flip Top FT 40V6UPNS; Plate processors — Nat/A-250; Electronic picture desk — Lf/AP Leaf Picture Desk; Scanners — Lf/Leafscan 35; Production cameras — LE/1-2-1, SCREEN/America 690-D; Automatic film processors — LE/LD 24AQ, SCREEN/America 220 DT; Color separation equipment (conventional) — Lf/AP Leaf Picture Desk; Digital color separation equipment — AG/PhotoScan, Ap/Power Mac, Adobe/Photoshop, V/Film Recorder.
PRESSROOM: Line 1 — 7-G/Urbanite single width; Line 2 — 1-Ik/Sheet Fed Press; Press drives — RKW, Fin, 1-Motor/D-C Current; Folders — 1-G/Half, 1-G/Quarter; Press control system — RKW, Fin. MAILROOM: Counter stackers — HL/Monitor H-T; Bundle tyer — OVL; Addressing machine — Video-Jet/InkJet. COMMUNICATIONS: Systems used — satellite. WIRE SERVICES: News — AP, SHNS, THO; Photos — AP; Syndicates — SHNS, THO; Receiving dishes — size-3m, AP. BUSINESS COMPUTERS: ATT, Oracle-Gen ledger; Accts payable; Applications: IBM; PCs & main system networked.

FORT ATKINSON

Jefferson County

'90 U.S. Census- 10,227; E&P '96 Est. 10,740

Daily Jefferson County Union (e-mon to fri)

Daily Jefferson County Union, 28 W. Milwaukee Ave.; PO Box 801, Fort Atkinson, WI 53538; tel (414) 563-5551; fax (414) 563-7298.

Circulation: 7,750(e); Sworn Oct. 4, 1994.

Price: 50¢(d); $65.00/yr.

Advertising: Open inch rate $6.50(e).

News Service: AP. **Politics:** Independent-Republican. **Established:** 1870.

Not Published: New Year; Memorial Day; Independence Day; Labor Day; Thanksgiving; Christmas.

Special Editions: FFA (Mar); Spring (Apr); Progress, Bridal (May, June, July); Fort Fest, Farm, Bridal (Aug); Winter, Gemuetlichkeit (Sept); Christmas (Dec).

CORPORATE OFFICER

President	W D Knox

GENERAL MANAGEMENT

Publisher	Brian Victor B Knox

ADVERTISING

Manager	Charles Frandson
Manager-Classified	Diane Niemeyer

MARKETING AND PROMOTION

Director-Marketing	Charles Frandson

CIRCULATION

Manager	Judy Schnell

NEWS EXECUTIVE

Editor	Christine Spangler

EDITORS AND MANAGERS

Books Editor	Brian Victor B Knox
City Editor	Randall Dullum
Editorial Page Editor	Christine Spangler
Farm Editor	Christine Spangler
Fashion/Society Editor	Christine Spangler
News Editor	Christine Spangler
Sports Editor	Jeff Seisser

Mechanical available: Offset; Black and 3 ROP colors; insert accepted — preprinted; page cut-offs — 22¾".

Mechanical specifications: Type page 13" x 21½"; E - 6 cols, 2 1/16", ⅛" between; A - 6 cols, 2 1/16", ⅛" between; C - 8 cols, 1 9/16", 1/16" between.

Commodity consumption: average pages per issue 35(d).

Equipment: EDITORIAL: Front-end hardware — 1-Mk; Other equipment — 2-AX/Ultra-Comp, 1-AX/Ultra-Count. CLASSIFIED: Front-end hardware — 1-Mk. PRODUCTION: Typesetters — 2-P/MK 1, 1-COM/7200; Plate exposures — 1-Douthitt/1400; Production cameras — 1-R/Cl; Automatic film processors — 1-Kk/420. PRESSROOM: Line 1 — 4-G/Community; Folders — 1-G/Community. MAILROOM: Counter stackers — 1-BG/Count-O-Veyor; Bundle tyer — 1-Bu, 3-Malow/Strap-tyer; Addressing machine — 1-MG/602. WIRE SERVICES: News — AP.

GREEN BAY

Brown County

'90 U.S. Census- 96,466; E&P '96 Est. 105,570
ABC-NDM (90): 269,388 (HH 100,385)

The Green Bay News-Chronicle (m-mon to fri; S)

The Green Bay News-Chronicle, 133 S. Monroe (54301); PO Box 2467, Green Bay, WI 54306; tel (414) 432-2941; fax (414) 432-8581.

Circulation: 7,034(m); 64,566(S); Sworn Sept. 25, 1995.

Price: 50¢(d); 50¢(S); $102.00/yr.

Advertising: Open inch rate $16.80(m); $16.80(S). **Representative:** Landon Associates Inc.

News Services: LAT-WP, NYT, UPI. **Politics:** Independent. **Established:** 1972.

Note: Sunday edition of this publication is a free circulation and is being audited by VAC.

Not Published: New Year; Memorial Day; Independence Day; Labor Day; Thanksgiving; Christmas.

Special Editions: Out Town (Jan); Progress Report, Home Improvement & Garden (Feb); Home Improvement & Garden (Mar); Seniors, Car Care, Home Improvement & Garden (Apr); Home Improvement & Garden (May); Bridal Showcase (June); Bridal Showcase, Home Improvement & Garden (Sept); Seniors, Monday Morning Football (Nov); Monday Morning Football (Dec).

Special Weekly Sections: Woman (fri); Sports Beat (S).

Magazine: Bay Beat (local, newsprint) (thur).

CORPORATE OFFICERS

President	Frank A Wood Jr
Vice Pres-Publications	Alan Rasmussen

GENERAL MANAGEMENT

Publisher	Frank A Wood Jr
Assoc Publisher	Pat Wood
General Manager	Ronald W Poppenhagen
Business Manager	Clyde P Baeten

Wisconsin I-443

ADVERTISING

Director-Sales/Marketing	Pat Wood
Manager-Classified	Kristin Van Emperin

CIRCULATION

Director	Scott DeBrux
Director	Dave Wood

NEWS EXECUTIVE

Editor	Ronald W Poppenhagen

EDITORS AND MANAGERS

News Editor	Tom Gunderson
Sports Editor	Scott Roscouius
Weekend Editor	Patti Rasmussen

Market Information: TMC.

Mechanical available: Offset; Black and 3 ROP colors; insert accepted — preprinted; page cut-offs — 13".

Mechanical specifications: Type page 10½" x 13"; E - 5 cols, 2 1/16", ⅛" between; A - 5 cols, 2 1/16", ⅛" between; C - 7 cols, 1⅝", ⅛" between.

Commodity consumption: Newsprint 1,500 short tons; width 28"; black ink 42,000 pounds; color ink 10,000 pounds; single pages printed 19,105; average pages per issue 40(d), 42(S).

Equipment: EDITORIAL: Front-end hardware — 6-Mk/TouchWriter Plus, Mk/Comp Plus; Printers — Ap/Mac LaserWriter, XIT/Clipper, QMS. CLASSIFIED: Front-end hardware — 3-Mk/TouchWriter Plus. DISPLAY: Adv layout systems — Ap/Mac Quadra; Front-end software — QuarkXPress, Multi-Ad/Creator, Aldus/PageMaker, Adobe/Illustrator. PRODUCTION: OCR software — Caere/OmniPage Pro; Typesetters — 2-COM/9000, 2-M/Linotron; Plate exposures — 2-Nu; Plate processors — 1-WL; Scanners — Ap/Mac Scanner; Production cameras — 2-B; Automatic film processors — 1-P.
PRESSROOM: Line 1 — 5-G/Community; Line 2 — 6-G/Community; Line 3 — 4-G/SSC; Folders — 3-G/2:1. MAILROOM: Counter stackers — 5-BG; Bundle tyer — 4-Bu; Addressing machine — 2-Am, 1-Ch, 1-Mg. WIRE SERVICES: News — LAT-WP, NYT, UPI; Photos — UPI; Stock tables — TMS; Syndicates — UPI; Receiving dishes — size-1m, UPI.

Green Bay Press-Gazette (e-mon to fri; m-sat; S)

Green Bay Press-Gazette, 435 E. Walnut; PO Box 19430, Green Bay, WI 54307-9430; tel (414) 435-4411; fax (414) 431-8499; e-mail pgnews@netnet.net. Gannett Co. Inc. group.

Circulation: 58,786(e); 58,786(m-sat); 87,815(S); ABC Sept. 30, 1995.

Price: 50¢(d); 50¢(sat); $1.50(S); $3.25/wk; $169.00/yr (carrier).

Advertising: Open inch rate $35.27(e); $35.27(m-sat); $46.40(S). **Representative:** Gannett National Newspaper Sales.

News Services: AP, GNS. **Politics:** Independent. **Established:** 1915.

Advertising not accepted: Mail order.

Special Editions: Bridal; Career Opportunities; People/Progress; Design-An-Ad; Recreation Guide; Fitness and Health; Home Improvement; Lawn & Garden; Graduation; Vacation; Showcase of Homes; Back-to-School; Fall Fashions; Prep Football; Packers Football; Home Furnishings; Recipe Contest; Prep Sports; Christmas Gift Guide; Quarterly Coupon Books.

Special Weekly Sections: Money Extra (tues); Lifestyle, Food (wed); Entertainment Extra (thur); Church Pages (sat); Home, Travel (S).

Magazines: USA Weekend, TV and Cable Week (own, newsprint), Puck Comics Weekly (S).

GENERAL MANAGEMENT

President/Publisher	William T Nusbaum
Controller	Douglas C Miller
Director-Human Resources	Sharon Hollingsworth

ADVERTISING

Director	James M Lobas
Manager-Classified	Linda R Greiwe
Manager-National	Dennis Tattum
Manager-Retail	Bill Gaier
Manager-Retail	Steve Lavin

MARKETING AND PROMOTION

Director-Market Development	David Hollingsworth

CIRCULATION

Director	Michael Prazma

NEWS EXECUTIVES

Editor	Claude J Werder
Managing Editor	Laurie E Holloway

EDITORS AND MANAGERS

Books Editor	Jean Perenboon
Consumer Interest Editor	Roger Schneider
Education Editor	Barbara Uebelacker
Environment/Ecology Editor	Barbara Uebelacker
Farm Editor	Tom Murphy
Fashion Editor	Jeff Ash
Films/Theater Editor	Warren Gerds
Food Editor	Jeff Ash
Librarian	Diane Robb
Madison Bureau Chief	Scott Hildebrand
Music Editor	Warren Gerds
News Editor	Dave Davenport
Opinion Page Editor	Bob Woessner
Photo Editor	John Robb
Radio/Television Editor	Warren Gerds
Real Estate Editor	Tom Content
Reader Contact Editor	Mike Blecha
Religion Editor	Jeff Ash
Society/Women's Editor	Dian Page
Sports Editor	Tony Walter
State Editor	Joanne Zipperer
Systems Editor	Jim Zima
Topics Editor-Metro	Barbara Uebelacker
Topics Editor-Lifestyle	Jeff Ash
Topics Editor-Money	Tom Content
Travel Editor	Mike Hoeft
Weekend Editor	Julie Pagel

MANAGEMENT INFORMATION SERVICES

Data Processing Manager	Monica Baures
Computer Technician	Mike Smits

PRODUCTION

Director	Brian Ambor
Manager-Pre Press	Denise Handrick

Market Information: Zoned editions; Split Run.

Mechanical available: DiLitho; Black and 3 ROP colors; insert accepted — preprinted, bags; page cut-offs — 23 9/16".

Mechanical specifications: Type page 13" x 22"; E - 6 cols, 2 1/16", ⅛" between; A - 6 cols, 2 1/16", ⅛" between; C - 9 cols, 1 5/16", 1/16" between.

Commodity consumption: Newsprint 6,000 metric tons; widths 54.50", 40.875", 27.25"; black ink 210,000 pounds; color ink 44,000 pounds; single pages printed 16,299; average pages per issue 37(d), 93(S); single plates used 44,000.

Equipment: EDITORIAL: Front-end hardware — 28-AT/7000; Front-end software — AT, Aldus/FreeHand, QuarkXPress; Printers — AU/APS, MON/82E; Other equipment — 4-Ap/Mac. CLASSIFIED: Front-end hardware — 17-AT; Front-end software — AT; Printers — MON/82E. DISPLAY: Adv layout systems — 10-Ap/Mac; Front-end software — Multi-Ad/Creator, Adobe/Photoshop, QuarkXPress; Printers — 2-AU/APS Software RIP & Imagesetter; Other equipment — 3-Umax Scanner, 1-Polaroid/Slide Scanner. PRODUCTION: Pagination software — QuarkXPress 3.5, AT; Typesetters — 2-MON/82E, 2-AU/Software RIP & Imagesetter; Plate exposures — 2-BKY/5KW; Plate processors — 1-WL/38D; Electronic picture desk — Lf/AP Leaf Picture Desk; Scanners — 1-RZ/4050E, 1-ECR/Autokon 1000, 1-X/1200 DPI, 3-Umax/Color 1200 DPI; Production cameras — 1-C/Marathon, 1-B/Admiral; Automatic film processors — 2-Kk, 5-LE; Film transporters — 4-LE; Color separation equipment (conventional) — 1-RZ; Digital color separation equipment — 1-Lf/AP Leaf Picture Desk, Adobe/Photoshop.
PRESSROOM: Line 1 — 6-G/Mark II double width, 2-G/Mark I double width; Press drives — CH/60 h.p.; Folders — 2-G/2:1; Reels and stands — G/3-Arm; Press control system — CH. MAILROOM: Counter stackers — 4-HL; Inserters and stuffers — HI/1472, S/NP630; Bundle tyer — 2-MLN/2A, 2-Dynaric, 1-Power Strap; Addressing machine — Dispensa-Matic-V4; Mailroom control system — Ic. ARS. HL/Spec 09. WIRE SERVICES: News — AP, GNS; Photos — AP; Stock tables — AP; Receiving dishes — size-10ft, AP. BUSINESS COMPUTERS: IBM/AS-400; Applications: Circ, Adv billing, Accts receivable, Gen ledger; PCs & main system networked.

JANESVILLE

Rock County

'90 U.S. Census- 52,133; E&P '96 Est. 53,757

The Janesville Gazette (e-mon to fri; m-sat; S)

The Janesville Gazette, 1 S. Parker Dr.; PO Box 5001, Janesville, WI 53547-5001; tel (608) 754-3311; fax (608) 754-8038. Bliss Communications Inc. group.

Circulation: 27,067(e); 27,067(m-sat); 28,385(S); Sworn Oct. 1, 1995.
Price: 50¢(d); 50¢(sat); $1.50(S); $3.80/wk (motor route), $3.65/wk (carrier); $187.72/yr.
Advertising: Open inch rate $25.08(e); $25.08(m-sat); $28.66(S).
News Services: AP, KRT. **Established:** 1845.
Not Published: New Year; Memorial Day; Independence Day; Labor Day; Thanksgiving; Christmas.
Special Editions: Progress Week (Jan); Mall Home Show, Bride's Section (Feb); Spring Car Care (Mar); Golf Directory, Home & Garden (Apr); Summer Fun Vacation Tab (May); Hats Off to Success (June); Back-to-School, Football (Aug); Fall Home Improvement, Parade of Homes (Sept); Winter Car Care, Auto Show (Oct); X'mas Opener (Nov); The Source Resource Guide (Dec).
Special Weekly Sections: Business (mon); Food (tues); Family, JNL Youth pages (wed); Horizons-Entertainment, Religion (fri); Health (sat); Food, Marketplace (S).
Magazines: JNL Kids Page (wed); Entertainment (thur); Local TV (sat); USA Weekend (S).
Broadcast Affiliates: WCLO-AM/WJVL-FM Janesville, WI; WBKV-AM/WBWI-FM West Bend, WI; WFHR-AM/WGLX-FM Wisconsin Rapids, WI.

CORPORATE OFFICERS
Board Chairman — Marshall W Johnston
President — Sidney H Bliss
Secretary — James E Warren
Treasurer — Robert J Lisser

GENERAL MANAGEMENT
Publisher — Sidney H Bliss
General Manager — David A Johnson

ADVERTISING
Manager-Retail — Denis Crotty
Manager-Classified — Dan White
Manager-National — Denis Crotty

MARKETING AND PROMOTION
Director-Marketing/Promotion — Wilson Y Leong

TELECOMMUNICATIONS
Audiotex Manager — Dan White

CIRCULATION
Director — Randy Hammer
Coordinator-Newspapers in Education — Jill Jensen

NEWS EXECUTIVES
Editor — Scott W Angus
Managing Editor — Grant VanderVelden

EDITORS AND MANAGERS
Area Editor — Teryl Franklin
Automotive Editor — Mike DuPre'
Business Editor — James Leute
City Editor — Frank Schultz
Editorial Page Editor — Gary Achterberg
Education Editor — Judy Immel
Entertainment/Food Editor — Mary Barber
Features Editor — Todd Mishler
Graphics Editor/Art Director — Tony DiNicola
Marketplace Editor — Margaret Collins
Photo Editor — Bill Olmsted
Religion Editor — Judy Immel
Special Sections Editor — Tony Ends
Sports Editor — David Wedeward
Sports Editor-Sunday — John McPoland
Sunday Gazette Editor — Greg Peck
Wire Editor — James Leute
Women's Editor — Rochelle Birkelo

MANAGEMENT INFORMATION SERVICES
Data Processing Manager — Pam Schmoldt

PRODUCTION
Manager-Systems — Tom Thren
Supervisor-Advertising — Don Francis
Foreman-Pressroom — Joe LaChance

Market Information: Zoned editions; TMC; Operate audiotex.
Mechanical available: Offset; Black and 3 ROP colors; insert accepted — preprinted; page cut-offs — 22¾".
Mechanical specifications: Type page 13" x 21½"; E - 6 cols, 2¹⁄₁₆", ⅛" between; A - 6 cols, 2¹⁄₁₆", ⅛" between; C - 9 cols, 1⅜", ¹⁄₁₆" between.
Commodity consumption: Newsprint 1,950 metric tons; widths 55", 41¼", 27½"; black ink 52,695 pounds; color ink 12,000 pounds; single pages printed 11,560; average pages per issue 30(d), 97(S); single plates used 26,000.
Equipment: EDITORIAL: Front-end hardware — Tandem/CLX; Other equipment — 1-Ap/Mac IIci, Ap/Power Mac 8100 Color Darkroom, Epson/Color Dye Subprinter. CLASSIFIED: Front-end hardware — SII; Other equipment — Teleclass, Micro Voice System. DISPLAY: Front-end hardware — 2-Ap/Mac 840AV, 2-Ap/Mac 6100; Front-end software — Adobe/Photoshop, Multi-Ad/Creator, QuarkXPress; Printers — GCC/1200p Laser Printer. PRODUCTION: Typesetters — 2-Pre Press/ Panther 14" w/Mac RIP; Platemaking systems — 1-3M/Pyrofax; Plate exposures — 2-Nu; Plate processors — 1-Stark; Electronic picture desk — Lf/AP Leaf Picture Desk, Ap/Mac Quadra 950; Scanners — 4-Epson/Flatbed, 1-HP/Flatbed, Kk/Neg Scanner; Production cameras — 1-B/Commodore; Automatic film processors — 1-DP; Color separation equipment (conventional) — Digi-Colour; Digital color separation equipment — Epson/ES-300C. PRESSROOM: Line 1 — 4-G/Metro; Folders — 1-G/2:1. MAILROOM: Counter stackers — 1-St/257, Id/NS440 (eds.), 1-Id/2000; Inserters and stuffers — GMA/SLS 1000; Bundle tyer — MLN/Spirit; Addressing machine — BH/1530; Other mailroom equipment — MM. LIBRARY: Electronic — SMS/Stauffer. WIRE SERVICES: News — AP, KRT; Photos — AP; Receiving dishes — size-9ft, AP. BUSINESS COMPUTERS: 1-HP/3000, HP/925LX; Applications: CJ: Circ, Adv billing, Accts receivable, Payroll, Gen ledger, Accts payable; PCs & micros networked; PCs & main system networked.

KENOSHA

Kenosha County

'90 U.S. Census- 80,352; E&P '96 Est. 82,412
ABC-CZ (90): 80,352 (HH 29,919)

Kenosha News

(m-mon to sat; S)

Kenosha News, 715 58th St.; Caller Box 190, Kenosha, WI 53141; tel (414) 657-1000; fax (414) 657-5101. United Communications Corp. group.
Circulation: 27,134(m); 27,134(m-sat); 29,744(S); ABC Sept. 30, 1995.
Price: 50¢(d); 50¢(sat); $1.50(S); $3.50/wk.
Advertising: Open inch rate $26.50(m); $26.50(m-sat); $28.00(S). **Representative:** Landon Associates Inc.
News Services: AP, LAT-WP, SHNS, KRT. **Politics:** Independent. **Established:** 1894.
Not Published: Christmas.
Special Editions: Tax Section, Bridal Section (Spring & Fall); Money Management; Home Improvement; Lawn & Garden; Spring Car Care; Fall Car Care; New Car Section.
Special Weekly Sections: Bulletin (mon); What's Up! (thur); TV Showtime (S).
Magazines: React (tues); Parade; Comics (S).
Broadcast Affiliates: KHSL-TV 12 Chico-Redding, CA; KEYC-TV 12 Mankato, MN; WWNY TV 7 Watertown, NY.

CORPORATE OFFICERS
President — Howard J Brown
Senior Vice Pres — Eugene W Schulte
Vice Pres/Publisher (Zion Benton News/Bargaineer) — Frank M Misureli
Vice Pres — Kenneth L Dowdell
Vice Pres — Ronald J Montemurro
Secretary/Treasurer — Eugene W Schulte
Asst Treasurer — Ronald J Montemurro

GENERAL MANAGEMENT
Publisher — Howard J Brown
General Manager — Eugene W Schulte
Controller — Fred E Ricker
Manager-Credit — Christopher S Cope
Manager-Computer Service — Gerald Kochman

ADVERTISING
Director — Frank M Misureli
Director-Public Service — Kenneth L Dowdell
Manager-Classified — Donald C Orth
Manager-Retail — James Hawkins
Coordinator-National — Charlotte Riley

TELECOMMUNICATIONS
Audiotex Manager — Kenneth L Dowdell

CIRCULATION
Manager — James Jones

NEWS EXECUTIVES
Editor — Richard D Martin
Managing Editor — James K Meyers

EDITORS AND MANAGERS
Amusements Editor — Kay Jones
Automotive Editor — Kay Jones
Building Editor — Dave Backman
Business Editor — Dave Backman
City Editor — Steve Lund
Columnist — Richard D Martin
Editorial Page Editor — James K Meyers
Editor-Kenosha Life — Elizabeth Snyder
Education Editor — David Engels
Films/Theater Editor — Kay Jones
Fashion/Women's Editor — Elizabeth Snyder
Food Editor — Elizabeth Snyder
Home Furnishings Editor — Elizabeth Snyder
Librarian — Michelle Arkens
News Editor — Karl Frederick
Photo Department Manager — John Sorensen
Radio/Television Editor — Kay Jones
Real Estate Editor — Kay Jones
Religion/Society Editor — Elizabeth Snyder
Sports Editor — David Marran
Weekend Editor — Kay Jones
Wire Editor — Les Ryshkus

MANAGEMENT INFORMATION SERVICES
Data Processing Manager — Gerald Kochman

PRODUCTION
Manager — Donald Kirschbaum
Manager-Systems — Michael Bain
Supervisor-Pre Press — John Larsen
Supervisor-Distribution Center — Robert Schneider
Engineer-Systems — Gerald Kochman
Foreman-Pressroom — James Hauke

Market Information: Zoned editions; Split Run; TMC; Operate audiotex.
Mechanical available: Offset; Black and 3 ROP colors; insert accepted — preprinted, any; page cut-offs — 22¾".
Mechanical specifications: Type page 13⅛" x 21½"; E - 6 cols, 2¹⁄₁₆", ⅛" between; A - 6 cols, 2¹⁄₁₆", ⅛" between; C - 9 cols, 1⅜", ¹⁄₁₆" between.
Commodity consumption: Newsprint 3,300 metric tons; widths 54¾", 41.06", 27.38"; average pages per issue 32(d), 56(S).
Equipment: EDITORIAL: Front-end hardware — SIA; Front-end software — Dewar/System IV; Other equipment — SIA/386 PC. CLASSIFIED: Front-end hardware — SIA; Front-end software — Dewar/System IV Classified. AUDIOTEX: Hardware — AT/2000; Software — Micro Voice/2000. DISPLAY: Adv layout systems — SCS/Layout 8000; Front-end hardware — 6-Ap/Mac Quadra 700; Front-end software — Multi-Ad/Creator; Other equipment — Umax/Scanner. PRODUCTION: Pagination software — QuarkXPress; Typesetters — 2-AU/APS6-108, 2-Dataproducts/LZR 2600; Plate exposures — 2-Nu/Flip Top FT40UPNS; Plate processors — 1-Nat/Super A-340; Electronic picture desk — 1-Lf/AP Leaf Picture Desk, 4-Ap/Mac; Scanners — X, 2-Lf/Leafscan 35; Production cameras — 1-B/3000, 1-C/Spartan II; Automatic film processors — 1-LE/LD 24A, 1-Glunz & Jensen/APS 6-108; Reproportion units — Typeflex/RP; Film transporters — 1-Glunz & Jensen. PRESSROOM: Line 1 — 6-G/Cosmo. MAILROOM: Counter stackers — 2-HL/Monitor HT II; Inserters and stuffers — 1-SLS/8-into-1; Bundle tyer — PSN/6, PSN/5; Addressing machine — 1-Am/1900. LIBRARY: Electronic — SMS/Stauffer Gold. COMMUNICATIONS: Systems used — satellite. WIRE SERVICES: News — AP, LAT-WP, SHNS, KRT; Photos — AP Photostream; Stock tables — TMS; Syndicates — KRT, LAT-WP, SHNS; Receiving dishes — AP. BUSINESS COMPUTERS: HP/3000 Series 937; Applications: Accounting, Circ, Adv; PCs & micros networked; PCs & main system networked.

LA CROSSE

La Crosse County

'90 U.S. Census- 51,003; E&P '96 Est. 53,911
ABC-CZ (90): 76,227 (HH 29,449)

La Crosse Tribune

(m-mon to sat; S)

La Crosse Tribune, 401 N. 3rd St.; PO Box 865, La Crosse, WI 54601; tel (608) 782-9710; fax (608) 782-8540. Lee Enterprises Inc. group.
Circulation: 34,626(m); 34,626(m-sat); 40,146(S); ABC Sept. 30, 1995.
Price: 50¢(d); 50¢(sat); $1.75(S); $16.00/4wk.
Advertising: Open inch rate $22.25(m); $22.25(m-sat); $24.40(S). **Representatives:** Landon Associates Inc.; Lee Group.
News Services: AP, KRT, SHNS. **Established:** 1904.
Not Published: Christmas.
Special Editions: Bridal (Jan); Progress, Financial (Feb); Building (Mar); Real Estate (Apr); Recreation & Vacation, Lawn & Garden (May); Graduation, Sunfish Days (June); Riverfest (July); Back-to-School, Fall Fashion, Football, Kornfest (Aug); Oktoberfest, Applefest (Sept); Baby Book, Automotive, Home Furnishings, Credit Unions (Oct); Christmas Opening, Basketball (Nov); Gift Guide (Dec).
Special Weekly Sections: Business, Onalska-Holmen Record, Sports Monday (mon); Food Day (tues); Health, Science (wed); Outdoors (thur); Kids (fri); Religion, Mutual Funds Report (sat); Travel, Real Estate, Automotive, Senior Citizens (S).
Magazines: Live!, Entertainment Magazine (thur); Television Magazine, Prime Time (sat); Parade (S).

GENERAL MANAGEMENT
Publisher — Jim P Santori
Manager-Human Resources — Meribeth Catania
Manager-Financial Services — David Burgess

ADVERTISING
Director — Thomas Kelley
Supervisor-Classified — Dianne Hauser

MARKETING AND PROMOTION
Coordinator-Marketing — Florence Heintz

TELECOMMUNICATIONS
Audiotex Manager — John Dial

CIRCULATION
Manager — Nicholas Nicks

NEWS EXECUTIVE
Editor — David Stoeffler

EDITORS AND MANAGERS
Business Editor — Reid Magney
City Editor — John Smalley
Editorial Page Editor — Marc Wehrs
News Editor — Ted Vollmer
Religion Editor — Gayda Hollnagel
Science/Technology Editor — Terry Rindfleisch
Sports Editor — Art Kabelowsky

MANAGEMENT INFORMATION SERVICES
Online Manager — John Dial
Data Processing Manager — Dave Burgess

PRODUCTION
Manager-Pre Press — Jim Pickett
Manager-Systems — Robert Spacek
Manager-Press/Plate — Lyle E Saddler

Market Information: Zoned editions; Split Run; TMC; Operate database; Operate audiotex.
Mechanical available: Offset; Black and 3 ROP colors; insert accepted — preprinted; page cut-offs — 22¾".
Mechanical specifications: Type page 13" x 21¾"; E - 6 cols, 2¹⁄₁₆", ⅛" between; A - 6 cols, 2¹⁄₁₆", ⅛" between; C - 9 cols, 1⅜", ¹⁄₁₆" between.
Commodity consumption: Newsprint 2,750 short tons; 2,560 metric tons; widths 27½", 13¾", 27"; black ink 73,600 pounds; color ink 20,800 pounds; single pages printed 12,000; average pages per issue 30(d), 56(S); single plates used 21,600.
Equipment: EDITORIAL: Front-end hardware — 1-HI/8300, 1-HI/PEN System, 4-HI/8000, 11-HI/8863a, 23-Zenith/PC; Front-end software — HI, Baseview/NewsEdit. CLASSIFIED: Front-end hardware — 1-HI/Cash System, 8-Zenith/PC; Front-end software — HI/Cash 3.5; AUDIOTEX: Hardware — VRI/Apex; Software — VRI/Custom. DISPLAY: Adv layout systems — 1-HI/8300, 3-HI/8000, 5-Ap/Mac Quadra, 2-Ap/Mac Quadra 950, 1-Ap/Mac Quadra 750; Front-end software — Multi-Ad/Creator, QuarkXPress 3.3, Aldus/FreeHand 4.0, Adobe/Illustrator 5.0; PRODUCTION: Pagination software — QuarkXPress 3.3; Typesetters — 2-AU/APS-108; Platemaking systems — Offset; Plate exposures — 2-Nu; Plate processors — 1-Nat; Scanners — 2-Microtek/ScanMaker II; Production cameras — 1-DAI, 1-C/1244; Automatic film processors — 3-Kk/214-K, 1-P, Wing-Lynch, LE/LD 2600A. PRESSROOM: Line 1 — 9-G/Urbanite single width; Line 2 — 4-Lincoln/ink pumps; Press drives — Fin; Folders — 1-G/2:1; Reels and stands — Stands; Press control system — Fin; Press registration system — Duarte. MAILROOM: Inserters and stuffers — MM/227E, MM/227; Bundle tyer — 2-MLN/ML2EE; Addressing machine — Ch/525E, BH/1530. LIBRARY: Electronic — SMS/Stauffer; Combination — 1-Recordak/MPG-TH. WIRE SERVICES: News — AP Datastream, AP Datafeatures; Photos — AP; Stock tables — AP; Syndicates — KRT, SHNS; Receiving dishes — size-10ft, AP. BUSINESS COMPUTERS: 1-IBM/AS400; Applications: Accounting, Circ; PCs & main system networked.

MADISON

Dane County

'90 U.S. Census- 191,262; E&P '96 Est. 212,563
ABC-CZ (90): 241,521 (HH 98,550)

Madison Newspapers Inc.

Madison Newspapers Inc., 1901 Fish Hatchery Rd.; PO Box 8056, Madison, WI 53713; tel (608) 252-6200; fax (608) 252-6203.
Representative: Landon Associates Inc.

Copyright ©1996 by the Editor & Publisher Co.

News Services: AP, UPI. **Established:** 1839 (Winsconsin State Journal), 1917 (Capital Times), 1948 (Madison Newspapers).
Special Editions: Apartment Living (Mar, June); Health; The Book of Business; Home Products; Spring Fashion; Spring Auto; Lawn & Garden; NIE; Wisconsin Travel; Golf Guide; Home Decorating/Remodeling; Parade of Homes; Fall Fashion; Answer Book; Football; Fall Home Improvement; Fall Auto Section; Holiday Gift Guide; Academic Scholars; Real Estate-Dane Co.
Special Weekly Sections: Business, Rhythm (Entertainment) (thur).

CORPORATE OFFICERS

Board Chairman	Clayton Frink
President	Philip Blake
Secretary	John H Lussier
Treasurer	Philip Blake

GENERAL MANAGEMENT

Vice Pres/General Manager	Michael Jameson
Publisher (The Capital Times)	Clayton Frink
Publisher (wisconsin State Journal)	Philip Blake

ADVERTISING

Director	Tim Rodriguez

MARKETING AND PROMOTION

Manager-Marketing/Promotion	Paul Spira

TELECOMMUNICATIONS

Director-Technology	Nathan Harper

CIRCULATION

Director-Customer Service	Phil Stoddard
Manager-Single Copy	Bill Herrichs
Supervisor-Customer Service	George Miller
Supervisor-Customer Service	Debbie McCarthy

MANAGEMENT INFORMATION SERVICES

Data Processing Manager	Brian Woolley
Online Manager	Nathan Harper

PRODUCTION

Manager-Technical Service	Al Chase
Asst Manager	Jerry Leek
Superintendent-Pressroom	Peter McKercher
Superintendent-Mailroom	Bob Niesen

Market Information: Zoned editions; Split Run; TMC; ADS; Operate database; Electronic edition.
Mechanical available: Offset; Black and 3 ROP colors; insert accepted — preprinted, samples, catalogs; page cut-offs — $22\frac{3}{4}$".
Mechanical specifications: Type page 13" x $21\frac{1}{2}$"; E - 6 cols, $2\frac{1}{16}$", $\frac{1}{8}$" between; A - 6 cols, $2\frac{1}{16}$", $\frac{1}{8}$" between; C - 10 cols, $1\frac{1}{4}$", $\frac{1}{16}$" between.
Commodity consumption: Newsprint 14,100 metric tons; widths 55", $41\frac{1}{4}$", $27\frac{1}{2}$"; black ink 325,000 pounds; color ink 100,000 pounds; single pages printed 31,700; average pages per issue 40(d), 104(S); single plates used 125,000.
Equipment: EDITORIAL: Front-end hardware — HI/Newsmaker, HI/Pagination; Front-end software — HI. CLASSIFIED: Front-end hardware — 33-Compaq/386, 3-Compaq/486, 2-PC/486 pagination terminal; Front-end software — Computext/CompuClass; Printers — Epson/FX 850. DISPLAY: Adv layout systems — HI/XP-21; Front-end hardware — Sun, Zenith/PC; Front-end software — HI; Other equipment — X/Scanner. PRODUCTION: Pagination software — HI/2100 Pagination; Typesetters — 3-AU/6; Plate exposures — 3-Nu; Plate processors — 2-WL, MAS; Electronic picture desk — Lf/AP Leaf Picture Desk; Production cameras — 3-SCREEN, C; Automatic film processors — 3-LE, DP; Digital color separation equipment — 1-CD.
PRESSROOM: Line 1 — 6-G/Offset Metro (3 color decks); Line 2 — 6-G/Offset Metro (3 color decks); Line 3 — 5-G/Community (1-Four H16A; 4-single width); Folders — 2-G/Metro 3:2, 1-G/Community SSE; Pasters — 12-G; Reels and stands — 12-G; Press control system — Fin. MAILROOM: Counter stackers — 7-Id/555; Inserters and stuffers — 2-HI/1372, 1-Mueller; Bundle tyer — 2-Dynaric/NP2; Wrapping singles — 4-Bu/Strapper; Addressing machine — 2-Ch/539, 5-CH, 4-Ideal. LIBRARY: Electronic — Vu/Text. COMMUNICATIONS: Digital ad delivery system — AP AdSend. BUSINESS COMPUTERS: IBM/AS400; Applications: Circ, Adv, Financial; PCs & micros networked; PCs & main system networked.

The Capital Times

(e-mon to fri; e-sat)

The Capital Times, 1901 Fish Hatchery Rd.; PO Box 8060, Madison, WI 53713; tel (608) 252-6400; web site http: //www.madison.com.
Circulation: 21,716(e); 23,541(e-sat); ABC Sept. 30, 1995.
Price: 50¢(d); 50¢(sat); $3.50/wk; $15.16/mo; $163.80/yr.
Advertising: Open inch rate $46.70(e); $46.70(e-sat); comb with Wisconsin State Journal (mS) $58.20. **Representative:** Landon Associates Inc.
News Services: AP, LAT-WP, SHNS. **Politics:** Independent. **Established:** 1917.
Note: For advertising, circulation and production personnel and detailed mechanical information, see Madison Newspapers Inc.

CORPORATE OFFICERS

President/Treasurer	Frederick W Miller
Exec Vice Pres/CEO	Clayton Frink
Vice Pres-Editorial	Dave Zweifel
Secretary	John H Lussier
Asst Secretary	Nancy B Gage
Asst Treasurer	Frederick H Gage

GENERAL MANAGEMENT

Publisher	Clayton Frink

ADVERTISING

Director	Tim Rodriguez

NEWS EXECUTIVES

Editor	Dave Zweifel
Assoc Editor	John Patrick Hunter
Assoc Editor	Phil Haslanger

EDITORS AND MANAGERS

Area News Chief	Jerry Ambelang
Books Editor	Phil Haslanger
Business Editor	Dennis Punzel
Capitol Bureau Editor	Matt Pommer
City Editor	Charles Sherman
Consumer Interest Editor	Dennis Punzel
Copy Desk Chief	Judie Kleinmaier
Editorial Page Editor	Phil Haslanger
Education Editor	Pamela Cotant
Higher Education Editor	Todd Moore
Environment/Ecology Editor	Mike Ivey
Fashion/Features Editor	Mary Bergin
Food Editor	Debra Carr-Elsing
Films/Theater Editor	Jake Stockinger
Librarian	Ron Larson
Music Editor	Kevin Lynch
News Editor	Steve Ray
Photo/Graphics Editor	Gary Neuenschwander
Chief Photographer	David Sandell
Political Editor	John Patrick Hunter
Radio/Television Editor	Samara Kalk
Real Estate Editor	Jonathan Silver
Religion Editor	Mary Bergin
Sports Editor	Joe Hart
Women's Editor	Mary Bergin

Market Information: Electronic edition.
Equipment: WIRE SERVICES: News — AP, CST, SHNS, Medill, LAT-WP; Photos — AP; Syndicates — United Features, Universal Press, Creators, United Media, Midwest Features Inc., TMS, King Features, WP, NAS; Receiving dishes — AP.

Wisconsin State Journal

(m-mon to fri; m-sat; S)

Wisconsin State Journal, 1901 Fish Hatchery Rd.; PO Box 8058, Madison, WI 53708; tel (608) 252-6100; fax (608) 252-6203; web site http://www.madison.com. Lee Enterprises Inc. group.
Circulation: 86,585(m); 97,671(m-sat); 163,096(S); ABC Sept. 30, 1995.
Price: 50¢(d); 50¢(sat); $1.50(S); $3.50/wk; $15.16/mo; $163.80/yr.
Advertising: Open inch rate $52.25(m); $52.25(m-sat); $88.20(S); comb with The Capital Times (e) $58.20. **Representative:** Landon Associates Inc.
News Services: AP, NYT, KRT. **Politics:** Independent. **Established:** 1839.
Note: For advertising, circulation, production personnel and detailed mechanical information, see Madison Newspapers Inc.
Special Weekly Sections: Senior Citizens (mon); Food, Zones (wed); Business Section, Entertainment (thur); TV/Cable, Real Estate/Home (S).
Magazines: Parade, Comics (S).

CORPORATE OFFICERS

Chairman of the Board/Treasurer	Philip Blake
President	Clayton Frink
Secretary	John H Lussier
Vice Pres	Michael Jameson
Asst Secretary/Treasurer	J Martin Nolman

GENERAL MANAGEMENT

Publisher	Philip Blake
General Manager	Michael Jameson
Controller	Pamela Wells
Director-Human Resources	Debbie Reed
Editor	Frank Denton

ADVERTISING

Director	Tim Rodrigues

MARKETING AND PROMOTION

Director-Marketing/Promotion	Paul Spira

NEWS EXECUTIVES

Editor	Frank Denton
Managing Editor	Clifford Behnke
Asst Managing Editor	Paul Fanlund
Assoc Editor	Thomas Still

EDITORS AND MANAGERS

Automotive Editor	Jennifer Sereno
Books Editor	Brian Howell
City Editor	David Stoeffler
Education Editor	David Stoeffler
Farm Editor	Jennifer Sereno
Films/Theater Editor	Brian Howell
Finance Editor	Jennifer Sereno
Garden/Home Furnishings Editor	Brian Howell
Librarian	Ron Larson
Music Editor	Brian Howell
Neighbors Editor	Rick Uhlman
News Editor	Ellen Heath
Photo Dept Manager	Roger Turner
Religion Editor	Brian Howell
School Editor	David Stoeffler
Sports Editor	Bill Brophy
Women's Editor	Brian Howell

MANAGEMENT INFORMATION SERVICES

Data Processing Manager	Brian Woolley

Market Information: Zoned editions; Split Run; TMC; ADS; Electronic edition.
Mechanical available: Black; insert accepted — preprinted.
Mechanical specifications: Type page 13" x $21\frac{1}{2}$"; E - 6 cols, $2\frac{1}{16}$", $\frac{1}{8}$" between; A - 6 cols, $2\frac{1}{16}$", $\frac{1}{8}$" between; C - 10 cols, $1\frac{1}{4}$", $\frac{1}{16}$" between.
Equipment: EDITORIAL: Front-end hardware — Sun/fileservers, Dell/Workstations; Front-end software — HI/Newsmaker 2.20; Printers — HP/Laser Printer; Other equipment — Dell/Latitude. CLASSIFIED: Front-end hardware — Computext/CompuClass, 33-Compaq/386; Front-end software — Computext/CompuClass 4.33; DISPLAY: Adv layout systems — DEC/Layout 80, HI/PLS System; Front-end hardware — Sun/fileservers, Dell/450L; Front-end software — HI/PLS 2.0; PRODUCTION: Pagination software — HI 2.0; Typesetters — AU/APS-108-S; Plate exposures — 2-Nu/FT40V6UPNS; Plate processors — WL/M-P38D; Electronic picture desk — Lf/AP Leaf Picture Desk; Scanners — CD/656; Production cameras — 1-C/Newspager, 2-DSA; Automatic film processors — E/24A, DP/28L; Color separation equipment (conventional) — 12-Ap/Mac, Adobe/Photoshop.
PRESSROOM: Line 1 — 12-G/Metro; Line 2 — 8-G/Community; Press drives — Fin; Folders — 2-G/Imperial 3:2, 1-G/Community SSC Quarter; Reels and stands — 12-G/Metro, 5-G/Metro; Press registration system — Web Tech/Auto Registration. MAILROOM: Counter stackers — 7-Id/N5550, BG/Count-O-Veyor; Inserters and stuffers — 2-HI/1372; Bundle tyer — 5-Dynaric/NP2; Addressing machine — 2-Ch/545. LIBRARY: Electronic — Vu/Text SAVE. WIRE SERVICES: News — AP, NYT, KRT, States News Service; Photos — AP; Stock tables — AP SelectStox I; Syndicates — King Features, Universal Press, United Features, TMS, Creators; Receiving dishes — AP.

MANITOWOC-TWO RIVERS

Manitowoc County

'90 U.S. Census- 48,550 (Manitowoc 35,520; Two Rivers 13,030); E&P '96 Est. 45,854 (Manitowac 32,917; Two Rivers 12,937)
ABC-CZ (90): 45,550 (HH 18,308)

Herald Times Reporter

(e-mon to sat; S)

Herald Times Reporter, 902 Franklin; PO Box 790, Manitowoc, WI 54220; tel (414) 684-4433; fax (414) 684-4416. Thomson Newspapers group.
Circulation: 18,421(e); 18,421(e-sat); 18,303(S); ABC Sept. 30, 1995.
Price: 50¢(d); 50¢(sat); $1.00(S); $2.85/wk; $12.35/mo; $148.20/yr.
Advertising: Open inch rate $15.20(e); $15.20(e-sat); $15.20(S). **Representative:** Thomson Newspapers.
News Services: AP, NEA. **Politics:** Independent. **Established:** 1872 (Reporter), 1898 (Herald-Times).
Not Published: New Year; Memorial Day; Independence Day; Labor Day; Christmas.
Special Weekly Sections: Consumer (tues); Adopt a Pet (wed); Entertainment, Dining, Outdoor, Recreation (thur); Church/Religion, Mature Lifestyle, Youth (fri); Health, Auto Service Directory, Food, Farm (S).
Magazines: TV Section, Color Comics (S).

GENERAL MANAGEMENT

Publisher/General Manager	Gary Omernick

ADVERTISING

Manager-Retail/Classified	Lowell Johnson

TELECOMMUNICATIONS

Audiotex Manager	Lowell Johnson

NEWS EXECUTIVES

Editor	Russ Budzisz
Asst Managing Editor	Dan Klatt

EDITORS AND MANAGERS

Columnist	Russ Budzisz
Editorial Page Editor	Russ Budzisz
Fashion/Food Editor	Russ Budzisz
Political/Real Estate Editor	Rob Young
Religion/Society Editor	Michelle Lange
Sports Editor	Thom Aiello
Women's Editor	Michelle Lange

MANAGEMENT INFORMATION SERVICES

Data Processing Manager	Gary Fick

PRODUCTION

Foreman-Composing	Basil Kennedy
Foreman-Pressroom	Jim Turner

Market Information: Zoned editions; TMC; Operate audiotex.
Mechanical available: Offset; Black and 3 ROP colors; insert accepted — preprinted, card stuffs; page cut-offs — $22\frac{3}{4}$".
Mechanical specifications: Type page 13" x $21\frac{1}{2}$"; E - 6 cols, $2\frac{1}{16}$", $\frac{1}{8}$" between; A - 6 cols, $2\frac{1}{16}$", $\frac{1}{8}$" between; C - 9 cols, $1\frac{3}{8}$", $\frac{1}{16}$" between.
Commodity consumption: width $27\frac{1}{2}$"; average pages per issue 22(d), 40(S).
Equipment: EDITORIAL: Front-end hardware — Mk; Printers — NewGen. CLASSIFIED: Front-end hardware — Mk; Printers — NewGen. DISPLAY: Adv layout systems — COM/MCS 100; Front-end hardware — HP; Front-end software — PBS. PRODUCTION: Typesetters — 4-Ap/Mac Quadra 950; Platemaking systems — Nu/Flip Top FT40U6UPNS; Plate exposures — SMS/Stauffer Scale 6; Plate processors — Nat; Electronic picture desk — Lf/AP Leaf Picture Desk; Scanners — ECR/Autokon 1000; Production cameras — Robinson, LE; Automatic film processors — LE/LD281Q, SCREEN; Color separation equipment (conventional) — Lf/Leafscan, ECR/Autokon 1000.
PRESSROOM: Line 1 — 6-G/Urbanite. MAILROOM: Bundle tyer — 1-Bu, 1-MLN; Addressing machine — 2-Am. WIRE SERVICES: News — AP; Syndicates — NEA; Receiving dishes — size-10ft, AP. BUSINESS COMPUTERS: Oracle, PBS; Applications: Adv, Circ, Payroll, Accts payable, Accts receivable; PCs & micros networked; PCs & main system networked.

MARINETTE, WI-MENOMINEE, MI

Marinette County, WI
Menominee County, MI

'90 U.S. Census- 21,241 (Marinette, WI 11,843; Menominee, MI 9,398); E&P '96 Est. 20,734 (Marinette, WI 11,896; Menominee, MI 8,838)

EagleHerald (e-mon to sat)

EagleHerald, 1809-27 Dunlap Ave.; PO Box 77, Marinette, WI 54143; tel (715) 735-6611; fax (715) 735-7580. Bliss Communications Inc. group.
Circulation: 11,772(e); 11,772(e-sat); Sworn Sept. 29, 1995.
Price: 50¢(d); 75¢(sat); $9.50/mo; $114.00/yr.
Advertising: Open inch rate $25.30(e); $25.30(e-sat). **Representative:** Landon Associates Inc.
News Service: AP. **Politics:** Independent. **Established:** 1867 (Herald Leader), 1871 (Eagle-Star), 1995 (EagleHerald).

Note: Effective July 10, 1995, the Marinette (WI) Eagle-Star (e-mon to sat) merged with the Menominee (MI) Herald Leader (e-mon to sat) to form the EagleHerald (e-mon to sat).
Not Published: New Year; Memorial Day; Independence Day; Labor Day; Thanksgiving; Christmas.
Special Editions: Community in Review (Feb); Home Improvement (Mar); Discover Us, Graduation '96 (May); Menominee County Fair (July); Waterfront Festival, Football Preview (Aug); Home Improvement (Sept); Health Care (Oct); M & M Game (Nov); Christmas Gift Guide, Last Minute Gift Guide (Dec).
Magazine: TV Week (sat).

CORPORATE OFFICERS

President Sidney H Bliss
Vice Pres Dennis J Colling
Secretary James E Warren
Treasurer Robert J Lisser

GENERAL MANAGEMENT

Publisher/General Manager Dennis J Colling
Business Manager Janice Schleihs

ADVERTISING

Manager Jim Hofer

CIRCULATION

Manager Wayne Jessel

NEWS EXECUTIVE

Editor Terri Lescelius

EDITORS AND MANAGERS

Presentation Editor Rob Becker
Regional Editor Dan Kitkowski
Sports Editor Jody Korch

MANAGEMENT INFORMATION SERVICES

Data Processing Manager Janice Schleihs

PRODUCTION

Manager-Press Roger Zink

Market Information: TMC; ADS.
Mechanical available: Offset; Black and 3 ROP colors; insert accepted — preprinted, any; page cut-offs — 22¾".
Mechanical specifications: Type page 13" x 21½"; E - 6 cols, 2 1/16", ⅛" between; A - 6 cols, 2 1/16", ⅛" between; C - 6 cols, 2 1/16", ⅛" between.
Commodity consumption: widths 27", 13½"; single pages printed 6,776; average pages per issue 22(d); single plates used 3,000.
Equipment: EDITORIAL: Front-end hardware — Mk/3000, IBM/PC; Front-end software — CText; Printers — Mk/Mycro-Comp AdWriter; Other equipment — 1-Ap/Mac. CLASSIFIED: Front-end hardware — Mk/3000. DISPLAY: Adv layout systems — 3-Ap/Mac, Mk/Mycro-Comp AdWriter. PRODUCTION: Platemaking systems — 1-3M/Deadliner-, 3M/Pyrofax; Production cameras — 1-Nu/Vertical 24, B; Color separation equipment (conventional) — 1-K. PRESSROOM: Line 1 — 6-G/Urbanite; Line 2 — 4-G/Community; Folders — 1-G/2:1, 1-G/4:1. MAILROOM: Bundle tyer — 2-Bu, 1-Sa/SR1A; Addressing machine — 1-Am/4000, 1-Am/1900, 1-Am/5000. COMMUNICATIONS: Systems used — satellite. WIRE SERVICES: News — AP; Receiving dishes — AP. BUSINESS COMPUTERS: IBM, Mk; Applications: Vision Data: Bus, Circ; PCs & micros networked; PCs & main system networked.

MARSHFIELD

Wood County

'90 U.S. Census- 18,859; **E&P '96 Est.** 19,607
ABC-CZ (90): 19,291 (HH 7,794)

Marshfield News-Herald

(e-mon to fri; m-sat)

Marshfield News-Herald, 111 W. 3rd; PO Box 70, Marshfield, WI 54449; tel (715) 384-3131; fax (715) 387-4175. Ogden Newspapers group.
Circulation: 14,793(e); 15,922(m-sat); ABC Sept. 30, 1995.
Price: 35¢(d); 50¢(sat).
Advertising: Open inch rate $15.25(e); $15.25(m-sat). **Representative:** Newspaper Marketing Group.
News Service: AP. **Politics:** Independent. **Established:** 1927.
Not Published: New Year; Memorial Day; Labor Day; Thanksgiving; Christmas.
Special Editions: Money, Finance, Taxes (Jan); Bridal, Valentine's (Feb); Spring Builders & Auto (Mar); Graduation, Dairyfest (May); Mad Market Days (July); Back-to-School, Football, Fairs (Aug); Fall Home Improvements (Sept); Fall Auto (Oct); Deer Hunting, Holiday Kick-off (Nov); Holiday Greetings, Basketball (Dec).
Special Weekly Sections: Farm Page, Entertainment Page (thur); Best Food Days, Church Page, TV Book, Home Improvement (sat); Business Page (daily).
Magazine: TV Listings (fri).

CORPORATE OFFICERS

President G Ogden Nutting
Vice Pres William C Nutting
Vice Pres Robert M Nutting
Secretary William O Nutting
Treasurer Duane D Wittman

GENERAL MANAGEMENT

Publisher James Eykyn
Manager-Education Service Bernice Bradley

ADVERTISING

Manager Karen Olson
Manager-National Karen Olson

CIRCULATION

Manager Bernice Bradley

NEWS EXECUTIVE

Editor William Heath

EDITORS AND MANAGERS

City Editor James Stern
Society Editor Amy Waldman
Sports Editor Daniel Kohn

PRODUCTION

Manager Richard Thomer

Market Information: Split Run; TMC.
Mechanical available: Offset; Black and 3 ROP colors; insert accepted — preprinted, anything 11¼" wide; 14" depth or less; page cut-offs — 21½".
Mechanical specifications: Type page 13½" x 22½"; E - 6 cols, 2 1/16", ⅛" between; A - 6 cols, 2 1/16", ⅛" between; C - 8 cols, 1½", ⅛" between.
Commodity consumption: Newsprint 650 short tons; width 27"; black ink 20,000 pounds; color ink 5,000 pounds; single pages printed 6,500; average pages per issue 20(d); single plates used 8,000.
Equipment: EDITORIAL: Front-end hardware — 1-COM. CLASSIFIED: Front-end hardware — 4-COM. DISPLAY: Adv layout systems — 2-Ap/Mac Radius Two Page Display, 1-Ap/Mac Radius Full Page Display. PRODUCTION: Typesetters — 2-Ap/Mac LaserWriter II; Platemaking systems — 1-Nu/Ultra Plus Flip Top FT40UPNS; Plate exposures — Nu/Ultra Plus; Plate processors — Nat/Super A-250; Production cameras — 1-B; Automatic film processors — LE/LD1800A; Digital color separation equipment — Ca/T-R 400 Densitometer. PRESSROOM: Line 1 — 6-G/Urbanite; Folders — 1-G. MAILROOM: Counter stackers — 1-BG/108; Bundle tyer — 2-Bu; Addressing machine — 2-Am/4000, St/labeler. WIRE SERVICES: News — Syndicates — AP; Receiving dishes — AP. BUSINESS COMPUTERS: NCR/Tower; Applications: Adv billing, Accts receivable, Gen ledger, Payroll, Accts payable; PCs & main system networked.

MENASHA

See APPLETON

MILWAUKEE

Milwaukee County

'90 U.S. Census- 628,088; **E&P '96 Est.** 628,878
ABC-NDM (90): 1,432,149 (HH 537,722)

Milwaukee Journal Sentinel

(m-mon to fri; m-sat; S)

Milwaukee Journal Sentinel, 333 W. State St.; PO Box 661, Milwaukee, WI 53201-0661; tel (414) 224-2000; fax (414) 224-2469; web site http://www.packerplus.com/.
Circulation: 309,137(m); 296,806(m-sat); 473,068(S); ABC Sept. 30, 1995.
Price: 50¢(d); 50¢(sat); $1.50(S); $1.85/wk.
Advertising: Open inch rate $217.99(m); $217.99(m-sat); $252.15(S). **Representative:** Newspapers First.
News Services: AP, GNN, KRT, LAT-WP, NYT. **Politics:** Independent. **Established:** 1837 (Sentinel), 1882 (Journal), 1995 (Journal Sentinel).
Note: Published by Journal Sentinel Inc., a subsidiary of Journal Communications. Effective Apr. 2, 1995, the Milwaukee Sentinel (m) merged with the Milwaukee Journal (eS) to become the Milwaukee Journal Sentinel (m-mon to sat; S).
Advertising not accepted: Certain medical and mail order.
Special Editions: Your Money, Boat Show, Year End Markets, Financial Planning/Taxes, Education, Weddings (Jan); Recreational Vehicles, Home Improvement, Auto (Feb); Home Show, Sports Show, Auto (Mar); Auto, Golf, Spring Garden (Apr); Spring Garden, Great Milwaukee Summer (May); First Time Homebuyers (June); Circus Parade, State Fair (July); Greater Milwaukee Open (Golf), Parade of Homes, Sports (Aug); Real Estate/Condos, Lawn & Garden, Fashion, Home Furnishings, Education (Sept); Weddings, Healthcare, Fall Auto, Pet Show (Oct); Auto Mil Bucks (Nov); Gift Guide, Wisconsin Business Development (Dec).
Special Weekly Sections: Business Tab (mon); Food (wed); Auto, New Construction (sat).
Magazines: Travel, Food/Cooking, Home, Health, Women, Books/Video (weekly); Parade, Sunday Magazine Network, Tribune TV Log (S).
Broadcast Affiliates: WSYM-TV Lansing, MI; KQRC-FM Kansas City, MO; KEZO-AM/FM/KKCD-FM Omaha, NE; KTNV-FM Las Vegas, NV; WTMJ-TV Milwaukee; WTMJ-AM/WTMJ-FM Milwaukee; WSAU-AM/WIFC-FM Wausau, WI.

CORPORATE OFFICERS

Chairman of the Board/CEO Robert A Kahlor
President Keith Spore
Senior Vice Pres/Editor Mary Jo Meisner
Senior Vice Pres-Human Resources Astrid Garcia
Senior Vice Pres-Advertising Everton Weeks
Senior Vice Pres-Circulation James Clark
Senior Vice Pres-Printing Kenneth Adams
Senior Vice Pres-Finance Todd Adams
Vice Pres-Marketing Services Cynthia Yomantas
Vice Pres-Legal Paul E Kritzer
Vice Pres-Circulation Marketing Mark Thomas
Vice Pres-Communications Robert Dye
Vice Pres-Info Technologies Peter Stockhausen
Vice Pres/Managing Editor Martin Kaiser

GENERAL MANAGEMENT

Labor Relations Manager James F Pepelnjak
Controller Claudia Booth

ADVERTISING

Senior Vice Pres Everton Weeks
Director-Display Kathleen Worthington-McQueary
Manager-Classified Rich Dobson
Manager-Business Ed Kirk

MARKETING AND PROMOTION

Manager-Marketing Service Cindy Yomantas

TELECOMMUNICATIONS

Info Service/Business Systems Jim Herzfeld
Audiotex Manager Jane Slaats

CIRCULATION

Senior Vice Pres James Clark
Vice Pres-Marketing Mark Thomas
Director-Operations James Boyd
Manager-Consumer Services Gloria Najera
Manager-Finance Lisa Haynes
Manager-Distribution Tom Pierce

NEWS EXECUTIVES

Editor Mary Jo Meisner
Managing Editor Martin Kaiser
Deputy Managing Editor Gerry Hinkley

EDITORS AND MANAGERS

Senior Editor-Administration Barbara Dembski
Senior Editor-Day News Carl Schwartz
Senior Editor-Night News David Vogel
Senior Editor-Night News Carolina Garcia
Senior Editor-Local News Jackie Jones
Senior Editor-Issues Celeste Williams
Senior Editor-Business George Stanley
Senior Editor-National Donald Walker
Senior Editor-Sports Garry D Howard
Senior Editor-Entertainment Diane Bacha
Senior Editor-Features Heidi Reuter
Senior Editor-Copy Desk Paul Sevart
Art Critic James Auer
Automotive Reporter Mark Savage
Cartoonist Stuart Carlson
Cartoonist Gary Markstein
City Editor Leonard Sykes
Columnist Euegene Kane
Columnist Dennis McCann
Columnist Joyce Evans
Columnist Bill Janz
Columnist Jay Reed
Columnist Michael Bauman
Drama Reporter Damien Jaques
Editorial Page Editor Kenneth P Roesslein
Deputy Editorial Page Editor Sue Ryon
Education Reporter Curtis Lawrence
Education Reporter Daynell Hooker
Education Reporter Tom Vanden Brook
Environment Reporter Don Behm
Fashion Reporter Cathy Fitzpatrick
Film Critic Duane Dudek
Food Editor Nancy Stohs
Graphics Editor Geoffrey Blaesing
Home Furnishing Reporter Cathy Fitzpatrick
Health Editor Neil Rosenburg
Librarian Rosemary Jensen
News Systems Editor Duane Freitag
Outdoor Writer Jay Reed
Photo Department Manager Alan King
Radio/Television Reporter Joanne Weintraub
Radio/Television Reporter Tim Cuprisin
Religion Reporter Jo Sandin
Science Reporter Mark Ward
State Editor Bruce Gill
Suburban Editor Mark Maley

MANAGEMENT INFORMATION SERVICES

Data Processing Manager Peter Stockhausen
Online Manager Dan Patrinos

PRODUCTION

Manager-Post Press Raymond Stoiber
Manager-Pre Press Gary Schell
Manager-Night Ed Muehlbauer
Manager-Advertising Services Fred Wolfgram
Manager-Maintenance Kenneth Kieck
Foreman-Pressroom John Garlock
Foreman-Camera/Platemaking Larry Scholl
Foreman-Mailroom Robert Jaeschke
Foreman-Composing Wallace Staver
Foreman-Paper/Ink Ervin Sadowski

Market Information: Zoned editions; Split Run; TMC; ADS; Operate database; Operate audiotex; Electronic edition.
Mechanical available: Black and 3 ROP colors; insert accepted — preprinted, product samples when pre-approved; page cut-offs — 22⅞".
Mechanical specifications: Type page 13" x 21 7/16"; E - 6 cols, 2 1/16", ⅛" between; A - 6 cols, 2 1/16", ⅛" between; C - 10 cols, 1¼", 1/16" between.
Commodity consumption: Newsprint 70,500 metric tons; widths 55", 41¼", 27½"; black ink 2,400,950 pounds; color ink 820,264 pounds; single pages printed 44,276; average pages per issue 46(d); single plates used 153,000.
Equipment: EDITORIAL: Front-end hardware — SII/Tandem; Front-end software — SII/Coyote; Printers — Data South. CLASSIFIED: Front-end hardware — SII/Tandem; Front-end software — SII; Printers — Data South. AUDIOTEX: Hardware — PEP. DISPLAY: Adv layout systems — CJ; Front-end hardware — DEC; Front-end software — CJ/Layout; Printers — HP/LaserJet II. PRODUCTION: Typesetters — 5-MON/Express, MAS/1000, 5-Konica/Processor; Plate exposures — 2-WL/Lith-X-Pozer III; Plate processors — 2-WL/38D, 1-WL/38D, 1-WL/S.A.X.; Scanners — DP/Highlighter 2000, 1-X/7650, 1-Howtek Desktop; Production cameras — 1-C/Marathon, 1-C/Olympia, 2-C/Newspager; Automatic film processors — 2-DP/26C, 1-DP/2, 4-DP/28C; Digital color separation equipment — CD/6461E, CD/Studio 3. PRESSROOM: Line 1 — 9-H/Colormatic; Line 2 — 9-H/Colormatic; Line 3 — 9-H/Colormatic; Line 4 — 9-H/Colormatic; Folders — 8-H/2:1; Pasters — Single V Type; Reels and stands — 36-H; Press control system — H/Reflex drive (w/Square D programmable controllers). MAILROOM: Counter stackers — 12-HL/Dual Carrier, 4-MST; Inserters and stuffers — 1-HI/1372P, 1-HI/1048P, 1-HI/1472P, 1-GMA/SLS-1000; Bundle tyer — 21-Dynaric; Wrapping singles — MRS, 2-Id, 22-Dynaric; Addressing machine — 1-St/Assembler, 1-KR/Quarter Folder. LIBRARY: Electronic — SII/Laser. WIRE SERVICES: News — AP, AP SelectStox; Stock tables — AP SelectStox. BUSINESS COMPUTERS: 2-DEC/6350; Applications: Ross: Payroll, Accts payable, Gen ledger; CJ.

MONROE

Green County

'90 U.S. Census- 10,241; **E&P '96 Est.** 10,530

The Monroe Evening Times

(e-mon to sat)

The Monroe Evening Times, 1065 4th Ave. W.; PO Box 230, Monroe, WI 53566-0230; tel (608) 328-4202; fax (608) 328-4217. Bliss Communications Inc. group.

Circulation: 6,917(e); 6,917(e-sat); Sworn Sept. 27, 1995.
Price: 50¢(d); 50¢(sat); $2.50/wk; $130.00/yr (carrier).
Advertising: Open inch rate $10.00(e); $10.00 (e-sat). Representative: Papert Companies.
News Service: AP. Politics: Republican. Established: 1898.
Not Published: New Year; Memorial Day; Independence Day; Labor Day; Thanksgiving; Christmas.
Advertising not accepted: Vending machines; Courses; Cash investment; Vacation.
Special Editions: Spring Bridal Edition, Progress Edition '96 (Jan); Chamber Home Show Edition, FHA/FFA, Chamber Spring Maxwell (Feb); Spring Car Care Edition, Home Improvement Edition, Ag Edition, Design-An-Ad Contest (Mar); Spring Sports, Easter "Eggstravaganza", Spring Day for the Handicapped (Apr); Dairy Breakfast, Law Day, Scholarship Pages, Graduation Special Section (May); Visitor's Guide, Chamber Picnic on the Square (June); Dairy Queen Pages, Balloon Rally Edition, Fair Edition (July); Fall Fashion, Fall Sports Section, Fire School Pages (Aug); Home Furnishings, Fall & Winter Bridal Edition, Cheese Days Festival, Arts and Entertainment Section (Sept); Chamber Great Pumpkin, Harvest Edition, Women at Work (Oct); Holiday Give-A-Way, Winter Sports Edition, Christmas Edition, Cookbook (Nov); Chamber Christmas Walk, 1st Baby Pages (Dec).
Special Weekly Sections: FOOD (mon); Business (tues); Senior Citizens (wed); Entertainment, Agriculture (thur); Religion (sat).
Magazines: Sports (mon); Food & Household Pages (wed).

CORPORATE OFFICERS
President	Sidney H Bliss
Vice Pres	Carl C Hearing
Secretary	James E Warren
Treasurer	Robert J Lisser

GENERAL MANAGEMENT
General Manager	Carl C Hearing
Manager-Office	Joan Gempeler

ADVERTISING
Manager-Retail	Gary Guralski
Manager-Classified	Gary Guralski

CIRCULATION
Manager	John A McNeil

NEWS EXECUTIVE
Editor	Judie Hintzman

EDITORS AND MANAGERS
Business Editor	Keith Ludolph
City/Metro Editor	Mary Jane Bestor
Editorial Page Editor	Judie Hintzman
Entertainment/Amusements Editor	Keith Ludolph
Farm/Agriculture Editor	Keith Ludolph
Features Editor	Mary Jane Bestor
News Editor	Mary Jane Bestor
Photo Editor	Heather Lisser
Religion Editor	Keith Ludolph
Sports Editor	Paul Krueger

PRODUCTION
Manager	Janeen Bruce

Market Information: Zoned editions; TMC; ADS.
Mechanical available: Offset; Black and 3 ROP colors; insert accepted — preprinted, hi fi; page cut-offs — 22¾".
Mechanical specifications: Type page 13" x 21½"; E - 6 cols, 2¹⁄₁₆", ⅛" between; A - 6 cols, 2¹⁄₁₆", ⅛" between; C - 9 cols, 1⅜", ¹⁄₁₆" between.
Commodity consumption: Newsprint 312 short tons; widths 27½", 34"; black ink 6,878 pounds; color ink 3,682 pounds; single pages printed 5,838; average pages per issue 17(d); single plates used 4,049.
Equipment: EDITORIAL: Front-end hardware — 10-Mk; Other equipment — 2-RSK/TRS 80, 2-RSK/Tandy 200. CLASSIFIED: Front-end hardware — 1-Mk; Printers — 1-TI. DISPLAY: Adv layout systems — 3-Ap/Power Mac, 1-Ap/Mac IIsi; Front-end software — Multi-Ad/Creator 3.6, QuarkXPress 3.3; Printers — Unity/1200. PRODUCTION: Pagination software — QuarkXPress 3.3; Typesetters — Unity/1200 XLO; Plate exposures — 1-B, 1-Nu; Plate processors — 1-Ic; Production cameras — 1-B; Automatic film processors — 1-P/26ML.
PRESSROOM: Line 1 — 7-G/Community; Folders — 1-G. MAILROOM: Counter stackers — 1-BG; Bundle tyer — 2-Bu; Addressing machine — 1-St/Paperman. LIBRARY: Electronic — Kk. WIRE SERVICES: News — AP; Receiving dishes — size-2½ft, AP. BUSINESS COMPUTERS: 5-ATT; Applications: SMS; Circ, Payroll, Print estimator, Bus mgmt, Accts receivable; PCs & main system networked.

NEENAH
See APPLETON

OSHKOSH
Winnebago County
'90 U.S. Census- 55,006; E&P '96 Est. 60,634
ABC-CZ (90): 65,257 (HH 24,382)

Oshkosh Northwestern
(m-mon to sat; S)
Oshkosh Northwestern, 224 State St.; PO Box 2926, Oshkosh, WI 54903; tel (414) 235-7700; fax (414) 235-1316.
Circulation: 23,854(m); 23,854(m-sat); 27,641(S); ABC Sept. 30, 1995.
Price: 50¢(d); 50¢(sat); $1.25(S); $3.09/wk (carrier); $148.20/yr (carrier), $160.40/yr (motor route).
Advertising: Open inch rate $19.60(m); $19.60(m-sat); $20.60(S). Representative: Landon Associates Inc.
News Services: AP, KRT. Politics: Republican. Established: 1868.
Advertising not accepted: 900 number betting lines.
Special Editions: Bridal (Jan); Home Plans (Feb); Progress Edition, Lawn-Garden-Home (Mar); Spring Sports (Apr); Mid-WI Fun Guide (May); Parade of Homes (June); Visitor's Guide, Experimental Aircraft (July); Football (Aug); Seniors, Answer Book, Home Improvement (Sept); Home Interiors, Restaurant Guide (Oct); Holiday Cookbook, Basketball (Nov); Holiday Gift Guide, Holiday Greetings (Dec).
Special Weekly Sections: Seniors (wed); Church (sat); Best Food Day, TV Guide, Business, Outdoors, Building, Travel, Art (S).
Magazine: Parade (S).

CORPORATE OFFICERS
President	Russell F Sprung
Secretary/Human Resources	Amy Sprister
Treasurer	Scott Altman

GENERAL MANAGEMENT
Publisher	Russell F Sprung

ADVERTISING
Director/Vice Pres-Marketing	James C Sprung
Manager-National	Lori Stubbe
Manager-Classified	Mark Shingler
Manager-Retail	John Nelson
Manager-Promotion	Judy Shingler
Special Sections	Dave Grey

CIRCULATION
Manager	Tom Biermann
Manager-Single Copy	Hadi Akhavein

NEWS EXECUTIVES
Exec Editor/Vice Pres-News	Thomas P Lee
Managing Editor	Stewart Rieckman

EDITORS AND MANAGERS
Business Editor	Sheila Storm
City Editor	Steve Pradarelli
Editorial Page Editor	Larry Peterson
Education Editor	Kelly Karpinski
Entertainment/Amusements Editor	Jim Lundstrom
Farm/Agriculture Editor	Doug Zellmer
Features Editor	Joe Dill
Graphics Artist	Jason Babler
News Editor	Joe Dill
Chief Photographer	Joe Sienkiewizz
Political/Government Editor	Steve Haas
Sports Editor	Mike Sherry

MANAGEMENT INFORMATION SERVICES
Manager-Info Systems	Julie Madson

PRODUCTION
Manager	Anton Putzer Jr
Manager-Composing	Sandra Smolinski
Manager-Pressroom	Don Taylor
Manager-Camera	James Swanke

Market Information: Zoned editions; TMC.
Mechanical available: Offset; Black and 3 ROP colors; insert accepted — preprinted; page cut-offs — 22¾".
Mechanical specifications: Type page 13" x 22"; E - 6 cols, 2¹⁄₁₆", ⅛" between; A - 6 cols, 2¹⁄₁₆", ⅛" between; C - 9 cols, 1⁵⁄₁₆", ⅛" between.
Commodity consumption: Newsprint 2,125 short tons; widths 55", 41¼", 27½"; black ink 36,600 pounds; color ink 11,119 pounds; single pages printed 13,576; average pages per issue 32(d), 36.65(sat), 63.53(S); single plates used 35,013.
Equipment: EDITORIAL: Front-end hardware — 17-Dewar/Discribe, 2-SII/386, 3-Compaq/386, 1-AST/386, 2-OTC/486, 6-OTC/386, 1-Ap/Mac 6100, 3-OT/Pentium; Front-end software — Dewar/Disc Net, Novell; Printers — 1-Okidata/193; Other equipment — Lf/AP Leaf Picture Desk, Lf/Leafscan 35. CLASSIFIED: Front-end hardware — 5-SII/386; Front-end software — Dewar/Disc Net; Printers — 1-Okidata/193. DISPLAY: Adv layout systems — 1-Dewar/Disc Net, Novell; Front-end hardware — 5-Ap/Mac 81100, 1-Ap/Mac Quadra 700, 1-Ap/Mac IIci, 1-Ap/Mac IIfx, 3-SII/386; Front-end software — Dewar, Novell, QuarkXPress, Aldus/FreeHand, Adobe/Photoshop; Printers — 1-AU/APS-6600; Other equipment — Syquest 44, PLI/128 floptical, 1-CD-Rom Player. PRODUCTION: Pagination software — Dewar/System IV; Typesetters — 2-AU/APS-6108; Plate exposures — 2-Nu/FT40V6UPNS; Plate processors — 1-Nat/A250, 1-Nat/A340; Electronic picture desk — Lf/AP Leaf Picture Desk; Scanners — 2-HP/ScanJet Plus, Umax/Power look, Microtek/35 ScanMaker; Production cameras — 1-SCREEN/260DL, 1-Nu/SST 2024; Automatic film processors — 1-P/26EL; Color separation equipment (conventional) — Lf/Leafscan 35; Digital color separation equipment — 1-RZ/4050E.
PRESSROOM: Line 1 — 5-HI/1660; Folders — 2-HI; Pasters — 5-MEG/D500; Press registration system — KFM. MAILROOM: Counter stackers — 2-Id/Marathoner; Inserters and stuffers — 1-GMA/SL 1000; Bundle tyer — 1-Dynaric. LIBRARY: Electronic — Nexis/NewsView. WIRE SERVICES: News — AP; Photos — AP; Stock tables — AP; Receiving dishes — size-10m, AP. BUSINESS COMPUTERS: 1-Sun/Sparcstation 20; Applications: SBS; Bus office; PBS, Media Plus: Circ; PCs & micros networked.

PORTAGE
Columbia County
'90 U.S. Census- 8,640; E&P '96 Est. 9,432

Daily Register (m-mon to sat)
Daily Register, 309 DeWitt St.; PO Box 470, Portage, WI 53901; tel (608) 742-2111; fax (608) 742-8346. Independent Media Group Inc. group.
Circulation: 4,172(m); 4,172(m-sat); Sworn Sept. 30, 1994.
Price: 50¢(d); 75¢(sat); $8.00/mo; $84.00/yr.
Advertising: Open inch rate $9.02(m); $9.02(m-sat); comb with Baraboo News Republic (mS) $22.25. Representative: Landon Associates Inc.
News Service: AP. Politics: Independent. Established: 1886.
Note: Effective Oct. 14, 1995, this publication changed its publishing plan from (m-mon to fri; S) to (m-mon to sat).
Not Published: New Year; Memorial Day; Independence Day; Labor Day; Christmas.
Special Editions: Progress, Car Care; Home Improvement; Back-to-School; Fall Sports; Hunting; Christmas Gift; Summer Fun Guide.

GENERAL MANAGEMENT
Publisher	David Gentry
Controller	Cheryl Troost

ADVERTISING
Director	Tom Dugan

CIRCULATION
Director	Michael Jeffery

NEWS EXECUTIVE
Editor	Tracy Moeller

EDITORS AND MANAGERS
Business Editor	Ken Pritchard
Lifestyle Editor	Kristin Gilpatrick
Sports Editor	Ray Halstead

PRODUCTION
Manager-Composing	Jason Sloaf
Manager-Press	John Barber
Asst Manager-Press	Al Zajda

Market Information: TMC.
Mechanical available: Offset; Black and 3 ROP colors; insert accepted — preprinted; page cut-offs — 22¾".
Mechanical specifications: Type page 13⅛" x 21½"; E - 6 cols, 2¹⁄₁₆", ⅛" between; A - 6 cols, 2¹⁄₁₆", ⅛" between; C - 9 cols, 1⅜", ¹⁄₁₆" between.
Commodity consumption: Newsprint 200 short tons; widths 27½", 28", 34"; black ink 6,500 pounds; color ink 1,000 pounds; single pages printed 5,032; average pages per issue 16(d); single plates used 6,000.
Equipment: EDITORIAL: Front-end hardware — 7-Mk. CLASSIFIED: Front-end hardware — 1-Mk. DISPLAY: Adv layout systems — Ap/Mac II, 1-Mk. PRODUCTION: Typesetters — 2-Ap/Mac LaserWriter Plus, Ap/Mac LaserWriter II NTX; Plate exposures — 2-Nu; Plate processors — 1-WL; Production cameras — 1-B; Automatic film processors — 1-P.
PRESSROOM: Line 1 — 5-G; Press control system — Fin. MAILROOM: Inserters and stuffers — 1-MM; Bundle tyer — 2-Bu; Addressing machine — 1-KR. WIRE SERVICES: News — AP; Receiving dishes — size-2ft, AP. BUSINESS COMPUTERS: 1-Goldstar; Applications: Circ mailing labels.

RACINE
Racine County
'90 U.S. Census- 84,298; E&P '96 Est. 84,408
ABC-CZ (90): 131,905 (HH 48,829)

The Journal Times
(m-mon to sat; S)
The Journal Times, 212 4th St., Racine, WI 53403; tel (414) 634-3322; fax (414) 631-1702. Lee Enterprises Inc. group.
Circulation: 35,242(m); 35,242(m-sat); 36,504(S); ABC Sept. 30, 1995.
Price: 50¢(d); 50¢(sat); $1.75(S); $4.00/wk; $15.60/mo; $179.40/yr.
Advertising: Open inch rate $33.27(m); $33.27(m-sat); $35.11(S). Representative: Landon Associates Inc.
News Services: AP, KRT. Established: 1856.
Advertising not accepted: Overseas travel employment; Envelope stuffing.
Special Weekly Sections: Business, Today's Living (mon); Food (tues); Health (wed); On the Town (thur); TV Times (fri); "Community", Religion (sat).
Magazine: Parade (S).

GENERAL MANAGEMENT
Publisher	Peter Selkowe
Director-Human Resources	Janet Tidwell
Controller	Nancy Fuchs

ADVERTISING
Manager-Retail	Rich Zinselmeier
Manager-Classified	Bill Werth

MARKETING AND PROMOTION
Manager-Marketing/Shoppers	James Wardrip

CIRCULATION
Manager	Jeff Schell

NEWS EXECUTIVE
Editor	Alan Buncher

EDITORS AND MANAGERS
Business/Finance Editor	Laura Summer Coon
City Editor	Dave Kraemer
Editorial Page Editor	Sean P Devlin
Features Editor	Barbara A Schuetz
Graphics Director	Theresa Schiffer
News Editor	Steven T Lovejoy
Photo Director	Mark Hertzberg
Sports Editor	Susan Shemanske

MANAGEMENT INFORMATION SERVICES
Online Manager	Bill Werth

PRODUCTION
Manager	Mike Rolland
Supervisor-Pressroom	Paul Betchkal
Supervisor-Electronic Copy Processing	Randy Schoedler
Supervisor-Mailroom	Tom Richie
Supervisor-Maintenance	Jay Draeger

Market Information: Zoned editions; TMC; Operate database.
Mechanical available: Flexo (direct); Black and 3 ROP colors; insert accepted — preprinted; page cut-offs — 22¾".
Mechanical specifications: Type page 13" x 21½"; E - 6 cols, 2¹⁄₁₆", ⅛" between; A - 6 cols, 2¹⁄₁₆", ⅛" between; C - 10 cols, 1¼", ¹⁄₁₆" between.
Commodity consumption: Newsprint 2,634 metric tons; widths 54", 40½", 27", 13.5"; black ink 98,747 pounds; color ink 22,974 pounds; single pages printed 13,678; average pages per issue 33(d), 48(S); single plates used 24,500.
Equipment: EDITORIAL: Front-end hardware — HI/8300, HI/PEN, 3-HI/8300; Front-end software — HI 8.0, XyWrite; Printers — Epson/FX

870; Other equipment — UTI, Cascado/OPI, Cascado/RIPs, 2-AG/AU 25, ECR/Autokon 1030 DE, Ap/Power Mac, Lf/AP Leaf Picture Desk. CLASSIFIED: Front-end hardware — HI/CASH; Front-end software — HI 3.6; Printers — Epson/DFX-5000; Other equipment — HI/CPAG. DISPLAY: Adv layout systems — HI/8300; Front-end hardware — 3-HI/8000, 1-HI/8903; Front-end software — HI 8.0; Printers — Epson/FX870; Other equipment — Pixel Craft/8000, Pixel Craft/4520, 2-Ap/Power Mac 7100, 2-Ap/Mac Centris 650, 1-Ap/Mac II ci, 1-Ap/Mac II, 1-Ap/Mac SE, 1-Ap/Mac SE30, 2-Ap/Mac LC, 1-Compaq/Page-Marc, 1-Ap/Mac LaserWriter, 1-Ap/Mac Laser-Writer NT, Xante/Accel-a-Writer 8200. PRODUCTION: Pagination software — HI/8300-8900 6.0, QuarkXPress, Adobe/Photoshop; OCR software — Caere/OmniPro 2.0; Typesetters — 2-AG/Avantra 25; Platemaking systems — Na; Plate exposures — 1-Bungess/Consulux, 1-Na/FX VII; Plate processors — 2-Na/40, 2-Na/FPII; Electronic picture desk — Lf/AP Leaf Picture Desk; Scanners — ECR/Autokon 1030, HP/ScanJet II, Pixel Craft/4520, Pixel Craft/8000, Lf/Leafscan 35, Polaroid/SprintScan; Production cameras — C/Spartan II, C/Spartan III; Automatic film processors — AG/On-line 025; Film transporters — C; Color separation equipment (conventional) — 1-Lf/AP Leaf Picture Desk, Nikon/35mm, ECR/Autokon, Cascade/OPI, AG/Avantras, Lf/Leafscan 35; Digital color separation equipment — 1-ECR/Autokon 1002-03, Cascade/OPI, QPS.

PRESSROOM: Line 1 — 1-MOT/Colormax double width (Flexo 1-5 Impression Unit); Line 2 — 1-MOT/Colormax double width (Flexo 1-5 Impression Unit); Line 3 — 1-MOT/Colormax double width (Flexo 1-3 Impression Unit); Press drives — PEC; Folders — 2-G/2:1; Reels and stands — G/Reels; Press control system — PEC/MOT. MAILROOM: Counter stackers — HL/HT Monitor; Inserters and stuffers — S/8-48, S/6-24; Bundle tyer — 1-Power Strap/PNS6, 1-Power Strap/PNS5, 1-MLN/2A; Addressing machine — Ch/Labeler, 515 base, 721 head. LIBRARY: Electronic — SMS/Stauffer Gold. COMMUNICATIONS: Digital ad delivery system — AP AdSend. WIRE SERVICES: News — AP Datastream, AP Datafeatures, AP, KRT; Photos — AP Photostream, AP; Stock tables — AP SelectStox; Syndicates — KRT; Receiving dishes — size-1m, AP. BUSINESS COMPUTERS: IBM/ASA 400; Applications: WordPerfect, Microsoft/Excel, Quattro/Pro, XYQUEST/XyWrite, Paradox; PCs & micros networked; PCs & main system networked.

RHINELANDER

Oneida County

'90 U.S. Census- 7,427; E&P '96 Est. 7,159

The Daily News

(e-mon to fri; S)

The Daily News, 314 Courtney St.; PO Box 778, Rhinelander, WI 54501; tel (715) 365-6397; fax (715) 365-6367. Scripps League Newspapers Inc. group.

Circulation: 6,560(e); 6,560(S); Sworn Sept. 26, 1995.

Price: 50¢(d); $1.00(S); $8.50/mo (in county), $9.25/mo (out of county); $87.00/yr (in county), $96.00/yr (out of county).

Advertising: Open inch rate $10.15(e); $10.15(S).

News Service: AP. **Politics:** Independent. **Established:** 1882.

Not Published: New Year; Memorial Day; Independence Day; Labor Day; Christmas.

Special Editions: Eye Care Feature, Financial Planning Section, ½ Price Ad Sale, Winter Bridal Edition (Jan); Valentine's Gift Guide, Baby Times Edition, Pet Parade Edition (Feb); Progress Edition (Mar); Spring Automotive Guide, Vacation and Travel Edition (Apr); Mother's Day Gift Guide, Spring Bridal Edition, Fun Country Tourist Guide (May); Father's Day Gift Guide, Advertising Sale, Say No to Drugs Coloring Book, Fun Country Tourist Guide (June); ½ Price Ad Sale, Fun Country Tourist Guide (July); Back-to-School Edition, Health and Fitness Guide, Home Energy Section, Fun Country Tourist Guide (Aug); Fall Automotive Guide, Oktoberfest, Fun Country Tourist Guide (Sept); ABC's of Business, Say No to Drugs Coloring Book, Home & Garden Section, Coupon Pages (Oct); Holiday Gift Guide, Holiday Songbook, Daily Gift Ideas, Thanksgiving Day Shoppers Edition (Nov); Holiday Gift Guides (II, III & IV) (Dec); Best Years Senior Publication (monthly).

Special Weekly Section: Northwoods Ad-Pak TMC (weekly).

Magazines: Fun Country Visitor's Guide (weekly, Memorial Day through Labor Day); Northwoods Ad-Pak-TMC 4100 (weekly); Best Years (monthly).

CORPORATE OFFICERS

Board Chairman/Treasurer E W Scripps
Vice Chairman/Corporate Secretary Betty Knight Scripps
President/Exec Vice Pres Roger N Warkins
Vice Pres-Finance Thomas E Wendel

GENERAL MANAGEMENT

Publisher/Editor Richard Timmons
Business Manager Jacqueline Clapper

ADVERTISING

Manager-Retail Dennis Piotrowski
Manager-National Richard Timmons

CIRCULATION

Manager Linda Wulf

NEWS EXECUTIVE

Managing Editor Meredyth Albright

PRODUCTION

Foreman-Composing Andrea Seidel
Foreman-Press/Plate Brian Dreifuerst

Market Information: TMC.

Mechanical available: Offset; Black and 3 ROP colors; insert accepted — preprinted, any; page cut-offs — 21½".

Mechanical specifications: Type page 14¼" x 22¾"; E - 6 cols, 2¹⁄₁₆", ⅛" between; A - 6 cols, 2¹⁄₁₆", ⅛" between; C - 6 cols, 2¹⁄₁₆", ⅛" between.

Commodity consumption: Newsprint 209 short tons; widths 27", 30"; single pages printed 5,014; average pages per issue 12(d), 32(S).

Equipment: EDITORIAL: Front-end hardware — 5-ScrippSat/PC; Front-end software — ScrippSat; Printers — 2-QMS/810. CLASSIFIED: Front-end hardware — ScrippSat; Front-end software — Synaptic; Printers — Okidata/393, QMS. DISPLAY: Adv layout systems — 2-ScrippSat/PC; Front-end hardware — ScrippSat; Front-end software — Archetype/Corel Draw; Printers — 2-QMS/810, 1-Unity/1800x60; Other equipment — Nikon/Coolscan, HP/3c ScanJet. PRODUCTION: Typesetters — 2-QMS/Laserprinter; Plate exposures — 1-Nu; Production cameras — 1-K/241, 1-K/V2 41; Automatic film processors — Kk; Digital color separation equipment — Adobe/Photoshop.

PRESSROOM: Line 1 — 4-G/Community; Folders — 1-G. MAILROOM: Bundle tyer — 1-Bu/69175. WIRE SERVICES: News — AP; Syndicates — SHNS; Receiving dishes — size-10ft, AP. BUSINESS COMPUTERS: 4-Mk/Acer; Applications: Payroll, Accts receivable, Accts payable, Circ, Class; PCs & micros networked; PCs & main system networked.

SHAWANO

Shawano County

'90 U.S. Census- 7,598; E&P '96 Est. 7,442

Shawano Leader

(e-mon to fri; S)

Shawano Leader, 1464 E. Green Bay St.; PO Box 416, Shawano, WI 54166; tel (715) 526-2121; fax (715) 524-3941. Independent Media Group Inc. group.

Circulation: 7,388(e); 7,388(S); VAC Mar. 31, 1995.

Price: 50¢(d); 75¢(S); $8.00/mo (carrier); $89.00/yr (carrier).

Advertising: Open inch rate $10.33(e); $10.33(S). **Representative:** Landon Associates Inc.

News Service: AP. **Politics:** Independent. **Established:** 1859.

Not Published: New Year; Memorial Day; Independence Day; Labor Day; Christmas.

Advertising not accepted: Adult only 900 numbers.

Special Editions: Finance (Jan); Wedding (Feb); Progress, Home Improvement, Farming (Mar); Vacation (Apr); Dairy (June); Fair, Sports (Aug); Christmas Opener, Codebook (Nov).

Special Weekly Sections: Entertainment (thur); Lifestyle (S).

Magazines: Seniors, Agriculture (tues); Education (wed); Religion, TV Guide (fri); Business, Food, Entertainment, Outdoors, Color Comics (S).

CORPORATE OFFICER

CEO Tony Alligretti

GENERAL MANAGEMENT

Vice Pres/Publisher Stephen P Staloch
Controller Barbara Jansen

ADVERTISING

Director Guy Huffman

CIRCULATION

Manager Dan Frazier

NEWS EXECUTIVE

Managing Editor Kent Tempus

EDITORS AND MANAGERS

Editorial Page Editor Kent Tempus
Entertainment/Amusements Editor Sherry B Rindt
Farm/Agriculture Editor Tim Ryan
Lifestyle Editor Sherry B Rindt
National Editor Kent Tempus
News Editor Kent Tempus
Outdoors Editor Nate Llewellyn
Photo Editor Nate Llewellyn
Political/Government Editor Kent Tempus
Religion Editor Sherry B Rindt
Sports Editor Denis Downey

MANAGEMENT INFORMATION SERVICES

Data Processing Manager Barbara Jansen

PRODUCTION

Manager Rod Christensen

Market Information: TMC.

Mechanical available: Offset; Black and 3 ROP colors; insert accepted — preprinted; page cut-offs — 22¾".

Mechanical specifications: Type page 13" x 21½"; E - 6 cols, 2¹⁄₁₆", ⅛" between; A - 6 cols, 2¹⁄₁₆", ⅛" between; C - 9 cols, 1⅓", ⅛" between.

Commodity consumption: Newsprint 270 short tons; widths 31", 27"; black ink 9,727 pounds; color ink 2,764 pounds; single pages printed 6,720; average pages per issue 14(d), 28(S); single plates used 10,692.

Equipment: EDITORIAL: Front-end hardware — Mk/6; Front-end software — Mk/1100 Plus; Printers — Ap/Mac LaserWriter Plus. CLASSIFIED: Front-end hardware — Mk; Front-end software — Mk; Printers — Ap/Mac LaserWriter Plus, HP/4 Laser; Other equipment — 2-Ap/Mac. PRODUCTION: Pagination software — Adobe/Photoshop, QuarkXPress, After Dark, Color Expert; Typesetters — Ap/Mac LaserWriter Plus, Linotype-Hell/Lino 560; Plate exposures — 1-Nu/Flip Top; Plate processors — Graham/Subtractive Development; Production cameras — B, AG; Automatic film processors — P, SCREEN/LD-220-QT; Color separation equipment (conventional) — Nikon/LS 3510, AG/Film Scanner.

PRESSROOM: Line 1 — 5-WPC; Line 2 — 3-WPC; Line 3 — 11-G/SCC Community; Folders — 2-WPC, 1-G/SSC; Pasters — 1-Enkel, 1-G/Community; Press control system — Phnuematic/RGS IV. MAILROOM: Counter stackers — Amerigraph/RS-12; Inserters and stuffers — KAN/320 3-into-1; Bundle tyer — MLN/in-line strappers; Wrapping singles — Bu, Sitma/5-into-1; Addressing machine — Ch/Video jet 4000 JsII, 3-Ch/label. WIRE SERVICES: News — AP. BUSINESS COMPUTERS: 1-IBM/Powerserver 320H, 4-Wyse/60. Applications: Circ, Prod, Bus, Adv.

SHEBOYGAN

Sheboygan County

'90 U.S. Census- 49,676; E&P '96 Est. 51,728
ABC-CZ (90): 49,676 (HH 19,703)

The Sheboygan Press

(e-mon to fri; m-sat; S)

The Sheboygan Press, 632 Center Ave.; PO Box 358, Sheboygan, WI 53082-0358; tel (414) 457-7711; fax (414) 457-0178. Thomson Newspapers group.

Circulation: 27,588(e); 27,588(m-sat); 29,006(S); ABC Sept. 30, 1995.

Price: 50¢(d); 50¢(sat); $1.25(S); $3.25/wk; $155.00/yr (carrier), $208.00/yr (mail).

Advertising: Open inch rate $25.00(e); $25.00(m-sat); $25.00(S). **Representative:** Landon Associates Inc.

News Services: AP, KRT. **Politics:** Independent. **Established:** 1907.

Not Published: New Year; Memorial Day; Independence Day; Labor Day; Thanksgiving; Christmas.

Special Editions: Bridal (Jan); Home Show, Auto Show (Mar); Farm (Apr); Building, Car Care (May); Football, County Fair (Aug); Building, Car Care (Oct); Christmas (Nov); Christmas Memories (Dec).

Special Weekly Section: Food (tues).

Magazines: TV Update; USA Weekend.

GENERAL MANAGEMENT

Controller Margaret E Krueger

ADVERTISING

Director David Llebelt
Asst Manager Donna Mueller

TELECOMMUNICATIONS

Audiotex Manager Tom Binder

CIRCULATION

Director-Sales & Marketing Michael Giuffre
Asst Director-Sales & Marketing Chris Seibel
Manager-Distribution Steve S Ewig

NEWS EXECUTIVES

Editor Robert L Schumacher
Managing Editor-News Robert Joslyn
Managing Editor-Presentation/Features Robert Farina

EDITORS AND MANAGERS

Business Editor Pat Tearney
City Editor Joseph Gulig
Community Editor Mary Eckhardt
County Government Pam Hinman
Education Editor Michael Lobash
Features Editor Gene Henschel
Librarian Janice Hildebrand
Municipal Government Editor Jami Lemke
Music/Drama Editor Gene Henschel
Outdoors Editor Barry Ginter
Photo Lab Bruce Halmo
Sports Editor Michael Knuth
State Editor Joseph Gulig
Wire Editor Wilson Ruff

PRODUCTION

Foreman-Composing James Splittgerber
Foreman-Pressroom Dennis Eirich

Market Information: TMC; Operate audiotex.

Mechanical available: Letterpress (stereo); Black and 3 ROP colors; insert accepted — preprinted; page cut-offs — 22¾".

Mechanical specifications: Type page 13" x 22¾"; E - 6 cols, 2¹⁄₁₆", ⅛" between; A - 6 cols, 2¹⁄₁₆", ⅛" between; C - 9 cols, 1⅜", ¹⁄₁₆" between.

Commodity consumption: Newsprint 2,080 short tons; widths 55", 41¼", 27⅞", 13¾"; black ink 64,200 pounds; color ink 6,525 pounds; single pages printed 11,929; average pages per issue 35(d), 60(S); single plates used 21,722.

Equipment: EDITORIAL: Front-end hardware — CText/PC; Front-end software — CText; Printers — Pre-Press/Panther; Other equipment — Ap/Mac IIci, Ap/Mac SE 30. CLASSIFIED: Front-end hardware — CText; Front-end software — CText; Printers — Pre-Press/Panther. DISPLAY: Front-end hardware — 4-Dewar/386 PC, 2-Dewar/PC 286, 3-CText/PC 386; Front-end software — CText 6.22, Dewar/Sys 3; Printers — Ap/Mac Printer IIXL. PRODUCTION: Pagination software — QuarkXPress 3.3; Typesetters — Tegra/Varityper 5100, 2-Panther/Plus, 1-V/4990; Platemaking systems — Na; Plate exposures — 1-Na, Na/Starlite; Plate processors — 1-Na, Na/NP 40; Electronic picture desk — Lf/AP Leaf Picture Desk; Scanners — Lf; Production cameras — 2-B, SCREEN/C690D, Braun/Commador; Automatic film processors — SCREEN/LD-281Q, SCREEN/LD-220 QT; Color separation equipment (conventional) — Panther/Plus.

PRESSROOM: Line 1 — 5-G/Headliner Anti-Friction double width Letterpress; Folders — 2-G/2:1; Reels and stands — Cline. MAILROOM: Bundle tyer — 1-Bu, 2-Wilton Pro/Standard 80; Addressing machine — KAN/550 2. LIBRARY: Electronic — SMS/Stauffer Gold. WIRE SERVICES: News — AP, KRT; Stock tables — AP; Receiving dishes — AP. BUSINESS COMPUTERS: CTS, IBM/36; Applications: Circ, Payroll, Accts payable, Accts receivable, Gen ledger; PCs & micros networked; PCs & main system networked.

Wisconsin I-449

STEVENS POINT

Portage County

'90 U.S. Census- 23,006; E&P '96 Est. 23,307
ABC-CZ (90): 33,566 (HH 11,953)

Stevens Point Journal

(e-mon to sat)

Stevens Point Journal, 1200 Third Ct.; PO Box 7, Stevens Point, WI 54481; tel (715) 344-6100; fax (715) 344-7229.

Circulation: 13,980(e); 13,980(e-sat); ABC Sept. 30, 1995.

Price: 50¢(d); 50¢(sat); $8.50/mo (carrier), $13.00/mo (mail).

Advertising: Open inch rate $13.52(e); $13.52(e-sat). **Representative:** Papert Companies.

News Services: AP, NYT. **Politics:** Independent. **Established:** 1873.

Not Published: New Year; Memorial Day; Independence Day; Labor Day; Thanksgiving; Christmas.

Advertising not accepted: Vending machines.

CORPORATE OFFICERS

President	Frank W Leahy
Vice Pres	Patrick Cashin
Secretary/Treasurer	James P Leahy

GENERAL MANAGEMENT

Publisher	Frank W Leahy
General Manager	James P Leahy
Business Manager	Charles Kadonsky

ADVERTISING

Director	Ken Brezinski
Manager-National	Ken Brezinski
Manager-Classified	Bonnie Quimby

CIRCULATION

Manager	Charles Kadonsky

NEWS EXECUTIVE

Editor	Bill Berry

EDITORS AND MANAGERS

City Editor	Debra Bradley
Farm/Outdoor Editor	Bill Berry
Picture Editor	Bill Berry
Sports Editor	Donald Friday
Wire Editor	Gene Kemmeter
Women's Editor	Trudy Stewart

PRODUCTION

Superintendent-Pressroom	Bernard Wisniewski

Market Information: TMC.

Mechanical available: Offset; Black and 4 ROP colors; insert accepted — preprinted; page cutoffs — 22".

Mechanical specifications: Type page 14½" x 21"; E - 6 cols, 2 1/16", 1/8" between; A - 6 cols, 2 1/16", 1/8" between; C - 8 cols, 1 2/3", 1/8" between.

Commodity consumption: average pages per issue 28(d).

Equipment: EDITORIAL: Front-end hardware — DEC. CLASSIFIED: Front-end hardware — DEC. PRODUCTION: Typesetters — 5-COM, 2-Linotype-Hell; Production cameras — 2-R; Automatic film processors — 2-P. PRESSROOM: Line 1 — 12-G/Community; Folders — 2-G; Pasters — 4-Enkel. MAILROOM: Counter stackers — 1-BG; Inserters and stuffers — 1-KAN; Bundle tyer — 4-Bu; Addressing machine — 2-Ch; Other mailroom equipment — 1-MM. COMMUNICATIONS: Digital ad delivery system — AP AdSend. WIRE SERVICES: News — AP, NYT. BUSINESS COMPUTERS: DEC/PDP 11-44.

SUPERIOR

Douglas County

'90 U.S. Census- 27,134; E&P '96 Est. 25,686

The Daily Telegram

(e-mon to fri; m-sat)

The Daily Telegram, 1226 Ogden Ave., Superior, WI 54880; tel (715) 394-4411; fax (715) 394-9404. Murphy Newspaper group.

Circulation: 10,516(e); 10,516(m-sat); Sworn Sept. 30, 1995.

Price: 50¢(d); 75¢(sat); $91.00/yr (carrier/mail), $104.00/yr (mail).

Advertising: Open inch rate $8.65(e); $8.65(m-sat). **Representative:** Papert Companies.

News Service: AP. **Politics:** Independent. **Established:** 1890.

Not Published: New Year; Memorial Day; Independence Day; Labor Day; Christmas.

Special Editions: Focus 2; Dollar Days; 2 City-wide Promotions; 2 Appliance; Fair; Building.

Special Weekly Sections: Best Food Day (wed); Church Page (fri); Teen Page, Bubble Gum Wrapper (sat).

Magazines: TV Pilot, USA Weekend (sat).

Broadcast Affiliates: KVEW-TV Kennewick, WA; KXLY-TV Spokane, WA; KXLY-FM Spokane, WA; KAPP-TV Yakima, WA; WISC-TV Madison, WI.

CORPORATE OFFICERS

President	John B Murphy
Vice Pres	Elizabeth Murphy Burns
Secretary	Lois L Wessman
Treasurer	George A Nelson
Vice Pres-Administration/Finance	George A Nelson

GENERAL MANAGEMENT

Publisher	John B Murphy
General Manager	William Holliday
Controller	Robert Wallace

ADVERTISING

Manager	Betty Porter

NEWS EXECUTIVES

Exec Editor	Leslee LeRoux
Asst Editor	Konnie LeMay

EDITORS AND MANAGERS

Amusements/Aviation Editor	Finley Stalvig
Books/Business Editor	Leslee LeRoux
Editorial Page Editor	Leslee LeRoux
Education Editor	Konnie LeMay
Farm Editor	Michael D Payton
Fashion Editor	Linda McGonegal
Films/Theater Editor	Finley Stalvig
Finance Editor	Leslee LeRoux
Food/Garden Editor	Linda McGonegal
Home Furnishings Editor	Linda McGonegal
Librarian/Music Editor	Finley Stalvig
News Editor	Leslee LeRoux
Photo Department Manager	Carl Knudson
Radio/Television Editor	Finley Stalvig
Real Estate Editor	Finley Stalvig
Religion Editor	Carl Knudson
School Editor	Konnie LeMay
Science Editor	Konnie LeMay
Society/Women's Editor	Linda McGonegal
Sports Editor	John Davy
Teen-Age/Youth Editor	Konnie LeMay
Travel Editor	Finley Stalvig

PRODUCTION

Director	Howard Mackey
Foreman-Composing	Dennis Corbin
Foreman-Mailroom	Mark Currie
Foreman-Pressroom	Louis Carlson

Market Information: TMC.

Mechanical available: Offset; Black and 3 ROP colors; insert accepted — preprinted; page cutoffs — 22¾".

Mechanical specifications: Type page 13" x 21½"; E - 6 cols, 2 1/16", 1/8" between; A - 6 cols, 2 1/16", 1/8" between; C - 9 cols, 1 3/8", 1/16" between.

Commodity consumption: Newsprint 985 short tons; widths 13¾", 27½"; black ink 14,100 pounds; color ink 1,510 pounds; single pages printed 7,416; average pages per issue 24(d), 28(sat); single plates used 9,189.

Equipment: EDITORIAL: Front-end hardware — DP, Cx; Front-end software — DP, Cx; Printers — Okidata. CLASSIFIED: Front-end hardware — DP, Cx; Front-end software — DP, Cx; Printers — TI/820. DISPLAY: Adv layout systems — SCS/Layout 8000; Front-end hardware — PC; Front-end software — SCS/Layout 8000; Printers — C.Itoh. PRODUCTION: Typesetters — 2-V/1000; Plate exposures — 1-Nu; Plate processors — Nat; Electronic picture desk — Lf/AP Leaf Picture Desk; Scanners — ECR/Autokon; Production cameras — R; Automatic film processors — LE; Color separation equipment (conventional) — Lf/Leafscan. PRESSROOM: Line 1 — 5-G/Urbanite; Press control system — Fin. MAILROOM: Counter stackers — Id; Inserters and stuffers — Amerigraph/848; Bundle tyer — EAM/Mosca, Dynaric; Addressing machine — Dispensa-Matic. WIRE SERVICES: News — AP; Photos — AP; Receiving dishes — size-8ft, AP. BUSINESS COMPUTERS: Vision Data, 10-PC; Applications: Vision Data: Accts receivable, Circ; PCs & micros networked; PCs & main system networked.

TWO RIVERS

See MANITOWOC

WATERTOWN

Jefferson and Dodge Counties

'90 U.S. Census- 12,388; E&P '96 Est. 9,205

Watertown Daily Times

(e-mon to fri; m-sat)

Watertown Daily Times, 113-115 W. Main St.; PO Box 140, Watertown, WI 53094-0140; tel (414) 261-4949; fax (414) 261-5102.

Circulation: 9,673(e); 9,673(m-sat); Sworn Sept. 29, 1995.

Price: 50¢(d); 50¢(sat); $94.80/yr (city & out of town carrier), $101.40/yr (in state), $104.00/yr (out of state), $100.00/yr (motor route).

Advertising: Open inch rate $8.41(e); $8.41(m-sat).

News Service: AP. **Politics:** Independent. **Established:** 1895.

Not Published: New Year; Memorial Day; Independence Day; Labor Day; Thanksgiving; Christmas.

Special Editions: Health & Fitness; Money; Senior Living; Design-An-Ad; Bridal; Spring Home Improvement; Car Care; Maxwell St.; Dining; Great Outdoors; Fall Home Improvement; Christmas Edition; Christmas Greetings.

Special Weekly Sections: Best Food Day (mon); Children's Page, Commerce Page (tues); Agri-Business (wed); Dining & Entertainment (thur); Commerce Page (fri).

Magazines: TV Section (fri); USA Weekend (sat).

CORPORATE OFFICERS

President	James M Clifford
Vice Pres	Patricia L Clifford
Secretary	Margaret A Krueger
Treasurer	Ralph H Krueger

GENERAL MANAGEMENT

Publisher/Editor	James M Clifford
Business Manager	Ralph H Krueger

ADVERTISING

Director-Retail & National	Judy Christian
Manager-Classified	Ray F Graglia

CIRCULATION

Director	Mark D Kuehl

NEWS EXECUTIVE

Managing Editor	Thomas Schultz

EDITORS AND MANAGERS

Editorial Page Editor	Thomas Schultz
Photo Editor	John Hart
Sports Editor	Steve Poellmann

Market Information: Zoned editions; Split Run; TMC.

Mechanical available: Offset; Black and 3 ROP colors; insert accepted — preprinted; page cutoffs — 22¾".

Mechanical specifications: Type page 13" x 21½"; E - 6 cols, 2.03", 1/6" between; A - 6 cols, 2.03", 1/6" between; C - 8 cols, 1½", 1/12" between.

Commodity consumption: Newsprint 560 short tons; width 28"; black ink 6,255 pounds; color ink 989 pounds; single pages printed 8,072; average pages per issue 24(d), 18(sat); single plates used 4,136.

Equipment: EDITORIAL: Front-end hardware — Ap/Mac; Front-end software — Baseview; Printers — Okidata, 3-Ap/Mac LaserWriter. CLASSIFIED: Front-end hardware — Ap/Mac; Front-end software — Baseview; Printers — Okidata. DISPLAY: Front-end hardware — Ap/Mac; Front-end software — QuarkXPress, Adobe/Illustrator; Printers — Ap/Mac LaserWriter. PRODUCTION: Pagination software — QuarkXPress 3.3, Adobe/Photoshop; Typesetters — AG/Accuset 1200; Plate exposures — 30-Nu/Flip Top FT40APRNS; Plate processors — Nat/A-250; Electronic picture desk — Ap/Mac Quadra 950, Adobe/Photoshop; Scanners — Ap/Mac One Scanner, Microtek/ScanMaker; Production cameras — B/Horizontal; Automatic film processors — Wing-Lynch/5; Color separation equipment (conventional) — Lf/Leafscan 35, Ap/Mac Quadra; Digital color separation equipment — AG/Accuset 1200. PRESSROOM: Line 1 — 5-G/Community; Line 2 — 1-G/Community; Line 3 — 1-G/Community; Folders — 1-G/Community. MAILROOM: Inserters and stuffers — 6-KAN/480; Bundle tyer — 2-Ty-Tech/TM45; Addressing machine — St/1600-2344. LIBRARY: Electronic — SMS/Stauffer Gold. COMMUNICATIONS: Digital ad delivery system — AP AdSend. WIRE SERVICES: News — AP Datafeatures, AP Newswire; Photos — AP Laserphoto; Receiving dishes — size-3m, AP. BUSINESS COMPUTERS: ATT/382-500; Applications: Accts receivable, Circ, Accts payable, Display billing, Class billing; PCs & micros networked; PCs & main system networked.

WAUKESHA

Waukesha County

'90 U.S. Census- 56,958; E&P '96 Est. 63,953
ABC-CZ (90): 56,958 (HH 21,235)

Waukesha County Freeman

(e-mon to fri; m-sat)

Waukesha County Freeman, 801 N. Barstow St.; PO Box 7, Waukesha, WI 53187; tel (414) 542-2501; fax (414) 542-6082. Thomson Newspapers group.

Circulation: 21,024(e); 21,024(m-sat); ABC Mar. 31, 1995.

Price: 50¢(d); 75¢(sat); $1.95/wk (carrier); $8.45/mo (carrier); $93.60/yr (carrier).

Advertising: Open inch rate $20.55(e); $20.55(m-sat).

News Services: AP, KRT. **Politics:** Independent-Conservative. **Established:** 1859.

Not Published: New Year; Memorial Day; Independence Day; Labor Day; Thanksgiving; Christmas.

Advertising not accepted: Objectionable.

Special Editions: National Hobby Month, License Plate Contest, MBA Home Builders Expo, National Eye Health Care Month, People's Choice Ballot, Jamboree, Brides, Adult Education, Child Care Directory, Winter Car Care, Super Bowl, Metro Assn. of Realtors, Home & Real Estate Expo, People's Choice Winners, Wacky Valentine's Date (Jan); Tax Directory, Valentine's Promotion, Downtown Waukesha Valentines, Boy Scouts Anniversary, President's Day Sale, Child Care Directory, Health/Medical Directory, Basketball, National FFA Week, Money Matters, A to Z, A Day in the Life of Waukesha County, Spring Fitness (Feb); National Women's History Month, Fish Fry, Tax Directory, Be Kind to Animals Week, Family/Locally owned Businesses, NCAA Men's Tournamnent, St. Pat's Promotion, Child Care Directory, Partners for Drug Free America, Health/Medical Directory, Coloring Book, Spring Home Improvement, Health File, Home & Landscape, Doctor's Day (Mar); Tax Directory, National Garden Month, Palm Sunday Church Directory, World Health Day, RV Campers, Easter Church Directory, Design-An-Ad, Golf Guide, Health/Medical Directory, MBA Spring Tour of Homes, ASE Mechanics, Earth Day, American Home Week, Professional Secretaries Week, Lawn & Garden, Pet Photo Contest, Planting Guide, Historic Preservation, Stress, Spring Fever (Apr); Draw your Mom Contest, National Beef/BBQ Month, National Home Decorating Month, National Pet Week, Financial Tab, Golf Directory, 101 Things to Do, Health/Medical Directory, Home and Landscaping, Safe Driving/Memorial Day, Power of Summer (May); Golf Guide, Sidewalk Sale, National Fresh Fruit/Vegetable Month, Draw your Dad Contest, Graduation Happy Ads, Graduation, Waukesha Co. Graduations, Flag Day, Father's Day Happy Ads, Summer Home Improvement, Health/Medical Directory, Family/Locally-Owned Business, Power of Summer (June); Antique Directory, Vacation Travel Guide, Family/Locally-owned Businesses, Nat'l Ice Cream Month, Nat'l Picnic Month, Waukesha County Fair, Health/Medical Directory, Home Furnishings, Education Guide, Golf Directory, Adopt A Pet, Health File, Lifesavers (July); Back-to-School, Sidewalk Sale, National Catfish Month, Antique Directory, Golf Directory, Fun on Water, MBA Parade of Home, Child Care Directory, Lifesavers, Resale Shops, Football Contest, Football Preview, Health/Medical Directory, A to Z (Aug); Baby Safety Month, Labor Day, National Chicken Month, Football Contest, Vacation Guide, All American Breakfast Month, Adult Dental Awareness Month, United Way, Fall Car Care, Fall Fun, Child Care Directory, Fall

Home Improvement, Local Entrepreneurs, Baby Photo Contest, Hunting/Fishing, Resource Guide, A to Z, Literacy Guide (Sept); National Restaurant Month, A to Z, Football Contest, MBA Fall Remodelers Tour, National Kitchen/Bath Month, National Pizza Month, Downtown Waukesha Fall Festival, National Boss Day, National Car Care Month, Credit Union Week, Child Care Directory, Emergency Medical Guide, Halloween, '97 Models, Adopt a Pet, Pamper Yourself, Business Spotlight, Women's Edition, Trick 'N' Treat Times (Oct); '97 Models, Football Contest, Christmas Parade, Decorate for the Holidays, Hot Spots, National Children's Book Week, Child Care Directory, Hometown Christmas, National Jewelry Month, Jaycee Parade, Spruce Up your Home, Wishbook, Where's the Need, Shop Downtown, A to Z, Holiday Fun (Nov); Christmas Gifting, Holiday Fun, Destination Downtown, Football Contest, Caroling Guide, Present Tense, Resource Directory, New Year's Entertainment Guide, Child Care Directory, Christmas Greetings, After Christmas Sale, Stress, Year in Review, Safe Driving for New Year, First Baby '97 Contest, New Year's Greeting (Dec); Freebate, Coupon Book, Crimestoppers, Mature Living (monthly).

Special Weekly Sections: House and Home, Food Section (thur); TV Freetime, Church Directory, Real Estate, Cruisin', Sports Weekend (sat).

Magazines: Freetime (own, newsprint), USA Weekend, 4-Color Comics, United Media Enterprise, Weekend Edition (sat).

GENERAL MANAGEMENT

Publisher David G Decker

ADVERTISING

Director Dave Perkins
Asst Manager Jon Denk

MARKETING AND PROMOTION

Manager-Marketing/Promotion Monica Mueller

CIRCULATION

Manager William Ney

NEWS EXECUTIVE

Managing Editor Roger Bartel

EDITORS AND MANAGERS

Amusements Editor Claire Beglinger
Automotive Editor Bruce Holan
Books/Music Editor Claire Beglinger
Business Editor Claire Beglinger
Editorial Page Editor Roger Bartel
Features Editor Claire Beglinger
Films/Theater Editor Claire Beglinger
Food Editor Claire Beglinger
Graphics Editor Mike Wroblewski
Librarian Patrice Shanks
News Editor Claire Beglinger
Photo Editor Todd Ponath
Radio/Television Editor Bruce Holan
Sports Editor Lee Fensin

PRODUCTION

Foreman-Press Tim Meyers

Market Information: Zoned editions; TMC.

Mechanical available: Web Offset; Black and 3 ROP colors; insert accepted — preprinted; page cut-offs — 22¾".

Mechanical specifications: Type page 13" x 21½"; E - 6 cols, 2", 3/16" between; A - 6 cols, 2", 3/16" between; C - 9 cols, 1⅜", 1/16" between.

Commodity consumption: Newsprint 1,800 short tons; widths 27½", 13¾"; black ink 52,000 pounds; color ink 2,800 pounds; average pages per issue 30(d); single plates used 16,000.

Equipment: EDITORIAL: Front-end hardware — CD/2330, 23-Cx/Magician Plus, 4-Cx/Magician, 6-RSK/Tandy 200. CLASSIFIED: Front-end hardware — CD/2330, 5-Cx/Magician Plus; Printers — 1-DEC/LA 180, 1-Facit/Line Printer. DISPLAY: Adv layout systems — 4-Cx/Magician Plus. PRODUCTION: Typesetters — 2-Tegra/Varityper; Platemaking systems — 1-Na/Twin Star; Plate exposures — 1-Dy/1240S; Production cameras — 1-B/1822; Automatic film processors — 1-ECR/Autokon. PRESSROOM: Line 1 — 8-G/Urbanite. COMMUNICATIONS: Facsimile — Savin/III. WIRE SERVICES: News — AP, KRT, TV Data; Receiving dishes — size-12ft, AP. BUSINESS COMPUTERS: 1-ATT/3B2-500; Applications: Circ, Adv billing, Accts receivable, Gen ledger, Payroll; PCs & main system networked.

WAUSAU

Marathon County

'90 U.S. Census- 37,060; E&P '96 Est. 41,902
ABC-CZ (90): 58,104 (HH 22,402)

The Wausau Daily Herald

(e-mon to fri; m-sat; S)

The Wausau Daily Herald, 800 Scott St.; PO Box 1286, Wausau, WI 54401; tel (715) 842-2101; fax (715) 848-9360. Gannett Co. Inc. group.

Circulation: 24,969(e); 27,175(m-sat); 32,079(S); ABC Sept. 30, 1995.

Price: 35¢(d); 35¢(sat); $1.25(S); $2.95/wk; $11.80/mo; $153.40/yr.

Advertising: Open inch rate $24.59(e); $24.59(m-sat); $27.26(S). **Representative:** Gannett National Newspaper Sales.

News Services: AP, GNS. **Politics:** Independent. **Established:** 1907.

Advertising not accepted: Advertising which discriminates.

Special Editions: Bridal (Jan); Progress, Home Show (Mar); Business Expo (Apr); Parade of Homes I (May); Logjam, Parade of Homes II (June); Sidewalk Sale (July); Wausau Guide, Artrageous, Home Improvement (Sept); Food/Lifestyle Expo, Fall Fashion (Oct); Holiday Shoppers (Nov); Gift Guide (Dec); Momentum, Real Estate, Guide (monthly); Coupon Clipper, Seniors (quarterly).

Special Weekly Sections: "Weekend" Entertainment, Outdoor Pages (thur); Church Page (fri); Homestyle, Farm Pages (sat); Outdoor Pages, Travel Pages (S).

Magazines: Focus (local, newsprint) (thur); TV Guide, Color Comics (S).

GENERAL MANAGEMENT

President/Publisher Michael S Scobey
Director-Human Resources Betty Donovan
Controller Bernadette Hollinger

ADVERTISING

Director Vic Brabender
Manager-Retail John Benetti
Manager-Classified/National Gayle Benazeski

MARKETING AND PROMOTION

Director-Market Development Mona Roth

CIRCULATION

Director Kevin Denny
Manager Danny Shrewsbury

NEWS EXECUTIVE

Managing Editor Jim Herman

EDITORS AND MANAGERS

Business Editor Rich Jackson
City Editor Sara Kuhl
Editorial Page Editor Tom Berger
Education Editor Will Henderson
Entertainment/Amusements Editor Sara Kuhl
Environment Editor Kelly Thayer
Farm/Food Editor Kelly Thayer
Fashion Editor Sara Kuhl
Features/Special Projects Editor Jamie Orcutt
Films/Theater Editor Jody Fraleigh
Health/Medical Editor Sara Kuhl
Librarian Debrah Siburt
Music/Radio Editor Jamie Orcutt
News Editor Peter Frank
Outdoors Editor Jim Lee
Photo Department Manager David Humphreys
Real Estate Editor Fred Hillman
Religion Editor Sara Kuhl
Sports Editor Steve Rupp
Teen-Age/Youth Editor Randy Riebe
Television Editor Jamie Orcutt
Travel Editor Barbara Shay
Women's Editor Sara Kuhl

MANAGEMENT INFORMATION SERVICES

Data Processing Manager Steve Koppa

PRODUCTION

Director Tom Leckenby
Manager-Pressroom Dave McDonald
Manager-Maintenance Jerry Borchardt
Manager-Distribution Center Joe Heinritz
Supervisor-Pre Press Marie Tiege
Supervisor-Pre Press (Night) Chris Paulson

Market Information: Zoned editions; Split Run; TMC; ADS.

Mechanical available: Offset; Black and 3 ROP colors; insert accepted — preprinted; page cut-offs — 22.75".

Mechanical specifications: Type page 13" x 21.5"; E - 6 cols, 2 1/16", ⅛" between; A - 6 cols, 2 1/16", ⅛" between; C - 9 cols, 1⅜", 1/16" between.

Commodity consumption: Newsprint 2,759 short tons; widths 54¾", 41", 27¼"; black ink 65,000 pounds; color ink 8,500 pounds; single pages printed 11,630; average pages per issue 26(d), 60(S); single plates used 40,000.

Equipment: EDITORIAL: Front-end hardware — Mk/6000; Front-end software — Mk/ACE II, Caere/OmniPage; Printers — Ap/Mac LaserPrinter; Other equipment — Mk. CLASSIFIED: Front-end hardware — PC/486s; Front-end software — FSI/Q-Sales; Printers — TI/810. DISPLAY: Adv layout systems — Ap/Mac; Front-end hardware — Ap/Mac; Front-end software — Multi-Ad/Creator, Aldus/FreeHand 3.0, QuarkXPress 3.1; Printers — HP, V/5000-5100, 1-ECR/1016 Imagesetter, 1-MON/Imagemaster 1000; Other equipment — CD, XYQUEST/44. PRODUCTION: Pagination software — QuarkXPress; Typesetters — 1-V/5000 controllers, 1-ECR/1016, 1-V/5100 Imager, 1-MON/Imagemaster 1000; Plate exposures — Nu, Ultra/Plus, Nu/FT40 APNS, Nu/FT46U6UPNS; Plate processors — Nat/A-250; Electronic picture desk — Lf/AP Leaf Picture Desk, Total Image Corporation/(PS-Link); Scanners — Nikon, AG/Color Focus, Microtek/XE; Production cameras — C/Spartan II; Automatic film processors — LE; Film transporters — LE; Color separation equipment (conventional) — Adobe/Photoshop.
PRESSROOM: Line 1 — 4-G/Metro double width (Hump on 2-10 side); Press drives — Fin; Folders — 1-G/2:1; Pasters — G/Flying Paster; Reels and stands — 4-G; Press control system — G; Press registration system — G. MAILROOM: Counter stackers — 2-HL/Dual Carrier; Inserters and stuffers — HI/1372, HI/624; Bundle tyer — 2-Power Strap; Addressing machine — Ch. WIRE SERVICES: News — AP; Photos — AP; Stock tables — AP SelectStox; Receiving dishes — AP. BUSINESS COMPUTERS: 1-IBM/AS-400; Applications: GNS.

WEST BEND

Washington County

'90 U.S. Census- 23,916; E&P '96 Est. 26,455
ABC-CZ (90): 23,916 (HH 8,686)

The Daily News

(e-mon to fri; m-sat)

The Daily News, 100 S. Sixth Ave.; PO Box 478, West Bend, WI 53095; tel (414) 338-0622; fax (414) 338-1984. Thomson Newspapers group.

Circulation: 10,981(e); 10,587(m-sat); ABC Sept. 30, 1995.

Price: 50¢(d); 50¢(sat); $2.15/wk; $9.10/mo (carrier), $10.30/mo (mail); $102.95/yr (carrier), $118.50/yr (mail), $109.20/yr (motor route).

Advertising: Open inch rate $12.54(e); $12.54(m-sat). **Representatives:** Landon Associates Inc.; Thomson Newspapers.

News Services: AP, THO (Washington Bureau). **Politics:** Independent. **Established:** 1855.

Note: Effective Aug. 26, 1995, this publication added a m-sat edition.

Special Editions: Agri-business; Home Improvement; Progress; Spring Car Care; Senior Citizens; Dairy; Back-to-School; Fall Home Improvement; New Cars; Christmas Gift Guide; Christmas Opening Edition; Christmas Countdown; County Fair Edition.

Special Weekly Sections: Business (mon); Food Section (wed); Business (thur); Real Estate & Home, Auto Section (sat).

Magazines: TV Leisure (thur); USA Weekend (sat).

GENERAL MANAGEMENT

Publisher Robert S Gallagher

ADVERTISING

Manager Barbara Swan

TELECOMMUNICATIONS

Audiotex Manager Barbara Swan

CIRCULATION

Manager-Sales Tom Huber

NEWS EXECUTIVE

Managing Editor Steve Sandberg

EDITORS AND MANAGERS

City Editor Dan Muckelbauer
News Editor DeAnn Laufenberg
Sports Editor Keith Schmidt

MANAGEMENT INFORMATION SERVICES

Data Processing Manager Edmund F Hulet III

PRODUCTION

Manager Edmund F Hulet III
Manager-Composing Carrie Whitfield
Manager-Pressroom Loran Marmes

Market Information: TMC; Operate audiotex.

Mechanical available: Offset; black; insert accepted — preprinted, smaller units than full-page, tabs, booklets; page cut-offs — 23 9/16".

Mechanical specifications: Type page 13" x 21½"; E - 6 cols, 2⅙", ⅛" between; A - 6 cols, 2⅙", ⅛" between; C - 9 cols, 1⅜", 1/16" between.

Commodity consumption: Newsprint 3,000 short tons; widths 27½", 34", 13¾"; black ink 200,000 pounds; color ink 5,000 pounds; single pages printed 4,960; average pages per issue 19.4(d); single plates used 7,000.

Equipment: EDITORIAL: Front-end hardware — Mk/6000; Front-end software — Mk/Ace II; Printers — 2-V/5100; Other equipment — Mk/Magitronic II. CLASSIFIED: Front-end hardware — 4-Mk/6000; Front-end software — Mk/Ace II; Printers — V/5100. DISPLAY: Adv layout systems — Ap/Mac IIci; Front-end hardware — Ap/Mac IIci; Front-end software — QPS, Aldus, Multi-Ad; Printers — V/5100, NewGen/Laser Printer. PRODUCTION: Typesetters — 3-COM/CRT MCS100; Platemaking systems — Nu/Flip Top FT40; Plate exposures — 1-Nu; Plate processors — 1-Nat/A-250; Electronic picture desk — Lf/AP Leaf Picture Desk; Scanners — 1-SCREEN/680C; Production cameras — SCREEN/Companica 680; Automatic film processors — LE/LD 24A; Color separation equipment (conventional) — Lf/AP Leaf Picture Desk, V.
PRESSROOM: Line 1 — 8-G/Community; Folders — G/SC, Manual; Press control system — Manual; Press registration system — Manual. MAILROOM: Bundle tyer — 1-Bu/St, 1-Power Strap; Addressing machine — 1-SAC/JR. COMMUNICATIONS: Systems used — satellite. WIRE SERVICES: News — AP; Photos — AP; Syndicates — THO; Receiving dishes — AP. BUSINESS COMPUTERS: 1-IBM/PC-XT, ATT; Applications: Adv billing, Payroll, Circ.

WISCONSIN RAPIDS

Wood County

'90 U.S. Census- 18,245; E&P '96 Est. 18,710
ABC-CZ (90): 30,515 (HH 11,860)

Daily Tribune

(e-mon to fri; m-sat)

Daily Tribune, 220 1st Ave. S.; PO Box 8090, Wisconsin Rapids, WI 54495-8090; tel (715) 423-7200; fax (715) 421-1545. Thomson Newspapers group.

Circulation: 14,142(e); 14,142(m-sat); ABC Sept. 30, 1995.

Price: 50¢(d); 50¢(sat); $8.95/mo; $101.40/yr.

Advertising: Open inch rate $13.35(e); $13.35(m-sat).

News Service: AP. **Politics:** Independent. **Established:** 1914.

Not Published: New Year; Memorial Day; Independence Day; Labor Day; Christmas.

Special Editions: Bridal Tab, January Coupon Specials, Super Bowl Specials (Jan); Badger State Games, Valentine's Gift Guide, Tax Guide, Senior Living, C. W. Homebuilders Home Show, Jaycee Sport Show, Locally-owned Businesses, Daytona 500 (Feb); Rapids Mall Boat Show, Boating Guide, NCAA Basketball Tourney, Design An Ad, Spring Car Care, Home Improvement Edition, Shape Up for Summer (Mar); Boating Guide, Home Improvement Edition, Easter Dining, Say "NO" to Drugs, Home & Garden Edition, Bridal Tab, Earth Day (Apr); Greatest Mom Contest, National Health Month, Graduation Tab, Women of the 90's, Memorial Day Coupons, Parade Previews, Youth Activities (May); Parade of Homes, Father's Day Honor Roll, Parade Pick-up, Fun-Filled Fourth, Riverfront Rendevous, Business Review (June); Sports Section, Water Ski Tourney, Ridikalas Daes (July); Discover Progress Editions, Rivercities Fun Fest, Sports Section, Back-to-School Edition, Fall Sports (Aug); Packer Tab, Sports Section, Fall Bridal Section, Fall Outdoors, United Way Tab, Home Improvement Edition (Sept); Sports Section, National Credit Union Week, Restaurant Tab, Fall Car Care, Homemaker's Tool (Oct); Sports Section, Gift Guide, Thanksgiving Dining, Thanksgiving Day Paper, Winter Sports, Let it Snow (Nov); Sports Section, Gift Guide, Sunday Special Edition, What Christmas Means to Me, New Year's Dining, First Baby Contest (Dec).

Special Weekly Sections: Weekend Sports (mon); Food (tues); Farm Page (wed); Dining & Entertainment (thur); Church & Religion (fri); Premier, Seniors Page (sat).

Copyright ©1996 by the Editor & Publisher Co.

Wyoming

GENERAL MANAGEMENT
Publisher — Randy Graf
Accountant — Steven Berlyn

ADVERTISING
Director — Helen Jungwith

CIRCULATION
Manager — Scott Skinner

NEWS EXECUTIVE
Editor — Thomas Enwright

EDITORS AND MANAGERS
Editorial Page Editor — Thomas Enwright
Food Editor — Nancy Quick
Librarian — Rosann Arndt
Living/Lifestyle Editor — Nancy Quick
News Editor — Mystique Macomber
Photo Chief — Steve Davis
Religion Editor — Nancy Quick
Sports Editor — Daniel Graf

PRODUCTION
Foreman-Composing — Tania Cota
Foreman-Pressroom — Bruce Leberg

Market Information: TMC.
Mechanical available: Offset; Black and 3 ROP colors; insert accepted — preprinted; page cut-offs — 22¾".
Mechanical specifications: Type page 13" x 21½"; E - 6 cols, 2 1/16", ⅛" between; A - 6 cols, 1 5/16", ⅛" between; C - 9 cols, 1 5/16", ⅛" between.
Commodity consumption: average pages per issue 22(d).
Equipment: EDITORIAL: Front-end hardware — 1-DEC; Front-end software — CText. CLASSIFIED: Front-end hardware — 3-DEC; Front-end software — CText. DISPLAY: Adv layout systems — Ap/Mac. PRODUCTION: Platemaking systems — 1-Na; Plate exposures — 1-BKY; Plate processors — 1-Na; Electronic picture desk — Lf/AP Leaf Picture Desk; Production cameras — 1-B; Automatic film processors — 1-P; Digital color separation equipment — Lf/AP Leaf Picture Desk.
PRESSROOM: Line 1 — 10-G/Community.
MAILROOM: Bundle tyer — 1-MLN. **LIBRARY:** Electronic — SMS. **WIRE SERVICES:** News — AP; Photos — AP; Receiving dishes — AP.

WYOMING

CASPER
Natrona County
'90 U.S. Census- 46,742; E&P '96 Est. 44,021
ABC-CZ (90): 49,719 (HH 19,714)

Star-Tribune
(m-mon to sat; S)
Star-Tribune, 170 Star Ln.; PO Box 80, Casper, WY 82602; tel (307) 266-0500; fax (307) 266-0501; e-mail ed@trib.com; web site http://www.trib.com/. Howard Publications group.
Circulation: 32,097(m); 32,097(m-sat); 35,263(S); ABC Sept. 30, 1995.
Price: 50¢(d); 50¢(sat); $1.25(S); $2.55/wk.
Advertising: Open inch rate $22.21(m); $22.21(m-sat); $24.41(S). **Representative:** Papert Companies.
News Services: AP, NYT. **Politics:** Independent. **Established:** 1914.
Not Published: Christmas.
Special Editions: Spring Home Improvement (Mar); Natrona County Visitor's Guide, Destination Wyoming (Apr); Casper Classic (June); Pulse of Progress, Destination Wyoming (July).
Special Weekly Sections: Food (wed); Church page (sat); Food, Wyoming Weekend (S); Markets (daily except mon).
Magazines: Wyoming TV Update, Color Comics, Parade (S).

CORPORATE OFFICER
President — Robert S Howard

GENERAL MANAGEMENT
Publisher — Robin W Hurless
Business Manager — Henry J Groenenberg

ADVERTISING
Director — Gary Hussman

CIRCULATION
Director — Maurice D Elhart

NEWS EXECUTIVE
Asst Managing Editor — Hugh Jackson

EDITORS AND MANAGERS
Books/Business Editor — Steve Wolgast
City Editor — Tom Rea
Editorial Page Editor — Charles Levendosky
News Editor — Steve Wolgast
Sports Editor — Ron Gullberg
State Editor — Paul Kraza

PRODUCTION
Foreman-Pressroom — Brian Compton
Foreman-Mailroom — Dan Sampson
Foreman-Composing — Connie Hehm

Market Information: TMC.
Mechanical available: Offset; Black and 3 ROP colors; insert accepted — preprinted; page cut-offs — 22¾".
Mechanical specifications: Type page 13" x 21½"; E - 6 cols, 2 1/16", ⅛" between; A - 6 cols, 2 1/16", ⅛" between; C - 9 cols, 1 ⅜", 1/16" between.
Commodity consumption: Newsprint 2,300 metric tons; widths 55", 41¼", 27½"; single pages printed 11,750.
Equipment: EDITORIAL: Front-end hardware — 1-Sun/Sparc. CLASSIFIED: Front-end hardware — 1-Sun/Sparc. DISPLAY: Adv layout systems — SCS, ECR/Pelbox. PRODUCTION: Typesetters — 2-ECR/Autokon Hyphen, 2-COM/8600; Plate exposures — 1-Nu; Plate processors — 1-Nat/A-340; Scanners — 2-Data Copy/730GS; Production cameras — 2-SCREEN/Companica; Automatic film proces-

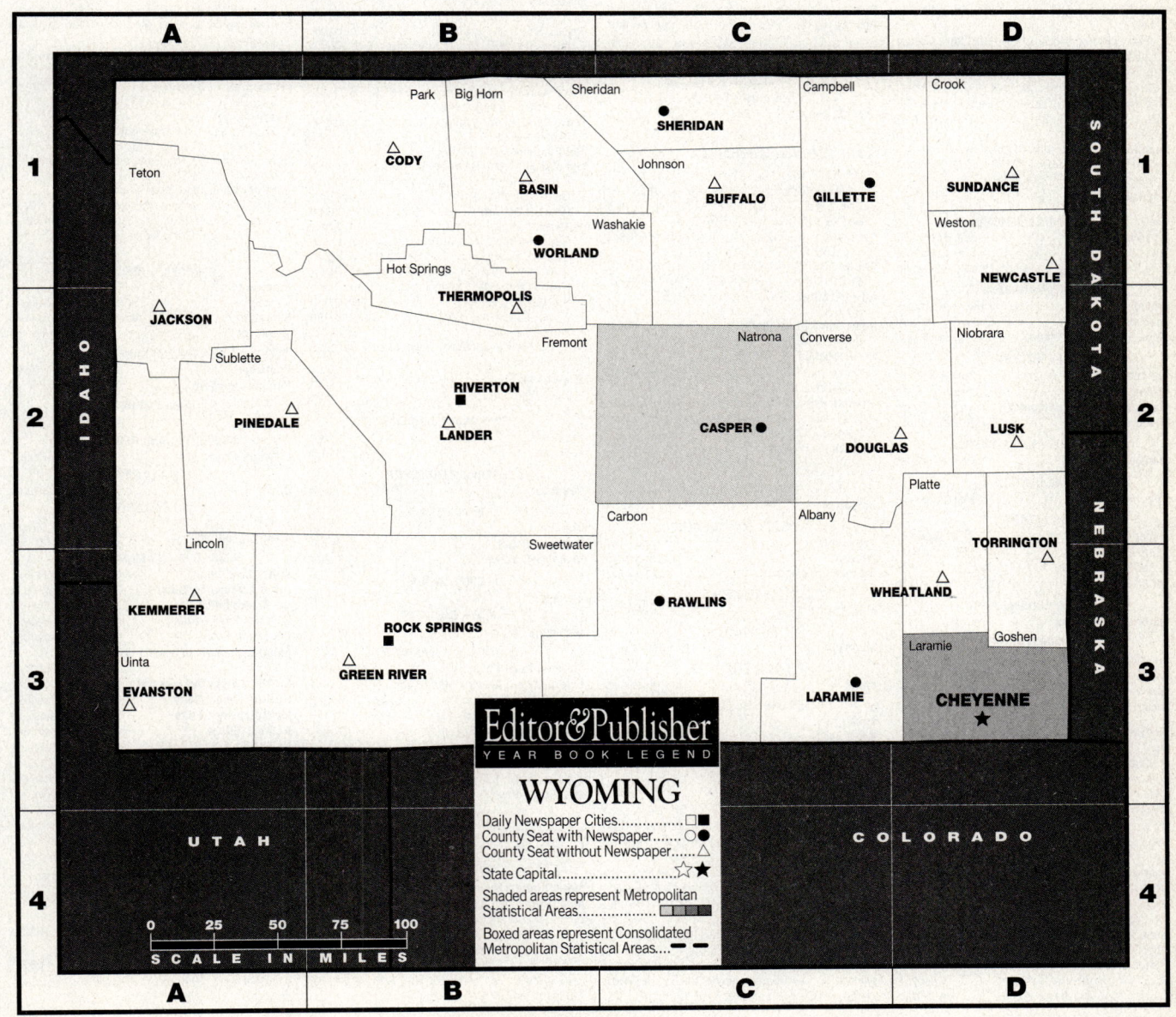

sors — 3-LE; Color separation equipment (conventional) — Nikon, Travell, LaCie.
PRESSROOM: Line 1 — 6-G/Cosmo offset; Pasters — 5-G; Reels and stands — 5-G. MAILROOM: Counter stackers — 3-HL; Inserters and stuffers — 2-MM; Bundle tyer — 2-MLN. COMMUNICATIONS: Facsimile — 1-Ricoh, 1-Fujitsu. WIRE SERVICES: News — AP, NYT; Stock tables — AP; Syndicates — AP. BUSINESS COMPUTERS: 2-Sun, 1-Unix/PC; Applications: Adv, Circ, Payroll, Accts payable; Word-Perfect; PCs & micros networked; PCs & main system networked.

CHEYENNE
Laramie County

'90 U.S. Census- 50,008; E&P '96 Est. 53,706
ABC-CZ (90): 53,840 (HH 21,073)

Wyoming Tribune-Eagle
(m-mon to sat; S)

Wyoming Tribune-Eagle, 702 W. Lincolnway, Cheyenne, WY 82001; tel (307) 634-3361. McCraken Newspapers group.

Circulation: 15,668(m); 15,668(m-sat); 17,978(S); ABC Sept. 30, 1995.

Price: 50¢(d); 50¢(sat); $1.25(S); $7.25/mo (carrier); $87.00/yr (carrier).

Advertising: Open inch rate $13.00(m); $13.00(m-sat); $13.00(S). **Representative:** Papert Companies.

News Services: NEA, AP, KRT. **Established:** 1867.

Special Editions: Working Woman (Jan); Senior Lifestyle (Feb); Bridal (Mar); Home Improvement (Apr); Tourism, Senior Lifestyles (May); Cheyenne Frontier Days (July); Football (Aug); Senior Lifestyles (Sept); New Car Show, Holiday Entertainment (Nov); Senior Lifestyles (Dec).

Special Weekly Sections: Foods (wed); Health (thur); Entertainment "TGIF" (fri); Religion (sat); Business, Finance (S).

Magazine: TV Week (S).

CORPORATE OFFICERS

Vice Pres	J Doug Reeves Jr
Treasurer	T Ray Cahalane
Vice Pres/Secretary	Ronald M Brown

GENERAL MANAGEMENT

President/Publisher	L Michael McCraken
Controller	Larry D Catalano
Manager-Business Office	Andy H Corbin

ADVERTISING

Director	Scott P Walker
Manager-Retail	James M Rath
Manager-Classified/Audiotex	Irene P Thien
Manager-National	Cynthia M Marek

MARKETING AND PROMOTION

Manager-Promotion	Katy Hinckley

CIRCULATION

Director	Mark V Bryan

NEWS EXECUTIVES

Managing Editor	Mary K Woolsey
Editor-Features	C J Putnam
Editor-Entertainment	Melissa L Jones
Editor-Sports	Ken C Pomponio

EDITOR AND MANAGER

Editorial Page Editor	Scott W Smith

PRODUCTION

Director	Richard M Moody
Asst Director	Thomas L Blumenshine
Foreman-Pressroom	Larry E Bechtholdt
Superintendent-Composing	Herbert R Bennett

Market Information: TMC; ADS; Operate audiotex.

Mechanical available: Offset; Black and 3 ROP colors; insert accepted — preprinted; page cut-offs — 22¾".

Mechanical specifications: Type page 13" x 21½"; E - 6 cols, 2 1/16", 1/8" between; A - 6 cols, 2 1/16", 1/8" between; C - 9 cols, 1 3/8", 1/16" between.

Commodity consumption: Newsprint 1,600 metric tons; widths 27½", 13¾"; black ink 36,800 pounds; color ink 6,000 pounds; single pages printed 11,206; average pages per issue 25(d), 27(sat), 63(S); single plates used 15,600.

Equipment: EDITORIAL: Front-end hardware — HAS, Cx; Front-end software — Cx. CLASSIFIED: Front-end hardware — HAS, Cx; Front-end software — Cx. AUDIOTEX: Hardware — TI/Micro 25mH 386 SX; Software — New Horizons/Info-Connect 1.3; Supplier name — TMS, VNN, AP StockQuote. DISPLAY: Adv layout systems — Ap/Mac; Front-end hardware — Ap/Mac, 3-Ap/Mac 700 Quadra, 2-Ap/Mac LC II, 1-Ap/Mac 800, 1-Ap/Mac 950, 2-Ap/Mac 8100; Front-end software — Multi-Ad/Creator, QuarkXPress, Adobe/Illustrator, Adobe/Photoshop; Printers — Linotype-Hell/Printer 60, Ap/Mac Apple Writer, Tegra/Varityper 5300 H, Panther/Pro. PRODUCTION: Typesetters — 2-V/5000V; Plate exposures — 2-Nu; Plate processors — Nat/A-250; Electronic picture desk — Lf/AP Leaf Picture Desk, Ap/Mac Centris 650; Scanners — ECR/Autokon, Microtek/Flatbed, Lf/Leafscan 45, Lf/Leafscan 35; Production cameras — C/Spartan III; Automatic film processors — P, AG; Reproportion units — ECR/Autokon; Film transporters — C; Color separation equipment (conventional) — Lf/AP Leaf Picture Desk; Digital color separation equipment — Lf/AP Leaf Picture Desk, Ap/Mac Centris 650, Ap/Mac 950, QPS.
PRESSROOM: Line 1 — 8-G/Urbanite 1010 (1 color unit); Press drives — Fin; Folders — 1-G/Urbanite SU; Press registration system — Duarte. MAILROOM: Counter stackers — QWI, BG; Inserters and stuffers — GMA/SLS 1000; Bundle tyer — MLN; Addressing machine — Mg; Other mailroom equipment — S/8 pocket of cover feeder. WIRE SERVICES: News — AP; Photos — AP; Stock tables — AP; Syndicates — LATS, NEA, KRT; Receiving dishes — size-10ft, AP, NSN. BUSINESS COMPUTERS: Sun/Sparc 10; Applications: PBS: Accounting, Adv Mgmt, Circ; PCs & main system networked.

GILLETTE
Campbell County

'90 U.S. Census- 17,635; E&P '96 Est. 20,831

The News-Record
(e-mon to fri; S)

The News-Record, 1201 W. 2nd St. (82716); Box 3006, Gillette, WY 82717; tel (307) 682-9306; fax (307) 686-9306.

Circulation: 6,290(e); 6,290(S); Sworn Sept. 25, 1994.

Price: 35¢(d); $1.00(S); $10.00/mo (mail); $22.50/3mo (carrier); $90.00/yr (carrier).

Advertising: Open inch rate $9.00(e); $9.00(S).

News Service: AP. **Politics:** Independent. **Established:** 1905.

Not Published: New Year; Memorial Day; Independence Day; Labor Day; Thanksgiving; Christmas.

Special Editions: Wyoming Tourism; National High School Rodeo; Cars; Weddings; Taxes; Football; Christmas.

Magazines: What's On (local entertainment and TV) (S); Health & Fitness Tab (monthly).

CORPORATE OFFICER

President	Betty Kennedy

GENERAL MANAGEMENT

Publisher	Ron Franscell
Publisher	Ann Franscell
Business Manager	Jack Wiley

ADVERTISING

Manager	Roxanne Viccaro

CIRCULATION

Manager	Helen Baker

NEWS EXECUTIVE

Editor	Ron Franscell

EDITORS AND MANAGERS

Business Editor	Deb Holbert
News Editor	Jim Frost
Sports Editor	Kathy Brown

PRODUCTION

Manager	Mike Urlaub

Market Information: TMC.

Mechanical available: Offset; Black and 3 ROP colors; insert accepted — preprinted; page cut-offs — 22¾".

Mechanical specifications: Type page 13" x 21"; E - 6 cols, 2 1/16", 1/8" between; A - 6 cols, 2 1/16", 1/8" between; C - 8 cols, 1½", 1/8" between.

Commodity consumption: Newsprint 235 metric tons; widths 27½", 13½"; black ink 11,750 pounds; color ink 720 pounds; single pages printed 7,600; average pages per issue 14(d), 24(S); single plates used 11,600.

Equipment: EDITORIAL: Front-end hardware — 9-Mk, 3-Ap/Power Mac 7100, 1-Ap/Power Mac 8100; Front-end software — QuarkXPress 3.31, Adobe/Photoshop 3.0, Adobe/FreeHand 4.0; Printers — ECR/Scriptsetter VRL 36. CLASSIFIED: Front-end hardware — 2-Mk. DISPLAY: Front-end hardware — 1-Ap/Power Mac 7100, 1-Ap/Power Mac 6115; Front-end software — QuarkXPress 3.31, Adobe/Photoshop 2.5 LE, Adobe/FreeHand 4.0; Printers — HP/LaserJet 4MV, ECR/Scriptsetter VRL 36. PRODUCTION: Pagination software — QuarkXPress 3.31; Typesetters — ECR/Scriptsetter VRL 36; Plate exposures — 1-Nu; Production cameras — 1-SCREEN/Companica; Automatic film processors — 1-LE.
PRESSROOM: Line 1 — 6-G; Folders — 1-G/2:1. MAILROOM: Bundle tyer — 1-Bu, Felins/F16, Allpack/351.610.001; Addressing machine — 1-El. COMMUNICATIONS: Facsimile — Tandy/fax 1000. WIRE SERVICES: News — AP; Stock tables — AP. BUSINESS COMPUTERS: PCs & micros networked; PCs & main system networked.

LARAMIE
Albany County

'90 U.S. Census- 26,687; E&P '96 Est. 28,798
ABC-CZ (90): 26,687 (HH 10,400)

Laramie Daily Boomerang
(m-tues to sat; S)

Laramie Daily Boomerang, 314 S. 4th St., Laramie, WY 82070; tel (307) 742-2176; fax (307) 721-2973. McCraken Newspapers group.

Circulation: 6,649(m); 6,649(m-sat); 6,925(S); ABC Sept. 30, 1995.

Price: 35¢(d); 35¢(sat); 75¢(S); $1.32/wk (carrier); $6.50/mo (carrier), $7.50/mo (motor route); $72.00/yr (carrier), $120.00/yr (mail).

Advertising: Open inch rate $7.80(m); $7.80(m-sat); $7.80(S).

News Service: AP. **Politics:** Independent. **Established:** 1881.

Not Published: Christmas.

Special Editions: Back-to-School, Health and Fitness, Chamber of Commerce Report (Jan); Brides (Feb); Spring Home Improvement (Mar); Car Care, Business Showcase (Apr); Annual Progress, High School Graduation Section (May); Senior Scene (June); Jubilee Edition, Crazy Days (July); University, Back-to-School, Albany County Fair Results (Aug); Brides, Hunting Guide (Sept); Car Care (Oct); Winter Recreation, Gift Guide, Basketball (Nov); Christmas Greeter, First Baby of the New Year (Dec).

Special Weekly Sections: Food (wed); Religion (sat); Food (S).

Magazines: Encore-TV and Entertainment (sat); USA Weekend (S).

CORPORATE OFFICERS

President	R R Allbaugh
Treasurer	R A Van Ekeren

GENERAL MANAGEMENT

Publisher	R A Van Ekeren

ADVERTISING

Director	Sheryn Pulse
Manager-Retail	Dorothy Soule
Manager-Classified	Cindy Keller

CIRCULATION

Manager	Brian Lane

NEWS EXECUTIVE

Managing Editor	Bob Wilson

EDITORS AND MANAGERS

Editorial Page Editor	Bob Wilson
Entertainment/Amusements Editor	Debra Thomsen
Environmental Editor	Robert Roten
Living/Lifestyles Editor	V J Bales
Sports Editor	Robert Hammond
Television/Film Editor	Debra Thomsen
Theater/Music Editor	Debra Thomsen
Women's Editor	V J Bales

PRODUCTION

Superintendent	Don Hofferber
Foreman-Composing	Jolene Hofferber
Foreman-Pressroom	N Jairell

Market Information: TMC.

Mechanical available: Offset; Black and 3 ROP colors; insert accepted — preprinted; page cut-offs — 22¾".

Mechanical specifications: Type page 12¾" x 21¼"; E - 6 cols, 2 1/16", 1/8" between; A - 6 cols, 2 1/16", 1/8" between; C - 6 cols, 2 1/16", 1/8" between.

Commodity consumption: Newsprint 320 short tons; width 27½"; black ink 5,900 pounds; single pages printed 7,500; average pages per issue 22(d), 30(S); single plates used 4,680.

Equipment: EDITORIAL: Front-end hardware — CD/2300, Cx; Front-end software — CD 3.0, HAS, CD/Magician Plus, CD/Page Magician; Other equipment — Epson/PC. CLASSIFIED: Front-end hardware — CD/2300, Cx; Front-end software — CD/2300, CD 3.0, HAS, CD/Magician Plus, Cx; Printers — TI/Omni 800. DISPLAY: Front-end hardware — 2-Ap/Mac Centris 650; Front-end software — QuarkXPress, Adobe/Photoshop, Fifth Generation Systems/Suitcase, CTA/Textpert; Printers — Linotype-Hell/Printer 60, LaserMaster/Unity 1000; Other equipment — Sharp/JX320 Scanner, PLI/Multisession CD Drive, PLI/Infinity 88 Removable. PRODUCTION: Typesetters — COM/8400; Automatic film processors — LE/PC13.
PRESSROOM: Line 1 — 6-G/Community. MAILROOM: Inserters and stuffers — 4-MM; Addressing machine — 1-Am. WIRE SERVICES: News — AP. BUSINESS COMPUTERS: 6-Epson, Wyse; Applications: SCO/Unix.

RAWLINS
Carbon County

'90 U.S. Census- 9,380; E&P '96 Est. 7,881

Rawlins Daily Times
(m-tues to sat)

Rawlins Daily Times, 6th & Buffalo Sts.; PO Box 370, Rawlins, WY 82301; tel (307) 324-3411; fax (307) 324-2797; e-mail nighthawx@aol.com. McCraken Newspapers group.

Circulation: 3,375(m); 3,375(m-sat); Sworn Oct. 13, 1995.

Price: 35¢(d); 35¢(sat); $1.75/wk; $7.00/mo; $49.00/yr (carrier), $59.50/yr (mail).

Advertising: Open inch rate $6.47(m); $6.47(m-sat). **Representative:** Papert Companies.

News Service: AP. **Politics:** Independent. **Established:** 1889.

Not Published: Days after holidays.

Special Editions: Home Improvement (Apr); Progress Edition (July); Fair (Aug); Hunter's Edition (Sept); Christmas Shopping Guide (Nov).

CORPORATE OFFICERS

President	Dave Perry
Vice Pres	William D McCraken
Secretary	Mary Charlotte Stout
Treasurer	Dave Perry

GENERAL MANAGEMENT

Publisher	Dave Perry
Purchasing Agent	Dave Perry

ADVERTISING

Director	Ed Walker

MARKETING AND PROMOTION

Manager-Promotion	Dave Perry

CIRCULATION

Director	Sue Cattles

NEWS EXECUTIVES

Editor	Dave Perry
Managing Editor	Charles H Bowlus

EDITORS AND MANAGERS

Action Line Editor	Charles H Bowlus
Business/Finance Editor	Charles H Bowlus
City/Metro Editor	Charles H Bowlus
Editorial Page Editor	Charles H Bowlus
Education Editor	Charles H Bowlus
Entertainment/Amusements Editor	Cynthia Blakesley
Graphics Editor/Art Director	Charles H Bowlus
Health/Medical Editor	Charles H Bowlus
Living/Lifestyle Editor	Cynthia Blakesley
National Editor	Charles H Bowlus
News Editor	Charles H Bowlus
Photo Editor	Charles H Bowlus
Political/Government Editor	Charles H Bowlus
Religion Editor	Charles H Bowlus
Science/Technology Editor	Charles H Bowlus
Sports Editor	Sam Amico
Television/Film Editor	Cynthia Blakesley
Women's Editor	Cynthia Blakesley

MANAGEMENT INFORMATION SERVICES

Data Processing Manager	Charles H Bowlus

PRODUCTION

Manager	Suzan Tanfield

Market Information: Zoned editions.

Mechanical available: Offset; Black and 3 ROP colors; insert accepted — preprinted, special arrangements; page cut-offs — 22⅝".

Mechanical specifications: Type page 10½" x 14"; E - 5 cols, 2¹⁄₁₆", ⅛" between; A - 5 cols, 2¹⁄₁₆", ⅛" between; C - 5 cols, 2¹⁄₁₆", ⅛" between.
Commodity consumption: Newsprint 43 metric tons; widths 30", 15"; black ink 1,840 pounds; color ink 50 pounds; single pages printed 4,700; average pages per issue 18(d), 20(sat).
Equipment: EDITORIAL: Front-end hardware — Mk/Newstouch AT; Printers — Ap/Mac LaserWriter II NTX. CLASSIFIED: Front-end hardware — Mk/Newstouch AT. DISPLAY: Adv layout systems — Ap/Power Mac 6100, Ap/Mac IIci, Ap/Mac IIvx. PRODUCTION: Pagination software — QuarkXPress 3.31; OCR software — Ofoto 2.0; Typesetters — Ap/Mac LaserWriter Pro 600, 2-Ap/Mac LaserWriter II; Platemaking systems — 1-B/Mercury; Scanners — Ap/Mac, Nikon/ScanTouch, Nikon/Coolscan; Production cameras — 1-Argyle/23; Automatic film processors — Kk/42A.
PRESSROOM: Line 1 — 6-HI/Cotrell V-15A; Folders — 1-HI. MAILROOM: Addressing machine — 1-Am/1900. WIRE SERVICES: News — AP; BUSINESS COMPUTERS: PCs & micros networked; PCs & main system networked.

RIVERTON
Fremont County
'90 U.S. Census- 9,202; E&P '96 Est. 8,888

The Riverton Ranger
(e-mon to fri)

The Riverton Ranger, 421 E. Main St.; PO Box 993, Riverton, WY 82501-0993; tel (307) 856-2244; fax (307) 856-0189.
Circulation: 6,858(e); Sworn Oct. 5, 1995.
Price: 50¢(d); $1.25/wk; $6.00/mo (carrier); $62.00/yr (mail, out of state).
Advertising: Open inch rate $9.80(e). **Representative:** Papert Companies.
News Service: AP. **Politics:** Independent. **Established:** 1906 (weekly), 1953 (semi-weekly), 1960 (daily).
Not Published: New Year; Memorial Day; Independence Day; Labor Day; Thanksgiving; Christmas.
Special Editions: Bridal (Jan); State Mining (June); Rendezvous-Balloon Rally (July); Fair and Rodeo (Aug); Fire Safety/Prevention (Oct); Christmas (Dec).
Magazines: EXTRA; Entertainment, TV Area-wide Schedule (fri).

CORPORATE OFFICERS

President	Robert A Peck
Secretary	Steven R Peck

GENERAL MANAGEMENT

Publisher	Robert A Peck
Co-Publisher	Steven R Peck
General Manager	Robert A Peck
Business Manager	Shirley Guthrie
Manager-Credit	Robert H Tyler
Purchasing Agent	Robert A Peck

ADVERTISING

Director	Anita Ellis

CIRCULATION

Manager	Carl Manning

NEWS EXECUTIVES

Assoc Editor	Carolyn B Tyler
Managing Editor	Chad Baldwin

EDITORS AND MANAGERS

Amusements/Automotive Editor	Steven R Peck
Columnist	Steven R Peck
Columnist	Carolyn B Tyler
Desk/Wire Editor	Chad Baldwin
Editorial Page Editor	Steven R Peck
Education Editor	Chad Baldwin
Fashion/Food Editor	Chad Baldwin
Home Furnishings/Society Editor	Shelley Ridenour
Photo Department Manager	Steven R Peck
Sports Editor	Chad Baldwin
Television/Film Editor	Steven R Peck
Theater/Music Editor	Steven R Peck

PRODUCTION

Manager	Paul Hugus
Foreman-Pressroom	Gilbert Wozney
Foreman-Composing	Gary Dieu

Market Information: TMC.
Mechanical available: Offset; Black and 3 ROP colors; insert accepted — preprinted, all; page cut-offs — 22¾".
Mechanical specifications: Type page 13" x 21½"; E - 6 cols, 2¹⁄₁₆", ⅛" between; A - 6 cols, 2¹⁄₁₆", ⅛" between; C - 6 cols, 2¹⁄₁₆", ⅛" between.
Commodity consumption: Newsprint 230 metric tons; widths 27½", 13¾"; black ink 4,950 pounds; color ink 500 pounds; single pages printed 7,974; average pages per issue 14(d); single plates used 3,987.
Equipment: EDITORIAL: Front-end hardware — 12-Synaptic/PC; Front-end software — Synaptic/Editorial; Printers — 2-Ap/Mac LaserWriter II, LaserMaster/1800; Other equipment — Ap/Mac Centris-Pagination Station, Ap/Mac Quadra Pagination Station. CLASSIFIED: Front-end hardware — 1-Synaptic/PC; Front-end software — Synaptic/Classified; Printers — LaserMaster/1800, LaserMaster/Pro 600; Other equipment — Polaroid/SprintScan, Microtek/Scanmaker. DISPLAY: Front-end hardware — Ap/Mac IIsi, Ap/Mac IIcx, Ap/Mac SE30, Data Copy/GS Plus; Front-end software — QuarkXPress 3.3, Adobe/Photoshop; Printers — 2-Ap/Mac LaserWriter. PRODUCTION: Typesetters — Ap/Mac LaserWriter; Plate processors — Nat; Production cameras — 1-Nu; Automatic film processors — P.
PRESSROOM: Line 1 — 6-G/Community offset; Folders — 1-G/Suburban. LIBRARY: Electronic — Folio Previews 2.0. WIRE SERVICES: News — AP; Receiving dishes — AP. BUSINESS COMPUTERS: 3-IBM/PC-XT, RSK/TRS-100; Applications: Accounting, Circ; PCs & micros networked.

ROCK SPRINGS
Sweetwater County
'90 U.S. Census- 19,050; E&P '96 Est. 18,712
ABC-CZ (90): 19,050 (HH 7,127)

Daily Rocket-Miner
(m-tues to sat)

Daily Rocket-Miner, 215 D St.; PO Box 98, Rock Springs, WY 82901; tel (307) 362-3736; fax (307) 382-2763.
Circulation: 7,729(m); 7,729(m-sat); ABC Sept. 30, 1995.
Price: 25¢(d); 25¢(sat); $54.00/yr (carrier/mail).
Advertising: Open inch rate $10.08(m); $10.08(m-sat).
News Services: AP, NEA. **Politics:** Independent-Democrat. **Established:** 1880.
Not Published: The day after: New Year; Memorial Day; Independence Day; Labor Day; Thanksgiving; Christmas.
Special Editions: Bridal (Feb); Western Wyoming Review of Progress (Mar); Western Wyoming Vacation (May).
Magazine: USA Weekend (sat).

CORPORATE OFFICERS

President	Charles E Richardson
Vice Pres	William D McCraken
Director	Anne W McCraken
Secretary	Patricia R Guthrie
Treasurer	Margaret E Richardson

GENERAL MANAGEMENT

Publisher	Charles E Richardson
Business Manager/Credit Manager	Patricia G Travis
Personnel Manager	Charles E Richardson
Purchasing Agent	Charles E Richardson

ADVERTISING

Director	Garry Gouger
Manager-Retail	Garry Gouger

CIRCULATION

Manager	Kelly White

NEWS EXECUTIVE

Managing Editor	Nick Motu

EDITORS AND MANAGERS

Amusements Editor	Charles E Richardson
Business/Finance Editor	Charles E Richardson
Consumer Interest/Education Editor	Charles E Richardson
Editorial Page Editor	Charles E Richardson
Environment/Food Editor	Charles E Richardson
Fashion/Society Editor	Nancy Vase
Music Editor	Charles E Richardson
News Editor	Bruce Yoder
Picture Editor	Bruce Yoder
Religion Editor	Nancy Vase
Sports Editor	William Gillespie
State Editor	Charles E Richardson

PRODUCTION

Foreman-Composing	Kristy James-Lacey
Foreman-Pressroom/Mailroom	Bruce Bell

Mechanical available: Offset; Black and 3 ROP colors; insert accepted — preprinted, most; page cut-offs — 22¾".
Mechanical specifications: Type page 16⅜" x 22½"; E - 7 cols, 2", ⅙" between; A - 9 cols, 1¾", ½" between; C - 9 cols, 1¾", ½" between.
Commodity consumption: widths 33½", 16¾"; average pages per issue 16(d), 16(sat).
Equipment: EDITORIAL: Front-end hardware — COM, HP; Other equipment — 6-COM/MDT350, 3-M/Correcterm, 1-COM/MCS 10. CLASSIFIED: Front-end hardware — Com; Other equipment — 3-M/Correcterm. DISPLAY: Adv layout systems — Com. PRODUCTION: Typesetters — 1-COM/4961, 2-COM/8400; Plate exposures — 1-B; Production cameras — 1-K/241.
PRESSROOM: Line 1 — 5-G/Community; Folders — 1-G. MAILROOM: Inserters and stuffers — 3-DG; Bundle tyer — 1-It/MS-AF, 1-Us/TE; Addressing machine — 2-Am/4000. WIRE SERVICES: News — AP; Receiving dishes — AP. BUSINESS COMPUTERS: 1-IBM; Applications: Accts receivable, Circ (Mail).

SHERIDAN
Sheridan County
'90 U.S. Census- 13,900; E&P '96 Est. 12,931
ABC-CZ (90): 13,900 (HH 5,857)

The Sheridan Press
(e-mon to fri; m-sat)

The Sheridan Press, 144 Grinnell; Box 2006, Sheridan, WY 82801; tel (307) 672-2431; fax (307) 672-7950. Seaton group.
Circulation: 6,322(e); 6,322(m-sat); ABC Sept. 30, 1995.
Price: 50¢(d); 50¢(sat); $7.50/mo, $8.75/mo (zone 3t); $77.50/yr (carrier/mail), $87.50/yr (zone 3t).
Advertising: Open inch rate $9.15(e); $9.15(m-sat). **Representative:** Papert Companies.
News Service: AP. **Politics:** Independent. **Established:** 1886.
Not Published: New Year; Memorial Day; Independence Day; Labor Day; Thanksgiving; Christmas.
Special Editions: Working Woman (Feb); Car Care (Apr); Big Horn Mountain Tourist and Recreation Guide (May); Sheridan-Wyo Rodeo (June); Hunting, Health (Sept); Fire Prevention (Oct); Christmas (Nov).
Special Weekly Section: "Options" (fri).

CORPORATE OFFICER

President	Edward L Seaton

GENERAL MANAGEMENT

Publisher	Keith D Kemper
Manager-Office	Linda Lightfoot
Director-Operations	Doug Edwards

ADVERTISING

Manager-Classified	Paul Deutsch
Manager-Local/National	Kathryn Fondyce

CIRCULATION

Manager	Sylvia Deutsch

NEWS EXECUTIVE

Managing Editor	Thomas Dreiling

EDITORS AND MANAGERS

Editorial Writer	Keith D Kemper
Sports Editor	Patrick Murphy

MANAGEMENT INFORMATION SERVICES

Data Processing Manager	Doug Edwards

PRODUCTION

Manager-Systems	Alvin Nielson
Foreman-Pressroom	Richard Schmidt

Market Information: TMC.
Mechanical available: Offset; Black and 3 ROP colors; insert accepted — preprinted, all; page cut-offs — 22¾".
Mechanical specifications: Type page 12¾" x 21½"; E - 6 cols, 2¹⁄₁₆", ⅛" between; A - 6 cols, 2¹⁄₁₆", ⅛" between; C - 7 cols, 1¾", ⅛" between.
Commodity consumption: Newsprint 377 metric tons; widths 13¾", 27½"; black ink 6,000 pounds; color ink 450 pounds; single pages printed 6,100; average pages per issue 18(d); single plates used 6,000.
Equipment: EDITORIAL: Front-end hardware — 3-Ap/Mac ci, 2-Ap/Mac Classic, 3-Ap/Mac SE 30; Front-end software — Baseview 1.1, QuarkXPress 3.3.1; Printers — LaserMaster/Unity; Other equipment — 2-Ap/Mac Classic, Ap/Power Mac Fileserver. CLASSIFIED: Front-end hardware — 1-Ap/Mac Quadra 650, 1-Ap/Power Mac, 1-Ap/Mac II, 1-Ap/Mac ci; Front-end software — Baseview 4.0; Printers — Ap/Mac NTX II. DISPLAY: Front-end hardware — 2-Ap/Power Mac; Front-end software — Multi-Ad/Creator 3.6.3, Adobe/Photoshop 3.0; Printers — XIT/Clipper. PRODUCTION: Pagination software — QuarkXPress 3.31; Typesetters — ECR/VRL 36; Plate exposures — 1-Nu; Scanners — 1-AG/Focus, 1-AG/Arcus II; Production cameras — Acti; Automatic film processors — LE.
PRESSROOM: Line 1 — 6-G/Community; Folders — 1-G/SC. MAILROOM: Bundle tyer — 1-Bu. WIRE SERVICES: News — AP Datastream, AP Datafeatures; Stock tables — AP; Syndicates — NEA; Receiving dishes — AP. BUSINESS COMPUTERS: 2-Compaq/486; Applications: BMF/Computer Services: Circ, Accounting.

WORLAND
Washakie County
'90 U.S. Census- 5,742; E&P '96 Est. 5,248
ABC-CZ (90): 5,742 (HH 2,211)

Northern Wyoming Daily News (m-tues to sat)

Northern Wyoming Daily News, 201 N. 8th St.; PO Box 508, Worland, WY 82401; tel (307) 347-3241, (307) 347-3242, (307) 347-4267. McCraken Newspapers group.
Circulation: 3,869(m); 3,869(m-sat); ABC Sept. 30, 1995.
Price: 25¢(d); 25¢(sat); $4.75/mo (carrier); $52.25/yr (mail).
Advertising: Open inch rate $6.41(m); $6.41(m-sat). **Representative:** Papert Companies.
News Service: AP. **Politics:** Independent. **Established:** 1905.
Not Published: Day after Christmas.
Special Editions: Big Horn Basin Progress; Barley Edition; Beet Edition; Trade Fair; Lawn & Garden; FFA; Bridal; Graduation; Welcome; Hunting; Car Care; Homemakers; Winter; Christmas Open; Christmas Greetings.
Magazine: Country Review (own, newsprint) (S).

CORPORATE OFFICERS

President	Hugh K Knoefel
Vice Pres	Ted O'Melia
Vice Pres	William D McCraken
Secretary	Ron Brown
Treasurer	Lee Lockhart

GENERAL MANAGEMENT

Publisher	Lee Lockhart

ADVERTISING

Manager	Dustin Fuller

CIRCULATION

Director	Dennis Koch

NEWS EXECUTIVE

Managing Editor	Tracey Deaton

EDITORS AND MANAGERS

Editorial Page Editor	Tracey Deaton
Education Editor	Tracey Deaton
Food Editor	Susan Lockhart
Librarian	Sean McMahon
People Page Editor	Deb Skalicky
Sports Editor	Duane Groshart

PRODUCTION

Superintendent	Nash Mercado

Market Information: TMC.
Mechanical available: Offset; Black and 3 ROP colors; insert accepted — preprinted; page cut-offs — 22¾".
Mechanical specifications: Type page 13" x 21½"; E - 6 cols, 2¹⁄₁₆", ⅛" between; A - 6 cols, 2¹⁄₁₆", ⅛" between; C - 6 cols, 2¹⁄₁₆", ⅛" between.
Commodity consumption: Newsprint 100 short tons; width 28"; black ink 4,500 pounds; color ink 200 pounds; single pages printed 4,548; average pages per issue 14(d); single plates used 1,200.
Equipment: EDITORIAL: Front-end hardware — DP/Imaging 2355. CLASSIFIED: Front-end hardware — DP/Imaging 2355. DISPLAY: Adv layout systems — 1-COM/350. PRODUCTION: Typesetters — 2-COM/US; Plate exposures — 1-Nu/Flip Top FT40; Production cameras — 1-SCREEN.
PRESSROOM: Line 1 — 4-G/Community; Folders — 1-G. MAILROOM: Bundle tyer — 1-Bu/BT 16 String Tyer; Addressing machine — 2-Wm. WIRE SERVICES: News — AP; Receiving dishes — AP. BUSINESS COMPUTERS: 2-IBM/Os 2; Applications: Bus record keeping, Payroll, Circ, Accts receivable, Accts payable; PCs & main system networked.

NATIONAL DAILIES & WEEKLIES
NEWSPAPERS PUBLISHED IN THE UNITED STATES FOR NATIONWIDE DISTRIBUTION

Capper's
(tues) (tabloid)

Stauffer Magazine Group, 1503 SW 42nd St., Topeka, KS 66609; tel. (913) 274-4300; fax (913) 274-4305; Morris Communications Corp. group.
Circulation: 349,413(m); ABC June 30, 1995.
Price: $1.50(d); $26.40/yr.
Advertising: Open inch rate $126.00(m).
Representatives: Fox & Associates.
News Service: AP. **Politics:** Independent.
Established: 1879.
Advertising not accepted: Liquor and cigarettes.

CORPORATE OFFICERS
President — Paul Simon
Vice Pres — E Van Anderson

GENERAL MANAGEMENT
General Manager — Donald R Keating

ADVERTISING
Director — Keith Chartier

CIRCULATION
Director — Dianne Graves

NEWS EXECUTIVE
Editor — Nancy Peavler

PRODUCTION
Operations Manager — Dennis Biswell

Market information: Zoned editions; Split run.
Mechanical available: Web Offset; black and 3 ROP colors; inserts accepted — preprinted, Add-a-card.
Mechanical specifications: Type page 10 ¾" x 12"; E - 5 cols, 1 ⅞"; ⅛" between.
Commodity consumption (estimated): Newsprint 955 short tons; width 48", 36", 24"; black ink 24,400 pounds; color ink 3,400 pounds; single pages printed 1,172; single plates used 3,400.
Equipment: PRODUCTION: typesetters — 3-HI/TXT; plate exposers — 2-N; plate processors — 2-WL; cameras — 1-C/Spartan, 1-C/Marathon; automatic film processors — 2-LE. PRESSROOM: Line 1 — 6-G/Mark II; folders — 2-G/2:1. MAILROOM: Counter stackers — 1-Id/330, 2-Id/440; stuffers — 1-HI/720P (overline); bundle tyers — 2-MLN; addressers — 2-AVY (online), 2-Ch. WIRE SERVICE: News — AP. BUSINESS COMPUTERS: Unisys/2200/100; applications: Profit-loss statements, Payroll, Label printing, Typesetting, Gen business; PCs & main system networked.

The Christian Science Monitor (m-mon to fri)
See Daily Newspaper Section under Boston, MA.

Grit (S) (tabloid)
Stauffer Magazine Group, 1503 SW 42nd St., Topeka, KS 66609; tel. (913) 274-4300; fax (913) 274-4305; Morris Communications Corp. group.
Circulation: 266,439(S); ABC June 30, 1995.
Price: $1.50(S); $26.50/yr.
Advertising: Open inch rate $126.00(S).
Representatives: Fox & Associates.
News Service: AP. **Politics:** Independent.
Established: 1882.
Special Editions: Health & Fitness; Recipe.

CORPORATE OFFICERS
President — Paul Simon
Vice Pres — E Van Anderson

GENERAL MANAGEMENT
General Manager — Donald R Keating

ADVERTISING
Director — Keith Chartier

CIRCULATION
Director — Dianne Graves

NEWS EXECUTIVE
Editor-in-Chief — Michael Scheibach

PRODUCTION
Operations Manager — Dennis Biswell

Market Information: Zoned editions; Split run.
Mechanical available: Web Offset; black and 3 ROP colors; inserts accepted — preprinted, Add-a-card or envelope.
Mechanical specifications: Type page 10 ¾" x 12"; E - 5 cols, 1 ⅞", ⅛" between; A - 5 cols, 1.9", 1/12" between; C - 5 cols, 1.9", 1/12" between.
Commodity consumption (estimated): Newsprint 863 short tons; width 48", 36", 24"; black ink 22,000 pounds; color ink 3,100 pounds; single pages printed 1,396; single plates used 1,706.
Equipment: EDITORIAL: Front-end hardware — 12-DD/UT2IT 0003, 1-Cp/170, 2-Cp/Alpha. CLASSIFIED: Front-end hardware — 5-DD. PRODUCTION: typesetters — 2-Linotype-Hell/Linotron 202; platemaking systems — 1-Polychrome; plate exposers — 1-BKY; cameras — 2-C, 1-Acti; automatic film processors — 2-LE; color separation equipment — 1-Ca. PRESSROOM: Line 1 — 4-HI/Lithomatis; Line 2 — 1-TKS/4-color; Line 3 — 1-HI/4-color; Line 4 — 1-H/4-color; folders — 1-HI/2:1, 1-HI/3:2. MAILROOM: Counter stackers — 1-Id; Bundle tyers — 3-Sa, 1-Tri-star, 1-MLN; wrappers — 2-MG. WIRE SERVICES: News — AP; receiving dishes — AP. BUSINESS COMPUTERS: Unisys/2200/100; applications: Circ, Gen ledger, Payroll; PCs & main system networked.

Investor's Business Daily (m-mon to fri)
See Daily Newspaper Section under Los Angeles, CA.

Journal of Commerce and Commercial (m-mon to fri)
See Daily Newspaper Section under NYC.

USA Today (m-mon to fri)
See Daily Newspaper Section under Arlington, VA.

The Wall Street Journal (m-mon to fri)
See Daily Newspaper Section under NYC.

DAILY TABLOID NEWSPAPERS

Kenai (AK) *Peninsula Clarion*
Kodiak (AK) *Daily Mirror*
Tucson (AZ) *Daily Territorial*
Los Angeles (CA) *Daily Commerce*
Palo Alto (CA) *Daily News*
Aspen (CO) *Daily News*
Aspen (CO) *Times*
Craig (CO) *Northwest Colorado Daily Press*
Denver (CO) *Rocky Mountain News*
Frisco (CO) *Summit Daily News*
La Junta (CO) *Tribune-Democrat*
Salida (CO) *Mountain Mail*
Steamboat Springs (CO) *Today*
Sterling (CO) *Journal-Advocate (Saturday Only)*
Telluride (CO) *Daily Planet*
Manchester (CT) *Journal Inquirer*
Milford (CT) *Citizen*
Kailua-Kona (HI) *West Hawaii Today*
Chicago (IL) *Defender*
Chicago (IL) *Sun-Times*
Watseka (IL) *Iroquois County's Times-Republic*
Jasper (IN) *Herald*
Boston (MA) *Christian Science Monitor*
Boston (MA) *Herald*
Dedham (MA) *Transcript*
Haverhill (MA) *Gazette (Saturday Only)*
Southbridge (MA) *News*
Waltham (MA) *News-Tribune*
Carrollton (MO) *Democrat*
Berlin (NH) *Daily Sun*
Berlin (NH) *Reporter*
Conway (NH) *Daily Sun*
Portsmouth (NH) *Herald (Monday Only)*
Trenton (NJ) *Trentonian*
Brooklyn (NY) *Daily Challenge*
Long Island (NY) *Newsday*
Middletown (NY) *Times Herald-Record*
New York (NY) *Daily News*
New York (NY) *Post*
Olean (NY) *Times-Herald (Saturday Only)*
Greenfield (OH) *Daily Times*
Alva (OK) *Review-Courier*
Cushing (OK) *Daily Citizen (Friday Only)*
Warren (OH) *Tribune Chronicle (Saturday Only)*
Wewoka (OK) *Times*
Woodward (OK) *News*
Portland (OR) *Daily Journal of Commerce*
Allentown (PA) *Morning Call (Saturday Only)*
Chester (PA) *Delaware County Daily Times*
Philadelphia (PA) *News*
Wilkes-Barre (PA) *Citizens' Voice*
Sunnyside (WA) *Daily Sun News*
Green Bay (WI) *News-Chronicle*
Rawlins (WY) *Daily Times*

1995 NEWSPRINT STATISTICS

ESTIMATED CONSUMPTION OF ALL U.S. USERS

	1995	1994	% Change
Twelve-month totals	11,593,000	11,695,000	-0.9

U.S. PUBLISHERS STOCK IN METRIC TONS

	Stocks	Days On-Hand
*December 1995	1,133,000	43
December 1994	879,000	33

*Includes strengthening of the sample base by the addition of more newspapers starting in March 1995.

SHIPMENTS

	U.S.A.	Canada	Exports	Total
From Canada				
Twelve Months 1995	5,802,700	1,183,600	2,259,200	9,245,500
Twelve Months 1994	5,906,300	1,111,200	2,419,300	9,436,800
From U.S.				
Twelve Months 1995	5,693,700	—	642,100	6,335,800
Twelve Months 1994	5,684,000	—	672,300	6,356,300

ESTIMATED CONSUMPTION OF ALL U.S. DAILY NEWSPAPERS

	1995	1994	% Change
Twelve-month totals	8,948,000	9,420,000	-5.0

PRODUCTION

	U.S.A.	Canada	North America
Twelve Months 1995	6,351,900	9,251,600	15,603,500
Twelve Months 1994	6,335,500	9,320,700	15,656,200

Sources: Newspaper Association of America
American Forest & Paper Association
Canadian Pulp and Paper Association

Copyright ©1996 by the Editor & Publisher Co.

GROUPS OF NEWSPAPERS UNDER COMMON OWNERSHIP

EDITOR'S NOTE: For the purpose of this listing, a "group" of daily newspapers is defined as two or more daily newspapers in different cities under the same principal ownership or control. In many groups each newspaper is a separate corporation, with little or no central direction of editorial policy.

A

Advance Publications — 950 Fingerboard Rd., Staten Island, NY 10305; tel (718) 981-1234; fax (718) 981-1456
Chairman — S I Newhouse; President — Donald E Newhouse.
New Orleans (LA) Times-Picayune (all day,S); Springfield (MA) Union-News (all day), Springfield (MA) Republican (S); Pascagoula (MS) Mississippi Press (e); Syracuse (NY) Herald-Journal (e), Syracuse (NY) Post-Standard (m), Syracuse (NY) Herald-American (S); Cleveland (OH) Plain Dealer (mS); Portland (OR) Oregonian (all day,S); Harrisburg (PA) Patriot (m), Harrisburg (PA) News (e), Harrisburg (PA) Patriot-News (S).
Alabama Group:
Birmingham (AL) News (eS), Huntsville (AL) Times (eS), Huntsville (AL) News (m), Mobile (AL) Press (e), Mobile (AL) Register (mS).
Booth Newspapers:
Ann Arbor (MI) News (mS), Bay City (MI) Times (eS), Flint (MI) Journal (eS), Grand Rapids (MI) Press (eS), Jackson (MI) Citizen Patriot (eS), Kalamazoo (MI) Gazette (eS), Muskegon (MI) Chronicle (eS), Saginaw (MI) News (eS).
UNYT + Plus: NJ-NY:
Jersey City (NJ) Jersey Journal (e), Newark (NJ) Star-Ledger (mS), Trenton (NJ) Times (mS); Staten Island (NY) Advance (eS).
Note: Advance Publications also owns Random House publishing, Condé Nast magazines, Parade and The New Yorker.

Alameda Newspaper Group — See MediaNews Inc.

Alta Group Newspapers — Alfred Rd; PO Box 627, Biddeford, ME 04005; tel (207) 282-1535; fax (207) 282-3138
President — Dennis Flaherty; Treasurer — Christopher McKenney.
Biddeford (ME) Journal Tribune (e); Milford (MA) Daily News (e); Little Falls (NY) Evening Times (e).

American Publishing Co. — See Hollinger International Inc.

Amos Press — PO Box 4129, Sidney, OH 45365-4129; tel (513) 498-2111; fax (513) 498-0806
President — Bruce Boyd.
Beavercreek (OH) News-Current (e), Fairborn (OH) Daily Herald (e), Sidney (OH) Daily News (e).
Note: Amos Suburban Newspapers division owns six weekly papers.

B

Ray Barnes Newspapers Inc. — 317 S. Anderson St.; PO Box 85, Elwood, IN 46036-2018; tel (317) 552-3355; fax (317) 552-3358
President — Jack Barnes.
Elwood (IN) Call-Leader (e), Elwood (IN) Tipton County Tribune (e); Kenton (OH) Times (e), Upper Sandusky (OH) Daily Chief Union (e).
Note: This group also owns one weekly newspaper.

A H Belo Corp. — 400 S. Record St. (75202); PO Box 655237, Dallas, TX 75265-5237; tel (214) 977-6606; fax (214) 977-6603
Chairman/President/CEO — Robert W Decherd; Vice Chairman/President-Broadcast Division — Ward L Huey Jr; President-Publishing Division — Burl Osborne; Sr. Vice Pres./Secretary/General Counsel — Michael J McCarthy; Sr. Vice Pres./CFO — Michael D Perry.
Owensboro (KY) Messenger-Inquirer (mS); Bryan-College Station (TX) Eagle (mS), Dallas (TX) Morning News (mS).
Note: Belo also owns Dallas/Fort Worth Suburban Newspapers Inc. (eight non-daily newspapers) and seven network-affiliated television stations.

Blade Communications Inc. — 541 N. Superior St., Toledo, OH 43660; tel (419) 245-6000
Co-Publisher-Toledo & Pittsburgh — John Robinson Block; Co-Publisher/President-Toledo & Pittsburgh — William Block Jr.
Toledo (OH) Blade (mS); Pittsburgh (PA) Post-Gazette (mS).

Bliss Communications Inc. — 1 S. Parker Dr.; PO Box 5001, Janesville, WI 53547-5001; tel (608) 754-3311; fax (608) 754-8038
Chairman — Marshall W Johnston; President/CEO — Sidney H Bliss; Secretary — James E Warren; Vice President/CFO — Robert J Lisser; Vice President-Technical Services — Charles A Flynn; Human Resources Director — Mary Jo Villa.
Ironwood (MI) Daily Globe (e); Janesville (WI) Gazette (e), Marinette (WI) Eagle-Herald (e), Monroe (WI) Evening Times (e).
Note: Bliss Communications owns shoppers in Wisconsin and three AM-FM radio stations (Robert S Dailey, General Manager).

Boone Newspapers Inc. — 1800 McFarland Blvd. N.E., Ste. 200; PO Box 2370, Tuscaloosa, AL 35403; tel (205) 752-3381; fax (205) 752-3392
Chairman — James B Boone Jr; President — John Mathew.
Alexander City (AL) Outlook (mS), Andalusia (AL) Star News (eS), Selma (AL) Times-Journal (mS), Troy (AL) Messenger (mS); Albert Lea (MN) Tribune (eS), Austin (MN) Daily Herald (eS), Fergus Falls (MN) Daily Journal (eS); Natchez (MS) Democrat (mS); Ironton (OH) Tribune (eS).

Boone/Narragansett (Michigan):
Dowagiac (MI) News (e), Niles (MI) Star (e).
Boone/Narragansett (Southwest):
Miami (OK) News-Record (eS); Alice (TX) Echo-News (eS), Brownwood (TX) Bulletin (eS), Stephenville (TX) Empire-Tribune (eS), Waxahachie (TX) Daily Light (eS).
Note: Boone Newspapers also owns 12 weekly and six semi-weekly publications. Operations in Oklahoma, Michigan and Texas are owned in partnership with Narragansett Capital Inc. with management by Boone Newspapers Inc.

Booth Newspapers — See Advance Publications.

Brehm Communication Inc. — 17065 Via del Campo, Ste. 200 (92127); PO Box 28429, San Diego, CA 92198; tel (619) 451-6200; fax (619) 451-3814
Chairman — W J Brehm; President — Bill Brehm Jr; General Manager — A Philip Tofani.
Bullhead City (AZ) Mohave Valley Daily News (m); Auburn (CA) Journal (m); Mt. Carmel (IL) Republican-Register (e); Princeton (IN) Clarion (m); Fort Madison (IA) Democrat (e), Keokuk (IA) Daily Gate City (e).
Note: This group also publishes over 50 weekly, semi-weekly and tri-weekly newspapers in Arizona, California, Illinois, Indiana, Iowa, Nevada and Utah.

Brown Publishing Co. — 8520 E. Kemper Rd., Cincinnati, OH 45249-1709; tel (513) 489-7227; fax (513) 489-7546
Chairman — Clarence J Brown; President/CEO — Mark R Policinski, Vice President — David Tyo Esq; Secretary — Joyce E Brown; Treasurer/Comptroller — John A Aston.
Circleville (OH) Herald (e), Logan (OH) Daily News (e), Urbana (OH) Daily Citizen (e), Van Wert (OH) Times-Bulletin (e), Washington Court House (OH) Record Herald (e), Wilmington (OH) News Journal (e).
Note: This group also owns eight weeklies and one magazine.

Bryan Newspapers — 300 4th Ave. S.E., Cullman, AL 35055; tel (205) 734-2131; fax (205) 734-7310/(205) 737-1020
Publisher — Robert Bryan.
Athens (AL) News Courier (mS), Cullman (AL) Times (mS).
Note: This group also publishes three weeklies in Alabama.

Buckner News Alliance — 2101 4th Ave., Ste. 2300, Seattle, WA 98121-2317; tel (206) 727-2727; fax (206) 727-NEWS
President — Philip F Buckner; Vice President — David B Martens; CFO/Treasurer — G B Brown.
York (PA) Daily Record (m); Pecos (TX) Enterprise (e).

Byrd Newspapers — 231 S. Liberty St.; PO Box 193, Harrisonburg, VA 22801; tel (540) 574-6200; fax (540) 433-9112
President — Harry F Byrd Jr.
Harrisonburg (VA) Daily News-Record (m), Winchester (VA) Star (e).
Note: This group also publishes weekly newspapers in Luray, Woodstock, Front Royal, Amherst, Lovingston, and Elkton, VA.

C

Calkins Newspapers — 8400 N. Bristol Pike, Levittown, PA 19057-5198; tel (215) 949-4011; fax (215) 949-4021
President — Grover Friend.
Willingboro (NJ) Burlington County Times (eS); Aliquippa-Ambridge-Beaver (PA) Beaver County Times (eS), Bristol-Levittown (PA) Bucks County Courier Times (mS), Doylestown (PA) Intelligencer/Record (mS), Uniontown (PA) Herald Standard (mS).

Capital Cities/ABC Inc. — 77 W. 66th St., New York, NY 10023; tel (212) 456-7777
Chairman/CEO — Thomas S Murphy; President/COO — Robert A Iger; Exec. Vice President — John B Fairchild; Sr. Vice President/CFO — Ronald J Doerfler; Sr. Vice Pres./President-Broadcast Group — Michael P Mallardi; Sr. Vice Pres./President-Publishing Group — Phillip J Meek; Sr. Vice Pres./President-Mutimedia Group — Stephen A Weiswasser; Sr. Vice Pres./President-ABC Television Network Group — David Westin; Sr. Vice Pres./President-Cable & Int'l. Broadcast Group — Herbert A Granath; Vice President/Controller/Asst. Secretary — Allan J Edelson; Vice President/Investor Relations — Joseph M Fitzgerald; Vice President/Executive Asst. to the Chairman — William J Wilkenson; Vice President/Taxes — James M Goldberg; Vice President — Steven M Bornstein; Vice President — Andrew E Jackson; Vice President — David S Loewith; Vice President/Corporate Communications — Patricia J Matson; Vice President/Labor Relations — Jeffrey Ruthizer; Vice President/Treasurer — David J Vondrak; Secretary — Philip R Farnsworth; Asst. Treasurer — Allen S Bomes; Vice Pres./President-Radio Division, Broadcast Group — James P Arcara; Vice Pres./General Counsel — Alan N Braverman; Vice Pres./President-Diversified Publishing Group — Ann Maynard Gray; Vice Pres./Director-Engineering, Broadcast Group — Robert O Niles; Vice Pres./President-Television Stations — Lawrence J Pollock; Director — Robert P Bauman; Director — Daniel B Burke; Director — Warren E Buffett; Director — Nicholas F Brady; Director — Frank T Cary; Director

---

GEORGE ROMANO

OVER FOUR DECADES
OF CONSTRUCTIVE SERVICE
TO THE NEWSPAPER INDUSTRY

6165 Via de la Tortola
Tucson, Arizona 85718

602-299-5292

Copyright ©1996 by the Editor & Publisher Co.

Newspaper groups

— John B Fairchild; Director — Leonard H Goldenson; Director — Robert A Iger; Director — Frank S Jones; Director — Ann Dibble Jordan; Director — John H Muller Jr; Director — Thomas S Murphy; Director — Wyndham Robertson; Director — M Cabell Woodward Jr.

Belleville (IL) News-Democrat (mS); Pontiac (MI) Oakland Press (e); Kansas City (MO) Star (mS); Albany (OR) Democrat-Herald (e), Ashland (OR) Daily Tidings (e); Wilkes-Barre (PA) Times Leader (mS); Fort Worth (TX) Star-Telegram (m,S).

Note: This group also owns and operates the ABC Television Network which provides news, entertainment and sports programming to approximately 224 affiliated stations nationwide. The Company's eight radio networks serve nearly 3,400 affiliated radio stations. It also owns 10 television stations and 18 radio stations. It holds the majority interest in ESPN and is also a partial owner of the Arts & Entertainment and Lifetime Cable programming services. It licenses, produces and distributes programming for cable and home video worldwide and to overseas broadcasters and theatrical distributors. This company publishes 78 weekly newspapers, 63 shopping guides, real estate magazines and various specialty and business periodicals and books.

Central Newspapers Inc. — 135 N. Pennsylvania St., Ste. 1200, Indianapolis, IN 46204-2400; tel (317) 231-9201
President/CEO — Louis Weil III; Exec Vice President — Eugene S Pulliam; Secretary — Marjorie C Tarplee; Chief Financial Officer — Thomas K MacGillivray; Controller — Robert Lowry.
Phoenix (AZ) Arizona Republic (mS), Phoenix (AZ) Gazette (e); Indianapolis (IN) Star (mS), Indianapolis (IN) News (e), Muncie (IN) Star (mS), Muncie (IN) Press (e), Noblesville (IN) Daily Ledger (e), Vincennes (IN) Sun-Commercial (eS).
Note: The Vincennes Sun-Commercial is published by Central Newspapers Inc. The other newspapers listed are published by separate corporations which Central Newspapers either directly or indirectly owns the controlling stock.

Chesapeake Publishing Corp. — 29088 Airpark Dr.; PO Box 600, Easton, MD 21601; tel (410) 822-1500; fax (410) 820-6518

John T. Cribb

Opportunity is now.

The market for sale of newspapers is quite active. Call us to discuss your options in an appraisal or sale.

BOLITHO-CRIBB
& Associates

Newspaper
Brokerage * Appraisal

<u>Established
1923</u>

John T. Cribb
1 Annette Park Drive
Bozeman, MT 59715
406-586-6621

Co-Chairman — Charles Calka; President — Thomas Bradlee; Treasurer — Stanley Wallace.
Easton (MD) Star Democrat (mS), Elkton (MD) Cecil Whig (m).
Note: This group also owns 28 non-daily newspapers and 22 specialty publications.

Chronicle Publishing Co. — 901 Mission St., San Francisco, CA 94103; tel (415) 777-7444
President-Parent Company — John B Sias; CEO — John B Sias.
San Francisco (CA) Chronicle (m), San Francisco (CA) Sunday Examiner & Chronicle (S); Bloomington (IL) Pantagraph (mS); Clinton (MA) Daily Item (e), Worcester (MA) Telegram & Gazette (mS).
Note: The San Francisco Sunday Examiner & Chronicle is published jointly with the Hearst Corporation. The Chronicle Publishing Co. also publishes three weeklies in Illinois.

Cleveland Newspapers Inc. — 525 Office Park Dr.; PO Box 530447, Birmingham, AL 35253-0447; tel (205) 870-1684
President — C Lee Walls Sr.
Jasper (AL) Mountain Eagle (eS); Cartersville (GA) Tribune News (e); Abilene (KS) Reflector-Chronicle (e), Hiawatha (KS) Daily World (e); Cleveland (MS) Bolivar Commercial (e), Monett (MO) Times (e), London (OH) Madison Press (e); Cleveland (TN) Banner (eS), Cookeville (TN) Herald-Citizen (e).
Note: The London (OH) Madison Press (Central Ohio Printing Corp.) is owned by Walls Newspapers Inc. in Birmingham, AL, and the majority of Walls Newspapers Inc. stock is owned by Cleveland Newspapers Inc.

Community Newspaper Co. — 254 Second Ave. (02194); PO Box 9113, Needham, MA 02192-9113; tel (617) 433-6700; fax (617) 433-6701
Chariman/CEO — Bill Elfers; Acting President — Paul Mucci; Exec. VP-Sales & Mktg. — David Bonfield; CFO — John Rehm.
Middlesex Community Newspapers: 33 New York Ave., Framingham, MA 01701; tel (508) 626-3800; fax (508) 626-4350
Publisher — Asa Cole; Editor-In-Chief — Andrea Haynes; Ad Director — Paul Farrell.
Dedham (MA) Daily Transcript (e), Framingham (MA) Middlesex News (eS), Waltham (MA) News-Tribune (e).
Note: Community Newspaper Co. has eight subsidiaries that publish over 110 non-daily newspapers in Massachusetts.

Consolidated Publishing Co. — 216 W. 10th St.; PO Box 189, Anniston, AL 36201; tel (205) 236-1551; fax (205) 231-0027
President — Phillip A Sanguinetti; Editor/Publisher — H Brandt Ayers.
Anniston (AL) Star (eS), Talladega (AL) Home (m).
Note: This group also publishes three weeklies.

Copley Press Inc. — 7776 Ivanhoe Ave.; PO Box 1530, La Jolla, CA 92038; tel (619) 454-0411; fax (619) 454-5014
Chairman/CEO — Helen K Copley; President/Exec. Comm./Director — David C Copley; Sr. Vice President/Exec. Comm./Director — Robert F Crouch; Vice President-Legal Affairs — Harold W Fuson Jr; Vice President/Finance/Secretary — Charles F Patrick; Vice President-Human Resources/Asst. Secretary — Carmi Hodge; Treasurer/Controller — Dean P Dwyer; Vice President — Roy E Bell; Vice President — Herbert G Klein; Vice President — John P Clarke; Vice President — Thomas J Wafer Jr.
Copley Newspapers:
San Diego (CA) Union-Tribune (mS), San Pedro (CA) News-Pilot (m), Santa Monica (CA) Outlook (m), Torrance (CA) Daily Breeze (mS).
Fox Valley Press: 3101 Rte. 30, Plainfield, IL 60544; tel (815) 439-5300
Aurora (IL) Beacon-News (eS), Elgin (IL) Courier-News (e), Joliet (IL) Herald-News (eS), Lincoln (IL) Courier (e), Springfield (IL) State Journal-Register (mS), Waukegan (IL) News-Sun (e).
Note: Copley Press subsidiaries also own and operate 31 weekly newspapers.

Cox Newspapers Inc. — 1400 Lake Hearn Dr. N.E. (30319); PO Box 105720, Atlanta, GA 30348; tel (404) 843-5000; fax (404) 843-7928

Chairman/CEO-Cox Enterprises Inc. (Parent Co.) — James C Kennedy; President — Jay R Smith; Sr Vice President — Brian G Cooper; Vice President-Circulation — Jay Campbell; Vice President-Advertising — Cathy B Coffey; Vice President-Operations — James A Cooper; Group Vice President — Michael Laosa; Sr. Vice President/Editor-in-Chief — Arnold S Rosenfeld; Vice President-Market Development — Peter M Winter; Controller-Newspaper Division — Buddy Solomon.
Chandler (AZ) Arizonan Tribune (mS), Gilbert (AZ) Tribune (mS), Mesa (AZ) Tribune (mS), Scottsdale (AZ) Progress Tribune (eS), Tempe (AZ) Daily News Tribune (mS), Yuma (AZ) Daily Sun (e); Grand Junction (CO) Daily Sentinel (eS), Daytona Beach (FL) News-Journal (mS), Palm Beach (FL) Daily News (mS), Palm Beach (FL) Post (mS); Atlanta (GA) Journal (e), Atlanta (GA) Constitution (m), Atlanta (GA) Journal & Constitution (S); Dayton (OH) Daily News (mS), Springfield (OH) News-Sun (mS); Austin (TX) American-Statesman (mS), Longview (TX) News-Journal (mS), Lufkin (TX) Daily News (eS), Nacogdoches (TX) Daily Sentinel (eS), Waco (TX) Tribune-Herald (mS).
Note: Cox Newspapers also has 47½% interest in the Daytona Beach (FL) News-Journal (mS) and has acquired 12½% interest in Agora-Gazeta of Warsaw, Poland, which publishes Gazeta Wyborcza.

D

Dix Communications — 212 E. Liberty St., Wooster, OH 44691; tel (216) 264-1125; fax (216) 263-5013
President — Albert E Dix; Vice President — Raymond Victor Dix; Vice President — Robert Victor Dix; Vice President — David E Dix; Vice President — Charles C Dix Jr; Treasurer — G Charles Dix II; Secretary — Robert C Dix Jr; Comptroller — Dale Gerber.
Frankfort (KY) State Journal (e); Alliance (OH) Review (e), Ashland (OH) Times-Gazette (e), Cambridge (OH) Jeffersonian (e), Defiance (OH) Crescent-News (e), Kent Ravenna (OH) Record-Courier (eS), Wooster (OH) Daily Record (e).
Note: Wooster Republican Printing Co. DBA Dix Communications publishes the above daily papers. This group also operates 18 weekly newspapers, four television stations and seven radio stations.

Donrey Media Group — 3600 Wheeler Ave.; PO Box 17017, Fort Smith, AR 72917-7017; tel (501) 785-9404; fax (501) 785-9479
Chairman — Jackson T Stephens; President/COO — Emmett Jones; Exec. Vice President/CFO — Darrell W Loftin; Vice President/Outdoor/TV/Cable Group — Ron Lamar; Vice President-Eastern Newspaper Group — Don Schneider; Vice President-Western Newspaper Group — David A Osborn.
Arkadelphia (AR) Daily Siftings Herald (e), Fort Smith (AR) Southwest Times Record (mS), Pine Bluff (AR) Commercial (mS), Springdale-Rogers (AR) Morning News of Northwest Arkansas (m); Chico (CA) Enterprise-Record (mS), Hemet (CA) News (mS), Lompoc (CA) Record (eS), Ontario (CA) Inland Valley Daily Bulletin (mS), Oroville (CA) Mercury-Register (e), Red Bluff (CA) Daily News (e), Redlands (CA) Daily Facts (eS), Ukiah (CA) Daily Journal (eS), Vallejo (CA) Times-Herald (mS), Woodland (CA) Daily Democrat (eS); Hilo (HI) Hawaii Tribune-Herald (mS), Kailua-Kona (HI) West Hawaii Today (mS); Washington (IN) Times-Herald (e); Clinton (IA) Herald (e), Oskaloosa (IA) Herald (e); Glasgow (KY) Daily Times (eS); Picayune (MS) Item (eS); Moberly (MO) Monitor-Index (e); Ely (NV) Daily Times (e), Las Vegas (NV) Review-Journal (mS); Alamogordo (NM) Daily News (eS), Asheboro (NC) Courier-Tribune (eS); Altus (OK) Times (eS), Bartlesville (OK) Examiner-Enterprise (eS), Blackwell (OK) Journal-Tribune (eS), Chickasha (OK) Daily Express (eS), Claremore (OK) Daily Progress (eS), Durant (OK) Daily Democrat (eS), Frederick (OK) Leader (eS), Guthrie (OK) Daily Leader (eS), Guymon (OK) Daily Herald (eS), Henryetta (OK) Daily Free-Lance (eS), Norman (OK) Transcript (eS), Okmulgee (OK) Daily Times (mS), Pauls Valley (OK) Daily Democrat (eS); Columbia (TN) Daily Herald (eS); Athens

We Deliver...

Dirks, Van Essen & Associates since 1985 has represented the sellers of 85 daily newspapers in 55 separate transactions. In the past year we have closed 11 transactions involving 29 daily newspapers:

	SELLER	PURCHASER	CIRCULATION
Raleigh (NC) News & Observer	Daniels Family	McClatchy Newspapers	155,000
15 Dailies in 8 States	Thomson Newspapers	American Publishing	151,900
Greenville (NC) Reflector	Whichard Family	Cox Enterprises	18,800
Jacksonville (IL) Journal-Courier Sedalia (MO) Democrat Barstow (CA) Desert Dispatch	Thomson Newspapers	Freedom Communications	15,300 13,500 7,700
Sterling-Rock Falls (IL) Gazette	Thomson Newspapers	Shaw Newspapers Dixon, IL	15,000
Worthington (MN) Daily Globe Mitchell (SD) Daily Republic Dickinson (ND) Press	Thomson Newspapers	Forum Communications Fargo, ND	13,400 12,300 7,900
Kerrville (TX) Times	Thomson Newspapers	Southern Newspapers Houston, TX	10,200
Shenandoah (PA) Herald	Goodson Newspapers	J.H. Zerbey Newspapers Pottsville, PA	9,400
Milford (CT) Citizen	Capital Cities/ABC	Journal Register Trenton, NJ	6,700
Southbridge (MA) News	Loren Ghiglione	John Coots and David Cutler	5,500
Fulton (MO) Sun	Stauffer Media	Capital News, Post-Tribune Jefferson City, MO	4,700

Dirks, Van Essen & Associates has concluded 16 years as the nation's most active firm in representing sellers of daily newspapers and non-daily groups. We are especially proud that more than 20 daily newspaper groups, having seen our work as prospective buyers, have engaged us in just the past seven years to assist them in divesting their own daily newspapers or non-daily groups. We are equally pleased that in the 84 transactions we have completed in the past 11 years, we have sold newspapers to 60 different buyers, demonstrating the depth of interest in newspaper companies and the breadth of our firm's ability to secure the highest possible price from the finest possible purchaser.

Lee E. Dirks
Formerly vice president and general manager of the Detroit Free Press; the nation's first full-time newspaper-stock analyst; Dow Jones newsman for eight years.

Owen Van Essen
Formerly business manager and part owner of the Worthington (MN) Daily Globe; joined Dirks, Van Essen & Associates in 1986.

DIRKS, VAN ESSEN & ASSOCIATES

123 E. Marcy St., Suite 207, Santa Fe, NM 87501

Phone: 505-820-2700   Fax: 505-820-2900

Newspaper groups

(TX) Daily Review (eS), Borger (TX) News-Herald (eS), Cleburne (TX) Times-Review (eS), Denison (TX) Herald (e), Gainesville (TX) Daily Register (eS), Jacksonville (TX) Daily Progress (eS), Kilgore (TX) News Herald (eS), Sherman (TX) Democrat (mS), Sweetwater (TX) Reporter (eS), Weatherford (TX) Democrat (eS); Aberdeen (WA) Daily World (eS).
Note: Donrey Media Group also owns five non-daily newspapers, one television station, five cable television franchises and 10 outdoor advertising facilities.

Dow Jones & Co. Inc. — 200 Liberty St., New York, NY 10281; tel (212) 416-2600
Chairman/CEO — Peter R Kann; President/COO — Kenneth L Burenga; President-International — Karen Elliot House; President-Business Informations Services — Dorothea Coccoli Palsho; Sr. Vice President/President-Magazines — James H Ottaway Jr; Vice President/Editor-WSJ — Robert L Bartley; Vice President/General Manager — Danforth Austin; Vice President-Marketing — Bernard T Flanagan; Vice President-Advertising-WSJ — Paul Atkinson; Vice President-Barron's — Robert Paradise; Vice President-Employee Relations — James Scaduto; Managing Editor-WSJ — Paul E Steiger; Sr. Vice President/General Counsel/Secretary — Peter G Skinner; Sr. VP/President-Dow Jones Telerate — Carl M Valenti; Director-Corporate Relations — Roger B May; Vice President/CFO — Kevin J Roche.
Note: Dow Jones publishes four regional editions of the Wall Street Journal Monday through Friday at 17 locations around the country; Barron's magazine; domestic and overseas newswires; a computerized news retrieval service; The Asian Wall Street Journal, The Wall Street Journal Europe & the National Business Employment Weekly, American Demographics and The Asian Wall Street Journal Weekly. Dow Jones also broadcasts radio and television news reports. Ottaway Newspapers Inc., a wholly owned subsidiary, publishes 19 daily community newspapers. Dow Jones Telerate Inc. provides electronic business information services around the world. Dow Jones Business Information Services provides news and information to corporations and consumers through a variety of electronic media.

E

Eagle Publishing Group — See MediaNews Inc.

Edwards Publications — 125 Eagles Nest Dr.; PO Box 1193, Seneca, SC 29679; tel (803) 882-3272
President — Bob L Edwards; Vice President — Jerry Edwards; Vice President — Steve Edwards; Secretary/Treasurer — Joyce L Edwards.
Cherokee (IA) Times (m), Spencer (IA) Daily Reporter (m), Stormlake (IA) Pilot-Tribune (m).
Note: Edwards also operates four weeklies and one bi-weekly in Iowa, two bi-weeklies in South Carolina, one weekly in Michigan plus 10 shoppers and 10 specialty publications in four states.

Emmerich Enterprises Inc. — PO Box 8050, Greenwood, MS 38930; tel (601) 453-5312; fax (601) 453-2908
President — J Wyatt Emmerich.
Clarksdale (MS) Press-Register (e), Greenwood (MS) Commonwealth (eS), McComb (MS) Enterprise-Journal (eS).
Note: This group also publishes eight weeklies and two semi-weeklies.

Evening Post Publishing Co. — 134 Columbus St., Charleston, SC 29403-4800; tel (803) 577-7111
Chairman — Peter Manigault; President — Ivan V Anderson Jr; Vice President — Travis O Rockey; Secretary — A M Wilcox; Asst. Secretary — Mary M Gilbreth; Treasurer — James W Martin.
Aiken (SC) Standard (mS), Charleston (SC) Post & Courier (mS).
Note: This group publishes the Buenos Aires (Argentina) Herald (mS), three non-daily newspapers in South Carolina and various non-sub. publications. It also operates nine television stations, Editors Press Service in New York and White Oak Forestry Corp. in Georgetown, SC.

F

Fackelman Newspapers — 2005 N. Pte. Alexis Dr., Tarpon Springs, FL 34689; tel (813) 942-2883; fax (813) 943-2207
President — Ann Nixon; Vice President-Operations — Marc Richard; Secretary — Ann Fackelman; Treasurer — Broward E Ratliff; Vice President-Investments — Frank E Nixon.
Jennings (LA) Daily News (e), Ruston (LA) Daily Leader (eS); Excelsior Springs (MO) Daily Standard (e), Maryville (MO) Daily Forum (e), Richmond (MO) Daily News (e).
Note: Fackelman Newspapers shares ownership of the Crowley (LA) Post-Signal (eS) with B I Moody III. In addition, this partnership owns three weekly newspapers in Louisiana. Fackelman Newspapers is also affiliated with two weeklies in Texas and one weekly in Florida.

Federated Media Corp. — 421 S. 2nd St; PO Box 2500, Elkhart, IN 46515; tel (219) 294-1661; fax (219) 294-4014
President — John Dille; Treasurer — Robert Watson; Publisher — Anthony H Biggs.
Elkhart (IN) Truth (eS), Greencastle (IN) Banner-Graphic (e).

Forum Communications Co. — 101 5th St., Fargo, ND 58107; tel (701) 235-7311
President/CEO — William C Marcil; Vice President — Lloyd G Case; Vice President — Charles Bohnet; Secretary/Treasurer — Jane B Marcil.
Willmar (MN) West Central Daily Tribune (e), Worthington (MN) Daily Globe (m); Dickinson (ND) Press (mS), Fargo (ND) Forum (mS); Mitchell (SD) Republic (e).
Note: This group publishes three weeklies, two bi-weeklies and also owns several television and radio stations and commercial printing operations.

Freedom Communications Inc. — 17666 Fitch (92714); PO Box 19549, Irvine, CA 92713; tel (714) 553-9292; fax (714) 474-4675
Chairman — Robert C Hardie; President Emeritus — D R Segal; President/CEO — James N Rosse; Sr. Vice Pres./CFO — David L Kuykendall; Sr. Vice Pres.-Orange County Newspapers — R David Threshie Jr; Sr. Vice Pres./President-Broadcast Division — Alan Bell; Sr. Vice Pres./President-Eastern Newspaper Division — Jonathan M Segal; Sr. Vice Pres./President-Western Newspaper Division — Scott Fischer; Vice President-Corporate Affairs/Secretary — Richard A Wallace; Vice President/Controller — Jeff Whitton; Vice President/President-Freedom Magazines Inc. — Samuel Wolgemuth; Vice President-Human Resources — Mark Ernst; Vice President-Risk Management — Penny Troup.
Barstow (CA) Desert Dispatch (e), Marysville-Yuba City (CA) Appeal-Democrat (mS), Porterville (CA) Recorder (e), Santa Ana (CA) Orange County Register (mS), Turlock (CA) Journal (e), Victorville (CA) Daily Press (mS); Colorado Springs (CO) Gazette Telegraph (mS); Fort Pierce (FL) Tribune (mS), Fort Walton Beach (FL) Northwest Florida Daily News (mS), Panama City (FL) News-Herald (mS); Jacksonville (IL) Journal-Courier (mS); Crawfordsville (IN) Journal Review (m), Seymour (IN) Tribune (e); Greenville (MS) Delta Democrat Times (eS), Sedalia (MO) Democrat (eS); Clovis (NM) News Journal (eS); Burlington (NC) Times-News (mS), Gastonia (NC) Gaston Gazette (mS), Jacksonville (NC) Daily News (mS), Kinston (NC) Free Press (eS), New Bern (NC) Sun Journal (mS); Lima (OH) News (mS); Brownsville (TX) Herald (mS), Harlingen (TX) Valley Morning Star (mS), McAllen (TX) Monitor (mS), Odessa (TX) American (mS), Pampa (TX) News (eS).
Note: Freedom Communications also owns and operates six television stations, 40 weekly and specialty publications, a cable television news channel and five magazines.

G

Gannett Co. Inc. — 1100 Wilson Blvd., Arlington, VA 22234; tel (703) 284-6000
Chairman/President/CEO — John J Curley; Vice Chairman/Chief Financial & Administrative Officer — Douglas H McCorkindale; President-Newspaper Division — Gary L Watson; Sr. Vice President-Newspaper Division — Carleton Rosenburgh; Group President-Atlantic Newspaper Group — Gary Sherlock; Sr. Group President-East Newspaper Group — Curtis Riddle; Group President-Gulf Coast Newspaper Group — Denise Bannister; Group President-Midwest Newspaper Group — Mary P Stier; Group President-Northwest Newspaper Group — Sara Bentley; Sr. Group President-Pacific Newspaper Group — Sue Clark-Jackson; Sr. Group President-Piedmont Newspaper Group — William deB Mebane; Sr. Group President-South Newspaper Group — Michael Coleman; Sr. Vice President/News-Newspaper Division — Phil Currie.
Montgomery (AL) Advertiser (mS); Mountain Home (AR) Baxter Bulletin (ms); Tucson (AZ) Citizen (e); Marin County (CA) Independent Journal (eS), Palm Springs (CA) Desert Sun (mS), Salinas (CA) Californian (m), San Bernardino (CA) County Sun (m), Tulare (CA) Advance-Register (e), Visalia (CA) Times-Delta (m); Fort Collins (CO) Coloradoan (mS); Norwich (CT) Bulletin (mS); Wilmington (DE) News Journal (mS); Brevard County (FL) Florida Today (mS), Fort Myers (FL) News-Press (mS), Pensacola (FL) News Journal (mS); Gainesville (GA) Times (eS), Moultrie (GA) Observer (mS); Honolulu (HI) Advertiser (mS); Boise (ID) Idaho Statesman (mS); Danville (IL) Commercial-News (eS), Rockford (IL) Register Star (mS), Lafayette (IN) Journal & Courier (mS), Marion (IN) Chronicle-Tribune (mS), Richmond (IN) Palladium-Item (eS); Des Moines (IA) Register (mS), Iowa City (IA) Press-Citizen (e); Louisville (KY) Courier-Journal (mS); Monroe (LA) News-Star (mS), Shreveport (LA) Times (mS); Battle Creek (MI) Enquirer (eS), Detroit (MI) News (eS), Lansing (MI) State Journal (mS), Port Huron (MI) Times Herald (eS); St Cloud (MN) Times (eS); Hattiesburg (MS) American (eS), Jackson (MS) Clarion-Ledger (mS); Springfield (MO) News-Leader (mS); Great Falls (MT) Tribune (mS); Reno (NV) Gazette-Journal (mS); Bridgewater (NJ) Courier-News (mS), Camden (NJ) Courier-Post (mS), Vineland (NJ) Daily Journal (e); Binghamton (NY) Press & Sun-Bulletin (mS), Elmira (NY) Star-Gazette (mS), Ithaca (NY) Journal (e), Mamaroneck (NY) Daily Times (eS), Mount Vernon (NY) Daily Argus (mS), New Rochelle (NY) Standard-Star (mS), Niagara Falls (NY) Niagara Gazette (mS), Nyack-Rockland (NY) Journal-News (mS), Ossining (NY) Citizen Register (eS), Peekskill (NY) Star (eS), Port Chester (NY) Daily Item (eS), Poughkeepsie (NY) Journal (mS), Rochester (NY) Democrat & Chronicle (mS), Rochester (NY) Times-Union (e), West Nyack-Rockland (NY) Rockland Journal-News (mS), Tarrytown (NY) Daily News (eS), Utica (NY) Observer-Dispatch (mS), West Nyack (NY) Rockland Journal-News (mS), White Plains (NY) Reporter Dispatch (eS), Yonkers (NY) Herald Statesman (mS); Asheville (NC) Citizen-Times (mS), Chillicothe (OH) Gazette (e), Cincinnati (OH) Enquirer (mS), Fremont (OH) News-Messenger (e), Gallipolis (OH) Tribune (e), Marietta (OH) Times (e), Pomeroy-Middleton (OH) Sentinel (e), Pomeroy-Middleton (OH) Times-Sentinel (S); Muskogee (OK) Daily Phoenix and Times-Democrat (mS), Salem (OR) Statesman Journal (mS), Chambersburg (PA) Public Opinion (e), Lansdale (PA) Reporter (e), Pittsburgh (PA) North Hills News Record (eS), Tarentum (PA) Valley News Dispatch (eS); Greenville (SC) News (mS), Greenville (SC) Piedmont (eS); Sioux Falls (SD) Argus Leader (mS), Clarksville (TN) Leaf-Chronicle (mS), Jackson (TN) Sun (mS), Nashville (TN) Tennessean (mS); El Paso (TX) Times (mS); Burlington (VT) Free Press (mS); Arlington (VA) USA TODAY

BROKER

•

APPRAISER

•

CONSULTANT

GERALD D. REILLY

12 TACONIC ROAD
GREENWICH, CONN. 06830
TELEPHONE: (203) 622-0599

... continuing a tradition of integrity and constructive service to publishers

Newspaper groups

I-459

(m), Staunton (VA) Daily News Leader (mS); Bellingham (WA) Herald (eS), Olympia (WA) Olympian (mS); Huntington (WV) Herald-Dispatch (mS), Point Pleasant (WV) Register (e); Green Bay (WI) Press-Gazette (eS), Wausau (WI) Daily Herald (eS); Agana (Guam) Pacific Daily News (mS); St Thomas (VI) Virgin Islands Daily News (m).
Note: Gannett owns non-daily publications in Arizona, Arkansas, California, Colorado, Florida, Georgia, Illinois, Indiana, Iowa, Michigan, Mississippi, Missouri, New Jersey, New York, Ohio, Oklahoma, Oregon, Pennsylvania, Vermont, Virginia, Washington, West Virginia, Wisconsin and the USA Weekend magazine. It operates 10 television and 11 radio stations and the largest outdoor advertising company in North America.

Guy Gannett Communications — One City Center; PO Box 15277, Portland, ME 04112-5277; tel (207) 828-8100; fax (207) 828-8160
Chairman — Madeleine G Gorson; Vice Chairman — John H Gannett; President/CEO — James B Shaffer; VP-Finance/CFO — James E Baker; VP-Human Resources — Jane N Begert; VP-Television — Michael L Bock; VP-Planning & Development — David S Burfeind; VP-New Media Strategies — J Willard Colston.
Augusta (ME) Kennebec Journal (m), Portland (ME) Maine Sunday Telegram (S), Portland (ME) Press Herald (m), Waterville (ME) Central Maine Morning Sentinel (m).
Note: The company also owns Minnesota Sun Publications (29 weeklies) and five television stations: WGME, Portland, ME; WGGB, Springfield, MA; WICS, Springfield, IL; KGAN, Cedar Rapids, IA; and WICD, Champaign, IL.

Goodson Newspaper Group — 1009 Lenox Dr.; PO Box 6590, Lawrenceville, NJ 08648; tel (609) 895-2600
President — David N Hurwitz; COO/Sr. Vice President — David B Carr; CFO/Sr. Vice President — Roy M Cockburn; Vice President-Labor — Michael J Tannler; Vice President-Finance — Benjamin J Kowalczyk.
Morristown (NJ) Daily Record (mS), Toms River (NJ) Ocean County Observer (mS); Kingston (NY) Daily Freeman (mS), Oneida (NY) Daily Dispatch (e); Massillon (OH) Independent (eS); Chester (PA) Delaware County Daily Times (mS), Pottstown (PA) The Mercury (mS).
Note: Goodson Newspaper Group also has four weekly publishing companies: Acme Newspapers (five in Ardmore, PA); Manahawkin Newspapers (seven in Manahawkin, NJ); Precision Publications (two in Toms River, NJ); Town Talk Newspapers (one in Media, PA).

Gray Communications — 126 N. Washington St. (31701); PO Box 48, Albany, GA 31720-0048; tel (912) 888-9390
CEO — John Williams; CFO — Bill Fielder.
Albany (GA) Herald (mS), Conyers (GA) Rockdale Citizen (e), Lawrenceville (GA) Gwinnett Daily Post (m).

H

Hagadone Corp. — PO Box C-6200, Coer d'Alene, ID 83814-1937; tel (208) 667-3431
President — Duane B Hagadone; Vice President — Bradley D Hagadone; Secretary — John R Barlow; Treasurer — Arthur S Flagan.
Coer d'Alene (ID) Press (mS), Kellogg (ID) Shoshone County News-Press (m), Sandpoint (ID) Bonner County Bee (m); Sioux City (IA) Journal (mS); Kalispell (MT) Inter Lake (eS); Moses Lake (WA) Columbia Basin Herald (e); Beloit (WI) News (e).
Note: The Sioux City (IA) Journal is owned jointly with Howard Publications.

Harris Enterprises Inc. — 1 N. Main St., Ste. 616 (67501); PO Box 190, Hutchinson, KS 67504-0190; tel (316) 694-5830; fax (316) 694-5834
Chairman — Lloyd Ballhagen; President — John Lee.
Burlington (IA) Hawk Eye (mS); Chanute (KS) Tribune (e), Garden City (KS) Telegram (e), Hays (KS) Daily News (mS), Hutchinson (KS) News (mS), Olathe (KS) Daily News (mS), Ottawa (KS) Herald (e), Parsons (KS) Sun (e), Salina (KS) Journal (mS).

Harte-Hanks Communications Inc. — 200 Concord Plaza Dr., Ste. 800 (78216); PO Box 269, San Antonio, TX 78291-0269; tel (210) 829-9000; fax (210) 829-9101
Chairman — Houston H Harte; President/CEO — Larry Franklin; Sr. Vice President/Legal Secretary — Donald R Crews; Sr. Vice President/CFO — Richard L Ritchie; Sr. Vice Pres./President-Harte-Hanks Newspapers — Stephen W Sullivan; Pres./Publisher-Caller Times, Corpus Christi, TX — Stephen W Sullivan; Sr. Vice Pres./President/CEO-Harte-Hanks Shoppers — Harry J Buckel; Sr. Vice Pres./President/CEO-Harte-Hanks Direct Mktg. — Richard M Hochhauser; Sr. Vice Pres./President/General Mgr.-KENS-TV — Michael J Conly; Vice President — Kevin J Barry; Vice President — Craig Combest; Vice President — Peter E Gorman; Vice President — Bill R Gulledge; Vice President — Frank Puckett Jr; Vice President — Charles R Dall'Acqua.
Anderson (SC) Independent-Mail (mS); Abilene (TX) Reporter-News (mS), Corpus Christi (TX) Caller-Times (mS), Plano (TX) Star Courier (mS), San Angelo (TX) Standard Times (mS), Wichita Falls (TX) Times Record News (mS).
Note: Harte-Hanks Communications Inc. also owns and operates a nationwide direct marketing company that provides a full range of specialized and coordinated direct marketing services, including database, integrated direct marketing, response management, targeted mail/data systems and transportation. Harte-Hanks owns and operates shoppers zoned into 582 separate editions reaching seven million households in four major markets, six daily newspapers, 25 non-daily publications, as well as KENS-TV (CBS affiliate in San Antonio) and KENS-AM Radio.

Hartman Newspapers Inc. — PO Box 1390, Rosenberg, TX 77471; tel (713) 342-8691; fax (713) 342-6968
President — J William Hartman; Sr. Vice President — Clyde C King Jr; Vice President/Secretary/Treasurer — Don F Jones; Vice President-Group Operations — Fred B Hartman.
Brenham (TX) Banner-Press (eS), Henderson (TX) Daily News (eS), McKinney (TX) Courier-Gazette (eS), Rosenberg (TX) Herald Coaster (eS), Terrell (TX) Tribune (eS).
Note: This group also includes three weekly and five semi-weekly newspapers.

Haskell Newspapers — 204 Broad St., Martinsville, VA 24115; tel (703) 638-8801
President — Robert H Haskell.
Sanford (FL) Herald (eS); Mayfield (KY) Messenger (e); Martinsville (VA) Bulletin (eS).
Note: This group also publishes one weekly newspaper.

Hearst Newspapers — 959 8th Ave., Hearst Magazine Bldg., New York, NY 10019; tel (212) 649-2000
Vice President/GM — Robert J Danzig; Sr. Vice President/CFO — Victor F Ganzi; National Editor — Joseph Kingsbury-Smith; Vice President/General Counsel — Jonathan E Thackeray; Marketing Development Mgr. — Buzz Wurzer; Director of Diversity — Maria Elena Torralva.
San Francisco (CA) Examiner (e), San Francisco (CA) Examiner & Chronicle (S); Edwardsville (IL) Intelligencer (e); Bad Axe (MI) Huron Daily Tribune (e), Midland (MI) Daily News (e); Albany (NY) Times-Union (mS); Beaumont (TX) Enterprise (eS), Houston (TX) Chronicle (mS), Laredo (TX) Morning News (mS), Midland (TX)

INVESTMENT BANKERS TO THE PUBLISHING, COMMUNICATIONS, MEDIA, BROADCASTING, INTERACTIVE DIGITAL MEDIA AND INFORMATION INDUSTRIES

Kevin M. Lavalla
Managing Director,
Newspaper Publishing

Veronis, Suhler & Associates, Inc., exclusively serves the media and communications industry providing media company owners investment banking services including: mergers, acquisitions, divestitures, recapitalizations, financing and valuations. Since its founding in 1981, VS&A has completed over 300 transactions totaling in excess of $18 Billion.

Kevin M. Lavalla, VS&A's Managing Director for Newspaper Publishing, has over 10 years experience in providing financial advisory services, including mergers and acquisitions, to daily and weekly newspapers, shoppers, local business, legal and specialty publications.

VERONIS, SUHLER & ASSOCIATES INC.

350 PARK AVENUE, NEW YORK, NEW YORK 10022
E-MAIL: lavallak@vsacomm.com • PHONE: (212) 935-4990 • FAX: (212) 935-0877

Copyright ©1996 by the Editor & Publisher Co.

Newspaper groups

Reporter-Telegram (eS), Plainview (TX) Daily Herald (eS), San Antonio (TX) Express News (mS); Seattle (WA) Post-Intelligencer (mS).
Note: The parent company, the Hearst Corp., also owns 13 monthly consumer magazines, more than 20 business publications, six television stations, seven radio stations and two book companies. The Hearst Corp. is also a partner in two cable programming networks, Lifetime and Arts & Entertainment and also owns King Features Syndicate. The San Francisco Sunday Examiner & Chronicle is owned by the Hearst Corp. and the Chronicle Publishing Co. The Seattle Times/Post Intelligencer is published every Sunday by the Seattle Times Corp. representing the Seattle Post-Intelligencer.

Hollinger International Inc. — 107-115 S. Emma St., West Frankfort, IL 62896; tel (618) 937-6411; fax (618) 932-6155
Chairman — David Radler; President/CEO — Larry J Perrotto; Vice Chairman — George R Sample; Exec. Vice President — John Satterwhite.
Fayetteville (AR) Northwest Arkansas Times (eS), Harrison (AR) Daily Times (e), Helena-West Helena (AR) Daily World (e), Malvern (AR) Daily Record (e), Newport (AR) Independent (e), Stuttgart (AR) Daily Leader (e); Yreka (CA) Siskiyou Daily News (e); Fort Morgan (CO) Times (e), Lamar (CO) Daily News (e), Sterling (CO) Journal Advocate (e); Naugatuck (CT) Daily News (e); New Smyrna Beach (FL) News & Observer (e); Blackfoot (ID) Morning News (m); Benton (IL) Evening News (e), Canton (IL) Daily Ledger (e), Carmi (IL) Times (e), Chicago (IL) Daily Southtown (mS), Chicago (IL) Sun-Times (mS), Du Quoin (IL) Evening Call (e), El Dorado (IL) Daily Journal (e), Flora (IL) Clay County Advocate (e), Harrisburg (IL) Daily Register (e), Marion (IL) Daily Republican (e), Monmouth (IL) Review Atlas (e), Olney (IL) Mail (e), Pontiac (IL) Daily Leader (e), West Frankfort (IL) Daily American (e); Columbia City (IN) Post & Mail (e), Decatur (IN) Daily Democrat (e), Greensburg (IN) Daily News (e), Hartford City (IN) News-Times (e), New Albany (IN) Tribune (e), Rensselaer (IN) Republican (e), Rushville (IN) Republican (e), Winchester (IN) News-Gazette (e); Atlantic (IA) News-Telegraph (e), Charles City (IA) Press (e); Atchison (KS) Daily Globe (e), Augusta (KS) Daily Gazette (e), Derby (KS) Daily Reporter (e), El Dorado (KS) Times (e), Leavenworth (KS) Times (eS), McPherson (KS) Sentinel (e); Corbin (KY) Times Tribune (e), Harlan (KY) Daily Enterprise (e), Middlesboro (KY) Daily News (e), Richmond (KY) Register (e); North Adams (MA) Transcript (e); Cheboygan (MI) Daily Tribune (m), Ionia (MI) Sentinel-Standard (e), Sault Ste. Marie (MI) Evening News (e), South Haven (MI) Daily Tribune (e); Crookston (MN) Times (e), Stillwater (MN) Gazette (e); Laurel (MS) Leader-Call (e), Meridian (MS) Star (mS), Starkville (MS) Daily News (e), West Point (MS) Daily Times-Leader (e); Boonville (MO) News Advertiser (e), Camdenton (MO) Lake Sun Leader (m), Carthage (MO) Press (e), Chillicothe (MO) Constitution-Tribune (e), Kirksville (MO) Daily Express (e), Macon (MO) Chronicle Herald (e), Mexico (MO) Ledger (e), Neosho (MO) Daily News (eS), Rolla (MO) Daily News (eS), Sikeston (MO) Standard Democrat (e), Waynesville (MO) Fort Gateway Guide (e); Beatrice (NE) Daily Sun (m), Sidney (NE) Telegraph (e); Bridgeton (NJ) Evening News (e), Millville (NJ) News (e); Herkimer (NY) Evening Telegram (e), Hornell (NY) Evening Tribune (e), North Tonawanda (NY) News (e), Olean (NY) Times Herald (eS), Oswego (NY) Palladium-Times (e), Salamanca (NY) Reporter (e), Wellsville (NY) Reporter (e); Newton (NC) Observer-News-Enterprise (e), Tarboro (NC) Daily Southerner (eS); Jamestown (ND) Sun (e), Valley City (ND) Times-Record (e); Portsmouth (OH) Daily Times (e), St. Mary's (OH) Evening Leader (e), Wapakoneta (OH) Daily News (e); Ada (OK) Evening News (eS), Woodward (OK) News (m); Bradford (PA) Era (m), Corry (PA) Journal (e), Honesdale (PA) Daily Independent (m), Kane (PA) Republican (e), Lewisburg (PA) Union County Journal (m), Milton (PA) Standard (e), Punxsutawney (PA) Spirit (m), Ridgeway (PA) Record (e), St. Marys (PA) Daily Press (e), Sayre (PA) Evening Times (e), Titusville (PA) Herald (m), Waynesboro (PA) Record Herald (e); Big Spring (TX) Herald (eS), Corsicana (TX) Daily Sun (eS), Del Rio (TX) News-Herald (eS), Greenville (TX) Herald Banner (mS), Huntsville (TX) Item (mS), Marshall (TX) News Messenger (eS), Mexia (TX) Daily News (e), Orange (TX) Leader (eS), Port Arthur (TX) News (mS), San Marcos (TX) Daily Record (e).
Note: Hollinger International (formerly American Publishing Co.) is a division of Canadian-based Hollinger Inc. Subsidiaries are Pioneer Press (48 non-daily newspapers in Illinois) and Star Publications (20 non-daily publications in Illinois).

Home News Enterprises — 332 Second St.; PO Box 3011, Columbus, IN 47202-3011; tel (812) 379-5612; fax (812) 379-5706
Chairman — Robert N Brown; President — Ned J Bradley; Vice President — Jeffrey N Brown; Exec. Asst. — Bettie R Burbrink.
Columbus (IN) Republic (e), Franklin (IN) Journal (e), Greenfield (IN) Reporter (e), Monticello (IN) Herald-Journal (e).

Hometown Communications — 2201-G Gault Ave. N.; PO Box 967, Fort Payne, AL 35967; tel (205) 845-2800; fax (205) 845-7784
President — Jim McGinnis.
Coffeyville (KS) Journal (eS), Pratt (KS) Tribune (e); Sturgis (MI) Journal (e); Fremont (NE) Tribune (e).
Note: This group also owns five weekly newspapers. Hometown is managed by McGinnis Communications.

Horvitz Newspapers Inc. — 1705 132nd Ave. NE; PO Box 90130, Bellevue, WA 98009-0130; tel (206) 455-2222; fax (206) 455-4989
CEO/President — Peter A Horvitz.
Maryville-Alcoa (TN) Daily Times (m); Bellevue (WA) Journal American (mS), Kent (WA) Valley Daily News (mS), Port Angeles (WA) Peninsula Daily News (eS).
Note: This company also owns three weekly newspapers in Washington state.

Howard Publications — Box 570, Oceanside, CA 92049; tel (619) 433-5771; fax (619) 433-2531
President — Robert S Howard; Vice President/Administration — Richard D Newell; Vice President — Thomas W Howard.
Escondido-Oceanside (CA) North County Times (mS), Temecula (CA) Californian (mS); Craig (CO) Press (e); Twin Falls (ID) Times-News (mS); Charleston (IL) Times Courier (m), Freeport (IL) Journal-Standard (e), Mattoon (IL) Journal-Gazette (m), Pekin (IL) Daily Times (e); Munster (IN) Times (mS); Waterloo (IA) Courier (eS); Maysville (KY) Ledger-Independence (m); Auburn (NY) Citizen-Advertiser (eS), Corning (NY) Leader (mS), Glens Falls (NY) Post-Star (mS); Carlisle (PA) Sentinel (e); Orangeburg (SC) Times & Democrat (mS); Casper (WY) Star-Tribune (mS).
Note: Howard Publications also owns 50% interest in the Sioux City (IA) Journal with Hagadone Corp.

Huckle Publishing Inc. — 6291 Peninsula Dr., Traverse City, MI 49686; tel (616) 929-3571
President — James Huckle.
Faribault (MN) Daily News (mS), Owatonna (MN) People's Press (mS).

I

Independent Media Group Inc. — Box 219, Watseka, IL 60970-0219; tel (815) 432-6066
President/CEO — Anthony A Allegretti; Controller — Gordon Cody.
Chippewa (WI) Herald-Telegram (eS), Baraboo (WI) News Republic (eS), Portage (WI) Daily Register (mS), Shawano (WI) Evening Leader (eS).
Note: Independent Media Group Inc. also owns one twice-weekly newspaper in Wisconsin.

Independent Newspapers Inc. (DE) — PO Box 7001, Dover, DE 19903; tel (800) 426-4192
Chairman/CEO — Joe Smyth; President-Delmarva — Tamra Brittingham; President-Arizona — Ed Dulin; President-Florida — Richard Hitt; Chief Financial Officer — Chris Engel.
Dover (DE) Delaware State News (mS), Lewes (DE) Daily Whale (mS), Okeechobee (FL) Daily News (mS); Cambridge (MD) Daily Banner (e).
Note: This group also publishes 10 weeklies and three monthlies in Arizona, two weeklies in Delaware, seven weeklies and one monthly in Florida and two weeklies and one monthly in Maryland.

Independent Newspapers Inc. (MI) — 100 Macomb Daily Dr.; PO Box 707, Mt Clemens, MI 48043; tel (313) 469-4510; fax (313) 469-4512
President/Publisher/CEO — J Gene Chambers.
Mt. Clemens (MI) Macomb Daily (e), Royal Oak (MI) Daily Tribune (e).
Note: This group also owns 12 weeklies.

Independent Publications Inc. — 945 Haverford Rd., Bryn Mawr, PA 19010; tel (215) 527-6330
President — William L McLean III; Vice President — Andrew T Bickford; Vice President/Treasurer — Charles E Catherwood.
Nashua (NH) Telegraph (eS), Geneva (NY) Finger Lakes Times (eS), Du Bois (PA) Courier-Express (e), Du Bois (PA) Tri County Sunday (S).

Inland Industries Inc. — PO Box 15999, Lenexa, KS 66215; tel (913) 492-9050
President/Chairman — Clark Murray; Vice Chairman — Wright (Bud) Coulson; Exec. Vice President — Jack D Burton.
Fairfield (IA) Daily Ledger (e), Mt Pleasant (IA) News (e), Washington (IA) Evening Journal (e); Kansas City (KS) Kansan (eS).
Note: Inland also owns and publishes weeklies in Belton and Harrisonville, MO, and Shawnee, KS, as well as a tri-weekly in Lee's Summit, MO. All Inland owned newspapers print and distribute separate TMC shoppers. In addition to its newspaper properties, Inland owns and operates Inland Newspaper Machinery Corp., Miller Cooper Ink and Graphic Supplies Co., Solna Web USA Inc., Inland Graphics International L.C. serving Latin America with offices in Miami and the 5 Star 5 Diamond C Lazy U Guest Ranch in Granby, CO.

J

Johnson Newspaper Corp. — 260 Washington St., Watertown, NY 13601; tel (315) 782-1000; fax (315) 782-2337
President/Treasurer — John B Johnson; Vice President/Secretary — Catherine C Johnson; General Manager — Kenneth A Holloway.
Batavia (NY) Daily News (e), Catskill (NY) Daily Mail (e), Malone (NY) Telegram (e), Watertown (NY) Daily Times (eS).

Carl A Jones Newspapers — PO Box 1717, Johnson City, TN 37605; tel (615) 929-3111
President — Tim P Jones; Secretary — John A Jones; Vice President — Carleton A Jones III; Treasurer — Alice J Torbett.
Johnson City (TN) Press (mS), Lebanon (TN) Democrat (m).
Note: This group also publishes six weekly newspapers.

Journal Newspapers Inc. — 2720 Prosperity Ave., Fairfax, VA 22034-1000; tel (703) 560-4000; fax (703) 846-8301
Chairman — Rupert Phillips; President — Karl Spain; Publisher — Ryan E Phillips; Sr. Editor — Jane Touzalin.
Lanham (MD) Prince George's Journal (m); Rockville (MD) Montgomery Journal (m); Alexandria (VA) Journal (m), Arlington (VA) Journal (m), Fairfax (VA) Journal (m), Manassas (VA) Prince William Journal (m).
Note: This group also publishes five weeklies in Virginia and five in Maryland.

Journal Register Co. — 50 W. State St., State Street Sq., Trenton, NJ 08608-1298; tel (609) 396-2200; fax (609) 396-2292

The Proven Professional.

Richard L. Hare

- Consultant to 300 dailies, weeklies, and shoppers in last 20 years
- Market wise in 50 states and Canada
- Expert manager, trainer
- Executive recruiter
- Successful broker and appraiser

Hare Associates, Inc.
62 Black Walnut Drive
Rochester, New York 14615
716/621-6873

Celebrating Twenty Years of Professional Service

Newspaper groups

President/CEO — Robert M Jelenic; Exec. Vice President/CFO/Treasurer — Jean B Clifton; Vice President-Technology — Allen J Mailman; Vice President-Marketing & Promotion — Trish K Dresser; Vice President-Production — William J Higginson; Vice President-Finance — John Collins; Vice President-Advertising — Michael J Lynch; Corporate Controller — Jeffrey P Krisel; Information Services Director — Douglas E Graham; Corporate Circulation Director — Anthony M Simmons; Corporate Communication Director — Diane B Pardee; Director of Internal Audit — Alan J Leslie.

Bristol (CT) Press (e), Middletown (CT) Press (m), New Britain (CT) Herald (e), New Haven (CT) Register (m), Torrington (CT) Register Citizen (m); Alton (IL) Telegraph (m); Fall River (MA) Herald News (m); Trenton (NJ) Trentonian (mS); Troy (NY) Record (mS); Dover-New Philadelphia (OH) Times Reporter (mS), Lake County (OH) News-Herald (mS), Lorain (OH) Morning Journal (mS); Norristown (PA) Times Herald (mS), Phoenixville (PA) Phoenix (m), West Chester (PA) Daily Local News (mS); Pawtucket (RI) Times (m), Woonsocket (RI) Call (mS).

Note: Journal Register Co. also publishes 94 non-daily publications with 2.2 million distribution: 40 weekly newspapers in the greater St. Louis area operating under Suburban Newspapers of Greater St. Louis Inc. (SNGSL); 40 weekly newspapers operating under Shoreling Newspapers, Imprint Newspapers and Elm City Newspapers; four real estate magazines operating under Gamer Publications in Connecticut; 10 weekly newspapers in the Philadelphia area; and four weekly newspapers in southern Rhode Island operating under Wilson Newspapers. In addition Journal Register Co. owns three commercial printing companies: Midwest Offset in Dover-New Philadelphia, OH; Mississippi Valley Offset in St. Louis, MO; and Imprint Printing in North Haven, CT. The company also operates a publishing industry software development company, Integrated Newspaper Systems Inc., in Trenton, NJ.

K

Kearns-Tribune Corp. — 400 Tribune Bldg., 8th Fl., Salt Lake City, UT 84111; tel (801) 237-2031; fax (801) 237-2022
President/Publisher — Dominic Welch; Vice President/Deputy Publisher — Thomas McCarthy.
Lewiston (ID) Tribune (mS), Moscow-Pullman (ID) Daily News (e); Sparks (NV) Tribune (eS); Salt Lake City (UT) Tribune (mS).
Note: This group also owns one weekly newspaper in Idaho.

Knight-Ridder Inc. — One Herald Plaza, Miami, FL 33132-1693; tel (305) 376-3800; fax (305) 376-3876
Chairman/CEO — P Anthony Ridder; President — John C Fontaine; Sr. Vice President-Finance/CFO — Ross Jones; Vice President-News — Clark Hoyt; Vice President-Operations — Frank McComas; Vice President-Corporate Relations — Polk Laffoon IV; Vice President-Technology — Larry Marbert; Vice President-Marketing — Jerome S Tilis; Vice President-News — Marty Claus; Vice President-Research — Virginia Fielder; Vice President/Secretary — Douglas C Harris; Vice President/President-BIS — David K Ray; Vice President-Finance & Administration — Tally Liu; Vice President/Controller — Gary Effren; Vice President-Supply — Homer E Taylor; Vice President-Operations — Peter Pitz; Vice President-Human Resources — Mary Jean Connors; Vice President/General Counsel — Cristina L Mendoza; Vice President/New Ventures — Sharon Studer.
Antioch (CA) Ledger-Dispatch (eS), Long Beach (CA) Press-Telegram (mS), Pleasanton (CA) Valley Times (mS), Richmond (CA) West County Times (mS), San Jose (CA) Mercury News (mS), Walnut Creek (CA) Contra Costa Times (mS), Boulder (CO) Daily Camera (m); Boca Raton (FL) News (mS), Bradenton (FL) Herald (mS), Miami (FL) Herald (mS), Tallahassee (FL) Democrat (mS); Columbus (GA) Ledger-Enquirer (mS), Macon (GA) Telegraph (mS), Milledgeville (GA) Union-Recorder (m); Fort Wayne (IN) News-Sentinel (e), Gary (IN) Post-Tribune (mS); Wichita (KS) Eagle (mS); Lexington (KY) Herald-Leader (mS); Detroit (MI) Free Press (mS); Duluth (MN) News-Tribune (mS), Saint Paul (MN) Pioneer Press (mS); Biloxi (MS) Sun Herald (mS); Charlotte (NC) Observer (mS); Grand Forks (ND) Herald (mS); Akron (OH) Beacon Journal (mS); Philadelphia (PA) Daily News (m), Philadelphia (PA) Inquirer (mS), State College (PA) Centre Daily Times (mS); Columbia (SC) State (mS), Myrtle Beach (SC) Sun News (mS); Aberdeen (SD) American News (mS).

L

Lancaster Management Inc. — 645 Walnut St.; PO Box 609, Gadsden, AL 35902; tel (205) 543-3417; fax (205) 543-3548
Chariman — James D Lancaster; President — Charles W Lancaster; Vice President — Michael F Schuver; Vice President — James D Lancaster Jr; Vice President — John W Roberts; Vice President — Peggy R Roberts.
Murray (KY) Ledger & Times (e); Branson (MO) Daily News (m); Hopewell (VA) News (e).
Note: Lancaster also publishes three weekly newspapers in Arkansas, five in Iowa, one in Mississippi and four in Missouri, as well as other non-daily publications in Georgia, Kentucky and Mississippi.

Landmark Communications Inc. — 150 W. Brambleton Ave., Norfolk, VA 23501; tel (804) 446-2010; fax (804) 446-2489
Chairman — Frank Batten; President/CEO — John O Wynne; Chief Operating Officer — Doug Fox; Vice President/Treasurer — James D Wagner; Vice Pres./Corporate Counsel — Becky Powhatan; Exec. Vice Pres./General Counsel — Louis F Ryan; Vice President/Controller — Colleen Pittman.
Crystal River (FL) Citrus County Chronicle (mS); Elizabethtown (KY) News-Enterprise (e); Westminster (MD) Carroll County Times (m); Los Alamos (NM) Monitor (e); Greensboro (NC) News & Record (mS); Norfolk (VA) Virginian-Pilot (mS), Roanoke (VA) Times (mS).
Note: Landmark also has a minority interest in the Capital-Gazette Communications Inc. in Annapolis, MD, and publishes 29 non-dailies, 23 shoppers, 15 specialty publications and 40 classified advertising/photo guide publications. It operates two television stations, the Weather Channel, a national cable network, the Travel Channel, Travel UK and Travel Channel-Latin America.

Lee Enterprises Inc. — 215 N. Main, 400 Putnam Bldg., Davenport, IA 52801-1924; tel (319) 383-2100; fax (319) 323-9608
Chairman — Lloyd G Schermer; President/CEO — Richard D Gottlieb; Vice President-Newspaper — Ron L Rickman; Vice President-Human Resources — Floyd Whellan; Vice President-Finance/Treasurer/CFO — Larry L Bloom.
Carbondale (IL) Southern Illinoisan (eS), Decatur (IL) Herald & Review (mS), Kewanee (IL) Star Courier (e); Davenport (IA) Quad-City Times (mS), Mason City (IA) Globe-Gazette (mS), Muscatine (IA) Journal (e), Ottumwa (IA) Courier (m); Winona (MN) Daily News (mS); Billings (MT) Gazette (mS), Butte (MT) Montana Standard (mS), Helena (MT) Independent Record (eS), Missoula (MT) Missoulian (mS), Lincoln (NE) Journal Star (m); Bismarck (ND) Tribune (eS); Corvallis (OR) Gazette-Times (mS); Rapid City (SD) Daily Journal (mS), La Crosse (WI) Tribune (eS), Madison (WI) Wisconsin State Journal (mS), Racine (WI) Journal Times (eS).
Note: This group owns and operates eight network-affiliated television stations, 19 daily newspapers and 39 weekly and specialty publications. It also manufactures graphic arts products for the newspaper industry through NAPP Systems Inc. in San Marcos, CA.

Lehman Communications Corp. — 350 Terry St.; PO Box 299, Longmont, CO 80502; tel (303) 776-2244
Publisher — Edward Lehman.
Canon City (CO) Daily Record (e), Longmont (CO) Daily Times-Call (eS), Loveland (CO) Daily Reporter-Herald (e).

Lewis Newspapers — 1209 State St.; PO Box 559, Lawrenceville, IL 62439; tel (618) 943-2331; fax (618) 943-3976
President — Larry H Lewis.
Lawrenceville (IL) Record (e), Robinson (IL) News (e).
Note: This group also owns two weekly newspapers.

Livermore Newspapers — 123 S. Broadway; PO Box 2470, Edmond, OK 73083; tel (405) 341-2121; fax (405) 340-7363
Chairman — E K Livermore Sr; President — E K Livermore Jr.
Edmond (OK) Sun (eS); Mineral Wells (TX) Daily Index (eS).

Lorain County Printing & Publishing Corp. — 225 East Ave.; PO Box 4010, Elyria, OH 44036; tel (216) 329-7000; fax (216) 329-7272
President — A D Hudnutt.
Elyria (OH) Chronicle-Telegram (eS), Medina (OH) Medina County Gazette (m).

M

Frank Mayborn Enterprises Inc. — 10 S. 3rd; PO Box 6114, Temple, TX 76501; tel (817) 778-4444
President — Sue Mayborn.
Killeen (TX) Daily Herald (mS), Temple (TX) Daily Telegram (mS).

McClatchy Newspapers — PO Box 15779, Sacramento, CA 95852; tel (916) 321-1855/(916) 321-1846
Chairman — James McClatchy; President/CEO — Erwin Potts; Vice President-Operations — William Honeysett; Vice President-Finance — James P Smith; Vice President-News — Gregory Favre.
Anchorage (AK) Daily News (mS); Fresno (CA) Bee (mS), Gilroy (CA) Dispatch (m), Hollister (CA) Freelance (m), Modesto (CA) Bee (mS), Sacramento (CA) Bee (mS); Beaufort (SC) Gazette (mS), Hilton Head Island (SC) Inland Packet (mS), Rock Hill (SC) The Herald (mS); Ellensburg (WA) Daily Record (m), Pasco-Kennewick-Richland (WA) Tri-City Herald (mS), Tacoma (WA) Morning News Tribune (mS).
Note: This group also owns and operates Legitech, a legislative voting tracking service operating in California, New York and Washington, DC. This group also publishes: Senior Spectrum, 14 senior citizen publications throughout California, Colorado, Nevada, Washington and Oregon; four weeklies in California; one weekly in Washington; and two weeklies, one monthly and one shopper in Southern California.

McNaughton Newspapers — 315 G St.; PO Box 1078, Davis, CA 95617; tel (916) 756-0800.
Davis (CA) Enterprise (eS), Fairfield (CA) Daily Republic (mS), Placerville (CA) Mountain Democrat (m).
Note: This group also owns one weekly newspaper.

Media General Inc. — 333 E. Grace St.; PO Box 85333, Richmond, VA 23293; tel (804) 649-6000; fax (804) 649-6898
Chairman — J Stewart Bryan III; Vice Chairman — James S Evans; President/CEO — J Stewart Bryan III; Sr. Vice President/CFO — M N Morton; President-Virginia Newspapers Inc. — Terry L Hall; Vice President/Business Mgr.-Virginia Newspapers Inc. — Robert E MacPherson; Vice President — Graham Woodlief; Vice President-Corporate Communications — Robert W Pendergast; Director-Information Services — Walter L Waleski Jr; Director-Research — Stephen T Shaw; Asst. Secretary/Dir.-Employee Benefits — D P Cooper; Controller — Steven Y Dickinson; Treasurer — Steven R Zacharias; Secretary/General Counsel — George L Mahoney.
Tampa (FL) Tribune (mS); Winston-Salem (NC) Journal (mS); Richmond (VA) Times-Dispatch (mS).

Virginia Newspapers Inc.:
President — Terry L Hall; Vice President/Business Mgr. — Robert E MacPherson.

John A. Park, Jr. & Associates

Expertise and reliability for owners considering the sale of their *newspapers*.

(919) 848-7202
Fax: (919) 848-7148
202 Springmoor Drive
Raleigh, NC 27615

Available for private, confidential consultation
Nationwide Personal Service

Charlottesville (VA) Daily Progress (mS), Culpeper (VA) Star-Exponent (mS), Lynchburg (VA) News & Advance (mS), Suffolk (VA) News-Herald (eS).

Note: Media General also owns 13 weeklies in West Central Florida and has 40% interest in Denver Newspapers Inc. (a division of MediaNews). Virginia Newspapers also operates several non-daily publications in Virginia.

MediaNews Inc. — 1560 Broadway, Ste. 1485, Denver, CO 80202; tel (303) 820-1952; fax (303) 820-1929
Chairman — Richard B Scudder; Vice Chairman/President/CEO — W Dean Singleton.
Fairbanks (AK) Daily News-Miner (mS); Denver (CO) Post (mS); Passaic (NJ) North Jersey Herald News (mS), Salem (NJ) Today's Sunbeam (mS), Woodbury (NJ) Gloucester County Times (eS); Las Cruces (NM) Sun-News (eS); Easton (PA) Express Times (mS), Johnstown (PA) Tribune Democrat (mS), York (PA) Dispatch (e); Woodbridge (VA) Potomac News (e).

Alameda Newspaper Group:
Alameda (CA) Times-Star (m), Fremont (CA) Argus (mS), Hayward (CA) Daily Review (mS), Oakland (CA) Tribune (mS), Pleasanton (CA) Tri-Valley Herald (mS).

New England Newspapers Inc.:
Pittsfield (MA) Berkshire Eagle (mS); Bennington (VT) Banner (m), Brattleboro (VT) Reformer (m).
Note: New England Newspapers (formerly Eagle Publishing) also operates the Manchester (VT) Journal weekly.

Media Services Group — 121 W. Summer St.; PO Box 1630, Greeneville, TN 37744; tel (423) 638-4181
Chairman — John M Jones; President — Gregg K Jones; Chief Operating Officer — Bruce Morrison.
Athens (TN) Post-Athenian (e), Greeneville (TN) Sun (e).
Note: This group also publishes four semi-weeklies, two tri-weeklies, one monthly business publication, one monthly running publication, one monthly outdoor publication and one quarterly tourism publication. Media Services Group also owns five radio stations.

KAMEN & CO.
GROUP SERVICES

Worldwide
Newspaper Management Consulting Firm

N.Y. (516) 379-2797
FL. (813) 786-5930

- Market Appraisals
- Restructurings
- Circulation Development
- Evaluations & Research
- Executive Search
- Newspaper Design
- Staff Training
- Conversions
- Market Development & Promotion
- Brokering/Negotiations

2355 Pershing Blvd., Suite 301
Baldwin, NY 11510

Mid-South Management Co. Inc. — PO Box 1634, Spartanburg, SC 29304; tel (803) 583-2907
Chairman/President — Phyllis B DeLapp; Vice President — Andrew M Babb; Secretary/Treasurer — Loretta W Conner.
La Grange (GA) Daily News (e); Laurinburg (NC) Exchange (e), Mt Airy (NC) News (e); Union (SC) Times (e); Williamson (WV) News (e).
Note: This group also owns and operates seven weeklies in North Carolina and Ohio.

Milliman Communications — 624 S. Cedar St; PO Box 160, Mason, MI 48854; tel (517) 676-9393; fax (517) 676-9402
Chairman — Richard Milliman; President — Teresa Fitzwater; Editor — Dirk Milliman.
Albion (MI) Recorder (e), Marshall (MI) Chronicle (mS), Three Rivers (MI) Commercial News (e).

Moffitt Newspapers — PO Box 8565, Roanoke, VA 24014; tel (703) 344-2489
Chairman/CEO — John F Moffitt; Vice President — Frank L Spicer; Vice President — W A Johnson.
Lewisburg (WV) Daily News (e), Welch (WV) Daily News (e).

Morgan City Newspapers Inc. — 1014 Front St.; PO Box 948, Morgan City, LA 70381; tel (504) 384-8370; fax (504) 384-4255
Owner/President/Publisher — Doyle E Shirley; Editor/Assoc. Publisher — Steve Shirley; General Mgr./Advertising Director — Andy Shirley; Managing Editor — Ted McManus; Circulation Mgr. — Kevin Fernandez.
Franklin (LA) Banner-Tribune (e), Morgan City (LA) Daily Review (e).

Morris Communications Corp. — PO Box 936, Augusta, GA 30913; tel (706) 724-0851
Chairman/CEO — William S Morris III; President — Paul Simon; Vice President — Edward B Skinner; Secretary/Treasurer — W A Herman III.
Juneau (AK) Empire (eS), Kenai (AK) The Peninsula Clarion (m); Jacksonville (FL) Florida Times-Union (mS), St. Augustine (FL) Record (eS); Amarillo (TX) Daily Times (m), Amarillo (TX) Globe-Times (e), Amarillo (TX) Sunday News-Globe (S), Lubbock (TX) Avalanche-Journal (mS).

Southeastern Newspapers Corp.:
Athens (GA) Banner-Herald (e), Athens (GA) Daily News (m), Athens (GA) Daily News & Banner-Herald (S), Augusta (GA) Chronicle (mS), Savannah (GA) Morning News (m), Savannah (GA) Evening Press (e), Savannah (GA) News-Press (S).

Stauffer Communications Inc.: Sixth & Jefferson, Topeka, KS 66607; tel (913) 295-1111
Conway (AR) Log Cabin Democrat (eS); Glenwood Springs (CO) Post (e); Winter Haven (FL) News Chief (eS); Arkansas City (KS) Traveler (e), Dodge City (KS) Daily Globe (m), Newton (KS) Kansan (e), Pittsburg (KS) Morning Sun (mS), Topeka (KS) Capital-Journal (mS); Hillsdale (MI) News (e), Holland (MI) Sentinel (eS); Brainerd (MN) Dispatch (eS); Blue Springs (MO) Examiner (e), Hannibal (MO) Courier-Post (m), Independence (MO) Examiner (e); Grand Island (NE) Independent (mS), York (NE) Daily News-Times (e); Ardmore (OK) Daily Ardmoreite (eS), Shawnee (OK) News Star (e); Yankton (SD) Press & Dakotan (e); Oak Ridge (TN) Oak Ridger (eS).

Note: The three Athens, GA, newspapers are published by Athens Newspapers Inc., a subsidiary of Southeastern Newspapers Corp. Morris Communications publishes six magazines and two non-daily papers in South Carolina and Texas.

Morris Newspaper Corp. — PO Box 8167, Savannah, GA 31412; tel (912) 233-1281; fax (912) 232-4639
President — Charles H Morris; Vice President/CFO — Eddie Brooks; Vice President/Secretary — Miriam Potter.
Manteca (CA) Bulletin (mS), Santa Clarita (CA) Signal & Enterprise (mS); Statesboro (GA) Herald (mS); Great Bend (KS) Tribune (eS); Murfreesboro (TN) Daily News-Journal (eS).
Note: This group also includes 20 weeklies, two bi-weeklies, seven tri-weeklies, eight shoppers, three television stations (two NBC affiliates, one ABC affiliate) and two commercial web press printing plants.

Murphy Newspaper Group — 1226 Ogden Ave., Superior, WI 54880; tel (715) 394-4411; fax (715) 394-9404
President — John B Murphy; Vice President — Elizabeth M Burns; Vice President-Finance — George A Nelson; Secretary — Lois L Wessman; Treasurer — Robert J Wallace.
Hibbing (MN) Tribune (eS), Virginia (MN) Mesabi News (eS); Ashland (WI) Press (m), Superior (WI) Telegram (e).

N

New York Times Co. — 229 W. 43rd St., New York, NY 10036; tel (212) 556-1234
Chairman — Arthur O Sulzberger; President — Lance R Primis; Sr. Vice President/CFO — Diane P Baker; Sr. Vice President/Deputy COO — David L Gorham; Sr. Vice President — Katharine P Darrow; Secretary — Laura J Corwin; Vice President/Corporate Controller — Frank R Gatti; Vice President/Tax — Thomas Nied; Vice President/General Counsel — Solomon B Watson IV; Vice President/Forest Products — Stephen Golden; Vice President/Human Resources — Leslie A Mardenborough; Vice President-Planning/Operations — Gordon Medencia; Vice President-Corporate Communications — Nancy Nielsen; Vice President-Internal Audit — Jack Hayon; Vice President-Broadcasting — C Frank Roberts; Treasurer — Richard G Thomas; Publisher — Arthur Sulzberger Jr; President/General Mgr. — Russell T Lewis; Exec. Vice President/Deputy General Mgr. — John M O'Brien; Exec. Vice President/Sales — William L Pollak; Vice President-Advertising — Janet L Robinson; Vice President-Advertising — Alexis Buryk; Sr. Vice President-Mktg. — James A Cutie; Publisher-Times Daily (AL) — Frank Helderman Jr; Publisher-Times (AL) — Roger N Hawkins; Publisher-News (AL) — Ron Sawyer; Publisher-News Press (CA) — P Steven Ainsley; Publisher-Press Democrat (CA) — Michael J Parman; Publisher-Sun (FL) — John Fitzwater; Publisher-Reporter (FL) — Don Caldwell; Publisher-Ledger (FL) — Don R Whitworth; Publisher-Star-Banner (FL) — Charles J Stout; Publisher-Daily News (FL) — John E Newhouse II; Publisher-Herald-Tribune (FL) — Lynn Matthews; Publisher-Daily Courier (LA) — H Miles Forrest; Publisher-Daily World (LA) — Aaron Parsons; Publisher-Daily Comet (LA) — Christopher Bond; Publisher-Times-News (NC) — Paul Bairstow; Publisher-Dispatch (NC) — Joe S Sink Jr; Publisher-Morning Star (NC) — John A Lynch; Publisher-Herald-Journal (SC) — David O Roberts.
Boston (MA) Globe (mS); New York (NY) Times (mS).

New York Times Regional Newspaper Group: 3414 Peachtree Rd. N.E., Ste. 1100, Atlanta, GA 30326; tel (404) 262-5656; fax (404) 262-5649
President — Jim Weeks.
Florence (AL) Times Daily (mS), Gadsden (AL) Times (mS), Tuscaloosa (AL) News (mS); Santa Barbara (CA) News-Press (mS), Santa Rosa (CA) Press Democrat (mS); Gainesville (FL) Sun (mS), Lake City (FL) Reporter (e), Lakeland (FL) Ledger (mS), Ocala (FL) Star-Banner (mS), Palatka (FL) Daily News (e), Sarasota (FL) Herald-Tribune (mS); Houma (LA) Daily Courier (eS), Opelousas (LA) Daily World (e), Thibodaux (LA) Daily Comet (e); Hendersonville (NC) Times-News (m), Lexington (NC) Dispatch (e), Wilmington (NC) Morning Star (m); Spartanburg (SC) Herald-Journal (mS).

Note: The New York Times Co. also publishes three non-daily newspapers in Florida and numerous magazines. It also owns six television and two radio stations. It is half-owner of the International Herald Tribune, which is printed in Europe, with the Washington Post Co. It has an interest in a Canadian newsprint mill and a partnership interest in Madison Paper Industries which produces supercalendered paper for magazines.

Newhouse Newspapers — See Advance Publications.

News Leader Inc. — 716 E. Napoleon; PO Box 1999, Sulphur, LA 70664; tel (318) 527-7055; fax (318) 528-3044
President — Al Gensheimer; Vice President — Ophelia Hayes.
De Ridder (LA) Beauregard Daily News (mS), Leesville (LA) Daily Leader (mS), Sulphur (LA) Southwest Daily News (mS).
Note: This group also owns five weekly newspapers.

News Media Corp. — 211 Hwy 38 E.; PO Box 46, Rochelle, IL 61068; tel (815) 562-2061; fax (815) 562-7048
President — John C Tompkins; Vice President — Michael Tompkins; Secretary — Michael Rand.
Watsonville (CA) Register-Pajaronian (e); Alamosa (CO) Valley Courier (e); Clinton (IL) Daily Journal (e).
Note: This group also owns three weekly newspapers in Illinois, five in West Virginia, seven in Colorado, one in Arizona, nine in Wyoming, and four in California.

Newspapers of New England — 1 Monitor Dr.; PO Box 1177, Concord, NH 03302-1177; tel (603) 224-5301 ext. 262; fax (603) 224-5301 ext. 256
Chairman — Donald R Dwight; President/Treasurer — George W Wilson; Controller — Michael P Kapusta.
Greenfield (MA) Recorder (e); Concord (NH) Monitor (m), Lebanon (NH) Valley News (m).
Note: This group also owns one weekly in New Hampshire.

Nixon Newspapers Inc. — 35 W. 3rd St.; PO Box 1149, Peru, IN 46970; tel (317) 473-3091; fax (317) 473-8428
President/CEO — John R Nixon; Exec Vice President/COO — Kenneth C Bronson; Vice President-Finance/CFO — John W Stackhouse; Secretary/Controller — Deborah M Huff.
Watseka (IL) Times-Republic (e); Brazil (IN) Times (e), Connersville (IN) News-Examiner (e), Frankfort (IN) Times (e), Michigan City (IN) News-Dispatch (e), New Castle (IN) Courier-Times (e), Peru (IN) Daily Tribune (e), Wabash (IN) Plain Dealer (e); Hammond (LA) Daily Star (e).
Note: This group also operates three non-daily newspapers in Illinois and Indiana.

O

Ogden Newspapers — 1500 Main St., Wheeling, WV 26003; tel (304) 233-0100
President/Publisher — G Ogden Nutting; Vice President/General Mgr. — Robert M Nutting; Vice President — William C Nutting; Secretary/Business Mgr. — William O Nutting; Treasurer/Controller — Duane D Wittman.
Cape Coral (FL) Breeze (e); Estherville (IA) Daily News (m), Fort Dodge (IA) Messenger (eS), Marshalltown (IA) Times-Republican (e), Webster City (IA) Freeman-Journal (e); Alpena (MI) News (e); Fairmont (MN) Sentinel (m), Marshall (MN) Independent (m), New Ulm (MN) Journal (mS); Dunkirk (NY) Evening Observer (e), Gloversville (NY) Leader-Herald (eS), Jamestown (NY) Post-Journal (eS), Saranac Lake (NY) Adirondack Enterprise (e); Minot (ND) Daily News (mS); Martins Ferry (OH) Times-Leader (eS), Tiffin (OH) Advertiser-Tribune (mS); Lewistown (PA) Sentinel (e), Williamsport (PA) Sun-Gazette (eS); Elkins (WV) Inter-Mountain (e), Martinsburg (WV) Journal (mS), Parkersburg (WV) Sentinel (e), Parkersburg (WV) News (mS), Wheeling (WV) Intelligencer (m), Wheeling (WV) News-Register (eS); Marshfield (WI) News-Herald (e).

Omaha World-Herald Co. — World-Herald Sq., Omaha, NE 68102; tel (402) 444-1000
Chief Executive Officer — John Gottschalk; Sr. Vice President/CFO — A William Kernen;

Copyright ©1996 by the Editor & Publisher Co.

Sr. Vice President — William Donaldson; Sr. Vice President — G Woodson Howe; Vice President — Richard R Seibert; Vice President — Terry J Kroeger.
Stockton (CA) Record (mS); Columbus (NE) Telegram (eS), Kearney (NE) Hub (e), Omaha (NE) World-Herald (meS); Carlsbad (NM) Current-Argus (eS); Brookings (SD) Daily Register (e), Huron (SD) Daily Plainsman (mS).

Ottaway Newspapers Inc. — Rte. 416; PO Box 401, Campbell Hall, NY 10916; tel (914) 294-8181; fax (914) 294-1659
Chairman — James H Ottaway Jr; President/CEO — Richard A Myers; Vice President-Newspaper Operations — Joseph Richter; Vice President-Newspaper Operations — Frank O King; Vice President-Newspaper Operations — Beverly Jackson; Vice President-News — David E Brace; Vice President-Finance and Law — Peter G Stone; Vice President-Production — Larry L Hoffman; Vice President-Financial Operations/Controller — William A Zurilla; Asst. Vice President-Risk Management/Treasurer — David P Stewart; Asst. Vice President-Employee Relations — Catherine D Paffenroth; Secretary — Robert D Sack.
Sun City (AZ) Daily News Sun (e); Santa Cruz County (CA) Sentinel (mS); Danbury (CT) News-Times (mS); Ashland (KY) Daily Independent (eS); Gloucester (MA) Daily Times (e), Hyannis (MA) Cape Cod Times (mS), New Bedford (MA) Standard-Times (mS), Newburyport (MA) Daily News (e), Salem (MA) Evening News (e); Traverse City (MI) Record-Eagle (mS); Mankato (MN) Free Press (m); Joplin (MO) Globe (mS); Middletown (NY) Times Herald-Record (mS), Oneonta (NY) Daily Star (m), Plattsburgh (NY) Press-Republican (mS); Medford (OR) Mail Tribune (mS); Sharon (PA) Herald (eS), Stroudsburg (PA) Pocono Record (mS), Sunbury (PA) Daily Item (mS).
Note: This group also publishes 13 non-daily newspapers and 18 shoppers. Ottaway Newspapers is a wholly-owned subsidiary of Dow Jones & Company Inc.

P

Park Communications Inc. — 333 W. Main St., Ste. 1700, Lexington, KY 40507; tel (606) 252-7275; fax (606) 252-2234
President — Wright M Thomas; Vice President-Newpapers — Ralph J Martin; Director-Advertising Sales-Newspapers — William Chuisano; Director-Circulation Sales-Newspapers — Dale Gerstenslager.
Warner Robins (GA) Sun (e), Warner Robins (GA) Sunday Sun (S); Burley (ID) South Idaho Press (eS); Effingham (IL) Daily News (e), Macomb (IL) Daily Journal (eS); Jeffersonville (IN) Evening News (e), Plymouth (IN) Pilot-News (e); Somerset (KY) Commonwealth-Journal (eS); Coldwater (MI) Daily Reporter (e); Bemidji (MN) Pioneer (mS); Hudson (NY) Register-Star (eS), Lockport (NY) Union-Star & Journal (e), Ogdensburg (NY) Courier Observer (m), Ogdensburg (NY) Journal (e), Ogdensburg (NY) Advance News (S); Aberdeen (NC) Citizen News-Record (eS), Clinton (NC) Sampson Independent (eS), Concord (NC) Tribune (eS), Eden (NC) Daily News (e), Elizabethtown (NC) Bladen Journal (m), Kannapolis (NC) Daily Independent (eS), Lumberton (NC) Robesonian (eS), Marion (NC) McDowell News (e), Morganton (NC) News-Herald (eS), Rockingham (NC) Daily Journal (e), Statesville (NC) Record & Ledger (e); Devils Lake (ND) Daily Journal (e); McAlester (OK) News-Capital & Democrat (eS), Sapulpa (OK) Daily Herald (eS); Manassas (VA) Journal Messenger (e), Waynesboro (VA) News-Virginian (e).
Note: This group also publishes 28 weekly newspapers and 48 shopping newspapers and owns nine television stations and 22 radio stations.

Paxton Media Group Inc. — 408 Kentucky Ave.; PO Box 2300, Paducah, KY 42002-2300; tel (502) 443-1771; fax (502) 442-8188
President/CEO — Fred Paxton; Chief Financial Officer — David Paxton; Vice President-Newspapers — Jay Frizzo.
Paragould (AR) Daily Press (mS), Russellville (AR) Courier-Democrat (mS), Searcy (AR) Daily Citizen (eS); Carrollton (GA) Times-Georgian (mS), Douglasville (GA) Douglas County Sentinel (m); Madisonville (KY) Messenger (mS), Paducah (KY) Sun (mS); Corinth (MS) Daily Corinthian (e); Henderson (NC) Daily Dispatch (mS), Lenoir (NC) News-Topic (e); Dyersburg (TN) State Gazette (mS), Sevierville (TN) Mountain Press (mS).
Note: Paxton Media Group Inc. also owns and operates an NBC-affiliated television station in Paducah, KY, and a number of weeklies in Arkansas, Mississippi, Georgia and Missouri.

Peoria Journal Star Inc. — 1 News Plaza, Peoria, IL 61643; tel (309) 686-3000; fax (309) 686-3052
Publisher — John McConnell; Vice President/Treasurer — Fred Bergia.
Peoria (IL) Journal Star (all day,S), Galesburg (IL) Register-Mail (e).

Pioneer Group — 502 N. State St., Big Rapids, MI 49307; tel (616) 796-4831; fax (616) 796-1152
President/CEO — Jack Batdorff; General Manager — John Batdorff II; Chief Financial Officer — Ruth Meikle; Editorial Director — Bob Diel; Circulation Director — Tony Walker.
Big Rapids (MI) Pioneer (m), Manistee (MI) News-Advocate (e).
Note: Pioneer Group also owns six weekly newspapers and six shoppers.

Pioneer Newspapers — 221 First Ave. W., Ste. 405, Seattle, WA 98119; tel (206) 284-4424
General Counsel/Vice President — Bradley F Henke; President — David R Lord; Secretary/Treasurer — DeLancey B Lewis; Controller — David P Sonnichsen.
Nampa/Caldwell (ID) Idaho Press-Tribune (eS), Pocatello (ID) Idaho State Journal (eS); Bozeman (MT) Daily Chronicle (eS), Havre (MT) Daily News (e); Klamath Falls (OR) Herald and News (eS); Logan (UT) Herald Journal (eS); Mt Vernon (WA) Skagit Valley Herald (e).
Note: Pioneer Newspapers also publishes weeklies in Idaho, Oregon and Washington.

Pryor Publishing Co. — 105 S. Adair (74361); PO Box 308, Pryor, OK 74362; tel (918) 825-3292; fax (918) 825-1965
General Manager — Henry Goodman; Editor — Terry Aylward.
Grove (OK) Source (m), Pryor (OK) Daily Times (eS).
Note: Pryor Publishing also owns four weekly newspapers.

Pulitzer Publishing Co. — 900 N. Tucker Blvd., St Louis, MO 63101; tel (314) 340-8402; fax (314) 340-3125
Chairman/President/CEO — Michael E Pulitzer; Sr. Vice President-Finance — Ronald H Ridgway; Sr. Vice President-Broadcasting Operations — Ken J Elkins; Sr. Vice President-Newspaper Operations — Nicholas G Penniman IV; Secretary — James V Maloney; Asst. Secretary — Nancy K Rankin; Vice President — R Jeffrey Edwards; Vice President — Thomas E Jackson; Treasurer — James M Vogelpohl; Asst. Treasurer — Jon H Holt; Vice President/Director-Operations — Marvin G Kanne; Vice President/Director-Advertising — Thomas L Rees; Vice President/Director-Circulation — Fred Matthias; Vice President/Director-Marketing — Lynne S Moeller.
Tucson (AZ) Arizona Daily Star (mS); St Louis (MO) Post-Dispatch (mS).
Note: Pulitzer Publishing Co. also owns nine television stations and two radio stations.

Q

Quincy Newspapers Inc. — PO Box 909, Quincy, IL 62306-0909; tel (217) 223-5100
President/Treasurer — Thomas A Oakley; Controller/Asst. Treasurer — David A Graff; Vice President-Administration/Asst. Secretary — Ralph M Oakley; Secretary — Allen M Oakley; Asst. Secretary/Asst. Treasurer — Peter A Oakley.
Quincy (IL) Herald-Whig (eS); Newton (NJ) Herald (eS).
Note: Quincy Newspapers Inc. also owns five television stations and two radio stations.

R

Red Wing Publishing Co. — 2760 N. Service Dr.; PO Box 82, Red Wing, MN 55066; tel (612) 388-8235; fax (612) 388-8912
Chairman-all Operations — Arlin Albrecht; Secretary/Director — Marilyn Albrecht.
International Falls (MN) Daily Journal (e), Red Wing (MN) Republican-Eagle (e).
Note: This group also operates 15 weeklies.

Robinson-Pettis Publishing — 112 S. Creek St.; PO Box 751, Holdenville, OK 74848; tel (405) 379-5411; fax (405) 379-5413
President — Bill Robinson.
Holdenville (OK) Daily News (eS), Wewoka (OK) Daily Times (eS).
Note: Robinson-Pettis also owns three weekly newspapers.

Rust Communications — 301 Broadway; PO Box 699, Cape Girardeau, MO 63702-0699; tel (314) 335-6611
President — Gary Rust; Chief Operating Officer — Wally Lage; Business Mgr. — Dick Caldwell.
Blytheville (AR) Courier News (eS); Cape Girardeau (MO) Southeast Missourian (mS), Dexter (MO) Daily Statesman (eS), Kennett (MO) Daily Dunklin Democrat (eS), Poplar Bluff (MO) Daily American Republican (eS).
Note: Rust Communications also owns a number of weeklies in Missouri and Arkansas.

S

Sandusky-Norwalk Newspapers — 537 E. Center, Ste. 201, Kingsport, TN 37660; tel (423) 392-0295; fax (423) 392-4627
Chairman/President — David A Rau; Vice President/Treasurer — Peter Vogt; Secretary — Susan White Smith; General Counsel/CFO — Peter Vogt.
Grand Haven (MI) Tribune (e); Norwalk (OH) Reflector (e), Sandusky (OH) Register (eS); Kingsport (TN) Times-News (mS); Ogden (UT) Standard-Examiner (eS).

Schurz Communications Inc. — 225 W. Colfax, South Bend, IN 46626; tel (219) 287-1001; fax (219) 287-2257
President — Franklin D Schurz Jr; Vice President — James S Schurz; Vice President — Scott C Schurz; Vice President — E Berry Smith; Chief Financial Exec./Treasurer — James G Young Jr; Vice President/Secretary — Mary Schurz; Asst. Secretary/Treasurer — Anne G Strantz.
El Centro (CA) Imperial Valley Press; Bedford (IN) Times-Mail (e), Bloomington (IN) Herald-Times (mS), South Bend (IN) Tribune (eS); Danville (KY) Advocate-Messenger (e); Hagerstown (MD) Herald (mS), Hagerstown (MD) Mail (e).

Scripps Howard — 312 Walnut, 28th Fl.; PO Box 5380, Cincinnati, OH 45201-5380; tel (513) 977-3000; fax (513) 977-3721
Chairman — Lawrence A Leser; President/CEO — William R Burleigh; Sr. Vice President-Corporate Development — Craig C Standen; Sr. Vice President-Cable Television — F Steven Crawford; Sr. Vice President-Finance/Administration — Daniel J Castellini; Sr. Vice President-Broadcasting — Frank Gardner; Sr. Vice President-Newspapers — Alan M Horton.
Birmingham (AL) Post-Herald (m); Monterey (CA) Monterey County Herald (m); Denver (CO) Rocky Mountain News (mS); Naples (FL) Daily News (mS), Stuart (FL) News (mS); Evansville (IN) Courier (mS); Covington (KY) Kentucky Post (e); Albuquerque (NM) Tribune (e); Cincinnati (OH) Post (e); Knoxville (TN) News-Sentinel (mS), Memphis (TN) Commercial Appeal (mS); El Paso (TX) Herald-Post (e).
John P Scripps Newspapers:
Redding (CA) Record Searchlight (eS), San Luis Obispo (CA) Telegram-Tribune (e), Ventura County (CA) Star (mS); Bremerton (WA) Sun (e).
Note: The Ventura County Star publishes six editions: Ventura County Star, Simi Valley Star, Moorpark Star, Thousand Oaks Star, as well as Oxnard and Camarillo editions. Scripps Howard also operates nine television stations, cable TV in nine states serving 754,000 basic subscribers. It is also a worldwide syndicator and licensor of news features and comics, including Peanuts. Scripps Howard News Service is located in Washington, DC; the legal office is in Cleveland, OH.

Scripps League Newspapers Inc. — HCR 1; Box 38, Charlottesville, VA 22901; tel (804) 973-3345; fax (804) 978-1637
Chairman/President/Treasurer — E W Scripps; Vice Chairman/Corp. Secretary — Betty Knight Scripps; Exec. Vice President — Roger N Warkins; Exec. Director-Special Projects — Barry H Scripps; Vice President-Finance — Thomas E Wendel.
Flagstaff (AZ) Arizona Daily Sun (eS); Banning (CA) Record-Gazette (e), Hanford (CA) Sentinel (eS), Napa Valley (CA) Register (eS), Santa Maria (CA) Times (eS), Taft (CA) Midway Driller (e); Lihue (HI) Garden Island (eS); De Kalb (IL) Daily Chronicle (eS); Haverhill (MA) Gazette (e); Park Hills (MO) Daily Journal (eS); Hamilton (MT) Ravalli Republic (m); Coos Bay (OR) World (eS), Dalles (OR) Chronicle (eS); Provo (UT) Daily Herald (eS); Newport (VT) Daily Express (e); Rhinelander (WI) Daily News (eS).
Note: Scripps League also owns and operates one weekly, one visitor's guide and a real estate publication in Arizona; seven weeklies, one semi-weekly, a visitor's guide and two real estate publications in California; two weeklies, two bi-weekly visitor's guides and a quarterly magazine in Hawaii; one weekly and one real estate publication in Illinois; one weekly in Kentucky; one weekly, one seniors' publication and one real estate publication in Massachusetts; one weekly and one real estate publication in Montana; two weeklies, one seniors' publication and one visitor's guide in Oregon; one weekly in Utah; and one weekly, one seniors' publication and

Setting the Standard for Publishing Executive Placement

GORDON WAHLS EXECUTIVE SEARCH

Now in our fourth successful decade we've become the premier name in the newspaper executive industry. Our dedication and persistence is shown by over 400 searches annually for people and companies nationwide.

Our fully qualified recruiters are ready to complete YOUR search, efficiently and confidentially. Call us today.

Walter Lynn
Vice President Publishing

(610) 565-0800
(800) 523-7112

GORDON WAHLS Executive Search

610 East Baltimore Pike
Media, PA 19063

All Position Fee Paid.

Copyright ©1996 by the Editor & Publisher Co.

Newspaper groups

one visitor's guide in Wisconsin. Scripps League publishes Napa Valley Appellation Magazine, distributed in the U.S., United Kingdom and France and the Japanese Beach Press, Tokyo. Scripps Diversified Enterprises Inc. owns Scripps: The Divided Dynasty, published by Donald I Fine Inc. A total of 54 publications.

Seaton Group — 218 W. 8th; PO Box 877, Coffeyville, KS 67337; tel (316) 251-2900
Chairman — Richard M Seaton.
Manhattan (KS) Mercury (eS), Winfield (KS) Daily Courier (e), Alliance (NE) Times-Herald (e), Hastings (NE) Tribune (e); Spearfish (SD) Black Hills Pioneer (e); Sheridan (WY) Press (e).

Seattle Times Co. — PO Box 70, Seattle, WA 98111; tel (206) 464-2329
President/COO — H Mason Sizemore.
Seattle (WA) Times (e), Walla Walla (WA) Union-Bulletin (eS), Yakima (WA) Herald-Republic (eS).
Note: Seattle Times Co. also publishes three non-daily newspapers in Washington state.

Shaw Newspapers — 444 Pine Hill Dr.; PO Box 487, Dixon, IL 61021; tel (815) 284-4000; fax (815) 284-9290
Chairman — E K Shaw; President/CEO — Thomas D Shaw; CFO/Secretary — Philip E Metka; Vice President — Robert A Shaw; Vice President — William E Shaw; Treasurer — Robert A Shaw.
Crystal Lake (IL) Northwest Herald (m), Dixon (IL) Telegraph (e), Geneva (IL) Kane County Chronicle (m), Sterling (IL) Daily Gazette (m), Geneva (IL) Kane County Chronicle (m); Creston (IA) News Advertiser (e), Newton (IA) Daily News (e).
Note: This group also owns eight non-daily newspapers, 10 shoppers, two business journals, one seniors magazine and one interactive service.

Shearman Newspapers — 4900 Hwy 90E; Box 2893, Lake Charles, LA 70602; tel (318) 433-3000; fax (318) 494-4008
President — Thomas B Shearman III; Vice President — Thomas B Shearman Jr; Secretary/Treasurer — Maynard Woodhatch.
Trinidad (CO) Chronicle News (e); Lake Charles (LA) American Press (mS); Hobbs (NM) News Sun (eS).

Small Newspaper Group Inc. — 8 Dearborn Sq., Kankakee, IL 60901; tel (815) 937-3300
Chairman — Jean Alice Small; President — Len Robert Small; Sr. Vice President/Secretary — Thomas P Small; Treasurer — Joseph E Lacaeyse.
Kankakee (IL) Daily Journal (eS), Moline (IL) Daily Dispatch (mS), Ottawa (IL) Daily Times (e), Rock Island (IL) Argus (eS), Streator (IL) Times-Press (e), La Porte (IN) Herald-Argus (e); Rochester (MN) Post-Bulletin (e).
Note: This group also publishes eight weeklies.

Smith Newspapers Inc. — PO Box 27, Fort Payne, AL 35967; tel (205) 845-5510
Chairman — Ben M Smith.
Linton (IN) Daily Citizen (e), Centerville (IA) Iowegian (m); Bastrop (LA) Daily Enterprise (m); Logan (WV) Banner (eS).
Note: This group also owns or manages 35 non-daily newspapers.

Southern Newspapers Inc. — 1050 Wilcrest Dr., Houston, TX 77042-1698; tel (713) 266-5481; fax (713) 266-1847
Chairman/President/CEO — Martha Ann Walls; Vice President/Secretary/COO — Lissa Walls Vahldiek; Vice President/Treasurer/CIO — B Cooper Walls; Vice President/Controller — Gerald Hoke; Exec. Vice President — Leon Brown; Vice President/Group Mgr. — James T Elsberry; Owner-Times-Journal (AL) — Lissa Walls Vahldiek; Owner-Review (NC) — Lissa W Walls Trust; Owner-Review (NC) — B Cooper Walls Trust; Owner-Tribune (TX) — B Cooper Walls.
Fort Payne (AL) Times-Journal (m), Scottsboro (AL) Sentinel (mS); Liberal (KS) Southwest Times (eS); Portales (NM) News Tribune (eS); Reidsville (NC) Review (eS); Bay City (TX) Tribune (e), Baytown (TX) Sun (eS), Freeport-Lake Jackson-Clute (TX) Brazosport Facts (mS), Kerrville (TX) Daily Times (eS), New Braunfels (TX) Herald-Zeitung (eS), Paris (TX) News (eS), Seguin (TX) Gazette-Enterprise (eS).
Note: Southern Newspapers Inc. also owns one weekly and two semi-weeklies in Texas, one semi-weekly in Georgia and one in New Mexico. The two Walls trusts also own a semi-weekly in North Carolina. The Fort Payne (AL) Times Journal, Reidsville (NC) Review, and Bay City (TX) Tribune are managed by Southern Newspapers Inc.

Stauffer Communications Inc. — See Morris Communications Corp.
Note: Stauffer Communications still operates television and radio stations through a trust.

Swift Newspapers — 437 W. Plumb Ln., Reno, NV 89509; tel (702) 333-7676; fax (703) 333-7677
Chairman — Phillip E Swift; President — Richard K Larson.
Grass Valley (CA) Union (e), Ridgecrest (CA) Daily Independent (eS), South Lake Tahoe (CA) Tribune (m), Frisco (CO) Summit Daily News (mS), Greeley (CO) Daily Tribune (eS), Vail (CO) Daily (mS); Carson City (NV) Nevada Appeal (mS); Roseburg (OR) News-Review (eS).
Note: This group also publishes 13 weekly and twice-weekly newspapers and three farm and ranch magazines.

T

Thomson Newspapers — Metro Center at One Station Pl., Stamford, CT 06902; tel (203) 425-2521; fax (203) 425-2516
President/CEO — Richard J Harrington; President/CEO-Great Lakes News Group — R Michael Sheppard; President/CEO-Western Group (US) — Joseph A Logan; President/CEO-Eastern Group (US) — Robert J Hively; President/CEO-Southern Group (US) — F Steve Sumner; President/CEO-Thomson Newspapers Canada — Samuel E Hindman; Publisher/CEO-The Globe and Mail — Roger P Parkinson; Sr. Vice Pres./CFO — Robert D Daleo; Sr. Vice Pres./Human Resources/Industrial Relations — Basil A Marraffa; Sr. Vice Pres.-New Media — Gerald Flake; Sr. Vice Pres.-Planning — J Kevin Reger; Vice Pres./Controller — Eric L Shuman; Vice. Pres.-Information Technology — Steven B Strout; Vice Pres.-Procurement — Robert Steinmetz.
Dothan (AL) Eagle (mS), Enterprise (AL) Ledger (mS), Opelika-Auburn (AL) News (mS); Eureka (CA) Times-Standard (eS), Pasadena (CA) Star-News (mS), West Covina (CA) San Gabriel Valley Tribune (mS), Whittier (CA) Daily News (mS); Bridgeport (CT) Connecticut Post (eS); Key West (FL) Citizen (eS), Marianna (FL) Jackson County Floridan (eS); Americus (GA) Times-Recorder (e), Cordele (GA) Dispatch (e), Dalton (GA) Daily Citizen-News (mS), Griffin (GA) Daily News (eS), Thomasville (GA) Times-Enterprise (e), Tifton (GA) Gazette (e), Valdosta (GA) Daily Times (mS); Mt. Vernon (IL) Register-News (e); Anderson (IN) Herald-Bulletin (mS), Kokomo (IN) Tribune (eS), Logansport (IN) Pharos-Tribune (eS), Terre Haute (IN) Tribune-Star (mS); Council Bluffs (IA) Daily Nonpareil (eS); Lafayette (LA) Daily Advertiser (mS); Cumberland (MD) Times-News (mS), Salisbury (MD) Daily News (mS); Fitchburg (MA) Sentinel & Enterprise (eS), Taunton (MA) Daily Gazette (e); Adrian (MI) Daily Telegram (e), Benton-Harbor-St. Joseph (MI) Herald-Palladium (eS), Escanaba (MI) Daily Press (e), Houghton (MI) Daily Mining Gazette (e), Iron Mountain (MI) Daily News (e), Marquette (MI) Mining Journal (eS); Portsmouth (NH) Herald (eS); Elizabeth City (NC) Daily Advance (eS), Monroe (NC) Enquirer-Journal (eS), Rocky Mount (NC) Telegram (mS), Shelby (NC) Star (eS), Ashtabula (OH) Star Beacon (mS), Bucyrus (OH) Telegraph-Forum (e), Canton (OH) Repository (eS), Coshocton (OH) Tribune (eS), East Liverpool (OH) Evening Review (e), Greenville (OH) Daily Advocate (e), Hamilton (OH) Journal-News (mS), Lancaster (OH) Eagle-Gazette (e), Marion (OH) Star (eS), Mansfield (OH) News Journal (eS), Middletown (OH) Journal (eS), Newark (OH) Advocate (e), Piqua (OH) Daily Call (e), Salem (OH) News (e), Steubenville (OH) Herald-Star (eS), Warren (OH) Tribune Chronicle (eS), Xenia (OH) Daily Gazette (e), Zanesville (OH) Times Recorder (mS); Enid (OK) News & Eagle (eS); Altoona (PA) Mirror (eS), Connellsville (PA) Daily Courier (e), Hanover (PA) Evening Sun (eS), Kittanning (PA) Leader Times (e), Lebanon (PA) Daily News (eS), Lock Haven (PA) Express (e), Meadville (PA) Tribune (eS), Monessan (PA) Valley Independent (e), New Castle (PA) News (e), Shamokin (PA) News-Item (e); Florence (SC) Morning News (ms); St. George (UT) Daily Spectrum (eS); Petersburg (VA) Progress-Index (eS); Beckley (WV) Register-Herald (mS), Bluefield (WV) Daily Telegraph (mS), Charleston (WV) Daily Mail (eS), Fairmont (WV) Times-West Virginian (mS), Weirton (WV) Daily Times (e); Appleton (WI) Post-Crescent (eS), Fond du Lac (WI) Reporter (eS), Manitowoc (WI) Herald Times Reporter (eS), Sheboygan (WI) Press (eS), Waukesha (WI) Freeman (e), West Bend (WI) News (e), Wisconsin Rapids (WI) Daily Tribune (e).

Eastern Group: One Thorn Run Center, 1187 Thorn Run Ext., Ste. 500, Coraopolis, PA 15108; tel (412) 262-7870
President/CEO-Eastern Group — Robert J Hively.

Southern Group: 600 N. Westshore Blvd., Ste. 700, Tampa, FL 33609; tel (813) 289-4455
President/CEO-Southern Group — F Steve Sumner.

Great Lakes Group: 330 S. Executive Dr., Ste. 204, Brookfield, WI 53005; tel (414) 796-1612
President/CEO-Great Lakes Group — R Michael Sheppard.

Western Group: 1210 Azusa Canyon, West Covina, CA 91790; tel (818) 962-8811
President/CEO — Joseph A Logan.

Thomson Newspapers Canada: 65 Queen St. W, Toronto, ON M5H 2MB; tel (416) 864-1710
President/CEO — Samuel E Hindman.

Times Mirror Co. — Times Mirror Sq., Los Angeles, CA 90053; tel (213) 237-3700/(213) 237-3727/(213) 237-3955; fax (213) 237-3751
Chairman — Robert F Erburu; Chief Executive Officer — Mark H Willes; Publisher/CEO-Los Angeles — Richard Schlosberg III; Sr. Vice President — Donald F Wright; Sr. Vice President — Curtis A Hessler; Sr. Vice President — Edward E Johnson; Sr. Vice President — Richard T Schlosberg III; Group VP-Medical/Scientific/Technical/College Publications — Patrick A Clifford; Group VP/President-Times Mirror Cable Television — Larry W Wangberg; Vice President/General Counsel — Thomas Unterman; Vice President-Strategic Development — Efrem Zimbalist III; Vice President/Chief Accounting Officer — Duane Storhaug; Vice President-Human Resources — James R Simpson; Vice President/CFO — James F Guthrie; Vice President-Adm./Comm. Affairs — Stephen C Meier; Vice President-Taxes — Jack L Plank; Vice President-Int'l./Asst. to the Chairman — Ann E Dilworth; Vice President/President-Times Mirror Training Group — John H Zenger; Vice President-Technology — Michael Liebhold; Secretary/Assoc. General Counsel — O Jean Williams; Editor-At-Large/Publisher/CEO-Times (CA) — David Laventhol; Publisher-Time/Advocate (CT) — William J Rowe; Publisher-Courant (CT) — Michael E Waller; Publisher/CEO-Newsday (NY) — Raymond A Jansen; Publisher-Morning Call (PA) — Gary K Shorts; Director-Corporate Communications — Martha Goldstein; Director-Investor Relations — Jean M Jarvis.
Costa Mesa (CA) Daily Pilot (m), Glendale (CA) News Press (m), Los Angeles (CA) Times (mS); Greenwich (CT) Time (all day, S), Hartford (CT) Courant (mS), Stamford (CT) Advocate (all day, S); Baltimore (MD) Sun Newspapers; Long Island (NY) Newsday (all day, S); Allentown (PA) Morning Call (mS).

Times Newspapers — Penn Ave. & Spruce Sts.; PO Box 3311, Scranton, PA 18505-3311; tel (717) 348-9100; fax (717) 348-9145
Publisher — E J Lynett Jr; Publisher — George Lynett; Publisher — William Lynett.

GENOVA, BURNS, TRIMBOLI & VERNOIA
ATTORNEYS AT LAW

Experienced in Daily Newspaper Operations and Management

Labor Relations, Employment Counselling, Employee Benefits, Employment-Related Litigation and Discrimination Defense on Behalf of Management

CONTACTS

ANGELO J. GENOVA
OR
MICHAEL E. HESTON
FORMER DIRECTOR OF PERSONNEL
GANNETT ROCHESTER NEWSPAPERS

Eisenhower Plaza II
354 Eisenhower Parkway
Livingston, New Jersey 07039
(201) 533-0777
(800) 301-0777

Scranton (PA) Times (eS), Scranton (PA) Tribune (m), Towanda (PA) Daily Review (m).
Note: This group also publishes two weeklies, six pennysavers and operates nine radio stations.

Times Publishing Inc. — 205 W. 12th St., Erie, PA 16534; tel (814) 870-1600; fax (814) 870-1615
President/Co-Publisher — Edward M Mead; Exec. Vice President/Co-Publisher — Michael Mead; Vice President/Asst. Secretary — Kevin Mead.
Lakeport (CA) Lake County Record Bee (m); Erie (PA) News (m), Erie (PA) Times (e), Erie (PA) Times News (S), Warren (PA) Times-Observer (m).
Note: Times Publishing also owns the Brown-Thompson group of five weekly newspapers in Pennsylvania and two twice-weeklies in northern California.

Tribune Co. — 435 N. Michigan Ave., 6th Fl., Chicago, IL 60611; tel (312) 222-3337
Chairman/President/CEO — John W Madigan; Exec. Vice President-Broadcasting — James C Dowdle; Exec. Vice President — Joseph D Cantrell; Sr. Vice President-Administration — John T Sloan; Sr. Vice President-Development — David D Hiller; Sr. Vice President/CFO — Donald C Grenesko; Sr. Vice President-Information Systems — John S Kazik; Vice President-Corporate Relations — Joseph A Hays; Vice President/Chief Counsel — James E Cushing; Vice President/Treasurer — David J Granat; Asst. Treasurer — Lisa M Featherer; Vice President/Controller — R Mark Mallory; Asst. Controller — Philip B Doherty; Vice President/Secretary — Stanley J Gradowski; Vice President-Marketing — M Catherine Jaros; Vice President-Development — Andrew J Oleszczuk; Vice President-Washington — Shaun M Sheehan; Vice President-Technology — James N Longson; President/CEO-Chicago Tribune Co. — Jack Fuller; President/Publisher-Sun Sentinel Co. — Scott C Smith; President/CEO-Sentinel Communications Co. — John P Puerner; President/Publisher-Daily Press — Jack W Davis Jr.
Fort Lauderdale (FL) Sun-Sentinel (mS), Orlando (FL) Sentinel (all day, S); Chicago (IL) Tribune (mS); Newport News (VA) Daily Press (mS).
Note: Tribune also owns Tribune Media Services, Compton's and Contemporary Books. It also owns eight television stations and five radio stations, produces and syndicates information and programming, publishes books and information in print and digital formats and has an ownership interest in one of Canada's largest newsprint manufacturers.

Tribune-Review Publishing Co. — Cabin Hill Dr., Greensburg, PA 15601; tel (412) 834-1151; fax (412) 838-5173

Chairman — Richard M Scaife; President — Edward H Harrell.
Greensburg (PA) Tribune-Review (mS), Irwin (PA) Standard Observer (e).

U

United Communications Corp. — 1209 Orange St., Wilmington, DE 19801; tel (414) 657-1000
President — Howard J Brown; Sr. Vice President — Eugene W Schulte.
Attleboro (MA) Sun-Chronicle (e); Kenosha (WI) News (e).
Note: This group also owns and operates two weekly newspapers, three shoppers and two television stations.

USMedia Group Inc. — PO Box 227, Crystal City, MO 63019; tel (314) 937-5200; fax (314) 937-7947
President — Eugene A Mace; Vice President — Alan Portner; Secretary — William J Ruhlman.
Madera (CA) Tribune (e), Merced (CA) Sun-Star (m), Paso Robles (CA) Country News-Press (e); Lemars (IA) Daily Sentinel (e); Colby (KS) Free Press (m), Goodland (KS) Daily News (e); Marshall (MO) Democrat-News (e), Nevada (MO) Daily Mail (e), Nevada (MO) Sunday Herald (S); McCook (NE) Daily Gazette (e).
Note: This group owns three weeklies in Arkansas, four in California, one in Idaho and one in Missouri.

V

Ventana Publishing — 283 S. Fir St.; PO Box 2315, Telluride, CO 81435; tel (970) 728-9788; fax (970) 728-9793
President — Mike Ritchey; Secretary — Tony Daranyi.
Telluride (CO) Daily Planet (m), Gunnison (CO) Country Times (m).
Note: Ventana also owns one weekly and one shopper.

W

Walls Investment Co. — 1050 Wilcrest Dr., Houston, TX 77042-1608; tel (713) 266-5481; fax (713) 266-1847
Owner — Carmage Walls.
Galveston (TX) County Daily News (mS), Texas City (TX) Sun (mS).

Washington Post Co. — 1150 15th St., NW, Washington, DC 20071; tel (202) 334-6620; fax (202) 334-6664
Chairman/CEO — Donald Graham; President/COO — Alan Spoon; Vice President — Martin Cohen; Vice President-Human Resources — Beverly Keil; Vice President-Planning/Development — Ross Hamachek;

Vice President-Communications — Guyon Knight; Publisher-Washington Post — Donald Graham; Vice President/General Counsel/Secretary — Diana M Daniels; Vice President/CFO — Jay Morse; Treasurer — Leonade D Jones.
Washington (DC) Post (mS); Everett (WA) Herald (eS).
Note: The Washington Post Co. is half owner, with the New York Times Co., of the International Herald Tribune, which is printed in Europe.

Wehco Media Inc. — PO Box 2221, Little Rock, AR 72203; tel (501) 378-3400
President/CEO — Walter E Hussman Jr; Controller — Allen W Berry; Secretary — Marilyn Augur; Asst. Secretary — Philip S Anderson.
Camden (AR) News (e), El Dorado (AR) News-Times (eS), Hot Springs (AR) Sentinel Record (mS), Little Rock (AR) Arkansas Democrat-Gazette (mS), Magnolia (AR) Banner News (e), Texarkana (AR-TX) Gazette (mS).

Western Communications Inc. — 1526 N.W. Hill St., Bend, OR 97701; tel (503) 382-1811; fax (503) 385-5802
Chairman — Elizabeth C McCool; President — Gordon R Black; Vice President-Finance — John Shaver.
Crescent City (CA) Triplicate (m); Baker City (OR) Herald (e), Bend (OR) Bulletin (e), LaGrande (OR) Observer (e).
Note: This group also publishes three weekly and one bi-weekly newspaper in Oregon.

Western Newspapers Inc. — 290 S. 1st Ave., Ste. 4, Yuma, AZ 85364; tel (520) 783-3311; fax (520) 783-3313
Chairman — Donald N Soldwedel; President — Joseph Soldwedel; Vice President/COO — Blake DeWitt; Financial Director — Diane Huff.
Kingman (AZ) Daily Miner (eS), Prescott (AZ) Daily Courier (eS).
Note: Western Newspapers shares ownership of the Lake Havasu City (AZ) Today's News-Herald (mS) with Wick Communications. Western also owns 12 non-daily newspapers, a commercial printing property in Yuma, AZ, and the Outdoor Advertising Co.

Western Publishing Co. — 101 S. Chestnut; PO Box 1228, North Platte, NE 69103; tel (308) 532-6783; fax (308) 532-3239
Chairman/President — James C Seacrest; Exec. Vice President/CEO — Eric R Seacrest; Vice President/Admin. of Finance — Richard Cole.
North Platte (NE) Telegraph (mS), Scottsbluff (NE) Star-Herald (mS).

Newspaper groups
I-465

Note: Western Publishing is owned by the families of James C Seacrest and the late Joe R Seacrest.

Westward Communications Inc. — 5005 LBJ Fwy., Ste 1040, Dallas, TX 75244; tel (214) 450-1717; fax (214) 450-1770
Chairman — Kenneth P Johnson; President — Will D Jarrett; Sr. Vice President/CFO — James Parke; Sr. Vice President-Operations — Harold Ruddle; Sr. Vice President-Marketing — John Wolf.
Conroe (TX) Courier (mS), Pasadena (TX) Citizen (mS).
Note: This group also publishes eight semi-weeklies and 35 weeklies. Westward also owns and operates the Southwest PR Newswire in Dallas.

Wick Communications — 333 W. Wilcox Dr., Ste. 302, Sierra Vista, AZ 85635; tel (520) 458-3973
President/Treasurer — Walter M Wick; Vice President/Secretary — Robert J Wick; Exec. Vice President — Lou Major Sr.
Bisbee (AZ) Review (eS), Douglas (AZ) Dispatch (e), Sierra Vista (AZ) Herald (eS), Tucson (AZ) Territorial (e); Bogalusa (LA) Daily News (eS), New Iberia (LA) Iberian (eS), Slidell (LA) Sentry-News; Roanoke Rapids (NC) Herald (eS); Wahpeton (ND) Daily News (mS), Williston (ND) Herald (eS); Ontario (OR) Argus-Observer (e).
Note: Wick shares ownership of the Lake Havasu City (AZ) Today's News-Herald (mS) with Western Newspapers Inc. This group also publishes 14 weekly newspapers and operates one radio station.

Witwer Newspapers — 112 N. Main St.; PO Box 39, Kendallville, IN 46755; tel (219) 347-0400
Chairman — George O Witwer; President — James Kroemer.
Auburn (IN) Star (e), Kendallville (IN) News-Sun (e).
Note: This group also publishes three weekly newspapers in Indiana.

Y

Yellowstone Newspapers — 401 S. Main; PO Box 665, Livingston, MT 59047; tel (406) 222-2000
President/GM — John Sullivan.
Livingston (MT) Enterprise (e), Miles City (MT) Star (e).
Note: This group also includes one monthly, two weekly and one bi-weekly publication, as well as broadcast and commercial printing properties.

AdMedia Corporate Advisors, Inc.

An Investment Banking and Strategic Advisory Firm Serving a Wide Range of Media, Advertising and Marketing Services Companies

Founded in 1990, *AdMedia* has a particular strength in newspaper and magazine publishing.

In six years the firm has assisted companies in this area with:

- mergers, acquisitions, divestitures
- strategic planning, market positioning shareholder relations, succession planning
- new debt and equity financings
- valuations

866 Third Avenue, 26th Floor, New York, NY 10022
Telephone: (212) 759-1870 • Facsimile: (212) 888-4960

PROFESSIONAL, BUSINESS AND SPECIAL SERVICE DAILIES

AGRICULTURE

Urner Barry's Price-Current
(mon to fri) (Agricultural Market News)
Urner Barry's Price-Current, PO Box 389, Toms River, NJ 08754-0389; tel (908) 240-5330; fax (908) 341-0891.
Circulation: 2,200(fr); Est. Oct. 25, 1995.
Price: $399.00/yr.
Advertising: Open inch rate $17.00. **Established:** 1858.

CORPORATE OFFICERS
President	Paul B Brown
Vice Pres	Bud O'Shaughnessy
Secretary	Rick Brown
Treasurer	Paul B Brown Jr
Director	Michael O'Shaughnessy

APPAREL, CLOTHING AND TEXTILES

Women's Wear Daily
(mon to fri)
Women's Wear Daily, 7 W. 34th St., New York, NY 10001; tel (212) 741-4340. Fairchild Publications (CapCities/ABC) group.
Circulation: 56,036(pd); 5,690(fr); ABC Mar. 31, 1995.
Price: $1.00(d); $89.00/yr.
Advertising: Open inch rate $211.00. **Established:** 1910.

CORPORATE OFFICERS
Chairman of the Board/Publisher	John B Fairchild
Senior Vice Pres/Group Publisher	Michael Coady
Group Vice Pres/Assoc Publisher	Patrick McCarthy
Vice Pres	Olivia Thompson

GENERAL MANAGEMENT
Publisher	Susan Hasson

NEWS EXECUTIVES
Exec Editor	Patrick McCarthy
Editor	Michael Coady

MECHANICAL PRODUCTION INFORMATION
Method of Printing: Offset.

BUILDING, CONSTRUCTION AND ENGINEERING

Dodge Construction News Chicago
(mon to fri) (Construction, Architecture)
Dodge Construction News Chicago, 180 N. Stetson Ave., Suite 910, Chicago, IL 60601; tel (312) 616-3282; fax (312) 616-3276. McGraw-Hill group.
Circulation: 800(pd); 4,200(fr); Sworn Sept. 20, 1995.
Price: $5.00(d); $1,200.00/yr.
Advertising: Open inch rate $830.00/page. **Established:** 1946.

GENERAL MANAGEMENT
Business Manager	Judy Arkin

NEWS EXECUTIVE
Managing Editor	Dennis M Halloran

EDITORS AND MANAGERS
Senior Editor	Jim Crockett
Art Director	H M Thompson

PRODUCTION
Supervisor	Mary J Cappello

MECHANICAL PRODUCTION INFORMATION
Method of Printing: Offset.

The Daily Journal
(mon to fri) (Construction, Legal, General Business)
The Daily Journal, 2000 S. Colorado Blvd., Suite 2000, Denver, CO 80222; tel (303) 756-9995; fax (303) 756-4465. McGraw-Hill group.
Circulation: 1,161(pd); 518(fr); Sworn Oct. 1, 1995.
Price: $10.00(d); $1,208.00/yr.
Advertising: Open inch rate $25.20 (display), $11.91 (classified). **Established:** 1897.

GENERAL MANAGEMENT
Publisher/Editor	Kristopher R Passey
Managing Editor	Mike Baker

CIRCULATION
Manager	John Roades

EDITORS AND MANAGERS
Senior Editor	Jack Phinney
Legal Editor	Lynn Burke
Project News Manager	Judy Ford

MECHANICAL PRODUCTION INFORMATION
Method of Printing: Offset.

Construction News Publishing Network "Green Sheet"
(mon to fri) (Construction)
Construction News Publishing Network "Green Sheet", 1333 Mayflower Ave., 3rd Fl. (91016-4066); PO Box 5050, Monrovia, CA 91017; tel (818) 932-6161; fax (818) 932-6163.
Circulation: 3,187(pd); Est. Aug. 31, 1992.
Price: $15.00(d); $1,460.00/yr.
Advertising: Open inch rate $33.55 (display), $5.00/line (classified). **Established:** 1865.

CORPORATE OFFICER
Publisher	Susan K Miller

NEWS EXECUTIVE
Editor	Maria Taylor

EDITORS AND MANAGERS
Desktop Publishing Manager	Mike Baker
Graphic Artist	Trudy Ung
Group Operations Manager	Gordon Watkins
Senior News Manager	Rock Rickert

PRODUCTION
Manager	Shirley Smith

MECHANICAL PRODUCTION INFORMATION
Method of Printing: Web Offset.

Daily Journal of Commerce
(mon to fri) (Building and Construction Municipal Bonds)
Daily Journal of Commerce, PO Box 52031, New Orleans, LA 70152; tel (504) 368-8900; fax (504) 368-8999.
Circulation: 2,000(pd); Est.
Price: $426.00/yr.
Advertising: Open inch rate $10.00.

CORPORATE OFFICER
President/Treasurer	Gaston Naquin

GENERAL MANAGEMENT
Publisher	Carlo Ragusa
Manager	Gaston Naquin

ADVERTISING
Director	Paul Serpas

NEWS EXECUTIVE
Editor	Carlo Ragusa

EDITOR AND MANAGER
Features Editor	Paul Serpas

Daily Pacific Builder
(mon to fri) (Construction)
Daily Pacific Builder, 221 Main St., 8th Fl., San Francisco, CA 94105; tel (415) 495-4200; fax (415) 495-0997. McGraw-Hill group.
Circulation: 5,000(pd); Est.
Price: $15.00(d); $1,611.00/yr.
Advertising: Open inch rate $31.50. **Established:** 1890.

CORPORATE OFFICER
Publisher	Douglas B Hebbard

GENERAL MANAGEMENT
Business Manager	Kassi Byington

NEWS EXECUTIVE
Senior Editor	Jim Elliott

PRODUCTION
Manager	Kelly Brennan

MECHANICAL PRODUCTION INFORMATION
Method of Printing: Offset.

Daily Commercial News and Construction Record
(mon to fri) (Construction and Building)
Daily Commercial News and Construction Record, 280 Yorkland Blvd., Willowdale, ON M2J 4Z6; tel (416) 494-4990; fax (416) 756-2767. Southam Communications Ltd. group.
Circulation: 4,758(pd); 326(fr); ABC Mar. 31, 1995.
Price: $675.00/yr (Canadian).
Advertising: Open inch rate $44.94 (Canadian). **Established:** 1927.

CORPORATE OFFICER
Publisher	Ian Hardy

ADVERTISING
Sales Manager-Display	Dave Watson
Inside Sales Manager	Susan Steele

CIRCULATION
Manager	Josie Vogel

EDITOR AND MANAGER
Editor	Scott Button

MECHANICAL PRODUCTION INFORMATION
Method of Printing: Offset.

COURT, LEGAL, BUSINESS COMMERCIAL AND FINANCIAL

Akron Legal News
(mon to fri) (Legal)
Akron Legal News, 60 S. Summit St., Akron, OH 44308; tel (216) 376-0917; fax (216) 376-7001.
Circulation: 870(pd); 10(fr); Sworn Oct. 1, 1995.
Price: 35¢(d); $65.00/yr; $25.00/3mo, $40.00/6mo.
Advertising: Open inch rate $4.50. **Established:** 1921.

GENERAL MANAGEMENT
Editor & Publisher	John L Burleson

MECHANICAL PRODUCTION INFORMATION
Method of Printing: Offset.

Daily Report
(mon to fri) (Law & Business)
Daily Reporter, 190 Pryor St. S.W., Atlanta, GA 30303-3685; tel (404) 521-1227.
Circulation: 5,232(pd); 544(fr); Sworn Sept. 29, 1995.
Price: $1.00(d); $220.00/yr.
Advertising: Open inch rate $1,200.00/page. **Established:** 1890.

GENERAL MANAGEMENT
Publisher	S Richard Gard Jr
Controller	Patricia Lipsey

ADVERTISING
Manager-Legal	Earl Higgins

CIRCULATION
Manager	Diane Beeching

NEWS EXECUTIVES
Editor	S Richard Gard Jr
Managing Editor	Carl Rauscher

MECHANICAL PRODUCTION INFORMATION
Method of Printing: Offset.

The Daily Record
(mon to sat) (Court & Commercial)
The Daily Record, 11-15 E. Saratoga St., Baltimore, MD 21202-2199; tel (410) 752-3849; fax (410) 752-2894. Dolan Media Co. group.
Circulation: 4,938(pd); 535(fr); Sworn Oct. 1, 1995.
Price: 50¢(d); $85.00/6mo; $155.00/yr.
Advertising: Open inch rate $16.00 (classified), $1,690 (full page display).
News Services: AP, PRN. **Established:** 1888.

CORPORATE OFFICER
President/Publisher	Richard H Groves

GENERAL MANAGEMENT
Exec Vice Pres	Leo Schaeffler
Senior Vice Pres	Frederick D Godman
Vice Pres-Marketing	Elisa C Graham
Vice Pres-Editor	Keith Girard

CIRCULATION
Vice Pres	Elisa C Graham

NEWS EXECUTIVE
Editor	Adam Ambrose

MECHANICAL PRODUCTION INFORMATION
Method of Printing: Offset.

Baton Rouge Daily Legal News
(mon to fri) (Court, Legal, Business, Commercial and Financial)
Baton Rouge Daily Legal News, 8252 W. El Cajon Dr., Baton Rouge, LA 70815; tel (504) 926-8882. Legal News Inc. group.
Circulation: 300(pd); Est.
Price: $2.00(d); $60.00/3mo.
Advertising: Open inch rate $3.00. **Established:** 1925.

ADVERTISING
Manager	Lisa S Cannon

EDITOR AND MANAGER
Editor	H M Mike Cannon

PRODUCTION
Manager	Chris Vaughn

MECHANICAL PRODUCTION INFORMATION
Method of Printing: Offset, tab.

Copyright ©1996 by the Editor & Publisher Co.

Special service dailies

I-467

Daily Bulletin
(mon to fri) (Legal, Banking and Real Estate)
Daily Bulletin, 125 Montague St., Brooklyn, NY 11201; tel (718) 624-0536; fax (718) 624-2716.
Circulation: 6,000(pd); Est. Apr. 2, 1993.
Price: 50¢(d); $150.00/yr.
Advertising: Open inch rate $5.00. **Established:** 1954.

GENERAL MANAGEMENT
Publisher .... J D Hasty

ADVERTISING
Manager-Legal .... Daniel Doctorow
Manager .... Patricia Higgins

EDITOR AND MANAGER
Editor .... Ed Goldstein

Broward Daily Business Review
(mon to fri) (Business, Real Estate & Law)
Broward Daily Business Review, One Southeast Third Ave., Suite 900; PO Box 010589, Miami, FL 33101; tel (305) 377-3721; fax (305) 374-8474.
Circulation: 3,245(pd); Sworn Sept. 14, 1995.
Price: $1.00; $3.00 (d-fri); $450.00/yr (Corporate), $169.00/yr (Small business or individual).
Advertising: Open inch rate $27.95.
News Services: PRN, Business Wire. **Established:** 1926.
Note: See Daily Business Review editions in Miami and Palm Beach, FL.

CORPORATE OFFICERS
Chairman of the Board .... Edward Wasserman
Exec Vice Pres .... Ruth Brown

GENERAL MANAGEMENT
Publisher .... Donna Trainer-Stutts
Assoc Publisher .... T Alicia Coya

ADVERTISING
Senior Account Representative .... Jane Biumi

CIRCULATION
Director .... Margarita Huerta

EDITORS AND MANAGERS
Editor in Chief .... Edward Wasserman
Exec Editor .... Mary Hladky

MECHANICAL PRODUCTION INFORMATION
Method of Printing: Offset.

Chicago Daily Law Bulletin
(mon to fri) (Legal & Credit)
Chicago Daily Law Bulletin, 415 N. State St., Chicago, IL 60610-4674; tel (312) 644-7800; fax (312) 644 4255.
Circulation: 6,268(pd); 95(fr); Sworn Sept. 27, 1995.
Price: 70¢(d); $170.00/yr.
Advertising: Open inch rate $26.40.
News Services: AP, NYT. **Established:** 1854.

CORPORATE OFFICERS
President .... Lanning Macfarland Jr
Exec Vice Pres .... Jeffrey Bope
Vice Pres .... Bernard Judge
Vice Pres .... Lanning Macfarland III
Vice Pres .... Brewster Macfarland
Treasurer .... James Banich

ADVERTISING
Senior Director-Sales & Marketing .... Jeffrey Bryan
Classified .... Sharon Foley

NEWS EXECUTIVES
Editor .... Bernard Judge
Managing Editor .... Stephen Brown

PRODUCTION
Plant Manager .... Richard Mpistolarides
Print Service Manager .... Fred Faulkner

MECHANICAL PRODUCTION INFORMATION
Method of Printing: Offset.

The Wall Street Journal Midwest Edition
(mon to fri) (Business News)
The Wall Street Journal, 1 S. Wacker Dr., Chicago, IL 60606; tel (312) 750-4000; fax (312) 750-4153.
Note: See listing in Daily Section under New York, NY.

Cincinnati Court Index
(mon to fri) (Legal)
Cincinnati Court Index, 215 E. Ninth St., Cincinnati, OH 45202; tel (513) 241-1450.
Circulation: 1,413(pd); 101(fr); Sworn Sept. 28, 1995.
Price: 25¢(d); $65.00/yr.
Advertising: Open inch rate $9.00.

CORPORATE OFFICERS
President .... Joe Shea
Vice Pres .... Harry E Gilligan

---

The Daily Legal News and Cleveland Recorder
(tues to sat) (Legal & Business)
The Daily Legal News and Cleveland Recorder, 2935 Prospect Ave., Cleveland, OH 44115-2688; tel (216) 696-3322; fax (216) 696-6329.
Circulation: 1,124(pd); 57(fr); Sworn Oct. 3, 1995.
Price: 30¢(d); $70.00/yr; $25.00/3mo, $40.00/6mo.
Advertising: Open inch rate $16.00. **Representatives:** Piano; PIO; NNA.
News Service: AP. **Established:** 1885.

GENERAL MANAGEMENT
Publisher .... Lucien B Karlovec Jr
Treasurer .... Charles E Bergstresser
Asst Publisher .... Jeffrey B Karlovec

ADVERTISING
Legal .... Richard Karlovec
Display .... Rae Szabo

CIRCULATION
Manager .... Richard Karlovec

NEWS EXECUTIVE
Editor/Managing Editor .... Lucien B Karlovec Jr

EDITOR AND MANAGER
News Editor .... John Lusk

PRODUCTION
Manager .... Ed Mattson

MECHANICAL PRODUCTION INFORMATION
Method of Printing: Offset.

Daily Transcript
(mon to fri) (Legal)
Daily Transcript, 22 N. Sierra Madre; PO Box 789, Colorado Springs, CO 80901; tel (719) 634-1593.
Circulation: 489(pd); 51(fr); Sworn Sept. 19, 1995.
Price: 75¢(d); $95.00/yr.
Advertising: Open inch rate $6.50.
News Services: CNS, LAT-WP, AP. **Established:** 1907.

CORPORATE OFFICER
President .... Fred Bernheim

ADVERTISING
Manager .... Mike Murt

EDITOR AND MANAGER
Editor .... Warren Wright

MECHANICAL PRODUCTION INFORMATION
Method of Printing: Offset.

The Daily Reporter
(mon to fri) (Commercial & Court News)
The Daily Reporter, 329 S. Front St., Columbus, OH 43215-5094; tel (614) 224-4835; fax (614) 224-8649.

Circulation: 4,483(pd); 148(fr); Sworn Oct. 1, 1995.
Price: 50¢(d); $80.00/yr.
Advertising: Open inch rate $18.00.
News Service: AP. **Established:** 1896.

GENERAL MANAGEMENT
Vice Pres/General Manager .... Dan L Shillingburg

ADVERTISING
Display .... Bud DeMoss
Display .... Suzanne Percy
Display .... Elena Bowman
Classified .... Tammy Freck

EDITOR AND MANAGER
Editor .... Barbara G James

PRODUCTION
Manager .... John F Wilson

MECHANICAL PRODUCTION INFORMATION
Method of Printing: Offset.

Daily Commercial Record
(mon to fri) (Business & Legal)
Daily Commercial Record, 706 Main St., Dallas, TX 75202; tel (214) 741-6366.
Circulation: 4,500(pd); Sworn Oct. 25, 1995.
Price: 80¢(d); $168.00/yr.
Advertising: Open inch rate $1.00/line. **Established:** 1888.

GENERAL MANAGEMENT
Publisher .... Mrs E Nuel Cates Sr

EDITOR AND MANAGER
Editor .... E Nuel Cates Jr

MECHANICAL PRODUCTION INFORMATION
Method of Printing: Offset.

The Wall Street Journal Southwest Edition
(mon to fri) (Business News)
The Wall Street Journal, 1233 Regal Row, Dallas, TX 75247.
Note: See listing in Daily Section under New York, NY.

Daily Court Reporter
(mon to fri) (Legal)
Daily Court Reporter, 120 W. Second St.; PO Box 340, Mid City Station, Dayton, OH 45402; tel (513) 222-6000; fax (513) 341-5020.
Circulation: 578(pd); 57(fr); Sworn Sept. 29, 1995.
Price: 50¢(d); $75.00/yr; $30.00/3mo, $50.00/6mo.
Advertising: Open inch rate $8.00. **Established:** 1917.

GENERAL MANAGEMENT
President/Publisher .... Jeffrey Foster
Office Manager .... Jean Prather

EDITOR AND MANAGER
Editor .... Chris Schmidt

The Daily Reporter
(mon to fri) (Legal)
The Daily Reporter, 201 S. Baltimore; PO Box 190, Derby, KS 67037; tel (316) 788-2835; fax (316) 788-0854. Hollinger International Inc. group.
Circulation: 2,148(pd); Est.
Price: 50¢(d); $6.50/mo; $78.00/yr.
Advertising: Open inch rate $6.73. **Representative:** American Publishing Co.
News Service: AP. **Established:** 1961.

CORPORATE OFFICERS
President .... Larry J Perrotto
Vice Pres .... Kenneth W Cape

GENERAL MANAGEMENT
Publisher .... Jimmie R Stephenson

ADVERTISING
Legal Manager .... Brenda Mello
Manager .... Faye Osonbaugh

CIRCULATION
Manager .... Tim Mello

EDITORS AND MANAGERS
Editor .... Sam Foster
Office Manager .... Letha M Stephenson

PRODUCTION
Manager .... Renee Browning

MECHANICAL PRODUCTION INFORMATION
Method of Printing: Offset.

The Detroit Legal News
(mon to fri) (Court & Commercial)
The Detroit Legal News, 2001 W. Lafayette, Detroit, MI 48216-1852; tel (313) 961-3949; fax (313) 961-7817.
Circulation: 1,398(pd); 326(fr); Sworn Oct. 1, 1995.
Price: 50¢(d); $125.00/yr.
Advertising: Open inch rate $15.00.
News Service: AP. **Established:** 1895.

GENERAL MANAGEMENT
Publisher .... Bradley L Thompson
Operations Manager .... Mary Jo Glonka

ADVERTISING
Manager .... Nan Borders

EDITORS AND MANAGERS
Editor .... Eric Pope
Legal Editor .... Jerry Harlan
Asst Legal Editor .... Constance Zwierzchowski
News Editor .... Chris Parks
News Editor .... Melanie Brown

MECHANICAL PRODUCTION INFORMATION
Method of Printing: Offset.

Fort Worth Commercial Recorder
(mon to fri) (Court & Commercial)
Fort Worth Commercial Recorder, 3032 S. Jones St.; PO Box 11038, Fort Worth, TX 76110; tel (817) 926-5351; fax (817) 926-5377. Ratcliff Publications Inc. group.
Circulation: 550(pd); 130(fr); Sworn Sept. 29, 1995.
Price: 75¢(d); $150.00/yr.
Advertising: Open inch rate $4.00. **Established:** 1903.

GENERAL MANAGEMENT
Publisher .... Genevieve Ratcliff

MECHANICAL PRODUCTION INFORMATION
Method of Printing: Offset.

Daily Court Review
(mon to fri) (Legal & Business)
Daily Court Review, 6807 Wynnwood; PO Box 1889, Houston, TX 77008; tel (713) 869-5434; fax (713) 869-8887.
Circulation: 949(pd); 12(fr); Est. Oct. 2, 1995.
Price: $1.25(d); $80.00/3mo; $195.00/yr.
Advertising: Open inch rate $16.75. **Representative:** NNA.
News Service: RN. **Established:** 1889.

GENERAL MANAGEMENT
Publisher Emeritus .... Earl M Morin Sr
Publisher/Editor .... E Milton Morin Jr

MECHANICAL PRODUCTION INFORMATION
Method of Printing: Offset.

Court & Commercial Record
(mon to fri) (Court & Commercial Newspaper)
Court & Commercial Record, 431 N. Pennsylvania, Indianapolis, IN 46204; tel (317) 636-0200.

Copyright ©1996 by the Editor & Publisher Co.

Special service dailies

Circulation: 796(pd); 80(fr); Sworn July, 31, 1995.
Price: 50¢(d); $89.00/yr.
Advertising: Open inch rate $12.50. **Established:** 1895.

CORPORATE OFFICER
Publisher .... Glenda J Jones
GENERAL MANAGEMENT
Business Manager .... Vivian Mercer
Administrative Asst .... Linda Blaylock
ADVERTISING
Director .... Greg Morris
CIRCULATION
Director .... Sheri Lindsay
NEWS EXECUTIVES
Editor .... Chris Banguis
Managing Editor .... Patricia J Pickett
PRODUCTION
Director .... Pat Kiefner
MECHANICAL PRODUCTION INFORMATION
Method of Printing: Offset.

Daily Record
(mon to fri) (Legal & Public Notice)
Daily Record, 3611 Troost Ave., Kansas City, MO 64109; tel (816) 931-2002; fax (816) 561-6675.
Circulation: 612(pd); 4(fr); Sworn Sept. 25, 1995.
Price: 40¢(d); $63.00/yr.
Advertising: Open inch rate $8.40. **Representative:** NNA. **Established:** 1888.

CORPORATE OFFICER
President .... Clifford B Smith
GENERAL MANAGEMENT
Co-Publisher .... Garrett L Smalley Jr
Secretary .... Robert W Smalley
General Manager/Treasurer ... Pamela Weaver
ADVERTISING
Legal .... Pamela Weaver

The Daily Record
(tues to sat) (Legal & Business News)
The Daily Record, 14710 Contrell Rd., Ste. B-8, Little Rock, AR 72212; tel (501) 868-4400; fax (501) 868-4844.
Circulation: 2,000(pd); Est.
Price: 50¢(d); $110.00/yr.
Advertising: Open inch rate $15.00. **Established:** 1925.

GENERAL MANAGEMENT
Publisher .... W F Rector Jr
ADVERTISING
Manager .... Rob Davis
EDITOR AND MANAGER
Editor .... Ralph S Mann
PRODUCTION
Manager .... Ralph S Mann
MECHANICAL PRODUCTION INFORMATION
Method of Printing: Web Press/Tab Size.

The Los Angeles Daily Journal
(mon to fri) (Court, Legal, Business, Commercial and Financial)
The Los Angeles Daily Journal, 915 E. First St., Los Angeles, CA 90012; tel (213) 229-5300; fax (213) 680-3682.
Circulation: 15,000(pd); Est. May 25, 1995.
Price: $2.00(d); $47.00/mo; $227.00/6mo; $389.00/yr.
Advertising: Open inch rate $19.28.
News Services: AP, NYT, CNS, McClatchy.
Established: 1888.

CORPORATE OFFICERS
Chairman of the Board .... Charles T Munger
Vice-Chairman of the Board ... J P Guerin
GENERAL MANAGEMENT
Publisher .... Gerald Salzman
ADVERTISING
Director .... Nell Fields
CIRCULATION
Manager .... Eric Lowenbach
NEWS EXECUTIVES
Editor .... Janet Shprintz
Managing Editor .... Stephen R Trousdale
EDITOR AND MANAGER
Open Forum Editor .... Ken Rutman
MECHANICAL PRODUCTION INFORMATION
Method of Printing: Offset.

Metropolitan News-Enterprise
(mon to fri) (Law)
Metropolitan News-Enterprise, 210 S. Spring St., Los Angeles, CA 90012; tel (213) 687-3886.
Circulation: 2,000(pd); Est. Mar. 31, 1993.
Price: 25¢(d); $139.00/yr.
Advertising: Open inch rate $6.00. **Established:** 1945.

GENERAL MANAGEMENT
Co-Publisher .... Rodger M Grace
Co-Publisher .... Jo-Ann W Grace
General Manager .... S John Babigan

The Daily Record
(mon to fri) (Court, Legal, Business, Commercial and Financial)
The Daily Record, PO Box 1062, Louisville, KY 40201; tel (502) 583-4471; fax (502) 585-5453.
Circulation: 373(pd); Est.
Price: 75¢(d); $150.00/yr; $50.00/3mo.
Advertising: Open inch rate $1.00/line (legal); 12.50/in (classified). **Established:** 1901.

CORPORATE OFFICERS
Publisher .... Connie J Cheak
Treasurer .... Pat Macdonald
Manager .... Jerry Ahlrica
NEWS EXECUTIVE
Managing Editor .... Leslie Wills
MECHANICAL PRODUCTION INFORMATION
Method of Printing: Offset.

The Daily News
(mon to fri) (Business/Finance)
The Daily News, 193 Jefferson (38103); PO Box 3663, Memphis, TN 38173-0663; tel (901) 523-1561; fax (901) 526-5813.
Circulation: 2,421(pd); 186(fr); Sworn Sept. 24, 1992.
Price: 50¢(d); $69.00/yr.
Advertising: Open inch rate $13.50.
News Service: CNS. **Established:** 1886.

CORPORATE OFFICERS
Chairman/Publisher .... L Peter Schutt Jr
Business Manager .... Ed Rains
EDITORS AND MANAGERS
Editor .... Leigh Ann Lane
Managing Editor .... Diana Lyons
Copy Editor .... Camille Gamble
MECHANICAL PRODUCTION INFORMATION
Method of Printing: Offset.

Miami Daily Business Review
(mon to fri) (Business, Real Estate & Law)
Miami Daily Business Review, One Southeast Third Ave., Suite 900; PO Box 010589, Miami, FL 33101; tel (305) 377-3721; fax (305) 374-8474.
Circulation: 5,730(pd); 24(fr); Sworn Sept. 14, 1995.
Price: $1.00; $3.00 (d-fri); $450.00/yr (Corporate), $169.00/yr (Small business or individual).
Advertising: Open inch rate $42.59.
News Services: PRN, Business Wire. **Established:** 1926.
Note: See Daily Business Review editions in Broward and Palm Beach, FL.

CORPORATE OFFICERS
Chairman of the Board .... Edward Wasserman
Chief Financial Officer .... Jim Pamplin
GENERAL MANAGEMENT
Publisher .... Donna Trainer-Stutts
Assoc Publisher .... T Alicia Coya
Marketing Director .... Amy Repine
CIRCULATION
Director .... Margarita Huerta
EDITORS AND MANAGERS
Editor in Chief .... Edward Wasserman
Exec Editor .... Craig Matters
MECHANICAL PRODUCTION INFORMATION
Method of Printing: Offset.

The Daily Reporter
(mon to fri) (Legal, Construction & Purchasing)
The Daily Reporter, 207 E. Michigan St.; PO Box 92933, Milwaukee, WI 53202-0933; tel (414) 276-0273; fax (414) 276-8057. Dolan Media Co. group.
Circulation: 2,209(pd); 186(fr); Sworn Sept. 28, 1995.
Price: 50¢(d); $109.00/yr.
Advertising: Open inch rate $11.25 (R.O.P. & classified), $1.75/line (legal).
News Service: AP. **Established:** 1897.

CORPORATE OFFICER
President/CEO .... James P Dolan
GENERAL MANAGEMENT
Vice Pres/Publisher .... Mark Stodder
CIRCULATION
Director .... Brian Clark
EDITOR AND MANAGER
Editor Emeritus .... Webster Woodmansee
PRODUCTION
Manager .... Jayne Michlie
MECHANICAL PRODUCTION INFORMATION
Method of Printing: Offset by Subcontract.

Finance and Commerce
(tues to sat) (Business & Legal)
Finance and Commerce, 615 S. 7th St.; PO Box 15045, Minneapolis, MN 55415; tel (612) 333-4244; fax (612) 333-3243.
Circulation: 1,000(pd); Sworn Sept. 1993.
Price: $1.00(d); $119.00/yr.
Advertising: Open inch rate $10.00.
News Service: AP. **Established:** 1887.

CORPORATE OFFICER
President/CEO .... Jim Dolan
GENERAL MANAGEMENT
Publisher .... Debra Quaal
Vice Pres .... Patrick Boulay
CIRCULATION
Manager .... Brian Clark
EDITOR AND MANAGER
Editor .... David Elmstrom
MECHANICAL PRODUCTION INFORMATION
Method of Printing: Web Offset.

American Banker
(mon to fri) (Financial)
American Banker, 1 State Street Plaza, New York, NY 10004; tel (212) 803-8200; fax (212) 843-9608. Thomson Financial Services group.
Circulation: 19,281(pd); ABC Sept. 30, 1995.
Price: $7.00(d); $750.00/yr. **Established:** 1836.

CORPORATE OFFICERS
President .... David S Branch
Vice Pres .... Mario G DiUbaldi
Assoc Publisher .... Carole Lambert
ADVERTISING
Director-Marketing .... Christine Feder
CIRCULATION
Director .... Micki LaPorte
Director-Sales .... John Perella
EDITORS AND MANAGERS
Senior Editor .... Debra Cope
Senior Editor .... Jeff Kutler
Senior Editor .... John Racine
Senior Editor .... Phil Roosevelt
PRODUCTION
Manager-Service .... Erwin Hambright
MECHANICAL PRODUCTION INFORMATION
Method of Printing: Web Offset.

Journal of Commerce & Commercial
(mon to fri) (Court, Legal, Business Commercial and Financial)
Journal of Commerce & Commercial, 2 World Trade Center, 27th Fl., New York, NY 10048; tel (212) 837-7000; fax (212) 837-7025.
Note: See listing in Daily Section under New York, NY.

New York Law Journal
(mon to fri) (Legal)
New York Law Journal, 111 8th Ave., New York, NY 10011; tel (212) 741-8300.
Circulation: 14,439(pd); ABC Sept. 30, 1995.
Price: $2.50(d); $420.00/yr.
Advertising: Open inch rate $8.10/line (classified). **Established:** 1888.

CORPORATE OFFICER
President/Publisher .... James A Finkelstein
GENERAL MANAGEMENT
Secretary/Assoc Publisher ... Nelson Seitel
Controller .... John Rago
ADVERTISING
Vice Pres/Director .... Edward Tyler
Manager-Classified .... Francis Fitts
Manager .... Carol Gauriglia
EDITOR AND MANAGER
Editor in Chief .... Ruth S Hochberger
PRODUCTION
Manager .... Arthur Michaels
MECHANICAL PRODUCTION INFORMATION
Method of Printing: Offset.

Standard & Poor's Dividend Record
(mon to fri) (Financial)
Standard & Poor's Dividend Record, 25 Broadway, New York, NY 10004; tel (212) 208-8369; fax (212) 412-0514. McGraw-Hill group.
Circulation: 1,546(pd); Sworn Oct. 25, 1995.
Price: $990.00/yr. **Established:** 1932.

CORPORATE OFFICER
President .... Harold W McGraw III
GENERAL MANAGEMENT
Publisher .... Ken Lutz
EDITOR AND MANAGER
Editor .... Anthony J Onofrio
MECHANICAL PRODUCTION INFORMATION
Method of Printing: Offset.

The Bond Buyer
(mon to fri) (Municipal Finance)
The Bond Buyer, One State Street Plaza, New York, NY 10004; tel (212) 803-8200. Thomson Financial Services group.

Special service dailies
I-469

Circulation: 3,500(pd); Est. Nov. 2, 1995.
Price: $11.00(d); $1,897.00/yr. Established: 1891.

CORPORATE OFFICER
President .... David S Branch
GENERAL MANAGEMENT
Publisher .... Thomas Curtin
ADVERTISING
Director .... Edward Meisner
CIRCULATION
Director .... Bob Bruning
NEWS EXECUTIVES
Editor in Chief .... Kieran Beer
Editor .... John Allan
Managing Editor .... Jim Murphy
PRODUCTION
Coordinator .... Joseph McDonald

Corporation Records, Daily News
(mon to fri) (Financial)
Corporation Records, Daily News, 25 Broadway, New York, NY 10004; tel (212) 208-8000. McGraw-Hill group.
Circulation: 3,318(pd); Est. Sept. 23, 1995.
Price: $1,350.00/yr. Established: Predecessor, 1914.

CORPORATE OFFICER
Chairman/CEO .... Joseph L Dionne
GENERAL MANAGEMENT
President/COO .... Harold W McGraw III
Exec Vice Pres/General Counsel/Secretary
.... Robert N Landes
Exec Vice Pres/CFO .... Robert J Bahash
Senior Vice Pres Treasury Operations
.... Frank D Penglase
Group Vice Pres Equity Services John C Zwingli
Senior Vice Pres-Equity Info Services
.... James G Branscome
EDITORS AND MANAGERS
Exec Editor-Market Scope/Daily News
.... Shauna Morrison
Editor .... John J Daly
Assoc Editor .... John Leigh
Assoc Editor .... Paula Schnorous

MECHANICAL PRODUCTION INFORMATION
Method of Printing: Offset.

The Wall Street Journal Eastern Edition
(mon to fri) (Business News)
The Wall Street Journal, 200 Liberty St., New York, NY 10281; tel (212) 416-2000.
Note: See listing in Daily Section under New York, NY.

The Inter-City Express
(mon to fri) (Government & Legal)
The Inter-City Express, 171 12th St., Suite 203, Oakland, CA 94607-4411; tel (510) 465-3121; fax (510) 465-1576.
Circulation: 852(pd); Est. Feb. 4, 1994.
Price: 50¢(d); $140.00/yr.

CORPORATE OFFICER
Publisher .... Nell Fields
ADVERTISING
Director .... Dan Gougherty
Manager-Legal .... Tonya Peacock
EDITORS AND MANAGERS
Editor .... Tom Barkley
Staff Writer .... Jonna Palmer
Support Staff .... Houay Keabouth
Support Staff .... Barbara Navarro
Support Staff .... Margaret Peacock
PRODUCTION
Design .... Ronald McNees

The Journal Record
(mon to fri) (Business & Legal)
The Journal Record, PO Box 26370, Oklahoma City, OK 73126-0370; tel (405) 235-3100; fax (405) 278-6946.

Circulation: 3,547(pd); 160(fr); Sworn Oct. 1, 1995.
Price: 50¢(d); $131.00/yr (in Oklahoma), $180.00/yr (outside Oklahoma).
Advertising: Open inch rate $14.70.
News Services: AP, NYT. Established: 1903.

CORPORATE OFFICER
Chairman of the Board .... Jim P Dolan
GENERAL MANAGEMENT
Publisher .... John Komonicki
Office Manager .... Pat Berry
ADVERTISING
Manager .... Mary Mélon
CIRCULATION
Manager .... Jan Weeks
EDITOR AND MANAGER
Managing Editor .... David Page
PRODUCTION
Manager .... Mary Powell

MECHANICAL PRODUCTION INFORMATION
Method of Printing: Offset.

Daily Record
(mon to fri) (Legal)
Daily Record, 3323 Leavenworth St., Omaha, NE 68105-1915; tel (402) 345-1303; fax (402) 345-2351.
Circulation: 1,100(pd); 114(fr); Sworn Oct. 2, 1995.
Price: $84.00/yr; $50.00/6mo.
Advertising: Open inch rate $7.25. Representative: NNA.
News Services: TMS, United Media, WP Writers Group, LATS. Established: 1886.

CORPORATE OFFICERS
President .... Ronald A Henningsen
Vice Pres .... Lynda K Henningsen
GENERAL MANAGEMENT
Publisher .... Ronald A Henningsen
ADVERTISING
Manager .... Lynda K Henningsen
CIRCULATION
Manager .... Diane Cloyd
NEWS EXECUTIVE
News Exec .... Charles Wieser
EDITOR AND MANAGER
Editor .... John P Elgsaer
PRODUCTION
Manager .... Brian Henningsen

MECHANICAL PRODUCTION INFORMATION
Method of Printing: Offset.

Palm Beach Daily Business Review
(mon to fri) (Business, Real Estate, and Law)
Palm Beach Daily Business Review, One Southeast Third Ave., 9th Fl. (33131); PO Box 010589, Miami, FL 33101; tel (305) 377-3721; fax (305) 374-8474.
Circulation: 2,362(pd); 34(fr); Sworn Sept. 14, 1995.
Price: $1.00 $3.00 (d-fri); $450.00/yr (Corporate), $169.00/yr (Small business or individual).
Advertising: Open inch rate $21.30. Established: 1926.
Note: See Daily Business Review editions in Broward and Miami, FL.

CORPORATE OFFICERS
Chairman of the Board ...... Edward Wasserman
Chief Financial Officer .... Jim Pamplin
GENERAL MANAGEMENT
Publisher .... Donna Trainer-Stutts
General Manager .... Deborah Mullin
Assoc Publisher .... T Alicia Coya
ADVERTISING
Sales Representative .... Sarah Huff
CIRCULATION
Director .... Margarita Huerta

EDITORS AND MANAGERS
Editor in Chief .... Edward Wasserman
Exec Editor .... Ken Cogburn

MECHANICAL PRODUCTION INFORMATION
Method of Printing: Offset.

The Wall Street Journal Western Edition
(mon to fri) (Business News)
The Wall Street Journal, 1701 Page Mill Rd., Palo Alto, CA 94304.
Note: See listing in Daily Section under New York, NY.

The Legal Intelligencer
(mon to fri) (Legal Community)
The Legal Intelligencer, 1617 John F. Kennedy Blvd., Suite 960, Philadelphia, PA 19103; tel (215) 557-2300; fax (215) 557-2301.
Circulation: 2,693(pd); 365(fr); Sworn Sept. 27, 1995.
Price: $3.00(d); $325.00/yr.
Advertising: Open inch rate $1.75/line.
News Service: AP. Established: 1843.

GENERAL MANAGEMENT
Chairman of the Board/Publisher
.... Raymond R Rafferty Jr
President/COO .... Jane Seagrave
Vice Pres-Sales .... Harry Alba
Vice Pres-Finance/CFO ..... Robert A Graham Jr
ADVERTISING
Director of Marketing .... Ana M Blanco
CIRCULATION
Director .... Ana M Blanco
NEWS EXECUTIVES
Editor in Chief .... Brian H Harris
Managing Editor .... Zan Hale
PRODUCTION
Manager .... Stephen Newman

MECHANICAL PRODUCTION INFORMATION
Method of Printing: Cold.

Pittsburgh Legal Journal
(mon to fri) (Legal)
Pittsburgh Legal Journal, 400 Koppers Bldg., 436 7th Ave., Pittsburgh, PA 15219; tel (412) 281-6566.
Circulation: 1,500(pd); 150(fr); Est. Oct. 26, 1995.
Price: $1.00(d).
Advertising: Open inch rate $8.00. Established: 1853.

NEWS EXECUTIVES
Editor in Chief .... Frederick N Egler Jr
Managing Editor .... James I Smith III

MECHANICAL PRODUCTION INFORMATION
Method of Printing: Offset.

Daily Journal of Commerce
(mon to fri) (Business)
Daily Journal of Commerce, 2840 N.W. 35th Ave.; PO Box 10127, Portland, OR 97210-0127; tel (503) 226-1311; fax (503) 224-7140.
Circulation: 3,453(pd); 100(fr); Sworn Oct. 1, 1995.
Price: $1.00(d); $92.00/6mo; $158.00/yr.
Advertising: Open inch rate $20.00. Established: 1872.

CORPORATE OFFICERS
President .... L M Smith
Vice Pres-Corporate Operations .. Phil Bridge
GENERAL MANAGEMENT
Publisher .... Dorothy H Smith

Vice Pres .... Peter Smith
Office Manager .... Jorja Orr
Director/Printing Sales .... Jack Geoghegan
Marketing/Classified .... Sherri Marx
ADVERTISING
Legal Manager .... Irwin J Caplan
CIRCULATION
Subscription Manager .... Sharon Perry
EDITORS AND MANAGERS
Editor .... Kevin Harden
Photography .... Greg Paul
PRODUCTION
Director .... Ali Hassannia
Pressroom Supervisor .... Jay Thompson

MECHANICAL PRODUCTION INFORMATION
Method of Printing: Offset.

Daily Shipping News
(mon to fri) (Foreign Trade, Transportation)
Daily Shipping News, 7831 S.E. Stark St., Suite 200, Portland, OR 97215; tel (503) 255-2142; fax (503) 255-2735.
Circulation: 510(pd); 72(fr); Sworn Sept. 25, 1995.
Price: 75¢(d); $165.00/yr.
Advertising: Open inch rate $7.00. Established: 1920.

GENERAL MANAGEMENT
Publisher .... Joseph Blaha
Chief Financial Officer ..... Robert A Graham Jr
ADVERTISING
Classified Manager .... Dorothy Nishida
Sales Representative .... Jim Egger
EDITORS AND MANAGERS
Editor .... Jim Egger
Vessel Movements Editor .... Laurie Woitte

MECHANICAL PRODUCTION INFORMATION
Method of Printing: Offset.

The Daily Record
(mon to fri) (Business, Legal)
The Daily Record, 11 Centre Park; PO Box 6, Rochester, NY 14601; tel (716) 232-6920.
Circulation: 1,744(pd); 222(fr); Sworn Sept. 29, 1995.
Price: $1.00(d); $65.00/3mo, $75.00/6mo; $119.00/yr.
Advertising: Open inch rate 90¢/line (agency rate), 75¢/line (retail rate). Representative: NNA. Established: 1908.

CORPORATE OFFICER
President/Publisher .... Johnson D Hay
GENERAL MANAGEMENT
Assoc Publisher .... Maria Biuso
General Manager .... Daniel Whaley
EDITORS AND MANAGERS
Editor .... Rogers E Gorman
Editorial Director .... Ginger Lamb

MECHANICAL PRODUCTION INFORMATION
Method of Printing: Offset.

The Daily Recorder
(mon to fri) (Legal, Government, Business/Real Estate, Construction)
The Daily Recorder, 1115 H St.; PO Box 1048 (95814), Sacramento, CA 95812-1048; tel (916) 444-2355; fax (916) 444-0636. Daily Journal Corp. group.
Circulation: 1,445(pd); 167(fr); Sworn Sept. 30, 1995.
Price: 50¢(d); $183.00/yr.
Advertising: Open inch rate $11.28 (display), $9.28 (classified). Established: 1911.

GENERAL MANAGEMENT
Publisher .... Geny De Vera-Gougherty

Copyright ©1996 by the Editor & Publisher Co.

Special service dailies

I-470

ADVERTISING
Commercial Sales — Dan Gougherty
Legal Sales — David A Fong
NEWS EXECUTIVE
Editor — Nora Lynn
EDITOR AND MANAGER
Reporter — Anne Marie Ternus
PRODUCTION
Editor — Heather Gordon
MECHANICAL PRODUCTION INFORMATION
Method of Printing: Offset.

The Daily Commercial Recorder
(mon to fri) (Legal & Business)
The Daily Commercial Recorder, 6222 N.W. International Hwy. 10, Suite 101, San Antonio, TX 78201; tel (210) 736-4450; fax (210) 736-5506.
Circulation: 476(pd); Est. Oct. 25, 1995.
Price: $1.00(d); $55.00/3mo; $125.00/yr.
Advertising: Open inch rate $15.10. Established: 1896.
CORPORATE OFFICER
President — William A Johnson
GENERAL MANAGEMENT
Publisher — Helen I Lutz
Assoc Publisher — Gregg R Rosenfield
Office Manager — Irene Palencia
Accountant — Susie D Cardenas
CIRCULATION
Manager — John Coldwater
EDITORS AND MANAGERS
Editor — Salwa Choucair
Legal Editor — Stella Orozco
PRODUCTION
Manager — Sylvia P Sepulveda
MECHANICAL PRODUCTION INFORMATION
Method of Printing: Offset.

San Diego Daily Transcript
(mon to fri)
San Diego Daily Transcript, PO Box 85469, San Diego, CA 92186-5469; tel (619) 232-4381; fax (619) 239-5716.
Note: See listing in Daily Section under San Diego, CA.

San Francisco Daily Journal
(mon to fri) (Government & Legal)
San Francisco Daily Journal, 1390 Market St., Suite 1210, San Francisco, CA 94102; tel (415) 252-0500; fax (415) 252-0288. Daily Journal Corp. group.
Circulation: 6,291(pd); 1,882(fr); Sworn Sept. 30, 1995.
Price: $1.00(d); $47.00/mo; $389.00/yr.
Advertising: Open inch rate $10.76. Established: 1893.
CORPORATE OFFICER
Assoc Publisher — Marguerite Jones
GENERAL MANAGEMENT
Business Manager — Kimberley Beeson
ADVERTISING
Manager — Linda Hubbell
CIRCULATION
Manager — Marguerite Jones
EDITORS AND MANAGERS
Editor — Philip D Hager
Managing Editor — Steven Ball
News Editor — Karen Hata

The Recorder
(mon to fri) (Court/Legal)
The Recorder, 625 Polk St., Suite 500, San Francisco, CA 94102; tel (415) 749-5400; fax (415) 749-5449.
Circulation: 6,872(pd); 852(fr); Sworn Oct. 2, 1995.
Price: $1.00(d); $6.58/wk; $28.50/mo; $342.00/yr. Established: 1877.
GENERAL MANAGEMENT
Assoc Publisher — Paul Gamble
Controller — Mark Lowe
CIRCULATION
Director — Pat Brubaker
Classified Director — Brian Witt
Legal Manager — Sandy Gibbons
Display Manager — Maria Sanen
EDITORS AND MANAGERS
Editor & Publisher — Peter E Scheer
Exec Editor — Susan Beck
MECHANICAL PRODUCTION INFORMATION
Method of Printing: Offset.

San Jose Post-Record
(mon to fri)
San Jose Post-Record, 90 N. First St., Suite 100, San Jose, CA 95113; tel (408) 287-4866; fax (408) 287-2544.
Circulation: 498(pd); 135(fr); Sworn Sept. 30, 1995.
Price: 25¢(d); $110.00/yr.
Advertising: Open inch rate $9.28 (display and classified), $10.50 (legal). Established: 1910.
CORPORATE OFFICER
Publisher — Fay Kenney
ADVERTISING
Manager-Legal — Veronica Espinoza
CIRCULATION
Manager — Veronica Espinoza
EDITOR AND MANAGER
Editor — Geoff Fein
PRODUCTION
Design — Lisa Churchill
MECHANICAL PRODUCTION INFORMATION
Method of Printing: Computer produced.

Seattle Daily Journal of Commerce
(mon to sat) (Business)
Seattle Daily Journal of Commerce, 83 Columbia St.; PO Box 11050, Seattle, WA 98104; tel (206) 622-8272; fax (206) 622-8416.
Circulation: 5,348(pd); 291(fr); Sworn Sept. 30, 1995.
Price: $1.00(d); $60.00/3mo; $95.00/6mo; $190.00/yr.
Advertising: Open inch rate $20.00. **Representatives:** NAA; NNA.
News Services: AP, Business Wire, PRN, NYT. Established: 1893.
CORPORATE OFFICERS
Corporate Officer — Monte Brown
Corporate Officer — D O Brown
Corporate Officer — Phil Brown
GENERAL MANAGEMENT
Publisher — Phil Brown
General Manager — John Mihalyo
ADVERTISING
Manager — John Mihalyo
Classified — Heather Mungton
Legal — Valerie Gallagher
CIRCULATION
Manager — Owen O'Neil
EDITORS AND MANAGERS
Editor — Phil Brown
Architecture Editor — Claire Enlow
Business Editor — Jon Savelle
City Editor — Jerry Craig
Construction Editor — Benn Minnick
Environmental Editor — Lucy Bodilly
Law & Court Editor — Jon Savelle
Real Estate Editor — Maude Scott
PRODUCTION
Manager — Mary Ann Swingler
MECHANICAL PRODUCTION INFORMATION
Method of Printing: Offset.

The Daily Legal News
(mon to fri) (Court, Legal, Business, Commercial and Financial)
The Daily Legal News Inc., 501 Texas St., Rm. M-103, Shreveport, LA 71101-5413; tel (318) 222-0213. Daily Legal News Inc. group.
Circulation: 483(pd); 35(fr); Sworn Sept. 28, 1995.
Price: $1.00(d); $22.00/mo; $264.00/yr.
Advertising: Open inch rate $45.00/mo (3 ½" x 1"). Established: 1920.
CORPORATE OFFICERS
President — Jared Z Evans
Secretary/Treasurer — Margaret P DeFoy
NEWS EXECUTIVES
Editor — Lee Ann Bryce
Managing Editor — Margaret P DeFoy

Sonoma County Daily Herald-Recorder
(mon to fri) (Legal, Court News & Recordings)
Sonoma County Daily Herald-Recorder, 1818 Fourth St.; PO Box 877, Santa Rosa, CA 95402; tel (707) 545-1166; fax (707) 545-6310. Daily Journal Corp. group.
Circulation: 350(pd); Est.
Price: $1.00(d); $188.00/yr.
Advertising: Open inch rate $8.16.
News Services: ACCN, AP. Established: 1899.
CORPORATE OFFICER
Publisher — Christine K Griego
GENERAL MANAGEMENT
Recordings — Nancy F Hamilton
Filings — Roberta J Nelson
ADVERTISING
Manager-Display — Dan Gougherty
Legal Notices — Christine K Griego
EDITORS AND MANAGERS
Los Angeles Editor — Lisa Churchill
Reporter/Calendars Editor — Erik H Cummins

Daily Events
(mon to fri) (Court & Legal)
Daily Events, 327 S. Patton; PO Box 1, Springfield, MO 65801-0001; tel (417) 866-1401; fax (417) 866-1491.
Circulation: 450(pd); Est.
Price: $1.00(d); $78.00/yr. **Representative:** ACCN Advertising Service.
GENERAL MANAGEMENT
Publisher — Earnest I Young
EDITOR AND MANAGER
Editor — Brenda Stewart
MECHANICAL PRODUCTION INFORMATION
Method of Printing: Digital Press Sheet.

The Courier Post
(mon to fri) (Legal News)
The Courier Post, 201 N. Main St., Suite 205; PO Box 1077, St. Charles, MO 63302-1077; tel (314) 421-1880; fax (314) 421-0436. Legal Communications Corp. (CapCities/ABC) group.
Circulation: 557(pd); 10(fr); Sworn Sept. 22, 1995.
Price: 50¢(d); $60.00/yr.
Advertising: Open inch rate $1.00.
News Service: RN. Established: 1969.
GENERAL MANAGEMENT
Publisher — Sara Sue Tedesco
Business Manager — John M Beck
Office Manager — Regina P Rickey
ADVERTISING
Manager — Susan Richard
CIRCULATION
Manager — Nancy S Comia-Hoffman
EDITOR AND MANAGER
Editor — William B Connaghan

PRODUCTION
Manager — John M Reno
MECHANICAL PRODUCTION INFORMATION
Method of Printing: Offset.

St. Joseph Daily Courier
(mon to fri) (Legal)
St. Joseph Daily Courier, 1014 S. 10th St., St. Joseph, MO 64503; tel (816) 279-3441.
Circulation: 220(pd); Sworn Oct. 4, 1995.
Price: 35¢(d); $5.35/mo; $46.00/yr.
CORPORATE OFFICER
President — Billy G Cunningham

The St. Louis Countain
(tues to sat) (Court, Legal, Business, Commercial and Financial)
The St. Louis Countain, 7777 Bonhomme, Suite 1205, St. Louis, MO 63105; tel (314) 421-1880. Legal Communications Corp. (CapCities/ABC) group.
Circulation: 925(pd); 82(fr); Sworn Sept. 22, 1995.
Price: $1.00(d); $187.00/yr.
Advertising: Open inch rate $5.00.
News Service: RN. Established: 1902.
GENERAL MANAGEMENT
Publisher — Sara Sue Tedesco
Business Manager — John M Beck
Information Services Manager — Janet M Watral
ADVERTISING
Manager — Susan Richard
CIRCULATION
Manager — Nancy S Comia-Hoffman
EDITOR AND MANAGER
Editor — William B Connaghan
PRODUCTION
Manager — John M Reno
MECHANICAL PRODUCTION INFORMATION
Method of Printing: Web Offset.

St. Louis Daily Record
(tues to sat) (Legal)
St. Louis Daily Record, 612 N. 2nd St., 4th Fl.; PO Box 88910, St. Louis, MO 63102; tel (314) 421-1880; fax (314) 421-0436. Legal Communications Corp. (CapCities/ABC) group.
Circulation: 824(pd); 79(fr); Sworn Sept. 22, 1995.
Price: 95¢(d); $187.00/yr.
Advertising: Open inch rate $5.00.
News Service: RN. Established: 1890.
GENERAL MANAGEMENT
Publisher — Sara Sue Tedesco
Information Services Manager — Janet M Watral
Business Manager — John M Beck
ADVERTISING
Manager — Susan Richard
CIRCULATION
Manager — Nancy S Comia-Hoffman
EDITOR AND MANAGER
Editor — William B Connaghan
PRODUCTION
Manager — John M Reno
MECHANICAL PRODUCTION INFORMATION
Method of Printing: Web Offset.

St. Louis Watchman Advocate
(mon to fri) (Court, Legal, Financial)
St. Louis Watchman Advocate, 200 S. Bemiston Ave., Suite 201, Clayton, MO 63105-1915; tel (314) 725-1515; fax (314) 725-1716.

Copyright ©1996 by the Editor & Publisher Co.

Special service dailies I-471

Circulation: 20,000(pd); Sworn Oct. 19, 1993.
Price: 50¢(d); $50.00/yr.
Advertising: Open inch rate $14.00. Established: 1881.

CORPORATE OFFICER
President/Publisher ..... Ronald W Kuper
ADVERTISING
Manager ..... Gabriela G Bethke
EDITOR AND MANAGER
Editor ..... Mary J McCormick

Saint Paul Legal Ledger
(tues to sat) (Legal, Business)
Saint Paul Legal Ledger, 46 E. 4th St., 640 Minnesota Bldg., St. Paul, MN 55101-1163; tel (612) 222-0059. Legal Ledger Inc. group.
Circulation: 537(pd); Sworn Sept. 29, 1995.
Price: 50¢(d); $50.00/6mo; $90.00/yr.
Advertising: Open inch rate $9.00. Established: 1927.

GENERAL MANAGEMENT
President/Publisher ..... Samuel E Lewis Jr
Mechanical Superintendent ..... Michael Lewis
Business Manager ..... Barbara St Martin
NEWS EXECUTIVE
Editor ..... Samuel E Lewis Jr
MECHANICAL PRODUCTION INFORMATION
Method of Printing: Offset.

Tacoma Daily Index
(mon to fri) (Court & Building News)
Tacoma Daily Index, 714 Pacific Ave., Tacoma, WA 98402; tel (206) 627-4853.
Circulation: 467(pd); 53(fr); Sworn Sept. 27, 1995.
Price: $50.00/yr.
News Service: ACCN Advertising Services.

GENERAL MANAGEMENT
Publisher/Editor ..... Marshall B Skidmore

Legal News
(mon to fri) (Court News)
Legal News, 218 Spitzer Building, Toledo, OH 43604; tel (419) 241-3333.
Circulation: 650(pd); Est.
Price: $75.00/yr.
Advertising: Open inch rate $8.00. Established: 1895.

GENERAL MANAGEMENT
Publisher/Editor ..... Allen C Foster
MECHANICAL PRODUCTION INFORMATION
Method of Printing: Offset Rotary.

The Daily Territorial
(mon to fri) (Legal & Business News)
The Daily Territorial, 1 W. Orange Grove Rd., Tucson, AZ 85704; tel (520) 297-1107; fax (520) 297-6253. Wick Communications Inc. group.
Circulation: 916(pd); 51(fr); Sworn Sept. 18, 1995.
Price: $1.00(d); $100.00/yr.
Advertising: Open inch rate $7.50. Established: 1930.

GENERAL MANAGEMENT
Publisher ..... Stephen E Jewett
ADVERTISING
Manager ..... David Stolar
EDITOR AND MANAGER
Editor ..... Cheri Cross-Bushenell
MECHANICAL PRODUCTION INFORMATION
Method of Printing: Offset.

Tulsa Daily Commerce & Legal News
(mon to fri) (Business, Finance & Legal)
Tulsa Daily Commerce & Legal News, 8545 E. 41st St., Tulsa, OK 74145; tel (918) 663-1414; fax (918) 664-8161. Retherford Publications Inc. group.
Circulation: 538(pd); 100(fr); Sworn Sept. 30, 1994.
Price: 50¢(d); $85.00/6mo (in Tulsa Co.), $115.00/6mo (in Oklahoma), $163.00/6mo (outside Oklahoma); $109.00/yr (in Tulsa Co.), $192.00/yr (in Oklahoma), $259.00/yr (outside Oklahoma).
Advertising: Open inch rate $7.50. Established: 1909.

GENERAL MANAGEMENT
President/Publisher ..... Bill R Retherford
Assoc Publisher ..... Tim R Retherford
Mechanical Superintendent ..... Bill Roberts
General Manager ..... Charles Cagle
ADVERTISING
Sales Representative ..... Monte Myrick
CIRCULATION
Operations Director ..... Bill Roberts
EDITORS AND MANAGERS
Editor/Managing Editor ..... Ralph Schaefer
Legal News Manager ..... Clifford White
MECHANICAL PRODUCTION INFORMATION
Method of Printing: Offset.

Daily Legal News
(mon to fri) (Legal)
Daily Legal News, 145 W. Commerce St., Youngstown, OH 44503; tel (216) 747-7777.
Circulation: 686(pd); 30(fr); Sworn Sept. 29, 1995.
Price: 35¢(d); $72.00/yr.
Advertising: Open inch rate $4.00. Established: 1924.

CORPORATE OFFICERS
President ..... James T Cover
Secretary/Treasurer ..... Richard F Demko
GENERAL MANAGEMENT
Co-Publisher ..... Richard F Demko
Co-Publisher ..... James T Cover
Office Manager ..... Mary Ann Shaffer
CIRCULATION
Manager ..... Mary Ann Shaffer
NEWS EXECUTIVES
Co-Editor ..... Richard F Demko
Co-Editor ..... James T Cover
EDITOR AND MANAGER
Reporter ..... Carol Ann Peebles
MECHANICAL PRODUCTION INFORMATION
Method of Printing: Offset (sheet fed).

ENTERTAINMENT

The Hollywood Reporter
(mon to fri) (Entertainment)
The Hollywood Reporter, 5055 Wilshire Blvd., Suite 600, Los Angeles, CA 90036; tel (213) 525-2000; fax (213) 525-2377.
Circulation: 23,789(pd); ABC Sept. 30, 1995.
Price: $1.25(d); $55.00/3mo; $115.00/6mo; $175.00/yr (domestic); $320.00/2yr.
Advertising: Open inch rate $44.00 (classified), $95.00 (display), $3,260.00 (full page display).
News Services: AP, DJ. Established: 1930.

CORPORATE OFFICERS
President ..... Arthur F Kingsbury
Vice Pres ..... Robert J Dowling
Chief Financial Officer ..... H Todd Hittle

GENERAL MANAGEMENT
Assoc Publisher ..... Lynne Segall
General Manager ..... Michael V Leonard Jr
ADVERTISING
Promotion Manager ..... C G O'Connor
CIRCULATION
Director ..... Pamela Anderson
NEWS EXECUTIVES
Editor in Chief ..... Robert J Dowling
Editor ..... David Morgan
Managing Editor ..... Howard Burns
EDITOR AND MANAGER
Washington DC Bureau Chief ..... Brooks Boliek
PRODUCTION
Manager ..... Robert Ford

Daily Variety
(mon to fri) (Entertainment)
Daily Variety, 5700 Wilshire Blvd., Suite 120, Los Angeles, CA 90036; tel (213) 857-6600.
Circulation: 26,582(pd); ABC Sept. 30, 1995.
Price: 75¢(d); $129.00/yr.
Advertising: Open inch rate $60.00.
News Services: DJ, AP. Established: 1933.

CORPORATE OFFICERS
President/Co-CEO ..... Terrence M McDermott
Chairman/Co-CEO ..... Robert L Krakoff
Senior Vice Pres/General Manager ..... John J Beni
GENERAL MANAGEMENT
Publisher ..... Michael Silverman
ADVERTISING
Director ..... Pattikay Lee
CIRCULATION
Distribution Manager ..... Jack Sunkes
EDITORS AND MANAGERS
Exec Editor ..... Stephen West
Editor-at-Large ..... Peter Pryor
Managing Editor ..... Jonathan Taylor
News Editor ..... Kinsey Lowe
PRODUCTION
Manager ..... Bob Butler
MECHANICAL PRODUCTION INFORMATION
Method of Printing: Offset.

METALS

American Metal Market
(mon to fri) (Metals)
American Metal Market, 825 7th Ave., New York, NY 10019; tel (212) 887-8550; fax (212) 887-8520. Chilton Co. (CapCities/ABC) group.
Circulation: 10,084(pd); ABC Sept. 30, 1995.
Price: $5.00(d); $575.00/yr, $395.00/yr (mon only).
Advertising: Open inch rate $60.00.
News Services: RN, DJ, AP, PRN, KRT. Established: 1882.

GENERAL MANAGEMENT
Publisher/Group Vice Pres ..... John L Lindsey
Business Manager ..... Georgia Steele
ADVERTISING
Director ..... Preston Gibson
CIRCULATION
Manager ..... Heidi Senecoff
NEWS EXECUTIVES
Editor in Chief ..... Michael Botta
Managing Editor ..... Robert Manas
EDITORS AND MANAGERS
Exec Editor ..... Ben Teplitz
Senior News Editor-Special Issues ..... Charles Berry

PRODUCTION
Manager ..... Julie Jacowleff
MECHANICAL PRODUCTION INFORMATION
Method of Printing: Web Offset.

REAL ESTATE

Daily Commerce
(mon to fri) (Commerce)
Daily Commerce, 915 E. First St., Los Angeles, CA 90054; tel (213) 229-5300.
Note: See listing in Daily Section under Los Angeles, CA

Inter-City Express
(mon to fri) (Real Estate)
Inter-City Express, PO Box 30157, Oakland, CA 94604; tel (415) 465-3121.
Circulation: 1,400(pd); Est.
Price: 50¢(d); $35.00/3mo; $90.00/yr.
Advertising: Open inch rate $4.84. Established: 1909.

GENERAL MANAGEMENT
Publisher ..... Helen B Fields
Marketing Director ..... M Z de Padua
NEWS EXECUTIVE
Editor ..... Michael Shokrian

SPORTS

Daily Racing Form
(mon to sat; S) (Thoroughbred Racing)
Daily Racing Form, 2231 Camelback Rd., Suite 100, Phoenix, AZ 85016; tel (602) 468-6500; fax (602) 468-6507.
Circulation: 60,500(pd); Est. Sept. 30, 1993.
Price: $3.00(d); $163.90/mo (1st class), $104.20/mo (2nd class); $1,966.50/yr (1st class), $1,250.30/yr (2nd class).
Advertising: Open inch rate $9.80.
News Services: RN, UPI. Established: 1894.
Note: Daily Racing Form publishes several editions nationwide. Circulation figures are estimated for total distribution.

CORPORATE OFFICERS
Chief Executive Officer ..... Jack Farnsworth
Chief Operating Officer ..... William Dow
GENERAL MANAGEMENT
Publisher ..... Jack Farnsworth
Vice Pres/General Manager ..... Stephen Adams
Office Manager ..... Diana Christianson
National Director-Communications ..... John Greco
Vice Pres-Track & Field Operations ..... Joseph Laskowski
ADVERTISING
Director-National ..... Richard Witt
Vice Pres-Marketing & Sales ..... Katherine Wilkins
CIRCULATION
National Director ..... Stephen Martin
NEWS EXECUTIVES
Editor in Chief ..... Neil Cook
Editor ..... George Bernet
Managing Editor ..... Duke Dosik
EDITORS AND MANAGERS
Bloodstock Editor ..... S H Fernando
Features Editor ..... Mike Mullaney
News Editor ..... Peter Berry
PRODUCTION
Vice Pres ..... Stephen Adams
Director-Printing ..... Stan Shulman
MECHANICAL PRODUCTION INFORMATION
Method of Printing: Offset.

Copyright ©1996 by the Editor & Publisher Co.

- **FIND THE INFORMATION YOU WANT INSTANTLY**
  With a CD-ROM drive linked to your PC, you'll have access to Year Book information instantly. A fully indexed, searchable database allows you to pull out Year Book data with the criteria you select.

- **IT'S EASY, IT'S FAST**
  The simple, menu-activated search-and-display capability of our CD-ROM makes finding data and compiling lists easier than ever.

- **SEARCH BY ANY FIELD**
  Your options are limitless! Sort newspapers by equipment use. Sort and rank by publication days and circulation. Search for special topic editions...

- **EXPORTABLE DATA**
  All the information can be exported to your PC in a wide range of formats, including Word Perfect, Lotus, DBF, ASCII, etc.

- **LISTING CAPABILITIES FOR MAILINGS**
  The CD-ROM can be purchased with listing capabilities, too. Customize mailing lists for each of your communications projects. Export data to your own label utility!

- **CD-ROM SECTIONS**
  The Year Book CD-ROM includes all the Year Book data for U.S. Dailies, U.S. Weeklies, Canadian Newspapers, Foreign Newspapers, Mechanical Equipment and Who's Where sections ...names of contacts and their areas of responsibility, plus other critical information about newspapers, newspaper suppliers and service companies.

SEARCH SOFTWARE: Dataware

COVERAGE DATES: Current

UPDATED: Annually

REQUIRES: IBM-PC or compatible, VGA or better Monitor, DOS 3.3 higher, Microsoft CD-ROM Extensions, 640K RAM, 3MB minimum, Hard Drive, CD-ROM Drive. Macintosh Plus or higher, Any monitor, V6.0.7, 7.0 or later, 2.5MB RAM minimum, 2MB available, Hard Drive, CD-ROM Drive.

CD-ROM without listing capabilities : $495
CD-ROM with listing capabilities : $895
Network versions are available.
Please call (212) 675-4380, ext. 509 for pricing.

Mail your order and payment to:
Editor & Publisher Year Book, 11 West 19th Street,
New York, NY 10011-4234.
Or to charge your order to your Visa/MC account, call
(212) 675-4380, ext. 509.

Payments must accompany all orders. NY, CA, DC, and Canada add appropriate tax. Please supply proper street address for UPS delivery. No deliveries will be made to P.O. boxes. All remittance must be in U.S. dollars.

For answers to technical questions about the CD-ROM, call (212) 675-4380, ext. 506.

More than 500,000 Newspaper Facts!

SECTION II

Weekly and Special Newspapers Published in the United States

Weekly newspapers	1-85
Alternative newspapers	86-87
Black newspapers	87-90
Ethnic newspapers	90-92
Gay and lesbian newspapers	92-93
Hispanic newspapers	93-95
Jewish newspapers	95-96
Military newspapers	96-98
Religious newspapers	98-100
College and university newspapers	101-112

LOOK–NO HANDS.

At Last–Fully Automated Sunday Completes, Comic Sections and TMC's. The Very Latest in Technology.
Only from SITMA.

Insert, Onsert, Quarter-Fold, Stack, Label, Bundle Wrap.

And Our Equipment And Service Is The Best News Of All.
(800) 728-1254

Newspaper publishers depend on reliable, efficient equipment to meet demanding schedules and incredible deadlines. SITMA equipment is up to the challenge of automating just about any production process you have in mind. And quality-built, SITMA equipment is backed by solid service and support with a 24-hour hot line and a comprehensive parts program. Give your productivity a boost. Call us today. And we'll deliver equipment and service that's front page news.

45 Empire Drive, St. Paul, MN 55103
Phone: (612) 222-2324
Fax: (612) 222-4652

WEEKLY NEWSPAPERS PUBLISHED IN THE UNITED STATES

This directory covers weekly community newspapers of general interest published up to three times a week. The list is arranged alphabetically by states and within each state, by the principal community or neighborhood served by each paper.

Then follows, in light italic type, the exact name of the paper.

Following the dash appears the paper's address, which may be in a different community from the area it serves. If only a zip code number appears (in parenthesis) it may be assumed that the community's name heading the entry along with the zip number forms a sufficient address.

The day or days of publication appear in abbreviated form. Circulations are shown as paid (pd) or free (fr), with the type of audit or report following: ABC - Audit Bureau of Circulations; CAC - Certified Audit of Circulations; CPVS - Community Papers Verification Service; VAC - Verified Audit Circulation; Sw - sworn statement of circulation; Est - estimate. Circulation figures are for Sept. 30, 1995, where they are available.

The amount in cents/dollars is the national advertising rate for one agate line/one inch, respectively (the open line/inch rate); N/A indicates advertising is not sold in agate line/open inch units; a "C" following the rate indicates that advertising is sold in combination with one or more weekly newspapers.

The names of the publisher, general manager, editor and managing editor follow the line rate where these are available.

Weekly papers of special interest (alternative, black, ethnic, gay & lesbian, hispanic, jewish, military, religious and college newspapers) are also included in this section.

ALABAMA

Abbeville: *Abbeville Herald* — 135-137 Kirkland St.; PO Box 609 (36310); Th; 1,989pd (Sw); $2.61; publisher & editor J Edward Dodd III; tel (334) 585-2331; fax (334) 585-6835

Albertville/Boaz: *The Sand Mountain Reporter* — 3760 US Hwy. 431; PO Box 190, Albertville (35950); Tu/Th/Sa; 13,500pd, 225fr (Sw); $7.32; publisher Michael Hudgins; editor Avis Holderfield; tel (205) 878-1311; fax (205) 878-2104

Andalusia/Opp/Florala/Red Level/Dozier/Gantt: *Covington Times Courier & Times Courier Plus* — 1033 E. Three Notch St., Andalusia (36420); W/F; 3,656pd, 15,677fr (Sw); $7.60; C; publisher Edward M Pace; editor James Walker; tel (334) 222-8541; fax (334) 222-1987

Arab: *The Arab Tribune* — 619 S. Brindlee Mountain Pkwy.; PO Box 605 (35016); W; 6,995pd, 193fr (Sw); $5.60; C; publisher Edwin H Reed; general manager Dannie Elmore; editor David Moore; tel (205) 586-3188; fax (205) 586-3188

Atmore: *The Atmore Advance* — 301 S. Main St.; PO Box 28 (36502); W/Su; 3,650pd, 25fr (Sw); $7.15; C; publisher & editor Michele Cox Gerlach; tel (334) 368-2123; fax (334) 368-2124

Auburn/Opelika/Lee Co.: *The Auburn Bulletin-Eagle* — 122 Tichenor Ave. (36830); PO Box 2240, Auburn (36831-3240); W/Su; 4,875pd, 15,991fr (Sw); $7.29; publisher Paul Sevaska; general manager & editor Stan Voit; tel (334) 821-7150; fax (334) 887-0037

Bay Minette: *The Baldwin Times* — Courthouse Sq.; PO Box 571 (36507); Th; 3,483pd (Sw); 35¢; publisher Meredith White; editor Tommy Leytham; managing editor Liz Springer; tel (334) 937-2511; fax (334) 937-2511

Birmingham: *Alabama Messenger* — 706 Frank Nelson Bldg. (35203); Sa; 1,343pd, 110fr (Est); 36¢; publisher Eleanor Abercrombie Foster; editor Karen W Abercrombie; managing editor Traci Smeraglia; tel (205) 252-3672; fax (205) 252-3639

Birmingham: *Over The Mountain Journal* — 3250 Independence Dr., Ste. 5 (35209); Th (bi-weekly); 39,600fr (Sw); $28.00; publisher Maurice G Wald; editor Carla Morrison; tel (205) 879-9686; fax (205) 879-4579

Brewton: *Brewton Standard* — 407 St. Nicholas (36426); PO Box 887 (36427); W; 5,200pd, 50fr (Est); $6.95; Su; 4,300pd, 50fr (Est); $6.95; C; publisher & editor David King; tel (334) 867-4876; fax (334) 867-4877

Camden: *Wilcox Progressive Era* — 16 Water St.; PO Box 100 (36726); W; 1,896pd, 600fr (Sw); $4.20; publisher & editor M Hollis Curl; tel (334) 682-4422; fax (334) 682-5163

Carrollton: *Pickens County Herald* — PO Box 390 (35447); W; 4,090pd, 18fr (Sw); $4.31; publisher Brian Hood; editor Douglas Sanders Jr; tel (205) 367-2217; fax (205) 367-2217

Centre: *Cherokee County Herald* — 107 W. 1st Ave. (35960); W; 4,118pd, 80fr (Est); $5.50; C; publisher Burgett H Mooney III; editor Paul W Dale; tel (205) 927-5037; fax (205) 927-4853

Centreville/Brent: *The Centreville Press* — 119 Court Sq. W.; PO Box 127, Centreville (35042); W; 3,900pd, 157fr (Est); $4.20; C; publisher Robert E Tribble; editor Judy M Farnetti; tel (205) 926-9769

Chatom: *Washington County News* — 305 Jordan St.; PO Box 510 (36518); W; 3,540pd, 30fr (Sw); $4.50; publisher James A Specht; general manager Shirley Helms; editor Frank Harwell; managing editor Sherrie Farabee; tel (334) 847-2599; fax (334) 847-3847

Choctaw Co.: *Choctaw Advocate* — 210 N. Mulberry St.; PO Box 475, Butler (36904); Th; 4,269pd, 67fr (Sw); $3.75; publisher & editor Tommy J Campbell; tel (205) 459-2858/2836; fax (205) 459-3000

Clanton/Chilton Co.: *Chilton County News* — PO Box 189, Clanton (35045-0189); Th; 1,875pd, 140fr (Sw); $5.32; publisher & editor Robert M Tucker; tel (205) 755-0110

Clanton/Jemison: *The Clanton Advertiser* — PO Box 1379, Clanton (35045); W/F/Su; 3,983pd, 196fr (Sw); 37¢; publisher & editor Michael R Kelley; general manager Stanley Allison; managing editor Trey Itughes; tel (205) 755-5747; fax (205) 755-5857

Clay Co.: *The Clay Times Journal* — PO Box 97, Lineville (36266); Th; 3,226pd, 92fr (Sw); $4.00; publisher & editor David Proctor; general manager Linda D McDonald; tel (205) 396-5760; fax (205) 396-5760

Clayton: *Clayton Record* — PO Box 69 (36016-0069); Th; 2,500pd (Est); $4.25; publisher & editor Bertie G Parish; managing editor Rebecca Beasley; tel (334) 775-3254; fax (334) 775-8554

Columbiana/Montevallo/Pelham/Hoover/Alabaster: *Shelby County Reporter* — Main St.; PO Box 947, Columbiana (35051); W; 7,940pd, 24,500fr (Sw); $10.50; C; publisher & editor Kim N Price; managing editor Leada D Franklin; tel (205) 669-3131; fax (205) 669-4217

Conecuh Co.: *The Evergreen Courant* — PO Box 440, Evergreen (36401); Th; 3,225pd, 285fr (Sw); $2.50; publisher Maurice G Bozeman; editor Robert Bozeman III; tel (334) 578-1492; fax (334) 578-1496

Cullman/Arab/Addison/Blountsville/Falkville/Jasper/Eva/Hanceville/Good Hope: *The Cullman Tribune* — 219 2nd Ave. S.E., Cullman (35055); Th; 13,400pd, 300fr (Est); $5.00; publisher Barbara Blalock; publisher & editor Delton Blalock; tel (205) 739-1351; fax (205) 739-4422

Dadeville: *Dadeville Record* — 103 N. Tallasee St.; PO Box 8 (36853); Th; 1,373pd, 21fr (Sw); 23¢; publisher Kenneth Boone; editor K A Turner; tel (205) 825-4231; fax (205) 234-6550

Demopolis/Marengo Co.: *The Demopolis Times* — 315 E. Jefferson St.; PO Box 860, Demopolis (36732); W/Su; 2,612pd, 82fr (Est); $5.90; publisher & editor Danny Smith; tel (334) 289-4017; fax (334) 289-4019

Eclectic: *Eclectic Observer* — PO Box 634 (36024); Th; 1,350pd, 100fr (Sw); $3.20; publisher Harold Whatley; editor Eric Burkett; tel (334) 541-3902; fax (334) 541-3903

Elba: *The Elba Clipper* — 419 W. Buford St.; PO Box A (36323); Th; 3,052pd, 45fr (Sw); $3.55; publisher John Ferrin Cox; editor Marvin McIlwain; tel (334) 897-2823; fax (334) 897-3434

Elmore Co.: *The Community Press* — 83 Deatsville Hwy.; PO Box 568, Millbrook (36054); Th; 1,305pd, 50fr (Sw); $3.50; publisher Lamar Smitherman; editor Steve Sawyer; tel (334) 285-6000; fax (334) 285-6001

Eufaula: *The Eufaula Tribune* — 514 E. Barbour St.; PO Box 628 (36027); W/Su; 5,966pd, 30fr (Sw); $4.76; C; publisher & editor Joel P Smith; managing editor Tom Davis; tel (334) 687-3506; fax (334) 687-3229

Fairhope/Daphne: *Fairhope Courier* — 325 Fairhope Ave.; PO Box 549, Fairhope (36533); W/Sa; 5,000pd (Sw); 35¢; publisher Meredith White; editor Tommy Leytham; tel (334) 928-2321; fax (334) 928-9963

Fayette: *The Times-Record* — 106 1st St. S.E.; PO Drawer 151 (35555); W; 4,487pd, 142fr (Est); $3.98; C; publisher Horace Moore; general manager & editor Michael James; tel (205) 932-6271; fax (205) 932-6998

Flomaton: *The Tri-City Ledger* — Hwy. 31 S.; PO Drawer F (36441); Th; 2,900pd, 30fr (Est); $2.14; publisher Bo Bolton; editor Joe Thomas; tel (334) 296-3491; fax (334) 296-3491

Florala: *Florala News* — 421 S. 5th St. (36442); Th; 2,139pd (Est); 12¢; publisher & editor Gary Woodham; managing editor Merl Woodham; tel (334) 858-3342; fax (334) 858-3786

Florence/Muscles Shoals: *Courier Journal* — 116 W. Mobile St.; PO Box 916, Florence (35631); W; 250pd, 57,547fr (Sw); $8.50; general manager Ronald T Regan; editor Thomas V Magazzu; tel (205) 764-4268; fax (205) 760-9618

Foley: *The Onlooker* — 217 N. McKenzie St.; PO Box 198 (36536); W/Sa; 147pd, 21fr (Est); $6.54; C; publisher Meredith White; editor Tommy Leytham; tel (334) 943-7712; fax (334) 943-3441

Ft. Deposit: *Lowndes Signal* — 118 Ellis St.; PO Box 384 (36032); Th; 1,680pd, 76fr (Sw); 20¢; publisher C B Cross Jr; editor F B Cross; tel (334) 227-4411; fax (334) 227-3441

Gardendale: *North Jefferson News* — PO Box 849 (35071); Th; 4,296pd, 66fr (ABC); $4.70; publisher Robert Bryan; editor Tim Lasseter; tel (205) 631-8716; fax (205) 631-9902

Geneva Co.: *Geneva County Reaper* — 803 Town Ave.; PO Box 160, Geneva (36340); W; 2,520pd, 340fr (Est); $4.50; C; publisher Moe Pujol; editor Jay Fellsberg; tel (334) 684-2280; fax (334) 684-3099

Georgiana: *Butler County News* — Miranda Ave.; PO Box 620 (36033); Th; 1,860pd, 105fr (Est); $1.25; publisher & editor R W Pride Jr; managing editor Teresa Lowe; tel (334) 376-2325; fax (334) 376-9302

Greene/Sumter Co.: *Greene County Democrat* — 214 Boligee St.; PO Box 598, Eutaw (35462); W; 1,836pd, 1,075fr (Sw); $7.50; C; publisher Carol Zippert; publisher & editor John Zippert; managing editor Laddi Jones; tel (205) 372-3373; fax (205) 372-2243

Greensboro: *The Greensboro Watchman* — 1005 Market St.; PO Drawer 550 (36744); Th; 2,700pd, 95fr (Sw); $5.50; publisher & editor Edward E Lowry Jr; managing editor Willie L Arrington; tel (334) 624-8323; fax (334) 624-8327

Greenville: *The Greenville Advocate* — 103 Hickory St.; PO Box 507 (36037); W/Sa; 5,230pd, 9,550fr (Est); $4.25; C; publisher Todd H Carpenter; managing editor Gregg Fuller; tel (334) 382-3111; fax (334) 382-7104

Guntersville: *The Advertiser-Gleam* — 2218 Taylor St.; PO Box 190 (35976); W/Sa; 12,001pd, 461fr (ABC); $6.10; C; publisher Porter Harvey; general manager Don Woodward; editor Sam Harvey; tel (205) 582-3232; fax (205) 582-3231

Haleyville/Winston Co.: *Northwest Alabamian* — Hwy. 195 E.; PO Box 430, Haleyville (35565); W/Sa; 6,890pd, 57fr (Sw); $4.40; C; publisher & editor Horace Moore; managing editor Melica Allen; tel (205) 486-9461; fax (205) 486-4849

Hanceville: *The Hanceville Herald* — 111 Commercial St.; PO Box 880 (35077); W; 1,800pd, 3,000fr (Est); $3.10; publisher & editor Jennifer Grantham; tel (205) 352-4775

Hartford: *Hartford News Herald* — PO Box 69 (36344); W; 1,105pd, 90fr (Est); $3.50; C; publisher Moe Pujol; editor Jay Felsberg; tel (334) 588-2996; fax (334) 684-3099

Hartselle: *The Hartselle Enquirer* — PO Box 929 (35640); W; 7,500pd, 7,000fr (Est); $5.25; publisher T L Beasley; editor C P Knight; tel (205) 773-1953; fax (205) 773-1953

Headland: *Headland Observer* — Hwy. 431 N., Rte. 2; PO Box 707 (36345); Th; 1,660pd, 28fr (Est); 21¢; C; publisher Michael A Mullens; editor Terry Grimes; managing editor Nancy Michel; tel (334) 693-3326; fax (334) 693-5224

Heflin: *The Cleburne News* — PO Box 6 (36264); Th; 3,450pd (Est); $5.00; C; publisher Henry A Jackson; general manager Minnie R Jackson; editor John A Jackson; tel (205) 463-2872; fax (205) 463-2872

Jackson: *The South Alabamian* — 1064 Coffeeville Rd.; PO Box 68 (36545); Th; 4,624pd, 45fr (Sw); $5.00; publisher Michael M Breedlove; editor Martha R Motes; tel (334) 246-4494; fax (334) 246-7486

Jacksonville: *Jacksonville News* — 203 Pelham Rd. S. (36265); W; 3,700pd (Est); $5.75; publisher Phillip A Sanguinetti; general manager & editor Julia Brock; tel (205) 435-5021; fax (205) 435-1028

LaFayette: *The LaFayette Sun* — PO Box 378 (36862); W; 2,800pd, 40fr (Sw); $4.25; publisher & editor Michael D Hand; tel (334) 864-8885; fax (334) 864-8310

Lamar Co.: *Lamar Leader* — 55071 Hwy. 17; PO Box 988, Sulligent (35586); W; 2,244pd, 63fr (Sw); $4.00; publisher & editor Don Dollar; general manager Becky Cox; tel (205) 698-8148; fax (205) 698-8146

Lamar/Pickens/Fayette Cos.: *West Alabama Gazette* — 100 Vernon St.; PO Box 249, Millport (35576); Th; 3,109pd, 91fr (Est); $4.11; publisher L Peyton Bobo; editor Barbara Bobo; tel (205) 662-4296; fax (205) 662-4740

Lauderdale Co.: *East Lauderdale News* — E. Lee St.; PO Box 179, Rogersville (35652); Th; 3,631pd, 390fr (Sw); $3.50; publishers & editors James B Cox & Phyllis D Cox; tel (205) 247-5565; fax (205) 247-1902

II-2 Alabama U.S. Weeklies

Leeds/Moody: *The Leeds News* — 720 Parkway Dr. N.E., Leeds (35094); Th; 3,248pd, 33fr (Sw); $6.05; publisher Robert Bryan; editor Rebecca Comer Gunter; tel (205) 699-2214; fax (205) 699-3157

Linden/Marengo: *The Democrat-Reporter* — PO Box 480040, Linden (36748); Tu; 6,896pd, 613fr (Sw); $6.00; publisher & editor Goodloe Sutton; tel (334) 295-5224

Luverne: *The Luverne Journal* — 406 Forest Ave.; PO Box 152 (36049); W; 3,500pd, 78fr (Sw); $4.75; publisher & editor Alvin Bland; general manager James Morgan; tel (334) 335-3541; fax (334) 335-3541

Madison: *Madison County Record* — 202 Main St.; PO Box 175 (35758); Th; 4,000pd, 8,500fr (Est); $7.50; C; publisher & editor Richard A Haston; tel (205) 772-8666; fax (205) 461-6397

Marion Co.: *Journal Record* — 401 State Hwy. 17; PO Box 1477, Hamilton (35570); W/Sa; 7,930pd, 56fr (Sw); $6.00; C; publisher Horace Moore; general manager & managing editor Les Walters; editor Ed Howell; tel (205) 921-3104; fax (205) 921-3105

Marion/Perry Co.: *Marion Times-Standard* — PO Box 418, Marion (36756); W; 139fr (Est); $3.10; publisher Robert E Tribble; general manager Lorrie Blankenship; editor Charley Ann Reichley; tel (334) 683-6318; fax (334) 683-4616

Monroeville/Monroe City: *The Monroe Journal* — 126 Hines St.; PO Box 826, Monroeville (36461); Th; 5,856pd, 372fr (Sw); $6.52; C; publisher Steve Stewart; editor Marilyn Handley; tel (334) 575-3282; fax (334) 575-3284

Montgomery: *Montgomery Independent* — 6005 Monticello Dr.; PO Box 241207 (36124-1207); Th; 5,819pd, 847fr (Sw); $7.50; C; publisher Donald Hatley; editor Wendi Lewis; tel (334) 213-7323; fax (334) 271-2143

Moulton/Lawrence: *The Moulton Advertiser* — 659 Main St.; PO Box 517, Moulton (35650); Th; 5,435pd, 108fr (Sw); $5.25; C; publisher & editor Luke Slaton; managing editor Deangelo McDaniel; tel (205) 974-1114; fax (205) 974-3097

Oneonta/Blount Co.: *The Blount Countian* — 217 3rd St. S.; PO Box 310, Oneonta (35121); W; 6,474pd, 157fr (Sw); $4.75; publisher & editor Molly Howard Ryan; managing editor Lisa Ryan; tel (205) 625-3231

Opp/Andalusia: *The Opp News* — 200 Covington Ave.; PO Box 409, Opp (36467); Th; 7,900pd, 200fr (Est); $5.00; publisher Randy Pebworth; editor Tracey Nelson; tel (334) 493-3595; fax (334) 493-4901

Ozark: *The Southern Star* — 428 E. Andrews Ave. (36360); PO Box 1729 (36361); W; 5,500pd, 6,000fr (Sw); $4.00; C; publisher & editor Joseph H Adams; tel (334) 774-2715; fax (334) 774-9619

Pell City/St. Clair Co.: *St. Clair News-Aegis* — 1820 2nd Ave. N.; PO Box 748, Pell City (35125); Th; 5,934pd, 54fr (ABC); 15¢; publisher Robert C Bryan; editor Gary Hanner; tel (205) 884-2310; fax (205) 884-2312

Phenix City: *The Phenix Citizen* — 1606 Broad St.; PO Box 1267 (36868); Th; 5,400pd, 8,926fr (Est); $4.25; publisher Jill Tigner; publisher & editor Mike Venable; tel (334) 298-0679; fax (334) 298-0690

Piedmont: *Piedmont Journal-Independent* — 115 N. Center Ave. (36272-2013); W; 3,500pd (Est); $4.38; publisher & editor Lane Weatherbee; tel (205) 447-2837; fax (205) 447-2837

Prattville/Autauga Co.: *The Prattville Progress* — 152 W. 3rd St.; PO Drawer C, Prattville (36067); W/Sa; 5,435pd, 88fr (Sw); $7.85; C; publisher Lamar Smitherman; editor Brightman Brock; tel (334) 365-6739; fax (334) 365-1400

Randolph: *The Randolph Leader* — 321 E. Main St.; PO Box 232, Roanoke (36274); W; 5,865pd, 3fr (Sw); 27¢; publisher & editor John W Stevenson; tel (334) 863-2819; fax (334) 863-4006

Red Bay: *The Red Bay News* — 109 4th Ave. S.; PO Box 1339 (35582); W; 3,263pd, 30fr (Sw); $4.60; publisher LaVale Mills; editor Tony Launius; tel (205) 356-2148; fax (205) 356-2787

Robertsdale: *The Independent* — 21764 Media Dr.; PO Box 509 (36567); Th; 3,921pd (Est); $5.42; C; publisher Meredith White; editor Tommy Leytham; managing editor Sheila Propp; tel (334) 947-7318; fax (334) 947-7652

Russellville/Franklin Co.: *Franklin County Times* — 142 Hwy. 43 Bypass; PO Box 1088, Russellville (35653); W/Su; 4,000pd (Sw); $6.90; C; publisher & editor Richard L Cameron; tel (205) 332-1881; fax (205) 332-1883

Samson: *Samson Ledger* — PO Box 66 (36477); W; 925pd, 75fr (Est); 9¢; C; publisher Moe Pujol; editor Jay Felsberg; tel (334) 898-2491; fax (334) 684-3099

Sheffield: *Sheffield Standard & Times* — 106 W. 5th St.; PO Box 1419, Tuscumbia (35674); Th; 4,508pd, 812fr (Est); 12¢; publisher & editor Jim Crawford Jr; managing editor Estelle Crawford-Whitehead; tel (205) 383-8471; fax (205) 383-8476

Sumter Co./W Alabama: *Sumter County Record-Journal* — 200 S. Washington St.; PO Drawer B, Livingston (35470); Th; 5,225pd, 200fr (Sw); $4.50; C; publisher & editor Tommy McGraw; tel (205) 652-6100; fax (205) 652-4466

Tallassee: *The Tallassee Tribune* — 301 Gilmer Ave.; PO Box 736 (36078); Th; 4,167pd, 32fr (Est); $4.00; publisher & editor Jack B Venable; tel (334) 283-6568; fax (334) 283-6569

Thomasville: *The Thomasville Times* — Hwy. 43 N.; PO Box 367 (36784); Th; 3,994pd, 125fr (Sw); $5.00; publisher Wells Bozeman; editor Dana T Dunn; tel (334) 636-2214; fax (334) 636-9822

Troy: *Troy Progress* — 906-A S. Brundidge St.; PO Box 188 (36081); Su; 12,701fr (CPVS); $8.00; C; publisher Rick Reynolds; tel (334) 566-9401; fax (334) 556-9403

Tuscumbia: *Colbert County Reporter* — 106 W. 5th St.; PO Box 1419 (35674); F; 4,000pd, 2,000fr (Est); $1.45; publisher & editor Jim Crawford Jr; managing editor Estelle Crawford-Whitehead; tel (205) 383-8471; fax (205) 383-8746

Tuskegee: *Tuskegee News* — 112 Eastside St.; PO Box 60 (36083); Th; 4,370pd, 273fr (Est); $6.76; C; publisher Paul R Davis; general manager Mike Smelley; editor Guy Rhodes; tel (334) 727-3020; fax (334) 727-3036

Union Springs: *Union Springs Herald* — PO Box 600 (36089); Th; 2,977pd (Sw); 13¢; publisher & editor Thomas May; tel (334) 738-2360; fax (334) 738-2342

Vernon: *Lamar Democrat* — 124 1st Ave. N.W.; PO Box 587 (35592); W; 3,243pd, 15fr (Est); $4.00; publisher Rex Rainwater; editor Howard L Reeves; tel (205) 695-7029; fax (205) 695-9501

W Alabama: *Greene County Independent* — 106 Main St., Eutaw (35462); Th; 1,025pd, 19fr (Sw); $4.00; publisher Betty C Banks; general manager Sharon Stuckey; editor Leewanna Parker; tel (205) 372-2232

Wetumpka/Elmore Co.: *The Wetumpka Herald* — 300 Green St.; PO Box 29, Wetumpka (36092); Th; 3,922pd, 52fr (Sw); $5.10; publisher Ellen T Williams; editor Gerald M Williams Sr; tel (334) 567-7811; fax (334) 567-3284

ALASKA

Bethel/Yukon/Kuskokwim/Delta in SW Alaska: *The Tundra Drums* — 660 3rd Ave.; PO Box 868, Bethel (99559); Th; 4,437pd, 398fr (Est); $8.44; C; publisher Christopher Casati; editor John Plestina; tel (907) 543-3500; fax (907) 543-3312

Chugiak/Eagle River: *The Chugiak-Eagle River Alaska Star* — 16941 N. Eagle River Loop Rd., Eagle River (99577); W/Sa; 6,010pd, 661fr (Sw); $14.80; C; publisher & editor Lee B Jordan; managing editor Stacy Simonet; tel (907) 694-2727; fax (907) 694-1545

Cordova: *The Cordova Times* — PO Box 200 (99574); Th; 1,294pd, 253fr (Est); $8.16; C; publisher Christopher Casati; editor John Woodbury; managing editor Cinthia Stimson; tel (907) 424-7181; fax (907) 424-5799

Delta Junction/Ft. Greely: *The Delta Wind* — PO Box 986, Delta Junction (99737); W; 1,090pd, 35fr (Est); $6.00; publisher Tri Delta Inc.; general manager & managing editor Loretta Schooley; editor Cathy Good; tel (907) 895-5115

Dillingham/Naknek/King Salmon/Bristol Bay: *The Bristol Bay Times* — PO Box 1770, Dillingham (99576); Th; 1,720pd, 286fr (Est); $8.16; C; publisher Christopher Casati; editor John Woodbury; managing editor Colleen Kelly; tel (907) 842-5572; fax (907) 842-5572

Homer: *Homer News* — 3482 Landings St. (99603); Th; 3,406pd, 20fr (ABC); $6.75; publisher Homer News Inc.; general manager & editor Mark Turner; tel (907) 235-7767; fax (907) 235-4199

Kotzbue/Barrow/NW Arctic/N Slope Boroughs: *The Arctic Sounder* — PO Box 290, Kotzebue (99752); Th; 2,120pd, 694fr (Est); $8.15; C; publisher Christopher Casati; editor Fern Greenbank; tel (907) 442-3213; fax (907) 442-2654

Matanuska/Susitna Borough: *The Frontiersman* — 1261 Seward Meridian, Wasilla (99654); W/F; 6,474pd, 479fr (ABC); $12.50; C; publishers Michael D Lindsey & Patricia P Lindsey; editor Victoria Naegele; tel (907) 376-5225; fax (907) 352-2277

Matanuska/Susitna Borough: *The Valley Sun* — 1261 Seward Meridian, Wasilla (99654); Tu; 34pd, 9,064fr (Est); $12.00; C; publishers Mike Lindsey & Pat Lindsey; general manager Steve Heide; editor Vicki Naegele; tel (907) 376-5225; fax (907) 352-2277

Nome/Seward Penisula: *The Nome Nugget* — 123 Front St.; PO Box 610, Nome (99762); Th; 3,150pd, 170fr (Sw); $11.00; C; publisher & editor Nancy L McGuire; tel (907) 443-5235; fax (907) 443-5112

Petersburg: *Petersburg Pilot* — 212 Harborway; PO Box 930 (99833); Th; 1,619pd, 34fr (Sw); $7.25; publisher Anne Loesch; publisher & editor Ronald J Loesch; tel (907) 772-9393; fax (907) 772-4871

Seward/Moose Pass/Hope: *The Seward Phoenix Log* — 315 4th Ave.; PO Box 89, Seward (99664); Th; 2,183pd, 121fr (Sw); $12.35; C; publisher Christopher Casati; editor John Woodbury; managing editor Dave Collins; tel (907) 224-8070; fax (907) 224-3157

Unalaska/Aleutian/Pribilof Islands: *The Dutch Harbor Fisherman* — Intersea Mall, Dutch Harbor (99692); Th; 1,132pd, 415fr (Sw); $12.35; C; publisher Christopher Casati; editor John Woodbury; managing editor Anntovza Sedjo; tel (907) 581-2092; fax (907) 581-2090

Valdez: *Valdez Vanguard* — 337 Fairbanks Dr.; PO Box 98 (99686-0098); W; 1,581pd, 125fr (Sw); $11.50; publisher Christopher Casati; general manager Eric Hancock; editor John Woodbury; managing editor Tony Bickert; tel (907) 835-2211; fax (907) 835-5101

Wrangell: *Wrangell Sentinel* — 312 Front St.; PO Box 798 (99929); Th; 1,381pd, 8fr (Sw); $6.50; publishers Alvin Bunch & Ann Kirkwood; editor Allen L Bird; tel (907) 874-2301; fax (907) 874-2303

ARIZONA

Ajo: *Ajo Copper News* — 10 Pajaro; PO Drawer 39 (85321); W; 2,169pd, 23fr (Est); $3.25; publisher Hollister David; editor Gabrielle David; tel (520) 387-7688; fax (520) 387-7505

Apache Junction: *Apache Junction Independent* — 201 W. Apache Trl., Ste. 708 (85220); W; 1,039pd, 17,222fr (VAC); $12.92; C; publisher Ed Dulin; editor James Files; tel (602) 982-7799; fax (602) 671-0016

Benson: *San Pedro Valley News-Sun* — 200 S. Ocotillo; PO Box 1000 (85602); W; 2,800pd, 50fr (Sw); $5.85; C; publisher Patricia Kohlman; editor Jim Tiffin; tel (520) 586-3382; fax (520) 586-2382

Bisbee: *The Bisbee News* — 99 Bisbee Rd., Ste. B (85603); Th; 32pd, 3,000fr (Sw); $6.00; publisher & general manager Dave Cartun; publisher & editor Mary Ellen Corbett; tel (520) 432-4400; fax (520) 432-4441

Bisbee: *The Bisbee Observer* — 7 Bisbee Rd., Ste. L (85603); Th; 1,936pd, 75fr (Sw); $5.25; publisher Ben Ketchum; editor Richard Senti; tel (520) 432-7254; fax (520) 432-4192

Bisbee/Hereford: *Brewery Gulch Gazette* — PO Drawer 48, Bisbee (85603); W; 273pd, 21fr (Sw); $3.50; publisher William C Epler; general manager Caryl Larkins; editor Gary Dillard; tel (520) 432-2244; fax (520) 432-2247

Buckeye: *Buckeye Valley News* — 122 S. 4th St.; PO Box 217 (85326); Th; 2,886pd, 18fr (Est); 24¢; publisher & editor Sharon Butler; tel (602) 386-4426; fax (602) 386-4427

Camp Verde: *The Journal* — PO Box 2048 (86322); W; 2,295pd, 244fr (Sw); $6.60; C; publisher Robert B Larson; editor Thomas L Brossart; tel (520) 567-3341; fax (520) 567-2373

Cave Creek/Carefree/N Scottsdale: *Foothills Sentinel* — 6045 Hidden Vly.; PO Box 1569, Cave Creek (85331); W; 3,341pd, 100fr (Sw); $9.35; C; publisher Tina Dwyer; editor James Dir; tel (602) 488-3436; fax (602) 488-4779

Chandler/Sun Lakes: *Chandler Independent* — 3150 N. Arizona Ave., Ste. 113, Chandler (85224); W; 189pd, 19,437fr (VAC); $13.16; C; publisher Ed Dulin; editor Linda Gronemann; tel (602) 497-0048; fax (602) 926-1019

Chino Valley: *Chino Valley Review* — PO Box 312, Prescott (86302); W; 101pd, 3,336fr (Sw); $4.50; C; publisher Robert Gilliland; editor Jim Garner; managing editor Ivan Murray; tel (520) 445-3333; fax (520) 445-4756

Coolidge: *Coolidge Examiner* — PO Box 15002, Casa Grande (85230-5002); W; 1,999pd, 10fr (Sw); $5.88; C; publisher Donovan M Kramer Jr; editor Dina Doolen; tel (520) 723-5441; fax (520) 723-7899

Cottonwood: *Cottonwood Journal Extra* — 830 S. Main St.; PO Box 2266 (86326); W; 4,850fr (Est); $6.00; C; publisher Robert B Larson; editor Thomas L Brossart; tel (520) 634-8551; fax (520) 282-6888

Eagar/Springerville: *The Round Valley Paper* — PO Box 867, Eagar (85925); W; 625pd, 417fr (Sw); $3.00; publisher & editor Glenn Jacobs; tel (520) 333-2033

E Mesa: *East Mesa Independent* — 201 W. Apache Trl., Ste. 708, Apache Junction (85220); W; 153pd, 35,563fr (VAC); $16.52; C; publisher Ed Dulin; editor Richard H Dyer; tel (602) 982-7799; fax (602) 671-0016

Eloy: *Eloy Enterprise* — PO Box 15002, Casa Grande (85230-5002); Th; 939pd, 7fr (Sw); $5.34; C; publisher Donovan M Kramer Jr; editor Joe Meahl; tel (520) 466-7333; fax (520) 836-0343

Florence: *Florence Reminder & Blade-Tribune* — PO Box 15002, Casa Grande (85230-5002); Th; 1,593pd, 7fr (Sw); $5.34; C; publisher Donovan M Kramer Jr; editor Timothy Housare; tel (520) 868-5897; fax (520) 836-0343

Fountain Hills/Rio Verde: *The Times of Fountain Hills & Rio Verde* — 16929 E. Enterprise Dr.; PO Box 17869, Fountain Hills (85269); W; 4,294pd, 15fr (Sw); $6.00; publisher L Alan Cruikshank; editor Michael Scharnow; tel (602) 837-1931; fax (602) 837-1951

Gilbert: *Gilbert Independent* — 3150 N. Arizona Ave., Ste. 113, Chandler (85224); W; 205pd, 14,288fr (VAC); $11.68; C; publisher Ed Dulin; general manager Karen Smith; editor Jeremy Handel; tel (602) 497-0048; fax (602) 926-1019

Glendale: *The Glendale Star* — 7122 N. 59th Ave. (85301); PO Box 7 (85311); Th; 6,315pd, 650fr (Sw); $6.00; C; publishers Darlene M Toops & William V Toops; general manager William E Toops; editor Michael G Hart; tel (602) 842-6000; fax (602) 842-6017

Globe: *San Carlos Apache Moccasin* — 298 N. Pine St. (85501); PO Box 31 (85502); Tu; 1,601pd, 37fr (Sw); $6.00; publisher & editor Ellen Kretsch; tel (520) 425-7121; fax (520) 425-7001

Globe/Miami: *Arizona Silver Belt* — 298 N. Pine; PO Box 31, Globe (85502); W; 5,405pd, 44fr (Sw); $12.79; C; publisher & editor Ellen Kretsch; tel (520) 425-7121; fax (520) 425-7001

Globe/Miami/San Carlos: *The Copper Country News* — 254 N. Broad St., Globe (85501); Tu; 34pd, 8,000fr (Est); $4.90; publisher & editor Donna Anderson; publisher Guy Anderson; tel (520) 425-0355; fax (520) 425-6535

U.S. Weeklies Arkansas II-3

ARKANSAS

Atkins: *The Atkins Chronicle* — 204 Ave. 1 N.E.; PO Box 188 (72823); W, 2,365pd, 201fr (Sw); $4.10; C; publisher Ginnie Tyson; publisher & editor Van A Tyson; managing editor Gail Murdoch; tel (501) 641-7161; fax (501) 641-1604

Bald Knob: *Bald Knob Banner* — 418 S. Helm; PO Drawer 1418 (72010); W, 1,053pd, 30fr (Est); 10¢; publisher & editor Sue Perdue; general manager & editor Teresa Tap; tel (501) 724-3863; fax (501) 724-5072

Beebe: *Beebe News* — 107 E. Center; PO Box O (72012); W, 2,220pd, 20fr (Est); $3.46; publisher & editor Lee McLane; tel (501) 882-5414; fax (501) 882-3576

Bella Vista Village: *The Weekly Vista* — 313 Town Center W., Bella Vista (72714); W, 4,826pd, 274fr (Est); $5.00; publisher Mike Brown; general manager Rollie Runions; editor Karen Roca; tel (501) 855-3724; fax (501) 855-6992

Booneville: *Booneville Democrat* — 72 W. 2nd St.; PO Box 208 (72927); W, 2,781pd, 75fr (Est); $4.25; publisher George Chance; editor William Landrum; tel (501) 675-4455; fax (501) 675-5457

Brinkley: *Brinkley Argus* — 308 W. Cedar St.; PO Box 711 (72021); W/Sa, 4,430pd, 11,000fr (Est); $4.70; C; publisher Flora Jean Elledge; general manager Kate Jacques; editor Thomas Jacques; tel (501) 734-1056; fax (501) 734-2302

Cabot: *Cabot Star-Herald* — 903 S. Pine; PO Box 1508 (72023); W, 6,068pd (Sw); $7.00; C; publisher Magie Enterprises Inc.; general manager Mark Magie; editor Shelly Moran; tel (501) 843-3534; fax (501) 843-6447

Calhoun Co.: *South Arkansas Accent* — Hwy. 167; PO Box 766, Hampton (71744); W, 1,485pd, 25fr (Est); $3.50; C; publisher & editor Ovid Goode; tel (501) 798-2236; fax (501) 798-2005

Carlisle: *Carlisle Independent* — 220 W. Main; PO Box 47 (72024); W, 1,400pd (Sw); $5.00; C; publisher Magie Enterprises Inc.; general manager Mark Magie; editor Shelly Moran; tel (501) 552-3111

Carroll Co.: *Eureka Springs Times-Echo* — PO Box 232, Eureka Springs (72632); Th; 3,085pd, 70fr (Est); $5.50; C; publisher LeRoy Gorell; editor Martha Campbell; tel (501) 253-9719; fax (501) 423-6640

Carroll Co.: *The Star Progress* — Oakview Dr.; PO Box 232, Berryville (72616); Th; 2,151pd, 66fr (Sw); $5.50; C; publisher LeRoy Gorell; editor Martha Campbell; tel (501) 423-6636; fax (501) 423-6640

Charleston: *Charleston Express* — 249 Main St.; PO Box 38 (72933); W; 2,135pd, 25fr (Est); 9¢; publisher Ken Richardson; editor Dolores James; tel (501) 965-7368; fax (501) 965-7206

Cherokee Vlg/Hardy: *The Cherokee Villager* — Town Center; PO Box 480, Cherokee Village (72525); W, 2,808pd, 85fr (Sw); $5.00; publisher & editor David Cox; tel (501) 257-2417; fax (501) 257-5487

Clarendon: *The Monroe County Sun* — PO Box 315 (72029); Th; 2,315pd, 95fr (Est); $4.00; publisher Flora Jean Elledge & Franklin H Elledge; general manager Kate Jacques; editor Marty Harper; tel (501) 747-3373; fax (501) 734-1494

Clarksville: *The Johnson County Graphic* — PO Box 289 (72830); W, 7,201pd, 28fr (Est); 36¢; publisher R L Fisher; general manager Ron Wylie; editor Margaret Wylie; tel (501) 754-2005; fax (501) 754-2098

Clinton: *Van Buren County Democrat* — 114 S. Court St.; PO Box 119 (72031); W, 4,913pd, 30fr (Est); $4.50; publisher & editor Jay W Jackson; publisher Patsy Jackson; tel (501) 745-5175; fax (501) 745-5175

Corning: *Clay County Courier* — 810 N. Missouri Ave.; PO Box 128 (72422); Th; 3,300pd (Est); 9¢; publisher & editor Jan V Rockwell; tel (501) 857-3531; fax (501) 857-5204

Cross/Woodruff/Poinsett/St. Francis/Crittenden Cos.: *The East Arkansas News Leader* — 702 N. Falls Blvd.; PO Box 308, Wynne (72396); W; 200pd, 22,137fr (Sw); $8.00; C; publisher David M Boger; general manager Sandra Boger; editor David Nichol; managing editor Fred Conley; tel (501) 238-2375; fax (501) 238-4655

Crossett: *The Ashley News Observer* — 102 Pine; PO Box 798 (71635); W; 4,950pd, 151fr (Sw); $6.38; C; publisher Larry W Johnson; editor Steve Sanders; tel (501) 364-5186; fax (501) 354-2116

Dardanelle: *Dardanelle Post-Dispatch* — 107 Harrison St.; PO Box 270 (72834); W, 2,044pd, 41fr (Est); 21¢; publisher Craig Martin; general manager & editor Robin Foster; tel (501) 229-2250; fax (501) 229-1159

De Queen: *De Queen Bee* — 404 De Queen Ave.; PO Box 1000 (71832); Th; 1,593pd, 87fr (Sw); $4.25; C; publisher Ray Kimball; general manager & editor Billy Ray McKelvy; tel (501) 642-2111; fax (501) 642-3138

De Witt: *De Witt Era-Enterprise* — 326 Court Sq.; PO Box 431 (72042); Th; 3,750pd (Est); $4.50; publishers Bill Braswell & James Braswell; editor Ann Cox; tel (501) 946-3241; fax (501) 946-1888

Decatur: *Decatur Herald* — PO Box 7 (72722); W; 1,200pd (Est); $6.35; publisher Mike Brown; editor James Garner; tel (501) 752-3675; fax (501) 736-2822

Des Arc: *White River Journal* — 424 Main St.; PO Box 1051 (72040-1051); Th; 2,518pd, 74fr (Sw); $3.35; publisher & editor Dean L Walls; tel (501) 256-4254

DeValls Bluff/Prairie: *DeValls Bluff Times* — PO Box 377, Hazen (72064); Th; 680pd, 14fr (Est); $2.40; publisher Betty L Woods; editor Bill Rutherford; tel (501) 255-4538; fax (501) 255-4534

Dumas/Desha/Lincoln/Drew: *Dumas Clarion* — 136 E. Waterman St.; PO Box C, Dumas (71639); W; 3,950pd, 50fr (Sw); $4.50; C; publisher Charlotte Schexnayder; editor Terry Hawkins; tel (501) 382-4925; fax (501) 382-6421

England: *England Democrat* — 121 E. Haywood; PO Drawer 250 (72046); W; 1,652pd, 12fr (Sw); $3.22; publisher & editor Jerry M Jackson; tel (501) 842-3111; fax (501) 842-3081

Eudora: *Eudora Enterprise* — 105 N. Court St.; PO Box 552, Lake Village (71653); W; 1,519pd (Est); 10¢; publisher & editor Steve Russell; tel (501) 265-2071; fax (501) 265-2807

Fordyce: *Fordyce News-Advocate* — 304 Spring St.; PO Box 559 (71742); W; 3,086pd, 164fr (Sw); $4.80; C; publisher & editor W R Whitehead Jr; tel (501) 352-3144; fax (501) 352-8091

Fulton/Sharp/Izard: *The News* — Hwy. 62/412 E.; PO Box 248, Salem (72576); Th; 3,016pd, 34fr (Sw); $5.00; C; general manager Janie Flynn; editor Max Cates; tel (501) 895-3207; fax (501) 895-4277

Gentry: *Gentry Courier-Journal* — 159 E. Main; PO Box 677 (72734); W; 2,000pd (Est); $6.35; publisher Mike Brown; editor James Garner; tel (501) 752-3675; fax (501) 736-2822

Glenwood: *Glenwood Herald* — 204 Broadway; PO Box L (71943); Th; 2,239pd, 50fr (Sw); $3.31; publisher Louie Graves; general manager & editor Mike McCoy; tel (501) 356-2111; fax (501) 356-4400

Gravette: *Gravette News Herald* — 123 E. Main; PO Box 640 (72736); W; 1,719pd (Sw); $3.00; publisher Scott Harrell; editor Robert D Evans; tel (501) 787-5300; fax (501) 787-5300

Green Forest: *Green Forest Tribune* — PO Box 139-D (72638); W; 1,263pd, 40fr (Sw); $4.40; publisher LeRoy Gorrell; editor Martha Campbell; tel (501) 423-6636; fax (501) 423-6640

Greenwood/S Sebastian: *Greenwood Democrat* — PO Box 398, Greenwood (72936); W; 2,569pd, 52fr (Sw); $4.09; C; publisher Cindy Wells; general manager Amy Lowdermilk; editor Donna R Forst; tel (501) 996-4494; fax (501) 996-4122

Copyright ©1996 by the Editor & Publisher Co.

II-4 Arkansas U.S. Weeklies

Gurdon: *The Gurdon Times* — 107 N. 2nd St.; PO Box 250 (71743); Th; 1,972pd, 44fr (Sw); $2.75; publisher & editor John Ragsdale; tel (501) 353-4482; fax (501) 887-2949

Hamburg: *Ashley County Ledger* — 107 N. Main St.; PO Box 471 (71646); W; 3,000pd (Est); 22¢; publisher & editor David Moyers; tel (501) 853-2424

Harrisburg: *The Modern News* — 216 Main St.; PO Box 400 (72432); W; 2,396pd, 49fr (Sw); $3.36; publisher Hazel Freeman; general manager & managing editor Charles D Nix; tel (501) 578-2121

Harrison: *Boone County Headlight* — 11 W. Rush Ave.; PO Box 40 (72601); Th; 1,672pd, 71fr (Sw); 24¢; publisher Jeff Christenson; general manager Jeff Dezort; editor Dwain Lair; tel (501) 741-2325; fax (501) 741-5632

Hazen: *Grand Prairie Herald* — 400 N. Front St.; PO Box 377 (72064); W; 1,500pd, 100fr (Est); $3.60; publisher Betty L Woods; editor Bill Rutherford; tel (501) 255-4538; fax (501) 255-4539

Heber Springs/Quitman: *Cleburne County Sun-Times* — 107-109 N. 4th St.; PO Box 669, Heber Springs (72543); W/F; 5,281pd, 82fr (Sw); $6.73; publisher Ed Trainor; editor Randy Kemp; tel (501) 362-2425; fax (501) 367-5877

Horseshoe Bend/Salem: *Easy Living News* — PO Box 223, Horseshoe Bend (72512); Th; 1,402pd, 108fr (Est); $4.50; publisher Thomas N Harris; editor Karen Johnson; tel (501) 670-5555; fax (501) 670-5566

Hot Springs Vlg.: *La Villa News* — 121 De Soto Center Dr., Hot Springs Village (71909); W; 4,196pd, 238fr (Sw); $5.00; C; publisher Rebecca Hodge Winburn; editor Randal Hunhoff; tel (501) 922-1900, (800) 833-4050; fax (501) 922-0958

Izard Co.: *White River Current* — 1100 E. 1st St.; PO Box 570, Calico Rock (72519); Th; 2,167pd, 33fr (Sw); $4.00; publisher & editor Jeannie Day; managing editor Margaret Waters; tel (501) 297-8300; fax (501) 297-8799

Jasper: *The Newton County Times* — PO Box 453 (72641); Th; 2,441pd (Sw); $2.14; publisher Jane Dunlap Christenson; editor Ruth Ann Wilson; tel (501) 446-2645; fax (501) 446-6286

Lake Village/Eudora: *Chicot Spectator* — 105 N. Court St.; PO Box 552, Lake Village (71653); W; 2,153pd (Est); 10¢; publisher & editor Steve Russell; tel (501) 265-2071; fax (501) 265-2807

Lewisville/Stamps/Bradley: *Lafayette County Democrat* — 107 Spruce St.; PO Box 507, Lewisville (71845); Th; 2,885pd, 3,600fr (Est); 19¢; publisher George R Wanstrath; editor Sue Terry; tel (501) 921-5711; fax (501) 921-5712

Lincoln: *The Lincoln Leader* — 119 W. Beans; PO Box 520 (72744); Th; 1,518pd, 159fr (Sw); $3.88; C; publisher & editor Boyce R Davis; tel (501) 824-3263; fax (501) 267-5540

Little River/Sevier: *Little River News* — 45 E. Commerce; PO Box 608, Ashdown (71822); Th; 3,509pd, 27fr (Sw); $5.45; publisher Gerald Stripling; publisher & editor James Williamson; tel (501) 898-3462

Little Rock/Pulaski Co.: *Little Rock Free Press* — PO Box 165118, Little Rock (72201); F; 20,000fr (Est); $27.53; publisher & editor Dotty Oliver; tel (501) 372-4719; fax (501) 372-4769

Lonoke: *Lonoke Democrat* — 402 N. Center St.; PO Drawer B (72086); W; 2,614pd (Sw); $6.00; C; publisher Magie Enterprises Inc.; general manager Mark Magie; editor Cone Magie; tel (501) 676-2463

Manila/Mississippi: *Northeast Arkansas Town Crier* — 100 W. Lake St.; PO Box 1326, Manila (72442); Tu; 2,929pd, 46fr (Est); $4.00; publisher & editor Nancy J Kemp; general manager Kaye Farrow; managing editor Melanie Sparkman; tel (501) 561-4634; fax (501) 561-3602

Marianna: *The Courier Index* — 12 W. Chestnut; PO Box 569 (72360); W; 2,390pd, 13fr (Sw); $6.00; publisher T Bonner McCollum; editor Robert Shearon; tel (501) 295-2521; fax (501) 295-9662

Marked Tree/Lepanto: *Tri-City Tribune* — 18 Elm St.; PO Box 490, Marked Tree (72365); Th; 1,900pd (Est); $3.30; publisher & editor John Boxley Jr; tel (501) 358-2993; fax (501) 358-4538

Marshall: *Marshall Mountain Wave* — 103 E. Main; PO Box 220 (72650); W; 4,099pd, 181fr (Sw); $4.40; publisher Jim Tilley; editor Debbie Horton; tel (501) 448-3321; fax (501) 448-5659

McCrory: *Woodruff Monitor-Leader-Advocate* — 301 Edmonds St.; PO Box 898 (72101); W; 1,950pd, 50fr (Est); $5.25; C; publisher Paula Davis; general manager Debbie Thompson; editor Bill Riddle; tel (501) 731-2561; fax (501) 731-5899

McGehee/Dermott: *McGehee-Dermott Times/News* — 205 N. 2nd; PO Box 290, McGehee (71654); W; 3,400pd, 9,879fr (Sw); $5.25; C; publishers James White Jr & Thomas White; managing editor James White; tel (501) 222-3922; fax (501) 222-3726

Mena: *Mena Star* — 501-7 Mena St.; PO Box 1307 (71953); Th; 2,637pd (Sw); $5.60; publisher Barney White; tel (501) 394-1900; fax (501) 394-1908

Monticello: *Advance-Monticellonian* — 314 N. Main St.; PO Box 486 (71655); W; 5,250pd (Sw); 25¢; publisher William F Jackson; editor Betty Evans; tel (501) 367-5325; fax (501) 367-6612

Morrilton: *Conway County Petit Jean Country Headlight* — 908 W. Broadway; PO Box 540 (72110); W; 6,523pd, 118fr (Sw); $7.70; publisher & editor Clifton Wells; general manager Eddy Hodge; managing editor Charlotte Hodge; tel (501) 354-2451; fax (501) 354-4225

Mt. Ida: *Montgomery County News* — West St.; PO Box 195 (71957); Th; 1,685pd, 45fr (Sw); $3.31; publisher Louie Graves; editor Mike McCoy; tel (501) 867-2010

Mountain View: *Stone County Leader* — 103 Main St.; PO Box 509 (72560); W; 3,060pd, 78fr (Sw); $4.45; C; publisher & editor James R Fraser; managing editor Lori Freeze; tel (501) 269-3841; fax (501) 269-2171

Murfreesboro: *Murfreesboro Diamond* — On The Square; PO Box 550 (71857); W; 1,682pd (Sw); $2.70; publisher Louie Graves; editor John L Balch; tel (501) 285-2723; fax (501) 285-3820

Nashville: *The Nashville News* — 418 N. Main; PO Box 297 (71852); M/Th; 4,189pd, 101fr (Sw); $7.70; C; publisher & editor Louie Graves; tel (501) 845-2010; fax (501) 845-5091

N Pulaski Co.: *The Times* — 26th & Willow Sts.; PO Box 428, North Little Rock (72115-0428); Th; 8,486pd, 337fr (Sw); $3.14; publisher David M Chism; editor Kitty Chism; tel (501) 758-2571; fax (501) 758-2597

Osceola: *The Osceola Times* — 112 N. Poplar (72370); Th; 2,500pd, 125fr (Sw); $3.50; C; publisher David Tennyson; editor Sandra Brand; tel (501) 563-2615; fax (501) 563-2616

Ozark: *The Spectator* — 207 W. Main (72949); W; 4,085pd (Est); 90¢; publisher Bob Bevil; editor Jo Eveld; tel (501) 667-2136; fax (501) 667-4365

Paris: *Paris Express-Progress* — PO Box 551 (72855); W; 4,000pd (Sw); $6.00; C; publisher William Hager; tel (501) 963-2901; fax (501) 963-3062

Pea Ridge/Benton: *The Times of Northeast Benton County* — 150-E S. Curtis Ave.; PO Box 25, Pea Ridge (72751); W; 1,636pd, 18fr (Sw); $3.25; publisher & editor Mike Freeman; tel (501) 451-1196

Perryville/Perry Co.: *Perry County Petit Jean Country Headlight* — Courthouse Sq.; PO Box 418, Perryville (72126); W; 2,040pd, 30fr (Sw); $8.25; publisher & editor Clifton Wells; general manager Eddy Hodge; managing editor Charlotte Hodge; tel (501) 354-2451; fax (501) 354-4225

Piggott: *The Piggott Times* — 209 W. Main St.; PO Box 59 (72454); W; 3,186pd, 130fr (Sw); 24¢; publisher & editor Ronald C Kemp; tel (501) 598-2201; fax (501) 598-5189

Pine Bluff: *Pine Bluff News* — 3900 B Miramar Dr.; PO Box 7806 (71611); F; 3,930pd, 54fr (Est); $4.90; publisher Mike Kellar; general manager Cindy Lee; editor Pat McHughes; tel (501) 879-5450; fax (501) 879-5636

Pocahontas: *Pocahontas Star Herald* — 109 N. Van Bibber; PO Box 608 (72455); Th; 6,100pd, 65fr (Est); $4.30; C; publisher Jan V Rockwell; editor Kathryn T Cheyne; tel (501) 892-4451; fax (501) 892-4453

Prairie Grove/Farmington: *The Prairie Grove Enterprise* — 114 N. Mock; PO Box 650, Prairie Grove (72753); Th; 2,000pd, 70fr (Sw); $3.50; C; publisher & editor Boyce R Davis; tel (501) 846-2191; fax (501) 267-5540

Prescott/Nevada Co.: *Nevada County Picayune* — 125 W. Main; PO Box 60, Prescott (71857); W; 2,500pd (Est); $5.00; publisher Betty Ragsdale; publisher & editor John R Ragsdale; tel (501) 887-2002; fax (501) 887-2949

Rector: *Clay County Democrat* — 306 Main St.; PO Box 366 (72461); W; 2,264pd, 93fr (Sw); $4.75; C; publisher Ronald E Kemp; editor Nancy J Kemp; tel (501) 595-3549; fax (501) 595-3611

Rison: *Cleveland County Herald* — 206 Main St.; PO Box 325 (71665); W; 2,565pd, 15fr (Sw); $3.50; publisher & editor Stan M Sadler; general manager Melody K Wilson; tel (501) 325-6412; fax (501) 325-6127

Sheridan/Grant Co.: *The Sheridan Headlight* — 101 E. Center St.; PO Box 539, Sheridan (72150); W; 4,050pd (Est); 19¢; publisher & editor Melody A Moorehouse; tel (501) 942-2142; fax (501) 942-2143

Sherwood: *Sherwood Voice* — 2902 E. Kiehl; PO Box 6166 (72124); Th; 1,566pd (Sw); $5.50; C; publisher Magie Enterprises Inc.; general manager Mark Magie; editor Amy Partain; tel (501) 835-4875; fax (501) 834-1425

Siloam Springs: *The Herald-Leader* — 101 N. Mount Olive; PO Box 370 (72761); W; 4,215pd, 18fr (Sw); $7.00; Su; 4,215pd, 18fr (Sw); $7.35; C; publisher Scott Harrell; editor Jami Jones; tel (501) 524-5144; fax (501) 524-3612

Smackover: *Smackover Journal* — 618 N. Broadway; PO Box 147 (71762); Th; 1,191pd, 24fr (Sw); $3.82; publisher Walter E Hussman Jr; general manager & editor Donna Faulkner; tel (501) 725-3131

S Sebastian Co.: *The Citizen* — PO Box 36, Mansfield (72944); W; 2,709pd, 85fr (Sw); $4.19; publisher & editor Marty Backus; tel (501) 928-5340; fax (501) 928-5340

Star City: *Lincoln Ledger* — 216 W. Bradley (71667); W; 2,278pd, 72fr (Sw); $3.00; publisher & editor Joe V Mason Sr; tel (501) 628-4161; fax (501) 628-3802

Trumann: *Trumann Democrat* — 200 Hwy. 463 S. (72472); W; 2,505pd, 20fr (Est); $3.25; publisher Charles Nix; general manager John Hampton; editor Joyce Jynes; tel (501) 483-6317

Van Buren/Alma: *Van Buren Press Argus-Courier* — 100 N. 11th St.; PO Box 369, Van Buren (72956); W/Sa; 4,950pd, 140fr (Sw); $5.25; publisher Ken Richardson; editor Roy Faulkenberry; tel (501) 474-5215; fax (501) 471-5607

Waldron/Scott Co.: *The Waldron News* — PO Box 745, Waldron (72958); W; 2,681pd, 7,081fr (Est); $2.70; C; publisher & editor Marty Backus; tel (501) 637-4161; fax (501) 637-4162

Walnut Ridge: *The Times Dispatch* — 225 W. Main St.; PO Box 389 (72476); W; 6,437pd, 39fr (Sw); 30¢; publisher & editor John A Bland; general manager Hope Segraves; tel (501) 886-2464; fax (501) 886-9369

Warren: *Warren Eagle Democrat* — 200 W. Cypress St. (71671); Tu; 4,395pd, 38fr (Est); 35¢; publisher & editor Robert L Newton; tel (501) 226-5831; fax (501) 226-6601

Washington Co.: *Washington County Observer* — 294 W. Main St.; PO Box 377, West Fork (72774); Th; 3,050pd, 75fr (Est); $3.50; C; publisher Boyce Davis; general manager & managing editor David Vanway; editor Velda Brotheron; tel (501) 839-2771; fax (501) 839-8535

White Hall: *White Hall Journal* — 6210 Dollarway Rd., Ste. 2A; PO Box 1166, Pine Bluff (71613-1166); W; 1,495pd, 818fr (Est); $4.58; publisher & editor Frank Lightfoot; tel (501) 247-4700; fax (501) 247-4755

Woodruff Co.: *Woodruff County Monitor* — 301 N. Edmonds Ave.; PO Box 898, McCrory (72101); W; 1,605pd, 45fr (Sw); $4.00; publisher Paula Davis; general manager Debbie Thompson; editor Bill Riddle; tel (501) 731-2263; fax (501) 731-5899

Wynne/Cross Co.: *Wynne Progress* — 702 N. Falls Blvd.; PO Box 308, Wynne (72396); F; 3,953pd, 250fr (Sw); $7.00; C; publisher David M Boger; editor David Nichol; managing editor Fred Conley; tel (501) 238-2375; fax (501) 238-4655

Yellville/Marion Co.: *The Mountain Echo* — Hwy. 62 & Church St.; PO Box 528, Yellville (72687); Th; 1,560pd, 75fr (Est); $5.00; C; publisher Chuck Pullums; general manager & editor Ray Davis; tel (501) 449-4257; fax (501) 449-6605

CALIFORNIA

Alameda: *Alameda Journal* — 1416 Park Ave. (94501); Tu/F; 352pd, 29,195fr (VAC); $16.00; C; publisher Cliff Benson; general manager Scott Connelly; editor Gloria J M Salvante; tel (510) 748-1666; fax (510) 748-1665

Aliso Viejo: *Aliso Viejo News* — 22481 Aspan, Lake Forest (92630); Th; 2,048pd, 3,886fr (Est); $33.53; C; publisher Orange County Register; editor Don Chapman; tel (714) 768-3631; fax (714) 454-7350

Amador Co.: *Amador Ledger-Dispatch* — 10776 Argonaut Ln.; PO Box 1328, Jackson (95642); M; 6,590pd, 17fr (Sw); $6.13; W/F; 6,590pd, 17fr (Sw); $8.18; C; publisher & editor Kathleen Newton; managing editor Joe Evans; tel (209) 223-1767; fax (209) 223-1264

Anaheim: *Anaheim Bulletin* — 1771 S. Lewis St. (92805); Th; 15pd, 60,237fr (Est); $15.59; publisher Dave Threshie; editor John Swanson; tel (714) 634-1567; fax (714) 704-3714

Anaheim Hills: *Anaheim Hills News* — 1771 S. Lewis St., Anaheim (92805); Th; 13pd, 13,488fr (Est); $7.63; publisher Dave Threshie; editor Joelle Collier; managing editor John Swanson; tel (714) 634-1567; fax (714) 704-3714

Anderson/Cottonwood: *Valley Post* — 2680 Gateway Dr.; PO Box 1148, Anderson (96007); Tu; 2,920pd, 8,100fr (Sw); $6.80; C; publisher Douglas P Hirsch; editor Loretta Carrico; tel (916) 365-2797; fax (916) 365-2829

Angels Camp/Murphys: *Calaveras Californian* — 1243 S. Main St.; PO Box 9, Angels Camp (95222); Th; 3,120pd, 2fr (Est); $2.60; C; publisher & editor John R Peterson; general manager Eric Peterson; managing editor Eleanor Peterson; tel (209) 736-2085; fax (209) 736-4147

Apple Vly.: *The Valley News* — 16925 Main St. (92345); PO Box 1147 (92307); F; 2,000pd, 400fr (Est); 17¢; publisher Jenny Jones; editor Joyce Bohannan; tel (619) 247-7359; fax (619) 244-6609

Arcata/McKinleyville: *The Union* — 613 H St.; PO Box 1146, Arcata (95521); W; 3,761pd, 14,000fr (Sw); $7.80; C; publisher Patrick O'Dell; editor Rosemary Wurst-Edmiston; tel (707) 826-8550; fax (707) 826-8556

Arroyo Grande: *Five Cities Times-Press-Recorder* — 1052 Grand Ave.; PO Box 460 (93420); W/F; 8,594pd, 283fr (VAC); $9.40; C; publisher & editor Dick Blankenburg; managing editor Mike Hodgson; tel (805) 489-4206; fax (805) 473-0571

Arvin: *Arvin Tiller* — 525 Bear Mt. Blvd.; PO Box 427 (93203); W; 2,295pd (Est); 18¢; publishers Donald L Reed & Frank W Reed; editor Flora Nichols; tel (805) 854-5594

Atascadero: *Atascadero News* — PO Box 6068 (93423); W/F; 7,148pd, 5,874fr (Sw); $7.30; C; publishers John A Porter & Judson D Porter; editor Lon Allan; managing editor James D Porter; tel (805) 466-2585; fax (805) 466-2714

Atwater/Winton/McSwain: *Atwater Signal* — 927 Atwater Blvd., Atwater (95301); W; 966pd, 11,841fr (Est); $9.52; C; publisher & editor David Wickenhauser; tel (209) 358-6431; fax (209)357-2968

Avalon/Catalina/Island Co.: *The Catalina Islander* — 615 Crescent Ave.; PO Box 428, Avalon (90704); F; 3,015pd, 2,000fr (Sw); $8.15; C; publisher & editor Sherri Walker; tel (310) 510-0500; fax (310) 510-2882

Avenal/Kettleman City: *Avenal Progress* — 141 E. King St., Avenal (93204); Th; 1,200pd (Est); $3.50; publisher & editor Bruce Pankratz; tel (209) 386-9385; fax (209) 935-5257

Azusa: *Azusa Herald* — 1210 N. Azusa Canyon Rd., West Covina (91790); Th; 3,100pd (Sw); $2.00; C; publisher Chuck Rathbun; editor John Irby; managing editor Rick Krzyzanowski; tel (818) 854-8700; fax (818) 856-2737

U.S. Weeklies California II-5

Banning/Beaumont/Cabazon/Calimesa/Cherry Vly.: *Community Adviser Newspaper* — 795 E. 6th St., Ste. N, Beaumont (92223); Th; 3,221pd, 10,779fr (Sw); $10.08; C; publisher Kenneth W Smith; editor Hal Lowe; tel (909) 845-9564; fax (909) 845-6713

Belmont/San Carlos: *Belmont & San Carlos Enquirer Bulletin* — 824 Cowan Rd., Burlingame (94010); Tu; 22,200fr (Sw); $15.25; C; publisher Colin Pratt; general manager Debbie Witten; editor Allen Clap; tel (415) 692-9406; fax (415) 692-7587

Beverly Hills: *Beverly Hills Independent* — 5215 Torrance Blvd., Torrance (90509); Th; 18,400fr (Est); $13.95; C; publisher Thomas J Wafer Jr; editor James M Box; tel (310) 540-5511; fax (310) 540-5391

Beverly Hills: *The Beverly Hills Courier* — 8840 Olympic Blvd. (90211); F; 2,500pd, 47,000fr (Est); $28.00; publisher & editor March Schwartz; tel (310) 278-1322; fax (310) 271-5118

Big Bear Lake: *Big Bear Grizzly* — 42007 Fox Farm Rd., Ste. 3B; PO Box 1789 (92315); Th; 8,968pd, 240fr (Sw); $11.15; C; publisher Jerry M Wright; editor John Emig; tel (909) 866-3456; fax (909) 866-2302

Bishop/Inyo: *Inyo Register* — 450 E. Line St.; PO Box 787, Bishop (93515); W/F/Su; 5,995pd, 135fr (Sw); $8.78; C; publishers Deane Funk & Pete Doughtie; editor Barbara Laughon; tel (619) 873-3535; fax (619) 873-3591

Blythe/Palo Verda Vly./Ettrenberg/Quartzsite: *Palo Verde Valley Times* — 231 N. Spring St.; PO Box 1159, Blythe (92226); W/F; 4,200pd, 124fr (Sw); $9.26; C; publisher Robin Mauser; editor Randy Sherman; tel (619) 922-3181; fax (619) 922-3184

Bodega Bay: *Bodega Bay Navigator* — 1580 Eastshore Rd.; PO Box 696 (94923); Th; 2,000pd (Sw); $7.00; publisher & general manager Joel Hack; publisher & editor Susan Sevilla; tel (707) 875-3574; fax (707) 875-3875

Bonsall: *Bonsall Messenger* — PO Box 1529, Valley Center (92082); Th; 1,208pd, 1,374fr (Est); $6.70; C; publisher Dale Good; editor David Ross; tel (619) 749-1112; fax (619) 746-1688

Boonville: *Anderson Valley Advertiser* — 14265 Hwy. 28; PO Box 459 (95415); W; 1,352pd, 57fr (Est); $1.61; publisher & editor Bruce Anderson; tel (707) 895-3016; fax (707) 895-3355

Brea: *Brea Progress* — 1771 S. Lewis St., Anaheim (92805); Th; 15pd, 11,168fr (Est); $7.34; publisher Dave Threshie; editor Mark Ducick; tel (714) 634-1567; fax (714) 704-3714

Buena Park: *Buena Park News* — 1771 S. Lewis St., Anaheim (92805); Th; 2pd, 6,894fr (Est); $7.63; publisher Dave Threshie; editor Erik Peterson; tel (714) 634-1567; fax (714) 704-3714

Burbank: *Burbank Leader* — 220 N. Glen Oaks Blvd., Ste. B (91502); W; 1,285pd, 30,605fr (VAC); $18.90; Sa; 1,506pd, 30,605fr (VAC); $18.90; C; publisher Judith B Kendall; editor William Lobdell; managing editor Paul Hubler; tel (818) 843-8700; fax (818) 954-9439

Burlingame/Hillsborough: *Hillsborough/Burlingame Boutique & Villager* — 824 Cowan Rd., Burlingame (94010); W; 3,100pd, 10,550fr (Sw); $15.25; C; publisher Colin Pratt; general manager Debbie Witten; editor Marc Burkhardt; tel (415) 692-9406; fax (415) 692-7587

Burney: *Intermountain News* — 36965 Main St.; PO Box 1030 (96013); W; 3,254pd, 85fr (Sw); $7.23; C; publisher & editor Craig Harrington; tel (916) 335-4533; fax (916) 335-5335

Calaveras Co.: *Calaveras Ledger-Dispatch* — 1248 S. Main St.; PO Box 1136, Angels Camp (95222); Tu; 3,640pd, 3,500fr (Est); $5.32; F; 3,640pd, 3,500fr (Est); $8.18; C; publisher & editor Kathleen Newton; managing editor Joe Evans; tel (209) 736-0921; fax (209) 736-9078

Calexico/Imperial Co.: *Calexico Chronicle* — 317 Heffenan (92231); PO Box 72, Calexico (92232); Th; 1,220pd, 879fr (Est); 20¢; publisher Lupe T Acuna; editor Hildy Carrillo-Rivera; tel (619) 357-3214; fax (619) 357-3811

Calistoga: *The Weekly Calistogan* — 1360 Lincoln Ave.; PO Box 385 (94515); Th; 1,605pd, 75fr (Sw); $7.83; C; publisher Bill Brenner; editor Pat Hampton; tel (707) 942-6242; fax (707) 942-4617

Cambria: *The Cambrian* — 2442 Main St.; PO Drawer 67 (93428); Th; 3,742pd, 50fr (Sw); $9.15; C; publisher John P Scripps Newspapers; editor Jay Thompson; tel (805) 927-8652; fax (805) 927-4708

Campbell: *Campbell Express* — 334 E. Campbell Ave. (95008-2012); W; 411pd, 6,597fr (Est); $7.14; publisher B J Hanchett; editor Kathryn Hanchett; tel (408) 374-9700; fax (408) 374-0813

Carlsbad: *Carlsbad Sun* — 2841 Loker Ave. E. (92008); Th; 279pd, 27,759fr (Est); $8.00; C; publisher Donna Medeiros; editor Terrie Lafferty Drago; tel (619) 431-4850; fax (619) 431-4888

Carmel/Carmel Vly./Pebble/Pacific Grove/Monterey: *The Carmel Pine Cone* — 4th & Mission Sts.; PO Box G-1, Carmel (93921); Th; 500pd, 12,000fr (Est); $15.10; C; publisher W A Chip Brown; editor Doug Thompson; tel (408) 624-0162; fax (408) 624-8076

Carpinteria/Summerland: *Coastal View* — 4856 Carpinteria Ave., Carpinteria (93013); W; 200pd, 6,000fr (Est); $9.00; publishers Gary L Dobbins & Michael Vanstry; publisher & editor Rosemarie Fanucchi; tel (805) 684-4428; fax (805) 684-4650

Carson: *Carson Star/South Bay Extra* — 5215 Torrance Blvd., Torrance (90509); Th; 23,220fr (Est); $17.68; C; publisher Thomas J Wafer Jr; editor James M Box; tel (310) 540-5511; fax (310) 540-5391

Caruthers Riverdale: *Caruthers-Easton Twin City Times* — 2452 W. Tahoe; PO Box 248, Caruthers (93609); W; 8,000fr (Est); 43¢; publisher & editor Dale Anderson; tel (209) 864-8923; fax (209) 864-3885

Ceres/Hughson/Keyes/S Modesto: *The Ceres Courier* — 2940 4th St.; PO Box 7, Ceres (95307); W/F; 4,062pd, 12,500fr (Sw); 42¢; C; publisher Darell Phillips; general manager Douglas Cox; editor Jeff Benziger; tel (209) 537-5032; fax (209) 537-0543

Chester: *Chester Progressive* — 242 Main St., Hwy. 36; PO Box 557 (96020); W; 2,732pd, 10fr (Sw); $4.50; C; publisher Michael C Taborski; editor Kristin Woods; tel (916) 258-3115; fax (916) 258-2365

Chino/Chino Hills: *Chino Champion* — 13179 9th St. (91710); PO Box 607, Chino (91708-0607); Th; 1,467pd, 15,232fr (VAC); $16.19; C; publisher & editor Allen P McCombs; general manager Bruce M Wood; managing editor Scott Moore; tel (909) 628-5501; fax (909) 591-6296

Chino Hills/Chino: *Chino Hills Champion* — 13179 9th St. (91710); PO Box 607, Chino (91708); Th; 500pd, 14,541fr (VAC); $16.19; C; publisher & editor Allen P McCombs; general manager Bruce M Wood; managing editor Scott Moore; tel (909) 628-5501; fax (909) 591-6296

Chowchilla: *The Chowchilla News* — 340 W. Robertson Blvd. (93610); W; 2,862pd, 28fr (Sw); $5.56; C; publisher & editor Jess Chambers; tel (209) 665-5751; fax (209) 665-5462

Chula Vista/S Bay: *Star-News* — 835 3rd Ave.; PO Box 1207, Chula Vista (91912); W; 20,000pd (Sw); $1.45; Sa; 24,000pd (Sw); $1.45; C; publisher Donna Medeiros; general manager Michael Sugamele; editor Rick Fitch; tel (619) 427-3000; fax (619) 424-6346

City Terrace/Los Angeles Co.: *City Terrace Comet-c/o Eastern Group Publications* — 2500 S. Atlantic Blvd., Bldg. B (90040); PO Box 33803, Los Angeles (90040); Th; 230pd, 4,730fr (Sw); $20.16; C; publisher & editor Dolores Sanchez; general manager Jonathan Sanchez; managing editor Tony Castro; tel (213) 263-5743; fax (213) 263-9169

Claremont: *Claremont Courier* — 111 S. College Ave. (91711); W/Sa; 5,240pd, 154fr (Sw); 51¢; C; publisher & editor Martin Weinberger; managing editor Patricia Yarborough; tel (909) 621-4761; fax (909) 621-4072

Clearlake: *Clear Lake Observer-American* — 4474 Old Hwy. 53; PO Box 6328 (95422); W/Sa; 3,275pd (Sw); $5.70; C; publisher John W Lowman; general manager Karen Streim; editor David D Stoneberg; tel (707) 994-6444; fax (707) 994-5335

Cloverdale: *Cloverdale Reveille Inc.* — 207 N. Cloverdale Blvd.; PO Box 157 (95425); W; 2,100pd, 105fr (Est); $4.50; publisher & editor Bonny J Hanchett; managing editor Roberta Lyons; tel (707) 894-3339

Clovis: *The Clovis Independent* — 1321 Railroad Ave.; PO Box 189 (93613); W; 3,953pd, 19,868fr (Est); $11.63; C; publisher & editor Earl Wright Jr; tel (209) 298-8081; fax (209) 298-0459

Coalinga/Avenal: *The Coalinga Record* — 152 E. Elm; PO Box 496, Coalinga (93210); W; 3,809pd, 2,690fr (Est); 43¢; publisher Dale Anderson; editor Bill Howell; tel (209) 935-2906; fax (209) 935-5257

Colfax: *Colfax Record* — 25 W. Church St.; PO Box 755 (95713); W; 1,557pd, 10fr (Est); 53¢; publisher Scott Little; editor Dan Foscalina; tel (916) 346-2232; fax (916) 346-2700

Colton/Grand Terrace: *The Colton Courier* — 1809 S. Commerce Ctr. W.; PO Box 6247, San Bernadino (92412); Th; 1,100pd, 10,400fr (Est); 27¢; publisher Bill Harrison; editor Lisa Cillarear; tel (909) 381-9898; fax (909) 384-0406

Colusa/Williams/Maxwell: *Colusa County Sun-Herald* — 825 Bridge St.; PO Box 89, Colusa (95932); M/W/F; 2,220pd, 5,213fr (Est); $6.45; publisher Darell Phillips; editors Jean-Pierre Cativiela & Kurt Schauppner; tel (916) 458-2121; fax (916) 458-5711

Corcoran: *Corcoran Journal* — 1012 Hale Ave.; PO Box 487 (93212); Th; 2,219pd, 26fr (Est); 20¢; publisher Robert Lyman; editor Jeanette Todd; tel (209) 992-3115; fax (209) 992-5543

Corning/S Tehama Co.: *Corning Observer* — 710 5th St.; PO Box 558, Corning (96021); M/W/F; 1,697pd, 2,172fr (Sw); $3.75; C; publisher Darell Phillips; editor Ty Phillips; tel (916) 824-5464; fax (916) 824-4804

Coronado: *Coronado Journal* — 1224 10th St., Ste. 102; PO Box 180008 (92118); F; 5,381pd, 181fr (Sw); $12.00; C; publisher Michael Sugamele; editor Kelly M Pyrek; tel (619) 435-3141; fax (619) 435-3051

Corte Madera/Larkspur: *Twin Cities Times* — 1050 Bridgeway; PO Box T, Sausalito (94966); Tu; 6,000pd (Est); $9.95; publisher Paul Anderson; general manager & editor Billie Anderson; editor Beth Anderson; tel (415) 924-8582; fax (415) 332-8714

Covina: *Covina Highlander Press Courier* — 1210 N. Azusa Canyon Rd., West Covina (91790); Th; 6,512pd, 12,950fr (Sw); $9.95; C; publisher Chuck Rathbun; editor John Irby; managing editor Rick Krzyzanowski; tel (818) 962-8811; fax (818) 856-2737

Crestline/Lake Gregory/Vly. of Enchantment: *Crestline Courier-News* — 24028 Lake Dr., Ste. C; PO Box 3307, Crestline (92325); Th; 3,462pd, 50fr (Est); $5.70; C; publisher Phil Jaffe; general manager Susan A Mosher; editor Matt Proietti; tel (909) 338-1893; fax (909) 338-4449

Culver City: *Culver City News-c/o Coastal Community Newspapers* — 4346 Sepulveda Blvd.; PO Box 5214 (90232); Th; 14,000fr (Sw); $25.00; C; publisher & editor Stephen Hadland; general manager Carol Layonc; managing editor Dave Myers; tel (310) 313-6733; fax (310) 313-6732

Culver City: *Culver City/Ladera Independent* — 5215 Torrance Blvd., Torrance (90509); Th; 30,100fr (Est); $13.95; C; publisher Thomas J Wafer Jr; editor James M Box; tel (310) 540-5511; fax (310) 540-5391

Cupertino: *Cupertino Courier* — 20465 Silverado Ave. (95014); W; 3,340pd, 15,012fr (Sw); $10.50; C; publisher David Cohen; general manager Kathy Wrightson; editor Caroline Leal; tel (408) 255-7500; fax (408) 252-3381

Cypress: *Cypress News* — 1771 S. Lewis St., Anaheim (92805); Th; 6,020fr (VAC); $6.94; C; publisher Dave Threshie; editor Erik Pedersen; tel (714) 634-1567; fax (714) 704-3714

Dana Point: *Dana Point News* — 22481 Aspan, Lake Forest (92630); Th; 12,195fr (VAC); $21.45; C; publisher Orange County Register; editor Steve Silberman; tel (714) 768-3631; fax (714) 454-7397

Del Mar/Solana Beach/Carmel Vly./Rancho Santa Fe: *Del Mar/Solana Beach/Carmel Valley/Rancho Santa Fe Sun* — 1228 Camino Del Mar, Del Mar (92014); Th; 358pd, 20,500fr (Est); $9.00; C; general manager Chris Blaisdale; editor Liam Truchard; managing editor Terrie Lafferty-Drago; tel (619) 792-3820; fax (619) 481-3312

Delano: *The Delano Record* — 1231 Jefferson St.; PO Box 938 (93216-0938); Th; 4,180pd, 135fr (Sw); $6.60; C; publishers Donald L Reed & Frank W Reed; general manager Lucille Blevins; editor Bob Schettler; tel (805) 725-0600; fax (805) 725-4373

Delhi: *Delhi Express* — PO Box 445 (95315); W; 3,000pd (Sw); $5.95; C; publisher John M Derby; editor Desiree Depui; tel (209) 358-5311; fax (209) 358-7108

Demair: *Demair Dispatch* — PO Box 65, Winton (95388); Th; 3,300pd (Est); 32¢; C; publisher John M Derby; managing editor Mae Branagh; tel (209) 358-5311; fax (209) 358-7108

Desert Hot Springs: *Desert Sentinel* — PO Box 338, Desert Hot Springs (92240); W; 2,290pd, 91fr (Sw); $10.95; C; publisher Robert J Dickey; general manager Linda Munsey; editor John Waters Jr; tel (619) 329-1411; fax (619) 329-3860

Diamond Bar: *Diamond Bar/Phillips Ranch Highlander* — 1210 N. Azusa Canyon Rd., West Covina (91790); Th; 9pd, 12,886fr (VAC); $7.55; C; publisher Chuck Rathbun; editor Frances Young; managing editor Rick Krzyzanowski; tel (818) 854-8700; fax (818) 854-8719

Dinuba/Cutler/Orosi: *The Dinuba Sentinel* — 145 S. L St.; PO Box 247, Dinuba (93618); Th; 3,335pd, 34fr (Sw); $5.80; C; publisher & editor Bob Raison; publisher Diane Raison; tel (209) 591-4632; fax (209) 591-1322

Dixon: *Dixon Tribune* — 145 E. A St. (95620); W/F/Su; 2,651pd, 2,240fr (Est); $6.10; C; publisher David Payne; editor Sherry Barkus; tel (916) 678-5594

Dorris/Malin/Merrill/Tulelake: *Butte Valley-Lost River Star* — 111 W. 3rd. St.; PO Box 708, Dorris (96023); W; 2,200pd, 800fr (Est); $1.25; publisher Carol McKay; publisher & editor Elizabeth Carleton; tel (916) 397-2601

Dos Palos: *Dos Palos Sun* — 1633 Center St. (93620); Th; 3,300fr (Est); $6.00; C; publisher & editor Bruce Pankratz; tel (209) 392-3921; fax (209) 392-2200

Dunsmuir: *The Dunsmuir News* — 924B N. Mount Shasta Blvd.; PO Box 127, Mount Shasta (96067); W; 1,326pd, 31fr (Sw); $3.90; publisher Genny Axtman; editor Steve Gerace; tel (916) 926-5214; fax (916) 926-4166

E Contra Costa Co.: *Brentwood News* — 654 3rd St.; PO Box 517, Brentwood (94513); Tu/F; 4,118pd, 580fr (VAC); $4.90; C; publisher George E Riggs; general manager Gloria Thomas; editor Pam Temby; tel (510) 634-2125; fax (415) 634-1149

E Los Angeles: *Mexican American Sun* — 2500 S. Atlantic Blvd., Bldg. B, Los Angeles (90040); Th; 267pd, 9,577fr (Sw); $20.16; C; publisher & editor Dolores Sanchez; general manager Jonathan Sanchez; managing editor Tony Castro; tel (213) 263-5743; fax (213) 263-9169

Easton/Caruthers: *The Twin City Times/Riverdale Free Press* — c/o Shannon Publications; PO Box 547, Lemore (93245); W; 303pd, 7,197fr (Est); 29¢; publisher & editor Dale Anderson; tel (209) 924-3488; fax (209) 924-5361

El Cerrito/Albany: *The Journal* — 6208 La Salle Ave.; PO Box 1624, El Cerrito (94530); Th; 230pd, 14,578fr (VAC); $18.10; C; publisher Warren (Chip) Brown; general manager Scott Connelly; editor Shannon Morgan; tel (510) 339-4060; fax (510) 339-4066

El Dorado Co.: *El Dorado Gazette, Georgetown Gazette & Town Crier* — 2775 Minersflat; PO Box 49, Georgetown (95634); Tu; 1,375pd, 29fr (Sw); $8.00; publisher & editor Mark Lantz; tel (916) 333-4481; fax (916) 333-0152

El Dorado Co.: *The Reporter* — PO Box 1028, Placerville (95667); W; 4,000pd, 2,000fr (Sw); $6.25; publisher & editor Frank Stephens; tel (916) 622-2280; fax (916) 622-6376

El Segundo: *El Segundo Herald* — 107 Sierra St.; PO Box 188 (90245); Th; 187pd, 14,000fr (Sw); $14.98; publisher Ben Pitcher; editor Linda Collins; tel (310) 322-1830; fax (310) 322-2787

Elk Grove: *Elk Grove Citizen* — 8970 Elk Grove Blvd. (95624); W/F; 8,634pd, 8,944fr (VAC); 25¢; publisher Roy Herburger; general manager Dean Davy; editor Janelle Deter; tel (916) 685-3945; fax (916) 686-6675

Encinitas: *Encinitas Sun* — 2841 Loker Ave. E., Carlsbad (92008); Th; 283pd, 19,196fr (Est); $8.00; C; publisher Richard Floco; general manager Chris Blaisdale; editor Tom Graves; tel (619) 634-1534; fax (619) 431-4888

II-6 **California** *U.S. Weeklies*

Escalon: *Escalon Times* — PO Box 98 (95320); W; 2,074pd, 69fr (Sw); $6.42; C; publisher Stanley L Cook; general manager William P Camp; editor John Branch; managing editor Steve Breen; tel (209) 838-7043; fax (209) 847-9750

Exeter: *The Sun* — 120 N.E.; PO Box 7 (93221-0007); W; 2,546pd, 164fr (Sw); $6.00; C; publisher Bill Brown; general manager John McNall; editor Bruce Whitworth; tel (209) 592-3171; fax (209) 592-4308

Fallbrook: *The Enterprise* — 232 S. Main St.; PO Box 397 (92028); Th; 6,882pd (ABC); $9.96; C; publisher G L (Don) Taylor; editor Betty Johnston; tel (619) 728-6116; fax (619) 723-4967

Felton: *The Valley Press* — 5901 Hwy. 9; PO Box V-1 (95018); W; 4,100pd, 250fr (Sw); $6.70; C; publisher Jack Fraser; editor Donna Jones; tel (408) 335-5321; fax (408) 438-4141

Ferndale/E River Vly./Mattole Vly.: *The Ferndale Enterprise* — 334 Main St.; PO Box 268, Ferndale (95536); Th; 1,335pd, 70fr (Sw); $5.50; publisher & editor Elizabeth Poston McHarry; tel (707) 786-4611

Fillmore/Piru: *Fillmore Herald* — 321 Central Ave.; PO Box 727, Fillmore (93016); Th; 2,967pd, 200fr (Sw); $5.00; publisher & editor Doug Huff; tel (805) 524-0153

Folsom: *Folsom Telegraph* — 555 Oakdale St., Ste. G1 (95630); W; 5,299pd, 2,748fr (Est); $7.80; C; publisher Dave Reese; editor Jim Duncan; tel (916) 985-2581; fax (916) 985-0720

Fort Bragg: *Fort Bragg Advocate-News* — 450 N. Franklin St.; PO Box 1188 (95437); Th; 5,138pd, 85fr (Est); $7.00; C; publisher Sharon Brewer; managing editor Katherine Lee; tel (707) 964-5642; fax (707) 964-0424

Fortuna/S Humboldt: *The Humboldt Beacon and Fortuna Advance* — 936 Main St.; PO Box 310, Fortuna (95540); Th; 3,855pd, 18fr (Est); $6.86; C; publisher Patrick O'Dell; editor Jack Hamilton; tel (707) 725-6166; fax (707) 725-4981

Foster City: *Foster City Progress* — 824 Cowan Rd., Burlingame (94010); W; 10,500fr (Est); $17.15; C; publisher Colin Pratt; general manager Debbie Whitten; editor Michelle O'Donnell; managing editor Marc Burkhardt; tel (415) 692-9406; fax (415) 692-7587

Fowler/Malaga: *Fowler Ensign* — 207 E. Merced, Fowler (93625); Th; 1,853pd, 99fr (Est); $4.25; C; publisher Fred Hall; editor John E Converse; managing editor Dawn Pearson; tel (209) 834-2535; fax (209) 834-4343

Fullerton: *Fullerton News-Tribune* — 1771 S. Lewis St., Anaheim (92805); Th; 18pd, 30,223fr (VAC); $10.38; C; publisher Dave Threshie; editor Bob Ziebell; tel (714) 634-1567; fax (714) 704-3714

Garberville/Redway: *Redwood Record* — 432 Maple Ln.; PO Box 10, Garberville (95542); Th; 1,809pd (Est); $4.04; C; publisher Patrick O'Dell; editor Judy Brill; tel (707) 923-2166; fax (707) 923-2168

Gardena/S Bay: *Gardena Valley News* — 16417 S. Western Ave.; PO Box 219, Gardena (90247); Th; 15,000pd (Est); $6.00; publisher George D Algie; editor Gary Kohatsu; tel (310) 329-6351; fax (310) 329-7501

Glendora: *Glendora Press* — 1210 N. Azusa Canyon Rd., West Covina (91790); Th; 15,025fr (Est); $8.20; C; publisher Chuck Rathbun; editor John Irby; managing editor Rick K Krzyzanowski; tel (818) 854-8700; fax (818) 854-8719

Gonzales: *Gonzales Tribune* — PO Box 648 (93926); W; 745pd, 10fr (Est); $4.95; publisher Harry F Casey; general manager Suzi Taylor; editor Bill Osterbrock; tel (408) 678-2660; fax (408) 678-3676

Greenville: *Indian Valley Record* — 222 Mill St.; PO Box 469 (95947); W; 926pd, 11fr (Sw); $4.50; C; publisher Michael C Taborski; editor Dave Keller; tel (916) 284-7800; fax (916) 284-7600

Gridley: *The Gridley Herald* — 630 Washington St.; PO Box 68 (95948); W/F; 3,000pd, 90fr (Sw); $5.80; C; publisher W D Burleson; editor Scott Williams; tel (916) 846-3661; fax (916) 846-4519

Gualala/Point Arena: *Independent Coast Observer* — PO Box 1200, Gualala (95445-1200); publisher Joanna McLaughlin; general manager & editor Stephen J McLaughlin; tel (707) 884-3501; fax (707) 884-1710

Gustine/Newman: *Gustine Press-Standard* — 375 5th St., Gustine (95322); Th; 2,000pd (Est); $6.50; publisher William Mattos; general manager Susan Mattos; editor Marie Rosemire; managing editor Dean Harris; tel (209) 854-6333; fax (209) 854-6111

Hacienda Heights: *Hacienda Heights Highlander* — 1210 N. Azusa Canyon Rd., West Covina (91790); Th; 14,350fr (Est); $7.80; C; publisher Chuck Rathbun; editor John Irby; managing editor Rick Krzyzanowski; tel (818) 962-8811; fax (818) 856-2737

Half Moon Bay/El Granada/Moss Beach/Miramar/Pescadero: *Half Moon Bay Review* — 714 Kelly Ave.; PO Box 68, Half Moon Bay (94019); W; 6,500pd, 4,700fr (Sw); $9.55; C; publisher & editor John Toth; managing editor Marc DesJardins; tel (415) 726-4424; fax (415) 726-7054

Hawthorne: *Hawthorne Community News* — 4346 Sepulveda Blvd., Culver City (90232); Th; 100pd, 17,000fr (Sw); $19.61; C; publisher & editor Steve Hadland; tel (310) 313-6733; fax (310) 313-6732

Healdsburg/Windsor: *Healdsburg Tribune* — 706 Healdsburg Ave.; PO Box 518, Healdsburg (95448); W; 4,433pd, 42fr (Est); $11.74; C; publisher & editor Mark Kilpatrick; general manager Kathy Roth; tel (707) 433-4451; fax (707) 431-2623

Hesperia/Victor Vly.: *Hesperia Valley Wide Resorter* — 16925 Main St.; PO Box 400937, Hesperia (92345); Th; 12,000fr (Est); $10.25; publisher Jenny Jones; editor Joyce Bohannan; tel (619) 244-0021; fax (619) 244-6609

Hilmar: *Hilmar Times* — PO Box 65, Winton (95388); W; 3,800pd (Sw); 32¢; C; publisher & editor John M Derby; tel (209) 358-5311; fax (209) 358-7108

Hollywood: *Hollywood Independent* — 4201 Wilshire Blvd., Ste. 600, Los Angeles (90010); W; 50,000fr (Est); $20.50; publisher Stephen C Laxineta; general manager Simon Tam; editor Brian Lewis; tel (213) 932-6397; fax (213) 932-8250

Holtville: *Holtville Tribune* — 523 Pine Ave. (92250); Th; 1,841pd, 31fr (Est); $3.45; C; publisher Stephen Larson; editor Cesar Soto; tel (619) 356-2995; fax (619) 356-4915

Hughson: *Hughson Chronicle* — 2435 Hughson St.; PO Box 130 (95326); Tu; 4,200pd (Sw); 25¢; publisher John M Derby; editor Sheila Raville; tel (209) 358-5311

Huntington Beach: *Huntington Beach Independent* — 18682 Beach Blvd., Ste. 160, Huntington Beach (92648); Th; 238pd, 54,345fr (Est); $23.10; C; publisher Tom Johnson; general manager & managing editor Steve Marble; editor Iris Yokoi; tel (714) 965-3030; fax (714) 965-7174

Idyllwild: *Idyllwild Town Crier* — 54185 Pine Crest Ave.; PO Box 157 (92549); W; 3,464pd, 215fr (Sw); $4.95; publisher & editor Gary Hutner; tel (909) 659-2145; fax (909) 659-2071

Imperial: *Imperial Valley Weekly* — 523 Pine Ave., Holtville (92250); Th; 1,000pd, 6,172fr (Sw); $4.35; C; publisher Stephen Larson; editor Cesar Soto; tel (619) 356-2995; fax (619) 356-4915

Imperial Beach: *Imperial Beach Times* — PO Box 1208 (91933); Th; 5,000fr (Est); $8.57; C; publisher & editor John Mahoney; tel (619) 429-5533; fax (619) 429-5556

Indian Wells Vly./Searles Vly.: *The News Review* — 109 N. Sanders, Ridgecrest (93555); W; 2,222pd, 10,728fr (Sw); $5.50; publisher Patricia Farris; editor Patti Farris Cosner; tel (619) 371-4301; fax (619) 371-4304

Indio: *Indio Post* — 86-632 Hwy. 111, Ste. B (92201); W; 3,536pd, 120fr (Est); 15¢; publisher Bob Dickey; general manager Linda Munsey; editor Dick Gazy; tel (619) 775-4200; fax (619) 342-7128

Inglewood: *Inglewood News c/o Coastal Community Media Newspapers* — 4043 Irving Pl., Culver City (90232); Th; 14,000fr (Sw); $19.61; C; publisher & editor Stephen Hadland; tel (310) 313-6733; fax (310) 313-6732

Irvine: *The Irvine World News* — 2712 McGaw; PO Box C-19512 (92714); Th; 795pd, 51,051fr (Est); $14.45; publisher Brian M Manning; general manager Tobey Anglin; editor Don Dennis; tel (714) 261-2435; fax (714) 261-2623

Julian: *Julian News* — PO Box 639 (92036); W; 2,500pd (Sw); $9.00; C; publisher & editor Michael Judson-Carr; general manager Kay Howley; tel (619) 765-2231; fax (619) 765-1838

Kerman/San Joaquin: *The Kerman News* — 652 S. Madera Ave.; PO Box 336, Kerman (93630); W; 1,650pd, 6,050fr (Est); 38¢; publisher & editor Mark Kilen; general manager & managing editor Esther Kilen; tel (209) 846-6689; fax (209) 846-8045

Kern River Vly.: *Kern Valley Sun* — 6474 Lake Isabella Blvd.; PO Box 3074, Lake Isabella (93240); W; 6,205pd, 75fr (Sw); $6.60; C; publisher & editor Bret Bradigan; managing editor Kim R Brown; tel (619) 379-3667; fax (619) 379-4343

King City: *The Rustler* — 116 S. 3rd St.; PO Box J (93930); W; 3,165pd, 100fr (Est); $8.70; C; publisher Bill Parsons; managing editor Suzi Taylor; tel (408) 385-4880; fax (408) 385-4799

Kingsburg: *The Kingsburg Recorder* — 1467 Marion St.; PO Box 126 (93631-0126); W; 2,531pd, 45fr (Sw); $11.00; C; publisher James Brock; editor Edwin E Jacobs; tel (209) 897-2993; fax (209) 897-4868

Klamath Trinity Vly.: *The Kourier* — 39060 Hwy. 299; PO Box 355, Willow Creek (95573); W; 2,810pd, 35fr (Est); 37¢; publisher & editor J F Garst Jr; tel (916) 629-2811

La Canada/Flintridge/La Crescenta: *La Canada Valley Sun* — 1061 Valley Sun Ln.; PO Box 38, La Canada Flintridge (91011); Th; 4,820pd, 672fr (Sw); $8.15; publisher Gerald Bean; editor Don Mazen; tel (818) 790-8774; fax (818) 790-5690

La Canada/Flintridge/Montrose/La Crescenta/Sunland/Tujunga: *The Foothill Leader* — 3527-A N. Verdugo Rd., Glendale (91208); W; 53pd, 34,436fr (VAC); $18.90; Sa; 54pd, 30,367fr (VAC); $18.90; C; publisher Judith B Kendall; editor William Lobdell; managing editor David Hertz; tel (818) 249-8090; fax (818) 249-6563

La Habra: *La Habra Star* — 1771 S. Lewis St., Anaheim (92805); Th; 4pd, 16,402fr (Est); $7.85; publisher Dave Threshie; editor Bob Ziebell; tel (714) 634-1567; fax (714) 704-3714

La Jolla: *La Jolla Light* — 450 Pearl St.; PO Box 1927 (92038); Th; 5,279pd, 407fr (Est); $21.85; C; publisher Donna Medeiros; general manager Jeff Harrison; editor Cynthia Queen; managing editor Arian Collins; tel (619) 459-4201; fax (619) 459-0977

La Palma: *La Palma News* — 1771 S. Lewis St., Anaheim (92805); Th; 1,670fr (VAC); $6.94; C; publisher Dave Threshie; editor Erik Pedersen; tel (714) 634-1567; fax (714) 704-3714

La Puente/Glendora/Hacienda Hts./Covina/W Covina: *La Puente Valley Journal* — 1210 N. Azusa Canyon Rd., West Covina (91790); Th; 9pd, 11,502fr (VAC); $6.75; C; publisher Chuck Rathbun; editor John Irby; managing editor Rick K Krzyzanowski; tel (818) 962-8811; fax (818) 854-8719

Lafayette/Orinda/Moraga: *Contra Costa Sun* — PO Box 599, Lafayette (94549); W; 8,017pd, 10fr (Sw); $18.35; publisher George E Riggs; editor Gayle Melvin; tel (510) 284-4444; fax (510) 284-1039

Laguna Beach: *Laguna Beach News* — 22481 Aspan, Lake Forest (92630); Th; 13,319fr (VAC); $21.45; C; publisher Orange County Register; editor Cathy Lawhon; tel (714) 768-3631; fax (714) 454-7350

Laguna Niguel: *Laguna Niguel News* — 22481 Aspan, Lake Forest (92630); Th; 18,557fr (VAC); $21.45; C; publisher Orange County Register; editor Cathy Lawhon; tel (714) 768-3631; fax (714) 454-7397

Lake Arrowhead: *Mountain News & Mountaineer* — 28200 Hwy. 189, Ste. 01-200; PO Box 2410 (92352); Th; 5,391pd, 143fr (Sw); $11.00; C; publisher Phil Jaffe; editor Matt Proietti; tel (909) 336-3555; fax (909) 337-5275

Lake Elsinore Vly.: *Lake Elsinore Valley Sun-Tribune* — 31900 Mission Trl., Ste. 120; PO Box 2108, Lake Elsinore Valley (92530); Th; 14,321pd, 1,087fr (Sw); $9.57; C; general manager Tom Paradis; editor Lowanna Maxwell; tel (714) 674-1535; fax (714) 674-0280

Lamont: *Lamont Reporter* — 9717 Main St.; PO Box 548 (93241); W; 250pd, 4,950fr (Est); $5.00; publishers Donald L Reed & Frank W Reed; editor Flora Nichols; tel (805) 845-3704; fax (805) 845-3705

Lancaster/Mojave/Acton: *Desert Mailer News* — 741 E. Ave. I, Lancaster (93535); Tu; 16,174fr (Sw); $3.61; C; publisher Jim Cullins; editor Gen Fortis; tel (805) 945-8671; fax (805) 942-6418

Lawndale: *Lawndale Tribune* — 4346 Sepulveda Blvd., Culver City (90232); Th; 6,000fr (Est); $16.47; C; publisher & editor Stephen Hadland; tel (310) 313-6733; fax (310) 313-6732

Leisure World: *Leisure World News* — 22481 Aspan, Lake Forest (92630); Th; 9,604pd, 1,105fr (VAC); $31.80; C; publisher Orange County Register; editor Cathy Lawhon; tel (714) 768-3631; fax (714) 454-7350

Lemon Grove: *Lemon Grove Review* — 3434 Grove St.; PO Box 127 (91946); Th; 673pd, 1,327fr (Est); $5.00; C; publisher & editor Steve Saint; tel (619) 469-0101

Lemoore: *Lemoore Advance* — PO Box 547 (93245); Th; 8,520fr (Est); 43¢; C; publisher & editor Dale Anderson; editor Glenn Faison; tel (209) 924-3488; fax (209) 924-6220

Lincoln/Placer Co.: *Lincoln News Messenger* — 627 5th St.; PO Box 368, Lincoln (95648); Th; 2,797pd, 10fr (Sw); $5.90; publisher Stacy Smithers; editor Troy Swauger; tel (916) 645-7733; fax (916) 645-2776

Linden/Stockton: *The Linden Herald* — 4950 N. Bonham St.; PO Box 929, Linden (95236); Th; 1,400pd, 9fr (Sw); $4.90; publisher & editor Brian Reilly; tel (209) 887-3112; fax (209) 887-3111

Lindsay: *Lindsay Gazette* — PO Box 308 (93247); W; 2,700pd (Est); 19¢; publisher Bill Brown; general manager John McNall; editor Michelle Rester; tel (209) 562-2585; fax (209) 562-2214

Livermore/Pleasanton: *The Independent* — PO Box 1198, Livermore (94550); W; 26,200fr (Sw); $21.40; publishers David T Lowell & Joan Kinney Seppala; editor Janet Armantrout; tel (510) 447-8700; fax (510) 447-0212

Livingston/Hilmar/Delhi: *The Chronicle* — 424 Main St., Livingston (95334); W; 261pd, 8,300fr (Est); $6.48; publisher David Wickenhauser; editor Michael McGuire; tel (209) 394-7939; fax (209) 394-7930

Lockeford/Clement/Wallace: *The Lockeford-Clements News* — 18540 N. Hwy. 88; PO Box 76, Lockeford (95237); W; 2,800pd (Sw); 25¢; publisher & editor Laura J Mays; tel (209) 727-5776

Long Beach: *The Reporter* — 3010 E. Anaheim St.; PO Box 4278 (90804); Tu/F; 429pd, 70fr (Sw); 25¢; C; publisher G B Pfanstiel; editor Sandra Miller; tel (310) 438-5641; fax (310) 438-7086

Loomis: *The Loomis News* — 3651 Taylor Rd.; PO Box 125 (95650); Th; 1,066pd, 141fr (Sw); $4.00; publisher Bud Pisarek; general manager Martha Garcia; tel (916) 652-7939; fax (916) 652-7879

Los Altos: *Los Altos Town Crier* — 138 Main St. (94022); W; 8,598pd, 7,114fr (Est); $12.88; C; publisher Paul Nyberg; editor Bruce Barton; tel (415) 948-4489; fax (415) 948-6647

Los Angeles: *Beverlywood/Rancho Park/Cheviot Hills News* — 4346 Sepulveda Blvd., Culver City (90232); Th; 12,000fr (Est); $19.61; C; publisher & editor Stephen Hadland; tel (310) 313-6733; fax (310) 313-6732

Los Angeles: *East Los Angeles/Brooklyn Belvedere Comet* — 2500 S. Atlantic Blvd., Bldg. B (90040); Th; 103pd, 3,878fr (Sw); $20.16; C; publisher & editor Dolores Sanchez; general manager Jonathan Sanchez; managing editor Tony Castro; tel (213) 263-5743; fax (213) 263-9169

Los Angeles: *Eastside Sun* — 2500 S. Atlantic Blvd., Bldg. B (90040); Th; 274pd, 19,077fr (Sw); $20.16; C; publisher & editor Dolores Sanchez; general manager Jonathan Sanchez; managing editor Tony Castro; tel (213) 263-5743; fax (213) 263-9169

Los Angeles Downtown Metropolitan: *Los Angeles Downtown News* — 1264 W. 1st St., Los Angeles (90026-5831); M; 45,000fr (Sw); $33.00; C; publisher & editor Sue Laris-Eastin; general manager Mary Staffa; managing editor Jack Skelley; tel (213) 481-1448; fax (213) 250-4617

U.S. Weeklies — California — II-7

Los Angeles/Hollywood/W Los Angeles/Culver City/Marina del Rey/Playa del Rey/Westchester: *Los Angeles Independent Newspaper Group* — 4201 Wilshire Blvd., Ste. 600, Los Angeles (90010); W; 64pd, 198,082fr (VAC); $79.41; Sa; 1pd, 54,004fr (VAC); $29.41; C; publisher Michael A Laxineta; general manager Simon Tam; editor Brian Lewis; tel (213) 932-6397; fax (213) 932-8250

Los Banos: *Los Banos Enterprise* — 1253 W. I St. (93635); W/Sa; 4,500pd (Est); $8.25; C; publisher Wolf Rosenberg; editor Mitch Naylor; tel (209) 826-3831; fax (209) 826-2005

Los Gatos: *Los Gatos Weekly-Times* — 245 Almendra Ave. (95030); W; 400pd, 19,300fr (Est); $14.00; C; publisher David Cohen; editor Dale Bryant; tel (408) 354-3110; fax (408) 354-3917

Lucerne Vly.: *Leader Publications* — PO Box 299 (92356); W; 1,860pd, 1,773fr (Est); $4.00; publisher Brehm Publications Co. Inc.; editor Bill Ewing; tel (619) 248-7878; fax (619) 248-2042

Malibu: *Malibu Surfside News* — 28990 Pacific Coast Hwy., Ste. 116-118; PO Box 903 (90265); Th; 9,990pd, 2,760fr (Sw); $15.00; publisher & editor Anne Soble; tel (310) 457-2112; fax (310) 457-9908

Malibu: *The Malibu Times* — 3864 Las Flores Canyon Rd.; PO Box 1127 (90265); Th; 900pd, 11,600fr (Est); $11.50; publisher & editor Arnold G York; tel (310) 456-5507; fax (310) 456-8986

Mammoth Lakes: *The Review Herald* — 1566 Tavern Rd., PO Box 110 (93546); Th/Su; 4,871pd, 35fr (Est); $8.13; C; publisher Deane Funk, editor Kelly DuFresne, managing editor Barbara Laughon; tel (619) 934-8544; fax (619) 934-7385

Mammoth Lakes/Mono Co.: *Mammoth Times Weekly* — 452 Old Mammoth Rd.; PO Box 3929, Mammoth Lakes (93546); Th; 1,500pd, 13,000fr (Sw); $8.75; C; publisher Wally Hofmann; general manager Sue Bouska; editor David Strumsky; tel (619) 934-3929; fax (619) 934-3951

Marina del Rey: *The Argonaut* — PO Box 11209 (90295-7209); Th; 19pd, 37,832fr (VAC); $23.40; publisher & editor David Asper Johnson; tel (310) 822-1629; fax (310) 822-2089

Mariposa/E Madera Cos.: *Mariposa Gazette* — 5081 Jones St., PO Box 38, Mariposa (95338-0038); Th; 5,109pd, 80fr (Est); $8.75; C; publisher Dalmar J Campbell; general manager R D Tucker; editor Ruth Campbell; managing editor Jerry Rankin; tel (209) 966-2500; fax (209) 966-3384

Mariposa/E Madera Cos.: *Mountain Life* — 5081 Jones St., PO Box 38, Mariposa (95338-0038); Tu; 10,000fr (Est); $8.75; C; publisher Dalmar J Campbell; general manager R D Tucker; editor Ruth Campbell; managing editor Jerry Rankin; tel (209) 966-2500; fax (209) 966-3384

Mendocino: *The Mendocino Beacon* — 45066 Ukiah St.; PO Box 225 (95460); Th; 2,088pd, 58fr (ABC); $4.90; C; publisher Sharon Brewer; managing editor Katherine Lee; tel (707) 937-5874; fax (707) 937-0825

Mendocino Co.: *Mendocino County Observer* — 50 Ramsey Rd.; PO Box 490, Laytonville (95454); F; 2,802pd, 109fr (Sw); $5.35; publisher & editor Jim Shields; tel (707) 984-6223; fax (707) 984-8118

Menifee: *Menifee Valley News* — 27070 Sun City Blvd.; PO Box 310, Sun City (92586); Th; 738pd, 6,970fr (Sw); $11.95; C; publisher Kathleen Williams-Boyer; editor Dennis Brosterhous; tel (909) 679-1195; fax (909) 679-2450

Menlo Park/Woodside: *The Country Almanac* — 3525 Alameda De Las Pulgas, Menlo Park (94025); W; 11,780pd, 9,520fr (Est); $1.10; publisher Tom Gibboney; editor Richard Hine; tel (415) 854-2626; fax (415) 854-0677

Merced: *Merced County Times* — PO Box 65, Winton (95388); Th; 5,600pd, 23,000fr (Sw); $7.95; C; publisher & editor John M Derby; tel (209) 358-5311

Middletown/Cobb/Clearlake: *Middletown Times Star* — 21152 Calistoga Ave.; PO Box 608, Middletown (95461); Th; 1,955pd, 266fr (Sw); $4.25; publisher & editor Teresa Sanders; tel (707) 987-3602; fax (707) 987-3901

Millbrae/San Bruno: *Millbrae/San Bruno Sun* — 824 Cowan Rd., Burlingame (94010); Tu; 1,320pd, 18,500fr (Sw); $15.25; C; publisher Colin Pratt; editor Tina Barseghien; managing editor Marc Burkhardt; tel (415) 692-9406; fax (415) 692-7587

Milpitas: *Milpitas Post* — 1615 A S. Main St. (95035); W; 3,019pd, 14,727fr (Est); $10.78; publishers Jimmy Chamoures & Mort Levine; editor Robert John Devincenzi; tel (408) 262-2454; fax (408) 263-9710

Mission Viejo: *Saddleback Valley News* — 22481 Aspan, Lake Forest (92630); W/F; 48,997fr (VAC); $33.53; C; publisher Orange County Register; editor Cathy Lawhon; tel (714) 768-3631; fax (714) 454-7397

Modoc Co.: *Modoc County Record* — 102 Carlos St.; PO Box 531, Alturas (96101); Th; 4,500pd, 100fr (Sw); $17.86; C; publisher Jane Holloway; publisher & editor Rick Holloway; tel (916) 233-2632; fax (916) 233-5113

Mojave/California City: *Mojave Desert News* — 8046 California City Blvd.; PO Box 2517, California City (93505); Th; 5,000pd, 1,500fr (Sw); $8.25; publisher Paul E Ingram III; editor Connie Baker; tel (619) 373-4812; fax (619) 373-2941

Montebello: *Montebello Comet* — 2500 S. Atlantic Blvd., Bldg. B, Los Angeles (90040); Th; 212pd, 3,932fr (Sw); $20.16; C; publisher & editor Dolores Sanchez; general manager Jonathan Sanchez; managing editor Tony Castro; tel (213) 263-5743; fax (213) 263-9169

Montebello: *Montebello Messenger* — 108 W. Beverly Blvd.; PO Box 578 (90640); Th; 1,341pd, 344fr (Est); 20¢; publisher & editor John Marty; tel (213) 721-1735

Monterey Park: *Monterey Park Comet* — 2500 S. Atlantic Blvd., Bldg. B, Los Angeles (90040); Th; 86pd, 4,415fr (Sw); $20.16; C; publisher & editor Dolores Sanchez; general manager Jonathan Sanchez; managing editor Tony Castro; tel (213) 263-5743; fax (213) 263-9164

Moreno Vly.: *The Valley Times* — 25873 Alessandro Blvd.; PO Box 9700 (92553); Th; 4,604pd, 180fr (Sw); $14.15; publisher Mel Harkavy; editor Larry Venus; tel (909) 242-7614; fax (909) 247-1920

Morgan Hill: *Morgan Hill Times* — 30 E. 3rd St.; PO Box 757 (95038); Tu/F; 3,269pd, 64fr (Sw); $7.25; publisher Paula Mabry; editor Walt Glines; tel (408) 779-4106; fax (408) 779-3886

Morro Bay/San Luis Obispo: *Central Coast Sun-Bulletin* — 1149 Market Ave.; PO Box 1387, Morro Bay (93443); W; 5,205pd, 6,987fr (VAC); $7.68; C; publisher Scripps Howard; general manager & editor Richard Palmer; tel (805) 772-7346; fax (805) 772-7044

Mount Shasta/McCloud: *Mount Shasta Herald* — 924 N. Mount Shasta Herald; PO Box 127, Mount Shasta (96067); W; 4,067pd, 79fr (Sw); $4.31; C; publisher Genny Axtman; editor Steve Gerace; tel (916) 926-5214; fax (916) 926-4166

Napa/St. Helena Calistoga: *Napa County Record* — 520 3rd St.; PO Box 88, Napa (94558); Th; 650pd, 6,000fr (Sw); $6.20; publisher David W Barker; editor Melodie Hilton; tel (707) 252-8877; fax (707) 226-3707

Needles: *Needles Desert Star* — 911 3rd St.; PO Box 427 (92363); W; 2,622pd, 175fr (Sw); $9.10; C; publisher Lalena Stewart; general manager & editor Robin Richards; tel (619) 326-2222; fax (619) 326-3480

Newman: *The West Side Index* — 1021 Fresno St.; PO Box 878 (95360); Th; 1,950pd, 25fr (Est); 17¢; C; publisher William H Mattos; general manager Susan Mattos; editor Dean Harris; tel (209) 862-2222; fax (209) 862-4133

Newman/Gustine: *Tuesday Review* — 1021 Fresno St.; PO Box 878, Newman (95360); Tu; 6,500fr (Est); $5.50; C; publisher William Mattos; general manager Susan Mattos; editor Dean Harris; tel (209) 862-2222; fax (209) 862-4133

Novato: *Novato Advance* — 1068 Machin Ave., PO Box 8 (94947); W; 6,643pd, 2,311fr (VAC); $14.62; C; publisher John Burns; editor John Jackson; tel (415) 892-1516; fax (415) 897-0940

Oakdale: *Oakdale Leader* — 122 S. 3rd Ave., PO Box 278 (95361); W; 4,937pd, 601fr (Sw); $9.35; C; publisher Stanley L Cook; general manager Williams P Camp; editor Steve Breen; tel (209) 847-3021; fax (209) 847-9750

Oakhurst/E Madera: *Sierra Star* — 49165 Rd. 426; PO Box 305, Oakhurst (93644); Th; 5,050pd, 20fr (Sw); $8.80; C; publisher Betty E Linn; editor Earlene Ward; tel (209) 683-4464; fax (209) 683-8102

Oakland: *Bay Area Press* — PO Box 10151 (94610); W; 9pd, 27,000fr (Est); 21¢; publisher & editor George Epstein; general manager Jan Miller; tel (510) 428-2000

Oakland: *The Montclarion* — 6208 La Salle Ave. (94611); Tu/F; 2,627pd, 27,445fr (VAC); $17.25; C; publisher Warren (Chip) Brown; general manager Scott Connelly; editor Chris Treadway; tel (510) 339-8777; fax (510) 339-4066

Ojai: *Ojai Valley News* — 408 Bryant Cir., Ste. A; PO Box 277 (93024); W/F; 6,331pd, 61fr (Sw); $8.00; C; publisher Ren L Adam; editor Timothy Dewar; tel (805) 646-1476; fax (805) 646-4281

Orange: *Orange City News* — 1771 S. Lewis St., Anaheim (92805); Th; 4pd, 36,994fr (Est); $11.42; publisher Dave Threshie; editor Joelle Collier; tel (714) 634-1567; fax (714) 704-3714

Orangevale: *Orangevale News* — 555 Oakdale St., Ste. G1, Folsom (95630); W; 1,495pd, 469fr (VAC); $7.70; C; publisher Dave Threshie; general manager Dave Reese; editor Jim Duncan; tel (916) 351-0112; fax (916) 985-0702

Orland: *Orland Press-Register* — 407 Walker St.; PO Box 847 (95963); M/W/F; 2,407pd, 45fr (Sw); $4.90; publisher Darell Phillips; editor Virginia Webster; managing editor Brooks Mancher; tel (916) 865-4433; fax (916) 865-3110

Pacific Palisades/Malibu: *Palisadian-Post & North Shore Shopper* — 839 Via De La Paz; PO Box 725, Pacific Palisades (90272); Th; 4,290pd, 13,700fr (Sw); $14.00; C; publisher Roberta Donohue; managing editor Bill Bruns; tel (310) 454-1321; fax (310) 454-1078

Pacifica: *Pacifica Tribune* — 59 Aura Vista; PO Box 1188 (94044); W; 7,477pd, 6,200fr (Sw); $12.90; C; publisher & editor Chris Hunter; tel (415) 359-6666; fax (415) 359-3821

Palm Desert: *Palm Desert Post* — 82-632 Hwy. 111, Ste. B, Indio (92201); W; 6,015pd, 3,382fr (Est); 54¢; publisher Bob Dickey; general manager Linda Munsey; editor Joan Boiko; tel (619) 775-4200; fax (619) 342-7128

Palos Verdes: *Palos Verdes Peninsula News* — 4010 Palos Verdes Dr. N., Ste. 208 (Roland Hills Estates); PO Box 2609, Palos Verdes Peninsula (90274); Th/Sa; 7,280pd, 10,072fr (Sw); 66¢; publisher Susan Frank; editor Gary Amo; managing editor Alan Gaford; tel (310) 377-6877; fax (310) 377-4522

Palos Verdes: *Peninsula Breeze/South Bay Extra* — 5215 Torrance Blvd., Torrance (90509); Th; 13,368fr (Est); $8.55; C; publisher Thomas J Wafer Jr; editor James M Box; tel (310) 540-5511; fax (310) 540-5391

Paradise/Magalia: *Paradise Post* — 5399 Clark Rd. (95969); PO Drawer 70, Paradise (95967); Tu/Th/Sa; 9,048pd, 8,800fr (Sw); $11.45; C; publisher Randy S Goldberg; editor Linda Meilink; tel (916) 877-4413; fax (916) 877-1326

Paramount: *The Paramount Journal* — 16460 Paramount Blvd.; PO Box 2055 (90723); Th; 3,000pd, 210fr (Est); $10.00; C; publisher & editor Don Plunkett; tel (213) 633-1234; fax (213) 630-8141

Pasadena: *Pasadena Weekly* — 50 S. Delacey Ave., Ste. 200 (91105); F; 38pd, 33,357fr (VAC); $19.00; publisher Jim P Laris; editor & managing editor Bill Evans; tel (818) 584-1500; fax (818) 795-0149

Paso Robles/Atascadero/N San Luis Obispo Co.: *Country News* — 77 Marquita Ave., Paso Robles (93446); W; 505pd, 18,321fr (Sw); $13.25; publisher Keith Berwick; editor Sheena Berwick; managing editor Scott Steepleton; tel (805) 237-6060; fax (805) 237-6066

Paso Robles/Templeton: *North County Journal* — 11th & Park Sts.; PO Box 757, Paso Robles (93447); W; 127pd, 5,700fr (Sw); $7.95; C; publisher Richard D Reddick; editor Irving Shear; tel (805) 238-6500; fax (805) 238-6504

Patterson/Westley: *Patterson Irrigator* — 26 N. 3rd St.; PO Box 157, Patterson (95363); Tu; 2,425pd, 3,450fr (Sw); $5.00; Th; 2,425pd (Sw); $4.00; publisher & editor Ronald Swift; tel (209) 892-6187; fax (209) 892-3761

Penasquitos: *Corridor News* — 13247 Poway Rd., Poway (92064); W; 790pd, 13,572fr (Sw); $10.90; C; publisher David W Calvert; general manager Ann Calvert; editor Steve Dreyer; tel (619) 748-0413; fax (619) 748-7695

Perris: *The Perris Progress* — 240 W. 4th St.; PO Box 128 (92572); W; 3,120pd, 20fr (Sw); $4.40; publisher Irene Hoban; publisher & editor John F Hoban; tel (909) 657-2181

Petaluma: *Argus-Courier* — 830 N. Petaluma Blvd.; PO Box 1091 (94952); Tu; 8,809pd, 796fr (VAC); $15.44; F; 8,809pd (VAC); $15.44; C; publisher Jack Morgan; editor Chris Samson; tel (707) 762-4541; fax (707) 765-6788

Placentia: *Placentia News-Times* — 1771 S. Lewis St., Anaheim (92805); Th; 8pd, 12,547fr (VAC); $6.80; publisher Dave Threshie; editor Gus Santoyo; tel (714) 634-1567; fax (714) 704-3714

Playa Del Rey: *Playa Del Rey News* — 4346 Sepulveda Blvd., Culver City (90232); Th; 3pd, 5,147fr (CPVS); $19.61; publisher & editor Steve Hadland; general manager Carol Layana; tel (310) 313-6733; fax (310) 313-6732

Point Reyes Station: *Point Reyes Light* — 11431 Hwy. 1; PO Box 210, Pt. Reyes Station (94956); Th; 4,021pd, 257fr (Sw); $12.10; publisher & editor David V Mitchell; general manager Don Schinske; tel (415) 663-8404; fax (415) 663-8458

Portola: *Portola Reporter* — 116 Commercial St. (96122); W; 2,075pd, 6fr (Sw); $4.50; publisher Michael Taborski; editor Terri Nacar; managing editor Dave Keller; tel (916) 832-4646; fax (916) 832-5319

Poway: *Poway News Chieftain* — 13247 Poway Rd. (92064); Th; 3,031pd, 10,381fr (VAC); $10.90; C; publisher David W Calvert; general manager Ann Calvert; editor Steve Dreyer; tel (619) 748-2311; fax (619) 748-7695

Quincy: *Feather River Bulletin* — 555 W. Main St.; PO Box B (95971); W; 3,247pd, 60fr (Sw); $4.50; C; publisher Michael C Taborski; editor Dave Keller; tel (916) 283-0800; fax (916) 283-3952

Ramona/Julian/Santa Ysabel: *Ramona Sentinel* — 611 Main St.; PO Box 367, Ramona (92065); Th; 5,252pd, 136fr (VAC); $10.29; C; publisher David W Calvert; general manager Ann Calvert; editor Maureen Robertson; tel (619) 789-1350; fax (619) 789-4057

Rancho Bernardo: *Rancho Bernardo News-Journal* — 11650 Iberia Pl., Ste. 215, San Diego (92128); Th; 697pd, 16,006fr (VAC); $10.90; C; publisher David W Calvert; general manager Ann Calvert; editor Steve Dreyer; tel (619) 487-5757; fax (619) 748-7695

Rancho Cardova: *The Grapevine Independent* — 3338 Mather Field Rd., Rancho Cordova (95670); Tu; 10,500pd, 2,000fr (Sw); $9.50; publisher Robert M Ling; editor Shelly Blanchard; tel (916) 361-1234; fax (916) 361-0491

Rancho Santa Margarita: *Rancho Santa Margarita News* — 22481 Aspan, Lake Forest (92630); W/F; 7,027fr (VAC); $33.53; C; publisher Orange County Register; editor Cathy Lawhon; tel (714) 768-3631; fax (714) 454-7397

Redondo Beach: *Redondo Reflex/South Bay Extra* — 5215 Torrance Blvd., Torrance (90509); Th; 24,436fr (Est); $15.47; C; publisher Thomas J Wafer Jr; editor James M Box; tel (310) 540-5511; fax (310) 540-5391

Redwood City: *Redwood City Tribune* — 824 Cowan Rd., Burlingame (94010); Tu; 25,150fr (Sw); $15.25; C; publisher Colin Pratt; general manager Debbie Witten; editor Klayton Jones; managing editor Marc Burkhardt; tel (415) 692-9406; fax (415) 692-7587

Reedley/Orange Cove: *The Reedley Exponent* — 1130 G St.; PO Box 432, Reedley (93654); Th; 4,045pd, 36fr (Est); $8.75; C; publisher Fred Hall; editor Budd Brockett; tel (209) 638-2244; fax (209) 638-5021

Rialto: *Rialto Record* — 1809 S. Commerce Ctr. W.; PO Box 6247, San Bernardino (92408); Th; 500pd, 17,079fr (Est); $10.30; publisher Bill Harrison; editor Lisa Cillarear; tel (909) 381-9898; fax (909) 384-0406

Rio Vista/Walnut Grove: *The River News-Herald & Isleton Journal* — 21 S. Front St.; PO Box 786, Rio Vista (94571); W; 2,726pd, 708fr (VAC); $5.50; publisher David L Payne; general manager Jennifer Deal; editor Michael Duffett; tel (707) 374-6431

Copyright ©1996 by the Editor & Publisher Co.

II-8 California *U.S. Weeklies*

Ripon/Salida: *The Ripon Record* — 130 W. Main St., Ripon (95366); W; 2,596pd, 4fr (Est); 23¢; publisher Antone E Raymus; general manager & editor Mike VandenBosh; managing editor Toni M Raymus; tel (209) 599-2194; fax (209) 823-7099

Riverbank: *The Riverbank News* — 6622 3rd St.; PO Box 887 (95367-2389); W; 1,130pd, 412fr (Sw); $7.13; C; publisher Stanley L Cook; general manager Williams P Camp; editor Marg Bilby; managing editor Steve Breen; tel (209) 847-3021; fax (209) 847-9750

Rocklin: *The Placer Herald* — 5903 B Sunset Blvd. (95677); Tu; 7,500fr (Est); $6.80; publisher Scott Little; general manager Cathy Krahn; editor Janis Dice; tel (916) 624-9713; fax (916) 624-7469

Rohnert Park: *The Community Voice* — 320 Professional Center Dr., Ste. 100; PO Box 2038 (94927); W; 4,000pd, 13,500fr (Est); $12.50; C; publisher Robert M Lynch; general manager Yatin Shah; editor Jud Snyder; tel (707) 584-2222; fax (707) 584-2233

Roseville: *The Press-Tribune* — 188 Cirby Way (95678); Tu; 13,295pd (ABC); $10.70; F/Su; 13,295pd (ABC); $10.60; publisher George E Riggs; general manager Carl Shaver; editor Traja Rosenthal; managing editor Nicholas Baptista; tel (916) 786-6500; fax (916) 783-1183

Rossmoor/Walnut Creek: *Rossmoor News* — 1006 Stanley Dollar Dr.; PO Box 2190, Walnut Creek (94595); W; 6,750pd, 750fr (Sw); $13.44; C; publisher Golden Rain Foundation; editor Maureen O'Rourke; tel (510) 988-7800; fax (510) 935-8348

Rowland Hts.: *Rowland Heights Highlander* — 1210 N. Azusa Canyon Rd., West Covina (91790); Th; 9,200fr (Sw); $6.00; C; publisher Chuck Rathbun; editor John Irby; managing editor Rick Krzyzanowski; tel (818) 854-8700; fax (818) 856-2737

St. Helena: *St. Helena Star* — 1328 Main St.; PO Box 346, St. Helena (94574); Th; 3,750pd, 50fr (Sw); $14.00; C; publisher Bill Brenner; editor Don Wegars; tel (707) 963-2731; fax (707) 963-8957

San Andreas: *Calaveras Prospect/Weekly-Citizen & Chronicle* — 109 E. St. Charles St.; PO Box 605 (95249); Th; 2,072pd, 3fr (Est); $3.15; C; publisher & editor John R Peterson; general manager Eric Peterson; tel (209) 754-4222

San Benito Co./Hollister: *The Pinnacle* — 341 Tres Pinos Rd., Ste. 201, Hollister (95023); Th; 500pd, 14,000fr (Sw); $7.45; publisher Pinnacle Publishing Co.; general manager Clifford A Cardoza; editor Marvin Snow; tel (408) 637-6300; fax (408) 637-8174

San Clemente: *Preview* — 22481 Aspan, Lake Forest (92630); Th; 130,000fr (Est); $47.80; C; publisher Stan Manning; editor Casey Jordan; managing editor Don Chapman; tel (714) 768-3631; fax (714) 492-0401

San Clemente: *Sun Post News* — 95 Ave. Del Mar; PO Box 367 (92672); Tu/Th/F; 7,483pd (Sw); $10.36; publisher Stan Manning; editor Morgan Sales; tel (714) 492-5121; fax (714) 492-0401

San Diego Co.: *San Diego Weekly News* — 7670 Opportunity Rd., Ste. 100, San Diego (92111); W; 20,000fr (Sw); $16.00; publisher & editor Bernardo Romanowsky; managing editor Stephen C Sterton; tel (619) 565-9135; fax (619) 565-4182

San Dimas: *San Dimas/La Verne Highlander* — 1210 N. Azusa Canyon Rd., West Covina (91790); Th; 6pd, 14,675fr (VAC); $7.20; C; publisher Chuck Rathbun; editor Frances Young; managing editor Rick Krzyzanowski; tel (818) 854-8700; fax (818) 856-2737

San Francisco Bay Area: *The Sun Reporter* — 1366 Turk St., San Francisco (94115); W; 10,794pd (Est); $57.00; publisher Garry Goodlet; editor Charles E Belle; tel (415) 931-5778; fax (415) 931-0214

San Francisco/San Mateo: *San Francisco Independent* — 1201 Evans Ave., San Francisco (94124); Tu; 372,650fr (Est); $77.90; F; 182,400fr (Est); $50.45; C; publisher Ted Fang; managing editor Susan Herbert; tel (415) 826-1100; fax (415) 826-5371

San Jose: *San Jose City Times* — 550 S. 1st St. (95113); W; 16,000fr (Est); $14.00; C; publisher David Cohen; tel (408) 298-8000; fax (408) 298-0602

San Jose: *Willow Glen Resident* — 550 S. 1st St. (95113); W; 19,000fr (Est); $14.00; C; publisher David Cohen; managing editor Barbara Wilcox; tel (408) 298-8000; fax (408) 298-0602

San Juan Capistrano: *Capistrano Valley News* — 22481 Aspan, Lake Forest (92630); Th; 9,251fr (VAC); $21.45; C; publisher Orange County Register; editor Steve Silberman; tel (714) 768-3631; fax (714) 454-7350

San Marcos: *San Marcos Courier* — 2841 Loker Ave. E., Carlsbad (92008); F; 514pd, 10,502fr (VAC); $9.50; C; publisher Donna Medeiros; general manager Chris Blaisdale; editor Terrie Lafferty Drago; tel (619) 431-4850; fax (619) 431-4888

San Marino: *San Marino Tribune* — 2260 Huntington Dr. (91108); Th; 2,773pd, 124fr (Sw); $6.34; publisher Clifton S Smith Jr; general manager Larry Londre; editor James Whelan; tel (818) 282-5707; fax (818) 457-6436

San Mateo: *San Mateo Weekly* — 824 Cowan Rd., Burlingame (94010); Tu; 30,370fr (Sw); $15.25; C; publisher Colin Pratt; editor Antonia Enters; managing editor Marc Burkhardt; tel (415) 692-9406; fax (415) 692-7587

San Rafael/Terra Linda: *Newspointer* — 1050 Bridgeway, Sausalito (94965); W; 12,000pd (Est); C; publisher Paul Anderson; general manager & managing editor Billie Anderson; editor Greg Risling; tel (415) 289-4040; fax (415) 332-8714

Sanger: *Sanger Herald* — 740 N St. (93657); Th; 3,000pd, 14,135fr (Est); $9.50; C; publisher Fred Hall; editor William Coleman; tel (209) 875-2511; fax (209) 875-2521

Santa Cruz Co.: *Good Times* — 1205 Pacific Ave.; PO Box 1885, Santa Cruz (95061); Th; 14pd, 41,916fr (VAC); $25.00; C; publisher Carole Atkinson; editor Erik Espe; tel (408) 458-1100; fax (408) 448-1295

Santa Cruz Co.: *Metro Santa Cruz* — 111 Union St., Santa Cruz (95060); Th; 37,454fr (VAC); $14.28; C; publisher Jeanne Howard; editor Buz Bezore; tel (408) 457-9000; fax (408) 457-5828

Santa Monica: *Outlook Mail* — 5215 Torrance Blvd., Torrance (90509); Th; 33,968fr (Est); $13.95; publisher Thomas J Wafer Jr; editor James M Box; tel (310) 540-5511; fax (310) 540-5391

Santee: *Santee Star* — 3434 Grove St. (91945); PO Box 127, Lemon Grove (91946); Th; 200pd, 4,000fr (Est); $12.50; publisher Steven Saint; tel (619) 469-0101

Saratoga: *Saratoga News* — 14375 Saratoga Ave., Ste. E2 (95070); W; 10,200fr (Est); $14.00; C; publisher David Cohen; editor Sue Fagalde Lick; tel (408) 867-6397; fax (408) 867-1010

Sausalito: *Marin Scope* — PO Box 1689 (94966); Tu; 1,750pd (Sw); $11.00; C; publisher Paul Anderson; editor Billie Anderson; tel (415) 332-3778; fax (415) 332-8714

Seal Beach/Huntington Harbor: *The Sun* — 216 Main St.; PO Box 755, Seal Beach (90740); Th; 196pd, 30,150fr (Est); $13.45; C; publisher Dar Brown; editor Dennis Kaiser; tel (310) 430-7555; fax (310) 430-3469

Seal Beach/Leisure World: *Leisure World Golden Rain News* — 13521 St. Andrews Dr.; PO Box 2338, Seal Beach (90740); Th; 6,705pd, 2,295fr (Sw); $10.60; publisher Golden Rain Foundation; managing editor David Saunders; tel (310) 430-0534; fax (310) 598-1617

Sebastopol/Sonoma Co.: *Sonoma West Times & News* — 130 S. Main St., Ste. 114; PO Box 521, Sebastopol (95472); W; 6,400pd, 4,000fr (Est); $12.12; publisher Rollie Atkinson; editor Barry Dugan; tel (707) 823-7845; fax (707) 823-7508

Selma: *The Selma Enterprise* — 2045 Grant St.; PO Box 100 (93662); W; 3,603pd, 100fr (Sw); $5.50; C; publisher James A Brock; editor Tim Sheehan; tel (209) 896-1976; fax (209) 896-9160

Shafter/Buttow Willow: *Shafter Press* — 107 E. Lerdo Hwy.; PO Bin A, Shafter (93263); W; 2,034pd, 40fr (Est); $5.75; publishers Donald L Reed & Frank W Reed; editor Roy Patrick; tel (805) 399-5925; fax (805) 746-5571

Shasta Lake: *Shasta Lake Bulletin* — 4138 Ashby Ct.; PO Box 8025 (96019); W; 958pd, 74fr (Sw); $3.75; publisher Craig Harrington; tel (916) 275-1716; fax (916) 275-1699

Sierra/Plumas/Nevada/Yuba Cos.: *The Mountain Messenger* — Main St.; PO Drawer A, Downieville (95936); Th; 2,950pd, 50fr (Sw); $5.50; publisher & editor Donald S Russell; tel (916) 289-3262; fax (916) 289-3262

Sierra Madre/Pasadena/Arcadia: *Sierra Madre News* — 9 Kersting Ct.; PO Box 37, Sierra Madre (91025-0037); Th; 3,255pd, 200fr (Sw); $5.00; publisher & editor Jan Reed; tel (818) 355-3324; fax (818) 355-2341

Signal Hill/Long Beach: *The Signal* — 2107 Cherry Ave., Ste. B, Signal Hill (90806); Th; 135pd, 20,825fr (VAC); $11.50; publisher & editor Thomas K Allen; managing editor Tiffany Montgomery; tel (310) 498-0707; fax (310) 498-7847

Soledad: *Soledad Bee* — PO Box 648 (93960); W; 1,378pd, 10fr (Est); $5.90; publisher Harry F Casey; general manager Suzi Taylor; editor Bill Osterbrock; tel (408) 678-2660; fax (408) 678-3676

Solvang: *Santa Ynez Valley News* — 423 2nd St.; PO Box 647 (93464); Th; 7,825pd, 100fr (Est); $9.70; C; publisher & editor Peg Johnson; general manager Lacinda Johnson; managing editor Bart Ortberg; tel (805) 688-5522; fax (805) 688-7685

Sonoma: *The Sonoma Index-Tribune* — 117 W. Napa St.; PO Box C (95476); Tu/F; 11,029pd, 218fr (Sw); $15.00; C; publisher Robert M Lynch; general manager Yatin Shah; editor William E Lynch; managing editor Joan Casserly; tel (707) 938-2111; fax (707) 938-1600

Sonoma Co.: *The Sonoma County Independent* — 540 Mendocino Ave., Santa Rosa (95401); Th; 391pd, 17,998fr (VAC); $19.00; publisher Bob Rucker; editor Greg Cahill; tel (707) 527-1200; fax (707) 527-1288

S Pasadena/San Marino: *South Pasadena Review* — 1024 Mission St.; PO Box 310, South Pasadena (91030); W; 5,000pd (Sw); $9.00; publisher William Ericson; editor Norma LeValley; tel (818) 799-2404, (213) 682-1412

Spring Vly.: *Spring Valley Bulletin* — PO Box 127, Lemon Grove (91946); Th; 200pd, 2,800fr (Sw); $5.00; C; publisher & editor Steve Saint; tel (619) 469-0101

Sun City: *Sun City News* — 27070 Sun City Blvd.; PO Box 310 (92586); Th; 3,220pd, 138fr (Sw); $11.95; C; publisher Kathleen Williams Boyer; editor Dennis Brosterhous; tel (909) 679-1191; fax (909) 679-2450

Sunnyvale: *Sunnyvale Sun* — 106B Murphy Ave. (94087); W; 100pd, 24,000fr (Est); $14.00; C; publisher David Cohen; editor Rebecca Smith; tel (408) 481-0174; fax (408) 481-0175

Susanville: *Lassen County Times* — 800 Main St. (96130); Tu; 6,128pd, 3,739fr (Est); $8.00; C; publisher Michael C Taborski; editor Dave Moller; managing editor Eve Devier; tel (916) 257-5321; fax (916) 257-0408

Tahoe City: *Tahoe World* — 241 N. Lake Blvd.; PO Box 138 (96145); Th; 4,421pd, 59fr (VAC); $9.35; C; publisher Bill Kunerth; editor Eric Henry; tel (916) 583-3488; fax (916) 583-7109

Tehachapi: *Tehachapi News & Tehachapi* — PO Box 230 (93561); W; 7,561pd, 426fr (Sw); $10.30; C; publishers Elizabeth Mead & William Mead; general manager Al Crisalli; editor Sheila Christensen; tel (805) 822-6828; fax (805) 822-4053

Temecula: *Rancho News* — 27645 Jefferson Ave., Ste. 104B; PO Box 237 (92593); Th; 22,807fr (VAC); $7.55; C; general manager Tom Paradis; editor Joe Hudon; tel (714) 676-5247; fax (714) 676-9343

Tiburon/Belvedere: *Ebbtide* — PO Box 1689, Sausalito (94966); Tu; 4,500fr (Sw); $9.25; C; publisher Paul Anderson; managing editor Billie Anderson; tel (415) 285-4040; fax (415) 332-8714

Tiburon/Belvedere: *The Ark* — 1550 Tiburon Blvd.; PO Box 1054, Tiburon (94920); W; 3,200pd, 50fr (Est); $8.00; publishers & editors Barbara Gnoss & Marilyn Kessler; general manager Ann Bidwell; tel (415) 435-2652; fax (415) 435-0849

Torrance: *Torrance Press-Herald Lifestyle* — 5215 Torrance Blvd. (90509); Th; 36,124fr (Est); $18.91; C; publisher Thomas J Wafer Jr; editor James M Box; tel (310) 540-5511; fax (310) 540-5391

Trona/Argus: *Trona Argonaut* — 13452 Lupine St. (93562); PO Box 306, Trona (93592); Th; 1,025pd, 2fr (Sw); $4.00; publisher Joe Sonia III; editor Margaret Ann Grams; tel (619) 372-4747; fax (619) 372-4748

Truckee/Donner Summit: *Sierra Sun* — 11105 Donner Pass Rd.; PO Box 2973, Truckee (96160); Th; 4,875pd, 67fr (VAC); $10.20; C; publisher Bill Kunerth; editor Peter Kostes; tel (916) 587-6061; fax (916) 587-3763

Tustin: *Tustin Weekly* — 181 El Camino Real, Ste. A (92680); F/Sa; 137pd, 30,724fr (VAC); $11.75; publisher Brien H Manning; general manager Tobey Anglin; editor Warren Esterline; tel (714) 832-9601; fax (714) 832-9693

Tustin/N Tustin: *The Tustin News* — 625 N. Grand Ave., Santa Ana (92701); Th; 1,674pd, 29,000fr (Est); $14.26; publisher Orange County Register; editor Paul Danison; managing editor Leon Teeboom; tel (714) 564-7072; fax (714) 565-6098

Twentynine Palms: *Desert Trail* — 6396 Adobe Rd.; PO Box 159, Twentynine Palms (92277); Th; 4,500pd, 10fr (Sw); $10.90; C; publisher Russell Cannon; general manager Christine Moore; editor John Manley; tel (619) 367-3577; fax (619) 367-1798

Valley Center: *Vly. Roadrunner* — PO Box 1529 (92082-1529); W; 3,162pd, 42fr (Sw); $6.00; C; publisher Dale Good; editor David Ross; tel (619) 749-1112; fax (619) 749-1688

Ventura Co.: *Ventura County & Coast Reporter* — 1567 Spinnaker Dr., Ste. 213, Ventura (93001); Th; 35,000fr (Sw); $14.00; publisher & editor Nancy Cloutier; tel (805) 658-7803; fax (805) 658-7803

Vista: *Vista Press* — 2841 Loker Ave. E., Carlsbad (92008); F; 3,147pd, 4,714fr (VAC); $10.60; publisher Donna Medeiros; general manager Chris Blaisdale; editor Terrie Lafferty Drago; tel (619) 431-4850; fax (619) 431-4888

Walnut: *Walnut Highlander* — 1210 N. Azusa Canyon Rd., West Covina (91790); Th; 10,050fr (Sw); $6.05; C; publisher Chuck Rathbun; editor John Irby; managing editor Rick Krzyzanowski; tel (818) 962-8811; fax (818) 856-2737

Waterford/Hickman: *Waterford News* — PO Box 70, Waterford (95386); Tu; 5,200fr (Sw); 32¢; publisher John M Derby; tel (209) 358-5311; fax (209) 358-7108

Weaverville: *Trinity Journal* — 218 Main St.; PO Box 340 (96093); W; 4,700pd, 20fr (Sw); $4.00; publisher Sarah Wenninger; editor Michael Wenninger; tel (916) 623-2055; fax (916) 623-2065

Weed: *Weed Press* — 924 N. Mount Shasta Blvd.; PO Box 127, Mount Shasta (96067); W; 1,559pd, 79fr (Est); $3.90; C; publisher Genny Axtman; editor Steve Gerace; tel (916) 926-5214; fax (916) 926-4166

W Covina: *West Covina Highlander* — 1210 N. Azusa Canyon Rd. (91790); Th; 79pd, 123,610fr (VAC); $12.50; publisher Chuck Rathbun; editor John Irby; managing editor Janice Luder; tel (818) 962-8811; fax (818) 856-2737

W Riverside: *Riverside County Record* — 8584 Limonite St.; PO Box 3187, Riverside (92519); Th; 950pd, 15,400fr (Est); $6.50; publisher & editor David H Barnes; tel (909) 685-6191; fax (909) 685-2961

W Sacramento: *The News-Ledger* — 816 W. Acres Rd.; PO Box 463 (95691); W; 2,318pd, 162fr (Sw); $5.75; publisher Michael P Garten; editor Steve Marschke; tel (916) 371-8030

Westchester: *Westchester News* — PO Box 5214, Culver City (90231-5214); Th; 15,000fr (Sw); $10.16; C; publisher & editor Steve Hadland; general manager Carol Layana; managing editor Dave Meyers; tel (310) 313-6727; fax (310) 313-6732

Westchester/Venice: *Westchester Observer/Marina News* — 5215 Torrance Blvd., Torrance (90509); Th; 29,000fr (Est); $13.95; C; publisher Thomas J Wafer Jr; editor James M Box; tel (310) 540-5511; fax (310) 540-5391

Western Orange Co.: *News-Enterprise* — 3622 Florista; PO Box 1010, Los Alamitos (90720); Th; 5,782pd, 797fr (Sw); $14.50; publisher Germaine R Erksine; general manager Ruthanne Binghman; tel (714) 527-8210; fax (714) 493-2310

Western Sonoma Co.: *Sonoma West Times & News* — 130 S. Main St.; PO Box 521, Sebastopol (95473); W; 2,000pd, 33fr (Est); $8.35; C; publisher Rollie Atkinson; editor Barry Dugan; tel (707) 869-3520; fax (707) 823-7508

Copyright ©1996 by the Editor & Publisher Co.

Westminster/Midway City: *Westminster Herald* — 7902 Westminster Blvd.; PO Box 428, Westminster (92864); Th; 3,400pd (Est); $8.40; publisher & editor Lloyd W Thomas; tel (714) 893-4501

Westwood: *Brentwood-Westwood Press/West L.A. Independent* — 5215 Torrance Blvd., Torrance (90509); Th; 49,600fr (Est); $13.95; C; publisher Thomas J Wafer Jr; editor James M Box; tel (310) 540-5511; fax (310) 540-5391

Westwood/Clear Creek: *Westwood Pinepress* — 201 3rd St.; PO Drawer Y, Westwood (96137); W; 709pd, 391fr (Est); $4.50; publisher Mike Taborski; editor Mary Hasselwander; tel (916) 256-2277; fax (916) 256-2277

Willits: *The Willits News* — 1424 S. Main; PO Box 628 (95490); W/F; 3,854pd, 126fr (Sw); $5.93; C; general manager Roy W Dufrain; editor Lillian Brown; tel (707) 459-4643; fax (707) 459-5313

Willows: *Willows Journal* — 1030 W. Wood St.; PO Box 731 (95988); M/F; 2,269pd (Est); $6.50; W; 4,136fr (Est); $7.75; publisher Darell Phillips; editor Brooks Mencher; tel (916) 934-6800; fax (916) 934-6815

Wilmington: *Harbor Extra* — 5215 Torrance Blvd., Torrance (90509); Th; 10,625fr (Est); $9.29; C; publisher Thomas J Wafer Jr; editor James M Box; tel (310) 540-5511; fax (310) 540-5391

Windsor/Sonoma Co.: *The Times* — PO Box 799, Windsor (95492); W; 1,500pd, 5,000fr (Est); $10.05; C; publisher & editor Mark Kilpatrick; general manager Kathy Roth; managing editor Gabe Fraire; tel (707) 838-9211; fax (707) 431-2623

Winters: *Winters Express* — 312 Railroad Ave.; PO Box 608 (95694); Th; 2,450pd, 600fr (Sw); $4.40; C; publisher Charles R Wallace; editor Debra Ramos; tel (916) 795-4551

Winton: *Winton Times* — 6950 Gerard St.; PO Box 65 (95388); Th; 1,300pd, 50fr (Est); 32¢; C; publisher John M Derby; editor Bob Anderson; tel (209) 358-5311; fax (209) 358-7108

Wrightwood/Phelan: *Mountaineer Progress* — 3936 Phelan Rd. (92371); PO Box 290130, Phelan (92329-0130); Th; 4,410pd, 135fr (Est); $9.95; C; publisher & editor John Hollis; tel (619) 868-3245; fax (619) 868-2700

Wyvernwood: *Wyvernwood Chronicle* — 2500 S. Atlantic Blvd., Bldg. B; PO Box 33803, Los Angeles (90040); Th; 9pd, 3,733fr (Sw); $20.16; C; publisher Dolores Sanchez; general manager Jonathan Sanchez; editor John Sanchez; managing editor Tony Castro; tel (213) 263-5743; fax (213) 263-5743

Yorba Linda: *Yorba Linda Star* — 1771 S. Lewis St., Anaheim (92805); Th; 15pd, 17,428fr (VAC); $7.36; C; publisher Dave Threshie; editor Gus Santoyo; tel (714) 634-1567; fax (714) 704-3714

Yucaipa/Calimesa: *Yucaipa & Calimesa News-Mirror* — 35154 Yucaipa Blvd.; PO Box 760, Yucaipa (92399); W; 6,320pd, 165fr (Sw); $13.60; C; publisher Steve Arthur; editor Bobbe Monk; tel (909) 797-9101; fax (909) 797-0502

Yucca Vly.: *Hi-Desert Star* — 56445 Twentynine Palms Hwy.; PO Box 880 (92286); W; 8,647pd, 275fr (Sw); $12.60; F; 9,897pd, 350fr (Sw); $12.60; Su; 10,444pd, 193fr (Sw); $12.60; C; publisher & editor Russell Cannon; managing editor Alisa Hicks; tel (619) 365-3315; fax (619) 365-2650

COLORADO

Akron/Otis/Anton/Lindon/Woodrow/Cope: *The Akron News-Reporter* — 69 Main St., Akron (80720); Th; 2,097pd, 33fr (Sw); $5.00; publisher Bonnie Miller; editor Karen Ashley; tel (970) 345-2296; fax (970) 345-6638

Arapahoe Co./Adams: *Aurora Sentinel* — 1730 S. Abilene St., Ste. 202 (80012); PO Box 440878, Aurora (80044); W; 7,192pd, 1,000fr (Sw); $16.95; C; publisher Karen Sowell; editor Jack Bacon; managing editor Dave Perry; tel (303) 750-7555; fax (303) 750-7699

Arapahoe/Jefferson Cos.: *The Englewood Herald* — 2329 W. Main St., Ste. 103, Littleton (80120); Th; 2,200pd, 1,000fr (Est); $10.60; C; publisher Gerard J Healey; editor Ann L Healey; managing editor Patty Burnett; tel (303) 794-7877; fax (303) 794-1909

Arapahoe/Jefferson Cos.: *The Highlands Ranch Herald* — 2329 W. Main St., Ste. 103, Littleton (80120); F; 12,000fr (Est); $13.25; C; publisher Gerard J Healey; editor Ann L Healey; managing editor Patty Burnett; tel (303) 794-7877; fax (303) 794-1909

Arapahoe/Jefferson Cos.: *The Littleton Independent* — 2329 W. Main St., Ste. 103, Littleton (80120); Th; 8,800pd, 1,200fr (Est); $15.25; C; publisher Gerard J Healey; editor Ann L Healey; managing editor Patty Burnett; tel (303) 794-7877; fax (303) 794-1909

Arvada: *Arvada Jefferson Sentinel* — 7405 Grandview Ave. (80002); Th; 5,214pd, 1,903fr (Sw); $15.32; C; publisher Robert E Cox; general manager Sidnie O'Connell; editor Jeff White; managing editor Kevin Duggan; tel (303) 239-9890; fax (303) 425-8757

Aspen/Roaring Fork Vly.: *The Aspen Times* — 310 E. Main St.; PO Box E, Aspen (81611); F; 7,700pd, 700fr (Sw); $6.50; C; publisher Loren Jenkins; managing editor Andy Stone; tel (970) 925-3414; fax (970) 925-6240

Bayfield/Ignacio: *Pine River Times* — 15 W. Mill St.; PO Box 830, Bayfield (81122-0830); Th; 1,329pd (Sw); $5.75; publisher & editor Ann McCoy; tel (970) 884-2331; fax (970) 884-4385

Berthoud/Larimer Co.: *The Old Berthoud Recorder* — 543 3rd St.; PO Box J, Berthoud (80513); Th; 3,200pd, 100fr (Est); $8.50; C; publisher Walter J Kinderman; editor Anne Benson; tel (970) 532-3715; fax (970) 532-3918

Brighton: *Brighton Standard Blade/Metro West* — PO Box 646 (80601); W/Sa; 2,849pd, 203fr (Sw); $7.00; C; publisher Terry Gogerty; editor Annette Riesel; tel (303) 659-1141; fax (303) 659-2901

Broomfield: *Broomfield Enterprise Sentinel* — 26 Garden Ctr., Ste. 4A (80020); Th; 500pd, 13,000fr (Est); $9.36; C; publisher Harold Higgins; general manager Jim Goasterland; editor Mikkel Kelly; tel (303) 466-3636; fax (303) 466-8168

Brush: *The Brush News-Tribune* — 109 Clayton St.; PO Box 8 (80723); W; 1,910pd, 72fr (Sw); $4.50; publisher & editor Darlene Doane; tel (970) 842-5516; fax (970) 842-5519

Buena Vista: *Chaffee County Times* — 101 Centennial Plz.; PO Box 2048 (81211); Th; 2,532pd, 30fr (Sw); $5.00; C; publisher Merle Baranczyk; editor Michael L Bullock; tel (719) 395-8621; fax (719) 395-8623

Burlington/Kit Carson Co.: *The Burlington Record* — 202 S. 14th St.; PO Box 459, Burlington (80807); Th; 3,350pd, 15fr (Sw); 30¢; publisher & editor Rol Hudler; tel (303) 346-5381; fax (719) 346-5514

Carbondale/Basalt/Aspen/Glenwood Springs: *Valley Journal* — 36 N. 4th St., Carbondale (81623-2012); Th; 4,628pd, 372fr (Sw); $7.00; publisher Bob Dundas; editor Pat Noel; tel (970) 963-3211; fax (970) 963-3259

Center: *Center Post-Dispatch* — 267 Worth St.; PO Box 1059 (81125); W; 563pd, 9fr (Est); $5.40; C; publisher Jay Byrne; editor Toni Vecchio; tel (719) 754-0055; fax (719) 852-3387

Central City/Black Hawk: *Weekly Register-Call* — 111 Eureka St.; PO Box 609, Central City (80427); F; 1,235pd, 23fr (Est); $6.00; publisher William C Russell Jr; editor Charlotte Taylor; tel (303) 582-5333; fax (303) 582-0332

Colorado Springs/El Paso: *Black Forest News* — 2545 E. Platt Pl., Colorado Springs (80909); Th; 1,600pd, 1,000fr (Sw); $3.75; publisher & editor Charles L R Mattson; tel (719) 473-4370

Commerce City: *Commerce City Express* — 7290 Magnolia Ave. (80022); Tu; 1,100pd, 10,500fr (Est); $5.00; publisher Terry Gogerty; editor June Younger; managing editor Michelle Dinges; tel (303) 288-7987; fax (303) 659-2900

Conejos Co.: *The Conejos County Citizen* — 517 Main St.; PO Box 79, La Jara (81140); W; 666pd, 7fr (Est); $5.40; C; publisher Jay Byrne; editor Toni Vecchio; tel (719) 274-4192; fax (719) 852-3387

Conifer/Morrison: *High Timber Times* — 43 Mount Evans Blvd., Pine (80470); W; 2,255pd, 26fr (Est); 44¢; publisher Kamal Eways; editor Tony Messenger; tel (303) 838-4884; fax (303) 674-4104

Cortez: *Cortez Montezuma Valley Journal* — 37 E. Main St.; PO Box O (81321); Tu/Th; 5,500pd, 48fr (Sw); $6.10; C; publisher R D Brown; editor Suzy Meyer; tel (970) 565-8527; fax (970) 565-8532

Cortez: *Cortez Sentinel* — 37 E. Main St.; PO Box O (81321); Sa; 5,854pd, 50fr (Sw); $6.10; C; publisher R D Brown; editor Suzy Meyer; tel (970) 565-8527; fax (970) 565-8532

Creede/Mineral Co.: *The Mineral County Miner* — 229 Adams St., Monte Vista (81144); Th; 956pd, 15fr (Est); $6.40; C; publisher Jay Byrne; editor Toni Vecchio; tel (719) 852-3531; fax (719) 852-3387

Crested Butte: *Crested Butte Chronicle & Pilot* — 500 Belleview; PO Box 369 (81224); Th; 3,650pd, 50fr (Est); $4.85; publisher Myles Arber; editor Lee Ervin; managing editor Michael Garren; tel (303) 349-6114; fax (303) 349-6116

Cripple Creek/Teller Co.: *The Gold Rush* — 1200 E. Hwy. 24; PO Box 340, Woodland Park (80866); Th; 885pd, 20fr (Est); $3.50; C; publisher Bruce Schlaubaugh; editor Paula Glover; tel (719) 687-3006

Deer Trail: *Tri-County Tribune* — 625 2nd Ave.; PO Box 220 (80105); Th; 525pd (Sw); 10¢; publisher Harry L Venter; tel (303) 769-4646

Del Norte: *The Del Norte Prospector* — 229 Adams St., Monte Vista (81144); Th; 609pd, 7fr (Est); $6.40; C; publisher Jay Byrne; editor Toni Vecchio; tel (719) 852-3531; fax (719) 852-3387

Delta Co.: *Delta County Independent* — 401 Meeker St.; PO Box 809, Delta (81416); W; 7,262pd, 80fr (Sw); $6.80; publishers Gladys Sunderland & Norman Sunderland; general manager Randy Sunderland; editor Pat Sunderland; tel (970) 874-4421; fax (970) 874-4424

Denver: *Colorado Statesman* — 1535 Grant St., Ste. 280 (80203); F; 2,139pd, 1,936fr (Est); $49.00; publisher & editor Jody Hope Strogoff; tel (303) 837-8600; fax (303) 837-9015

Denver: *Herald Dispatch* — 47 S. Federal Blvd. (80219); Th; 2,184pd, 285fr (Est); 25¢; publisher & editor J Ivanhoe Rosenberg; tel (303) 936-7776; fax (303) 936-0994

Denver: *The Colorado Leader* — 3480 W. 1st Ave. (80219); Sa; 1,755pd (Est); $4.50; publisher & editor James Eitzen; tel (303) 922-0589

Dove Creek: *Dove Creek Press* — 390 N. Main; PO Box 598 (81324); Th; 1,010pd, 57fr (Est); 22¢; publisher Doug Funk; editor Linda Funk; tel (303) 677-2214

Eads: *Kiowa County Press* — 1208 Maine St.; PO Box 248 (81036); F; 927pd, 25fr (Est); $3.66; publisher & editor Chris Sorensen; tel (719) 438-5352

Eagle/Gypsum/Vail/Avon/Aspen/Glenwood Springs: *The Eagle Valley Enterprise* — 11 Eagle Park E. Dr.; PO Box 450, Eagle (81631); Th/Su; 14,200pd, 200fr (Sw); $8.26; C; publisher & editor Gojan Nikolich; tel (970) 328-6656; fax (970) 328-6393

E El Paso/Elbert Cos.: *Ranchland News* — 115 Sioux Ave.; PO Box 307, Simla (80835); Th; 3,852pd, 137fr (Est); $5.45; publisher & editor Monty Gaddy; general manager Becky Gaddy; tel (719) 541-2288; fax (719) 541-2289

Eaton/Ault/Pierce: *North Weld Herald* — 206 1st St., Eaton (80615); Th; 2,197pd (Est); 34¢; publisher Bruce J Bormann; general manager Brenda L Bormann; editor Linda Kirtley; tel (303) 454-3466; fax (303) 454-3467

Estes Park: *Estes Park Trail-Gazette* — 251 Moraine Ave.; PO Box 1707 (80517); W/F; 5,641pd, 58fr (Sw); $9.24; publisher & editor Terence K Licence; managing editor Timothy E Asbury; tel (970) 586-3356; fax (970) 586-9532

Evergreen: *The Canyon Courier* — 4009 S. Colorado Hwy. 74; PO Box 430 (80439); W; 7,934pd, 94fr (Sw); $10.95; C; publisher Kamal Eways; editor Tony Messenger; tel (303) 674-5534; fax (303) 674-4104

Flagler: *The Flagler News* — 321 Main Ave.; PO Box 188 (80815); Th; 1,350pd, 60fr (Sw); $3.08; publisher & editor Thomas E Bredehoft; general manager Jean Bredehoft; tel (719) 765-4466; fax (719) 765-4517

Florence: *The Florence Citizen* — 200 S. Pikes Peak (81226); Th; 1,468pd, 30fr (Est); 24¢; publishers Nelda M Cruzen & Robert B Cruzen; editor Robert Wood; tel (719) 784-6383

Fort Lupton: *Fort Lupton Press* — PO Box 646, Brighton (80601); W; 908pd, 4,321fr (Est); $5.00; Sa; 908pd, 26fr (Est); $5.00; C; publisher Annette Riesel; editor Chuck Ballou; tel (303) 857-4440; fax (303) 857-6801

Fountain Vly.: *El Paso County Advertiser & News* — 120 Ohio St.; PO Box 400, Fountain (80817); W; 1,751pd, 22fr (Est); $9.90; publisher Kathryn Wiese; editor Karen Johnson; managing editor Patty St Louis; tel (719) 382-5611; fax (719) 382-5614

Fowler: *The Fowler Tribune* — 112 E. Cranston (81039); Th; 1,452pd, 32fr (Sw); $4.75; publisher Charles W Buck; publisher & editor Wilma W Gager; tel (719) 263-5311; fax (719) 263-5549

Frederick: *Frederick Farmer & Miner* — 204 Oak St.; PO Box 400 (80530); W; 734pd, 134fr (Sw); 21¢; publisher & editor Mike Neilsen; tel (303) 833-2331

Fruita/Loma/Mack/Mesa Co.: *Fruita Times* — 217 E. Aspen Ave., Fruita (81521-2285); F; 1,243pd, 32fr (Sw); $4.41; publisher & editor Eugene Thomas; tel (970) 858-3924; fax (970) 858-7658

Golden Jefferson: *The Golden Transcript* — 1000 10th St.; PO Box 987, Golden (80401); Tu/Th; 2,920pd, 1,218fr (VAC); $14.00; C; publisher Robert Short; editor Jacque Scott; tel (303) 279-5541; fax (303) 279-7157

Granby/Grand Lake: *Sky-Hi News* — 424 E. Agate Ave.; PO Box 408, Granby (80446); Th; 3,380pd, 215fr (Est); 34¢; publisher & editor Patrick Brower; tel (303) 887-3334; fax (303) 887-3204

Greenhorn Vly.: *Greenhorn Valley News* — PO Box 41, Colorado City (81019); Th; 1,000pd, 74fr (Sw); $5.00; publisher & editor Becky Minnis; publisher Steve Minnis; tel (719) 676-3304; fax (719) 676-3135

Greenwood Vlg./Cherry Hills/Littleton/Englewood: *The Villager* — 8933 E. Union, Ste. 230, Greenwood Village (80111); Th; 2,675pd, 1,340fr (Sw); $27.78; C; publisher Gerri Sweeney; publisher & editor Robert F Sweeney; general manager Saundra Dorrance; tel (303) 773-8313; fax (303) 773-8456

Haxtun: *Haxtun Herald* — 217 S. Colorado; PO Box 128 (80731); Th; 1,191pd, 50fr (Sw); $5.14; publisher & editor Jean Gray; tel (970) 774-6118

Hayden: *Hayden Valley Press* — 126 Walnut St.; PO Box E (81639); Th; 540pd, 15fr (Est); $3.00; publisher Carol Brett-Beumer; editor Stefka White; tel (970) 824-7031; fax (970) 824-6810

Holyoke: *Holyoke Enterprise* — 130 N. Interocean; PO Box 297 (80734); Th; 2,002pd, 15fr (Est); $4.40; publishers Elna Johnson & Loral Johnson; editor Brenda Brandt; tel (970) 854-2811

Hugo/Limon/Arriba/Lincoln: *Eastern Colorado Plainsman* — 329 4th St.; PO Box 98, Hugo (80821); Th; 1,355pd, 45fr (Est); $5.00; publisher & editor Becky Osterwald; tel (719) 743-2371

Idaho Springs/Georgetown: *Clear Creek Courant* — 1634 Miner St.; PO Box 2020, Idaho Springs (80452); W; 2,114pd, 11fr (Sw); $6.00; publishers & editors Carol Wilcox & Cary Stiff; tel (303) 567-4491; fax (303) 567-4492

Jackson Co.: *Jackson County Star* — 417 5th St.; PO Box 397, Walden (80480); Th; 1,240pd, 30fr (Sw); $7.25; publishers Chard Smith & Dusty Smith; editor Terry Myers; managing editor Marlon Trick; tel (970) 723-4404; fax (970) 723-4404

Jefferson Co.: *Columbine Community Courier* — 9719 W. Coal Mine Ave., Unit N; PO Box 621093, Littleton (80162); W; 24,500fr (Sw); $14.70; publisher Kamal P Eways; editor Tony Messenger; tel (303) 933-2233; fax (303) 933-4449

Johnstown/Milliken: *The Johnstown Breeze* — 7 S. Parish; PO Box 400, Johnstown (80534); Th; 1,241pd, 15fr (Est); 34¢; publisher Clyde Briggs; editor Ardis Briggs; tel (970) 587-4525

Julesburg/Ovid/Sedgwick: *Julesburg Advocate* — 108 Cedar St.; PO Box 46, Julesburg (80737); Th; 1,853pd, 30fr (Sw); $3.60; publisher & managing editor Sandi Austin; tel (970) 474-3388; fax (970) 474-3389

Kersey/Gill/La Salle/Gilcrest/Platteville: *The Voice* — 326 1st St.; PO Box 130, Kersey (80644); Th; 1,045pd, 20fr (Sw); $4.83; publishers Idella M Noel & James P Noel; editor Junita Johannes; tel (970) 356-7176; fax (970) 356-7176

Kiowa: *Elbert County News* — PO Box 1270 (80117); Th; 2,765pd, 30fr (Sw); $4.74; C; publisher J Tom Graham; editor Rich Bangs; managing editor Matthew Vuletich; tel (303) 688-3128; fax (303) 660-0240

Kremmling: *Middle Park Times* — 114 N. 3rd St.; PO Box 476 (80459); Th; 1,068pd, 22fr (Sw); $5.00; C; publisher Patrick Brower; editor Jeff Truchot; tel (970) 724-3350; fax (970) 724-3449

La Junta: *Arkansas Valley Journal* — 7 W. 5th St.; PO Box 500 (81050); Th; 5,805pd, 219fr (Est); $5.60; publisher Daniel R Hyatt; general manager Pat Ptolmey; editor Susan Russell; tel (719) 384-8121; fax (719) 384-2867

La Salle: *La Salle Leader* — PO Box 646, Brighton (80601); Sa; 300pd, 1,800fr (Sw); $3.00; publishers Annette Riesel & Terry Gogerty; tel (303) 659-2522

La Veta/Cuchara: *The La Veta/Cuchara Signature* — PO Box 154, La Veta (81055-0154); Th; 1,116pd, 5fr (Sw); $5.00; publisher & editor Richard D Carpenter; tel (719) 742-5591

Lafayette: *Lafayette News* — 1285 Centaur Village Dr.; PO Box 488 (80026); W/Sa; 1,982pd, 52fr (Sw); $6.50; C; publisher Douglas E Conarroe; editor Percy A Conarroe; managing editor Cynthia Campbell; tel (303) 665-6515

Lakewood/Metro Jefferson Co.: *The Jefferson Sentinel* — 1224 Wadsworth Blvd., Lakewood (80215); Th; 9,000pd, 2,000fr (Sw); $27.56; C; publisher Robert E Cox; general manager Sidnie O'Connell; editor Ben Miller; tel (303) 239-9890; fax (303) 239-9808

Las Animas: *Bent County Democrat* — 516 Carson Ave.; PO Box 467 (81054); Th; 1,617pd (Sw); $3.70; publisher & editor Jack L Lowe; tel (719) 456-1333; fax (719) 456-1420

Leadville: *Leadville Herald Democrat* — 717 Harrison Ave.; PO Box 980 (80461); Th; 2,800pd, 100fr (Sw); $4.80; C; publisher Merle Baranczyk; general manager & editor Grant Dunham; tel (719) 486-0641; fax (719) 486-0611

Limon: *The Limon Leader* — 801 Main Ave.; PO Box 1300 (80828); Th; 2,541pd, 66fr (Sw); $5.00; publisher John N Thomas; editor Luci Reimer; tel (719) 775-2064; fax (719) 775-9082

Louisville: *Louisville Times* — 916 Main St. (80027); W/Sa; 2,781pd, 153fr (Sw); $6.50; C; publisher Douglas E Conarroe; managing editor Cynthia Campbell; tel (303) 666-6576

Lyons/Boulder Co.: *The Old Lyons Recorder* — 430 Main St.; PO Box 1729, Lyons (80540); Th; 2,100pd, 600fr (Sw); $8.50; C; publisher Walter J Kinderman; editor Patricia Kinderman; tel (303) 823-6625; fax (303) 823-6633

Mancos: *Mancos Times-Tribune* — 135 Grand Ave.; PO Box 397 (81328); W; 844pd, 9fr (Sw); $3.25; C; publisher R D Brown; editor Julie Powell; tel (970) 533-7766; fax (970) 565-8532

Manitou Springs: *Pikes Peak Journal* — 22 Ruxton (80829); F; 1,390pd, 135fr (Sw); $4.50; C; publisher & editor John G Graham; managing editor Jeanne Davant; tel (719) 685-9201

Meeker: *The Meeker Herald* — 178 Main St.; PO Box 720 (81641); Th; 2,045pd, 50fr (Sw); $5.35; publisher & editor Glenn R Troester; general manager Donna L Troester; tel (970) 878-4017; fax (970) 878-4016

Metro Jefferson Co.: *The Jefferson Sentinel* — 1224 Wadsworth Blvd., Lakewood (80215); Th; 6,725pd, 2,916fr (Sw); $17.40; C; publisher Robert E Cox; general manager Sidnie O'Connell; editor Ben Miller; managing editor Kevin Duggan; tel (303) 239-9890; fax (303) 239-9808

Monte Vista: *The Monte Vista Journal* — 229 Adams St. (81144); W; 2,086pd, 33fr (Est); $7.40; C; publisher Jay Byrne; editor Toni Vecchio; tel (719) 852-3531; fax (719) 852-3387

Montezuma Co.: *Dolores Star* — 211 Railroad Ave.; PO Box 660, Dolores (81323); Th; 1,290pd, 29fr (Sw); $4.20; publisher Sam Green; editor Melinda Green; tel (970) 882-4486

Monument/Woodmoor: *The Tribune* — 238 Washington St.; PO Box 488, Monument (80132); Th; 3,163pd, 107fr (Sw); $6.50; publisher & editor William H Kezziah Jr; tel (719) 481-3423; fax (719) 481-4172

Nederland: *The Mountain-Ear* — 20 Lakeview Dr., Ste. 208; PO Box 99 (80466); Th; 1,936pd, 16fr (Sw); $6.60; publisher & editor Kay Turnbaugh; tel (303) 258-7075

Northglenn/Thornton: *Northglenn-Thornton Sentinel* — 7380 Lowell Blvd.; PO Box 215, Westminster (80030); Th; 4,729pd, 236fr (Sw); $14.00; C; publisher Bruce G Harper; editor Karen Brown; tel (303) 426-6000; fax (303) 430-1676

Norwood/Nucla/Naturita: *San Miguel Basin Forum* — PO Box 9, Nucla (81424); Th; 1,403pd, 15fr (Est); $4.37; publisher & editor Roger Culver; tel (970) 864-7425; fax (970) 864-7856

Ordway/Olney Springs/Crowley Co./Sugar Co.: *Ordway New Era* — 223 Main St.; PO Box 578, Ordway (81063); Tu; 803pd, 8fr (Est); $3.50; publisher Daniel R Hyatt; editor Susan S Russell; tel (719) 267-3576; fax (719) 267-4661

Ouray/Ridgway: *Ouray County Plaindealer* — 333 6th Ave.; PO Box 607, Ouray (81427); Th; 1,929pd, 35fr (Sw); $6.00; C; publisher & editor David Mullings; tel (970) 325-4412; fax (970) 325-4413

Pagosa Springs/Archuleta: *The Pagosa Springs Sun* — 466 Pagosa St.; PO Box 9, Pagosa Springs (81147); Th; 3,552pd, 10fr (Sw); $5.70; publisher & editor David C Mitchell; tel (970) 264-2101

Palisade/Clifton: *The Palisade Tribune* — 124 W. 3rd St.; PO Box 8, Palisade (81526); Th; 1,100pd, 3,000fr (Sw); $7.50; publisher Robert F Sweeney; editor Robert C Dougherty; tel (970) 464-5614

Park Co.: *Park County Republican & Fairplay Flume* — 5138 Park County Rd. 64; PO Box 460, Bailey (80421); F; 2,355pd, 57fr (Sw); $5.00; C; publisher Merle Baranczyk; editor Stephen Millard; managing editor Carol Wilburn; tel (303) 838-4423, (303) 838-2108; fax (303) 832-8414

Parker/Castle Rock: *Parker Trail* — PO Box 905, Castle Rock (80104); Th; 758pd, 200fr (Sw); $9.00; publisher & editor Bob Lombardi; publisher Dawn Achhorner; tel (303) 660-2360; fax (303) 660-1740

Pine/Morrison: *High Timber Times* — 43 Mount Evans Blvd., Pine (80470); Th; 1,562pd (Est); $10.95; publisher Kamal Eways; editor Tony Messenger; tel (303) 838-4884; fax (303) 838-6007

Rangely: *Rangely Times* — 713 E. Main St.; PO Box 460 (81648); Th; 1,042pd, 39fr (Sw); $4.25; C; publisher Bernard Yaeger; general manager Peggy Rector; managing editor Lavella Justus; tel (970) 675-5033; fax (970) 675-8709

Rifle: *The Citizen Telegram* — 132 E. 3rd Rifle Co.; PO Box 111 (81650); W; 2,858pd, 158fr (Sw); $7.00; publisher Community Newspapers of Colorado; general manager Barbara Donily; editor Suzanna Hart; tel (970) 625-3245; fax (970) 625-3628

Saguache: *The Saguache Crescent* — 316 4th St.; PO Box 195 (81149); Th; 645pd, 13fr (Sw); $4.27; publisher Dean I Coombs; editor Marie O Coombs; managing editor Margaret Batchelder; tel (719) 655-2620

Silverton: *The Silverton Standard and The Miner* — 1257 Greene St.; PO Box 8 (81443); Th; 1,360pd, 3fr (Est); $5.50; publisher & editor Jon Denious; publisher Sharon Denious; tel (970) 387-5477

Snowmass Village/Pitkin Co.: *Snowmass Sun* — 16 Kearns Rd., Ste. 211; PO Box 5770, Snowmass Village (81615); W; 1,954pd, 154fr (Sw); $7.00; publisher & editor Jim Pokrandt; tel (970) 923-5829; fax (970) 923-2571

South Fork: *The South Fork Times* — 229 Adams St., Monte Vista (81144); Th; 770pd, 7fr (Est); $5.40; C; publisher Jay Byrne; editor Toni Vecchio; tel (719) 852-3531; fax (719) 852-3387

Steamboat Springs/Routt Co.: *Steamboat Pilot* — 1041 Lincoln Ave.; PO Box 774827, Steamboat Springs (80477); Th; 6,135pd, 279fr (Sw); $8.20; C; publisher Suzanne Antinoro; editor Tom Ross; tel (970) 879-1502; fax (970) 879-2888

Stratton: *Stratton Spotlight* — 124 Colorado Ave.; PO Box 287 (80836); Tu; 506pd, 35fr (Sw); $3.75; publisher Stratton Publishing Co.; editor Linda Coles; tel (719) 348-5913; fax (719) 348-5948

Summit Co.: *Summit County Journal* — 40 W. Main St.; PO Box 709, Frisco (80443); W; 2,632pd, 1,201fr (Sw); $7.95; C; publisher Robert Brown; general manager Michael Kirschbaum; editor T Alex Miller; tel (970) 668-0750; fax (970) 668-0755

Telluride: *The Telluride Times-Journal* — 123 S. Spruce St.; PO Box 1765 (81435); Th; 3,403pd, 766fr (VAC); $7.50; publisher Thomas Bonfietti; editor Margo Hecker; tel (970) 728-4301, (970) 728-4488; fax (970) 728-6090

Vail Vly.: *Vail Trail* — 41184 Hwys. 6 & 24; PO Drawer 6200, Vail (81658); F; 9,585pd, 4,365fr (Sw); $8.20; publisher & editor Allen Knox; managing editor Tara Flanagan; tel (303) 949-4004; fax (303) 949-0199

Walsenburg: *Huerfano World* — 111 W. 7th St.; PO Box 191 (81089); Th; 2,900pd, 50fr (Sw); $8.60; publisher & editor Jay D Crook; tel (719) 738-1720; fax (719) 738-1727

Watkins/Bennett/Strasburg/Byers/Deer Trail: *Eastern Colorado News* — 1522 Main St.; PO Box 555, Strasburg (80136); Th; 1,074pd, 40fr (Sw); $4.75; publisher & editor Mike Galarneau; tel (303) 622-4417; fax (303) 622-9717

Westcliffe: *Wet Mountain Tribune* — 404 Main St.; PO Box 300 (81252); Th; 2,534pd, 21fr (Sw); $6.44; publisher & editor Jim Little; tel (719) 783-2361; fax (719) 783-2879

Westminster: *Westminster Window* — 7380 Lowell Blvd.; PO Box 215 (80030); Th; 3,357pd, 346fr (Sw); $14.00; C; general manager Bruce G Harper; editor Karen Brown; tel (303) 426-6000; fax (303) 430-1676

Wiggins/Orchard/Weldona/Hoyt: *The Wiggins Courier* — 213 Dickinson; PO Box 98, Wiggins (80654); Th; 676pd, 30fr (Sw); $3.00; publisher Verna Segelke; editor Darlene Ruyle; tel (970) 483-7460; fax (970) 483-7313

Windsor: *Windsor Beacon* — 425 Main St. (80550); Th; 2,867pd, 77fr (Sw); $4.50; publisher Roger Lipker; general manager Ruth Lipker; editor Todd Vess; tel (970) 686-9646; fax (970) 686-9647

Winter Park: *Winter Park Manifest* — PO Box 409 (80482); Th; 2,900pd (Est); $6.25; C; publisher Patrick Brower; editor Harry Williamson; tel (303) 726-5721; fax (303) 726-8789

Woodland Park/Ute Pass: *Ute Pass Courier* — 1200 E. Hwy. 24; PO Box 340, Woodland Park (80866); Th; 4,000pd (Sw); $5.94; C; publisher Bruce Schlabaugh; managing editor Paula Glover; tel (719) 687-3006

Wray/Eckley/Yuma/Idalia/Haigler: *Wray Gazette* — 411 Main St.; PO Box 7, Wray (80758); W; 3,110pd, 40fr (Sw); $4.50; publishers Jeanette B Rieb & Ronald C Rieb; tel (970) 332-4846; fax (970) 332-4065

CONNECTICUT

Avon: *Avon News* — 20 Isham Rd., West Hartford (06107); Th; 2,415pd, 6fr (Est); $6.69; C; publisher Jim Normandin; editor John Misselwitz; tel (203) 236-3571; fax (203) 236-0490

Bethany/Orange/Woodbridge: *The Bulletin* — 349 New Haven Ave.; PO Box 589, Milford (06460); Th; 9,600fr (Est); $7.70; C; publisher William Rush; editor Cindy MacAulay; tel (203) 876-6800; fax (203) 877-4772

Bloomfield: *Bloomfield Journal* — 20 Isham Rd., West Hartford (06107); F; 2,246pd, 4fr (Est); $6.26; publisher Jim Normandin; editor Lynn Woike; tel (203) 236-3571; fax (203) 236-0490

Branford/N Branford: *Branford Review* — 230 E. Main St.; PO Box 829, Branford (06405); Tu/Sa; 5,442pd, 171fr (Est); 34¢; C; publisher & editor Marianne Cipriano; tel (203) 488-2535; fax (203) 481-4125

Bridgeport: *Bridgeport News* — PO Box 298, Trumbull (06611); Th; 19,752fr (Sw); $13.00; publisher Benjamin W Gumm; editor Brad Durrell; tel (203) 268-6234; fax (203) 452-1068

Brookfield: *Brookfield Journal* — 132 Danbury Rd. (New Milford 06776); PO Box 268 (06804); F; 2,243pd, 124fr (Est); $9.75; C; publisher Trip Rothschild; general manager & editor Art Cummings; managing editor Jan Howard; tel (203) 775-2533; fax (203) 354-2645

Cheshire: *Cheshire Herald* — 125 Commerce Ct., Ste. 11; PO Box 247 (06410); Th; 6,431pd, 397fr (Est); $5.92; publisher Joseph J Jakubisyn; general manager Maureen Jakubisyn; editor Clarke W Hammersley; tel (203) 272-5316; fax (203) 250-7145

Clinton/Killingworth: *Clinton Recorder* — 16D W. Main St.; PO Box 914, Clinton (06413); Tu/Sa; 5,000pd, 5,386fr (Est); $3.03; publisher William Rush; editor Michael Lemansky; managing editor Kim Ryan; tel (860) 669-5727; fax (860) 664-4531

Colchester/Salem/E Haddam/E Hampton/Hebron/Marlborough/Lebanon/Portland: *The Regional Standard* — 139 S. Main St.; PO Box 510, Colchester (06415); F; 8,469pd (Est); $7.50; C; publisher William Rush; editor Karen Barretta; managing editor Kim Ryan; tel (860) 537-2341; fax (860) 537-1768

Cromwell: *Cromwell Chronicle* — 211 Shunpike Rd., Ste. 5 (06416); F; 7,000fr (Sw); $6.00; publisher & editor Ron Nolan; tel (203) 635-1819; fax (203) 632-7203

Darien: *Darien News-Review* — 6 Squab Ln. (06820); Th; 7,067pd, 2,069fr (Sw); $15.12; C; publisher B V Brooks; general manager Kevin Lalley; editor Janet Cummings; managing editor Tim Mahin; tel (203) 655-7476; fax (203) 655-1442

E Hartford: *The East Hartford Gazette* — 54 Connecticut Blvd. (06108); Th/F; 8,858pd, 10,553fr (Est); $8.10; publisher Vance C Brown; editor William Doak; tel (203) 289-6468; fax (203) 289-6469

E Haven: *The Advertiser* — 349 New Haven Ave.; PO Box 589, Milford (06460); Th; 9,800fr (Est); $7.70; publisher William Rush; editor Denise Madera; tel (203) 876-6800; fax (203) 877-4772

Easton: *Easton Courier* — PO Box 298, Trumbull (06611); Th; 3,396fr (CAC); $7.00; C; publisher Benjamin W Gumm; editor Don Eng; tel (203) 268-6234; fax (203) 452-1068

Fairfield/Southport: *Fairfield Citizen-News* — 220 Carter Henry Dr., Fairfield (06430); W/F; 10,624pd, 2,974fr (ABC); $18.20; C; publisher B V Brooks; editor Patricia Hines; managing editor Laura A Nailen; tel (203) 255-4561; fax (203) 255-0456

Fairfield/Southport/Easton: *Fairfield Minuteman* — 877 Post Rd. E.; PO Box 3119, Westport (06880); Th; 25,000fr (Est); $13.00; C; publisher Mark Owades; editor John Schwing; managing editor Ed Silverstein; tel (203) 226-8877; fax (203) 221-7540

Farmington: *Farmington News* — 20 Isham Rd., West Hartford (06107); Th; 2,247pd, 3fr (Est); $6.19; C; publisher Jim Normandin; editor Kelly Callaghan; tel (203) 236-3571; fax (203) 236-0490

Glastonbury/Marlborough: *Glastonbury Citizen* — 87 Nutmeg Ln.; PO Box 373, Glastonbury (06033); Th; 8,900pd, 500fr (Est); $8.00; C; publisher James Hallas; general manager John Ultee; editor Kathleen Stack; tel (860) 633-4691; fax (860) 657-3258

Greater Southbury Area: *Voices Sunday-The Weekly Star* — 90 Middle Quarter Mall; PO Box 689, Woodbury (06798); Su; 133pd, 20,669fr (CAC); $12.88; C; publisher Rudy Mazurosky; editor Miriam Schlicht & Pattie Wesley; tel (203) 263-2116; fax (203) 266-0199

Greenwich: *Greenwich News* — 36 Sherwood Pl. (06830); PO Box 7879 (06836); Th; 6,791pd, 8,210fr (Sw); $23.10; C; publisher B V Brooks; editor Carolyn Ryzswicz; managing editor Timothy Dumas; tel (203) 869-1777; fax (203) 869-1168

Guilford: *Shore Line Times* — Times Bldg. (06437); W/F; 8,612pd, 131fr (Est); 34¢; publisher William Rush; editor Silvio Albino; managing editor Kim Ryan; tel (203) 453-2711; fax (203) 458-6576

Hamden: *Hamden Chronicle* — 349 Haven Ave.; PO Box 589, Milford (06460); Th; 10,000fr (Est); $7.70; publisher William Rush; editor Leslie Drost; tel (203) 876-6800; fax (203) 877-4772

Hartford: *The Hartford News* — 191 Franklin Ave. (06114); W; 25,000fr (Sw); $10.00; publisher & editor Jon B Harden; publisher Lynne Lumsden; general manager & managing editor Andy Hart; tel (860) 296-6128; fax (860) 296-8769

Hartford: *The Reminder* — Old Town Rd.; PO Box 27, Vernon (06066); Tu; 110,000fr (Est); $24.00; publisher & editor Kenneth Hovland Jr; general manager George Cunningham; tel (860) 875-3366; fax (860) 875-2089

Kent Co./S Kent: *Kent Good Times Dispatch* — PO Box 430, Kent (06757); F; 1,076pd, 34fr (CAC); $5.45; C; publisher Walter N Rothschild; editor Lesly Ferris; tel (860) 927-4621; fax (860) 927-4622

Lakeville/Salisbury/Cornwall/Norfolk/Canaan/ Kent/Falls Vlg.: *The Lakeville Journal* — 33 Bissell St.; PO Box 353, Lakeville (06039); Th; 5,707pd (Sw); $9.95; C; publisher A Whitney Ellsworth; editor David Parkbil; managing editor Kathryn Boughton; tel (860) 435-9873; fax (860) 435-0146

Lewisboro: *The Lewisboro Ledger* — 16 Bailey Ave.; PO Box 1019, Ridgefield (06877); Th; 1,650pd, 33fr (CAC); $5.00; C; publisher Thomas B Nash; editor Jack Sanders; tel (203) 438-6544; fax (203) 438-6014

Litchfield: *Litchfield Enquirer* — PO Box 547 (06759); F; 7,247pd, 34fr (Sw); $9.90; C; publisher Walter N Rothschild; editor Art Cummings; managing editor John McKenna; tel (860) 567-8766; fax (860) 567-0005

Litchfield Co.: *The Litchfield County Times* — 32 Main St., New Milford (06776); F; 10,712pd, 2,906fr (Sw); $13.50; publisher Arthur L Carter; editor Kenneth Paul; managing editor Douglas Clement; tel (203) 355-4141; fax (203) 354-8706

Milford: *Milford Mirror* — PO Box 298, Trumbull (06611); Th; 16,301fr (Est); $12.60; C; publisher Benjamin W Gumm; editor Jill Dion; tel (203) 268-6234; fax (203) 452-1068

Milford: *Milford Reporter* — 349 New Haven Ave.; PO Box 589 (06460); F; 20,053fr (Est); 79¢; publisher William Rush; editor Leslie Drost; tel (203) 876-6800; fax (203) 877-4772

Monroe: *Monroe Courier* — PO Box 298, Trumbull (06611); Th; 3,752pd, 375fr (Est); $7.40; C; publisher Benjamin W Gumm; editor John Voket; tel (203) 268-6234; fax (203) 452-1068

New Canaan: *New Canaan Advertiser* — 42 Vitti St.; PO Box 605 (06840); Th; 6,446pd, 430fr (ABC); 45¢; publisher V Donald Hersam Jr; general manager Marty Hersam; editor Edmond J Chrostowski; tel (203) 966-9541; fax (203) 966-8006

New Milford: *New Milford Times* — 132 Danbury Rd.; PO Box 1139 (06776); F; 6,920pd, 401fr (Est); $11.00; C; publisher Trip Rothschild; editor Art Cummings; tel (860) 354-2261; fax (860) 354-2645

New Milford/Brookfield: *Housatonic Weekend/Litchfield Weekend* — 132 Danbury Rd.; PO Box 1139, New Milford (06776); F; 19,948fr (CAC); $13.75; C; publisher Trip Rothschild; editor Art Cummings; managing editor Leigh Greiser; tel (860) 354-2261; fax (860) 354-2645

Newington: *Newington Town Crier* — 20 Isham Rd., West Hartford (06107); F; 3,413pd (Sw); $8.44; C; publisher Jim Normandin; editor Linda Levinson; tel (203) 236-3571; fax (203) 236-0490

Newtown: *The Newtown Bee* — 5 Church Hill Rd. (06470); F; 6,883pd, 87fr (Sw); $5.90; C; publisher & editor R Scudder Smith; managing editor Curtiss Clark; tel (203) 426-3141; fax (203) 426-1394

N Haven/Wallingford: *The Post* — 349 New Haven Ave.; PO Box 589, Milford (06460); Th; 4,500fr (Est); $7.70; publisher William Rush; editor Leslie Drost; tel (203) 876-6800; fax (203) 877-4772

Old Lyme/Old Saybrook: *Pictorial Gazette* — 162 Main St.; PO Drawer O, Old Saybrook (06475); Tu; 6,648pd, 1,380fr (Est); $7.80; Sa; 12,000pd, 1,330fr (Est); $10.25; C; publisher William Rush; editor Doreen Madden; managing editor Kimberly Potter Ryan; tel (860) 388-3441; fax (860) 388-5613

Portland/S Glastonbury: *River East News Bulletin* — PO Box 373, Glastonbury (06033); F; 17,000fr (Est); $6.00; publisher & editor James Hallas; tel (860) 633-7691; fax (860) 657-3258

Redding: *The Redding Pilot* — 16 Bailey Ave.; PO Box 1019, Ridgefield (06877); Th; 2,047pd, 43fr (CAC); $7.35; C; publisher Thomas B Nash; editor Jack Sanders; tel (203) 438-6544; fax (203) 544-9153

Ridgefield: *The Ridgefield Press* — 16 Bailey Ave.; PO Box 1019 (06877); Th; 6,497pd, 114fr (CAC); $7.35; C; publisher Thomas B Nash; editor Jack Sanders; tel (203) 438-6544; fax (203) 438-6014

Rocky Hill: *Rocky Hill Post* — 20 Isham Rd., West Hartford (06107); F; 1,735pd, 2fr (Sw); $4.96; C; publisher James F Normandin; editors Linda Levinson & Melanie Winters; tel (860) 236-3571; fax (860) 236-0490

Shelton: *Huntington Herald* — PO Box 298, Trumbull (06611); W; 10,653fr (CAC); $10.30; C; publisher Benjamin W Gumm; editor Tom Henry; tel (203) 268-6234; fax (203) 452-1068

Simsbury: *Simsbury News* — 20 Isham Rd., West Hartford (06107); Th; 2,855pd (Est); $8.11; C; publisher Jim Normandin; editor Kelly Callaghan; tel (203) 236-3571; fax (203) 236-0490

Simsbury/Farmington/Avon: *Farmington Valley Herald* — 1522 Hopmeadow St.; PO Box 477, Simsbury (06070); Th; 5,786pd, 547fr (Est); $8.14; publisher James Normandin; general manager Michael Vanacore; editor Robin Vinci; tel (860) 658-4471; fax (860) 658-2898

Southbury: *Voices* — 90 Middle Quarter Mall; PO Box 383 (06488); W; 523pd, 25,006fr (CAC); $12.88; C; publisher Rudy Mazurosky; editors Miriam Schlicht & Pattie Wesley; tel (203) 263-2116; fax (203) 266-0199

Southington: *The Observer* — 213 Spring St.; PO Box 648 (06489-0648); Th; 4,756pd, 34fr (CAC); $7.50; publisher Anthony L Urillo; editor Steve Mauren; tel (860) 621-6751; fax (860) 621-1841

Stratford: *Stratford Bard* — 349 New Haven Ave.; PO Box 589, Milford (06460); Th; 18,000fr (Est); $9.00; publisher William Rush; editor Dorothy Eurle; tel (203) 876-6800; fax (203) 877-4772

Stratford: *Stratford Star* — PO Box 298, Trumbull (06611); Th; 16,635fr (CAC); $12.00; C; publisher Benjamin W Gumm; editor Jack Terceno; managing editor Lorraine Bukowski; tel (203) 268-6234; fax (203) 452-1068

Thomaston/Plymouth: *Thomaston Express* — 44 Union St.; PO Box 250, Thomaston (06787); Th; 1,628pd, 27fr (Est); $4.41; publisher James F Normandin; general manager Michael Vanacore; editor Michael Chaiken; tel (860) 283-4355; fax (860) 283-4356

Trumbull: *Trumbull Times* — PO Box 332, Monroe (06468); Th; 6,672pd, 484fr (CAC); $11.40; C; publisher Benjamin W Gumm; editor Tom Ebersold; managing editor Lorraine Bukowski; tel (203) 268-6234; fax (203) 452-1068

Watertown: *Town Times* — 1192 Main St.; PO Box 1 (06795); Th; 264pd, 8,702fr (CAC); $11.06; C; publisher Rudy Mazurosky; editor Tommy Valuckas; tel (860) 274-8851; fax (860) 945-3116

W Hartford: *West Hartford News* — 20 Isham Rd. (06107); Th; 11,000fr (Est); $10.00; C; publisher Jim Normandin; editor Keith Griffin; tel (203) 236-3571; fax (203) 236-0490

W Haven: *West Haven News* — 349 New Haven Ave.; PO Box 589, Milford (06460); Th; 5,000pd (Est); 30¢; publisher William Rush; editor Ed Crowder; tel (203) 876-6800; fax (203) 877-4772

Weston: *The Weston Forum* — 16 Bailey Ave.; PO Box 1019, Ridgefield (06877); W; 85pd, 3,568fr (CAC); $7.35; C; publisher Thomas B Nash; editor Jack Sanders; tel (203) 438-6544; fax (203) 438-3395

Westport/Weston: *Westport Minuteman* — 877 Post Rd. E.; PO Box 3119, Westport (06880); Th; 18,000fr (Est); $13.00; C; publisher Mark Owades; editor Lise Connell; managing editor Thane Gravel; tel (203) 226-8877; fax (203) 221-7540

Westport/Weston: *Westport News* — 136 Main St., Westport (06880); W/F; 10,419pd, 2,793fr (ABC); $18.20; C; publisher B V Brooks; editor Woody Klein; managing editor Gary Larkin; tel (203) 226-6311; fax (203) 454-2765

Wethersfield: *Wethersfield Post* — 20 Isham Rd., West Hartford (06107); F; 4,694pd, 2fr (Sw); $11.18; C; publisher James Normandin; editor Melanie Winters; tel (860) 236-3571; fax (860) 236-0146

Wilton: *The Wilton Bulletin* — 196 Danbury Rd.; PO Box 367 (06897); W; 4,612pd, 82fr (CAC); $7.35; C; publisher Thomas B Nash; editor Jack Sanders; tel (203) 438-6544

Windsor: *Windsor Journal* — 20 Isham Rd., West Hartford (06107); F; 2,400pd (Est); $8.58; C; publisher Jim Normandin; editor Paul Angilly; tel (203) 236-3571; fax (203) 236-0490

Windsor Locks: *Windsor Locks Journal* — 20 Isham Rd., West Hartford (06107); F; 1,629pd (Sw); $4.66; C; publisher James F Normandin; editor Paul Angilly; tel (860) 236-3571; fax (860) 236-0490

DELAWARE

Central Sussex Co.: *The Sussex Post* — Midway Shopping Ctr.; PO Box 37, Lewes (19958); W; 53pd, 18,612fr (VAC); $8.60; C; publisher Tamra Brittingham; editor Andrew West; tel (302) 934-9261; fax (302) 934-8590

Dover: *Dover Post* — 609 E. Division St.; PO Box 664 (19903); W; 2,276pd, 26,290fr (Est); $8.80; C; publisher Jim Flood Sr; general manager Jim Flood Jr; editor Don Flood; tel (302) 678-3616; fax (302) 678-8291

Georgetown: *The Sussex Countian* — 115 N. Race St. (19947); W; 3,896pd, 50fr (Est); $5.95; C; publisher Jim Flood; general manager Caroline O'Neal; editor Lance Keeler; managing editor William Spencer; tel (302) 856-0026; fax (302) 856-0925

Harrington: *The Harrington Journal* — 110 Center St.; PO Box 239 (19952); W; 3,500pd, 400fr (Est); $1.64; publisher Larry Effingham; general manager Ron MacArthur; editor Carol Ann Porter; tel (302) 398-3206; fax (302) 398-3824

Middletown/Odessa: *The Middletown Transcript* — 24 W. Main St., Middletown (19709); W; 2,936pd, 116fr (Sw); $2.05; C; publisher Jim Flood; editor Alysia Moticha; tel (302) 378-9531; fax (302) 378-0647

Milford: *The Chronicle* — 10-16 S.W. Front St.; PO Box 297 (19963); W; 8,500pd, 3,000fr (Est); $7.65; C; publisher & editor Ron MacArthur; tel (302) 422-1200; fax (302) 422-1211

Newark/Glasgow/Bear: *Newark Post* — 153 E. Chesnut Hill Rd., Newark (19713); F; 6,857pd, 4,036fr (Sw); $8.75; C; publisher James B Streit Jr; editor David Scott; tel (302) 737-0724; fax (302) 737-9019

Rehoboth Beach/Lewes/Bethany Beach/Fenwick: *Delaware Beachcomber* — 3719 Hwy. 1; PO Box 309, Rehoboth Beach (19971); W; 20,000fr (Est); $10.00; C; publisher Brian Hunt; general manager Jane Meleady; editor Terry Plowman; tel (302) 227-9466; fax (302) 227-9469

Rehoboth Beach/Lewes/Bethany Beach/Fenwick: *Delaware Coast Press* — 3719 Hwy. 1; PO Box 309, Rehoboth Beach (19971); W; 11,000fr (Est); $8.65; C; publisher Brian Hunt; general manager Jane Meleady; editor Terry Plowman; tel (302) 227-9466; fax (302) 227-9469

Seaford/Laurel/Delmar: *The Leader/State Register* — 616 Water St., Seaford (19973); W/F; 10,000pd (Est); $9.20; C; publisher Bryant Richardson; editor Tony Windsor; tel (302) 629-5505; fax (302) 629-6700

Smyrna/Clayton: *Smyrna/Clayton Sun-Times* — 45 W. Commerce St.; PO Box 327, Smyrna (19977); W; 2,635pd, 376fr (VAC); $5.95; C; publisher Jim Flood Sr; general manager Don Flood; editor Ben Mace; tel (302) 653-2083; fax (302) 653-8821

SE Sussex Co.: *The Wave* — Rte. 1, Lem Hickman Plz.; PO Box 1420, Bethany Beach (19930); W; 10,500fr (Sw); $8.75; publisher John D Backe; general manager Susan Lyons; editor Steve Hoegnomann; tel (302) 537-1881; fax (302) 537-9705

Wilmington: *The Dialog* — 1925 Delaware Ave.; PO Box 2208 (19899); Th; 48,500pd (Sw); $7.00; publisher & editor Robert L Johnston; general manager Daniel Medinger; tel (302) 573-3109; fax (302) 573-2397

FLORIDA

Amelia Island: *New-Leader* — 511 Ash St.; PO Box 766, Fernandina Beach (32034); W; 9,308pd, 46fr (Sw); $10.78; publisher Foy Maloy; general manager Mary Hurst; tel (904) 261-3696; fax (904) 261-3698

Apopka/Altamonte Springs: *The Planter* — 439 W. Orange Blossom Trl.; PO Box 880, Apopka (32704-0880); Th; 10,000fr (Sw); $8.00; C; publisher John E Ricketson; general manager Neoma R DeGard; editor John Peery; tel (407) 886-2777; fax (407) 889-4121

Apopka/Orange: *Apopka Chief* — 439 W. Orange Blossom Trl.; PO Box 880, Apopka (32704-0880); F; 3,079pd, 148fr (Sw); $7.50; C; publisher John E Ricketson; general manager Neoma R DeGard; editor John Peery; tel (407) 886-2777; fax (407) 889-4121

Arcadia: *The Arcadian* — 207 W. Oak St.; PO Box 670 (33821); Th; 5,000pd, 3,200fr (Est); $8.59; C; publisher Donna S Thomas; editor Ginger Riggs; tel (941) 494-2434; fax (941) 494-3533

Arcadia/DeSoto: *DeSoto Sun-Herald* — 207 W. Oak St.; PO Box 670, Arcadia (33821); W; 5,547pd, 4,000fr (Est); $6.70; publisher Donna S Thomas; editor Wade Hill; tel (941) 494-7600; fax (941) 494-3533

Auburndale/Lake Alfred: *Auburndale Star* — 213 E. Lake Ave.; PO Box 126, Auburndale (33823); Th; 3,250pd (Est); 45¢; publisher Joe Ben Oller; editor Max Robinson; managing editor Garry Maitland; tel (813) 688-8500; fax (813) 686-7079

Avon Park: *The News-Sun/Avon Park* — 203 W. Main St. (33825); W; 4,506pd, 18fr (Est); $5.80; C; publisher Judy D Robinette; editor David Brown; tel (941) 453-5500

Bartow: *The Polk County Democrat* — 190 S. Florida Ave. (33830); PO Box 120 (33831); M/Th; 3,939pd, 490fr (Sw); $6.15; C; publisher & editor S L Frisbie IV; tel (813) 533-4183; fax (813) 533-0402

Bay Co.: *Beach-Bay News* — 17214 Back Beach Rd., Panama City Beach (32413); Th; 8,000pd (Est); $5.25; C; publisher Gary Woodham; general manager & editor Paul Cox; tel (904) 234-6990; fax (904) 234-3054

Belle Glade/Pahokee: *The Sun* — 417 N.W. 16th St., Ste. 6; PO Box 2226, Belle Glade (33430); Th; 2,100pd (Est); $8.81; C; publisher & editor Brenda Bunting; tel (407) 996-4404; fax (407) 996-2209

Belleview: *Voice of South Marion* — 11412 S.E. US Hwy. 301; PO Box 700 (32620); W; 1,610pd, 45fr (Est); 22¢; publisher Jim Waldron; editor Sandy Waldron; tel (904) 245-3161

Beverly Hills: *Beverly Hills Visitor* — 4 Beverly Hills Blvd.; PO Box 640850 (34464); Su; 5,500fr (Est); $4.00; C; publisher Gerard Mulligan; general manager & editor Kathie Stewart; tel (904) 746-4292; fax (904) 746-5401

Boca Grande: *The Boca Beacon* — 431 Park Ave.; PO Box 313 (33921); F; 4,000pd, 3,000fr (Sw); $6.58; publisher & editor Dusty Hopkins; tel (813) 964-2995; fax (813) 964-0372

Boca Grande/Englewood: *Gasparilla Gazette* — 301 Park Ave.; PO Box 929, Boca Grande (33921); F; 5,000pd (Sw); $5.20; C; publisher Harry Pappas; editor Lynne Hendricks; tel (813) 964-2728; fax (813) 964-2850

Boca Raton: *Boca Monday* — 601 Fairway Dr.; PO Box 1189, Deerfield Beach (33441); M; 6pd, 26,315fr (VAC); $21.25; C; publisher Bruce Warshal; editor Richard Haydan; tel (954) 698-6397; fax (954) 429-1207

Boca Raton: *Boca Raton Thursday Times* — 601 Fairway Dr.; PO Box 1189, Deerfield Beach (33441); Th; 6pd, 25,659fr (VAC); $18.55; publisher Bruce Warshal; editor Richard Haydan; tel (954) 698-6397; fax (954) 429-1207

Boca Raton: *West Boca Times* — 601 Fairway Dr.; PO Box 1189, Deerfield (33441); W; 6pd, 19,561fr (VAC); $14.10; publisher Scott Patterson; editor Richard Haydan; tel (954) 698-6397; fax (954) 429-1207

Bonita Springs: *Bonita Banner* — 9102 Bonita Beach Rd.; PO Box 40 (33923); W; 427pd, 31,703fr (Sw); $8.85; Sa; 235pd, 31,703fr (Sw); $8.85; publisher Collier County Publishing Co.; general manager Steve Akers; editor Don Goodwin; managing editor Cathy Hollopeter; tel (813) 992-2110; fax (813) 922-7819

Boynton Beach: *The Boynton Beach Times* — 601 Fairway Dr.; PO Box 1189, Deerfield Beach (33441); Th; 7pd, 24,584fr (VAC); $15.90; publisher Scott Patterson; editor Richard Haydan; tel (954) 698-6397; fax (954) 429-1207

Brandon/Seffner/Valrico: *The Brandon News* — 1401 Oakfield Dr., Brandon (33511-4854); W; 42,500fr (Sw); $11,76; C; general manager Carla Rockwell; editor D'Ann White; tel (813) 689-7764; fax (813) 689-9545

Branford: *The Branford News* — Main St.; PO Box 148 (32008); Th; 1,800pd, 20fr (Sw); $3.65; C; publisher Shirley W Hatch; editor George Petrena; tel (904) 935-1427; fax (904) 935-3043

Broward Co.: *Broward News* — 767 S. State Rd. 7 (441), Ste. 1; The Forest Office Complex, West Bldg., Margate (33068); Th; 30,000fr (Est); $11.00; C; publisher Harvey Lustig; general manager Shelly Lazarus; editor Mort Luxner; tel (305) 977-7770; fax (305) 977-7779

Broward Co.: *Community News* — 6836 Stirling Rd., Hollywood (33024); W; 71,526fr (VAC); $35.00; publisher Roger Clark; editor Francesca Nasto-Kramer; tel (954) 963-4000; fax (954) 964-4006

Bunnell/Palm Coast: *The Flagler/Palm Coast News-Tribune* — 2 McCormick Dr., Bunnell (32110-9987); W/Sa; 8,738pd, 913fr (Sw); $8.05; C; publisher Tippen Davidson; general manager Georgia Kaney; managing editors Carl Laundrie & Nick Klasne; tel (904) 437-2491; fax (904) 437-0139

Calhoun/Liberty Co.: *The Calhoun Liberty Journal* — Summers Rd.; PO Box 536, Bristol (32321); W; 1,600pd, 3,700fr (Sw); $4.50; C; publisher Johnny Eubanks; editor Teresa Eubanks; tel (904) 643-3333; fax (904) 643-3334

Callahan/Hilliard/Yulee: *Nassau County Record* — 213 W. Brandies Ave.; PO Box 609, Callahan (32011); Th; 4,329pd, 46fr (Sw); $4.80; publisher Jennifer Wise; general manager Wanda Council; editor Winn Hardin; tel (904) 879-2727; fax (904) 879-5155

Captiva: *Captiva Current* — 2340 Periwinkle Way (Sanibel 33957); PO Box 549 (33954); F; 4,000fr (Est); $4.80; C; editor Ralf Kircher; tel (941) 472-1580; fax (941) 472-8398

Carrabelle: *The Carrabelle Times* — PO Box 393 (32322); Th; 866pd, 60fr (Est); $4.00; publisher Robert A Lindsay; general manager & editor John F Lee; tel (904) 697-2222

Carrollwood: *Carrollwood News* — 10029 N. Dale Mabry, Tampa (33618); W; 39,000fr (Sw); $11.32; general manager Carla Rockwell; editor Kevin Kaley; tel (813) 264-0170; fax (813) 265-1723

Cedar Key/Levy: *Cedar Key Beacon* — 6050 D St.; PO Box 532, Cedar Key (32625-4913); Th; 1,500pd (Sw); $3.00; publisher Mike Raftis; general manager & managing editor Connie Raftis; tel (904) 543-5701; fax (904) 543-5928

Chattahoochee: *Twin City News* — 314 Washington St.; PO Box 505 (32324); Th; 1,503pd, 51fr (Sw); $3.75; publisher & editor Stan Ramsey; tel (904) 663-2255; fax (904) 663-8102

Chiefland/Levy: *Chiefland Citizen* — W. Park Ave.; PO Box 980, Chiefland (32644); Th; 3,222pd, 32fr (Sw); $5.25; C; publisher Christopher Wilson; general manager & editor Wihlena V Wilson; tel (904) 493-1553; fax (904) 493-9336

Chipley/Bonita: *Washington County News* — 112 Railroad Ave.; PO Box 627, Chipley (32428); M/Th; 2,896pd, 34fr (Sw); $4.80; C; publisher & editor Maurice Pujol Jr; tel (904) 638-0212; fax (904) 638-4601

Clermont/Groveland: *South Lake Press* — 737 8th St. (34711); PO Box 120868, Clermont (34712-0868); Th; 2,115pd, 503fr (Sw); $5.25; publisher Janet Gillis; general manager Tom McEntire; editor Eric Walker; tel (904) 394-2183; fax (904) 394-8001

Clewiston: *Clewiston News* — 626 W. Sugarland Hwy.; PO Box 1236 (33440); W; 2,453pd, 171fr (Est); $7.84; C; publisher Richard Hitt; general manager Kelly Milicezic; tel (941) 983-9148; fax (941) 983-7537

Coastal: *Pelican Press* — 230 Avda. Madera, Sarasota (34242); Th; 21,000fr (Est); $10.00; C; publisher John B Davidson; general manager Sally Baxter; editor Anne Johnson; tel (813) 349-4949; fax (813) 346-7118

Cocoa: *The Tribune* — PO Box 419000, Melbourne (32941); W; 39,518fr (Est); $15.95; C; publisher Michael Coleman; managing editor Harry McNamara; tel (407) 242-3801; fax (407) 242-0760

Coral Springs/Broward: *Coral Springs/Parkland Forum* — 9660 W. Sample Rd., Ste. 203, Coral Springs (33065); Th; 71pd, 28,499fr (VAC); $24.75; C; publisher Suzanne Pemper; editor Bill Lovell; managing editor Van A Gosselin; tel (954) 752-7474; fax (954) 752-7855

Crescent City/Georgetown: *Putnam County Courier-Journal* — 330 N. Summit St., Crescent City (32112); W; 2,350pd, 7,600fr (Est); $5.25; publisher William T Laurie; general manager & editor Howard Phillips; tel (904) 698-1644; fax (904) 698-1994

Crestview: *North Okaloosa Bulletin* — 301 N. Main St.; PO Box 447 (32536); W; 17pd, 13,650fr (CPVS); $4.60; publisher & managing editor James J Knudsen; editor Linn McGee; tel (904) 682-6524; fax (904) 682-2246

Cross City: *Dixie County Advocate* — Cedar St.; PO Box 5030 (32628); Th; 1,840pd, 54fr (Est); 85¢; publisher & editor Skipper Jones; managing editor Sue Chewning; tel (904) 498-3312; fax (904) 498-0420

Cutler Co.: *Cutler Courier* — 10700 Caribbean Blvd., 201, Miami (33189); F; 25,000fr (Sw); $16.00; publisher Ann Healy; publisher & managing editor James D Healy; general manager Marilee Davis; editor Scott Turick; tel (305) 253-4339; fax (305) 253-7179

Deerfield Beach/Lighthouse: *Deerfield Beach-Lighthouse Point Observer* — 43 N.E. 2nd St., Deerfield Beach (33441); Th; 30,000fr (Est); $7.00; publisher J David Eller; editor Judith V Wilson; tel (954) 428-9045; fax (954) 428-9096

Deerfield Beach: *Deerfield Times* — 601 Fairway Dr.; PO Box 1189 (33441); Th; 7pd, 15,541fr (VAC); $12.75; publisher Scott Patterson; editor Kevin Brady; managing editor Richard Haydan; tel (954) 698-6397; fax (954) 429-1207

DeLand/Orange City/DeBary: *The DeLand Beacon/West Volusia Beacon* — 141 E. Indiana Ave.; PO Box 753, DeLand (32721-0753); W; 4,200pd, 500fr (Est); $6.00; publisher Mustard Seed Publishing Co. Inc.; general manager Joann Kramer; editor Barb Shepherd; managing editor Eileen Burns Everett; tel (904) 734-4622; fax (904) 734-4641

Delray Beach: *The Delray Beach Times* — 601 Fairway Dr.; PO Box 1189, Deerfield Beach (33441); M/Th; 5pd, 14,986fr (VAC); $12.75; publisher Scott Patterson; editor Kevin Brady; managing editor Richard Haydan; tel (954) 698-6397; fax (954) 429-1207

Destin/Okaloosa Co./Walton Co.: *The Destin/Walton Log* — 1225 Airport Rd.; PO Box 957, Destin (32540); W/Sa; 8,200pd, 150fr (Est); $8.82; publisher Michael A Levi; editor Bill Runge; tel (904) 837-2828; fax (904) 654-5982

E Pasco: *Pasco News* — 13032 S. Hwy. 301; PO Box 187, Dade City (33525); Th; 4,200pd, 36,000fr (Sw); 24¢; C; publisher J W Owens; editor June Hamory; tel (904) 567-5639; fax (904) 567-5640

Eustis: *Eustis News* — 4645 Hwy. 19A, Mount Dora (32757); Th; 6,000pd (Est); 23¢; publisher Mike Tabor; general manager Marianne Witt; editor C J Woodring; tel (904) 357-3199; fax (904) 357-3202

Everglades City: *Everglades Echo* — 2301 CR 951, Ste. C, Naples (33999); Tu; 684pd, 100fr (Sw); $4.00; C; publishers Roy Tuff & Russell Tuff; general manager Maria Tuff; editor Kaydee Tuff; tel (813) 353-0444; fax (813) 353-9040

Florida Keys/Monroe Co.: *Florida Keys Keynoter* — 3015 Overseas Hwy.; PO Box 500158, Marathon (33050); W; 8,482pd, 340fr (Est); $11.95; Sa; 9,542pd, 340fr (Est); $11.95; C; publisher Tom Schumaker; editor Tom Tuell; tel (305) 743-5551; fax (305) 743-9586

Fort Lauderdale: *Eastsider* — 601 Fairway Dr.; PO Box 1189, Deerfield Beach (33441); W; 5pd, 26,337fr (VAC); $18.45; publisher Scott Patterson; editors Kevin Brady & Steven Reiskind; managing editor Richard Haydan; tel (954) 698-6397; fax (954) 429-1207

Fort Meade: *The Fort Meade Leader* — 25 W. Broadway; PO Box 893, Ft. Meade (33841); Tu/F; 1,187pd, 69fr (Sw); $4.85; C; publisher & editor S L Frisbie IV; tel (941) 285-8625; fax (941) 285-7634

Fort Myers Beach: *Fort Myers Beach Bulletin* — 19260 San Carlos Blvd.; PO Box 2867, Fort Myers Beach (33932); F; 14,000fr (Est); $7.10; C; publisher & managing editor Michael Pistella; general manager Joel Jenkins; editor June Preston; tel (941) 463-4421; fax (941) 463-1402

Fort Myers/Fort Myers Beach: *Fort Myers Beach Observer* — 15501 McGregor Blvd.; PO Box 08730, Fort Myers (33908); W; 13,500fr (Est); $8.20; C; publisher Harold Pappas; general manager Wendy Murray; editor Dawn Grodsky; tel (941) 482-7111; fax (941) 482-6365

Fort Myers/Fort Myers Beach: *Fort Myers Observer* — 15501 McGregor Blvd.; PO Box 08730, Fort Myers (33908); W; 16,000fr (Est); $7.90; C; publisher Harold Pappas; general manager Wendy Murray; editor Dawn Grodsky; tel (941) 482-7111; fax (941) 482-6365

Franklin Co.: *The Apalachicola Times* — 265 N. Water St.; PO Box 820, Apalachicola (32320); Th; 1,149pd, 40fr (Est); $4.00; C; publisher Robert Lindsay; general manager & editor John F Lee; tel (904) 653-8868; fax (904) 653-8036

Frostproof: *The Frostproof News* — PO Box 67 (33843); Th; 1,383pd, 65fr (Est); $5.46; C; publisher Richard Hitt; general manager Sonny H Stalls; editor Amy Stealey; tel (813) 635-2171; fax (813) 635-4265

Gainesville: *The Record/The Farm d'Ranch* — PO Box 806 (32602); Th; 5,000pd (Est); $9.68; publisher Constance D Rowe; general manager J B Rowe III; editor Dick Canaday; tel (904) 377-2444; fax (904) 338-1986

Gasden Co.: *Havana Herald* — 103 W. 7th Ave., Havana (32333); Th; 2,200pd, 25fr (Est); $3.01; publisher & editor John N Bert; managing editor Billy Blackman; tel (904) 539-6586; fax (904) 539-0454

Golden Gate: *Golden Gate Gazette* — 2301 CR 951, Ste. C, Naples (33999); Tu; 4,500pd (Est); $9.00; C; publishers Roy Tuff & Russell Tuff; general manager Maria Tuff; editor Kaydee Tuff; tel (813) 353-0444; fax (813) 353-9040

Graceville: *The Graceville News* — 1004 10th Ave.; PO Box 187 (32440); Th; 1,700pd, 10fr (Sw); $3.36; publisher John Ferrin Cox; editor Sharon Taylor; tel (904) 263-6015

Greater Orlando: *The Weekly* — 807 S. Orlando Ave., Ste. R, Winter Park (32789); Th; 50,000fr (Est); $45.00; C; publisher Ron Williams; general manager George Biggers; editor Jeff Truesdell; tel (407) 645-5888; fax (407) 645-2547

Greater Seminole: *Seminole Beacon* — 10621 117th Dr. N., Largo (34643); Th; 37,200fr (Est); $6.69; publisher Linda Dominick; editor Gretchen Cain; tel (813) 397-5563; fax (813) 397-5900

Green Cove Springs: *Clay County Crescent* — 1564 Kingsley Ave., Orange Park (32067); Th; 3,300pd, 150fr (Est); 55¢; C; publisher Joyce Lydon; editor Sandy Mulvihill; tel (904) 264-3200; fax (904) 269-6958

Gulf Breeze/Pensacola: *The Gulf Breeze Sentinel* — 1200 Gulf Breeze Pkwy.; PO Box 967, Gulf Breeze (32561); Th; 2,694pd, 164fr (Sw); $12.00; C; publisher & editor Marlin M Osborn; tel (904) 934-1200; fax (904) 932-8765

Hallandale: *Hallandale Digest* — 224 S. Dixie Hwy.; PO Box 1310 (33009); Th; 41,000fr (Est); $11.50; publisher & editor Peter Bluesten; general manager Dan Bluesten; managing editor Larry Bluesten; tel (954) 457-8029; fax (954) 457-1284

Hamilton Co.: *The Jasper News* — 102 N.E. 2nd Ave.; PO Drawer D, Jasper (32052); Th; 2,082pd, 30fr (Est); $5.25; C; publisher Michael F Coulter; general manager Wycliff Wynn; editor Gail Newsome; tel (904) 792-2487; fax (904) 792-3009

Hardee Co.: *The Herald-Advocate* — 115 S. 7th Ave.; PO Box 338, Wauchula (33873); Th; 5,536pd, 53fr (Sw); $3.90; publisher & editor Jim Kelly; managing editor Cynthia Krahl; tel (813) 773-3255

Hernando Co.: *Hernando Today* — 15299 Cortez Blvd., Brooksville (34613); W; 10,945pd, 19,861fr (CPVS); $16.00; F; 10,575pd, 1,136fr (CPVS); $6.76; Sa; 10,945pd, 19,861fr (CPVS); $9.73; C; publisher Duane L Chichester; editor Robert Nolte; tel (904) 544-5280; fax (904) 799-3688

High Springs/Alachua/Newberry: *The High Springs Herald* — 5 N.W. 1st St.; PO Box 745, High Springs (32643); Th; 3,327pd, 62fr (Sw); $7.00; publisher Ed Barber; general manager Carol Chidlow; editor Bo Turner; tel (904) 454-1297; fax (904) 454-4559

Highland City: *Highlands Press* — PO Box 963 (33846); W; 2,350pd, 150fr (Sw); $4.50; C; publisher & editor William M Histed; tel (813) 425-3411

Holmes Co.: *Holmes County Times* — 105 E. Virginia Ave.; PO Box 67, Bonifay (32425); W; 2,404pd, 12fr (Sw); $4.00; C; publisher & editor Maurice Pujol Jr; tel (904) 547-9414; fax (904) 638-4601

Homestead/S Dade: *South Dade News Leader* — 15 N.E. 1st Rd.; PO Box 900340, Homestead (33090); M/W; 10,609pd (Est); $16.90; F; 10,609pd (Sw); $16.90; C; publisher Glenn A Martin; managing editor Yolanda Ulrich; tel (305) 245-2311; fax (305) 248-0596

Immokalee/La Belle: *Immokalee Bulletin* — 22 Fort Thompson Ave.; PO Box 518, La Belle (33935); W; 29pd, 3,500fr (Est); $3.45; publisher Sonny H Stalls; editor Patty Brant; tel (941) 657-6000; fax (941) 675-1445

Indian River Co.: *Sebastian Sun* — 1617 14th Ave., Vero Beach (32960); F; 500fr (Est); $5.50; C; publisher Mark Schumann; editor Nic Powell; tel (407) 589-4566; fax (407) 589-3431

Indian River Co.: *Vero Beach Sun* — 1617 14th Ave., Vero Beach (32960); Th; 19,595fr (Sw); $9.00; C; publisher Mark Schumann; editor Nic Powell; tel (407) 589-4566; fax (407) 589-3431

Jacksonville: *The Jacksonville Advocate* — 6172 Pettiford Dr. W. (32209); M; 28,620pd (Sw); $15.50; publisher & editor Isiah J Williams III; general manager Emily Timmons; tel (904) 764-4740; fax (904) 766-5542

Jacksonville Beach: *The Beaches Leader* — 1114 Beach Blvd.; PO Box 50129, Jacksonville Beach (32250); W/F; 12,146pd, 54fr (Sw); $12.20; C; publisher Thomas H Wood; editor Kathleen Bailey; tel (904) 249-9033

Jefferson Co./Monticello: *Jefferson County Press* — 209 N. Cherry St.; PO Box 979, Monticello (32345-0979); Th; 100fr (Sw); $2.00; C; publisher & editor Dorothy L Miller; tel (904) 997-2560; fax (912) 498-1420

Jupiter/Tequesta: *The Jupiter Courier* — 800 W. Indiantown; PO Box 1486, Jupiter (33458); W/Su; 7,739pd, 410fr (Est); $11.67; C; publisher E W Scripps Co.; general manager Charles E Scripps Jr; managing editor Kevin Henistock; tel (407) 746-5111; fax (407) 743-0673

Key Biscayne: *The Islander News* — 104 Crandon Blvd., Ste. 301 (33149); Th; 2,599pd, 744fr (Sw); $21.00; publisher & editor Nancye Ray; general manager Gloria Chapman; tel (305) 361-3333; fax (305) 361-5051

Keystone Hts.: *Lake Region Monitor* — 135 Call St.; PO Drawer A, Starke (32091); Th; 2,100pd (Est); 16¢; publisher John Miller; editor Lesley Peters; tel (904) 473-2210; fax (904) 964-8628

La Belle: *Caloosa Belle* — 22 Fort Thompson Ave.; PO Box 518 (33935); W; 6,800fr (Est); $4.00; publisher Sonny H Stalls; editor Patty Brant; tel (941) 657-6000; fax (941) 675-1445

Lady Lake/Belleview/Wildwood/Fruitland Park: *The Tri-County Sun* — 1200 Avda. Central, Lady Lake (32159); F; 24,000fr (Sw); $8.00; C; publisher Hank Crockett; editor Ad Carpenter; tel (904) 753-1119; fax (904) 753-2380

Lake Panasoffkee/Sumter: *The Sumter Journal* — Hwy. 470; PO Box 546, Lake Panasoffkee (33538); Th; 2,000pd (Est); $1.80; publisher Ed Lasky; general manager Shirley Lasky; editor Jim Burris; tel (904) 793-6222; fax (904) 793-5530

Lake Placid: *Lake Placid Journal* — 232 N. Main St.; PO Box 696 (33852); Th; 4,890pd (Est); 40¢; publisher Mathew Delaney; general manager Monte Delaney; editor Constance Delaney; tel (941) 465-2522; fax (941) 699-0331

Lake Wales: *Lake Wales News* — 140 E. Stuart Ave. (33853-4198); Th; 2,662pd, 214fr (Sw); 25¢; publisher & editor Owen B Brice; tel (813) 676-3467

Lake Worth: *Lake Worth Herald and Coastal Observer* — 130 S. H St.; PO Box 191 (33460); Th; 1,108pd, 38,000fr (Sw); $10.45; C; publisher Karl J Easton Jr; editor Jay Kravetz; tel (407) 585-9387; fax (407) 585-5434

Lehigh Acres: *Lehigh Acres News-Star* — 1250 Business Way; PO Box 908 (33970-0908); W; 8,140pd, 6,988fr (Est); $6.00; publisher Patricia Derneau; editor Tom Wason; tel (941) 369-2191; fax (941) 369-1396

Leon: *Tallahassean* — 1230 N. Adams St., Tallahassee (32303); F; 13,375pd, 1,439fr (Sw); $9.60; publisher Sylvia Jordan; editor Cathie Pope-Johnson; managing editor Karen Groves; tel (904) 224-3805; fax (904) 561-6651

Live Oak: *Suwannee Democrat* — 123 W. Conner St.; PO Box 370 (32060); W/Sa; 4,800pd, 28fr (Est); 35¢; C; publisher Michael F Coulter; general manager Wycliff Wynn; managing editor Garry Ferrell; tel (904) 362-1734; fax (904) 362-7281

Longboat Key: *Longboat Observer, Inc.* — 5570 Gulf of Mexico Dr.; PO Box 8100 (34228); Th; 1,500pd, 18,500fr (Est); $9.00; publisher & editor Matthew G Walsh; tel (813) 383-5509; fax (813) 383-7193

MacClenny: *The Baker County Press* — 104 5th St. S.; PO Box 598 (32063); Th; 5,400pd, 25fr (Est); 35¢; C; publisher & editor James C McGauley; tel (904) 259-2400; fax (904) 259-6502

Madison Co.: *Madison County Carrier* — Hwy. 53 S.; PO Drawer 772, Madison (32341); W; 4,500pd (Sw); $5.00; C; publisher Tommy Greene; general manager Emerald Kinsley; editor Harvey Greene; tel (904) 973-4141; fax (904) 973-4121

Madison Co.: *Madison County Press* — 305 Range St.; PO Box 299, Madison (32340-0299); Th; 150pd, 150fr (Sw); $2.00; C; publisher & editor Dorothy L Miller; tel (904) 973-6397; fax (912) 498-1420

Madison Co.: *Madison Enterprise-Recorder* — 111 S.E. Shelby St.; PO Box 772, Madison (32340); F; 2,000pd, 125fr (Sw); $4.00; C; publisher Tommy Greene; general manager Emerald Kinsley; editor Harvey Greene; tel (904) 973-6361; fax (904) 973-6494

Mandarin/NW St. Johns Co.: *Mandarin News & St. Johns River Pilot* — 11148-4 San Jose Blvd.; PO Box 24541, Mandarin (32223); Th; 6,000pd (Est); $8.76; C; publisher Tom Wood; editor Linda Gilbertson; managing editor Kathleen Feindt Bailey; tel (904) 262-5076

Marathon/Big Pine: *The Keys Advertiser* — 9709 Overseas Hwy., Marathon (33050-3342); W; 9,000fr (Est); $6.25; C; publisher Winston A Burrell; general manager Kathleen Bryan; tel (305) 743-8766; fax (305) 743-9977

Marco Island/Naples: *Marco Island Eagle* — 579 Elkcam Cir.; PO Box 579, Marco Island (33969); W; 10,743pd, 344fr (ABC); $10.50; publisher Cheryl Ferrara; editor Ron Delhomme; managing editor Fran Stahl; tel (813) 394-7592; fax (813) 394-8552

Margate/Coconut Creek: *Margate/Coconut Creek Forum* — 9660 W. Sample Rd., Ste. 203, Coral Springs (33065); Th; 7pd, 21,017fr (VAC); $19.40; C; publisher Suzanne Pemper; editor Bill Lovell; managing editor Van A Gosselin; tel (954) 752-7474; fax (954) 752-7855

Mayo: *The Mayo Free Press* — PO Box 248 (32066); Th; 1,500pd, 50fr (Est); $2.00; publisher Shirley Hatch; general manager Martha Taylor; editor Bonnie Adams; tel (904) 294-1210; fax (904) 294-2666

Miami: *Community Newspapers* — 6796 S.W. 62nd Ave.; PO Box 1970, South Miami (33143); M/W/Th/F; 782pd, 260fr (Sw); $31.00; publisher Grant Miller; editor Michael Miller; managing editor David Berkowitz; tel (305) 665-8214; fax (305) 661-0954

Miami: *Kendall News Gazette* — 6796 S.W. 62nd Ave., South Miami (33143); M/Th; 16,500fr (Sw); $19.45; C; publisher Grant Miller; editor Michael Miller; tel (305) 669-7355; fax (305) 661-0954

Miami/Dade Co.: *Miami Today* — 710 Brickell Ave.; PO Box 1368, Miami (33101); Th; 489pd, 31,044fr (BPA); $112.00; publisher & editor Michael Lewis; tel (305) 358-2663

Millsborough Co.: *Community Connections* — 3210 E. 7th Ave., Tampa (33605); Th; 20,000fr (Est); $6.00; publisher Roland Manteiga; general manager Patrick Manteiga; managing editor Fritz Wandell; tel (813) 248-3921; fax (813) 247-5357

Milton/Santa Rosa: *Santa Rosa Press Gazette* — 531 S.W. Elva St., Milton (32570); M/Th; 5,785pd, 67fr (Sw); $9.65; C; publisher Jimmie D Hill; editor Jim Fletcher; tel (904) 623-2120; fax (904) 623-2007

Monticello: *Monticello News* — 100 W. Dogwood St.; PO Box 428 (32344); W/F; 2,669pd, 30fr (Est); $4.98; publisher Ron Cichon; general manager Shirley Rudd; editor Lazaro Aleman; tel (904) 997-3568; fax (904) 997-3774

Moore Haven: *Glades County Democrat* — 626 W. Sugarland Hwy.; PO Box 1236, Clewiston (33440); Th; 933pd, 56fr (Est); $5.37; C; publisher Richard Hitt; general manager Kelly Milicezic; editor Anne Deuschle; tel (941) 946-0511; fax (941) 983-7537

Mount Dora: *The Mount Dora Topic* — 4645 Hwy. 19A (32757); Th; 3,087pd, 220fr (Est); $2.28; publisher Mike Tabor; general manager Marianne Witt; editor C J Woodring; tel (904) 357-3199; fax (904) 357-3202

Mulberry/Bradley/Lakeland: *Mulberry Press* — 1020 N. Church Ave., Hwy. 37-N, Mulberry (33860-2040); W; 2,975pd, 15fr (Sw); $4.50; C; publisher & editor William M Histed; tel (813) 425-3411; fax (813) 425-3411

New Port Richey: *West Pasco Press* — 6214 US Hwy. 19 (34652); W; 1,291pd, 44fr (Est); 22¢; publisher Rich Litowchak; editor W E Matner Jr; tel (813) 849-7500; fax (813) 847-2902

Niceville: *The Bay Beacon* — 203 W. John Sims Pkwy., Ste. 2 (32578); W; 100pd, 12,256fr (Sw); $6.35; publisher & editor Stephen W Kent; tel (904) 678-1080; fax (904) 729-3225

NE Florida: *The Northeast Florida Advocate* — 6172 Pettiford Dr. W., Jacksonville (32209-1842); Th; 35,236fr (Est); $25.00; publisher & editor Isiah J Williams III; general manager Emily Timmons; tel (904) 765-8982; fax (904) 766-5542

Orlando/W Orange: *The West Orange Times* — 720 S. Dillard St. (34787); PO Box 770309, Winter Garden (34777-0309); Th; 7,575pd, 250fr (Sw); $6.50; publisher Andrew C Bailey; editor Mary Anne Swickerath; tel (407) 656-2121; fax (407) 656-6075

Osceola Co./Kissimmee/St. Cloud: *Osceola News-Gazette* — 108 Church St. (34741); PO Box 422068, Kissimmee (34742); Th/Sa; 1,120pd, 27,130fr (Sw); $7.65; C; publisher Dan L Autrey; editor Bill Orben; managing editor Tom Germond; tel (407) 846-7600; fax (407) 846-8516

Oviedo/Winter Springs: *The Oviedo Voice* — 169 W. Broadway, Oviedo (32765); Th; 2,010pd, 800fr (Sw); $6.00; publisher James R Noles Sr; general manager Stephen M Combs; editor Darrell Johnson; tel (407) 366-9181; fax (407) 366-7580

Pensacola: *Escambia Sun Press* — 3610 Barrancas Ave. (32507); Th; 3,500pd (Est); $2.14; publisher Michael J Driver; general manager Kathie Wall; managing editor Denise Messer; tel (904) 456-3121; fax (904) 456-0103

Perry: *Perry News-Herald* — 123 S. Jefferson; PO Box 888 (32347); F; 4,101pd, 250fr (Sw); $5.00; publisher Donald D Lincoln; general manager & managing editor Susan H Lincoln; editor Aaron Portwood; tel (904) 584-5513; fax (904) 838-1566

Perry: *Taco Times* — PO Box 888 (32347); W; 5,050pd (Est); $5.00; publisher Donald D Lincoln; general manager & managing editor Susan H Lincoln; editor Aaron Portwood; tel (904) 584-5513; fax (904) 838-1566

Pinellas: *The Suncoast News* — 6214 US Hwy. 19, New Port Richey (34652); W; 89pd, 151,000fr (Sw); $52.45; Sa; 89pd, 134,000fr (Sw); $52.45; C; publisher & editor Gwen Stevenson; general manager Richard A Litowchak; tel (813) 849-7500; fax (813) 847-2902

Pinellas Co.: *Pinellas News* — 533 4th St. N.; PO Box 1507, St. Petersburg (33731-1507); F; 2,289pd, 614fr (Sw); $8.00; C; publisher & editor Robert Potter; tel (813) 894-2411; fax (813) 894-2522

Plant City: *Plant City Courier* — 102 S. Evers St. (33566-5455); Th; 3,926pd (Est); $8.22; C; general manager Carla Rockwell; editor Bob McClure; tel (813) 752-3113; fax (813) 754-3725

Polk City/Lakeland/Auburndale: *Polk City Press* — PO Box 444, Polk City (33868); W; 2,200pd, 100fr (Sw); $5.50; C; publisher & editor William M Histed; tel (813) 956-4033

Pompano Beach: *The Pompano Ledger* — 660 S. Federal Hwy. (33062); Th; 23,000pd (Sw); $12.95; publisher Karen M Foley; editor Edward J Foley; managing editor Elaine Pasmore; tel (954) 946-7277

Ponte Vedra: *Ponte Vedra Recorder* — PO Box 501 (32004); F; 5,000pd, 6,000fr (Sw); $13.50; publisher Timothy Bradford; editor Grace Hayes; tel (904) 285-2915; fax (904) 249-6555

Port St. Joe: *The Star* — 306 William Ave.; PO Box 308 (32456); Th; 2,506pd, 25fr (Est); 12¢; publisher & editor Wesley R Ramsey; tel (904) 227-1278

Quincy: *Gadsden County Times* — 15 S. Madison St.; PO Box 790 (32351); Th; 3,286pd, 1,958fr (Sw); $5.88; C; publisher Frederick C Drew; editor Alice Dupont-Smith; tel (904) 627-7649; fax (904) 627-7191

Ruskin/Riverview/Gibsonton/Summerfield: *East Bay Breeze* — 1507 Sun City Center Plz., Sun City Center (33570-5300); W; 15,200fr (Sw); $7.43; general manager Carla Rockwell; editor Penny Fletcher; managing editor Lee Landenberger; tel (813) 634-3007; fax (813) 634-8420

Sanibel/Captiva: *Island Reporter* — 2340 Periwinkle Way; PO Box 809, Sanibel (33957); F; 8,500pd, 563fr (Est); $7.75; C; publisher Gulfcoast Weeklies; editor Ralf Kircher; tel (941) 472-1587; fax (941) 472-8398

Sanibel/Captiva: *The Sanibel-Captiva Islander* — 2407 Periwinkle Way; PO Box 56, Sanibel Island (33957); Tu; 4,021pd, 643fr (Sw); $6.15; C; publisher Joel Jenkins; general manager Harry Pappas; editor Louis Rom; tel (813) 472-5185; fax (813) 472-5302

Sebring: *The News-Sun* — 2227 U.S. 27 S. (33870); W; 19,212pd, 657fr (ABC); $6.75; Su; 18,643pd, 336fr (ABC); $6.75; publisher Judy D Robinette; editor David Brown; tel (941) 385-6155

S Brevard Co.: *Barefoot Bay Sun* — 1617 14th Ave., Vero Beach (32960); F; 4,600fr (Sw); $5.50; C; publisher Mark Schumann; editor Nic Powell; tel (407) 589-4566; fax (407) 589-3431

Starke: *Bradford County Telegraph* — 135 W. Call St.; PO Drawer A (32091); Th; 5,400pd (Est); 32¢; publisher John Miller; editor Marcia Goodge; tel (904) 964-6305; fax (904) 964-8628

Sumter Co.: *Sumter County Times* — 204 E. McCollum Ave., Bushnell (33513); Th; 5,000pd (Est); $4.75; publisher Gerard Mulligan; editor Bob Reichman; tel (904) 793-2161; fax (904) 793-1486

Sun City Center/Hillsborough: *The Sun* — 1507 Sun City Center Plz., Sun City Center (33570-5300); W; 205pd, 11,500fr (Sw); $9.85; C; publisher Carla Rockwell; editor Penny Fletcher; managing editor Lee Landenberger; tel (813) 634-9258; fax (813) 634-8420

Sunrise: *Sunrise Times* — 601 Fairway Dr.; PO Box 1189, Deerfield Beach (33441); F; 14pd, 47,833fr (VAC); $15.35; publisher Scott Patterson; editor Bill Lovell; managing editor Richard Haydan; tel (954) 698-6501; fax (954) 698-6719

Tallahassee: *Tallahassee Advertiser* — 1209 Commercial Park Dr.; PO Box 3696 (32315-3696); Th; 6,450pd, 126fr (Est); $9.00; C; publisher & editor John V Whitman Jr; tel (904) 385-3547; fax (904) 385-6177

Tamarac/N Lauderdale Forum: *Tamarac/North Lauderdale Forum* — 601 Fairway Dr.; PO Box 1189, Deerfield Beach (33441); F; 14pd, 39,615fr (VAC); $21.25; C; publisher Suzanne Pemper; editor Bill Lovell; managing editor Van A Gosselin; tel (954) 698-6501; fax (954) 698-6719

Tampa: *The Free Press* — 1010 W. Cass St. (33606); publisher Janet Harrison; general manager & managing editor John Harrison; editor Betty Stewart; tel (813) 254-5888; fax (813) 251-0511

Tampa: *Town 'n Country News* — 7512 Paula Dr., Ste. 105-B (33615); W; 22,800fr (Sw); $9.89; general manager Carla Rockwell; editor Rebecca Pividal; managing editor Lee Landenberger; tel (813) 249-0725; fax (813) 249-0825

Temple Terrace: *Temple Terrace News* — 1401 Oakfield Dr., Brandon (33511-4854); W; 24,000fr (Sw); $9.75; general manager Carla Rockwell; editor Shirley Adema; managing editor Lee Landenberger; tel (813) 689-7764; fax (813) 689-9545

Titusville: *Star-Advocate* — PO Box 41900, Melbourne (32941); W; 9,100pd, 19,414fr (Est); $6.50; publisher Michael Coleman; managing editor Harry McNamara; tel (407) 242-3801; fax (407) 242-0760

Trenton: *Gilchrist County Journal* — PO Box 127 (32693); Th; 3,430pd (Est); 7¢; publisher & editor J Min Ayers; tel (904) 463-7135; fax (904) 463-7393

Union Co.: *Union County Times* — 135 W. Call St.; PO Drawer A, Starke (32091); Th; 2,150pd (Est); $3.60; C; publisher & managing editor John Miller; editor Linda Griffis; tel (904) 964-6305; fax (904) 964-8628

Upper Florida Keys: *The Reporter* — 91655 Overseas Hwy.; PO Box 1197, Tavernier (33070); Th; 7,900pd (Est); $1.78; publisher Dagny Wolff; editor James C Rubino; tel (305) 852-3216; fax (305) 852-8249

Venice/N Port/Englewood: *The Venice Gondolier* — 200 E. Venice Ave., Venice (34285); W; 9,870pd, 15,500fr (Sw); $12.75; Sa; 10,595pd, 15,500fr (Sw); $12.75; C; publisher Bob Vedder; editor John Edmondson II; tel (813) 484-2611; fax (813) 485-3036

Wakulla Co.: *The Wakulla News* — Hwy. 319; PO Box 307, Crawfordville (32326); Th; 4,500pd, 30fr (Sw); $4.85; publisher Wakulla Publishing Co.; general manager William Phillips; editor Stacie M Phillips; managing editor Shannon Tumbull; tel (904) 926-7102; fax (904) 926-3815

Wellington/Royal Palm Beach: *Wellington/Royal Palm Beach Forum* — 11320 Fortune Cir., Ste. G-32, Wellington (33414); W; 21,695fr (VAC); $16.15; C; publisher Barbara Turner; editor J B Thompson; tel (407) 791-7790; fax (407) 791-7593

Wellington/Royal Palm Beach/Loxahatchee: *The Town Crier* — 12794 W. Forest Hill Blvd., Ste. 14, Wellington (33414); W; 20,000fr (Est); $13.00; C; publisher & editor Bob Markey Jr; managing editor Jean Firpo; tel (407) 793-7606; fax (407) 793-6090

Williston: *Williston Sun-Suwanee Valley News* — PO Drawer Q (32696); Th; 2,380pd, 55fr (Sw); $2.00; publisher Bess E Williams; editor Nick Williams; tel (904) 528-6397

Winter Park/Maitland: *Winter Park-Maitland Observer* — 609 Executive Dr. (32789); PO Box 2426, Winter Park (32790); Th; 10,000pd (Est); $10.00; C; publisher Gerhard J W Munster; editor Carole Arthurs; tel (407) 628-8500

Zephyrhills/E Pasco Co.: *Zephyrhills News* — 38333 5th Ave. (33541); PO Box 638, Zephyrhills (33539); Th; 3,568pd, 215fr (Sw); $8.85; C; publisher Janet Gillis; tel (813) 782-1558; fax (813) 788-7987

GEORGIA

Adairsville/Kingston: *The North Bartow News* — PO Box 374, Adairsville (30103); W; 293pd, 5,447fr (Sw); $2.75; C; publisher Charles E Hurley; editor Shelia Mullinax; tel (770) 773-3754; fax (770) 773-3754

Adel: *Adel News-Tribune* — 109 Anderson; PO Box 1060, Fort Valley (31030); W; 3,140pd, 204fr (Sw); $3.80; C; publisher Robert E Tribble; general manager Chuck Morley; editor Cindy Morley; tel (912) 825-2432; fax (912) 825-4130

Alma: *Alma Times-Statesman* — 402 12th St.; PO Box 428 (31510); Th; 3,270pd, 60fr (Sw); $3.20; C; publisher & editor Helen Gardner & Max Gardner; tel (912) 632-7201; fax (912) 632-4156

Alpharetta/Roswell: *The Alpharetta-Roswell Neighbor* — PO Box 449, Marietta (30061); W; 119pd, 37,250fr (Sw); $22.25; C; publisher Otis A Brumby Jr; editor Peggie Reeves; tel (770) 428-9411; fax (770) 428-7945

Alpharetta/Roswell: *The Revue* — 319 N. Main St., Alpharetta (30201); F; 24,000fr (Est); $15.00; publisher Ray Appen; editor Hatcher Hurd; tel (770) 442-3278; fax (770) 475-1216

Ashburn/Sycamore/Rebecca/Turner Co.: *Wiregrass Farmer* — 109 Gordon St.; PO Box 309, Ashburn (31714); W; 2,800pd, 30fr (Sw); $3.85; publisher & editor Ben Baker; tel (912) 567-3655; fax (912) 567-4402

Athens/Clark Cos.: *The Athens Observer* — 288 N. Lumpkin; PO Box 112, Athens (30613); Th; 8,435pd (Est); 63¢; C; publisher O L McBroom; general manager Jesse Jenkins; tel (706) 353-9300; fax (706) 353-1008

II-14 **Georgia** *U.S. Weeklies*

Atkinson Co.: *Atkinson County Citizen* — 520 Austin Ave.; PO Box 398, Pearson (31642); Th; 1,200pd (Sw); $2.00; publisher & editor Patsy W Kirkland; tel (912) 422-3824; fax (912) 422-6050

Augusta/Hephzibah/Martinez/Evans/Grovetown/Harlem/Appling: *Columbia News Times* — PO Box 204178, Martinez (30917-4178); W; 15,500pd (Sw); $5.95; F; 15,500pd (Est); $5.95; C; publisher Phillip Blanchard; general manager & editor Karl N Haywood; tel (706) 863-6165; fax (706) 863-9080

Bainbridge: *The Post-Searchlight* — 301 N. Crawford St.; PO Box 277 (31717); W/Sa; 6,021pd, 284fr (Sw); $4.52; publisher S M Griffin Jr; general manager Scott Forsyth; managing editor Teresa Brown; tel (912) 246-2827, (800) 521-5232; fax (912) 246-7665

Barnesville: *Barnesville Herald-Gazette* — 509 Greenwood St.; PO Box 220 (30204); Tu; 5,000pd, 20fr (Sw); $3.60; publisher & editor Walter B Geiger Jr; tel (770) 358-0754; fax (770) 358-0756

Barrow Co.: *The Winder News* — 189 W. Athens St.; PO Drawer C, Winder (30680); W; 6,858pd, 9fr (CAC); $7.90; publisher Debbie Burgamy; editor LeAnne Bell; tel (770) 867-7557; fax (770) 867-1034

Bartow Co.: *Bartow Neighbor* — 16 Wall St., Carterville (30120); W; 17,300fr (Est); $123.10; publisher Otis A Brumby Jr; editor Masie Underwood; tel (770) 386-0872; fax (770) 422-9533

Baxley/Alma: *The Baxley News-Banner* — 300 Parker St.; PO Box 409, Baxley (31513); W; 4,027pd, 80fr (Sw); $4.40; publisher & editor Helen Gardner & Max Gardner; tel (912) 367-2468; fax (912) 367-0277

Blackshear/Patterson: *The Blackshear Times* — 638 Gordon St.; PO Box 410, Blackshear (31516); W; 3,070pd, 40fr (Sw); $3.50; publisher & editor Robert M Williams Jr; general manager Cheryl Williams; tel (912) 449-6693; fax (912) 449-1719

Blairsville: *North Georgia News* — 259 Cleveland St. (30512); PO Box 2029 (30514); W; 5,148pd, 17fr (Est); 15¢; publisher Wanda R West; general manager & managing editor Donna Corn; editor Kenneth West; tel (706) 745-6343; fax (706) 745-1830

Blakely/Early Co.: *Early County News* — 115 College St.; PO Box 748, Blakely (31723); Th; 3,651pd, 99fr (Sw); 28¢; publisher William W Fleming; general manager Judy Fleming; editor Kathy Pando; tel (912) 723-4376; fax (912) 723-6097

Blue Ridge/Fannin Co.: *The News Observer* — APD 515 Appalachian Pl.; PO Box 989, Blue Ridge (30513); W; 8,000pd, 1,500fr (Sw); $7.35; publisher & editor J Glenn Harbison; tel (706) 632-2019; fax (706) 632-2577

Boston: *Georgia South* — 101 N. Main St.; PO Box 69 (31626); Th; 1,300pd, 4,700fr (Sw); $7.00; C; publisher & editor Dorothy L Miller; tel (912) 498-6397; fax (912) 498-1420

Bowdon: *The Bowdon Bulletin* — 118 City Hall Ave. (30108); Th; 2,915pd, 70fr (Est); 70¢; publisher Dawn Weatherby; editor Denise Turner; managing editor Julianne Foster; tel (770) 258-2838, (770) 258-2146; fax (770) 258-9747

Brooks Co.: *Quitman Free Press* — 112 N. Lee St.; PO Box 72, Quitman (31643); W; 3,087pd, 60fr (Est); 18¢; publisher & editor Wendell Tidwell; general manager Ann Knight; tel (912) 263-4615; fax (912) 263-5282

Bryan Co.: *Richmond Hill-Bryan County News* — Ste. 140-C Ford Village; PO Box 1239, Richmond Hill (31324); W; 2,940pd, 10fr (Sw); $4.75; C; publisher Robert M Williams Jr; general manager & editor Vicky Whitehead; tel (912) 756-2668; fax (912) 756-5907

Buena Vista/Ellaville: *Patriot Citizen* — PO Box 108, Buena Vista (31803); Th; 1,250pd (Sw); $3.50; C; publisher Robert E Tribble; editor Ron Provencher; tel (708) 846-3188

Calhoun: *Calhoun Times and Gordon County News* — 215 W. Line St.; PO Box 8 (30701); W/Sa; 8,309pd, 175fr (Sw); $5.18; C; publisher B H Mooney III; general manager Ed Lewis; editor Mitch Talley; tel (706) 629-2231; fax (706) 625-0899

Camden Co./Nassau: *Camden County Tribune* — 707 Osborne St.; PO Box 470, St. Marys (31558); W; 5,920pd, 235fr (Sw); $4.85; C; publisher Linn Hudson; editor Allison Schaefers; tel (912) 882-4927; fax (912) 882-6519

Camilla/Pelham: *Camilla Enterprise* — 13 S. Scott; PO Box 365, Camilla (31730); W/F; 3,788pd, 33fr (Est); 18¢; publisher & editor Roger Ann Jones; tel (912) 336-5265; fax (912) 336-8476

Cartersville: *The Herald-Tribune* — 251 S. Tenn. St.; PO Box 70 (30120); Tu; 334pd (Sw); $5.00; C; publisher & editor Charles E Hurley; general manager Kevin Atwill; managing editor Kevin Atwill; tel (770) 382-4545; fax (770) 382-2711

Cedartown: *The Cedartown Standard* — 213 Main St.; PO Box 308 (30125); Tu/Th; 2,993pd, 8fr (Sw); $6.00; C; publisher B H Mooney III; editor James Penney; tel (770) 748-1520

Chamblee/Dunwood: *Dunwoody/Chamblee/Doraville-DeKalb Neighbor* — PO Box 449, Marietta (30060); W; 35pd, 22,950fr (Sw); $21.50; C; publisher Otis A Brumby Jr; editor Steve Rosenburg; tel (770) 428-9411; fax (770) 422-9533

Chatsworth: *Chatsworth Times* — N. 3rd Ave.; PO Box 130 (30705); W; 3,354pd (Est); 14¢; publisher & editor David Shelton; tel (706) 695-4646; fax (706) 695-7181

Chattooga Co./Summerville: *The Summerville News* — Rome Blvd.; PO Box 310, Summerville (30747); Th; 7,445pd, 60fr (Est); $19.64; publisher & editor Winston Eugene Espy; general manager David Espy; tel (706) 857-2494; fax (706) 857-2393

Cherokee Co.: *Cherokee Tribune* — PO Box 966, Canton (30114); W/Su; 7,187pd, 425fr (Sw); $10.50; C; publisher James L Hilliard; managing editor Rebecca Johnston; tel (770) 479-1441; fax (770) 479-3505

Clarke/Oconee/Madison: *Suburban Review* — PO Box 912, Athens (30603-0912); W; 30,000fr (Est); $12.05; C; editor Anisha Frizzell; tel (706) 549-0123; fax (706) 543-5234

Claxton/Hagar/Bellville: *Claxton Enterprise* — 14 S. Newton; PO Box 218, Claxton (30417); Th; 3,183pd, 350fr (Est); 22¢; publisher & editor Mitchell E Peace; general manager Pamela E Peace; tel (912) 739-2132; fax (912) 739-2140

Cleveland/Helen: *White County News* — 13 E. Jarrard St., Cleveland (30528); Th; 2,397pd, 183fr (Sw); $3.95; C; publisher Rhonda Wilcox; general manager John Solesbee; tel (706) 865-4718; fax (706) 865-3048

Cobb Co.: *Austell-Mableton-Powder Springs Neighbor* — PO Box 449, Marietta (30061); Th; 24pd, 21,800fr (Sw); $19.80; C; publisher Otis A Brumby Jr; editor Rodney Shumake; tel (770) 428-9411; fax (770) 428-7945

Cochran: *The Cochran Journal* — 104 Cherry St.; PO Drawer 232 (31014); W; 3,458pd, 42fr (Sw); $3.85; C; publisher Bob Tribble; general manager & managing editor Joe Whitfield; tel (912) 934-6303; fax (912) 934-6800

College Park: *The Atlanta News Leader* — 4006 Riverdale Ct. (30337); Th; 5,000pd, 5,000fr (Sw); $11.29; C; publisher Creed W Pannell Jr; general manager Teresa Morrison; editor Lee Haven; managing editor Serena McCoy; tel (404) 907-8949; fax (404) 907-1267

Commerce/Jackson: *The Commerce News* — PO Box 419, Commerce (30529); W; 3,481pd, 140fr (Est); $2.80; publisher Herman Buffington; general manager & editor Mark Beardsley; tel (706) 335-2927; fax (706) 335-4531

Cornelia: *The Northeast Georgian* — 119 Level Grove; PO Box 1555 (30531); Tu; 8,100pd, 50fr (Est); $4.50; publisher John D Solesbee; editor Steve Avery; tel (706) 778-2400; fax (706) 778-4114

Covington/Newtown Co.: *The Covington News* — 1166 Usher St., Covington (30209); Th/Sa; 6,097pd, 18fr (Sw); $7.35; C; publisher Ron Stokes; general manager Johnny Elmore; editor Ross Norton; tel (770) 787-6397; fax (770) 786-6451

Crawfordville: *The Advocate Democrat* — 107 N. Main St.; PO Box 149, Greensboro (30642-0149); Th; 800pd, 8fr (Est); $2.50; C; publisher & editor Carey Williams Jr; tel (706) 453-7988; fax (706) 453-2311

Cumming/Forsyth/Dawson: *Forsyth County News* — 121 Dahlonega St.; PO Box 210, Cumming (30128); W; 13,012pd, 95fr (CAC); $11.50; Su; 13,155pd, 95fr (CAC); $11.50; C; publisher Dennis Stockton; editor Karleen Chalker; tel (770) 887-3126; fax (770) 889-6017

Cuthbert/Fort Gaines: *The Cuthbert Times and News Record* — Dawson St.; PO Box 261, Cuthbert (31740); Th; 1,613pd, 245fr (Sw); $3.32; C; publisher Joel P Smith; editor Tom Davis; tel (912) 732-2731; fax (205) 687-3229

Dade Co.: *Dade County Sentinel* — 5 W. Church St.; PO Box 277, Trenton (30752); W; 4,373pd, 48fr (Sw); $5.00; publisher & editor William E Gifford; tel (706) 657-6182; fax (706) 657-4970

Dahlonega: *The Dahlonega Nugget* — 1020 W. Main St.; PO Box 36 (30533); Th; 5,025pd, 25fr (Est); $3.45; publisher John D Solesbee; editor Joseph Kisselburg; tel (706) 864-3613; fax (706) 864-4360

Dallas/Paulding Co.: *Dallas New Era* — 121 W. Spring St.; PO Box 530, Dallas (30132); Th; 6,900pd (Sw); $3.00; publisher J S Parker & J T Parker; editor T E Parker; tel (770) 445-3379/5726

Danielsville/Madison Co.: *Danielsville Monitor* — Court House Sq.; PO Box 279, Danielsville (30633); F; 1,563pd, 6fr (Sw); $1.96; publisher & editor Jere C Ayers; tel (706) 795-3102, (706) 783-2553; fax (706) 783-2553

Darien/McIntosh Co.: *The Darien News* — 101 Broad St.; PO Box 496, Darien (31305); Th; 2,933pd, 26fr (Sw); $3.50; publishers Mr Charles M Williamson Jr & Mrs Charles M Williamson Jr; editor Kathleen Russell; tel (912) 437-4251; fax (912) 437-2299

Dawson/Terrell: *The Dawson News* — 139 W. Lee St.; PO Box 350, Dawson (31742); Th; 2,725pd, 30fr (Sw); $4.50; C; publisher & editor Tommy Rountree; tel (912) 995-2175; fax (912) 995-3713

Dawsonville: *Dawson County Advertiser & News* — Main St.; PO Box 225 (30534); Th; 3,394pd, 50fr (Sw); $3.45; publisher Don Waldrip; editor Chyrl Waldrip; tel (706) 265-2345; fax (706) 265-7842

De Kalb Co.: *Decatur-DeKalb News/Era* — 739 DeKalb Industrial Way, Decatur (30033); Th; 9,179pd, 301fr (CAC); $8.56; publisher Gerald W Crane; editor John Sell; tel (404) 292-3536

De Kalb Co.: *Decatur/Tucker/Stone Mountain-DeKalb Neighbor* — PO Box 449, Marietta (30060); W; 45pd, 51,445fr (CAC); $35.70; C; publisher Otis A Brumby Jr; tel (770) 428-9411; fax (770) 422-9533

De Kalb Co./N Atlanta: *The Champion* — 4178 Snapfinger Wds. Dr., Decatur (30035); PO Box 361500, Decatur (30036-1500); W; 4,678pd, 8,893fr (CPVS); $10.25; publisher Carolyn Jernigan-Glenn; general manager Dr Earl D Glenn; editor Alonia Jernigan; tel (404) 284-4010; fax (404) 284-4167

Dodge Co./Eastman: *The Dodge County News* — 218 Main St. S.E.; PO Box 69, Eastman (31023-0069); W; 4,625pd, 100fr (Sw); $3.45; publisher & editor Chuck Eckles; general manager Cindy Eckles; tel (912) 374-0360; fax (912) 374-0361

Donalsonville: *Donalsonville News* — 120 W. 2nd St.; PO Box 338 (31745); Th; 3,349pd, 81fr (Sw); $2.66; C; publisher & editor Waldo L McLeod; tel (912) 524-2343; fax (912) 524-2343

Douglas/Coffe Co.: *The Douglas Enterprise* — 1823 S. Peterson Ave.; PO Box 551, Douglas (31533); W; 7,756pd, 5fr (Sw); $6.00; Su; 7,756pd (Sw); $6.00; C; publisher Jim Merritt; general manager Mary Onley; editor Thomas Frier Jr; tel (912) 384-2323; fax (912) 383-0218

Douglas/Poulding Cos.: *Tri-County News* — PO Box 1586, Douglasville (30133); W; 30,000fr (Est); $6.89; C; publisher Dawn Weatherby; general manager Leonard Woolsey; editor Bill Fordham; tel (770) 942-6571; fax (770) 949-7556

Douglasville: *The Douglas Neighbor* — PO Box 449, Marietta (30061); W; 31pd, 22,950fr (Sw); $19.80; C; publisher Otis A Brumby Jr; editor Joe Baggett; tel (770) 428-9411; fax (770) 428-7945

Dunwoody/Chamblee/S Springs/Roswell/Alpharetta: *Crier Newspapers* — 17 Dunwoody Park, Ste. 101; PO Box 888044, Dunwoody (30338); W; 20,000fr (Sw); $15.89; publisher Susan Courtemanche; general manager Jim Hart; editor Lenore Whitley; tel (770) 394-4147; fax (770) 394-0019

E Cobb: *East Cobb Neighbor* — PO Box 499, Marietta (30061); Th; 26pd, 45,900fr (Sw); $23.85; C; publisher Otis A Brumby Jr; editor Rodney Shumake; tel (770) 428-9411; fax (770) 422-9533

Elbert Co.: *The Elbert County Examiner* — 4 S. Public Sq.; PO Box 960, Elberton (30635); Tu; 3,709pd, 172fr (Sw); $4.25; publisher & editor Linton Johnson; tel (706) 283-8500; fax (706) 283-9700

Elbert Co.: *The Elberton Star* — 14 N. Oliver St.; PO Box 280, Elberton (30635); W; 4,308pd, 60fr (Sw); $5.10; publisher & managing editor Paula Pennell; editor Carolyn Cann; tel (706) 283-3100; fax (706) 283-7841

Ellijay/Gilmer Co.: *Times-Courier* — 13 River St.; PO Box 1076, Ellijay (30540); Th; 6,219pd, 35fr (Sw); $3.75; publisher George N Bunch III; editor George N Bunch Jr; tel (706) 635-4313; fax (706) 635-7006

Fayetteville: *Fayette County News* — 180 Church St.; PO Box 96 (30214); W/F; 4,596pd (Sw); $3.95; Su; 15,588pd (Sw); $3.95; C; publisher Robert E Tribble; general manager Gary Cornwell; editor Pat Cooper; tel (770) 461-6317; fax (770) 460-8172

Fayetteville: *Fayette Neighbor* — PO Box 449, Marietta (30061); Th; 32pd, 20,150fr (Sw); $14.95; C; publisher Otis A Brumby Jr; editor Rob Richardson; tel (770) 461-1136; fax (770) 422-9533

Fitzgerald: *The Herald-Leader* — 202-204 E. Central Ave.; PO Box 40 (31750); W; 5,480pd, 75fr (Sw); $4.50; publisher & editor Gerald W Pryor; managing editor Barbara Ashe; tel (912) 423-9331; fax (912) 423-6533

Folkston: *Charlton County Herald* — 102 1/2 W. Love St.; PO Box 398 (31537); W; 2,950pd, 100fr (Sw); $2.90; publisher & editor David L Thompson; general manager C Sherry Lloyd; tel (912) 496-3585; fax (912) 496-4585

Forest Park: *South Fulton Neighbor* — 5300 Frontage Rd., Ste. B (30050); W; 27,000fr (Est); $123.10; C; publisher Otis A Brumby Jr; editor Martha Barksdale; tel (404) 363-8484; fax (404) 363-0212

Forsyth/Monroe Co.: *The Monroe County Reporter* — 30 E. Johnston St.; PO Box 795, Forsyth (31029); W; 4,500pd, 6,000fr (Est); 48¢; C; publisher & editor Jackson Daniel; tel (912) 994-2358; fax (912) 994-2359

Fort Vly.: *The Leader-Tribune* — 109 Anderson Ave.; PO Box 1060 (31030); W; 4,750pd, 9,600fr (Est); $4.20; C; general manager & editor Chuck Morley; tel (912) 825-2432; fax (912) 825-4130

Franklin Co.: *Franklin County Citizen* — 12150 Augusta Rd.; PO Box 580, Lavonia (30553); Th; 5,081pd, 39fr (Est); $4.35; C; publisher & editor Greg T Pitts; tel (706) 356-8557; fax (706) 356-2008

Franklin Co.: *The News Leader* — PO Box 26, Royston (30662); W; 2,262pd, 40fr (Sw); $3.78; C; publisher Peggy Vickery; editor Joe Edwards; tel (706) 245-7351; fax (706) 245-5991

Glennville: *Glennville Sentinel* — 105 Barnard St.; PO Box 218 (30427); Th; 3,300pd, 35fr (Sw); $3.95; publisher & editor Pam S Waters; tel (912) 654-2515; fax (912) 654-2527

Gray: *Jones County News* — 111 Clinton St.; PO Box 1538 (31032); Th; 3,200pd, 45fr (Sw); 18¢; publisher G B Moore III; editor Tasi Moore; tel (912) 986-3929; fax (912) 986-1935

Greene Co.: *The Herald Journal* — 107 N. Main St.; PO Box 149, Greensboro (30642); Th; 4,200pd, 48fr (Est); $2.50; C; publisher & editor Carey Williams Jr; tel (706) 453-7988; fax (706) 453-2311

Greenville: *Meriwether Vindicator* — PO Box A (30222); F; 1,850pd, 47fr (Sw); $3.50; C; publisher Robert E Tribble; editor Micky D'Avey; tel (706) 846-3188

Hamilton/Harris Co.: *Harris County Journal* — PO Box 75, Hamilton (31816); Th; 2,600pd, 30fr (Sw); $3.50; C; publisher Robert E Tribble; editor David Eakin; tel (404) 846-3188

Haralson Co.: *The Haralson Gateway Beacon* — PO Box 685, Bremen (30110); Th; 5,392pd, 67fr (Est); $6.45; C; publisher Dawn Weatherby; editor Rhonda Hancock; managing editor Julianne Foster; tel (770) 537-2434; fax (770) 537-0826

Hartwell: *The Hartwell Sun* — 138 N. Forrest Ave.; PO Box 700 (30643); W; 5,835pd, 65fr (Sw); $5.35; C; publisher Peggy Vickery; editor Wassie Vickery; tel (706) 376-8025; fax (706) 376-3016

Hawkinsville: *Hawkinsville Dispatch and News* — 329 Commerce St.; PO Box 30 (31036); W; 2,975pd, 40fr (Est); $3.40; publisher Charlie C Southerland; editor Riley Troill; tel (912) 783-1291; fax (912) 783-1293

U.S. Weeklies **Georgia** **II-15**

Hazlehurst/Jeff Davis Co.: *Jeff Davis County Ledger* — 122 Railroad St.; PO Box 338, Hazlehurst (31539); W; 3,449pd, 72fr (Est); 27¢; publisher & editor Thomas H Purser; general manager Carolyn Thompson; tel (912) 375-4225; fax (912) 375-3704

Henry Co.: *The Henry Herald* — 32 Macon St.; PO Box 233, McDonough (30253); W; 6,615pd, 190fr (Est); $7.00; F; 6,615pd, 190fr (Est); $6.35; C; publisher & editor Joe Hiett; tel (770) 957-9161; fax (770) 954-0282

Hiawassee/Young Harris: *Towns County Herald* — PO Box 365, Hiawassee (30546); Th; 3,000pd, 20fr (Est); $4.20; publisher Wanda R West; editor Carl Vanzuro; tel (706) 896-4454; fax (706) 745-1830

Hinesville: *The Coastal Courier* — 125 S. Main St.; PO Box 498 (31313); Su/W/F; 5,119pd, 192fr (Est); $7.00; C; publisher Mark Griffin; editor Pat Watkins; tel (912) 876-0156; fax (912) 368-6329

Hogansville: *Hogansville Herald* — PO Box 426 (30230); Th; 975pd (Sw); $3.10; publisher Robert E Tribble; general manager Mike Hale; editor Laurie J Lewis; tel (706) 846-3188; fax (706) 846-2206

Homerville: *Clinch County News* — 210 E. Dame Ave.; PO Box 377 (31634); W; 2,100pd, 70fr (Est); 14¢; publisher Robert Williams; editor Len Robbins; tel (912) 487-5337; fax (912) 487-3227

Jackson/Butts Co.: *Jackson Progress-Argus* — 129 S. Mulberry St.; PO Box 249, Jackson (30233); W; 4,191pd, 53fr (Sw); $6.25; C; publisher W Herman Cawthon; general manager Sandra O'Neal; editor Larry Stanford; tel (770) 775-3107; fax (770) 775-3855

Jasper: *Pickens County Progress* — 94 N. Main St.; PO Box 67 (30143); Th; 5,910pd, 90fr (Est); $2.75; publisher John R Pool; editor Martha E Pool; managing editor William E Pool; tel (706) 692-2457; fax (706) 692-9738

Jefferson: *The Jefferson Reporter* — Estelle St.; PO Box 277, Wrens (30833); W; 1,750pd, 20fr (Est); $3.69; publishers Joyce Drinkwater & Marcus Drinkwater; general manager Dianne Stewart; editor Jennifer Newton; tel (706) 547-6629; fax (706) 547-2259

Jefferson/Commerce: *The Jackson Herald* — 33 Lee St.; PO Box 908, Jefferson (30549); W; 7,939pd, 278fr (Sw); $5.31; C; publisher Herman Buffington; general manager & editor Mike Buffington; tel (706) 367-5233; fax (706) 367-8056

Jesup/Wayne: *The Press-Sentinel* — 252 W. Walnut St.; PO Box 607, Jesup (31545); W/Su; 6,067pd, 248fr (Est); $6.30; C; publisher J H (Sandy) Sanders Jr; editor Drew Davis; tel (912) 427-3757; fax (912) 427-4092

Jonesboro/Forest Park: *The Clayton Neighbor* — 5300 Frontage Rd., Ste. B, Forest Park (30050); W; 42pd, 41,398fr (Sw); $25.40; publisher Otis A Brumby Jr; editor John Marsh; tel (770) 428-9411; fax (770) 422-9533

Kennesaw/Acworth: *Kennesaw-Acworth-Neighbor* — PO Box 449, Marietta (30061); Th; 28pd, 18,200fr (Sw); $17.55; C; publisher Otis A Brumby Jr; editor Rodney Shumake; tel (770) 428-9411; fax (770) 422-9533

Kingsland: *The Southeast Georgian* — PO Box 1429 (31548); W; 4,068pd, 35fr (Est); 23¢; publisher & editor Mark Jicha; tel (912) 729-5231; fax (912) 729-1589

LaFayette: *Walker County Messenger* — 120 E. Patton St.; PO Box 766 (30728-0766); W/F; 4,158pd, 50fr (Sw); $6.00; C; publisher Burgett H Mooney III; editor Don Stilwell; tel (706) 638-1859; fax (706) 368-7045

Lake Oconee/Greene/Morgan/Putnam Cos.: *The Lake Oconee Free Press* — 131 E. Jefferson; PO Box 191, Madison (30650-0191); Sa; 8,706pd, 159fr (Sw); $4.90; C; publisher & editor Adelaide W Ponder; publisher W Graham Ponder; general manager Billy Arthur; managing editor Patrick Yost; tel (706) 342-2424; fax (706) 342-1300

Lakeland/Valdosta: *Lanier County News* — 335 W. Church St.; PO Box 278, Lakeland (31635); W; 850pd, 200fr (Est); 17¢; publisher & editor Ann Knight; tel (912) 896-2233; fax (912) 896-7237

Lee Co.: *The Lee County Ledger* — 124 4th St.; PO Box 715, Leesburg (31763); Th; 1,940pd, 33fr (Sw); $2.25; publisher Derryl Quinn; editor Charles Quinn; tel (912) 759-2413

Lexington: *The Oglethorpe Echo* — PO Box 268 (30648); Th; 2,750pd, 30fr (Est); 25¢; publisher Ralph B Maxwell; editor Ralph B Maxwell Jr; tel (706) 743-5510/3111

Lincolnton: *The Lincoln Journal* — 204 Peachtree St.; PO Box 399 (30817); Th; 2,300pd, 50fr (Est); $2.35; C; publisher & editor Sparky Newsome; general manager Terri Lang; tel (706) 359-3229; fax (706) 359-2884

Louisville/Jefferson Co.: *News & Farmer & Wadely Herald* — 615 Mulberry St.; PO Box 487, Louisville (30434); W; 3,150pd, 9fr (Est); $3.69; publisher Joyce Drinkwater; editor Jennifer Newton; tel (912) 625-7722; fax (706) 547-2259

Ludowici: *The Ludowici News* — 8 S. McDonald St.; PO Box 218 (31316); Th; 1,012pd, 54fr (Est); $2.24; C; publisher Ken Buchanan; editor Joe Parker; tel (912) 545-2103; fax (912) 487-4092

Madison Co.: *Comer News* — 422 Main St.; PO Box 7, Comer (30629); Th; 1,650pd, 7fr (Sw); $1.96; publisher & editor Jere C Ayers; managing editor Virginia O'Kelley; tel (706) 783-2553; fax (706) 783-2553

Manchester: *Manchester Star-Mercury* — Warm Springs Hwy.; PO Box 426 (31816); W; 3,600pd, 24fr (Sw); $4.20; C; publisher Robert E Tribble; general manager Mike Hale; editor Micky D'Avy; tel (706) 846-3188; fax (706) 846-2206

McDuffie/Warren/Columbia: *The McDuffie Progress* — 101 Church St.; PO Box 1090, Thomson (30824); Su/W; 4,518pd, 128fr (Sw); $4.50; C; publisher Ted Delaney; editor Wesley King; tel (706) 595-1601; fax (706) 597-8974

McRae: *The Telfair Enterprise* — 237 W. Oak St.; PO Box 269 (31055); W; 3,107pd, 55fr (Sw); $3.90; publisher Sarah J Bowen; editor Ed Bowen Jr; tel (912) 868-6015; fax (912) 868-5486

Meriwether Co.: *Meriwether Free Press* — 116 E. Court Sq.; PO Box 925, Greenville (30222); W; 2,425pd, 25fr (Sw); $3.60; publisher & editor Lee N Howell; tel (706) 672-1753; fax (706) 672-1977

Metro Augusta: *The Metropolitan Spirit* — PO Box 3809, Augusta (30914); Th; 20,000fr (Est); $16.00; publisher & editor David Vantrease; tel (706) 738-1142; fax (706) 733-6663

Metter: *The Metter Advertiser* — 15 S. Rountree St.; PO Box 8 (30439); W; 2,719pd, 182fr (Sw); $3.71; C; publisher & editor Carvy Snell; tel (912) 685-6566; fax (912) 685-4901

Miller Co.: *Miller County Liberal Inc.* — 157 E. Main St.; PO Box 37, Colquitt (31737-0037); Th; 2,815pd, 85fr (Est); $3.50; publisher & editor Terry Toole; general manager Betty Jo Toole; managing editor Debra Jones; tel (912) 758-5549; fax (912) 758-5540

Montgomery Co.: *The Montgomery Monitor* — Rte. 1; PO Box 279, Ailey (30410); W; 1,708pd, 36fr (Est); 27¢; C; publisher & editor James T Windsor; general manager Bonnie Williamson; tel (912) 529-6624; fax (912) 537-2076

Monticello/Jasper Co.: *The Monticello News* — 237 Washington St.; PO Box 30, Monticello (31064); Th; 2,388pd, 38fr (Est); $3.25; publisher William T Hughes Jr; editor Kathy Pope; tel (770) 468-6511; fax (770) 468-6576

Morgan/Greene/Putnam: *The Madisonian* — 131 E. Jefferson; PO Box 191, Madison (30650); Th; 4,519pd, 104fr (Sw); $4.65; C; publisher & editor Adelaide W Ponder; publisher W Graham Ponder; general manager Billy Arthur; managing editor Patrick Yost; tel (706) 342-2424; fax (706) 342-1300

Nahunta: *Brantley Enterprise* — PO Box 454 (31553); Th; 2,000pd (Est); $2.75; publisher Ken Buchanan; general manager Cheri Knox; tel (912) 462-6776; fax (912) 462-6776

Nashville: *The Berrien Press* — 200 E. McPherson St.; PO Box 455 (31639); W; 3,989pd, 54fr (Sw); $3.50; publisher & editor Donald F Boyd; tel (912) 686-3523; fax (912) 686-7771

Newnan: *The Newnan Times-Herald* — 16 Jefferson St.; PO Box 1052 (30264); W/Sa; 13,655pd, 215fr (Est); $5.50; C; publisher William Thomasson; editor Marianne C Thomasson; tel (770) 253-1576; fax (770) 253-2538

Ocilla: *Ocilla Star* — 102 E. 4th St.; PO Box 25 (31774); W; 2,188pd, 90fr (Sw); $2.70; publisher & editor Frances M Bradford; general manager & managing editor Elizabeth Wilcox; tel (912) 468-5433; fax (912) 468-5045

Paulding Co.: *Paulding Neighbor* — PO Box 449, Marietta (30061); Th; 30pd, 14,700fr (Sw); $13.00; C; publisher Otis A Brumby Jr; editor Stan Hardegree; tel (770) 428-9411; fax (770) 422-9533

Peachtree City: *This Week in Peachtree City* — 111 Petrol Pt., Ste. C; PO Box 2468 (30269); W/F; 4,906pd (Sw); $3.95; Su; 8,860pd (Sw); $3.95; C; publisher Robert E Tribble; general manager & editor Gary Cornwell; tel (770) 487-7729; fax (770) 460-8172

Pelham/Mitchell Co.: *The Pelham Journal* — 310 W. Railroad S., Pelham (31779); W; 3,371pd, 10fr (Est); 17¢; publisher & editor Roger Jones; general manager Susan Sowel; tel (912) 294-3661; fax (912) 336-8476

Perry: *The Houston Home Journal* — 807 Carroll St.; PO Drawer M (31069); W; 4,500pd, 6,000fr (Est); 44¢; C; publisher & editor J J Johnson; tel (912) 987-1823; fax (912) 988-1181

Pike Co.: *Pike County Journal and Reporter* — PO Box 789, Zebulon (30295); Tu; 2,245pd (Est); $2.65; publisher & editor Laura Geiger; tel (706) 567-3446; fax (706) 567-8814

Putnam Co.: *The Eatonton Messenger* — 111 N. Jefferson Ave.; PO Box 4027, Eatonton (31024); Th; 3,480pd, 100fr (Sw); 18¢; C; publisher Mrs Battle Smith; editor Gary Jones; tel (706) 485-3501; fax (706) 485-4166

Rabun Co.: *The Clayton Tribune* — Main & Oak Crescent Sts.; PO Box 425, Clayton (30525); Th; 6,500pd, 50fr (Sw); $5.45; C; publisher Russell Majors; editor Dorsey Martin; tel (706) 782-3312; fax (706) 782-4230

Richland/Lumpkin/Preston: *Stewart-Webster Journal* — U.S. 27-A St.; PO Box 426, Manchester (31816); Th; 1,875pd, 11fr (Sw); $3.50; C; publisher Robert E Tribble; general manager & managing editor Mike Hale; editor Ron Provencher; tel (706) 846-3188; fax (706) 846-2206

Ringgold: *The Catoosa County News* — 105 Maple St. (30736); W; 3,550pd, 60fr (Sw); $6.00; C; publisher Burgett H Mooney III; editor Richard L Ball; tel (706) 935-2621; fax (706) 965-5934

Roberta/Crawford: *The Georgia Post* — 341 & D.E. Agency; PO Box 860, Roberta (31078-0860); Th; 1,500pd (Est); $2.00; publisher & editor Walter B Geiger; managing editor Celia Martin; tel (912) 836-3195

Rockdale: *The Rockdale Neighbor* — 580 Fairground St.; PO Box 449, Marietta (30060); Th; 32pd, 16,200fr (Sw); $14.65; C; publisher Otis A Brumby Jr; editor Vala Peyton; tel (770) 428-9411; fax (770) 422-9533

Rockmart: *Rockmart Journal* — PO Box 609 (30153); W; 3,172pd, 24fr (Est); $5.80; publisher Burgett H Mooney III; editor James A Thaxton; tel (770) 684-7811

St. Simons Island/Sea Island: *The Islander* — 520 Wesley Oaks Cir.; PO Box 20539, St. Simons Island (31522); M; 2,292pd, 155fr (Sw); $5.39; publisher E J Permar; general manager & editor Matthew J Permar; tel (912) 265-9654; fax (912) 638-2764

Sandersville: *The Sandersville Progress* — 118 E. Haynes St.; PO Box 431 (31082); W; 4,529pd, 100fr (Est); 21¢; publisher Robert Tribble; general manager & editor Robert Garrett; tel (912) 552-3161; fax (912) 552-5177

Shasta/Modoc/Lassen Cos.: *The Mountain Echo* — 43152 Hwy. 299 E.; PO Box 224, Fall River Mills (96028); Tu; 2,837pd, 65fr (Sw); $6.50; publisher & editor Walt Caldwell; general manager Lisa Bullmore; tel (916) 336-6262; fax (916) 336-6262

Smyrna: *The Smyrna/Vinings Neighbor* — PO Box 449, Marietta (30061); Th; 25pd, 12,000fr (Sw); $18.35; C; publisher Otis A Brumby Jr; editor Rodney Shumake; tel (770) 428-9411; fax (770) 422-9533

Soperton: *The Soperton News* — Main & 2nd Sts.; PO Box 537 (30457); W; 2,737pd, 44fr (Est); 27¢; C; publisher & editor James T Windsor; tel (912) 529-6624; fax (912) 529-6624

S De Kalb: *South De Kalb Neighbor* — 3060 Mercer University Dr., Ste. 210, Atlanta (30341); W; 9pd, 35,866fr (CAC); $46.20; C; publisher Otis A Brumby Jr; editor Steve Rosenberg; tel (770) 454-9388; fax (770) 454-9131

Sparta/Hancock Co.: *The Sparta Ishmaelite* — 109 Broad St.; PO Box 308, Sparta (31087); Th; 2,060pd, 70fr (Sw); $2.80; C; publisher & editor R Allen Haywood; general manager Christy Griffin; tel (706) 444-5330; fax (706) 444-5330

Stockbridge/McDonough: *Henry Neighbor* — 5300 Frontage Rd., Ste. B, Forest Park (30050); Th; 52pd, 19,675fr (Sw); $14.00; publisher Otis A Brumby Jr; editor Valerie Graves; tel (404) 363-8484; fax (404) 363-0212

Summerville: *The Chattooga Press* — PO Box 485 (30747); W; 10,322fr (Est); $6.00; C; publisher Burgett H Mooney III; editor Pam Purcell; tel (706) 857-5433; fax (706) 232-9632

Swainsboro/Emanuel Co.: *The Blade* — W. Moring St.; PO Box 938, Swainsboro (30401); M/W; 5,646pd, 80fr (Sw); $4.06; C; publisher William C Rogers Jr; editor Ruby Fagler; tel (912) 237-9971; fax (912) 237-9451

Sylvania/Sereven Co.: *The Sylvania Telephone* — 208 N. Main St.; PO Box 10, Sylvania (30467); Th; 3,915pd, 35fr (Est); $3.90; publisher Eric Denty; editor Dan Johnson; managing editor Lee Thompson; tel (912) 564-2045; fax (912) 564-7055

Sylvester/Worth Co.: *The Sylvester Local News* — 103 E. Kelly St.; PO Box 387, Sylvester (31791); W; 3,741pd, 20fr (Est); $2.75; publisher & editor Marian A Sumner; tel (912) 776-7713; fax (912) 776-4607

Talbotton: *Talbotton New Era* — PO Box 248 (31816); Th; 1,200pd, 20fr (Sw); $3.50; C; publisher Robert E Tribble; editor Micky D'Avy; tel (706) 846-3188

Tattnall Co.: *Tattnall Journal* — 110 Folsom St.; PO Box 278, Reidsville (30453); Th; 3,660pd, 107fr (Sw); $4.36; publisher & editor Russell B Rhoden; managing editor Wilton R Rhoden; tel (912) 557-6761; fax (912) 557-4132

Telfair Co.: *The Telfair Times* — PO Box 459, Helena (31037); W; 1,800pd, 200fr (Est); $2.75; C; publisher Martin A Crowe; editor Elizabeth Garrett; tel (912) 868-5776; fax (912) 868-7255

Thomaston: *The Thomaston Times* — 621 E. Main St.; PO Box 430 (30286); M/W/F; 6,036pd, 250fr (Est); $4.38; C; publisher & editor Chris Smith; general manager Elmo Jackson; managing editor Kim Madlom; tel (706) 647-5414; fax (706) 647-2833

Toccoa: *The Toccoa Record* — 151 W. Doyle St.; PO Drawer 1069 (30577); Th; 6,742pd, 72fr (Est); 19¢; publisher & editor C A Hamilton; managing editor Tom Law; tel (706) 886-9476; fax (706) 886-2161

Vidalia/Lyons: *The Advance-Progess* — 205 1st St.; PO Box 669, Vidalia (30474); W; 6,500pd, 204fr (Sw); $4.10; C; publisher William F Ledford Sr; general manager William F Ledford Jr; tel (912) 537-3131; fax (912) 537-4899

Vienna: *Vienna News-Observer* — 115 E. Union; PO Box 186 (31092); Th; 2,562pd, 118fr (Est); 14¢; publisher Robert E Tribble; general manager Peggy King; editor Mrs C Raymond King; tel (912) 268-2096; fax (912) 268-1924

Villa Rica: *The Villa Rican* — PO Box 757 (30180); Th; 2,514pd, 26fr (Sw); $4.05; C; publisher Dawn Weatherby; editor Frank X Ellis; managing editor Julianne Foster; tel (770) 459-5166; fax (770) 459-4804

Vinings: *Northside-Sandy Springs Neighbor* — PO Box 449, Marietta (30061); W; 267pd, 29,800fr (Sw); $27.25; C; publisher Otis A Brumby Jr; editor Fay Edmundson; tel (770) 428-9411; fax (770) 422-9533

Walton Co.: *Walton Tribune* — 124 N. Broad; PO Box 808, Monroe (30655); W/Su; 6,172pd (Est); $6.76; C; publisher & editor Robert O Hale; managing editor Wes Swietek; tel (770) 267-8371; fax (770) 267-7780

Washington/Wilkes Co.: *The News-Reporter* — 116 W. Robert Toombs Ave.; PO Box 340, Washington (30673); Th; 4,745pd, 130fr (Est); $3.75; publisher & editor P Smythe Newsome Sr; general manager & managing editor Sparky Newsome; tel (706) 678-2636; fax (706) 678-3857

Watkinsville: *The Oconee Enterprise* — 26 Barnett Shoals; PO Box 535 (30677); Th; 3,622pd, 4fr (Sw); $5.00; publisher Vinnie Williams; general manager Maridee Williams; managing editor Joe Feeney; tel (706) 769-5175; fax (706) 769-8532

Waynesboro: *The True Citizen* — 610 Academy Ave.; PO Box 948 (30830); Th; 4,551pd, 46fr (Sw); $4.50; C; publisher Roy F Chalker Jr; general manager Bonnie K Taylor; editor Jimmy Ezzell; managing editor Dianne Vickrey; tel (706) 554-2111; fax (706) 554-2437

Wheeler Co.: *The Wheeler County Eagle* — Farm Bureau Bldg.; PO Box 409, Alamo (30411); W; 1,616pd, 161fr (Est); $3.78; publisher & editor James T Windsor; tel (912) 529-6624; fax (912) 529-6624

Wilkinson Co.: *Wilkinson County News* — 100 High Hill St.; PO Box 205, Irwinton (31042); Th; 2,344pd, 108fr (Est); $2.00; publisher Joe Boone; editor Edwin M Boone; tel (912) 946-2218; fax (912) 946-7226

Wrightsville: *The Wrightsville Headlight* — 102 W. Elm St.; PO Box 290 (31096); Th; 1,817pd, 67fr (Sw); $3.25; C; publisher Robert Tribble; general manager Robert Garrett; editor Katherine Cummings; tel (912) 864-3528; fax (912) 864-2166

HAWAII

Hawaii Kai/Kuliouou: *Hawaii Kai Sun Press* — 45-525 Luluku Rd., Kaneohe (96744); Th; 8,400fr (Est); $10.19; C; publisher Ken Berry; general manager Christopher McMahon; editor Bill Stone; managing editor James Gonser; tel (808) 235-5881; fax (808) 247-7246

Kauai: *Kauai Times* — 3133 B Oihana St.; PO Box 231, Lihue, Kauai (96766); W/Su; 21,000fr (Est); $13.85; publisher & editor Roy Callaway; managing editor Sue Dixon Strong; tel (808) 245-8825; fax (808) 246-9195

Mililani/Wahiawa/Waipio Gentry/Waipahu (Central): *Central Sun Press* — 562 California Ave., Wahiawa (96786); Th; 16,125fr (Est); $9.08; C; publisher Ken Berry; editor Scott Ishikawa; tel (808) 622-3966; fax (808) 621-1738

Windward/Lkaneohe/Kailua/Kahalau: *Windward Sun Press* — 45-525 Luluku Rd., Kaneohe (96744); Th; 27,456fr (Est); $10.42; C; publisher Ken Berry; editor Eloise Aguiar; tel (808) 235-5881; fax (808) 247-7246

IDAHO

Aberdeen: *The Aberdeen Times* — 31 S. Main St.; PO Box X (83210); W; 855pd, 20fr (Sw); $4.10; C; publisher Erma Crompton; editor Virginia Anderson; tel (208) 397-4440; fax (208) 226-5295

American Falls: *Power County Press* — 174 Idaho St.; PO Box 547 (83211); W; 2,000pd (Sw); $5.85; C; publisher Erma Crompton; general manager & editor Brett Crompton; tel (208) 226-5294; fax (208) 226-5295

Arco/Mackay: *Arco Advertiser* — 146 S. Front St.; PO Box 803, Arco (83213); Th; 1,787pd, 15fr (Sw); $3.75; publisher & editor Donald L Cammack; managing editor Charles L Cammack; tel (208) 527-3038; fax (208) 527-8210

Bonners Ferry: *Bonners Ferry Herald* — 7183 Main St.; PO Box 539 (83805); W; 3,000pd, 204fr (Est); $4.35; publisher & editor David Keyes; tel (208) 267-5521; fax (208) 267-5523

Buhl: *Buhl Herald* — 126 S. Broadway; PO Box 312 (83316-0312); W; 2,745pd, 33fr (Sw); $4.15; publisher Robert M Bailey; editor Sandra Wisecaver; tel (208) 543-4335; fax (208) 543-6834

Cambridge/Midvale: *The Upper Country News-Reporter* — 155 Superior St.; PO Box 9, Cambridge (83610); Th; 1,091pd, 30fr (Est); $2.53; publisher & editor R Stuart Dopf; tel (208) 257-3515

Challis: *Challis Messenger* — 310 N. Main; PO Box 405 (83226); Th; 1,876pd, 18fr (Sw); $3.95; publisher & editor Peggy Parks; tel (208) 879-4445

Cottonwood: *Cottonwood Chronicle* — 503 King St.; PO Box 157 (83522); Th; 986pd, 28fr (Sw); 32¢; publisher Robert E Wherry; editor Greg A Wherry; tel (208) 962-3851; fax (208) 962-7131

Driggs/Tetonia/Victor: *Teton Valley News* — 80 E. Little Ave.; PO Box 49, Driggs (83422-0049); Th; 1,705pd, 30fr (Est); $5.50; publisher Fred A McCabe; general manager Tammy van Leerdam; editor Jeanne Anderson; tel (208) 354-8101; fax (208) 354-8621

Emmett/Gem Co.: *Messenger-Index* — 120 N. Washington St.; PO Box 577, Emmett (83617); W; 3,918pd, 467fr (Est); $5.94; C; publisher James T Barnes Jr; general manager Kathy Steed; editor Wendy Brown; managing editor Tom Goff; tel (208) 365-6066; fax (208) 365-6068

Fremont Co.: *Fremont County Herald-Chronicle* — 44 N. Bridge St.; PO Box 568, St. Anthony (83445); Tu/Th; 1,985pd, 74fr (Sw); $4.20; C; publisher Roger O Porter; editor Lauren McKeeber; tel (208) 624-4455; fax (208) 356-8312

Gooding: *Gooding County Leader* — 200 Main St. (83330); W; 1,631pd, 11fr (Sw); $5.00; C; publisher Patricia Nance; general manager Norma Devoe; editor Mary Ann Hagen; managing editor Pat Marcantonio; tel (208) 934-4449; fax (208) 934-4440

Grangeville/Idaho Co.: *Idaho County Free Press* — 318 E. Main; PO Box 690, Grangeville (83530); W; 3,772pd, 68fr (Sw); $8.25; publisher Andrew McNab; editor Jance Tong; tel (208) 983-1070; fax (208) 983-1336

Hailey/Sun Vly.: *Wood River Journal* — 112 S. Main St.; PO Box 988, Hailey (83333); W; 2,000pd, 10,450fr (Sw); $8.90; publisher & editor Dan Gorham; managing editor Wayne Adair; tel (208) 788-3444; fax (208) 788-0083

Homedale/Marsing/Owyhee: *The Owyhee Avalanche* — 20 E. Idaho Ave.; PO Box 97, Homedale (83628); W; 1,250pd, 38fr (Est); $4.25; publisher & editor Joe E Aman; tel (208) 337-4681; fax (208) 337-4867

Jefferson/Clark Cos.: *The Jefferson Star* — PO Box 37, Rigby (83442); W; 2,176pd, 100fr (Sw); $5.25; C; publisher Ken Carr; tel (208) 745-8701

Jerome: *North Side News* — 133 E. Main St.; PO Box 468 (83338); W; 1,251pd, 11fr (Sw); $5.00; C; publisher Patricia Nance; general manager Norma DeVoe; editor Jeanne Vandiver; managing editor Patricia Marcantonio; tel (208) 324-3391

Kamiah/Kooskia/Nezperce/Craigmont/Winchester/Reubens: *The Clearwater Progress* — 615 4th St.; PO Box 428, Kamiah (83536-0428); W; 1,650pd, 62fr (Sw); $4.00; publisher Bill Glenn; general manager Mary Bruder; editor Jeff St Peter; tel (208) 935-0838; fax (208) 935-0973

Kendrick: *The Kendrick Gazette* — PO Box 177 (83537); Th; 850pd, 20fr (Est); $2.00; publisher & editor William A Roth; tel (208) 289-5731

Ketchum/Sun Vly./Hailey/Bellvue/Blaine Co.: *Idaho Mountain Express* — 591 1st Ave. N.; PO Box 1013, Ketchum (83340); W; 2,089pd, 39fr (Sw); $8.45; publisher Pam Morris; editor Barbara Perkins; tel (208) 726-8060; fax (208) 726-2329

McCall/New Meadows/Donnelly/Cascade: *The Star-News* — 1000 1st St.; PO Box 985, McCall (83638); Th; 5,166pd, 51fr (Sw); $6.25; publisher & editor Tom Grote; tel (208) 634-2123; fax (208) 634-4950

Meridian/Eagle/Star: *The Valley News* — 815 E. 1st St.; PO Box 299, Meridian (83680); Th; 1,300pd, 19,000fr (Est); $7.95; publisher Tere Foley; editor Laren Roberts; tel (208) 888-1941; fax (208) 888-1097

Minidoka Co.: *Minidoka County News* — 518 6th St.; PO Box 454, Rupert (83350); W; 1,176pd, 5fr (Est); $4.00; C; publisher Kary Miller; editor Judy Albertson; tel (208) 436-4201; fax (208) 436-4556

Montpelier: *The News-Examiner* — 847 Washington; PO Box 278 (83254); W; 1,653pd, 26fr (Sw); $4.16; C; publishers J Walter Ross & Wayne D Bell; general manager & editor Rosa S Moosman; tel (208) 847-0552; fax (208) 847-0553

Moscow (ID)/Whitman Co. (WA): *Palouse Living* — 409 S. Jackson; PO Box 8187, Moscow (83843); Tu; 14,500fr (Est); $8.90; C; publisher & editor Randy C Frisch; tel (208) 882-5561; fax (208) 883-8205

Mountain Home: *Mountain Home News* — 195 S. 3rd E.; PO Box 1330 (83647); W; 4,000pd, 88fr (Sw); $5.95; C; publisher Coleen Swenson; editor Kelly Everitt; tel (208) 587-3331; fax (208) 587-9205

Nezperce/Craigmont: *Lewis County Herald* — 517 Oak St.; PO Box 159, Nezperce (83543-0159); Th; 1,007pd, 16fr (Sw); 32¢; publisher Patricia E Wherry; publisher & editor Robert E Wherry; tel (208) 937-2671

Oldtown/Priest River: *The Gem State Miner* — 317 S. Union Ave.; PO Box 222, Priest River (83856); W; 810pd, 5fr (Est); $4.95; C; publisher & editor Fred J Willenbrock; tel (208) 437-4275; fax (509) 447-9222

Orofino: *Clearwater Tribune* — 161 Main St.; PO Box 71 (83544); Th; 3,250pd, 15fr (Sw); $3.75; C; publisher & editor Cloann Wilkins McNall; managing editor Marcie Stanton; tel (208) 476-4571; fax (208) 476-0765

Payette Co.: *Independent Enterprise* — 21 S. Main St.; PO Box 519, Payette (83661); W; 1,852pd, 63fr (Sw); $6.30; publisher Eugene Rhinehart; editor Julie Mitchell; tel (208) 642-3357; fax (503) 889-3347

Post Falls: *The Post Falls Tribune* — 318 Spokane St.; PO Box 39 (83854); Th; 3,018pd, 65fr (Est); $3.95; publisher & editor Kerri Thoreson; tel (208) 773-7502; fax (208) 773-7002

Preston: *Preston Citizen* — 77 S. State; PO Box 472 (83263); W; 3,250pd, 300fr (Est); $4.41; publishers Walter Ross & Wayne D Bell; editor Necia Seamons; tel (208) 852-0155; fax (208) 852-0158

Priest River/Oldtown: *Priest River Times* — Cottonwood Village; PO Box 10, Priest River (83856); W; 1,650pd, 8,000fr (Sw); 50¢; publisher & editor Linda Jordan; tel (208) 448-2431; fax (208) 448-2938

Rexburg: *The Rexburg Standard-Journal* — 23 S. 1st St.; PO Box 10 (83440); Tu/Th; 4,048pd, 50fr (Est); 43¢; publisher & editor Roger O Porter; tel (208) 356-5441; fax (208) 356-8312

St. Maries/Harrison/Claria: *Saint Maries Gazette-Record* — 127 S. 7th, St. Maries (83861); W; 3,621pd (Est); $4.28; publisher Daniel H Hammes; editor Robert M Hammes; tel (208) 245-4538; fax (208) 245-4011

Salmon: *The Recorder-Herald* — 519 Van Dreff St.; PO Box 310 (83467); Th; 3,358pd, 61fr (Sw); $4.80; publisher Rick Hodges; editor Jewell Tracy; tel (208) 756-2221; fax (208) 756-2222

Shelley/Firth/Basalt: *Shelley Pioneer* — 154 E. Center; PO Box P, Shelley (83274); Th; 1,690pd, 20fr (Sw); 24¢; C; publisher & editor Ken Carr; general manager Crystal Foster; tel (208) 357-7661

Shoshone: *Lincoln County Journal* — 108 N. Rail St. W.; PO Box 704 (83352); W; 644pd, 10fr (Sw); $5.00; publisher Patricia Nance; general manager Norma Devoe; editor Jane King; managing editor Pat Marcantonio; tel (208) 886-2740

Shoshone Co.: *Idaho News Observer* — 602 Cedar St., Ste. 201; PO Box 1235, Wallace (83873); W; 1,600pd, 200fr (Sw); $4.00; publisher & editor Paul Friend; general manager Barbara Friend; tel (208) 753-0203; fax (208) 753-0303

Soda Springs: *Caribou County Sun* — 169 S. 1st W.; PO Box 815 (83276); Th; 2,681pd, 155fr (Sw); $5.15; publisher & editor Mark Steele; tel (208) 547-3260; fax (208) 547-4422

Weiser/Midvale/Cambridge: *Weiser Signal American* — 18 E. Idaho St.; PO Box 709, Weiser (83672); M/W; 2,423pd, 10fr (Sw); $7.00; publisher James R Simpson; editor Rob Ruth; tel (208) 549-1717; fax (208) 549-1718

ILLINOIS

Addison/Bensenville/Wood Dale: *The Press* — 112 S. York St., Elmhurst (60126); W/F; 4,157pd, 905fr (Sw); $9.83; C; publishers Jack Cruger & Peter C Cruger; tel (708) 834-0900; fax (708) 530-3349

Albion/Edwards Co.: *Journal-Register* — 19 W. Main St., Albion (62806); Th; 2,921pd, 25fr (Sw); $3.80; publisher Krista Harms; editor Dean Bunting; tel (618) 445-2355; fax (618) 445-3459

Albion/W Salem/Olney: *Edwards County Independent Times* — 108 N. Albion St.; PO Box 427, West Salem (62476); W; 500pd, 4,000fr (Sw); $4.20; C; publisher & editor Harry E Bradham; tel (618) 456-8808

Algonquin: *Algonquin Countryside* — 200 James St., Barrington (60010); Th; 2,313pd (ABC); $46.00; C; publisher Thomas J Neri; editor Jo Hansen; managing editor Tom Scott; tel (708) 381-9200; fax (708) 381-5840

Alsip/Crestwood: *The Alsip/Crestwood/Blue Island Star* — 1526 Otto Blvd.; PO Box 157, Chicago Heights (60411); Th/Su; 2,027pd, 961fr (ABC); $23.21; C; publisher Norman A Rosinski; editor Lester Sons; tel (708) 755-6161; fax (708) 755-9112

Alsip/Garden Homes: *Alsip Express* — 3840 W. 147th St.; PO Box 548, Midlothian (60445); Th; 4,300pd, 500fr (Sw); $6.44; C; publisher Walter Lysen; editor Gerald Gibbons; tel (708) 388-2425; fax (708) 385-7811

Altamont: *The Altamont News* — 118 N. Main; PO Box 315 (62411-0315); Tu; 1,875pd, 54fr (Est); $2.65; publisher & editor Joe Baker; tel (618) 483-6176; fax (618) 483-5117

Amboy: *The Amboy News* — 219 E. Main St.; PO Box 162 (61310); Th; 2,229pd, 36fr (Sw); $2.48; publisher & editor John A Koski; tel (815) 857-2311; fax (815) 857-2517

Antioch: *Antioch News-Reporter* — 30 S. Whitney; PO Box 268, Grayslake (60030); Th; 4,881pd, 14fr (Sw); $7.50; C; publisher & editor William H Schroeder; managing editor Rhonda Burke; tel (708) 223-8161; fax (708) 223-8810

Arcola: *Arcola Record-Herald* — 118 E. Main St. (61910); Th; 3,024pd (Est); 18¢; publisher & editor Don Rankin; tel (217) 268-4959; fax (217) 268-4815

Arenzville/Concord/Chapin: *Triopia Tribune* — Rte. 100; PO Box 320, Bluffs (62621); W; 429pd, 270fr (Est); $3.45; C; publisher & editor Dallas M Warrum; general manager Elaine J Warrum; tel (217) 754-3369; fax (217) 754-3369

Ashland: *Ashland Sentinel* — 116 N. Hardin St.; PO Box 418 (62612); Th; 828pd (Est); 65¢; publisher & editor Barbara Hill Nowack; tel (217) 476-3332; fax (217) 476-3332

Ashley: *Ashley News* — PO Box 184, Du Quion (62832); Th; 293pd, 10fr (Est); 9¢; publisher Call Publishing Co. Du Quoin; general manager Steve Fisher; editor John Croessman; tel (618) 542-2133; fax (618) 542-2726

Ashton/Franklin Grove: *The Ashton Gazette* — 813 Main St.; PO Box 287, Ashton (61006); Th; 905pd, 10fr (Sw); $2.50; C; publisher David W Townsend; editor Dara L Townsend; tel (815) 453-2551

Assumption/Moweaqua/Macon: *Golden Prairie News* — 301 S. Chestnut, Assumption (62510); W; 2,152pd, 28fr (Sw); $3.00; publisher & editor Willard Raymond; tel (217) 226-3721; fax (217) 226-3579

Astoria: *The Astoria South Fulton Argus* — 100 N. Pearl; PO Box 427 (61501); W; 2,500pd (Est); $3.47; publisher Thomas B Stevens; editor Merrie Jean Parry; tel (309) 329-2151; fax (309) 329-2344

Atkinson: *The Atkinson Annawan News* — PO Box 727 (61235); Th; 2,200pd (Est); 17¢; publisher Anita Bird; editor Sheryl Plumley; tel (309) 936-7215; fax (309) 936-7150

Atwood: *The Atwood Herald* — 107 N. Main; PO Box 589 (61913); Th; 910pd, 30fr (Sw); 24¢; publisher Mike Brothers; editor Kim Barnett; tel (217) 578-3213; fax (217) 578-2833

Auburn: *Auburn Citizen* — 110 N. 5th St.; PO Box 50 (62615); Th; 1,342pd, 110fr (Sw); $3.50; C; publisher & editor Joseph Michelich Jr; tel (217) 438-6155

Augusta: *The Augusta Eagle/Tri-County Scribe* — 602 Main St.; PO Box 257 (62311); W; 1,550pd, 30fr (Sw); $2.21; C; publisher John T Flack; publisher & managing editor Lea A Flack; tel (217) 392-2715

Barrington/Deer Park: *Barrington Courier-Review* — 200 James St., Barrington (60010); Th; 7,397pd (ABC); $70.00; C; publisher Thomas J Neri; editor Jo Hansen; managing editor Bob Nelander; tel (708) 381-9200; fax (708) 381-5840

Barry/Pike Co.: *The Paper* — 725 Bainbridge St., Barry (62312); W; 2,000pd, 53fr (Sw); $2.50; publisher & editor Debra J Harshman; tel (217) 335-2112; fax (217) 335-2112

Bartlett: *The Bartlett Examiner* — 4N 781 Gerber Rd. (60103); W; 9,000pd (Est); $10.75; publisher Randall Petrik; editor Nadia R Kanhai; tel (708) 830-4145; fax (708) 830-2531

Bartlett/Roselle/Itasca/Glen Ellyn/Wheaton: *The Bartlett Press* — 112 S. York St., Elmhurst (60126); Th; 875pd, 49fr (Sw); $9.83; C; publishers Jack Cruger & Peter C Cruger; editor Rick Nagel; tel (708) 834-0900; fax (708) 530-3349

U.S. Weeklies **Illinois** **II-17**

Beecher: *Beecher Herald* — 120 W. North St.; PO Box 429, Peotone (60468); W; 1,322pd, 56fr (Est); $2.55; publisher Gilbert L Russell; general manager Chris Russell; tel (708) 946-2151; fax (708) 258-6295

Beecher City/Cowden/Stewardson/Strasburg/Shumway: *Beecher City Journal* — 104 S. Charles St.; PO Box 38, Beecher (62414); M; 1,571pd, 55fr (Sw); $3.50; publisher & editor P J Ryan; managing editor Cherie Ryan; tel (618) 487-5634

Belleville: *Belleville Journal* — 219 N. Illinois (62222); W; 34,009fr (CAC); $12.90; Su; 32,981fr (CAC); $12.90; C; general manager Larry Johnson; editor Bonita Tillman; managing editor Scott Queen; tel (618) 277-7000; fax (618) 277-7018

Benld/Gillespie/Wilsonville/Sawyerville/Eagarville/Mt. Clare: *Enterprise* — 216 E. Central; PO Box 137, Benld (62009); Th; 2,200pd, 45fr (Est); $1.75; publisher & editor Dan Fisher; general manager Mag Fisher; tel (217) 835-4868; fax (217) 839-2577

Bensenville: *Bensenville Press* — 112 S. York St., Elmhurst (60126); W/F; 84pd, 893fr (VAC); $9.83; C; publishers Jack Cruger & Pete Cruger; tel (708) 834-0900

Berwyn/Cicero: *Cicero-Berwyn-Stickney Forest View Life* — 2601 S. Harlem Ave., Berwyn (60402); Su/W/F; 23,334pd, 2,470fr (CAC); $16.38; publisher Jack R Kubik; general manager Larry Randa; editor Robert Lifka; tel (708) 242-1234; fax (708) 484-7778

Blandinsville/McDonough: *Blandinsville Star-Gazette* — 103 S. Main St.; PO Box 79, Blandinsville (61420); Th; 583pd, 10fr (Est); $2.80; publisher Joe Acklin; editor Kalyn Hainline; tel (309) 652-3328; fax (309) 462-3221

Bloomingdale: *Bloomingdale Press* — 112 S. York St., Elmhurst (60126); Th; 1,014pd, 2,315fr (Sw); $9.83; C; publishers Jack Cruger & Peter C Cruger; editor Rick Nagel; tel (708) 834-0900; fax (708) 530-3349

Bloomington: *Twin City Community News* — 202 N. Center St.; PO Box 1625 (61702); W; 29,000fr (Sw); $11.95; publisher J C Brown; editor Katy O'Grady-Pyne; tel (309) 827-8555; fax (309) 829-6926

Blue Mound: *Blue Mound Leader* — PO Box 318 (62513-0318); Th; 778pd, 222fr (Sw); 40¢; C; publisher & editor Cynthia L Stuart; tel (217) 692-2323

Bluffs: *Bluffs Times* — Rte. 100; PO Box 320 (62621); W; 384pd, 275fr (Est); $3.45; C; publisher & editor Dallas M Warrum; general manager Elaine J Warrum; tel (217) 754-3369; fax (217) 754-3369

Bolingbrook: *Bolingbrook Metropolitan* — 112 S. York St., Elmhurst (60126); Th; 1,572pd, 575fr (Sw); $9.36; C; publishers Jack Cruger & Pete Cruger; general manager Vince Saputo; editor Mike Helenthal; tel (708) 834-0900; fax (708) 257-5640

Bolingbrook: *The Bolingbrook Sun* — 339 N. Schmidt Rd. (60440); W/F; 4,839pd, 17fr (ABC); $7.50; C; publisher James J Tezak; editor Tim West; tel (708) 759-9169; fax (708) 759-1726

Bourbonnais/Bradley/Monee: *The Herald/Country Market* — 500 Brown Blvd., Bourbonnais (60914); Tu; 4,377pd, 26,744fr (Sw); $10.88; C; publisher & editor Toby Olszewski; general manager Jon Olszewski; managing editor Mary Bedell; tel (815) 933-1131; fax (815) 933-3785

Braceville: *Braceville Express* — 111 S. Water St.; PO Box 327, Wilmington (60481); W; 500fr (Sw); $6.50; publisher George H Fisher; editor Eric D Fisher; tel (815) 476-7966; fax (815) 476-7002

Braidwood: *Braidwood Journal* — 273 S. Broadway; PO Box 99, Coal City (60416); W; 882pd, 43fr (Est); $1.50; C; publisher & editor Sheridan R Bailey; general manager Mitch Bailey; tel (815) 458-6246; fax (815) 634-2815

Breese: *The Breese Journal* — 623-625 N. 2nd St.; PO Box 405 (62230); Th; 5,622pd, 85fr (Est); $5.34; C; publisher Steve Mahlandt; editor Dave Mahlandt; tel (618) 526-7211; fax (618) 526-2590

Bridgeport: *Bridgeport News* — 3252 S. Halstead St., Chicago (60608); W; 300pd, 25,000fr (Est); $1.65; publisher Joseph Feldman; editor Janice Racinowski; tel (312) 842-5883; fax (312) 842-5097

Bridgeport: *Bridgeport Leader-Times* — 131 E. Olive St.; PO Box 317 (62417); Th; 1,551pd, 370fr (Sw); $3.55; C; publisher Charlotte Valbert & Louis H Valbert; editor Ray Price; tel (618) 945-2111; fax (618) 945-2131

Bridgeview/Burbank: *Bridgeview Independent* — 3840 W. 147th St.; PO Box 548, Midlothian (60445); W; 600pd, 3,100fr (Est); $6.44; C; publisher Walter H Lysen; editor Gerald Gibbons; tel (708) 388-2425; fax (708) 385-7811

Buffalo Grove/Long Grove: *Buffalo Grove Countryside* — 2201 Waukegan Rd., Ste. E-175, Bannockburn (60015); Th; 5,500pd (ABC); $54.00; C; publisher Thomas J Neri; editor Jo Hansen; managing editor Arnold Grahl; tel (708) 381-9200; fax (708) 317-1022

Bunker Hill: *Gazette-News* — 150 N. Washington (62014); Th; 1,281pd, 55fr (Est); $2.20; publisher & editor John Galer; tel (618) 585-4411

Burnham/Calumet City: *The Burnham/Calumet City Star* — 1526 Otto Blvd.; PO Box 157, Chicago Heights (60411); Th/Su; 1,104pd, 928fr (Est); $5.38; C; publisher Norman A Rosinski; general manager James S Meidell; editor Lester Sons; managing editor Frank Shuftan; tel (708) 755-6161; fax (708) 755-9112

Bushnell: *McDonough-Democrat* — 358 E. Main St.; PO Box 269 (61422); M; 1,988pd (Est); 30¢; publisher & editor William Lorton; tel (309) 772-2129; fax (309) 772-3994

Cahokia/Dupo: *Cahokia-Dupo Journal* — 212 W. Locust, Columbia (62236); W; 12,895fr (Est); $6.24; Su; 12,405fr (Est); $6.24; C; publisher & editor Marge Wilson; general manager & managing editor Dan Brown; tel (618) 281-7691; fax (618) 281-7693

Cahokia/Dupo/Columbia: *Cahokia-Dupo Herald* — 713 Range Lane; PO Box 1638, Cahokia (62206); W; 35pd, 16,500fr (Est); $8.80; C; publisher Mark J Schmersahl; editor Chris Orlet; tel (618) 337-7300; fax (618) 332-1348

Cairo: *Cairo Citizen* — 711 Washington Ave.; PO Box 33 (62914); Th; 3,100pd (Est); $4.50; C; publisher Jerry L Reppert; general manager & managing editor Jim West; editor David McNeely; tel (618) 734-4242; fax (618) 734-4244

Calhoun Co.: *The Calhoun News* — 310 S. County Rd.; PO Box 367, Hardin (62047); W; 2,675pd, 25fr (Sw); $6.59; C; publisher James F Campbell; general manager & editor James B Campbell; tel (618) 576-2244; fax (618) 576-2245

Cambridge: *Cambridge Chronicle* — 119 W. Exchange St.; PO Box 132 (61238); Th; 974pd, 17fr (Sw); $3.60; publisher & editor Thomas C Terry; tel (309) 937-3303

Carlinville: *Macoupin County Enquirer Inc.* — 125 E. Main St.; PO Box 200 (62626); Th; 4,395pd, 400fr (Sw); $2.75; C; publisher & editor Chris Schmitt; tel (217) 854-2534; fax (217) 854-2535

Carlyle: *Union Banner* — 671 10th St.; PO Box 220 (62231); W; 4,880pd, 25fr (Est); $4.60; C; publisher & editor Warren Dempsey; general manager Mike Langham; tel (618) 594-3131; fax (618) 594-3115

Carol Stream: *Carol Stream Press* — 112 S. York St., Elmhurst (60126); Th; 1,824pd, 4,085fr (Sw); $9.83; C; publishers Jack Cruger & Peter C Cruger; editor Rick Nagel; tel (708) 834-0900

Carol Stream: *The Carol Stream Examiner* — 4N 781 Gerber Rd., Bartlett (60103); W; 7,700pd (Est); $10.75; publisher Randall Petrik; editor Robin Anne; tel (708) 830-4145

Carroll Co.: *Carroll County Review* — 809 Main St.; PO Box 369, Thomson (61285); W; 2,262pd, 53fr (Sw); $5.00; publisher Jonathan K Whitney; editor William Gengenbach; tel (815) 259-2131; fax (815) 259-3226

Carrollton: *Gazette-Patriot* — 428 N. Main St.; PO Box 231 (62016); Th; 1,701pd, 60fr (Sw); $4.75; C; publisher Albert W Scott II; editor Albert W Scott III; tel (217) 942-3626; fax (217) 942-3699

Cary/Fox River Grove: *Cary-Grove Countryside* — 200 James St., Barrington (60010); Th; 3,016pd (ABC); $46.00; C; publisher Thomas J Neri; editor Jo Hansen; tel (708) 381-9200; fax (708) 381-5840

Cass Co.: *Illinoian Star* — 1210 Wall St., Beardstown (62618); Th; 1,953pd, 47fr (Sw); $7.12; C; publisher William Mitchell; general manager Pat Wellenkamp; editor Sally Leal; tel (217) 323-1010; fax (217) 323-5402

Cerro Gordo/Bement: *The News-Record* — 221 E. South St.; PO Box 49, Cerro Gordo (61818); W; 1,228pd (Sw); $4.12; publisher & editor Joe Lenhart; tel (217) 763-3541; fax (217) 763-5001

Chatham: *Chatham Clarion* — 456 N. Main (62629); Th; 1,728pd, 12fr (Sw); $3.50; C; publisher Joseph Michelich Jr; editor Paul Eisenberg; managing editor Jill Michelich; tel (217) 483-2614; fax (217) 483-3988

Chicago: *Booster* — 1115 W. Belmont (60657); W; 10,678pd (Sw); $36.70; C; publisher Lee Mortenson; editor Bill Santamour; tel (312) 281-7500; fax (312) 281-0740

Chicago: *Chicago Independent Bulletin* — 2037 W. 95th St. (60643); Th; 500pd, 61,500fr (CPVS); $11.43; publisher & editor Hurley L Green Sr; tel (312) 783-1040

Chicago: *Chicago's Northwest Side Press* — 4941 Milwaukee Ave. (60630); W; 41,000fr (Sw); $19.74; publishers Bette Nadig & Glenn Nadig; general manager Brian Nadig; editor Randy Ericson; tel (312) 286-6100

Chicago: *Harlem-Foster Times* — 7331 N. Lincoln Ave., Lincolnwood (60646); W; 2,769pd, 221fr (Est); $30.94; C; publisher Lee Mortensen; general manager Si Smith; editor Bill Santamour; managing editor Terry Kruszczak; tel (708) 329-2000; fax (708) 329-2060

Chicago: *Harlem-Irving Times* — 7331 N. Lincoln, Lincolnwood (60646); W; 3,306pd, 2,346fr (Est); $30.94; C; publisher Lee Mortenson; general manager Si Smith; editor Bill Santamour; managing editor Terry Kruszczak; tel (708) 329-2000; fax (708) 329-2060

Chicago: *Inside Publications* — 4710 N. Lincoln (60625); W; 48,600fr (Sw); $20.00; publisher Ronald Roenigk; editor Nancy Amdur; tel (312) 878-7333; fax (312) 878-0959

Chicago: *Inside Lincoln Park* — 4710 N. Lincoln (60625); W; 30,000fr (Est); $20.00; C; publisher Ronald Roenigk; editor Nancy Amdur; tel (312) 878-7333; fax (312) 878-0959

Chicago: *Inside Lake View* — 4710 N. Lincoln (60625); W; 20,000fr (Est); $20.00; C; publisher Ronald Roenigk; editor Nancy Amdur; tel (312) 878-7333; fax (312) 878-0959

Chicago: *Inside Ravenswood* — 4710 N. Lincoln (60625); W; 20,000fr (Est); $20.00; C; publisher Ronald Roenigk; editor Nancy Amdur; tel (312) 878-7333; fax (312) 878-0959

Chicago: *Jefferson Park/Portage Park/Bel-Cragin Times* — 7331 N. Lincoln Ave., Lincolnwood (60053); Th; 4,486pd, 591fr (Est); $30.94; C; publisher Lee Mortensen; general manager Si Smith; editor Bill Santamour; managing editor Terry Kruszczak; tel (708) 329-2000; fax (708) 329-2060

Chicago: *Journal* — 4937 Milwaukee Ave. (60630); Tu; 1,000fr (Sw); $6.86; publishers Bette Nadig & Glenn Nadig; general manager Brian Nadig; editor Randy Erickson; tel (312) 286-6100

Chicago: *Lincoln Park/Lake View/Near North/Downtown Skyline* — 1115 W. Belmont (60657); Th; 804pd, 24,625fr (Est); $36.70; C; publisher Lee Mortenson; editor Bill Santamour; tel (312) 281-7500; fax (312) 281-0740

Chicago: *Near North News* — 222 W. Ontario St., Ste. 502 (60610); Sa; 7,520pd, 80fr (Sw); $10.50; publisher & editor Arnie Matanky; tel (312) 787-2677; fax (312) 787-2680

Chicago: *North Center/Lincoln Belmont/Lakeview Booster* — 7331 N. Lincoln Ave., Lincolnwood (60646); W; 5,111pd, 3,286fr (Est); $16.80; C; publisher Lee Mortenson; general manager Si Smith; editor Bill Santamour; managing editor Phil Dunn; tel (708) 329-2000; fax (708) 329-2060

Chicago: *Reporter* — 4941 N. Milwaukee (60630); Sa; 13,000fr (Sw); $9.10; C; publishers Bette Nadig & Glenn Nadig; general manager Brian Nadig; editor Randy Erickson; tel (312) 286-6100

Chicago: *Scottsdale-Ashburn Independent* — 3840 W. 147th St.; PO Box 548, Midlothian (60445); Th; 200pd, 5,600fr (Est); 30¢; C; publisher Walter H Lysen; editor Gerald Gibbons; tel (708) 388-2425; fax (708) 385-7811

Chicago: *Southwest News-Herald* — 6225 S. Kedzie Ave. (60629); Th; 12,586pd (ABC); 48¢; publisher James Vondrak; general manager Naheta Jablonski; editor Joseph Boyle; tel (312) 476-4800; fax (312) 476-7811

Chicago: *The North Loop News* — 1332 N. Halsted St. (60622-2632); Th; 24,700fr (Est); $13.33; publisher Anne E Albanese; editor Michelle C Albanese; managing editor Deborah Madden; tel (312) 787-5396; fax (312) 787-1616

Chicago Hts./Steger: *Chicago Heights Star* — 1526 Otto Blvd.; PO Box 157 (60411); Th; 62,662pd (ABC); $13.54; Su; 65,569pd (ABC); $13.54; publisher Norman A Rosinski; general manager James S Meidell; editor Lester Sons; managing editor Frank S Shufton; tel (708) 755-6161; fax (708) 755-9112

Chicago Ridge: *Chicago Ridge Citizen* — 3840 W. 147th St.; PO Box 548, Midlothian (60445); Th; 3,600pd, 500fr (Est); 38¢; publisher Walter Lysen; editor Gerald Gibbons; tel (708) 388-2425; fax (708) 385-7811

Chicago Ridge/Worth: *The Chicago Ridge/Worth Star* — 1526 Otto Blvd.; PO Box 157, Chicago Heights (60411); Th; 62,758pd (ABC); $64.10; Su; 65,995pd (ABC); $64.10; C; publisher Norman A Rosinski; general manager James S Meidell; editor Lester Sons; managing editor Frank Shuftan; tel (708) 755-6161; fax (708) 755-9112

Chicago Suburbs: *Morton Grove/Niles Life* — 7331 N. Lincoln Ave., Lincolnwood (60646); Th; 6,330pd, 5,145fr (Est); $20.33; C; publisher Lee Mortenson; general manager Si Smith; editor William Santamour; managing editor Marcy Marzaki; tel (708) 329-2000; fax (708) 329-2060

Chicago/Edgebrook: *Edgebrook Times Review* — 130 S. Prospect Ave., Park Ridge (60068); Th; 1,332pd (Est); $50.00; C; publisher Thomas J Neri; editor Anne Lunde; tel (708) 696-3133; fax (708) 696-3229

Chillicothe: *Illinois Valley Advertiser* — 1008 N. 4th St. (61523); W; 4,131fr (Est); $5.77; C; publisher Ted Fleming; general manager & editor Beth Gehrt; tel (309) 274-2185; fax (309) 274-2741

Christopher: *The Progress* — 112 N. Victor; PO Box A (62822); Th; 2,110pd, 50fr (Est); $6.50; Su; 7,500fr (Est); $6.50; C; publisher G David Green; editor Del Rea; tel (618) 724-9423; fax (618) 724-9510

Cissna Park: *The Cissna Park News* — 119 W. Garfield; PO Box 8 (60924); Th; 1,557pd (Sw); $2.50; C; publisher & editor Rick A Baier; tel (815) 457-2245

Claredon Hills: *The Claredon Hills-DuPage Progress* — 922 Warren Ave., Downers Grove (60515); Th; 332pd, 5,622fr (CAC); $6.46; C; publisher & editor C J Winter; publisher P K Winter; managing editor Jennifer Parello; tel (708) 969-0188; fax (708) 969-0258

Clarendon Hills: *Clarendon Hills Doings* — 118 W. 1st St.; PO Box 151, Hinsdale (60522-0151); W/F; 10,043pd, 250fr (Sw); $14.00; C; publisher & editor J Peter Teschner; general manager James Slonoff; managing editor Pamela Lannom; tel (708) 887-0600; fax (708) 887-9646

Clayton: *Clayton Enterprise* — PO Box 200, Camp Point (62320); Tu; 250pd (Est); $2.50; publisher & editor James L Taylor; tel (217) 593-6515; fax (217) 593-7720

Coal City: *The Coal City Courant* — 273 S. Broadway; PO Box 99 (60416); W; 2,449pd, 12fr (Est); $1.40; C; publisher & editor Sheridan R Bailey; general manager Mitch Bailey; tel (815) 634-2102; fax (815) 634-2815

Collinsville: *Collinsville Journal* — 113 E. Clay St. (62234); W; 20,224fr (Est); $11.75; Su; 19,404fr (Est); $11.75; publisher Nicole Vaughn; general manager Scott Spone; editor Martin Richter; managing editor Scott Queen; tel (618) 344-0264; fax (618) 344-3611

Collinsville: *The Collinsville Herald* — 113 E. Clay St. (62234); Th; 5,522pd (Est); $7.49; publisher Nicole Vaughn; general manager Scott Spone; editor Martin Richter; managing editor Scott Queen; tel (618) 344-0264; fax (618) 344-3611

Columbia/Waterloo: *Monroe County Clarion Journal* — 212 W. Locust, Columbia (62236); W; 13,973fr (CAC); $5.98; Su; 7,979fr (CAC); $5.98; publisher Dan Braun; editors Joan Lecht & Marge Wilson; managing editor Scott Queen; tel (618) 281-7691; fax (618) 281-7693

Countryside: *Countryside Press* — 112 S. York Rd., Elmhurst (60126); Th; 149pd, 58fr (VAC); $8.53; C; publisher Jack Cruger & Pete Cruger; tel (708) 834-0900

II-18 Illinois U.S. Weeklies

Crawford Co.: *Robinson Argus* — 205 S. Franklin St.; PO Box 253, Robinson (62454); Th; 1,403pd, 20fr (Est); 17¢; publisher Carol Smith Scarpone; editor Sam Scarpone; tel (618) 544-2174

Dallas City: *Dallas City Enterprise* — 386 Oak St.; PO Box 455 (62330); Th; 1,186pd, 24fr (Est); $1.65; publisher Stephen Kempher; editor Susan Kempher; tel (217) 852-3511; fax (217) 852-3210

Darien: *The Darien Dupage Progress* — 922 Warren Ave., Downers Grove (60515); Th; 691pd, 9,496fr (CAC); $9.35; C; publisher & editor C J Winter; publisher P K Winter; managing editor Jennifer Parello; tel (708) 969-0188; fax (708) 969-0228

Darien: *Darien Metropolitan* — 223 Main St., Lemont (60440); Th; 4,830pd (Est); 47¢; publisher Jack Cruger; general manager Vince Saputo; editor Mike Helenthal; tel (708) 739-2300; fax (708) 257-5640

Decatur: *Decatur Tribune* — 240 N. Park St.; PO Box 1490 (62525); W; 5,300pd (Sw); $5.00; publisher & editor Paul Osborne; tel (217) 422-9702; fax (217) 422-7320

Deerfield/Bannockburn: *Deerfield Review* — 2201 Waukegan Rd., Ste. E-175, Bannockburn (60015); Th; 6,108pd (ABC); $64.00; publisher Thomas J Neri; general manager Peter Neill; editor Carol Goddard; managing editor Arnold Grahl; tel (708) 317-0500; fax (708) 317-1022

Delavan/S Tazewell Co.: *The Delavan Times* — 314 Locust St.; PO Box 199, Delavan (61734); W; 1,425pd, 15fr (Sw); $2.00; publisher & editor Ruth M Larimore; tel (309) 244-7111

Des Plaines: *Des Plaines Journal* — 622 Graceland Ave. (60016); W/Su; 14,672pd (Est); 78¢; publisher Richard C Wessell Sr; editor Todd C Wessell; tel (708) 299-5511; fax (708) 298-8549

Des Plaines: *Des Plaines Times* — 130 S. Prospect Ave., Park Ridge (60068); Th; 8,067pd (Est); $50.00; C; publisher Thomas J Neri; editor Joyce Diebel; tel (708) 696-3133; fax (708) 696-3229

Divernon: *Divernon News* — 110 N. 5th St.; PO Box 50, Auburn (62530); Th; 345pd, 11fr (Sw); $3.50; C; publisher & editor Joseph Michelich Jr; managing editor Jill Michelich; tel (217) 438-6155; fax (217) 438-6156

Dongola: *Dongola Tri-County Record* — 130 Front St.; PO Box 189 (62926); Th; 1,105pd, 42fr (Sw); $3.15; publisher & editor Burman P Eddleman; tel (618) 827-4353

Douglas Co.: *The Tuscola Review Inc.* — 115 W. Sale St.; PO Box 350, Tuscola (61953); Tu; 3,366pd, 21fr (Sw); 31¢; C; publisher Robert D Hastings; editor Randy H Hastings; tel (217) 253-2358; fax (217) 253-3265

Downers Grove: *The Downers Grove Reporter* — 922 Warren Ave. (60515); W; 6,056pd, 497fr (CAC); $9.30; F; 5,638pd, 18,349fr (CAC); $13.64; C; publisher & editor C J Winter; publisher P K Winter; managing editor Jennifer Parello; tel (708) 969-0188; fax (708) 969-0228

Downers Grove/Clarendon Hills/Lemont: *Lemont Reporter* — 922 Warren Ave., Downers Grove (60515); W; 808pd, 6,755fr (CAC); $5.95; C; publishers C J Winter & P K Winter; editor Bernie Biernacki; managing editor Jennifer Parello; tel (708) 257-1090; fax (708) 257-1093

Durand/Davis/Lake Sommerset/Brodhead/E Freeport: *Durand/Stephenson Gazette* — 2124 Harlem Rd.; PO Box 15340, Rockford (61132); W; 979pd, 3,437fr (Sw); $6.63; C; publisher Brian Gay; general manager Randy Johnson; editor Michele Thomas; tel (815) 877-4044; fax (815) 654-4857

Dwight: *Dwight Star & Herald* — 204 E. Chippewa St.; PO Box 159 (60420); Th; 2,370pd, 30fr (Sw); $2.60; C; publisher Scott McGraw; general manager Thomas C Doran; editor Jody Bourne; tel (815) 584-3007

Earlville: *The Earlville Leader* — 124 W. Railroad St.; PO Box 606 (60518); W; 1,115pd, 8fr (Sw); $2.50; publisher Earle E Frame; editor Lynn Henrikson; tel (815) 246-6911

E Dubuque: *East Dubuque Register* — 141 Sinsinawa Ave. (61025); F; 1,500pd, 60fr (Est); $3.25; publisher Thomas Werner; editor Thomas H Berryman; tel (815) 747-3171; fax (815) 747 3215

E Peoria: *East Peoria Courier* — 100 Detroit Ave.; PO Box 250, Morton (61550-0250); W; 198pd, 11,256fr (Est); $8.02; C; publisher Ted J Fleming; managing editor Jill Peterson; tel (309) 676-2511; fax (309) 266-7385

E St. Louis: *East St. Louis Journal* — 212 W. Locust, Columbia (62236); W/Su; 20,990fr (CAC); $13.36; publisher Mike Viola; general manager Dan Braun; editor Scott Queen; tel (618) 281-7691; fax (618) 281-7693

Edinburg: *The Herald-Star* — 103 S. Easton; PO Box 50 (62531); W; 664pd, 34fr (Sw); $2.00; publisher & editor Glenn W Luttrell; tel (217) 623-5523; fax (217) 623-4216

Edwards Co.: *West Salem Times Advocate* — 108 N. Albion St.; PO Box 427, West Salem (62476); F; 1,350pd, 4,000fr (Sw); $4.20; C; publisher & editor Harry E Bradham; tel (618) 456-8808

Edwardsville: *Edwardsville Journal* — 113 E. Clay St., Colinsville (62234); W; 12,467fr (CAC); $12.17; publisher Nicole Vaughn; general manager Scott Spone; editor Martin Richter; managing editor Scott Queen; tel (618) 344-0264; fax (618) 344-3611

Elburn: *The Elburn Herald* — 123 N. Main St.; PO Box L (60119); Th; 2,500pd, 15fr (Est); 80¢; publisher Richard L Cooper; editor Louise B Cooper; managing editor Kim M Boyd; tel (708) 365-6446; fax (708) 365-2251

Elk Grove: *Elk Grove Times* — 200 James St., Barrington (60010); Th; 766pd (Est); $60.00; C; publisher Thomas J Neri; editor Brian Rausch; tel (708) 381-9200; fax (708) 381-5840

Elmhurst: *The Elmhurst Press* — 112 S. York St. (60126); W/F; 7,165pd, 412fr (VAC); $11.00; C; publishers Jack Cruger & Peter C Cruger; editor Rick Nagel; tel (708) 834-0900; fax (708) 530-3349

Elmwood: *Tri-County News-Elmwood Gazette* — 116 S. Magnolia; PO Box 289 (61529); Th; 305pd (Est); $2.00; publisher & editor DeEllda Swindler; tel (309) 742-2521; fax (309) 742-2511

Elmwood Park: *Elm Leaves* — 1148 Westgate Ave., Oak Park (60301); W; 3,789pd (ABC); $50.00; C; publisher Thomas J Neri; editor Rick Behren; tel (708) 383-3200; fax (708) 383-3678

Elmwood Park: *Elmwood Park Post* — 6008 W. Belmont Ave., Chicago (60634); F; 4,000fr (Sw); $1.25; publisher Arthur Diaz; editor Jackie Pledger; tel (312) 283-7900; fax (312) 283-7761

Elmwood Park: *Elmwood Park/River Grove Times* — 7331 N. Lincoln Ave., Lincolnwood (60646); Th; 1,486pd, 382fr (Est); $30.94; C; publisher Lee Mortenson; general manager Si Smith; editor Bill Santamour; managing editor Terry Kruszczak; tel (708) 329-2000; fax (708) 329-2060

Emington/Saunemin/Cullon: *Emington Joker* — 204 E. Chippewa; PO Box 159, Dwight (60420); Th; 476pd, 10fr (Est); $1.95; C; publisher Scott McGraw; general manager & editor Thomas C Doran; tel (815) 584-3007

Erie: *The Review* — 100 E. Main; PO Box 31, Morrison (61270); W; 2,000pd, 17fr (Sw); 27¢; C; publisher Anthony M Komlanc Jr; editor Judy James; tel (815) 772-7244

Evanston: *Evanston Review* — 1600 Orrington Ave., Ste. 500 (60201); Th; 13,996pd (ABC); $85.00; C; publisher Thomas J Neri; editor Gary Taylor; tel (708) 866-6501; fax (708) 866-0965

Evergreen Park: *Evergreen Park Courier* — 3840 W. 147th St.; PO Box 548, Midlothian (60445); Th; 5,290pd, 525fr (Est); $6.44; publisher Walter Lysen; editor Gerald Gibbons; tel (708) 388-2425; fax (708) 385-7811

Fairbury/Forrest/Chatsworth/Chenoa/Colfax/Gridley: *The Blade* — 125 W. Locust; PO Box 78, Fairbury (61739); W; 3,400pd (Sw); $5.85; publisher R A Westerfield; editor Peg Reynolds; tel (815) 692-2366; fax (815) 692-3782

Fairfield: *Wayne County Press* — 213 E. Main St.; PO Box F (62837); M/Th; 8,465pd, 60fr (Sw); $7.14; publisher Thomas Mathews Jr; editor Penny Shreve; tel (618) 842-2662; fax (618) 842-7912

Fairview Hts.: *Fairview Heights/O'Fallon Journal* — 219 N. Illinois, Belleville (62222); W; 6,110fr (Est); $11.54; Su; 5,627fr (Est); $11.54; C; general manager Larry Johnson; editor Bonita Tillman; managing editor Scott Queen; tel (618) 277-7000; fax (618) 277-7018

Fairview Hts./O'Fallon: *Fairview Heights Tribune* — 314 E. Church St.; PO Box C, Mascoutah (62258-0189); Th; 1,250pd (Sw); $3.25; C; publisher Greg Hoskins; managing editor Les Hostetler; tel (618) 566-8282; fax (618) 566-8283

Farina: *Farina News* — 109 N. Walnut; PO Box H (62838); Th; 1,133pd (Est); 9¢; publisher & editor Shirley Ann Quick; tel (618) 245-6216

Farmer City: *Farmer City Journal* — 221 S. Main St.; PO Box 80 (61842-0080); W; 1,380pd (Est); $4.80; C; publisher Newspaper Div./Chronicle Pub. Co. Group; editor & managing editor Steve Hoffman; tel (309) 928-2193; fax (309) 928-2194

Fisher: *The Fisher Reporter* — 118 S. 3rd St.; PO Box 400 (61843-0400); W; 1,099pd, 12fr (Sw); $3.10; publisher & editor Kenneth M Sparks; publisher Robert Sparks; tel (217) 897-1525

Flanagan: *The Flanagan Home Times* — 112 S. Main St.; PO Box 158 (61740); W; 861pd (Sw); $3.50; C; publisher Richard Westerfield; general manager & editor Debbie Evans; tel (815) 796-2271

Forest Park: *Forest Park Review* — 141 S. Oak Park Ave., Oak Park (60302); W; 2,458pd, 71fr (Sw); $6.67; C; publisher Dan Haley; editor Paige Fumo; tel (708) 366-0600; fax (708) 524-0447

Forreston: *Forreston Journal* — 313 Main St. (61030); Th; 967pd, 24fr (Est); $3.25; publisher Bill Shaw; general manager Earleen Hinton; editor Bruce Harrison; tel (815) 938-3320; fax (815) 732-4238

Fox Lake/Spring Grove: *The Fox Lake Press* — 30 S. Whitney St.; PO Box 268, Grayslake (60030); Th; 5,340pd, 19fr (Est); $7.50; C; publisher & editor William H Schroeder; managing editor Rhonda Burke; tel (708) 223-8161; fax (708) 223-8810

Frankfort/Mokena/New Leno: *Frankfort-Mokena Star* — 1526 Otto Blvd.; PO Box 157, Chicago Heights (60411); Th/Su; 3,572pd, 1,426fr (Est); $8.03; publisher Norman A Rosinski; editor Lester Sons; tel (708) 687-8400; fax (708) 755-9112

Franklin Park: *Franklin Park Herald-Journal* — 1148 Westgate Ave., Oak Park (60301); W; 3,725pd (ABC); $50.00; C; publisher Thomas J Neri; editor Rick Behren; tel (708) 383-3200; fax (708) 383-3678

Franklin Park: *Franklin Park Post* — 6008 W. Belmont Ave., Chicago (60634); F; 2,000fr (Sw); $1.25; publisher Arthur Diaz; editor Jackie Pledger; tel (312) 283-7900; fax (312)-283-7761

Franklin/Murrayville: *Franklin Times* — 208 Main St.; PO Box 237, Franklin (62638); Th; 485pd, 120fr (Sw); $2.75; C; publisher & editor Ira J Lionts; general manager Allan Kifner; managing editor Denise Smith; tel (217) 675-2461; fax (217) 675-2461

Freeburg: *The Freeburg Tribune* — 10 S. Monroe St.; PO Box 98 (62243); Th; 2,572pd (Sw); $4.55; publisher & editor Harold G Carpenter; tel (618) 539-3320

Fulton/Albany: *Fulton Journal* — 408 10th Ave.; PO Box 30, Fulton (61252); W; 2,095pd, 8fr (Est); 20¢; publisher Doris Kramer; publisher & editor Henry Kramer; tel (815) 589-2424; fax (815) 589-2568

Galena: *The Gazette* — 309 S. Main St.; PO Box 319 (61036); W; 5,500pd, 11,400fr (Sw); $6.50; publisher & editor P Carter Newton; tel (815) 777-0019; fax (815) 777-3809

Galesburg: *The Galesburg Post* — 80 S. Cherry St. (61401); Th; 1,940pd, 45fr (Sw); $1.50; C; publisher Mary A Creighton; editor John P Creighton; tel (309) 343-5617

Galva: *The Galva News* — 214 Exchange St.; PO Box GG (61434); W; 2,196pd (Est); 10¢; publisher Don Cooper; general manager Lowell McKirgan; editor Rob Clark; tel (309) 932-2103; fax (309) 932-3282

Galva: *The Wrova Shopper* — 214 S. Exchange St.; PO Box GG (61434); W; 1,139pd (Est); $2.85; publisher Don Cooper; editor Rob Clark; tel (309) 932-2103; fax (309) 932-3282

Gardner/S Wilmington/Braceville: *Gardner Chronicle* — 204 E. Chippewa St.; PO Box 159, Dwight (60420); W; 837pd, 10fr (Sw); $1.95; C; publisher Scott McGraw; general manager Thomas C Doran; editor Lisa Hofman; tel (815) 584-3007

Geneseo: *Geneseo Republic* — 108 W. 1st (61254); F; 3,134pd, 31fr (Sw); $4.45; C; publisher Thomas C Terry; general manager Marnie Roman; editor Lisa Hammer; tel (309) 944-2119; fax (309) 944-6161

Geneva: *The Geneva Republican* — 6 James St.; PO Box 708 (60134); Th; 3,750pd, 50fr (Est); $10.50; publisher & editor Wayne G Woltman; managing editor Tim Unzicker; tel (708) 232-2324; fax (708) 232-9974

Genoa/Kingston/Kirkland: *Genoa-Kingston-Kirkland News* — 216 W. State St., Sycamore (60178); W; 1,185pd, 35fr (Sw); $8.48; C; publisher Robert F Coleman; editor Debbie McDaniel; tel (815) 784-5138; fax (815) 899-4329

Gibson City: *Gibson City Courier* — 310 N. Sangamon Ave.; PO Box 549 (60936); W; 2,171pd, 25fr (Est); $5.48; C; publisher Dennis C Kaster; editor Doris Benter; tel (217) 784-4244; fax (217) 784-4246

Gillespie: *Area News* — 112 W. Chestnut; PO Box 209 (62033); Th; 2,954pd (Est); $28.00; publisher & editor David Ambrose; publisher Patty Ambrose; tel (217) 839-2130; fax (217) 839-2139

Gilman: *The Gilman Star* — 203 N. Central St.; PO Box 7 (60938); W; 2,705pd, 41fr (Est); $2.21; C; publisher & editor John T Elliott; tel (815) 265-7332; fax (815) 265-7880

Girard: *The Girard Gazette* — 169 W. Jackson St.; PO Box 339, Virden (62690); W; 1,211pd, 17fr (Sw); $3.50; C; publishers Charles E Jones & Dorothy Jones; editor Norris E Jones; tel (217) 627-2115; fax (217) 965-4512

Glasford: *The Glasford Gazette* — 401 Main St. (61533-0260); Th; 1,206pd (Est); $3.22; publisher & editor Bill Wadkins; tel (309) 389-2811

Glen Ellyn/Wheaton: *The Glen Ellyn News* — 460 Pennsylvania Ave., Glen Ellyn (60137); W/F; 6,600pd, 400fr (Est); $8.24; C; publisher Stuart S Stone; editor Michael Vaughn; tel (708) 469-0100; fax (708) 469-4472

Glencoe: *Glencoe News* — 3701 W. Lake Ave., Glenview (60025); Th; 2,278pd (ABC); $50.00; publisher Thomas J Neri; editor Elaine Fandell; tel (708) 486-9200; fax (708) 486-7451

Glendale Hts.: *Glendale Heights Press* — 112 S. York St., Elmhurst (60126); Th; 1,017pd, 579fr (Sw); $9.83; C; publishers Jack Cruger & Peter C Cruger; editor Rick Nagel; tel (708) 834-0900; fax (708) 530-3349

Glenview: *Glenview Announcements* — 3701 W. Lake Ave. (60025); Th; 7,728pd (ABC); $64.00; publisher Thomas J Neri; editor Cathy Backer; tel (708) 486-9200; fax (708) 486-7451

Golden: *New Era* — PO Box 200, Camp Point (62320); Tu; 500pd (Est); $2.50; publisher & editor James L Taylor; tel (217) 593-6515; fax (217) 593-7720

Granite City: *Granite City Journal* — 1815 Delmar Ave. (62040); W; 22,505fr (Est); $12.17; Su; 21,680fr (Est); $12.17; publisher Suburban Journals; general manager Larry Johnson; editor Bob Slate; managing editor Scott Queen; tel (618) 877-7700; fax (618) 876-4240

Granite City: *Press Record* — 1815 Delmar Ave. (62040); Th; 6,643pd (Est); $12.17; publisher Suburban Journals; general manager Larry Johnson; editor Bob Slate; managing editor Scott Queen; tel (618) 877-7700; fax (618) 876-4240

Grayslake: *Grayslake Times* — 30 S. Whitney St.; PO Box 268 (60030); Th; 4,181pd, 15fr (Est); $7.50; C; publisher & editor William H Schroeder; managing editor Rhonda Burke; tel (708) 223-8161; fax (708) 223-8810

Grayslake/Gages Lake: *Grayslake Review* — 2201 Waukegan Rd., Ste. E-175, Bannockburn (60015); Th; 3,538pd (ABC); $50.00; C; publisher Thomas J Neri; general manager Peter Neill; editor Carol Goddard; managing editor Jerry Wallis; tel (708) 317-0500; fax (708) 317-1022

Grayville: *Mercury-Independent* — 105 E. North St.; PO Box 220 (62844); Th; 1,963pd, 25fr (Est); 18¢; publisher Steve Raymond; editor Karen Lourens; tel (618) 375-3131; fax (618) 445-3459

Great Lakes Naval Training: *Great Lakes Bulletin* — 30 S. Whitney St.; PO Box 268, Grayslake (60030); F; 22,000fr (Est); $16.75; C; publisher William H Schroeder; editor Jeff Brown; tel (708) 223-8161; fax (708) 223-8810

Greenup/Cumberland Co.: *Greenup Press* — 104 E. Cumperland; PO Box 127, Greenup (62428); W; 1,686pd, 44fr (Sw); $4.00; publisher & editor William J McMorris; tel (217) 923-3704; fax (217) 923-3704

Greenview/Athens: *Menard County Review* — Rte. 2; PO Box 77B, Athens (62613); Th; 1,500pd, 12fr (Sw); $2.10; C; publisher Jane Cutright; editors Carolyn Miller & Sue Kennebeck; tel (217) 636-8453/968-5511/632-2236; fax (217) 632-2237

Greenville/Bond Co.: *The Greenville Advocate* — 305 S. 2nd St.; PO Box 10, Greenville (62246); Tu/Th; 4,926pd, 53fr (Sw); $5.50; C; publisher & editor Duane Reeves; tel (618) 664-3144

Gurnee: *Gurnee Review* — 2201 Waukegan Rd., Ste. E-175, Bannockburn (60015); Th; 3,983pd (ABC); $50.00; C; publisher Thomas J Neri; general manager Peter Neill; editor Carol Goddard; managing editor Jerry Wallis; tel (708) 317-0500; fax (708) 317-1022

Gurnee: *The Gurnee Press* — 30 S. Whitney St.; PO Box 268, Grayslake (60030); Th; 4,714pd, 14fr (Est); $7.50; C; publisher & editor William H Schroeder; managing editor Rhonda Burke; tel (708) 223-8161; fax (708) 223-8810

Hampshire/Kane Co.: *Hampshire Register-News* — PO Box 337, Hampshire (60140); W; 1,425pd, 17fr (Sw); $10.45; C; publisher Roger Coleman; editor Gary Koehler; tel (708) 683-2627; fax (815) 899-4329

Hancock Co.: *Hancock County Journal-Pilot* — 31 N. Washington St.; PO Box 478, Carthage (62321); W; 3,785pd, 142fr (Sw); $5.00; C; publisher Bill Ferguson; managing editor Tom Martin; tel (217) 357-2149; fax (217) 357-2177

Hanna City: *Hanna City-Trivoli Index* — 401 Main St., Glasford (61533-0260); Th; 330pd (Est); $3.22; publisher & editor Bill Wadkins; tel (309) 389-2811

Hanover Park: *The Hanover Park Examiner* — 4N 781 Gerber Rd., Bartlett (60103); W; 5,600pd (Est); $10.75; publisher Randall Petrik; editor Robin Anne; tel (708) 830-4145; fax (708) 830-2531

Hardin Co.: *Hardin County Independent* — 25-27 W. 1st St.; PO Box 328, Elizabethtown (62931); Th; 2,389pd, 100fr (Sw); $2.80; publisher & editor Noel E Hurford; tel (618) 287-2361

Harvard: *Harvard Star* — 5404 W. Elm St., McHenry (60050); W; 1,178pd (Est); $7.05; C; publisher David M Stamps; general manager Albert (Bo) Smith; tel (815) 385-2231; fax (815) 385-2231

Harvey/Markham/Dixmoor: *Harvey-Markham Star* — 1526 Otto Blvd.; PO Box 157, Chicago Heights (60411); Th/Su; 4,122pd, 163fr (Est); $7.32; publisher Norman A Rosinski; general manager James S Meidell; editor Lester Sons; managing editor Frank Shuftan; tel (708) 755-6161; fax (708) 755-9112

Havana: *Mason County Democrat* — 219 W. Market (62644); W; 3,900pd (Est); $7.00; publisher Robert L Martin Jr; editor Wendy J Martin; tel (309) 543-3311; fax (309) 543-6844

Hazel Crest/Country Club: *Hazel Crest-Country Club Hills Star* — 1526 Otto Blvd.; PO Box 157, Chicago Heights (60411); Su/Th; 3,793pd, 162fr (Est); $7.36; publisher Norman A Rosinski; general manager James S Meidell; editor Lester Sons; managing editor Frank Shuftan; tel (708) 755-6161; fax (708) 755-9112

Henry/Marshall: *Henry News Republican* — 709 3rd St.; PO Box 190, Henry (61537); W; 2,019pd, 681fr (Sw); $4.25; C; publisher & editor George Ziegler; tel (309) 364-3250; fax (309) 364-3858

Herrin: *The Spokesman* — 106 N. 14th St.; PO Box 128 (62948); Th; 1,818pd, 115fr (VAC); 30¢; Su; 10,030fr (VAC); 30¢; publisher G David Green; editor John Homan; tel (618) 942-5000; fax (618) 942-4630

Herscher: *The Herscher Press* — 204 E. Chippewa St.; PO Box 159, Dwight (60420); Th; 898pd, 12fr (Sw); $1.95; C; publisher Scott McGraw; general manager Thomas C Doran; editor Myke Feinman; tel (815) 584-1270

Heyworth: *Heyworth Star* — 105 S. Buchanan St. (61745); Th; 1,096pd (Est); 25¢; publisher & editor James M Beveridge; tel (309) 473-2414

Hickory Hills: *Hickory Hills Citizen* — 3840 W. 147th St., Midlothian (60445); Th; 2,700pd, 400fr (Est); $6.44; C; publisher Walter H Lysen; editor Gerald Gibbons; tel (708) 388-2425; fax (708) 385-7811

Highland: *Highland News Leader* — 1 Woodcrest Professional Park; PO Box 250 (62249); M/Th; 8,000pd (Sw); $7.25; publisher Steve Holt; general manager Kay Maue; tel (618) 654-2366; fax (618) 654-1181

Highland Park/Highwood: *Highland Park News* — 2201 Waukegan Rd., Ste. E-175, Bannockburn (60015); Th; 7,735pd (ABC); $64.00; C; publisher Thomas J Neri; editor Carol Goddard; managing editor Kyle Leonard; tel (708) 317-0500; fax (708) 317-1022

Hillsboro: *Hillsboro Journal* — 431 S. Main St.; PO Box 100 (62049); M/Th; 6,513pd, 36fr (Est); $5.25; C; publisher John M Galer; editor Phillip C Galer; tel (217) 532-3933; fax (217) 532-3632

Hillsboro/Litchfield: *The Montgomery County News* — Court House Sq.; PO Box 250, Hillsboro (62049); M/W/F; 4,788pd, 60fr (Est); $2.86; publisher Nancy Slepicka; editor Richard Slepicka; tel (217) 532-3929; fax (217) 532-3522

Hillside/Berkeley: *West Cook County Press* — 112 S. York St., Elmhurst (60126); Th; 486pd, 162fr (Sw); $8.18; publishers Jack Cruger & Peter C Cruger; editor Rick Nagel; tel (708) 834-0900; fax (708) 530-3349

Hillside/Berkeley: *West Proviso Herald* — 1148 Westgate Ave., Oak Park (60301); W; 2,313pd (ABC); $58.00; C; publisher Thomas J Neri; editor Tom Ganz; tel (708) 383-3200; fax (708) 383-3678

Hinsdale/Clarendon Hills/Oak Brook/Darien/Burr Ridge/Willowbrook/Oakbrook Terrace/Western Springs/Indian Head Park: *The Doings* — 118 W. 1st St.; PO Box 151, Hinsdale (60522); W/F; 10,043pd, 267fr (Sw); $14.00; C; publisher & editor J Peter Teschner; general manager James Slonoff; managing editor Pamela Lannom; tel (708) 887-0600; fax (708) 887-9646

Hoffman Estates: *Hoffman Estates Review* — 200 James St., Barrington (60010); Th; 3,518pd (ABC); $60.00; C; publisher Thomas J Neri; editor Jo Hansen; managing editor Brian Rausch; tel (708) 381-9200; fax (708) 381-5840

Homer Twp.: *The Homer Township Star* — 1526 Otto Blvd.; PO Box 157, Chicago Heights (60411); Th; 62,758pd (ABC); $5.98; Su; 65,995pd (ABC); $5.98; C; publisher Norman A Rosinski; general manager James S Meidell; editor Lester Sons; managing editor Frank Shuftan; tel (708) 755-6161; fax (708) 755-9112

Homewood/Flossmoor: *Homewood Flossmoor Star* — 1526 Otto Blvd.; PO Box 157, Chicago Heights (60411); Th/Su; 7,785pd, 241fr (Est); $9.43; publisher Norman A Rosinski; general manager James S Meidell; editor Lester Sons; managing editor Frank Shuftan; tel (708) 755-6161; fax (708) 755-9112

Hoopeston: *Chronicle* — 308 E. Main St.; PO Box 190 (60942); Tu/F; 2,200pd, 10fr (Sw); $3.45; C; publisher Bette D Schmid; editor JoAnn Gocking; tel (217) 283-5111; fax (217) 283-5846

Hyde Park/Kenwood: *Hyde Park Herald* — 5240 S. Harper Ave., Chicago (60615); W; 5,919pd, 174fr (Sw); $33.66; publisher Bruce Sagan; editor Florence Goold; tel (312) 643-8533; fax (312) 643-8542

Illiopolis: *Illiopolis Sentinel* — 550 Mary St.; PO Box 477 (62539); Th; 865pd, 60fr (Sw); $2.24; publisher & editor Frank J Bell; tel (217) 486-7321

Itasca: *Itasca Press* — 112 S. York Rd., Elmhurst (60126); Th; 655pd, 21fr (VAC); $9.83; C; publishers Jack Cruger & Peter C Cruger; tel (708) 834-0900

Joliet Area/Will Co.: *Farmers Weekly Review* — 100 Manhattan Rd., Joliet (60433); Th; 8,774pd, 22fr (Sw); $8.00; publisher & editor Patrick J Cleary; tel (815) 727-4811; fax (815) 727-5570

Kinmundy: *Kinmundy Express* — 210 S. Madison; PO Box 220 (62854); Th; 843pd (Est); 9¢; publisher Rudolph D Slane; editor Judith Slane; tel (618) 547-3111

Knoxville: *The Knoxville Journal* — 80 S. Cherry St., Galesburg (61401); Th; 1,125pd, 5fr (Sw); $1.50; C; publisher & editor John P Creighton; publisher Mary A Creighton; tel (309) 343-5617

La Grange/La Grange Park/Countryside: *La Grange Press* — 112 S. York St., Elmhurst (60126); Th; 484pd, 2,972fr (Sw); $8.53; C; publishers Jack Cruger & Peter C Cruger; editor Rick Nagel; tel (708) 834-0900; fax (708) 530-3349

La Grange/W Cook Co.: *Suburban Life Citizen* — 709 Enterprise Dr., Oak Brook (60521-8824); W/Sa; 25,119pd, 3,127fr (CAC); $16.38; publishers Jack R Kubik; editor Bill Conkis; managing editor Joe DeRosier; tel (708) 368-1100; fax (708) 368-1199

La Harpe: *Hancock County Quill* — PO Box 465 (61450); W; 1,310pd, 50fr (Sw); 18¢; C; publisher Dessa L Rodeffer; general manager Lucille Rodeffer; tel (217) 659-3316

Lacon/Toluca/Sparland: *Lacon Home Journal* — 204 S. Washington St., Lacon (61540); W; 1,940pd (Sw); $3.50; publisher & editor William H Sondag; tel (309) 246-2865; fax (309) 246-3214

Lake Forest/Lake Bluff: *Lake Forester* — 2201 Waukegan Rd., Ste. E-175, Bannockburn (60015); Th; 6,516pd (ABC); $64.00; C; publisher Thomas J Neri; editor Carol Goddard; managing editor Kyle Leonard; tel (708) 317-0500; fax (708) 317-1022

Lake Villa: *Lake Villa Record* — 30 S. Whitney St.; PO Box 268, Grayslake (60030); Th; 2,979pd, 12fr (Est); $7.50; C; publisher & editor William H Schroeder; managing editor Rhonda Burke; tel (708) 223-8161; fax (708) 223-8810

Lake Villa/Lindenhurst: *The Review* — 2201 Waukegan Rd., Ste. E-175, Bannockburn (60015); Th; 2,208pd (ABC); $50.00; C; publisher Thomas J Neri; general manager Peter Neill; editor Carol Goddard; managing editor Jerry Wallis; tel (708) 317-0500; fax (708) 317-1022

Lake Zurich: *Lake Zurich Enterprise* — 30 S. Whitney; PO Box 268, Grayslake (60030); Th; 3,396pd, 325fr (Est); $7.50; C; publisher & editor William H Schroeder; managing editor Rhonda Burke; tel (708) 223-8161; fax (708) 223-8810

Lake Zurich/Kildeer/Wauconda: *Lake Zurich Courier* — 200 James St., Barrington (60010); Th; 3,405pd, 200fr (ABC); $46.00; C; publisher Thomas J Neri; editor Jo Hansen; managing editor Tom Scott; tel (708) 381-9200; fax (708) 381-5840

Lansing/Lynwood: *The Lansing/Lynwood Star* — 1526 Otto Blvd.; PO Box 157, Chicago Heights (60411); Th/Su; 1,633pd, 1,120fr (Est); $4.74; C; publisher Norman A Rosinski; general manager James S Meidell; editor Lester Sons; managing editor Frank Shuftan; tel (708) 755-6161; fax (708) 755-9112

Lawrence Co.: *Lawrence County News* — 1209 State St.; PO Box 559, Lawrenceville (62439); W; 413pd (Est); 10¢; publisher Larry H Lewis; tel (618) 943-2331; fax (618) 943-3976

Lawrence/Richland Cos.: *The Sumner Press* — 216 S. Christy; PO Box 126, Sumner (62466); Th; 1,805pd, 250fr (Sw); $2.60; publisher Sumner Press Inc.; editor JoAnn Dowty; tel (618) 936-2212; fax (618) 936-2858

Le Roy/Downs/Ellsworth: *The Le Roy Journal* — 119 E. Center St.; PO Box 30, Le Roy (61752-0030); W; 1,306pd (Est); $4.70; publisher Newspaper Div./Chronicle Pub. Co. Group; editor Sue Bratcher; managing editor Steve Hoffman; tel (309) 962-4441; fax (309) 962-2037

Leaf River/Byron/Oregon/Stillman Vly./ Rochelle: *Northern Ogle County Tempo* — 2124 Harlem Rd.; PO Box 15340, Loves Park (61111); Tu; 1,750pd, 4,738fr (Sw); $6.65; C; publisher Brian Gay; general manager Randy Johnson; editor Michele Thomas; tel (815) 877-4044; fax (815) 654-4857

Lebanon: *Lebanon Advertiser* — 309 W. St. Louis St. (62254-0126); W; 1,620pd, 11fr (Sw); 25¢; publisher Harrison Leon Church; editor Helen S Church; tel (618) 537-4498

Lebanon: *Lebanon Herald* — 314 E. Church St.; PO Drawer C, Mascoutah (62258-0158); Th; 1,200pd (Sw); $3.25; C; publisher Greg Hoskins; managing editor Les Hostetler; tel (618) 566-8282; fax (618) 566-8283

Lemont: *Lemont Metropolitan* — 112 S. York St., Elmhurst (60126); Th; 3,474pd (Sw); $8.53; C; publishers Jack Cruger & Peter C Cruger; editor Mike Galati; tel (708) 834-0900

Lena: *Northwestern Illinois Farmer* — 119 W. Railroad; PO Box 536 (61048); W; 11,345pd, 85fr (Sw); $7.00; publisher Patrick Mattison; editor Norman Templin; tel (815) 369-2811; fax (815) 369-2816

Lewistown: *Fulton Democrat* — 165 W. Lincoln (61542); W; 3,850pd, 2,600fr (Sw); 11¢; publisher Robert L Martin Jr; editor Ruth Lynn; tel (309) 547-3055; fax (309) 543-6844

Leyden/Proviso Twps.: *Northlake Star Sentinel* — 1440 W. North Ave., Ste. 206, Melrose Park (60160); W; 1,080pd, 1,119fr (Est); 45¢; publisher & editor David Roberts; tel (708) 345-1750; fax (708) 345-1795

Liberty/Payson: *The Liberty Bee-Times* — 19 E. Hannibal; PO Box 198, Liberty (62347); W; 1,200pd, 35fr (Sw); 25¢; C; publisher James Elliott; editor Marcia Elliott; tel (217) 645-3033; fax (217) 645-3083

Libertyville: *Libertyville News* — 30 S. Whitney St.; PO Box 268, Grayslake (60030); Th; 3,081pd, 15fr (Est); $7.50; C; publisher & editor William H Schroeder; managing editor Rhonda Burke; tel (708) 223-8161; fax (708) 223-8810

Libertyville/Green Oaks: *Libertyville Review* — 2201 Waukegan Rd., Ste. E-175, Bannockburn (60015); Th; 4,110pd (ABC); $50.00; C; publisher Thomas J Neri; editor Carol Goddard; managing editor Sheila Richard; tel (708) 317-0500; fax (708) 317-3551

Lincolnwood: *Lincolnwood Life* — 7331 N. Lincoln Ave. (60646); Th; 1,295pd, 478fr (CAC); $36.70; C; publisher Lee Mortenson; general manager Si Smith; editor Bill Santamour; managing editor Marcy Marzuka; tel (708) 329-2000; fax (708) 329-2060

Lincolnwood: *Lincolnwood Review* — 1600 Orrington Ave., Evanston (60201); Th; 1,575pd (Est); $50.00; publisher Thomas J Neri; editor Peter Neill; managing editor Dan Obermaier; tel (708) 866-5250; fax (708) 866-0965

Lindenhurst: *Lindenhurst News* — 30 S. Whitney St.; PO Box 268, Grayslake (60030); Th; 2,832pd, 11fr (Est); $7.50; C; publisher & editor William H Schroeder; managing editor Rhonda Burke; tel (708) 223-8161; fax (708) 223-8810

Lisle: *The Lisle Reporter* — 922 Warren Ave., Downers Grove (60515); Th; 6,867fr (Est); $7.35; C; publisher & editor C J Winter; publisher P K Winter; managing editor Jennifer Parello; tel (708) 969-0188; fax (708) 969-0258

Lisle: *The Lisle Sun* — 9 W. Jackson; PO Box 269, Naperville (60566-0269); W/F; 3,581pd (ABC); $6.75; C; publisher James J Tezak; editor Timothy J West; tel (708) 355-0063; fax (708) 355-2432

Loda: *Loda Times* — 218 N. Market St.; PO Box 73, Paxton (60957); W; 320pd, 5fr (Sw); $6.10; C; publisher Paul E Anderson; general manager Toni Swan; editor Robert Maney; managing editor David Hinton; tel (217) 379-4313; fax (217) 379-3104

Lombard: *Lombardian* — 613 S. Main St. (60148); W; 10,000pd, 4,500fr (Est); 44¢; publisher Scott D MacKay; editor Bonnie MacKay; tel (708) 627-7010; fax (708) 627-7027

Lombard: *The Lombard Spectator* — 112 S. York St., Elmhurst (60126); W/F; 1,503pd, 7,007fr (Sw); $10.06; C; publishers Jack Cruger & Peter C Cruger; editor Rick Nagel; tel (708) 834-0900; fax (708) 530-3349

Mahomet: *The Mahomet Citizen* — 427 E. Main St. (61583-0919); W; 2,202pd (Sw); $3.55; publisher & editor Erik Anderson; tel (217) 586-2512; fax (217) 586-4821

Manhattan: *Manhattan American* — 120 W. North St.; PO Box 429, Peotone (60468); Th; 854pd, 55fr (Est); $1.55; publisher Gilbert L Russell; editor Barbara Daugherty; tel (708) 946-2151; fax (708) 258-6295

Manito: *Manito Review* — 104 N. Broadway; PO Box 560 (61546); Tu; 3,250fr (Est); $3.50; C; publisher & editor Victor Rickard; general manager Betty Wilson; tel (309) 968-6705; fax (309) 968-7486

Manteno: *The Manteno News* — 415 S. Locust; PO Box 578 (60950); Th; 1,744pd, 36fr (Sw); $2.50; C; publisher Gilbert Russell; general manager Mary LaMore; managing editor Betty Knauth; tel (815) 468-6397; fax (815) 468-7577

Marengo: *Marengo Star* — 5404 W. Elm St., McHenry (60050); W; 1,055pd (Est); $7.05; C; publisher David M Stamps; general manager Albert (Bo) Smith; tel (815) 385-2231; fax (815) 385-2237

Marissa/New Athens/Lenzburg/Darmstadt: *The Journal Messenger* — 615 E. Lyons (62257); Th; 1,909pd, 79fr (Sw); $3.95; C; publisher Bart McDowell; editor Michael Huck; tel (618) 295-2812; fax (618) 295-3422

Mascoutah: *Herald* — 314 E. Church St.; PO Drawer C (62258-0189); Th; 2,250pd (Sw); $3.25; C; publisher Greg Hoskins; managing editor Les Hostetler; tel (618) 566-8282; fax (618) 566-8283

Matteson/Richton Park: *Matteson-Richton Park Star* — 1526 Otto Blvd.; PO Box 157, Chicago Heights (60411); Th; 62,758pd (ABC); $7.12; Su; 65,995pd (ABC); $7.12; C; publisher Norman A Rosinski; general manager James S Meidell; editor Lester Sons; managing editor Frank Shuftan; tel (708) 755-6161; fax (708) 755-9112

Maywood/Broadview: *Maywood Herald* — 1148 Westgate Ave., Oak Park (60301); W; 3,208pd (ABC); $58.00; C; publisher Thomas J Neri; editor Tom Ganz; tel (708) 383-3200; fax (708) 383-3678

McHenry: *McHenry Star* — 5404 W. Elm St. (60050); W; 12,150fr (Est); $7.90; C; publisher David M Stamps; general manager Albert (Bo) Smith; tel (815) 385-2231; fax (815) 385-2237

McLeansboro/Mt. Vernon/Carmi/Dahlgren/Benton/Dale/Broughton/Fairfield/Wayne City: *McLeansboro Times Leader* — 123 S. Jackson St.; PO Box 479, McLeansboro (62859); W; 3,021pd, 13fr (Sw); $4.10; C; publisher Charles E Deitz; general manager Kathy Metcalf; editor Ken Dare; tel (618) 643-2387

Melrose Park/Stone Park: *The Melrose Park Herald* — 1148 Westgate Ave., Oak Park (60301); W; 2,264pd (ABC); $58.00; C; publisher Thomas J Neri; editor Tom Ganz; tel (708) 383-3200; fax (708) 383-3678

Melvin/Roberts: *Ford County Press* — 115 W. Main; PO Box 195, Melvin (60952); Th; 965pd, 19fr (Sw); $2.25; C; publisher & editor Fred W Thackeray; tel (217) 388-7721

Mendon: *Dispatch-Times* — PO Box 200, Camp Point (62320); Tu; 845pd (Est); 20¢; publisher & editor James L Taylor; tel (217) 936-2295; fax (217) 593-7720

Mendota: *Mendota Reporter* — 702 Illinois Ave.; PO Box 100 (61342); W; 4,271pd, 265fr (Sw); $6.75; C; publisher Thomas Cross; general manager Jeff Ohlendorf; editor Kip Cheek; tel (815) 539-9396; fax (815) 539-7862

Mercer Co.: *The Times Record* — 113-115 S. College Ave.; PO Box 309, Aledo (61231); W; 4,000pd, 11,000fr (Est); $8.40; C; general manager Ray McGrew; tel (309) 582-5112; fax (309) 582-5319

Meredosia: *Meredosia Budget* — Rte. 100; PO Box 320, Bluffs (62665); W; 421pd, 275fr (Est); $3.45; C; publisher & editor Dallas M Warrum; managing editor Elaine J Warrum; tel (217) 754-3369; fax (217) 754-3369

Metamora: *Metamora Herald* — 214 E. Partridge (61548); Th; 2,382pd, 45fr (Est); 16¢; publisher & editor Melvin Nielson; general manager & managing editor Stephanie Vanlaningham; tel (309) 367-2335; fax (309) 367-4277

Metropolis: *The Metropolis Planet* — 111 E. 5th St.; PO Box 820 (62960); W; 5,417pd, 116fr (Sw); $5.60; C; publisher & editor Clyde Wills; tel (618) 524-2141; fax (618) 524-4727

Midlothian: *Star Super Saver II* — 1526 Otto Blvd.; PO Box 157, Chicago Heights (60411); Su; 10,701fr (Est); $1.90; publisher Norman A Rosinski; general manager James S Meidell; editor Lester Sons; managing editor Frank Shuftan; tel (708) 755-6161; fax (708) 755-9112

Midlothian/Tinley Park/Crestwood/Posen/Markham: *Midlothian-Bremen Messenger* — 3840 W. 147th St.; PO Box 548, Midlothian (60445); Th; 11,000pd, 1,106fr (Est); $6.44; publisher Walter H Lysen; editor Gerald Gibbons; tel (708) 388-2425; fax (708) 385-7811

Milford: *Milford Herald-News* — 18 S. Axtel Ave.; PO Box 200 (60953); W; 1,300pd, 30fr (Est); $2.00; publisher & editor John O Hallock; tel (815) 889-4321

Millstadt/Belleville: *Millstadt Enterprise Journal* — 212 W. Locust, Columbia (62236); W; 415pd, 4,135fr (Est); $5.70; publisher Dan Braun; editor Marge Wilson; managing editor Scott Queen; tel (618) 281-7691; fax (618) 281-7693

Minier: *Olympia Review* — 102 S. Main St.; PO Box 710 (61759); Tu; 4,498fr (Est); $4.50; publisher & editor Victor Rickard; tel (309) 392-2414; fax (309) 392-2169

Minonk: *Minonk News-Dispatch* — 224 E. 5th St.; PO Box 68 (61760); Th; 671pd (Sw); $4.60; C; publisher Mark Barra; editor J W Shults; tel (309) 432-2505; fax (309) 432-2506

Momence: *The Momence Progress-Reporter* — 110 W. River St.; PO Box 289 (60954); Th; 2,440pd, 62fr (Est); $2.25; publisher H Gene Lincoln; editor M Sue Lincoln; tel (815) 472-2000; fax (815) 472-3877

Monee: *Monee Moniter* — 120 W. North St.; PO Box 429, Peotone (60468); Th; 561pd, 37fr (Est); $2.40; publisher Gilbert L Russell; general manager Chris Russell; tel (708) 258-3473; fax (708) 258-6295

Mont Clare: *Mont Clare Post* — 6008 W. Belmont Ave., Chicago (60634); F; 1,500fr (Sw); $1.25; publisher Arthur Diaz; editor Jackie Pledger; tel (312) 283-7900; fax (312) 283-7761

Monticello: *Piatt County Journal-Republican* — 118 E. Washington St.; PO Box 110 (61856); W; 3,668pd, 39fr (Sw); $6.10; C; publisher Dennis C Kaster; editor Maggie Schwarzentraub; tel (217) 762-2511; fax (217) 352-1722

Morrison: *Whiteside News-Sentinel* — 100 E. Main St. (61270); Tu; 3,000pd, 24fr (Sw); 27¢; publisher & editor Anthony M Komlanc Jr; tel (815) 772-7244

Morrisonville: *The Morrisonville Times* — 511 Carlin St. (62546); W; 1,163pd, 50fr (Est); 13¢; publishers John Lennon & Julia Lennon; editor Terri Deao; tel (217) 526-3323; fax (217) 526-3323

Morton: *Tazewell News/Tazewell News Extra* — 100 Detroit Ave.; PO Box 250 (61550-0250); W; 3,629pd, 5,729fr (Est); $8.95; Sa; 3,629pd (Est); $8.95; C; publisher Ted J Fleming; editor DeWayne Bartles; tel (309) 263-2211; fax (309) 266-7385

Morton Grove: *Morton Grove Champion* — 1600 Orrington Ave., Evanston (60201); Th; 3,636pd (ABC); $46.00; C; publisher Thomas J Neri; editor Dan Obermaier; tel (708) 866-5250; fax (708) 866-0965

Morton/Tremont: *Courier* — 184 E. Washington, Morton (61550); W; 8,650fr (Est); $5.73; C; publisher & editor Roger Hagel; tel (309) 263-7414; fax (309) 444-8505

Mt. Carroll: *Mirror-Democrat* — 308 N. Main St.; PO Box 191, Mt. Carroll (61053); W; 1,975pd, 10fr (Sw); $6.00; C; publisher & editor Robert W Watson; general manager Pam Cross; tel (815) 244-2411; fax (815) 244-2965

Mt. Greenwood: *Mount Greenwood Express* — 3840 W. 147th St.; PO Box 548, Midlothian (60445); Th; 8,729pd, 800fr (Est); 38¢; C; publisher Walter H Lysen; editor Gerald Gibbons; tel (708) 388-2425; fax (708) 385-7811

Mt. Morris: *Mount Morris Times* — 121A S. 4th; PO Box 8, Oregon (61061); Th; 1,025pd, 35fr (Est); $4.77; publisher Bill Shaw; general manager Earleen Hinton; editor Ginger Riehle; tel (815) 732-6166; fax (815) 732-4238

Mt. Prospect: *Mount Prospect Times* — 130 S. Prospect Ave., Park Ridge (60068); Th; 5,512pd (Est); $46.00; C; publisher Thomas J Neri; editor Joyce Diebel; tel (708) 696-3133; fax (708) 696-3229

Mt. Pulaski: *The Weekly-News* — 217 S. Washington St., Mt. Pulaski (62548); Th; 1,462pd (Sw); $6.00; C; publisher & editor Michael Lakin; tel (217) 792-5557

Mt. Sterling/Brown Co.: *The Democrat Message* — 110 W. Main; PO Box 71, Mt. Sterling (62353); Tu; 2,400pd, 25fr (Est); 19¢; publisher Joan Coulson; general manager & managing editor Warren Coulson; tel (217) 773-3371; fax (217) 773-3369

Mt. Zion/Dalton City: *The Mt. Zion Region News* — 130 Wildwood Dr.; PO Box 79, Mt. Zion (62549); Th; 1,650pd, 20fr (Sw); $5.50; C; publisher Mike Brothers; editor Erin Brothers; tel (217) 864-4212; fax (217) 864-4711

Mundelein: *Mundelein Review* — 2201 Waukegan Rd., Ste. E-175, Bannockburn (60015); Th; 2,702pd (ABC); $50.00; C; publisher Thomas J Neri; editor Sheila Richard; tel (708) 317-0500; fax (708) 317-1022

Mundelein: *The Mundelein News* — 30 S. Whitney St.; PO Box 268, Grayslake (60030); Th; 3,162pd, 13fr (Est); $7.50; C; publisher & editor William H Schroeder; general manager William M Schroeder; managing editor Rhonda Burke; tel (708) 223-8161; fax (708) 223-8810

Murphysboro: *Murphysboro American* — 1400 Walnut; PO Box 550 (62966); M; 1,766pd, 8,695fr (VAC); $6.14; Th; 1,760pd (VAC); $6.14; C; publisher & editor Tom Tiernan; general manager John Fleming; tel (618) 684-5833; fax (618) 684-5080

Naperville: *Naperville Metroplitan* — 112 S. York St., Elmhurst (60126); Th; 6,000fr (Sw); $8.83; C; publishers Jack Cruger & Pete Cruger; tel (708) 834-0900

Naperville: *The Naperville Sun* — 9 W. Jackson; PO Box 269 (60566-0269); W/F; 19,846pd, 391fr (ABC); $10.25; Su; 19,406pd, 383fr (ABC); $10.25; C; publisher James J Tezak; editor Timothy J West; tel (708) 355-0063; fax (708) 355-2432

Nashville/Washington Co.: *The Nashville News* — 211 W. St. Louis St.; PO Box 47, Nashville (62263); W; 5,675pd, 50fr (Sw); $4.75; publisher & editor Richard Tomaszewski; tel (618) 327-3411; fax (618) 327-3299

Nauvoo: *Nauvoo News Independent* — 1245 MulHolland St.; PO Box 415 (62354); W; 636pd, 63fr (Sw); $4.50; publisher Jane Langford; editor Kathy Wallace; tel (217) 453-6771; fax (217) 453-2707

Neoga: *Neoga News* — 579 Chestnut Ave.; PO Box 387 (62447); Th; 1,400pd (Est); 14¢; general manager Barbara Banning; tel (217) 895-2234

New Athens: *Journal Messenger* — RR1; PO Box 406 (62264); Th; 2,400pd (Est); $3.95; C; publisher Quad County Typesetting Co.; editor Michael Huck; tel (618) 475-2166

New Baden/Trenton: *Clinton County News* — 314 E. Church St.; PO Drawer C, Mascoutah (62258); Th; 1,131pd (Sw); $3.25; C; publisher Greg Hoskins; managing editor Les Hostetler; tel (618) 566-8282; fax (618) 566-8283

New Berlin/Loami/Curran/Berlin: *New Berlin Bee* — 104 S. Carwright; PO Box 50, Pleasant Plains (62677); F; 875pd (Sw); 11¢; publisher & editor Al Swettman Jr; tel (217) 626-1711

Newman: *The Newman Independent* — S. Broadway; PO Box 417 (61942); Th; 950pd (Est); 24¢; publisher & editor Laura Sarins; tel (217) 837-2414

Newton: *Press-Mentor* — 101 S. Jackson; PO Box 151 (62448); M/Th; 4,135pd, 50fr (Sw); $5.60; publisher & editor Don Hecke; managing editor Paula Lidy; tel (618) 783-2324; fax (618) 783-2325

Niantic/Harristown: *County Line Observer* — 116 Montgomery St.; PO Box 477, Illiopolis (62539); F; 350pd, 15fr (Sw); $2.20; publisher & editor Frank J Bell; tel (217) 486-7321

Niles: *Niles Herald-Spectator* — 130 S. Prospect Ave., Park Ridge (60068); Th; 2,666pd (ABC); $46.00; C; publisher Pioneer Press; publisher Thomas J Neri; editor Carroll Salman; tel (708) 696-3133; fax (708) 696-3229

Niles/Morton Grove/Skokie: *The Bugle* — 8746 N. Shermer Rd., Niles (60648); Th; 8,896pd, 135fr (Est); $1.30; C; publisher David Besser; editor Diane Miller; tel (708) 966-3900; fax (708) 966-0198

Nokomis: *Free Press-Progress* — 112 W. State St.; PO Box 130 (62075); W; 2,194pd, 15fr (Sw); $2.45; C; publisher Thomas J Phillips Jr; editor Fred Christner; tel (217) 563-2115; fax (217) 563-7464

Norridge/Harwood Heights: *Norridge-Harwood Heights News* — 130 S. Prospect Ave., Park Ridge (60068); Th; 3,202pd (ABC); $46.00; C; publisher Pioneer Press; publisher Thomas J Neri; editor Caroll Salman; tel (708) 696-3133; fax (708) 696-3229

North Town/Rogers Park/Edgewater/Ravenswood/Albany Park: *Lerner News Star* — 7331 N. Lincoln Ave., Lincolnwood (60646); W; 9,974pd, 3,813fr (Est); $27.40; C; publisher Lee Mortenson; general manager Si Smith; editor Bill Santamour; managing editor Phill Dunn; tel (708) 329-2000; fax (708) 329-2060

Northbrook: *Northbrook Star* — 3701 W. Lake Ave., Glenview (60025); Th; 7,518pd (ABC); $64.00; publisher Thomas J Neri; editor Cathy Backer; tel (708) 486-9200; fax (708) 486-7457

Northern Co.: *Madison County Chronicle* — 117 E. Wall; PO Box 490, Worden (62097); Th; 826pd, 10fr (Sw); $3.90; publisher John M Galer; general manager & editor Vera Eckhardt; tel (618) 459-3655; fax (618) 459-3655

Northlake: *Northlake Herald-Journal* — 3701 N. Lake Ave., Glenview (60025); W; 1,940pd (ABC); $50.00; C; publisher Thomas J Neri; editor Rick Behren; tel (708) 251-4300; fax (708) 256-9024

Northlake: *Northlake Post* — 6008 W. Belmont Ave., Chicago (60634); F; 2,000fr (Sw); $1.25; publisher Arthur Diaz; editor Jackie Pledger; tel (312) 283-7900; fax (312) 283-7761

NW Chicago: *Edison-Norwood Times Review* — 130 S. Prospect Ave., Park Ridge (60068); Th; 5,701pd (Est); $50.00; C; publisher Thomas J Neri; editor Anne Lunde; tel (708) 696-3133; fax (708) 696-3229

NW Chicago: *Northwest Leader* — 6008 W. Belmont, Chicago (60634); W; 13,100pd, 400fr (Sw); $25.00; C; publisher Arthur Diaz; editor Jackie Pledger; tel (312) 283-7900; fax (312) 283-7761

Norwood: *Norridge/Harwood Heights/Norwood Park Times* — 7331 N. Lincoln Ave., Lincolnwood (60646); W; 3,660pd, 1,489fr (Est); $30.94; C; publisher Lee Mortenson; general manager Si Smith; editor Bill Santamour; managing editor Terry Kruszczak; tel (708) 329-2000; fax (708) 329-2060

O'Fallon: *O'Fallon Progress* — 612 E. State St.; PO Box 970 (62269); W; 3,600pd, 60fr (Sw); $9.50; C; publisher Cecil (Bud) Ross; managing editor Jennifer Gammage; tel (618) 632-3643; fax (618) 632-6438

Oak Brook: *Oak Brook Doings* — 118 W. 1st St.; PO Box 151, Hinsdale (60522-0151); W/F; 10,043pd, 250fr (Sw); $14.00; C; publisher & editor J Peter Teschner; general manager James Slonoff; managing editor Pamela Lannom; tel (708) 887-0600; fax (708) 887-9646

Oak Brook: *Oakbrook Terrace Press* — 112 S. York St., Elmhurst (60126); W/F; 223pd, 809fr (Sw); $10.06; C; publisher Jack Cruger & Peter C Cruger; tel (708) 834-0900; fax (708) 530-3349

Oak Brook: *Suburban Life* — 709 Enterprise Dr. (60521-8814); W/Sa; 9,250pd, 19,785fr (CAC); $21.00; C; publishers Jack R Kubik; managing editor Joseph DeRosier; tel (708) 368-1100; fax (708) 368-1199

Oak Forest/Midlothian: *The Oak Forest/Midlothian Star* — 1526 Otto Blvd.; PO Box 157, Chicago Heights (60411); Th/Su; 3,313pd, 886fr (Est); $5.98; publisher Norman A Rosinski; general manager James S Meidell; editor Lester Sons; managing editor Frank Shuftan; tel (708) 755-6161; fax (708) 755-9112

Oak Lawn: *Oak Lawn Independent* — 3840 W. 147th St.; PO Box 548, Midlothian (60445); Th; 11,900pd, 900fr (Sw); $6.44; C; publisher Walter H Lysen; editor Gerald Gibbons; tel (708) 388-2425; fax (708) 385-7811

Oak Lawn/Evergreen Park: *The Oak Lawn Star* — 1526 Otto Blvd.; PO Box 157, Chicago Heights (60411); Th/Su; 2,213pd, 1,398fr (Est); $10.21; C; publisher Norman A Rosinski; general manager James S Meidell; editor Lester Sons; managing editor Frank Shuftan; tel (708) 755-6161; fax (708) 755-9112

Oak Park: *Oak Leaves* — 1148 Westgate Ave. (60301); W; 11,525pd (ABC); $79.00; C; publisher Thomas J Neri; editor Randy Blaser; tel (708) 383-3200; fax (708) 383-3678

Oak Park/River Forest: *Wednesday Journal of Oak Park & River Forest* — 141 S. Oak Park Ave., Oak Park (60302); W; 7,424pd, 6,618fr (VAC); $20.08; C; publisher Dan Haley; editor Paula Krapf; tel (708) 524-8300; fax (708) 524-0447

Odell: *Odell Times* — 204 E. Chippewa St.; PO Box 159, Dwight (60420); Th; 409pd, 10fr (Est); $1.95; C; publisher Scott McGraw; general manager & editor Thomas C Doran; tel (815) 584-3007

Okawville: *The Okawville Times* — 109 E. Walnut; PO Box 68 (62271); W; 2,000pd (Sw); $3.00; publisher Gary W Stricker; editor Debby Stricker; tel (618) 243-5563

Oregon: *Oregon Republican-Reporter* — 121A S. 4th; PO Box 8 (61061); Th; 1,300pd, 39fr (Est); $4.77; publisher Bill Shaw; general manager Earleen Hinton; editor Jim Henry; tel (815) 732-6166; fax (815) 732-4238

Oregon: *The Ogle County Life* — 200 N. 3rd St., Ste. B; PO Box 378 (61061); M; 13,000fr (Sw); $7.85; C; publisher Thomas Cross; general manager John Shank; editor Doug Olesen; tel (815) 732-2156; fax (815) 732-6154

Orland Park: *Orland Township Messenger* — 3840 W. 147th St.; PO Box 548 (60445); Th; 200pd, 3,000fr (Est); 38¢; C; publisher Walter Lysen; editor Gerald Gibbons; tel (708) 388-2425; fax (708) 385-7811

Orland Park/Orland Hills: *The Star* — 1526 Otto Blvd.; PO Box 157, Chicago Heights (60411); Su/Th; 3,079pd, 801fr (Est); $6.56; publisher Norman A Rosinski; editor Lester Sons; tel (708) 614-4700; fax (708) 755-9112

Oswego/Montgomery: *Ledger-Sentinel* — 64 S. Main; PO Box 669, Oswego (60543); Th; 3,272pd, 26fr (Est); $5.08; C; publisher Jeffrey A Farren; editor Roger A Matile; tel (708) 554-8573; fax (708) 553-7085

Ottawa/Grand Ridge/Utica: *The Thrif-T-Nikel Weekly* — 801 Canal St.; PO Box 279, Ottawa (61350); W; 16pd, 14,148fr (Est); $6.72; C; publisher Steven F Gray; editor Linda Walter; tel (815) 433-5595; fax (815) 433-5596

Palatine/Inverness: *Palatine Countryside* — 200 James St., Barrington (60010); Th; 6,776pd (ABC); $60.00; C; publisher Thomas J Neri; editor Robert Loerzel; tel (708) 381-9200; fax (708) 381-5840

Palmyra: *Northwestern News* — 169 W. Jackson; PO Box 440, Virden (62690); W; 853pd, 31fr (Sw); $3.50; C; publishers Charles E Jones & Dorothy Jones; editor Norris Jones; tel (217) 965-3355; fax (217) 965-4512

Palos Heights: *The Regional News* — 12243 S. Harlem Ave. (60463); Th; 15,889pd, 50fr (Sw); $14.00; publisher Charles Richards; managing editor Rich Parmeter; tel (708) 448-4000

Palos Heights/Palos Hills: *The Palos Area Star* — 1526 Otto Blvd.; PO Box 157, Chicago Heights (60411); Th/Su; 990pd, 711fr (Est); $10.21; C; publisher Norman A Rosinski; general manager James S Meidell; editor Lester Sons; managing editor Frank Shuftan; tel (708) 755-6161; fax (708) 755-9112

Palos Hills/Hickory Hills: *Palos Citizen* — 3840 W. 147th St.; PO Box 548, Midlothian (60445); Th; 4,371pd, 450fr (Sw); $6.44; publisher Walter Lysen; editor Gerald Gibbons; tel (708) 388-2425; fax (708) 385-7811

Park Forest/Olympia Fields: *Park Forest Star* — 1526 Otto Blvd.; PO Box 157, Chicago Heights (60411); Th/Su; 6,446pd, 225fr (Est); $8.76; publisher Norman A Rosinski; general manager James S Meidell; editor Lester Sons; managing editor Frank Shuftan; tel (708) 755-6161; fax (708) 755-9112

Park Ridge: *Park Ridge Herald-Advocate* — 130 S. Prospect Ave. (60068); Th; 8,895pd (ABC); $50.00; C; publisher Thomas J Neri; editor Carroll Salman; tel (708) 696-3133; fax (708) 696-3229

Pawnee: *Pawnee Post* — 110 N. 5th St.; PO Box 50, Auburn (62615); Th; 580pd, 10fr (Sw); $3.50; C; publisher & editor Joseph Michelich Jr; managing editor Jill Michelich; tel (217) 438-6155; fax (217) 438-6156

Paxton: *Paxton Weekly Record* — 218 N. Market; PO Box 73 (60957); W; 2,040pd, 30fr (Sw); $6.10; publisher Paul E Anderson; general manager Toni Swan; editor Robert Maney; managing editor David Hinton; tel (217) 379-4313; fax (217) 379-3104

Pecatonica/Winnebago/Seward: *Pecatonica/Winnebago Gazette* — 2124 Harlem Rd.; PO Box 15340, Loves Park (61111); W; 2,145pd, 4,996fr (Sw); $6.63; C; publisher Brian Gay; general manager Randall Johnson; managing editor Melanie Bradley; tel (815) 877-4044; fax (815) 654-4857

Peoria: *The Observer* — 1616 W. Pioneer Pkwy. (61615); W; 300pd, 22,000fr (Sw); $12.14; C; publisher Ted J Fleming; general manager David Zoeller; editor Rick Wade; tel (309) 692-4910; fax (309) 692-6447

Peoria Hts./Richwoods: *Peoria Heights Herald* — 1334 E. Samuel Ave.; PO Box 9184, Peoria Heights (61614); F; 90pd, 950fr (Sw); $6.00; publisher & editor Jim Mansfield; tel (309) 685-3814

Peotone: *Peotone Vedette* — 120 W. North St.; PO Box 429 (60468); W; 2,318pd, 98fr (Est); $2.50; publisher Gilbert L Russell; general manager Chris Russell; tel (708) 258-3473; fax (708) 258-6295

Petersburg: *The Petersburg Observer* — 235 E. Sangamon; PO Box 350 (62675); Th; 3,002pd, 25fr (Sw); $2.40; C; publisher & editor Jane Cutright; tel (217) 632-2236; fax (217) 632-2237

Philo: *Southern Champaign Co. Today* — 5 S. Main St.; PO Box 20, Villa Grove (61956); W; 2,750fr (Sw); $3.00; publisher & editor Jeffrey W Holmes; tel (217) 832-4201; fax (217) 832-4001

Pike Co.: *Pike Press* — 115 W. Jefferson; PO Box 70, Pittsfield (62363); W; 7,773pd, 77fr (Sw); $7.50; C; publisher & editor Julie Boren; tel (217) 285-2191; fax (217) 285-5222

Pinckneyville: *Pinckneyville Democrat* — 105B S. Main St.; PO Box 99 (62274); W; 1,921pd, 122fr (Sw); $3.95; C; publisher Bart McDowell; general manager Debbie Smith; editor John Sheley; tel (618) 357-2811; fax (618) 357-3429

Plainfield/NW Will Co.: *The Enterprise* — 519 Lockport St.; PO Box 127, Plainfield (60544); W; 5,078pd, 80fr (Sw); $6.75; C; publishers Beverly Perry & Wayne Perry; editor Deborah Danielski; tel (815) 436-2431; fax (815) 436-2592

Plano: *Plano Record* — PO Box 186 (60545); Th; 987pd, 16fr (Est); $4.07; C; publisher Jeffery A Farren; editor Kathleen M Farren; tel (708) 553-7034; fax (708) 553-7085

Pleasant Hill/Pike Co.: *The Weekly Messenger* — 111 S. Main St.; PO Box 340, Pleasant Hill (62366); W; 1,490pd, 10fr (Sw); $5.23; C; publisher & editor James B Campbell; tel (217) 734-2345; fax (217) 734-2346

Pleasant Plains: *The Pleasant Plains Press* — 104 S. Cartwright; PO Box 50 (62677); F; 525pd (Sw); 11¢; publisher & editor Al Swettman Jr; tel (217) 626-1711

Polo: *Tri-County Press* — 113 N. Franklin; PO Box 97 (61064); Th; 1,611pd, 35fr (Est); $3.25; C; publisher Bill Shaw; general manager Earleen Hinton; editor Andrea Mills; tel (815) 946-2364; fax (815) 732-4238

Pope Co.: *Herald-Enterprise* — Jefferson & Monroe Sts.; PO Box 400, Golconda (62938); Th; 1,875pd, 145fr (Sw); $2.50; publisher & editor Virginia Brenner; tel (618) 683-3531; fax (618) 683-3831

Port Byron: *The Review* — 201 N. Main St.; PO Box 575 (61275); W; 2,255pd, 13fr (Sw); $5.25; publisher Anthony M Komlanc Jr; editor Judy James; tel (309) 659-2761; fax (309) 659-2761

Princeton/Spring Vly.: *Bureau County Republican* — 316 S. Main St.; PO Box 340, Princeton (61356); Tu/Th/Sa; 6,679pd, 54fr (Sw); $7.50; C; publisher Sam R Fisher; editor Lori Hamer; tel (815) 875-4461; fax (815) 875-1235

Princeville: *Tri-County News/The Princeville Telephone Edition* — 116 S. Magnolia; PO Box 289, Elmwood (61529); W; 350pd (Est); $2.00; publisher DeEllda Swindler; editor Linda S Swindler; tel (309) 742-2521; fax (309) 742-2511

Prophetstown: *Prophetstown Echo* — 342 Washington St. (61277); Tu; 1,975pd, 113fr (Est); $2.75; publisher & editor Neil Robinson; managing editor Jody Robinson; tel (815) 537-5107

Proviso Twp.: *Proviso Star-Sentinel* — 1440 W. North Ave., Ste. 210, Melrose Park (60160); W; 8,749pd, 9,537fr (Est); 45¢; publisher & editor David Roberts; tel (708) 345-1750; fax (708) 345-1795

Pulaski/Johnson/Massac Co.: *The Pulaski Enterprise* — 315 1st St.; PO Box 459, Mounds (62964); W; 2,469pd, 2,320fr (Sw); $14.40; publisher Edward A Taylor Jr; editor Lottie M Taylor; tel (618) 745-6267

Putnam Co.: *Putnam County Record* — PO Box 48, Granville (61326); W; 2,955pd, 450fr (Sw); $4.50; C; publisher & editor Elin A Arnold; tel (815) 339-2321

Ramsey: *Ramsey News-Journal* — 217 S. Superior St.; PO Box 218 (62080); Th; 1,831pd, 74fr (Sw); $4.60; publisher R J Mueller Sr; editor B J Mueller; tel (618) 423-2411/2514

Randolph/Perry/Jackson Cos.: *The County Journal* — PO Box 369, Percy (62272); Th; 6,683pd, 87fr (Sw); $5.75; C; publishers & editors Gerald Willis & Larry Willis; tel (618) 497-8273; fax (618) 497-2607

Rankin: *Rankin Independent* — PO Box 8, Cissna Park (60924); Th; 485pd (Sw); $2.50; C; publisher Rick A Baier; editor Mary Ann Scott; tel (815) 457-2245

Rantoul: *Rantoul Press* — 1332 E. Harmon Dr.; PO Box 909 (61866-0909); W; 4,642pd, 6,914fr (CPVS); $10.89; C; publisher Dennis C Kaster; editor Chris Slack; tel (217) 892-9613; fax (217) 892-9451

Raymond: *The Panhandle Press* — Pentagon Plz.; PO Box 15 (62560-0015); W; 1,026pd, 17fr (Sw); $3.50; C; publishers Charles E Jones & Dorothy Jones; editor Norris Jones; tel (217) 229-4412/965-3355; fax (217) 965-4512

Raymond: *The Raymond News* — 327 E. Broad St. (62560); Th; 612pd, 18fr (Est); 13¢; publisher & editor Phillip Galer; tel (217) 229-3421; fax (217) 532-3632

Red Bud: *North County News* — 124 S. Main St.; PO Box 68 (62278); Th; 3,882pd, 12fr (Est); 10¢; publisher Victor L Mohr; general manager & managing editor Mike Mohr; editor Jane Lucht; tel (618) 282-3803; fax (618) 282-6134

Reddick/Essex: *Reddick-Essex Courier* — 204 E. Chippewa St.; PO Box 159, Dwight (60420); Th; 387pd, 12fr (Sw); $2.64; C; publisher Scott McGraw; general manager Thomas C Doran; editor Myke Feinman; tel (815) 584-1270

Ridgway: *The Ridgway News* — Main St.; PO Box 160 (62984); Th; 1,050pd (Sw); $3.75; publisher & editor Jim Doyle; tel (618) 272-4961

River Forest: *Forest Leaves* — 1148 Westgate Ave., Oak Park (60301); W; 2,413pd (ABC); $79.00; C; publisher Thomas J Neri; editor Randy Blaser; tel (708) 383-3200; fax (708) 383-3678

River Grove: *River Grove Messenger* — 1148 Westgate Ave., Oak Park (60301); W; 1,405pd (Est); $50.00; C; publisher Thomas J Neri; editor Rick Behren; tel (708) 383-3200; fax (708) 383-3678

River Grove: *River Grove Post* — 6008 W. Belmont Ave., Chicago (60634); F; 1,452pd, 1,300fr (Sw); $1.25; publisher Arthur Diaz; editor Jackie Pledger; tel (312) 283-7900; fax (312) 283-7761

Roanoke: *The Roanoke Review* — 105 E. Broad St. (61561); Th; 1,146pd (Sw); $4.10; publisher Mark Barra; editor Cheryl Wolfe; tel (309) 923-5841; fax (309) 467-4563

Rochelle: *Farmer's Report* — 211 Hwy. 38 E. (61068); W; 2,500pd, 8,000fr (Sw); 31¢; publisher Tom Cross; editor Jeff Robertson; tel (815) 562-4174; fax (815) 562-2161

Rochelle: *The Rochelle News-Leader* — 211 Hwy. 38 E. (61068); Tu/Su; 3,781pd, 569fr (Sw); $7.15; Th; 3,832pd, 618fr (Sw); $7.15; publisher C Thomas Cross; editor Jeff Robertson; tel (815) 562-4171; fax (815) 562-2161

Rochester: *Rochester Times* — 129 S. John St. (62653); Th; 755pd, 2fr (Sw); $3.50; C; publisher & editor Joseph Michelich Jr; managing editor Jill Michelich; tel (217) 498-8080; fax (217) 498-8089

Rockford/Loves Park/Machesney Park: *Rockford Journal* — 2124 Harlem Rd.; PO Box 15340, Rockford (61132); W; 283pd, 20,308fr (Sw); $12.22; C; publisher Brian Gay; general manager Randy Johnson; editor Janine Nunes; tel (815) 877-4044; fax (815) 654-4857

Rockton/Roscoe/Shirland: *North Suburban Herald* — 2124 Harlem Rd.; PO Box 15340, Loves Park (61111); W; 2,867pd, 5,996fr (Sw); $9.18; C; publisher Randall Johnson; editor Janine Nunes; tel (815) 877-4044; fax (815) 654-4857

Rolling Meadows: *Rolling Meadows Review* — 200 James St., Barrington (60010); Th; 2,166pd (ABC); $46.00; C; publisher Thomas J Neri; editor Jo Hansen; managing editor Robert Loerzel; tel (708) 381-9200; fax (708) 381-5840

Romeoville: *Romeoville Metropolitan* — 112 S. York St., Elmhurst (60126); Th; 301pd, 157fr (Sw); $9.36; C; publishers Jack Cruger & Pete Cruger; general manager Vince Saputo; editor Mike Helenthal; tel (708) 834-0900; fax (708) 257-5640

Romeoville: *Romeoville Sun* — 339 N. Schmidt Rd., Bolingbrook (60440); W/F; 1,413pd (ABC); $7.50; C; publisher James J Tezak; editor Tim West; tel (708) 759-9169; fax (708) 759-1726

Roselle: *Roselle Press* — 112 S. York St., Elmhurst (60126); Th; 672pd, 879fr (Sw); $8.30; C; publishers Jack Cruger & Pete Cruger; editor Karen Rizzo; tel (708) 834-0900

Rosemont: *Rosemont Times* — 130 S. Prospect Ave., Park Ridge (60068); Th; 1,370pd (Est); $46.00; C; publisher Thomas J Neri; editor Anne Lunde; tel (708) 696-3133; fax (708) 696-3229

Roseville: *Roseville Independent* — 140 N. Main St.; PO Box 140 (61473); Th; 955pd (Est); $1.25; publisher Joe Acklin; editor Phil Gerding; tel (309) 426-2255; fax (309) 462-3221

Round Lake: *The Round Lake News* — 30 S. Whitney St.; PO Box 268, Grayslake (60030); Th; 4,912pd, 17fr (Sw); $7.50; C; publisher & editor William H Schroeder; managing editor Rhonda Burke; tel (708) 223-8161; fax (708) 223-8810

Rushville: *The Rushville Times* — 110 E. Lafayette; PO Box 226 (62681); W; 3,612pd, 88fr (Est); $3.25; publishers Beverly Perry & Wayne Perry; editor Alan Icenogle; tel (217) 322-3321; fax (217) 322-2770

St. Clair Co.: *County Journal* — 219 N. Illinois, Belleville (62222); W; 6,550fr (CAC); $8.27; C; publisher Mark Gehrs; general manager Larry Johnson; editor Bonita Tillman; managing editor Scott Queen; tel (618) 277-7000; fax (618) 277-7018

St. Clair/Madison Cos.: *The Legal Reporter* — 612 E. State St.; PO Box 970, O'Fallon (62269); W; 1,126pd, 75fr (Sw); $7.50; C; publisher Cecil F Ross; editor Jennifer Gammage; tel (618) 632-3643; fax (618) 632-6438

St. Elmo: *St. Elmo Banner* — PO Box 10, St. Elmo (62458); Tu; 1,073pd, 7fr (Est); 18¢; C; publisher & editor Joe Baker; tel (618) 483-6176; fax (618) 483-5177

Salem: *Salem Times-Commoner* — 120 S. Broadway; PO Box 548 (62881); M/W/F; 5,116pd, 96fr (Sw); $6.08; C; publisher Francis Rees; editor Lela Colclasure; tel (618) 548-3330; fax (618) 548-3593

Sandwich/Kendall Co./La Salle Co.: *Fox Valley Shopping News* — PO Box 609, Yorkville (60560); W; 26,300fr (Est); $6.19; publisher & editor Dick Whitfield; tel (708) 553-7431; fax (708) 553-0310

Savanna: *Savanna Times-Journal* — 330 Main St.; PO Box 218 (61074); Tu; 2,050pd, 10fr (Sw); 27¢; publisher & editor Robert W Watson; general manager Patt Shepherd; tel (815) 273-2277; fax (815) 273-2715

Schaumburg: *Schaumburg Review* — 200 James St., Barrington (60010); Th; 6,611pd (ABC); $60.00; C; publisher Thomas J Neri; editor Brian Rausch; tel (708) 381-9200; fax (708) 381-5840

Schiller Park: *Schiller Park Post* — 6008 W. Belmont Ave., Chicago (60634); F; 1,827fr (Sw); 95¢; publisher Arthur Diaz; editor Jackie Pledger; tel (312) 283-7900

Seneca/Marseilles/Ottawa: *The Town and Country* — PO Box 898, Seneca (61360); W; 12,787pd (Est); $8.20; C; publisher & editor Steven F Gray; managing editor Lillian Friecke; tel (815) 433-5595; fax (815) 433-5596

Shawneetown: *The Gallatin Democrat* — 106 1/2 Lincoln Blvd.; PO Box 545 (62984); Th; 2,050pd, 50fr (Sw); $3.75; publisher & editor Jim Doyle; tel (618) 269-3147; fax (618) 269-3297

Sheffield: *Sheffield Bulletin* — 622 S. Mason St. (61361); Th; 1,341pd, 20fr (Est); 15¢; publisher & editor Julia A Nestler; tel (815) 454-2072; fax (815) 454-2268

Skokie/Lincolnwood: *Skokie Review* — 1600 Orrington Ave., Evanston (60201); Th; 7,402pd (ABC); $50.00; C; publisher Thomas J Neri; editor Peter Neill; managing editor Dan Obermaier; tel (708) 866-5250; fax (708) 866-0965

Sorento: *The Sorento News* — PO Box 38 (62049); Th; 426pd, 8fr (Sw); $4.00; C; publisher John M Galer; editor Philip C Galer; tel (217) 532-3933; fax (217) 532-3632

S Holland/Dolton/Thornton: *South Holland-Dolton Star* — 1526 Otto Blvd.; PO Box 157, Chicago Heights (60411); Th/Su; 3,335pd, 1,652fr (Est); $7.21; publisher Norman A Rosinski; general manager James S Meidell; editor Lester Sons; managing editor Frank Shuftan; tel (708) 755-6161; fax (708) 755-9112

Sparta: *Sparta News-Plaindealer* — 116 W. Main St.; PO Box 217 (62286); W; 5,000pd, 250fr (Sw); $7.38; publisher Bart McDowell; general manager Debbie Smith; editor Mike Springston; tel (618) 443-2145; fax (618) 443-2780

Spring Vly.: *Bureau County Republican* — 316 S. Main St.; PO Box 340, Princeton (61356); Tu/Th/Sa; 7,110pd, 63fr (Sw); 14¢; C; publisher Sam R Fisher; editor Lori Hamer; tel (815) 875-4461; fax (815) 875-1235

Staunton/Livingston/Worden/New Douglas: *Staunton Star-Times* — 108 W. Main; PO Box 180, Staunton (62088); Th; 3,545pd, 175fr (Sw); $5.05; publisher & editor Walter F Haase; tel (618) 635-2000; fax (618) 635-5281

Steeleville: *Steeleville Ledger* — 108 N. Sparta St. (62288); Th; 1,572pd, 37fr (Sw); $3.55; C; publisher & editor Clent H Webster; tel (618) 965-3417/3418; fax (618) 965-3548

Stockton/Warren: *Stockton/Warren Gazette* — 119 S. Main; PO Box 35, Stockton (61085); W; 1,535pd, 44fr (Est); 22¢; publisher P Carter Newton; general manager Carol Tucker; tel (815) 947-2311; fax (815) 947-2578

II-22 Illinois U.S. Weeklies

Stronghurst: *The Henderson County Quill* — 102 N. Broadway; PO Box 149 (61480); W; 1,689pd, 50fr (Sw); $3.75; C; publisher Belva M Bell; publisher & editor Dessa L Rodeffer; tel (309) 924-1871; fax (309) 924-1212

Suburban Chicago: *The Skokie Life* — 7331 N. Lincoln Ave., Lincolnwood (60646); Th; 3,933pd, 1,849fr (Est); $36.70; C; publisher Lee Mortenson; general manager Si Smith; editor Bill Santamour; managing editor Marcy Marzuka; tel (708) 329-2000; fax (708) 329-2060

Sullivan: *News-Progress* — 100 W. Monroe St.; PO Box 290 (61951); M/W; 3,786pd, 83fr (Sw); $5.65; publisher Marion E Best; editor Daniel Hagen; tel (217) 728-7381; fax (217) 728-2020

Summit/Justice: *Des Plaines Valley News* — 6257 Archer Rd.; PO Box 348, Summit (60501); Th; 4,000pd, 500fr (Est); $6.00; C; publisher & editor John C Noonan; managing editor Vanessa Holloway; tel (708) 594-9340; fax (708) 594-9494

Sycamore/DeKalb: *Sycamore News* — 216 W. State St., Sycamore (60178); W; 6,577fr (Est); $8.48; C; publisher Roger F Coleman; editor Kim Kubiak; managing editor Gary Koehler; tel (815) 899-6397; fax (815) 899-4329

Teutopolis: *Teutopolis Press-Dieterich Special Gazette* — PO Box 667 (62467); W; 1,737pd, 26fr (Sw); $3.80; C; publisher & editor Don Hecke; general manager & managing editor Joyce Probst; tel (217) 857-3116; fax (217) 857-3623

Tinley Park: *Tinley Park Star* — 1526 Otto Blvd.; PO Box 157, Chicago Heights (60411); Su/Th; 3,673pd, 577fr (Est); $5.21; publisher Norman A Rosinski; general manager James S Meidell; editor Lester Sons; managing editor Frank Shuftan; tel (708) 755-6161; fax (708) 755-9112

Tolono: *The County Star* — 101 E. Holden St.; PO Box N (61880); Th; 1,231pd (Sw); 20¢; publisher Marajen Stevick Chinigo; general manager Jerry Myers; editor Tim Mitchell; tel (217) 485-4010; fax (217) 485-4010

Tonica: *The Tonica News* — PO Box 67 (61370); F; 769pd, 50fr (Sw); $3.50; C; publisher & editor Elin A Arnold; tel (815) 442-8419

Tower Hill/Pana/Rosamond/Ramsey/Ohlman/Millersville/Oconee/: *Pana News-Palladium* — 205 S. Locust St.; PO Box 200, Pana (62557); M/Th; 4,435pd, 82fr (Sw); $2.75; C; publisher Thomas J Phillips Jr; editor & managing editor Thomas R Latonis; tel (217) 562-2113; fax (217) 562-3729

Trenton: *The Trenton Sun* — 15 W. Broadway; PO Box 118 (62293); W; 1,460pd, 10fr (Est); 10¢; publisher & editor Michael Conley; tel (618) 224-9422; fax (618) 224-9422

Union Co.: *The Gazette-Democrat* — 112 Lafayette St.; PO Box 529, Anna (62906); Th; 4,883pd (ABC); $6.55; C; publisher Jerry L Reppert; general manager James West Jr; editor Geof Skinner; tel (618) 833-2158; fax (618) 833-5813

University Park/Crete/Beecher: *Crete-University Park Star* — 1526 Otto Blvd.; PO Box 157, Chicago Heights (60411); Su/Th; 3,677pd, 130fr (Est); $6.16; publisher Norman A Rosinski; general manager James S Meidell; editor Lester Sons; managing editor Frank Shuftan; tel (708) 755-6161; fax (708) 755-9112

Vandalia: *The Leader-Union* — 229 S. 5th St.; PO Box 315 (62471); W/F; 5,644pd, 35fr (Sw); $5.74; C; publisher David R Bell; managing editor Rich Bauer; tel (618) 283-3374; fax (618) 283-0977

Vernon Hills: *Vernon Hills Review* — 2201 Waukegan Rd., Ste. E-175, Bannockburn (60015); Th; 2,161pd (ABC); $50.00; C; publisher Thomas J Neri; editor Sheila Richard; tel (708) 317-0500; fax (708) 317-1022

Vernon Hills/Lincolnshire/Riverwoods/Prairie View/Long Grove/Buffalo Grove: *Vernon Hills News* — 30 S. Whitney St.; PO Box 268, Grayslake (60030); Th; 2,810pd, 5fr (Sw); $7.50; C; publisher & editor William H Schroeder; managing editor Rhonda Burke; tel (708) 223-8161; fax (708) 223-8810

Vienna: *The Vienna Times* — PO Box 457 (62995); Th; 2,508pd, 55fr (Sw); $2.88; C; publisher & editor Don Sanders; tel (618) 658-4321; fax (618) 658-4321

Villa Grove: *Villa Grove News* — 5 S. Main St.; PO Box 20 (61956); Th; 1,493pd, 79fr (Sw); $3.00; publisher & editor Jeffrey W Holmes; tel (217) 832-4201; fax (217) 832-4001

Villa Park: *The Villa Park Argus* — 112 S. York St., Elmhurst (60126); W/F; 2,202pd, 378fr (Sw); $10.06; C; publishers Jack Cruger & Peter C Cruger; editor Rick Nagel; tel (708) 834-0900; fax (708) 530-3349

Villa Park: *Villa Park Review* — 613 S. Main St., Lombard (60148); W; 7,000pd, 3,000fr (Est); 44¢; publisher Scott D MacKay; editor Margaret Fitzpatrick; tel (708) 627-7010; fax (708) 627-7027

Virden: *The Virden Recorder* — 169 W. Jackson St.; PO Box 339 (62690); W; 1,999pd, 15fr (Sw); $4.00; C; publishers Charles E Jones & Dorothy Jones; editor Norris E Jones; tel (217) 965-3355; fax (217) 965-4512

Virginia/Chandlerville: *Virginia Gazette* — 117 E. Springfield, Virginia (62691); W; 1,127pd, 45fr (Sw); $4.80; C; publisher William Mitchell; editor Nikky Kaul; tel (217) 452-3513; fax (217) 452-3382

Walnut: *The Walnut Leader* — 110 Jackson St.; PO Box 280 (61376-0280); M; 1,752pd, 18fr (Est); $2.52; publisher Gary Brooks; editor Linda Brooks; tel (815) 379-9290; fax (815) 379-2659

Warren/Newport Twps.: *Warren Newport Press* — 30 S. Whitney St.; PO Box 268, Grayslake (60030); Th; 2,791pd, 10fr (Sw); $7.50; C; publisher & editor William H Schroeder; managing editor Rhonda Burke; tel (708) 223-8161; fax (708) 223-8810

Warrenville: *Warrenville Free Press* — 100 Arbor Ave., W. Chicago (60815); Th; 4,400pd (Est); $10.00; publisher & editor Wayne G Woltman; tel (708) 231-0500; fax (708) 231-6813

Washburn: *The Washburn Leader* — 214 E. Partridge, Metamora (61548); Th; 843pd, 30fr (Est); 11¢; publisher & editor Melvin Nielsen; general manager & managing editor Stephanie Vanlaningham; tel (309) 367-2335; fax (309) 367-4277

Washington: *Washington Reporter* — 100 Detroit Ave.; PO Box 250, Morton (61550-0250); W; 171pd, 7,914fr (Est); $5.28; C; publisher Ted J Fleming; managing editor Jeanette Kendall; tel (309) 444-2513; fax (309) 266-7385

Washington/Sunnyland: *Courier* — 100 Ford Ln., Washington (61571); W; 22,000fr (Sw); $7.50; C; publisher & editor Roger Hagel; tel (309) 444-3139; fax (309) 444-8505

Waterloo: *The Waterloo Republic-Times* — 222 S. Main St.; PO Box 147 (62298); W; 4,000pd, 7fr (Sw); $7.50; C; publisher Mark J Schmersahl; general manager Karen Domyan; editor Marvin Courtner; tel (618) 939-3814; fax (618) 939-3815

Wauconda Lake/Island Lake: *The Wauconda Leader* — 30 S. Whitney St.; PO Box 268, Grayslake (60030); Th; 4,122pd, 10fr (Sw); $7.50; C; publisher & general manager & editor William H Schroeder; managing editor Rhonda Burke; tel (708) 223-8161; fax (708) 223-8810

Waverly: *Waverly Journal* — 130 S. Pearl St.; PO Box 78 (62692); F; 1,188pd, 20fr (Est); $3.94; publisher & editor Ann Pacatte; tel (217) 435-9221; fax (217) 435-4511

W Chicago: *The West Chicago Press* — 100 Arbor Ave. (60185); Th; 4,700pd (Est); $11.00; publisher & editor Wayne G Woltman; tel (708) 231-0500; fax (708) 231-6813

Westchester: *Westchester News* — 112 S. York St., Elmhurst (60126); Th; 869pd, 1,124fr (Sw); $8.18; C; publishers Jack Cruger & Peter C Cruger; editor Rick Nagel; tel (708) 562-0900

Westchester: *Westchester Herald* — 1148 Westgate Ave., Oak Park (60301); W; 1,197pd (ABC); $58.00; C; publisher Thomas J Neri; editor Tom Ganz; tel (708) 383-3200; fax (708) 383-3678

Westmont: *The Westmont-DuPage Progress* — 922 Warren Ave., Downers Grove (60515); Th; 993pd, 6,136fr (CAC); $8.94; C; publisher & editor C J Winter; publisher P K Winter; managing editor Jennifer Parello; tel (708) 969-0188; fax (708) 969-0228

Wheaton: *Wheaton Press* — 112 S. York St., Elmhurst (60126); Th; 214pd, 231fr (Sw); $9.83; C; publishers Jack Cruger & Peter C Cruger; editor Rick Nagel; tel (708) 834-0900; fax (708) 530-3349

Wheaton: *The Wheaton Sun* — 9 W. Jackson St.; PO Box 269, Naperville (60566-0269); W/F; 4,605pd, 1,268fr (ABC); $5.25; C; publisher James J Tezak; editor Timothy J West; tel (708) 355-0063; fax (708) 355-2432

Wheaton/Glen Ellyn: *The Wheaton Leader* — 460 Pennsylvania Ave., Glen Ellyn (60137); W; 500pd, 9,000fr (Est); $9.75; C; publisher Stuart S Stone; editor Darlene Ostrowski; managing editor Michael Vaughn; tel (708) 668-7957; fax (708) 469-4472

Wheeling: *Wheeling Countryside* — 2201 Waukegan Rd., Ste. E-175, Bannockburn (60015); Th; 2,111pd (ABC); $60.00; C; publisher Thomas J Neri; editor Arnold Grahl; tel (708) 317-0500; fax (708) 317-1022

White Hall/Greenfield: *Greene Prairie Press* — 112 E. Sherman; PO Box 261, White Hall (62092); Th; 2,687pd, 112fr (Est); 17¢; publisher Elmer Fedder; general manager Rose Marie Summers; editor Merrilyn Fedder; tel (217) 374-2871; fax (217) 742-3596

Wicker Park/W Town: *Wicker Park/West Town Extra* — 3918 W. North Ave., Chicago (60647); Th; 82pd, 37,944fr (VAC); $46.99; C; publisher & editor Mary Montgomery; tel (312) 252-3534; fax (312) 252-6031

Williamsfield: *Tri-County News/Williamsfield Times Edition* — 116 S. Magnolia; PO Box 289, Elmwood (61529); Th; 457pd (Est); $2.00; C; publisher & editor DeEllda Swindler; tel (309) 742-2521; fax (309) 742-2511

Willowbrook: *The Willowbrook-DuPage Progress* — 922 Warren Ave., Downers Grove (60515); Th; 2,350fr (Est); $5.00; C; publisher & editor C J Winter; publisher P K Winter; managing editor Jennifer Parello; tel (708) 969-0188; fax (708) 969-0258

Wilmette: *Wilmette Life* — 3701 W. Lake Ave., Glenview (60025); Th; 7,441pd (ABC); $64.00; publisher Thomas J Neri; editor Elaine Fandell; tel (708) 486-9200; fax (708) 486-7451

Wilmington: *Wilmington Advocate* — 273 S. Broadway; PO Box 99, Coal City (60416); W; 990pd, 22fr (Est); $1.40; publisher & editor Sheridan R Bailey; general manager Mitch Bailey; tel (815) 634-2102; fax (815) 634-2815

Wilmington: *Wilmington Free Press* — 111 S. Water St.; PO Box 327 (60481); W; 1,718pd, 11fr (Sw); $4.25; publisher George H Fisher; managing editor Eric D Fisher; tel (815) 476-7966; fax (815) 476-7002

Winchester/Alsey: *The Winchester Times* — 4 S. Hill, Winchester (62694); Th; 1,905pd, 65fr (Est); 17¢; C; publisher & editor Elmer Fedder; general manager Merrilyn Fedder; tel (217) 742-3313; fax (217) 742-3596

Windsor: *Shelby County News-Gazette* — 1108 Maine; PO Box 86 (61957-0086); W; 890pd, 15fr (Sw); $2.95; C; publisher Peggy A Hartman; editor Jerry D Hartman; tel (217) 459-2121; fax (217) 459-2121

Winfield: *The Winfield Press* — 100 Arbor Ave., West Chicago (60185); Th; 600pd (Est); $11.00; publisher & editor Wayne G Woltman; tel (708) 231-0500; fax (708) 231-6813

Winnetka: *Winnetka Talk* — 2201 Waukegan Rd., Ste. E-175, Bannockburn (60015); Th; 5,253pd (ABC); $64.00; C; publisher Thomas J Neri; editor Peter Neill; tel (708) 317-0500; fax (708) 317-1022

Wonder Lake: *Wonder Lake Star* — 5404 W. Elm St., McHenry (60050); W; 4,200fr (Est); $4.30; C; publisher David M Stamps; general manager Albert (Bo) Smith; tel (815) 385-2231; fax (815) 385-2237

Wood Dale: *Wood Dale Press* — 112 S. York St., Elmhurst (60126); W/F; 683pd, 10fr (Sw); $9.83; C; publishers Jack Cruger & Pete Cruger; editor Don Hammontree; tel (708) 834-0900

Woodford Co.: *The Woodford County Journal* — 126 S. Main; PO Box 36, Eureka (61530); Th; 1,751pd, 17fr (Sw); $4.60; C; publisher Mark Barra; editor Arlene Franks; tel (309) 467-3314; fax (309) 467-4563

Woodford Co.: *Roanoke Review* — 105 E. Broad St.; PO Box 200, Roanoke (61561); Th; 1,008pd, 9fr (Sw); $4.60; C; publisher Mark Barra; editor Cheryl Wolfe; tel (309) 923-5841; fax (309) 923-4563

Woodridge: *The Woodridge Progress* — 922 Warren Ave., Downers Grove (60515); Th; 1,465pd, 7,271fr (CAC); $9.92; C; publisher & editor C J Winter; publisher P K Winter; managing editor Jennifer Parello; tel (708) 969-0228; fax (708) 969-0258

Woodstock: *Woodstock Star* — 5404 W. Elm St., McHenry (60050); W; 9,950fr (Est); $7.90; C; publisher David M Stamps; general manager Albert (Bo) Smith; tel (815) 385-2231; fax (815) 385-2237

Worth: *Worth Citizen* — 3840 W. 147th St., Midlothian (60445); Th; 2,750pd, 500fr (Est); 38¢; C; publisher Walter Lysen; editor Gerald Gibbons; tel (708) 388-2425; fax (708) 385-7811

Worth/Palos Hills/Oak Lawn/Evergreen Park/Chicago Ridge/Hickory Hills: *The Reporter* — 12247 S. Harlem Ave., Palos Heights (60463); Th; 16,100pd, 75fr (Sw); $14.00; publisher Charles Richards; editor Jack Murray; tel (708) 448-6161

Yates City: *Tri-County News/Yates City Banner Edition* — 116 S. Magnolia; PO Box 289, Elmwood (61529); Th; 64pd (Est); $2.00; publisher DeEllda Swindler; editor Linda S Swindler; tel (309) 742-2521; fax (309) 742-2511

Yorkville: *Kendall County Record* — 222 S. Bridge; PO Box J (60560); Th; 3,349pd, 50fr (Est); $3.22; C; publisher Jeffrey A Farren; editor Kathleen M Farren; tel (708) 553-7034; fax (708) 553-7085

Zion/Winthrop Harbor: *Zion Benton News* — 2719 Elisha Ave.; PO Box 111, Zion (60099); Th; 4,000pd (Est); 24¢; publisher Frank Misureli; editor Mona Shannon; tel (708) 746-9000; fax (708) 746-9150

INDIANA

Albion: *Albion New Era* — 407 S. Orange St.; PO Box 25 (46701); W; 1,835pd, 85fr (Sw); $3.50; C; publisher Robert L Allman; editor Joy Y LeCount; tel (219) 636-2727; fax (219) 636-2042

Alexandria: *Alexandria Times-Tribune* — 1 Harrison Sq.; PO Box 330 (46001); W; 2,055pd, 30fr (Sw); $1.96; publisher Jack L Barnes; editor Linda Ferris; tel (317) 724-4469; fax (317) 724-4460

Angola: *Herald-Republican* — 45 S. Monument Pl.; PO Box 180 (46703); W/F; 6,590pd, 38fr (Sw); $6.85; C; publisher Roger J Huntzinger; editor Rick Martinez; tel (219) 665-3117; fax (219) 665-2322

Aurora: *The Journal-Press* — 126 W. High St.; PO Box 328, Lawrenceburg (47025); Tu; 7,089pd, 56fr (Sw); $5.75; C; publisher John W Reiniger; editor Joe Awad; tel (812) 537-0063; fax (812) 537-5576

Austin/Scott Co.: *The Austin Chronicle* — 183 E. McClain Ave.; PO Box 159, Scottsburg (47170); Sa; 1,250pd, 25fr (Est); 17¢; publisher Joe Green; general manager & managing editor Bob Hollis; editor Mark Grigsby; tel (812) 752-2611; fax (812) 752-6486

Batesville/Oldenburg: *The Herald Tribune* — 4 W. Pearl St.; PO Box 89, Batesville (47006); W/Sa; 4,037pd, 332fr (Sw); $7.25; C; publisher Beverly A Schultz; editor Don Krause; tel (812) 934-4343; fax (812) 934-6406

Benton Co.: *The Benton Review* — 102 E. 5th St.; PO Box 527, Fowler (47944-0527); W; 3,000pd, 20fr (Sw); $2.50; publisher & editor Karen Moyars; tel (317) 884-1902; fax (317) 884-8110

Berne: *Berne Tri Weekly News* — 153 S. Jefferson St.; PO Box 324 (46711); M/W/F; 2,283pd, 32fr (Sw); $4.00; C; publisher Charles W Marks; editor Tony Mellencamp; tel (219) 589-2101; fax (219) 589-8614

Bicknell: *North Knox News* — PO Box 98 (47512); Tu/Th/Sa; 1,200pd (Est); $4.32; publisher Michael Quayle; editor Carol Guinnup; tel (812) 735-2222; fax (812) 735-2244

Bicknell: *South Knox Independent* — PO Box 98 (47512); W; 100pd (Est); $1.75; publisher Michael Quayle; editor Carol Guinnup; tel (812) 735-2222; fax (812) 735-2244

Bloomfield: *Bloomfield News* — 29-31 W. Main St.; PO Box 311 (47424); Th; 495pd, 151fr (Sw); $3.00; C; publisher & editor William C Miles; general manager Richard Hamlin; managing editor Gayle Robbins; tel (812) 384-4684; fax (812) 384-3741

Boonville: *The Boonville Standard* — 204 W. Locust St.; PO Box 71 (47601); W; 4,301pd (Sw); $7.20; C; publisher Myra Teal; editor David Pearce; tel (812) 897-2330; fax (812) 897-3703

Boonville: *Warrick Enquirer* — 204 W. Locust St.; PO Box 266 (47601); F; 3,085pd, 9fr (Sw); $4.38; C; publisher Myra Teal; general manager & editor David Pearce; tel (812) 897-2330; fax (812) 897-3703

U.S. Weeklies **Indiana** **II-23**

Boswell: *Boswell Enterprise* — 105 N. Clinton St.; PO Box 614 (47921); F; 335pd (Sw); $2.50; publisher Anna Mary Krebs; publisher & editor Cecil Krebs; tel (317) 869-5536

Bourbon: *Bourbon News-Mirror* — 116 E. Center St.; PO Box 47 (46504); Th; 1,321pd, 6fr (Sw); $2.11; publisher Pilot Co. Inc.; editor Sheron Knepp; tel (219) 342-5143

Bremen: *Bremen Enquirer* — 126 E. Plymouth St. (46506); W; 1,527pd, 6fr (Sw); $3.13; C; publisher Park Newspapers Inc.; general manager Robert Noren; editor Holly Fuchs; tel (219) 546-2941; fax (219) 546-3599

Broad Ripple/Glendale: *North Side Topics* — 957 Logan St.; PO Box 1478, Noblesville (46060); Th; 89pd, 4,841fr (Sw); $6.63; C; publisher David Lewis; editor Tom Jekel; managing editor Lee Ann Peake; tel (317) 773-1210; fax (317) 773-3872

Brook: *Brook Reporter* — 117 N. Van Rensselaer St., Rensselaer (47978); Th; 861pd (Sw); 13¢; C; publisher Douglas S Caldwell; editor William F Kaye; tel (219) 866-5111; fax (219) 866-3775

Brookston: *Prairie Review* — 208 S. Prairie St.; PO Box 189 (47923); Th; 523pd, 8fr (Sw); $3.00; publisher & editor Pamela Hughes; tel (317) 563-3631; fax (317) 563-3631

Brookville/Franklin Co.: *The Brookville Democrat* — 533 Main; PO Box 38, Brookville (47012); W; 4,055pd, 62fr (Sw); $3.50; publisher Whitewater Publications Inc.; editor John L Estridge; tel (317) 647-4221; fax (317) 647-4811

Brookville/Franklin Co.: *The Brookville American* — 531 Main St.; PO Box 38, Brookville (47012); W; 852pd, 20fr (Sw); $18.00; C; publisher Gary L Wolf; editor John L Estridge; tel (317) 647-4811; fax (317) 647-4811

Butler: *The Butler Bulletin* — 108 E. Main St. (46721); Tu; 1,547pd, 26fr (Est); 41¢; publisher & editor Joe W Shelton Jr; tel (219) 868-5501

Carmel: *Carmel News Tribune* — 957 Logan St.; PO Box 1478, Noblesville (46060); W; 116pd, 16,888fr (Sw); $10.13; C; publisher David Lewis; editor Tom Jekel; managing editor Patricia White; tel (317) 773-1210; fax (317) 773-3872

Carroll Co.: *Carroll County Comet* — 14 E. Main St.; PO Box 26, Flora (46929); W; 5,004pd, 34fr (Sw); $7.56; publisher Joe Moss; publisher & editor Susan Scholl; tel (219) 967-4135; fax (219) 967-4657

Castleton: *Castleton Banner* — 957 Logan St.; PO Box 1478, Noblesville (46060); W; 21pd, 9,473fr (Sw); $10.13; C; publisher David Lewis; editor Tom Jekel; managing editor Lee Ann Peake; tel (317) 773-1210; fax (317) 773-3872

Centerville: *The Centerville Crusader* — PO Box 26 (47330-0026); W; 1,238pd, 40fr (Est); $3.00; publishers Nancy Kinder & Peggy Patterson; tel (317) 825-2496; fax (317) 825-4613

Charlestown/Sellersburg: *The Leader* — 490 E. State Rd. 60; PO Box 38, Pekin (47165); W; 39pd, 11,084fr (VAC); $3.75; publisher Joe Green; editor Mark Grigsby; tel (812) 967-3176; fax (812) 967-3194

Cicero/Arcadia/Atlanta: *Heights Herald* — 957 Logan St.; PO Box 1478, Noblesville (46060); Th; 38pd, 3,325fr (Sw); $4.61; C; publisher David Lewis; editor Tom Jekel; managing editor Karen Peterson; tel (317) 773-1210; fax (317) 773-3872

Clark Co.: *Clark County Journal* — 221 Spring St.; PO Box 867, Jeffersonville (47130-0867); W; 95pd, 12,980fr (Sw); $2.25; C; publisher Park Newspapers Inc.; general manager Tom Lindley III; editor John Gilkey; tel (812) 283-6636; fax (812) 284-7080

Clay City: *The News* — 717 Main St.; PO Box 38 (47841); W; 2,000pd, 1fr (Sw); $3.25; publisher & editor Rhonda G Riggle; tel (812) 939-2163; fax (812) 939-2286

Corydon/Harrison Co.: *The Corydon Democrat* — 301 N. Capitol Ave.; PO Box 220, Corydon (47112-0220); W; 8,017pd, 210fr (Sw); $5.50; C; publisher Dennis L Huber; editor Randy West; tel (812) 738-2211; fax (812) 738-1909

Crawford Co.: *Clarion News* — 301 N. Capitol Ave.; PO Box 220, Corydon (47112-0220); W; 1,780pd, 15,000fr (Est); $4.35; publisher Dennis L Huber; editor Sara B Combs; tel (812) 738-4552; fax (812) 738-1909

Crothersville/Jackson Co.: *Crothersville Times* — 110 E. Howard St.; PO Box 141, Crothersville (47229); W; 1,131pd, 28fr (Sw); $2.00; C; publisher & editor Curt Kovener; tel (812) 793-2188; fax (812) 793-2188

Crown Point: *Lake County Star* — 15 N. Court St.; PO Box 419 (46307); Tu/Th; 3,030pd, 156fr (Sw); $7.50; C; publisher Douglas Caldwell; general manager Dan Sprung; managing editor Rick Dal Corobbo; tel (219) 663-4212; fax (219) 663-0137

Culver/Lake Maxinkuckee: *The Culver Citizen* — 107 S. Main; PO Box 90, Culver (46511); W; 1,540pd, 50fr (Sw); $4.07; C; publisher Frederick A Karst; editor Judith L Karst; tel (219) 842-3229; fax (219) 935-0083

Dale/Spencer Co.: *The Dale News* — PO Box 38, Ferdinand (47532); F; 1,175pd, 22fr (Est); $2.50; C; publishers Kathy Tretter & Miriam Ash & Paul Ash; publisher & editor Richard Tretter; tel (812) 367-2041; fax (812) 367-2371

Danville: *The Republican* — 6 E. Main St.; PO Box 149 (46122); Th; 1,000pd (Sw); $3.00; publisher & editor Betty Jean Weesner; tel (317) 745-2777

Demotte/Jasper: *Kankakee Valley Post-News* — 827 S. Halleck St.; PO Box 110, Demotte (46310); Th; 3,010pd, 15fr (Est); $3.89; publisher Doug Caldwell; general manager & editor Joan Whitaker; tel (219) 987-5111; fax (219) 987-5119

Dunkirk: *Dunkirk News and Sun* — 212 S. Main St.; PO Box 59 (47336); W; 1,031pd, 11fr (Sw); $2.75; C; publisher John C Ronald; editor Robert Banser; tel (317) 768-6022; fax (219) 726-8143

Ellettsville: *The Journal* — 211 N. Sale St.; PO Box 98, Elletsville (47429-0098); W; 2,465pd, 35fr (Est); $3.00; C; publisher John T Gillaspy; general manager John A Gillaspy; managing editor Gina M Hawkins; tel (812) 876-2254; fax (812) 876-2853

Fairmount/Summitville: *The News-Sun* — 122 S. Main St.; PO Box 25, Fairmount (46928); W; 123pd, 4,250fr (Sw); $5.00; publisher & editor Jim Terhune; tel (317) 948-4164; fax (317) 948-4164

Ferdinand/Dubois Co.: *The Ferdinand News* — 113 W. 6th St.; PO Box 38, Ferdinand (47532); Th; 3,018pd, 54fr (Sw); $2.25; C; publishers Kathy Tretter & Miriam Ash & Paul Ash; publisher & editor Richard Tretter; tel (812) 367-2041; fax (812) 367-2371

Fishers: *Fishers Sun Herald* — 957 Logan St.; PO Box 1478, Noblesville (46060); W; 47pd, 9,882fr (Sw); $9.21; C; publisher David Lewis; editor Tom Jekel; managing editor Karen Peterson; tel (317) 773-1210; fax (317) 773-3872

Ft. Branch/Owensville: *South Gibson Star Times* — 203 S. McCreary St.; PO Box 70, Fort Branch (47648); Tu; 2,700pd, 1fr (Est); 40¢; C; publishers Frank Heuring & Rachael Heuring; editor Mike Rasche; tel (812) 753-3553; fax (812) 753-4251

Fountain/Warren Cos.: *Fountain County Neighbor* — 1322 E. Main St.; PO Box 30, Attica (47918); Tu/F; 1,860pd, 17fr (Sw); $3.85; C; publisher Bette D Schmid; managing editor Matthew Gilbert; tel (317) 762-2411; fax (317) 762-2163

Francesville/Medaryville: *Francesville Tribune* — PO Box 458, Francesville (47946); Th; 885pd, 10fr (Sw); $3.50; publisher Donald H Ames; editor Darlene J Ames; tel (219) 567-2221

Franklin: *The Franklin Challenger* — 152 S. Madison Ave.; PO Box 708, Greenwood (46142); Th; 150pd, 100fr (Sw); $2.50; C; publisher & editor Don Guerrettaz; tel (317) 888-3376; fax (317) 888-3377

French Lick: *Springs Valley Herald* — PO Box 311 (47432); W; 2,950pd, 66fr (Sw); $4.55; publisher Dorothy Ballard; general manager Doug Gromer; editor Ruth Marshall; tel (812) 936-9630

Garrett/Keyser/Butler Twp.: *The Garrett Clipper* — 106 S. Randolph St.; PO Box 59, Garrett (46738); M/Th; 2,200pd (Sw); $2.80; publisher R Wayne Bartels; editor Patricia A Bartels; tel (219) 357-4123; fax (219) 357-4124

Gas City/Jonesboro: *Twin City Journal-Reporter* — 239 E. Main St., Gas City (46933); W; 1,949pd, 21fr (Sw); $3.50; C; publisher & editor Cynthia Eschbach Payne; tel (317) 674-0070; fax (317) 674-0071

Geist: *Geist Gazette* — 957 Logan St.; PO Box 1478, Noblesville (46060); W; 21pd, 5,215fr (Sw); $5.62; C; publisher David Lewis; editor Tom Jekel; managing editor Lee Ann Peake; tel (317) 773-1210; fax (317) 773-3872

Goshen/Elkhart Cos.: *Paper-Goshen* — PO Box 188, Milford (46542); Tu; 30,068fr (VAC); $7.30; C; publisher Della Baumgartner; general manager Ron Baumgartner; editor Jeri Seely; tel (219) 658-4111; fax (219) 658-4701

Greensburg/Decatur Co.: *The Greensburg Times* — 135 S. Franklin St.; PO Box 106, Greensburg (47240); F; 455pd, 3fr (Sw); $2.38; publisher Phillip Hart; editor Jeff Emsweller; tel (812) 663-3111; fax (812) 663-2985

Greenwood/Franklin/Indianapolis: *Greenwood and Southside Challenger* — 152 S. Madison Ave.; PO Box 708, Greenwood (46142); W; 635pd, 5fr (Sw); $5.00; C; publisher & editor Don Guerrettaz; tel (317) 888-3376; fax (317) 888-3377

Hagerstown: *The Hagerstown Exponent* — 99 S. Perry St. (47346-1521); W; 2,294pd, 3fr (Sw); $6.05; C; publisher & editor Bob Hansen; publisher & managing editor Pat Hansen; tel (317) 489-4035; fax (317) 489-5323

Hazleton: *White River News* — PO Box 127 (47640); Th; 450pd, 360fr (Sw); $3.55; publishers Charlotte Valbert & Louis H Valbert; editor Hazel H Degenhart; tel (812) 784-2341; fax (812) 945-2321

Hendricks Co.: *Hendricks County Flyer* — 202 N. Mill St.; PO Box 6, Plainfield (46168); M; 6,317pd, 25,783fr (Est); $11.50; C; publisher W Jack McCarthy; editor Tim Evans; tel (317) 839-5129; fax (317) 839-6546

Hendricks Co.: *The Westside Flyer* — 202 N. Mill St.; PO Box 6, Plainfield (46168); M; 766pd, 10,734fr (Est); $7.75; C; publisher W Jack McCarthy; editor Tim Evans; tel (317) 839-5129; fax (317) 839-6546

Hobart: *Hobart Gazette* — 3161 E. 84th Pl., Merrillville (46410); W; 4,615pd, 725fr (VAC); $5.80; C; publisher Thomas Paar; editor Steve Euvino; tel (219) 942-0521; fax (219) 942-0820

Hope: *The Star-Journal* — 311 Washington St.; PO Box 65 (47246); Th; 1,370pd, 40fr (Est); $3.00; publisher Charles T Biggs; general manager Jean Elliot; tel (812) 546-6113; fax (812) 546-6114

Jackson Co.: *The Jackson County Banner* — 116 E. Cross St.; PO Box G, Brownstown (47220); Tu; 3,885pd, 2fr (Sw); $4.60; Th; 3,727pd, 2fr (Sw); $4.60; publisher Kenneth Layton; general manager & editor Joe Persinger; tel (812) 358-2111; fax (812) 358-5606

Jasonville: *The Jasonville Leader* — PO Box 125 (47438); Th; 750pd, 50fr (Sw); $3.00; publisher & editor Nancy Enstrom; tel (812) 665-3145

Kentland/Newton Co.: *The Newton County Enterprise* — 305 E. Graham St.; PO Box 107, Kentland (47951); W; 1,817pd, 37fr (Sw); $2.75; C; publisher Bette D Schmid; editor Carla Waters; tel (219) 474-5532; fax (219) 474-5354

Kewanna: *The Observer* — 110 E. Main St.; PO Box 307 (46939); Th; 500pd, 68fr (Sw); $2.00; publisher Joe Good; editor Karen Good; tel (219) 653-2101

Knightstown: *Tri-County Banner* — PO Box 116 (46148); W; 2,320pd, 8fr (Est); $3.98; publisher Ty Swincher; editor Eric M Cox; tel (317) 345-2111; fax (317) 345-2186

La Crosse: *The Regional News* — PO Box 358 (46348); Th; 2,954pd, 5,100fr (Est); $4.96; publisher Richard N Slater; editor Susan Slater Wright; tel (219) 785-2234; fax (219) 785-2442

LaGrange: *LaGrange News* — PO Box 148 (46761); W; 4,612pd, 15fr (Est); 31¢; publisher William Connelly; editor Guy Thompson; tel (219) 463-2166; fax (219) 463-2734

LaGrange: *LaGrange Standard* — PO Box 148 (46761); W; 5,450pd, 15fr (Est); 31¢; publisher William Connelly; editor Guy Thompson; tel (219) 463-2166; fax (219) 463-2734

Lake Co.: *Crown Point Register* — 15 N. Court St.; PO Box 419, Crown Point (46307); Th; 243pd (Sw); $7.00; C; publisher Douglas S Caldwell; general manager Dan Sprung; managing editor Rick Dal Corobbo; tel (219) 663-4212; fax (219) 663-0137

Lake Station: *Lake Station Herald* — 3161 E. 84th Pl., Merrillville (46410); Th; 1,355pd, 119fr (VAC); $5.80; C; publisher Thomas Paar; editor Steve Euvino; tel (219) 942-0521; fax (219) 942-0820

Lapel: *The Lapel Post* — 209 W. 9th St.; PO Box 967 (46051); Th; 900pd (Sw); $3.25; publisher Brent A Smith; publisher & editor Deborah L Smith; tel (317) 534-4900

Lawrence: *Lawrence Times* — 957 Logan St.; PO Box 1478, Noblesville (46060); W; 25pd, 7,337fr (Sw); $9.31; C; publisher David Lewis; editor Tom Jekel; managing editor Lee Ann Peake; tel (317) 773-1210; fax (317) 773-3872

Lawrence Twp.: *The Lawrence Township Journal* — 7962 Pendleton Pike, Lawrence (46226); W; 3,000pd, 4,500fr (Sw); $5.00; publisher Joseph E Zainey; general manager & editor Shelly Zainey; tel (317) 542-8149; fax (317) 542-1137

Lawrenceburg: *The Dearborn County Register* — 126 W. High St.; PO Box 328 (47025); Th; 8,771pd, 63fr (Sw); $6.25; C; publisher John W Reiniger; editor Gene McCann; managing editor Joe Awad; tel (812) 537-0063; fax (815) 537-5576

Liberty: *Union County Review* — 10-12 N. Market; PO Box 30 (47353); Tu; 4,140fr (Est); $4.00; C; publisher Gary Wolf; editor Vivian Risch; tel (317) 458-5114; fax (317) 458-5115

Liberty: *The Liberty Herald* — 10-12 N. Liberty Herald; PO Box 30 (47353); Th; 2,600pd, 41fr (Est); $3.50; C; publisher Gary Wolf; editor Vivian Risch; tel (317) 458-5114; fax (317) 458-5115

Ligonier: *Advance-Leader* — PO Box 30 (46767); Th; 997pd, 20fr (Sw); $4.15; publisher James D Kroemer; editor Gary Kauffman; tel (219) 894-3102; fax (219) 894-3104

Lowell/Cedar Lake: *Lowell Tribune* — 116 Clark St.; PO Box 248, Lowell (46356); W; 4,500pd, 8,000fr (Sw); $5.95; C; publisher & editor Lyle H Pilcher; tel (219) 696-7711; fax (219) 696-7713

Madison: *The Weekly Herald* — 310 Courier Sq. (47250); F; 364pd, 3fr (Sw); $8.26; publisher & editor Jane W Jacobs; tel (812) 265-3641

Martin/Pike/Paviess Cos.: *Hoosier Express* — Memorial @ N.E. 14th St.; PO Box 517, Washington (47501); Tu; 8,300fr (Est); $3.25; C; publisher F Wendall Gooch; general manager & editor Michael E Crosley; managing editor Pat Morrison; tel (812) 254-7322; fax (812) 254-7837

Martin/Pike/Paviess Cos.: *Tri-County News* — Memorial @ N.E. 14th St.; PO Box 517, Washington (47501); Th; 3,000pd, 400fr (Est); $2.85; C; publisher F Wendall Gooch; general manager & editor Michael E Crosley; managing editor Pat Morrison; tel (812) 254-7322; fax (812) 254-7837

Merrillville: *Merrillville Herald* — 3161 E. 84th Pl. (46410); Th; 6,268pd, 819fr (VAC); $5.80; C; publisher Thomas Paar; editor Rory Holscher; tel (219) 942-0521; fax (219) 942-0820

Middlebury: *The Middlebury Independent* — PO Box 68 (46540-0068); W; 871pd, 5fr (Est); 14¢; publisher William Connelly; editor Guy Thompson; tel (219) 463-2166; fax (219) 463-2734

Middletown: *The Middletown News* — 469 Locust St.; PO Box 96 (47356); Th; 1,745pd (Sw); 35¢; publisher Jack N White; editor Cheryl Hines; tel (317) 354-2221; fax (317) 354-2221

Mishawaka/S Bend: *The Mishawaka Enterprise* — 410 Lincoln Way E., Ste. 6 (46544); PO Box 584, Mishawaka (46546-0584); Th; 2,000pd (Est); $4.25; publisher Ecom Publishing; editor William Nich; tel (219) 255-4789; fax (219) 255-4789

Mitchell: *The Mitchell Tribune* — 122 N. 7th St.; PO Box 378 (47446); W; 2,384pd, 150fr (Est); $2.40; publisher Becky Grissom; publisher & editor Norman Grissom; general manager & managing editor Juanita Mosier; tel (812) 849-2075; fax (812) 849-2911

Monon/Brookston: *Monon News* — 108 W. 4th St.; PO Box 98, Monon (47959); Th; 1,223pd, 5fr (Sw); 10¢; C; publisher & editor Sue Hughes; tel (219) 253-6234; fax (219) 253-6234

Monroeville: *The Monroeville News* — 115 E. South St.; PO Box 429 (46773); W; 997pd, 19fr (Est); $3.02; publisher Mark Miller; editor Lois Ternet; tel (219) 623-3316; fax (219) 724-7981

Montpelier: *The Montpelier Herald* — 107 E. High St. (47359); Th; 482pd, 7fr (Est); 42¢; publisher & editor Thomas L Laymon; tel (317) 728-5322

Mooresville: *The Times* — 23 E. Main St.; PO Box 308 (46158); W; 6,793pd, 25fr (Sw); $6.05; C; publisher Sharon Clipp; editor Steve Heath; tel (317) 831-0280; fax (317) 831-7068

Morocco: *The Courier* — 173 E. State; PO Box 138 (47963); Tu; 1,193pd, 10fr (Sw); $3.32; publisher Douglas S Caldwell; editor William F Kaye; tel (219) 866-5111; fax (219) 866-3775

II-24 **Indiana** *U.S. Weeklies*

Mt. Vernon: *Mount Vernon Democrat* — 425 Main St.; PO Box 767 (47620); W; 3,696pd, 33fr (Est); $5.17; C; publisher News Publication Co. Inc.; general manager & editor Mike Warren; tel (812) 838-4811; fax (812) 838-3696

Nappanee: *Nappanee Advance News* — 158 W. Market St.; PO Box 230 (46550); W; 2,191pd, 6fr (Sw); 27¢; C; publisher Plymouth Pilot Co.; editor Bob Noren; managing editor Barbara Keiser; tel (219) 773-3127; fax (219) 773-7573

Nashville: *Brown County Democrat* — 136 N. Van Buren St.; PO Box 277 (47448-0277); W; 4,259pd, 57fr (ABC); $3.35; C; publisher Bruce Gregory Temple; general manager & editor Michael S Lewis; tel (812) 988-2221; fax (812) 988-1570

New Castle: *The Henry County News Republican* — 206 S. 14th St.; PO Box 528 (47362); W; 1,600pd, 100fr (Est); 25¢; publisher Ty Swincher; editor Eric M Cox; tel (317) 529-9060; fax (317) 521-9329

New Palestine: *New Plestine Press* — 25 W. Mill St.; PO Box 407 (46163); Th; 2,000pd (Sw); $4.00; publisher Victor L Tucker; editor Barbara Tucker; managing editor Jenny L Gruehr; tel (317) 861-4242; fax (317) 861-4201

Newburgh: *Newburgh Chandler Register* — 501 State St.; PO Box 535 (47629); W; 2,608pd (Sw); $7.20; C; publisher Myra Teal; general manager Mary Anne Robling; editor David Pearce; tel (812) 853-3366; fax (812) 853-8685

Noblesville: *The Noblesville Times* — 954 E. Conners St.; PO Box 100 (46060); Th; 350pd, 54fr (Est); $2.75; publisher Martha C Hudler; editor Don Alexander; tel (317) 773-3970

N Manchester: *The News-Journal* — 112 W. Main St.; PO Box 324 (46962); W; 2,395pd, 1,100fr (Sw); $7.30; publisher Worth Weller; general manager Ric Rogers; editor Estelle Rodis-Brown; tel (219) 982-6383; fax (219) 982-8233

N Vernon: *North Vernon Plain Dealer* — 528 E. O & M Ave.; PO Box 410 (47265); Th; 6,925pd, 17fr (Sw); $4.40; publisher & editor Barbara King; tel (812) 346-3973

N Vernon: *The North Vernon Sun* — 528 E. O & M Ave.; PO Box 410 (47265); Tu; 5,788pd, 17fr (Sw); $4.40; publisher & editor Barbara King; tel (812) 346-3973

NE Washington Twp.: *Nora News Dispatch* — 957 Logan St.; PO Box 1478, Noblesville (46060); W; 10pd, 8,189fr (CAC); $10.05; C; publisher David Lewis; editor Tom Jekel; managing editor Lee Ann Peake; tel (317) 773-1210; fax (317) 773-3872

NW Washington Twp.: *North Meridian Observer* — 957 Logan St.; PO Box 1478, Noblesville (46060); W; 21pd, 7,479fr (Sw); $9.59; C; publisher David Lewis; editor Tom Jekel; managing editor Lee Ann Peake; tel (317) 773-1210; fax (317) 773-3872

Oakland City: *Oakland City Journal* — PO Box 187 (47660); W; 1,700pd, 3,600fr (Sw); $7.01; C; publisher Gary Blackburn; editor Peggy Whetstone; tel (812) 749-3913; fax (812) 386-6199

Odon: *The Odon Journal* — 102 W. Main St.; PO Box 307 (47562); W; 2,674pd, 49fr (Est); $2.63; publisher & editor John L Myers; general manager Sue Myers; tel (812) 636-7350; fax (812) 636-7359

Orleans: *The Progress Examiner* — 233 S. 2nd; PO Box 225 (47452); W; 1,850pd, 37fr (Sw); $2.25; publisher & editor John F Noblitt; managing editor Nancy Wright; tel (812) 865-3242; fax (812) 865-3242

Ossian: *The Ossian Journal* — 105 N. Jefferson St.; PO Box 365 (46777); Th; 409pd, 9fr (Sw); 31¢; publisher & editor James C Barbieri; tel (219) 622-4108; fax (219) 622-4108

Paoli/Orange Cos.: *Paoli News* — PO Box 190, Paoli (47454); Th; 2,678pd, 104fr (Sw); $2.85; C; publisher F Wendell Gooch; publisher & editor Helen M Gooch; general manager Arthur Hampton; managing editor Brenda Cornwell; tel (812) 723-2572; fax (812) 723-2592

Paoli/Orange Cos.: *Paoli Republican* — PO Box 190, Paoli (47454); Tu; 2,823pd, 105fr (Sw); $2.85; C; publisher & editor F Wendell Gooch; publisher Helen M Gooch; general manager Arthur Hampton; managing editor Brenda Cornwell; tel (812) 723-2572; fax (812) 723-2592

Perry/Spencer Cos./Hancock Co. (KY): *The Perry County News* — 537 Main St.; PO Box 309, Tell City (47586); M/Th; 7,560pd, 30fr (Sw); $5.65; C; general manager Phil Junker; editor Mary Jeanne Schumacher; tel (812) 547-3424; fax (812) 547-2847

Pike Co.: *The Press-Dispatch* — 820 Poplar St.; PO Box 68, Petersburg (47567); Th; 5,286pd (ABC); $3.29; publishers Frank Heuring & Rachel Heuring; editor Andy Heuring; tel (812) 354-8500; fax (812) 354-2014

Pike Twp.: *Pike Register* — 957 Logan St.; PO Box 1478, Noblesville (46060); W; 34pd, 8,212fr (Sw); $10.13; C; publisher David Lewis; editor Tom Jekel; managing editor Lee Ann Peake; tel (317) 773-1210; fax (317) 773-3872

Plainfield/Avon: *The Weekend Flyer* — 202 N. Mill St.; PO Box 6, Plainfield (46168); Th; 2,718pd, 814fr (Sw); $6.75; C; publisher W Jack McCarthy; editor Tim Evans; tel (317) 839-5129; fax (317) 839-6546

Portage: *Portage Journal-Press* — 2583 Portage Mall (46368); Th; 6,268pd, 819fr (VAC); $5.80; C; publisher Thomas Paar; editor Jim Masters; tel (219) 762-9564; fax (219) 763-1602

Posey Co.: *The Posey County News* — PO Box 250, Poseyville (47633); Tu; 4,800pd, 50fr (Sw); 21¢; publisher & editor James A Kohlmeyer; tel (812) 874-2813, (812) 985-7989; fax (812) 985-7989

Remington: *Remington Press* — 117 N. Van Rensselaer St., Rensselaer (47978); Th; 1,067pd (Sw); $2.85; C; publisher Douglas S Caldwell; editor William F Kaye; tel (219) 866-5111; fax (219) 866-3775

Ripley Co.: *Osgood Journal* — 115 S. Washington St.; PO Box 158, Versailles (47042); Tu; 4,660pd, 46fr (Sw); $4.50; publisher Linda Chandler; editor Laura Creech; tel (812) 689-6364; fax (812) 689-6508

Ripley Co.: *Versailles Republican* — 115 S. Washington St.; PO Box 158, Versailles (47042); Th; 4,770pd, 46fr (Sw); $4.50; publisher Linda Chandler; editor Laura Creech; tel (812) 689-6364; fax (812) 689-6508

Rising Sun: *The Ohio County News* — 235 Main St.; PO Box 128 (47040); Th; 878pd, 7fr (Sw); $3.50; C; publisher John Reiniger; general manager & editor Tim Hillman; tel (812) 438-2011; fax (812) 438-3228

Rising Sun: *The Rising Sun Recorder* — 235 Main St.; PO Box 128 (47040); Th; 1,328pd, 23fr (Sw); $3.50; C; publisher John Reiniger; general manager & editor Tim Hillman; tel (812) 438-2011; fax (812) 438-3228

Rockville: *Parke County Sentinel* — 125 W. High St.; PO Box 187 (47872); W; 3,988pd, 49fr (Sw); 22¢; publisher Richard E Harney; editor Larry Bemis; tel (317) 569-2033; fax (317) 569-1424

Royal Center: *Royal Center Record* — 111 S. Chicago; PO Box 638 (46978); Th; 802pd, 50fr (Sw); $3.00; publisher Stephen E Fisher; editor Bobbi S Fisher; tel (219) 643-3165; fax (219) 643-9440

Salem: *The Salem Leader* — 117-119 E. Walnut St.; PO Box 509 (47167); Tu; 5,081pd, 324fr (Sw); $4.50; C; publisher Rodger J Grossman; general manager Nancy G Thomas; editor Cecil J Smith; tel (812) 883-3281; fax (812) 883-4446

Salem: *The Salem Democrat* — 117-119 E. Walnut St.; PO Box 509 (47167); Th; 5,023pd, 268fr (Sw); $4.50; C; publisher Rodger J Grossman; general manager Nancy G Thomas; editor Cecil J Smith; tel (812) 883-3281; fax (812) 883-4446

Salem: *The Washington County Edition* — 490 E. State Rd. 60; PO Box 38, Pekin (47165); W; 10,442fr (VAC); $3.75; publisher Joe Green; editor Mark Grigsby; tel (812) 967-3176; fax (812) 967-3194

Salem/New Albany: *The Banner-Gazette* — 490 E. State Rd. 60; PO Box 38, Pekin (47165); W; 101pd, 15,711fr (VAC); $5.35; C; publisher Joe Green; editor Mark Grigsby; tel (812) 967-3176; fax (812) 967-3194

Scott Co.: *Scott County Journal* — 183 E. McClain; PO Box 159, Scottsburg (47170); Sa; 3,801pd, 20fr (Est); $3.47; C; publisher Joe Green; editor Mark Grigsby; managing editor Bob Hollis; tel (812) 752-2611; fax (812) 752-2611

Scottsburg: *The Giveaway* — 490 E. State Rd. 60; PO Box 38, Pekin (47165); W; 108pd, 16,079fr (VAC); $5.85; C; publisher Joe Green; editor Mark Grigsby; tel (812) 967-3176; fax (812) 967-3194

Scottsburg/Scott Co.: *The Chronicle* — 183 E. McClain; PO Box 159, Scottsburg (47170); Sa; 983pd, 11fr (Est); $3.47; publisher Joe Green; editor Mark Grigsby; tel (812) 752-2611; fax (812) 752-2611

Sheridan: *Sheridan News* — 957 Logan St., Noblesville (46060); Th; 1,166pd, 9fr (Sw); $4.61; C; publisher David Lewis; editor Tom Jekel; managing editor Karen Peterson; tel (317) 773-1210; fax (317) 773-3872

Shoals: *The Shoals News* — 3rd and High Sts.; PO Box 240 (47581); W; 2,612pd, 53fr (Sw); $3.00; publisher & editor Stephen A Deckard; tel (812) 247-2828; fax (812) 247-2243

S Whitley/Pierceton: *Tribune-News* — 113 S. State St., South Whitley (46787); W; 1,488pd, 25fr (Sw); $4.50; publisher John David Tranter; editor Linda Tranter; tel (219) 723-4771; fax (219) 723-4771

Spencer: *The Owen Leader* — 114 E. Franklin St.; PO Box 22 (47460); Th; 367pd, 25fr (Est); $2.75; publisher John T Gillaspy; general manager Chris Ranard; editor Tom Douglas; tel (812) 829-3936; fax (812) 829-4666

Spencer Co.: *The Journal-Democrat* — 541 Main St.; PO Box 6, Rockport (47635-0006); Th; 5,534pd, 15fr (Sw); $4.34; C; publisher & editor Stilla Janosa McMahon; tel (812) 649-9196, (812) 649-4440; fax (812) 649-9197

Starke/Pulaski Cos.: *The Leader* — 4 S. Main St.; PO Box 38, Knox (46534); W; 4,300pd (Est); $4.30; C; publisher Frank Alan; editor Melissa Andrade; tel (219) 772-2101; fax (219) 772-7041

Syracuse/Milford/N Webster: *The Mail-Journal* — 206 S. Main St.; PO Box 188, Milford (46542-0188); W; 2,775pd, 49fr (Sw); $4.60; C; publisher Della Baumgartner; general manager Ron Baumgartner; editor Jeri Seely; tel (219) 658-4111; fax (219) 658-4701

Tippecanue Co.: *Lafayette Leader* — 22 N. 2nd St.; PO Box 620, Lafayette (47902); Th; 4,175pd, 200fr (Sw); 17¢; publisher Dennis Dunn; editor Lynn Holland; tel (317) 423-2624; fax (317) 423-4495

Vevay: *The Switzerland Democrat* — 111 W. Market St.; PO Box 157 (47043); Th; 527pd, 4fr (Sw); $3.50; C; publisher & editor Don R Wallis Jr; managing editor Pat Lanman; tel (812) 427-2311

Vevay: *Vevay Reveille-Enterprise* — 111 W. Market St.; PO Box 157 (47043); Th; 2,889pd, 25fr (Sw); $3.50; C; publisher & editor Don R Wallis Jr; managing editor Pat Lanman; tel (812) 427-2311

Wakarusa: *Wakarusa Tribune* — PO Box 507 (46573); W; 1,390pd, 66fr (Sw); $4.60; C; publisher Mary Grantner; editor Bill Nich; tel (219) 862-2179; fax (219) 862-2179

Walkerton/N Liberty: *Walkerton Independent News* — 601 Roosevelt Rd., Walkerton (46574); Th; 2,400pd (Est); 13¢; publisher & editor Susan Urbin; tel (219) 586-3139

Warren/Benton/Fountain Cos.: *The Review-Republican* — 38 N. Monroe St.; PO Box 216, Williamsport (47993); Th; 3,036pd, 42fr (Sw); $2.50; publisher Mary Ann Akers; editor Lee Anne Akers; tel (317) 762-3322; fax (317) 762-6418

Westfield: *Westfield Enterprise* — 957 Logan St.; PO Box 1478, Indianapolis (46280); W; 29pd, 4,129fr (Sw); $4.61; C; publisher David Lewis; editor Tom Jekel; managing editor Patricia White; tel (317) 773-1210; fax (317) 773-3872

Westville: *Westville Indicator* — PO Box 828 (46391); Th; 490pd, 150fr (Est); $4.86; publisher Richard N Slater; editor Susan Slater Wright; tel (219) 785-2234; fax (219) 785-2442

Winamac: *The Pulaski County Journal* — 114 W. Main (46996); W; 3,700pd, 7,600fr (Sw); $3.45; C; publisher Douglas F Haley; general manager Laura Haley; editor Keenan Lane; tel (219) 946-6628

Wolcott: *The New Wolcott Enterprise* — 125 W. Market St.; PO Box 78 (47995); Th; 799pd, 54fr (Sw); $2.85; publisher & editor Richard M Wheeler; general manager Barbara Lawson; tel (219) 279-2167; fax (219) 279-2167

Worthington/Greene Co.: *The Worthington Times* — 12 S. Lessie; PO Box 45, Worthington (47471); F; 900pd, 100fr (Est); $3.00; publisher & editor Anna Rochelle; tel (812) 875-2141; fax (812) 875-3630

Zionsville/Boone Cos.: *Zionsville Times-Sentinal* — 250 S. Elm; PO Box 838, Zionsville (46077); W; 3,750pd (Est); $5.30; publisher Jay Endress; editor Paula Endress; tel (317) 873-6397; fax (317) 873-6259

IOWA

Ackley: *World Journal* — 712 Main St.; PO Box 5 (50601); W; 2,390pd, 1,780fr (Est); $2.60; C; publisher & editor David Enerson; tel (515) 847-2592; fax (515) 847-2592

Adair/Casey: *The Adair News* — 403 Audubon St.; PO Box 8, Adair (50002); Th; 1,675pd, 15fr (Est); $2.80; publisher W E Littler III; editor W E Littler Jr; tel (515) 742-3241; fax (515) 742-3489

Adel: *Dallas County News & Roundup Inc.* — PO Box 156 (50003); Tu/Th; 3,659pd, 41fr (Est); $3.50; C; publisher J B Tiedemann; general manager Jim Bradley; editor Laura Gift; managing editor Helen Brengren; tel (515) 993-4233; fax (515) 993-4235

Afton: *Afton Star-Enterprise* — 274 N. Douglas; PO Box 128 (50830); Th; 1,180pd, 40fr (Sw); $2.75; publisher & editor Donna G Haight; tel (515) 347-8721

Akron: *Akron Register Tribune* — PO Box 407 (51001); W; 1,524pd, 14fr (Sw); $4.00; C; publisher & editor Carter A Pitts; tel (712) 568-2551

Albia: *Albia Union-Republican* — 109-111 Benton Ave. E. (52531); Th; 3,500pd, 300fr (Sw); $3.45; C; publisher & editor David A Paxton; tel (515) 932-7121; fax (515) 932-2822

Algona/Kossuth Co.: *The Algona Upper Des Moines* — 14 E. Nebraska St.; PO Box 400, Algona (50511); Th; 5,123pd, 78fr (Est); $4.65; C; publisher Dick Plum; editor Carol Andersen; tel (515) 295-3535; fax (515) 295-7217

Allison: *Butler County Tribune Journal* — 308 N. Main; PO Box 8 (50602); Th; 1,792pd, 27fr (Est); $2.24; publisher & editor Jerry A Platter; tel (319) 267-2731; fax (319) 267-2731

Alta: *Alta Advertiser* — 212 1/2 Main St.; PO Box 22 (51002); W; 680pd (Est); $3.28; publisher & editor Dolores L Ober; publisher Larry Ober; general manager Diana Otto; tel (712) 284-2300; fax (712) 434-2363

Altoona/Mitchellville/Bondurant/Runnells/Pleasant Hill: *Altoona Herald Mitchellville Index* — 809 8th St. S.W., Ste. C; PO Box 427, Altoona (50009); Th; 2,985pd, 8,000fr (Est); $4.71; C; publisher Tom Hawley; general manager Amy Duncan; editor Diane Taylor; tel (515) 967-4224; fax (515) 967-0553

Anamosa/Jones Co.: *Anamosa Journal-Eureka* — 208 W. Main; PO Box 108, Anamosa (52205); Th; 2,652pd, 6,240fr (Sw); $3.36; C; publisher Larry Woellert; tel (319) 462-3511; fax (319) 462-4540

Anita/Wiota/Cumberland/Massena: *Anita Tribune* — 860 Main St.; PO Box 216, Anita (50020); Th; 1,567pd, 50fr (Sw); $3.25; publisher & editor Gene Andrews; tel (712) 762-4188

Ankeny: *Ankeny Today* — 1932 S.W. 3rd St.; PO Box 608 (50021-0608); Th; 1,507pd, 114fr (Sw); $5.88; C; publisher & editor R Buckman Brock; general manager Ron Sampson; tel (515) 964-9375; fax (515) 964-3105

Armstrong: *Armstrong Journal* — Hwy. 15 N.; PO Box 285 (50514); W; 878pd (Sw); $3.50; publisher & editor Jerry D Wiseman; tel (712) 864-3460

Audubon/Exira/Brayton: *Audubon County Advocate Journal* — 301 Broadway; PO Box 247, Audubon (50025); F; 2,415pd, 57fr (Sw); $3.85; publisher Keith McGlade; editor Jeff Oakley; tel (712) 563-2661; fax (712) 563-3118

Aurelia: *The Aurelia Sentinel* — 231 Main St.; PO Box 428 (51005); W; 1,200pd, 10fr (Est); $1.15; publisher & editor Dolores L Ober; tel (712) 434-2312; fax (712) 434-2363

Avoca: *The Avoca Journal-Herald* — 217 Elm St.; PO Box 308 (51521); Th; 1,682pd, 35fr (Sw); $3.06; C; publisher & editor Donald L Nielson; general manager Marc Rechtenbach; managing editor Rich Price; tel (712) 343-2154; fax (712) 343-2262

Bagley: *Bagley Gazette* — PO Box 158 (50026); Th; 1,029pd, 30fr (Est); 13¢; publisher & editor Ken Robinson; managing editor Luann Waldo; tel (712) 651-2321; fax (712) 651-2599

Bancroft/Lakota/Ledyard: *The Bancroft Register* — 103 W. Ramsey; PO Box 175, Bancroft (50517); W; 1,107pd, 20fr (Sw); $4.40; publisher Jerry D Wiseman; tel (515) 885-2531; fax (515) 885-2771

U.S. Weeklies **Iowa** **II-25**

Bayard/Bagley: *The News Gazette* — PO Box 130, Bayard (50029); Th; 2,235pd, 65fr (Est); $4.42; publisher & editor Ken Robinson; managing editor Luann Waldo; tel (712) 651-2321; fax (712) 651-2599

Bedford: *The Bedford Times-Press* — 313 Main St. (50833); W; 2,000pd (Sw); $2.50; publishers Colleen Larimer & Randall Larimer; tel (712) 523-2525; fax (712) 523-3230

Belle Plaine: *Belle Plaine Union* — 832 12th St.; PO Box 208 (52208); W; 1,474pd (Est); $5.78; C; publisher Don E Magdefrau; editor James Magdefrau; tel (319) 444-2520; fax (319) 444-2522

Bellevue: *Bellevue Herald-Leader* — 118 S. 2nd St. (52031); Th; 2,800pd, 30fr (Est); $3.65; C; publisher Douglas D Melvold; editor Lowell Carlson; tel (319) 872-4159; fax (319) 872-4298

Belmond: *The Belmond Independent* — 215 E. Main St.; PO Box 126 (50421-0126); Th; 2,400pd (Sw); $2.75; publishers Dirk J Van Der Linden & Lee H Van Der Linden; tel (515) 444-3333

Bettendorf: *Bettendorf News* — 1704 State St.; PO Box L (52722); Th; 2,268pd, 1,662fr (Sw); $7.50; publisher Robert A Fusie; general manager Michael Gulledge; managing editor Dardre Cox Baker; tel (319) 355-2644; fax (319) 355-0956

Blairstown: *South Benton Star-Press* — 832 12th St. (52209); Th; 1,457pd (Est); $5.78; C; publisher Don E Magdefrau; editor James Magdefrau; tel (319) 444-2520; fax (319) 444-2522

Bloomfield: *The Bloomfield Democrat* — 207-209 S. Madison (52537); Tu; 2,677pd, 44fr (Est); 27¢; C; publisher & editor C Gary Spurgeon; tel (515) 664-2334; fax (515) 664-2316

Breda: *Breda News* — 103 Main St.; PO Box 183 (51436); W; 732pd (Est); $1.07; editor Diane Lucas; tel (712) 673-2318

Britt: *The Britt News-Tribune* — 42 W. Center St. W.; PO Box 38 (50423); W; 1,455pd, 43fr (Sw); 16¢; C; publisher Martin Bunge; general manager & editor Willy Klein; tel (515) 843-3851; fax (515) 843-3307

Brooklyn: *The Brooklyn Chronicle* — 110 N. Jackson; PO Box AG (52211); W; 1,396pd (Sw); $4.20; publisher & editor Chuck V Dunham; tel (515) 522-9288; fax (515) 522-7527

Brooklyn: *The Free Press* — PO Box 468 (52211); W; 1,574pd, 20fr (Sw); $5.18; publisher Daniel J DeBettignies; general manager Daniel J Bett; editor Mike Thomson; tel (515) 522-7155; fax (515) 522-7909

Buffalo Center: *Buffalo Center Tribune* — 124 N. Main St.; PO Box 367 (50424); Th; 1,595pd, 34fr (Sw); $2.87; publisher & editor Merlyn R Elman; tel (515) 562-2606; fax (515) 562-2636

Carlisle: *The Carlisle Citizen* — 220 S. 1st; PO Box 370 (50047); Th; 1,512pd (Est); $3.58; publisher Robert Klein; editor Polly Thiel; tel (515) 989-0525; fax (515) 989-0743

Cascade: *Cascade Pioneer-Advertiser* — 116 1st Ave. W.; PO Box 9 (52033); Th; 3,600pd, 30fr (Est); 25¢; publisher Bob LeMay; editor Bob Howie; tel (319) 852-3217; fax (319) 852-7188

Central City: *Linn News-Letter* — 38 4th St. N.; PO Box A (52214); Tu; 2,362pd, 182fr (Sw); $3.50; publisher & editor Vern McShane; tel (319) 438-1313

Chariton: *Chariton Herald-Patriot* — 817 Braden Ave. (50049); Th; 3,369pd, 19fr (Sw); $5.00; C; publisher Norval J Lowe; editor Caroline Ruden; tel (515) 774-2137; fax (515) 774-2139

Chariton: *The Chariton Leader* — 817 Braden Ave. (50049); Tu; 3,361pd, 19fr (Sw); $5.00; C; publisher Norval J Lowe; editor Caroline Ruden; tel (515) 774-2137; fax (515) 774-2139

Charter Oak/Ute: *Charter Oak-Ute NEWSpaper* — PO Box 187, Mapleton (51034); Th; 783pd (Est); $2.55; C; publisher & editor Edward M Lyon; tel (712) 678-3571; fax (712) 882-1330

Clarinda: *The Clarinda Herald-Journal* — 205 E. Main St.; PO Box 278 (51632); W; 3,800pd, 75fr (Sw); $5.25; publisher & editor Wayne Matheny; tel (712) 542-2181; fax (712) 542-5424

Clarion: *Clarion Wright County Monitor* — 107 2nd Ave. N.E.; PO Box 153 (50525); Th; 1,733pd, 14fr (Sw); $3.63; publisher & editor Barbara A Dorsey; tel (515) 532-2871; fax (515) 532-2354

Clarksville: *The Clarksville Star* — 114 S. Main St. (50619); Th; 1,058pd, 31fr (Est); $2.24; publisher & editor Jerry A Platter; tel (319) 278-4641

Clayton/Fayette: *Strawberry Pt. Press Journal* — 107 W. Mission; PO Box 70, Strawberry Point (52076); W; 1,925pd, 40fr (Sw); 14¢; publisher & editor Harry L Nolda; tel (319) 933-4370; fax (319) 933-4370

Clear Lake: *Clear Lake Mirror-Reporter* — 12 N. 4th St. (50428); W; 2,290pd, 96fr (Sw); $5.75; publisher Michael J Finnegan; editor Marianne Morf; tel (515) 357-2131; fax (515) 357-2133

Colfax/Baxter/Mingo: *Jasper County Tribune* — 7 Walnut St.; PO Box 7, Colfax (50054); Th; 2,190pd, 50fr (Est); 12¢; publisher & editor Allyn Arthur; tel (515) 674-3591

Columbus Jct.: *The Columbus Gazette* — 207 Main St.; PO Box 267 (52738); W; 1,370pd, 40fr (Sw); $4.20; C; publisher Darwin K Sherman; general manager Penny Rauscher; editor Linda Wenger; tel (319) 728-2413; fax (319) 728-3272

Conrad: *The Record* — 104 N. Main St.; PO Box 190 (50621); Th; 1,176pd, 33fr (Sw); $3.08; C; publisher & editor Helen Kopsa; tel (515) 366-2020; fax (515) 366-2020

Coon Rapids: *Coon Rapids Enterprise* — 504 Main St. (50058); Th; 1,467pd, 33fr (Est); 9¢; publisher & editor Charles Nixon; tel (712) 684-2821; fax (712) 684-2821

Corning: *Adams County Free Press* — 800 Davis Ave. (50841); Th; 2,648pd, 49fr (Sw); $3.64; publisher & editor Dan Field; tel (515) 322-3161; fax (515) 322-3162

Corydon: *Corydon Times Republican* — 205 W. Jackson (50060); Tu; 3,011pd (Est); $1.65; publisher Rhonda Bennett; editor Tammy Courter; tel (515) 872-1234; fax (515) 872-1965

Cresco: *Times-Plain Dealer* — 214 N. Elm; PO Box 350 (52136); W; 3,690pd, 49fr (Sw); $4.62; publisher H Denis Moore; editor Ken Becker; tel (319) 547-3601; fax (319) 547-4602

Dayton: *Dayton Review* — 24 E. Skillet St.; PO Box 6 (50530); W; 844pd, 35fr (Sw); $3.00; publisher Darlene Diehl; publisher & editor James A Diehl; tel (515) 547-2811; fax (515) 547-2337

Decorah: *Decorah Public Opinion* — 107 E. Water St.; PO Box 350 (52101); Tu; 6,322pd, 105fr (Sw); $4.50; C; publisher John Anundsen; editor Richard M Fromm; tel (319) 382-4221; fax (319) 382-5949

Decorah: *The Decorah Journal* — 107 E. Water St.; PO Box 350 (52101); Th; 6,302pd, 105fr (Sw); $4.50; C; publisher John Anundsen; editor Richard M Fromm; tel (319) 382-4221; fax (319) 382-5949

Denison: *Denison Bulletin* — 1410 Broadway; PO Box 550 (51442); Tu; 3,950pd, 64fr (Est); $10.15; C; publisher Richard Knowles; editor Charles Signs; tel (800) 657-5889; fax (712) 263-2125

Denison: *Denison Review* — 1410 Broadway; PO Box 550 (51442); Sa; 3,890pd, 224fr (Est); $10.15; C; publisher Richard Knowles; editor Charles Signs; tel (800) 657-5889; fax (712) 263-2125

Denver: *Forum* — 144 E. Franklin; PO Box 509 (50622); W; 852pd (Sw); $3.55; publisher & editor Robert Adams; tel (319) 984-6179; fax (319) 984-6282

DeWitt: *The DeWitt Observer* — 512 7th St.; PO Box 118 (52742); W/Sa; 4,326pd, 53fr (Sw); $7.40; C; publisher Robert Parrott; general manager & editor Mary Rueter; tel (319) 659-3121; fax (319) 659-3778

Donnellson: *Donnellson Star* — PO Box 66, West Point (52656); Th; 400pd, 40fr (Est); $5.40; C; publisher Ray Fullenkamp; editor Christy Holtkamp; managing editor Lorene A Fedler; tel (319) 837-6722; fax (319) 837-6128

Doon/Lyon Co./Sioux Co.: *Doon Press* — R.R. 1; PO Box 1, Doon (51235); Th; 3,610pd (Est); 21¢; publisher & editor Harold Aardema; tel (712) 726-3313; fax (712) 726-3134

Dows: *Dows Advocate* — 104 W. Ellsworth St.; PO Box 139 (50071); Th; 789pd, 29fr (Sw); $2.35; publisher & editor Sharon J Walbaum; tel (515) 852-3640; fax (515) 852-3571

Dunlap: *Dunlap Reporter* — 114 Iowa Ave. (51529); Th; 1,330pd, 28fr (Sw); $2.95; publisher & editor Charles Walker; tel (712) 643-5380; fax (712) 643-2173

Dyersville/Dubuque Co.: *Dyersville Commercial* — 137 1st Ave. E.; PO Box 128, Dyersville (52040); W; 3,870pd, 139fr (Sw); $3.60; C; publisher & editor Robert H LeMay; tel (319) 875-7131; fax (319) 875-2279

Dysart: *The Dysart Reporter* — 317 Main St.; PO Box 70 (52224); Th; 883pd, 23fr (Est); 11¢; publisher Mike Schlessinger; editor Sharon Treloar; tel (319) 476-3550; fax (319) 478-2813

Eagle Grove: *Eagle Grove Eagle* — 314 W. Broadway; PO Box 6 (50533); W; 2,364pd, 65fr (Sw); $4.70; C; publisher Gary L Milks; editor Carolyn Burns; tel (515) 448-4745; fax (515) 448-3182

Early/Odebolt/Arthur/Nemaha/Schaller/Kiron: *The Chronicle* — 109 E. 2nd; PO Box 119, Early (50535); Th; 754pd, 20fr (Est); 15¢; publisher Robert L Miller; general manager Glo Huisgenga; editor Nancy Hendrickson; tel (712) 273-5681

Eddyville: *Eddyville Tribune* — PO Box 228 (52553); Th; 477pd, 20fr (Est); 18¢; publisher Jack Arnold; general manager A Zaccamundeo; editor Beverly Lehman; tel (515) 969-4846; fax (515) 933-4241

Edgewood/Clayton: *Reminder* — PO Box 58, Edgewood (52042); Tu; 1,490pd, 17fr (Est); $3.58; publisher Donna Skattum; publisher & editor Roger Skattum; tel (319) 928-6876

Eldon/Batavia: *Beacon Forum* — PO Box 429, Eldon (52544); Th; 478pd, 37fr (Sw); 18¢; C; publisher Jack Arnold; general manager A Zaccamundeo; editor Ruth Arnold; tel (515) 652-7612; fax (515) 933-4241

Eldora: *Eldora Herald-Ledger* — 1513 Edgington Ave.; PO Box 471 (50627); Tu; 2,696pd, 78fr (Sw); $6.72; publisher A J Schafer; editor Virginia Stiles; tel (515) 858-5051; fax (515) 858-5541

Eldora: *Hardin County Index* — 1513 Edgington Ave.; PO Box 471 (50627); F; 2,696pd, 78fr (Sw); $5.32; publisher A J Schafer; editor Virginia Stiles; tel (515) 858-5051; fax (515) 858-5541

Eldridge: *The North Scott Press* — 214 N. 2nd St.; PO Box B (52748); W; 5,265pd, 21fr (Sw); $6.50; publisher William F Tubbs; editor Charles S Campbell; tel (319) 285-8111; fax (319) 285-8114

Elgin: *The Elgin Echo* — 247 Center St.; PO Box 97 (52141); W; 1,735pd (Est); 14¢; C; publisher & editor Janell Bradley; tel (319) 426-5591

Elk Horn: *Elk Horn Kimballton Review* — 4238 Main St.; PO Box 10 (51531); Th; 1,290pd, 17fr (Est); $1.25; publisher & editor Jeanette Wilkerson; tel (712) 764-4818; fax (712) 764-4818

Elkader: *The Clayton County Register* — 106 Cedar St. N.W.; PO Box 130 (52043); W; 2,456pd, 148fr (Sw); $5.10; publisher Robert P Griffith; editor Robert Andersen; tel (319) 245-1311; fax (319) 245-1312

Emmetsburg: *The Democrat* — 1901 Main St. (50536); Tu/Th; 2,146pd, 20fr (Est); $4.50; C; publisher John Schmidt; editor Jane Whitmore; tel (712) 852-2323; fax (712) 852-3184

Emmetsburg: *The Reporter* — 1901 Main St.; PO Box 73 (50536); Tu; 2,146pd, 20fr (Est); $4.50; C; publisher John Schmidt; editor Jane Whitmore; tel (712) 852-2323; fax (712) 852-3184

Essex: *Essex Independent* — PO Box 59 (51638); Th; 508pd, 16fr (Sw); $3.92; C; publisher Gregg K Knowles; editor Robert D Jackson; tel (712) 379-3313

Everly/Royal: *Everly-Royal News* — Main St.; PO Box 77, Everly (51338); Th; 851pd, 30fr (Sw); $4.18; publishers Billie S Robinson & Edward Robinson; editor Will Robinson; tel (712) 834-2388; fax (712) 728-2223

Fontanelle/Bridgewater/Greenfield/Massena: *Fontanelle Observer* — 313 5th St.; PO Box 248, Fontanelle (50846); W; 895pd, 29fr (Sw); $3.00; publisher The Fontanelle Observer, Inc; editor Clark BreDahl; tel (515) 745-3161

Forest City: *The Forest City Summit* — 105 S. Clark St.; PO Box 350 (50436); Tu; 3,300pd, 7,400fr (Sw); $5.05; C; publisher Martin Bunge; editor Cynthia A Carter; tel (515) 582-2112; fax (515) 582-4442

Fremont: *Fremont Gazette* — 114 Main St.; PO Box 9 (52561); Th; 645pd, 30fr (Est); 18¢; publisher Jack Arnold; general manager Chris Arnold; editor Mark Kime; tel (515) 933-4241; fax (515) 933-4341

Fremont Co.: *Sidney Argus-Herald* — 604 S. Main St.; PO Box 190, Sidney (51652); Th; 1,285pd, 25fr (Sw); $3.54; publisher Ellen West Longman; editor Dennis Bateman; tel (712) 374-2251; fax (712) 374-2677

Garner/Hancock Co.: *The Garner Leader/Signal* — 365 State St., Hancock (50438); W; 2,316pd, 40fr (Est); 21¢; publisher William F Schrader; editor Patricia Ginapp; tel (515) 923-2684; fax (515) 923-2685

George: *Lyon County News Inc.* — 113 E. Michigan Ave.; PO Box 68 (51237); Th; 1,115pd, 45fr (Sw); $3.00; publisher & managing editor Faye Trei; editor Cheryl Koerselman; tel (712) 475-3351; fax (715) 475-3353

Gladbrook/Garwin/Lincoln: *Northern-Sun Print* — 423 2nd St.; PO Box 340, Gladbrook (50635); F; 1,164pd, 50fr (Sw); $3.92; publisher Leroy A Moser; general manager & editor Gregg A Moser; managing editor Jeanne Paustian; tel (515) 473-2102; fax (515) 473-2102

Glenwood: *The Opinion-Tribune* — 116 S. Walnut; PO Box 191 (51534); W; 3,667pd, 43fr (Sw); $3.94; C; publisher Lois Helms; editor Joe Foreman; tel (712) 527-3191; fax (712) 527-3193

Glidden: *The Glidden Graphic* — 111 Idaho St.; PO Box 607 (51443); W; 955pd, 28fr (Sw); $2.75; publisher Frederick G Morain; general manager & editor Cynthia S Kerkhoff; tel (712) 659-3144

Gowrie: *The Gowrie News* — PO Box 473 (50543); W; 1,720pd, 15fr (Est); $1.95; publisher Robert Patton; editor Nancy Vogt; tel (515) 352-3325; fax (515) 352-3309

Graettinger: *The Graettinger Times* — 102 E. Robins Ave.; PO Box 118 (51342-0118); W; 819pd, 7fr (Sw); $3.50; C; publisher & editor Peter B Olson; tel (712) 859-3780

Greene: *Greene Recorder* — 219 N. 2nd St.; PO Box 370 (50636); W; 1,225pd, 68fr (Sw); $2.80; publisher Fred J Hawker; editor Sylvia J Hawker; tel (515) 823-4525

Greenfield: *Adair County Free Press* — 108 E. Iowa St.; PO Box 148 (50849); W; 2,920pd, 140fr (Sw); $4.00; C; publisher & editor Kenneth H Sidey; tel (515) 743-6121; fax (515) 743-6122

Grinnell: *Grinnell Herald-Register* — 813 5th Ave.; PO Box 360 (50112-0360); M/Th; 3,005pd, 355fr (Sw); $6.25; publisher & editor A J Pinder; managing editors Jeanne B Pinder & Larry Pinder; tel (515) 236-3113; fax (515) 236-5135

Grundy Center: *Grundy Register* — 601 G Ave.; PO Box 245 (50638-0245); Th; 3,110pd, 189fr (Est); $3.64; publisher A Ralph Kothenbeutel; editor Deb Werkman; tel (319) 824-6958; fax (319) 824-6288

Guthrie Co.: *Guthrie Center Times* — 205 State St.; PO Box 217, Guthrie Center (50115); W; 2,022pd, 17fr (Est); $4.20; publisher & editor Scott P Gonzales; tel (515) 747-2297; fax (515) 747-2208

Guttenberg: *Guttenberg Press* — PO Box 937 (52052); W; 2,700pd (Est); $4.00; publisher Robert LeMay; general manager Carl Neiers; editor Dorothy Wendel; tel (319) 252-2421; fax (319) 252-2277

Hamburg: *Hamburg Reporter* — 1009 Main St. (51640); Th; 1,685pd (Est); $3.60; publisher & editor John D Field; tel (712) 382-1234; fax (712) 382-1234

Hampton: *Hampton Chronicle* — 9 2nd St. N.W.; PO Box 29 (50441); Th; 3,772pd, 69fr (Sw); $4.75; C; publisher Joseph P Roth; editor Brad Hicks; tel (515) 456-2585; fax (515) 456-2587

Hampton: *Hampton Times* — 9 2nd St. N.W.; PO Box 29 (50441); Tu; 3,755pd, 43fr (Sw); $4.66; C; publisher Joseph P Roth; editor Brad Hicks; tel (515) 456-2585; fax (515) 456-2587

Harlan/Shelby Co.: *News-Advertiser* — 1114 7th St.; PO Box 721, Harlan (51537); F; 4,965pd, 50fr (Sw); $4.01; C; publishers Alan Mores & Leo Mores & Steven Mores; editor Bob Bjoin; tel (712) 755-3111; fax (712) 755-3324

Harlan/Shelby Co.: *Harlan Tribune* — 1114 7th St.; PO Box 721, Harlan (51537-0721); Tu; 4,965pd, 50fr (Sw); $4.87; C; publishers Alan Mores & Steven Mores; editor Bob Bjoin; tel (712) 755-3111; fax (712) 755-3324

Hartley: *The Hartley Sentinel* — 71 1st St. S.E. (51346); Th; 1,565pd, 35fr (Sw); $4.58; publishers Billie S Robinson & Edward Robinson; editors Doris Vezina & W R Vezina Jr; tel (712) 728-2223; fax (712) 728-2223

II-26 **Iowa** *U.S. Weeklies*

Hawarden: *The Independent* — 820 Central Ave.; PO Box 31 (51023); Th; 1,490pd, 42fr (Est); $1.61; publisher & editor Larry U Meints; tel (712) 552-1051; fax (712) 552-2503

Hedrick: *Hedrick Journal* — PO Box 215 (52563); Th; 645pd, 36fr (Est); 18¢; publisher Jack Arnold; general manager A Zaccamundeo; editor Big Dee Emry; tel (515) 653-2344; fax (515) 933-4241

Hopkinton: *Delaware County Leader* — 101 1st St.; PO Box 128 (52237-0128); Th; 1,516pd (Est); 9¢; publishers Mary Helle & Roger Helle; editor Cathy Harris; tel (319) 926-2626; fax (319) 926-2045

Hospers/Sioux/Orange City: *Siouxland Press* — 207 Main St., Hospers (51238); W; 1,755pd, 90fr (Est); $2.00; publishers & editors Harlan Rouse & Katie Rouse; tel (712) 752-8401; fax (712) 752-8405

Hudson: *The Hudson Herald* — 411 Jefferson St. (50643); Th; 1,375pd, 25fr (Sw); $2.80; publisher & editor Clifford Murray; tel (319) 988-3855; fax (319) 988-3855

Hull: *Sioux County Index-Reporter* — 1217 Main St.; PO Box 420 (51239); W; 1,221pd, 25fr (Sw); $5.00; C; publisher New Century Press Inc.; general manager Jim Houck; editor Russ Goold; tel (712) 439-1075; fax (712) 439-2001

Humboldt: *Humboldt Independent* — 512 Summer Ave.; PO Box 157 (50548); Th; 4,269pd, 98fr (Sw); $4.90; publisher James Gargano; editor Jeffrey Gargano; tel (515) 332-2514; fax (515) 332-1505

Ida Grove: *The Ida County Courier* — 210 2nd St.; PO Box 249 (51445); W; 2,430pd, 70fr (Sw); $4.30; C; publisher Roger D Rector; editor Beth Wolterman; tel (712) 364-3131; fax (712) 364-3010

Independence/Buchanan: *Independence Bulletin-Journal* — 116 5th Ave. N.E.; PO Box 290, Independence (50644); W/Sa; 3,806pd, 70fr (Sw); $5.75; C; publisher & editor Marty Van Ee; tel (319) 334-2557; fax (319) 334-6752

Indianola: *The Record-Herald and Indianola Tribune* — 203 W. Salem; PO Box 259 (50125); W; 5,150pd, 245fr (Sw); $6.37; C; publisher Tom Hawley; editor Deb Belt; tel (515) 961-2511; fax (515) 961-4833

Inwood: *West Lyon Herald* — 211 Main St. (51246); W; 1,460pd, 55fr (Sw); $3.78; C; publisher New Century Press Inc.; general manager Jim Houck; editor Jane Ver Stag; tel (712) 753-2258; fax (712) 753-4864

Iowa Falls: *Times-Citizen* — 406 Stevens St.; PO Box 640 (50126); W/Sa; 3,489pd, 20fr (Sw); $5.00; C; publisher Mark H Hamilton; general manager J E Martin; managing editor Elaine Loring; tel (515) 648-2521; fax (515) 648-4765

Iowa Falls: *Times-Citizen Weekend* — 406 Stevens St.; PO Box 640 (50126); W; 4,200pd, 9,000fr (Est); $5.00; publisher Mark H Hamilton; general manager J E Martin; editor Elaine Loring; tel (515) 648-2521; fax (515) 648-4765

Ireton: *Ireton Examiner* — PO Box 218 (51027); Th; 641pd, 23fr (Sw); $3.57; C; publisher Denice Ping; editor Ardis Eilts; tel (712) 278-2092; fax (712) 278-2840

Jefferson: *Jefferson Herald* — 214 N. Wilson; PO Box 440 (50129); Th; 3,259pd, 37fr (Sw); $3.50; C; publisher & editor Frederick G Morain; general manager David Goyan; tel (515) 386-4161; fax (515) 386-4162

Jefferson: *The Bee* — 214 N. Wilson; PO Box 440 (50129); Tu; 350pd, 8,210fr (Est); $4.85; C; publisher & editor Frederick G Morain; general manager David Goyan; tel (515) 386-4161; fax (515) 386-4162

Jesup: *Citizen Herald* — 930 6th St.; PO Box 545 (50648); W; 1,217pd (Sw); $4.85; publisher & editor Kim Edward Adams; tel (319) 827-1128; fax (319) 827-1125

Jewell: *South Hamilton Record-News* — 602 Main St.; PO Box 130 (50130); Th; 1,700pd, 40fr (Est); $2.45; publisher & editor Kenneth Scott Ervin; tel (515) 827-5931

Kalona: *Kalona News* — 419 B Ave.; PO Box 430 (52247-0430); Th; 3,050pd, 70fr (Sw); $4.25; publisher & editor Ronald C Slechta; tel (319) 656-2273; fax (319) 656-2299

Kanawha/Klemme/Britt: *Kanawha Reporter* — 101 N. Main St.; PO Box 190, Kanawha (50447); Th; 900pd, 50fr (Sw); $2.26; publisher & editor Rodger Tveiten; tel (515) 762-3994; fax (515) 762-3994

Keokuk Co.: *The Sigourney News-Review* — 114 E. Washington St.; PO Box 285, Sigourney (52591); W; 2,786pd, 21fr (Sw); $3.80; C; publisher Kenneth Chaney; tel (515) 622-3110; fax (515) 622-2766

Keota: *The Keota Eagle* — 310 E. Broadway; PO Box 18 (52248); W; 1,227pd, 40fr (Est); $2.00; publisher Kenneth Chaney; editor Angie Corr; tel (515) 636-2309; fax (515) 622-2766

Kingsley: *Kingsley News-Times* — 1 W. 2nd St.; PO Box 445 (51028-0445); W; 972pd, 175fr (Sw); $3.50; publisher & editor Tom Stangl; tel (712) 378-2770; fax (712) 378-2770

Knoxville: *The Knoxville Journal-Express* — 122 E. Robinson; PO Box 458 (50138); W/F; 3,500pd, 190fr (Sw); $6.15; C; publisher Jack Crook; editor Abigail St John; tel (515) 842-2155; fax (515) 842-2929

La Porte City: *The Progress-Review* — 313 Main St. (50651); W; 1,445pd, 16fr (Est); 15¢; publisher Robert J Wagner; editor Diane Roberts; tel (319) 342-2429; fax (319) 342-2433

Lake City: *The Lake City Graphic* — 103 N. Center; PO Box 121 (51449); W; 1,598pd, 10fr (Est); $2.25; publisher & editor Daniel E Jackson; tel (712) 464-3188

Lake Mills: *Lake Mills Graphic* — 204 N. Mill (50450); W; 2,975pd (Est); $2.94; publisher & editor Harris D Honsey; tel (515) 592-4222; fax (515) 592-6397

Lake Park: *Lake Park News* — 204 Market St.; PO Box 157 (51347); Th; 607pd, 12fr (Est); $2.50; C; publisher Michael Kuehn; editor Bobbie McBride; tel (712) 832-3131; fax (712) 832-3131

Lake View: *Lake View Resort* — 313 Main St.; PO Box 470 (51450); W; 1,343pd, 50fr (Est); $5.21; publisher Tessie McKinney; general manager Penny Garrels; editor Marcia Haakenson; tel (712) 657-8588; fax (712) 657-2495

Lamoni: *Lamoni Chronicle* — 116 N. Linden; PO Box 40 (50140); W; 1,400pd (Est); $1.45; publisher & editor David Allen; tel (515) 784-6397; fax (515) 784-7669

Lamont: *Lamont Leader* — PO Box 299 (50650); Th; 900pd, 50fr (Est); 16¢; publisher & editor Eleanor McGraw Riley; tel (319) 924-2361

Lansing/New Albin/De Soto (WI)/Harper's Ferry/Waterville: *Allamakee Journal* — 231 Main; PO Box 280, Lansing (52151); W; 1,700pd, 50fr (Est); $3.39; C; publisher Tom Johnson; editor Christopher Pothoven; tel (319) 538-4665; fax (319) 538-4665

Laurens: *The Laurens Sun* — 119 S. 3rd; PO Box 125 (50554-0125); Th; 1,420pd, 12fr (Sw); $2.90; C; publisher William H Chaffee; editor Mrs William H Chaffee; tel (712) 845-4541

Leon: *The Leon Journal-Reporter* — 110 N. Main (50144); W; 2,300pd (Sw); $3.54; C; publishers Gary D Lindsey & William R Lindsey; editor Margaret Lindsey; tel (515) 446-4151

Lime Springs: *Lime Springs Herald* — PO Box 187 (52155); Th; 830pd, 28fr (Sw); $2.80; C; publisher Eileen M Evans; editor Alfred R Evans; tel (319) 566-2687; fax (507) 324-5267

Logan/Harrison Co.: *The Logan Herald-Observer* — 112 S. 4th Ave.; PO Box 148, Logan (51546); W; 2,140pd, 35fr (Sw); $3.60; publisher Eugene A Bloom; editor Gerald D Bloom; tel (712) 644-2705; fax (712) 647-3081

Lone Tree/Johnson: *Reporter* — PO Box 235, Lone Tree (52755); Th; 955pd, 24fr (Est); $3.01; publisher Phil Prichard; editor Cate Spears; tel (319) 629-5207

Louisa Co.: *Wapello Republican* — 301 James L Hodges Ave. S.; PO Box 306, Wapello (52653); Th; 2,494pd, 8fr (Sw); $3.78; C; publisher Mary C Hodges; publisher & general manager Michael A Hodges; editor Kris Songer; tel (319) 523-4631; fax (319) 523-8167

Lowden/Clarence: *Sun-News* — 518 Main St.; PO Box O, Lowden (52255); Th; 1,106pd (Sw); $2.52; C; publisher Sally I Taylor; editor Pat Kroemer; tel (319) 944-5387; fax (319) 886-6466

Madrid: *Madrid Register-News* — 102 S. Main (50156); Th; 2,000pd (Est); $1.43; publisher & editor Dennis W Wilcox; tel (515) 795-2730; fax (515) 795-2012

Malvern: *The Malvern Leader* — PO Box 129 (51551); Th; 1,370pd, 20fr (Est); $2.25; publisher & editor Mark Siekman; tel (712) 624-8512; fax (712) 624-9041

Manchester/Delaware Co.: *The Manchester Press* — PO Box C, Manchester (52057); Tu; 4,731pd, 22fr (Est); $6.88; C; publisher & editor Larry K Woellert; tel (319) 927-2020; fax (319) 927-4945

Manilla/Crawford: *The Manilla Times* — 459 Main St.; PO Box 365, Manilla (51454); Th; 966pd, 28fr (Sw); $2.74; publisher & editor Ronald A Colling; tel (712) 654-2911; fax (712) 654-2911

Manly: *Manly Signal* — 103 E. Elmore; PO Box 250 (50456); Th; 1,140pd (Sw); $2.75; publisher & editor Scott L Keil; tel (515) 454-2216; fax (515) 454-2216

Manning: *The Manning Monitor* — 411 Main St.; PO Box 346 (51455); Th; 1,560pd, 30fr (Sw); $3.25; C; publisher & editor Ronald A Colling; tel (712) 653-3854

Manson: *Manson Journal* — 1018 Main St.; PO Box 40 (50563); Th; 2,047pd, 16fr (Est); 13¢; publisher Gary Dudley; editor Ron Sturgis; tel (712) 469-3381; fax (712) 469-2648

Mapleton: *Mapleton Press* — 504 Main; PO Box 187 (51034); Th; 2,120pd, 80fr (Est); $3.95; C; publisher & editor Edward M Lyon; tel (712) 882-1101; fax (712) 882-1330

Maquoketa: *Maquoketa Sentinel-Press* — 108 W. Quarry St.; PO Box 1150 (52060); W/Sa; 5,050pd, 50fr (Est); $3.85; C; publisher Douglas D Melvold; editor Kirsten McLaughlin; tel (319) 652-2441; fax (319) 652-6094

Marcus: *Marcus News* — 401 Main; PO Box 445 (51035); Th; 1,593pd (Sw); $3.20; publisher & editor Keith Clarkson; tel (712) 376-4712

Marengo: *Marengo Pioneer-Republican* — 100 W. Main St.; PO Box 208 (52301); Th; 2,443pd (Est); $5.78; C; publisher Michael T Simmons; general manager Daniel J DeBettignies; managing editor G Alan Sieve; tel (319) 642-5506; fax (319) 642-5509

Marion/Alburnett/Springville/Hiawatha: *Marion Times* — 720 11th St.; PO Box 506, Marion (52302); Th; 1,500pd, 12,636fr (Sw); $9.00; C; publisher Bob Le May; general manager & editor Bill Harper; tel (319) 377-7037; fax (319) 377-9535

McGregor/Marquette: *North Iowa Times* — 134 Main St., McGregor (52157); W; 750pd (Sw); $2.75; publishers Bob LeMay & Jack Howe; tel (319) 873-2210

Mediapolis: *The Mediapolis News* — PO Box 548 (52637); Th; 1,713pd, 137fr (Est); 15¢; publishers Dave Tapp & Phyillis Tapp; general manager Joyce Swafford; editor Kendra Jahn; tel (319) 394-3174; fax (319) 394-3134

Milford: *Milford Mail* — 916 10th St.; PO Box 238 (51351); Th; 943pd (Sw); $3.25; C; publisher Michael Kuehn; editor Doris Welle; tel (712) 338-4712; fax (712) 338-4712

Missouri Vly./Logan/Modale/Mondamin: *Valley Times-News* — 501 E. Erie; PO Box 159 (51555); W/F; 2,200pd, 30fr (Sw); $5.52; C; publisher Mark A Rhoades; general manager Mike Wendorf; managing editor Pete Graham; tel (712) 642-2791; fax (712) 642-2595

Monona/Luana/Farmersburg: *Monona Billboard* — 200 S. Main St.; PO Box 628, Monona (52159); Tu; 2,346pd, 35fr (Est); $2.10; publisher Gerald J Carroll; general manager & editor Marcia Carroll; tel (319) 539-4300; fax (319) 539-4780

Monroe/Otley/Reasnor: *Monroe Legacy* — 209 N. Commerce; PO Box 340, Monroe (50170); Th; 793pd, 1fr (Est); $2.30; publisher & editor Kathleen Burman; tel (515) 259-2708

Montezuma: *The Montezuma Republican* — 406 E. Main; PO Box 100 (50171); W; 2,119pd, 18fr (Sw); $3.85; C; publisher Daniel J DeBettignies; editor Susan Green; tel (515) 623-5116; fax (515) 623-5580

Monticello: *The Monticello Express* — 111 E. Grand St.; PO Box 191 (52310); W; 3,206pd, 25fr (Sw); $3.75; publisher Robert F Goodyear; editor Craig Neises; tel (319) 465-3555

Moravia: *Moravia Union* — 103 E. Chariton; PO Box 468 (52571); W; 1,037pd, 6fr (Est); $3.10; C; publisher & editor Patty Brown; tel (515) 724-3224

Morman Trial Community: *The Humeston New Era* — PO Box 377, Humeston (50123); Tu; 900pd, 5fr (Sw); $2.00; C; publisher Norval J Lowe; general manager & editor Virginia Sponsler; managing editor Rhonda Bennett; tel (515) 877-3951; fax (515) 872-1965

Morning Sun: *Morning Sun News-Herald* — PO Box 67 (52640); Th; 789pd (Est); $2.21; C; publisher & editor Michael A Hodges; general manager Marge Kimble; tel (319) 868-7509; fax (319) 523-8167

Mount Ayr/Ringgold Co.: *Mount Ayr Record-News* — 122 W. Madison; PO Box 346, Mount Ayr (50854); Th; 2,714pd, 130fr (Sw); $2.84; publisher & editor H Alan Smith; tel (515) 464-2440; fax (515) 464-2229

Mount Vernon: *The Sun* — 113 1st St. W.; PO Box 129 (52314); Th; 2,203pd, 13fr (Sw); $5.75; C; publisher & editor Dennis F Herrick; managing editor Stacy Haynes Moore; tel (319) 895-6216

Nashua/Plainfield/Ionia: *The Nashua Reporter & Weekly Post* — 216 Main St.; PO Box 67, Nashua (50658); W; 1,202pd (Sw); $2.60; publishers & editors C L Conklin & W Orric; tel (515) 435-4151

Neola: *Gazette* — 107 4th St.; PO Box 7 (51559); Th; 1,816pd (Sw); 13¢; publisher & editor Maureen R Olsen; tel (712) 485-2276

Nevada: *Nevada Journal* — 1133 6th St.; PO Box 89 (50201); Th; 3,039pd, 100fr (Sw); $5.20; C; editor Marlys Barker; tel (515) 382-2161; fax (515) 382-4299

New Hampton/Chicksaw Co.: *New Hampton Tribune* — 10 N. Chestnut Ave.; PO Box 380, New Hampton (50659); Th; 3,500pd (Sw); $3.00; C; publisher Daniel T Feuling; editor Beverly Kolthoff; tel (515) 394-2111; fax (515) 394-2113

New Hampton/Chicksaw Co.: *New Hampton Economist* — 10 N. Chestnut Ave.; PO Box 380, New Hampton (50659); Tu; 3,500pd (Est); $3.00; C; publisher Daniel T Feuling; editor Beverly Kolthoff; tel (515) 394-2111; fax (515) 394-2113

New London: *New London Journal* — 138 W. Main (52645); Th; 1,045pd, 4fr (Est); $1.25; publisher Mary Hodges; publisher & editor Mike Hodges; tel (319) 367-2366

New Sharon: *New Sharon Star* — 103 N. Main; PO Box 90 (50207); Th; 896pd, 23fr (Est); $3.74; publisher Jack Arnold; editor Cyndy Hanselman; tel (515) 637-2632

Newell/Marathon/Buena Vista Co./Albert City: *Buena Vista County Journal* — 220 S. Fulton St.; PO Box 666, Newell (50568-0666); W; 1,073pd, 60fr (Sw); $2.75; publishers Glenn C Schreiber & Wanda Schreiber; general manager Connie Reinert; editor Dale Garlock; tel (712) 272-4417; fax (712) 272-3323

Nora Springs: *Nora Springs Advertiser* — 34 S. Hawkeye Ave.; PO Box 335 (50458); W; 1,635pd, 10fr (Est); $3.00; C; publisher & editor Dan Cutler; tel (515) 749-5317

N English: *North English Record* — PO Box 160 (52316); Th; 783pd (Est); $5.78; C; publisher Michael Simmons; general manager Daniel J DeBettignies; editor Craig Crombaugh; managing editor G Alan Sieve; tel (319) 664-3237; fax (319) 642-5509

Northwood: *The Northwood Anchor* — 801 Central Ave.; PO Box 105 (50459); W; 1,998pd, 12fr (Sw); $4.35; publisher Lloyd O Madson; editor Stuart B Madson; tel (515) 324-1051; fax (515) 324-2432

Norwalk: *North Warren Town and County News* — PO Box 325 (50211); Th; 1,501pd, 36fr (Sw); $3.28; publisher Dorothy Graham; editor Sally Huntoon; tel (515) 981-0406

Oakland/Hancock/Carson/Macedonia: *The Herald* — 107 N. Main St.; PO Box 556, Oakland (51560); W; 1,150pd, 12fr (Sw); $3.06; C; publisher Donald L Nielson; editor Rich Price; tel (712) 482-6768; fax (712) 482-5520

Ocheyedan/Melvin/May City/Harris: *The Ocheyedan Press-Melvin News* — 859 Main St.; PO Box 456, Ocheyedan (51354); W; 1,386pd, 27fr (Est); $3.15; C; publisher Bob Reiste; general manager Arlyn Pedley; editor Jan Reiste Pedley; tel (712) 758-3140; fax (712) 758-3186

Onawa: *Onawa Democrat* — PO Box 418 (51040-0418); Th; 2,793pd, 29fr (Sw); $3.10; publishers & editors Fredrick W Wonder II & William A Wonder; tel (712) 423-2411; fax (712) 423-2411

Onawa/Soldier/Moorhead: *The Onawa Sentinel* — 1014 9th St.; PO Box 208, Onawa (51040); Th; 1,199pd, 20fr (Est); $3.25; publisher & editor Verlee Sawyer; tel (712) 423-2021; fax (712) 423-3038

Orange City/Alton: *Sioux County Capital-Democrat* — 113 Central S.E., Orange City (51041); W; 2,390pd, 65fr (Est); $3.50; C; publisher Dale H Pluim; general manager Bob Hulstein; editor Doug Calsbeek; tel (712) 737-4266; fax (712) 737-3896

Copyright ©1996 by the Editor & Publisher Co.

U.S. Weeklies **Kansas** II-27

Osage/Mitchell Co.: *Mitchell County Press-News* — 112 N. 6th St.; PO Box 60, Osage (50461); W; 3,304pd, 70fr (Sw); $4.90; C; publisher & editor Paul Bunge; managing editor Larry Kershner; tel (515) 732-3721; fax (515) 732-5689

Osceola/Clarke Co.: *Osceola Sentinel-Tribune* — 115 E. Washington; PO Box 447, Osceola (50213); Th; 3,807pd, 55fr (Sw); $4.22; publisher & editor Frank Morlan; publisher Sally T Morlan; tel (515) 342-2131/2132; fax (515) 342-2060

Ossian/Winneshiek Co.: *Ossian Bee* — 107 W. Main St.; PO Box 96, Ossian (52161); W; 1,135pd, 33fr (Est); $2.52; publisher & editor Dirk Amundson; general manager Marlys Amundson; tel (319) 532-9113; fax (319) 532-9081

Panora: *Guthrie County Vedette* — 111 E. Main St.; PO Box 38 (50216); W; 1,412pd, 12fr (Sw); $1.80; publisher & editor Scott P Gonzales; general manager Gordon Castile; tel (515) 755-2115; fax (515) 755-2425

Parkersburg/Aplington/New Hartford: *Parkersburg Eclipse-News-Review* — 503 Coates St.; PO Box 501, Parkersburg (50665); W; 2,235pd, 70fr (Sw); 21¢; publisher & editor Leon M Thorne; tel (319) 346-1461; fax (319) 346-1461

Paullina: *Paullina Times* — 144 E. Broadway; PO Box 637 (51046); Th; 1,318pd, 10fr (Sw); $4.00; C; publisher & editor Mike Otto; tel (712) 448-3622; fax (712) 448-3622

Pella: *Pella Chronicle* — 739 Franklin St.; PO Box 126 (50219); Th; 3,040pd, 18fr (Est); $4.25; publisher Jack Crook; general manager Pat Reeves; editor Barry Johnson; tel (515) 628-3882; fax (515) 628-3905

Perry: *Perry Chief* — 1323 2nd St.; PO Box 98 (50220); Th; 2,885pd, 36fr (Sw); $5.16; C; publisher Stephen R Whitehead; general manager Lori Lott; managing editor Denise Pierce; tel (515) 465-4666; fax (515) 465-3087

Peterson: *The Peterson Patriot* — 202 Main St.; PO Box 126 (51047); Th; 560pd, 10fr (Sw); $2.75; publisher Roger E Stoner; editor Jane F Stoner; tel (712) 295-7711; fax (712) 295-6705

Pocahontas/Fonda/Rolfe: *Pocahontas Record-Democrat* — 128 N. Main St.; PO Box 128, Pocahontas (50574); Tu; 2,090pd, 44fr (Sw); $4.00; C; publisher & editor Glenn C Schreiber; tel (712) 335-3553; fax (712) 335-3856

Postville: *Postville Herald-Leader* — 112 N. Lawler; PO Box 100 (52162); W; 1,500pd (Est); $3.57; C; publisher Tom Johnson; editor Sharon Drahn; tel (319) 864-3333; fax (319) 864-3400

Prairie City: *Prairie City News* — 108 E. Jefferson; PO Box 249 (50228); Th; 1,055pd, 24fr (Sw); $2.96; publisher & editor Orian Woods; tel (515) 994-2349; fax (515) 994-3169

Preston: *Preston Times* — 4 N. Stephens St.; PO Box 9 (52069); W; 867pd, 25fr (Est); 16¢; publisher Terry Mertens; editor Jerry Mertens; tel (319) 689-3841

Primghar: *O'Brien County Bell* — 105 1st St. N.E.; PO Box 478 (51245); Th; 987pd (Sw); $2.65; publisher & editor Deborah Fisch; tel (712) 757-4055; fax (712) 757-4055

Red Oak: *The Red Oak Express* — 2012 Commerce Dr.; PO Box 377 (51566); Tu; 4,714pd, 15fr (Sw); $5.20; C; publisher Jane Magneson; editor Jan Castle Renander; tel (712) 623-2566; fax (712) 623-2568

Reinbeck: *Reinbeck Courier* — 406 Grundy Ave.; PO Box O (50669-0177); Th; 1,667pd, 171fr (Sw); $3.60; C; publisher Leroy A Moser; editor Gregg A Moser; tel (319) 345-2031; fax (319) 345-6767

Remsen: *Remsen Bell-Enterprise* — 257 Washington St.; PO Box 209 (51050); Th; 1,301pd (Sw); $2.57; publisher & editor Noel N Ahmann; tel (712) 786-1196

Riceville: *Riceville Recorder* — Lock Box A (50466); Th; 1,490pd (Est); 8¢; publisher M E Messersmith; editor Bea Messersmith; tel (515) 985-2142

Richland: *The Plainsman-Clarion* — PO Box 188 (52585); Th; 1,435pd (Est); $2.66; C; publisher Michael Hodges; editor Trisha Ulin; tel (319) 456-6641

Ringsted: *Ringsted Dispatch* — Hwy. 15 N.; PO Box 285, Armstrong (50514); W; 421pd (Sw); $4.40; publisher & editor Jerry D Wiseman; tel (712) 864-3460

Rock Rapids: *The Lyon County Reporter* — 310 1st Ave.; PO Box 28 (51246); W; 2,686pd, 30fr (Sw); $4.94; C; publisher Jim Houck; editor Jodie A Hoogendoorn; tel (712) 472-2525; fax (712) 472-3414

Rock Vly.: *Rock Valley Bee* — 1442 Main St. (51247); Tu; 1,389pd, 4,200fr (Est); 20¢; C; publisher Don Johnson; publisher & editor Pearl Johnson; tel (712) 476-2795; fax (712) 476-2796

Ruthven: *Ruthven Zipcode* — PO Box 327 (51358-0327); W; 325pd, 6fr (Sw); $3.50; C; publisher & editor Peter B Olson; tel (712) 859-3780

Sac City: *The Sac Sun* — 1405 W. Main St.; PO Box 426 (50583); Tu; 1,829pd, 85fr (Sw); $3.10; C; general manager Dorothy Kruskop; editor Teesie McKinney; tel (712) 662-7161; fax (712) 662-4198

Sac/Carrol Cos.: *Auburn Enterprise & Tri-County Special* — PO Box E, Auburn (51433); W; 371pd, 7,500fr (Est); $2.57; publisher & editor Delbert C Morenz; tel (712) 688-2216

Saint Ansgar: *St. Ansgar Enterprise Journal* — 205 W. 4th St.; PO Box 310, St. Ansgar (50472); Th; 1,268pd, 65fr (Sw); $3.20; publisher David Padwin; general manager Vickie Bruggman; tel (515) 736-4541; fax (515) 736-2399

Sanborn: *The Sanborn Pioneer* — 121 Main St.; PO Box 280 (51248); Th; 1,002pd, 25fr (Sw); $2.75; publisher & editor Dorothy Chrisman; tel (712) 729-3201

Schaller/Early/Nemaha/Galva: *Schaller Herald* — 203 S. Main; PO Box 129, Schaller (51053); W; 875pd (Sw); $4.02; publisher & editor Betty Bailey; tel (712) 275-4229

Schleswig: *The Schleswig Leader* — PO Box 70 (51461); Th; 940pd, 50fr (Est); $2.05; C; publisher & editor Edward M Lyon; general manager Elaine Teut; tel (712) 676-3414

Scranton: *Scranton Journal* — PO Box 187 (51462); W; 580pd, 35fr (Est); 13¢; publisher Central Iowa Publishers Inc.; editor Luann Waldo; tel (712) 651-2321; fax (712) 651-2599

Sergeant Bluff: *The Sergeant Bluff Advocate* — 405 4th St.; PO Box 712 (51054); Th; 828pd, 15fr (Sw); $2.00; publisher Bruce Morrison; editor Anne Morrison; tel (712) 943-4600; fax (712) 943-4600

Seymour/Promise/Plano/Cincinnati/Nama/Corydon/Centerville: *The Seymour Herald* — 116 N. 4th St., Seymour (52590); Th; 1,556pd, 50fr (Sw); $2.00; publisher & editor Karen Young; publisher Ken Banks; tel (515) 898-7554

Sheldon: *The N'West Iowa Review* — 227 9th St.; PO Box 160 (51201); Sa; 4,555pd, 386fr (Sw); $6.93; publisher Peter W Wagner; general manager Jeff Wagner; managing editor Jeff Grant; tel (712) 324-5347; fax (712) 324-2345

Sheldon: *The Sheldon Mail-Sun* — 227 9th St.; PO Box 160 (51201); W; 2,466pd, 25fr (Sw); $7.76; publisher Peter W Wagner; general manager Jeff Wagner; managing editor Jeff Grant; tel (712) 324-5347; fax (712) 324-2345

Sibley: *The Osceola County Gazette-Tribune* — 201 9th St. (51249); W; 1,983pd, 45fr (Est); $5.25; C; publisher & editor Jay Mohr; tel (712) 754-2551; fax (712) 754-2552

Sioux Center: *Sioux Center News* — 32 3rd St. N.W.; PO Box 238 (51250); Tu; 2,421pd, 141fr (Sw); $4.50; C; publishers B J Overlie & Warren Overlie; editor Gordon Wolf; tel (712) 722-0741; fax (712) 722-0744

Sioux Rapids: *Sioux Rapids Bulletin Press* — 208 Main St.; PO Box T (50585); W; 1,156pd (Est); $4.50; publisher Bob Madsen; editor Barb Meister; tel (712) 283-2500

Slater/Huxley/Kelly/Cambridge/Collins/Maxwell/Baxter/Elkhart: *The Tri-County Times* — 312 Main St.; PO Box 237, Slater (50244); W; 3,459pd, 60fr (Sw); $5.00; publisher & editor Edwin W Rood; managing editor Sharon Rood; tel (515) 685-3412

Solon/Ely/Swisher: *The Solon Economist* — PO Box 249, Solon (52333); W; 1,065pd, 65fr (Sw); 15¢; publisher Brian Fleck; editor Marietta Beuter; tel (319) 644-2233; fax (319) 644-1356

Spirit Lake: *Spirit Lake Beacon* — 1706 Ithaca Ave.; PO Box AE (51360); Th; 3,639pd, 11fr (Sw); $4.60; C; publisher Michael J Kuehn; editor Sue Lave; tel (712) 336-1211; fax (712) 336-1219

Stacyville (IA)/Adams (MN): *The Monitor Review* — S. Broad St.; PO Box 276, Stacyville (50476); Th; 1,269pd, 26fr (Sw); $3.83; publishers & editors Bob Adams & Kim Edward Adams; tel (515) 737-2119; fax (515) 737-2119

State Center/Melbourne: *Enterprise-Record* — 130 W. Main; PO Box 634, State Center (50247); Th; 1,230pd, 37fr (Sw); $3.62; C; publisher & editor John C Strawn II; tel (515) 483-2120; fax (515) 483-2938

Storm Lake: *Storm Lake Times* — 220 W. Railroad St.; PO Box 487 (50588-0401); W/Sa; 2,350pd (Sw); $6.00; publisher John Cullen; editor Art Cullen; tel (712) 732-4991; fax (712) 732-4331

Story City/Roland: *The Story City Herald* — 423 Broad St.; PO Box 233, Story City (50248); W; 2,164pd, 56fr (Sw); $4.50; publishers & editors Laura Urbanek & Todd Thorson; tel (515) 733-4318; fax (515) 733-4319

Stuart/Guthrie: *The Stuart Herald* — 1317-1319 N. 2nd; PO Box D, Stuart (50250); Th; 1,169pd, 66fr (Sw); $2.75; C; publisher Alan Taylor; editor Vicki Taylor; tel (515) 523-1010; fax (515) 523-2825

Sully: *Diamond Trail News* — 303 7th Ave.; PO Box 186 (50251); W; 1,741pd, 25fr (Sw); $3.00; publisher Mark Davitt; managing editor Margaret Vanderweerdt; tel (515) 594-4488; fax (515) 594-4498

Sumner: *Sumner Gazette* — 106 E. 1st St.; PO Box 208 (50674); Th; 1,969pd, 65fr (Est); $3.49; C; publisher & editor Cal C Milnes; publisher Katy Milnes; tel (319) 578-3351

Sutherland: *The Sutherland Courier* — 130 W. 2nd St. (51058); Th; 674pd, 15fr (Sw); $4.00; C; publisher & editor Mike Otto; tel (712) 446-3450; fax (712) 446-3450

Swea City: *Swea City Herald-Press* — PO Box 428 (50590); W; 640pd (Sw); $4.40; publisher & editor Jerry D Wiseman; tel (515) 272-4660

Tabor: *Tabor Beacon-Enterprise* — PO Box 299 (51653); Th; 1,145pd, 20fr (Est); $1.07; publisher & editor Mark Siekman; tel (712) 629-2255

Tama/Toledo/S Tama Co.: *Toledo Chronicle* — 220 W. 3rd St.; PO Box 118, Tama (52342); Tu/Th; 2,778pd, 45fr (Est); $3.40; publisher D Michael Schlesinger; general manager Bill Christensen; editor Nancy Dostal; tel (515) 484-2841; fax (515) 484-5705

Tama/Toledo/S Tama Co.: *The Tama News-Herald* — 220 W. 3rd St.; PO Box 118, Tama (52339); Th; 3,304pd, 45fr (Sw); $3.25; publisher D Michael Schlesinger; general manager Bill Christensen; editor Nancy Dostal; tel (515) 484-2841; fax (515) 484-5705

Thompson: *The Thompson Courier* — PO Box 318 (50478); Th; 846pd (Sw); 10¢; C; publisher Martin Bunge; editor Kim Norstrud; managing editor Cynthia A Carter; tel (515) 584-2770

Thornton/Rockwell: *Southern County News* — PO Box 96, Thornton (50479); Th; 1,000pd (Est); $3.50; publisher & editor William Schrader; tel (515) 998-2712; fax (515) 998-2712

Tipton: *The Tipton Conservative and Advertiser* — W. 5th St.; PO Box 271 (52772); W; 4,768pd, 30fr (Sw); $4.50; C; publisher Herbert E Clark; general manager & editor Stuart Clark; managing editor Sally I Taylor; tel (319) 886-2131; fax (319) 886-6466

Titonka: *Titonka Topic* — 147 Main St. N.; PO Box 329 (50480); Th; 840pd, 10fr (Sw); $2.68; publisher & editor Lanita Kardoes; tel (515) 928-2723; fax (515) 928-2506

Traer: *The Traer Star-Clipper* — 625 2nd St. (50675); Th; 3,052pd, 90fr (Est); 10¢; publisher Mike Schlesinger; editor Ellen Young; tel (319) 478-2323; fax (319) 478-2818

Tripoli: *Tripoli Leader* — 204 S. Main St.; PO Box 29 (50676); W; 1,467pd, 21fr (Sw); $3.08; publisher & editor Robert J Sassman; tel (319) 882-4207; fax (319) 882-4200

Urbandale: *Urbandale News* — 3805 69th St.; PO Box 3616 (50322); Th; 3,489pd, 10fr (Sw); $6.00; C; publisher Kevin Brown; editor Adam Jones; tel (515) 276-0265; fax (515) 276-5004

Vail/Arcadia/Westside: *The Observer* — PO Box 188, Vail (51465); Th; 1,074pd, 14fr (Sw); 12¢; C; publisher Robert L Miller; editor Cleone Podey; tel (712) 677-2438

Van Buren Co.: *Van Buren Register* — PO Box 477, Keosauqua (52565); Th; 2,951pd, 11fr (Est); $2.52; C; publisher & editor Russell Ebert; tel (319) 293-3197; fax (319) 293-3198

Victor: *Victor Echo* — 205 Washington St.; PO Box 81 (52347); W; 380pd, 30fr (Sw); $2.80; publisher & editor Chuck V Dunham; tel (319) 647-2333; fax (319) 522-2527

Villisca/Stamton/Nodaway: *Villisca Review & Stanton Viking* — 409 S. 3rd Ave.; PO Box 6, Villisca (50864); Th; 1,350pd, 22fr (Sw); $2.25; publisher & editor Carolyn Cole Gage; tel (712) 826-2142; fax (712) 826-8888

Walnut Co.: *The Walnut Bureau* — 225 Antique City Dr.; PO Box 468, Walnut (51577); Th; 660pd, 14fr (Sw); $1.80; publisher & editor Nicholas R Hoffman; tel (712) 784-3575

Waukon: *Waukon Standard* — 15 1st St. N.W.; PO Box 286 (52172); Tu; 4,050pd (Est); $1.05; publisher Tom Johnson; editor Richard Schilling; tel (319) 568-3431; fax (319) 568-4242

Waverly/Janesville/Readlyn/Shell Rock/Plainfield/Bremer Co.: *The Bremer County Independent/Waverly Democrat* — 311 W. Bremer Ave.; PO Box 858, Waverly (50677); Tu/Th; 6,426pd, 25fr (Sw); $4.75; C; publisher Jayne A Thomas Hall; editor Raymond Locke; tel (319) 352-3334; fax (319) 352-5135

W Bend/Rodman/Ottosen: *West Bend Journal* — 223 Broadway; PO Box 47, West Bend (50597); Th; 1,066pd, 11fr (Sw); $2.50; publishers & editors Angela Schmidt & Neal Schmidt; tel (515) 887-4141

W Branch: *West Branch Times* — 105 S. Downey St.; PO Box 368 (52358); Th; 1,276pd, 38fr (Est); $5.00; publisher Deb Owen; publisher & editor Mike Owen; tel (319) 643-2131

W Burlington/Danville/Middletown: *Des Moines County News* — 204 Broadway; PO Box 177 (52655); Th; 1,900pd, 15fr (Est); $3.57; C; publisher Michael A Hodges; editor Ramona Nahorney; tel (319) 752-8328; fax (319) 523-8167

W Des Moines: *Western Express* — 2221 E. Ovid (50313); PO Box 4826, Des Moines (50306); F; 807pd, 7fr (Sw); $5.20; publisher Roger Smed; editor Dave DeValois; tel (515) 262-1190; fax (515) 262-2267

W Liberty: *The West Liberty Index* — 112 E. 3rd St.; PO Box 96 (52776); Th; 2,134pd, 7fr (Sw); $4.34; publisher Wally Johnson; general manager & editor Diane Beranak; tel (319) 627-2814; fax (319) 627-2110

W Point: *West Point Bee* — PO Box 66 (52656); Th; 675pd, 40fr (Est); $5.40; publisher Ray Fullencamp; editor Christy Holtkamp; managing editor Lorene A Fedler; tel (319) 837-6722; fax (319) 837-6128

W Union: *Fayette County Union* — 119 S. Vine St. (52175); W; 3,872pd, 4,000fr (Est); 24¢; C; publisher & editor Gerald H Blue; tel (319) 422-3888

Williamsburg: *Williamsburg Journal Tribune* — PO Box 690 (52361); Th; 1,764pd (Est); $5.78; C; publisher Michael T Simmons; general manager Daniel J DeBettignies; editor Todd Kimm; managing editor G Alan Sieve; tel (319) 668-1240; fax (319) 642-5509

Wilton/Durant/Moscow/Stockton: *Wilton-Durant Advocate News* — 101 W. 4th St.; PO Box 415, Wilton (52778); Th; 2,634pd, 32fr (Sw); $5.75; publisher William F Tubbs; general manager Nancy Peirce; editor Craig Dueker; tel (319) 732-2029; fax (319) 732-3144

Winfield/Wayland: *Winfield Beacon/Wayland News* — 107 E. Elm St.; PO Box F, Winfield (52659); Th; 1,760pd, 45fr (Sw); $3.00; publisher & editor M Catherine Lauderdale; tel (319) 257-6813; fax (319) 257-6902

Winterset/Madison Co.: *Winterset Madisonian* — 112 W. Court Ave.; PO Box 350, Winterset (50273); W; 3,827pd, 23fr (Est); $4.11; C; publisher Ted C Gorman; editor Chris Dorsey; tel (515) 462-2101; fax (515) 462-2102

Winthrop: *The Winthrop News* — PO Box A (50682); Th; 1,500pd, 10fr (Est); 32¢; C; publisher & editor Esther Brockling; general manager Steve Fister; tel (319) 935-3027; fax (319) 935-3082

Woodbine: *Woodbine Twiner* — 509 Walker St.; PO Box 16 (51579); W; 1,326pd (Sw); $4.14; publisher & editor Eugene A Bloom; tel (712) 647-2821; fax (712) 647-3081

Zearing: *Tri-County News* — 117 W. Main St.; PO Box 156 (50278); Th; 814pd (Est); $2.17; publisher & editor William H Britten; tel (515) 487-7661

KANSAS

Alma/McFarland/Paxico/Maple Hill: *The Signal Enterprise* — 323 Missouri; PO Box 158, Alma (66401); Th; 1,245pd, 30fr (Sw); $2.50; C; publisher & editor Ervan D Stuewe; publisher Pamela K Stuewe; tel (913) 765-3327

Alta Vista/Dwight/White City: *The Prairie Post* — 108 E. MacKenzie St.; PO Box 326, White City (66872-0326); Th; 1,100pd (Est); $2.20; C; publisher & editor Joann Kahnt; tel (913) 349-5516; fax (913) 349-5516

Altamont: *Altamont Journal* — 403 Commercial St., Oswego (67356); Th; 261pd (Est); 6¢; publishers Charles R Crowell & Robert O Crowell; editor Charles Crowell; tel (316) 784-5722

Anderson Co.: *The Anderson Countian* — 112 W. 6th St.; PO Box 409, Garnett (66032); Th; 3,036pd, 30fr (Sw); $4.67; publisher & editor Garold Dane Hicks; tel (913) 448-3121

Anderson Co.: *The Garnett Review* — 112 W. 6th St.; PO Box 409, Garnett (66032); M; 3,036pd, 30fr (Sw); $4.67; publisher & editor Garold Dane Hicks; tel (913) 448-3121

Andover: *The Journal-Advocate* — PO Box 453 (67002); Th; 1,876pd, 61fr (Sw); $6.00; publisher Kay L Palmer; editor Kathy Campbell; tel (316) 733-2002

Anthony/Harper/Attica: *Anthony Republican & Bulletin* — 121 E. Main; PO Box 31, Anthony (67003); W; 3,090pd, 27fr (Sw); $3.00; publisher & editor James W Dunn; general manager Vera L Dunn; tel (316) 842-5129; fax (316) 842-5120

Ashland: *The Clark County Clipper* — 705 Main St.; PO Box 457 (67831); Th; 1,260pd, 30fr (Est); $2.50; publisher & editor Amber Woodruff; tel (316) 635-2312; fax (316) 635-2643

Baldwin: *The Baldwin Ledger* — 814 High St.; PO Box 66, Baldwin City (66006); Th; 2,000pd, 6,000fr (Sw); $4.95; C; publisher Doris Downing Miller & Monte Miller; managing editor Chad Lawhorn; tel (913) 594-6424; fax (913) 594-3080

Baxter Springs: *The Baxter Springs Citizen* — 1010 Military Ave.; PO Box 657 (66713); Tu/F; 2,105pd, 25fr (Sw); $4.80; C; publisher Jeffrey L Nichols; managing editor Brent Fisher; tel (316) 856-2115; fax (316) 856-3162

Belle Plaine/Udall: *The Belle Plaine News* — 431 Merchant; PO Box 128, Belle Plaine (67013); Th; 884pd, 30fr (Sw); $3.50; C; publisher William Sam Clester; editor Marian Phipps; tel (316) 488-2234; fax (316) 488-3241

Belleville: *Farmer Stockman of the Midwest* — 1817 U.S. 81 Frontage Rd.; PO Box 349 (66935); M; 5,564pd, 104fr (Sw); $10.50; publisher & editor Merle M Miller; tel (913) 527-2224; fax (913) 527-2225

Belleville: *The Belleville Telescope* — 1817 U.S. 81 Frontage Rd.; PO Box 349 (66935); Th; 4,116pd, 136fr (Sw); $6.30; publisher Merle M Miller; editor Mark L Miller; tel (913) 527-2244; fax (913) 527-2225

Bird City/McDonald: *The Bird City Times* — 312 Bird Ave.; PO Box 167, Bird City (67731); Th; 625pd, 3fr (Sw); $3.05; C; publishers Cynthia Haynes & Steve Haynes; general manager & editor Karen Krien; managing editor Debby Miller; tel (913) 734-2621; fax (913) 332-3001

Bonner Springs: *Bonner Springs-Edwardsville Chieftain* — 128 Oak St.; PO Box 256 (66012); Th; 2,909pd, 205fr (Est); $3.30; publisher & editor Clausie W Smith; tel (913) 422-4048

Brown/Atchison Cos.: *The Horton Headlight* — 133 W. 8th St.; PO Box 269, Horton (66439); Th; 2,066pd, 39fr (Est); $1.45; publisher Ethel Mae Foley; general manager & editor Susan Higley; tel (913) 486-2512; fax (913) 486-2512

Burden: *The Cowley County Reporter* — 414 Main St.; PO Box 97 (67019); Th; 596pd, 22fr (Sw); $2.35; C; publisher Martin Hellar; editor Ann Alexander; tel (316) 438-2370; fax (316) 438-2370

Burlington: *Coffey County Today* — 324 Hudson St.; PO Box A (66839-0218); M/W/F; 2,105pd, 41fr (Sw); $4.34; C; publisher Glenn R German; editor Mark Petterson; tel (316) 364-5325; fax (316) 364-2607

Caldwell: *Caldwell Messenger* — 111 S. Main St.; PO Box 313 (67022); W; 1,460pd, 15fr (Est); $2.55; publisher & editor Damon F Weber; tel (316) 845-2320; fax (316) 845-6461

Caney: *Caney Chronicle* — 202 W. 4th; PO Box 186 (67333); W; 1,795pd, 53fr (Sw); 22¢; C; publisher & editor Rudy M Taylor; tel (316) 879-2156

Canton/Galva/Roxbury: *The Canton Pilot* — 137 N. Main; PO Box 495, Canton (67428); Th; 594pd, 27fr (Est); 24¢; publisher Canton Pilot Inc.; tel (316) 628-4430

Cawker City: *Cawker City Ledger* — 128 Wisconsin; PO Box 7 (67430); Th; 1,053pd (Sw); $1.60; publisher & editor Darrel E Miller; general manager & managing editor Ruth Miller; tel (913) 781-4831; fax (913) 454-3866

Chapman: *The Chapman Advertiser and Enterprise Journal* — 437 N. Marshall; PO Box E (67431); Th; 922pd, 54fr (Sw); $4.10; C; publisher John G Montgomery; general manager & managing editor Roland E Waechter; editor Julie Hamel; tel (913) 922-6856; fax (913) 762-4584

Cherryvale: *Cherryvale Chronicle* — 115 N. Labette; PO Box 156 (67335); W; 1,600pd (Est); $3.25; C; publisher Rudy M Taylor; editor Andy Taylor; tel (316) 336-2100; fax (316) 336-2101

Chetopa: *Chetopa Advance* — PO Box 207 (67336); Th; 1,215pd, 13fr (Sw); 9¢; publisher Charles Crowell; publisher & editor Robert Crowell; tel (316) 236-7591; fax (316) 795-4712

Cimarron: *Cimarron Jacksonian* — PO Box 528 (67835); Tu; 1,223pd (Est); 13¢; publisher Jerry Anderson; editor Kirk Anderson; tel (316) 855-3902

Clearwater/Andale/Cheney/Clearwater/Colwich/Garden Plaine/Goddard/Haven: *Times Sentinel* — 101 N. Main St.; PO Box 507, Cheney (67025); Th; 3,600pd, 25fr (Est); $5.50; C; publishers Amy Crouch & Paul Rhodes; general manager Carol Carr; editor Tim Pouncey; tel (316) 542-3111; fax (316) 542-3283

Clifton: *The Clifton News-Tribune* — 107 E. Parallel; PO Box K (66937); Th; 532pd, 16fr (Sw); $2.00; C; publisher & editor Everett R Daves; tel (913) 455-3466

Clyde: *Clyde Republican* — 305 Washington; PO Box 397 (66938-0397); Th; 880pd, 51fr (Est); $2.50; publisher & editor Margene Cash; tel (913) 446-2201

Coldwater: *The Western Star* — 113 S. Central; PO Box 518 (67029-0518); Th; 1,158pd, 30fr (Sw); $2.50; publisher & editor Dennies D Andersen; tel (316) 582-2101

Columbus: *The Weekly Modern Light* — 215 S. Kansas; PO Box 231 (66725); Tu; 284pd, 5fr (Sw); N/A; publisher Jay Lacy; editor Alan Storey; tel (316) 429-2773

Conway Springs: *Conway Springs Star and The Argonia Argosy* — PO Box 158 (67031); Th; 1,559pd, 54fr (Est); 15¢; publisher & editor Raymond J Cline; tel (316) 456-2473

Cottonwood Falls/Chase Co.: *Chase County Leader-News* — 306 Broadway; PO Box K, Cottonwood Falls (66845-0436); Th; 1,259pd, 50fr (Sw); $3.50; publisher & editor Jerry Schwilling; publisher Karen Schwilling; tel (316) 273-6391; fax (316) 273-8674

Courtland: *Courtland Journal-Empire* — 420 Main St. (66939-0318); Th; 700pd, 20fr (Sw); 77¢; publishers C Mainquist & R Mainquist; tel (913) 374-4428

Delphos/Glasco: *The Delphos Republican* — 213 E. Main St.; PO Box 457, Glasco (67445); Th; 362pd (Sw); $2.25; C; publisher George Tatro; publisher & editor Royanne Tatro; tel (913) 568-2565

Dighton: *The Dighton Herald* — 113 E. Long St.; PO Box 637 (67839); W; 1,250pd, 48fr (Sw); 13¢; C; publishers & editors Barbara E Gardner & Jim W Gardner; tel (316) 397-5347

Doniphan Co.: *The Kansas Chief* — 113 S. Main St.; PO Box 157, Troy (66087); Th; 1,500pd, 25fr (Sw); $3.25; publisher & editor Steven C Tetlow; general manager & managing editor Ranae Tetlow; tel (913) 985-2456; fax (913) 985-3841

Downs: *The Downs News & Times* — PO Box 157 (67437); Th; 1,071pd, 79fr (Sw); $3.20; C; publisher Darrel E Miller; general manager & editor Ruth Miller; tel (913) 454-3514; fax (913) 454-3866

Ellinwood/Great Bend: *Ellinwood Leader* — 105 N. Main; PO Box 487, Ellinwood (67526); Th; 1,369pd, 654fr (Sw); $3.40; publisher John M Settle; editor Deborah McLaughlin; tel (316) 564-3116

Ellis: *The Ellis Review* — 1018 Washington; PO Box 227 (67637); Th; 1,319pd, 38fr (Est); $2.25; publisher & editor Bill Gasper; managing editor Connie Fox; tel (913) 726-4583

Ellsworth Co.: *The Ellsworth Reporter* — 220 Court St.; PO Box 7, Ellsworth (67439); Th; 2,888pd, 12fr (Sw); $3.78; C; publisher Dorothy A Gaston; publisher & editor Karl K Gaston; tel (913) 472-3103; fax (913) 472-3268

Erie: *The Erie Record* — 317 S. Main St.; PO Box 159 (66733-0159); Th; 1,403pd, 6fr (Sw); $2.44; publisher & editor Leah Kensinger; tel (316) 244-3371

Eskridge/Dover/Harveyville: *Flint Hills Independent* — PO Box 27, Eskridge (66423); Th; 2,375pd (Sw); $7.50; C; publisher & editor Sam Elliott; tel (913) 449-7272; fax (913) 449-2411

Eudora: *Eudora News* — 729 Main; PO Box 419 (66025); W; 1,141pd, 97fr (Sw); $3.85; publisher Bert Hull; editor Vickie Hull; tel (913) 542-2747

Eureka: *The Eureka Herald* — 106 W. 2nd; PO Box 590 (67045); Th; 3,750pd, 50fr (Est); $4.00; publisher & editor Richard W Clasen; tel (316) 583-5721

Everest: *The Everest World* — 607 Utah, Hiawatha (66424); Th; 240pd, 25fr (Sw); $1.90; C; publisher Barry A Stokes; editor Virginia Regier; tel (913)742-2111; fax (913) 742-2276

Frankfort: *Frankfort Area News* — PO Box 156 (66427); Tu; 776pd (Sw); $3.00; publishers & editors Betty Suther & LaVonne Farrell; tel (913) 292-4726; fax (913) 292-4522

Fredonia: *Wilson County Citizen* — 406 N. 7th St.; PO Box 330 (66736); M/Th; 3,941pd, 69fr (Sw); $3.75; C; publishers & editors Joseph Relph & Rita Relph; managing editor Mina DeBerry; tel (316) 378-4415; fax (316) 378-4688

Galena: *Galena Sentinel Times* — 115 N. Main (66739); W; 1,204pd, 122fr (Est); 13¢; publisher David F Nelson; editor Frances C Secrist; tel (316) 783-5034; fax (316) 783-1388

Gardner: *Gardner News* — PO Box 303 (66030); W; 1,400pd, 20fr (Sw); $4.75; C; publisher Rhonda Humble; editor Janet Swanson; tel (913) 884-7615; fax (913) 884-6707

Gardner/Spring Hill/Edgerton: *Spring Hill New Era/The Gardner News* — PO Box 303, Gardner (66030); W; 850pd, 50fr (Est); $5.50; W; 2,000pd, 150fr (Est); $5.50; C; publisher Rhonda Humble; editor Janet Swanson; tel (913) 856-7615; fax (913) 856-6707

Garnett/Anderson: *Garnett Review* — PO Box 409, Garnett (66032); M; 4,137pd, 22fr (Est); 41¢; publisher & editor Dane Hicks; tel (913) 448-3121

Girard/Pittsburg/Frontenac/Arma: *The Girard Press* — 102 S. Ozark; PO Box 126, Girard (66743); Tu; 2,850pd (Sw); $2.90; publisher Ed McKechnie; managing editor Janet Gilliland; tel (316) 724-4426; fax (316) 724-4493

Glasco: *The Glasco Sun* — 213 E. Main St.; PO Box 457 (67445); Th; 816pd (Sw); $2.25; publisher & editor Royanne Tatro; editor George Tatro; tel (913) 568-2565

Grant Co.: *The Ulysses News* — 218 N. Main St.; PO Box 706, Ulysses (67880); Th; 2,854pd, 16fr (Est); 30¢; publisher Michael A Pace; general manager Carla Waechter; editor Shirley Pace; managing editor Michael Alcala; tel (316) 356-1201; fax (316) 356-4610

Greensburg/Kiowa Co.: *Kiowa County Signal* — PO Box 368, Greensburg (67054); W; 1,300pd, 30fr (Est); $3.30; C; publisher J K Phillips II; general manager Ronda Brown; tel (316) 723-2115

Gridley: *Gridley Gleam* — 659 Blackbird Rd.; PO Box 93 (66852); Th; 440pd, 13fr (Est); $1.30; publisher & editor T J Watson; tel (316) 836-3152; fax (316) 836-3401

Hanover: *Hanover News* — PO Box 278 (66945); F; 1,234pd (Est); 9¢; publisher Dora Sand; publisher & editor R L Sand; tel (913) 337-2242

Herington: *The Herington Times* — 7 N. Broadway; PO Box 310 (67449); Th; 2,639pd, 50fr (Sw); $5.25; publisher & editor Larry Byers; tel (913) 258-2211; fax (913) 258-2400

Hesston: *Hesston Record* — 109 N. Main; PO Box 340 (67062); Th; 1,074pd, 130fr (Sw); 24¢; publishers & editors Bob Latta & Loretta Latta; tel (316) 327-4831; fax (316) 327-4830

Highland: *Highland Vidette* — 312 W. Main St.; PO Box 98 (66035); Th; 1,262pd, 7fr (Est); 10¢; publisher & editor Glenn Sutherland; tel (913) 442-3791

Hill City: *The Hill City Times* — 110 N. Pomeroy; PO Box 308 (67642-0308); Tu; 2,506pd, 20fr (Sw); $3.86; publisher Robert Boyd; editor James Logback; tel (913) 674-5700; fax (913) 674-3678

Hillsboro: *The Hillsboro Star-Journal* — 104 S. Main St.; PO Box A (67063); W; 2,749pd, 30fr (Sw); $4.00; publisher & editor Stacy Stenseng; general manager Stacy Klassen; managing editor Rusty Stenseng; tel (316) 947-3975; fax (316) 947-3883

Holton/Jackson Co.: *The Holton Recorder* — 109 W. 4th St.; PO Box 311, Holton (66436); M/Th; 4,850pd (Sw); $4.25; publisher Bryan McDaniel; editor Leslie C McDaniel; tel (913) 364-3141; fax (913) 364-3422

Howard/Molina/Lougton: *Elk County Citizen-Advance News* — 125 S. Wabash; PO Box 248, Howard (67349); W; 2,075pd, 30fr (Sw); 19¢; C; publisher Martin Hellar; editor Janis Sinclair; tel (316) 374-2101; fax (316) 374-2102

Hoxie: *The Hoxie Sentinel* — 640 Main St.; PO Box 78 (67740); Th; 1,826pd, 52fr (Sw); $3.00; publisher & editor Bill Gasper; tel (913) 675-3321; fax (913) 675-3421

Hugoton: *The Hugoton Hermes* — 522 S. Main; PO Box 849 (67951); Th; 2,144pd, 95fr (Sw); $4.50; publisher Donald Goering; editor Sherill Goering; tel (316) 544-4321; fax (316) 544-7321

Independence: *The Independence News* — 210 W. Main St. (67301); Sa; 500pd, 500fr (Sw); $5.00; publisher & editor John F Vermillion; tel (316) 331-4950

Jefferson Co.: *Valley Falls Vindicator* — 416 Broadway; PO Box 187, Valley Falls (66088); Th; 2,464pd, 27fr (Sw); $3.50; C; publisher Wilson-Davis Publications Inc.; editor Clarke Davis; tel (913) 945-3257; fax (913) 945-3444

Jetmore/Hodgeman Co.: *The Jetmore Republican* — PO Box 337, Jetmore (67854); Th; 1,004pd, 10fr (Est); $3.00; publishers Jerry Anderson & Mark Anderson; general manager & editor Jerry Buxton; tel (316) 357-8316; fax (316) 357-8464

Johnson Co.: *The Sun Newspapers* — 7373 W. 107th St., Overland Park (66212); W/F; 550pd, 95,072fr (Est); $30.35; publishers Stan Rose & Steve Rose; editor Jack Lovelace; tel (913) 381-1010; fax (913) 381-9889

Johnson/Stanton Co.: *Johnson Pioneer* — 103 N. Main St.; PO Box 10, Johnson (67855); Th; 717pd, 27fr (Sw); $2.25; publisher & editor Ronda Ford; tel (316) 492-6244

Kansas City: *Wyandotte West/Suburban Advertiser* — 7735 Washington Ave.; PO Box 12003 (66112); W; 12,300fr (Sw); $10.36; Th; 2,208pd, 631fr (Sw); $10.36; C; publisher & editor Murrel Bland; tel (913) 788-5565; fax (913) 788-9812

Kearny Co.: *The Lakin Independent* — 118 N. Main; PO Box 45, Lakin (67860); Th; 1,630pd, 30fr (Sw); 25¢; publisher Monte Canfield; editor Kathy McVey; tel (316) 355-6162

Kingman: *Kingman Journal* — PO Box 353 (67068); Tu; 3,298pd (Sw); $3.15; publisher & editor Robert L McQuin; tel (316) 532-3151; fax (316) 532-3152

Kingman: *Kingman Leader-Courier* — PO Box 353 (67068); F; 3,298pd, 60fr (Sw); $3.15; publisher & editor Robert L McQuin; tel (316) 532-3151; fax (316) 532-3152

Kinsley/Lewis/Offerle/Belpre: *Edwards County Sentinel* — 218 E. 6th St.; PO Box 39, Kinsley (67547); Th; 1,600pd (Est); $4.00; publishers & editors Cathy Woolard & David L Kazmaier; tel (316) 659-2080

Kiowa: *The Kiowa News* — 614 Main St. (67070); Th; 1,592pd, 44fr (Sw); 17¢; publisher & editor Rex Zimmerman; tel (316) 825-4229; fax (316) 825-4229

La Crosse/Rush/Ellis/Barton/Ness/Pawnee Cos.: *The Rush County News* — 112 W. 8th St.; PO Box 60, La Crosse (67548); Th; 2,087pd, 34fr (Sw); $3.95; publisher & editor Duane Engel; publisher & managing editor Mary Engel; tel (913) 222-2555; fax (913) 222-2557

Lebanon: *The Lebanon Times* — 409 Walnut; PO Box 158 (66952); Th; 480pd (Sw); 7¢; publisher Darrel E Miller; editor Phyllis Bell; tel (913) 389-6631

Leoti: *Leoti Standard* — 114 S. 4th; PO Box N (67861); W; 1,628pd, 30fr (Sw); $42.51; publisher Jerry Anderson; editor Linda Geyer; tel (316) 375-2631; fax (316) 375-2184

LeRoy/Lebo/Waverly/Hartford/Melvern: *This Week* — PO Box 151, Burlington (66839); W; 1,247pd, 43fr (Sw); $3.43; C; publisher Glenn R German; editor Mark Petterson; tel (316) 364-8610; fax (316) 364-2607

Lincoln/Beverly/Barnard/Sylvan Grove: *Lincoln Sentinel-Republican* — 141 W. Lincoln Ave.; PO Box 67, Lincoln (67455); Th; 2,013pd, 32fr (Sw); $21.00; publisher Pat Rasmussen; publisher & editor Ray Rasmussen; tel (913) 524-4200

Lindsborg/Gypsum/Assaria/Marquette/Falun/Smolan: *The Lindsborg News-Record* — 114 S. Main St.; PO Box 31, Lindsborg (67456); Th; 2,997pd, 136fr (Sw); $3.70; publisher John G Montgomery; editor Marty Hardy; tel (913) 227-3348; fax (913) 227-3740

U.S. Weeklies Kentucky II-29

Linn: *Linn-Palmer Record* — 405 2nd St.; PO Box 324 (66953); Th; 1,056pd, 15fr (Est); 10¢; publisher & editor Tom M Mall; tel (913) 348-5481

Logan: *The Logan Republican* — 101 E. Main St.; PO Box 97 (67646-0097); Th; 1,000pd (Est); $3.00; publisher & editor V Gottschalk; tel (913) 689-4339

Louisburg/Miami: *Louisburg Herald* — 15 S. Broadway; PO Box 99, Louisburg (66053); Th; 1,975pd (Est); $2.66; publishers Gladys Hawkins & Webster Hawkins; general manager & editor Tom Bassing; tel (913) 837-4321; fax (913) 837-4322

Lucas/Sylvan Grove: *Lucas-Sylvan News* — 203 S. Main St.; PO Box 337, Lucas (67648); Th; 854pd, 22fr (Sw); $2.35; publisher Craig D Langdon; editor Carolyn Schultz; tel (913) 525-6355

Madison: *The Madison News* — 118 S. 3rd St.; PO Box 248 (66860); Th; 778pd, 15fr (Sw); $2.94; publisher Frances Gilman; editor Stephen Gilman; tel (316) 437-2433; fax (316) 437-2433

Manhattan: *Grass & Grain* — 16th & Yuma Sts.; PO Box 1009 (66502); Tu; 15,640pd, 922fr (Sw); $8.00; publisher Dean Coughenour; editor Beth Gaines-Riffel; tel (913) 539-7558; fax (913) 539-2679

Mankato: *The Jewell County Post* — 111 E. Main St.; PO Box 305, Mankato (66956); Th; 1,167pd (Est); $2.50; publisher Joe Beach; editor Lesa Peroutek; tel (913) 378-3191; fax (913) 378-3782

Marion Co.: *Marion County Record* — 117 S. 3rd St.; PO Box 278, Marion (66861); W; 3,150pd, 10fr (Sw); $4.50; publisher & editor Bill Meyer; tel (316) 382-2165; fax (316) 382-2262

Marquette: *Marquette Tribune* — PO Box 308 (62464); W; 700pd (Sw); $2.82; publisher Karl K Gaston; editor Nyla Rawson; tel (913) 546-2266; fax (913) 546-2266

Marshall Co.: *Telegraph* — 113 Commercial; PO Box 236, Waterville (66548); Th; 550pd, 100fr (Est); $3.00; publisher William M Hays; editor Liz Anderson; tel (913) 363-2061, (913) 325-2219

Marysville/Marshall Co.: *Marysville Advocate* — 107 S. 9th; PO Box 271, Marysville (66508); Th; 5,907pd, 102fr (Sw); $4.75; publisher & editor Howard Kessinger; publisher Sharon Kessinger; tel (913) 562-2317; fax (913) 562-5589

Meade: *Meade County News* — 105 S. Fowler; PO Box 310 (67864); W; 1,350pd (Est); $2.90; publisher Jerry Anderson; editor Tom Kuhns; tel (316) 873-2118; fax (316) 873-5456

Medicine Lodge: *Barber County Index* — 106 W. 1st St.; PO Box 349 (67104); W; 2,350pd (Sw); $1.95; publisher Jim Phillips; editor James Emrick; tel (316) 886-5617; fax (316) 886-5104

Medicine Lodge/Sharon/Isabel/Sun City/Lake City/Kiowa/Hazelton/Hardtner/Nashville: *Gyp Hill Premiere* — 110 N. Main St., Medicine Lodge (67104); M; 1,460pd, 39fr (Est); $3.00; publisher Kevin J Noland; general manager Ronda D Noland; editor Tate W Henke; tel (316) 886-5654; fax (316) 886-5655

Miltonvale: *Miltonvale Record* — 12 Spruce St. (67466); Th; 729pd, 25fr (Sw); $2.00; publisher & editor Richard R Phelps; tel (913) 427-2680; fax (913) 429-2216

Minneapolis: *Minneapolis Messenger* — 108 N. Concord; PO Box 249 (67467); Th; 2,200pd, 33fr (Est); $2.80; publisher & editor John Wilson; tel (913) 392-2129; fax (913) 392-2026

Minneola/Clark: *The Minneola Record* — PO Box 456, Minneola (67865); Th; 562pd, 14fr (Est); $1.92; publisher & editor Amber Woodruff; tel (316) 885-4710; fax (316) 635-2643

Morton Co.: *Elkhart Tri-State News* — 546 Morton; PO Box 777, Elkhart (67950); Th; 1,630pd, 10fr (Sw); 18¢; publisher & editor Karen Brady; tel (316) 697-4716

Moundridge/Inman/Buhler: *The Ledger* — PO Box 720, Moundridge (67107); Th; 1,925pd (Sw); $3.67; publisher Jerry Davies; editor Joel Morris; tel (316) 345-6353; fax (316) 345-2170

Mt. Hope/Andale/Colwich/Garden Plain/Bentley/Maize: *The Mount Hope Clarion* — 101 S. Ohio; PO Box 337, Mount Hope (67108); Th; 1,498pd, 149fr (Sw); $4.00; C; publisher Billy Chance; editor Delores A Weve; tel (316) 667-2697; fax (316) 667-2406

Mulberry/Arcadia: *The Mulberry Advance* — 919 Military; PO Box 267, Mulberry (66756); F; 109pd, 25fr (Sw); 16¢; publisher & editor Darvin E Weaver; tel (316) 764-3831

Mullinville: *Merchant's Directory* — 215 W. Wall; PO Box 168 (67109-0168); W; 347pd (Sw); $2.00; publisher & editor Howard Kendall; tel (316) 548-2678

Mulvane/Rose Hill: *The Mulvane News* — 204 W. Main St.; PO Box 157, Mulvane (67110); Tu/Th; 1,750pd, 4,850fr (Sw); $8.50; C; publisher & editor Michael Robinson; tel (316) 777-4233

Natoma: *The Independent Record* — 418 Main St.; PO Box 160 (67651); Th; 1,052pd, 54fr (Sw); $2.10; publisher & editor Della Richmond; tel (913) 885-4582

Neodesha/Wilson Co.: *Neodesha Derrick* — 501 Main St.; PO Box 356, Neodesha (66757); Th; 1,569pd, 99fr (Sw); $3.50; publisher & editor Jo Anne Hartley Harper; tel (316) 325-3000; fax (316) 325-2880

Ness City/Ness Co.: *Ness County News* — PO Box C, Ness City (67560); Th; 2,407pd, 32fr (Sw); $2.80; publisher & editor John Clarke; tel (913) 798-2213; fax (913) 798-2214

Norwich: *The Norwich News* — 309 W. Spring Ave.; PO Box 194, Conway Springs (67031); W; 245pd (Sw); $2.88; publisher A J Bozarth; editor Pam Adams; tel (316) 456-2232

Oakley/Grinnell/Winona: *The Oakley Graphic* — 118 Center, Oakley (67748); W; 1,860pd, 79fr (Est); $3.08; publisher Jerry Anderson; editor Barbara Glover; tel (913) 672-3228; fax (913) 672-3229

Oberlin: *The Oberlin Herald* — 170 S. Penn Ave. (67749-2243); W; 2,777pd, 36fr (Sw); $4.20; C; publisher Cynthia Haynes; publisher & editor Steve Haynes; managing editor Connie Grafel; tel (913) 475-2206; fax (913) 475-2800

Osage Co.: *Osage County Chronicle* — PO Box 65, Burlingame (66413); Th; 5,100pd (Sw); $4.15; publisher & editor K Kurt Kessinger; tel (913) 654-3621; fax (913) 654-3438

Osawatomie/Linn/Franklin: *Osawatomie Graphic* — 635 Main St.; PO Box 99, Osawatomie (66064); Th; 4,929pd (Sw); $5.00; C; publisher Webster Hawkins; editor Carol Chitwood; tel (913) 755-4151; fax (913) 755-6544

Osborne/Downs Alton: *Osborne County Farmer* — 210 W. Main St.; PO Box 130, Osborne (67473); Th; 2,728pd, 100fr (Sw); $3.40; publisher Dale Worley; editor Sandra A Trail; tel (913) 346-5424; fax (913) 346-5400

Oskaloosa/Leavenworth: *Oskaloosa Independent* — 607 Delaware; PO Box 278, Oskaloosa (66066); Th; 1,875pd, 29fr (Sw); 20¢; C; publisher & editor Clarke Davis; tel (913) 863-2520; fax (913) 863-2730

Ottawa: *Ottawa Times* — 401 S. Main St., Ste. 1; PO Box 246 (66067); Th; 1,177pd, 50fr (Sw); $3.75; C; publisher Jim Hitch; general manager Kent Ramsey; editor Bill Gray; tel (913) 242-9200; fax (913) 242-9595

Oxford/Geuda Springs: *The Oxford Register* — PO Box 128, Belle Plaine (67013); Th; 364pd, 17fr (Sw); $4.12; C; publisher William Sam Clester; editor Marian Phipps; tel (316) 455-3535; fax (316) 488-3241

Paola: *The Miami County Republic* — 121 S. Pearl St.; PO Box 389 (66071); M/W; 5,785pd, 20fr (Sw); $4.40; publisher & editor Phil McLaughlin; tel (913) 294-2311; fax (913) 294-5318

Parsons/Oswego/Chetopa/Cherryvale/Edna/Altamont/St. Paul/Mound Vly./Erie/McCune/Bartlett/Thayer/Welch: *Parsons News* — 1930 Clark; PO Box 937, Parsons (67357); Th; 1,426pd, 346fr (Sw); $4.80; publisher & editor Virginia L Tippet; managing editor Tracey Tippet; tel (316) 421-2990; fax (316) 421-2990

Peabody/Burns/Florence: *The Gazette-Bulletin* — 117 N. Walnut; PO Box 129, Peabody (66866-0129); Th; 1,233pd, 9fr (Sw); $2.50; publisher Shirley B Krause; editor William V Krause; tel (316) 983-2185

Phillipsburg: *Phillips County Review* — 257 F; PO Box 446 (67661); Th; 3,350pd, 150fr (Est); $3.95; publisher Ronald K Lower; editor Perry Hanson; tel (913) 543-5242; fax (913) 543-6563

Plainville/Palco/Zurich: *Plainville Times* — 400 W. Mill St.; PO Box 40, Plainville (67663); Th; 2,274pd, 40fr (Sw); $2.66; publisher & editor Carol Van Dyke; tel (913) 434-4525; fax (913) 434-4525

Pleasanton/Linn Co.: *The Linn County News* — 808 Main St.; PO Box 478, Pleasanton (66075); Th; 3,000pd (Est); $4.50; publisher Michael Crawford; editor Melody Berry; tel (913) 352-6235; fax (913) 352-6607

Pottawatomie/Wabaunsee Cos.: *Wamego Smoke Signal* — 407 Lincoln Ave.; PO Box 267, Wamego (66547); W; 133pd, 10,583fr (Est); $4.50; C; publisher John Grey Montgomery; general manager James Gibbons; tel (913) 456-2602; fax (913) 456-8484

Quinter: *Gove County Advocate* — PO Box 365 (67752); W; 1,699pd, 129fr (Sw); $3.00; publisher Roxanne K Broeckelman; publisher & editor Tom W Broeckelman; tel (913) 754-3651; fax (913) 754-3878

Russell: *The Russell Record* — 802 N. Maple St. (67665); M/Th; 3,303pd, 80fr (Sw); 18¢; publisher Allan D Evans; editor Irene Jepsen; tel (913) 483-2111; fax (913) 483-4012

Sabetha: *The Sabetha Herald* — PO Box 208 (66534); W; 2,542pd, 50fr (Sw); $3.75; publisher Bryan McDaniel; editor Elvyn Jones; tel (913) 284-3300; fax (913) 284-2320

St. Francis: *The Saint Francis Herald* — 310 W. Washington; PO Box 1050, St. Francis (67756); Th; 1,832pd, 4fr (Sw); $3.65; C; publishers Cynthia Haynes & Steve Haynes; general manager & editor Karen Krien; tel (913) 332-3162; fax (913) 332-3001

St. John/Hudson/Macksville/Stafford: *St. John News* — 318 N. Main; PO Box 488, St. John (67576); W; 1,371pd, 14fr (Sw); $3.30; C; publisher J K Phillips II; editor Lisa Stevens John; tel (316) 549-3201

St. Marys/Pottawatomie: *St. Marys Star* — 517 W. Bertrand; PO Box 190, St. Marys (66536-0190); Tu; 2,005pd, 65fr (Sw); $2.96; publisher & editor Anita H Janssen; tel (913) 437-2935/2333; fax (913) 437-2095

Sedan: *The Sedan Times-Star* — 226 E. Main; PO Box 417 (67361); W; 2,450pd (Est); $3.65; publisher Martin Hellar; editor Paula Richard; tel (316) 725-3176; fax (316) 725-3272

Seneca/Nemaha Co.: *The Seneca Courier-Tribune* — 512 Main; PO Box 100, Seneca (66538); W; 3,192pd (Sw); $4.00; C; publisher & editor Dan Diehl; managing editor Matt Diehl; tel (913) 336-2175

Sharon Springs: *The Western Times* — 110 N. Main St.; PO Box 269 (67758); Th; 1,253pd, 25fr (Sw); $2.95; publisher Jackie Walker; editor Barry Walker; tel (913) 852-4900

Shawnee/Lenexa/Merriam/De Soto/Lake Quivira: *The Journal Herald* — 11004 Johnson Dr., Shawnee (66203); W; 3,842pd, 1,258fr (Sw); $5.25; publisher & editor Chuck Robinson; general manager Justin Cothran; tel (913) 631-2550; fax (913) 631-6552

Smith Co.: *Smith County Pioneer* — 201 S. Main St.; PO Box 266, Smith Center (66967); Th; 3,509pd, 54fr (Sw); $3.85; publisher & editor Darrel E Miller; publisher Ruth Miller; managing editor Linda Riedy; tel (913) 282-3371; fax (913) 282-6383

S Haven: *The South Haven New Era* — 309 W. Spring Ave.; PO Box 194, Conway Spring (67031); W; 414pd, 14fr (Sw); $2.88; publisher A J Bozarth; editor Nina Barker; tel (316) 456-2232

Spearville: *Spearville News* — 400 Main; PO Box 127 (67876); Th; 1,000pd, 6fr (Sw); 80¢; publisher & editor L A Vierthaler; tel (316) 385-2200; fax (316) 385-2610

Stafford Co.: *Stafford Courier* — 114 E. Broadway; PO Box 276, Stafford (67578); W; 1,750pd (Sw); 15¢; publishers Frank D Smiley & Marilyn A Smiley; editor Mary A Stackhouse; tel (316) 234-5241; fax (316) 234-5242

Sterling: *Sterling Bulletin* — PO Box 97 (67579); Th; 1,425pd, 10fr (Sw); $2.52; C; publishers Ed Howell & Melissa Howell; editor Betty Childs; tel (316) 278-2114; fax (316) 234-2330

Sublette/Satanta/Copeland: *The Haskell County Monitor-Chief* — 116 S. Inman St.; PO Box 700, Sublette (67877); W; 940pd, 8fr (Sw); 40¢; C; publisher Jerry Anderson; editor Charity Horinek; tel (316) 675-2204; fax (316) 675-8717

Syracuse/Coolidge/Kendall: *The Syracuse Journal* — 50 W. Hwy. 50; PO Box 1137, Syracuse (67878); W; 1,528pd, 17fr (Sw); $2.80; publisher Jim Frantz; general manager & editor Linda Frantz; tel (316) 384-5640; fax (316) 384-5228

Tonganoxie: *The Tonganoxie Mirror* — PO Box 920 (66086); W; 2,461pd (Sw); $4.50; publisher & editor Don Waterman; publisher Mary Waterman; managing editor Brian Waterman; tel (913) 845-2222; fax (913) 845-9451

Tribune: *Greeley County Republican* — 507 Broadway; PO Box 610 (67879); W; 1,640pd, 14fr (Est); $2.66; publishers & editors Dan M Epp & Jan Epp; tel (316) 376-4264; fax (316) 376-2433

Turon/Reno Co.: *The Record* — 117 N. Burns; PO Box 38, Turon (67583-0038); Th; 771pd, 26fr (Sw); $2.10; publisher Larry Green; editor Joan Green; tel (316) 497-6448

Vly. Center: *Ark Valley News* — 210 W. Main St.; PO Box 218 (67147); Th; 2,026pd, 50fr (Sw); $27.85; publishers & editors Les Anderson & Nancy Anderson; tel (316) 755-0821; fax (316) 755-0644

Wakeeney: *Western Kansas World* — 205 Main St.; PO Box 218 (67672); Th; 1,969pd, 276fr (Sw); $2.60; publisher Jack Millard; publisher & editor Jerry Millard; tel (913) 743-2155; fax (913) 743-5340

Wamego: *The Wamego Times* — PO Box 247 (66547); Th; 5,000pd (Est); $3.55; publisher Karl K Gaston; publisher & editor Mark Portell; tel (913) 456-7838; fax (913) 456-9668

Washington Co.: *The Washington County News* — PO Box 316, Washington (66968); Th; 3,050pd, 1fr (Sw); $4.00; publisher & editor William M Hays; general manager Theresa Livingston; tel (913) 325-2219; fax (913) 325-3255

Wathena: *The Wathena Times* — 317 St. Joseph St.; PO Box 368 (66090); Th; 1,815pd, 25fr (Est); $2.91; publisher Ethel Mae Foley; editor Dana Foley; tel (913) 989-4415; fax (913) 989-4416

Westmoreland: *Westmoreland Recorder* — 106 N. 2nd; PO Box 128 (66549); Th; 1,000pd (Est); $2.64; publisher & editor Richard E Smith; tel (913) 457-3411

Wilson: *Wilson World* — N. Main; PO Box 526 (67439); Th; 755pd, 6fr (Sw); 18¢; C; publisher Karl K Gaston; editor James Bednarz; tel (913) 658-2235

Woodson Co.: *Yates Center News* — 113 S. Main St.; PO Box 285, Yates Center (66783); Th; 1,998pd, 12fr (Sw); $3.50; publisher & editor Randall C Braden; tel (316) 625-2181

KENTUCKY

Adair: *Adair Progress* — 98 Grant Ln.; PO Box 595, Columbia (42728); Th; 3,842pd, 261fr (Sw); $4.37; publisher Donna Crowe; general manager J U Rogers; editor Paul B Hayes; tel (502) 384-6471; fax (502) 384-6474

Adair: *Columbia News* — 98 Grant Ln.; PO Box 595, Columbia (42728); Tu; 3,076pd, 186fr (Sw); $4.37; publisher Donna Crowe; general manager J U Rogers; editor Paul B Hayes; tel (502) 384-6471; fax (502) 384-6474

Albany/Clinton: *Clinton County News* — 116 Washington St.; PO Box 360, Albany (42602); Th; 3,417pd, 14fr (Est); $3.43; publisher & editor Alan B Gibson; tel (606) 387-5144; fax (606) 387-7949

Barbourville/Knox Co.: *The Mountain Advocate* — 214 Knox St.; PO Box 190, Barbourville (40906); Th; 6,073pd, 50fr (Est); $5.88; C; publisher Cecil H Wilson; editor Richard Trimble; tel (606) 546-9225; fax (606) 546-3175

Bardstown: *The Kentucky Standard* — 110 W. Stephen Foster Ave.; PO Box 639 (40004-0639); M/W/F; 8,400pd (Est); $6.78; C; publisher Steve Lowery; editor Tim Ballard; managing editor Teresa Rice; tel (502) 348-9003; fax (502) 348-1971

Bardwell: *The Carlisle County News* — 122 Front St.; PO Box 309 (42023); Th; 2,052pd, 77fr (Est); $2.00; publisher Chris McGehee; general manager Greg Leneave; editor Kay Preston; tel (502) 628-5490; fax (502) 628-3167

Barren Co.: *Glasgow Republican* — 100 Commerce Dr.; PO Box 399, Glasgow (42142); W; 111pd, 1,889fr (Est); $3.10; C; publisher William J Tinsley; editor Francis Bastien; tel (502) 678-5171; fax (502) 678-5052

Beaver Dam: *Ohio County Messenger* — 115 N. Main St.; PO Box 187 (42320); W; 2,400pd, 35fr (Est); $2.00; publisher Mrs Andy Anderson; general manager Tressi Brown; editor Dave McBride; tel (502) 274-4949; fax (502) 754-9484

II-30 **Kentucky** *U.S. Weeklies*

Bedford/Trimble: *Trimble Banner-Democrat* — West St.; PO Box 68, Bedford (40006); Th; 1,706pd, 30fr (Sw); $3.09; C; publisher Dorothy Abernatny; general manager Mable Richmond; editor Lauren Yates; tel (502) 255-3205; fax (502) 255-7797

Benton: *Tribune-Courier* — 308 E. 12th St.; PO Box 410 (42025); W; 7,192pd, 428fr (Sw); $5.05; C; publisher Jerry Lyles; editor Greg Travis; tel (502) 527-3162; fax (502) 527-4567

Berea: *The Berea Citizen* — 711 Chestnut St.; PO Box 207 (40403); Th; 3,531pd, 15fr (Est); $3.35; publisher & editor Mike French; general manager Letta Jackson; tel (606) 986-0959; fax (606) 986-0960

Boone Co.: *The Boone County Recorder* — 7736 U.S. 42, Ste. D-4, Florence (41042); Th; 5,984pd, 107fr (Est); $6.75; C; publisher Gene A Clabes; editor Amy Charley; tel (606) 283-0404; fax (606) 283-2536

Breckinridge Co.: *Breckinridge County Herald-News* — U.S. 60 E.; PO Box 6, Hardinsburg (40143); W; 5,697pd, 93fr (Est); $4.09; publisher Brucie Beard; general manager & managing editor Nancy Beard; editor David Platt; tel (502) 756-2109; fax (502) 756-1003

Brooksville: *Bracken County News* — 216 Frankfort St.; PO Box 68 (41004-0068); Th; 2,331pd, 92fr (Est); 15¢; publisher Kathy Day; editor Libby Estill; tel (606) 735-2198; fax (606) 735-2199

Brownsville: *Edmonson News* — 101 S. Main St.; PO Box 69 (42210-0069); Th; 4,000pd (Est); $4.20; publisher & editor William Canty; tel (502) 597-3115; fax (502) 597-3115

Bullitt Co.: *The Pioneer News* — 455 N. Buckman St.; PO Box 98, Shepherdsville (40165); M/W; 4,953pd, 561fr (Est); $6.12; C; publisher & editor Thomas Barr; tel (502) 543-2288; fax (502) 955-9704

Burkesville/Cumberland Co.: *Cumberland County News* — Public Sq.; PO Box 307, Burkesville (42717); W; 2,547pd, 95fr (Sw); $3.85; C; publisher Patsy Judd; editor Cyndi Pritchett; tel (502) 864-3891; fax (502) 864-3497

Butler Co.: *The Green River Republican & The Butler County Banner* — 119 N. Main; PO Box 219, Morgantown (42261); W; 5,144pd (Est); $2.50; publisher Roger Givens; general manager Rita Flener; editor Deborah Givens; tel (502) 526-4151; fax (502) 526-3111

Cadiz: *The Cadiz Record* — 50 Nunn Blvd.; PO Box 311 (42211); W; 4,169pd, 28fr (Sw); $4.00; C; publisher Walter Dear; general manager Jan Witty; editor Matt Sanders; tel (502) 522-6605; fax (502) 522-3001

Campbell Co.: *Campbell County Recorder* — 654 Highland Ave., Ste. 27, Fort Thomas (41075); Th; 3,030pd, 23fr (Est); $6.00; C; publisher Gene Clabes; editor Steve Olding; tel (606) 781-4421; fax (606) 233-2536

Campbellsville: *Central Kentucky News-Journal* — 428 Woodlawn Ave.; PO Box 1138 (42719-2938); M/Th; 6,780pd, 58fr (Sw); $5.49; C; publisher Richard Robards; editor Stan McKinney; tel (502) 465-8111; fax (502) 465-2500

Campton: *The Wolfe County News* — 270 Main St.; PO Box 129 (41301); F; 2,654pd, 34fr (Sw); $2.69; C; publisher Earl W Kinner Jr; editor J B Stamper; tel (606) 662-6145; fax (606) 662-4010

Carlisle: *The Carlisle Mercury* — 234 N. Locust St.; PO Box 272 (40311); Th; 2,234pd, 20fr (Est); $3.10; publisher Park Newspapers Inc.; editor Leigh Stone; tel (606) 289-2464; fax (606) 289-7900

Carrollton: *The News-Democrat* — 422 Main St.; PO Box 60 (41008); W; 3,477pd, 17fr (Sw); $4.27; C; publisher Davette Baker Baxter; tel (502) 732-4261; fax (502) 732-0453

Cave City/Glasgow: *The Progess* — 604 E. Broadway; PO Box 546, Cave City (42127); Th; 4,491pd, 2,068fr (Sw); $6.55; publisher Aubrey C Wilson; publisher & editor Dorothy D Wilson; managing editor Aubrey C Wilson Jr; tel (502) 773-3401; fax (502) 773-8950

Central City/Greenville: *Leader-News* — 1730 W. Everly Bros. Blvd.; PO Box 471, Central City (42330); W; 8,038pd, 88fr (Sw); 14¢; publisher Mrs Andy Anderson; general manager Legon McDonald; editor Carolyn Hillard; tel (502) 754-3000; fax (502) 754-9484

Central City/Muhlenberg: *The Times-Argus* — 202 W. Broad St.; PO Box 31, Central City (42330); W; 2,213pd, 114fr (Sw); $3.00; publisher & editor Mark Stone; general manager Debbie Harris; managing editor Richard Deavers; tel (502) 754-2331; fax (502) 754-1805

Clinton: *The Hickman County Gazette* — 308 S. Washington; PO Box 200 (42031); Th; 2,175pd, 25fr (Sw); 15¢; publisher Larry Lewis; editor Gaye Bencini; tel (502) 653-3381; fax (502) 653-3322

Cumberland: *The Tri-City News* — PO Box 490 (40823); W; 2,009pd, 39fr (Sw); $4.50; publisher & editor Paul J Wilder; general manager Delores A Jackson; tel (606) 589-2588; fax (606) 589-2589

Cynthiana: *Cynthiana Democrat* — 412 Webster Ave.; PO Box 160 (41031); Th; 5,206pd, 15fr (Est); $4.31; C; publisher George William Jacobs; editor Becky Barnes; tel (606) 234-1035; fax (606) 234-8096

Danville/Harrodsburg/Stanford/Lancaster/Nicholasville: *Danville Examiner* — 226 N. 2nd St., Danville (40422); F; 10,758pd (Sw); $3.50; publisher J Peter Frank; editor A C Frank; managing editor Steele Harmon; tel (606) 236-8541

Dawson Springs: *The Dawson Springs Progress* — 131 S. Main St.; PO Box 460 (42408); Th; 2,924pd, 35fr (Sw); $3.22; publisher & editor Jed Dillingham; publisher & managing editor Scott N Dillingham; tel (502) 797-3271; fax (502) 797-3271

Elizabethtown: *Hardin County Independent* — 609 E. Dixie Ave. (42701); Th; 3,264pd, 30fr (Sw); $5.75; publisher & editor Gerald Lush; tel (502) 737-5585

Elkton: *The Todd County Standard* — 102 Public Sq.; PO Box 308 (42220); W; 2,372pd (Sw); $4.00; publisher & editor Michael C Finch; tel (502) 265-2439; fax (502) 265-2571

Falmouth/Butler/Foster/Demossville/California: *The Falmouth Outlook* — 210 Main St.; PO Box 111, Falmouth (41040); Tu; 4,039pd, 50fr (Sw); $5.99; C; publisher & editor Debbie Dennie; tel (606) 654-3333; fax (606) 654-4365

Fleming/Morgan/Bath Rowan: *The Shopping News* — 722 W. 1st St., Morehead (40351); W; 9,100pd (Est); $3.80; C; publisher Park Newspapers Inc.; editor Shirley Smith; tel (606) 784-4116; fax (606) 784-7337

Flemingsburg/Fleming Co.: *Flemingsburg Gazette* — 111 Mt. Sterling Ave.; PO Box 32, Flemingsburg (41041); Tu; 3,581pd, 760fr (Est); $3.50; publisher Jean R Denton; publisher & editor Lowell O Denton; general manager Patricia Bloomfield; managing editor Virginia Filoe; tel (606) 845-9211; fax (606) 845-9211

Franklin: *Franklin Favorite* — 103 N. High St.; PO Box 309 (42135); Th; 5,200pd, 290fr (Sw); $4.24; publisher Henry D Stone; editor Charles Portmann; tel (502) 586-4481; fax (502) 586-6031

Fulton (KY)/S Fulton (TN): *The Fulton Leader/The Fulton Shopper* — 304 E. State Line; PO Box 1200, Fulton (42041); Th; 2,716pd, 32fr (Sw); $3.92; C; publisher & editor William Mitchell; managing editor Rita Mitchell; tel (502) 472-1121; fax (502) 472-1129

Gallatin Co.: *The Gallatin County News* — 211 3rd St.; PO Box 435, Warsaw (41095); W; 2,500pd, 37fr (Est); $3.25; publisher Denny K Warnick; general manager & editor Kelley Warnick; tel (606) 567-5051; fax (606) 567-6397

Georgetown: *Georgetown News-Graphic* — 481 Cherry Blossom Way; PO Box 461 (40324); W/Sa; 5,780pd, 622fr (Est); $5.33; publisher Mike Scogin; editor Kristi Lopez; managing editor Byron Brewer; tel (502) 863-1111; fax (502) 863-6296

Grant Co.: *Grant County News* — 151 N. Main St.; PO Box 247, Williamstown (41097); Th; 3,742pd, 23fr (Sw); $4.25; C; publisher Ken Stone; editor Jamie Baker-Nantz; tel (606) 824-3343; fax (606) 824-5888

Grayson/Carter: *Grayson Journal-Enquirer* — 113 S. Hord St., Grayson (41143); W; 3,945pd, 45fr (Est); $3.55; C; publisher Park Newspapers Inc.; editor Larry Bobblitt; tel (606) 474-5101; fax (606) 474-0013

Greensburg: *Greensburg Record-Herald* — 102 W. Court St., Ste. 130; PO Box 130 (42743); W; 4,238pd, 100fr (Est); $4.64; publisher Walter C Gorin; editor J O Brown Jr; tel (502) 932-4381; fax (502) 932-4441

Greenup Co.: *The Greenup News* — 207 Harrison St., Greenup (41144); Th; 5,171pd, 76fr (Est); $3.21; publisher Park Newspapers Inc.; editor Mason Branham; tel (606) 473-9851; fax (606) 473-7591

Harrodsburg: *The Harrodsburg Herald* — 101 W. Broadway; PO Box 68 (40330); Th; 6,088pd (ABC); $5.04; publisher & editor Bill Randolph; general manager Chris Freeman; managing editor Gary Moyers; tel (606) 734-2726; fax (606) 734-0737

Hartford/Ohio Co.: *The Ohio County Times-News* — 108 W. Center St.; PO Box 226, Hartford (42347); Th; 6,154pd, 75fr (Est); 26¢; publisher Mrs Andy Anderson; general manager Doris Hicks; editor Dave McBride; tel (502) 298-7100; fax (502) 298-9572

Hawesville/Lewisport: *The Hancock Clarion* — 32 Main St.; PO Box 39, Hawesville (42348); Th; 3,723pd, 106fr (Sw); $4.25; publisher & editor Donn K Wimmer; tel (502) 927-6945; fax (502) 927-6947

Hazard: *The Herald Voice* — 380 Main St.; PO Box 869 (41701); Th; 5,057pd (Sw); $7.61; publisher & editor Jack G Thomas; tel (606) 436-5771; fax (606) 436-3140

Hazard: *Perry County News* — Taxi Alley; PO Box 600 (41701); Th; 3,500pd, 184fr (Sw); $5.00; publisher Shirley Slaven; editor & managing editor Randy Walters; tel (606) 439-4953; fax (606) 439-4928

Hickman/Fulton Co.: *Hickman Courier Inc.* — 1232 Moscow Ave.; PO Box 70, Hickman (42050); Th; 2,270pd, 50fr (Sw); $3.75; publisher Paul Westphelling Jr; general manager Barbara Atwill; editor John O Jones; tel (502) 236-2726; fax (502) 236-2726

Hodgenville: *The LaRue County Herald News* — 40 Shawnee Dr. (42748); W; 3,975pd, 25fr (Est); $3.95; publisher & editor Debbie Polly; tel (502) 358-3118; fax (502) 358-4852

Hyden: *The Leslie County News* — 100 Main St.; PO Box 917 (41749); Th; 2,321pd, 53fr (Est); $4.80; publisher Vernon Baker; editor Bill Conway; tel (606) 672-3399; fax (606) 672-7409

Hyden: *Thousandsticks News* — 100 Main St.; PO Box 917 (41749); Tu; 2,341pd, 28fr (Est); $4.80; publishers Reba Baker & Vernon Baker; editor Bill Conway; tel (606) 672-3399; fax (606) 672-7409

Inez: *The Mountain Citizen* — Main St., Cain Bldg.; PO Box 1029 (41224); W; 5,000pd, 100fr (Sw); $3.90; publisher & managing editor Lisa Stayton; general manager Roger Smith; editor Mike Sisco; tel (606) 298-7570; fax (606) 298-3711

Irvine: *Citizen Voice & Times* — 108 Court St.; PO Box 660 (40336); Th; 4,685pd, 13,700fr (Sw); $4.26; C; publisher Guy Hatfield; general manager Cheryl Lockett; editor Allen Blair; tel (606) 723-5161; fax (606) 723-5509

Jackson: *Beattyville Enterprise* — 149 E. Main St.; PO Box 126, Beattyville (41311-0126); W; 2,805pd (Est); 22¢; publisher Lois Kilburn; editor Susan Hobbs; tel (606) 464-2444; fax (606) 464-2444

Jackson: *Jackson Times* — 1001 College Ave. (41339); Th; 4,330pd, 25fr (Est); 22¢; publisher Jeanne Dzierzek; editor Jack Neice; tel (606) 666-2451; fax (606) 666-5757

Jenkins: *The Letcher County Community Press* — Rte. 805; PO Box 156, Cromona (41810); W; 2,919pc, 20fr (Est); 14¢; publisher & editor Charles W Whitaker; managing editor William M Whitaker; tel (606) 855-4541; fax (606) 855-9290

Kenton Co.: *Kenton County Recorder* — 7736 U.S. 42, Ste. D-4, Florence (41042); Th; 1,344pd, 103fr (Est); $6.75; C; publisher Gene A Clabes; editor Amy Charley; tel (606) 283-0404; fax (606) 283-2536

Knott Co.: *Troublesome Creek Times* — Main St.; PO Box 700, Hindman (41822); W; 4,357pd, 135fr (Sw); $4.15; publisher & editor Ron Daley; tel (606) 785-5134; fax (606) 785-0105

La Grange/Oldham Co.: *The Oldham Era* — 204 S. 1st St.; PO Box 5, La Grange (40031); Th; 7,000pd, 5fr (Sw); $6.25; C; publisher Dorothy L Abernathy; editor Kit Millay-Fullenlove; tel (502) 222-7183; fax (502) 222-7194

Lancaster: *Garrard County News* — 33 Public Sq.; PO Box 292 (40444); Th; 3,891pd, 17fr (Sw); $2.80; publisher & editor Jack Penchoff; tel (606) 792-2203; fax (606) 792-4839

Lancaster: *Lancaster Central Record* — 106 Richmond St.; PO Box 492 (40444); Th; 2,811pd, 38fr (Est); $1.65; publisher Jim Cox; editor Marguerite W Whittaker; tel (606) 792-2831; fax (606) 792-3448

Laurel Co.: *The Sentinel-Echo* — PO Box 830, London (40743); M/W/F; 6,032pd, 371fr (Sw); $5.69; C; publisher & editor Darrell C Hathcock; tel (606) 878-7400; fax (606) 878-7404

Lawrenceburg/Anderson Co.: *Anderson News* — 133 Main St.; PO Box 116, Lawrenceburg (40342); W; 5,757pd, 72fr (Est); $4.61; C; publisher & editor Don White; tel (502) 839-6906; fax (502) 839-3118

Leitchfield/Grayson Co.: *Grayson County News-Gazette* — 208 S. Main St.; PO Box 305, Leitchfield (42755); M/Th; 5,342pd, 147fr (Est); $4.22; C; publisher Park Newspapers of Lexington; general manager & editor Carol Bond; tel (502) 259-9622; fax (502) 259-5537

Livingston Co.: *Livingston Ledger* — U.S. 60 & Mill St.; PO Box 129, Smithland (42081); Th; 2,492pd, 30fr (Est); $14.29; C; publisher Chris McGehee; editor Greg Leneave; tel (502) 928-2128; fax (502) 442-5220

Louisa: *The Tri-Rivers Advertiser* — 106 Pocahontas; PO Box 129 (41230); Su; 20,874fr (Sw); 20¢; publisher & editor C D Watts; tel (606) 638-9957; fax (606) 638-9949

Louisa/Lawrence Co.: *The Big Sandy News* — 101 Main Cross St.; PO Box 766, Louisa (41230); W; 3,546pd, 50fr (Sw); $4.20; publisher Allen Perry; general manager Marjorie P Hale; editor Jerry Pennington; tel (606) 638-4581; fax (606) 638-9949

Lyon Co.: *The Herald-Ledger* — 214 Commerce St.; PO Box 577, Eddyville (42038); W; 2,750pd, 24fr (Est); $2.50; C; publisher & editor Cindy Riley; tel (502) 388-2269; fax (502) 388-5540

Manchester: *The Manchester Enterprise* — 103 3rd St.; PO Box 449 (40962); Th; 7,100pd (Est); $5.25; C; publisher Glenn Gray; general manager Missy Walker; editor Mark Hoskins; tel (606) 598-2319; fax (606) 598-2330

Marion: *The Crittenden Press* — 125 E. Bellville St.; PO Box 191 (42064-0191); Th; 4,075pd, 128fr (Sw); 22¢; publisher Nancy Mick; editor Chris Evans; tel (502) 965-3191; fax (502) 965-2516

Martin Co.: *The Martin County Sun* — Court St.; PO Box 1314, Inez (41224); Tu; 2,325pd, 60fr (Est); $3.10; publisher & editor Mark Grayson; managing editor Jama Trivett; tel (606) 298-4612; fax (606) 298-4411

McCreary Co.: *The McCreary County Record* — Courthouse Sq.; PO Box 9, Whitley City (42653); Tu; 4,934pd, 65fr (Sw); $3.95; publisher Park Newspapers of the Cumberlands Inc.; general manager J T Stratton; editor Ken Shmidheiser; tel (606) 376-5356/5357; fax (606) 376-5357

McLean Co.: *McLean County News* — 165 E. 2nd St.; PO Box 266, Calhoun (42327); Th; 3,163pd, 21fr (Est); $3.95; C; publisher Steve Austin; general manager Teresa Revlett; managing editor Amy Grewe; tel (502) 273-3287; fax (502) 273-3544

Meade/Hardin/Breckinridge: *The Meade County Messenger* — 235 Main St.; PO Box 678, Brandenburg (40108); W; 5,746pd, 50fr (Sw); $4.95; C; publisher Kay McGehee; editor Janice Fulps; tel (502) 422-2155; fax (502) 422-2110

Menifee Co.: *Menifee County News* — 722 W. 1st St., Morehead (40351); W; 799pd, 10fr (Est); $3.80; C; publisher Park Newspapers Inc.; editor Shirley Smith; tel (606) 784-4116; fax (606) 784-7337

Menifee Co.: *Shopping News* — 722 W. 1st St., Morehead (40351); W; 8,094fr (Est); $3.80; publisher Park Newspapers Inc.; editor Shirley Smith; tel (606) 784-4116; fax (606) 784-7337

Metcalfe Co.: *Herald-News* — Public Sq.; PO Box 87, Edmonton (42129); Tu; 2,487pd, 34fr (Sw); $3.60; C; publisher & editor Clay Scott; publisher Patsy Judd; tel (502) 432-3291; fax (502) 432-4414

Monroe Co.: *Monroe County Citizen* — 301 N. Main, Ste. 2, Tompkinsville (42167); Tu; 1,968pd, 699fr (Sw); $6.55; publishers Aubrey C Wilson & Dorothy D Wilson; editor Aubrey C Wilson Jr; tel (502) 487-8666; fax (502) 773-8950

Monroe Co.: *Tompkinsville News* — 105 N. Main, Tompkinsville (42167); Th; 4,350pd, 167fr (Sw); $3.25; C; publisher & managing editor Blanche B Trimble; editor Gina Kinslow; tel (502) 487-5576/8024; fax (502) 487-8839

Montgomery Co.: *Mt. Sterling Advocate* — 40 S. Bank St.; PO Box 406, Mt. Sterling (40353); Th; 5,834pd, 40fr (Sw); $7.60; C; publisher Douglas S Taylor; editor Glen Greene; tel (606) 498-2222; fax (606) 498-2228

Monticello: *The Wayne County Outlook* — 109 E. Columbia Ave.; PO Box 432 (42633); W; 6,000pd, 25fr (Est); $5.50; publisher Lois Yoakum; editor Melodie Phelps; tel (606) 348-3338; fax (606) 348-8848

Copyright ©1996 by the Editor & Publisher Co.

LOUISIANA

Amite: *Amite Tangi-Digest* — 120 N.E. Central Ave.; PO Box 698 (70422); Th; 3,400pd (Est); $4.00; managing editor Carol Brooke; tel (504) 748-7156; fax (504) 748-7104

Arcadia/Trade Area: *Bienville Democrat* — 723 N. Railroad Ave.; PO Box 29, Arcadia (71001); Th; 2,700pd, 150fr (Est) $4.05; C; publisher Wayne E Dring; editor Wayne R Dring; tel (318) 263-2922; fax (318) 263-8897

Ascension: *Gonzales Weekly* — PO Box 38, Gonzales (70737); F; 6,984pd, 101fr (Est); $5.62; publisher Crawford A Bishop; general manager & editor Arlene E Bishop; tel (504) 647-4569; fax (504) 644-8238

Assumption Parish: *Assumption Pioneer* — 501 Assumption St.; PO Drawer 428, Napoleonville (70390); Th; 2,600pd (Est) $2.25; publisher Philip Gianelloni; tel (504) 369-7153; fax (504) 369-7153

Avoyelles: *Avoyelles Journal* — PO Box 523, Marksville (71351); W; 16,500pd (Est); $9.50; Su; 16,500pd (Est) $7.50; publisher & editor Randy DeCuir; tel (318) 253-5413; fax (318) 253-7223

Baker: *The Observer* — 5240 Groom Rd. (70714); Th; 1,737pd, 25fr (Est) $4.70; C; publisher Jack Roberts; editor Bill Catchings; tel (504) 775-2315; fax (504) 774-9212

Basile: *Basile Weekly* — 610 Stagg Ave.; PO Box 578 (70515); Th; 1,239pd, 99fr (Est); $2.80; C; publisher & editor Darrel B LeJeune; tel (318) 432-6807; fax (318) 432-6807

Bossier City: *Bossier Press Tribune* — 409 Barksdale Blvd.; PO Box 6267 (71111); F; 4,982pd, 27,450fr (Est); $6.15; C; publisher Robert E Barton; editor Nancy Cook; tel (318) 747-7900; fax (318) 747-5298

Bunkie: *The Bunkie Record* — 803 Evergreen Hwy.; PO Box 179 (71322); Th; 1,900pd (Sw); $3.85; C; publisher Avoyelles Publishing Co.; editor Garland Forman; tel (318) 346-7251

Cameron: *Cameron Pilot* — 203 E. Harrison; PO Box 995, DeQuincy (70633); Th; 2,230pd, 15fr (Sw); $4.40; publisher & editor Jerry Wise; publisher Joy Wise; tel (318) 786-8004; fax (318) 786-8131

Catahoula Parish: *Catahoula News Booster* — 103 3rd St.; PO Box 188, Jonesville (71343); Th; 1,588pd, 10fr (Sw) $4.00; publisher Bill Clifton; editor Fred Ferrington; tel (318) 339-7242; fax (318) 339-7243

Church Point: *Church Point News* — 315 N. Main; PO Drawer 319 (70525); W; 2,100pd (Est); $3.50; publisher Willie Pitre; editor Diana Daigle; tel (318) 684-5711

Claiborne Parish: *Claiborne Banner* — 604 N. Main, Homer (71040); Tu; 2,659pd, 30fr (Sw); $3.20; C; publisher Wayne Dring; editor Paige Reeder; tel (318) 624-1212; fax (318) 624-1212

Clinton/Jackson/Wilson/Ethel/Norwood/E Feliciana Parish: *The Watchman* — PO Box 368, Clinton (70722); Th; 3,500pd, 36fr (Est); $3.95; publisher Jack Roberts; editor Bill Catchings; tel (504) 683-5195; fax (504) 683-4276

Colfax/Grant Co.: *Colfax Chronicle* — 505 2nd St.; PO Box 248, Colfax (71417-0248); Th; 2,803pd, 165fr (Sw); $5.00; publisher & managing editor W Dru Richards; editor Helen Richards; tel (318) 627-3711; fax (318) 627-3019

Columbia/Caldwell/LaSalle: *The News Journal* — U.S. 165 S.; PO Box 911, Columbia (71418); M; 7,765fr (Sw); $3.50; publisher Sammy J Franklin; general manager Becky Stapleton; editor T Craig Franklin; tel (318) 649-7136; fax (318) 649-7776

Concordia Parish: *Concordia Sentinel* — 1308 N. 1st St.; PO Box 312, Ferriday (71334); W; 4,140pd, 50fr (Sw); $3.50; C; publisher & editor Sam Hanna; tel (318) 757-3646; fax (318) 757-3001

Coushatta/Red River Parish: *Coushatta Citizen* — 1703 Ringgold Ave.; PO Box 1365, Coushatta (71019-2006); Th; 2,302pd, 27fr (Est); $4.51; C; publisher Marsha Loftin, editor J M Jones; tel (318) 932-4201; fax (318) 932-4285

Covington/Mandeville: *St. Tammany Farmer* — 321 N. New Hampshire St.; PO Box 269, Covington (70434); Th; 4,139pd (Sw); $5.95; publisher St. Tammany Farmer Inc.; general manager Vera Hardman; editor Ron Barthet; tel (504) 892-2323; fax (504) 892-2325

De Quincy: *The De Quincy News* — 203 E. Harrison; PO Box 995 (70633); W; 3,385pd, 15fr (Sw); $4.40; publisher & editor Jerry Wise; publisher Joy Wise; tel (318) 786-8004; fax (318) 786-8131

Delhi: *The Delhi Dispatch* — 703 Broadway; PO Box 608 (71232); Th; 1,500pd, 39fr (Est); $2.50; C; publisher & editor Gene Sloninger; tel (318) 878-2444; fax (318) 728-5991

Donaldsonville: *The Donaldsonville Chief* — 402 Railroad Ave.; PO Box 309 (70346); Th; 2,664pd, 190fr (Est); $4.40; C; publisher & editor Ella Metrejean; general manager Theresa Cavalier; managing editor Juanita Quaid; tel (504) 473-3101; fax (504) 473-4060

Eunice: *Eunice News* — 251 N. 2nd St.; PO Box 989 (70535); Th/Su; 3,398pd, 8,200fr (Sw); $4.99; publisher Willie Pitre; editor Jerry Hoffpauir; tel (318) 457-3061; fax (318) 457-3122

Farmerville: *Farmerville Gazette* — 102 N. Washington; PO Box 722 (71241); Th; 5,600pd (Est); 15¢; publisher Carlton White; general manager Bettye White; editor Donna Miller; tel (318) 368-9732; fax (318) 368-7331

Franklin Parish: *The Franklin Sun* — 604 Prairie St.; PO Box 550, Winnsboro (71295); W; 5,868pd, 52fr (Est); 22¢; publisher & editor Sam Hanna; tel (318) 435-4521; fax (318) 435-9220

Franklinton: *The Era-Leader* — 1137 Main St.; PO Drawer F (70438); W; 3,491pd (Sw); $4.90; C; publisher Steve Kuperstock; tel (504) 839-9077; fax (504) 839-9077

Hammond: *The Hammond Vindicator* — PO Box 2848 (70404); Th; 967pd (Est); $4.39; publisher Louisiana State Newspapers; general manager Carol A Brooke; tel (504) 748-7156; fax (504) 748-7104

Homer: *Homer Guardian-Journal* — 620 N. Main St.; PO Box 119 (71040); Th; 3,400pd (Est); 15¢; publisher Geraldine H Hightower; general manager Hilda H Spillers; editor Janice McIntyre; tel (318) 927-3541; fax (318) 927-3542

Jeanerette: *The Jeanerette Enterprise* — 808 E. Main St.; PO Box 327 (70544); W; 28pd, 4,200fr (Est); $1.07; publisher Will Chapman; editor Karma Champagne; tel (318) 276-5171; fax (318) 367-9640

Jena/La Salle Parish: *The Jena-Times Olla-Tullos Signal* — 107 N. 3rd St.; PO Drawer 1384, Jena (71342); W; 4,390pd, 45fr (Sw); $4.80; publisher & editor Sammy J Franklin; tel (318) 992-4121; fax (318) 992-2287

Jonesboro/Hodge: *The Jackson Independent* — 624 Hudson Ave.; PO Box 520, Jonesboro (71251); Th; 3,499pd, 62fr (Sw); $4.30; publisher & editor T L Colvin Jr; managing editor T L Colvin III; tel (318) 259-2551; fax (318) 259-8537

Kaplan: *The Kaplan Herald* — 219 N. Cushing Ave.; PO Box 236 (70548); W; 3,200pd, 11,000fr (Sw); $4.00; C; publisher David Clevenger; general manager Mike Hebert; editor Judy T Mire; tel (318) 643-8002; fax (318) 643-1382

Kentwood/Tangipahoa: *The Kentwood News-Ledger* — 212 Ave. F; PO Box AD, Kentwood (70444); Th; 1,525pd (Est); $4.39; C; publisher Louisiana State Newspapers; general manager Carol A Brooke; editor Sylvia D Jackson; tel (504) 229-8607; fax (504) 748-7104

Kinder: *Kinder Courier News* — 9th and 4th Aves.; PO Drawer AK (70648); Th; 1,631pd, 10,771fr (Est); $3.80; publisher & editor Mark Leibson; general manager Rebekah Evans; tel (318) 738-5642; fax (318) 738-5630

Lake Providence: *Banner-Democrat* — 313 Lake St.; PO Box 828 (71254-2688); Th; 2,130pd, 48fr (Sw); $3.50; publisher & editor A C Carlton; general manager Jimmy Neighbours; tel (318) 559-2750; fax (318) 559-2750

LaPlace: *LaPlace L'Observateur* — 116 Newspaper Dr.; PO Box 1010 (70069-1010); W/Sa; 5,000pd (Est); $6.25; C; publisher J Kennon; editor Michael Stout; tel (504) 652-9545; fax (504) 652-3885

Livingston Parish: *Denham Springs-Livingston Parish News* — 688 Hatchell Ln.; PO Box 1529, Denham Springs (70726); Th/Su; 9,927pd, 52fr (Sw); $6.50; C; publisher Jeff M David; editor Mike Dowty; tel (504) 665-5176; fax (504) 667-0167

Logansport: *Logansport Interstate-Progress* — PO Box 158 (71049); Th; 1,391pd, 53fr (Est); 15¢; C; publisher Keenan C Gingles; general manager & editor Tracy McKee; tel (318) 697-5521; fax (318) 697-5521

Lutcher/St. James: *The News-Examiner* — 2290 Texas St.; PO Drawer 460, Lutcher (70071); Th; 3,571pd, 376fr (Sw); $3.50; publisher Wilbur Reynaud; general manager & editor Huey Stein; tel (504) 869-5784; fax (504) 869-4386

Madison Parish: *Madison Journal* — 300 S. Chestnut St., Tallulah (71282); W; 2,737pd, 8fr (Sw); $3.75; publisher C G Sanders; editor Pat Kelly; tel (318) 574-1404; fax (318) 574-4219

Mamou: *The Mamou Acadian Press* — PO Box 360 (70554); Th; 2,600fr (Sw); $3.31; publisher David L Ortego; editor Bernice Ardoin; tel (318) 363-2103; fax (318) 363-2841

Mandeville/Covington: *The News-Banner* — PO Drawer 90, Covington (70433); W/F/Su; 1,078pd, 20,709fr (Est); $8.50; publisher Floyd Burckel; editor Barbara Danahay; tel (504) 892-7980; fax (504) 892-8242

Mansfield/Desoto Parish: *Mansfield Enterprise* — 202 Adams St.; PO Box 840, Mansfield (71052); Th; 4,800pd, 10fr (Sw); $5.04; publisher Keenan C Gingles; editor Vickie Welborn; tel (318) 872-4120; fax (318) 872-6038

Marksville/Avoyelles: *The Marksville Weekly News* — PO Box 523, Marksville (71351); Th; 1,800pd (Est); $3.00; publisher Randy DeCuir; tel (318) 253-5413; fax (318) 253-7223

Oakdale/Allen Parish: *The Oakdale Journal* — 122 E. 6th Ave.; PO Box 668, Oakdale (71463); Th; 1,557pd, 15fr (Est); $3.70; C; publisher Willie Pitre; editor Barbara Doyle; tel (318) 335-0635; fax (318) 335-0431

Ouachita Parish: *The Ouachita Citizen* — 810 Natchitoches; PO Box 758, West Monroe (71291); Th; 5,900pd, 11,000fr (Sw); $9.00; C; publisher Robert E Borton; general manager Bill Lea; editor Mark Rainwater; tel (318) 322-3161; fax (318) 325-2285

Plaquemine: *Plaquemine Post/South* — 58650 Belleview Dr.; PO Box 589 (70764); Th; 5,822pd, 105fr (Sw); $3.92; publisher Joyce S Hebert; editor Ellie Hebert; tel (504) 687-3288; fax (504) 687-1814

Plaquemines Parish: *Placquemines Gazette* — 7952 Hwy. 23; PO Box 700, Belle Chasse (70037); F; 3,117pd, 23fr (Sw); $4.40; publisher & editor Dale Benoit; publisher Norris Babin; managing editor Monet Pastorek; tel (504) 392-1619; fax (504) 393-9327

Plaquemines Parish: *Plaquemines Watchman* — 7952 Hwy. 23; PO Box 700, Belle Chasse (70037); Tu; 3,117pd, 23fr (Sw); $4.40; publisher & editor Dale Benoit; publisher Norris Babin; tel (504) 392-1619; fax (504) 393-9327

Pointe Coupee: *The Pointe Coupee Banner* — 123 St. Mary; PO Box 400, New Roads (70760); Th; 5,145pd, 36fr (Sw); $5.00; publishers Brent Roy & E M White & Mary LaCour; editor Brian Costello; tel (504) 638-7155; fax (504) 638-8442

Ponchatoula: *The Drum* — PO Box 1399 (70454); W; 5,000fr (Est); $3.00; publisher & editor Eddie Ponds; tel (504) 386-6537

Ponchatoula/Hammond: *The Ponchatoula Times* — 145 W. Pine, Ste. A; PO Box 743, Ponchatoula (70454); Th; 2,911pd, 925fr (Sw); $3.95; publisher & editor Bryan T McMahon; publisher Terry Ann McMahon; tel (504) 386-2877; fax (504) 386-0458

Ponchatoula/Tangipahoa: *The Enterprise* — 240 E. Pine St.; PO Box 218, Ponchatoula (70454); W; 1,873pd, 220fr (Sw); $2.45; publisher & editor Don Ellzey; tel (504) 386-6537

Rayne: *The Rayne-Acadian Tribune* — 108 N. Adams Ave.; PO Box 260 (70578); Th; 4,543pd, 14fr (Sw); $3.50; C; publisher Milo A Nickel; general manager & editor Steven Bandy; tel (318) 334-3186; fax (318) 334-8474

Rayne: *The Rayne Independent* — 201 E.S. 1st St.; PO Box 428 (70578); Th; 3,675pd, 200fr (Sw); $3.60; publisher & editor Jo Cart; general manager Walter T Cart; tel (318) 334-2128; fax (318) 334-2120

Rayville/Richland Parish: *Richland Beacon-News* — 110 N. Louisa; PO Box 209, Rayville (71269); Th; 2,271pd, 64fr (Est); $4.25; C; publisher Terry Stockton; editor William C Hardin; tel (318) 728-6467; fax (318) 728-5991

Ringgold: *Ringgold Record* — PO Box 708 (71068-0708); W; 6,338pd (Est); $3.32; C; publisher & editor Wayne R Dring; tel (318) 894-6397; fax (318) 894-6397

Sabine Parish: *The Sabine Index* — 850 San Antonio Ave.; PO Box 850, Many (71449); W; 5,953pd, 10fr (CAC); $6.02; C; publisher Robert Gentry; editor Shannon Clements; tel (318) 256-3495; fax (318) 256-9151

St. Charles Parish: *St. Charles Herald-Guide* — 14236 US Hwy. 90; PO Box 1199, Boutte (70039); Th/Su; 6,100pd (Sw); $5.65; publisher Tony Taylor; editor Shell Armstrong; tel (504) 758-2795; fax (504) 758-7000

St. Helena Parish: *The St. Helena Echo* — Hamberlin St.; PO Box 190, Greensburg (70441); Th; 1,004pd, 15fr (Sw); $2.00; publisher Louisiana State Newspapers; general manager Willie Pitre; editor Donna DeLee Womack; managing editor Carol Brooke; tel (504) 222-4541; fax (504) 748-7104

St. Martin Parish: *Breaux Bridge Banner* — 214 N. Main; PO Box 69, St. Martinville (70582); W; 8,000fr (Est); $5.11; publisher & editor Henri C Bienvenu; tel (318) 394-6232/332-3562; fax (318) 394-7511

St. Martin Parish: *Teche News* — 214 N. Main St.; PO Box 69, St. Martinville (70582); W; 6,327pd, 49fr (Sw); $5.11; publisher & editor Henri C Bienvenu; tel (318) 394-6232; fax (318) 394-7511

SW Bienville Parish: *Ringgold Progress* — 217 Mill St.; PO Box 708, Ringgold (71001); Tu; 6,833fr (Sw); $4.51; C; publisher Wayne E Dring; general manager Margaret Hershberger; tel (318) 894-6397; fax (318) 263-8897

Springhill: *Springhill Press & News-Journal* — 127 N. Main St.; PO Box 668 (71075); W; 4,600pd, 8,900fr (Sw); $4.25; C; publisher & editor Steve Colwell; managing editor Vicky Darst; tel (318) 539-3511; fax (318) 539-3512

Vacherie: *The Enterprise* — 2681 Hwy. 20; PO Box 9 (70090); W; 1,700pd (Est); 20¢; publisher Wilbur Reynaud; editor Huey Stein; tel (504) 265-2120; fax (504) 265-2120

Vermilion Parish/Gueydan: *Gueydan Journal* — 301 Main; PO Box 536, Gueydan (70542); Th; 986pd, 15fr (Sw); $5.00; C; publisher & editor Meceal Hollier Smith; tel (318) 536-6016/9997

Ville Platte: *Ville Platte Gazette* — 145 Court St.; PO Box 220 (70586); Th/Su; 3,416pd, 36fr (Sw); $4.96; C; publisher Louisiana State Newspapers; general manager David L Ortego; editor Bill Juneau; tel (318) 363-3939; fax (318) 363-2841

Vinton: *Vinton News* — 1803 Penny; PO Box 946 (70668); W; 1,100pd (Est); 11¢; publisher Erbon W Wise; editor Brenda Merchant; tel (318) 589-7650; fax (318) 528-3044

Vivian/Caddo: *Caddo Citizen* — 105 W. Louisiana Ave.; PO Box 312, Vivian (71082); W; 3,431pd, 49fr (Est); $3.50; publisher & editor Linda Murray; tel (318) 375-3294; fax (318) 375-4578

Welsh: *The Welsh Citizen* — 119 S. Elm St.; PO Box 796 (70591); Tu; 2,025pd, 25fr (Est); $2.42; publisher Nancy J Cormier; editor Alex Arceneaux; tel (318) 734-2891

W Baton Rouge/Bernville: *West Side Journal* — 668 N. Jefferson; PO Box 260, Port Allen (70767); Th; 3,789pd, 139fr (Est); $4.48; publisher Loretta Decuir; general manager Stephanie Husers; tel (504) 343-2540; fax (504) 344-0923

W Carroll Parish: *The West Carroll Gazette* — 512 S. Constitution Ave.; PO Drawer 1007, Oak Grove (71263); W; 2,200pd, 100fr (Sw); $4.25; C; publisher North Louisiana Publishing Co.; general manager Terry Stockton; editor Johney S Turner; tel (318) 428-3207; fax (318) 428-2747

W Feliciana Parish: *St. Francisville Democrat* — 9707 Royal St.; PO Drawer 1876, St. Francisville (70775); Th; 1,438pd (Est); $5.45; general manager Jack Roberts; editor Susan A Bush; tel (504) 635-3366

Westlake/Moss Bluff: *Westlake/Moss Bluff News* — 905 McKinley; PO Box 127, Westlake (70669); W; 1,719pd, 9,000fr (Est); $7.65; C; publisher Erbon W Wise; editor Cliff Seiber; tel (318) 436-0583; fax (318) 528-3044

Winn Parish: *Winn Parish Enterprise-News American* — 1005 Lafayette; PO Box 750, Winnfield (71483); W; 4,026pd, 32fr (Sw); $4.84; publisher & editor Bob Holeman; tel (318) 628-2712

Zachary: *The Plainsman-News* — 5145 Main St., Ste. C (70791); Th; 1,671pd, 12fr (Est); $4.70; C; publisher Jack Roberts; editor Bill Catchings; tel (504) 654-6841; fax (504) 775-2341

MAINE

Bangor: *The Weekly* — 631 Hammond St.; PO Box 2237 (04402-2237); Sa; 38,600fr (Sw); $17.00; C; general manager Roger Tremblay; editor Jeff Shula; tel (207) 942-2913; fax (207) 947-7508

Belfast/Waldo Co.: *The Republican Journal* — 33 High St.; PO Box 327, Belfast (04915); Th; 6,193pd, 60fr (Sw); $5.95; C; publisher David E Morse; editor Tom Groening; tel (207) 338-3333; fax (207) 338-5498

Biddeford/Saco/Old Orchard Beach: *Biddeford-Saco-OOB Courier* — 5 Washington St., Ste. 12; PO Box 1894, Biddeford (04005); Th; 150pd, 22,000fr (Sw); $8.50; C; publisher & editor David Flood; tel (207) 282-4337; fax (207) 282-4339

Blue Hill/Brooklin/Brooksville/Sedgewick/Surrey: *The Weekly Packet* — Main St.; PO Box 646, Blue Hill (04614); Th; 1,962pd, 42fr (Sw); $7.00; C; publisher & editor R Nathaniel W Barrows; managing editor Ellen Bouraem; tel (207) 374-2341; fax (207) 374-2343

Boothbay Harbor/Wiscasset: *The Boothbay Register* — 95 Townsend Ave.; PO Box 357 (04538); Th; 4,825pd, 161fr (Est); $5.50; C; publisher Marylouise Cowan; editor Kevin G Burnham; managing editor Mary D Brewer; tel (207) 633-4620; fax (207) 633-7123

Bridgton: *The Bridgton News* — 42 Main St.; PO Box 244 (04009); Th; 6,576pd, 47fr (Sw); $4.50; publisher H A Shorey III; general manager Stephen E Shorey; editor Wayne E Rivet; tel (207) 647-2851

Calais/Noodland/Princeton: *The Calais Advertiser* — 14 Church St.; PO Box 660, Calais (04619); Th; 4,300pd (Est); $3.30; publisher & editor Ferguson Calder; general manager Stephanie Higgins; tel (207) 454-3561; fax (207) 454-3458

Camden: *The Camden Herald* — 69 Elm St.; PO Box 248 (04843); Th; 4,980pd, 150fr (Sw); $6.00; publisher William S Patten; editor Amy Rawe; tel (207) 236-8511; fax (207) 236-2816

Caribou/Limestone: *Aroostook Republican and News* — 159 Bennet Dr.; PO Box 608, Caribou (04736); W; 4,490pd, 27fr (Sw); $6.50; C; editor Martha Lawstrom; tel (207) 496-3251; fax (207) 492-4351

Castine/Penobscot/Orland: *Castine Patriot* — Water St.; PO Box 205, Castine (04421); Th; 1,442pd, 37fr (Est); $6.25; C; publisher & editor R Nathaniel W Barrows; tel (207) 326-9300; fax (207) 326-4383

Damariscotta/Newcastle/Bristol/Bremen/Waldoboro/Nobleboro/Wiscasset/ S Bristol/Jefferson/Whitefield/Edgecomb: *The Lincoln County News* — PO Box 36, Damariscotta (04543); Th; 6,863pd, 49fr (Sw); $4.00; C; publisher Christopher Roberts; editor Judi Finn; tel (207) 563-3171; fax (207) 563-3127

Dexter/Dover/Milo: *Eastern Gazette* — 380-382 Main St.; PO Box 306, Dexter (04930); M; 600pd, 13,400fr (Sw); $7.75; publisher Janice Shank; publisher & editor Robert H Shank; general manager Michele Lancaster; tel (207) 924-7402; fax (207) 924-6215

Dover-Foxcroft: *The Piscataquis Observer* — Union Sq.; PO Box 30 (04426); W; 4,155pd, 50fr (Sw); $6.90; editor Martha M Lostrom; managing editor Tom Lizotte; tel (207) 564-8355; fax (207) 564-7056

Ellsworth: *The Ellsworth American* — 63 Main St.; PO Box 509 (04605); Th; 10,911pd, 280fr (Sw); $10.00; publisher Alan L Baker; editor James Russell Wiggins; managing editor Katherine Heidinger; tel (207) 667-2576; fax (207) 667-7656

Falmouth/Yarmouth/Cumberland/Freeport/N Yarmouth: *The Forecaster* — 317 Foreside Rd.; PO Box 66797, Falmouth (04105); Th; 11,500pd, 6,000fr (Est); $11.50; publisher Marian L McCue; editor John Lovell; tel (207) 781-3661; fax (207) 781-2060

Fort Fairfield: *Fort Fairfield Review* — PO Box 411 (04742); W; 1,986pd, 12fr (Sw); $4.25; publisher David S Henley; editor Marcia Reed; tel (207) 472-3111

Franklin Co.: *Franklin Journal & Farmington Chronicle* — Wilton Rd.; PO Box 750, Farmington (04938); Tu; 4,098pd, 10fr (Sw); $4.50; F; 4,822pd, 10fr (Sw); $4.50; C; publisher Janet K Warner; managing editor Dan Vlossak; tel (207) 778-2075; fax (207) 778-6970

Hancock Co.: *The Ellsworth Weekly* — 81 Main St.; PO Box 1122, Ellsworth (04605); Sa; 10,000fr (Est); $5.00; C; publisher David E Morse; editor Earl Brechlin; tel (207) 667-5514; fax (207) 667-0693

Houlton: *Houlton Pioneer Times* — 23 Court St.; PO Box 456 (04730); W; 5,820pd, 27fr (Est); $6.00; C; editor Martha M Lostrom; tel (207) 532-2281; fax (207) 532-2403

Kennebunk/York Co.: *York County Coast Star* — US Rte. 1 S.; PO Box 979, Kennebunk (04043); W; 11,175pd (ABC); $14.75; publishers Lou McGrew & Neil P Collins; editor John Martins; tel (207) 985-2961; fax (207) 985-9050

Lincoln: *Lincoln News* — PO Box 35 (04457); Th; 5,560pd, 25fr (Sw); $4.50; publisher & editor M Sheila Tenggren; managing editor Kevin Tenggren; tel (207) 794-6532; fax (207) 794-2004

Lincoln Co.: *Lincoln County Weekly* — Main St.; PO Box 1287, Damariscotta (04543); Th; 5,000pd (Est); $4.00; C; publisher David E Morse; editor Joan Grant; tel (207) 563-5006; fax (207) 563-3615

Lincoln/Sagadahoc: *Coastal Journal* — 97 Commercial St.; PO Box 575, Bath (04530); W; 95pd, 30,000fr (Sw); $10.60; general manager Scott H Kessel; editor Michelle Friedland; tel (207) 443-6241; fax (207) 443-5605

Livermore Falls/Jay: *Livermore Falls Advertiser* — 59 Main St.; PO Box B (04254); Th; 2,846pd, 7fr (Sw); $4.15; C; publisher Janet K Warner; editor Mitch Thomas; tel (207) 897-4321; fax (207) 778-6970

Machias: *Machias Valley News Observer* — 31 Broadway St.; PO Box 357 (04654); W; 3,148pd, 63fr (Sw); $4.90; editors Eugene M Townsend & Jay B Hinson; managing editor Nancy Hayward; tel (207) 255-6561; fax (207) 255-4058

Madawaska: *St. John Valley Times* — 696 W. Main St.; PO Box 419 (04756); W; 5,815pd, 64fr (Sw); $4.77; publisher & editor Emery L Labbe; general manager & managing editor Don Levesque; tel (207) 728-3336; fax (207) 728-3825

Millinocket/E Millinocket: *The Katahdin Times* — 202 Penobscot Ave.; PO Box 330, Millinocket (04462); Tu; 4,121pd, 50fr (Est); $6.15; publisher David S Henley; editor Barbara M Waters; tel (207) 723-8118; fax (207) 723-4434

Mt. Desert Island: *Bar Harbor Times* — 76 Cottage St.; PO Box 68, Bar Harbor (04609); Th; 7,264pd, 106fr (Sw); $7.50; C; publisher David E Morse; editor Earl Brechlin; tel (207) 288-3311; fax (207) 288-5813

Norway/Paris/Oxford/Hebron/Harrison/Waterford: *Advertiser Democrat* — 2 Bridge St.; PO Box 269, Norway (04268); Th; 6,250pd, 100fr (Sw); $4.50; C; publisher Howard A James; general manager Judy James; editor Katherine Munro; tel (207) 743-7011; fax (207) 743-2256

Old Town/Orono: *Penobscot Times* — 400 N. Main St.; PO Box 568, Old Town (04468); Th; 3,254pd, 193fr (Sw); 25¢; publisher David C Wollstadt; editor Robert Diebold; tel (207) 827-4451

Oxford Co.: *The Bethel Oxford County Citizen* — Main St.; PO Box 109, Bethel (04217); W; 3,240pd, 80fr (Est); $3.50; C; publisher Edward M Snook; editor Michael Daniels; tel (207) 824-2444; fax (207) 824-2426

Piscataquis/N Somerset Co.: *The Moosehead Messenger* — Greenville-Shirley Rd.; PO Box 418, Greenville (04441-0418); W; 4,000pd (Sw); $3.50; publisher & editor Andrew L Jensen; tel (207) 695-3077; fax (207) 695-3780

Presque Isle: *Presque Isle Star-Herald* — 40 North St., Ste. B; PO Box 510 (04769); W; 6,494pd, 48fr (Est); $6.00; C; editor Martha M Lostrom; tel (207) 768-5431; fax (207) 764-7585

Rockland: *The Courier-Gazette* — 1 Park Dr.; PO Box 249 (04841); Tu; 7,924pd, 195fr (Est); $7.50; Th; 8,618pd, 195fr (Est); $7.50;

Sa; 8,483pd, 195fr (Est); $7.50; C; publisher David E Morse; editor Michael J McGuire; managing editor Stephen Betts; tel (207) 594-4401; fax (207) 596-6981

Rumford/Mexico: *Rumford Falls Times* — 71 Canal St.; PO Box 490, Rumford (04276); W; 4,405pd, 26fr (Sw); 20¢; publisher Howard James; general manager & managing editor Bruce Little; editor Gregory T Davis; tel (207) 364-7893; fax (207) 369-0170

Sanford: *The Sanford News* — 6 School St.; PO Box D (04070); Tu; 7,027pd (Est); $8.07; C; general manager Barbara Caouette; editor Buzz Dietterle; tel (207) 324-5986; fax (207) 490-1431

Scarborough: *Scarborough Leader* — 27 Gorham Rd. (04070); Sa; 8,000fr (Sw); $6.95; C; publisher Carolyn Flood; tel (207) 883-5944; fax (207) 883-6351

Somerset Co.: *Somerset Gazette* — 2 Island Ave., Skowhegan (04976); M; 10,000fr (Sw); $7.75; publisher & editor Gail Lombardi; tel (207) 474-0606; fax (207) 474-0303

Stonington/Deer Isle: *Island Ad-Vantages* — PO Box 36, Stonington (04681); Th; 2,267pd, 870fr (Sw); $7.00; C; publisher & editor R Nathaniel W Barrows; managing editor Ellen Booraem; tel (207) 367-2200; fax (207) 374-2439

Waldo Co.: *The Waldo Independent* — 47 Church St.; PO Box 228, Belfast (04915); Th; 5,201pd, 31fr (Sw); $5.85; editor Toni Mailloux; tel (207) 338-5100; fax (207) 338-1810

Waldo/Knox/Lincoln Co: *Midcoast Encore* — 1 Park Dr.; PO Box 249, Rockland (04841); M; 44,513fr (Est); $8.95; C; publisher David E Morse; editor Michael J McGuire; managing editor Beth Rowan; tel (207) 594-4401; fax (207) 596-6981

Washington Co.: *The Downeast Coastal Press* — HCR 69; PO Box 287, Cutler (04626); Tu; 2,962pd, 25fr (Sw); $3.30; C; publisher & editor Frederick Hastings; tel (207) 259-7751; fax (207) 259-7751

Westbrook: *American Journal* — 4 Dana St. (04092); W; 6,889pd, 173fr (Sw); $10.00; publisher & editor Harry T Foote; managing editor Raymond M Foote; tel (207) 854-2577; fax (207) 854-0018

Windham/Gorham/Westbrook/Standish/Gray/Casco/Raymond/Naples: *The Suburban News* — 778 Roosevelt Trl., Windham (04062); Tu; 8,500fr (Est); $7.00; publishers G William Diamond & Gary Cooper & Ray Roux; editor Kay Soldier; tel (207) 892-1166; fax (207) 892-1171

Winthrop/E Winthrop: *Community Advertiser* — 324-A Maine Ave., Farmingdale (04344); M; 8,418fr (Est); $6.00; publisher & editor Keith E Peters; tel (207) 582-8486; fax (207) 582-4530

Wiscasset: *The Wiscasset Newspaper* — 95 Townsend Ave.; PO Box 357, Boothbay Harbor (04538); Th; 987pd, 97fr (Est); $5.50; C; publisher Marylouise Cowan; editor Judith Sutter; managing editor Mary D Brewer; tel (207) 633-4620

York/York Harbor/York Beach/Cape Neddick/Ogunquit: *York Weekly* — 17 Woodbridge Rd.; PO Box 7, York (03909); W; 5,100pd, 100fr (Sw); $8.50; publisher & editor James E Carter; tel (207) 363-4343; fax (207) 351-2849

MARYLAND

Arbutus: *Arbutus Times* — 835 Frederick Rd., Baltimore (21228); W; 3,978pd, 278fr (CAC); $23.56; C; publisher S Zeke Orlinsky; editor Jim Joyner; managing editor Len Lazrick; tel (410) 788-4500; fax (410) 788-4103

Baltimore City: *Baltimore Messenger* — 409 Washington Ave., Towson (21204); W; 54pd, 12,951fr (CAC); $18.67; C; publisher S Zeke Orlinsky; general manager Jean Moon; editor Elizabeth Eck; managing editor Len Lazrick; tel (410) 337-2400; fax (410) 337-2490

Baltimore Co.: *Northeast Times Booster* — 409 Washington Ave., Towson (21204); W; 13pd, 18,719fr (CAC); $20.44; C; publisher S Zeke Orlinsky; general manager Jean Moon; editor Blaise Willig; managing editor Len Lazrick; tel (410) 337-2400; fax (410) 337-2490

Baltimore Co.: *Jeffersonian* — 409 Washington Ave., Towson (21204); Th; 5,516pd, 828fr (Sw); $27.11; C; publisher S Zeke Orlinsky; general manager Jean Moon; editor Angela Borneman; managing editor Len Lazrick; tel (410) 337-2400; fax (410) 337-2490

Baltimore Co.: *Northeast Times Reporter* — 409 Washington Ave., Towson (21204); W; 14pd, 16,714fr (CAC); $20.44; C; publisher S Zeke Orlinsky; general manager Jean Moon; editor Blaise Willig; managing editor Len Lazrick; tel (410) 337-2400; fax (410) 337-2490

Bowie: *Bowie Blade-News* — 6000 Laurel-Bowie Rd., Ste. 101; PO Box 770 (20715); Th; 13,779pd, 367fr (ABC); 71¢; publisher Philip Merrill; general manager & editor John L Rouse; tel (301) 262-3700; fax (301) 464-7027

Brunswick/Jefferson/Lovettsville: *The Brunswick Citizen* — 2 S. Maryland Ave., Brunswick (21716); Th; 3,500pd (Sw); $5.85; C; publisher Pete Maynard; editor Scott Edie; tel (301) 834-7722

Calvert Co.: *Calvert Independent* — 424 Solomons Island Rd.; PO Box 910, Prince Frederick (20678); W; 8,772pd, 80fr (Sw); C; publisher Charlie Mister; editor Richard McIntire; tel (410) 535-1575; fax (301) 855-9070

Caroline Co.: *The Times Record* — 219 Market St.; PO Box 160, Denton (21629); W; 4,157pd (CAC); $6.60; publisher Larry Effingham; editor Peter Howell; tel (410) 479-1800; fax (410) 479-3174

Catonsville: *Catonsville Times* — 835 Frederick Rd., Baltimore (21228); W; 7,127pd, 558fr (CAC); $27.11; C; publisher S Zeke Orlinsky; editor Jim Joyner; managing editor Len Lazrick; tel (410) 788-4500; fax (410) 788-4103

Chestertown: *Kent County News* — 217 High St.; PO Box 30 (21620); F; 7,796pd, 193fr (Sw); $8.45; C; general manager Mary Burton; editor Patricia K McGee; tel (410) 778-2011; fax (410) 778-6522

Columbia: *Columbia Flier* — 10750 Little Patuxent Pkwy. (21044); Th; 129pd, 33,570fr (CAC); $43.11; C; publisher S Zeke Orlinsky; general manager Jean Moon; editor Tom Graham; managing editor Len Lazrick; tel (410) 730-3620; fax (410) 730-7053

Crisfield: *The Crisfield Times* — 914 W. Main St.; PO Box 230 (21817); W; 3,156pd, 93fr (Sw); 16¢; publisher Jim Ritch; editor Barbara Pastuszak; tel (410) 968-1188; fax (410) 968-1197

Damascus: *The Damascus Courier-Gazette* — 1200 Quince Orchard Blvd., Gaithersburg (20878); W; 18pd, 7,579fr (VAC); $7.60; C; publisher William Schlossenberg; editor Tom Grant; tel (301) 948-3120; fax (301) 670-7183

Dorchester Co.: *The Dorchester Star* — 300 Academy St.; PO Box 176, Cambridge (21613); F; 11,500fr (Sw); $6.55; C; publisher Larry Effingham; editor Gail Dean; tel (410) 228-0222; fax (410) 228-0685

Dundalk: *The Dundalk Eagle* — 4 N. Center Pl.; PO Box 8936 (21222); Th; 20,998pd, 2,708fr (Sw); $12.60; publisher Kimbel E Oelke; general manager Mary G Oelke; editor Deborah Cornely; tel (410) 288-6060; fax (410) 288-2712

Eastern Montgomery Co.: *Burtonsville Free Press* — 615 Main St., Laurel (20707-4005); W; 25pd, 22,239fr (CAC); $25.78; C; publisher S Zeke Orlinski; editor Jim Joyner; managing editor Len Lazrick; tel (301) 725-2000; fax (301) 725-7344

Gaithersburg: *The Gaithersburg Gazette* — 1200 Quince Orchard Blvd. (20878); W; 209pd, 41,440fr (VAC); $19.40; C; publisher William Schlossenberg; editor Georgia MacDonald; tel (301) 948-3120; fax (301) 670-7183

Glen Burnie/Northern Anne Arundel Co.: *The Maryland Gazette* — 306 Crain Hwy. S.W. (21061); W; 36,584pd, 988fr (Sw); $43.18; Sa; 36,584pd, 988fr (Sw); $30.86; publisher Philip Merrill; editor Robert Mosier; tel (410) 766-3700; fax (410) 768-5189

Greenbelt: *Greenbelt News Review* — PO Box 68 (20768); Th; 100pd, 10,400fr (Sw); $7.10; publisher Diane Oberg; editor Mary Lou Williamson; tel (301) 474-4131

Hancock: *The Hancock News* — 263 Pennsylvania Ave. (21750); W; 8,550fr (Est); $4.60; C; publisher James S Buzzerd; general manager Sandy Buzzerd; editor J Warren Buzzerd; tel (301) 678-6255; fax (301) 678-5520

Harford Co.: *The Aegis* — 10 Hayes St.; PO Box 189, Bel Air (21014); W; 35,816pd, 1,626fr (ABC); $16.45; C; publisher John D Worthington IV; editor Ted Hendricks; tel (410) 838-4400; fax (410) 638-0357

Harford Co.: *The Weekender* — PO Box 189, Bel Air (21014); F; 83,640fr (Est); $30.00; publisher John D Worthington; editor Ted Hendricks; tel (410) 838-4400; fax (410) 638-0357

Havre De Grace/Aberdeen: *The Record* — 316 St. John St.; PO Box 210, Havre De Grace (21078); F; 4,588pd, 467fr (ABC); $10.46; publisher John D Worthington; editor Ted Hendricks; managing editor Lois Schwalenberg; tel (410) 939-4040; fax (410) 939-2390

Howard Co.: *Howard County Times* — 10750 Little Patuxent Pkwy., Columbia (21044); Th; 15,814pd, 2,385fr (CAC); $28.00; C; publisher S Zeke Orlinsky; general manager Mike Esses; editor Tom Graham; tel (410) 730-3620; fax (410) 730-7053

Laurel: *Laurel Leader* — 615 Main St. (20707); Th; 406pd, 26,698fr (CAC); $35.11; C; publisher S Zeke Orlinsky; editor Joe Murchison; tel (301) 725-2000; fax (301) 317-8736

Lexington Park/St. Mary's Co.: *The Enterprise* — Rte. 235, Esperanza Shopping Center; PO Box 700 (20653); W/F; 15,627pd, 35fr (Est); $12.65; C; publisher Ralph Martin; general manager Dave Palmer; editor Rick Boyd; managing editor Donnie Morgan; tel (301) 862-2111; fax (301) 737-2896

Lower Worcester Co.: *Worcester County Messenger* — 129 Market St.; PO Box 388, Pocomoke City (21851); W; 3,200pd (Sw); $8.55; C; publisher John D Backe; general manager & editor Bill Kerbin; tel (410) 957-1700; fax (410) 957-4314

Middletown/Myersville: *The Middletown Valley Citizen* — 1220 Marker Rd., Middletown (21769); Th; 1,500pd (Est); $4.40; C; editor Julie Maynard; tel (301) 371-9399

Oakland: *The Garrett County Weekender* — 109 S. 3rd St.; PO Box 475 (21550); F; 16,718pd (Sw); $4.92; publisher Terry Horn; general manager Lori Remenick; editor Cindy Stacy; managing editor Lance White; tel (301) 334-9172; fax (301) 359-0377

Oakland: *The Republican* — PO Box 326 (21550); Th; 11,550pd, 37fr (ABC); 25¢; publisher Robert B Sincell; editor Donald W Sincell; tel (301) 334-3963; fax (301) 334-5904

Ocean City: *Maryland Coast-Dispatch* — PO Box 467, Berlin (21811); F; 25,000fr (Est); $5.00; publisher Dick Lohmeyer; editor Greg Ford; tel (410) 641-4561; fax (410) 641-0966

Ocean City Coastal Area: *Maryland Beachcomber* — 214 16th St.; PO Box 479, Ocean City (21842); F; 25,000fr (Est); $10.00; C; publisher Darel La Prade; editor Bill Hitchcock; managing editor Joe Harris; tel (410) 289-6834; fax (410) 289-6838

Ocean City/Worcester Co.: *Maryland Times-Press* — 214 16th St.; PO Box 479, Ocean City (21842); W; 5,429pd, 971fr (Sw); $9.30; C; publisher Darel La Prade; editor Joseph Harris; tel (410) 289-6834; fax (410) 289-6838

Olney: *Olney Gazette* — 1200 Quince Orchard Blvd., Gaithersburg (20878); W; 11pd, 12,976fr (VAC); $8.80; publisher Gary Socha; editor Judy Hruz; tel (301) 948-3120; fax (301) 570-8854

Overlea/Parkville/Fullerton: *The North East Avenue* — 8902 Belair Rd., Baltimore (21236); Th; 19,960fr (CPVS); $8.40; C; publisher Kenneth C Coldwell Sr; managing editor Jackie Nickel; tel (410) 256-7777; fax (410) 256-7765

Owings Mills: *Owings Mills Times* — 409 Washington Ave., Towson (21204); Th; 123pd, 31,021fr (Sw); $18.22; C; publisher S Zeke Orlinsky; general manager Jean Moon; editor Dan Gainor; managing editor Len Lazrick; tel (410) 337-2400; fax (410) 337-2490

Perry Hall/White Marsh/Parkville/Rosedale/Carney/Cub Hill: *The Times-Herald* — 2300 York Rd., Ste. 216, Timonium (21093); Th; 32,000fr (Sw); $11.43; publisher Marina Brockmann; editor Jim Gordon; tel (410) 453-0092; fax (410) 453-0065

Perry Hall/White Marsh/Carney/Kingsville: *The Perry Hall Avenue* — 8902 Belair Rd., Baltimore (21236); W; 17,960fr (CPVS); $8.40; C; publisher Kenneth C Coldwell Sr; editor Jackie Nickel; tel (410) 256-7777; fax (410) 256-7765

Prince Frederick/Calvert Co.: *The Recorder* — 234 Merrimac Ct.; PO Box F, Prince Frederick (20678); W/F; 7,470pd, 13fr (Est); $7.27; C; publisher Ralph Martin; general manager Jeannie Green; editor Kevin Conron; tel (410) 535-1214; fax (410) 535-5883

Prince George's Co.: *The Prince George's Sentinel* — 9458 Lanham-Severn Rd., Ste. 203, Seabrook (20706); W; 2,617pd, 130fr (Sw); $22.75; C; publisher Lynn Kapiloff; editor James McCormick; tel (301) 306-9500; fax (301) 306-9596

Queen Anne's Co.: *Queen Anne's Record-Observer* — 114 Broadway; PO Box 410, Centreville (21617); F; 4,287pd, 51fr (Est); $5.97; publisher Larry Effingham; editor William Kirby; tel (410) 758-1400; fax (410) 758-1701

Rockville: *Rockville Gazette* — 1200 Quince Orchard Blvd., Gaithersburg (20878); W; 71pd, 32,066fr (VAC); $14.72; publisher Gary Socha; editor Judy Hruz; tel (301) 948-3120; fax (301) 670-7183

Somerset Co.: *Somerset Herald* — 11763 Somerset Ave.; PO Box 310, Princess Anne (21853); W; 3,000pd (Sw); $7.40; C; publisher John D Backe; general manager & editor Richard Crumbacker; tel (410) 651-1600; fax (410) 651-3785

S Prince George's Co.: *South County Current* — 14760 Main St. (20772); PO Box 30, Upper Marlboro (20773); W; 21,000fr (Sw); $9.87; C; publisher Ralph Martin; general manager Dale Foster; editor Joe Norris; tel (301) 627-2833; fax (301) 627-2835

SE Baltimore Co./Essex/Middle River/Chase/Rosedale: *The Avenue News* — 442 Eastern Blvd.; PO Box 7889, Baltimore (21221); Th; 36,540fr (CPVS); $15.60; C; publisher Kenneth C Coldwell Sr; editor Jackie Nickel; tel (410) 687-7775; fax (410) 687-7881

Towson: *Towson Times* — 409 Washington Ave. (21204); W; 158pd, 36,820fr (CAC); $29.78; C; publisher S Zeke Orlinsky; general manager Jean Moon; editor Paul Milton; managing editor Len Lazrick; tel (410) 337-2400; fax (410) 337-2490

Upper Marlboro: *The Enquirer-Gazette* — 14760 Main St. (20772); PO Box 30 (20773); Th; 3,820pd, 1,002fr (CAC); $4.99; publisher Ralph Martin; general manager Dale Foster; editor Joe Norris; tel (301) 627-2833; fax (301) 627-2835

Waldorf: *The Maryland Independent* — 14760 Main St. (20772); PO Box 30, Upper Marlboro (20773); W/F; 24,474pd, 327fr (CAC); $12.82; C; publisher Ralph Martin; general manager Dale Foster; editor Joe Norris; tel (301) 627-2833; fax (301) 627-2835

Wicomico: *Salisbury News & Advertiser* — 1501 Court Plaza, Ste. 27, Salisbury (21801); W; 250pd, 13,500fr (Est); $9.75; publisher James Ritch; editor Robin Adamopoulos; tel (410) 749-0272; fax (410) 749-5073

MASSACHUSETTS

Abington: *Abington Standard C/O Associated Newspapers* — 7 Cabot Pl.; PO Box 441, Stoughton (02072); W; 756pd, 5fr (Sw); $5.75; C; publisher Richard R Dailey; editor Michael Lenney; tel (617) 341-1111; fax (617) 341-1111

Abington/Rockland: *Abington/Rockland Mariner* — 165 Enterprise Dr., Marshfield (02050); Th; 2,124pd, 101fr (CAC); $11.30; C; publisher Margaret Smoragiewiecz; managing editor David Levine; tel (617) 837-3500; fax (617) 837-9619

Acton/Boxborough: *The Beacon* — 150 Baker Ave. Extension; PO Box 9191, Concord (01742-9191); Th; 5,473pd, 57fr (CAC); $15.75; C; publisher Mark O'Neil; editor Dorris Hillberg; managing editor Marlene Switzer; tel (508) 369-2800; fax (508) 371-9058

Allston/Brighton: *Allston-Brighton Citizen Journal* — PO Box 659, Boston (02258); Th; 6,583pd, 5,417fr (Est); $15.50; C; publisher Robert L Marchione; general manager John McSherry; editor Chris Price; tel (617) 254-0334; fax (617) 254-5081

Amesbury: *Amesbury News* — 16 Millyard St. (01913); F; 3,557pd, 799fr (Sw); $9.65; C; publisher Charles F Goodrich; editor Donna Greene; managing editor Jim Malone; tel (508) 388-2406; fax (508) 388-7972

Amherst/Hadley/Sunderland: *Amherst Bulletin* — 55 University Dr., Amherst (01002); F; 108pd, 13,229fr (Sw); $9.67; C; publishers Charles W DeRose & Peter L DeRose; editor Nick Grabbe; tel (413) 549-2000; fax (413) 585-5222

II-34 **Massachusetts** *U.S. Weeklies*

Andover: *The Andover Townsman* — 33 Chestnut St.; PO Box 1986 (01810); Th; 7,053pd, 367fr (Sw); $9.50; publisher Irving E Rogers Jr; general manager Michael A Masessa Jr; editor Perry C Colmore; tel (508) 475-1943; fax (508) 470-2819

Arlington: *The Arlington Advocate* — 33 New York Ave.; PO Box 9149, Framingham (01701); Th; 10,088pd, 495fr (CAC); $13.15; C; publisher Asa Cole; editor Tom Rose; tel (617) 643-7900; fax (617) 641-5567

Ashland: *Ashland TAB* — 1254 Chestnut St., Newton (02164); Tu; 3,630fr (Est); $9.75; C; publisher Stephen Cummings; editor John Wilpers; tel (617) 969-0340; fax (617) 969-3302

Athol: *Athol/Orange Town Crier* — PO Box 1435, Greenfield (01302); F; 11,920fr (Est); $5.95; C; publisher Roger G Miller; general manager Bob LaPierre; editor Jim Gilday; tel (413) 774-7226; fax (413) 774-6809

Auburn/S Worcester: *Auburn News* — 25 Elm St., Southbridge (01550); W; 2,717pd, 63fr (Sw); $8.45; C; publisher John Coots; editor David Cutler; tel (508) 764-4325; fax (508) 832-2431

Avon: *Avon Messenger C/O Associated Newspapers* — 7 Cabot Pl.; PO Box 441, Stoughton (02072); W; 375pd, 50fr (Sw); $5.75; C; publisher & editor Richard R Dailey; managing editor Michael Lenney; tel (617) 341-1111; fax (617) 341-1111

Ayer: *The Public Spirit* — 69 Fitchburg Rd.; PO Box 362 (01432); W; 4,800pd, 500fr (Sw); $8.35; C; publisher Frank J Hartnett Sr; editor Frank J Hartnett Jr; tel (617) 772-0777

Barnstable: *Cape Cod News* — 5 Namskaket Ave., Orleans (02653); Th; 11,773fr (Est); $10.90; publisher Victoria Ogden; editor Mark Skala; tel (508) 255-2121; fax (508) 240-0333

Barnstable Co.: *The Register* — 5 Namskaket Ave., Orleans (02653); Th; 11,987pd (Est); $11.15; C; publisher Victoria Ogden; editor Mark Skala; tel (508) 255-2121; fax (508) 240-0333

Barnstable/Hyannis: *Barnstable Patriot* — 326 Main St.; PO Box 1208, Hyannis (02601); Th; 2,098pd, 206fr (Sw); $7.20; publishers Anne G Sennott & Robert F Sennott; editor David B Still II; tel (508) 771-1427; fax (508) 790-3997

Barre: *The Barre Gazette* — 5 Exchange St.; PO Box 448 (01005); Th; 2,033pd, 65fr (Sw); $5.35; C; publishers Patrick H Turley & Thomas A Turley; editor Marilyn A Haynes; tel (508) 355-4000; fax (508) 355-6274

Bedford: *Bedford Minuteman* — 150 Baker Ave. Extension, Concord (01742-9191); Th; 3,166pd (Est); $11.35; C; publisher Mark O'Neil; editor Richard Lodge; tel (508) 369-2800; fax (508) 369-7089

Belchertown/Granby/Amherst: *The Sentinel* — 10 S. Main St.; PO Box 601, Belchertown (01007); Th; 8,500fr (Est); $6.50; C; publisher Thomas A Turley; general manager David Anderson; tel (413) 323-7040, (413) 323-5999; fax (413) 323-9424

Belmont: *The Belmont Citizen-Herald* — 33 New York Ave.; PO Box 9149, Framingham (01701); Th; 5,843pd, 338fr (CAC); $12.60; C; publisher Asa Cole; editor Chris Begley; tel (617) 643-7900; fax (617) 641-5567

Berkshire Co.: *The Advocate/The South Advocate* — 38 Spring St.; PO Box 95, Williamstown (01267); W; 503pd, 21,000fr (Sw); $8.75; C; publisher Ellen Joy Bernstein; general manager Gail E King; editor Mark Rondeau; tel (413) 458-9000; fax (413) 458-5715

Berkshire Co.: *The Berkshire Record C/O Record Building* — 21 Elm St., Great Barrington (01230); Th; 4,250pd (Est); $8.80; C; publisher Anthony Prisendorf; editor Donna Prisendorf; tel (413) 528-5380; fax (413) 528-5943

Billerica: *Billerica Minuteman* — 150 Baker Ave. Extension, Concord (01742-9191); Th; 4,953pd (Est); $11.75; C; publisher Mark O'Neil; editor Richard Lodge; tel (508) 369-2800; fax (508) 369-7089

Blackstone Valley: *Blackstone Valley Tribune* — 60 Church St.; PO Box 210, Whitinsville (01588); W; 4,469pd (Sw); $10.10; C; publisher John Coots; editor Deborah E Gauthier; tel (508) 234-5686; fax (508) 234-7506

Bolton: *The Bolton Common* — PO Box 8 (01740); F; 2,376pd, 245fr (Sw); $7.00; C; publishers Edward Miller & Kathleen Cushman; general manager Barbara Kemp; editor Bill Latimer; tel (508) 779-5113

Boston: *Boston Post Gazette* — 5 Prince St.; PO Box 135 (02113); F; 25,000fr (Sw); $20.00; publisher & editor Pamela Donnaruma; tel (617) 227-8929

Boston: *Boston TAB* — 254 2nd Ave., Needham (02194); Tu; 17,540fr (VAC); $12.35; C; publisher Kirk Davis; editor George Donnelly; tel (617) 433-8200; fax (617) 433-8201

Boston: *Boston Citizen Journal* — PO Box 659 (02258); Th; 22,000fr (Est); $15.50; C; publisher Robert L Marchione; editor Bill Kelly; tel (617) 254-0334; fax (617) 254-5081

Bourne: *Bourne Courier* — 5 Namskaket Ave., Orleans (02653); Th; 2,057pd (Est); $6.30; C; publisher Victoria Ogden; editor Mark Skala; tel (508) 255-2121; fax (508) 240-0333

Boylston/W Boylston: *The Banner* — PO Box 306, West Boylston (01583); Th; 1,595pd, 64fr (Sw); $6.20; C; publisher Frank Hewitt; editor Lisa Drueke; managing editor Jan Gottesman; tel (508) 835-4865; fax (508) 368-1151

Braintree: *Braintree Gazette C/O Associated Newspapers* — 7 Cabot Pl.; PO Box 441, Stoughton (02072); W; 1,100fr (Sw); $5.75; C; publisher & editor Richard R Dailey; managing editor Michael Lenney; tel (617) 341-1111; fax (617) 314-1111

Braintree: *Braintree Forum* — 720 Union St.; PO Box 850911 (02184); W; 3,657pd, 242fr (CAC); $8.00; C; publisher Margaret Smoragaewicz; editor Cathy Conley; tel (617) 843-2937; fax (617) 849-3319

Brockton: *Brockton News-Tribune C/O Associated Newspapers* — 7 Cabot Pl.; PO Box 441, Stoughton (02072); W; 2,450fr (Sw); $5.75; C; publisher & editor Richard R Dailey; managing editor Michael Lenney; tel (617) 341-1111; fax (617) 341-1111

Brockton/Metro S Brockton: *Chronicle (A Weekly News/Magazine) C/O Associated Newspapers* — 7 Cabot Pl.; PO Box 441, Stoughton (02072); W; 7,000fr (Sw); $10.25; C; publisher & editor Richard R Dailey; managing editor Michael Lenney; tel (617) 341-1111; fax (617) 314-1111

Brookline: *Brookline Citizen Journal* — 101 N. Beacon (Allston, 02134); PO Box 659, Boston (02258); Th; 5,565pd, 6,435fr (Est); $15.50; C; publisher Robert L Marchione; general manager John McSherry; editor Chris Price; tel (617) 254-0334; fax (617) 254-5081

Brookline: *Brookline TAB* — 1254 Chestnut St., Newton (02164); Tu; 19,574fr (Est); $24.70; C; publisher Stephen Cummings; editor John Wilpers; tel (617) 969-0340; fax (617) 969-3302

Burlington: *Burlington Union* — 150 Baker Ave. Extension, Concord (01742-9191); Th; 3,106pd (Est); $11.75; C; publisher Mark O'Neil; editor Richard Lodge; tel (508) 369-2800; fax (508) 369-7089

Cambridge: *Cambridge TAB* — 1254 Chestnut St., Newton (02164); Tu; 15,932fr (Est); $19.75; C; publisher Stephen Cummings; editor John Wilpers; tel (617) 969-0340; fax (617) 969-3302

Cambridge: *Cambridge Chronicle* — 364 Cummings Park, Woburn (02144); Th; 12,099pd (Est); $18.25; C; publisher Frank E Yetter; editor George Donnelly; tel (617) 937-8000; fax (617) 937-0262

Canton: *Canton Citizen* — 40 Revere St.; PO Box 291 (02021); Th; 2,106pd, 178fr (Sw); $6.50; publisher & editor Beth Erickson; tel (617) 821-4418; fax (617) 821-4419

Canton: *Canton Journal* — 12 Revere St.; PO Box 254 (02021); Th; 2,747pd, 260fr (CAC); $8.00; C; publisher Margaret Smoragaewicz; editor Jim Woodworth; tel (617) 828-0006; fax (617) 828-9039

Canton: *Canton Register C/O Associated Newspapers* — 7 Cabot Pl.; PO Box 441, Stoughton (02072); W; 725fr (Sw); $5.75; C; publisher & editor Richard R Dailey; managing editor Michael Lenney; tel (617) 341-1111; fax (617) 341-1111

Cape Cod: *The Cape Codder* — 5 Namskaket Rd., Orleans (02653); Tu/F; 14,988pd (Est); $14.65; publisher Victoria Ogden; editor Mark Skala; tel (508) 255-2121; fax (508) 240-0333

Carlisle: *Carlisle Mosquito* — PO Box 616 (01741); F; 1,800fr (Est); $7.00; editor Jackie Frey; tel (508) 369-8313; fax (508) 369-3569

Carver: *Carver Reporter C/O MPG Newspapers* — 9 Long Pond Rd.; PO Box 959, Plymouth (02362-0959); W; 83pd, 4,220fr (CAC); $7.01; publisher Phyllis J Hughes; editor Mark Pothier; tel (508) 746-5555; fax (508) 747-2148

Charlestown: *The Charlestown Patriot & Somerville Chronicle* — 1 Thompson Sq.; PO Box 54 (02129); Th; 4,500pd (Sw); $4.20; publisher & editor Gloria S Conway; tel (617) 241-9511; fax (617) 241-9511

Chatam/Harwich/Orleans: *The Cape Cod Chronicle* — 60-C Munson Meeting Way, Chatam (02633); Th; 7,695pd, 326fr (Sw); $8.50; C; publisher & editor Henry C Hyora; managing editor William Galuim; tel (508) 945-2220; fax (508) 945-2579

Chelmsford: *Chelmsford Independent* — 150 Baker Ave. Extension, Concord (01742-9191); Th; 4,134pd (Est); $11.75; C; publisher Mark O'Neil; editor Richard Lodge; tel (508) 369-2800; fax (508) 369-7089

Chelsea: *Chelsea Record* — 327 Broadway, Revere (02151); W/F; 2,576pd, 340fr (CAC); $6.05; C; publishers Lou McGrew & Neil P Collins; general manager Stephen Quigley; editor Edmund Coletta Jr; tel (617) 284-2400; fax (617) 289-5352

Cheshire: *Jaffrey-Rindge Chronicle* — 20 Front St.; PO Box 248, Winchendon (01475); W; 787pd, 2fr (Sw); $7.05; C; publisher Martha J O'Connor; editor Ron Muse; tel (508) 297-0050; fax (508) 297-2177

Chicopee/Holyoke/Granby: *Chicopee Herald Weekly* — 143 E. Main St. (01020); PO Box 950, Chicopee (01014); Th; 31,030fr (Sw); $11.77; publisher John Maslar; editor Joanne Despard; tel (413) 592-1400; fax (413) 592-5286

Cohasset: *Cohasset Mariner* — 165 Enterprise Dr.; PO Box 682, Marshfield (02050); Th; 1,802pd (Est); $8.00; C; publisher Margaret Smoragaewicz; editor Pat Desmond; tel (617) 837-3500; fax (617) 837-9619

Concord/Carlisle: *The Concord Journal* — 150 Baker Ave. Extension, Ste. 305; PO Box 9191, Concord (01742-9191); Th; 5,660pd, 52fr (CAC); $15.75; C; publisher Mark O'Neil; editor Lucille Daniel; managing editor Marlene Switzer; tel (508) 369-2800; fax (508) 371-9058

Danvers: *Danvers Herald* — 152 Sylvan St.; PO Box 293 (01923); Th; 5,354pd, 790fr (CAC); $9.65; publisher Charles F Goodrich; editor Howard Iverson; managing editor Jim Malone; tel (508) 774-0505; fax (508) 774-0450

Dartmouth/Westport: *The Chronicle* — 45 Slocum Rd.; PO Box 268, South Dartmouth (02748); W; 5,933pd, 108fr (Sw); $9.95; C; publisher Warren G Hathaway; general manager Raymond P Hopkins; editor Susan Gonsalves; tel (508) 992-1522; fax (508) 992-1620

Dorchester: *Dorchester Argus-Citizen* — 1205 Hyde Park Ave.; PO Box 67, Hyde Park (02136); Th; 2,375pd, 350fr (Sw); 52¢; C; publisher Susan H Pollock; editor David Johnson; tel (617) 361-6500; fax (617) 361-8909

Dorchester/Mattapan: *The Reporter* — 304 Neponset Ave., Dorchester (02122); Th; 4,000pd (Est); $8.00; C; publisher Marc Forry; editor Edward W Forry; tel (617) 436-1222; fax (617) 825-5516

Dover: *Dover Tab* — 1254 Chestnut St., Newton (02164); Tu; 2,226fr (Est); $8.40; C; publisher Stephen Cummings; editor John Wilpers; tel (617) 969-0340; fax (617) 969-3302

Dover/Sherborn: *Dover-Sherborn Suburban Press* — 992 Great Plain Ave.; PO Box 358, Needham (02192); Th; 2,997pd (Est); $11.10; C; publisher William Barrett; editor Phil Maddocks; managing editor Liz Banks; tel (617) 444-1706; fax (617) 444-1795

Dracut: *Dracut Dispatch* — 434 Textile Ave.; PO Box 1 (01826); Th; 4,143pd (Sw); $7.00; publisher William J Themelis; editor Geraldine Katin; tel (508) 957-0007; fax (508) 957-1051

Duxbury: *Duxbury Clipper* — PO Box 1656 (02331); W; 4,500pd, 200fr (Est); $4.90; C; publisher & editor John Henry Cutler; tel (617) 934-2811; fax (617) 934-5917

Duxbury: *Duxbury Reporter C/O MPG Newspapers* — 9 Long Pond Rd.; PO Box 959, Plymouth (02362-0959); W; 57pd, 5,389fr (CAC); $7.01; C; publisher Phyllis J Hughes; editor Mark Pothier; tel (508) 746-5555; fax (508) 747-2148

E Boston: *East Boston Sun Transcript* — 327 Broadway, Revere (02151); W; 6,000fr (CAC); $6.75; C; publishers Lou McGrew & Neil P Collins; general manager Stephen Quigley; editor Peter Nagle; managing editor Edmund Coletta Jr; tel (617) 284-2400; fax (617) 289-5352

E Bridgewater: *East Bridgewater Citizen C/O Associated Newspapers* — 7 Cabot Pl.; PO Box 441, Stoughton (02072); W; 416pd (Sw); $5.75; C; publisher & editor Richard R Dailey; managing editor C MacDonald; tel (617) 341-1111; fax (617) 341-1111

E/W Bridgewater: *Bridgewater Independent* — 232 Bedford St.; PO Box 156, Bridgewater (02324); Th; 2,017pd (Est); $5.35; C; publisher John A Anderson III; editor Terry Egan; tel (508) 697-2881; fax (508) 947-1763

E/W Bridgewater: *East Bridgewater Star* — 232 Bedford St.; PO Box 156, Bridgewater (02324); Th; 66pd, 33fr (Est); $5.35; C; publisher John A Anderson III; editor Terence F Egan; tel (508) 697-2881; fax (508) 947-1763

Easton: *Easton Bulletin C/O Associated Newspapers* — 7 Cabot Pl.; PO Box 441, Stoughton (02072); W; 1,321pd, 100fr (Sw); $5.75; C; publisher & editor Richard R Dailey; managing editor Michael Lenney; tel (617) 341-1111; fax (617) 341-1111

Easton: *Easton Journal* — 28A S. Main St., Sharon (02067); F; 64pd, 5,334fr (CAC); $7.58; C; publisher Kirk Davis; editor Tom Glynn; managing editor Ellen Albanese; tel (508) 230-7964; fax (617) 784-6724

Everett: *Everett Leader Herald News Gazette* — 28 Church St.; PO Box 108 (02149); Th; 15,000fr (Sw); $6.00; publisher Martin J McDonough; editor Joseph Curnane Jr; tel (617) 387-4570; fax (617) 387-0409

Fairhaven/Acushnet: *The Advocate* — 9 Long Pond Rd.; PO Box 959, Plymouth (02362-0959); Th; 2,136pd, 4fr (CAC); $7.92; C; publisher Phyllis J Hughes; editor Mark Pothier; tel (508) 748-1123; fax (508) 748-1128

Falmouth/Mashpee/Bourne: *The Enterprise* — 50 Depot Ave.; PO Box 647, Falmouth (02541); Tu/F; 9,412pd, 130fr (ABC); $9.25; C; publishers & editors Margaret Hough Russell & William Henry Hough; managing editor Janice Walford; tel (508) 548-4700; fax (508) 540-8407

Foxboro: *The Foxboro Reporter* — 36 Mechanic St.; PO Box 289 (02035); Th; 4,245pd, 90fr (Est); $6.25; C; publisher Paul A Rixon; editor Jeffrey Peterson; tel (508) 543-4851; fax (508) 543-4888

Framingham: *Framingham TAB* — 1254 Chestnut St., Newton (02164); Tu; 16,935fr (Est); $17.20; C; publisher Stephen Cummings; editor John Wilpers; tel (617) 969-0340; fax (617) 969-3302

Franklin/Medway/Millis: *The Country Gazette* — PO Box 612, Franklin (02038); W; 32,138fr (CAC); $25.88; C; publisher Kirk Davis; editor Mary Van Doren; managing editor Ellen Albanese; tel (508) 528-2600; fax (508) 528-2676

Georgetown: *Georgetown Record* — 2 Washington St.; PO Box 192, Ipswich (01938); Th; 1,797pd, 123fr (Sw); $9.65; C; publisher Charles F Goodrich; editor Ted Wadsworth; managing editor Jim Malone; tel (508) 774-0505; fax (508) 774-6365

Great Barrington: *The Berkshire Courier* — 620 S. Main St.; PO Box 150, Great Barrington (01230); Th; 4,916pd, 80fr (Est); $7.00; publisher John W P Mooney; editor Eileen W Mooney; tel (413) 528-3020; fax (413) 528-5702

Greenfield: *Greenfield Town Crier* — 393 Main St.; PO Box 1435 (01302); F; 21,048fr (Sw); $7.80; C; publisher Roger G Miller; general manager Robert LaPierro; editor James Gildea; tel (413) 774-7226; fax (413) 774-6809

Halifax/Plympton: *Halifax/Plympton Reporter C/O MPG Newspapers* — 9 Long Pond Rd.; PO Box 959, Plymouth (02362-0959); Th; 1,329pd, 2fr (CAC); $6.43; C; publisher Phyllis Hughes; editor Mark Pothier; tel (508) 746-5555; fax (508) 747-2148

Hamilton: *Hamilton-Wenham Chronicle* — 152 Sylvan St.; PO Box 293, Danvers (01923); W; 2,926pd, 177fr (Sw); $9.65; C; publisher Charles F Goodrich; editor Sasha Paulsen; managing editor Jim Malone; tel (508) 774-0505; fax (508) 774-6365

Hanover: *Hanover Branch C/O Associated Newspapers* — 7 Cabot Pl.; PO Box 441, Stoughton (02072); W; 342pd, 50fr (Sw); $5.75; C; publisher & editor Richard R Dailey; managing editor Michael Lenney; tel (617) 341-1111; fax (617) 341-1111

U.S. Weeklies **Massachusetts** **II-35**

Hanover: *Hanover Mariner* — 165 Enterprise Dr.; PO Box 682, Marshfield (02050); W; 2,182pd, 132fr (CAC); $8.00; C; publisher Margaret Smoragaewicz; editor Judy Enright; tel (617) 837-3500; fax (617) 837-9619

Hanson: *Hanson Town Crier C/O Associated Newspapers* — 7 Cabot Pl.; PO Box 441, Stoughton (02072); W; 286pd, 25fr (Sw); $5.75; C; publisher & editor Richard R Dailey; managing editor Michael Lenney; tel (617) 341-1111; fax (617) 341-1111

Harvard: *Harvard Post* — 53 Bolton St.; PO Box 308 (01451); F; 2,635pd, 21fr (Sw); $7.00; C; publishers Edward Miller & Kathleen Cushman; general manager Barbara Kemp; editor Ann Levison; tel (508) 456-8122

Harwich: *Harwich Oracle* — 5 Namskaket Rd., Orleans (02653-0039); Th; 3,829fr (Est); $8.90; C; publisher Victoria Ogden; editor Mark Skala; tel (508) 255-2121; fax (508) 240-0333

Hingham: *Hingham Journal* — 73 South St. (02043); Th; 4,443pd (Est); $8.00; C; publisher Margaret Smoragaewicz; editor Mary Ford; tel (617) 749-0031; fax (617) 740-8955

Hingham: *Hingham Mariner* — 165 Enterprise Dr.; PO Box 682, Marshfield (02050); Th; 3,996pd, 447fr (CAC); $8.00; C; publisher Margaret Smoragaewicz; editor Mary Ford; tel (617) 837-3500; fax (617) 837-9619

Holbrook: *Holbrook Sun* — 720 Union St. (02184); PO Box 355 (02343); W; 1,790pd, 92fr (CAC); $8.00; C; publisher Margaret Smoragaewicz; editor Cathy Conley; tel (617) 767-4000; fax (617) 849-3319

Holbrook: *Holbrook Times C/O Associated Newspapers* — 7 Cabot Pl.; PO Box 441, Stoughton (02072); W; 452pd, 50fr (Sw); $5.75; C; publisher & editor Richard R Dailey; managing editor Michael Lenney; tel (617) 341-1111; fax (617) 341-1111

Holden/Paxton/Rutland/Princeton/Sterling: *The Landmark* — 1650 Main St.; PO Box 546, Holden (01520); Th; 8,070pd, 319fr (Sw); $7.56; publisher & managing editor Joanne G Root; editor Jim Keogh; tel (508) 829-5981; fax (508) 829-5984

Holliston: *Holliston TAB* — 1254 Chestnut St., Newton (02164); Tu; 3,654fr (Est); $9.75; C; publisher Stephen Cummings; editor John Wilpers; tel (617) 969-0340; fax (617) 969-3302

Hudson: *Hudson Sun* — 230 Maple St., Marlboro (01752); Th; 3,500pd (Est); $12.60; publisher Asa Cole; editor John Towne; tel (508) 485-7830; fax (508) 490-7450

Hull: *The Hull Times* — 667 Nantasket Ave.; PO Box 477 (02045); Th; 3,533pd, 42fr (Sw); $5.00; publishers Sherry Larkin & Susan Ovans; editor Christopher Haraden; tel (617) 925-9266; fax (617) 925-0336

Huntington: *Country Journal* — 5 Main St.; PO Box 429 (01050); Th; 2,834pd, 16fr (Sw); $4.75; publisher & editor Margot Locke; tel (413) 667-3211; fax (413) 667-3011

Hyde Park: *Hyde Park Tribune* — 1261 Hyde Park Ave. (02136); Th; 4,215pd, 425fr (Sw); $7.00; C; publisher Susan H Pollock; editor David Johnson; tel (617) 361-6500; fax (617) 361-8909

Ipswich: *Ipswich Chronicle* — 2 Washington St.; PO Box 192 (01938); Th; 4,966pd, 270fr (Sw); $9.65; C; publisher Charles F Goodrich; editor Janet Mackay-Smith; managing editor Jim Malone; tel (508) 774-0505; fax (508) 774-6365

Jamaica Plain/Roxbury: *Jamaica Plain Citizen* — 1261 Hyde Park Ave., Hyde Park (02136); Th; 2,669pd, 350fr (Sw); $7.00; C; publisher Susan H Pollock; editor David Johnson; tel (617) 361-6500; fax (617) 361-8909

Kingston: *Kingston Mariner* — 165 Enterprise Dr.; PO Box 682, Marshfield (02050); W; 3,000fr (Est); $8.00; C; publisher Margaret Smoragaewicz; editor Paula Woodhull; tel (617) 837-3500; fax (617) 827-9619

Kingston: *Kingston Reporter C/O MPG Newspapers* — 9 Long Pond Rd.; PO Box 959, Plymouth (02362-0959); Th; 180pd, 3,395fr (CAC); $7.01; C; publisher Phyllis Hughes; editor Mark Pothier; tel (508) 746-5555; fax (508) 747-2148

Lexington: *Lexington Minuteman* — 150 Baker Ave. Extension, Concord (01742-9191); Th; 8,093pd (Est); $15.75; C; publisher Mark O'Neil; editor Richard Lodge; tel (508) 369-2800; fax (508) 369-7089

Lincoln: *Lincoln Journal* — 150 Baker Ave. Extension; PO Box 9191, Concord (01742-9191); Th; 1,545pd, 36fr (CAC); $9.50; C; publisher Mark O'Neil; editor Brad Skillman; managing editor Marlene Switzer; tel (508) 369-2800; fax (508) 371-9058

Littleton: *Littleton Independent* — 150 Baker Ave. Extension, Concord (01742-9191); Th; 1,844pd (Est); $9.50; C; publisher Mark O'Neil; editor Richard Lodge; tel (508) 369-2800; fax (508) 369-7089

Lynn: *Lynn Sunday Post* — 617 Chestnut St. (01904); Su; 4,517pd (Sw); $9.65; publisher Frank Yetter; editor Susan Hershey; managing editor Jim Malone; tel (617) 592-4600; fax (617) 592-1811

Lynnfield: *The Lynnfield Villager* — 55 Salem St.; PO Box 186 (01940); W; 1,168pd, 121fr (CAC); $4.60; C; publisher Albert E Sylvia; editor Albert E Sylvia Jr; tel (617) 334-6319

Malden: *Malden Observer* — 40 W. Foster St., Melrose (02176); Th; 12,512fr (Est); $9.65; publisher Frank Yetter; managing editor Peter Chianca; tel (617) 665-4000; fax (617) 665-2195

Manchester: *The Manchester Cricket* — 50 Summer St.; PO Box 357 (01944); F; 2,427pd, 90fr (Sw); $7.00; publisher Daniel F Slade; editor Daniel B Slade; tel (508) 526-7131; fax (508) 526-8193

Mansfield: *Mansfield Reporter C/O Associated Newspapers* — 7 Cabot Pl.; PO Box 441, Stoughton (02072); W; 925fr (Sw); $5.75; C; publisher & editor Richard R Dailey; managing editor Michael Lenney; tel (617) 341-1111; fax (617) 341-1111

Mansfield/Sharon/Norton: *The Mansfield News* — 154 Copeland Dr.; PO Box 109, Mansfield (02048); F; 3,181pd, 456fr (CAC); $7.04; C; publisher Kirk Davis; editor Donna Whitehead; managing editor Ellen Albanese; tel (508) 339-8977; fax (508) 339-0340

Marblehead: *The Marblehead Reporter* — 40 South St.; PO Box 468 (01945); Th; 10,957fr (Sw); $12.45; C; publisher Charles F Goodrich; editor Diana Montgomery; managing editor Jim Malone; tel (617) 631-7700; fax (617) 639-2830

Marion/Mattapoisett/Rochester: *The Sentinel* — 9 Long Pond Rd.; PO Box 959, Plymouth (02362-0959); Th; 2,505pd, 9fr (CAC); $7.92; C; publisher Phyllis Hughes; editor Mark Pothier; tel (508) 748-1123; fax (508) 748-1128

Marlboro: *Marlboro Enterprise* — 230 Maple St. (01752); Th; 4,700pd (Est); $12.60; publisher Asa Cole; editor John Towne; tel (508) 485-7830; fax (508) 490-7450

Marshfield: *Marshfield Mariner* — 165 Enterprise Dr.; PO Box 682 (02050); W; 4,033pd, 306fr (CAC); $8.00; C; publisher Margaret Smoragaewicz; editor Jane Lane; tel (617) 837-3500; fax (617) 837-9619

Marshfield: *Marshfield Reporter MPG Newspapers* — 9 Long Pond Rd.; PO Box 959, Plymouth (02362-0959); Th; 69pd, 6,458fr (CAC); $7.01; C; publisher Phyllis J Hughes; editor Mark Pothier; tel (508) 746-5555; fax (508) 747-2148

Martha's Vineyard: *The Martha's Vineyard Times* — 14 Beach Rd.; PO Box 518, Vineyard Haven (02568); Th; 3,690pd, 9,071fr (Sw); $13.70; publisher & editor Doug Cabral; tel (508) 693-6100; fax (508) 693-6000

Martha's Vineyard: *Vineyard Gazette* — 34 S. Summer St.; PO Box 66, Edgartown (02539-0066); Tu/F; 13,572pd, 10fr (Sw); $16.75; publisher & general manager Mary Jo Reston; publisher & editor Richard F Reston; tel (508) 627-4311; fax (508) 627-7444

Mashpee: *Mashpee Messenger* — 5 Namskaket Ave., Orleans (02653); Th; 2,393fr (Est); $5.55; C; publisher Victoria Ogden; editor Mark Skala; tel (508) 255-2121; fax (508) 240-0333

Maynard: *The Maynard Beacon* — 150 Baker Ave. Extension; PO Box 9191, Concord (01742-9191); Th; 2,605pd (Est); $15.75; C; publisher Mark O'Neil; editor Richard Lodge; managing editor Marlene Switzer; tel (508) 369-2800; fax (508) 369-7089

Medfield: *Medfield Suburban Press* — 992 Great Plain Ave.; PO Box 358, Needham (02192); Th; 3,403pd (Sw); $11.10; C; publisher William Barrett; editor Susan Davis; managing editor Liz Banks; tel (617) 444-1706; fax (617) 444-1795

Medford: *Medford Transcript* — 57 High St. (02155); W; 4,749pd, 813fr (CAC); $8.13; C; publishers Lou McGrew & Neil Collins; editor Ed Coletta; tel (617) 396-1982; fax (617) 393-0166

Melrose: *Melrose Free Press* — 40 W. Foster St. (02176); Th; 6,384pd, 701fr (Sw); $9.65; C; publisher Frank E Yetter; managing editor Peter Chianca; tel (617) 665-4000; fax (617) 665-2195

Merrimack Valley: *Merrimack Valley Sunday* — 16 Millyard, Amesbury (01913); Sa; 9,202fr (Sw); $9.65; publisher Charles F Goodrich; editor Donna Greene; managing editor Jim Malone; tel (508) 388-2406; fax (508) 388-7972

Middleboro/Lakeville/Raynham/Bridgewater/Taunton: *Capeway News* — PO Box 1348, Middleboro (02346); Tu; 44,817fr (Est); $16.50; publisher Maureen Sullivan; editor Terry Egan; tel (508) 947-1111; fax (508) 947-1763

Middleboro/Lakeville/Raynham/Bridgewater/Taunton: *Middleboro Gazette* — 148 W. Grove St.; PO Box 551, Middleboro (02346); Th; 5,423pd, 215fr (Sw); $9.95; C; publisher Warren G Hathaway; general manager Raymond Hopkins; editor Jane Lopes; tel (617) 947-1760

Millis: *Millis Suburban Press* — 992 Great Plain Ave.; PO Box 358, Needham (02192); Th; 2,667pd (Sw); $11.10; C; publisher William Barrett; editor Linda Halfrey; managing editor Liz Banks; tel (617) 444-1706; fax (617) 444-1795

Milton: *Milton Record Transcript* — 26 High St. (02187); F; 4,839pd, 175fr (Sw); $6.90; C; publisher & editor Daniel Horgan; tel (617) 698-6563; fax (617) 689-7827

Milton: *Milton Townsman C/O Associated Newspapers* — 7 Cabot Pl.; PO Box 441, Stoughton (02074); W; 1,000fr (Sw); $5.75; C; publisher & editor Richard R Dailey; managing editor Michael Lenney; tel (617) 341-1111; fax (617) 341-1111

Nantucket: *The Inquirer and Mirror* — Milestone; PO Box 1198 (02554); Th; 10,449pd, 203fr (Sw); $8.75; publisher & editor Marianne Staton; tel (508) 228-0001; fax (508) 325-5089

Nantucket: *Nantucket Beacon* — 64 Old South Rd.; PO Box 2610 (02584); W; 5,140pd, 545fr (Est); $8.70; C; publisher Edward R Leach; editor Mark E Vogler; tel (508) 228-8455; fax (508) 228-8994

Natick: *Natick Bulletin* — 992 Great Plain Ave.; PO Box 358, Needham (02192); Th; 3,769pd, 283fr (Sw); $11.10; C; publisher William Barrett; editor Joyce Bain; managing editor Liz Banks; tel (617) 444-1706; fax (617) 444-1795

Natick: *Natick TAB* — 1254 Chestnut St., Newton (02164); Tu; 8,719fr (Est); $12.00; C; publisher Stephen Cummings; editor John Wilpers; tel (617) 969-0340; fax (617) 969-3302

Needham: *Needham Times* — 992 Great Plain Ave.; PO Box 358 (02192); Th; 11,895fr (Est); $15.60; C; publisher William Barrett; editor Jon-Paul Potts; managing editor Liz Banks; tel (617) 444-1706; fax (617) 444-1795

Needham: *The Needham Chronicle* — 33 New York Ave.; PO Box 9149, Framingham (01701); W; 162pd, 10,286fr (CAC); $9.25; C; publisher Asa Cole; editor M R F Buckley; tel (617) 433-7839; fax (617) 433-7835

Newton: *Newton TAB* — 1254 Chestnut St. (02164); Tu; 24,418fr (Est); $25.00; C; publisher Stephen Cummings; editor John Wilpers; tel (617) 969-0340; fax (617) 969-3302

Newton: *The Newton Graphic* — 33 New York Ave.; PO Box 9149, Framingham (01701); Th; 305pd, 26,558fr (CAC); $10.10; C; publisher Asa Cole; editor Ellen Ishkanian; tel (617) 398-8000; fax (617) 398-8010

Norfolk: *Norfolk Suburban Press* — 992 Great Plain Ave.; PO Box 358, Needham (02192); Th; 2,651pd, 428fr (Sw); $11.10; C; publisher William Barrett; editor Joe Peters; managing editor Liz Banks; tel (617) 444-1706; fax (617) 444-1795

N Andover: *North Andover Citizen* — 3 1st St. (01845); Th; 3,919pd, 1,089fr (Sw); $9.65; C; publisher Charles F Goodrich; editor Karen Fioretti; managing editor Jim Malone; tel (508) 685-5128; fax (508) 685-3782

N Attleboro/Plainville: *The Free Press* — 34 N. Washington St.; PO Box 1047, North Attleborough (02761); W; 9,349fr (Sw); $7.00; publisher & editor Douglas R Reed; publisher F William Hentschel; tel (508) 699-6755; fax (508) 699-8545

N Boston Suburbs: *North Shore Sunday* — 152 Sylvan St.; PO Box 293, Danvers (01923); Su; 40pd, 85,885fr (Sw); $33.20; publisher Charles F Goodrich; editor Taylor Armerding; managing editor Jim Malone; tel (508) 774-0505; fax (508) 774-6365

N Reading: *North Reading Transcript* — 7 Bow St.; PO Box 7 (01864); Th; 3,875pd, 133fr (CAC); $5.25; C; publisher Albert E Sylvia Jr; editor Robert Turosz; tel (508) 664-4761; fax (508) 664-4954

N/S Grafton: *The Grafton News* — N. Grafton Shopping Center; PO Box 457, North Grafton (01536); W; 3,389pd, 40fr (Sw); $4.50; publisher & editor Charles N Bolack; tel (508) 839-2259; fax (508) 839-5235

Norton: *Norton Courier C/O Associated Newspapers* — 7 Cabot Pl.; PO Box 441, Stoughton (02072); W; 800fr (Sw); $5.75; C; publisher & editor Richard R Dailey; managing editor Michael Lenney; tel (617) 341-1111; fax (617) 341-1111

Norton: *Norton Mirror* — 154 Copeland Dr.; PO Box 109, Mansfield (02048); F; 1,247pd, 698fr (CAC); $6.72; C; publisher Kirk Davis; editor Donna Whitehead; managing editor Ellen Albanese; tel (508) 339-8977; fax (508) 339-0340

Norwell: *Norwell Mariner* — 165 Enterprise Dr.; PO Box 682, Marshfield (02050); W; 2,048pd, 162fr (CAC); $8.00; C; publisher Margaret Smoragaewicz; editor Judy Enright; tel (617) 837-3500; fax (617) 837-9619

Palmer/Brimfield/Holland: *Palmer Journal-Register* — 24 Water St., Palmer (01069); Th; 5,100pd (Sw); $5.35; C; publishers Patrick H Turley & Thomas A Turley; editor Tina McNaughton; tel (413) 283-8393; fax (413) 289-1977

Peabody/Lynnfield: *Peabody & Lynnfield Weekly News* — 10 1st Ave.; PO Box 6039, Peabody (01960); Th; 27,500fr (Sw); $12.00; publisher Richard Ayer; editor Robert Curtin; tel (508) 532-5880; fax (508) 532-4250

Pembroke: *Pembroke Mariner* — 165 Enterprise Dr.; PO Box 682, Marshfield (02050); W; 1,221pd, 80fr (CAC); $8.00; C; publisher Margaret Smoragaewicz; editor Paula Woodhull; tel (617) 837-3500; fax (617) 837-9619

Pembroke: *Pembroke Reporter C/O MPG Newspapers* — 9 Long Pond Rd.; PO Box 959, Plymouth (02362-0959); Th; 1,334pd, 5fr (CAC); $6.43; C; publisher Phyllis Hughes; editor Mark Pothier; tel (508) 746-5555; fax (508) 747-2148

Pepperell: *Times Free Press* — 69 Fitchburg Rd.; PO Box 362, Ayer (01432); W; 11,000pd, 500fr (Est); $8.35; C; publisher Frank Hartnett Sr; editor Frank J Hartnett Jr; tel (508) 772-0777; fax (508) 772-4012

Pittsfield: *The Pittsfield Gazette* — 141 North St.; PO Box 2236 (01202); Th; 600pd, 7,400fr (Sw); $6.75; publisher & editor Jonathan Levine; tel (413) 443-2010; fax (413) 443-2445

Plymouth: *Old Colony Memorial C/O MPG Newspapers* — 9 Long Pond Rd.; PO Box 959 (02362-0959); Th; 12,852pd, 54fr (CAC); $17.62; C; publisher Phyllis J Hughes; editor Mark Pothier; tel (508) 746-5555; fax (508) 747-2148

Provincetown/Well Fleet: *The Advocate* — 100 Bradford St.; PO Box 93, Provincetown (02657); Th; 6,323pd, 374fr (Sw); $13.25; publisher & editor Peter Steele; tel (508) 487-1170; fax (508) 487-3878

Quincy: *Quincy Sun* — 1372 Hancock St. (02169); Th; 5,835pd, 470fr (Sw); $7.00; publisher Henry W Bosworth Jr; editor Robert H Bosworth; tel (617) 471-3100

Randolph: *Randolph Herald C/O Associated Newspapers* — 7 Cabot Pl.; PO Box 441, Stoughton (02072); W; 876pd, 100fr (Sw); $6.76; C; publisher Richard R Dailey; editor Michael Lenney; tel (617) 341-1111; fax (617) 341-1111

Randolph: *Randolph Mariner* — 720 Union St., Braintree (02184); Th; 1,122pd, 95fr (CAC); $8.00; C; publisher Margaret Smoragaewicz; editor Jim Woodworth; tel (617) 961-4141; fax (617) 828-9039

Raynham: *Raynham Journal C/O Associated Newspapers* — 7 Cabot Pl.; PO Box 441, Stoughton (02072); W; 348pd, 50fr (Sw); $5.75; C; publisher & editor Richard R Dailey; managing editor Michael Lenney; tel (617) 341-1111; fax (617) 341-1111

Reading/N Reading/Wilmington: *The Suburban News* — 100 Main St.; PO Box 1001, Reading (01867); Sa; 21,000fr (Sw); $20.95; C; publisher Richard Dailey; general manager Christine MacDonald; editor Rose Thompson; tel (617) 944-4444; fax (617) 944-4494

II-36 Massachusetts U.S. Weeklies

Revere: *The Revere Journal* — 327 Broadway (02151); W; 7,016pd, 467fr (CAC); $8.65; C; publishers Lou McGrew & Neil P Collins; general manager Stephen Quigley; editor David Procopio; managing editor Ed Coletta; tel (617) 284-2400; fax (617) 289-5352

Rockland: *Rockland Standard C/O Associated Newspapers* — 7 Cabot Pl.; PO Box 441, Stoughton (02072); W; 892pd, 100fr (Sw); $5.75; C; publisher & editor Richard R Dailey; managing editor Michael Lenney; tel (617) 341-1111; fax (617) 341-1111

Rockland: *South Shore News* — 65 Grove St.; PO Box 309 (02370); M; 70,729fr (Est); $19.50; publisher Paul Mack; managing editor Marc Songini; tel (617) 878-5100; fax (617) 878-1318

Roslindale: *Parkway Transcript* — 33 New York Ave.; PO Box 9149, Framingham (01701); W; 3,174pd, 285fr (CAC); $10.50; C; publisher Asa Cole; editor James Harder; tel (617) 329-5008; fax (617) 326-9675

Sandwich: *Sandwich Broadsider* — 5 Namskaket Ave., Orleans (02653); W; 3,911pd (Est); $8.90; C; publisher Victoria Ogden; editor Mark Skala; tel (508) 255-2121; fax (508) 240-0333

Saugus: *Saugus Advertiser* — 40 W. Foster St., Melrose (02176); Th; 4,844pd, 842fr (Sw); $11.55; publisher Charles F Goodrich & Frank Yetter; editor Dawn Souza; tel (617) 665-4000; fax (617) 665-2195

Scituate: *Scituate Mariner* — 165 Enterprise Dr.; PO Box 682, Marshfield (02050); Th; 3,355pd, 150fr (CAC); $8.00; C; publisher Margaret Smoragaewicz; editor Mailyn Jackson; tel (617) 837-3500; fax (617) 837-9619

Sharon: *Sharon Sentinel C/O Associated Newspapers* — 7 Cabot Pl.; PO Box 441, Stoughton (02072); W; 302pd, 50fr (Sw); $5.75; C; publisher & editor Richard R Dailey; managing editor Michael Lenney; tel (617) 341-1111; fax (617) 341-1111

Sharon: *The Sharon Advocate* — 28A S. Main St. (02067); F; 4,008pd, 318fr (CAC); $7.61; C; publisher Kirk Davis; editor Ellen Albanese; managing editor Tom Glynn; tel (617) 784-2131; fax (617) 784-6724

Shelburne Falls: *Shelburne Falls and West County News* — 73 Bridge St.; PO Box 218 (01370); F; 2,520pd, 17fr (Sw); $5.90; publisher & editor Richard Matthews; tel (413) 625-9417; fax (413) 625-2158

Sherborn: *Sherborn TAB* — 1254 Chestnut St., Newton (02164); Tu; 1,735fr (Est); $8.40; C; publisher Stephen Cummings; editor John Wilpers; tel (617) 969-0340; fax (617) 969-3302

Somerset/Swansea: *The Spectator* — 780 County St.; PO Box 427, Somerset (02726); W; 7,181pd, 349fr (CAC); $9.95; C; publisher Warren G Hathaway; general manager Raymond P Hopkins; editor Lisa Paulo Anaesy; tel (508) 674-4656; fax (508) 677-1210

Somerville: *Somerville Journal* — 364 W. Cummings Park, Woburn (01801); Th; 10,365pd (Est); $18.25; C; publisher Frank Yetter; editor George Donnelly; tel (617) 937-8000; fax (617) 937-0262

Southborough: *Southborough Villager* — 230 Maple St., Marlboro (01752); Th; 1,232pd (Est); $6.85; C; publisher Asa Cole; editor Glenda Hazard; tel (508) 485-5200; fax (508) 485-2133

Spencer/The Brookfield: *New Leader* — 135 Main St., Spencer (01562); Th; 2,989pd, 25fr (Sw); $6.85; C; publisher Rose Malagrida; editor Laurie Griggs; tel (508) 885-9402; fax (508) 885-4213

Stoneham: *The Stoneham Independent* — 377 Main St. (02180); W; 4,566pd, 28fr (Sw); $6.50; C; publisher Peter M Haggerty; editor Jeff Gutridge; tel (617) 438-1660; fax (617) 438-6762

Stoughton: *Stoughton Chronicle C/O Associated Newspapers* — 7 Cabot Pl.; PO Box 441 (02072); W; 1,459pd, 100fr (Sw); $5.75; C; publisher & editor Richard R Dailey; managing editor Michael Lenney; tel (617) 341-1111; fax (617) 341-1111

Stoughton: *Stoughton Journal* — 165 Enterprise Dr., Marshfield (02050); Th; 1,604pd, 37fr (CAC); $11.30; C; publisher Margaret Smoragiewicz; managing editor David Levine; tel (617) 837-3500; fax (617) 8379619

Sudbury: *Sudbury TAB* — 1254 Chestnut St., Newton (02164); Tu; 4,153fr (Est); $11.75; C; publisher Stephen Cummings; editor John Wilpers; tel (617) 969-0340; fax (617) 969-3302

Sudbury: *Sudbury Town Crier* — 33 New York Ave.; PO Box 9149, Framingham (01701); Th; 3,423pd, 98fr (CAC); $7.00; C; publisher Asa Cole; editor Lee Ann Jacob; tel (617) 433-7825; fax (617) 433-7835

Swampscott: *The Swampscott Reporter* — 40 South St.; PO Box 468, Marblehead (01945); Th; 3,988pd, 499fr (Sw); $12.45; publisher Charles F Goodrich; editor Susan Hershey; managing editor Jim Malone; tel (617) 631-7700; fax (617) 639-2830

Taunton: *Taunton Patriot C/O Associated Newspapers* — 7 Cabot Pl.; PO Box 441, Staughton (02072); W; 1,150fr (Sw); $5.75; C; publisher & editor Richard R Dailey; managing editor Michael Lenney; tel (617) 341-1111; fax (617) 341-1111

Tewksbury: *Tewksbury Advertiser* — 2 Survey Cir., North Billerica (01862); Th; 2,696pd, 988fr (CAC); $9.50; C; publisher Mark O'Neil; editor Lawrence M Walsh; managing editor Marlene Switzer; tel (508) 667-2156; fax (508) 262-9947

Topsfield: *Tri-Town Transcript* — 58 Main St.; PO Box 301 (01983); Th; 4,886pd, 675fr (Sw); $9.65; publisher Charles F Goodrich; editor Faye Raynard; managing editor Jim Malone; tel (508) 887-2727; fax (508) 887-2727

Townsend/Ashby/Pepperell/Lunenburg: *Main Street Trilogy* — 8 Jefts St.; PO Box 571, Townsend (01469); W; 6,400pd (Sw); $6.50; publisher Mary Flora Hale; editor David Henshaw; tel (508) 597-5465; fax (508) 597-5365

Wakefield: *Wakefield Observer* — 40 W. Foster St., Melrose (02176); F; 6,951fr (CAC); $9.65; C; publisher Frank Yetter; managing editor Peter Chianca; tel (617) 665-4000; fax (617) 665-2195

Walpole: *The Walpole Times* — PO Box 388 (02081); Th; 5,499pd, 46fr (Est); $6.90; publisher H D Lang; editor Paul Pronovost; tel (508) 668-0243; fax (508) 668-5174

Ware: *Ware River News* — 4 Church St.; PO Box 120 (01082); Th; 3,743pd, 150fr (Sw); $6.30; C; publishers Patrick H Turley & Thomas A Turley; editor Glenn H Ickler; tel (413) 967-3505; fax (413) 967-6009

Wareham: *Wareham Courier C/O MPG Newspapers* — 9 Long Pond Rd.; PO Box 959, Plymouth (02362-0959); Th; 5,439pd, 19fr (CAC); $9.89; C; publisher Phyllis J Hughes; editor Mark Pothier; tel (508) 295-0027; fax (508) 748-1128

Watertown: *Watertown Press* — 364 W. Cummings Park, Woburn (01801); Th; 4,385pd (Est); $12.60; C; publisher Frank Yetter; editor George Donnelly; tel (617) 937-8000; fax (617) 937-0262

Watertown: *Watertown Sun* — 33 New York Ave.; PO Box 9149, Framingham (01701); W; 2,957pd, 506fr (CAC); $8.50; C; publisher Asa Cole; managing editor Ellen Ishkanian; tel (617) 398-8000; fax (617) 398-8010

Wayland: *Wayland TAB* — 1254 Chestnut St., Newton (02164); Tu; 3,435fr (Est); $11.75; C; publisher Stephen Cummings; editor John Wilpers; tel (617) 969-0340; fax (617) 969-3302

Wayland/Weston: *Wayland-Weston Town Crier* — 33 New York Ave.; PO Box 9149, Framingham (01701); Th; 5,282pd, 184fr (CAC); $8.00; C; publisher Asa Cole; editor Lee Ann Jacob; tel (617) 433-7825; fax (617) 433-7835

Webster: *The Patriot* — 15 Sutton Rd.; PO Box 310 (01570); W; 3,000pd (Sw); $6.00; C; publisher Paul O'Donnell; editor Sally Patterson; tel (508) 943-8784; fax (508) 943-8129

Webster/Oxford/Thompson: *The Times* — 7 Main St.; PO Box 900, Webster (01570); W; 4,576pd, 398fr (Sw); $8.95; C; publisher Ernest A Mayotte; editor Martin Fey; tel (508) 943-4800; fax (508) 987-0002

Wellesley: *The Wellesley Townsman* — 33 New York Ave.; PO Box 9149, Framingham (01701); Th; 7,172pd, 403fr (CAC); $10.00; C; publisher Asa Cole; editor Cathy Brauner; tel (617) 235-4000; fax (617) 235-8687

Wellesley: *Wellesley TAB* — 1254 Chestnut St., Newton (02164); Tu; 6,646fr (Est); $12.80; C; publisher Stephen Cummings; editor John Wilpers; tel (617) 969-0340; fax (617) 969-3302

W Bridgewater: *West Bridgewater Times C/O Associated Newspapers* — 7 Cabot Pl.; PO Box 441, Stoughton (02072); W; 293pd, 50fr (Sw); $5.75; C; publisher & editor Richard R Dailey; managing editor Michael Lenney; tel (617) 341-1111; fax (617) 341-1111

W Roxbury: *West Roxbury Transcript* — 33 New York Ave.; PO Box 9149, Framingham (01701); W; 4,705pd, 309fr (CAC); $10.50; C; publisher Asa Cole; editor James Harder; tel (617) 329-5008; fax (617) 326-9675

W Springfield: *West Springfield Record* — 516 Main St.; PO Box 357 (01089); Th; 5,317pd, 2fr (Sw); $2.45; publisher & editor Tom Coburn; tel (413) 736-1587; fax (413) 739-2477

Westboro/Hopkinton/Upton: *Westborough News* — 10 E. Main St., Westboro (01581); F; 2,097pd, 531fr (Sw); $7.50; publisher & editor Phyllis T Jones; tel (508) 366-1511; fax (508) 366-5265

Westford: *Westford Eagle* — 150 Baker Ave. Extension, Concord (01742-9191); Th; 4,282pd (Est); $11.35; C; publisher Mark O'Neil; editor Richard Lodge; tel (508) 369-2800; fax (508) 369-7089

Weston: *Weston TAB* — 1254 Chestnut St., Newton (02164); Tu; 2,730fr (Est); $12.80; C; publisher Stephen Cummings; editor John Wilpers; tel (617) 969-0340; fax (617) 969-3302

Westwood: *Westwood Suburban Press* — 992 Great Plain Ave.; PO Box 358, Needham (02192); Th; 4,934pd, 412fr (Est); $11.10; C; publisher William Barrett; editor Sheri Giglio; managing editor Liz Banks; tel (617) 444-1706; fax (617) 444-1795

Weymouth: *Weymouth Dispatch C/O Associated Newspapers* — 7 Cabot Pl.; PO Box 441, Stoughton (02072); W; 700fr (Sw); $5.75; C; publisher & editor Richard R Dailey; managing editor Michael Lenney; tel (617) 341-1111; fax (617) 341-1111

Weymouth: *Weymouth News* — PO Box 330 (02188); W; 4,136pd, 229fr (CAC); $8.00; C; publisher Margaret Smoragaewicz; editor Patsy Murray; tel (617) 837-3500; fax (617) 849-3319

Whitman: *Whitman Times C/O Associated Newspapers* — 7 Cabot Pl.; PO Box 441, Stoughton (02072); W; 502pd, 50fr (Sw); $5.75; C; publisher & editor Richard R Dailey; managing editor Michael Lenney; tel (617) 341-1111; fax (617) 341-1111

Wilmington: *Town Crier* — PO Box 939 (01887); W; 5,492pd, 48fr (CAC); $5.25; publisher Larz F Neilson; editor Jeff Nazzaro; tel (508) 658-2346; fax (508) 658-2266

Wilmington: *Wilmington Advertiser* — 2 Survey Cir., North Billerica (01862); Th; 243pd, 4,267fr (CAC); $9.50; C; publisher Mark O'Neil; editor Tim Kane; managing editor Marlene Switzer; tel (508) 667-2156; fax (508) 262-9947

Winchendon: *The Winchendon Courier* — 20 Front St.; PO Box 248 (01475); W; 2,307pd, 4fr (Sw); $7.05; C; publisher John Coots; editor Ron Muse; tel (508) 297-0050; fax (508) 297-2177

Winchester: *The Winchester Star* — 27 Waterfield Rd. (01890); Th; 4,716pd, 791fr (Est); $11.50; C; publisher Asa Cole; editor Nancy Schwalbert; tel (617) 729-6100; fax (617) 729-3837

Winthrop: *Winthrop Sun-Transcript* — 193 Winthrop St. (02152); Th; 4,089pd, 339fr (Sw); $6.05; C; publishers Lou McGrew & Neil P Collins; editor Edmund Colletta Jr.; tel (617) 846-3700; fax (617) 289-5352

Woburn/Winchester/Stoneham: *Woburn Advocate* — 200 W. Cummings Park, Woburn (01801); Th; 8,976pd, 4,511fr (Sw); $13.45; C; publisher Frank Yetter; managing editor Dyke Hendrickson; tel (617) 937-8000; fax (617) 937-0262

MICHIGAN

Ada/Cascade/Forest Hills: *Ada/Cascade/Forest Hills Advance* — 2141 Port Sheldon Rd.; PO Box 9, Jenison (49429); W; 137pd, 12,184fr (VAC); $6.54; C; publisher Joel Holland; editor Mike Wyngarden; tel (616) 669-2700; fax (616) 669-1162

Alcona Co.: *Alcona County Review* — 111 Lake St.; PO Box 548, Harrisville (48740); W; 2,700pd, 39fr (Est); $3.75; publisher & editor Cheryl L Peterson; tel (517) 724-6384; fax (517) 724-6655

Allegan Co.: *Penasee Globe* — 133 E. Superior; PO Box 445, Wayland (49348); W; 4,153pd, 17,128fr (Sw); 36¢; C; publisher Ron Carlson; editor Nila Aamoth; tel (616) 792-2271; fax (616) 792-2030

Allegan Co.: *The Allegan County News* — 235 North St.; PO Box 189, Allegan (49010); Th; 4,996pd, 146fr (Sw); 33¢; C; publisher Cheryl Kaechele; general manager Peggy Hotchkiss; editor Allan Bassler; tel (616) 673-5534; fax (616) 673-5535

Allen Park/Melvindale: *The Allen Park/Melvindale News-Herald* — One Heritage Pl., Ste. 100, Southgate (48195); W; 7,856pd, 4,095fr (Est); $51.80; Su; 7,318pd, 973fr (Est); $51.80; C; publisher Fredrick G Manuel; editor Karl Ziomek; tel (313) 246-0800; fax (313) 284-2028

Allendale: *Ottawa Advance* — 2141 Port Sheldon Rd.; PO Box 9, Jenison (49429); Tu; 68pd, 8,279fr (VAC); $7.14; C; publisher Joel Holland; editor Mike Wyngarden; tel (616) 669-2700; fax (616) 669-1162

Antrim Co.: *Antrim County News* — 206 N. Bridge St.; PO Box 337, Bellaire (49615); W; 5,500pd (Sw); $6.65; C; publisher John G Tarrant; general manager Jeffrey Hallberg; editor Keith Matheny; tel (616) 533-8523

Arenac Co.: *Arenac County Independent* — 203 E. Cedar St.; PO Box 699, Standish (48658); W; 6,200pd, 44fr (Sw); $5.50; publisher Robert Edward Perlberg; general manager Gerald Stahl; editor Ben Welmers; tel (517) 846-4531; fax (517) 846-9868

Armada: *Armada Times* — 23061 E. Main St.; PO Box 915 (48005); W; 1,716pd, 219fr (Sw); $3.75; publisher & editor Katherine Steffen; tel (810) 784-5551; fax (810) 784-8710

Atlanta: *The Montmorency County Tribune* — 12625 State St.; PO Box 186 (49709); W; 4,850pd, 50fr (Sw); $5.95; C; publisher & editor Thomas C Young; tel (517) 785-4214; fax (517) 785-3118

Baraga Co.: *L'Anse Sentinel* — 202 N. Main St.; PO Box 5, L'Anse (49946); W; 4,246pd (Sw); 37¢; publisher Ed Danner; editor Barry Drue; tel (906) 524-6194

Bay City/Bay Co.: *Bay City Democrat & Bay County Legal News* — 309 9th St.; PO Box 278, Bay City (48707-0278); Th; 778pd, 43fr (Est); 18¢; publisher & editor Scott E DeVeau; general manager Carol DeVeau; tel (517) 893-6344; fax (517) 893-2991

Bear Lake: *Manistee County Pioneer Press* — 7710 Lake St.; PO Box 218 (49614); W; 1,900pd (Est); $1.25; publisher Terry Fitzwater; general manager & editor Pauline Jaquish; tel (616) 864-3311; fax (616) 864-3898

Belleville/Van Buren: *The Belleville Enterprise* — 35540 Michigan Ave.; PO Box 578, Wayne (48184); Th/Su; 1,568pd, 1,428fr (Sw); $12.24; C; publisher Mike Wilcox; editor Joan Dyer-Zinner; tel (313) 729-4000; fax (313) 729-6088

Berrien Springs/St. Joseph: *The Journal Era* — 101 W. Ferry St.; PO Box 98 (49103-0098); W; 2,500pd, 10,000fr (Est); $4.25; C; publisher Mike Perry; editor Kathy Pullano; tel (616) 473-5421; fax (616) 471-1362

Birmingham/Bloomfield: *The Birmingham-Bloomfield Eccentric* — 805 E. Maple (48009); PO Box 3011, Birmingham (48012); M/Th; 13,003pd, 2,580fr (CAC); $87.86; C; publisher John Reddy; general manager Steve Pope; editor Joe Bauman; managing editor Bob Sklar; tel (810) 644-1100; fax (810) 644-1314

Blissfield: *Blissfield Advance* — 121 Newspaper St. (49228); W; 2,792pd, 42fr (Sw); $4.50; C; publisher Paul J Heidbreder; editor Walt Walkowski; tel (517) 486-2400/4290

Boyne City/E Jordan: *The Boyne Citizen* — 112 S. Park St.; PO Box A, Boyne City (49712); Th; 412fr (Sw); $6.16; publisher & editor Hugh Conklin; general manager Susan Garwood; managing editor Susan Conklin; tel (616) 582-6761; fax (616) 582-6762

Brighton: *Brighton Argus* — 113 E. Grand River (48116); W; 11,027pd, 83fr (CAC); $9.74; C; publisher Richard Perlberg; editor Buddy Moorehouse; tel (810) 227-0171; fax (810) 227-0175

Bronson: *Bronson Journal* — 113 W. Chicago St.; PO Box 38 (49028); Th; 1,884pd, 119fr (Sw); $3.75; C; publisher & editor Scott D McGraw; managing editor Doug Olson; tel (517) 369-5085; fax (517) 369-2225

Brooklyn: *The Exponent* — 160 S. Main St.; PO Box 428 (49230); Tu; 1,262pd, 10,972fr (Est); $4.40; publisher Matt Schepeler; editor Joyce Brown; tel (517) 592-2122; fax (517) 592-3241

U.S. Weeklies **Michigan** **II-37**

Brown City: *Brown City Banner* — 4241 Main St.; PO Box 250 (48416); W; 2,037pd, 313fr (Sw); $5.50; C; publisher Ernest E Slade; editor Bernice Hillman; tel (810) 346-2753; fax (810) 346-2579

Buchanan/Bridgman/Baroda: *Berrien County Record* — 109 Days Ave.; PO Box 191, Buchanan (49107); W; 1,918pd, 226fr (Sw); $5.35; publisher & editor Donald W Holmes; tel (616) 695-3878; fax (616) 695-3880

Byron Center: *Byron Center/Dorr Advance* — 2141 Port Sheldon Rd.; PO Box 9, Jenison (49429); Tu; 11pd, 7,889fr (Sw); $5.22; C; publisher Joel Holland; editor Mike Wyngarden; tel (616) 669-2700; fax (616) 669-1162

Caledonia: *Caledonia/Gaines Twp. Advance* — 2141 Port Sheldon Rd.; PO Box 9, Jenison (49429); Tu; 2pd, 7,273fr (Sw); $4.20; C; publisher Joel Holland; editor Mike Wyngarden; tel (616) 669-2700; fax (616) 669-1162

Camden: *Camden Publications* — 331 E. Bell St. (49232); W; 23,400pd (Sw); $6.95; publisher Kurt Greenhoe; editor John Snyder; tel (517) 368-0365; fax (517) 368-5131

Canton: *Canton Observer* — 744 Wing St., Plymouth (48170); M/Th; 848pd, 4,401fr (CAC); $87.86; C; publisher Banks Dishman; general manager Steve Pope; editor Jeff Counts; managing editor Susan Rosiek; tel (313) 459-2700; fax (313) 459-4224

Canton: *The Canton Eagle* — 35540 Michigan Ave.; PO Box 578, Wayne (48184); Th; 1,065pd, 8,000fr (Sw); $12.44; Su; 1,065pd, 6,705fr (Sw); $12.44; C; publisher Mike Wilcox; editor Joan Dyer-Zinner; tel (313) 729-4000; fax (313) 729-6088

Carson City/Crystal: *Carson City Gazette* — 211 W. Main St.; PO Box 820, Carson City (48811); M; 275pd, 8,939fr (Est); $4.15; C; publisher John Stafford; general manager John Norton; editor Barbara Sutherland; tel (517) 584-3967; fax (517) 584-3591

Cass City/Thumb: *Cass City Chronicle* — 6550 Main St.; PO Box 115, Cass City (48726); W; 3,504pd, 32fr (Sw); 16¢; publisher John Haire; general manager Clarke Haire; editor Tom Montgomery; tel (517) 872-2010; fax (517) 872-2010

Cassopolis/Vandalia: *Cassopolis Vigilant* — PO Box 128, Cassopolis (49031); Th; 1,164pd, 14fr (Sw); $4.65; publisher Thomas J Rattenbury; editor Jaime Courtney; tel (616) 445-2656; fax (616) 683-2175

Cedar Springs: *Cedar Springs Post* — 36 E. Maple St.; PO Box 370 (49319); Th; 6,000pd, 6,000fr (Est); $5.20; C; publisher Lois Allen; general manager Kim Blake; editor Terry Riggle; tel (616) 696-3655; fax (616) 696-9010

Central Lake/E Jordan/Ellsworth: *The Torch* — Corner Main & Maple St.; PO Box 575, Central Lake (49622); W; 1,000pd, 200fr (Sw); $2.70; C; publisher John Tarrant; general manager Jeff Hallberg; editor Deb Saygers Hobbs; tel (616) 544-2345; fax (616) 544-2408

Charlevoix: *Charlevoix Courier* — 112 Mason St.; PO Box 117 (49720); W; 1,747pd, 113fr (Sw); $20.02; C; publisher Kirk Shaller; general manager Ken Winter; editor Scott Swanson; tel (616) 547-6558; fax (616) 547-4992

Chelsea: *The Chelsea Standard* — 114 N. Main St. (48118); Th; 4,909pd, 75fr (Sw); $4.00; publisher & editor Brian Hamilton; tel (313) 475-1371; fax (313) 475-1413

Chesterfield/New Baltimore/Richmond: *The Chesterfield Review/The Review/Independent Press* — 68834 S. Main St., Richmond (48062); M; 225pd, 20,945fr (Est); $9.80; C; publisher John Johnson; general manager Alice Brandel; editors Jeff Payne & Jim Hopper; tel (810) 727-3745; fax (810) 727-3929

Clare: *The Clare Sentinel* — 112 W. 4th St.; PO Box 237 (48617); Tu; 110pd, 9,116fr (Sw); $7.00; publisher & editor Alfred R Bransdorfer; general manager Mary C Bransdorfer; tel (517) 386-9937; fax (517) 386-9938

Clare/Farwell: *Clare County Review* — 431 N. McEwan St., Clare (48617); Su; 110pd, 9,116fr (Sw); $7.00; publisher & editor Patricia Maurer; tel (517) 386-4414; fax (517) 386-2412

Clarkston: *Clarkston News* — 5 S. Main St. (48346); W; 4,355pd, 110fr (Sw); $7.70; C; publisher James A Sherman; editor Annette Kingsbury; tel (810) 625-3370

Clarksville: *Clarksville Record* — 129 Division, Freeport (49325); Th; 600pd (Est); $1.55; publishers & editors Christy Geiger & Ron Geiger; tel (616) 765-8511

Climax: *The Climax Crescent* — 150 N. Main St. (49034); F; 759pd, 52fr (Sw); 95¢; publisher & editor Bruce Rolfe; tel (616) 746-4331

Clinton: *The Clinton Local* — 108 Tecumseh St.; PO Box B (49236); Th; 2,000pd (Sw); 16¢; publisher & editor Maryann Habrick; tel (517) 456-4100; fax (517) 456-6372

Colon: *Colon Express* — 216 E. State St.; PO Box 816 (49040); W; 1,111pd, 27fr (Sw); $2.40; publisher & editor Skip Plath; tel (616) 432-3488

Croswell: *Sanilac Jeffersonian* — 14 Wells St. (48422); M; 695pd, 7,000fr (Sw); 32¢; C; publisher John D Johnson; editor Carol Seifferlein; tel (810) 679-4500; fax (810) 679-4504

Crystal Falls/Alpha/Amasa: *Diamond Drill* — 229 Superior Ave.; PO Box 150, Crystal Falls (49920); W; 3,215pd, 110fr (Sw); $3.75; publisher Rudolph Dalpra; editor Robert Dalpra; tel (906) 875-6633; fax (906) 875-3021

Davison: *Davison Index* — 220 N. Main St.; PO Box 100 (48423); W; 9,500pd (Est); $5.82; C; publisher James A Sherman Jr; editor Don Schelske; tel (810) 653-3511

Dearborn: *Dearborn Times-Herald* — 13730 Michigan Ave.; PO Box 706 (48126); W; 17,902pd, 1,250fr (Sw); $15.50; C; publisher Frank H Bewick; editor Thomas J Edwards; tel (313) 584-4000; fax (313) 584-1357

Dearborn/Dearborn Heights: *Press & Guide Newspapers* — 15340 Michigan Ave.; PO Box 484, Dearborn (48126); Th; 24,104pd, 19,948fr (Est); $32.10; C; publisher Robert A Riddell; managing editor Gary Woronchak; tel (313) 943-4250; fax (313) 846-5531

Dearborn Hghts./Dearborn: *Heights Times-Herald* — 13730 Michigan Ave.; PO Box 706, Dearborn (48126); W; 5,773pd, 1,106fr (Sw); $10.50; C; publisher Frank H Bewick; editor Thomas J Edwards; tel (313) 584-4000; fax (313) 584-1357

Decatur: *Decatur Republican* — 121 S. Phelps; PO Box 36 (49045); Th; 1,767pd, 49fr (Sw); 11¢; publisher & editor David D Moormann; tel (616) 423-2411

Deckerville/Carsonville: *The Deckerville Recorder* — 3520 Main St.; PO Box 519, Deckerville (48427); Tu; 1,324pd, 172fr (Sw); $2.50; publisher & editor Douglas Regentin; tel (810) 376-3805; fax (810) 376-4058

Detroit: *Detroit Monitor* — 33490 Groesbeck, Fraser (48026); Th; 47,000fr (Sw); $12.00; publisher Joseph R Zerilli; editor Horst Mann; tel (810) 296-6007; fax (810) 296-6072

DeWitt/Bath/Laingsburg: *DeWitt/Bath Review* — 215 N. Clinton Ave., St. Johns (48879); Su; 122pd, 7,970fr (Est); $5.76; C; publisher Pres Odette; general manager Pete Cantine; editor Al Wilson; tel (800) 544-4094; fax (517) 224-4452

Dexter: *The Dexter Leader* — 114 N. Main St., Chelsea (48118-1502); Th; 2,590pd, 48fr (Sw); $3.30; publisher & editor Brian Hamilton; tel (313) 475-1371; fax (313) 475-1413

Durand/Vernon/Bancroft/Bryon/Gaines: *Durand Express* — 219 N. Saginaw St.; PO Box 168, Durand (48429); Th; 2,122pd, 58fr (Sw); $5.50; C; publisher Owen A Rood; general manager John Pilmore; editor Bryan Myrkle; tel (517) 288-3164; fax (517) 288-4666

E Grand Rapids: *Cadence Newspaper* — 705 Bagley St. S.E. (49506); W; 3,000pd, 2,500fr (Est); $5.70; publisher Joel Holland; managing editor Mike Wyngarden; tel (616) 454-9456; fax (616) 454-4666

E Grand Rapids: *East Grand Rapids/Cadence Advance* — 2141 Port Sheldon Rd.; PO Box 9, Jension (49429); W; 1,081pd, 3,451fr (VAC); $7.44; C; publisher Joel Holland; editor Mike Wyngarden; tel (616) 669-2700; fax (616) 669-1162

E Jordan: *East Jordan Journal* — PO Box 405 (49727); W; 1,000pd (Est); $2.60; publisher John Tarrant; general manager Jeff Hallberg; editor Deb Saygers Hobbs; tel (616) 536-0044; fax (616) 533-6803

E Lansing/Haslett/Okemos: *Towne Courier* — 624 S. Cedar St.; PO Box 160, Mason (48854); Sa/Su; 4,480pd, 12,350fr (Sw); $10.00; C; publisher & editor Richard L Milliman II; tel (517) 676-9393; fax (517) 676-9402

E Michigan: *The Valley Farmer* — 905 S. Henry St., Bay City (48706); Th; 1,975pd, 198fr (Sw); $4.30; publisher David Hebert; editor Mark Schanhals; tel (517) 893-6507

E Tawas/Tawas City: *Iosco County News Herald* — 101 W. State St.; PO Box 72, East Tawas (48730); W; 7,770pd, 25fr (Sw); $4.62; C; publisher J Berkeley Smith; editor Neal R Miller; tel (517) 362-3456; fax (517) 362-6601

Edwardsburg: *Edwardsburg Argus* — PO Box 128, Cassopolis (49031); Th; 820pd, 10fr (Sw); $4.65; publisher Thomas J Rattenbury; editor Jamie Courtney; tel (616) 663-6085; fax (616) 683-2175

Elk Rapids/Antrim: *Town Meeting* — 212 River St.; PO Box 335, Elk Rapids (49629-0335); W; 1,850pd, 40fr (Sw); $2.70; C; publisher John G Tarrant; editor Amy Whitaker; tel (616) 264-9711; fax (616) 264-5191

Evart: *Evart Review* — 125 N. Main St. (49631); W; 1,505pd, 12fr (Sw); $3.50; publisher John A Batdorff; general manager John A Batdorff II; editor Jim Crees; managing editor Jim Bruskotter; tel (616) 734-5587; fax (616) 734-2123

Farmington: *Farmington Observer* — 36251 Schoolcraft Rd. (48150); PO Box 2428, Birmingham (48151); M/Th; 2,136pd, 8,611fr (CAC); $87.68; C; publisher Phil Power; general manager Steven Pope; editor Susan Rosiek; managing editor Robert Sklar; tel (313) 591-2300; fax (313) 591-7279

Fennville: *The Fennville Edition of Allegan County News* — 235 North St.; PO Box 189, Allegan (49010); Th; 1,261pd (Est); $4.14; publisher & editor Cheryl Kaechele; editor Allan Bassler; tel (616) 673-5534; fax (616) 673-5535

Fenton: *The Independent* — 2141 Port Sheldon Rd., Jenison (49428); Th; 75pd, 10,588fr (VAC); 33¢; publisher Joel Holland; editor Dennis Setter; tel (810) 733-2239; fax (810) 733-2688

Fowlerville: *The Fowlerville Review* — 323 E. Grand River Ave., Howell (48843); W; 6,772fr (CAC); $4.72; publisher Phil Power; general manager Richard Perlberg; editor Maria Stuart; managing editor Buddy Moorehouse; tel (517) 548-2000; fax (517) 548-3005

Frankenmuth: *Frankenmuth News* — 231 Hubinger; PO Box 252 (48734); W; 4,950pd, 25fr (Sw); $4.48; publisher Steven Grainger; general manager Gretchen Rau; editor Scott Wenzel; tel (517) 652-3246; fax (517) 652-3247

Frankfort: *The Benzie County Record-Patriot* — 417 Main St.; PO Box 673 (49635); W; 3,998pd, 102fr (Sw); $4.00; C; publisher Terence J Fitzwater; editor Roland Halliday; tel (616) 352-9659; fax (616) 352-7874

Freeport: *Freeport News* — 129 Division St.; PO Box 25 (49325); Th; 688pd (Est); $8.57; publishers & editors Christy Geiger & Ron Geiger; tel (616) 765-8511

Fremont: *Fremont Times-Indicator* — 44 W. Main St.; PO Box 7 (49412); W; 10,000pd (Est); 25¢; publisher & editor Richard C Wheater; tel (616) 924-4400; fax (616) 924-4066

Garden City: *Garden City Observer* — 36251 Schoolcraft Rd. (48150); PO Box 2428, Livonia (48151); M/Th; 548pd, 4,155fr (CAC); $87.86; C; publisher Phil Power; general manager Steven Pope; editor Susan Rosiek; managing editor Robert Sklar; tel (313) 591-2300; fax (313) 591-7279

Gaylord: *Gaylord Herald Times* — 2066 S. US 27; PO Box 598 (49735); Th; 7,010pd, 140fr (Sw); $8.31; C; publisher James L Grisso; editor Chris Jenkins; tel (517) 732-1111; fax (517) 732-3490

Gladwin/Beaverton: *Gladwin County Record* — 700 E. Cedar Ave.; PO Box 425, Gladwin (48624); W; 7,242pd, 60fr (Sw); $5.75; publisher & editor Ronald A Przystas; tel (517) 426-9411; fax (517) 426-2023

Grand Ledge: *The Grand Ledge Independent* — 219 S. Bridge St. (48837); Tu; 388pd, 8,466fr (CAC); $6.15; C; publisher Lee Beam; managing editor Michelle Rabidoux; tel (517) 627-6085; fax (517) 627-3497

Grand Rapids: *Grand Rapids Advance* — 2141 Port Sheldon Rd.; PO Box 9, Jenison (49429); Tu; 56pd, 12,035fr (VAC); $7.74; C; publisher Joel Holland; editor Mike Wyngarden; tel (616) 669-2700; fax (616) 669-1162

Grass Lake: *The News* — 1220 Francis St.; PO Box 806, Jackson (49204); Tu; 2,681pd (Est); 50¢; publisher & editor Ben Wade; editor Patricia Reithmiller; tel (517) 787-0450

Grayling/Crawford Co.: *Crawford County Avalanche* — 102 Michigan Ave.; PO Box 490, Grayling (49738); Th; 4,810pd, 65fr (Sw); 25¢; publisher Howard Madsen; general manager Linda Golnick; editor Terry Wright; tel (517) 348-6811; fax (517) 348-6806

Grosse Ile Twp./Wayne: *Ile Camera* — 8801 Macomb St.; PO Box 233, Grosse Ile (48138); F; 3,181pd, 105fr (Sw); $6.30; publisher Fredrick G Manuel; editor Michael Raveane; managing editor Karl Ziomek; tel (313) 676-0515; fax (313) 676-0638

Grosse Pointe: *Grosse Pointe News* — 96 Kercheval Ave., Grosse Pointe Farms (48236); Th; 17,045pd (ABC); $13.69; publisher Robert G Edgar; editor John Minnis; tel (313) 882-3500; fax (313) 882-1585

Hamtramck/Warren: *The Citizen* — 11901 Jos. Campau, Hamtramck (48212); Th; 10,055pd, 150fr (Est); $11.50; publisher Karen Spang; editor Charles Sercombe; tel (313) 365-9500

Harbor Beach: *The Harbor Beach Times* — 123 N. 1st St. (48441); Th; 3,200pd (Est); 90¢; publisher & editor Mike Murphy; tel (517) 479-3605; fax (517) 479-9697

Harbor Springs: *Harbor Light* — 211 E. 3rd St. (49740); W; 1,568pd, 43fr (Sw); $8.90; C; publisher Kevin O'Neill; general manager & editor Charles O'Neill; tel (616) 526-2191; fax (616) 526-7634

Hart/Shelby: *Oceana's Herald Journal* — 123 State St.; PO Box 190, Hart (49420); Th; 6,575pd, 275fr (Sw); $7.65; C; publisher Richard Lound; editor Mary Sanford; tel (616) 873-5620; fax (616) 873-4775

Hastings: *The Hastings Banner* — 1952 N. Broadway; PO Box B (49058); Th; 8,000pd, 54fr (Est); $2.55; C; publisher Melvin F Jacobs; general manager Frederic J Jacobs; editor David T Young; tel (616) 948-8051; fax (616) 945-5192

Holly: *Northwest Oakland County Herald Advertiser* — 4048 Grange Hall Rd. (48442); Th; 12,000fr (Est); 24¢; publisher & editor Alan C Campbell; tel (810) 634-8219

Homer/Litchfield: *The Homer Index* — 122 E. Main St., Homer (49245); W; 1,754pd, 40fr (Sw); $2.90; publisher & editor Mike Warner; publisher & general manager Sharon Warner; tel (517) 568-4646; fax (517) 568-4346

Houghton Lake/Roscommon: *The Houghton Lake Resorter* — 4049 W. Houghton Lake Dr.; PO Box 248, Houghton Lake (48629); Th; 7,879pd, 55fr (Sw); $5.27; publisher & editor Thomas W Hamp; tel (517) 366-5341; fax (517) 366-4472

Howell: *The Livingston County Press* — 323 E. Grand River Ave. (48843); W; 13,769pd, 80fr (CAC); $11.74; C; publisher Phil Power; general manager Richard Perlberg; editor Maria Stuart; managing editor Buddy Moorehouse; tel (517) 548-2000; fax (517) 548-3005

Imlay City: *Tri-City Times* — PO Box 278 (48444); W; 5,771pd, 1,229fr (Est); 27¢; publishers Delores Heim & Martin Heim; general manager Randy Jorgensen; editor Cathy Barringer Rourke; tel (810) 724-2615; fax (810) 724-8552

Indian River: *Straitsland Resorter* — 3691 Club Rd.; PO Box 579 (49749); Th; 3,130pd, 65fr (Sw); $3.80; publisher Joan J Hoffman; tel (616) 238-7362

Inkster: *The Inkster Ledger-Star* — 35540 Michigan Ave.; PO Box 578, Wayne (48184); Th; 1,580pd, 1,607fr (Sw); $12.24; Su; 1,580pd, 1,607fr (CAC); $12.24; publisher Mike Wilcox; editor Joan Dyer-Zinner; tel (313) 729-4000; fax (313) 729-6088

Iron Co.: *Iron River Reporter* — 801 W. Adams; PO Box 311, Iron River (49935); W; 4,640pd, 145fr (Est); $4.45; C; general manager Jay Barry; managing editor Ed Erikson III; tel (906) 265-9927; fax (906) 265-5755

Ithaca/St. Louis/Gratiot Co.: *Gratiot County Herald* — 123 N. Main St.; PO Box 10, Ithaca (48847); Th; 5,666pd, 168fr (Sw); $6.65; C; publisher Tom MacDonald; editor Randy Williams; tel (517) 875-4151; fax (517) 875-3159

Jenison/Grandville: *Grand Valley Advance* — 2141 Port Sheldon Rd.; PO Box 9, Jenison (49429); Tu; 6,131pd, 17,069fr (VAC); $9.36; C; publisher Joel Holland; editor Mike Wyngarden; tel (616) 669-2700; fax (616) 669-1162

Jonesville: *Jonesville Independent* — 253 E. Chicago St.; PO Box 96 (49250); W; 790pd, 73fr (Sw); $2.50; C; publisher & editor Scott D McGraw; managing editor Doug Olson; tel (517) 849-9880; fax (514) 849-7401

Kalkaska: *Kalkaska Leader & Kalkaskian* — 318 N. Cedar (49646); W; 4,075pd (Sw); $6.16; C; publisher John G Tarrant; general manager Jeffrey Hallberg; editor Sharon Coppock; tel (616) 258-4600

Kentwood: *Kentwood Advance* — 2141 Port Sheldon Rd., Jenison (49429); Tu; 60pd, 15,183fr (VAC); $8.46; C; publisher Joel Holland; editor Mike Wyngarden; tel (616) 669-2700; fax (616) 669-1162

Kinross/Pickford/Rudyard/Cedarville/Hessel/De Tour/Stalwart/Barbeau/Goetzville: *The Community Voice* — 348 Davis Ct., Kincheloe (49788); Th; 80pd, 5,100fr (Sw); $6.00; C; publisher & editor Jim MacLaren; general manager Barb MacLaren; tel (906) 495-5207; fax (906) 495-5604

Lake City/Missaukee Co.: *Waterfront of Missaukee County Inc.* — 101 N. Main St.; PO Box U, Lake City (49651); Tu; 2,663pd, 96fr (Est); $4.70; publisher & editor Robert C Redman; tel (616) 839-4315; fax (616) 839-4994

Lake Co.: *Lake County Star* — 851 S. Michigan Ave., PO Box 399, Baldwin (49304); Th; 2,446pd, 76fr (Sw); $3.35; publisher John (Jack) A Batdorff; general manager John Batdorff II; editor Kathy Carper; managing editor Judy Hale; tel (616) 745-4635; fax (616) 745-7733

Lakeview: *Lakeview Enterprise* — 327 Lincoln Ave.; PO Box 500 (48850); W; 1,370pd, 12fr (Sw); $3.50; C; publisher John (Jack) A Batdorff; general manager John A Batdorff II; editor Mike K Taylor; managing editor Jim Bruskotter; tel (517) 352-6026; fax (517) 352-8210

Lapeer: *The County Press* — 1521 Imlay City Rd.; PO Box 220 (48446); W; 17,040pd (ABC); $17.79; Su; 14,834pd (ABC); $17.79; C; publisher Ernest E Slade; editor Mark Haney; tel (810) 664-0811; fax (810) 664-5852

Leelanau Co.: *The Leelanau Enterprise and Tribune* — 112 Chandler St.; PO Box 527, Leland (49654); Th; 7,646pd, 25fr (Sw); $5.90; publisher & editor R C Kerr; managing editor W O'Brien; tel (616) 256-9827

Leslie/Rives/Tompkin/Onondaga/Bunkerhill: *Leslie Local Independent* — 109 Carney St.; PO Box 617, Leslie (49251); Tu; 1,800pd (Est); $3.97; publisher S-G Publications Inc.; general manager Joan Hill; editor Larry Hook Jr; tel (517) 589-8228; fax (517) 589-8526

Lincoln Park/Southgate/Ecorse: *The Lincoln Park/Southgate/Ecorse/River Rouge News-Herald* — 1 Heritage Pl., Ste. 100, Southgate (48195); W; 14,769pd, 8,619fr (Est); $51.80; Su; 13,952pd, 1,420fr (Est); $51.80; C; publisher Fredrick G Manuel; editor Karl Ziomek; tel (313) 246-0800; fax (313) 284-2028

Livonia: *Livonia Observer* — 744 Wing St., Plymouth (48170); M/Th; 16,615pd, 10,102fr (CAC); $87.86; C; publisher Banks Dishman; general manager Steven Pope; editor Jeff Counts; managing editor Susan Rosiek; tel (313) 459-2700; fax (313) 459-4224

Lowell: *Lowell Ledger* — 105 N. Broadway; PO Box 128 (49331); W; 2,500pd, 200fr (Est); $2.62; publisher Roger Brown; editor Thad Kraus; tel (616) 897-9261; fax (616) 897-4809

Manchester: *The Manchester Enterprise* — 109 E. Main St.; PO Box 37 (48158); Th; 1,800pd, 60fr (Sw); 31¢; publisher & editor Emory W Garlick; general manager T M Benedict; managing editor M Chartrand; tel (313) 428-8173; fax (313) 428-9044

Manistee: *Manistee Observer* — 75 Maple St.; PO Box 317 (49660); Su; 1,200pd, 16,500fr (Sw); $6.00; C; publisher Terence J Fitzwater; editor Ken Grabowski; tel (616) 723-3592; fax (616) 723-4733

Manistique/Schoolcraft Co.: *Pioneer-Tribune* — 212 Walnut St., Manistique (49854); Th; 3,800pd, 60fr (Sw); $2.86; publisher & editor Leanne C Trebilcock; tel (906) 341-5200

Marcellus: *Marcellus News* — 149 E. Main St.; PO Box 277 (49067); Th; 1,387pd (Est); 11¢; publisher & editor Donald Moormann; tel (616) 646-2101

Marion: *The Marion Press* — 108 E. Main St.; PO Box D (49665); W; 1,941pd, 10fr (Sw); 14¢; publisher & editor James D Blevins; general manager Sheron Wonsey; tel (616) 743-2481; fax (616) 743-9501

Marlette: *The Marlette Leader* — 3051 Main St.; PO Box 338 (48453); W; 1,948pd, 10fr (Sw); $5.35; publisher H Allen Wamsley; editor John Frazier; tel (517) 635-2435; fax (517) 635-3769

Marysville/St. Clair: *Blue Water Voice* — 242 S. Water St., Marine City (48039); W; 11,400fr (Est); $9.00; C; publisher Voice Communications Corp.; general manager Joseph Stabile; editor Donna Remer; tel (810) 765-4059; fax (810) 765-1166

Marysville/St. Clair: *Downriver Voice* — 31950 23 Mile Rd.; PO Box 760, Marine City (48059); W; 11,400fr (Est); $9.00; C; publisher Voice Communications Corp.; general manager Joe Stabile; editor Donna Remer; tel (810) 949-7900; fax (810) 949-2217

Marysville/St. Clair: *Macomb Voice* — 31950 23 Mile Rd.; PO Box 760, New Baltimore (48047); W; 4,000pd (Est); $8.10; C; publisher Voice Communications Inc.; general manager Joseph Stabile; editor Donna Remer; tel (810) 949-7900; fax (810) 949-2217

Mason/Ingham/Dansville/Holt/Lansing: *Ingham County News* — 624 S. Cedar; PO Box 160, Mason (48854); W; 2,250pd (Sw); $6.00; C; publisher & editor Richard L Milliman II; tel (517) 676-9393; fax (517) 676-9402

Mayville/Fostoria/Silverwood: *Mayville Monitor* — 6071 Fulton St.; PO Box 299, Mayville (48744-0299); Th; 1,268pd (Sw); $3.50; publisher & managing editor Debra Langford; publisher & editor Gale Langford; tel (517) 843-6441; fax (517) 843-0054

Middleville/Caledonia: *The Sun & News* — 1952 N. Broadway; PO Box 188, Hastings (49058); Tu; 148pd, 8,000fr (Est); $3.50; C; publisher R G Edgar; editor David T Young; tel (616) 945-9554; fax (616) 945-5192

Milan: *The Milan Area Leader* — 37 E. Main St.; PO Box 17 (48160); W; 2,668pd, 101fr (Sw); 26¢; publisher & general manager & managing editor Glenna Jones; editor Warren Hale; tel (313) 439-8118; fax (313) 439-8150

Milford: *Milford Times* — 405 N. Main St.; PO Box 339 (48381); Th; 5,623pd, 103fr (Sw); $8.83; C; publisher & editor Frank J Eichenlaub; general manager Richard Perlberg; tel (810) 685-1507; fax (810) 685-2892

Minden City: *The Minden City Herald* — 1524 Main St. (48456); Th; 1,500pd (Est); 70¢; publisher & editor Paul Engel; tel (517) 864-3630; fax (517) 864-5363

Morenci: *Morenci Observer* — 120 North St. (49256); W; 2,479pd, 74fr (Sw); $4.10; publisher & editor David G Green; tel (517) 458-6811

Mt. Clemens: *The Clinton-Fraser-Mt. Clemens-Macomb-Harrison Advisor* — 48075 Van Dyke; PO Box 168, Utica (48317); Tu; 100,860fr (CAC); $28.25; C; publisher Wayne Oehmke; editor Don Chamberlain; tel (810) 731-1000; fax (810) 731-8172

Mt. Morris/Clio: *Genesee County Herald* — G10098 N. Dort Hwy.; PO Box 127, Mount Morris (48458); W; 1,009pd, 134fr (Sw); $5.85; publishers Jeffery C Harrington & Michael J Harrington; editor Stephen Lee; tel (810) 686-3840; fax (810) 686-9181

Munising/Alger Co.: *The Munising News* — 113 W. Superior St.; PO Box 38, Munising (49862); W; 3,020pd, 42fr (Sw); $4.17; C; publishers Esley Mattson & John Williams; editor Verl Dan Wilson; tel (810) 387-3282

Nashville/Vermontville: *Maple Valley News* — 1952 N. Broadway; PO Box 188, Hastings (49058); Tu; 148pd, 3,200fr (Est); $2.20; C; publisher R G Edgar; managing editor David T Young; tel (616) 945-9554; fax (616) 945-5192

New Baltimore: *The Bay Voice* — 31950 23 Mile Rd.; PO Box 760 (48047); W; 24,600fr (Est); $12.90; C; publisher Voice Communications Corp.; general manager Joseph Stabile; editor Donna Remer; tel (810) 949-7900; fax (810) 949-2217

New Buffalo/Bridgman/Chikaming/Michiana: *New Buffalo Times* — 102 S. Whittaker; PO Box 369, New Buffalo (49117); W; 6,000pd (Est); $5.00; publisher & editor Mary Beth Moriarty; general manager Tarena Adams; tel (616) 469-1100; fax (616) 469-4812

New Buffalo/Three Oaks: *Harbor County News* — 122 N. Whittaker St., New Buffalo (49117); Th; 10,500fr (Est); $5.00; publisher Don J Manaher; editor Phyllis Kelly; tel (616) 469-1410; fax (616) 469-3029

Newberry: *The Newberry News* — 316 Newberry Ave.; PO Box 46 (49868); W; 3,450pd, 35fr (Sw); $2.30; publisher & editor Nancy Diem; tel (810) 293-8401; fax (810) 293-8815

N Macomb Co.: *The Countryman* — 124 W. St. Clair; PO Box 96, Romeo (48065-0096); W; 5,906pd, 7,125fr (VAC); $7.55; C; publisher & editor Melvin E Bleich; tel (810) 752-3524

N Macomb Co.: *The Romeo Observer* — 124 W. St. Clair; PO Box 96, Romeo (48065-0096); W; 5,779pd, 545fr (ABC); $7.55; C; publisher & editor Melvin E Bleich; tel (810) 752-3524

Northeast/Grand Rapids: *Northfield Advance* — 2141 Post Sheldon Rd.; PO Box 9, Jenison (49429); W; 82pd, 19,406fr (VAC); $8.58; C; publisher Joel Holland; editor Mike Wyngarden; managing editor Len Lazrick; tel (616) 669-2700; fax (616) 669-1162

Northern Oakland Co./SE Genesee Co./SW Lapeer: *Reminder Newspapers* — 48 South St., Ste. 101; PO Box 560, Ortonville (48462); Th; 68,610pd, 46,743fr (Est); $73.75; Su; 3,947pd, 6,239fr (Est); $8.75; C; general manager Kerry Davis; editor Allan P Adler; tel (810) 627-2843; fax (810) 627-3473

Norway: *Norway Current* — 723 Main St.; PO Box 66 (49870); W; 1,500pd (Sw); $3.00; C; publisher L A Underhill; editor Vicki Underhill; tel (906) 563-5212; fax (906) 563-5904

Onaway: *Onaway Outlook* — Washington Ave.; PO Box 176 (49765); W; 2,300pd, 61fr (Est); $1.25; publisher Richard Milliman; editor Joe Hefele; tel (517) 733-6543

Ontonagon: *The Ontonagon Herald* — 326 River St.; PO Box 98 (49953); W; 3,475pd, 70fr (Sw); $4.50; publisher & editor Maureen Guzek; tel (906) 884-2826; fax (906) 884-2939

Orion Twp.: *The Lake Orion Review* — 666 S. Lapeer Rd.; PO Box 108, Oxford (48371); W; 3,257pd, 28fr (Est); 25¢; C; publisher James A Sherman; editor Brad Kadrich; tel (810) 628-4801; fax (810) 628-9750

Oscoda: *Oscoda Press* — 310 S. State; PO Box 663 (48750); W; 5,900pd (Sw); $3.65; C; publisher J Berkeley Smith; tel (517) 739-2054; fax (517) 739-3201

Otsego/Plainwell: *The Union Enterprise* — 352 12th St.; PO Box 417, Plainwell (49080); C; publisher & managing editor Cheryl Kaechele; editor Allan Bassler; tel (616) 685-9571/5985

Owosso/Durand/Chesaning: *Independent Advisor* — 1907 W. M-21, Owosso (48867); Su; 38,529fr (Sw); $11.20; C; publisher Michael Flores; editor Bill Constine; tel (517) 723-1118; fax (517) 725-1834

Oxford: *Oxford Leader* — 666 S. Lapeer Rd.; PO Box 108 (48371); W; 3,513pd, 36fr (Sw); $4.40; C; publisher James A Sherman Jr; editor Brad Kadrich; tel (810) 628-4801; fax (810) 628-9550

Parma/Concord/Hanover/Horton/Spring Arbor/Sandstone/Pulaski/Tompkins: *West County Press* — 123 W. Main; PO Box 279, Parma (49269); W; 1,480pd, 20fr (Est); $2.35; publisher Matt Schepeler; editor Ed Freumbl; tel (517) 531-4542; fax (517) 531-3576

Paw Paw: *Courier-Leader* — 32280 E. Red Arrow Hwy.; PO Box 129 (49079); F; 4,131pd (Sw); $2.50; C; publisher & editor Felix A Racette; general manager Steven A Racette; tel (616) 657-3072; fax (616) 657-5723

Perry/Morrice/Shiftsburg: *Shiwassee County Journal* — 130 N. Main St.; PO Box 107, Perry (48872); Th; 1,018pd, 33fr (Sw); $5.50; C; publisher Owen A Rood; general manager John Pilmore; editor Bryan Merkle; tel (517) 625-3181; fax (517) 288-4666

Pigeon/Sebewaing: *The Newsweekly* — 7232 E. Michigan Ave.; PO Box 589, Pigeon (48755); Tu; 6,044pd, 591fr (Sw); $4.60; C; publisher & editor Mark W Rummel; tel (517) 453-3100; fax (517) 453-3877

Pinckney: *Pinckney Post* — 323 E. Grand River Ave. (48843); PO Box 230, Howell (48843-0230); W; 8,008fr (CAC); $4.72; publisher Roland Peterson; general manager Rich Perlberg; editor Buddy Moorehouse; tel (517) 548-2000; fax (517) 548-3005

Plymouth: *Plymouth Observer* — 744 Wing St. (48170); M/Th; 5,00pd, 3,557fr (CAC); $87.86; C; publisher Banks Dishman; general manager Steven Pope; editor Jeff Counts; managing editor Susan Rosiek; tel (313) 459-2700; fax (313) 459-4224

Plymouth/Canton: *The Community Crier* — 821 Penniman Ave., Plymouth (48170-1624); W; 5,203pd, 14,192fr (Sw); $26.11; publisher W Edward Wendover; editor Rob Kirkbride; tel (313) 453-6900

Portland: *Portland Review and Observer* — 1138 Grand River Ave.; PO Box 349 (48875); M; 122pd, 6,114fr (Sw); $5.95; C; publisher Lee Beam; editor Nan Simons; tel (800) 646-6397; fax (517) 627-3497

Redford: *Redford Observer* — 36251 Schoolcraft Rd. (48150); PO Box 2428, Livonia (48151); M/Th; 7,598pd, 4,097fr (CAC); $87.86; C; publisher Phil Power; general manager Steven Pope; editor Susan Rosiek; managing editor Robert Sklar; tel (313) 591-2300; fax (313) 591-7279

Reed City: *Reed City Herald News* — 101 W. Slosson; PO Box 117 (49677); Th; 2,065pd, 30fr (Sw); $3.50; publisher John (Jack) A Batdorff; general manager John Batdorff II; editor David Barber; managing editor Jim Bruskotter; tel (616) 832-5566; fax (616) 832-5558

Richmond/Armada/Memphis: *The North Macomb Voice* — 69089 Main St., Richmond (48062); W; 9,636fr (Est); $8.10; C; general manager Joseph Stabile; editor Donna Remer; tel (810) 727-7558; fax (810) 727-4413

Rochester: *The Rochester Eccentric* — 36251 Schoolcraft Rd. (48150); PO Box 2428, Livonia (48151); M/Th; 3,570pd, 7,316fr (CAC); $87.86; C; publisher Phil Power; general manager Steven Pope; editor Susan Rosiek; managing editor Robert Sklar; tel (313) 591-2300; fax (313) 591-7279

Rochester/Rochester Hills: *The Rochester Clarion* — 313 Main St.; PO Box 9, Rochester (48307); Th; 10,000pd (Sw); $14.45; C; publisher Donald R Seed; editor Greg Normand; tel (810) 651-4141; fax (810) 651-8243

Rockford: *Rockford Squire* — 51 E. Bridge St. (49341); Th; 6,700fr (Est); $5.70; C; publisher Roger C Allen; general manager Kathy Thomas; editor Todd Halterman; tel (616) 866-4465; fax (616) 866-3810

Rockford/Belmont: *Rockford/Cedar Springs Advance* — 2141 Port Sheldon Rd.; PO Box 9, Jenison (49429); Tu; 94pd, 13,534fr (VAC); $6.00; C; publisher Joel Holland; editor Mike Wyngarden; managing editor Len Lazrick; tel (810) 669-2700; fax (810) 669-1162

Rogers City: *Presque Isle County Advance* — 104 S. 3rd St.; PO Box 50 (49779); Th; 4,200pd (Est); $5.00; C; publisher Richard L Milliman; general manager & editor Richard W Lamb; tel (517) 734-2105; fax (517) 734-3053

Romeo: *The Romeo-Washington Bruce Advisor* — 48075 Van Dyke; PO Box 168, Utica (48317); Tu; 5,540fr (CAC); $10.85; C; publisher Wayne Oehmke; editor Don Chamberlain; tel (810) 731-1000; fax (810) 731-8172

Romulus: *The Romulus Roman* — 35540 W. Michigan Ave.; PO Box 578, Wayne (48184); Th/Su; 1,674pd, 1,312fr (Sw); $12.24; C; publisher Mike Wilcox; editor Joan Dyer-Ziner; tel (313) 729-4000; fax (313) 729-6088

Roscommon: *The Roscommon County Herald-News* — 905 Lake St.; PO Box 8 (48653); Su; 14,000pd (Est); $5.25; C; publisher Robert Edward Perlberg; editor Phil Bendily; managing editor Cindy Gibbs; tel (517) 275-5100; fax (517) 275-5449

Saginaw: *The Saginaw Press* — 410 Hancock St.; PO Box 1836 (48605-1836); F; 567pd, 5fr (Sw); $4.48; publisher Saginaw Publishing Co.; editor George W Baxter III; tel (517) 793-8070; fax (517) 793-7225

Saginaw/Thomas James Twps.: *The Township Times* — 2089 Wieneke Rd., Saginaw (48603); W; 4,100pd, 88fr (Sw); $8.25; C; publishers Daniel Lea & Ed Belles; managing editor Robert Grnak; tel (517) 799-3200; fax (517) 799-7085

St. Clair Shores/Roseville: *St. Clair Shores-Roseville-East Detroit Advisor* — 48075 Van Dyke; PO Box 168, Utica (48318); Tu; 100,860fr (CAC); $18.10; C; publisher Wayne Oehmke; editor Don Chamberlain; tel (810) 731-1000; fax (810) 731-8172

St. Clair Shores/Roseville: *The Connection* — 96 Kercheval Ave., Grosse Pointe (48236); Th; 35,127fr (Est); $16.62; C; publisher Robert G Edgar; editor John Minnis; tel (313) 882-0294; fax (313) 882-1585

St. Ignace/Mackinac: *The St. Ignace News* — 359 Reagon St.; PO Box 277, St. Ignace (49781); Th; 6,159pd, 98fr (Sw); $6.86; publisher & editor Wesley H Maurer Jr; general manager Richard M Hayden; tel (810) 643-9150; fax (818) 643-9122

St. Johns: *Clinton County News* — 215 N. Clinton Ave., St. Johns (48879); Su; 245pd, 12,018fr (Sw); $8.06; C; publisher Pres Odette; general manager Pete Cantine; editor Al Wilson; tel (800) 544-4094; fax (517) 224-4452

Saline/Milan: *The Saline Reporter* — 106 W. Michigan Ave., Saline (48176); W; 4,385pd, 125fr (Sw); $5.65; C; publisher Fred Manuel; editor Thomas S Kirvan; tel (313) 429-7380; fax (313) 429-3621

Sanilac Co.: *Sanilac County News* — 432 S. Sandusky Rd., Sandusky (48471); Tu/W; 9,000pd, 16,000fr (Sw); $7.25; C; publisher John D Johnson; editor Eric Levine; tel (810) 648-4000; fax (810) 648-4002

Saugatuck: *The Commercial Record* — 790 Lake St.; PO Box 246 (49453); Th; 1,915pd,

102fr (Sw); $4.14; C; publisher Cheryl Kaechele; editor Donita Hunt; tel (616) 857-2570; fax (616) 857-4637

Sheperd/Isabella/Gratiot: *The Shepherd Argus* — 213 W. Wright Ave.; PO Box 459, Shepherd (48883); W; 2,000pd (Est); $4.50; publisher George E Grim; general manager John A Grim; editor Geraldine Grim; tel (517) 828-6360; fax (517) 828-5361

S Lyon: *South Lyon Herald* — 101 N. Lafayette (48178); Th; 5,125pd, 33fr (CAC); $8.06; C; publisher Rich Perlberg; editor Rick Byrne; tel (810) 437-2011; fax (810) 437-9460

Southfield: *Southfield Eccentric* — 36251 Schoolcraft Rd. (48150); PO Box 2428, Livonia (48151); M/Th; 5,548pd, 6,798fr (CAC); $87.86; C; publisher Phil Power; general manager Steven Pope; editor Susan Rosiek; managing editor Robert Sklar; tel (313) 591-2300; fax (313) 591-7279

Southgate: *The News-Herald Newspapers* — 1 Heritage Pl., Ste. 100 (48195); W; 57,309pd, 31,096fr (Est); $51.80; Su; 51,069pd, 6,492fr (Est); $51.80; C; publisher Fredrick G Manuel; editor Karl Ziomek; tel (313) 246-0828; fax (313) 284-2028

SW Berrien Co.: *Southcounty Gazette* — 505 W. Locust; PO Box 303, Three Oaks (49128); Th; 1,661pd, 38fr (Sw); $4.00; C; publisher Michael Hojnacki; editor Marisue Hojnacki; tel (616) 756-2421; fax (616) 756-7220

Sparta/Kent City: *Sparta/Kent City Advance* — 2141 Port Sheldon Rd.; PO Box 9, Jenison (49429); Tu; 28pd, 11,917fr (Sw); $4.98; C; publisher Joel Holland; editor Mike Wyngarden; managing editor Len Lazrick; tel (810) 669-2700; fax (810) 669-1162

Springport: *Springport Signal* — 104 Maple St.; PO Box 157 (49284); Th; 200pd, 2,000fr (Est); $2.66; publisher & editor Robert A Doner; tel (517) 857-2500; fax (517) 857-2887

Sterling Hts./Utica: *Sterling Heights/Utica/Shelby Source Newspaper* — 48075 Van Dyke; PO Box 168, Utica (48317); W/Su; 159pd, 50,984fr (CAC); $24.85; C; publisher Wayne Oehmke; editor Don Chamberlain; tel (810) 731-1000; fax (810) 731-8172

Stockbridge/Munith/Leslie: *The Town Crier* — 510 Water St.; PO Box 548, Stockbridge (49285); Tu; 1,706pd, 20fr (Est); $5.00; publisher Charlotte Camp; general manager Mary Bachman; editor Ruth Wellman; tel (517) 851-7833; fax (517) 851-4641

Taylor/Romulus: *The Taylor/Romulus News-Herald* — 1 Heritage Pl., Ste. 100, Southgate (48195); W; 10,325pd, 5,996fr (Est); $51.80; Su; 8,961pd, 1,477fr (Est); $51.80; C; publisher Fredrick G Manuel; editor Karl Ziomek; tel (313) 246-0800; fax (313) 284-2028

Tecumseh: *The Tecumseh Herald* — 110 E. Logan St.; PO Box 218 (49286); Th; 5,060pd, 30fr (Sw); 32¢; publisher James C Lincoln; editor James L Lincoln Jr; tel (517) 423-2174; fax (517) 423-6258

Troy: *The Troy Eccentric* — 36251 Schoolcraft Rd. (48150); PO Box 2428, Livonia (48151); M/Th; 4,510pd, 6,133fr (CAC); $87.86; C; publisher Phil Power; general manager Steven Pope; editor Susan Roseik; managing editor Robert Sklar; tel (313) 591-2300; fax (313) 591-7279

Tuscola Co.: *The Vassar Pioneer Times* — 113 S. Main St.; PO Box 69, Vassar (48768); W; 1,257pd, 16fr (Est); $4.71; publisher H Allen Wamsley; editor Sandy Walker; tel (517) 823-8579; fax (517) 823-8778

Tuscola Co.: *Tuscola County Advertiser* — 344 N. State St.; PO Box 106, Caro (48723); W; 9,222pd, 16fr (Sw); $5.96; C; publisher Brett McLaughlin; editor Dean Bohn; tel (517) 673-3181; fax (517) 673-5662

Union City: *Register-Tribune* — 314 N. Broadway St.; PO Box 8 (49094); Th; 1,236pd, 76fr (Sw); $3.00; C; publisher & editor Scott D McGraw; managing editor Doug C Olson; tel (517) 741-8451

Union Lake/Oakland Co.: *Spinal Column Newsweekly* — 7196 Cooley Lake Rd.; PO Box 14, Union Lake (48387-0014); W; 35,185fr (Sw); $1.07; publisher James W Fancy; editor Tim Dmoch; tel (810) 360-6397; fax (810) 360-4711

Upper Peninsula of MI: *Porcupine Press* — PO Box 200, Chatham (49816); W; 4,350pd (Sw); $5.75; publisher & editor Michael J Van Den Branden; tel (906) 439-5111; fax (906) 439-5337

Vicksburg/Schoolcraft: *The Commercial Express* — 109 S. Main St.; PO Box 154, Vicksburg (49097); W; 2,000pd (Sw); $3.86; C; publisher & editor Jan Rabbers; tel (616) 649-2333; fax (616) 649-2335

Wakefield: *Wakefield News* — 405 Sunday Lake St. (49968); Th; 1,355pd, 48fr (Sw); $2.50; publisher & editor Henry R Backman; tel (906) 224-9561

Walker: *Walker/Westside Advance* — 2141 Port Sheldon Rd.; PO Box 9, Jenison (49429); Tu; 438pd, 23,427fr (Sw); $10.26; C; publisher Joel Holland; editor Mike Wyngarden; managing editor Len Lazrick; tel (810) 669-2700; fax (810) 669-1162

Warren: *Warren Advisor* — 48075 Van Dyke; PO Box 168, Utica (48318); Tu; 100,860fr (CAC); $12.05; C; publisher Wayne Oehmke; editor Don Chamberlain; tel (810) 731-1000; fax (810) 731-8172

Waterford: *Waterford Spinal Column* — 7196 Cooley Lake Rd. (Waterford 48327); PO Box 14, Union Lake (48387); W; 13,520pd (Sw); 55¢; C; publisher James W Fancy; editor Tim Dmoch; tel (810) 360-6397; fax (810) 360-4711

Wayne: *The Wayne Eagle* — 35540 W. Michigan Ave.; PO Box 578 (48184); Th/Su; 1,798pd, 2,056fr (Sw); $12.24; C; publisher Mike Wilcox; editor Joan Dyer-Zinner; tel (313) 729-4000; fax (313) 729-6088

W Bloomfield: *The West Bloomfield/Lakes Eccentric* — 36251 Schoolcraft Rd. (48150); PO Box 2428, Livonia (48151); M/Th; 3,870pd, 6,970fr (CAC); $87.86; C; publisher Phil Power; general manager Steven Pope; editor Susan Rosiek; managing editor Robert Sklar; tel (313) 591-2300; fax (313) 591-7279

W Branch: *Ogemaw County Herald* — 215 W. Houghton Ave.; PO Box 247 (48661); Th; 5,962pd, 76fr (Sw); $5.00; C; publisher Robert E Perlberg; editor Dennis Mansfield; managing editor Cindy Gibbs; tel (517) 345-0044

W Lansing: *Delta-Waverly News Herald* — 219 S. Bridge St.; PO Box 70, Grand Ledge (48837); W; 10,135fr (CAC); $5.46; C; publisher Lee Beam; editor Nancy Zeimen; tel (517) 627-6085; fax (517) 627-3497

Westland: *The Westland Eagle* — 35540 Michigan Ave.; PO Box 578, Wayne (48184); Th/Su; 2,136pd, 10,091fr (Sw); $17.80; C; publisher Mike Wilcox; editor Joan Dyer-Zinner; tel (313) 729-4000; fax (313) 729-6088

Westland: *Westland Observer* — 36251 Schoolcraft Rd. (48150); PO Box 2428, Livonia (48151); M/Th; 4,922pd, 6,404fr (CAC); $87.86; C; publisher Phil Power; general manager Steven Pope; editor Susan Rosiek; managing editor Robert Sklar; tel (313) 591-2300; fax (313) 591-7279

Whitehall/Montague/Rothbury/Twin Lake/N Muskegon: *White Lake Beacon* — 432 Spring St.; PO Box 98, Whitehall (49461); M; 500pd, 10,900fr (Est); $7.65; C; publisher Richard Lound; editor Greg Means; tel (616) 894-5356; fax (616) 894-2174

Williamston/Webbenville: *The Enterprise* — 624 S. Cedar; PO Box 160, Mason (48854); W; 1,450pd, 34fr (Sw); $6.00; C; publisher & editor R L Milliman II; tel (517) 676-9393; fax (517) 676-9402

Woodhaven/Brownstown Twp./Riverview/Flatrock/Rockwood/Gibraltar/Huron Twp.: *News-Herald* — 1 Heritage Pl., Ste. 100, Southgate (48195); W; 10,934pd, 7,517fr (Est); $51.80; Su; 9,899pd, 1,710fr (Est); $51.80; C; publisher Fredrick G Manuel; editor Karl Ziomek; tel (313) 246-0800; fax (313) 284-2028

Wyandotte/Trenton: *The Wyandotte/Trenton News-Herald* — 1 Heritage Pl., Ste. 100, Southgate (48195); W; 13,425pd, 4,869fr (Est); $51.80; Su; 10,939pd, 912fr (Est); $51.80; C; publisher Fredrick G Manuel; editor Karl Ziomek; tel (313) 246-0800; fax (313) 284-2028

Wyoming: *Wyoming Advance* — 2141 Port Sheldon Rd.; PO Box 9, Jenison (49429); Tu; 1,309pd, 21,291fr (Sw); $9.96; C; publisher Joel Holland; editor Mike Wyngarden; managing editor Len Lazrick; tel (810) 669-2700; fax (810) 669-1162

Yale/Avoca/Emmett/Brown City: *Yale Expositor* — 21 S. Main St.; PO Box 158, Yale (48097); W; 2,520pd, 24fr (Sw); $5.00; publisher Arthur W Brown; editor Bonnie Brown; tel (810) 387-2300; fax (810) 387-2300

Zeeland: *Zeeland Record* — 16-20 S. Elm St.; PO Box 39 (49464); Th; 2,000pd (Sw); $4.50; publisher Paul Van Koevering; editor Kurtis Van Koevering; tel (616) 772-2131

MINNESOTA

Ada: *Norman County Index* — 307 W. Main St.; PO Box 148 (56510); Tu; 2,302pd, 27fr (Sw); $4.06; publisher J R Pfund; editor Ross D Pfund; tel (218) 784-2541; fax (218) 784-2551

Adams/Mower: *Adams Monitor Review* — PO Box 283, Adams (55909); Th; 1,269pd, 26fr (Sw); $3.83; publishers Kim Edward Adams & Robert Adams; tel (507) 582-3542; fax (507) 582-3542

Adrian: *Nobles County Review* — 100 Maine Ave.; PO Box 160 (56110); W; 1,300fr (Est); $2.75; publisher Jerry Johnson; editor Patricia Johnson; tel (507) 483-2213; fax (507) 483-2219

Aitkin/McGregor/Palisade: *Aitkin Independent Age* — 213 Minnesota Ave. N.; PO Box 259, Aitkin (56431); W; 5,601pd, 95fr (Sw); $4.05; C; publisher Seward County Independent Inc.; general manager Andrew M Skaj; editor Ann Schwartz; tel (218) 927-3761; fax (218) 927-3763

Albany/Stearns: *Stearns-Morrison Enterprise* — 561 Railroad Ave.; PO Box 310, Albany (56307); Tu; 2,326pd, 2,300fr (Est); $3.15; publisher & editor Carole J Larson; publisher Don R Larson; editor Michael Kosik; tel (612) 845-2700; fax (612) 256-3363

Alden: *Alden Advance* — 150 E. Main; PO Box 485 (56009); Th; 1,100pd, 25fr (Est); $2.16; publisher David Gehrke; editor Jim Gehrke; tel (507) 874-3440

Alexandria: *Echo-Press* — 225 7th Ave. E.; PO Box 549 (56308); W/F; 10,089pd, 55fr (Sw); $8.20; C; publisher Jon Haaven; editor Al Edenloff; tel (612) 763-3133; fax (612) 763-3258

Anoka/Coon Rapids: *Anoka County Union* — 4101 Coon Rapids Blvd., Coon Rapids (55443); F; 6,500pd, 93fr (Sw); $3.95; C; publisher Elmer L Andersen; editor Peter Bodley; tel (612) 421-4444; fax (612) 421-4315

Appleton: *The Appleton Press* — 241 W. Snelling (56208); Tu; 2,488pd (Sw); 17¢; publisher Curtis Johnson; editor Loren Johnson; tel (612) 289-1323; fax (612) 289-2702

Arlington: *Arlington Enterprise* — 402 W. Alden St. (55307); W; 1,978pd, 76fr (Est); 15¢; publisher Gail M Kill; editor Kurt Menk; tel (612) 964-5547; fax (612) 964-5547

Askov/Finlayson: *Askov American* — Kontor Bldg.; PO Box 275, Askov (55704); Th; 1,800pd, 150fr (Sw); $3.88; publisher Cynthia Heiller; publisher & editor David Heiller; tel (612) 838-3151; fax (612) 838-3152

Bagley: *Farmers Independent* — 102 N. Main St.; PO Box 130 (56621); W; 2,693pd, 20fr (Sw); $2.75; C; publisher Farmers Publishing Co.; general manager & editor Tom Burford; tel (218) 694-6265; fax (218) 694-6015

Balaton: *Balaton Press Tribune* — 220 Central Ave. S.; PO Box 310 (56115); W; 909pd, 23fr (Sw); 13¢; C; publisher & editor Katherine M Swift; tel (507) 734-5421

Battle Lake: *Battle Lake Review* — 114 Lake Ave. N.; PO Box 98 (56515); W; 2,170pd, 149fr (Sw); $3.60; C; publisher & editor Jon Tamke; tel (218) 864-5952; fax (218) 864-5212

Baudette: *The Baudette Region* — 219 1st Ave. N.E.; PO Drawer C (56623); W; 2,187pd, 3fr (Sw); $3.80; publisher & editor John C Oren; tel (218) 634-1722; fax (218) 634-1224

Benson: *Swift County Monitor & News* — 101 S. 12th St.; PO Box 227 (56215); W; 3,309pd (Sw); 23¢; publisher & editor Reed W Anfinson; tel (612) 843-4111; fax (612) 843-3246

Bird Island: *Bird Island Union* — 750 Ash Ave.; PO Box 160 (55310); W; 1,050pd (Sw); $3.20; C; publisher John Hubin; publisher & editor Ken Hubin; managing editor Bren McDowell; tel (612) 365-3266; fax (612) 365-3266

Biwabik/Rural Gilbert: *The Biwabik Times* — 211 N. Main St.; PO Box 169, Biwabik (55708); Th; 1,160pd, 55fr (Sw); 10¢; publisher & editor Kitty Anderson; tel (218) 865-6265; fax (218) 865-6265

Blackduck: *The American* — 209 Main St.; PO Box M (56630); Su; 1,337pd, 2,907fr (Sw); $3.80; C; publisher Omar Forberg; general manager Paula Bauman; editor Karin Parker; tel (218) 835-4211; fax (218) 835-4211

Blaine/Anoka: *Blaine-Spring Lake Park Life* — 4101 Coon Rapids Blvd., Coon Rapids (55433); F; 1,756pd, 40fr (Sw); $2.80; publisher Elmer Anderson; editor Carolyn Thompson; managing editor Peter Bodley; tel (612) 421-4444; fax (612) 421-4315

Blooming: *Prairie Times* — 411 E. Main St.; PO Box 247, Blooming Prairie (55917); W; 2,275pd (Est); 12¢; publisher & editor Elsie Slinger; tel (507) 583-4431; fax (507) 583-4445

Blue Earth/Winnebago: *Faribault County Register* — 125 N. Main St.; PO Box 100, Blue Earth (56013); M; 3,232pd, 55fr (Sw); $7.26; C; publisher Darwin Oordt; general manager Kelly Anderson; editor Kyle J MacArthur; tel (507) 526-7324; fax (507) 526-4080

Bovey: *Scenic Range News* — 314 2nd St.; PO Box 70 (55709); Th; 1,831pd, 14fr (Sw); 14¢; publisher & editor Douglas D Deal; publisher Ethel Deal; tel (218) 245-1422

Brooklyn Park: *Brooklyn Park Sun Post* — 4080 W. Broadway Ave., Ste. 113, Minneapolis (55422-5605); W; 1,260pd, 15,455fr (Sw); $16.60; C; publisher Donald W Thurlow; general manager Edward Shur; editor Michael Garlitz; managing editor Yvonne Klinnert; tel (612) 536-7500; fax (612) 537-3367

Brooten: *Bonanza Valley Voice* — PO Box 280 (56316); Th; 857pd, 54fr (Est); 75¢; publisher & editor Howard J Johnson; tel (612) 346-2400; fax (612) 346-2237

Browerville/Clarissa/Cushing/Eagle Bend/Long Prairie/Staples: *Browerville Blade* — 121 W. 6th St.; PO Box 245, Browerville (56438); W; 1,771pd, 46fr (Sw); $2.50; publisher Peter Quirt; editor Theresa Quirt; tel (612) 594-2911; fax (612) 594-6111

Browns Vly./Traverse: *Valley News* — 329 W. Broadway; PO Box 339, Browns Valley (56219); Tu; 1,218pd, 15fr (Est); $3.00; publisher & editor Eugene Labs; tel (612) 695-2570

Brownton/McLeod/Stewart: *Brownton Bulletin* — 134 44th Ave. N.; PO Box 309, Brownton (55312); W; 971pd, 28fr (Est); $2.50; C; publisher McLeod Publishing Co.; editor Lori Copler; tel (612) 328-4444

Buffalo: *Wright County Journal-Press* — 108 Central Ave.; PO Box 159 (55313); Th; 5,719pd, 95fr (Sw); $4.06; C; publisher & editor J P McDonnell Jr; tel (612) 682-1221; fax (612) 682-5458

Buffalo Lake/Hector/Cosmo: *The Buffalo Lake News Mirror* — 100 Main N., Buffalo Lake (55314); W; 2,800pd (Est); 20¢; C; publishers & editors John Hubin & Ken Hubin; tel (612) 833-2001; fax (612) 833-2001

Burnsville/Dakota Co.: *Dakota County Tribune* — PO Box 1439, Burnsville (55337); Th; 982pd, 102fr (CAC); 63¢; publishers Daniel H Clay & Joseph R Clay; general manager Bob Temple; editor Brenda Haugen; managing editor Evelyn Hoover; tel (612) 894-1111; fax (612) 894-1859

Byron: *Byron Review* — 505 E. Frontage Rd.; PO Box 39 (55920); Tu; 1,100pd, 18fr (Sw); $3.00; publisher Garry Borgen; publisher & editor Susan Paynic; tel (507) 775-6180; fax (507) 775-6703

Caledonia: *The Caledonia Argus* — 121 W. Main St.; PO Box 227 (55921); W; 2,907pd, 34fr (Sw); $2.15; C; publisher & editor Thomas Murphy; tel (507) 724-3475

Cambridge/E Center: *The Cambridge Star* — 741 2nd Ave. S.E., Cambridge (55008); W; 641pd, 9,311fr (VAC); $7.25; publisher James J Schmitz; editor Linda Nayce; tel (612) 689-1181; fax (612) 689-1185

Canby: *Canby News* — 123 1st St. E.; PO Box 129 (56220); W; 2,847pd, 70fr (Sw); $3.55; publisher & editor Don Beman; publisher Ellie Beman; tel (507) 223-5303; fax (507) 223-5404

Cannon Falls: *Cannon Falls Beacon* — 120 S. 4th St.; PO Box 366 (55009); Th; 4,000pd, 200fr (Sw); $4.65; C; publisher & editor G Richard Dalton; tel (507) 263-3991; fax (507) 263-2300

Cass/Hubbard Cos.: *The Pilot-Independent* — 408 Minnesota Ave. W.; PO Box 190, Walker (56484); Th; 3,620pd, 180fr (Est); $15.50; C; publisher Joseph R Sherman; editor Paul Nye; tel (218) 547-1000; fax (218) 547-3000

Cass Lake: *The Cass Lake Times* — 218 2nd St. N.W.; PO Box 398 (56633); Th; 1,250pd, 11fr (Sw); $2.90; publisher & editor Victor W Olson; tel (218) 335-2290

II-40 Minnesota U.S. Weeklies

Champlin/Dayton: *Champlin-Dayton Press* — 33 2nd St. N.E.; PO Box 280, Osseo (55369); Tu; 1,924pd, 3,817fr (Est); $4.00; C; publisher Don R Larson; editor Carole J Larson; managing editor Peggy Bakken; tel (612) 425-3323

Chanhassen: *Chanhassen Villager* — 80 W. 78th St., Ste. 170; PO Box 99 (55317); Th; 164pd, 4,317fr (Est); $7.95; C; publisher Mark Weber; general manager Stan Rolfsrud; editor Dean Trippler; tel (612) 934-5045; fax (612) 934-7960

Chaska: *Chaska Herald* — PO Box 113 (55318); Th; 3,740pd, 265fr (Sw); $6.95; C; publisher Stan Rolfsrud; editor LaVonne Barac; tel (612) 448-2650; fax (612) 448-3146

Chatfield: *The Chatfield News* — 13 3rd St. S.E., Ste. 4 (55923); W; 1,760pd, 1fr (Sw); $2.75; C; publisher & editor Michael Grieve; tel (507) 867-3870

Chisholm/Hibling: *The Tribune Press-Free Press* — 216 W. Lake St., Chisholm (55719); Tu/Th; 3,075pd, 10fr (Est); $3.24; publisher & editor Veda Ponikvar; tel (218) 254-4432; fax (218) 254-4432

Chokio: *Chokio Review* — PO Box 96 (56221); Th; 957pd (Sw); $2.64; publishers Michele Heiberg & Owen Heiberg; general manager & editor Rhonda Asmus; tel (612) 324-2405; fax (612) 324-2777

Circle Pines/Lino Lakes: *Quad Community Press* — 4779 Bloom Ave., White Bear Lake (55110); Tu; 2,410pd, 5,398fr (VAC); $9.00; C; publisher Eugene D Johnson; managing editor Paul Wahl; tel (612) 429-7781; fax (612) 429-1242

Clara City: *The Clara City Herald* — 34 E. Center Ave.; PO Box 458 (56222); W; 1,622pd, 40fr (Est); $2.50; publisher Ted Almen; editor John G White; tel (612) 847-3130; fax (612) 847-2630

Claremont: *Claremont News* — 115 Elm St.; PO Box B (55924); W; 460pd, 55fr (Sw); N/A; publisher & editor Virginia M Sendle; tel (507) 528-2173

Clarkfield/Granite Falls: *Granite Falls-Clarkfield Advocate-Tribune* — 138 8th Ave.; PO Box 99, Granite Falls (56241); Th; 4,200pd (Est); $4.00; C; publisher Tim Douglas; editor Tim Johnson; tel (612) 564-2126; fax (612) 564-4293

Clinton: *The Northern Star* — PO Box 336, Ortonville (56278); Th; 1,974pd, 20fr (Sw); $4.00; C; publisher James D Kaercher; editor Lois Torgerson; tel (612) 325-5152; fax (612) 839-3761

Cloquet/Carlton Co.: *The Pine Knot* — 1418 Hwy. 33 S.; PO Box 236, Cloquet (55720); M/Th; 4,500pd, 25fr (Sw); $6.45; C; publisher & editor Scott L Elwood; tel (218) 879-6761; fax (218) 879-6696

Comfrey/Darfur: *The Comfrey Times* — 112 W. Brown; PO Box 218, Comfrey (56019); Th; 950pd, 35fr (Sw); $2.40; publisher & editor G P Richter; tel (507) 877-2281

Coon Rapids: *Coon Rapids Herald* — 4101 Coon Rapids Blvd. (55433); F; 3,244pd, 65fr (Est); 20¢; publisher Elmer Anderson; editor Peter Bodley; tel (612) 421-4444; fax (612) 421-4315

Cottage Grove: *The Washington County Bulletin* — 7163 E. Pt. Douglas Rd.; PO Box 99 (55016); W; 4,367pd, 153fr (Sw); 40¢; publisher Steve Messick; general manager Jeffrey Patterson; editor Keith Neis; tel (612) 459-3434; fax (612) 459-9491

Cottonwood/Belview/Echo/Vesta/Hanley Falls: *Tri-County News* — 74 W. Main; PO Box 76, Cottonwood (56229); W; 1,900pd, 25fr (Est); 30¢; C; publisher Jeff Meyer; editor Rae Yost; tel (507) 423-6239; fax (507) 423-6230

Crosby: *Crosby-Ironton Courier* — 12 E. Main; PO Box 67 (56441); W; 4,209pd, 45fr (Est); $6.58; publisher T M Swensen; editor Dina McDonough; managing editor Amy Sharpe; tel (218) 546-5029; fax (218) 546-8352

Dassel/Cokato: *Enterprise & Dispatch* — 261 Atlantic Ave. W.; PO Box 340, Dassel (55325); Tu; 2,990pd, 55fr (Sw); $4.00; publisher & editor Carolyn H Holje; general manager Dan Holje; tel (612) 275-2192; fax (612) 275-2193

Dawson: *Dawson Sentinel* — 674 Chestnut St.; PO Box 1015 (56232); Th; 2,209pd, 15fr (Sw); $2.90; publisher & editor Dave Hickey; tel (612) 769-2497; fax (612) 769-2459

Deer River/Bigfork: *The Western Itasca Review* — 15 1st St. N.E.; PO Box 427, Deer River (56636); Th; 1,621pd, 44fr (Sw); $2.70; C; publisher & editor Bob Barnacle; general manager Karen Miller; tel (218) 246-8533; fax (218) 246-8540

Delano: *Delano Eagle* — 300 Railroad Ave.; PO Box 168 (55328); M; 711pd, 2,100fr (CAC); $5.60; C; publisher Don R Larson; general manager Peggy Bakken; editor Carole Larson; managing editor Jeff Borowicz; tel (612) 972-6171; fax (612) 425-2945

Detroit Lakes: *The Becker County Record* — 511 Washington Ave.; PO Box 826 (56501); Su; 712pd, 11,778fr (VAC); $7.50; publisher Dennis Winskowski; editor Jamie Marks-Erickson; tel (218) 847-3151; fax (218) 847-9409

Detroit Lakes: *The Detroit Lakes Tribune* — 511 Washington Ave.; PO Box 826 (56502); Th; 5,407pd, 295fr (Sw); $6.90; publisher Dennis Winskowski; editor Jamie Marks-Erickson; tel (218) 847-3151; fax (218) 847-9409

Dodge Center: *Dodge Center Star-Record* — 40 W. Main St.; PO Box 279 (55927); Tu; 1,350pd, 42fr (Sw); $2.85; publisher & editor Larry Miller; tel (507) 374-6531; fax (507) 374-9327

Duluth: *Budgeteer Press* — 5807 Grand Ave. (55807); Su; 1,738pd, 48,212fr (Est); $14.50; publisher & editor Richard F Palmer; tel (218) 624-3665; fax (218) 624-7927

Eagan: *Eagan Sun Current* — 7831 E. Bush Lake Rd., Bloomington (55439); W; 15,400fr (Est); $18.60; C; publisher Donald W Thurlow; editor Edward Shur; managing editor Yvonne Klinnert; tel (612) 896-4700; fax (612) 896-4728

Eagle Bend/Bertha/Clarissa/Hewitt: *Independent News Herald* — 310 Main St.; PO Box 188, Clarissa (56440); W; 2,354pd, 184fr (Sw); $3.90; publishers & editors Diane Silbernagel & Ernie Silbernagel; tel (218) 756-2131; fax (218) 756-2126

E Grand Forks/Polk: *The Exponent* — 1010 Central Ave. N.E.; PO Box 285, East Grand Forks (56721); W; 2,174pd, 4fr (Sw); $3.05; publisher & general manager Julie Nordine; publisher & managing editor Rollin Bergman; editor Pete Myszkowski; tel (218) 773-2808; fax (218) 773-9212

Eden Prairie: *Eden Prairie News* — 7901 Flying Cloud Dr., Ste. 150; PO Box 44220 (55344); Th; 7,247pd, 3,841fr (Sw); $9.35; C; publisher & editor Mark Weber; tel (612) 829-0265; fax (612) 829-0917

Eden Valley: *The Eden Valley Journal Patriot* — 299 State St.; PO Box 347 (55329); W; 1,700pd, 19fr (Sw); $3.00; publisher & editor Steve Swenson; tel (612) 453-2460

Edgerton: *Edgerton Enterprise* — 831 Main St.; PO Box 397 (56128); W; 1,977pd, 67fr (Sw); $3.00; publisher & editor Melvin DeBoer; tel (507) 442-6161; fax (507) 442-6161

Elbow Lake: *Grant County Herald* — 35 Central Ave. N.; PO Box 2019 (56531); W; 2,500pd, 20fr (Est); 20¢; publisher David Simpkins; editor Christopher A Ray; tel (218) 685-5326; fax (218) 685-5327

Elk River Region: *Elk River Star News* — 647 Main St.; PO Box 330, Elk River (55330); W; 592pd, 13,348fr (CPVS); $6.75; C; publisher Elmer L Andersen; general manager & editor Don Heinzman; tel (612) 441-3500; fax (612) 441-6401

Ellendale/Geneva/Clarks Grove/Hope: *Our Community News* — 2nd St. at 6th Ave.; PO Box 37, Ellendale (56026); Th; 1,060pd, 38fr (Est); $2.25; publisher Orville Langlie; editor Mavis Langlie; tel (507) 684-2315; fax (507) 684-2315

Ely: *Ely Echo* — 2 E. Sheridan (55731); M; 4,511pd, 60fr (Sw); $5.90; publisher Anne Wognum; general manager Nick Wognum; editor Bob Cary; tel (218) 365-3141; fax (218) 365-3142

Ely: *Elysian Enterprise* — PO Box 119, Elysian (56028); Th; 602pd, 60fr (Sw); $2.75; publisher Charles Wann; general manager & editor Jay Schneider; tel (507) 267-4323; fax (507) 362-4458

Erskine/Mentor: *The Erskine Echo* — 309 1st St.; PO Box A, Erskine (56535); W; 959pd, 23fr (Sw); $3.25; publisher & editor Robert Hole; tel (218) 687-3775

Excelsior/Shorewood/Deephaven/Tonka Bay: *Excelsior/Shorewood Sun Sailor* — 7831 E. Bush Lake Rd., Bloomington (55439); W; 8,500pd (Est); $14.60; C; publisher Don Thurlow; general manager Ed Shur; editor Sandra Brand; tel (612) 896-4700; fax (612) 896-4728

Fairfax/Franklin: *Fairfax Standard* — 102 S.E. 1st St.; PO Box 589, Fairfax (55332); W; 1,362pd, 20fr (Sw); $3.20; C; publisher Charles H Warner; editor Steven J Palmer; tel (507) 426-7235; fax (507) 426-7235

Farmington: *The Farmington Independent* — 320 3rd St.; PO Box 192 (55024); Th; 1,625pd, 10fr (Sw); $5.70; publisher & editor Doug Heikkila; tel (612) 460-6606; fax (612) 463-7730

Fertile: *The Fertile Journal* — Mill St.; PO Box 128 (56540); W; 1,737pd, 10fr (Est); $1.43; publisher & editor Michael D Moore; tel (218) 945-6120; fax (218) 945-6205

Floodwood: *The Forum* — 112 W. 7th Ave.; PO Box 286 (55736); F; 1,305pd, 75fr (Sw); $3.54; publisher & editor Nancy J Raihala; tel (218) 476-2232; fax (218) 476-2232

Foley: *Benton County News* — 220 Broadway; PO Box 187 (56329); Tu; 2,592pd (Est); 12¢; C; publisher & editor Ronald Youso; tel (612) 968-7220; fax (612) 968-7220

Forest Lake: *The Times* — 880 S.W. 15th St. (55025-1381); Th; 3,986pd, 24fr (Sw); $5.70; C; publisher Elmer L Andersen; general manager Howard D Lestrud; editor Cliff Buchan; tel (612) 464-4601; fax (612) 464-4605

Fosston: *The Thirteen Towns* — 116 2nd St. N.W.; PO Box 505 (56542); M; 3,000pd, 6,000fr (Sw); $4.50; C; publisher C & K Publishing Inc.; editor David S Carr; tel (218) 435-1313; fax (218) 435-1309

Fridley/Arden Hills/Roseville/Falcon Heights: *Focus News* — 2819 Hamline Ave., Roseville (55113); Th; 52,707fr (Sw); $29.00; C; publisher Richard Roberts; general manager Colette Kaecher Roberts; tel (612) 633-3434; fax (612) 633-9550

Fulda: *Fulda Free Press* — 128 N. St. Paul Ave.; PO Box 439 (56131); W; 1,400pd (Est); $2.75; C; publisher & editor Gerald D Johnson; tel (507) 425-2303; fax (507) 435-2501

Gaylord: *Gaylord Hub* — PO Box 208 (55334); Th; 2,171pd, 16fr (Est); $3.25; publisher & editor James E Deis; tel (612) 237-2476; fax (612) 237-2476

Gibbon: *The Gibbon Gazette* — PO Box 456 (55335); Th; 900pd, 29fr (Sw); $2.75; C; publisher Charles H Warner; editor Lynda Sabo; tel (507) 834-6966

Glencoe/McLeod: *The McLeod County Chronicle* — 716 E. 10th St.; PO Box 188, Glencoe (55336); W; 3,018pd, 50fr (Sw); $4.28; C; publisher William Ramige; editor Rich Glennie; tel (612) 864-5518

Glenwood: *Pope County Tribune* — 108 S. Franklin; PO Box 157 (56334); M; 4,153pd, 75fr (Est); 23¢; C; publisher & editor John R Stone; tel (612) 634-4571

Gonvick: *Leader Record* — 2nd & Main St.; PO Box 159 (56644); W; 1,888pd, 61fr (Est); $3.25; C; publisher Richard D Richards; editor Corrine J Richards; tel (218) 487-5225; fax (218) 487-5251

Grand Marais: *Cook County News-Herald* — 11-1/2 Broadway; PO Box 757 (55604); M; 4,920pd, 10fr (Sw); $4.50; publisher & editor Jack Becklund; publisher Patti Becklund; tel (218) 387-1025; fax (218) 387-2539

Grand Rapids: *Grand Rapids Herald-Review* — 301 1st Ave. N.W.; PO Box 220 (55744); W/Su; 8,310pd, 200fr (Est); $6.50; C; publisher & editor Charles R Johnson; tel (218) 326-6623; fax (218) 326-6626

Grygla: *The Grygla Eagle* — PO Box 17 (56727); W; 650pd, 30fr (Sw); 16¢; C; publisher Richard D Richards; general manager & editor Joy Nordby; tel (218) 294-6220; fax (218) 294-6220

Hallock/Kittson Co.: *Kittson County Enterprise* — 109 S. 3rd St.; PO Box 730, Hallock (56728); W; 1,924pd, 40fr (Sw); $5.00; publisher Keith O Axvig; general manager & managing editor Gail Norland; editor Cindy Gleason; tel (218) 843-2868; fax (218) 843-2312

Hancock: *The Hancock Record* — 564 6th St.; PO Box 425 (56244); W; 1,000pd (Est); 10¢; publisher James Morrison; editor Katie Erdman; tel (612) 392-5527; fax (612) 589-4357

Hanska: *The Hanska Herald* — PO Box 45 (56041-0045); Th; 762pd, 26fr (Sw); $2.30; publisher Norman L Becken; editor Bernice Becken; managing editor N Ross Becken; tel (507) 439-6214

Hastings: *Hastings Star Gazette* — 741 Spiral Blvd.; PO Box 277 (55033); Th; 5,863pd, 33fr (Sw); $4.93; C; publisher Steven R Messick; editor Doug Schultz; tel (612) 437-6153

Hawley/Glyndon: *The Hawley Herald* — PO Box 709, Hawley (56549); M; 2,266pd, 25fr (Est); $4.25; C; publisher Eugene Prim; general manager & editor Linda Walter; tel (218) 483-3306; fax (218) 483-4457

Hayfield: *The Hayfield Herald* — PO Box 85 (55940); Tu; 1,750pd, 20fr (Sw); $2.65; publisher & editor Larry Miller; tel (507) 477-2232; fax (507) 374-9327

Henderson: *Henderson Independent* — PO Box 8 (56044); Th; 1,075pd, 85fr (Sw); $2.90; publisher Paul M Malchow; general manager & editor Sarah Johnson Malchow; tel (612) 248-3223

Hendricks: *The Hendricks Pioneer* — 100 S. Main St.; PO Box 5 (56136); W; 1,318pd, 150fr (Est); 21¢; publisher & editor Marlan Thompson; tel (507) 275-3197

Henning/Ottertail/Vining: *The Henning Advocate* — 400 Douglas Ave.; PO Box 35, Henning (56551); W; 1,404pd, 10fr (Sw); 22¢; publishers Andrew Barr & Debra Barr; editor Jerry Barney; tel (218) 583-2935; fax (218) 583-2909

Herman Norcross: *The Herman Review* — 408 Berlin Ave.; PO Box E, Herman (56248); Th; 1,260pd (Sw); $2.88; C; publisher Michele Heiberg; managing editor Helen Brunkow; tel (612) 677-2229

Heron Lake/Okabena: *The Tri-County News* — 931 2nd Ave.; PO Box 227, Heron Lake (56138); W; 907pd, 19fr (Est); $3.00; publisher Gerald D Johnson; editor Carol Schreiber; tel (507) 793-2327; fax (507) 793-2327

Hills/Beaver Creek/Steen: *Hills Cresent* — PO Box 457, Hills (56138); Th; 770pd, 30fr (Sw); $2.25; publisher Preston Ver Meer; editor Chad Mickelson; managing editor Renae Larson; tel (507) 962-3230; fax (507) 962-3211

Hinckley: *Hinckley News* — 115 E. Main St. (55037); Th; 1,816pd, 32fr (Sw); 16¢; publisher Pat O'Donovan; editor Tim Burkhardt; tel (612) 384-6188; fax (612) 384-6188

Hopkins: *Hopkins Sun Sailor* — 7831 E. Bush Lake Rd., Bloomington (55439); W; 10,175pd (Est); $21.20; C; publisher Don Thurlow; general manager Ed Shur; editor Mike Smith; tel (612) 896-4700; fax (612) 896-4728

Howard Lake/Waverly: *Howard Lake Herald* — 817 6th St.; PO Box 190, Howard Lake (55349); M; 1,425pd, 20fr (Est); $3.60; C; publisher William C Ramige; general manager Dale Kovar; editor Chris Schanus; tel (612) 543-2131; fax (612) 543-2135

Hutchinson: *The Hutchinson Leader* — 36 Washington Ave. W. (55350); Tu/Th; 5,226pd, 120fr (Sw); $5.06; publisher Wayne Kasich; editor Richard Crawford; tel (612) 587-5000; fax (612) 587-6104

Isanti Co.: *Isanti County News* — PO Box 352, Cambridge (55008); Th; 2,950pd, 46fr (Est); $3.65; publisher Elmer L Andersen; editor Evelyn Puffer; tel (612) 689-1981; fax (612) 689-4372

Isle: *Mille Lacs Messenger* — Main St.; PO Box 26 (56342); W; 5,990pd (Sw); $5.50; C; publisher Richard Norlander; general manager Kevin Anderson; editor James Baden; tel (612) 676-3123; fax (612) 676-8450

Ivanhoe/Hendricks: *The Ivanhoe Times* — 315 N. Norman; PO Box 100, Ivanhoe (56142); Th; 1,020pd, 10fr (Sw); $3.00; publisher & editor Brent Beck; publisher & general manager Ellen Beck; tel (507) 694-1246

Jackson: *Jackson County Pilot* — 310 2nd St.; PO Box 208 (56143-0208); Th; 2,270pd, 100fr (Est); $5.91; C; publisher James V Keul; editor Jerrod Igou; tel (507) 847-3771; fax (507) 847-5822

Janesville: *Janesville Argus* — 107 N. Main St.; PO Box 220 (56048-0220); W; 1,313pd, 23fr (Sw); $2.62; C; publisher & editor Judy A Winter; tel (507) 234-6651; fax (507) 234-6390

Jasper: *Jasper Journal* — PO Box 188 (56144-0188); M; 927pd, 6fr (Sw); $2.45; publisher Charles L Draper; general manager Delores Quissell; editor Elaine Sestak; tel (507) 348-4176; fax (507) 825-2168

Jordan: *Jordan Independent* — 109 Rice St. (55352); Th; 1,451pd, 138fr (Est); $4.50; C; publisher Stan Rolfsrud; editor Charlene J Koepp; tel (612) 492-2224

Karlstad: *North Star News* — 204 Main St. S. (56732); Th; 2,880pd, 31fr (Est); $3.43; publisher & editor Julie Nordine; publisher Rollin Bergman; tel (218) 436-2157; fax (218) 436-3271

Kasson: *Dodge County Independent* — 105 1st Ave. N.W.; PO Box 367 (55944); W; 1,976pd, 38fr (Sw); $3.50; C; publisher Folmer Carlsen; editor Randy Carlsen; tel (507) 634-7503

Kenyon: *The Kenyon Leader* — 638 2nd St. (55946); W; 1,906pd, 43fr (Sw); $3.08; publisher Robert D Noah; editor Douglas Noah; tel (507) 789-6161; fax (507) 789-6161

U.S. Weeklies **Minnesota** II-41

Kerkhoven: *Kerkhoven Banner* — 1003 Atlantic Ave.; PO Box 148 (56252); Th; 1,412pd, 61fr (Sw); $3.00; C; publisher & editor Theodore J Almen; tel (612) 264-3071; fax (612) 264-3070

Kiester/Bricelyn: *The Courier-Sentinel* — 405 W. Center St.; PO Box 250, Kiester (56051); Th; 1,923pd, 17fr (Sw); $3.10; publisher & editor Cynthia A Matson; tel (507) 294-3400

Kimball: *Tri-County News* — PO Box 220 (55353); Th; 1,370pd, 25fr (Sw); $2.35; C; publishers Sharon Schumacher & Steven Prinsen; editor Janet Robinson; tel (612) 398-5000; fax (612) 274-2301

La Crescent/Hokah/Houston/Dakota/Brownsville: *Houston County News* — 306 Main St.; PO Box 205, La Crescent (55947); Th; 1,917pd, 17fr (Sw); $3.95; C; publishers & editors Jean Silberman & Tom van der Linden; tel (507) 895-2940; fax (507) 895-2942

Lafayette: *Lafayette Nicollet Ledger* — 631 Main Ave.; PO Box 212 (56054); Th; 1,187pd, 11fr (Sw); 15¢; publisher & editor Doug Hanson; tel (507) 228-8985; fax (507) 228-8779

Lake Benton: *Lincoln County Valley Journal* — 115 S. Center St.; PO Box 218 (56149); W; 1,600pd, 450fr (Est); $1.14; publisher & editor Marlin Thompson; tel (507) 368-4214

Lake City: *The Lake City Graphic* — 107 S. Lakeshore Dr.; PO Box 469 (55041); Th; 3,191pd (Sw); 39¢; C; publisher Dennis Schumacher; editor Rick Ousky; tel (612) 345-3316; fax (612) 345-4200

Lake Crystal: *Lake Crystal Tribune* — 101 W. Humphrey; PO Box 240 (56055); W; 1,874pd, 33fr (Sw); $3.10; publisher & editor Don R Marben; tel (507) 726-2133

Lake Park: *Lake Park Journal* — PO Box 75 (56554); M; 979pd, 11fr (Sw); 15¢; C; publisher Eugene Prim; editor Carolyn Anderson; managing editor Linda Walters; tel (218) 238-6872; fax (218) 238-6872/483-4457

Lakefield/Jackson/Okabena: *Lakefield Standard* — 403 Main St.; PO Box 249, Lakefield (56150); W; 1,846pd, 41fr (Sw); $3.15; C; publisher Jim Keul; editor Mark Erickson; tel (507) 662-5555; fax (507) 662-6770

Lakeville/Dakota: *Lakeville Life & Times* — 20777 Holyoke Ave. W.; PO Box 549, Lakeville (55044); Sa; 31pd, 17,396fr (CPVS); $10.86; publisher & editor Richard M Sherman; managing editor Jonette Hubred; tel (612) 469-2181; fax (612) 469-2184

Lamberton/Revere/Wanda: *Lamberton News* — 218 Main; PO Box 308, Lamberton (56152); W; 1,654pd, 46fr (Sw); $3.00; publisher & editor J G Dietl; tel (507) 752-7181; fax (507) 752-7181

Le Center: *The Le Center Leader* — 62 E. Minnesota St. (56057); W; 1,848pd, 50fr (Est); $5.60; C; publisher Steve Jessop; tel (612) 357-2233; fax (612) 357-6656

Le Roy: *Le Roy Independent* — 135 E. Main St.; PO Box 89 (55951); Th; 1,200pd, 22fr (Sw); $2.80; C; publisher & editor Eileen M Evans; managing editor Alfred R Evans; tel (507) 324-5325; fax (507) 324-5267

Le Sueur: *News-Herald* — 101 Bridge St. (56058); W; 2,025pd, 45fr (Sw); $5.30; C; publisher David M Gordon; editor Daryl Thul; tel (612) 665-3332; fax (612) 665-3334

Lewiston: *Lewiston Journal* — PO Box 608 (55952); Tu; 1,373pd (Est); 18¢; publisher Timothy M Mack; editor Susan Schossou-Halter; tel (507) 523-2119; fax (507) 523-2891

Lindstrom/Chicago City: *Chicago County Press* — 1265 Lake Blvd.; PO Box 748, Lindstrom (55045); Th; 3,750pd, 95fr (Sw); $5.55; C; publisher & editor John Silver; tel (612) 257-5115; fax (612) 257-5500

Litchfield: *Independent Review* — 217 Sibley Ave. N.; PO Box 921 (55355); Th; 4,650pd, 150fr (Est); 14¢; publisher & editor Stan Roeser; general manager Vern Madson; tel (612) 693-3266; fax (612) 693-9177

Little Canada: *Little Canada Press* — 4779 Bloom Ave., White Bear Lake (55110); Tu; 102pd, 3,006fr (VAC); $6.75; C; publisher Eugene D Johnson; managing editor Paul Wahl; tel (612) 429-7781; fax (612) 429-1242

Little Falls/Morrison Co.: *Morrison County Record* — 216 S.E. 1st St., Little Falls (56345); Su; 502pd, 16,170fr (Est); $5.94; C; publisher Carolyn Hoheisel; editor Robert Wright; tel (612) 632-2345; fax (612) 632-2348

Long Prairie/Todd Co.: *The Long Prairie Leader* — 21 3rd St. S.; PO Box 479, Long Prairie (56347); Tu; 3,341pd, 288fr (Est); 25¢; publisher Gary R Brown; editor Sue Farmer; tel (612) 732-2151; fax (612) 732-2152

Luverne: *The Rock County Star Herald* — 117 W. Main St.; PO Box 837 (56156-0837); Th; 3,118pd, 26fr (Est); $5.60; C; publisher Roger S Tollefson; editor Lori Ende; tel (507) 283-2333; fax (507) 283-2335

Mabel/Preston/Harmony: *News Record* — 102 Fillmore St. W.; PO Box 307, Mabel (55954); Th; 1,618pd (Sw); $3.30; C; publisher David A Phillips; editor Melissa Vander Plas; tel (507) 493-5204; fax (507) 493-5204

Madelia: *Madelia Times-Messenger* — 112 W. Main St.; PO Box 159 (56062); Tu; 2,050pd (Sw); $4.50; C; publisher Michael J Whalen; editor Bruce Lindquist; tel (507) 642-3636; fax (507) 642-3535

Madison: *The Western Guard* — 216 6th Ave.; PO Box 183 (56256); W; 3,200pd, 15fr (Sw); $4.80; C; publisher & editor Richard Gail; tel (612) 598-7521; fax (612) 598-7523

Madison Lake/Eagle Lake/St. Clair: *Lake Region Times* — 512 Main St.; PO Box 128 (56063-0128); W; 918pd, 13fr (Est); $1.96; C; publisher & editor Marie Groebner; tel (507) 243-3031; fax (507) 243-3122

Mahnomen: *The Mahnomen Pioneer* — PO Box 219 (56557); W; 2,775pd, 10fr (Est); $3.20; publisher Patrick D Kelly; general manager Brian Kelly; editor Sue Gruman; tel (218) 935-5296

Maple Lake: *Maple Lake Messenger* — 218 Division St.; PO Box 817 (55358); W; 1,500pd, 67fr (Sw); $2.40; publisher & editor Harold Brutlag; tel (612) 963-3813; fax (612) 963-6114

Mapleton/Blue Earth: *Maple River Messenger* — 309 Main St.; PO Box 425, Mapleton (56065); W; 1,017pd, 8fr (Est); $2.35; publisher Kenneth Warner; tel (507) 524-3212

Maplewood: *Maplewood Review* — 2515 7th Ave. E., North St. Paul (55109); W; 1,024pd, 140fr (VAC); $17.60; C; publishers Jeffery R Enright & N T Lillie; editor Holly Wenzel; managing editor Mary Lee Hagert; tel (612) 777-8800; fax (612) 777-8288

Marine on St. Croix/New Scandia: *Country Messenger* — 21070 Olinda Trl. N., Scandia (55073); W; 1,658pd, 143fr (Sw); $4.80; publisher & editor Kay L Hempel; tel (612) 433-3845; fax (612) 433-3158

McLeod/Sibley/Renville/Carver Cos.: *The Glencoe Enterprise* — 831 11th St.; PO Box 97, Glencoe (55336); Th; 2,370pd, 50fr (Sw); $4.25; publisher & editor Annamarie Tudhope; tel (612) 864-4715

Melrose: *Melrose Beacon* — 408 E. Main St.; PO Box 186 (56352); M; 2,160pd, 2,456fr (Est); $3.60; publishers Carole J Larson & Don R Larson; editor Michael Kosik; tel (612) 256-3240

Milaca: *Mille Lacs County Times* — 225 S.W. 2nd St.; PO Box 9 (56353); W; 3,132pd, 12fr (Sw); $2.75; publisher Elmer L Andersen; general manager Lois Ploeger; editor Gary Larson; managing editor Jeff Hage; tel (612) 983-6111; fax (612) 983-6112

Milan: *The Milan Standard-Watson Journal* — PO Box 190 (56262); W; 670pd, 10fr (Est); $1.50; publisher & editor Loren Johnson; general manager Leslie Ehrenberg; tel (612) 734-4458; fax (612) 289-2702

Minneapolis/St. Paul: *Minnesota Sun Publications* — 7831 E. Bush Lake Rd., Bloomington (55439); W/Su; 274,000fr (Sw); $90.70; C; publisher Don Thurlow; general manager & editor Ed Shur; tel (612) 896-4700; fax (612) 896-4754

Minneapolis/St. Paul: *Skyway News and Freeway News* — 15 S. 5th St., Ste. 800, Minneapolis (55402); Tu; 55,000fr (Sw); $33.81; C; publisher Mari Adamson-Bray; editors Becky Sisco & Greg Erickson; managing editor Dawn Johnson; tel (612) 375-9222; fax (612) 375-9208

Minnesota Lake: *Minnesota Lake Tribune* — Main St.; PO Box 308 (56068); Th; 900pd, 25fr (Sw); 10¢; publisher & editor Kenneth Hiscock; tel (507) 462-3575

Minnetonka: *Minnetonka Sun Sailor* — 7831 E. Bush Lake Rd., Bloomington (55439); W; 10,807pd (Est); $16.90; C; publisher Don Thurlow; general manager Ed Shur; editor Jason Kulhanek; tel (612) 896-4700; fax (612) 896-4728

Montevideo/Milan/Watson: *Montevideo American-News* — 223 S. 1st St.; PO Box 736, Montevideo (56265); Th; 4,420pd, 18fr (Sw); 41¢; C; publisher Patrick A Schmidt; editor John Givan; tel (612) 269-2156; fax (612) 269-2159

Montgomery: *Montgomery Messenger* — 310 1st St. S.; PO Box 49 (56069); Th; 2,051pd, 20fr (Sw); $1.65; C; publisher E Charles Wann; editor Karen Simon; tel (612) 364-8601; fax (612) 364-8602

Monticello: *Monticello Times* — 116 E. River St.; PO Box 548 (55362); Th; 2,596pd, 281fr (Sw); $5.40; C; publisher & editor Donald Q Smith; tel (612) 295-3131; fax (612) 295-3080

Moose Lake: *Star Gazette* — PO Box 449 (55767); Th; 2,884pd (Sw); $3.75; publisher & editor Jerry DeRungs; tel (218) 485-4406

Moose Lake/Carlton: *Arrowhead Leader* — 321 Elm Ave.; PO Box 506, Moose Lake (55767); M; 2,484pd (Sw); $2.85; publisher & managing editor Robert Hanson; editor Pat Macaulay; tel (218) 485-8420; fax (218) 485-8420

Mora/Kanabec Co.: *Kanabec County Times* — 106 N.W. Railroad Ave., Mora (55051); Th; 2,900pd (Est); $3.65; C; publisher Wade Weber; editor Lee Ostrom; tel (612) 679-2661; fax (612) 679-2663

Morgan: *Morgan Messenger* — PO Box 38 (56266); W; 1,067pd, 50fr (Sw); $2.25; publisher & editor Victor Walter Olson; tel (507) 249-3130

Morris: *Morris Sun* — 108 E. 6th St.; PO Box 470 (56267); Tu; 3,558pd, 56fr (Sw); $4.62; C; publisher Morris Tribune Inc.; editor James S Morrison; tel (612) 589-2525

Morris: *Morris Tribune* — 108 E. 6th St.; PO Box 470 (56267); Th; 3,577pd, 56fr (Sw); $4.62; C; publisher Morris Tribune Inc.; editor James S Morrison; tel (612) 589-2525

Mound: *The Laker* — 2310 Commerce Blvd.; PO Box 82 (55364); M; 1,900pd (Est); 32¢; publisher James D Berreth; general manager & editor Bill Holm; tel (612) 472-1140; fax (612) 472-0516

Mountain Lake: *Mountain Lake Observer-Advocate* — PO Box 429 (56159); W; 2,250fr (Sw); $3.40; publisher & editor Charles B Paulson; publisher Marcia Paulson; tel (507) 427-2725; fax (507) 427-2724

Murray: *Fulda Free Press* — 118 N. St. Paul Ave.; PO Box 439, Fulda (56131); W; 1,400pd (Sw); 14¢; C; publisher & editor Gerald Johnson; tel (507) 425-2303; fax (507) 425-2501

Nashwauk: *Eastern Itascan* — 310 Central Ave. (55769-1132); Th; 1,402pd, 53fr (Sw); $2.50; C; publisher Brian Oftelie; editor Bill Proznik; tel (218) 885-2100

Nevis/Akeley/Laporte: *Northwood Press* — PO Box 28, Nevis (56467); Th; 1,435pd, 41fr (Sw); $3.25; publisher & editor Victor Woodrow Olson; tel (218) 652-3475

New Brighton/Mounds View: *New Brighton-Mounds View Bulletin* — 909 7th Ave. N.W.; PO Box 120608, New Brighton (55112); W; 167pd, 10,653fr (VAC); $18.00; C; publisher & general manager Jeffery R Enright; publisher N T Lillie; editor James Schwartz; managing editor Mary Lee Hagert; tel (612) 633-2777; fax (612) 633-3846

New Hope/Golden Valley: *New Hope-Golden Valley Sun-Post* — 7831 E. Bush Lake Rd., Bloomington (55439); W; 1,559pd, 12,370fr (Sw); $19.40; C; publisher Don Thurlow; general manager & editor Ed Shur; tel (612) 896-4700; fax (612) 896-4754

New London: *New London* — PO Box 250 (56273); M; 1,214pd, 36fr (Sw); $4.58; C; publisher James C Hensley; editor Bev Ahlquist; tel (612) 796-2945; fax (612) 796-6375

New Prague: *The New Prague Times* — 200 E. Main St.; PO Box 25 (56071); Th; 4,080pd, 85fr (Sw); $4.75; publisher E Charles Wann; editor Lois Suel Wann; tel (612) 758-4435; fax (612) 758-4135

New Richland/Waldorf: *New Richland Star* — 212 N. Broadway; PO Box 248, New Richland (56072); W; 2,071pd, 28fr (Sw); 80¢; publisher & editor Margaret A Engesser; tel (507) 465-8112

New York Mills: *New York Mills Herald* — PO Box 158 (56567); Th; 1,950pd (Sw); $4.83; C; publisher & editor Michael A Parta; tel (218) 385-2275

N Branch/Branch/Rush City: *ECM Post Review* — 612 Main St.; PO Box 366, North Branch (55056-0336); Th; 2,341pd (Sw); $7.80; C; publisher Elmer L Andersen; editor Twyla L Ring; tel (612) 674-7025; fax (612) 674-7026

N St. Paul: *Ramsey County Review* — 2515 7th Ave. E. (55109); W; 1,210pd, 131fr (VAC); $17.60; C; publishers Jeffery R Enright & N T Lillie; editor Holly Wenzel; managing editor Mary Lee Hagert; tel (612) 777-8800; fax (612) 777-8288

Northfield: *Northfield News* — 115 W. 5th St.; PO Box 58 (55057); W/F; 5,865pd, 250fr (Est); $5.95; C; publisher Robert Bradford; general manager Richard Kleber; editor David Welch; tel (507) 645-5615; fax (507) 645-6005

Northome: *Northome Record and Mizpah Message* — Main St.; PO Box 25 (56661); Tu; 890pd, 46fr (Sw); $3.50; publisher & editor Kathryn E Elhard; tel (218) 897-5278

Norwood: *Norwood-Young America Times* — PO Box 67 (55368); Th; 2,433pd, 41fr (Est); 21¢; publisher James D Berreth; editor Tim Larson; tel (612) 467-2271; fax (612) 467-2294

Oakdale/Lake Elmo: *Oakdale Lake Elmo Review* — 2515 7th Ave. E., North St. Paul (55109); W; 758pd, 28fr (VAC); $17.60; C; publishers Jeffery R Enright & N T Lillie; editor Holly Wenzel; managing editor Mary Lee Hagert; tel (612) 777-8800; fax (612) 777-8288

Oklee: *The Oklee Herald* — PO Box 9 (56742); W; 1,131pd (Est); $2.92; C; publisher Richard D Richards; editor Marilyn Whyte; tel (218) 796-5181; fax (218) 487-5251

Olivia: *Olivia Times-Journal* — 816 E. Lincoln (56277); M; 1,787pd, 27fr (Sw); $3.80; C; publisher Rose Hettig; editor Patricia Kelly; tel (612) 523-2032; fax (612) 523-2033

Ortonville: *The Ortonville Independent* — 29 N.W. 2nd St.; PO Box 336 (56278); Tu; 3,236pd, 90fr (Sw); $4.50; C; publisher James D Kaercher; editor Suzette Kaercher; tel (612) 839-6163; fax (612) 839-3761

Osakis: *Osakis Review* — 28 E. Main St.; PO Box 220 (56360); Tu; 1,307pd, 28fr (Sw); $3.85; C; publisher John J Olson; editor Roberta J Olson; tel (612) 859-2143; fax (612) 859-2054

Osseo/Maple Grove: *Osseo-Maple Grove Press* — 33 2nd St. N.E.; PO Box 280, Osseo (55369); W; 5,118pd, 7,339fr (Est); $4.80; C; publisher Don R Larson; editor Carole J Larson; managing editor Peggy Bakken; tel (612) 425-3323

Park Rapids: *Park Rapids Enterprise* — 402 Pleasant; PO Box 111 (56470); W/Sa; 6,150pd, 120fr (Sw); $7.00; publisher Dennis Winskowski; general manager Michael Gravdahl; editor Lu Ann Hurd-Lof; tel (218) 732-9242; fax (218) 732-8757

Paynesville: *The Paynesville Press* — 211 Washburne Ave.; PO Box 54 (56362-0054); Tu; 2,745pd, 224fr (Sw); $4.55; C; publisher Peter J Jacobson; editor Linda Stelling; tel (612) 243-3772

Pelican Rapids/Rothsay: *Pelican Rapids Press* — 29 W. Mill; PO Box L, Pelican Rapids (56572); W; 3,436pd, 14fr (Sw); $4.50; publisher & editor Gary E Peterson; publisher Richard Peterson; tel (218) 863-1421; fax (218) 863-1423

Pequot Lakes: *Lake Country Echo* — 127 W. Lake St.; PO Box 240 (56472); Th; 3,930pd, 65fr (Sw); $4.50; C; publisher Peter T Anderson; editor Louis Hoglund; tel (218) 568-8521; fax (218) 568-5407

Perham: *Enterprise-Bulletin* — 135 E. Main St.; PO Box 288 (56573); Th; 3,207pd, 50fr (Est); $5.41; publisher Michael A Parta; general manager Jennifer Parta; editor Charles R Johnson; tel (218) 346-5900; fax (218) 346-5901

Pine City: *Pine City Pioneer* — 405 2nd Ave. E. (55063); Th; 3,227pd, 104fr (Est); $5.20; publisher Dianne Kiel Arnold; editor Cindy Rolain Frets; tel (612) 629-6771; fax (612) 629-6772

Pine River/Backus: *Pine River Journal* — 215 Norway Ave.; PO Box 370, Pine River (56474); W; 2,241pd, 26fr (Sw); $3.15; C; publisher Peter T Anderson; editor Louis Hoglund; tel (218) 587-2360; fax (218) 587-2331

Pipestone: *Pipestone County Star* — 101 2nd St. N.E.; PO Box 277 (56164); Th; 3,727pd, 111fr (Est); $5.40; publisher & editor Charles L Draper; tel (507) 825-3333; fax (507) 825-2168

Plainview: *Plainview News* — 409 W. Broadway; PO Box 457 (55964); Tu; 2,466pd, 10fr (Sw); 14¢; publisher Timothy M Mack; editor Janet M Mack; tel (507) 534-3121; fax (507) 534-3920

Plymouth: *Plymouth Sun Sailor* — 7831 E. Bush Lake Rd., Bloomington (55439); Th; 3,453pd, 13,619fr (Sw); $22.00; C; publisher Don Thurlow; general manager Ed Shur; editor Sally Thompson; tel (612) 896-4700; fax (612) 896-4728

Princeton: *Princeton Union-Eagle* — 208 N. LaGrande Ave., PO Box 278 (55371); Th; 3,469pd, 71fr (Sw); $3.95; C; publisher Elmer L Andersen; general manager Timothy J Enger; editor Luther J Dorr; tel (612) 389-1222; fax (612) 389-1728

Prior Lake: *Prior Lake American* — 14093 Commerce Ave.; PO Box 538 (55372); Sa; 580pd, 6,347fr (Est); $9.20; C; publisher Laurie Hartman; general manager Stan Rolfsrud; editor Jim Riccioli; tel (612) 447-6669; fax (612) 447-6671

Proctor: *Proctor Journal* — 215 5th St. (55810-1686); Th; 1,923pd, 15fr (Est); $3.00; publisher Sam Schlepper; general manager Diane Giuliani; tel (218) 624-3349; fax (218) 624-7037

Raymond/Prinsburg: *The News* — 204 Spicer St.; PO Box 157, Raymond (56282); W; 1,159pd, 18fr (Est); $2.58; C; publisher & editor William H Paterson; tel (612) 967-4244

Red Lake Falls: *The Gazette* — 105 Main Ave. S.; PO Box 370 (56750); W; 1,446pd, 69fr (Sw); $5.50; publisher & general manager & managing editor Keith O Axvig; editor Dorin Anderson; tel (218) 253-2594; fax (218) 253-4114

Redwood Falls: *The Redwood Falls Gazette* — 140 E. 2nd St.; PO Box 299 (56283); Tu/Th; 5,042pd, 165fr (Sw); $5.75; publisher & editor Rick Peterson; tel (507) 637-2929; fax (507) 637-3175

Renville/Danube/Sacred Heart: *Renville County Star Farmer News* — 110 N.W. Dupont Ave.; PO Box 468, Renville (56284); W; 2,151pd (Sw); $4.10; publisher & editor Daniel A Licklider; tel (612) 329-3324

Rockford/Wright: *Rockford Newsleader* — 8240 Bridge St., Rockford (55373); M; 5,400pd (CPVS); $2.75; publishers Kathy Windom & Larry Windom; tel (612) 477-6884

Roseau Co.: *Roseau Times-Region* — 106 Center St. W.; PO Box 220, Roseau (56751); F; 4,100pd, 33fr (Est); $5.00; C; publisher E Neil Mattson; general manager Jodi Wiskow; editor Dick Melvin; tel (218) 463-1521; fax (218) 463-1530

Roseville/Little Canada/Falcon Hts.: *Roseville Review* — 2515 7th Ave. E., North Saint Paul (55109); Tu; 16,443fr (VAC); $11.50; C; publishers Jeffery R Enright & N T Lillie; editor Amelia Swisher; managing editor Mary Lee Hagert; tel (612) 777-8800; fax (612) 777-8288

Rushford/Peterson: *Tri-County Record* — 212 S. Mill St.; PO Box 429, Rushford (55971); Th; 1,607pd, 5fr (Sw); $3.47; C; publishers & editors Darlene J Schober & Myron J Schober; tel (507) 864-7700

Ruthton: *Buffalo Ridge Gazette* — 320 Aetna St.; PO Box 70 (56170); W; 481pd, 20fr (Sw); $2.94; publisher Charles Hunt; general manager Pamela Hunt; managing editor Lorry Sanderson; tel (507) 658-3919; fax (507) 247-5502

St. Anthony: *St. Anthony Bulletin* — 909 7th Ave. N.W.; PO Box 120608, New Brighton (55112); W; 51pd, 2,454fr (VAC); $18.00; C; publisher & general manager Jeffery R Enright; publisher N T Lillie; editor James Schwartz; managing editor Mary Lee Hagert; tel (612) 633-2777; fax (612) 633-3846

St. Charles: *St. Charles Press* — PO Box 617, St. Charles (55972); Tu; 1,950pd, 1,735fr (Est); $4.50; C; publisher Timothy M Mack; editor Julie Smith; tel (507) 932-3663; fax (507) 932-5537

St. James: *Plaindealer* — 604 1st Ave. S.; PO Box 67, St. James (56081); Th; 3,015pd, 40fr (Est); $5.40; C; publisher R Joseph Flanagan; editor Greg Gelsen; tel (507) 375-3161; fax (507) 375-3221

St. Louis Park: *St. Louis Park Sun Sailor* — 7831 E. Bush Lake Rd., Bloomington (55439); W; 16,250pd (Est); $21.20; C; publisher Don Thurlow; general manager Ed Shur; editor Heather Gay; tel (612) 896-4700; fax (612) 896-4728

St. Michael/Rockford: *North Crow River News* — 33 2nd St. N.E.; PO Box 280, Osseo (55369); Tu; 2,292pd, 2,595fr (Est); $4.60; publisher Don R Larson; editor Carole J Larson; managing editor Peggy Bakken; tel (612) 425-3323

St. Michael/Rockford: *Rockford Area News* — 33 2nd St. N.E.; PO Box 280, Osseo (55369); Tu; 2,859fr (Est); $2.60; publisher Don R Larson; editor Carole J Larson; tel (612) 425-3323

St. Michael/Rockford: *South Crow River News* — 33 2nd St. N.E.; PO Box 280, Osseo (55369); Tu; 1,040pd (Est); $2.60; publisher Don R Larson; editor Carole J Larson; tel (612) 425-3323

St. Paul: *East Side Review* — 2515 7th Ave. E., North St. Paul (55109); M; 20,120fr (Est); $13.50; C; publishers Jeffery R Enright & N T Lillie; editor Maggie Tacheny; managing editor Mary Lee Hagert; tel (612) 777-8800; fax (612) 777-8288

St. Peter: *St. Peter Herald* — 311 S. Minnesota Ave.; PO Box 446, St. Peter (56082); Th; 3,317pd, 60fr (Est); 30¢; C; publisher Peggy Palmer; editor Bill Floyd; tel (507) 931-4520; fax (507) 931-4522

Sanborn: *Sanborn Sentinel* — PO Box 38 (56083); Th; 591pd, 15fr (Sw); 80¢; publisher & editor Walter Olson; tel (507) 648-3288; fax (507) 249-3130

Sandstone: *Pine County Courier* — 414 N. Main St.; PO Box 230 (55072-0230); Th; 1,878pd, 88fr (Est); $3.19; publisher & editor Richard A Coffey; tel (612) 245-2368; fax (612) 245-2438

Sauk Centre: *Sauk Centre Herald* — 522 Sinclaire Lewis Ave. (56378); Tu; 3,464pd, 7,000fr (Est); $3.30; C; publisher & managing editor David Simpkins; editor Carol Moorman; tel (612) 352-6577; fax (612) 352-5647

Sauk Rapids: *Sauk Rapids Herald* — 7 2nd Ave. S.; PO Box 8 (56379); W; 1,382pd (Est); 10¢; publisher & editor Ronald Doroff; tel (612) 251-1971

Sebeka/Menahga: *The Review Messenger* — PO Box 309, Sebeka (56477); W; 3,356pd, 174fr (Sw); $4.60; publisher John F Bloomquist; editor Timothy M Bloomquist; tel (218) 837-5005/5558; fax (218) 837-5560

Shakopee: *Shakopee Valley News* — 327 Marshall Rd.; PO Box 8 (55379); Th; 3,248pd, 224fr (Sw); $6.75; C; publisher & editor Stan Rolfsrud; tel (612) 445-3333; fax (612) 445-3333

Sherburn: *The West Martin Weekly News* — 10 N. Main St.; PO Box 820 (56171); W; 1,671pd, 102fr (Sw); $3.40; C; publisher & editor Harwood Schaffer; publisher Polly Anna Schaffer; tel (507) 764-6681; fax (507) 764-2756

Shoreview: *Shoreview* — 4779 Bloom Ave., White Bear Lake (55110); Tu; 148pd, 8,627fr (VAC); $9.00; C; publisher Eugene D Johnson; managing editor Paul Wahl; tel (612) 429-7781; fax (612) 429-1242

Shoreview/Arden Hills/Vadnais Hts./N Oaks: *Shoreview/Arden Hills Bulletin* — 909 7th Ave. N.W.; PO Box 120608, New Brighton (55112); W; 93pd, 15,580fr (VAC); $18.00; C; publisher & general manager Jeffery R Enright; publisher N T Lillie; editor James Schwartz; managing editor Mary Lee Hagert; tel (612) 633-2777; fax (612) 633-3846

Silver Lake: *Silver Lake Leader* — 421 Main St.; PO Box 343 (55381); Th; 1,371pd, 43fr (Sw); 80¢; publisher Kenneth Merrill; editor Dorothy Merrill; tel (612) 327-2216

Slayton: *Murray County Herald* — 2734 Broadway; PO Box 263 (56172); M; 2,000pd (Sw); 16¢; publisher Will Beers; general manager Jonah Beers; editor Randy Beers; tel (507) 836-8726; fax (507) 836-8942

Sleepy Eye: *Sleepy Eye Herald-Dispatch* — 115 2nd Ave. N.E.; PO Box 499 (56085); Th; 3,720pd, 250fr (Sw); $5.65; C; publisher & editor Larry Dobson; tel (507) 794-3511; fax (507) 794-5031

S St. Paul/W St. Paul/Inver Grove Hts./Mendota: *South-West Review* — 2515 7th Ave. E., North St. Paul (55109); Su; 24,915fr (VAC); $14.70; C; publishers Jeffery R Enright & N T Lille; editor Lori Sater; managing editor Mary Lee Hagert; tel (612) 777-8800; fax (612) 777-8288

Spicer: *Spicer Free Press* — 14288 Hwy. 23 N.; PO Box 910 (56288); M; 938pd, 15fr (Sw); $4.58; C; publisher Jim Hensley; editor Bev Ahlquist; tel (612) 796-2945; fax (612) 796-6375

Spring Grove: *Spring Grove Herald* — 119 Maple Dr.; PO Box 68 (55974); Tu; 1,500pd, 80fr (Sw); $2.40; publisher B A Onsgard; editor F W Onsgard; tel (507) 498-3868

Spring Valley: *Spring Valley Tribune* — 141 S. Broadway; PO Box 112 (55975-0112); W; 1,836pd, 5fr (Sw); $3.30; C; publisher David A Phillips; editor Cheryl Brandner; tel (507) 346-7365; fax (507) 346-7366

Springfield: *Springfield Advance-Press* — 13 S. Marshall Ave.; PO Box 78 (56087); W; 2,239pd, 39fr (Est); $3.50; C; publisher P C Hedstrom; editor Doris M Weber; tel (507) 723-4225; fax (507) 723-4400

Staples/Motley/Pillager: *The Staples World* — 224 N. 4th St.; PO Box 100, Staples (56479); Th; 2,704pd, 36fr (Sw); $4.30; C; publisher Russ Devlin; general manager Brenda Halvorson; editor Tom Crawford; tel (218) 894-1112; fax (218) 894-3570

Starbuck: *The Starbuck Times* — 504 Wollan St.; PO Box 457 (56381); W; 1,912pd, 172fr (Sw); $3.50; publisher & editor Ron Lindquist; tel (612) 239-2244; fax (612) 239-4214

Stephen/Argyle: *Messenger Banner* — 586 Pacific Ave.; PO Box 48, Stephen (56757); Th; 1,960pd, 155fr (Est); $3.00; publisher & editor E L Anderson; tel (218) 478-2210

Stewartville: *Stewartville Star* — 102 N. Main St.; PO Box 35 (55976); Tu; 2,200pd, 2,700fr (Sw); $3.50; C; publisher & editor Sandy Forstner; tel (507) 533-4271; fax (507) 533-4272

Stillwater: *St. Croix Valley Press* — 4779 Bloom Ave., White Bear Lake (55110); Th; 345pd, 10,875fr (VAC); $10.10; C; publisher Eugene D Johnson; managing editor Paul Wahl; tel (612) 429-7781; fax (612) 429-1242

Storden/Jeffers: *The Storden-Jeffers Times Review* — 316 America St.; PO Box 39, Storden (56174-0039); Th; 620pd, 47fr (Sw); $3.25; publisher George Parrish; editor Sharon Evers; tel (507) 445-3400; fax (507) 445-3104

Thief River Falls: *Northern Watch* — 324 N. Main Ave.; PO Box 100, Thief River Falls (56701-0100); F; 408pd, 21,910fr (Sw); $8.00; C; publisher John Mattson; editor Marvin Lundin; tel (218) 681-4450; fax (218) 681-4455

Thief River Falls: *Thief River Falls Times* — 324 N. Main Ave.; PO Box 100, Thief River Falls (56701); Tu; 5,589pd, 114fr (Sw); $5.50; C; publisher John P Mattson; editor Marvin Lundin; tel (218) 681-4450; fax (218) 681-4455

Tower: *The Tower News* — PO Box 447 (55790); Th; 1,950pd, 50fr (Sw); $3.50; publisher Anthony Sikora; editor Phyllis D Burgess; tel (218) 753-3170

Tracy: *Tracy Headlight-Herald* — 207 4th St.; PO Box 1188 (56175); W; 2,261pd, 24fr (Sw); 24¢; publisher & editor Seth Schmidt; tel (507) 629-4300; fax (507) 629-4301

Truman: *The Truman Tribune* — 118 Ciro St. E.; PO Box 98 (56088); W; 1,118pd, 15fr (Sw); $3.75; C; publisher & editor Vickie K Greiner; tel (507) 776-2751; fax (507) 776-2751

Twin Vly./Gary: *The Twin Valley Times/Gary Graphic* — 101 Main Ave. W.; PO Box 478, Twin Valley (56584); Tu; 1,441pd, 5fr (Sw); $3.75; C; publisher & managing editor Rod Thoreson; tel (218) 584-5195; fax (218) 584-5196

Two Harbors/Silver Bay: *Lake County News-Chronicle* — PO Box 158, Two Harbors (55616); Th; 2,936pd, 46fr (Sw); $1.43; publisher George Williams; editor Forrest Johnson; tel (218) 834-2141

Tyler: *Tyler Tribute* — 151 N. Tyler St.; PO Box Q (56178-0466); Th; 1,610pd, 70fr (Sw); $3.85; publisher & editor Charles R Hunt; tel (507) 247-5502; fax (507) 247-5502

Ulen: *The Ulen Union* — 112 N. P Ave. E.; PO Box 248 (56585); W; 1,355pd, 35fr (Est); $1.55; publisher & editor David G Evans; tel (218) 596-8813

Vadnais Heights: *Vadnais Heights Press* — 4779 Bloom Ave., White Bear Lake (55110); W; 831pd, 3,138fr (VAC); $23.15; C; publisher Eugene D Johnson; managing editor Paul Wahl; tel (612) 429-7781; fax (612) 429-1242

Verndale: *The Verndale Sun* — 21 1st Ave. S.W.; PO Box E (56481); W; 816pd, 53fr (Sw); 69¢; C; publishers Peter Quirt & Theresa Quirt; editor Aaron Quirt; tel (218) 445-5779; fax (218) 445-5779

Waconia: *The Waconia Patriot* — 8 Elm St. S.; PO Box 5 (55387); Th; 3,250pd (Est); 25¢; publisher James D Berreth; general manager Robert Ackerwold; editor Keith Anderson; tel (612) 442-4414; fax (612) 442-4428

Wadena: *Wadena Pioneer Journal* — 314 S. Jefferson; PO Box 31 (56482); Th; 3,750pd, 93fr (Est); $5.30; publisher Randy Mohs; editor Miranda Bryant; tel (218) 631-2561; fax (218) 631-1621

Wanamingo: *The News Record* — 225 Main St.; PO Box 97, Zumbrota (55992); W; 4,300pd, 9,000fr (Est); $5.25; publisher & editor David A Grimsrud; tel (507) 732-7617; fax (507) 732-7619

Warren: *Warren Sheaf* — 127 W. Johnson Ave.; PO Box 45 (56762); W; 3,062pd, 78fr (Sw); $4.00; publisher & editor E Neil Mattson; tel (218) 745-5174; fax (218) 745-5175

Warroad City/Roseau Co.: *The Warroad Pioneer* — 109 E. Lake St.; PO Box E, Warroad (56763); Tu; 2,380pd, 73fr (Est); $2.75; C; publishers Julie Nordine & Rollin Bergman; managing editor Pamela Pederson; tel (218) 386-1594; fax (218) 386-1072

Waseca: *Waseca County News* — 213 2nd St. N.W.; PO Box 465 (56093); Tu/Th; 3,506pd, 32fr (Sw); $5.52; C; publisher & editor Tom West; managing editor Lisa Meyers; tel (507) 835-3380; fax (507) 835-3435

Waterville: *Lake Region Life* — 115 S. 3rd St. (56096); Th; 1,573pd, 65fr (Est); $4.00; C; publisher & editor Jay Schneider; tel (507) 362-4495; fax (507) 362-4458

Wayzata/Orono/Long Lake: *Wayzata/Orono/Long Lake Sun Sailor* — 7831 E. Bush Lake Rd., Bloomington (55439); W; 13,172pd (Est); $22.00; C; publisher Don Thurlow; general manager Ed Shur; editor Greg Krakau; tel (612) 896-4700; fax (612) 896-4728

Wells: *Wells Mirror* — 40 W. Franklin (56097); W; 1,985pd, 71fr (Sw); $3.00; C; publisher Michael Johnson; editor Tracy Madden; tel (507) 553-3131; fax (507) 553-3132

W Concord: *West Concord Enterprise* — 236 W. Main; PO Box 8 (55985); W; 776pd, 43fr (Sw); $3.00; publisher & editor Virginia M Sendle; tel (507) 527-2492; fax (507) 527-2492

Wheaton/Traverse Co.: *Wheaton Gazette* — 1114 Broadway, Wheaton (56296); Tu; 2,908pd, 15fr (Est); 18¢; publisher & editor William N Kremer; managing editor Michael P Kremer; tel (612) 563-8146; fax (612) 563-8147

White Bear Lake/Birchwood: *The White Bear Press* — 4779 Bloom Ave. (55110); W; 7,793pd, 11,159fr (VAC); $20.30; C; publisher Eugene D Johnson; managing editor Paul Wahl; tel (612) 429-7781; fax (612) 429-1242

Williams/Baudette/Roosevelt: *The Northern Light* — Main St.; PO Box 157, Williams (56686); Tu; 1,296pd, 38fr (Sw); $2.50; publishers Julie Nordine & Rollin Bergman; editor Jaime DeLarge; tel (218) 783-6875; fax (218) 783-3651

Windom: *Cottonwood County Citizen* — 260 10th St.; PO Box 309 (56101); Th; 3,475pd, 188fr (Est); $5.70; publisher Kim M Anderson; editor Rahn Larson; tel (507) 831-3455; fax (507) 831-3740

Winona: *Winona Post* — 64 E. 2nd St.; PO Box 27 (55987); W; 24,694fr (CPVS); $9.98; Su; 21,004fr (CPVS); $9.98; publisher John Edstrom; general manager Patrick Marek; editor Frances Edstrom; tel (507) 452-1262; fax (507) 454-6409

Winsted/Lester Prairie: *Winsted Lester Prairie Journal* — 151 Main Ave. W.; PO Box 129, Winsted (55395); M; 1,440pd, 25fr (Sw); $3.70; C; publisher William Ramige; general manager & editor Dale Kovar; tel (612) 485-2535; fax (612) 543-2135

Winthrop: *The Winthrop News* — 110 N. Carver St.; PO Box L (55396); W; 1,410pd (Est); 70¢; publisher Doug Hanson; editor Shirley Sommer; tel (507) 647-5357; fax (507) 647-5358

Wood Lake: *The Wood Lake News* — 250 3rd St.; PO Box 219 (55297-0219); W; 885pd (Sw); $2.50; publisher & editor Corinne F Stelter; tel (507) 485-3141

Woodbury/S Maplewood: *Woodbury-South Maplewood Review* — 2515 7th E., North St. Paul (55109); Tu; 9,515fr (VAC); $7.20; C; publishers Jeffery R Enright & N T Lillie; editor Andy Wind; managing editor Mary Lee Hagert; tel (612) 777-8800; fax (612) 777-8288

Zumbrota: *News-Record* — 225 Main St.; PO Box 97 (55992); W; 4,300pd, 50fr (Sw); $2.14; publisher & editor David A Grimsrud; tel (507) 732-7617

MISSISSIPPI

Ackerman/French Camp/Weir: *The Choctaw Plaindealer* — 139 E. Main; PO Drawer 910, Ackerman (39735); Th; 2,500pd, 100fr (Est); 25¢; C; publisher Robert A Anderson Sr; editor Donna McKey; tel (601) 285-6248; fax (601) 285-6695

Amory/Smithville/Hatley: *Amory Advertiser* — 113 S. Main; PO Box 519, Amory (38821); W; 4,965pd, 266fr (Est); $3.40; C; publisher Barry Burleson; editor Chris Wilson; tel (601) 256-5647; fax (601) 256-5701

Baldwyn: *Baldwyn News* — 102 W. Main St.; PO Box 130 (38824); W; 1,687pd, 20fr (Sw); 17¢; publisher John Haynes; general manager & editor Edwina Carpenter; tel (601) 365-3232; fax (601) 365-3232

Batesville: *The Panolian* — 174 Hwy. 51 N.; PO Box 393 (38606-0393); W; 9,765pd, 300fr (Sw); $5.50; publisher & editor Tawanda Tankersely; tel (601) 563-4591; fax (601) 563-5610

Bay St. Louis/Waveland/Diamondhead: *Sea Coast Echo* — 124 Court St.; PO Box 2009, Bay St. Louis (39521-2009); Th/Su; 6,398pd, 118fr (Sw); $5.90; publisher & editor Ellis Cuevas; general manager Randy Ponder; managing editor Richard Meek; tel (601) 467-5473; fax (601) 467-0333

Bay Springs: *The Jasper County News* — PO Box 449 (39422); W; 2,950pd, 74fr (Sw); $4.50; C; publisher Ronnie L Buckley; editor Kevin Williamson; tel (601) 764-3104/3105; fax (601) 764-3106

Belmont: *The Belmont and Tishomingo Journal* — 430 N. 2nd St.; PO Box 70 (38827); Th; 2,006pd, 57fr (Sw); $4.20; C; publisher M Wayne Mitchell; editor Catherine Mitchell; tel (601) 454-7196; fax (601) 454-7196

Belzoni: *The Belzoni Banner* — 115 Jackson St.; PO Box 610 (39038); W; 1,910pd, 50fr (Sw); $2.80; publisher & editor Mary W Toney; general manager Julian Toney III; tel (601) 247-3373; fax (601) 247-3373

Benton Co.: *Southern Advocate* — 114 Church St.; PO Box 157, Ashland (38603-0157); Th; 1,162pd (Sw); $2.00; publisher & editor Granville P Harrison Jr; tel (601) 224-6681; fax (601) 224-6681

Biloxi/Harrison: *Biloxi-D'Iberville Press* — PO Box 194, Biloxi (39533); W; 6,870pd, 1,000fr (Est); $6.60; C; publisher C R Stein; editor Walter Fountain; tel (601) 392-3307; fax (601) 392-7043

Booneville/Prentiss Co.: *The Banner-Independent* — 210 Main St.; PO Box 10, Booneville (38829); Th; 5,397pd, 85fr (ABC); $6.45; editor Duane Cross; tel (601) 728-6214; fax (601) 728-1636

Bruce: *The Calhoun County Journal* — 207 N. Newberger; PO Box 278 (38915); W; 3,350pd, 118fr (Est); $4.25; publisher S Gale Denley; editors Joanne Denley & Lisa Denley; tel (601) 983-2570; fax (601) 983-7667

Calhoun City/Derma/Verdaman: *The Monitor-Herald* — 200 S. Main St.; PO Box 69, Calhoun City (38916); Th; 2,832pd, 80fr (Sw); $3.65; publisher & editor Kenny Hoblitzell; tel (601) 628-5241; fax (601) 628-4651

Canton: *Madison County Herald* — 159 E. Center St.; PO Box 119 (39046); Th; 3,809pd, 29fr (Est); $5.36; editor Ken Wilbanks; managing editor Bill Zimmerman; tel (601) 859-1221; fax (601) 859-9409

Carrollton: *The Conservative* — Lexington Ave.; PO Box 345, Carrollton (38917); Th; 992pd, 14fr (Est); $4.25; publisher & editor Tim Beeland; tel (601) 283-1131

Carthage: *The Carthaginian* — 122 W. Franklin St.; PO Box 457 (39051); Th; 5,169pd, 59fr (Sw); $4.75; publisher John Keith; general manager Brenda Lewis; editor Mildred Dearman; managing editor E Waid Prather; tel (601) 267-4501; fax (601) 267-5290

Charleston/Tallahatchie: *Sun Sentinel* — S. Court Sq.; PO Box 250, Charleston (38921); Th; 2,303pd, 99fr (Sw); $4.50; publisher & editor Clay McFerrin; tel (601) 647-8462

Clinton/Hinds: *Clinton News* — 311 E. Jefferson; PO Box 66, Clinton (39056); Th; 300pd, 9,900fr (Sw); $5.00; C; publisher Duane McAllister; editor Bill Zimmerman; tel (601) 924-7142; fax (601) 924-7976

Collins/Covington Co.: *The News-Commercial* — 104 1st St. S.; PO Drawer 1299, Collins (39428); W; 3,142pd, 25fr (Sw); $2.50; publisher & editor Jamie Arrington; tel (601) 765-8275; fax (601) 765-6952

Columbia/Marion Co.: *The Columbian-Progress* — 318 2nd St.; PO Box 1171, Columbia (39429); Th/Sa; 4,115pd, 36fr (Est); $5.30; publisher & editor Ken Prillhart; managing editor Laurie Bultman; tel (601) 736-2611; fax (601) 736-4507

Crystal Springs: *The Meteor* — 201 E. Georgetown St.; PO Box 353 (39059); W; 3,615pd, 1,385fr (Est); $4.62; publisher & editor Henry Carney; tel (601) 892-2581; fax (601) 892-2249

De Kalb: *Kemper County Messenger* — Main St.; PO Box 546 (39328); Th; 1,500pd, 85fr (Est); $1.95; publisher James L Sledge Jr; general manager Jayne Jowers; editor Jeff Jowers; tel (601) 743-5760; fax (601) 743-2760

DeSoto Co.: *DeSoto Times* — PO Box 100, Hernando (36832); Th; 6,559pd, 234fr (Sw); $7.00; publisher & editor William Bailey; managing editor Nora Bentley; tel (601) 429-6397; fax (601) 429-5229

Eupora/Mathiston: *Webster Progress-Times* — 124 Dunn St.; PO Drawer D, Eupora (39744); W; 2,049pd (Sw); $4.00; publisher & general manager Timothy R James; tel (601) 258-7532; fax (601) 258-6474

Fayette/Jefferson Co.: *Fayette Chronicle* — 429 N. Main St.; PO Box 536, Fayette (39069); Th; 1,950pd, 35fr (Est); $3.00; publisher Charles K Shepard; editor Charles B Shepard; tel (601) 786-3661; fax (601) 786-3661

Franklin Co.: *Franklin Advocate* — 111 Main St.; PO Box 576, Meadville (39653); W; 2,971pd, 12fr (Sw); $4.00; publisher & editor David Webb; tel (601) 384-2484; fax (601) 384-2276

Fulton/Itawamba Co.: *The Itawamba County Times* — 106 W. Main St.; PO Drawer 1549, Fulton (38843); W; 5,257pd, 73fr (Sw); $5.67; C; publisher & editor Rubye Del Harden; general manager Phyllis Zettler; managing editor Susan Harp; tel (601) 862-3141; fax (601) 862-7804

Gauthier: *Gauthier Independent* — 3880 Gauthier-Vancleave Rd.; PO Box 158 (39553); Th; 588pd, 52fr (Sw); $5.65; C; publisher & general manager James B Ricketts; tel (601) 497-4571

Gloster: *Wilk-Amite Record* — Main St.; PO Box 130 (39638); F; 1,811pd, 10fr (Est); $4.00; publisher & editor David Webb; general manager Louise McKenzie; tel (601) 225-4531; fax (601) 384-2276

Greene Co.: *Greene County Herald* — Main St. at Capital St.; PO Box 220, Leakesville (39451); Th; 2,803pd, 52fr (Est); 16¢; publisher John F Turner; editor Leola Turner; tel (601) 394-5070; fax (601) 394-5070

Hazlehurst/Wesson/Crystal Springs: *Copiah County Courier* — 103 S. Ragsdale Ave.; PO Box 351, Hazlehurst (39083); W; 3,829pd, 203fr (Sw); $5.56; C; publisher & editor James W Lambert Jr; tel (601) 894-3141; fax (601) 894-3144

Holly Springs/Marshall: *South Reporter* — 157 S. Center St.; PO Box 278, Holly Springs (38635); Th; 5,122pd, 25fr (Sw); $4.90; C; publisher & editor Walter W Webb; tel (601) 252-4261; fax (601) 252-3388

Holmes Co.: *Holmes County Herald* — 308 Court Sq.; PO Box 60, Lexington (39095-0060); Th; 3,241pd, 151fr (Est); $3.75; publisher & editor Bruce Hill; general manager Libby Hill; tel (601) 834-1151; fax (601) 834-1074

Houston: *Times Post* — 219 N. Jackson St.; PO Box 629 (38851); W; 3,914pd, 5,300fr (Sw); 17¢; C; publisher & editor Kenny Hoblitzell; tel (601) 456-3771; fax (601) 456-5202

Indianola: *The Enterprise-Tocsin* — 114 Main St.; PO Box 650 (38751); Th; 4,542pd, 63fr (Est); $3.26; publisher & editor Jim D Abbott; tel (601) 887-2222; fax (601) 887-2999

Iuka: *Tishomingo County News* — 120 W. Front St.; PO Box 70 (38852); Th; 3,882pd, 116fr (Sw); $4.50; publisher John H Biggs; editor Charlotte McVay; tel (601) 423-2211; fax (601) 423-2214

Jackson/Hinds/Madison: *Northside Sun* — 246 Briarwood; PO Box 16709, Jackson (39236); Th; 8,665pd, 548fr (Sw); $9.11; publisher J Wyatt Emmerich; editor Jimmye Sweat; tel (601) 957-1122; fax (601) 957-1533

Kosciusko: *The Star-Herald* — PO Box 1228 (39090); Th; 7,541pd, 250fr (Sw); 18¢; C; publisher Neal H Turnage; editor Jack Weatherly; tel (601) 289-2251; fax (601) 289-2254

Leland: *Leland Progress* — 103 E. 3rd St.; PO Box 72 (38756); Th; 1,241pd, 50fr (Est); $3.25; publisher & editor Jeremy Weldon; tel (601) 686-4081; fax (601) 686-4081

Liberty: *The Southern Herald* — 258 Main St.; PO Box 674 (39645); Th; 1,180pd, 15fr (Est); $2.80; publisher & editor Richard H Stratton; tel (601) 657-4818; fax (601) 657-4818

Louisville: *Winston County Journal* — 119 N. Court St.; PO Box 469 (39339); W; 4,197pd, 42fr (Sw); $7.46; publisher & editor Jerry Shiverdecker; tel (601) 773-6241; fax (601) 773-6242

Lucedale: *George County Times* — PO Box 238 (39452); Th; 5,000pd, 100fr (Est); 14¢; publisher & editor O G Sellers; tel (601) 947-2967

Madison/Ridgeland/Canton/Jackson/Flora: *Madison County Journal* — 210 W. Jackson St.; PO Box 219, Ridgeland (39153); Th; 2,586pd, 482fr (Sw); $6.10; C; publisher & editor James E Prince III; tel (601) 853-4222; fax (601) 856-9419

Magee/Mendenhall: *The Magee Courier* — 206 N. Main Ave.; PO Box 338, Magee (39111-0338); Th; 3,400pd, 85fr (Sw); $7.58; C; publisher & editor John Pat Brown; general manager Pat Brown; managing editor Miriam May; tel (601) 849-3434; fax (601) 849-6828

Magnolia: *The Magnolia Gazette* — PO Box 152 (39652); W; 1,380pd (Est); $4.39; publisher Louisiana State Newspapers; general manager Carol Brooke; editor Chellette Simmons; tel (601) 783-2441; fax (504) 748-7104

Marks: *Quitman County Democrat* — PO Box 328 (38646); Th; 2,060pd, 72fr (Est); 79¢; publishers & editors John Fleming & Josephine Fleming; tel (601) 326-2181; fax (601) 326-6077

Mendenhall/Simpson Co.: *Simpson County News* — 120 Court Ave., Mendenhall (39114); Th; 1,950pd, 74fr (Est); $7.58; C; publisher & editor John Pat Brown; managing editor Miriam May; tel (601) 847-2525; fax (601) 849-6828

Monroe Co.: *Aberdeen Examiner* — 209 E. Commerce St.; PO Box 279, Aberdeen (39730); W; 5,162pd, 67fr (Est); 29¢; publisher & editor Barry Burleson; general manager Rubye Del Hardin; tel (601) 369-4507; fax (601) 369-4508

Monticello: *Lawrence County Press* — 534 Broad St.; PO Box 549 (39654); W; 3,428pd, 20fr (Sw); $5.00; publisher & editor John H Carney Jr; tel (601) 587-2781

New Albany: *New Albany Gazette* — 713 Carter Ave.; PO Box 300 (38652); W/F; 5,715pd, 145fr (Est); $3.94; C; publisher New Albany Publishing Co.; general manager Kenneth Jones; editor Betty Jo Stewart; tel (601) 534-6321; fax (601) 534-6355

Newton Co.: *The Newton Record* — 120 S. Main St.; PO Box 60, Newton (39345); W; 2,335pd, 31fr (Sw); $4.95; C; publisher & editor J E Strange; tel (601) 683-2001; fax (601) 683-2360

Noxubee Co.: *Macon Beacon* — 403 S. Jefferson; PO Box 32, Macon (39341); Th; 2,795pd, 77fr (Sw); $2.95; C; publisher & editor R Scott Boyd; tel (601) 726-4747; fax (601) 726-4742

Ocean Springs: *Ocean Springs Record* — 715 Cox Ave.; PO Box 1650 (39566-1650); Th; 3,169pd, 334fr (Sw); $5.65; C; publisher & editor James B Ricketts; tel (601) 875-2791; fax (601) 875-9569

Okolona: *Okolona Messenger* — 249 Main St. (38860); Th; 1,086pd, 19fr (Est); $2.50; publisher & editor Murry Blankenship; tel (601) 447-5501; fax (601) 447-5024

Olive Branch/DeSoto Co.: *DeSoto County Tribune* — 8885 Goodman Rd.; PO Box 486, Olive Branch (38654); W; 4,384pd, 90fr (Sw); $8.65; C; publisher D W Jones; editor Tyler Chow; tel (601) 895-6220; fax (601) 895-4377

Panola Co.: *The Southern Reporter* — 203 S. Main St.; PO Box 157, Sardis (38666-0157); Th; 2,125pd, 343fr (Sw); $4.32; publisher & editor J Crisler Fletcher; tel (601) 487-1551; fax (601) 487-1552

Philadelphia: *The Neshoba Democrat* — 439 Beacon St.; PO Box 30 (39350); W; 7,084pd, 85fr (Sw); $5.00; C; publisher & editor Stanley Dearman; tel (601) 656-4000; fax (601) 656-6379

Pontotoc: *Pontotoc Progress* — PO Box 210 (38863); Th; 6,232pd, 221fr (Sw); $5.75; publisher Gary Andrews; editor David Helms; tel (601) 489-3511; fax (601) 489-6714

Poplarville: *The Poplarville Democrat* — 109 W. Pearl St.; PO Box 549 (39470); Th; 1,736pd, 30fr (Sw); $4.00; publisher Dave Sims; editor Larry Stringer; tel (601) 795-2247; fax (601) 798-8602

Port Gibson: *The Port Gibson Reveille* — 708 Main St.; PO Box 1002 (39150); Th; 2,151pd, 49fr (Sw); $3.80; publisher & editor Edgar T Crisler Jr; tel (601) 437-5103; fax (601) 437-4410

Prentiss/Bassfield: *Prentiss Headlight* — 1020 3rd St.; PO Box 1257, Prentiss (39474); W; 2,803pd, 25fr (Est); $3.32; C; publisher William O Jacobs; editor Patsy Speights; tel (601) 792-4221; fax (601) 792-4222

Purvis: *Lamar County News* — Pump St.; PO Box 429 (39475); Th; 1,048pd, 94fr (Est); 14¢; publisher Larry Sanford; editor Mitch Deaver; tel (601) 794-2765; fax (601) 796-3542

Quitman/Clarke: *Clarke County Tribune* — PO Box 900, Quitman (39355); W; 3,735pd, 50fr (Est); $4.00; C; publisher James T Speed; general manager Mary C Speed; editor Cindy Baxley; tel (601) 776-3726; fax (601) 776-5793

Raleigh/Taylorsville: *Smith County Reformer* — PO Box 380, Taylorsville (39168); W; 2,965pd, 720fr (Sw); $4.50; C; publisher Ronnie L Buckley; editor Belinda Singleton; tel (601) 785-6525; fax (601) 785-6525

Rankin Co.: *Rankin County News* — PO Box 107, Brandon (39042); W; 5,293pd (Est); $5.00; C; publisher & editor Marcus R Bowers Jr; tel (601) 825-8333; fax (601) 825-8334

Richton: *Richton Dispatch* — 110 Walnut St.; PO Drawer X (39476); Th; 1,430pd, 25fr (Sw); 12¢; publisher & editor Larry A Wilson; general manager Dean Wilson; tel (601) 788-6031; fax (601) 788-6031

Ripley: *Southern Sentinel* — 113 N. Commerce St.; PO Box 558 (38663); W/Sa; 7,110pd, 62fr (Sw); $4.75; publisher & editor Ronald H Prince; managing editor Kenny Goode; tel (601) 837-8111; fax (601) 837-4504

Rolling Fork: *Deer Creek Pilot* — PO Box 398 (39159); Th; 1,500pd, 50fr (Est); $2.80; publisher & editor Ray Mosby; tel (601) 873-4354; fax (601) 873-4355

Scott Co.: *Scott County Times* — 311 Smith St.; PO Box 89, Forest (39074); W; 4,902pd, 134fr (Sw); $6.50; C; publisher & editor Sidney L Salter; managing editor Leilani Pope; tel (601) 469-2561; fax (601) 469-2004

Senatobia/Tate Co.: *The Democrat* — 219 E. Main St.; PO Box 369, Senatobia (38668); Tu; 4,060pd, 165fr (Sw); $5.50; C; publisher Joe Lee III; editor Sarah Bondurant; tel (601) 562-4414; fax (601) 562-8866

Tunica: *The Tunica Times* — 991 Magnolia St.; PO Box 308 (38676); Th; 1,834pd, 172fr (Sw); $3.65; publisher & editor Brooks N Taylor; tel (601) 363-1511; fax (601) 363-1511

Tylertown: *The Tylertown Times* — 727 Beulah Ave.; PO Box 72 (39667); Th; 3,620pd, 63fr (Est); $3.95; publisher & editor Carolyn Dillon; tel (601) 876-5111; fax (601) 876-5280

Union: *The Union Appeal* — 105 Main St.; PO Box 10 (39365); W; 2,950pd (Est); $3.50; publisher & editor Jack R Tannehill; managing editor John Muse; tel (601) 774-9433; fax (601) 774-8301

Water Vly.: *North Mississippi Herald* — PO Box 648 (38965); Th; 2,701pd, 102fr (Sw); $4.00; publisher & editor Ed Shearer III; general manager Betty Shearer; tel (601) 473-1473

Waynesboro/Wayne Co.: *The Wayne County News* — 608 Station St.; PO Box 509, Waynesboro (39367-0509); Th; 4,333pd, 79fr (Sw); $3.95; publisher Jeff Mosley; tel (601) 735-4341; fax (601) 735-1111

Wiggins: *Stone County Enterprise* — 143 1st St.; PO Box 157 (39577); W; 2,900pd, 55fr (Sw); $4.50; C; publisher & editor Don Groves; tel (601) 928-4802; fax (601) 928-2191

Winona: *The Winona Times* — 321 Summit St.; PO Box 151 (38967); Th; 3,602pd, 61fr (Sw); $4.25; publisher & editor Tim Beeland; tel (601) 283-1131

Woodville/Centerville: *The Woodville Republican* — 425 Depot St.; PO Box 696, Woodville (39669); Th; 2,800pd, 75fr (Sw); $2.94; publisher & editor Andrew J Lewis; tel (601) 888-4293; fax (601) 888-6151

Yalobusha Co.: *The Coffeeville Courier* — 1119 Main St.; PO Drawer G, Coffeeville (38922); Th; 2,100pd, 50fr (Sw); $1.75; publisher Gerald H Denley; managing editor Sarah H Williams; tel (601) 675-2446

Yazoo Co.: *The Yazoo Herald* — 1035 Grand Ave.; PO Box 720, Yazoo City (39194); W/Sa; 3,816pd, 33fr (Est); $4.97; publisher & editor Roy Thomas; tel (601) 746-4911; fax (601) 746-4915

MISSOURI

Adrian/Bates Co.: *The Adrian Journal* — 39 E. Main; PO Box 128, Adrian (64720); Th; 1,500pd (Sw); $4.25; C; publisher Linda G Oldfield; publisher & editor Stephen M Oldfield; tel (816) 297-2100; fax (816) 297-2149

II-44 Missouri U.S. Weeklies

Advance: *Advance Statesman* — PO Box 310 (63730); W; 1,779pd, 75fr (Est); 90¢; publisher Barbara Hill; general manager Judy Frederich; editor Jan Morgan; tel (314) 722-5322; fax (314) 722-5322

Albany/Stanberry: *The Albany Ledger* — Smith & Clay Sts.; PO Box 247, Albany (64402); W; 2,300pd, 45fr (Sw); $3.20; publishers Jack T Pitzer & Tanya L Pitzer; editor Jim Avey; tel (816) 726-3997; fax (816) 726-3997

Appleton City: *Appleton City Journal* — PO Box 7 (64724); Th; 1,725pd, 64fr (Est); $3.60; C; publisher Jack Krier; editor Mike Crawford; tel (816) 476-5566; fax (816) 476-5566

Arcadia Vly./Iron Co./Ironton/Pilot Knob/Belleview: *Mountain Echo* — 110 N. Main; PO Box 25, Ironton (63650); W; 2,856pd, 44fr (Sw); $4.65; C; publisher Judy Schaaf; general manager Lisa Yancey; editor Mark Cheaney; tel (314) 546-3917; fax (314) 546-3919

Archie: *The Archie News* — PO Box 344 (64725); Th; 300pd (Sw); $5.25; C; publishers Linda G Oldfield & Stephen G Oldfield; tel (816) 297-2100

Arnold: *Jefferson County Journal* — 27 Fox Valley Center (63010); W; 19,675fr (CAC); $13.42; Su; 19,330fr (CAC); $13.42; publisher Jefferson County Publications; general manager Joe Michelson; editor Lois Kendall; managing editor John Winkleman; tel (314) 296-2800; fax (314) 296-3224

Ash Grove/Walnut Grove/Willard/Bois D'Arc/Everton/Dadeville/Halltown: *Ash Grove Commonwealth* — 105 Main St.; PO Box 277 (65604); Th; 1,586pd, 3,725fr (Sw); 13¢; C; publisher & editor F Dal Mason; publisher Mrs F Dal Mason; tel (417) 751-2322

Aurora/Marionville/Verona: *Aurora Advertiser* — 226 W. Church; PO Box 509, Aurora (65605); M/F; 3,465pd (Sw); $4.15; W; 3,465pd, 6,800fr (Sw); $4.50; C; publisher Paul E Donley; editor Kim McCully; tel (417) 678-2115; fax (417) 678-2117

Ava: *Douglas County Herald* — PO Box 577 (65608); Th; 4,900pd, 50fr (Est); $2.75; publisher J E Curry; editor Keith Moore; tel (417) 683-4181

Ballwin/Manchester/Winchester: *Press Journal* — 1714 Deer Tracks Trl., St. Louis (63131); W; 32,160fr (Sw); $13.34; Su; 31,492fr (Sw); $13.34; C; general manager Laurie Salmo; editor Mary Shapiro; managing editor Dan Barger; tel (314) 821-2462; fax (314) 821-0843

Barry Co.: *Barry County Advertiser* — 904 West St.; PO Box 488, Cassville (65625); W; 11,500fr (Est); $4.00; publisher Jean Melton; general manager & managing editor Russ Melton; editor Jennie Herrin; tel (417) 847-4475/3155; fax (417) 847-4523

Bates Co.: *News-Xpress* — 5 N. Main St.; PO Box 210, Butler (64730); F; 3,726pd, 109fr (Sw); $5.05; C; publisher Jim Peters; editor C A Moore; tel (816) 679-6127; fax (816) 679-4905

Belle/Linn: *The Belle Banner/Tri-County Newspapers* — 307 S. Alvarado Ave.; PO Box 711, Belle (65013); W; 1,658pd, 170fr (Sw); 16¢; C; publisher & editor Ron J Lewis; tel (314) 859-3328; fax (314) 859-6274

Bellefontaine Neighbors/Jennings/Flordell Hills: *North County East Journal* — 4305 Woodson Rd., St. Louis (63134); W; 47,495fr (CAC); $13.94; Su; 46,458pd (CAC); $13.94; general manager Rick Jarvis; editor Dan Barger; managing editor Ann Nicholson; tel (314) 426-2222; fax (314) 426-4911

Belton/Raymore: *The Star-Herald* — 419 Main St.; PO Box 379, Belton (64012); Th; 4,269pd, 28fr (Est); $6.00; C; publisher & editor Mark Fox; tel (816) 331-5353; fax (816) 322-2943

Bethany/Harrison Co.: *Bethany Republican-Clipper* — 214 N. 16th St.; PO Box 351, Bethany (64424); W; 4,000pd, 16,000fr (Sw); 27¢; C; publisher & editor Philip Conger; tel (816) 425-6325; fax (816) 425-3441

Bland/Owensville: *The Bland Courier/Tri-County Newspapers* — 307 S. Alvarado Ave.; PO Box AA, Belle (65013); W; 783pd, 70fr (Sw); 16¢; C; publisher Kurt J Lewis; editor Ron J Lewis; tel (314) 646-3312; fax (314) 859-6274

Bloomfield: *The Bloomfield Vindicator* — 300 N. Prairie St.; PO Box L (63825); W; 1,525pd, 60fr (Sw); $3.50; publisher & editor Barbara Hill; general manager Vicci Lang; tel (314) 568-3310; fax (314) 624-7449

Bolivar: *Herald-Free Press* — 335 S. Springfield St.; PO Box 330 (65613); W; 7,235pd, 40fr (Sw); $5.05; C; publisher Dave Berry; editor Judy Kallenbach; tel (417) 326-7636; fax (417) 326-8701

Bollinger Co.: *The Banner-Press* — 103 Walnut St.; PO Box 45, Marble Hill (63764); Th; 4,416pd, 34fr (Sw); $4.10; publisher Wally Lage; general manager Dale Chronister; editor Jim McIntosh; tel (314) 238-2821

Boone Co.: *Boone County Journal* — PO Box 197, Ashland (65010); Th; 1,510pd, 103fr (Est); $3.00; publisher Dick Flink; publisher & editor Jane Flink; tel (314) 657-2334; fax (314) 657-2002

Boonville: *The Record* — 412 High St. (65233); Tu; 265pd, 10,000fr (Sw); $7.60; publisher Scott J Jackson; editor Steve Thomas; tel (816) 882-5335; fax (816) 882-2256

Bourbon: *Bourbon Beacon* — 120 N. Pine St.; PO Box 300 (65441); Th; 850pd (Est); $2.20; publisher & editor Mary Warden; tel (314) 732-4410

Bowling Green: *The Bowling Green Times* — 106 W. Main; PO Box 110 (63334); W; 2,800pd, 23fr (Sw); $4.05; C; publisher & editor Kate B Dickson; tel (314) 324-2222; fax (314) 324-3991

Braymer: *Braymer Bee* — 306 Shouse St.; PO Box 308 (64624); Th; 1,345pd, 72fr (Est); $1.25; publisher Anne Tezon; editor Patty Pryor; tel (816) 645-2217; fax (813) 645-2217

Brunswick: *The Brunswicker* — 118 E. Broadway; PO Box 188 (65236); Th; 1,826pd, 95fr (Est); $2.72; publisher & editor Larry M Baxley; publisher Susan K Baxley; tel (816) 548-3171; fax (816) 388-6688

Buffalo: *Buffalo Reflex* — 114 E. Lincoln; PO Box 770 (65622); W; 4,414pd, 50fr (Sw); $4.00; C; publisher & editor James E Hamilton; tel (417) 345-2224; fax (417) 345-2235

Cabool: *Cabool Enterprise* — 525 Main St.; PO Box 40 (65689); Th; 1,995pd (Sw); 11¢; publishers C Russell Wood & Joanne M Wood; editor Dala Whittaker; tel (417) 962-4411; fax (417) 962-4455

Cameron: *The Citizen Observer* — BB Hwy.; PO Box 70 (64429); Th; 2,324pd, 85fr (Sw); $2.70; C; publisher & editor Craig Watkins; general manager Scott Gordon; tel (816) 632-6543; fax (816) 632-4508

Campbell: *Campbell Citizen* — 406 W. Grand; PO Box 186 (63933); W; 1,560pd, 40fr (Est); 18¢; publisher & editor Ronald Kemp; tel (314) 246-2531

Canton/Lewis Co.: *The Canton Press-News Journal* — 130 N. 4th St.; PO Box 227, Canton (63435); Th; 3,400pd (Sw); $2.38; publisher David Steinbeck; editor Daniel Steinbeck; tel (314) 288-5668

Carrollton: *Carrollton Democrat* — Hwy. 65 S.; PO Box 69 (64633); Tu/F; 2,579pd, 61fr (Sw); $4.35; C; publisher Frank W Mercer; editor Jon E Flatland; tel (816) 542-0881; fax (816) 542-2580

Caruthersville: *The Tuesday Democrat-Argus* — 111 E. 5th St.; PO Box 1059 (63830); Tu; 2,417pd, 26fr (Sw); $4.15; publisher John Rust; general manager Sheila Ralph; editor Jennifer Dodson; tel (314) 333-4336; fax (314) 333-2307

Caruthersville: *The Wednesday Democrat-Argus* — 111 E. 5th St.; PO Box 1059 (63830); W; 2,301pd, 26fr (Sw); $3.85; publisher John Rust; general manager Sheila Ralph; editor Jennifer Dodson; tel (314) 333-4336; fax (314) 333-2307

Cassville: *Cassville Democrat* — 600 Main St.; PO Box 486 (65625); W; 3,393pd, 70fr (Est); $3.60; publisher & editor Lisa Schlichtman; publisher Mike Schlichtman; general manager Darlene Wierman; tel (417) 847-2610; fax (417) 847-3092

Centralia/Sturgeon: *The Centralia Fireside Guard* — 118 W. Sneed; PO Box 7, Centralia (65240); W; 3,183pd, 900fr (Est); 29¢; publisher Jeff Hedberg; editors Charles A Hedberg & Janann Hedberg; tel (314) 682-2133; fax (314) 682-3361

Chariton Co.: *Chariton Courier* — PO Box 318, Marceline (64658); Th; 570pd, 80fr (Est); $2.65; C; publisher Ivan Buckman; general manager Bill Evans; tel (816) 376-3508; fax (816) 376-2757

Charleston: *The Enterprise-Courier* — 206 S. Main St.; PO Box 69 (63834); Th; 2,600pd, 350fr (Est); 26¢; publisher Mildred Wallhausen; general manager Kelly Golightly; editors Jim Anderson & Liz Anderson; tel (314) 683-3351; fax (314) 683-2217

Chesterfield/Clarkson Valley/Widwood: *Chesterfield Journal* — 1714 Deer Tracks Trl., St. Louis (63131); W; 14,899fr (Est); $9.26; Su; 14,595fr (Est); $9.26; C; general manager Laurie Salmo; editor Mary Shapiro; managing editor Dan Barger; tel (314) 821-2462; fax (314) 821-0843

Clarence: *Clarence Courier* — 106 E. Maple St.; PO Drawer 10 (63437); W; 1,562pd, 118fr (Sw); $3.00; C; publisher & editor Dennis Williams; tel (816) 699-2344; fax (816) 699-2194

Clinton/Henry Co.: *Clinton Eye* — 212 S. Washington; PO Box 586, Clinton (64735); Th; 665pd, 20fr (Est); $4.50; C; publisher & editor Kathleen White Miles; general manager Dan Miles; tel (816) 885-2281; fax (816) 885-2265

Cole Camp: *Cole Camp Courier* — 401 1/2 W. Main; PO Box 280 (65325); Th; 1,000pd (Sw); $2.25; publisher James E Dickerson; editor Diana Ball; tel (816) 668-4418; fax (816) 668-4418

Concordia/Emma/Alma/Blackburn/Waverly: *The Concordian* — 714 Main St.; PO Box 999, Concordia (64020-0999); W; 2,938pd, 63fr (Sw); $3.20; C; publisher & editor Gary L Beissenherz; tel (816) 463-7522; fax (816) 463-7942

Crane/Stone Co.: *The Crane Chronicle/Stone County Republican* — 108 Main; PO Box A, Crane (65633-0401); Th; 2,816pd, 15fr (Sw); $3.50; editor Dolores M Shiveley; tel (417) 723-5248; fax (417) 723-8490

Crestwood/Sunset Hills/Fenton: *Southwest County Journal* — 4210 Chippewa, St. Louis (63116); W; 29,690fr (Est); $13.89; Su; 28,546fr (Est); $13.89; C; publisher Don Miller; general manager Laurie Salmo; editors Jim Merkel & Kevin Carbery; managing editor Lois Kendall; tel (314) 664-2700; fax (314) 664-8533

Creve Coeur/Des Peres: *West County Journal* — 1714 Deer Tracks Trl., St. Louis (63131); W/Su; 28,844fr (Est); $12.75; C; publisher Don Miller; editor Regina DeLuca; managing editor Dan Barger; tel (314) 821-2462; fax (314) 821-0843

Cuba: *The Cuba Free Press* — 110 S. Buchanon; PO Box 568 (65453); Th; 3,573pd, 42fr (Sw); $2.85; C; publisher Delma Pascoe; publisher & editor Percy Pascoe; tel (314) 885-7460; fax (314) 885-3803

Daviess Co.: *Gallatin North Missourian* — 203 N. Main; PO Box 37, Gallatin (64640); W; 2,596pd (Sw); $3.25; C; publisher & editor Darryl Wilkinson; tel (816) 663-2154; fax (816) 663-2498

De Soto: *Family Gazette* — 320 S. Main (63020); W; 5,000fr (Est); $7.50; publisher & editor Lee Khorl; tel (314) 337-0800; fax (314) 337-0800

Dixon: *Dixon Pilot* — 302 Locust; PO Drawer V (65459); Th; 2,800pd (Est); $3.00; publisher Rick Blackburn; general manager Connie Blackburn; editor Ralph Nelson; tel (314) 759-2127

Doniphan: *The Prospect-News* — 110 Washington St.; PO Box 367 (63935); W; 5,379pd (Est); 16¢; C; publisher Don Schrieber; editor Barbara Horton; tel (314) 996-2103

Drexel: *Drexel Star* — 130 Main St.; PO Box 378 (64742); Th; 1,080pd (Est); $3.00; publisher Stephen M Oldfield; editor Ellen Glaze; tel (816) 657-2222; fax (816) 657-2045

Dunklin/New Madrid: *Delta News Journal & Press Merit* — 127 W. Main; PO Box 701, Malden (63863); Tu; 1,000pd, 33,000fr (Est); $5.00; C; publisher Barbara Hill; editor Tim Gage; managing editor Lorraine Heiser; tel (314) 276-5148/4523; fax (314) 276-3687

E Prairie: *The East Prairie Eagle* — 116 E. Chestnut; PO Box 10 (63845); W; 2,398pd, 25fr (Est); $3.64; C; publisher Mildred Wallhausen; general manager & editor Liz Anderson; tel (314) 649-3541; fax (314) 683-2217

Edina: *The Edina Sentinel* — 205 N. Main; PO Box 270 (63537-0270); W; 1,925pd, 60fr (Est); 82¢; publisher & editor Hazel Bledsoe Smith; tel (816) 397-2226; fax (816) 397-2227

El Dorado Springs: *El Dorado Springs Sun* — 125 N. Main; PO Box 71, El Dorado Springs (64744); Th; 4,354pd, 50fr (Sw); $2.50; publisher Kimball S Long; editor Kenneth W Long; tel (417) 876-3841; fax (417) 876-3348

El Dorado Springs: *The Star* — 105 S. Main St.; PO Box 269, El Dorado Springs (64744); Th; 492pd, 2fr (Sw); $3.60; C; publisher & editor Larry Brownlee; publisher Patsy Brownlee; general manager Mae McNeece; tel (417) 876-2500; fax (417) 876-5986

Eldon: *Eldon Advertiser* — 415 S. Maple; PO Box 315 (65026); Th; 5,064pd, 55fr (Sw); $3.25; C; publisher Dane Vernon; general manager Tim Flora; editor Virginia Duffield; tel (314) 392-5658

Ellington: *Reynolds County Courier* — Main St.; PO Box 130 (63638); Th; 2,662pd, 20fr (Sw); $5.45; publisher & editor Harold T Ellinghouse; publisher Mary B Stivers; tel (314) 663-2243; fax (314) 663-2763

Elsberry: *The Elsberry Democrat* — 312 Broadway (63343); W; 1,380pd, 2fr (Est); $2.40; editor Margaret Ann Herring; tel (314) 898-2318; fax (314) 898-2173

Eminence/Winona/Mountain View/Summersville: *Current Wave* — Main St.; PO Box J, Eminence (65466); W; 1,950pd, 24fr (Sw); $4.00; publisher & editor Roger Dillon; general manager Rita Johnson; tel (314) 226-3335; fax (314) 226-3335

Fairfax: *The Fairfax Forum* — 128 Main St.; PO Box 17 (64446); Th; 879pd (Sw); $2.16; editor Nancy Gaines; tel (816) 686-2741

Farmington/St. Francois: *The Press-Leader* — 218 N. Washington; PO Box 70, Farmington (63640); Tu; 3,978pd, 20,300fr (Sw); $7.77; Th/Sa; 3,978pd (Sw); $7.77; publisher Mark Griggs; editor Mike Myers; tel (314) 756-8927; fax (314) 756-9160

Faucett/Rural Buchanan Co.: *Buchanan County News* — PO Box 217, Faucett (64448); W; 1,850pd, 80fr (Sw); $4.00; publisher Jim McPherson; editor Beth McPherson; tel (816) 238-3996; fax (816) 238-0036

Fayette: *The Democrat-Leader* — 202 E. Morrison; PO Box 32 (65248-0032); Sa; 2,410pd, 92fr (Sw); $2.98; publisher & editor H Denny Davis; tel (816) 248-2235; fax (816) 248-1200

Fayette: *The Fayette Advertiser* — 202 E. Morrison; PO Box 32 (65248-0032); W; 2,410pd, 92fr (Sw); $2.98; publisher & editor H Denny Davis; tel (816) 248-2235; fax (816) 248-1200

Ferguson/Berkeley/Normandy: *North County Journal West* — 4305 Woodson Rd., Woodson Terrace (63134); W; 51,995fr (CAC); $17.06; Su; 50,678fr (CAC); $17.06; general manager Rick Jarvis; editor Dan Barger; tel (314) 426-2222; fax (314) 426-4911

Festus: *News Democrat Journal* — 998 E. Gannon Dr.; PO Box 309 (63028); W; 23,221fr (CAC); $12.43; Su; 22,894fr (CAC); $12.43; general manager Joe Nicholson; editor John Winkleman; managing editor Steve Taylor; tel (314) 296-1800; fax (314) 931-2638

Florissant Vly.: *Florissant Valley Reporter* — 525 St. Francois, Ste. 9 (63031); PO Box 69, Florissant (63032); Tu; 7,283pd (Sw); $9.00; publisher & editor David L Reynolds; tel (314) 839-1111

Glasgow: *Glasgow Missourian* — 109 Market St.; PO Box 248 (65254); Th; 1,510pd, 22fr (Sw); $2.80; publishers & editors Joseph O Young & Ruth Young; managing editor Barbara Audsley; tel (816) 338-2195; fax (816) 338-2494

Granby/Diamond: *Newton County News* — 312 N. Main St.; PO Box 50, Granby (64844); Th; 1,500pd, 10fr (Sw); $3.00; publisher & editor Newton E Renfro; general manager Toni Carnes; tel (417) 472-3100; fax (417) 472-6311

Grandview/Jackson: *Jackson County Advocate* — 500 Main St.; PO Box A, Grandview (64030); Th; 6,505pd, 167fr (Sw); $6.00; publisher & editor James Turnbaugh Jr; tel (816) 761-6200

Grant City: *The Times Tribune* — 309 S. Front St. (64456); W; 1,929pd, 40fr (Est); $3.50; publisher & editor Tom Ellingsworth; tel (816) 564-3603

Greenfield: *Vedette & Advocate* — 6 N. Main; PO Box 216 (65661); Th; 2,454pd, 50fr (Sw); $3.50; C; editor Marlene DeClue; tel (417) 637-2712; fax (417) 637-2232

Hale: *Hale Tribune* — 4th & Walnut St.; PO Box 86 (64643); Th; 500pd (Est); $1.85; publisher Frank Jackson; editor Debbie Gilson; tel (816) 565-2401; fax (816) 542-2580

Hamilton: *Hamilton Advocate* — 105 N. Davis St.; PO Box 187 (64644); W; 1,860pd, 43fr (Sw); $3.70; C; publisher & editor Anne L Tezon; tel (816) 583-2116; fax (816) 583-2118

Harrisonville/Cass Co.: *The Cass County Democrat-Missourian* — 301 S. Lexington; PO Box 329, Harrisonville (64701); F; 5,860pd, 76fr (Sw); $5.75; C; publisher & editor William E James; managing editor Emery Styron; tel (816) 380-3228; fax (816) 380-7650

Hayti: *The Friday Democrat-Argus* — 111 E. 5th St.; PO Box 1059, Caruthersville (63830); F; 2,345pd, 26fr (Sw); $3.85; publisher John Rust; general manager Sheila Ralph; editor Jennifer Dodson; tel (314) 333-4336; fax (314) 333-2307

Hermann: *The Advertiser-Courier* — 136 E. 4th St.; PO Box 350 (65041); W; 4,921pd, 61fr (Est); 16¢; publisher Jim Gierke; editor Don Kruz; tel (314) 486-5418; fax (314) 486-5524

Hickory Co.: *The Index* — PO Box 127, Hermitage (65668); Th; 4,053pd (Sw); $4.20; publisher Earl Jenkins; editor Don Ginnings; tel (417) 745-6404; fax (417) 745-2222

Higginsville: *Higginsville Advance* — 3002 Highway Blvd.; PO Box 422 (64037); W/F; 2,835pd, 69fr (Sw); $5.10; C; publisher Jack Krier; general manager Beverly Mackie; editor Heather Hoflander; tel (816) 584-3611; fax (816) 584-7966

High Ridge: *Meramec Journal* — 2 Burian Plz. (63049); W; 15,149fr (CAC); $13.52; Su; 14,599fr (CAC); $13.52; publisher & editor John Winkleman; general manager Joe Nicholson; tel (314) 376-6511; fax (314) 677-3220

Holden: *The Holden MH Progress* — 117 2nd St.; PO Box 8 (64040); Th; 1,600pd, 50fr (Sw); $4.30; C; publisher & editor Rusty Hartwell; tel (816) 732-5552; fax (816) 732-4696

Holt Co.: *Mound City News* — 511 State St.; PO Box 175, Mound City (64470); Th; 2,409pd (Sw); $4.00; publishers & editors Chris Boultinghouse & Linda Boultinghouse; tel (816) 442-5423; fax (816) 442-5423

Holt Co.: *Times Observer* — 119 W. Nodaway, Oregon (64473); Th; 1,436pd, 11fr (Sw); $3.00; publisher Wilma J Ripley; editor Robert E Ripley; tel (816) 446-3331; fax (816) 446-3409

Hopkins: *The Hopkins Journal* — 411 E. Barnard St.; PO Box 170 (64461); W; 1,420pd (Sw); 12¢; publisher Paul E Thompson; editor Darla Thompson; tel (816) 778-3205; fax (816) 778-3345

Houston: *Houston Herald-Republican* — 113 N. Grand; PO Box 70 (65483); Th; 4,200pd, 5,700fr (Sw); $3.30; C; publisher Robert L Davis; editor Brad Gentry; tel (417) 967-2000; fax (417) 967-2096

Houston: *Houston Republican* — 113 N. Grand; PO Box 70 (65483); Th; 775pd (Est); $3.10; publisher Robert L Davis; editor Brad Gentry; tel (417) 967-3358; fax (417) 967-2096

Humansville: *Humansville Star-Leader* — PO Box 215 (65674); Th; 1,715pd, 9fr (Est); $2.05; publisher Jack Krier; editor Michael Crawford; tel (417) 754-2228; fax (417) 754-2228

Huntsville/Higbee: *Randolph County Times-Herald* — 101 N. Main, Huntsville (65259); W; 500pd, 20fr (Est); $3.60; C; publisher Bob Cunningham; editor Thelma Bryan; tel (816) 277-3211; fax (816) 263-3626

Jackson: *Cash-Book Journal* — 210 W. Main St.; PO Box 369 (63755); W; 8,300pd (Sw); $6.50; publisher Gerald Jones; editor David Bloom; tel (314) 243-3515; fax (314) 243-3517

Jamesport: *Tri-County Weekly* — PO Box 137 (64648); Th; 1,470pd (Est); $2.50; publisher & editor Natha McAllister; tel (816) 684-6515; fax (816) 684-6515

Kahoka: *The Media* — 178 W. Main St.; PO Box 230 (63445); W; 2,650pd (Sw); 82¢; publisher & editor Hazel Bledsoe Smith; tel (816) 727-3395; fax (816) 727-2475

Kansas City: *Press Dispatch* — 7007 N.E. Parvin Rd. (64117); W; 1,951pd, 785fr (Sw); $20.16; C; publisher H Guy Townsend III; editor Linn Brown; tel (816) 454-9660; fax (816) 454-7523

Kansas City: *Wednesday Magazine* — 7007 N.E. Parvin Rd. (64117); W; 375pd, 33,895fr (Sw); $20.16; C; publisher H Guy Townsend III; managing editor David Knopf; tel (816) 454-9660; fax (816) 454-7523

Kansas City/Clay Co.: *Clay Dispatch-Tribune* — 7007 N.E. Parvin Rd., Kansas City (64117); W; 9,690pd, 25,792fr (Sw); $20.16; C; publisher H Guy Townsend III; editor Linn Brown; tel (816) 454-9660; fax (816) 454-7523

Kansas City/Platte Co.: *Platte Dispatch-Tribune* — 7007 N.E. Parvin Rd., Kansas City (64117); W; 1,974pd, 10,850fr (Sw); $20.16; C; publisher H Guy Townsend III; editor Linn Brown; tel (816) 454-9660; fax (816) 454-7523

Kearney/Holt: *The Kearney Courier* — 102 Jefferson; PO Box 138, Kearney (64060); Th; 2,084pd (Est); $2.85; publisher & editor Richard N Whipple; general manager Kathy Whipple; managing editor Gene Gentrup; tel (816) 628-6010; fax (816) 628-4422

Kimberling City: *Kimberling City Table Rock Gazette* — PO Box 432 (65686); Th; 925pd, 1,467fr (Sw); $5.50; publisher LeRoy Gorrell; editor Martha Campbell; tel (417) 739-4695; fax (501) 423-6640

King City: *The Tri-County News* — 108 N. Connecticut; PO Box 428 (64463); F; 1,574pd, 40fr (Est); $2.50; publisher & editor Robert E Cobb; tel (816) 535-4313

Knob Noster: *Knob Noster Item* — PO Box 188 (65336); Th; 1,129pd, 10fr (Sw); $3.50; publisher & editor Stan Hall; tel (816) 563-3606

La Belle: *La Belle Star* — PO Box 66 (63447); W; 787pd, 99fr (Est); 45¢; publisher & editor Hazel Bledsoe Smith; publisher Robert B Smith; tel (816) 462-3848

La Plata/Atlanta Areas: *The Home Press* — 107 N. Gex St.; PO Box 149, La Plata (63549); W; 1,175pd, 43fr (Est); $3.00; publisher & editor Lois A Bragg; tel (816) 332-4431; fax (816) 332-4431

Ladue/Huntleigh/Frontenac: *West County Journal* — 1714 Deer Tracks Trl., St. Louis (63131); W; 28,844fr (CAC); $12.32; Su; 28,020fr (CAC); $12.32; editor Regina DeLuca; managing editor Dan Barger; tel (314) 821-2462; fax (314) 821-0843

Lamar/Barton/Dade: *Lamar Democrat* — 900 Gulf St.; PO Box 458, Lamar (64759); W; 3,196pd, 181fr (Sw); $4.50; Sa; 3,273pd, 750fr (Sw); $4.50; publisher & editor Douglas D Davis; tel (417) 682-5529; fax (417) 682-5595

Lawson/Excelsior Springs: *The Lawson Review* — 405 N. Pennsylvania; PO Box 125, Lawson (64062); W; 1,700pd (Sw); $3.50; publisher R Cress Hewitt; editor David Blyth; tel (816) 296-3412; fax (816) 296-3412

Lee's Summit: *Lee's Summit Journal* — 415 S. Douglas St.; PO Box 387 (64063); M/F; 6,360pd, 156fr (Sw); $8.70; C; publisher W Ferrell Shuck; editor Ken Hatfield; tel (816) 524-2345; fax (816) 524-5136

Lemay/Mehlville/Carondelet/Oakville: *Naborhood Link News* — 416 Lemay Ferry Rd., St. Louis (63125); W; 34,500pd, 211fr (Sw); $7.75; publisher Vernon G Schertel; editor Vernon E Schertel; tel (314) 631-4321; fax (314) 631-4322

Lexington/Lafayette: *News* — 925 Main St.; PO Box 279, Lexington (64067); W/F; 2,015pd, 30fr (Est); $2.08; publisher Frank Mercer; general manager Nancy Wisdom; editor Rick Stalder; tel (816) 259-2266; fax (816) 259-4870

Liberal/Mindenmines: *Liberal News* — 106 Main; PO Box 6, Liberal (64762); Th; 811pd, 3fr (Est); $3.00; publishers & editors Darvin E Weaver & Ruth Ann Weaver; general manager Beth Workman; tel (417) 843-5315

Liberty: *Liberty Tribune-News* — 7007 N.E. Parvin Rd., Kansas City (64117); W; 216pd, 10,000fr (Sw); $20.16; C; publisher H Guy Townsend III; editor Angie Borgedalin; tel (816) 454-9660; fax (816) 454-7523

Liberty/Excelsior Springs/Kearney/Holt/Orrick/Missouri City: *Liberty Shopper News* — 12 N. Main St., Liberty (64068); W; 19,025fr (VAC); $7.20; C; publisher Randall E Battagler; editor Jason Offutt; tel (816) 781-1044; fax (816) 781-1755

Licking: *Licking News* — 122 S. Main St.; PO Box 297 (65542); Th; 2,223pd, 39fr (Sw); $2.70; publisher & editor G Eugene Derrickson; tel (314) 674-2412; fax (314) 674-2412

Lincoln: *The Lincoln New Era* — 401 1/2 W. Main; PO Box 280, Cole Camp (65325); Th; 300pd, 10fr (Est); $2.25; C; publisher James R Dickerson; editor Diana Ball; tel (816) 668-4418; fax (816) 668-4418

Lincoln Co.: *Troy Free Press* — 615 E. Cherry, Troy (63379); W; 6,500pd (Est); 13¢; publisher Pat Whiteside; editor Greg Ochoa; tel (314) 528-9550

Louisiana: *The Louisiana Press-Journal* — 3406 W. Georgia St.; PO Box 466 (63353); W; 3,024pd, 21fr (Sw); $3.85; C; publisher & editor Walt Gilbert; general manager Jim Gierke; tel (314) 754-5566; fax (314) 754-4749

Madison Co.: *Democrat News* — 131 S. Main; PO Box 471, Fredericktown (63645); Th; 3,400pd (Sw); $5.00; C; publisher Mary Cissell; editor Alan Kopitsky; tel (314) 783-3366; fax (314) 783-6890

Malden: *Big Nickel Advertiser* — 127 W. Main; PO Box 701 (63863); Th; 30,000fr (Sw); $3.50; C; publisher Barbara Hill; editor Tim Gage; managing editor Lorraine Heiser; tel (314) 276-3708; fax (314) 276-3687

Mansfield: *The Mansfield Mirror/Wright Co. Republican* — 300 E. Commercial St.; PO Box 197 (65704); Th; 2,072pd, 27fr (Est); 12¢; publisher Dean DeVries; general manager & editor Larry Dennis; tel (417) 924-3226; fax (417) 924-3227

Marceline/Linn Cos.: *The Marceline Press* — 123 S. Kansas; PO Box 318, Marceline (64658); Th; 1,904pd, 100fr (Sw); $3.10; C; publisher Ivan Buckman; general manager Bill Evans; editor Cathy Lenny; tel (816) 376-3508; fax (816) 376-2757

Marshfield: *The Marshfield Mail* — 211 N. Clay St.; PO Drawer A (65706); W; 5,012pd, 93fr (Sw); $3.65; C; publisher Gordon Nordquist; general manager & editor Deanna A Barker; tel (417) 468-2013; fax (417) 859-7930

Marthasville: *The Marthasville Record* — 203 W. South St.; PO Box 77 (63357); Th; 755pd, 8fr (Sw); $4.27; publishers & editors Mabel Eichmeyer & Rueben Eichmeyer; tel (314) 433-2223

Maysville: *DeKalb County Record-Herald* — PO Box 98 (64469); W; 1,743pd, 73fr (Est); 17¢; publisher Terry Pearl; editor Chrissy Jestes; tel (816) 449-2121; fax (816) 449-2808

McDonald Co.: *McDonald County News-Gazette* — PO Box 266, Pineville (64856); W; 1,431pd, 169fr (Est); 14¢; C; publisher & editor George Pogue; general manager Robert Stout; tel (417) 223-4377/4675; fax (417) 223-4049

McDonald Co.: *McDonald County Press* — PO Box 266, Pineville (64856); W; 961pd, 121fr (Est); 12¢; publisher & editor George Pogue; general manager Robert Stout; tel (417) 223-4675; fax (417) 223-4049

Memphis: *Memphis Democrat* — 121 S. Main St. (63555); Th; 2,780pd (Est); 12¢; publisher & editor Tom Ellingsworth; tel (816) 465-7016

Milan/Sullivan Co.: *The Milan Standard* — 105 S. Market St., Milan (63556); Th; 4,008pd, 25fr (Sw); $4.20; publisher & editor Robert W Wilson; tel (816) 265-4244; fax (816) 265-3180

Miller/Lawrence: *The Miller Press* — 6 N. Main St. (65682); PO Box 236, Miller (65707); Th; 476pd, 29fr (Sw); $3.25; C; publisher & editor Marlene DeClue; tel (417) 452-3792; fax (417) 637-2232

Moniteau Co.: *California Democrat* — 319 S. High; PO Box 126, California (65018); W; 3,774pd, 8fr (Sw); $6.15; publisher Ray Grimes; editor Connie Bestgen; tel (314) 796-2135; fax (314) 796-4220

Monroe: *Monroe City News* — PO Box 187 (63456); Th; 2,487pd, 20,532fr (Est); 18¢; publisher & editor Linda Geist; tel (314) 735-4538; fax (314) 735-4020

Montgomery City: *Montgomery Standard* — 115 W. 2nd St.; PO Box 190 (63361); W; 3,331pd, 73fr (Sw); $2.50; publisher & editor John Fisher; tel (314) 564-2339

Mt. Vernon: *The Lawrence County Record* — 312 S. Hickory; PO Box 348 (65712); Th; 3,270pd, 35fr (Sw); $2.20; C; publisher & editor Kathy S Fairchild; publisher Steve Fairchild; tel (417) 466-2185

Mountain Grove: *Mountain Grove News-Journal* — 150 E. 1st St.; PO Box 530 (65711); W; 3,135pd, 75fr (Sw); $4.30; publisher Dean DeVries; general manager Sandy Anderson; editor Doug Berger; tel (417) 926-5148

Mountain View: *Mountain View Standard* — 168 Elm; PO Box 52 (65548); W; 7,600pd, 550fr (Est); 22¢; publisher & editor Brian Hood; tel (417) 934-2025; fax (417) 934-6481

Nevada: *The Nevada Herald* — 131 S. Cedar; PO Box 247 (64772); Su; 4,550pd, 120fr (Sw); $5.50; C; publisher & editor Tom Larimer; tel (417) 667-3344; fax (417) 667-8121

New Madrid: *The Weekly Record* — 218 Main St. (63869); F; 1,400pd (Sw); $3.25; publisher & editor Clement Cravens; tel (314) 748-2120

Norborne: *Norborne Democrat-Leader* — 106 S. Pine; PO Box 101 (64668); Th; 1,100pd (Est); $3.20; publishers Jack Krier & Kathy Krier; editor Margaret A Brown; tel (816) 594-3712

N Kansas City/N St. Louis Co.: *Northland News* — 12 N. Main, Liberty (64068); W; 23,359fr (VAC); $7.20; C; publisher Randall E Battagler; editor Jason Offutt; tel (816) 781-1044

N St. Louis Co.: *Community News* — 5748 Helen Ave., St. Louis (63136); W; 25,000fr (Sw); $20.00; publisher Robert J Huneke Jr; general manager & editor Charles R Bockskopf; tel (314) 261-5555; fax (314) 261-2776

O'Fallon/Lebanon: *O'Fallon Journal* — 216 E. Elm St., O'Fallon (63366); W; 12,453fr (CAC); $7.28; F/Su; 12,290fr (CAC); $7.28; general manager Rick Jarvis; editor Scott Queen; tel (314) 240-4949; fax (314) 240-7913

Oakville/Mehlville: *Oakville/Mehlville Journal* — 4210 Chippewa, St. Louis (63116); W; 20,210fr (Est); $12.38; Su; 20,012fr (Est); $12.38; C; publisher Don Miller; general manager Laurie Salmo; editor Jim Merkel; managing editor Lois Kendall; tel (314) 664-2700; fax (314) 664-8533

Odessa/Wellington/Bates City/Mayview/Napoleon: *The Odessan* — 204 W. Mason; PO Box 40, Odessa (64076); Th; 3,980pd, 65fr (Sw); $3.35; publisher Betty S Spaar; general manager Leanna Thompson; editor Carol Conrow; tel (816) 230-5311; fax (816) 230-5313

Osage Co.: *Unterrified Democrat* — 300 E. Main St.; PO Box 109, Linn (65051); W; 4,750pd, 5fr (Sw); $4.25; publisher Jerrilynn S Voss; editor Paul A Slater; tel (314) 897-2109

Osceola/St. Clair: *St. Clair Co. Courier* — 3rd & Pine Sts.; PO Box 406, Osceola (64776); Th; 2,165pd, 100fr (Est); $3.60; C; publisher Jack Krier; editor Michael Crawford; tel (417) 646-2211; fax (417) 646-8015

Overland/St. Ann/Vinita: *County Star Journal West* — 4305 Woodson Rd., Woodson Terrace (63134); W; 12,421fr (CAC); $9.10; Su; 11,971fr (CAC); $9.10; general manager Rick Jarvis; editor Dan Barger; tel (314) 426-2222; fax (314) 426-4911

Owensville/Gerald/Belle: *Gasconade County Republican* — 106 E. Washington Ave.; PO Box 540, Owensville (65066); W; 3,107pd, 83fr (Sw); $3.50; C; publisher Don Warden; publisher & editor Thomas C Warden; tel (314) 437-2323; fax (314) 437-3033

Ozark Co.: *Ozark County Times* — 3rd St.; PO Box 188, Gainesville (65655); W; 3,925pd, 7,300fr (Sw); $3.90; C; publisher Walt Sanders; editor Bruce Roberts; tel (417) 679-4641; fax (417) 679-3423

Ozark/Nixa/Christian Co.: *Christian County Headliner News* — 427 E. South St.; PO Box 490, Ozark (65721); W; 5,229pd, 20fr (Sw); $5.50; C; publisher Roger Frieze; editor Chris Wrinkle; tel (417) 581-3541; fax (417) 581-3577

Pacific: *Tri-County Journal* — 111 W. St Louis St. (63069); W; 10,969fr (CAC); $13.00; general manager Mona Von Trapp; editor Danette Thompson; tel (314) 257-3943; fax (314) 227-1272

Palmyra: *Palmyra Spectator* — 304 S. Main; PO Box 391 (63461); W; 2,628pd, 75fr (Sw); $3.50; publisher & editor Mark Cheffey; tel (314) 769-3111; fax (314) 769-3554

Paris/Monroe: *Monroe Co. Appeal* — 230 N. Main St.; PO Box 207, Paris (65275); Th; 2,200pd, 12fr (Est); $3.25; publisher Richard J Fredrick; managing editor Cheryl Gholson; tel (816) 327-4192; fax (816) 327-4847

Parkville/Riverside/Rural S Platte Co.: *Platte County Gazette* — 12 N. Main, Liberty (64068); W; 301pd (VAC); $7.20; C; publisher Randall E Battagler; editor Scott McIntosh; managing editor Jason Ossutt; tel (816) 781-1044; fax (816) 741-9593

Perry Co.: *The Republic-Monitor* — 10 W. Maries St.; PO Box 367, Perryville (63775); Tu/Th; 5,811pd (Sw); $5.25; C; publisher & editor Randall J Pribble; tel (314) 547-4567; fax (314) 547-1643

Perry/Ste. Genevieve Cos.: *Perryville Sun Times* — PO Box 344, Perryville (63775); W; 1,880pd, 40fr (Sw); $4.25; publisher Elmo L Donze; editor John Meacham; tel (314) 547-8005/6780; fax (314) 547-8005

Pierce City: *Leader-Journal* — 105 W. Commercial (65723); Th; 704pd, 60fr (Est); 70¢; publisher & editor Linda Elderton; tel (417) 476-2232; fax (417) 476-2232

Platte City: *The Landmark* — 252 Main St.; PO Box 410 (64079); Th; 1,725pd, 50fr (Est); $3.82; publisher Ethel Mae Foley; editor Ivan Foley; tel (816) 858-2313; fax (816) 858-2313

Platte City/Weston/Dearborn/Cauden Pt./Edgerton/Farley: *The Platte County Citizen* — 416 Branch St., Hwy. 92, Platte City (64079); W; 3,942pd, 170fr (Sw); $6.00; publishers Paul D Campbell & Rebecca K Campbell; editor Steve Smith; tel (816) 858-5154; fax (816) 858-2154

Plattsburg: *The Clinton County Leader* — 102 E. Maple (64477); Tu; 2,166pd, 4fr (Est); $2.80; publisher & editor J W Tinnen; tel (816) 539-2111; fax (816) 539-3530

Pleasant Hill: *Pleasant Hill Times* — 126 1st St.; PO Box 8 (64080); W; 2,700pd (Est); 16¢; C; publisher & editor F Kirk Powell; general manager Jan Powell; managing editor Kerry Warman; tel (816) 987-2138; fax (816) 987-5699

Portageville: *Missourian-Review* — PO Box 456 (63873); Th; 1,329pd, 12fr (Est); $2.00; C; publisher & editor Erwin Lloyd; tel (314) 379-5355; fax (314) 688-2225

Potosi: *The Independent-Journal* — 119 E. High St.; PO Box 340 (63664); Th; 5,250pd, 127fr (Sw); $3.40; publisher & editor Neil Richards; publisher Ruby Richards; tel (314) 438-5141; fax (314) 438-4472

Princeton: *The Post-Telegraph* — 704 Main St.; PO Box 286 (64673); Th; 2,680pd, 51fr (Est); $3.15; C; publisher John Roberts; general manager Patsy J Colt; editor Preston J Cole; tel (816) 748-3266; fax (816) 748-4747

Puxico/Stoddard: *Weekly Press* — 144 E.L. Hawk St.; PO Box 277, Puxico (63960); W; 2,310pd, 40fr (Est); $3.25; publisher & editor Cletis R Ellinghouse; tel (314) 222-3243; fax (314) 222-3243

Ralls Co.: *Ralls County Herald-Enterprise* — 415 Main St.; PO Box 426, New London (63459); Th; 1,350pd, 30fr (Est); $3.65; publisher & editor Bob Anderson; publisher Carol Anderson; tel (314) 985-5531

Raytown: *Raytown Dispatch-Tribune* — 7007 N.E. Parvin Rd., Kansas City (64117); W; 5,838pd, 19,559fr (Sw); $20.16; C; publisher H Guy Townsend III; general manager Len Egdish; editor Don Ledford; tel (816) 454-9660; fax (816) 454-7523

Raytown/Kansas City/Independence: *Raytown Post* — 10212 E. 63rd St.; PO Box 9338, Raytown (64133); W; 96pd, 18,904fr (Sw); $9.90; publisher & editor Lee Gray; tel (816) 353-5545

Republic: *The Republic Monitor* — 206 N. Main (65738); Th; 2,250pd (Est); 13¢; publisher Darren Sumner; general manager Vicky Haynes; editor Glynette Hubach; tel (417) 732-2525; fax (417) 732-2980

Rich Hill/Hume: *Rich Hill Mining Review* — 120 N. Six M; PO Box 49, Rich Hill (64779); Th; 1,750pd (Sw); $2.50; publisher & editor Randy Bell; tel (417) 395-4131; fax (417) 395-2171

Richland: *Richland Mirror* — PO Box 757 (65556); Th; 2,200pd (Est); 15¢; publisher & editor Gail Wright; general manager Brenda Shelton; tel (314) 765-3391; fax (314) 765-3235

Rock Hill/Maplewood/Brentwood: *Mid-County Journal* — 1714 Deer Tracks Trl., St. Louis (63131); W; 14,357fr (Est); $10.71; Su; 13,454fr (Est); $10.71; editor Neal Learner; managing editor Dan Barger; tel (314) 821-2462; fax (314) 821-0843

Rock Port: *Atchison County Mail* — 300 Main St.; PO Box 40 (64482-0040); Th; 2,550pd, 30fr (Sw); $3.00; publishers & editors Marilyn Farmer & William W Farmer; general manager Michael P Farmer; managing editor William C Farmer; tel (816) 744-6245; fax (816) 744-2645

St. Charles Co.: *St. Charles Journal* — 1529 Old Hwy. 94-S, Ste. 108, St. Charles (63303); W; 24,936fr (CAC); $18.75; F/Su; 24,067fr (CAC); $18.75; general manager Rick Jarvis; editor Scott Queen; tel (314) 724-1111; fax (314) 946-5955

St. Francois Co.: *The Green Sheet* — 218 N. Washington; PO Box 70, Farmington (63640); Tu; 20,900fr (Est); $5.40; publisher Mark Griggs; tel (314) 756-8927; fax (314) 756-9160

St. James: *St. James Leader-Journal* — 125 W. Springfield, St. James (65559); W; 2,500pd, 5,500fr (Sw); $3.50; publisher & editor Joe Arnold; tel (314) 265-3321; fax (314) 265-3197

St. Louis: *Central West End Journal* — 1714 Deer Tracks Trl., St. Louis (63131); W; 7,385fr (Est); $7.54; C; editor Neal Learner; managing editor Dan Barger; tel (314) 821-2462; fax (314) 821-0843

St. Louis: *South City Journal* — 4210 Chippewa, St. Louis (63116); W; 23,090fr (Est); $11.25; C; publisher Don Miller; general manager Laurie Salmo; editor Glen Sparks; managing editor Lois Kendall; tel (314) 664-2700; fax (314) 664-8533

St. Louis Co.: *North Side Journal* — 4305 Woodson Rd., St. Louis (63134); Th; 46,600fr (CAC); $14.98; C; general manager Rick Jarvis; editor Dan Barger; managing editor Ann Nicholson; tel (314) 426-2222; fax (314) 426-4911

St. Louis Co.: *County Star Journal East* — 4305 Woodson Rd., St. Louis (63134); W/Su; 28,256fr (Est); $11.45; C; general manager Rick Jarvis; editor Dan Barger; tel (314) 426-2222; fax (314) 426-4911

St. Peters/Harvester/Dardeene: *St. Peters Journal* — 1529 Old Hwy. 94-S, Ste. 108, St. Charles (63303); Su; 24,067fr (CAC); $10.92; W; 28,831fr (CAC); $10.92; general manager Rick Jarvis; editor Scott E Queen; tel (314) 724-1111; fax (314) 946-5955

Ste. Genevieve: *Ste. Genevieve Herald* — 330 Market St.; PO Box 447, Ste. Genevieve (63670); W; 4,494pd, 89fr (Sw); $5.10; publisher Robert J Burr; managing editor B Jean Rissover; tel (314) 883-2222; fax (314) 883-2833

Salem: *The Salem News* — PO Box 798 (65560); Tu/Th; 3,774pd, 38fr (Sw); $4.60; C; publisher June Vickery; publisher & editor W Ray Vickery; tel (314) 729-4126; fax (314) 729-4920

Salisbury/Chariton: *Salisbury Press-Spectator* — 111 S. Broadway; PO Box 313, Salisbury (65281-0313); Th; 2,275pd, 55fr (Est); $2.90; C; publisher & general manager Larry M Baxley; publisher Susan K Baxley; editor Lucy Vaughn; tel (816) 388-6131; fax (816) 388-6688

Sarcoxie: *Sarcoxie Record* — 101 N. 6th St.; PO Box 400 (64862); Th; 900pd (Est); $2.70; C; publisher & editor Linda Elderton; tel (417) 548-3311; fax (417) 548-3312

Savannah/Andrew Co.: *Savannah Reporter and Andrew County Democrat* — 115 S. 4th; PO Box 299, Savannah (64485); Th; 3,565pd, 9fr (Est); $4.00; publisher Larry Miller; publisher & editor Twila Miller; tel (816) 324-3149; fax (816) 324-3632

Schuyler Co.: *The Excelsior* — PO Box 250, Lancaster (63548); W; 1,792pd (Sw); $3.24; publisher & editor Ann Bunch; tel (816) 457-3707; fax (816) 457-3707

Scott Co.: *Scott County News* — 113 S. Main St.; PO Box 97, Chaffee (63740); Su; 7,700fr (Est); $4.50; C; publisher Wally Lage; general manager Jim Litwicki; editor Jim Obert; tel (314) 887-3636; fax (314) 887-3637

Sedalia/Pettis: *Central Missouri News* — 406 S. Ohio St., Sedalia (65301); W; 5,650pd (Sw); $5.00; publisher Greg Melton; editor Peter F Daniels; tel (816) 827-2425; fax (816) 827-2427

Senath: *Dunklin County Press* — 114 Commercial St.; PO Box 356 (63876); W; 1,502pd (Sw); $3.50; C; publisher & editor Ronald C Kemp; managing editor Dawn Jackson; tel (314) 738-2604; fax (314) 738-2604

Seneca: *Seneca News-Dispatch* — PO Box E (64865); Th; 1,676pd, 50fr (Est); 70¢; publisher & editor Diane Collins; tel (417) 776-2236; fax (417) 776-2204

Seymour: *Webster County Citizen* — 221 S. Commercial; PO Box 190 (65746); W; 1,925pd, 15fr (Sw); $3.00; C; publishers & editors Gary Sosniecki & Helen Sosniecki; tel (417) 935-2257

Shelbina: *Shelbina Democrat* — 115 S. Center; PO Box 138 (63468); W; 2,668pd (Est); 12¢; publisher & editor Cecelia Gilbert; tel (314) 588-2133; fax (314) 588-2134

Shelby Co.: *Shelby County Herald* — 106 E. Main; PO Box 225, Shelbyville (63469); W; 2,105pd, 40fr (Sw); $3.08; publisher & editor W Rogers Hewitt; tel (314) 633-2261; fax (314) 633-2133

Sheridan/Worth Co.: *Quad River News* — R.R. 1; PO Box 16, Sheridan (64486); W; 724pd (Est); $2.50; publisher & editor Joe Stark; tel (816) 799-3735/3162; fax (816) 564-3707

Slater/E Saline Co.: *The Slater News-Rustler* — 105 N. Main; PO Box 26, Slater (65349); Th; 1,749pd, 40fr (Sw); $2.80; publisher Kathryn Dohrman; editor Angie Magore; managing editor Cindy R Williams; tel (816) 529-2888

Smithville: *The Smithville Lake Democrat-Herald* — 110 N. Bridge St.; PO Box 269 (64089-0269); W; 2,340pd, 130fr (Sw); $4.00; C; publisher David (Scoop) Peery; general manager Kathy Atkins; tel (816) 532-4444; fax (816) 532-4918

S St. Louis: *South County Journal* — 4210 Chippewa, St. Louis (63116); W; 24,217fr (Est); $12.43; Su; 23,742fr (Est); $12.43; C; publisher Don Miller; general manager Laurie Salmo; editor Kevin Carberry; managing editor Lois Kendall; tel (314) 664-2700; fax (314) 664-8533

S St. Louis: *South Side Journal* — 4210 Chippewa, St. Louis (63116); W/Su; 38,210fr (Est); $14.43; C; publisher Don Miller; general manager Laurie Salmo; editor Glen Sparks; managing editor Lois Kendall; tel (314) 664-2700; fax (314) 664-8533

SW St. Louis: *South West City Journal* — 4210 Chippewa, St Louis (63116); W/Su; 26,990fr (Est); $13.99; C; publisher Don Miller; general manager Laurie Salmo; editor Glen Sparks; managing editor Lois Kendall; tel (314) 664-2700; fax (314) 664-8533

Steele: *The Steele Enterprise* — 227 W. Main St.; PO Box 90 (63877); Th; 2,001pd, 431fr (Sw); $3.50; publisher & editor David Tennyson; editor Karen Tennyson; tel (314) 695-3415; fax (314) 695-2114

Steelville: *The Steelville Star-Crawford Mirror* — PO Box BG (65565); W; 3,311pd, 13fr (Est); $2.05; C; publishers Delma Pascoe & Percy Pascoe; editor Ava Viehman; tel (314) 775-5454; fax (314) 885-3803

Stockton: *Cedar County Republican/Stockton Journal* — 108 S.E. Arcade; PO Box C (65785); W; 2,632pd, 93fr (Est); $3.30; C; publisher Jeff Jasper; editor Anita Todd; tel (417) 276-4211

Stover/Morgan Co.: *Morgan County Press* — 2nd & Maple; PO Box 130, Stover (65078); W; 1,409pd, 279fr (Sw); $2.20; C; publisher Dane Vernon; editor Connie Vibrock; tel (314) 377-4616; fax (314) 377-4512

Sullivan: *Sullivan Independent News* — PO Box 268 (63080); W; 6,900pd, 100fr (Est); 11¢; publisher & editor Kathy Abell; managing editor Fern Wittell; tel (314) 468-6511; fax (314) 468-4046

Tarkio: *The Tarkio Avalanche* — 107 N. 3rd St.; PO Box 278 (64491); Th; 1,467pd, 120fr (Sw); $2.75; publishers & editors Joy L Johnson & William W Johnson; tel (816) 736-4111; fax (816) 706-5700

Thayer/Oregon Co.: *South Missourian-News* — 101 Chestnut St., Thayer (65791); W; 1,246pd, 32fr (Sw); $5.00; C; publisher Janie Flynn; editor Max Cates; managing editor Jan Sisk; tel (417) 264-3085; fax (417) 264-3814

Tipton Area: *Tipton Times* — 123 W. Moniteau; PO Box U, Tipton (65081); Th; 1,908pd (Sw); $2.80; C; publisher Dane Vernon; editor Becky Holloway; tel (816) 433-5721; fax (816) 433-2222

Tuscumbia: *Miller County Autogram Sentinel* — 409-15 S. Maple St.; PO Box 315, Eldon (65026); Th; 1,727pd (Sw); $2.20; C; publisher Dane Vernon; general manager Tim Flora; editor Virginia Duffield; tel (314) 392-5658

Unionville: *Unionville Republican* — 111 S. 16th; PO Box 365 (65565); W; 3,143pd, 189fr (Est); $2.73; publisher & editor Ron Kinzler; tel (816) 947-2222; fax (816) 947-2223

University City/Olivette: *Citizen Journal* — 1714 Deer Tracks Trl., St. Louis (63131); W; 23,047fr (Est); $7.54; Su; 22,659fr (Est); $7.54; publisher Journal Register Co.; editor Neal Learner; managing editor Dan Barger; tel (314) 821-2462; fax (314) 821-0843

Van Buren: *The Current Local* — 614 Main St.; PO Box 100 (63965-0100); Th; 2,300pd (Sw); $3.50; publishers Alan Turley & Marjorie Turley; editor Steve Turley; tel (314) 323-4515

Vandalia: *The Vandalia Leader-Press* — 108 W. State; PO Box 239 (63382); W; 2,500pd (Sw); $2.90; publisher Lora D Steiner; editors Mary K Steiner & William C Steiner; tel (314) 594-2222/3322; fax (314) 594-6741

Versailles/Morgan Co.: *The Versailles Leader-Statesman* — 104 W. Jasper; PO Box 348, Versailles (65084-0348); Th; 3,456pd, 89fr (Sw); $3.00; C; publisher Dane Vernon; editor Duane Johnson; tel (314) 378-5441; fax (314) 378-4292

Vienna: *Maries County Gazette-Adviser* — Courthouse Sq. (65582); W; 1,772pd (Est); $2.50; C; publisher & editor Kurt Lawis; tel (314) 422-3441; fax (314) 422-3441

Warrensburg/Johnson Co.: *Standard-Herald* — 132 W. Pine St.; PO Box 7, Warrensburg (64093); W; 10,000fr (Est); $5.55; C; publisher Jack Krier; general manager Fred J Rich; editor Jason Baldwin; tel (816) 747-3135; fax (816) 747-7800

Warrenton: *Warrenton News-Journal* — 111 W. Main (63383); W; 11,747fr (CAC); $4.75; general manager Rich Coleman; editor Scott Queen; managing editor Marie Hollenbeck; tel (314) 456-3481; fax (314) 456-3388

Warsaw: *Benton County Enterprise* — 107 Main; PO Box 128 (65355); Th; 4,151pd, 29fr (Est); 95¢; publisher & editor Mahlon K White; general manager Heidi Polliver; tel (816) 438-6312; fax (816) 438-3464

Washington/Union: *Washington Missourian* — 14 W. Main St.; PO Box 336, Washington (63090); W; 14,540pd, 208fr (ABC); $6.75; Sa; 12,572pd, 182fr (ABC); $6.75; C; publisher Thomas L Miller; publisher & editor William L Miller; tel (314) 239-7701; fax (314) 239-0915

Waverly: *The Waverly Times* — 65 & 24 Highway S.; PO Box 69 (64096); W; 803pd, 15fr (Est); 80¢; publisher Jack Krier; editor Jon E Flatland; managing editor Frank Mercer; tel (816) 542-0881; fax (816) 542-2580

Wayne Co.: *Wayne County Journal-Banner* — 101 W. Elm St.; PO Box 97, Piedmont (63957); Th; 4,933pd, 60fr (Sw); $5.60; publisher & editor Harold T Ellinghouse; publisher Mary B Stivers; tel (314) 223-7122; fax (314) 223-7871

Webb City/Carl Junction: *Webb City Sentinel/Wise Buyer* — 8 S. Main St.; PO Box 150, Webb City (64870); W/F; 1,641pd, 10,000fr (Est); $5.32; publisher & editor Bob Foos; publisher Merle Lortz; managing editor Kathleen Schrader; tel (417) 673-2421; fax (417) 673-5308

Webster Groves/Kirkwood/Meachan Park: *Webster-Kirkwood Journal* — 1714 Deer Tracks Trl., St. Louis (63131); W; 26,065fr (CAC); $13.42; Su; 25,454fr (CAC); $13.42; editor Regina DeLuca; managing editor Dan Barger; tel (314) 821-2462; fax (314) 821-0843

Wellsville: *Optic-News* — 123 W. Hudson; PO Box 73 (63384); Tu; 1,932pd (Sw); $2.20; publisher John Fisher; editor Gay Hagan; tel (314) 684-2929

Wentzville: *The Wentzville Union and St. Charles County Record* — 201 N. Main, Ste. 205 (63301); PO Box 1077, St. Charles (63302); F; 1,367pd, 175fr (Est); $1.45; publisher Sue Tedesco; general manager Regina Ricky; editor Will Connaghan; tel (314) 327-6279; fax (314) 949-6973

Wentzville/New Melle/Augusta: *Wentzville Journal* — 501 E. Pearce Blvd., Wentzville (63385); W; 9,025fr (CAC); $6.92; F; 8,822fr (CAC); $6.92; Su; 8,825fr (CAC); $6.92; general manager Rick Jarvis; editor Tammy Tucker; managing editor Scott Queen; tel (314) 327-6463; fax (314) 327-6411

W Franklin Co.: *New Haven Leader* — 103B Hwy. 100 W.; PO Box 168, New Haven (63068); W; 2,800pd, 89fr (Sw); $3.75; C; editor Steve Roth; tel (314) 237-3222; fax (314) 237-7222

Weston: *Weston Chronicle* — 605 Main St.; PO Box 6 (64098-0006); W; 1,691pd (Est); $3.20; publisher Jim McPherson; editor Beth McPherson; tel (816) 640-2251; fax (816) 386-2251

Wheaton: *The Wheaton Journal* — 109 E. Santee; PO Box 100 (64874); Th; 400pd, 15fr (Est); $2.60; publisher & editor David Moore; publisher Tina Moore; tel (417) 652-3828

Willard: *Cross Country Times* — East Center; PO Box 216 (65781); W; 1,200pd, 8,500fr (Est); $4.00; C; publisher Roger Frieze; editor Greg Martin; tel (417) 742-2539; fax (417) 742-4070

Willow Springs: *Willow Springs News* — 705 E. Main St. (65793); W; 1,250pd, 152fr (Sw); $4.25; C; publisher & editor Brian R Hood; tel (417) 469-2192; fax (417) 934-6481

Windsor: *The Windsor Review* — 205 S. Main St. (65360); W; 2,800pd, 8,800fr (Sw); $4.65; C; publisher James R Dickerson; managing editor Diana Ball; tel (816) 647-2121; fax (816) 647-2122

MONTANA

Anaconda/Deer Lodge Co.: *Anaconda Leader* — 121 Main St., Anaconda (59711); W/F; 4,170pd, 59fr (Sw); $4.76; publisher Dean A Neitz; editor Dick Crockford; tel (406) 563-5283; fax (406) 563-5284

U.S. Weeklies Nebraska II-47

Baker: *Fallon County Times* — 115 S. Main St.; PO Box 679 (59313); Th; 1,602pd, 49fr (Est); $3.00; C; publisher Darlene Hornung; editor Jody Strand; tel (406) 778-3344; fax (406) 778-3345

Belt/Stockett/Highwood: *The Eagle* — 211 Castner St., Ste. 4; PO Box 200, Belt (59412); W; 1,085pd, 52fr (Sw); $2.75; publisher Curtis E Wall; editor Curtis H Wall; tel (406) 277-4473; fax (406) 277-4473

Big Sandy: *The Mountaineer* — Johames Ave.; PO Box 529 (55920); W; 902pd, 99fr (Est); $2.50; C; publisher & editor James L Rettig; tel (406) 378-2176; fax (406) 378-2176

Big Timber/Sweet Grass: *The Big Timber Pioneer* — 111 W. 1st St.; PO Box 190, Big Timber (59011); F; 1,820pd, 70fr (Sw); $5.00; C; publisher Dale C Oberly; editor Beccy Oberly; tel (406) 932-5299; fax (406) 932-4931

Bigfork: *The Bigfork Eagle* — 8293 Hwy. 35; PO Box 406 (59911); W; 2,250pd, 2,450fr (Sw); $5.50; publisher & editor Marc Wilson; managing editor Virginia Wilson; tel (406) 837-5131

Boulder: *The Boulder Monitor* — 104 W. Centennial; PO Box 66 (59632); Th; 1,250pd (Sw); $3.50; publisher Vernon A Sutherlin; editor Denise Sutherlin; tel (406) 225-3821; fax (406) 225-3747

Browning: *Glacier Reporter* — 208 N. Piegan; PO Box R (59417); Th; 2,400pd (Est); 22¢; publisher Brian Kavanagh; general manager Marlene Augare; editor John McGill; tel (406) 338-2090; fax (406) 338-2410

Carter Co.: *The Ekalaka Eagle* — PO Box 66, Ekalaka (59324); F; 1,035pd (Est); 16¢; publisher M Brice Lambert; editor Lois Lambert; tel (406) 775-6245; fax (406) 775-8750

Cascade: *Cascade Courier* — 12 Central; PO Box 308 (59421); W; 643pd, 12fr (Est); 16¢; publisher & editor Patrick C Travis; tel (406) 468-9231; fax (406) 468-9231

Chester: *Liberty County Times Inc.* — Hwy. 2 E.; PO Box 689 (59522); W; 1,632pd, 17fr (Est); $2.50; publisher Albert Larson; general manager John Hutchison; editor Jeanne Larson; tel (406) 759-5355

Chinook/Blaine: *Chinook Opinion* — PO Box 97, Chinook (59523); W; 1,648pd, 48fr (Sw); $2.60; C; publisher & editor Michael D Perry; tel (406) 357-2680; fax (406) 357-2959

Choteau/Teton Co.: *Choteau Acantha* — 216 1st Ave. N.W.; PO Box 320, Choteau (59422); W; 2,003pd, 23fr (Sw); $3.00; publisher Jeffrey O Martinsen; editor Melody Martinsen; tel (406) 466-2403

Columbia Falls: *Hungry Horse News* — 926 Nucleus Ave.; PO Box 189 (59912); Th; 7,000pd, 50fr (Sw); $8.60; publisher & editor Brian M Kennedy; tel (406) 892-2151; fax (406) 892-5600

Columbus/Absarokee: *The Stillwater County News* — 508 E. Pike Ave.; PO Box 659, Columbus (59019); W; 2,200pd (Sw); $9.00; publisher James E Moore; general manager & editor Tricia Elpel; tel (406) 322-5212; fax (406) 322-5391

Conrad/Brady/Valier: *Independent Observer Inc.* — 7 3rd Ave. S.E.; PO Box 966, Conrad (59425); W; 2,305pd, 70fr (Sw); $4.29; publisher John H Lee; editor Buck Traxler; tel (406) 278-5561; fax (406) 278-5562

Culbertson: *The Searchlight* — PO Box 496 (59218); Th; 1,089pd, 20fr (Sw); $2.50; publisher Mamie Downs; editor Ila Mae Forbregd; tel (406) 787-5821

Cut Bank: *Cut Bank Pioneer Press* — 217 W. Main; PO Box 478 (59427); W; 2,865pd, 30fr (Est); $3.80; publisher Brian Kavanagh; editor LeAnne Kavanagh; tel (406) 873-2201; fax (406) 873-2443

Cut Bank/Browning: *Western Breeze* — 32 S. Central Ave.; PO Box 1253, Cut Bank (59427); Tu/F; 1,680pd, 80fr (Sw); $5.00; C; publisher & editor James M O'Day; tel (406) 873-4128; fax (406) 873-4129

Deer Lodge: *Silver State Post* — 312 Missouri Ave.; PO Box 111 (59722); W; 1,800pd (Est); $4.48; publisher Eric Boshart; publisher & editor Kathryn Boshart; tel (406) 846-2424; fax (406) 846-2453

Dillon: *Dillon Tribune Examiner* — 22 S. Montana St.; PO Box 911 (59725); W; 2,759pd, 108fr (Est); $5.05; publisher & editor John M Barrows; tel (406) 683-2331; fax (406) 683-2332

Eureka: *Tobacco Valley News* — PO Box 307 (59917); Th; 2,101pd, 13fr (Est); $6.05; publisher Robin Newman; publisher & editor Steve Newman; tel (406) 296-2514; fax (406) 296-2515

Fairfield: *Sun Times* — 409 Central Ave.; PO Box 578 (59436); W; 2,450pd (Est); $3.50; C; publisher & editor Jim L Anderson; tel (406) 467-2334; fax (406) 467-3354

Flathead Co.: *Kalispell News* — 38 6th Ave. W.; PO Box 9050, Kalispell (59904); F; 3,623pd, 728fr (Sw); $5.85; C; publisher Marjean Thomas; editor Frank Thomas; tel (406) 755-6767; fax (406) 755-5449

Forsyth/Colstrip: *The Independent Enterprise* — 183 N. 9th Ave.; PO Box 106, Forsyth (59327); Th; 1,368pd, 23fr (Sw); $4.50; C; editor Pat Corley; tel (406) 356-2149

Ft. Benton/Chouteau Co.: *The River Press* — 1114 Front St.; PO Box 69, Fort Benton (59442); W; 2,110pd, 107fr (Est); $3.50; publishers Esther Tichenor & Stan Tichenor; editor Tim Burmeister; tel (406) 622-3311; fax (406) 622-5446

Gallatin Co.: *High Country Independent Press* — 220 S. Broadway, Belgrade (59714); Th; 2,025pd, 200fr (Sw); $5.72; publisher & editor Devon Hubbard Sorlie; tel (406) 388-6762; fax (406) 388-6072

Glendive: *Glendive Ranger-Review* — 119 W. Bell St.; PO Box 61 (59330); Th/Su; 3,493pd, 20fr (Sw); $4.75; C; publisher Jerry Zander; managing editor Merv Mecklenburg; tel (406) 365-3303; fax (406) 365-5435

Hardin: *Big Horn County News* — 204 N. Center Ave. (59034-1908); W; 2,506pd, 52fr (Est); $7.50; C; publisher James E Moore II; editor Debra Cliff; tel (406) 665-1008; fax (406) 665-1012

Harlem/Blaine Co.: *Harlem News* — PO Box 278, Harlem (59526); W; 1,404pd, 31fr (Est); $2.30; publisher Mary Perry; publisher & editor Michael D Perry; tel (406) 353-2441; fax (406) 357-2959

Harlowton: *The Times Clarion* — 111 S. Central; PO Box 307 (59036-0307); Th; 1,649pd, 17fr (Sw); $3.25; publisher Audrey J Miller; publisher & editor Gerald H Miller; tel (406) 632-5633; fax (406) 632-5644

Laurel: *Laurel Outlook* — 415 E. Main St.; PO Box 278 (59044); W; 2,720pd, 100fr (Est); $4.95; publisher Milton Wester; editor Steve Barlow; tel (406) 628-4412; fax (406) 628-8260

Lewistown: *Lewistown News-Argus* — 521 W. Main; PO Box 900 (59457); W/Su; 4,677pd, 117fr (Sw); $6.18; publisher David C Byerly; editor Dori Jacobs; tel (406) 538-3401; fax (406) 538-3405

Libby/Troy: *Western News* — 311 California Ave.; PO Box 1377, Libby (59923); W/F; 4,161pd, 28fr (Est); $4.80; publisher H M McMahon; editor Roger Morris; tel (406) 293-4124; fax (406) 293-7187

Malta: *The Phillips County News* — 18 S. 1st St.; PO Box 850 (59538); W; 2,705pd, 52fr (Est); $3.50; C; publisher Bonnie Starr; publisher & editor Curtis H Starr; general manager & managing editor Todd Hancock; tel (406) 654-2020; fax (406) 654-1410

Philipsburg/Drummond: *The Philipsburg Mail* — 123 E. Broadway; PO Box 160, Philipsburg (59858); W; 1,327pd, 19fr (Est); $4.00; publisher & editor Jim Tracy; publisher & general manager Lee Tracy; tel (406) 859-3223; fax (406) 859-3223

Plentywood: *Plentywood Herald* — 150 N. Main; PO Box 397 (59254); W; 2,300pd (Est); $2.95; publisher Tim Polk; general manager Marvel Hellegaard; editor Joe Nistler; tel (406) 765-2190; fax (406) 765-2190

Polson/Ronan/Pablo/Arlee/Charlo/St. Ignatius: *Lake County Leader* — 213 Main St.; PO Box 1091, Polson (59860); Th; 5,332pd, 190fr (Est); $5.98; C; publisher John Schnase; editor Rich Stripp; tel (406) 883-4343; fax (406) 883-4349

Red Lodge: *Carbon County News* — 202 S. Hauser; PO Box 970 (59068); W; 3,200pd, 6fr (Sw); $7.00; C; publisher James E Moore II; editor Shelley Beaumong; tel (406) 446-2222; fax (406) 446-2225

Roundup: *The Roundup Record-Tribune/Winnett Times* — 24 Main St.; PO Box 350 (59072); W; 2,421pd, 105fr (Sw); $4.13; publisher Eric N Rasmussen; editor Louise G Rasmussen; tel (406) 323-1105; fax (406) 323-1761

Scobey/Daniels Co.: *Daniels County Leader* — 23 Main; PO Box 850, Scobey (59263); Th; 1,296pd, 30fr (Est); 10¢; publisher & editor Larry C Bowler; tel (406) 487-5303

Shelby: *The Shelby Promoter* — 119 Maple Ave.; PO Box 610 (59474); Th; 2,478pd, 64fr (Sw); 32¢; publisher Brian Kavanagh; editor Sharon Dunham; tel (406) 434-5171; fax (406) 434-5955

Sheridan Co.: *Sheridan County News* — 115 N. Main; PO Box 397, Plentywood (59254); W; 2,000pd, 100fr (Sw); $3.92; publisher Tim Polk; general manager Marvel Hellegaard; editor Joe Nistler; tel (406) 765-2190; fax (406) 765-2190

Sidney: *Sidney Herald* — 310 2nd Ave. N.E. (59270); W/Sa; 4,225pd (Est); $5.60; C; publisher Richard Schneider; editor Mary Borseth; tel (406) 482-2403; fax (406) 482-7802

Stanford: *Judith Basin Press* — 117 Central; PO Box 507 (59479); W; 1,050pd, 50fr (Est); 15¢; publisher Lance D Davis; editor Boni L Schmit; tel (406) 566-2471

Superior: *Mineral Independent* — 106 2nd Ave. W.; PO Box 98 (59872); Th; 1,077pd, 20fr (Sw); $2.50; C; publisher Marveen Peters; editor Joe L Rapier; tel (406) 822-3329; fax (406) 822-4406

Terry: *The Terry Tribune* — 203 Logan Ave.; PO Box 127 (59349); W; 1,030pd, 31fr (Est); $2.64; publisher John Watson; editor Dave Schwarz; tel (406) 637-5513; fax (406) 637-2149

Thompson Falls: *Sanders County Ledger* — 603 Main St.; PO Box 219 (59873); Th; 3,100pd, 50fr (Sw); $3.00; publisher Bina Eggensperger; publisher & editor Tom Eggensperger; tel (406) 827-3421; fax (406) 827-4375

Three Forks: *Three Forks Herald* — PO Box 586 (59752); W; 1,350pd (Est); $2.50; publisher Jim Jewett; editor Jo Jewett; tel (406) 285-3414

Townsend: *Townsend Star* — 314 Broadway; PO Box 1011 (59644); W; 1,450pd, 45fr (Sw); $3.50; C; publisher & editor Jeff Stoffer; general manager Kate Murphy; tel (406) 266-3333; fax (406) 266-5440

Valier: *The Valierian* — 811 Choteau St.; PO Box 308 (59486); Th; 547pd, 6fr (Sw); $2.00; publisher & editor Lois Green; tel (406) 279-3719; fax (406) 279-3686

Valley Co.: *Glasgow Courier* — 341 3rd Ave. S.; PO Box 151, Glasgow (59230); Th; 4,028pd, 79fr (Sw); $5.35; publisher John Stanislaw; editor Scott Ross; tel (406) 228-9301; fax (406) 228-2665

W Yellowstone: *The West Yellowstone News* — 309 Canyon St.; PO Box 969 (59758); Th; 1,892pd, 4fr (Sw); $5.25; publisher Gary Stevenson; editor Gayle Mansfield; tel (406) 646-9719; fax (406) 646-4023

White Sulphur Springs: *The Meagher County News* — 13 E. Main; PO Box 349 (59645); Th; 1,088pd (Sw); $3.20; publisher Patricia M Rademacher; publisher & editor Verle L Rademacher; tel (406) 547-3831; fax (406) 547-3832

Whitefish: *The Whitefish Pilot* — 312 2nd St.; PO Box 488 (59937); Th; 4,800pd, 47fr (Est); $8.25; publisher Brian M Kennedy; general manager Jolene Shima; tel (406) 862-3505; fax (406) 862-3636

Whitehall/Boulder: *Whitehall Ledger* — 15 W. Legion Ave.; PO Box L, Whitehall (59759); Th; 1,149pd, 16fr (Sw); $4.12; C; publisher Gary W Stevenson; editor Jon Anderson; tel (406) 287-5301; fax (406) 287-5352

Wibaux: *The Wibaux Pioneer-Gazette* — 120 S. Wibaux St.; PO Box 218 (59353); Th; 968pd, 18fr (Sw); $2.40; publisher & editor Frank Datta; tel (406) 795-2218; fax (406) 795-2218

Wolf Pt.: *Herald-News* — PO Box 639 (59201); Th; 3,105pd, 36fr (Est); $3.00; publisher Mamie Downs; general manager Harry Downs; editor Greg Little; tel (406) 653-2222; fax (406) 653-2222

Worden/Custer/Shepherd/Huntley/Pompeys Pillar/Ballantine/Billing Heights/Montana: *The Yellowstone County News* — 1348 Main, Ste. 201, Billings Heights (59105); Th; 1,000pd, 200fr (Sw); $5.00; publisher Pete Robison; publisher & general manager Rebecca Tescher Robison; editor Jan Falstad; tel (406) 245-1624; fax (406) 254-1687

NEBRASKA

Ainsworth: *Ainsworth Star-Journal* — 327 N. Main; PO Box 145 (69210); W; 2,956pd (Est); $2.60; publisher Kathy S Worrell; publisher & editor Rodney B Worrell; tel (402) 387-2844; fax (402) 387-1234

Albion/Boone Co.: *Albion News* — 328 W. Church St.; PO Box 431, Albion (68620-0431); W; 2,876pd, 75fr (Sw); $3.65; publisher & editor Jean Kaup; tel (402) 395-2115; fax (402) 395-2772

Alma: *Harlan County Journal* — 713 W. Main St.; PO Box 9 (68920); Th; 2,286pd, 56fr (Sw); $3.10; publisher Marilyn Lingg; publisher & editor Wayne Lingg; tel (308) 928-2143

Arapahoe/Edison/Hendley/Holbrook: *Arapahoe Public Mirror* — 420 Nebraska Ave.; PO Box 660, Arapahoe (68922); Th; 1,473pd, 9fr (Sw); $3.25; C; publisher T M (Ted) Gill; editor Gayle Gill Schutz; tel (308) 962-7261; fax (308) 962-7262

Arlington: *Arlington Citizen* — 16th & Front Sts.; PO Box 328, Blair (68008); W; 917pd, 23fr (Est); $3.45; publisher Kenneth H Rhoades; general manager Mark Rhodes; editor Carrie Larkins; tel (402) 426-2121; fax (402) 426-2227

Arnold: *Arnold Sentinel* — PO Box 136 (69120); Th; 10,450pd, 20fr (Sw); $4.50; publisher Arthur M French; editor Marcia R Hora; tel (308) 848-2511

Arthur: *The Arthur Enterprise* — PO Box 165 (69121); Th; 425pd, 40fr (Sw); $2.50; publisher Robert J Crouse; editor Karen A Sizer; tel (308) 764-2402

Ashland: *The Ashland Gazette* — 1518 Silver St.; PO Box 127 (68003); Th; 1,918pd, 64fr (Sw); $3.22; publisher Zean E Carney; editor Cheryl Warren; tel (402) 944-3397; fax (402) 944-3398

Atkinson: *The Atkinson Graphic* — 407 E. State St.; PO Box 159 (68713); Th; 2,155pd, 30fr (Sw); $3.10; publisher & editor Jerry Hollingsworth; general manager Roxanne Hollingsworth; tel (402) 925-5411

Auburn: *Auburn Press-Tribune* — 830 Central Ave.; PO Box 250 (68305); Tu; 3,344pd, 93fr (Est); $4.20; publisher Mark Cramer; editor Darrell Wellman; tel (402) 274-3185; fax (402) 274-3273

Auburn: *Nemaha County Herald* — 830 Central Ave.; PO Box 250 (68305-0250); F; 3,245pd, 89fr (Sw); $4.20; publisher Mark Cramer; editor Darrell Wellman; tel (402) 274-3185; fax (402) 274-3273

Aurora: *Aurora News-Register* — 1320 K St.; PO Box 70 (68818); W; 3,795pd, 70fr (Sw); $4.50; publisher Ronald L Furse; editor Hadley Fruits; tel (402) 694-2131; fax (402) 694-2133

Bartlett/Ericson/Spalding: *Wheeler County Independent* — 757 H St.; PO Box 547, Burwell (68823); W; 337pd, 15fr (Sw); $3.50; C; publisher & editor Kendall Neiman; publisher Steve DeLashmutt; tel (308) 346-4504; fax (308) 346-4018

Bassett: *Rock County Leader* — 118 Clark St.; PO Box 488 (68714); W; 1,650pd (Est); $1.65; publisher & editor Billy G Fegley; tel (402) 684-3771; fax (402) 684-2857

Bayard: *The Bayard Transcript* — 336 Main St.; PO Box 626 (69334); W; 1,092pd, 33fr (Est); $2.66; publisher & editor Jeanne Heath; tel (308) 586-1313

Beaver City: *Times-Tribune* — 903 O St.; PO Box 258 (68926-0258); Th; 1,011pd (Est); $2.70; publisher Frankie John; tel (308) 268-2205

Bellevue/Offut A.F.B.: *Bellevue Leader* — 604 Fort Crook Rd.; PO Box 1219, Bellevue (68005); W; 6,522pd, 18,000fr (Sw); $12.60; C; publisher Dixie Cavner; editor Ron Petak; tel (402) 733-7300; fax (402) 733-9116

Benkelman: *The Benkelman Post and News-Chronicle* — 513 Chief St.; PO Box 800 (69021-0800); W; 1,570pd, 9fr (Sw); $5.15; publisher Glenda M Bartholomew; editor Jan M Cady; tel (308) 423-2337; fax (308) 423-5555

Bertrand: *The Bertrand Herald* — 615 Minor Ave.; PO Box 425 (68927); Th; 800pd, 75fr (Sw); $4.00; publisher & editor Robert Engle; editor Genevive Engle; tel (308) 472-3217

Blair: *The Blair Enterprise* — 16th & Front Sts.; PO Box 328 (68008); Th; 4,156pd, 156fr (Sw); $6.10; C; publishers Kenneth H Rhoades & Mark Rhoades; editor Kathy Schwartz; tel (402) 426-2121; fax (402) 426-2227

Blair: *The Pilot-Tribune* — 16th & Front Sts.; PO Box 328 (68008); Tu; 4,156pd, 156fr (Est); $6.10; C; publishers Kenneth H Rhoades & Mark Rhoades; editor Kathy Schwartz; tel (402) 426-2121

Bloomfield: *The Bloomfield Monitor* — 110 N. Broadway; PO Box 367 (68718); Th; 1,669pd (Est); 22¢; publisher & editor Joseph M Skrivan; general manager Mary Ellen Skrivan; tel (402) 373-2332

II-48 **Nebraska** *U.S. Weeklies*

Blue Hill: *The Blue Hill Leader* — 514 W. Gage St.; PO Box 38 (68930); W; 1,533pd, 37fr (Sw); $2.66; C; publisher & editor Leland Ostdiek; tel (402) 756-2077; fax (402) 756-2097

Bridgeport: *Bridgeport News-Blade* — 801 Main St.; PO Box 400 (69336); W; 1,850pd (Est); $2.28; publisher Wendelin P Lummel; editor Oneva M Lummel; tel (308) 262-0675; fax (308) 262-0675

Broken Bow: *Custer County Chief* — 305 S. 10th Ave.; PO Box 190 (68822-0190); M; 3,165pd, 26fr (Sw); $5.50; Th; 3,165pd, 26fr (Sw); $4.50; C; publisher Charles Najacht; editor Jeffrey Bielser; tel (308) 872-2471; fax (308) 872-2415

Burwell: *The Burwell Tribune* — 757 H St.; PO Box 547 (68823); W; 1,367pd, 39fr (Sw); $3.50; C; publisher & editor Kendall Neiman; publisher Steve DeLashmutt; tel (308) 346-4504; fax (308) 346-4018

Butte: *The Butte Gazette* — PO Box 6 (68722); Th; 541pd, 21fr (Sw); 12¢; publisher & editor Leon O Wells; tel (402) 775-2431

Cairo/Boclus/Dannebrog: *Cairo Record* — PO Box 540, Cairo (68824); Th; 832pd, 60fr (Sw); $2.50; publisher Timothy J Mohanna; editor Rosalie Stutzman; tel (308) 485-4284; fax (308) 485-4286

Callaway: *The Callaway Courier* — 204 E. Morse St.; PO Box 338 (68825); W; 940pd, 25fr (Est); 50¢; C; publisher & editor Michael Wendorff; tel (308) 836-2200

Cambridge: *Cambridge Clarion* — 415 Nelson St.; PO Box 70 (69022); Th; 1,482pd, 70fr (Sw); $1.05; publisher & editor Allan Gaskill; tel (308) 697-3326

Cedar Rapids: *Cedar Rapids Press* — 102 S. Cedar; PO Box D, Spalding (68665); M; 617pd, 10fr (Sw); $2.25; publisher & editor David Bopp; tel (308) 497-2153

Central City: *Republican-Nonpareil* — 802 C Ave.; PO Box 26 (68826); Th; 2,900pd (Est); 18¢; C; publisher & editor Robert M Jensen; tel (308) 946-3081; fax (308) 946-3082

Chadron: *The Chadron Record* — 248 W. 2nd St.; PO Box 1141 (69337); Tu/F; 2,851pd, 100fr (Sw); $7.80; C; publisher & editor Christopher Spencer; tel (308) 432-5511; fax (308) 432-2385

Chappell: *Chappell Register* — 273 Vincent Ave.; PO Box 528 (69129); Th; 1,315pd, 10fr (Sw); $2.02; publisher & editor Michael Talbott; tel (308) 874-2207; fax (308) 874-2207

Cherry Co.: *Midland News* — 146 W. 2nd St.; PO Box 448, Valentine (69201); Tu; 1,500pd, 119fr (Est); $3.75; C; publisher Butch Hovendick; editor Missy Walm; tel (402) 376-2833; fax (402) 376-1946

Chester/Hubbell/Byron: *Chester Herald* — 510 Thayer; PO Box 338, Chester (68327-0338); W; 750pd (Sw); $3.00; publisher James M Williams; general manager & editor Christine Williams; tel (402) 324-5764; fax (402) 324-5764

Clearwater: *Clearwater Record-Ewing News* — Main St.; Box 98 (68726-0098); Th; 868pd, 15fr (Est); $1.70; publisher & editor Deborah D Bauer; tel (402) 887-4840; fax (402) 887-4711

Coleridge/Cedar: *Coleridge Blade* — 107 W. Broadway; PO Box 8, Coleridge (68727-0008); W; 929pd, 13fr (Sw); $2.25; publishers & editors Elizabeth Yost & Robert Yost; tel (402) 283-4267

Colfax Co.: *Colfax County Press* — 242 Pine St.; PO Box 166, Clarkson (68629); W; 1,473pd, 61fr (Sw); $2.44; publisher & editor T A Evans; general manager Helen Evans; tel (402) 892-3544; fax (402) 892-3141

Cozad: *Cozad Free Press* — PO Box 6 (69130); Th; 450pd (Est); $4.25; publisher Dean Dorsey; tel (308) 784-3644; fax (308) 784-3647

Cozad: *The Tri-City Trib* — PO Box 6 (69130); Th; 2,850pd (Est); $4.25; publisher Dean Dorsey; tel (308) 784-3644; fax (308) 784-3647

Crawford/Harrison: *Crawford Clipper/Harrison Sun* — 435 2nd St., Crawford (69337); Th; 1,279pd, 5fr (Sw); 15¢; publisher & editor Twila Vogl; managing editor Diane Clark; tel (308) 665-2310; fax (308) 665-2310

Creighton: *Creighton News* — 816 Main St.; PO Box 55 (68729); W; 1,440pd, 13fr (Sw); $2.35; publisher News Publishing Co.; general manager Sid Charf; editor David Sonnenfelt; tel (402) 358-5220

Crete: *The Crete News* — 1201 Linden Ave.; PO Box 40 (68333); W; 4,227pd, 80fr (Sw); $3.30; publisher & editor Lloyd Reeves; publisher Trudy Reeves; tel (402) 826-2147; fax (402) 826-5072

Crofton: *The Crofton Journal* — 108 W. Main St.; PO Box 224 (68730); Th; 900pd (Est); 17¢; publisher Kevin Henseler; publisher & editor Tweeter Henseler; tel (402) 388-4355; fax (402) 388-4336

Curtis/Eustis: *Hi-Line Enterprise* — 208 Center Ave.; PO Box 85, Curtis (69025); Th; 1,400pd, 40fr (Est); $3.00; C; publisher Dale Crawford; editor Charles E Greenlee; tel (308) 367-4144; fax (308) 367-8616

David City/Butler Co.: *The Banner-Press* — 331 E St.; PO Box 407, David City (68632); Th; 4,201pd, 54fr (Est); $4.20; publisher & editor Zean E Carney; tel (402) 367-3054; fax (402) 367-3055

Dawson Co.: *Lexington Clipper-Herald* — 114 W. 5th; PO Box 599, Lexington (68850-0599); W/Sa; 4,672pd, 6,000fr (Est); 11¢; C; publisher Peter J Cook; editor Melody M Loughry; tel (308) 324-5511; fax (308) 324-5240

Deshler: *Deshler Rustler* — 706 4th St.; PO Box 647 (68340); W; 1,804pd, 526fr (Sw); $3.00; publisher & editor Harold W Struve; tel (402) 365-7221; fax (402) 365-7243

Dodge/Snyder: *Dodge Criterion* — 140 Oak St.; PO Box 68, Dodge (68633); W; 1,347pd, 11fr (Sw); 22¢; publishers & editors Kathy Kauffold & Ken H Kauffold; tel (402) 693-2415

Doniphan: *The Doniphan Herald* — 320 4th St.; PO Box 173 (68832-0173); Th; 712pd, 23fr (Sw); $2.60; publisher & editor Deborah A Doty; tel (402) 845-2728

Elgin: *The Elgin Review* — 116 S. 2nd St.; PO Box 359 (68636); W; 1,367pd, 4fr (Sw); $2.25; publishers & editors James E Dickerson & Julianne K Dickerson; tel (402) 843-5500; fax (402) 843-5422

Elkhorn/Waterloo/Valley: *The Douglas County Post Gazette* — 113 Hillrise Center; PO Box 677, Elkhorn (68022); Tu; 2,470pd, 5,400fr (Est); $7.15; publisher Penny Overmann; editor Mark Thiessen; tel (402) 289-2329; fax (402) 289-0861

Elwood: *The Elwood Bulletin* — 308 Smith Ave.; Box 115 (68937); W; 1,217pd, 25fr (Est); 14¢; C; publisher T M Gill; editor Kathy Beck; tel (308) 785-2251

Eustis: *Eustis News* — 208 Center Ave.; PO Box 85 (69028); Th; 345pd, 15fr (Sw); $3.00; C; publisher Dale Crawford; editor Charles E Greenlee; tel (308) 486-3191; fax (308) 367-8616

Exeter: *Fillmore County News* — 181 E. Senaca St.; PO Box 115 (68351); Tu; 735pd (Est); $2.20; C; publisher W A Bonta; editor Margie J Bonta; tel (402) 266-5161

Fairbury: *Fairbury Journal-News* — 516 5th St.; PO Box 415 (68352); Tu/F; 5,110pd, 12fr (Est); $4.00; publisher F A Arnold; editor Denise Andersen; tel (402) 729-6141; fax (402) 729-3892

Fall City: *Journal* — 1810 Harlan St.; PO Box 128 (68355); Tu/F; 4,205pd, 212fr (Sw); $3.75; publisher George W Schock; editor Bill Schock; managing editor Scott Schock; tel (402) 245-2431; fax (402) 245-4404

Franklin/Bloomington: *Franklin County Chronicle* — 707 15th Ave.; PO Box 271, Franklin (68939); Tu; 1,210pd, 13fr (Sw); $2.00; publisher & editor Kim L Naden; tel (308) 425-3481; fax (308) 425-6823

Friend: *Sentinel* — PO Box 228 (68359); Th; 1,290pd (Est); $2.95; publishers Jerry Ryan & Jim Ryan; editor Sharon Ryan; tel (402) 947-2391

Fullerton: *Nance County Journal* — 416 4th St.; PO Box 10 (68638); W; 1,107pd, 300fr (Sw); $3.50; C; publisher & editor William H Thompson; general manager Vic Wassermann; managing editor Barb Micek; tel (308) 536-3100; fax (308) 536-3100

Garden Co./Oshkosh: *Garden County News* — 204 Main St.; PO Box 290, Oshkosh (69154-0290); Th; 1,570pd, 70fr (Sw); $2.42; C; publisher & editor James E McKeeman; tel (308) 772-3555

Geneva: *Nebraska Signal* — 131 N. 9th; PO Box 233 (68361-0233); W; 3,250pd (Sw); $5.50; publisher John Edgecombe Jr; editor Claudia Bohn; tel (402) 759-3117; fax (402) 759-4214

Genoa: *The Genoa Leader-Times* — 524 Willard Ave.; PO Box 427 (68640); W; 852pd, 168fr (Est); $1.65; publisher & editor T A Evans; general manager Martha Shockley; tel (402) 993-2205

Gering: *Gering Courier* — 1428 10th St.; PO Box 70 (69341); Th; 2,118pd, 43fr (Sw); $27.00; publisher & editor Carol Ann Lewis; general manager Jack D Lewis; tel (308) 436-2222; fax (308) 436-7127

Gibbon: *The Gibbon Reporter* — 10 LaBarre St.; PO Box 820 (68840-0820); W; 1,097pd, 36fr (Est); $1.80; publisher Steven L Glenn; editor Laura Kozin; tel (308) 468-5393

Gordon: *Gordon Journal* — PO Box 270 (69343); W; 2,626pd (Est); $1.25; publisher Morris Evans; editor Suzanne Evans; tel (308) 282-0118

Gothenburg: *The Gothenburg Times* — 406 10th St.; PO Box 385 (69138); W; 2,306pd, 67fr (Sw); $3.15; publishers Greg Viergutz & Kathi Viergutz; tel (308) 537-3636; fax (308) 537-7554

Grand Island: *West Nebraska Register* — 804 W. Division; PO Box 608 (68802); F; 16,746pd, 133fr (Sw); $7.56; publishers Bishop Lawrence McNamara; editors Marilyn Zastrow & Mary Parlin; tel (308) 382-4660; fax (308) 382-4746

Gretna: *Gretna Guide* — 620 N. Highway 6; PO Box 240 (68028); W; 1,095pd, 96fr (Sw); 21¢; publisher & editor Mike Overmann; publisher Penny Overmann; tel (402) 332-3232; fax (402) 332-4733

Gretna: *The Gretna Breeze* — 138 N. Washington; PO Box 460940, Papillion (68128-0940); Th; 332pd, 20fr (Sw); $2.76; C; publisher Jim Nagen; editor Cathy Tibbels; tel (402) 339-3331; fax (402) 339-8562

Hartington: *Cedar County News* — 102 W. Main St.; PO Box 977 (68739); W; 2,485pd, 5fr (Est); $3.80; publisher Peggy Year; publisher & editor Rob Dump; tel (402) 254-3997; fax (402) 254-3998

Hayes Co.: *The Hayes Center Times-Republican Inc.* — PO Box 7, Hayes Center (69032); Th; 867pd, 20fr (Sw); $5.39; publisher G B Crapson; editor Kathy Broz; tel (308) 286-3325

Hebron/Thayer Co.: *Hebron Journal-Register* — 318 Lincoln Ave.; PO Box 210, Hebron (68370); W; 3,232pd, 118fr (Est); $4.75; publisher & editor Kim Johnson; tel (402) 768-7214; fax (402) 768-7354

Hemingford: *The Ledger* — 714 Box Butte Ave.; PO Box 7 (69348); Th; 1,220pd, 22fr (Est); $2.35; publisher & editor Brian C Kuhn; tel (308) 487-3334; fax (308) 487-3347

Henderson: *The Henderson News* — 1021 N. Main St.; PO Box 606 (68371); Th; 965pd, 31fr (Sw); $3.50; publisher Jan Edgecombe; editor Jerry Jacobitz; tel (402) 723-5861; fax (402) 723-5863

Hooper/Scribner: *Rustler Sentinel* — 204 N. Main; PO Box 24, Hooper (68031-0024); W; 2,008pd, 33fr (Sw); $5.00; publisher Dick Lindberg; general manager & editor Kathy Lodl; tel (402) 654-2218; fax (402) 654-2130

Howells: *Howells Journal* — 137 3rd St.; PO Box 335 (68641); W; 1,200pd (Est); $2.52; publisher Chris Chebuhar; editor Cheryl Chebuhar; tel (402) 986-1777

Humboldt/Dowson/Table Rock: *Humboldt Standard* — West Square; PO Box 627, Humboldt (68376-0627); Th; 1,535pd, 15fr (Sw); $3.40; C; publisher & editor Jack Cooper; tel (402) 862-2200; fax (402) 862-2200

Hyannis: *Grant County News* — PO Box 308 (69350); Th; 705pd, 10fr (Sw); 11¢; publisher & editor Sharon M Wheelock; tel (308) 458-2425; fax (308) 458-2425

Imperial: *Imperial Republican* — 622 Broadway; PO Box 727 (69033); Th; 2,256pd, 20fr (Sw); $3.65; publisher Elna Johnson; publisher & editor Loral Johnson; tel (308) 882-4453; fax (308) 882-5167

Indianola: *Indianola News* — 115 N. 4th St.; PO Box 130 (69034-0130); Th; 355pd, 2fr (Sw); $2.73; publisher & editor Mary Marsh; tel (308) 364-2130

Kenesaw/Juniata/Heartwell/Prosser/Holstein: *Kenesaw Clarion* — PO Box 366, Kenesaw (68956); F; 500pd (Sw); $3.00; C; publisher Clipper Publishing; general manager Steven L Glenn; editor Cheryl A Kluver; tel (402) 751-2652; fax (308) 647-6788

Keya Paha Co.: *Springview Herald* — W. L St.; PO Box 369, Springview (68778-0369); Th; 785pd, 39fr (Sw); $2.67; C; publisher & editor Karen A Kurzenberger; managing editor Donna L Ludemann; tel (402) 497-3651; fax (402) 497-2651

Kimball: *Western Nebraska Observer* — 118 E. 2nd St.; PO Box 700 (69145-0700); Th; 2,211pd, 15fr (Sw); $3.90; publisher Sherry Pinkerton; editor Jeff Stahla; tel (308) 235-3631; fax (308) 235-3632

Laurel: *Advocate* — 106 E. 2nd; PO Box 688 (68745); W; 1,094pd (Sw); $1.62; publisher Duane L Weber; editor Tanya Lute; tel (402) 256-3200; fax (402) 748-3354

Lawrence: *Lawrence Locomotive* — 111 N. Calvert St.; PO Box 188 (68957); Th; 870pd (Sw); $2.10; C; publisher & editor Allen Ostdiek; tel (402) 756-7284

Leigh: *Leigh World* — PO Box 278 (68643); W; 954pd, 20fr (Sw); 15¢; publisher & editor T A Evans; general manager Linda Beagle; tel (402) 487-2218; fax (402) 892-3141

Lyons: *Lyons Mirror Sun* — 214 Main St.; PO Box 59 (68038); Th; 1,129pd, 6fr (Sw); $3.25; C; publisher Dewaine Gahan; editor Anne O'Mara; tel (402) 687-2616

Madison: *The Madison Star-Mail* — 211 S. Main St.; PO Box 487 (68748); Th; 1,432pd (Est); $3.15; publisher & editor Christopher J Zavadil; tel (402) 454-3818

Meadow Grove: *Meadow Grove News* — 209 Main; PO Box 5 (68752); Th; 500pd, 30fr (Sw); 89¢; publisher Leslie D Falter; editor Judy Cleveland; tel (402) 634-2332

Milford: *Milford Times* — 510 1st St.; PO Box 723 (68405-0723); W; 961pd, 10fr (Est); 19¢; publisher & editor Frances Seeley; publisher George R Seeley; tel (402) 761-2911

Minden/Kearney Co.: *The Minden Courier* — 317 N. Minden Ave.; PO Box 379, Minden (68959); Tu; 2,546pd, 27fr (Sw); $3.85; publishers JoAnn Edgecombe & John Edgecombe; editor Julienne Gasseling; tel (308) 832-2220; fax (308) 832-2221

Mitchell: *The Index* — 1269 Center Ave. (69357); W; 1,636pd, 150fr (Est); $2.00; publisher & editor Jeanne Heath; tel (308) 623-1322

Mullen: *Hooker County Tribune* — 306 N.W. 1st; PO Box 125 (69152); Th; 875pd, 34fr (Sw); $3.30; publisher & editor Lanita Evans; tel (308) 546-2242

Neligh: *The Neligh News and Leader* — 419 Main St.; PO Box 46 (68756); W; 2,585pd, 38fr (Est); $1.15; publisher & editor Cindy Charf; tel (402) 887-4840; fax (402) 887-4711

Nelson: *Nelson Gazette* — 63 E. 4th; PO Box 285 (68961); Th; 975pd (Est); 13¢; publisher & editor James A Menke; tel (402) 225-2301

Newman Grove: *Newman Grove Reporter* — PO Box 476 (68758); W; 1,235pd (Est); $2.50; publisher & editor Kevin P Dugan; tel (402) 447-6012

Niobrara: *Niobrara Tribune* — PO Box 256 (68760); Th; 500pd (Est); 11¢; publishers Kevin Henseler & Tweeter Henseler; editor LaReta Eranstiter; tel (402) 857-3737; fax (402) 388-4336

N Bend/Morse Bluff: *North Bend Eagle* — 721 Main St.; PO Box 100, North Bend (68649); W; 1,467pd, 5fr (Sw); $3.50; publishers & editors Cheryl Chehubar & Chris Chehubar; tel (402) 652-8312

O'Neill: *Holt County Independent* — PO Box 360 (68763); Th; 4,725pd, 20fr (Sw); $4.08; publisher & editor George A Miles; managing editor Burns McCulloh; tel (402) 336-1221; fax (402) 336-1222

Oakland: *Oakland Independent* — 217 Oakland Ave.; PO Box 85 (68045-0085); Th; 1,700pd, 8fr (Sw); $4.00; C; publisher Bobbie Gahan; publisher & editor Dewaine Gahan; tel (402) 685-5624; fax (402) 685-5625

Ogallala: *Keith County News* — 116 W. A; PO Box 359 (69153); M/W; 3,987pd, 116fr (Sw); $5.25; publisher & editor Jack Pollock; managing editor Tom Huddleson; tel (308) 284-4046; fax (308) 284-4046

Omaha Suburbs: *Suburban Signal* — PO Box 460940, Papillion (68128-0940); W; 10,835pd (Est); $7.36; C; publisher James Nagen; editor Cathy Tibbels; tel (402) 339-3331; fax (402) 339-8562

Orchard: *The Orchard News* — 235 Windom St.; PO Box 130 (68764); Th; 740pd, 10fr (Sw); $1.50; publisher & editor Janice Mosel; tel (402) 893-2535

Ord: *The Ord Quiz* — 305 S. 16th St.; PO Box 197 (68862); Th; 2,779pd, 85fr (Sw); $4.40; C; publisher Kerry E Leggett; editor Doug Barber; tel (308) 728-3262; fax (308) 728-5715

Osceola: *Polk County News* — 421 N. Polk; PO Box 258 (68651); Th; 606pd, 20fr (Est); 8¢; publisher & editor William H Thompson; tel (402) 747-2431; fax (402) 764-5341

Copyright ©1996 by the Editor & Publisher Co.

Osmond: *The Osmond Republican* — PO Box 428 (68765); W; 897pd, 61fr (Sw); $2.75; publisher & editor Duane L Weber; tel (402) 748-3666; fax (402) 748-3354

Overton/Elm Creek: *The Beacon-Observer* — 504 C. St.; PO Box 330, Overton (68863); W; 1,566pd, 30fr (Sw); $3.60; publisher & editor Norman G Taylor; publisher Polly A Taylor; tel (308) 987-2451; fax (308) 987-2452

Oxford/Orleans: *Oxford Standard* — 104 W. South Railway; PO Box 125, Oxford (68967); Th; 1,092pd, 55fr (Sw); $2.59; publisher & editor James R Cooley; publisher Maria H Cooley; tel (308) 824-3582

Palmer: *Palmer Journal* — 218 Stanwick; PO Box 218 (68864-0218); Th; 702pd (Est); 6¢; publisher & managing editor Dale D Kirkpatrick; general manager & editor Kyle Kirkpatrick; tel (308) 894-3025

Papillion/La Vista: *The Papillion Times* — 138 N. Washington St.; PO Box 460940, Papillion (68128-0940); Th; 3,990pd, 56fr (Sw); $4.91; C; publisher Jim Nagen; editor Cathy Tibbels; tel (402) 339-3331; fax (402) 339-8562

Pawnee City Co.: *The Pawnee Republican* — 600 G St.; PO Box 111, Pawnee City (68420); Th; 1,834pd, 52fr (Sw); 32¢; publisher & editor Beverly J Puhalla; publisher Ronald J Puhalla; tel (402) 852-2575; fax (402) 852-2565

Pender: *The Pender Times* — 313 Main St. (68047); Th; 1,184pd, 75fr (Sw); 14¢; publisher & editor Norvin Hansen; tel (402) 385-3013

Petersburg: *Petersburg Press* — PO Box 177 (68652); W; 630pd, 11fr (Est); $2.55; publisher Mike Sunderland; tel (402) 386-5384

Pierce: *Pierce County Leader* — PO Box 129 (68767); Th; 2,129pd, 30fr (Est); 10¢; publisher Leslie D Falter; editor Randee D Falter; tel (402) 329-4665; fax (402) 329-6337

Plainview: *The Plainview News* — 508 W. Locust Ave.; PO Box 9 (68769-0009); W; 1,814pd (Sw); $2.70; publisher Leonard J Warneke; editor Dennis Meyer; tel (402) 582-4921; fax (402) 582-4922

Plattsmouth/Cass Co.: *Plattsmouth Journal* — 410 Main St.; PO Box 250, Plattsmouth (68048); M/Th; 5,518pd, 247fr (Sw); $5.30; publisher Louis Prohaska; editor Kevin Larson; tel (402) 296-2141; fax (402) 296-3401

Ponca: *Nebraska Journal-Leader* — 110 East St.; PO Box 545 (68770); Th; 1,271pd, 28fr (Est); 13¢; publisher & editor Richard D Volkman; tel (402) 755-2204

Ralston/Millard: *Ralston Recorder* — 138 N. Washington; PO Box 460940, Papillion (68128-0940); Th; 1,726pd, 29fr (Sw); $3.66; C; publisher Jim Nagen; editor Cathy Tibbels; tel (402) 331-6300; fax (402) 339-8562

Randolph/Cedar: *Times* — PO Box 380, Randolph (68771); W; 1,350pd, 53fr (Sw); $1.90; publisher Duane L Weber; editor Angie Nordhues; tel (402) 337-0488; fax (402) 748-3354

Ravenna: *The Ravenna News* — 322 Grand Ave.; PO Box 110 (68869); W; 2,000pd, 25fr (Est); 14¢; C; publishers George A Peterson & T M (Ted) Gill; editor Nancy Jackson; tel (308) 452-3411; fax (308) 452-3511

Red Cloud: *The Red Cloud Chief* — 309 N. Webster St.; PO Box 466 (68970); Th; 1,905pd, 55fr (Sw); 18¢; C; publisher & editor Robert A Hanson; managing editor Charles Mittan; tel (402) 746-3700; fax (402) 746-2368

Rushville/Hay Springs: *Sheridan County Star* — PO Box 450, Rushville (69360); W; 1,400pd, 23fr (Sw); $2.75; publisher Gayle Davis; tel (308) 327-2601; fax (308) 327-2613

St. Edward: *The St. Edward Advance* — 3rd & Beaver; PO Box 287, St. Edward (68660); Th; 786pd, 28fr (Sw); $2.55; publisher & editor Stephanie A Dawson; tel (402) 678-2771

St. Paul: *The Phonograph-Herald* — PO Box 27, St. Paul (68873); W; 2,452pd, 6fr (Sw); $2.60; publisher Mildred I Thompson; editor Connie M Thompson; tel (308) 754-4401; fax (308) 754-4498

Sargent/Milburn/Comstock/Arcadia: *Sargent Leader* — 757 H St.; PO Box 547, Burwell (68823); Th; 704pd, 25fr (Est); $2.20; publisher & editor Kendall Neiman; publisher Steve DeLashmutt; tel (308) 527-4210; fax (308) 527-4210

Schuyler/Colfax: *The Schuyler Sun* — 1112 C St.; PO Box 506, Schuyler (68661); Th; 3,471pd, 75fr (Sw); $4.65; C; publisher Francis C Svoboda; editor Michael F Rea; tel (402) 352-2424; fax (402) 352-3332

Scotia/N Loup: *The Scotia Register* — 305 E. Main St.; PO Box 306, Scotia (68875-0306); Th; 574pd, 12fr (Sw); $5.00; publishers & editors Mary A Medbery & Wilber D Medbery; tel (308) 245-4125

Scottsbluff: *The Business Farmer-Stockman* — 1617 Ave. A; PO Box 770 (69363-0770); F; 2,864pd (Est); $4.22; C; publisher & editor Penny Yenkel; tel (308) 635-2045; fax (308) 635-2348

Seward Co.: *Seward County Independent* — 129 S. 6th; PO Box 449, Seward (68434); W; 3,840pd, 99fr (Est); 27¢; C; publisher Mark Rhoades; editor Lori Shriner; tel (402) 643-3676; fax (402) 643-6774

Shelton: *The Shelton Clipper* — 113 C St.; PO Box 520 (68876); W; 1,001pd, 2fr (Sw); $1.15; publisher Steven L Glenn; general manager Jana Walker; editor Laura Kozin; tel (308) 647-5158; fax (308) 647-6788

Sherman Co.: *Sherman County Times* — 822 O St.; PO Box 430, Loup City (68853); Th; 1,768pd, 6fr (Est); $3.50; publisher Beverly J Peterson; publisher & editor George A Peterson; tel (308) 745-1260

S Sioux City: *South Sioux City Star* — 2520 Dakota Ave.; PO Box 157, South Sioux City (68776); Th; 4,600pd, 78fr (Sw); $8.24; publisher Kent Broyhill; editor Peggy Williams; tel (402) 494-4264; fax (402) 494-2414

Southern Lancaster Co./Western Otoe/Northern Gage: *The Voice News* — 118 Locust St.; PO Box 148, Hickman (68372-0148); Th; 2,100pd, 57fr (Sw); $5.50; publishers & editors Bill Bryant & Linda Bryant; tel (402) 792-2255

Spalding: *Spalding Enterprise* — 102 S. Cedar; PO Box D (68665); Th; 981pd, 15fr (Sw); $2.25; publisher & editor David Bopp; tel (308) 497-2153

Spencer: *The Spencer Advocate* — PO Box 187 (68777); Th; 1,040pd, 27fr (Sw); $1.90; publisher & editor Leon O Wells; tel (402) 589-1010; fax (402) 589-1010

Springfield: *The Springfield Monitor* — 138 N. Washington St.; PO Box 460940, Papillon (68128-0940); Th; 580pd, 20fr (Sw); $2.80; C; publisher Jim Nagen; editor Cathy Tibbels; tel (402) 339-3331; fax (402) 339-8562

Stanton: *Stanton Register* — 907 Ivy St.; PO Box 719 (68779); W; 1,514pd, 20fr (Sw); $2.66; publisher & editor Marlin G Waechter; tel (402) 439-2173

Stapleton: *Stapleton Enterprise* — PO Box 98 (69163); Th; 970pd (Sw); $2.40; publisher Arthur M French; editor Marcia R Hora; tel (308) 636-2444

Superior/Nelson/Mankato (KS): *The Superior Express* — 148 E. 3rd St.; PO Box 408, Superior (68978); Th; 4,258pd, 117fr (Sw); $4.00; publisher & editor Bill Blauvelt; tel (402) 879-3291; fax (402) 879-3293

Sutherland: *The Courier-Times* — 824 1st St.; PO Box 367 (69165); Th; 1,075pd (Sw); $3.00; publisher & editor Trenda Seifer; tel (308) 386-4617

Sutton/Clay Co.: *Clay County News* — 207 N. Saunders; PO Box 405, Sutton (68979); Th; 2,955pd, 50fr (Sw); $3.40; publishers Donald L Russell & Linda A Russell; editor Bill Brown; tel (402) 773-5576; fax (402) 773-5577

Syracuse: *Syracuse Journal-Democrat* — 123 W. 17th St.; PO Box O (68446); Th; 2,723pd, 126fr (Est); $3.75; C; publisher William R Welsh; general manager Janet Mason; editor David Swanson; tel (402) 269-2135; fax (800) 456-5158

Taylor/Almeria: *Taylor Clarion* — 757 H St.; PO Box 547, Burwell (68823); W; 434pd, 14fr (Sw); $3.50; C; publisher & editor Kendall Neiman; publisher Steve DeLashmutt; tel (308) 346-4504; fax (308) 346-4018

Tecumseh: *The Tecumseh Chieftain* — 241 Clay St.; PO Box 809 (68450); Th; 2,624pd, 19fr (Sw); $4.00; publisher Michael Kunzman; publisher & general manager Teri Pendell; editor Ann Wickett; tel (402) 335-3394; fax (402) 335-3496

Tekamah/Herman/Decatur/Craig: *Burt County Plaindealer* — 707 S. 13th; PO Box 239, Tekamah (68061); Tu; 2,127pd, 192fr (Sw); $3.50; publisher Joe Zink; managing editor Brenda S Cornelius; tel (402) 374-2225; fax (402) 374-2739

Tilden/Meadow Grove: *The Tilden Citizen* — 202 E. 2nd; PO Box 280, Tilden (68781); W; 1,314pd, 25fr (Est); $1.05; publisher & editor Leslie D Falter; tel (402) 368-5315

Trenton/Hitchcock Co.: *Hitchcock County News* — 346 Main; PO Box 278, Trenton (69044); W; 1,279pd, 20fr (Sw); $5.39; publisher & editor G B Crapson; general manager Virginia Scarbrough; tel (308) 334-5226; fax (308) 334-5226

Tryon: *The Tryon Graphic* — PO Box 8 (69167-0008); Th; 550pd (Sw); $3.00; publisher Arthur M French; editor Audrey French; tel (308) 587-2433

Valentine: *Valentine Newspaper* — 610 N. Main; Box 450 (69201); W; 2,600pd (Est); $3.30; publisher Marjorie Dover; publisher & editor Ray K Dover; tel (402) 376-3742

Wahoo/Ashland/Brainard: *Wahoo Newspaper* — 564 N. Broadway; PO Box 147, Wahoo (68066); Th; 4,047pd, 51fr (Est); $4.06; C; publisher & editor Zean E Carney; tel (402) 443-4162; fax (402) 443-4459

Wakefield: *The Wakefield Republican* — 224 Main St.; PO Drawer 110 (68784); Th; 1,250pd, 4fr (Sw); $2.75; publishers & editors Linda H Rischmueller & William H Rischmueller; tel (402) 287-2323

Wauneta: *The Wauneta Breeze* — 324 Tecumseh; PO Box 337 (69045); Th; 1,093pd, 23fr (Sw); $3.50; publisher & editor Lori Pankonin & Russ Pankonin; tel (308) 394-5389; fax (308) 394-5931

Wausa/Environs: *The Wausa Gazette* — 603 E. Broadway; PO Box G, Wausa (68786); Th; 1,050pd, 41fr (Sw); $2.40; publisher & editor Robert P Reinhardt; tel (402) 586-2661

Waverly: *The News* — 14210 Kenilworth; PO Box 100 (68462); Th; 1,675pd, 150fr (Sw); $3.60; publisher & editor Marilyn J Carney; publisher Zean E Carney; tel (402) 786-2344; fax (402) 786-2344

Wayne: *The Wayne Herald* — 114 Main; PO Box 70 (68787); Th; 2,400pd (Est); $4.95; C; publisher & editor Lester J Mann; general manager Linda Granfield; tel (402) 375-2600; fax (402) 375-1888

W Point: *West Point News* — 134 E. Grove; PO Box 40 (68788); W; 3,859pd, 100fr (Est); $4.55; C; publisher Tom Kelly; editor Willis Mahannah; tel (402) 372-2461; fax (402) 372-3530

Wilbur/Saline Cos.: *Wilber Republican* — 206 W. 3rd; PO Box 457, Wilber (68343); W; 1,500pd (Est); $2.73; publisher & editor Kent M Korinek; tel (402) 821-2586; fax (402) 821-3308

Wisner/Beemer/Bancroft/Pilger: *Wisner News-Chronicle* — 1014 Ave. E.; PO Box 460, Wisner (68791); Th; 2,281pd, 30fr (Sw); $4.27; publisher & editor Theodore M Huettmann; tel (402) 529-3229; fax (402) 529-3279

Wolbach: *The Wolbach Messenger* — PO Box 38 (68882); Th; 447pd, 1fr (Sw); 8¢; publisher Mildred I Thompson; editor Connie M Thompson; tel (308) 246-5268; fax (308) 754-4498

Wood River: *The Wood River Sunbeam* — 108 W. 9th; PO Box 356 (68883-0356); W; 1,083pd, 9fr (Sw); $3.50; publishers & editors Charlene Hoschouer & Douglas G Hoschouer; tel (308) 583-2241

Wymore/Odell: *Wymore Arbor State* — 206 S. 7th St.; PO Box 327, Wymore (68466); Th; 1,666pd, 78fr (Sw); $3.30; publisher Keith Clarkson; editor Michelle Casebeer; tel (402) 645-3344; fax (402) 645-3345

NEVADA

Boulder City: *Boulder City News* — 1227 Arizona St.; PO Box 60065 (89006); Th; 4,575pd, 10fr (Sw); $3.50; C; publisher Mike O'Callaghan; general manager Timothy O'Callaghan; editor Roy Theiss; tel (702) 293-2302; fax (702) 294-0977

Dayton/Fernley/Silver Springs: *Fernley Leader/ Dayton Courier* — PO Box 841, Yerington (89447); W; 2,600pd (Sw); $4.75; C; publisher Bob Sanford; publisher & general manager Jim Sanford; editor Laura Tennant; managing editor David Sanford; tel (702) 463-4242; fax (702) 463-5547

Death Valley: *Death Valley Gateway Gazette* — 1330 Highway 160, Ste. 6, Pahrump (89048); Th; 5,000pd (Est); $5.94; general manager David Downing; editor Beverly Robinson; tel (702) 727-5583; fax (702) 727-7142

Douglas Co.: *The Record-Courier* — 1218 W. Eddy St., Gardnerville (89410); W/Sa; 6,500pd, 181fr (Sw); $9.75; C; publisher Tim Huether; editor Kurt Hildebrand; managing editor Sheila Gardner; tel (702) 782-5121; fax (702) 882-2556

Elko Co.: *Elko Independent* — 276 11th St.; PO Box 309, Elko (89083); W; 1,706pd, 360fr (Sw); $5.00; C; publisher & editor Kay McMullen Thompson; general manager Samuel C McMullen; managing editor Sean S Thompson; tel (702) 738-3611; fax (702) 738-1453

Eureka: *Eureka Sentinel* — 150 Main St.; PO Box 193, Tonopah (89049); Th; 550pd, 50fr (Est); $4.06; publisher & editor William G Roberts; tel (702) 482-3365; fax (702) 482-5042

Hawthorne: *Mineral County Independent News* — 501 D St.; PO Box 1270 (89415-1270); W; 2,690pd, 70fr (Sw); $5.00; publisher Frank Hughes; publisher & editor Ted Hughes; publisher Tony Hughes; tel (702) 945-2414; fax (702) 945-1270

Incline Village/Kings Bch: *North Lake Tahoe Bonanza* — 917 Tahoe Blvd., Ste. 100; PO Box 7820 (89450); W/F; 1,346pd, 4,815fr (Sw); $10.56; publisher & editor Jeffrey Ackerman; tel (916) 546-2506; fax (916) 546-2507

Laughlin: *Laughlin Nevada Times* — 3100 S. Needles Hwy., Ste. 700; PO Box 29909 (89028); W; 10,000fr (Sw); $12.30; C; publisher Lalena Stewart; editor Bill Hoban; tel (702) 298-6090; fax (702) 298-3626

Lincoln Co.: *Lincoln County Record* — 1001 Ranch (Caliente 89008); PO Box 507, Pioche (89043-0507); Th; 1,506pd, 29fr (Sw); $4.50; publisher & editor Connie Simkins; tel (702) 726-3333; fax (702) 726-3331

Pahrump: *Pahrump Valley Times* — 2160 E. Calvada Blvd. (89048); W/F; 5,720pd, 533fr (Sw); $6.75; publisher & editor Rich Thurlow; general manager Connie Coon; tel (702) 727-5102; fax (702) 727-5309

Pershing Co.: *Lovelock Review-Miner* — 230 Main St.; PO Box 620, Lovelock (89419); Th; 1,397pd, 11fr (Sw); $4.26; publisher & editor Gwen Bogh Carter; tel (702) 273-7245; fax (702) 273-0500

Tonopah: *Times-Bonanza/Goldfield News* — 150 Main St.; PO Box 193 (89049); Th; 2,700pd, 100fr (Sw); $4.62; publisher & editor William G Roberts; tel (702) 482-3365; fax (702) 482-5042

Wendover/Wells/Eureka: *High Desert Advocate* — 1940 Plateau Way; PO Box 3190, Wendover (89883); W; 3,550pd, 100fr (Sw); $6.25; publisher Harry Copelan; editor Howard Copelan; tel (702) 664-2300; fax (702) 664-3311

Yerington: *Mason Valley News* — 41 N. Main St.; PO Box 841 (89447); F; 3,850pd, 83fr (Sw); $5.60; C; publisher Bob Sanford; publisher & general manager Jim Sanford; editor Dave Sanford; tel (702) 463-4242/2856; fax (702) 463-5547

NEW HAMPSHIRE

Alton: *Granite State Vacationer* — 563 Central Ave., Dover (03870); W; 50,000fr (Est); $12.00; C; publisher Tri-Town Publisher Inc.; editor Buzz Dietterle; tel (603) 742-3700; fax (603) 742-6442

Bedford/Merrimack: *Bedford-Merrimack Bulletin* — 15 Elm St.; PO Box 280, Goffstown (03045); Th; 10,205fr (Est); $8.00; C; publisher Nackey S Loeb; general manager & editor Jeffrey A Rapsis; tel (603) 497-4123; fax (603) 497-5017

Bristol: *The Record Enterprise* — PO Box 248 (03222); W; 2,105pd, 76fr (Est); 24¢; publisher Tom Hepner; editor Bill York; tel (603) 744-3330; fax (603) 744-5875

Carroll Co.: *Carroll County Independent* — Moultonville Rd.; PO Box 38, Center Ossipee (03814); W; 4,692pd, 89fr (Sw); $8.70; C; publisher Jacob J Burghardt; general manager Edward Engler; editor Frank Gospodarek; tel (603) 539-4111; fax (603) 539-5564

Concord/Manchester/Keene: *New Hampshire Week In Review* — 202 W. Main St.; PO Box 917, Hillsboro (03244); M; 22,000fr (Est); $12.75; publisher Leigh Bosse; editor Joyce Bosse; tel (603) 464-3388; fax (603) 464-4106

Derry/Londonderry: *Derry News* — 46 W. Broadway, Derry (03038); W/F; 10,389pd, 210fr (Sw); $11.45; C; publisher Allan B Rogers Jr; editor Robert Wallack; tel (603) 437-7000; fax (603) 432-4510

Dover/Rollinsford/Somersworth: *Dover Times* — 270 Central Ave., Dover (03820); Th; 5,579fr (CAC); $7.90; C; publisher Lou McGrew; editor John F J Sullivan; tel (603) 742-7209; fax (603) 742-7606

Durham/Newmarket: *The Tri-Town Transcript* — 563 Central Ave.; PO Box 519, Dover (03820); Th; 7,000pd (Est); $7.45; C; publisher Paul Dietterle; general manager Bonnie Dubois; editor Carolyn Handy; tel (603) 742-3700; fax (603) 742-6442

Exeter: *The Exeter News-Letter* — 7 Portsmouth Ave. (Stratham, 03885); PO Box 250 (03833); Tu/F; 7,253pd, 178fr (Est); $10.25; C; publisher John Tabor; editor Thomas P Lynch; tel (603) 772-6000; fax (603) 772-3830

Franklin/Tilton: *Franklin-Tilton Telegram* — 448 Central St.; PO Box 100, Franklin (03235); Th; 1,660pd, 300fr (Est); $4.75; publisher & editor Thomas Caldwell; tel (603) 934-6560; fax (603) 934-6536

Goffstown/New Boston/Weare/Dunbarton: *Goffstown News* — 15 Elm St.; PO Box 280, Goffstown (03045); Th; 7,000fr (Est); $8.00; C; publisher Nackey S Loeb; general manager & editor Jeffrey A Rapsis; tel (603) 497-4123; fax (603) 497-5017

Greater Nashua: *1590 Broadcaster* — 502 W. Hollis St.; PO Box 548, Nashua (03061); W; 62,551fr (Est); 71¢; C; publisher Maurice Parent; editor Donald Dillaby; tel (603) 889-1590; fax (603) 883-4344

Hampton/Hampton Falls/N Hampton/Seabrook/Rye: *The Hampton Union* — 7 Portsmouth Ave. (Stratham, 03885); PO Box 250, Exeter (03833); Tu; 6,355pd, 111fr (ABC); $10.80; F; 6,355pd, 111fr (ABC); $15.40; C; publisher John Tabor; editor Thomas P Lynch; tel (603) 772-6000; fax (603) 772-3830

Hooksett/Allenstown/Epsom/Pembroke: *Suncook-Hooksett Banner* — 1100 Hooksett Rd. Community Plz.; PO Box 280, Hooksett (03106); Th; 7,665fr (Est); $8.00; C; publisher Nackey S Loeb; general manager & editor Jeffrey A Rapsis; managing editor James B Van Anglen; tel (603) 626-6397; fax (603) 626-6144

Hudson/Litchfield/Nashaw/Londonderry/Tyngsboro (MA): *Hudson/Litchfield News* — 222 Central St., Ste. 5, Hudson (03051-4494); F; 11,152fr (Sw); $7.50; publisher Fideie Bernasconi; editor Diane Thoms; tel (603) 880-1516; fax (603) 880-1516

Kingston/Newton/Fremont: *Kingstonian* — 7 Portsmouth Ave. (Stratham, 03885); PO Box 250, Exeter (03833); Sa; 1,995pd (Est); $9.85; C; publisher John Tabor; editor Thomas P Lynch; tel (603) 772-6000; fax (603) 772-3830

Lancaster: *The Coos County Democrat* — 79 Main St.; PO Box 28 (03584); W; 6,898pd, 70fr (Sw); $5.50; C; publisher John D Harrigan; editor Eugene Ehlert; tel (603) 788-4939; fax (603) 788-3022

Littleton/Lisbon: *The Courier* — 365 Union St.; PO Box 230, Littleton (03561); W; 6,205pd, 92fr (Sw); 24¢; C; publisher Thomas C Hepner; editor Tim McCarthy; tel (603) 444-3927; fax (603) 444-3920

Meredith/Center Harbor/Moultonboro/Sandwich: *Meredith News* — 5 Water St.; PO Box 729, Meredith (03253); W; 3,916pd, 64fr (Sw); $4.80; publisher C Allen Gable; general manager David French; editor Rudy VanVeghten; tel (603) 279-4516; fax (603) 279-3331

Merrimack/Bedford/Amherst: *The Village Crier* — 579 D.W. Highway; PO Box 1000, Merrimack (03054); Tu; 7,500fr (Est); $5.40; publisher Seth Heywood; general manager Carolyn Kallan; editor Lucille F Heywood; tel (603) 424-7610

Milford/Amherst/Mt. Vernon/Wilton: *The Milford Cabinet and Wilton Journal* — 4 School St.; PO Box 180, Milford (03055); W; 8,900pd, 78fr (Sw); $9.00; C; publisher Frank P Manley; editor Robert Mackintosh; tel (603) 673-3100; fax (603) 673-8250

New London/Newport: *The Argus-Champion* — 86 Sunapee St.; PO Box 509, Newport (03773); W; 5,700pd, 183fr (Est); $7.75; C; publisher William Galloway; general manager Claire Piaggi; editor Jeff Shippee; tel (603) 863-1776; fax (603) 863-0066

Peterborough: *Monadnock Ledger* — 20 Grove St.; PO Box 36 (03458); Th; 6,761pd, 121fr (Sw); $7.30; publisher Heather McKernan; editor Mary J Kopp; tel (603) 924-7172; fax (603) 924-3681

Peterborough/Jaffrey: *The Peterborough Transcript* — 43 Grove St., Peterborough (03458); Th; 6,000pd, 125fr (Est); $7.15; C; publisher Joseph D Cummings; editor John Franklin; tel (603) 924-3333; fax (603) 924-7946

Plaistow/Hampstead/Atkinson/Sandown/Danville: *Plaistow/Hampstead News* — 7 Portsmouth Ave. (Stratham 03885); PO Box 250, Exeter (03833); Sa; 2,604pd (Est); $9.85; C; publisher John Tabor; editor Thomas P Lynch; tel (603) 772-6000; fax (603) 772-3830

Plymouth/Baker River: *The Record-Enterprise* — 111 Main St.; PO Box 148, Plymouth (03264); W; 6,336pd, 75fr (Sw); $4.75; C; publisher Thomas C Hepner; general manager & editor William York; managing editor Brian McCarthy; tel (603) 536-1311; fax (603) 536-8940

Raymond: *Raymond Times* — 7 Portsmouth Ave.; PO Box 250, Exeter (03833); Sa; 1,671pd (Est); $9.35; C; publisher John Tabor; editor Thomas P Lynch; tel (603) 772-6000; fax (603) 772-3830

Rochester: *Rochester Times* — 77 N. Main St. (03867); Th; 7,720fr (CAC); $7.90; C; publisher Lou McGrew; editor John Nolan; tel (603) 332-2300; fax (603) 330-0718

Salem/Windham/Pelham: *Salem Observer* — 380 Main St.; PO Box 720, Salem (03079); W; 5,329pd, 69fr (Est); $8.76; publisher Arthur J Mueller Jr; editor Monique Duhamel; tel (603) 893-4356

Wolfeboro: *The Granite State News* — Endicott St.; PO Box 879 (03894); W; 4,766pd, 54fr (Sw); $8.70; C; publisher Jacob J Burghardt; general manager Edward Engler; editor Jeanne B Tempest; tel (603) 569-3126; fax (603) 569-4743

Wolfeboro: *Lakes Region Courier* — PO Box 1630 (03894); Th; 4,917fr (CAC); $7.90; C; publisher Lou McGrew; editor Mark Smith; tel (603) 569-6550; fax (603) 569-3053

NEW JERSEY

Asbury Park/Avon/Bradley Beach/Neptune/Neptune City/Ocean Grove: *Ocean Grove & Neptune Times* — 41 Pilgrim Pathway; PO Box 5, Ocean Grove (07756); Th; 4,494pd, 600fr (Sw); $5.00; publisher & editor Gregory D Hunt; general manager Kevin Sheehan; tel (908) 775-0007; fax (908) 774-4480

Atco/Berlin/Clementon/Winslow Twp.: *Record-Breeze* — 134 Kings Hwy. E., Haddonfield (08033); Th; 2,143pd, 830fr (Sw); $8.45; C; publisher Jane Parr; general manager John Brookover; editor Albert Countryman Jr.; managing editor John Worthington; tel (609) 354-0200; fax (609) 216-1220

Belleville: *Belleville Post* — 266 Liberty St.; PO Box 110, Bloomfield (07003); Th; 144pd, 3,337fr (Sw); $15.00; C; publisher David Worrall; editor Thomas Canavan; tel (908) 686-7700; fax (908) 686-7700

Belleville: *The Belleville Times* — 155 A Washington Ave.; PO Box 56 (07109); Th; 6,110pd (Est); $15.95; C; publisher Frank A Orechio; editor Richard Dickon; tel (201) 759-3200; fax (201) 667-3904

Belvidere: *The News* — 206 Greenwich St.; PO Box 265 (07823); W; 1,127pd, 57fr (Sw); 24¢; publisher Rosemarie Maio; editor Ejvind Boccolini; tel (908) 475-1848; fax (908) 852-9320

Bergen Co.: *Press Journal* — PO Box 631, Englewood (07631); Th; 6,880pd, 3,280fr (Est); $12.95; C; publisher William Cohen; editor Eleanor Marra; tel (201) 871-6900

Bergenfield/Alpine: *Twin-Boro News* — 19 Legion Dr., Bergenfield (07621); W; 28,428fr (CAC); $8.58; publisher Horace W Spafford; editor Janice Friedman; tel (201) 384-0998; fax (201) 384-2832

Bernardsville: *Bernardsville News* — 17 Morristown Rd. (07924); W; 8,570pd, 434fr (CAC); $14.25; C; publisher Cortlandt Parker; editor Charles T Zavalick; managing editor Phil Nardone; tel (908) 766-3900; fax (908) 766-6365

Blairstown: *The Blairstown Press* — PO Box 425 (07825); W; 3,793pd, 182fr (Est); $5.46; publisher Rosemarie Maio; editor Paul Avery; managing editor Dan Herschberg; tel (908) 362-6161; fax (908) 362-9223

Bloomfield: *Bloomfield Life* — 106 Broad St.; PO Box 1879 (07003); Th; 4,710pd (Est); $15.25; C; publisher Frank A Orechio; editor Steve Galvacky; tel (201) 748-9700; fax (201) 667-3904

Bloomfield: *The Independent Press of Bloomfield* — 266 Liberty St.; PO Box 110 (07003); Th; 3,292pd, 235fr (Sw); $15.00; C; publisher David Worrall; editor Thomas Canavan; tel (908) 686-7700; fax (908) 686-4169

Bordentown/Florence: *Register-News* — 137 Farnsworth Ave.; PO Box 189, Bordentown (08505-0189); Th; 7,877pd, 100fr (Sw); $7.27; publisher Hershel M Brown; editor Jennifer L Collins; tel (609) 298-7111; fax (609) 298-7107

Bound Brook: *Bound Brook Chronicle* — 44 Veterans Memorial Dr. E.; PO Box 699, Somerville (08876); Th; 3,740pd (Est); $12.35; publisher Louis Barsony; editor Michael Deak; managing editor Andrew Simpson; tel (908) 722-3000; fax (908) 526-2509

Brick Twp.: *Brick Township Town News/Sampler* — 526 Jackson Ave.; Box 1111, Brick (08723); Th; 127pd, 4,975fr (Sw); $4.25; publisher & editor Edward C Mueller; tel (908) 477-9110; fax (908) 477-8305

Brielle/Belmar/Manasquan/Sea Girt/Spring Lake/Spring Lake He: *The Coast Star* — 13 Broad St., Manasquan (08736); Th; 7,380pd, 55fr (Sw); $4.25; publisher & editor James M Manser; managing editor Dawn D'Aries; tel (908) 223-0076

Byram/Hopatcong/Stanhope: *Sussex County Chronicle* — Waterloo Rd.; PO Box 52, Stanhope (07874-0523); W; 1,875pd (Sw); $7.95; C; publisher Rosemarie Maio; managing editor Shawn Cupolo; tel (201) 691-9530; fax (908) 852-9320

Caldwell: *The Progress* — 6 Brookside Ave.; PO Box 72 (07006); Th; 8,192pd, 388fr (ABC); $10.75; C; publisher John A Sullivan III; editor Jean E Conlon; tel (201) 226-8900; fax (201) 226-0553

Cape May Area/Lower Twp.: *Cape May Star and Wave* — 513 Washington Mall, Cape May (08204); Th; 6,559pd, 51fr (Sw); $5.50; publisher Ralph J Cooper; editor Mary Keely; tel (609) 884-3466; fax (609) 884-2893

Cape May Co.: *Cape May County Herald/Lower Township Lantern/Cape May Herald-Dspt.* — 1508 Rte. 47 S.; PO Box 400, Rio Grande (08242); W; 28,754pd (Sw); $13.80; C; publisher Arthur R Hall; general manager Gary Rudy; editor Joseph R Zelnik; tel (609) 886-8600; fax (609) 886-1879

Cape May Co.: *Cape May County Gazette Leader* — 1212 Atlantic Ave.; PO Box 469, Wildwood (08260); W; 4,500pd, 30,000fr (Sw); $9.00; C; publisher Rick Travis; editor Rob Seitzinger; tel (609) 522-3423; fax (609) 522-7451

Chatham: *The Chatham Courier* — 27 Bowers Ln. (07928); Th; 3,660pd, 74fr (Est); $10.90; C; publisher Cortlandt Parker; editor Heather MacGregor; managing editor Gene Robbins; tel (201) 635-0639; fax (201) 635-6081

Cherry Hill/Haddonfield: *Courier Post/This Week* — 301 Cuthbert Blvd.; PO Box 5300, Cherry Hill (08034); Th; 32,807pd, 114,998fr (Est); $13.01; C; publisher Bob Collins; editor Tom Engelman; tel (609) 663-4200; fax (609) 663-7664

Clark: *Clark Eagle* — 1291 Stuyvesant Ave.; PO Box 3109, Union (07083); Th; 652pd, 39fr (CAC); $13.00; C; publisher David Worrall; editor Thomas Canavan; tel (908) 686-7700; fax (908) 686-4169

Clark: *Clark Patriot* — 219 Central Ave.; PO Box 1061, Rahway (07065); Th; 1,137pd, 200fr (Sw); $9.10; C; publisher & editor Ellen Vigilante; managing editor Linda Koenig; tel (908) 574-1200; fax (908) 388-4143

Clementon/Berlin/Lindenwold: *The Record-Breeze* — PO Box 67, Blackwood (08012); Th; 5,000pd, 500fr (Sw); $7.35; C; publisher Jane Parr; general manager James Wyatt; editor John Worthington; tel (609) 234-0200; fax (609) 227-1207

Clifton: *Dateline Journal* — 10 Park Place, Butler (07405); W; 30,100fr (CAC); $23.71; Su; 24,150fr (CAC); $23.71; C; publisher Richard Vezza; editor Albina Sportelli; managing editor Carol Nysmom; tel (201) 772-7003; fax (201) 838-1495

Clifton/Wayne/Paterson/Passaic/Parsippany/E Hanover/Montclai: *The North Jersey Prospector* — 85 Crooks Ave., Clifton (07011); Th; 54,408pd, 20,000fr (Sw); 90¢; publisher Alex Bidnik; editor Blanche Kubat; managing editor Alex Bidnik Jr; tel (201) 773-8300

Collingswood Haddon Twp.: *The Retrospect* — 732 Haddon Ave.; PO Box 296, Collingswood (08108); F; 4,086pd, 117fr (Sw); 47¢; publisher & editor Kenneth W Roberts; tel (609) 854-1400

Cranbury/Monroe: *The Cranbury Press* — 397 Ridge Rd.; PO Box 309, Dayton (08810); W; 3,593pd, 139fr (Est); $11.00; publisher James B Kilgore; general manager Michael O'Hara; editor Helene Ragovin; tel (908) 329-9214; fax (908) 329-9286

Cranford/Kenilworth: *Cranford Chronicle* — 102 Walnut Ave.; PO Box 626, Cranford (07016); W; 2,450pd, 121fr (CAC); $15.00; C; publisher Louis Barsony; editor Ed Carroll; managing editor Michael Deak; tel (908) 276-6000; fax (908) 276-6220

Cumberland Co.: *Cumberland Reminder* — 211 N. Buck St.; PO Box 1600, Millville (08332); W; 20,022fr (Sw); $5.25; publisher Darrell Kopp; editor Karen L Keirsey; tel (609) 825-8811; fax (609) 884-1100

Denville: *Neighbor News* — 435 E. Main St., Rte. 53 (07834); W; 33,991fr (CAC); $22.55; C; publisher Salvatore Paci; editor Cathleen Whittaker; tel (201) 586-3012; fax (201) 586-3449

Denville/Rockaway: *Citizen of Morris County* — 124 E. Main St.; PO Box 7, Denville (07834); W; 6,262pd, 898fr (Est); 22¢; publisher & editor George S Mitchell; tel (201) 627-0400; fax (201) 627-0403

E Brunswick: *Sentinel* — 7 Edgeboro Rd. (08816); W; 558pd, 49,892fr (Sw); $6.45; C; publisher Kevin L Wittman; editor Gregory Bean; managing editor Darren Smith; tel (908) 254-7000; fax (908) 254-0486

E Orange: *East Orange Record* — 170 Scotland Rd.; PO Box 849, Orange (07051); Th; 2,606pd, 98fr (Sw); $13.00; C; publisher David Worrall; editor Thomas Canavan; tel (908) 686-7700; fax (908) 686-4169

Egg Harbor City: *Egg Harbor News* — 315 W. Main St.; PO Box 596, Hammonton (08037); Th; 1,100pd, 40fr (Sw); $8.25; publisher Ron Jacovini; editor Norlynne Lubrano; tel (609) 561-2300; fax (609) 561-2249

Elmer: *Elmer Times* — 21 State St.; PO Box 1160 (08318); Th; 2,100pd (Sw); 13¢; publisher & editor Pamela S Brunner; tel (609) 358-6171

Englewood/Closter: *Press Journal* — PO Box 631, Englewood (07631); Th; 6,880pd, 3,280fr (Est); $12.95; C; publisher William Cohen; editor Eleanor Marra; tel (201) 871-6900; fax (201) 947-6968

Englewood/Teaneck: *Suburbanite* — 231 Herbert Ave., Closter (07624); W; 10pd, 53,203fr (CAC); $12.32; publisher Joe Giosio; editor David Savastano; tel (201) 784-0266; fax (201) 784-2594

Fair Lawn: *The News Beacon* — 12-38 River Rd. (07410); Th; 925pd, 184fr (Est); $9.75; publisher Sherwood L Spitz; editor Pete Kelly; tel (201) 791-8400; fax (201) 843-2388

Fair Lawn/Elmwood Park/Saddle Brook: *Fair Lawn/Elmwood Park/Saddle Brook Shopper* — 12-38 River Rd., Fair Lawn (07410); W; 25,418fr (CAC); 45¢; editor Erik Englund; tel (201) 791-8400; fax (201) 794-3259

Fairview: *Bergen Free Press* — 155 S. Broad Ave. (07022); W/Th/F; 11,000fr (Est); 29¢; publisher Salvatore Cangiano; editor David Cangi; tel (201) 945-5597

Florham Park: *Florham Park Eagle* — 155 Main St., Madison (07940); Th; 3,400pd (Est); $10.90; publisher Cortlandt Parker; editor Gene Robbins; tel (201) 377-2000; fax (201) 377-7721

Fort Lee/Palisades Park/Cliffside Park: *Bergen News Palisades* — 111 Grand Ave.; PO Box 616, Palisades Park (07650); W; 36,839fr (CAC); $43.11; C; publisher William Cohen; editor Eleanor Marra; tel (201) 947-5000; fax (201) 947-6968

Franklin Twp.: *The Franklin News-Record* — 300 Witherspoon St., Princeton (08542); F; 5,625fr (Est); $5.40; C; publisher James B Kilgore; general manager Michael O'Hara; editor Cindy Naylor; tel (908) 359-0850; fax (908) 359-3930

Franklin Twp.: *The Sentinel* — N. Delsea Dr.; PO Box 367, Franklinville (08322); Th; 4,200pd (Est); $6.65; publisher & editor James R Kinkade; tel (609) 694-1600; fax (609) 694-0469

Freehold/W Monmouth: *News Transcript* — 25 Kilmer Dr., Ste. 109, Morganville (07751); W; 355pd, 26,678fr (CAC); $6.45; C; publisher Kevin L Wittman; editor Gregory Bean; managing editor Mark R Rosman; tel (908) 972-6740; fax (908) 972-6746

Frenchtown: *Delaware Valley News* — 207 Harrison St.; PO Box 244 (08825-0244); Th; 3,816pd, 19fr (ABC); $12.00; C; publisher Catherine T Langley; editor Nick DiGiovanni; managing editor Jay Langley; tel (908) 996-4047; fax (908) 996-2238

Garfield: *Garfield-Wellington Shopper* — 12-38 River Rd., Fair Lawn (07410); W; 27,133fr (CAC); 45¢; editor Erik Englund; tel (201) 791-8400; fax (201) 791-3259

Garfield/Wallington/Saddle Brook: *The Messenger* — Harrison & McArthur Aves., Garfield (07026); Th; 1,400pd (Est); $5.35; publisher Nancy C Huffman; editor James A Huffman; tel (201) 473-1927; fax (201) 546-4233

Glen Ridge: *The Glen Ridge Paper* — 266 Liberty St.; PO Box 110, Bloomfield (07003); Th; 1,515pd, 137fr (CAC); $15.00; C; publisher David Worrall; editor Thomas Canavan; tel (908) 686-7700; fax (908) 686-4169

Glen Ridge: *Glen Ridge Voice* — 855A Bloomfield Ave. (07028); Th; 2,458pd (Est); $14.00; publisher Frank A Orechio; editor Howard Klausner; tel (201) 748-0700; fax (201) 667-3904

Gloucester City/Brooklawn/Mt. Ephraim/Westville: *Gloucester City News* — 34 S. Broadway; PO Box 151 (08030); Th; 4,752pd, 73fr (Sw); $5.25; publisher & editor William E Cleary; tel (609) 456-1199; fax (609) 456-1330

Hackettstown/Washington: *The Star Gazette* — 106 E. Moore St.; PO Box 500, Hackettstown (07840); Th; 4,468pd, 13fr (CAC); $6.86; publisher Rosemarie Maio; editor Dan Hirshberg; tel (908) 852-1212; fax (908) 852-9320

Haledon: *Haledon/North Haledon/Prospect Park Shopper* — 12-38 River Rd., Fair Lawn (07410); W; 6,752fr (CAC); 25¢; editor Erik Englund; tel (201) 791-8400; fax (201) 794-3259

Hamilton: *The Hamilton Observer* — 300 Witherspoon St.; PO Box 350, Princeton (08542); F; 4,618fr (Est); $11.00; publisher James B Kilgore; general manager Michael O'Hara; editor Cindy Naylor; tel (609) 924-3244; fax (609) 921-3842

Hammonton: *Hammonton News* — 115 12th St.; PO Box 596 (08037); Th; 6,011pd, 100fr (Sw); 35¢; C; publisher Ronald Jacovini; editor Norlynne Lubrano; tel (609) 561-2300

Hanover/Whippany/Cedar Knolls: *Hanover Eagle/Regional Weekly News* — PO Box 160, Madison (07940); Th; 4,000pd (Est); $10.90; C; publisher Cortlandt Parker; editor Jim Lent; tel (201) 377-2000; fax (201) 377-7721

Hasbrouck Hts.: *The Observer* — 194 Blvd.; PO Box 445, Hasbrouck Heights (07604); W; 2,825pd, 75fr (Est); 50¢; publisher Hasbrouck Heights Publishing Co.; editor Rose Heck; tel (201) 288-0333; fax (201) 288-1847

Hazlet/Matawan/Middletown: *The Independent* — 7 Edgeboro Rd., East Brunswick (08816); W; 1,014pd, 28,237fr (Est); $28.33; publisher Kevin Wittman; editor Gregory Bean; managing editor Paul Fiorilla; tel (908) 254-7000; fax (908) 254-0256

Highland Park: *Highland Park Herald* — 44 Veterans Memorial Dr. E.; PO Box 699, Somerville (08876); F; 2,509pd (Est); $12.35; C; publisher Louis Barsony; editor David Block; tel (908) 732-3000; fax (908) 526-2509

Hightstown/E Windsor: *Windsor-Hights Herald* — Warren Plz. Ctr., Rte. 130 S., Hightstown (08520); W; 4,762pd, 150fr (Est); $18.50; publisher James B Kilgore; general manager Michael O'Hara; editor Frank Herick; tel (609) 448-3005; fax (609) 448-8044

Hillsborough Twp.: *Hillsborough Beacon* — 307 Omni Dr.; PO Box 695, Hillsborough (08876); Th; 3,883pd, 150fr (Est); $20.80; C; publisher James B Kilgore; general manager Michael O'Hara; editor Jon F Steele; tel (908) 359-0850; fax (908) 359-3930

Hillside: *Hillside Leader* — 1291 Stuyvesant Ave.; PO Box 3109, Union (07083); Th; 1,074pd, 31fr (CAC); $10.00; publisher David Worrall; editor Thomas Canavan; tel (908) 686-7700; fax (908) 686-4169

Hoboken: *The Hoboken Reporter* — 1400 Washington St.; PO Box 3086 (07030); Su; 14,592fr (CAC); $30.00; C; publisher Joseph Barry; general manager Lucha M Malato; editor Michael Richardson; tel (201) 798-7800; fax (201) 798-0018

Hopewell: *Hopewell Valley News* — PO Box 8 (08525); Th; 3,059pd, 141fr (Est); $11.00; publisher James B Kilgore; general manager Michael O'Hara; editor Ruth P Luse; tel (609) 466-1190; fax (609) 466-2123

Hudson Co.: *Hudson Current* — 1400 Washington St.; PO Box 3086, Hoboken (07030); Th; 10,080fr (Est); $30.00; C; publisher Joseph Barry; general manager Lucha M Malato; editor Michael Richardson; tel (201) 798-7800; fax (201) 798-0018

Hunterdon Co.: *Hunterdon County Democrat* — 18 Minneakoning Rd.; PO Box 32, Flemington (08822-0032); Th; 24,170pd, 200fr (ABC); $25.95; C; publisher Catherine T Langley; general manager Edward J Mack; editor Jay Langley; managing editor Rick Epstein; tel (908) 782-4747; fax (908) 782-6572

Hunterdon Co.: *Hunterdon Observer* — 18 Minneakoning Rd.; PO Box 32, Flemington (08822-0032); Sa; 40,561fr (Sw); $16.85; C; publisher Catherine T Langley; managing editor Sallie Graziano; tel (908) 782-4747; fax (908) 782-6572

Irvington: *Irvington Herald* — 463 Valley St.; PO Box 158, Maplewood (07040); Th; 1,517pd, 118fr (CAC); $13.00; C; publisher David Worrell; editor Thomas Canavan; tel (908) 686-7700; fax (908) 686-4169

Jersey City: *The Jersey City Reporter* — 1400 Washington St.; PO Box 3086, Hoboken (07030); Su; 13,785fr (CAC); $30.00; C; publisher Joseph Barry; general manager Lucha M Malato; editor Michael Richardson; tel (201) 798-7800; fax (201) 798-0018

Kenilworth: *Kenilworth Leader* — 1291 Stuyvesant Ave.; PO Box 3109, Union (07083); Th; 619pd, 22fr (CAC); $15.00; C; publisher David Worrall; editor Thomas Canavan; tel (908) 686-7700; fax (908) 686-4169

Lacey: *The Lacey Beacon* — 345 E. Bay Ave., Manahawkin (08050); Th; 2,565pd, 7fr (Sw); $21.26; C; publisher Peter Lindquist; editor Jan Zollinger; tel (609) 597-3211; fax (609) 597-0341

Lambertville/W Amwell Twp./Stockton: *The Beacon* — PO Box 8, Hopewell (08525); W; 3,008pd, 203fr (Est); $8.50; C; publisher James B Kilgore; general manager Michael O'Hara; editor Mae Rhine; tel (609) 397-3000; fax (609) 397-5801

Landing: *Roxbury Register* — PO Box 252 (07850); Th; 2,692pd (Est); $9.50; publishers Cortlandt Parker & Nancy Parker; editor Phil Garber; tel (201) 770-1304; fax (201) 895-4234

Lawrence Twp.: *The Lawrence Ledger* — PO Box 8, Hopewell (08525); Th; 2,993pd, 91fr (Est); $11.00; C; publisher James B Kilgore; general manager Michael O'Hara; editor Thomas Lederer; tel (609) 466-8650; fax (609) 466-2123

Ledgewood/W Morris/Roxbury/Mt. Arlington: *The Star Journal* — PO Box 455, Ledgewood (07852); W; 2,219pd, 89fr (Sw); $6.75; C; publisher Rosemarie Maio; editor Lynn Apolinaro; tel (201) 584-7176; fax (908) 852-9320

Linden: *Linden Leader* — 1291 Stuyvesant Ave.; PO Box 3109, Union (07083); Th; 1,906pd, 1,167fr (CAC); $13.00; C; publisher David Worrall; editor Thomas Canavan; tel (908) 686-7700; fax (908) 686-4169

Livingston: *West Essex Tribune* — 495 S. Livingston Ave.; PO Box 65 (07039-0065); Th; 7,249pd, 121fr (ABC); $9.75; C; publisher & editor E Christopher Cone; managing editor Nancy B Dinar; tel (201) 992-1771; fax (201) 992-7015

Lodi/Maywood/Rochelle Park: *Lodi/Maywood/Rochelle Park Shopper* — 12-38 River Rd., Fair Lawn (07410); W; 27,133fr (CAC); 45¢; editor Erik Englund; tel (201) 791-8400; fax (201) 794-3259

Long Branch (Central Shore): *Atlanticville* — 184 Broadway; PO Box 59, Long Branch (07740); Th; 8,100pd, 600fr (Sw); $10.50; publisher Michael Booth; general manager Shannon Booth; editor Dan Mintz; managing editor Ben Forrest; tel (908) 870-9338; fax (908) 870-6800

Lyndhurst: *Commercial Leader* — 251 Ridge Rd. (07071); W; 3,243pd (Est); 24¢; publisher John Savino; editor Jolyn Garner; tel (201) 438-8700; fax (201) 438-9022

Madison: *Madison Eagle* — 155 Main St. (07940); Th; 3,400pd (Est); $10.90; C; publisher Cortlandt Parker; editor Gene Robbins; tel (201) 377-2000; fax (201) 377-7721

Manahawkin: *The Mailbag* — 345 E. Bay Ave. (08050); F; 51,138fr (Sw); $25.75; publisher Peter J Lindquist; editor Jan Zollinger; tel (609) 597-3211; fax (609) 597-0341

Manahawkin/Long Beach/Long Beach Island: *Beach Haven Times* — 345 E. Bay Ave., Manahawkin (08050); W; 7,077pd, 16fr (Sw); $21.26; publisher Peter J Lindquist; editor Jan Zollinger; tel (609) 597-3211; fax (609) 597-0341

Manville: *The Manville News* — 307 Omni Dr., Hillsborough (08876); Th; 1,141pd, 70fr (Est); $11.00; C; publisher James B Kilgore; general manager Michael O'Hara; editor Jon F Steele; tel (908) 359-0850; fax (908) 359-3930

Maplewood/S Orange: *News-Record of Maplewood & South Orange* — 463 Valley St.; PO Box 158, Maplewood (07040); Th; 5,855pd, 1,042fr (CAC); $13.00; C; publisher David Worrall; editor Thomas Canavan; tel (908) 686-7700; fax (908) 686-4169

Mays Landing: *Atlantic County Record* — PO Box 475 (08330); Th; 1,200pd, 461fr (Est); $8.50; publisher Ron Jacovini; editor Norlynne Lubrano; tel (609) 641-3100; fax (609) 646-0561

Mays Landing: *Record Journal* — PO Box 475 (08330); Th; 10,000pd (Est); $8.90; publisher Ron Jacovini; editor Norlynne Lubrano; tel (609) 641-3100; fax (609) 646-0561

Maywood/Rochelle Park: *Our Town* — 58 W. Pleasant Ave., Maywood (07607); Th; 3,208pd, 100fr (Sw); $7.50; publisher James Panos; publisher & editor Katherine J Panos; tel (201) 843-5700

Medford: *The Central Record* — Old Marlton Pike; PO Box 1027 (08055-0127); Th; 12,000pd, 1,100fr (Sw); $8.78; publisher Patricia E Haughey; editor Joseph A Panella; tel (609) 654-5000; fax (609) 654-8237

Mendham/Chester: *Observer Tribune* — 530 E. Main St.; PO Box 600, Chester (07930); Th; 6,820pd, 272fr (CAC); $16.75; C; publisher Cortlandt Parker; editor Garry Herzog; tel (908) 879-4100; fax (908) 879-6141

Metuchen/Edison: *Metuchen/Edison Review* — 44 Veterans Memorial Dr. E.; PO Box 699, Somerville (08876); F; 5,582pd (Est); $12.35; C; publisher Louis Barsony; editor Dave Pilla; tel (908) 722-3000; fax (908) 526-2509

Middlesex/Dunellan: *The Chronicle* — 44 Veterans Memorial Dr. E.; PO Box 699, Somerville (08876); Th; 2,745pd (Est); $12.35; C; publisher Louis Barsony; editor Dave Pilla; tel (908) 722-3000; fax (908) 526-2509

Middletown/Hazlet: *The Courier* — 320 Kings Hwy. E.; PO Box 399, Middletown (07748); Th; 8,565pd, 350fr (Est); $8.50; publisher John Famulary; editor Bonnie Walling; tel (908) 957-0070; fax (908) 957-0143

Millburn/Short Hills: *The Item of Millburn & Short Hills* — 100 Millburn Ave., Millburn (07041); Th; 5,505pd, 139fr (Est); $11.40; C; publisher Barbara A Lewis; editor Carter J Bennett; tel (201) 376-1200; fax (201) 376-8556

Monroe Twp./Sicklerville/Williamstown: *Plain Dealer* — PO Box 67, Blackwood (08012); W; 2,630pd, 214fr (Est); 34¢; C; publisher Jane Parr; general manager James Wyatt; editor John Worthington; tel (609) 228-7300; fax (609) 227-1207

Monroe/Spotswood/Jamesburg/Helmetta: *Monroe Sentinel* — 7 Edgeboro Rd., East Brunswick (08816); W; 9,800pd (Est); $18.33; publisher Kevin L Wittman; editor Gregory Bean; managing editor Darren Smith; tel (908) 254-7000; fax (908) 254-0256

Montclair: *The Montclair Times* — 114 Valley Rd. (07042); Th; 22,349pd, 973fr (Sw); $15.45; C; publisher Barbara A Lewis; editor Lucinda Smith; tel (201) 746-1100; fax (201) 746-8131

Morristown/Morris Plains: *Morris News-Bee* — PO Box 160, Madison (07940); Th; 3,000pd (Est); $5.00; publisher Cortlandt Parker; editor James Lent; tel (201) 538-1000; fax (201) 377-7721

Mt. Laurel/Maple Shade: *Mount Laurel Progress Press* — 306-08 E. Main St., Maple Shade (08052); Th; 1,200pd, 1,200fr (Est); 35¢; publisher & editor Frank E Gerkens Jr; tel (609) 779-7788

Mt. Olive Twp.: *Mount Olive Chronicle* — 336 Rte. 46, Budd Lake (07828); Th; 173pd, 9,019fr (CAC); $14.25; C; publisher Cortlandt Parker; editor Phil Garber; tel (201) 691-8181; fax (201) 691-2396

Mountainside: *Mountainside Echo* — 1291 Stuyvesant Ave.; PO Box 3109, Union (07083); Th; 758pd, 54fr (CAC); $13.00; C; publisher David Worrall; editor Thomas Canavan; tel (908) 686-7700; fax (908) 686-4169

Netcong: *News-Leader* — 26 Main St.; PO Box 637 (07857); W; 1,658pd, 93fr (Sw); $5.46; publisher Rosemarie Maio; editor Shawn Cupolo; tel (201) 347-0300; fax (908) 852-9320

New Egypt: *The New Egypt Press* — 58 Main St.; PO Box 188 (08533); Th; 3,600pd, 300fr (Sw); $7.35; C; publisher Intercounty Newspaper Group; general manager Christina Holien; editor Sam Depalma; managing editor Hollis Painting; tel (609) 758-2112; fax (609) 758-1816

N Arlington: *North Arlington Leader* — 251 Ridge Rd., Lyndhurst (07071); W; 2,378pd (Est); $9.90; publisher John Savino; editor Thom Ammarito; tel (201) 438-8700; fax (201) 438-9022

N Bergen: *The North Bergen/North Hudson Reporter* — 1400 Washington St.; PO Box 3086, Hoboken (07030); Su; 28,400fr (CAC); $30.00; C; publisher Joseph Barry; general manager Lucha M Malato; editor Michael Richardson; tel (201) 798-7800; fax (201) 798-0018

N Brunswick Twp.: *North Brunswick Post* — 397 Ridge Rd.; PO Box 309, Dayton (08810); F; 2,160pd, 84fr (Est); $11.00; publisher James B Kilgore; general manager Michael O'Hara; editor Helene Ragovin; tel (908) 329-0260; fax (908) 329-9286

N Brunswick Twp.: *North Brunswick Sentinel* — 7 Edgeboro Rd., East Brunswick (08816); Th; 9,000pd (Est); $18.33; publisher Kevin L Wittman; editor Gregory Bean; managing editor Paul Fiorilla; tel (908) 254-7000; fax (908) 254-0256

N Plainfield: *Green Brook-North Plainfield Journal* — 44 Veterans Memorial Dr. E.; PO Box 699, Somerville (08876); W; 3,740pd (Est); $12.35; C; publisher Louis Barsony; editor Lorie Russo; tel (908) 722-3000; fax (908) 526-2509

Northeastern Monmouth Co.: *The Two River Times* — 3 E. Front St., Red Bank (07701); Th; 8,000pd, 12,000fr (Est); $11.90; publisher Claudia Ansorge; editor Cort Smith; tel (908) 219-5788; fax (908) 747-7213

Northern Hunterdon Co.: *Hunterdon Review* — PO Box 5308, Clinton (08809); W; 4,565pd, 306fr (CAC); $14.50; publisher Cortlandt Parker; editor Richard Hartten; tel (908) 735-4081; fax (908) 735-2945

Northfield/Linwood/Somers Pt./Egg Harbor Twp./Ocean City: *The Current* — 11 Devins Ln., Pleasantville (08232); F; 800pd, 19,000fr (Sw); $11.25; C; publisher Robert M McCormick; general manager Sharon Litton; editor Bernadette Suski-Harding; tel (609) 272-7470; fax (609) 272-7460

Nutley: *Nutley Journal* — 266 Liberty St.; PO Box 110, Bloomfield (07003); Th; 699pd, 1,596fr (CAC); $15.00; C; publisher David Worrall; editor Thomas Canavan; tel (908) 686-7700; fax (908) 686-4169

Nutley: *The Nutley Sun* — 800 Bloomfield Ave.; PO Box 281 (07110); Th; 7,064pd (Est); $16.75; C; publisher Frank A Orechio; editor Juliann Walsh; tel (201) 667-2100; fax (201) 667-3904

Ocean City: *The Sentinel-Ledger* — 112 8th St. (08226); Th; 9,920pd, 156fr (ABC); 68¢; publisher Ralph Cooper; editor John H Andrus II; tel (609) 399-5411; fax (609) 399-0416

Ocean Co.: *Advance News* — 2048 Rte. 37, W. Rd. 1, Lakehurst (08733); W; 17,660pd, 1,885fr (Sw); 28¢; C; publisher Jerri T Varelli; editor Stephen Crosson; tel (908) 657-8936; fax (908) 657-2970

Old Bridge/Sayreville/Parlin: *Surburban* — 7 Edgeboro Rd., East Brunswick (08816); W; 21,000pd (Est); $6.45; publisher Kevin L Wittman; editor Gregory Bean; managing editor Darren Smith; tel (908) 254-7000; fax (908) 254-0486

Orange: *Orange Transcript* — 170 Scotland Rd.; PO Box 849 (07051); Th; 1,305pd, 83fr (CAC); $13.00; C; publisher David Worrall; editor Thomas Canavan; tel (908) 686-7700; fax (908) 686-4169

Paramus/Pascack Valley: *The Post Review* — 50 Eisenhower Dr. (07652); Su; 3,436pd, 193fr (Sw); $26.70; publisher Sherwood L Spitz; editor Ellen Walsh; tel (201) 368-0100 Ext. 1009; fax (201) 843-3794

Pascack Vly.: *Community Life* — Sturbridge Commons, 345 Kinderkamack Rd.; PO Box 697, Westwood (07675); W/Sa; 462pd, 26,284fr (Sw); $14.90; C; publisher Sherwood L Spitz; general manager Jerry Jastrab; editor Barbara J Stewart; tel (201) 664-2501; fax (201) 664-1332

II-52 **New Jersey** *U.S. Weeklies*

Passaic/Clifton/Garfield: *The Passaic Citizen* — 298 Passaic St., Passaic (07055); Th; 4,000pd (Est); $10.00; publisher Henry Helstoski; editor Helen Gately; tel (201) 779-7500

Passaic/Morris Co.: *Suburban Trends* — 10 Park Pl., Butler (07405); W/Su; 14,608pd, 998fr (Est); $18.50; C; publisher Richard Vezza; editor Jack Carle; tel (201) 838-9000; fax (201) 838-1495

Paulsboro/Pitman/Gibbstown/Glassboro: *The News & World Report* — 3 2nd Ave.; PO Box 332, Pitman (08071-0332); F; 2,300pd, 5,000fr (Sw); $5.61; C; publisher & editor Andrew Wolfe; managing editor Daniel Interrante; tel (609) 589-5957; fax (609) 582-8117

Pennington: *Pennington Post/Intercounty Newspaper* — 12 N. Main St.; PO Box 703 (08534); Th; 2,468pd, 206fr (Sw); $8.45; C; publisher Jane Parr; general manager & managing editor Art Thompson; editor Sean Duffy; tel (609) 737-3379; fax (609) 737-8126

Perth Amboy: *Perth Amboy Gazette* — 219 Central Ave.; PO Box 1061, Rahway (07065); Th; 259pd, 6,741fr (Est); $11.90; C; publisher & editor Ellen Vigilante; managing editor Linda Koenig; tel (908) 574-1200; fax (908) 388-4143

Phillipsburg: *The Free Press* — 198 Chambers St.; PO Box 827 (08865-0827); Th; 3,042pd (Sw); $4.95; C; publisher Timothy Sowecke; general manager John Goretti; editor Michael O'Connor; tel (908) 859-4444; fax (908) 859-3084

Piscataway: *Piscataway Review* — 44 Veterans Memorial Dr. E.; PO Box 699, Somerville (08876); F; 4,588pd (Est); $12.35; C; publisher Louis Barsony; editor Sylvie Mulvane; tel (908) 722-3000; fax (908) 526-2509

Pleasantville/Linwood: *Mainland Journal* — PO Box 231, Pleasantville (08232); Th; 6,200pd, 20fr (Est); $8.50; publisher Ron Jacovini; editor Norlynne Lubrano; tel (609) 641-3100; fax (609) 646-0561

Pt. Pleasant Beach: *The Leader* — 707 Arnold Ave.; PO Box 1771, Pt. Pleasant Beach (08742); Th; 4,416pd, 325fr (Sw); $8.00; C; publisher Tom Bateman; editor Jeannie Tomaselli; tel (908) 899-1000; fax (908) 899-2135

Princeton: *Town Topics* — 4 Mercer St.; PO Box 664 (08542); W; 6,507pd, 6,403fr (Sw); $7.25; publisher & editor Donald C Stuart III; tel (609) 924-2200

Princeton/Plainsboro/Montgomery/Junction/W Windsor: *The Princeton Packet* — 300 Witherspoon St.; PO Box 350, Princeton (08542); Tu/F; 13,813pd, 596fr (Est); $28.00; C; publisher James B Kilgore; general manager Michael O'Hara; editor Randy Bergmann; tel (609) 924-3244; fax (609) 921-2714

Rahway: *Rahway News-Record* — 219 Central Ave.; PO Box 1061 (07065); Th; 1,477pd, 400fr (Sw); $9.10; C; publisher & editor Ellen Vigilante; managing editor Linda Koenig; tel (908) 574-1200; fax (908) 388-4143

Rahway: *Rahway Progress* — 1291 Stuyvesant Ave.; PO Box 3109, Union (07083); Th; 431pd, 83fr (CAC); $13.00; C; publisher David Worrall; editor Thomas Canavan; tel (908) 686-7700; fax (908) 686-4169

Rahway: *The Atom Tabloid* — 219 Central Ave.; PO Box 1061 (07065); W; 24pd, 22,316fr (Est); $20.58; C; publisher & editor Ellen Vigilante; managing editor Linda Koenig; tel (908) 574-1200; fax (908) 388-4143

Ramsey/Mahwah: *The Reporter* — PO Box 264, Ramsey (07446); F; 4,468pd, 2,138fr (Est); $9.00; C; publisher William Cohen; editor Eleanor Marra; tel (201) 825-3737; fax (201) 947-6968

Ramsey/Suffern (NY): *The Home And Store News* — 6A E. Main St.; PO Box 329, Ramsey (07446-0329); W; 25,900fr (Sw); $10.20; C; publisher Arthur R Aldrich; general manager Jo Bosakowski; editor Eleanor Harman; tel (201) 327-1212; fax (201) 327-3684

Randolph/Mine Hill Twps.: *The Randolph Reporter* — 2 W. Hanover Ave., Ste. 112, Randolph (07869); Th; 3,771pd, 53fr (CAC); $14.25; C; publisher Cortlandt Parker; editor Claire Swedberg; tel (201) 895-2601; fax (201) 895-4234

Ridgewood: *The Ridgewood News* — 50 Eisenhower Dr., Paramus (07652); Th; 8,916pd, 193fr (ABC); $26.70; publisher Sherwood L Spitz; editor Ellen Walsh; tel (201) 368-0100 Ext. 1009; fax (201) 843-3794

Ridgewood: *The Sunday News* — 75 N. Maple Ave. (07450); Tu; 8,795pd, 566fr (ABC); $26.70; publisher Sherwood L Spitz; editor Ellen Walsh; tel (201) 612-5200; fax (201) 612-0723

Roselle: *Roselle Spectator* — 1291 Stuyvesant Ave.; PO Box 3109, Union (07083); Th; 651pd, 33fr (CAC); $13.00; C; publisher David Worrall; editor Thomas Canavan; tel (908) 686-7700; fax (908) 686-4169

Roselle Park: *Roselle Park Leader* — 1291 Stuyvesant Ave.; PO Box 3109, Union (07083); Th; 975pd, 41fr (CAC); $18.00; C; publisher David Worrall; editor Thomas Canavan; tel (908) 686-7700; fax (908) 686-4169

Rutherford: *The South Bergenite* — 71 Union Ave., Ste. 107 (07070); W; 35,603fr (Sw); $3.02; publisher Richard J Vezza; editor Edward Kensik; managing editor Michelle Rosa; tel (201) 933-1166; fax (201) 933-5496

Scotch Plains/Fanwood: *The Times* — PO Box 368, Scotch Plains (07076); Th; 2,233pd (Sw); $9.00; publisher Kurt C Bauer; editor Paul J Peyton; tel (908) 232-4407; fax (908) 232-0473

Scotch Plains/Fanwood: *Scotch Plains-Fanwood Press* — 102 Walnut Ave.; PO Box 626, Cranford (07016); Th; 3,656pd (Sw); $12.35; C; publisher John J O'Brien; editor Edward Carroll; managing editor Michael Deak; tel (908) 276-6000; fax (908) 276-6220

Seaside Heights: *Ocean County Review* — 906 B Grand Central Ave., Lavallette (08735); PO Box 8 (08751); W; 6,241pd, 122fr (Sw); $8.00; C; publisher Rockfleet Media Inc.; general manager Thomas R Bateman; tel (908) 793-0147; fax (908) 793-6740

Secaucus: *Home News* — 766 Irving Pl.; PO Box 1100 (07094); Th; 3,360pd, 60fr (Sw); 24¢; publisher & editor Gretchen Henkel; tel (201) 867-2071; fax (201) 865-3806

Secaucus: *Secaucus Reporter* — 1400 Washington St.; PO Box 3086, Hoboken (07030); Su; 5,649fr (CAC); $30.00; C; publisher Joseph Barry; general manager Lucha M Malato; editor Michael Richardson; tel (201) 798-7800; fax (201) 798-0018

Somerset: *The Hills-Bedminster Press* — 44 Veterans Memorial Dr. E.; PO Box 699, Somerville (08876); W; 2,500pd (Est); $12.35; C; publisher Louis Barsony; editor Michael Deak; tel (908) 722-3000; fax (908) 526-2509

Somerset Co.: *Franklin Focus* — 44 Veterans Memorial Dr. E.; PO Box 699, Somerville (08876); Th; 11,410pd (Est); $12.35; C; publisher Louis Barsony; editor Lorie Russo; tel (908) 722-3000; fax (908) 526-2509

Somerset/Franklin Twp.: *The Somerset Spectator* — PO Box 5717, Somerset (08875-5717); Th; 3,376pd, 2,100fr (Sw); $11.00; publisher Helen Reilly; editor Nancy Michell; managing editor Paul Aquaro; tel (908) 247-8700; fax (908) 247-3709

Somerville/Manville: *Somerset Messenger-Gazette* — 44 Veterans Memorial Dr. E.; PO Box 699, Somerville (08876); Th; 14,432pd (Est); $17.70; C; publisher John J O'Brien; editor Michael Deak; managing editor Andrew Simpson; tel (908) 722-3000; fax (908) 526-2509

S Amboy/Sayreville: *The Citizen* — 157 Luke St.; PO Box 3095, South Amboy (08879); Th (bi-weekly); 2,431pd, 1,583fr (Sw); $10.50; publisher James A Gotti; editor Joseph Sainato; managing editor Joann Knueppel; tel (908) 727-2000; fax (908) 727-1880

S Brunswick: *The Central Post* — 397 Ridge Rd.; PO Box 309, Dayton (08810); Th; 4,319pd, 113fr (Est); $20.80; C; publisher James B Kilgore; general manager Michael O'Hara; editor Helene Ragovin; tel (908) 329-0260; fax (908) 329-9286

S Brunswick: *South Brunswick Sentinel* — 7 Edgeboro Rd., East Brunswick (08816); Th; 9,000pd (Est); $18.33; publisher Kevin L Wittman; editor Gregory Bean; managing editor Paul Fiorilla; tel (908) 254-7000; fax (908) 254-0256

S Plainfield: *South Plainfield Reporter (Forbes Newpapers)* — 44 Veterans Memorial Dr. E.; PO Box 699, Sommerville (08876); Th; 3,666pd (Est); $12.35; C; publisher Louis Barsony; editor Sylvie Mulvane; tel (908) 722-3000; fax (908) 526-2509

Springfield: *Springfield Leader* — 1291 Stuyvesant Ave.; PO Box 3109, Union (07083); Th; 1,625pd, 95fr (CAC); $13.00; C; publisher David Worrall; editor Thomas Canavan; tel (908) 686-7700; fax (908) 686-4169

Stafford/Barnegat: *The Beacon* — 345 E. Bay Ave., Manahawkin (08050); Th; 4,454pd, 8fr (CAC); $7.60; C; publisher J Peter Lindequist; editor Jan Zollinger; tel (609) 597-3211; fax (609) 597-0341

Summit: *The Summit Herald* — 80 South St., New Providence (07974); Sa; 2,106pd, 93fr (CAC); $8.70; publisher Michael J Kelly; editor Patricia E Meola; tel (908) 464-1025; fax (908) 464-9085

Summit: *Summit Observer* — 1291 Stuyvesant Ave.; PO Box 3109, Union (07508); Th; 1,000pd, 200fr (CAC); $13.00; C; publisher David Worrall; editor Raymond Worrall; managing editor Tom Canavan; tel (908) 686-7700

Summit/New Providence/Millburn-Short Hills/Berkeley Hts./The Chathams/Madison/Long Hill Twp.: *Independent Press* — 80 South St., New Providence (07974); W; 502pd, 38,494fr (CAC); $19.50; publisher Michael J Kelly; editor Christopher Moore; tel (908) 464-1025; fax (908) 464-9085

Teaneck/Ridgefield Park/Fort Lee: *Sun Bulletin* — 111 Grand Ave.; PO Box 616, Palisades Park (07650); F; 9,562pd, 5,635fr (Est); $15.40; C; publisher William Cohen; editor Eleanor Marra; managing editor Sue Perkins; tel (201) 947-5000; fax (201) 947-6968

Toms River/Bricktown: *Ocean County Reporter* — 8 Robbins St., Toms River (08753); Th; 327pd, 96,465fr (CAC); $29.95; C; publisher Robert J Juzwiak; tel (908) 349-1501; fax (908) 240-0545

Tuckerton/Little Egg Harbor: *The Tuckerton Beacon* — 345 E. Bay Ave., Manahawkin (08050); Th; 3,800pd, 6fr (CAC); $21.26; C; publisher Peter Lindquist; editor Jan Zollinger; tel (609) 597-3211; fax (609) 597-0341

Union: *Union Leader* — 1291 Stuyvesant Ave.; PO Box 3109 (07083); Th; 5,505pd, 2,575fr (CAC); $15.00; C; publisher David Worrall; editor Thomas Canavan; tel (908) 686-7700; fax (908) 686-4169

Union Co.: *Suburban News/Elizabeth City News* — PO Box 2309, Westfield (07090); W/Su; 97,987fr (CAC); $41.82; C; publisher Richard F Harknett; editor Ellen Fox-Tamblyn; tel (908) 396-4500; fax (908) 396-4770

Vailsburg/Newark: *Vailsburg Leader* — 463 Valley St.; PO Box 158, Maplewood (07040); Th; 85pd, 3fr (CAC); $13.00; C; publisher David Worrall; editor Thomas Canavan; tel (908) 686-7700; fax (908) 686-4169

Verona/Cedar Grove: *Verona-Cedar Grove Times* — 685 Bloomfield Ave., Ste. 101, Verona (07044); Th; 5,435pd, 275fr (ABC); $11.25; C; publisher Barbara A Lewis; editor Ward Miele; tel (201) 239-0900; fax (201) 746-8131

Warren/Watchung: *Echoes-Sentinel* — 256 Mercer St., Sterling (07980); W; 5,106pd (ABC); $10.60; publisher Cortlandt Parker; editor Jeff French; tel (908) 647-0412; fax (908) 647-7679

Washington Twp.: *The News Report* — Black Horse Pike & Rte. 42, Turnersville (08012); PO Box 64, Blackwood (08012-0067); Th; 2,841pd, 611fr (Sw); $8.45; C; editor Mark Peters; managing editor John Worthington; tel (609) 228-7300; fax (609) 227-1207

Wayne/Pompton Lakes/Fairfield/Lincoln/Park Pequannock: *The Independent News* — 206 Wanaque Ave., Pompton Lakes (07442); Th; 80,000fr (Est); $25.15; publisher & editor Joseph Nicastro; publisher Ronald Higgins; tel (201) 839-7200; fax (201) 839-7569

Weehawken: *The Weehawken Reporter* — 1400 Washington St.; PO Box 3086, Hoboken (07030); Su; 5,350fr (CAC); $9.75; C; publisher Joseph Barry; general manager Lucha M Malato; editor Michael Richardson; tel (201) 798-7800; fax (201) 798-0018

W Orange: *West Orange Chronicle* — 170 Scotland Rd.; PO Box 849, Orange (07051); Th; 4,664pd, 403fr (CAC); $13.00; C; publisher David Worrall; editor Thomas Canavan; tel (908) 686-7700; fax (908) 686-4169

W Windsor/Plainsboro: *West Windsor-Plainsboro Chronicle* — PO Box 189, Princeton Junction (08550); Th; 2,971pd, 50fr (Sw); $6.00; publisher & editor Samuel L Earle; tel (609) 799-6601; fax (609) 799-3450

Western Monmouth Co.: *The Messenger-Press* — Warren Pl., Rte. 130 S., Hightstown (08520); Th; 3,358pd, 501fr (Est); $11.00; C; publisher James B Kilgore; general manager Michael O'Hara; editor Frank Herick; tel (609) 448-2100; fax (609) 448-8044

Westfield: *The Westfield Leader* — 50 Elm St.; PO Box 250 (07091); Th; 5,568pd, 500fr (Sw); $9.00; publisher Kurt C Bauer; editor Paul J Peyton; tel (908) 232-4407; fax (908) 232-0473

Westfield: *The Westfield Record* — 102 Walnut Ave.; PO Box 626, Cranford (07016); Th; 118pd, 9,133fr (CAC); $12.35; C; publisher Louis Barsony; editor Edward Carroll; managing editor Michael Deak; tel (908) 276-6000; fax (908) 276-6220

Wood-Ridge/Moonachie: *Wood-Ridge Independent* — 210 Hackensack St.; PO Box 242, Wood-Ridge (07075); W; 1,401pd, 63fr (Sw); $6.00; publisher & editor Bob Hannon; tel (201) 935-1612

NEW MEXICO

Albuquerque: *Health City Sun* — 900 Park Ave. S.W.; PO Box 1517 (87103); F; 1,500pd, 220fr (Est); $10.00; C; publisher Francisco Collado; editor Alicia Alvarez; managing editor Lori Chavez; tel (505) 243-3210; fax (505) 842-5464

Angel Fire/Colfax Co./Red River: *Sangre de Cristo Chronicle* — Centro Plz.; PO Drawer I, Angel Fire (87710); Th; 2,230pd, 25fr (Sw); 53¢; publisher Guy H Wood; publisher & managing editor Marcia T Wood; tel (505) 377-2358

Cibola Co.: *Cibola County Beacon* — 300 N. 2nd, Grants (87020); W; 3,225pd, 7,500fr (Sw); $6.30; F; 3,225pd (Sw); $6.30; C; publisher Brett Burke; editor J D Meisner; tel (505) 287-4411; fax (505) 287-7822

Clayton/Mosquero/Texline: *Union County Leader* — 15 N. 1st St.; PO Box 486, Clayton (88415); W; 2,563pd, 34fr (Sw); $5.50; publisher & editor Nick Payton; tel (505) 374-2587; fax (505) 374-8117

Dona Ana/Sierra/Catron/Luna/Hidalgo/Otero/Valencia/Socorro: *The Courier* — 115 W. Hall St.; PO Box 910, Hatch (87937); Th; 8,000pd (Est); $8.00; C; publisher Rio Valley Publishing Co.; editor Susan Christy; tel (505) 267-3546; fax (505) 267-3019

Espanola: *Rio Grande Sun* — 238 N. Railroad; PO Box 790 (87532); Th; 11,269pd, 41fr (Est); $6.35; publisher Robert E Trapp; editor Michael Kaemper; tel (505) 753-2126

Estancia Valley: *Estancia Valley Citizen* — 400 S. 5th St.; PO Box 288, Estancia (87016-0288); Th; 2,209pd, 75fr (Sw); $7.06; publisher Carolyn Appelman; editor Morrow Hall; tel (505) 384-2744

Ft. Sumner: *De Baca County News* — 412 Ave. C; PO Box 448 (88119); Th; 1,341pd, 12fr (Est); $4.20; C; publisher Scot Stinnett; editor Lisa Stinnett; tel (505) 355-2462; fax (505) 355-7253

Gallup: *The Gallup Weekly Paper* — 206A W. Hill (87301); W; 25,000fr (Est); $8.00; C; publisher Bret Burke; general manager Marcy White; tel (505) 863-6753; fax (505) 863-6736

Jal: *The Jal Record* — 309 Main St.; PO Drawer Y309 (88252); Th; 1,271pd, 26fr (Est); $3.00; publisher Rick McLaughlin; editor Velma Taylor; tel (505) 395-2516; fax (915) 586-2562

Las Cruces: *Las Cruces Bulletin* — 1210 E. Madrid; PO Box 637 (88004); Th; 535pd, 20,965fr (Sw); $12.65; publisher & editor Stephen Klinger; tel (505) 524-8061; fax (505) 526-4621

Lea Co.: *The Hobbs Flare* — 114 E. Dunam St.; PO Box 1095, Hobbs (88240); Th; 3,700pd, 50fr (Sw); $3.95; C; publisher & editor Rick McLaughlin; general manager Donetta Black; managing editor John Winklemann; tel (505) 393-5141; fax (505) 393-1831

Lincoln Co.: *Lincoln County News* — 309 Central Ave.; PO Drawer 459, Carrizozo (88301); Th; 1,803pd, 98fr (Sw); $4.85; publisher Peter Aguilar; publisher & editor Ruth Hammond; tel (505) 648-2333

Lordsburg: *Lordsburg Liberal* — 211 Shakespeare St. (88045); F; 2,700pd (Est); $3.08; publisher & editor Christina Ely; tel (505) 542-3471; fax (505) 542-3473

Raton: *The Raton Range* — 208 S. 3rd St.; PO Box 1068 (87740); Tu/F; 2,908pd, 20fr (Sw); $5.75; C; publisher Curtis Williams; managing editor Todd Wildermuth; tel (505) 445-2721; fax (505) 445-2723

U.S. Weeklies **New York** II-53

Rio Rancho/Albuquerque: *The Observer* — 1594 Sara Rd. S.E.; PO Box 15878, Rio Rancho (87124); W; 2,457pd, 15,274fr (VAC); $9.90; publisher & editor Michael J Ryan; managing editor Mary Beth King; tel (505) 892-8080; fax (505) 892-5719

Ruidoso: *The Ruidoso News* — 104 Park Ave.; PO Box 128 (88345); M/Th; 5,103pd, 129fr (Sw); $7.25; C; publisher Keith Green; general manager Karen Payton; editor Joanna Dodder; tel (505) 257-4001; fax (505) 257-7053

Santa Rosa: *Santa Rosa News* — 108 5th; PO Box Drawer F (88435); Th; 1,550pd, 200fr (Sw); $4.20; publisher & editor Darrel Freeman; tel (505) 472-5454

Socorro: *Defensor Chieftain* — 200 Winkler S.W.; PO Box Q (87801); W/Su; 2,897pd, 30fr (Sw); $6.56; C; publisher Keith Green; editor Gwen Roath; tel (505) 835-0520; fax (505) 835-1837

Taos/Angel Fire/Questa: *The Taos News* — 120 Camino de la Placita; PO Box U, Taos (87571); Th; 10,635pd, 211fr (ABC); $11.80; publisher George Fellows; editor Deborah Ensor; tel (505) 758-2241; fax (505) 758-9647

Truth or Consequences: *Sierra County Sentinel* — 1747 E. 3rd; PO Box 351 (87901); W; 4,173pd (Sw); $2.85; publisher Myrna Baird; tel (505) 894-3088; fax (505) 894-3998

Truth or Consequences: *The Herald* — 1204 N. Date; PO Box 752 (87901); W; 4,385pd (Sw); $3.00; publisher Bob Tooley & Mike Tooley; editor Jim Streicher; tel (505) 894-2143; fax (505) 894-7824

Tucumcari Area: *Quay County Sun* — 902 S. 1st St.; PO Box 1408, Tucumcari (88401-1408); W/Sa; 3,506pd, 15fr (Est); $4.10; publisher & editor Ron Wilmot; managing editor Kristi Saatmann; tel (505) 461-1952; fax (505) 461-1965

Valencia Co.: *Valencia County News-Bulletin* — 1837 Sosimo Padilla Blvd.; PO Box 25, Belen (87002); W/Sa; 6,200pd, 70fr (Sw); $7.50; C; publisher Chris Baker; editor Sandy Battin; tel (505) 864-4472; fax (505) 864-3549

NEW YORK

Adams/Delmar Co./Colonie: *Colonie Spotlight* — PO Box 5349, Colonie (12205); W; 2,653pd, 1,347fr (Est); $9.40; C; publisher & editor Richard A Ahlstrom; managing editor Eric Bryant; tel (518) 439-4949; fax (518) 439-0609

Adams/S Jefferson Co.: *Jefferson County Journal* — 7 Main St.; PO Box 68, Adams (13605-1215); W; 3,000pd (Sw); $3.50; publisher & editor Karl A Fowler; tel (315) 232-4586, (315) 232-2141; fax (315) 232-4586

Akron/Newstead: *Akron Bugle* — 7263 Downey Rd., Akron (14001); Th; 1,624pd, 44fr (Sw); $3.50; publisher & editor Marilyn J Kasperek; tel (716) 542-9615

Albion: *Albion Advertiser* — 116 N. Main St. (14411-1232); W; 2,511pd, 43fr (Sw); $4.53; C; publisher & editor Owen P Toale; tel (716) 589-4455; fax (716) 589-4488

Alden: *Alden Advertiser* — 13200 Broadway (14004); Th; 3,459pd, 129fr (Sw); $5.75; publisher Weisbeck Publishing & Printing Inc.; general manager Leonard A Weisbeck Jr; editor Leonard A Weisbeck Sr; tel (716) 937-9226

Alexandria Bay: *Thousand Islands Sun* — Rte. 12; PO Box 277 (13607); W; 6,397pd, 25fr (Est); $4.60; publisher T.I. Printing Co. Inc.; editor Jeanne R Snow; tel (315) 482-2581; fax (315) 482-6315

Alfred: *The Alfred Sun* — 773 Rte. 244; PO Box 811 (14802); Th; 812pd, 23fr (Sw); $2.75; publisher & editor David L Snyder; tel (607) 587-8110

Amenia: *The Harlem Valley Times* — Front St.; PO Box 316, Millbrook (12545); Th; 3,459pd, 440fr (Est); $6.30; C; publishers Hamilton Meserve & Helen Meserve; editor Bob Lomicky; tel (914) 677-8241; fax (914) 677-6337

Amherst: *Amherst Bee* — 5564 Main St. (14221); PO Box 150, Buffalo (14231-0150); W; 10,368pd, 215fr (Sw); $12.40; C; publisher Trey Measer; editor Michele Darstein; managing editor Dave Sherman; tel (716) 632-4700; fax (716) 633-8601

Amityville: *The Amityville Record* — 85 Broadway (11701); W; 2,370pd, 150fr (Sw); $6.00; C; publisher Alfred James; publisher & managing editor Carolyn James; editor Jim Custer; tel (516) 264-0077; fax (516) 264-5310

Arcade/Yorkshire: *Arcade Herald* — 12 Liberty St., Arcade (14009); Th; 4,597pd, 100fr (Sw); $6.79; publisher & editor Kathleen L Mason; tel (716) 496-5013/492-2525; fax (716) 492-2667

Avon/Geneseo/Caledonia/Levonoia: *The Lake & Valley Clarion* — 38 Main St.; PO Box 9, Geneseo (14454); Th; 1,175pd, 410fr (Sw); $5.00; publisher & editor Corrin Strong; managing editor Hal Legg; tel (716) 243-3530; fax (716) 243-3764

Babylon/Islip Twps.: *The Beacon* — 65 Deer Park Ave.; PO Box 670, Babylon (11702); Th; 5,000pd, 400fr (Sw); 75¢; publishers Edward P Mangano & John Mangano; editor Terry Bouquet; tel (516) 587-5612; fax (516) 587-0198

Baldwin: *Baldwin Herald* — 379 Central Ave., Lawrence (11559); W; 1,882pd, 1,618fr (Sw); $10.22; C; publishers Clifford Richner & Stuart Richner; editor Allison Zisko; managing editor Fran Evans; tel (516) 569-4000; fax (516) 569-4942

Baldwin/Freeport: *The Baldwin Citizen* — PO Box 521, Baldwin (11510); W; 5,110pd, 300fr (Est); 82¢; publisher Barry Manning; editor David Abolafia; managing editor Patricia G Hornell; tel (516) 739-6400; fax (516) 739-5404

Baldwinsville: *The Messenger* — 9 E. Genesee St.; PO Box 270 (13027); W; 7,150pd (Est); $6.85; C; publisher Stewart F Hancock; general manager Richard K Keene; editor Larry Rulison; managing editor Jim Arnold; tel (315) 635-3921

Ballston Spa: *Ballston Journal* — 72 W. High St. (12020); W; 2,147pd, 25fr (Sw); 43¢; C; publisher & editor Charles Hogan; tel (518) 885-4341

Bath: *The Steuben Courier-Advocate* — 10 W. Steuben St. (14810); Su; 11,606fr (Est); 25¢; publisher Colleen Neeley; editor Mark Raven; tel (607) 776-2121; fax (607) 776-3967

Bayside/Bay Terrace/Oakland Gordon: *The Bayside Times* — 41-02 Bell Blvd., 2nd Fl., Bayside (11361); Th; 11,124pd (Sw); 80¢; C; publisher & editor Steven Blank; managing editor Roz Liston; tel (718) 229-0300; fax (718) 225-7117

Beacon: *Beacon Free Press* — 84 E. Main St., Wappingers Falls (12590); W; 8,069fr (Sw); $7.35; C; publisher Albert M Osten; editor Bill Parsons; tel (914) 297-3723; fax (914) 297-6810

Bellmore: *Bellmore Life* — 2818 Merrick Rd. (11710); W; 3,830pd, 601fr (ABC); $12.46; C; publisher Linda Laursen Toscano; editor Paul Laursen; tel (516) 826-0333; fax (516) 826-0814

Bennington Co. (VT): *The Northshire Free Press* — 14 E. Main St.; PO Box 330, Granville (12832); Sa; 6,300fr (Sw); $7.45; C; publisher John M Manchester; editor Stella Wood; tel (518) 642-1234; fax (518) 642-1344

Bethpage: *Bethpage Tribune* — 329 Broadway; PO Box 399 (11714); F; 558pd, 100fr (Sw); 40¢; publisher & editor Linda Mangano; tel (516) 681-0442; fax (516) 681-6517

Boonville: *Boonville Herald & Adirondack Tourist* — E. Schuyler St.; PO Box 372 (13309); W; 2,927pd, 247fr (Sw); $3.50; publisher & editor Mrs Livingston Lansing; general manager Teresa E Freeman; managing editor Sandra Hrim; tel (315) 942-4449

Brewster: *Brewster Times* — 83 E. Lake Blvd.; PO Drawer H, Mahopac (10541); W; 8,200pd (Est); 57¢; publisher & editor Don Hall; tel (914) 628-8400; fax (914) 628-8400

Brockport: *The Brockport Post* — 4 S. Main St., Pittsford (14534); Tu; 1,600pd (Est); $6.30; C; publisher & editor Andrew D Wolfe; general manager John S Wolfe; tel (716) 924-4040; fax (716) 637-5637

Bronx: *Bronx Press-Review* — 170 W. 233rd St. (10463); Th; 10,990pd, 297fr (Est); 65¢; C; publisher Andrew Wolf; editor Sondra Levin; tel (718) 543-5200; fax (718) 543-4206

Bronx: *Co-op City News* — 135 Dreiser Loop (10475); Th; 8,299pd, 3,506fr (Est); $9.42; C; publisher Christopher G Hagedorn; editor Paula Young; tel (914) 636-7400; fax (914) 636-2957

Bronx: *Parkchester News* — 135 Dreiser Loop (10475); F; 12,200fr (Est); $9.42; C; publisher Christopher G Hagedorn; editor Karol Nielsen; tel (914) 636-7400; fax (914) 636-2957

Bronx: *The Bronx News* — 135 Dreiser Loop (10475); Th; 6,000pd, 4,000fr (Est); $6.50; C; publisher Christopher G Hagedorn; editor Karol Nielsen; tel (718) 671-1234; fax (914) 636-2957

Bronxville: *Bronxville Review-Press Reporter* — 1 Odell Plz., Yonkers (10701); Th; 2,122pd (Sw); $15.29; C; publisher Gary F Sherlock; editor Diane S Zeeman; tel (914) 696-8245; fax (914) 696-8208

Brookhaven Twp.: *Brookhaven Review* — 127 E. Main St.; PO Box 925, Smithtown (11787); Th; 2,415pd, 835fr (Sw); 30¢; publisher & editor Sal Diperi; managing editor Terry Gilberti; tel (516) 265-3500; fax (516) 265-3504

Brookhaven/Riverhead: *Community Journal* — Rte. 25 A & Dogwood Dr.; PO Box 619, Wading River (11792); W; 7,500pd (Est); $7.00; publisher & editor Bernadette Budd; tel (516) 929-8882

Brooklyn: *Bay News* — 1733 Sheepshead Bay Rd. (11235); M; 14,912pd (Sw); $14.12; C; publisher Edward E Luster; general manager Dan Holt; editor Ken Brown; tel (718) 769-4400; fax (718) 769-5048

Brooklyn: *Bay Ridge Courier* — 1733 Sheepshead Bay Rd. (11235); M; 9,150pd, 2,038fr (Sw); $14.12; publisher Edward E Luster; general manager Dan Holt; editor Ken Brown; tel (718) 769-4400; fax (718) 769-5048

Brooklyn: *Brooklyn Graphic* — 1733 Sheepshead Bay Rd. (11235); M; 7,840pd, 2,415fr (Sw); $14.12; C; publisher Edward E Luster; general manager Dan Holt; editor Ken Brown; tel (718) 769-4400; fax (718) 769-5048

Brooklyn: *Brooklyn Heights Press & Cobble Hill News* — 125 Montague St., Brooklyn Heights (11201); Th; 19,500pd (Est); 82¢; publisher J D Hasty; editor John Gardiner; tel (718) 624-0536; fax (718) 624-2716

Brooklyn: *Brooklyn Phoenix* — 125 Montague St., Brooklyn Heights (11201); F; 18,000pd (Est); 65¢; publisher & editor Fred Halla; tel (718) 624-0528/3609; fax (718) 624-2716

Brooklyn: *Canarsie Digest* — 1733 Sheepshead Bay Rd. (11235); M; 8,645pd, 1,602fr (Sw); $14.12; C; publisher Edward E Luster; general manager Dan Holt; editor Ken Brown; tel (718) 769-4400; fax (718) 769-5048

Brooklyn: *Flatbush Life* — 1733 Sheepshead Bay Rd. (11235); M; 13,284pd, 675fr (Sw); $14.12; C; publisher Edward E Luster; editor Dan Holt; tel (718) 769-4400; fax (718) 769-5048

Brooklyn: *Harbor Watch (Metro New York)* — 1733 Sheepshead Bay Rd. (11235); F; 35,000fr (Est); $15.60; publisher Dan Holt; editor Ken Brown; managing editor Emily DiCenso; tel (718) 769-4400; fax (718) 769-5048

Brooklyn: *Home Reporter and Sunset News* — 8723 3rd Ave. (11209); Th; 9,696pd, 150fr (Sw); $1.00; publisher J Frank Griffin; editor Sara M Otey; tel (718) 238-6600; fax (718) 238-6630

Brooklyn: *Kings Courier* — 1733 Sheepshead Bay Rd. (11235); M; 13,846pd, 2,652fr (Sw); $14.12; C; publisher Edward E Luster; general manager Dan Holt; editor Ken Brown; tel (718) 769-4400; fax (718) 769-5048

Brooklyn: *The Brooklyn Paper* — 26 Court St. (11242); F; 2,700pd, 7,300fr (Sw); 75¢; publisher Ed Weintrob; editor Howard Altschiller; tel (718) 834-9161; fax (718) 834-9278

Brooklyn: *The Brooklyn Spectator* — 8723 3rd Ave. (11209); Tu; 8,888pd, 50fr (Sw); 85¢; publisher J Frank Griffin; editor Sara M Otey; tel (718) 238-6600; fax (718) 238-6630

Brooklyn: *The Brooklyn Times* — 8723 3rd Ave. (11209); Th; 4,403pd, 50fr (Sw); 78¢; publisher & editor J Frank Griffin; tel (718) 238-6600; fax (718) 238-6630

Broome Co.: *The Valley News* — 3128 Watson Blvd., Endwell (13760); F; 5,000pd (Sw); $12.95; C; publisher Brad Manchester; general manager Richard Maynard; managing editor Mary Pat Hyland; tel (607) 757-0753; fax (607) 757-0784

Buffalo: *South Buffalo News* — 2703 S. Park Ave., Lackawanna (14218); W; 5,300pd (Est); $7.80; publisher & editor William Delmont; managing editor George Delmont; tel (716) 823-8222; fax (716) 821-0550

Camillus/Jordan-Elbridge: *Camillus Advocate* — PO Box 270, Baldwinsville (13027); W; 3,475pd (Sw); $5.55; C; publisher Stewart Hancock; general manager Richard Keene; editor Kathryn Loomis; managing editor Jim Arnold; tel (315) 635-3921; fax (315) 637-3124

Canaan/Bennington: *The Taconic Valley Echo* — Rte. 22; PO Box 270, Berlin (12022); Th; 2,000pd, 56fr (Sw); $4.35; publisher Ralph de Leon; editor Marilyn Conlin; managing editor Vivienne Jaffe; tel (518) 658-2777; fax (518) 658-2266

Canarsie: *Canarsie Courier* — 1142 E. 92nd St.; PO Box 81 Canarsie Station, Brooklyn (11236); Th; 9,962pd, 125fr (Sw); 73¢; publisher Mary Samitz; editor Charles Rogers; tel (718) 257-0600; fax (718) 272-0870

Canastota: *Canastota Bee-Journal* — 114 Canal St.; PO Box 228 (13032); W; 2,524pd, 25fr (Sw); $3.05; publisher Stewart Hancock; editor Kathy Hogan; tel (315) 697-7142

Carmel/Buster: *The Puttnam Courier Trader* — 73 Gleneida Ave.; PO Box 220, Carmel (10512); Th; 4,945pd, 212fr (CAC); $9.95; publisher John Norton; editor Barbara Gallo-Farrell; tel (914) 225-3633; fax (914) 225-1914

Carthage: *Carthage Republican Tribune* — PO Box 549 (13619); W; 2,550pd, 18fr (Sw); $3.50; C; publisher & editor Ramon D Hansen; tel (315) 493-1270; fax (315) 493-1271

Cazenovia: *Cazenovia Republican* — 72 Albany St.; PO Box 301 (13035); W; 3,744pd (Est); $5.90; C; publisher Stewart F Hancock; general manager Richard Keene; editor Jennifer Kovalich; managing editor Jim Arnold; tel (315) 655-3415; fax (315) 655-3415

Centereach: *The Mid Island News* — PO Box 21 (11720); Th; 2,149pd (Sw); $7.15; C; publisher & editor Bernard Paley; tel (516) 265-2100; fax (516) 265-6237

Central Sq.: *The Citizen Outlet* — 80 N. Jefferson St.; PO Box 129, Mexico (13114); Tu; 5,490pd (Est); 27¢; publisher & editor Mark Backus; tel (315) 963-7813; fax (315) 963-4087

Chautauqua Co.: *Quality Guide* — 41 E. Main St.; PO Box 38, Westfield (14787); M; 9,302fr (Est); 26¢; publisher Donald L Meyer; editor Bob Houston; tel (716) 326-3163

Cheektowaga: *Cheektowaga Bee* — 5564 Main St. (14221); PO Box 150, Buffalo (14231-0150); Th; 1,708pd, 45fr (Sw); $8.80; C; publisher Trey Measer; editor Michele Darstein; managing editor Dave Sherman; tel (716) 632-4700; fax (716) 633-8601

Cheektowaga: *Cheektowaga Times* — 343 Maryvale Dr. (14225); Th; 4,457pd, 250fr (Sw); $8.05; publisher & editor Eve J Allis; general manager Margaret Bourdette; tel (716) 892-5323; fax (716) 892-4925

Chemung Co.: *Chemung Valley Reporter* — 126 S. Main St.; PO Box 474, Horseheads (14845); Th; 1,400pd, 100fr (Sw); $7.50; C; publisher Patricia Powers; general manager Jerry Brown; editor Martha Horton; managing editor Linda Gudas; tel (607) 739-3001; fax (607) 739-2935

Chittenango/Bridgeport: *Chittenango-Bridgeport Times* — PO Box 270, Baldwinsville (13037); W; 2,126pd (Sw); $3.75; C; publisher Stewart Hancock; general manager Richard Keene; editor Kate Brennan; managing editor Jim Arnold; tel (315) 687-3887

Clarence: *Clarence Bee* — 5564 Main St. (14221); PO Box 150, Buffalo (14231-0150); W; 4,352pd, 170fr (Sw); $10.60; C; publisher Trey Measer; editor Michele Darstein; managing editor Dave Sherman; tel (716) 632-4700; fax (716) 633-8601

Clinton: *The Clinton Courier* — 32 College St.; PO Box 294 (13323-0294); W; 2,065pd, 30fr (Sw); $4.50; publisher Cynthia Z Kershner; editor Charles J Kershner; tel (315) 853-3490; fax (315) 853-3522

Cobleskill: *Times-Journal* — 19 Division St.; PO Box 339 (12043); W; 6,659pd, 76fr (Est); 44¢; publisher James Poole; editor Patsy Nichosia; tel (518) 234-2515; fax (518) 234-7898

Columbia Co.: *The Independent Of Columbia & Rensselaer Counties* — Rte. 23; PO Box 246, Hillsdale (12529); M/Th; 9,300pd, 100fr (Sw); $11.15; publisher Tony Jones; editor Vicki Simons; managing editor Ray Fashona; tel (518) 325-4400; fax (518) 325-4497

Commack: *Commack News* — PO Box 21 (11725); Th; 4,627pd (Sw); $7.15; C; publisher & editor Bernard Paley; tel (516) 265-2100; fax (516) 265-6237

Conklin/Kirkwood: *The Country Courier* — 1035 Conklin Rd.; PO Box 208, Conklin (13748); W; 1,650pd (Sw); $2.50; C; publisher Donald Einstein; editor Elizabeth Einstein; tel (607) 775-0472; fax (607) 775-5863

Copyright ©1996 by the Editor & Publisher Co.

Cooperstown/Oneonta: *Freeman's Journal* — 89 Main St.; PO Box 591 (13326); Su; 4,651pd, 60fr (Est); $1.06; C; publisher Robert C Miller; editor Dan Sheridan; tel (607) 547-2545; fax (607) 547-5587

Cornwall: *Cornwall Local* — 35 Hasbrouck Ave.; PO Box B (12518); W; 2,961pd, 69fr (Sw); $8.17; C; publisher Joseph Gill; editors Fred Brennan & Patricia Abramo; tel (914) 534-7771; fax (914) 534-3855

Coxsackie/Athens: *Greene County News* — PO Box 39-RR #1, West Coxsackie (12192-9718); Th; 2,123pd, 89fr (Est); 14¢; publisher John B Johnson; general manager Anthony Panetta; editor Annibar Jensis; tel (518) 731-8189; fax (518) 731-8180

Cuba/Allegany Co./Wellsville: *Cuba Patriot & Free Press* — 34 Water St., Cuba (14727); W; 2,559pd, 96fr (Sw); $3.90; C; publisher Christina Arden-Hopkins; editor John Arden-Hopkins; tel (716) 968-2580; fax (716) 968-2622

Dansville/Wayland/Nunda: *Genesee Country Express* — 113 Main St., Dansville (14437); Th; 2,896pd, 88fr (Sw); $5.00; C; publisher Frederick W Kurtz; editor Brian Langen; tel (716) 335-2271; fax (716) 335-6957

Delaware Co.: *Delaware County Times* — 56 Main St., Delhi (13753); F; 1,800pd, 200fr (Est); $3.50; publisher Donald F Bishop II; general manager & editor Linda Jones; tel (607) 746-2176; fax (607) 746-3135

Delaware/Western Sullivan: *The Reporter* — 181 Delaware St.; PO Box 359, Walton (13856); W; 6,992pd, 114fr (Sw); $6.70; publisher Melissa C Rowell; tel (607) 865-4131; fax (607) 865-7586/8983

Delmar/Bethlehem/Colonie: *The Spotlight* — 125 Adams St.; PO Box 100, Delmar (12054); W; 6,115pd, 915fr (Sw); $11.70; C; publisher & editor Richard A Ahlstrom; managing editor Susan Graves; tel (518) 439-4949; fax (518) 439-0609

Depew: *Depew Bee* — 5564 Main St. (14221); PO Box 150, Buffalo (14231-0150); Th; 1,486pd, 29fr (Sw); $10.60; C; publisher Trey Measer; editor Michele Darstein; managing editor Dave Sherman; tel (716) 632-4700; fax (716) 633-8601

Deposit: *The Deposit Courier* — Courier Bldg. 138 Front St. (13754); W; 2,078pd, 55fr (Sw); 14¢; C; publisher & editor Hilton A Evans; tel (607) 467-2191; fax (607) 467-5330

Dewitt: *Dewitt Times* — 7-9-11 E. Genesee St.; PO Box 270, Baldwinsville (13027); W; 1,123pd, 150fr (Sw); $4.00; C; publisher Stewart Hancock; general manager Richard Keene; editor Chris Donlon; managing editor Jim Arnold; tel (315) 637-3921; fax (315) 635-3914

Dundee Area: *The Dundee Observer* — 45 Water St.; PO Box 127, Dundee (14837); W; 2,630pd, 370fr (Sw); $3.85; publisher & editor Mary Geo Tomion; tel (607) 243-8351; fax (607) 243-5833

E Aurora: *East Aurora Advertiser* — 710 Main St.; PO Box 5 (14052); Th; 4,440pd, 340fr (Sw); $7.40; C; publisher & editor Grant M Hamilton; general manager Sandra Cunningham; tel (716) 652-0320

E Aurora/Elma: *East Aurora Bee* — 5564 Main St. (14221); PO Box 150, Buffalo (14231-0150); Th; 7,444pd, 3,603fr (Sw); $12.40; C; publisher Trey Measer; editor Michele Darstein; managing editor Dave Sherman; tel (716) 632-4700; fax (716) 633-8601

E Fishkill: *East Fishkill Record* — PO Drawer H, Mahopac (10541); Th; 3,100pd (Est); 40¢; publisher & editor Don Hall; tel (914) 628-8400

E Hampton: *The East Hampton Star* — 153 Main St.; PO Box 5002 (11937); Th; 14,177pd, 435fr (ABC); $19.00; C; publisher Arthur L Carter; editor Helen S Rattray; managing editor Jack Otter; tel (516) 324-0002; fax (516) 324-7943

E Meadow/Westbury/Levittown: *Meadowbrook Times* — 379 Central Ave., Lawrence (11559); W; 1,490pd, 510fr (Sw); $7.28; C; publishers Clifford Richner & Stuart Richner; editor Hannah Bennett; managing editor Fran Evans; tel (516) 569-4000; fax (516) 569-4942

E Rochester: *East Rochester Post-Herald* — 666 Phillips Rd., Victor (14564); Th; 1,100pd (Est); $6.30; C; publisher & editor Andrew D Wolfe; general manager John S Wolfe; tel (716) 924-4040; fax (716) 924-7734

E Rockaway/Lynbrook: *East Rockaway/Lynbrook Observer* — 100 E. 2nd St., Ste. 202, Mineola (11501); W; 2,635pd, 250fr (Sw); 82¢; C; publisher Barry Manning; editor Pat Horwell; tel (516) 739-6400; fax (516) 739-5404

Elizabethtown/Westport: *Valley News* — 1 High St.; PO Box 338, Elizabethtown (12932); W; 3,593pd (Sw); $6.75; C; publisher Daniel E Alexander; general manager Ed Coats; editor Fred Herbst; tel (518) 873-6368; fax (518) 873-6360

Ellenville: *Ellenville Press* — 7 Cape Ave.; PO Box 31 (12428); W; 1,200pd, 51fr (Sw); 40¢; publisher & editor Minnie L Wainer; tel (914) 647-7222; fax (914) 647-7443

Elma: *Elma Review* — PO Box 118 (14059); W; 1,030pd, 11fr (Sw); $6.92; C; publisher & editor Grant M Hamilton; general manager Sandra Cunningham; tel (716) 652-0320

Elmont/Franklin Sq.: *Three Village Times* — 132 E. 2nd St.; PO Box 1578, Mineola (11501); F; 1,648pd, 623fr (Sw); $5.60; C; editor Bob Clark; managing editor Danny McCue; tel (516) 747-8282; fax (516) 742-5867

Far Rockaway: *Rockaway Journal* — 3791 Central Ave., Lawrence (11559); W; 1,540pd, 760fr (Sw); $7.28; C; publishers Clifford Richner & Stuart Richner; editor Seena Weisman; managing editor Fran Evans; tel (516) 569-4000; fax (516) 569-4942

Farmingdale/N Massapequa: *Farmingdale Observer* — 132 E. 2nd St.; PO Box 1578, Mineola (11501-3510); F; 3,052pd, 1,002fr (Sw); $5.60; C; publisher Karl V Anton Sr; editor Christina Leonard; managing editor Danny McCue; tel (516) 747-8282; fax (516) 742-5867

Fayetteville/Manlius: *Fayetteville-Manilus Eagle Bulletin* — 117 Highbridge St.; PO Box 65, Fayetteville (13066); W; 6,167pd, 560fr (Sw); $6.31; C; publisher Stewart F Hancock; general manager Richard K Keene; editor Chris Donlon; managing editor Jim Arnold; tel (315) 635-3921; fax (315) 637-3124

Fishkill: *Fishkill Standard* — PO Drawer H, Mahopac (10541); Th; 6,200pd (Est); 40¢; publisher & editor Don Hall; tel (914) 628-8400

Floral Park: *Floral Park Dispatch* — 132 E. 2nd St.; PO Box 1578, Mineola (11501); F; 1,076pd, 457fr (Sw); $5.60; C; publisher Karl V Anton Sr; editor Danny McCue; tel (516) 747-8282; fax (516) 742-5867

Floral Park/Bellerose: *The Gateway* — 139 Tulip Ave.; PO Box 227, Floral Park (11002); W; 12,000pd, 11fr (Sw); 75¢; publisher & editor Carla Cohen; tel (516) 775-2700

Flushing/Kew Gardens: *The Flushing Times* — 41-02 Bell Blvd., 2nd Fl., Bayside (11361); Th; 4,851pd (Sw); 60¢; C; publisher & editor Steven Blank; managing editor Roz Liston; tel (718) 229-0300; fax (718) 229-7117

Ft. Plain: *Courier-Standard-Enterprise* — 41 Main St.; PO Box 351 (13339); W; 4,365pd, 175fr (Sw); 33¢; publisher Richard Barker; general manager Kevin McClary; editor Robert Lindsay; tel (518) 993-2321; fax (518) 993-4919

Franklin Sq./Garden City: *Franklin Square Bulletin* — 139 Tulip Ave.; PO Box 227, Franklin Square (11001); Th; 8,700pd, 43fr (Sw); 75¢; C; publisher & editor Carla Cohen; tel (516) 775-7700

Freeport/Baldwin: *Freeport-Baldwin Leader* — 1840 Merrick Ave., Merrick (11566); Th; 2,202pd, 296fr (Sw); $6.86; C; publisher Linda Laursen Toscano; editor Paul Laursen; tel (516) 378-3133; fax (516) 378-0287

Freeport/Roosevelt: *Long Island Graphic* — 379 Central Ave., Lawrence (11559); Th; 860pd, 200fr (Est); $6.86; C; publishers Clifford Richner & Stuart Richner; editor Jean Graham; managing editor Fran Evans; tel (516) 569-4000; fax (516) 569-4942

Fresh Meadows/Jamaica Estates/Hollis Hills: *The Fresh Meadows Times* — 41-02 Bell Blvd., 2nd Fl., Bayside (11361); Th; 1,397pd (Sw); 60¢; C; publisher & editor Steven Blank; managing editor Roz Lester; tel (718) 229-0300; fax (718) 225-7117

Fulton: *Fulton Patriot* — 117 Oneida St. (13069); Tu; 600pd, 5,500fr (Est); $5.00; publisher & editor Vincent R Caravan; tel (315) 598-6397

Fulton: *The Valley News* — 117 Oneida St. (13069); M/Th; 8,757pd, 148fr (Sw); $6.89; publisher & editor Vincent R Caravan; tel (315) 598-6397

Garden City: *Garden City News* — 821 Franklin Ave. (11530); F; 6,741pd (Est); 29¢; publisher Robert L Morgan Jr; editor Meg Norris; tel (516) 294-8900; fax (516) 294-8924

Garden City/Stewart Manor: *Garden City Life* — 132 E. 2nd St.; PO Box 1578, Mineola (11501); W; 2,241pd, 1,050fr (Sw); $5.60; C; publisher Karl V Anton Sr; editor Robert Clarke; managing editor Danny McCue; tel (516) 747-8282; fax (515) 742-5867

Gates/Chili/Scottsville/Spencerport: *Gates-Chili News* — 2361 Chili Ave., Rochester (14624); W; 8,700pd, 1,000fr (Sw); $6.22; publisher Patricia M Smith; general manager Chris Ayotte; editor Michael Murphy; tel (716) 247-9200; fax (716) 247-9210

Geneseo: *Community Publications Inc.* — PO Box 66 (14454); Th; 11,900pd (Est); 6.50; C; publisher & editor A O'Byrne; tel (716) 786-3179

Glen Cove/Glen Head/Sea Cliff/Glenwood Landing/Locust Vly./Brookville: *Glen Cove Record Pilot* — 132 E. 2nd St.; PO Box 1578, Mineola (11501); Th; 5,126pd, 1,128fr (Sw); $5.60; C; publisher Karl V Anton Sr; editor Karl V Anton Jr; managing editor Danny McCue; tel (516) 747-8282; fax (516) 742-5867

Glen Oaks/Bellerose/N Shore Towers/Floral Park/New Hyde: *The Glen Oaks Ledger* — 41-02 Bell Blvd., 2nd Fl., Bayside (11361); Th; 1,504pd (Sw); 60¢; C; publisher & editor Steven Blank; managing editor Roz Liston; tel (718) 229-0300; fax (718) 225-7117

Glendale/Ridgewood: *Forest Hills/Rego Park Times* — 55-51 69th St.; PO Box 376, Maspeth (11378); Th; 1,320pd, 165fr (Est); $9.50; C; publisher & editor Walter H Sanchez; general manager Lora Sanchez; tel (718) 639-7000; fax (718) 429-1234

Glendale/Ridgewood: *Glendale Register* — 55-51 69th St.; PO Box 376, Maspeth (11378); Th; 1,320pd, 165fr (Est); $9.50; C; publisher & editor Walter H Sanchez; general manager Lora Sanchez; tel (718) 639-7000; fax (718) 429-1234

Glendale/Ridgewood: *Jackson Heights News* — 55-51 69th St.; PO Box 376, Maspeth (11378); Th; 385pd, 12,000fr (Est); $9.50; C; publisher & editor Walter H Sanchez; general manager Lora Sanchez; tel (718) 639-7000; fax (718) 429-1234

Glendale/Ridgewood: *Long Island City/Astoria Journal* — 55-51 69th St.; PO Box 376, Maspeth (11378); Th; 300pd, 14,000fr (Est); $9.50; C; publisher & editor Walter H Sanchez; general manager Lora Sanchez; tel (718) 639-7000; fax (718) 429-1234

Glens Falls/Lake George: *The Chronicle* — PO Box 153, Glens Falls (12801); Th; 700pd, 24,300fr (Sw); $16.00; publisher Patricia Maddock; editor Mark Frost; tel (518) 792-1126

Goshen/Chester: *Independent Republican* — 132 W. Main St.; PO Drawer A, Goshen (10924); W; 3,192pd, 250fr (Sw); $4.00; publisher Betty Jane Wright; editor Eileen Farley; tel (914) 294-6111; fax (914) 294-0532

Gouverneur/Dekalb/Fowler: *The Tribune-Press* — 74 Trinity; PO Box 268, Gouverneur (13642); W; 3,724pd, 301fr (Est); $3.70; C; publisher & editor M Dan McClelland; general manager Elizabeth Bell; tel (315) 287-2100; fax (315) 287-2101

Grand Island: *Island Dispatch* — 1854 C Whitehaven Rd.; PO Box 130 (14072-0130); F; 2,963pd, 459fr (Sw); $7.62; C; publisher Arthur Mazenauer; editor Michele Ramstetter; tel (716) 773-7676; fax (716) 773-7190

Granville: *The Granville Sentinel* — 14 E. Main St.; PO Box 330 (12832); W; 3,350pd, 50fr (Sw); $7.45; C; publisher John Manchester; editor Stella Wood; tel (518) 642-1234; fax (518) 642-1344

Great Neck: *Great Neck News* — 634 Middleneck Rd. (11021); F; 7,000pd (Est); 39¢; publisher & editor Robert L Morgan; tel (516) 487-1100

Great Neck/Lake Success: *Great Neck Record* — 132 E. 2nd St.; PO Box 1578, Mineola (11501); Th; 5,319pd, 988fr (Sw); $12.21; C; publisher Karl V Anton Sr; editor Wendy Kreitzman; managing editor Danny McCue; tel (516) 747-8282; fax (516) 742-5867

Greece: *The Greece Post* — 4 S. Main St., Pittsford (14534); Tu; 8,500pd (Est); $8.25; C; publisher & editor Andrew D Wolfe; general manager John S Wolfe; tel (716) 924-4040; fax (716) 924-7734

Greene: *The Chenango American/Whitney Point Reporter/Oxford Review-Times* — 12 S. Chenango St.; PO Box 566 (13778); Tu; 2,586pd, 131fr (Sw); 15¢; C; publisher Kenneth S Paden; editor Peter S Mansheffer; tel (607) 656-4511; fax (607) 563-7118

Greenpoint: *Greenpoint Gazette& Advertiser* — 597 Manhattan Ave., Brooklyn (11222); W; 5,000pd (Est); $5.00; publishers & editors Ralph Carrano & Adelle Haines; tel (718) 389-6067; fax (718) 349-3471

Greenville: *The Greenville Local* — 164 Main St.; PO Box 307, Ravena (12143); Th; 1,500pd (Sw); $3.25; publisher Richard Bleezarde; editor Stacey Miezels; tel (518) 756-2030/2087; fax (518) 756-8555

Greenwich Vlg./Lower Manhattan: *The Villager* — 80 8th Ave., New York (10011); W; 12,140pd, 5,000fr (Est); $20.00; publisher Elizabeth Butson; editor Thomas G Butson; tel (212) 229-1890; fax (212) 229-2790

Greenwich/Salem/Argyle/Easton/Cambridge/Schuylerville/Shusha: *The Journal-Press* — 35 Salem St.; PO Box 185, Greenwich (12834); Th; 2,509pd, 103fr (Sw); $4.50; publisher & managing editor Sally B Tefft; general manager Culver S Tefft; editor Patricia Conner; tel (518) 692-2266

Greenwood Lake/W Milford: *The Greenwood Lake News and West Milford News* — Windermere Ave.; PO Box 1117, Greenwood Lake (10925); W; 2,816pd, 186fr (Sw); $8.00; publisher Ann Chaimowitz; editor Ron Nowak; tel (914) 477-2575; fax (914) 477-2577

Guilderland/New Scotland: *Altamont Enterprise and Albany County Post* — 123 Maple Ave.; PO Box 654, Altamont (12009); Th; 6,656pd, 150fr (Sw); $9.00; publisher James E Gardner; editor Christopher Sanford; tel (518) 861-6641/5005; fax (518) 861-5105

Halesite: *Halesite Gazette* — 38 Glades Way (11743); Th; 1,550pd, 3,441fr (Sw); $5.43; publisher & editor Lawrence J Michael; tel (516) 547-0668

Hamburg/Twps. of Boston: *The Sun and Erie County Independent* — 46 Buffalo St.; PO Box 590, Hamburg (14075); Th; 9,429pd (Sw); 47¢; publishers Karl Kluckhohn & William Haws; editor Eileen Hotho; tel (716) 649-4040; fax (716) 649-6374

Hamilton Co.: *Hamilton County News* — Rte. 8/30; PO Box 166, Speculator (12164); Tu; 3,454pd (Sw); $6.35; C; publisher Frank W Gappa; general manager Kevin McClary; managing editor Cristine Knapp Meixner; tel (518) 548-6898; fax (518) 548-5305

Hamilton/Morrisville: *The Mid-York Weekly* — 55 Utica St.; PO Box 318, Hamilton (13346); Th; 2,998pd, 263fr (Est); $2.35; publisher Robert W Tenney; editor Caroly Godfrey; tel (315) 824-2150; fax (315) 824-4220

Hancock: *The Hancock Herald* — PO Box 519 (13783); W; 2,375pd (Sw); 14¢; publisher Kenneth S Paden; editor Sally Zegers; tel (607) 637-3591; fax (607) 637-4383

Hastings-on-Hudson: *The Enterprise* — 5 Boulanger Plz.; PO Box 278 (10706); F; 4,575pd, 250fr (Sw); $11.76; publisher Deborah G White; editor Terri Salvatore; tel (914) 478-2787; fax (914) 478-2863

Haverstraw/Clarkstown: *The Rockland County Times* — 11 New Main St., Haverstraw (10927); Th; 8,000pd (Est); $7.90; publisher & editor Evelyn Davis; tel (914) 429-2000; fax (914) 429-8990

Hempstead: *The Hempstead Beacon* — 1 Jonathan Ave., Hicksville (11801); Th; 4,800pd (Sw); 35¢; publisher Peter Hoegl; editor Sheila Hoegl Noeth; tel (516) 931-1400

Henrietta: *The Henrietta Post* — 666 Phillips Rd., Victor (14564); W; 2,500pd (Est); $6.30; C; publisher & editor Andrew D Wolfe; general manager John S Wolfe; tel (716) 924-4040; fax (716) 924-7734

Hicksville: *Hicksville Illustrated News* — 132 E. 2nd St.; PO Box 1578, Mineola (11501); Th; 4,457pd, 1,368fr (Sw); $12.21; publisher Karl V Anton Jr; editor Tricia Clarke; tel (516) 747-8282; fax (516) 742-5867

Hicksville: *Hicksville Mid-Island Times* — 81 E. Barclay St. (11801); F; 2,289pd (Est); 29¢; publisher Robert L Morgan Jr; editor Meg Norris; tel (516) 931-0012

Highland Falls: *The News of the Highlands* — 163-165 Main St.; PO Box 278 (10928); W; 1,752pd, 1,048fr (Est); 15¢; publisher News of the Highlands Inc.; general manager Joseph V Gill; editor Frederick W Brennan; tel (914) 446-4519; fax (914) 446-0532

Hunter/Greene/Ulster Co.: *The Mountain Eagle* — Railroad Ave.; PO Box 968, Tannersville (12485); Th; 5,000pd (Sw); $6.95; publisher & editor Paul Smart; tel (518) 589-7007; fax (518) 589-7028

Huntington: *The Long-Islander* — 313 Main St.; PO Box 1805 (11743); Th; 8,103pd, 3,892fr (Sw); publisher Jim Koutsis; editor Peter Sloggatt; tel (516) 427-7000; fax (516) 427-5820

Huntington/Northport: *The Record* — 322 Main St.; PO Box 1805, Huntington (11743); W; 4,277pd (Sw); C; publisher James Koutsis; editor Peter Sloggatt; tel (516) 427-7000; fax (516) 427-5820

Hyde Park: *Hyde Park Townsman* — Front St.; PO Box 316, Millbrook (12545); Th; 2,416pd, 99fr (Est); $6.90; C; publishers Hamilton Meserve & Helen Meserve; editor Diane Zucker; tel (914) 677-8241; fax (914) 677-6337

Interlaken: *The Interlaken Review* — PO Box N, Trumansburg (14886); W; 351pd, 42fr (Sw); 18¢; publisher James Bilinski; editor Brock Delworth; tel (607) 532-9239; fax (607) 387-9421

Irondequoit: *Irondequoit Press* — 657 Titus Ave., Rochester (14617); Tu; 7,700pd (Est); $8.25; C; publisher & editor Andrew D Wolfe; general manager John S Wolfe; tel (716) 924-4040; fax (716) 342-6146

Islip: *Islip News* — PO Box 940, Central Islip (11722); Th; 2,187pd (Sw); $7.15; C; publisher Bernard Paley; editor David Ambro; tel (516) 265-2100; fax (516) 265-6237

Jericho: *Jericho News Journal* — 81 E. Barclay St., Hicksville (11801); F; 685pd (Est); 29¢; publisher Robert L Morgan Jr; editor Meg Norris; tel (516) 931-0012

Jericho/Syosset: *Syosset/Jericho Tribune* — 132 E. 2nd St.; PO Box 1578, Mineola (11501); F; 3,158pd, 753fr (Sw); $5.60; C; publisher Karl V Anton Jr; editor Kathy Gerber; tel (516) 747-8282; fax (516) 742-5867

Kenmore/Tonawanda: *Ken-Ton Bee* — 5564 Main St. (14221); PO Box 150, Buffalo (14231-0150); W; 1,574pd, 69fr (Sw); $8.80; C; publisher Trey Measer; editor Michele Darstein; managing editor Dave Sherman; tel (716) 632-4700; fax (716) 633-8601

Lackawanna: *Lackawanna Front Page* — 2703 S. Park Ave. (14218); W; 6,500pd, 15fr (Est); $7.80; publisher & editor William Delmont; tel (716) 823-8222; fax (716) 821-0550

LaGrange/Union Vale/Beekman/Pleasant Vly.: *The Voice-Ledger* — Front St.; PO Box 316, Millbrook (12545); Th; 2,992pd, 72fr (Sw); $6.30; publishers Hamilton Meserve & Helen Meserve; editor Diane Zucker; managing editor Gene Lomoriella; tel (914) 677-8241; fax (914) 677-6337

LaGrangeville: *LaGrangeville La Grange Independent* — 85 E. Lake Blvd.; PO Drawer H, Mahopac (10541); W; 2,500pd (Est); 40¢; publisher & editor Don Hall; tel (914) 628-8400; fax (914) 628-8400

Lake Placid: *The Lake Placid News* — 412 S. Main St.; PO Box 111 (12946); F; 4,000pd (Est); $5.70; C; publisher Catherine Moore; editor Julie Stowell; tel (518) 523-4401; fax (518) 523-1351

Lancaster: *Lancaster Bee* — 5564 Main St. (14221); PO Box 150, Buffalo (14231-0150); Th; 3,716pd, 46fr (Sw); $10.60; C; publisher Trey Measer; editor Michele Darstein; managing editor Dave Sherman; tel (716) 632-4700; fax (716) 633-8601

Lawrence/Cedarhurst/Woodmere/Hewlett/Inwood/Atlantic Beach: *Nassau Herald* — 379 Central Ave., Lawrence (11559); Th; 10,228pd, 2,422fr (Sw); $13.30; C; publishers Clifford Richner & Stuart Richner; editor Randi Kreiss; managing editor Fran Evans; tel (516) 569-4000; fax (516) 569-4942

Levittown: *Levittown Tribune* — 132 E. 2nd St.; PO Box 1578, Mineola (11530); Th; 3,290pd, 764fr (Sw); $5.60; C; publisher Karl V Anton Jr; editor Neil McKenna; managing editor Danny McCue; tel (516) 747-8282; fax (516) 742-5867

Lewiston/Porter: *Lewiston Porter Sentinel* — 1854 C Whitehaven Rd.; PO Box 130, Grand Island (14072-130); Sa; 8pd, 12,170fr (Sw); $13.86; C; publisher Arthur Mazenauer; editor Michelle Ramstetter; tel (716) 773-7676; fax (716) 773-7190

Little Neck/Douglaston: *The Little Neck Ledger* — 41-02 Bell Blvd., 2nd Fl., Bayside (11361); Th; 3,477pd (Sw); 60¢; C; publisher & editor Steven Blank; managing editor Roz Liston; tel (718) 229-0300; fax (718) 225-7117

Liverpool: *Review* — 9 E. Genesee St.; PO Box 270, Baldwinsville (13027); W; 4,926pd, 311fr (Est); $5.65; C; publisher Stewart F Hancock; general manager Richard K Keene; editor David Tyler; managing editor Jim Arnold; tel (315) 635-3921

Locust Valley: *The Leader* — 160 Birch Hill Rd.; PO Box 468 (11560); Th; 3,200pd, 80fr (Est); 68¢; publisher & editor Edith Hay Wyckoff; tel (516) 676-1434; fax (516) 671-7442

Long Beach/Pt. Lookout: *Long Beach Herald* — 379 Central Ave., Lawrence (11559); Th; 4,116pd, 2,984fr (Sw); $10.50; C; publishers Clifford Richner & Stuart Richner; editor Michael Harrison; managing editor Fran Evans; tel (516) 569-4000; fax (516) 569-4942

Loudonville/Newtonville/Menands: *The Loudonville Weekly* — 125 Adams St., Delmar (12054); W; 5,000fr (Sw); $7.65; C; publishers & editors Richard Ahlstrom; managing editor Eric Bryant; tel (518) 439-4949; fax (518) 439-0609

Lowville: *Journal and Republican* — 7556 State St. (13367); W; 6,032pd, 22fr (Sw); $7.95; publisher Pamela J Spry; editor Gordon Allen; tel (315) 376-3525; fax (315) 376-4136

Lynbrook/E Rockaway/Malverne: *Lynbrook Herald* — 379 Central Ave., Lawrence (11559); W; 3,391pd, 2,709fr (Sw); $10.22; C; publishers Clifford Richner & Stuart Richner; editor Fran Evans; tel (516) 569-4000; fax (516) 569-4942

Lyons/Newark/Sodus/Maledon/Palmyra/Ontario/Sodas Pt./William: *Wayne County Star* — 36B Canal St.; PO Box 430, Lyons (14489); W/Sa; 3,879pd, 99fr (Est); $2.80; C; publisher Christopher M Palermo; editor Mary K Henderberg; tel (315) 946-9701; fax (315) 946-4382

Mahopac: *Putnam County Press* — 83 E. Lake Blvd.; PO Drawer H (10541); W; 3,200pd (Sw); 57¢; publisher & editor Don Hall; tel (914) 628-8400; fax (914) 628-8400

Malverne/Lynbrook: *The Malverne-Lynbrook Community Times* — PO Box 116, Malverne (11565); Th; 2,544pd, 240fr (Est); 57¢; publisher Barry S Manning; editor Patricia Horwell; tel (516) 739-6400; fax (516) 739-5404

Manhasset/Munsey Park: *Manhasset Press* — 132 E. 2nd St.; PO Box 1578, Mineola (11501); Th; 3,801pd, 304fr (Sw); $7.85; C; publisher Karl V Anton Jr; editor Eileen Brennan; managing editor Danny McCue; tel (516) 747-8282; fax (516) 742-5867

Manhattan: *Chelsea Clinton News* — 242 W. 30th St., New York (10010); Th; 6,053pd, 200fr (Sw); $19.70; C; publisher Robert S Trentlyon; general manager Laura Chamberlain; editor Larry O'Connor; tel (212) 268-2552; fax (212) 268-2935

Manhattan: *New York Town & Village* — 1 Madison Ave., New York (10010); Th; 5,500pd, 4,000fr (Est); $13.50; publisher Charles G Hagedorn; editor Christopher G Hagedorn; managing editor Todd Maisel; tel (212) 679-1234

Manhattan: *Our Town Newspaper* — 242 W. 30th St., 5th Fl., New York (10001); W; 120,000fr (CPVS); $4.82; publisher & editor Tom Allon; tel (212) 268-8600; fax (212) 268-0164

Manhattan: *The Westsider* — 242 W. 30th St., New York (10001); Th; 8,143pd, 200fr (Sw); $21.70; C; publisher Robert S Trentlyon; general manager Laura Chamberlain; editor Larry O'Connor; tel (212) 268-2552; fax (212) 268-2935

Marcellus: *Marcellus Observer* — PO Box 270, Baldwinsville (13027); W; 1,418pd (Est); $5.45; C; publisher Stewart Hancock; general manager Richard Keene; editor Amber Spain; managing editor Jim Arnold; tel (315) 635-3921; fax (315) 635-3914

Margaretville: *Catskill Mountain News* — Main St.; PO Box 290 (12455); W; 4,950pd, 97fr (Sw); $5.75; publisher Richard D Sanford; editor Diane Galusha; tel (914) 586-2601; fax (914) 586-2366

Maspeth/Glendale: *Queens Ledger* — 55-51 69th St.; PO Box 376, Maspeth (11378); Th; 10,890pd (Est); $9.50; C; publisher & editor Walter H Sanchez; general manager Lora Sanchez; tel (718) 639-7000; fax (718) 429-1234

Massapequa: *Massapequa Post* — 1045-B Park Blvd., Massapequa Park (11762); W; 3,800pd, 100fr (Sw); $7.50; C; publishers Alfred James & Carolyn James; editor M T Capone; tel (516) 798-5100; fax (516) 798-5296

Massapequa: *Massapequan Observer* — 132 E. 2nd St.; PO Box 1578, Mineola (11501); F; 1,878pd, 631fr (Sw); $5.18; C; publisher Karl V Anton Sr; editor Terry Robinson; managing editor Danny McCue; tel (516) 747-8282; fax (516) 742-5867

Mayville: *Mayville Sentinel* — 41 E. Main St.; PO Box 38, Westfield (14787); Th; 1,050pd, 25fr (Est); $3.30; C; publisher Ogden Newspapers Inc.; general manager & editor Bob Houston; tel (716) 326-3163; fax (716) 326-3165

Merrick: *Merrick Life* — The Community Newspapers; 1840 Merrick Ave. (11566); Th; 5,845pd, 980fr (ABC); $13.02; C; publisher Linda Laursen Toscano; editor Paul Laursen; tel (516) 378-5320; fax (516) 378-0287

Merrick: *The Merrick Beacon* — 1 Jonathan Ave., Hicksville (11801); F; 4,700pd (Est); $4.90; C; publisher Peter Hoegl; editor Sheila Hoegl Noeth; tel (516) 931-1400

Mexico: *Independent Mirror* — N. Jefferson St.; PO Box 129 (13114); Tu; 2,969pd (Est); 27¢; publisher Mark H Backus; editor Rose Ann Parsons; tel (315) 963-7813; fax (315) 963-4087

Millbrook/Union Vale: *Millbrook Round Table* — Front St.; PO Box 316, Millbrook (12545); Th; 2,076pd, 49fr (Sw); $6.30; C; publishers Hamilton Meserve & Helen Meserve; editor Diane Zucker; tel (914) 677-8241; fax (914) 677-6337

Millerton/NE Amenia: *The Millerton News* — Main St.; PO Box AD, Millerton (12546); Th; 773pd, 41fr (Sw); $9.95; publisher A Whitney Ellsworth; editor David N Parker; managing editor Kathryn Boughton; tel (518) 789-4401; fax (518) 435-4802

Mineola/New Hyde Park: *New Hyde Park Illustrated* — 132 E. 2nd St.; PO Box 1578, Mineola (11501); F; 2,153pd, 847fr (Sw); $5.60; C; publisher Karl V Anton Jr; editor Margaret Whitely; managing editor Danny McCue; tel (516) 747-8282; fax (516) 742-5867

Mineola/Williston Park: *Mineola American* — 132 E. 2nd St.; PO Box 1578, Mineola (11501); W; 3,359pd, 1,080fr (Sw); $5.60; publisher Karl V Anton Sr; editor Maggie Whitley; managing editor Danny McCue; tel (516) 747-8282; fax (516) 742-5867

Monroe Co.: *Perinton-Fairport Post* — 666 Phillips Rd.; PO Box C, Fishers (14453); Th; 4,500pd (Est); $7.70; publisher Andrew D Wolfe; general manager John S Wolfe; tel (716) 924-4040; fax (716) 924-7734

Monroe/Woodbury: *The Photo News* — 45 Gilbert St., Monroe (10950); W; 4,833pd, 1,100fr (Sw); $10.00; C; publisher & editor Stan Martin; tel (914) 782-4000; fax (914) 782-1711

Moravia: *Moravia Republican-Register* — 6 Central St.; PO Box 591 (13118); W; 545pd, 200fr (Sw); 32¢; publisher & editor B F McGuerty III; tel (315) 497-1551

Naples: *The Naples Record* — 23 Mill St.; PO Box 370 (14512); W; 1,302pd, 25fr (Sw); $2.25; publisher & editor Michael C Fowler; tel (716) 374-5260; fax (716) 374-8590

New Berlin: *The New Berlin Gazette* — 13 West St. (13411); Th; 2,337pd (Sw); 10¢; publisher & editor James Austin; general manager Gayle Austin; tel (607) 847-6131

New Paltz/Highland/Rosendale/Gardiner/Plattekill: *The Herald* — 71 Main St.; PO Box 537, New Paltz (12561); Th; 2,550pd, 150fr (Est); $11.50; C; publisher Geddy Sveikauskas; general manager Diane Consello-Brandes; editor Julie O'Corozine; tel (914) 255-7000; fax (914) 255-7005

New Windsor: *The Sentinel* — PO Box 406, Vails Gate (12584); Th; 2,413pd, 35fr (Sw); 21¢; publisher & editor Everett W Smith; general manager Rich Durbin; tel (914) 562-1218

New York: *People's Weekly World* — 235 W. 23rd St. (10011); Th; 66,000pd, 1,700fr (Sw); $15.00; publisher Longview Publishing Co.; editor Tim Wheeler; tel (212) 924-2523; fax (212) 645-5436

New York: *The New York Observer* — 54 E. 64th St. (10021); W; 38,500pd (Est); $20.00; publisher Arthur L Carter; editor Peter Kaplan; tel (212) 755-2400; fax (212) 980-2087

New York/New Jersey/Connecticut: *New York Harbor Watch* — 1733 Sheepshead Bay Rd., Brooklyn (11235); F; 5,220pd, 28,580fr (Est); $15.40; publisher & editor Dan Holt; tel (718) 769-4400; fax (718) 769-5048

Newark: *The Courier-Gazette* — 613 S. Main St. (14513); F; 2,983pd, 33fr (Sw); 27¢; C; publisher John H Van Dusen; editor Sandra Marcano; tel (315) 331-1000; fax (315) 331-1053

Newfield: *Newfield News* — 51 E. Main St., Trumansburg (14886); W; 475pd, 30fr (Est); $2.50; publisher James Bilinski; editor Brock Delworth; tel (607) 387-3181; fax (607) 387-9421

Niagara/Wheatfield: *Niagara-Wheatfield Tribune* — 1854 C Whitehaven Rd.; PO Box 130, Grand Island (14072-0130); Th; 6pd, 13,487fr (Sw); $15.25; C; publisher A Skip Mazenauer; editor Michele Ramstetter; tel (716) 773-7676; fax (716) 773-7190

N Creek: *The North Creek News-Enterprise* — Ski Bowl Rd.; PO Box 85 (12853); Th; 1,755pd, 111fr (Sw); 13¢; publisher & editor Jerry L Gardner; tel (518) 251-3012; fax (518) 251-4147

N Syracuse: *Star-News* — 486 S. Main St.; PO Box 270 (13212); W; 6,275pd (Sw); $7.60; C; publisher Stewart F Hancock; general manager Richard K Keene; editor Maria Forastiero; managing editor Jim Arnold; tel (315) 635-3921

Northern Westchester: *The Patent Trader* — Rtes. 121 & 35; PO Box 1000, Cross River (10518); Th; 6,222pd, 2,766fr (CAC); $24.00; publisher & editor Carll Tucker; managing editor Evan Brandt; tel (914) 763-3200; fax (914) 763-3911

Northport: *Observer* — 160 Main St.; PO Box 60 (11768); Th; 7,901pd (Sw); $7.15; C; publisher Bernard Paley; editor David Ambro; tel (516) 261-6124; fax (516) 265-6237

Northport: *The Northport Journal* — 322 Main St., Huntington (11743); Th; 2,500pd (Sw); $5.60; C; publisher Jim Koutsis; editor George Wallace; tel (516) 427-7000; fax (516) 427-5820

Oceanside/Island Park: *Oceanside-Island Park Herald* — 379 Central Ave., Lawrence (11559); Th; 3,445pd, 1,805fr (Sw); $10.22; C; publishers Clifford Richner & Stuart Richner; editor Jennifer White; managing editor Fran Evans; tel (516) 569-4000; fax (516) 569-4942

Oceanside/Rockville Ctr.: *The Oceanside-Rockville Centre Beacon* — 216 E. 2nd St., Mineola (11501); Th; 4,530pd, 620fr (Sw); 82¢; publisher Barry S Manning; editor Florence Bialick; managing editor Patricia Horwell; tel (516) 739-6400; fax (516) 739-5404

Ogdensburg: *Advance News* — PO Box 409 (13669); Su; 10,563pd, 134fr (Sw); $5.18; publisher Dorothy Park; editor Charles W Kelly; tel (315) 393-1000; fax (315) 393-5108

Old Forge: *Adirondack Echo* — 5 Main St. (13420); F; 3,000pd (Sw); 90¢; publisher David W Bartlett; editor Patrick Russell; tel (315) 369-3747

Oneida/Southern Oneida Co./Northern Madison Co.: *The Waterville Times* — 128 E. Main St.; PO Box C, Waterville (13480); W; 2,165pd, 15fr (Sw); $3.00; publisher & editor Mary C Cleary; tel (315) 841-4105; fax (315) 841-4104

Orchard Park: *Orchard Park Bee* — 5564 Main St. (14221); PO Box 150, Buffalo (14231-0150); Th; 7,629pd, 3,417fr (Sw); $12.40; C; publisher Trey Measer; editor Michele Darstein; managing editor Dave Sherman; tel (716) 632-4700; fax (716) 633-8601

Orchard Park/Boston/Colden/Aurora/Elma/Holland/Marilla/Wales: *The Southtowns Citizen* — 6519 E. Quaker St., Orchard Park (14127); F; 3,500pd, 400fr (Sw); $11.20; publisher & editor Christopher Coleman; tel (716) 662-0001; fax (716) 667-3002

Oyster Bay/E Norwich/Oyster Bay Cove/Bayville: *Oyster Bay Enterprise Pilot* — 132 E. 2nd St.; PO Box 1578, Mineola (11501); Th; 1,892pd, 492fr (Sw); $5.60; C; publisher Karl V Anton Sr; editor Dagmar Karpi; managing editor Danny McCue; tel (516) 747-8282; fax (516) 742-5867

Oyster Bay Twp.: *Oyster Bay-Syosset Guardian* — 102 Audrey Ave.; PO Box 28, Oyster Bay (11771); F; 2,700pd, 50fr (Est); 64¢; publisher Estate of Edwina Snow; editor Gloria R O'Rourke; tel (516) 922-4215; fax (516) 922-4227

Palmyra/Macedon/Marion/Gawanda/Walwerth: *The Courier-Journal* — 612 E. Main St.; PO Box 235, Palmyra (14522); W; 2,371pd, 61fr (Sw); $4.75; C; publisher Lawrence Lucieer; general manager Thomas L Klemann; editor Stephen P Buchiere; tel (315) 597-6655; fax (315) 597-6947

Patchogue: *Islip Bulletin* — PO Box 780 (11772); Th; 2,200pd (Est); $11.44; publisher John T Tuthill; editor Kevin Molloy; tel (516) 475-1000; fax (516) 475-1565

Patchogue: *Long Island Advance* — PO Box 780 (11772); Th; 8,000pd (Est); $14.00; publisher John T Tuthill; editor Kevin Molloy; tel (516) 475-1000; fax (516) 475-1565

Pawling/Holmes/Patterson: *News-Chronicle* — 3 Memorial Ave., Pawling (12564); W; 1,241pd, 83fr (CAC); $6.90; C; publisher John Norton; managing editors Bernadette Shustak & Betty Tani; tel (914) 855-1100; fax (914) 855-1106

II-56 **New York** *U.S. Weeklies*

Peekskill/Cortlandt Cos.: *Peekskill Herald* — 927 South St.; PO Box 2250, Peekskill (10566); Th; 3,426pd, 70fr (Sw); $11.40; publisher Regina Clarkin O'Leary; editor Kathy Daley; tel (914) 737-7747

Pelham/Pelham Manor: *The Pelham Weekly* — 306 5th Ave., Pelham (10803); F; 1,000pd, 30fr (Sw); $6.25; publisher & editor Margaret A Klein; tel (914) 738-8717; fax (914) 738-9608

Penfield: *Penfield Post-Republican* — 666 Phillips Rd., Victor (14564); W; 3,800pd (Est); $7.70; C; publisher & editor Andrew D Wolfe; general manager John S Wolfe; tel (716) 924-4040; fax (716) 924-7734

Penn Yan: *Penn Yan Chronicle-Express* — 138 Main St. (14527); W; 4,082pd (Sw); $5.25; C; publisher Gregg K Morris; editor Jim Kidd; tel (315) 536-4422; fax (315) 536-0682

Perry: *Perry Herald* — 12 Borden Ave.; PO Box 219 (14530); Th; 955pd, 22fr (Sw); $3.85; publisher Randy White; editor Susan Cady White; tel (716) 237-2212; fax (716) 237-2211

Phoenix: *Phoenix Register* — N. Jefferson St.; PO Box 129, Mexico (13114); Tu; 3,104pd (Est); 27¢; publisher & editor Mark Backus; tel (315) 963-7813; fax (315) 963-4087

Pine Plains/Stanford: *Register Herald* — Front St.; PO Box 316, Millbrook (12545); Th; 1,567pd, 38fr (Sw); $6.30; C; publishers Hamilton Meserve & Helen Meserve; editor Diane Zucker; tel (914) 677-8241; fax (914) 677-6337

Pittsford/Brighton: *Brighton-Pittsford Post* — 666 Phillips Rd.; PO Box C (14453), Victor (14564); W; 12,500pd (Est); $12.10; C; publisher & editor Andrew D Wolfe; general manager John S Wolfe; tel (716) 924-4040; fax (716) 924-7734

Plainview/Old Bethpage: *Plainview/Old Bethpage Herald* — 132 E. 2nd St.; PO Box 1578, Mineola (11501); F; 1,322pd, 447fr (Sw); $5.60; C; publisher Karl V Anton Jr; editor Kathy Gierber; managing editor Danny McCue; tel (516) 747-8282; fax (516) 742-5867

Plattsburgh: *Plattsburgh Free Trader* — 1 High St.; PO Box 338, Elizabethtown (12932); Tu; 14,500fr (Est); $7.50; C; publisher Daniel E Alexander; general manager Ed Coats; editor Fred Herbst; tel (518) 561-8144; fax (518) 873-6360

Port Chester/Rye Brook: *Port Chester Guide* — 145 Irving Ave.; PO Box 1309, Port Chester (10573); W; 1,550pd, 450fr (Sw); $5.50; publisher Robert B Sorensen; editor Anne Vaccaro Brady; tel (914) 939-1164; fax (914) 939-6908

Port Chester/Rye Brook: *Westmore News* — 38 Broad St., Port Chester (10573-4197); Th; 2,312pd, 712fr (Sw); $7.06; publisher Richard Abel; editor Jananne Abel; tel (914) 939-6864; fax (914) 939-6877

Port Jefferson/Port Jefferson Sta.: *The Port Times-Record* — 185 Rte. 25A; PO Box 707, Setauket (11733); Th; 6,559pd, 572fr (Sw); $11.66; C; publisher Leah S Dunaief; general manager Johness Watts Kuisel; editor Denise Alfieri; tel (516) 751-7744

Port Jervis: *The Gazette* — 84-88 Fowler St. (12602); F; 8,200pd (Sw); $6.00; general manager Brad Lipe; editor Janis Osborne; tel (914) 856-5383; fax (914) 858-8484

Port Washington: *Port Washington News* — 132 E. 2nd St.; PO Box 1578, Mineola (11501); Th; 6,501pd, 329fr (Sw); $5.60; C; publisher Karl V Anton Jr; editor Christina Cronin Southard; managing editor Danny McCue; tel (516) 747-8282; fax (516) 742-5867

Poughkeepsie: *Spackenkill Sentinel* — 84 E. Main St., Wappingers Falls (12590); W; 4,003fr (Sw); $5.88; C; publisher Albert M Osten; editor Bill Parsons; tel (914) 297-3723; fax (914) 297-6810

Putnam Co.: *The Putnam Courier-Trader* — 73 Gleneida Ave.; PO Box 220, Carmel (10512); Th; 4,984pd, 312fr (CAC); $9.95; C; publisher John Norton; managing editor Barbara Gallo-Farrell; tel (914) 225-3633; fax (914) 225-1914

Queens: *Floral Park Bulletin* — 139 Tulip Ave.; PO Box 227, Floral Park (11001); Th; 8,500pd (Sw); 75¢; publisher & editor Carla Cohen; tel (516) 775-2700

Queens Co.: *Queens Tribune* — 174-15 Horace Harding Expwy., Fresh Meadows (11365); Th; 2,000pd, 144,000fr (Est); $35.00; C; publisher Michael Schenkler; editor David Oats; tel (718) 357-7400; fax (718) 357-9417

Queens Co.: *The Queen Courier* — 214-07 42nd Ave., Bayside (11361); Th; 6,000pd, 80,000fr (Est); $16.00; publisher & managing editor Victoria Schneps; editor Tamara Hartman; tel (718) 224-5863; fax (718) 224-5441

Queens Co.: *Times Newsweekly* — 66-58 Fresh Pond Rd.; PO Box 299, Ridgewood (11386); Th; 23,425pd, 800fr (Sw); $12.50; publisher & editor Maureen E Walthers; managing editor James P Devlin; tel (718) 821-7500; fax (718) 456-0120

Ravena/Coeymans/Sekirk: *The News-Herald* — 164 Main St.; PO Box 307, Ravena (12143); Th; 3,800pd (Est); $3.31; C; publisher Richard G Bleezarde; editor Stacey Miezels; tel (518) 756-2030/2087; fax (518) 756-8555

Red Creek/Wolcott: *Post-Herald* — 6784 Main St.; PO Box 199, Red Creek (13143); Th; 3,065pd, 38fr (Sw); $4.25; C; publisher Christopher M Palermo; editor Charles Itzin; tel (315) 754-6229; fax (315) 754-6431

Rensselaer Co./Northern Columbia: *The Taconic Valley Echo* — PO Box 270, Berlin (12022); Th; 1,825pd, 53fr (Sw); $1.94; publisher & editor Ralph deLeon; tel (518) 658-3212/18; fax (518) 658-2266

Rhinebeck: *The Gazette Advertiser* — Front St.; PO Box 316, Millbrook (12545); W; 3,169pd, 138fr (Est); $6.30; C; publishers Hamilton Meserve & Helen Meserve; editor Diane Zucker; tel (914) 677-8241; fax (914) 677-6337

Riverdale: *The Riverdale Press* — 6155 Broadway, Bronx (10471); Th; 11,809pd, 900fr (Sw); $21.25; C; publisher & editor Bernard L Stein; publisher & general manager Richard L Stein; tel (718) 543-6065; fax (718) 584-4038

Riverhead/Brookhaven: *The News-Review* — 7785 Rte. 25; PO Box 1500, Mattituck (11952); Th; 4,739pd, 135fr (Sw); $12.17; C; publishers Joan Gustavson & Troy Gustavson; general manager Doug Gillen; editor Jeff Miller; managing editor Ruth Jernick; tel (516) 298-3200; fax (516) 298-3287

Rockaway Peninsula: *The Wave of Long Island* — 88-08 Rockaway Beach Blvd.; PO Box 97, Rockaway Beach (11693); F; 11,737pd, 75fr (Sw); $7.00; publisher Leon S Locke; general manager Sanford Bernstein; tel (718) 634-4000; fax (718) 945-0913

Rockland Co.: *Rockland Review* — 55 Virginia Ave.; PO Box 211, West Nyack (10994-0211); W; 35,000fr (Sw); $15.75; C; publisher Cynthia Cockerill; editor Sandra Frederichs; tel (914) 358-0222; fax (914) 358-1162

Rockville Centre: *The Rockville Centre News & Owl* — 216 E. 2nd St., Mineola (11501); Th; 3,697pd, 300fr (Est); 57¢; publisher Barry Manning; editor Helen L Shrimpton; managing editor Patricia Horwell; tel (516) 739-6400; fax (516) 739-5404

Rockville Centre: *Rockville Centre Herald* — 379 Central Ave., Lawrence (11559); Th; 3,096pd, 2,404fr (Sw); $10.22; C; publishers Clifford Richner & Stuart Richner; editor Jeff Kluewer; managing editor Fran Evans; tel (516) 569-4000; fax (516) 569-4942

Rocky Pt./Miller Pl./Shoreham/Wading River/Sound Beach/Ridge: *The Village Beacon-Record* — PO Box 707, Setauket (11733); Th; 5,067pd (Sw); $9.29; C; publisher Leah S Dunaief; general manager Johness Watts Kuisel; editor Denise Alfieri; tel (516) 751-7744

Roslyn/E Hills: *Roslyn News* — 132 E. 2nd St.; PO Box 1578, Mineola (11501); Th; 2,435pd, 821fr (Sw); $5.60; C; publisher Karl V Anton Jr; editor Joseph Scotchie; managing editor Danny McCue; tel (516) 747-8282; fax (516) 742-5867

Rouses Pt.: *The North Countryman* — 1 High St.; PO Box 338, Elizabethtown (12932); W; 4,500fr (Sw); $6.50; C; publisher Daniel E Alexander; general manager Ed Coats; editor John Gereau; tel (518) 873-6368; fax (518) 873-6360

Rutland Co. (VT): *The Lakes Region Free Press* — 14 E. Main St.; PO Box 330, Granville (12832); Sa; 7,431fr (Est); $7.10; C; publisher John M Manchester; editor Stella Wood; tel (518) 642-1234; fax (518) 642-1344

Sag Harbor: *Sag Harbor Express* — Main St.; PO Box 1690 (11963); Th; 2,000pd (Est); 25¢; C; publisher Gardner Cowles; editor Brian Boyan; tel (516) 725-1700; fax (516) 725-1584

St. James/Nissequogue/Smithtown/Nesconset/Kings Park: *The Times (St. James, Smithtown, Nesconset)* — 185 Rte. 25A; PO Box 707, Setauket (11733); Th; 7,470pd, 577fr (Sw); $9.29; C; publisher Leah S Dunaief; general manager Johness Watts Kuisel; editor Marie Muirtagh; tel (516) 751-7744

Saugerties: *The Old Dutch Post Star* — 45 Partition St.; PO Box 149 (12477); Su; 3,531pd, 739fr (Est); $6.00; publisher Frederick W Lee; editor Tim Johnson; managing editor Paul Scott; tel (914) 246-4985; fax (914) 246-5108

Sayville/Suffolk Co.: *Suffolk County News* — 23 Candee Ave.; PO Box 367, Sayville (11782); Th; 3,686pd, 71fr (Sw); 49¢; C; publisher John T Tuthill; general manager Josephine LaBarca; editor Kevin Molloy; managing editor Anthony Howard; tel (516) 589-6200; fax (516) 589-3246

Scarsdale: *Scarsdale Inquirer* — 14 Harwood Ct.; Ste. 510; PO Box 418 (10583); F; 6,295pd, 385fr (Sw); $16.47; C; publisher Deborah G White; editor Linda Leavitt; tel (914) 725-2500; fax (914) 725-1552

Seaford: *Seaford/Wantagh Observer* — 2262 Centre Ave., Bellmore (11710); Th; 4,700pd, 500fr (Est); 28¢; publisher & editor Jackson B Pokress; tel (516) 679-9888

Seneca Co.: *The Reveille/Between the Lakes* — 2024 Rtes. 5 & 20; PO Box 557, Seneca Falls (13148); Th; 1,610pd, 55fr (Sw); $5.40; publisher Joseph L Siccardi; editor Howard Van Kirk; tel (315) 568-6400; fax (315) 568-4200

Setauket/Stony Brook/Old Field/Poquott: *The Village Times* — 185 Rte. 25A; PO Box 707, Setauket (11733); Th; 9,323pd, 576fr (Sw); $11.17; C; publisher Leah S Dunaief; general manager Johness Watts Kuisel; editor Joan Cipriano; tel (516) 751-7744

Shelter Island: *Shelter Island Reporter* — PO Drawer 3020, Shelter Island Heights (11965); Th; 2,804pd, 115fr (Sw); $5.25; publisher Gardner Cowles III; editor Elizabeth A Bonora; tel (516) 749-1000; fax (516) 749-0144

Sherburne: *Sherburne News* — 17 E. State St. (13460); W; 2,000pd (Sw); $2.50; publisher & editor John M McDaniel; tel (607) 674-6071; fax (607) 674-6071

Sherman/Clymer: *Chautauqua News* — 41 E. Main St.; PO Box 38, Westfield (14787); Th; 996pd, 18fr (Sw); $3.10; publisher Donald L Meyer; editor Robert Houston; tel (716) 326-3163; fax (716) 326-3165

Sidney: *Tri-Town News* — 5 Winkler Rd.; PO Box 388 (13838); W; 4,730pd, 14fr (Sw); $4.00; C; publisher Kenneth S Paden; editor Nancy Sue Burns; tel (607) 563-3526; fax (607) 563-7118

Skaneateles/Marcellus: *Skaneateles Press* — 2 Fennell St.; PO Box 550, Skaneateles (13152); W; 3,352pd, 150fr (Est); $4.07; C; publisher Stewart Hancock; editor Amber Spain; tel (315) 685-8338; fax (315) 685-8338

Smithtown: *The Smithtown News* — 1 Brooksite Dr.; PO Box 805 (11787); Th; 9,957pd (Sw); $7.15; C; publisher Bernard Paley; editor David Ambro; tel (516) 265-2100; fax (516) 265-6237

Smithtown Twp.: *Smithtown Messenger* — 127 E. Main St.; PO Box 925, Smithtown (11787); Th; 4,530pd (Est); $6.25; publisher & editor Sal Diperi; managing editor Terry Gilberti; tel (516) 265-3500; fax (516) 265-3504

S Queens: *The Forum of South Queens* — 137-05 Cross Bay Blvd., Ozone Park (11417); F; 25,000fr (Est); $7.00; C; publisher Thomas LaVecchia; editor Dennis Waszak; tel (718) 845-3221; fax (718) 738-7645

Southampton: *The Southampton Press* — PO Box 1207 (11968); Th; 10,137pd, 369fr (Sw); $1.18; C; publisher Donald H Louchheim; editor Peter B Boody; tel (516) 283-4100; fax (516) 283-4927

SE Queens: *Queens Village Times* — 41-02 Bell Blvd., Bayside (11361); Th; 1,085pd (Sw); 60¢; C; publisher & editor Steven Blank; managing editor Roz Liston; tel (718) 229-0300; fax (718) 225-7117

Southold Town/Shelter Island: *The Suffolk Times* — 7785 Main Rd.; PO Box 1500, Mattituck (11952); Th; 9,550pd, 200fr (Sw); $15.55; C; publishers Joan Gustavson & Troy Gustavson; general manager Doug Gillen; editor Jeff Miller; managing editor Tim Kelly; tel (516) 298-3200; fax (516) 298-3287

Southold/Riverhead: *The Traveler-Watchman* — Traveler St.; PO Box 725, Southold (11971); Th; 19,209pd, 112fr (Sw); $8.60; publisher Emanuel Kontokosta; editor Joey MacLellan; tel (516) 765-3425; fax (516) 727-1992

Spencer: *Random Harvest* — PO Box N, Trumansburg (14886); W; 450pd, 50fr (Est); $1.75; publisher James Bilinski; editor Brock Dillworth; tel (607) 387-3181; fax (607) 387-9421

Spring Creek Sun: *Spring Creek Sun* — 1540 Van Siclen Ave., Brooklyn (11239); F; 10,500fr (Sw); $12.00; publisher & editor Michael Horowitz; tel (718) 642-2718; fax (718) 642-7301

Springville/Concord/Ashford/Colden/Boston/E Otto: *Springville Journal* — 33 E. Main St.; PO Box 99, Springville (14141); Th; 3,556pd, 812fr (Sw); $5.80; C; publishers Karl Kluckhohn & William Haws; editor David C Pierce; tel (716) 592-4550; fax (716) 592-4663

Staten Island: *Staten Island Register* — 2100 Clove Rd. (10305); Tu; 16,800pd, 2,800fr (Sw); $35.00; publisher Joanne Lent; editor Bill Franz; managing editor Diane Sclafans; tel (718) 447-4700; fax (718) 816-7719

Suffolk Co.: *Suffolk Life Newspapers* — 1461 Rte. 58; PO Box 167, Riverhead (11901); W; 550pd, 496,582fr (CAC); $140.00; C; publisher & editor David J Willmott Sr; general manager Sheryl Heather; managing editor Lou Grasso; tel (516) 369-0800; fax (516) 369-5930

Suffolk Co.: *Three Village Herald* — PO Box 703, East Setauket (11733); W; 7,833pd, 192fr (Sw); $9.93; C; publisher Gardner Cowles III; editor Susan Bridson; tel (516) 751-1550; fax (516) 751-8592

Sullivan Co.: *Sullivan County Democrat* — 33 Main St.; PO Box 308, Callicoon (12723); Tu/F; 8,500pd, 160fr (Sw); $6.96; publisher Fred W Stabbert Jr; editor Laurie Ramie; tel (914) 887-5200; fax (914) 887-5386

Syracuse/Cortland: *Onondaga Valley News* — 250 Bear St. W.; PO Box 4970, Syracuse (13221); M; 5,490pd, 4,768fr (Sw); $6.18; C; publisher A Loren Colburn; editor Suzanne Bedford; tel (315) 472-7825; fax (315) 478-1434

Ticonderoga: *The Times of Ticonderoga* — 162 Montcalm St.; PO Box 471 (12883); M; 8,565pd, 15fr (Sw); $6.30; publisher Daniel E Alexander; general manager Ed Coats; editor John Gereau; tel (518) 585-6204; fax (518) 585-2209

Tioga Co.: *The Owego News* — 32-34 Lake St., Owego (13827); F; 2,500pd (Sw); N/A; C; publisher Brad Manchester; general manager Richard Maynard; managing editor Mary Pat Hyland; tel (607) 687-6397; fax (607) 687-7811

Trumansburg: *Ovid Gazette* — PO Box N (14886); W; 426pd, 61fr (Est); $7.25; C; publisher James Bilinski; editor Brock Dillworth; tel (607) 387-3181; fax (607) 387-9421

Trumansburg: *The Trumansburg Free Press* — PO Box N (14886); W; 1,286pd, 98fr (Sw); $6.70; C; publisher James Bilinski; editor Brock Dillworth; tel (607) 387-3181; fax (607) 277-1012

Tupper Lake/Long Lake/Piercefield/Childwold/Newcomb: *Tupper Lake Free Press* — 136 Park St.; PO Box 1210, Tupper Lake (12986); W; 3,448pd, 89fr (Sw); $4.34; publisher & editor Dan McClelland; general manager Betty Bell; tel (518) 359-2166; fax (518) 359-2295

Ulster Co.: *New Paltz News* — 108 Vineyard Ave.; PO Box 458, Highland (12528); W; 4,163pd, 25fr (Sw); $5.00; C; publisher & editor T Craig McKinney; tel (914) 691-2000; fax (914) 691-8601

Ulster Co.: *Southern Ulster Pioneer* — 108 Vineyard Ave.; PO Box 458, Highland (12528); W; 4,163pd, 25fr (Sw); $5.00; C; publisher & editor T Craig McKinney; tel (914) 691-2000; fax (914) 691-8601

Uniondale: *The Uniondale Beacon* — 1 Jonathan Ave., Hicksville (11801); F; 5,000pd (Sw); $4.90; C; publisher Peter Hoegl; editor Sheila Hoegl Noeth; tel (516) 931-1400

Upper Delaware Valley: *The River Reporter* — 8 Main St.; PO Box 150, Narrowsburg (12764); Th; 3,423pd, 132fr (Sw); $5.00; publisher Stuart Communications Inc.; general manager Laurie Stuart; editor Pam Chergotis; tel (914) 252-7414; fax (914) 252-3298

Valley Stream: *Valley Stream Herald* — 379 Central Ave., Lawrence (11559); Th; 6,855pd, 2,145fr (Sw); $10.50; C; publishers Clifford Richner & Stuart Richner; editor Carol Sutton; managing editor Fran Evans; tel (516) 569-4000; fax (516) 569-4942

Valley Stream: *Valley Stream Maileader* — 216 E. 2nd St.; PO Box 159 (11582), Mineola (11501); Th; 8,513pd, 800fr (Est); 57¢; publisher Barry S Manning; editor Andrea S Halbfinger; managing editor Patricia G Horwell; tel (516) 739-6400; fax (516) 739-5404

Vestal: *Vestal Town Crier* — 1035 Conklin Rd.; PO Box 208, Conklin (13748); W; 1,200pd (Sw); $4.50; C; publisher Donald Einstein; editor Elizabeth Einstein; tel (607) 775-0472; fax (607) 775-5863

Victor: *The Perinton-Fairport Post* — 666 Phillips Rd. (Victor 14564); PO Box C, Fishers (14453); W; 4,500pd (CAC); $7.70; C; publisher & editor Andrew D Wolfe; general manager & managing editor John S Wolfe; tel (716) 924-4040; fax (716) 924-7734

Wantagh/Seaford: *The Citizen* — 2818 Merrick Rd., Bellmore (11710); Th; 3,039pd, 255fr (ABC); $11.06; C; publisher Linda Laursen Toscano; editor Paul Laursen; tel (516) 826-0812; fax (516) 826-0814

Wappingers Falls/E Fishkill/Fishkill/Hopewell Junction: *Southern Dutchess News* — 84 E. Main St., Wappingers Falls (12590); W; 13,962pd, 13,175fr (Sw); $13.82; C; publisher Albert M Osten; editor Bill Parsons; tel (914) 297-3723; fax (914) 297-6810

Warrensburg: *Warrensburg-Lake George News* — 166 Main St.; PO Box 130 (12885); W; 2,833fr (Est); 10¢; publisher Dan Alexander; editor Fred Herbst; managing editor John Gereau; tel (518) 623-3411; fax (518) 623-9264

Warwick: *The Warwick Advertiser* — 9 Main St.; PO Box 190 (10990); W; 4,888pd, 100fr (Sw); $10.00; C; publisher & editor Stan Martin; tel (914) 986-2061

Warwick: *Warwick Valley Dispatch* — 2 Oakland Ave. (10990); W; 3,109pd, 300fr (Est); 15¢; publisher & editor Betty Jane Wright; tel (914) 986-2216; fax (914) 987-1180

Washington/Northern Rensselaer/Eastern Saratoga Cos.: *The North Country Free Press* — 14 E. Main St.; PO Box 330, Granville (12832); M; 20,000fr (Sw); $8.95; C; publisher John M Manchester; editor Stella Wood; tel (518) 642-1234; fax (518) 642-1344

Washingtonville/Chester: *Orange County Post* — 15 Goshen Ave.; PO Box 341 (10992); Tu; 2,842pd, 150fr (Est); 22¢; publisher & editor John M Spear; tel (914) 496-3611; fax (914) 496-1715

Watkins Glen/Schuyler Co.: *The Watkins Review & Express* — 210 N. Franklin St.; PO Box 112, Watkins Glen (14891); W; 2,874pd (Sw); $3.45; publisher Gary Herzig; editor Glenda Gephart; tel (607) 535-2711; fax (607) 535-2500

Wayne Co.: *Wayne County Mail* — 210 Empire Blvd., Webster (14580); Th; 1,976pd, 224fr (Est); 24¢; publisher James J Gertner; editor Jennifer Callus; tel (716) 671-1533; fax (716) 671-7067

Webster: *The Webster Post* — 40 North Ave. (14580); W; 2,700pd (Est); $6.30; C; publisher & editor Andrew D Wolfe; general manager John S Wolfe; tel (716) 872-2221; fax (716) 872-0494

Webster: *Webster Herald* — 2010 Empire Blvd. (14580); W; 4,761pd, 64fr (Est); $2.81; C; publisher & editor James J Gertner; tel (716) 671-1533; fax (716) 671-7067

W Hempstead: *West Hempstead Beacon* — 1 Jonathan Ave., Hicksville (11801); F; 5,200pd (Sw); $4.90; C; publisher Peter Hoegl; editor Sheila Hoegl Noeth; tel (516) 931-1400

W Seneca: *West Seneca Bee* — 5564 Main St. (14221); PO Box 150, Buffalo (14231-0150); Th; 3,504pd, 300fr (Sw); $16.00; C; publisher Trey Measer; managing editor Dave Sherman; tel (716) 632-4700; fax (716) 633-8601

W Suburban Rochester: *Suburban News* — 1835 N. Union St.; PO Box F, Spencerport (14559); M; 60pd, 31,585fr (CPVS); $13.59; C; publisher Keith A Ryan; editor Evelyn Dow; tel (716) 352-3411; fax (716) 352-4811

W Winfield: *The West Winfield Star* — PO Box 6 (13491); W; 1,221pd, 20fr (Est); 10¢; publisher & editor Wallace Brown; tel (315) 822-3001

Westbury/Carle Place: *Westbury Times* — 132 E. 2nd St.; PO Box 1578, Mineola (11501); Th; 2,777pd, 968fr (Sw); $5.60; C; publisher Karl V Anton Sr; editor Danny McCue; tel (516) 747-8282; fax (516) 742-5867

Westfield: *The Westfield Republican* — 41 E. Main St.; PO Box 38 (14787); Th; 1,295pd, 15fr (Est); $3.10; C; publisher & editor Bob Houston; tel (716) 326-3163; fax (716) 326-3165

Westhampton Beach/Hampton Bays: *The Hampton Chronicle-News* — PO Box 1071, Westhampton Beach (11978); Th; 6,784pd, 206fr (Sw); $1.04; C; publisher Donald H Louchheim; editor W Michael Pitcher; tel (516) 288-1100; fax (516) 288-4965

Whitehall: *The Whitehall Times* — 14 E. Main St.; PO Box 330 (12832); Th; 2,000pd, 75fr (Sw); $7.45; C; publisher John M Manchester; editor Stella Wood; tel (518) 642-1234; fax (518) 642-1344

Whitestone/College Pt.: *The Whitestone Times* — 41-02 Bell Blvd., 2nd Fl., Bayside (11361); Th; 3,680pd (Sw); 60¢; C; publisher & editor Steven Blank; managing editor Roz Liston; tel (718) 229-0300; fax (718) 229-7117

Williamson: *The Williamson Sun & Sentinel* — 4048 Circle Dr.; PO Box 31 (14589-0031); Th; 1,600pd (Est); $2.30; publisher & editor Jean T Cooper; tel (315) 589-4421

Williston Park: *New Hyde Park Herald Courier* — 105 Hillside Ave. (11596); F; 2,030pd (Est); 29¢; publisher & editor M Norris; tel (516) 746-0240

Williston Park: *Williston Times* — 105 Hillside Ave. (11596); F; 2,300pd, 150fr (Est); 39¢; publisher & editor M Norris; tel (516) 746-0240

Windsor/Harpursville: *The Windsor Standard* — 1035 Conklin Rd.; PO Box 208, Conklin (13748); W; 1,297pd, 89fr (Sw); $2.50; C; publisher Donald Einstein; editor Elizabeth Einstein; tel (607) 775-0472; fax (607) 775-5863

Woodhaven: *Leader/Observer* — 80-34 Jamaica Ave. (11421); Th; 5,672pd, 300fr (Est); $9.00; publisher Walter H Sanchez; general manager Scott M Hamilton; tel (718) 296-2200; fax (718) 429-1234

Woodmere: *South Shore Record* — 990 Railroad Ave.; PO Box 330 (11598); Th; 10,513pd, 2,490fr (Sw); 72¢; publisher & editor Florence B Schwartzberg; tel (516) 374-9200; fax (516) 374-9209

Woodside/Long Island City/Sunnyside: *Woodside Herald* — 43-11 Greenpoint Ave., Sunnyside (11104); F; 14,000pd (Est); $5.40; publisher & editor Joseph Sabba; tel (718) 729-3444; fax (718) 729-8614

Woodstock: *Ulster County Townsman* — 18 Rock City Rd.; PO Box 308 (12498); Th; 4,500pd, 150fr (Sw); 12¢; publisher & editor J Blake Killin; tel (914) 679-2145; fax (518) 589-7028

Yonkers: *Yonkers Home News & Times* — 40 Larkin Plz. (10701); Th; 19,215fr (CPVS); $10.00; publisher Ralph R Martinelli; editor Louise Montclare; tel (914) 965-4000; fax (914) 965-2892

Yorktown: *The North County News* — 1520 Front St., Yorktown Heights (10598); W; 9,506pd, 126fr (ABC); $6.88; publisher Cynthia Smith; managing editor Nancy Haggerty; tel (914) 962-4748; fax (914) 962-6763

NORTH CAROLINA

Albemarle: *Stanly News and Press* — 237 W. North St.; PO Box 488 (28002); Tu/Th; 10,848pd, 250fr (Sw); 67¢; Su; 10,685pd, 250fr (Sw); 67¢; C; publisher J LaJeune Waggoner; editor David Deese; tel (704) 982-2121; fax (704) 983-7999

Alleghany Co.: *The Alleghany News* — 108 S. Main St.; PO Box 8, Sparta (28675); Th; 3,900pd, 45fr (Sw); $3.25; C; publisher Alleghany News Publishing Inc.; general manager & managing editor Ron Brown; editor Lynn Worth; tel (910) 372-8999; fax (910) 372-5707

Alleghany/Grayson Cos.: *The Blue Ridge Sun* — W. Whitehead St.; PO Box 757, Sparta (28675); W; 2,750pd, 25fr (Sw); $2.30; C; publisher & editor M B Richardson; managing editor Kathy M Anders; tel (910) 372-5490

Andrews: *The Andrews Journal* — 2nd St.; PO Box 250 (28901); Th; 2,406pd, 65fr (Sw); $5.29; C; publisher Vickie Creasman; editor Jeff Robinson; tel (704) 321-4271; fax (704) 321-5890

Apex: *Apex Herald* — 616 W. Chatham St.; PO Box 1539 (27502); W; 3,177pd (Sw); $6.75; C; publisher Jim Small; editor Mark Todd; tel (919) 362-8356; fax (919) 362-1369

Archdale/Trinity: *The Archdale Trinity News* — 324 Greenoak Dr.; PO Box 4553, Archdale (27263-4553); Th; 3,689pd, 15fr (Sw); $3.55; C; publisher Bennie Harden; editor Michael Feeney; tel (910) 434-2716; fax (910) 841-5165

Ashe Co.: *The Jefferson Post* — 203 S. 2nd St.; PO Box 808, West Jefferson (28694); Tu/Th; 6,481pd, 170fr (Sw); $5.10; C; publisher & editor Sandra G Hurley; tel (910) 246-7164; fax (910) 246-7165

Asheboro/Randolph Co.: *The Randolph Guide* — 431 Fayetteville St.; PO Box Drawer 1044, Asheboro (27204-1044); W; 2,239pd, 550fr (Sw); $5.50; C; publisher Robert M Derr Jr; general manager & editor Kathi Keys; tel (910) 625-5576; fax (910) 625-5577

Belmont/Mt. Holly: *Banner News* — 812 Woodlawn Ave., Belmont (28012); W; 3,069pd, 45fr (Sw); $5.88; C; publisher David Crawley; general manager Mike Shehan; managing editor Jim Heffner; tel (704) 827-7526; fax (704) 827-1037

Bessemer City: *Bessemer City Record* — E. King St. & Canterbury Rd.; PO Box 769, Kings Mountain (28086); W; 879pd, 10fr (Sw); $5.35; C; publisher David Crawley; editor Gary Stewart; tel (704) 739-7496; fax (704) 739-0611

Black Mountain: *Black Mountain News* — 130 Center Ave.; PO Box 9 (28711); Th; 3,178pd, 107fr (Sw); $3.85; publisher & editor James E Aycock; tel (704) 669-8727; fax (704) 669-8619

Blowing Rock: *The Blowing Rocket* — Sunset Dr.; PO Box 1026 (28605); Th; 3,000pd, 200fr (Sw); $3.00; C; publisher William Cummings; editor Jerry Burns; tel (704) 295-7522; fax (704) 295-7507

Boone: *The Mountain Times* — PO Box 1815 (28607); Th; 240pd, 15,100fr (VAC); $5.00; publisher & editor Kenneth Ketchie; tel (704) 264-6397; fax (704) 264-8536

Boone: *Watauga Democrat* — 474 Industrial Park Dr.; PO Box 3050 (28607); M/W/F; 8,576pd, 2,562fr (Sw); $7.40; publisher Armfield Coffey; editor Tim Smith; tel (704) 264-3612; fax (704) 262-0282

Burgaw: *The Pender Chronicle* — 110 Courthouse Ave.; PO Box 726 (28425); W; 4,787pd, 50fr (Sw); $3.75; publisher & editor H L Oswald; tel (910) 259-2504; fax (910) 259-2504

Burgaw: *The Pender Post* — PO Box 955 (28425); W; 4,700pd, 200fr (Sw); $4.00; publisher & editor Patrick A Thomas; tel (910) 259-9111; fax (910) 259-9112

Burnsville: *Times Journal* — PO Box 280 (28714); W; 5,356pd, 300fr (Sw); $4.65; publisher & editor Jody Higgins; general manager Pat Randolph; tel (704) 682-2120; fax (704) 682-3701

Butner/Creedmoor: *The Butner-Creedmoor News* — 418-20 N. Main St.; PO Box 726, Creedmoor (27522); Th; 3,968pd, 79fr (Sw); $5.25; publisher & editor Harry R Coleman; managing editor Bebe Coleman; tel (919) 528-2393; fax (919) 528-0288

Canton/Candler: *The Enterprise* — 119 Main St.; PO Box 268, Canton (28716); W; 1,800pd (Sw); $4.25; publisher Kenneth F Wilson; editor Peggy Gosselin; tel (704) 648-2381

Carolina/New Hanover: *The Island Gazette* — PO Box 183, Carolina Beach (28428); W; 3,500pd, 325fr (Est); $5.00; publisher Beattie McKee; publisher & editor Roger McKee; tel (910) 458-8156

Cary: *The Cary News* — 212 E. Chatham St.; PO Box 4949 (27519-4949); W/Sa; 11,521pd, 100fr (Est); $11.70; publisher Jack Andrews; editor Jane Paige; tel (919) 460-2600; fax (919) 460-6034

Caswell Co.: *Caswell Messenger* — 137 Main St.; PO Box 100, Yanceyville (27379); W; 4,500pd, 40fr (Sw); $6.05; C; publisher Charles A Womack Jr; general manager Patti Gwynn; editor Gordon Bendall; tel (910) 694-4145; fax (910) 694-5637

Chapel Hill: *The Chapel Hill News* — 505 W. Franklin St.; PO Box 870 (27516); W; 85pd, 20,537fr (Sw); $10.60; F; 85pd, 20,455fr (Sw); $10.60; Su; 129pd, 20,608fr (Sw); $10.60; C; publisher & editor Ted Vaden; managing editor Richard Hart; tel (919) 932-2000; fax (919) 968-4953

Charlotte/Mecklenburg: *The Leader* — 801 E. Trade St., 2nd Fl. (28202); PO Box 30486, Charlotte (28230); F; 40,000fr (Sw); $32.00; publisher Stan Kaplan; general manager & editor Richard Hinshaw; managing editor Sis Kaplan; tel (704) 331-4842; fax (704) 347-0358

Charlotte/Mecklenburg: *The Mecklenburg Times* — 400 E. Trade St., Ste. 301; PO Box 36306, Charlotte (28205); Tu/F; 855pd, 45fr (Sw); $5.50; publisher John F Kurie; general manager June D Powell; editor Jill Purdy; tel (704) 377-6221; fax (704) 377-6214

Cherryville: *The Eagle* — 107 E. Main St.; PO Box 699 (28021); W; 2,299pd, 31fr (Sw); $5.35; C; publisher David Crawley; managing editor James Heffner; tel (704) 435-6752; fax (704) 435-8293

Chowan Co.: *The Chowan Herald* — 421 S. Broad St.; PO Box 207, Edenton (27932); Th; 4,378pd, 93fr (Sw); $4.25; publisher E N Manning; editor Cliff Clark; tel (919) 482-4418; fax (919) 482-4410

Clayton: *Clayton News-Star* — 322 W. Main St.; PO Box 157 (27520); Tu; 3,193pd, 60fr (Sw); $4.82; C; publisher Ralph E Delano; editor Michelle Moore; tel (919) 553-7234; fax (919) 553-5858

Clemmons/Lewisville: *The Clemmons Courier* — PO Box 765, Clemmons (27012); Th; 2,760pd, 50fr (Sw); $5.00; C; publisher & editor Dwight Sparks; tel (910) 766-4126

Cleveland Co.: *Cleveland Times* — 205 S. Washington St.; PO Box 1029, Shelby (28151); Th; 1,354pd, 5fr (Sw); $5.35; C; publisher David Crawley; editor Gary Stewart; tel (704) 481-8202; fax (704) 481-1031

Columbia: *East Carolina Reminder* — PO Box 1788, Washington (27889); W; 4,730fr (Sw); $3.75; publisher Ashley B Futrell Jr; editor Mark Inabinett; tel (919) 946-2144; fax (919) 946-9797

Danbury/Stokes Co.: *The Danbury Reporter* — PO Box 647, Walnut Cove (27052); W; 5,078pd, 30fr (Sw); $5.90; C; publisher Turk Tergliafera; editor Denise Styers Petree; tel (910) 591-8191; fax (910) 591-4379

Denton: *Denton Record* — 142 W. Salisbury St.; PO Box 308 (27239-0308); Th; 2,303pd, 34fr (Sw); $3.60; publishers & editors Ed Wallace & Venus Wallace; tel (704) 869-4575

Elkin/Jonesville: *The Tribune/The Tribune Advertiser* — 214 E. Main St.; PO Box 1009, Elkin (28621); M/W/F; 5,950pd, 160fr (Sw); $5.30; C; publisher R Fletcher Good IV; editor Bill Watson; tel (910) 835-1513; fax (910) 835-8742

Fairmont: *The Times-Messenger* — 107 W. Thompson St.; PO Box 684 (28340); Th; 1,106pd, 653fr (Sw); $2.80; publisher Herald Publishing Co. of N.C.; editor Betty Overturf; tel (910) 628-7125

Farmville: *Farmville Enterprise* — 126 Main St.; PO Box 247 (27828); W; 2,905pd, 29fr (Sw); $3.15; C; publisher & editor Robert A Stephens; tel (919) 753-4126; fax (919) 753-4127

Forsyth Co.: *The Weekly Independent* — 8170 Depot St.; PO Box 806, Rural Hall (27045); Th; 1,500pd, 100fr (Sw); $4.25; C; publisher Turk Tergliafera; editor Laura Knight; tel (910) 969-6076/9548; fax (910) 969-9390

Four Oaks/Johnston: *Four Oaks-Benson News in Review* — 113 S. Market St.; PO Box 9, Benson (27504-0009); W; 4,500pd (Est); $4.10; publisher Ralph E Delano; general manager Norman Delano; editor Carey Wilson; tel (919) 894-3331; fax (919) 894-1069

Franklin/Macon Co.: *The Franklin Press* — 246 Depot St.; PO Box 350, Franklin (28734); W/F; 7,541pd, 21fr (Sw); $9.00; publisher Kenneth Hudgins; editor Scott McRae; tel (704) 524-2010; fax (704) 524-8821

Fremont/Wayne: *Wayne-Wilson News Leader* — 113 N. Wilson St.; PO Box 158, Fremont (27830); W; 720pd, 63fr (Sw); $3.59; C; publisher & editor Barry Merrill; tel (919) 242-6301; fax (919) 965-5903

Fuquay-Varina/Wake: *Fuquay-Varina Independent* — PO Box 669, Fuquay-Varina (27526); W; 4,385pd (Est); $6.75; C; publisher James S Smale; editor Suzette Rodriquez; tel (919) 552-5675; fax (919) 552-7564

Garner: *Garner News* — 503-L US Hwy. 702; PO Box 466 (27529); W; 5,155pd (Sw); $6.75; C; publisher James S Smale; tel (919) 772-8747, (919) 772-1166; fax (919) 779-7824

Gates Co.: *Gates County Index* — PO Box 146, Gatesville (27938); W; 2,450pd, 60fr (Sw); $9.00; publisher Park Newspapers Inc.; general manager Joseph N Vaughan; editor Helene Knight; managing editor Joe Vaughan; tel (919) 357-0960; fax (919) 332-3940

Graham Co.: *The Graham Star* — 129 By Pass; PO Box 68, Robbinsville (28771); Th; 3,207pd, 24fr (Sw); $4.50; C; publisher Weaver Carringer; editor Kate Henry; tel (704) 479-3383; fax (704) 479-3383

Graham/Alamance Co.: *The Alamance News* — 114 W. Elm St.; PO Box 431, Graham (27253); Th; 7,252pd, 843fr (ABC); $6.89; publisher & editor Thomas E Boney Jr; tel (910) 228-7851

Havelock/Cherry Pt.: *The Havelock News* — 230 Stonebridge Sq.; PO Box 777, Havelock (28532); Th; 3,000pd, 21fr (Sw); $4.97; publisher Joe R Browning; editor Tom Kovac; tel (919) 444-1999; fax (919) 447-0897

Hertford Co.: *The News Herald* — 801 Parker Ave.; PO Box 1325, Ahoskie (27910); M/W/F; 6,276pd, 30fr (Sw); $4.92; publisher & editor Joseph N Vaughan; managing editor Jay Jenkins; tel (919) 332-2123; fax (919) 332-3940

Hertford/Perquimans Co.: *The Perquimans Weekly* — 119 W. Grubb St.; PO Box 277, Hertford (27944); Th; 1,781pd, 73fr (Sw); $4.16; publisher Richard D Brown; editor Susan Harris; tel (919) 426-5728; fax (919) 335-4415

Hickory/Catawba: *The Hickory News* — PO Box 2650, Hickory (28603); Th; 4,260pd, 450fr (Sw); $4.95; C; publisher & editor Charles H Deal; tel (704) 328-6164; fax (704) 322-6398

Highlands: *The Highlander* — PO Box 249 (28741); Tu/F; 3,700pd, 40fr (Est); $5.83; publisher & editor Ralph W Morris; tel (704) 526-4114; fax (704) 526-3658

Hillsborough: *The News of Orange County* — 106 S. Churton St.; PO Box 580 (27278); W; 4,174pd, 100fr (Sw); $6.00; C; publisher Charles A Womack Jr; general manager David Jones; editor Jonathan Butler; tel (919) 732-2171; fax (919) 732-4852

Jamestown/Guilford: *Jamestown News* — 107-B Wade St.; PO Box 307, Jamestown (27282); W; 1,860pd, 20fr (Est); $5.00; C; publisher & editor Charles A Womack III; tel (910) 841-4933; fax (910) 841-4953

Johnston Co.: *The Smithfield Herald* — 125 S. 4th St.; PO Box 1417, Smithfield (27577); Tu/F; 14,169pd, 753fr (Sw); $9.50; publisher Eddie Thorndyke; managing editor Scott Bolejack; tel (919) 934-2176; fax (919) 989-7093

Kenly/Johnston: *Kenly News* — 201 W. 2nd St.; PO Box 39, Kenly (27542); W; 2,927pd, 180fr (Sw); $3.50; publisher & editor Richard D Stewart; tel (919) 284-2295; fax (919) 284-6397

Kernersville/Walkertown: *Kernersville News* — 300 E. Mountain; PO Box 337, Kernersville (27284); Tu; 13,900fr (Sw); $15.41; Th; 6,000pd (Sw); $10.93; Sa; 6,000pd (Sw); $7.97; C; publisher John Owensby; editor John Staples; tel (910) 993-2161

King/Stokes Co.: *The King Times-News* — 141 Pineview Dr.; PO Box 545, King (27021); Th; 5,850pd, 360fr (Sw); $7.10; C; publisher Turk Tergliafera; editor Karen McConkey; tel (910) 983-3109; fax (910) 983-8203

Kings Mountain: *Kings Mountain Herald* — E. King; PO Box 769 (28086); Th; 4,021pd, 95fr (Sw); $5.88; C; publisher David Crawley; editor Gary Stewart; tel (704) 739-7496; fax (704) 739-0611

LaGrange: *Weekly Gazette* — 108 S. Caswell St. (28551); W; 1,220pd, 25fr (Sw); $3.00; publisher & editor Glenn Penuel; tel (919) 566-3028; fax (919) 566-3345

Lillington: *Harnett County News* — 407 Main St.; PO Box 939 (27546); W; 2,851pd (Est); $3.75; C; publisher Harnett County News Inc.; editor David Snipes; tel (910) 893-5121; fax (910) 893-6128

Lincolnton: *Lincoln Times-News* — 119 W. Water St.; PO Box 40 (28092); M/W/F; 10,407pd (Sw); $7.05; C; publisher & editor Jerry G Leedy; general manager Jerilyn L Setser; managing editor Kathryn Yarbro; tel (704) 735-3031; fax (704) 735-3037

Littleton/Lake Gaston: *The Littleton Observer* — 101 E. South Main St.; PO Box 417, Littleton (27850); Th; 1,000pd, 50fr (Sw); $4.00; publisher Hal Sharpe; editor Patrick Brannan; tel (919) 586-6397

Louisburg/Franklinton/Youngsville: *The Franklin Times* — 109 S. Bickett Blvd.; PO Box 119, Louisburg (27549); W/Sa; 7,420pd, 416fr (Sw); $6.49; publisher & editor Gary R Cunard; tel (919) 496-6503; fax (919) 496-1689

Madison/Mayodan: *The Messenger* — 208 W. Murphy St.; PO Box 508, Madison (27025); W/F; 4,994pd, 41fr (Sw); $5.00; C; publisher & editor Bruce Webb; tel (910) 548-6047; fax (910) 548-2853

Manteo/Dare: *The Coastland Times* — 501 Budleigh St.; PO Box 400, Manteo (27954); Tu/Th; 8,956pd, 50fr (Sw); $5.60; Su; 8,957pd, 50fr (Sw); $5.60; publisher Times Printing Co. Inc.; editor Francis W Meekins; managing editor David L Schulty; tel (919) 473-2105; fax (919) 473-1515

Mars Hill: *Mountain Advisor* — 106-108 N. Main; PO Box 190 (28754); F; 5,471pd, 650fr (Sw); $2.65; publisher & editor Ed Howard; tel (704) 689-4612; fax (704) 689-4511

Martin Co.: *The Enterprise* — 108 W. Main St.; PO Box 387, Williamston (27892); Tu/Th; 5,261pd, 35fr (Sw); $4.00; C; publisher Dallas F Coltrain; managing editor Bobby Burns; tel (919) 792-1181; fax (919) 792-1921

Mebane/Haw River/Efland: *The Mebane Enterprise* — 106 N. 4th St., Mebane (27302); W; 1,332pd, 154fr (Sw); $5.50; C; publisher Charles A Womack Jr; general manager Lynn Brooks; editor Kitty Brandon; tel (919) 563-3555; fax (919) 563-9242

Mecklenburg/Lake Norman: *The Mecklenburg Gazette* — 108 S. Main St.; PO Box 549, Davidson (28036); W; 4,500pd (Sw); $3.72; publisher Park Newspapers Inc.; general manager Nick Carrington; managing editor Carolyn Knauer; tel (704) 892-8809; fax (704) 892-8810

Mocksville/Davie Co.: *Davie County Enterprise Record* — 171 S. Main St.; PO Box 525, Mocksville (27028); Th; 7,843pd, 32fr (Sw); $5.50; C; publisher & editor Dwight Sparks; tel (704) 634-2129

Montgomery Co.: *Montgomery Herald* — 139 Bruton St.; PO Box 426, Troy (27371); W; 6,890pd, 157fr (Sw); $5.70; publisher R Guy Hankins; editor Gary L Evans; tel (910) 576-6051; fax (910) 576-1050

Mooresville/Lake Norman: *Mooresville Tribune* — 147 E. Center Ave.; PO Box 300, Mooresville (28115); W; 7,647fr (Sw); $5.35; C; publisher Park Newspapers Inc.; general manager Nick Carrington; managing editor Annette Privette; tel (704) 664-5554; fax (704) 664-3614

Morehead City/Beaufort: *Carteret County News-Times* — 4034 Arendell St.; PO Box 1679, Morehead City (28557); W/F; 11,884pd (Est); $9.00; Su; 12,317pd (ABC); $9.00; C; publisher & general manager Lockwood Phillips; publisher & editor Walter D Phillips; managing editor Loyd Little; tel (919) 726-7081; fax (919) 726-6016

Mt. Olive: *Mount Olive Tribune* — 301 W. Highway 55; Box 709 (28365); Tu/F; 4,086pd, 103fr (Sw); $5.90; publisher Sterling Pierce; editor Steve Herring; tel (919) 658-9456; fax (919) 658-9559

Murphy: *Cherokee Scout* — 1st Church St.; PO Box 190 (28906); W; 7,681pd, 175fr (Sw); $7.36; C; publisher Weaver Carringer; editor Patty Little; tel (704) 837-5122; fax (704) 837-5832

Nash Co.: *The Nashville Graphic* — 106 N. Boddie St.; PO Box 1008, Nashville (27856); W/F; 2,691pd, 192fr (Sw); $5.00; C; publisher & editor Hal C Sharpe; general manager Sam Taylor; tel (919) 459-7101; fax (919) 459-3052

Newland: *Avery Journal* — PO Box 1330 (28657); Th; 6,981pd, 280fr (Sw); $5.00; publisher Mike Blanton; editor Bertie Burleson; tel (704) 733-2448; fax (704) 733-0639

N Wake: *The Wake Weekly* — 229 E. Owen Ave. (27587); PO Box 1919, Wake Forest (27588); Th; 7,048pd, 30fr (Sw); $8.15; publisher R W Allen; editor Margaret G Allen; tel (919) 556-3182; fax (919) 556-2233

N Wilkesboro/Wilkes Co.: *The Journal-Patriot* — 711 Main St.; PO Box 70, North Wilkesboro (28659); M/Th; 17,400pd, 270fr (Sw); 33¢; C; publishers JC Hubbard Jr & John W Hubbard; editor Charles Williams; tel (910) 838-4117; fax (910) 838-9864

Oxford/Granville Co.: *Oxford Public Ledger* — 200 W. Spring St.; PO Box 643, Oxford (27565); M/Th; 6,390pd, 60fr (Sw); $4.50; publisher Charles Critcher; editor Johnny Whitfield; tel (919) 693-2646; fax (919) 693-3704

Pamlico: *The Pamlico News* — PO Box 510, Oriental (28571); W; 3,560pd, 60fr (Est); $4.00; publisher Henry G Winfrey; editor Sallie R Winfrey; tel (919) 249-1555; fax (919) 249-0857

Person Co.: *The Courier-Times Inc.* — 109 Clayton Ave.; PO Box 311, Roxboro (27573); W/Sa; 7,697pd, 67fr (Sw); $5.60; publisher Jerry M Clayton; editor Neal Rattican; tel (910) 599-0162; fax (910) 597-2773

Plymouth/Roper/Creswell: *The Roanoke Beacon* — 210 W. Water St.; PO Box 726, Plymouth (27962); W; 4,478pd (Sw); $3.14; publisher Hope G Jones; editor Doward N Jones Jr; tel (919) 793-2123

Polk Co.: *Polk County News Journal* — PO Box 576, Columbus (28722); W; 2,500pd, 220fr (Sw); $3.85; C; publisher John F Lawrence; editor Robert Balme; tel (704) 894-3220

Princeton/Johnston: *Princeton News-Leader* — 109 Center St.; PO Box 597, Princeton (27569); W; 776pd, 267fr (Sw); $3.59; C; publisher & editor Barry Merrill; tel (919) 936-9891; fax (919) 965-5903

Raeford: *The News Journal* — 119 W. Elwood Ave.; PO Box 550 (28376); W; 4,500pd, 132fr (Sw); $5.04; C; publisher Louis H Fogleman Jr; general manager & editor Ken MacDonald; tel (910) 875-2121; fax (910) 875-7256

Ramseur/Randolph Co.: *The Bulletin* — 741 Liberty St.; PO Drawer 1060, Ramseur (27316-1060); Th; 1,803pd, 84fr (Sw); $5.25; C; publisher & editor Chip Womick; tel (910) 824-2231; fax (910) 625-5577

Randelman/Randolph Co.: *The Randleman Reporter* — 125 W. Academy, Randleman (27317); W; 1,198pd, 163fr (Sw); $5.25; C; publisher Robert M Derr Jr; general manager & editor Sandra Cooper; tel (910) 498-4151; fax (910) 498-4152

Red Springs: *The Red Springs Citizen* — W. 4th Ave.; PO Box 72 (28377); W; 2,700pd, 5,000fr (Est); $3.00; C; publisher Stewart McLeod; editor Barbara Rhodes; tel (910) 843-8171, (910) 843-4631; fax (910) 865-4995

Richlands/Beulaville: *Richlands-Beulaville Advertiser News* — 107 N. College St.; PO Box 699, Wallace (28466); W; 2,299pd, 20fr (Sw); $3.75; publisher H L Oswald III; general manager A L Reyer; tel (910) 285-2178; fax (910) 285-3179

Robersonville: *The Weekly Herald* — PO Box 387, Williamston (27892); W; 530pd, 10fr (Sw); $2.45; publisher Dallas F Coltrain; editor Bobby Burns; tel (919) 792-1181; fax (919) 792-1921

Rutherford Co.: *County News Enterprise* — 218 W. 1st St.; PO Box 800, Rutherfordton (28139-0800); W; 9,000fr (Est); $5.60; publisher Jim Duffy; editor Jean Gordon; tel (704) 287-3327; fax (704) 287-9371

St. Pauls/Parkton: *The St. Pauls Review* — 220 W. Broad St.; PO Box 265, St. Pauls (28384); Th; 2,850pd (Est); $3.00; C; publisher Stewart McLeod; editor Paul Terry; tel (910) 865-4179; fax (910) 865-4995

Scotland Neck/Enfield: *Commonwealth Progress* — 1701 Main St.; PO Box 40, Scotland Neck (27874); W; 1,300pd, 5,000fr (Est); $7.00; publisher Joe Vaughan; editor Sylvia Hughes; tel (919) 826-2111; fax (919) 826-2111

Selma: *The Johnstonian-Sun* — 101 N. Webb St.; PO Box 278 (27576); Th; 2,122pd, 504fr (Sw); $3.59; C; publisher & editor Barry W Merrill; tel (919) 965-2033; fax (919) 965-5903

Shallotte: *The Brunswick Beacon* — 106 Cheers St.; PO Box 2558 (28459); Th; 14,222pd, 10fr (Sw); $6.76; publisher Carolyn H Sweatt & Edward M Sweatt; editor Lynn Sweatt Carlson; tel (910) 754-6890; fax (910) 754-5407

Siler City: *The Chatham News* — 303 W. Raleigh; PO Box 290 (27344); Th; 4,745pd, 175fr (Sw); $4.40; publisher & editor Alan D Resch; tel (919) 663-3232; fax (919) 663-4042

Snow Hill: *Snow Hill Standard Laconic* — 402 S.E. 2nd St.; PO Box 128 (28580); W; 3,226pd, 651fr (Est); $3.70; publisher Nelson D Adams; editor Peggy Greene; tel (919) 747-3883; fax (919) 747-7656

Southern Pines/Moore Co.: *The Pilot* — 145 Pennsylvania Ave.; PO Box 58, Southern Pines (28388); M/Th; 15,980pd (Sw); $4.25; publisher & editor Sam Ragan; tel (910) 692-7271; fax (910) 692-9382

Southport/Long Beach: *The State Port Pilot* — 105 S. Howe St.; PO Box 10548, Southport (28461-0548); W; 7,704pd, 35fr (Sw); $5.75; publisher The State Port Pilot Inc.; editor Ed Harper; tel (910) 457-4568; fax (910) 457-9427

Spring Hope/Bailey/Middlesex: *Spring Hope Enterprise & The Bailey News* — 113 Ash St.; PO Box 399, Spring Hope (27882); Th; 2,370pd, 700fr (Sw); $6.00; publisher & editor Ken Ripley; tel (919) 478-3651; fax (919) 478-3075

Spruce Pine Mitchell: *Mitchell News-Journal* — 401 Locust Ave.; PO Box 339, Spruce Pine (28777); W; 6,279pd (Sw); $6.25; publisher Rick Bacon; editor Rachel Hoskins; tel (704) 765-2071; fax (704) 765-1616

Swansboro/Cape Carteret/Emerald Isle/Cedar Pt./Bogue/Kubert: *Tideland News* — 101-2 Church St.; PO Box 1098, Swansboro (28584); W; 2,171pd, 327fr (Sw); $4.10; C; publisher Eleanore D Phillips; editor J Sharpe Williams Jr; tel (910) 326-5066; fax (910) 326-1165

Sylva/Jackson: *The Sylva Herald & Ruralite* — 24 E. Main St.; PO Box 307, Sylva (28779); Th; 6,954pd, 46fr (Sw); $5.32; publisher J A Gray; editor Angela Griffin Nicholas; tel (704) 586-2611; fax (704) 586-2637

Tabor City/Loris (SC): *The Tabor City Tribune* — Highway 701 Business N.; PO Box 67, Tabor City (28463); W; 2,702pd, 748fr (Est); $3.50; publisher W Horace Carter; editor Deuce Niven; tel (910) 653-3153; fax (910) 653-9440

Taylorsville: *The Taylorsville Times* — 106 E. Main St.; PO Box 279 (28681); W; 6,606pd, 82fr (Sw); $3.70; publisher Lee Sharpe; editor David Icenhour; tel (704) 632-2532; fax (704) 632-8233

Thomasville/Davidson Co.: *The Thomasville Times* — 512 Turner St.; PO Box 549, Thomasville (27360); Tu/Th/Sa; 6,434pd, 212fr (ABC); $7.95; publisher Robert M Schoolfield; editor Sarah Sue Ingram; tel (910) 472-9500; fax (910) 476-7272

Transylvania Co.: *The Transylvania Times* — 100 N. Broad St.; PO Box 32, Brevard (28712); M/Th; 7,638pd, 91fr (Sw); $4.50; publisher & editor Stella A Trapp; tel (704) 883-8156; fax (704) 883-8158

Trenton: *The Jones Post* — PO Box 1788, Washington (77889); Th; 668pd (Sw); $2.25; publisher Ashley B Futrell Jr; editor Mark Inabinett; tel (919) 946-2144; fax (919) 946-9797

Union/Anson Cos.: *The Home News* — 123 E. Union St.; PO Box 100, Marshville (28103); Th; 139fr (Sw); $3.95; publisher Beaver Dam Press Inc.; editor Rosemary Osborn; tel (704) 624-5068

Valdese/E Burke Co.: *The Valdese News* — PO Box 280, Morgantown (28680-0280); W; 585pd, 1,800fr (Sw); $2.90; C; publisher & editor H Eugene Willard; tel (704) 437-2161; fax (704) 437-5372

Wadesboro/Anson: *The Anson Record* — 210 E. Morgan St.; PO Box 959, Wadesboro (28170); W; 6,800pd, 15fr (Est); $5.20; C; publisher Michael C Leonard; editor Sandra Z Bruney; tel (704) 694-2161; fax (704) 694-7060

Wake Forest: *The Wake Weekly* — 229 E. Owen Ave.; PO Box 1919 (27588); Th; 7,047pd, 200fr (Sw); $8.15; publisher Robert W Allen Sr; editor Margaret G Allen; managing editor James W Allen; tel (919) 556-3182; fax (919) 556-2233

Wallace: *Wallace Enterprise* — 113-115 N. College St.; PO Box 699 (28466); M/Th; 6,034pd (Sw); $5.00; publisher H L Oswald; editor Sammie W Carter; tel (910) 285-2178; fax (910) 285-3179

Warrenton: *The Warren Record* — 123 S. Main St.; PO Box 70 (27589-0070); W; 5,636pd, 35fr (Sw); $4.00; publisher Record Printing Co.; editor Howard F Jones; tel (919) 257-1200; fax (919) 257-1413

Warsaw: *Warsaw-Faison News* — Clark Shopping Center, College St.; PO Box 427 (28398); Th; 3,385pd, 200fr (Sw); $3.75; publisher H L Oswald; editor Sammie W Carter; tel (910) 293-4534; fax (910) 285-3179

Waynesville/Haywood Co.: *The Mountaineer* — 413 N. Main St.; PO Drawer 129, Waynesville (28786); M/W/F; 11,460pd, 236fr (ABC); $8.75; C; publisher Kenneth F Wilson; editor Scott McLeod; tel (704) 452-0661; fax (704) 452-0665

Wendell/Knightdale: *Gold Leaf Farmer* — 10 S. Main St.; PO Box 400, Wendell (27591); Th; 2,630pd, 225fr (Sw); $5.67; C; publisher Mark Wilson; editor Matt Shaw; tel (919) 365-6262; fax (919) 269-8383

Whiteville/Columbus Co.: *The News Reporter* — 127 W. Columbus St.; PO Box 707, Whiteville (28472); M/Th; 9,134pd, 440fr (Est); $6.25; C; publisher & editor James C High; tel (910) 642-4104; fax (910) 642-1856

Windsor: *Bertie Ledger-Advance* — 124 S. King St.; PO Drawer 69 (27983-0069); Th; 3,885pd, 27fr (Sw); $3.35; publisher & editor Laura Harrell; tel (919) 794-3185; fax (919) 794-2835

Yadkin Co./Elkin: *The Enterprise* — PO Box 1460, Yadkinville (27055); W; 14,238fr (Est); $5.90; C; publisher Turk Tergliafera; editor Barbara Harding; tel (910) 679-4900; fax (910) 679-7355

Yadkinville: *The Yadkin Ripple* — 115 Jackson St.; PO Box 7 (27055); Th; 5,800pd, 100fr (Sw); $4.00; publisher Craig Rutledge; editor Charles Mathis; tel (910) 679-2341; fax (910) 679-2340

Zebulon: *The Zebulon Record* — 110 Arendell Ave.; PO Box 1167 (27597); Th; 3,252pd, 137fr (Est); $5.67; C; publisher Mark Wilson; editor Marty Coward; tel (919) 269-6101; fax (919) 269-8383

NORTH DAKOTA

Aneta: *Aneta Star* — PO Box 157, Fordville (58231); Th; 497pd (Est); 14¢; C; publisher Gunnard Ness; editor Truman Ness; tel (701) 229-3641; fax (701) 229-3217

Ashley: *The Ashley Tribune* — 119 W. Main St.; PO Box 178 (58413); W; 1,728pd, 27fr (Sw); $3.25; C; publishers Thomas E Lovik & Wanda L Lovik; managing editor Patrick Kellar; tel (701) 288-3531; fax (701) 288-3531

Beach: *The Golden Valley News* — 97 E. Main; PO Box 156 (58621); Th; 1,160pd, 50fr (Sw); $5.00; C; publisher Dennis K Kelly; general manager & editor Mary Melvin; tel (701) 872-3755; fax (701) 872-3756

Benson Co.: *Benson County Farmers Press* — 120 B Ave. N.; PO Box 98, Minnewaukan (58351); W; 2,649pd, 415fr (Sw); $3.90; publisher & editor Richard M Peterson; tel (701) 473-5436; fax (701) 473-5436

Beulah: *Beulah Beacon* — 324 2nd Ave. N.E. (58523); W; 2,448pd, 44fr (Sw); $4.50; C; publisher Mike Gackle; general manager Ken Beauchamp; editor Nancy Northrup; tel (701) 873-4381; fax (701) 873-2383

Bottineau: *The Bottineau Courant* — 419 Main St.; PO Box 29 (58318); Tu; 3,481pd, 91fr (Est); $3.63; publisher Mike Getzloff; editor Terry Aman; tel (701) 228-2605; fax (701) 228-5864

Bowbells: *Burke County Tribune* — PO Box 40 (58721); W; 1,583pd, 77fr (Sw); 26¢; publisher & editor Rhoda Greenup; tel (701) 377-2626

Bowman: *Bowman County Pioneer* — PO Drawer F (58623-0018); F; 1,700pd (Est); $3.75; publisher Jeff Schumacher; editor Angie Kelly; tel (701) 523-5623; fax (701) 523-3441

Cando: *Towner County Record Herald* — 423 Main St. (58324); Sa; 2,100pd, 75fr (Est); $3.64; publisher & editor R G Denison; tel (701) 968-3223; fax (701) 968-3345

Carson/Grant Co./Sioux-Flasher/Cannon Ball/Salem Selfridge: *Carson Press* — 119 Main; PO Box 100, Elgin (58533); W; 997pd (Sw); $3.00; publisher & editor Duane Schatz; publisher Gail Schatz; tel (701) 584-2900

Casselton: *Cass County Reporter* — 122 N. 6th Ave.; PO Box 190 (58012); W; 3,106pd, 50fr (Sw); $4.22; publishers Cheryl Kelly & Shaun Kelly; general manager Grace Thoemke; editor Michael L Utt; tel (701) 347-4493; fax (701) 347-4495

Cavalier: *The Cavalier Chronicle* — 207 Main St. W.; PO Box 20 (58220); W; 2,871pd, 20fr (Est); 24¢; C; publisher & editor Lynn Schroeder; tel (701) 265-8844; fax (701) 265-8089

Center: *Center Republican* — PO Box 340, Washburn (58577); Th; 647pd, 18fr (Est); $4.00; C; publisher Mike Gackle; editor Lucille Gullickson; tel (701) 462-8126; fax (701) 462-8128

Cooperstown/Griggs Co.: *Griggs County Sentinel-Courier* — PO Box 525, Cooperstown (58425); F; 1,800pd, 106fr (Est); $3.60; publisher Bill Devlin; editor Lois Saxberg; tel (701) 797-3331; fax (701) 797-3476

Crosby: *The Journal* — 217 N. Main; PO Box E (58730); W; 2,900pd, 30fr (Sw); $5.00; publisher & editor Steve Andrist; tel (701) 965-6088

Drayton: *Valley News & Views* — PO Box 309 (58225); Th; 859pd, 17fr (Est); $3.75; publisher & editor Lyle VanCamp; general manager Roberta VanCamp; tel (701) 454-6333; fax (701) 454-6333

Drayton/Gilby: *Drayton Express* — PO Box 157, Fordville (58231); Th; 650pd (Est); 14¢; C; publisher Gunnard Ness; editor Truman Ness; tel (701) 229-3641; fax (701) 229-3217

Edgeley: *Edgeley Mail* — PO Box 278 (58433); W; 1,154pd, 57fr (Sw); $4.00; publisher & editor Patty Wood Bartle; tel (701) 493-2261

Edmore: *Edmore Herald* — Main St. (58330); Th; 534pd (Est); 14¢; C; publisher Gunnard Ness; editor Truman Ness; tel (701) 229-3641; fax (701) 229-3217

Elgin/Carson/New Leipzig-Raleigh/Sheilds/Grant Co.: *The Grant County News* — 119 Main; PO Box 100, Elgin (58533); W; 1,376pd (Sw); $3.00; publisher & editor Duane Schatz; publisher Gail Schatz; tel (701) 584-2900; fax (701) 584-2900

Ellendale: *Dickey County Leader* — 216 Main St.; PO Box 9 (58436); Th; 1,225pd, 44fr (Est); $4.05; C; publisher Kelly Publishing Inc.; editor Livy Hird; tel (701) 349-3222; fax (701) 349-3229

Enderlin: *Enderlin Independent* — 209 4th Ave. (58027); W; 1,000pd, 49fr (Sw); $3.25; C; publisher & editor Ruth E McCleerey; tel (701) 437-3131; fax (701) 437-3131

Fairmount/Hankinson/Lidgerwood/Wynemere: *Richland County News-Monitor* — PO Box 190, Hankinson (58041); W; 2,800pd (Est); $4.30; C; publisher Newell Grant; editor Karen Leshovsky; tel (701) 242-7696; fax (701) 242-7406

Finley/Steele Co.: *Steele County Press* — PO Box 475, Finley (58230); Sa; 1,550pd, 3,800fr (Est); $4.30; publisher & editor William R Devlin; tel (701) 524-1640; fax (701) 524-2221

Fordville: *Fordville Tri-County Sun* — PO Box 157 (58231); Th; 876pd (Est); 14¢; C; publisher Gunnard Ness; editor Truman Ness; tel (701) 229-3641; fax (701) 229-3217

Garrison: *McLean County Independent* — 91 N. Main St.; PO Box 309 (58540-0309); W; 3,385pd, 77fr (Sw); $4.50; publisher Donald C Gackle; general manager Michael W Gackle; editor Alan Reed; tel (701) 463-2201; fax (701) 463-7487

Grafton: *The Walsh County Record* — 402 Hill Ave.; PO Box 471 (58237-0471); Tu; 3,834pd, 132fr (Sw); $4.35; C; publisher Jackie L Thompson; editor John A Strand; tel (701) 352-0640

Harvey: *The Herald-Press* — 1015 Lincoln Ave. (58341); M; 3,734pd (Est); 17¢; publisher Charles Eldredge; general manager Janine Schmitz; tel (701) 324-4646

Hatton/Traill: *Hatton Free Press* — PO Box 157, Fordville (58231); Th; 823pd, 23fr (Est); $2.83; publisher Gunnard Ness; editor Truman Ness; tel (701) 229-3641; fax (701) 229-3217

Hazen: *The Hazen Star* — 26 E. Main; PO Box 508 (58545); Th; 2,152pd, 34fr (Est); $3.85; C; publisher BHG Inc.; general manager Ken Beauchamp; editor Lauren Donovan; tel (701) 748-2255

Hebron: *Hebron Herald* — 102 S. Park St.; PO Box 9 (58638); W; 1,136pd, 46fr (Sw); $4.00; publisher Jane Brandt; tel (701) 878-4494; fax (701) 878-4494

Hillsboro/Traill Co.: *Hillsboro Banner* — 20 W. Caledonia Ave.; PO Box 39, Hillsboro (58045); M; 1,426pd, 35fr (Sw); $5.22; publisher Gorman King Jr; general manager Ruth Johnson; editor Valerie Coit; tel (701) 436-4241; fax (701) 436-4245

Kenmare: *The Kenmare News* — 20 N.W. 2nd St.; PO Box 894 (58746); W; 2,370pd, 20fr (Est); $3.00; publisher & editor Terry Froseth; tel (701) 385-4275; fax (701) 385-4395

Kidder Co.: *The Steele Ozone-Press* — PO Box 350, Steele (58482); W; 1,596pd (Sw); $3.90; publisher & editor Bruce Kalmbach; tel (701) 475-2513

Killdeer/Halliday: *Dunn County Herald* — 318 S.E. Central Ave.; PO Box 609, Killdeer (58640-0609); F; 1,302pd, 22fr (Sw); $4.81; C; publisher & editor Flyyn J Ell; general manager Gloria Kukla; tel (701) 764-5312; fax (701) 764-5049

Kulm: *Kulm Messenger* — PO Box J (58456); W; 941pd, 37fr (Sw); $3.25; C; publisher & editor Gerald P Harris; tel (701) 647-2411

La Moure Co.: *La Moure Chronicle* — 11 S. Main St.; PO Box 196, La Moure (58458); W; 1,295pd, 15fr (Sw); $3.25; C; publishers & editors Gerald P Harris & Ruth Harris; tel (701) 883-5393

Langdon/Cavalier Co.: *Cavalier County Republican* — 710 3rd St., Langdon (58249); M; 2,414pd, 97fr (Sw); $5.75; publisher & editor Marv Baker; tel (701) 256-5311; fax (701) 256-5841

Larimore: *Larimore Leader* — PO Box 157, Fordville (58231); Th; 731pd (Est); 14¢; C; publisher Gunnard Ness; editor Truman Ness; tel (701) 229-3641; fax (701) 229-3217

Linton: *Emmons County Record* — 201 N. Broadway; PO Box 38 (58552); Tu; 2,645pd, 65fr (Sw); $3.75; publisher & editor Allan C Burke; publisher Leah Burke; tel (701) 254-4537; fax (701) 254-4909

Lisbon: *The Ransom County Gazette* — 310 Main St.; PO Box 473 (58054); M; 3,115pd, 65fr (Est); $1.85; publisher & editor Sean W Kelly; general manager Cheryl Kelly; tel (701) 683-4128; fax (701) 683-4129

Mandan/Morton: *The Morton Co. & Mandan News* — 303 1st St. N.E.; PO Box 908, Mandan (58554); Th; 1,954pd, 100fr (Est); $6.50; C; publisher Ken Elias; editor Richard Hinton; tel (701) 663-6823; fax (701) 662-2442

Mayville/Portland: *Traill County Tribune* — 130 S. Center Ave.; PO Box 567, Mayville (58257); Sa; 2,458pd, 5fr (Sw); $5.00; publisher Tom Dutcher; editor Jeri Hird Dutcher; tel (701) 786-3281; fax (701) 786-3287

McVille: *McVille Messenger* — PO Box 157, Fordville (58231); Th; 484pd (Est); $2.83; C; publisher Gunnard Ness; editor Truman Ness; tel (701) 229-3641; fax (701) 229-3217

Medora: *Billings County Pioneer* — PO Box 156, Beach (58621); Th; 650pd, 40fr (Est); $3.75; C; publisher Dennis Kelly; general manager & editor Mary Melvin; tel (701) 872-3755; fax (701) 872-3756

Michigan: *Nelson County Arena* — PO Box 157, Fordville (58231); Th; 996pd (Est); 14¢; C; publisher Gunnard Ness; editor Truman Ness; tel (701) 229-3641; fax (701) 229-3217

Mohall/Lansford/Sherwood: *Renville County Farmer* — 112 Main St. W.; PO Box 98, Mohall (58761); W; 1,599pd, 59fr (Sw); $4.20; C; publisher & editor Gloria Abrahamson; general manager LaVonne Erckson; tel (701) 756-6363; fax (701) 756-7136

Napoleon: *Napoleon Homestead* — 323 Main St.; PO Box 29 (58561); W; 1,840pd, 20fr (Sw); $3.90; publisher Jerome Schwartzenberger; editor Terry Schwartzenberger; tel (701) 754-2212; fax (701) 754-2212

Nelson: *Lakota American* — 201 Main St.; PO Box 507, Lakota (58344); W; 1,420pd, 14fr (Sw); $2.60; publisher & editor Lyle Pederson; tel (701) 247-2482; fax (701) 247-2482

New England/Regent/Mott/Amidon/Marmarth: *The Herald* — PO Box 517, New England (58647); F; 1,750pd (Est); $3.75; C; publisher Jeff Schumacher; tel (701) 579-4530; fax (701) 579-4180

New Rockford: *The New Rockford Transcript* — 632 1st Ave. N.; PO Box 752 (58356); Sa; 1,757pd, 94fr (Sw); 25¢; C; publisher Craig Voigt; editor Edward Hov; tel (701) 947-2417; fax (701) 947-2418

New Salem: *New Salem Journal* — I-94 & Highway 31, Exit 27; PO Box 416 (58563); W; 1,680pd (Est); 16¢; publisher Doug Rapsavage; publisher & editor Rocky Rapsavage; tel (701) 843-7567; fax (701) 843-7623

New Town/Keene/Mandaree/Parshall/Fort Berthold Reservation: *New Town News* — 313 Main St.; PO Box 730, New Town (58763); Th; 1,047pd, 37fr (Sw); $4.50; C; publisher BHG Inc.; editor Gale Kaas; tel (701) 627-4829; fax (701) 627-4021

Northwood: *The Gleaner* — 22 N. Main; PO Box C (58267); W; 2,291pd, 373fr (Est); 18¢; publisher & editor David L Pfeifle; tel (701) 587-6126; fax (701) 587-5219

Oakes/Dickey Co.: *The Oakes Times* — PO Box 651, Oakes (58474); Th; 1,351pd, 35fr (Sw); $5.65; C; publisher Kelly Publishing Inc.; editor Mary Schmitz; tel (701) 742-2361; fax (701) 742-2207

Park River: *The Walsh County Press* — PO Box 49 (58270); Sa; 1,718pd, 900fr (Sw); $6.50; C; publisher Harry W Kelly; editor Holly Anderson; tel (701) 284-6333; fax (701) 284-6091

Parshall: *Mountrail County Record* — 24 Main St.; PO Box 8 (58770); W; 1,037pd, 46fr (Est); 11¢; publisher Mike Gackle; editor Ellena Anderson; tel (701) 862-3515; fax (701) 862-3514

Pembina: *Pembina New Era* — PO Box 157, Fordville (58231); Th; 964pd (Est); 14¢; publisher Gunnard Ness; editor Truman Ness; tel (701) 229-3641; fax (701) 229-3217

Rolla: *Turtle Mountain Star* — 11 N.E. 1st St.; PO Box 849 (58367); M; 4,250pd (Est); 24¢; publisher & editor Roger Bailey; tel (701) 477-6495; fax (701) 477-3182

Rugby: *Pierce County Tribune* — 219 S. Main; PO Box 385 (58368); M; 2,847pd, 254fr (Sw); 31¢; publisher & editor Mark L Carlson; tel (701) 776-5252; fax (701) 776-2159

Sargent Co.: *The Teller* — 427 Main St.; PO Box 247, Milnor (58060); F; 1,867pd, 43fr (Sw); $2.75; C; publishers & editors Janet Bradbury & Richard Bradbury; tel (701) 427-9472

Slope/Hettinger Cos.: *The Herald* — 744 Main St.; PO Box 517, New England (58647); F; 1,200pd (Est); $3.75; publisher Jeff Schumacher; general manager Darlene Gullickson; tel (701) 579-4530; fax (701) 579-4180

Stanley/Mountrail: *Mountrail County Promoter, Inc.* — 117 Main St.; PO Box 99, Stanley (58784); W; 2,310pd, 90fr (Est); $3.50; publisher & editor Donald Kilen; tel (701) 628-2333; fax (701) 628-2694

Towner: *The Mouse River Journal* — PO Box 268 (58788); W; 2,300pd (Est); $5.00; publisher Dennis Kelly; general manager & editor William Domres; tel (701) 537-5610; fax (701) 537-5493

Turtle Lake/Mercer: *The McLean County Journal* — 210 Main St.; PO Box 220, Turtle Lake (58575-0220); Th; 848pd, 55fr (Sw); $3.60; publisher & editor Gerald W Anderson; tel (701) 448-2649; fax (701) 448-2649

Underwood/McLean: *Underwood News* — PO Box 340, Underwood-Washburn (58577); W; 695pd, 22fr (Est); $4.50; C; publisher BHG Inc.; editor Linda Hermanson; tel (701) 442-5535; fax (701) 462-8128

Washburn: *Leader-News* — PO Box 340 (58577); Th; 1,810pd, 55fr (Est); $4.50; C; publisher Mike Gackle; editor Joe Froelich; tel (701) 462-8126; fax (701) 462-8128

Watford City: *The McKenzie County Farmer* — 109 N. Main St.; PO Box 587 (58854-0587); W; 2,231pd, 26fr (Sw); $5.00; publisher & editor Neal A Shipman; tel (701) 842-2351; fax (701) 842-2352

W Fargo: *West Fargo Pioneer* — 322 Sheyenne St.; PO Box 457 (58078); W; 3,052pd, 51fr (Est); $3.50; publisher Donovan C Witham; editor Tom Jensen; tel (701) 282-2443; fax (701) 282-9248

Westhope/Antler/Newburg: *Standard* — 207 Main St.; PO Box 267, Westhope (58793-0267); W; 627pd, 30fr (Est); $3.00; publisher & editor Linda D Sisk; tel (701) 245-6461

Williston: *The Plains Reporter* — 14 4th St. W.; PO Box 1447 (58801); W; 14,500fr (Sw); $3.97; C; publisher Don Mrachek; general manager Ben Forthun; editor Ruth Newman; tel (701) 572-2165; fax (701) 572-1965

Wilton: *The Wilton News* — PO Box 340, Washburn (58577); W; 1,400pd (Est); 12¢; publisher Mike Gackle; editor Joe Froelich; tel (701) 462-8126; fax (701) 462-8128

Wishek: *The Wishek Star* — 511 Beaver Ave.; PO Box 275 (58495); W; 1,680pd, 45fr (Sw); $3.25; C; publisher & editor Thomas E Lovik; editor Wanda L Lovik; tel (701) 452-2331; fax (701) 452-2340

OHIO

Ada: *Ada Herald* — 309 S. Main St.; PO Box 117 (45810); W; 2,752pd, 47fr (Est); $4.14; publisher Larry R Joseph; editor Jon Umphress; tel (419) 634-6055; fax (419) 634-0912

Adams/Brown/Highland: *The Manchester Signal* — 414 E. 7th St., Manchester (45144); Th; 3,797pd, 28fr (Sw); $3.75; C; publisher & editor William G Woolard Jr; tel (513) 549-2800; fax (513) 549-3611

Amelia/Batavia/Monroe/Mt. Carmel/Pierce/Union/Withamsville: *Western Community Journal* — 394 Wards Corner Rd., Ste. 160, Loveland (45140); W; 6,138pd, 10,957fr (CAC); $9.60; C; publisher Thomas E Niehaus; editor Gary L Presley; tel (513) 753-1111; fax (513) 753-1117

Amherst: *Amherst News-Times* — 155 N. Leavitt Rd.; PO Box 67 (44001); W; 2,130pd, 199fr (Sw); $5.95; C; publisher Tom Smith; general manager Scott Swanson; editor Kathleen Koshar; tel (216) 988-2801; fax (216) 774-2167

Anderson Tulp: *Forest Hills Journal* — 394 Wards Corner Rd., Ste. 160, Loveland (45140); W; 7,465pd, 8,583fr (CAC); $12.65; C; publisher Thomas E Niehaus; editor Gary L Presley; tel (513) 753-1111; fax (513) 753-1117

Andover: *Pymatuning Area News* — Public Sq.; PO Box 458 (44003); W; 1,789pd, 150fr (Sw); $8.25; C; publisher John Lampson; general manager Jeff Lampson; editor James Mallory; tel (216) 293-6097; fax (216) 293-7374

II-60 **Ohio** *U.S. Weeklies*

Antwerp: *Antwerp Bee-Argus* — 113 N. Main St.; PO Box 278 (45813); W; 1,320pd, 50fr (Sw); $4.00; publisher James S Temple; general manager June L Temple; editor Sandra K Temple; managing editor Rodger S Temple; tel (419) 258-8161; fax (419) 258-9365

Archbold: *Archbold Buckeye* — 207 N. Defiance St. (43502); W; 3,212pd, 80fr (Sw); $6.90; publisher Ross William Taylor; general manager Sharon S Taylor; tel (419) 445-4466; fax (419) 445-4177

Archbold: *Archbold Farmland News* — 104 Depot St.; PO Box 240 (43502); Tu; 7,322pd, 627fr (Sw); $8.50; publisher O Roger Taylor; editor Jeremy J Rohrs; tel (419) 445-9456; fax (419) 445-4444

Attica: *Attica Hub* — 26 N. Main St.; PO Box 516 (44807); Th; 1,993pd, 62fr (Sw); $3.00; C; publisher Seneca Publishing; editor Dawn Martin; tel (419) 426-3491; fax (419) 426-3491

Auburn/Bainbridge/S Russell/Russell: *West Geauga Sun* — 5510 Cloverleaf Pkwy., Cleveland (44125-4887); Th; 11,161pd, 700fr (Est); $18.90; C; publisher Gerald H Gordon; editor Mary Jane Skala; tel (216) 524-0830; fax (216) 524-7792

Auglaize/Mercer/Shelby: *The Community Post* — 72 N. Main St.; PO Box 155, Minster (45865); Th; 2,282pd, 50fr (Sw); $4.05; publisher Sandy Bruns; editor Sharon Gotts Chalk; tel (419) 628-2369; fax (419) 628-4712

Aurora: *Aurora Advocate* — 1619 Commerce Dr.; PO Box 1549, Stow (44224-0549); W; 300pd, 5,210fr (Sw); $5.76; C; publisher David E Dix; general manager Richard M Sekella; editor Ken Lahmers; managing editor Jim Flick; tel (216) 688-0088; fax (216) 688-1588

Austintown: *Austintown Leader* — 25 N. Canfield-Niles Rd. (44515); F; 6,000fr (Est); $7.00; C; general manager & editor Robbin Durda; tel (216) 792-7729; fax (216) 792-7791

Austintown: *Austintown Town Crier* — Tribune Box 47; PO Box 1431, Warren (44482-1431); Sa; 14,000fr (Est); $10.95; publisher Larry Dorshner; editor Paul Smith; managing editor Emily Webster; tel (216) 841-1619; fax (216) 841-1717

Avon Lake/N Ridgeville: *The Sun* — 5510 Cloverleaf Pkwy., Cleveland (44125-4887); Th; 4,696pd, 2,445fr (ABC); $9.35; C; publisher Gerald H Gordon; editor Kevin Burns; tel (216) 524-0830; fax (216) 524-7792

Avon/Sheffield Village: *The Press* — 158 Lear Rd.; PO Box 300, Avon Lake (44012); W; 5,320pd, 7,222fr (Sw); 71¢; C; publisher R J Hemmer Jr; editor Marcella Grande; tel (216) 933-5100; fax (216) 933-7904

Barberton/Norton: *Barberton Herald* — 70 4th St. N.W.; PO Box 831, Barberton (44203); Th; 7,400pd, 97fr (Est); $10.50; C; publisher & editor Dave Richardson; managing editor Carl Bako; tel (216) 753-1068

Barnesville: *Barnesville Enterprise* — 162 E. Main St.; PO Box 30 (43713); W; 4,382pd, 63fr (Sw); $4.50; C; publisher Robert Dix; editor Bruce A Yarnall; tel (614) 425-1912; fax (614) 425-2545

Batavia/Monroe/New Richmond/Ohio/Pierce/Williamsburg: *Clermont Community Newspapers* — 394 Wards Corner Rd., Ste. 160, Loveland (45140); W; 1,403pd, 6,199fr (CAC); $4.73; C; publisher Thomas E Niehaus; editor Gary L Presley; tel (513) 753-1111; fax (513) 753-1117

Bedford: *Bedford Sun Banner* — 5510 Cloverleaf Pkwy., Cleveland (44125-4887); Th; 5,080pd, 515fr (ABC); $9.25; C; publisher Gerald H Gordon; editor Mark Morilak; tel (216) 524-0830; fax (216) 524-7792

Bedford: *Bedford Times-Register* — 711 Broadway; PO Box 46059 (44146-0059); Th; 3,300pd (Sw); $7.32; C; publisher David E Dix; general manager Richard M Sekella; editor Jim Flick; tel (216) 232-4055; fax (216) 232-8861

Beechwold/Clintonville: *The Booster* — 5257 Sinclair Rd.; PO Box 29912, Columbus (43229); W; 3,660pd, 14,630fr (CAC); $8.10; C; publisher James A Toms; editor Martin M Rozenman; managing editor Joe Meyer; tel (614) 785-1212; fax (614) 842-4760

Bellville/Butler: *Bellville Star & Tri-Forks Press* — 88 Main St., Bellville (44813); Th; 1,766pd, 14fr (Sw); $3.75; publisher William Kreeger; managing editor Doug Shephard; tel (419) 886-2291; fax (419) 886-2704

Belpre: *River Cities News* — 307 Washington Blvd. (45714); F; 5,000fr (Sw); $3.90; publisher & editor Paul Arvidson; tel (614) 423-1170; fax (614) 423-1170

Berea: *The News Sun* — 5510 Cloverleaf Pkwy., Cleveland (44125-4887); Th; 16,856pd, 735fr (ABC); $18.80; C; publisher Gerald H Gordon; editor Linda Kinsey; tel (216) 524-0830; fax (216) 524-7792

Bethel/Felicity: *The Bethel Journal-Press* — 4440 Glen Este-Withamsville Rd., Ste. 800, Cincinnati (45242); Th; 1,635pd (CAC); $3.25; C; publisher Thomas E Niehaus; editor Gary L Presley; tel (513) 734-4017; fax (513) 734-7509

Bexley: *Bexley News* — 5257 Sinclair Rd.; PO Box 29912, Columbus (43229); W; 993pd, 4,960fr (CAC); $6.35; C; publisher James A Toms; editor Martin Rozenman; managing editor Joe Meyer; tel (614) 785-1212; fax (614) 842-4760

Bexley: *Bexley This Week* — PO Box 341890, Columbus (43234); M; 6,492fr (Est); $6.95; C; publisher Consumer News Services Inc.; editor Ben Cason; managing editor Craig McDonald; tel (614) 841-1781; fax (614) 841-0767

Blanchester/Wilmington: *The Star-Republican* — 202 E. Main St.; PO Box 235, Blanchester (45107); M; 22,720fr (Sw); $8.14; publisher Clarence Graham; editor Rose Cooper; tel (513) 783-2421; fax (513) 382-4392

Bloomville: *The Bloomville Gazette* — 26 N. Main St.; PO Box 516, Attica (44807); Th; 360pd, 29fr (Sw); $3.00; C; publisher Seneca Publishing; editor Dawn Martin; tel (419) 426-3491; fax (419) 426-3491

Blue Ash/Montgomery: *Northeast Surburban Life Press* — 394 Wards Corner Rd., Ste. 160, Loveland (45140); W; 3,011pd, 5,116fr (CAC); $7.60; C; publisher Thomas E Niehaus; managing editor Gary L Presley; tel (513) 683-5115; fax (513) 677-4690

Bluffton: *The Bluffton News* — 101 N. Main St.; PO Box 49 (45817); Th; 3,000pd (Sw); $5.00; C; publisher Thomas M Edwards; editor Fred Steiner; tel (419) 358-8010; fax (419) 358-5027

Boardman: *Boardman Town Crier* — Tribune Box 47; PO Box 1431, Warren (44482-1431); Sa; 17,000fr (Est); $13.30; publisher Larry Dorshner; editor Linda Joseph; managing editor Emily Webster; tel (216) 841-1619; fax (216) 841-1717

Botkins/Anna/Jackson: *Shelby-County Review* — 8 Willipie St., Wapakoneta (45895); Tu; 4,516fr (Est); $4.12; C; publisher Dianna Epperly; editor Nina Lee; tel (419) 738-2128; fax (419) 738-5352

Brecksville/Independence: *The Sun Courier* — 5510 Cloverleaf Pkwy., Cleveland (44125-4887); Th; 6,933pd, 802fr (ABC); $13.65; C; publisher Gerald H Gordon; editor Carol Kovach; tel (216) 524-0830; fax (216) 524-7792

Brooklyn: *Brooklyn Sun Journal* — 5510 Cloverleaf Pkwy., Cleveland (44125-4887); Th; 9,485pd, 420fr (ABC); $13.80; C; publisher Gerald H Gordon; editor Carol Kovach; tel (216) 524-0830; fax (216) 524-7792

Brookville: *Brookville Star* — 14 Mulberry St.; PO Box 100 (45309); W; 200pd, 6,000fr (Sw); $5.00; publisher Joe E Gordon; editor Jim Hoffman; tel (513) 833-2545

Brown Co.: *The Brown County Press* — 106 S. High St.; PO Box 453, Mt. Orab (45154); M; 14,350fr (Sw); $5.60; C; publisher William C Latham; editor Eunice Ott; tel (513) 444-3441; fax (513) 444-2652

Brunswick: *Brunswick Sun Times* — 5510 Cloverleaf Pkwy., Cleveland (44125-4887); Th; 6,460pd, 748fr (ABC); $11.80; C; publisher Gerald H Gordon; editor Glenn Wojciak; tel (216) 524-0830; fax (216) 524-7792

Cadiz: *Harrison News-Herald* — 136 S. Main St.; PO Box 127 (43907); M; 5,745pd, 235fr (Sw); $5.36; publisher Patricia O'Grady; editor Charles Peterson; tel (614) 942-2118; fax (614) 942-4667

Canal Fulton: *The Signal* — 117 N. Canal St.; PO Box 546 (44614); Su; 12,000fr (Est); $7.50; publisher John Blanchflower; editor Marsha Kolega; tel (216) 854-4549; fax (216) 854-1928

Canal Winchester: *The Times* — 5257 Sinclair Rd.; PO Box 29912, Columbus (43229); W; 2,067pd, 392fr (CAC); $6.50; C; publisher James A Toms; editor Martin Rozenman; managing editor Joe Meyer; tel (614) 785-1212; fax (614) 842-4760

Canfield: *Canfield Town Crier* — Tribune Box 47; PO Box 1431, Warren (44482-1431); Sa; 7,400fr (Est); $8.55; publisher Larry Dorschner; editor Mike Hill; managing editor Emily Webster; tel (216) 841-1619; fax (216) 841-1717

Carey: *The Progressor Times* — 1198 E. Findlay St.; PO Box 37 (43316); W; 3,200pd (Est); $2.25; C; publisher & editor Stephen C Zender; tel (419) 396-7567; fax (419) 396-7527

Carrollton: *The Free Press Standard* — 43 E. Main St.; PO Box 37 (44615); Th; 7,656pd, 246fr (Sw); $5.99; publisher Maynard Buck Jr; general manager Bill Peterson; editor Carol McIntire; managing editor Don Rutledge; tel (216) 627-5591; fax (216) 627-3195

Centerville/Bellbrook: *Centerville-Bellbrook Times* — 3085 Woodman Dr., Ste. 170, Kettering (45420); W; 21,650fr (Est); $9.29; Sa; 2,495pd (Est); $9.29; C; publisher Mark E Raymond; editor Mark Kellam; tel (513) 294-7000; fax (513) 294-2981

Chagrin Falls: *Chagrin Herald Sun* — 5510 Cloverleaf Pkwy., Cleveland (44125-4887); Th; 1,870pd, 332fr (ABC); $18.90; C; publisher Gerald H Gordon; editor Mary Jane Skala; tel (216) 524-0830; fax (216) 524-7792

Chagrin Falls/Bentleyville/Moreland Hills/Orange Village: *Chagrin Valley Times* — 525 E. Washington St.; PO Box 150, Chagrin Falls (44022); Th; 9,992pd, 3,518fr (Sw); $22.50; C; publisher Harold K Douthit III; general manager Carole A Vigliotti; editor David Lange; tel (216) 247-5335; fax (216) 247-5615

Cincinnati: *Delhi Press* — 5552 Cheviot Rd. (45247); W; 8,907pd, 11,504fr (Est); $14.93; C; publisher Anthony E Schad; editor Nancy Daly; tel (513) 923-3111; fax (513) 923-1806

Cincinnati: *Hilltop News-Press* — 5552 Cheviot Rd. (45247); W; 5,912pd, 14,383fr (CAC); $13.66; C; publisher Anthony E Schad; editor Eric Spangler; managing editor Nancy Daly; tel (513) 923-3111; fax (513) 923-1806

Cincinnati: *Northwest Press* — 5552 Cheviot Rd. (45247); W; 8,507pd, 9,529fr (CAC); $10.74; C; publisher Anthony E Schad; editor Eric Spangler; managing editor Nancy Daly; tel (513) 923-3111; fax (513) 923-1806

Cincinnati: *Tri-County Press* — 5552 Cheviot Rd. (45247); W; 2,112pd, 6,834fr (CAC); $7.03; C; publisher Anthony E Schad; editor Nancy Daly; tel (513) 923-3111; fax (513) 923-1806

Cincinnati: *Western Hills Press* — 5552 Cheviot Rd. (45247); W; 10,079pd, 24,647fr (CAC); $15.65; C; publisher Anthony E Schad; editor Nancy Daly; tel (513) 923-3111; fax (513) 923-1806

Clermont Co.: *Community Journal Press North* — 394 Wards Corner Rd., Ste. 160, Loveland (45140); W; 1,597pd, 4,931fr (Sw); $4.50; C; publisher Thomas E Niehaus; editor Gary L Presley; tel (513) 753-1111; fax (513) 753-1117

Clermont Co.: *The Clermont Sun* — 465 E. Main St.; PO Box 366, Batavia (45103); Th; 3,141pd, 370fr (Sw); $6.50; C; publisher William C Latham; editor Jean Kowalski; tel (513) 732-2511; fax (513) 732-6344

Cleveland Hts.: *The Sun Press* — 5510 Cloverleaf Pkwy., Valley View (44125-4887); Th; 19,778pd, 995fr (ABC); $25.25; C; publisher Gerald H Gordon; editor Mary Jane Skala; tel (216) 524-0830; fax (216) 524-7792

Clintonville: *Clintonville This Week* — PO Box 432890, Columbus (43234); M; 14,914fr (Est); $8.20; C; publisher Consumer News Services Inc.; editor Ben Cason; managing editor Craig McDonald; tel (614) 841-1781; fax (614) 841-0767

Clyde: *The Clyde Enterprise* — 107 S. Main St.; PO Box 29 (43410); W; 2,452pd, 40fr (Sw); $4.20; publisher Gazette Publishing Inc.; general manager Jack Trainor; editor John Brewer; tel (419) 547-9194; fax (419) 547-9726

Coldwater/S Mercer Co.: *Mercer County Chronicle* — 116 W. Main St., Coldwater (45828); W; 2,655pd, 175fr (Sw); $4.60; publisher & editor Bonnie J Van DeMark; tel (418) 678-2324; fax (419) 678-4659

Columbia Sta.: *Rural-Urban Record* — 24487 Squires Rd.; PO Box 966, Columbia Station (44028); M; 148pd, 14,608fr (Est); $5.50; publisher & editor Leonard Boise; general manager Lee Boise; tel (216) 236-8982

Columbiana: *The Columbiana Heritage* — PO Box 448 (44408); F; 600pd, 400fr (Est); $5.95; publisher Geoffrey Goll; editor Sue Picklesimer; tel (216) 482-0600; fax (216) 482-1400

Columbus: *News East* — 5257 Sinclair Rd.; PO Box 29912 (43229); W; 33pd, 16,435fr (CAC); $8.00; C; publisher James A Toms; editor Martin Rozenman; managing editor Joe Meyer; tel (614) 785-1212; fax (614) 842-4760

Columbus Grove/Pandora: *Putnam County Vidette* — 111 E. Sycamore St.; PO Box 127, Columbus Grove (45830); W; 800pd, 49fr (Sw); $4.15; C; publisher Gary Hirt; general manager Brady Glick; editor Paul K Muckley; tel (419) 659-2173; fax (419) 659-2760

Conneaut: *The Courier* — 218 Washington St.; PO Box 212 (44030); W; 2,500pd, 40fr (Sw); $8.25; C; publisher John Lampson; general manager Jeff Lampson; editor Patrick Williams; tel (216) 593-6030; fax (216) 593-6061

Continental: *Continental News Review* — 201 N. Main St.; PO Box 995 (45831); W; 1,075pd (Est); $3.50; publisher & editor Nyle Stateler; tel (419) 596-3897

Covington/Bradford/W Milton Trading Zones: *Stillwater Valley Advertiser* — 395 S. High St.; PO Box 69, Covington (45318); Tu/W; 10,508fr (Sw); $7.14; C; publisher & editor Gary L Godfrey; tel (513) 473-2028; fax (513) 473-3299

Crestline: *The Crestline Advocate* — 312 N. Seltzer St.; PO Box 226 (44827); W; 2,230pd, 50fr (Sw); $4.34; publisher Mark N Brouwer; editor Joseph J Petti; tel (419) 683-3355

Cuyahoga Falls: *Cuyahoga Falls News-Press* — 1619 Commerce Dr.; PO Box 1549, Stow (44224-0549); Su; 1,200pd, 23,200fr (Sw); $7.68; C; publisher David E Dix; general manager Richard M Sekella; editor Ellin Walsh; managing editor Bev Ocasek; tel (216) 688-0088; fax (216) 688-1588

Dalton/Kidron/Orrville: *The Dalton Gazette & Kidron News* — 41 W. Main St.; PO Box 495, Dalton (44618); W; 1,202pd, 4fr (Sw); $5.00; publisher & editor Francis Woodruff; tel (216) 828-8401; fax (216) 828-8401

Darke Co.: *The Early Bird* — 5312 Sebring Warner Rd., Greenville (45331); Su; 16pd, 26,532fr (CAC); $13.50; publisher Carol L Ball; editor Norma Jenkins; tel (513) 548-3330; fax (513) 548-3376

Deer Park/Kenwood/Sycamore Twp.: *Suburban Life Press* — 394 Wards Corner Rd., Ste. 160, Loveland (45140); W; 3,747pd, 7,585fr (CAC); $10.50; C; publisher Thomas E Niehaus; editor Gary L Presley; tel (513) 683-5115; fax (513) 677-4690

Delaware: *Delaware This Week* — PO Box 341890, Columbus (43234); Su; 18,655fr (Sw); $8.55; C; publisher Consumer News Services Inc.; editor Ben Cason; managing editor Craig McDonald; tel (614) 841-1781; fax (614) 841-0767

Delta: *The Delta Atlas* — 212 Main St. (43515); W; 1,572pd, 201fr (Sw); $2.80; publisher & editor Bernice T Mack; tel (419) 822-3231

Deshler: *The Deshler Flag* — 107 E. Main St. (43516); Th; 1,500pd (Est); $3.65; C; publisher Donald J Mickens; general manager John Mickens; editor Carol Paulson; tel (419) 278-2816

Dresden: *Dresden Transcript* — 17 E. 9th; PO Box 105 (43821); Th; 4,700pd (Sw); $5.00; C; publisher & editor Alfred E Lewis; general manager Maryam Lewis; tel (614) 754-1608; fax (614) 754-1609

Dublin: *Dublin News* — 5257 Sinclair Rd.; PO Box 29912, Columbus (43229); W; 5,427pd, 10,094fr (CAC); $7.20; C; publisher James A Toms; editor Martin Rozenman; managing editor Joe Meyer; tel (614) 785-1212; fax (614) 842-4760

Dublin: *Dublin Villager* — PO Box 341890, Columbus (43234); M; 22,756fr (Sw); $8.35; C; publisher Consumer News Services Inc.; editor Ben Cason; managing editor Craig McDonald; tel (614) 841-1781; fax (614) 841-0767

E Cincinnati: *Eastside Weekend* — 4700 Duke Dr., Ste. 130, Mason (45040); Th; 50,000fr (ABC); $225.00; publisher & editor Susan McHugh; tel (513) 459-1711; fax (513) 459-1722

E Cleveland: *Sun Scoop Journal* — 5510 Cloverleaf Pkwy., Cleveland (44125-4887); Th; 4,815pd, 505fr (ABC); $9.40; C; publisher Gerald H Gordon; editor Mark Morilak; tel (216) 524-0830; fax (216) 524-7792

E Columbus: *Eastside This Week* — PO Box 341890, Columbus (43234); M; 17,007fr (Est); $8.20; C; publisher Consumer News Services Inc.; editor Ben Cason; managing editor Craig McDonald; tel (614) 841-1781; fax (614) 841-0767

U.S. Weeklies **Ohio** **II-61**

E Columbus: *The Eastside Messenger* — 3378 Sullivant Ave., Columbus (43204); M; 47,616fr (CAC); $14.75; C; publisher Earl F Moore Sr; general manager Philip F Daubel; editor Ken Drenten; tel (614) 272-5422; fax (614) 272-0684

Edgerton: *The Edgerton Earth* — PO Box 445 (43517); Th; 1,301pd, 74fr (Sw); $2.95; publishers & editors Dean Howard & Mary Howard; tel (419) 298-2369; fax (419) 298-2360

Edon: *The Edon Commercial* — PO Box 218 (43518-0218); W; 693pd, 58fr (Sw); $3.00; publishers & editors Dean Howard & Mary Howard; tel (419) 272-2413; fax (419) 298-2360

Euclid: *Euclid Sun Journal* — 5510 Cloverleaf Pkwy., Cleveland (44125-4887); Th; 12,020pd, 729fr (ABC); $17.95; C; publisher Gerald H Gordon; editor Mark Morilak; tel (216) 524-0830; fax (216) 524-7792

Fairfield: *Fairfield Echo* — 5120 Dixie Hwy. (45014); W; 18,325fr (Est); $6.00; publisher Robert Murphy; editor Emily York; tel (513) 829-7900; fax (513) 829-7950

Fayette: *The Fayette Review* — 118 W. Main St.; PO Box 219 (43521); Th; 1,089pd, 120fr (Est); $3.30; publisher Yvonne J Potter; editor Donald I Potter; tel (419) 237-2591

Franklin/Carlisle/Hunter: *The Franklin Chronicle* — 42 E. 4th St.; PO Box 99, Franklin (45005); Tu; 1,274pd, 1,619fr (Est); $6.00; C; publisher Carl Esposito; editor Dan Darragh; managing editor Ed Richter; tel (513) 746-3691; fax (513) 746-6013

Fredericktown: *Knox County Citizen* — 42 N. Main St.; PO Box 240 (43019); Th; 1,385pd, 162fr (Sw); $4.50; publisher Hirt Publishing Co.; general manager William Kreeger; tel (614) 694-4016; fax (614) 694-4555

Fulton Co.: *The Expositor* — 201 N. Fulton St., Wauseon (43567); Tu/Th; 4,353pd, 51fr (Sw); $8.97; C; publisher Robert M Krumm; editor Brian Liskai; tel (419) 335-2010

Gahanna: *Gahanna News* — 5257 Sinclair Rd.; PO Box 29912, Columbus (43229); W; 399pd, 11,756fr (CAC); $6.50; publisher James A Toms; editor Martin Rozenman; managing editor Joe Meyer; tel (614) 785-1212; fax (614) 842-4760

Gahanna: *New Albany This Week* — PO Box 341890, Columbus (43234); M; 2,640fr (Sw); $5.50; C; publisher Consumer News Services Inc.; editor Ben Cason; managing editor Craig McDonald; tel (614) 841-1781; fax (614) 841-0767

Gahanna: *Rocky Fork Enterprise* — 110 N. High St.; PO Box 30769 (43230); W; 4,821pd, 286fr (Sw); $8.00; publisher Consumer News Services Inc.; editor Ben Cason; tel (614) 471-1600; fax (614) 471-1764

Garfield/Maple Heights: *The Garfield-Maple Sun* — 5510 Cloverleaf Pkwy., Cleveland (44125-4887); Th; 10,491pd, 861fr (ABC); $18.00; C; publisher Gerald H Gordon; editor Carol Kovach; tel (216) 524-0830; fax (216) 524-7792

Genoa/Oregon/Toledo/Northwood/Woodville/Oak Harbor/Walbridge: *Suburban Press & Metro Press* — 1550 Woodville; PO Box 169, Millbury (43447); M; 92pd, 35,829fr (Sw); $20.16; C; publisher Harold K Douthit III; general manager John Szozda; managing editor Scott Carpenter; tel (419) 836-2221; fax (419) 836-1319

Georgetown/Brown: *Georgetown News Democrat* — 210 S. Main St.; PO Box 149, Georgetown (45121); W; 5,800pd, 60fr (Est); $3.78; publisher Joan R Wood; general manager Julie Richmond; editor David Wood; tel (513) 378-6161; fax (513) 378-2004

German Vlg.: *German Village Gazette* — 5257 Sinclair Rd.; PO Box 29912, Columbus (43229); Th; 29pd, 4,235fr (CAC); $6.30; C; publisher James A Toms; editor Martin Rozenman; managing editor Joe Meyer; tel (614) 785-1212; fax (614) 842-4760

Germantown/Farmersville: *The Germantown Press* — 50 W. Center St.; PO Box 115, Germantown (45327); Th; 2,438pd, 100fr (Est); $4.85; publisher & editor Dolores A Grunwald; general manager Dixie Neatherton; tel (513) 855-2300

Grandview: *Grandview This Week* — PO Box 340890, Columbus (43234); M; 6,008fr (Est); $6.95; C; publisher Consumer News Services Inc.; editor Ben Cason; managing editor Craig McDonald; tel (614) 841-1781; fax (614) 841-0767

Grandview Heights: *Tri-Village News* — 5257 Sinclair Rd.; PO Box 29912, Columbus (43229); W; 1,635pd, 3,913fr (CAC); $6.20; publisher James A Toms; editor Martin Rozenman; managing editor Joe Meyer; tel (614) 785-1212; fax (614) 842-4760

Granville/Licking Co.: *The Granville Sentinel* — 110 E. Elm St.; PO Box 357, Granville (43023); Th; 2,000pd, 50fr (Est); $4.25; C; publisher & editor Sherry Bech Paprochi; tel (614) 587-3397; fax (614) 587-3398

Greenwich/N Fairfield: *Greenwich Enterprise Review* — 9 Main St.; PO Box 7, Greenwich (44837); Tu; 12,251fr (Sw); $3.38; C; publisher & editor Ken C Gove; general manager Karla Souslin; managing editor Lynne Phillips; tel (419) 752-3854; fax (419) 933-2031

Grove City: *Grove City News* — 5257 Sinclair Rd.; PO Box 29912, Columbus (43229); Th; 25pd, 9,240fr (CAC); $6.45; C; publisher James A Toms; editor Martin Rozenman; managing editor Joe Meyer; tel (614) 785-1212; fax (614) 842-4760

Grove City: *The Grove City Record* — 4048 Broadway; PO Box 339 (43123); W; 5,355pd, 156fr (Sw); $7.75; publisher Consumer News Services Inc.; editor Bob Monds; tel (614) 875-2307; fax (614) 875-6028

Harrison: *Harrison Press* — 607 Harrison Ave.; PO Box 610 (45030); W; 5,875pd, 41fr (Sw); $5.25; C; publisher John W Reiniger; editor Jerry Andrew Blair; tel (513) 367-4582; fax (513) 367-4593

Hartville: *The Hartville News* — 316 E. Maple St.; PO Box 428 (44632); W; 2,868pd, 21fr (Est); $3.40; publisher Knowles Press Inc.; editor Rosalee Haines; managing editor Jackie Vaughn; tel (216) 877-9345; fax (216) 877-1364

Heath/Newark: *Ace News* — 619 Industrial Pkwy.; PO Box 2312, Heath (43056-1524); Th; 4,500pd, 500fr (Est); $4.90; publisher Ronald P Boeckman; editor Jean Carrelli; tel (614) 522-8566

Hicksville: *The News Tribune* — 147 E. High St.; PO Box 303 (43526); W; 2,148pd, 74fr (Sw); $4.50; publishers & editors Mary Ann Barth & Michael G Barth; tel (419) 542-7764; fax (419) 542-7370

Hilliard: *Hilliard Northwest News* — 5257 Sinclair Rd.; PO Box 29912, Columbus (43229); W; 2,347pd, 12,485fr (CAC); $6.85; C; publisher James A Toms; editor Martin Rozenman; managing editor Joe Meyer; tel (614) 785-1212; fax (614) 842-4760

Hilliard: *Hilliard This Week* — PO Box 341890, Columbus (43234); M; 19,664fr (Sw); $7.35; C; publisher Consumer News Services Inc.; editor Ben Cason; managing editor Craig McDonald; tel (614) 841-1781; fax (614) 841-0767

Hillsboro/Highland Co.: *The Press Gazette* — 209 S. High St.; PO Box 40, Hillsboro (45133); Tu/Th; 5,218pd, 55fr (Sw); $3.70; C; publisher Phillip A Roberts; editor Liz Johnson; managing editor Rory Ryan; tel (513) 393-3456; fax (513) 393-2059

Huber Heights: *Huber Heights Courier* — 7089 Taylorsville Rd., Dayton (45424); W; 6,091pd, 4,130fr (Sw); $7.56; C; publisher Vernon T Bowling; general manager David E Copen; editor Charles Vosskuehler; tel (513) 236-4990

Hudson: *Hudson Hub-Times* — 1619 Commerce Dr.; PO Box 1549, Stow (44224-1549); W/Su; 500pd, 8,000fr (Sw); $6.00; C; publisher David E Dix; general manager Richard M Sekella; editor Debbie DiMascio; managing editor Bev Ocasek; tel (216) 688-0088; fax (216) 688-1588

Hyde Park/Oakley/Fairfax: *Eastern Hills Journal Press* — 394 Wards Corner Rd., Ste. 160, Loveland (45140); W; 150pd, 12,192fr (CAC); $12.11; C; publisher Thomas E Niehaus; managing editor Gary L Presley; tel (513) 683-5115; fax (513) 677-4690

Jackson: *Jackson Journal-Herald* — 295 Broadway; PO Box 270 (45640); W/F/Su; 5,987pd (Sw); $6.72; C; publisher Dale Gardner; editor Pete Wilson; tel (614) 286-2187; fax (614) 286-5854

Jackson Twp./Perry Twp./Canal Fulton: *The Sun Journal* — 7215 Whipple Ave. N.W., North Canton (44720); Th; 4,000pd (Est); $6.35; C; publisher Stark Journal Inc.; general manager Bernie Clements; editor Mark Knapik; managing editor Mike McNulti; tel (216) 966-1121; fax (216) 966-1202

Jefferson: *The Gazette* — 46 W. Jefferson St.; PO Box 166 (44047); W; 2,316pd, 400fr (Sw); $8.25; C; publisher John Lampson; general manager Jeff Lampson; editor Lucille Donelly; tel (216) 576-9115; fax (216) 576-2735

Jefferson Co./Toronto/Wintersville: *Citizen Tribune* — 2204 Powell Ave., Steubenville (43952); Th; 848pd, 28fr (Sw); $4.00; C; publisher & editor Patrick J O'Hara; editor Dolly O'Hara; tel (614) 537-3776

Johnstown: *Johnstown Independent* — 73 S. Main St.; PO Box 455 (43031); W; 2,185pd, 8fr (Sw); $5.90; publisher Consumer News Services Inc.; editor Mary Rob Clodfelter; tel (614) 967-2045; fax (614) 855-2857

Kettering/Oakwood: *Kettering-Oakwood Times* — 3085 Woodman Dr., Ste. 170, Kettering (45420); W; 26,500fr (Est); $9.88; Sa; 2,650pd (Est); $9.88; C; publisher Mark E Raymond; editor Nick Blizzard; tel (513) 294-7000; fax (513) 294-2981

Lakewood: *Lakewood Sun Post* — 5510 Cloverleaf Pkwy., Cleveland (44125-4887); Th; 11,690pd, 736fr (ABC); $20.05; C; publisher Gerald H Gordon; editor Kevin Burns; tel (216) 524-0830; fax (216) 524-7792

Lebanon: *Sunday Western Star* — 200 Harmon Ave.; PO Box 29 (45036); Su; 15,700fr (Est); $8.34; C; publisher Fred E Gibson; editor Thomas Barr; tel (513) 932-3010; fax (513) 932-6056

Lebanon: *The Western Star* — 200 Harmon Ave.; PO Box 29 (45036); W; 8,350pd, 139fr (Sw); $8.34; C; publisher Fred E Gibson; editor Thomas Barr; tel (513) 932-3010; fax (513) 932-6056

Leesburg: *Leesburg Citizen* — 345 Jefferson St.; PO Box 118, Greenfield Highland (45135); Th; 1,396pd, 58fr (Sw); $2.25; C; publisher Jack Schluep; general manager Gary Schluep; editor Teresa Wisecup; tel (513) 981-2141; fax (513) 981-2880

Lewisburg: *The Lewisburg Leader* — 10 S. Main St., West Alexandria (45381); Th; 982pd, 40fr (Est); 26¢; publisher & editor John McCarroll Keefe; tel (513) 839-4733; fax (513) 839-5351

Liberty Center/Deshler: *The Liberty Press* — PO Box 6, Liberty Center (43532); Th; 1,235pd, 41fr (Sw); $3.75; C; publisher Donald J Mickens; editor Kaye Lingruen; tel (419) 533-2401

Lisbon: *The Lisbon Heritage* — PO Box 448, Columbiana (44408-0448); F; 1,000pd (Est); $5.95; C; publisher Geoffrey Goll; editor Sue Picklesimer; tel (216) 482-0600; fax (216) 482-1400

London/Madison Co.: *The Madison Messenger* — 78 S. Main St., London (43140); M; 11,653fr (CAC); $6.05; C; publisher Earle F Moore Sr; general manager Jim Durban; editor Kristy Zurbrick; managing editor Ken Drenten; tel (614) 852-0809; fax (614) 852-0814

Lorain Co.: *The Lorain County Times* — 1443 Colorado Ave.; PO Box 516, Lorain (44052); Th; 1,020pd, 980fr (Sw); $11.60; C; publisher & editor Eleanor J Gottschalk; tel (216) 288-1111; fax (216) 356-0515

Loudonville/Perrysville: *The Loudonville Times* — 425 E. Haskell St., Loudonville (44842); Tu; 2,102pd, 50fr (Sw); $4.20; publisher Jon Truax; editor Jim Brewer; tel (419) 994-4166; fax (419) 994-4617

Louisville/Nimishillen Twp./E Canton: *The Louisville Herald* — 308 S. Mill; PO Box 170, Louisville (44641-0170); Th; 3,288pd (Sw); $4.06; publisher Paul M Clapper; editor Frank H Clapper; tel (216) 875-5610; fax (216) 875-4475

Loveland: *The Loveland Herald Press* — 394 Wards Corner Rd., Ste. 160 (45140); W; 2,290pd, 2,526fr (CAC); $5.00; C; publisher Thomas E Niehaus; managing editor Gary L Presley; tel (513) 683-5115; fax (513) 677-4690

Lynchburg: *Lynchburg News* — 345 Jefferson St., Greenfield Highland (45123); Th; 683pd, 115fr (Sw); $2.25; publisher Jack Schluep; general manager Gary Schluep; editor Teresa Wisecup; tel (513) 981-2141; fax (513) 981-2880

Malvern/Brown Twp.: *Malvern Community News* — 177 Curry St., Minerva (44657); Th; 1,057pd, 25fr (Sw); $2.85; C; publisher Charles C Dix Jr; general manager Robert Shaffer; editor Sarah Reed; tel (216) 868-3408; fax (216) 868-3273

Maple Heights: *Maple Heights Press* — 711 Broadway; PO Box 46059, Bedford (44146-0059); Th; 3,100pd, 75fr (Est); $7.56; C; publisher David E Dix; general manager Richard M Sekella; editor Jim Flick; tel (216) 232-4055; fax (216) 232-8861

Marion: *Marion Newslife Advertiser* — 1260 Delaware Ave.; PO Box 514 (43301-0514); Su; 31,994fr (Est); $10.71; C; publisher & editor Steven Phillips; tel (614) 387-7255; fax (614) 387-7142

Mason/Kings Mills/Landen: *Community Press of Mason* — 394 Wards Corner Rd., Ste. 160, Loveland (45140); W; 175pd, 7,888fr (CAC); $4.30; publisher Thomas E Niehaus; managing editor Gary L Presley; tel (513) 683-5115; fax (513) 677-4690

Mayfield/Mayfield Heights/S Euclid: *The Sun Messenger* — 5510 Cloverleaf Pkwy., Cleveland (44125-4887); Th; 14,357pd, 742fr (ABC); $21.60; C; publisher Gerald H Gordon; editor Mark Morilak; tel (216) 524-0830; fax (216) 524-7792

McArthur: *The Vinton County Courier* — 104 N. Market St.; PO Box 468 (45651); Sa; 4,000pd (Est); $4.27; C; publisher & editor Bill Gardner; tel (614) 596-5393; fax (614) 596-5393

McConnelsville/Morgan: *Morgan County Herald* — 89 W. Main St.; PO Box 268, McConnelsville (43756); W; 4,727pd, 31fr (Sw); $5.60; publisher Jack L Barnes; editor Don Keller; tel (614) 962-3377

Mechanicsburg: *The Mechanicsburg Telegram* — 30 S. Oak St.; PO Box 390, London (43140); W; 550pd (Sw); $5.00; C; publisher Donald L Hartley; editor Bill McCullick; tel (614) 852-1616; fax (614) 852-1620

Medina: *The Medina Sun* — 5510 Cloverleaf Pkwy., Cleveland (44125-4887); Th; 12,117fr (Est); $9.00; C; publisher Gerald H Gordon; editor Glenn Wojciak; tel (216) 524-0830; fax (216) 524-7792

Miamisburg/Miami Twp./W Carrollton: *Miamisburg News* — 230 S. 2nd St.; PO Box 108, Miamisburg (45342); W; 7,026pd, 37fr (Sw); $8.12; C; publisher Kimm Mote; editor Jim Pickering; tel (513) 866-3331; fax (513) 866-6011

Milford: *Milford Advertiser-Press* — 394 Wards Corner Rd., Ste. 160, Loveland (45140); W; 3,539pd, 5,223fr (CAC); $6.21; C; publisher Thomas E Niehaus; editor Gary L Presley; tel (513) 753-1111; fax (513) 753-1117

Millersburg/Holmes Co.: *The Holmes County Hub* — 25 N. Clay St.; PO Box 151, Millersburg (44654); Th; 3,631pd, 321fr (Sw); $8.80; C; publisher Raymond Victor Dix; editor Jeanine Kendle; managing editor C Ken Blum; tel (216) 674-1811; fax (216) 674-3780

Minerva: *Minerva Leader* — 177 Curry St.; PO Box 30 (44657); Th; 3,141pd, 41fr (Est); $4.30; publisher Charles C Dix Jr; general manager Robert C Shaffer; editor Sarah Reed; tel (216) 868-5222; fax (216) 868-3273

Monroe Co.: *Monroe County Sentinel* — 323 Eastern Ave.; PO Box 470, Woodsfield (43793-0470); M; 6,600fr (Sw); $3.00; C; publisher & editor William E Moore; tel (614) 472-1631; fax (614) 472-1110

Monroe Co.: *"The Spirit of Democracy"* — 323 Eastern Ave.; PO Box 470, Woodsfield (43793-0470); F; 800pd (Sw); $3.00; C; publisher & editor William E Moore; tel (614) 472-1631; fax (614) 472-1110

Montgomery/Green Cos.: *Amos Suburban Newspapers* — 3085 Woodman Dr., Ste. 170, Dayton (45420); W/Sa; 23,200pd, 68,500fr (Est); $25.92; C; publisher Mark E Raymond; editor William Flanagan Jr; tel (513) 294-7000; fax (513) 294-2981

Montpelier: *Montpelier Leader-Enterprise* — 319 W. Main St.; PO Box 149 (43543); W; 1,415pd, 55fr (Sw); $4.75; publishers Christopher Cullis & Ford Cullis; editor David Belden; tel (419) 485-3113; fax (419) 485-3114

Morrow/N Delaware Cos.: *Morrow County Independent* — 123 E. Main St.; PO Box 66, Cardington (43315); W; 1,300pd, 126fr (Est); $2.70; publisher William Kreeger; editor Susie Dye; tel (419) 864-6046; fax (419) 947-7241

Mt. Gilead: *The Morrow County Sentinel* — 255 Neal Ave.; PO Box 149 (43338); W; 4,038pd, 140fr (Sw); $6.60; publisher William W Kreeger; editor Allen Gress; tel (419) 946-3010; fax (419) 947-7241

Mt. Sterling: *The Tribune* — 30 S. Oak St.; PO Box 390, London (43140); M; 6,733fr (Sw); $5.00; C; publisher Donald L Hartley; editor Bill McCullick; tel (614) 852-1616; fax (614) 852-1620

New Carlisle: *The New Carlisle Sun* — 225 S. Main St.; PO Box 225 (45344); W; 5,600pd (Est); $5.35; C; publisher Vernon T Bowling; editor Gary Gregory; tel (513) 845-3861; fax (513) 667-8987

Copyright ©1996 by the Editor & Publisher Co.

New Concord: *New Concord Area Leader* — 831 Wheeling Ave.; PO Box 10, Cambridge (43725); F; 1,250pd (Est); $2.78; C; publisher R C Dix; editor Lisa L Short; tel (614) 435-3531; fax (614) 432-6219

New Lebanon: *The New Lebanon Advertiser* — 10 S. Main St., West Alexandria (45381); M; 8,500fr (Est); $5.00; publisher & editor John McCarroll Keefe; tel (513) 839-4733; fax (513) 839-5351

New Lexington/Perry Co.: *Perry County Tribune* — 117 S. Main St.; PO Box 312, New Lexington (43764); W; 3,754pd, 466fr (Est); $3.85; publisher Gary L Hirt; general manager Dave Shubert; editor Carl W Burnett Jr; tel (614) 342-4121; fax (614) 342-4131

New London: *New London Record* — 211 W. Main St.; PO Box 110 (44851-2110); Th; 2,931pd (Est); $4.33; publisher Thomas Mezick; editor Terry Wilson; tel (419) 929-3411; fax (419) 929-3800

New Washington: *New Washington Herald* — 625 S. Kibler St.; PO Box 367 (44854); Th; 1,392pd, 81fr (Sw); $1.90; publisher Herald Printing Co.; editor Robert L Bordner; managing editor Bonnie Ackerman; tel (419) 492-2133; fax (419) 492-2128

Newcomerstown: *Newcomerstown News* — 140 W. Main St.; PO Box 30 (43832); W; 3,299pd, 24fr (Sw); $4.00; C; publisher Jerry Wolfram; editor Ray H Booth; tel (614) 498-7117; fax (614) 432-5624

Noble Co.: *The Journal & The Noble County Leader* — 309 Main St.; PO Box 315, Caldwell (43724); M; 4,645pd, 155fr (Sw); 22¢; publisher & editor David Evans; tel (614) 732-2341; fax (614) 732-7288

N Baltimore/Hoytville: *The North Baltimore News* — 114 N. Main St.; PO Box 67 (45872); Th; 983pd, 92fr (Est); $3.50; C; publisher Thomas M Edwards; editor Bev Hogue; tel (419) 257-2771; fax (419) 257-3058

N Canton/Lake Twp./Plain Twp.: *The Sun Journal* — 7215 Whipple Ave. N.W. (44720); W; 4,000pd (Est); $6.35; publisher Stark Journal Inc.; general manager Bernard W Clements; editor Mark Knapik; managing editor Mike McNulti; tel (216) 966-1121; fax (216) 966-1202

N Columbus: *Northland This Week* — PO Box 341890, Columbus (43234); M; 25,951fr (Est); $9.30; C; publisher Consumer News Services Inc.; editor Ben Cason; managing editor Craig McDonald; tel (614) 841-1781; fax (614) 841-0767

N Olmsted/Westlake: *Sun Herald* — 5510 Cloverleaf Pkwy., Cleveland (44125-4887); Th; 16,958pd, 1,048fr (ABC); $23.60; C; publisher Gerald H Gordon; editor Kevin Burns; tel (216) 524-0830; fax (216) 524-7792

N Ridgeville: *The Press & Light* — 34100 Center Ridge Rd.; PO Box 89 (44039); W; 1,500pd, 2,500fr (Sw); $7.00; C; publisher Harold K Douthit III; general manager Toni Musgrove; editor Carol Klear; tel (216) 327-7543; fax (216) 327-2499

Northern Portage Co.: *The Gateway Press* — 9276 S.R. 14, Streetsboro (44241); W; 17,000fr (Sw); $7.50; publisher Record Publishing Co.; general manager Rich Sekella; editor Laura White; tel (216) 626-5558; fax (216) 626-5550

Northfield/Macedonia/Sagamore Hills: *Nordonia Hills Sun* — 5510 Cloverleaf Pkwy., Cleveland (44125-4887); Th; 3,471pd, 200fr (Est); $10.60; C; publisher Gerald H Gordon; editor Carol Kovach; tel (216) 524-0830; fax (216) 524-7792

Northfield/Macedonia/Sagamore Hills: *The News Leader* — 711 Broadway; PO Box 46059, Bedford (44146); W; 300pd, 9,100fr (Est); $6.24; C; publisher David E Dix; general manager Richard M Sekella; editor Erica Peterson; tel (216) 232-4055; fax (216) 232-8861

Northland: *The Northland News* — 5257 Sinclair Rd.; PO Box 29912, Columbus (43229); W; 7,736pd, 13,383fr (CAC); $9.10; C; publisher James A Toms; editor Martin M Rozenman; managing editor Joe Meyer; tel (614) 785-1212; fax (614) 842-4760

NW Columbus: *Northwest Columbus News* — 5257 Sinclair Rd.; PO Box 29912, Columbus (43229); W; 1,390pd, 5,240fr (CAC); $6.50; C; publisher James A Toms; editor Martin M Rozenman; managing editor Joe Meyer; tel (614) 785-1212; fax (614) 785-4760

Norton: *Sun Banner Pride* — PO Box 209, Wadsworth (44282); Th; 2,704pd, 350fr (ABC); $9.30; publisher Sun Newspapers Inc.; editor Charles Aukerman; tel (216) 725-1147; fax (216) 725-2314

Oak Harbor: *The Exponent* — 264 W. Water St.; PO Box 70 (43449); W; 2,500pd, 200fr (Est); $5.00; publisher Catherine Freed; general manager Raymond Herb; editor Kimra Traynor Herb; tel (419) 898-5361; fax (419) 898-0501

Oberlin: *Oberlin News-Tribune* — 42 S. Main St.; PO Box 29 (44074); Tu; 1,978pd, 143fr (Sw); $5.95; C; publisher Tom Smith; general manager Scott Swanson; editor Kathleen Koshar; tel (216) 775-1611; fax (216) 774-2167

Ontario/Lexington/Madison: *Tribune Courier & The Madison Tribune* — 347 Allen Dr.; PO Box 127, Ontario (44862); Th; 2,221pd, 64fr (Sw); $9.10; publisher Frank Stumbo; general manager & editor John J Kirschenheiter; managing editor Betty E Stumbo; tel (419) 529-2847; fax (419) 529-2847

Orwell/Grand Valley: *The Valley News* — 46 W. Jefferson St.; PO Box 166, Jefferson (44047); W; 1,151pd, 75fr (Sw); $8.25; C; publisher John Lampson; general manager Jeff Lampson; editor Doris Cook; managing editor Mark Owens; tel (216) 576-9115; fax (216) 576-2735

Oxford: *The Oxford Press* — 15 S. Beech St. (45056); Th; 3,862pd (Sw); $6.81; C; publisher William Cusack; editor Robert A Ratterman Jr; tel (513) 523-4139; fax (513) 523-1935

Pandora: *Pandora Times* — PO Box 167 (45877); W; 194pd, 15fr (Sw); $4.15; C; publisher Gary Hirt; general manager Brady Glick; editor Paul K Muckley; tel (419) 659-2173; fax (419) 659-2760

Parma: *Parma Sun Post* — 5510 Cloverleaf Pkwy., Cleveland (44125-4887); Th; 27,794pd, 993fr (ABC); $26.65; C; publisher Gerald H Gordon; editor Linda Kinsey; tel (216) 524-0830; fax (216) 524-7792

Pataskala: *The Pataskala Standard* — 350 S. Main St.; PO Box 7 (43062-0009); W; 4,486pd, 25fr (Sw); $4.25; C; publisher & editor T W Caw; general manager Margaret Caw; tel (614) 927-2991; fax (614) 927-2930

Paulding Co.: *Paulding Progress* — 113 S. Williams; PO Box 180, Paulding (45879); W; 3,743pd, 100fr (Sw); $4.55; publisher & editor Anna Brewster; tel (419) 399-4015; fax (419) 399-4030

Perrysburg: *Perrysburg Messenger-Journal* — 117 E. 2nd St.; PO Box 267 (43552); W; 5,654pd, 882fr (Sw); $5.20; C; publisher & editor Robert C Welch; tel (419) 874-4491

Pickerington: *Pickerington This Week* — PO Box 341890, Columbus (43234); M; 14,958fr (Est); $7.20; C; publisher Consumer News Services Inc.; editor Ben Cason; managing editor Craig McDonald; tel (614) 841-1781; fax (614) 841-0767

Pickerington: *The Pickerington Times-Sun* — 5257 Sinclair Rd.; PO Box 29912, Columbus (43229); W; 1,952pd, 4,872fr (CAC); $6.50; C; publisher James A Toms; editor Martin Rozenman; managing editor Joe Meyer; tel (614) 785-1212; fax (614) 842-4760

Plain City: *Plain City Advocate* — 30 S. Oak St.; PO Box 390, London (43140); Tu; 1,750pd (Sw); $5.00; C; publisher Donald L Hartley; editor Bill McCullick; tel (614) 852-1616; fax (614) 852-1620

Poland: *Poland Town Crier* — Tribune Box 47; PO Box 1431, Warren (44482-1431); Sa; 9,400fr (Est); $9.55; publisher Larry Dorshner; editor David Dutchek; managing editor Emily Webster; tel (216) 841-1619; fax (216) 841-1717

Port Clinton: *Port Clinton Beacon* — 106 W. Perry St.; PO Box 87 (43452); Th; 350pd, 16,132fr (Sw); $11.00; C; publisher & editor John Schaffner; tel (419) 732-2154; fax (419) 734-5382

Powell: *Olentangy Valley News* — 5257 Sinclair Rd.; PO Box 29912, Columbus (43229); W; 792pd, 4,900fr (CAC); $5.95; publisher James A Toms; editor Martin Rozenman; managing editor Joe Meyer; tel (614) 785-1212; fax (614) 842-4760

Powell: *Powell This Week* — PO Box 341890, Columbus (43234); M; 5,551fr (Sw); $5.50; C; publisher Consumer News Services Inc.; editor Ben Cason; managing editor Craig McDonald; tel (614) 841-1781; fax (614) 841-0767

Preble Co.: *County-Register* — 542 N. Barron St.; PO Box 120, Eaton (45320); Su; 12,919fr (Est) $4.80; C; publisher James R Hardin; editor Deron Newman; tel (513) 456-5553; fax (513) 456-3558

Preble Co.: *The Register-Herald* — 542 N. Barron St.; PO Box 120, Eaton (45320); W; 6,300pd, 58fr (Est); $4.12; C; publisher James R Hardin; editor Deron Newman; tel (513) 456-5553; fax (513) 456-3558

Putnam Co.: *Putnam County Sentinel* — 232 E. Main St.; PO Box 149, Ottawa (45875-0149); W; 7,911pd, 119fr (Sw); $3.98; C; publisher Gary L Hirt; general manager Brady M Glick; editor Nancy J Kline; tel (419) 523-5709

Randolph Twp./Englewood: *Englewood Independent* — 107 W. National Rd., Englewood (45322); W; 9,500pd (Est); $5.80; C; publisher Vernon T Bowling; general manager David E Copen; editor Steve D Drew; tel (513) 836-2610; fax (513) 836-1940

Reynoldsburg: *Reynoldsburg News* — 5257 Sinclair Rd.; PO Box 29912, Columbus (43229); W; 235pd, 11,071fr (CAC); $6.50; C; publisher James A Toms; editor Martin Rozenman; managing editor Joe Meyer; tel (614) 785-1212; fax (614) 842-4760

Reynoldsburg: *Reynoldsburg This Week* — PO Box 341890, Columbus (43234); M; 14,771fr (Sw); $7.20; C; publisher Consumer News Services Inc.; editor Ben Cason; managing editor Craig McDonald; tel (604) 841-1781; fax (604) 841-0767

Richwood: *Richwood Gazette* — 26 S. Franklin; PO Box 187 (43344-0187); W; 2,857pd, 16fr (Est); $4.90; publisher David Behrens; general manager Charlene Jolliff; editor Susan Leeper; tel (614) 943-2214

Ripley: *Ripley Bee* — 110 Waterworks Rd.; PO Box 97 (45167); W; 2,500pd, 500fr (Est); 15¢; publisher & editor Morgan Ross Jr; tel (513) 392-4321; fax (513) 392-4124

Rossford: *The Rossford Record Journal* — 117 E. 2nd St.; PO Box 267, Perrysburg (43552-0267); Th; 1,759pd, 374fr (Sw); $3.50; C; publisher & editor Robert C Welch; tel (419) 874-4491

Sebring: *Sebring Times* — 185 W. Ohio (44672); Th; 400pd, 75fr (Est); $3.30; C; publisher G Charles Dix II; editor K C Held; tel (216) 938-2060; fax (216) 821-8258

Sharonville/W Chester: *Suburban Press/Westchester Press* — PO Box 62359, Sharonville (45262); Th; 5,600pd (Sw); $6.45; C; publisher & editor James H Dygert; tel (513) 671-3000

Solon: *Solon Herald Sun* — 5510 Cloverleaf Pkwy., Cleveland (44125-4887); Th; 3,848pd, 242fr (ABC); $18.90; C; publisher Gerald H Gordon; editor Mary Jane Skala; tel (216) 524-0830; fax (216) 524-7792

Solon: *Solon Times* — 525 E. Washington St.; PO Box 150, Chagrin Falls (44022); Th; 3,048pd, 1,319fr (Sw); $22.50; publisher Harold K Douthit III; general manager Carole A Vigliotti; editor David Lange; tel (216) 247-5335; fax (216) 247-5615

S Cleveland: *The Leader* — 4818 Turney Rd., Garfield Heights (44125); Th; 6,500pd, 100fr (Est); $4.75; C; publisher & editor William E Kleinschmidt; tel (216) 883-0300; fax (216) 271-7447

S Columbus: *Southside This Week* — PO Box 341890, Columbus (43234); M; 24,907fr (Est); $8.35; C; publisher Consumer News Services Inc.; editor Ben Cason; managing editor Craig McDonald; tel (614) 841-1781; fax (614) 841-0767

SE Columbus: *The Southeast Messenger* — 3378 Sullivant Ave., Columbus (43204); M; 27,442fr (CAC); $9.15; C; publisher Earle F Moore Sr; general manager Philip F Daubel; editor Lorri Lowe; managing editor Ken Drenten; tel (614) 272-5422; fax (614) 272-0684

SE Stark Co.: *The Press-News* — PO Box 304, Minerva (44657-0304); Th; 2,450pd (Sw); $3.35; C; publisher G Charles Dix II; editor Karen Mundy; tel (216) 868-5222/3505; fax (216) 868-3273

SW Columbus: *Grove City Southwest Messenger* — 3378 Sullivant Ave., Columbus (43204); M; 16,460fr (CAC); $7.70; C; publisher Earl F Moore Sr; general manager Philip F Daubel; editor Harold Stevens; managing editor Ken Drenten; tel (614) 272-5422; fax (614) 272-0684

Spencerville: *The Journal News* — 126 N. Broadway; PO Box 8 (45887); Th; 2,080pd (Sw); $5.15; publisher Doris Beebe; editor Richard Beebe; tel (419) 647-4981

Springboro/Franklin: *The Star Press* — 25 E. Central Ave.; PO Box F, Springboro (45066); Tu/Su; 13,000pd (Est); $6.85; publisher Fred E Gibson; editor Terry Baver; tel (513) 748-2550; fax (513) 748-1165

Stow/Munroe Falls: *Stow Sentry* — 1619 Commerce Dr.; PO Box 1549, Stow (44224-0549); Su; 1,800pd, 12,200fr (Sw); $6.84; C; publisher David E Dix; general manager Richard M Sekella; editor Jeri Jewett; tel (216) 688-0088; fax (216) 688-1588

Streetsboro/Mantua/Hiram/Garrettsville/Shalersville: *Gateway News* — 9276 State Rte. 14, Streetsboro (44241); W; 14,000fr (Sw); $5.88; C; publisher David E Dix; general manager Richard M Sekella; editor Laura White; tel (216) 626-5558; fax (216) 626-5550

Strongsville: *Strongsville Sun Star* — 32 Park St., Brea (44017); Th; 9,155pd, 60fr (CAC); $9.50; C; publisher Gerald Gordon; editor Linda Kinsey; tel (216) 243-3725; fax (216) 243-4905

Strongsville/N Royalton: *The Sun Star* — 5510 Cloverleaf Pkwy., Cleveland (44125-4887); Th; 11,480pd, 756fr (ABC); $14.65; C; publisher Gerald H Gordon; editor Linda Kinsey; tel (216) 524-0830; fax (216) 524-7792

Struthers/Campbell/Lowellville: *The Journal* — 23 Lowellville Rd., Struthers (44471); Th; 5,000pd (Est); $5.00; publisher Lawrence V McCarthy; editor Karen S Spaite; tel (216) 755-2155

Stryker/W Unity: *The Advance Reporter* — 719 E. Jackson St., West Unity (43570); W; 2,006pd (Est); $14.29; publisher Regis L Spielvogel; editor Lee Spielvogel; tel (419) 924-2382; fax (419) 924-2382

Sugarcreek/Amish: *The Budget* — 134 N. Factory St.; PO Box 249, Sugarcreek (44681); W; 19,966pd, 1,161fr (Sw); $7.35; publisher Albert Spector; editor George Smith; managing editor Fannie Erb; tel (216) 852-4634; fax (216) 852-4421

Sunbury: *The Sunbury News* — 40 S. Vernon St.; PO Box 59 (43074); Th; 3,186pd, 37fr (Sw); $4.00; publisher The Delaware Gazette Publishing Co.; general manager Art Ruth; editor Susan Wright; tel (614) 965-3891; fax (614) 965-3992

Swanton/E Fulton Co.: *Swanton Enterprise* — 97 N. Main St.; PO Box 180, Swanton (43558); Tu; 1,611pd, 15fr (Sw); $7.60; C; publisher Tom Smith; general manager Robert Krumm; editor Debbie Katterheinrich; tel (419) 826-3580; fax (419) 826-3590

Sycamore: *Mohawk Leader* — 1198 E. Findlay St.; PO Box 368 (44882); W; 4,500pd (Est); 20¢; C; publisher & editor Stephen C Zender; tel (419) 396-7567; fax (419) 396-7527

Sylvania: *Sylvania Herald* — 4444 W. Alexis Rd.; PO Box 8830, Toledo (43623); W; 2,230pd (Est); $16.42; C; publisher Allen C Foster; editor Chris McKeon; tel (419) 475-6000; fax (419) 472-7774

Tallmadge: *Tallmadge Express* — 1619 Commerce Dr.; PO Box 1549, Stow (44224-0549); Su; 450pd, 6,100fr (Est); $6.00; C; publisher David E Dix; general manager Richard M Sekella; editor Sy O'Neill; tel (216) 688-0088; fax (216) 688-1588

Tipp City: *Tipp City Herald* — 1455 W. Main St.; PO Box 430 (45371-2803); W; 3,162pd, 45fr (Sw); $5.80; C; publisher Vernon T Bowling; general manager David Coven; editor Thomas Barnett; tel (513) 667-2214; fax (513) 667-8987

Toledo: *West Toledo Herald* — 4444 W. Alexis Rd. (43623); W; 23,097pd, 250fr (Est); $16.42; C; publisher Allen C Foster; editor Michael Brice; tel (419) 475-6000

Twinsburg: *The Bulletin* — 711 Broadway; PO Box 46059, Bedford (44146-0059); Th; 600pd, 6,500fr (Sw); $6.00; C; publisher David E Dix; general manager Richard M Sekella; editor Linda Hoy; tel (216) 232-4055; fax (216) 232-8861

Twinsburg: *The Twinsburg Sun* — 5510 Cloverleaf Pkwy., Cleveland (44125-4887); Th; 2,038pd, 200fr (Est); $10.60; C; publisher Gerald H Gordon; editor Carol Kovach; tel (216) 524-0830; fax (216) 524-7792

Union Co.: *Union County This Week* — PO Box 341890, Columbus (43234); Su; 13,645fr (Sw); $7.20; C; publisher Consumer News Services Inc.; editor Ben Cason; managing editor Craig McDonald; tel (614) 841-1781; fax (614) 841-0767

Upper Arlington: *The Upper Arlington News* — 5257 Sinclair Rd.; PO Box 29912, Columbus (43229); W; 7,815pd, 7,734fr (CAC); $9.10; C; publisher James A Toms; editor Martin Rozenman; managing editor Joe Meyer; tel (614) 785-1212; fax (614) 842-4760

Upper Arlington: *Upper Arlington* — PO Box 341890, Columbus (43234); M; 24,848fr (Sw); $9.30; C; publisher Consumer News Services Inc.; editor Ben Cason; managing editor Craig McDonald; tel (614) 841-1781; fax (614) 841-0767

Utica: *The Utica Herald* — 120 S. Main St.; PO Box 515 (43080); Th; 2,102pd, 7fr (Est); $3.20; publisher Nelson A Smith; editor Alan Reed; tel (614) 892-2771

Vermilion: *Vermilion Photojournal* — 630 N. Main; PO Box 23 (44089); Tu; 3,358pd, 486fr (Sw); $7.00; C; publisher Harold K Douthit III; editor Karen Cornelius; tel (216) 967-5268; fax (216) 967-1912

Versailles: *The Versailles Policy* — 13 E. Main St.; PO Box 74 (45380); W; 2,130pd, 101fr (Sw); $4.00; C; publisher & editor Scott Langston; tel (513) 526-9131; fax (513) 526-9131

Wadsworth/Norton: *Sun Banner Pride* — 5510 Clovercraf Pkwy.; PO Box 209, Cleveland (44125-4887); Th; 4,458pd, 350fr (ABC); $10.65; C; publisher Gerald H Gordon; editor Charles Aukerman; tel (216) 524-0830; fax (216) 524-7792

Waverly/Pike Co.: *The News Watchman* — 101 W. 2nd St.; PO Box 151, Waverly (45690); Tu/Th; 3,702pd (Sw); $5.12; C; publisher P Dale Gardner Jr; editor Betty McAdow; tel (614) 947-2149; fax (614) 947-1344

Wellington: *Wellington Enterprise* — PO Box 38 (44090); Tu; 2,796pd, 62fr (Sw); $5.60; publisher Tom Smith; general manager Scott Swanson; editor Jody Greene; managing editor Roger Roser; tel (216) 647-3171; fax (216) 647-3172

Wellston: *Wellston Sentry* — 22 S. Ohio Ave.; PO Box 310 (45692); Tu/Th; 1,880pd (Est); $5.12; C; publisher P Dale Gardner; editor Bob Farley; tel (614) 384-6786; fax (614) 286-5854

Wellston/Oakhill/Jackson/McArthur/Hamdem: *The Wellston Telegram* — 12 S. Ohio Ave.; PO Box 111, Wellston (45692); Th; 500pd, 4,800fr (Sw); $5.00; C; publisher & editor Steven P Keller; tel (614) 384-6102; fax (614) 384-3063

W Alexandria: *The Twin Valley News* — 105 S. Main St. (45381); Th; 890pd, 60fr (Est); 26¢; publisher & editor John McCarroll Keefe; tel (513) 839-4733; fax (513) 839-5351

W Chester/Liberty: *Community Press of West Chester* — 394 Wards Corner Rd., Ste. 160, Loveland (45140); W; 301pd, 14,582fr (CAC); $4.52; C; publisher Thomas E Niehaus; managing editor Gary L Presley; tel (513) 683-5115; fax (513) 677-4690

W Chester/Liberty Twp./Mason: *Pulse-Journal* — 1074 Reading Rd., Mason (45040); W; 25,050fr (Sw); $6.80; C; publisher Rhonda L Ford; editor Mary L Hitt; tel (513) 398-8856; fax (513) 459-7965

W Cleveland: *West Side Sun News* — 5510 Cloverleaf Pkwy., Cleveland (44125-4887); Th; 17,556pd, 804fr (ABC); $18.50; C; publisher Gerald H Gordon; editor Kevin Burns; tel (216) 524-0830; fax (216) 524-7792

W Columbus: *The Westside Messenger* — 3378 Sullivant Ave., Columbus (43204); M; 42,528fr (CAC); $14.60; C; publisher Earle F Moore Sr; general manager Philip F Daubel; editor Dan Trittschuh; managing editor Ken Drenten; tel (614) 272-5422; fax (614) 272-0684

W Columbus: *Westside This Week* — PO Box 341890, Columbus (43234); M; 13,126fr (Est); $7.20; C; publisher Consumer News Services Inc.; editor Ben Cason; managing editor Craig McDonald; tel (614) 841-1781; fax (614) 841-0767

W Milton: *West Milton Record* — 2 S. Miami St.; PO Box 277 (45383); W; 3,000pd (Est); $5.20; C; publisher Vernon Bowling; editor Karen Katzcuback; tel (513) 698-4451; fax (513) 667-8987

Westerville: *The Public Opinion* — 5257 Sinclair Rd.; PO Box 29912, Columbus (43229); F; 3,629pd, 1,382fr (Sw); $4.25; C; publisher James A Toms; editor Martin Rozenman; managing editor Joe Meyer; tel (614) 785-1212; fax (614) 842-4760

Westerville: *Westerville News* — 5257 Sinclair Rd.; PO Box 29912, Columbus (43229); W; 7,005pd, 11,058fr (CAC); $7.25; C; publisher James A Toms; editor Martin Rozenman; managing editor Joe Meyer; tel (614) 785-1212; fax (614) 842-4760

Westerville: *Westerville This Week* — PO Box 341890, Columbus (43234); M; 27,103fr (Sw); $8.80; C; publisher Consumer News Services Inc.; editor Ben Cason; managing editor Craig McDonald; tel (614) 841-1781; fax (614) 841-0767

Westlake/Bay Village: *Westlaker Times* — 21010 Center Ridge Rd., Rocky River (44146); Th; 1,558pd, 1,442fr (Sw); $11.60; C; publisher & editor Eleanor J Gottschalk; managing editor Aaron Buckholz; tel (216) 356-0920; fax (216) 356-0515

Westlake/N Olmsted/Bay Village/Fairview Park/Rocky River: *West Life* — 27006 Center Ridge Rd.; PO Box 45014, Westlake (44145); W; 15,120pd, 750fr (Est); $11.00; C; managing editor Mary Slama; tel (216) 871-5797; fax (216) 871-3824

Westland/New Rome/W Point/Galloway: *Westland News* — 5257 Sinclair Rd.; PO Box 29912, Columbus (43229); Th; 7pd, 16,852fr (Sw); $8.40; publisher James A Toms; editor Martin Rozenman; managing editor Joe Meyer; tel (614) 785-1212; fax (614) 842-4760

Wheelersburg: *The Scioto Voice* — 8019 Hayport Rd.; PO Box 400 (45694); Th; 3,570pd, 785fr (Sw); $4.85; publisher & editor James G Kegley; general manager Shawn Jordan; tel (614) 574-8494; fax (614) 574-2329

Whitehall: *Whitehall News* — 5257 Sinclair Rd.; PO Box 29912, Columbus (43229); W; 61pd, 8,313fr (CAC); $6.20; C; publisher James A Toms; editor Martin Rozenman; managing editor Joe Meyer; tel (614) 785-1212; fax (614) 842-4760

Willard: *Willard Times-Junction* — 211 Myrtle Ave.; PO Box 368 (44890-0368); M/Th; 3,416pd, 50fr (Sw); $5.92; C; publisher & editor Ken C Gove; general manager Karla Souslin; managing editor Jim Fairchild; tel (419) 935-0184; fax (419) 933-2031

Willshire: *Photo Star* — 307 State St.; PO Box B (45898); Tu; 275pd, 12,725fr (Est); $3.50; publisher Judith Bunner; editor John D Bunner; tel (419) 495-2696; fax (419) 495-2143

Woodsfield: *Monroe County Beacon* — 103 E. Court; PO Box 70 (43793); Th; 5,559pd, 144fr (Sw); $4.65; C; publisher & editor Kristina Vineyard; tel (614) 472-0734; fax (614) 472-0735

Worthington: *Worthington Suburbia News* — 5257 Sinclair Rd.; PO Box 29912, Columbus (43229); W; 6,983pd, 11,210fr (CAC); $8.10; C; publisher James A Toms; editor Martin Rozenman; managing editor Joe Meyer; tel (614) 785-1212; fax (614) 842-4760

Worthington: *Worthington This Week* — PO Box 341890, Columbus (43234); M; 24,781fr (Sw); $8.80; C; publisher Consumer News Services Inc.; editor Ben Cason; managing editor Craig McDonald; tel (614) 841-1781; fax (614) 841-0767

Yellow Springs: *Yellow Springs News* — 253 1/2 Xenia Ave.; PO Box 187 (45387); Th; 1,732pd, 39fr (Sw); $5.50; publisher Karen Hernandez; general manager Doug Hinkley; editor Amy Harper; tel (513) 767-7373

Youngstown/Boardman: *Boardman News* — 6221 Market St., Youngstown (44512); Th; 4,650pd, 100fr (Est); $5.00; publisher Jack A Darnell; editor John A Darnell; tel (216) 758-2658; fax (216) 758-2658

OKLAHOMA

Afton/Fairland: *The Afton-Fairland American* — 7 N. Main St.; PO Box 339, Fairland (74343); Th; 1,050pd, 20fr (Est); 14¢; publisher & editor John Link; tel (918) 676-3484; fax (918) 256-7100

Alfalfa Co.: *The Cherokee Messenger & Republican* — 216 S. Grand; PO Box 245, Cherokee (73728); Th; 2,296pd, 63fr (Sw); $3.80; publisher Larry Hammer; general manager Steve Booher; editor Carol Angle; tel (405) 596-3344

Allen: *The Allen Advocate* — 101 W. Broadway; PO Drawer 465 (74825); Th; 1,415pd, 50fr (Est); 11¢; publisher & editor Bill Robinson; tel (405) 857-2687; fax (405) 857-2573

Antlers: *Antlers American* — 106 E. Main St.; PO Box 578 (74523); W; 3,266pd, 50fr (Sw); $4.10; publisher & editor Joe H Cain; publisher Linda Cain; tel (405) 298-3314; fax (405) 298-3316

Apache: *The Apache News* — 121 E. Evans; PO Box 778 (73006); Th; 1,230pd, 35fr (Est); 16¢; publisher Stan Wright; editor Joye Wright; tel (405) 588-3862; fax (405) 588-3167

Arnett: *Ellis County Capital* — 323 E. Renfrow; PO Box 236 (73832); Th; 1,180pd, 50fr (Sw); $3.50; publisher Anita Denson; publisher & editor Jerry L Denson; tel (405) 885-7788

Atoka: *Atoka County Times* — 100 E. 2nd; PO Box 330 (74525); W; 3,933pd (Est); $4.30; publisher Louise Cain; editor Kenneth Hamilton; tel (405) 889-3319; fax (405) 889-2300

Barnsdall: *Barnsdall Times* — 118 N. 5th St.; PO Box 469 (74002); Th; 1,225pd, 87fr (Sw); $2.52; publisher & editor Robert L Evans; tel (918) 847-2916

Beaver: *The Herald-Democrat* — 108 S. Douglas; PO Box 490 (73932-0490); Th; 2,000pd, 2,335fr (Sw); $3.25; C; publisher & editor Joe Lansden; tel (405) 625-3241

Bethany: *The Tribune* — 3813 N. College; PO Box 40 (73008); Th; 2,758pd, 5fr (Est); $5.95; publisher Ken Brett Wesner; general manager Terry Barnett; editor Lyne Gardner; tel (405) 789-1962; fax (405) 789-4253

Bixby: *Bixby Bulletin* — 8545 E. 41st St., Tulsa (74145); Th; 1,445pd, 71fr (Sw); $6.85; publisher Bill R Retherford; general manager Charles E Cagle; editor Mike McCarty; managing editor Ralph Schaefer; tel (918) 663-1414; fax (918) 664-8161

Boise City/Cimarron Co.: *The Boise City News* — 105 W. Main; PO Box 278, Boise City (73933-0278); W; 1,712pd, 73fr (Est); $3.43; publisher & editor Jim Rosebery; tel (405) 544-2222; fax (405) 544-3281

Bristow: *The Bristow News* — 112 W. 6th Ave.; PO Box 840 (74010); W; 3,231pd, 25fr (Sw); $5.50; publisher Bristow Publishers Inc.; general manager Roberta A Williams; tel (918) 367-2282; fax (918) 367-2724

Bristow: *The Record-Citizen* — 112 W. 6th Ave.; PO Box 840 (74010); Sa; 3,134pd, 25fr (Sw); $5.50; publisher Bristow Publishers Inc.; general manager Roberta A Williams; tel (918) 367-2282

Broken Arrow: *Broken Arrow Ledger* — 110 W. Kenosha (74012); Tu/Th; 3,731pd, 81fr (Sw); $7.50; Su; 3,731pd, 81fr (Sw); $9.40; C; publisher Bill R Retherford; general manager Charles Cagle; editor Wayne Bishop; managing editor Ralph Schaefer; tel (918) 258-7171

Broken Bow: *Broken Bow News* — 108 N. Broadway (74728); W/Su; 2,193pd, 70fr (Est); $1.05; publisher Bruce Willingham; editor Tisha Holladay; tel (405) 584-6210; fax (405) 584-9466

Bryan Co.: *Bryan County Star* — 111 W. Main; PO Box 1427, Durant (74702); Th; 6,000pd, 300fr (Est); 13¢; publisher & editor Cecil Plyler; tel (405) 924-6499; fax (405) 924-7685

Buffalo: *Harper County Journal* — 3 W. Turner; PO Drawer 240 (73834); W; 1,213pd, 3fr (Sw); $3.19; C; publisher Jerry Anderson; editor Terrie F Balcomb; tel (405) 735-2526; fax (405) 735-2527

Carnegie: *Carnegie Herald* — 14 W. Main; PO Box 129 (73015); W; 1,860pd, 40fr (Est); $3.50; publisher Donald Cooper; publisher & editor Lori Cooper; tel (405) 654-1443; fax (405) 654-1608

Carter Co.: *The Carter County Courier* — 619 W. Broadway, Ardmore (73401); W; 5,000pd, 100fr (Sw); $6.00; C; publisher Tim McCullers; general manager Lillian Scheppers; editor Jon Parker; managing editor Michael McCullers; tel (405) 226-6397; fax (405) 226-8381

Catoosa: *Port of Catoosa Times-Herald* — 650 S. Cherokee; PO Box 40 (74015); W; 3,560pd (Est); $3.25; publisher Eula Kester; general manager Angie Hixson; managing editor John Kester; tel (918) 266-3664; fax (918) 266-3666

Chandler: *Lincoln County News* — 718 Manvel Ave.; PO Box 248 (74834); Th; 4,048pd, 32fr (Sw); $3.80; C; publisher Stephen E Mathis; general manager P Dawn Mathis; editor Nancy Hart; tel (405) 258-1818; fax (405) 258-1824

Checotah: *McIntosh County Democrat* — 201 W. Okmulgee; PO Box 385, Checotah (74426); Th; 2,995pd, 70fr (Est); 20¢; publisher Jim Lonsdale; general manager Connie Morris; editor Don Campbell; tel (918) 473-2313; fax (918) 473-6541

Chelsea: *Chelsea Reporter* — 245 W. 6th St.; PO Box 6 (74016); Th; 1,753pd, 29fr (Sw); $3.00; publisher & editor Robert A Herring; tel (918) 789-2331

Choctaw/Nicoma Park: *Choctaw/Nicoma Park Free Press* — 6301 Tinker Diagonal (73110); PO Box 30338, Midwest City (73140-3338); Th; 1,747pd, 89fr (Sw); $5.60; C; publisher & editor Richard R Hefton; tel (405) 737-3050; fax (405) 733-2068

Clayton/Pushmataha Co.: *Clayton Today* — PO Box 246, Clayton (74536); Th; 1,300pd (Est); $2.50; publishers Mitch Mullin & Sandy Mullin; general manager & editor Virginia Weaver; managing editor Linda Madlock; tel (918) 569-4741; fax (918) 569-4741

Coalgate: *The Coalgate Record-Register* — 115 N. Main; PO Box 327 (74538); W; 2,062pd, 35fr (Est); $3.50; C; publisher & editor Bill Robinson; publisher Dayna Robinson; general manager Helen Langdon; tel (405) 927-2355; fax (405) 927-3800

Collinsville: *Collinsville News* — 8545 E. 41st St., Tulsa (74145); W; 1,816pd, 40fr (Sw); $6.85; publisher Bill R Retherford; general manager Charles E Cagle; editor Nancy Schuette; managing editor Ralph Schaefer; tel (918) 663-1414; fax (918) 664-8161

Comanche: *Comanche Times* — 400 N. Hwy. 81 (73529); Th; 1,221pd, 35fr (Sw); $2.50; publisher & editor Steve Bolton; publisher Tracy Bolton; tel (405) 439-6500; fax (405) 439-6500

Cordell/Washita Co.: *The Cordell Beacon* — 115 E. Main St.; PO Box 220, Cordell (73632); W; 4,136pd (Sw); $3.50; publisher Ken Wesner; editor Jason McCarty; tel (405) 832-3333; fax (405) 832-3335

Corn: *Washita County Enterprise* — 202 W. Main; PO Box 68 (73024); Th; 900pd (Est); 14¢; publisher James Resneder; editor Flo Richardson; tel (405) 343-2513; fax (405) 343-2513

Cotton Co.: *Walters Herald* — 112 E. Colorado St.; PO Box 247, Walters (73572); Th; 2,770pd, 30fr (Est); $3.64; publisher & editor Scott Wesner; tel (405) 875-3326; fax (405) 875-3150

Covington/Marshall: *Covington Record* — PO Drawer L, Covington (73730); Th; 584pd, 54fr (Sw); $3.50; C; publisher Covington Publishing Co.; editors Janet Smith & Nancy Miller; tel (405) 864-7612

Coweta/Porter/Haskell: *Coweta America* — 107 S. Broadway, Coweta (74429); W; 2,745pd, 34fr (Sw); $6.85; C; publisher Bill R Retherford; general manager Charles E Cagle; editor Christi Wheeland; managing editor Ralph Schaefer; tel (918) 486-4444; fax (918) 664-8161

Crescent: *The Logan County News* — 215 S. 1st; PO Box 1630, Guthrie (73044); W; 4,200pd (Est); $5.00; F/Su; 4,000pd (Est); $5.00; publisher & editor David Ulrich; tel (405) 282-7093; fax (405) 282-2140

Cyril/Cement: *The Cyril News* — 102 Main; PO Box 10, Cyril (73029); Th; 1,090pd, 95fr (Sw); 15¢; publisher & editor Earl Reeves; tel (405) 464-2410

Davis/Murray Co.: *The Davis News* — 321 E. Main; PO Box 98, Davis (73030); Th; 1,760pd, 39fr (Sw); $3.50; publisher & editor Sharon R Chadwick; tel (405) 369-2807; fax (405) 369-2574

Del City: *Del City Sun* — 6301 Tinker Diagonal; PO Box 30338 (73140); Th; 1,404pd, 19fr (VAC); $5.60; C; publisher & editor Richard R Hefton; tel (405) 737-3050; fax (405) 733-2068

El Reno: *El Reno Tribune* — 201 N. Rock Island; PO Box 9 (73036-0009); W; 4,084pd, 11,300fr (Sw); $4.70; Su; 4,084pd (Sw); $4.70; publisher & editor Ray T Dyer; publisher & general manager Sean E Dyer; tel (405) 262-5180; fax (405) 262-5180

Eldorado: *The Eldorado Courier* — 507 W. Main St.; PO Box 10 (73537); Th; 655pd, 25fr (Est); 55¢; publisher & editor James B Hynum; tel (405) 633-2376

Erick: *Beckham County Democrat* — PO Box 49 (73645); Th; 1,039pd (Sw); $2.24; publishers & editors Charles R Shultz & Helen Shultz; tel (405) 526-3392

Eufaula/McIntosh: *Indian Journal* — 109 S. Main; PO Box 689, Eufaula (74432); Th; 3,600pd (Est); $3.33; publisher & editor Connie Morris; tel (918) 689-2191; fax (918) 689-2377

Eufaula/McIntosh: *Lake Eufaula World* — Rte. 4; PO Box 183, Eufaula (74432); Th; 3,981pd, 300fr (Sw); $3.10; publisher & editor Connie Morris; tel (918) 689-5291; fax (918) 689-5492

Fairview: *Fairview Republican* — 112 N. Main; PO Box 497 (73737); Th; 3,117pd, 45fr (Sw); $4.00; C; publisher Hoby Hammer; editor Liz Bennett; tel (405) 227-4439

II-64 **Oklahoma** *U.S. Weeklies*

Fletcher: *Fletcher Herald* — 424 W. Cole St.; PO Box 469 (73541); Th; 1,030pd, 69fr (Sw); 11¢; publisher Kent Herring; editor Joretta Herring; tel (405) 549-6045; fax (405) 549-6045

Ft. Cobb: *The Fort Cobb News* — 314 Main; PO Box 250 (73038); Th; 797pd, 13fr (Sw); 13¢; publisher & editor John J Jackson; tel (405) 643-2331

Frederick: *The Frederick Press* — 117 N. 9th St.; PO Box 367 (73542); Th; 2,283pd, 50fr (Est); $4.00; publisher Shelby Miller; managing editor Sharen Housley; tel (405) 335-3893; fax (405) 335-5400

Freedom: *The Freedom Call* — PO Box 172 (73842); Th; 480pd (Est); 60¢; publisher & editor Linda Carrico; tel (405) 621-3578

Gage: *Gage Record* — 323 E. Renfrow; PO Box 236, Arnett (73832); Th; 415pd, 20fr (Sw); $3.00; publisher Anita Denson; publisher & editor Jerry L Denson; tel (405) 885-7788

Garber/Billings: *Garber-Billings News* — 516 Main St.; PO Box 9, Garber (73738); Th; 683pd, 35fr (Sw); $3.00; publisher & editor Vickie Hogan; tel (405) 863-2240; fax (405) 863-2240

Geary: *Geary Star* — 114 W. Main St. (73040); Th; 1,016pd, 46fr (Est); $2.94; publisher & editor Fred Bingham; general manager Elesha Bingham; tel (405) 884-2424; fax (405) 884-2308

Glenpool: *Glenpool Post* — 8545 E. 41st St., Tulsa (74145); W; 737pd, 47fr (Sw); $6.85; C; publisher Bill R Retherford; general manager Charles Cagle; editor Sally McGrew; managing editor Ralph Schaefer; tel (918) 663-1414

Grandfield/Chattanooga/Devol/Randlett: *The Big Pasture News* — PO Box 608, Grandfield (73546); Sa; 878pd, 15fr (Sw); $2.10; publisher & editor Phyllis Branham; tel (405) 479-5757

Granite: *The Granite Enterprise* — 311 N. Main; PO Box 128 (73547); Th; 824pd, 8fr (Sw); $2.85; publisher Patti Locklear; general manager David Locklear; editor Tena Hahn Locklear; managing editor Jan Locklear; tel (405) 535-2166; fax (405) 535-2166

Grove: *The Grove Sun* — 14 W. 3rd St.; PO Box 969 (74344); W/Su; 7,700pd, 10fr (Est); $6.40; publisher & editor M Gerald Stone; managing editor Don Cease; tel (918) 786-9051; fax (918) 786-2156

Guthrie: *Guthrie Register News* — 107 W. Harrison; PO Box 879 (73044); W; 6,000pd (Sw); $4.80; publisher Robert Hager; editor Tara Frick; tel (405) 282-2222

Harrah/Newalla: *The Harrah Herald* — 6301 Tinker Diagonal; PO Box 30338, Midwest City (73140); Th; 747pd, 45fr (VAC); $5.60; C; publisher & editor Richard R Hefton; tel (405) 737-3050; fax (405) 733-2068

Hartshorne/Pittsburg Co.: *Hartshorne Sun* — 1130 Penn Ave.; PO Box 330, Hartshorne (74547-0330); Th; 1,264pd, 62fr (Sw); $4.42; general manager Owen Jones; editor Jim Nicholson; tel (918) 297-2577; fax (918) 297-2577

Healdton/Fox/Ratliff City/Velma: *The Healdton Herald* — 439 W. Main St.; PO Box 250, Healdton (73438); Th; 1,755pd, 18fr (Sw); $3.50; C; publisher & managing editor Cleo Chaffin; publisher & editor Ken Chaffin; tel (405) 229-0132; fax (405) 229-0132

Heavener: *The Heavener Ledger* — 507 E. 1st St.; PO Box 38 (74937-0038); Th; 4,000pd, 250fr (Sw); 15¢; publisher & editor Jack Johnson; publisher James A Johnson; tel (918) 653-2425; fax (918) 653-7305

Hennessey: *The Hennessey Clipper* — 117 S. Main; PO Box 338 (73742); Th; 1,440pd, 140fr (Sw); $4.50; publisher William B Walter; editor Barbara A Walter; tel (405) 853-4888; fax (405) 853-6297

Hinton: *Hinton Record* — 108 E. Main; PO Box 959 (73047); Th; 642pd, 6fr (Sw); 14¢; C; publisher & editor Tim Curtin; managing editor Debra Potts; tel (405) 542-6644; fax (405) 542-3746

Hollis: *The Hollis News* — 119 W. Broadway; PO Box 709 (73550); Th; 1,864pd, 51fr (Sw); $2.66; publisher Tom Higley; general manager & editor Judy Webb; tel (405) 688-9271/3376; fax (405) 688-2261

Hominy: *The Hominy News/Progress* — 115 W. Main St.; PO Box 38 (74035); W; 1,612pd, 35fr (Est); $2.75; C; publishers D Jo Ferguson & Larry Ferguson; general manager Ramona Brown; tel (918) 885-2101

Hugo/Ft. Towson/Boswell/Soper/Grant: *Choctaw County Times* — 300 N. B St., Hugo (74743); W; 2,500pd, 500fr (Est); $3.00; C; publisher & managing editor Linda Rabon; general manager Deborah Brock; editor Pat Ray; tel (405) 326-8353; fax (405) 326-5388

Hydro: *The Hydro Review* — 104 E. Main St.; PO Box 188 (73048); W; 642pd, 6fr (Sw); 14¢; C; publisher & editor Tim Curtin; tel (405) 663-2237; fax (405) 663-2137

Inola/Rogers Co.: *Inola Independent* — 16 W. Commercial; PO Box 999, Inola (74036); W; 1,300pd, 50fr (Sw); $2.25; publisher Robert L Evans; editor Yvonne M Evans; tel (918) 543-8786; fax (918) 543-2881

Jay/Colcord/Kansas/Oaks: *Delaware County Journal* — 254 5th St.; PO Box 1050, Jay (74346); W; 2,118pd, 30fr (Sw); $4.00; C; publisher M Gerald Stone; editor John Reid III; tel (918) 253-4322; fax (918) 786-2156

Jenks: *Jenks Journal* — 8545 E. 41st St., Tulsa (74145); Th; 1,341pd, 77fr (Sw); $6.85; C; publisher Bill R Retherford; general manager Charles Cagle; managing editor Ralph Schaefer; tel (918) 663-1414

Jones/Spencer Luther: *The Oklahoma County News* — 6301 Tinker Diagonal; PO Box 30338, Midwest City (73140); Th; 970pd, 41fr (VAC); $5.60; C; publisher & editor Richard R Hefton; tel (405) 737-3050; fax (405) 733-2068

Kingfisher: *The Kingfisher Times & Free Press* — 323 N. Main; PO Box 209 (73750); W/Su; 3,926pd, 120fr (Sw); $4.30; publisher & editor Gary Reid; tel (405) 375-3220; fax (405) 375-3222

Konawa: *Konawa Leader* — 103 N. Broadway; PO Box 157 (74849); Th; 1,550pd (Sw); 90¢; publisher Max Gallagher; general manager & editor Ed Gallagher; tel (405) 925-3187; fax (405) 925-3187

Laverne: *Laverne Leader Tribune* — 205 S. Broadway; PO Box 370 (73848); W; 1,277pd, 21fr (Sw); 11¢; publisher Jerry Anderson; editor Sonya Harris; tel (405) 921-3391; fax (405) 921-3392

Lindsay: *Lindsay News* — 117 S. Main St.; PO Box 768 (73052); Th; 3,200pd (Est); 13¢; publisher & editor Meredon Cable; general manager Darrell Cable; managing editor Melissa Hughes; tel (405) 756-4461; fax (405) 756-4461

Lone Grove/Carter Co.: *The Lone Grove Ledger* — Ledger Center Hwy. 70; PO Box 577, Lone Grove (73443-0577); W; 1,018pd, 100fr (Sw); $3.45; publisher Gary K Hicks; editor Linda Hicks; tel (405) 657-6492

Madill: *The Madill Record* — 211 Plaza; PO Box 529 (73446); Th; 4,001pd, 102fr (Est); $4.50; publisher Mark A Codner; general manager Sherry Codner; editor Julia Davis; tel (405) 795-3355; fax (405) 795-3530

Mangum: *The Mangum Star-News* — 110 E. Lincoln; PO Box 340 (73554); Th; 3,150pd (Sw); 15¢; publisher & editor Michael Bush; tel (405) 782-3321; fax (405) 782-2198

Mannford/Jennings: *Mannford Eagle* — 8545 E. 41st St., Tulsa (74145); W; 1,264pd, 52fr (Sw); $3.41; C; publisher Bill R Retherford; general manager Charles Cagle; editor Jerri DeWeese; managing editor Ralph Schaefer; tel (918) 663-1414

Marietta: *Marietta Monitor* — 104 W. Main St.; PO Box 330 (73448); F; 3,280pd, 30fr (Sw); $2.25; publisher Willis Choate; editor Wilma Choate; tel (405) 276-3255; fax (405) 276-2118

Marlow: *The Marlow Review* — 316 W. Main; PO Box 153 (73055); Th; 3,700pd, 10fr (Sw); 18¢; publisher & editor Harbour Whitaker; tel (405) 658-6657

Maysville: *The Maysville News* — 402 Williams St.; PO Box 617 (73057); Th; 1,041pd, 20fr (Est); $2.38; publisher & editor Kenneth R Wood; tel (405) 867-4457; fax (405) 867-5115

McLoud: *The McLoud News* — 109 N. Main; PO Box 517 (74851); Th; 1,400pd, 50fr (Est); $4.80; publisher & editor Larry Thornjon; tel (405) 964-2920; fax (405) 964-2930

Medford: *The Medford Patriot-Star and Grant County Journal* — 116 1/2 W. Cherokee; PO Box 49 (73759); W; 1,837pd, 48fr (Sw); 14¢; publisher & editor R D Cowger; publisher Rose Cowger; tel (405) 395-2212

Meeker/Lincoln Co.: *The Meeker News* — 620 Main St.; PO Box 686, Meeker (74855); Th; 1,350pd, 18fr (Est); $2.52; publisher Judy Friskup; editor Kent Friskup; tel (405) 279-2363; fax (405) 279-3850

Midwest City: *The Midwest City Sun* — 6301 Tinker Diagonal; PO Box 30338 (73140); Th; 4,566pd, 37fr (VAC); $7.42; C; publisher & editor Richard R Hefton; tel (405) 737-3050; fax (405) 733-2068

Midwest City: *The Sunday Sun* — 6301 Tinker Diagonal; PO Box 30338 (73140); Su; 10,124pd, 30fr (VAC); $11.80; C; publisher & editor Richard R Hefton; tel (405) 737-3050; fax (405) 733-2068

Minco/Grady Co.: *Minstrel* — 305 W. Main St.; PO Box 448, Minco (73059); Th; 800pd, 25fr (Est); $2.52; publisher & editor Marshall Settle; tel (405) 352-4221; fax (405) 224-2711

Moore/S Oklahoma City: *Moore American* — 623 N. Broadway (73160); PO Box 6739, Moore (73153); F; 3,285pd, 630fr (Sw); $5.80; C; publisher Oran Redden; editor Bob Doucette; tel (405) 794-5555; fax (405) 799-8046

Mooreland: *Mooreland Leader* — PO Box 137 (73852); Th; 918pd, 45fr (Sw); $2.54; publisher & editor Tim Schnoebelen; tel (405) 994-5410; fax (405) 994-5409

Mustang/Canadian Co.: *The Mustang News* — 464 N. Financial Center Ter.; PO Box 67, Mustang (73064); Th; 3,143pd, 150fr (Sw); $3.95; C; publisher Kathy Crout; general manager Robert Crout; editor Mike Clark; tel (405) 376-4571; fax (405) 376-3722

Newcastle/McClain Co.: *Newcastle Pacer* — 120 N.E. 2nd, Ste. 102; PO Box 429, Newcastle (73065); Th; 1,450pd, 72fr (Sw); $2.75; publisher & general manager Jocile Leyerle; publisher & editor Marvin Leyerle; tel (405) 387-5277; fax (405) 387-9863

Newkirk: *The Newkirk Herald Journal* — 121 N. Main; PO Box 131 (74647-0131); Th; 1,463pd (Sw); $4.78; publisher & editor Robert W Lobsinger; tel (405) 362-2140

Nowata Co.: *The Nowata Star* — 213 N. Maple, Nowata (74048); W; 2,240pd (Sw); $4.62; publisher David Reid; editor Dave Altman; tel (918) 273-2446

Okarche/Canadian Co.: *Chieftain* — 118-A N. Main St.; PO Box 468, Okarche (73762); Th; 1,000fr (Est); $2.00; publisher & editor Roger Pugh; managing editor Kevin Young; tel (405) 373-1616; fax (405) 373-1636

Okeene: *Okeene Record* — PO Box 664 (73763); Th; 1,009pd, 25fr (Sw); $3.75; publishers Connie Miller & Mack Miller; editor Pamela Davis; tel (405) 822-4401; fax (405) 822-3051

Okemah: *Okemah News Leader* — 602 W. Broadway; PO Box 191 (74859); Th/Su; 2,867pd, 17fr (Sw); $3.50; publisher & editor Guy Mason; tel (918) 623-0123; fax (918) 623-1024

Oklahoma City: *Friday* — 10801 N. Quail Plaza Dr.; PO Box 20340 (73156); F; 8,052pd, 84fr (VAC); $8.68; C; publisher & editor J Leland Gourley; general manager Vicki Gourley; managing editor Gordon Walker; tel (405) 755-3311

Oklahoma City: *The Capitol Hill Beacon* — 124 W. Commerce (73109); Th; 526pd, 13,838fr (VAC); 81¢; publisher & editor David Sellers; tel (405) 232-4151; fax (405) 235-0818

Okmulgee Co./Morris: *The Morris News* — 112 S. 4th St.; PO Box 113, Morris (74445); W; 985pd, 14fr (Sw); $3.00; publisher & editor Herman L Thompson; tel (918) 733-4898; fax (918) 733-4153

Olustee: *Eldorado Courier* — PO Box 56, El Dorado (73537); Th; 450pd, 25fr (Est); 55¢; publisher & editor Wilma Jo Bassel; tel (405) 633-2376

Oologah/Rogers Co.: *Oologah Lake Leader* — 109 S. Maple; PO Box 460, Oologah (74053-0460); Th; 1,788pd, 35fr (Sw); $4.92; publisher Faith Wylie; publisher & editor John Wylie II; managing editor Carolyn Estes; tel (918) 443-2428

Owasso: *Owasso Reporter* — 8545 E. 41st St., Tulsa (74145); Th; 3,982pd, 67fr (Sw); $7.50; publisher Bill R Retherford; general manager Charles E Cagle; editor Peggy Robinson; managing editor Ralph Schaefer; tel (918) 663-1414; fax (918) 664-8161

Pawhuska: *Pawhuska Journal-Capital* — 700 Kihekah; PO Box 238 (74056); W/Sa; 1,863pd, 37fr (Sw); $4.30; publisher & editor Jim Butcher; tel (918) 287-1590; fax (918) 287-1804

Pawnee/Pawnee Co.: *Pawnee Chief* — 6th & Illinois Sts.; PO Box 370, Pawnee (74058); W; 2,719pd, 176fr (Sw); $3.50; publisher & editor D Jo Ferguson; tel (918) 762-2552; fax (918) 762-2554

Perkins: *Perkins Journal* — 122 S. Main St.; PO Box 40 (74059); Th; 2,325pd, 25fr (Est); 21¢; publisher & editor R V Clark; tel (405) 547-2411; fax (405) 547-2411

Picher: *Tri-State Tribune* — 120 N. Connell Ave.; PO Box 307 (74360); Th; 5,910pd, 90fr (Est); 16¢; publisher Eula Kester; editor John R Kester; tel (918) 673-1085; fax (918) 673-1140

Piedmont/Canadian Co.: *The Piedmont-Surrey Gazette* — 113 Monroe Ave. N.W., Piedmont (73078); Th; 891pd, 27fr (Sw); $3.94; publisher & managing editor Roger Pugh; editor Kevin Young; tel (405) 373-1616; fax (405) 373-1636

Prague: *Times-Herald* — 1123 Broadway; PO Box U (74864-1100); Th; 2,306pd, 10fr (Sw); $2.90; publisher & editor Charles McCormick; managing editor Sharon Maggard; tel (405) 567-3933; fax (405) 567-3934

Pryor: *The Pryor Jeffersonian* — 105 S. Adair; PO Box 308 (74362); W; 3,352pd (Est); $3.75; publisher Henry L Goodman; editor Terry Alward; tel (918) 825-1300; fax (918) 825-1965

Purcell: *Purcell Register* — 225 W. Main St.; PO Box 191 (73080); Th; 5,684pd, 103fr (Est); $6.30; publisher & editor John D Montgomery; general manager Grace E Montgomery; managing editor Bill Moakley; tel (405) 527-2126; fax (405) 527-3299

Ringling: *The Ringling Eagle* — 103 E. Main St.; PO Box 626 (73456-0626); Th; 1,151pd, 20fr (Sw); $3.50; publisher & editor Melissa Grace; managing editor Mary Grace; tel (405) 662-2221

Rush Springs: *The Rush Springs Gazette* — 220 W. Blakely; PO Box 597 (73082); Th; 1,200pd, 25fr (Est); $1.82; C; publisher Conn Goodwin; publisher & editor Karen Goodwin; tel (405) 476-2525

Ryan: *The Ryan Leader* — 606 Washington St.; PO Box 220 (73565); Th; 567pd, 45fr (Sw); $1.75; publisher Tracy Mesler; editor Addie Williams; tel (405) 757-2281

Sallisaw: *Sequoyah County Times* — 111 N. Oak (74955); Th/Su; 6,367pd, 318fr (Sw); $5.50; publisher James Mayo; editor Sally Maxwell; tel (918) 775-4433; fax (918) 775-3023

Sand Springs: *Sand Springs Leader* — 8545 E. 41st St., Tulsa (74145); W; 3,720pd, 70fr (Sw); $8.50; Su; 3,720pd, 70fr (Sw); $6.00; C; publisher Bill R Retherford; general manager Charles Cagle; editor Jill Reeves; managing editor Ralph Schaefer; tel (918) 663-1414

Sayre: *Sayre Record* — 711 N. 4th St. (73662); W; 1,689pd, 20fr (Sw); $2.60; publisher Brad Spitzer; editor Dayva Spitzer; tel (405) 928-5540; fax (405) 928-5550

Sayre/Beckham Co.: *The Sayre Journal* — 110 N. 4th St.; PO Box 340, Sayre (73662-0340); Th; 1,981pd, 18fr (Sw); $2.86; C; publisher & editor Tom Higley; general manager & managing editor Sonya M Blackshear; tel (405) 928-3372; fax (405) 928-3211

Sentinel: *Sentinel Leader* — 307 E. Main St.; PO Box 37 (73664); Th; 1,350pd, 25fr (Est); $3.36; publisher & editor Mark Schoonmaker; managing editor Emma Schoonmaker; tel (405) 393-4348; fax (405) 393-4349

Shattuck: *Northwest Oklahoman* — 329 S. Main St.; PO Box 460 (73858); Th; 1,349pd, 28fr (Sw); $3.00; publisher & editor Neil Colbert; tel (405) 938-2533; fax (405) 938-5240

Shawnee: *Shawnee American* — 106 W. Main St. (74801); PO Box 1592 (74802-1592); F; 105pd (Sw); 70¢; publisher Jim Clifton; editor Marguerite Clifton; tel (405) 275-1000

Shawnee: *The Shawnee Sun* — 114 N. Broadway; PO Box 3578 (74802-3578); Th; 1,245pd, 150fr (Sw); $5.50; C; publisher & editor Wayne Trotter; tel (405) 275-3891; fax (405) 598-3891

Shidler: *Shidler Review* — 213 Cosden Ave.; PO Box 6 (74652); Th; 1,269pd, 10fr (Est); 35¢; publisher & editor Brenda Lawless; tel (918) 793-3841; fax (918) 793-3841

Skiatook: *Skiatook Journal* — 8545 E. 41st St., Tulsa (74145); W; 2,312pd, 48fr (Sw); $6.85; publisher Bill R Retherford; general manager Charles E Cagle; editor Donna Pearce; managing editor Ralph Schaefer; tel (918) 663-1414; fax (918) 664-8161

Snyder: *Kiowa County Democrat* — 610 E St.; PO Box 305 (73566); Th; 1,253pd, 22fr (Sw); $3.00; publisher & editor O T Brooks; tel (405) 569-2684; fax (405) 569-2640

Spiro: *Spiro Graphic* — 212 S. Main St.; PO Box 190 (74959); Th; 2,659pd, 152fr (Sw); $3.58; C; publisher Jim Fienup; editor John Clark; tel (918) 962-2075; fax (918) 962-3531

Stigler: *Stigler News-Sentinel* — 204 S. Broadway; PO Box 549 (74462); Th; 4,020pd, 150fr (Est); 24¢; publisher Linus G Williams; editor Sharon M Johnson; tel (918) 967-4655; fax (918) 967-4289

Stilwell: *Stilwell Democrat Journal* — 118 N. 2nd St.; PO Box 508 (74960); Th; 6,000pd, 58fr (Sw); $3.50; publisher Brad Sugg; general manager & managing editor Jean Price; editor Jim Monroe; tel (918) 696-2228; fax (916) 696-7066

Stroud/Lincoln Creek: *Stroud American* — 315 W. Main St.; PO Box 400, Stroud (74079); Th; 2,451pd, 49fr (Sw); 13¢; publisher & editor Billie F Brown; tel (918) 968-2581; fax (918) 968-3864

Sulphur: *Sulphur Times-Democrat* — 115 W. Muskogee; PO Box 131 (73086); W; 3,644pd, 160fr (Est); $2.40; publisher & editor James John; general manager & managing editor Kathy John; tel (405) 622-2102; fax (405) 622-2937

Talihina: *Talihina American* — 205 N.W. 5th; PO Box 37, Wilburton (74578); Th; 1,610pd, 10fr (Sw); $3.40; publishers Mitch Mullin & Sandy Mullin; editor Ann Driver; tel (918) 567-2390; fax (918) 567-2390

Tecumseh: *The Tecumseh Countywide News* — 101 N. Broadway; PO Box 38 (74873); Th; 1,937pd, 50fr (Sw); $6.00; C; publisher & editor Gloria Trotter; tel (405) 598-3793

Thomas: *Thomas Tribune* — 115 W. Orient; PO Box 10 (73669); Th; 1,750pd (Sw); $3.29; publisher Harold Gleason; editor Sondra Buckaloo; tel (405) 661-3525

Tishomingo: *Johnston County Capital-Democrat* — 103 N. Neshoba; PO Box 400 (73460); W; 3,019pd, 24fr (Sw); $3.00; publisher & editor Ray Lokey; tel (405) 371-2356; fax (405) 371-9648

Tonkawa: *The Tonkawa News* — 108 N. 7th St.; PO Box 250 (74653); Th; 1,800pd, 45fr (Sw); $5.00; publisher & editor H Lyle Becker; tel (405) 628-2532; fax (405) 628-4044

Tulsa: *Southwest Tulsa News* — 8545 E. 41st St. (74145); Th; 1,397pd, 49fr (Sw); $6.25; publisher Bill R Retherford; general manager Charles E Cagle; editor David Breed; managing editor Ralph Schaefer; tel (918) 663-1414; fax (918) 664-8161

Tuttle: *The Tuttle Times* — PO Box 180 (73089); W; 1,435pd, 40fr (Est); $2.80; C; publisher Marshall Settle; editor David Settle; tel (405) 381-3173; fax (405) 224-2711

Valliant: *Valliant Leader* — 119 N. Dalton; PO Box 89 (74764); W; 1,650pd, 50fr (Sw); $3.22; publisher & editor Peter A Wilson; tel (405) 933-4579; fax (405) 933-4900

Vici: *Vici Beacon News* — PO Box 117, Seiling (73663); Th; 1,325pd, 6fr (Sw); $3.75; publishers Connie Miller & Mack Miller; editor Kathy Morris; tel (405) 922-4296; fax (405) 922-7777

Wagoner: *Wagoner Tribune* — 221 E. Cherokee (74467); Th; 3,187pd, 25fr (Sw); $7.50; C; publisher Bill R Retherford; managing editor Ralph Schaefer; tel (918) 485-5505; fax (918) 485-8442

Wakita: *Wakita Herald* — 104 W. Main St.; PO Box 26 (73771); Th; 466pd, 6fr (Sw); $1.60; publisher & editor Miriam Draper; tel (405) 594-2440

Watonga: *The Watonga Republican* — 104 E. Main St.; PO Box 30 (73772); Th; 642pd, 6fr (Sw); $4.50; C; publisher & managing editor Tim Curtin; editor Darrell Rice; tel (405) 623-4922; fax (405) 623-4925

Waukomis: *Waukomis Oklahoma Hornet* — 124 N. Main St.; PO Box 669 (73773); Th; 550pd (Est); $1.85; publisher R Jack Christy Jr; editor David Christy; tel (405) 758-3255; fax (405) 758-3255

Waurika: *Waurika News-Democrat* — 117 W. Broadway (73573); Th; 1,839pd, 28fr (Est); $3.40; publisher Alexander J Hruby; general manager & editor Jeff Hall; tel (405) 228-2316; fax (405) 228-3647

Waynoka: *Woods County Enterprise* — 109 N. Main St. (73860); Th; 893pd, 15fr (Sw); $3.50; publisher Jeff Shultz; editor Anette Shultz; tel (405) 824-2171; fax (405) 824-2172

Weleetka/Pharoah/Dustin/Wetumka/Henryetta/Okemah: *The Weleetkan* — 110 W. 9th; PO Box 427, Weleetka (74880); F; 880pd, 45fr (Sw); $2.80; publisher & editor William A Morgan; managing editor Polly Everett; tel (405) 786-2224; fax (405) 452-3329

Wellston: *The Wellston News* — 307 Cedar; PO Box 249 (74881); Th; 410pd, 10fr (Est); $2.50; C; publisher Herb Stingley; editor Jean Stingley; tel (405) 356-2478; fax (405) 356-2478

Westville: *Westville Reporter* — 122 S. Williams St.; PO Box 550 (74965); Th; 2,019pd, 70fr (Sw); $2.50; publisher Boyce R Davis; editor Scott Davis; tel (501) 723-5445; fax (501) 824-5540

Wetumka: *The Hughes County Times* — 120 S. Main St.; PO Box 38 (74883); Th; 2,100pd, 60fr (Est); $3.78; publisher & editor William A Morgan; tel (405) 452-3294; fax (405) 452-3329

Wilson: *Wilson Post-Democrat* — 439 W. Main; PO Box 250, Healdton (73438); Th; 689pd, 7fr (Sw); $2.94; C; publisher & managing editor Cleo Chaffin; publisher & editor Ken Chaffin; tel (405) 229-0132; fax (405) 229-0132

Wynnewood: *Wynnewood Gazette* — 210 S. Dean A. McGee; PO Box 309 (73098-0309); Th; 1,530pd, 90fr (Sw); $3.50; publisher & editor Ms Larry G Russell; tel (405) 665-4333; fax (405) 665-4334

Yale: *The Yale News* — 103 N. Main St.; PO Box 307 (74085); Th; 876pd, 28fr (Sw); $2.70; publishers & editors Beth Ray & Homer Ray; tel (918) 387-2125; fax (918) 387-2866

Yukon: *The Yukon Review* — 110 S. 5th St.; PO Box 851400 (73085); W/Sa; 4,670pd (VAC); $6.00; publishers Karen Grigsby & Randel Grigsby; general manager Randy Anderson; editor Conrad Dudderar; tel (405) 354-5264; fax (405) 354-3044

OREGON

Aloha: *Aloha Breeze* — 150 S.E. 3rd Ave.; PO Box 588, Hillsboro (97123); W; 6,000fr (Sw); $5.10; publisher Walter V McKinney; general manager James Dehning; editor Val Hess; tel (503) 648-1131; fax (503) 648-9191

Baker City/Baker Co.: *Record-Courier* — 1718 Main St.; PO Box 70, Baker City (97814); Th; 4,239pd, 58fr (Est); $5.25; C; publisher & editor Byron C Brinton; tel (503) 523-5353

Bandon: *Bandon Western World* — 1185 Baltimore St.; PO Box 248 (97411); W; 2,603pd, 275fr (Sw); 54¢; publisher & editor William Ketsdever; tel (503) 347-2423; fax (503) 347-2424

Beaverton/Tigard: *Beaverton Valley Times/ Times Publications* — 6975 S.W. Sandburg Rd., 2nd Fl. (Tigard 97223); PO Box 370, Beaverton (97075); Th; 8,500pd (Sw); $8.65; C; publisher Steve Clark; editor Michael Kelly; tel (503) 684-0360; fax (503) 620-3433

Burns/Hines Co./Harney Co.: *Burns Times-Herald* — 355 N. Broadway, Burns (97720); W; 2,995pd, 21fr (Sw); $7.00; C; publisher Donna Clark; editor Pauline Braymen; tel (503) 573-2022; fax (503) 573-3915

Canby/Wilsonville: *The Canby Herald/ Wilsonville Spokesman* — 241 N. Grant St.; PO Box 1108, Canby (97013); W; 4,334pd, 67fr (Sw); $5.25; C; publisher William D Cassel; editor Cam Sivesind; tel (503) 266-6831; fax (503) 266-6836

Central Linn Co.: *The Times* — 109 Spalding Ave.; PO Box 278, Brownsville (97327); W; 1,799pd, 62fr (Est); $4.20; publisher & editor Russ Neilsen; tel (503) 466-5311; fax (503) 466-5312

Clackamas: *Clackamas Review* — 1915 S.E. Harrison (Milwaukee 97222); PO Box 1520 (97015); Th; 6,000pd (Sw); $8.00; publisher Richard Skayhan; editor Charles Deister; tel (503) 786-1996; fax (503) 786-6977

Clatskanie: *Clatskanie Chief* — 97 Conyers St.; PO Box 8 (97016); Th; 2,450pd, 25fr (Sw); $3.50; publisher & editor Deborah Steele Hazen; tel (503) 728-3350; fax (503) 728-3350

Coquille Valley: *Coquille Valley Sentinel* — PO Box 400, Coquille (97423); W; 1,995pd, 84fr (Sw); $4.00; C; publisher Frederick Taylor; general manager Dorothy Taylor; tel (503) 396-3191; fax (503) 396-3624

Cottage Grove: *Cottage Grove Sentinel* — 116 N. 6th St.; PO Box 35 (97424); W; 5,600pd, 9fr (Est); $7.40; C; publisher & editor Jody Rolnick; tel (503) 942-3325; fax (503) 942-3328

Creswell: *The Creswell Chronicle* — 244 W. Oregon Ave.; PO Box 428 (97426); W; 875pd, 58fr (Sw); $5.81; publisher & editor Gerri O'Rourke; tel (503) 895-2197

Crook Co.: *Prineville Central Oregonian* — 558 N. Main, Prineville (97754); Tu/Th; 3,739pd, 75fr (Sw); $6.50; C; publisher James O Smith; general manager Bill Schaffer; managing editor Bill Sheehy; tel (541) 447-6205; fax (541) 447-1754

Curry Co.: *Curry Coastal Pilot* — 507 Chetco Ave.; PO Box 700, Brookings (97415); W/Sa; 7,030pd, 59fr (Sw); $5.50; C; publisher Judith Zelmer Smith; editor Jerry Teague; tel (541) 469-3123; fax (541) 469-4679

Dallas/Polk Co./Monmouth/Independence: *The Polk County Itemizer-Observer* — 147 S.E. Court St.; PO Box 108, Dallas (97338); W; 6,235pd, 29fr (Sw); $7.50; C; publisher Nancy J Adams; managing editor Virginia Henderson; tel (503) 623-2373; fax (503) 623-2395

Dayton: *Dayton Tribune* — 408 4th St.; PO Box 69 (97114); Th; 426pd, 21fr (Sw); $1.68; publisher & editor George Meitzen; tel (503) 864-2310; fax (503) 864-2310

Drain/Yoncalla/Elkton: *Drain Enterprise* — 309 1st St.; PO Box 26, Drain (97435); Th; 1,357pd, 27fr (Sw); $3.36; publisher Betty Anderson; editor Sue Anderson; tel (503) 836-2241

Enterprise/Joseph/Wallowa: *Wallowa County Chieftain* — 106 N.W. 1st; PO Box 338, Enterprise (97828); Th; 4,200pd (Sw); $6.75; publisher Donald L Swart; editor Richard W Swart; tel (503) 426-4567; fax (503) 426-3921

Estacada: *Clackamas County News* — 313 S.W. Hwy. 224; PO Box 549 (97023); W; 2,150pd, 35fr (Est); $8.75; C; publisher & editor William H James; tel (503) 630-3241; fax (503) 630-5840

Florence: *The Siuslaw News* — 148 Maple; PO Box 10 (97439); W; 6,875pd, 105fr (Est); $5.25; C; publishers Beverly Holman & Paul R Holman; editor Robert Serra; tel (503) 997-3441; fax (503) 997-7979

Forest Grove: *Forest Grove News Times* — PO Box 408 (97116); W; 5,200pd, 3,700fr (Est); $7.25; C; publishers J Brian Monihan; editor Jim Hart; tel (503) 357-3181; fax (503) 359-8456

Gilliam/Wheeler Cos.: *The Times-Journal* — 319 S. Main St.; PO Box 746, Condon (97823); Th; 1,630pd, 40fr (Sw); $4.25; C; publisher Janet L Stinchfield; publisher & editor McLaren E Stinchfield; tel (503) 384-2421

Gold Beach: *Curry County Reporter* — 510 N. Ellensburg Ave.; PO Box 766 (97444); W; 3,270pd, 62fr (ABC); $4.90; publisher & editor Betty Van Leer; publisher Robert Van Leer; managing editor Molly Walker; tel (503) 247-6643; fax (503) 247-6644

Grant Co.: *The Blue Mountain Eagle* — 741 W. Main St.; PO Box 69, John Day (97845); Th; 3,900pd, 100fr (Sw); $5.00; publisher East Oregonian Publishing Co.; general manager Karla Averett; editor Loren Russell; tel (503) 575-0710; fax (503) 575-1244

Gresham: *Gresham Outlook* — 1190 N.E. Division; PO Box 747 (97030); W/Sa; 10,661pd, 156fr (Sw); $14.50; C; publisher William R Hunter; editor Lloyd Woods; tel (503) 665-2181; fax (503) 665-2187

Heppner: *The Heppner Gazette Times* — 147 W. Willow St.; PO Box 337 (97836); W; 1,458pd, 56fr (Sw); $4.25; publisher & editor April Sykes; publisher David Sykes; tel (503) 676-9228

Hermiston: *The Hermiston Herald* — 193 E. Main St.; PO Box 46 (97838); Tu; 4,278pd, 62fr (Sw); $7.70; publisher Dan Zimmerman; editor Michael Kane; tel (503) 567-6457; fax (503) 567-4125

Hillsboro: *Hillsboro Argus* — 150 S.E. 3rd Ave.; PO Box 588 (97123); Tu/Th; 14,370pd, 740fr (Sw); $8.40; C; publisher Walter V McKinney; general manager James Dehning; editor Val Hess; tel (503) 648-1131; fax (503) 648-9191

Hood River: *Hood River News* — 419 State St.; PO Box 390 (97031); W/Sa; 5,418pd, 88fr (Sw); $6.75; C; publisher James A Kelly; general manager Joe Deckard; editor Mike Doke; tel (503) 386-1234; fax (503) 386-6796

Illinois Valley: *Illinois Valley News* — 319 S. Redwood Hwy.; PO Box M, Cave Junction (97523); W; 3,332pd, 25fr (Sw); $3.50; C; publisher & editor Robert R Rodriguez; tel (503) 592-2541

Jefferson: *Jefferson Review* — 115 S. 2nd St.; PO Box 330 (97352); Th; 850pd (Est); $3.00; publisher & editor Jack Gillespie; tel (503) 327-2241; fax (503) 327-2241

Junction City: *Tri-County News* — 445 W. 6th St.; PO Box 395 (97448); Th; 2,073pd, 41fr (Sw); $5.95; C; publishers Joe Cannon & Louise Cannon; editor Judy Hunt; tel (503) 998-3877; fax (503) 935-4082

Keizer: *Keizertimes* — 142 Chemawa Rd. N. (97303); Th; 3,800pd, 6,200fr (Sw); $8.50; C; publisher Les Zaitz; publisher & editor Scott Callister; tel (503) 390-1051

Lake Oswego: *Lake Oswego Review* — 111 A Ave.; PO Box 548 (97034); Th; 7,665pd, 752fr (Est); $7.40; C; publisher Bob Bigelow; editor Jennifer Brandlon; managing editor Dana Haynes; tel (503) 635-8811; fax (503) 635-8817

Lakeview/Lake Co.: *Lake County Examiner* — 305 N. F St.; PO Box 271, Lakeview (97630); Th; 2,744pd, 40fr (Est); $6.00; general manager Tillie Flynn; managing editor Erik Hogstrom; tel (503) 947-3378; fax (503) 947-4359

Lebanon: *Lebanon Express* — 90 E. Grant; PO Box 459 (97355); W; 4,800pd (Est); $7.25; publisher Mary Jo Parker; editor Brooke Brannon; tel (503) 258-3151; fax (503) 259-3569

Lincoln City: *The News Guard* — 930 S.E. Hwy. 101; PO Box 848 (97367); W; 5,704pd, 19fr (Est); $5.25; C; publisher & editor James Moore; managing editor Steve Mims; tel (503) 265-7287/994-2178; fax (503) 994-7613

Madras: *The Madras Pioneer* — 241 S.E. 6th; PO Box W (97741); W; 3,800pd, 100fr (Est); $5.00; C; publisher Tony Ahern; editor Susan Matheny; tel (503) 475-2275; fax (503) 475-3710

McKenzie River Valley: *McKenzie River Reflections* — 59059 Old McKenzie Hwy., McKenzie Bridge (97413); F; 1,200pd (Sw); $4.75; publisher Kenneth Engleman; managing editor Louise Engleman; tel (503) 822-3358; fax (503) 822-3358

McMinnville: *News-Register* — 611 E. 3rd St.; PO Box 727 (97128); Tu/Th/Sa; 9,995pd, 440fr (Sw); $9.50; publisher & editor Jon E Bladine; general manager Guy Euevengham; managing editor Yvette Saavinen; tel (503) 472-5114; fax (503) 472-9151

Mill City: *The Mill City Enterprise* — PO Box 348 (97360); Th; 1,256pd, 43fr (Est); $2.75; publisher & editor Gale Hann; tel (503) 897-2772; fax (503) 897-2335

Milton-Freewater: *Valley Times* — 205 N. Main St.; PO Box 170 (97862); W; 2,200pd, 4,800fr (Sw); $5.75; publisher Terry Hager; editor Nick Peterson; tel (503) 938-0702; fax (503) 938-0691

Molalla: *Molalla Pioneer* — 217 E. Main St.; PO Box 168 (97038); W; 3,290pd, 50fr (Sw); $6.00; C; publisher William D Cassel; general manager Jan LaFollette; editor Mike Lucas; tel (503) 829-2301; fax (503) 829-2317

Monmouth/Independence: *Itemizer Observer* — PO Box 108, Dallas (97338); W; 2,465pd, 56fr (Est); $7.00; C; publisher Nancy Adams; editor Virginia Henderson; tel (503) 623-2375; fax (503) 623-2395

Myrtle Pt.: *Myrtle Point Herald* — 408 Spruce St.; PO Box 606 (97458); W; 1,777pd, 255fr (Sw); $6.75; publisher & editor Laura Isenhart; tel (503) 572-2717; fax (503) 572-2828

Newberg/St. Paul/Dundee/Sherwood: *Newberg Graphic* — 109 N. School St.; PO Box 700, Newberg (97132); W; 6,100pd, 4,900fr (Sw); $6.90; Sa; 6,100pd (Sw); $6.90; C; publisher & editor David Thouvenel; managing editor Gary Allen; tel (503) 538-2181; fax (503) 538-1632

Newport/Lincoln Co.: *News-Times* — PO Box 965, Newport (97365); W/F; 9,431pd, 301fr (Sw); $7.75; publisher Mary Jo Parker; editor Leslie O'Donnell; tel (503) 265-8571; fax (503) 265-3103

N Willamette Valley: *North Willamette News* — 217 E. Main St.; PO Box 168, Molalla (97038); W; 3,131fr (Sw); $8.50; C; publisher William D Cassel; editor Mike Lucas; tel (503) 829-2301; fax (503) 829-2317

Oakridge/Westfir: *Dead Mountain Echo* — 48013 Hwy. 58; PO Box 900, Oakridge (97463); Th; 1,099pd, 70fr (Sw); $6.00; publisher Larry D Roberts; editor David Rauzi; tel (503) 782-4241; fax (503) 782-3323

Pendleton/Umatilla Co.: *The Pendleton Record* — PO Box 69, Pendleton (97801); Th; 828pd (Est); $5.50; publisher Marguerite Maznaritz; editor Richard E Maznaritz; tel (503) 276-2853

Philomath: *Benton Bulletin* — 1324 Main St.; PO Box 340 (97370); Th; 1,162pd, 19fr (Sw); $4.62; C; publisher Joe Cannon; editor John Butterworth; tel (503) 929-3043; fax (503) 929-3043

Port Orford/N Curry Co.: *Port Orford News* — 519 W. 10th St.; PO Box 5, Port Orford (97465); W; 1,241pd, 9fr (Sw); $4.25; publisher Louis L Felsheim; editor Paul L Peterson; tel (503) 332-2361; fax (503) 332-8101

Portland: *Portland Observer* — 47 N.E. Martin L. King Blvd.; PO Box 3137 (97211); W; 10,900pd, 720fr (Sw); $14.50; publisher Joyce Washington; editor Chuck Washington; tel (503) 288-0033; fax (503) 288-0015

Redmond: *The Redmond Spokesman* — 226 N.W. 6th; PO Box 788 (97756); W; 4,149pd, 40fr (Sw); $7.70; C; publisher Carl Vertrees; editor Scott Maben; tel (503) 548-2184; fax (503) 548-3203

Reedsport: *Reedsport Courier* — 174 N. 16th; PO Box 268 (97467); Th; 2,800pd (Est); $6.49; publisher & editor Carl Olson; tel (503) 271-3633; fax (503) 271-3138

Rogue River/Evans Valley/Gold Hill: *Rogue River Press* — 105 Gardiner St.; PO Box 1485, Rogue River (97537); W; 1,844pd, 409fr (Sw); $5.15; publisher & editor Dave Ehrhardt; tel (503) 582-1707; fax (503) 582-0201

St. Helens/Scappoose/Warren: *The Chronicle and Sentinel-Mist* — 195 S. 15th St.; PO Box 1153, St. Helens (97051); W/Sa; 6,200pd, 26fr (Est); $4.60; C; publisher Pamela Petersen; editor Greg Cohen; tel (503) 397-0116; fax (503) 397-4093

Sandy: *Sandy Post* — PO Box 68 (97055); W; 2,557pd, 28fr (Sw); $13.40; C; publisher William R Hunter; editor Lloyd Woods; tel (503) 668-5548; fax (503) 668-7951

Scappoose/St. Helens: *The South County Spotlight* — 52644 N.E. 1st St.; PO Box C, Scappoose (97056); W; 4,128pd, 692fr (Est); 19¢; C; publisher & editor Art Heerwagon; publisher Sally Heerwagon; tel (503) 543-6387; fax (503) 543-6380

Seaside/S Clatsop Co.: *Seaside Signal* — 113 N. Holladay Dr.; PO Box 848, Seaside (97138); Th; 3,408pd, 56fr (Est); $7.69; C; publisher & editor Kevin Widdison; tel (503) 738-5561; fax (503) 738-5672

Sheridan/Willamina: *The Sun* — 136 E. Main; PO Box 68, Sheridan (97378); W; 2,210pd, 30fr (Sw); $8.10; publisher & editor George Robertson; tel (503) 843-2312

Silverton/Mt. Angel: *Silverton Appeal Tribune/Mt. Angel News* — PO Box 35, Silverton (97381); W; 4,417pd, 31fr (Sw); $7.36; C; publisher Brad Senison; editor Ben Mobius; tel (503) 873-8385; fax (503) 873-8064

S Douglas Co.: *Umpqua Free Press* — 119 S. Main St.; PO Box 729, Myrtle Creek (97457); Th; 2,749pd, 20fr (Est); $4.80; publisher & editor Robert F Scherer; publisher Sharon W Scherer; tel (503) 863-5233; fax (503) 863-5234

Springfield: *Springfield News* — 1887 Laura St.; PO Box 139 (97477); W; 9,900pd, 182fr (Est); $9.85; Sa; 11,235pd, 182fr (Est); $9.85; C; publisher J Mark Garber; managing editor Rob Romig; tel (503) 746-1671; fax (503) 746-0633

Stayton: *The Stayton Mail* — 400 N. 3rd St.; PO Box 400 (97383); W; 3,784pd, 14fr (Sw); $8.55; C; publisher & editor Howard (Bill) Woodall Jr; tel (503) 769-6338

Sutherlin/Oakland/Umpqua: *The Sun Tribune* — 104 E. Central; PO Box 430, Sutherlin (97479-0430); Th; 1,127pd, 27,000fr (Sw); $6.50; C; publisher Ronald J Stewart; general manager Kris Kennedy; editor Linda Schnell; tel (503) 459-2261; fax (503) 459-1542

Sweet Home: *The New Era* — 1313 Main; PO Box 39 (97386); W; 3,000pd, 5,000fr (Est); $6.95; publisher & editor Alex Paul; publisher Debra Paul; tel (503) 367-2135; fax (503) 367-2137

The Dalles/Wasco/Sherman: *The Dalles Reminder* — PO Box 984, The Dalles (97058); F; 2,800pd, 15,200fr (Sw); $9.85; C; publisher Marilyn Roth; editor Dan Spatz; tel (503) 298-8545; fax (503) 298-8547

Tigard: *Tigard Times/Times Publications* — 6975 S.W. Sandburg Rd., 2nd Fl. (97223); Th; 5,500pd (Est); $6.75; C; publisher Steve Clark; editor Michael Kelly; tel (503) 684-0360; fax (503) 620-3433

Tillamook Co.: *Headlight-Herald* — 1908 2nd St.; PO Box 444, Tillamook (97141); W; 7,709pd, 134fr (Sw); $7.69; C; publisher Linda Shaffer; editor Scott Frank; tel (503) 842-7535; fax (503) 842-8842

Vale: *The Malheur Enterprise* — 227 A St. W.; PO Box 310 (97918); W; 2,119pd, 65fr (Sw); $7.50; publisher Za Dean Auyer; editor W G Auyer; tel (503) 473-3377; fax (503) 473-3268

Veneta: *West-Lane News* — 25027 Dunham; PO Box 188 (97487); Th; 2,488pd, 27fr (Sw); $6.65; C; publishers Joe Cannon & Louise Cannon; editor Judy Hunt; tel (503) 935-1882; fax (503) 935-4082

Warrenton/Astoria: *The Columbia Press* — 926 E. Harbor Ct.; PO Box 130, Warrenton (97146); F; 1,500pd (Sw); $5.00; C; publisher & editor Gary Nevan; publisher Julia Nevan; tel (503) 861-3331

Woodburn: *Woodburn Independent* — 650 N. 1st St.; PO Box 96 (97071); W; 5,100pd, 15,100fr (Sw); $7.00; C; publisher Lester R Reitan; editor Nikki DeBuse; tel (503) 981-3441; fax (503) 981-1253

PENNSYLVANIA

Albion: *The Albion News* — 16 Market St.; PO Box 7 (16401); W; 3,105pd, 120fr (Sw); $5.50; publisher John Lampson; editor Vickie Canfield Peters; tel (814) 756-4133; fax (814) 756-5643

Aliquippa: *News* — 1181 Airport Rd.; PO Box 629 (15001-0629); Th; 67,180fr (Sw); $17.38; publisher Raymond A Palket; editor Ione Morgan; tel (412) 375-6611; fax (412) 375-1011

Ambler: *Ambler Gazette* — 290 Commerce Dr.; PO Box 1628, Ft. Washington (19034); W; 10,136pd, 160fr (Est); $20.12; C; publisher Arthur W Howe IV; editor Fred D Behringer; tel (215) 542-0200; fax (215) 643-9475

Apollo: *Apollo News Record* — 134 Grant Ave., Vandergriff (15690); W; 1,744pd, 25fr (Est); $10.50; C; publisher Don Cole; editor Jo-Jo Bodnar; tel (412) 567-5656; fax (412) 568-3818

Ardmore: *Main Line Life* — 110 Ardmore Ave. (19003); Th; 799pd, 17,947fr (CAC); $11.20; C; publisher Arthur W Howe; editor David Burket; tel (610) 896-9555; fax (610) 896-9560

Bangor: *Slate Belt Hometown News* — 13-15 Main St. (18013); Th; 2,000fr (Est); $2.50; publisher & editor Cathleen McFall; tel (610) 588-2196

Barnesboro: *The Barnesboro Star* — 520 Philadelphia Ave.; PO Box 158 (15714); W; 5,242pd (Est); $4.70; C; publisher Frank K Noll; general manager Michael Shuma; editor Connie Scanlan; managing editor Jerry Kane; tel (814) 948-6210; fax (814) 948-7563

Bath/Northampton/Nazareth: *The Home News* — 120 S. Walnut St.; PO Box 39, Bath (18014); Th; 4,150pd, 40fr (Sw); 28¢; publisher & editor William J Halbfoerster; general manager David W Halbfoerster; tel (610) 837-0107; fax (610) 837-0482

Beaver: *Central News* — 1181 Airport Rd.; PO Box 629, Aliquippa (15001-0629); Th; 16,964fr (Sw); $12.80; C; publisher Raymond A Palket; editor Ione Morgan; tel (412) 375-6611; fax (412) 375-1011

Bedford: *Bedford Inquirer* — 424 W. Penn St.; PO Box 671 (15522); F; 337pd, 8fr (Sw); $2.25; publisher & editor Edward K Frear; general manager Don Hopf; tel (814) 623-1151; fax (814) 623-5055

Bedford/S Blair Cos.: *The Guide* — 100 Masters Ave.; PO Box 328, Everett (15537); Sa; 56pd, 29,476fr (Est); $9.00; publisher Kenneth L Holtzinger; tel (814) 652-5191; fax (814) 652-9544

Bethlehem: *Bethlehem Star* — 531 Main St.; PO Box 1067 (18018); Th; 20,000fr (Est); $10.50; C; publisher Tim Sowecke; general manager David McCollum; editor Joe Lyons; tel (610) 867-5000; fax (610) 866-1771

Birdsboro: *The News of Southern Berks* — 124 N. Chestnut St.; PO Box 565, Boyertown (19512); W; 1,895pd, 210fr (Sw); $5.90; C; publisher James C Webb; editor Kathrine Ritz; managing editor Jeffery Bell; tel (610) 367-6041; fax (610) 369-0233

Boyertown: *Boyertown Area Times* — 124 N. Chestnut St.; PO Box 565 (19512); Th; 6,103pd, 269fr (Sw); $8.40; C; publisher James C Webb; editor Jeff Bell; tel (610) 367-6041; fax (610) 369-0233

Bradford: *Bradford Journal-Miner* — 265 S. Ave.; PO Box 17 (16701); Th; 5,500pd (Sw); $5.95; publisher Grant Nichols; editor Debi Nichols; tel (814) 362-6563

Bradford/Sullivan/Wyoming/Susquehanna Cos.: *The Rocket-Courier* — 302 State St.; PO Box 187, Wyalusing (18853); Th; 5,042pd, 52fr (Sw); $6.00; C; publisher W David Keeler; general manager Nancy Keeler; editor Wesley Skillings; tel (717) 746-1217; fax (717) 746-7737

Brentwood/Baldwin: *South Hills Record* — 3623 Brownsville Rd., Pittsburgh (15227); Th; 3,954pd, 131fr (Est); $10.23; publisher Thomas Bova; editor Jeff Jones; managing editor Edith Hughes; tel (412) 884-3111; fax (412) 884-3106

Bridgeville: *Bridgeville Area News* — 8 E. Mall Plz., Carnegie (15106); W; 1,654pd, 67fr (Est); $5.98; publisher Thomas Bova; editor Donna Seiling; tel (412) 276-4000; fax (412) 276-0865

Bristol: *Bristol Pilot* — 2100 Frost Rd.; PO Box 232 (19007); Th; 2,351pd, 820fr (Sw); $10.00; C; publisher Art Thompson; editor Kathleen Fratti; tel (215) 788-1682; fax (215) 788-6328

Brookville: *Jeffersonian Democrat* — 301 Main St.; PO Box 498 (15828); Th; 3,920pd, 83fr (Sw); $5.25; publisher W Dock Lias; editor Randon W Bartley; tel (814) 849-5339; fax (814) 849-4333

Canton: *The Canton Independent Sentinel* — 41 Lycoming St.; PO Box 128 (17724); W; 1,800pd, 45fr (Est); $2.80; publisher John Shaffer; editor Andrea Sutton; tel (717) 673-5151; fax (717) 673-4315

Carbondale: *Carbondale News* — 41 N. Church St. (18407); W; 6,048pd, 30fr (Sw); $4.80; C; publisher Philip T Heth; editor Tom Fontana; tel (717) 282-3300; fax (717) 282-3950

Carnegie: *The Signal-Item* — 8 E. Mall Plz. (15106); W; 3,545pd, 78fr (Est); $9.80; publisher Thomas Bova; editor Donna Seiling; managing editor Edith Hughes; tel (412) 276-4000; fax (412) 276-0865

Catasauqua/Whitehall: *Catasauqua Dispatch* — 420 Howertown Rd., Catasauqua (18032); Th; 750pd (Sw); 23¢; publisher & editor Marlin E Wolf; tel (610) 264-9451

Chestnut Hill/Wyndmoor/Erdenheim/Mt. Airy: *Chestnut Hill Local* — 8434 Germantown Ave., Philadelphia (19118); Th; 8,450pd, 375fr (Sw); $12.23; publisher Chestnut Hill Community Association; editor Marie Reinhart Jones; tel (215) 248-8800; fax (215) 248-8814

Clarion: *Clarion News* — 645 Main St.; PO Box 647 (16214); Tu/Th; 5,817pd, 68fr (Sw); 15¢; publisher Patrick Boyle; editor Paul M Hambke; tel (814) 226-7000; fax (814) 226-7518

Clarks Summit: *Abington Journal* — 211 S. State St. (18411); W; 2,661pd, 182fr (Sw); $6.15; C; publisher Ronald A Bartizek; editor Kenneth Books; tel (717) 587-1148

Collegeville/Trappe: *The Independent* — 350 Walnut St.; PO Box 39, Collegeville (19426); Tu; 1,694pd, 62fr (Est); $4.50; publisher John Stewart; editor James Stewart; tel (610) 489-3001; fax (610) 489-8633

Conneautville/Mercer/Crawford/Clarion/Venango Cos.: *Conneautville Courier* — PO Box K, Springboro (16435); F; 1,200pd, 216,968fr (Sw); $68.00; C; publisher Herbert O Haas; general manager & editor Jessie Haas; tel (814) 587-2033; fax (814) 587-3720

Conshohocken: *The Recorder* — 700 Fayette St. (19428); Th; 3,900pd, 700fr (Sw); $7.35; publisher Fred Donaldson; general manager Michael Cooper; editor Nancy O'Brien; tel (610) 828-4600; fax (610) 941-0547

Coraopolis/Moon Twp.: *The Record* — 705 5th Ave., Coraopolis (15108); W; 1,079pd, 106fr (Est); 53¢; publisher Thomas Bova; editor Harry Funk; managing editor Edith Hughes; tel (412) 264-4140; fax (412) 264-8269

Coraopolis/Sewickley: *Star News* — 1181 Airport Rd.; PO Box 629, Aliquippa (15001-0629); Th; 12,396fr (Sw); $12.80; C; publisher Raymond A Palket; editor Ione Morgan; tel (412) 375-6611; fax (412) 375-1011

Coudersport: *Potter Leader-Enterprises* — PO Box 29 (16915); W; 10,405pd, 200fr (Est); $3.85; publisher Joseph A Majot; editor Teri McDowell; tel (814) 274-8044; fax (814) 274-8120

Cranberry Twp.: *Cranberry Journal* — 20232 Perry Hwy. (16066); W; 263pd, 4,434fr (Est); $5.55; publisher Thomas Bova; editor James Bender; managing editor Edith Hughes; tel (412) 776-4422; fax (412) 776-4492

Dallas: *The Dallas Post* — 607 Main Rd.; PO Box 366 (18612); W; 2,515pd, 176fr (Sw); $6.15; C; publisher & editor Ronald A Bartizek; tel (717) 675-5211

Delaware Co.: *News of Delaware County* — Manoa Shopping Ctr., Havertown (19083); W; 19,230pd, 20,289fr (CAC); $19.74; C; publisher Deborah Shaw; managing editor Joan Connor Toenniessen; tel (610) 446-8700; fax (610) 449-0419

Doylestown: *Doylestown Patriot* — 350 S. Main St.; PO Box 2246 (18901); Th; 1,384pd, 764fr (Sw); $10.00; C; publisher Art Thompson; editor Gwen Stockwell-Rushton; tel (215) 340-9811; fax (215) 340-1306

Doylestown/Newtown: *Bucks County Sunday Telegraph* — 390 Easton Rd., Horsham (19044-2592); Su; 125pd, 7,350fr (Est); 80¢; publisher Matthew H Petersohn; editor Sandra L Petersohn; tel (215) 345-0820

Duncannon: *Duncannon Record* — PO Box A (17020); Th; 2,579pd, 30fr (Sw); $3.15; C; publisher Rick White; editor Wade Fowler; managing editor Gary Thomas; tel (717) 834-4616

Dushore/Sullivan Co.: *The Sullivan Review* — Main & Water Sts.; PO Box 305, Dushore (18614-0305); Th; 6,819pd, 54fr (Sw); $4.50; publisher & editor Stefana H Shoemaker; publisher T W Shoemaker; tel (717) 928-8136/8403; fax (717) 928-8006

E Montgomery Co.: *Progress of Montgomery County* — 390 Easton Rd., Horsham (19044-2592); W; 251pd, 17,000fr (Est); 80¢; publisher Matthew H Petersohn; editor Sandra L Petersohn; tel (215) 675-8250

E Montgomery Co.: *The Globe* — 101 Greenwood Ave., Jenkintown (19046); W; 1,579pd, 1,032fr (CAC); $12.72; C; publisher Arthur W Howe; editor Fred D Behringer; managing editor Warren W Patton; tel (215) 885-1345; fax (215) 643-1257

E Pittsburgh: *The Free Press* — 522 Braddock Ave., Braddock (15104); Th; 220pd, 20,200fr (Sw); $8.00; publisher & editor Anthony R Munson; tel (412) 271-0622; fax (412) 351-1593

Ebensburg/Cambria Co.: *Ebensburg News Leader* — 975 Rowena Dr.; PO Box 777, Ebensburg (15931); W; 2,200pd, 28fr (Est); $2.40; C; publisher Frank K Noll; general manager Genne Stepp; editor Ken Piper; tel (814) 472-4110; fax (814) 472-2275

Ebensburg/Central Cambria Co.: *The Mountaineer-Herald* — 113 S. Center St.; PO Box 359, Ebensburg (15931); W; 3,026pd, 87fr (Sw); $3.92; publisher David E Thompson; editor Kathleen P Nikolishen; tel (814) 472-8240; fax (814) 472-6946

Edinboro/Cambridge Springs: *Independent Enterprise* — 109 Erie St., Ste. 5, Edinboro (16412); Su; 3,279pd, 13fr (Sw); $7.49; C; publisher Mark E Laskowski; editor Cheryl Cross; managing editor Peggy Machinski; tel (814) 734-1234; fax (814) 734-8973

Elizabethtown: *Elizabethtown Chronicle* — 25 Center Sq.; PO Box 189 (17022); Th; 3,005pd, 657fr (Sw); $5.70; C; publisher Wanda S Reid; editor Michael Givler; tel (717) 367-7152; fax (717) 367-3655

Emmaus: *The East Penn Press* — 1633 N. 26th St., Allentown (18104); W; 6,001pd, 822fr (Sw); $3.60; C; publisher Fred L Masenheimer; general manager Joye Jackson; editor Julia Paxson; tel (610) 740-0944; fax (610) 740-0947

Emporium: *Cameron County Echo* — 300 S. Broad St.; PO Box 308 (15834); Tu; 3,761pd, 48fr (Est); 30¢; publisher Barbara A Brown; editor David A Brown; tel (814) 486-3711; fax (814) 486-0990

Ephrata/Cocalico: *The Ephrata Review* — 1 E. Main St.; PO Box 527, Ephrata (17522); W; 9,000pd, 828fr (Sw); $10.00; publisher Lancaster County Weeklies Inc.; general manager Robert G Campbell; editor Andrew Fasnaght; tel (717) 733-6397; fax (717) 733-6058

Fairview/Girard: *Cosmopolite Herald* — 139 E. Main St., Girard (16417); Su; 2,900pd, 5,700fr (Sw); $7.49; C; general manager Mark E Laskowski; editor Valerie Myers; managing editor Peggy Machinski; tel (814) 774-9648; fax (814) 774-0328

Folsom: *Ridley Press* — 3245 Garrett Rd., Drexel Hill (19026); Th; 7,000pd (Est); $6.00; publisher Press Publishing Co.; editor Theodore B Cannon; managing editor Helen Reilly; tel (610) 259-4141

Forest City: *The Forest City News* — 636 Main St. (18421); W; 3,247pd, 91fr (Sw); $2.90; publisher John P Kameen; editor Patricia M Striessky; tel (717) 785-3800; fax (717) 785-9840

Forest Co.: *Forest Press* — 165 Elm St.; PO Box 366, Tionesta (16353); W; 4,600pd (Est); $3.60; publisher Edwin R Patrick; editor Virginia Patrick; tel (814) 755-4900; fax (814) 755-4429

U.S. Weeklies Pennsylvania II-67

Franklin Park: *North Journal* — 20232 Perry Hwy., Cranberry Township (16066); Th; 167pd, 7,601fr (Est); 41¢; publisher Thomas Bova; editor James Bender; managing editor Edith Hughes; tel (412) 776-4422; fax (412) 776-4492

Germantown: *The Leader And Germantown Papers* — 2385 W. Cheltenham Ave., Ste. 182, Philadelphia (19150); W; 15,000fr (Sw); $6.95; C; publisher Fred Donaldson; editor Marshall Rothman; tel (215) 885-4111; fax (215) 885-0226

Germantown District: *Germantown Courier* — 6622 Germantown Ave., Philadelphia (19119); W; 81pd, 19,603fr (CAC); $14.67; C; publisher Deborah Shaw; editor Sharon Bender; tel (215) 848-4300; fax (215) 848-9160

Glenside: *Glenside News* — 101 Greenwood Ave., Jenkintown (19046); W; 2,862pd, 30fr (CAC); $20.12; C; publisher Arthur W Howe IV; editor Warren Patton; tel (215) 885-1345; fax (215) 884-9112

Greater Pittston: *Greater Pittston Gazette* — 49 Broad St., Pittston (18640); Th; 2,200pd, 1,000fr (Est); $3.95; publisher & editor Joe Valenti; managing editor Chris Kocher; tel (717) 654-1260; fax (717) 655-8942

Greencastle: *The Echo Pilot* — PO Box 159 (17225); W; 2,151pd, 41fr (Est); 35¢; publisher Wayne E Baumbaugh; editor Sharon G Baumbaugh; tel (717) 597-2164; fax (717) 597-2164

Grove City: *Allied News* — 201 Erie St.; PO Box 190 (16127); W; 4,926pd, 18fr (Est); $9.80; C; publisher John L Lima; general manager John N Galands; editor Brian David; tel (412) 458-5010; fax (412) 458-1609

Hamburg/Berks: *Hamburg Item* — 3rd & State Sts.; PO Box 31, Hamburg (19526); W; 3,739pd, 39fr (Est); $3.01; publisher & editor Avery D Piersons; general manager Bill Colunil; managing editor Bob Work; tel (610) 562-7515; fax (610) 562-7516

Hatboro/Montgomery Co.: *Public Spirit* — 101 N. York Rd., Hatboro (19040); W; 5,968pd, 4,116fr (CAC); $20.12; C; publisher Arthur W Howe IV; editor Andrew Hussie; tel (215) 675-3430; fax (215) 675-9024

Havertown: *Haverford Press* — 3732 W. Chester Pike; PO Box 249, Newton Sq. (19073); W; 2,432pd, 725fr (Sw); $6.25; C; publisher Reese J Crowe Jr & Richard L Crowe; editor William W Lawrence; tel (610) 356-6664/3820; fax (610) 353-5321

Hawley/Lake Wallenpaupack: *The News Eagle* — 522 Spring St., Hawley (18428); Tu/Th/Sa; 5,606pd, 156fr (Est); $4.50; publisher James D Dyson; editor John C Dyson Jr; tel (717) 226-4547; fax (717) 226-4548

Hellertown: *The Valley Voice* — 800 Main St.; PO Box 147 (18055-0147); F; 1,685pd (Sw); $10.20; publisher Ann Marie Gonsalves; editor Charles Schenk; tel (610) 838-2066; fax (610) 838-6598

Hershey/Hummelstown: *Hershey Chronicle* — 513 W. Chocolate Ave.; PO Box 556, Hershey (17033); Th; 3,682pd, 319fr (Sw); $5.70; C; publisher Wanda S Reid; editor Kristy Kramer; tel (717) 533-2900; fax (717) 531-2561

Hershey/Hummelstown: *The Sun* — 115-117 S. Water St.; PO Box C, Hummelstown (17036); W; 5,874pd, 258fr (Sw); $4.76; publisher Rosemary K Jackson; editor William S Jackson; tel (717) 566-3251; fax (717) 566-6196

Huntingdon Valley: *The Far Northeast Citizen-Sentinel* — 1102 Churchill Rd., Philadelphia (19118-1601); W; 480pd, 13,520fr (Sw); 80¢; publisher Matthew H Petersohn; editor Sandra L Petersohn; tel (215) 632-2700

Jeannette: *The Jeannette Spirit* — 107 S. 2nd St. (15644); W; 1,807pd, 35fr (Sw); $6.02; C; publisher H Ralph Hernley; general manager Joseph F Soforic; editor Gregory L Stock; tel (412) 527-2868; fax (412) 887-5115

Jefferson Co.: *Jefferson County Neighbors* — PO Box 444, Punxsutawney (15767); W; 1,469pd, 1,450fr (Est); $4.10; publisher William C Anderson; editor Wick Divibiss; tel (814) 938-8740; fax (814) 938-3794

Jenkintown: *Times Chronicle* — 101 Greenwood Ave. (19046); W; 6,814pd, 66fr (CAC); $20.12; C; publisher Arthur W Howe IV; editor Warren Patton; tel (215) 885-1345; fax (215) 884-9112

Johnsonburg: *The Johnsonburg Press Inc.* — 517 Market St.; PO Box 10 (15845); W; 2,004pd, 25fr (Sw); $5.25; publisher & editor Frances Fowler; tel (814) 965-2503; fax (814) 965-2504

Kensington/Bridesburg/Fish Town/Penn Treaty/Port Richmond: *Guide Newspapers* — 2022 E. Allegheny Ave., Philadelphia (19134); Th/F; 17pd, 46,213fr (CAC); $22.96; C; publisher & editor H Robert Jacobs; tel (215) 423-1000; fax (215) 426-4438

King of Prussia: *King of Prussia Courier* — 134 N. Wayne Ave.; PO Box 409, Wayne (19087); W; 569pd, 7,530fr (CAC); $14.25; C; publisher William Burgess; editor Dennis Daylor; tel (610) 688-3000; fax (610) 254-8522

King of Prussia: *The Colonial* — 416 Egypt Rd. (19403); W; 2,614pd, 1,148fr (CAC); $7.96; C; publisher Arthur W Howe IV; editor Gillian Gordon; tel (610) 630-6200

King of Prussia: *The Post* — 416 Egypt Rd., Norristown (19403); W; 168pd, 5,532fr (CAC); $8.72; C; publisher Arthur W Howe IV; editor Lisa Lombardo; tel (610) 630-6200

Kutztown: *The Patriot* — PO Box 346 (19530); Th; 4,449pd, 73fr (Sw); $6.00; publisher Jacob R Esser; editor Tony Phyrillas; tel (610) 683-7343; fax (610) 683-5616

Lackawanna Co./Wayne Co./Moscow/Hamlin: *The Villager* — R.R. 2; PO Box 2186 B, Moscow (18444); W; 3,280pd, 1,035fr (Sw); $4.60; C; publisher Philip T Heth; editor Nicole Boni; tel (717) 842-8789; fax (717) 842-9841

Lancaster Co.: *Lancaster Farming Inc.* — 1 E. Main St., Ephrata (17522); Sa; 49,989pd, 1,330fr (Est); $9.24; publisher Lancaster Farming Inc.; editor Everett Newswanger; tel (717) 626-1164; fax (717) 733-6058

Laural Highlands: *The New Republic* — 145 Center St.; PO Box 239, Meyersdale (15552); Th; 3,400pd, 18fr (Sw); $4.10; C; publisher Edward B Dunlap; general manager Linda A Gindlesperger; editor Scott Shumaker; tel (814) 634-8321; fax (814) 634-5556

Leechburg: *Leechburg Advance* — 134 Grant Ave., Vandergrift (15690); W; 5,732pd, 14fr (Est); $10.50; C; publisher Don Cole; editor Jo-Jo Bodnar; tel (412) 567-5656; fax (412) 568-3818

Ligonier: *The Ligonier Echo* — 112 W. Main St. (15658); W; 4,105pd, 52fr (Sw); $6.30; C; publisher H Ralph Hernley; general manager Joseph F Soforic; editor Richard P Schwab; tel (412) 238-2111; fax (412) 887-5115

Lititz: *The Lititz Record Express* — 22 E. Main St.; PO Box 366 (17543); Th; 6,551pd, 190fr (Sw); $6.50; C; publisher Lancaster County Weeklies Inc.; general manager Robert L Campbell; editor Rick Reitz; tel (717) 626-2191; fax (717) 733-6058

Lower Bucks Co.: *Bucks County Tribune* — PO Box 375, Feasterville (19053-0375); W; 1,320pd, 15,200fr (Sw); $16.80; C; publisher Matthew H Petersohn; editor Sandra L Petersohn; tel (215) 675-6600

Lower Merion/Radnor Twp.: *Main Line Times* — 311 E. Lancaster Ave., Ardmore (19003); Th; 13,320pd, 536fr (ABC); $18.22; C; publisher Deborah Shaw; editor Daniel A Eisenhoth; tel (610) 642-4300; fax (610) 645-7620

Luzerne Co.: *West Side Weekly* — 950 Wyoming Ave., Forty Fort (18704); Th; 3,000pd (Sw); $4.95; publisher & editor Dotty Martin; tel (717) 287-8484; fax (717) 287-1983

Malvern/Exton: *The Suburban Advertiser* — 134 N. Wayne Ave.; PO Box 409, Wayne (19087); Th; 97pd, 17,516fr (CAC); $15.80; C; publisher William Burgess; editor Brad Wilson; tel (610) 688-3000; fax (610) 524-1997

Manayunk/Roxborough/E Falls/Andorra: *The Review* — 6220 Ridge Ave., Philadelphia (19128); W; 14,000pd, 9,500fr (Sw); $13.50; C; publisher Fred Donaldson; general manager John Foderaro; editor George Beetham; tel (215) 483-7300; fax (215) 483-2073

Marcus Hook: *Marcus Hook Press* — 3245 Garrett Rd., Drexel Hill (19026); Th; 3,500pd (Sw); $6.00; publisher Press Publishing Co.; editor P A Girard; managing editor M M Girard; tel (610) 259-4141

Mc Donald: *The Record-Outlook* — 116 E. Lincoln Ave., McDonald (15057); W; 3,257pd, 31fr (Est); 17¢; publisher & editor Eliza A Northrop; tel (412) 926-2111; fax (412) 926-2123

McConnellsburg: *Fulton County News* — 417 E. Market St.; PO Box 635 (17233); Th; 6,418pd, 40fr (Sw); $4.30; publisher Jamie S Greathead; editor Bob Saul; tel (717) 485-4513; fax (717) 485-5187

Middleburg: *Middleburg Post* — 14 W. Market; PO Box 356 (17842); Tu; 3,413pd, 45fr (Sw); $3.30; C; publisher Anton M VanBuren; managing editor Wade Fowler; tel (717) 837-6065; fax (717) 837-0776

Middletown: *Press and Journal* — 20 S. Union St.; PO Box 310 (17057); W; 10,500pd, 894fr (Est); 70¢; publisher & editor Joseph C Sukle Jr; tel (717) 944-4628; fax (717) 944-2083

Mifflinburg: *Mifflinburg Telegraph* — 358 Walnut St.; PO Box 189 (17844); W; 80pd, 741fr (Sw); $4.00; publisher John Stamm; editor Connie Sanders; tel (717) 966-2255; fax (717) 966-9706

Mifflintown/Juniata Co: *Juniata Sentinel* — Old Rte. 22 W. of Mifflintown; PO Box 127, Mifflintown (17059); W; 7,501pd, 294fr (Sw); $7.00; publisher William A Gilliland; editor Polly D Digon; tel (717) 436-8206; fax (717) 436-5174

Milford: *Pike County Dispatch* — 105 W. Catharine St.; PO Box 186 (18337-0186); Th; 5,986pd, 208fr (Sw); $5.25; publisher & editor Sue Doty Lloyd; managing editor Rick Freeman; tel (717) 296-6641; fax (717) 296-2610

Millcreek Twp.: *Millcreek Sun* — 2126 Filmore Ave., Erie (16506); Su; 3,279pd, 13fr (Sw); $7.49; C; publisher Mark E Laskowski; editor Claudia Mosso; managing editor Peggy Machinski; tel (814) 833-7459; fax (814) 838-9802

Monroeville/Pitcairn: *Times Express* — 610 Beatty Rd., Monroeville (15146); W; 4,746pd, 66fr (Est); $10.77; publisher Thomas Bova; editor Edith Hughes; tel (412) 856-7400; fax (412) 856-7954

Montgomery Co.: *Montgomery Post/Montgomery Newspapers* — 290 Commerce Dr.; PO Box 1628, Fort Washington (19034); W; 1,675pd, 3,843fr (CAC); $7.96; C; publisher Arthur W Howe IV; editor Fred Behringer; tel (215) 675-3430; fax (215) 643-9475

Montgomery Co.: *The Montgomery County Observer* — 1050 DeKalb Pike, Blue Bell (19422); W; 6,000pd, 15,000fr (Est); $11.50; publisher & editor Francis Laping; tel (610) 277-6342

Montgomeryville: *Montgomeryville Spirit* — 215 Front St., Souderton (18964-0459); W; 1,643pd, 14,064fr (CAC); $9.40; C; publisher Arthur W Howe IV; editor Fred D Behringer; tel (215) 723-4801; fax (215) 643-9475

Morrisons Cove: *Morrisons Cove Herald* — 113 N. Market St., Martinsburg (16662); Th; 6,228pd, 120fr (Est); $4.00; publisher & editor David L Snyder; tel (814) 793-2144; fax (814) 793-4882

Mt. Airy District: *Mt. Airy Times Express* — 6622 Germantown Ave., Philadelphia (19119); W; 22pd, 14,010fr (CAC); $9.56; C; publisher Deborah Shaw; editor Sharon Bender; tel (215) 848-4300; fax (215) 848-9160

Mt. Pleasant: *The Mount Pleasant Journal* — 23-33 S. Church St. (15666); W; 5,382pd, 56fr (Sw); $7.67; C; publisher H Ralph Hernley; general manager Joseph F Soforic; editor Paul S Brittain; tel (412) 547-5722; fax (412) 887-5115

Mountaintop: *Mountaintop Eagle* — 85 S. Main Rd.; PO Box 10 (18707); W; 2,670pd, 50fr (Sw); $6.00; publisher & editor Stephanie Grubert; managing editor Kathy Flower; tel (717) 474-6397; fax (717) 474-9272

Muncy/Hughesville: *The Luminary* — PO Box 432, Muncy (17756); W; 1,178pd, 12fr (Sw); $2.50; publisher Thomas C Briley; editor Vivian Daily; tel (717) 546-8555; fax (717) 584-5399

Murrysville: *Murrysville Area Star* — 610 Beatty Rd., Monroeville (15146); W; 1,133pd, 4,306fr (Est); 45¢; publisher Thomas Bova; editor Edith Hughes; tel (412) 856-7400; fax (412) 856-7954

Nanty Glo: *The Nanty Glo Journal* — 975 Roberts St.; PO Box 256 (15943); W; 3,088pd (Est); $2.95; C; publisher Frank K Noll; general manager Gene Stepp; editor Ken Piper; tel (814) 749-8631; fax (814) 749-8632

New Bethlehem/Rimersburg: *The Leader-Vindicator* — 435 Broad St.; PO Box 158, New Bethlehem (16242); W; 5,159pd, 53fr (Sw); $5.00; publisher James R Shaffer; editor Joe Shaw; tel (814) 275-3131; fax (814) 275-3531

New Bloomfield: *Perry County Times* — 51 N. Church St.; PO Box 130 (17068); Th; 5,501pd, 51fr (Sw); $4.12; C; publisher Rick White; editor Wade Fowler; managing editor Gary Thomas; tel (717) 582-4305; fax (717) 582-7933

New Brighton/Beaver Falls: *North News* — 1181 Airport Rd.; PO Box 629, Aliquippa (15001-0629); Th; 13,562fr (Sw); $12.80; C; publisher Raymond A Palket; editor Ione Morgan; tel (412) 375-6611; fax (412) 375-1011

New Hope: *The New Hope Gazette* — 170 Old York Rd.; PO Box 180 (18938); Th; 3,126pd, 165fr (Sw); $10.00; C; publisher Art Thompson; editor Bridget Wingert; tel (215) 862-9415; fax (215) 862-2160

New Wilmington/Pulaski: *The Globe* — 129 W. Neshannock Ave., New Wilmington (16142); W; 1,800pd (Est); $3.43; publisher Richard Steinlechner; general manager Paul Mirkovich; editor Norma Steinlechner; tel (412) 946-3501; fax (412) 946-2097

Newtown: *The Advance of Bucks County* — PO Box 910 (18940); W; 4,965pd, 606fr (Sw); $10.00; C; publisher & editor Art Thompson; tel (215) 968-2244; fax (215) 968-3501

Newtown Square/Marple Twp./Media/Middletown: *County Press* — 3732 W. Chester Pike; PO Box 249, Newtown Square (19073); W; 6,950pd, 1,093fr (Sw); $6.75; C; publishers Reese J Crowe Jr & Richard L Crowe; editor William W Lawrence; tel (610) 356-6664; fax (610) 353-5321

Newville: *Valley Times-Star* — 23 Big Spring Ave.; PO Box 160 (17241); W; 3,017pd, 75fr (Est); $2.24; C; publisher Kenneth Wolfrom; editor Barbara Thompson; tel (717) 776-3197; fax (717) 776-9290

N Dauphin Co.: *The Upper Dauphin Sentinel* — 510 Union St.; PO Box 250, Millersburg (17061-0250); Tu; 8,639pd, 135fr (Est); $6.72; publisher Ben L Kocher; editor Duane E Good; tel (717) 692-4737; fax (717) 692-2420

North East: *North East Breeze* — 39 S. Lake St. (16428); Su; 3,005pd, 4,805fr (Sw); $7.49; C; publisher Mark E Laskowski; editor Roger Coda; managing editor Peggy Machinski; tel (814) 725-4557; fax (814) 725-1981

N New Castle Co./Delaware/Hockessin (DE)/Newark (DE): *Brandywine Chronicle* — 5000 Limestone Rd.; PO Box 520, Oxford (19363); Th; 5,000fr (Sw); $7.00; C; publisher AD PRO Inc.; editor Andrew H Lieberman; tel (610) 932-2444; fax (610) 932-2246

N Versailles/White Oak/E McKeesport/Wilmerding/Wall/Pitcairn: *Community News* — PO Box 280, Irwin (15642); W; 20,575fr (Sw); $6.90; C; publisher Richard T Rae; editor Craig J Smith; tel (412) 523-6588; fax (412) 523-6805

NE Philadelphia: *Northeast Times Newspaper* — 2512 Metropolitan Dr., Trevose (19053); W/Th; 1,722pd, 241,114fr (CAC); $31.32; C; publisher Robert T Smylie; editor John Scanlon; tel (215) 355-9009; fax (215) 355-4812

NE Philadelphia: *The Northeast Breeze* — 54 Park Ave., Rockledge (19046); Th; 22,400fr (Sw); $10.50; C; publisher Fred Donaldson; general manager Barbara Huggett; editor Bob Kent; tel (215) 379-5500; fax (215) 379-5555

NW Washington Co.: *The Record Enterprise* — 11 Main St., Burgettstown (15021); W; 2,622pd, 27fr (Est); $4.45; C; publisher Cornerstone Publications; editor Eliza A Northrop; tel (412) 947-4700; fax (412) 947-5674

Northern Lancaster Co.: *The Shopping News* — 615 E. Main St.; PO Box 456, Ephrata (17522); W; 34,434fr (CAC); $6.00; publisher John Hocking; general manager Julie Fetter; tel (717) 738-1151; fax (717) 733-3900

Norwin Heights: *Norwin Star* — 610 Beatty Rd., Monroeville (15416); W; 319pd, 16fr (Est); $6.96; publisher Kevin Aylmer; editor Frances Volpe; managing editor Edith Hughes; tel (412) 856-7400; fax (412) 856-7954

Oakmont/Plum/Verona: *The Advance Leader* — 610 Beatty Rd., Monroeville (15146); W; 1,707pd, 25fr (Est); $9.62; publisher Thomas Bova; editor Edith Hughes; tel (412) 856-7400; fax (412) 856-7954

Oxford: *The Oxford Tribune* — 322 Hodgson St. (19363); W; 1,500pd, 100fr (Est); $9.10; publisher Chesapeake Publishing; general manager Jeff Mezzatesta; editors Eric Magill & Kerin D Magill; tel (610) 932-8886; fax (610) 932-2808

Parkesburg: *Parkesburg Post* — 22 E. State St., Quarryville (17566); Th; 1,559pd, 64fr (Est); $4.00; publisher Donald Althouse; editor Fran Maye; tel (610) 786-2992; fax (610) 786-8679

Patton: *Union Press Courier* — 452 Magee Ave.; PO Box 116 (16668); Th; 5,000pd, 225fr (Est); $4.50; C; publisher Frank Cammarata; editor Gretchen Smith; tel (814) 674-3666; fax (814) 674-3628

Penn Hills/Churchill: *The Progress* — 610 Beatty Rd., Monroeville (15146); W; 3,652pd, 26fr (Est); 63¢; publisher Thomas Bova; editor Edith Hughes; tel (412) 856-7400; fax (412) 856-7954

Pennsburg: *Town and Country* — Rte. 663 & Dotts St.; PO Box 5 (18073); Th; 5,125pd, 2fr (Est); $6.94; C; publisher Suzanne A Bush; editor Anthony Noel; tel (215) 679-9561; fax (215) 679-9563

II-68 Pennsylvania U.S. Weeklies

Perkasie/Sellersville: *Perkasie News-Herald* — 320 S. 7th St.; PO Box 127, Perkasie (18944); W; 6,850pd, 250fr (Sw); $6.60; publisher Charles W Baum; editor John A Gerner; tel (215) 257-6839; fax (215) 257-8701

Perry Co.: *The News-Sun* — PO Box 128, Newport (17074); W; 3,192pd, 47fr (Sw); $3.63; C; publisher Rick White; editor Wade Fowler; managing editor Gary Thomas; tel (717) 582-4305

Philadelphia/Cheltenham: *The Leader* — 2385 W. Cheltenham Ave. Ste. 182, c/o Intercounty Newspaper, Philadelphia (19150); W; 29,000pd (Est); 89¢; C; publisher Fred Donaldson; editor Marshall Rothman; tel (215) 885-4111; fax (2150 885-0226

Pine Grove: *Press-Herald* — 181 S. Tulpehocken St. (17963); Th; 2,960pd, 168fr (Est); $5.75; C; publisher Fred V Knecht; general manager & managing editor William K Knecht II; editor Paula Schaeffer; tel (717) 345-4455; fax (717) 345-8467

Pittston: *Sunday Dispatch* — 109 New St.; PO Box 451 (18640); Su; 13,850pd (Est); 24¢; publisher John Watson; general manager Bill Watson III; editor Dave Janoski; tel (717) 655-1418; fax (717) 883-1266

Port Allegany: *Port Allegany Reporter-Argus* — PO Box 129 (16743); W; 1,975pd, 120fr (Est); 30¢; publisher Joseph Majot; editor Teri McDowell; tel (814) 642-2811; fax (814) 642-7169

Port Royal: *The Times* — 111 W. 4th St. (17082); W; 3,650pd, 15fr (Est); 40¢; publisher & editor David E Wade; tel (717) 527-2213

Portage: *The Portage Dispatch* — 722 Delancey Dr.; PO Box 395 (15946); W; 5,272pd (Est); $4.95; C; publisher Frank K Noll; general manager Gene Neral; editor Ken Piper; tel (814) 736-9666; fax (814) 736-9666

Quaker Vly. School District: *The Sewickley Herald* — 509 Hegner Way, Sewickley (15143); W; 3,345pd, 165fr (Est); 76¢; C; publisher Thomas Bova; editor Frank Tiboni; managing editor Edith Hughes; tel (412) 741-8200; fax (412) 741-8200

Quakertown/Upper Bucks Co./Philadelphia/Delaware Vly.: *Quakertown Free Press* — 312 W. Broad St., Free Press Bldg.; PO Box 100, Quakertown (18951); Tu/F; 7,500pd, 3,000fr (Sw); $6.55; C; publisher C M (Ty) Meredith IV; general manager Traci Wornham; editor James McFadden; managing editor Kate Kane; tel (215) 536-6820; fax (215) 536-7201

Quarryville: *The Sun-Ledger* — 22 E. State St. (17566); W; 2,498pd (Est); $13.20; C; publisher Donald Althouse; editor Fran Maye; tel (717) 786-2992; fax (717) 786-8679

Renovo/Lock Haven: *The Record* — 129 5th St., Renovo (17764); W; 2,376pd (Sw); $3.00; publisher Frank O'Reilly; general manager John Lipez; editor Buck O'Reilly; tel (717) 923-1500

Rockledge/Chettenham: *The Breeze* — 54 Park Ave., Rockledge (19046); Th; 379pd, 49fr (Est); 16¢; publisher & editor Bob Kent; general manager Barbara Huggett; tel (215) 379-5500; fax (215) 379-5555

Royersford: *The Valley Item* — 290 Commerce Dr. (Fort Washington 19034); PO Box 38, Schwenksville (19473); Th; 1,190pd, 12fr (CAC); $5.96; C; publisher Arthur W Howe IV; editor Chris Hennessey; tel (215) 948-4850

Royersford/Spring City: *Spring-Ford Reporter* — Park Towne Plz.; PO Box 28, Royersford (19468); W; 1,855pd, 3,028fr (CAC); $7.96; C; publisher Art Howe; managing editor Alethea Lynch; tel (610) 948-4850; fax (610) 948-5914

Saxton: *The Broad Top Bulletin* — 900 6th St.; PO Box 188 (16678); W; 3,178pd (Sw); $3.50; publisher & editor Jon D Baughman; tel (814) 635-2851

Schuylkill Haven: *The Call* — 960 E. Main St.; PO Box 178, Schuylkill Haven (17972); Th; 4,750pd, 250fr (Sw); $6.80; C; publisher Fred V Knecht; general manager & managing editor William K Knecht II; editor LaJeune Steidle; tel (717) 385-3120; fax (717) 385-0725

Scottdale: *The Independent-Observer* — 229 Pittsburgh St. (15683-0222); W; 2,844pd, 43fr (Sw); $6.30; C; publisher H Ralph Hernley; general manager Joseph F Soforic; editor Marshall L Forys; tel (412) 887-6101; fax (412) 887-5115

Selinsgrove: *Selinsgrove Times Tribune* — PO Box 30 (17870); W; 1,440pd, 60fr (Sw); $4.00; C; publisher Anton M VanBuren; editor Robert Hufnagle; managing editor Wade Fowler; tel (717) 374-4408; fax (717) 374-6080

Sharpsburg/Aspinwall: *The Herald* — 101 Emerson Ave., Aspinwall (15215); W; 5,330pd, 42fr (Est); $12.00; C; publisher Scott M Brown; editor Matthew Clark; tel (412) 782-2121; fax (412) 782-1195

Shippensburg: *The News-Chronicle* — 1011 Ritner Hwy.; PO Box 100 (17257); M/Th; 6,069pd, 84fr (Sw); $5.35; C; publisher Kenneth E Wolfrom; general manager Robert Riggs; editor James Curtis; tel (717) 532-4101; fax (717) 532-3020

Souderton: *Souderton Independent* — 21 S. Front St.; PO Box 459 (18964-0459); W; 5,073pd, 50fr (CAC); $7.96; C; publisher Arthur W Howe IV; editor Barbara McClennen; tel (215) 723-4801; fax (215) 723-8779

S Chester Co.: *Chester County Press* — 5000 Limestone Rd.; PO Box 520, Oxford (19363); W; 13,125pd, 1,441fr (Sw); $11.20; C; publisher Andrew H Lieberman; general manager Randall S Lieberman; editor Monika Weiss; managing editor Cathy Ash; tel (610) 932-2444; fax (610) 932-2246

S Huntingdon Co.: *The Valley Log* — Water St.; PO Box 219, Orbisonia (17243-0219); W; 3,061pd, 70fr (Sw); $2.50; publisher C Arnold McClure; editor Terry Dillman; tel (814) 447-5506; fax (814) 447-3050

S Suburban Pittsburgh: *The Advertiser* — 3801 Washington Rd.; PO Box 929, McMurray (15317); Th; 34,136fr (CAC); $15.35; C; publisher William B Northrop Jr; editor Debbie Popp; tel (412) 561-0700; fax (412) 941-8685

S Suburban Pittsburgh: *The Almanac* — 3801 Washington Rd.; PO Box 929, McMurray (15317); W; 31,215fr (CAC); $15.35; C; publisher William B Northrop Jr; editor Debbie Popp; tel (412) 561-0700; fax (412) 941-8685

SE Chester Co.: *The Kennett Paper* — 116 S. Union St., Kennett Square (19348); Th; 4,372pd, 1,688fr (Sw); $9.50; publisher James G Blaine; editor David Thomas; managing editor Mary Hutchings; tel (610) 444-6590; fax (610) 444-4931

Springfield: *Springfield Press* — 204 Ballymore Rd.; PO Box 291 (19064); W; 6,200pd, 270fr (Sw); $6.75; C; publisher Reese J Crowe Jr; editor Dottie Koetzle; tel (610) 544-6660; fax (610) 544-4530

Springfield Twp.: *Springfield Sun* — 290 Commerce Dr.; PO Box 1628, Fort Washington (19034); Th; 2,601pd, 45fr (CAC); $20.12; C; publisher Arthur W Howe IV; editor Fred D Behringer; tel (215) 542-0200; fax (215) 643-9475

Strasburg: *Strasburg Weekly News* — 140 W. Main St.; PO Box 249 (17579); F; 782pd, 79fr (Sw); $1.60; publisher Gerald S Lestz; editor Gail E Anderson; tel (717) 687-7721; fax (717) 392-1341

Susquehanna Co.: *The Susquehanna County Independent* — 24 S. Main St., Montrose (18801); W; 3,485pd, 121fr (Sw); $8.40; publisher Elizabeth (Boots) Taylor; editor Teri Olcott; tel (717) 278-6397; fax (717) 278-4305

Susquehanna Co.: *The Susquehanna County Transcript* — 214-216 Exchange St., Susquehanna (18847); W; 6,700pd, 320fr (Sw); 16¢; publisher & editor Charles Ficarro; tel (717) 853-3134; fax (717) 853-4707

Swarthmore: *The Swarthmorean* — 107 Rutgers Ave., Ste. 1; PO Box 59 (19081); F; 2,054pd, 50fr (Est); 24¢; publisher & editor Beth Gross; publisher Donald W Delson; tel (610) 543-0900; fax (610) 543-3790

Tower City: *West Schuylkill Herald* — 613 E. Grand Ave.; PO Box C (17980); Th; 1,800pd, 150fr (Est); $4.20; publisher Fred V Knecht; editor June B Reibsane; managing editor William Knecht; tel (717) 647-2191; fax (717) 647-2420

Troy: *Troy Gazette-Register* — 11 Canton St.; PO Box 126 (16947); Th; 1,200pd (Est); $2.75; publisher Troy Gazette Register Inc.; general manager Kathy Morris; editor Shirley Lewis; tel (717) 297-3024; fax (717) 297-2954

Tunkhannock: *New Age-Examiner* — 16 E. Tioga St.; PO Box 59 (18657); Tu/F; 4,950pd, 51fr (Est); $6.20; C; publisher James E Towner; editor Mary Baldwin; tel (717) 836-2123; fax (717) 836-3378

Union City: *Times-Leader* — 8230 W. High St. Ext.; PO Box 151 (16438); Su; 3,453pd, 6,793fr (Sw); $7.49; C; publisher Mark E Laskowski; editor John Finnerty; managing editor Peggy Machinski; tel (814) 438-7666; fax (814) 438-2898

Upper Darby: *Upper Darby Press* — 3245 Garrett Rd., Drexel Hill (19026); Th; 4,000pd (Sw); $6.00; C; publisher Press Publishing Co.; editor Philippe A Girard; tel (610) 259-4141

Valley View: *The Citizen-Standard* — 100 W. Main St.; PO Box 147 (17983); W; 4,752pd, 70fr (Sw); $6.26; C; publisher Gregory J Zyla; managing editor Tom Mitchell; tel (717) 682-9081; fax (717) 682-8734

Vandergrift/Apollo: *The News-Citizen* — 134 Grant Ave., Vandergrift (15690); W; 2,219pd, 32fr (Est); $10.50; C; publisher Don Cole; editor Jo-Jo Bodnar; tel (412) 567-5656; fax (412) 568-3818

Washington/Wheeling (WV): *Weekly Recorder* — 256 Main St.; PO Box F, Claysville (15323); F; 2,950pd, 39fr (Sw); $4.00; publisher & editor Douglas R Teagarden; general manager Susan Burd; tel (412) 663-7742

Wayne Co.: *The Weekly Almanac* — 709 Church St., Honesdale (18431); Tu; 3,500pd, 50fr (Sw); $4.65; publisher & editor James A Kalbaugh; publisher & general manager Judie G Kalbaugh; tel (717) 253-9270; fax (717) 253-8937

Wayne/Main Line/Berwyn/Paoli: *The Suburban & Wayne Times* — 134 N. Wayne Ave.; PO Box 409, Wayne (19087); Th; 12,048pd, 155fr (ABC); $16.70; publisher William Burgess; editor James Lewis; tel (610) 688-3000; fax (610) 254-8522

Wellsboro/Tioga Co.: *The Wellsboro Gazette* — 25 E. Ave.; PO Box 118, Wellsboro (16901); W; 7,227pd (Sw); $4.95; C; publisher Donald J Fryday; editor Jeff Fetzer; tel (717) 724-2287; fax (717) 724-2278

W Newton: *The Times-Sun* — 205 E. Main St. (15089); W; 2,865pd, 43fr (Sw); $6.30; C; publisher H Ralph Hernley; general manager Joseph F Soforic; editor Colleen A Pollock; tel (412) 872-6800; fax (412) 887-5115

Westfield/Galeton: *Free Press-Courier* — 129 Main St.; PO Box 127, Westfield (16950); W; 2,735pd (Est); $3.00; C; publisher Tioga Printing Corp.; editor Elizabeth Stierly; managing editor Marie Pepero; tel (814) 367-2230; fax (814) 367-2230

Westmoreland/Indiana Cos.: *The Dispatch* — 101 W. Market St.; PO Box 37, Blairsville (15717); F; 16,500pd, 1,500fr (Sw); $10.65; C; publisher Richard M Scaife; general manager & editor John M Jennings; tel (412) 459-6100; fax (412) 459-7366

White Haven/Weatherly: *The Journal-Herald* — 211 Main St., White Haven (18661); Th; 1,765pd, 20fr (Sw); $3.00; C; publishers Clara Holder & Jay Holder; general manager Seth Isenberg; editor Ruth Isenberg; tel (717) 443-9131

Willow Grove: *Willow Grove Guide* — 101 N. York Rd., Hatboro (19040); W; 1,331pd, 1,345fr (CAC); $20.12; C; publisher Arthur W Howe IV; editor Andrew Hussie; tel (215) 675-3430; fax (215) 675-9024

Woodland Hills: *Woodland Area Progress* — 610 Beatty Rd., Monroeville (15416); W; 1,984pd, 57fr (Est); $14.39; publisher Kevin Aylmer; editor Bob Wertz; managing editor Edith Hughes; tel (412) 856-7400; fax (412) 856-7954

Yardley: *Yardley News* — 10 Penn Valley Dr.; PO Box 910 (18940); Th; 5,518pd, 147fr (Sw); $10.00; C; publisher Art Thompson; editor Jeffrey Werner; tel (215) 493-2794; fax (215) 321-0527

Yardley/Lower Makefield: *Yardley News* — 10 Penn Valley Dr., Yardley (19067); Th; 4,900pd, 600fr (Sw); $7.35; C; publisher Art Thompson; editor Jeff Werner; tel (215) 493-2794; fax (215) 321-0527

Yeadon: *The Yeadon Times* — 719 Church Ln.; PO Box 5305 (19050); Th; 1,800pd, 300fr (Est); 15¢; publisher & editor Frank Davenport; tel (610) 623-6088

York: *York Sunday News* — 205 N. George St. (17401); PO Box 2807 (17405); Su; 91,460pd (ABC); $39.00; C; publisher & editor James D Sneddon; tel (717) 854-1575; fax (717) 843-2958

Youngwood/New Stanton: *The Adviser* — 229 Pittsburgh St., Scottdale (15683); W; 2,530fr (Sw); $6.30; C; publisher H Ralph Hernley; general manager Joseph F Soforic; editor Jonna Stairs; tel (412) 547-5722; fax (412) 887-5115

RHODE ISLAND

Barrington: *Barrington Times* — 139 Main St. (02885); PO Box 227 (02806); W; 5,258pd, 35fr (CAC); $5.50; C; publisher R S Bosworth Jr; general manager Matthew D Hayes; editor Monica Allen; tel (401) 245-6000

Block Island: *The Block Island Times* — 460 Chapel St.; PO Box 278 (02807); Sa; 1,950pd, 150fr (Sw); $14.50; publisher & editor Peter Wood; general manager Erica Tonner; managing editor Katie Mulvaney; tel (404) 466-2222; fax (404) 466-2222

Bristol: *Bristol Phoenix* — 1 Bradford St.; PO Box 90 (02809); Th; 6,627pd, 45fr (CAC); $5.50; C; publisher R S Bosworth Jr; general manager Matthew D Hayes; editor Gisela Medek; tel (401) 253-6000

Cranston: *Cranston Herald* — 798 Park Ave. (02910); Th; 3,491pd, 76fr (CAC); $8.00; C; publisher & managing editor John I Howell Jr; general manager Richard Fleischer; editor Steve Lowenthal; tel (401) 781-4240; fax (401) 732-3110

E Greenwich: *The East Greenwich Pendulum* — 580 Main St.; PO Box 350 (02818); Th; 2,936pd, 53fr (CAC); $7.10; C; publisher Marc Romanow; editor Ann Davidson; tel (401) 884-4665; fax (401) 884-9819

Jamestown: *Jamestown Press* — 42 Narragansett Ave. (02835); Th; 300pd, 5,700fr (Sw); $8.25; publisher & editor Jeffrey J McDonough; managing editor Chris Irby; tel (401) 423-3200; fax (401) 423-1661

Newport Co.: *Newport This Week* — 38 Bellevue Ave.; PO Box 159, Newport (02840); Th; 300pd, 12,000fr (Est); 66¢; publisher Lisette Prince; editor John Pantalone; tel (401) 847-7766; fax (401) 846-4974

N Kingstown: *The Standard-Times* — 113 W. Main St. (02852); Th; 5,510pd, 99fr (CAC); $8.95; C; publisher Marc Romanow; editor Rudy Hempe; tel (401) 294-4576; fax (401) 294-9736

Portsmouth: *Sakonnet Times* — 2829 E. Main Rd.; PO Box 131 (02871); Th; 6,593pd, 59fr (CAC); $5.50; C; publisher R S Bosworth Jr; general manager & managing editor Matthew D Hayes; editor Bruce Burdett; tel (401) 683-1000; fax (401) 683-6688

S Kingstown: *The Narragansett Times* — 187 Main St.; PO Box 232, Wakefield (02880); W; 9,272pd, 138fr (CAC); $11.20; F; 10,000pd (Est); $11.20; C; publisher Marc Romanow; editor Betty Cotter; tel (401) 789-9744; fax (401) 783-5610

Warren: *Warren Times-Gazette* — 139 Main St.; PO Box 50 (02885); W; 3,081pd, 32fr (CAC); $5.50; C; publisher & editor William Rupp; general manager Matthew D Hayes; tel (401) 245-6002

Warwick: *The Warwick Beacon* — 1944 Warwick Ave. (02889); Tu/Th; 10,438pd, 264fr (Sw); $10.00; C; publisher & managing editor John I Howell Jr; general manager Richard Fleischer; editor Marcia O'Brien; tel (401) 732-3100; fax (401) 732-3110

SOUTH CAROLINA

Abbeville: *Press & Banner* — 107 W. Pickens St.; PO Box 769 (29620); W; 5,000pd (Est); $1.64; editor John R West; tel (803) 459-5461; fax (803) 459-5463

Allendale Co.: *The Allendale County Citizen-Leader* — 307 N. Main; PO Box 98, Allendale (29810); Tu; 2,150pd, 20fr (Est); $2.97; C; publisher Eric Denty; general manager & editor Bill Goodson; tel (803) 584-3441; fax (803) 584-3442

Bamberg Co.: *The Advertizer-Herald* — 102 McGee St.; PO Box 929, Bamberg (29003); Th; 4,100pd, 82fr (Est); 22¢; publisher & editor Betty S Kilgus; general manager & managing editor Carol Barker; tel (803) 245-5204; fax (803) 245-3900

Barnwell/Williston: *The People-Sentinel* — 1810 Main St.; PO Box 1255, Barnwell (29812); W; 5,052pd, 136fr (Est); $5.25; C; publisher Eric Denty; general manager Bill Goodson; editor Sharon Taylor; tel (803) 259-3501; fax (803) 259-2703

Batesburg/Leesville: *The Twin City-News* — 114 E. Columbia Ave.; PO Box 311, Batesburg (29006); Th; 4,364pd, 50fr (Sw); $3.75; publisher Sara Bruner; editor Virginia Sprinkle; tel (803) 532-6203; fax (803) 532-6204

Belton/Honea Path: *News-Chronicle* — 31 Main St.; PO Box 167, Honea Path (29654); W; 4,600pd (Sw); 90¢; publisher B F Ellison Jr; editor Elaine Ellison-Rider; tel (803) 369-7154, (803) 338-6124; fax (803) 338-1109

Belton/Honea Path: *The Belton & Honea Path* — Public Sq.; PO Box 606, Belton (29627-0606); W; 3,100pd, 30fr (Est); 22¢; publisher B F Ellison Jr; editor Elaine Ellison-Rider; tel (803) 338-6124; fax (803) 338-1109

Bennettsville: *Marlboro Herald-Advocate* — 100 Fayetteville Ave.; PO Drawer 656 (29512); M/Th; 6,800pd (Est); $5.58; C; publisher & editor W L Kinney Jr; tel (803) 479-3815; fax (803) 479-7671

Berkeley Co.: *Berkeley Independent* — 320 E. Main St.; PO Box 427, Moncks Corner (29461); W; 9,387pd, 85fr (Sw); $5.35; publisher & editor H Allen Morris; tel (803) 761-6397; fax (803) 899-6996

Bishopville/Lee Co.: *Lee County Observer* — 218 N. Main St.; PO Box 567, Bishopville (29010); W; 3,775pd, 25fr (Est); $3.45; publisher J W (Dick) Scott Jr; editor Carpenter King; tel (803) 484-9431; fax (803) 484-5055

Calhoun Falls: *The Calhoun Falls News* — 107 W. Pickins St.; PO Box 769, Abbeville (29620); W; 1,825pd, 100fr (Est); $5.00; editor John R West; tel (803) 459-5461; fax (803) 459-5463

Camden/Kershaw: *Chronicle Independent* — 909 W. DeKalb St.; PO Box 1137, Camden (29020); M/F; 7,135pd, 636fr (Sw); $6.50; W; 7,135pd, 14,136fr (Sw); $6.50; publisher & editor Glenn Tucker; publisher Michael Mischner; tel (803) 432-6157; fax (803) 432-7609

Charleston/Berkely: *The Charleston Chronicle* — 1109 King St.; PO Box 20548, Charleston (29413-0548); W; 1,543pd, 4,408fr (CPVS); $7.70; publisher & editor James J French Sr; tel (803) 723-2785; fax (803) 577-6099

Cherokee Co.: *Blacksburg Times & Cherokee Tribune* — 112 W. Cherokee St.; PO Box 155, Blacksburg (29702); W; 1,900pd (Sw); $2.00; C; publisher & editor Gene McKown; general manager Linda Northy; tel (803) 839-2621; fax (803) 839-2621

Cherokee Co.: *The Cherokee Chronicle* — 423 N. Linestone St.; PO Box 729, Gaffney (29342); Tu/Th; 4,962pd, 44fr (Est); $4.75; publisher Tommy E Martin; general manager Beth Ballantyne; editor Charles W Wyatt; tel (803) 488-1016; fax (803) 488-1443

Chester: *The News & Reporter* — 104 York St.; PO Box 250 (29706); W; 6,034pd, 80fr (Sw); $5.11; F; 5,726pd, 84fr (Sw); $5.11; C; publisher William J Aultman; editor L D McKeown; tel (803) 385-3177; fax (803) 581-2518

Chesterfield/Marlboro Co.: *The Cheraw Chronicle* — 114 Front St.; PO Box 191, Cheraw (29520); Th; 5,400pd, 196fr (Est); $5.85; C; publisher & editor Margaret E Jackson; tel (803) 537-5261; fax (803) 537-4518

Clemson/Pendleton: *The Messenger* — 210 W. 1st St. (29678); PO Box 547, Seneca (29679); W/F; 3,229pd, 125fr (Est); $4.75; C; publisher Steve Edwards; editor Dan Brannan; tel (803) 882-2375/654-2451; fax (803) 882-2381

Clinton: *Clinton Chronicle* — 513 N. Broad St.; PO Box 180 (29325); W; 4,945pd, 155fr (Sw); $5.75; publisher Larry Franklin; editor Rick Hendricks; tel (803) 833-1900; fax (803) 833-1902

Clover: *The Clover Herald* — 20 W. Liberty St.; PO Box 38 (29710); Th; 2,300pd, 5fr (Sw); 23¢; C; publisher Ray G Jimison; editor Mike Faulkenberry; tel (803) 684-9903; fax (803) 628-0300

Conway/Horry Co.: *The Horry Independent* — 2510 Main St.; PO Box 740, Conway (29526); Th; 5,600pd, 125fr (Sw); $5.95; publisher Steve Robertson; editor Kathy Ropp; tel (803) 248-6671; fax (803) 248-6024

Darlington: *The News and Press* — 117 S. Main St.; PO Box 513 (29532); W; 5,675pd, 30fr (Sw); $4.76; publisher Morrell L Thomas Jr; editor Jim Fille; tel (803) 393-3811; fax (803) 393-6811

Dillon: *The Dillon Herald* — 501 N. 2nd Ave.; PO Box 1288 (29536); Tu/Th; 6,477pd, 475fr (Sw); $4.97; publisher Herald Publishing Co. Inc.; editor Paul Jones; tel (803) 774-3311; fax (803) 841-1930

Edgefield: *The Edgefield Advertiser* — 119 Courthouse Sq.; PO Box 628 (29824); W; 500pd (Sw); $1.75; publisher & editor W W Mims; tel (803) 637-3540

Edgefield Co./Johnston: *The Citizen News* — 201 Main St.; PO Box 448, Edgefield (29824); Th; 2,772pd, 257fr (Sw); $4.45; C; publisher Bettis C Rainsford; general manager Joanne Rainsford; editor Steven E Parham; tel (803) 637-5306; fax (803) 637-6066

Fort Mill/N Lancaster Co.: *Fort Mill Times* — 116 Main St.; PO Box 250, Fort Mill (29716-0250); W; 5,100pd, 875fr (Sw); $6.25; publisher John E Mantle; editor Jerry P McGuire; tel (803) 547-2353; fax (803) 547-2321

Gaffney/Blacksburg: *The Gaffney Ledger* — 1604 Baker Blvd.; PO Box 670, Gaffney (29342); M/W/F; 9,992pd, 129fr (Sw); $7.05; publisher Louis C Sossamon; editor Cody Sossamon; managing editor Klonie Jordan; tel (803) 489-1131; fax (803) 487-7667

Georgetown: *The Georgetown Times* — 615 Front St.; PO Drawer G (29442); M/W/F; 5,867pd, 90fr (Sw); $5.10; C; publisher Cathy Wilkerson; editor Jesse Tullos; tel (803) 546-4148; fax (803) 546-2395

Georgetown: *Times Mid-Week* — 615 Front St.; PO Drawer G (29442); Tu; 15,550fr (Est); $7.20; C; publisher Cathy Wilkerson; editor Jesse Tullos; tel (803) 546-4148; fax (803) 546-2395

Goose Creek/Ladson: *The Goose Creek Gazette* — 549B College Park Rd. (29456); PO Box 304, Goose Creek (29445); W; 4,723pd, 51fr (Est); $2.75; publisher Bill Collins; general manager Barbara Dobson; tel (803) 572-0511; fax (803) 572-0312

Greer: *The Greer Citizen* — 105 Victoria St.; PO Box 70 (29652); W; 10,903pd, 55fr (Sw); $5.50; publisher & editor Leland E Burch; publisher Walter M Burch; tel (803) 877-2076; fax (803) 877-3563

Hampton: *Hampton County Guardian* — 200 Lee Ave.; PO Box 625 (29924); Th; 5,200pd, 230fr (Est); $3.65; C; publisher Eric Denty; editor Laura J McKenzie; tel (803) 943-4645; fax (803) 943-9365

Hardeeville: *Hardeeville Times* — 200 W. Main St.; PO Box 788, Ridgeland (29936); W; 673pd (Sw); $5.50; C; publisher & editor Larry Miller; publisher Renee Miller; managing editor Jessica Jenkins; tel (803) 726-6161/6041; fax (803) 726-8661

Hartsville: *The Hartsville Messenger* — 207 E. Carolina Ave.; PO Box 1865 (29550); M/W; 6,233pd, 738fr (Est); $3.90; publisher H D Osteen Jr; editor Dennie Truesdale; tel (803) 332-6545; fax (803) 332-1341

Hemingway/Johnsonville: *Weekly Observer* — N. Main St.; PO Drawer 309, Hemingway (29554); Th; 2,800pd, 100fr (Est); $2.35; publisher & editor Russ Pace; tel (803) 558-3323; fax (803) 558-9601

Holly Hill/Santee: *The Observer* — 605 Gardner Blvd.; PO Box 715, Holly Hill (29059); W; 2,366pd, 92fr (Sw); $3.85; publisher & editor William M Owens; general manager Jean S Felkel; tel (803) 496-3242; fax (803) 496-3242

Inman: *Inman Times* — PO Drawer 7 (29349); W; 2,250pd (Est); 11¢; publisher Milton C Smith; editor Hilda Morrow; tel (803) 472-9548; fax (803) 472-3363

Irmo/NW Columbia: *The Lake Edition* — PO Box 1015, Irmo (29063); W; 4,000pd (Sw); 18¢; publishers Jackie Black & Sam Bruce; editor Paul Younghaus; tel (803) 551-1551; fax (803) 892-5757

Jasper Co.: *Jasper County Sun & Hardeeville Times* — 200 W. Main St.; PO Box 788, Ridgeland (29936); W; 1,688pd, 10fr (Sw); $5.50; C; publisher & editor Larry Miller; publisher Renee Miller; managing editor Jessica Jenkins; tel (803) 726-6161/6041; fax (803) 726-8661

Kershaw: *The Kershaw News-Era* — 103 S. Hart St.; PO Box 398 (29067); W; 1,775pd, 15fr (Est); 11¢; publisher & editor Jim McKeown; tel (803) 475-6095; fax (803) 475-9473

Kingstree/Williamsburgh: *The News* — 107 E. Mill St.; PO Box 574, Kingstree (29556); W; 4,863pd, 37fr (Est); $3.75; C; publisher Vickey Nexsen Boyd; editor Linda Brown; tel (803) 354-7454; fax (803) 354-6530

Lake City: *News & Post* — 103 W. Main St.; PO Box 428 (29560); W; 3,450pd, 7,800fr (Sw); 16¢; C; publisher Janice W Saunders; editor Thom Anderson; tel (803) 394-3571; fax (803) 394-5057

Lancaster Co.: *The Lancaster News* — 701 N. White St.; PO Box 640, Lancaster (29720); W/F/Su; 12,750pd, 31fr (Sw); $7.25; C; publisher David Ernest; general manager Buddy Aultman; editor Benjamin R Hamm; tel (803) 283-1133; fax (803) 283-8969

Landrum/Inman: *The News Leader* — 146 N. Trade Ave.; PO Box 9, Landrum (29356-0009); Tu; 2,568pd, 151fr (Est); $3.30; C; publisher & editor John F Lawrence; tel (803) 457-3337; fax (803) 472-6900

Laurens Co.: *Laurens County Advertiser* — 226 W. Laurens St.; PO Box 490, Laurens (29360); W; 8,050pd, 150fr (Sw); $6.20; F; 7,500pd, 150fr (Sw); $6.20; Sa; 17,700fr (Sw); $6.80; C; publisher W James Brown; tel (803) 984-2586; fax (803) 984-4039

Lexington Co.: *Dispatch-News* — 115 E. Main St.; PO Box 1317, Lexington (29072); W; 7,805pd, 200fr (Est); $5.30; publisher Eric Denty; editor Pam Chamberlin; tel (803) 359-3195; fax (803) 359-1378

Lexington Co.: *Lexington County Chronicle* — PO Box 9, Lexington (29071); W; 4,588pd, 914fr (Sw); $6.00; publisher MacLeod Bellune; editor Jerry Bellune; tel (803) 359-7633; fax (803) 359-2936

Liberty: *The Monitor* — 205 Russell St.; PO Box 709, Easley (29641); W; 1,381pd, 46fr (Sw); $2.65; publisher Jerry Vickery; editor Warren Wise; tel (803) 843-9378; fax (803) 855-6825

Loris: *The Loris Scene* — 4103 Main St.; PO Box 326 (29569); W; 2,138pd, 95fr (Est); $3.00; publisher Ricky A Hardee; general manager & editor Marti Cartrette; tel (803) 756-1447; fax (803) 756-7800

Manning: *The Manning Times* — 4 S. Brooks St.; PO Box 576 (29102); Th; 3,100pd, 250fr (Sw); 17¢; publisher & editor J Alan Young; tel (803) 435-8422; fax (803) 435-4189

Marion/Mullins: *Marion Star & Mullins Enterprise* — 211 Railroad Ave.; PO Box 880, Marion (29571); W; 7,000pd, 5,500fr (Sw); $6.75; publisher Robert Rider; editor Tracy Telford; managing editor Don Smith; tel (803) 423-2050; fax (803) 423-2542

McCormick Co.: *McCormick Messenger* — 120 S. Main St.; PO Box 98, McCormick (29835); Th; 1,863pd, 103fr (Est); $4.25; publisher McCormick Media Inc.; editor Janelle Collins; tel (803) 465-3311; fax (803) 465-3528

Mt. Pleasant/Isle of Palms/Sullivans Island: *Moultrie News* — 1558-B Ben Sawyer Blvd.; PO Box 2014, Mt. Pleasant (29464); Th; 16,000fr (Est); $5.00; C; publisher Charles P Diggle Sr; general manager & editor Chuck Diggle; tel (803) 849-1778; fax (803) 849-0214

Mullins: *The Enterprise* — 135 N. Main St.; PO Box 429 (29574); W; 5,000pd (Est); 16¢; publisher Robert Rider; editor Don Smith; tel (803) 464-9579

Myrtle Beach/N Myrtle Beach/Horry Co.: *The Times* — 203 N. Kings Hwy.; PO Box 725, North Myrtle Beach (29597); Th; 10,725pd, 500fr (Est); $6.18; C; publisher Pauline L Lowman; editor Polly Lowman; tel (803) 249-3525; fax (803) 249-7012

Newberry: *The Newberry Observer & Herald & News* — 1716 Main St. (29108); M/W/F; 6,387pd, 90fr (Sw); $8.66; C; publisher & editor Ollie Moye; tel (803) 276-0625; fax (803) 276-1517

N Augusta/Belvedere: *The Post* — PO Box 7800 (29841); W; 800pd, 15,000fr (Est); $6.15; C; publisher Bettis C Rainsford; general manager Joanne Rainsford; editor Steven E Parham; tel (803) 279-1000; fax (803) 279-7654

N Augusta/Belvedere: *The Star* — 106 E. Buena Vista Ave.; PO Box 6095 (29841); Th; 2,848pd, 33fr (Est); 25¢; publisher & editor Miriam L Woodring; tel (803) 279-2793; fax (803) 278-5149

Oconee Co.: *The Seneca Journal/Tribune* — 210 N.W. 1st St. (29678); PO Box 547, Seneca (29679); W/Sa; 8,800pd, 400fr (Est); $5.00; C; publisher Steve Edwards; editor Dan Brannan; tel (803) 882-2375; fax (803) 882-2381

Pageland: *Pageland Progressive-Journal* — Hwy. 9 E.; PO Box 218 (29728); Tu; 3,915pd, 7fr (Sw); $2.50; publisher & editor Brian K Hough; tel (803) 672-2358; fax (803) 672-5593

Pawleys Island: *Coastal Observer* — Commerce Ln., Waccamaw Park; PO Box 1170 (29585); Th; 3,792pd, 125fr (Sw); $5.00; publisher & editor Charles R Swenson; tel (803) 237-8438; fax (803) 237-8439

Pickens: *The Pickens Sentinel* — 109 Garvin St.; PO Box 95 (29671); W; 6,707pd, 83fr (Sw); $5.98; publisher Jerry Alexander; general manager Don Hunt; managing editor Brian Garner; tel (803) 878-2453; fax (803) 878-2454

Pickens Co.: *The Easley Progress* — 205 Russell St.; PO Box 709, Easley (29641); W; 8,480pd, 162fr (Sw); $5.90; C; publisher Jerry Vickery; general manager Bonnie Lesley; editor Chris Eldridge; managing editor Warren Wise; tel (803) 855-0355; fax (803) 855-6825

Richland Co.: *The Star-Reporter* — 716 Santee Ave.; PO Box 292, Columbia (29205); Th; 1,034pd, 8,825fr (Sw); $8.83; publisher W Miller Montgomery; editor Mimi Maddock; tel (803) 771-0219; fax (803) 252-6397

St. George: *Dorchester Eagle-Record* — 5549 Memorial Blvd.; PO Box 278, St. George (29477); Th; 3,200pd (Est); $3.35; publisher Doris Owens; publisher & editor William M Owens; tel (803) 563-3121

St. Matthews/Calhoun Co.: *The Calhoun Times* — 111A W. Bridge; PO Box 176, St. Matthews (29135); Th; 2,000pd, 20fr (Est); $2.09; publisher & editor Edwin C Morris; tel (803) 874-3137; fax (803) 874-4154

Saluda: *Standard Sentinel* — 302 N. Main St.; PO Box 676 (29138); Th; 3,749pd (Est); 15¢; publisher & editor Ralph B Shealy; tel (803) 445-2527; fax (803) 445-8679

Simpsonville/Mauldin: *Tribune-Times* — 911 S.E. Main St.; PO Box 1179, Simpsonville (29681); W; 6,033pd, 195fr (Sw); $6.18; publisher Multimedia; general manager Sudie Buchanan; editor Ernie Kastner; tel (803) 967-9580; fax (803) 967-9585

Summerville: *Summerville Journal-Scene* — 104 E. Doty Ave.; PO Box 715 (29483); W/F; 8,533pd, 715fr (Sw); 30¢; publisher & editor William C Collins; tel (803) 873-9424; fax (803) 873-9432

Walhalla: *Keowee Courier* — 111 Short St.; PO Box 528 (29691); W; 6,000pd, 206fr (Est); $3.85; C; publisher Robert E Tribble; general manager Mitch Tribble; editor Ashton Hester; tel (803) 638-5856; fax (803) 647-5405

Walterboro/Colleton Co.: *The Press & Standard* — 113 Washington St., Walterboro (29488); Tu/F; 6,500pd, 17,500fr (Sw); $5.50; C; publisher Taylor Smith; editor Katrina McCall; tel (803) 549-2586; fax (803) 549-2446

Ware Shoals/Greenwood: *The Observer* — 730 N. Greenwood; PO Box 176, Ware Shoals (29622); W; 2,950pd, 50fr (Est); $2.00; publisher S Daniel Branyon; editor Faye Branyon; tel (803) 456-7772; fax (803) 456-7122

Westminster: *The Westminster News* — Main St.; PO Box 278, Westminster (29693); W; 3,775pd, 50fr (Est); 22¢; publisher Robert E. Tribble; editor Mitch Tribble; tel (803) 647-5404; fax (803) 647-5405

Williamston/Piedmont: *The Journal* — 106 W. Main St.; PO Box 369, Williamston (29697); W; 4,416pd (Est); $5.07; publisher W C Meade; editor Sharon Crout; tel (803) 847-7361; fax (803) 847-9879

Winnsboro/Fairfield Co.: *The Herald Independent* — 127 N. Congress St.; PO Box 90, Winnsboro (29180); Th; 4,512pd, 213fr (Sw); $5.56; C; publisher Lamon Warnock; editor Pauline Patrick; tel (803) 635-4016; fax (803) 635-2948

Woodruff: *Woodruff News* — 110 N. Main St.; PO Box 249 (29388); Th; 3,800pd, 50fr (Est); $3.25; C; publisher & editor Milton C Smith; tel (803) 476-3513

York: *Yorkville Enquirer* — 20 W. Liberty St.; PO Box 30 (29745); Th; 2,561pd (Sw); 23¢; C; publisher Ray G Jimison; editor Gene Graham; tel (803) 684-9903; fax (803) 628-0300

SOUTH DAKOTA

Alcester/Union Co.: *Alcester Union* — PO Box 227, Alcester (57001); Th; 923pd, 28fr (Sw); $3.15; publisher Donald Brose; editor Mary Etta Brose; tel (605) 934-2640

Alexandria: *The Alexandria Herald* — 531 Main St.; PO Box 450 (57311); Th; 663pd, 22fr (Sw); $2.25; C; publisher & editor David L Stoltz; tel (605) 239-4521; fax (605) 239-4521

Arlington: *The Arlington Sun* — 208 S. Main; PO Box 370 (57212); W; 1,292pd, 50fr (Est); 11¢; publisher R G Sturges; editor Tim Sturges; tel (605) 983-5491; fax (605) 983-5715

Copyright ©1996 by the Editor & Publisher Co.

Armour: *The Armour Chronicle* — 624 S. Main; PO Box 129 (57313); Tu; 913pd, 10fr (Sw); $4.35; C; publisher Mary Neugebauer; publisher & editor Renee Van Der Werff; tel (605) 724-2747

Artesian: *Artesian Commonwealth* — PO Box 218, Woonsocket (57385-0218); Th; 310pd, 8fr (Sw); $2.35; publisher Gerald W Klaas; editor Gloria K Klaas; tel (605) 796-4221; fax (605) 796-4221

Avon: *Avon Clarion* — 103 N. Main; PO Box 345 (57315); W; 1,007pd (Est); 11¢; publisher & editor Jackson S Brodeen; managing editor Clair R Brodeen; tel (605) 286-3919; fax (605) 286-3712

Baltic: *Baltic Beacon* — 414 4th St.; PO Box 99, Dell Rapids (57022); W; 343pd, 13fr (Est); $3.75; C; publisher Jim Wilber; editor Shaun Marko; tel (605) 428-5441; fax (605) 428-5992

Belle Fourche: *Belle Fourche Bee* — 1004 5th Ave. (57717); Sa; 395pd, 20fr (Est); 20¢; C; publisher Dixon Media; editor Timothy Velder; tel (605) 892-2528; fax (605) 892-2529

Beresford: *Beresford Republic* — 111 N. 3rd; PO Box 111 (57004); Th; 1,470pd (Sw); $3.00; publisher & editor M Jill Sundstrom; tel (605) 763-2006; fax (605) 763-5503

Bonesteel: *Bonesteel Enterprise* — PO Box 170 (57317); Th; 550pd (Est); $3.00; publisher & editor Carol A Perlenfein; tel (605) 654-2678

Bowdle: *Bowdle Pioneer* — 3039 Main St.; PO Box 368 (57428); Th; 736pd, 12fr (Sw); 14¢; C; publisher Lawrence Gauer; editor Mary Lou Gauer; tel (605) 285-6101; fax (605) 285-6520

Brandon/Valley Springs: *Brandon Valley Challenger* — 1300 E. Rushmore; PO Box 257, Brandon (57005); W; 881pd, 27fr (Sw); $3.75; publisher James Wilber; editor Alicia P Thiele; tel (605) 582-6025; fax (605) 582-6025

Bridgewater: *Bridgewater Tribune* — 440 N. Main; PO Box 250 (57319); Th; 900pd (Sw); $3.00; publisher Danny Schwans; general manager Rhonda Glanzer; editor Troy Schwans; tel (605) 729-2251; fax (605) 425-2547

Britton: *Britton Journal* — 706 7th St.; PO Box 69 (57430); W; 2,040pd, 59fr (Sw); $2.82; publisher & editor Charles L Card; tel (605) 448-2281; fax (605) 448-2282

Bryant: *The Bryant Dakotan* — 101 Main; PO Box 127 (57221-0127); W; 605pd, 25fr (Sw); $2.85; publisher & editor Linda M Walters; managing editor Ruth Noem; tel (605) 628-2551; fax (605) 628-2551

Buffalo: *Nation's Center News* — 507 W. 5th; PO Box 107 (57720); W; 1,592pd, 32fr (Est); $2.20; publisher Linda Stephens; publisher & editor Wally Stephens; general manager LaVerne E Helms; tel (605) 375-3228; fax (605) 375-3318

Burke: *The Burke Gazette* — 825 Main St.; PO Box 359 (57523); Tu; 1,620pd, 10fr (Sw); $3.11; publisher & editor C J Fahrenbacher; tel (605) 775-2612; fax (605) 775-2612

Canistota: *Canistota Clipper* — Main St.; PO Box 128 (57012); Th; 798pd, 10fr (Sw); $2.48; publisher & editor Matt Anderson; general manager Mary Ann Feterl; tel (605) 296-3181; fax (605) 296-3289

Canova: *Canova Herald* — Main St.; PO Box 128, Canistota (57012); W; 579pd, 10fr (Est); 60¢; publisher & editor Matt Anderson; general manager Mary Ann Feterl; tel (605) 296-3181; fax (605) 296-3289

Canton: *Sioux Valley News* — 213 E. 5th; PO Box 255 (57013); Th; 2,272pd, 33fr (Sw); 14¢; C; publisher Bruce Farus; editor Eric Hohman; tel (605) 987-2631; fax (605) 987-2631

Castlewood: *The Hamlin County Republican* — 123 E. Main; PO Box 50 (57223-0050); W; 775pd (Est); $2.35; publisher & editor Greg Archer; managing editor LeAnne Archer; tel (605) 793-2293; fax (605) 793-9140

Centerville: *Centerville Journal* — 529 Broadway; PO Box H (57014); Th; 826pd (Sw); $3.00; publisher & editor M Jill Sundstrom; tel (605) 563-2351; fax (605) 763-5503

Chamberlain: *The Chamberlain Register* — 120 S. Main; PO Box 550 (57325); Th; 2,803pd, 60fr (Est); 19¢; publisher Pat Hays & Rod Hays; editor Brian Gehring; tel (605) 734-6360

Clark Co.: *Clark County Courier* — 117 E. 1st, Clark (57225); W; 2,420pd, 30fr (Sw); 23¢; publisher Bert Moritz & David Moritz; editor Bill Krikac; tel (605) 532-3654; fax (605) 532-5424

Clear Lake: *Clear Lake Courier* — 416 3rd Ave. S.; PO Box 830 (57226-0830); W; 1,580pd, 65fr (Sw); $3.25; publisher & editor Gary DeJong; tel (605) 874-2499; fax (605) 874-2642

Corsica: *Corsica Globe* — PO Box 45 (57328); W; 1,093pd, 51fr (Sw); $3.65; publisher & editor Mary Neugebauer; tel (605) 946-5489; fax (605) 946-5179

Custer: *Custer County Chronicle* — 602 Mount Rushmore Rd.; PO Box 551 (57730); W; 2,174pd, 36fr (Est); $1.05; C; publisher Terri Tuggle; editors Alice Anderson & Jim Anderson; tel (605) 673-2217; fax (605) 673-3321

De Smet: *The De Smet News* — 220 Calumet Ave.; PO Box 69 (57231); W; 1,572pd, 17fr (Sw); $3.60; C; publisher & editor Dale Blegen; tel (605) 854-3331; fax (605) 854-3332

Deadwood/Lead/Spearfish/Whitewood: *The Lawrence County Centennial* — 68 Sherman St.; PO Box 512, Deadwood (57732); W/Sa; 2,500pd, 25fr (Est); $4.75; C; publisher Bill Derby; editor George Ledbetter; tel (605) 578-3305; fax (605) 578-2023

Dell Rapids/Trent/Baltic: *Dell Rapids Tribune* — 414 E. 4th St.; PO Box 99, Dell Rapids (57022); W; 1,214pd, 58fr (Est); $3.75; C; publisher Jim Wilber; editor Shaun Marko; tel (605) 428-5441; fax (605) 428-5992

Delmont: *The Delmont Record* — PO Box 129, Armour (57313); W; 220pd, 10fr (Sw); $4.35; C; publisher Mary Neugebauer; publisher & editor Renee Van Der Werff; tel (605) 779-3301

Deuel Co.: *Gary Interstate* — PO Box 128, Gary (57237); Th; 386pd (Sw); $2.50; publisher & editor Naomi Blaschko; tel (605) 272-5731; fax (605) 272-5768

Dewey Co.: *Eagle Butte News* — 210 N. Main; PO Box 210, Eagle Butte (57625); Th; 1,810pd, 40fr (Est); 17¢; publisher Jack L Stoner; editor Pauline Webb; tel (605) 964-2100; fax (605) 964-2100

Doland: *Times-Record* — PO Box 223, Turton (57477); Th; 807pd (Est); 50¢; publisher & editor Alina Becker; tel (605) 897-6636; fax (605) 897-6636

Dupree/Ziebach Co.: *West River Progress* — 411 S. Main; PO Box 158, Dupree (57623); Th; 647pd, 6fr (Sw); $3.36; C; publisher & editor Jack L Stoner; general manager Evelyn Anderson; tel (605) 365-5145; fax (605) 365-5145

Edgemont: *Edgemont Herald Tribune* — 410 2nd Ave. (57735); W; 939pd, 70fr (Est); 90¢; publisher & editor Barbara F Bryan; tel (605) 662-7201

Elk Point/Jefferson: *The Leader-Courier* — 108 W. Main; PO Box 310, Elk Point (57025); Th; 1,808pd, 30fr (Est); $18.85; publisher & editor Scott Munger; tel (605) 356-2632; fax (605) 356-3626

Elkton: *Elkton Record* — 205 Elk St.; PO Box K (57026); Th; 900pd, 57fr (Est); $2.50; publisher Chris Schumacher; editor Emile Moore; tel (605) 542-4831; fax (605) 627-9310

Emery: *The Emery Enterprise* — 152 3rd St.; PO Box 244 (57332); Th; 518pd, 17fr (Sw); $2.25; publisher & editor David L Stoltz; tel (605) 449-4420; fax (605) 239-4521

Estelline: *Estelline Journal* — PO Box 159 (57234); Th; 900pd (Sw); $2.35; C; publisher & editor Greg Archer; general manager Lee Anne Archer; tel (605) 873-2475; fax (605) 793-9140

Eureka: *Northwest Blade* — 713 7th St.; PO Box 797 (57437-0797); W; 1,743pd, 30fr (Sw); $3.24; publisher Arlo C Mehlhaff; editor Bonnie L Mehlhaff; tel (605) 284-2631; fax (605) 284-2501

Faith: *The Faith Independent* — 112 N. Main; PO Box 38 (57626); W; 995pd, 60fr (Est); 14¢; publisher & editor John Hipps; tel (605) 967-2161; fax (605) 967-2160

Faulkton: *Faulk County Record* — 121 8th Ave. S.; PO Box 68 (57438); W; 1,700pd, 3fr (Sw); $2.36; publisher & editor Jim Moritz; publisher Jody Moritz; tel (605) 598-6525; fax (605) 598-4355

Flandreau: *Moody County Enterprise* — 107 2nd Ave. W.; PO Box 71 (57028); W; 2,398pd, 23fr (Sw); $3.15; C; publisher & editor Charles F Cecil; general manager Roger Janssen; tel (605) 997-3725; fax (605) 997-3194

Frederick: *Brown County Independent* — 303 3rd Ave.; PO Box 557 (57441-0557); Th; 907pd, 23fr (Est); $5.50; C; publisher Paul Irvin Kosel; editor Stacy Seaman Bretsch; tel (605) 329-2538; fax (605) 329-2538

Freeman/Marion/Dolton: *The Freeman Courier* — 215 S. Main; PO Box 950, Freeman (57029); W; 2,300pd, 50fr (Est); $2.50; publisher & editor Tim Waltner; tel (605) 925-7033

Garretson/Sherman: *Garretson Weekly* — 512 Main Ave.; PO Box 310, Garretson (57030-0310); Th; 1,210pd, 15fr (Sw); $2.76; publisher & editor Margie Martens; tel (605) 594-6315

Geddes: *Charles Mix County News* — Main St.; PO Box 257 (57342); Th; 626pd, 1fr (Sw); $2.45; publisher & editor Harold J Jaeger; tel (605) 337-2571

Gettysburg/Potter Co.: *Potter County News* — 110 S. Exene; PO Box 190, Gettysburg (57442); Th; 2,100pd, 50fr (Est); $2.56; publisher Jack L Stoner; editor Barb Boyer; tel (605) 765-2464; fax (605) 765-2465

Gregory: *Times-Advocate* — 623 Main; PO Box 378 (57533); W; 3,832pd (Est); $4.40; publisher & editor Nelson L Miller; general manager Sally Miller; tel (605) 835-8089; fax (605) 835-8089

Groton: *Groton Regional Independent* — 16 N. Main; PO Box 588 (57445-0588); Th; 1,000pd, 48fr (Est); $5.50; C; publisher & editor Paul Irvin Kosel; tel (605) 397-2676; fax (605) 397-8671

Hartford: *The Area News* — Main St.; PO Box 128, Canistota (57012); Th; 618pd (Sw); $2.76; publisher & editor Matt Anderson; general manager Mary Ann Feterl; tel (605) 296-3181; fax (605) 296-3289

Hayti/Lake Norden/Hazel/Lake Poinsett: *Herald-Enterprise* — Main St.; PO Box 207, Hayti (57241); W; 925pd, 35fr (Est); $2.60; C; publisher & editor Greg Archer; general manager LeeAnne Archer; tel (605) 783-3636; fax (605) 793-9140

Highmore: *Highmore Herald* — 211 Iowa St.; PO Box 435 (57345); Th; 1,425pd, 25fr (Sw); $2.96; C; publisher & editor Mary Ann Morford; tel (605) 852-2927; fax (605) 852-2927

Hill City: *Penninton County Prevalier-News* — 114 Main St.; PO Box 266 (57745); W; 1,079pd, 20fr (Sw); $3.30; C; publisher Terri Tuggle; general manager Alice Anderson; editor Don Gerken; tel (605) 574-2538

Hot Springs: *Hot Springs Star* — 107 N. Chicago; PO Box 1000 (57747); Tu; 2,251pd, 25fr (Sw); $4.00; publisher & editor Gregory R Corr; tel (605) 745-4170; fax (605) 745-3161

Hoven/Tolstoy: *The Hoven Review* — PO Box 37, Hoven (57450); Th; 972pd (Sw); $2.58; C; publisher & editor Leona C Wager; tel (605) 948-2110

Howard: *Miner County Pioneer* — PO Box P (57349); Th; 1,902pd, 65fr (Sw); $3.12; C; publisher & editor Danny Schwans; tel (605) 772-5644; fax (605) 772-5644

Hudson: *The Hudsonite* — PO Box 227, Alcester (57001-0227); Th; 371pd, 19fr (Est); $2.24; publisher Donald Brose; editor Mary Etta Brose; tel (605) 934-2640

Humboldt/Minnehaha Co.: *The Journal* — PO Box 128, Canistota (57012); Th; 545pd (Est); $2.76; C; publisher & editor Matt Anderson; tel (605) 296-3181; fax (605) 296-3289

Hurley: *The Hurley Leader* — PO Box 218 (57036); Th; 583pd, 22fr (Est); 11¢; publisher Craig Steenslang; editor Kay Schooler; tel (605) 238-5229; fax (605) 238-5229

Ipswich: *The Ipswich Tribune* — 103 Main; PO Box 7 (57451); W; 917pd, 3fr (Sw); $2.35; publisher D E Gibson; editor Tena Gibson; tel (605) 426-6471; fax (605) 426-6471

Irene: *The Tri-County News* — 303 W. Main; PO Box 6 (57037-0006); Th; 703pd, 23fr (Sw); $2.25; publisher & editor Pam Buchholz; tel (605) 263-3339; fax (605) 263-3339

Isabel: *The Isabel Dakotan* — 403 N. Main St.; PO Box 207 (57633); Th; 563pd, 29fr (Sw); $8.50; publisher Myron L Lofgren; editor Sarah A Lofgren; tel (605) 466-2258

Java: *Selby Record* — 4411 Main St.; PO Box 421, Selby (57472-0421); W; 1,326pd, 17fr (Sw); $3.00; publisher Allan Burke; publisher & editor Leah P Burke; general manager Leanda Staebner; tel (605) 649-7866; fax (605) 649-7054

Kadoka: *Kadoka Press* — 218 S. Main; PO Box 309 (57543); Th; 1,066pd, 37fr (Est); $2.20; publisher Don Ravellette; editor Rhonda Dennis; tel (605) 837-2259; fax (605) 837-2312

Kimball: *Brule County News* — Main St.; PO Box 46 (57355-0046); Th; 1,297pd, 16fr (Est); $2.60; publisher Rod Hays; editor Darla J Viereck; tel (605) 778-6253; fax (605) 778-6959

Lake Andes: *The Lake Andes Wave* — 209 S. Main; PO Box 187, Wagner (57380); W; 332pd (Est); $2.50; publisher & editor Carol Harrell; publisher Donald Harrell; tel (605) 384-5616; fax (605) 384-5955

Lake Preston: *Lake Preston Times* — 301 N. Main; PO Box 368 (57249); Th; 1,184pd, 35fr (Sw); $2.90; C; publisher Dale Blegen; editor Shelley Slaight; tel (605) 847-4421

Langford: *Langford Bugle* — PO Box 107 (57454); W; 629pd, 8fr (Est); $1.60; publisher Charles L Card; editor Shirley Schneider; tel (605) 448-2281; fax (605) 448-2282

Lemmon: *The Lemmon Leader* — 213 Main; PO Box 180 (57638); Tu; 1,950pd, 28fr (Est); 16¢; C; publisher & editor Alice A Farstad; tel (605) 374-3751; fax (605) 374-5295

Lennox: *The Lennox Independent* — 114 S. Main St. (57039); Th; 2,070pd, 35fr (Est); 13¢; publisher & editor Kris Vanzee; tel (605) 647-2284; fax (605) 647-2467

Leola: *McPherson County Herald* — PO Box 170 (57456); W; 804pd, 39fr (Sw); $6.50; publisher & editor Mary Hoffman; tel (605) 439-3131; fax (605) 439-3131

Lyman Co.: *Lyman County Herald* — 124 Main; PO Box 280, Presho (57568); W; 796pd, 20fr (Est); 14¢; publisher Robert Cameron; general manager Pat McNaughton; editor Helen Cameron; tel (605) 895-2505; fax (605) 895-2505

Marion/Monroe/Dolton: *Marion Record* — 211 N. Broadway; PO Box 298, Marion (57043); Th; 900pd, 25fr (Est); 12¢; publisher & editor James Wilson; tel (605) 648-3821; fax (605) 648-3821

Martin: *Bennett County Booster II* — PO Box 610 (57551); W; 2,220pd, 54fr (Sw); $4.25; publisher & editor Dale Lewis & Mary Lewis; tel (605) 685-6866; fax (605) 685-6535

McIntosh: *Corson County News* — 204 1st Ave. W.; PO Box 788, McLaughlin (57642); W; 820pd (Est); 70¢; publisher Lavonne Lofgren; general manager Marlo Utter; editor Merle E Lofgren; tel (605) 823-4490; fax (605) 823-4632

McLaughlin: *McLaughlin Messenger* — 204 1st Ave. W.; PO Box 788 (57642); Th; 736pd (Est); 70¢; publisher Lavonne Lofgren; general manager Marlo Utter; editor Merle E Lofgren; tel (605) 823-4490; fax (605) 823-4632

Menno: *The Hutchinson Herald* — 154 E. Poplar; PO Box 537 (57045); W; 1,055pd, 43fr (Sw); $3.24; publisher & editor William J Headley; tel (605) 387-5158; fax (605) 387-5148

Milbank/Grant/Roberta: *Grant County Review* — 225 S. Main St.; PO Box 390, Milbank (57252-0390); W; 4,420pd, 17fr (Est); $4.41; publisher & editor Phyllis Dolan Justice; general manager Clarence Justice; tel (605) 432-4516

Miller/Hand Co.: *The Miller Press* — 114 W. 3rd St.; PO Box 196, Miller (57362); M; 2,231pd, 19fr (Sw); 24¢; C; publisher & editor Gary L McFarlane; tel (605) 853-3575; fax (605) 853-2478

Mission: *Todd County Tribune* — W. Hwy. 18; PO Box 229 (57555-0229); W; 1,883pd, 47fr (Sw); $4.00; C; publisher & editor Margaret Figert; tel (605) 856-4469; fax (605) 856-2428

Mobridge: *The Mobridge Tribune* — 111 W. 3rd St. (57601); W; 3,595pd, 18fr (Sw); $4.70; C; publisher & editor Larry Atkinson; tel (605) 845-3646; fax (605) 845-7659

Montrose: *Montrose Herald* — Main St.; PO Box 128, Canistota (57012); F; 554pd (Sw); $2.48; publisher & editor Matt Anderson; general manager Mary Ann Feterl; tel (605) 296-3181; fax (605) 296-3289

Murdo/Draper/Okaton/Jones: *Murdo Coyote* — PO Box 465, Murdo (57559); Th; 710pd, 5fr (Sw); 35¢; C; publisher & editor Clarice Roghair; publisher Melvin Roghair; tel (605) 669-2529

Newell: *Valley Irrigator* — 119 3rd St.; PO Box 167 (57760); W; 1,031pd, 100fr (Est); 20¢; C; publisher & editor Tim Velder; general manager Ruth Anderson; tel (605) 456-2585; fax (605) 456-2585

Onida: *Onida Watchman* — PO Box 205 (57564); Th; 1,037pd, 30fr (Sw); 12¢; publisher & editor Parker Knox; tel (605) 258-2724; fax (605) 224-9210

Parker/Turner Co.: *The New Era* — 242 N. Main St.; PO Box 579, Parker (57053-0579); W; 1,782pd, 20fr (Est); $1.88; publisher Jim Houck; editor Jill Meier; tel (605) 297-4419; fax (605) 297-4015

Parkston: *Parkston Advance* — PO Box J (57366); Th; 1,598pd (Est); 70¢; publisher Edward J Ehler; tel (605) 928-3111

U.S. Weeklies **Tennessee** **II-71**

Philip: *The Pioneer-Review* — 185 S. Center Ave.; PO Box 788 (57567); Th; 1,615pd, 35fr (Sw); $4.25; C; publisher Don Ravellette; editor Andrea Cook; tel (605) 859-2516; fax (605) 859-2410

Pierre: *The Times* — 333 W. Dakota; PO Box 878 (57501); Th; 1,069pd, 27fr (Sw); $4.30; publisher Terry J Hipple; editor Dana Hess; tel (605) 224-7301; fax (605) 224-9210

Plankinton: *South Dakota Mail* — 116 N. Main St.; PO Box 367 (57368); Th; 1,015pd (Est); $2.00; publisher & editor Adeline E Van Genderen; tel (605) 942-7770; fax (605) 942-7770

Platte: *The Platte Enterprise* — PO Box 546 (57369); Th; 1,950pd, 20fr (Est); 10¢; publisher & editor Ralph Nachtigal; general manager Sharon Huizenga; tel (605) 337-3101; fax (605) 337-3543

Pollock/Herreid: *Prairie Pioneer* — Main St.; PO Box 218, Pollock (57648-0218); Th; 1,942pd, 15fr (Est); $2.15; publishers Allan C Burke & Leah P Burke; general manager Brenda Larson; editor Waynette Geigle; tel (605) 889-2320; fax (605) 889-2361

Rapid City: *Indian Country Today* — 1920 Lombardy Dr. (57701); PO Box 2180 (57709); W; 14,200fr (Est); $9.64; C; publisher Tim Giago; editors Avis Little Eagle & Dan Anderson; tel (605) 341-0011; fax (605) 341-6940

Redfield: *The Redfield Press* — 16 E. 7th Ave.; PO Box 440 (57469); W; 3,458pd, 58fr (Est); $4.00; publisher Walter Mundstock; editor David Lias; tel (605) 472-0822; fax (605) 472-3634

Roscoe/Hosmer: *The Roscoe-Hosmer Independent* — 103 Main; PO Box 7, Ipswich (57451); W; 605pd, 2fr (Sw); $2.10; publisher D E Gibson; editor Tena Gibson; tel (605) 426-6471; fax (605) 426-6471

Rosholt: *The Rosholt Review* — PO Box 136 (57260); W; 1,260pd, 25fr (Sw); $2.12; publisher Burl Cook; editor Kathleen Cook; tel (605) 537-4276; fax (605) 537-4858

Salem: *The Salem Special* — 135 S. Main; PO Box 220 (57058); Th; 1,850pd, 81fr (Sw); $3.00; publisher & editor Troy Schwans; tel (605) 425-2361; fax (605) 425-2547

Scotland: *Scotland Journal* — 630 1st St.; PO Box 388 (57059); W; 1,111pd, 60fr (Sw); $2.92; publisher Marvin A Blaha; general manager & editor Patty Mogck; tel (605) 583-4419; fax (605) 583-4406

Selby/Java/Akaska/Glenham: *Selby Record* — 4411 Main St.; PO Box 421, Selby (57472-0421); Th; 1,326pd, 17fr (Sw); $2.90; publishers Allan C Burke & Leah P Burke; editor Sandy Bond; tel (605) 649-7866

Sisseton: *Sisseton Courier* — 117 E. Oak; PO Box 169 (57262); W; 3,201pd, 90fr (Est); $4.41; publisher & editor Harley E Deutsch; tel (605) 698-7642; fax (605) 698-3641

S Shore: *South Shore Gazette* — Main St.; PO Box 96 (57263); Th; 480pd (Est); $2.17; publisher & editor Marvin M Anderson; tel (605) 756-4200

Springfield: *Springfield Times* — 712 8th St.; PO Box 465 (57062); W; 633pd, 24fr (Est); $2.44; publisher Marvin Blaha; editor Zoa Libis; tel (605) 369-2441

Stickney: *The Stickney Argus* — 207 Main St.; PO Box 37 (57375); W; 652pd, 31fr (Est); $2.35; publisher & editor Barbara Howard; tel (605) 732-4555

Sturgis: *Meade County Times-Tribune* — 1238 Main St.; PO Box 69 (57785); W; 3,861pd, 11,200fr (Sw); $4.50; C; publisher Bill Derby; editor Phil Johnson; tel (605) 347-2503; fax (605) 347-2321

Sturgis/Meade Co.: *Black Hills Press* — 1238 Main; PO Box 69, Sturgis (57785); Sa; 3,711pd, 200fr (Sw); $4.50; C; publisher Bill Derby; editor Phil Johnson; tel (605) 347-2503; fax (605) 347-2321

Timber Lake/Dewey Co.: *Timber Lake Topic* — 806 Main St.; PO Box 10, Timber Lake (57656); Th; 1,450pd, 31fr (Sw); $2.50; C; publishers & editors Jim Nelson & Kathy Snyder Nelson; tel (605) 865-3546; fax (605) 865-3787

Tripp: *The Tripp Star Ledger* — PO Box D (57376); W; 606pd (Est); 85¢; publisher & editor Scott Ehler; tel (605) 935-6015

Tyndall: *Tribune & Register* — 114 Pearl St.; PO Box 520 (57066); W; 1,480pd, 48fr (Est); $2.92; publisher Marvin A Blaha; editor Becky Tycz; tel (605) 589-3242; fax (605) 589-3448

Vermillion: *Plain Talk* — PO Box 256 (57069); F; 2,452pd, 30fr (Est); 18¢; publishers Stephen W Michels & William H Willroth IV; tel (605) 624-2695; fax (605) 624-2696

Viborg: *Viborg Enterprise* — 100 N. Main; PO Box 398 (57070); Th; 1,100pd (Est); $2.75; publisher Craig Steenslang; editor Kay Schooler; tel (605) 326-5212; fax (605) 326-5212

Volga: *The Volga Tribune* — 222 Kasan Ave. (57071); Th; 1,046pd, 37fr (Est); $2.50; publisher Chris Schumacher; editor Amy Hinderaker; tel (605) 627-9471; fax (605) 627-9310

Wagner: *Post & Announcer* — 209 S. Main; PO Box 187 (57380); W; 1,750pd, 1,820fr (Est); $2.50; publisher & editor Carol M Harrell; publisher Donald Harrell; tel (605) 384-5616; fax (605) 384-5955

Wakonda/Clay Co.: *Wakonda Times* — PO Box 256, Vermillion (57069); F; 500pd (Est); $2.70; publishers Stephen W Michels & William Willroth IV; tel (605) 624-2695; fax (605) 624-2696

Wall: *Pennington County Courant* — 212 4th Ave.; PO Box 435 (57790); Th; 1,020pd, 35fr (Sw); $4.25; C; publisher Don Ravellette; general manager Belle Ravellette; editor Dave Maack; tel (605) 279-2565; fax (605) 279-2965

Waubay: *Waubay Clipper* — 546 Main St. (57273); M; 875pd, 26fr (Est); 70¢; publisher & editor Linda M Walters; tel (605) 947-4501; fax (605) 947-4501

Webster: *Reporter and Farmer* — 624 Main (57274); M; 3,862pd, 16fr (Est); 23¢; publisher & editor Larry Ingalls; tel (605) 345-3356; fax (605) 345-3739

Wessington: *Times-Enterprise* — PO Box 107 (57381); Th; 443pd, 4fr (Sw); 60¢; publisher Gary McFarlane; publisher & editor Paula McFarlane; general manager Janice McGirr; tel (605) 458-2253; fax (605) 853-2478

Wessington Springs/Jerauld: *True Dakotan/Alpena Journal* — PO Box T, Wessington Springs (57382); Tu; 166pd (Est); $2.25; publishers & editors Dennis P Wenzel & J Craig Wenzel; tel (605) 539-1281; fax (605) 539-9315

White: *Tri-City Star* — PO Box 336 (57276); Th; 524pd, 23fr (Est); $2.50; publisher Chris Schumacher; editor Bernice Patrick; tel (605) 629-8341; fax (605) 627-9310

White Lake: *Aurora County Standard and White Lake Wave* — PO Box 37, Stickney (57375); W; 367pd, 22fr (Est); $2.35; publisher & editor Barbara Howard; tel (605) 732-4555

White River: *Mellette County News* — PO Box 229, Mission (57555-0229); W; 267pd, 7fr (Sw); $4.00; C; publisher & editor Margaret Figert; managing editor Phyllis Littau; tel (605) 259-3642; fax (605) 856-2428

Wilmot/Corona: *Wilmot Enterprise* — 805 Main St.; PO Box 37, Wilmot (57279); W; 805pd, 25fr (Sw); $3.50; publisher & editor Cheryl Rondeau-Bassett; tel (605) 938-4651; fax (605) 938-4683

Winner/Tripp Co.: *Winner Advocate* — 125 W. 3rd; PO Box 71, Winner (57580); W; 4,000pd, 65fr (Est); $5.75; publisher Mylan Schroeder; editor Dan Bechtold; tel (605) 842-1481; fax (605) 842-1979

Wolsey: *Wolsey News* — PO Box 107, Wessington (57381); Th; 380pd, 5fr (Sw); 13¢; C; publisher Gary L McFarlane; publisher & editor Paula McFarlane; general manager Janice McGirr; tel (605) 458-2253; fax (605) 853-2478

Woonsocket: *Woonsocket News* — Dumont Ave.; PO Box 218 (57385); Th; 1,330pd, 10fr (Sw); $2.76; publisher Gerald W Klaas; editor Gloria K Klaas; tel (605) 796-4221; fax (605) 796-4221

Yankton: *Missouri Valley Observer* — PO Box 858 (57078); Th; 2,300pd, 60fr (Est); 25¢; publisher & editor Brian Hunhoff; tel (605) 665-0484

TENNESSEE

Alamo/Crockett Co.: *The Crockett Times* — 128 W. Main; PO Box 160, Alamo (38001); Th; 3,941pd, 12fr (Sw); $4.50; publisher Robert B Sims; editor Patricia Sims; tel (901) 696-4558; fax (901) 696-4550

Ashland City: *Ashland City Times* — 1100 N. Main St.; PO Box 158 (37015); W; 4,996pd, 39fr (CAC); $3.06; C; publisher Gene Washer; editor Jill Cecil; tel (615) 792-4230; fax (615) 792-3671

Bartlett: *Bartlett Express* — 2874 Shelby St.; PO Box 34967 (38184-0967); Th; 6,189pd, 19fr (Sw); $8.25; publisher & editor John H Murchison; tel (901) 388-1500; fax (901) 386-3157

Blountville: *Sullivan County News* — 3200 Highway 126; PO Box 490 (37617); Th; 2,646pd, 165fr (Sw); $6.33; editor David McGee; tel (423) 323-5700; fax (423) 323-1681

Bolivar: *Bolivar Bulletin-Times* — 410 W. Market St.; PO Box 152 (38008); W; 5,539pd, 166fr (Sw); $5.25; C; publisher Richard F Fry; general manager Kay Zawacki; editor Anne Ingle; tel (901) 658-3691; fax (901) 658-7222

Brentwood: *Brentwood Journal* — 750 Old Hickory Blvd., Ste. 150, Bldg. 2 (37027-7938); Th; 11,000pd (Est); $8.00; C; publisher Lee Denmark; editor Lauren Lexa; tel (615) 371-6154; fax (615) 377-3130

Brownsville/Haywood Co.: *Brownsville States-Graphic* — 42 S. Washington; PO Box 198, Brownsville (38012); Th; 4,190pd, 51fr (Sw); $3.50; C; publisher & editor C T Smith; general manager Carlton Veirs; tel (901) 772-1172; fax (901) 772-2255

Byrdstown: *Pickett County Press* — 23 Courthouse Sq., Main St.; PO Box 268 (38549); Th; 1,764pd, 11fr (Sw); $3.00; publisher & editor James E Hill; tel (615) 864-3675; fax (615) 864-3675

Camden/Benton: *The Camden Chronicle* — 144 W. Main St.; PO Box 527, Camden (38320); W; 4,254pd, 57fr (Sw); $2.40; publisher Lisa Richardson; general manager Elton Hatley; editor Don Kelley; tel (901) 584-7200; fax (901) 584-4943

Carthage: *Carthage Courier* — 509 N. Main; PO Box 239 (37030); Th; 4,545pd, 24fr (Est); 24¢; C; publisher Scott Winfree; editor Eddie West; tel (615) 735-1110; fax (615) 735-0635

Celina/Clay Co.: *Citizen-Statesman* — E. Lake Ave.; PO Box F, Celina (38551); Tu; 2,176pd, 173fr (Est); $3.40; publisher Patsy Judd; editor Michelle Watson; tel (615) 243-2235; fax (615) 243-2232

Centerville: *Hickman County Times* — 104 N. Central Ave.; PO Box 100 (37033); M; 5,899pd, 80fr (Est); $2.52; C; publisher Jim Crawford Jr; editor Brad Martin; tel (615) 729-4282; fax (615) 729-4282

Chattanooga: *Hamilton County Herald* — 6129 Airways Blvd.; PO Box 21279 (37421); F; 308pd, 72fr (Est); $2.82; publisher & editor Earl Williams; general manager Harry McAllister; tel (423) 892-1336; fax (423) 899-6393

Clinton/Anderson Co.: *The Courier-News* — 233 N. Hicks St.; PO Box 270, Clinton (37716); W; 5,985pd, 135fr (Sw); $7.60; Su; 5,985pd, 135fr (Sw); $8.85; C; publisher & editor Doug Morris; managing editor Rick Hooper; tel (423) 457-2515; fax (423) 457-1586

Cocke: *Newport Plain Talk* — 145 E. Broadway; PO Box 279, Newport (37821); M/W/F; 9,581pd, 72fr (Sw); $6.80; C; publisher & editor David Popiel; publisher John M Jones Jr; managing editor Gilbert Soesbee; tel (423) 623-6171

Collierville: *The Collierville Herald* — 139 N. Main St.; PO Box 427 (38017); Th; 4,809pd, 369fr (Sw); 15¢; publisher & editor Van Pritchartt; general manager Tom Spain; tel (901) 853-2241

Collierville/Germantown: *Independent* — 215 S. Center St.; PO Box 939, Collierville (38027-0939); Th; 4,718pd, 294fr (Est); $5.00; C; publisher Shoppers Press of Memphis; managing editor Linda McGregor Scott; tel (901) 853-7060

Crossville: *Crossville Chronicle* — 312 S. Main St.; PO Box 449 (38555); Tu; 7,460pd, 11,315fr (Sw); $6.30; W; 7,460pd (Sw); $5.30; F; 7,460pd, 140fr (Sw); $5.30; C; publisher Pauline D Sherrer; editor Mike Moser; tel (615) 484-5145; fax (615) 456-7683

Crossville: *Cumberland Times* — US Hwy. 127 N.; PO Box 745 (38555); Th; 2,249pd, 15fr (Est); $4.25; C; publisher & editor Denny Lepley; tel (615) 484-7510; fax (615) 456-1312

Decatur Co.: *The News-Leader* — 113 S. Tennessee Ave.; PO Box 340, Parsons (38363); W; 4,106pd, 25fr (Sw); 13¢; publisher & editor Mary S Alexander; publisher Sam Kennedy; tel (901) 847-6354; fax (901) 847-9120

Dickson Co.: *The Dickson Herald* — 104 Church St.; PO Box 587, Dickson (37055); W; 9,000pd, 11,000fr (Est); $6.33; F; 9,000pd (Est); $6.33; publisher Gene Washer; general manager Debbie Tyler; editor Chris Norman; tel (615) 446-2811; fax (615) 446-5560

Dover/Erin: *The Stewart-Houston Times* — 8 Main St.; PO Box 250, Erin (37061); Tu; 4,989pd, 542fr (Est); $4.88; publisher F Gene Washer; editor M J McMillan; tel (615) 289-3345; fax (615) 289-4191

Dunlap: *The Dunlap Tribune* — 155A Ranklin Ave. S.; PO Box 487 (37327); Th; 2,423pd, 15fr (Sw); 24¢; C; publisher Amy Sue Hale; editor Linda Faye Rogers; tel (423) 949-2505; fax (423) 949-5297

Dyer/Rutherford/Kenton: *The Tri-City Reporter* — 101 N. Main; PO Box 266, Dyer (38330); Th; 2,935pd, 75fr (Sw); $3.00; publisher Tri-City Reporter Inc.; editor April Jackson; tel (901) 692-3506; fax (901) 692-4844

E Shelby: *East Shelby Review* — 16814 Highway 64; PO Box 423, Sommerville (38068); W; 4,800fr (Est); $4.50; C; publisher & editor Don L Dowdle; managing editor Rhonda Wilson; tel (901) 465-4042; fax (901) 465-5493

Erwin: *The Erwin Record* — 218 Gay St.; PO Drawer 700 (37650); Tu; 4,483pd, 25fr (Est); $3.92; publisher & editor Thomas D Harris; tel (423) 743-4112; fax (423) 743-6125

Etowah: *Etowah Enterprise* — 718 Ohio Ave.; PO Box A (37331); W; 1,600pd, 289fr (Sw); $6.99; publisher & editor Richard McCoy; tel (423) 263-5411

Farragut/W Knoxville: *Press Enterprise* — 11863 Kingston Pike, Knoxville (37922); W; 400pd, 16,600fr (Est); $8.95; publisher Elaine Grove; editor David Spates; tel (423) 675-6397; fax (423) 675-1675

Fayetteville: *Elk Valley Times/Observer & News* — 418 N. Elk Ave.; PO Box 9 (37334); W; 8,400pd, 402fr (Sw); 35¢; publisher & editor Lucy Carter; tel (615) 433-6151; fax (615) 433-6151

Franklin/Brentwood: *The Review Appeal* — 121 2nd Ave. N.; PO Box 681988, Franklin (37068-1988); W/F/Su; 8,245pd, 76fr (Sw); $10.40; C; general manager L Lee Denmark; editor Ron Taylor; tel (615) 794-2555; fax (615) 790-0522

Franklin/Brentwood: *The Williamson Leader* — 128 Holiday Ct., Ste. 121 (37067); PO Box 729, Franklin (37065-0729); Th; 6,500pd, 25fr (Sw); 43¢; C; publisher & editor Bailey Leopard; managing editor Philip Betbeze; tel (615) 794-4564; fax (615) 794-9581

Gainesboro: *Jackson County Sentinel* — Anderson-Haile Bldg.; PO Box 37 (38562); W; 2,968pd, 25fr (Sw); 10¢; publisher Richard F Knight; editor Elise B Roberts; tel (615) 268-9725; fax (615) 268-9725

Gallatin/Portland: *The News-Examiner* — 1 Examiner Ct.; PO Box 1387, Gallatin (37066); M/W/F; 10,204pd, 242fr (CAC); $9.15; C; publisher Bob Atkins; general manager Fred Brooks; editor Steve Rogers; tel (615) 452-2561; fax (615) 452-9110

Grainger Co.: *Grainger County News* — Cherry St.; PO Box 218, Rutledge (37861); Th; 2,709pd (Sw); $2.75; publisher Linda Witt; tel (423) 828-5254

Halls: *Halls Graphic* — 145 E. Jackson; PO Box 289, Ripley (38063); W; 1,444pd, 12fr (Est); $1.95; C; publisher & editor William A Klutts; general manager Terry Ford; tel (901) 635-1771; fax (901) 635-2111

Hardin Co.: *The Courier* — 801 Main St.; PO Box 340, Savannah (38372-0339); Th; 8,805pd, 20fr (Sw); $3.50; publisher Kathryn Craddock; editor Jim Thompson; tel (901) 925-6397

Harriman City: *The Harriman Record* — PO Box 610, Kingston (37763-0610); Tu; 415pd, 8fr (Sw); $2.26; publisher Dave Commons; editor Darrell Richardson; tel (423) 882-1313; fax (423) 376-1945

Hawkins Co.: *Rogersville Review* — 207 Washington St.; PO Box 100, Rogersville (37857); W/Sa; 7,084pd, 15fr (Est); $3.90; publisher & editor Ellen M Addison; managing editor Tammy Cheek; tel (423) 272-7325/7422; fax (423) 272-7889

Henderson: *Chester County Independent* — 218 S. Church St.; PO Box 306 (38340); Th; 4,500pd, 10fr (Sw); $3.50; C; publisher & editor Scott Whaley; tel (901) 989-4624; fax (901) 989-5008

Hendersonville: *The Hendersonville Star News* — 110 Sanders Ferry Rd.; PO Box 68 (37075); W; 140pd, 13,256fr (CAC); $9.15; F; 120pd, 13,085fr (CAC); $9.15; C; publisher Bob Atkins; general manager Judi McMinn; editor Mike McClanhan; tel (615) 824-8480; fax (615) 824-3126

Hohenwald: *Lewis County Herald* — 31 E. Linden Ave.; PO Box 69 (38462); Th; 3,485pd, 15fr (Sw); $1.60; publisher & editor Byrne K Dunn; tel (615) 796-3191; fax (615) 796-2153

Humboldt: *The Courier Chronicle* — 2606 E. End Dr.; PO Box 448 (38343); W; 3,255pd, 400fr (Sw); $3.70; C; publisher J Frank Warmath; editor Martha W Dodson; tel (901) 784-2531; fax (901) 784-2533

Huntingdon: *Carroll County News-Leader* — 163 Court Sq.; PO Box 389 (38344); W; 7,000pd, 4,900fr (Sw); 14¢; publisher Dennis M Richardson; editor Shirley Nanney; tel (901) 986-2253; fax (901) 986-3585

Jamestown: *Fentress Courier* — 206 Gaudin St.; PO Box 1198 (38556); W; 4,850pd (Sw); $3.00; C; publisher & editor Bill Bowdon; tel (615) 879-4040; fax (615) 879-7716

Jasper: *Jasper Journal* — 6615 Highway 41; PO Box 398 (37347); Tu; 4,408pd (Est); $2.94; publisher Allen Kirk; editor Linda Rector; tel (423) 942-2433; fax (423) 942-8835

Jefferson Co.: *Jefferson Standard-Banner* — 122 W. Andrew Johnson Hwy.; PO Box 310, Jefferson City (37760); Tu/Th; 5,321pd, 3,024fr (CAC); $4.40; C; publisher Tom Gentry; editor Dale Gentry; tel (423) 475-2081

Jellico: *The Advance-Sentinel* — 220 N. 1st St.; PO Box 1261, La Follette (37766-1261); W; 1,026pd, 150fr (Sw); 15¢; publisher Larry K Smith; editor Rex Hickey; tel (423) 562-8468; fax (423) 566-7060

La Follette: *La Follette Press* — 220 N. 1st St.; PO Box 1261 (37766); Th; 7,323pd, 15fr (Sw); $3.85; publisher Larry K Smith; editor Charles Winfrey; tel (423) 562-8468; fax (423) 566-7060

Lafayette: *Macon County Times* — 200 Times Ave.; PO Box 69 (37083); W; 5,534pd, 577fr (Sw); $4.70; publisher & editor J Truett Langston; tel (615) 666-2440; fax (615) 666-4909

Lake City: *The Town Crier* — PO Box 505 (37769); Tu; 1,512pd, 50fr (Est); 13¢; publisher Larry Smith; editor Rex Hickey; tel (423) 426-2220; fax (423) 566-7060

Lawrenceburg: *The Democrat-Union* — 238 Hughes St.; PO Box 685 (38464); Tu; 8,500pd (Est); $4.50; F; 10,000pd (Est); $4.50; publisher Jim Crawford Jr; editor Charlie Crawford; managing editor Bobby Crawford; tel (615) 762-2222; fax (615) 762-4191

Lebanon: *The Wilson World* — 115 E. Main St.; PO Box 857 (37088-0857); Th; 5,024pd, 175fr (Sw); $5.70; publisher & editor Tommy A Bryan; tel (615) 444-6008; fax (615) 444-6018

Lewington: *Lexington Progress* — 60 S. Broad St.; PO Box 210, Lexington (38351); W; 6,094pd, 25fr (Sw); 13¢; publisher Tom Franklin; general manager & editor Mike Reed; tel (901) 968-6397; fax (901) 968-9560

Lewisburg: *Lewisburg Tribune* — 116 E. Ewing St.; PO Box 2608 (37091); Th; 6,510pd, 72fr (Sw); $3.25; publisher Thomas H Hawkins; editor Betty Orr; tel (615) 359-1188; fax (615) 359-1847

Lewisburg: *Marshall Gazette* — 116 E. Ewing St.; PO Box 2608 (37091); Tu; 6,510pd, 72fr (Sw); $3.25; publisher Thomas H Hawkins; editor Betty Orr; tel (615) 359-1188; fax (615) 359-1847

Linden/Perry Co.: *Buffalo River Review* — 115 S. Mill St.; PO Box 914, Linden (37096); W; 2,666pd, 188fr (Sw); 12¢; publisher Sam Kennedy; general manager Bill Haxton; editor Randy Mackin; tel (615) 589-2169; fax (615) 589-3858

Livingston: *Livingston Enterprise* — 203 S. Church St.; PO Box 129 (38570); W; 5,400pd, 95fr (Est); 10¢; C; publisher Richard F Knight; editor Allie Collins; tel (615) 823-1274; fax (615) 268-9125

Loudon Co.: *The News-Herald* — 508 E. Broadway; PO Box 310, Lenoir City (37771); M/Th; 7,374pd, 42fr (Sw); $7.12; publisher Bobby J Buckner; editor Linda Brewer; tel (423) 986-6581; fax (423) 988-3261

Lynchburg: *Moore County News* — 223 Hiles St.; PO Drawer 500 (37352); Th; 1,500pd, 20fr (Sw); $3.62; publisher & editor Marilyn Craig; tel (615) 759-7302; fax (615) 759-7302

Manchester/Coffee Co.: *Manchester Times* — 300 N. Spring St.; PO Box 191, Manchester (37355); W; 6,300pd, 4,500fr (Est); 29¢; publisher Chuck Cunningham; editor Rob Long; tel (615) 728-7577; fax (615) 728-7614

Marion Co.: *South Pittsburg Hustler* — 307 1/2 Elm Ave.; PO Box 765, South Pittsburg (37380); Th; 3,750pd, 13,330fr (Est); $3.10; publisher & editor Jim Shanks; general manager Chris Long; managing editor Beenea Hyatt; tel (423) 837-6312; fax (423) 837-8715

Martin/Weakley: *Weakley County Press* — 235 Lindell; PO Box 410, Martin (38237); Tu/Th; 5,700pd, 300fr (Sw); 16¢; publisher David Critchlow Jr; managing editor Joe Lofaro; tel (901) 587-3144; fax (901) 587-3147

Maynardville/Luttrell/Sharps Chapel/Andersonville/Heiskell/Corryton/New Tazewell: *Union News Leader* — 150 Court St.; PO Box 866, Maynardville (37807); Tu; 2,200pd, 150fr (Sw); $4.25; publisher Chris Upton; general manager Mary Ann Collins; editor Elbra Davis; managing editor Linda Johnson; tel (423) 992-3392; fax (423) 992-6861

McKenzie/Tri County Area: *McKenzie Banner* — 3 Banner Row; PO Box 100, McKenzie (38201); W; 6,108pd, 192fr (Sw); $3.75; C; publisher Ramona Washburn; editor Joel T Washburn; tel (901) 352-3323; fax (901) 352-3322

McMinnville: *Southern Standard* — 105 College St.; PO Box 150 (37110); W/F/Su; 8,190pd, 409fr (Sw); $5.55; publisher William R Fryar; general manager Pat Zechman; editor Mike McGee; tel (615) 473-2191; fax (615) 473-6823

McMinnville: *Warren County News* — 105 College St.; PO Box 150 (37110); Tu; 6,700fr (Est); $1.65; publisher William R Fryar; general manager Pat Zechman; editor Mike McGee; tel (615) 473-2191; fax (615) 473-6823

Milan/Bradford/Atwood/Medina/Gibson/Lavinia: *Milan Mirror-Exchange* — 1104 S. Main St.; PO Box 549, Milan (38358); Tu; 5,475pd, 50fr (Sw); $3.25; publisher & editor Bob Parkins; general manager & managing editor Melanie Day; tel (901) 686-1632; fax (901) 686-9005

Millington: *The Millington Star* — 5107 Easley St.; PO Box 305 (38083-0305); W; 2,780pd, 19fr (Sw); $4.75; C; publisher & editor Harry L Hix Jr; tel (901) 872-2286; fax (901) 872-2965

Monroe Co.: *Monroe County Advocate/Democrat* — 609 Sweetwater/Vonore Rd.; PO Box 389, Sweetwater (37874); W; 14,657pd, 91fr (Sw); $5.35; Su; 14,657pd, 91fr (Sw); $6.85; C; publisher Thomas G Wilson III; editor Ann Wallace; tel (423) 337-7101; fax (423) 337-5932

Monroe/McMinn/Blount: *The Tellico Laker* — 509 Cook St.; PO Box 8, Madisonville (37354); F; 4,366pd, 107fr (Sw); $5.35; C; publisher Thomas G Wilson III; editor Ann Wallace; tel (423) 442-4575; fax (423) 442-1416

Morgan Co.: *Morgan County News* — 224 Maiden St.; PO Box 346, Wartburg (37887); Th; 4,250pd, 49fr (Sw); $4.34; C; publisher Dave Commons; editor Judy Underwood; tel (423) 346-6225; fax (423) 346-5788

Mt. Juliet: *Mt. Juliet News* — 3735 N. Mt. Juliet Rd. (37122); Th; 5,000pd (Sw); $5.00; C; publisher & general manager Brad Rowlett; publishers James Page & Mike Redden; editor Camille Moffitt; tel (615) 754-6397; fax (615) 754-0406

Mountain City/Johnson Co.: *The Tomahawk Inc.* — 118 S. Church St.; PO Box 90, Mountain City (37683); W; 5,051pd, 223fr (Est); $3.50; publisher Carleton A Jones; general manager Lee Stagar; editor Deidra J Smith; tel (423) 727-6121; fax (423) 727-4833

Nashville: *Nashville Record* — 222 2nd Ave. N., Ste. 215 (37201); Th; 1,267pd, 305fr (Sw); 41¢; publisher Bob Atkins; general manager Henrietta Haywood Shell; editor Barbara McCaskill; tel (615) 256-8288; fax (615) 242-2370

Nashville: *Westview* — 8120 Sawyer Brown Rd.; PO Box 210183 (37221); Th; 4,333pd, 560fr (Sw); $8.50; C; publisher Evelyn Underwood; editor Paula Underwood Winters; tel (615) 646-6131; fax (615) 662-0946

Newbern: *Dyer County Tennessean* — 113 Jefferson; PO Box 187 (38059); Th; 3,225pd, 25fr (Sw); $4.50; publisher Cynthia Mitchell; publisher & editor Vyron Mitchell Jr; tel (901) 627-3247; fax (901) 627-6145

Oneida: *Scott County News* — 224 S. Alberta Ave.; PO Box 4399 (37841); Th; 6,800pd (Est); 16¢; publisher Sheila Erwin; editor Richard Magyar Jr; tel (615) 569-8351; fax (615) 569-4500

Pikeville: *The Bledsonian-Banner* — 108 W. Spring St.; PO Box 370 (37367); Th; 2,682pd, 64fr (Sw); 24¢; publisher Amy Sue Hale; editor Ruth Burton; tel (423) 447-2996; fax (423) 447-2997

Polk Co./Copper Basin: *Polk County News/Citizen Advance* — Main St.; PO Box 129, Benton (37307); W; 3,031pd, 158fr (Sw); $3.80; publisher Randolph E Buehler Sr; editor Ingrid A Buehler; tel (423) 338-2818; fax (423) 338-4574

Portland: *The Portland Leader* — 109 S. Broadway; PO Box J (37148); W; 2,482pd, 95fr (Est); $3.50; C; publisher Wanda Rogers; managing editor Byron Edwards; tel (615) 325-9241; fax (615) 325-9243

Pulaski: *Giles Free Press* — 308 W. College; PO Box E (38478); Th; 7,673pd, 724fr (Sw); $6.30; publisher S Hershel Lake; editor Joe Collins; managing editor Dana Keeton; tel (615) 363-3544; fax (615) 363-4319

Pulaski: *The Pulaski Citizen* — 308 W. College; PO Box 308 (38478); Tu; 7,657pd, 671fr (Sw); $6.30; publisher S Hershel Lake; editor Joe Collins; managing editor Dana Keeton; tel (615) 363-3544; fax (615) 363-4319

Rhea Co.: *The Herald-News* — 3687 Rhea County Hwy.; PO Box 286, Dayton (37321-0286); W; 4,870pd, 69fr (Sw); $6.85; Su; 4,870pd, 69fr (Sw); $9.06; publisher Ed Emens; editor John Carpenter; tel (423) 775-6111; fax (423) 775-8218

Ripley: *The Lauderdale County Enterprise* — 145 E. Jackson; PO Box 289 (38063-0289); Th; 4,632pd, 43fr (Est); $2.70; publisher & editor William A Klutts; general manager Terry Ford; tel (901) 635-1771; fax (901) 635-2111

Ripley/Lauderdale Co.: *The Lauderdale Voice* — 299 Cleveland St.; PO Box 249, Ripley (38063); W; 3,050pd, 35fr (Sw); 17¢; publisher John H Murchison; editor Jay Heath; tel (901) 635-1238; fax (901) 635-3394

Roane Co.: *The Roane County News* — 204 Franklin St.; PO Box 610, Kingston (37763); M/W/F; 8,205pd, 45fr (Sw); $6.24; C; publisher Dave Commons; editor Darrell Richardson; tel (615) 376-3481; fax (615) 376-1945

Rockwood: *The Rockwood Times* — 204 Franklin St.; PO Box 610, Kingston (37763); Tu; 558pd, 12fr (Sw); $2.52; C; publisher Dave Commons; editor Darrell Richardson; tel (615) 354-9162

Scott Co.: *Independent Herald* — 415 N. Alberta St., Oneida (37841-3002); Th; 3,989pd, 36fr (Est); $3.65; publisher & editor Paul Roy; tel (615) 569-6343; fax (615) 569-9566

Selmer/McNairy Co.: *Independent Appeal* — 111 N. 2nd St.; PO Box 220, Selmer (38375); Th; 6,459pd, 150fr (Sw); $2.52; publisher William J Rail; editor Mark Dean; tel (901) 645-5346; fax (901) 645-3591

Smithville: *The Smithville Review* — 106 S. 1st St.; PO Box 247 (37166); W; 3,992pd, 429fr (Sw); $3.75; publisher William R Fryar; editor Dennis Stanley; tel (615) 597-5485; fax (615) 597-5489

Smyrna/LaVergne: *The Rutherford Courier* — 103 N. Front St.; PO Box 127, Smyrna (37167); Th; 2,969pd, 61fr (Sw); $5.60; C; publisher William R Fryar; general manager Nilla Rinehart; editor Patrick Gross; tel (615) 459-3868; fax (615) 459-3878

Somerville/Fayette Co.: *Fayette County Review* — 16814 Highway 64; PO Box 423, Somerville (38068); W; 2,868pd, 10fr (Sw); $2.95; C; publisher & editor Don L Dowdle; managing editor Mike Cody; tel (901) 465-4042; fax (901) 465-5493

Somerville/Fayette Co.: *The Fayette Falcon* — 101 W. Court Sq.; PO Box 39, Somerville (38068); W; 3,310pd, 155fr (Sw); $3.20; C; publisher Somerville Publishing Co. Inc.; general manager & editor Butch Rhea; tel (901) 465-3567; fax (901) 465-3568

Sparta: *The Sparta Expositor* — 34 W. Bockman Way; PO Box 179 (38583); M/Th; 5,400pd, 6,000fr (Sw); $31.07; C; publisher & editor Suzanne Dickerson; tel (615) 836-3284

Springfield: *Robertson County Times* — 505 W. Court Sq.; PO Box 637 (37172); W; 9,348pd (Sw); $4.91; publisher Hugh B Braddock; editor Tom Beesley; tel (615) 384-3567; fax (615) 384-1221

Tazewell/New Tazewell: *Claiborne Progress* — 1714 Main St.; PO Box B, Tazewell (37879); W; 6,945pd, 24fr (Sw); $5.70; C; publisher J T Hurst; editor Ron Morgan; tel (615) 626-3222; fax (615) 626-6868

Tipton Co.: *The Covington Leader* — 2001 Highway 51 S.; PO Box 529, Covington (38019-0529); W; 7,302pd, 414fr (Sw); $4.30; publisher & managing editor George T Whitley; editor Rodney Eubank; tel (901) 476-7116; fax (901) 476-0373

Tiptonville: *The Lake County Banner* — 315 Church St. (38079); W; 3,031pd, 179fr (Sw); 35¢; publisher Richard S Jones; general manager & editor Evan S Jones; tel (901) 253-6666; fax (901) 253-6667

Tracy City/Grundy Co.: *Grundy County Herald* — 123 Oak St.; PO Box 189, Tracy City (37387); Th; 4,800pd (Est); $4.95; publisher & editor Dawn J Brothers; tel (615) 592-2781; fax (615) 598-5812

Trenton: *The Herald Gazette* — 111 E. 1st St.; PO Box 7 (38382); W; 4,375pd, 125fr (Est); 19¢; C; publishers David Critchlow & J Frank Warmath; editor Danny Jones; tel (901) 855-1711; fax (901) 855-9587

Trousdale Co.: *The Hartsville Vidette* — 111 Marlene St.; PO Box 47, Hartsville (37074); Th; 1,889pd, 33fr (Sw); $2.50; publisher Carleton A Jones; editor Angelene Anderson; tel (615) 374-3556

Tullahoma: *The Tullahoma News* — 505 Lakeway Pl.; PO Box 400 (37388); W/F/Su; 7,720pd, 95fr (Sw); $5.81; publisher Terry Craig; general manager Dot Clark; editor Bob Kyer; managing editor Betty Dement; tel (615) 455-4545; fax (615) 455-9299

Washington Co.: *Herald and Tribune* — 702 Jackson Blvd.; PO Box 277, Jonesborough (37659); W; 3,340pd, 195fr (Sw); $3.60; publisher John A Jones; general manager H Don Miller; editor Kelly Arnold; tel (423) 753-3136; fax (423) 753-6528

Waverly: *The News-Democrat* — 302-A W. Main St.; PO Box 626 (37185); F; 3,495pd, 174fr (Sw); $4.10; C; publisher Bill Ridings; editor Richard McCoy; tel (615) 296-2426; fax (615) 296-5156

Waynesboro: *The Wayne County News* — 119 E. Hollis St.; PO Box 156 (38485); W; 6,542pd, 24fr (Sw); $2.45; publisher & editor Nelle Bailey Cole; managing editor Kathy Brison; tel (615) 722-5429; fax (615) 722-5429

Weakley Co.: *Dresden Enterprise and Sharon Tribune* — 113 Wilson St.; PO Box 139, Dresden (38225-0139); W; 6,300pd (Sw); $3.25; C; publisher Ramona Washburn; general manager & editor Jeff Washburn; tel (901) 364-2234; fax (901) 364-5774

Winchester/Franklin Co.: *Herald-Chronicle* — 906 Dinah Shore Blvd., Winchester (37398); M/Th; 9,200pd, 4,700fr (Sw); $5.95; C; publisher Charles Sons; general manager Davis Sons; editor Eddie Medley; tel (615) 967-2272; fax (615) 967-2299

Woodbury: *Cannon Courier* — 210 W. Water St. (37190); Tu; 3,618pd, 100fr (Est); 10¢; publishers & editors Andy Bryson & Susan Bryson; general manager Teresa Stoetzel; tel (615) 563-2512; fax (615) 563-2519

TEXAS

Abernathy: *Abernathy Weekly Review* — 916 Ave. D; PO Box 160 (79311-0160); F; 959pd, 37fr (Sw); $2.65; publisher & editor Scott Luce; tel (806) 298-2033

Alamo Heights: *The North San Antonio Times* — 8603 Botts Ln.; PO Box 17947, San Antonio (78217); Th; 4,153pd, 5,000fr (Sw); $8.75; C; publisher Bob Jones; editor Steve Henry; tel (210) 828-3321; fax (210) 828-3787

Albany: *The Albany News* — 49 S. Main St.; PO Box 278 (76430); Th; 1,805pd, 12fr (Sw); $3.75; publisher & editor Donnie Lucas; managing editor Melinda Lucas; tel (915) 762-2201; fax (915) 762-3201

Allen: *The Allen American* — 705 N. Greenville Ave., Ste. 100; PO Box 27 (75013); W; 3,591pd, 374fr (VAC); $5.00; Sa; 3,895pd, 374fr (VAC); $5.00; C; publisher Lynn Dickerson; general manager Debbie Tackett; editor Tim Watterson; managing editor Brenda Welchlin; tel (214) 727-3352; fax (214) 727-8215

Alpine/Marathon/Terlinqua: *Alpine Avalanche* — 112 N. 5th St.; PO Box 719, Alpine (79831); Th; 4,205pd, 23fr (Sw); $5.19; C; publisher & editor Burnic Lawrence; tel (915) 837-3334; fax (915) 837-7181

U.S. Weeklies **Texas** **II-73**

Alvin/Brazoria Co.: *Sun* — 201 E. House St.; PO Box 1407, Alvin (77512-1407); M; 1,899pd, 212fr (VAC); $6.42; C; publisher & editor Jim Schwind; tel (713) 331-4421; fax (713) 585-3504

Alvin/Liverpool: *Alvin Journal* — 2206 E. Broadway (77588); PO Box 1830, Pearland (77581); W; 15,000fr (Sw); $5.83; C; publisher Louis Blackmon; editor Wesley Busch; tel (713) 485-2785; fax (713) 485-4464

Amherst: *Amherst Press* — PO Box 370 (79312); Su; 406pd, 24fr (Sw); $2.20; publisher Bruce A Peel; editor Grata Reber; tel (806) 385-6444; fax (806) 385-5234

Anahuac/Chambers Co.: *Anahuac Progress* — 209 Wilcox St.; PO Box 100, Anahuac (77514); W; 1,304pd, 321fr (VAC); $5.05; C; publisher & editor Ernie E Zieschang; general manager & managing editor Keith Kathan; tel (409) 267-6131; fax (409) 336-3345

Andrews: *Andrews County News* — 210 E. Broadway (79714); Th/Su; 3,402pd, 135fr (Sw); $3.50; C; publisher James Roberts; editor Don Ingram; tel (915) 523-2085; fax (915) 523-9492

Angleton: *The Angleton Times* — 700 Western Ave. (77515); PO Box 936 (77516); W/Sa; 2,474pd, 235fr (Sw); $5.10; publisher Ken E Wilson; editor Tommy Crow; tel (409) 849-8581; fax (409) 849-0230

Aransas Pass/Port Aransas: *Aransas Pass Progress* — 346 S. Houston St.; PO Box 2100, Aransas Pass (78335); W; 2,721pd, 82fr (Sw); $5.00; C; publisher Richard P Richards; managing editor John Lowman; tel (512) 758-5391; fax (512) 758-5393

Aransas/San Patricio Co.: *The Herald* — 2307 Highway 35 N. (78382); PO Box 1448, Rockport (78381); Th; 3,579pd (Est); $6.00; publisher W W Janecek; editor Linda Bechtol; tel (512) 729-1828; fax (512) 729-9060

Argyle: *Argyle Sun* — 275 Market; PO Box 879, Lake Dallas (75065); Th; 1,650fr (Est); $5.00; editor Cliff Gaines; tel (817) 497-4141

Arlington: *Arlington Citizen-Journal* — PO Box 1088 (76004); Su; 71,820pd (ABC); $19.56; publisher Michael Tully; editor Mike Blackman; tel (817) 548-5400; fax (817) 261-1193

Arlington: *Arlington News* — 1000 Ave. H E.; PO Box 1087 (76011); Th/Su; 4,302pd, 1,069fr (CAC); $21.68; F; 20,150fr (Sw); $21.68; C; publisher Daniel L Crowe; editor Russ Rian; tel (817) 695-0500; fax (817) 695-0555

Atlanta/Cass Co.: *The Atlanta Citizens Journal* — 306 W. Main St.; PO Box 1188, Atlanta (75551); W/Su; 3,771pd, 51fr (Sw); $6.98; C; publisher William R Owney; tel (903) 796-7133; fax (903) 796-3294

Austin: *The Bellville Times* — 106 E. Palm; PO Box 98, Bellville (77418); Th; 3,929pd, 44fr (Sw); $6.00; publisher & editor James R Maler; tel (512) 865-3131

Azle: *Azle News* — 1121 S.E. Parkway; PO Box 1409 (76020); Th; 4,147pd, 196fr (Sw); $3.60; C; publisher & editor Bob Buckel; tel (817) 237-1184; fax (817) 238-9617

Ballinger: *The Ballinger Ledger* — 810 Hutchings Ave.; PO Box 111 (76821); Th; 2,050pd, 32fr (Est); $5.00; publisher Boles Publishing; general manager Jean Boles; editor Roeneal Boles; tel (915) 365-3501; fax (915) 365-5389

Bandera Co.: *Bandera Bulletin* — 1105 Cedar St.; PO Box 697, Bandera (78003); W; 4,461pd, 12fr (Sw); $3.00; publisher Sean French; editor Caroline Edwards; tel (210) 796-3718; fax (210) 796-4885

Bastrop: *Bastrop Advertiser & County News* — 908 Water St.; PO Box 459 (78602); Th/Su; 4,539pd, 6fr (Sw); $6.45; C; publisher Steve Taylor; editor Davis McAuley; tel (512) 321-2557; fax (512) 321-1680

Beeville: *Beeville Bee-Picayune* — 111 N. Washington St.; PO Box 10 (78104-0010); W/Sa; 5,502pd, 98fr (Sw); $6.55; C; publisher Fred C Latcham Jr; general manager George Geoffrey Latcham; editor Fred C Latcham III; tel (512) 358-2550; fax (512) 358-5323

Belton: *Belton Journal* — 314 E. Central; PO Box 180 (76513); Th; 3,071pd, 415fr (Sw); $6.25; publisher James J Herring; editor Richard Stone; tel (817) 939-5754; fax (817) 937-2333

Big Lake: *The Big Lake Wildcat* — 309 2nd St.; PO Box 946 (76932); Th; 1,292pd, 73fr (Sw); $3.25; publisher J L Werst Jr; editor David L Werst; tel (915) 884-2215; fax (915) 884-5771

Big Sandy/Hawkins: *Big Sandy & Hawkins Journal and Tri-Area News* — PO Box 897, Big Sandy (75755); W; 1,342pd, 21fr (Sw); 20¢; publisher Jim Bardwell; editor Charlotte Heldenbrand; tel (214) 636-4351; fax (214) 636-5091

Blanco: *Blanco County News* — PO Box 429 (78606); W; 1,850pd, 35fr (Sw); 13¢; publisher & editor Roy C McNett; tel (210) 833-4812; fax (210) 833-4246

Blossom/Lamar Co.: *The Blossom Times* — PO Box 5, Blossom (75416); Th; 360pd, 10fr (Sw); $3.05; publisher Nanalee Nichols; editor Thomas Nichols; tel (903) 652-4205; fax (903) 652-4205

Boerne: *Boerne Star* — 282 N. Main St.; PO Box 820 (78006-0820); W; 4,223pd, 95fr (Sw); $4.25; publisher & editor Leon Aldridge; tel (210) 249-2441; fax (210) 249-2441

Bogata/Red River Co.: *The Bogata News* — 306 Main St.; PO Box 306, Bogata (75435); Th; 1,311pd, 30fr (Sw); $3.00; publisher & editor Nanalee Nichols; tel (903) 632-5322; fax (903) 652-4205

Booker/Darrouzett/Follett: *The Booker News* — 204 S. Main St.; PO Drawer G, Booker (79005); Th; 1,119pd, 27fr (Sw); $2.30; publisher & editor Ben Boren; tel (806) 658-4732

Bowie: *The Bowie News* — 218 W. Tarrant; PO Box 831 (76230); Th/Su; 3,800pd, 550fr (Est); $4.80; publisher Jim Winter; general manager K Williams; editor Barbara Beckwith; tel (817) 872-2247; fax (817) 872-4812

Bowie Co.: *Bowie County Citizens Tribune* — 129 E. North Front, New Boston (75570); Th/Su; 12,500pd (Est); $6.65; C; publisher Mary Ann Pope; tel (903) 628-5801; fax (903) 628-2551

Brady: *The Brady Herald* — 201 S. Bridge St.; PO Box 1151 (76825); Tu; 3,389pd, 68fr (Sw); $4.20; publisher & editor Larry B Smith; tel (915) 597-2959; fax (915) 597-1434

Brady: *The Brady Standard* — 201 S. Bridge St.; PO Box 1151 (76825); Th; 3,453pd, 74fr (Sw); $4.20; publisher & editor Larry B Smith; tel (915) 597-2959; fax (915) 597-1434

Breckenridge: *Breckenridge American* — 114 E. Elm; PO Box 871 (76424); W/Sa; 3,502pd, 57fr (Sw); $5.35; publisher Virgil E Moore III; editor Herrel Hallmark; tel (817) 559-5412; fax (817) 559-3491

Bremond: *Bremond Press* — 301 S. Main St.; PO Box 490 (76629); F; 1,262pd, 60fr (Sw); $2.00; publisher & editor Betty Yezak; tel (817) 746-7033

Bridgeport: *The Bridgeport Index* — 916 Halsell St.; PO Box 1150 (76426); Th; 1,935pd, 40fr (Est); 35¢; publisher Harlan Bridwell; editor Joann Pritchard; tel (817) 683-4021; fax (817) 683-3841

Bronte: *The Bronte Enterprise* — 116 Main St.; PO Drawer O (76933); F; 782pd, 15fr (Est); 13¢; publisher & editor Hal Spain; tel (915) 473-2001; fax (915) 473-4800

Brownfield: *Brownfield News* — 409 W. Hill; PO Box 1272 (79316); W/Su; 3,610pd, 60fr (Sw); 14¢; publisher & editor Lynn Brisendine; tel (806) 637-4535; fax (806) 637-3795

Buda/Kyle/Manchaca: *Hays County Free Press* — FM 2770 at Mountain City Sta.; PO Box 339, Buda (78610); Th; 2,374pd, 79fr (Sw); $4.38; publisher & editor Bob Barton; general manager Sandra Grizzle; tel (512) 268-7862/262-6397; fax (512) 268-0262

Buffalo: *The Buffalo Press* — 300 E. Commerce; PO Box B (75831); W; 1,586pd, 3,200fr (Est); $3.10; publisher Holly H Rogers; editor Rolf Hinton; tel (214) 322-4248; fax (214) 322-4023

Buna: *East Texas Banner* — 104 N. Kellie St.; PO Drawer B, Kirbyville (75956); Th; 3,300pd (Sw); $4.41; publisher Joe Herndon; tel (409) 423-2696; fax (409) 423-4793

Burkburnett: *Informer Star* — 417 Ave. C; PO Box 906 (76354); Th; 2,755pd, 30fr (Est); $3.50; publisher & editor Sean C McBeath; tel (817) 569-2191

Burleson: *Burleson Star* — 319 N. Burleson Blvd. (76028); PO Box 909 (76097); M/Th; 6,140pd, 54fr (Est); $4.50; C; publisher & editor James Moody; tel (817) 295-0486; fax (817) 295-5278

Burnet: *Burnet Bulletin* — 101 E. Jackson; PO Box 160 (78611); W; 3,691pd, 20fr (Sw); $5.00; C; publisher & editor Darin Brock; tel (512) 756-6136

Caldwell: *Burleson County Citizen Tribune* — 205 W. Buck St. (77836); Th; 3,364pd, 36fr (Sw); $4.50; publisher & editor Sam Preuss; tel (409) 567-3286; fax (409) 567-7898

Cameron/Rockdale: *Cameron Herald* — 108 E. 1st St.; PO Box 1230, Cameron (76520); Th; 3,615pd, 125fr (Sw); 25¢; C; publisher & editor Wayne Green; tel (817) 697-6671; fax (817) 697-4902

Canadian: *The Canadian Record* — 211 Main; PO Box 898 (79014); Th; 1,644pd, 72fr (Sw); $3.00; publisher & editor Nancy Ezzell; editor Laurie Ezzell Brown; tel (806) 323-5321/6461; fax (806) 323-6102

Canton: *Canton Herald* — 103 E. Tyler; PO Box 577 (75103); Th; 5,508pd, 11fr (Est); $4.12; publisher Glenn McNeill Jr; general manager Betsy McNeill; editor Linda Brown; tel (903) 567-4000; fax (903) 873-4321

Canyon Lake: *Times Guardian/Chronicle* — 1151 FM 2673 (Sattler 78133); PO Box 2098 (78130); W; 1,745pd, 35fr (Sw); $5.25; C; publisher & editor Janis Davis; managing editor Robert Stewart; tel (210) 907-3882; fax (210) 964-2771

Canyon/Randall Co.: *The Canyon News* — 1500 5th Ave.; PO Box 779, Canyon (79015); Th/Su; 3,850pd, 412fr (Sw); $4.25; publisher Brad Tooley; editor Kimberly Burk; tel (806) 655-7121; fax (806) 655-0823

Carrizo Springs: *Carrizo Springs Javelin* — 604 N. 1st; PO Box 188 (78834); W; 1,856pd, 100fr (Sw); 15¢; publisher George Willems; editor John Willems; tel (210) 876-2318; fax (210) 876-2620

Carrollton/Farmers Branch: *The Market* — 1165 S. Stemmons, Ste. 100, Lewisville (75067); Th; 760pd, 21,933fr (Est); $9.00; C; publisher Lynne Dickerson; editor Tim Waterson; tel (214) 436-3566; fax (214) 219-0719

Carthage: *Panola Watchman* — 109 W. Panola St.; PO Box 518 (75633); W/Su; 4,606pd, 80fr (Est); $6.75; C; publisher Bill Holder; editor Ted Leach; tel (903) 693-7888; fax (903) 693-5857

Castroville: *The News Bulletin* — 407 Paris St. (78009); Th; 2,213pd (Sw); $4.50; C; publisher & editor Thomas Barnes; tel (210) 538-2556; fax (210) 538-2447

Cedar Hill: *Cedar Hill Today* — 1701 N. Hampton (DeSoto 75115); PO Box 381029, Duncanville (75138-1029); Th; 2,511pd, 2,404fr (Sw); $6.70; C; publisher Richard Collins; managing editor Phil Major; tel (214) 298-4211; fax (214) 298-6369

Cedar Park: *Hill Country News* — PO Box 1777 (78613); W; 1,675pd, 1,527fr (Sw); 18¢; publisher Don Moore; editor Tom Burke; tel (512) 258-4127; fax (512) 258-4752

Celina: *Celina Record* — 211 W. Pecan; PO Box 308 (75009); Th; 1,076pd, 70fr (Sw); $3.00; publishers & editors Cue Lewis & David Lewis; tel (214) 382-2341; fax (214) 382-2341

Center/Shelby Co.: *The Light and Champion* — 137 San Augustine St.; PO Box 1989, Center (75935); Tu/F; 4,379pd, 301fr (Sw); $6.40; C; publisher Bob Windham; editor Candace Velvin; tel (409) 598-3377; fax (409) 598-6394

Chandler/Brownsboro: *Chandler & Brownsboro Statesman* — PO Box 168, Brownsboro (75756); W; 1,446pd (Sw); $2.50; publisher Roger C Perry; editor Elaine C Reichard; tel (903) 852-7641

Chico: *Chico Texan* — 716 Halsell St.; PO Box 1150, Bridgeport (76426); Th; 455pd, 40fr (Est); 25¢; publisher Harlan Bridwell; editor Joann Pritchard; tel (817) 683-4021; fax (817) 683-3841

Childress: *Childress Index* — 226 Main St.; PO Box 1210 (79201); Tu/Th/Su; 3,142pd, 115fr (Est); 14¢; publisher Morris Higley; editor Chris Blackburix; tel (817) 937-2525; fax (817) 937-2239

Chillicothe: *Valley News* — PO Box 129 (79225); Th; 465pd, 18fr (Sw); $1.99; publisher & editor Larry Crubtree; tel (817) 852-5232

Cisco/Eastland Co.: *The Cisco Press* — 700 Conrad Hilton Ave.; PO Box 470, Cisco (76437); Th/Sa; 1,575pd, 50fr (Sw); $4.00; C; publisher Houston V O'Brien; editor Richard Kurklin; tel (817) 442-2244; fax (817) 629-2092

Clarksville/Red River Co.: *The Clarksville Times* — 106 E. Main St.; PO Box 1018, Clarksville (75426); Th; 2,710pd (Est); $8.00; publisher Robert B Palmer; editor Ben E Black; tel (903) 427-5616; fax (903) 427-5617

Claude: *Claude News* — 130 Trice; PO Box 210 (79019); Th; 831pd (Est); 50¢; publisher Steve Sirmon; editor Charity Sirmon; tel (806) 226-3461

Clear Lake City: *The Citizen* — 17511 El Camino Real (77058); PO Box 57907, Webster (77598); W; 11,850fr (VAC); $12.22; F; 2,813pd, 49fr (VAC); $12.22; C; publisher Mike Allison; editor Lori Williams; tel (713) 488-1108; fax (713) 286-0750

Cleveland: *Cleveland Advocate* — 106 W. Hanson St.; PO Box 1628 (77327); W; 2,400pd, 32fr (Est); $7.03; publisher Diana Lobner; editor Jimmy Galvan; tel (713) 592-2626; fax (713) 592-2629

Clifton: *Clifton Record* — 310 W. 5th St.; PO Box 353 (76634); W; 3,217pd, 24fr (Sw); $4.10; publisher James W Smith; publisher & editor W Leon Smith; tel (817) 675-3336; fax (817) 675-4090

Clyde: *Clyde Journal* — 95 S. 1st St.; PO Drawer W (79510); W; 2,250pd, 40fr (Sw); 20¢; publisher Don Tabor; editor Daniel Tabor; tel (915) 893-4244; fax (915) 893-2780

Coleman: *Chronicle & Democrat-Voice Inc.* — 208 W. Pecan St.; PO Box 840 (76834-0840); Tu/Th; 3,224pd, 70fr (Sw); $4.10; publishers & editors Brett Autry & Stan Brudney; tel (915) 625-4128; fax (915) 625-4129

Colorado City/Mitchell: *Colorado City Record* — 156 E. 2nd St.; PO Box 92, Colorado City (79512); Th; 3,900pd, 100fr (Est); $4.60; publisher & editor Earl Plagens; tel (915) 728-3413; fax (915) 728-3414

Columbus/Colorado Co.: *The Colorado County Citizen* — 513 Spring St.; PO Box 548, Columbus (78934); W; 3,925pd (Est); $4.00; publisher & editor M L (Tex) Rogers; tel (409) 732-2304; fax (409) 732-8804

Commerce: *Commerce Journal* — 1219 Washington St.; PO Box 1291 (75428); W/Su; 2,508pd, 67fr (Est); $6.16; publisher Albert Vaughan; editor Warren Morrison; tel (903) 886-3196; fax (903) 886-3198

Copperas Cove: *Copperas Cove Leader-Press* — 115 W. Ave. D; PO Box 370 (76522); Th; 2,214pd, 56fr (Sw); $5.20; publisher David G Landmann; editor Connie G Landmann; tel (817) 547-4207; fax (817) 542-3299

Corpus Christi: *Nueces County Record-Star* — 104 N. 5th St.; PO Box 1192, Robstown (78380); Th; 7,291pd (Sw); $6.26; publisher & editor Sam F Keach; managing editor Julie Martinez; tel (512) 387-4511; fax (512) 387-2276

Corrigan: *Corrigan Times* — 202 E. Front St.; PO Box 115-V (75939); Th; 1,350pd (Est); $3.22; publisher Alvin Holley; editor Greg Peak; tel (409) 398-2535; fax (409) 327-7156

Corsiciana/Navarro Co./Freestone Co.: *Richland Chambers Progress* — 110 S. Colket; PO Box 280, Kernes (75144); Th; 9,000fr (Est); $4.50; C; publisher Don L Dowdle; editor Debbie Bailey; tel (903) 396-7788; fax (903) 396-2728

Crane: *The Crane County News Inc.* — 401 S. Gaston St. (79731-2621); Th; 1,570pd, 70fr (Sw); $6.00; C; publisher Paula Nichols; publisher & editor Skip Nichols; tel (915) 558-3541; fax (915) 558-2676

Crockett/Houston Co.: *Houston County Courier* — 102 S. 7th; PO Box 551, Crockett (75835); Th/Su; 5,763pd (Sw); $4.50; C; publisher Bassett Keller; editor LaDeanne Smith; tel (409) 544-2238; fax (409) 544-4088

Crosby Co./Ralls/Lorenzo/Crosbyton: *Crosby County News & Chronicle* — 109 W. Aspen, Crosbyton (79322-2501); F; 1,404pd, 62fr (Sw); $3.22; publisher & editor Ben Gillespie; tel (806) 675-2881; fax (806) 675-2855

Cross Plains: *Cross Plains Review* — 155 E. 8th St.; PO Box 519 (76443); W; 1,465pd, 35fr (Est); $3.00; C; publisher Don Tabor; editor Vanda King; tel (817) 725-6111; fax (817) 725-7225

Crowell: *The Foard County News and Crowell Index* — 108 S. 1st St.; PO Box 489 (79227-0489); Th; 1,424pd, 42fr (Sw); $3.00; publisher & editor Leslie Hopkins; tel (817) 684-1355; fax (817) 684-1700

Crystal City: *Zavala County Sentinel* — 202 E. Nueces St.; PO Drawer G (78839); Th; 2,280pd, 50fr (Sw); $3.50; publisher & editor M Dale Barker; tel (210) 374-3465; fax (210) 374-5771

Cuero: *Cuero Record* — 119 E. Main St.; PO Box 351 (77954-0351); W; 2,722pd, 147fr (Sw); $4.50; publisher & editor Glenn Rea; tel (512) 275-3464; fax (512) 275-3131

Daingerfield/Lone Star/Hughs Springs: *The Bee* — 707 Linda Dr.; PO Drawer M, Daingerfield (75638); W; 2,654pd, 53fr (Sw); $4.95; publisher & editor Donald M Cooper; tel (903) 645-3940; fax (903) 645-3731

Copyright ©1996 by the Editor & Publisher Co.

Dallas: *Suburban Tribune* — 3008 Balch Springs Rd., Ste. F, Balch Springs (75180); Th; 2,248pd, 898fr (Sw); $6.50; publisher & editor Ken Milstead; tel (214) 286-4000

Dallas: *The White Rocker News* — 10809 Garland Rd.; PO Box 180698 (75218); Th; 3,406pd, 384fr (Sw); $10.50; publisher & editor Retta Hanie; tel (214) 327-9335

Dallas/Oak Cliff: *Oak Cliff Tribune* — 400 S. Zang, Ste. C 101; PO Box 4650, Dallas (75208); Th; 9,470pd, 600fr (Est); $15.00; publisher Joe Whitney; editor Kathie Majors; tel (214) 943-7755; fax (214) 943-7775

De Kalb: *De Kalb News* — 145 N.W. Johnson (75559); Th; 2,800pd (Est); $6.65; publisher & editor Harold R Pope; editor Roger Pope; tel (214) 667-2509

Decatur/Wise Co.: *Wise County Messenger* — 115 S. Trinity; PO Box 149, Decatur (76234); Th/Su; 5,001pd, 29fr (Sw); $5.05; C; publisher Roy J Eaton; general manager Mark A Jordon; editor Julie Porter; tel (817) 627-5987; fax (817) 627-1004

Deer Park: *Deer Park Progress* — 102 W. Pasadena Blvd.; PO Box 369 (77536); W; 11,000fr (VAC); $11.20; Su; 4,000pd (VAC); $11.20; C; publisher Larry Power; editor Mary Ellen Wilson; tel (713) 479-2760; fax (713) 479-3415

Dell City/Hudspeth Co.: *Hudspeth County Herald & Dell Valley Review* — 290 Trail W. Park; PO Box 659, Dell City (79837); F; 760pd, 10fr (Sw); $4.00; publisher & editor Mrs James Lynch; tel (915) 964-2426; fax (915) 964-2426

Denver City: *Denver City Press* — 321 N. Main St.; PO Box 1240 (79323); Th/Su; 2,046pd, 3fr (Est); 20¢; publisher Gene Snyder; editor Earl Moseley; tel (806) 592-2141

Deport: *Deport Times* — Main St.; PO Box 98 (75435); Th; 1,172pd, 10fr (Sw); $3.05; publisher & editor Nanalee Nichols; tel (903) 652-4205; fax (903) 652-4205

DeSoto: *DeSoto Today* — 1701 N. Hampton (75115); PO Box 381029, Duncanville (75138-1029); Th; 3,357pd, 4,807fr (Sw); $7.70; C; publisher Richard Collins; managing editor Phil Major; tel (214) 298-4211; fax (214) 298-6369

Devine: *The Devine News* — 216 S. Bright St.; PO Box 508 (78016); Th; 3,600pd (Sw); $4.50; publisher Charlie Pat DuBose; general manager Kathleen Calame; editor L Kitty DuBose; tel (210) 665-2211

Devine/Lytle/Medina Co.: *Medina Valley Times* — 15207 Adams St.; PO Box 1570, Lytle (78052); Th; 3,255pd, 44fr (Sw); $5.00; C; publisher & editor Thomas A Barnes; tel (210) 772-3672; fax (210) 772-3507

Diboll: *The Free Press* — 201 N. Temple Dr.; PO Box 700 (75941); Th; 3,526pd, 187fr (Sw); $4.00; editor Gary Willmon; tel (409) 829-1801; fax (409) 829-1811

Dimmitt/Hart/Nazareth: *The Castro County News* — 108 W. Bedford; PO Box 67, Dimmitt (79027); Th; 2,538pd, 15fr (Est); $3.50; publisher & editor Don Nelson; tel (806) 647-3123; fax (806) 647-3112

Donley Co.: *The Clarendon News* — 103 Kearney; PO Box 1110, Clarendon (79226); Th; 1,452pd (Sw); $2.75; publisher & editor Robert C Williams; tel (806) 874-2259

Dripping Springs: *Century News* — PO Box 49, Wimberley (78676); W; 97pd, 2,430fr (Sw); $5.20; C; publisher Mary V Saunders; managing editor Harrell King; tel (512) 847-2202; fax (512) 847-9054

Dripping Springs/Hays Co.: *Dripping Springs Dispatch* — Railroad 12 & Highway 290, Promenade Ctr., Ste. 4; PO Box 550, Dripping Springs (78620); Th; 1,282pd, 81fr (Sw); $4.71; C; publisher & editor Dale Roberson; tel (512) 858-7893; fax (512) 858-4828

Duncanville: *Duncanville Today* — 1701 N. Hampton (75115); PO Box 381029 (75138-1029); Th; 5,020pd, 3,557fr (Sw); $8.20; C; publisher Richard Collins; managing editor Phil Major; tel (214) 298-4211; fax (214) 298-6369

Eagle Lake: *Eagle Lake Headlight* — 220 E. Main St.; PO Box 67 (77434-0067); Th; 2,080pd, 38fr (Sw); $3.78; publisher & editor Jeannine Fearing; tel (409) 234-5521

Eagle Pass: *Eagle Pass News-Guide & Sunday News* — 1342 Main St.; PO Box 764 (78852); Th/Su; 2,665pd, 47fr (Sw); $3.15; publisher Rex S McBeath; editor Mrs A W McBeath; tel (210) 773-2309; fax (210) 773-3398

Earth/Lamb Co.: *Earth Weekly News* — PO Box 568, Earth (79031); F; 800pd, 150fr (Est); $2.70; publisher Barbara Goodwin; editor Twyla Woodring; tel (806) 257-3314

E Bernard: *East Bernard Tribune* — PO Box X (77435); W; 1,960pd (Est); $1.03; publisher L M Preuss; editor Fred Chambers; tel (409) 335-4014; fax (409) 335-4014

Eastland: *Eastland Telegram* — 215 S. Seaman; PO Box 29 (76448); Th/Su; 2,805pd, 250fr (Sw); $4.00; C; publisher & editor Houston V O'Brien; tel (817) 629-1707

Eden: *The Eden Echo* — 135 Market St.; PO Box V (76837); Th; 1,021pd, 30fr (Est); 20¢; publisher Allen Amos; editor Kathy Amos; tel (915) 869-3561

Edgewood: *Edgewood Enterprise* — PO Box 7 (75117); Th; 1,246pd, 4fr (Est); $2.40; C; publisher Sandy Hill; editor Glenda Lee; tel (903) 896-4401; fax (903) 962-3660

El Campo: *El Campo Leader-News* — 203 E. Jackson St.; PO Box 1180 (77437); W/Sa; 6,114pd, 13fr (Sw); $5.95; publisher Fred V Barbee Jr; editor Chris F Barbee; tel (409) 543-3363; fax (409) 543-0097

Electra: *Electra Star-News* — 207 N. Waggoner; PO Box 1192 (76360); Th; 1,812pd, 79fr (Est); $3.00; C; publisher & editor Jeannette Miller; tel (817) 495-2149; fax (817) 495-2627

Elgin: *Elgin Courier* — 105 N. Main; PO Box 631 (78621); Th; 2,958pd, 50fr (Sw); $5.70; C; publisher & editor Beverly Daughtry; tel (512) 285-3333

Ellis Co.: *The Press* — 113 S. Dallas; PO Box 426, Ennis (75120); F; 4,200pd (Est); $3.75; publisher & editor Sherry Williams; tel (214) 875-9015; fax (214) 875-9047

Emory/Rains Co.: *Rains County Leader* — 103 N. Texas St.; PO Box 127, Emory (75440); Th; 3,100pd, 50fr (Est); $3.15; publisher & editor Kathleen Hill Becknell; tel (903) 473-2653; fax (903) 473-2653

Ennis/Ellis Co.: *Ellis County News* — 213 N. Dallas St.; PO Box 100, Ennis (75119); Th; 717pd, 100fr (Est); 50¢; publisher & editor Charles E Gentry; tel (214) 875-3801; fax (214) 875-9747

Everman: *Everman Times* — 833 E. Enon; PO Box 40230 (76140); Th; 406pd, 55fr (Sw); $4.40; C; publisher & editor Gene S Blessing; general manager William E Blessing; tel (817) 478-4661; fax (817) 483-4661

Fairfield: *The Fairfield Recorder* — 101 E. Commerce (75840); Th; 3,197pd, 23fr (Est); $4.00; publisher & editor Joe Reavis; tel (903) 389-3334

Falfurrias/Premont/Encino: *Falfurrias Facts* — 219 E. Rice; PO Box 619, Falfurrias (78355); Th; 1,663pd, 21fr (Est); $2.50; publisher & editor Marcelo Silva; tel (512) 325-2200; fax (512) 325-2200

Falls Co.: *Marlin Democrat* — 211 Fortune St.; PO Box 112, Marlin (76661); W; 2,469pd, 70fr (Est); $4.28; C; publisher Roberta McDaniel; editor Brentron Scaggs; tel (817) 883-2554; fax (817) 883-6553

Farmers Branch/Carrollton: *Metrocrest News* — 1720 Josey, Ste. 100, Carrollton (75006); Th; 356pd, 34,195fr (CAC); $23.68; C; publisher Daniel L Crowe; editor Rodger Cramer; tel (214) 418-9999; fax (214) 418-1620

Farmersville: *Farmersville Times* — 101 S. Main; PO Box 512 (75442); Th; 2,183pd, 68fr (Est); $3.75; publisher Robert Harty Jr; editor Bob Poole; tel (214) 782-6171; fax (214) 782-7023

Farwell/Texico (NM): *The State Line Tribune* — 404 3rd St.; PO Box 255, Farwell (79325); F; 1,254pd (Est); $2.90; publisher & editor Mike Pomper; tel (806) 481-3681

Flatonia: *The Flatonia Argus* — 214 S. Penn St.; PO Box 468 (78941); W; 1,440pd, 38fr (Est); 80¢; publisher Paul Prause; editor Don Clark; tel (512) 865-3510; fax (512) 865-2455

Floresville/Wilson Co.: *Floresville Chronicle-Journal* — 1433 3rd St.; PO Box 820, Floresville (78114); Th; 4,274pd, 75fr (Est); $3.50; C; publisher Joe H Fietsam; general manager James J Fietsam; editor Mrs Joe H Fietsam; tel (210) 393-2111; fax (210) 393-9012

Floyd Co.: *Floyd County Hesperian* — 111 E. Missouri St., Floyd (79235-2821); Th; 2,422pd, 26fr (Sw); $2.80; publisher & editor Alice Towery Gilroy; tel (806) 983-3737; fax (806) 983-3141

Forney: *The Forney Messenger* — 113 1/2 W. Old Highway 80; PO Box 936 (75126); Th; 1,555pd (Est); $3.00; publisher & editor Cary L Griffin; tel (214) 552-3121; fax (214) 552-3599

Ft. Bend: *Fort Bend Mirror* — PO Box 1267, Sugar Land (77478-1267); Th; 1,065pd, 168fr (VAC); $4.00; publisher Clyde King; editor Cheryl Skinner; tel (713) 242-9104; fax (713) 342-3219

Ft. Stockton: *The Fort Stockton Pioneer* — 210 N. Nelson St.; PO Box 1528 (79735); Th; 3,384pd, 130fr (Est); $4.70; publisher & editor John Cordsen; tel (915) 336-2281; fax (915) 336-6432

Franklin/Robertson Co.: *Franklin News Weekly* — 200 Dechard; PO Box 935, Franklin (77856); Th; 1,200pd, 41fr (Est); $4.00; C; publisher & editor Billie McNair; tel (409) 828-3221; fax (409) 828-5536

Frankston/Lake Palestine: *The Frankston Citizen* — 112 W. Main St.; PO Box 188, Frankston (75763); Th; 1,638pd, 126fr (Sw); $3.90; publisher & editor Joe W Tindel; tel (903) 876-2218; fax (903) 876-4974

Fredericksburg: *Fredericksburg Standard Radio Post* — 108 E. Main St.; PO Box 473 (78624); W; 9,432pd, 56fr (Sw); $7.20; publisher Arthur H Kowert; general manager & editor Terry Collier; tel (210) 997-2155; fax (210) 997-9955

Freer/Duval Co.: *The Freer Press* — 309 E. Hahl St.; PO Box 567, Freer (78357); W; 948pd, 36fr (Sw); $2.90; publisher & editor Lataine Wright Dillard; managing editor Mell Rose Gandy; tel (512) 394-7402; fax (512) 394-5386

Freestone Co.: *The Teague Chronicle* — 319 Main St.; PO Box 631, Teague (75860); Th; 2,173pd, 100fr (Est); $4.00; publisher Patricia Massey; editor Steve Massey; tel (817) 739-2141

Friendswood: *Friendswood Journal* — PO Box 1448 (77546); W; 3,100pd, 5,000fr (Est); $5.80; C; publisher Ron Gervais; editor Michael Smith; tel (713) 485-2785; fax (713) 485-4464

Friendswood/Alvin: *Friendswood Reporter News* — 2404 S. Park, Pearland (77581); W; 2,000pd, 8,000fr (Sw); $4.25; C; publisher & managing editor Laura Emmons; general manager Linda Knight; editor Joan Cummings; tel (713) 485-7501; fax (713) 485-6397

Friona: *The Friona Star* — 916 Main; PO Box 789 (79035); Sa; 1,550pd, 102fr (Sw); $4.00; C; publisher & editor Bill Ellis; tel (806) 247-2211; fax (806) 247-2211

Frisco: *Frisco Enterprise* — 6827 Main St.; PO Box 800 (75034); F; 3,800pd (Est); $4.00; publisher Harlan Bridwell; editor Donna Zambiasi; tel (214) 377-2141; fax (214) 335-2356

Fritch/Hutchinson Cos.: *The Eagle Press* — 709 W. Broadway; PO Box 1659, Fritch (79036); F; 1,500pd (Sw); $3.00; publisher & editor Debra Wells; publisher Derrol Wells; tel (806) 857-2123; fax (806) 857-2123

Gail/Borden Co.: *The Borden Star* — 100 Kincaid Ave.; PO Box 137, Gail (79738); W; 504pd, 10fr (Est); $2.00; publisher & editor Clarajane Dyess; tel (806) 756-4402; fax (806) 756-4310

Garland: *Garland News* — 613 State St. (75040); Th/Su; 8,637pd, 90fr (CAC); $21.68; F; 15,600fr (Sw); $21.68; C; publisher Daniel L Crowe; editor Ray Leszcynski; tel (214) 272-6591; fax (214) 487-0655

Garrison: *Garrison In The News* — PO Box 278 (75946); Th; 1,144pd, 15fr (Est); 10¢; publisher & editor Joanne Barton; tel (409) 347-2322; fax (409) 347-3203

Gatesville: *The Gatesville Messenger and Star-Forum* — 116 S. 6th St.; PO Box 799 (76528); Th; 5,400pd, 62fr (Sw); $2.25; publisher Marshall Day; editor Larry Kennedy; tel (817) 865-5212; fax (817) 865-2361

Georgetown: *The Sunday Sun* — 707 Main St.; PO Box 39 (78627); Su; 6,792pd, 198fr (Sw); $5.95; publisher Clark Thurmond; editor Linda Scarbrough; managing editor Brian Pearson; tel (512) 930-4824; fax (512) 863-2474

Georgetown: *The Williamson County Sun* — 707 Main St.; PO Box 39 (78626); W; 6,720pd, 198fr (Sw); $5.95; publisher Clark Thurmond; editor Linda Scarbrough; managing editor Brian Pearson; tel (512) 930-4824; fax (512) 863-2474

Giddings: *Giddings Times & News* — 170 N. Knox Ave.; PO Box 947 (78942); W; 5,800pd, 40fr (Sw); $7.50; publisher & editor L M (Buddy) Preuss III; managing editor David True; tel (409) 542-2222; fax (409) 542-9410

Gilmer: *Gilmer Mirror* — 214 E. Marshall St.; PO Box 250 (75644); W/Sa; 5,861pd, 70fr (Sw); $5.25; publisher & editor Sarah L Greene; general manager William R Greene; tel (903) 843-2503; fax (903) 843-5123

Gladewater: *Gladewater Mirror* — 201 S. Dean; PO Box 1352 (75647); W; 1,772pd (Sw); $5.00; C; publisher Bill Woodall; editor Judy Imman; tel (903) 845-2235; fax (903) 845-2237

Glen Rose: *Glen Rose Reporter* — 100 S.W. Vernon; PO Box 2009 (76043); W; 2,203pd, 122fr (Est); $2.10; publisher & editor Dan McCarty; tel (817) 897-2282; fax (817) 897-9423

Goldthwaite/Mills Co.: *Goldthwaite Eagle* — 1002 Fisher St.; PO Box 249, Goldthwaite (76844); Th; 2,355pd, 25fr (Sw); $5.00; publisher & editor Frank Bridges; tel (915) 648-2244/3563; fax (915) 648-3417

Goliad Co.: *Texan Express* — 302 S. Commercial; PO Box 1, Goliad (77963); W; 2,011pd, 26fr (Est); $3.00; publisher & editor Martha Mullenix; tel (512) 645-2330; fax (512) 645-2812

Gonzales: *The Gonzales Inquirer* — PO Box 616 (78629-0616); Tu/Th; 4,000pd (Est); $3.60; publisher David Tuma; editor Charles Wood; tel (210) 672-2861; fax (210) 672-7029

Gorman/Carbon/Desdemona: *Gorman Progress* — 106 S. Kent St.; PO Box 68, Gorman (76454); Th; 1,017pd, 37fr (Sw); $2.65; publisher Lonnie Joe Bennett; editor Herman Bennett; tel (817) 734-2410; fax (817) 734-2799

Graham/Young Co.: *The Graham Leader* — 620 Oak; PO Box 600, Graham (76450); W/Su; 4,723pd, 10fr (Sw); $4.60; publisher James R Gray; editor Lewis Simmons; tel (817) 549-7800; fax (817) 549-4364

Granbury: *Hood County News* — 1501 S. Morgan; PO Box 879 (76048); W/Sa; 9,714pd, 36fr (Sw); $6.16; C; publisher Jerry Tidwell; general manager Joe Thompson; editor Roger Enlow; tel (817) 573-7066; fax (817) 573-6579

Grand Prairie: *Grand Prairie News* — 1000 Ave. H E., Arlington (76011); Th/Su; 6,112pd, 227fr (CAC); $21.68; F; 8,814fr (Sw); $21.68; C; publisher Daniel L Crowe; editor Herb Booth; tel (817) 695-0500; fax (817) 695-0555

Grand Saline: *The Grand Saline Sun* — 116 N. Main St.; PO Drawer G (75140); Th; 2,275pd, 50fr (Sw); $3.94; C; publisher Sandy Hill; editor Jan Adamson; tel (903) 962-4275; fax (903) 962-3660

Grandview: *Grandview Tribune* — 102 E. Criner; PO Box 440 (76050); F; 1,000pd, 200fr (Sw); $2.50; C; publisher Jack Magness Jr; general manager Diane Magness; tel (817) 866-3391

Granger: *Granger News* — 108 W. Clark; PO Box 50, Bartlett (76511); Th; 834pd (Sw); $2.70; C; publisher & editor Gayle Bielss; tel (817) 527-4424; fax (817) 527-4333

Grapevine: *The Grapevine Sun* — 332 S. Main St.; PO Box 400 (76099); Th/Su; 1,113pd, 15,942fr (Est); $5.70; C; publisher Fred Patterson; general manager Tom Bateman; editor Les Cockrell; tel (817) 488-8561; fax (817) 488-5339

Groesbeck/Thornton/Kosse: *The Groesbeck Journal* — 115 N. Ellis St.; PO Box 440, Groesbeck (76642); Th; 4,870pd, 50fr (Sw); 16¢; C; publisher & editor Thomas E Hawkins; tel (817) 729-5103; fax (817) 729-5555

Groom/McLean/Claude: *The Groom News* — 84 Broadway; PO Box 460, Groom (79039); Th; 1,087pd (Est); 13¢; publisher Phillip J Miller; editor Donna Burton; tel (806) 248-7333

Groveton: *Groveton News* — 203 E. 1st; PO Box 730 (75845); Th; 1,950pd, 25fr (Est); 13¢; publisher Alvin Holley; editor Valerie Collins; tel (409) 642-1726/1891; fax (409) 642-1195

Gun Barrel City: *Cedar Creek Pilot* — 828 W. Main (75147); Th/Su; 6,022pd, 55fr (Sw); $4.80; publisher Dan Dwelle; general manager Ann Rounsavall; editor Chip Souza; tel (903) 887-8051

Gun Barrel City: *Cedar Creek Progress* — 110 S. Colket; PO Box 280, Kerens (75144); Th; 7,000fr (Sw); $4.50; C; publisher Don L Dowdle; editor Debbie Bailey; tel (903) 396-7788; fax (903) 396-2728

Hallsville: *Hallsville Herald* — 100 Texas Ave. (75692); PO Box 930 (75650); Th; 624pd, 27fr (Est); $3.75; publisher & editor Mike Elswick; managing editor Annie Britt; tel (903) 687-3204; fax (903) 687-3291

Hamilton: *Herald News* — 112 E. Main; PO Box 833 (76531); Th; 3,670pd, 100fr (Est); 14¢; publisher & editor Kenneth Miller; publisher R B Miller Jr; tel (817) 386-3145; fax (817) 386-3001

Hamlin: *The Hamlin Herald* — 350 S. Central; PO Box 339 (79520); Th; 1,255pd (Est); $3.00; publisher & editor Rick Craig; tel (915) 576-3606; fax (915) 576-3607

Hardin Co./Lumberton/Silsbee: *Hardin County News* — PO Box 8204, Lumberton (77711); W; 17,000fr (Sw); $7.95; publisher John Butters; managing editor Tony Flowers; tel (409) 755-4912; fax (409) 755-7654

Hart: *Hart Beat* — 407 Broadway; PO Box 350 (79043-0350); F; 450pd, 10fr (Est); $3.00; publisher & editor Neoma Wall Williams; tel (806) 938-2640; fax (806) 938-2216

Haskell: *The Haskell Free Press* — 401 S. 1st St.; PO Box 1058 (79521); Th; 2,672pd, 24fr (Sw); $4.25; publisher John McDougal; editor Joyce Jones; tel (817) 864-2686; fax (817) 864-2686

Hawley/Jones Co.: *Jones County Journal* — PO Box 810, Hawley (79525); Th; 156pd (Est); $3.06; publisher & editor Jennifer Craig; tel (915) 537-2251

Hearne: *The Hearne Democrat* — 112 3rd St.; PO Box 433 (77859); Th; 3,250pd, 45fr (Est); 80¢; C; publisher Chap Harriman; editor Michelle Harriman; tel (409) 279-3411; fax (409) 279-5401

Hebbronville: *Hebbronville Enterprise* — 308 E. Galbraith; PO Box 759 (78361); Th; 700pd, 400fr (Est); $4.00; publisher & editor Tony Salinas; managing editor Alfredo Cardenas; tel (512) 527-3261; fax (512) 527-4545

Hempstead/Waller: *The Waller County News-Citizen* — 905 12th St.; PO Box 556, Hempstead (77445); W; 2,450pd (Sw); $5.97; C; publisher & editor Jim Belew; tel (409) 826-3361; fax (409) 826-3360

Henrietta: *The Clay County Leader Inc.* — 114 W. Ikard; PO Box 10 (76365); Th; 3,074pd, 86fr (Est); $3.50; publisher & editor Phil Major; tel (817) 538-4333

Hico: *The Hico News-Review* — 109 W. 1st; PO Drawer D (76457); W; 600pd, 23fr (Sw); $2.25; publisher Cindy Outlaw; editor Laura Kestner; tel (817) 796-4325; fax (817) 796-2548

Highland Park/University Park: *Northside People* — 6116 N. Central Expy., Ste. 230, Dallas (75206); Th; 1,341pd, 17,410fr (VAC); $23.00; C; publisher & editor Raymond Wilkerson; managing editor Tom Boone; tel (214) 739-2244; fax (214) 363-6948

Highland Park/University Park: *Park Cities News* — 8115 Preston, Ste. 120 LB 10, Dallas (75225-6307); Th; 4,100pd, 3,700fr (Sw); $19.50; publisher & editor Marjorie B Waters; general manager Thomas R Waters; managing editor Peter H Waters; tel (214) 369-7570; fax (214) 369-7736

Highland Park/University Park: *Park Cities People* — 6116 N. Central Expy., Ste. 230, Dallas (75206); Th; 4,310pd, 2,197fr (VAC); $19.20; C; publisher & editor Raymond Wilkerson; managing editor Tom Boone; tel (214) 739-2244; fax (214) 363-6948

Highlands/Crosby: *The Highlands Star/Crosby Courier* — 210 Kernohan (77532); PO Box 405, Highlands (77562); Th; 898pd, 500fr (Sw); $4.00; publisher & editor Gilbert Hoffman; managing editor Theresa Lamson; tel (713) 266-3444; fax (713) 977-1188

Hillsboro: *The Reporter* — 335 Country Club Rd.; PO Box 569 (76645); M/Th; 5,140pd, 60fr (Sw); $5.90; publisher & editor Roger Galle; tel (817) 582-3431; fax (817) 582-3800

Hondo/Medina Co.: *Hondo Anvil Herald* — 1601 Ave. K; PO Box 400, Hondo (78861); Th; 3,917pd, 10fr (Sw); $5.00; C; publishers Jeff Berger & William E Berger; editor Frances Guinn; tel (210) 426-3346; fax (210) 426-3348

Honey Grove: *Honey Grove Signal Citizen* — 550 N. 6th; PO Box 300 (75446); F; 1,714pd, 62fr (Sw); $3.00; C; publisher Carl Ryser; general manager & managing editor Betty Ryser; editor Marita Nichols; tel (903) 378-2396; fax (903) 378-3926

Houston: *Houston Forward Times* — 4411 Almeda Rd.; PO Box 2962 (77001); W; 50,592pd, 1,035fr (Est); $14.28; C; publisher Lenora Carter; general manager Henrietta Smith; editor Bud Johnson; tel (713) 526-4727; fax (713) 526-3170

Houston: *Metro Weekender* — 4411 Almeda Rd.; PO Box 2962 (77001); F; 73,500fr (Est); $14.28; C; publisher Lenora Carter; general manager Henrietta Smith; editor Bud Johnson; tel (713) 526-4727; fax (713) 526-3170

Houston Co.: *Crockett Houston County Courier* — 102 S. 7th; PO Box 551, Crockett (75835); Th/Su; 5,604pd, 172fr (Sw); $4.15; C; publisher Bassett Keller; editor LaDeanne Smith; tel (409) 544-2238; fax (409) 544-4088

Howe: *The Howe Enterprise* — 106 E. Haning St.; PO Box 488 (75459-0488); Th; 657pd, 36fr (Sw); $3.75; publisher Dale Rideout; editor Lana Rideout; tel (903) 532-6012

Humble/Kingwood/Porter: *Humble Echo* — 20202 Highway 59; PO Box 2705, Humble (77338); W; 43,378fr (Est); $18.43; publisher Kelly Roberts; editor Norm Rowland; tel (713) 446-3733; fax (713) 446-0201

Hurst/Euless/Bedford/N Richland Hills/Watauga: *Mid-Cities News* — 1000 Ave. H E., Arlington (76011); Th/Su; 5,288pd, 1,913fr (CAC); $21.68; F; 1,913fr (Sw); $21.68; C; publisher Daniel L Crowe; editor L James Kunke; tel (817) 695-0560; fax (817) 695-0555

Idalou: *Idalou Beacon* — 818 Frontage Rd.; PO Box 887 (79329); Th; 493pd, 21fr (Sw); $2.90; publisher & editor Scott Luce; tel (806) 892-2233

Ingleside: *Ingleside Index* — 346 S. Houston St. (78336); PO Box 2100, Aransas Pass (78335); Th; 763pd, 55fr (Sw); $3.95; C; publisher Richard P Richards; editor John Lowman; tel (512) 758-5391; fax (512) 758-5393

Iowa Park: *Iowa Park Leader* — 112 W. Cash; PO Box 430 (76367); Th; 2,669pd (Est); $2.25; publisher & editor Bob Hamilton; tel (817) 592-4431; fax (817) 592-4431

Irving: *Irving News* — 1000 Ave. H E., Arlington (76011); Th/Su; 8,218pd, 3fr (CAC); $21.68; F; 10,800fr (Sw); $21.68; C; publisher Daniel L Crowe; editor Miles Moffeit; tel (817) 695-0500; fax (817) 695-0555

Jack Co.: *Jack County Herald* — 200 W. Belknap; PO Drawer 70, Jacksboro (76458); Th; 2,650pd (Est); $2.80; publisher Jim Gray; editor Craig Holamon; tel (817) 567-2616; fax (817) 567-2071

Jack Co.: *Jacksboro Gazette-News* — 200 W. Belknap; PO Drawer 70, Jacksboro (76458); M; 2,027pd, 54fr (Sw); $3.10; publisher James R Gray; tel (817) 567-2616; fax (817) 567-2071

Jackson Co.: *Jackson County Herald/Tribune* — 306 N. Wells; PO Box 8, Edna (77957); W; 4,248pd, 127fr (Sw); $5.75; publisher & editor Bert C West; tel (512) 782-3547; fax (512) 782-6002

Jasper: *The Jasper News-Boy* — 302 N. Wheeler St.; PO Box 1419 (75951-1419); W; 5,354pd, 31fr (Est); $6.71; Su; 8,300pd (Est); $4.20; publisher Willis Webb; editor Gary Hanlon; tel (409) 384-3441; fax (409) 384-8803

Jefferson: *Jefferson Jimplecute* — 205 W. Austin; PO Drawer J (75657); Th; 2,173pd, 8fr (Est); $3.70; publisher Joe Wayne Dennis; editor Lou Anne Suber; tel (903) 665-2462; fax (903) 665-3802

Jewett: *The Jewett Messenger* — Highway 79 & 2nd St.; PO Box 155 (75846); W; 1,676pd (Est); $3.00; publisher L D Pettey Jr; editor Carolyn Pettey; tel (903) 626-4296; fax (903) 626-4065

Johnson City: *The Record-Courier* — 205 Nugent; PO Box 205 (78636); Th; 1,408pd, 20fr (Est); $4.60; publisher & editor Robyn Henderson; tel (210) 868-7181; fax (210) 868-7182

Jones Co.: *Western Observer* — 1120 W. Court Plz., Anson (79501); Th; 1,520pd, 19fr (Est); 63¢; C; publisher & editor Donald Dawes; tel (915) 823-3253; fax (915) 823-3224

Joshua: *Joshua Tribune* — PO Box 1169 (76058); Th; 999pd, 35fr (Sw); $3.00; publisher James Moody; editor Don Eierdam; tel (817) 295-0486; fax (817) 295-5278

Junction: *The Junction Eagle* — 215 N. 6th St.; PO Box 226 (76849); W; 1,975pd (Sw); $4.00; publisher Whittemore Cooper; editor Roy Cooper; tel (915) 446-2610; fax (915) 446-4025

Karnes Co.: *Kenedy Advance-Times* — 110 S. Market St.; PO Box 129, Karnes City (78118); W; 1,953pd, 89fr (Est); $3.50; publisher & editor Bill DeFries; tel (210) 780-3924; fax (210) 780-3711

Karnes Co.: *The Karnes Citation* — 110 S. Market St.; PO Box 129, Karnes City (78118); W; 2,396pd, 44fr (Est); $3.50; publisher & editor Bill DeFries; tel (210) 780-3924; fax (210) 780-3711

Katy: *The Katy Times* — PO Box 678 (77492-0678); W/Su; 7,281pd, 517fr (VAC); $5.75; publisher Ken Steger; editor Dave Mundy; tel (713) 391-3141; fax (713) 391-2030

Kaufman: *The Kaufman Herald* — 300 N. Washington (75142); Th; 3,351pd (VAC); $6.90; publisher Bill Jordan; general manager Les Linebarger; editor Pam High; tel (214) 932-2171; fax (214) 932-2172

Keller/Roanoke: *The Keller Citizen* — 538 E. Price; PO Box 615, Keller (76244); Tu; 260pd, 13,863fr (Sw); $7.00; publisher William C Lewis; general manager Sandra S Lewis; editor Roy Kron; tel (817) 431-2231; fax (817) 431-2231

Kennedale: *The Kennedale News* — PO Box 406 (76060); Th; 383pd, 50fr (Sw); $4.40; C; publisher & editor Gene S Blessing; general manager William E Blessing; tel (817) 478-4661; fax (817) 483-0493

Kerens: *The Kerens Tribune* — PO Box 280 (75144); Th; 1,000pd (Sw); $2.77; publisher Don Dowdle; editor Loyd Cook; tel (903) 396-2261; fax (903) 396-2728

Kerrville/Kerr Co.: *The Mountain Sun* — 516 Quinlan St.; PO Box 1249, Kerrville (78028); W; 6,900pd (Sw); $4.90; publisher William H Williams; editor Lew Williams; managing editor Gary Taylor; tel (210) 257-3300; fax (210) 257-3329

Kingsville: *Kingsville Record and Bishop News* — PO Box 951 (78364-0951); W; 5,788pd (ABC); $5.75; Su; 6,249pd (ABC); $5.75; publisher & editor Bob Odom; tel (512) 592-4304; fax (512) 592-1015

Knox City: *Knox County News* — PO Box 9 (79529); Th; 1,147pd, 36fr (Sw); $3.50; publisher & editor Stacy Angle Thompson; tel (817) 658-3142; fax (817) 658-3142

Kress: *The Kress Chronicle* — Rte. 3 Box 4A (79052); Th; 340pd, 10fr (Sw); $2.75; publisher Kay Lyn Young; tel (806) 684-2637; fax (806) 684-2236

Kyle: *The Kyle Eagle* — Corner Stone Park, Corner of Railroad 12 & 3237 (Wimberly 78676); PO Box 1209 (78640); W; 2,887fr (Est); $5.59; publisher Mary Saunders; managing editor Harrell King; tel (512) 268-0562; fax (512) 847-9054

La Grange/Fayette Co.: *The Fayette County Record* — 127 S. Washington; PO Box 400, La Grange (78945); Tu/F; 5,966pd (Sw); $3.75; publisher & editor Richard L Barton Jr; tel (409) 968-3155; fax (409) 968-6767

La Marque/W Texas City: *La Marque Times/The Santa Fe Newspapers Inc.* — 1118 Bayou Rd.; PO Box 158, La Marque (77568); W; 2,700pd, 1,300fr (Sw); $5.85; C; publisher Harry Monych; editor Joanne Stephens; tel (409) 935-2431; fax (409) 925-1399

La Porte: *The Bay Shore Sun & Bayshore Sun Extra* — 1200 Highway 146 S., Ste. 180; PO Box 1414 (77572); W; 2,989pd, 7,300fr (Est); $6.25; Su; 2,989pd (Est); $4.10; publisher & editor John Black; tel (713) 471-1234; fax (713) 471-5763

La Vernia: *La Vernia News* — 128 E. Chihuahua; PO Box 129 (78121-0129); Th; 813pd, 69fr (Est); $3.25; publisher & editor Betsy Melenesk; tel (210) 779-3751; fax (210) 779-3751

Ladonia: *Ladonia News* — 550 N. 6th; PO Box 187 (75449-1321); F; 582pd, 53fr (Sw); $2.50; C; publisher Carl Ryser; editor Marita Nichols; managing editor Betty Ryser; tel (214) 977-8222

Lake Dallas/Corinth: *Lake Cities Sun* — 275 Market St.; PO Box 879, Lake Dallas (75065); W; 826pd, 413fr (Sw); $5.00; publisher Terry Lantrip; editor Cliff Gaines; tel (817) 497-4141

Lake Jackson/Clute: *The Brazorian News* — PO Box 98, Lake Jackson (77566); Su; 3,000pd (Est); $6.00; publisher Tommy Anderson; editor Bob White; tel (409) 297-6512; fax (409) 297-3451

Lamesa: *Lamesa Press-Reporter* — 523 N. 1st St.; PO Box 710 (79331); W/Su; 4,093pd, 59fr (Sw); $3.35; publisher & editor Russel Skiles; tel (806) 872-2177; fax (806) 872-2623

Lampasas Co.: *Lampasas Dispatch Record* — 416 S. Live Oak St.; PO Box 631, Lampasas (76550); M/Th; 3,462pd, 223fr (Sw); $5.18; publisher Fred Lowe; editor Jim Lowe; tel (512) 556-6262; fax (512) 556-3278

Lancaster: *Lancaster Today* — 1701 N. Hampton (75115); PO Box 381029, Duncanville (75138-1029); Th; 2,320pd, 1,730fr (Sw); $6.70; C; publisher Richard Collins; editor Chuck Blum; managing editor Mark Victry; tel (214) 298-4211; fax (214) 298-6369

Las Colinas: *Las Colinas Business News* — 1000 Ave. H E., Arlington (76011); Th; 8,846fr (Sw); $21.68; C; publisher Daniel L Crowe; editor Miles Moffeit; tel (817) 695-0500; fax (817) 695-0555

Lavaca Co.: *Lavaca County Tribune-Herald* — 108 S. Texana St.; PO Box 427, Hallettsville (77964); W; 4,050pd (Est); $4.00; publisher Larry Rothbauer; editor Henry Jasek; tel (512) 798-2481; fax (512) 798-9902

Leakey: *Real American* — PO Box 1140 (78873); W; 15,000pd, 100fr (Est); $3.95; publisher & editor Patricia Thurmond; tel (210) 232-5204; fax (210) 232-5630

Leonard: *The Leonard Graphic* — 121 W. Fannin St.; PO Box A (75452); Th; 1,150pd, 20fr (Est); $1.63; publishers & editors David Johnson & Jeannie Johnson; tel (903) 587-3303

Levelland: *Levelland & Hockley County News-Press* — 711 Austin St.; PO Drawer 1628 (79336); W/Su; 4,547pd, 74fr (Sw); $5.25; publisher & editor Stephen A Henry; tel (806) 894-3121; fax (806) 894-7957

Lewisville/Flower Mound/Highland Vlg.: *Lewisville News* — 131 W. Main St.; PO Box 639, Lewisville (75067); W/F/Su; 456pd, 20,950fr (Sw); $7.55; C; publisher Fred Patterson; editor Dawn E Cobb; managing editor Tom Bateman; tel (214) 436-5551; fax (214) 436-6849

Liberty/Dayton: *The Liberty Vindicator* — 301 Vera Ln.; PO Box 9189, Liberty (77575); W/Su; 3,430pd, 867fr (Sw); $6.70; publisher & editor Ernie E Zieschang; managing editor Britt Hall; tel (409) 336-3611; fax (409) 336-3345

Lindale/Hide-A-Way Lake: *The Lindale News* — 401 S. Main St.; PO Box 187, Lindale (75771); Th; 2,164pd, 43fr (Sw); $4.00; publisher Tom Boone; editor Janet Ragland; tel (903) 882-3232; fax (903) 882-8194

Linden: *Cass County Sun* — 306 W. Main St.; PO Box 920 (75563); W; 650pd, 9fr (Est); $5.13; C; publisher William R Owney; editor Melody Brunble; tel (903) 756-7396; fax (903) 796-3038

Lipscomb Co.: *Lipscomb County Limelight* — 301 S. Main; PO Box 248, Follett (79034); W; 1,000pd (Est); 15¢; publisher & editor Terri Martin; tel (806) 653-2871; fax (806) 653-2631

Littlefield: *Lamb County Leader News* — 313 W. 4th St.; PO Box 310 (79339); W/Su; 2,362pd, 75fr (Sw); $5.00; publishers Pat Henry & Stephen A Henry; editor Joella Lovvorn; tel (806) 385-4481; fax (806) 385-4640

Livingston/Rock Co.: *Polk County Enterprise* — 100 Calhoun St.; PO Box 1276, Livingston (77351); Th/Su; 7,361pd, 47fr (Est); 30¢; publisher Alvin Holley; editor Barbara White; tel (409) 327-4357; fax (409) 327-7156

Llano Co.: *The Llano News* — 813 Berry; PO Box 187, Llano (78643); Th; 3,061pd, 47fr (Sw); $4.40; publisher & editor Walter L Buckner; general manager Jimmy Stevenson; tel (915) 247-4433; fax (915) 247-4433

Lockhart: *Lockhart Post-Register* — 111 S. Church St.; PO Box 929 (78644); Th; 3,875pd, 20fr (Sw); $5.50; publisher Dana Garrett; editor Annie Dahel; tel (512) 398-4886; fax (512) 398-4888

Lockney/Floyd Co./Floydada: *The Floyd County Hesperian Beacon* — 111 E. Missouri St., Floydada (79235); Th; 2,555pd, 23fr (Est); $2.80; publisher & editor Alice Towery Gilroy; tel (806) 983-3737

Luling: *The Luling Newsboy and Signal* — 415 E. Davis St.; PO Box 352 (78648); Th; 1,846pd, 36fr (Sw); $4.00; publisher & editor Karen G McCrary; tel (210) 875-2116; fax (210) 875-2124

Mabank/Gunbarrel City/Eustace/Kemp/Tool/Seven Points/Payne Springs/Malakoff/Trinidad: *The Monitor/Leader* — 1316 S. 3rd St.; PO Box 48, Mabank (75147); Th/Su; 5,600pd (Sw); $5.45; C; publisher Charlotte Whitaker; general manager Jim McKee; editor Janice Arnsdorff; tel (903) 887-4511; fax (903) 887-4510

Madisonville: *Madisonville Meteor* — 205 N. Madison; PO Box 999 (77864); W; 3,259pd, 40fr (Sw); $4.41; publisher & editor Edna Keasling; tel (409) 348-3505; fax (409) 348-3338

Malakoff/Trinidad/Caney City/Cross Roads/Star Harbor/Cayuga/Payne Springs/Eustacek/Gunbarrel City/Seven Points/Tool/Kemp/Mabank: *The Malakoff News* — 103 S. Terry; PO Box 509, Malakoff (75148); Th; 1,600pd (Est); $4.00; publisher Loretta Humble; editor Mike Hannigan; tel (903) 489-0531; fax (903) 489-2543

Mansfield/S Arlington: *Mansfield News-Mirror* — 119 N. Main; PO Box 337, Mansfield (76063-0337); M/Th; 3,950pd, 50fr (Sw); $5.50; publisher & editor Jerry T Ebensberger; tel (817) 473-4451; fax (817) 473-0730

Marble Falls: *Burnet Bulletin* — 101 E. Jackson; PO Box 160, Burnet (78611); W; 3,733pd, 14fr (Sw); $5.00; C; general manager Darin Brock; tel (512) 756-6136; fax (512) 756-8911

Marble Falls: *The Highlander* — 208 Main; PO Box 1000 (78654); Tu/F; 5,879pd, 14fr (Sw); $6.00; C; publisher Ron Prince; managing editor Billy Berkenbile; tel (210) 693-4367; fax (210) 693-3650

Marfa/Presidio/Alpine/Ft. Davis: *The Big Bend Sentinel* — 110 N. Highland; PO Box P, Marfa (79843); Th; 2,334pd, 5fr (Sw); $2.75; C; publisher & editor Robert L Halpern; general manager Rosario Salgado Halpern; managing editor Teresa Salgado; tel (915) 729-4342; fax (915) 729-4601

Mart: *Mart Texan* — 514 Texas Ave.; PO Box 150 (76664); Th; 2,500pd (Est); $1.25; publisher & editor Thomas Hawkins; tel (817) 876-3808

Mason Co.: *Mason County News* — 110 Live Oak; PO Drawer Q, Mason (76856); W; 2,638pd, 5fr (Sw); $3.00; C; publisher & editor G W Lyon; tel (915) 347-5757; fax (915) 347-5668

Mathis: *The Mathis News* — 620 E. San Patricio (78368); Th; 1,970pd, 35fr (Est); $5.10; C; publishers James F Tracy Jr & John H Tracy; editor Charles E Sullivan; tel (512) 547-3274; fax (512) 547-3275

McAllen/Edinburg/Mission: *Valley Town Crier* — 1811 N. 23rd St., McAllen (78501); W; 100,145fr (Sw); $19.50; C; publisher Mike McKinney; editor Alma Navarro; tel (210) 682-2423; fax (210) 631-6371

McCamey: *McCamey News* — 520 Burleson; PO Drawer E (79752); Th; 965pd, 50fr (Est); $3.31; publisher & editor Wayne Greer; tel (915) 652-3312; fax (915) 652-8995

McGregor: *McGregor Mirror & Crawford Sun* — 311 S. Main St.; PO Box 415 (76657-0415); Th; 2,086pd, 7fr (Sw); 21¢; publisher Bonnie Mullens; publisher & editor Charles Mooney; publisher Mynette Taylor; tel (817) 840-2091

McLean: *The McLean News* — 210 N. Main (79057); Th; 1,179pd, 14fr (Sw); $1.32; publisher Phillip J Miller; editor Charlotte Whattey; tel (806) 779-2141

Memphis: *Memphis Democrat* — 617 Main; PO Box 190 (79245); Th; 2,000pd, 65fr (Est); $2.80; publisher & editor Billy A Combs; tel (806) 259-2441; fax (806) 259-2441

Menard: *Menard News & Messenger* — 220 Gay St.; PO Box 248 (76859); Th; 1,266pd (Sw); $3.25; publisher Dan Feather Jr; editor Dorothy Kerns; tel (915) 396-2243

Mercedes: *The Mercedes Enterprise* — 230 S. Texas Ave.; PO Box 657 (78570); W; 1,724pd, 6fr (Sw); $3.80; publisher & editor Robert Hinds; tel (210) 565-2425; fax (210) 565-2570

Merkel: *The Merkel Mail* — 910 N. 1st St.; PO Box 428 (79536); W; 1,545pd, 20fr (Est); $3.00; publisher & editor Cloy A Richards; publisher Melanie Richards; tel (915) 928-5712; fax (915) 928-5712

Miami/Roberts Co.: *The Miami Chief* — 401 E. Commercial St.; PO Box 396, Miami (79059-0396); Th; 606pd, 20fr (Sw); $2.82; publisher Clarence Traughber; publisher & editor Valda Traughber; tel (806) 868-2521; fax (806) 868-5381

Midlothian: *Midlothian Today* — 1701 N. Hampton (75115), Duncanville (75138-1029); Th; 1,153pd (Sw); $4.25; C; publisher Richard Collins; editor Tracey Layton; managing editor Mark Victry; tel (214) 298-4211; fax (214) 298-6369

Midlothian: *The Midlothian Mirror* — 214 W. Ave. F; PO Box 70 (76065); Th; 1,743pd, 157fr (Est); $3.50; publisher Barham Alderdice; editor Sunny Alderdice; tel (214) 775-3322

Miles: *Miles Messenger* — 104 Robinson St.; PO Box 307 (76861); Th; 542pd, 10fr (Sw); $3.50; publisher & editor Donna Glass; tel (915) 468-3611

Mineola: *Mineola Monitor* — 130 E. Broad; PO Box 210 (75773); W; 2,727pd, 33fr (Sw); $5.70; C; publisher Bill Woodall; editor Doris Newman; tel (903) 569-2442; fax (903) 569-9201

Mission/Hidalgo: *Progress Times* — 1217 N. Conway; PO Box 353, Mission (78572); W; 2,910pd, 1,978fr (Sw); $9.00; C; publisher & editor June K Brann; general manager James Brunson; tel (210) 585-4893; fax (210) 585-2304

Missouri City: *Fort Bend Mirror* — PO Box 1267, Sugarland (77487); W; 5,801pd, 223fr (Est); 22¢; Th; 2,700pd (Est); $4.00; publisher Clyde King; editor Cheryl Skinner; tel (713) 242-9104; fax (713) 342-3219

Monahans: *Monahans News* — 107 W. 2nd; PO Box 767 (79756); Th; 3,947pd, 53fr (Sw); $4.00; C; publisher & editor Pearson Cooper; tel (915) 943-4313; fax (915) 943-4314

Moody/Bruceville/Eddy: *The Moody Courier* — 827 S. Highway 317; PO Box 38, Moody (76557); Th; 865pd, 35fr (Sw); $3.50; publisher Bill C Foster; general manager & editor Anna Belle Madson; tel (817) 853-2801; fax (817) 853-2819

Moore Co.: *The Moore County News-Press* — 7th & Meredith Sts.; PO Box 757, Dumas (79029); Th/Su; 4,791pd, 209fr (Sw); $5.70; C; publisher & editor Mike Coggins; managing editor Todd Hepler; tel (806) 935-4111; fax (806) 935-2348

Morton/Whiteface/Bledsoe/Maple/Enochs: *Morton Tribune* — 107 N.W. 1st; PO Box 1016, Morton (79346); Th; 972pd (Sw); $3.25; publisher David Sahlin; editor Sherrill Taylor Sahlin; tel (806) 266-5576

Moulton: *The Moulton Eagle* — 208B Westmoore St.; PO Box G (77975); Th; 1,350pd (Est); $2.80; publisher Bob Anderson; editor Dianna Polaske; tel (512) 596-4871; fax (512) 596-4871

Mt. Enterprise: *Mount Enterprise Progress* — PO Drawer 250 (75681); F; 493pd, 19fr (Est); 90¢; publisher & editor Mrs Joe R Compton; tel (903) 822-3511

Mt. Vernon/Franklin Co.: *Mt. Vernon Optic-Herald* — 106 S. Kaufman St.; PO Drawer H, Mount Vernon (75457); Th; 2,982pd, 10fr (Sw); $4.00; publisher Robert W Wright; editor Lillie Cates Bush; managing editor Pat Wright; tel (903) 537-2228; fax (903) 537-2227

Muenster/Lindsay: *Muenster Enterprise* — 117 E. 1st; PO Box 190, Muenster (76252); F; 1,866pd, 55fr (Sw); $4.60; publisher & editor Dave Fette; tel (817) 759-4311; fax (817) 759-4110

Muleshoe: *Bailey County Journal* — 304 W. 2nd; PO Box 449 (79347); Su; 2,075pd, 150fr (Sw); $3.30; publisher Scot Stinnett; general manager Lisa Stinnett; editor Rick White; tel (806) 272-4536

Muleshoe: *Muleshoe Journal* — 304 W. 2nd; PO Box 449 (79347); Th; 2,075pd, 150fr (Sw); $3.30; publisher Scot Stinnett; general manager Lisa Stinnett; editor Rick White; tel (806) 272-4536

Munday: *Munday Courier* — 111 E. B St.; PO Box 130 (76371-0130); W; 1,285pd, 39fr (Sw); $3.50; publisher Michael L Waggoner; editor Cynthia White; tel (817) 422-4314; fax (817) 422-4314

Naples/Omaha: *The Monitor* — 207 Main St.; PO Box 39, Naples (75568-0039); W; 2,000pd, 36fr (Sw); $3.78; publisher & editor Morris G Craig; tel (903) 897-2281; fax (903) 897-2095

Navasota/Grimes Co.: *The Navasota Examiner* — 115 Railroad St.; PO Box 751, Navasota (77868-0751); Th; 5,341pd, 85fr (Sw); $4.75; publisher & editor Clark J Whitten; publisher Robert H Whitten; tel (409) 825-6484; fax (409) 825-2230

Needville: *Gulf Coast Tribune* — 3115 School St.; PO Box 488 (77461); Th; 1,194pd, 67fr (Sw); $3.20; publisher & editor David E Toney; tel (409) 793-6560; fax (409) 793-4260

New Ulm: *The New Ulm Enterprise* — Highway 109 St.; PO Box 128 (78950); Th; 1,274pd, 12fr (Est); 15¢; publisher & editor Raymond L Dungen Jr; tel (409) 992-3351; fax (409) 992-3352

Newton Co.: *Newton County News* — 112 Coutmail; PO Box 65, Newton (75966); Th; 2,400pd, 4,100fr (Sw); $4.00; C; publisher & editor Glenn A Mitchell; tel (409) 379-2416; fax (409) 379-2416

Nocona: *Nocona News* — 104 E. Walnut; PO Box 539 (76255); Th; 2,653pd, 56fr (Sw); 24¢; publishers & editors Linda Mesler & Tracy Mesler; tel (817) 825-3201

Normangee: *The Normangee Star* — 100 W. Main; PO Box 249 (77871); Th; 1,184pd, 75fr (Sw); $2.94; publisher Bille G Bouldin; editor Patrick Martin; tel (409) 396-3391; fax (409) 396-6651

NW Houston: *The Leader* — 3500A E. TC Jester; PO Box 924487, Houston (77292); W; 83,427fr (CAC); $1.18; C; publisher Terry Burge; editor Diane Hess; tel (713) 686-8494; fax (713) 686-0970

O'Donnell: *O'Donnell Index-Press* — 702 8th St.; PO Box 457 (79351); W; 550pd, 20fr (Sw); $5.00; C; publisher & editor Stephanie Stephens; tel (806) 428-3591

Odem: *The Odem-Edroy Times* — PO Drawer B, Sinton (78387); Th; 560pd, 30fr (Sw); $4.25; C; publishers James F Tracy Jr & John H Tracy; editor Jim Mc Elhaney; tel (512) 364-1270; fax (512) 364-3833

Olney: *The Olney Enterprise* — 213 E. Main; PO Box 577 (76374); Th; 2,497pd, 19fr (Sw); $2.80; publisher & editor David H Penn; tel (817) 564-5558

Olton: *Olton Enterprise* — 716 Main St.; PO Drawer E (79064); Su; 1,100pd, 70fr (Sw); $3.25; publisher & editor Sue Cannon; tel (806) 285-2631

Orange Co.: *Opportunity Valley News* — 200 W. Front; PO Box 1028, Orange (77630); W; 23,000fr (Sw); $8.57; C; publisher Jan Bronley; editor Belinda Dyer; tel (409) 883-3571; fax (409) 883-6342

Overton/New London/Arp: *The Overton Press* — 120 E. Henderson St.; PO Box 99, Overton (75684); Th; 1,913pd, 35fr (Sw); $4.75; publisher & editor Molly Zimmerman; tel (903) 834-6178; fax (903) 834-6179

Ozona: *Ozona Stockman* — 1000 Avenue E.; PO Box 370 (76943); W; 1,755pd, 15fr (Est); 23¢; publisher John S Moore; editor Linda Moore; tel (915) 392-2551; fax (915) 392-2439

Paducah: *The Paducah Post* — 819 9th St.; PO Drawer E (79248); Tu; 1,595pd, 14fr (Est); $2.99; publisher & editor Jimmye C Taylor; tel (806) 492-3585; fax (806) 492-3585

Paint Rock: *The Concho Herald* — 104 Robinson St.; PO Box 307, Miles (76861-0307); Th; 128pd (Sw); $3.50; publisher & editor Donna Glass; tel (915) 468-3611

Palacios: *Palacios Beacon* — 453 Commerce; PO Box 817 (77465); W; 1,652pd, 26fr (Sw); $4.00; publisher & editor Nicholas M West; tel (512) 972-3009; fax (512) 972-2610

Panhandle: *Panhandle Herald* — 319 Main St.; PO Box 429 (79068); Th; 1,235pd, 39fr (Sw); 18¢; publishers Jean Miller & Joseph J Miller; editor Betty N Biggs; managing editor Donna Huff; tel (806) 537-3634; fax (806) 537-3780

Parker Co.: *Moneysaver* — 512 Palo Pinto St., Weatherford (76086); Tu; 25,000fr (Est); $6.75; C; publisher Jane Ramos Trimble; editor Tim Wood; tel (817) 594-7447; fax (817) 594-9734

Pearland: *Pearland Journal* — 2206 E. Broadway, Ste. A; PO Box 1830 (77588); W; 2,940pd, 60fr (Est); $4.24; C; publisher Ron Gervais; editor Michael Smith; tel (713) 485-2785; fax (713) 485-4464

Pearland/Alvin: *Pearland Reporter News* — 2404 S. Park, Pearland (77581); W; 2,000pd, 8,000fr (Sw); $4.25; C; publisher & managing editor Laura Emmons; general manager Linda Knight; editor Joan Cummings; tel (713) 485-7501; fax (713) 485-6397

Pearsall/Dilley/Cotulla: *Frio-Nueces Current* — 220 S. Oak; PO Box 1208, Pearsall (78061); Th; 4,260pd, 75fr (Sw); $4.75; publisher William E Dozier Jr; editor Joseph E Casanova; tel (210) 334-3644; fax (210) 334-3647

Perryton: *The Perryton Herald* — 401 S. Amber St.; PO Box 989 (79070); Th/Su; 3,311pd, 108fr (Sw); $3.60; publisher Jim Hudson; editor Mary H Dudley; tel (806) 435-3631; fax (806) 435-2420

Petersburg: *Petersburg Post* — 1520 Main St.; PO Box 248 (79250); F; 639pd, 32fr (Sw); $3.00; publisher & editor Chris Pierson; tel (806) 667-3841; fax (806) 667-3619

Pharr: *The Advance News* — 1101 N. Cage Blvd., Twin Palms Plz., Ste. 1C (78577); W; 8,309pd, 5,000fr (Sw); $7.25; publisher & editor Greg Wendorf; tel (210) 783-0036; fax (210) 787-8824

Pittsburg: *The Pittsburg Gazette* — 112 Quitman St. (75686); Th; 2,759pd, 33fr (Sw); $5.72; C; publisher Debbie Knox; editor Susan Taft; tel (903) 856-6629; fax (903) 856-0510

Pleasanton: *Pleasanton Express* — 114 Goodwin; PO Drawer 880 (78064); W; 7,901pd, 80fr (Est); $7.15; C; publishers Bill Wilkerson & Judy Wilkerson; managing editor David Wilkerson; tel (210) 569-2341; fax (210) 569-6100

Port Aransas/Mustang Island: *Port Aransas South Jetty* — 141 W. Cotter; PO Box 1116, Port Aransas (78373); Th; 3,907pd, 85fr (Sw); $5.50; publisher & editor Mary Judson; publisher & general manager Murray Judson; tel (512) 749-5131; fax (512) 749-5137

Port Isabel/S Padre Island: *Port Isabel-South Padre Press* — 101 Maxan; PO Box 308, Port Isabel (78578); M/Th; 4,438pd, 99fr (Sw); $4.65; C; publisher Ben Brooks; managing editor David Hamerly; tel (210) 943-5545; fax (210) 943-4782

Port Lavaca/Calhoun Co.: *The Calhoun County Wave Extra* — 107 E. Austin; PO Box 88, Port Lavaca (77979); W; 4,000fr (Sw); $3.75; C; publisher & editor Steve Bales; tel (512) 552-9788; fax (512) 552-3108

Port Neches/Nederland/Groves/Port Arthur: *Mid County Chronicle* — 2112 Nederland Ave.; PO Box 2140, Nederland (77627); W; 230pd, 25,203fr (Sw); $9.84; publisher John Butters; editor Regina Throp; tel (409) 722-0479; fax (409) 729-7626

Portland/Gregory: *Portland News* — 101 Cedar Pl., Ste. G, Portland (78374); Th; 2,500pd, 50fr (Sw); $5.95; C; publishers James F Tracy Jr & John H Tracy; editor Rusty Weller; tel (512) 643-1566; fax (512) 364-3833

Post: *The Post Dispatch* — 123 E. Main (79356); Th; 1,645pd, 55fr (Est); $4.00; publisher & editor Wesley W Burnett; tel (806) 495-2816; fax (806) 495-2059

Pottsboro/Grayson Co.: *Pottsboro Press* — 706 Highway 120 N.; PO Box 837, Pottsboro (75076-0837); W; 1,853pd, 5fr (Sw); $3.45; publishers Bob Conary & Lori Conary; editor Melissa Hill; tel (903) 786-4051; fax (903) 786-9336

Princeton: *Princeton Herald* — 101 S. Main, Farmersville (75407); Th; 1,040pd, 60fr (Sw); $3.00; publisher Robert Harty Jr; editor Bob Poole; tel (214) 736-6311; fax (214) 782-7023

Quanah: *Tribune-Chief* — 310 Mercer St. (79252); Th/Su; 1,320pd, 5fr (Sw); $2.50; publisher Larry L Crabtree; editor Carol Whitmire; tel (817) 663-5333; fax (817) 663-5073

Quitaque/Turkey: *The Valley Tribune* — 44B Main St.; PO Box 478, Quitaque (79255); Th; 865pd, 20fr (Sw); $2.45; C; publisher Jimmye C Taylor; editor Eunice McFall; tel (806) 455-1101; fax (806) 455-1222

Quitman: *Wood County Democrat* — 111 W. Lipscomb; PO Box 308 (75783); W; 4,300pd, 100fr (Est); $5.40; C; publisher Nell French; tel (903) 763-4522; fax (903) 763-2313

Ranger/Eastland Co.: *Ranger Times* — 211 Elm St.; PO Box 118, Ranger (76470); Th/Su; 766pd, 23fr (Est); $3.00; publisher Houston V O'Brien; editor Sheila McCoy; tel (817) 647-1101; fax (817) 629-2092

Rankin: *Rankin News* — 815 Grand (79778); Th; 710pd (Sw); 14¢; publisher Katie Hutchens; editor Hal Hutchens; tel (915) 693-2873; fax (915) 693-2873

Raymondville/Willacy Co.: *Raymondville Chronicle & Willacy County News* — 192 N. 4th St.; PO Box 369, Raymondville (78580); W; 3,005pd, 20fr (Sw); $8.40; publisher & editor Paul E Whitworth; general manager Edie Whitworth; managing editor Mark Whitworth; tel (210) 689-2421; fax (210) 689-6575

Refugio Co.: *Refugio County Advantage Press* — 412 N. Alamo; PO Drawer 200, Refugio (78377-0200); W; 2,595pd, 24fr (Sw); $4.40; publisher & editor Martha Lamson; tel (512) 526-2397; fax (512) 526-2398

Richardson: *Richardson News* — 409 Belle Grove, Ste. 101 (75080); Th/Su; 6,823pd, 496fr (CAC); $21.68; F; 7,319fr (Sw); $21.68; C; publisher Daniel L Crowe; editor Lois Brown; tel (214) 234-3199; fax (214) 234-6906

U.S. Weeklies **Texas** **II-77**

Riesel: *Riesel Rustler* — 412 S. 16th St. (Waco 76706); PO Box 100 (76682); F; 934pd (Sw); $2.10; publisher Roger Jones; editor Norman S White Jr; tel (817) 896-2311; fax (817) 753-3884

Rio Grande City: *Rio Grande Herald* — 109-A N. Britton Ave.; PO Box 452, Rio Grande (78882); Th; 2,750pd (Sw); 18¢; publisher Pearl A Mathis; general manager Rosie M Briseno; editor Kenneth Roberts; tel (210) 487-2819; fax (210) 383-3172

Rising Star: *The Rising Star* — 105 N. Main St.; PO Box 129 (76471-0127); Th; 778pd, 96fr (Sw); $42.00; C; publisher Houston V O'Brien; editor Elaine Coleman; tel (817) 643-4141; fax (817) 629-2092

Robert Lee/Bronte: *The Observer Enterprise* — 707 Austin; PO Box 1329, Robert Lee (76945); F; 1,553pd, 32fr (Sw); 15¢; publisher Hal Spain; editor Joan Davis; managing editor JoNell Blair; tel (915) 453-2433; fax (915) 453-4643

Rochester/Rule: *Twin Cities News* — 207 4th St.; PO Box 280, Rochester (79544); Th; 772pd, 17fr (Sw); $2.50; publisher & editor Patsy Rogers; tel (817) 743-3322; fax (817) 743-3322

Rockdale/Thorndale/Milano/Lexington: *The Rockdale Reporter & Messenger* — 221-225 E. Cameron Ave.; PO Box 552, Rockdale (76567-2972); Th; 4,433pd, 129fr (Sw); $4.50; publisher & editor J W Cooke; tel (512) 446-5838; fax (512) 446-5317

Rockport: *Rockport Pilot* — 1002 Wharf St.; PO Box 730 (78382); W/Sa; 4,100pd (Est); $5.20; publisher Mike Provst; editor Mary Hoekstra; tel (512) 729-9900; fax (512) 729-8903

Rocksprings/Edwards Co.: *The Texas Mohair Weekly* — 411 Well; PO Box 287, Rocksprings (78880); Th; 881pd, 25fr (Sw); $4.00; publishers & editors Carolyn Anderson & O D Anderson; tel (210) 683-3130

Rockwall/Royse City/Heath: *The Rockwall Journal-Success* — 114 N. San Jacinto St.; PO Box 127, Rockwall (75087); Tu/F; 3,521pd, 223fr (Sw); $5.25; publisher Glen Smith; editor William O Cawley; tel (214) 722-5191; fax (214) 722-6920

Roma/Star: *The South Texas Reporter* — 101 La Fragua St.; PO Drawer 1005, Roma (78584); Th; 3,400pd (Est); $3.50; publisher Arnulfo Guerra; general manager Elena V Guerrero; editor Raul Guerra; tel (210) 849-1757; fax (210) 849-1757

Rosebud/Lott: *The Rosebud News* — 331 Main St.; PO Box 516, Rosebud (76570); Th; 2,128pd, 61fr (Sw); $3.50; publishers Jack C Killgore & John R Killgore; editor Andrea K Macal; tel (817) 583-7811; fax (817) 583-4000

Round Rock: *Round Rock Leader* — 105 S. Blair; PO Box 459 (78680-0459); M/Th; 5,309pd, 401fr (Sw); $5.80; C; publisher Kenneth H Long; editor Will Hampton; tel (512) 255-5827; fax (512) 255-3733

Rowena: *Rowena Press* — 104 Robinson St.; PO Box 307, Miles (76861-0307); Th; 73pd (Sw); $2.30; publisher & editor Donna Glass; tel (915) 468-3611

Rusk/Alto/Wells: *Cherokeean/Herald* — 618 N. Main St.; PO Box 475, Rusk (75785); Th; 3,325pd, 35fr (Sw); $4.00; publisher E H Whitehead; editor Marie Whitehead; tel (903) 683-2257; fax (903) 683-5104

Sabinal/E Uvalde Co.: *The Sabinal Sampler* — 1601 Ave. K; PO Box 400, Hondo (78861); W; 800fr (Sw); $6.00; C; publishers Jeff Berger & William E Berger; tel (210) 426-3346; fax (210) 426-3348

Sabine Co.: *Sabine County Reporter* — 211 Worth St.; PO Box 700, Hemphill (75948); W; 3,249pd, 53fr (Sw); $3.95; publisher & editor Stephanie Corley; tel (409) 787-2172; fax (409) 787-4300

St. Jo: *The Saint Jo Tribune* — 105 Howell; PO Drawer 160 (76265); Th; 832pd, 51fr (Sw); $2.50; publisher Rebecca Smith; editor C E Cole; managing editor Dee Cole; tel (817) 995-2586

San Antonio: *North San Antonio Recorder-Times* — 8603 Botts Ln.; PO Box 17947 (78217); Th; 83,700fr (Est); $23.00; publisher Bob Jones; editor Steve Henry; tel (210) 828-3321; fax (210) 828-3787

San Antonio: *North San Antonio Times* — 8603 Botts Ln.; PO Box 17947 (78217); Th; 10,100pd (Est); $13.50; publisher Bob Jones; editor Steve Henry; tel (210) 828-3321; fax (210) 828-3787

San Augustine Co.: *San Augustine Tribune* — 315 W. Columbia St.; PO Drawer M, San Augustine (75972); Th; 4,874pd, 70fr (Sw); $3.25; publisher & editor Arlan Hays; tel (409) 275-2181

San Benito: *San Benito News* — 356 N. Sam Houston; PO Box 1791 (78586); W/Su; 4,787pd, 200fr (Sw); $4.65; C; publisher Jim Elam; managing editor Martha McClain; tel (210) 399-2436; fax (210) 233-9604

San Saba Co.: *The San Saba News & Star* — 505 E. Wallace; PO Box 815, San Saba (76877); Th; 2,394pd, 70fr (Sw); $3.87; C; publisher Donald Sloan; editor Wahnee Stallings; tel (915) 372-5115; fax (915) 372-3973

Sanderson: *Sanderson Times* — 124 W. Oak; PO Box 748 (79848); Th; 1,000pd, 25fr (Est); $2.00; publisher & editor J A Gilbreath; tel (915) 345-2442; fax (915) 345-2442

Sanger: *Sanger Courier* — 201 S. Stemmons; PO Box 68 (76266); Th; 1,689pd (Est); 29¢; publisher Roy L Lemons; editor Blake Lemons; tel (817) 458-7429; fax (817) 458-3691

Santa Anna: *Santa Anna News* — PO Box 399 (76878); Th; 927pd, 20fr (Sw); $2.65; publisher & editor Polly Warnock; tel (915) 348-3545

Schulenburg: *The Schulenburg Sticker* — 405 N. Main St.; PO Box 160 (78956-0160); Th; 2,876pd, 37fr (Sw); $4.00; publisher Maxine Vyvjala; editor Diane Prause; managing editor Darrell Vyvjala; tel (409) 743-3450; fax (409) 743-4609

Seagraves: *Gaines County News* — 206 Main St.; PO Box 815 (79359); Th; 998pd, 20fr (Sw); $2.75; C; publisher & editor Linda Ayres; tel (806) 546-2320

Sealy: *Sealy News* — 111 Main St.; PO Box 480 (77474); Th; 4,231pd, 44fr (Sw); $4.20; C; publisher Jim Grimes; editor Wilma Petrusek; tel (409) 885-3562; fax (409) 885-3562

Seminole: *Seminole Sentinel* — 406 S. Main St.; PO Box 1200 (79360); W/Su; 2,035pd, 20fr (Sw); $3.36; publisher M Gene Dow; editor Dave J Fisher; tel (915) 758-3667; fax (915) 758-2136

Seymour: *Baylor County Banner* — 109 E. Morris St.; PO Box 912 (76380); Th; 2,308pd, 26fr (Sw); $3.30; publisher & editor Earl Gwinn; tel (817) 888-2616; fax (817) 888-3610

Shamrock: *The Shamrock Texan* — 115 N. Main St.; PO Box 589 (79079); Th; 1,760pd, 60fr (Sw); $3.26; publisher & editor Kip Pease; tel (806) 256-2131; fax (806) 256-5403

Shepherd/Coldspring: *San Jacinto News-Times* — PO Box 237, Shepherd (77371); Th; 1,859pd, 17fr (Sw); $16.00; publisher Alvin Holley; editor Martha Charrey; tel (409) 628-6851; fax (409) 327-7156

Shiner: *The Shiner Gazette* — 713 N. Ave. D; PO Box 727 (77984); Th; 2,689pd, 69fr (Sw); $4.75; publisher L M (Buddy) Preuss III; general manager Robert Anderson; editor Myra Lampley; managing editor Agnes Sedlmeyer; tel (512) 594-3346; fax (512) 594-3346

Silsbee/Lumbertown/Fred: *The Silsbee Bee* — 410 Highway 96 S.; PO Box 547, Silsbee (77656); Th; 6,220pd, 326fr (Sw); $4.70; publisher & editor Danny Reneau; general manager Janet Reneau; tel (409) 385-5278; fax (409) 385-5270

Sinton: *San Patricio County News* — 113-117 S. Rachal; PO Drawer B (78387-0167); Th; 2,010pd, 50fr (Sw); $5.95; C; publisher & editor James F Tracy Jr; publisher John H Tracy; tel (512) 364-1270; fax (512) 364-3833

Slaton: *The Slatonite* — 139 S. 9th; PO Box 667 (79364-0667); Th; 2,350pd, 25fr (Sw); $3.60; publisher & editor James R Davis Jr; tel (806) 828-6201; fax (806) 828-6202

Smithville: *Smithville Times* — 303 Main St.; PO Box 659 (78957); Th; 2,525pd, 116fr (Sw); $5.25; C; publisher J Tom Graham; editor Graham Baker; tel (512) 237-4655; fax (512) 237-5443

Sonora: *The Devil's River News* — 216 E. Main St. (76950); Th; 1,315pd, 25fr (Sw); $4.36; C; publisher Cam Campbell; editor Stephanie Campbell; tel (915) 387-2507; fax (915) 387-5691

S Padre Island/Rio Grande Valley: *The Coastal Current* — 1004 Padre Blvd.; PO Box 2429, South Padre Island (78597); F; 10,000fr (Est); $4.95; C; publisher Jonathan Deeley; editor Lori Todd; tel (210) 761-9341; fax (210) 761-1436

Spearman/Hansford: *Hansford County Reporter-Statesman* — 213 Main; PO Box 458, Spearman (79081); Th; 1,606pd, 20fr (Sw); $2.90; publishers & editors Chad Davis & Dezi Torres; tel (806) 659-3434; fax (806) 659-3368

Springtown: *Springtown Epigraph* — PO Box 557 (76082); Th; 1,667pd, 110fr (Sw); $2.75; C; publisher & editor Bob Buckel; tel (817) 220-7217; fax (817) 238-9617

Spur: *The Texas Spur* — 424 Burlington Ave.; PO Box 430 (79370); Th; 2,004pd, 30fr (Sw); 16¢; publisher & editor Grady Joe Harrison; tel (806) 271-3381

Stamford: *Stamford American* — 112 E. Hamilton; PO Box 1207 (79553); Th; 2,293pd, 25fr (Sw); $3.08; C; publisher Lewis Alambar; general manager Becky Alambar; editor Chandra Mathis; tel (915) 773-3621; fax (915) 773-3622

Sterling City: *Sterling City News-Record* — 305 W. Side Elm; PO Box 608 (76951); F; 1,067pd (Est); $2.80; publisher & editor Evelyn Douthit; tel (915) 378-3251; fax (915) 378-2030

Stratford: *The Stratford Star* — 309 N. Main; PO Box 8 (79084); Th; 927pd, 38fr (Sw); $3.50; publisher & editor Martha Robertson; tel (806) 396-5885; fax (806) 396-5885

Sudan: *Sudan Beacon News* — PO Box 190 (79371); Su; 300pd (Est); $2.50; publisher George Goodwin; editor Annette Scheller; tel (806) 227-2183

Taft: *Taft Tribune* — 325 Green Ave. (78390); W; 1,200pd, 30fr (Sw); $5.10; C; publishers James F Tracy & John H Tracy; editor Belinda Tracy; tel (512) 528-2515; fax (512) 364-3833

Tahoka: *Lynn County News* — 1617 Main; PO Box 1170 (79373); Th; 1,520pd, 22fr (Sw); $3.50; publisher & editor Juanell Jones; publisher & general manager Vondell Elliott; tel (806) 998-4888

Talco: *Talco Times* — Main St.; PO Box 98 (75435); Th; 422pd, 10fr (Sw); $3.05; publisher & editor Nanalee Nichols; tel (903) 652-4205; fax (903) 652-4205

Thorndale: *Thorndale Champion* — 211 W. 3rd St.; PO Box 1040, Taylor (76574); Th; 1,012pd, 10fr (Sw); $3.00; C; publisher Robert Swonke; editor Don McAlister; tel (512) 352-8535; fax (512) 352-2227

Three Rivers/Live Oak/George West: *The Progress* — U.S. 281; PO Box 848, Three Rivers (78071); W; 3,205pd, 14fr (Sw); $3.10; publisher & editor Collis D Sellman; tel (512) 786-3022; fax (512) 786-3671

Throckmorton Co.: *Throckmorton Tribune* — PO Box 847, Throckmorton (76083); Th; 1,051pd, 214fr (Est); $14.00; publisher & editor Cecil Mayes; publisher Joyce Mayes; tel (817) 849-7951; fax (817) 849-3069

Trenton/Leonard/Bonham/Whitewright: *Trenton Tribune* — 115 Hamilton; PO Box 43, Trenton (75490); Tu; 1,129pd (Est); $3.36; publisher & editor Tom M Holmes; tel (903) 989-2325

Trinity: *The Trinity Standard* — 125 Main St.; PO Box 712 (75862); Th; 2,384pd, 18fr (Sw); $3.20; publisher Alvin Holley; editor Stan Nolen; tel (409) 594-2126; fax (409) 594-7547

Tulia: *Tulia Herald* — 115 S. Austin; PO Drawer 87 (79088); Th; 2,920pd, 30fr (Sw); $2.84; publisher & editor Chris Russett; tel (806) 995-3535; fax (806) 995-3536

Universal City Area: *Herald* — 122 E. Byrd; PO Box 2789 (78148); W; 143pd, 32,000fr (Sw); $10.12; publisher Robert L Jones II; editor Gary Gossett; tel (210) 658-7424; fax (210) 658-0390

Uvalde: *The Uvalde Leader-News* — 110 N. East St.; PO Box 740 (78802); Th/Su; 5,959pd, 85fr (Sw); $5.50; publisher Craig K Garnett; editor Bill Cockerill; tel (210) 278-3335; fax (210) 278-9191

Van Horn: *Van Horn Advocate* — 701 W. Broadway; PO Box 8 (79855); Th; 961pd, 14fr (Sw); $2.90; publisher Larry Simpson; general manager & managing editor Dawn Simpson; editor Jeff McCoy; tel (915) 283-2003; fax (915) 283-2920

Van Zandt Co.: *Van Zandt News* — 109 N. 5th; PO Box 60, Wills Point (75169); Su; 4,218pd, 83fr (Est); $4.12; publisher & managing editor Glenn McNeill Jr; general manager Betsy McNeill; editor Greg Wells; tel (903) 873-2525; fax (903) 873-4321

Vega/Oldham Co.: *The Vega Enterprise* — 116 S. Main; PO Box 130, Vega (79092); Th; 655pd, 10fr (Sw); $3.00; publisher & editor Quincy Taylor; tel (806) 267-2230

Vidor: *The Vidorian* — 450 W. Bolivar; PO Box 1236 (77662); Th; 1,587pd, 21fr (Sw); $4.06; C; publisher A Merle Luker; managing editor Randall Luker; tel (409) 769-5428; fax (409) 769-2600

Waco/McLennon Co.: *The Waco Citizen* — 1020 N. 25th St.; PO Box 3280, Waco (76707); W/Su; 10,000pd (Est); $10.00; C; publisher Marla Hanson; general manager David P Mowery; editor John Hasselmeier; tel (817) 754-3511; fax (817) 754-3541

Wallis: *Wallis News-Review* — 6109 Commerce; PO Box 668 (77485); Th; 1,120pd, 10fr (Est); $2.52; publisher Raymond L Dungen Jr; editor Lucille Jeneb; tel (409) 478-6412

Waskom/E Harrison: *Waskom Review* — 100 Texas Ave.; PO Box 727, Waskom (75692-0727); Th; 612pd, 36fr (Est); $4.50; publisher Mike Elswick; managing editor Annie Britt; tel (903) 687-2100/3204; fax (903) 687-3291

Weimar: *The Weimar Mercury* — 200 W. Main St.; PO Box 277 (78962); Th; 3,262pd, 96fr (Est); $2.70; publisher & editor Bruce Beal; tel (409) 725-9595

Wellington: *Wellington Leader* — 913 West Ave.; PO Box 992 (79095); Th; 2,450pd, 60fr (Est); $3.60; publisher Henry W Wells; editor Virginia Robey; managing editor Melanie A Jeffrey; tel (806) 447-2559; fax (806) 447-2463

West: *The West News* — 214 W. Oak; PO Box 38 (76691); Th; 3,000pd (Sw); 14¢; publisher Linn A Pescaia; editor Larry Knapek; tel (817) 826-3718

W Columbia: *The Brazoria County News* — 113 E. Bernard; PO Box 488 (77486); Th; 10,300fr (Est); $4.75; publisher & editor David E Toney; tel (409) 345-3127

Wharton: *Wharton Journal-Spectator* — 115 W. Burleson St.; PO Box 111 (77488); W/Sa; 4,595pd, 48fr (Sw); $5.25; publisher Fred V Barbee Jr; general manager & editor Larry Jackson; tel (409) 532-8840; fax (409) 532-8845

Wheeler: *The Wheeler Times* — PO Box 1080 (79096); Th; 1,138pd, 25fr (Sw); 11¢; publisher & editor Louis C Stas; tel (806) 826-3123; fax (806) 826-3048

White Deer/Skellytown: *White Deer News* — 209 Main St.; PO Box 728, White Deer (79097); Th; 670pd, 50fr (Sw); $3.70; publisher Joseph J Miller; managing editor Donna Huff; tel (806) 883-4881

White Settlement: *White Settlement Bomber News* — 7820 Wyatt Dr., Fort Worth (76108); Th; 1,000pd, 5,000fr (Est); $10.50; C; publisher & editor Janice Underwood; managing editor Charlsea Littlefield; tel (817) 246-2473; fax (817) 246-2474

Whitesboro: *News-Record* — 130 E. Main St.; PO Box 68 (76273); Th; 2,665pd, 38fr (Sw); $5.50; publisher & editor Jim Davison; tel (903) 564-3565; fax (903) 564-9655

Whitewright: *The Whitewright Sun* — 121 Grand Ave.; PO Box 218 (75491); Th; 855pd, 21fr (Sw); $3.31; publisher Dennis Combs; general manager & editor Clara Combs; tel (903) 364-2276; fax (903) 364-2276

Whitney: *Whitney Messenger* — 111 N. Colorado; PO Box 1195 (76692); W; 1,300pd (Sw); $5.00; C; publisher Charlene Bunch; editor Sandy Youngblood; tel (817) 694-3713; fax (817) 694-3522

Wills Pt.: *Wills Point Chronicle* — 109 N. 5th St.; PO Box 60 (75169); F; 3,561pd, 834fr (Est); $4.12; publisher & managing editor Glenn McNeill Jr; general manager Betsy McNeill; editor Wilbur Callaway; tel (903) 873-2525; fax (903) 873-4321

Wimberley: *The Wimberley View* — Cornerstone Park, Ste. A; PO Box 49 (78676); W/Sa; 827pd, 2,200fr (Sw); $5.59; publisher Mary Saunders; managing editor Harrell King; tel (512) 847-2202; fax (512) 847-9054

Winkler Co.: *The Winkler County News* — 109 S. Poplar; PO Drawer A, Kermit (79745); Th; 3,700pd, 61fr (Sw); $3.98; C; publisher & editor Rick McLaughlin; managing editor Bert Brewer; tel (915) 586-2561; fax (915) 586-2562

Winnsboro: *The Winnsboro News* — 105 E. Locust St.; PO Box 87 (75494); Th; 4,114pd, 4fr (Sw); $4.85; publisher & editor Thomas F Pendergast; managing editor Karen W Pendergast; tel (903) 342-5247; fax (903) 342-3266

II-78 Texas U.S. Weeklies

Winters: *The Winters Enterprise* — 104 N. Main (79567); Th; 1,707pd, 10fr (Sw); $4.00; publisher & editor Jean Boles; tel (915) 754-4958; fax (915) 754-4628

Wolfe City/Celeste/Commerce/Greenville/Bonham: *The Wolfe City Mirror* — 209 W. Main; PO Drawer F, Wolfe City (75496); Th; 805pd, 12fr (Sw); $3.25; publisher & editor Lorrie Dorner; general manager JoAnn Page; tel (903) 496-7297; fax (903) 496-2421

Wylie/Sachse/Murphy: *The Wylie News* — 113 Oak St.; PO Box 369, Wylie (75098); W; 2,513pd, 318fr (Est); $3.50; publisher Chad Engbrock; editor Margaret Cook; tel (214) 442-5515/2623; fax (214) 442-4318

Yoakum: *Herald-Times* — 312 Lott St.; PO Box 798 (77995); W; 3,200pd (Est); $4.60; C; publisher Bob Anderson; editor John Carroll; tel (512) 293-5266; fax (512) 293-5267

Yorktown: *DeWitt County View* — 120 S. Riedel St.; PO Box 275 (78164); W; 2,003pd, 91fr (Sw); $3.50; publishers & editors John E Janacek & Mary Janacek; tel (512) 564-2122

Yorktown/Dewitt Co.: *Yorktown News* — 117 S. Church St.; PO Box 398, Yorktown (78164); W; 1,832pd, 75fr (Sw); 16¢; publisher & editor Lee Roy Griffin Jr; tel (512) 564-2242

Zapata: *Zapata County News* — Highway FM496 W.; PO Box 216 (78076-0216); Th; 2,754pd, 100fr (Sw); $3.65; C; publisher Bob McVey; editor Kate McVey; tel (210) 765-6931; fax (210) 765-9058

UTAH

American Fork/Alpine/Highland: *Citizen* — 59 W. Main St.; PO Box 7, American Fork (84003); W; 4,100pd (Sw); $7.00; C; publisher Brett R Bezzant; editor Barbara Christiansen; managing editor Marc Haddock; tel (801) 756-7669; fax (801) 756-5274

Beaver: *Beaver Press* — 40 E. Center St.; PO Box 351 (84713); Th; 1,375pd (Est); 10¢; publisher Robert L Draper; editor Marlow L Draper; tel (801) 438-2891; fax (801) 438-8804

Brigham City: *Box Elder News Journal* — 55 S. 100 W.; PO Box 370 (84302); W; 5,015pd, 4,811fr (Sw); $7.50; C; publisher Charles C Claybaugh; editor Sarah Yates; tel (801) 723-3471; fax (801) 723-5247

Castle Dale/Emery Co.: *Emery County Progress* — PO Box 589, Castle Dale (84513); Tu; 1,762pd, 18fr (Sw); $4.00; C; publisher Kevin Ashby; editor Larry Davis; tel (801) 381-2431; fax (801) 381-5431

Coalville/Kamas: *Summit County Bee* — 17 S. Main; PO Box 7, Coalville (84017); Th; 1,445pd, 41fr (Sw); 12¢; C; publishers Richard M Buys & Susan F Buys; managing editor Tom Noffsinger; tel (801) 336-5501; fax (801) 654-5085

Davis Co.: *Davis County Clipper* — 1370 S. 500 W.; PO Box 267, Bountiful (84010); Tu/F; 10,130pd, 40fr (Est); $8.95; C; publisher & editor R Gail Stahle; managing editor Judith Jensen; tel (801) 295-2251; fax (801) 295-3044

Davis Co.: *The Lakeside Review* — 2146 N. Main, Layton (84041); Tu; 18,935pd (Est); $16.65; Sa; 18,935pd (Est); $10.05; publisher Scott Trundell; editor April Adams; tel (801) 776-4951; fax (801) 773-7284

Delta: *Millard County Chronicle* — 40 N. 300 W.; PO Box 249 (84624); Th; 2,350pd (Sw); $21.43; publisher & editor Susan B Dutson; tel (801) 864-2400; fax (801) 864-2214

Delta/Fillmore: *Millard County Gazette* — PO Box 908, Fillmore (84631); Tu; 4,410fr (Est); $5.75; publisher & editor Dale E Whipple; tel (801) 743-6983; fax (801) 743-6983

Ephraim: *Ephraim Enterprise* — 35 S. Main, Manti (84642); Th; 500pd (Est); $3.00; C; publisher & editor Max E Call; general manager David E Call; tel (801) 835-4241; fax (801) 835-1493

Eureka: *Eureka Reporter* — 98 N. Church St.; PO Box 150 (84628-0150); F; 420pd, 15fr (Sw); 11¢; publisher Martin W Conover; editor Grace Bernini; tel (801) 433-6933

Fillmore: *Millard County Chronicle Progress* — 29 W. 100 South; PO Box 288 (84631); W; 24,000pd (Est); $4.50; publisher & editor Susan B Dutson; tel (801) 743-5340, (801) 864-2400; fax (801) 864-2214

Gunnison: *Gunnison Valley News* — 47 S. Main; PO Box 189 (84634); W; 940pd, 40fr (Sw); 22¢; publisher Jim Olsen; general manager & editor Lori Olsen; tel (801) 528-3111; fax (801) 528-7634

Heber City: *Wasatch Wave* — 675 W. 100 South; PO Box 128 (84032); W; 3,024pd, 60fr (Sw); 16¢; publisher Richard M Buys; managing editor Tom Noffsinger; tel (801) 654-1471; fax (801) 654-5085

Kanab: *Southern Utah News* — 26 N. Main St. (84741); W; 1,800pd, 5fr (Sw); $4.00; publisher Dennis Brunner; publisher & editor Dixie Brunner; tel (801) 644-2900; fax (801) 644-2926

Kaysville/Fruit Heights/Layton/Clearfield/Sunset/Syracuse/W Point/Clinton: *Kaysville Today* — 197 N. Main, Layton (84041); W; 32,633fr (Est); $11.95; C; publisher & editor R Gail Stahle; managing editor Judith Jensen; tel (801) 547-9800; fax (801) 295-3044

Lehi: *Lehi Free Press* — 59 W. Main St.; PO Box 7, American Fork (84003); W; 2,200pd (Sw); $7.00; C; publisher Brett R Bezzant; editor Russ Daly; managing editor Marc Haddock; tel (801) 756-7669; fax (801) 756-5274

Magna: *Magna Times* — 8980 W. 2700 S. (84044); Th; 1,914pd, 75fr (Est); 14¢; publisher & editor J Howard Stahle; tel (801) 250-5656; fax (801) 250-5685

Manti: *Manti Messenger* — 35 S. Main (84642); Th; 700pd (Est); $3.00; publisher & editor Max E Call; general manager David E Call; tel (801) 835-4241; fax (801) 835-1493

Monticello/Blanding: *The San Juan Record* — 49 S. Main; PO Box 879, Monticello (84535); W; 2,129pd, 34fr (Sw); $3.36; publisher & editor Bill Boyle; tel (801) 587-2277; fax (801) 587-2277

Morgan Co.: *Morgan County News* — PO Box 190, Morgan (84050); F; 1,350pd, 29fr (Est); 15¢; publisher & editor Ken Adams; publisher Marie Adams; tel (801) 829-3451; fax (801) 829-4073

Mt. Pleasant: *The Pyramid* — 49 W. Main (84647); W; 2,367pd, 46fr (Sw); $4.25; C; publisher Martin W Conover; editor Penny Hamilton; tel (801) 462-2134; fax (801) 462-2459

Nephi: *The Times News* — PO Box 77 (84648); W; 1,391pd, 62fr (Sw); $3.25; publisher Allan R Gibson; editor Mariann C Gibson; tel (801) 623-0525; fax (801) 623-4735

Orem: *Orem-Geneva Times* — 546 S. State (84058); W; 3,500pd (Est); $3.95; publisher Brent R Sumner; editor Reva Bowen; tel (801) 225-1340; fax (801) 225-1341

Panguitch: *Garfield County News* — 120 N. Tropic; PO Box 127, Tropic (84776); Th; 2,050pd, 35fr (Est); 22¢; publisher Katie Thomas; editor Nancy Twitchell; tel (801) 679-8730; fax (801) 679-8847

Park City: *Park Record* — 1670 Bonanza Dr.; PO Box 3688 (84060); Th; 8,500pd, 110fr (Sw); $7.71; publisher Andy Bernhard; editor Sena Flanders; tel (801) 649-9014; fax (801) 649-4942

Payson/Santaquin: *The Payson Chronicle* — 12 S. Main, Payson (84651); W; 1,400pd, 100fr (Sw); $3.10; publisher & editor Michael Olson; tel (801) 465-9221; fax (801) 465-9221

Pleasant Grove: *Pleasant Grove Review* — 59 W. Main St.; PO Box 7, American Fork (84003); W; 2,900pd (Sw); $7.00; C; publisher Brett R Bezzant; editor Marcella Walker; managing editor Marc Haddock; tel (801) 756-7669; fax (801) 756-5274

Price/Carbon Co.: *Sun Advocate* — 76 W. Main St.; PO Box 870, Price (84501); Tu/Th; 5,002pd, 40fr (Sw); $5.60; C; publisher Kevin Ashby; editor Lynnda Johnson; tel (801) 637-0732; fax (801) 637-2716

Richfield: *The Richfield Reaper* — 65 W. Center; PO Box 730 (84701); W; 5,360pd, 139fr (Sw); $12.50; C; publisher Mark G Fuellenbach; editor Hal Edwards; tel (801) 896-5476; fax (801) 896-8123

Roosevelt: *Uintah Basin Standard* — 268 S. 200 East (84066); Tu; 3,933pd, 95fr (Sw); $4.00; C; publisher Craig Ashby; editor Lezlee Whiting; tel (801) 722-5131; fax (801) 722-4140

Salina: *Salina Sun* — 3 E. Main; PO Box 85 (84654); W; 925pd, 50fr (Sw); $4.50; C; publisher Jim Olsen; general manager Lora Peterson; editor Lori Olsen; tel (801) 529-7839; fax (801) 529-7727

Salt Lake City: *Private Eye Weekly* — 60 W. 400 South (84101); Th; 43,000fr (Sw); $31.30; publisher John Saltas; editor Tom Walsh; tel (801) 575-7003; fax (801) 575-6106

Salt Lake Vly.: *The Green Sheet* — PO Box 267, Bountiful (84011); Th; 6,251pd, 18,811fr (Est); $3.93; publisher Gail Stahle; editor Judy Jensen; tel (801) 296-6500; fax (801) 295-3044

Spanish Fork: *Spanish Fork Press* — 280 N. Main (84660); Th; 2,295pd, 180fr (Sw); 30¢; publisher & editor Lane Henderson; tel (801) 798-9770; fax (801) 798-9770

Springville: *Springville Herald* — 161 S. Main (84663); W; 2,600pd, 43fr (Sw); 21¢; C; publisher Martin W Conover; general manager M Craig Conover; editor Pat Conover; tel (801) 489-5651; fax (801) 489-7021

Tooele Co.: *Tooele Transcript-Bulletin* — 58 N. Main; PO Box 390, Tooele (84074); Tu/Th; 6,103pd, 430fr (Sw); $4.95; C; publisher Scott Dunn; editor Mike Call; tel (801) 882-0050; fax (801) 882-6123

Tremonton/Garland: *The Leader* — 119 E. Main St., Tremonton (84337); W; 2,750pd, 18fr (Est); $4.97; publisher Greg Madson; editor Diana Hunsaker Myers; tel (801) 257-5182; fax (801) 257-6175

Vernal: *Vernal Express* — 54 N. Vernal Ave.; PO Box 1000 (84078); W; 4,288pd, 34fr (Sw); $6.00; C; publisher Jack R Wallis; editor Steven R Wallis; tel (801) 789-3511; fax (801) 789-8690

VERMONT

Addison Co.: *The Valley Voice* — 3 Court St., Middlebury (05753); M; 8,800pd (Est); $5.00; publisher Cheryl Denett; editor Michael Cameron; tel (802) 388-6366; fax (802) 388-6368

Barton: *The Chronicle* — Water St.; PO Box O (05822); W; 8,039pd, 235fr (Sw); $7.75; publisher & editor Chris Braithwaite; managing editor Elizabeth A Landolt; tel (802) 525-3531

Bellows Falls: *Bellows Falls Town Crier* — PO Box 459 (05101); F; 21pd, 11,432fr (CAC); $6.20; C; publisher Roger G Miller; general manager & editor Stephen F Crimmin; tel (802) 463-9591; fax (802) 463-9818

Bennington Co.: *Vermont News Guide* — PO Box 1265, Manchester Center (05255); Tu; 275pd, 16fr (Sw); $6.70; C; publisher & editor Jack Quinn; tel (802) 362-3535; fax (802) 362-5368

Bradford: *Journal Opinion* — The Mill; PO Box 378 (05033); Tu/W; 4,183pd, 154fr (Sw); $5.50; publisher & editor Robert F Huminski; general manager Connie Sanville; managing editor Charles Glazer; tel (802) 222-5281; fax (802) 222-5438

Brattleboro: *Brattleboro Town Crier* — PO Box 537 (05302); F; 20pd, 11,882fr (CAC); $6.20; C; publisher William P Bedard; editor Suzette Pepin; tel (802) 257-7771; fax (802) 257-2211

Essex/Essex Junction: *The Essex Reporter* — PO Box 116, Essex Junction (05453); Th; 7,500fr (Est); $7.00; C; publisher & editor Bill Scheer; tel (802) 878-5282

Franklin Co.: *County Courier* — 209 Main St.; PO Box 398, Enosburg Falls (05450); Th; 3,248pd, 70fr (Sw); $5.16; publisher Alison Dubilier; publisher & editor Mathias Dubilier; tel (802) 933-4375; fax (802) 933-4907

Grand Isle Co./Milton/Swanton/Rouses Pt. (NY)/Champlain (NY): *The Islander* — 21 Sunset View Rd.; PO Box 212, South Hero (05486); Tu; 7,000fr (Sw); $4.00; publisher Elaine S Fowler; publisher & editor George D Fowler; tel (802) 372-5600; fax (802) 372-5600

Hardwick/Greensboro: *Hardwick Gazette* — Main St.; PO Box 367, Hardwick (05843); W; 3,024pd, 33fr (Sw); $5.00; publisher & editor Ross Connelly; editor Susan M Jarzyna; tel (802) 472-6521

Killington: *The Mountain Times* — Rte. 4 Sherburne Flats; PO Box 183 (05751); Th; 310pd, 10,000fr (Est); $6.25; publisher & editor Royal W Barnard; general manager Veronica Barnard; tel (802) 773-6970; fax (802) 773-4482

Ludlow/Springfield: *The Black River Tribune* — 110A Main St.; PO Box 156, Ludlow (05149); W; 2,246pd, 125fr (Sw); $4.25; publisher William A Hunter; editor Janet Upton; tel (802) 228-8817; fax (802) 228-8000

Mad River Valley: *The Valley Reporter* — Mad River Green; PO Box 119, Waitsfield (05673); Th; 2,801pd, 98fr (Sw); $5.92; C; publisher & editor Alvan R Benjamin; general manager Patricia A Clark; managing editor Lisa A Loomis; tel (802) 496-3928

Manchester: *Manchester Journal* — Memorial Ave.; PO Box 569 (05255-0569); W; 2,684pd, 5fr (Sw); $8.70; C; publisher Mark Nesbit; managing editor Adam R Tschorn; tel (802) 362-2222; fax (802) 362-5327

Middlebury/Vergennes/Bristol/Brandon: *Addison County Independent* — 4 Maple St.; PO Box 31, Middlebury (05753); M; 6,350pd, 2,650fr (Sw); $7.05; Th; 6,832pd, 127fr (Sw); $7.05; publisher & editor Angelo S Lynn; tel (802) 388-4944; fax (802) 388-3100

Morrisville/Lamoille Co.: *News & Citizen* — Brooklyn St.; PO Box 369, Morrisville (05661); Th; 3,440pd, 20fr (Sw); 21¢; C; publisher Bradley A Limoge; editor Paulette Wallace; tel (802) 888-2212; fax (802) 888-2173

Northfield/Roxbury: *Northfield News* — 10 East St., Northfield (05663); Th; 1,431pd, 71fr (Est); $3.55; publisher & editor Ingrid M Wilson; publisher James L Wilson; tel (802) 485-3681; fax (802) 485-7909

Randolph/Orange Co.: *The Herald of Randolph* — 30 Pleasant St.; PO Box 309, Randolph (05060); Th; 5,750pd (ABC); $6.24; publisher & editor M Dickey Drysdale; tel (802) 728-3232; fax (802) 728-9275

Springfield/Chester: *Springfield Reporter* — 151 Summer St., Springfield (05156); W; 1,680pd, 75fr (Sw); $3.65; publisher & editor Rodney W Arnold; tel (802) 885-2246; fax (802) 885-9821

Stowe: *The Stowe Reporter* — 49 School St.; PO Box 489 (05672); Th; 5,507pd, 50fr (Sw); $5.80; C; publisher D T Elliman; editor Gregory J Popa; tel (802) 253-2101; fax (802) 253-8332

Washington/Orange Cos.: *The World* — 82 Barre-Montpelier Rd., Barre (05641); W; 48pd, 25,580fr (CAC); $7.50; publishers Deborah Phillips & Gary Hass; editor Vernon Davis; tel (802) 479-2582; fax (802) 479-7916

Williston: *Williston Whistle* — 702 Williston Rd.; PO Box 1158 (05495); Th; 4,000fr (Sw); $7.50; publishers & editors Marianne Apfelbaum & Paul Apfelbaum; tel (802) 879-4839, (802) 878-0051; fax (802) 879-4839

Wilmington/Dover: *Deerfield Valley News* — Rte. 100; PO Box 310, West Dover (05356); Th; 3,000pd, 2,500fr (Sw); $6.40; C; publisher & editor Randy L Capitani; managing editor Sarah Wolfe; tel (802) 464-3388; fax (802) 464-7255

Windsor: *Windsor Chronicle* — 83 Hartland St., Ste. 4 (05089-1432); Th; 1,695pd, 50fr (Est); $4.75; publisher & editor Fredrick Straka; publisher Olga Straka; tel (802) 674-2975

Woodstock/Windsor Co.: *Vermont Standard* — Rte. 4; PO Box 88, Woodstock (05091); Th; 3,519pd, 240fr (Sw); $4.75; publisher Phillip C Camp; editor Kevin M Forrest; tel (802) 457-1313; fax (802) 457-3639

VIRGINIA

Abingdon/Washington Co.: *Abingdon Virginian* — 170 E. Main St., Abingdon (24210); W; 3,725pd, 573fr (Sw); $7.50; publisher & editor Martha M Weisfeld; tel (540) 628-2962

Abingdon/Washington Co.: *Washington County News* — 143 W. Main St. (24210); PO Box 399, Abingdon (24212); W; 5,088pd, 40fr (Sw); $4.56; publisher Bill Thomas; editor Dan Kegley; tel (540) 628-7101; fax (540) 628-9396

Accomack Co.: *Chincoteague Beacon* — 21222 Fairground Rd.; PO Box 288, Tasley (23441); W; 6,500fr (Sw); $5.25; C; publisher John D Backe; general manager Darel La Prade; editor Bill Sterling; tel (804) 787-1200; fax (804) 787-9567

Accomack Co.: *Eastern Shore News* — 21222 Fairground Rd. (Tasley 23441); PO Box 249, Onley (23418); W; 13,600pd (Sw); $10.15;

U.S. Weeklies **Virginia** II-79

Sa; 11,000pd (Sw); $8.15; C; publisher John D Backe; general manager & editor Bill Sterling; tel (804) 787-1200; fax (804) 787-9567

Alexandria: *The Alexandria Gazette Packet* — 1700 Diagonal Rd., Ste. 410 (22314); Th; 1,180fr (CAC); $18.90; C; publisher Jerry Vernon; editor Christa Watters; managing editor Mary Ann Weber; tel (703) 838-0302; fax (703) 548-2228

Amelia/Prince Edward: *Amelia Bulletin Monitor* — PO Box 123, Amelia (23002); Th; 8,200pd (Est); $7.00; publisher Ann Salster; editor Michael D Salster; tel (804) 561-3655; fax (804) 561-2065

Amherst Co.: *Amherst New Era Progress* — 113 2nd St.; PO Box 90, Amherst (24521); Th; 5,006pd (ABC); 27¢; publisher Thomas T Byrd; general manager Shelby Ferguson; editor Nancy Crutchfield; tel (804) 946-7195; fax (804) 946-2684

Appomattox: *Times-Virginian* — 507 Court St.; PO Box 2097 (24522); W; 3,900pd (Est); $6.00; publisher Zan Womack; general manager Cindy W Smith; editor Lewis Wood; tel (804) 352-8215; fax (804) 352-2216

Arlington Co.: *Arlington Courier* — 3440 N. Fairfax Dr. (22101); PO Box 7560, Arlington (22207); W; 1,056pd, 26,687fr (Sw); $15.73; C; publisher David R Dear Jr; tel (703) 522-9898; fax (703) 522-8788

Bedford Co.: *Bedford Bulletin/The Bullet* — 402 E. Main St.; PO Box 331, Bedford (24523); M; 20,300fr (Est); $7.04; W; 8,073pd (Est); $6.37; C; general manager Jay Bondurant; editor Rebecca Jackson-Clause; tel (540) 586-8612; fax (540) 586-0834

Bedford/Franklin Co.: *Smith Mountain Eagle* — PO Box 231, Moneta (24121); W; 3,424pd, 88fr (Sw); $6.30; publisher Charles Womack Jr; general manager Dianne White; editor Rob Lyon; tel (540) 297-1222; fax (540) 297-1944

Berryville: *The Clarke Courier* — 16 W. Main St.; PO Box 32 (22611); W; 2,027pd, 173fr (Sw); $7.20; C; publisher Arthur W Arundel; general manager Betty J Murray; editor Val Van Meter; tel (540) 955-1111; fax (540) 955-1334

Big Stone Gap/Appalachia: *The Post* — 215 Wood Ave.; PO Box 250, Big Stone Gap (24219); W; 4,667pd, 131fr (ABC); $6.15; C; publisher Robbie G Tate; general manager & managing editor Jeff Moore; tel (540) 523-1141; fax (540) 523-1175

Blackstone: *Courier-Record* — 207 S. Main; PO Box 450 (23824); Th; 6,315pd, 50fr (Sw); $5.60; publisher & editor Doug Coleburn; tel (804) 292-3019; fax (804) 292-5966

Bland Co.: *Bland Messenger* — 460 W. Main St., Wytheville (24382); Th; 1,842pd, 20fr (Sw); $5.75; C; publisher & editor D Gregory Rooker; tel (540) 228-6611, (800) 655-1406; fax (540) 228-7260

Botetourt: *The Fincastle Herald* — Herald Sq.; PO Box 127, Fincastle (24090); W; 5,366pd, 285fr (Sw); $5.32; C; publisher Ray L Robinson; general manager Edwin L McCoy; editor Edwin Taylor; tel (540) 473-2741; fax (540) 344-1404

Brookneal/Campbell Co.: *Union Star* — 241 Main St.; PO Box 180, Brookneal (24528); W; 2,947pd, 20fr (Sw); $5.30; C; publisher Charles A Womack Jr; general manager Cynthia Rutledge; editor Paula Bryant; tel (804) 376-2795; fax (804) 376-2676

Burke: *Burke Times* — 1760 Reston Pkwy., Ste. 411, Reston (22090); Th; 13,532fr (CAC); $16.95; C; publisher Arthur W Arundel; general manager Peter Arundel; editor Marcia McAllister; managing editor Janet Rems; tel (703) 437-5400; fax (703) 437-6019

Caroline Co.: *The Caroline Progress* — 121 Courthouse Ln.; PO Box 69, Bowling Green (22427); W; 3,586pd, 30fr (Est); $7.90; C; publisher Edward Carroll; general manager Karen Oyler; editor Jay Plotkin; tel (804) 633-5005; fax (804) 633-6740

Centreville: *The Centreville Times* — 1760 Reston Pkwy., Ste. 411, Reston (22090); Th; 189pd, 10,929fr (CAC); $13.30; C; publisher Arthur W Arundel; general manager Peter Arundel; editor Marcia McAllister; managing editor Janet Rems; tel (703) 437-5400; fax (703) 437-6019

Chantilly: *The Chantilly Times* — 1760 Reston Pkwy., Ste. 411, Reston (22090); Th; 101pd, 6,307fr (CAC); $13.30; C; publisher Arthur W Arundel; general manager Peter Arundel; editor Marcia McAllister; managing editor Janet Rems; tel (703) 437-5400; fax (703) 437-6019

Charlottesville City: *Charlottesville Albemarle Observer* — 100 South St. W.; PO Box 617 (22902-0617); Th; 3,601pd, 6,883fr (CAC); $8.00; publisher J Gray Ferguson; general manager Kimberly Robbins; managing editor Cory Reiss; tel (804) 295-0124; fax (804) 293-4047

Chatham/Pittsylvania Co.: *Star-Tribune* — 30 N. Main St.; PO Box 111, Chatham (24531); W; 8,225pd, 59fr (Sw); $6.50; C; publisher Charles A Womack Jr; editor Tim Davis; tel (804) 432-2791; fax (804) 432-4033

Chesapeake: *The Chesapeake Post* — 1024 N. Battlefield Blvd. (23320); PO Box 1327 (23327); F; 8,425pd, 1,740fr (Est); $6.05; publisher Hanes Byerly; editor Victoria Edwards; tel (804) 547-4571; fax (804) 548-0390

Christiansburg/Radford: *The News Messenger* — 3325 N. Franklin St.; PO Box 419, Christiansburg (24073); W/Sa; 5,097pd, 8,614fr (Sw); $8.87; general manager Mike Williams; editor Gene Morrell; tel (540) 382-6171; fax (540) 382-3009

Clarksville/Chase City: *The News-Progress* — 306 Virginia Ave.; PO Box 1015, Clarksville (23927); M/W; 5,919pd, 510fr (Est); $3.70; publisher Keith A Shelton; editor D E Loftis Jr; managing editor Cathy Cochelin; tel (804) 374-2451; fax (804) 372-3911, (804) 374-2074

Clintwood/Dickenson: *The Dickenson Star* — Main St.; PO Box 707, Clintwood (24228); W; 6,677pd, 111fr (Est); $4.20; C; publisher Robbie G Tate; general manager Johnny Teglas; editor Jenay Tate; tel (540) 926-8816; fax (540) 926-8827

Craig Co.: *The New Castle Record* — Main St.; PO Box 116, New Castle (24127); W; 1,334pd, 37fr (Sw); $4.55; C; publisher & editor Ray L Robinson; managing editor Edwin L McCoy; tel (540) 864-5944; fax (540) 389-2930

Crewe/Burkeville: *The Crewe-Burkeville Journal* — 107 W. Carolina Ave.; PO Box 108, Crewe (23930); Th; 6,200pd, 150fr (Est); $4.00; publisher & editor Jim R Eanes; tel (804) 645-7534; fax (804) 645-1848

Culpeper: *Culpeper News* — 605 S. Main St. (22701); Th; 5,800pd, 200fr (Est); 47¢; publisher Joseph McCaffrey; general manager David King; editor Vince Vala; tel (540) 825-3232; fax (540) 825-5670

Denbigh/Newport News: *Denbigh Gazette* — 4824 George Washington Hwy.; PO Box 978, Yorktown (23692); Th; 5,000pd, 6,000fr (Sw); $7.35; C; publisher D Gaither Perry; general manager Carol Ivy; editor Vic Johnston; tel (804) 898-7225; fax (804) 890-0119

Drakes Branch: *Charlotte Gazette* — Main St.; PO Box 214 (23937); Th; 3,050pd, 50fr (Est); $2.50; publisher Dorothy C Tucker; editor Otis O Tucker III; tel (804) 568-3341; fax (804) 568-3731

Emporia: *Independent-Messenger* — 441 S. Main St.; PO Box 786 (23847); Th/Su; 5,899pd, 360fr (Sw); $8.00; C; publisher Hanes Byerly; general manager Tom Page; editor Jamie Brown; tel (804) 634-4153; fax (804) 634-0783

Fairfax: *Fairfax Times* — 1760 Reston Pkwy., Ste. 411, Reston (22090); Th; 18,200fr (CAC); $16.95; C; publisher Arthur W Arundel; general manager Peter Arundel; editor Marcia McAllister; managing editor Janet Rems; tel (703) 437-5400; fax (703) 437-6019

Fairfax Station: *Fairfax Station Times* — 1760 Reston Pkwy., Ste. 411, Reston (22090); Th; 4,550fr (CAC); $16.95; C; publisher Arthur W Arundel; general manager Peter Arundel; editor Marcia McAllister; managing editor Janet Rems; tel (703) 437-5400; fax (703) 437-6019

Falls Church: *Falls Church News-Press* — 929 W. Broad St. (22046); Th; 7,500fr (Sw); $10.15; publisher Nicholas F Benton; tel (703) 532-3267; fax (703) 532-3396

Farmville/Prince Edward/Buckingham/Cumberland: *The Farmville Herald* — 114 North St.; PO Box 307, Farmville (23901-0307); W/F; 8,400pd, 88fr (Sw); $6.50; Su; 7,400pd, 50fr (Sw); $6.50; C; publisher Steven E Wall; editor J K Woodley III; tel (804) 392-4151; fax (804) 392-6298

Fauquier: *The Fauquier Times-Democrat* — 39 Culpeper St.; PO Box 631, Warrenton (22186); W; 14,895pd, 568fr (ABC); $13.00; C; publisher Arthur W Arundel; general manager John T Toler; editor Lou Hatter; tel (540) 347-4222; fax (540) 349-8676

Fauquier Co.: *The Fauquier Citizen* — 50 Culpeper St.; PO Box 3430, Warrenton (22186); F; 7,680pd (Est); $13.75; publisher Ellen F Emerson; publisher & editor Lawrence K Emerson; tel (540) 347-5522; fax (540) 347-7363

Floyd Co.: *The Floyd Press* — 710 E. Main St.; PO Box 155, Floyd (24091); Th; 4,118pd, 49fr (Sw); $3.92; publisher William Sumner; general manager Dorothy Sumner; editor Wanda Combs; tel (540) 745-2127; fax (540) 745-2126

Franklin/Southampton: *The Tidewater News* — 1000 Armory Dr.; PO Box 497, Franklin (23851); Th/Su; 8,990pd, 172fr (Sw); $8.20; C; publisher Hanes Byerly; general manager Ron Wilmot; editor Jim Hekel; managing editor Jamie Brown; tel (804) 562-3187; fax (804) 562-6795

Front Royal/Warren Co.: *The Warren Sentinel* — 429 N. Royal Ave.; PO Box 1297, Front Royal (22630); Th; 5,897pd (ABC); $4.40; C; publisher Thomas T Byrd; general manager Sara Woodard; editor Michele Sullivan; tel (540) 635-4174; fax (540) 635-7478

Galax: *The Gazette* — 108 W. Stuart Dr.; PO Box 68 (24333); M/W/F; 8,083pd, 682fr (Sw); $6.77; C; publisher Chuck Burress; editor Amy Hauslohner; tel (540) 236-5178; fax (540) 236-0756

Gate City/Scott Co.: *Scott County Virginia Star* — 103 E. Jackson St.; PO Box 218, Gate City (24251); W; 5,277pd, 145fr (Sw); $5.06; publisher & editor Rex E McCarty; tel (540) 386-7027; fax (540) 386-2354

Gloucester/Mathews: *Gloucester Mathews Gazette-Journal* — 6625 Main St.; PO Box J, Gloucester (23061); Th; 10,666pd, 197fr (Sw); $8.00; publisher John Warren Cooke; editor Elsa C Verbyla; tel (804) 693-3101; fax (804) 693-7844

Goochland Co.: *The Goochland Gazette* — 3052 River Rd. W.; PO Box 139, Goochland (23063); Sa; 2,459pd (Sw); $8.50; C; publisher JGF Media Inc.; general manager Deborah Crook; editor McGregor McCance; tel (804) 556-3135; fax (804) 556-4237

Great Falls: *Great Falls Current* — 6819 Elm St.; PO Box 580, McLean (22101); Th; 4,268fr (Sw); $11.31; C; publisher & editor David R Dear Jr; managing editor Cort Kirkwood; tel (703) 356-3320; fax (703) 556-0825

Greene Co.: *The Greene County Record* — PO Box 66, Stanardsville (22973); Th; 2,984pd, 52fr (Est); $4.22; publisher Peter S Yates; general manager Charlotte Gallihugh; editor Jeff Poole; tel (804) 985-2315; fax (804) 985-8356

Grundy/Buchanan Co.: *The Virginia Mountaineer* — 105 Main St.; PO Drawer 2040, Grundy (24614); Th; 8,640pd, 82fr (Sw); $6.44; publisher & editor Lodge Compton; general manager Sam Baottey; managing editor Cathy St Clair; tel (540) 935-2123; fax (540) 935-2125

Hanover Co.: *The Herald Progress* — 11293 Air Park Rd., Ashland (23005); M; 8,075pd (ABC); $8.00; Th; 8,541pd, 379fr (ABC); $8.00; publisher & editor J Malcolm Pace III; general manager Stephen T Pace; tel (804) 798-9031; fax (804) 798-9036

Herndon: *The Herndon Times* — 1760 Reston Pkwy., Ste. 411, Reston (22090); Th; 220pd, 12,543fr (CAC); $19.00; publisher Arthur W Arundel; general manager Peter Arundel; editor Marcia McAllister; managing editor Janet Rems; tel (703) 437-5400; fax (703) 437-6019

Highland/Bath Cos.: *The Recorder* — 3 Water St.; PO Box 10, Monterey (24465); F; 5,090pd, 10fr (Sw); $3.95; publisher & editor Christy Pugh; tel (540) 468-2147; fax (540) 468-2048

Hillsville/Carroll Co.: *The Carroll News* — 1026 W. Stuart Dr.; PO Box 487, Hillsville (24343); W; 6,220pd, 180fr (Sw); $7.01; C; publisher Ina L Horton; editor Wendy L Turner; tel (540) 728-7311; fax (540) 728-4119

Independence: *The Declaration* — 304 Davis St.; PO Box 70 (24348-0070); W; 2,457pd, 125fr (Sw); $6.10; C; publisher & editor John E North; tel (540) 773-2222; fax (540) 773-2287

King George: *The Journal* — PO Box 409 (22485); W; 4,000pd, 2,772fr (Est); $8.00; C; publisher & editor Ruth Herrink; tel (540) 775-2024; fax (540) 775-4099

Lancaster Co.: *Rappahannock Record* — 27 Main St.; PO Box 400, Kilmarnock (22482); Th; 7,812pd, 85fr (Sw); $6.50; publishers Betty Lee Gaskins & Fredrick A Gaskins; editor John C Wilson; tel (804) 435-1701; fax (804) 435-2632

Lawrenceville: *Brunswick Times-Gazette* — 213 Main St.; PO Box 250 (23868); W; 3,666pd, 117fr (Est); 20¢; publisher Hanes Byerly; general manager Tom Page; editor Mike Bollinger; tel (804) 848-2114

Lebanon/Russell: *The Lebanon News* — 308 Main St.; PO Box 1268, Lebanon (24266); W; 5,510pd, 90fr (Est); $4.90; publisher & editor Jerry E Lark; tel (540) 889-2112; fax (540) 889-5017

Lexington: *The News-Gazette* — 20 W. Nelson St.; PO Box 1153 (24450); W; 9,364pd (ABC); $6.85; C; publisher M W Paxton IV; editor Daryl Woodson; tel (540) 463-3113; fax (540) 464-6397

Loudoun Co.: *Eastern Loudoun Times* — 1760 Reston Pkwy., Ste. 411, Reston (22090); Th; 78pd, 15,840fr (CAC); $13.35; C; publisher Arthur W Arundel; general manager Peter Arundel; editor Marcia McAllister; managing editor Janet Rems; tel (703) 437-5400; fax (703) 437-6019

Loudoun Co.: *Loudoun Times-Mirror* — 9 E. Market St., Leesburg (22075); W; 17,374pd, 1,906fr (Est); $15.65; C; publisher Arthur W Arundel; managing editor Patti Snodgrass; tel (703) 777-1111; fax (703) 771-0036

Louisa/Fluvanna: *The Central Virginian* — 101 Elm Ave.; PO Box 464, Louisa (23093); Th; 7,000pd, 30fr (Sw); $7.05; publisher & editor Hilda D Miller; tel (540) 967-0368; fax (540) 967-0457

Lovingston/Nelson Co.: *Nelson County Times* — 113 2nd St.; PO Box 90, Amherst (24521); Th; 4,288pd (ABC); 22¢; publisher Thomas T Byrd; editor Jim Manner; tel (804) 946-7195

Madison Co.: *Madison County Eagle* — 110 Berry Hill Rd., Orange (22960); Th; 3,802pd, 10fr (Sw); $7.60; C; publisher Peter S Yates; general manager Charlotte Gallihugh; editor Jeff Poole; tel (540) 672-1266; fax (540) 672-5831

Marion: *Smyth County News & Messenger* — Cherry & Sheffey Sts.; PO Box 640 (24354); W; 7,574pd, 33fr (Est); $9.25; Sa; 7,574pd, 33fr (Est); $6.20; C; publisher Debbie C Maxwell; editor Tim Thornton; tel (540) 783-5121; fax (540) 783-9713

McLean/Tyson Corner: *The McLean Providence Journal & Fairfax Herald* — 6819 Elm St.; PO Box 580, McLean (22101); Th; 1,479pd, 12,075fr (Sw); $12.93; C; publisher & editor David R Dear Jr; managing editor Cort Kirkwood; tel (703) 356-3320; fax (703) 556-0825

Mechanicsville: *Mechanicsville Local* — 7235 Stonewall Pkwy.; PO Box 1118 (23111); W; 188pd, 15,816fr (CAC); $14.90; C; publisher JGF Media Inc.; general manager Deborah Crook; editor McGregor McCance; managing editor Bob Rayner; tel (804) 746-1235; fax (804) 730-0476

Middlesex Co.: *The Southside Sentinel* — 276 Virginia St.; PO Box 549, Urbanna (23175); Th; 5,239pd, 128fr (Sw); $6.50; publisher & editor Frederick A Gaskins; managing editor John Thomas Hardin; tel (804) 758-2328; fax (804) 758-5896

Montross/Colonial Beach: *Westmoreland News* — 3 Courthouse Ln.; PO Box 699, Montross (22520); Th; 4,454pd, 21fr (Sw); $6.45; C; publisher William C O'Donovan; general manager & editor Lynn E Norris; tel (804) 493-8096; fax (804) 493-8009

Norton/Wise Co.: *The Coalfield Progress* — 725 Park Ave. S.E.; PO Box 380, Norton (24273); Tu; 7,356pd (ABC); $8.38; Th; 8,134pd (ABC); $8.38; C; publisher Robbie G Tate; general manager Johnny Teglas; editor Jenay Tate; tel (540) 679-1101; fax (540) 679-5922

Orange Co.: *Orange County Review* — 110 Berry Hill Rd., Orange (22960); Th; 6,901pd, 18fr (Est); $9.75; C; publisher Peter S Yates; general manager Charlotte Gallihugh; editor Jeff Poole; tel (540) 672-1266; fax (540) 672-5831

Page Co.: *Page News and Courier* — 17 S. Broad St.; PO Box 707, Luray (22835); Th; 7,356pd (ABC); $6.30; publisher Page-Shenandoah Newspaper Corp.; editor John D Waybright Jr; tel (540) 743-5123; fax (540) 743-4779

Pearisburg/Giles Co.: *Virginian Leader* — 511 Mountain Lake Ave.; PO Drawer C, Pearisburg (24134); W; 6,181pd, 102fr (Sw); $4.50; publisher Kenneth Rakes; editor Roger Mullins; tel (540) 921-3434; fax (540) 921-2563

Pennington Gap: *Powell Valley News* — 125 E. Morgan Ave.; PO Box 459 (24277); W; 7,409pd, 121fr (Sw); $5.60; C; publisher & editor Donald R Watson; general manager Rick L Watson; managing editor Louise Carver; tel (540) 546-1210; fax (540) 546-5468

Poquoson City: *The Poquoson Post* — 4824 George Washington Hwy.; PO Box 978, Yorktown (23692); W; 3,000pd, 1,000fr (Sw); $7.35; C; publisher D Gaither Perry; general manager Carol Ivy; editor Kathy Lee Hull; tel (804) 898-7225; fax (804) 890-0119

Portsmouth: *The Portsmouth Times* — 1024 N. Battlefield Blvd. (23320); PO Box 1327, Chesapeake (23327); F; 7,410pd, 1,746fr (Sw); $5.25; C; publisher Hanes Byerly; editor Victoria Edwards; tel (804) 547-4571; fax (804) 548-0390

Rappahannock Co.: *Rappahannock News* — 249 Main St.; PO Box 59, Washington (22747); Th; 2,825pd, 117fr (ABC); $8.25; C; publisher Arthur W Arundel; general manager Barbara C Wayland; editor Sharon Kilpatrick; tel (540) 675-3349; fax (540) 675-3088

Reston/Herndon/Vienna: *The Reston Times/ Herndon Times* — 1760 Reston Pkwy., Ste. 411, Reston (22090); W; 366pd, 15,474fr (CAC); $19.00; C; publisher Arthur W Arundel; general manager Peter Arundel; editor Marcia McAllister; managing editor Janet Rems; tel (703) 437-5400; fax (703) 437-6019

Richlands: *Richlands News-Press* — 1206 2nd St.; PO Box 818 (24641); W; 2,952pd, 149fr (Sw); $9.72; C; publisher William H Hall; editor Charles Boothe; tel (540) 963-1081; fax (540) 963-0123

Richmond Co.: *Northern Neck News* — 5 Court St.; PO Box 8, Warsaw (22572); W; 4,454pd, 21fr (Sw); $5.35; C; publisher W C O'Donovan; editor John Peters; tel (804) 333-3655; fax (804) 333-0033

Rockbridge Co./Buena Vista/Lexington: *Rockbridge Weekly* — 128 W. 21st St.; PO Box 791, Buena Vista (24416); W; 13,300fr (Sw); 30¢; publisher & editor Jerry Clark; tel (540) 261-8000; fax (540) 261-8030

Rockingham/Page Cos.: *The Valley Banner* — 157 Spotswood Ave.; PO Box 126, Elkton (22827); Th; 4,489pd (ABC); $5.85; C; publisher Rockingham Publishing Co.; general manager & editor Randolph C Murphey IV; tel (540) 298-9444; fax (540) 298-2560

Rocky Mount/Franklin Co.: *The Franklin News-Post* — 121 Main St.; PO Box 250, Rocky Mount (24151-0250); M; 7,530pd, 25fr (Sw); $10.06; W/F; 7,530pd (Sw); $10.06; publisher R B Hundley; editor Melinda Williams; tel (540) 483-5113; fax (540) 483-8013

St. Paul/Castlewood/Dante: *Clinch Valley Times* — 16541 Russell St.; PO Box 817, St. Paul (24283-0817); W; 2,599pd, 42fr (Sw); $3.95; publisher Allen Gregory; publisher & editor Ann Y Gregory; tel (540) 762-7671; fax (540) 762-0929

Salem: *Salem Times Register* — 1633 W. Main St.; PO Box 1125 (24153); Th; 4,030pd, 381fr (Sw); $5.32; C; publisher Ray L Robinson; editor Christian Moody; managing editor Edwin L McCoy; tel (540) 389-9355; fax (540) 389-2930

Smithfield: *The Times* — 228 Main St. (23430); PO Box 366 (23431); W; 4,866pd, 95fr (Sw); $4.85; publisher & editor John B Edwards; tel (804) 357-3288; fax (804) 357-0404

S Boston/Halifax Co.: *The South Boston Gazette-Virginian* — 3201 Halifax Rd.; PO Box 524, South Boston (24592); M/W/F; 10,900pd, 173fr (Sw); 36¢; publisher & editor Keith A Shelton; tel (804) 572-3945; fax (804) 572-1173

S Hill: *The South Hill Enterprise* — 914 W. Danville St.; PO Box 60 (23970); W; 8,287pd, 66fr (Sw); $4.20; publisher South Hill Publishing Co. Inc.; editor Frank L Nanney Jr; tel (804) 447-3178; fax (804) 447-5931

Springfield: *Springfield Times Courier* — 1760 Reston Pkwy., Ste. 411, Reston (22090); Th; 14pd, 22,144fr (CAC); $16.95; publisher Arthur W Arundel; general manager Peter Arundel; editor Marcia McAllister; managing editor Janet Rems; tel (703) 437-5400; fax (703) 437-6019

Stuart: *The Bull Mountain Bugle* — PO Box 308 (24171); W; 3,800pd, 100fr (Sw); $3.50; publisher Bob Martin; editor Cindy Griffith; tel (540) 694-7117; fax (540) 694-5510

Stuart/Patrick Co.: *The Enterprise* — 22 E. Main St.; PO Box 348, Stuart (24171-0348); W; 3,990pd, 210fr (Sw); $3.25; publisher Gail M Harding; editor Nancy Lindsey; tel (540) 694-3101; fax (540) 694-3102

Sussex/Surry Cos.: *Sussex-Surry Dispatch* — 228 Fleetwood St.; PO Box 370, Wakefield (23888); W; 2,823pd, 25fr (Sw); $6.25; C; publisher William O'Donovan; general manager & managing editor Lorrie Smith; editor Brian Rafferty; tel (804) 899-3551; fax (804) 899-7312

Tappahannock: *Rappahannock Times* — 622 Charlotte St.; PO Box 1025 (22560); Th; 4,514pd, 280fr (Sw); $4.10; publisher W A Cleaton; editor Chris Rose; tel (804) 443-2200; fax (804) 443-9684

Tazewell: *Clinch Valley News* — 1206 2nd St., Richlands (24641); W; 3,361pd, 36fr (Est); $7.50; C; publisher William H Hall; editor Charles Boothe; managing editor Jim Talbert; tel (540) 963-1081; fax (540) 963-0123

Victoria/Kenbridge: *Kenbridge-Victoria Dispatch* — PO Box 40, Victoria (23974); Th; 3,400pd (Sw); $3.40; publisher & editor Dorothy C Tucker; tel (804) 696-5550; fax (804) 696-2958

Vienna: *The Vienna Times* — 1760 Reston Pkwy., Ste. 411, Reston (22090); Th; 218pd, 12,671fr (CAC); $13.30; C; publisher Arthur W Arundel; general manager Peter Arundel; editor Marcia McAllister; managing editor Janet Rems; tel (703) 437-5400; fax (703) 437-6019

Vinton: *The Vinton Messenger* — 118 E. Lee Ave.; PO Box 508 (24179); Th; 2,407pd, 28fr (Est); 31¢; C; publisher Ray L Robinson; general manager Nita Echols; editor John Warren; managing editor Edwin McCoy; tel (540) 343-0720; fax (540) 343-2648

Virginia Beach: *The Virginia Beach Sun* — 1024 N. Battlefield Blvd. (23320); PO Box 1327, Chesapeake (23327); W; 7,659pd, 1,440fr (Est); $6.05; publisher Hanes Byerly; editor Victoria Edwards; tel (804) 547-4571; fax (804) 548-0390

W Point/King William/New Kent/King/Queen: *The Tidewater Review* — 702 Main St.; PO Box 271, West Point (23181); W; 3,549pd, 121fr (Sw); $6.75; C; publisher W C O'Donovan; general manager & managing editor R E Spears III; tel (804) 843-2282; fax (804) 843-4404

Williamsburg: *The Virginia Gazette* — 216 Ironbound Rd.; PO Box 419 (23187); W/Sa; 14,500pd (Est); $9.95; C; publisher & editor William C O'Donovan; managing editor Susan Q Bruno; tel (804) 220-1736; fax (804) 220-1665

Woodstock: *The Shenandoah Valley-Herald* — 207 N. Main St.; PO Box 507 (22664); W; 6,230pd, 22fr (ABC); $6.35; C; publisher Richard R J Morin; editor C L Earehart; tel (540) 459-4078; fax (540) 459-4077

Wythe Co.: *Southwest Virginia Enterprise* — 460 W. Main St., Wytheville (24382); W; 6,612pd, 32fr (Sw); $8.50; Sa; 6,612pd, 32fr (Sw); $7.75; C; publisher & editor D Gregory Rooker; tel (540) 228-6611, (800) 655-1406; fax (540) 228-7260

Yorktown/York Co.: *York Town Crier* — 4824 George Washington Hwy.; PO Box 978, Yorktown (23692); W; 4,500pd, 500fr (Sw); $7.35; C; publisher D Gaither Perry; general manager Carol Ivy; editor Beth Meisner; tel (804) 898-7225; fax (804) 890-0119

WASHINGTON

Anacortes: *Anacortes American* — 901 6th St.; PO Box 39 (98221); W; 3,752pd (Sw); $7.50; C; publisher & editor Duncan Frazier; tel (360) 293-3122; fax (360) 293-5000

Arlington/Smokey Pt.: *The Times* — 423 N. Olympic Ave., Arlington (98223); W; 2,727pd, 9,943fr (Est); $9.85; C; publisher Sim Wilson; editor Sarah Arney; tel (360) 435-5757; fax (360) 435-0999

Bainbridge Isle: *Bainbridge Review* — 221 Winslow Way W.; PO Box 10817 (98110); W; 4,248pd, 61fr (Sw); $11.50; C; publisher Chris Allen; editor Jack Swanson; managing editor Kevin Dwyer; tel (206) 842-6613; fax (206) 842-5867

Battle Ground: *The Reflector* — 21914 N.E. 112th Ave.; PO Box 2020 (98604); W; 998pd, 18,982fr (VAC); $9.00; C; publisher & editor Marvin F Case; tel (360) 687-5151; fax (360) 687-5162

Blaine/Birch Bay: *The Banner/Pacific News Corp.* — 335 H St., (98230); PO Box 1712, Blaine (98231); Th; 120pd, 7,500fr (Est); $10.50; publisher Egon Nielsen; editor Theresa Thinnes; tel (360) 332-6397; fax (360) 332-2100

Bonney Lake: *The Lakes Observer* — 1007 Main St.; PO Box 428 (98390); W; 1,217pd, 320fr (Sw); 42¢; publisher Gregory L Gordon; editor William Ostlund; tel (206) 863-8172

Bremerton/Silverdale: *Central Kitsap Reporter* — 2817 Wheaton Way, Ste. 104; PO Box 2588, Bremerton (98310-0334); W; 598pd, 21,747fr (CAC); $12.65; C; publisher Michael Shepard; editor Michael Wagar; tel (360) 373-7969; fax (360) 373-7481

Brewster: *Brewster Quad City Herald* — 525 W. Main Ave.; PO Box 37 (98812); Th; 2,500pd (Est); 18¢; publisher & editor Ike Vallance; tel (509) 689-2507; fax (509) 689-2508

Buckley: *Buckley Bulletin* — 1007 Main St.; PO Box 428, Sumner (98390); W; 876pd, 518fr (Sw); 42¢; publisher Gregory L Gordon; editor William Ostlund; tel (360) 863-8697

Burien/Tukwila/Des Moines: *Highline News/Des Moines News* — 207 S.W. 150th St.; PO Box 48119, Burien (98148); W; 7,864pd, 42,981fr (Sw); $20.00; Sa; 7,534pd, 11,181fr (Sw); $20.00; C; publisher Craig Dennis; editor Rob Smith; tel (206) 242-0100; fax (206) 241-2788

Camas/Washougal: *Camas-Washougal Post Record* — 425 N.E. 4th Ave.; PO Box 1013, Camas (98607); Tu; 4,200pd, 4,000fr (Sw); $4.50; C; publisher Mike Gallagher; editor Craig Clohessy; tel (360) 834-2141; fax (360) 834-3423

Cashmere: *Cashmere Valley Record* — 201 Cottage Ave.; PO Box N (98815); W; 1,544pd, 77fr (Sw); $5.10; C; publishers Jeff Gauger & Liz Gauger; tel (509) 782-3781; fax (509) 548-4789

Castle Rock/Cowlitz Co.: *Cowlitz County Advocate* — 27 Cowlitz St. W.; PO Box 368, Castle Rock (98611); Tu; 92pd, 4,097fr (VAC); $8.50; C; publisher Johnny L Hayden; editor Cheryll Borgaard; tel (360) 274-6663; fax (360) 274-6664

Cathlamet: *Wahkiakum County Eagle* — 77 Main St.; PO Box 368 (98612-0368); Th; 1,611pd, 38fr (Sw); $3.10; publisher Robert Nelson; editor Rick Nelson; tel (360) 795-3391; fax (360) 795-3983

Chelan: *Lake Chelan Mirror* — 315 E. Woodin Ave.; PO Box 249 (98816); W; 3,300pd (Est); $4.70; publisher & editor Richard T Gavin; tel (509) 682-2213

Cheney: *Cheney Free Press* — 1616 W. 1st St.; PO Box 218 (99004); Th; 3,450pd, 4,950fr (Est); 50¢; publisher Bill Ifft; editor Kevin Hanson; tel (509) 235-6184; fax (509) 235-2887

Chewelah/Springdale/Addy: *The Chewelah Independent* — E. 309 Main; PO Box 5, Chewelah (99109); Th; 2,197pd, 149fr (Est); $3.75; publisher Nancy Blake; editor Liz Riley; tel (509) 935-8422; fax (509) 935-8426

Cle Elum: *Northern Kittitas County Tribune* — 221 Pennsylvania; PO Box 308 (98922); Th; 3,022pd, 3fr (Sw); $3.00; publisher Walter R Larson; editor Mary Lou Larson; tel (509) 674-2511

Colfax: *Whitman County Gazette* — 211 N. Main St. (99111); Th; 4,272pd, 46fr (Est); $5.00; publisher Gordon Forgey; editor Jerry Jones; tel (509) 397-4333; fax (509) 397-4527

Colville: *Statesman-Examiner* — PO Box 271 (99114); W; 6,904pd, 25fr (Sw); $8.20; C; publisher Don Birch; editor Chris K Cowbrough; tel (509) 684-4567; fax (509) 684-3849

Coulee City: *The News-Standard* — 405 W. Main; PO Box 488 (99115); Th; 662pd (Est); $3.25; publisher Gary Page; publisher & editor Margi Page; tel (509) 632-5402; fax (509) 632-8791

Davenport: *Davenport Times* — 506 Morgan; PO Box 66 (99122); Th; 2,226pd (Sw); $5.00; C; publisher Kyp Graber; editor Kathy Hedgecock; tel (509) 725-0101

Dayton: *Dayton Chronicle* — 358 E. Main; PO Box 6 (99328); W; 1,850pd (Est); $5.88; publisher & editor Jack Williams; tel (509) 382-2221

Deer Park: *Tribune* — N. 104 Main St.; PO Box 400 (99006); W; 1,799pd, 58fr (Sw); $6.25; C; publisher Barbara Hanna; editor Tom Costigan; tel (509) 276-5043; fax (509) 276-2041

Douglas Co.: *The Douglas County Empire Press* — 102 W. Locust; PO Box 430, Waterville (98858); Th; 10pd, 1,834fr (Est); $3.80; publisher Gary Page; publisher & editor Margi Page; tel (509) 745-8313; fax (509) 745-8313

Eastsound/Friday Harbor: *The Islands' Sounder* — PO Box 758, Eastsound (98245); W; 4,648pd, 267fr (Sw); $8.45; C; publisher Jay Brodt; editor Ted Grossman; tel (360) 376-4500; fax (360) 376-4501

Enumclaw/Buckley: *Enumclaw Courier-Herald/Buckley News Banner* — 1627 Cole St.; PO Box 157, Enumclaw (98022); W; 6,389pd, 100fr (Sw); $9.79; publisher Jack Darnton; editor Paul Schmidt; tel (360) 825-2555; fax (360) 825-1092

Ephrata: *Grant County Journal* — 29 Alder S.W.; PO Box 998 (98823); M/Th; 2,818pd (Sw); 38¢; publisher Jeffrey G Fletcher; editor Joe Dennis; managing editor Randy Bracht; tel (509) 754-4636; fax (509) 754-5112

Everett: *Everett News* — PO Box 499, Snohomish (98290); W; 7,000pd, 30,000fr (Est); 80¢; publisher David H Mach; editor Leslie Hynes; tel (360) 568-4121; fax (360) 568-1484

Federal Way: *Federal Way News* — 1634 S. 312th St. (98003); W; 6,057pd, 40,518fr (Sw); $20.00; Sa; 6,152pd, 14,190fr (Sw); $20.00; C; publisher Craig Dennis; editor Brad Broberg; tel (206) 839-0700

Ferndale/Blaine: *Westside Record-Journal* — 2008 Main St.; PO Box 38, Ferndale (98248); W; 2,800pd, 5,750fr (Sw); $11.55; C; publisher Michael D Lewis; general manager Kimberly Winjum; editor Josh Barnhill; tel (360) 384-1411; fax (360) 671-9083

Forks: *Forks Forum & Peninsula Herald* — 490 Forks Ave.; PO Box 300 (98331); W; 890pd, 4,210fr (Est); $5.03; C; publisher Brown M Maloney; editor Don Gronning; tel (360) 374-2281; fax (360) 374-5739

Gig Harbor: *The Peninsula Gateway* — 7521 Pioneer Way; PO Box 407 (98335); W; 10,532pd, 280fr (Sw); $11.70; C; publisher Thomas C Taylor; editor Tony Hazarian; tel (206) 851-9921; fax (206) 851-3939

Goldendale/Klickitat Co.: *Goldendale Sentinel* — 117 W. Main, Goldendale (98620-9526); Th; 2,875pd (Est); $5.50; C; publisher Andrew McNab; general manager Brent T DeLaPaz; editor Robert Kelly; tel (509) 773-3777; fax (509) 773-4737

Grand Coulee: *The Star* — 03 Midway Ave.; PO Box 150 (99133); W; 1,889pd, 22fr (Sw); $5.25; publisher & editor Scott Hunter; tel (509) 633-1350; fax (509) 633-3828

Grandview: *Grandview Herald* — 107 Division St. (98930); W; 2,440pd, 41fr (Sw); $5.47; C; publisher John L Fournier Jr; editor Cathy Masters; tel (509) 882-3712; fax (509) 882-2833

Issaquah: *Issaquah Press* — 45 Front St. S.; PO Box 1328 (98027); W; 7,290pd, 11,193fr (VAC); $12.00; C; publisher Deborah L Berto; editor Dave Hansen; tel (206) 392-6434; fax (206) 391-1541

Kelso/Longview: *Kelso-Longview Advocate* — 1105-A 15th St., Longview (98632); Tu; 33pd, 24,655fr (VAC); $11.50; C; publisher Johnny L Hayden; editor Cheryll Borgaard; tel (360) 636-3636; fax (360) 636-1318

Kirkland: *Kirkland Courier* — 14796 N.E. 95th St. (Redmond 98052); PO Box 3238 (98083); W; 569pd, 15,517fr (VAC); $15.00; C; publisher Kim Nolan; general manager Robert Munford; editor Mike Lee; managing editor Daven Rosener; tel (206) 861-4660; fax (206) 881-9567

LaConner Area: *Channel Town Press* — 306 Morris St.; PO Box 575, LaConner (98257); W; 1,810pd, 15fr (Sw); $5.00; publisher Audrey M Pentz; general manager & managing editor Pattie A Johns; tel (360) 466-3315

Copyright ©1996 by the Editor & Publisher Co.

Lakewood/Steilacoom/DuPont: *The Lakewood Journal* — 9105 Bridgeport Way S.W., Tacoma (98499); Th; 945pd, 12,688fr (CAC); $13.55; C; publisher Jim Long; editor Walter Neary; tel (360) 584-8080; fax (360) 584-6098

Langley: *South Whidbey Record* — 201 2nd & Anthes Aves.; PO Box 387 (98260); W/Sa; 5,700pd (Est); $9.50; publisher Gregg McConnell; editor Jim Larsen; tel (360) 221-5300; fax (360) 221-6474

Leavenworth: *The Leavenworth Echo* — 215 14th St.; PO Box 39 (98826-0039); W; 2,370pd, 30fr (Sw); $5.50; C; publishers Jeff Gauger & Liz Gauger; tel (509) 548-5286; fax (509) 548-4789

Lewis Co.: *Lewis County News* — 320 N.W. Pacific Ave., Chehalis (98532); W; 81pd, 22,212fr (VAC); $11.50; C; publisher Johnny L Hayden; editor Bonita Meyers; tel (360) 740-0445; fax (360) 740-0443

Long Beach/S Pacific Co.: *Chinook Observer* — 212 S. Oregon St.; PO Box 427, Long Beach (98631-0427); Tu; 6,166pd, 20fr (Est); $5.50; publisher East Oregonian Publishing Co.; general manager George Potter; editor Matt Winters; tel (360) 642-8181; fax (360) 642-8105

Lynden/Everson: *Lynden Tribune* — 113 N. 6th St.; PO Box 153, Lynden (98264); W; 6,200pd, 7,700fr (Sw); $14.90; C; publisher Michael D Lewis; editor Dave Brumbaugh; tel (360) 354-4444; fax (360) 734-0575

Lynwood/Edmonds/Mill Creek/Mountlake Terrace: *The Enterprise* — 7300 196th St.; PO Box 977, Lynnwood (98036); W; 206pd, 44,170fr (VAC); $20.30; C; publisher Joe Pitt; editor Tom Pearce; tel (206) 775-7521; fax (206) 774-8622

Magnolia: *Magnolia News* — 225 W. Galer St., Seattle (98119); W; 413pd, 7,281fr (VAC); $122.00; C; publisher Mike Dillon; editor Jack Arends; tel (206) 282-0900; fax (206) 285-1085

Maple Valley/Ravensdale: *Voice of the Valley* — PO Box 307, Maple Valley (98038); W; 12,600fr (Est); $7.00; publisher & editor Saundra Hipple; tel (206) 432-9696; fax (206) 432-0701

Marysville: *The Globe* — PO Box 145 (98270); W; 3,245pd, 15,212fr (Est); $9.85; publisher Sim Wilson; editor Dan Buchanan; tel (360) 659-1300; fax (360) 658-0350

Marysville/Arlington: *North Snohomish Weekly* — PO Box 3187, Arlington (98223); Th; 22,857fr (Sw); $15.10; C; publisher Leighton P Wood; editor Kristen Kinnamon; tel (360) 653-8000; fax (360) 653-9848

Mercer Island: *Mercer Island Reporter* — 7845 S.E. 30th St.; PO Box 38 (98040); W; 4,782pd, 408fr (Est); $11.80; C; publisher Howard Mullenary; general manager & editor Jane Meyer; tel (206) 232-1215; fax (206) 232-1284

Methow Vly.: *Methow Valley News* — 201 Glover St.; PO Box 97 (98856); W; 2,885pd, 57fr (Sw); $5.70; publisher R Lee Hicks; editor Mary Rea; tel (509) 997-7011; fax (509) 977-3277

Monroe/Sultan: *Monroe Monitor/Valley News* — 113 W. Main St.; PO Box 399, Monroe (98272); W; 3,336pd, 208fr (Est); $5.90; publisher & editor Ken Robinson; tel (360) 794-7116; fax (360) 794-6202

Montesano/Aberdeen/Hoquiam: *Montesano Vidette* — 109 W. Marcy St.; PO Box 671, Montesano (98563); Th; 2,400pd (Est); $3.50; publisher C E Pritchard; editor H R (Sam) Pritchard; tel (360) 249-3311

Morton/Mineral/Randle/Mossyrock/Onalaska: *The Morton Journal* — 278 Main St.; PO Drawer M, Morton (98356-0077); W; 2,695pd, 22fr (Sw); $5.75; C; publishers Franklin DeVaul & Judith DeVaul; general manager Kathy Lyons; editor Steven Smith; tel (360) 496-5993; fax (360) 496-5993

Newport/Pend Oreille Co.: *The Newport Miner* — 317 S. Union Ave.; PO Box 349, Newport (99156); W; 3,891pd, 15fr (Est); $4.95; C; publisher & editor Fred J Willenbrock; tel (509) 447-2433; fax (509) 447-9222

N Bend/Snoqualmie/Fall City/Preston/Carnation/Duvall: *Snoqualmie Valley Reporter* — 231 N. Bend Blvd. N.; PO Box 349, North Bend (98045); W; 3,486pd, 938fr (Est); $8.54; C; publisher Howard Mullenary; general manager & editor Mark Briggs; tel (206) 888-9435; fax (206) 888-9439

N Franklin Co.: *Franklin County Graphic* — 346 S. Columbia Ave.; PO Box 160, Connell (99326); Th; 200pd, 2,506fr (Est); $4.25; C; publisher & editor Duane W Ruser; general manager & managing editor Kathy Valdez; tel (509) 234-3181; fax (509) 234-3182

N Seattle: *The North Central Outlook* — 2314 3rd Ave., Seattle (98121); W; 1,198pd, 7,502fr (VAC); $20.00; C; publisher Brenda French; editor Linnea Lundgren; tel (206) 461-1300; fax (206) 461-1340

Oak Harbor: *Crosswind* — PO Box 10 (98277); F; 8,368fr (CAC); $12.65; C; publisher Gregg McConnell; editor Eileen Brown; tel (360) 675-6611

Oak Harbor: *Whidbey News Times* — 3098-300 Ave. W.; PO Box 10 (98277); W/Sa; 8,344pd, 260fr (CAC); $12.65; C; publisher Gregg McConnell; editor David Fisher; tel (360) 675-6611; fax (360) 679-2695

Ocean Shores/Ocean City/Copalis Beach/Copalis Crossing/Pacific Beach/Taholah: *The North Coast News* — 739 Pt. Brown Ave. N.W.; PO Box 272, Ocean Shores (98569); W; 910pd, 5fr (Sw); $6.90; C; publisher Phyllis J Porter; general manager Bob Focht; editor Tom Hyde; tel (360) 289-2441

Odessa: *The Odessa Record* — 1 W. 1st Ave.; PO Box 458 (99159); Th; 1,250pd (Sw); $4.00; publisher & editor Donald E Walter; tel (509) 982-2632; fax (509) 982-2651

Omak/Okanogan: *The Omak-Okanogan County Chronicle* — 618 Okoma Dr.; PO Box 553, Omak (98841-0553); W; 5,680pd, 248fr (Est); $9.40; C; publisher & editor John E Andrist & Mary Koch; tel (509) 826-1110; fax (509) 826-5819

Oroville/Tonasket: *Okanogan Valley Gazette-Tribune* — PO Box 250, Oroville (98844-0250); Th; 2,959pd, 38fr (Est); 26¢; publisher Robert E Davis; editor Gary A DeVon; tel (509) 476-3602; fax (509) 476-3054

Othello: *The Outlook* — PO Box 0 (99344); W; 2,205pd, 5,750fr (Est); 26¢; C; publisher Bill Edlin; editor Mark Grim; tel (509) 488-3342; fax (509) 488-3345

Pierce Co.: *The South Pierce County Dispatch* — 109 Center St.; PO Box 248, Eatonville (98328); W; 3,400pd, 16,600fr (Est); 44¢; publisher James Martin-Almy; tel (360) 832-4411; fax (360) 832-6606

Pomeroy: *East Washingtonian* — 933 Main St.; PO Box 70 (99347); W; 1,700pd (Est); $4.35; publisher & editor Michael Tom; publisher Teresa M Tom; tel (509) 843-1313; fax (509) 843-3911

Port Orchard/S Kitsap Co.: *Port Orchard Independent* — 1035 Bethel Rd.; PO Box 27, Port Orchard (98366); W/Sa; 2,029pd, 15,633fr (Sw); $12.65; C; publisher Michael Shepard; editor Patrick Jenkins; tel (360) 876-4414; fax (360) 292-9521

Port Townsend: *Port Townsend Jefferson County Leader* — 226 Adams St.; PO Box 552 (98368); W; 9,496pd, 38fr (Sw); $8.20; publisher & editor Frank W Garred; general manager Scott Wilson; tel (360) 385-2900

Poulsbo/N Kitsap: *Kitsap County Herald* — 19062 Highway 305, Ste. 203; PO Box 278, Poulsbo (98370); W/Sa; 1,591pd, 7,807fr (Sw); $11.50; C; publisher Douglas Weese; general manager Kim Pisz; editor Ray Miller; managing editor Kevin Dwyer; tel (360) 779-4464; fax (360) 682-1107

Prosser: *Prosser Record-Bulletin* — 613 7th St.; PO Box 750 (99350); W; 3,411pd, 61fr (Sw); $5.47; C; publisher John L Fournier Jr; editor Cathy Masters; tel (509) 786-1711; fax (509) 786-1779

Puyallup/Eastern Pierce: *Pierce County Herald/Herald Sampler* — PO Box 517, Puyallup (98371); Tu/F; 16,000pd, 24,000fr (Est); $14.65; C; publisher Gale Robinette; editor George M Pica; tel (206) 841-2481; fax (206) 840-8231

Queen Anne: *Queen Anne News* — 225 W. Galer St., Seattle (98119); W; 1,408pd, 11,238fr (VAC); $9.25; C; publisher Mike Dillon; editor Jack Arends; tel (206) 282-0900; fax (206) 285-1085

Quincy: *Quincy Valley Post Register* — PO Box 217 (98848); Th; 2,000pd, 90fr (Est); 19¢; publisher Charles Fournier; general manager Rosemary Cassal; editor Mark Martinez; tel (509) 787-4511; fax (509) 787-2682

Rainier/Columbia Cos.: *New Rainier Review* — 27 Cowlitz St. W.; PO Box 368, Castle Rock (98611); Tu; 20pd, 3,545fr (VAC); $7.25; C; publisher Johnny L Hayden; editor Cheryll Borgaard; tel (360) 274-6663; fax (360) 274-6664

Raymond/S Bend: *The Willapa Harbor Herald* — 333 3rd St.; PO Box 706, Raymond (98577); W; 3,986pd, 50fr (Sw); $5.92; C; publishers & editors Lora Nicholson & Meredith Nicholson; tel (360) 942-3466; fax (360) 942-3487

Redmond: *Redmond Sammamish Valley New* — 14796 N.E. 95th St. (98052); W; 606pd, 16,615fr (VAC); $15.00; C; publisher Kim Nolan; general manager Robert Munford; editor Mike Lee; managing editor Daven Rosener; tel (206) 883-7187; fax (206) 881-9567

Ritzville: *The Ritzville Adams County Journal* — 216 W. Railroad Ave.; PO Box 288 (99169-0288); Th; 1,896pd, 46fr (Est); $3.50; publisher Dee Ruser; publisher & editor Duane W Ruser; tel (509) 659-1020; fax (509) 659-0842

Royal City/Mattawa: *Royal Review* — PO Box 219, Royal City (99357); W; 1,125pd, 35fr (Est); $3.75; publisher & editor Andrew Perkins; publisher Rachel Perkins; tel (509) 346-9723; fax (509) 346-9453

San Juan Co.: *The Journal of the San Juan Islands* — 580 Guard St.; PO Box 519, Friday Harbor (98250); W; 5,081pd, 175fr (Sw); $10.25; publisher John McKenna; editor Mike Hagan; tel (360) 378-4191; fax (360) 378-4103

Seattle: *Capitol Hill Times* — 2314 3rd Ave. (98121); W; 1,001pd, 15,809fr (VAC); $20.00; C; publisher Brenda French; editor Dennis Pauley; tel (206) 461-1300; fax (206) 461-1340

Seattle: *University Herald* — 2314 3rd Ave. (98121); W; 1,844pd, 9,940fr (VAC); $20.00; C; publisher Brenda L French; editor Linnea Lundgren; tel (206) 461-1300; fax (206) 461-1340

Sedro-Woolley/Burlington: *Courier Times* — 807 Metcalf St.; PO Box 32, Sedro-Wooley (98284); Th; 2,500pd, 2,500fr (Sw); $6.50; publisher Vernon Barr; general manager Fred Slipper; editor Cookson Beecher; tel (360) 855-1641; fax (360) 855-1652

Sequim: *The Sequim Gazette* — 147 W. Washington; PO Box 1750 (98382); W; 7,950pd, 80fr (Sw); $9.65; publisher Brown M Maloney; general manager Sue Ellen Riesau; editor Jim Manders; tel (360) 683-3311; fax (360) 683-6670

Shelton: *Shelton-Mason County Journal* — 227 W. Cota St.; PO Box 430 (98584); Th; 9,874pd, 74fr (Est); $8.00; publisher & editor Henry Gay; tel (360) 426-4412

Skagit Co.: *The Skagit Argus* — 413 Gates St.; PO Box 739, Mount Vernon (98273); W; 3,677pd, 635fr (Sw); $7.60; publisher Dan Berentson; editor Tony Flynn; tel (360) 336-6555; fax (360) 336-3176

Snohomish: *Snohomish County Tribune* — PO Box 499 (98291); W; 2,682pd, 36,000fr (Est); 95¢; C; publisher David H Mach; editor Leslie Hynes; tel (360) 568-4121; fax (360) 568-1484

Snoqualmie/Fall City: *Snoqualmie Valley Record* — 8124 Falls Ave. S.E.; PO Box 300, Snoqualmie (98065); Th; 5,000pd (Est); $5.00; publisher Robert Scott; editor Brian Kelly; tel (206) 888-2311; fax (206) 888-2427

S Seattle: *Beacon Hill News/South District Journal* — 2314 3rd Ave., Seattle (98121); W; 3,009pd, 14,979fr (VAC); $20.00; C; publisher Brenda L French; tel (206) 461-1300; fax (206) 461-1340

S Spokane/N Whitman Co.: *The Standard-Register* — N. 125 Crosby St.; PO Box 988, Tekoa (99033); F; 1,800pd, 2,000fr (Sw); $4.00; C; publisher Tim Flock; editor Bonita Lawhead; tel (509) 284-5782

Spokane Vly.: *Spokane Valley News* — 10623 E. Sprague Ave., Ste. A, Spokane (99206); W; 3,916pd, 162fr (Est); $13.00; C; publisher & editor Rob Allen; tel (509) 926-8341; fax (509) 927-1154

Spokane Vly.: *The Valley Herald* — 8940 E. Sprague Ave., Spokane (99212); Th; 2,000pd, 500fr (Est); $12.00; publisher Clark E Hager Sr; editor Charlie Plumb; tel (509) 924-2440; fax (509) 928-3168

Sprague/Harrington: *Sprague Advocate* — S. 113 C St.; PO Box 327, Sprague (99032); Th; 450pd, 12fr (Sw); $3.45; publisher & editor Tess Canaday; tel (509) 257-2928

Stanwood/Camano Island: *Stanwood/Camano News* — 9005 271st St. N.W.; PO Box 999, Stanwood (98292); Tu; 3,489pd (Est); $7.60; publisher & editor Dave Pinkham; tel (360) 629-2155; fax (360) 629-4211

Stevenson: *The Skamania County Pioneer* — 138 N.W. 2nd St.; PO Box 219 (98648); W; 2,484pd, 109fr (Est); $2.95; publishers Marilyn Kelly & Pat Diehl; editor Lynn Blaisdell; tel (509) 427-8444; fax (509) 427-4229

Sumner: *The News Review* — 1007 Main St.; PO Box 428 (98390); W; 2,235pd, 21fr (Sw); 42¢; publisher Gregory L Gordon; editor William Ostlund; tel (206) 863-8171

Tenino: *The Tenino Independent* — 297 W. Sussex Ave.; PO Box 4004 (98589); W; 1,050pd, 4,000fr (Est); 30¢; publishers Franklin DeVaul & Judith DeVaul; editor Glen Dickason; tel (360) 264-2500; fax (360) 264-2955

Toppenish: *Toppenish Review* — 11 E. Toppenish Ave.; PO Box 511 (98948); W; 3,100pd, 3,700fr (Est); $3.25; publisher James Flint; editor Ted Escobar; tel (509) 865-4055; fax (509) 865-2655

Vancouver: *Cover Story* — 701 W. 8th St.; PO Box 180 (98666); Tu; 59,391pd, 42,166fr (Est); $37.11; C; publisher Scott Campbell; editor Tom Koenninger; tel (360) 694-3391; fax (360) 699-6033

Vashon/Maury Island: *Vashon-Maury Island Beachcomber* — 17500 99th Ave. S.W.; PO Box 447, Vashon Island (98070); W; 4,340pd, 149fr (Sw); $6.95; publisher Linda Martin; editor Allison Arthur; tel (206) 463-9195; fax (206) 463-6122

Waitsburg: *The Times* — 139 Main St.; PO Box 97 (99361); Th; 1,830pd, 20fr (Est); $5.10; publisher Jane A Smith; publisher & editor Ron D Smith; tel (509) 337-6631; fax (509) 337-6045

Wapato: *Wapato Independent* — PO Box 67 (98951); W; 1,900pd (Est); $2.75; publisher James Flint; editor Steven McFadden; tel (509) 877-3322; fax (509) 865-2577

W Seattle: *West Seattle Herald* — 3500 S.W. Alaska, Seattle (98126); W; 12,122pd, 16,549fr (Est); $15.50; publisher Jerry Robinson; general manager Roger Hollings; editor Adam Worcester; tel (206) 932-0300; fax (206) 937-1223

White Salmon/Bingen: *The Enterprise* — 220 E. Jewett; PO Box 218, White Salmon (98672); Th; 2,700pd, 37fr (Sw); $4.35; C; publisher Elaine Bakke; editor D C Jesse Burkhardt; tel (509) 493-2112; fax (509) 493-2399

Whitman Co.: *Palouse Living* — S. 107 Grand (99163); PO Box 8187, Moscow (83843); Tu; 14,316fr (Sw); $6.30; C; publisher & editor Randy C Frisch; tel (208) 882-5561; fax (208) 883-8205

Wilbur: *Wilbur Register* — PO Box 186 (99185); Th; 1,646pd, 115fr (Est); $3.00; publisher & editor Frank Stedman; tel (509) 647-5551; fax (509) 647-5552

Woodinville/Bothell/Kenmore: *Northshore Citizen* — PO Box 647, Bothell (98041); W; 7,000pd, 18,000fr (Est); $13.00; C; publisher Howard Mullenary; editor John R Merrill; tel (206) 486-1231; fax (206) 483-3286

Woodland/Kalama/Ridgefield/Upper Clark Co.: *The Lewis River News/Kalama Bulletin* — 435 Davidson Ave.; PO Box 39, Woodland (98674); W; 137pd, 7,546fr (VAC); $8.95; C; publisher Johnny L Hayden; editor Larry Martinez; tel (360) 225-8287; fax (360) 225-8289

Yelm/Rainier/Roy/McKenna: *The Nisqually Valley News* — 207 Yelm Ave. W.; PO Box 597, Yelm (98597); W/Th; 2,520pd, 10fr (Est); $7.00; C; publisher Denny Waller; editor Fiona Reeves; tel (360) 458-2681; fax (360) 458-5741

WEST VIRGINIA

Berkeley Springs: *The Morgan Messenger* — 104 Mercer St.; PO Box 567, Berkeley Springs (25411); W; 2,909pd, 2,400fr (Est); $3.80; C; publisher James S Buzzerd; editor J Warren Buzzerd; managing editor John Douglas; tel (304) 258-1800; fax (304) 258-8441

Braxton Co.: *Braxton Democrat-Central* — 205 Main St., Sutton (26601); F; 3,926pd, 100fr (Est); $3.00; publisher & managing editor Craig A Smith; editor Joan Bias; tel (304) 765-5555; fax (304) 765-5555

Brooke Co.: *The Brooke County Review* — 319 Charles St.; PO Box 591, Wellsburg (26070); Th; 2,000pd, 400fr (Sw); $4.00; publisher & editor J W George Wallace; tel (304) 737-0946; fax (304) 737-0297

Buckhannon: *Record Delta* — 7 N. Locust St.; PO Box 550 (26201); M/W/F; 3,865pd, 122fr (Sw); $8.51; publisher Mark E Davis; managing editor Jim Warner; tel (304) 472-2800; fax (304) 472-0537

Calhoun Co.: *The Calhoun Chronicle* — PO Box 400, Grantsville (26147); Th; 3,300pd (Est); 18¢; publisher Carl R Morris; general manager Sandi Marshall; editor Newton Nichols; tel (304) 354-6917; fax (304) 354-7142

Charles Town/Jefferson Co.: *Spirit of Jefferson Advocate* — 210 N. George St.; PO Box 966, Charles Town (25414); Th; 4,894pd, 77fr (Sw); $6.00; publisher Jefferson Publishing Co. Inc.; general manager R Meade Dorsey; editor Edward W Dockeney Jr; tel (304) 725-2046

Clay/Clay Co.: *Clay County Free Press* — 115 Main St., PO Box 180, Clay (25043); W; 3,894pd, 140fr (Sw); $4.40; publisher & editor Clinton N Nichols; tel (304) 587-4250; fax (304) 587-2213

Elizabeth: *Wirt County Journal* — PO Box 309 (26143); W; 2,515pd, 45fr (Est); 20¢; publisher James McGoldrick; general manager & editor Joyce Moller; tel (304) 275-8981; fax (304) 684-2426

Fayette Plateau: *The Fayette Tribune* — 417 Main St.; PO Box 139, Oak Hill (25901); M/Th; 5,917pd (Est); $5.83; publisher Tom James; general manager Debby McNeal; editor Cheryl Keenan; tel (304) 469-3373; fax (304) 469-4105

Glenville: *The Glenville Democrat* — 206 E. Main St.; PO Box 458 (26351); Th; 2,100pd, 25fr (Sw); $3.50; C; publisher & editor David H Corcoran; tel (304) 462-7309

Glenville: *The Glenville Pathfinder* — 109 E. Main St.; PO Box 430 (26351); Th; 1,200pd, 8fr (Sw); $3.50; C; publisher & editor David H Corcoran; tel (304) 462-7309; fax (304) 462-7300

Grafton: *The Mountain Statesman* — 914 W. Main St.; PO Box 218 (26354); M/W/F; 2,584pd, 20fr (Sw); $7.50; C; publisher Mark Davis; general manager & managing editor James L Clark; editor Marvin Gelhausen; tel (304) 265-3333; fax (304) 265-3342

Guyandotte: *Guyandotte Voice* — 6202 S. Main St.; PO Box 4508, Chapmanville (25508); Th; 980pd, 60fr (Sw); $4.25; publisher Logan Media Inc.; editor Jerry Godby; tel (304) 855-3588; fax (304) 855-3589

Harrisville: *Ritchie Gazette & The Cairo Standard* — 112-116 E. Main St.; PO Box 215 (26362-0215); Th; 3,632pd, 40fr (Sw); $4.46; publisher & editor Delores J Smith; general manager Judith D Newbrough; tel (304) 643-2221

Hinton: *Hinton News* — 210 2nd Ave.; PO Box 1000 (25951); Tu; 4,329pd (Est); $5.20; publisher & editor Fred Long; tel (304) 466-0005

Huntington/Barboursville: *The Cabell Record* — 2085 U.S. Rte. 60; PO Box 186, Culloden (25510); Th; 1,554pd, 184fr (Sw); $4.40; C; publisher & editor William O Robinson; tel (304) 743-1222; fax (304) 562-6214

Iaeger: *The Industrial News* — PO Drawer 180 (24844); W; 2,500pd, 20fr (Est); $2.35; publisher & editor W A Johnson; general manager & managing editor Ruby McCoy; tel (304) 938-2142; fax (304) 436-3146

Jackson Co.: *The Jackson Star News* — 237 Washington St.; PO Box 10, Ravenswood (26164); W; 5,850pd, 50fr (Sw); $5.15; Sa; 14,000fr (Sw); $5.15; C; publisher & editor Gregory Matics; tel (304) 273-9333; fax (304) 273-3401

Keyser: *The Weekender-The Mountain Echo* — 24 Armstrong St.; PO Box 879 (26726); Sa; 6,314pd, 76fr (Est); 21¢; C; publisher Jim Tetrick; editor R Michael Johnson; tel (304) 788-3333; fax (304) 788-3398

Kingwood/Preston Co.: *Preston County Journal* — 110 W. Main St.; PO Box 587, Kingwood (26537); W/Sa; 5,299pd (Est); $4.50; publisher Gary A Bolyard; general manager Dennis Peters; editor Tina M Bolyard; managing editor Carol Peters; tel (304) 329-0090; fax (304) 329-2450

Lincoln Co.: *The Lincoln Journal Inc.* — 328 Walnut St.; PO Box 308, Hamlin (25523); W; 5,246pd (Sw); $7.85; C; publisher Thomas A Robinson; general manager Patty Pritchard; editor L Christopher Prichard; tel (304) 824-5101; fax (304) 824-5210

Lincoln Co.: *The Lincoln News Sentinel* — 328 Walnut St.; PO Box 308, Hamlin (25523); W; 1,250pd, 25fr (Sw); $7.85; C; publisher Thomas A Robinson; general manager Patty Pritchard; editor L Christopher Prichard; tel (304) 824-5101; fax (304) 824-5210

Lincoln Co.: *The Lincoln Times* — 328 Walnut St.; PO Box 308, Hamlin (25523); Sa; 10,400fr (Sw); $7.85; C; publisher Thomas A Robinson; general manager Patty Pritchard; editor L Christopher Prichard; tel (304) 824-5101; fax (304) 824-5210

Madison/Danville: *Coal Valley News* — PO Box 508, Madison (25130); W; 6,000pd, 12,200fr (Est); $3.75; publisher & editor F Keith Davis; managing editor Connie Cumbridge; tel (304) 369-1165; fax (304) 369-1166

Madison/Danville: *Hometown News* — PO Box 597, Madison (25130); W; 4,455pd, 7fr (Est); $3.80; publisher & editor Janet Yeager; tel (304) 369-5175; fax (304) 369-5176

Marlinton/Pocahontas Co.: *The Pocahontas Times* — 810 2nd Ave.; PO Box 117, Marlinton (24954); Th; 6,347pd, 89fr (Sw); $3.50; publisher Pocahontas Times Inc.; editor William P Mc Neel; managing editor Pamela E Pritt; tel (304) 799-4973

Mason Co.: *Tri-County News* — PO Box 468, Mason (25260); Sa; 16,000fr (Est); $4.40; publisher Robert L Wingett; general manager Larry Boyer; editor Mindy Carnes; managing editor Larry Ewing; tel (614) 446-2342; fax (614) 446-3008

Monroe Co.: *Monroe Watchman* — 400 Main St.; PO Box 179, Union (24983); Th; 4,000pd (Est); $1.78; publisher & editor H H Mohler; tel (304) 772-3016

Moorefield: *The Moorefield Examiner and Weekender* — 132 Main St.; PO Box 380 (26836); W/Sa; 3,517pd, 119fr (Est); $2.25; publisher & editor Phoebe F Heishman; general manager David Heishman; tel (304) 538-2342; fax (304) 538-7294

Mullens/Wyoming Co.: *The Mullens Advocate* — 217 Moran Ave., Mullens (25882); W; 2,565pd, 231fr (Sw); 23¢; publisher Tony Johnson; general manager & managing editor Eva E Smith; tel (304) 294-4144

New Cumberland: *Hancock County Courier* — Jefferson St.; PO Box 547 (26047); Th; 1,902pd, 120fr (Sw); $3.70; publisher & editor Hugh C Tate Sr & Joyce L Frain; tel (304) 564-3131; fax (304) 564-3131

New Martinsville: *Wetzel Chronicle* — 1100 3rd St.; PO Box 289, New Martinsville (26155); W; 6,721pd, 106fr (Est); 22¢; C; publisher Kenneth H Sickle; editor Don Smith; tel (304) 455-3300; fax (304) 455-1275

Parsons/Tucker Co.: *The Parsons Advocate* — 212 Main St.; PO Box 403, Parsons (26287); W; 3,650pd, 85fr (Sw); $3.25; publisher George Smith; publisher & editor Mariwyn M Smith; tel (304) 478-3533; fax (304) 478-4658

Petersburg: *Grant County Press* — PO Box 39 (26847); Tu; 5,210pd (Sw); $4.25; publisher Potomac Valley Press Inc.; editor Bill Fouch; tel (304) 257-1844; fax (304) 257-1691

Philippi: *The Barbour Democrat* — PO Box 459 (26416); W; 4,655pd, 157fr (Est); $2.93; publisher & editor Robert A Byrne; tel (304) 457-2222; fax (304) 457-2703

Piedmont/Westernport/Luke: *The Piedmont Herald* — 34 Railroad St.; PO Box 68, Piedmont (26750); Tu; 2,151pd, 134fr (Est); $1.70; publishers & editors Margaret J Hood & William T Hood; editor Bob Fike; tel (304) 355-2381; fax (304) 355-2383

Pineville/Wyoming Co.: *The Independent Herald* — PO Box 100, Pineville (24874-0100); W; 3,391pd, 766fr (Est); $2.75; publisher Charles Cline; editor Ron Mullens; tel (304) 732-6060; fax (304) 732-8228

Pleasants Co.: *Pleasants County Leader* — 206 George St.; PO Box 27, St. Marys (26170); Sa; 1,994pd (Sw); 35¢; C; publisher & editor James McGoldrick; tel (304) 684-2424; fax (304) 684-2426

Pleasants Co.: *St. Marys Oracle* — 206 George St.; PO Box 27, St. Marys (26170); W; 2,976pd, 40fr (Sw); 35¢; C; publisher & editor James McGoldrick; tel (304) 684-2424; fax (304) 684-2426

Princeton: *Princeton Times* — 109 Thorn St.; PO Box 1199 (24740); Th; 1,938pd, 19fr (Sw); $6.65; C; publisher Steve Smith; general manager & editor Jerry Morgan; tel (304) 425-8191; fax (304) 487-1632

Rainelle/Greenburg Co./Pocahontas/Summers/Monroe/Mercer: *Meadow River Post* — 204C W. Washington St., Lewisberg (24901); Th; 6,800pd, 4,700fr (Est); $6.77; publisher Robert Hammond; editor Dan Page; tel (304) 645-1915; fax (304) 645-4853

Richwood: *Nicholas County News Leader* — 4 Railroad Ave.; PO Box 591 (26261); W; 4,685pd, 100fr (Est); 25¢; publisher Jay Comstock; general manager & editor Russell L McCauley; tel (304) 846-2666; fax (304) 846-4972

Ritchie Co.: *Pennsboro News* — 409 Main St.; PO Box 368, Pennsboro (26415); W; 2,752pd, 32fr (Sw); $2.80; publisher James McGoldrick; general manager Randa Gregg; tel (304) 659-2441; fax (304) 659-2441

Romney: *Hampshire Review* — 25 S. Grafton St.; PO Drawer 1036 (26757); W; 4,932pd, 10fr (Est); 25¢; publisher Cornwell & Ailes Inc.; general manager Nora Kimble; editor Charles See; managing editor Lana Bean; tel (304) 822-3871; fax (304) 822-4487

Shinnston: *Shinnston News & Harrison County Journal* — 223 Pike St.; PO Box 187 (26431); Th; 3,300pd, 25fr (Sw); $5.00; C; publisher Kim Gemondo; publisher & editor Mike Queen; tel (304) 592-1030; fax (304) 592-0603

Sistersville: *Tyler Star-News* — 727 Wells St.; PO Box 191 (26175); W; 3,782pd, 120fr (Sw); 22¢; C; publisher Kenneth H Sickle; editor Charles Mason; tel (304) 652-4141; fax (304) 652-1454

Spencer/Roane Co.: *Roane County Reporter* — 210 E. Main St.; PO Box 647, Spencer (25276-0647); Th; 2,321pd, 41fr (Sw); $5.64; C; publisher & editor David J Hedges; managing editor Jim Cooper; tel (304) 927-2360; fax (304) 927-2361

Spencer/Roane Co.: *The Times Record* — 210 E. Main St.; PO Box 647, Spencer (25276-0647); Th; 3,485pd, 61fr (Sw); $5.64; C; publisher David J Hedges; editor Jim Cooper; tel (304) 927-2360; fax (304) 927-2361

Sutton/Braxton Co.: *Braxton Citizens' News* — 501 Main St.; PO Box 516, Sutton (26601); Tu; 6,057pd, 73fr (Sw); $4.10; publisher Ed Given; editor Delbert Thayer; tel (304) 765-5193; fax (304) 765-2754

Terra Alta: *The Preston County News* — 110 W. Main St.; PO Box 587, Kingwood (26537); W/Sa; 4,678pd (Est); $4.50; publisher Gary A Bolyard; general manager Dennis Peters; editor Tina M Bolyard; managing editor Carol Peters; tel (304) 329-0090; fax (304) 329-2450

Upper Kanawka Vly.: *Montgomery Herald* — 406 Lee St.; PO Box 240, Montgomery (25136); W; 4,700pd (Sw); $5.83; publisher Tom James; editor Cheryl Keenan; tel (304) 442-4156; fax (304) 442-8753

Wayne: *Wayne County News* — 310 Central Ave. (25570); W; 5,800pd (Est); 36¢; publisher & editor Tom George; managing editor Terry Ranson; tel (304) 272-3433; fax (304) 522-3910

Webster Springs: *Webster Echo* — 219 Back Fork St.; PO Box 749 (26288); W; 2,910pd, 67fr (Sw); 23¢; publisher & editor D Boyd Dotson Jr; managing editor Elizabeth Tracy; tel (304) 847-5828; fax (304) 847-5991

Webster Springs: *Webster Republican* — 219 Back Fork St.; PO Box 749 (26288); W; 1,177pd, 30fr (Sw); 15¢; publisher D Boyd Dotson III; editor Elizabeth Tracey; tel (304) 847-5828; fax (304) 847-5991

W Union: *The Herald Record* — 202 E. Main St. (26456); Tu; 3,193pd, 15fr (Est); $2.00; publisher & editor Virginia Nicholson; tel (304) 873-1600; fax (304) 873-2811

W Virginia: *West Virginia Hillbilly* — 4 Railroad Ave., Richwood (26261); Th; 3,000pd, 3,000fr (Est); $7.25; publisher & editor Russell L McCauley; tel (304) 846-2029; fax (304) 846-4972

Weston/Lewis Co.: *Weston Democrat* — 238 Main Ave.; PO Box 968, Weston (26452); W; 7,926pd, 80fr (Sw); $2.90; publisher Robert Billeter; editor George Whelan; tel (304) 269-1600; fax (304) 269-4035

Winfield: *Putnam Democrat* — 10 Main St.; PO Box 179 (25213); Th; 1,275pd, 75fr (Est); 24¢; C; publisher & editor William O Robinson; tel (304) 586-2451; fax (304) 586-2451

WISCONSIN

Abbotsford/Colby: *Tribune-Phonograph* — 103 W. Spruce St.; PO Box 677, Abbotsford (54405); W; 2,416pd, 23fr (Sw); $5.65; C; publisher J A O'Leary; general manager Carol O'Leary; editor Chuck Runnoe; tel (715) 223-2342; fax (715) 223-3505

Adams Co.: *The Adams County Times/The Friendship Reporter* — 116 S. Main St.; PO Box 99, Adams (53910); W; 4,000pd (Est); $4.95; publisher & editor Richard A Hannagan; tel (608) 339-7844; fax (608) 339-3903

Albany/Brooklyn/Juda: *Albany Herald* — 200 Oak St.; PO Box 70, Albany (53502); Th; 2,500pd, 300fr (Sw); $1.95; publisher & editor George Martin; tel (608) 862-3224

Algoma: *Algoma Record-Herald* — 602 3rd St.; PO Box 68 (54201); W; 3,070pd, 25fr (Sw); $4.75; C; publisher Frank A Wood Jr; general manager Larry Wilken; managing editor Lee Lawrenz; tel (414) 487-2222

Amery/Polk Co.: *Amery Free Press* — 215 S. Keller Ave.; PO Box 338, Amery (54001); Tu; 5,000pd (Est); $4.50; C; publisher Palmer H Sondreal; general manager Steve Sondreal; editor Jerry Sondreal; tel (715) 268-8101; fax (715) 268-8125

Amherst/Amherst Junction/Nelsonville: *Tomorrow River Times* — 112 Christy St.; PO Box 236, Amherst (54406); Th; 657pd, 5fr (Sw); $5.00; C; publisher Trey Foerster; general manager Mary Foerster; editor Sharon Van Ryzin; tel (715) 445-3415; fax (715) 445-3988

Arcadia: *The Arcadia News-Leader* — 625 Dettloff Dr.; PO Box 220 (54612); Th; 2,295pd, 15fr (Est); $3.80; C; publisher Charles E Blaschko; editor Peter Filla; tel (608) 323-3366; fax (608) 323-2185

Argyle: *Argyle Agenda* — 101 State St.; PO Drawer 426 (53504); Th; 866pd, 78fr (Est); $4.85; C; editor Nancy Ostby; tel (608) 543-3773; fax (608) 527-5285

Athens/Edgar/Marathon: *The Record Review* — 103 W. Spruce St.; PO Box 677, Abbotsford (54465); W; 1,734pd, 4fr (Sw); $5.65; C; publisher J A O'Leary; general manager Carol O'Leary; editor Peter Weinschenk; tel (715) 223-2342; fax (715) 223-3505

Augusta: *Augusta Area Times* — PO Box 465 (54722); W; 1,396pd, 35fr (Sw); $4.00; publisher Michael D Jensen; editor Beth Ellie; tel (715) 286-2655; fax (715) 597-2705

Baldwin/Woodville/Hammond: *The Baldwin Bulletin* — 805 Main St., Baldwin (54002); Tu; 2,821pd (Sw); $3.40; C; publisher Peter Hawley; editor Thomas Hawley; tel (715) 684-2484; fax (715) 684-4937

Barron: *County News-Shield* — 219 E. LaSalle Ave.; PO Box 100 (54812); W; 3,544pd (Est); 15¢; publisher Jim Bell; editor Robert Groshong; tel (715) 537-3117; fax (715) 537-5640

Belleville: *Belleville Recorder* — 38 River St.; PO Box 50 (53508); Th; 1,375pd, 10fr (Est); $4.25; publisher & managing editor Stuart Shapiro; tel (608) 424-3232

Berlin: *Berlin Journal* — 301 June St.; PO Box 10 (54923); Th; 3,314pd (Est); $5.20; C; publisher R M Gonyo; general manager Ty Gonyo; editor James L Wolff; tel (414) 361-1515; fax (414) 361-1518

Berlin: *Fox Lake Representative* — 301 June St. (Fox Lake 53933); PO Box 10 (54923); Th; 577pd (Est); $5.20; C; publisher R M Gonyo; general manager T Y Gonyo; editor James L Wolff; tel (414) 361-1515; fax (414) 361-1518

Black Earth: *News-Sickle-Arrow* — 1126 Mills St.; PO Box 286 (53515); Th; 2,580pd (Est); 32¢; publisher Dan Witte; general manager Judy Bergum; editor John Donaldson; tel (608) 767-3655; fax (608) 767-2222

U.S. Weeklies **Wisconsin** **II-83**

Blair/Taylor/Ettrick: *Blair Press* — 109 N. Gilbert; PO Box 187, Blair (54616); Th; 2,150pd (Sw); $5.00; C; publisher Elizabeth Hjornevik; publisher & editor Gerald R Hjornevik; tel (608) 989-2531; fax (608) 989-2531

Blanchardville: *Blade-Atlas* — 300 S. Main St.; PO Box 116 (53516); Th; 1,145pd, 15fr (Est); $3.85; publisher & editor John P Reilly; publisher T Michael Reilly; managing editor Gary McKenzie; tel (608) 523-4284; fax (608) 523-1019

Bloomer: *Bloomer Advance Inc.* — 1210 15th Ave.; PO Box 25 (54724); Tu; 3,400pd, 30fr (Est); $4.75; publisher Al Bauer; editor Todd Schmidt; tel (715) 568-3100; fax (715) 568-3111

Boscobel: *The Boscobel Dial* — 805 Wisconsin Ave. (53805); Th; 6,117pd, 29fr (Sw); $3.30; C; publisher James S Small; editor David Krier; tel (608) 375-4458; fax (608) 375-2369

Brillion/Reedsville: *The Brillion News* — 425 W. Ryan St., Brillion (54110); Th; 1,958pd, 5fr (Sw); $3.75; C; publisher Noel Zander; publisher & editor Zane C Zander; managing editor Ted Pennekamp; tel (414) 756-2222; fax (414) 756-2701

Brodhead: *Independent-Register* — 922 W. Exchange St.; PO Box 255 (53520); W; 2,093pd, 76fr (Sw); $4.22; C; publisher Kim Markham; editor Dan Markham; tel (608) 897-2193; fax (608) 897-4137

Brookfield: *Brookfield News* — 11063 W. Bluemound Rd. (53226); PO Box 13155, Wauwatosa (53213); Th; 6,241pd, 141fr (Sw); $11.60; publisher Wayne P Toske; general manager Janet Raach; editor Nancy Bialek; managing editor Jeannie Wieland; tel (414) 778-5000; fax (414) 778-5012

Burlington: *Burlington Standard Press* — 140 Commerce St.; PO Box 437 (53105); W/Su; 7,848pd, 7,548fr (Sw); $9.10; C; publisher Robert W Branen; editor Pete Wicklund; tel (414) 763-3511; fax (414) 763-2238

Cadott: *The Cadott Sentinel* — PO Box 70 (54727); Th; 1,250pd, 53fr (Est); $5.50; publisher Trygg J Hansen; editor Heather Hill; tel (715) 289-4978; fax (715) 239-6200

Cambridge: *Cambridge News* — 201 W. North; PO Box 8 (53523); Th; 1,890pd, 46fr (Sw); 31¢; C; publisher Dennis L Hawkes; editor Barbro McGinn; tel (608) 423-3213; fax (608) 648-8187

Campbellsport: *Campbellsport News* — 101 N. Fond du Lac; PO Box 138 (53010); Th; 2,191pd, 11fr (Est); 14¢; C; publisher & editor Gerald F Ninnemann; tel (414) 533-8338; fax (414) 533-5579

Cashton: *The Cashton Record* — 713 Broadway St.; PO Box 100 (54619); W; 1,500pd (Est); 11¢; publisher Gerald Eddy; general manager & editor Rose Eddy; tel (608) 654-7330; fax (608) 654-7330

Chetek: *The Chetek Alert Inc.* — 312 Knapp St.; PO Box 5 (54728); Th; 3,402pd, 20fr (Sw); $4.10; publisher & editor Melodee A Eckerman; publisher Paul H Lange; tel (715) 924-4118; fax (715) 924-4122

Chilton: *Chilton Spirit* — 52 W. Main St.; PO Box 82 (53014); Th; 1,500pd (Sw); $3.60; C; publishers Joe Mathes & Mark Sherry & Mike E Mathes; editor Todd Weber; tel (414) 849-4773; fax (414) 894-2161

Chilton: *Chilton Times-Journal* — 19 E. Main St.; PO Box 227 (53014); Th; 5,020pd, 50fr (Sw); $4.80; C; publisher Gary Vercauteren; editor Deb Weiger; tel (414) 849-7036; fax (414) 849-4651

Clinton: *The Clinton Topper* — 400 B Front; PO Box 569 (53525); Th; 1,590pd, 204fr (Sw); $3.80; C; publisher Henry Schroeder; editor Robert L Gard; tel (608) 676-4111/4664; fax (608) 676-4664

Clintonville: *Tribune-Gazette* — 13 11th St.; PO Box 270 (54929); Th; 3,535pd, 69fr (Est); $6.47; C; publisher & managing editor Scott D McGraw; general manager Jeff C Hoffman; tel (715) 823-3151; fax (715) 823-7479

Colfax: *The Colfax Messenger* — 511 Railroad; PO Box 517 (54730); W; 1,479pd, 15fr (Sw); $3.85; C; publisher & editor Ellis Bloomfield; tel (715) 962-3535; fax (715) 962-3535

Columbus: *Columbus Journal* — PO Box 188 (53925); M; 2,483pd (Est); $4.79; C; publisher Marshall Bernhagen; editor Patty Hoselton; tel (414) 623-3160; fax (414) 623-9383

Cornell/Holcombe: *The Cornell & Lake Holcombe Courier* — 121 Main St.; PO Box 546, Cornell (54732-0546); Th; 1,551pd, 59fr (Sw); $5.75; C; publisher Trygg J Hansen; editor Heather Hill; tel (715) 239-6688; fax (715) 239-6200

Crandon: *Forest Republican* — 108-110 W. Madison St.; PO Box 367 (54520); W; 3,793pd (Est); 80¢; publisher & editor Russell H Steel; general manager Arlet Steel; tel (715) 478-3315; fax (715) 478-5385

Cuba City: *Tri-County Press* — 301 S. Main St.; PO Box 869 (53807); Th; 2,667pd, 17fr (Sw); $4.25; C; publisher William S Hale; general manager Gloria Landon; editor Craig Kowalski; tel (608) 744-2107; fax (608) 744-2108

Cudahy/St. Francis: *Cudahy-St. Francis Reminder-Enterprise* — PO Box 13155, Wauwatosa (53213); Th; 5,703pd, 193fr (Sw); $11.60; publisher Wayne P Toske; general manager Janet Raasch; editor Candy Doyle; managing editor Jeannie Wieland; tel (414) 778-5000; fax (414) 778-5012

Cumberland: *Cumberland Advocate* — 1375 2nd Ave.; PO Box 637 (54829); W; 3,026pd, 100fr (Sw); $4.50; C; publisher Craig Bucher; publisher & editor Sharon Bucher; tel (715) 822-4469; fax (715) 822-4451

Darlington: *Republican-Journal* — 316 S. Main St.; PO Box 20 (53530); Th; 3,900pd, 14fr (Est); $6.00; publisher Brian A Lund; editor Cindy Lund; tel (608) 776-4425; fax (608) 776-4301

De Pere/S Brown Co.: *De Pere Journal* — 126 S. Broadway; PO Box 188, De Pere (54115); Th; 3,777pd, 30fr (Sw); $6.60; publisher Paul J Creviere; editor Marie Creviere; tel (414) 336-4221

Deerfield/Dane: *The Independent* — 7 S. Main St., Deerfield (53531); Th; 1,501pd, 27fr (Est); $5.65; C; publisher Brian Knox; general manager Charles Frandson; editors Mary Pohlman & Pam Chickoring; tel (608) 764-5515; fax (608) 764-8214

Delavan: *The Delavan Enterprise* — 1436 Mound Rd.; PO Box 366 (53115); W; 5,200pd (Est); $5.40; publisher Delavan Enterprise; general manager John Hawerson; editor Tom Sheehan; tel (414) 728-3411; fax (414) 728-5706

Denmark: *The Denmark Press* — 138 Main St.; PO Box 610 (54208); Tu; 1,941pd, 245fr (Sw); $3.85; publisher Frank A Wood; editor Jeff Kralovetz; tel (414) 863-2154; fax (414) 863-6102

Dodgeville: *The Dodgeville Chronicle* — 106 W. Merrimac St.; PO Box 96 (53533); Th; 5,632pd, 75fr (Est); 14¢; publishers & editors J Patrick Reilly & T Michael Reilly; tel (608) 935-2331; fax (608) 935-9531

Dousman: *Kettle Moraine Index* — PO Box 218 (53118); Th; 1,725pd (Sw); $7.37; C; publisher Gary J Jasiek; editor Scott Peterson; tel (414) 367-3272; fax (414) 367-7414

Durand: *The Courier-Wedge* — PO Box 190 (54736); Th; 4,300pd, 36fr (Est); 15¢; publisher Michael Stumpf; editor Mary Trettin; tel (715) 672-4252; fax (715) 672-4254

Eagle River/Three Lakes/Vilas Co.: *Vilas County News Review* — 330 W. Division St.; PO Box 1929, Eagle River (54521); W; 8,670pd, 80fr (Sw); $8.50; C; publisher Byron McNutt; editor Kurt Krueger; tel (715) 479-4421; fax (715) 479-6242

E Troy: *The East Troy News* — 2100 Church St. (53120-0047); W; 2,395pd, 55fr (Est); $6.00; publisher Robert W Branen; editor Richard Berg; tel (414) 642-7451; fax (414) 642-5934

Eau Claire: *The Country Today* — 611 S. Farwell; PO Box 570 (54702); W; 33,937pd, 2,785fr (Sw); $17.00; C; publisher Pieter Graaskamp; editor Jim Massey; tel (715) 833-9270; fax (715) 833-9273

Edgerton: *Edgerton Reporter* — 21 N. Henry St. (53534); W; 3,602pd, 2,122fr (Est); 39¢; C; publisher Diane Everson; publisher & editor Helen V Everson; tel (608) 884-3367; fax (608) 884-8187

Elkhorn/Geneva Lakes Area: *The Elkhorn Independent* — 11 W. Walworth St.; PO Box 200, Elkhorn (53121-0200); Th; 3,434pd, 17fr (Sw); $7.35; publisher Robert W Branen; editor Nancy Jacobsen; tel (414) 723-2250; fax (414) 723-7424

Elm Grove: *Elm Grove Elm Leaves* — PO Box 13155, Wauwatosa (53213); Th; 1,493pd, 32fr (Sw); $11.60; publisher Wayne P Toske; general manager Janet Raasch; editor Nancy Bialek; managing editor Jeannie Wieland; tel (414) 778-5000; fax (414) 778-5012

Elmwood: *Elmwood Argus* — 216 S. McKay Ave.; PO Box 69, Spring Valley (54767); Th; 475pd, 17fr (Sw); $1.70; C; publisher & editor Duane Kelley; tel (715) 778-4395/8395

Elroy: *Tribune-Keystone* — 249 Main St. (53929); W/Sa; 2,073pd (Est); $6.03; C; publisher Tony Allegretti; editor Bill Smith; tel (608) 462-8224; fax (608) 462-5678

Evansville: *Evansville Review* — 8409 U.S. Highway 14 N.; PO Box 77 (53536); W; 1,460pd, 1,990fr (Est); 11¢; C; publisher Frank H Gildner Jr; editor M Vivian Gildner; tel (608) 882-5220; fax (608) 882-5221

Fennimore: *Fennimore Times* — 1150 Lincoln Ave. (53809); W; 1,747pd, 2fr (Est); $3.35; C; publisher William S Hale; editor Matt Johnson; tel (608) 822-3912; fax (608) 822-3916

Fitchburg: *Fitchburg Star* — 2934 Fish Hatchery Rd., Ste. 226, Verona (53713-5012); Th; 531pd, 45fr (Sw); $4.02; C; publisher & editor Henry W Schroeder; managing editor Chuck Nowlan; tel (608) 273-3576/845-9559; fax (608) 845-9550

Florence Co.: *The Florence Mining News* — 140 Florence Ave.; PO Box 79, Florence (54121); W; 1,838pd, 7fr (Est); $4.33; publisher & editor Nancy Gomez; tel (715) 528-3276; fax (715) 696-3400

Fox Pt./Bayside: *Fox Point/Bayside/River Hills Herald* — PO Box 13155, Wauwatosa (53213); Th; 9,043pd, 335fr (Sw); $11.60; publisher Wayne P Toske; general manager Janet Raasch; editor Mary Schuchmann; managing editor Jeannie Wieland; tel (414) 778-5000; fax (414) 778-5012

Franklin/Hales Corners: *Franklin-Hales Corners Hub* — PO Box 13155, Wauwatosa (53213); Th; 4,112pd, 138fr (Sw); $11.60; publisher Wayne P Toske; general manager Janet Raasch; editor Candy Doyle; managing editor Jeannie Wieland; tel (414) 778-5000; fax (414) 768-5837

Frederic: *The Inter-County Leader* — 303 N. Wisconsin Ave.; PO Box 490 (54837); W; 4,393pd, 143fr (Est); 18¢; publisher Doug Panek; editor Gary B King; tel (715) 327-4236; fax (715) 327-4870

Galesville/Ettrick/Trempealeau: *Galesville Republican* — 19852 Court Ave.; PO Box 695, Galesville (54630); Th; 1,811fr (Sw); $4.50; C; publisher John Graf; tel (608) 582-2330

Gays Mills/Soldiers Grove: *Crawford County Independent Kickapoo Scout* — PO Box 188, Gays Mills (54631); Th; 2,431pd, 23fr (Sw); 25¢; publisher James S Small; general manager Jean Roth; tel (608) 735-4413; fax (608) 735-6414

Germantown: *Germantown Banner-Press* — PO Box 13155, Wauwatosa (53213); Th; 2,335pd, 49fr (Sw); $11.60; publisher Wayne P Toske; general manager Janet Raasch; editor Nancy Bialek; managing editor Jeannie Wieland; tel (414) 778-5000; fax (414) 778-5012

Glendale: *Glendale Herald* — PO Box 13155, Wauwatosa (53213); Th; 9,043pd, 335fr (Sw); $11.60; publisher Wayne P Toske; general manager Janet Raasch; editor Mary Schuchmann; managing editor Jeannie Wieland; tel (414) 778-5000; fax (414) 778-5012

Glenwood City/Boyceville: *Glenwood City Tribune* — 215 Oak St.; PO Box 38, Glenwood City (54013); W; 2,785pd, 37fr (Sw); 29¢; publisher & editor Carlton De Witt; managing editor Shawn De Witt; tel (715) 265-4646; fax (715) 265-7496

Glidden: *The Glidden Enterprise* — 342 Grant St.; PO Box 128 (54527); W; 1,406pd, 75fr (Sw); $3.02; publisher & editor Matthew J Hart Jr; tel (715) 264-3481

Grant Co./Lancaster: *Grant County Herald Independent* — 208 W. Cherry St.; PO Box 310, Lancaster (53813); Tu; 4,165pd (Sw); $6.59; C; publisher William S Hale; editor John D Ingebritsen; tel (608) 723-2151; fax (608) 723-7272

Grantsburg/Siren/Webster: *Burnett County Sentinel* — 114 Madison Ave.; PO Box 397, Grantsburg (54840-0397); W; 4,191pd, 62fr (Sw); $4.10; C; publisher & editor Byron Higgin; general manager Wanda Larson; tel (715) 463-2341; fax (715) 463-5138

Green Lake: *Green Lake Reporter* — PO Box 10 (54941); Th; 1,417pd (Est); $4.60; C; publisher R M Gonyo; general manager T Y Gondo; editor James L Wolff; tel (414) 361-1515; fax (414) 361-1518

Greendale: *Greendale Village Life* — PO Box 13155, Wauwatosa (53213); Th; 3,001pd, 61fr (Sw); $11.60; publisher Wayne P Toske; general manager Janet Raasch; editor Dave Rank; managing editor Jeannie Wieland; tel (414) 778-5000; fax (414) 778-5012

Greenfield: *Greenfield Observer* — PO Box 13155, Wauwatosa (53213); Th; 3,392pd, 246fr (Sw); $11.60; C; publisher Wayne P Toske; editor Janet Raasch; managing editor Jeanne Wieland; editor Mary Lou Stover; tel (414) 778-5000; fax (414) 768-5837

Hammond/St. Croix/Roberts: *Central St. Croix News* — 815 Davis St.; PO Box 206, Hammond (54015); W; 1,020pd (Est); $3.25; publisher & editor Barbara Gardner; tel (715) 796-2355; fax (715) 796-2355

Hartford: *The Hartford Times-Press* — 225 N. Main St.; PO Box 222 (53027); Th; 6,722pd, 28fr (Est); $3.46; C; publisher & editor John E McLoone; tel (414) 673-3500; fax (414) 673-5260

Hartland/Pewaukee/Delafield: *Lake Country Reporter* — 440 Cardinal Ln.; PO Box 200, Hartland Lake (53029); Tu/Th; 8,011pd (CPVS); $9.67; C; publisher Gary J Jasiek; editor Scott Peterson; tel (414) 367-3272; fax (414) 367-7414

Hayward: *Sawyer County Record* — 220 W. 1st St.; PO Box 191 (54843); W; 7,040pd, 9,800fr (Est); $5.50; C; publisher Gary Pennington; editor Kris Sorenson; tel (715) 634-4881; fax (715) 634-8191

Hillsboro: *Sentry-Enterprise* — 839 Water Ave.; PO Box 469 (54634); Th; 1,994pd, 107fr (Sw); $5.69; C; publisher & editor John W Knowles; tel (608) 489-2264; fax (608) 489-2348

Horicon: *Horicon Reporter* — 319 E. Lake St.; PO Box 148 (53032); Th; 1,879pd, 40fr (Sw); $3.46; publisher Andrew Johnson; editor Edward J Zagorski III; tel (414) 485-2016; fax (414) 485-4820

Hudson: *The Hudson Star-Observer* — 226 Locust St.; PO Box 147 (54016); Th; 5,858pd (Sw); $7.08; C; publisher Steve Dzubay; editor Douglas W Stohlberg; managing editor Bob Zientara; tel (715) 386-9333; fax (715) 386-9891

Independence: *News-Wave* — 23703 Washington St.; PO Box 47 (54747); Th; 1,055pd (Est); $4.41; publisher & editor O J Evenson; tel (715) 985-3815; fax (715) 985-9330

Iola/Scandinavia: *The Iola Herald* — 165 N. Main St.; PO Box 235, Iola (54945); Th; 1,331pd, 5fr (Sw); $5.00; C; publisher Trey Foerster; general manager Mary Foerster; editor Sharon Van Ryzin; tel (715) 445-3415; fax (715) 445-3988

Iron Co.: *Iron County Miner* — 216 Copper St.; PO Box 8, Hurley (54534); Th; 2,430pd, 114fr (Sw); $3.80; publisher & editor Ernest Moore; tel (715) 561-3405

Jackson Co.: *Banner Journal* — 409 E. Main St., Black River Falls (54615); W; 4,400pd, 100fr (Est); $6.50; C; publisher Dan Witte; general manager Kathy Potter; editor Jeanette Ruxton; tel (715) 284-4304; fax (715) 284-4634

Juneau Co.: *Juneau County Star-Times* — 500 La Crosse St.; PO Box 220, Mauston (53948); W; 5,100pd (Est); $3.09; Sa; 5,100pd, 20fr (Est); $3.09; C; publisher & editor Patrick Peckham; tel (608) 847-6224; fax (608) 847-5457

Juneau/Hustisford: *Dodge County Independent-News* — 122 S. Main St.; PO Box 167, Juneau (53588); Th; 1,559pd, 152fr (Est); $3.44; publisher Scott Fitzgerald; editor Bonnie Fitzgerald; tel (414) 386-2421; fax (414) 386-2422

Kaukauna: *Kaukauna Times* — 1900 Crooks Ave.; PO Box 109 (54130); Tu/Th; 5,754pd, 354fr (Est); $6.15; C; publisher Glenn P Hansen; general manager Lyle J Hansen; editor Joyce Schubring; tel (414) 766-4651; fax (414) 766-4736

Kenosha Co.: *Westosha Report* — 316 N. Lake Ave.; PO Box 992, Twin Lakes (53181); M; 7,239pd, 6,476fr (Sw); $9.10; C; publisher Robert W Branen; editor Diane Jahnke; tel (414) 877-2813; fax (414) 877-3619

Kenosha Co./NW Lake Co. (IL): *Bulletin* — 715-58 St., Lower Level, Kenosha (53140); M; 70,000fr (Sw); $7.45; C; publisher Howard J Brown; editor Darren Hillock; tel (414) 656-1101, (800) 846-1101; fax (414) 656-1255

Copyright ©1996 by the Editor & Publisher Co.

II-84 **Wisconsin** *U.S. Weeklies*

Kewaskum: *Kewaskum Statesman* — 250 Main St.; PO Box 98 (53040); Tu; 3,050pd (Est); $3.30; C; publisher & editor Lana L Kuehl; general manager Cheyl A Kuehl; managing editor A R Kuehl; tel (414) 626-3312; fax (414) 626-2626

Kewaunee: *Kewaunee Enterprise* — 206 Ellis St.; PO Box 86 (54216); Th; 1,600pd, 10fr (Sw); $4.75; C; publisher Frank A Wood; general manager Larry Wilken; editor Mabel Temby; tel (414) 388-3175; fax (414) 388-0609

La Farge: *The Epitaph-News* — 308 Main St. (54639); Th; 1,672pd, 20fr (Est); 18¢; publisher & editor April Paul; tel (608) 625-2451; fax (608) 627-1838

Ladysmith: *Ladysmith News* — 120 W. 3rd St. S.; PO Box 189 (54848-0189); Th; 5,796pd, 69fr (Est); $5.30; C; publisher T D Bell; editor John Terrill; tel (715) 532-5591

Lake Geneva: *Lake Geneva Regional News* — 315 Broad St.; PO Box 937 (53147); Th; 5,623pd, 52fr (Sw); $6.60; publisher Don Bearder; general manager Douglas A Bearder; managing editor Dennis Martin; tel (414) 248-4444; fax (414) 248-4476

Lake Mills: *The Lake Mills Leader* — 322 N. Main St.; PO Box 60 (53551); Th; 2,940pd, 35fr (Sw); $5.46; C; publisher Dennis L Hawkes; editor Arlys J Hawkes; tel (414) 648-2334; fax (414) 648-8187

Lodi: *The Lodi Enterprise* — 146 S. Main St. (53555); Th; 2,109pd, 25fr (Est); 34¢; publisher & editor Bill Haupt; publisher Jan Haupt; tel (608) 592-3261; fax (608) 592-3866

Loyal/Spencer/Greenwood: *The Tribune Record-Gleaner* — 318 N. Main St.; PO Box 187, Loyal (54446); W; 3,585pd, 199fr (Sw); $6.40; publishers Florence J Berglund & Robert E Berglund; editor Dean Lesar; tel (715) 255-8531; fax (715) 255-8357

Luxemburg: *Luxemburg News* — PO Box 130 (54217); Th; 1,150pd (Est); 80¢; publisher Frank Wood; general manager Larry Wilken; editor Lee Lawrenz; tel (414) 845-2525; fax (414) 845-2525

Manawa/Odgensburg: *Manawa Advocate* — 165 N. Main St.; PO Box 235, Iola (54945); Th; 638pd, 5fr (Sw); $5.00; C; publisher Trey Foerster; general manager Mary Foerster; editor Sharon Van Ryzin; tel (715) 445-3415; fax (414) 445-3988

Marion/Tigeston: *The Marion Advertiser* — 109 N. Main St.; PO Box 268, Marion (54950); Th; 2,816pd (Est); $1.25; publisher Daniel S Brandenburg; editor Patsy R Brandenburg; tel (715) 754-5444

Markesan/Kingston/Dalton: *The Herald* — 51 E. John St., Markesan (54936); Th; 1,778pd, 28fr (Est); $4.79; C; publisher Marshall Bernhagen; editor Kevin Kirsh; tel (414) 398-2334; fax (414) 398-3835

Mayville: *The Mayville News* — 126 Bridge St.; PO Box 271 (53050); Th; 4,091pd, 49fr (Est); $4.61; C; publisher Andrew Johnson; editor Ken Thomas; tel (414) 387-2211; fax (414) 387-5515

McFarland: *Community Life* — 6041 Monona Dr., Monona (53716); W; 148pd, 571fr (Est); 33¢; C; publisher Henry Schroeder; editor Lee Kelstinsky; tel (608) 221-1544; fax (608) 221-0463

Medford: *The Star News* — 116 S. Wisconsin Ave.; PO Box 180 (54451); W; 6,779pd, 174fr (Est); $8.85; C; publisher J A O'Leary; editor Don Woerpel; tel (715) 748-2626; fax (715) 748-2699

Menomonee Falls: *Menomonee Falls News* — PO Box 13155, Wauwatosa (53213); Th; 4,938pd, 154fr (Est); $11.60; publisher Wayne P Toske; general manager Janet Raasch; editor Nancy Bialek; managing editor Jeannie Wieland; tel (414) 778-5000; fax (414) 778-5012

Menomonie/Dunn Co.: *Dunn County News* — 710 Main St.; PO Box 40, Menomonie (54751); W; 4,223pd, 32fr (VAC); $5.85; Su; 4,052pd, 32fr (VAC); $7.40; C; publisher Jeff Becker; editor Peg Zaemisch; tel (715) 235-3411; fax (715) 235-0936

Merrill/Lincoln Co.: *Foto News* — 805 E. Main St.; PO Box 606, Merrill (54452); W; 15,103pd (Sw); $7.68; publisher & editor L James O'Day; general manager & managing editor Lauree O'Day; tel (715) 536-7121

Middleton: *Middleton Times-Tribune* — 7507 Hubbard Ave.; PO Box 6220006 (53562); Th; 2,284pd, 44fr (Est); 17¢; publisher Dan Witte; editor Mike Keeny; tel (608) 836-1601; fax (608) 836-3759

Milton: *The Milton Courier* — 513 Vernal Ave.; PO Box 69 (53563); Th; 3,058pd, 58fr (Est); $4.50; publisher Brian Victor B Knox; editor Doug Welch; tel (608) 868-2442; fax (608) 868-4664

Milwaukee: *City Edition* — 777 N. Jefferson (53202); Th; 30,000fr (Sw); $25.00; publisher Carol S Weiss; editor Jeff White; tel (414) 273-8696; fax (414) 273-3633

Milwaukee: *The Milwaukee Courier* — 2431 W. Hopkins St.; PO Box 06279 (53206); Sa; 15,000fr (Est); $10.46; C; publisher Carole Geary; general manager & editor Walter Jones; tel (414) 449-4860; fax (414) 449-4872

Mineral Pt.: *Democrat Tribune* — 334 High St. (53565); Th; 1,211pd, 15fr (Est); $3.70; publisher J Patrick Reilly & T Michael Reilly; editor Jeanie Lewis; tel (608) 987-2141; fax (608) 935-9531

Minocqua: *Lakeland Times* — Chippewa St.; PO Box 790 (54548); Tu/F; 10,434pd (Sw); $5.45; C; publisher Donald Walker; general manager Dean Acheson; editor Dean Bortz; tel (715) 356-5236; fax (715) 358-2121

Mondovi: *Mondovi Herald-News* — 123 W. Main; PO Box 67 (54755); Th; 3,415pd, 10fr (Est); $3.65; publisher Perry Nyseth; editor Cindy Gibson; tel (715) 926-4970; fax (715) 926-4928

Monona/Madison: *The Community Herald* — 6041 Monona Dr., Monona (53716); W; 1,491pd, 25fr (Sw); $7.00; C; publisher Henry W Schroeder; editor Lisa Avelleyra; tel (608) 221-1544; fax (608) 221-0463

Montello: *The Marquette County Tribune* — 120 Underwood Ave.; PO Box 188 (53949); Th; 4,540pd, 41fr (Sw); $5.70; publishers Daniel Witte & Mark Witte; editor Mary Faltz; tel (608) 297-2424; fax (608) 297-9293

Monticello: *Monticello Messenger* — 105 E. North Ave.; PO Box 36 (53570); W; 800pd, 10fr (Est); 21¢; C; publisher Dan Witte; editor Ann Schmidt; tel (608) 938-4855; fax (608) 527-5285

Mosinee: *Mosinee Times* — 407 3rd St. (54455); Th; 2,431pd, 20fr (Sw); 19¢; publisher & editor John Durst; tel (715) 693-2300; fax (715) 643-1574

Mt. Horeb: *Mount Horeb Mail* — 118 E. Main (53572); Th; 2,133pd, 10fr (Est); $6.97; C; publishers Dan Witte & Mark Witte; editor Judy Brick; tel (608) 437-5553; fax (608) 437-3443

Mukwonago/Eagle/E Troy: *Mukwonago Chief* — 555 Bay View Rd.; PO Box 204, Mukwonago (53149); W; 4,222pd, 23fr (CPVS); $7.48; C; publisher Terri Blazek; editor Jim Flaherty; tel (414) 363-4045; fax (414) 363-8573

Muskego: *Muskego Sun* — PO Box 13155, Wauwatosa (53213); Th; 2,939pd, 49fr (Sw); $11.60; publisher Wayne P Toske; general manager Janet Raasch; editor Dave Rank; managing editor Jeannie Wieland; tel (414) 778-5000; fax (414) 778-5012

Neillsville: *The Clark County Press* — 614 Hewett; PO Box 149 (54456); W; 3,429pd, 33fr (Est); $4.00; C; publishers Dan Witte & Mark Witte; editor Nick Kuzjak; tel (715) 743-2600; fax (715) 743-5460

New Berlin: *New Berlin Citizen* — PO Box 13155, Wauwatosa (53213); Th; 3,708pd, 173fr (Sw); $11.60; publisher Wayne P Toske; general manager Janet Raasch; editor Nancy Bialek; managing editor Jeannie Wieland; tel (414) 778-5000; fax (414) 778-5012

New Glarus: *New Glarus Post* — 407 2nd St.; PO Box 65 (53574); W; 1,639pd, 90fr (Sw); $1.55; publisher Dan Witte; editor Ann Schmidt; tel (608) 527-5252; fax (608) 527-5285

New Holstein: *New Holstein Reporter* — 2118 Wisconsin Ave.; PO Box 177 (53061); Th; 1,855pd, 177fr (Sw); $3.60; C; publisher Joe Mathes; publisher & editor Mark Sherry; publisher Mike E Mathes; tel (414) 898-4276; fax (414) 894-2161

New London: *Press-Star* — 416 N. Water St.; PO Box 283 (54961); F; 2,366pd, 120fr (Sw); $7.98; C; publisher & editor Bill Melendes; tel (414) 982-4321; fax (414) 982-7672

New Richmond: *The News* — PO Box 98 (54017); Th; 5,641pd, 100fr (Est); $6.25; publisher Michael J Burke; editor Don Stoner; tel (715) 246-6881; fax (715) 246-7117

Niagara: *Niagara Journal* — N22847 Lincoln; PO Box 217 (54151); Tu; 1,100pd, 150fr (Sw); $2.50; publisher & editor Gary Molle; managing editor Beth Molle; tel (715) 251-3638

Oak Creek: *Oak Creek Pictorial* — PO Box 13155, Wauwatosa (53213); Th; 4,201pd, 125fr (Sw); $11.60; publisher Wayne P Toske; general manager Janet Raasch; editor Candy Doyle; managing editor Jeannie Wieland; tel (414) 778-5000; fax (414) 778-5012

Oconomowoc: *Oconomowoc Enterprise* — 212 E. Wisconsin Ave.; PO Box B (53066); W; 5,791pd (Sw); $7.90; C; publisher Steven Jahn; editor Pat Walker; tel (414) 567-5511; fax (414) 567-4422

Oconto: *Oconto County Reporter* — 648 Brazeau Ave.; PO Box 200 (54153); W; 4,397pd, 533fr (Est); 12¢; publisher & editor William T Borneman; tel (414) 834-4242; fax (414) 834-4878

Oconto Falls/Gillett: *Oconto County Times-Herald* — 107 S. Main St.; PO Box 128, Oconto Falls (54154); W; 4,998pd, 208fr (Sw); $7.80; C; publisher & editor Roger F Shellman; tel (414) 846-3427; fax (414) 846-3430

Omro: *Omro Herald* — 300 June St. (54963); Th; 954pd (Sw); $5.20; C; publisher R M Gonyo; general manager T Y Gonyo; editor James L Wolff; tel (414) 685-2707; fax (414) 361-1518

Onalaska: *Onalaska Community Life* — 205 Green St.; PO Box 367 (54650); Th; 1,188pd, 57fr (Sw); $5.50; C; publisher Gretchen Skoloda; editor David Skoloda; tel (608) 781-6700; fax (608) 526-4853

Ontario/Norwalk/Wilton: *The County Line Connection* — PO Box 7, Ontario (54651); Th; 1,250pd, 20fr (Sw); $3.00; publisher & editor Karen Parker; tel (608) 337-4232; fax (608) 337-4857

Oregon: *Oregon Observer* — 112 Janesville St.; PO Box 26 (53575); Th; 2,570pd, 70fr (Est); $9.40; publisher & editor Henry W Schroeder; managing editor Debra Harvall; tel (608) 251-3252; fax (608) 251-0582

Orfordville: *Journal & Footville News* — 124 E. Spring St.; PO Box 248 (53576); W; 861pd (Est); $4.27; publisher & editor George E Stewart; managing editor Betty Stewart; tel (608) 879-2211; fax (608) 879-2211

Osceola: *Osceola Sun* — 108 Cascade St.; PO Box 248 (54020); Tu; 1,995pd, 4fr (Sw); $3.85; publisher Jeff Holmquist; publisher & editor Julie Holmquist; tel (715) 294-2314; fax (715) 755-3314

Osseo: *The Tri-County News* — 51119 Omaha St.; PO Box 460 (54758); W; 1,661pd, 8fr (Sw); 18¢; publisher Michael D Jensen; managing editor Beth Ellie; tel (715) 597-3313; fax (715) 597-2705

Owen/Withee: *O-W Enterprise* — 1006 Division St.; PO Box F, Withee (54498); W; 970pd, 100fr (Est); $6.00; publisher & editor Larry Shimono; tel (715) 229-2103; fax (715) 229-2104

Ozaukee Co.: *News Graphic* — PO Box 47, Cedarburg (53012); M/Th; 9,432pd (ABC); 34¢; C; publisher Philip Paige; editor Mark Jaeger; tel (414) 375-5100; fax (414) 375-5107

Palmyra: *Palmyra Enterprise* — PO Box M (53156); Th; 1,154pd, 25fr (Est); $3.35; C; publisher & editor Tom Coe; tel (414) 495-2171; fax (414) 495-2171

Park Falls: *Park Falls Herald* — 259 2nd Ave. N.; PO Box 410 (54552); Th; 3,363pd, 15fr (Est); $5.75; C; publisher & editor Kenneth P Dischler; tel (715) 762-4940; fax (715) 762-2757

Peshtigo/Marinette Co.: *Peshtigo Times* — PO Box 187, Peshtigo (54157); W; 10,587pd, 789fr (Sw); $5.50; C; publisher Mary Ann Gardon; editor Leo J Pesch; tel (715) 582-4541; fax (715) 582-4662

Phillips/Price: *The Bee* — 115 N. Lake Ave.; PO Box 170, Phillips (54555); Th; 4,646pd, 23fr (Sw); $5.40; C; publisher Ted Kempkes; editor Ray Rivard; tel (715) 339-3036; fax (715) 339-4300

Pierce Co.: *Pierce County Herald* — 126 S. Chestnut St.; PO Box 300, Ellsworth (54011); W; 4,197pd, 275fr (Sw); $4.66; publisher Jay V Griggs; editor Bill Kirk; tel (715) 273-4334; fax (715) 273-4335

Platteville/Grant: *Platteville Journal* — 1190 W. Hwy. 151; PO Box 266, Platteville (53818); Tu/Th; 4,300pd, 2,300fr (Sw); $2.85; C; publisher & editor Richard Brockman; general manager Renee Baker; tel (608) 348-3006; fax (608) 348-7979

Plymouth/Western Sheboygan Co.: *The Review* — 113 E. Mill St.; PO Box 317, Plymouth (53073); Tu/Th; 6,803pd, 52fr (Est); $5.95; C; publisher & editor Barry S Johanson & M Christine Johanson; tel (414) 893-6411; fax (414) 893-5505

Polk Co.: *The County Ledger-Press* — 105 Main St.; PO Box 129, Balsam Lake (54810); Th; 7,270pd, 177fr (Est); 44¢; publisher Thos C Miller; editor Linda Peterson; tel (715) 485-3121; fax (715) 485-3037

Port Washington: *Ozaukee Press* — 125 E. Main St.; PO Box 249 (53074); Th; 6,720pd, 530fr (Sw); $9.65; C; publisher & editor William F Schanen III; tel (414) 284-3494; fax (414) 284-0067

Poynette: *The Poynette Press* — 125 N. Main St.; PO Box 37 (53955); W; 1,598pd (Est); $5.30; publisher Molly Emerson; editor Richard Emerson; tel (608) 635-2565; fax (608) 846-9664

Prairie du Chien Area: *Courier Press* — 132 S. Beaumont; PO Box 149, Prairie du Chien (53821); M; 3,800pd (Est); $5.85; W; 3,900pd (Est); $5.85; C; publisher E B Howe; editor William H Howe; tel (608) 326-2441

Prescott: *The Prescott Journal* — 311 Dakota St.; PO Box 157 (54021); Th; 3,767pd, 253fr (Est); $4.25; C; publisher & editor Gary B Rawn; tel (715) 262-5454; fax (715) 262-5474

Princeton: *Princeton Times-Republic* — PO Box 147 (54968); Th; 1,494pd (Est); $4.60; C; publisher R M Gonyo; general manager T Y Gonyo; editor James L Wolff; tel (414) 295-6261; fax (414) 361-1518

Randolph: *The Advance* — 115 Williams St. (53956); W; 1,802pd, 40fr (Est); $4.50; C; publisher Marshall Bernhagen; editor John Wiersma; tel (414) 326-5151; fax (414) 326-3529

Random Lake: *The Sounder* — 405 2nd St.; PO Box 346 (53075-0346); Th; 2,828pd, 56fr (Sw); $3.67; publisher Ray Scholler; general manager & editor Gary Feider; tel (414) 994-9244; fax (414) 994-4817

Reedsburg: *Times-Press* — 117 S. Walnut; PO Box 269 (53959); W/Sa; 3,000pd (Est); $7.87; editor Peter Margolies; tel (608) 524-4336; fax (608) 524-4337

Rice Lake: *Rice Lake Chronotype* — 28 S. Main St.; PO Box 30 (54868); W; 9,291pd, 118fr (Sw); $5.75; C; publisher Warren L Dorrance; editor Sam Finazzo; tel (715) 234-2121; fax (715) 234-5232

Richland Center: *The Richland Observer* — 172 E. Court St. (53581); Th; 5,339pd (Est); $3.25; publisher & editor Erik R Olson; tel (608) 647-6141

Ripon: *The Ripon Commonwealth Press* — 646 S. Douglas St.; PO Box 344 (54971); W; 3,541pd (Sw); $5.10; C; publisher Tim Lyke; editor Pam Arens; tel (414) 748-3017; fax (414) 748-3028

River Falls: *River Falls Journal* — 112 E. Walnut St.; PO Box 25 (54022); Th; 4,387pd, 86fr (Sw); $6.91; C; publisher Steve Dzubay; general manager Rory Palm; editor Phil Pfuehler; tel (715) 425-1561; fax (715) 425-5666

Sauk City/Prairie du Sac: *Sauk Prairie Star* — 801 Water St.; PO Box 606, Sauk City (53583); Th; 3,450pd, 40fr (Est); 30¢; publishers Dan Witte & Mark Witte; editor Dan Satran Jr; tel (608) 643-3444; fax (608) 643-4988

Seymour/Black Creek/Shiocton: *Times Press* — 205 N. Main; PO Box 128, Seymour (54165); Th; 2,243pd (Sw); 35¢; C; publisher Add Inc.; general manager Ken Hodgden; editor Bettyann Kowalski; tel (414) 833-2517; fax (414) 833-2454

Sharon: *The Sharon Reporter* — 213 Baldwin St.; PO Box 508 (53585); W; 744pd (Sw); $5.20; C; publisher Robert F Branen; general manager Daniel A Snow; editor Mabel Jackson; tel (414) 736-4380

Sheboygan Falls: *The Sheboygan Falls News* — PO Box 183 (53085); W; 2,138pd, 11fr (Est); $2.95; C; publishers Barry S Johanson & M Christine Johanson; editor Sandra Kimball; tel (414) 467-6591; fax (414) 893-5505

Shell Lake: *Washburn County Register* — PO Box 455 (54871); Th; 1,946pd, 67fr (Est); $4.25; publisher Connie A Parenteau; publisher & editor Marc E Parenteau; tel (715) 468-2314; fax (715) 468-2314

Copyright ©1996 by the Editor & Publisher Co.

Shorewood: *Shorewood Herald* — PO Box 13155, Wauwatosa (53213); Th; 9,165pd, 394fr (Sw); $11.60; publisher Wayne P Toske; general manager Janet Raasch; editor Mary Schuchmann; managing editor Jeannie Wieland; tel (414) 778-5000; fax (414) 778-5012

S Milwaukee: *South Milwaukee Voice Graphic* — PO Box 13155, Wauwatosa (53213); Th; 4,249pd, 200fr (Sw); $11.60; publisher Wayne P Toske; general manager Janet Raasch; editor Candy Doule; managing editor Jeannie Wieland; tel (414) 778-5000; fax (414) 778-5012

Sparta/Cashton/Norwalk/Tomah: *Monroe County Democrat* — 114 W. Oak St.; PO Box 252, Sparta (54656); Th; 5,192pd, 108fr (Sw); $5.10; publisher & editor William V Gleiss; tel (608) 269-3186; fax (608) 269-6876

Sparta/Cashton/Norwalk/Tomah: *The Sparta Herald* — 114 W. Oak St.; PO Box 252, Sparta (54656-0252); M; 4,910pd, 95fr (Sw); $5.10; publisher & editor T C Radde; tel (608) 269-3186; fax (608) 269-6876

Spooner/Washburn Co.: *Spooner Advocate* — 509 Front St.; PO Box 338, Spooner (54801); Th; 5,085pd, 25fr (Sw); $4.25; C; publisher Janet I Krokson; editor Bill Thornley; tel (715) 635-2181; fax (715) 635-2186

Spring Green: *The Weekly Home News* — 120 N. Worcester St.; PO Box 39 (53588); W; 2,255pd (Est); 15¢; publishers James Schwanke & Linda Schwanke; editor Donald Greenwood; tel (608) 588-2508; fax (608) 588-2509

Spring Vly: *Spring Valley Sun* — S. 216 McKay Ave.; PO Box 69 (54767); W; 700pd (Est); $1.90; C; publisher & editor Duane Kelley; tel (715) 778-4395

Stanley: *The Stanley Republican* — 131 E. 1st Ave.; PO Box 114 (54768); Th; 2,565pd (Est); 27¢; publisher & editor B J Fazendin; tel (715) 644-3319; fax (715) 644-5452

Stoughton: *Stoughton Courier-Hub* — 301 W. Main St.; PO Box 577 (53589-0577); Th; 4,138pd (Sw); $5.80; C; publisher Walter L Handy; editor Eric Neuwirth; tel (608) 873-6671; fax (608) 873-3473

Stratford: *Stratford Journal* — PO Box 5 (54484); W; 615pd (Sw); $5.18; publisher & editor Paul Hale; tel (715) 687-4112

Sturgeon Bay/Door Co.: *Door County Advocate* — 233 N. 3rd Ave.; PO Box 130, Sturgeon Bay (54235); Tu/F; 11,646pd, 100fr (Sw); $6.15; publisher Frank A Wood Jr; general manager Chris Wood; editor Richard McCord; tel (414) 743-3321; fax (414) 743-5817

Sun Prairie: *The Star* — 14 Columbus St.; PO Box 645 (53590); Th; 4,491pd, 179fr (Est); $6.67; C; publisher Hometown News Limited Partnership; general manager Penny Weisner; editor Chris Mertes; tel (608) 837-2521; fax (608) 825-4460

Sussex: *Sussex Sun* — 440 Cardinal Ln.; PO Box 200, Hartland (53029); Tu; 2,722pd (Sw); $7.37; C; publisher Gary J Jasiek; editor Sandra Wolken; tel (414) 367-3272; fax (414) 367-7414

Thorp: *The Thorp Courier* — 403 N. Washington; PO Box 487 (54771); Th; 2,802pd, 57fr (Sw); $5.00; C; publisher & editor Mark J LaGasse; tel (715) 669-5525; fax (715) 669-5596

Three Lakes: *The Three Lakes News* — 330 W. Division St.; PO Box 1929, Eagle River (54521); W; 1,264pd, 15fr (Sw); $8.50; C; publisher Byron McNutt; editor Kurt Krueger; tel (715) 479-4421; fax (715) 479-6242

Tomah: *The Tomah Journal* — 1108 Superior Ave.; PO Box 190 (54660-0190); Th; 5,405pd (Sw); $7.98; C; publisher & editor John R Kenny; managing editor John Froelich; tel (608) 372-4123; fax (608) 372-2791/3064

Tomah: *Tomah Monitor Herald* — 1108 Superior Ave.; PO Box 190 (54660); M; 5,405pd (Sw); $7.98; C; publisher & editor John R Kenny; managing editor John Froelich; tel (608) 372-4123; fax (608) 372-2791/3064

Tomahawk: *Tomahawk Leader* — 315 W. Wisconsin Ave.; PO Box 345 (54487); Tu; 4,838pd, 14fr (Sw); $6.00; C; publisher & editor Kathleen A Tobin; publisher Larry M Tobin; tel (715) 453-2151

Turtle Lake: *Turtle Lake Times* — PO Box 88 (54889); Th; 1,137pd (Est); 70¢; publisher James P Slack; editor Anne L Slack; tel (715) 986-4675

Union Grove: *Westine Report* — 1113 Main St.; PO Box 54 (53182); W; 2,587pd (Sw); $7.50; C; publisher Robert W Branen; general manager Richard H Leipzig; editor Roselyn Calek; tel (414) 878-1300; fax (414) 763-2238

Valders: *Valders Journal* — 204 N. Liberty St.; PO Box 400 (54245); Th; 2,129pd (Sw); $4.51; publisher Marion F Brockman; editor Brian D Thomsen; tel (414) 775-4431; fax (414) 775-4474

Verona: *The Verona Press* — 120 W. Verona Ave.; PO Box 6 (53593); Th; 1,669pd, 52fr (Sw); $6.72; C; publisher & editor Henry W Schroeder; managing editor Debra Harvall; tel (608) 845-9559; fax (608) 845-9550

Viroqua/Vernon Co.: *Vernon County Broadcaster* — 122 W. Jefferson St.; PO Box 472, Viroqua (54665-0472); Th; 5,654pd, 50fr (Sw); $5.65; C; publishers Mary Hollister & Peter Hollister; managing editor Mary Bormann Hollister; tel (608) 637-3137; fax (608) 637-8557

Walworth/Fontana/Linn: *The Times* — 325 Kenosha St.; PO Box 129, Walworth (53184); W; 3,871pd, 210fr (Est); $5.40; C; publisher Robert R Branen; general manager Daniel A Snow; editor Kent Johnson; tel (414) 275-2166; fax (414) 275-5259

Washburn/Cable/Bayfield: *The County Journal* — PO Box 637, Washburn (54891); Th; 3,396pd, 25fr (Sw); $4.80; publisher Eric Erickson; editor Darrell Pandergrass; tel (715) 373-5500; fax (715) 373-5546

Waterford/Norway/Wind Lake/Rochester: *Waterford Post* — 224-A N. Milwaukee; PO Box 297, Waterford (53185); Su; 1,438pd, 299fr (Est); $6.00; C; publisher Southern Lakes Media Inc.; general manager Rich Leipzig; editor Tim Franklin; tel (414) 534-4668; fax (414) 763-2238

Waterloo/Marshall: *The Courier* — 114 N. Monroe St.; PO Box 6, Waterloo (53594); Th; 1,466pd, 80fr (Sw); $6.65; C; publisher Victor B Knox; general manager Charles Frandson; managing editor Alan Kay; tel (414) 478-2188; fax (414) 478-3618

Waunakee: *Waunakee Tribune* — 105 South St.; PO Box 128 (53597); Th; 3,300pd (Est); $8.58; C; publisher Anita I Drake; publisher & editor Arthur M Drake; tel (608) 849-5227; fax (608) 849-4225

Waupaca: *Waupaca County Post* — 717 10th St.; PO Box 152 (54981); Th; 7,624pd, 455fr (Sw); $5.25; C; publisher Scott B Turner; general manager Donald Edmunds; editor Loren Sperry; tel (715) 258-5546; fax (715) 258-8162

Waupun/Brandon/Fox Lake: *Leader-News* — 520 E. Main; PO Box 111, Waupun (53963); W; 645pd, 457fr (Sw); $6.12; C; publisher Marshall Bernhagen; editor Kevin Passon; tel (414) 324-5555; fax (414) 324-8582

Wautoma/Waushara Co.: *The Waushara Argus* — Hwy. 21 & 73 E.; PO Box 838, Wautoma (54982); W; 6,360pd, 40fr (Sw); 26¢; C; publisher & editor Mary Kunosch; tel (414) 787-3334; fax (414) 787-2883

Wauwatosa: *Wauwatosa News-Time* — PO Box 13155 (53213); Th; 6,330pd, 419fr (Sw); $11.60; publisher Wayne P Toske; general manager Janet Raasch; editor Dave Rank; managing editor Jeannie Wieland; tel (414) 778-5000; fax (414) 778-5012

W Allis: *West Allis Star* — PO Box 13155, Wauwatosa (53213); Th; 3,722pd, 338fr (Est); $11.60; publisher Wayne P Toske; general manager Janet Raasch; editor Dave Rank; managing editor Jeannie Wieland; tel (414) 778-5000; fax (414) 778-5012

W Salem: *La Crosse County Countryman* — 153 S. Leonard St.; PO Box 847 (54669); Th; 2,000pd, 30fr (Sw); $5.72; publisher Bill Griffith; editor Ron Marose; tel (608) 786-1950

Westby: *The Times* — 5 E. 1st; PO Box 140 (54667); Th; 1,890pd, 30fr (Sw); $3.60; C; publisher Mary Bormann Hollister; general manager Peter Hollister; editor Eric Wuennenberg; tel (608) 634-4317; fax (608) 637-8557

Weyauwega: *Weyauwega Chronicle* — 105 W. Wisconsin St.; PO Box 80 (54983); Th; 3,101pd, 187fr (Sw); $4.40; publisher Scott B Turner; editor Kenneth Handwiche; tel (414) 867-2158; fax (715) 258-8162

Whitefish Bay: *Whitefish Bay Herald* — PO Box 13155, Wauwatosa (53213); Th; 9,821pd, 446fr (Sw); $11.60; publisher Wayne P Toske; general manager Janet Raasch; editor Mark Schuchmann; managing editor Jeannie Wieland; tel (414) 778-5000; fax (414) 778-5012

Whitehall: *Whitehall Times* — 1410 Main St.; PO Box 95 (54773); Th; 2,208pd, 52fr (Est); $6.10; publisher Robert O Gauger; general manager Charles A Gauger; editor Scott Bruce Thomson; tel (715) 538-4765; fax (715) 538-4540

Whitewater: *Whitewater Register* — 101 W. Whitewater St.; PO Box 327 (53190); Th; 2,855pd, 153fr (Est); $3.96; C; publisher Tom Coe; editor Tim Sobie; tel (414) 473-3363; fax (414) 473-5635

Winneconne: *Winneconne News* — 908 E. Main St.; PO Box 370 (54986); W; 1,655pd (Sw); 15¢; publisher John A Rogers; editor Margaret E Rogers; tel (414) 582-4541

Winter: *Sawyer County Gazette* — Main St.; PO Box 68 (54896); W; 2,111pd, 14fr (Sw); $2.50; publisher & editor Meredith Rickert; tel (715) 266-2511; fax (715) 266-2511

Wisconsin Dells: *Wisconsin Dells Events* — 716 Elm St.; PO Box 116 (53965); W/Sa; 3,000pd (Est); $6.77; publisher Anthony Allegretti; editor Kay James; tel (608) 254-8327; fax (608) 254-8328

Wisconsin Statewide: *Wisconsin State Farmer* — 717 10th St.; PO Box 152, Waupaca (54981); F; 24,917pd, 4,325fr (Sw); $8.60; publisher Scott B Turner; general manager Donald Edmunds; editor Carla Gunst; tel (715) 258-5546; fax (715) 258-8162

Wittenberg: *Enterprise & News* — 110 W. Vinal St.; PO Box 190 (54499); Th; 1,482pd, 10fr (Est); $2.75; publisher Wittenberg Press Inc.; editor Gordy Boldig; tel (715) 253-2737; fax (715) 253-2700

Wonewoc/Elroy: *The Wonewoc Reporter* — PO Box 98, Wonewoc (53968); W; 2,073pd, 20fr (Est); $6.92; Sa; 2,073pd (Est); $6.03; publisher Anthony Allegretti; editor Bill Smith; tel (608) 462-8224; fax (608) 462-5678

Woodville: *The Woodville Leader* — 130 S. Main (54028); W; 850pd (Est); $3.25; publisher & editor Rueben Heim; tel (715) 698-2401; fax (715) 698-2952

WYOMING

Afton: *Star Valley Independent* — 360 S. Washington; PO Box 129 (83110); Th; 3,210pd (Est); 25¢; publisher & editor Dan Dockstader; tel (307) 886-5727; fax (307) 886-5742

Basin: *Basin Republican Rustler* — 409 W. C St.; PO Box 640 (82410); Th; 1,371pd, 10fr (Sw); $4.00; C; publisher & editor Eric D Adams; publisher Linda M Adams; tel (307) 568-2458

Bridger Valley: *Uinta County Pioneer* — 1718 Center St.; PO Box 538, Lyman (82937); F; 1,536pd (Sw); $4.97; C; publisher Debbie Smith; editor Gerry Forbes; tel (307) 787-3229; fax (307) 787-6795

Buffalo: *Buffalo Bulletin* — 58 N. Lobban; PO Box 730 (82834); Th; 4,210pd, 55fr (Sw); $5.00; publisher & editor Jim Hicks; tel (307) 684-2223; fax (307) 684-7431

Casper: *Casper Journal* — 2000 Fairgrounds Rd. (82604); PO Box 1427 (82602); Sa; 1,525pd, 500fr (Sw); 25¢; publisher Chris Zukin; editor Mark Whitmarsh; tel (307) 265-3870; fax (307) 265-3870

Cody: *The Cody Enterprise* — 1549 Sheridan Ave.; PO Box 1090 (82414); M/W; 5,738pd, 117fr (Sw); $8.00; publisher & editor Bruce E McCormack; tel (307) 587-2231; fax (307) 587-5208

Douglas: *The Douglas Budget* — 310 Center St.; PO Box 109 (82633); W; 2,987pd, 51fr (Sw); $6.50; C; publisher & editor Matt Adelman; tel (307) 358-2965; fax (307) 358-4454

Dubois/Fremont: *Dubois Frontier* — 103 S. 1st, Dubois (82513); Th; 1,400pd, 75fr (Est); $3.40; publisher Shirley Sanderson; editor Margery DeSpain; tel (307) 455-2525; fax (307) 455-3163

Evanston/Uinta Co.: *Uinta County Herald* — 1565 S. Hwy. 150, Ste. D; PO Box 210, Evanston (82930); Tu/F; 4,006pd, 65fr (Sw); $8.75; C; publisher Michael Jensen; editor Shawn Hubble; tel (307) 789-6560; fax (307) 789-2700

Glenrock: *Glenrock Independent* — 207 S. 4th; PO Box 9 (82637); Th; 1,300pd (Est); 14¢; publisher Nerwin O Reed; general manager Jana Reed Tyler; managing editor Randy D Stalker; tel (307) 436-2211; fax (307) 436-8803

Green River: *Green River Star* — 520 Wilkes Dr., Ste. 6 (82935); Th; 2,863pd, 120fr (Est); 39¢; C; publisher & editor Keith Bray; tel (307) 875-3103; fax (307) 875-8778

Greybull: *Greybull Standard & Tribune* — 614 Greybull Ave. (82426); Th; 1,561pd, 37fr (Sw); $4.25; C; publisher & editor Eric D Adams; tel (307) 765-4485; fax (307) 765-9640

Jackson: *Jackson Hole Guide* — 185 N. Glenwood; PO Box 648 (83001); W; 7,915pd, 212fr (Est); $9.00; C; publisher Fred A McCabe; general manager Alison Wolverton; editor Tom Hacker; managing editor Linda Fantin; tel (307) 733-2430; fax (307) 733-7841

Jackson Hole: *Jackson Hole News* — 1225 Maple Way; PO Box 7445, Jackson (83001); W; 7,323pd, 55fr (Est); 45¢; C; publisher Michael Sellett; editor Angus Thuermer Jr; tel (307) 733-2047; fax (307) 733-2138

Kemmerer: *The Kemmerer Gazette* — 708 J.C. Penney Dr.; PO Box 30 (83101); Th; 2,000pd (Sw); $4.20; publisher Mark Steele; editor Donald Kominsky; tel (307) 877-3347; fax (307) 877-3736

Lander: *Wyoming State Journal* — 453 Main; PO Box 900 (82520); M/W; 4,475pd, 2,600fr (Est); $5.00; publisher William C Sniffin; editor Cynthia Beckwith; tel (307) 332-2323; fax (307) 332-9332

Lovell/Byron/Cowley: *The Lovell Chronicle* — 234 E. Main; PO Box 787, Lovell (82431); Th; 2,135pd, 70fr (Est); $4.00; publisher & editor David H Peck; tel (307) 548-2217

Lusk: *The Lusk Herald* — 227 S. Main St.; PO Box 30 (82225); W; 1,280pd (Est); $4.75; C; publisher Bill Hansen; general manager Denise Barrs; tel (307) 334-2867; fax (307) 334-2514

Moorcroft/Gillette: *Moorcroft Leader* — 304 Riley; PO Box 67, Moorcroft (82721-0067); Th; 856pd, 115fr (Sw); $2.50; publisher & editor Edith Shepherd; tel (307) 756-3371; fax (307) 756-9827

Newcastle/Weston Co.: *News Letter Journal* — 14 W. Main; PO Box 40, Newcastle (82701); Th; 2,370pd (Est); $5.68; publisher & editor Robert Hicks; tel (307) 746-2777; fax (307) 746-2660

Pinedale/Big Piney: *The Pinedale Roundup* — 11 Mill St.; PO Box 100, Pinedale (82941); Th; 2,882pd, 12fr (Est); $5.00; C; publisher Fred A McCabe; editor Janet Montgomery; tel (307) 367-2123; fax (307) 367-6623

Powell: *The Powell Tribune* — 128 S. Bent St.; PO Box 70 (82435); Tu/Th; 4,000pd (Sw); 36¢; publisher Dave Bonner; managing editor Dennis Davis; tel (307) 754-2221; fax (307) 754-4873

Saratoga: *Saratoga Sun* — 116 E. Bridge St.; PO Box 489 (82331); W; 1,503pd, 20fr (Sw); $5.50; C; publisher Gary W Stevenson; editor Toby F Marlatt; tel (307) 326-8311; fax (307) 326-5108

Shoshoni: *Shoshoni Pioneer* — 310 W. 6th; PO Box 420 (82649); Th; 780pd (Est); $3.75; publisher & editor Troi Williams; tel (307) 876-2627

Sundance: *The Sundance Times* — 311 Main; PO Box 400 (82729); Th; 1,352pd, 30fr (Sw); $3.70; publisher & editor Howard Allen; tel (307) 283-3411

Thermopolis: *Thermopolis Independent Record* — 431 Broadway; PO Box 31 (82443); Th; 2,387pd, 32fr (Sw); $5.15; publisher & editor Patrick H Schmidt; tel (307) 864-2328; fax (307) 864-5711

Torrington/Goshen Co.: *The Torrington Telegram* — 2025 Main; PO Box 1058, Torrington (82240); W/F; 2,880pd, 65fr (Est); $5.45; C; publisher Bill Hansen; editor Cary Berry; tel (307) 532-2184; fax (307) 532-2283

Upton: *Weston County Gazette* — 723 2nd St.; PO Box 526 (82730); Th; 870pd (Est); 10¢; publisher & editor Clarence Woodard; tel (307) 468-2642; fax (307) 468-2642

Wheatland: *Platte County Record-Times* — 1007 8th St.; PO Box 969 (82201); W; 2,540pd, 10fr (Est); $3.85; publisher & editor Jim Wood; tel (307) 322-2627; fax (307) 322-9612

ALTERNATIVE NEWSPAPERS PUBLISHED IN THE UNITED STATES

ARIZONA

Phoenix/Maricopa Co.: *New Times* — 1201 E. Jefferson (85034); PO Box 2510, Phoenix (85002); Tu; 237pd, 134,843fr (VAC); $33.00; publisher Michele Laven; general manager Don Lineberg; editor John Mecklin; managing editor Jeremy Voas; tel (602) 271-0040; fax (602) 495-9954

Tucson Metro: *Tucson Weekly* — 201 W. Cushing; PO Box 2429, Tucson (85702); Th; 75pd, 36,360fr (VAC); $13.37; publisher & editor Douglas Riggers; tel (520) 792-3630; fax (520) 792-2096

CALIFORNIA

Butte/Glenn/Tehama Co.: *Chico News & Review* — 353 E. 2nd St., Chico (95928); Th; 79pd, 39,887fr (VAC); $20.14; C; publisher Jeff Von Kaenel; general manager Ron Slack; editor Robert Speer; tel (916) 894-2300; fax (916) 894-0143

Greater Los Angeles: *Los Angeles Reader* — 5550 Wilshire Blvd., Ste. 301, Los Angeles (90036); F; 64pd, 81,552fr (Sw); $47.25; publisher & editor James E Vowell; managing editor Erik Himmelsbach; tel (213) 965-7430; fax (213) 933-0281

Los Angeles: *LA Weekly* — 6715 Sunset Blvd. (90028); Th; 3,298pd, 161,815fr (Est); $56.04; C; publisher Mike Sigman; general manager Paulette Taix; editor Sue Horton; managing editor Mary Melton; tel (213) 465-9909; fax (213) 465-0444

Los Angeles: *Los Angeles View* — 2342 Sawtelle Blvd. (90064); F; 57pd, 60,286fr (VAC); $49.00; C; publisher James Sogg; editor Alex Demyanenko; managing editor Danny Feingold; tel (310) 477-0403; fax (310) 477-8428

Los Angeles Harbor Area: *Random Lengths* — 1117 S. Pacific Ave.; PO Box 731, San Pedro (90733); Th; 1,500pd, 28,500fr (Sw); $16.50; C; publisher James Preston Allen; general manager S K Matsumiya; editor Jim Elmendorf; managing editor Mike Easterbrook; tel (310) 519-1442; fax (310) 832-1000

Marin Co.: *Pacific Sun* — 21 Corte Madera Ave.; PO Box 5553, Mill Valley (94942); W; 105pd, 39,148fr (VAC); $20.00; publisher & editor Steve McNamara; managing editor Linda Xiques; tel (415) 383-4500; fax (415) 383-4159

Metro San Diego: *San Diego Reader* — 1703 India St. (92101); PO Box 85803, San Diego (92186); Th; 28pd, 134,084fr (VAC); $36.99; publisher & editor Jim Holman; tel (619) 235-3000; fax (619) 231-0489

Monterey Co.: *Coast Weekly* — 668 Williams Ave., Seaside (93955); Th; 42,000fr (Sw); $12.76; publisher Bradley Zeve; editor Jill Duman; managing editor Chuck Thurman; tel (408) 394-5656; fax (408) 394-2909

Oakland/Berkeley: *East Bay Express* — 931 Ashby Ave., Berkeley (94710); F; 65,000fr (Est); $24.00; publisher Nancy Banks; editor John Raeside; tel (510) 540-7400; fax (510) 540-7700

Orange Co.: *OC Weekly* — 151 Kalmus Dr., Ste. H-10, Costa Mesa (92626); Th; 50,000fr (Est); $17.73; publisher Michael Sigman; editor Will Swaim; managing editor Wyn Hilty; tel (714) 708-8400; fax (714) 708-8404

Palo Alto/Menlo Park: *Palo Alto Weekly* — 703 High St.; PO Box 1610, Palo Alto (94302); W/F; 26,275pd, 22,675fr (Sw); $34.35; C; publisher William S Johnson; editor Paul Gullixson; tel (415) 326-8210; fax (415) 326-3928

Sacramento: *Sacramento News & Review* — 1015 20th St. (95814); Th; 68pd, 80,837fr (VAC); $34.46; C; publisher Jeff vonKaenel; general manager David Comden; editor Melinda Welsh; tel (916) 498-1234; fax (916) 498-7910

San Francisco Bay Area: *San Francisco Bay Guardian* — 520 Hampshire St., San Francisco (94110); W; 2,159pd, 78,000fr (VAC); $42.00; publisher & editor Bruce B Brugmann; tel (415) 255-3100; fax (415) 255-8955

San Francisco Bay Area: *SF Weekly* — 425 Brannan St., San Francisco (94107); W; 53pd, 76,331fr (VAC); $40.00; publisher Scott Price; editor Andrew O'Hehir; managing editor Chris Borris; tel (415) 541-0700; fax (415) 777-1839

San Luis Obispo/Northern Santa Barbara Co.: *New Times* — 197 Santa Rosa St., San Luis Obispo (93405); W; 26pd, 37,277fr (VAC); $13.50; C; publisher & general manager Bev Johnson; publisher & editor Steve Moss; managing editor Richard Jackoway; tel (805) 546-8208; fax (805) 546-8641

Santa Barbara Co.: *Santa Barbara Independent* — 1221 State St., Ste. 200, Santa Barbara (93101); Th; 40,000fr (Sw); $15.00; publisher George Thurlow; editor Marianne Partridge; tel (805) 965-5205; fax (805) 965-5518

Santa Clara Co./Silicon Vly: *Metro* — 550 S. 1st St., San Jose (95113); Th; 86,000fr (Est); $38.00; C; publisher David Cohen; editor Steve Buel; managing editor Dan Pulcrano; tel (408) 298-8000; fax (408) 271-3521

South Bay: *Easy Reader* — 832 Hermosa Ave.; PO Box 427, Hermosa Beach (90254); Th; 22pd, 70,000fr (Sw); $20.00; publisher & editor Kevin Cody; tel (310) 372-4611; fax (310) 318-6292

COLORADO

Colorado Springs: *Colorado Springs Independent* — 121 E. Pikes Peak, Ste. 445 (80903); W; 25pd, 23,465fr (VAC); $10.68; publisher John Weiss; editor Kathe Eastburn; tel (719) 577-4545; fax (719) 577-4107

Metro Denver/Boulder Area: *Denver Westword* — 1612 18th St., Ste. 150 (80202); PO Box 5970, Denver (80217); W; 107,058fr (ABC); $25.50; C; publisher Amy Cobb; editor Patricia Calhoun; managing editor Andy Van de Voorde; tel (303) 296-7744; fax (303) 296-5416

CONNECTICUT

Fairfield Co.: *The Fairfield County Weekly* — 1 Dock St., 5th Fl., Stamford (06902); Th; 49,981fr (VAC); $35.00; C; publisher Barbara Hess; editor Lorraine Gengo; managing editor Elizabeth Hilts; tel (203) 406-2406; fax (203) 406-1099

Hartford: *Hartford Advocate* — 100 Constitution Plz. (06103); Th; 59,935fr (Sw); $35.00; C; publisher Francis J Zankowski; editor Russ Hoyle; managing editor Janet Reynolds; tel (860) 548-9300; fax (860) 548-9335

New Haven: *New Haven Advocate* — 1 Long Wharf Dr. (06511); W; 161pd, 54,950fr (VAC); $36.00; C; publisher Gail Thompson; editor Oosh Mamis; tel (203) 789-0010; fax (203) 787-1418

DISTRICT OF COLUMBIA

Washington: *Washington City Paper* — 2390 Champlain St. N.W. (20009); F; 92,316fr (ABC); $38.00; publisher Thomas K Yoder; general manager Amy Austin; editor David Carr; tel (202) 332-2100; fax (202) 462-8323

FLORIDA

Greater Miami: *Miami New Times* — 330 N. Biscayne Blvd., Ste. 1000; PO Box 011591, Miami (33101); W; 30pd, 80,244fr (VAC); $22.00; publisher Hal Smith; editor Jim Mullin; tel (305) 372-0004; fax (305) 372-3446

Jacksonville: *Folio Weekly* — 9456 Philips Hwy., Ste. 11 (32256); Tu; 29pd, 30,531fr (VAC); $26.73; publisher Sam Taylor; editor Bob Snell; tel (904) 260-9770; fax (904) 260-9773

Tampa/St. Petersburg/Clearwater: *Weekly Planet* — 402 Reo St., Ste. 218 (33609); PO Box 20132, Tampa (33622-0132); Th; 75,000fr (Est); $23.85; publishers Ben Eason & Terry Garrett; general manager Gia Coppi; managing editor Susan Dix Tibbits; tel (813) 286-1600; fax (813) 289-8010

GEORGIA

Atlanta/Gwinnet Co./Cobb Co.: *Creative Loafing* — 750 Willoughby Way N.E., Atlanta (30312); Sa; 294pd, 110,730fr (VAC); $37.50; publisher Deborah Eason; editor Tony Paris; tel (404) 688-5623; fax (404) 522-1532

IDAHO

Boise: *Boise Weekly* — 280 N. 8th St., Ste. 30 (83702); PO Box 1657 (83701); Th; 12,180fr (VAC); $18.67; publishers Andy Hedden-Nicely & Debi Hedden-Nicely & Larry G Ragan; editor David Madison; tel (208) 344-2055; fax (208) 342-4733

ILLINOIS

Chicago Lakefront: *Chicago Reader* — 11 E. Illinois, Chicago (60611); F; 985pd, 133,105fr (ABC); $47.00; publisher Jane Levine; editor Alison True; tel (312) 828-0350; fax (312) 828-9926

Metro Chicago: *New City* — 770 N. Halsted St., Ste. 208, Chicago (60622); Th; 43pd, 54,375fr (VAC); $32.29; publisher & editor Brian J Hieggelke; publisher & general manager Jan Hieggelke; managing editor Frank Sennett; tel (312) 243-8786; fax (312) 243-8802

Springfield: *Illinois Times* — 610 S. 7th; PO Box 3524 (62708); Th; 112pd, 31,046fr (VAC); $35.00; publisher & editor Fletcher F Farrar Jr; managing editor William Furry; tel (217) 753-2226; fax (217) 753-2281

INDIANA

Bloomington: *Bloomington Voice* — 3902 B S. Oldstate Rd. 37 (47401); Th; 6pd, 14,463fr (VAC); $15.50; C; publisher Bill Craig; editor Diane Aden Hayes; managing editor Greg Jefferson; tel (812) 331-0963; fax (812) 331-0863

Indianapolis/Marion Co.: *NUVO* — 811 E. Westfield Blvd., Indianapolis (46220); W; 49,137fr (VAC); $25.36; publisher Kevin McKinney; editor Harrison Ullmann; managing editor Susan Gilman; tel (317) 254-2400; fax (317) 254-2405

Richmond: *Main Event* — 99 S. Perry St., Hagerstown (47346-1521); W; 8,500fr (Est); $5.95; C; publisher & editor Bob Hansen; general manager Ken B Smith; tel (317) 489-4035; fax (317) 489-5323

LOUISIANA

New Orleans/Jefferson/Orleans Parish: *Gambit-New Orleans Weekly* — 3923 Bienville St., New Orleans (70119); M; 99pd, 36,733fr (VAC); $4.67; C; publisher Margo DuBos; editor Allen Johnson; tel (504) 486-5900; fax (504) 488-7263

MAINE

Maine: *Maine Times* — 561 Congress St., Portland (04101); W; 14,705pd, 617fr (Est); $32.35; publisher W E Rawlings; editor Randy Wilson; tel (207) 828-5432; fax (207) 828-5438

Portland: *Casco Bay Weekly* — 561 Congress St. (04101); Th; 30,000fr (Sw); $14.78; publisher Seth Sprague; editor Wayne Curtis; tel (207) 775-6601; fax (207) 775-1615

MARYLAND

Baltimore Metro: *Baltimore City Paper* — 812 Park Ave., Baltimore (21201); W; 91,500fr (Sw); $31.50; publisher Don Farley; editor Sono Motoyoma; tel (410) 523-2300; fax (410) 523-2222

MASSACHUSETTS

Boston: *Boston Phoenix* — 126 Brookline Ave. (02215); Th; 78,000pd, 50,000fr (Sw); $5.40; publisher Stephen M Mindich; editor Peter Kadzis; tel (617) 536-5390; fax (617) 536-1463

Northampton/Amherst/Pioneer Vly: *Valley Advocate* — 87 School St., Hatfield (01301); Th; 26,908fr (VAC); $25.00; C; publisher Joleen Benedict; editor Tom Mudd; tel (413) 247-9301; fax (413) 247-5439

Springfield: *Springfield Advocate* — 1127 Main St. (01103); Th; 65,000fr (VAC); $16.00; C; publisher Catherine Nelson; editor Kitty Axelson; tel (413) 781-1900; fax (413) 781-1906

Worcester: *Worcester Magazine* — 172 Shrewsberry St. (01614); W; 36pd, 39,683fr (VAC); $18.90; C; publisher Catherine Nelson; editor Jay Whearley; tel (508) 799-0511; fax (508) 755-8860

MICHIGAN

Detroit: *The Metro Times* — 733 St. Antoine (48226); W; 101,100fr (ABC); $31.50; publisher Ron Williams; editor Desiree Cooper; tel (313) 961-4060; fax (313) 961-6598

MINNESOTA

Minneapolis/St. Paul: *City Pages* — 401 N. 3rd St., Ste. 550 (55401); PO Box 59183, Minneapolis (55459); W; 100,161fr (VAC); $41.10; publisher Tom Bartel; editor Steve Perry; managing editor Monika Bauerlein; tel (612) 375-1015; fax (612) 372-3737

Twin Cities: *Twin Cities Reader* — 10 S. 5th St., Ste. 200, Minneapolis (55402); W; 74pd, 95,823fr (VAC); $29.95; publisher Jeffrey H Litt; editor Claude Peck; tel (612) 321-7300; fax (612) 321-7333

MISSOURI

Kansas City: *Pitch Weekly* — 3535 Broadway, Ste. 400 (64111); Th; 67,158fr (VAC); $35.00; publisher Hal Brody; editor Bruce Rodgers; managing editor Jeff Drake; tel (816) 561-6061; fax (816) 756-0502

Kansas City, MO-KS: *Kansas City New Times* — 207 Westport Rd., Ste. 201, Kansas City (64111); Th; 10pd, 45,000fr (Sw); $8.89; C; publisher & editor J P O'Connor; general manager Jennifer Williams; managing editor David Madole; tel (816) 753-7880; fax (816) 561-6252

Metro St. Louis: *The Riverfront Times* — 1221 Locust, Ste. 900, St. Louis (63103); T/W; 326pd, 99,630fr (VAC); $41.95; publisher & editor Raymond P Hartmann; managing editor Safir Ahmed; tel (314) 231-6666; fax (314) 231-9040

NEW MEXICO

Santa Fe Co.: *Santa Fe Reporter* — 132 E. Marcy St. (87501); PO Box 2306, Santa Fe (87504); W; 246pd, 25,000fr (Sw); $15.25; publisher Hope Aldrich; editor Robert Mayer; tel (505) 988-5541; fax (505) 988-5348

NEW YORK

Albany/Saratoga/Schenectady/Troy: *Metroland* — 4 Central Ave., Albany (12210); Th; 33,000fr (Sw); $30.47; publisher & editor Stephen Leon; general manager Lisa Hoenig; tel (518) 463-2500; fax (518) 463-3712

Ithaca: *Ithaca Times* — 109-111 N. Cayuga St.; PO Box 27 (14851); Th; 83pd, 20,880fr (Est); $17.50; publisher James Bilinski; managing editor Jay Wrolstad; tel (607) 277-7000; fax (607) 277-1012

Manhattan: *New York Press* — 295 Lafayette St., 9th Fl, New York (10012); W; 52pd, 81,848fr (VAC); $29.75; publisher & editor Russ Smith; tel (212) 941-1130; fax (212) 941-7824

New York: *The Village Voice* — 36 Cooper Sq. (10003-7118); W; 121,126pd, 28,327fr (ABC); N/A; publisher David Schneiderman; general manager Ava Seave; editor Karen Durbin; managing editor Doug Simmons; tel (212) 475-3333; fax (212) 598-0629

Rochester: *City Newspaper* — 250 N. Goodman St. (14607-1199); Th; 1,638pd, 17,744fr (VAC); $13.00; publisher & editor Mary Anna Towler; publisher William Towler; tel (716) 244-3329; fax (716) 244-1126

Syracuse/Onondaga Co.: *Syracuse New Times* — 1415 W. Genesee St., Syracuse (13204-2156); W; 559pd, 44,543fr (Sw); $24.00; publisher Arthur Zimmer; general manager Gregg A Gambell; editor Mike Greenstein; tel (315) 422-7011; fax (315) 422-1721

Westchester Co.: *The Westchester County Weekly* — 1 Dock St., 5th Fl., Stamford (06902); Th; 19,979fr (VAC); $27.00; C; publisher Barbara Hess; editor Lorraine Gengo; managing editor Elizabeth Hilts; tel (203) 406-2406; fax (203) 406-1099

NORTH CAROLINA

Asheville/Buncombe Co.: *Mountain Xpress* — 2 Wall St.; PO Box 144, Asheville (28802); W; 12,513fr (VAC); $13.00; publisher & editor Jeff Fobes; general manager Carey Watson; tel (704) 251-1333; fax (704) 251-1311

Charlotte: *Creative Loafing* — 1620 S. Blvd., Ste. 3A (28203); W; 35,000fr (Est); publisher Carolyn Butler; editor John Grooms; tel (704) 375-2121; fax (704) 375-3960

Copyright ©1996 by the Editor & Publisher Co.

Raleigh/Durham/Chapel Hill: *The Independent Weekly* — 2810 Hillsborough Rd.; PO Box 2690, Durham (27715); W; 381pd, 45,962fr (VAC); $22.00; publisher Steve Schewel; general manager Jewel Wheeler; editor Gillian Floren; tel (919) 286-1972; fax (919) 286-4274

OHIO

Athens Co.: *The Athens News* — 14 N. Court St.; PO Box 543, Athens (45701); M/Th; 14pd, 15,158fr (CPVS); publisher Bruce Mitchell; editor Terry Smith; tel (614) 594-8219; fax (614) 592-5695

Cincinnati/Oxford/Dayton: *Everybody's News* — 1310 Pendleton St., Ste. 700, Cincinnati (45210); F; 42,000fr (Sw); $8.00; publisher Donna Goodwin; editor Randy Katz; managing editor Erma P Sanders; tel (513) 381-2606; fax (513) 287-8643

Cleveland: *Cleveland Free Times* — 1846 Coventry Rd., Ste. 100 (44118-1682); W; 32,522fr (VAC); $20.00; publisher Randy Siegel; editor Cindy Barber; managing editor Eric Broder; tel (216) 321-2300; fax (216) 321-4456

Columbus: *The Other Paper* — PO Box 29913 (43229); Th; 50,000fr (Sw); N/A; publisher Max S Brown; editor Danny Russell; tel (614) 847-3800; fax (614) 848-3838

Columbus/Central Ohio: *Columbus Guardian* — 400 Dublin Ave., Ste. 100, Columbus (43215); Th; 41,909fr (VAC); $13.00; C; publisher Ron Williams; editor Mimi Morris; tel (614) 469-1510; fax (614) 469-1508

Greater Columbus: *Columbus Alive* — 689 N. High St., Columbus (43215); Th; 42,500fr (Est); $25.00; publisher Phil Miller; editor Pat Schmucki; tel (614) 221-2449; fax (614) 221-2456

OKLAHOMA

Oklahoma City Metro: *Oklahoma Gazette* — 801 N.W. 36th St.; PO Box 54649, Oklahoma City (73154-1649); Th; 45,275fr (ABC); $14.86; publisher Bill Bleakley; editor Mike Easterling; tel (405) 528-6000; fax (405) 528-4600

OREGON

Eugene: *Eugene Weekly* — 1251 Lincoln St. (97401); Th; 25,000fr (VAC); $22.00; publisher Sonja Snyder; editor Lois Wadsworth; tel (503) 484-0519; fax (503) 484-4044

Portland: *Willamette Week* — 822 S.W. 10th Ave. (97205); W; 900pd, 73,715fr (VAC); $33.72; publisher Richard H Meeker; general manager Barbara McDonald; editor Mark L Zusman; managing editor Les Harper; tel (503) 243-2122; fax (503) 243-1115

PENNSYLVANIA

Allegheny Co.: *In Pittsburgh Newsweekly* — 2100 Wharton St., Ste. 300, Pittsburgh (15203-1942); W; 100pd, 55,000fr (Est); $28.59; publisher John Burnstein; general manager Amy Jaffe; editor Dan Cook; managing editor Patricia G Barnes; tel (412) 488-1212; fax (412) 488-1217

Greater Center City/Suburb Philadelphia/S Jersey: *Philadelphia City Paper* — 206 S. 13th St., Philadelphia (19107); Th; 85,000fr (Est); $12.35; publisher & editor Bruce Schimmel; general manager Paul Curci; managing editor David Y Warner; tel (215) 735-8444; fax (215) 732-9033

Philadelphia/Mainline: *Philadelphia Weekly* — 1701 Walnut St., Philadelphia (19103); W; 61,900fr (CPVS); $13.48; publisher Michael Cohen; editor Tim Whitaker; tel (215) 563-7400; fax (215) 563-6799

RHODE ISLAND

Rhode Island Statewide: *Providence Phoenix* — 150 Chestnut St., Providence (02903); Th; 60,000fr (Est); $29.00; C; publishers Stephen M Mindich & Steve Brown; editors Lou Papineau & Peter Kadzis; tel (401) 273-6397; fax (401) 273-0920

TENNESSEE

Memphis: *Memphis Flyer* — 460 Tennesse St.; PO Box 687 (38103); Th; 40pd, 51,000fr (Sw); $15.46; publisher Kenneth Neill; general manager Cheryl Bader; editor Dennis Freeland; managing editor Steve Russell; tel (901) 521-9000; fax (901) 521-0129

Nashville: *The Nashville Scene* — 209 10th Ave. S., Ste. 222 (37203-4101); Th; 49,531fr (ABC); $38.35; C; publisher Albie Del Favero; editor Bruce Dobie; tel (615) 244-7989; fax (615) 244-8578

TEXAS

Austin: *Austin Chronicle* — 4000 N. 1H-35 (78751); PO Box 49066 (78765); F; 267pd, 77,6454fr (VAC); $29.12; C; publisher Nick Barbaro; editor Louis Black; managing editor Jennifer Scoville; tel (512) 454-5766; fax (512) 458-6910

Dallas Observer: *Dallas Observer* — 2130 Commerce Ave., Dallas (75201); Th; 100,000fr (Sw); 55¢; C; publisher Lee Newquist; general manager Jared Rosckes; editor Peter Elkind; managing editor Glen Warchol; tel (214) 757-9000; fax (214) 757-8590

Houston: *Houston Press* — 2000 W. Loop S., Ste. 1900 (77027); Th; 77,294fr (ABC); $105.26; publisher Terry Coe; general manager Carol Flagg; editor Jim Simmon; managing editor Mitchell Shields; tel (713) 624-1400; fax (713) 624-1444

San Antonio: *San Antonio Current* — 8750 Tesoro Dr., Ste. 1 (78217); Th; 11pd, 28,116fr (Sw); $9.57; publisher Bob Walton; editor Mike Hood; tel (512) 828-7660; fax (512) 828-7883

Texas Statewide: *The Texas Observer* — 307 W. 7th St., Austin (78701); Bi-wkly; 5,505pd, 90fr (Sw); $25.00; publisher Geoff Rips; editor Lou Dubuse; managing editor Michael King; tel (512) 477-0746; fax (512) 474-1175

UTAH

Salt Lake City: *Private Eye* — 68 W. 400 S. (84101); Th; 43,000fr (Sw); $8.73; publisher John Saltas; managing editor Tom Walsh; tel (801) 575-7003; fax (801) 575-6106

VERMONT

Burlington/Chittenden: *Vermont Times* — 3 Webster Rd.; PO Box 940, Shelburne (05482-0940); W; 678pd, 39,322fr (Sw); $22.50; Bi-Mthly; 7,000fr (Est); $15.00; publisher & editor Linda D Birner; publishers Nancy Chioffi & Nat Winthrop; general manager Cheryl Strickland; editor Dan Hickey; tel (802) 985-2400; fax (802) 985-2490

WASHINGTON

E Seattle (suburban area): *Eastsideweek* — 1008 Western Ave., Ste. 300, Seattle (98104); W; 34,381fr (ABC); $31.00; C; publisher Skip Berger; editor Knute Berger; managing editor John Arthur Wilson; tel (206) 827-5550; fax (206) 467-4377

Greater Seattle Area: *Seattle Weekly* — 1008 Western Ave., Ste. 300, Seattle (98101); W; 33,500pd (Est); $47.75; publisher David Brewster; editor Knute Berger; managing editor Katherine Koberg; tel (206) 623-0500; fax (206) 467-4377

WISCONSIN

Madison: *Isthmus* — 101 King St. (53703); F; 855pd, 59,090fr (VAC); $31.45; publisher Vincent P O'Hern; editor Marc Eisen; tel (608) 251-5627; fax (608) 251-2165

Milwaukee: *Shepherd Express Weekly News* — 1123 N. Water St. (53202); Th; 262pd, 51,310fr (VAC); $17.50; C; publisher Doug Hissom; editor Scott Kerr; managing editor Julie Wichman; tel (414) 276-2222; fax (414) 276-3312

BLACK NEWSPAPERS PUBLISHED IN THE UNITED STATES

ALABAMA

Birmingham: *Birmingham Times (Est. 1964)* — 115 3rd Ave. W. (35204); PO Box 10503 (35202); Th; 10,000pd (CPVS); $10.52; publisher Dr Jesse J Lewis; editor Keith Walters; tel (205) 251-5158; fax (205) 323-2294

Birmingham: *Birmingham World (Est. 1932)* — 407 15th St. N. (35203); PO Box 2285 (35201); Th; 11,500pd (Sw); $12.50; publisher Joe Dickson; editor Marcel Hopson; tel (205) 251-6523; fax (205) 328-6729

Eutaw: *Greene County Democrat (Est. 1984)* — 214 Boligee St.; PO Box 598 (35462); W; 1,479pd, 1,341fr (CPVS); $6.75; publisher Carol Zippert; publisher & editor John Zippert; general manager Laddie Jones; tel (205) 372-3373; fax (205) 372-2243

Florence: *Florence Shoals News-Leader (Est. 1980)* — 412 S. Court St., Ste. 206 (35630); PO Box 427 (35630); W; 5,000pd (Sw); $8.50; publisher & editor William R Liner; tel (205) 766-5542; fax (205) 760-1117

Huntsville: *Speakin' Out Weekly (Est. 1980)* — 1300 Meridian St. (35801); W; 10,000pd (Sw); $7.25; publisher & editor William Smothers; tel (205) 551-1020; fax (205) 551-0607

Mobile: *Inner City News (Est. 1976)* — 212 S. Dr Martin Luther King Dr.; PO Box 1545 (36633-1545); Th; 5,000pd (Est); $17.74; publisher & editor Charles W Porter; tel (334) 452-9329; fax (334) 452-9330

Mobile: *Mobile Beacon and Alabama Citizen (Est. 1943)* — 2311 Coastarides St. (36601); PO Box 1407 (36633); Sa; 4,462pd, 20fr (Est); $8.64; publisher Lancie M Thomas; editor Cleretta T Blackmon; tel (334) 479-0629

Mobile: *New Times (Est. 1981)* — 156 S. Broad St. (36602); Th; 5,000pd (Sw); $10.00; publisher & editor Leophus Lyde; tel (334) 432-0356; fax (334) 432-8320

Montgomery: *Montgomery/Tuskegee Times (Est. 1977)* — 150 W. Fairview Ave. (36105); W; 5,000pd (Sw); publisher & editor Al Dixon; tel (334) 262-5026; fax (334) 262-5026

ARIZONA

Phoenix: *Arizona Informant (Est. 1971)* — 1746 E. Madison St., Ste. 2 (85034); W; 7,806pd (Sw); $20.83; publisher Charles Campbell; general manager Clovis Campbell Jr; editor Clovis Campbell Sr; tel (602) 257-9300

ARKANSAS

Little Rock: *Arkansas State Press (Est. 1941)* — 221 W. 2nd St., Ste. 608 (72201); Th; 5,000pd (Est); $15.00; C; publisher & editor Janetta Kearney; tel (501) 371-9991; fax (501) 371-9128

CALIFORNIA

Bakersfield: *Bakersfield News Observer (Est. 1977)* — 1219 20th St. (93385); PO Box 3624 (93385); W; 49,047pd (CPVS); $16.00; publisher Joseph Coley; editor Ellen Cleek; tel (805) 324-9466; fax (805) 324-9472

Berkeley: *California Voice (Est. 1919)* — 1366 Turk St., San Francisco (94115); Su; 37,330pd (CPVS); $17.00; publisher Gary Goodlett; editor Gary Raynaldo; managing editor Amelia Ashley-Ward; tel (415) 931-5778; fax (415) 931-0214

Compton: *Compton Bulletin (Est. 1970)* — 349 W. Compton Blvd. (90220); W; 32,516pd, 42,484fr (CPVS); $25.00; publisher O Ray Watkins; editor Betty Wilson; tel (310) 635-6776

Fresno: *California Advocate (Est. 1967)* — 452 Fresno St. (93706); PO Box 11826 (93775); W; 2,250pd (Sw); $14.00; publisher Mark Kimber; editor Pauline Kimber; tel (209) 268-0941; fax (209) 266-6947

Lemon Grove: *San Diego Monitor (Est. 1988)* — 3750 Olive Ave. (91945); Th; 2,000pd, 5,000fr (Sw); publisher & editor Willie Morrow; tel (619) 263-1603

Los Angeles: *Central-News Wave Group (Est. 1919)* — 2621 W. 54th St. (90043); W; 280,000pd (Sw); $16.50; publisher C Z Wilson; editor Alice Marshall; tel (213) 290-3000; fax (213) 293-2136

Los Angeles: *Firestone Park News (Est. 1924)* — 4053 Marlton Ave. (90008); PO Box 19027A (90019); Th; 23,933pd (Est); $14.00; publisher Clifford Young; editor Lela Ward Oliver; tel (213) 291-9486; fax (213) 291-2123

Los Angeles: *Herald Dispatch (Est. 1952)* — 4053 Marlton Ave. (90008); PO Box 19027A (90019); Th; 34,633pd, 257fr (Est); $16.00; publisher Clifford Young; editor Lela Ward Oliver; tel (213) 291-9486; fax (213) 291-2123

Los Angeles: *Los Angeles Sentinel (Est. 1933)* — 3800 Crenshaw Blvd. (90008); Th; 18,682pd, 672fr (ABC); $22.50; publisher Kenneth Thomas; editor Marshall Lowe; managing editor Marsha Mitchell-Bray; tel (213) 299-3800; fax (213) 299-3896

Los Angeles: *Watts Star Review (Est. 1875)* — 4053 Marlton Ave. (90008); PO Box 19027A (90019); Th; 29,877pd (Est); $15.00; publisher Clifford Young; editor Lela Ward Oliver; tel (213) 291-9486; fax (213) 291-2123

Oakland: *Post Group (Est. 1963)* — 630 20th St.; PO Box 1350 (94612); W/Su; 114,437pd (CPVS); $14.05; publishers Thomas L Berkeley & Velda Berkeley; editor Gail Berkeley; tel (510) 763-1120; fax (510) 763-9670

Pasadena: *Pasadena Journal-News (Est. 1989)* — 1541 N. Lake Ave., Ste. A (91104); Th; 8,000pd (Sw); $12.00; publisher Joe C Hopkins; publisher & editor Ruthie Hopkins; tel (818) 798-3972; fax (818) 798-3282

Riverside: *Black Voice News (Est. 1973)* — 3583 Main St. (92501); PO Box 1581 (92502); Th; 8,000pd (CPVS); $19.50; publisher & editor Cheryl Brown; publisher Hardy Brown; tel (909) 682-6070/889-0506; fax (909) 276-0877

Sacramento: *Observer Group (Est. 1962)* — 3540 4th Ave.; PO Box 209 (95801); Th; 49,000pd, 49,818fr (Est); $41.00; publisher & editor William H Lee; general manager & managing editor Kathryn C Lee; tel (916) 452-4781; fax (916) 452-7744

San Bernardino: *Precinct Reporter (Est. 1965)* — 1677 W. Baseline St. (92411); Th; 55,000pd (Est); $22.50; publisher & editor Brian Townsend; tel (909) 889-0597; fax (909) 889-1706

San Bernardino: *The American News (Est. 1969)* — 1583 W. Baseline St.; PO Box 7010 (92411); Th; 10,000pd (Sw); $9.85; publishers Samuel Martin Sr & Willie Mae Martin; editor Samuel Martin Jr; tel (909) 889-7677

San Diego: *Voice & Viewpoint (Est. 1961)* — 1729 N. Euclid Ave. (92105); PO Box 95 (92112); Th; 18,000pd (CPVS); $12.50; publisher & editor John Warren; managing editor Gerri Adams-Warren; tel (619) 266-2233; fax (619) 266-0533

San Francisco: *San Francisco Metro Reporter Group (Est. 1975)* — 1366 Turk St. (94115); Su; 111,118pd (CPVS); $15.00; publisher Gary Goodlett; editor Amelia Ashley-Ward; tel (415) 931-5778; fax (415) 931-0214

San Francisco: *The Sun Reporter (Est. 1942)* — 1366 Turk St. (94115); Th; 12,000pd (ABC); $15.00; publisher Gary Goodlett; editor Amelia Ashley-Ward; tel (415) 931-5778; fax 14159310214

COLORADO

Denver: *Denver Weekly News (Est. 1971)* — 2937 Welton St.; PO Box 5008 (80217); Th; 6,000pd, 4,000fr (Sw); $13.44; publisher F Cosmo Harris; general manager Ruth Cockrell; editor Gordon Jackson; tel (303) 292-5158; fax (303) 292-5344

CONNECTICUT

Hartford: *Inquirer Group (Est. 1975)* — 3281 Main St. (06120); PO Box 1260 (06101); W; 125,000pd (Est); $11.25; publisher William R Hales; editor Monique Jarvis; tel (860) 522-1462; fax (860) 522-3014

II-88 Black newspapers

DISTRICT OF COLUMBIA

Washington: *Capitol Spotlight (Est. 1953)* — 529 14th St. N.W., Ste. 2101 (20045); Th; 20,000pd (Est); $12.50; publisher & editor Betty Brooks; tel (202) 745-7858; fax (202) 745-7860

Washington: *News Dimensions (Est. 1992)* — 1221 Massachusetts Ave. N.W., Ste. 522 (20005); F; 400pd, 24,600fr (Est); $8.00; publisher & editor Barry Murray; tel (202) 628-2300; fax (202) 628-0550

Washington: *Washington Afro-American and Tribune (Est. 1892)* — 1612-14th St. N.W. (20009); F; 8,709pd (Sw); $19.30; C; publisher Frances L Murphy II; editor Lawanza Spears; tel (202) 332-0080; fax (202) 939-7461

Washington: *Washington Informer (Est. 1964)* — 3117 Martin Luther King Jr Ave. S.E. (20032); Th; 27,000pd (Sw); $11.80; publisher Dr Calvin W Rolark; editor Denise Rolark Barnes; tel (202) 561-4100; fax (202) 574-3785

Washington: *Washington New Observer (Est. 1957)* — 811 Florida Ave. N.W. (20001); Th; 10,000pd (Est); $4.85; publisher & editor Robert B Newton; general manager Lauren P Newton; tel (202) 232-3060; fax (202) 232-1711

Washington: *Washington Sun (Est. 1967)* — 830 Kennedy St. N.W. (20011); Th; 45,000pd (Est); N/A; publisher & editor J C Cooke; managing editor Mae Lynn; tel (202) 882-1021

FLORIDA

Daytona Beach: *Daytona Times (Est. 1978)* — 427 S. Martin Luther King Blvd. (32114); PO Box 1110 (32115); Th; 14,544pd (CPVS); $19.11; publisher Charles W Cherry Sr; editor Charles W Cherry Jr; tel (904) 253-0321; fax (904) 254-7510

Ft. Lauderdale: *The Broward Times* — 1001 W. Cypress Creek Rd., Ste. 111 (33309); F; 25,000pd (Est); $13.50; C; publisher Keith A Clayborne; general manager Bernadette Bostwick; editor Mara Kissin; tel (954) 351-9070; fax (954) 351-3099

Ft. Lauderdale: *Westside Gazette (Est. 1971)* — 701 N.W. 18th Ave.; PO Box 5304 (33311); Th; 30,494pd, 5,880fr (CPVS); $12.10; publisher Levi Henry; general manager Dorothy Dillard; editor Yvonne Henry; managing editor Pamela Lewis; tel (954) 523-5115; fax (954) 522-2553

Ft. Myers: *Community Voice (Est. 1988)* — 3046 Lafayette St. (33916); Th; 12,000pd (Est); $15.00; publisher & editor Charles Weaver; tel (941) 337-4444

Jacksonville: *The Florida Star (Est. 1951)* — 5196-C Norwood Ave., Ste. C; Gateway Mall (32203); W; 9,622pd (CPVS); $14.00; publisher Mary W Simpson; editor Ron Williams; managing editor P Erica Simpson; tel (904) 766-8834; fax (904) 765-1673

Jacksonville/St. Augustine/Ponte Verda/Neptune Beach/Atlanti: *Jacksonville Free Press (Est. 1986)* — 1603-I Edgewood Ave. W.; PO Box 43580, Jacksonville (32203-3580); W; 24,200pd (Sw); $18.55; publisher Rita Perry; general manager R J Eggleton; editor Sylvia Perry; managing editor Rosella Carter; tel (904) 634-1993; fax (904) 384-0235

Miami: *Miami Times (Est. 1923)* — 900 N.W. 54th St.; PO Box 270200 (33127); Th; 19,961pd, 239fr (ABC); $21.00; publishers Garth C Reeves & Rachel J Reeves; editor Mohamed Hamaludin; tel (305) 757-1147; fax (305) 756-0771

Orlando: *Orlando Times (Est. 1975)* — 4403 Vineland Blvd. (32811); PO Box 5339 (32855); Th; 11,000pd (Sw); $10.00; publisher & editor Calvin Collins; general manager L H Collins; tel (305) 841-1044

Pensacola: *New American Press (Est. 1979)* — 619 N. Devillers St.; PO Box 13626 (32501); Th; 31,778pd (CPVS); $32.40; publisher Angelina LeRoy; general manager Walter LeRoy; editor Bobbie Weaver; tel (904) 432-8410; fax (904) 434-5023

Pensacola: *Pensacola Voice (Est. 1971)* — 213 E. Yonge St. (32503); Th; 32,186pd (CPVS); $22.50; publisher Les Humphrey; editor Cheryl Johnson; tel (904) 434-6963; fax (904) 469-8745

St. Petersburg: *Weekly Challenger (Est. 1967)* — 2500 E. 9th St. S., Ste. F (33705); Th; 22,000pd (Sw); $11.75; publisher Cleveland Johnson Jr; editor Cynthia Armstrong; tel (813) 896-2922; fax (813) 896-2568

Tallahassee: *Capitol Outlook (Est. 1964)* — 602 N. Adams St.; PO Box 11335 (32301); Th; 12,000pd (CPVS); $27.65; publisher & editor Roosevelt Wilson; general manager Cathy Wilson; tel (904) 681-1852; fax (904) 681-1093

Tampa: *Florida Sentinel-Bulletin (Est. 1945)* — 2207 21st Ave. (33605); PO Box 3363 (33601); Tu/F; 23,000pd (CPVS); $12.00; publisher C Blythe Andrews Jr; general manager Sybil Andrews-Wells; editor Gwendolyn Hayes; tel (813) 248-1921; fax (813) 248-4507

W Palm Beach: *Florida Photo News and Image (Est. 1955)* — PO Box 1583-46 (33402); Th; 4,000pd, 1,000fr (Est); $9.10; publisher & editor Yasmin Cooper; tel (407) 833-4511; fax (407) 833-0711

GEORGIA

Albany: *Albany Southwest Georgian (Est. 1938)* — 310 S. Jackson St. (31701); PO Box 1943 (31702); Th; 16,000pd (Sw); $6.00; publisher A C Searles; editor Tom Searles; tel (912) 436-2156; fax (912) 435-6860

Atlanta: *Atlanta Daily World Inc.* — 145 Auburn Ave. N.E. (30335-1201); Su/Tu/Th; 18,000pd (Est); $11.90; publisher & editor C A Scott; tel (404) 659-1110

Atlanta: *Atlanta Inquirer (Est. 1960)* — 947 Martin Luther King Dr. N.W.; PO Box 92367 (30314); Th; 51,101pd, 9,622fr (CPVS); $25.20; C; publisher John B Smith; editor David L Stanley; managing editor Christopher Weems; tel (404) 523-6086; fax (404) 523-6088

Atlanta: *Atlanta Voice (Est. 1966)* — 633 Pryor St. (30312); PO Box 92487 (30314); Th; 103,000pd (Sw); $45.00; publisher Janis Ware; editor Stan Washington; tel (404) 524-6426; fax (404) 523-7853

Augusta: *The Metro Courier (Est. 1983)* — 314 Walton Way (30901); PO Box 2385 (30903); W; 18,791pd, 574fr (Est); $13.82; publisher & editor Barbara A Gordon; tel (706) 724-6556; fax (706) 722-7104

College Park: *Atlanta-News Leader (Est. 1990)* — 4006 Riverdale Ct. (30337); W; 5,000pd, 5,000fr (Sw); $11.29; C; editor Carla Harper; managing editor Lee Haven; tel (770) 907-8949; fax (770) 907-1267

Columbus: *The Columbus Times (Est. 1958)* — 2230 Buena Vista Rd.; PO Box 2845 (31906); Tu; 20,000pd (Sw); $14.24; publisher Ophelia Mitchell; editor Carol Gerdes; managing editor Helmet Gerdes; tel (706) 324-2404; fax (706) 596-0657

Decatur: *The Champion* — PO Box 361500 (30036-1500); W; 8,258pd, 1,742fr (CPVS); $10.00; publisher Carolyn Jernigan-Glenn; editor Alonia Jernigan; tel (404) 284-4010; fax (404) 284-4167

Macon: *Macon Courier (Est. 1974)* — 1055 Walnut St. (31201); PO Box 52201 (31208); W; 15,000pd (Sw); $16.20; publisher & editor Melvyn J Williams; tel (912) 746-5605; fax (912) 742-4274

Savannah: *Savannah Herald (Est. 1945)* — 1803 Barnard St.; PO Box 486 (31402); W; 8,500pd (Sw); $9.50; publisher & editor Floyd Adams Jr; tel (912) 232-4505; fax (912) 232-4079

Savannah: *The Savannah Tribune (Est. 1974)* — 916 W. Montgomery St. (31401); PO Box 2066 (31402); Th; 10,000pd (Sw); $12.00; publisher & editor Shirley James; general manager Joeleene Hayes; tel (912) 233-6128; fax (912) 232-8666

ILLINOIS

Chicago: *Chicago Citizen (Est. 1965)* — 412 E. 87th St. (60619); Th; 50,000pd (CPVS); $54.80; publisher William A Garth; editor Lisa Ely; tel (312) 487-7700; fax (312) 487-7931

Chicago: *Chicago Crusader (Est. 1940)* — 6429 S. Martin Luther King Dr. (60637); Th; 55,173pd, 147fr (Sw); $9.86; publisher Dorothy R Leavell; general manager John L Smith; editor Dorothy R Leavell; tel (312) 752-2500; fax (312) 752-2817

Chicago: *Chicago Daily Defender (Est. 1905)* — 2400 S. Michigan Ave. (60616); M/F; 23,489pd, 28,214fr (ABC); $17.84; publisher Frederick D Sengstacke; general manager Eugene Scott; editor John H Sengstacke; managing editor Michael Brown; tel (312) 225-2400; fax (312) 225-9231

Chicago: *Independent Bulletin (Est. 1972)* — 2037 W. 95th St. (60643); Th; 400pd, 62,000fr (Sw); $11.43; publisher & editor Hurley Green Sr; tel (312) 783-1040

Chicago: *Muslim Journal (Est. 1960)* — 910 W. Van Buren, Ste. 100 (60607); F; 20,000pd (Est); $13.38; publisher & editor Ayesha K Mustafaa; tel (312) 243-7600; fax (312) 243-9778

Chicago: *Tri-City Journal (Est. 1978)* — 18 S. Michigan Ave., Ste. 1006 (60603); Th; 50,000pd (CPVS); publisher & editor Ibn Sharrieff; tel (312) 346-8123; fax (312) 606-0860

Decatur: *African-American Voice (Est. 1969)* — 625 E. Wood St. (62523); W; 19,000pd (Sw); $5.00; publisher Horace G Livingston Jr; general manager Vanessa Jones; editor Leo Livingston; tel (217) 423-2231; fax (217) 423-5860

E St. Louis: *East St. Louis Monitor (Est. 1963)* — 1501 State St.; PO Box 2137 (62205); Th; 4,987pd, 321fr (CPVS); $14.60; publisher Anne Jordan; general manager Clyde Jordan Jr; editor Ernest Merser; managing editor Frazier Garner; tel (618) 271-0468

INDIANA

Ft. Wayne: *Ft. Wayne Frost Illustrated (Est. 1968)* — 3121 S. Calhoun St. (46807); Tu; 2,295pd, 32fr (CPVS); $14.50; publisher Edward N Smith; editor Edna M Smith; tel (219) 745-0552; fax (219) 745-9503

Gary: *Gary American* — 2268 Broadway; PO Box 1199 (46407); F; 9,000pd, 2,000fr (Est); $9.00; C; publisher & editor Fred Harris; managing editor Dinah Biggs; tel (219) 883-4903

Gary: *Gary Crusader (Est. 1961)* — 1549 Broadway (46407); Th; 27,783pd (Sw); $7.84; publisher & editor Dorothy R Leavell; tel (219) 885-4357; fax (219) 883-3317

Gary: *Gary Info (Est. 1963)* — 1953 Broadway (46407); Th; 40,000pd (CPVS); $10.52; publisher & editor Imogene Harris; tel (219) 882-5591; fax (219) 886-1090

Indianapolis: *Indiana Herald (Est. 1959)* — 2170 N. Illinois Ave. (46202); Th; 10,000pd (Sw); $16.38; publisher & editor Mary Tandy; managing editor Mary Bryant; tel (317) 923-8291; fax (317) 923-8292

Indianapolis: *Indianapolis Recorder (Est. 1895)* — 2901 N. Tacoma Ave.; PO Box 18267 (46218); Th; 7,645pd, 244fr (Sw); $10.21; publisher William G Mays; general manager Charles M Blair; managing editor Connie Gaines Hays; tel (317) 924-5143; fax (317) 924-5148

KANSAS

Kansas City: *Kansas State Globe (Est. 1983)* — 5121 Parallel Pkwy. (66104); PO Box 171274 (66117); Th; 30,000pd (Est); $18.14; publisher Jordan Publishing Co.; editor Doretha Jordan; tel (913) 596-1008; fax (913) 287-4506

KENTUCKY

Louisville: *The Louisville Defender (Est. 1933)* — 1720 Dixie Hwy. (40210); PO Box 2557 (40201); Th; 3,200pd (CAC); $8.80; publisher Consumer Communications Industries; general manager Clarence Leslie; editor Yvonne Coleman; tel (502) 772-2591; fax (502) 772-8655

LOUISIANA

Alexandria: *Alexandria News Weekly (Est. 1959)* — 1746 Mason St. (71301); PO Box 608 (71309); Th; 10,000pd (Sw); $8.00; publisher & editor Alice Coleman; tel (318) 443-7664

Monroe: *Monroe Dispatch (Est. 1975)* — 2301 Desiard St. (71201); PO Box 4823 (71211); Th; 12,500pd (Sw); $7.75; publisher Frank Detiege Sr; editor Irma Detiege; tel (318) 387-3001

Monroe: *Monroe Free Press (Est. 1969)* — 216 Collier (71202); PO Box 1442 (71210); Th; 14,000pd (Est); $8.00; C; publisher & editor Roosevelt Wright; tel (318) 388-1310

New Orleans: *Louisiana Weekly (Est. 1925)* — 1001 Howard Ave., Ste. 2600; PO Box 53008 (70113); M; 3,134pd, 848fr (ABC); $12.95; publisher Henry B Dejoie Sr; general manager Bertel Dejoie; editor Henry B Dejoie Jr; managing editor CC Campbell; tel (504) 524-5563; fax (504) 527-5826

New Orleans: *New Orleans Data News Weekly* — 3501 Napolean Ave. (70125); Th; 20,000pd (Est); $17.50; publisher Terry B Jones; editor Sharon Womble; tel (504) 822-4433; fax (504) 821-0320

Shreveport: *Shreveport Sun (Est. 1920)* — 2224 Jewella Rd.; PO Box 38357 (71133-8357); Th; 5,000pd (Est); $8.92; publisher & editor Sonya C Landry; tel (318) 631-6222; fax (318) 635-2822

MARYLAND

Baltimore: *Baltimore Afro-American (Est. 1892)* — 2519 N. Charles St. (21218); PO Box 1857 (21203); F; 10,938pd (ABC); $29.26; C; publisher John J Oliver Jr; general manager Frances M Draper; editor James Williams; tel (410) 554-8200; fax (410) 554-8213

Baltimore: *Baltimore Times (Est. 1986)* — 12 W. 25th St. (21218); Th; 40,000fr (Sw); $24.30; C; publisher Joy Bramble; general manager Freddie Howard; editor Ernie Boston; tel (410) 366-3900; fax (410) 243-1627

MASSACHUSETTS

Boston: *Bay State Banner (Est. 1965)* — 68 Fargo St. (02210); Th; 10,561pd, 68fr (Sw); $9.90; publisher & editor Melvin B Miller; managing editor Robin Washington; tel (617) 357-4900

MICHIGAN

Benton Harbor: *Citizen (Est. 1978)* — 175 W. Main St.; PO Box 216 (49002); Su; 42,000pd (Est); $20.50; publisher Charles Kelly; editor Teresa Kelly; tel (616) 927-1527; fax (616) 927-2023

Detroit: *Michigan Chronicle (Est. 1936)* — 479 Ledyard St. (48201-2687); W; 28,319pd (ABC); $29.57; publisher & general manager Samuel Logan; editor Robert McTyre; managing editor Carol Archer; tel (313) 963-5522; fax (313) 963-8788

Ecorse: *Ecorse Telegram* — 4122 10th St. (48229); Th; 12,000fr (Sw); $12.50; publisher & editor J C Wall; tel (313) 928-2955

Grand Rapids: *Afro-American Gazette (Est. 1990)* — 1014 Franklin St. (49507); M; 8,670fr (ABC); $75.54; publisher Patricia E Grier; editor Walter L Mathis Sr; tel (616) 243-0577; fax (616) 243-6844

Grand Rapids: *Grand Rapids Times (Est. 1957)* — 2016 Eastern Ave.; PO Box 7258 (49510); F; 5,000pd (Sw); $14.80; publisher & editor Patricia Pulliam; managing editor Yergan Pulliam; tel (616) 245-8737; fax (616) 245-1026

Highland Park: *Michigan Citizen (Est. 1978)* — 12541 2nd St.; PO Box 03560 (48203); F; 46,200pd (Est); $18.70; publisher Charles Kelley; general manager Bernice Brown; editor Teresa Maxwell Kelley; managing editor Kascene Barks; tel (313) 869-0033; fax (313) 869-0430

Jackson: *Blazer News (Est. 1962)* — 3419 S. Meridian Rd. (49203); PO Box 806 (49204); W; 6,000fr (Est); $12.60; publisher Ben Wade; editor Ruth Wade; tel (517) 787-0450; fax (517) 787-2907

MINNESOTA

Minneapolis: *Minneapolis Spokesman (Est. 1934)* — 3744 4th Ave. S. (55409); Th; 16,000pd (Sw); $17.59; publisher & editor Launa Q Newman; general manager Wallace Jackman; tel (612) 827-4021; fax (612) 827-0577

Minneapolis: *St. Paul Recorder (Est. 1936)* — 3744 4th Ave. S.; PO Box 40100, St. Paul (55104-9838); Th; 10,000pd (Sw); $17.59; publisher & editor Launa Q Newman; general manager Wallace Jackman; tel (612) 224-4886; fax (612) 827-0577

St. Paul: *Insight News (Est. 1974)* — 422 University Ave., Ste. 8 (55103); M/Tu/W; 899pd, 27,750fr (Est); $18.00; C; publisher Al McFarlane; general manager Covelle Houston; editor Brandt Williams; tel (612) 227-8968; fax (612) 227-0521

MISSISSIPPI

Jackson: *Jackson Advocate (Est. 1940)* — 300 N. Farish St. (39202); PO Box 3708 (39207); Th; 13,000fr (CPVS); $27.00; publisher & editor Charles W Tisdale; managing editor Brad Franklin; tel (601) 948-4122; fax (601) 948-4125

Black newspapers II-89

Meridian: *Mississippi Memo Digest (Est. 1961)* — 2511 5th St.; PO Box 5782 (39301); W; 3,000pd (Sw); $9.50; publisher & editor Robert E Williams; tel (601) 693-2372

MISSOURI

Kansas City: *Kansas City Globe (Est. 1972)* — 615 E. 29th St.; PO Box 090410 (64109); F; 10,500pd (Est); $12.95; publisher & editor Marion Jordan; tel (816) 531-5253; fax (816) 531-5256

Kansas City: *The Call (Est. 1919)* — 1715 E. 18th St. (64108); PO Box 410-477 (64141); F; 17,010pd (ABC); $9.10; publisher & editor Lucille H Bluford; managing editor Donna F Stewart; tel (816) 842-3804; fax (816) 842-4420

St. Louis: *Evening Whirl (Est. 1964)* — PO Box 5088 (63147); Tu; 9,450pd (Sw); $12.50; publisher & editor Benjamin Thomas; general manager Martha Greene; tel (314) 388-3888; fax (314) 383-7335

St. Louis: *St. Louis American (Est. 1928)* — 4144 Lindell Blvd., Ste. B5 (63108-2927); Th; 198pd, 1,299fr (CAC); $32.87; publisher Donald Suggs; editor Bennie G Rogers; managing editor Eric Clark; tel (314) 533-8000; fax (314) 533-0038

St. Louis: *St. Louis Argus (Est. 1912)* — 4595 Martin Luther King Dr. (63113); Th; 30,000pd (CPVS); $14.29; publisher Dr Eugene Mitchell; editor Donald Thompson; tel (314) 531-1323; fax (314) 361-6421

St. Louis: *St. Louis Metro Sentinel (Est. 1968)* — 2900 N. Market; PO Box 7969 (63106); Th; 2,500pd, 22,500fr (Sw); $16.59; C; publisher & editor Michael C Williams; general manager L Eutz; tel (314) 531-2101; fax (314) 531-4442

NEVADA

Las Vegas: *Las Vegas Sentinel-Voice (Est. 1980)* — 900 E. Charleston Blvd. (89104); Th; 5,000pd (Est); $14.00; publisher & editor Ramon Savoy; tel (702) 380-8100; fax (702) 380-8102

NEW JERSEY

Teaneck: *The Connection (Est. 1982)* — 362 Cedar Ln., Ste. C; PO Box 2122 (07666); Th; 8,100pd, 33,000fr (Sw); $35.00; publisher & editor Ralph F Johnson; tel (201) 801-0771; fax (201) 801-0492

NEW YORK

Brooklyn: *City Sun (Est. 1984)* — 44 Court St., Ste. 307 (11201); PO Box 020560 (11202); W; 52,600pd (ABC); $47.50; publisher Andrew W Copper; managing editor Maitefa Angaza; tel (718) 624-5959; fax (718) 596-7429

Brooklyn: *New York Daily Challenge/Afro Times (Est. 1972)* — 1360 Fulton St. (11216); Mon-Fri/Wknd; 78,000pd (CPVS); publisher Thomas H Watkins Jr; general manager Jean Wells; editor Dawad Philip; tel (718) 636-9119; fax (718) 857-9115

Brooklyn: *The New American* — 1360 Fulton St. (11216); Th; 44,747pd, 12,916fr (CPVS); $43.00; publisher Thomas H Watkins Jr; general manager Jean Wells; editor Elenore Branch; tel (718) 636-9119; fax (718) 857-9115

Buffalo: *Buffalo Challenger (Est. 1962)* — 1303 Fillmore Ave. (14211); W; 10,000pd (Sw); $14.00; publisher & editor Barbara Banks; tel (716) 897-0442; fax (716) 897-3307

Buffalo: *Buffalo Criterion (Est. 1925)* — 623-25 William St. (14206); S; 10,000pd (Sw); $11.67; publisher & editor Frank E Merriweather; general manager Francis Gist; managing editor Evelyn Ferguson; tel (716) 882-9570; fax (716) 882-9570

Fresh Meadows: *The New York Voice Inc. (Est. 1958)* — 61-17 190th St., Ste. 206 (11365); Th; 90,000pd (CAC); $37.13; publisher Kenneth Drew; general manager Tempsey Lawson; editor Rozaan S Mohamed; tel (718) 264-1500; fax (718) 264-7708

Hempstead: *Economic Forum (Est. 1981)* — PO Box 2132 (11551-2132); F; 5,000pd (Sw); $5.50; publisher Robert Hugo Adams; tel (516) 486-0986

Metro New York: *New York Beacon (Est. 1975)* — 15 E. 40th St., Ste. 402, New York (10016); F; 55,000pd (Est); $35.00; publisher Walter Smith Jr; editor Miatta Haj Smith; tel (212) 213-8585

New York: *New York Amsterdam News (Est. 1909)* — 2340 Frederick Douglass Blvd. (10027); Th; 30,994pd, 1,110fr (ABC); $41.70; publisher Wilbert A Tatum; general manager Selvin Michael; editor William Egyir; tel (212) 932-7400; fax (212) 222-3842

NORTH CAROLINA

Charlotte: *Charlotte Post* — 1531 Camden Rd. (28203); PO Box 30144 (28230); Th; 5,000pd (Sw); $8.55; publisher Gerald O Johnson; editor Herb White; tel (704) 376-0496; fax (704) 342-2160

Concord/Salisbury/Statesville: *Piedmont Sun (Est. 1989)* — 1670 E. Broad St., Ste. 165, Statesville (28677); Th; 5,000fr (Sw); $5.00; C; publisher Irdell Pub.; publisher & editor L Melissa Smith; tel (704) 636-8932; fax (704) 873-1054

Durham: *Carolina Times (Est. 1927)* — 923 Old Fayetteville St. (27701); PO Box 3825 (27702); Th; 4,500pd (Sw); $6.00; publisher & editor Vivian Austin Edmonds; general manager Kenneth W Edmonds; tel (919) 682-2913; fax (919) 682-2913

Greensboro: *Carolina Peacemaker (Est. 1967)* — 400 Summit Ave.; PO Box 20853 (27420); Th; 27,500pd (Sw); $14.00; publisher John Marshall Kilimanjaro; editor William Howard; managing editor C Vickie Kilimanjaro; tel (910) 274-6210; fax (910) 273-5103

Raleigh: *The Carolinian (Est. 1940)* — 649 Maywood Ave.; PO Box 25308 (22603); M; 17,000pd (Sw); $8.00; Th; 17,000pd (Sw); $9.40; C; publisher & editor Prentice Monroe; managing editor Cash Michaels; tel (919) 834-5558

Wilmington: *The Challenger (Est. 1987)* — 514 Princess St.; PO Drawer 1679 (28402); Th; 2,500pd, 2,500fr (Est); $10.00; publisher Kathy Grear; editor Leonard Johnson; tel (910) 762-1337; fax (910) 763-6304

Wilmington: *Wilmington Journal (Est. 1927)* — 412 S. 7th St. (28401); PO Box 1618 (28402); Th; 5,471pd, 2,848fr (CPVS); $5.00; publisher & editor Katherine Jervay Tate; general manager Vernice Hamilton; tel (910) 765-5502; fax (910) 343-1334

Winston-Salem: *Winston Salem Chronicle (Est. 1974)* — 617 N. Liberty St. (27101); PO Box 1636 (27102); Th; 6,982pd, 279fr (ABC); $9.37; publisher Ernest H Pitt; editor John Hinton; tel (910) 722-8624; fax (910) 723-9173

OHIO

Akron: *Akron Reporter (Est. 1969)* — 1046 S. Arlington (44306); PO Box 2042 (44309); Tu; 35,000pd (Sw); $21.50; publisher William R Ellis Jr; editor Carlton D Ellis; tel (216) 773-4196

Cincinnati: *Cincinnati Herald (Est. 1956)* — 863 Lincoln Ave. (45206); Th; 25,000pd (CPVS); $11.50; publisher William Spillers; general manager Erica Salter; editor James Clingman; tel (513) 221-5440; fax (513) 221-2959

Cleveland: *Call and Post (Est. 1920)* — 1949 E. 105th St.; PO Box 6237 (44101); W; 30,000pd (Est); $32.51; publisher John Bustamante; editor Shelley Shockley; tel (216) 791-7600; fax (216) 791-6568

Columbus: *Columbus Call and Post (Est. 1962)* — 109 Hamilton Ave. (43203); PO Box 2606 (43216); Th; 15,000pd (Sw); $17.80; publisher John Bustamante; editor Amos H Lynch Sr; tel (614) 224-8123; fax (614) 224-8517

Toledo: *Toledo Journal (Est. 1975)* — 3021 Douglas Rd.; PO Box 2536 (43606); W; 17,972fr (CPVS); $18.92; C; publisher Sandra S Stewart; editor Myron A Stewart; tel (419) 472-4521

Youngstown: *The Buckeye Review (Est. 1937)* — 1555 Belmont Ave. (44504); F; 2,000pd (Sw); $6.50; publisher & editor Mike McNair; tel (216) 743-2250; fax (216) 746-2340

OKLAHOMA

Oklahoma City: *Black Chronicle (Est. 1979)* — 1528 N.E. 23rd St. (73111); PO Box 17498 (73136); Th; 28,927pd (Sw); $13.44; publisher & editor Russell M Perry; general manager Laurel Talley; managing editor Albert J Lindsey; tel (405) 424-4695; fax (405) 424-6708

Oklahoma City: *Ebony Tribune (Est. 1986)* — 800 N.E. 36th St. (73105); F; 1,000pd, 5,000fr (Sw); $11.00; publisher & editor Lecia D Swain; tel (405) 525-9885; fax (405) 525-9822

Tulsa: *The Oklahoma Eagle (Est. 1921)* — 624 E. Archer St. (74120); PO Box 3267 (74101); Th; 12,800pd (Sw); $9.30; publishers Edward L Goodwin & James O Goodwin; general manager Jerry Goodwin; editor Mike Staniford; tel (918) 582-7124; fax (918) 582-8905

OREGON

Portland: *Portland Observer (Est. 1970)* — 4747 N.E. Martin Luther King Blvd. (97211); PO Box 3137 (97208); W; 12,000pd, 18,000fr (Est); $14.00; publisher Joyce Washington; editor Chuck Washington; tel (503) 288-0033; fax (503) 288-0015

Portland: *The Skanner (Est. 1975)* — 2337 N. Williams Ave. (97227); PO Box 5455 (97228); Th; 10,500pd (Sw); publisher Bernie Foster; editor Bobbie Foster; tel (503) 287-3562; fax (503) 284-5677

PENNSYLVANIA

Philadelphia: *Philadelphia Metro (Est. 1978)* — 526 S. 16th St. (19146); Th; 98,000fr (VAC); $66.27; publisher Robert W Boyle; editor Irving Randolph; tel (215) 893-4050; fax (215) 735-3612

Philadelphia: *Philadelphia Tribune (Est. 1884)* — 526 S. 16th St. (19146); Tu; 26,400pd, 98,000fr (Est); $66.27; F; 10,600pd, 98,000fr (Est); $66.27; C; publisher Robert W Boyle; editor Irving Randolph; tel (215) 893-4050; fax (215) 735-3612

Philadelphia: *The Philadelphia New Observer (Est. 1975)* — 1930 Chestnut St., Ste. 900; PO Box 30092 (19103); W; 10,303pd, 70,697fr (Sw); $24.00; publisher & editor J H Warren III; tel (215) 665-8400; fax (215) 665-8914

Philadelphia: *The Philadelphia Sunday Sun* — 628 W. Rittenhouse St. (19144); Su; 20,000pd (Sw); $24.00; C; publisher & editor J Whyatt Mondesire; general manager Harriet Garrett; managing editor Leonard Davidson; tel (215) 848-7864; fax (215) 848-7893

Philadelphia: *Scoop USA (Est. 1960)* — 1220 N. Broad St. (19121-5139); F; 28,000fr (Sw); $14.00; publisher & editor R Sonny Driver; managing editor Stephanie Turner; tel (215) 232-5974; fax (215) 232-5974

Pittsburgh: *New Pittsburgh Courier (Est. 1905)* — 315 E. Carson St. (15219); W/Sa; 30,628pd, 1,200fr (Sw); $16.45; C; publisher John Sengstacke; general manager & editor Rod Doss; managing editor Ed Davis; tel (412) 481-8302; fax (412) 481-1360

RHODE ISLAND

Providence: *The Providence American (Est. 1986)* — 131 Washington St. (02903); W; 200pd, 4,479fr (CPVS); $15.00; C; publisher & editor Frank Graham; tel (401) 351-8860; fax (401) 351-8865

SOUTH CAROLINA

Charleston: *Charleston Chronicle (Est. 1971)* — 1109 King St. (29403); PO Box 20548 (29413-0548); W; 6,000fr (CPVS); $7.70; publisher & editor J John French; tel (803) 723-2785; fax (803) 577-6099

Charleston: *Coastal Times (Est. 1983)* — 2106 Mt. Pleasant St., Ste. 3 (29403); W; 1,000pd, 4,000fr (Sw); $5.95; publisher James E Clyburn; editor Mignon Clyburn; tel (803) 723-5318; fax (803) 723-5326

Columbia: *Carolina Panorama* — 2346 E. Two Notch Rd. (29203); PO Box 11205 (29211); Th; 6,000pd (Sw); $8.00; publisher Nat Abraham Jr; editor Nat Abraham Sr; tel (803) 256-4015; fax (803) 256-4015

Columbia: *South Carolina Black Media Group (Est. 1973)* — 1310 Harden St. (29204); PO Box 11128 (29211); Th; 75,000pd (CPVS); $5.34; publisher Isaac Washington; editor Bernard Legette; tel (803) 799-5252; fax (803) 799-7709

TENNESSEE

Memphis: *Tri State Defender (Est. 1951)* — 124 E. Calhoun Ave. (38103); PO Box 2065 (38101); Th; 15,000pd (CPVS); $15.50; publisher John H Sengstacke; editor Audrey Parker-McGhee; tel (901) 523-1818; fax (901) 523-1820

Nashville: *Nashville Pride (Est. 1988)* — 1215 9th Ave. N. (37208); F; 20,000pd (Sw); $15.86; publisher Larry Davis; editor C Ailene Lydia; managing editor Geraldine Heath; tel (615) 255-9800; fax (615) 255-9802

TEXAS

Austin: *Austin Sun* — 6448 Hwy. 290 E., Ste. G 101 (78723); F; 20,000fr (CPVS); $26.50; C; publisher Dorris Ellis; editor Shuronda Robinson; managing editor Richard J Smith; tel (512) 467-2881; fax (512) 467-2890

Austin: *Nokoa - The Observer (Est. 1987)* — 1154-B Angelina St. (78702); PO Box 1131 (78767); F; 247pd, 7,253fr (Est); $15.95; publisher & editor Akwasi Evans; managing editor Joe Washington; tel (512) 499-8713; fax (512) 499-8740

Austin: *The Villager (Est. 1973)* — 1123-A Rosewood Ave. (78702); F; 6,000pd (Est); $10.00; publisher & editor T L Wyatt; managing editor Bobbie Hall; tel (512) 476-0082; fax (512) 476-0179

Dallas: *Dallas Examiner (Est. 1986)* — 1111 Dragon St.; PO Box 3720 (75207); Th; 20,000pd (Est); $24.00; publisher Molley Finch Belt; editor Anthony Curley; tel (214) 948-9175; fax (214) 651-7251

Dallas: *Dallas Post Tribune Inc. (Est. 1949)* — 2726 S. Beckley Ave. (75224); Th; 18,000pd (CPVS); $15.50; publisher & editor Theodore Lee Jr; managing editor Dorothy Lee; tel (214) 946-7678; fax (214) 946-6823

Dallas: *Dallas Weekly (Est. 1953)* — 3101 Martin Luther King Blvd. (75215); PO Box 15832 (75212); Th; 76pd, 13,474fr (VAC); $19.57; publisher & editor Jim Washington; tel (214) 428-8958

Houston: *Forward Times (Est. 1960)* — 4411 Almeda Rd.; PO Box 8346 (77004); W; 60,000pd (CPVS); $19.60; publisher Lenora Carter; general manager Henrietta Smith; editor George Bud Johnson; tel (713) 526-4727; fax (713) 526-3170

Houston: *Houston Defender (Est. 1930)* — 2626 S. Loop W., Ste. 360 (77054); PO Box 8005 (77288); Su; 30,000pd (Est); $24.95; publisher & editor Sonceria Messiah-Jiles; managing editor Marilyn Marshall; tel (713) 663-6996; fax (713) 663-7116

Houston: *Houston Informer & Texas Freeman (Est. 1893)* — 4209 Dowling St. (77004); PO Box 3086 (77253); Tu; 23,000pd (Sw); $40.18; publisher Lorenza P Butler Jr; general manager William Hadnott; editor George McElroy; tel (713) 527-8261; fax (713) 524-7028

Houston: *Houston Metro* — 4411 Almeda Rd.; PO Box 8346 (77288-8346); W/F; 60,000pd (CPVS); $14.28; publisher Lenora Carter; general manager Henrietta Smith; editor George Bud Johnson; tel (713) 526-4727; fax (713) 526-3170

Houston: *Houston Sun (Est. 1983)* — 1520 Isabella (77004-4042); PO Box 8041 (77288-8041); Th; 20,000pd, 10,000fr (Est); $36.50; C; publisher & editor Dorris Ellis; publisher & general manager Lonal Robinson; tel (713) 524-4474; fax (713) 524-0089

Lubbock: *Southwest Digest (Est. 1977)* — 902 E. 28th St. (79404); PO Box 2553 (79408); Th; 10,000pd (Sw); $12.00; publishers & editors Eddie Richardson & T J Patterson; tel (806) 762-3612; fax (806) 762-4605

San Antonio: *San Antonio Informer (Est. 1988)* — 333 S. Hackberry St. (78203-1257); Th; 4,000pd (Est); $5.00; publisher Tommy Moore; editor Virginia Moore; tel (210) 227-8300; fax (210) 223-4111

San Antonio: *San Antonio Register (Est. 1930)* — 235 St. Charles (78202); PO Box 1598 (78296); Th; 7,200pd (Sw); $4.50; publisher & editor Edwin Glosson; general manager James Washington; tel (210) 222-1721; fax (210) 227-3455

San Antonio: *Snap News (Est. 1947)* — 1609 E. Houston St. (78202); Th; 10,000pd (Sw); $4.00; publisher Eugene Coleman; editor Betty Page; managing editor Diane Wilson; tel (210) 224-0706; fax (210) 223-1500

VIRGINIA

Charlottesville: *Albermarle Tribune (Est. 1954)* — 406 7th St. N.E.; PO Box 3428 (22902); Th; 4,000pd (Sw); $10.40; publisher & editor Agnes White; tel (804) 979-0373; fax (804) 971-5821

Copyright ©1996 by the Editor & Publisher Co.

Norfolk: *Journal and Guide (Est. 1900)* — 362 Campostella Rd. (23523); PO Box 209 (23501); W; 19,000pd, 6,000fr (CPVS); $16.05; publisher Brenda H Andrews; editor Leonard Colzin; tel (804) 543-6531; fax (804) 543-7620

Petersburg: *Southside Virginia Star (Est. 1989)* — 618 E. Washington St.; PO Box 402 (23803); Th; 1,600pd (Sw); publisher Paul C Bland; editor Kamala Haywood; tel (804) 862-9611; fax (804) 861-6325

Richmond: *Richmond Afro-American (Est. 1939)* — 2606-08 W. Cary St. (23220); W; 563pd, 30,037fr (CAC); $21.31; publisher John J Oliver Jr; general manager Tracey Jeter; editor Ruth Richey; tel (804) 342-2376; fax (804) 342-0013

Richmond: *Richmond Free Press (Est. 1992)* — 101 W. Broad St. (23220); PO Box 27709 (23261); Th; 144pd, 24,589fr (VAC); $15.80; publisher & editor Raymond H Boone; tel (804) 644-0496; fax (804) 643-7519

Richmond: *Richmond Voice (Est. 1985)* — 214 E. Clay St., Ste. 202 (23219); W; 15,000pd, 18,000fr (CPVS); $10.53; publisher & editor Jack Green; tel (804) 644-9060; fax (804) 644-5617

Roanoke: *Roanoke Tribune (Est. 1939)* — 2318 Melrose Ave. N.W. (24017); Th; 2,900pd, 275fr (Sw); $5.04; publisher & editor Claudia A Whitworth; tel (540) 343-0326; fax (540) 343-0326

WASHINGTON

Seattle: *Facts News (Est. 1961)* — 2765 E. Cherry St.; PO Box 22015 (98122); W; 13,000pd (VAC); $9.85; publisher & editor Elizabeth Beaver; tel (206) 324-0552; fax (206) 324-1007

Seattle: *Seattle Medium (Est. 1970)* — 2600 S. Jackson; PO Box 22047 (98144); W; 50,000pd (CPVS); $21.00; publisher Chris Bennett; general manager Prisilla Hailey; editor Connie Cameron; tel (206) 627-1103; fax (206) 322-6518

Seattle: *Tacoma True-Citizen* — PO Box 22047 (98122); Th; 16,000pd (CPVS); publisher Chris Bennett; editor Connie Cameron; tel (206) 627-1103; fax (206) 322-6518

WISCONSIN

Milwaukee: *Community Journal (Est. 1976)* — 3612 N. Martin Luther King Dr. (53212); W/F; 4,096pd, 800fr (CPVS); $27.96; publisher Patricia O Thomas; general manager Robert Thomas; editor Michael Holt; managing editor Tom Mitchell; tel (414) 265-5300; fax (414) 265-1536

Milwaukee: *Milwaukee Courier (Est. 1961)* — 2431 W. Hopkins (53206); Sa; 14,000fr (Est); $10.20; publishers Carol Greary & Faith Colas; editor Walker Jones; tel (414) 449-4860; fax (414) 449-4872

Milwaukee: *Milwaukee Star (Est. 1963)* — 3815 N. Teutonia Ave.; PO Box 06279 (53206); Th; 5,000fr (Est); $7.00; C; publisher Carole Geary; editor Walker Jones; tel (414) 449-4870; fax (414) 449-4872

ETHNIC NEWSPAPERS PUBLISHED IN THE UNITED STATES

AFGHAN

Hayward: *Omaid Weekly (Hope) (Est. 1992) (Dari/Farsi)* — 27368 Marigold (94545), PO Box 4611, Hayward, CA 94540; M; 1,700pd (Sw); $4.00; publisher Mohammad Q Koshan; general manager Kaweem M Koshan; editor Mohammad Q Koshen; tel (510) 786-2030; fax (510) 786-2030

ALBANIAN

Bronx: *Illyria (English/Albanian)* — 2321 Hughes Ave., Bronx, NY 10458; W/Sa; 11,927pd, 136fr (Est); $15.00; publisher Harry Bajraktari; editors Deborah Jo Argus & Sinan Kamberaj; tel (718) 220-2000

S Boston: *Liria (Liberty) (Est. 1941) (English/Albanian)* — 409 W. Broadway, PO Box 477, South Boston, MA 02127; Mthly; 1,200pd, 50fr (Est); $14.00; C; publisher Free Albania Organization; general manager Al Sofi; editor Shkelqim Beqari; managing editor Van Christo; tel (617) 269-5192; fax (617) 269-6420

ARABIC

Detroit: *American-Arab Message (English/Arabic)* — 17514 Woodward Ave., Detroit, MI 48203; F; 67,000pd (Sw); $17.75; publisher & editor Iman M A Hussein

Jacksonville: *The Syrian-Lebanese Star (Est. 1963)* — 4251 University Blvd. S., Ste. 201, Jacksonville, FL 32216; Mthly; $15.00; publisher & editor Alvin M Coplan; tel (904) 737-6996

Los Angeles: *Beirut Times (Est. 1985) (Arabic/English)* — PO Box 93475, Los Angeles, CA 90093; Tu; 15,000fr (Est); $20.00; C; publisher & editor Michel B Abssi; managing editor Suletman Hawatmeh; tel (213) 469-4354; fax (213) 469-4988

New York: *Action* — 230 E. 44th St., PO Box 416, New York, NY 10017; M; 5,000pd, 10,000fr (Est); $15.00; publisher David Howie; editor Dr M T Mehdi; tel (212) 972-0460; fax (212) 682-1405

ARMENIAN

Fresh Meadows: *Armenian Reporter International (Est. 1967) (English)* — PO Box 600, Fresh Meadows, NY 11365; Th; 5,200pd (Est); 32¢; C; publisher Armenian Reporter International Inc.; editor Sylva A Boghosian; managing editor Aris Sevag; tel (718) 380-1200

Glendale: *California Courier (Est. 1958) (English)* — PO Box 5390, Glendale, CA 91221; Th; 1,800pd, 200fr (Sw); $8.10; publisher Harut Sassounian; editor Serge Samoniantz; tel (818) 409-0949

Watertown: *The Armenian-Mirror Spector (English)* — 755 Mt. Auburn St., Watertown, MA 02272; W; 3,327pd $6.00; publisher Baikar Association Inc.; editor Ara Kalaydjian; tel (617) 924-4420

Watertown: *Armenian Weekly (Est. 1934) (English)* — 80 Bigelow Ave., Watertown, MA 02172; Sa; 2,550pd, 100fr (Est); $6.00; publisher Hairenik Assoc. Inc.; general manager John Megerdichian; editor Vahe Habeshian; tel (617) 926-3974; fax (617) 926-1750

Watertown: *Baikar-Armenian Weekly* — PO Box 302, Watertown, MA 02272; Mthly; 1,300pd (Est); 30¢; publisher Baikar Assoc. Inc.; editor Krikor Keusseyan; tel (617) 924-4420; fax (617) 924-3860

Watertown: *Hairenik (Fatherland) (Est. 1899) (English)* — 80 Bigelow Ave., Watertown, MA 02172; Th; 2,200pd, 100fr (Est); $5.00; publisher Hairenik Assoc. Inc.; editor Vatche Proudian; tel (617) 926-3974

BULGARIAN

Ft. Wayne: *Macedonian Tribune (Makedonska Tribuna) (Est. 1927) (English/Bulgarian)* — 124 W. Wayne, Fort Wayne, IN 46802; Bi-Wkly Th; 1,320pd, 64fr (Sw); $10.00; publisher Macedonian Patriotic Organization; tel (219) 422-5900; fax (219) 422-1348

CHINESE

Boston: *Sampan (Est. 1976) (Chinese/English)* — 90 Tyler St., Boston, MA 02111; Bi-wkly; 6,000pd, 6,000fr (Est); $8.00; C; publisher Chao-ming Lee; editor Robert O'Malley; tel (617) 426-9492; fax (617) 482-2316

Edison: *New Jersey China Times (Est. 1995) (Chinese)* — 1668 Rte. 27, Ste. 2, Edison, NJ 08817; M; 20,000fr (Est); $12.44; C; publisher Chinese Commercial Journal; general manager Wei Yang; general manager & managing editor Xiao-Yin Mao; editor Yong Li; tel (908) 572-3335, (212) 343-9717; fax (908) 572-5072

Flushing: *Pacific Times (Est. 1987) (English/Taiwan/Chinese)* — 132-45 41st Rd., Flushing, NY 11355; F; 15,000pd, 20,000fr (Est); $40.00; publisher Dr Clisff Yang; editor Dr K C Wang; managing editor C Ti Chen; tel (718) 461-7668; fax (718) 461-7668

Honolulu: *United Chinese Press* — 100 N. Beretania St., Ste. 204, Honolulu, HI 96817; M/Sa; 3,000pd (Est); 19¢; publisher United Chinese Press Ltd.; editor K K Liu; tel (808) 536-6883

Houston: *Southern Chinese Daily News (Est. 1979) (Chinese/English)* — 12129 Bellaire Blvd., Houston, TX 77072; Tu-Su; 450pd, 15,000fr (Est); $5.00; C; publisher Wea H Lee; general manager Emerson Chu; editor Yin Cheng Fang; tel (713) 498-4310; fax (713) 498-2728/(713)498-2724

Houston: *US Asia News (Chinese/English)* — 12129 Bellaire Blvd., Ste. 201, Houston, TX 77072; Sa; 8,000pd, 7,000fr (Est); $10.00; publisher Wea H Lee; general manager Emerson Chu; editor Mike H He; tel (713) 498-4310; fax (713) 498-2728/2724

New York: *China Daily Distribution Corp. (Est. 1981) (English)* — 1 World Trade Ctr., Ste. 3369, New York, NY 10048; M-Sa; 200,000pd, 300fr (Est); $76.50; publisher China Daily; editor Zhu Yinghuang; tel (212) 488-9677; fax (212) 488-9493

New York: *China Tribune (Est. 1943)* — 396 Broadway, Ste. 1002, New York, NY 10013; Tu/Sa; 9,985pd, 250fr (Est); $5.00; publisher Mr. Chu; editor Mr. Lum; tel (212) 925-6790

New York: *The United Journal (Est. 1952) (English)* — 83-85 White St., New York, NY 10013; M/Sa; 33,000pd (Sw); 55¢; C; publisher Chin Fu Woo; general manager & editor Yuk Tsun Wang; managing editor Edward Lee & Leon Lam; tel (212) 513-1440; fax (212) 693-1392

San Francisco: *Chinese Times (Est. 1924) (Chinese)* — 686 Sacramento St., San Francisco, CA 94111; M/Sa; 12,000pd (Est); 40¢; publisher Chinese Times Pub. Co. Inc.; editor M K Lee; tel (415) 982-6206; fax (415) 982-3387

Seattle: *Northwest Asian Weekly (Est. 1983) (Chinese)* — 414 8th Ave. S., Seattle, WA 98104-3002; Th; 4,000pd, 11,000fr (Sw); $20.00; C; publisher Assunta Ng; general manager George Liu; editor Deni Luna; tel (206) 223-0623; fax (206) 223-0626

Seattle: *Seattle Chinese Post (Est. 1983) (Chinese)* — 414 8th Ave. S., Seattle, WA 98104-3002; Th; 4,000pd, 11,000fr (Sw); $20.00; C; publisher Assunta Ng; general manager George Liu; editor Frank Soup; tel (206) 223-0623; fax (206) 223-0626

Whitestone: *World Journal (Est. 1976) (Chinese)* — 141-07 20th Ave., Whitestone, NY 11357; Daily; 250,000pd, 2,500fr (Est); $7.00; publisher T W Wang Inc.; editor Jacob K J Ma; tel (718) 746-9006; fax (718) 746-6509

CROATIAN

Chicago: *Danica (Est. 1912)* — 4851 Drexel Blvd., Chicago, IL 60615; W; 3,000pd (Est); publisher Croatian Center Assoc.; editor Rev Timothy Majic

Chicago: *Nasa Nada (Est. 1921)* — 4848 S. Ellis Ave., Chicago, IL 60615; Mthly; 6,218pd (Est); publisher Croatian Catholic Union; editor Rev Ivo Sivric

Pittsburgh: *Zajednicar (Est. 1904) (English/Croatian)* — 100 Delaney Dr., Pittsburgh, PA 15235; W; 38,000fr (Est); publisher Croatian Fraternal Union of America; editor Edward J Verlich; tel (412) 351-3909; fax (412) 823-1594

CZECH

Granger: *Nasinec (Fellow Countryman) (Est. 1914) (Czech/English)* — 206 E. Davilla St., PO Box 636, Granger, TX 76530; M; 670pd (Sw); $2.25; publisher & editor Joe D Vrabel; tel (512) 859-2238

Temple: *Vestnik (Est. 1920)* — 204 N. Davis St., PO Box 100, Temple, TX 76503; W; 14,000pd (Est); publisher Stillhouse Hollow Publishers; editor Rudy J Sefcik

CZECH/SLOVAK

Berwyn: *Denni Hlasatel (Czechoslovak Daily Herald) (Est. 1891) (Czech/Slovak)* — 6426 W. Cermak Rd., Berwyn, IL 60402; W/Su; 5,000pd, 150fr (Sw); $6.50; C; publisher & editor Josef Kucera; tel (708) 749-1891/(708) 749-1898; fax (708) 749-1935

DANISH

Burbank: *Bien (The Bee) (Est. 1882) (Danish)* — 1527 W. Magnolia Blvd., Burbank, CA 91506; Th; 5,280pd (Est); 50¢; publisher & editor Poul Dalby Andersen; tel (818) 845-7300

Hoffman Estates: *Den Danske Pioneer (Est. 1872) (Danish/English)* — 1582 Glen Lake Rd., Hoffman Estates, IL 60195; Bi-Wkly; 3,000pd (Est); $7.50; publisher Chris Steffensen

DUTCH

Lynden: *The Windmill Herald (Dutch/English)* — PO Box 313, Lynden, WA 98264-0313; W; 12,700pd (Est); $19.80; publisher A A Van der Heide; tel (604) 532-1733; fax (604) 532-1734

ESTONIAN

New York: *Vaba Eesti Sona (Free Estonian Word) (Estonian/English)* — 243 E. 34th St., New York, NY 10016; Th; 3,800pd (Est); $11.00; publisher The Nordic Press Inc.; editor Harald Raudsepp; tel (212) 686-3356; fax (212) 686-3356

FILIPINO

New York: *The Filipino Reporter (Est. 1972) (Tagalog/English)* — 19 W. 34th St., Ste. 602, New York, NY 10001; F; 47,000pd, 2,000fr (Est); $1.10; publisher & editor Libertito Pelayo; tel (212) 967-5784; fax (212) 967-5848

S San Francisco: *Philippine News (English)* — 371 Allerton Ave., South San Francisco, CA 94080; W; 112,783pd (Est); $10.00; publisher Alex A Esclamado; editor Cherie Moreno; tel (415) 872-3000; fax (415) 872-0217

FINNISH

Brooklyn: *New Yorkin Uutiset (Est. 1906) (English)* — 4422 8th Ave., Brooklyn, NY 11220; Tu; 1,800pd, 300fr (Est); $10.00; publisher Finnish Newspaper Co. Inc.; editor Anita Valkama Rothovius; tel (718) 435-0800; fax (718) 871-7230

Fitchburg: *Raivaaja (Pioneer) (Est. 1905) (Bilingual)* — 147 Elm St., PO Box 600, Fitchburg, MA 01420; W; 2,000pd (Est); 35¢; publisher Raivaaja Pub. Co.; editor Marita Cauthen; tel (508) 343-3822; fax (308) 345-1007

Superior: *Tyomies-Eteenpain (Est. 1903) (Finnish/English)* — 1720 Tower Ave., PO Box 549, Superior, WI 54880; Th; 300pd (Est); $4.00; C; publisher Tyomies Society; general manager Weikko Jarvi; editor Mai-Lis Keskela; tel (715) 394-4961; fax (715) 394-7655

Superior: *The Finnish-American Reporter (Est. 1986) (English)* — 1720 Tower Ave., PO Box 549, Superior, WI 54880; Mthly; 2,500pd, 500fr (Est); $6.00; C; publisher Tyomies Society; general manager Weikko Jarvi; editor Lynn Maria Laitala; tel (715) 394-4961; fax (715) 394-7655

FRENCH

New York: *France-Amerique (Est. 1943) (French)* — 1560 Broadway, Ste. 511, New York, NY 10036-1525; W; 18,000pd, 4,000fr (Est); $35.00; publisher Trocadero Publishing; general manager John Cedric Pedersen; editor Jean-Louis Turlin; tel (212) 221-6700; fax (212) 221-6997

Copyright ©1996 by the Editor & Publisher Co.

Ethnic newspapers II-91

San Francisco: *Journal Francais d'Amerique (Est. 1979)* — 1051 Divisadero St., San Francisco, CA 94115; Bi-Wkly; 30,000pd (Est); N/A; publisher Marie Galanti; editor Anne Prah-Perochon; tel (415) 921-5100; fax (415) 921-0213

San Francisco: *France Today (English)* — 1051 Divisadero St., San Francisco, CA 94115; Monthly; 14,000pd, 4,000fr (Est); $7.36; publisher Marie Galanti; editor Elizabeth Bell; tel (800) 851-7785; fax (415) 921-0213

GERMAN

Blaine: *Pazifische Rundschau (Pacific Review) (Est. 1965) (German)* — PO Box 1770, Blaine, WA 98231-1770; Bi-Wkly Sa; 12,390pd, 110fr (Est); $28.00 (US); 24.50 (CAN); C; publisher Ackermann's Advertising & News; editor Baldwin Ackermann; tel (360) 270-2923; fax (360) 273-9365

Chicago: *Abendpost/Sonntagpost (Est. 1889)* — 55 E. Jackson St., Chicago, IL 60604; Tu/F/Su; N/A; publisher Abendpost Co.; tel (800) 288-0089

Cleveland: *Waechter Und Anzeiger (Est. 1852)* — 4164 Lorian Ave., Cleveland, OH 44113; F; 3,295pd (Est); publisher Waechter Und Anzeiger Pub. Co.; editor Stefan Deubel

Kenilworth: *New Jersey Freie Zeitung* — 500 S. 31st St., Kenilworth, NJ 07033; F; 6,500pd (Sw); $14.00; publisher & editor Eberhard Schweizer; tel (908) 245-7995; fax (908) 245-7997

Los Angeles: *California-Staats Zeitung (Est. 1890) (German)* — 1201 N. Alvarado St., PO Box 26308, Los Angeles, CA 90026; F; 19,254pd, 221fr (Sw); $12.00; C; publisher Stephanie Teichmann; editor Rainer Jacobs; tel (213) 413-5500; fax (213) 413-5469

New York: *Aufbau (Reconstruction) (Est. 1934) (German/English)* — 2121 Broadway, New York, NY 10023; Bi-Wkly F; 10,000pd (Est); $21.00; publisher New World Club Inc.; publisher Jerry Brunwell; editor Uwe Westphal; managing editor Monika Ziegler; tel (212) 873-7400; fax (212) 496-5736

New York: *Staats-Zeitung Und Herold (Est. 1834) (English/German)* — 160 W. 71st St., New York, NY 10023; Wknd; 6,850pd, 1,450fr (Sw); $21.70; publisher Jes Rau; general manager Katrin Hecker-MacLeod; editor Sabina Ellert; tel (212) 875-8914; fax (212) 875-0534

Philadelphia: *Philadelphia Gazette-Democrat* — 9940 Haldeman Ave., Philadelphia, PA 19115; Sa; 2,355pd 75¢; publisher Erwin Steuer; editor Otto Leukert

Troy: *Nordamerikaniche Wochenpost (Est. 1854) (English/German)* — 1120 E. Long Lake Rd., Troy, MI 48098; Sa; 30,012pd (Est); $1.20; publisher Beth Knuth; editor Kroon Brigit; tel (810) 641-9944; fax (810) 641-9946

GREEK

Astoria: *Campana (Greek American Review) (Est. 1917) (English/Greek)* — 30-96 42nd St., Astoria, NY 11103; Bi-Wkly; 9,000pd, 300fr (Sw); $5.00; publisher & editor Costas Athanasiades; tel (718) 278-3014; fax (718) 278-3023

Boston: *Hellenic Chronicle (Est. 1950) (English)* — 5 Franklin Commons, Framingham, MA 01701; Th; 22,100pd (Est); $14.50; publisher A A Agris; editor Nancy Argis Savage; managing editor George Anagnostos; tel (508) 820-9700; fax (508) 820-0952

Chicago: *Greek Star (Est. 1904) (English)* — 4710 N. Lincoln Ave., Chicago, IL 60625; Th; 7,800pd (Est); $12.00; publisher United Hellenic American Congress; editor Diane Lymberopoulos; tel (312) 878-7331; fax (312) 878-0959

Chicago: *Greek Press (Est. 1911) (English/Greek)* — PO Box 99, Wood Dale, IL 60191; Su; 13,200pd, 200fr (Est); 72¢; publisher National Greek Press Publishing Co.; editor Aris Angelopoulos; tel (708) 766-2955; fax (708) 766-3069

Long Island City: *Proini (Morning) (Est. 1976) (English)* — 25-50 Crescent St., Long Island City, NY 11102; M-Sa; 32,000pd, 5,000fr (Est); $8.50; publisher & editor Fannie Petallides; tel (718) 626-7676; fax (718) 626-7830

Long Island City: *The National Herald (Est. 1915) (Greek)* — 41-17 Crescent St., Long Island City, NY 11101; M-F; 45,000pd (Est); 80¢; Sa; 55,000pd (Est); 80¢; publisher Anthony H Diamataris; tel (718) 784-5255; fax (718) 472-0510

New York: *Hellenic Times (Greek/English)* — 823 11th Ave., New York, NY 10019; Bi-Wkly; 15,000pd, 100fr (Est); 64¢; publisher John Catsimatidis; editor Jimmy Kapsalis; tel (212) 986-6881; fax (212) 977-3662

HUNGARIAN

Akron: *Amerikai-Kanadai Magyar Elet (American-Canadian Hungarian Life) (Est. 1959) (English)* — 2637 Copley Rd., Akron, OH 44321; Sa; 11,850pd, 4,150fr (Est); $10.00; publisher Buda Publishing Co.; editor Elizabeth Schmidt; tel (312) 625-8774

Los Angeles: *Californiai Magyarsag (California Hungarians) (English)* — 207 S. Western Ave., Ste. 201, PO Box 74773, Los Angeles, CA 90004; F; 7,500pd (Sw); $5.00; publisher & editor Maria Fenyes; tel (213) 463-3473; fax (213) 384-7642

New York: *Amerikai Magyar Szo (American Hungarian Word) (Est. 1954) (Hungarian)* — 130 E. 16th St., New York, NY 10003-3593; Th; 1,250pd, 150fr (Sw); $10.00; publisher Hungarian Word Inc.; editor Joseph Garai; tel (212) 254-0397; fax (212) 254-0397

Thousand Oaks: *Magyarok Vasarnapja (Hungarians' Sunday) (Est. 1894) (Hungarian)* — 2226 N. Three Springs Dr., PO Box 4442, Thousand Oaks, CA 91359; Bi-Wkly Su; 8,000pd, 1,000fr (Sw); $4.00; C; publisher & editor Lorant Szasz; general manager Elizabeth Szasz; tel (818) 707-1548; fax (818) 597-9867

INDIAN (ASIA)

Emeryville: *India-West (Est. 1975) (English)* — 5901 Christie Ave., Ste. 301, Emeryville, CA 94608; F; 11,788pd, 1,376fr (Sw); $15.00; publisher Ramesh P Murarka; editor Bina A Murarka; tel (510) 652-3552; fax (510) 652-7968

New York: *India Abroad* — 43 W. 24th St., New York, NY 10010-3205; F; 52,571pd, 4,332fr (ABC); $28.00; C; publisher & editor Gopal Raju; tel (212) 929-1727; fax (212) 627-9503

New York: *India Monitor (Est. 1991) (English)* — 303 5th Ave., Ste. 1503, New York, NY 10016; Su; 27,000fr (Est); $24,00; publisher & editor Venugopal Naidu; tel (212) 889-6878; fax (212) 889-6798

New York: *News India-Times (Est. 1969)* — 244 5th Ave., Ste. 402, New York, NY 10001; Tu; 68,500pd (Sw); $25.00; publisher & editor John Perry; general manager T J Mathew; tel (212) 481-3110; fax (212) 889-5774

INDIAN (NATIVE AMERICAN)

Flagstaff: *Navajo Hopi Observer (Est. 1980)* — 2608 N. Steves Blvd., Flagstaff, AZ 86004; W; 211pd, 11,500fr (Sw); $8.64; C; publisher & editor Linda Ritchie; tel (520) 526-3881; fax (520) 527-0217

Flathead Indian Reservation/Pablo: *Char-Koosta News (Est. 1953) (English)* — 51396 Hwy. 93 N., PO Box 278, Pablo, MT 59855; F; 3,665pd, 151fr (Sw); $3.75; publisher & editor Ron Bick

Lake Traverse Reservation: *Sota Iya Ye Ypai (Est. 1968)* — PO Box 628, Agency Village, SD 57262; W; 850pd (Sw); $2.66; publisher Sisseton-Wahpeton Sioux Tribe; general manager & managing editor Charles D Floro; tel (605) 938-4452; fax (605) 938-4452

Luc du Flambeau: *Lac du Flambeau News (Est. 1993) (English)* — 418 Little Pines Rd., PO Box 67, Lac du Flambeau, WI 54538; Mthly; 250pd, 11,750fr (Est); $7.50; publisher Lac du Flambeau Band of Lake Superior Chippewa; editor Mike Bassett; tel (715) 588-9272; fax (715) 588-9408

Rapid City: *Indian Country Today (Est. 1981)* — PO Box 2180, Rapid City, SD 57709; W; 14,000pd (Est); $9.97; publisher Tim Giago; editor Pam Stillman; tel (605) 341-0011; fax (605) 341-6940

IRISH

New York: *Irish Echo (Est. 1928) (English)* — 309 5th Ave., New York, NY 10016; Sa; 59,292pd, 294fr (Sw); $19.00; C; publisher Claire Grimes; editor Tom Connelly; tel (212) 686-1266; fax (212) 686-1756

New York: *The Irish People (English)* — 363 7th Ave., New York, NY 10001; W; 12,000pd (Est); $5.00; publisher The Irish People Inc.; editor Martin Galvin; tel (212) 947-7022; fax (212) 947-1916

New York: *Irish Voice (Est. 1987) (English)* — 432 Park Ave. S., Ste. 1503, New York, NY 10016; W; 85,000pd (Est); 50¢; publisher Niall O'Dowd; editor Patrick Farrelly; tel (212) 684-3366; fax (212) 779-1198

ISRAELI

New York: *The Jerusalem Post International Edition (Est. 1932) (English)* — 211 E. 43rd St., New York, NY 10017; W; 50,000pd (Est); $55.00; publisher Yehuda Levy; editor David Bar-Illan; tel (212) 599-3666; fax (212) 599-4743

ITALIAN

Newark: *Italian Tribune News (Est. 1931) (English)* — 427 Bloomfield Ave., Newark, NJ 07107; Th; 25,000pd (Est); $15.28; publisher Ace Alagna; editor Joan Alagna; tel (201) 485-6000; fax (201) 485-8967

Philadelphia: *Sons of Italy Times (Est. 1913)* — 414 Walnut St., Philadelphia, PA 19106; Bi-Wkly; 15,000pd (Est); $7.00; C; publisher Order Sons of Italy in America; editor John B Acchione III; tel (215) 592-1713; fax (215) 592-9152

St. Louis: *Il Pensiero (The Thought) (Est. 1904) (Italian/American)* — 10001 Stonell Dr., St. Louis, MO 63123; publisher & general manager Antonio Lombardo; editor A Gandolfo; managing editor L Lombardo; tel (314) 638-3446; fax (314) 638-8222

Totowa: *The Italian Voice (La Voce Italiana) (Est. 1932) (English)* — PO Box 9, Totowa, NJ 07511-0009; Th; 7,000pd, 100fr (Est); $7.35; publisher & editor Cesarina A Earl; tel (201) 942-5028/(201) 942-2814

Westwood: *America Oggi (Est. 1988) (Italian)* — 55 Bergenline Ave., Westwood, NJ 07675; Daily; 60,000pd (Est); $21.00; C; publisher Gruppo Editoriale Oggi Inc.; editor Andrea Mantineo; tel (201) 358-6697; fax (212) 268-0379

JAPANESE

Chicago: *Chicago Shimpo (Japanese/English)* — 4670 N. Manor Ave., Chicago, IL 60625; W/F; 5,000pd (Est); $10.00; publisher Takeo F Sugano; editor Art Morimitsu & Kayoko Kawaguchi; tel (312) 478-6170; fax (312) 478-9360

Honolulu: *The Hawii Hochi (Japanese/English)* — PO Box 17430, Honolulu, HI 96817-0430; Daily; 7,200pd (Est); N/A; publisher Paul S Yempuku; editor Mitsunori Shoji; tel (808) 845-2255

Honolulu: *Japanese Beach Press (Est. 1971) (Japanese)* — 2222 Kalakaua Ave., Ste. 1004, PO Box 2039, Honolulu, HI 96805; Bi-Wkly F; 100pd, 35,000fr (Est); $15.50; C; publisher Roy Callaway; general manager & editor Atsuko Chambers; tel (808) 926-4410; fax (808) 926-4822

Los Angeles: *The Rafu Shimpo (L.A. Japanese Daily News) (Est. 1903) (Japanese/English)* — 259 S. Los Angeles St., Los Angeles, CA 90012; M-Sa; 21,397pd, 5fr (Sw); $11.00; publisher Michael Komai; editors Naomi Hirahara & Tareshi Ota; tel (213) 629-2231; fax (213) 627-0737

Monterey Park: *Pacific Citizen (Japanese/English)* — 2 Coral Cir., Ste. 204, Monterey Park, CA 91755; F; 23,946pd, 287fr (Est); $1.42; publisher Japanese American Citizens League; editor Richard Suenaga; tel (213) 725-0083; fax (213) 725-0064

San Francisco: *Hokubei Mainichi (English/Japanese)* — 1746 Post St., San Francisco, CA 94115; Tu-Sa; 10,000pd, 125fr (Est); 86¢; publisher Akira Matsuo; editor Atsuyo Hiramato; tel (415) 567-7324; fax (415) 567-3926

San Francisco: *Nichibet Times (Est. 1946) (English/Japanese)* — 2211 Bush St., PO Box 3098, San Francisco, CA 94119; Tu-Sa; 8,115pd (Est); 39¢; publisher Nichi Bei Times Co.; editors I Namekawa (Jpse.) & Michi Onuma (Eng.); tel (415) 921-6820; fax (415) 921-0770

Seattle: *The Hokubei Hochi (North American Post) (Est. 1946) (Japanese)* — 662 1/2 S. Jackson St., PO Box 3173, Seattle, WA 98104; M/W/F; 1,785pd, 16fr (Sw); $23.50; C; publisher Mick Matsuzawa; general manager Minoru Barada; editor Akiko Kusunose; tel (206) 623-0100; fax (206) 625-1424

Seattle: *The Northwest Nikkei (Est. 1989) (English)* — 662 1/2 S. Jackson St., PO Box 3173, Seattle, WA 98114; Mthly; 10,000pd (Est); $9.50; publisher Tomro Moriguchi; general manager Mick Matsuzawa; editor S Taniguchi; tel (206) 623-0100; fax (206) 625-1424

KOREAN

Chicago: *Korea Times (Est. 1971) (Korean)* — 4447 N. Keozie Ave., Chicago, IL 60625; Daily; 10,000pd, 5,000fr (Est); Th; 12,000fr (Sw); $12.50; publisher & editor J C Wall; publisher Yong W Kim; editor Kil Won Yook; tel (312) 463-1050; fax (312) 267-3336

Los Angeles: *Korea Times (Korean/English)* — 141 N. Vermont Ave., Los Angeles, CA 90004; Daily; 45,000pd (Est); F; 5,000pd (Sw); $14.80; publisher Jae Min Chang; publisher & editor Patricia Pulliam; editors Kap S Lee & Tom Byun; managing editors Sun D Kim & Yergan Pulliam; tel (213) 487-5323

New York: *Korea Times (Est. 1967) (Korean/English)* — 42-22 27th St., Long Island City, NY 11101; M-Sa; 20,000pd (Est); M; 8,670fr (ABC); $75.54; publishers Andrew H Ohm & Patricia E Grier; editors Kee Young Lee & Walter L Mathis Sr; tel (718) 482-1111; fax (718) 706-1086

New York: *The Korea Herald/U.S.A. (Est. 1953) (English)* — 150 W. 51st St., Ste. 1426, New York, NY 10019; F; 46,200pd (Est); $18.70; Tu/Su; 5,000pd (Est); N/A; publisher Charles Kelley; publisher & editor K J Choi; general manager Bernice Brown; editor Teresa Maxwell Kelley; managing editor Kascene Barks; tel (212) 582-5205

LITHUANIAN

Addison: *Sandara (The League) (English/Lithuanian)* — 208 W. Natoma Ave., PO Box 241, Addison, IL 60101; Bi-mthly; 1,200pd, 200fr (Est); $3.60; publisher Lithuanian National League of America Inc.; editor Grozvydas J Lazauskas; tel (708) 543-8198; fax (312) 735-8793

Brooklyn: *Darbininkas (The Worker) (Est. 1915) (English/Lithuanian)* — 341 Highland Blvd., Brooklyn, NY 11207; F; 16,000pd (Est); 17¢; C; publisher Franciscan Fathers; general manager Rev Francis Giedgaudas; editor Rev Dr Cornelius Bucmys; tel (718) 827-1352; fax (718) 827-2964

Brooklyn: *Vienybe (Unity) (Est. 1886)* — 192 Highland Blvd., Brooklyn, NY 11207; Bi-Wkly; 2,000pd, 20fr (Est); $2.50; publisher Son Joseph Tyslaiva; editor Jonas Valaitis; tel (718) 277-7257

Chicago: *Draugas (The Lithuanian Daily "Friend") (Est. 1909) (Lithuanian)* — 4545 W. 63rd St., Chicago, IL 60629; Tu-Sa; 5,526pd, 100fr (Sw); $5.00; publisher Lithuanian Catholic Press Society; general manager Pijus V Stoncius; editor Danute Bindokas; tel (312) 585-9500; fax (312) 585-8284

Chicago: *Vilnis (Est. 1923)* — 3116 S. Halsted St., Chicago, IL 60608; Bi-Wkly; 1,500pd (Est); publisher Workers Publishing Assoc. Inc.; editor Stanley J Jokubka

Cleveland: *Dirva (The Lithuanian National Newspaper)* — 19807 Cherokee Ave., PO Box 1919, Cleveland, OH 44119-0191; Th; 3,500pd (Est); $4.00; publisher Viltis Inc.; editor B Gaidziunas; tel (216) 431-6344; fax (216) 531-8428

New York: *Tevyne (Fatherland) (Est. 1896) (English/Lithuanian)* — 307 W. 30th St., New York, NY 10001; 10x/yr; 2,227pd, 60fr (Est); N/A; publisher Lithuanian Alliance of America; general manager Genevieve Meiliunas; editor Vytautas Kasniunas; tel (212) 563-2210

Wilkes-Barre: *Mic Garsas (Est. 1917) (Lithuanian/English)* — 71-73 S. Washington St., Wilkes-Barre, PA 18701; Mthly; 2,000pd (Est); N/A; publisher Lithuanian Catholic Alliance; editor Florence Eckert; tel (717) 823-8876

NORWEGIAN

Brooklyn: *Nordisk Tidende/Norway Times (Est. 1891) (Bilingual)* — 481-81 St., Brooklyn, NY 11209; Th; 5,000pd (Est); $2.65; C; publisher Norse News Inc.; editor Tom Roren; tel (718) 238-1100; fax (718) 921-9648

Copyright ©1996 by the Editor & Publisher Co.

Seattle: *Western Viking (Norwegian/English)* — 2405 N.W. Market St., Seattle, WA 98107; F; 4,500pd (Est); 50¢; publisher & editor Dr Alf L Knudsen; tel (206) 784-4617; fax (206) 784-4856

POLISH

Baldwin: *Polish American World (Est. 1959) (English)* — 3100 Grand Blvd., Baldwin, NY 11510-4815; F; 5,000pd, 5,000fr (Est); $6.00; publisher H R Glinka; general manager Helen Poster; editor Linda Romalewski; managing editor Edward Dmuchowski; tel (516) 223-6514; fax (516) 223-6514

Brooklyn: *Dzlennik Nowojorski (New York Daily) (Est. 1993) (Polish)* — 861 Manhattan Ave., Stes. 5 & 6, Brooklyn, NY 11222; Daily; 40,000fr (Est); $10.00; publisher Michael Kuchejda; tel (718) 389-0666; fax (718) 389-6422

Buffalo: *Polish-American Journal (Est. 1911) (English)* — 1275 Harlem Rd., Buffalo, NY 14206; Mthly; 18,750pd, 500fr (Est); $12.50; publisher Panagraphics Inc.; editor Mark A Kohan; managing editor Paulette T Kulbacki; tel (716) 893-5771; fax (716) 893-5783

Chicago: *Dzlennik Chicagowski (Chicago Daily) (Est. 1990) (Polish)* — 5242 W. Diversy Ave., Chicago, IL 60639; Daily; 40,000fr (Est); $10.00; publisher Michael Kuchejda; tel (312) 283-1898; fax (312) 283-1675

Chicago: *Polish Daily News (Dziennik Zwaizkowy) (Est. 1908) (English/Polish)* — 5711 N. Milwaukee, Chicago, IL 60646; M-F; 8,616pd, 555fr (Sw); 75¢; publisher Edward Moskal; general manager Emily Leszczynski; editor Wojciech Bialasiewicz; tel (312) 763-3343; fax (312) 763-3825

Chicago: *Zgoda (Harmony) (Est. 1881) (Polish/English)* — 6100 N. Cicero Ave., Chicago, IL 60646-4385; publisher Polish National Alliance of N. America; editor Wojciech A Wierzewski, Ph.D.; tel (312) 286-0500 ext. 373; fax (312) 286-0842

Clifton: *Post Eagle (Est. 1962) (English)* — 800 Van Houten Ave., PO Box 2127, Clifton, NJ 07015; W; 16,500pd (Sw); $8.00; publisher Post Pub. Co. Inc.; editor Chester Grabowski; managing editor Christine Witmyer; tel (201) 473-5414; fax (201) 473-3211

Hamtramck: *Swiat Polski (Polish World) (Est. 1904) (Polish)* — 11903 Joseph Campeau, Hamtramck, MI 48212; W; 4,300pd, 700fr (Sw); $27.00; C; managing editor Lillian F Szymanski; tel (313) 365-1990; fax (313) 365-0850

Jamesburg: *Glos Narodu (Voice of the People) (Est. 1901)* — 410 Matchaponix Ave., Jamesburg, NJ 08831; Th; 19,000pd (Est); N/A; publisher & editor Romuald Waszkielewicz

Jamesburg: *Obywatel Amerykanski (Est. 1920)* — 410 Matchaponix Ave., Jamesburg, NJ 08831; Th; 14,900pd (Est); publisher Romuald Waszkeilewicz Co. Inc.; editor Romuald Waszkeilewicz

Jamesburg: *Polak Amerykanski (Est. 1920)* — 410 Matchaponix Ave., Jamesburg, NJ 08831; Th; 4,900pd (Est); publisher Romuald Waszkielewicz Co. Inc.; editor Romuald Waszkielewicz

New York: *Polish-American Daily News (Nowy Dziennik) (Est. 1971) (Polish)* — 333 W. 38th St., New York, NY 10018; M-Sa; 38,000pd, 1,000fr (Est); $1.00; C; publisher & editor B Wierzbianski; general manager T Rydzaj; managing editor T Deptula; tel (212) 594-2266; fax (212) 594-2383

Scranton: *Rola Boza (God's Field) (Est. 1923) (English/Polish)* — 1008 Pittston Ave., Scranton, PA 18505; Bi-Wkly; 7,380pd, 123fr (Est); N/A; publisher Polish National Catholic Church; editor Bishop Anthony M Rysz; managing editor Prime Bishop John Swantik; tel (717) 346-9131; fax (717) 346-2188

Scranton: *Straz (The Guard) (Est. 1897) (English/Polish)* — 1002 Pittston Ave., Scranton, PA 18505; Th; 10,000pd (Est); $3.50; publisher Polish National Union of America; editor Mitchell Grochowski; tel (717) 344-1513

Sheboygan: *Horyzonty (Est. 1988) (Polish)* — PO Box 976, Sheboygan, WI 53081; F; 2,200pd, 300fr (Est); $7.00; publisher Artex Publishing Inc.; editor Leszek Zielinski; tel (414) 458-9987; fax (414) 458-9987

St. Paul: *Nowiny Minnescockie* — 440 Thomas St., St. Paul, MN 55103; F; 1,672pd (Est); N/A; publisher Minnesota Polish Pub. Co. Inc.; editor J M Koleski

Stevens Point: *Gwiazda Polarna (Bilingual)* — 2619 Post Rd., Stevens Point, WI 54481; Sa; 12,225pd, 95fr (Est); $11.00; publisher Point Publications Inc.; editor Malgorzata Terentiew; tel (715) 345-0744; fax (715) 345-1913

PORTUGUESE

Fall River: *O Jornal (Est. 1975) (Portuguese)* — 410 2nd St., PO Box 1149, Fall River, MA 02722; Th; 17,000fr (Sw); $13.00; C; publisher & editor Kathleen B Castro; tel (508) 675-0321/(508) 675-0322; fax (508) 678-1798

Hayward: *Voz de Portugal (English)* — 368-70 "A" St., Hayward, CA 94541; Bi-Wkly; 4,500pd (Est); publisher & editor Lourenco Costa Aguiar; tel (510) 537-9503

New York: *Folha do Brasil (Est. 1991) (Portuguese)* — 16 W. 46th St., 7th Fl., New York, NY 10036; Tu; 50,000pd (Est); $9.50; publisher Moses Aspan Esq.; editor Sergio R Cesario; tel (212) 869-7038; fax (212) 730-2089

Newark: *Luso Americano (Portuguese American Newspaper) (Est. 1928) (Portuguese/English)* — 88 Ferry St., Newark, NJ 07105; W/F; 33,460pd (Sw); $5.00; publisher & editor A S Matinho; tel (201) 589-4600; fax (201) 589-3848

San Pablo: *Jornal Portugues (Portuguese Journal) (Est. 1888) (Bilingual)* — 1912 Church Ln., San Pablo, CA 94806; Th; 2,107pd, 300fr (Sw); $5.00; publisher Albert C Pacciorini; editor Alberto S Lemos; managing editor Maria C Leal; tel (510) 237-0888; fax (510) 237-3790

RUSSIAN

Huntingdon Vly.: *The Far Northeast Citizen-Sentinel (Est. 1961) (Russian/English)* — 1102 Churchill Rd., Philidelphia, PA 19038; W; 480pd, 13,520fr (Sw); $16.80; publisher Matthew H Petersohn; editor Sandra L Petersohn; tel (215) 632-2700

New York: *Novoye Russkoye Slovo (English)* — 111 5th Ave., 5th Fl., New York, NY 10003-1005; M-Sa; 60,000pd, 120fr (Est); $1.25; publisher Novoye Russkoye Slove Pub. Corp.; editor Andrei Sedych; tel (212) 387-0299

Philadelphia: *Truth (Bilingual)* — 1733 Spring Garden St., Philadelphia, PA 19130; Mthly; 3,000pd (Est); $3.50; publisher Russian Brotherhood Organization of USA; editor Stephen P Kopestonsky

San Francisco: *Russian Life Daily (Russian)* — 2458 Sutter St., San Francisco, CA 94115; Tu-Sa (m); 1,500pd (Est); $2.40; publisher Russian Life Inc.; tel (415) 921-5380; fax (415) 921-8726

SERBIAN

Pittsburgh: *American Srbobran (Est. 1927) (English)* — 1 5th Ave., 7th Fl., Pittsburgh, PA 15222; W; 4,000pd, 200fr (Est); $2.50; publisher Serb National Federation; editor Robert Rade Stone; tel (412) 612-6600

SLOVAK

E Orange: *Sokol Times (Est. 1920)* — 276 Prospect St., East Orange, NJ 07019; Mthly; 6,000fr (Est); N/A; publisher Sokol U.S.A.; editor Anna L Sopoci; tel (201) 676-0280; fax (201) 676-3348

Middletown: *Jednota (Union) (English)* — Jednote & Rosedale Ave., PO Box 350, Middletown, PA 17057; W; 725pd, 34,290fr (Est); 16¢; publisher First Catholic Slovak Union; editor Joseph R Kristofik; tel (717) 944-0461

Middletown: *Zornicka (English)* — 315 Oak Hill Dr., Middletown, PA 17057; Mthly; 4,200pd (Est); N/A; publisher Ladies PA Slovak Catholic Union; editor Ed Kovac Jr; tel (717) 944-6308

Passaic: *Katolicky Sokol/Slovak Catholic Falcon (Est. 1911) (English)* — 205 Madison St., Passaic, NJ 07055; W; 12,000pd (Est); publisher Slovak Catholic Sokol; editor Daniel F Tanzone; tel (201) 777-4010; fax (201) 779-8245

Pittsburgh: *Narodne Noviny (English/Slovak)* — 2325 E. Carson St., Pittsburgh, PA 15203; Monthly; 150pd, 12,500fr (Est); publisher National Slovak Society; editor Joseph Stefka; tel (412) 488-1890; fax (412) 488-0327

SLOVENIAN

Burr Ridge: *Prosveta (Enlightenment) (Est. 1916) (English)* — 247 W. Allegheny Rd., Imperial, PA 15126-9774; W; 19,700pd (Sw); $7.00; publisher Slovene National Benefit Society; editor Jay Sedmak; tel (412) 695-1100; fax (412) 695-1555

Cleveland: *Amerikanski Slovenec-Glasilo KSKJ (The American Slovenian-Voice of American Slovenian Catholic) (Est. 1891) (English/Slovene)* — 708 E. 159th St., Cleveland, OH 44110; W; 10,800pd (Est); $5.00; publisher American Slovenian Catholic Union; editor John T Nemec; tel (216) 541-7243; fax (216) 361-4088

Cleveland: *Ameriska Domovina (Slovene)* — 6117 St. Clair Ave., Cleveland, OH 44103; M-F (m); 9,000pd (Est); publisher American Home Pub. Co.; editor James V Debevec; tel (216) 431-0628

SWEDISH

Brooklyn: *Norden (Est. 1896)* — 754-4th Ave., Brooklyn, NY 11329; Th; 900pd, 1,000fr (Est); 35¢; publisher Norden News Inc.; editor Erik R Hermans; tel (718) 788-0900

Downey: *California Veckoblad (California Weekly News) (Est. 1910) (English)* — 10921 Paramount Blvd., Downey, CA 90241-3616; F; 2,800pd, 300fr (Est); 35¢; C; publisher & editor Mary A Hendricks; general manager & managing editor Jane Hendricks; tel (310) 862-4880

New York: *Nordstjernan-Svea (Est. 1872) (English/Swedish)* — 123 W. 44th St., Ste. 12C, New York, NY 10036; Th; 6,000pd (Est); $21.00; publisher Ulf E Martensson; editor Alvalene P Karlsson; tel (212) 944-0776; fax (212) 944-0763

San Francisco: *Vestkusten (The West Coast) (Est. 1886) (Bilingual)* — 237 Ricardo Rd., Mill Valley, CA 94941-2517; Bi-Mthly; 1,398pd, 898fr (Sw); $6.00; publisher Barbro Sachs Osher; editor Karin W Person; managing editor Bridget Strimberg-Brink; tel (415) 381-5149; fax (415) 381-9664

SWISS

New York: *Swiss American Review (French/German/Italian/English)* — 608 5th Ave., Ste. 609, New York, NY 10020; W; 3,500pd (Est); publisher Swiss American Review Inc.; editor Karl Vonlanthen; tel (212) 247-0459; fax (212) 397-2473

San Francisco: *Schweizer-Journal (Swiss Journal) (Est. 1918) (English)* — 548 Columbus Ave., PO Box 330082, San Francisco, CA 94133; Bi-Wkly; 4,000pd, 100fr (Est); $20.00; publisher Swiss Journal Co. Inc.; editors Anthony Muschi & Louis Muschi; tel (415) 362-8072; fax (415) 362-3159

TURKISH

New York: *Hurriyet (English/Turkish)* — 500 5th Ave., Ste. 1021, New York, NY 10110; M-Sa; 5,800pd (Est); $15.00; publisher Erol Simavi; editor Dogan Uluc; tel (212) 921-8880; fax (212) 391-4017

UKRAINIAN

Jersey City: *Svoboda Ukrainian Daily (Liberty) (Est. 1983) (English)* — 30 Montgomery St., Jersey City, NJ 07302; Tu-Sa; 13,000pd (Sw); $12.00; C; publisher The Ukrainian National Assoc. Inc.; editor Zenon Snylyk; tel (201) 434-0237; fax (201) 451-5486

Jersey City: *The Ukrainian Weekly (Est. 1933) (English)* — 30 Montgomery St., Jersey City, NJ 07302; Su; 10,500pd (Est); $10.00; publisher The Ukrainian National Assoc. Inc.; editor Romana Hadzewycz; tel (201) 434-0237; fax (201) 451-5486

UKRAINIAN/ENGLISH

Philadelphia: *America Ukrainian Catholic Daily (Est. 1912) (Bilingual)* — 817 N. Franklin St., Philadelphia, PA 19123; Tu/Th/Sa; 4,080pd, 200fr (Est); $2.52; publisher Providence Assoc. of Ukrainian Catholics in America; editor Osip Roshka; tel (215) 627-0233; fax (215) 238-1933

GAY & LESBIAN NEWSPAPERS PUBLISHED IN THE UNITED STATES

CALIFORNIA

Sacramento/N California: *Dad Guess What Newspaper* — 1725 "L" St., Sacramento (95814); Bi-Mthly; 7,000fr (Est); $15.00; C; publisher & editor Linda D Birner; general manager Cheryl Strickland; tel (916) 441-6397; fax (916) 441-6422

Sacramento/N California: *Mom Guess What Newspaper* — 1725 "L" St., Sacramento (95814); Bi-Mthly; 2,000pd, 7,000fr (Est); $15.00; C; publisher & editor Linda D Birner; general manager Cheryl Strickland; tel (916) 441-6397; fax (916) 441-6422

San Diego/Orange Co./Los Angeles: *Gay & Lesbian Times* — 3911 Normal St., San Diego (92103); Th; 400pd, 24,000fr (Sw); $12.40; C; publisher Michael G Portantino; editor Chris DiEdoardo; managing editor Corri Plank; tel (619) 299-6397; fax (619) 299-3430

San Francisco: *Bay Area Reporter* — 395 9th St. (94103-3831); Th; 35,500fr (Sw); $19.85; C; publisher Bob Ross; general manager Michael Yamashita; tel (415) 861-5019; fax (415) 861-8144

San Francisco: *San Francisco Bay Times* — 525 Bryant St. (94107); Bi-Wkly Th; 43,000fr (Est); N/A; C; publisher & editor Kim Corsaro; tel (415) 227-0800; fax (415) 227-0890

San Francisco: *San Francisco Sentinel* — 285 Shipley St. (94107); Th; 5,250pd, 29,750fr (Est); $15.00; publisher & editor Ray Chalker; tel (415) 281-3745; fax (415) 281-3745 ext. 137

COLORADO

Denver: *Out Front* — 244 Washington St. (80203); Bi-Wkly; 11,000fr (Sw); $7.99; publisher Q Publishing Group Ltd.; publisher Greg Montoya; editor Sam Gallegos; managing editor Madeleine Ingraham; tel (303) 778-7900; fax (303) 778-7978

DISTRICT OF COLUMBIA

Washington: *The Washington Blade* — 1408 "U" St., N.W. (20009-3916); F; 2,515pd, 41,195fr (VAC); $32.00; publisher Don Michaels; general manager James Lamont; editor Lisa Keen; managing editor Mark Sullivan; tel (202) 797-7000; fax (202) 797-7040

GEORGIA

Atlanta: *Southern Voice* — 1095 Zonolite Rd. (30306); Th; 350pd, 19,650fr (Est); $13.28;

Copyright ©1996 by the Editor & Publisher Co.

publisher Leigh Vanderels; general manager Gary Kaupman; editor Devon Clayton; tel (404) 876-1819; fax (404) 876-2709

IDAHO

Idaho: *Diversity News* — PO Box 323, Boise (83701); Mthly; 400pd, 1,600fr (Sw); $6.00; publisher The Gay & Lesbian Community Center Inc.; editor Rich Keefe; managing editor Bob Dunn; tel (208) 323-0805; fax (208) 323-0805

ILLINOIS

Chicago: *Outlines* — 3059 N. Southport (60657); Mthly; 1,500pd, 20,500fr (Est); publisher & editor Tracy Baim; tel (312) 871-7610; fax (312) 871-7609

INDIANA

Indiana/Kentucky/Ohio: *The Word* — 225 E. North St.; Tower 1, Ste. 2800, Indianapolis (46204); Last Tu/Month; 14,000fr (Sw); $6.95; C; publisher Ted Fleischaker; general manager & editor Don Newton; tel (317) 632-8840; fax (317) 687-8840

MARYLAND

Baltimore: *Baltimore Alternative* — 36 W. 25th St. (21218); PO Box 2351 (21203); Mthly; 15,000fr (Sw); $16.40; publisher & managing editor Charles Mueller; general manager Garey Lambert; editor Rawley Grau; tel (410) 235-3401; fax (410) 889-5665

MINNESOTA

Minneapolis: *Equal Time* — 310 E. 38th St., Ste. 207 (55409); W; 1,000pd, 24,000fr (Est); $20.00; publisher Lavender Inc.; editor Ruby Dichtorman; tel (612) 823-3836; fax (612) 823-2615

MISSOURI

St. Louis: *The Lesbian and Gay News Telegraph* — PO Box 14229-A (63178); publisher & editor Jim Thomas; tel (314) 664-6411; fax (314) 664-6303

NEW YORK

New York: *New York Native* — 28 W. 25th St., 4th Fl. (10010); PO Box 1475 (10008); M; 9,000pd, 3,000fr (Sw); $15.36; publisher & editor Charles Ortleb; general manager Ray Nocera; managing editor Neenya Ostrum; tel (212) 627-2120; fax (212) 727-9321

New York: *Stonewall News* — 28 W. 25th St., 4th Fl. (10010); PO Box 1475 (10008); M; 1,000pd, 11,000fr (Est); $10.14; publisher & editor Charles Ortleb; general manager Ray Nocera; managing editor Neenya Ostrum; tel (212) 627-2120; fax (212) 727-9321

Rochester: *Empty Closet* — 179 Atlantic Ave. (14607-1255); Mthly; 2,000pd, 4,000fr (Est); $3.30; publisher Gay Alliance of Genesee Valley; editor Susan Jordan; tel (716) 244-9030; fax (716) 244-8246

NORTH CAROLINA

Charlotte: *Q Notes* — 4037 E. Independence Blvd., Ste. 611 (28205); PO Box 221841 (28222); Mthly; 13,500fr (Sw); $3.72; publisher Jim Yarbrough; editor David Stout; tel (704) 531-9988; fax (704) 531-1361

Raleigh: *Front Page* — 309 W. Martin St. (27601); PO Box 27928 (27611); Bi-Wkly; 250pd, 12,000fr (Est); $5.96; publisher James Baxter; tel (919) 829-0181; fax (919) 829-0830

OHIO

Columbus: *Stonewall Union Reports* — PO Box 10814 (43201-7814); Mthly; 1,500pd, 3,500fr (Est); publisher Stonewall Union; editor Mike Dittmer; tel (614) 299-7764; fax (614) 299-4408

OREGON

Portland: *Just Out* — PO Box 14400 (97214); Bi-Mthly; 12,500fr (Est); $17.50; publisher & managing editor Renee LaChance; tel (503) 236-1252; fax (503) 236-1257

Salem: *Community News* — PO Box 663 (97308); Mthly; 480pd, 12,000fr (Sw); $3.60; C; publisher Chuck Simpson; general manager Julie Adams; editor Ron Hall; tel (503) 363-0006

PENNSYLVANIA

Delaware Valley: *Au Courant Newsmagazine* — PO Box 42741, Philadelphia (19101); Tu; 12,000fr (Sw); $7.56; publisher & managing editor Scott Mallinger; tel (215) 790-1179; fax (215) 790-9721

Philadelphia: *Philadelphia Gay News* — 505 S. 4th St. (19147); F; 902pd, 12,299fr (VAC); $9.90; publisher Mark A Segal; editor Al Patrick; tel (215) 625-8501; fax (215) 925-6437

TENNESSEE

Memphis: *Triangle Journal News* — 3434 Philsdale; PO Box 11485 (38111); Last F/Month; 56pd, 4,000fr (Sw); $3.02; C; publisher Printers Ink; general manager & editor Allen Cook; editor John Stilwell; tel (901) 454-1411; fax (901) 454-1411

TEXAS

Austin: *The Texas Triangle* — 1615 W. 6th St. (78703); Th; 30,000fr (Sw); $17.50; publisher & editor Kay Longcope; general manager Barbara Wohlgemuth; managing editor David Elliot; tel (512) 476-0576; fax (512) 472-8154

Dallas: *Dallas Voice* — 3000 Carlisle, Ste. 200 (75204); F; 12,000fr (Sw); $8.32; publisher Robert Moore; editor Dennis Vercher; tel (214) 754-8710; fax (214) 969-7271

Houston: *Houston Voice* — 811 Westheimer, Ste. 105 (77006); Th; 300pd, 9,000fr (Est); $19.00; publisher Crad Duren; general manager Jack Leonard; editor Sheri Cohen Darbonne; tel (713) 529-8490; fax (713) 529-9531

VERMONT

Vermont: *Out in the Mountains* — 109 S. Winooski Ave.; PO Box 177, Burlington (05402); Mthly; 500pd, 2,500fr (Est); $10.00; publisher Out in the Mountains Inc; editor Fred Kuhr; tel (802) 655-5638

VIRGINIA

Norfolk: *Our Own Community Press* — 739 Yarmouth St. (23510); Mthly; 12,000fr (Est); publisher Alicia Herr; editor Patrick Evans; tel (804) 625-0700; fax (804) 625-6024

WASHINGTON

Seattle: *Seattle Gay News* — PO Box 22007 (98122); F; 30,000fr (Est); $28.00; publisher George Bakan; editor Sally J Clark; tel (206) 324-4297; fax (206) 322-7188

WISCONSIN

Milwaukee: *Wisconsin Light* — 1843 N. Palmer St. (53212); W; 3,000pd (Est); Bi-Wkly Th; 350pd, 11,000fr (Est); publisher Jerry Johnson; editors Rev Timothy Majic & Terry Boughner, Ph.D.; tel (414) 372-2773; fax (414) 289-0789

HISPANIC NEWSPAPERS PUBLISHED IN THE UNITED STATES

ARIZONA

Pheonix: *El Sol De Arizona (Est. 1939) (English/Spanish)* — 2226 W. Northern Ave., Ste. C-208, Phoenix (85021); F; 200pd, 25,000fr (Est); $10.40; C; publisher Ray Flores; managing editor Christine Flores; tel (602) 995-6162; fax (602) 995-6168

Yuma: *Bajo El Sol (Est. 1991) (Spanish)* — 2055 Arizona Ave., PO Box 271, (85366); F; 15,000fr (Sw); $6.20; publisher Sam Pepper; editor Maria Chavoya; tel (520) 783-3333; fax (520) 343-1004

CALIFORNIA

Acton/Agua Dulce: *Acton/Agua Dulce News (Est. 1982) (English/Spanish)* — 3212 Country Way, PO Box 57, Acton (93510); Th; 5,300pd 575fr, (Sw); $11.93; C; publisher John Joyce; tel (805) 269-1169; fax (805) 269-2139

Bakersfield: *El Mexicalo (Est. 1980) (English/Spanish)* — 931 Niles St., (93305); Th; 5,000pd, 10,000fr (CVPS); $13.86; C; publisher Esther H Manzano; general manager Erlinda H Manzano; editor Tony H Manzano; tel (805) 323-9334; fax (805) 323-6951

Bakersfield: *El Popular - Bakersfield (Est. 1983) (Spanish)* — 1206 California Ave., (93304); Th; 25,000pd, 1,000fr (Est); $15.00; publisher & editor Raul R Comacho Sr; tel (805) 325-1351

Escondido: *Hispanos Unidos (Est. 1987) (Spanish)* — PO Box 462016, (92046-2016); F; 35pd, 16,965fr (Est); $16.00; publisher & editor Jaime A Castaneda; tel (619) 740-9561; fax (619) 747-1626

Fresno: *El Popular Newspaper Group of California (Est. 1983) (Spanish)* — 1206 California Ave., Bakersfield (93304); F; 24,476pd, 1,524fr (Sw); $13.50; C; publisher & editor Raul M Camacho Jr; managing editor Hector Manuel Salazar; tel (209) 264-5763; fax (805) 325-1351

Los Angeles: *Eastern Group (Est. 1948) (Spanish/English)* — 2500 S. Atlantic Blvd., Bldg. B, (90040); Th; 1,496pd, 66,518fr (Sw); $20.16; C; publisher Dolores Sanchez; general manager Jonathan Sanchez; editor John Sanchez; managing editor Tony Castro; tel (213) 263-5743; fax (213) 263-9169

Los Angeles: *La Opinion (Est. 1926) (Spanish)* — 411 W. 5th St., PO Box 15093, (90013); Daily; 105,918pd (Est); $20.00; publisher Jose I Lozano; editor Monica Lozano; managing editor Gerardo Lopez; tel (213) 622-8332; fax (213) 896-2151

Los Angeles: *La Prensa de Los Angeles (Est. 1966) (Spanish)* — 8033 Sunset Blvd., Ste. 704, (90046); Th; 45,000pd (Est); $18.00; C; editor Carlos Groppa; tel (213) 654-6268

Los Angeles: *Novedades (Est. 1991) (Spanish)* — 1241 Soto St., Ste. 203-M, (90023); Th; 77,000fr (Est); $28.25; C; publisher John DiCarlo; general manager Laura Herrera; editor Angel Morales; tel (213) 881-6515; fax (213) 881-6524

Los Angeles: *LA Voz Libre (Est. 1981) (Spanish)* — 3107 W. Beverly Blvd., Ste. 1, (90057); Th; 1,100pd, 43,400fr (Est); $20.00; C; publisher & editor Angel M Prada; general manager Jose M Martinez; managing editor Jose Albuerne; tel (213) 388-4639; fax (213) 388-2053

Los Angeles/Orange Co.: *La Guia Familiar (Est. 1979) (Spanish)* — 15844 Strather St. (91406), PO Box 9190, Van Nuys (91409); Th; 246,000fr (Sw); $61.25; C; publisher & editor Victor Field; general manager Arthur Lerner; editor Diane Flores Lerner; tel (818) 781-2605; fax (818) 781-2625

Los Angeles/Orange Co.: *Tu Mundo Artistico (Est. 1982) (Spanish)* — 15844 Strathern St (91406), PO Box 9190, Van Nuys (91409); Th; 105,000fr (Sw); $34.50; C; publisher & editor Victor Field; general manager Arthur Lerner; editor Diane Flores Lerner; tel (818) 781-2605; fax (818) 781-2625

Los Angeles/Orange Co.: *Variedades (Est. 1991) (Spanish)* — 15844 Strathern St. (91406), PO Box 9190, Van Nuys (91409); Th; 200,000fr (Sw); $61.25; C; publisher & editor Victor Field; general manager Arthur Lerner; editor Diane Flores Lerner; tel (818) 781-2605; fax (818) 781-2625

Oakland: *El Mundo (Est. 1963) (Bilingual)* — 630 20th St., (94612); Th; 31,950fr (CVPS); $12.00; publisher Thomas L Berkley; general manager Jeff Douvel; editor Ana Parker; tel (510) 287-8200; fax (510) 763-9670

Orange Co.: *Excelsior (Est. 1992) (Spanish)* — 915 E. Katella Ave., Anaheim (92805); F; 54,142fr (VAC); $24.70; publisher Joseph L Arbona Sr; editor D Miguel Jimenez; tel (714) 978-1151; fax (714) 978-2212

Sacramento: *El Hispano (Est. 1968) (Bilingual)* — 928 2nd St., Ste. 300 (95814), PO Box 2856, (95812); W; 3,000pd, 17,000f (Est); $11.53; publisher & editor Pedro Chavez; general manager & managing editor Bel Larenas; tel (916) 442-0267; fax (916) 442-2818

Sacramento: *Sacramento el Popular (Est. 1983) (Spanish)* — 831 "E" St., Ste. 16, Sacaramento (95814); F; 21,497pd, 4,503fr (Sw); $13.50; C; publisher & editor Raul M Camacho Jr; tel (800) 995-8626; fax (805) 325-1351

Salinas: *El Sol (Est. 1968) (Spanish)* — 230 Capitol St. (93901), PO Box 1610, (93902); Th; 14,700fr (Sw); $13.00; C; publisher & editor Oscar Parodi; tel (408) 757-8118; fax (408) 757-1006

San Diego: *Ahora Now (Est. 1980) (Bilingual)* — 675 E. San Ysidro Blvd., (92073); Th; 10,000fr (Est); $16.00; publisher Bertha Alicia Gonzalez; editor Mario Ramirez; tel (619) 428-2277; fax (619) 428-0871

San Diego: *La Prensa San Diego (Est. 1976) (Spanish/English)* — 1950 5th Ave., Stes. 1,2 & 3, (92101-2309); C; publisher La Prensa Munoz Inc.; publisher Daniel L Munoz Sr; editor Daniel H Munoz Jr; tel (619) 231-2873; fax (619) 231-9180

San Fernando Vly.: *Vecinos Del Valle (Est. Spanish)* — c/o Daily News, PO Box 4200, Woodland Hills (91365-4200); W; 2pd, 46,924fr (VAC); $11.00; C; publisher Los Angeles Daily News; general manager Truman Beasby; editor Aida Ferrarone; tel (818) 713-3229; fax (818) 723-3029

San Francisco: *El Bohemio News (Est. 1971) (Spanish/English)* — 3133 22nd St., (94110); Wkly; 29,057fr (CVPS); $21.00; publisher & editor Fernando Rosado; tel (415) 647-1924; fax (415) 824-7248

San Francisco: *El Latino (Est. 1992) (Spanish)* — 262 Monterey Blvd., (94131); W; 14,574pd (VAC); $12.00; publisher Ricardo Ron; editor Roberto Heller; managing editor Carla Gomez; tel (415) 334-2061; fax (415) 334-2068

San Francisco: *El Tecolote (Est. 1970) (English)* — 766 Valencia St., (94110); Mthly; 250pd, 10,000fr (Est); $10.00; C; publisher Accion Latino; editor Juan Gonzales; tel (415) 252-5957; fax (415) 252-5701

San Francisco: *Horizontes (Horizons) (Est. 1983) (Spanish)* — 2601 Mission St., 9th Fl., (94110); F; 300pd, 19,700fr (Sw); $17.00; publisher & editor Juan J Pifarre; managing editor Alberto Maxwell; tel (415) 641-6051; fax (415) 282-3320

San Francisco: *Tiempo Latino (Est. 1977) (Spanish)* — 3288 21st St., Box 9, (94110); W; 30,000fr (Sw); $15.00; publisher & managing editor Gail E Neira; tel (415) 821-4452

San Jose: *El Observador (Est. 1980) (Spanish/English)* — 777 N. 1st St., Ste. 420 (95112-6311), PO Box 1990, (95109); W; 192pd, 17,819fr (VAC); $22.80; C; publishers Betty Morales & Hilbert Morales; editor Graciela P Michael; tel (408) 295-4272; fax (408) 295-0188

San Jose: *La Oferta Review (Spanish)* — 1376 N. 4th St., (95112-4713); W; 700pd, 31,640fr (Est); $24.81; Sa; 700pd, 31,640fr $24.81; publisher Franklin G Andrade; editor Mary J Andrade; tel (408) 729-6397; fax (408) 729-3278

Sanger: *El Sol de Valle (Est. 1986) (Spanish/English)* — 718 "N" St., (93657); W; 51pd, 21,257fr (VAC); $16.50; publisher & editor Kevin Kennedy; tel (209) 875-8771; fax (209) 875-7083

Southern California: *Variedades HTMC (Est. 1993) (Spanish)* — 15844 Strathern St., PO Box 9190, Van Nuys (91406); Th; 541,000fr (Sw); $90.50; C; publisher & editor Victor Field; general manager Arthur Lerner; editor Diane Flores Lerner; tel (818) 781-2605; fax (818) 781-2625

Stockton: *La Nacion (Est. 1984)* — 2250 Stewart St., Ste. 8, (95205); Th; 25,000pd $9.00; publisher Porfirio Perez; editor Manuel Tobias; tel (209) 943-5143; fax (209) 943-0625

COLORADO

Denver: *La Voz Newspaper (Est. 1974) (Spanish/English)* — 2885 W. 3rd Ave., (80219); W; 736pd, 12,396fr (CVPS); $12.00; publisher & editor Wanda M Padilla; general manager Cliff Bautsch; managing editor Sandra Tores; tel (303) 936-8556; fax (303) 922-9632

FLORIDA

Hialeah: *La Voz de la Calle (Est. 1981) (English)* — 4696 E. 10th St., PO Box 3187, (33013); F; 20,000fr (Est); $7.00; publisher & editor Vincent Rodriguez; tel (305) 687-5555

Hialeah: *Sol de Hialeah (Est. 1969) (Spanish)* — 436 Palm Ave., (33010); Th; 24,000fr (Est); $7.00; publisher & editor Angela Martinez; tel (305) 887-8324

Hillsborough Co.: *Community Connections (Est. 1987) (Spanish/English)* — 3210 E. 7th Ave., PO Box 5536, Tampa (33605); Th; 20,000fr (Sw); $6.00; publisher & editor Patrick Manteiga; tel (813) 248-3921; fax (813) 247-5357

Homestead: *La Voz Hispana de South Dade (Est. 1992) (Spanish)* — 15 N.E. 1st Rd., (33030); Th; 5,000fr (Est); $11.90; publisher Glenn A Martin; editor Yolanda Ulrich; tel (305) 245-2311; fax (305) 248-0596

Longwood: *La Prensa (Est. 1981) (Spanish)* — 685 S.C.R. 427, (32750-6403); Th; 19,160fr (CVPS); $12.00; C; publisher & general manager & editor Manuel A Toro; managing editor Dora Casanova de Toro; tel (407) 767-0070; fax (407) 767-0070

Miami: *Diario Las Americas (Est. 1953) (Spanish)* — 2900 39th St. N.W., (33142); Tu-Sa; 66,174pd, 70,214fr (Est); $28.00; publisher & editor Horacio Aguirre; tel (305) 633-3341; fax (305) 635-7668

Miami: *El Nuevo Herald (Est. 1976) (English)* — 1 Herald Plz., (33132-1693); Su; 99,528pd (Est); $32.10; publisher Roberto Suarez; editor Carlos Verdecia; tel (305) 376-3535; fax (305) 376-2378

Miami: *El Nuevo Patria (The New Homeland) (Est. 1959) (Spanish)* — 850 N. Miami Ave., Ste. 102 (33136), PO Box 2-Jose Marti Station, (33135); Th; 7,800pd, 21,200fr (Sw); $13.90; publisher Eladio Jose Armesto; general manager Miriam Gonzalez; editor Dr Carlos Diaz Lujan; managing editor Dr Jose Enrique Puente; tel (305) 530-8787; fax (305) 577-8989

Miami: *La Prensa Centroamericana (Est. 1987) (Spanish)* — 10404 W. Flagler St., Ste. 4, (33174); Th; 600pd, 6,400fr (Sw); $9.80; C; publisher & managing editor Filemon Ortega; general manager Francisco A Ortega; editor Lena Gutierrer; tel (305) 551 3292; fax (305) 551-6678

Miami: *Libre Semanal (Free Weekly) (Est. 1966) (Spanish)* — 904 S.W. 23rd Ave., (33135); F; 4,700pd, 10,300fr (CVPS); $10.00; publisher Demetrio Perez, Jr; tel (305) 643-4200; fax (305) 649-2767

Miami: *Viva Semanal (Spanish)* — 2960 Coral Way, (33145); W; 58,269fr (VAC); $24.50; publisher Amancio Suarez; general manager Rudy Robayna; editor Beatriz Parga; tel (305) 445-4011; fax (305) 443-4805

Miami Shores: *La Voz Catolica (Est. 1982) (Spanish)* — 9401 Biscayne Blvd., PO Box 38-1059, (33138); Mthly; 39,237pd, 405fr (Sw); $21.84; publisher The Voice-La Voz Publishing Co.; editor Araceli M Cantero; tel (305) 758-3399

Palm Beach Co.: *La Voz Hispana (Est. 1991) (Spanish)* — 3242 S. Dixie Hwy., W. Palm Beach (33405-1510); C; publisher Raul Rio; editor Dr Joaquin Freire; managing editor Hector A Diaz; tel (407) 659-1833; fax (407) 833-8174

Port St. Lucie: *Alma Latina (Spanish Soul) (Est. 1990) (Spanish)* — 265 S.W. Port St. Lucie Blvd., Ste. 154, Victoria Sq., (34984); Bi-Mthly F; 7,000fr (Est); $10.00; publisher & editor Annie Del Rosario; tel (407) 878-4365; fax (407) 879-4002

Tampa: *La Gaceta (Est. 1922) (Spanish)* — 3210 E. 7th Ave., PO Box 5536, (33675); F; 18,200pd (Sw); $8.50; publisher & editor Roland Manteiga; general manager Patrick Manteiga; tel (813) 248-3921; fax (813) 247-5357

Tampa: *Nuevo Siglo (Est. 1990) (Spanish)* — 4809 N. Armenia Ave., Ste. 115, (33603); Th; 4,000pd, 18,000fr (Est); $8.00; publisher Neris Ramon Palacios; general manager Rosmeli Palacios; managing editor Ledis Palacios; tel (813) 872-6692; fax (813) 877-6444

ILLINOIS

Chicago: *Back of the Yards Journal/El Periodico (Est. 1932) (Spanish/English)* — 4642 S. Damen Ave., (60609-3252); W; 1,000pd, 47,000fr (CVPS); $7.50; C; publisher Patrick J Salmon; general manager & managing editor Susan Strohacker; editor Robert Lukens; tel (312) 927-7200

Chicago: *El Imparcial Newspaper (Est. 1986) (Spanish)* — 3615 W. 26th St., 2nd FL, PO Box 23390, (60623); Th; 25,380fr (CVPS); $10.50; publisher & editor Alicia C Santelices; general manager Lucia Soto; managing editor Carmen R Gomez; tel (312) 542-4444, (708) 484-1188; fax (708) 484-0202

Chicago: *El Heraldo (Est. 1975) (English/Spanish)* — 1525 W. Grand Ave., (60622); Th; 15,000fr (Sw); $18.43; publisher Marta Foster; editor Gonzalo Sanchez; tel (312) 455-0300; fax (312) 666-NEWS (6397)

Chicago: *El Manana Daily News (Est. 1971)* — 2700 S. Harding Ave., (60623); Daily; 45,000pd (Est); $25.41; publisher Gorki C Tellez; editor Humberto Perrales; tel (312) 521-9137; fax (312) 521-5351

Chicago: *El Observador (The Observer) (Est. 1991) (Spanish)* — 9500 S. Commercial Ave., (60617); F; 15,000fr (Sw); $12.50; publisher & editor Gaspar Rojas; tel (312) 768-1622; fax (312) 768-9366

Chicago: *Extra Bilingual Community Newspapers (Est. 1980) (English/Spanish)* — 3918 W. North Ave., (60647); Th; 82pd, 37,944fr (VAC); $38.72; C; publisher Mila Tellez; general manager Steve Weimer; editor Mary Montgomery-Clifford; tel (312) 252-3534; fax (312) 252-6031

Chicago: *La Raza Newspaper (Est. 1970) (Spanish)* — 3909 N. Ashland Ave., (60613); Th; 13,062pd, 6,435fr (CAC); $60.00; publisher Luis Rossi; general manager Carlos Buitrago; editor Gabriela Bustamante; tel (312) 525-6285/9400; fax (312) 525-6449

Chicago: *The Lawndale News/Su Noticiero Bilingue (Est. 1940) (English/Spanish)* — 2300 S. Kedvale, (60623); Th; 150pd, 150,636fr (CVPS); $45.00; Su; 150pd, 29,340fr (CVPS); $45.00; publisher Lynda Nardini; general manager Robert Nardini; editor Hayley Carlton; tel (312) 762-2266; fax (312) 762-5076

Chicago: *Logan Square/Buckton Extra (Bilingual)* — 3918 W. North Ave., (60647); Th; (VAC); $38.72; publisher Mila Tellez; editor Miguel Alba; tel (312) 252-3534; fax (312) 252-6031

Chicago: *Northeast Extra (Bilingual)* — 3918 W. North Ave., (60647); W; 6,200fr (Est); $19.17; publisher Mila Tellez; editor Ricardo Vela; tel (312) 252-3534; fax (312) 252-6031

Chicago: *Northwest Extra (Est. 1980) (English/Spanish)* — 3918 W. North Ave., (60647); W; 12,265fr (Est); $38.72; publisher Mila Tellez; general manager Steve Weimer; tel (312) 252-3534; fax (312) 252-6031

Chicago: *Pilsen/Little Village/Lawndale Extra (Bilingual)* — 3918 W. North Ave., (60647); F; 2,330pd (Est); $8.65; publisher Mila Tellez; editor Ricardo Vela; tel (312) 252-3534; fax (312) 252-6031

Chicago: *Southwest Extra (Est. 1980) (English/Spanish)* — 3918 W. North Ave., (60647); Th; 12,365fr (Est); $39.72; publisher Mila Tellez; general manager Steve Weimer; tel (312) 252-3534; fax (312) 252-6031

Chicago: *Wicker Park/East Town Extra (Bilingual)* — 3918 W. North Ave., (60647); Th; (Est); publisher Mila Tellez; editor Mary Montgomery; tel (312) 252-3534; fax (312) 252-6031

Cicero: *Momento (Est. 1984) (Bilingual)* — 5600 W. Cermak Rd., (60650); Th; 30,000fr (Est); $17.50; publisher Carmen Aguilar; editor Julio C Montoya; tel (312) 522-0288

KANSAS

Garden City: *La Semana en el suroeste de Kansas (Est. 1991) (Spanish)* — 310 N. 7th, PO Box 958, (67846); Tu; 2,340fr (Sw); $3.50; publisher James E Bloom; editor Itzel Stewart; tel (316) 275-8500; fax (316) 275-5165

LOUISIANA

Metairie: *Aqui New Orleans (Est. 1987) (Bilingual)* — 4324 Veterans Blvd., Ste. 205, (70006); M; 20,000fr (Est); publisher & editor Amaury Almaguer; tel (504) 456-6122; fax (504) 456-6150

MASSACHUSETTS

Andover: *El Carillon (Est. 1991)* — PO Box 1868, (01810); Bi-Wkly Tu; 20,000pd (Est); publisher & editor Pablo Navarro; tel (508) 688-8889

Boston: *El Mundo (Est. 1972) (Spanish)* — 20 Columbia St., Cambridge (02139); Th; 27,000pd (Est); $1.21; C; publisher & editor Alberto Vasallo; tel (617) 876-4293; fax (617) 876-2132

Boston/Worcester/Lawrence/Chelsea/Rhode Island: *La Semana (Est. 1978) (Spanish/English)* — 911 Massachussetts Ave. (Boston 02118), PO Box 850, Dorchester (02125); Th; 9,667fr (CVPS); $21.00; publisher & editor Peter N Cuenca; tel (617) 541-2222; fax (617) 427-6227

NEVADA

Las Vegas: *El Mundo (Est. 1980) (Spanish)* — 845 N. Eastern Ave., (89101); Sa; 16,000fr (Est); $13.50; C; publisher Eddie Escobedo Sr; general manager Eddie Escobedo Jr; editor Frank Corro; managing editor Hector Soso; tel (702) 649-8553; fax (702) 649-7429

NEW JERSEY

Elizabeth: *La Voz (Est. 1976)* — 948 Elizabeth Ave., PO Box 140, (07201); Bi-Wkly; 38,000pd (Est); $9.00; publisher & editor Abel-Garcia Berry; tel (908) 352-6654; fax (908) 352-9735

Hudson Co.: *El Nuevo Hudson (Est. 1995) (Spanish)* — 30 Journal Sq., Jersey City (07306); W/Sa; 10,000pd (Est); $1.00; C; publisher Scott Ring; tel (201) 217-2478

Union City: *Continental Newspaper (Est. 1980) (Spanish)* — 503 47th St., (07087); Th; 38,000pd (Sw); $35.00; C; publisher Abeiardo Morva; general manager M Ofelia Dones; editor Mario Ciria Jr; managing editor Veronica Romero; tel (201) 864-9505; fax (201) 864-9456

Union City: *La Tribuna Publication Inc. (Est. 1962) (Spanish/English)* — 300 36th St., PO Box 805, (07087); Bi-Mthly; 53,000pd (Est); $16.80; publisher Ruth Molenaar; general manager Soraya Molenaar; editor Lionel Rodriquez; tel (201) 863-3310/(201) 617-1360; fax (201) 617-0042

NEW MEXICO

Albuquerque: *El Hispano News (Est. 1966) (Spanish)* — 900 Park Ave. S.W., PO Box 986, (87103); F; 5,771pd, 400fr (Sw); $10.00; C; publisher A B Collado; editor Sara Garcia; managing editor Francisco Collado; tel (505) 243-6161; fax (505) 842-5464

Espanola: *Rio Grande Sun (Est. 1956) (English)* — 238 N. Railroad, PO Box 790, (87532); Th; 10,602pd, 41fr (Sw); $6.35; publisher & editor Robert E Trapp; managing editor Robert B Trapp; tel (505) 753-2126; fax (505) 753-2140

Taos: *The Taos News (Est. 1959)* — 123 Camino de la Placitas, PO Box U, (87571); Th; 10,635pd (ABC); $10.95; publisher George Fellows; editor Deborah Ensor; tel (505) 758-2241; fax (505) 758-9647

NEW YORK

Franklin Square: *Nueva Americana (Est. 1993) (Spanish)* — 1145 Arlington Ave., (11010); W; 25,000fr (Sw); $11.50; publisher Margerita Chavez; editor Arturo Chavez; tel (516) 352-6009; fax (516) 352-5924

New York: *El Diario La Prensa (Est. 1913)* — 143-155 Varick St., (10013); Daily; 48,000pd (Sw); $35.75; C; publisher Carlos D Ramirez; editor Juan Garcia; tel (212) 807-4600; fax (212) 633-6201

New York: *Impacto (Est. 1968) (Spanish)* — 853 Broadway, Ste. 811, (10003); W; 57,500pd (Est); $34.46; C; publisher Carlos G Carrillo; editor Armando Bermudez; tel (212) 505-0288; fax (212) 598-9414

New York: *La Tribuna Hispana-NY/NJ (The Hispanic Tribune of NY and NJ) (Est. 1988) (Spanish)* — 19A W. Columbia St., Hempstead (11550), PO Box 801, Westbury (11590); Th; 2,000pd, 28,000fr (Sw); $15.50; C; publisher Emilio A Ruiz; general manager Diana Patino; editor Luis Aguilar; tel (516) 486-6457; fax (516) 292-3972

New York: *La Voz Hispana (The Hispanic Voice) (Est. 1976)* — 159 E. 116th St., (10029); Th; 60,000pd, 5,000fr (Est); $1.65; publisher Nick Lugo Jr; editor J Del Rio; tel (212) 348-8200

New York: *Noticias del Mundo (Est. 1980)* — 401 5th Ave., (10016); Daily; 24,714pd, 314fr (Est); $25.48; publisher Phillip Sanchez; editor Jose Cardinali; tel (212) 684-5656; fax (212) 889-0024

Woodside: *Resumen Newspaper (Est. 1971) (Spanish)* — 69-08 Roosevelt Ave., (11377-2934); publisher Fernando F Rojas; general manager Jasmina Abria; editor Fernando J Rojas; managing editor Jose Romero Jr; tel (718) 899-8603; fax (718) 899-7616

PENNSYLVANIA

Upper Darby: *El Hispano (Est. 1976) (Spanish)* — 8605 Westchester Pike, (19082); Th; 1,200pd, 30,800fr (Sw); $28.00; publisher & managing editor Aaron G Lopez; editor Sara Lopez; tel (610) 789-5512; fax (610) 789-5524

TEXAS

Amarillo: *El Mensajero (Est. 1989) (Spanish)* — 814 S. Lamar, PO Box 895, (79105); Tu; 200pd, 15,000fr (CVPS); $10.53; publisher El Mensajero Inc.; editor Dr Ramon Godoy; tel (806) 371-7084; fax (806) 371-7090

Brownsfield: *The Brownsville Herald (Est. 1934) (English/Spanish)* — 1135 E. Van Buren, PO Box 351, Brownsville (78522); Daily; 17,657pd (Est); $5.87; publisher Douglas Hardie; editor Lavice Laney; tel (210) 542-4301

Carrizo Springs: *Javelin (Est. 1884) (English)* — 604 N. 1st St., PO Box 188, (78834); Th; 3,000pd (Est); $3.50; publisher George Willems; editor John Willems; tel (210) 876-2318; fax (210) 876-2620

Corpus Christi: *La Verdad (Est. 1942)* — 910 Francesca St., (78405); publisher Santos de la Paz; editor Samuel Kelson

Dallas: *El Sol de Texas (Est. 1966) (Spanish)* — 4210 Spring Valley Rd. (75244), PO Box 803402, (75380-3402); Th; 500pd, 26,000fr (Est); $15.00; C; publisher Charles D Orten; publisher & editor Rogelio I Santillan; general manager Charles Orten; tel (214) 386-9120; fax (214) 386-7125

Dallas/Ft. Worth: *El Heraldo News (Est. 1992) (Spanish)* — 2995 LBJ Fwy., Ste.218, Dallas (75234); F; 22,000fr (Est); $15.00; publisher Jose Torres Jr; general manager Consuelo Torres; editor Jesus Padilla; tel (214) 484-9901; fax (214) 484-9902

Ft. Worth: *El Informador Hispano (Est. 1987) (Spanish)* — 3100 N. Main, PO Box 163661, (76161); F; 850pd, 29,150fr (Sw); $15.00; publisher Frederick L Garcia; general manager Elida Lopez; editor Orestes Galleguillos; tel (817) 626-8624; fax (817) 626-1855

Houston: *Semana Newspaper (The Week) (Est. 1993) (Spanish)* — 6802 Bintliff Dr. (77074), PO Box 742149, (77274-2149); W; 125,000fr (Sw); $37.00; publisher Mario G Duenas; editor Raul Alonso; tel (713) 774-4652, (713) 774-4666; fax (713) 774-4666

Laredo: *El Tiempo de Laredo (Est. 1926) (English)* — 111 Esperanza, PO Box 2129,

(78041); Su; 20,000pd (Est); $17.35; Tu; 20,000pd (Est); $14.80; publisher Bill Green; editor Odie Arambula; tel (210) 728-2500; fax (210) 724-3036

Lubbock/Midland/Odessa: *El Editor-Lubbock (Est. 1977) (English/Spanish)* — 1502 Ave. "M", PO Box 11250, Lubbock (79408); Th; 15,000fr (Sw); $16.00; C; publisher & editor Bidal Aguero; general manager Olga Riojas-Aquero; managing editor Olga Riojas-Aguero; tel (806) 763-3841; fax (806) 741-1110

McAllen: *El Periodico USA (Est. 1986) (Spanish)* — 4200 N. Bicentennial Dr., (78504); W; 1,000pd, 113,000fr (Est); $30.00; publisher & editor Jose Luis B Garza; tel (210) 631-5628; fax (210) 631-0832

Midland: *Nueva Vista (Est. 1990) (Spanish/English)* — 201 E. Illinois, PO Box 1650, (79701); Th; 23,596pd (Est); $12.50; C; publisher Charles A Spence; general manager J R Ruiz; tel (915) 682-5311; fax (915) 6823793

Midland: *El Editor Permian Basin (Est. 1977) (English/Spanish)* — 1401 Rankin Hwy., (79701); W; 6,180pd, 4,200fr (Sw); $16.00; C; publisher & editor Manuel J Orona; general manager Kim Gomez; managing editor Bidal Aguero; tel (915) 570-0405; fax (915) 687-3972

Presido: *The International Presido Paper (Spanish)* — PO Box Y, (79845-1245); Th; 1,000pd (Sw); $2.60; publisher & editor Robert Halpern; general manager & managing editor Rosario Salgado-Halpern; tel (915) 729-4342; fax (915) 729-4601

Roma: *Roma Star (Est. 1995) (English/Spanish)* — PO Box 3008, (78584); W; 1,623pd, 350fr (Est); $3.00; C; publisher Bob McVey; general manager Irma Martinez; editor Kate McVey; tel (210) 849-7403; fax (210) 765-9058

San Antonio: *La Prensa De San Antonio (Est. 1989) (English/Spanish)* — 113 Lexington Ave., (78205); F; 4,640pd, 57,360fr (Sw); $18.00; publisher Tino Duran; general manager Robert Sanchez; editor Frank Alvarez; managing editor Rolando Romero; tel (210) 242-7900; fax (210) 242-7901

JEWISH NEWSPAPERS PUBLISHED IN THE UNITED STATES

ARIZONA

Phoenix: *Jewish News of Greater Phoenix (Est. 1948)* — 1625 E. Northern Ave., Ste. 106; PO Box 26590 (85068); F; 5,106pd, 785fr (Sw); $24.00; publisher & editor Florence Eckstein; tel (602) 870-9470; fax (602) 870-0426

CALIFORNIA

Los Angeles: *B'nai B'rith Messenger (Est. 1897)* — 2510 W. Pico Blvd.; PO Box 35915 (90035); F; 67,000pd, 250fr (Est); $4.03; publisher A L Butler; tel (213) 487-7514

Los Angeles: *Central California Jewish Heritage* — 2130 S. Vermont Ave. (90007); Mthly; 13,500pd (Est); $16.00; publisher Herb Brin; editor Dan Brin; tel (213) 737-2122; fax (213) 737-1021

Los Angeles: *Heritage Southwest Jewish Press (Est. 1914)* — 2130 S. Vermont Ave. (90007); F; 13,500pd (Sw); $16.50; publisher Herb Brin; editor Dan Brin; tel (213) 737-2122; fax (213) 737-1021

Los Angeles: *The Jewish Journal of Greater Los Angeles (Est. 1986)* — 3660 Wilshire Blvd., Ste. 204 (90010); F; 52,822pd, 750fr (Sw); $37.65; publisher Ed Brennglass; editor Gene Lichtenstein; managing editor Marlene Marks; tel (213) 738-7778; fax (213) 386-9501

Los Angeles: *Orange County Jewish Heritage* — 2130 S. Vermont Ave. (90007); F; 13,500pd (Est); $16.00; publisher Herb Brin; editor Dan Brin; tel (213) 737-2122; fax (213) 737-1021

Los Angeles: *San Diego Jewish Press Heritage* — 2130 S. Vermont Ave. (90007); F; 13,500pd (Est); $16.00; publisher Herb Brin; editor Dan Brin; tel (213) 737-2122; fax (213) 737-1021

San Diego: *San Diego Jewish Times (Est. 1979)* — 4731 Palm Ave. (91941-3519); PO Box 3619, La Mesa (91944); Bi-Wkly F; 15,153pd, 499fr (Sw); $32.00; publisher Garry L Rosenberg; editor Carol A Rosenberg; tel (619) 463-5515

San Francisco: *Jewish Bulletin of Northern California (Est. 1946)* — 225 Bush St., Ste. 1480 (94104); F; 25,083pd, 581fr (Sw); $28.25; publisher & editor Marc S Klein; general manager Nora Contini; managing editor Sherwood Weingarten; tel (415) 263-7200; fax (415) 263-7222

COLORADO

Denver: *Intermountain Jewish News Inc. (Est. 1913)* — 1275 Sherman St., Ste. 214 (80203-2299); F; 50,000pd (Sw); $38.34; publisher Miriam Goldberg; editor Rabbi Hiller Goldberg; managing editor Larry Hankin; tel (303) 861-2234; fax (303) 832-6942

CONNECTICUT

W Hartford: *Connecticut Jewish Ledger* — 740 N. Main St. (06117); F; 30,000pd, 110fr (Est); $39.00; publisher NRG Connecticut Ltd. Partnership; editor Jonathan S Tobin; tel (860) 231-2424; fax (860) 231-2428

DELAWARE

Delaware: *The Jewish Voice* — 100 W. 10th St., Ste. 301, Wilmington (19801-1645); F; 3,200pd, 1,000fr (Est); $7.00; C; publisher The Jewish Federation of Delaware; editor Daniel Weintraub; tel (302) 427-2100; fax (302) 427-2438

FLORIDA

Ft. Lauderdale: *Hi-Riser (Est. 1965)* — 601 Fairway Dr.; PO Box 1189, Deerfield Beach (33441); Th; 9pd, 18,923fr (VAC); $18.45; publisher Scott Patterson; editors Kevin Brady & Steven Reiskind; managing editor Richard Haydan; tel (305) 698-6397; fax (305) 429-1207

Ft. Lauderdale: *Jewish Journal Broward (North-JA) (Est. 1978)* — 601 Fairway Dr.; PO Box 1189, Deerfield Beach (33441); W; 26pd, 22,040fr (VAC); $24.17; C; publisher Bruce Warshal; editor Andrew Polin; managing editor Alan Goch; tel (954) 698-6501; fax (954) 429-1207

Miami: *Jewish Journal, Dade (Est. 1978)* — 601 Fairway Dr.; PO Box 1189, Deerfield Beach (33441); F; 24pd, 20,123fr (VAC); $26.50; C; publisher Rabbi Bruce S Warshal; editor Andrew Polin; managing editor Alan Goch; tel (954) 698-6397; fax (954) 429-1207

Miami: *Miami Hi-Riser (Est. 1995)* — 601 Fairway Dr.; PO Box 1189, Deerfield Beach (33441); Tu; 25,000fr (Est); $17.50; publisher Scott Patterson; editors Kevin Brady & Steven Reiskind; managing editor Richard Haydan; tel (954) 698-6501; fax (954) 698-6719

Palm Beach: *Jewish Journal Palm Beach North* — 601 Fairway Dr.; PO Box 1189, Deerfield Beach (33441); Tu; 15pd, 22,930fr (VAC); $25.88; C; publisher Bruce Warshal; editor Andrew Polin; managing editor Alan Goch; tel (945) 698-6397; fax (945) 429-1207

Palm Beach: *Jewish Journal Palm Beach South* — 601 Fairway Dr.; PO box 1189, Deerfield Beach (33441); Tu; 21,870fr (VAC); $25.88; C; publisher Rabbi Bruce S Warshal; general manager Jan Giglio; editor Andrew Polin; managing editor Alan Goch; tel (954) 698-6501; fax (954) 429-1207

GEORGIA

Atlanta: *Atlanta Jewish Times (Est. 1925)* — 1575 Northside Dr. N.W., Ste. 470 (30318); F; 8,717pd, 348fr (Est); $21.00; C; publisher Daniel Chovenac; editor Neil Rubin; tel (404) 352-2400; fax (404) 355-9388

ILLINOIS

Chicago: *JUF (Jewish United Fund)* — 1 S. Franklin St., Ste. 722 (60606); Mthly; 55,000pd (Est); $1.85; publisher Jewish United Fund; editor Joseph Aaron; tel (312) 346-6700; fax (312) 855-2470

INDIANA

Indianapolis: *The Indiana Jewish Post & Opinion* — 2120 N. Meridian St. (46202); W; 4,325pd (Est); $12.00; publisher Gabriel Cohen; editor Ed Stattmann; tel (317) 927-7800; fax (317) 927-7807

Indianapolis: *National Jewish Post & Opinion (Est. 1932)* — 2120 N. Meridian St. (46202); W; 17,965pd (Est); $16.80; publisher & editor Gabriel Cohen; managing editor Ed Stattman; tel (317) 927-7800; fax (317) 927-7807

KANSAS

Overland Park: *Kansas City Jewish Chronicle (Est. 1920)* — 7373 W. 107th St. (62212); F; 10,000pd (Sw); $30.80; publisher & editor Steve Rose; tel (913) 648-4620

KENTUCKY

Louisville: *The Kentucky Jewish Post & Opinion* — 1551 Bardstown Rd (40205); W; 3,910pd (Est); $8.00; publisher Gabriel Cohen; editor Julie D Segal; tel (502) 459-1914; fax (502) 459-1915

MARYLAND

Baltimore: *Jewish Times (Est. 1919)* — 2104 N. Charles (21218); F; 20,000pd (Sw); $30.00; C; publishers Charles A Buerger & Susan A Patchen; editor Michael Davis; tel (410) 752-3504; fax (410) 539-0882

MASSACHUSETTS

Boston: *The Boston Jewish Times (Est. 1945)* — 15 School St. (02108); Th; 1,400pd, 209fr (Est); $6.00; publisher Rabbi Dr Yitzchok Aharon Korff; managing editor Frank C Scott; tel (617) 367-9100; fax (617) 367-9310

Boston: *The Jewish Advocate (Est. 1902)* — 15 School St. (02108); F; 26,500pd, 2,500fr (Est); $25.50; publisher Rabbi Dr Yitzchok Aharon Korff; managing editor Frank C Scott; tel (617) 367-9100; fax (617) 367-9310

Boston: *Zion's Herald* — 566 Commonwealth Ave., United Methodist Center (02115); F; 6,500fr (Sw); $7.00; publisher Boston Wesleyan Association; tel (617) 266-3900

Springfield: *Jewish Weekly Press (Est. 1945)* — 85-A Mill St; PO Box 1569 (01101); Th; 1,350pd, 1,200fr (Sw); $11.00; publishers Gail Glickman White & Kenneth Glickman White; tel (413) 739-4771

MICHIGAN

Southfield: *The Detroit Jewish News (Est. 1942)* — 27676 Franklin Rd. (48034); F; 19,066pd, 414fr (Sw); $28.00; C; publisher Arthur Horwitz; editor Phil Jacobs; tel (810) 354-6060; fax (810) 354-6069

MINNESOTA

Minneapolis: *American Jewish World (Est. 1912)* — 4509 Minnetonka Blvd. (55416); F; 6,000pd (Sw); $15.00; publisher Rabbi Marc Liebhaber; editor Marshall Hoffman; tel (612) 920-7000; fax (602) 920-6205

MISSOURI

St. Louis: *Saint Louis Jewish Light (Est. 1963)* — 12 Millstone Campus Dr. (63146); W; 14,800pd (Sw); $16.00; publisher Robert Cohn; editor Linda Matz Mantle; tel (314) 432-3353; fax (314) 432-0515

NEBRASKA

Omaha: *Jewish Press (Est. 1920)* — 333 S. 132nd St. (68154); F; 3,700pd (Est); 95¢; publisher Jewish Federation of Omaha; editor Morris Maline; tel (402) 334-8200; fax (402) 334-5422

NEW JERSEY

Pleasantville: *The Jewish Record (Est. 1939)* — 1525 S. Main St. (08232); F; 10,500pd (Sw); $9.80; publisher Martin Korik; tel (609) 383-0999

Teaneck: *Jewish Standard (Est. 1935)* — 1086 Teaneck Rd. (07666); F; 18,000pd (Sw); publisher James Janoff; editor Rebecca Boroson; tel (201) 837-8818

Westfield: *Jewish Horizon* — 812 Central Ave. (07090); Th; 13,000pd (Sw); editor Fran Gold; tel (908) 654-0077

Whippany: *Metrowest Jewish News (Est. 1947)* — 901 Rte. 10 (07981-1157); Th; 25,000pd, 1,000fr (Est); $31.45; publisher Susan B Milberg; general manager Amir Cohen; editor David Twersky; managing editor Debra Rubin; tel (201) 887-3900; fax (201) 887-4152

NEW YORK

Albany: *The Jewish World (Est. 1965)* — 1104 Central Ave. (12205); Th/F; 3,456pd, 319fr (Sw); $9.94; publisher Sam S Clevenson; editor Laurie J Clevenson; tel (518) 459-8455; fax (518) 459-5289

Brooklyn: *Der Yid* — 13 Hooper St. (11211); Th; 38,000pd, 2,400fr (Est); $12.00; publisher Der Yid Publication Association; editors Aron Friedman & Rabbi Sender Deutsch; tel (718) 797-3900; fax (718) 797-1985

Brooklyn: *The Jewish Press (Est. 1961)* — 338 3rd Ave. (11215-1897); F; 92,167pd, 15,587fr (Est); $84.00; publisher Rabbi Sholom Klass; editor Arnold Fine; tel (718) 330-1100; fax (718) 935-1215

Brooklyn: *Tablet (Est. 1908)* — 653 Hicks St. (11231); Sa; 85,003pd, 1,420fr (ABC); $1.75; publisher The Tablet Publishing Co. Inc.; tel (718) 858-3838; fax (800) 486-3838

Buffalo: *Buffalo Jewish Review (Est. 1918)* — 15 E. Mohawk St. (14203); F; 4,200pd (Sw); $9.80; publisher Arnold Weiss; editor Harlan C Abbey; tel (716) 854-2192

Great Neck: *Jewish Tribune of Rockland County* — 115 Middle Neck Rd. (11021); Th; 14,000pd (Est); $12.00; publisher Jerome W Lippman; editor Naomi Lippman; tel (516) 829-4000; fax (516) 829-4776

Great Neck: *Long Island Jewish World* — 115 Middle Neck Rd. (11021); F; 32,063pd (Sw); $24.00; publisher Jerome W Lippman; editor Naomi Lippman; tel (516) 829-4000

New York: *The Brooklyn Jewish Week* — 1501 Broadway (10036); F; 13,431pd, 162fr (Est); $92.00; publisher Gary Rosenblatt; tel (212) 921-7822

New York: *Haddoar (Post) (Est. 1921)* — 47 W. 34th St., Ste. 609 (10001-3012); F; 3,500pd (Est); $1.20; publisher Haddar Association, Inc.; editor Shlomo Shamir; tel (212) 629-9443; fax (212) 629-9472

New York: *Jewish Forward* — 45 E. 33rd St. (10016); F; 10,000pd (Est); $2.00; publisher Forward Association Inc.; general manager Harold Ostroff; editor Mordecai Strigler; tel (212) 889-8200

New York: *Jewish Telegraphic Agency Community News Reporter* — 330 7th Ave., 11th Fl. (10001-5010); F; N/A; publisher Jewish Telegraphic Agency Inc.; tel (212) 643-1890; fax (212) 643-8498

New York: *Jewish Telegraphic Agency Daily News Bulletin* — 330 7th Ave., 11th Fl. (10001-5010); Daily; N/A; publisher Jewish Telegraphic Agency Inc.; tel (212) 643-1890; fax (212) 643-8498

New York: *Jewish Telegraphic Agency Weekly News Digest*—330 7th Ave., 11th Fl. (10001-5010); F; 2,523pd, 50fr (Est); N/A; publisher Mark J Joffe; editor Lisa Hostein; managing editor Kenneth Bandler; tel (212) 643-1890; fax (212) 643-8498

New York: *The Jewish Week* — 1501 Broadway, Ste. 505 (10036); F; 84,888pd, 15,560fr (ABC); $92.00; publisher & editor Gary Rosenblatt; managing editor Robert Goldblum; tel (212) 921-7822; fax (212) 921-8420

New York: *The Long Island Jewish Week* — 1501 Broadway (10036); F; 21,966pd, 259fr (Est); $92.00; publisher Gary Rosenblatt; tel (212) 921-7822

New York: *The Queens Jewish Week* — 1501 Broadway (10036); F; 15,753pd, 116fr (Est); $92.00; publisher Gary Rosenblatt; tel (212) 921-7822

New York: *The Westchester Jewish Week* — 1501 Broadway (10036); F; 15,661pd, 192fr (Est); $92.00; publisher Gary Rosenblatt; tel (212) 921-7822

New York: *Yiddisher Kemfer (Est. 1906)*—275 7th Ave. (10001-6708); F; 3,000pd (Est); $5.00; publisher Labor Zionist Letters Inc.; editor Mordecai Strigler; tel (212) 675-7808

Vly. Stream: *Jewish Journal (Est. 1969)*—210 E. Sunrise Hwy., Ste. 304 (11581); F; 47,000pd, 33,000fr (Sw); $1.40; publisher Harold Singer; tel (516) 561-6900; fax (516) 561-6971

NORTH CAROLINA

Charlotte: *Star of Zion* — 401 E. 2nd St.; PO Box 31005 (28231); Th; 8,000pd, 200fr (Sw); $10.00; C; publisher AMEZ Publishing House; general manager Anthony Brown; editor Dr. Morgan W Tann; managing editor Dr Marie P Tann; tel (704) 377-4329; fax (704) 377-2809

OHIO

Cincinnati: *The American Israelite (Est. 1854)* — 906 Main St., Ste. 505 (45202); Th; 6,800pd (Sw); publisher Millard Mack; tel (513) 621-3145

Cleveland: *The Cleveland Jewish News (Est. 1964)*—3645 Warrensville Ctr. Rd. (44122); F; 16,000pd, 500fr (Sw); $23.00; publisher Harry Scharp; editor Cynthia Dettelback; managing editor Ellen Harris; tel (216) 991-8300; fax (216) 991-9556

Columbus: *Ohio Jewish Chronicle (Est. 1921)* — 2862 Johnstown Rd. (43219); PO Box 30965 (43230); Th; 2,481pd, 322fr (Sw); $8.25; publisher Stephen Pinsky; managing editor Judith P Franklin; tel (614) 337-2055; fax (614) 337-2059

Dayton: *Dayton Jewish Chronicle (Est. 1962)*—6929 N. Main St. (45415); Th; 2,000pd (Sw); $7.50; publisher & editor Leslie Cohen Zukowsky; tel (513) 278-0783; fax (513) 223-5687

OREGON

Portland: *The Jewish Review* — 6800 S.W. Beavertown-Hillsdale Hwy., Ste. C (97225); Semi-Mthly; 7,000pd (Sw); $10.80; publisher Jewish Federation of Portland; tel (503) 292-4913

PENNSYLVANIA

Huntingdon Vly.: *Jewish Times (Est. 1927)* — 103 A Tomlinson Rd. (19006); Th; 32,500pd, 1,000fr (Est); $24.95; publisher Jewish Federation of Greater Philadelphia; general manager Jerry Parishy; editor Matthew Schuman; tel (215) 938-1177; fax (215) 938-0692

Philadelphia: *Jewish Exponent (Est. 1887)* — 226 S. 16th St. (19102); F; 62,000pd (ABC); $47.15; publisher & editor Al Erlick; tel (215) 893-5700; fax (215) 546-3957

Pittsburgh: *The Jewish Chronicle (Est. 1962)*—5600 Baum Blvd. (15206); Th; 12,000pd (Est); $12.10; Th; 19,000pd (Est); N/A; publisher & editor Romuald Waszkielewicz; general manager Barbara Befferman; editor Joel Roteman; managing editor Iris Samson; tel (412) 687-1000; fax (412) 687-5119

TENNESSEE

Memphis: *Hebrew Watchman* — 4646 Poplar Ave., Ste. 232 (38117); Th; 17,000fr (Sw); $13.00; Th; 3,000pd (Sw); $60.00; publishers & editors Herman I Goldberger & Kathleen B Castro; tel (901) 763-2215

TEXAS

Dallas: *Texas Jewish Post (Est. 1947)*—11333 N. Central Expwy., Ste. 213 (75243); Mthly; 3,000pd (Est); $3.50; Th; 4,188pd, 355fr (Est); $23.08; publisher & editor Jimmy Wisch; editor Stephen P Kopestonsky; tel (817) 927-2831; fax (817) 429-0840

Houston: *Jewish Herald-Voice (Est. 1908)* — PO Box 153 (77001-0153); Th; 6,852pd, 100fr (Est); $22.00; publisher Joseph W Samuels; editor Jeanne F Samuels; tel (713) 630-0391; fax (713) 630-0404

WASHINGTON

Seattle: *Jewish Transcript (Est. 1924)*—2031 3rd Ave., Ste. 200 (98121); Semi-Mthly; 3,667pd, 312fr (Sw); $15.70; publisher Jewish Federation of Greater Seattle; general manager Karen Chachkes; editor Craig Degginger; tel (206) 441-4553; fax (206) 441-2736

WISCONSIN

Milwaukee: *The Wisconsin Jewish Chronicle (Est. 1921)* — 1360 Prospect Ave. (53202); F; 3,119pd, 2,115fr (Est); $13.80; publisher Milwaukee Jewish Federation; tel (414) 271-2992; fax (414) 271-0487

MILITARY NEWSPAPERS PUBLISHED IN THE UNITED STATES

ALABAMA

Ft. McClellan (Army): *McClellan News* — Bldg. 51, Buckner Cir., Ft. McClellan (36205-5000); W; 7,500fr (Est); $7.25; publisher Jacksonville News; publisher Julia Brock; editor Sgt Paul McGuire; tel (205) 848-5574/3643; fax (205) 848-6169

Ft. Rucker: *Army Flier* — Fort Rucker; PO Box 1140, Enterprise (36331); F; 10,000fr (Sw); $8.53; C; publisher Mark Cullen; editor Maj Steve Eisenhart; tel (334) 347-9533; fax (334) 347-0825

Maxwell-Gunther AFB: *Maxwell-Gunther Dispatch*—152 W. 3rd St.; PO Drawer C, Prattville (36067); F; 13,500fr (Est); $18.76; publisher The Advertiser Co.; publisher Lamar Smitherman; editor Sgt William Dunlap; tel (205) 365-6739; fax (205) 365-1400

Redstone Arsenal (Army): *Redstone Rocket* — 3311 Bob Wallace Ave., Ste. 102, Huntsville (35805); W; 18,000fr (Est); publisher Sara Grant; tel (205) 539-9828; fax (205) 539-9866

ALASKA

North Pole: *Goldpanner* — PO Box 55757 (99705); F; 3,600fr (Est); publisher Rick Corsi; tel (907) 488-0669

ARIZONA

Ft. Huachuca (Army): *Huachuca Scout* — 200 E. Wilcox Dr., Sierra Vista (85635); Th; 13,700fr (Est); publisher Five Star Publishing; publisher Roxanne Prusia; tel (602) 458-3340; fax (602) 458-9938

Luke AFB: *Tallyho* — 7122 N. 59th Ave.; PO Box 7 (85311), Glendale (85301); F; 500pd, 10,000fr (Est); $7.00; C; publisher Pueblo Publishers Inc.; general manager William E Toops; tel (602) 842-6000; fax (602) 842-6017

Yuma MCAS (Marine): *Cactus Comet* — PO Box 271, Yuma (85364); Th; 3,000fr (Est); $6.92; C; publisher Sun Printing Co.; publisher Samuel J Pepper; tel (520) 726-3333; fax (520) 343-1009

ARKANSAS

Little Rock AFB: *Air Scoop* — C/O Arkansas Democrat Gazette, Capitol & Sts. (72201); PO Box 2221, Little Rock (72203); F; 11,000fr (Est); $8.50; publisher Wehco Commercial Printing; general manager Marleen Eddleman; tel (501) 378-3582; fax (501) 399-3663

CALIFORNIA

Alameda NAS: *Carrier* — 2411 S. Old Crow Canyon Rd., San Ramon (94583); F; 10,000fr (Est); N/A; publisher Coast Publishing; publisher Mike Digulla; tel (415) 838-7933

Camarillo/Oxnard/Ventura: *Seabee Coverall* — 2864 Sailor Ave.; PO Box 2970, Ventura (93002-2970); Bi-Wkly/F; 8,000fr (Est); $7.90; publisher Jill E Holden; general manager Martha Garcia; editor & managing editor Doris Lance; tel (805) 642-4008; fax (805) 642-6530

Camarillo/Oxnard/Ventura: *Missile* — 43424 Copeland Cir., Ste. D, Lancaster (93535); Th; 8,000fr (Est); $7.50; C; publisher Jill E Holden; editor Pat Hollenbaugh; tel (805) 945-5634; fax (805) 723-7757

Camp Pendleton (Marine): *Scout*—1722 S. Hill St., Oceanside (92054); Th; 30,000fr (Est); publisher Southcoast Newspapers Inc.; publisher Tony Pallotto; tel (619) 433-7333

Coronado NAB (Navy): *Gator* — 1224 10th St.; PO Box 8, Coronado (92118); F; 3,000fr (Est); publisher Coronado Journal; publisher Pat Cavanaugh; tel (619) 435-3141; fax (619) 435-3051

Edwards AFB: *Desert Wings*—43424 Copeland Cir., Ste. D (93535); PO Box 1332, Lancaster (93584); F; 10,000fr (Est); $11.55; C; publisher Aerotech News; publisher Paul J Kinison; editor TSgt True Carr USAF; tel (805) 945-5634; fax (805) 723-7757

El Centro NAF: *Sandpaper* — PO Box 278, Jacumba (92034); Bi-Wkly/F; 1,100fr (Est); publisher David Alvernaz; tel (619) 766-4785

El Toro MCAS (Marine): *Flight Jacket*—23811 Via Fabricante, Mission Viejo (92691); F; 13,000fr (Est); publisher Golden West Publ.; publisher Ray Ellis; tel (714) 768-3631

Fleet Reserve Assn BR 9: *Fantail Report*—1224 10th St.; PO Box 8, Coronado (92118); Mthly/Th; 5,000fr (Est); publisher Coronado Journal; publisher Pat Cavanaugh; tel (619) 435-3141; fax (619) 435-3051

Ft. Irwin: *Tiefort Telegraph* — Bldg. 983, Inner Loop Rd. (92310); F; 6,500fr (Est); $7.95; publisher Cmd Gen Paul Kinison; editor Sgt James Thompson; tel (619) 380-4511; fax (619) 380-4511

Lompoc: *Space & Missile Times* — 115 N. "H" St.; PO Box 578 (93438) (93436); F; 8,467fr (Est); $13.55; C; publisher The Lompoc Record; publisher Ron Hoffer; managing editor SSgt Timothy Hoffman; tel (805) 736-2313; fax (805) 736-5654

March AFB: *Beacon* — 3512 14th St., Riverside (92501); F; 7,500fr (Est); publisher The Press Enterprise; publisher Don Brower; tel (714) 782-7701

Mare Is. Naval Shipyard: *Grapevine*—440 Curtola Pkwy., Vallejo (94590); publisher Vallejo Times Herald; publisher Ron Rhea; tel (707) 644-1141

Marine Corps: *Observation Post* — 56445 29 Palms Hwy.; PO Box 880, Yucca Valley (92286); F; 8,600fr (Sw); $12.25; C; publisher Hi-Desert Publisher; publisher Hal J Paradis; tel (619) 365-3315; fax (619) 365-2650

NAS Moffett Field: *Moffett News*—2411 S. Old Crow Canyon Rd., San Ramon (94583); Th; 8,000fr (Est); publisher Composite Graphics; publisher Mike Digulla; tel (510) 838-7933

Nav. Res. Readiness Comm.: *Ready Now*—1224 10th St.; PO Box 8, Coronado (92118); Mthly/F; 5,000fr (Est); publisher Coronado Journal; publisher Pat Cavanaugh; tel (619) 435-3141; fax (619) 435-3051

Naval Station San Diego: *Signal Bridge*—1025 Rosecrans St., San Diego (92106); F; 28,000fr (Est); publisher West Coast Community Newspapers; tel (619) 226-8501; fax (619) 226-0573

N Island NAS: *North Islander*—1224 10th St.; PO Box 8, Coronado (92118); Mthly/F; 10,000fr (Est); publisher Coronado Journal; publisher Pat Cavanaugh; tel (619) 435-3141; fax (619) 435-3051

Ridgecrest (Navy): *Rocketeer* — 224 E. Ridgecrest Blvd.; PO Box 7, Ridgecrest (93555); Bi-Wkly/Th; 9,500fr (Est); publisher Steve Boster; editor Barry McDonald; tel (619) 939-3354; fax (619) 939-2796

San Diego: *Compass*—615 Murray Canyon Rd., Ste. 805 (92108); F; 56,000fr (Sw); $25.00; publisher Southcoast Newspapers Inc.; publisher Jim Missett; tel (619) 682-7200; fax (619) 439-8430

San Diego SB NTC (Navy): *Hoist* — 1224 10th St.; PO Box 8, Coronado (92118); F; 6,000fr (Est); publisher Coronado Journal; publisher Heidi Benson; tel (619) 435-3141; fax (619) 435-3051

COLORADO

Lowry AFB: *Lowry Airman*—7380 Lowell Blvd.; PO Box 215, Westminster (80030); F; 14,500fr (Est); publisher Aurora Pub. Co.; publisher Roy Robinson; tel (303) 426-6000

Peterson AFB: *Space Observer* — 22 N. Sierra Madre Ave., Colorado Springs (80903); Th; 7,500fr (Est); $9.00; publisher Gowdy-Printcraft Press Inc.; publisher John Bernheim; editor Kathy Pulverante; tel (719) 634-1593; fax (719) 632-0762

CONNECTICUT

New London SB (Navy): *Dolphin* — 120 N. Fair St., Guilford (06437); Th; 20,000fr (Est); publisher Shoreline Newspapers; publisher John C Peterson; tel (203) 453-2711

DELAWARE

Dover AFB: *The Airlifter* — PO Box 737, Dover (19903); F; 7,000fr (Est); $6.30; publisher Delaware St. News; publisher Tamra Brittingham; editor TSgt Russ Maheras; tel (302) 674-3600; fax (302) 674-4752

FLORIDA

Cecil Field (Navy): *Airwinger* — PO Box 111, N.A.S. Cecil Field (32215-0111); Th; 7,000fr (Est); publisher ADD Inc.; publisher Regina Hodges; tel (904) 778-6055; fax (904) 778-5833

Coastal Systems (Navy): *Coastal Courier* — 501 W. 11th St. (32401); PO Box 1940, Panama City (32402); Bi-Wkly/F; 3,500fr (Sw); $5.40; publisher Karen Hanes; editor Ken Hoffman; tel (904) 387-3566; fax (904) 763-4636

Eglin AFB: *Eglin Eagle* — 2101 W. Government St., Pensacola (32501); F; 16,500fr (CAC); $14.50; publisher PEC Printing & Publishing; editor SSgt Mike Spaits; tel (904) 438-5421; fax (904) 434-2785

Hurlburt Field (AFB): *Commando* — PO Box 2949, Ft. Walton Beach (32549); F; 5,500fr (Est); publisher NW Florida Daily News; publisher Marvin Debolt; tel (904) 863-1111

Kings Bay NSB: *Kings Bay Periscope* — 4511 Lexington Ave., Jacksonville (33210); F; 10,310fr (Sw); $6.50; publisher Ultra Type; publisher Ellen S Rykert; editor Joc Stacy Byington; tel (904) 389-4293; fax (904) 389-2234

Copyright ©1996 by the Editor & Publisher Co.

Macdill AFB: *Thunderbolt* — 1401 Oakfield Dr., Brandon (33511-4654); F; 8,800fr (Est); $11.15; publisher Sunbelt Newspapers Inc.; general manager Carla Rockwell; editors Lorrenda D Thorton & Shelly R Boedicker; tel (813) 689-7764; fax (813) 689-9545

Mayport Naval Station: *The Mirror* — PO Box 280032, Naval Station, Mayport (32228-0032); F; 9,650fr (Sw); $8.23; publisher The Beaches Leader Inc.; publisher Tom Wood; editor Hal Newsome; tel (904) 270-5226; fax (904) 270-5329

NAS Pensacola: *Gosport* — 2101 W. Government St., Pensacola (32501); F; 14,500fr (CAC); $16.50; publisher PEC Printing & Publishing; editor Art Giberson; tel (904) 438-5421; fax (904) 434-2785

NAS Whiting Field: *Whiting Tower* — 2101 W. Government St.; PO Box 1232, Pensacola (32501); F; 3,500fr (CAC); $7.50; publisher PEC Printing & Publishing; publisher John Thompson; editor Kay Frank; tel (904) 438-5421; fax (904) 434-2785

Orlando Naval Tr. Center: *The Navigator* — 1405 Poinsettia Dr., Ste. G-5, Delray Beach (33444-1250); Th; 22,500fr (Est); publisher SGS Publications; publisher Doug Bose; tel (407) 872-1870

Patrick AFB/Cape Can. AFS: *Missileer* — PO Box 419000, Melbourne (32941-9000); F; 8,200fr (Est); $6.30; publisher Mike Coleman; editor Harry McNamara; tel (407) 242-3846; fax (407) 242-6618

Tyndall AFB: *Gulf Defender* — 501 W. 11th St. (32401); PO Box 1940, Panama City (32402); F; 7,000fr (CAC); $6.15; publisher Freedom Newspapers Communications Inc.; publisher Karen Hanes; editor Sr Airman Jason Tudor; tel (904) 747-5000; fax (904) 763-4636

GEORGIA

Ft. Benning (Army): *The Bayonnet* — 1819 S. Lumpkin Rd., Columbus (31903); F; 24,000fr (Sw); $16.90; publisher The Advertiser Co.; publisher Maj Gen John W Hendrix; general manager Gibson Pryor; editor Agatha Hudson Jones; tel (706) 682-3346; fax (706) 682-3268

Ft. Gordon (Army): *Sentinel* — PO Box 948, Waynesboro (30830); Th; 13,000fr (CAC); $8.00; publisher Roy F Chalker Jr.; editor Roger Dotson; tel (706) 554-2111; fax (706) 554-2437

Ft. Stewart & Hunter: *Patriot* — 123 S. Main St., Hinesville (31313); Th; 17,000fr (Est); $9.70; publisher MNC of Hinesville; general manager Mark Griffin; editor Sgt J W Sternickel; tel (912) 368-0526; fax (912) 368-6329

Robins AFB: *Robins Rev-up* — PO Box 6129, Warner Robins (31095); F; 18,000fr (Est); publisher The Daily Sun; publisher Gary McDuffie; tel (912) 923-6432

Waynesboro: *Fort Gordon Signal* — 610 Academy Ave.; PO Box 948 (30830); Th; 18,500fr (Est); $8.00; C; publisher Roy F Charles Jr; general manager Bonnie K Taylor; tel (706) 724-2122; fax (706) 724-2437

HAWAII

Hickham AFB: *Hawaiian Falcon* — 45-525 Luluku Rd., Kaneohe (96744); F; 8,000fr (Sw); $10.11; C; publisher Community Publications; publisher Ken Berry; general manager Chris McMahon; tel (808) 235-5881

Kaneohe Bay MCAS (Marine): *Hawaii Marine* — 45-525 Luluku Rd., Kaneohe (96744); F; 8,550fr (Sw); $10.11; publisher Community Publications; publisher Ken Berry; general manager Chris McMahon; tel (808) 235-5881; fax (808) 247-4629

Pearl Harbor (Navy): *Hawaii Navy News* — 45-525 Luluku Rd., Kaneohe (96744); Th; 16,000fr (Sw); $11.89; publisher Community Publications; publisher Ken Berry; general manager Chris McMahon; tel (808) 235-5881; fax (808) 247-4629

IDAHO

Mountain Home AFB: *The Gunfighter* — 5325 Kendall St., Boise (83706); F; 7,000fr (Est); $5.50; publisher Graphic Arts Pub.; publisher Reed Hansen; general manager Rich Swensen; editor Elaine Mattson; managing editor Scott Sturkel; tel (800) 365-3020; fax (208) 376-0434

ILLINOIS

Glenview NAS: *Glenviews* — Bldg. 41, NAS, Glenview (60025); Mthly; 6,478fr (Est); publisher Pioneer Press Inc.; editor JO2 Kathy Pfeifer; tel (708) 657-2107

Scott Air Force Base: *The Scott Flier* — 314 E. Church St.; PO Drawer C, Mascoutah (62258); Th; 4,200fr (Sw); $3.25; C; publisher Greg Hoskins; managing editor Les Hostetler; tel (618) 566-8282; fax (618) 566-8283

KANSAS

Ft. Leavenworth (Army): *Fort Leavenworth Lamp* — 102 E. Olive; PO Box 126, Lansing (66043); F; 8,500fr (Est); publisher Lansing Pub. Inc.; publisher Sandy Hattock; tel (913) 684-5267

Ft. Riley (Army): *Fort Riley Post* — PO Box 129, Junction City (66441); F; 11,500fr (CAC); $6.10; publisher Maj Gen William Hartzog; editor Sgt Michelle Rafuse; tel (913) 762-5000; fax (913) 762-4584

McConnell AFB: *Contrails* — 3821 W. 20th St. N., Wichita (67203); F; 5,300fr (Est); $10.00; publisher Mercia Publishing Enterprises; editor SSgt Tom Saunders; tel (316) 942-5010; fax (316) 942-5010

KENTUCKY

Ft. Campbell (Army): *Fort Campbell Courier* — 1618 E. 9th St.; PO Box 1087, Hopkinsville (42240); Th; 23,000fr (Est); $6.99; publisher Kentucky New Era; publisher Robert Carter; editor Lee Elder; tel (502) 887-3220; fax (502) 887-3222

Ft. Knox (Army): *Inside the Turrett* — 408 W. Dixie Ave., Elizabethtown (42701); Th; 20,896fr (Est); $6.60; publisher Mike Anders; editor Larry Barnes; tel (502) 769-1200; fax (502) 765-7318

LOUISIANA

Ft. Polk (Army): *Guardian* — 716 E. Napolean St. (70663); PO Box 1999, Sulphur (70664); Tu/F; 16,000fr (Est); $15.30; C; publisher News Leader Inc.; publisher Al Gensheimer; general manager George Jinks; tel (318) 527-7075; fax (318) 528-3044

New Orleans NAS: *Nolair News* — 835 Convention Center Blvd., New Orleans (70130); Mthly; 4,000fr (Est); publisher News on Wheels; publisher Kenny Nagim; tel (504) 524-3785; fax (504) 523-4835

MAINE

Brunswick (Navy): *The Patroller* — 6 Industry Rd.; PO Box 10, Brunswick (04011); Th; 4,700fr (Est); $6.00; publisher Campbell B Niven; general manager Daniel Snow; editor James C Womack; tel (207) 729-3311; fax (207) 729-5728

Loring AFB: *Limelite* — PO Box 510, Presque Island (04769); Th; 6,150fr (Est); publisher Northeast Regional Publishing Co.; publisher Herb Andrews; tel (800) 924-9041

MARYLAND

Aberdeen Proving Ground: *APG News* — 10 S. Hays St.; PO Box 1890, Bel Air (21078); W; 12,500fr (Est); $9.07; C; publisher Homestead Pub. Co.; publisher John Worthington IV; editor Karen Jolley Drewen; tel (410) 838-4409; fax (410) 838-2843

Andrews AFB: *Capital Flyer* — 9030 Comprint Ct., Gaithersburg (20877); F; 15,000fr (Sw); $12.17; C; publisher Comprint Inc.; publisher Elaine Brady; editor Sgt Guthrie; tel (301) 948-1520; fax (301) 948-1967

Annapolis Naval Academy: *Trident* — 9030 Comprint Ct., Gaithersburg (20877); F; 2,712pd, 11,000fr (Est); $11.24; C; publisher Comprint Inc.; editor Leo Mehalic; tel (301) 948-1520; fax (301) 948-1967

Assoc. of the U.S. Army: *Basecamp Briefs* — 9030 Comprint Ct., Gaithersburg (20877); Qtrly/Th; 8,000fr (Sw); $8.86; C; publisher Comprint Inc.; publisher Elaine Brady; editor Mike Kelley; tel (301) 948-1520; fax (301) 948-1967

Bethesda Medical Center: *The Journal* — 9030 Comprint Ct., Gaithersburg (20877); Th; 11,000fr (Sw); $11.24; C; publisher Comprint Inc.; general manager Elaine Brady; editor Kevin Sforza; tel (301) 948-1520; fax (301) 948-1967

Bolling AFB D.C.: *AFDW Beam* — 9030 Comprint Ct., Gaithersburg (20877); Th; 15,000fr (Sw); $12.17; C; publisher Comprint Inc.; publisher Elaine Brady; editor Sgt Darrell Green; tel (301) 948-1520; fax (301) 948-1967

Fort Belvoir (Army): *Eagle* — 9030 Comprint Ct., Gaithersburg (20877); Th; 17,000fr (Sw); $12.17; C; publisher Comprint Inc.; publisher Elaine Brady; editor Mary Binder; tel (301) 948-1520; fax (301) 948-1967

Ft. Detrick: *Fort Detrick Standard* — 9030 Comprint Ct., Gaithersburg (20877); Bi-Wkly/F; 5,500fr (Est); $8.86; C; publisher Comprint Inc.; editor Ann Duble; tel (301) 948-1520; fax (301) 948-1967

Ft. McNair/Pentagon: *Pentagram* — 9030 Comprint Ct., Gaithersburg (20877); F; 31,000fr (Sw); $21.01; C; publisher Comprint Inc.; publisher Elaine Brady; editor Tom Mani; tel (301) 948-1520; fax (301) 948-1967

Ft. Meade: *Soundoff!* — 1075 Little Patuxent Pkwy., Columbia (21044); Th; 3pd, 14,836fr (CAC); $27.11; publisher S Zeke Orlinsky; general manager Jean Moon; editor Kathy Vantran; tel (410) 730-3620; fax (410) 730-7053

Marine HQ D.C.: *Henderson Hall News* — 9030 Comprint Ct., Gaithersburg (20877); F; 5,500fr (Est); $8.86; C; publisher Comprint Inc.; general manager Elaine Brady; editor Sgt Reed; tel (301) 948-1520; fax (301) 948-1967

Patuxent NAS: *Tester* — 9030 Comprint Ct., Gaithersburg (20877); F; 12,500fr (Sw); $12.17; C; publisher Comprint Ct.; publisher Elaine Brady; editor Fred Bradshaw; tel (301) 948-1520; fax (301) 948-1967

Walter Reed Army Med Ctr.: *Stripe* — 9030 Comprint Ct., Gaithersburg (20877); F; 10,000fr (Sw); $11.24; C; publisher Comprint Inc.; publisher Elaine Brady; editor Beverly Chidell; tel (301) 948-1520; fax (301) 948-1967

Washington Navy Yard: *Sea Services Weekly* — 9030 Comprint Ct., Gaithersburg (20877); F; 10,000fr (Sw); $11.24; C; publisher Comprint Inc.; publisher Elaine Brady; tel (301) 948-1520; fax (301) 948-1967

MASSACHUSETTS

Ft. Devens (Army): *Fort Devens Dispatch* — 69 Finchburg Rd., Ayer (01432); W; 5,000fr (Est); publisher Public Spirit; publisher Frank Hartnett; tel (508) 772-0777

Hanscom AFB: *Hansconian* — 33 New York Ave., Framingham (01701); F; 8,500fr (Sw); $7.00; C; publisher Middlesex News; publisher Asa Cole; editor Sgt Renee E Hearkell; tel (617) 433-7900; fax (617) 433-7875

Mass. Military Residence: *Otis Notice* — PO Box 571, Osterville (02655); Mthly; 5,500fr (Sw); $6.00; publisher LuJean Printing Co. Inc.; publisher Luke P Lally; editor Pauline L Judge; tel (508) 428-8900; fax (508) 428-8524

MICHIGAN

K.I. Sawyer AFB: *Northern Light* — 1010 W. Washington, Marquette (49855); F; 4,200fr (CAC); $4.50; publisher Action Shopper-News; editor Sgt Jim Hughes; tel (906) 228-8920

Wurtsmith AFB: *Klaxon* — PO Box 548, Wurtsmith (48740); Th; 1,600fr (Est); publisher Jim Dunn; tel (517) 724-6384; fax (517) 724-6655

MISSISSIPPI

Keesler AFB: *Keesler News* — 205 DeBuys Rd., Gulfport (39507); PO Box 4567, Biloxi (39531); F; 14,000fr (Est); $11.55; C; publisher Gulf Publishing; publisher Roland Weeks Jr.; editor Perry Jennifer; tel (601) 896-2100; fax (601) 896-2362

Meridian NAS: *Skyline* — 814 22nd Ave.; PO Box 1591, Meridian (39302); W; 3,500fr (Sw); $4.75; publisher American Publishing; publisher Jerry Strader; general manager John Bohl; editor Susan Junkins; managing editor Steve Swogentensky; tel (601) 693-1551; fax (601) 485-1275

MISSOURI

Ft. Leonard Wood (Army): *Essayons* — 103 E. Business Rte. I-44; PO Box 831 SRB, St. Robert (65583); Th; 250pd, 8,800fr (Est); $7.60; C; publisher Lebanon Publishing Co.; publisher Karla Fudge; editor Rick Brunk; tel (314) 336-3435; fax (314) 336-4471

Whiteman Air Force Base: *The Missouri Warrior* — 700 S. Massachusetts; PO Box 848, Sedalia (65302); F; 5,300fr (Sw); $3.65; publisher Frank Lyon; tel (816) 826-1000; fax (816) 826-2413

NEBRASKA

Offutt AFB: *Air Pulse* — 604 Fort Crook Rd.; PO Box 1219, Bellevue (68005); F; 13,500fr (Sw); $13.24; C; publisher Dixie Cavner; tel (402) 733-7300; fax (402) 733-9116

NEW JERSEY

Burlington Co./Fort Dix: *The Fort Dix Post* — 4284 Rte. 130, Willingboro (08046); F; 9,122fr (CAC); $10.04; C; publisher Stanley M Ellis; editor Carolee Nisbet; tel (609) 871-8085; fax (609) 877-2706

McGuire AFB: *The McGuire Airtides* — 4282 Rte. 130, Willingboro (08046); F; 9,576fr (CAC); $10.04; C; publisher Stanley M Ellis; editor SSgt Mary McHale; tel (609) 871-8085; fax (609) 877-2706

Picatinny Arsenal (Army): *Voice* — 435 E. Main St.; PO Box 1244, Denville (07834); Th (Bi-Wkly); 8,500fr (Sw); N/A; publisher Neighbor News Inc.; publisher Salvatore Paci; tel (201) 586-3012; fax (201) 586-3449

NEW MEXICO

Cannon AFB: *Mach Meter* — 101 E. 1st St., Portales (88130); F; 5,100fr (Est); publisher The Portales News Tribune; publisher Marshall Stinnett; tel (505) 356-4481; fax (505) 356-3630

Holloman AFB/Otero Co.: *Sunburst* — 1200 N. White Sands, Ste. 124, Alamogordo (88310); F; 8,500fr (Est); C; publisher Ruidoso News; publisher Sammy Lopez; managing editor Susan Pitts; tel (505) 437-5727; fax (505) 437-3300

White Sands Missile Range: *Missile Ranger* — 256 W. Las Cruces Ave.; PO Box 1749 (88004), Las Cruces (88005); F; 6,000fr (Est); $5.75; C; publisher George S Smith; editor Sue Hannon; tel (505) 523-4581; fax (505) 523-7913

NEW YORK

Ft. Drum (Army): *Fort Drum Sentinel* — 82 Public Sq., Watertown (13601); Th; 12,000fr (Sw); $7.80; publisher Johnson News Corp.; general manager Robert O'Marah; editor Lisa Reape; tel (315) 778-3638; fax (315) 782-3955

Griffiss AFB Rome: *Mohawk Flyer* — PO Box 471, Rome (13442-0471); F; 8,800fr (Est); $4.35; C; publisher Rome Sentinel Company; tel (315) 337-4000; fax (315) 337-4704

Plattsburgh AFB: *Champlaner* — 170 Margaret St., Plattsburgh (12901); F; 5,000fr (Est); publisher Press Republican; publisher Brenda Tallman; tel (518) 561-2300

U.S. Mil. Academy (Army): *Pointer View* — 45 Gilbert St., Monroe (10956); F; 8,000fr (Est); publisher Stan Martin; editor Irene Brown; tel (914) 782-4000; fax (914) 782-1711

NORTH CAROLINA

Army Reserve: *Griffon (The)* — 4801 E. Independence Blvd., Ste. 1110, Charlotte (28212); Qtrly; 5,000fr (Est); publisher Knight Publications Inc.; publisher R B Knight; tel (704) 568-7804; fax (704) 563-4286

Camp Lejune (USMC): *Globe* — 122 Branchwood Shpg. Ctr.; 825 Gum Branch Rd., Ste. 125, Jacksonville (28540); Th; 28,500fr (Est); publisher & general manager Lynn Freeman; editor Beth Stanz; tel (919) 938-7467; fax (919) 938-2722

Charleston AFB (SC): *Airlift Dispatch* — PO Box 35050, Fayetteville (28303); F; 7,500fr (Est); $6.50; publisher Carl S Coulthard; editor Sgt Alex Smith; tel (919) 487-3500; fax (919) 487-4320

Craven Co.: *Windsock* — 230 Stonebridge; PO Box 777, Havelock (28532); Th; 13,000fr (Sw); $9.97; C; publisher Joe R Browning; tel (919) 447-2346; fax (919) 447-0897

Fayetteville: *Fort Bragg Paraglide* — PO Box 35395 (28303); Th; 25,000fr (CAC); $13.58; publisher Dickson Press Inc.; editor SSgt Mark Martello; tel (919) 864-0666; fax (919) 864-8911

Jacksonville: *Rotovue* — 122 Branchwood Shpg. Ctr. (28540); Bi-Wkly/F; 8,300fr (Est); publisher ENC Publications; publisher Lynne Freeman; tel (919) 938-7467

Pope AFB (NC): *Tiger Times* — PO Box 35050, Fayetteville (28303); F; 5,000fr (Est); $5.00; publisher Carl S Coulthard; editor Sgt Garrett Reed; tel (919) 487-3500; fax (919) 487-4320

Seymour Johnson AFB: *The Scope* — 1510 Wright Ave., Ste. 200, Goldsboro (27531-2468); F; 5,400fr (Est); $4.00; publisher Wayne Printing Co.; editor SSgt Lee Roberts; tel (919) 736-5170; fax (919) 736-6654

NORTH DAKOTA

Grand Forks AFB: *Grafton* — 402 Hill Ave., Grafton (58237); Th; 6,500fr (Est); publisher Morgan Publishing; tel (701) 352-0640

Minot AFB: *Sentry* — PO Box 309, Garrison (58540); F; 7,000fr (CAC); $7.50; publisher BHG Inc.; tel (701) 463-2201; fax (701) 463-7487

OHIO

Newark AFB: *On Target* — 120 S. Main St.; PO Box 515, Utica (43080); Bi-Wkly/Th; 2,400fr (Est); publisher Utica Herald; publisher Nelson A Smith; tel (614) 892-2771

South Dayton: *The Oakwood Register* — PO Box 572, Dayton (45409); Tu; 5,200fr (Sw); $9.50; publisher Delores E Winkler; editor Sherry Heinzerling; tel (513) 294-2662; fax (513) 294-8375

Veterans/Civil Service: *Golden Eagle* — PO Box 572, Dayton (45409); Mthly; 200pd, 22,000fr (CAC); $8.50; publisher Delores E Winkler; editor Brian Barr; tel (513) 294-2662; fax (513) 294-8375

OKLAHOMA

Altus AFB: *The Patriot* — 218 W. Commerce St., Altus (73531); C; publisher Donrey Media Group; publisher Lyle M Exstrom; tel (405) 482-1221; fax (405) 482-5709

Ft. Sill (Army): *Cannonneer* — 3rd & "A" Ave; PO Box 2069, Lawton (73502); Th; 14,600fr (Sw); $7.25; publishers Don Bentley & Stephen Bentley; tel (405) 353-0620; fax (405) 585-5103

Tinker AFB: *Tinker Take-Off* — 621 N. Robinson (73102); PO Box 26370 (73126), Oklahoma City F; 28,000fr (Est); $17.50; publisher Journal Record Publishing; publisher Dan Hogan; general manager Mike Dinger; editor Darla Booker; managing editor Ed Shannon; tel (405) 278-6005; fax (405) 278-6096

RHODE ISLAND

Newport (Navy): *Newport Navalog* — 101 Malbone Rd., Newport (02840); F; 7,200fr (CAC); $11.24; publisher Sherman Publishing Co.; editor Richard Alexander; tel (401) 849-3300; fax (401) 849-3306

SOUTH CAROLINA

Charleston AFB: *Airlift Spirit* — 1852 I Wallace School Rd., Charleston (29407); publisher Cross Creek Publishing Inc.; publisher Carl Coulthard; tel (803) 763-1800; fax (919) 487-4320

Charleston Naval Base: *Bow Hook* — 1850 Ben Sawyer Blvd; PO Box 2014, Mt Pleasant (29465); F; 8,000fr (Est); $5.00; C; publisher Community Press Inc.; publisher Charles P Diggle; editor Melissa Melcher; tel (803) 849-1778; fax (803) 849-0214

Ft. Jackson (Army): *Fort Jackson Leader* — PO Box 6932, Columbia (29260-6932); Th; 12,000fr (Est); publisher Harvey Moss; editor Sgt Robert Edwards; tel (803) 782-2554; fax (803) 782-8133

Shaw AFB/Sumter S.C.: *The Spirit* — 909 W. Dekalb St.; PO Box 1137, Camden (29020); F; 7,700fr (Est); $8.28; publisher Camden Media Co.; tel (803) 432-6157; fax (803) 432-7609

SOUTH DAKOTA

Ellsworth AFB: *Plainsman* — 105 New York St.; PO Box 1102, Ellsworth (57701); F; N/A; publisher Base Publishing; publisher Joel Weaver; tel (605) 348-9150

TENNESSEE

Bartlett: *Bartlett Express* — 2874 Shelby St., Ste. 201 (38134); W; 6,178pd (CAC); $12.40; publisher Express Publishing; publisher Buddy Murchison; tel (901) 386-3157

Cordova: *Cordova Beacon* — 2874 Shelby St., Ste. 201, Bartlett (38134); W; 10,000pd (CAC); $12.40; publisher Buddy Murchison; tel (901) 386-3157

TEXAS

Carswell AFB: *Carswell Sentinel* — 3412 Marquita Dr., Fort Worth (76116); F; 12,000fr (Est); publisher Target Marketing Publishing; publisher Stanley Cole; tel (817) 560-2396; fax (817) 560-2328

Dyess AFB: *Dyess Peacemaker* — 100 Cypress; PO Box 3653, Abilene (79604); C; publisher Reporter Publishing Co.; Harte-Hanks; publisher Frank Pucket; general manager Kay Davis; tel (915) 676-6779; fax (915) 672-8734

Ft. Bliss (Army): *Fort Bliss Monitor* — 1420 Geronimo, El Paso (79925); Th; 20,000fr (Est); publisher Laven & Associates Ltd.; tel (915) 772-0934; fax (915) 772-1594

Ft. Hood (Army): *Fort Hood Sentinel* — 10 S. 3rd; PO Box 6114, Temple (75503-6114); Th; 22,500fr (Sw); $5.85; publisher Mayborn Enterprises; publisher Sue Mayborn; general manager Charles R Harrell; tel (817) 778-4444; fax (817) 778-4444 Ext. 271

Ft. Sam Houston (Army): *News Leader* — 122 E. Byrd; PO Box 2789, Universal City (78148); F; 10,000fr (Est); publisher Prime Time Inc./Herald Newspaper Group; publisher Bob Jones; tel (512) 658-7424

Kelly AFB: *Kelly Observer* — 7137 Military Dr. W.; PO Box 27040, San Antonio (78227); Th; 22,000fr (Est); $10.50; C; publisher Jim Berg Publications; publisher Jim Berg; editor Frank Garcia; tel (210) 675-4500; fax (210) 675-4577

Laughlin AFB: *Border Eagle* — PO Drawer 4020, Del Rio (78841-4020); F; 2,900fr (Est); publisher Del Rio News Herald; publisher Joe San Miguel; tel (512) 775-1551; fax (512) 774-2610

Randolph AFB: *Wingspread* — 122 E. Byrd; PO Box 2789, Universal City (78148); F; 10,000fr (Est); publisher Prime Time Inc./Herald Newspaper Group; publisher Bob Jones; tel (512) 658-7424

Red River Army Depot: *Red River Review* — 129 E. North Front, New Boston (75570); Mthly; 15,200fr (Est); publisher Carla Pope; tel (903) 628-2329/5801; fax (903) 628-2551

UTAH

Davis/Weber Cos.: *Hill Top Times* — 1152 W. Riverdale Rd. (Ogden 84405); PO Box 445, Roy (84067); Th; 600pd, 21,500fr (Sw); $7.75; C; publisher Bill Mulvay; general manager Anne M Johnson; editor Frances Kosa Kowsky; managing editor Bill Orndoff; tel (801) 394-9655; fax (801) 394-7058

VIRGINIA

Army: *Blue Ridger* — 516 E. Randolph Rd.; PO Box 481, Hopewell (23860); Qtrly; 4,000fr (Est); $25.00; publisher & editor Andy Prustok; tel (804) 458-8511; fax (804) 458-8511

Ft. Eustis/Ft. Story (Army): *The Wheel* — 2509 Walmer Ave.; PO Box 10304, Norfolk (23513); Th; 10,000fr (Sw); $9.68; C; publisher Military Newspapers of Virginia; publishers Jean Casey Lindley & William C Eisenbeiss; editor Jerry W Rogers; tel (804) 857-1212; fax (804) 853-1634

Ft. Lee (Army): *The Fort Lee Traveller* — PO Box 481, Hopewell (23860); Th; 9,300fr (CAC); $5.80; publisher & editor Andy Prustok; tel (804) 458-8511; fax (804) 458-8511

Ft. Lee (Army): *Traveller* — 2509 Walmer Ave.; PO Box 10304, Norfolk (23513); F; 10,000fr (Sw); $6.92; C; publisher Military Newspapers of Virginia; publishers Jean Casey Lindley & William C Eisenbeiss; editor Starlene R Parizek; tel (804) 857-1212; fax (804) 853-1634

Ft. Monroe (Army): *Casemate* — 2509 Walmer Ave.; PO Box 10304, Norfolk (23513); Bi-Wkly F; 5,000fr (Sw); $6.56; C; publisher Military Newspapers of Virginia; publishers Jean Casey Lindley & William C Eisenbeiss; editor Connie Smalls; tel (804) 857-1212; fax (804) 853-1634

International Defense Community: *Defense News* — 6883 Commercial Dr., Springfield (22159); M; 36,377pd, 3,133fr (Sw); $125.00; C; publisher Jack Kerrigan; editor Sharon Denny; managing editor Greg Couteau; tel (703) 642-7330; fax (703) 642-7386

Langley Air Force Base: *The Flyer* — 4824 George Washington Hwy.; PO Box 978, Yorktown (23692); F; 13,500fr (Sw); $8.75; C; publisher D Gaither Perry; general manager Carol Ivy; editor C J O'Dell; tel (804) 898-7225; fax (804) 890-0119

Naval Weapons Station: *The Booster* — 2509 Walmer Ave.; PO Box 10304, Norfolk (23513); Mthly/F; 5,000fr (Sw); $6.04; C; publisher Military Newspapers of Virginia; publishers Jean Casey Lindley & William C Eisenbeiss; editor J Thomas Black; managing editor Jim Starling; tel (804) 857-1212; fax (804) 853-1634

Navy/USMC: *Navy Times* — 6883 Commercial Dr., Springfield (22159); M; 87,137pd, 4,521fr (ABC); publisher Army Times Publishing; editor Tobias Naegele; tel (703) 750-8636

Navy/USMC/USCG/Hampton Roads: *Soundings* — 2509 Walmer Ave.; PO Box 10304, Norfolk (23513); W; 45,000fr (Sw); $14.24; C; publisher Military Newspapers of Virginia; publisher Jean Casey Lindley & William C Eisenbeiss; editor Dave Stump; tel (804) 857-1212; fax (804) 853-1634

Norfolk Naval Base: *The Flagship* — 150 W. Brambleton Ave., Norfolk (23510); Tu; 20,750pd, 250fr (Sw); Th; 40,000fr (Est); $20.75; publisher Commonwealth Printing Co.; publisher J Lorne Peachey; general manager Daniel Sykes; editor JO2 Don Kennedy; tel (804) 446-2750; fax (804) 627-3829

Oceana NAS: *Jet Observer* — 2509 Walmer Ave.; PO Box 10304, Norfolk (23513); Bi-Wkly Th; 8,000fr (Sw); $8.52; C; publisher Military Newspapers of Virginia; publishers Jean Casey Lindley & William C Eisenbeiss; editor Annette Hall; tel (804) 857-1212; fax (804) 853-1634

Quantico MCB (USMC): *Quantico Sentry* — PO Box 2470, Woodbridge (22193); F; 12,000pd (Est); $13.75; Th; 21,926pd, 182fr (Sw); $7.50; C; publisher Potomac News; publishers Andy Mick & Most Rev David B Thompson; editors Earl Hicks & Philip M Bowman; tel (703) 878-8000; fax (703) 878-3993

WASHINGTON

Ft. Lewis: *Northwest Airlifter* — 10507-4 Gravelly Lake Dr. S.W. (98499); PO Box 98801, Tacoma (98498); F; 8,200fr (Sw); $12.30; C; publisher Military News Publishers; publisher Tom Swarner; editor Ken Swarner; tel (206) 584-1212; fax (206) 581-5962

Ft. Lewis: *The Ranger* — 10507-4 Gravelly Lake Dr. S.W. (98499); PO Box 98801, Tacoma (98498); Th; 116,000pd (Sw); $60.00; Th; 22,000fr (Sw); $12.30; C; publisher Military News Publishers; publisher Tom Swarner; editor Ken Swarner; tel (206) 584-1212; fax (206) 581-5962

Ft. Lewis (Army): *Northwest Guardian* — 9105 Bridgeport Way S.W., Tacoma (98499); W; 60,000pd, 200fr (Est); $22.00; Th; 9pd, 15,972fr (CAC); $12.90; publisher Brett Carlson; editors Sgt Kim Simmons & WM Fletcher Allen; tel (206) 584-5818; fax (206) 584-6098

WYOMING

F E Warren AFB: *Sentinel* — 1810 Westland Rd., Cheyenne (82001); Th; 15,700pd (Sw); $8.40; F; 4,500fr (Est); publisher Lindsay Publishing; publishers Father J Peter Sartain & Jim Wood; tel (307) 632-5666

RELIGIOUS NEWSPAPERS PUBLISHED IN THE UNITED STATES

ALABAMA

Birmingham: *One Voice (Est. 1971)* — 8131 4th Ave. S. (35206); PO Box 10822 (35202); F; 16,129pd, 254fr (Sw); $5.10; publisher Rev John T Igoe; tel (205) 838-8305

Mobile: *The Catholic Week* — PO Box 349 (36601); F; 14,300pd, 254fr (Sw); $7.88; publisher Most Rev Oscar H Lipscomb; tel (334) 432-3529

ARKANSAS

Little Rock: *Arkansas Catholic (Est. 1911)* — 2500 N. Tyler St. (72207); PO Box 7417 (72217); Sa; 5,600pd, 525fr (Est); $14.00; publisher Most Rev Andrew J McDonald, DD; editor Malea Walters; managing editor Most Rev Francis I Malone, JCL; tel (501) 664-0340; fax (501) 664-9075

CALIFORNIA

Los Angeles: *The Tidings (Est. 1895)* — 1530 W. 9th St. (90015); F; 40,978pd, 957fr (Sw); $21.88; publisher Cardinal Roger M Mahony; tel (213) 251-3360

Sacramento: *Catholic Herald (Est. 1908)* — 5890 Newman Ct. (95819-2698); W; 49,983pd (Est); $18.00; C; publisher Bishop William Weingand; editor Julie Sly; tel (916) 452-3344; fax (916) 452-2945

San Diego: *Southern Cross (Est. 1912)* — PO Box 81869 (92138-1869); Bi-Wkly; 17,806pd, 1,542fr (Sw); $20.00; publisher Bishop Robert H Brom; editor Larry Montali Jr; tel (619) 490-8266; fax (619) 490-8355

COLORADO

Denver: *Denver Catholic Register (Est. 1900)* — 200 Josephine St. (80206); W; 83,411pd, 500fr (Sw); $30.80; publisher Most Rev J Francis Stafford; tel (303) 388-4411

CONNECTICUT

Hartford: *The Catholic Transcript (Est. 1898)* — 785 Asylum Ave. (06105-2886); F; 14,446pd, 3,823fr (Sw); $13.55; publisher Most Rev Daniel A Cronin; general manager Scott K Parmelee; editor Janet Alampi; managing editor Rev John P Gatzak; tel (860) 527-1175; fax (860) 947-6397

DELAWARE

Wilmington: *The Dialog (Est. 1965)* — PO Box 2208 (19899) (19806); Th; 48,056pd (Est); $17.10; publisher Most Rev Robert E Mulvee; tel (302) 573-3109

DISTRICT OF COLUMBIA

Washington: *Catholic Standard (Est. 1951)* — 5001 Eastern Ave.; PO Box 4464 (20017); Th; 44,918pd, 390fr (Sw); $28.00; publisher Ron Rhea; general manager Thomas H Schmidt; editor Mark Zimmerman; tel (301) 853-4599; fax (301) 853-3349

Washington: *El Pregonero (Est. 1977)* — 5001 Eastern Ave.; PO Box 4464 (20017); Th; 349pd, 23,023fr (Sw); $18.70; general manager Thomas H Schmidt; editor Oscar Reyes; tel (301) 853-4504

FLORIDA

Orlando: *The Florida Catholic (Est. 1939)* — 498 S. Lake Destiny Dr., Ste. 32810; PO Box 609512 (32860-9512); Mthly/F; 10,000fr (Est); F; 134,474pd, 1,377fr (Sw); $41.00;

Religious newspapers II-99

C; publishers Most Rev Norbert M Dorsey & Pat Cavanaugh; general manager & editor Deagon Henry Libersat; managing editor Gary Morton; tel (407) 660-9141; fax (407) 660-2977

Palm Beach Gardens: *The Florida Catholic (Est. 1985)* — 9995 N. Military Trl. (33410); F; 11,000pd, 4,000fr (Sw); $1.90; Th; 8,000fr (Est); publishers Mike Digulla & Most Rev J Keith Symons; tel (407) 775-9527

Pensacola: *The Florida Catholic (Est. 1984)* — PO Drawer 17329 (32522); F; 10,000pd (Sw); $1.90; Bi-Wkly/Th; 9,500fr (Est); publishers Bishop John M Smith & Steve Boster; editor Barry McDonald; tel (904) 432-5215

Santa Rosa Co.: *Santa Rosa Press Gazette (Est. 1907)* — 531 S.W. Elva St., Milton (32570); M/Th; 5,056pd, 61fr (Sw); $10.50; F; 56,000fr (Sw); $25.00; C; publishers Jimmie D Hill & Jim Missett; general manager Carol Barnes; editor Jim Fletcher; tel (904) 623-3616; fax (904) 623-2007

Tampa: *The Florida Catholic (Est. 1939)* — PO Box 18081 (33679); F; 23,180pd (Sw); $1.90; F; 8,467fr (Est); $13.55; publishers David McNamara & Ron Hoffer; managing editor SSgt Timothy Hoffman; tel (813) 879-7978

Venice: *The Florida Catholic (Est. 1984)* — PO Box 2006 (34284); F; 12,568pd (Sw); $7.35; F; 14,500fr (Est); tel (813) 484-9543

GEORGIA

Atlanta: *The Georgia Bulletin* — 680 W. Peachtree N.W. (30308-1984); Th; 20,000fr (Est); Th; 54,360pd (Est); $17.06; publisher John C Peterson; editor Gretchen Keiser; managing editor Kathi Stearns; tel (404) 888-7832; fax (404) 888-7849

Atlanta: *Wesleyan Christian Advocate* — 159 Ralph McGill Blvd. N.E.; PO Box 54455 (30308-0455); F; 29,301pd, 123fr (Sw); $24.00; F; 7,000fr (Est); $6.30; publisher Tamra Brittingham; editor Mark A Westmoreland & TSgt Russ Maheras; tel (404) 659-8809; fax (404) 659-1727

Waynesboro: *The Southern Cross (Est. 1920)* — 601 E. 6th St. (30830); Th; 10,370pd (Sw); $54.00; publisher Most Rev Raymond W Lessard; tel (770) 554-3539

HAWAII

Honolulu: *Hawaii Catholic Herald (Est. 1936)* — 1184 Bishop St. (96813); Bi-Wkly F; 10,500pd (Sw); $13.45; Th; 7,000fr (Est); publishers Most Rev Joseph A Ferrario & Regina Hodges; tel (808) 533-1791

IDAHO

Boise: *Idaho Catholic Register (Est. 1958)* — 303 Federal Way (83705-5925); F; 12,630pd, 160fr (Sw); $7.65; Bi-Wkly/F; 3,500fr (Sw); $5.40; publishers Bishop Tod David Brown & Karen Hanes; general manager Lenn George; editors Colette Cowman & Ken Hoffman; tel (208) 342-1311; fax (208) 342-0224

ILLINOIS

Belleville: *The Messenger (Est. 1907)* — 2620 Lebanon Ave.; PO Box 327 (62221); F; 16,500fr (CAC); $14.50; F; 17,500pd, 343fr (Sw); $9.15; publisher Most Rev James P Keleher; editor SSgt Mike Spaits; tel (618) 235-9601

Chicago: *The New World (Est. 1892)* — 1144 Jackson Blvd. (60607); F; 33,793pd, 673fr (Est); $55.00; F; 5,500fr (Est); publishers Joseph Cardinal Bernardin & Marvin Debolt; general manager Robert L Gaskill; editor Rev Thomas C Widner, SV; managing editor Mary Claire Gart; tel (312) 243-1300; fax (312) 243-1526

Chicago: *The Sentinel (Est. 1912)* — 150 N. Michigan, Ste. 2025 (60601); F; 10,310fr (Sw); $6.50; Th; 50,000pd (Est); $17.50; publisher Ellen S Rykert; publisher & editor Jack Fishbein; general manager Larry Pines; editor Joc Stacy Byington; managing editor Ruth Marcus; tel (312) 407-0060; fax (312) 407-0096

Peoria: *The Catholic Post (Est. 1934)* — 409 N.E. Monroe; PO Box 1722 (61656); F; 32,750pd, 330fr (Sw); $13.25; F; 8,800fr (Est); $11.15; publisher Msgr R G Peters; general manager Carla Rockwell; editors Lorrenda D Thorton & Shelly R Boedicker; tel (309) 673-3603

Springfield: *Catholic Times (Est. 1896)* — 1615 W. Washington St.; PO Box 3187 (62708-3187); W; 40,172pd, 114fr (Sw); $18.73; F; 9,650fr (Sw); $8.23; publishers Bishop Daniel L Ryan & Tom Wood; editors Dave Bakke & Hal Newsome; tel (217) 698-8500; fax (217) 698-0619

INDIANA

Evansville: *The Message (Est. 1970)* — 4200 N. Kentucky Ave. (47711); PO Box 4169 (47724-0169); F; 12,302pd, 75fr (Sw); $5.80; F; 14,500fr (CAC); $16.50; publisher Most Rev Gerald A Gettelfinger; editors Art Giberson & Paul R Leingang; tel (812) 424-5536; fax (812) 421-1334

Ft. Wayne: *The Todays Catholic (Est. 1926)* — 150 E. Doan Dr.; PO Box 11169 (46856); Su; 14,834pd (Sw); $67.00; F; 3,500fr (CAC); $7.50; publishers John Thompson & Most Rev John Michael D'Arcy; general manager Mary Dolores Dahm; editors John Antenbouck & Kay Frank; managing editor Murray Mubley; tel (219) 456-2824/(219) 456-2900; fax (219) 744-1473

Huntington: *Our Sunday Visitor (Est. 1912)* — 200 Noll Plz. (46750); Su; 104,000pd (Sw); $84.00; Th; 22,500fr (Est); C; publishers Doug Bose & Robert P Lockwood; general manager Greg Erlandson; editor David Scott; managing editor Richard Beemer; tel (219) 356-8400; fax (219) 356-8472

Indianapolis: *The Criterion (Est. 1960)* — 1400 N. Meridian St.; PO Box 1717 (46206); F; 59,442pd, 5,890fr (Sw); $9.54; F; 8,200fr (Est); $6.30; publishers Daniel Conway & Mike Coleman & Most Rev Daniel Mark Buechlein; editors Harry McNamara & John F Fink; tel (317) 236-1570

Lafayette: *The Catholic Moment (Est. 1945)* — 610 Lingle Ave.; PO Box 1603 (47902); F; 24,000fr (Sw); $16.90; Su; 26,099pd, 87fr (Sw); $9.00; publishers Maj Gen John W Hendrix & Most Rev William L Higi; general manager Gibson Pryor; editors Agatha Hudson Jones; Thomas A Russell; managing editor Caroline Bodle Mooney; tel (317) 742-2050; fax (317) 742-7513

Merrillville: *Northwest Indiana Catholic (Est. 1987)* — 9292 Broadway (46410-7088); Th; 13,000fr (CAC); $8.00; Su; 19,440pd (Sw); $8.25; publishers Bishop Dale J Melczek & Roy F Chalker Jr.; editors Brian T Oszewski & Roger Dotson; tel (219) 769-9292; fax (219) 738-9034

IOWA

Davenport: *The Catholic Messenger (Est. 1882)* — 736 Federal St.; PO Box 460 (52805-0460); Th; 21,545pd, 200fr (Sw); $7.08; publisher Most Rev William Franklin; editor Rev Francis Henricksen; tel (319) 323-9959; fax (319) 323-6612

Dubuque: *The Witness (Est. 1921)* — 1229 Mt. Loretta; PO Box 917 (52004); Th; 17,000fr (Est); $9.70; Su; 18,761pd, 100fr (Sw); $4.75; publisher Most Rev Daniel W Kucera OSB; general manager Mark Griffin; general manager & managing editor Msgr Thomas J Ralph; editor Sgt J W Sternickel; tel (319) 588-0556; fax (319) 556-5464

Sioux City: *The Globe (Est. 1953)* — 1825 Jackson St.; PO Box 5079 (51102); F; 18,000fr (Est); Th; 25,476pd, 250fr (Sw); $10.00; publishers Gary McDuffie & Most Rev Lawrence D Soens; tel (712) 255-2550

KANSAS

Dodge City: *The Southwest Kansas Register (Est. 1966)* — 910 Central Ave.; PO Box 137 (67801); Bi-Mthly; 6,255pd (Sw); $5.00; F; 8,000fr (Sw); $10.11; publisher Ken Berry; publisher & editor Tim Wenzl; general manager Chris McMahon; tel (316) 227-1500; fax (316) 227-1570

Wichita: *The Catholic Advance (Est. 1901)* — 424 N. Broadway (67202-2377); Th; 16,000fr (Sw); $11.89; Th; 29,598pd (Sw); $11.77; publishers Ken Berry & Most Rev Eugene J Gerber; general manager Chris McMahon; tel (316) 269-3965

KENTUCKY

Erlanger: *The Messenger (Est. 1926)* — 947 Donaldson Rd.; PO Box 18068 (41018-0068); F; 14,032pd, 500fr (Sw); $8.95; C; publisher Msgr Donald Hellmann; general manager & editor Jerry Enderle; managing editor Jean Bach; tel (606) 283-6270; fax (606) 283-6334

Louisville: *The Record (Est. 1879)* — 1200 S. Shelby St. (40203); Th; 63,372pd (Sw); $17.25; F; 7,000fr (Est); $5.50; publisher Reed Hansen; general manager Rich Swensen; editors Elaine Mattson & Joseph E Duerr; managing editor Scott Sturkel; tel (502) 636-0296

Louisville: *Western Recorder (Est. 1826)* — 10701 Shelbyville Rd.; PO Box 43969 (40253); Tu; 46,969pd (Sw); $20.00; Mthly; 6,478fr (Est); publisher Board of Directors of Western Recorder Inc.; editors JO2 Kathy Pfeifer & Marv Knox; managing editor Mark Wingfield; tel (502) 244-6470; fax (502) 244-6474

LOUISIANA

New Orleans: *Clarion Herald (Est. 1963)* — 1000 Howard Ave., Ste. 400 (70113); PO Box 53247 (70153) Th; 55,111pd, 937fr (Est); $26.75; publisher Most Rev Francis B Schulte; general manager & editor Peter Finney Jr; managing editor Florence Herman; tel (504) 524-1618; fax (504) 596-3020

Schriever: *The Bayou Catholic (Est. 1879)* — 1801 Hwy. 311 (70395); W; 19,550pd, 83fr (Sw); $14.60; publisher Louis G Aguirre; tel (504) 868-7720; fax (504) 868-3215

MAINE

Brunswick: *The Church World (Est. 1930)* — Industry Rd.; PO Box 698 (04011); Th; 6,848pd (Est); $7.50; F; 8,500fr (Est); publisher Roman Catholic Bishop of Portland; tel (207) 729-8753

MARYLAND

Baltimore: *Catholic Review* — 320 Cathedral St.; PO Box 777 (21203); F; 11,500fr (CAC); $6.10; W; 67,070pd, 2,550fr (Sw); $22.00; publishers Archbishop William H Keeler & Maj Gen William Hartzog; editor Sgt Michelle Rafuse; tel (410) 547-5380

Silver Spring: *Adventist Review* — 12501 Old Columbia Pike (20904-6600); Th; 42,000pd, 281fr (Sw); F; 5,300fr (Est); $10.00; publisher Review & Herald Publishing Assoc.; tel (301) 791-7000

Washington, DC: *Catholic Standard (Est. 1951)* — 5001 Eastern Ave., Hyattsville (20782); Th; 44,918pd, 390fr (Sw); $27.75; publisher Cardinal James A Hickey; general manager Thomas H Schmidt; editor Mark V Zimmermann; tel (301) 853-4599; fax (301) 853-3349

MASSACHUSETTS

Boston: *The Pilot* — 49 Franklin St. (02110); Th; 20,896fr (Est); $6.60; F; 33,962pd, 110fr (Est); $21.00; publisher Mike Anders; editors Larry Barnes & Rev Peter V Conley; tel (617) 482-4316; fax (617) 482-5647

Fall River: *The Anchor (Est. 1957)* — 887 Highland Ave.; PO Box 7 (02722-0007); F; 29,266pd, 400fr (Sw); $10.25; publisher Most Rev Sean P O'Malley; general manager Rosemary Dussautt; editor Rev John F Moore; tel (508) 675-7151; fax (508) 675-7048

Worcester: *The Catholic Free Press (Est. 1951)* — 47 Elm St. (01609); F; 18,511pd, 187fr (Est); $18.60; Th; 6,150fr (Est); publishers Herb Andrews & Most Rev Daniel P Reily, DD, Pub.; general manager & editor Gerard E Goggins; tel (508) 757-6387; fax (508) 756-8315

MICHIGAN

Detroit: *The Michigan Catholic (Est. 1872)* — 305 Michigan Ave. (48226); W; 12,500fr (Est); $9.07; F; 25,200pd (Est); $13.84; publishers Archbishop Adam J Maida & John Worthington IV; editor Karen Jolley Drewen; tel (313) 244-8000

Flint: *The Catholic Times (Est. 1991)* — 1045 Darling St.; PO Box 8 (48532); F; 15,000fr (Sw); $12.17; F; 7,977pd, 114fr (Sw); $6.25; C; publisher Elaine Brady; general manager Mark A Myczkowiak; editors Barbara Kelly & Sgt Guthrie; tel (810) 767-6525; fax (810) 767-6567

Grand Rapids: *The Banner* — 2850 Kalamazoo Ave. S.E. (49560); F; 2,712pd, 11,000fr (Est); $11.24; M; 35,000pd, 500fr (Est); $65.00; publisher CRC Publications; editors John Suk & Leo Mehalic; managing editor Harvey Smit; tel (616) 246-0732; fax (616) 246-0834

Saginaw: *The Catholic Weekly (Est. 1939)* — 1520 Court St.; PO Box 1405 (48605); F; 11,887pd, 322fr (Sw); $7.28; Qtrly/Th; 8,000fr (Sw); $8.86; C; publisher Elaine Brady; general manager Mark A Myczkowiak; editors Kathleen Sucha & Mike Kelley & Paul E Seman; tel (517) 793-7661; fax (517) 793-7663

MINNESOTA

St. Cloud: *St. Cloud Visitor (Est. 1938)* — 305 N. 7th Ave., Ste. 206; PO Box 1068 (56302); Th; 15,000fr (Sw); $12.17; Th; 41,063pd, 166fr (Est); $8.25; publisher Diocese of St. Cloud; tel (612) 251-3022

St. Paul: *Catholic Bulletin* — 244 Dayton Ave. (55102); Th; 17,000fr (Sw); $12.17; Th; 30,000pd (Sw); $34.00; publishers Dennis W Heaney & Elaine Brady; editor Mary Binder; tel (612) 291-4444

MISSISSIPPI

Biloxi: *Gulf Pine Catholic (Est. 1983)* — 870 Nativity Dr.; PO Box 1189 (39533-1189); F; 4,585pd, 15fr (Sw); $7.00; C; publisher Bishop Joseph L Howze; editor Shirley M Henderson; tel (601) 374-8318; fax (601) 435-7949

Jackson: *Mississippi Today (Est. 1954)* — 237 E. Amite St.; PO Box 2130 (39225-2130); F; 13,106pd, 312fr (Est); $10.50; Bi-Wkly/F; 5,500fr (Est); $8.86; publisher Most Rev William R Houck; editors Ann Duble & Janna Avalon; tel (601) 969-1880; fax (601) 960-8455

Mississippi: *The Baptist Record (Est. 1877)* — PO Box 530, Jackson (39205); Th; 107,000pd, 870fr (Est); $34.00; F; 31,000fr (Sw); $21.01; publisher Elaine Brady; editors Guy Henderson & Tom Mani; tel (601) 968-3800

S Mississippi: *Gulf Pine Catholic (Est. 1983)* — 870 Nativity Dr. (39531); PO Box 1189, Biloxi (39533-1189); F; 4,916pd, 15fr (Sw); $7.00; F; 5,500fr (Est); $8.86; publisher Most Rev Joseph Lawson Howze; general manager Elaine Brady; editors Sgt Reed & Shirley M Henderson; tel (601) 374-8318; fax (601) 435-7949

MISSOURI

Jefferson City: *The Catholic Missourian (Est. 1958)* — PO Box 1107 (65102); F; 12,500fr (Sw); $12.17; F; 21,000pd (Sw); $9.10; publishers Bishop Michael F McAuliffe & Elaine Brady; editor Fred Bradshaw; tel (314) 635-9127; fax (314) 635-2286

Jefferson City: *Word and Way (Est. 1863)* — 400 E. High St. (65101); Th; 52,999pd, 995fr (Est); $29.00; publisher Missouri Baptist Convention; managing editor Tim Palmer; tel (314) 635-7931; fax (314) 659-7436

Kansas City: *National Catholic Reporter Publishing Co. Inc. (Est. 1964)* — 115 E. Armour Blvd.; PO Box 419281 (64141-6281); F; 10,000fr (Sw); $11.24; Th; 47,911pd, 397fr (Sw); $55.00; publishers Elaine Brady & William McSweeney Jr; editor Thomas C Fox; tel (816) 531-0538; fax (816) 968-2268

St. Louis: *Reporter* — 1333 S. Kirkwood Rd. (63122-7295); W; 5,000fr (Est); Mthly; 62,079pd, 1,334fr (Sw); $100.00; publisher Frank Hartnett; publisher & editor Rev David Mahsman; managing editor Bruce Kueck; tel (314) 965-9000

St. Louis: *St. Louis Review (Est. 1941)* — 462 N. Taylor Ave. (63108); Mthly; 5,500fr (Sw); $6.00; F; 96,611pd (Est); $22.88; publishers Bishop Edward J O' Donnell & Luke P Lally; editor Pauline L Judge; tel (314) 531-9700; fax (314) 531-2269

Springfield: *The Mirror (Est. 1965)* — 601 S. Jefferson (65806-3143); F; 16,900pd (Est); $13.50; F; 4,200fr (CAC); $4.50; editors Rev Mark G Boyer & Sgt Jim Hughes; tel (417) 866-0841; fax (417) 866-1140

NEBRASKA

Grand Island: *West Nebraska Register (Est. 1930)* — 804 W. Division; PO Box 608 (68802); Th; 1,600fr (Est); F; 17,500pd (Sw); $7.56; publishers Jim Dunn & Most Rev Lawrence J McNamara; tel (308) 382-4660

Lincoln: *Southern Nebraska Register (Est. 1932)* — 3400 Sheridan Blvd.; PO Box 80329 (68506); F; 14,000fr (Est); F; $11.55; F; 22,341pd, 110fr (Est); $67.00; publishers Most Rev Fabian W Bruskeitz & Roland Weeks Jr.; editor Perry Jennifer; tel (402) 488-0090

Omaha: *The Catholic Voice (Est. 1903)* — 6060 Northwest Radial Hwy.; PO Box 4010 (68104-0010); W; 3,500fr (Sw); $4.75; F; 69,497pd, 6fr (Sw); $25.00; publishers Jerry Strader & Most Rev Elden F Curtiss; general manager John Bohl; editors Stephen M Kent & Susan Junkins; managing editor Steve Swogentensky; tel (402) 558-6611; fax (402) 558-6614

NEW JERSEY

Camden: *Catholic Star Herald (Est. 1951)* — 1845 Haddon Ave. (08103); Th; 250pd, 8,800fr (Est); $7.60; F; 47,000pd (Sw); $18.90; publishers Karla Fudge & Most Rev James T McHugh; editor Rick Brunk; tel (609) 756-7910

Clifton: *The Beacon (Est. 1967)* — 597 Valley Rd. (07013); PO Box 1887 (07015-1887); Th; 33,712pd (Sw); $23.53; F; 5,300fr (Sw); $3.65; publishers Bishop Frank J Rodimer & Frank Lyon; tel (201) 279-8845

E Orange: *The Catholic Advocate (Est. 1951)* — 37 Evergreen Pl. (07018-2153); F; 13,500fr (Sw); $13.24; W; 25,351pd, 1,000fr (Sw); $16.50; publishers Dixie Cavner & Robert B Dylak; managing editor Steve Peter; tel (201) 678-0212

Trenton: *The Monitor (Est. 1953)* — 315 Lowell Ave.; PO Box 3095 (08619); Th; 34,228pd, 466fr (Est); $17.50; Bi-Wkly/Th; 8,500fr (Sw); N/A; publishers Most Rev John C Reiss JCD & Salvatore Paci; tel (609) 586-7400

NEW YORK

Albany: *The Evangelist (Est. 1926)* — 40 N. Main Ave. (12203); Th; 59,495pd, 350fr (Sw); $16.80; F; 8,500fr (Est); publishers Bishop Howard J Hubbard & Sammy Lopez; general manager Barbara R Oliver; editor James P Breig; managing editor Susan Pitts; tel (518) 453-6688; fax (518) 453-6793

Atlantic Beach/Cedarhurst/Hewlett/Inwood/Lawrence/N Woodmer: *Nassau Herald (Est. 1924)* — 379 Central Ave., Lawrence (11559-1607); Th; 10,494pd, 2,130fr (Est); $13.30; C; publisher Clifford Richner; general manager Stuart Richner; editor Randy Kreiss; managing editor Fran Evans; tel (516) 569-4000; fax (516) 569-4942

Conklin: *The Independent Baptist Voice* — 1035 Conklin Rd.; PO Box 208 (13748); F; 5,000fr (Est); W; 682pd, 25fr (Sw); $2.25; C; publishers Brenda Tallman & Donald Einstein; tel (607) 775-0472

New York: *America (Est. 1909)* — 106 W. 56th St. (10019); Sa; 35,694pd, 368fr (Sw); $58.50; F; 8,000fr (Est); publisher America Press Inc.; publisher Stan Martin; general manager James Santora; editors George W Hunt & Irene Brown; managing editor Robert C Collins; tel (212) 581-4640; fax (212) 399-3596

New York: *Aufbau (Est. 1934)* — 2121 Broadway (10023); Bi-Wkly/F; 30,000pd (Sw); $16.80; Qtrly; 5,000fr (Est); publishers Jerry Brunell & R B Knight; tel (212) 873-7400

New York: *Catholic New York (Est. 1981)* — PO Box 5133 (10150-5133); Th; 129,669pd, 942fr (ABC); $34.30; F; 7,500fr (Est); $6.50; publisher Ecclesiastical Communication Corp.; tel (212) 688-2399

New York: *The Forward (Est. 1990)* — 45 E. 33rd St. (10016); F; 20,000pd (Est); $30.00; C; publisher & editor Seth Lipsky; managing editor Jonathan Mahler; tel (212) 889-8200; fax (212) 447-4606

Oceanside/Island Park: *Oceanside/Island Park Herald (Est. 1967)* — 379 Central Ave., Lawrence (11559-1607); Th; 3,719pd, 1,830fr (Est); $10.22; C; publisher Clifford Richner; general manager Stuart Richner; editor Jennifer White; managing editor Fran Evans; tel (516) 569-4000; fax (516) 569-4942

Ogdenburg: *North Country Catholic* — 308 Isabella St.; PO Box 326 (13669); M; 9,339pd (Est); $9.60; publisher Diocese of Ogdenburg; tel (315) 393-2540

Rochester: *Catholic Courier (Est. 1889)* — 1150 Buffalo Rd. (14624); Bi-Wkly/Th; 2,400fr (Est); Th; 49,627pd, 2,663fr (Sw); $34.12; publishers Most Rev Matthew H Clark & Nelson A Smith; editor Karen M Franz; tel (716) 328-4340

Rockville Center: *Long Island Catholic (Est. 1962)* — 99 N. Village Ave.; PO Box 9009 (11571-9009); W; 122,235pd, 783fr (ABC); $39.50; Mthly; 200pd, 22,000fr (CAC); $8.50; publishers Delores E Winkler & Most Rev John R McGann; editors Brian Barr & Elizabeth O'Connor; managing editor Richard Mauter; tel (516) 594-1000; fax (516) 594-1092

Syracuse: *Catholic Sun (Est. 1892)* — 421 S. Warren St. (13202); Th; 34,853pd, 303fr (Est); $24.60; publishers Bishop James Moynihan & Lyle M Exstrom; managing editor Anne Checkosky; tel (315) 422-8153; fax (315) 422-7549

Vestal: *The Reporter* — 500 Clubhouse Rd. (13850); F; 28,000fr (Est); $17.50; Th; 3,000pd (Sw); $7.25; publishers Dan Hogan & Marc Goldberg; general manager Mike Dinger; editor Darla Booker; managing editor Ed Shannon; tel (607) 724-2360

Woodmere: *South Shore Record (Est. 1953)* — Railroad Ave.; PO Box 330 (11598); Th; 17,153pd (Sw); $13.44; publisher Florence B Schwartzberg; tel (516) 374-9200

NORTH CAROLINA

Greensboro: *North Carolina Christian Advocate (Est. 1855)* — PO Box 508 (27402-0508); Tu; 15,956pd (Sw); $10.00; F; 8,000fr (Est); $5.00; publisher Methodist Board of Publication Inc.; tel (910) 272-1196

Raleigh: *Biblical Recorder* — PO Box 26568 (27611); Th; 12,000fr (Est); Sa; 65,000pd (Est); $31.50; publisher Harvey Moss; editors R G Puckett & Sgt Robert Edwards; tel (919) 847-2127

Raleigh: *The North Carolina Catholic* — 300 Cardinal Gibbons Dr. (27606-2198); Su; 32,700pd (Sw); $17.00; F; 7,700fr (Est); $8.28; publisher Bishop F Joseph Gossman; tel (919) 821-9720

OHIO

Cincinnati: *The Catholic Telegraph (Est. 1831)* — 100 E. 8th St. (45202); F; 28,993pd, 144fr (Sw); $35.79; W; 6,178pd (CAC); $12.40; publishers Buddy Murchison & Most Rev Daniel E Pilarczyk; tel (513) 421-3131

Cincinnati: *Christian Standard (Est. 1866)* — 8121 Hamilton Ave. (45231); publishers Buddy Murchison & Eugene H Wigginton; editor Sam Stone; tel (513) 931-4050; fax (513) 931-0904

Cleveland: *Catholic Universe Bulletin* — 1027 Superior Ave. N.E., Chancery Bldg., 4th Fl. (44114); F; 12,000fr (Est); F (Bi-Wkly); 41,150pd (Sw); $21.50; publishers Bishop Anthony M Pilla & Stanley Cole; tel (216) 696-6525; fax (216) 696-6519

Columbus: *The Catholic Times (Est. 1951)* — PO Box 636 (43216-0636); Th; 20,000fr (Est); F; 28,684pd, 80fr (Est); $12.50; publisher Most Rev James A Griffin; editor Fr Thomas Kessler; tel (614) 224-5195

OKLAHOMA

Oklahoma City: *Baptist Messenger (Est. 1912)* — PO Box 12130 (73157-2130); Th; 100,000pd (Est); $42.00; Th; 22,000fr (Est); $10.50; publisher Jim Berg; general manager & editor Glenn A Brown; editor Frank Garcia; tel (405) 942-3800; fax (405) 942-3075

OREGON

Portland: *Catholic Sentinel (Est. 1870)* — 5536 N.E. Hassalo St.; PO Box 18030 (97218-0030); F; 15,973pd, 572fr (Sw); $17.95; F; 2,900fr (Est); publishers Joe San Miguel & John Limb; general manager Dan Humphries; editor Robert Pfohman; tel (503) 281-1191

PENNSYLVANIA

Erie: *Lake Shore Visitor (Est. 1874)* — 429 E. Grandview Blvd.; PO Box 10668 (16514-0668); Mthly; 15,200fr (Est); F; 19,591pd, 213fr (Est); $11.00; publishers Carla Pope & Donald W Trautman; managing editor Gary C Loncki; tel (814) 824-1160; fax (814) 824-1128

Greensburg: *The Catholic Accent (Est. 1951)* — 723 E. Pittsburgh St.; PO Box 850 (15601); Qtrly; 4,000fr (Est); $25.00; Th; 48,641pd, 428fr (Sw); $10.00; publisher & editor Andy Prustok; publisher Most Rev Anthony G Bosco; tel (412) 834-4010

Philadelphia: *The Catholic Standard & Times (Est. 1833)* — 222 N. 17th St. (19103); Bi-Wkly F; 5,000fr (Sw); $6.56; Th; 59,779pd (Sw); $28.00; publishers Cardinal Anthony Bevilacqua & Jean Casey Lindley & William C Eisenbeiss; editor Connie Smalls; tel (215) 587-3660/(215) 587-3661; fax (215) 587-3979

Pittsburgh: *Pittsburgh Catholic (Est. 1844)* — 135 1st Ave., Ste. 200 (15222-1506); F; 113,784pd, 1,037fr (Sw); $20.92; M; 87,137pd, 4,521fr (ABC); publisher Pittsburgh Catholic Pub Associates; tel (412) 471-1252; fax (412) 471-4228

Scottdale: *Gospel Herald* — 616 Walnut Ave. (15683); Tu; 20,750pd, 250fr (Sw); publisher J Lorne Peachey; tel (412) 887-8500

RHODE ISLAND

Providence: *Providence Visitor (Est. 1875)* — 184 Broad St. (02903); Th; 30,385pd, 2,021fr (Sw); $13.23; W; 45,000fr (Sw); $14.24; publishers Jean Casey Lindley & Most Rev Louis E Gelineau & William C Eisenbeiss; editors Dave Stump & Michael Brown; managing editor Rev Stanley T Nakowicz; tel (401) 272-1010; fax (401) 421-8418

SOUTH CAROLINA

Charleston: *The New Catholic Miscellany (Est. 1951)* — 119 Broad St. (29401); PO Box 818 (29402) Th; 21,926pd, 182fr (Sw); $7.50; publisher Most Rev David B Thompson; editor Philip M Bowman; tel (803) 724-8375; fax (803) 724-8368

Columbia: *South Carolina United Methodist Advocate* — 4908 Colonial Dr., Ste. 207 (29203-6070); Th; 14,000pd (Sw); $12.00; publisher Willie Teague; tel (803) 786-9486

Edgefield: *Edgefield Advertiser (Est. 1836)* — 119 Courthouse Dr.; PO Box 628 (29824); W; 375pd, 17fr (Sw); $1.75; publisher & editor W W Mims; tel (803) 637-3540; fax (803) 637-0602

Greenville: *The Baptist Courier (Est. 1869)* — 100 Manly St.; PO Box 2168 (29602); Th; 116,000pd (Sw); $60.00; publisher The Baptist Courier Inc.; tel (803) 232-8736

TENNESSEE

Brentwood: *Baptist & Reflector (Est. 1835)* — 5001 Maryland Way; PO Box 728 (37024); W; 60,000pd, 200fr (Est); $22.00; publisher Tennessee Baptist Convention; editor WM Fletcher Allen; tel (615) 371-2003; fax (615) 371-2080

Memphis: *Common Sense (Est. 1975)* — PO Box 41679 (38104); Th; 15,700pd (Sw); $8.40; publisher Father J Peter Sartain; tel (901) 722-4770

Nashville: *Tennessee Register (Est. 1937)* — 2400 21st Ave. S. (37212); Bi-Wkly; 17,000pd, 400fr (Est); $8.75; publisher Most Rev Edward Kmiec; general manager & editor Anthony J Spence; tel (615) 383-6393; fax (615) 292-8411

TEXAS

Corpus Christi: *South Texas Catholic (Est. 1966)* — 1200 Lantana (78407); Bi-Wkly/F; 4,100pd, 11,900fr (Est); $10.00; publisher Most Rev Rene H Gracida; tel (512) 289-1752; fax (512) 289-1783

Dallas: *Baptist Standard (Est. 1888)* — 2343 Lone Star Dr.; PO Box 660267 (75226-0267); W; 198,913pd, 2,104fr (Est); $110.00; publisher Presnall H Wood; tel (214) 630-4571; fax (214) 638-8535

Dallas: *The National Christian Reporter* — PO Box 660275 (75266-0275); F; 13,000pd, 82fr (Est); $15.00; publisher The Newspaper Div/United Methodist Comm Council; tel (214) 630-6495

Dallas: *The Texas Catholic (Est. 1952)* — 3725 Blackburn; PO Box 190347 (75219-4489); Bi-Wkly/F; 44,600pd, 400fr (Est); $37.00; publisher Most Rev Charles V Grahmann DD; editor Bronson Havard; tel (214) 528-8792; fax (214) 528-3411

Dallas: — PO Box 660275 (75266-0275); Mthly; 26,667pd (Est); $15.00; publisher The Newspaper Div/United Methodist Comm Council; tel (214) 630-6495

Dallas: *The United Methodist Reporter (Est. 1847)* — PO Box 660275 (75266-0275); F; 270,109pd, 1,064fr (Sw); $103.50; publisher The Newspaper Div/United Methodist Comm Council; tel (214) 630-6495

Dallas: *The United Methodist Review* — PO Box 660275 (75266-0275); Bi-Wkly; 121,226pd, 258fr (Est); $48.00; publisher The Newspaper Div/United Methodist Comm Council; tel (214) 630-6495

Ft. Worth: *North Texas Catholic (Est. 1985)* — 800 W. Loop 820 S. (76108); F; 25,405pd, 206fr (Sw); $15.00; publisher Bishop Joseph P Delaney; tel (817) 560-3300

UTAH

Salt Lake City: *Intermountain Catholic (Est. 1899)* — 27 "C" St.(84103); PO Box 2489 (84110-2489); F; 13,672pd, 24fr (Sw); $8.00; publisher Roman Catholic Bishop of Salt Lake City; editor Barbara S Lee; managing editor Anne M Ibach; tel (801) 328-8641; fax (801) 328-9680

VIRGINIA

Arlington: *Arlington Catholic Herald* — 200 N. Glebe Rd., Ste. 614 (22203); Th; 45,000pd (Sw); $20.72; publisher Bishop John R Keating; tel (703) 841-2590

Richmond: *The Presbyterian Outlook (Est. 1943)* — 3711 Saunders Ave. (23227); PO Box 85623 (23285-5623); M; 11,511pd, 226fr (Sw); $31.00; publisher The Presbyterian Outlook Foundation Inc.; editor Robert H Bullock Jr; tel (804) 359-8442; fax (804) 353-3639

Richmond: *Religious Herald (Est. 1828)* — PO Box 8377 (23226-0377); Th; 32,000pd (Sw); $20.00; publisher The Religious Herald Pub Assoc Inc.; editor Michael J Clingenpeel; tel (804) 672-1973; fax (804) 672-2051

WASHINGTON

Seattle: *The Progress (Est. 1897)* — 910 Marion St. (98104); Th; 15,178pd, 1,582fr (Est); $14.00; publisher The Archdiocese of Seattle; tel (206) 441-4553; fax (206) 382-3487

WEST VIRGINIA

Wheeling: *The Catholic Spirit* — PO Box 951 (26003-0119); Bi-Wkly/F; 4,569pd, 85fr (Sw); $9.38; publisher Most Rev Bernard W Schmitt; tel (304) 233-0880

WISCONSIN

La Crosse: *Times Review* — 3710 E. Ave. S.; PO Box 4004 (54602-4004); Th; 25,332pd, 100fr (Sw); $10.00; publisher Bishop John F Paul; tel (608) 788-1524

Madison: *Catholic Herald-Madison Edition (Est. 1948)* — 702 Blackhawk Ave.; PO Box 5913 (53705); Th; 29,000pd (Est); $15.00; publisher Bishop William H Bullock; tel (608) 233-8060

Milwaukee: *Catholic Herald (Est. 1878)* — 3501 S. Lake Dr.; PO Box 07913 (53207-0913); Th; 76,801pd, 3,301fr (Sw); $48.00; publishers Archbishop Rembert G Weakland & Ethel M Gintoft; general manager M JDesmond; editor Thomas J Smith; tel (414) 769-3478

Superior: *Catholic Herald (Est. 1954)* — 1512 N. 12th St.; PO Box 969 (54880); Th; 20,000pd (Sw); $13.00; publisher Bishop Raphael M Fliss; editor Sam M Lucero; tel (715) 392-8268

Copyright ©1996 by the Editor & Publisher Co.

COLLEGE & UNIVERSITY NEWSPAPERS

STUDENT NEWSPAPERS PUBLISHED WEEKLY OR DAILY

EDITOR'S NOTE: The following list of college and university newspapers was provided to Editor & Publisher by American Passage Media Corporation, Carleton W. Bryant, Vice President, (800) 426-5537. Advertising numbers are national open column inch rates reported to American Passage. Only the primary paper at each college or university is listed.

ALABAMA

Alabama A&M Univ.: *Maroon & White* — PO Box 991, Normal (35762); 5,000; $12.73; editor Charlotte Hinson; tel (205) 851-5620; Format: 6x15

Alabama State Univ.: *Hornet Tribune* — 915 S. Jackson, Montgomery (36195); 2,500; $10.91; editor Alberta Perry; tel (334) 293-4419; Format: 6x14.5

Auburn Univ.: *Auburn Plainsman* — B-100 Union Bldg., Auburn (36849); H; 19,500; $11.15; editor Jan Waters; tel (334) 844-4130/4139; Format: 6x21

Auburn Univ.: *Aumnibus* — Auburn Univ At Montgomery, Montgomery (36117-3596); W; 1,800; $9.09; editor Brian Miller; tel (334) 244-3569; Format: 5x13

Birmingham Southern College: *Hilltop News* — Box A-46, Birmingham (35254); 2,000; $12.73; tel (205) 458-6080; Format: 5x16

Jacksonville State Univ.: *Chanticleer* — 180 Self Hall, Box 3060, Jacksonville (36265); H; 7,000; $9.51; editor Michael Canada; tel (205) 782-5712; Format: 5x13

Jefferson State Community College: *Pioneer* — 2601 Carson Rd., Birmingham (35215); 5,000; $12.11; tel (205) 856-6095/6096; Format: 4x12

Samford Univ.: *Samford Crimson* — SU Box 2269, Birmingham (35229); W; 4,800; $21.63; editor Amy Walker; tel (205) 870-2474/2998/2011; Format: 5x16

Spring Hill College: *Springhillian* — Spring Hill College, Mobile (36608); 2,000; $8.00; tel (334) 380-3850; Format: 5x13

Troy State Univ.: *Tropolitan* — Wallace Hall, Troy (36082); H; 4,000; $8.00; editor Kristy Galbraith; tel (334) 670-3327; Format: 4x13

Tuskegee Univ.: *Campus Digest* — Kresge Center, #318, Tuskegee (36088); 4,500; $8.00; editor Derrick Dortch; tel (334) 727-8263; Format: 5x13

Univ. of Alabama: *Kaleidoscope* — Box 76 University Center, Birmingham (35294); T; 8,000; $12.73; editor Marcus Nelson; tel (205) 934-3354; Format: 6x21.5

Univ. of Alabama: *Exponent* — University Center, Huntsville (35899); W; 4,500; $11.26; editor Gricel Ocasio; tel (205) 895-6090; Format: 6x21

Univ. of Alabama: *Crimson White* — 923 University Blvd., Tuscaloosa (35487); MWHF; 15,000; $13.18; editor Saun Kelly; tel (205) 348-7839; Format: 6x21.5

Univ. of Montevallo: *Alabamian* — Information Services, Montevallo (35115); 2,500; $9.09; editor D Scott Mauldin; tel (205) 665-6222; Format: 6x21.5

Univ. of North Alabama: *Flor-Ala* — Box 5300 University Station, Florence (35632); H; 4,500; $8.00; editor Shannon Heupel; tel (205) 760-4363/4427; Format: 6x21

Univ. of South Alabama: *Vanguard* — PO Box U-25100, Mobile (36688); M; 6,500; $10.00; tel (334) 460-6442; Format: 6x21

ALASKA

Alaska Pacific Univ.: *APU Journal* — 4101 University Dr., Anchorage (99508-4672); 1,000; $9.04; tel (907) 564-8304; Format: 5x16

Univ. of Alaska: *Northern Light* — Campus Center, Rm. 215, Anchorage (99508); M; 5,000; $12.28; editor Scott Gere; tel (907) 786-1318; Format: 4x16

Univ. of Alaska: *Sunstar* — Wood Center, Fairbanks (99775-6640); T; 4,500; $29.09; editor Tony Jacob; tel (907) 474-7540; Format: 4x14.5

ARIZONA

Arizona State Univ.: *State Press* — Mathews Center, Tempe (85287-1502); MTWHF; 18,000; $17.91; tel (602) 965-6555; Format: 6x16

Central Arizona College: *The Cactus* — Wodruff & Overfield Rds., Coolidge (85228); 3,500; $8.00; editor Bonnie Warren-Kertz; tel (602) 426-4455; Format: 5x13

Embry Riddle Aero Univ.: *Horizon* — 3200 Willow Creek Rd., Prescott (86301); 2,000; $8.18; editor Laura Wilson; tel (602) 776-3891; Format: 6x21

Glendale Community College: *The Voice* — 6000 W. Olive, Glendale (85302-3090); 5,000; $10.91; editor Alan Miller; tel (602) 435-3820; Format: 6x16

Grand Canyon Univ.: *Canyon Echoes* — 3300 W. Camelback Rd., Phoenix (85061-1097); T; 2,000; $9.13; editors Laura Dobbins & Steve Gardner; tel (602) 589-2569; Format: 5x12.75

Mesa Community College: *Mesa Legend* — 1833 W. Southern Ave., Mesa (85202); 15,000; $10.00; editor Riley Stauen; tel (602) 461-7330/7329; Format: 6x20.5

Northern Arizona Univ.: *Lumberjack* — Bldg. #18, Rm. 107, Flagstaff (86011); H; 13,000; $12.55; editor Simone Tothe; tel (520) 523-2570; Format: 6x21

Pima Community College: *Aztec Press* — 2202 W. Anklam Rd., Tucson (85709); W; 8,500; $16.36; tel (520) 884-6800; Format: 6x16

Univ. of Arizona: *Arizona Daily Wildcat* — Student Union Bldg., Rm. 5, Tucson (85721); MTWHF; 20,000; $17.55; editor Christine Verges; tel (520) 621-1714/1686; Format: 6x16

ARKANSAS

Arkansas State Univ.: *Herald* — PO Box 1930, State University (72467); TF; 8,000; $11.37; tel (501) 972-3075; Format: 6x21.5

Arkansas Tech Univ.: *Arka-Tech* — Highway 7, Russellville (72801); M; 2,500; $8.00; editor Connie Bilbo; tel (501) 968-0390; Format: 5x13.5

Harding Univ.: *Bison* — Sta. A, Box 1192 Searcy (72143); F; 3,500; $9.09; tel (501) 279-4055; Format: 4x12

Henderson State Univ.: *The Oracle* — Box 7693, Arkadelphia (71999); F; 3,000; $8.00; editor Jasper Ballew; tel (501) 230-5221; Format: 6x14

Hendrix College: *The Profile* — 1601 Harkrider, Conway (72032); H; 1,200; $9.09; editor Margie Allsbrook; tel (501) 450-1269; Format: 5x13

John Brown Univ.: *Three Fold Advocate* — PO Box 2501, Siloam Springs (72761); M; 1,000; $8.00; tel (501) 524-3131 ext. 189; Format: 5x12.5

Southern Arkansas Univ.: *The Bray* — Box 1400 Sau, Magnolia (71753); H; 2,500; $8.00; editor Chauntel Lane; tel (501) 235-4268; Format: 6x13

Univ. of Arkansas: *Arkansas Traveler* — 747 W. Dickson, Fayetteville (72701); MWF; 10,000; $19.09; editor Anson Low; tel (501) 575-3887; Format: 5x14

Univ. of Arkansas: *The Ualr Forum* — 2801 S. University Ave., Little Rock (72204); M; 5,000; $9.77; editor Krystal Adams; tel (501) 569-3326; Format: 5x15

Univ. of Arkansas: *Arkansawyer* — 211 L.A. Davis Union, Pine Bluff (71601); 3,000; $9.09; editor Demorris Williams; tel (501) 543-8502; Format: 5x13

Univ. of Central Arkansas: *Echo* — UCA PO Box 5038, Conway (72035); H; 7,000; $8.64; editor Sara Greene; tel (501) 450-5885/5886; Format: 5x15.5

CALIFORNIA

Allan Hancock College: *The Oracle* — 800 S. College Dr., Santa Maria (93454); 1,500; $8.00; editor Doug Di Franco; tel (805) 922-6966 ext. 3220; Format: 5x13

American River College: *The Current* — 4700 College Oak, Sacramento (95841); M; 5,000; $12.73; editor Emily Cauch; tel (916) 484-8304; Format: 5x16

Antelope Vly. College: *Crusader* — 3041 W. Ave. K, Lancaster (93536); H; 2,500; $14.54; editor Karen Perry; tel (805) 943-3241 ext. 359; Format: 5x15.5

Azusa Pacific Univ.: *Clause* — 901 E. Alosta, Azusa (91702-7001); F; 2,000; $14.09; editor Adam Bosler; tel (818) 815-6000 ext. 3515; Format: 4x16

Bakersfield College: *Renegade Rip* — 1801 Panorama Dr., Bakersfield (93305); F; 7,500; $8.50; tel (805) 395-4323; Format: 6x21

Biola Univ.: *Chimes* — 13800 Biola Ave., La Mirada (90639); F; 2,700; $14.08; editor Emily Smith; tel (310) 903-4880; Format: 5x16

Cabrillo College: *The Voice* — 6500 Soquel Dr., Aptos (95003); M; 5,000; $9.69; tel (408) 479-6293; Format: 6x20

Cal Poly State Univ.: *Mustang Daily* — Graphic Arts Bldg., Rm. 226, San Luis Obispo (93407); MTWHF; 6,000; $16.37; editor April Karys; tel (805) 756-1143; Format: 5x16

California Baptist College: *Banner* — 8432 Magnolia Ave., Riverside (92504); 1,000; $9.09; tel (714) 689-5771; Format: 5x12

California Institute of Tech.: *California Tech* — 40-58 Sac, Pasadena (91125); F; 3,500; $12.36; editor Tom Grundy; tel (818) 395-6154; Format: 5x16.5

California Lutheran Univ.: *The Echo* — 60 Olsen Rd., Thousand Oaks (91360); W; 1,900; $10.91; tel (805) 493-3865; Format: 4x16

California State Poly Univ.: *Poly Post* — 3801 W. Temple Ave., Pomona (91768); T; 6,500; $11.82; editor Taylor Vaughan; tel (909) 869-3528; Format: 6x21

California State Univ.: *The Runner* — 9001 Stockdale Hwy., Bakersfield (93311-1099); W; 3,000; $18.18; editor Bob Christie; tel (805) 664-2165; Format: 4x13

California State Univ.: *Rainbow* — 1000 E. Victoria St., Carson (90746); H; 3,000; $15.00; editor Don Sergler; tel (310) 516-3687; Format: 4x13

California State Univ.: *Orion* — 1st & Normal, Chico (95929); W; 10,000; $13.50; editor Stacia Lay; tel (916) 898-5625; Format: 6x21

California State Univ.: *Daily Collegian* — Keats Campus Bldg., Ste. 42, Fresno (93740-0042); MTHF; 3,500; $9.09; tel (209) 278-5731; Format: 5x11.25

California State Univ.: *Daily Titan* — Humanities 211, Fullerton (92634); TWHF; 6,000; $12.00; tel (714) 773-3373; Format: 6x21

California State Univ.: *The Pioneer* — Dept of Mass Communication, Hayward (94542); H; 10,000; $14.54; tel (510) 885-3526; Format: 5x16

California State Univ.: *Daily Forty Niner* — 1331 Palo Verde, Long Beach (90840-4601); MTWH; 10,000; $18.00; tel (310) 985-8001/5177; Format: 6x16

California State Univ.: *University Times* — 5151 State University Dr., Los Angeles (90032); MH; 7,000; $14.00; editor Amy Dam; tel (213) 343-4220; Format: 6x16

California State Univ.: *Daily Sundial* — 18111 Nordhoff St., Northridge (91330-8258); MTWH; 9,000; $14.00; tel (818) 885-2998; Format: 7x16

California State Univ.: *State Hornet Newspaper* — 6000 J St., Sacramento (95819-6102); TF; 12,000; $14.54; editor Susan List; tel (916) 278-5587/7248; Format: 6x20.5

California State Univ.: *Chronicle* — 5500 University Pkwy., San Bernardino (92407); W; 5,000; $18.18; tel (909) 880-5931; Format: 5x12

California State Univ.: *The Signal* — 801 W. Monte Vista Ave., Turlock (95382); W; 4,500; $8.80; editor Armida Sadivar; tel (209) 667-3411; Format: 4x13

Cerritos College: *Talon Marks* — 11110 E. Alondra Blvd., Norwalk (90650); 7,500; $14.54; editor Nancy Ballard; tel (310) 860-2451 ext. 2617; Format: 4x13

Chabot College: *Spectator* — 2555 Hesperian Blvd., Hayward (94545); H; 6,000; $10.91; editor John Henel; tel (510) 783-4151/786-6919; Format: 5x16

Chaffey College: *Mountain Breeze* — 5885 Haven Ave., Alta Loma (91737); 3,000; $10.38; editor Henry Salazar; tel (909) 941-2182; Format: 4x15

Chapman Univ.: *Panther* — 333 N. Glassell, Orange (92666); M; 1,600; $10.91; editor Paula Yakubic; tel (714) 744-7616; Format: 5x16

Citrus College: *Clarion* — 1000 W. Foothill Blvd., Glendora (91740); 3,000; $9.09; editor Kathryn Dunn; tel (818) 914-8587; Format: 5x15

Claremont Colleges: *Collage* — Huntley Bookstore Bsmt., Claremont (91711); H; 6,000; $12.44; editor Joanne Helkenn; tel (909) 624-1887; Format: 4x13.5

College of Marin: *Echo Times* — 835 College Ave., Kentfield (94904); 3,000; $9.09; tel (415) 485-9690; Format: 5x14

College of Notre Dame: *The Argonaut* — 1500 Ralston Ave., Belmont (94002); 2,000; $8.00; tel (415) 508-3677; Format: 4x11.5

College of San Mateo: *San Matean* — Burlingame (94010); 3,000; $13.62; tel (415) 692-9406; Format: 5x16

College of The Canyons: *Canyon Call* — 26455 Rockwell Canyon Rd., Valencia (91355); W; 3,000; $10.00; editor Rehan Hyder; tel (805) 259-7800 ext. 318; Format: 5x16

College of The Sequoias: *Campus* — 915 S. Mooney, Visalia (93277); F; 2,100; $8.00; tel (209) 730-3844; Format: 6x21.5

Contra Costa College: *The Advocate* — 2600 Mission Bell Dr., San Pablo (94806); F; 2,500; $8.00; editor Genoa Barrow; tel (510) 235-7800 ext. 225; Format: 6x21

Cypress College: *The Charger Chronicle* — 9200 Valley View, Cypress (90630); W; 4,000; $10.50; tel (714) 828-7590; Format: 5x16

Diablo Vly. College: *Inquirer* — 321 Golf Club Rd., Pleasant Hill (94523); F; 5,000; $9.54; tel (510) 685-1230 ext. 313; Format: 6x21

E. LA College: *Campus News* — 1301 Brooklyn Ave., Monterey Park (91754); W; 5,000; $8.18; editor Robert Martinez; tel (213) 265-8819; Format: 6x21

El Camino College: *Warwhoop* — 16007 Crenshaw Blvd., Torrance (90506); H; 8,000; $13.50; editor Michelle Cecena; tel (310) 660-3328; Format: 6x21

Evergreen Vly. College: *The Flyer* — 3095 Yurba Beuna, San Jose (95121); 2,000; $14.54; tel (408) 274-7900 ext. 6682; Format: 4x16

Foothill College: *Foothill Sentinel* — 12345 El Monte Rd., M-24, Los Altos Hills (94022); 4,000; $9.23; tel (415) 949-7372; Format: 5x16.5

Fresno City College: *Rampage* — 1101 E. University, Fresno (93741); 4,000; $8.00; editor Steve Sauer; tel (209) 442-8262; Format: 5x16

Fullerton College: *Hornet* — 321 E. Chapman Ave., Fullerton (92632); M; 5,000; $11.82; editor Gwen Struve; tel (714) 992-7154; Format: 6x21

Gavilan College: *The Rambler* — 5055 Santa Teresa Blvd., Gilroy (95020); 2,000; $8.18; editors Virginia Acton & Michael Duran; tel (408) 848-4827; Format: 5x16

Glendale Community College: *El Vaquero* — 1500 N. Verdugo Rd., Glendale (91208); 3,500; $9.73; editor Michael Redding; tel (818) 240-1000 ext. 5352; Format: 5x16

Golden Gate Univ.: *The Gateway* — 536 Mission St., San Francisco (94105-2968); 4,000; $10.00; editor Sandra Davis; tel (415) 442-7878; Format: 5x15.25

Golden West College: *The Western Sun* — 15744 Golden West St., Huntington (92647); H; 6,000; $10.91; tel (714) 895-8256; Format: 6x21.5

Grossmont College: *The Summit* — 8800 Grossmont College Dr., El Cajon (92020); H; 3,000; $9.51; editor Stephanie Macys; tel (619) 465-1700 exts. 270/271; Format: 5x16

Holy Names College: *HNC Newspaper* — 3500 Mountain Blvd., Oakland (94619-9989); F; 1,000; $12.73; editor Christine Renner; tel (510) 436-1045; Format: 5x14

Copyright ©1996 by the Editor & Publisher Co.

Humboldt State Univ.: *Lumberjack* — Nelson Hall, E. 6, Arcata (95521); W; 6,000; $8.00; tel (707) 826-3259; Format: 5x14

Laney College: *Laney Tower* — 900 Fallon St., Oakland (94607); 4,000; $12.00; tel (510) 464-3459/3460; Format: 5x16

Loma Linda Univ.: *Today* — University Relations Office, Loma Linda (92354); 4,000; $8.00; editor Richard Weismeyer; tel (909) 824-4526; Format: 5x16

Long Beach City College: *Viking* — 4901 E. Carson, Long Beach (90808); H; 6,000; $11.00; editor Joe Cabera Zermeno; tel (310) 420-4284; Format: 5x16

LA City College: *Collegian* — 855 N. Vermont Ave., Los Angeles (90029); 5,000; $8.00; tel (213) 953-4268; Format: 6x21

LA Pierce College: *The Roundup* — 6201 Winnetka Ave., Woodland Hills (91371); W; 5,000; $12.73; tel (818) 719-6483; Format: 6x21

LA Southwest College: *Explorer* — 1600 W. Imperial Hwy., Los Angeles (90047); 4,000; $8.00; tel (213) 777-2225 ext. 376; Format: 5x15

LA Trade Tech. College: *Trade Winds* — 400 W. Washington Blvd., Los Angeles (90015); 5,000; $14.00; editor Shafeeq Qarsim; tel (213) 744-9046; Format: 5x13.5

LA Vly. College: *Valley Star* — 5800 Fulton Ave., Van Nuys (91401-4096); H; 7,000; $10.69; tel (818) 781-1200 ext. 239; Format: 6x21

Los Medanos College: *Lmc Experience* — 2700 E. Leland Rd., Pittsburg (94565); F; 2,000; $8.00; tel (510) 439-2181 ext. 357; Format: 6x21

Loyola Law School: *Loyola Reporter* — 1441 W. Olympic Blvd., Los Angeles (90015); 1,000; $15.00; editor David Bleistein; tel (213) 736-8117; Format: 4x16

Loyola Marymount Univ.: *Los Angeles Loyolan* — 7101 W. 80th St., Los Angeles (90045); W; 3,100; $12.73; editor James Keane; tel (310) 338-7509/2879; Format: 5x16

Mcgeorge School of Law: *Dialogue* — 3200 5th Ave., Sacramento (95817); 1,000; $17.71; editor Melissa Korber; tel (916) 736-1077; Format: 3x13

Menlo College: *The Oak* — 1000 El Camino Real, Atherton (94025); 2,500; $10.35; editor Susan Larson; tel (415) 688-3710/306-5381; Format: 4x16

Mills College: *Mills Weekly* — 5000 Macarthur Blvd., Oakland (94613-1399); H; 1,200; $10.91; tel (510) 430-2246; Format: 5x16

Modesto Jr College: *Focus* — College Ave., Modesto (95350); T; 3,500; $9.09; tel (209) 575-6224; Format: 5x13

Moorpark College: *Reporter* — 7075 Campus Rd., Moorpark (93021); M; 7,500; $9.09; tel (805) 378-1440/1553; Format: 6x21.5

Mt San Antonio College: *The Mountaineer* — 1100 N. Grand Ave., Walnut (91789); 6,000; $10.91; tel (909) 594-5611 ext. 4597; Format: 5x15

Occidental College: *The Occidental* — 1600 Campus Rd., Box F40, Los Angeles (90041); F; 2,000; $11.82; editor Timothy Suing; tel (213) 259-2896; Format: 5x16

Ohlone College: *Ohlone Monitor* — 43600 Mission Blvd., Rm. 5310, Fremont (94539-0390); H; 3,200; $8.30; tel (510) 659-6075/6074; Format: 5x16

Orange Coast College: *Coast Report* — 2701 Fairview Rd., Costa Mesa (92626); W; 8,000; $10.50; tel (714) 432-5673/5094; Format: 6x21

Oxnard College: *Campus Observer* — 4000 S. Rose, Oxnard (93033); 3,000; $10.91; tel (805) 986-5836; Format: 5x13

Pacific Union College: *Campus Chronicle* — Campus Center, Angwin (94508); 2,000; $8.00; tel (707) 965-7121; Format: 4x13.75

Palomar College: *Telescope* — 1140 W. Mission Rd., San Marcos (92069); F; 4,000; $10.90; tel (619) 744-1150 ext. 2450; Format: 5x16

Pasadena City College: *The Courier* — 1570 E. Colorado Blvd., Rm. CC220, Pasadena (91106-2003); H; 10,000; $12.27; editor Enrico Piazza; tel (818) 585-7979; Format: 6x21

Pepperdine Univ.: *Graphic* — 24255 Pacific Coast Hwy., Malibu (90265); H; 2,800; $16.37; tel (310) 456-4318/4311; Format: 6x20.5

Point Loma Nazarene College: *The Point* — 3900 Lomaland Dr., San Diego (92106-2899); W; 2,200; $12.73; editor Molly Yanity; tel (619) 221-2444; Format: 4x16

Pomona College: *The Student Life* — Edmunds Student Union, Claremont (91711); F; 2,400; $10.60; editor Brian Arbour; tel (909) 621-8555 ext. 2269; Format: 6x22

Rancho Santiago College: *El Don* — 17th St. at Bristol, Santa Ana (92706); F; 4,000; $10.60; tel (714) 564-5617; Format: 5x14

Rio Hondo College: *El Paisano* — 3600 Workman Mill Rd., Whittier (90608); W; 3,000; $8.00; tel (310) 908-3453; Format: 6x21

Sacramento City College: *Express* — 3835 Freeport Blvd., Sacramento (95822); H; 3,000; $8.00; editor Dana Oland; tel (916) 558-2562; Format: 5x15

Saddleback College: *Lariat* — 28000 Marguerite Pkwy., Mission Viejo (92692); 6,000; $10.91; tel (714) 582-4688; Format: 6x21

San Bernardino Vly. College: *Warrior* — 701 S. Mt. Vernon Ave., San Bernardino (92410); 2,000; $8.00; tel (909) 888-6511 ext. 1530; Format: 4x15.5

San Diego City College: *City Times* — 1313 12th Ave., San Diego (92101); 2,000; $9.09; tel (619) 230-2437; Format: 3x10

San Diego Mesa College: *Mesa Press* — 7250 Mesa College Dr., San Diego (92111-4998); M; 2,000; $9.10; tel (619) 627-2630; Format: 3x10

San Diego State Univ.: *Daily Aztec* — PSFA Bldg., Rm. 358, San Diego (92182); MTWHF; 13,000; $21.13; editor Josh Suchon; tel (619) 594-7292/6977; Format: 4x16

San Francisco State Univ.: *Golden Gater* — 1600 Holloway Ave., San Francisco (94132); TH; 10,000; $15.27; tel (415) 338-3123; Format: 6x21

San Joaquin Delta College: *Impact* — 5151 Pacific Ave., Stockton (95207); F; 2,000; $8.00; editor Eric Giese; tel (209) 474-5288/5156; Format: 5x15

San Jose City College: *The Times* — 2100 Moorpark Ave., San Jose (95128); 2,500; $9.09; tel (408) 298-2181 ext. 3849; Format: 5x15.75

San Jose State Univ.: *Spartan Daily* — 1 Washington Sq., San Jose (95192-0149); MTWHF; 7,500; $15.06; editor Joanne Dominque; tel (408) 924-3270/3283; Format: 6x21

Santa Barbara City Coll: *Channels* — 721 Cliff Dr., Santa Barbara (93109-2394); F; 4,000; $17.82; editor Elise Johnson; tel (805) 965-0581 ext. 2826; Format: 5x16

Santa Clara Univ.: *The Santa Clara* — Box 1190, Santa Clara (95053); H; 4,500; $12.00; editor Tim O'Conner Fraser; tel (408) 554-4445/4764; Format: 5x15.5

Santa Monica College: *Corsair* — 6101 W. Centinela Ave., Culver City (90230); W; 5,000; $16.00; tel (310) 215-3534; Format: 6x20

Santa Rosa Jr College: *The Oakleaf* — 1501 Mendocino Ave., Santa Rosa (95401); H; 6,300; $14.55; tel (707) 527-4254/4505; Format: 5x16

Shasta College: *Lance* — PO Box 6006, Redding (96099); 4,500; $10.45; editor Susan Deuel; tel (916) 225-4744; Format: 5x14

Solano Community College: *The Tempest* — 4000 Suisun Valley Rd., Suisun City (94585); H; 2,000; $10.91; tel (707) 864-7000 ext. 361; Format: 5x12.5

Sonoma State Univ.: *Sonoma State Star* — Student Union, Rohnert Park (94928); T; 4,000; $14.54; editor Paul Chambers; tel (707) 664-2714; Format: 5x13

Southwestern College: *Southwestern Sun* — 900 Otay Lakes Rd., Chula Vista (91910); 6,000; $8.19; editor Jeff Sanford; tel (619) 482-6368; Format: 6x22

Southwestern School of Law: *Commentator* — 675 S. Westmoreland Ave., Los Angeles (90005); 2,000; $11.36; tel (213) 738-6873; Format: 4x16

St Marys College: *The Collegian* — PO Box 3010, Moraga (94575); H; 4,000; $18.18; editor Brian Thomas; tel (510) 631-4279; Format: 4x16

Stanford Univ.: *The Stanford Daily* — Storke Publications Bldg., Stanford (94305); MTWHF; 13,500; $18.17; editor Sara Katz; tel (415) 723-2555 ext. 402; Format: 6x21

US International Univ.: *Envoy* — 10455 Pomerado Rd., San Diego (92131); 2,000; $13.64; tel (619) 635-4540; Format: 5x16

Univ. of California: *Daily Californian* — 600 Eshleman Hall, Berkeley (94720); TF; 23,000; $25.87; editor Bita Bowman; tel (510) 548-8300/8080; Format: 5x16

Univ. of California: *California Aggie* — 25 Lower Freeborn, Davis (95616); MTWHF; 13,000; $14.46; editor Todd Perlman; tel (916) 752-0365; Format: 6x21

Univ. of California: *New University* — 3100 Gateway Commons, Irvine (92717); M; 12,000; $21.38; editor Phat X Chiern; tel (714) 824-4285/4284; Format: 5x15.5

Univ. of California: *Guardian* — 9500 Gilman Dr., Ms 0316, La Jolla (92093-0316); MH; 13,000; $15.91; editor Tedd Ladd; tel (619) 534-3466/3967; Format: 5x16

Univ. of California: *Daily Bruin* — 225 Kerckhoff Hall, Los Angeles (90024); MTWHF; 25,000; $25.91; editor Roxanne Marquez; tel (310) 206-7562/0905; Format: 5x16

Univ. of California: *Highlander* — Riverside, 92521 (T); 10,000; $13.73; tel (909) 787-5039/3617; Format: 6x14

Univ. of California: *Daily Nexus* — PO Box 13402-Ucen, Santa Barbara (93107); MTWHF; 11,500; $14.68; editor Suzanne Gardner; tel (805) 893-3828/3820; Format: 6x16.5

Univ. of California: *City On A Hill* — Stonehouse UCSC, Santa Cruz (95064); H; 12,000; $15.00; editor Jennifer Webster Burnham; tel (408) 459-4359; Format: 5x13

Univ. of La Verne: *Campus Times* — 1950 3rd St., Laverne (91750); F; 1,600; $9.09; tel (909) 392-2712; Format: 4x16

Univ. of Redlands: *Bulldog* — Gannett Center, Redlands (92374); M; 2,000; $7.40; editor Susi Knadler; tel (909) 335-5139; Format: 5x12.5

Univ. of San Diego: *Vista* — Alcala Park, San Diego (92110); H; 4,000; $19.27; editor Joey Santos; tel (619) 260-4714; Format: 4x16

Univ. of San Francisco: *Foghorn* — 2130 Fulton St., San Francisco (94117-1080); H; 4,000; $21.82; editor Kent German; tel (415) 666-6122; Format: 4x16

Univ. of San Francisco Law: *Forum* — Ignatian Heights, San Francisco (94117-1080); 800; $8.22; editor Alison Simms; tel (415) 666-2672; Format: 5x15.5

Univ. of Southern California: *Daily Trojan* — Student Union 404, Los Angeles (90089-0895); MTWHF; 10,000; $13.00; editor Michelle Ladd; tel (213) 740-2707; Format: 5x16

Univ. of The Pacific: *Pacifican* — 3601 Pacific Ave., Stockton (95211); H; 4,500; $18.18; editor Kate Lamping; tel (209) 946-2114; Format: 6x20

Ventura College: *Ventura College Press* — 4667 Telegraph Rd., Ventura (93003); W; 2,700; $10.91; editor Sandy Davis; tel 8056546400 ext. 1380; Format: 6x21

W Los Angeles College: *Oiler* — 4800 Freshman Dr., Culver City (90230); 6,000; $14.14; tel (310) 287-4319; Format: 4x13.5

W Vly. College: *Norseman* — 14000 Fruitvale Ave., Saratoga (95070); 3,000; $10.00; tel (408) 741-2043; Format: 6x21

Westmont College: *Horizon* — 955 La Paz Rd., Santa Barbara (93108); F; 2,000; $10.91; editor Joanne Spiritosanto; tel (805) 565-6301; Format: 5x16.75

Whittier College: *Quaker Campus* — Box 8613, Whittier (90608); H; 2,000; $8.42; editor Jamine Leigh Kramer; tel (310) 907-4254; Format: 5x16

COLORADO

Adams State College: *South Coloradan* — College Center, Alamosa (81102); H; 2,500; $8.00; editor Maggie Kanne; tel (719) 589-7904; Format: 5x15

Aims Community College: *The Aims Angle* — 5401 W. 20th St., Greeley (80634); W; 2,000; $8.00; tel (303) 330-8008 ext. 450; Format: 3x10

Arapahoe Community College: *Rapp Street Journal* — 2500 W. College Dr., Littleton (80160-9002); 3,000; $9.09; tel (303) 797-5666; Format: 5x16

Colorado College: *The Catalyst* — Worner Center, Colorado Springs (80903); F; 2,500; $9.70; editor Chad Nitta; tel (719) 389-6675; Format: 5x15

Colorado School of Mines: *Mines Oredigger* — 16th & Maple, Golden (80401); T; 3,000; $9.09; editor Matt Lampros; tel (303) 273-3352; Format: 6x21

Colorado State Univ.: *Rocky Mt Collegian* — Lory Student Center, Fort Collins (80523); MTWHF; 12,000; $12.55; editor Mindy Varner; tel (303) 491-1146; Format: 6x21.5

Front Range Community College: *Front Page* — 3645 W. 112th Ave., Westminster (80030); 2,500; $9.09; editor Perry Swanson; tel (303) 466-8811 ext. 534; Format: 5x16

Ft. Lewis College: *Independent* — 119 Cub, Durango (81301); F; 4,000; $13.64; editor Duane Roberson; tel (970) 247-7405; Format: 6x21

Mesa State College: *Criterion* — 1175 Texas, Grand Junction (81502); H; 5,000; $11.82; editor Mark Borgard; tel (790) 248-1255; Format: 5x16

Metropolitan State College: *The Metropolitan* — Auraria Student Union, Denver (80204); F; 5,000; $10.00; editor Louis Landa; tel (303) 556-8361; Format: 4x14

Northeastern Jr College: *Plainsman Pathway* — 100 College Dr., Sterling (80751); 1,400; $8.00; tel (303) 522-6600; Format: 5x14

Red Rocks Community College: *Red Rocks Journal* — 13300 W. 6th Ave., Golden (80401-5398); 2,000; $9.10; editor Cheryl Jung; tel (303) 988-6160 ext. 371; Format: 4x16

Regis Univ.: *Highlander* — 3333 Regis Blvd., Denver (80221-1099); W; 1,200; $13.64; editor Nandini Stocker; tel (303) 964-5391; Format: 5x16

US Air Force Academy: *Falcon Flyer* — 22 N.Sierra Madre, Colorado Springs (80903); H; 7,500; $10.99; editor Doug Roth; tel (719) 634-1593; Format: 6x16

Univ. of Colorado: *Colorado Daily* — 839 Pearl St., Boulder (80302); MTWHF; 19,000; $21.46; editor Clint Talbott; tel (303) 443-6272/442-3914; Format: 6x14

Univ. of Colorado: *The Scribe* — 1420 Austin Bluffs Pkwy., Colorado Sprgs (80933); W; 2,000; $10.00; editor John Stevens; tel (719) 593-3469; Format: 5x16

Univ. of Colorado: *Advocate* — 955 Lawrence St., Denver (80204); W; 3,000; $15.45; editor Jeffrey Georgeson; tel (303) 556-8321/2535; Format: 4x14

Univ. of Denver: *The Clarion* — 2050 E. Evans Ave., Denver (80208); H; 4,000; $14.55; editor Kristin Branch; tel (303) 871-3929; Format: 5x16

Univ. of Northern Colorado: *Mirror* — University Center, Greeley (80639); MWF; 7,000; $11.36; editor John Gimlin; tel (303) 351-4487; Format: 5x16

Univ. of Southern Colorado: *USC Today* — 2200 Bonforte Blvd., Pueblo (81001); W; 4,000; $8.00; editor Georgeanne Nelson; tel (719) 549-2812; Format: 5x15.75

Western State College: *Top Of The World* — Student Union, Rm. 204, Gunnison (81231); T; 2,000; $10.00; editor Keith Carlsen; tel (303) 943-3062; Format: 5x17

CONNECTICUT

Central Connecticut State Univ.: *Central Recorder* — 1615 Stanley St., New Britain (06050); W; 6,000; $8.65; tel (203) 832-3744; Format: 5x16

Connecticut College: *College Voice* — Box 5351, New London (06320); T; 3,500; $9.09; editor April Ondis; tel (203) 439-2813; Format: 5x16

Eastern Connecticut State Univ.: *Campus Lantern* — Student Center, Rm. 215, Willimantic (06226-2295); W; 2,800; $11.18; editor Rob; tel (203) 465-4445; Format: 4x15

Fairfield Univ.: *The Mirror* — Box AA, Fairfield (06430); H; 3,500; $9.64; editor Laura White; tel (203) 254-4000 ext. 2533; Format: 4x16

Housatonic Community Technical College: *Horizons* — 510 Barnum Ave., Bridgeport (06608); 1,000; $8.00; tel (203) 579-6442; Format: 4x15

Manchester Community College: *Live Wire* — 60 Bidwell St., Manchester (06040); 2,000; $9.09; editor Kym Soper; tel (203) 647-6057; Format: 5x15

Naugatuck Vly. Community Tech College: *The Comm Tech News* — 750 Chase Park Way, Waterbury (06708); 2,000; $8.00; tel (203) 596-8651; Format: 4x13

Norwalk Community College: *Soundings* — 333 Wilson Ave., Norwolk (06854); 2,500; $9.66; tel (203) 857-7115; Format: 4x16

Quinnipiac College: *Chronicle* — 275 Mt. Carmel Ave., Hamden (06518); H; 3,100; $9.09; editor Kim Phipps; tel (203) 288-5251 ext. 8358; Format: 5x16

Sacred Heart Univ.: *Spectrum* — 5151 Park Ave., Fairfield (06432); H; 2,500; $10.91; editor Jonathan Mccarthy; tel (203) 371-7945; Format: 5x16

Copyright ©1996 by the Editor & Publisher Co.

S. Central Community College: *The Raven* — 60 Sargent Dr., New Haven (06511); 3,000; $8.00; editor Terri Kenny; tel (203) 789-6942; Format: 5x15

Southern Connecticut State Univ.: *Southern News* — Student Center, Box 58 New Haven (06515); H; 6,000; $8.73; editor Chris Rukan; tel (203) 392-6928; Format: 4x16

Trinity College: *Tripod* — Box 1310, Hartford (06106); T; 3,000; $10.69; editor Jim Barr; tel (203) 297-2584/2000; Format: 4x17

Univ. of Bridgeport: *The Scribe* — 244 University Ave., Bridgeport (06602); H; 3,200; $8.00; editor Susie Morray; tel (203) 576-4382; Format: 5x16

Univ. of Connecticut: *The Daily Campus* — 11 Dog Ln., Storrs (06268); MTWHF; 10,000; $11.36; editor Kara Martinson; tel (203) 486-3407; Format: 5x16

Univ. of Hartford: *Informer* — 200 Bloomfield Ave., West Hartford (06117); H; 4,000; $8.18; editor Lauren Oettinger; tel (203) 768-4723; Format: 5x16

Univ. of New Haven: *The Charger Bulletin* — 300 Orange Ave., West Haven (06516); H; 5,000; $14.54; editor George R Ribellino Jr; tel (203) 932-7182; Format: 4x16

Wesleyan Univ.: *Argus* — Wesleyan Sta., Middletown (06457); TF; 3,200; $9.24; tel (203) 685-3325/3316; Format: 5x16

W. Connecticut State Univ.: *Westconn Echo* — 181 White St., Memorial Hall, Danbury (06810); T; 4,500; $12.12; editor Judy Hankison; tel (203) 837-8285; Format: 4x15

Yale Univ.: *Yale Daily News* — 241-A Yale Sta., New Haven (06520); MTWHF; 5,000; $18.18; editor Jeff Glasser; tel (203) 432-2400; Format: 6x21

DELAWARE

Delaware State Univ.: *Hornet* — Box 732, Dover (19901); 2,500; $17.26; editor Kaylyn Kendall; tel (302) 739-5179; Format: 5x14.5

Univ. of Delaware: *The Review* — B-1 Student Center, Newark (19716); TF; 14,000; $16.37; editor Jim Miller; tel (302) 831-1398; Format: 6x21

Wesley College: *The Whetstone* — Box 60, Dover (19901); 1,500; $8.00; tel (302) 736-2378; Format: 5x14

DISTRICT OF COLUMBIA

American Univ.: *Eagle* — 227 Mary Graydon Ctr., Washington (20016); M; 7,500; $14.54; editor Erik Diehn; tel (202) 885-1410/1414; Format: 6x21

Catholic Univ. of America: *Tower* — University Center W., Ste. 200, Washington (20064); F; 5,000; $12.73; editor Christopher Tompkins; tel (202) 319-5778; Format: 5x14

Gallaudet Univ.: *The Buff & Blue* — Ely Center, Rm. 333, Washington (20002); F; 2,000; $9.09; editor Katherine De Lorenzo; tel (202) 651-5000/5280; Format: 4x14

George Washington Univ.: *GW Hatchet* — 2140 G St. N.W., Washington (20052); MH; 10,000; $18.63; editor Jared Sher; tel (202) 994-7079; Format: 5x14

Georgetown Univ.: *The Hoya* — 37th & O Sts. N.W., Washington (20057); TF; 8,400; $20.00; editor Francine Fredeman; tel (202) 687-3947; Format: 6x20

Howard Univ.: *Hilltop* — 2251 Sherman Ave. N.W., Washington (20001); F; 10,000; $16.36; editor Jennifer Golson; tel (202) 806-6866; Format: 6x21

Trinity College: *Trinity Times* — Box A-331, Washington (20017); 1,000; $9.09; editor Beth Nohmy; tel (202) 939-5000 ext. 5332; Format: 5x15

FLORIDA

Barry Univ.: *Barry Buccaneer* — 11300 N.E. 2nd Ave., Miami Shores (33161); 2,000; $9.09; tel (305) 899-3093; Format: 4x15

Bethune-Cookman College: *Voice Of The Wildcats* — Student Center, 2nd Fl., Daytona Beach (32114-3099); 3,000; $8.00; tel (904) 255-1401 ext. 424; Format: 4x13

Brevard Community College: *Capsule* — 1519 Clearlake Rd., Cocoa (32922); 4,000; $14.54; tel (407) 632-1111 ext. 4230; Format: 4x15

Broward Community College: *The Observer* — 1000 Coconut Creek Blvd., Pompano Beach (33066); 10,000; $9.09; editor Eileen Solen; tel (305) 973-2237; Format: 5x16

Eckerd College: *The Triton Tribune* — Box B, St. Petersburg (33711); W; 2,200; $8.00; editor Amy Fisher; tel (813) 864-8416; Format: 5x16

Embry Riddle Aero Univ.: *Avion* — Avion Newspaper, Daytona Beach (32114-3917); W; 8,000; $13.25; editor Chad Troutvetter; tel (904) 226-6051; Format: 6x20

Florida A&M Univ.: *Famuan* — Tucker Hall, Rm. 309, Tallahassee (32307); H; 5,000; $14.54; tel (904) 599-3840; Format: 4x16

Florida Atlantic Univ.: *Free Press* — 777 Glades Rd., Boca Raton (33431); MTWH; 6,000; $14.54; editor Ross Levy; tel (407) 367-3766; Format: 5x13

Florida Institute of Tech.: *Crimson* — 150 W. University Blvd., Melbourne (32901); F; 1,500; $9.36; editor Gus Abdon; tel (407) 768-8000 ext. 8024; Format: 5x16

Florida International Univ.: *The Beacon* — Student Center 253, North Miami (33181); W; 8,000; $10.00; tel (305) 940-5611; Format: 5x16

Florida Southern College: *Southern* — Communications Dept., Lakeland (33801-5698); F; 2,000; $9.09; editor Eric Barton; tel (813) 680-4168; Format: 5x12

Florida State Univ.: *Florida Flambeau* — PO Box 20287, Tallahassee (32316); MTWHF; 21,000; $23.91; editor Che Odom; tel (904) 681-6692 ext. 29; Format: 5x13

Hillsborough Community College: *Hawkeye* — PO Box 5096, Tampa (33675); 6,000; $17.00; editor Christopher Carrothers; tel (813) 253-7662; Format: 4x16

Jacksonville Univ.: *Navigator* — PO Box 281014, Jacksonville (32211); F; 1,500; $8.18; editor Jeremy Cohen; tel (904) 745-7526; Format: 6x21

Lake Sumter Community College: *Angler* — 9501 US Hwy. 441, Leesburg (34788); F; 1,200; $8.00; tel (904) 323-3629; Format: 4x12

Miami-Dade Community College: *Falcon Times* — 11380 N.W. 27th Ave., Miami (33167); W; 3,000; $15.14; tel (305) 237-1255; Format: 3x16

Miami-Dade Community College S.: *Catalyst* — 11011 S.W. 104th St., Miami (33176); H; 3,750; $21.82; tel (305) 237-2323; Format: 3x15

Nova Southeastern Univ.: *The Knight* — 3301 College Ave., Ft. Lauderdale (33314); 2,000; $9.55; editor Jason Domasky; tel (305) 452-1553; Format: 4x12

Pensacola Jr College: *Corsair* — Bldg. 4, Office 469, Pensacola (32505-7382); 7,000; $11.92; editors Mike Ensley & Orin Fletcher; tel (904) 484-1455/1458; Format: 5x12.5

Rollins College: *The Sandspur* — 1000 Holt Ave., Winter Park (32789); W; 2,500; $11.82; editor Theresa Greenlees; tel (407) 646-2696; Format: 5x16

St Petersburg Jr College: *The Wooden Horse* — 6455 29th St. N., St. Petersburg (33733); 6,000; $12.00; tel (813) 341-3756/4929; Format: 5x15

Stetson Univ.: *Stetson Reporter* — 421 N. Woodland Blvd., Deland (32720); T; 1,500; $8.00; editor Davina Yetter; tel (904) 822-7224; Format: 5x20

Univ. of Florida: *Independent Florida Alligator* — Box 14257, Gainesville (32604); MTWHF; 32,000; $23.00; tel (904) 376-4482; Format: 5x13

Univ. of Miami: *Miami Hurricane* — University Center, Coral Gables (33146); TF; 10,000; $14.54; editor William Wachsberger; tel (305) 284-4401; Format: 6x22.5

Univ. of N. Florida: *Spinnaker* — 4567 St. Johns Bluff Rd., Jacksonville (32224); 3,000; $10.91; editor Tom Kopacz; tel (904) 646-2727; Format: 5x16.5

Univ. of S. Florida: *Oracle* — CPR 472, Tampa (33620); MTWHF; 15,000; $20.91; editor Jamal Thalji; tel (813) 974-2560/2620; Format: 5x13

Univ. of Tampa: *Minaret* — Box 2757, Tampa (33606); F; 2,000; $8.82; editor Marie Miller; tel (813) 253-3333 ext. 462; Format: 5x15

Univ. of W. Florida: *Voyager* — Bldg. 36, Rm. 108, Pensacola (32514); T; 3,500; $15.16; editor Samuel Holmes; tel (904) 474-2191; Format: 4x13

Valencia Community College: *The Paper* — PO Box 3028, Mail Code 3-8, Orlando (32825); 6,000.00; $10.45; tel (407) 299-5000 ext. 2370; Format: 5x16

GEORGIA

Agnes Scott College: *The Profile* — E. Collebe Ave., Decatur (30030); F; 1,000; $8.00; tel (404) 371-6851; Format: 5x14

Armstrong State College: *Ink Well* — 11935 Abercorn St., Savannah (31419-1997); 2,500; $9.09; editor Ron Speir Jr.; tel (912) 927-5351; Format: 4x13

Atlanta Univ. Center: *The AUC Digest* — 117 Vine St. S.W., Atlanta (30314); M; 13,000; $20.52; editor Lo Jelks; tel (404) 523-6136; Format: 4x13.5

Augusta College: *Bell Ringer* — 2500 Walton Way, Augusta (30910); M; 3,400; $10.91; editor Brad Poole; tel (706) 737-1600; Format: 5x14

Berry College: *Campus Carrier* — Box 520, Mount Berry (30149); T; 2,000; $8.00; editor Mark Hopkins; tel (706) 236-2294; Format: 5x12

Clark Atlanta Univ.: *Panther* — 240 James P Brawley Dr., Atlanta (30314); M; 5,000; $14.55; editor Tara Gunter; tel (404) 880-8077; Format: 6x15.5

Dekalb Community College: *The Dekalb Collegian* — 555 N. Indian Creek Dr., Clarkston (30021); 5,000; $8.00; editor Mark Hoerrer; tel (404) 298-3881; Format: 5x16

Emory Univ.: *Emory Wheel* — Dobbs University Center, Atlanta (30322); TF; 7,500; $14.45; editor Marcy Lamm; tel (404) 727-6178; Format: 5x14

Georgia College: *The Colonnade* — PO Box 3128, Milledgeville (31061); H; 2,000; $8.00; editor Penny Alligood; tel (912) 453-4511; Format: 5x15

Georgia Institute of Tech.: *Technique* — 353 Ferst Dr., Rm. 137, Atlanta (30332-0290); F; 11,000; $11.82; editor Chris Carson; tel (404) 894-2830; Format: 5x15

Georgia Southern Univ.: *George-Anne* — Landrum, Box 8001, Statesboro (30460); TH; 7,000; $11.69; editor Enoch Autry; tel (912) 681-5418; Format: 6x21

Georgia State Univ.: *Signal* — University Center, Rm. 200, Atlanta (30303); T; 15,000; $14.54; editor Derrick Peavy; tel (404) 651-3623/2242; Format: 5x15

Kennesaw State College: *The Sentinel* — Student Center 234, Kennesaw (30144); W; 4,500; $10.00; editor Marty Dye; tel (404) 423-6470; Format: 6x21.5

Lagrange College: *Hilltop News* — 601 Broad St., Lagrange (30240); 1,000; $8.00; editor Andy Mccullough; tel (706) 812-7246; Format: 5x13

Macon College: *Commuter* — K Bldg., Rm. 210, Macon (31297); 5,000; $8.00; editor Thomas Wyatt; tel (912) 757-3605; Format: 5x14

Medical College of Georgia: *Beeper* — 3054 Angela St., Augusta (30907); W; 10,000; $21.82; editor Christine Deriso; tel (706) 860-5455; Format: 5x12

Mercer Univ.: *Mercer Cluster* — 1400 Coleman Ave., Macon (31207); 1,700; $8.00; editor Michael Ray; tel (912) 752-2871; Format: 5x14

Oglethorpe Univ.: *Stormy Petrel* — Box 450, Atlanta (30319); 1,000; $8.10; editor Ryan Queen; tel (404) 364-8425; Format: 5x14

Savannah State College: *Tigers Roar* — Kennedy Hall, Rm. 144, Savannah (31404); 2,000; $8.00; editor Mrs Jerrie Hewitt; tel (912) 356-2265; Format: 5x16

Southern College of Tech.: *The Sting* — 1100 S. Marietta Pkwy., Marietta (30060); 4,000; $9.09; editor Andrew Newton; tel (404) 528-7310; Format: 5x14

Spelman College: *Spelman Spotlight* — PO Box 1234, Atlanta (30314-4399); 3,000; $8.00; tel (404) 525-1743; Format: 4x14

Univ. of Georgia: *Red And Black* — 123 N. Jackson, Athens (30601); MTWHF; 16,000; $22.73; tel (706) 543-1791; Format: 6x21

Valdosta State Univ.: *Spectator* — VSC, Box 7164, Valdosta (31698); H; 4,500; $8.00; editor Rex Gambill; tel (912) 333-5686; Format: 6x21.5

Wesleyan College: *The Pioneer* — 4760 Forsyth Rd., Macon (31297-4299); H; 1,000; $8.00; editor Beth Milstead; tel (912) 757-5100; Format: 5x14

W Georgia College: *West Georgian* — Maple St., Bldg. D, Carrollton (30118); W; 4,500; $8.64; tel (770) 836-6527; Format: 5x13

HAWAII

Brigham Young Univ.: *Ke Alaka'i* — Campus Box 1920, Laie (96762); W; 2,500; $12.82; editor Leeann Lambert; tel (808) 293-3696; Format: 5x15

Chaminade Univ.: *Silversword* — 3140 Waialae Ave., Honolulu (96816); 1,000; $8.00; editor Dennis Bautista; tel (808) 735-4791; Format: 4x13

Kapiolani Community College: *Kapio* — 4303 Diamond Head Rd., Honolulu (96816); T; 3,000; $9.09; tel (808) 734-9120; Format: 5x15

Univ. of Hawaii at Hilo: *Ke Kalahea* — 200 W. Kawili St., Hilo (96720-4091); T; 4,500; $16.82; editor Eric Lee; tel (808) 933-3504; Format: 5x14

Univ. of Hawaii at Manoa: *Ka Leo O Hawaii* — Kaleo Bldg., Honolulu (96822); MTWHF; 14,000; $14.00; editor Ryan Ozawa; tel (808) 956-8238; Format: 5x16

IDAHO

Albertson College: *Coyote* — 2112 Cleveland Blvd., Caldwell (83605); 700; $8.00; editor Eric Ellis; tel (208) 459-5608; Format: 4x16

Boise State Univ.: *Arbiter* — 1910 University Dr., Boise (83725); T; 5,000; $18.18; editor Adam Rush; tel (208) 345-8204; Format: 5x14

Idaho State Univ.: *Bengal* — 1065 S. 8th Ave. Pocatello (83209); H; 5,000; $9.09; editor Janet Howard; tel (208) 236-3990; Format: 5x16

Lewis-Clark State College: *Pathfinder* — 8th Ave. & 6th St., Lewiston (83501-2698); W; 1,000; $8.00; editor Laurell Haapanen; tel (208) 799-2470/2256; Format: 5x12

Northern Idaho College: *The Sentinel* — 1000 W. Garden Ave., Coeur D'Alene (83814); 2,000; $8.00; editor Mark Jerome; tel (208) 769-3300 ext. 389; Format: 4x12

NW Nazarene College: *Crusader* — Box C, Nampa (83686); T; 1,200; $9.09; editor Andrew Zirschky; tel (208) 467-8656; Format: 4x12

Ricks College: *Scroll* — Spori Bldg., Rm. 160 Rexburg (83460); W; 5,000; $8.00; editor Dave Turnbull; tel (208) 356-2900; Format: 5x13

Univ. of Idaho: *Idaho Argonaut* — Student Union Bldg., Moscow (83844-4271); TF; 8,500; $11.46; editor Shelby Depp; tel (208) 885-7794; Format: 5x15.75

ILLINOIS

Augustana College: *Observer* — Augustana, Box 204, Rock Island (61201); F; 3,000; $8.00; editor Julie Wilde; tel (309) 794-7485; Format: 5x15.5

Barat College: *The Journaux* — 700 E. Westleigh Rd., Lake Forest (60045); 800; $8.00; editor Denise Banis; tel (708) 234-3000 ext. 688; Format: 5x17

Bradley Univ.: *Bradley Scout* — Sisson Hall 319, Peoria (61625); F; 5,600; $8.97; editor Sara Bender; tel (309) 677-3057; Format: 5x15

Chicago State Univ.: *Tempo* — 95th & King Dr. RUC 100, Chicago (60628); 5,000; $8.00; editor Sharonda Holmes; tel (312) 995-3699; Format: 5x15

College of Dupage: *Courier* — 22nd & Lambert Rd., Glen Ellyn (60137); F; 7,000; $10.46; tel (708) 858-2800 ext. 2379; Format: 4x16

College of Lake Co.: *Chronicle* — 19351 W. Washington, Grayslake (60030); 3,750; $10.91; editor Tiffany Gleaner; tel (708) 223-3634; Format: 4x15

Columbia College: *Chronicle* — Chicago (60605); M; 5,000; $8.00; editor Art Golab; tel (312) 663-1600 ext. 5343; Format: 5x16

Concordia College: *Spectator* — 7400 W. Augusta St., River Forest (60305); 1,000; $18.18; editor Julie Frank; tel (708) 771-8300 ext. 3191; Format: 4x14

Depaul Univ.: *Depaulia* — 2345 N. Clifton Ave., B14, Chicago (60614); F; 7,500; $16.27; editor Zack Martin; tel (312) 325-7441; Format: 5x16

Devry Institute: *Hard Copy* — 3300 N. Campbell Ave., Chicago (60618); 1,000; $11.48; tel (312) 929-8500 ext. 2017; Format: 4x11

Eastern Illinois Univ.: *Daily Eastern News* — 127 Buzzard Bldg., Charleston (61920); MTWHF; 8,900; $12.73; tel (217) 581-2812; Format: 5x16

Elgin Community College: *ECC-Observer* — 1700 Spartan Dr., Elgin (60123); 4,000; $12.82; editor Brett Ferguson; tel (708) 697-1000 ext. 7426; Format: 5x14

Elmhurst College: *The Leader* — Box 321, Elmhurst (60126); H; 1,400; $8.00; editor Thomas Isberg; tel (708) 617-3320/3721; Format: 5x15

Governers State Univ.: *GSU Innovator* — Stenunkel Rd., University Park (60466); 3,000; $8.00; editor Steve Reid; tel (708) 534-5000 exts. 5318/4517; Format: 5x16

Greenville College: *Papyrus* — 315 E. College Ave., Greenville (62246); 1,100; $8.00; tel (618) 664-1840 ext. 4506; Format: 5x16

Harold Washington College: *Herald* — 30 E. Lake St., Chicago (60601); 3,000; $9.09; tel (312) 553-5895; Format: 4x16

Illinois Benedictine College: *Candor* — 5700 College Rd., Lisle (60532); T; 1,200; $10.91; editor Joe Ursitti; tel (708) 960-1500 ext. 4406; Format: 5x15

Illinois Institute of Tech.: *Technology News* — 3241 S. Federal St., Chicago (60616); M; 3,500; $11.81; editor Catherine Bertucci; tel (312) 567-3085; Format: 5x16

Illinois State Univ.: *Daily Vidette* — Edwards Annex, Normal (61761); MTWHF; 13,500; $12.99; editor Carla Eskew; tel (309) 438-7685/8742; Format: 5x16

Illinois Wesleyan Univ.: *Argus* — PO Box 2900, Bloomington (61701); F; 2,700; $9.09; editor Dave Brown; tel (309) 556-3036; Format: 5x13

Joliet Jr College: *Blazer* — 1216 Houbolt Ave., Joliet (60436); 3,000; $8.71; editor John Wielgat; tel (815) 729-9020 ext. 2313; Format: 5x15

Kennedy-King College: *Kennedy-King Press* — 6800 S. Wentworth, Chicago (60621); 2,000; $11.37; editor Donna Chipman; tel (312) 602-5432; Format: 5x15

Knox College: *Knox Student* — Box 83, Galesburg (61401); 1,300; $8.00; editors Nicole Havelka & Rob Clark; tel (309) 343-0112 ext. 418; Format: 5x16

Lake Forest College: *The Stentor* — 555 N. Sheridan Rd., Lake Forest (60045-2399); W; 1,000; $9.09; editor Jacob Fenske; tel (708) 735-5215; Format: 5x14

Lake Land College: *Lighthouse* — 5001 Lake Land Blvd., Mattoon (61938); 2,000; $8.00; editor Wendy Nichols; tel (217) 235-3131; Format: 4x16

Lewis Univ.: *The Flyer* — Rte. 53, Box 10, Romeoville (60441); H; 1,500; $8.00; editor Jim Caswell; tel (815) 838-0500 ext. 234; Format: 4x16

Lincoln Land Community College: *The Lamp* — Shepherd Rd., Springfield (62794); 2,000; $8.00; tel (217) 786-2311; Format: 5x16.5

Loyola Univ.: *Loyola Phoenix* — 6525 N. Sheridan Rd., Chicago (60626); W; 6,000; $16.36; editor Victoria Higgins; tel (312) 508-3922; Format: 4x16

Macmurray College: *The Daily Other* — Jacksonville, 62650 (MTWHF); 700; $8.00; editor Shelby Seville; tel (217) 479-7049/7000; Format: 3x11

Malcolm X College: *Malcolm X Press* — 1900 W. Van Buren, Chicago (60612); 3,000; $8.00; tel (312) 850-7321; Format: 4x16

Mchenry County Community Coll: *Tartan* — 8900 US Hwy. 14, Crystal Lake (60012); H; 2,000; $8.00; tel (815) 455-8571; Format: 4x15

Monmouth College: *The Oracle* — College Box 941, Monmouth (61462); T; 1,000; $10.90; editor Amy Bradshaw; tel (309) 457-3456/2333; Format: 4x13

Moraine Vly. Community College: *Glacier* — 10900 S. 88th Ave., Palos Hills (60465); 5,000; $12.05; editor Kim Kappel; tel (708) 974-4300 exts. 4177/4178; Format: 4x16

Morton College: *Collegian* — Rm. 218-C, Cicero (60650); 1,500; $8.00; editor John Kramer; tel (708) 656-8000 ext. 376; Format: 5x16

N Central College: *NCC Chronicle* — 30 N. Brainard, Naperville (60566-1017); 1,400; $9.09; editor Karen Duda; tel (708) 637-5422; Format: 5x16

N Park College: *College News* — 3225 W. Foster Ave., Chicago (60625); F; 1,500; $10.82; editor Eric Sharaga; tel (312) 244-5618; Format: 5x16

Northeastern Illinois Univ.: *Northeastern Independent* — 5500 N. St. Louis, Chicago (60625); 4,000; $15.00; editor Kim Dudash; tel (312) 794-2812; Format: 5x16

Northern Illinois Univ.: *Northern Star* — CLB 130, Dekalb (60115); MTWHF; 16,000; $15.28; editor Leslie Rogers; tel (815) 753-0101; Format: 5x16

Northwestern Univ.: *Daily Northwestern* — 1999 Sheridan Rd., Evanston (60208); MTWHF; 8,500; $12.84; tel (708) 491-7206; Format: 4x16

Oakton Community College: *Occurrence* — 1600 E. Golf Rd., Des Plaines (60016); 3,500; $14.55; editor Marcy Blackwelder; tel (708) 635-1678; Format: 5x16

Olivet Nazarene Univ.: *Glimmer Glass* — Box 6024, Kankakee (60901); 2,000; $10.81; editor Lori Brooks; tel (815) 939-5315; Format: 6x21

Parkland Community College: *Prospectus* — Rm. X-155, Champaign (61821-1899); W; 6,000; $13.64; editor Tina Henderson; tel (217) 351-2216; Format: 5x16

Prairie State College: *Student Review* — 202 S. Halstead St., Chicago Heights (60411); 1,500; $8.00; tel (708) 709-3612; Format: 5x14

Principia College: *Principia Pilot* — Elsah, (62028); F; 1,500; $12.73; tel (618) 374-2131 ext. 5039; Format: 4x13

Rock Vly. College: *Valley Forge* — 3301 N. Mulford Rd., Rockford (61111); 2,500; $8.00; editor Suzan La Salla; tel (815) 654-4458; Format: 5x16

Roosevelt Univ.: *Roosevelt Torch* — 430 S. Michigan Ave., Chicago (60605); M; 4,000; $10.00; editor Chris; tel (312) 341-3669; Format: 5x16

Rosary College: *The Reporter* — 7900 W. Division, River Forest (60305); 2,000; $10.45; editor Jennifer Utterback; tel (708) 524-6035; Format: 5x13

St Xavier Univ.: *Xavierite* — 3700 W. 103rd St., Chicago (60655); 2,000; $10.90; editor Jessi Virtusio; tel (312) 298-3381; Format: 5x16

Sangamon State Univ.: *SSU News* — Shepherd Rd., Springfield (62794); W; 2,000; $9.09; editor Stephanie Mclelland; tel (217) 786-6397; Format: 5x16

S Suburb College Cook Co.: *Courier* — South Holland (60473); 10,000; $10.91; editor Mike Krasl; tel (708) 596-2000 ext. 336; Format: 5x16

Southern Illinois Univ.: *Daily Egyptian* — Communications Bldg., Carbondale (62901); MTWHF; 22,000; $16.09; editor Lloyd Goodman; tel (618) 536-3311 ext. 212; Format: 5x16

Southern Illinois Univ.: *Alestle* — University Center, Box 1167, Edwardsville (62026-1167); TH; 5,000; $10.82; editor Paul Williams; tel (618) 692-3528; Format: 5x13.5

Triton College: *Fifth Avenue Journal* — 2000 5th Ave., River Grove (60171); 5,000; $11.19; tel (708) 456-0300 ext. 3318; Format: 5x17

Univ. of Chicago: *Chicago Maroon* — Ida Noyes Hall, Rm. 305, Chicago (60637); TF; 11,500; $16.36; editor Duncan Brown; tel (312) 702-9555; Format: 4x16

Univ. of Illinois: *Daily Illini* — 57 E. Green, Champaign (61820); MTWHF; 10,000; $16.00; editor Michelle Collins; tel (217) 333-8618; Format: 5x16

Univ. of Illinois: *Chicago Flame* — 117 S. Morgan, Chicago (60607); T; 18,000; $16.37; editor John Cline; tel (312) 421-0480; Format: 5x16

Waubonsee Community College: *Insight* — Rte. 47 at Harter Rd., Sugar Grove (60554); 2,000; $8.00; tel (708) 466-4811 ext. 555; Format: 4x16

Western Illinois Univ.: *Western Courier* — PO Box 6009, Macomb (61455); MWF; 6,000; $12.73; editor Crystal Andrus; tel (309) 298-1876; Format: 5x15.75

Wheaton College: *Wheaton Record* — CPO 588, Wheaton College, Wheaton (60187); F; 3,200; $13.64; editor Elesha Hodge; tel (708) 752-5077; Format: 5x15

Wilbur Wright College: *Wright News* — 4300 N. Narragansett, Chicago (60634); 3,500; $9.09; editor Melissa Clay; tel (312) 481-8555; Format: 5x15

William Rainey Harper College: *Harbinger* — 1200 W. Algonquin Rd., Palatine (60067-7398); 4,000; $14.55; editor Jim Walaitis; tel (708) 925-6460; Format: 5x16

INDIANA

Anderson Univ.: *Andersonian* — 1100 E. 5th St., Anderson (46012-3462); H; 2,800; $8.00; editor David Baird; tel (317) 641-4341; Format: 5x16

Ball State Univ.: *Daily News* — W. Quadrangle, Rm. 135, Muncie (47306); MTWHF; 14,000; $13.36; editor Andy Paras; tel (317) 285-8256; Format: 6x21.5

Butler Univ.: *Butler Collegian* — 4600 Sunset Ave., Indianapolis (46208); W; 3,000; $10.91; editor Karen Mellon; tel (317) 283-9358/9713; Format: 5x16

Depauw Univ.: *Depauw* — Depauw Center For Contemp Media, Greencastle (46135); TF; 3,500; $12.73; editor Aaron Luchetti; tel (317) 658-5977; Format: 5x13

Earlham College: *Earlham Word* — Box E-492, Richmond (47374); 1,200; $8.00; editor Lori Southerland; tel (317) 983-1569; Format: 5x12

Goshen College: *Goshen College Record* — Goshen (46526); F; 1,500; $8.00; tel (219) 535-7398/7587; Format: 5x13

Indiana State Univ.: *Indiana Statesman* — HMSU 726, Terre Haute (47809); MWF; 8,000; $13.18; editor Mark Stalcup; tel (812) 237-3025/3037; Format: 5x13

Indiana Univ.: *Indiana Daily Student* — Ernie Pyle Hall, Rm. 120, Bloomington (47405); MTWHF; 20,000; $19.97; tel (812) 855-0763; Format: 6x21

Indiana Univ.: *Preface* — 1700 Mishawaka Ave., South Bend (46615); 2,500; $12.73; tel (219) 237-4325; Format: 5x13

Indiana Univ. NW: *Northwest Phoenix* — 3400 Broadway, Gary (46408); 2,500; $10.91; editor Mary Sachta; tel (219) 980-6795; Format: 6x21

Indiana Univ. SE: *Southeast Horizon* — 4201 Grant Line Rd., New Albany (47150); T; 3,000; $8.37; editor Chris Adams; tel (812) 941-2253; Format: 4x13

Indiana Wesleyan Univ.: *The Journal* — 4201 Washington St., Marion (46953); 1,000; $8.00; editor Mari Beth Tackett; tel (317) 674-6901 ext. 2745; Format: 5x17

Indiana-Purdue Univ.: *Communicator* — Walb Union, Rm. 215, Fort Wayne (46805); H; 5,000; $10.25; tel (219) 481-6583; Format: 6x21.5

Indiana-Purdue Univ.: *Sagamore* — 425 University Blvd., Indianapolis (46202); M; 13,000; $19.80; editor Brian Moore; tel (317) 274-3456; Format: 6x20.75

Manchester College: *Oak Leaves* — Box 101, North Manchester (46962); H; 1,250; $8.00; editor Heather Waymire; tel (219) 982-5317; Format: 5x13

Marian College: *The Carbon* — 3200 Cold Springs Rd., Indianapolis (46222); 800; $8.00; editor Eileen M. Nyikos; tel (317) 929-0123; Format: 4x17

Purdue Univ.: *Purdue Exponent* — 460 Northwestern Ave., West Lafayette (47906-0506); MTWHF; 20,000; $11.20; editor Christine Thompson; tel (317) 743-1111 ext. 108; Format: 6x16

Purdue Univ.-Calumet: *Purdue Chronicle* — Chronicle Office - C344H, Hammond (46323); W; 5,000; $10.00; editor Nelly Aguilara; tel (219) 989-2547/2548; Format: 5x16

Rose Hulman Inst of Tech: *The Rose Thorn* — 5500 Wabash Ave., Terre Haute (47803-3999); F; 1,200; $8.64; editor Chad Zigler; tel (812) 877-1511 ext. 255; Format: 5x16

St Mary-Of-The-Woods: *The Woods Student* — Le Fer Hall, Box 406, St Mary-Of-The-Woods (47876); 1,600; $8.63; editor Elaine Yaw; tel (812) 535-5132/5179; Format: 4x11

Taylor Univ.: *The Echo* — 610 S. Adams, Upland (46989); F; 2,400; $8.00; tel (317) 998-5359; Format: 5x14

Univ. of Evansville: *University Crescent* — 1800 Lincoln Ave., Evansville (47702); F; 3,500; $11.82; tel (812) 479-2846; Format: 5x12

Univ. of Indianapolis: *The Student Reflector* — 1400 E. Hanna Ave., Indianapolis (46227); 1,200; $13.64; editor Sara Bastin; tel (317) 788-3269/3445; Format: 4x11.25

Univ. of Notre Dame: *The Observer* — PO Box Q, Notre Dame (46556); MTWHF; 13,000; $10.91; editor Joan Lucas; tel (219) 631-6900; Format: 5x16

Univ. of Southern Indiana: *The Shield* — 8600 University Blvd., Evansville (47712); W; 4,500; $10.02; editor Jeffrey Anderson; tel (812) 464-1870; Format: 5x14

Valparaiso Univ.: *The Torch* — 816 Union St., Valparaiso (46383); F; 4,000; $9.09; editor Amy Gannaway; tel (219) 464-5426/464-6665; Format: 5x16

Vincennes Univ.: *The Trailblazer* — Shircliff Humanities Center (SH-15), Vincennes (47591-5201); F; 5,500; $4.00; tel (812) 888-4451/4554; Format: 4x14

Wabash College: *Bachelor* — Board Of Publications, Crawfordsville (47933); H; 1,100; $11.82; editor Ezra Ball; tel (317) 364-4213; Format: 4x11.5

IOWA

Briar Cliff College: *Cliff News* — 3303 Rebecca St., Sioux City (51104); 1,000; $8.00; tel (712) 279-5443/5459; Format: 5x16

Central Univ. of Iowa: *The Ray* — Pella, (50219); W; 2,500; $8.00; tel (515) 628-5239/4151; Format: 5x16

Clarke College: *Courier* — 1550 Clarke Dr., Dubuque (52001); F; 1,200; $10.90; tel (319) 588-6300; Format: 4x14

Coe College: *Coe Cosmos* — Box 568, Cedar Rapids (52402); F; 1,100; $18.18; tel (319) 399-8646; Format: 5x13

Cornell College: *The Cornellian* — 600 1st St. W., Mt. Vernon (52314); W; 1,600; $8.00; editor A Earley; tel (319) 895-4430; Format: 5x16

Dordt College: *The Diamond* — Sioux City Center, (51250); 900; $8.00; tel (712) 722-3771 ext. 6431; Format: 4x13

Drake Univ.: *Times-Delphic* — 2507 University Ave., Des Moines (50311); TF; 3,200; $10.91; editor Tawny Colaizy; tel (515) 271-2148; Format: 5x16

Graceland College: *Tower* — Box 1545, Lamoni (50140); F; 1,100; $8.00; editor Gevin Booth; tel (515) 784-5261; Format: 4x16.5

Grand View College: *Grand Views* — 1331 Grandview Ave., Des Moines (50316); F; 1,500; $8.18; tel (515) 263-2806; Format: 4x13

Grinnell College: *Scarlet & Black* — Grinnell College, Box T-1, Grinnell (50112); F; 2,000; $10.91; editor Dan Buettner; tel (515) 269-3325; Format: 5x13

Iowa State Univ.: *Iowa State Daily* — Hamilton Hall, Rm. 108, Ames (50011); MTWHF; 16,000; $15.28; editor Troy Mccullough; tel (515) 294-4121; Format: 6x21

Iowa Wesleyan: *The Courier* — 601 N. Main, Mount Pleasant (52641); 1,000; $8.00; editor Martha Jacobs; tel (319) 385-8021 ext. 368; Format: 6x21.5

Iowa Western Community College: *Western Chronicle* — 2700 College Blvd., Council Bluffs (51503); 2,500; $9.09; editor Libby Rocha; tel (712) 325-3200 ext. 416; Format: 5x12.5

Kirkwood Community College: *Communique* — 6301 Kirkwood Blvd. S.W., Cedar Rapids (52406); 5,000; $9.09; editor David Savage; tel (319) 398-5589/5444; Format: 4x16

Luther College: *College Chips* — 700 College Dr., Decorah (52101); H; 2,200; $10.91; tel (319) 387-1044; Format: 3x11

Morningside College: *Collegian Reporter* — 1501 Morningside Ave., Sioux City (51106); M; 1,000; $8.00; editors Chris Dixon & Douglas Rants; tel (712) 274-5171; Format: 5x12.25

Muscatine Community College: *The Calumet* — 152 Colorado St., Muscatine (52761); 2,000; $8.00; editor Mary Shield; tel (319) 263-8250 ext. 137; Format: 4x16

Northwestern College: *The Beacon* — Box 249, Orange City (51041); F; 900; $8.00; editor J Macier; tel (712) 737-1608; Format: 5x14

St Ambrose Univ.: *The Buzz: On Campus* — 518 W. Locust, Davenport (52803); 2,200; $9.54; editor Kami Keehner; tel (319) 383-8718; Format: 8x21

Teikyo-Marycrest Univ.: *The Crest* — 1607 W. 12th St., Davenport (52804); H; 1,200; $9.09; editor Kim Brown; tel (319) 326-9595; Format: 6x20

Univ. of Iowa: *Daily Iowan* — 201 Communications Center, Iowa City (52242); MTWHF; 20,500; $20.33; editor Kirsten Scharnberg; tel (319) 335-5791; Format: 6x21

Univ. of Northern Iowa: *Northern Iowan* — 112 Maucker Union, Cedar Falls (50614-0166); TF; 9,000; $15.45; tel (319) 273-2157; Format: 5x15

Upper Iowa Univ.: *Collegian* — Po Box 1857, Fayette (52142); H; 600; $8.00; tel (319) 425-5212; Format: 4x15

Wartburg College: *Wartburg Trumpet* — Mcelroy Communication Arts Center, Waverly (50677); M; 2,300; $14.73; tel (319) 352-8289; Format: 5x16

KANSAS

Baker Univ.: *Baker Orange* — 300 Pulliam Journalism Center, Baldwin (66006); F; 1,500; $8.00; editor Anji Gandhi; tel (913) 594-6451 ext. 559; Format: 5x14

Bethany College: *Bethany Messenger* — Union Box 7, Lendsborg (67456); F; 1,500; $8.00; editor Eric Yonkey; tel (913) 227-3311 ext. 234; Format: 5x13

Butler Co. Community College: *Lantern* — Towardo & Haverhill, El Dorado (67042); H; 3,000; $8.00; editor Scott Harper; tel (316) 321-5083 ext. 170; Format: 4x15

Emporia State Univ.: *Bulletin* — 1200 Commerical, Emporia (66801); M; 4,000; $8.18; editor Jameson Watkins; tel (316) 343-1200 ext. 5201; Format: 6x21

Ft. Hays State Univ.: *University Leader* — 600 Park St., Hays (67601-4099); TF; 4,800; $10.00; editor Squire Boone; tel (913) 628-5884/5301; Format: 6x21

Johnson Co. Community College: *Campus Ledger* — 12345 College Blvd., Overland Park (66210); W; 4,500; $16.36; editor Brad Seitter; tel (913) 469-8500 exts. 3190/3193; Format: 6x21

Kansas City Community College: *The Advocate* — 7250 State Ave., Kansas City (66112); 3,000; $8.00; tel (913) 334-1100 exts. 229/237; Format: 4x16

Kansas State Univ.: *Kansas State Collegian* — Student Publications, Manhattan (66506); MTWHF; 14,000; $11.09; editor Neil Anderson; tel (913) 532-6555/6560; Format: 6x21

Pittsburg State Univ.: *Collegio* — Student Union Bldg., Pittsburg (66762); T; 6,000; $10.00; editor Adam Murphy; tel (316) 235-4816; Format: 6x21

St Mary College: *The Taper* — 4100 S. 4th St., Leavenworth (66048-5082); 1,000; $9.09; editor Rachel Umscheid; tel (913) 682-5151 ext. 315; Format: 4x17

Univ. of Kansas: *Daily Kansan* — 119 Stauffer-Flint Hall, Lawrence (66045); MTWHF; 14,500; $13.09; editor Colleen Mccian; tel (913) 864-4358; Format: 6x21

Washburn Univ.: *The Review* — 1700 College, Topeka (66621); F; 2,500; $10.91; editor Stephanie Taylor; tel (913) 233-3211; Format: 6x21

Wichita State Univ.: *Sunflower* — Campus Box 134, Wichita (67208); MWF; 10,000; $12.36; editor Nancy Hart; tel (316) 689-3640; Format: 4x15

KENTUCKY

Asbury College: *The Collegian* — N. Lexington Dr., Wilmore (40390); F; 3,000; $8.00; editor Katherine Lehman; tel (606) 858-3511 ext. 2283; Format: 5x14

Bellarmine College: *Concord* — Newburg Rd., Louisville (40205-0671); W; 2,500; $12.42; editor Jennifer Newton; tel (502) 452-8157; Format: 5x13

Berea College: *Pinnacle* — CPO 2302, Berea (40404); 2,000; $8.00; editor Chris Capley; tel (606) 986-9341 ext. 6577; Format: 5x13

Centre College of Kentucky: *Centre College Cento* — 600 W. Walnut St., Danville (40422); 1,300; $8.00; editor Robert Alford; tel (606) 238-6726; Format: 6x22.5

Eastern Kentucky Univ.: *Eastern Progress* — 117 Donovan Annex, Richmond (40475-0941); H; 10,000; $8.18; editor Don Perry; tel (606) 622-1881; Format: 6x21.5

Georgetown College: *Georgetonian* — 400 E. College St., Georgetown (40324-1696); F; 1,500; $8.00; editor Cathy Jones; tel (502) 863-8150; Format: 6x17

Kentucky State Univ.: *The Thorobred News* — Carver Hall 124, Frankfort (40601); 2,200; $8.00; editor Calvin Wilson; tel (502) 227-5927; Format: 4x13

Morehead State Univ.: *The Trail Blazer* — UPO 1024, Morehead (40351); W; 6,500; $10.91; editor Kristi Phillips; tel (606) 783-2601; Format: 6x21

Murray State Univ.: *Murray State News* — 2609 University Sta., Murray (42071-3301); F; 5,000; $11.05; editor Allison Millikan; tel (502) 762-4478/4491; Format: 6x21

Northern Kentucky Univ.: *The Northerner* — University Center, Rm. 209, Highland Heights (41076); W; 7,500; $10.91; editor Jerry Floyd; tel (606) 572-5260/5232; Format: 6x20

Paducah Community College: *The Signal* — Box 7380, Paducah (42001); W; 800; $8.00; editor Gale Weaver; tel (502) 554-9200; Format: 4x14

Spalding Univ.: *The Spectrum* — 851 S. 4th St., Louisville (40203); 1,000; $8.00; editor Dianne Carter; tel (502) 585-9911 ext. 238; Format: 5x12

Thomas More College: *The Utopian* — 333 Thomas More Pkwy., Crestview Hills (41017); 1,000; $10.38; editor Scott Kramer; tel (606) 344-3605; Format: 4x14

Univ. of Kentucky: *Kentucky Kernel* — 026 Journalism Bldg., Lexington (40506-0042); MTWHF; 17,000; $16.37; editor Lance Williams; tel (606) 257-2872/2871; Format: 6x21.5

Univ. of Louisville: *The Louisville Cardinal* — Old Student Center, Louisville (40292); H; 13,000; $10.91; editor Michael Lindenberger; tel (502) 852-0701; Format: 6x21

Western Kentucky Univ.: *College Heights Herald* — 122 Garrett Center, Bowling Green (42101); TH; 12,000; $9.00; tel (502) 745-2653; Format: 5x16

LOUISIANA

Centenary College: *Conglomerate* — PO Box 41188, Shreveport (71104); 1,300; $10.38; editor Si Sikes; tel (318) 869-5269; Format: 4x14

Delgado Community College: *The Dolphin* — 615 City Park Ave., New Orleans (70119); 2,000; $8.00; tel (504) 483-4061; Format: 4x13

Grambling Univ.: *Gramblinite* — PO Box 45, Grambling (71245); H; 8,500; $11.82; editor Monica Hughes; tel (318) 274-2304; Format: 6x20

Louisiana College: *Wildcat* — 1140 College Dr., Pineville (71359-0606); F; 1,000; $10.63; tel (318) 487-7211; Format: 4x14

Louisiana State Univ.: *Daily Reveille* — 39 Hodges Hall, Baton Rouge (70803); TWHF; 19,000; $11.64; tel (504) 388-1697; Format: 5x16

Louisiana State Univ.: *Almagest* — 1 University Pl., Shreveport (71115); F; 1,200; $8.64; tel (318) 797-5328; Format: 4x12

Louisiana Tech Univ.: *Tech Talk* — PO Box 10258, Ruston (71272-0045); H; 10,000; $8.00; tel (318) 257-4949/4946; Format: 6x21.25

Loyola Univ.: *Loyola Maroon* — Box 64, New Orleans (70118); F; 3,500; $15.83; editor Christopher Raphael; tel (504) 865-3536; Format: 4x13.5

LSU College At Alexandria: *The Paper Tiger* — 8100 Hwy. 71 S., Alexandria (71302); 2,000; $9.09; tel (318) 473-6452; Format: 3x9

LSU College At Eunice: *The Bayou Bengal* — PO Box 1129, Eunice (70535); 900; $8.00; tel (318) 457-7311 ext. 218; Format: 5x13

McNeese State Univ.: *Contraband* — McNeese University, PO Box 91375, Lake Charles (70609-1375); W; 4,500; $13.64; editor Catherine Bonds; tel (318) 475-5645; Format: 6x21.5

Nicholls State Univ.: *Nicholls Worth* — NSU, PO Box 2010, Thibodaux (70310); H; 6,000; $8.00; editor Toyna Danos; tel (504) 448-4259; Format: 5x13

NE Louisiana Univ.: *Pow Wow* — 700 University Ave., Sub 249, Monroe (71209); F; 7,000; $8.00; editor Jeff Welch; tel (318) 342-5454/5456; Format: 6x21

Northwestern State Univ.: *Current Sauce* — Rm. 103, Natchitoches (71457); T; 3,500; $8.00; editor Jane Baldwin; tel (318) 357-5213/5456; Format: 6x21

Southeastern Louisiana Univ.: *Lions Roar* — #3017, Hammond (70402-0877); H; 5,500; $8.00; editor Adam Daigle; tel (504) 549-3731; Format: 6x21.5

Southern Univ.: *Digest* — PO Box 10188, Baton Rouge (70813); F; 8,000; $14.44; tel (504) 771-2230/2231; Format: 5x14

Tulane Univ.: *Tulane Hullabaloo* — University Center, New Orleans (70118); F; 5,000; $18.18; editor Brittany Troop; tel (504) 865-5658; Format: 6x21

Univ. of New Orleans: *Driftwood* — University Center, Rm. 218, New Orleans (70148); H; 8,000; $14.18; editor Mary E Lopz; tel (504) 286-6377/6378; Format: 6x21.5

Univ. of Southwestern Louisiana: *The Vermilion* — PO Box 44813, Lafayette (70504); F; 10,000; $9.09; editor Tanya Anderson; tel (318) 482-6960; Format: 4x12

Xavier Univ. of Louisiana: *Xavier Herald* — 7325 Palmetto St., New Orleans (70125); 3,500; $18.18; editor Gregory Lee; tel (504) 483-7474; Format: 4x14

MAINE

Bates College: *Bates Student* — Chase Hall, Lewiston (04240); F; 3,000; $10.91; editor Jennifer Lacher; tel (207) 795-7494; Format: 4x15

Bowdoin College: *Orient* — 12 Cleaveland St., Brunswick (04011); F; 3,000; $8.64; tel (207) 725-3300; Format: 4x15

Colby College: *Colby Echo* — Roberts Union, Waterville (04901); H; 5,000; $11.37; tel (207) 872-3349; Format: 5x15.25

Univ. of Maine: *Maine Stream* — Student Center, Farmington (04938); 1,000; $8.00; tel (207) 778-7330; Format: 5x14

Univ. of Maine: *Maine Campus* — Lord Hall, Ste. 7A, Orono (04469); MWF; 4,500; $18.10; editor Katy Breenan; tel (207) 581-1273; Format: 4x15

Univ. of Southern Maine: *University Free Press* — 92 Bedford St., Portland (04103); M; 5,000; $10.91; editor Justin Leonard; tel (207) 780-4085; Format: 5x15

MARYLAND

Anne Arundel Community College: *Campus Crier* — 101 College Pkwy., Arnold (21012); 4,000; $10.78; editor Steve Stalling; tel (410) 541-2803/2338; Format: 5x13.5

Bowie State Univ.: *Bowie State Spectrum* — Communications Dept., Bowie (20715); M; 3,000; $18.18; tel (301) 464-7251; Format: 5x14

Catonsville Community College: *The Red & Black* — 800 S. Rolling Rd., Catonsville (21228); 4,000; $8.00; editor Janon Fisher; tel (410) 455-4485/4322; Format: 5x12

Cecil Community College: *The Seahawk* — 1000 North East Rd., North East (21901); 500; $8.00; tel (410) 287-6060 ext. 325; Format: 3x13.5

Charles Co. Community College: *The Hawkeye* — PO Box 910, La Plata (20646); 1,500; $8.00; editor Chris Baker; tel (301) 934-2251 ext. 537; Format: 5x12.5

College of Notre Dame of Maryland: *Columns* — 4701 N. Charles St., Baltimore (21210); F; 1,500; $8.00; tel (301) 532-5580; Format: 5x15

Columbia Union College: *Columbia Journal* — Columbia Union College, Takoma Park (20912); 1,200; $8.00; editor Camille Lofters; tel (301) 891-4111; Format: 5x13

Coppins State College: *Courier* — 2500 W. North Ave., Baltimore (21216); 4,000; $8.00; tel (410) 383-5857; Format: 4x15

Essex Community College: *The Montage* — 7201 Rossville Blvd., Baltimore County (21237); 4,000; $10.91; tel (410) 780-6576; Format: 4x13

Frostburg State Univ.: *The Bottom Line* — 232 Lane Center, Frostburg (21532); TH; 2,500; $8.00; editor Rick Carter; tel (301) 687-4326/4000; Format: 5x13

Goucher College: *Quindecim* — Box 1437, Towson (21204); 1,500; $11.32; tel (410) 337-6413; Format: 5x15

Hood College: *Hood Today* — Rosemont Ave., Frederick (21701-9988); 1,100; $8.00; editor Sheila Dronsfield; tel (301) 696-3641; Format: 5x12

Howard Community College: *Howard CC Times* — 10901 Little Patuxent Pkwy., Columbia (21044); 4,000; $8.00; editor Michael Mohen; tel (410) 964-4937; Format: 5x14

Johns Hopkins Univ.: *News-Letter* — 3400 N. Charles St., Baltimore (21218); F; 7,000; $14.54; editor Maximilian Barteau; tel (410) 516-6000; Format: 6x21

Loyola College: *Greyhound* — 100 W. Cold Spring Ln., Baltimore (21210); T; 3,000; $14.55; editor Jen Brennan; tel (410) 617-2867; Format: 6x21.5

Montgomery College: *Spur* — 51 Mannakee St., Rockville (20850); 4,000; $11.82; tel (301) 251-7176; Format: 4x14

Morgan State Univ.: *Spokesman* — Hillen & Coldspring, Baltimore (21239); 3,000; $9.09; editor Fiona Williams; tel (410) 319-3454; Format: 5x12.75

Mt St Mary's College: *The Mountain Echo* — 16300 Old Emmitsburg Rd., Emmitsburg (21727-7799); 2,500; $9.09; editor Vince Chesney; tel (301) 447-5246; Format: 4x12.25

Mt Vernon College: *Post Impressions* — 2100 Foxhall Rd. N.W., Washington (20007); 600; $11.42; tel (202) 625-0400; Format: 2x10

Prince Georges Community College: *The Owl* — 301 Largo Rd., Largo (20772-2199); 4,000; $16.36; tel (301) 322-0905; Format: 4x14

St John's College: *The Gadfly* — Box 2800, Annapolis (21404); H; 800; $10.91; editor Nathan Jongewaard; tel (410) 263-2371; Format: 3x10

St Mary's College of Maryland: *Point News* — Charles Hall, St. Mary's City (20686); T; 2,500; $10.91; editor Chris Heun; tel (301) 862-0213; Format: 5x15

Salisbury State College: *Flyer* — 1101 Camden Ave., Rm. 229, Salisbury (21801); T; 3,500; $8.00; tel (410) 543-6191; Format: 5x13

Towson State Univ.: *Towerlight* — University Union, Rm. 313, Towson (21204); H; 10,000; $10.71; editor David Wharen; tel (410) 830-2288; Format: 5x13

Univ. of Baltimore: *Ubique* — 1420 N. Charles St., Baltimore (21201); 3,000; $10.47; editor Stacey Maddern; tel (410) 837-4029; Format: 4x13

Univ. of Maryland: *Retriever* — 5401 Wilkens Ave., Baltimore (21228); T; 5,000; $11.64; editor Pam Hawsley; tel (410) 455-1260/1264; Format: 6x21.5

Univ. of Maryland: *Diamondback* — PO Box U, College Park (20742); MTWHF; 19,000; $19.29; editor B.J. Sanford; tel (301) 314-8000; Format: 6x21.25

Univ. of Maryland Eastern Shore: *Hawks Message* — Eastern Shore, Princess Anne (21853); 1,000; $18.18; tel (410) 651-6443/2200; Format: 3x17

Villa Julie College: *The Villager* — Green Spring Valley Rd., Stevenson (21153); 1,600; $8.38; tel (410) 486-7000; Format: 5x13

Western Maryland College: *Phoenix* — 2 College Hill, Westminster (21157); 1,500; $10.91; tel (410) 751-8600; Format: 5x14

MASSACHUSETTS

American International College: *Yellow Jacket* — 1000 State St., Springfield (01109); W; 1,200; $9.00; tel (413) 737-7000 ext. 265; Format: 4x13

Amherst College: *Amherst Student* — Box 1816, Amherst (01002-5000); W; 3,500; $9.09; editor Nick Catoggio; tel (413) 542-2304; Format: 5x16

Assumption College: *Le Provocateur* — 500 Salisbury St., Worcester (01609); 1,500; $12.60; editor Dave Nordman; tel (508) 752-5615 ext. 155; Format: 5x15

Babson College: *Babson Free Press* — Box 140, Babson Park (02157); H; 2,000; $9.09; editor Lawrence Gauti; tel (617) 239-4229; Format: 5x13

Bentley College: *Vanguard* — La Cava Capus Center, Rm. 169B, Waltham (02154); H; 5,000; $15.00; editor Kristen Dupee; tel (617) 891-3497; Format: 5x16

Boston College: *The Heights* — 113 Mcelroy Commons, Chestnut Hill (02167); M; 10,000; $12.75; editor Mike Hoffman; tel (617) 552-2220; Format: 5x16

Boston Univ.: *Daily Free Press* — 842 Commonwealth Ave., Boston (02215); MTWHF; 12,000; $16.91; editor Mike Kaunzelman; tel (617) 232-6841; Format: 5x16

Brandeis Univ.: *The Justice* — Usdan 7, Waltham (02254); T; 4,500; $11.82; editor Jeremy Markowitz; tel (617) 736-3750; Format: 5x16

Bridgewater State College: *The Comment* — Adrian Rondileau Campus Center, Bridgewater (02325); H; 3,500; $8.00; editor Susanna Sinclair; tel (508) 697-1719; Format: 5x16

Bristol Community College: *Byline* — 777 Elsbree St., Fall River (02720); 2,000; $8.00; editor Victoria Orlando; tel (508) 678-2811 ext. 2132; Format: 4x14

Bunker Hill Community College: *The Third Rail* — Student Activities, Boston (02129); 4,000; $12.73; editor Kim Binshaw; tel (617) 228-2258; Format: 5x16

Cape Cod Community College: *Main Sheet* — Rte. 132, West Barnstable (02668); 3,500; $19.89; editors Marcia Macinnis & Andrew Ojala; tel (508) 362-2131 ext. 4323; Format: 6x15

Clark Univ.: *The Scarlet* — Box B-13, Worcester (01610); H; 3,000; $12.00; editor Dan Stractman; tel (508) 793-7508; Format: 4x15

College of The Holy Cross: *Crusader* — PO Box 32A, Worcester (01610); F; 4,000; $10.00; editor Anne Donahue; tel (508) 793-2668; Format: 4x16

Dean College: *The Dean Journal* — 99 Main St., Franklin (02038); 1,700; $15.45; editor Peter Wootton; tel (508) 528-9100 ext. 390; Format: 4x13

Eastern Nazarene College: *Campus Camera* — 23 E. Elm St., Quincy (02170); 1,000; $9.00; editor Allison Wilson; tel (617) 773-6350 ext. 3577; Format: 5x16

Emerson College: *Berkeley Beacon* — 130 Beacon St., Boston (02116); H; 2,500; $16.37; editor Dan Vlossak; tel (617) 578-8687; Format: 5x13.5

Fitchburg State College: *Strobe* — 160 Pearl St., Fitchburg (01420); W; 2,500; $9.69; tel (508) 665-3647; Format: 5x15

Framingham State College: *Gatepost News* — 100 State St., Framingham (01701); F; 2,000; $12.73; editor Suzanne Mcdonald; tel (508) 626-4605/875-1287; Format: 5x15

Hampshire College: *The Phoenix* — 893 West St., Amherst (01002-5001); F; 1,500; $13.64; tel (413) 549-4600 ext. 4650; Format: 4x13

Harvard Univ.: *Harvard Crimson* — 14 Plympton St., Cambridge (02138); MTWHFS; 3,500; $11.36; editor Andrew Wright; tel (617) 576-6600; Format: 6x21

Holyoke Community College: *Phoenix Press* — 303 Homestead Ave., Holyoke (01040); 10,000; $8.00; tel (413) 538-7000 ext. 534; Format: 3x9.5

Massachusetts Institute of Tech.: *The Tech* — 84 Massachusetts Ave., Cambridge (02139); TF; 9,000; $12.19; editor Dan Stevenson; tel (617) 258-8324; Format: 5x16

Massasoit Community College: *The Voice* — 1 Massasoit Blvd., Brockton (02402); 2,000; $11.36; editor Richard Pepp; tel (508) 588-9100 ext. 1485; Format: 5x15.5

Merrimack College: *Argus* — 315 Turnpike Rd., North Andover (01845); 1,000; $8.00; editor Linda Dainis; tel (508) 837-5000 exts. 4523/4279; Format: 5x16

Middlesex Community College: *Campus Report* — Springs Rd., Bedford (01730); 4,000; $18.18; tel (617) 280-3761; Format: 5x13

Mt Holyoke College: *The Mount Holyoke News* — PO Box 3215, South Hadley (01075); H; 3,500; $9.09; editor Elizabeth Cook; tel (413) 538-3223/4272; Format: 5x16

Nichols College: *Bison* — Center Rd., Dudley (01571-5000); 1,000; $10.69; editor Meredith Ford; tel (508) 943-1560 ext. 113; Format: 4x17

N Adams State College: *Beacon* — Church St, North Adams (01247); H; 2,200; $9.54; tel (413) 664-4511 ext. 404; Format: 4x13

Northeastern Univ.: *Northeastern News* — 360 Huntington Ave., Boston (02115); W; 10,000; $14.55; editor David L. Schutz; tel (617) 373-4343; Format: 5x16

Northern Essex Community College: *Necc Observer* — 100 Elliott St., Haverhill (01830); 3,000; $9.09; tel (508) 374-3900 ext. 2634; Format: 4x16

Salem State College: *Salem State Log* — 352 Lafayette St., Salem (01970); 4,500; $10.90; editor Michael Strong; tel (508) 741-6448; Format: 4x16

Simmons College: *Simmons News* — 300 The Fenway, Boston (02115); H; 2,500; $8.00; tel (617) 738-3189; Format: 4x17

Smith College: *Sophian* — Capen Annex, Northampton (01063); H; 4,000; $10.00; editor Julia Hayden; tel (413) 585-4972/5628; Format: 4x16

Springfield College: *The Student* — 263 Alden St., Box 1700, Springfield (01109); H; 2,300; $8.52; editor Adam Mehan; tel (413) 748-3132/3000; Format: 4x16

Stonehill College: *Summit* — 320 Washington St., North Easton (02357); 2,400; $8.00; editor Angela Dion; tel (508) 230-7830; Format: 5x16

Suffolk Univ.: *Suffolk Journal* — 41 Temple St., Boston (02114); W; 2,000; $8.00; editor Dan Coakley; tel (617) 573-8323; Format: 5x17

Tufts Univ.: *Tufts Daily* — Curtis Hall, Medford (02155); MTWHF; 5,000; $12.73; editor David Meyers; tel (617) 627-3090; Format: 5x16

Univ. of Massachusetts: *Daily Collegian* — 113 Campus Center, Amherst (01003); MTWHF; 17,000; $19.00; editor Andrew Davidson; tel (413) 545-3500; Format: 8x21

Univ. of Massachusetts: *Mass Media* — Harbor Campus, Boston (02125); T; 12,000; $12.73; editor Atha Demopoulos; tel (617) 287-7995; Format: 4x15.75

Univ. of Massachusetts: *Connector* — 426 Fox Hall, Lowell (01854); T; 4,000; $10.00; editor Tracy Beauchesne; tel (508) 934-5009; Format: 5x16

Univ. of Massachusetts: *The Torch* — Old Westport Rd., North Dartmouth (02747); F; 2,000; $10.02; editor Allison Chown; tel (508) 999-8158; Format: 4x16

Wellesley College: *Wellesley News* — 300 OBillings Hall, Wellesley (02181); W; 3,500; $15.45; editor Lisa Sargent; tel (617) 431-7520; Format: 4x16

Wentworth Institute: *Spectrum* — 550 Huntington Ave., Boston (02115); 2,000; $8.00; tel (617) 442-9010 ext. 367/452; Format: 4x16

Western New England College: *Westerner* — 1215 Wilbraham Rd., Springfield (01119); 3,000; $8.00; editor William Stevens; tel (413) 782-1580; Format: 5x13.5

Westfield State College: *The Owl* — Box 210, Westfield (01086); M; 4,000; $8.00; tel (413) 568-3311 ext. 5431; Format: 5x16

Wheaton College: *Wheaton Wire* — Box W1081, Norton (02766); H; 2,000; $8.00; editor Jen Williams; tel (508) 286-3821; Format: 5x16

Williams College: *Williams Record* — Baxter Hall, Williamstown (01267); T; 3,900; $10.46; editor Barbara Shreve; tel (413) 597-2289; Format: 6x21

Worcester Poly Institute: *Newspeak* — WPI, Box 2700, Worcester (01609); T; 2,000; $9.91; editor Kristen Greene; tel (508) 831-5464; Format: 4x16

Worcester State College: *Student Voice* — Student Center, Rm. 217, Worcester (01602); W; 2,500; $10.00; editor Eric Johnson; tel (508) 754-2313; Format: 5x16

MICHIGAN

Albion College: *The Pleiad* — Baldwin Hall, Albion (49224); F; 2,600; $8.19; editor Christa Loffelman; tel (517) 629-1651/1503; Format: 5x14

Calvin College: *Chimes* — Grand Rapids, 49546 (F); 4,000; $12.73; editor Tim Steen; tel (616) 957-7031; Format: 5x15

Central Michigan Univ.: *CM Life* — Anspach Hall, Rm. 8, Mount Pleasant (48859); MWF; 14,000; $19.00; editor Marjory Raymer; tel (517) 774-3493; Format: 6x21

Delta College: *Delta Collegiate* — Office B-101, University Center (48710); H; 3,500; $10.00; tel (517) 686-9337; Format: 5x14

Eastern Michigan Univ.: *Eastern Echo* — 121 Goodison Hall, Ypsilanti (48197-2260); MWF; 10,000; $11.17; editor Amy Colegrove; tel (313) 487-1010; Format: 6x21

Ferris State Univ.: *Ferris Torch* — Starr Rm. 221, Big Rapids (49307); TH; 7,000; $9.27; editor Darcie Smith; tel (616) 592-2609; Format: 5x14

Grand Rapids Community College: *Collegiate* — 143 Bostwick N.E., Grand Rapids (49503); 3,000; $10.91; editor Don Lee; tel (616) 771-4157/4000; Format: 5x15.5

Grand Vly. Univ.: *Lanthorn* — 1 Campus Landing, Allendale (49401); W; 6,000; $12.00; tel (616) 895-2460; Format: 5x16

Henry Ford Community College: *Mirror* — 5101 Evergreen Rd., C-4K, Dearborn (48128); 3,000; $9.09; editor Tamie Jovanelly; tel (313) 845-9639; Format: 5x16

Hillsdale College: *Collegian* — 33 E. College, Hillsdale (49242); H; 1,650; $9.09; editor Kip Oren; tel (517) 437-7341; Format: 5x15

Hope College: *Anchor* — De Witt Center, Holland (49423); W; 2,500; $10.18; editor Heather Mumby; tel (616) 394-7877; Format: 5x16

Kalamazoo College: *The Index* — 1200 Academy St., Kalamazoo (49007); W; 1,200; $8.00; editor Mark Crilley; tel (616) 337-7216; Format: 5x15

Lake Superior State Univ.: *Compass* — 107 Walker Cisler Center, Sault St. Marie (49783); 2,000; $8.18; editor Rich Walker; tel (906) 635-2551; Format: 5x16

Lansing Community College: *The Lookout* — 430 N. Capitol, Lansing (48901); 7,000; $10.91; editor Erin Oakley; tel (517) 483-1290; Format: 5x16

Lawrence Technological Univ.: *Tech News* — 21000 W. Ten Mile Rd., Southfield (48075); 3,000; $8.00; tel (810) 356-0200 ext. 2200; Format: 5x13

Michigan State Univ.: *State News* — 301 MAC, Ste. 105, East Lansing (48823-4376); MTWHF; 35,000; $26.37; editor Rachel Perry; tel (517) 353-6400/355-3447; Format: 6x21

Michigan Tech. Univ.: *Tech Lode* — Memorial Union Bldg., Houghton (49931); F; 5,500; $8.00; tel (906) 487-2404; Format: 6x21

Mott Community College: *MCC Post* — 1401 E. Court St., Flint (48502-2392); 4,200; $8.00; editor Jody O'Hara; tel (810) 762-5616/0247; Format: 5x13.5

Nazareth College: *The Mirror* — 3333 Gull Rd., Kalamazoo (49001-1282); 1,000; $9.09; tel (616) 349-4200 ext. 267; Format: 3x17

Northern Michigan Univ.: *Northwind* — Lee Hall, Marquette (49855); H; 6,000; $9.45; editor Amy Goodrich; tel (906) 227-2545; Format: 5x13

Oakland Univ.: *Oakland Post* — 36 Oakland Center, Rochester (48309-4401); W; 5,000; $12.73; editor Rob Snell; tel (810) 370-4269/4267; Format: 6x21

Saginaw Vly. State Univ.: *Valley Vanguard* — 7400 Bay Rd., University Center (48710); 2,500; $10.91; editor Sharon Covieo; tel (517) 790-4248; Format: 4x15

Schoolcraft College: *Schoolcraft Connection* — DPCC, 4th Fl., Livonia (48152); 5,000; $9.09; editor Mary Wertz; tel (313) 462-4422; Format: 5x16

Spring Arbor College: *Crusader* — 106 Main St., Spring Arbor (49283); W; 1,000; $8.00; editor Heather Campbell; tel (517) 750-1200 ext. 334; Format: 5x13

St Clair Co. Community College: *Erie Square Gazette* — 323 Erie St., Port Huron (48060); H; 2,000; $8.18; editor Jennifer O'Brien; tel (810) 984-3881 ext. 5733; Format: 5x12.8

Univ. of Detroit Mercy: *Varsity News* — 3800 Puritan, Detroit (48221); W; 5,000; $9.09; editor Kristy Dressler; tel (313) 993-3300; Format: 6x20.5

Univ. of Michigan: *Michigan Daily* — Student Publications, Ann Arbor (48109); MTWHF; 16,500; $17.82; editor Jessie Halladay; tel (313) 764-0431; Format: 6x22

Univ. of Michigan: *Michigan Journal* — 4901 Evergreen, Dearborn (48128); M; 5,000; $10.00; editor Amy B. Quinn; tel (313) 593-5428; Format: 4x12.5

Univ. of Michigan: *Michigan Times* — UCEN, Rm. 381, Flint (48502-2186); 4,000; $8.73; editor Cynthia West; tel (810) 762-3475; Format: 5x15

Wayne State Univ.: *The South End* — 6001 Cass Ave., Detroit (48202); MTWHF; 10,000; $9.09; editor Doug Levy; tel (313) 577-3498; Format: 5x14

Western Michigan Univ.: *Western Herald* — 1523 Student Service Bldg., Kalamazoo (49008); MTWH; 12,500; $15.27; editor J.D. Pierce; tel (616) 387-2107; Format: 6x21

MINNESOTA

Augsburg College: *Augsburg Echo* — 731 21st Ave. S., Minneapolis (55454); H; 2,000; $9.09; editors Rob Voedisch & Sarah Jankowski; tel (612) 330-1102; Format: 5x16

Bemidji State Univ.: *Northern Student* — Box 24, Bemidji (56601); W; 4,000; $8.00; editor Devlyn Brooks; tel (218) 755-2987; Format: 5x16

Bethel College: *Clarion* — 3900 Bethel Dr., St. Paul (55112); 2,100; $14.26; editor Penny Johnson; tel (612) 638-6214; Format: 4x15.5

Carleton College: *Carletonian* — 1 N. College St., Northfield (55057); F; 2,900; $9.09; tel (507) 663-4158; Format: 6x21

College of St Benedict: *Independent* — Box 1556, St. Joseph (56374); H; 4,000; $8.00; editor Sara Burnett; tel (612) 363-5041; Format: 5x14

College of St Catherine: *The St. Catherine Wheel* — 2004 Randolph Ave., St. Paul (55105); 2,500; $10.00; editor Tracy Olson; tel (612) 690-6535; Format: 5x16

College of St Scholastica: *CSS Cable* — 1200 Kenwood, Duluth (55811); F; 1,500; $9.09; editor Jessica Mcdonald; tel (218) 723-6187; Format: 4x15

Concordia College: *Concordian* — Concordia College ,FPO 104, Moorhead (56562); F; 4,000; $8.18; editor Heather Hauschild; tel (218) 299-3827; Format: 5x16

Concordia College: *The Sword* — Hamline & Marshall, St. Paul (55104); 1,500; $9.09; editor Erica Wentzel/Anne Roth; tel (612) 641-8483; Format: 4x15.25

Gustavus Adolphus College: *The Gustavian Weekly* — GAC, St. Peter (56082); F; 2,500; $8.00; tel (507) 933-7636; Format: 5x15

Hamline Univ.: *Oracle* — Hamline University, 1536 Hewitt, St. Paul (55104); F; 1,500; $9.10; editor Jennifer Thorson; tel (612) 641-2268/2718; Format: 5x16

Lakewood Community College: *The Leader* — 3401 Century Ave., White Bear Lake (55110); 1,500; $8.00; tel (612) 779-3371; Format: 4x14

Macalester College: *Macalester Weekly* — 1600 Grand Ave., St. Paul (55105); F; 1,600; $9.09; tel (612) 696-6684; Format: 4x15

Mankato State Univ.: *Reporter* — MSU, Box 38, Mankato (56002); TH; 7,500; $8.00; editor Renee Berg; tel (507) 389-1776; Format: 5x15

Moorhead State Univ.: *Advocate* — Comstock Memorial Union, Moorhead (56563); H; 5,000; $8.00; editor Sarah Jackson; tel (218) 236-2365/2551; Format: 5x15

Northland Community College: *Northern Light* — Highway 1 E., Thief River Falls (56701); 750; $8.00; editor Elizabeth Perfecto; tel (218) 681-0701 ext. 180; Format: 5x14

Rochester Community College: *Echo* — E. Highway 14, Rochester (55904); 2,400; $14.55; editor Matthew Evans; tel (507) 285-7247; Format: 5x15

St Cloud State Univ.: *University Chronicle* — 13 Stewart Hall, St. Cloud (56301); TF; 7,000; $9.54; editor Kim Wimpsitt; tel (612) 255-3943/4086; Format: 5x15

St John's Univ.: *The Record* — Box 1285, Collegeville (56321); 4,000; $8.00; editor Matthew Selby/Tom Mccarthy; tel (612) 363-2540; Format: 4x16

St Olaf College: *Manitou Messenger* — St Olaf College, Northfield (55057); F; 3,000; $9.50; editor Rachel Vogt/Brooke Bonneville; tel (507) 646-3275; Format: 6x21.5

SW State Univ.: *The Impact* — Ste. 157, Marshall (56258); 2,000; $8.00; editor Pete Reinert; tel (507) 537-6228; Format: 5x15

Univ. of Minnesota: *UMD Statesman* — 118 Kirby Student Center, Duluth (55812); H; 6,000; $15.00; editor Ron Hustvedt; tel (218) 726-8154/7112; Format: 5x15

Univ. of Minnesota: *Minnesota Daily* — 720 Washington Ave. S.E., Ste. 349, Minneapolis (55414); MTWHF; 25,000; $20.89; editor Pam Louwagie; tel (612) 627-4080; Format: 5x16

Univ. of Minnesota: *University Register* — Minority Resource Center, Morris (56267); H; 1,600; $8.00; editor Wade West; tel (612) 589-6078; Format: 5x15

Winona State Univ.: *Winonan* — Kryzsko Commons, Winona (55987); W; 5,000; $10.90; editor David Boehler; tel (507) 457-5677; Format: 6x21

MISSISSIPPI

Delta State Univ.: *Delta Statement* — Box D-3, Cleveland (38733); H; 2,500; $8.00; editor Laura Williams; tel (601) 846-4715; Format: 4x13

Jackson State Univ.: *Blue & White Flash* — Mass Comm. Bldg., Jackson (39217); H; 2,500; $12.73; editor Shantella Sherman; tel (601) 968-2167; Format: 6x21.5

Millsaps College: *Purple & White* — Box 15424-Campbell Center, Jackson (39210); H; 1,200; $8.00; tel (601) 974-1211; Format: 5x14

Mississippi College: *Mississippi Collegian* — MC, Box 4171, Clinton (39058); 2,000; $8.00; tel (601) 925-3244; Format: 5x14

Mississippi State Univ.: *Reflector* — Student Media Center, Miss State (39762-5407); TF; 13,000; $18.18; editor Alison Stamps; tel (601) 325-2374; Format: 6x21

Mississippi Univ. For Women: *Spectator* — Box W1030, Columbus (39701); H; 2,500; $8.00; tel (601) 329-7268; Format: 5x12.5

Mississippi Vly. State Univ.: *Delta Devils Gazette* — Box 309-Journalism, Itta Bena (38941); 2,000; $8.00; editor Calandra Jefferson; tel (601) 254-9041 ext. 6333; Format: 5x13

Univ. of Mississippi: *Daily Mississippian* — Farley Hall, University (38677); MTWHF; 11,000; $10.46; editor Melanie Simpson; tel (601) 232-5391/5632; Format: 5x16

Copyright ©1996 by the Editor & Publisher Co.

Univ. of Southern Mississippi: *Student Printz* — SS Box 5088, Hattiesburg (39406); TH; 6,500; $12.73; editor Scott Rouse; tel (601) 266-4267/5188; Format: 5x12.5

MISSOURI

Central Missouri State Univ.: *Mule Skinner* — Martin Bldg. 30, Warrensburg (64093); H; 6,500; $8.00; tel (816) 543-4051; Format: 6x21

Devry Institute: *The Turning Point* — 11224 Holmes Rd., Kansas City (64131); M; 1,000; $10.00; editor Suzette Statz; tel (816) 941-0430 ext. 348; Format: 2x10

Evangel College: *The Lance* — 1111 N. Glenstone, Springfield (65802); F; 1,600; $9.09; editor Erin Cole; tel (417) 865-2815 ext. 7238; Format: 5x16

NE Missouri State Univ.: *Index* — Sub Media Center, Kirksville (63501); H; 6,000; $10.91; editor Kevin Poortinga; tel (816) 785-4319/4449; Format: 6x21

NW Missouri State Univ.: *Northwest Missourian* — 2 Wells Hall, Maryville (64468); H; 8,000; $9.09; tel (816) 562-1635/1224; Format: 6x21

Penn Vly. Community College: *Scout* — 3201 S.W. Traffic Light, Kansas City (64111); 3,000; $8.00; tel (816) 759-4000; Format: 4x13.5

St Louis Community College: *Montage* — 11333 Big Bend, Kirkwood (63122); 5,000; $10.91; editor Jim Buchanan; tel (314) 984-7955; Format: 4x14

St Louis Univ.: *University News* — 20 N. Grand Blvd., St. Louis (63103); F; 8,000; $12.73; editor Bill Fronczak; tel (314) 977-2813; Format: 6x21.5

SE Missouri State Univ.: *Capaha Arrow* — 1 University Plz., Cape Girardeau (63701); W; 6,000; $8.00; editor Tamara Zellars; tel (314) 651-2540; Format: 5x15.25

SW Missouri State Univ.: *Southwest Standard* — 901 S. National, Springfield (65804); W; 15,000; $17.73; editor Sean Kliethermes; tel (417) 836-5524; Format: 6x21

Stephens College: *Stephens Life* — Box 2014, Columbia (65215); F; 2,000; $9.09; tel (314) 876-7254; Format: 5x13

Univ. of Missouri: *Maneater* — A038 Brady Commons, Columbia (65211); TF; 13,000; $14.37; editor Patrick Strawbridge; tel (314) 882-8356/8357; Format: 5x16

Univ. of Missouri: *University News* — 5327 Holmes, Kansas City (64110); M; 8,000; $12.73; editor Sashi Sabaratnam; tel (816) 235-1386/1393; Format: 5x16

Univ. of Missouri: *Missouri Miner* — 103 Norwood Hall, Rolla (65401); W; 4,500; $8.18; editor Christopher Goo; tel (314) 341-4235; Format: 5x13

Univ. of Missouri: *The Current* — 8001 Natural Bridge Rd., St. Louis (63121); M; 6,000; $12.27; editor Micheal O'Brien; tel (314) 516-5175/5316; Format: 6x21

Washington Univ.: *Student Life* — Womens Bldg., Rm. 42, Campus Box 1039, St. Louis (63130); TF; 8,000; $10.91; editor Melissa Schwarzberg; tel (314) 935-6713; Format: 6x21

Webster Univ.: *Journal* — 470 E. Lockwood, St. Louis (63119-3194); H; 3,500; $11.45; editor Chuck Bolinger; tel (314) 961-2660 ext. 7538; Format: 4x14.5

Westminster College: *Columns* — 500 Westminster Ave., Fulton (65251); 800; $8.00; tel (314) 642-3361 ext. 397; Format: 4x13

MONTANA

Montana College of Mineral Science & Tech.: *The Technocrat* — Montana Tech., Box 70, Butte (59701); F; 1,500; $9.09; editor Jennifer Nelson; tel (406) 496-4241; Format: 5x16

Montana State Univ.: *Retort* — Box B, Billings (59101); 2,000; $10.82; tel (406) 657-2194; Format: 5x16

Montana State Univ.: *Exponent* — Strand Union Bldg., Bozeman (59717); TF; 7,500; $16.27; editor Tawna Mitchell; tel (406) 994-2611; Format: 5x13

Northern Montana College: *Nomoco* — PO Box 7751, Havre (59501-7751); TH; 1,000; $8.00; editor Becky Petrick; tel (406) 265-4112; Format: 4x10

Univ. of Montana: *Montana Kaimin* — Journalism Bldg. J-206, Missoula (59812); TWHF; 6,000; $14.55; editor Kevin Crough; tel (406) 243-6541; Format: 5x16.5

NEBRASKA

Creighton Univ.: *Creightonian* — 203 Hitchcock Center, Omaha (68178-0119); F; 4,500; $12.70; editor Dan Bratetic; tel (402) 280-2539; Format: 4x15.5

Midland Lutheran College: *The Midland* — 900 N. Clarkson, Fremont (68025); F; 1,800; $9.09; editor Kathleen Healy; tel (402) 721-5487 ext. 6378; Format: 5x16.5

Nebraska Wesleyan Univ.: *Cornerstone* — SMB 1122, Lincoln (68504); F; 1,300; $9.09; editor Tim Blankenship; tel (402) 465-2417; Format: 5x14

Union College: *Clock Tower* — 3800 S. 48th St., Lincoln (68506); 850; $8.00; editor Leland Krum; tel (402) 488-2331 ext. 2091; Format: 3x9.5

Univ. of Nebraska: *Antelope* — Thomas Hall, Rm. 101, Kearney (68849); H; 4,500; $8.00; editor Joe Kurtz; tel (308) 865-8488; Format: 6x21.5

Univ. of Nebraska: *Daily Nebraskan* — 1400 R St., Lincoln (68588-0448); MTWHF; 16,000; $20.00; editor Chris Hain; tel (402) 472-2589/1769; Format: 5x16.5

Univ. of Nebraska: *The Gateway* — 60th & Dodge Sts., Annex 26, Omaha (68182); TF; 6,000; $9.45; editor Veronica Burgher; tel (402) 554-2470/2494; Format: 6x15.5

Wayne State College: *Wayne Stater* — Newspaper Office, Wayne (68787); W; 4,200; $8.00; tel (402) 375-7489/2200; Format: 5x15.5

NEVADA

Community College of Southern Nevada: *Reflections* — 3200 E. Cheyenne Ave., N1A, North Las Vegas (89030); 3,000; $10.91; tel (702) 651-4339; Format: 4x12

Univ. of Nevada: *The Rebel Yell* — Las Vegas, 89154 (H); 6,000; $12.73; editor Teresa Hinds; tel (702) 895-3878; Format: 5x16

Univ. of Nevada: *Sagebrush* — Asun/Sagebrush Office, Reno (89557); TF; 6,000; $12.73; editor John Clark; tel (702) 784-6589/4033; Format: 6x21

NEW HAMPSHIRE

Dartmouth College: *The Dartmouth* — 6175 Robinson Hall, Hanover (03755); MTWHF; 2,500; $10.85; tel (603) 646-2600; Format: 5x12.5

Franklin Pierce College: *Pierce Arrow* — The Manor, Rindge (03461); W; 1,000; $8.00; editor Alison Smith; tel (603) 899-4170; Format: 5x13

Keene State College: *Equinox* — Elliot Hall, Keene (03431); W; 4,000; $9.09; tel (603) 358-2401; Format: 5x13

New England College: *The New Englander* — Nec-Office Of Student Programs, Henniker (03242); 3,500; $8.00; editor Alicia Fonash; tel (603) 428-2243; Format: 4x16

Notre Dame College: *De Notre* — 2321 Elm St., Manchester (03104); 1,500; $8.00; tel (603) 669-4298 ext. 255; Format: 4x14

Plymouth State College: *The Clock* — College Union Bldg., Plymouth (03264); H; 3,600; $8.00; editor Jamie Hamlin; tel (603) 535-2279/5000; Format: 5x15

St Anselm College: *St Anselm Crier* — 87 St. Anselm College Dr., Manchester (03102); 1,800; $13.64; editor Craig Maccormack; tel (603) 641-7016; Format: 5x13

Univ. of New Hampshire: *New Hampshire* — Memorial Union B, Rm. 153, Durham (03824); TF; 8,000; $18.00; editor Jeffry Glenn; tel (603) 862-1323; Format: 5x13.75

NEW JERSEY

Atlantic Community College: *Atlantic Review* — 5100 Blackhorse Pike, Mays Landing (08330); 5,000; $8.31; tel (609) 343-5109; Format: 5x14

Bergen Community College: *Monitor* — 400 Paramus Rd., Paramus (07652); 4,500; $8.00; editor Anthony Deprospo Jr.; tel (201) 447-3029; Format: 4x15

Bloomfield College: *Collective Voice* — Bloomfield College, Bloomfield (07003); 2,000; $8.00; editor Angelique Tindal; tel (201) 748-9000 exts. 420/260; Format: 4x16

Brookdale Community College: *The Stall* — Newman Springs Rd., Lincroft (07738); 7,000; $8.00; editor Scott Poris; tel (908) 842-1900 ext. 2266; Format: 5x15

Burlington Co. College: *The Source* — Pemberton-Browns Mill Road, Pemberton (08068); 2,000; $8.00; editor Julia Welsh; tel (609) 894-9311 ext. 588; Format: 4x16

Camden Co. College: *Campus Press* — PO Box 200, Blackwood (08012); 5,000; $13.64; editor Edward Mergenthal; tel (609) 227-7200 ext. 202; Format: 4x15

Centenary College: *Centenary College Quill* — 400 Jefferson St., Hackettstown (07840-0089); 500; $9.09; editor Rachael Bigelow; tel (908) 852-1400 ext. 243; Format: 5x14

Cook College Rutgers Univ.: *Green Print* — Cook Campus Center, New Brunswick (08903); W; 4,500; $8.00; editor Sean Carr; tel (908) 932-9481; Format: 5x16

County College of Morris: *Youngtown Edition* — SCC #140, 214 Center Grove Rd., Randolph (07869); W; 3,500; $15.00; tel (201) 328-5224/5469; Format: 6x16

Douglass College: *Caellian* — 202 College Hall, New Brunswick (08903); H; 3,000; $8.00; editor Anne Baney; tel (908) 846-7871/9822; Format: 4x16

Drew Univ.: *The Acorn* — 36 Madison Ave., Madison (07940); F; 2,000; $8.00; tel (201) 408-3451; Format: 5x17

Essex Co. College: *Ecco* — 303 University Ave., Newark (07102); 3,000; $14.55; tel (201) 877-3177; Format: 5x16

Fairleigh Dickinson Univ.: *Metro* — 285 Madison Ave., Madison (07940); W; 3,000; $12.57; editor Maurice Brooks; tel (201) 593-8580/8582; Format: 5x17

Fairleigh Dickinson Univ.: *Equinox* — 1000 River Rd., Teaneck (07666); H; 8,500; $15.38; editor Joe Orlando; tel (201) 692-2046; Format: 5x17

Gloucester County College: *Gazette* — Tanyard Rd., Sewell (08080); 4,500; $8.00; editor D'Borah Michel; tel (609) 468-5000 ext. 206; Format: 5x15.75

Jersey City State College: *Knight Examiner* — 2039 Kennedy Blvd., Jersey City (07305-1597); 3,000; $18.18; tel (201) 200-3575; Format: 5x15

Mercer Co. Community College: *College Voice* — 1200 Old Trenton Rd., Trenton (08690); 1,500; $14.73; editor Nicole Glonek; tel (609) 586-4800 ext. 405; Format: 5x14

Middlesex Community College: *Quo Vadis* — PO Box 3050, Edison (08818-3050); F; 4,900; $9.33; editor Dana Sartaiw; tel (908) 548-6000 ext. 3443; Format: 3x10

Monmouth College: *Outlook* — College Center, 3rd Fl., West Long Branch (07764); H; 3,600; $8.00; tel (908) 571-3481; Format: 5x15.5

Montclair State Univ.: *Montclarion* — Student Center Annex, Upper Montclair (07043); H; 6,000; $12.73; editor Kevin Colligan; tel (201) 655-5237/5169; Format: 4x14.5

New Jersey Institute of Tech.: *The Vector* — 150 Bleeker St., Newark (07102); T; 4,000; $17.00; editor Jaime Alejandro; tel (201) 596-3611; Format: 5x15

Ocean Co. College: *Viking News* — College Dr., Toms River (08754-2001); H; 4,000; $8.00; editor Andy Nasto; tel (908) 255-0481; Format: 5x16

Princeton Univ.: *Daily Princetonian* — PO Box 469, Princeton (08542); MTWHF; 2,500; $11.00; editor Shirley Leung; tel (609) 924-7570/9219200; Format: 5x15.75

Ramapo College of New Jersey: *Ramapo News* — 505 Ramapo Valley Rd., Mahwah (07430-1680); H; 3,000; $11.82; editor Brook Caska; tel (201) 825-1749; Format: 5x15

Rider Univ.: *Rider News* — 2083 Lawrenceville Rd., Lawrenceville (08648-3099); F; 3,500; $12.73; editor Kin Widenor; tel (609) 896-5337; Format: 4x14

Rowan College of New Jersey: *Glassboro Whit* — Pub Suite Student Center, Rte. 322, Glassboro (08028); H; 6,000; $8.00; tel (609) 256-4533; Format: 5x16

Rutgers Univ.: *Gleaner* — 326 Penn St., Camden (08102); W; 4,000; $8.00; editor Mathew Appleton; tel (609) 225-6354; Format: 5x15

Rutgers Univ.: *Medium* — LPO 16405, New Brunswick (08903-5064); W; 8,000; $10.00; editor Lee Carpenter; tel (908) 445-4721; Format: 5x16

Rutgers Univ.: *Daily Targum* — 126 College Ave., Ste. 431, New Brunswick (08903); MTWHF; 17,000; $22.51; editor Karen Averbach; tel (908) 932-7051; Format: 5x16

Rutgers Univ.: *Observer* — 350 Dr. Martin Luther King Blvd., Newark (07102); T; 3,000; $11.96; editor Tawana Murphy; tel (201) 648-5358/5859; Format: 5x15

Seton Hall Univ.: *Setonian* — 400 S. Orange Ave., South Orange (07079); H; 5,000; $11.45; editor Maria Perotin; tel (201) 761-9083; Format: 5x15

St Peter's College: *Pauw Wow* — 2641 Kennedy Blvd., Jersey City (07306); 3,000; $12.12; editor Jeanette Masferrer; tel (201) 915-9146; Format: 4x16

Stevens Institute of Tech.: *Stute* — Castle Point Sta., Hoboken (07030); F; 2,500; $19.60; editor Mike Andreano; tel (201) 659-0143; Format: 5x16

Stockton State College: *Argo* — G-206 College Center, Pomona (08240); F; 2,500; $11.37; editor Vaughn Watson; tel (609) 652-4560/4205(MESSAGE); Format: 4x12.5

Sussex Community College: *The College Hill* — College Hill, Newton (07860); 1,000; $18.18; tel (201) 579-5400; Format: 4x17

Trenton State College: *The Signal* — Hill Wood Lakes, Trenton (08650-4700); T; 6,000; $10.82; editor Christine Ott; tel (609) 771-2499/2424; Format: 5x14

Union Co. College: *The Scroll* — 1033 Springfield Ave., Cranford (07016); 5,000; $8.18; editor James Howard; tel (908) 709-7161; Format: 5x14

Univ. College of Rutgers University: *Evening Watch* — Rutgers Student Center, New Brunswick (08903); 5,000; $8.00; editor Kay Schechter; tel (908) 828-1762; Format: 5x16

Upsala College: *The Gazette* — Upsala College, East Orange (07019); 1,000; $8.64; tel (201) 266-7708; Format: 4x15

William Paterson College: *The Beacon* — 300 Pompton Rd., Wayne (07470); M; 8,000; $13.64; editor Yoni Greenbaum; tel (201) 595-3265; Format: 5x14

NEW MEXICO

Eastern New Mexico Univ.: *Chase* — Station 39, Portales (88130); H; 3,000; $8.00; editor Donia Dunlap; tel (505) 562-2756; Format: 5x13

New Mexico Highlands Univ.: *La Mecha* — Motimer Hall, NMHU 210, Las Vegas (87701); H; 1,750; $8.00; editor Raymond Sanchez; tel (505) 454-3463/3454; Format: 5x10.5

New Mexico State Univ.: *Round Up* — Box CC, University Park (88003); MWF; 15,000; $19.85; editor Sam Bradley; tel (505) 646-6397; Format: 5x13

Univ. of New Mexico: *Daily Lobo* — Albuquerque, 87131-2061 (MTWHF); 14,500; $13.49; tel (505) 277-5656; Format: 5x16

NEW YORK

Adelphi Univ.: *Delphian* — 308 University Center, Garden City (11530); W; 4,800; $10.91; tel (516) 877-6935; Format: 5x14

Alfred Univ.: *Fiat Lux* — Powell Campus Center, Alfred (14802); 2,500; $8.18; editor Darcia Harris; tel (607) 871-2192; Format: 5x16

Barnard College: *Barnard Bulletin* — Macintosh Center, Rm. 105, New York (10027); W; 2,500; $21.64; editor Catherine Pajak; tel (212) 854-2119; Format: 3x10.5

Baruch College: *The Ticker* — 360 PAS, 17 Lexington Ave., New York (10010); 10,000; $10.91; editor Eric Torsen; tel (212) 802-6799; Format: 5x15

Bronx Community College: *The Communicator* — 181st St. & University Ave., Bronx (10453); 8,000; $27.29; tel (718) 220-6404; Format: 5x18

Brooklyn College: *Kingsman* — Ave. H & Bedford Ave., Brooklyn (11210); M; 10,000; $18.18; editor Edward Fruchtman; tel (718) 434-0875/951-4293; Format: 6x15

Broome Community College: *Generations* — PO Box 1017, Binghamton (13902); 2,000; $9.09; editor Bill Frobe; tel (607) 778-5110; Format: 5x16

Canisius College: *Griffin* — 2001 Main St., Buffalo (14208-1098); F; 3,500; $9.10; editor Brian Kantz; tel (716) 888-2195/2187; Format: 5x15

City College of New York: *Campus* — NAC, Rm. 1-119, New York (10031); 2,500; $9.09; editor Vincent Louis; tel (212) 650-8177/8178; Format: 5x15

Clarkson Univ.: *Integrator* — Cheel Campus Center, Potsdam (13699); M; 9,500; $9.09; editor Wayne Devoid; tel (315) 265-9051; Format: 5x16

Colgate Univ.: *Maroon-News* — Student Union, Hamilton (13346); F; 4,300; $10.00; editor Cory Fellows; tel (315) 824-7327/7745; Format: 5x16

College of Mt St Vincent: *Mountimes* — PO Box 75, Riverdale (10471); M; 1,000; $8.00; editor Maria Elena Baker; tel (212) 405-3471; Format: 5x15

College of New Rochelle: *Tatler* — Campus Activities Office, New Rochelle (10805); W; 1,100; $14.55; tel (914) 654-5207; Format: 5x15

College of St Rose: *The Chronicle* — 432 Western Ave., Albany (12203); 1,500; $8.00; tel (518) 454-5192; Format: 4x14

College of Staten Island: *College Voice* — 2800 Victory Blvd., Staten Island (10314); 5,000; $15.58; editor Michael Garofalo; tel (718) 982-3091; Format: 4x14

Columbia Univ.: *Daily Spectator* — 1125 Amsterdam Ave., New York (10025); MTWHF; 10,000; $22.54; editor Elizabeth Berke; tel (212) 854-9550; Format: 6x15

Cooper Union: *Cooper Pioneer* — Cooper Sq., New York (10003); 2,000; $13.18; editor Laurie Friedman; tel (212) 353-4133; Format: 4x13.5

Cornell Univ.: *Cornell Daily Sun* — 119 S. Cayuga St., Ithaca (14850); MTWHF; 5,000; $10.36; editor Andrew Morse; tel (607) 273-3606; Format: 5x16

Corning Community College: *Crier* — 1 Academic Dr., Corning (14830); 3,000; $8.14; tel (607) 962-9339; Format: 4x14

Culinary Institute of America: *La Papilotte* — PO Box 53, Hyde Park (12538); 2,000; $8.00; tel (914) 452-9600; Format: 4x14.5

CUNY NYC Tech. College: *New Tech Times* — 300 Jay St., Brooklyn (11201); 7,000; $18.47; editor Marisela Guzman; tel (718) 260-5453; Format: 5x15

CW Post Campus - LIU: *Pioneer* — 199 Hillwood Commons, Brookville (11548); W; 7,000; $18.18; editor Vito Formica; tel (516) 299-2619/2618; Format: 5x15

Dowling College: *Lions Voice* — Idlehour Blvd., Oakdale (11769); T; 3,000; $8.18; editor Phil Paranicas; tel (516) 244-3028; Format: 4x14

Dutchess Community College: *Dutchess Chronicle* — Pendell Rd., Poughkeepsie (12601); 2,000; $9.09; editor Judy Sunderland; tel (914) 471-4500 ext. 4831; Format: 4x15

Elmira College: *Octagon* — EC Octagon Office, Box 916, Elmira (14901); H; 1,000; $8.19; editor Tyrone Marsh; tel (607) 735-1917; Format: 4x12.5

Erie Community College-North: *North Star* — Main & Young Rd., Williamsville (14221); 5,000; $8.00; editor Michael J. Schmid; tel (716) 851-1597; Format: 5x13.5

Fashion Inst of Tech: *W27* — Suite A728, New York (10001); 4,500; $20.61; editor Drew Hindes/Dana Pusateri; tel (212) 760-7610/7798; Format: 4x15

Fordham Univ.: *The Ram* — E. Fordham Rd., Bronx (10458); H; 10,000; $10.45; editor Catherine Sabatos; tel (718) 817-4379; Format: 5x17

Fordham Univ. Lincoln Center.: *Observer* — 113 W. 60th St., Box 18, New York (10023); 5,000; $14.78; editor John Stocker; tel (212) 636-6016; Format: 4x16

Hamilton College: *The Spectator* — 198 College Hill Rd., Clinton (13323); F; 3,500; $8.00; editor James D'Aleo; tel (315) 859-4100; Format: 5x16

Hartwick College: *The Hilltops* — Daily Star, PO Box 250, Oneonta (13820); F; 1,800; $8.00; editor Ken Hall; tel 6074321000 ext. 39; Format: 5x12.5

Hobart & William Smith College: *Herald* — SF-92, Geneva (14456); F; 2,000; $9.78; tel (315) 789-4933; Format: 4x16

Hofstra Univ.: *Chronicle* — 203 Student Center, Hempstead (11550-1022); H; 6,500; $16.24; editor Dan Kline; tel (516) 463-6965; Format: 4x14

Houghton College: *The Houghton Star* — CPO Box 378, Houghton (14744); 1,000; $8.00; editor Heather Dale; tel (716) 567-9200; Format: 5x16

Hudson Valley Community College: *Hudsonian* — 80 Vandenburgh Ave., Troy (12180); 2,000; $12.99; tel (518) 270-7187; Format: 4x14

Hunter College: *Hunter Envoy* — 695 Park Ave., New York (10021); 15,000; $13.45; editors Wilford Haywood & Frantz Barbier; tel (212) 772-4252/4251; Format: 5x14

Iona College: *Ionian* — 715 North Ave., New Rochelle (10801); T; 2,000; $9.09; editor Angela Ciminello; tel (914) 633-2370; Format: 5x15

Ithaca College: *Ithacan* — 953 Danby Rd., Ithaca (14850-7258); H; 6,000; $10.91; editor Kevin Harlin; tel (607) 274-3207/3208; Format: 5x16

John Jay College: *Lex Review* — 445 W. 59th St., New York (10019); 9,000; $17.27; tel (212) 237-8307; Format: 4x16

Kingsborough Community College: *Scepter* — 2001 Oriental Blvd., Brooklyn (11235); 4,000; $18.18; editor Thomas Vellios; tel (718) 368-5603; Format: 4x15

Lehman College: *Meridian* — Bedford Park Blvd. W., Bronx (10468); 8,000; $21.82; editor Denise Stephens; tel (718) 960-4966; Format: 4x15

Lemoyne College: *Dolphin* — 16 Loyola Hall, Syracuse (13214); H; 2,500; $10.91; editor Anne Marie Henning; tel (315) 445-4542; Format: 4x16

Long Island Univ.-Brooklyn: *Seawanhaka* — 1 Univ Plaza, Brooklyn (11201); T; 4,000; $22.73; tel (718) 488-1591; Format: 4x16.5

Long Island Univ.-Southampton: *Windmill* — Southampton Campus, Southhampton (11968); T; 3,000; $8.00; tel (516) 283-4000; Format: 5x15

Manhattan College: *Quadrangle* — Manhattan College Pkwy., Riverdale (10471); H; 2,000; $14.55; editor James Vreeland; tel (718) 920-0270; Format: 4x14

Manhattanville College: *Touchstone* — 125 Purchase St., Purchase (10577); 1,500; $10.22; tel (914) 694-2200 ext. 6509; Format: 4x15.5

Marist College: *The Circle* — 290 North Rd., Poughkeepsie (12601); T; 3,100; $8.00; tel (914) 575-3000 ext. 2429; Format: 5x15.5

Marymount College: *Cormont* — Box 2, Tarrytown (10591); 1,500; $8.00; editor Arnella Ford; tel (914) 631-3200 ext. 292; Format: 4x16.5

Marymount Manhattan College: *Imp* — 221 E. 71st St., New York (10021); 1,000; $21.82; editor Marina Nicoletti; tel (212) 517-0493; Format: 3x11

Medgar Evers College: *Adafi* — 1150 Carroll St., Brooklyn (11225); 3,500; $8.50; editor Andrianne Payson; tel (718) 270-6426; Format: 4x17

Mt St Marys: *Clarion* — 330 Powell Ave., Newburgh (12550-3598); F; 2,000; $8.00; tel (914) 561-0800 ext. 176; Format: 5x14

Nassau Community College: *Vignette* — College Union, Garden City (11530); M; 8,000; $17.27; editor Arthur Zackiewicz; tel (516) 572-7227; Format: 4x14

Nazareth College: *The Gleaner* — 4245 East Ave., Rochester (14610); 3,000; $10.61; editor Stephen Mccaffrey; tel (716) 586-2525 ext. 342; Format: 5x16

New York Institute of Tech.: *Off The Circle* — 1855 Broadway, Rm. 502A, New York (10023); 1,500; $8.00; editor Dexter Mobley; tel (212) 261-1566; Format: 4x14

New York Institute of Tech.: *Campus Slate* — Student Government Bldg., Old Westbury (11568); M; 3,500; $10.71; editor Stefanie Fredella; tel (516) 686-7690; Format: 4x15

New York Univ.: *Washington Square News* — 566 Laguardia Pl., Rm. 914, New York (10012); MTWHF; 25,000; $18.36; editor David Barkhyner; tel (212) 998-4300; Format: 5x16

Niagara Univ.: *Niagara Index* — PO Box 1919, Niagara Falls (14109); F; 2,000; $14.54; editor Megan Dwan; tel (716) 286-8512; Format: 5x13.5

Onondaga Community College: *Overview* — Rte. 173, Syracuse (13215); H; 3,000; $8.00; tel (315) 469-7741 ext. 2278; Format: 4x16

Pace Univ.: *Pace Press* — 41 Park Row, 8th Fl., New York (10038); 12,000; $14.91; editor Jessica Campbell; tel (212) 346-1553; Format: 5x15.5

Pace Univ.: *New Morning* — 861 Bedford Rd., Pleasantville (10570-2799); 3,000; $12.27; editor Anthony Gandia; tel (914) 773-3401; Format: 5x15

Polytechnic Univ.: *The Reporter* — Box 625, Brooklyn (11201); 5,000; $18.18; editor Josianne D'Arbouet; tel (718) 260-3845/3800/3944; Format: 4x15

Pratt Institute: *Prattler* — 215 Willoughby Ave., Brooklyn (11205); 2,500; $9.82; editor Jean Shin; tel (718) 636-3525; Format: 5x14

Queens College: *QC Quad* — 65-30 Kissena Blvd., Flushing (11367-0904); M; 7,500; $16.36; editor Andrew Watson; tel (718) 520-9030; Format: 4x14

Queensborough Community College: *Communique* — 56th Ave. & Springfield Blvd., Bayside (11364); 8,000; $11.36; editor Laura Payne; tel (718) 631-6233; Format: 3x16

Rensselaer Poly Institute: *Polytechnic* — Rensselaer Union, Box 35, Troy (12180-3590); W; 9,000; $19.00; editor Nancy Ortins; tel (518) 276-6770; Format: 5x16

Roberts Wesleyan College: *The Beacon* — 2301 Westside Dr., Rochester (14624); 1,500; $8.18; tel (716) 594-6110; Format: 4x14.5

Rochester Institute of Tech.: *Reporter Magazine* — 37 Lomb Memorial Dr., Rochester (14623-0887); F; 13,000; $13.64; editor Christine Koenig; tel (716) 475-2214; Format: 3x10

Rockland Community College: *Outlook* — 145 College Rd., Suffern (10901); 5,000; $12.73; tel (914) 574-4389/356-6261; Format: 4x17

Russell Sage College: *Quill* — Box 2116, Troy (12180); H; 1,000; $23.92; tel (518) 270-2259; Format: 3x14

St Bonaventure Univ.: *The Bona Venture* — Drawer X, St. Bonaventure (14778); F; 3,500; $9.09; editor Micheal Hill; tel (716) 375-2227; Format: 6x21.5

St Francis College: *The Voice* — 180 Remsen St., Brooklyn (11201); 1,500; $8.00; tel (718) 522-2300 ext. 258; Format: 4x14

St John's Univ.: *The Torch* — 8000 Utopia Pkwy., Jamaica (11439); W; 6,000; $15.58; editor Jason Boland; tel (718) 990-6756; Format: 4x14

St Lawrence Univ.: *Hill News* — EJ Noble University Center, Canton (13617); F; 4,000; $8.00; tel (315) 379-5139/5140; Format: 5x14

St Thomas Aquinas: *The Thoma* — Rural Rte. 340, Sparkill (10976); 1,000; $16.36; editor Christy Norris; tel (914) 398-4075; Format: 5x15

Siena College: *The Promethean* — Foy Campus Center, Loudonville (12211); TH; 3,000; $8.19; editor Kristi Lombardi; tel (518) 783-2560; Format: 4x16

Skidmore College: *Skidmore News* — Saratoga Springs (12866); H; 3,000; $16.36; tel (518) 584-5000 ext. 2585; Format: 4x15.5

State Univ. College of NY: *Record* — 1300 Elmwood Ave., Buffalo (14222); TF; 4,000; $8.00; editor Margaret Coghlan; tel (716) 878-4539; Format: 5x16

State Univ. College of NY: *Dragon Chronicle* — 111 Corey Union, Cortland (13045); T; 5,000; $8.00; editor Jim Furiosi; tel (607) 753-2805; Format: 5x16

State Univ. College of NY: *The Leader* — S107 Campus Center, Fredonia (14063); M; 5,000; $9.09; editor Michelle Kromm; tel (716) 673-3369; Format: 4x15

State Univ. College of NY: *Lamron* — Mac Vittie Union Box 42, Geneseo (14454); H; 3,500; $9.09; editor Torye Mullin; tel (716) 245-5896; Format: 5x16

State Univ. College of NY: *Oracle* — Sub 417, New Paltz (12561); H; 10,000; $8.00; editor Hal Koplan; tel (914) 257-3030/3031; Format: 5x16

State Univ. College of NY: *State Times* — Hunt Union, Oneonta (13820); H; 5,000; $9.09; editor Michelene Potter; tel (607) 436-2492; Format: 5x12

State Univ. College of NY: *Oswegonian* — 15B Hewitt Union, Oswego (13126); H; 7,500; $8.00; tel (315) 341-3600; Format: 5x13

State Univ. College of NY: *Cardinal Points* — Agell College Center, Plattsburgh (12901); H; 6,000; $9.09; editor Howard Gussak; tel (518) 564-2174/2175; Format: 5x15

State Univ. College of NY: *The Load* — 735 Anderson Hill Rd., Purchase (10577); 3,000; $8.00; tel (914) 251-6993; Format: 4x15

State Univ. College of NY A&T: *Campus Voice* — Farrell Hall, Delhi (13753); 3,000; $9.34; tel (607) 746-4270; Format: 5x15

State Univ. of New York: *Pipe Dream* — Box 2002 University Union, Binghamton (13901); TF; 9,000; $10.00; editor Monica Luraschi; tel (607) 777-2257; Format: 6x16

State Univ. of New York: *Stylus* — 219 Holmes Hall, Brockport (14420); W; 5,500; $9.55; editor Greg Hardy; tel (716) 395-5623/2230; Format: 5x16

State Univ. of New York: *Spectrum* — Student Union, Ste. 132, Buffalo (14260); MWF; 12,000; $11.82; editor Bonnie Butkas; tel (716) 645-2152/2468; Format: 5x16

State Univ. of New York: *Catalyst* — Box 210, Old Westbury (11568); 1,500; $8.00; tel (516) 876-3208; Format: 4x14

State Univ. of New York: *Statesman* — PO Box A E, Stony Brook (11790/11794); MH; 9,000; $8.00; editor Tom Masse; tel (516) 632-6480; Format: 6x14

State Univ. of NY College of Tech.: *Tor Echo* — 110A Orvis Center, Alfred (14802); T; 2,500; $8.00; tel (607) 587-8110/4427; Format: 5x16

State Univ. of NY College of Tech.: *Rambler* — Roosevelt Hall, Farmingdale (11735); 3,000; $10.39; editor Karen Musgrave; tel (516) 420-2611; Format: 3x14

Stern College For Women: *The Observer* — 245 Lexington Ave., New York (10016); 5,000; $8.00; editor Rachel Schenker; tel (212) 340-7715; Format: 5x14

SUCNY/Potsdam College: *The Racquette* — 119 Barrington Student Union, Potsdam (13676); H; 3,500; $8.00; editor Mark Mayer; tel (315) 267-3287; Format: 5x14

Suffolk Community College: *The Compass* — 533 College Rd., Selden (11784); 3,500; $11.55; tel (516) 451-4826; Format: 4x13.25

SUNY Institute of Tech.: *Factory Times* — PO Box 3050, Utica (13504-3050); 1,000; $9.09; tel (315) 792-7426; Format: 4x16

Syracuse Univ.: *Daily Orange* — 744 Ostrom Ave., Syracuse (13210); MTWHF; 9,000; $15.44; editor David Franecki; tel (315) 443-2314; Format: 5x15.75

US Military Academy: *Pointer View* — Computer Graphics, Newburgh (12550); F; 8,000; $17.51; editor Irene Brown; tel (914) 561-7500; Format: 6x15

Union College: *Concordiensis* — Box 2577 Union College, Schenectady (12308); H; 3,000; $10.91; editor Heather Reynolds; tel (518) 388-6155; Format: 5x16

Univ. at Albany State Univ. NY: *Albany Student Press* — 1400 Washington Ave., Albany (12222); F; 10,000; $10.91; editor Susan Craine; tel (518) 442-5665; Format: 5x16

Univ. of Rochester: *Campus Times* — Box CPU 277086, River Sta., Rochester (14627-7086); H; 6,000; $10.18; tel (716) 275-5943; Format: 5x16

Utica College-Syracuse Univ.: *Tangerine* — Box 55, Utica (13502); F; 1,700; $8.18; editor Tom Mcginty; tel (315) 792-3067; Format: 4x15.5

Vassar College: *Miscellany News* — Box 165, Poughkeepsie (12601); F; 2,800; $8.60; editor Jessica Thaler; tel (914) 437-5348; Format: 5x15

Wagner College: *Wagnerian* — 631 Howard Ave., Staten Island (10312); H; 2,000; $8.00; editor Mike Hoffman; tel (718) 390-3191; Format: 4x10

Wells College: *Onyx* — Public Relations Office, Aurora (13026); 500; $8.00; editor Jen Dimond; tel (315) 364-3209; Format: 5x10

Westchester Community College: *The Viking* — 75 Grasslands Rd., Valhalla (10595); 7,000; $8.18; tel (914) 785-6768; Format: 5x13

Yeshiva Univ.: *The Commentator* — 500 W. 185th St., New York (10033); 5,000; $11.36; editor Owen Cuyrulnik; tel (212) 740-2155; Format: 4x15

York College: *Pandoras Box* — 94-20 Guy R Brewer Blvd., Jamaica (11451); 5,000; $16.96; editor Baraka Dorsey; tel (718) 262-2529; Format: 4x15

NORTH CAROLINA

Appalachian State Univ.: *Appalachian* — ASU Drawer 9025, Student Union, 2nd Fl., Boone (28608); TH; 7,000; $8.00; tel (704) 262-2157/2212; Format: 6x21

Campbell Univ.: *Campbell Times* — PO Box 241, Buies Creek (27506); H; 2,500; $10.18; tel (800) 334-4111 ext. 1524; Format: 5x12

Davidson College: *Davidsonian* — Box 219, Davidson (28036); M; 3,500; $8.00; editor Harrison Roberts; tel (704) 892-2148; Format: 5x15.5

Duke Univ.: *Chronicle* — 101 W. Union Bldg., Durham (27708-0858); MTWHF; 15,000; $19.64; editor Allison Stuebe; tel (919) 684-3811; Format: 6x14

E Carolina Univ.: *East Carolinian* — Student Pubs Bldg., Greenville (27858); TH; 12,000; $11.82; editor Stephanie Lassiter; tel (919) 328-2000; Format: 6x21.5

Elon College: *Pendulum* — Campus Box 2800, Elon College (27244); H; 2,600; $8.00; editor Erick Gill; tel (910) 584-2185; Format: 5x12

Fayetteville State Univ.: *The Bronco's Voice* — 1200 Murchison Rd., Fayetteville (28301-4298); 3,000; $11.82; editor Roger Harris; tel (910) 486-1357/1111; Format: 4x12

Fuqua School of Business: *Over The Counter* — Fuqua School of Business, Durham (27708); 800; $8.00; editor Steve Church; tel (919) 660-7888; Format: 4x14

Guilford College: *Guilfordian* — PO Box 17717, Greensboro (27410); F; 1,700; $8.00; editor Jacob Stohler; tel (919) 292-5511 ext. 2306; Format: 5x14

Meredith College: *Meredith Herald* — 3800 Hillsborough St., Raleigh (27607-5298); W; 1,600; $8.00; tel (919) 829-2824; Format: 5x14

North Carolina A&T State Univ.: *Register* — Box E-25, Greensboro (27411); M; 5,000; $8.00; editor Lori Riddick; tel (910) 334-7700/7701/7702; Format: 6x21

North Carolina Central Univ.: *Campus Echo* — NCCU English Department, Durham (27701); 2,000; $8.00; tel (919) 560-6504; Format: 6x21

North Carolina State Univ.: *Technician* — NCSU Box 8608, Raleigh (27695-8608); MWF; 18,000; $16.82; editors Ron Batche & Jean Lorscheider; tel (919) 515-2029; Format: 6x21

Pembroke State Univ.: *The Pine Needle* — 1937 Paladin St., Pembroke (28372); 1,800; $8.00; editor Philip Pickard; tel (910) 521-4214; Format: 6x21.5

Salem College: *The Salemite* — Winston-Salem (27108); 650; $8.00; tel (919) 721-2825/2812; Format: 5x12

Univ. of North Carolina: *Daily Tar Heel* — CB 5210, Box 49, Chapel Hill (27514); MTWHF; 20,000; $18.18; editor Thanassis Cambanis; tel (919) 962-0175; Format: 6x21

Univ. of North Carolina: *University Times* — Student Media Mrktg, Charlotte (28223-0001); H; 7,000; $12.73; editor Todd Ward; tel (704) 547-2160; Format: 6x16

Univ. of North Carolina: *Carolinian* — 201 Elliot Hall, Box 10, Greensboro (27412); H; 4,500; $13.38; editor Jeff Whittlow; tel (910) 334-5752/5753; Format: 4x16

Univ. of North Carolina: *Seahawk* — 601 S. College Rd., Wilmington (28403); H; 4,000; $11.82; editor June Oranits; tel (910) 395-3789; Format: 6x21.5

Wake Forest Univ.: *Old Gold & Black* — 518 Benson Univ Cntr, Winston Salem (27109); H; 5,500; $8.00; editor Brian Uzwiak; tel (910) 759-5279; Format: 6x21

Western Carolina Univ.: *Western Carolinian* — PO Box 66, Cullowhee (28723); H; 6,000; $9.00; editor Blake Frizzell; tel (704) 227-7267; Format: 4x13

NORTH DAKOTA

Bismarck State College: *Mystician* — 1500 Edwards Ave., Bismarck (58501); 2,400; $8.00; tel (701) 224-5467; Format: 5x14

Dickinson State Univ.: *Western Concept* — Box 165, Dickinson (58601); 300; $8.00; tel (701) 227-2846; Format: 3x9.5

Jamestown College: *Collegian* — Box 6045, Jamestown (58405); 1,000; $8.00; editor Lisa Grinsteiner; tel (701) 252-3467 ext. 2579; Format: 5x15

Minot State Univ.: *Red And Green* — 500 University Ave. W., Minot (58707); W; 3,000; $6.82; tel (701) 857-3355; Format: 4x15

North Dakota State Univ.: *Spectrum* — 357 Memorial Union, Fargo (58105); TF; 7,500; $8.00; editor Krista Olstad; tel (701) 231-8994; Format: 5x16

Univ. of North Dakota: *Dakota Student* — Box 8177-Univ Station, Grand Forks (58202); TF; 7,000; $8.00; editor Greg Pinski; tel (701) 777-2677; Format: 5x16

Valley City College: *The Viking News* — Box 697, Valley City (58072); 1,175; $8.00; tel (701) 845-0463; Format: 5x13

OHIO

Antioch College: *Antioch Record* — 795 Livermore St., Yellow Springs (45387); F; 1,200; $8.40; tel (513) 767-6418; Format: 4x13

Ashland Univ.: *Collegian* — College Ave., Ashland (44805); H; 2,400; $8.00; editor T.J. Moraco; tel (419) 289-4142 ext. 5310; Format: 4x13

Baldwin Wallace College: *The Exponent* — 275 Eastland Rd., Berea (44017-2088); W; 3,500; $8.00; editor Grant Gatchet; tel (216) 826-2272; Format: 5x17

Bowling Green State Univ.: *Bg News* — 204 W. Hall, Bowling Green (43403); MTWHF; 11,200; $10.46; tel (419) 372-2606; Format: 6x21

Capital Univ.: *The Chimes* — 2199 E. Main St., Columbus (43209); H; 2,300; $8.00; editor Amy Taylor; tel (614) 236-6716; Format: 5x14

Case Western Reserve Univ.: *Observer* — 11111 Euclid Ave., Cleveland (44106); F; 7,000; $15.45; editor Sarah Willen; tel (216) 368-2916; Format: 5x14

Cedarville College: *Cedars* — 251 N. Main, Cedarville (45314); W; 2,000; $8.00; tel (513) 766-7991; Format: 5x13.5

Cleveland State Univ.: *Cauldron* — 2121 Euclid, Cleveland (44115); MH; 7,500; $11.36; editor Bill Thompson; tel (216) 687-2270; Format: 4x13

College of Mt St Joseph: *MSJ Dateline* — College Of Mt St. Joseph, Cincinnati (45233-1672); 1,000; $14.54; editor Brian Turner; tel (513) 244-4627; Format: 4x15

College of Wooster: *The Wooster Voice* — 3187 Lowry Center, PO Box C, Wooster (44691); F; 2,000; $12.27; editors Lauren Cohen & Jason Gindele; tel (216) 263-2598; Format: 5x13

Cuyahoga Community College-E: *High Point* — 4250 Richmond Rd., Warrensville To (44122); 1,500; $12.73; editor Isha Tell; tel (216) 987-2344/6000; Format: 5x15.5

Cuyahoga Community College-Metro: *Mosaic* — 2900 Community College Ave. Sc120, Cleveland (44115); 3,500; $8.00; tel (216) 987-4231; Format: 4x13

Cuyahoga Community College-W: *Spectrum* — 11000 Pleasant Valley Rd., Parma (44130); 2,000; $10.00; editor Brian Giguere; tel (216) 987-5530; Format: 4x15

Denison Univ.: *The Denisonian* — Slayter Hall, Granville (43023); H; 2,500; $9.09; editor John D.Carroll; tel (614) 587-6378; Format: 5x16

Franciscan Univ. Steubenville: *Troubadour* — Franciscan Way, Steubenville (43952); H; 1,500; $12.72; editor Mike Niewodowski; tel (614) 283-6257; Format: 5x13.5

Heidelberg College: *Kilikilik* — 67 Greenfield St., Tiffin (44883); F; 1,000; $8.00; editor Eden Terenzini; tel (419) 448-2180; Format: 5x16

Hiram College: *Advance* — Kennedy Center, Hiram (44234); 1,200; $14.50; editor Roger Adkins; tel (216) 569-3211 ext. 5203; Format: 5x15

John Carroll Univ.: *Carroll News* — University Heights, Cleveland (44118); H; 4,500; $11.82; editor Melissa Tilk; tel (216) 397-4398; Format: 5x15.5

Kent State Univ.: *Daily Kent Stater* — Taylor Hall, Rm. 101, Kent (44242); TWHF; 14,000; $12.27; tel (216) 672-2586; Format: 6x21

Kenyon Coll: *Collegian* — Gund Commons, Gambier (43022); H; 2,000; $9.09; editor Greg Nold; tel (614) 427-5307/5661; Format: 4x15

Lakeland Community College: *Lakelander* — State Rte. 306 & I 90, Mentor (44060); 2,500; $10.91; editor Melina Champine; tel (216) 953-7264; Format: 4x13

Marietta College: *Marcolian* — 215 5th St., Marietta (45750); H; 4,000; $10.91; editor Jennifer Pesci; tel (614) 376-4555; Format: 6x21.5

Miami Univ.: *Miami Student* — 337 Shriver Center, Oxford (45056); TF; 10,000; $11.82; editor Jennifer Markiewicz; tel (513) 529-2210; Format: 5x16

Mt Union College: *Dynamo* — 1972 Clark Ave., Alliance (44601); F; 1,200; $10.91; tel (216) 823-2884; Format: 5x12

Muskingum College: *Black & Magenta* — Montgomery Hall, New Concord (43762); F; 2,000; $8.00; editor Kim Masteuar; tel (614) 826-8296; Format: 5x13

Oberlin College: *Oberlin Review* — Wilder Box 90, Oberlin (44074); F; 3,500; $11.97; editor Nicholas Riccardi; tel (216) 775-8123; Format: 5x16

Ohio State Univ.: *Ohio State Lantern* — 242 W. 18th Ave., Rm. 281, Columbus (43210); MTWHF; 30,000; $18.18; tel (614) 292-2031; Format: 6x21

Ohio Univ.: *The Post* — Baker Center Ground Fl., Athens (45701); MTWHF; 14,000; $10.37; editor Joe Shavtis; tel (614) 593-4010/4018; Format: 6x21.5

Ohio Wesleyan Univ.: *Transcript* — Slocum Hall, Delaware (43015-2373); W; 1,600; $8.89; editor Seth Daniel; tel (614) 368-3006; Format: 5x12.5

Otterbein College: *Tan & Cardinal* — N. Grove & W. College, Westerville (43081); H; 1,600; $9.09; editor Heather Rutz; tel (614) 823-1159; Format: 4x14

Sinclair Community College: *The Clarion* — 444 W. 3rd St., Dayton (45402); T; 5,000; $10.00; editor Christy Gilpin; tel (513) 226-2744/2500; Format: 6x13

Univ. of Akron: *Buchtelite* — 302 E. Buchtel Ave., Akron (44325-4602); TH; 15,000; $16.27; editor Eric Barnes; tel (216) 972-6347; Format: 6x21

Univ. of Cincinnati: *News Record* — 201C Tangeman Univ Ctr., Cincinnati (45221); MWHF; 10,000; $9.19; tel (513) 556-5900; Format: 6x21

Univ. of Dayton: *Flyer News* — 232 Kennedy Union, Dayton (45469-0626); TF; 5,000; $15.45; editor Meg Artman; tel (513) 229-3226; Format: 5x13

Univ. of Toledo: *The Collegian* — 2801 W. Bancroft, Toledo (43606); MH; 13,000; $18.11; editor Andrew Curliss; tel (419) 537-4468; Format: 6x21

Wilberforce Univ.: *Mirror* — Bickett Rd. & Rte. 42, Wilberforce (45384); 1,000; $8.00; tel (513) 376-2911 ext. 658; Format: 4x16

Wilmington College: *The Hourglass* — Box 660, Wilmington (45177); H; 1,250; $8.00; editor Shannon Hill; tel (513) 382-6661 ext. 332; Format: 4x14

Wittenberg Univ.: *Torch* — PO Box 720, Springfield (45501); T; 3,000; $8.00; editor Barbara Myers; tel (513) 327-6151; Format: 5x13.5

Wright State Univ.: *Guardian* — 046 University Center, Dayton (45435); W; 6,000; $14.91; tel (513) 873-5537; Format: 5x13

Xavier Univ.: *Xavier Newswire* — University Center, Cincinnati (45207); W; 3,000; $9.09; tel (513) 745-3130; Format: 5x13

Youngstown State Univ.: *Jambar* — 410 Wick Ave., Youngstown (44555); TF; 6,000; $13.64; tel (216) 742- 3094/3095; Format: 5x16

OKLAHOMA

Cameron Univ.: *Cameron Collegian* — 2800 W. Gore, Lawton (73505); F; 3,000; $8.00; tel (405) 581-2260/2261; Format: 4x12

E Central Univ.: *East Central Journal* — Fentem Hall, Ada (74820); H; 3,000; $8.00; tel (405) 332-8000 ext. 250; Format: 5x12

Langston Univ.: *Gazette* — Box 837, Lanston (73050); F; 3,000; $8.00; tel (405) 466-2231; Format: 5x16

Northeastern State Univ.: *The Northeastern* — The Northeastern, Tahlequah (74464-7098); W; 5,000; $8.00; tel (918) 456-5511 ext. 2890; Format: 5x13

Northwestern Oklahoma: *Northwestern News* — Alva, 73717 (H); 1,900; $8.00; tel (405) 327-1700 exts. 291/242; Format: 5x15

Oklahoma Baptist Univ.: *Bison* — 500 W. University, Shawnee (74801); W; 2,000; $8.00; editor Torey Lightcap; tel (405) 275-2850 ext. 2236/2128; Format: 5x14

Oklahoma City Community College: *The Pioneer* — 7777 S. May Ave., Oklahoma City (73159); M; 3,500; $12.73; editor Jessica Halliburton; tel (405) 682-1611 ext. 7674; Format: 5x13

Oklahoma City Univ.: *Campus* — 2501 N. Blackwelder, Oklahoma City (73106); F; 1,200; $8.18; tel (405) 521-5128; Format: 4x14.5

Oklahoma State Univ.: *Daily O'Collegian* — 109 Paul Miller Bldg., Stillwater (74078); MTWHF; 10,000; $13.00; tel (405) 744-7371; Format: 6x21

Oral Roberts Univ.: *Oracle* — LRC 225, Tulsa (74171); M; 5,000; $10.00; tel (918) 495-6346; Format: 4x13

Southeastern Oklahoma State Univ.: *Southeastern* — SOSU Box 4237, Durant (74701-0609); W; 3,000; $8.00; tel (405) 924-0121 ext. 2696; Format: 6x21

Southwestern Oklahoma State Univ.: *Southwestern Newspaper* — 100 Campus Dr., Weatherford (73096); 2,500; $8.00; editor Chip Chandler; tel (405) 774-3065; Format: 4x10

Univ. of Central Oklahoma: *Vista* — 100 N. University Dr., Edmond (73034); TH; 5,000; $8.00; editor Jennifer Palmer; tel (405) 341-2980 ext. 5916/5549; Format: 5x14

Univ. of Oklahoma: *Oklahoma Daily* — 860 Van Vleet Oval, Norman (73019-0270); MTWHF; 14,000; $14.49; editor Joy Mathis; tel (405) 325-2521; Format: 6x21

Univ. of Tulsa: *Tulsa Collegian* — 600 S. College Ave., Tulsa (74104); W; 4,000; $9.09; editor Julie Molenda; tel (918) 631-2355/3818/3084; Format: 6x21.5

OREGON

Central Oregon Community College: *Broadside* — 2600 N.W. College Way, Bend (97701); 2,000; $9.09; editor Terry S. Cranford; tel (503) 382-2743/3835121; Format: 5x13

Chemeketa Community College: *Courier 4* — PO Box 14007, Salem (97309); F; 3,500; $14.54; tel (503) 399-5134; Format: 5x15

Clackamas Community College: *Clackamas Print* — 19600 S. Molalla Ave., Oregon City (97045); W; 2,000; $8.00; editor Heidi Branstator; tel (503) 657-6958 ext. 2310; Format: 5x16

Eastern Oregon State College: *The Eastern Voice* — Hoke College Ctr. 320, La Grande (97850); 2,000; $8.00; editor Tracy Terrel; tel (503) 962-3386/3526; Format: 5x13

George Fox Coll: *The Crescent* — Newberg (97132); 1,600; $8.00; editor Pat Johnson; tel (503) 538-8383 ext. 4103; Format: 5x16

Lane Community College: *The Torch* — 4000 E. 30th Ave., Eugene (97405); F; 4,000; $9.09; tel (503) 747-4501 ext. 2654; Format: 5x15

Lewis & Clark College: *Pioneer Log* — Box 21 LC, Portland (97219); F; 3,100; $10.91; editor Rich Pizor; tel (503) 768-7146; Format: 5x16

Linfield College: *The Linfield Review* — 900 S. Baker St., Mcminnville (97128); F; 1,700; $8.00; editor Jennifer Jones; tel (503) 472-7715; Format: 5x16

Linn-Benton Community College: *Commuter* — 6500 S.W. Pacific Blvd., Albany (97321); W; 2,000; $8.00; editor Steve Garett; tel (503) 928-2361 ext. 373; Format: 4x16

Mt Hood Community College: *Advocate* — 26000 S.E. Stark, Gresham (97030); F; 2,500; $8.00; editor Beth Allen; tel (503) 667-7250; Format: 5x16

Oregon Inst of Technology: *The Edge* — College Union Bldg., Klamath Falls (97601); F; 2,100; $8.00; editor Darin Rutledge; tel (503) 885-1835; Format: 5x12.5

Oregon State Univ.: *OSU Daily Barometer* — Memorial Union E. 118, Corvallis (97331-1617); MTWHF; 10,500; $11.51; editor Liz Foster; tel (503) 737-6373; Format: 6x16.25

Pacific Univ.: *Pacific Index* — UC Box 586 Pacific University, Forest Grove (97116); 1,500; $8.00; tel (503) 357-6151 ext. 2655; Format: 5x16.5

Portland Community College: *The Bridge* — 12000 S.W. 49th Ave., Portland (97280); H; 5,000; $14.55; editor Oro N Bull; tel (503) 244-6111 ext. 4181; Format: 5x16

Portland State Univ.: *Vanguard* — PO Box 751, Portland (97207); TWHF; 10,000; $11.82; tel (503) 725-5686; Format: 6x16

Reed College: *Quest* — 3203 S.E. Woodstock Blvd., Portland (97202-8199); T; 1,400; $11.36; tel (503) 777-7707; Format: 5x17

Southern Oregon State College: *Siskiyou* — 1250 Siskiyou Blvd., Ashland (97520); M; 3,000; $8.00; tel (503) 552-6307/6306; Format: 5x21.5

SW Oregon Community College: *Southwester* — 1988 Newmark Ave., Coos Bay (97420); F; 1,000; $8.00; editor Beth Kuhn; tel (503) 888-7333; Format: 6x13

Univ. of Oregon: *Oregon Daily Emerald* — PO Box 3159, Eugene (97403); MTWHF; 10,000; $16.37; editor David Thorn; tel (503) 346-3712/5511; Format: 5x15

Univ. of Portland: *The Beacon* — 5000 N. Willamette Blvd., Portland (97203-5798); H; 2,000; $12.73; editor Nancy Nilles; tel (503) 283-7376/7372; Format: 5x16

Western Oregon State: *Western Star* — Werner College Center, Monmouth (97361); F; 3,000; $9.10; tel (503) 838-8347; Format: 5x16

Willamette Univ.: *Collegian* — 900 State St., Salem (97301); F; 2,500; $12.28; editor Ryan Beckwith; tel (503) 370-6053; Format: 5x16

Copyright ©1996 by the Editor & Publisher Co.

PENNSYLVANIA

Albright College: *Albrightian* — ACC Box 107, Reading (19612-5234); 1,300; $17.27; editor Tara Scanio; tel (610) 921-7558; Format: 4x16

Allegheny College: *Campus* — Allegheny College, Box 12 Meadville (16335); H; 2,700; $8.00; editor Jeff Weis; tel (814) 332-5386; Format: 5x16

Allentown College: *The Desales Minstrel* — Allentown College, Center Valley (18034); 1,000; $8.00; editor Michael Gerchufsky; tel (610) 282-1100 ext. 249; Format: 4x16

Beaver College: *The Tower* — 450 S. Easton Rd., Glenside (19038); 1,000; $14.54; editor Michelle Maier; tel (215) 572-2171; Format: 5x15

Behrend College: *The Collegian* — Station Rd., Erie (16563-0906); H; 2,500; $9.09; tel (814) 898-6488; Format: 5x15

Bloomsburg Univ.: *The Voice* — Kehr Union, Box 97, Bloomsburg (17815); H; 5,000; $10.45; editor Peter Mayes; tel (717) 389-4457/4557; Format: 6x21

Bucknell Univ.: *The Bucknellian* — Box C-3952, Lewisburg (17837); H; 5,500; $9.48; editor Jeff Boulter; tel (717) 524-1085; Format: 6x21.5

Bucks Co. Community College: *Centurion* — Swamp Rd., Newtown (18940); W; 2,500; $11.82; editor Ed Ozalas; tel (215) 968-8273; Format: 4x15.5

Cabrini College: *Loquitur* — 610 King Of Prussia Rd., Radnor (19087); F; 1,300; $9.69; editor Heather Mcallister; tel (610) 971-8412; Format: 4x15

California Univ.: *California Times* — 211 Student Union, Bldg. B, California (15419); F; 5,000; $8.00; tel (412) 938-4319; Format: 5x16

Carnegie Mellon Univ.: *Tartan* — Carnegie Student Center, Pittsburgh (15213-3890); M; 7,000; $9.09; editor Andrew Sprune; tel (412) 268-2111; Format: 6x21

Cedar Crest College: *Crestiad* — 100 College Dr., Allentown (18104); 800; $8.00; editor Stacey L. Nelson; tel (610) 437-4471; Format: 5x12

Chatham College: *The Communique* — Box 596, Pittsburgh (15232-2814); 900; $8.00; tel (412) 365-1622; Format: 4x14

Cheyney Univ.: *Record* — Student Activities, Cheyney (19319); 1,400; $8.00; editor Heather Flynn; tel (610) 399-2250/2195; Format: 4x14.5

Clarion Univ.: *The Clarion Call* — 270 Gemmel Ctr., Clarion (16214); H; 6,000; $8.18; editor Michelle Sporer; tel (814) 226-2380; Format: 5x12.5

Community College of Allegheny: *Boyce Campus Collegian* — 595 Beatty Rd., Monroeville (15146); 1,500; $8.00; editor Rick Johnson; tel (412) 325-6730; Format: 5x14

Community College of Allegheny: *Forum* — 1750 Clariton Rd., Rte. 885, West Mifflin (15122); 2,000; $8.00; editor Patrick Kincaid; tel (412) 469-6352; Format: 5x14

Community College of Philadelphia: *Student Vanguard* — 1700 Spring Garden St., Philadelphia (19130); 4,000; $8.18; editor Michael Moffa; tel (215) 751-8200 ext. 8201; Format: 5x16

Delaware Co. Community College: *Communitarian* — Rte. 252, Media (19063); 2,000; $9.09; editor Stan Wielosik; tel (610) 359-5348; Format: 4x12.5

Delaware Valley College: *Rampages* — Rte. 202, Doyleston (18901); 750; $10.50; editor Adam Kaplan; tel (215) 345-1500 ext. 2238; Format: 4x16

Dickinson College: *The Dickinsonian* — Holland Union, Box 4, Carlisle (17013); H; 2,400; $8.81; editor Rob Burk; tel (717) 245-1410; Format: 4x13

Drexel Univ.: *The Triangle* — 32nd & Chestnut Sts., Philadelphia (19104); F; 7,000; $11.00; editor John Gruber; tel (215) 895-2585; Format: 5x15

Duquesne Univ.: *Duquesne Duke* — 417 DPCC, Pittsburgh (15282); H; 4,000; $10.91; editor Jennifer Weeks; tel (412) 396-6629; Format: 5x14

Eastern College: *Waltonian* — Box 1000, St. Davids (19087); 1,000; $8.00; editor Joleen Senter; tel (610) 341-1710; Format: 4x12

Edinboro Univ.: *Spectator* — University Center, Edinboro (16444); F; 4,500; $9.09; editor Carol Anne Minor; tel (814) 732-2266/2270; Format: 5x13

Elizabethtown College: *Etownian* — 1 Alpha Dr., Elizabethtown (17022); F; 2,500; $10.04; editor Grant Gegwich; tel (717) 361-1132; Format: 5x14

Franklin & Marshall College: *College Reporter* — PO Box 3003, Lancaster (17604-3303); M; 3,000; $11.82; editors David Wertheimer & Amiee Henderson; tel (717) 291-4095; Format: 5x15.5

Gannon Univ.: *The Gannon Knight* — Box 638, Erie (16541); M; 4,000; $8.00; editor Lauren Bordner; tel (814) 871-7688; Format: 5x13

Gettysburg College: *Gettysburgian* — Box 434, Gettysburg (17325); H; 3,200; $11.82; editor Will Siss; tel (717) 337-6449; Format: 5x12

Grove City College: *Collegian* — 100 Campus Dr., Grove City (16127); F; 2,200; $8.00; editor Rebecca Beinlich; tel (412) 458-2193/3302; Format: 5x16

Harrisburg Community College: *The Fourth Estate* — 3300 Cameron St. Rd., Harrisburg (17110); T; 3,500; $10.91; editor Paula Hammond; tel (717) 780-2582; Format: 6x21

Haverford College: *Bi-College News* — 370 Lancaster Ave., Haverford (19041); F; 2,800; $11.82; tel (610) 526-7323; Format: 5x16

Indiana Univ. Pennsylvania: *Penn* — 319 Pratt Dr., Indiana (15701); MWF; 11,000; $12.64; editor Jennifer Blackwell; tel (412) 349-6160; Format: 5x16

Juniata College: *Juniatian* — 1700 Moore St., Huntington (16652); H; 1,500; $8.00; editor Jonathan Bell; tel (814) 643-4310 ext. 340; Format: 5x14

Kings College: *Crown* — 133 N. Franklin, Box 1695, Wilkes-Barre (18711); 2,000; $12.73; editor Tara Conn; tel (717) 826-5900 ext. 659; Format: 5x12

Kutztown Univ.: *Keystone* — 114 N. Student Center, Kutztown (19530); W; 4,000; $8.00; editor Ben Herr; tel (610) 683-4454; Format: 6x21

La Salle Univ.: *La Salle Collegian* — 1900 W. Olney Ave., Philadelphia (19141); W; 2,500; $12.00; editor Brian Howard; tel (215) 951-1398; Format: 5x16

Lafayette College: *The Lafayette* — Box 9470, Easton (18042); F; 2,600; $9.09; editor Yvonne Koulouthros; tel (610) 250-5354; Format: 5x16

Lehigh Univ.: *Brown & White* — Univ Ctr. #29, Bethlehem (18015-3065); TF; 7,000; $9.09; editor Lori Montemurro; tel (610) 758-4184/4181; Format: 4x15

Lincoln Univ.: *Lincolnian* — English Dept., Lincoln University (19352); F; 1,500; $8.00; editor Sheyna Peterson; tel (610) 932-8300 ext. 515; Format: 4x14

Lock Haven Univ. of PA: *Eagle Eye* — Parsons Union Bldg., Lock Haven (17745); F; 2,000; $9.09; editor Jennifer Bowes; tel (717) 893-2334; Format: 4x13

Luzerne Co. Community College: *The Outlook* — 1333 S. Prospect Rd., Nanticoke (18634-3899); 3,000; $8.00; editor Matt Solovey; tel (717) 821-0905; Format: 5x13

Mansfield Univ.: *Flashlight* — Student Activities, Mansfield (16933); W; 2,200; $8.00; tel (717) 662-4986/4000; Format: 5x16

Marywood College: *The Wood Word* — 2300 Adams Ave., Scranton (18509); 2,000; $10.91; editor Eric Pochas; tel (717) 348-6209/969-1974; Format: 6x21

Mercyhurst College: *Merciad* — Lower Level Baldwin Hall, Erie (16546); H; 2,000; $8.00; editor Joseph Legler; tel (814) 824-2376; Format: 5x16

Messiah College: *Swinging Bridge* — PO Box 1313, Grantham (17027); H; 2,800; $8.00; editor Del Schwartzentruber; tel (717) 766-2511 ext. 343; Format: 5x12

Millersville Univ.: *The Snapper* — Advertising, Millersville (17551); W; 4,500; $10.91; editor Greg Swartz; tel (717) 872-3516/3672; Format: 6x21

Montgomery Community College: *Mustang* — 340 Dekalb Pike, Blue Bell (19422); 2,500; $8.40; editor Michelle Geiser; tel (215) 628-4352; Format: 5x13

Moravian College: *Comenian* — Box 13, Bethlehem (18018); W; 1,500; $8.20; editor Deanna Moyer; tel (610) 866-1682; Format: 5x15

Muhlenberg College: *Muhlenberg Weekly* — Basement Martin Luther Hall, Allentown (18104-5586); F; 1,400; $6.82; editor Jessica Gullickson; tel (610) 821-3187; Format: 5x12

Penn State Univ.-Ogontz: *Campus News* — 1600 Woodland Rd., Abington (19001); 2,000; $8.00; editor Amy Zurzola; tel (215) 881-7300; Format: 4x16

Pennsylvania State Univ.: *Daily Collegian* — National Ad Department, University Park (16801); MTWHF; 19,300; $15.00; tel (814) 865-2531; Format: 6x21.5

Philadelphia College of Textiles: *Text* — Schoolhouse, Philadelphia (19144-5487); 2,000; $8.00; tel (215) 951-2892; Format: 3x16

Point Park College: *Globe* — 201 Wood St., Pittsburgh (15222); H; 2,100; $9.09; editor Dawn Pennington; tel (412) 392-4740/4734; Format: 5x14

Rosemont College: *The Rambler* — Montgomery Ave., Rosemont (19010); 400; $8.00; editor Holly Morton; tel (610) 527-0200; Format: 4x16

St Francis College: *Loretto* — Box 2030, Loretto (15940); F; 1,500; $8.00; editor Chris Donnelly; tel (814) 472-3038; Format: 5x13

St Josephs Univ.: *The Hawk* — 5600 City Ave., Philadelphia (19131); F; 3,000; $9.09; editor Sean Sullivan; tel (610) 660-1079; Format: 5x16

St Vincent College: *The Review* — PO Box A, Latrobe (15650); 1,000; $8.00; editor Tami Zavolta; tel (412) 539-9761 ext. 513; Format: 4x10.5

Shippensburg Univ.: *Slate* — Cumberland Union Bldg., Shippensburg (17257); T; 3,500; $9.09; tel (717) 532-1778 ext. 1707; Format: 5x12.5

Slippery Rock Univ.: *Rocket* — Eisenberg Classroom Bldg., Rm. 220, Slippery Rock (16057); F; 3,800; $8.00; tel (412) 738-2643; Format: 5x14

Susquehanna Univ.: *The Crusader* — Susquehanna University, Selinsgrove (17870); F; 2,300; $8.00; editor Monica Hoyer; tel (717) 372-4298; Format: 6x21.5

Swarthmore College: *Phoenix* — 500 College Ave., Swarthmore (19081-1397); F; 2,600; $10.91; editor Ben Stern; tel (610) 328-8172/8173; Format: 5x16

Temple Univ.: *Temple News* — 13th St. & Montgomery Ave., Philadelphia (19122); TWHF; 10,000; $14.54; editor J.M. Martino; tel (215) 204-6041/6098; Format: 5x12.5

Thiel College: *Thielensian* — Box 1654, Greenville (16125); T; 1,200; $8.00; editor Paul Machi; tel (412) 589-2197; Format: 5x14

Univ. of Pennsylvania: *Daily Pennsylvanian* — 4015 Walnut St, Philadelphia (19104); MTWHF; 14,000; $15.46; editor Jordana Horn; tel (215) 898-6581; Format: 6x21

Univ. of Pittsburgh: *The Source* — 300 Campus Dr., Bradford (16701); 1,200; $8.00; tel (814) 362-7682; Format: 5x12.5

Univ. of Pittsburgh: *Advocate* — 140 Biddle Hall, Johnstown (15904); T; 2,800; $12.73; editor Chris Boekhe; tel (814) 269-7470; Format: 5x13

Univ. of Pittsburgh: *Pitt News* — 426 William Pitt Union, Pittsburgh (15260); MTWH; 14,000; $15.91; editor Mark Gordon; tel (412) 648-7978/7879/7875; Format: 5x16

Univ. of Scranton: *Aquinas* — Mail Rm. Box D, Scranton (18510); H; 5,000; $14.54; editor Alexandra Gojic; tel (717) 941-7464; Format: 5x13

Ursinus College: *Grizzly* — E. Main St., Collegeville (19426); T; 2,500; $8.00; editor Marc Ellman /Mark Leiser; tel (610) 409-3513; Format: 5x12

Villanova Univ.: *Villanovan* — Dougherty Hall, Villanova (19085); F; 7,500; $10.90; editor Kathleen Cooney/Sean Kelly; tel (610) 519-7206; Format: 5x16

Washington & Jefferson: *The Red And Black* — Student Center, Washington (15301); H; 1,300; $8.00; editor Alex Chotkowski; tel (412) 223-6049; Format: 6x21

West Chester Univ.: *Quad* — 331 Wayne Hall, West Chester (19383); T; 6,500; $11.82; editor Bod Gardner; tel (610) 436-2375; Format: 5x15

Westminster College: *Westminster Holcad* — 101 Old Main, New Wilmington (16172); H; 1,800; $8.00; tel (412) 946-7223/7224; Format: 4x13

Widener Univ.: *Dome* — 1 University Pl., Chester (19013); F; 2,500; $14.82; editor Carla Maratci; tel (610) 499-4421; Format: 4x14

Wilkes Univ.: *Beacon* — Box 111, Wilkes-Barre (18766); H; 2,000; $9.09; editor Lynn Marie Rosencrantz; tel (717) 831-5000 ext. 2962; Format: 5x13

York College of Pennsylvania: *The Spartan* — Country Club Rd., York (17403-3426); T; 2,500; $8.00; editor Heather Odeay; tel (717) 846-7788 ext. 312; Format: 5x13

RHODE ISLAND

Brown Univ.: *Brown Daily Herald* — 195 Angell St., Providence (02906); MTWHF; 4,100; $18.18; editor Justin Pritchard; tel (401) 351-3260; Format: 5x16

Bryant College: *Archway* — Box 7, Smithfield (02917); H; 4,000; $10.80; editor Sue Martoue; tel (401) 232-6028; Format: 5x15.5

Johnson & Wales Univ.: *Campus Herald* — 8 Abbott Park Pl., Providence (02903); M; 4,500; $10.00; editor Brendi Baran; tel (401) 598-2804; Format: 4x14.75

Providence College: *Cowl* — Box 2981 Friar Sta., Providence (02918); H; 3,800; $10.91; editor Theresa Edo; tel (401) 865-2214; Format: 5x16

Rhode Island College: *Anchor* — 600 Mt. Pleasant, Providence (02908); M; 5,000; $8.18; editor John Valerio; tel (401) 456-8280/8544; Format: 5x16

Rhode Island School of Design: *Independent* — Box 1930, Providence (02912); H; 2,500; $9.09; tel (401) 863-1993; Format: 5x16

Roger Williams Univ.: *The Messenger* — 1 Old Ferry Rd., Bristol (02809-2921); 2,500; $8.00; editor Kary Andrews; tel (401) 254-3276/3076/253-1040; Format: 5x16.5

Univ. of Rhode Island: *Good 5 Cent Cigar* — Memorial Union, Rm. 139, Kingston (02881); TWHF; 6,500; $10.91; editor Kari Lyons; tel (401) 792-2914; Format: 6x16

SOUTH CAROLINA

Citadel Military College: *The Brigadier* — Dept. of Student Activities, Charleston (29409); F; 4,000; $9.09; editor Gary Brown; tel (803) 953-5111; Format: 6x20.5

Clemson Univ.: *Tiger* — 906 University Union, Clemson (29632-2337); F; 12,000; $13.90; editor Mike Burns; tel (803) 656-2167/2152/1652; Format: 5x16

Coastal Carolina Univ.: *Chanticleer* — Hwy. 544 E., PO Box 1954, Conway (29526); T; 2,500; $10.91; editor Jennifer Hyland; tel (803) 349-2330; Format: 6x13

Converse College: *The Conversationalist* — PO Box 566, Spartanburg (29301); 1,000; $9.09; tel (803) 596-9503; Format: 5x16

Erskine College: *Tower Times* — PO Box 338, Due West (29639); F; 1,200; $8.00; tel (803) 379-2131; Format: 5x13

Furman Univ.: *The Paladin* — Box 28584, Greenville (29613); F; 3,000; $10.91; tel (803) 294-2077; Format: 5x16

South Carolina State Univ.: *Collegian* — 300 College St. N.E., Orangeburg (29117); 5,000; $8.00; tel (803) 536-7522; Format: 6x21

The College of Charleston: *Cougar Pause* — Stern Center, Charleston (29424); 4,000; $14.54; editor James Handcock; tel (803) 953-8119; Format: 6x20

Univ. of South Carolina: *The Gamecock* — 1400 Greene St., Russell House #323, Columbia (29208); MWF; 10,000; $14.45; editor Wendy Hudson; tel (803) 777-4249; Format: 6x21.5

Univ. of South Carolina: *The Carolinian* — Hodge Center, 2nd Fl., Spartanburg (29303); F; 2,500; $10.29; editor James Compton; tel (803) 599-2138; Format: 5x12.5

Winthrop Univ.: *Johnsonian* — Box 6800, Rock Hill (29733); T; 3,700; $12.28; editor Danielle Kiracofe; tel (803) 323-3419; Format: 5x16

SOUTH DAKOTA

Augustana College: *Augustana Mirror* — Box 794, Sioux Falls (57197); H; 2,000; $9.09; editor Sarah Green; tel (605) 336-4423; Format: 5x21.25

Black Hills State Univ.: *BHSU Today* — 1200 University, Spearfish (57799-9003); M; 1,500; $8.19; tel (605) 642-6389; Format: 4x16

Dakota State Univ.: *Eastern* — Beadle Hall, Madison (57042); 800; $8.00; editor Brenda Eitemiller; tel (605) 256-5267; Format: 4x15

Huron Univ.: *The Alph'O'Mega* — 333 9th St. S2, Sioux Falls (57350); 600; $8.00; tel (605) 352-8721; Format: 5x18

Mt Marty College: *Moderator* — 1100 W. 5th, Yankton (57078); H; 1,000; $8.00; editor Julie Schmidt; tel (605) 668-1543; Format: 5x13

Sioux Falls College: *The Vessel* — 1501 S. Prairie, Sioux Falls (57105); 500; $8.00; tel (605) 331-6774; Format: 5x16

South Dakota School Mines & Tech.: *The Tech* — Surbeck Center, Rapid City (57701-3995); 1,500; $9.09; tel (605) 394-2653; Format: 4x16

South Dakota State Univ.: *SDSU Collegian* — USU 069 Box 2815, Brookings (57007); 7,000; $20.65; editor Jason Hove; tel (605) 688-6164; Format: 6x21.5

Univ. of South Dakota: *Volante* — University Exchange, Box 141, Vermillion (57069); W; 6,500; $11.82; editor Shana Barber; tel (605) 677-6469; Format: 6x21

TENNESSEE

Austin Peay State Univ.: *The All State* — 610 Drane St., Clarksville (37044); W; 4,000; $12.36; editor Kiezha Smith; tel (615) 648-7376; Format: 6x21.5

Belmont Univ.: *The Belmont Vision* — 1900 Belmont Blvd., Nashville (37212); 3,000; $12.73; editor Cree Lawson; tel (615) 385-6433; Format: 5x14

Christian Brothers Univ.: *The Cannon* — 650 E. Parkway South, Memphis (38104); 1,200; $8.18; editor Elizabeth Ousset; tel (901) 722-0387; Format: 4x13

E Tennessee State Univ.: *East Tennessean* — Box 70688, Johnson City (37614-0002); MH; 6,000; $10.91; tel (615) 929-5363/4387; Format: 5x13

Fisk Univ.: *Fisk Forum* — 17th Ave. N., Nashville (37203); 1,000; $8.00; tel (615) 329-8706; Format: 4x13

Maryville College: *Highland Echo* — PO Box 2820, Maryville (37801); H; 1,000; $8.00; tel (615) 981-8243; Format: 5x13

Middle Tennessee State Univ.: *Sidelines* — Box 42, Murfreesboro (37132); MH; 8,000; $8.50; tel (615) 898-2815; Format: 5x14

Rhodes College: *The Sou'Wester* — 2000 N. Parkway, Memphis (38112); H; 2,000; $8.18; editors Jason Carmel & Welch Suggs; tel (901) 726-3970; Format: 4x14.5

State Tech. Institute: *Sidewinder* — 5983 Macon Cove, Memphis (38134-3673); 3,000; $8.00; editor Tina Bodenheimer; tel (901) 383-4178; Format: 4x12

Tennessee State Univ.: *Meter* — Otis F Payne Center., Rm. 304, Nashville (37209); 4,000; $12.11; editor Nadine Bewry; tel (615) 963-5652; Format: 4x12

Tennessee Tech. Univ.: *Tech Oracle* — Box 5072, Cookeville (38505); F; 6,000; $8.00; tel (615) 372-3060; Format: 6x21.5

Union Univ.: *Cardinal & Cream* — 45 By Pass, Jackson (38305); 1,300; $8.00; editor Ashley Blair; tel (901) 668-1818; Format: 5x13.5

Univ. of Memphis: *Daily Helmsman* — Campus Box 528194, Memphis (38152); TWHF; 9,500; $14.45; editor Michael Thompson; tel (901) 678-2191; Format: 5x15

Univ. of Tennessee: *University Echo* — University Center, Rm. 111, Chattanooga (37403); TH; 4,200; $8.00; editor Deborah Dryer; tel (615) 785-2146; Format: 4x13

Univ. of Tennessee: *The Daily Beacon* — 11 Communications Bldg., Knoxville (37996); MTWHF; 16,200; $15.91; tel (615) 974-5206; Format: 6x21

Univ. of Tennessee: *The Pacer* — Gooch Hall, Rm. 314, Martin (38237); H; 5,000; $8.00; editor Jeriane Thompson; tel (901) 587-7780; Format: 5x13

Univ. of The South: *Sewanee Purple* — Student Post Office, Sewanee (37375); 2,000; $8.00; tel (615) 598-1204; Format: 6x12.5

Vanderbilt Univ.: *Hustler* — Sta. B, Box 1504, Nashville (37235); TF; 8,500; $13.36; editor Ryan Underwood; tel (615) 322-7347; Format: 5x14

TEXAS

Abilene Christian Univ.: *The Optimist* — ACU Sta., Box 7892, Abilene (79699); WF; 3,800; $8.00; editor Sharla Stephens; tel (915) 674-2463; Format: 6x21

Amarillo College: *Ranger* — PO Box 447, Amarillo (79178); F; 2,500; $8.00; editor Brad Garrett; tel (806) 371-5290; Format: 6x20.25

Angelo State Univ.: *Ram Page* — Box 10899, San Angelo (76909); H; 4,500; $18.18; editor Raju Sekhri; tel (915) 942-2040/2130/2323; Format: 6x21.5

Austin College: *A C Observer* — Ste. 61598, PO Box 1177, Sherman (75090); 1,200; $8.00; tel (903) 813-2296; Format: 4x13

Baylor Univ.: *Lariat* — 1217 MI Cooper, 2nd Fl., Waco (76798); TWHF; 7,500; $18.18; editor Tracey Sutherland; tel (817) 755-3407; Format: 4x12.75

Brookhaven College: *Courier* — 3939 Valley View, Farmers Branch (75244-4997); M; 2,500; $8.00; editors Lauri Bingham & Darla Bean; tel (214) 620-4787; Format: 4x16

Del Mar College: *The Foghorn* — 101 Baldwin, Corpus Christi (78404); W; 5,000; $9.09; editor Veronica Garcia; tel (512) 886-1246; Format: 6x14

Devry Institute: *The Current Flow* — 4801 Regent Blvd., Rm. 270, Irving (75063); 400; $8.00; tel (214) 929-6777 ext. 241; Format: 4x11

E Texas State Univ.: *The East Texan* — Box 4104, Commerce (75429-1901); H; 4,000; $10.91; tel (903) 886-5244; Format: 5x16.5

Eastfield College: *Eastfield Et Cetera* — 3737 Motley Dr., Mesquite (75150); M; 3,000; $12.73; editor Cory Johnson; tel (214) 324-7130; Format: 4x14

El Paso Community College: *El Conquistador* — Box 20500, El Paso (79998); 5,000; $8.18; editor Gilbert Cornwell; tel (915) 594-2500; Format: 5x16

Hardin-Simmons Univ.: *The Brand* — 2200 Hickory, Abilene (79698); 1,000; $9.09; editor Marlin Bowman; tel (915) 670-1438; Format: 3x10.5

Houston Baptist Univ.: *Collegian* — 7502 Fondren Rd., Houston (77074-3298); 2,500; $16.36; editor Leslie Tripp; tel (713) 995-3218; Format: 5x15

Houston Community College: *The Egalitarian* — Central Campus, Houston (77004); W; 7,000; $8.82; editor Scott Williams; tel (713) 630-7252/7253; Format: 5x13

Incarnate Word College: *The Logos* — 4301 Broadway, San Antonio (78209); 3,000; $9.55; editor Alex Garcia; tel (210) 829-3964; Format: 4x16

Kilgore College: *The Flare* — 1100 Broadway Rm. 203, Kilgore (75662); F; 3,000; $8.00; editor Kendall Webb; tel (903) 983-8194; Format: 6x20.5

Lamar Univ.: *University Press* — PO Box 10055 LUS, Beaumont (77710); WF; 7,000; $10.00; tel (409) 880-8102; Format: 6x21.5

Lee College: *Lantern* — 511 S. Whiting, Baytown (77522-0818); 2,000; $8.00; editor Bobby Horn Jr.; tel (713) 425-6506; Format: 6x21

Letourneau Univ.: *Yellow Jacket* — 2100 S. Mobberly, Longview (75607); F; 1,400; $10.91; editor Linda Dixon; tel (903) 753-0231; Format: 5x14

Lubbock Christian Univ.: *Campus Edition* — 5601 W. 19th St., Lubbock (79407-2099); 1,000; $10.91; tel (806) 792-3221; Format: 5x13

Mcmurry Univ.: *War Whoop* — MCM Sta., Box 248, Abilene (79697); 1,000; $8.00; tel (915) 691-6375; Format: 5x13

Midwestern State Univ.: *The Wichitan* — Box 160, Wichita Falls (76308); T; 2,700; $9.09; tel (817) 689-4704; Format: 6x21

N Harris Co. College: *The Paper* — 2700 W. Thorne Dr., Houston (77070); 5,500; $11.82; tel (713) 443-5670/5578; Format: 4x13

Our Lady of the Lake Univ.: *Lakefront* — 411 S.W. 24th St., San Antonio (78207-4689); 1,000; $8.00; tel (210) 434-6711 ext. 445; Format: 5x13

Palo Alto College: *The Paladin* — 1400 W. Villaret, San Antonio (78224); 2,500; $8.00; editor Rosario Ybarra; tel (210) 921-5022; Format: 4x17

Prairie View A&M Univ.: *The Panther* — Hilliard Hall, Rm. 216, Prairie View (77446-2876); H; 4,500; $14.54; tel (409) 857-2132; Format: 6x21

Rice Univ.: *Rice Thresher* — Ley Student Center, 2nd Fl., Houston (77005); F; 6,000; $13.64; editor Charles Klein; tel (713) 527-4801; Format: 5x16

Richland College: *Richland Chronicles* — 12800 Abrams Rd., Dallas (75243); 4,000; $10.91; editor Scott Russell; tel (214) 238-6079/6068; Format: 6x21

St Edwards Univ.: *Hilltop Views* — 3001 S. Congress, Austin (78704-6489); 3,000; $10.27; editor Melissa Valenzueh; tel (512) 448-8426; Format: 5x16

St Mary's Univ.: *Rattler* — 1 Camino Santa Maria, San Antonio (78228); W; 2,700; $12.73; editor Maria Elena Rodriguez; tel (210) 436-3401; Format: 5x13

St Phillip's College: *Tiger* — 1801 Martin Luther King, San Antonio (78203); 2,000; $8.00; tel (210) 531-3244; Format: 4x13.75

Sam Houston State Univ.: *Houstonian* — PO Box 2178, Huntsville (77341); TH; 6,000; $18.07; editor Jenn Cansler; tel (409) 294-1495; Format: 6x21

San Antonio College: *Ranger* — 1300 San Pedro Ave., San Antonio (78284); F; 7,000; $8.00; editor Estella Duran; tel (210) 733-2278; Format: 6x21

San Jacinto College: *San Jacinto Times* — 8060 Spencer Hwy., Pasadena (77505); M; 6,000; $9.00; tel (713) 478-2752; Format: 6x21

S Plains College: *Plainsman Press* — 1400 College Ave., Levelland (79336); W; 2,000; $9.09; editor Erin Spencer; tel (806) 894-9611 ext. 435; Format: 4x13

Southern Methodist Univ.: *Daily Campus* — 3140 Dyer St., Ste. 314, Dallas (75275); TWHF; 4,500; $20.91; editor Richard Lytle; tel (214) 768-4509/4555; Format: 6x21

SW Texas Jr College: *Southwest Texan* — 2401 Garner Field Rd., Uvalde (78801); 3,000; $8.00; tel (210) 278-4401 ext. 222; Format: 5x13

SW Texas State Univ.: *University Star* — Old Main, Rm. 102, San Marcos (78666); TWHF; 10,000; $11.82; tel (512) 245-3487; Format: 6x13

Southwestern Univ.: *The Megaphone* — SU State, Box 6048, Georgetown (78626); H; 1,000; $8.00; editor Steve Mendenhal; tel (512) 863-1347; Format: 5x13

Stephen F Austin Univ.: *Pine Log* — PO Box 13049, SFA Station, Nacogdoches (75962); TF; 7,000; $8.00; editor Leslie Conder; tel (409) 468-4703; Format: 6x21

Tarleton State Univ.: *J-Tac* — Box T-518, Tarleton Station, Stephenville (76402); H; 3,500; $8.00; tel (817) 968-9490; Format: 6x21

Tarrant Co. Jr College: *The Collegian* — 828 Hardwood Rd., Hurst (76054-3299); W; 15,000; $11.82; editor Kevin Hendricks; tel (817) 788-6619; Format: 6x21

Texarkana College: *TC News* — 2500 N. Robison Rd., Texarkana (75501); 2,500; $8.00; editor Mary Gillette; tel (903) 838-4541 ext. 364; Format: 4x12

Texas A&M Univ.: *Battalion* — 230 Reed Mcdonald Bldg., College Station (77843); MTWHF; 23,000; $23.64; editor Chris Whitley; tel (409) 845-2696; Format: 6x21

Texas A&M Univ. Kingsville: *The South Texan* — Sta. 1, Campus Box 123, Kingsville (78363); F; 5,000; $8.00; editor Leah Daniels; tel (512) 595-3707/3700; Format: 5x13

Texas Christian Univ.: *Daily Skiff* — TCU Box 32929, Ft. Worth (76129); TWHF; 4,000; $10.91; editor John Lumpkin; tel (817) 921-7426; Format: 6x21.5

Texas Lutheran College: *Lone Star Lutheran* — 1000 W. Court, Seguin (78155); F; 1,000; $8.00; editor Josh Norman; tel (210) 372-8073; Format: 5x16

Texas Southern Univ.: *Herald* — 3100 Cleburne, Houston (77004); 10,000; $9.09; editor Dawn Monroe; tel (713) 639-1976/527-7315; Format: 5x13

Texas Tech Univ.: *Univ. Daily* — Box 43081, Lubbock (79409-3081); MTWHF; 14,000; $16.91; editor Kristie Davis; tel (806) 742-3384; Format: 6x21

Texas Wesleyan Univ.: *Rambler* — 1201 Wesleyan, Ft. Worth (76105); W; 1,000; $9.09; editor Kim Laster; tel (817) 531-4871; Format: 6x15

Texas Woman's Univ.: *The Lasso* — 1322 Oakland St., Denton (76201); W; 3,000; $9.09; tel (817) 898-2183; Format: 5x13

Trinity Univ.: *Trinitonian* — Box 62, San Antonio (78212-7200); F; 3,500; $10.91; editor Liz Phillips; tel (210) 736-8555; Format: 5x13

Trinity Valley Community College: *TVCC News-Journal* — 500 S. Prairieville St., Athens (75751); F; 3,000; $8.00; tel (903) 675-6358; Format: 5x14

Tyler Jr College: *Tjc News* — 1400 Devine St., Tyler (75701); H; 3,500; $8.00; editor Linda Zeigler; tel (903) 510-2335; Format: 5x12.5

Univ. of Dallas: *University News* — Box 690, Irving (75062); M; 2,000; $12.72; editor Kimberly Mackinnon; tel (214) 721-5089/255-0108; Format: 5x13

Univ. of Houston: *Daily Cougar* — 151 Communications, Houston (77204); MTWHF; 13,000; $11.82; editor Melinda Mcbride; tel (713) 743-5345/5340; Format: 5x16

Univ. of Houston-Clear Lake: *Uhclidian* — 2700 Bay Area Blvd., Houston (77058); M; 3,000; $9.09; editor Edwina Lewis; tel (713) 283-2570; Format: 5x13.75

Univ. of Houston-Downtown: *Dateline* — Suite 260 South, Houston (77002); 8,000; $19.09; editor Maria Panis; tel (713) 221-8569; Format: 4x14

Univ. of N Texas: *North Texas Daily* — PO Box 5156, Denton (76201-5156); TWHF; 11,000; $8.00; editor Jennifer Huckabay; tel (817) 565-2853; Format: 6x21

Univ. of St Thomas: *Cauldron* — 3800 Montrose Blvd., Houston (77006); $1,500.00; $11.87; editor David Summerlin; tel (713) 525-3579; Format: 5x14

Univ. of Texas: *Shorthorn* — University Center, S.W. Corner, Arlington (76019-0038); MTWHF; 14,000; $14.50; editor John Dycus; tel (817) 272-3188; Format: 6x21

Univ. of Texas: *Daily Texan* — 2500 Whitis Ave., Austin (78713); MTWHF; 28,000; $25.18; tel (512) 471-3851/1865/6221; Format: 6x21.5

Univ. of Texas: *The Pan American* — Student Publications, UC 322, Edinburg (78539); H; 9,000; $10.91; tel (210) 381-2541; Format: 6x21

Univ. of Texas: *Prospector* — 500 University Ave. W., El Paso (79902); TH; 9,000; $12.28; tel (915) 747-5161; Format: 5x16

Univ. of Texas: *UTD Mercury* — Student Union, Rm. 2.108, Richardson (75083-0688); M; 4,000; $10.91; editor Patrick Nichols; tel (214) 883-2286; Format: 5x13

Univ. of Texas: *Paisano* — 14547 Roadrunner Way, San Antonio (78249); T; 6,000; $13.64; editor Melissa Tennies; tel (210) 690-9301; Format: 4x14

Univ. of Texas: *UT Tyler Patriot* — 3900 University Blvd., Tyler (75701-6699); 3,000; $8.00; tel (214) 566-7255; Format: 6x21

Univ. of Texas Permain Basin: *Mesa Journal* — PO Box 8087, Odessa (79762); 1,800; $9.38; editor Chris Kirkes; tel (915) 367-2118; Format: 5x16

W Texas State Univ.: *Prairie* — WT State, Box 747, Canyon (79016); W; 4,500; $8.00; editor Sara Rath; tel (806) 656-2413; Format: 5x15

Western Texas College: *Western Texan* — S. College Ave., Snyder (79549); 2,000; $8.00; tel (915) 573-8511 ext. 273; Format: 4x13

Wiley College: *Wildcat Prowler* — 711 Rosborough-Springs Rd., Marshall (75670); 2,000; $8.00; tel (903) 938-8341 ext. 239; Format: 5x13

UTAH

Brigham Young Univ.: *Daily Universe* — 538 Elwc, Provo (84602); MTWHF; 18,500; $17.64; tel (801) 378-2957; Format: 6x21

College of Eastern Utah: *The Eagle* — 451 E. 400 North, Price (84501); 1,500; $8.00; editor Maryanne Southards; tel (801) 637-2120 ext. 213; Format: 5x13

Dixie College: *Dixie Sun* — 225 S. 700 East, St. George (84770); F; 1,500; $8.00; editor Mindy Ford; tel (801) 673-4811 ext. 346; Format: 5x13

Salt Lake Community College: *Horizon* — PO Box 30808, Salt Lake City (84130-0808); T; 5,500; $9.64; tel (801) 957-4019; Format: 5x17

Southern Utah Univ.: *University Journal* — Box 9384, Cedar City (84720); MWF; 4,200; $11.27; editor Larry Baker; tel (801) 586-7748; Format: 5x13

Univ. of Utah: *Daily Utah Chronicle* — 240 Union Bldg., Salt Lake City (84112); MTWHF; 19,000; $18.18; tel (801) 581-7041; Format: 5x16

Utah State Univ.: *The Utah Statesman* — Taggert Student Center, Logan (84322-0165); MWF; 7,000; $8.63; tel (801) 797-1743; Format: 5x13

Utah Valley State College: *College Times* — Box 1609, Orem (84058); W; 3,500; $9.09; editor Shiela Banister; tel (801) 222-8617; Format: 5x13

Weber State Univ.: *Signpost* — Box 2110, Ogden (84408-2110); MWF; 5,000; $8.18; tel (801) 626-6359; Format: 5x16

Westminster College: *The Forum* — 1840 S. 1300 East, Salt Lake City (84105); T; 1,000; $8.18; editor Dave Neisler; tel (801) 488-4156; Format: 5x13

VERMONT

Castleton State College: *The Cairn* — Campus Center., Castleton (05735); W; 2,000; $9.10; editor Bridgett Taylor; tel (802) 468-5611 ext. 228; Format: 5x15

Lyndon State College: *Critic* — LSC Box L-966, Lyndonville (05851); H; 2,000; $8.00; tel (802) 626-9371 ext. 215; Format: 4x16

Middlebury College: *Middlebury Campus* — Hepburn Annex, Drawer 30, Middlebury (05753); H; 3,500; $8.00; editor Shamoil Shipchandler; tel (802) 388-3711 ext. 5736; Format: 5x16

Copyright ©1996 by the Editor & Publisher Co.

Norwich Univ.: *Norwich Guidon* — Communications Center, Northfield (05663); TH; 3,000; $8.00; editor Ritva Carlson; tel (802) 485-2554; Format: 5x15

St Michaels College: *Defender* — Box 275, Colchester (05439); W; 4,000; $8.25; tel (802) 654-2421; Format: 5x16

Univ. of Vermont: *Vermont Cynic* — Billings Center, Burlington (05405-0040); H; 8,000; $25.45; editor Laura Bernardini; tel (802) 656-4412; Format: 5x15

VIRGINIA

Christopher Newport Univ.: *The Captain's Log* — 50 Shoe Ln., Newport News (23606); M; 2,500; $9.09; editor Robin Harris; tel (804) 594-7196; Format: 4x15

Clinch Valley College: *Highland Cavalier* — CVC Box 5637, Wise (24293); T; 1,600; $8.00; tel (703) 328-0212; Format: 4x21

College of William & Mary: *Flat Hat* — PO Box 320, Williamsburg (23186); F; 5,000; $9.20; editor Mike Hadley; tel (804) 221-3283; Format: 6x21

George Mason Univ.: *Broadside* — 4400 University Dr., Fairfax (22030-4444); MH; 8,000; $16.33; editor Brian Ragan; tel (703) 993-2945; Format: 5x15.5

Hampden-Sydney College: *Hampden-Sydney Tiger* — Box 635, Hampden-Sydney (23943); 2,000; $10.91; editor T Marshall Manson; tel (804) 223-6318; Format: 5x18

Hampton Univ.: *Hampton Script* — PO Box 6237, Hampton (23668); 4,000; $11.82; editor Kent Walker; tel (804) 727-5385; Format: 4x12

James Madison Univ.: *Breeze* — Anthony-Seeger Hall, Harrisonburg (22807); MH; 8,500; $14.55; editor Allison Boyce; tel (540) 568-6127; Format: 4x12.75

Liberty Univ.: *Liberty Champion* — 3765 Candler's Mtn. Rd. 2E, Lynchburg (24506-8001); T; 5,000; $8.00; editor Shannon Harrington; tel (804) 582-2128; Format: 6x21

Longwood College: *Rotunda* — LC Box 2901, Farmville (23909); F; 2,500; $8.20; editor Al Biddlecomb; tel (804) 395-2120; Format: 6x21

Lynchburg College: *The Critograph* — Box 6146, Lynchburg (24501); T; 2,000; $8.55; editor Karen Roberts; tel (804) 522-8301; Format: 5x12

Mary Washington College: *Bullet — MWC*, Box 604, Fredericksburg (22401); T; 3,200; $8.00; editor Lori Betourne; tel (703) 372-3588; Format: 6x21

Marymount Univ.: *The Blue Banner* — 2807 N. Glebe Rd., Arlington (22207); 1,800; $9.09; tel (703) 284-1611; Format: 4x14

Norfolk State Univ.: *Spartan Echo* — 2401 Corprew Ave., Norfolk (23504); F; 6,000; $18.18; editor Angela Moore; tel (804) 683-8562/8446; Format: 4x14

Old Dominion Univ.: *Mace And Crown* — Webb Center, Rm. 2101, Norfolk (23529); W; 6,500; $13.18; editor Selina Gwaltney; tel (804) 683-3452; Format: 4x14

Radford Univ.: *Tartan* — Heth Hall, 2nd Fl., Radford (24142); H; 5,000; $12.73; editor Justin Brown; tel (540) 831-5474; Format: 5x13

Randolph Macon College: *The Yellow Jacket* — Office Of Public Relations, Ashland (23005-5506); T; 1,500; $8.00; editor Shawn Pickrell; tel (804) 752-7214; Format: 4x15

Randolph-Macon Womens College: *Sundial* — Box 396, Lynchburg (24503); M; 1,000; $8.00; tel (804) 846-7392 ext. 4299; Format: 6x21

Roanoke College: *Brackety Ack* — Box 293, Salem (24153); F; 1,200; $8.64; editor Tom Gibbons; tel (703) 375-2327; Format: 5x14

Sweet Briar College: *Sweet Briar News* — PO Box 258, Sweet Briar (24595); H; 1,000; $8.00; tel (804) 381-6360; Format: 5x12

US Naval Academy: *Trident* — Comprint, Alexandria (21402); 12,000; $18.58; editor Leon Mahalic; tel (703) 548-9893; Format: 6x13

Univ. of Richmond: *Collegian* — 327 Tyler Haynes Commons, Richmond (23173); H; 4,000; $8.00; editor Katie Masterson; tel (804) 289-8825; Format: 5x14

Univ. of Virginia: *Cavalier Daily* — Basement Newcomb Hall, Charlottesville (22904); MTWHF; 10,000; $10.82; editor Michael Sampson; tel (804) 924-1085; Format: 6x21

Virginia Commonwealth Univ.: *Commonwealth Times* — Box 2010, Richmond (23284-2010); MWF; 5,000; $16.89; editor Melenie Irvin; tel (804) 828-1058; Format: 4x12.5

Virginia Military Institute: *Vmi Cadet* — Box 7, Lexington (24450); F; 1,700; $8.00; editor Matt Howell; tel (540) 463-3537; Format: 5x13

Virginia State Univ.: *The Statesman* — Box 9063, Petersburg (23806); 3,000; $11.00; editor Frances Melson; tel (804) 524-5298; Format: 5x13.75

Virginia Tech.: *Collegiate Times* — 363 Squires Student Center, Blacksburg (24061); TF; 14,000; $14.27; editor Terry Pudalind; tel (540) 231-9864; Format: 6x21

Washington & Lee Univ.: *Ring-Tum-Phi* — PO Box 899, Lexington (24450); H; 2,500; $8.00; editor Michelle Brien; tel (703) 462-4060; Format: 6x21.5

WASHINGTON

Bellevue Community College: *Advocate* — PO Box 92700, Bellevue (98007-6484); H; 2,500; $9.09; tel (206) 641-2433; Format: 4x17.5

Big Bend Community College: *Tumbleweed Times* — 7662 Chanute St. , Moses Lake (98837-3299); 1,500; $8.00; editor Leonard Johnson; tel (509) 762-6248; Format: 5x14

Central Washington Univ.: *Observer* — 400 E. 8th Ave., Ellensburg (98926-7435); H; 6,000; $9.54; tel (509) 963-1026; Format: 5x16

Clark College: *Independent* — 1800 E. Mcloughlin Blvd., Vancouver (98663); F; 2,500; $13.91; tel (360) 992-2879; Format: 5x14.5

Eastern Washington Univ.: *Easterner* — MS-58, Cheney (99004); H; 5,000; $13.63; editor Patrick Heald; tel (509) 359-7010/6270; Format: 5x15

Everett Community College: *Clipper* — 801 Wetmore, Everett (98201); 2,000; $12.45; tel (206) 388-9419; Format: 5x14

Gonzaga Univ.: *The Bulletin* — E. 723 Boone Ave., Spokane (99258); F; 4,000; $16.36; tel (509) 328-4220 ext. 2239; Format: 6x20

Grays Harbor Community College: *Timberline* — College Heights, Rm. 322, Aberdeen (98520); 1,000; $12.73; tel (360) 532-9020; Format: 6x21.5

Green River Community College: *Current* — 12401 S.E. 320th St., Auburn (98002); 1,500; $9.09; editor Carrin Hargraves; tel (206) 833-9111 ext. 267; Format: 3x11

Highline Community College: *Thunderword* — PO Box 98000, Midway (98198-9800); 2,500; $9.09; editor Marlin Bowman; tel (206) 878-3710; Format: 3x9.5

Lower Columbia College: *Logos* — PO Box 3010, Longview (98632); F; 1,500; $12.73; tel (360) 577-3412; Format: 4x13

Olympic College: *The Olympian* — 1600 Chester Ave., Bremerton (98310-1699); 1,750; $8.00; tel (360) 478-4667; Format: 4x13.5

Pacific Lutheran Univ.: *The Mooring Mast* — University Center, Tacoma (98447); F; 3,200; $9.54; editor Kimberly Lusk; tel (206) 535-7492; Format: 5x16

Peninsula College: *Buccaneer* — 1502 E. Lauridsen, Port Angeles (98362); 2,000; $11.68; editor Darcy Chappel; tel (360) 417-6470; Format: 6x21

Pierce College: *Pioneer* — 9401 Farwest Dr. S.W., Tacoma (98498); 3,000; $8.18; tel (206) 964-6513/6604; Format: 5x16

Seattle Central Community College: *City Collegian* — 1701 Broadway, Seattle (98122); H; 3,500; $9.00; tel (206) 587-6959; Format: 5x16

Seattle Pacific Univ.: *Falcon* — The Media House, Seattle (98119); W; 2,500; $13.19; editor Jason Macpherson; tel (206) 281-2104; Format: 6x16

Seattle Univ.: *Spectator* — Broadway at Madison, Seattle (98122); H; 3,200; $15.00; tel (206) 296-6474; Format: 5x15.5

Shoreline Community College: *Ebbtide* — 16101 Greenwood Ave. N., Seattle (98133); 3,500; $9.09; tel (206) 546-4730; Format: 5x14.5

Skagit Valley Community College: *Cardinal* — 2405 E. College Way, Mt Vernon (98273); 2,500; $9.09; tel (360) 428-1296; Format: 4x13

S. Puget Sound Community College: *Sounds* — Student Newspaper, Olympia (98512); 2,000; $13.64; tel (360) 754-7711 ext. 414; Format: 4x16

S Seattle Community College: *Sentinel* — 6000 16th Ave. S.W., Seattle (98106-1499); F; 1,500; $9.09; editor Dan Thompson; tel (206) 764-5333; Format: 4x16

Spokane Community College: *Reporter* — 1810 N. Greene St., Spokane (99207); 2,500; $8.00; tel (509) 533-7171; Format: 5x15

Spokane Falls Community College: *Sfcc Communicator* — Bldg. 5 Rm. 112/Ms 3050, Spokane (99204); 3,000; $9.55; tel (509) 533-3602; Format: 5x16

Tacoma Community College: *Challenge* — 5900 S. 12th St., Tacoma (98465); 2,700; $8.00; editor John Mcnama; tel (206) 566-5042/6045; Format: 5x13.5

The Evergreen State College: *Cooper Point Journal* — Cab 316, Olympia (98505); H; 3,500; $16.00; editor Reynor Padilla; tel (360) 866-6000 ext. 6054; Format: 4x16

Univ. of Puget Sound: *Puget Sound Trail* — 1500 N. Warner, Tacoma (98416); H; 2,000; $10.90; editor Tony Cesario; tel (206) 756-3278; Format: 5x15.5

Univ. of Washington: *Daily* — 144 Communications Bldg., Seattle (98195); MTWHF; 18,000; $12.91; editor Hans Ruegamer; tel (206) 543-2336/7666; Format: 5x16

Walla Walla College: *The Collegian* — Walla Walla College, College Place (99324); H; 2,200; $8.00; editor Sally Pershall; tel (509) 527-2971/2985; Format: 5x12.5

Washington State Univ.: *Daily Evergreen* — Administration Way, Pullman (99165); MTWHF; 14,000; $15.51; tel (509) 335-3552; Format: 5x16

Western Washington Univ.: *Western Front* — College Hall, Bellingham (98225); TF; 7,000; $12.27; tel (360) 650-3161; Format: 5x15

Whatcom Community College: *Horizon* — 237 W. Kellogg Rd., Bellingham (98225); 3,500; $9.09; editor Anya Bronsema; tel (360) 676-2170 ext. 226; Format: 5x20

Whitman College: *The Pioneer* — 200 Boyer St., Walla Walla (99362); H; 1,500; $11.04; editor Jason Copeland; tel (509) 527-5372; Format: 4x14

Whitworth College: *Whitworthian* — Box 4302, Spokane (99251); T; 1,700; $10.00; editor Cindy Brett; tel (509) 466-3248; Format: 5x15

Yakima Valley Community College: *The Hub Caps* — PO Box 1647, Yakima (98907); M; 2,500; $18.36; editor Donna Hill; tel (509) 575-2442; Format: 3x8.5

WEST VIRGINIA

Alderson Broaddus College: *The Battler Columns* — Campus Box 515A, Philippi (26416); 1,200; $8.00; tel (304) 457-1700; Format: 5x12.5

Fairmont State College: *Columns* — LRC, Rm.110, Fairmont (26554); H; 4,000; $8.00; tel (304) 367-4740; Format: 5x12

Marshall Univ.: *Parthenon* — 311 Smith Hall, Huntington (25755); TWHF; 7,500; $10.28; tel (304) 696-2273; Format: 5x16

Shepherd College: *Picket* — Miller Office Complex, Shepherdstown (25443); 4,000; $12.72; editor Tracie Bronson; tel (304) 876-5377; Format: 5x13.5

Univ. of Charleston: *Golden Reporter* — 2300 Maccorkle Ave. S.E., Charleston (25304-1099); 1,000; $8.00; editor Steffanie Myers; tel (304) 357-4745; Format: 6x17

West Virginia Institute of Tech.: *Tech Collegian* — Student Service Center, Montgomery (25136); W; 2,500; $8.18; tel (304) 442-3371/3180; Format: 4x13.5

West Virginia State College: *Yellow Jacket* — Campus Box 175, Institute (25112); H; 1,500; $8.00; tel (304) 766-3212; Format: 5x17.5

West Virginia Univ.: *Daily Athenaeum* — 284 Prospect St, Morgantown (26506-6427); MTWHF; 15,000; $14.25; editor Eric Corrado; tel (304) 293-2593; Format: 6x21

West Virginia Wesleyan: *Pharos* — WVWC 59 College Ave., Buckhannon (26201); F; 1,200; $8.00; editor Sarah Gould; tel (304) 473-8004; Format: 5x12.5

Wheeling Jesuit College: *Spokesman* — Box 416, Wheeling (26003); 700; $8.00; tel (304) 243-2000 ext. 452; Format: 5x17

WISCONSIN

Alverno College: *Alpha* — 3401 S. 39th St., Milwaukee (53215); 1,500; $12.13; tel (414) 382-6299/6000; Format: 4x15.5

Beloit College: *Round Table* — Box 109, Beloit (53511); F; 2,000; $10.00; tel (608) 363-2475; Format: 5x13

Carthage College: *The Arrow* — Box 1313, Kenosha (53140-1900); H; 1,800; $8.00; editor Kristin Jacobson; tel (414) 551-6150; Format: 5x16.5

Edgewood College: *On The Edge* — 855 Woodrow, Madison (53711); 650; $8.00; editor Susan Pierce; tel (608) 257-4861 ext. 2257; Format: 5x16

Lawrence Univ.: *Lawrentian* — Box 599, Appleton (54912); 1,650; $14.54; editor Brian Drier; tel (414) 832-6768; Format: 5x14

Madison Area Tech. College: *Slant* — 3550 Anderson St., Madison (53704); 10,000; $8.00; editor Norman Engvall; tel (608) 246-6809; Format: 4x15

Marquette Univ.: *Marquette Tribune* — 1131 W. Wisconsin, Milwaukee (53233); TH; 8,500; $15.00; editor Laura Ugnarski; tel (414) 288-1738/7057; Format: 5x16

Milwaukee Area Tech. College: *The Matc Times* — 700 W. State St., Milwaukee (53233); 8,500; $15.45; editor Kris Kingston; tel (414) 297-6268/6600; Format: 5x18.5

Milwaukee School of Engineering: *Ingenium* — 1025 N. Broadway St., Milwaukee (53202-3109); 2,500; $12.73; editor Brian Gillespie; tel (414) 277-7255; Format: 4x15.5

Ripon College: *College Days* — Harwood Union, Ripon (54971); 1,400; $8.27; editor Brad Browne; tel (414) 748-8105; Format: 3x9

St Norbert College: *SNC Times* — Apac Box 27, De Pere (54115-2099); W; 1,500; $8.00; editor Chris Thiede; tel (414) 337-3268; Format: 5x15

Univ. of Wisconsin: *Spectator* — 175 Hibbard Hall, Eau Claire (54701); MH; 7,500; $10.90; editor Jody Chromey; tel (715) 836-4366; Format: 6x21.5

Univ. of Wisconsin: *Fourth Estate* — Student Life SS 1905, Green Bay (54311-7001); H; 3,000; $8.46; editor Cory Kaisler; tel (414) 465-2719; Format: 5x16

Univ. of Wisconsin: *UW Parkside Ranger* — Box 2000, Kenosha (53141-2000); H; 4,000; $11.18; tel (414) 595-2287/2278; Format: 5x16

Univ. of Wisconsin: *Racquet* — 1725 State St., Lacrosse (54601); H; 5,000; $9.55; editor Mary Biron; tel (608) 785-8381; Format: 5x16

Univ. of Wisconsin: *Badger Herald* — 550 State St., Madison (53703); MTWHF; 17,000; $13.64; editor Richie Schwartz; tel (608) 257-4712; Format: 6x21

Univ. of Wisconsin: *Stoutonia* — 114 Memorial Student Union, Menomonie (54751); H; 5,500; $12.37; editor Erica Kalkofen; tel (715) 232-2272; Format: 5x16

Univ. of Wisconsin: *UWM Post* — Union Box 88, PO Box 413, Milwaukee (53211); MH; 10,000; $10.91; editor Brian Huber; tel (414) 229-4578; Format: 5x16

Univ. of Wisconsin: *Advance Titan* — Radford Hall 11, Oshkosh (54901); H; 11,000; $16.36; editor Erin Mallone; tel (414) 424-3049; Format: 5x15.5

Univ. of Wisconsin: *Exponent* — 1 University Plz., Platteville (53818); H; 4,000; $8.00; tel (608) 342-1471/1353; Format: 5x16

Univ. of Wisconsin: *Student Voice* — 216 S. Hall, River Falls (54022); H; 4,000; $9.45; tel (715) 425-3118/3624; Format: 6x21

Univ. of Wisconsin: *Pointer* — 104 CAC,UW, Stevens Point (54481); H; 4,000; $12.18; editor Stepanie Sprangers; tel (715) 346-3707/2249; Format: 5x15.5

Univ. of Wisconsin: *Promethean* — HFAC 1184, Superior (54880); F; 2,500; $10.00; editor Laure-Elina Benard; tel (715) 394-8335; Format: 4x21

Univ. of Wisconsin: *Royal Purple* — 266 E. University Center, Whitewater (53190); W; 7,000; $9.54; editor Eric Fritz; tel (414) 472-5100; Format: 5x16

Viterbo College: *Lumen* — 815 S. 9th St., La Crosse (54601); 1,500; $8.00; tel (608) 791-0468/0469; Format: 5x15

Waukesha Co. Tech. Institute: *Technique* — 800 W. Main, Pewaukee (53072); 1,500; $8.00; tel (414) 691-5308; Format: 4x17

WYOMING

Casper College: *Chinook* — 125 College Dr., Casper (82601); 3,000; $8.64; editor Paula Unger; tel (307) 268-2591; Format: 5x13

Laramie Co. Community College: *Wingspan* — Fine Arts Bldg., Rm. 176, Cheyenne (82007); 2,500; $8.00; tel (307) 778-1304; Format: 3x10

Univ. of Wyoming: *Branding Iron* — University Sta., PO Box 4238, Laramie (82071); TWHF; 7,000; $10.91; editor Steve Bahiner; tel (307) 766-6190/6336; Format: 5x13

SECTION III

Newspapers Published in Canada

Daily newspapers	1-25
Weekly newspapers	26-34
Ethnic newspapers	35
Tabloid newspapers	35
Newspaper groups under common ownership	36

DAILY NEWSPAPERS PUBLISHED IN CANADA

ALBERTA

CALGARY

'91 Census- 710,675 (Metro Area 754,030); E&P '96 Est. 780,139 (Metro Area 785,914)
ABC-CZ (91): 710,677 (HH 262,370)

Calgary Herald
(m-mon to thur; m-fri; m-sat)
Sunday Herald (S)

Calgary Herald, 215 16 St. S.E.; Box 2400, Stn. M, Calgary, AB T2P 0W8; tel (403) 235-7100; fax (403) 235-7575; web site http://www.southam.com/calgaryherald. Southam Newspapers group.
Circulation: 112,735(m); 156,961(m-fri); 130,061(m-sat); 110,018(S); ABC Sept. 30, 1995.
Price: 50¢(d); $1.00(fri); $1.00(sat); 50¢(S); $13.50/mo; $162.00/yr.
Advertising: Modular rate $3.98(m); $4.58(m-fri); $4.25(m-sat); $3.98(S). **Representative:** Southam Newspapers.
News Services: CP, AP, RN, LAT-WP, DJ, SOU, CSM. **Politics:** Independent. **Established:** 1882.
Not Published: New Year; Good Friday; Victoria Day; July 1; Civic Holiday (Aug); Labor Day; Thanksgiving; Christmas.
Special Editions: Ski Week, Weddings (Jan); Investment Guide I, Investment Guide II (Feb); Auto Show, Auto Show Guide, Better Business Bureau, Spring Fashions (Mar); Golf, Fun & Sun (Apr); House & Garden (May); Pre-Stampede, Environment Week, Home Electronics (June); Stampede Edition (July); Back-to-School Fashion, Learning, Reader's Choice (Aug); Fall Fashion, Stitches (Sept); Furniture Sale I, Furniture Sale II, Furniture Sale III, Science & Technology (Oct); Gift Guide I, Ski '96, Home Electronics (Nov); Gift Guide II, Gift Guide III (Dec).
Special Weekly Sections: Small Business (mon); Wheels (fri).
Magazines: TV Times (fri); Comics (sat).

CORPORATE OFFICERS
President/CEO — William Ardell
Vice Pres — Kevin Peterson

GENERAL MANAGEMENT
Publisher — Kevin Peterson
Director-Internal Operations — Murray Ball
Administration & Credit Manager — R Edey

ADVERTISING
Manager-Retail — Gary Cobb
Sales Manager-Classified/National — Kathleen O'Halloran

MARKETING AND PROMOTION
Director-Marketing Resources — Sharon Henwood

TELECOMMUNICATIONS
Audiotex Manager — Dave Haynes

CIRCULATION
Director-Reader, Sales & Service — Georges Ritchot

NEWS EXECUTIVES
Editor — Crosbie Cotton
Managing Editor — Steve Roberts
Asst Managing Editor — Gary Park

EDITORS AND MANAGERS
Books Editor — K McGoogan
Cartoonist — Vance Rodewalt
City & Life Editor — Ron Nowell
Columnist — Don Braid
Columnist — Don Martin
Columnist — Allan Maki
Columnist — Tom Keyser
Columnist — Bill Gold
Columnist — Susan Ruttan
Editorial Page Editor — Joan Crockett
Editorial Writer — Bob Bragg
Editorial Writer — Chuck Frank
Editorial Writer — Roman Cooney
Editorial Writer — David Trigueiro
Education Reporter — Lisa Dempster
Education Reporter — Andy Marshall
Entertainment Editor — Al Rach
Editorial Page Editor — Joan Crockett
Finance Editor — Ken Hull
Homes/Travel Editor — Beth Burgess
Librarian — Karen Crosby
Music Editor — Eric Dawson
Music — James Muritech
Photo Editor — Peter Brosseau
Radio/Television Reporter — Bob Blakey
Sports Editor — Mark Tremblay

MANAGEMENT INFORMATION SERVICES
Data Processing Manager — Brian Jamieson

PRODUCTION
Vice Pres-Manufacturing — Al Rudd
Manager-Operations (Night) — Norm Semmens
Manager — Brian Biswanger
Manager-Pre Press/Info Technology — Brian Jamieson
Foreman-Pressroom — Ted Reis
Foreman-Plate Making — Mike Bears
Foreman-Distribution Center — Tom Smith
Supervisor-Systems Support — Mike Cochrane

Market Information: Zoned editions; Split Run; TMC; Operate audiotex.
Mechanical available: Offset; Black and 3 ROP colors; insert accepted — preprinted, stitched in TV Times magazine; page cut-offs — 23 9/16".
Mechanical specifications: Type page 11½" x 22⅛"; E - 5 cols, 2.18", .16" between; A - 10 cols, 1.08", .16" between; C - 10 cols, 1.08", .16" between.
Commodity Consumption (estimated): Newsprint 19,578 metric tons; widths 139cm, 104cm, 69cm; black ink 150,192 kg; color ink 84,105 kg; single pages printed 29,300; average pages per issue 70(d), 50(S); single plates used 150,000.

Equipment: EDITORIAL: Front-end software — QPS, Copy Desk; Printers — QMS/11 x 17. CLASSIFIED: Front-end hardware — Cybergraphics. AUDIOTEX: Hardware — Micro Voice/Blackbox; Software — Micro Voice; Supplier name — PEP, Comstock. DISPLAY: Adv layout systems — SCS/Layout 8000; Front-end hardware — Ap/Macs; Front-end software — Multi-Ad/Creator, QuarkXPress. PRODUCTION: Pagination software — QPS 1.1, QuarkXPress, Multi-Ad/Creator; Typesetters — 3-AU/APS-108 C-6 RIPS; Plate exposers — 2-WL/Lith-X-Pozer, 2-N/Flip Top; Plate processors — 1-Hoechst/N-322, 1-WL; Electronic picture desk — CD; Scanners — 1-Lf/Leafscan 45, 2-Nikon/3510, 1-Microtek/60025, 1-Sharp/JX-600; Production cameras — 1-C/Marathon, 1-C/Spartan; Automatic film processors — 2-LE/24A, 2-LE/18, 2-P/online 24"; Film transporters — 2-P, 1-LE; Color separation equipment (conventional) — 1-Lf/Leafscan 45, 2-Nikon/3510, 1-Microtek/60025, 1-Sharp/JX-600, Ap/Mac, Linotype-Hell, Topez; Digital color separation equipment — Adobe/Photoshop, Lindcolor 3.2.1.
PRESSROOM: Line 1 — 9-G/Metro double width; Line 2 — 9-G/Metro double width; Line 3 — 9-G/Metro; Press drives — Fin; Folders — G; Pasters — G/Metro; Reels and stands — G/Metro; Press control system — G/PCS. MAILROOM: Counter stackers — 4-QWI/300, 2-QWI/350; Stuffers — 3-Fg; Bundle tyer — 3-MLN, 4-MLN/MLN IIA, 2-Constellation; Wrapping singles — 1-St/PM 720; Addressing machine — 6-Dm. LIBRARY: Electronic Infomart/(offsite), Text Apple Search, T-ONE Merlin/Photos. COMMUNICATIONS: Digital ad delivery system — Ap/Remote Access, First Class/Bulletin Board. WIRE SERVICES: News — CP; Photos — RN, CP, AP, SOU; Stock tables — CP; receiving dishes — size-2m. BUSINESS COMPUTERS: 3-DEC/VAX 4000-100; Applications: In-house; PCs & micros networked; PCs & main system networked.

EXPLANATION OF SYMBOLS AND ABBREVIATIONS FOR CANADIAN DAILIES

CITY POPULATIONS, ETC.
Population figures, except where otherwise shown, are from the 1991 Statistics Census. Population estimates for 1996 are provided when available.
ABC definitions follow lines of urban development, trading habit or political boundary. Publishers may report their circulation by **city zone** and **retail trading zone**, or by **newspaper designated market**. These are established with approval of the Audit Bureau of Circulations.
ABC-city zone (ABC-CZ) - Area described as the corporate city center or target area or circulation.
Newspaper Designated Market (ABC-NDM) - The geographical area which a newspaper considers to be the market it serves. Publisher members have the option of reporting circulation according to just the new NDM or in combination with a City Zone and/or Retail Trading Zone figure.
HH - Households.

NEWSPAPER PUBLICATION AND CIRCULATION
(d) - daily
(m) - morning
(e) - evening
(S) - Sunday
(all day) - several editions published through the day.

CIRCULATION
Figures preceded by "ABC" indicate net paid (excluding bulk) circulation from ABC publisher's statement for period ending Sept. 30, 1995, unless otherwise noted.

All other figures are from newspapers' sworn postal statements of Sept. 30, 1995, unless otherwise noted.

ADVERTISING RATES
Maximum rate Modular agate line for general (national) display advertising is shown where available for each edition of the paper and for combination between editions and other daily papers.

NEWS SERVICES
AP - Associated Press
AFP - Agence France-Presse
CP - Canadian Press
CN - Capitol News Service
CNS - Copley News Service
CQ - Congressional Quarterly Service
CSM - Christian Science Monitor
DJ - Dow Jones
GNS - Gannett News Service
HN - Hearst Newspapers
KRT - Knight Ridder-Tribune
LAT-WP - Los Angeles Times-Washington Post News Service
NEA - Newspaper Enterprises Association
NNS - Newhouse News Service
NYT - New York Times News Service
ONS - Ottaway News Service
PNS - Pacific News Service
RN - Reuters News Agency
SHNS - Scripps-Howard Newspaper Service
SNS - Sterling News Service
SOU - Southam News Service
THO - Thomson News Service
UPI - United Press International

For table of abbreviations of equipment and manufacturer, see front pages.
For informaton on Canadian Newspaper Units (CNU), see front pages.

The Calgary Sun
(m-mon to sat)
The Sunday Sun (S)

The Calgary Sun, 2615-12th St., N.E., Calgary, AB T2E 7W9; tel (403) 250-4200. Toronto Sun Publishing Corp. group.
Circulation: 67,521(m); 67,521(m-sat); 99,603(S); ABC Sept. 30, 1995.
Price: 35¢(d); 35¢(sat); 75¢(S); $2.50/wk; $130.00/yr.
Advertising: Modular rate $2.71(m); $2.78(m-sat); $2.91(S).
News Services: CP, UPI, RN, GNS, CNW. **Politics:** Independent. **Established:** 1980.
Note: Corporate rates are offered on a collective basis between the Edmonton, Calgary and Toronto markets.
Not Published: Good Friday; Christmas.

GENERAL MANAGEMENT
Publisher — Ken King
General Manager — Lester Pyette
Controller — Don Liddell

ADVERTISING
Director — Gordon Norrie

MARKETING AND PROMOTION
Director — Michele McDonald

CIRCULATION
Director — Joe King

NEWS EXECUTIVES
Editor in Chief — Bob Poole
Managing Editor — Chris Nelson

EDITORS AND MANAGERS
City Editor — Sean McCann
Graphics Editor — Randy Hill

MANAGEMENT INFORMATION SERVICES
Manager-Management Info Services — Mark Hall

PRODUCTION
Manager — Trent Anderson

Market Information: TMC.
Mechanical available: Offset; Black and 3 ROP colors; insert accepted — preprinted; page cut-offs — 22¾".
Mechanical specifications: Type page 10¼" x 14¼"; E - 6 cols, 1.58", ⅙" between; A - 8 cols, 1 3/16", ⅙" between; C - 8 cols, 1 3/16", ⅙" between.
Commodity Consumption (estimated): Newsprint 8,200 metric tons; widths 13.5", 27", 40.5"; single pages printed 35,000; average pages per issue 88(d), 80(sat), 170(S); single plates used 52,000.

Equipment: EDITORIAL: Front-end hardware — 3-Sun/Sparc 10-52, 1-Sun/Sparc 10-41; Front-end software — P.INK; Printers — 2-Chelgraph/PPT-600, 1-QMS/860 Print System, AU/APS 2000, Canon/Color Copier; Other equipment — 5-Edit/112B, 10-Ap/Power Book 150, 17-Ap/Mac Quadra 610, 16-Ap/Mac Quadra 650, 10-Ap/Mac Quadra 700, 8-Ap/Mac Quadra 800, 4-Ap/Mac Quadra 840 AV, 2-Ap/Power Mac 7100, 2-Ap/Power Mac 8100. CLASSIFIED: Front-end hardware — DEC/PDP 1170; Front-end software — Composition Systems; Other equipment — 9-CT/90. DISPLAY: Adv layout systems — 7-Ap/Mac Quadra 700, 3-Ap/Power Mac 7100, 2-Ap/Mac Quadra 800; Front-end software — Multi-Ad/Creator, QuarkXPress 3.3, Scitex Adobe/Photoshop; Printers — ECR/VR30; Other equipment — 2-HP/Scanner, Scitex. PRODUCTION: Typesetters — 3-III/3850, Harlequin, 4-DEC/Alpha w/AU RIPs; Plate exposers — 2-Olec/Plateburner, 1-KFM/TD-33; Plate processors — 2-Polychrome; Electronic picture desk — CD/Solo; Scanners — Scitex/Smart Plus, Scitex/340L, Howtek/D4000; Production cameras — C/Spartan II, 1-AG; Automatic film processors — 1-LE/LBQ-24E, 3-P; Film transporters — 3-P/SC2050; Digital color separation equipment — Nikon/LS3510, Kk/RFS 2035.
PRESSROOM: Line 1 — 3-G/HO (mono), 4-G/decks; Press drives — Allen Bradley; Folders — G/Imperial; Pasters — 6-G/CT50 RTP; Reels and stands — 6-G/CT-50. MAILROOM: Counter stackers — 3-HL, 2-QWI; Stuffers — 1-HI, 1-S; Bundle tyer — 2-Dynaric, 2-MLN; Wrapping

Copyright ©1996 by the Editor & Publisher Co.

III-2 Alberta

singles — 1-QWI, 1-NJP, 1-SH; Addressing machine — Dm; Other mailroom equipment — KAN/Quarter Folder. LIBRARY: Electronic — Vu/Text. WIRE SERVICES: News — CP, RN, GNS; Stock tables — CP; receiving dishes — CP. BUSINESS COMPUTERS: PCs & micros networked; PCs & main system networked.

EDMONTON

'91 Census- 616,740 (Metro Area 839,920); E&P '96 Est. 667,740 (Metro Area 874,129)
Journal
ABC-CZ (91): 694,466 (HH 260,263)
Sun
ABC-NDM (91): 808,929 (HH 297,337)

The Edmonton Journal

(m-mon to thur; m-fri; m-sat; S)

Edmonton Journal, 10006 101 St.; PO Box 2421, Edmonton, AB T5J 2S6; tel (403) 429-5100. Southam Newspaper group.

Circulation: 147,060(m); 178,010(m-fri); 147,060(m-sat); 135,779(S); ABC Sept. 30, 1995.

Price: 50¢(d); 75¢(fri); 75¢(sat); 75¢(S); $3.00/wk; $13.00/mo; $156.00/yr.

Advertising: Modular rate $7.78(m); $8.55(m-fri); $8.55(m-sat); $7.78(S). **Representative:** Southam Newspaper Group.

News Services: SNS, AP, CP, RN, NYT, KRT, LAT-WP. **Politics:** Independent. **Established:** 1903.

Not Published: New Year; Good Friday; Victoria Day; July 1; Civic Holiday (Aug); Labour Day; Thanksgiving Day; Christmas Day.

Advertising not accepted: Fraudulent or offensive.

Special Editions: Your Money, Today's Bride (Jan); International Auto Show (Feb); Spring Fashions (Mar); Spring Clean Up, Home Show Guide, Tee to Green (Apr); Electronics/Photo, Bikes (May); Vacation Planning Guide (June); Klondike Days Guide (July); Courses & Classes, Dance & Music, Lively Arts (Aug); Edmonton Home Show, Furniture & Appliance Sale, Fall Fashions (Sept); Renovation Month, Computer Buying Guide, Home Electronics (Oct); Canadian Finals Rodeo, Guide to Christmas I (Nov); Courses & Classes, Guide to Christmas II, Guide to Christmas III (Dec).

Special Weekly Sections: Money (mon); Flair (tues); Food (wed); Computers & Technology (thur); What's On, Wheels (fri); Homes, Travel, Insight, Careers (sat); Insight (S).

Magazines: TV Times; Comics (tab).

CORPORATE OFFICER

President Linda Hughes

GENERAL MANAGEMENT

Publisher Linda Hughes
Vice Pres Finance David Becker
Credit Supervisor David Marshall
Vice Pres Marketing Patricia Hutchison
Vice Pres Human Resources Ken Wickenberg

ADVERTISING

Vice Pres-Sales John Connolly
Manager-National Sales Gordon Deeks
Manager-Retail Sales Gordon Deeks
Manager-Classified Cathy Townshend

TELECOMMUNICATIONS

Audiotex Manager Paul DeGroot

CIRCULATION

Vice Pres-Reader Sales & Service Dave Reidie
Director-Distribution Paul Dunn
Director-Reader Sales and Service Dennis Skulsky

NEWS EXECUTIVES

Editor in Chief Murdoch Davis
Editorial Board Chairman Duart Farquharson
Managing Editor Sheila Pratt
Asst Managing Editor Allan Mayer
Asst Managing Editor Roy Wood

EDITORS AND MANAGERS

Business Editor Peter Collum
Editorial Cartoonist Malcolm Mayes
City Editor Kathy Kerr
Films Editor Marc Horton
Fashion Editor Chris Standring
Food Editor Judy Schultz
Leisure & Entertainment Editor Bob Remington
Librarian Elaine Mantua
Photo Editor Steve Makris
Radio/Television Editor Bob Remington
Sports Editor Wayne Moriarty
Travel Editor Judy Schultz

MANAGEMENT INFORMATION SERVICES

Data Processing Manager Michael Carpenter

PRODUCTION

Vice Pres Manufacturing Fred Castle
Asst Manager Locke Boros
Foreman-Pressroom Ken Muir

Market Information: Zoned editions; Split Run; TMC; Operate database; Operate audiotex.

Mechanical available: Offset; Black and 3 ROP colors; insert accepted — preprinted; page cut-offs — 23 9/16".

Mechanical specifications: Type page 13½" x 23 9/16"; E - 6 cols, 2 1/16", ⅛" between; A - 6 cols, 2 1/16", ⅛" between; C - 10 cols, 1¼", ⅛" between.

Commodity Consumption (estimated): Newsprint 22,300 metric tons; widths 54.13", 40.55", 26.97"; black ink 414,000 kg; color ink 167,600 kg; single pages printed 20,976; average pages per issue 64.5(d), 58(S); single plates used 125,000.

Equipment: EDITORIAL: Front-end hardware — PC/386, PC/486, Ap/Mac 950, Ap/Power PC 8100, Ap/Power PC 7100, Ap/Power PC 6100, Ap/PowerBook 270C, Ap/PowerBook 230; Front-end software — XYQUEST/XyWrite, Novell/Netware, QPS, Adobe/Illustrator, Copy Desk, Adobe/Photoshop; Printers — HP/451MX, Graphic Enterprises/Tabloid Printer. CLASSIFIED: Front-end hardware — Cybergraphics, PC/386, DEC/VAX 4000, Ap/Mac; Front-end software — VMS, Pathworks, Multi-Ad, QPS, Adobe/Illustrator; Printers — Ap/Mac LaserWriter IIg; Other equipment — AU/APS 6-108C. AUDIOTEX: Hardware — PC/486; Software — Proprietary. DISPLAY: Adv layout systems — Ap/Mac, SCS/Layout 8000; Front-end hardware — Ap/Mac Quadra 700, Ap/Mac Quadra 800, Ap/Mac Quadra 950, Ap/Power PC 8100; Front-end software — Multi-Ad/Creator, QuarkXPress, Adobe/Illustrator, Adobe/Photoshop; Printers — Ap/LaserWriter, Canon/color copier, LaserMaster/Unity; Other equipment — CD-Rom, Canon/Digital Still Camera, Alpha/NT RIP. PRODUCTION: Pagination software — Southam/Ad Trak, AU/Softpip; Typesetters — 2-MON/Express Laser, 2-AU/APS-6-108C, 1-AU/APS-6-108FC; Plate exposers — 3-N/Flip Top FT40UPNS; Plate processors — 3-Hoechst/Futura 860; Electronic picture desk — CD; Scanners — Kk/Negative, Nikon/Negative, PixelCraft, AG, Microtek; Production cameras — C/Spartan, C/Marathon, 2-Escofot; Automatic film processors — 3-LE, 2-Kk; Film transporters — 1-LE; Color separation equipment (conventional) — 2-DAI/Newscolor.
PRESSROOM: Line 1 — 9-G/Metroliner (5 half decks); Line 2 — 9-G/Metroliner (5 half decks); Line 3 — 9-G/Metroliner (5 half decks); Press control system — G/PCS. MAILROOM: Counter stackers — 6-HL/Monitor; Stuffers — 3-Fg/Drum; Bundle tyer — 6-Power Strap, 13-MVP; Wrapping singles — Manual. LIBRARY: Electronic — Southam/Infomart. COMMUNICATIONS: Satellite. WIRE SERVICES: News — CP, Canada News Wire; Stock tables — CP; receiving dishes — AP, Southam. BUSINESS COMPUTERS: 4-DEC/VAX 4000, 785-DEC/VAX 11; Applications: Circ, Adv billing, Accts receivable, Gen ledger, Payroll; PCs & micros networked; PCs & main system networked.

The Edmonton Sun

(m-mon to sat)

Sunday Sun (S)

The Edmonton Sun, #250, 4990-92 Avenue, Edmonton, AB T6B 3A1; tel (403) 468-0100. Toronto Sun Publishing Corp. group.

Circulation: 74,542(m); 74,542(m-sat); 113,893(S); ABC Sept. 30, 1995.

Price: 50¢(d); 50¢(sat); 75¢(S); $2.90/wk.

Advertising: Modular rate $3.15(m); $3.15(m-sat); $3.71(S). **Representatives:** Toronto Sun Publishing; Vancouver Western Corp.

News Services: RN, CP, AP, SHNS. **Established:** 1978.

Note: Corporate rates are offered on a collective basis between the Edmonton, Calgary and Toronto markets.

Not Published: Apr 9; Dec 25.

Special Weekly Sections: Car Market, Express (mon); Car Market (fri); Travel (sat); Homes, Showcase, Sunday (entertainment & lifestyle section) (S); Sports (daily).

Magazines: Saturday Home Improvement (monthly-sat); Local Magazine (newsprint), TV Magazine, Comics (S); Modern Woman (monthly-last Sunday).

CORPORATE OFFICERS

Board Chairman Lionel H Schipper
President Paul V Godfrey
Vice Pres-Finance Bruce Jackson

GENERAL MANAGEMENT

Publisher Craig Martin
General Manager David Black
Chief Accountant Gunther Motsch

ADVERTISING

Director Ken Brown
Classified Manager Gord Schwinghamer
Manager-Retail John Caputo

MARKETING AND PROMOTION

Promotion Director Sandi Maday

CIRCULATION

Director Larry Leclair
Manager-Promotion Kim Torrance

NEWS EXECUTIVES

Editor in Chief Paul Stanway
Editor Vicky MacLean
Managing Editor Graham Dalziel

EDITORS AND MANAGERS

Business/Finance Editor Dan Healing
Cartoonist Fred Curatolo
City Editor Erik Floren
Columnist Linda Slobodian
Columnist Donna Marie Artuso
Columnist Neil Waugh
Columnist Anne Alexander
Express Editor Jeff Craig
Features Editor Tom Elsworthy
Librarian John Sinclair
News Editor Tony Salloway
Photo Department Manager Gary Bartlett
Television Editor Neal Watson
Sports Editor Scott Haskins
Wire Editor Gary Poignant

MANAGEMENT INFORMATION SERVICES

Info Service Manager George Giusti
Data Processing Manager/Research Analyst Shayne Sundholm

PRODUCTION

Manager Joe Celino
Manager-Pre Press Will Stephani
Foreman-Pressroom Robert Taylor

Market Information: Split Run; Operate database; Operate audiotex.

Mechanical available: Offset; Black and 3 ROP colors; insert accepted — preprinted; page cut-offs — 22¾".

Mechanical specifications: Type page 11¼" x 13½"; E - 8 cols, 1.17", .139" between; A - 8 cols, 1.17", .139" between; C - 8 cols, 1.17", .139" between.

Commodity Consumption (estimated): Newsprint 11.5 metric tons; widths 30", 45", 60"; black ink 222,224 pounds; color ink 57,697 pounds; single pages printed 25,882; average pages per issue 82(d), 56(sat), 152(S); single plates used 42,500.

Equipment: EDITORIAL: Front-end hardware — 50-Ap/Mac; Front-end software — QuarkXPress 3.3, P.INK/Database 2030, P.INK/Software 2.3.2; Printers — 1-NewGen, 2-QMS, 2-HP/LaserJet, 1-Tektronix/Phaser III pix; Other equipment — 2-Ricoh/fax. CLASSIFIED: Front-end hardware — CSI; Front-end software — CSI, CJ; Other equipment — Ricoh/fax. DISPLAY: Adv layout systems — CJ; Front-end hardware — 1-Ap/Mac ci; Front-end software — Mk/Managing Editor; Printers — 2-HP/LaserJet III. PRODUCTION: Typesetters — 2-APPS, 2-QMS, 1-ECR/Pelbox, 2-III/3850, 1-Tektronix/PX1; Plate exposers — 3-N/Flip Top; Plate processors — 2-Howson, 1-WL; Electronic picture desk — CD; Scanners — 1-Impro, 1-Howtek/Drum, 1-Howtek/Scanmaster Plus, 1-Pixel Craft/Scanner; Production cameras — 2-C/Spartan Horizontal; Automatic film processors — 2-LE/24, 2-P/24" On-line to III.
PRESSROOM: Line 1 — G/Metro (7 units; 3 half decks); Folders — 1-G/Double. MAILROOM: Counter stackers — 3-G/Stackmaster, 3-Id; Stuffers — 2-S/72P; Bundle tyer — 2-MLN, MLN/News 90; Wrapping singles — 3-Cyclops; Addressing machine — 3-MVP/BW50, 1-AVY/Labeler. LIBRARY: Combination — REM/200. COMMUNICATIONS: Facsimile — 2-CD/Pagefax Writer; Satellite. WIRE SERVICES: News — CP, AP, RN, SHNS, GNS; Photos — CP, AP, RN; Stock tables — TSE, VSE, ASE; Syndicates — Canada News Wire, United Media, LATS, Toronto Star, Creators, Universal Press; receiving dishes — CP. BUSINESS COMPUTERS: 3-IBM; PCs & main system networked.

FORT McMURRAY

'91 Census- 34,705; E&P '96 Est. 36,579
ABC-Town of Pub. (91): 34,706 (HH 11,295)

Fort McMurray Today

(e-mon to thur; e-fri)

Fort McMurray Today, 8550 Franklin Ave.; Bag 4008, Fort McMurray, AB T9H 3G1; tel (403) 743-8186; fax (403) 790-1006. Bowes Publishers Limited (Toronto Sun Publishing) group.

Circulation: 4,891(e); 7,107(e-fri); ABC Sept. 30, 1995.

Price: 75¢(d); $1.25(fri); $8.50/mo; $95.01/yr; $4.25 (bi-weekly).

Advertising: Modular rate 88¢(e); 88¢(e-fri).

News Service: CP. **Politics:** Independent. **Established:** 1974.

Not Published: Official holidays.

Special Editions: Brides, Minor Hockey Week (Jan); Your Money (Feb); Slogan & Logo Contest (Mar); Graduation, Mystery Face, Spring Wheels (Apr); Mother's Day, Forestry Week, Home & Garden, Tourist Guide, Trade Show Guide (May); Father's Day, Safety Week, Environment (June); Summer Sizzler (July); InterPlay, Back-to-School (Aug); Fall Trade Show, Energy Update, School's Back (Sept); Home Plan, Fire Prevention Week, Small Business Profile (Oct); Light the City Contest, Christmas Song Book, Christmas Gift Guide (Nov); Impaired Driving, Christmas Greetings, Child's Christmas Eve, New Year's Baby (Dec).

Magazines: Fort McMurray Today; TV Scene; Pony; Local TV listings; Syndicated; Newsprint.

GENERAL MANAGEMENT

Publisher/General Manager Tim O'Rourke

ADVERTISING

Manager-Retail Sandi Christensen

CIRCULATION

Manager/Supervisor Juliet Normand

NEWS EXECUTIVE

Managing Editor Darrell Skidnuk

EDITORS AND MANAGERS

City Editor Randy Provencal
Features Editor Margaret Huff
Sports Editor Bob Nyen

Market Information: Split Run; TMC.

Mechanical available: Offset; Black and 3 ROP colors; insert accepted — preprinted, most; page cut-offs — 22¾".

Mechanical specifications: Type page 13" x 21¼"; E - 6 cols, 2 1/16", ⅛" between; A - 6 cols, 2 1/16", ⅛" between; C - 9 cols, 1⅓", ⅛" between.

Commodity Consumption (estimated): Newsprint 160 metric tons; widths 27½", 13¾", 34"; black ink 8,992 pounds; color ink 2,240 pounds; single pages printed 5,020; average pages per issue 20(d); single plates used 4,400.

Equipment: EDITORIAL: Front-end hardware — Ap/Mac; Front-end software — Microsoft, QPS. CLASSIFIED: Front-end hardware — Ap/Mac; Front-end software — Baseview, QPS. DISPLAY: Adv layout systems — Ap/Mac; Front-end hardware — Ap/Mac, NEC/600; Front-end software — Mk/Ad Touch, Ap/Mac SE IIs. PRODUCTION: Typesetters — 2-M/Linotron 202W, Ap/Mac IIci; Plate exposers — 1-N; Plate processors — 1-Ic; Production cameras — 1-Acti; Automatic film processors — 1-P, 1-Fuji.
PRESSROOM: Line 1 — 7-G/Community; Folders — 1-G/Suburban 2:1. MAILROOM: Counter stackers — 1-BG/Count-O-Veyor; Bundle tyer — 2-Weld Loc/SP-505; Addressing machine — Bostich, Polar, CAT. COMMUNICATIONS: Facsimile — Canon/Fax; Satellite. WIRE SERVICES: News — CP; receiving dishes — CP. BUSINESS COMPUTERS: 4-NCR/Tower; PCs & micros networked; PCs & main system networked.

GRANDE PRAIRIE

'91 Census- 28,270; E&P '96 Est. 30,543
ABC-CZ (91): 28,271 (HH 9,855)

Daily Herald-Tribune

(e-mon to thur; e-fri)

Daily Herald-Tribune, 10604 100th St.; Bag 3000, Grande Prairie, AB T8V 6V4; tel (403) 532-1110; fax (403) 532-2120. Bowes Publishers Limited (Toronto Sun Publishing) group.

Circulation: 8,210(e); 12,157(e-fri); ABC Sept. 30, 1995.
Price: 60¢(d); 80¢(fri); $8.50/mo; $95.00/yr.
Advertising: Modular rate $1.00(e); $1.00(e-fri).
News Service: CP. **Politics:** Independent. **Established:** 1910.
Not Published: Legal holidays.
Special Editions: Business Review (Feb); On The Land (Mar); Tourist Book (Apr); Spring And Fall Car Care Sections; Today's Women; Visitor's Guide; Homes (last fri each month).
Magazines: TV Magazine; Color comics.

CORPORATE OFFICERS
Board Chairman Bruce Jackson
President W R Dempsey

GENERAL MANAGEMENT
Publisher/Business Manager Peter Woolsey

ADVERTISING
Sales Manager Brian Smart

CIRCULATION
Manager Mrs Val Hunt

NEWS EXECUTIVES
Editor Bill Scott
Managing Editor David Lassner

EDITOR AND MANAGER
City Editor Don Moon

PRODUCTION
Superintendent Brenda Haggerty
Office Manager Pat Olson

Market Information: Split Run; TMC; Operate database.
Mechanical available: Offset; Black and 3 ROP colors; insert accepted — preprinted; page cutoffs — 23".
Mechanical specifications: Type page 13¾" x 21¼"; E - 6 cols, $2\frac{1}{16}$", ⅛" between; A - 6 cols, $2\frac{1}{16}$", ⅛" between; C - 9 cols, 1⅓", ⅛" between.
Commodity Consumption (estimated): Newsprint 600 metric tons; widths 28"; black ink 7,000 kg; color ink 350 kg; single pages printed 8,263; average pages per issue 24(d); single plates used 7,500.
Equipment: EDITORIAL: Front-end hardware — Mk. CLASSIFIED: Front-end hardware — Mk; Front-end software — Ap/Mac. DISPLAY: Adv layout systems — 5-Ap/Mac; Front-end software — Ap/Mac, QPS, Aldus/PageMaker; Other equipment — 1-Mk, Datacopy. PRODUCTION: Pagination software — QPS 3.2; Typesetters — ECR/PelBox; Plate exposers — 1-Ultralite/2500, 1-N/Flip Top; Plate processors — 1-Nat, N; Production cameras — 1-Acti; Automatic film processors — 2-P.
PRESSROOM: Line 1 — 10-G/Community (8 down; 2 stack; Balloon former); Line 2 — RKW. MAILROOM: Counter stackers — 1-BG, CH; Bundle tyer — 1-Sa, 2-Sivaron; Addressing machine — 1-Am, 1-IBM. COMMUNICATIONS: Facsimile — Canon. WIRE SERVICES: News — CP; receiving dishes — CP. BUSINESS COMPUTERS: 2-NCR.

LETHBRIDGE

'91 Census- 60,975; E&P '96 Est. 65,196
ABC-CZ (91): 60,974 (HH 23,320)

The Lethbridge Herald

(e-mon to sat; S)

The Lethbridge Herald, 504 7th St. S.; PO Box 670, Lethbridge, AB T1J 3Z7; tel (403) 328-4411; fax (403) 328-4536; email lherald@lis.ab.ca; web site http://www.lis.ca.ab/lherald. Thomson Newspapers group.
Circulation: 21,417(e); 21,417(e-sat); 19,641(S); ABC Sept. 30, 1995.
Price: 75¢(d); 75¢(sat); 75¢(S); $3.10/wk; $12.40/mo; $161.20/yr.
Advertising: Modular rate $1.63(e); $1.63(e-sat); $1.63(S). **Representative:** Thomson Newspapers.
News Services: CP, CSM, THO. **Politics:** Independent. **Established:** 1907.
Not Published: New Year; Good Friday; Victoria Day; August Civic Holiday; Labor Day; Thanksgiving; Christmas.
Special Editions: Business in Review; Report '96; Recipe Round Up; AG-Expo; Home Trades Fair; Car Care; Small Business; Year-end Review Car Care; Year-end Review Vacation (Holiday); Cook Book.
Special Weekly Sections: Real Estate Showcase (digest/pony tab size) (thur); TV Scene (digest/pony tab size) (fri).
Magazines: TV Scene; Cover Story; Seniors.

CORPORATE OFFICER
President Sam Hindman

GENERAL MANAGEMENT
Publisher/General Manager D R Doram
Controller T Horii
Credit Manager T Horii
Education Service Manager S Simpson

ADVERTISING
Manager Ryan McAdams
Manager-National Ryan McAdams

TELECOMMUNICATIONS
Audiotex Manager T Horii

CIRCULATION
Manager S Simpson

NEWS EXECUTIVE
Managing Editor Bill Whitelaw

EDITORS AND MANAGERS
Agriculture Editor Ric Swihart
Books Editor Bill Whitelaw
Business Editor Ric Swihart
City Editor Gord Smiley
Editorial Page Editor Bill Whitelaw
Entertainment Editor Pat Sullivan
News Editor Gary Harker
Outdoors Editor Garry Allison
Photo Department Manager David Rossiter
Sports Editor Randy Jensen
Travel Editor Bill Whitelaw

PRODUCTION
Foreman Composing Room J Price
Foreman-Pressroom L Chogi
Foreman-Mailroom R Parascak

Market Information: Zoned editions; TMC; ADS; Operate audiotex; Electronic edition.
Mechanical available: Offset; Black and 3 ROP colors; insert accepted — preprinted; page cutoffs — 22¾".
Mechanical specifications: Type page 12⅝" x 21½"; E - 6 cols, $2\frac{1}{16}$", ⅛" between; A - 6 cols, $2\frac{1}{16}$", ⅛" between; C - 10 cols, 1½", $\frac{1}{16}$" between.
Commodity Consumption (estimated): Newsprint 1,723 metric tons; widths 25"; 34"; black ink 45,000 pounds; color ink 4,500 pounds; single pages printed 152,000; average pages per issue 39.40(d); single plates used 24,120.
Equipment: EDITORIAL: Front-end hardware — 2-DEC/486-33 Mhz dx MTE Fileserver; Front-end software — CText, QPS, SMS, CText/AFM; Printers — 2-Genicom/Model 3810 SP; Other equipment — 4-RSK/Tandy 100. CLASSIFIED: Front-end hardware — DEC/486-33 Mhz dx MTE Fileserver; Front-end software — CText/AFM, CText/Standard Class System, Hydrafax; Printers — Genicom/3810 SP. DISPLAY: Adv layout systems — SCS/Layout 8000(6.06); Front-end hardware — Ap/Mac, DEC; Front-end software — QPS 3.2, Adobe/Photoshop 2.5, Adobe/Illustrator 5.0, Archetype/Designer, Multi-Ad/Creator 3.5; Printers — 2-Ap/Mac LaserPrinter, 1-QMS/Printer. PRODUCTION: Pagination software — QuarkXPress, Microsoft/Windows 3.1; Typesetters — 2-V/6000; Plate exposers — 2-N; Plate processors — Nat/A-250; Production cameras — C/Spartan III; Automatic film processors — LE; Shrink lenses — 2-CK Optical. PRESSROOM: Line 1 — 7-G/Urbanite (1-3 color unit); Press control system — Fin. MAILROOM: Bundle tyer — 3-MLN/2; Wrapping singles — 1-MLN/MS-7; Addressing machine — 1-Am. WIRE SERVICES: News — CP Datafile; Photos — CP; Stock tables — CP Datastocks; Syndicates — THO; receiving dishes — size-6ft, CP. BUSINESS COMPUTERS: IBM/Sys 34.

MEDICINE HAT

'91 Census- 43,625; E&P '96 Est. 46,757
ABC-CZ (91): 43,625 (HH 16,975)

Medicine Hat News

(e-mon to sat)

Medicine Hat News, 3257 Dunmore Rd. S.E.; PO Box 10, Medicine Hat, AB T1A 7E6; tel (403) 527-1101; fax (403) 527-6029. Southam Newspapers group.
Circulation: 13,808(e); 13,808(e-sat); ABC Sept. 30, 1995.
Price: 50¢(d); 50¢(sat); $2.25/wk; $112.50/yr.
Advertising: Modular rate 65¢(e); 65¢(e-sat). **Representative:** Southam Newspapers.
News Services: CP, NYT, SOU. **Politics:** Independent. **Established:** 1885.
Special Editions: Progress, Agriculture (Mar); Homes & Gardens (Apr); Tourist (May); Stampede (July); Education (Aug); Fall Shopping (Sept); Car Care (Oct); Christmas (Dec).

CORPORATE OFFICER
President William Ardell

GENERAL MANAGEMENT
Publisher John Weimer
Business Manager Ron Turner

ADVERTISING
Director-Sales/Service Clarence Heringer

MARKETING AND PROMOTION
Manager-Marketing Clarence Heringer
Manager-Newspaper Promotion Susan Guerra

CIRCULATION
Manager-Readers Sales/Service Perry Gagley

NEWS EXECUTIVE
Managing Editor Gordon Wright

EDITORS AND MANAGERS
Photo Department Manager Frank Webber
Society Editor Angela Stubbs

PRODUCTION
Manager W B Hartley

Market Information: Split Run; TMC.
Mechanical available: Offset; Black and 3 ROP colors; insert accepted — preprinted; page cutoffs — 22¾".
Mechanical specifications: Type page 13" x $21\frac{9}{16}$"; E - 6 cols, $2\frac{1}{16}$", ⅛" between; A - 6 cols, $2\frac{1}{16}$", ⅛" between; C - 6 cols, $2\frac{1}{16}$", ⅛" between.
Commodity Consumption (estimated): Newsprint 660 metric tons; widths 27", 13½"; black ink 7,500 kg; single pages printed 8,409; average pages per issue 27.8(d); single plates used 8,000.
Equipment: EDITORIAL: Front-end hardware — 23-RSK/Tandy 3000, 9-RSK/Tandy 4000, VGM/100; Front-end software — CText/Ventura; Printers — 2-Ap/Mac NTX; Other equipment — Cornerstone/Monitors. CLASSIFIED: Front-end hardware — 5-RSK/Tandy 3000, VGM/100; Front-end software — CText. DISPLAY: Adv layout systems — 4-Ap/Mac II, 1-Ap/Mac si, 1-Ap/Mac Quadra 650, 1-Ap/Mac SE 30, 1-Ap/Mac SE; Printers — 2-Ap/Mac IIg, 1-QMS/860 plus; Other equipment — HP/ScanJet IIC scanner, Abaton/300. PRODUCTION: Typesetters — SII/LaserWriter NTX; Plate exposers — 1-3M/Pyrofax; Electronic picture desk — CD; Production cameras — 1-B/Caravel; Automatic film processors — AG/5400; Shrink lenses — CK Optical/SQU-7. PRESSROOM: Line 1 — 10-G/Community. MAILROOM: Stuffers — KAN/480; Bundle tyer — 2-Sa/S1120, 1-MLN, 1-Ca. WIRE SERVICES: News — CP, SNS; Photos — CP; receiving dishes — CP. BUSINESS COMPUTERS: Applications: Payroll, Circ, Adv; PCs & micros networked.

RED DEER

'91 Census- 58,135; E&P '96 Est. 62,813
ABC-CZ (91): 58,134 (HH 21,450)

Red Deer Advocate

(e-mon to thur; e-fri; e-sat)

Red Deer Advocate, 2950 Bremner Ave.; PO Bag 5200, Red Deer, AB T4N 5G3; tel (403) 343-2400; fax (403) 341-4772. Trinity (N.A.) Holdings Inc. group.
Circulation: 19,756(e); 23,947(e-fri); 19,756(e-sat); ABC Sept. 30, 1995.
Price: 61¢(d); 89¢(fri); 89¢(sat); $20.05/mo (mail), $10.90/mo (carrier); $237.54/yr (mail), $124.26/yr (carrier, prepaid).
Advertising: Modular rate $1.67(e); $1.78(e-fri); $1.67(e-sat).
News Services: CP, AP, SHNS. **Politics:** Independent. **Established:** 1901.
Not Published: New Year; Good Friday; Labor Day; Thanksgiving; Christmas; Victoria Day; Canada Day; Heritage Day.
Special Edition: Wide range of specials.
Special Weekly Sections: Local Sports (mon); Community Focus (tues); Wheels (wed); Food (thur); Homes, Travel, Religion, Books, Finance (sat); Entertainment, Outdoor, Gardening (seasonal).
Magazines: TV Today (fri); Color Comics (sat).

GENERAL MANAGEMENT
Publisher Howard Janzen
Controller Bonnie Thiele

ADVERTISING
Manager-Retail Bob Carey

MARKETING AND PROMOTION
Manager-Marketing & Promotion Greg Lutes

CIRCULATION
Manager Allan Melbourne

NEWS EXECUTIVE
Managing Editor Joe McLaughlin

MANAGEMENT INFORMATION SERVICES
Management Info Services Manager David Lucas

PRODUCTION
Manager Derek Olinek

Market Information: Split Run; TMC.
Mechanical available: offset; Black and 3 ROP colors; insert accepted — preprinted, envelopes & cards 8" x 11"; page cut-offs — 22¾".
Mechanical specifications: Type page 11.7" x 21½"; E - 6 cols, $1\frac{13}{16}$", ⅛" between; A - 6 cols, $1\frac{13}{16}$", ⅛" between; C - 9 cols, 1⅛", ⅛" between.
Commodity Consumption (estimated): Newsprint 45 grams short tons; 1,500 metric tons; widths 30", 10¼"; black ink 50,000 pounds; color ink 20,000 pounds; single pages printed 9,010; average pages per issue 24(d), 32(sat); single plates used 15,000.
Equipment: EDITORIAL: Front-end hardware — Ap; Front-end software — QPS, Baseview/NewsEdit; Printers — Ap/Mac LaserPrinter; Other equipment — 2-X/Copier. CLASSIFIED: Front-end hardware — IBM; Front-end software — Graph-X. DISPLAY: Adv layout systems — Ap; Front-end hardware — Ap; Front-end software — QPS, Multi-Ad; Printers — Ap/Mac LaserPrinter; Other equipment — Syquest/drives. PRODUCTION: Plate exposers — 2-N; Plate processors — WL/300; Electronic picture desk — CD; Scanners — Nikon; Production cameras — 1-Acti/24B, 1-Acti/204; Automatic film processors — P/26 RTR; Color separation equipment (conventional) — CD, Adobe/Photoshop.
PRESSROOM: Line 1 — 40-G/Suburban, 32-G/Urbanite single width; Folders — 2-G; Reels and stands — 2-G/Urbanite, 2-G/Suburban. MAILROOM: Counter stackers — KAN; Stuffers — 2-KAN/480 Inserting Machines; Bundle tyer — 2-Gd/Oval Strapping Model EX-415; Wrapping singles — 1-Poly-Bag; Other mailroom equipment — MM/Saddle Stitcher. LIBRARY: Combination — Non-electronic Filing. COMMUNICATIONS: Facsimile — Canon. WIRE SERVICES: News — NAS, DF, CN Laser Photo, CP (2 lines), CAN Newswire, Envoy 80 Govt. Services; Stock tables — CP, Datastox; Syndicates — SHNS; CP. BUSINESS COMPUTERS: Sun/Sparc 20; Applications: Sun PBS; PCs & micros networked; PCs & main system networked.

BRITISH COLUMBIA

CRANBROOK

'91 Census- 16,445; E&P '96 Est. 17,745
ABC-CZ (91): 16,447 (HH 6,230)

The Daily Townsman

(e-mon to fri)

The Daily Townsman, 822 Cranbrook St. N., Cranbrook, BC V1C 3R9; tel (604) 426-5201; fax (604) 426-5003; web site http://www.sterlingnews.com/cranbrook. Sterling Newspapers (Hollinger Inc.) group.
Circulation: 4,397(e); ABC Sept. 30, 1995.
Price: 51¢(d); $7.00/mo; $84.00/yr.
Advertising: Modular rate 86¢(e).
News Service: SNS. **Politics:** Independent. **Established:** 1946 (Daily 1969).
Special Edition: Community Update (Mar).
Special Weekly Section: East Kootenay Weekly (wed).
Magazines: Real Estate; TV Guide (fri).

GENERAL MANAGEMENT
Publisher Nigel Lark

ADVERTISING
Director Cina Wales

CIRCULATION
Director Laura Butler

NEWS EXECUTIVE
Editor David Sands

PRODUCTION
Manager M Barnhardt

III-4 British Columbia

Market Information: TMC.
Mechanical available: Web Offset; Black and 3 ROP colors; insert accepted — preprinted, all sizes up to 13" x 10"; page cut-offs — 22½".
Mechanical specifications: Type page 13" x 21⅜"; E - 6 cols, 2¹⁄₁₆", ⅛" between; A - 6 cols, 2¹⁄₁₆", ⅛" between; C - 6 cols, 2¹⁄₁₆", ⅛" between.
Commodity Consumption (estimated): average pages per issue 12(d).
Equipment: EDITORIAL: Front-end hardware — 5-Ap/Mac II; Front-end software — QuarkXPress. CLASSIFIED: Front-end hardware — 2-Ap/Mac II. DISPLAY: Adv layout systems — Multi-Ad; Front-end hardware — 5-Ap/Mac II; Front-end software — Multi-Ad/Creator. PRODUCTION: Production cameras — 1-N; Automatic film processors — P.
PRESSROOM: Line 1 — 6-HI/Offset. MAILROOM: Addressing machine — Okidata/Printer. WIRE SERVICES: News — Sterling News Service. BUSINESS COMPUTERS: PCs & micros networked.

DAWSON CREEK

'91 Census- 10,980; E&P '96 Est. 11,874

Peace River Block News

(e-mon to fri)

Peace River Block News, 901-100 Ave., Dawson Creek, BC V1G 1W2; tel (604) 782-4888; fax (604) 782-6770; email jhainsw@pris.bc.ca; web site http://www.sterlingnews.com/peace. Sterling Newspapers (Hollinger Inc.) group.
Circulation: 2,548(e); Sworn June 22, 1995.
Price: 60¢(d); $105.00/yr.
Advertising: Modular rate 92¢(e).
News Service: Sterling News Service. **Established:** 1930.
Special Editions: Transportation; Bridal; Progress; Farming; Christmas; Vacation; Tourist.

GENERAL MANAGEMENT
Publisher Margaret Forbes
ADVERTISING
Director Brian Bredesen
NEWS EXECUTIVE
Editor Jeremy Hainsworth

Market Information: Zoned editions; Split Run; TMC.
Mechanical available: Offset; Black and 3 ROP colors; insert accepted — preprinted; page cut-offs — 21".
Mechanical specifications: Type page 13" x 21⅜"; E - 6 cols, 2¹⁄₁₆", ⅛" between.
Commodity Consumption (estimated): Newsprint 265 metric tons; widths 27½"; black ink 2,200 pounds; color ink 725 pounds; single pages printed 4,975; average pages per issue 12(d); single plates used 11,000.
Equipment: EDITORIAL: Front-end hardware — Ap/Mac; Printers — Ap/Mac LaserWriter II. CLASSIFIED: Front-end hardware — 1-Ap/Mac; Printers — Ap/Mac LaserWriter II. DISPLAY: Adv layout systems — 4-Ap/Mac; Printers — Ap/Mac LaserWriter IIg. PRODUCTION: Pagination software — QuarkXPress 3.3; OCR software — COM/Headliner; Plate processors — Ajex International; Production cameras — K; Automatic film processors — P.
PRESSROOM: Line 1 — KP. MAILROOM: Counter stackers — KAN; Stuffers — 1-KAN/Inserter; Bundle tyer — 1-Weld Loc. COMMUNICATIONS: Facsimile — 1-Savin. WIRE SERVICES: News — Sterling News Service. BUSINESS COMPUTERS: Laser 4865x-25.

FORT ST. JOHN

'91 Census- 14,155; E&P '96 Est. 15,401
ABC-CZ (91): 14,156 (HH 5,180)

Alaska Highway Daily News

(e-mon to fri)

Alaska Highway Daily News, 9916 98th St., Fort St. John, BC V1J 3T8; tel (604) 785-5631; fax (604) 785-3522; email theeditor.ahn@awinc.com; web site http://sterling.com/alaska. Sterling Newspapers (Hollinger Inc.) group.
Circulation: 2,998(e); ABC Sept. 30, 1995.
Price: 60¢(d); $6.50/mo (carrier); $85.00/yr (mail), $66.00/yr (carrier), $150.00/yr (foreign).
Advertising: Modular rate 93¢(e).
News Service: SNS. **Politics:** Independent. **Established:** weekly 1943, daily 1976.
Not Published: Statutory Holidays.
Special Edition: Weekly regional (S w/TMC).

GENERAL MANAGEMENT
Publisher Bruce Lantz
ADVERTISING
Manager Sandy Lavac
CIRCULATION
Manager Bert Gammage
NEWS EXECUTIVE
Managing Editor Tom Wilkinson
EDITOR AND MANAGER
Sports Editor John Geary

Market Information: TMC.
Mechanical available: Offset; Black and 3 ROP colors; insert accepted — preprinted; page cut-offs — 22¾".
Mechanical specifications: Type page 13" x 21½"; E - 6 cols, 2¹⁄₁₆", ⅛" between; A - 6 cols, 2¹⁄₁₆", ⅛" between; C - 8 cols, 1½", ⅛" between.
Commodity Consumption (estimated): average pages per issue 16(d).
Equipment: EDITORIAL: Front-end hardware — 1-Mk/Linotype, RSK, 1-Ap/Mac, 3-Mk/1100, Mk/1100 Plus, 1-Mk/1100 2 Plus, 1-Mk/Remote 1100 2 Plus. CLASSIFIED: Front-end hardware — 1-Mk/1100. PRODUCTION: Typesetters — 2-COM/Unisetter-High Range; Plate exposers — 1-N/Flip Top; Scanners — COM; Production cameras — 1-B/Caravel; Automatic film processors — 1-Rapidoprint/DD 2666. MAILROOM: Bundle tyer — 1-Tom/Tying machine; Addressing machine — RSK/Tandy-3000. WIRE SERVICES: News — SNS. BUSINESS COMPUTERS: RSK/Tandy 3000; Applications: Billing, Carriers - ABC Audit report data, Circ.

KAMLOOPS

'91 Census- 67,060; E&P '96 Est. 74,029
ABC-CZ (91): 67,057 (HH 24,735)

Kamloops Daily News

(e-mon to sat)

Kamloops Daily News, 393 Seymour St., Kamloops, BC V2C 6P6; tel (250) 372-2331; fax (604) 374-3884; web site http://www.netshop.bc.ca/dailynews/html. Southam Newspapers group.
Circulation: 16,078(e); 16,078(e-sat); ABC Sept. 30, 1995.
Price: 55¢(d); 55¢(sat).
Advertising: Modular rate 85¢(e); 85¢(e-sat).
News Services: CP, SOU. **Established:** 1937.
Magazines: Spotlight; TV Time.

GENERAL MANAGEMENT
Publisher Brian Butterf
Controller Kelvin Stretch
ADVERTISING
Manager Gord Wilkinson
CIRCULATION
Manager Dale Brin
NEWS EXECUTIVE
Editor M G Rothenburger
PRODUCTION
Manager Pat Grove-White

Market Information: TMC.
Mechanical available: Offset; Black and 3 ROP colors; insert accepted — preprinted; page cut-offs — 22¾".
Mechanical specifications: Type page 13" x 21½"; E - 6 cols, 2¹⁄₁₆", ⅛" between; A - 6 cols, 2¹⁄₁₆", ⅛" between; C - 6 cols, 2¹⁄₁₆", ⅛" between.
Commodity Consumption (estimated): Newsprint 1,400 metric tons; widths 27½", 32", 34"; black ink 26,400 pounds; color ink 3,725 pounds; single pages printed 10,000; average pages per issue 33.5(d); single plates used 7,000.
Equipment: EDITORIAL: Front-end hardware — RSK/Tandy 3000 Network, CText, RSK/Tandy 4000-Ventura; Front-end software — RSK/Tandy VGM 100. CLASSIFIED: Front-end hardware — 2-Ap/Mac SE, RSK/Tandy 3000 Network, CText; Front-end software — RSK/Tandy VGM 100; Other equipment — 1-Ap/Mac LaserPrinter NTX. DISPLAY: Adv layout systems — 1-Ap/Mac II, SCS/Layout 8000; Front-end software — DEC/VT-100; Other equipment — 1-Abaton/Flatbed scanner. PRODUCTION: Typesetters — 2-Ap/Mac Laser-Printer NTX, 5-Ap/Mac II, 1-Ap/Mac SE; Plate exposers — 3M/Pyrofax; Production cameras — C, DS/Vertical 670, Acti/225-Horizontal; Automatic film processors — Danagraph/Processor; Color separation equipment (conventional) — WDS.
PRESSROOM: Line 1 — 12-G/Community; Folders — 2-G/SE. MAILROOM: Stuffers — KAN/320-6 Station; Bundle tyer — 2-Gd/Constellation. COMMUNICATIONS: Facsimile — Ricoh/Rapicom 320; satellite. WIRE SERVICES: News — CP, SOU, CP Stocks, CP Agate (Sports); Service Bureau Via Satellite. BUSINESS COMPUTERS: MAI, Service Bureau Via Satellite, PCs; Applications: Accts payable, Accts receivable, Payroll, Gen ledger, Equipment file, Circ.

KELOWNA

'91 Census- 75,950; E&P '96 Est. 87,518
ABC-CZ (91): 71,496 (HH 27,971)

The Daily Courier

(e-mon to fri; m-sat; S)

The Daily Courier, 550 Doyle Ave., Kelowna, BC V1Y 7V1; tel (604) 762-4445; fax (604) 762-3866; email metro@ok.bc.ca, cybered@ok.bc.ca (internet editor); web site http://www.ok.bc.ca. Thomson Newspapers group.
Circulation: 17,119(e); 17,119(m-sat); 16,369(S); ABC Sept. 30, 1995.
Price: 50¢(d); 75¢(sat); 50¢(S); $2.75/wk.
Representative: Thomson Newspapers.
News Services: CP, AP, THO, RN, AFP, CSM. **Politics:** Independent. **Established:** 1904.
Note: Advertising is based on a group modular agate line rate of $2.32. Individual newspaper rate not made available.
Not Published: Statutory holidays.
Advertising not accepted: Sexually suggestive or discriminating.
Special Weekly Sections: Golf (wed); Enviroment, Fashion (thur); Seniors (fri); Arts, Weekend Outings (sat); Cookin', Travel, Trends (S).
Magazines: Westside Weekly (wed); TV Scene, Westside Weekly (fri).

GENERAL MANAGEMENT
Publisher/General Manager Jonathan Franklin
Accountant Sandra Dinan
Office Manager Debbi Beauchamp
ADVERTISING
Manager Malcolm Gunn
Manager-Special Projects Ron Harding
Manager-Supervisor Classified Maxine Grigg
MARKETING AND PROMOTION
Director-Marketing Paul Moore
CIRCULATION
Director Gerry Jackson
Asst Manager Dean Warner
NEWS EXECUTIVES
Editor Al Hogan
Managing Editor-News Jeff Melnychuk
EDITORS AND MANAGERS
Business Editor Tom Wilson
Editorial Page Editor Dave Henshaw
Entertainment Editor Andre Wetjen
Life Editor Karin Maltby
Metro Editor Allan Coyle
Photo Editor Kip Fransz
Sports Editor Lorne White
Westside Editor David Marsden
MANAGEMENT INFORMATION SERVICES
Manager-Info Service Jack Morrison
PRODUCTION
Manager-Pre Press Grant Hallgrimson
Foreman Don Whiting
Foreman-Press Bob Warner

Market Information: Zoned editions; TMC; ADS; Electronic edition.
Mechanical available: Offset; Black and 3 ROP colors; insert accepted — preprinted; page cut-offs — 21½".
Mechanical specifications: Type page 13" x 21¼"; E - 6 cols, 2¹⁄₁₆", ⅛" between.
Commodity Consumption (estimated): Newsprint 1,560 short tons; widths 28", 33"; black ink 39,600 pounds; color ink 15,840 pounds; single pages printed 400,000; average pages per issue 28(d), 40(S); single plates used 16,800.
Equipment: EDITORIAL: Front-end hardware — Ap/Mac; Front-end software — QuarkXPress 3.3; Printers — Panther/Pro, DEC/VT 1200. CLASSIFIED: Front-end hardware — Ap/Mac, DEC/PC; Front-end software — QuarkXPress, CText. DISPLAY: Adv layout systems — Mk/Ad Director; Front-end hardware — PBS; Printers — ATT/477, DEC/VT 400. PRODUCTION: Pagination software — QuarkXPress 3.3; OCR software — Caere/OmniPage 3.0; Typesetters — Panther/Pro 46; Electronic picture desk — CD; Scanners — Nikon/3510 AF, Polaroid/SprintScan, Microtek; Automatic film processors — Fuji/360F Graphic Processor, Kodamatic/520 Processor; Shrink lenses — APO/Nikkor 480mm; Color separation equipment (conventional) — ECR/Autokon 1000-DE; Digital color separation equipment — Ap/Mac.
PRESSROOM: Line 1 — 6-G/Community, 2-G/Community (VOP;Balloon); Press drives — Fin/50 Hp & 60 Hp motors; Folders — G/SC 518; Press control system — Fin. MAILROOM: Bundle tyer — 3-Gd/Oval Strap; Addressing machine — 1-ATT. COMMUNICATIONS: Facsimile — Canon/L 770 Fax. WIRE SERVICES: News — CP, THO; Photos — CP; Syndicates — Miller, United Features, Toronto Star, LATS, NYT, SHNS; receiving dishes — CP.

KIMBERLEY

'91 Census- 6,530; E&P '96 Est. 6,896

The Daily Bulletin

(e-mon to fri)

The Daily Bulletin, 335 Spokane St., Kimberley, BC V1A 1Y9; tel (604) 427-5333; fax (604) 427-5336; web site http://www.sterlingpress.com/kimberley. Sterling Newspapers (Hollinger Inc.) group.
Circulation: 1,822(e); Sworn May, 1994.
Price: 47¢(d).
Advertising: Modular rate 75¢(e).
News Service: SNS. **Politics:** Independent. **Established:** 1932.
Not Published: Statutory holidays.
Special Editions: Special Merchant Shopping Events; Julyfest; K.I.O.T.A.C.; Winterfest.
Special Weekly Sections: East Kootenay Weekly (wed); Real Estate Guide (wkly).

GENERAL MANAGEMENT
Publisher Bev Middlebrook
ADVERTISING
Salesperson Bev Middlebrook
CIRCULATION
Director Betty Ann Helland
NEWS EXECUTIVE
Editor Crystalee Dovan
PRODUCTION
Manager B Barnhardt

Market Information: Split Run; TMC.
Mechanical available: Offset; Black and 3 ROP colors; insert accepted — preprinted; page cut-offs — 23".
Mechanical specifications: Type page 12¾" x 21⅜"; E - 6 cols, 2¹⁄₁₆", ⅛" between; A - 6 cols, 2¹⁄₁₆", ⅛" between; C - 6 cols, 2¹⁄₁₆", ⅛" between.
Commodity Consumption (estimated): average pages per issue 12(d).
Equipment: EDITORIAL: Front-end hardware — Ap/Mac II. WIRE SERVICES: News — Sterling News Service. BUSINESS COMPUTERS: PCs & micros networked.

NANAIMO

'91 Census- 60,130; E&P '96 Est. 68,982
ABC-CZ (91): 60,129 (HH 23,735)

Nanaimo Daily Free Press

(m-mon to sat)

Nanaimo Daily Free Press, 223 Commercial St.; Box 69, Nanaimo, BC V9R 5K5; tel (604) 753-3451; fax (604) 753-8730; email freepress@island.ner. Thomson Newspapers group.
Circulation: 12,700(m); 12,700(m-sat); ABC Sept. 30, 1995.
Price: 70¢(d); 60¢(sat); $2.30/wk; $119.60/yr.
Advertising: Modular rate $1.17(m); $1.17(m-sat). **Representative:** Thomson Newspapers.
News Service: CP. **Established:** 1874.
Note: Effective Aug. 8, 1995, this publication changed its publishing plan from (e-mon to sat) to (m-mon to sat)
Special Weekly Section: TV Scene (fri).
Magazines: Island Seniors, Nanaimo Homes (monthly).

GENERAL MANAGEMENT
Publisher/General Manager James W Rice
ADVERTISING
Manager Rick Methor
CIRCULATION
Manager Susan Fowler
NEWS EXECUTIVE
Managing Editor John Kimantas

Copyright ©1996 by the Editor & Publisher Co.

British Columbia III-5

EDITOR AND MANAGER
City Editor Walter Cordery
PRODUCTION
Foreman-Composing F Wright

Market Information: Split Run; ADS.
Mechanical available: Offset; Black and 3 ROP colors; insert accepted — preprinted; page cut-offs — 21½".
Mechanical specifications: Type page 14¼" x 21½"; E - 6 cols, 2", ⅛" between; A - 6 cols, 2", ⅛" between; C - 9 cols, 1⅜", ⅛" between.
Commodity Consumption (estimated): Newsprint 1,100 metric tons; average pages per issue 18(d).
Equipment: EDITORIAL: Front-end hardware — COM/One System; Printers — 3-AX; Other equipment — Ap/Mac. CLASSIFIED: Front-end hardware — COM. DISPLAY: Other equipment — COM. PRODUCTION: Scanners — COM; Production cameras — 1-B; Automatic film processors — 1-Caravelle; Color separation equipment (conventional) — CD; Digital color separation equipment — Nikon.
PRESSROOM: Line 1 — 9-G/Community; Folders — G/Quarter, G/2:1. WIRE SERVICES: News — CP; Photos — CP; receiving dishes — CP. BUSINESS COMPUTERS: ATT.

NELSON

'91 Census- 8,760; E&P '96 Est. 9,593
ABC-CZ (91): 8,760 (HH 3,525)

Nelson Daily News
(e-mon to fri)

Nelson Daily News, 266 Baker St., Nelson, BC V1L 4H3; tel (604) 352-3552; fax (604) 352-2418; web site http://www.sterling news.com/nelson. Sterling Newspapers (Hollinger Inc.) group.
Circulation: 4,272(e); ABC Mar. 31, 1995.
Price: 75¢(d); $9.10/mo; $101.65/yr.
Advertising: Modular rate $1.02(e). **Representative:** Sterling Newspapers.
News Service: Sterling News Service. **Politics:** Independent. **Established:** 1902.
Not Published: Dec 26 and statutory holidays.
Special Editions: Nelson Fact Book, Environmentally Speaking (Jan); Bridal Guide, Environmentally Speaking, Nelson in Review (Feb); Kootenay Country Trade Contractor & Home Improvement Guide, Hunting & Fishing Guide, Seniors (The Golden Outlook), Environmentally Speaking (Mar); Kootenay Visitor, Kootenay Country Coupon Book, Environmentally Speaking (Apr); Tee-Rific Golf Newspaper, Kootenay Circle Tour Trip Tips, Chamber of Commerce/Daily News "Get Lost in Nelson" Map, Environmentally Speaking, Seniors (The Golden Outlook) (May); Graduation Supplement, Kootenay Pictorial, Canada Day Celebration, Mid-Summer Bonspiel Guide, Environmentally Speaking, Tee-Rific Golf Newspaper (June); RCMP/Police Salute To Law Enforcement, Nelson Daily News Crossword Book, Environmentally Speaking, Tee-Rific Golf Newspaper (July); End of Summer (Back-to-School), Nelson Daily News Take Out Food Guide, Environmentally Speaking, Tee-Rific Golf Newspaper (Aug); Nelson & Area Clubs & Organizations-Fall 1996, Kootenay Visitor, Environmentally Speaking, Seniors (The Golden Book) (Sept); Kootenay Country Trade Contractor & Home Improvement Guide, Hunting & Fishing Guide, Environmentally Speaking, Bridal Guide (Oct); Kootenay Holly-Days Gift Guides, Environmentally Speaking (Nov); Environmentally Speaking, Seniors (The Golden Outlook), Shop 'Til You Drop, Santa's Letters, Christmas Greetings, Christmas Song Book, Holiday Cookbook (Dec).
Magazine: West Kootenay Advertiser.

CORPORATE OFFICER
President David Radler
GENERAL MANAGEMENT
Publisher L R (Verne) Shaull
Office Manager Gwen Thompson
ADVERTISING
Manager Colin Seed
CIRCULATION
Manager Mike McKinney
NEWS EXECUTIVE
Managing Editor David Howe
EDITOR AND MANAGER
Sports Editor Bruce Fuhr
PRODUCTION
Supervisor Warren Garner
Foreman-Pressroom Keiron Chapman

Market Information: Zoned editions; TMC.
Mechanical available: Offset; Black and 3 ROP colors; insert accepted — preprinted, catalogs-single envelopes.
Mechanical specifications: Type page 13" x 21½"; E - 6 cols, 2¹⁄₁₆", ⅛" between; A - 8 cols, 2¹⁄₁₆", ⅛" between; C - 8 cols, 1½", ⅛" between.
Commodity Consumption (estimated): Newsprint 480 metric tons; widths 27¾", 13⅝", 34"; single pages printed 4,680; average pages per issue 24(d); single plates used 17,000.
Equipment: EDITORIAL: Front-end software — Ap/Mac. CLASSIFIED: Printers — 2-AX, 2-Ap/Mac Plus LaserPrinter. DISPLAY: Adv layout systems — 2-Ap; Printers — 1-Ap/LaserPrinter. PRODUCTION: Typesetters — 3-Ap, 1-Ap/LaserPrinter; Plate exposers — 2-N; Plate processors — 1-Nat; Production cameras — 2-B; Automatic film processors — 1-LE; Shrink lenses — 1-CK Optical/SQU-7.
PRESSROOM: Line 1 — 5-G/Community; Folders — 1-G. MAILROOM: Bundle tyer — 2-Sa; Addressing machine — 1-Ap, 1-Wm. WIRE SERVICES: News — SNS; Syndicates — SNS. BUSINESS COMPUTERS: 1-Ap, 1-IPC/TVM.

PENTICTON

'91 Census- 27,260; E&P '96 Est. 30,587
ABC-CZ (91): 28,517 (HH 12,210)

Penticton Herald
(m-mon to sat)

Penticton Herald, 186 Nanaimo Ave. W., Penticton, BC V2A 1N4; tel (604) 492-4002; fax (604) 492-2403. Thomson Newspapers group.
Circulation: 8,639(m); 8,639(m-sat); ABC Sept. 30, 1995.
Price: 50¢(d); 75¢(sat); $2.40/wk; $10.40/mo; $117.00/yr.
Representative: Canadian Newspapers Limited.
News Service: CP. **Politics:** Independent. **Established:** 1910.
Note: Advertising is based on a group modular agate line rate of $2.32. Individual newspaper rate not made available.
Not Published: Jan 1; Apr 1; May 23; July 1; Aug 1; Sept 5; Oct 10; Nov 11; Dec 25; Dec 26.
Advertising not accepted: At newspaper's discretion.
Special Editions: Progress, Home Improvement (Mar); Home Improvement (Apr, Sept.).
Special Weekly Section: Food (mon).
Magazines: Weekly TV, Weekly Real Estate Tab (thur).

GENERAL MANAGEMENT
Publisher/General Manager Jane Howard-Coady
ADVERTISING
Manager Andre Martin
CIRCULATION
Manager Jerry Jackson
NEWS EXECUTIVE
Managing Editor Mike Turner
PRODUCTION
Foreman-Pressroom Grant Hallgrimson

Market Information: TMC; ADS.
Mechanical available: Offset; Black and 3 ROP colors; insert accepted — preprinted, coupons, envelopes, small catalogues; page cut-offs — 21½".
Mechanical specifications: Type page 13" x 21½"; E - 6 cols, 2¹⁄₁₆", ⅛" between; A - 6 cols, 2¹⁄₁₆", ⅛" between; C - 9 cols, 1⅓", ⅛" between.
Commodity Consumption (estimated): Newsprint 330 metric tons; widths 27½", 13¾"; black ink 2,400 pounds; color ink 200 pounds; single pages printed 6,400; average pages per issue 20(d); single plates used 13,000.
Equipment: EDITORIAL: Front-end hardware — Ap/Mac; Front-end software — QPS. CLASSIFIED: Front-end hardware — CText. DISPLAY: Adv layout systems — Mk/Ad Manager; Front-end hardware — Ap/Mac; Front-end software — QuarkXPress. PRODUCTION: Pagination software — QPS; Typesetters — Panther; Production cameras — Acti; Automatic film processors — Fuji.
PRESSROOM: Press control system — Manual. MAILROOM: Bundle tyer — 1-Gd/OVL; Addressing machine — ATT. LIBRARY: Combination — Bound Files, 1-Microfilm Machine. WIRE SERVICES: News — CP; Syndicates — CP, AP, Star Features, TV Data, Toronto Star, United Features, Miller; receiving dishes — CP. BUSINESS COMPUTERS: ATT, Primax/212; Applications: All Functions; PCs & micros networked; PCs & main system networked.

PORT ALBERNI

'91 Census- 18,405; E&P '96 Est. 19,691
ABC (91): 18,403 (HH 7,065)

Alberni Valley Times
(e-mon to fri)

Alberni Valley Times, 4918 Napier St.; PO Box 400, Port Alberni, BC V9Y 7N1; tel (604) 723-8171; fax (604) 723-0586; email avtimes@port.island.net; web site http://port.island.net/~avtimes. Sterling Newspapers (Hollinger Inc.) group.
Circulation: 6,295(e); ABC Sept. 30, 1995.
Price: 56¢(d); $9.00/mo; $108.00/yr.
Advertising: Modular rate $1.09(e).
News Service: SNS. **Politics:** Conservative. **Established:** 1967.
Not Published: Statutory holidays; Easter Monday.
Special Editions: Car Care (Spring & Fall); Travel (Feb); Progress, New Auto Supplement (Mar); Vacation (May); Salmon Derby (July, Aug); New Auto Supplement (Oct); Remembrance Day (Nov); Christmas (Dec).
Magazine: Weekender Magazine (own, offset) (fri).

CORPORATE OFFICER
President David R Radler
GENERAL MANAGEMENT
Publisher/General Manager N Hannaford
Credit Manager N Hannaford
Purchasing Agent R Atterbury
CIRCULATION
Manager J Richardson
NEWS EXECUTIVE
Managing Editor Rob Diotte
EDITOR AND MANAGER
Sports Editor Gary Banys
PRODUCTION
Manager R Atterbury
Foreman-Composing R Atterbury
Pressroom D Houle

Market Information: TMC.
Mechanical available: Offset; Black and 3 ROP colors; insert accepted — preprinted; page cut-offs — 21".
Mechanical specifications: Type page 13⅛" x 21"; E - 6 cols, 2", ¼" between; A - 6 cols, 2", ¼" between; C - 8 cols, 1½", ¼" between.
Commodity Consumption (estimated): Newsprint 250 short tons; widths 27½", 29"; single pages printed 3,600; average pages per issue 18(d).
Equipment: EDITORIAL: Front-end hardware — Ap/Mac Plus System. CLASSIFIED: Printers — Ap/Mac LaserWriter. DISPLAY: Front-end hardware — Ap/Mac LC III System; Printers — Ap/Mac LaserWriter, Ap/Mac ImageWriter. PRODUCTION: Typesetters — 3-Ap/Mac, Ap/Mac LaserWriter; Production cameras — 2-K/V. BUSINESS COMPUTERS: PCs & micros networked.

PRINCE GEORGE

'91 Census- 69,655; E&P '96 Est. 75,046
ABC-CZ (91): 69,653 (HH 24,130)

The Prince George Citizen
(m-mon to thur; m-fri; m-sat)

The Prince George Citizen, 150 Brunswick St.; PO Box 5700, Prince George, BC V2L 5K9; tel (604) 562-2441; fax (604) 562-7453. Southam Newspapers group.
Circulation: 17,240(m); 19,680(m-fri); 17,240(m-sat); ABC Sept. 30, 1995.
Price: 80¢(d); $1.00(fri); 80¢(sat); $12.20/mo.
Advertising: Modular rate 86¢(m); 90¢(m-fri); 86¢(m-sat).
News Service: CP. **Politics:** Independent. **Established:** 1916.
Note: Effective June 12, 1995, this publication changed its publishing plan from (e-mon to thur; fri; sat) to (m-mon to thur; fri; sat)
Magazine: TV Times (fri).

CORPORATE OFFICER
President Andrew Prozes
GENERAL MANAGEMENT
Publisher Bob McKenzie
Director-Finance Del Laverdure
ADVERTISING
Director Lu Verticchio
CIRCULATION
Director-Reader Sales Tim Emsky
NEWS EXECUTIVE
Editor Roy Nagel
EDITORS AND MANAGERS
City Editor M Allen
Editorial Page Editor Roy Nagel
News Editor P Miller
MANAGEMENT INFORMATION SERVICES
Data Processing Manager John Black
PRODUCTION
Manager-Manufacturing C Lampert
Foreman-Pressroom R Baird

Market Information: Split Run; TMC; Operate database.
Mechanical available: Offset; Black and 3 ROP colors; insert accepted — preprinted; page cut-offs — 22¾".
Mechanical specifications: Type page 11½" x 21½"; E - 5 cols, 2¼", ⅜" between; A - 10 cols, 1¹⁄₁₆", ⅛" between; C - 6 cols, 1¾", ⅛" between.
Commodity Consumption (estimated): Newsprint 1,600 metric tons; widths 25"; black ink 48,500 pounds; color ink 8,000 pounds; single pages printed 9,350; average pages per issue 34(d); single plates used 10,000.
Equipment: EDITORIAL: Front-end hardware — CText, QuarkXPress, 2-RSK/Tandy 4000, 27-RSK/Tandy 3000 (PC LAN), 7-RSK/Tandy 4000 (PC LAN). CLASSIFIED: Front-end hardware — CText, 9-RSK/Tandy 3000 (PC LAN); Printers — 1-Ap/LaserWriter II NTX. DISPLAY: Adv layout systems — Multi-Ad/Creator, QuarkXPress, SCS/Layout 8000; Front-end hardware — Ap/Mac II, Ap/PowerMac PC 7100-66; Front-end software — Multi-Ad/Creator 3.6, QuarkXPress 3.3; Printers — Ap/Mac LaserWriter, 2-AU/APS-6-108; Other equipment — 4-CD-Rom, 4-Scanner, 1-Canon/IX-12F. PRODUCTION: Pagination software — QuarkXPress 3.3; OCR software — Canon; Typesetters — AU/APS-6-108; Plate exposers — 2-B/MV; Plate processors — 1-WL/30-A; Electronic picture desk — CD; Production cameras — 1-C/Auto Companica 690C; Automatic film processors — 1-LE; Color separation equipment (conventional) — WDS; Digital color separation equipment — Adobe/Photoshop.
PRESSROOM: Line 1 — 6-G/11RB single width; Folders — 1-G. MAILROOM: Counter stackers — 1-BG/109, 1-MM/310; Stuffers — 1-MM/227; Bundle tyer — 2-MLN; Other mailroom equipment — 1-MM/1528. WIRE SERVICES: News — CP; Stock tables — CP; Syndicates — SOU; receiving dishes — size-3m, CP. BUSINESS COMPUTERS: DEC/PDP 11-44; Applications: Gen ledger, Payroll, Accts payable.

PRINCE RUPERT

'91 Census- 16,620; E&P '96 Est. 18,053
ABC-CZ (91): 16,620 (HH 5,790)

The Daily News (e-mon to fri)

The Daily News, 801 2nd Ave. West, Prince Rupert, BC V8J 1H6; tel (604) 624-6781; fax (604) 624-2851; email prdnews @kaien.awinc.com; web site http://www.sterlingnews.com/rupert. Sterling Newspapers (Hollinger Inc.) group.
Circulation: 3,485(e); ABC Mar. 30, 1995.
Price: 50¢(d); $7.48/mo; $90.00/yr.
Advertising: Modular rate 92¢(e).
News Service: SNS. **Politics:** Independent. **Established:** 1910.
Special Editions: Community Update (Apr); Northwest Host (May).
Magazine: TV Magazine (thur).

GENERAL MANAGEMENT
Publisher Leslie Yates
ADVERTISING
Manager Karen Myers
CIRCULATION
Manager Margaret Clark
NEWS EXECUTIVE
Editor Scott Crowson
PRODUCTION
Foreman Trevor Kayzer

Market Information: Zoned editions; TMC.
Mechanical available: Offset; Black and 3 ROP colors; insert accepted — preprinted; page cut-offs — 21½".
Mechanical specifications: Type page 13¼" x 21½"; E - 6 cols, 2¹⁄₁₆", ⅛" between.

III-6 British Columbia

Commodity Consumption (estimated): widths 27", 34"; single pages printed 4,000; average pages per issue 16(d); single plates used 4,800.
Equipment: EDITORIAL: Front-end hardware — Ap/Mac; Front-end software — Microsoft/Word, QPS. CLASSIFIED: Front-end hardware — Ap/Mac; Front-end software — Microsoft/Word, QPS, Claris/FileMaker Pro. DISPLAY: Adv layout systems — Ap/Mac; Front-end software — QPS, Multi-Ad, Ap/Mac. PRODUCTION: Typesetters — QMS/860; Platemaking systems — B; Scanners — COM.
PRESSROOM: Line 1 — G/Community. BUSINESS COMPUTERS: Ap/Mac.

TRAIL

'91 Census- 7,915; E&P '96 Est. 8,431
ABC-CZ (91): 9,733 (HH 4,210)

Trail Daily Times
(e-mon to fri)

Trail Daily Times, 1163 Cedar Ave., Trail, BC V1R 4B8; tel (604) 368-8551; web site http://www.sterlingnews.com/trail. Sterling Newspapers (Hollinger Inc.) group.
Circulation: 5,220(e); ABC Sept. 30, 1995.
Price: 70¢(d); $8.00/mo; $96.00/yr.
Advertising: Modular rate $1.02(e).
News Service: SNS. **Established:** 1895.
Special Weekly Section: West Kootenay Advertiser (mon).

GENERAL MANAGEMENT
Publisher Raymon Picco
Office Manager Barbara Blatchford
ADVERTISING
Manager Bill Pettigrew
CIRCULATION
Manager Terry Finlay
NEWS EXECUTIVE
Managing Editor Tracy Konschuk
EDITORS AND MANAGERS
City Editor Ray Mazleck
Home Furnishings Editor Nancy Rode
Women's Editor Nancy Rode
PRODUCTION
Foreman-Composing Warren Garner

Market Information: Split Run; TMC.
Mechanical available: Offset; Black and 3 ROP colors; insert accepted — preprinted.
Mechanical specifications: Type page 13¼" x 21½"; E - 6 cols, $2\frac{1}{16}$", ⅛" between.
Commodity Consumption (estimated): average pages per issue 16(d).
Equipment: EDITORIAL: Front-end hardware — Ap/Mac Plus, 6-HI/1020 & 1030; Printers — Ap/LaserWriter. PRODUCTION: Typesetters — 1-COM/7200, 2-COM/4961, 1-COM/Unisetter; Production cameras — 1-AG; Automatic film processors — 1-Kk.

VANCOUVER

'91 Census- 471,875 (Metro Area 1,602,505); E&P '96 Est. 519,200 (Metro Area 1,738,196)
ABC-CZ (91): 953,287 (HH 387,290)

Pacific Press Limited

Pacific Press Limited, 2250 Granville St., Vancouver, BC V6H 3G2; tel (604) 732-2944; fax (604) 732-2308. Southam Newspapers group.
Established: 1957.
Note: The Vancouver Sun and the Province are owned by Pacific Press Limited which operates accounting, mechanical, advertising, circulation, promotion and human resources departments for both. The editorial departments of these two newspapers are independent and competitive under their respective editors-in-chief.

CORPORATE OFFICERS
President & Publisher Don Babick
Vice Pres-Advertising Ron Clark
Vice Pres-Human Resources Andy Smith
Vice Pres-Finance Don Ross
Vice Pres-Production Jack Ferguson
Vice Pres-Marketing John Bardawill
GENERAL MANAGEMENT
Publisher Don Babick
Director-Communications Don MacLachlan
Credit Manager Derek Burrows
ADVERTISING
Manager-Operations Jim Chapman
MARKETING AND PROMOTION
Vice Pres Advertising Ron Clark
TELECOMMUNICATIONS
Manager-Info Systems Dick Thomas
CIRCULATION
Vice Pres-Reader Sales & Service Mike Pellant
Manager-Administration and Systems Nick Tataren
PRODUCTION
Vice Pres Jack Ferguson
Asst Director Bill Osborne
Manager Bill Vennels
Night Manager Jack Lymburner
Asst Manager John Weidenbacher
General Foreman-Pressroom Doug Martin
Chief Engineer Frank Hakkaart
Mailing Bernard Edwards

Mechanical available: Letterpress (Direct); Flexo; Black and 3 ROP colors; insert accepted — preprinted; page cut-offs — $23\frac{9}{16}$".
Commodity Consumption (estimated): Newsprint 49,500 metric tons; widths 55", 41¼", 27½"; black ink 2,500,000 pounds; color ink 200,000 pounds; single plates used 220,000.
Equipment: CLASSIFIED: Front-end hardware — CSI/AMS, 65-CSI/112-B. DISPLAY: Adv layout systems — 20-Ap/Mac II; Front-end hardware — SCS/Layout 8000, 12-CSI/112-B. PRODUCTION: Typesetters — 2-MON/Mk2, 2-MON/Express; Platemaking systems — 2-Na/NP120-, 1-Na/NP40-, 2-HE/SR100; Plate exposers — 2-WL/Lith-X-Pozer; Plate processors — 2-WL/Lithoplater; Scanners — 2-ECR/Autokon 1000; Production cameras — 1-C/Marathon, 2-C/Newspager, 1-DAI; Automatic film processors — 1-P/ML24, 2-Le/2600, 4-LE/LD24; Film transporters — 2-C; Color separation equipment (conventional) — 1-Newscolour/3000; Digital color separation equipment — 2-Howtek/Colorscan.
PRESSROOM: Line 1 — 21-G/MK I (Granville Plant); Line 2 — 9-G/MK I (Granville Plant); Line 3 — 10-MAN/Flexoman (Surrey Plant); Line 4 — 10-MAN/Flexoman (Surrey Plant); Folders — 4-G/(Granville Plant), 2-MAN/(Surrey Plant); Pasters — 24-G, 6-Cline/CC (Granville), 16-H/(Surrey); Reels and stands — 24-G, 6-Cline/CC (Granville), 16-H/(Surrey). MAILROOM: Counter stackers — 6-Id/NS550, 6-Id/2000, 6-Id/2100; Stuffers — 3-Fg, 4-GMA/SLS 1000; Bundle tyer — 2-OVL/JP 80, 6-MLN, 4-OVL/JP-40; Wrapping singles — 3-Constellation/K101; Addressing machine — 4-Dm. LIBRARY: Electronic — Basis. BUSINESS COMPUTERS: 1-DEC/VAX 11-785, 2-DEC/VAX 8600; Applications: Circ, Adv billing, Accts receivable, Gen ledger, Payroll, Miscellaneous; PCs & micros networked; PCs & main system networked.

The Province
(m-mon to fri; S)

The Province, 2250 Granville St., Vancouver, BC V6H 3G2; tel (604) 732-2222; fax (604) 732-2720. Southam Newspapers group.
Circulation: 153,758(m); 190,100(S); ABC Sept. 30, 1995.
Price: 75¢(d); $1.00(S); $11.00/mo.
Advertising: Modular rate $3.95(m); $4.39 (m-fri); $4.99(S). **Representatives:** Southam Newspapers; Cresmer, Woodward, O'Mara & Ormsbee.
News Services: CP, UPI, SHNS, NNS, KRT. **Politics:** Independent. **Established:** 1898.
Note: The Province (mS) and the Vancouver Sun (m) have a combination rate of $9.43 (m-mon-thur), $11.00 (m-fri) and $11.54 (m-sat & S) per Agate line. For advertising, circulation, promotion, accounting, human resources, mechanical, personnel and production specificiations, see Pacific Press Limited.
Not Published: New Year; Good Friday; Victoria Day; Canada Day; B.C. Day; Labor Day; Thanksgiving; Remembrance Day; Christmas; Boxing Day.
Magazine: Color Comics (S).

CIRCULATION
Vice Pres-Reader Sales & Service Mike Pellant
Manager-Administration & Systems Nick Tataren
Manager-Sales Stephen Hastings
Manager-Single Copy Geoff Lay
Manager-Customer Service Rick Russell
NEWS EXECUTIVES
Editor in Chief Michael Cooke
Managing Editor Neil Graham
Deputy Managing Editor-Days Vivienne Sosnowski
EDITORS AND MANAGERS
Business/Finance Editor Lorne Smith
City Editor Joey Thompson
Columnist Bob Stall
Columnist Jeani Read
Columnist Shane McCune
Columnist Brian Kieran
Editorial Writer Paul Schratz
Editorial Page Editor James McNulty
Living Editor Renee Blackstone
News Editor Bill Holden
News Editor-Features Garry Steckles
Photo Editor John Denniston
Showcase Editor Peter Clough
Sports Editor Malcom Kirk
PRODUCTION
Vice Pres Jack Ferguson
Asst Director Bill Osborne
Manager Bill Vennels
Chief Engineer Frank Hakkaart

Mechanical available: Letterpress (Direct); Flexo; Black and 3 ROP colors; insert accepted — preprinted; page cut-offs — $23\frac{9}{16}$".
Mechanical specifications: Type page 10¾" x 13"; E - 5 cols, $2\frac{1}{16}$", ⅛" between; A - 5 cols, $2\frac{1}{16}$", ⅛" between; C - 8 cols, 1¼", $\frac{1}{16}$" between.
Commodity Consumption (estimated): single pages printed 39,000; average pages per issue 120(d), 172(S).
Equipment: EDITORIAL: Front-end hardware — CSI/NMS, Ap/Mac; Front-end software — CSI/E-1128, Ap/Mac, QuarkXPress 3.1; Other equipment — 4-TM/2277, 6-RSK/100. CLASSIFIED: Front-end hardware — CSI. DISPLAY: Adv layout systems — SCS/Layout 8000; Front-end hardware — 32-Ap/Mac; Front-end software — Multi-Ad/Creator 3.7; Printers — QMS/860, Ap/LaserWriter II, MON/Laser Express; Other equipment — AG/Scanner, 3-MON/Software RIP 2000. PRODUCTION: Pagination software — Ap/Mac, QuarkXPress 3.1; Typesetters — 3-MON/Laser Express 1200, 3-MON/Software RIP 2000, 2-Color Central/Spooler; Platemaking systems — Hercules; Plate exposers — Hercules; Plate processors — Hercules; Electronic picture desk — CD; Scanners — Howtek, ECR/Autokon; Automatic film processors — LE; Color separation equipment (conventional) — Howtek; Digital color separation equipment — MON. LIBRARY: Electronic — Infoline. WIRE SERVICES: News — CP, AP, UPI; Stock tables — CP; receiving dishes — size-1.5m, UPI.

The Vancouver Sun
(m-mon to thur; m-fri; m-sat)

The Vancouver Sun, 2250 Granville St., Vancouver, BC V6H 3G2; tel (604) 732-2111; fax (604) 732-2323. Southam Newspapers group.
Circulation: 185,535(m); 244,106(m-fri); 249,919(m-sat); ABC Sept. 30, 1995.
Price: 75¢(d); $1.00(fri); $1.00(sat); $10.00/mo.
Advertising: Modular rate $6.52(m); $7.82(m-fri); $7.82(m-sat). **Representatives:** Southam Newspapers; Cresmer, Woodward, O'Mara & Ormsbee.
News Services: SOU, CP, AP, RN, TSS, NYT. **Politics:** Independent. **Established:** 1886.
Note: The Vancouver Sun (m) and the Province (mS) have a combination rate of $9.43 (m-mon-thur), $11.00 (m-fri) and $11.54 (m-sat & S) per Agate line. For advertising, circulation, promotion, accounting, human resources, mechanical, personnel and production specifications see Pacific Press Limited.
Not Published: New Year; Good Friday; Victoria Day; Canada Day; B.C. Day; Labor Day; Thanksgiving; Remembrance Day; Christmas; Boxing Day.
Advertising not accepted: All advertising accepted, provided advertising meets reasonable standards of decency and is not libelous in nature or contrary to laws of Canada.
Magazines: TV Times (fri); Colour Comics (sat).

CIRCULATION
Vice Pres-Reader Sales & Service Mike Pellant
Manager-Administration Systems Nick Tataren
Manager-Sales Stephen Hastings
Manager-Single Copy Geoff Lay
Manager-Customer Service Rick Russell
NEWS EXECUTIVES
Editor in Chief John Cruickshank
Deputy Managing Editor-Features & Administration Shelley Fralic
Deputy Managing Editor-News Gary Mason
EDITORS AND MANAGERS
Arts & Entertainment Editor Bart Jackson
Books Editor Marke Andrews
Business Editor Gerald Proselandis
Cartoonist Roy Peterson
Columnist Archie McDonald
Columnist Vaughn Palmer
Columnist Elizabeth Aird
Columnist-Sports Archie McDonalds
Columnist Trevor Lautens
Columnist Steve Hume
Drama Critic Barbara Crook
Editorial Page Editor Patricia Graham
Editorial Services Deb Millward
Entertainment Editor Bart Jackson
Foreign Editor Steve Jackson
Food Writer Eve Johnson
Life Editor Valerie Casselton
Movies Critic Peter Birnie
Music Critic-Rock Katherine Monk
Music Critic-Classical Michael Scott
National Editor Larry Emrick
Chief News Editor Nick Palmer
New Homes Editor Steve Whysall
Saturday Review Editor Max Wyman

Mechanical available: Letterpress (direct); Flexo; Black and 3 ROP colors; insert accepted — preprinted; page cut-offs — $23\frac{9}{16}$".
Mechanical specifications: Type page 13" x 22"; E - 6 cols, $2\frac{1}{16}$", ⅛" between; A - 6 cols, $2\frac{1}{16}$", ⅛" between; C - 10 cols, 1¼", $\frac{1}{16}$" between.
Commodity Consumption (estimated): single pages printed 22,000; average pages per issue 62(d), 108(sat).
Equipment: EDITORIAL: Front-end hardware — CSI/NMS, Ap/Mac; Front-end software — CSI/E112B, Ap/Mac, QuarkXPress 3.1; Other equipment — 4-TM/2277 Remote Terminal, 6-RSK/100. CLASSIFIED: Front-end hardware — CSI. DISPLAY: Adv layout systems — SCS/Layout 8000; Front-end hardware — 32-Ap/Mac; Front-end software — Multi-Ad/Creator 3.7; Printers — QMS/860, Ap/LaserWriter II, MON/Laser Express; Other equipment — AG/Flatbed Scanner, Color Central/Spooler, 3-MON/Software RIP 2000. PRODUCTION: Pagination software — Ap/Mac, QuarkXPress 3.1; Typesetters — 2-Color Central/Spooler, 3-MON/Laser Express 1200, 3-MON/Software RIP 2000; Platemaking systems — Na; Plate exposers — Na; Plate processors — Na; Electronic picture desk — CD; Scanners — Howtek, ECR/Autokon; Automatic film processors — LE; Film transporters — CD/PageFax; Color separation equipment (conventional) — Howtek; Digital color separation equipment — MON. MAILROOM: Counter stackers — 6-Id/2100; Mailroom control system — Id. LIBRARY: Electronic — Infoline. WIRE SERVICES: News — CP, NYT, RN; Stock tables — CP. BUSINESS COMPUTERS: PCs & micros networked; PCs & main system networked.

VERNON

'91 Census- 23,510; E&P '96 Est. 26,428
ABC-CZ (91): 32,532 (HH 12,911)

Vernon Daily News
(m-mon to sat)

Vernon Daily News, 3309 31st Ave.; PO Box 4000, Vernon, BC V1T 6N8; tel (604) 545-0671; fax (604) 545-7193. Thomson Newspapers group.
Circulation: 6,882(m); 6,882(m-sat); ABC Sept. 30, 1994.
Price: 50¢(d); 50¢(sat).
Representative: Thomson Newspapers.
News Service: CP. **Established:** 1891.
Note: Advertising is based on a group modular agate line rate of $2.32. Individual newspaper rate not made available.
Not Published: Christmas; Boxing Day; Remembrance Day; Thanksgiving; Labor Day; Good Friday; New Year; Dominion Day; Victoria Day; B.C. Day.
Special Edition: Vacation Guide (May).
Magazines: After 50 (Seniors) (mon); Food Fair (wed); Spotlight (entertainment) (thur); TV Scene (TV tab) (fri); Okanagan Sunday (sat).

GENERAL MANAGEMENT
Publisher/General Manager Kirk Mearas
Business Manager Elsie Twamley
ADVERTISING
Manager Les Matthews
CIRCULATION
Manager Ian Jensen
NEWS EXECUTIVE
Managing Editor Bill McIntrye

Market Information: TMC; ADS.
Mechanical available: Offset; Black and 3 ROP colors; insert accepted — preprinted; page cut-offs — 22¾".

Copyright ©1996 by the Editor & Publisher Co.

Mechanical specifications: Type page 13" x 21½"; E - 6 cols, 2 1/16", 1/8" between; A - 6 cols, 2 1/16", 1/8" between; C - 9 cols, 1 3/8", 1/8" between.
Commodity Consumption (estimated): single pages printed 5,608; average pages per issue 18(d); single plates used 18,960.
Equipment:
PRESSROOM: Line 1 — 8-G/Community. WIRE SERVICES: News — CP, THO. BUSINESS COMPUTERS: ATT; Applications: Accts receivable, Accts payable, Payroll, Circ, Business; PCs & main system networked.

VICTORIA

'91 Census- 71,230 (Metro Area 287,985); E&P '96 Est. 77,863 (Metro Area 312,748)
ABC-NDM (91): 288,071 (HH 119,460)

Times-Colonist
(m-mon to sat; S)

Times-Colonist, 2621 Douglas St.; PO Box 300, Victoria, BC V8T 4M2; tel (604) 380-5211; fax (604) 380-5255; email timesc @interlink.bc.ca; web site http://www.com/timesc. Thomson Newspapers group.
Circulation: 73,991(m); 73,991(m-sat); 73,235(S); ABC Sept. 30, 1995.
Price: 70¢(d); $1.00 (fri); $1.00(sat); $1.00(S); $3.50/wk; $15.21/mo; $172.00/yr.
Advertising: Modular rate $3.38(m); $3.38(m-sat); $46.06(S). **Representatives:** Thomson Newspapers; Cresmer, Woodward, O'Mara & Ormsbee.
News Services: CP, LAT-WP, NYT, CSM. **Politics:** Independent. **Established:** Colonist-1858, Times-1884.
Not Published: Statutory Holidays.
Advertising not accepted: Anything of spurious or misleading nature.
Special Edition: Seniors "Fifty+" (1st mon/mo).
Special Weekly Sections: Travel (sat); Homes (S).
Magazines: "TV Scene" Magazine (fri); Comic (S).

GENERAL MANAGEMENT
Publisher Paul Willcocks
General Manager Peter Baillie
Director-Finance Al Shiraishi
Credit Manager Joanne Wainwright
Accounting Manager Jeanette Schuitima
Business Systems Manager Don Stewart

ADVERTISING
Director B E Hobbs
Manager-Retail D B Thompson
Manager-Classified R S Gibbons

CIRCULATION
Manager-Sales John Crerar
Manager-Distribution Rav Pallan
Manager-Reader Services Matt McGeachie

NEWS EXECUTIVES
Managing Editor David A Brown
Asst Managing Editor Jody Patterson

EDITORS AND MANAGERS
Art Editor Adrian Chamberlain
Art Editor Michael D Reid
Business/Finance Editor Norman Gidney
Business/Finance Editor Stew Lang
City Editor Jack Knox
Columnist Lon Wood
Columnist Jim Gibson
Editorial Writer Paul Minvielle
Editorial Writer Paul Moss
Garden Editor Helen Chesnut
Librarian Doreen Ash
Music/Drama Editor Adrian Chamberlain
Music/Drama Editor Michael D Reid
Real Estate Jack Knox
Sports Columnist Ernie Fedoruk
Sports Editor David Senick

MANAGEMENT INFORMATION SERVICES
Data Processing Manager Don Stewart

PRODUCTION
Manager-Pre Press Julien Phillips
Manager-Systems Julien Phillips
Foreman-Composing Bill Mitchell
Foreman-Pressroom Doug Shillington
Foreman-Stereo John Heryet
Foreman-Mailroom Lonnie Restell
Manager-Maintenance George Porter

Market Information: Split Run; TMC; ADS; Electronic edition.
Mechanical available: Offset; Black and 3 ROP colors; insert accepted — preprinted; page cut-offs — 22¾".
Mechanical specifications: Type page 13" x 22⅛"; E - 6 cols, 2 1/16", 1/8" between; A - 6 cols, 2 1/16", 1/8" between; C - 10 cols, 1¼", 1/16" between.
Commodity Consumption (estimated): Newsprint 7,244 metric tons; widths 54", 40.5", 27"; black ink 57,172 kg; color ink 30,025 kg; single pages printed 16,858; average pages per issue 44(d), 40(S); single plates used 58,000.
Equipment: EDITORIAL: Front-end hardware — CText/PCs, CText/fileserver, IBM/386, IBM/fileserver; Front-end software — CText/3party. CLASSIFIED: Front-end hardware — CText/PCs, CText/fileservers, IBM/386, IBM/fileserver; Front-end software — CText/3party. DISPLAY: Adv layout systems — CText/Adept; Front-end hardware — PC/486 servers; Front-end software — CText/3party; Printers — V/5500 paper, V/5510 film. PRODUCTION: Pagination software — Ap/Mac, QuarkXPress; OCR software — Caere/Omni-Page; Typesetters — 2-V/5000 C Film, 2-V/11x17, 1-V/Full page; Platemaking systems — Offset; Plate exposers — 2-N; Plate processors — 2-WL; Electronic picture desk — CD; Scanners — 2-ECR/Autokon-1000 DE; Production cameras — 2-C/Spartan III; Automatic film processors — 1-LE/24LDQ, 1-DP/24L; Shrink lenses — Animorfic; Color separation equipment (conventional) — CD/Picture Desk, Ap/Mac, Gateway, Intersep; Digital color separation equipment — CD/Picture Desk Leafax. PRESSROOM: Line 1 — 9-G/Urbanite Colorliner (35 couples); Press drives — Allan Bradley; Folders — 2-G/2:3; Pasters — Automatic; Reels and stands — RTP/50; Press control system — G/APCS. MAILROOM: Stuffers — 2-MM/Bi-Liner 308; Bundle tyer — 2-OVL/JP-80; Addressing machine — 1-LinePrinter. LIBRARY: Electronic — CText, SMS, IBM/368 fileserver. WIRE SERVICES: News — CP, LAT-WP, NYT, THO; Stock tables — CP. BUSINESS COMPUTERS: HP/9000-H50; Applications: Lotus/1-2-3 Microsoft/Word Microsoft/Windows WordPerfect Fox/Pro Oracle: Accts payable, Gen ledger; PBS: Accts receivable, Adv, Circ; PCs & micros networked; PCs & main system networked.

MANITOBA

BRANDON

'91 Census- 38,570; E&P '96 Est. 39,260
ABC-CZ (91): 38,567 (HH 15,335)

Brandon Sun
(e-mon to sat)

Brandon Sun, 501 Rosser Ave., Brandon, MB R7A 0K4; tel (204) 727-2451; fax (204) 725-0976. Thomson Newspaper group.
Circulation: 18,204(e); 18,204(e-sat); ABC Sept. 30, 1995.
Price: 50¢(d); 50¢(sat); $2.50/wk (carrier); $130.00/yr (carrier), $256.80/yr (mail).
Advertising: Modular rate $1.39(e); $1.39(e-sat). **Representative:** Thomson Newspapers.
News Services: CP, Thomson. **Politics:** Independent. **Established:** 1882.
Note: Effective Sept. 22, 1995, this publication changed its publishing plan from (e-mon to sat; S) to (e-mon to sat)

GENERAL MANAGEMENT
Publisher Rob Forbes
Business Manager Dave Grennan

ADVERTISING
Manager-Sales Gord Derouin

CIRCULATION
Manager Dale Robson

NEWS EXECUTIVE
Managing Editor Brian Marshall

EDITORS AND MANAGERS
Life/Style Editor Ken Coleman
Sports Editor Mike Jones

PRODUCTION
Manager Bill Chester
Foreman-Composing R Gouldie
Foreman-Pressroom R Smith

Market Information: TMC.
Mechanical available: Offset; Black and 3 ROP colors; insert accepted — preprinted; page cut-offs — 22¾".
Mechanical specifications: Type page 13" x 22"; E - 6 cols, 2 1/16", 1/8" between; A - 6 cols, 2 1/16", 1/8" between; C - 6 cols, 2 1/16", 1/8" between.
Commodity Consumption (estimated): Newsprint 909 metric tons; widths 27½", 13¾"; black ink 25,000 pounds; color ink 2,600 pounds; single pages printed 6,900; average pages per issue 23(d); single plates used 4,500.
Equipment: EDITORIAL: Front-end hardware — 1-Ik/Minitek II; Other equipment — 2-Te/Remote Terminal, 2-RSK/TRS 100, 1-RSK/TRS 200. CLASSIFIED: Front-end hardware — Ik/Minitek II. DISPLAY: Adv layout systems — Ik/Minitek II; Front-end hardware — 8-ZC/Model 40, 1-Xenotron. PRODUCTION: Typesetters — 2-M/Linotron 202; Plate exposers — 1-N/Ultra-Plus; Plate processors — 1-Ic, 1-Enco; Production cameras — 2-N/2024; Automatic film processors — 1-LE/24A. PRESSROOM: Line 1 — 10-HI/V15D. MAILROOM: Counter stackers — 2-BG/105; Stuffers — 1-KAN/320, 1-KAN/480; Bundle tyer — 2-Constellation. WIRE SERVICES: News — CP; receiving dishes — CP. BUSINESS COMPUTERS: IBM/Sys 36; Applications: Business; PCs & micros networked; PCs & main system networked.

FLIN FLON

'91 Census- 7,115; E&P '96 Est. 7,208

The Reminder
(e-mon to thur; e-fri)

The Reminder, 10 North Ave., Flin Flon, MB R8A 0T2; tel (204) 687-7339; fax (204) 687-4473.
Circulation: 3,600(e); 3,900 (e-fri); Sworn Sept. 30, 1995.
Price: 40¢(d); 60¢(fri); $108.00/yr (in Canada), $150.00/yr (outside Canada).
Advertising: Modular rate 56¢(e).
News Service: CP. **Politics:** Independent. **Established:** 1946.
Not Published: Important holidays.
Special Edition: Christmas.

CORPORATE OFFICER
President Randy Daneliuk

GENERAL MANAGEMENT
Publisher Randy Daneliuk

ADVERTISING
Manager Sharon Salthammer

CIRCULATION
Manager Randy Daneliuk

NEWS EXECUTIVE
Editor Randy Daneliuk

EDITOR AND MANAGER
News Editor John Chipman

PRODUCTION
Foreman-Pressroom Randy Daneliuk

PORTAGE LA PRAIRIE

'91 Census- 13,185; E&P '96 Est. 13,432
ABC-CZ (91): 7,156 (HH 5,040)

The Daily Graphic
(e-mon to sat)

The Daily Graphic, 1941 Saskatchewan Ave. W.; Box 130, Portage la Prairie, MB R1N 3B4; tel (204) 857-3427; fax (204) 239-1270. Bowes Publishers Limited (Toronto Sun Publishing) group.
Circulation: 4,149(e); 4,149(e-sat); ABC Sept. 30, 1995.
Price: 45¢(d); 45¢(sat); $104.00/yr.
Advertising: Modular rate 80¢(e); 80¢(e-sat).
News Service: CP. **Politics:** Independent. **Established:** 1895.
Not Published: New Year; Good Friday; Victoria Day; July 1; Civic Holiday; Labor Day; Nov 11; Thanksgiving; Christmas; Boxing Day.
Special Editions: Fair Edition; Back-to-School; Bride Issue; Christmas Greetings; Minor Hockey Week; Agricultural Edition; Energy Issue; Auto; Christmas Song Sheets; Gift Guide; Central Plains Info; Get to Know Us; Shop Portage; New Year's Greetings; New Year's Baby; Cookbook.
Special Weekly Section: TV Guide (thur).
Magazine: TV Log.

GENERAL MANAGEMENT
Publisher Tom Tenszen

ADVERTISING
Manager Tom Tenszen

CIRCULATION
Supervisor C Miller

NEWS EXECUTIVE
Managing Editor Simon Blake

EDITOR AND MANAGER
City Editor Andrew Maxwell

MANAGEMENT INFORMATION SERVICES
Data Processing Manager Mae Barter

PRODUCTION
Supervisor-Press Rene Coté
Supervisor-Composing Alison Blake

Market Information: TMC.
Mechanical available: Offset; Black and 3 ROP colors; insert accepted — preprinted; page cut-offs — 21".
Mechanical specifications: Type page 14½" x 21"; E - 6 cols, 2⅛", 1/8" between; A - 6 cols, 2⅛", 1/8" between; C - 6 cols, 2⅛", 1/8" between.
Commodity Consumption (estimated): Newsprint 525.7 metric tons; widths 14", 15.5", 28", 31", 34"; black ink 14,784 pounds; color ink 916 pounds; single pages printed 5,550; average pages per issue 14(d); single plates used 7,560.
Equipment: EDITORIAL: Front-end hardware — Ap/Mac; Front-end software — Ap/Mac. CLASSIFIED: Front-end hardware — Ap/Mac; Front-end software — Ap/Mac. DISPLAY: Adv layout systems — Ap/Mac Desktop; Front-end software — Ap/Mac. PRODUCTION: OCR software — Ap/Mac; Typesetters — 2-L/101 Laser; Plate exposers — 1-B; Plate processors — 1-Nat; Scanners — LE; Production cameras — 1-Kk; Automatic film processors — 1-Kk, 1-LE. PRESSROOM: Line 1 — 7-G/Community; Folders — G/SSC, G/SC. MAILROOM: Counter stackers — 2-BG/Count-O-Veyor; Bundle tyer — MLN, Constellation; Addressing machine — St/Label Mailer, IBM/Label System 36. COMMUNICATIONS: Facsimile — X. WIRE SERVICES: News — CP; receiving dishes — CP. BUSINESS COMPUTERS: IBM/Sys 36; Applications: Business.

WINNIPEG

'91 Census- 616,790 (Metro Area 652,355); E&P '96 Est. 636,408 (Metro Area 673,158)
Free Press
ABC-NDM (91): 140,954 (HH 47,340)
Sun
ABC-NDM (91): 616,790 (HH 241,165)

Winnipeg Free Press
(m-mon to fri; m-sat; S)

Winnipeg Free Press, 1355 Mountain Ave., Winnipeg, MB R2X 3B6; tel (204) 697-7000; fax (204) 697-7356; email city-desk@freepress.mb.ca; web site http://www.freepress.mb.ca/freepress. Thomson Newspapers group.
Circulation: 134,493(m); 207,718(m-sat); 143,478(S); ABC Sept. 30, 1995.
Price: 50¢(d); $1.25(sat); 50¢(S); $3.25/wk; $161.20/yr (carrier).
Advertising: Modular rate $5.95(m); $7.60(m-sat); $5.95(S). **Representative:** Cresmer, Woodward, O'Mara & Ormsbee.
News Services: CP, AP, KRT, NYT, LAT-WP, SHNS, THO. **Politics:** Independent. **Established:** 1872.
Not Published: Jan 1; Apr 9; May 24; July 1; Aug 2; Sept 6; Oct 11; Nov 11; Dec 25.
Magazines: T.V. Scene (offset) (sat); Close-Up (tab) (S).

GENERAL MANAGEMENT
Publisher H R Redekop
Credit Manager Kurt Enns

ADVERTISING
Director P Nixdorf

MARKETING AND PROMOTION
Director Promotion Tess Bernatki-Byrd

NEWS EXECUTIVES
Exec Editor Duncan McMonagle
Asst Managing Editor John Sullivan
Asst Managing Editor (Night) Pat Flynn

EDITORS AND MANAGERS
Art Director Gordon Preece
Book Editor Morley Waker
Business Editor John Douglas
Cartoonist Dale Cummings
City Editor Maureen Houston
Design & Graphics Editor Paul Pihichyn
Editorial Page Editor Brian Cole
Films Editor Paul McKie
Food Editor Ilana Ismon
Garden Editor Gerry Oliver
Librarian Joan Williamson
Special Sections Editor Gord Arnold
Sports Editor Julian Rachey
Tempo Editor Gail Cabana-Coldwell
Washington DC Bureau David MacDonald

III-8 Manitoba

PRODUCTION

Manager Stephan M Majorki
Foreman-Pressroom Bob Skazyk
Foreman-Mailroom Jack Bartell

Market Information: Zoned editions; Split Run; TMC.
Mechanical available: Letterpress (direct); Black and 3 ROP colors; insert accepted — preprinted; page cut-offs — 23 9/16".
Mechanical specifications: Type page 13" x 22 1/8"; E - 6 cols, 2 1/16", 1/8" between; A - 6 cols, 2 1/16", 1/8" between; C - 10 cols, 1 1/4", 1/8" between.
Commodity Consumption (estimated): Newsprint 21,697 metric tons; widths 54", 40 1/2", 27"; black ink 880,320 pounds; color ink 103,600 pounds; single pages printed 24,180; average pages per issue 63(d), 32(S); single plates used 140,000.
Equipment: EDITORIAL: Front-end hardware — 1-CSI/PDP 11-70, 1-HAS/2330; Front-end software — HAS/Magician Plus, MeD/CSI-103, MeD/CSI-105. CLASSIFIED: Front-end software — MeD/CSI-107. PRODUCTION: Typesetters — 2-MGD/Metroset, 3-COM; Platemaking systems — 2-Na/Superstar; Plate exposers — 2-Na/News Printer II; Scanners — 2-ECR/Autokon; Production cameras — 2-C/SP-3; Automatic film processors — 2-DP/24L, 2-LE/PC18, 1-Fuji; Film transporters — 2-C.
PRESSROOM: Line 1 — 7-G/Mark I; Line 2 — 7-G; Line 3 — 7-G/Mark I; Folders — 4-G; Pasters — 7-G/Digital, 14-Cline; Reels and stands — 7-G, 14-Cline; Press control system — Hurletron. MAILROOM: Counter stackers — 2-CH/MK-IV, 1-SH/257S; Stuffers — 1-S/24P; Bundle tyer — 7-MLN; Wrapping singles — 1-St. WIRE SERVICES: News — CP, CP Data Specials; Stock tables — CP; receiving dishes — CP. BUSINESS COMPUTERS: 1-IBM/Sys 34; Applications: Circ, Adv billing, Accts receivable, Gen ledger, Payroll; PCs & main system networked.

The Winnipeg Sun

(m-mon to sat; S)

The Winnipeg Sun, 1700 Church Ave., Winnipeg, MB R2X 3A2; tel (204) 694-2022; fax (204) 694-2347. Quebecor Inc. group.
Circulation: 46,990(m); 46,990(m-sat); 62,092(S); ABC Sept. 30, 1995.
Price: 35¢(d); 50¢(fri); 50¢(sat); 50¢(S); $2.80/wk; $135.00/yr.
Advertising: Modular rate $1.80(m); $1.80(m-sat); $2.25(S).
News Service: CP. **Politics:** Independent. **Established:** 1980.
Not Published: New Year; Good Friday; Victoria Day; Canada Day; Civic Holiday; Christmas.
Special Weekly Section: Midweek Extra (wed).
Magazines: Friday Plus Tab; Saturday Scene; Preview Television Magazine, Sunday Magazine Tab (S).

CORPORATE OFFICER

Vice Pres Richard Boyer

GENERAL MANAGEMENT

Publisher John Cochrane
Controller Norm Shelton
General Manager Bob Doroz

ADVERTISING

Director of Sales John Ross
Classified Sales Manager Linda Shaver
National Sales Manager Marshall Lank

MARKETING AND PROMOTION

Prom Director Patricia Watts Stevens

CIRCULATION

Director Ronald V Keith

NEWS EXECUTIVE

Managing Editor Mark Stevens

EDITORS AND MANAGERS

Assignments Editor Glenn Cheater
Entertainment Editor John Kendle
Films Editor Randall King
Librarian Denette Ruff
Music Editor John Kendle
News Editor Dave Komosky
Political Editor Don MacGillvray
Radio/Television Editor Denise Duguay
Sports Editor Wayne Parks
Photo Editor Bruce Rapinchuk

PRODUCTION

Manager Art Wilks

Mechanical available: Offset; Black and 3 ROP colors; insert accepted — preprinted, y; page cut-offs — 22 3/4".
Mechanical specifications: Type page 10 7/16" x 14 1/4"; E - 7 cols, 1 7/16", 3/16" between; A - 7 cols, 1 7/16", 3/16" between; C - 7 cols, 1 7/16", 3/16" between.
Commodity Consumption (estimated): Newsprint 2,500 metric tons; widths 30", 34"; black ink 58,000 pounds; color ink 15,000 pounds; single pages printed 16,075; average pages per issue 40(d), 64(S); single plates used 15,000.
Equipment: EDITORIAL: Front-end hardware — Ap/Mac; Front-end software — QuarkXPress 3.31; CLASSIFIED: Front-end hardware — Ap/Mac; Front-end software — Baseview. DISPLAY: Adv layout systems — Ap/Mac; Front-end hardware — COM/MD7 350 MCS with preview. PRODUCTION: Typesetters — COM/MCS work stations, Ap/Mac SE; Platemaking systems — N/Flip Top-, Amerigraph; Plate exposers — B; Plate processors — Enco/N-263; Scanners — Hel/DB-300, COM/8400; Production cameras — DS/240, B/4000; Automatic film processors — 2-Kk/readimeters; Film transporters — P.
PRESSROOM: Line 1 — 8-G/Urbanite (3 color units); Folders — 2-G/Half, 2-G/Quarter; Pasters — Enkel; Press control system — Fin. MAILROOM: Counter stackers — 1-G/Stackmaster; Bundle tyer — MLN. WIRE SERVICES: News — CP; Photos — CP; Stock tables — Dataphone; Syndicates — Universal Press, Toronto Star; receiving dishes — CP. BUSINESS COMPUTERS: DEC/486-66, DEC/P5; Applications: Accpac; PCs & micros networked; PCs & main system networked.

NEW BRUNSWICK

CARAQUET

'91 Census- 4,610; E&P '96 Est. 4,750
ABC-NDM (91): 88,101 (HH 29,170)

L'Acadie Nouvelle

(m-mon to fri)

L'Acadie Nouvelle, 476 Boul. St.-Pierre Ouest; CP 5536, Caraquet, NB E1W 1B7; tel (506) 727-4444; fax (506) 727-7620.
Circulation: 17,761(m); ABC September 30, 1995.
Price: 70¢(d); $170.00/yr.
Advertising: Modular rate $1.20(m).
News Service: CP. **Established:** 1984.
Special Weekly Sections: Women, Seniors (mon); Business, Seniors (tues); Food, Seniors (wed); Car, Seniors (thur); Television, Show (sat); Seniors (S).

GENERAL MANAGEMENT

Publisher Gilles Gagne

ADVERTISING

Manager Hache Gilles

CIRCULATION

Manager Jacques Lanteigne

NEWS EXECUTIVES

Editor Nelson Landry
Managing Editor Claude Boucher

PRODUCTION

Manager Claudine Hache

Market Information: Split Run.
Mechanical available: Offset; Black and 3 ROP colors; insert accepted — preprinted, y; page cut-offs — 14 3/16".
Mechanical specifications: Type page 10 3/8" x 12 1/8"; E - 5 cols, 1.92", 1/6" between; A - 5 cols, 1.92", 1/6" between; C - 7 cols, 1 1/3", 1/6" between.
Commodity Consumption (estimated): Newsprint 850 metric tons; widths 28 5/8"; single pages printed 9,240; average pages per issue 42(d); single plates used 4,400.
Equipment: EDITORIAL: Front-end hardware — COM, Ap/Mac; Front-end software — Mk. CLASSIFIED: Front-end hardware — PC; Front-end software — Informatel. DISPLAY: Front-end hardware — Ap/Mac; Front-end software — QuarkXPress, Adobe/Illustrator; Printers — AG/Selectset 5000. PRODUCTION: Typesetters — COM/Lino Type; Plate exposers — N/Flip Top FT40AP; Plate processors — Enco/Negative Plate Processor Model N-322; Automatic film processors — Eskofot; Color separation equipment (conventional) — AG/Color Scanner.
PRESSROOM: Line 1 — 6-HI/D-150. MAILROOM: Bundle tyer — 2-OVL, 1-Nichiro Kogyo/Model EX311; Addressing machine — 4-Wm. COMMUNICATIONS: Facsimile — Meridian; Satellite; Fiber Optic. WIRE SERVICES: News — CP, Canada News Wire; Photos — CP; receiving dishes — CP. BUSINESS COMPUTERS: IBM; Applications: AccPac; PCs & micros networked.

FREDERICTON

'91 Census- 46,465; E&P '96 Est. 48,222
ABC-CZ (91): 50,974 (HH 19,910)

The Daily Gleaner

(e-mon to sat)

The Daily Gleaner, 12 Prospect St. West; PO Box 3370, Fredericton, NB E3B 5A2; tel (506) 452-6671; fax (506) 452-7405. Summit Publishing group.
Circulation: 30,090(e); 30,090(e-sat); ABC Sept. 30, 1995.
Price: 55¢(d); 55¢(sat); $2.30/wk (carrier); $118.00/yr (carrier).
Advertising: Modular rate $1.32(e); $1.32(e-sat).
News Service: CP. **Politics:** Independent. **Established:** 1889.
Not Published: New Year; Good Friday; Victoria Day; Canada Day; New Brunswick Day; Labor Day; Thanksgiving; Remembrance Day; Boxing Day; Christmas Day.
Advertising not accepted: Cigarette advertising.
Special Editions: Progress Section; Bridal Fashion Section; Gardening Section; Spring Car Care; Home Improvement Section; Consumer Electronics; National Forest Week; Creative Youth; Oromocto Pioneer Days; Canada Day; Woodstock Old Home Week; Northside Section; Armed Forces Day; Continuing Education; Fredericton Exhibition; Energy Section; Fall Fashion; Fredericton Canadians; Fall Car Care; Rotary Radio Auction; Winter Vacation; First Snow of Winter; Downtown Section; Christmas Greetings Section; First Baby of the Year; Continuing Education; Hunting Section.
Special Weekly Sections: Sports Plus B/S (tues); Cars Plus B/S (wed).
Magazines: Real Estate Guide (mon); TV/Radio Guide (fri); Today's Woman (sat); Business In New Brunswick (monthly).

CORPORATE OFFICER

President Tom Crowther

GENERAL MANAGEMENT

Publisher Calvin MacIntosh
General Manager Calvin MacIntosh
Comptroller Kevin Chase

ADVERTISING

Manager Dana Clowater

CIRCULATION

Manager Robert MacFarlane

NEWS EXECUTIVES

Editor Steve Benteau
Managing Editor Steve Benteau
Asst Managing Editor Kathy Jenkins
Asst Managing Editor Anne Moores

EDITORS AND MANAGERS

Book Page Editor Ann Moores
City Editor Kathy Jenkins
Editorial Page Editor Steve Benteau
Fashion/Women's Editor Christy English
Front Page Editor Anne Moores
Sports Editor Dave Ritchie

PRODUCTION

Foreman Composing George Miles
Foreman Pressroom Kevin Scott
Mailroom Foreman Robert MacFarlane

Market Information: Split Run.
Mechanical available: Offset; Black and 3 ROP colors; insert accepted — preprinted; page cut-offs — 22 5/8".
Mechanical specifications: Type page 13" x 21 1/2"; E - 6 cols, 2 1/16", 1/8" between; A - 6 cols, 2 1/16", 1/8" between; C - 6 cols, 2 1/16", 1/8" between.
Commodity Consumption (estimated): Newsprint 2,100 metric tons; widths 27 1/2"; black ink 51,350 pounds; color ink 7,850 pounds; single pages printed 11,720; average pages per issue 40(d); single plates used 26,850.
Equipment: EDITORIAL: Front-end hardware — 23-AT/7000; Front-end software — AT/7000; Other equipment — 2-CD/Electronic Picture Desk. CLASSIFIED: Front-end hardware — 6-AT/7000; Front-end software — AT/7000. PRODUCTION: Typesetters — 2-Cx/Supersetter; Plate exposers — 1-BKY, 1-N; Plate processors — 2-LE/1800; Electronic picture desk — 2-CD; Scanners — RZ/210S; Production cameras — C/Spartan II; Film transporters — 1-C; Color separation equipment (conventional) — 1-Newscolor/3000; Digital color separation equipment — RZ/210S Color Scanner.
PRESSROOM: Line 1 — 8-G/Urbanite, 4-G/Urbanite; Folders — G/2:1; Reels and stands — 2-G/4 High. MAILROOM: Bundle tyer — 2-Gd; Addressing machine — 2-Panasonic/1925S PC. LIBRARY: Electronic — 1-Canon/Microfilm reader-printer. COMMUNICATIONS: Facsimile — 3-Panafax. WIRE SERVICES: News — CP Newstream; receiving dishes — CP. BUSINESS COMPUTERS: 3-MAI/2500, 2-Panasonic/FX 1925S PC, 2-Toshiba/T2200SX; Applications: Adv billing, Accts receivable, Gen ledger, Payroll, Accts payable; PCs & micros networked; PCs & main system networked.

MONCTON

'91 Census- 57,010; E&P '96 Est. 58,780
ABC-CZ (91): 83,743 (HH 31,225)

The Times-Transcript

(e-mon to fri; e-sat)

The Times Transcript, 939 Main St. (E1C 8P3); PO Box 1001, Moncton, NB E1C 1G8; tel (506) 859-4900; fax (506) 859-4899. Summit Publishing group.
Circulation: 41,535(e); 54,777(e-sat); ABC Sept. 30, 1995.
Price: 55¢(d); 67¢(sat); $2.65/wk; $256.80/yr.
Advertising: Modular rate $1.74(e); $1.83(e-sat).
News Service: CP. **Politics:** Independent. **Established:** Transcript-1882, Times-1877.
Not Published: New Year; Good Friday; Victoria Day; Dominion Day; New Brunswick Day; Labour Day; Remembrance Day; Thanksgiving; Christmas.

GENERAL MANAGEMENT

Publisher/General Manager T M Bembridge
Controller Ralph Seely

MARKETING AND PROMOTION

Manager-Marketing Ann Kenny

CIRCULATION

Manager Paul Drisdelle

NEWS EXECUTIVE

Managing Editor John Wells

EDITORS AND MANAGERS

Editorial Writer Norbert Cunningham
News Editor Edith Robb

PRODUCTION

Manager John Ross

Market Information: Zoned editions; Split Run; TMC.
Mechanical available: Offset; Black and 3 ROP colors; insert accepted — preprinted; page cut-offs — 22 1/4".
Mechanical specifications: Type page 13" x 21 1/2"; E - 6 cols, 2 1/16", 1/8" between; A - 6 cols, 2 1/16", 1/8" between; C - 9 cols, 1 1/3", 1/8" between.
Commodity Consumption (estimated): Newsprint 2,843 metric tons; widths 27 1/2", 41 3/10", 55"; black ink 43,500 pounds; color ink 15,500 pounds; single pages printed 11,690; average pages per issue 38(d); single plates used 30,600.
Equipment: EDITORIAL: Front-end hardware — HI. CLASSIFIED: Front-end hardware — HI. DISPLAY: Front-end hardware — Ap/Mac; Front-end software — QuarkXPress 3.3, Multi-Ad/Creator 3.5.2, Adobe/Photoshop 2.5.1, Adobe/Illustrator 3.2; Printers — V/5100, Ap/Mac LaserWriter Pro, MON/Express Master 3850. PRODUCTION: OCR software — Caere/OmniPage 2.1; Platemaking systems — Kk; Plate exposers — 1-N; Plate processors — Kk/Aqua-image; Scanners — RZ, Nikon; Production cameras — Konica; Automatic film processors — Fuji; Reproportion units — 2-ECR/Autokon 100; Color separation equipment (conventional) — Controlux, Fuji/Color Art.
PRESSROOM: Line 1 — G/Headliner; Line 2 — G/Headliner; Line 3 — G/Headliner; Line 4 — G/Headliner; Line 5 — G/Headliner; Line 6 — G/Headliner; Press drives — Allen Bradley; Folders — G/3:2, G/Jaw; Pasters — 6-G/RT-50. MAILROOM: Counter stackers — 2-HL; Stuffers — 2-MM. COMMUNICATIONS: Facsimile — 3-X/400, 1-X/410. WIRE SERVICES: News — CP; Photos — CP; Stock tables — CP. BUSINESS COMPUTERS: MAI.

Copyright ©1996 by the Editor & Publisher Co.

SAINT JOHN
Including Lancaster

'91 Census- 74,970 (Metro Area 124,980); E&P '96 Est. 76,117 (Metro Area 128,431)
ABC-NDM (91): 100,457 (HH 39,330)

The Telegraph-Journal
(m-mon to fri; m-sat)
St. John Times Globe
(e-mon to fri)

The Telegraph-Journal/St. John Times Globe, 210 Crown St.; PO Box 2350, Saint John, NB E2L 3V8; tel (506) 632-8888; fax (506) 648-2654. New Brunswick Publishing Co. Ltd. group.

Circulation: 28,377(m); 28,842(e); 60,909 (m-sat); ABC Sept. 30, 1995.

Price: 65¢(d); $1.00(sat); $2.60/wk (m/e) (carrier); $130.00/yr (m/e) (carrier).

Advertising: Modular rate $2.25(m); $2.25(e); $2.24(m-sat). **Representative:** Canadian Media Connection.

News Services: NYT, SOU, UPI, DJ. **Politics:** Independent. **Established:** 1868.

Not Published: Christmas.

Special Editions: January Discount, Women in Business, Winter Car Care, Health & Recreation, Home Improvement (Jan); Brides Edition, RRSP, Business & Industrial Review (Feb); Spring Fashions, Home Improvement (Mar); Time for Thought, Car Care, Salute to Volunteers, New Homes, Lawn & Garden (Apr); National Forest Week Port Days, Vacation PEI (May); National Transportation Week, NB Travel Guide, Super Discount Days, Farming New Brunswick (June); Nova Scotia Vacationland, Loyalist Days (July); Festival by the Sea, NB Travel Guide, Back-to-School, Focus on Education, Atlantic Nat'l Exhibition (Aug); Moose Hunting, Fall Fashion, Duck Hunting, Home Improvement (Sept); Fire Prevention, Co-op Week, Seniors Today, Small Business Week, Winter Car Care (Oct); Crime Prevention, Remembrance Day, Christmas Carols, Favorite Christmas Recipes (Nov); Christmas Greetings, Report on Education (Dec).

Special Weekly Sections: Sports Week (mon); The Reader (sat).

Magazines: Real Estate Guide (tues); Showtime TV Guide (fri); Travel, Book Page, People Page, N.B. Reader (sat).

Broadcast Affiliates: Radio CHSJ.

GENERAL MANAGEMENT
Exec Vice Pres/General Manager Bruce W Phinney
Publisher/Editor in Chief Neil Reynolds
Controller Dianne Peters

ADVERTISING
Director-Sales/Marketing Charles Fraser

MARKETING AND PROMOTION
Director-Sales/Marketing Charles Fraser

CIRCULATION
Manager Richard M Russell

NEWS EXECUTIVES
Editor in Chief/Publisher Neil Reynolds
Managing Editor (St. John Times Globe) Carolyn Ryan
Managing Editor (Telegraph Journal) Scott Anderson

EDITORS AND MANAGERS
Editorial Page Editor (Telegraph Journal) Don Cayo
Sports Editor Peter McGuire

MANAGEMENT INFORMATION SERVICES
Systems Manager James Kennedy

PRODUCTION
Manager Philip Tetreault

Market Information: TMC; ADS.

Mechanical available: Letterpress (direct); Black and 3 ROP colors; insert accepted — preprinted, product samples; page cut-offs — $23\frac{9}{16}$".

Mechanical specifications: Type page 13" x 22"; E - 6 cols, $2\frac{1}{16}$", $\frac{1}{8}$" between; A - 6 cols, $2\frac{1}{16}$", $\frac{1}{8}$" between; C - 6 cols, $2\frac{1}{16}$", $\frac{1}{8}$" between.

Commodity Consumption (estimated): Newsprint 3,483 metric tons; widths 56", $40\frac{1}{2}$", 28"; black ink 18,759 pounds; color ink 2,139 pounds; single pages printed 18,183; average pages per issue 30(d), 50(sat); single plates used 35,169.

Equipment: EDITORIAL: Front-end hardware — Ap/Mac Quadra 650's, Ap/Mac Classic's, Ap/Mac II fx's; Front-end software — Mk/SpeedWriter 2.0.67, Mk/PageSpeed 3.0b16, Solo Browser, SMS/Stauffer Gold; Printers — Okidata/OL850, Ap/LaserWriter, DataProducts/LZR 2600 Proofer; Other equipment — Sun/Sparc 2. CLASSIFIED: Front-end hardware — Ap/Mac LC's; Front-end software — Mk/Class Speed 3.1.b20, 4th Dimension 2.2.3; Printers — Okidata/OL840; Other equipment — Sun/Sparc 2. DISPLAY: Front-end hardware — Ap/Mac II fx's, Ap/Mac Quadra 700; Front-end software — Mk/AdSpeed 3.0b16 DB, QuarkXPress, Adobe/TypeStyler; Printers — QMS/PS-815 MR Laser, Ap/Laser-Writer II, AG/TabScript 300, Tektronix/Phaser III. PRODUCTION: Pagination software — DTI/AdSpeed, Mk/PageSpeed 3.0, DTI; OCR software — Caere/OmniPage 2.1, Adobe/Photoshop; Typesetters — Ap/Mac IIfx, Ap/Mac Quadra 700, Ap/Mac Quadra 650, AU/APS-3850; Platemaking systems — Na; Plate exposers — 2-He/Auto Film; Electronic picture desk — CD; Scanners — Kk/RFS 2035 Film Scanner, AG/Focus II (B&W), Imager/Pro Quickscan 8000; Automatic film processors — LE/L2600; Color separation equipment (conventional) — C, Ap/Mac; Digital color separation equipment — DTI/AdSpeed. PRESSROOM: Line 1 — 7-H/3277; Folders — 2-H; Press control system — GE. MAILROOM: Counter stackers — 3-HPS; Stuffers — 1-Amerigraph; Bundle tyer — 5-Gd/Ovalstrapping; Addressing machine — 1-KAN; Mailroom control system — 1-HPS. LIBRARY: Electronic — SMS/Stauffer Gold, SMS/Stauffer Remote. WIRE SERVICES: News — Photos — RN; Syndicates — Toronto Star, NYT, NEA, King Features, SOU; receiving dishes — UPI, RN, CP, SOU. BUSINESS COMPUTERS: Mk/Acer 386's, Compaq/486's, Sun/Sparc 2, Wyse/60 Terminals; Applications: WordPerfect: Purchase orders, Payroll, Accounting; Sun PBS/Media Plus Lotus; PCs & micros networked.

NEWFOUNDLAND

CORNER BROOK

'91 Census- 22,410; E&P '96 Est. 23,127
ABC-CZ (91): 23,029 (HH 7,590)

The Western Star
(e-mon to sat)

The Western Star, West St.; PO Box 460, Corner Brook, NF A2H 6E7; tel (709) 634-4348; fax (709) 634-9824. Thomson Newspapers group.

Circulation: 10,344(e); 10,344(e-sat); ABC Sept. 30, 1995.

Price: 56¢(d); $1.00(sat); $11.60/mo (carrier); $150.80/yr (carrier).

Advertising: Modular rate $1.02(e); $1.02(e-sat). **Representative:** Thomson Newspapers.

News Service: CP. **Politics:** Independent. **Established:** 1900.

Not Published: New Year; Good Friday; Empire Day; Dominion Day; Labor Day; Thanksgiving; Armistice Day; Christmas.

Special Edition: Christmas.

GENERAL MANAGEMENT
Publisher John Cheek
Controller Andrew Hunt
Credit Manager Andrew Hunt
Purchasing Agent Andrew Hunt

ADVERTISING
Manager Andrew Robertson
Manager-Classified Andrew Robertson

CIRCULATION
Manager David Hampton

NEWS EXECUTIVE
Managing Editor R Williams

EDITORS AND MANAGERS
City Editor John Mayo
Editorial Page Editor Ray Sweetapple
Sports Editor Don Bradshaw

PRODUCTION
Foreman Tim Chell

Market Information: TMC.

Mechanical available: Offset; Black and 1 ROP color.

Mechanical specifications: Type page $14\frac{1}{8}$" x 21"; E - 6 cols, $2\frac{1}{16}$", $\frac{1}{8}$" between.

Commodity Consumption (estimated): average pages per issue 40(d).

Equipment: EDITORIAL: Front-end hardware — HI. CLASSIFIED: Front-end hardware — HI. PRODUCTION: Typesetters — 2-COM/Unisetter. MAILROOM: Bundle tyer — 1-Whig, 1-Gd; Addressing machine — 1-Am.

SAINT JOHN'S

'91 Census- 95,770 (Metro Area 171,860); E&P '96 Est. 97,660 (Metro Area 184,968)
ABC-CZ (91): 95,770 (HH 32,570)

The Evening Telegram
(e-mon to fri; m-sat; S)

The Evening Telegram, Columbus Dr.; PO Box 5970, St. John's, NF A1C 5X7; tel (709) 364-6300; fax (709) 364-9333. Thomson Newspapers group.

Circulation: 39,703(e); 63,228(m-sat); 39,202(S); ABC Sept. 30, 1995.

Price: 60¢(d); $1.00(sat); 60¢(S); $3.30/wk; $14.30/mo; $171.60/yr, $52.00/yr (sat only), $72.80/yr (sat & S only).

Advertising: Modular rate $1.93(e); $2.44(e-sat); $1.84(S). **Representative:** Thomson Newspapers.

News Services: CP, AP, RN, AFP, THO. **Established:** 1879.

Special Editions: Fishing; Vacation; Back-to-School; Hunting; Christmas; Cook Book; Business Review and Forecast.

Magazine: TV Guide Tab.

GENERAL MANAGEMENT
Publisher Miller H Ayre
General Manager Miller H Ayre
Comptroller Larry A Kelly

ADVERTISING
Manager Dan Johnson
Manager-Retail Sales Sean Nugent

MARKETING AND PROMOTION
Manager-Marketing Jeanette Payne

CIRCULATION
Manager Lon Lovestone
Manager-Home Delivery Sales Chris Hodder
Manager-Single Copy Sales Dan Butler

NEWS EXECUTIVE
Managing Editor Joseph Walsh

EDITORS AND MANAGERS
Assoc Editor/Editorial Page Editor Moira Baird
News Editor Bretton Loney
Sports Editor Robin Short

PRODUCTION
Manager Boyd Cranford
Foreman-Pressroom L Chaytor

Market Information: Split Run; TMC.

Mechanical available: Offset; Black and 3 ROP colors; insert accepted — preprinted; page cut-offs — $21\frac{1}{2}$".

Mechanical specifications: Type page 13" x $21\frac{1}{2}$"; E - 6 cols, $2\frac{1}{16}$", $\frac{1}{8}$" between; A - 6 cols, $2\frac{1}{16}$", $\frac{1}{8}$" between; C - 9 cols, $1\frac{1}{3}$", $\frac{1}{8}$" between.

Commodity Consumption (estimated): Newsprint 3,200 short tons; widths 54.3", 40.7", 22.2"; black ink 40,800 pounds; color ink 8,000 pounds; single pages printed 12,475; average pages per issue 48(d), 32(S); single plates used 16,000.

Equipment: EDITORIAL: Front-end hardware — 2-HAS/CPU, Ap/Mac Quadra 840 AU, Ap/Power Mac 6100, 17-Ap/Mac Performa 580, 6-Ap/Power Mac 7200-90; Front-end software — Baseview/NewsEdit Pro IQue; Printers — 3-Ap/Mac LaserPrinter 360, 2-Panther/Pro 36 Imagesetters; Other equipment — 3-Umax/1260 Scanners. CLASSIFIED: Front-end hardware — HAS/Magician Terminals, 7-Ap/Mac 5200CD; Front-end software — Class Manager Pro. DISPLAY: Adv layout systems — 2-HAS/Ad Pro; Front-end hardware — HAS/Terminal, 4-Ap/Mac 7200-90; Front-end software — QuarkXPress 3.3, Multi-Ad 3.7, Adobe/Typestyler 2.0, Adobe/Illustrator 5.5, Adobe/Photoshop 3.02, Adobe/Streamline 3.07; Printers — LaserMaster/Unity 1200XL, Lexmark/4079, Ap/Mac Personal Laser NT, 2-HP/LaserJet 4MV. PRODUCTION: Pagination software — QuarkXPress 3.3; Typesetters — 3-COM/8600, 2-Panther/Pro 36, 2-Ap/Mac 8000-100 w/Adobe/CPSI; Platemaking systems — 1-3M/Pyrofax (imager & fuser); Plate exposers — 1-N/(standby); Plate processors — WL; Electronic picture desk — CD, 2-Ap/Mac 7200-90; Scanners — CD, 2-Nikon/3510 Slide, 1-Nikon/Coolscan, 3-Umax/1260 Flatbed; Production cameras — 1-N/SST 2024 C, ECR/Autokon 1000. PRESSROOM: Line 1 — 1-G/Cosmo (offset) double width; Line 2 — 1-G/Cosmo (offset) double width; Line 3 — 1-G/Cosmo (offset) double width; Line 4 — 1-G/Cosmo (offset) double width; Line 5 — 1-G/Cosmo (offset) double width; Line 6 — GAM double width; Line 7 — GAM double width; Press drives — G; Folders — G; Pasters — G; Reels and stands — G, Enkel; Press control system — G. MAILROOM: Counter stackers — 1-MSI; Bundle tyer — 2-Gd/Q; Addressing machine — 1-Am/6250. LIBRARY: Combination — Digital Archival/Phrasea w/CD. COMMUNICATIONS: Facsimile — Gentner/distribution amplifier. WIRE SERVICES: News — AP, CP; receiving dishes — CP. BUSINESS COMPUTERS: IBM; Applications: Microsoft/Windows Word Perfect, Lotus Microsoft/Excel; PCs & micros networked; PCs & main system networked.

NOVA SCOTIA

AMHERST

'91 Census- 9,745; E&P '96 Est. 10,064
ABC-CZ (91): 9,742 (HH 3,880)

Amherst Daily News
(m-mon to fri)
The Citizen (m-sat)

Amherst Daily News, 10 Lawrence St.; PO Box 280, Amherst, NS B4H 3Z2; tel (902) 667-5102; fax (902) 667-0419.

Circulation: 4,062(m); 6,333(m-sat); ABC Sept. 30, 1995.

Price: 55¢(d); 60¢(sat); $2.50/wk (carrier); $100.00/yr (mail), $82.00/yr (carrier).

Advertising: Modular rate 69¢(m); 69¢(m-sat).

News Service: CP. **Politics:** Independent. **Established:** 1893.

Special Editions: Valentine (Feb); Christmas (Dec); Home Show; Maple Syrup; Trade & Industry; Kids Stuff; Spring; Fishing; Outdoors; Environment; Graduation; Blueberry.

Magazines: Nightlife; TV Guide.

CORPORATE OFFICERS
President Earl J Gouchie
Vice Pres Mary Conrad
Secretary/Treasurer Vince Arbing

GENERAL MANAGEMENT
General Manager Earl J Gouchie

ADVERTISING
Manager Richard Spicer

CIRCULATION
Manager Donald Griffiths

NEWS EXECUTIVE
Editor John Conrad

PRODUCTION
Superintendent Greg Landry
Foreman-Composing Greg Landry

Market Information: Split Run.

Mechanical available: Offset; Black and 3 ROP colors; insert accepted — preprinted; page cut-offs — $22\frac{3}{4}$".

Mechanical specifications: Type page $12\frac{7}{8}$" x $21\frac{1}{2}$"; E - 6 cols, $2\frac{1}{16}$", $\frac{1}{8}$" between; A - 6 cols, $2\frac{1}{16}$", $\frac{1}{8}$" between; C - 6 cols, $2\frac{1}{16}$", $\frac{1}{8}$" between.

Commodity Consumption (estimated): widths 35", $27\frac{1}{2}$", $13\frac{3}{4}$"; average pages per issue 16(d).

Equipment: EDITORIAL: Front-end hardware — COM/8600, COM/110, RSK/Tandy; Front-end software — COM. CLASSIFIED: Front-end software — COM/PE. DISPLAY: Front-end hardware — Ap/Mac. PRODUCTION: Typesetters — COM; Plate exposers — N/Ultra Plus; Plate processors — Nat/A-250; Automatic film processors — P/26 TQ. PRESSROOM: Line 1 — 8-HI/Cotrell JF25B V-15A; Folders — HI/1:1; Reels and stands — 6-HI/Standard. MAILROOM: Bundle tyer — 2-AMP/Cyclop Rotant N; Addressing machine — 4-Wm/Chauncy. WIRE SERVICES: News — CP. BUSINESS COMPUTERS: RSK.

HALIFAX

'91 Census- 114,455 (Metro Area 320,500); E&P '96 Est. 118,199 (Metro Area 335,018)
Chronicle-Herald and Mail Star
ABC-NDM (90): 330,105 (HH 121,690)
Daily News
ABC-NDM (91): 330,846 (HH 122,125)

The Chronicle-Herald
(m-mon to sat)
The Mail-Star (e-mon to sat)

The Chronicle-Herald, 1650 Argyle St.; PO Box 610, Halifax, NS B3J 2T2; tel (902) 426-2811; fax (902) 426-1164; email herald@fox.nstn.ca; web site http://www.herald.ns.ca.in newscentre.

Circulation: 96,723(m); 43,597(e); 96,723 (m-sat); 43,597(e-sat); ABC Sept. 30, 1995.
Price: 60¢(d); 65¢(sat); $2.43/wk (inc. GST); $10.65/mo (inc. GST); $120.48/yr (inc. GST).
Advertising: Modular rate $4.02(m); $4.02(e); $4.02(m-sat); $4.02(e-sat).
News Services: CP, NYT, London Telegraph. **Politics:** Independent. **Established:** Herald-1875, Mail-1879.
Not Published: New Year; Labor Day; Christmas.
Special Editions: Industrial Review & Forecast Tab (Jan); Spring Brides Tab, Travel Tab (Feb); Today's Woman (Apr); Wheels Tab (May); Discover Nova Scotia Tab, National Ski-Week, National Photo Month, National Forestry Month (June); Home Sweet Home Tab (Sept).
Special Weekly Sections: Sports (mon); Everybody's Business (tues); Living Today (Food, Fashions, Lifestyles) (wed); Thursday! (Entertainment) (thur); This NovaScotian, C Books, Collecting, Historical Interest, Bird Watching, Columns (fri); Travel, Viewpoint (World Events, Investigative Reports) (sat); Science; New York Times Crossword.
Magazines: Mayflower-entertainment TV (tues); Homes (wed); Comics (sat).

CORPORATE OFFICERS
CEO G W Dennis
Vice Pres/Secretary P Devine

GENERAL MANAGEMENT
Publisher G W Dennis
Vice Pres Sarah Dennis
Vice Pres/General Manager A J Ripley
Vice Pres/Personnel Manager R J Capon
Comptroller H Hall

ADVERTISING
Manager Fred Buckland
Sales Manager-Classified Tara O'Blenis
Sales Manager-Display Eric Lawson

MARKETING AND PROMOTION
Manager Richard M Russell

TELECOMMUNICATIONS
Audiotex Manager Richard M Russell

CIRCULATION
Manager Scott Boyle

NEWS EXECUTIVES
Managing Editor J S Purves
Deputy Managing Editor T O'Neil

EDITORS AND MANAGERS
Books Editor Christine Soucie
Business Editor Roger Taylor
Night Editor J Howitt
Sports Editor M Flemming

MANAGEMENT INFORMATION SERVICES
Online Manager Alberta Dube

Market Information: Zoned editions; Split Run; TMC; ADS; Operate database; Operate audiotex; Electronic edition.
Mechanical available: Letterpress (direct); Black and 3 ROP colors; insert accepted — preprinted; page cut-offs — 22¾".
Mechanical specifications: Type page 13" x 21¼"; E - 6 cols, 2.03", ⅙" between; A - 6 cols, 2.03", ⅙" between; C - 10 cols, 1.23", 1⁄12" between.
Commodity Consumption (estimated): widths 54", 40½", 27"; average pages per issue 48(d); single plates used 73,000.
Equipment: EDITORIAL: Front-end hardware — DEC/TMS, Ap/Mac Quadra; Printers — DEC/LA 120; Other equipment — 2-CD/EPD, NewsView/Text Archive System, PhotoView/Image Archive System, ECP/Pagination System. CLASSIFIED: Front-end hardware — DEC/CMS; Printers — 3-DEC/LA-120; Other equipment — Classified Pagination. AUDIOTEX: Hardware — PEP, Brite Voice System, Micro Voice; Software — PEP, Unix/V-386 3.2, Ingres, VoicePrint/9000 2.4.2.1; Supplier name — Brite Voice Systems. DISPLAY: Adv layout systems — SCS/Layout 8000; Front-end hardware — DEC/VAX; Front-end software — SCS/Layout 8000; Printers — DEC/LP25. PRODUCTION: Pagination software — ECP 9C; OCR software — Caere/OmniPage Pro; Typesetters — 3-Ultre/Recorders; Platemaking systems — Na; Plate exposers — 1-Na/Master Printer, 1-Na/Starlite; Plate processors — 2-Na/NP-80; Electronic picture desk — 2-CD; Scanners — HP/ScanJet IIc, 1-ECR/Autokon 1000, 1-ECR/Autokon 1000DE, 2-ECR/Autokon 8400; Production cameras — 2-C/Newspager; Automatic film processors — 4-LE; Reproportion units — 4-ECR/Autokon, 5-C/Breeze, 3-Bitcaster; Color separation equipment (conventional) — 5-C/Breeze; Digital color separation equipment — Nikon/LS3500. PRESSROOM: Line 1 — 6-H; Line 2 — 5-Crabtree; Press drives — GE; Folders — 4-H/2:1; Reels and stands — 6-H, 5-Crabtree/double reels; Press control system — GE. MAILROOM: Counter stackers — SH/251, SH/257, GPS/5000, SH/251, SH/257, GPS/5000; Stuffers — GMA/SLS 1000; Bundle tyer — 1-MLN/2A, 1-MLN/2A, 1-MLN/2A; Wrapping singles — 2-K/Pac; Addressing machine — 2-Wm/Stamping machines. LIBRARY: Electronic — NewsView/Folioview, PhotoView/ Image Archive. WIRE SERVICES: News — CP Datafile, CP Dataspecials, NYT, TV Data, Daily Telegraph; Stock tables — CP Stocks, Fundata; Syndicates — TV Data, NYT; receiving dishes — size-4ft, CP. BUSINESS COMPUTERS: DEC/Alpha; Applications: VMS: Accounting, Circ, Inventory, Accts payable, Circ; UMS/Open: Custom Applications; PCs & micros networked; PCs & main system networked.

The Daily News
(m-mon to sat; S)

The Daily News, 11 Thornhill Dr.; PO Box 8330 Station A, Halifax, NS B3K 5M1; tel (902) 468-1222; fax (902) 468-3609; email dnews@atcon.com; web site http://www.cfn.cs.dal.ca/media/todaysnews/todaysnews.html. Newfoundland Capital Corp. group.
Circulation: 26,857(m); 26,857(m-sat); 43,021(S); ABC Sept. 30, 1995.
Price: 55¢(d); 55¢(sat); 75¢(S); $2.93/wk (home delivery); $170.42/6 mos (mail).
Advertising: Modular rate $1.11(m); $1.11(m-sat); $1.44(S).
News Services: CP, Southam, SHNS. **Politics:** Independent. **Established:** Weekly-1974, Daily-1979.
Not Published: Christmas; New Year.
Magazines: Bedford Sackville Weekly News (wed); New Dartmouth News (thur).
Broadcast Affiliates: KIXX/Q 104/SUN FM.

CORPORATE OFFICER
President/Publisher Mark Richardson

GENERAL MANAGEMENT
Publisher Mark Richardson
Vice Pres-Finance Bart Henneberry

ADVERTISING
Manager Deane Hennigar
Manager Classified Bob Scott
Vice Pres-Sales Rick MacPherson

MARKETING AND PROMOTION
Marketing Director Carole McDougall

CIRCULATION
Vice Pres-Operations John Landry

NEWS EXECUTIVES
Editor in Chief Douglas MacKay
Managing Editor Bill Turpin

EDITORS AND MANAGERS
Business Editor John McLeod
Entertainment Editor Sandy MacDonald
News Editor Joan Westen
Sports Editor Dave Whynacht
Sunday Editor Shane Ross

MANAGEMENT INFORMATION SERVICES
Data Processing Manager Derrick Wong

PRODUCTION
Manager Paul Bruce
Consultant Don Reid

Market Information: Electronic edition.
Mechanical available: Offset; Black and 3 ROP colors; insert accepted — preprinted; page cut-offs — 15".
Mechanical specifications: Type page 10¼" x 14"; E - 5 cols, 4½", .42" between; A - 7 cols, 1 5⁄16", 3⁄16" between; C - 7 cols, 1 5⁄16", 3⁄16" between.
Commodity Consumption (estimated): Newsprint 3,000 metric tons; widths 15", 30", 34"; black ink 50,000 pounds; single pages printed 25,000; average pages per issue 52(d), 88(S); single plates used 9,000.
Equipment: EDITORIAL: Front-end hardware — 18-Ap/Mac; Printers — 2-CG/8600, V/printer, V/6000, V/3200, V/Selectpress 600; Other equipment — 9-PC. CLASSIFIED: Front-end hardware — 4-IBM/PC; Front-end software — III/Tecs-2. PRODUCTION: Typesetters — 2-COM/8600; Platemaking systems — 1-Ingenuity/Film Miser; Plate exposers — N/631; Direct-to-plate imaging — 3M/Pyrofax Imager-Fuser; Production cameras — Danagraph/602A, Danagraph/902A, Photoace/260D; Automatic film processors — Danagraph/DG 2600, LE/PC 13; Color separation equipment (conventional) — Digi-Colour/DC-4000. PRESSROOM: Line 1 — 1-DEV/3 high; Line 2 — 4-G/Community; Line 3 — 4-G/Community; Folders — 1-G/Community, 1-G/SSC. MAILROOM: Counter stackers — HI/Graphics; Bundle tyer — 2-G/Minimax, 1-Samuel, 4-Strapex. LIBRARY: Electronic — SMS/Stauffer Gold, Infomart/Dialog. WIRE SERVICES: News — CP, SOU, SHNS; Photos — CP; Stock tables — CP; receiving dishes — size-4 ½ft, CP. BUSINESS COMPUTERS: IBM/System 38; Applications: Accts receivable, Circ; PCs & micros networked; PCs & main system networked.

NEW GLASGOW

'91 Census- 9,905; E&P '96 Est. 10,163
ABC-CZ (91): 22,327 (HH 8,355)

The Evening News
(e-mon to sat)

The Evening News, 352 East River Rd., New Glasgow, NS B2H 5E2; tel (902) 752-3000; fax (902) 752-1945. Thomson Newspapers group.
Circulation: 9,904(e); 9,904(e-sat); ABC Sept. 30, 1995.
Price: 55¢(d); 75¢(sat); $2.75/wk; $133.55/yr.
Advertising: Modular rate $1.02(e); $1.02(e-sat).
News Services: CP, THO. **Established:** 1911.
Not Published: New Year; Good Friday; Victoria Day; Canada Day; Labor Day; Thanksgiving; Remembrance Day; Christmas.
Special Editions: Business and Industrial Review, Car Care, Fishing (Apr); Brides (May); Hunting, Cookbook (Sept); Fire Prevention, Car Care (Oct).
Magazines: Business, Seniors (monthly); Real Estate (every 2 weeks).

GENERAL MANAGEMENT
Publisher/General Manager Lee Ballantyne

ADVERTISING
Manager Jim Kwiatkowski

CIRCULATION
Representative David Battist

NEWS EXECUTIVE
Managing Editor Doug MacNeil

EDITOR AND MANAGER
City Editor Heather Fiske

Market Information: TMC; ADS.
Mechanical available: Offset; Black and 3 ROP colors; insert accepted — preprinted; page cut-offs — 22¾".
Mechanical specifications: Type page 13¼" x 21½"; E - 6 cols, 2 1⁄16", ⅛" between; A - 6 cols, 2 1⁄16", ⅛" between; C - 9 cols, 1⅓", ⅛" between.
Commodity Consumption (estimated): Newsprint 300 metric tons; widths 27½", 13¾"; single pages printed 5,000; average pages per issue 16(d).
Equipment: EDITORIAL: Front-end software — Mk. CLASSIFIED: Front-end software — Mk. DISPLAY: Front-end software — Mk. PRODUCTION: Typesetters — Mk; Production cameras — B. PRESSROOM: Line 1 — 8-G/Community. MAILROOM: Bundle tyer — Gd; Addressing machine — Mailrite/Computer. WIRE SERVICES: News — CP. BUSINESS COMPUTERS: ATT, Samsung; Applications: Payroll, Billing, Accts Receivable, Circ; PCs & micros networked; PCs & main system networked.

SYDNEY

'91 Census- 26,065; E&P '96 Est. 26,304
ABC-CZ (91): 35,309 (HH 12,923)

Cape Breton Post
(m-mon to sat)

Cape Breton Post, 255 George St.; PO Box 1500, Sydney, NS B1P 6K6; tel (902) 564-5451; fax (902) 562-7077. Thomson Newspapers group.
Circulation: 30,279(m); 30,279(m-sat); ABC September 30, 1995.
Price: 50¢(d); 70¢(sat); $3.20/wk; $13.86/mo; $166.40/yr.
Advertising: Modular rate $1.74(m); $1.74(m-sat). **Representative:** Thomson Newspapers.
News Services: CP, THO. **Politics:** Independent. **Established:** 1900.
Not Published: New Year; Good Friday; Victoria Day; Civic Holiday; Labor Day; Thanksgiving; Armistice Day; Canada Day; Christmas; New Year.
Special Editions: Year End; Fishing; Home Improvement; Brides; Tourist; Labor Day; Hunting; Automobile; Industrial; Winter Sports; Summer Sports; Triple Play of Summer; Vacation/Tourist Guides.
Special Weekly Sections: Just Saturday, Celebrations.
Magazines: TV Scene (fri); Cover Story (entertainment tab) (sat).

GENERAL MANAGEMENT
Publisher/General Manager Peter Kapyrka
Business Manager Jobe Williams

ADVERTISING
Director Kelly Madden

TELECOMMUNICATIONS
Audiotex Manager Bill Crawley

CIRCULATION
Manager Tom McCarron

NEWS EXECUTIVE
Editor Fred Jackson

EDITORS AND MANAGERS
City Editor Doyle MacKinnon
Editorial Page Editor Doug McGee

PRODUCTION
Manager-Composing Ron Evely
Manager-Press Guy Belisle

Market Information: TMC; ADS; Operate audiotex.
Mechanical available: Offset; Black and 3 ROP colors; insert accepted — preprinted; page cut-offs — 21".
Mechanical specifications: Type page 13" x 21½"; E - 6 cols, 2 1⁄16", ⅛" between; A - 6 cols, 2 1⁄16", ⅛" between; C - 9 cols, 1⅜", 1⁄16" between.
Commodity Consumption (estimated): Newsprint 1,447.1 metric tons; widths 27½", 13¾"; black ink 1,750 kg; color ink 4,409 kg; single pages printed 8,466; average pages per issue 28(d), 44(sat); single plates used 6,348.
Equipment: EDITORIAL: Front-end hardware — HAS/H552, 17-Ap/Mac Preforma 580, 9-Ap/Power Mac 7100, 2-Ap/Power 8100, 2-Ap/Mac PowerBook 520; Front-end software — Baseview/NewsEdit IQUE, Baseview, QuarkXPress, Achieving; Printers — Xante/1200 dpi; Other equipment — Polaroid/Slide Scanners, 2-Umax/Scanner. DISPLAY: Front-end hardware — 4-Ap/Power Mac 1800; Front-end software — Metro/AdCreation Tool Kit, QuarkXPress, Adobe/Photoshop, Adobe/Illustrator. PRODUCTION: Pagination software — QuarkXPress w/Metro/Ad Creation Tool Kit; Typesetters — 2-COM/8600; Production cameras — N/18x24. PRESSROOM: Line 1 — 8-G/Urbanite; Folders — 1-G. MAILROOM: Counter stackers — 1-MSI; Bundle tyer — 3-Constellation; Addressing machine — 1-Am. COMMUNICATIONS: Satellite. WIRE SERVICES: News — CP; Photos — CP; receiving dishes — CP. BUSINESS COMPUTERS: 1-HAS System, 2-AT&T System; Applications: HP Lotus Microsoft/Windows.

TRURO

'91 Census- 11,680; E&P '96 Est. 11,884
ABC-CZ (91): 18,500 (HH 7,413)

The Daily News
(e-mon to fri; m-sat)

The Daily News, 6 Louise St.; PO Box 220, Truro, NS B2N 5C3; tel (902) 893-9405; fax (902) 893-0518. Thomson Newspapers group.
Circulation: 8,009(e); 9,918(m-sat); ABC Sept. 30, 1995.
Price: 50¢(d); $1.00(sat); $2.50/wk (carrier); $130.08/yr.
Advertising: Modular rate $1.01(e); $1.01(m-sat). **Representative:** Thomson Newspapers.
News Service: CP. **Politics:** Independent. **Established:** 1891.
Not Published: Statutory holidays; New Year; Good Friday; Victoria Day; Canada Day; Civic Holiday; Labor Day; Thanksgiving; Christmas.
Special Editions: Industrial (Mar); Brides (May); Stay & Play (June); Stay & Play (July); Stay & Play, N.S. Prov. Exhibition (Aug); Fashion, Automotive (Spring); Outdoors (Summer); Fashion, Automotive, Energy (Fall); Outdoors, Energy (Winter); Cookbooks (Christmas); Downtown Christmas (6 editions); Christmas Carols; Year-Ender.
Magazines: TV News, RE Showcase (sat); Cover Story (S).

GENERAL MANAGEMENT
Publisher/General Manager Leith W Orr
Accountant Bernadine Hyson

ADVERTISING
Manager Bruce Pearson

MARKETING AND PROMOTION
Manager-Marketing/Promotion Bruce Pearson

CIRCULATION
Manager Lowell Sherry

NEWS EXECUTIVE
Managing Editor Bill McGuire

EDITOR AND MANAGER
Assignment Editor Charles Beckwith
MANAGEMENT INFORMATION SERVICES
Data Processing Manager Dave Conrad
PRODUCTION
Manager Dave Conrad

Market Information: Zoned editions; TMC; ADS.
Mechanical available: Offset; Black and 3 ROP colors; insert accepted — preprinted, packaging, booklets, samples; page cut-offs — 22¾".
Mechanical specifications: Type page 13" x 21"; E - 6 cols, 2.07", 1/16" between; A - 6 cols, 2.07", 1/16" between; C - 9 cols, 1⅓", 1/16" between.
Commodity Consumption (estimated): Newsprint 400 short tons; 375 metric tons; widths 27.5", 14⅞"; black ink 5,300 kg; color ink 350 kg; single pages printed 6,300; average pages per issue 22(d); single plates used 3,760.
Equipment: EDITORIAL: Front-end hardware — Mk; Front-end software — Mk. CLASSIFIED: Front-end hardware — Mk; Front-end software — Mk; Printers — Mk. DISPLAY: Front-end hardware — Mk; Front-end software — Mk; Printers — Mk. PRODUCTION: Plate processors — 1-Nat/A-340; Production cameras — Companica/640.
PRESSROOM: Line 1 — 4-G/Community SC280, 2-G/Community SC280. MAILROOM: Bundle tyer — 1-Gd/Oval Strapper. WIRE SERVICES: News — CP; receiving dishes — size-6ft, CP. BUSINESS COMPUTERS: ATT; Applications: Business; PCs & micros networked; PCs & main system networked.

ONTARIO

BARRIE

'91 Census- 62,730; E&P '96 Est. 71,893
ABC-CZ (91): 62,728 (HH 22,635)

The Examiner (e-mon to sat)

The Examiner, 16 Bayfield St.; PO Box 370, Barrie, ON L4M 4T6; tel (705) 726-6537; fax (705) 726-7706. Sterling Newspapers (Hollinger Inc.) group.
Circulation: 11,148(e); 11,148(e-sat); ABC Sept. 30, 1995.
Price: 50¢(d); 75¢(sat); $3.10/wk (carrier); $150.00/yr (carrier), $238.60/yr (mail).
Advertising: Modular rate $1.13(e); $1.13(e-sat). **Representative:** Thomson Newspapers.
News Service: CP. **Politics:** Independent. **Established:** 1864 (daily 1958).
Not Published: Christmas; Good Friday.
Special Editions: Real Estate; Job Market; TV Scene.

GENERAL MANAGEMENT
Publisher/General Manager Ron Laurin
Business Manager Mary Ellis
ADVERTISING
Director Tim Cote
Manager-Classified Kim Block
CIRCULATION
Manager Rick Hann
NEWS EXECUTIVE
Managing Editor Michel Beaudin
EDITORS AND MANAGERS
City Editor Don Wilcox
Sports Editor Steve Hardy

Market Information: Zoned editions; Split Run; TMC.
Mechanical available: Offset; Black and 3 ROP colors; insert accepted — preprinted; page cut-offs — 21½".
Mechanical specifications: Type page 13" x 21½"; E - 6 cols, 2 1/16", ⅛" between; A - 6 cols, 2 1/16", ⅛" between; C - 9 cols, 1⅓", ⅛" between.
Commodity Consumption (estimated): average pages per issue 19(d).
Equipment: EDITORIAL: Printers — 3-TTS. PRODUCTION: Typesetters — 7-L.

BELLEVILLE

'91 Census- 37,240; E&P '96 Est. 39,240
ABC-CZ (91): 37,243 (HH 15,325)

The Intelligencer (e-mon to fri; m-sat; S)

The Intelligencer, 45 Bridge St. E.; PO Box 5600, Belleville, ON K8N 1L5; tel (613) 962-9171; fax (613) 962-9652. Sterling Newspapers (Hollinger Inc.) group.
Circulation: 18,019(e); 18,019(m-sat); 16,347(S); ABC Sept. 30, 1995.
Price: 50¢(d); 93¢(sat); 93¢(S); $3.20/wk (carrier); $166.40/yr (carrier), $320.00/yr (mail).
Advertising: Modular rate $1.17(e); $1.17(m-sat); $1.17(S). **Representative:** Thomson Newspapers.
News Services: CP, AP, THO. **Politics:** Independent. **Established:** 1870.
Not Published: New Year; Canada Day; Civic Holiday; Thanksgiving; Christmas; Victoria Day; Good Friday; Easter Sunday; Labour Day.
Special Editions: Progress; Car Care; Home Improvement.
Special Weekly Sections: Prime Time-Seniors (mon); Pulse (tues); Cookin' (wed); Dressing Up (thur).
Magazines: Weekly Real Estate; Color Comics; TV Magazine; Weekly Auto Market.

GENERAL MANAGEMENT
Publisher/General Manager Peter E Leichnitz
Accountant Joe Gillis
ADVERTISING
Manager Valerie Andrews
CIRCULATION
Manager Ron Prins
NEWS EXECUTIVE
Managing Editor Nick Palmer
EDITORS AND MANAGERS
City Editor Brian O'Meara
Sports Editor Ady Vos
Women's Editor Linda O'Connor
PRODUCTION
Foreman-Pressroom Brian Jones

Market Information: Split Run; TMC; ADS.
Mechanical available: Offset; Black and 3 ROP colors; insert accepted — preprinted; page cut-offs — 21½".
Mechanical specifications: Type page 13" x 21½"; E - 6 cols, 2 1/16", ⅛" between; A - 6 cols, 2 1/16", ⅛" between; C - 9 cols, 1¼".
Commodity Consumption (estimated): average pages per issue 22(d), 28(sat), 22(S).
Equipment: EDITORIAL: Front-end hardware — CText, CD/EPD, ECR/Autokon Graphic System; Other equipment — Nikon/Color Scanners. CLASSIFIED: Front-end hardware — CText, 6-COM. PRODUCTION: Typesetters — 2-COM. PRESSROOM: Line 1 — 7-G/Urbanite. MAILROOM: Bundle tyer — 2-Gd; Addressing machine — 2-Am. WIRE SERVICES: News — receiving dishes — CP. BUSINESS COMPUTERS: ATT.

BRANTFORD

'91 Census- 82,000; E&P '96 Est. 87,647
ABC-CZ (91): 81,997 (HH 30,460)

The Expositor (m-mon to sat)

The Expositor, 53 Dalhousie St.; PO Box 965, Brantford, ON N3T 5S8; tel (519) 756-2020; fax (519) 756-9481. Southam Newspapers group.
Circulation: 25,763(m); 25,763(m-sat); ABC Sept. 30, 1995.
Price: 60¢(d); $1.00 (fri); $1.00(sat); $3.20/wk; $166.00/yr (carrier).
Advertising: Modular rate $1.941(m); $1.941 (m-sat). **Representative:** Southam Newspapers.
News Services: CP, SOU. **Politics:** Independent. **Established:** 1852.
Note: All printing and production for The Brantford Expositor is done by the Hamilton Spectator, Hamilton, Ontario. Effective May 15, 1995, this publication changed its publishing plan from (e-mon to sat) to (m-mon to sat)
Not Published: New Year; Good Friday; Victoria Day; Canada Day; Civic Holiday; Labor Day; Thanksgiving; Christmas.
Special Editions: Financial; Home & Garden; Brides; Spring & Fall Fashion; Spring & Fall Car Care; Vacation Guide; Fifty Plus; Home Entertainment; Year End Review; Christmas Gift Guides; Community Guide; Environment; Parenting; Small Business; Technology.
Special Weekly Sections: Sports (mon); Crossroads (wed); Homes (fri).
Magazines: TV Times (fri); Comics (sat); Community Guide (annual).

CORPORATE OFFICERS
President William Ardell
Secretary/Treasurer John G Craig
GENERAL MANAGEMENT
Publisher W R (Bill) Findlay
Business Manager J R Ferris
Comptroller W Wiesel
ADVERTISING
Manager David Weber
Manager-Sales Steve Welch
Manager-Sales Toby Tyler
MARKETING AND PROMOTION
Manager-Marketing & Promotion Susan Kellas Azzopardi
CIRCULATION
Manager Susan Kellas Azzopardi
Supervisor-Sales David Elliott
NEWS EXECUTIVES
Managing Editor David Schultz
News Editor Susan Johnston
EDITORS AND MANAGERS
Auto Editor James Fleming
Books Editor Dennis Marcella
City Editor Peter DePodesta
Editorial Page Editor Albert Vandermey
Education Susan Bailey
Fashion/Women's Editor Mary-Anne Davies
Features Editor Dennis Marcella
Food Editor Mary-Anne Davies
Librarian Lyn Colwell
Music Editor Dennis Marcella
Political Editor Peter Fitzpatrick
Radio/Television Editor Dennis Marcella
Real Estate Editor James Fleming
Sports Editor Ed O'Leary
Teenage Youth Editor Susan Bailey
PRODUCTION
Manager David Weber
Coordinator-Technology T Kerby

Market Information: TMC.
Mechanical available: Offset; Black and 3 ROP colors; insert accepted — preprinted; page cut-offs — 22".
Mechanical specifications: Type page 11½" x 22"; E - 5 cols, 1½", ⅛" between; A - 9 cols, 2⅛", 1/12" between; C - 8 cols, 1 17/24", 1/12" between.
Commodity Consumption (estimated): Newsprint 1,919 metric tons; widths 55"; black ink 20,000 pounds; color ink 12,000 pounds; single pages printed 10,000; average pages per issue 34(d); single plates used 21,120.
Equipment: EDITORIAL: Front-end hardware — RSK/Tandy, PC, Ap/Mac Quadras; Front-end software — CText, QuarkXPress; Printers — ECR/PelBox Imagesetter; Other equipment — Umax/600 DPI Scanner. CLASSIFIED: Front-end hardware — RSK/Tandy, PC; Front-end software — CText; Printers — Ap/Mac Laser-Writer II NTX. DISPLAY: Adv layout systems — SCS/Layout 8000; Front-end hardware — Ap/Mac Quadras; Front-end software — QuarkXPress 3.31, Aldus/FreeHand 5.0, Adobe/Photoshop 3.01; Printers — 3-Ap/Mac LaserWriter II NTX, 2-ECR/PelBox Imagesetter, QMS/860 600dpi laser; Other equipment — Nikon/35mm Scanner, 1-Umax/1200 DPI Scanner, 3-Umax/600 DPI Scanner, 1-Pixelcra Ft/11x17 Scanner. PRODUCTION: Pagination software — SCG/Ad Trac System, SCS/Linx, QuarkXPress 3.31; OCR software — Calera/Wordscan; Typesetters — 2-ECR/Pelbox 1045C; Electronic picture desk — CD, Ap/Mac Quadra 840 AV; Scanners — Ap/Mac Quadra 700, Nikon, Umax; Production cameras — C/Spartan II; Automatic film processors — 3-LE; Film transporters — LE; Color separation equipment (conventional) — Ap/Mac, Adobe/Photoshop 3.01; Digital color separation equipment — Nikon/LS3510AF. WIRE SERVICES: News — CP, SOU; receiving dishes — size-12ft, CP. BUSINESS COMPUTERS: DEC/9200, PC; PCs & micros networked; PCs & main system networked.

BROCKVILLE

'91 Census- 21,580; E&P '96 Est. 22,741
ABC-CZ (91): 21,582 (HH 9,095)

The Brockville Recorder and Times (e-mon to sat)

The Brockville Recorder and Times, 23 King St. W.; PO Box 10, Brockville, ON K6V 5T8; tel (613) 342-4441; fax (613) 342-4456.
Circulation: 15,952(e); 15,952(e-sat); ABC Sept. 30, 1995.
Price: 60¢(d); $1.00(fri); 75¢(sat); $3.30/wk; $14.30/mo; $171.60/yr (carrier).
Advertising: Modular rate $1.20(e); $1.20(e-sat).
News Services: CP, AP, RN. **Politics:** Independent. **Established:** 1821, daily-1873.
Advertising not accepted: All tobacco products as ROP.
Special Editions: Industrial Showcase, Winter Sale Section (Jan); Women in Business, Bridal Edition (Feb); Spring Home Improvement, Spring Fashions (Mar); Boating '96, Spring Car Care, Spring Sale Section (Apr); Garden/Pool/Patio, Youth '96 (May); Riverfest '96 (June); Riverfest Review, Summer Sale Section (July); Leeds-Grenville Agriculture (Aug); Hunting & Fishing, Fall Home Improvement, Fall Fashions (Sept); Home Energy, Fall Car Care, Fall Sale Section (Oct); Consumer Electronics, Christmas Gift Guide (Nov); Christmas Gift Guide, Christmas Greetings, Year-End Review (Dec); Pursuit (Health & Wellness tab) (monthly).
Special Weekly Sections: TV Travel Times; Real Estate (tab).

CORPORATE OFFICERS
President Hunter S Grant
Secretary Janet Higgs
Vice Pres/Treasurer W S Watson
GENERAL MANAGEMENT
Co-Publisher Mrs Perry S Grant Beverley
Co-Publisher Hunter S Grant
General Manager Hunter S Grant
Asst General Manager Robert Erickson
Credit Manager Sharon Holmes
Education Service Manager Barbara Milks
ADVERTISING
Manager Chris Murphy
MARKETING AND PROMOTION
Manager-Marketing & Promotion Barbara Milks
TELECOMMUNICATIONS
Audiotex Manager Steve Clark
CIRCULATION
Manager Stan Butler
NEWS EXECUTIVE
Editor in Chief Mrs Perry S Grant Beverley
EDITORS AND MANAGERS
City Editor Don Swayne
Asst City Editor Barry Raison
Editorial Page Editor Doug Coward
Editorial Writer Doug Coward
Farm Editor Mark Calder
Fashion/Food Editor Perry S Grant Beverley
Film/Theater Editor Deanna Lysko
Librarian Huguette Babcock
Music Editor Deanna Lysko
Photo Department Manager David Erwin
Picture Editor Phil Kall-Shewan
Radio/Television Editor Phil Kall-Shewan
Real Estate Editor Roy Lewis
Sports Editor Ron Smith
Travel Editor Phil Kall-Shewan
Women's Editor Perry S Grant Beverley
PRODUCTION
Foreman-Composing L T J Smith
Foreman-Pressroom Robert A Webster
Photo Lab David Erwin
Photographer Deanna Lysko
Photographer Mark Lysko

Market Information: Zoned editions; Split Run; TMC; Operate audiotex.
Mechanical available: Offset; Black and 3 ROP colors; insert accepted — preprinted, up to 13½"x11½"; page cut-offs — 22⅜".
Mechanical specifications: Type page 11½" x 21⅜"; E - 6 cols, 1¾", ⅛" between; A - 6 cols, 1¾", ⅛" between; C - 6 cols, 1¾", ⅛" between.
Commodity Consumption (estimated): Newsprint 800 short tons; 900 metric tons; widths 25", 12½"; 33", 16½"; black ink 20,000 pounds; color ink 300 pounds; single pages printed 9,261; average pages per issue 30(d); single plates used 21,000.
Equipment: EDITORIAL: Front-end hardware — 19-Ap/Power Mac 7100-80, Ap/Mac Performa 580; Front-end software — QuarkXPress, Baseview/Extension; Printers — Okidata/320. CLASSIFIED: Front-end hardware — 5-Ap/Power Mac 6100-66; Front-end software — Baseview/ClassFlow, Baseview/Class Manager; Printers — Okidata/393-320, Star/NX1001. DISPLAY: Front-end hardware — 3-Ap/Mac ci, 1-Ap/Mac fx, 1-Ap/Mac II, 1-Ap/Power Mac PC 8180, 2-PC, Ap/Mac 6100; Front-end software — Multi-Ad/Creator, QuarkXPress, Adobe/Photoshop, Archetype/Corel Draw; Printers — Canon/Bubble Jet BJC 800. PRODUCTION: Pagination software — Baseview/Extension, QuarkXPress; Typesetters — 2-XIT/Clipper, 2-XIT/Schooner; Plate exposers — 1-N/Flip Top FT40APR; Plate processors — 1-AZO; Electronic picture desk — CD/486 Newsline; Scanners — LE/480; Production cameras — Escofot/480; Automatic film processors — Wing Lynch/Model 5, AG/Rapidline 28; Digital color separation equipment — Nikon/LS3500AF, Microtek/600ZS, AG/Scanner.

III-12 Ontario

PRESSROOM: Line 1 — 8-G/Community, 1-G/Community (w/Color Hump); Folders — G/SSC; Press Registration Systems Duarte. MAILROOM: Bundle tyer — 1-GD, OVL/R101, Cyclops. LIBRARY: Electronic — SMS/Staufer. COMMUNICATIONS: Facsimile — 1-X, 1-Panasonic. WIRE SERVICES: News — CP; Photos — CP; Syndicates — AP, CP; receiving dishes — AP, CP. BUSINESS COMPUTERS: IBM/AS-400; Applications: Adv billing, Accts receivable, Gen ledger, Billing, Circ, Database; PCs & micros networked; PCs & main system networked.

BURLINGTON
See HAMILTON

CAMBRIDGE

'91 Census- 92,775; E&P '96 Est. 101,870
ABC-CZ (91): 92,772 (HH 31,865)

The Cambridge Reporter
(e-mon to sat)

The Cambridge Reporter, 26 Ainslie St. S., Cambridge, ON N1R 5T2; tel (519) 621-3810; fax (519) 621-8239. Sterling Newspapers (Hollinger Inc.) group.
Circulation: 10,070(e); 10,070(e-sat); ABC March 31, 1995.
Price: 50¢(d); 75¢(sat); $2.40/wk (carrier); $114.40/yr (carrier), $350.00/yr (mail).
Advertising: Modular rate $1.11(e); $1.11(e-sat). **Representative:** Thomson Newspapers.
News Service: CP. **Politics:** Independent. **Established:** 1846.
Not Published: New Year; Good Friday; Christmas.
Advertising not accepted: Liquor, according to Provincial laws; certain patent medicine.
Special Editions: Progress (Mar); Vacation Guide (May, June, Aug); Cookbook (Oct).
Magazines: Business Magazine (monthly); TV Scene Magazine, Cover Story (weekly).

GENERAL MANAGEMENT
Publisher/General Manager Steve Rhodes
Accountant Maggy Portelli
CIRCULATION
Manager Steve Campbell
NEWS EXECUTIVE
Managing Editor Christina Jonas
PRODUCTION
Foreman-Pressroom Don Moon

Market Information: TMC.
Mechanical available: Offset; Black and 3 ROP colors; insert accepted — preprinted; page cutoffs — 22¾".
Mechanical specifications: Type page 13" x 21½"; E - 6 cols, 2 1/16", ⅞" between; A - 6 cols, 2 1/16", ⅛" between; C - 9 cols, 2 1/16", ⅛" between.
Commodity Consumption (estimated): Newsprint 700 metric tons; widths 27¼"; black ink 11,800 pounds; color ink 564 pounds; single pages printed 9,336; average pages per issue 26(d); single plates used 10,000.
Equipment: EDITORIAL: Front-end hardware — 14-HAS. CLASSIFIED: Front-end hardware — 3-HAS, 5-IBM/II. PRODUCTION: Typesetters — DEC; Plate exposers — 1-N/Plate Maker; Plate processors — 1-WL/30B; Production cameras — 1-C/Spartan II; Automatic film processors — 1-P/Pakorol.
PRESSROOM: Line 1 — G/Urbanite. MAILROOM: Bundle tyer — 1-Gd/Tristar; Addressing machine — 1-EI/3001. WIRE SERVICES: News — AP, CP; Syndicates — THO. BUSINESS COMPUTERS: 1-Phillips; Applications: Circ, Adv billing, Accts receivable, Gen ledger, Payroll.

CHATHAM

'91 Census- 43,560; E&P '96 Est. 45,880
ABC-CZ (91): 43,557 (HH 16,400)

The Chatham Daily News
(e-mon to sat)

The Chatham Daily News, PO Box 2007, Chatham, ON N7M 5M6; tel (519) 354-2000; fax (519) 436-0949. Thomson Newspapers group.
Circulation: 15,988(e); 15,988(e-sat); ABC Sept. 30, 1995.
Price: 55¢(d); 55¢(sat); $2.70/wk; $11.27/mo; $135.20/yr (carrier).
Advertising: Modular rate $1.05(e); $1.05(e-sat). **Representative:** Thomson Newspapers.
News Services: AP, CP, RN. **Politics:** Independent. **Established:** 1865.
Not Published: New Year; Good Friday; May 24; Thanksgiving; Christmas.
Special Editions: Progress; Building; Farm; Cookbook; Brides Vacation; Baby; Business Women; Car Care; Seniors.
Special Weekly Section: Business Today (tues).
Magazines: Real Estate (mon); TV Scene (fri).

GENERAL MANAGEMENT
Publisher/General Manager Everett A Burgess
Credit Manager Pam Botari
ADVERTISING
Manager Everett A Burgess
Manager-Classified Dick Chisholm
MARKETING AND PROMOTION
Manager-Promotion Everett A Burgess
CIRCULATION
Manager Shawn Shatford
NEWS EXECUTIVE
Editor Jim Blake
EDITORS AND MANAGERS
Amusements Editor Randy Cocte
Books Editor Jim Blake
Business/Finance Editor Rod Hilts
Fashion/Society Editor Bill Reddick
Films/Theater Editor Randy Cocte
Food Editor Bill Reddick
Music Editor Randy Cocte
News Editor Rod Hilts
Photo Department Manager Daniel Janisse
Picture Editor Daniel Janisse
Teen-Age Youth Editor Randy Cocte
PRODUCTION
Foreman-Composing Ian Hackson
Foreman-Pressroom Brian Tremblay

Market Information: TMC; ADS.
Mechanical available: Offset; Black and 3 ROP colors; insert accepted — preprinted; page cutoffs — 22¾".
Mechanical specifications: Type page 13" x 21½"; E - 6 cols, 2 1/16", ⅛" between; A - 6 cols, 2 1/16", ⅛" between; C - 9 cols, 1⅓", ⅛" between.
Commodity Consumption (estimated): widths 27"; average pages per issue 23(d).
Equipment: EDITORIAL: Front-end hardware — 2-Hx/HS43, 1-DEC/PDP-1104; Front-end software — Hx. CLASSIFIED: Front-end hardware — 1-Hx/HS43, 3-Hx. PRODUCTION: Typesetters — 2-COM; Plate exposers — 1-N; Plate processors — 1-Nat; Scanners — 2-Hx; Production cameras — 1-B; Automatic film processors — 1-Richmond.
PRESSROOM: Line 1 — 7-G/Urbanite. MAILROOM: Bundle tyer — 1-Gd, 1-WT; Addressing machine — 1-EI. COMMUNICATIONS: Satellite. WIRE SERVICES: News — CP; Stock tables — CP, Toronto Stock Exchange; receiving dishes — CP. BUSINESS COMPUTERS: PCs & main system networked.

COBOURG

'91 Census- 15,080; E&P '96 Est. 16,463
ABC-CZ (91): 15,079 (HH 5,870)

Cobourg Daily Star
(e-mon to fri)

Cobourg Daily Star, 415 King St.; PO Box 400, Cobourg, ON K9A 4L1; tel (905) 372-0131; fax (905) 372-4966. St. Catharines Standard Ltd. group.
Circulation: 5,463(e); ABC June 30, 1993.
Price: 60¢(d); $2.65/wk; $11.50/mo; $136.00/yr.
Advertising: Modular rate 83¢(e). **Politics:** Independent. **Established:** Weekly-1831, Daily-1976.
Not Published: New Year; Good Friday; Victoria Day; Dominion Day; Civic Holiday; Labor Day; Thanksgiving; Christmas; Boxing Day.

GENERAL MANAGEMENT
Publisher/Chief Operating Officer Chuck Burke
Asst to the Publisher Cheryl McMenemy
ADVERTISING
Director James Bovaird
CIRCULATION
Manager Barbara Weightman
NEWS EXECUTIVE
Managing Editor Jim T Grossmith
PRODUCTION
Manager Bob Bell

Market Information: TMC.
Mechanical available: Offset; Black and 3 ROP colors; insert accepted — preprinted.
Mechanical specifications: Type page 13½" x 21½"; E - 6 cols, 2 1/16", ⅛" between.
Commodity Consumption (estimated): Newsprint 500 metric tons; widths 34", 28"; black ink 7,181 pounds; color ink 700 pounds; average pages per issue 26(d).
Equipment: EDITORIAL: Front-end hardware — Mk; Front-end software — Mk. CLASSIFIED: Front-end software — Mk. PRODUCTION: Platemaking systems — LE/Processor, lk.

CORNWALL

'91 Census- 47,135; E&P '96 Est. 49,373
ABC-CZ (91): 47,317 (HH 18,360)

Standard-Freeholder
(e-mon to sat)

Standard-Freeholder, 44 Pitt, Cornwall, ON K6J 3P3; tel (613) 933-3160; fax (613) 933-7521. Thomson Newspapers group.
Circulation: 17,883(e); 17,883(e-sat); ABC Sept. 30, 1995.
Price: 56¢(d); 80¢(sat); $2.95/wk; $153.40/yr (carrier).
Advertising: Modular rate $1.17(e); $1.17(e-sat). **Representative:** Thomson Newspapers.
News Services: CP, AP. **Politics:** Independent. **Established:** Freeholder-1844, Standard-1886.
Advertising not accepted: Escort ads; 976 advertising.
Special Editions: Brides (Feb); Progress (Mar); Automotive, Home & Garden, Vacation (Apr); Car Care (Oct).
Special Weekly Section: Hometown (sat).
Magazine: TV Section (thur).

GENERAL MANAGEMENT
Publisher/General Manager Milton Ellis
Controller/Credit Manager E Lidstowe
Purchasing Agent Milton Ellis
ADVERTISING
Director Tim Creswell
Manager-Classified Peter Padbury
CIRCULATION
Director A Jesmer
NEWS EXECUTIVE
Editor Craig Elson
EDITORS AND MANAGERS
Amusements/Auto Editor Craig Elson
Books Editor Craig Elson
Editorial Page Editor Craig Elson
Films/Theater Editor Craig Elson
Food/Home Editor Craig Elson
Photo Department Manager Craig Elson
Science/Sports Editor Craig Elson
Society/Women's Editor Craig Elson
PRODUCTION
Foreman-Composing D Hamill
Foreman-Pressroom, Stereo D Roosenboom

Market Information: Zoned editions; Split Run; TMC.
Mechanical available: Offset; Black and 3 ROP colors; insert accepted — preprinted, max. of 36 pages-limit 6 inserts per issue; page cutoffs — 22¾".
Mechanical specifications: Type page 13" x 21½"; E - 6 cols, 2 1/16", ⅛" between; A - 6 cols, 2 1/16", ⅛" between; C - 9 cols, 1⅓", ⅛" between.
Commodity Consumption (estimated): Newsprint 600 metric tons; widths 27½"; black ink 14,400 pounds; color ink 1,200 pounds; single pages printed 7,590; average pages per issue 25(d).
Equipment: EDITORIAL: Front-end hardware — HI; Front-end software — HI. CLASSIFIED: Front-end hardware — HI; Front-end software — HI. PRODUCTION: Typesetters — 2-COM; Plate processors — 1-Nat; Production cameras — 7-B.
PRESSROOM: Line 1 — 8-G/Community. MAILROOM: Stuffers — 1-Gd; Bundle tyer — 1-Gd; Addressing machine — 1-EI/3001. COMMUNICATIONS: Facsimile — 1-Sharp. WIRE SERVICES: News — Syndicates — CP, AP; receiving dishes — CP. BUSINESS COMPUTERS: 1-ATT; PCs & main system networked.

FORT FRANCES

'91 Census- 8,890; E&P '96 Est. 9,272

The Daily Bulletin
(e-mon; tues; thur; fri)

Fort Frances Daily Bulletin, 116 First St. East; PO Box 339, Fort Frances, ON P9A 1K2; tel (807) 274-5373; fax (807) 274-7286; email fftimes@ocna.org; Fort Frances Times Ltd. group.
Circulation: 2,776(e); Sworn May 30, 1993.
Price: 30¢(d); $3.25/2 wks; $80.00/yr.
Advertising: Modular rate 76¢(e). **Established:** 1930.
Advertising not accepted: As determined by publisher.
Special Editions: Phone Book (Jan); Farm Agriculture (Apr); Outdoor Living (May); Fun in the Sun (June); B.A.S.S. Tournament (July); Farm Agriculture (Oct); Christmas Shopping (Nov).
Special Weekly Section: Food Recipe (thur).

CORPORATE OFFICERS
President James R Cumming
General Manager Doland G Cumming
GENERAL MANAGEMENT
Publisher James R Cumming
ADVERTISING
Manager D Logan
CIRCULATION
Manager L Plumridge
NEWS EXECUTIVE
Editor Michael Behan
EDITORS AND MANAGERS
Business/Education Editor Jody Miller
Government/Political Editor Jeremy Loome
Sports Editor Robert Drinkwater
PRODUCTION
Manager Don Cumming

Mechanical available: Offset; Black and 3 ROP colors; insert accepted — preprinted; page cutoffs — 16".
Mechanical specifications: Type page 10 13/16" x 15"; E - 5 cols, 2 1/16", ⅛" between; A - 5 cols, 2 1/16", ⅛" between; C - 5 cols, 2 1/16", ⅛" between.
Commodity Consumption (estimated): Newsprint 23 short tons; 21 metric tons; widths 32", 16"; single pages printed 2,110; average pages per issue 10(d); single plates used 550.
Equipment: EDITORIAL: Front-end hardware — Ap/Mac; Front-end software — Ap/Mac; Printers — Ap/LaserWriter II NT, LaserMaster/Unity 1200 XLO. CLASSIFIED: Front-end hardware — Ap/Mac; Front-end software — Ap/Mac, Baseview/Class Manager. DISPLAY: Adv layout systems — Ap/Mac; Front-end hardware — Ap/Mac; Front-end software — Ap/Mac. PRODUCTION: Pagination software — QPS; OCR software — XD/Copy GS Plus; Typesetters — 1-V; Plate exposers — 1-B/2500; Plate processors — 1-Encomatic; Scanners — XD/Copy GS Plus, 1-Datacopy/GS Plus; Production cameras — 1-DS/CD240, DAI; Automatic film processors — 1-P.
PRESSROOM: Line 1 — 4-HI/Cotrell V15 AB. MAILROOM: Counter stackers — 1-BG/Count-O-Veyor; Bundle tyer — 1-Bu; Addressing machine — 1-Am, 1-Gp. COMMUNICATIONS: Facsimile — 1-Ricoh. BUSINESS COMPUTERS: 2-IBM/PC, 2-Wyse, 1-NCR/Tower; Applications: Circ, Billing, Gen ledger, Accts receivable, Accts payable, Payroll; PCs & micros networked.

GUELPH

'91 Census- 87,980; E&P '96 Est. 95,496
ABC-CZ (91): 87,976 (HH 32,415)

The Daily Mercury
(e-mon to sat; S)

The Daily Mercury, 8-14 Macdonnell St.; PO Box 3604, Guelph, ON N1H 6P7; tel (519) 822-4310; fax (519) 767-1681. Sterling Newspapers (Hollinger Inc.) group.
Circulation: 15,521(e); 16,655(e-sat); 15,362(S); ABC March 31, 1995.
Price: 60¢(d); 75¢(sat); 75¢(S); $2.60/wk (carrier); $377.25/yr (mail).
Advertising: Modular rate $1.21(e); $1.21(e-sat); $1.21(S). **Representative:** Thomson Newspapers.
News Service: CP. **Politics:** Independent. **Established:** 1854.
Not Published: Eight statutory Canadian Holidays.
Special Editions: Progress; Cookbook; Home Improvement; Fashion; Travel; Auto; Dining; Financial Planning; Brides; Stereo; Club Activities.

GENERAL MANAGEMENT
Publisher/General Manager Stephen Rhodes
Credit Manager Kathy Elliott
Purchasing Agent Kathy Elliott
ADVERTISING
Manager-Classified Ron Drillen
CIRCULATION
Manager Martin Doherty

Ontario III-13

NEWS EXECUTIVE

Managing Editor Ed Cassavoy

EDITORS AND MANAGERS

Assignment Editor-News Bonnie Ewen Pyke
Editorial Page Editor Rolf Pederson
Editorial Writer Rolf Pederson
Education Richard Dooley
Fashion/Women's Editor Rosemary Anderson
Librarian Marg Lynch
Sports Editor Rob Massey
Wire Editor Myrna Ferris

PRODUCTION

Foreman-Composing Ken Pullen
Foreman-Pressroom Don Moon
Foreman-Mailroom Wendy Millson

Market Information: Split Run; TMC.
Mechanical available: Offset; Black and 3 ROP colors; insert accepted — preprinted; page cut-offs — 22¾".
Mechanical specifications: Type page 13" x 21½"; E - 6 cols, 2$\frac{1}{16}$", ⅛" between; A - 6 cols, 2$\frac{1}{16}$", ⅛" between; C - 9 cols, 1⅓", ⅛" between.
Commodity Consumption (estimated): Newsprint 995 metric tons; widths 54"; average pages per issue 28(d).
Equipment: EDITORIAL: Front-end hardware — HAS, HI. CLASSIFIED: Front-end hardware — 4-HAS. PRODUCTION: Platemaking systems — 1-N; Plate exposers — 1-N; Production cameras — 1-B, 1-N; Automatic film processors — 1-B.
PRESSROOM: Line 1 — 7-G; Folders — 1-G. MAILROOM: Bundle tyer — 1-Gd; Addressing machine — 1-Am. LIBRARY: Combination — Microfiche. WIRE SERVICES: News — CP; Syndicates — CP. BUSINESS COMPUTERS: ATT; Applications: Payroll, Billing; PCs & main system networked.

HAMILTON-BURLINGTON

'91 Census- 448,075 (Hamilton 318,500; Burlington 129,575) (Metro Area 599,760); E&P '96 Est. 476,187 (Hamilton 336,173; Burlington 140,014) (Metro Area 625,689)
ABC-NDM (91): 559,760 (HH 221,315)

The Spectator

(m-mon to fri; m-sat)

The Spectator, 44 Frid St., Hamilton, ON L8N 3G3; tel (905) 526-3333. Southam Newspapers group.
Circulation: 109,083(m); 136,245(m-sat); ABC Sept. 30, 1995.
Price: 75¢(d); $1.50(sat); $3.50/wk (carrier); $15.20/mo; $172.90/yr.
Advertising: Modular rate $5.56(m); $6.06(m-sat). **Representative:** Southam Newspapers.
News Services: CP, UPI, LAT-WP, AP. **Politics:** Independent. **Established:** 1846.
Note: Effective Oct. 1, 1995, this publication changed its publishing plan from (e-mon to sat) to (m-mon to sat)
Not Published: New Year; Good Friday; Victoria Day; Dominion Day; Civic Holiday; Labor Day; Thanksgiving; Christmas.
Special Editions: Bridal Guide (Jan); Autofile I, Dining Guide (Feb); Autofile II, Spring Fashion (Mar); Spring Home Improvement, Autofile III, Volunteer (Apr); Autofile IV (May); Autofile V, Summer Leisure/Sound of Music (June); Autofile VI (July); Autofile VII (Aug); Canadian Open, Autofile VIII, Fall Fashion, Fall Bridal, Fall Home Improvement (Sept); Autofile IX (Oct); Autofile X, Gift Guide I (Nov); Gift Guide II (Dec).
Special Weekly Sections: Automotive (thur); Real Estate, Travel (sat).
Magazines: Sports, Business, Lifestyle, Entertainment (daily); Business and Your Money (tues); Food Section (wed); Ego Section, Auto Section (thur); Travel, Real Estate Tab, Weekend Section (sat).

CORPORATE OFFICER

Vice Pres Andrew Prozes

GENERAL MANAGEMENT

Publisher Andrew Prozes
Vice Pres-Finance/General Manager Jack Nelson
Controller Claire Bentzen-Bilkvist
Purchasing J Camilleri
Business Manager I McLeod
Human Resources Manager Gerry Custeau
Director-New Media/Info Technology Susan Emigh

ADVERTISING

Director Anne Antony
Manager-Internal Sales/Marketing Mike Desrosiers
Manager-AD Services Ron Dupius
Manager-Automotive/Real Estate Doris Irvine
Manager-Local Accounts Julia Kamula

MARKETING AND PROMOTION

Manager-Marketing Services John Hay

CIRCULATION

Director-Reader Sales & Service Terry Willows
Reader Sales & Service Manager Distribution Gary Myers
Reader Sales & Service Supervisor (Burlington Zoned Edition) Al Lennie

NEWS EXECUTIVES

Editor Rob Austin
Editor-Burlington Zoned Edition Brent Lawson
Managing Editor-Days John Gibson
Managing Editor-Nights Gerry Nott

EDITORS AND MANAGERS

Business Editor Steve McNeill
Editorial Page Editor Gary Hall
Editorial Writer Gord McNulty
Editorial Writer Peter Van Harten
Education Christine Cox
Food Editor Suzanne Bourret
Librarian/Senior Info Technician Tami Danciu
Metro Editor Dana Robbins
Chief Photographer Ron Albertson
Radio/Television Writer Eric Kohanik
Religion/Ethics Writer Casey Korstanje
Life Editor Michele Steeves
Sports Editor Tim Doyle
Theater Writer Stew Brown
Travel Editor Dan Kislenko
Wire Editor Ron Levett

PRODUCTION

Manager Tom Curd
Electronic Manager Bill Cooke
Manager-Printing Service Dave Potter

Market Information: Split Run; TMC; ADS; Operate audiotex; Electronic edition.
Mechanical available: Offset; Black and 3 ROP colors; insert accepted — preprinted, min. 50lbs. bookstack single sheet, max. ⅜" thickness; page cut-offs — 23$\frac{9}{16}$".
Mechanical specifications: Type page 11.5" x 22¼"; E - 6 cols, 2$\frac{1}{16}$", ⅛" between; A - 10 cols, 1$\frac{1}{16}$", $\frac{1}{12}$" between; C - 10 cols, 1$\frac{1}{16}$", $\frac{1}{12}$" between.
Commodity Consumption (estimated): Newsprint 16,500 metric tons; widths 50", 37.5", 25"; black ink 333,000 pounds; color ink 100,000 pounds; single pages printed 17,500; average pages per issue 50(d); single plates used 90,000.
Equipment: EDITORIAL: Front-end hardware — SDC, 2-HI/PLS; Front-end software — SDC/Text II, Computek, HI/PLS; Other equipment — Ap/Mac Graphics System. CLASSIFIED: Front-end hardware — Cybergraphics, DEC/VAX 4000, PCs; Front-end software — Cybergraphics, HI/PLS. AUDIOTEX: Hardware — QNX/24 line; Supplier name — Brite Voice Systems. DISPLAY: Adv layout systems — Ap/Mac IIsi; Front-end hardware — HI/8900, Ap/Mac Quadra 700, Ap/Mac Quadra 950, Microtek/Scanners, Ap/Mac IIsi, Abaton/Scan 300-85; Front-end software — HI/Layout, QuarkXPress, Multi-Ad/Creator, Aldus/Freehand, Adobe/Photoshop, Ofoto, Broderbund/TypeStyler; Printers — HP/Laserwriter II; Other equipment — Ap/Mac Quadra 900. PRODUCTION: Pagination software — QuarkXPress 3.3, Adobe/Photoshop; Typesetters — 2-AU/APS 6, 1-AU/3850; Plate exposers — Ovac/Twin Drawer, KFM/PlatXPress, III/Automatic w/KFM/Vision Bender; Plate processors — 2-Azoplate/N8605N; Production cameras — 1-C/1211, 1-C/1270; Automatic film processors — 2-LE/LD-24A, 2-LE/PC-18; Film transporters — LE; Shrink lenses — 2-CK Optical; Color separation equipment (conventional) — Pixel Craft; Digital color separation equipment — DSA/608.
PRESSROOM: Line 1 — 8-G/Metro 3183(3 half decks) double width; Line 2 — 8-G/Metro 3184(3 half decks) double width; Line 3 — 8-G/Metro 3185(3 half decks) double width; Folders — 4-G/3:2; Pasters — G; Reels and stands — G. MAILROOM: Counter stackers — 4-St/2578-88, 2-HL/Monitor, 1-HL/HT, 1-HL/HT2; Stuffers — 4-GMA/SLS 1000 (8-into-1); Bundle tyer — 4-MLN/2, 1-MLN/2EE, 2-Power Strap/PSN5, 2-Power Strap/PSN6; Wrapping singles — 1-Cr/39163-661, 1-St/1530 Bagger-Sealer, 2-Ideal/ALS 2500. WIRE SERVICES: News — CP; Stock tables — CP; Syndicates — SOU; receiving dishes — size-1.2m, CP. BUSINESS COMPUTERS: 2-DEC/VAX 6220; Applications: Accts receivable, Gen ledger, Adv, Circ, Human resources, Payroll, Accts payable; PCs & main system networked.

INGERSOLL

See WOODSTOCK

KENORA

'91 Census- 9,780; E&P '96 Est. 10,248
ABC-NDM (91): 15,910 (HH 5,990)

Daily Miner & News

(e-mon to fri)

Daily Miner & News, 33 Main St.; PO Box 1620, Kenora, ON P9N 3X7; tel (807) 468-5555; fax (807) 468-4318. Bowes Publishers Limited (Toronto Sun Publishing) group.
Circulation: 4,721(e); ABC Sept. 30, 1995.
Price: 65¢(d); $110.00/yr (carrier/mail).
Advertising: Modular rate 88¢(e).
News Service: CP. **Politics:** Independent. **Established:** 1881 (daily 1952).
Not Published: Statutory Holidays.
Special Editions: Our Community (Feb, Oct).

GENERAL MANAGEMENT

Publisher Mitch Wolfe

ADVERTISING

Manager Ted Weiss
Manager-National Jim Blight

CIRCULATION

Manager Bob Stewart

NEWS EXECUTIVE

Editor Fred Rinne

Market Information: Zoned editions; Split Run; TMC.
Mechanical available: Offset; Black and 3 ROP colors; insert accepted — preprinted; page cut-offs — 22¾".
Mechanical specifications: Type page 13" x 21¼"; E - 6 cols, 2$\frac{1}{16}$", ⅛" between; A - 6 cols, 2$\frac{1}{16}$", ⅛" between; C - 9 cols, 1⅓", ⅛" between.
Commodity Consumption (estimated): widths 28", 14⅜"; 34"; average pages per issue 16(d).
Equipment: EDITORIAL: Front-end hardware — Ap/Mac, 7-Mk. CLASSIFIED: Front-end hardware — Ap/Mac. PRODUCTION: Plate exposers — 1-N; Scanners — Ap/Mac; Production cameras — 1-Acti.
PRESSROOM: Line 1 — 5-G/Community; Folders — 1-G. MAILROOM: Bundle tyer — 1-Samuel, 1-Gd; Addressing machine — 1-Am. COMMUNICATIONS: Satellite. WIRE SERVICES: News — CP; receiving dishes — size-12 ft, CP. BUSINESS COMPUTERS: PCs & main system networked.

KINGSTON

'91 Census- 56,595; E&P '96 Est. 59,533
ABC-NDM (91): 99,783 (HH 33,300)

The Kingston Whig-Standard

(m-mon to fri; m-sat)

The Kingston Whig-Standard, 306 King St. East; PO Box 2300, Kingston, ON K7L 4Z7; tel (613) 544-5000; fax (613) 530-4119. Southam Newspapers group.
Circulation: 27,963(m); 36,150(m-sat); ABC Sept. 30, 1995.
Price: 60¢(d); $1.49(sat); $3.40/wk (carrier); $17.38/mo (motor route), $14.73/mo (carrier); $176.80/yr (carrier), $208.65/yr (motor route).
Advertising: Modular rate $2.26(m); $2.26(m-sat).
News Services: CP, AP, SOU. **Politics:** Independent-Liberal. **Established:** 1926.
Not Published: New Year; Good Friday; Victoria Day; Dominion Day; Civic Holiday; Labor Day; Thanksgiving; Christmas.
Special Editions: Managing Your Money (Jan); Brides, Managing Your Money (Feb); Spring Thing (Mar); Home & Garden, Spring Fashion (Apr); Vacation Guide '96 (May); Dining Guide, Bargain Sale (July); Back-to-School (Aug); Home & Garden, Fall Activity Guide, Fall Fashion (Sept); Managing Your Money, Small Business, Women in Business (Oct); Festival of Trees, Christmas Section (Nov); Year End Review, Baby of the Year (Dec); Mutual Fund (monthly).
Special Weekly Sections: Health (mon); Small & Growing Business, Fashion (tues); Food (wed); Technology, Entertainment (thur); Entertainment (fri); Companion/Travel (sat).
Magazine: TV Times (sat).

GENERAL MANAGEMENT

Vice Pres-Advertising & Reader Sales Fred Laflamme
Director-Manufacturing & Computer Systems Raymond Dunn
Publisher Bill Peterson
Human Resources Manager Sheldon MacNeil
Business Manager Catriona Ross
Education Service (Newspapers in Education) Elizabeth Wilson

ADVERTISING

Manager-Classified Ted Raaflaub
Asst Manager-Retail/National Jutta Witteveen
Coordinator Co-op Gary Burrows
Supervisor-Special Sections Debbie Tindal

MARKETING AND PROMOTION

Manager-Promotion/Community Service Elizabeth Wilson

NEWS EXECUTIVE

Managing Editor Lynn Messerschmidt

EDITORS AND MANAGERS

City & Regional Editor Jack Chiang
Editorial Page Editor Steve Lukits
News Editor Rob Tripp
News Features Editor Tim Gordanier
Sports Editor Tim Gordanier

Market Information: TMC; Electronic edition.
Mechanical available: Offset; Black and 3 ROP colors; insert accepted — preprinted; page cut-offs — 23¾".
Mechanical specifications: Type page 11¾" x 21½"; E - 5 cols, 2.18", $\frac{3}{16}$" between; A - 10 cols, 1.08", $\frac{1}{16}$" between; C - 5; 8 cols, 2.25"; 1.36" between.
Commodity Consumption (estimated): Newsprint 2,377 metric tons; widths 25", 12½"; black ink 24,203 kg; color ink 9,600 kg; single pages printed 11,510; average pages per issue 38(d); single plates used 21,600.
Equipment: EDITORIAL: Front-end hardware — Ap/Mac; Front-end software — QPS; Printers — QMS/860. CLASSIFIED: Front-end hardware — 1-Cybergraphics; Front-end software — Cybergraphics; Printers — QMS/860. DISPLAY: Adv layout systems — SCS/Layout 8000; Front-end hardware — Ap/Mac; Front-end software — QuarkXPress, Aldus/FreeHand, Adobe/Illustrator; Printers — Ap/LaserWriter II NTX, 2-AU/APS-6-108; Other equipment — ECR/Autokon Scanner, Nikon/Scanner, Imapro/Scanner, Kk/Scanner. PRODUCTION: Pagination software — QuarkXPress; OCR software — Caere/OmniPage; Typesetters — 2-AU/APS 6-108C; Plate exposers — N/Flip Top Ultra Plus; Plate processors — Azoplate/N263A; Scanners — 1-ECR/Autokon 1000; Production cameras — 2-C/Spartan III; Automatic film processors — Z/2600R; Film transporters — 1-C.
PRESSROOM: Line 1 — 10-G/Urbanite; Press drives — Allen Bradley/Twin DC Driver; Folders — 1-Z, 1-SU/Jaw Folder w/ ¼ Folder; Pasters — 7-Enkel; Press control system — Allen Bradley/Console; Press Registration Systems—Pin System. MAILROOM: Counter stackers — 2-HL/HT II; Stuffers — GMA/SLS-1000; Bundle tyer — 1-OVL, 2-OVL/JP-40; Addressing machine — 2-Wm; Mailroom control system — PMS-6; Other mailroom equipment — 2-MM/Saddle Stitcher H325. LIBRARY: Electronic — Informat. COMMUNICATIONS: Remote imagesetting — 1-T. WIRE SERVICES: News — CP; Photos — CP; Stock tables — CP; receiving dishes — size-3ft,10ft, CP, SNN. BUSINESS COMPUTERS: 5-IBM/PC, Service Bureau; Applications: Circ, Adv billing, Accts receivable, Payroll, Financial statements, Budget, Linage and contract statistics, Accts payable; PCs & micros networked; PCs & main system networked.

KIRKLAND LAKE

'91 Census- 10,440; E&P '96 Est. 10,516
ABC-CZ (91): 10,440 (HH 4,405)

Northern Daily News

(e-mon to sat)

Northern Daily News, 8 Duncan Ave.; PO Box 1030, Kirkland Lake, ON P2N 3L4; tel (705) 567-5321; fax (705) 567-6162. Thomson Newspapers group.
Circulation: 5,319(e); 5,319(e-sat); ABC Sept. 30, 1995.

Price: 55¢(d); 75¢(sat); $2.55/wk (carrier); $132.60/yr (carrier/mail).
Advertising: Modular rate 93¢(e); 93¢(e-sat). **Representative:** Thomson Newspapers.
News Service: CP. **Politics:** Independent. **Established:** 1922 (daily 1946).
Not Published: Statutory holidays.

GENERAL MANAGEMENT
Publisher/General Manager Syl Belisle
Business Manager/Purchasing Agent Beth Rutan

ADVERTISING
Manager Marilyn Sayer

CIRCULATION
Manager Darrin Smith

NEWS EXECUTIVE
Managing Editor Tim Kelly

PRODUCTION
Foreman-Composing/Pressroom Bob Aube

Market Information: Split Run; TMC.
Mechanical available: Offset; Black and 3 ROP colors; insert accepted — preprinted; page cut-offs — 21½".
Mechanical specifications: Type page 13" x 21½"; E - 6 cols, $2\frac{1}{16}$", ⅛" between; A - 6 cols, $2\frac{1}{16}$", ⅛" between; C - 9 1½" cols, ⅛".
Commodity Consumption (estimated): average pages per issue 12(d).
Equipment: EDITORIAL: Front-end software — Mk. CLASSIFIED: Front-end software — Mk. PRODUCTION: Typesetters — Mk. MAILROOM: Bundle tyer — 1-BST.

KITCHENER-WATERLOO

'91 Census- 239,465 (Kitchener 168,285; Waterloo 71,180)(Metro Area 356,420); E&P '96 Est. 261,672 (Kitchener 182,243; Waterloo 79,429)(Metro Area 380,121)
ABC-CZ (91): 239,463 (HH 88,530)

The Record

(e-mon to fri; m-sat)

The Record, 225 Fairway Rd., Kitchener, ON N2G 4E5; tel (519) 894-2231; fax (519) 894-3912. Southam Newspapers group.
Circulation: 69,606(e); 87,558(m-sat); ABC Sept. 30, 1995.
Price: 60¢(d); $1.25(sat); $12.00/mo (carrier); $132.00/yr (carrier).
Advertising: Modular rate $3.62(e); $4.06(m-sat). **Representatives:** Newspaper Mktg Bureau; Bardal, Gosbee & Assoc.
News Services: CP, LAT-WP. **Politics:** Independent. **Established:** 1878.
Not Published: New Year; Good Friday; Victoria Day; July 1; Civic Holiday; Labor Day; Thanksgiving; Christmas.
Advertising not accepted: Mail order.
Special Weekly Section: Small Business Section (wed).
Magazines: Entertainment Tab (thur); TV Times (sat).

GENERAL MANAGEMENT
Publisher Wayne MacDonald
Business Manager Peter Hamberger
Research Manager Janice Respondek
Community Relations Manager Owen Lackenbaver

TELECOMMUNICATIONS
Audiotex Manager Dwight Storring

CIRCULATION
Manager E A MacLeod

NEWS EXECUTIVES
Editor Carolyne Rittinger
Assoc Editor Al Coates
Managing Editor Don McCurdy

EDITORS AND MANAGERS
Agriculture Editor Mike Strathder
Art/Theatre Editor Rob Ried
Assignment Desk Brenda Moerle
Books Editor Joe Sinasac
Business Editor Ian Darling
Business Reporter Mike Srathdee
Cambridge Civic/General Reporter Chris Aagaard
City Editor Frank Etherington
Asst City Editor Jon Fear
Columnist Brian Caldwell
Columnist Luisa D'Amato
Courts Reporter Gene McCarthy
Editorial Page Editor Frits Roos
Education Diane Wood
Education Priti Yelaja
Entertainment Editor Phil Bast
Environment Reporter John Roe
Fashion/General Reporter Miles Socha
Finance Reporter Tom Nunn
Food Editor Carol Jankowski
Gender Issues Reporter Rose Simone
General Assignment Reporter Barb Aggerholm
Health Editor Carol Jankowski
Home Furnishings Carol Jankowski
Humor/Youth Beat Reporter Joel Rubinoff
Kitchener & Regional Gov't Catherine Thompson
Labor Reporter Carol Goodwin
Librarian Michael Fox
Living Section Editor Carol Jankowski
Multicultural Reporter Liz Monteiro
Municipal Gov't Kevin Crowley
Music Editor Phil Bast
Photo Coordinator Brian Clark
Police Tony Reinmart
Police Fran Barrick
Queen's Park Greg Crone
Radio/Television Columnist Bonnie Malleck
Real Estate (Homes) Editor Dave Pink
Religion/Classical Music Reporter Pauline Durichen
Social Service Reporter Beth Gallagher
Sports Editor Mickey Mowbray
Travel Editor Malcolm Aird

MANAGEMENT INFORMATION SERVICES
Online Manager Bob South

PRODUCTION
Manager David Zwaniga
Manager-Systems George Styles
Manager-Distribution Kevin Brooks
Manager-Press Peter Rudat

Market Information: Split Run; TMC; Operate database; Operate audiotex.
Mechanical available: Letterpress (direct); Black and 3 ROP colors; insert accepted — preprinted, brochures, envelopes; page cut-offs — $23\frac{9}{16}$".
Mechanical specifications: Type page 13" x 22¼"; E - 6 cols, $2\frac{1}{16}$", ⅛" between; A - 6 cols, $2\frac{1}{16}$", ⅛" between; C - 6 cols, $2\frac{1}{16}$", ⅛" between.
Commodity Consumption (estimated): Newsprint 7,000 short tons; 6,300 metric tons; widths 50", 25", 37½"; black ink 300,000 pounds; color ink 46,000 pounds; single pages printed 17,600; average pages per issue 56(d), 80(sat); single plates used 35,000.
Equipment: EDITORIAL: Front-end hardware — Ap/Mac, PC; Front-end software — QuarkXPress, QPS; Printers — 2-DEC/LA120. CLASSIFIED: Front-end hardware — 2-DEC/VAX 4000-60; Front-end software — Cybergraphics; Printers — HP/LaserJet IV. DISPLAY: Adv layout systems — SCS/Layout 8000; Front-end hardware — DEC/VAX 6310; Front-end software — SCS/Layout 8000; Printers — C.Itoh/300, 1-Mannesman/660, 1-Mannesman/690. PRODUCTION: OCR software — Calera/Wordscan; Typesetters — 2-ECR/1045CS, 2-V, 1-Printer/60, 1-III/3850; Platemaking systems — Na; Plate exposers — 2-Na/Starlite; Plate processors — 2-Na/Superstar, 1-Na/NP80; Electronic picture desk — CD; Scanners — HP/ScanJet Plus, 1-C/Newspager, 1-ECR/2650.
PRESSROOM: Line 1 — 8-G/Mark V; Press drives — Fin; Folders — 1-G/Imperial 3:2 double & inverted; Pasters — 8-G/Automatic; Reels and stands — 8-G/Automatic; Press Registration Systems PC. MAILROOM: Counter stackers — 4-G/5000, HL; Stuffers — 2-GMA/SLS1000 (8:2), 2-St/940 (1:1); Bundle tyer — 2-MLN/2A-82432, 1-MLN/MLOAE-16977; Wrapping singles — 3-St/LW600, 1-RKW/G. LIBRARY: Electronic — Infomart. COMMUNICATIONS: Facsimile — PB, Konica. WIRE SERVICES: News — CP Datafile; Stock tables — Toronto Stock Exchange; Syndicates — WP; receiving dishes — size-1.8m, CP. BUSINESS COMPUTERS: DEC/VAX 6310; Applications: Accts payable, Gen ledger, Adv, Circ; PCs & micros networked; PCs & main system networked.

LINDSAY

'91 Census- 16,700; E&P '96 Est. 18,305
ABC-CZ (91): 16,696 (HH 6,680)

Lindsay Daily Post

(e-mon to fri)

Lindsay Daily Post, 15 William St. N., Lindsay, ON K9V 3Z8; tel (705) 324-2114; fax (705) 324-0174. Sterling Newspapers (Hollinger Inc.) group.
Circulation: 7,943(e); ABC Sept. 30, 1995.
Price: 50¢(d); $101.40/yr (mail).
Advertising: Modular rate 86¢(e). **Representative:** Thomson Newspapers. **Politics:** Independent. **Established:** 1895.

GENERAL MANAGEMENT
Publisher/General Manager Jamie Milne
Accountant Lois Clarke

ADVERTISING
Manager Paul Ramsay

CIRCULATION
Manager Joan Allan

NEWS EXECUTIVE
Managing Editor Joe Hornyak

EDITOR AND MANAGER
Sports Editor Bruce Corcoran

Market Information: TMC.
Mechanical available: Offset; Black and 2 ROP colors; insert accepted — preprinted; page cut-offs — 22¾".
Mechanical specifications: Type page 11⅜" x 21½"; E - 6 cols, 1¾", ⅛" between; A - 6 cols, 1¾", ⅛" between; C - 6 cols, 1¾", ⅛" between.
Commodity Consumption (estimated): Newsprint 400 metric tons; widths 28", 14"; average pages per issue 62(d).
Equipment: EDITORIAL: Front-end hardware — 3-COM. PRODUCTION: Typesetters — Ap/Mac; Plate exposers — 1-N/Flip Top FT 40 V2UP; Production cameras — 1-K/18" x 24"; Automatic film processors — LE/22. PRESSROOM: Line 1 — 4-G/Community, 1-G/Stacked Unit; Folders — G/SC. MAILROOM: Bundle tyer — Weld Loc/SP 500; Addressing machine — Am/Farrington NL-25 Newspaper Labeler. BUSINESS COMPUTERS: 3-IBM/PC; Applications: Adv, Circ, Accounting.

LONDON

'91 Census- 303,165 (Metro Area 381,525); E&P '96 Est. 329,260 (Metro Area 421,276)
ABC-NDM (91): 137,706 (HH 47,350)

The London Free Press

(m-mon to fri; m-sat)

The London Free Press, 369 York St.; PO Box 2280, London, ON N6A 4G1; tel (519) 679-1111; fax (519) 667-4528; web site http://www.mediawb.com.
Circulation: 106,129(m); 135,718(m-sat); ABC Sept. 30, 1995.
Price: 56¢(d); $1.26(sat); $2.94/wk; $11.76/mo; $144.18/yr.
Advertising: Modular rate $5.07(m); $5.33(m-sat). **Representative:** Newspaper Mktg Bureau.
News Services: CP, AP, RN, KRT. **Politics:** Independent. **Established:** 1849.
Not Published: Christmas.
Special Editions: Winter Blowout (Jan); Cuisine, Winter Blowout (Feb); Style, Boat Show, Auto Show (Mar); Baseball Annual, Travel Show, Home & Garden Show, Enviroguide, Fit (Apr); Backyard, Wheel World, Travel Ontario (May); Seniors Guide (June); Style (Sept); Indoors (Oct); Ski, Discover Winter, Home for the Holidays (Nov); Gift Guide (Dec).
Special Weekly Sections: Forum, Travel (sat).
Magazines: Business Monday (mon); TV-Times, Comics, Homes (sat).
Broadcast Affiliates: CFPL AM/FM; CKNX AM/FM.

CORPORATE OFFICERS
Board Chairman J B Pearson
President/Publisher R A Green
Group Vice Pres & Corporate Secretary M G Walker

GENERAL MANAGEMENT
Credit Manager S Dimarco
Director-Human Resources/Oper J L Loebach

ADVERTISING
Director Ken West

MARKETING AND PROMOTION
Director-Marketing M F Pierce
Customer Service Manager Michelle Grantham

CIRCULATION
Sales Manager Susan Cornell

NEWS EXECUTIVES
Editor Philip R McLeod
Exec Editor J A Bembridge
Assoc Editor-News & Information Mary Nesbitt
Assoc Editor-Opinion & Commentary Helen Connell

EDITORS AND MANAGERS
Arts & Entertainment Editor Herb Shoveller
Art Director Bill McGrath
Business Editor John Miner
Homes Editor Clare Dear
London/Regional Editor Gary May
News Design Editor Dale Stolk
Our Times Editor Tess Kalinowski
Sections Editor Emilie Smith
Sports Editor James Reaney
Travel Editor Doug English

PRODUCTION
Manager Bill Stewart
Manager Paul Gartlen
Director-Operations & Human Resources J L Loebach
Director-Info Systems Maureen Brown
Distribution Supervisor Steve Mann
Building Maintenance Supervisor Cecil Johnston
Electronic Pre Press Team Leader Colin Grantham

Market Information: Zoned editions; Split Run; TMC.
Mechanical available: Offset; Letterpress (direct); Black and 3 ROP colors; insert accepted — preprinted, broadsheet, tabloid, quarter fold, mini; page cut-offs — $23\frac{9}{16}$".
Mechanical specifications: Type page 13" x 22¼"; E - 6 cols, $2\frac{1}{16}$", ⅛" between; A - 6 cols, $2\frac{1}{16}$", ⅛" between; C - 6 cols, $2\frac{1}{16}$", ⅛" between.
Commodity Consumption (estimated): Newsprint 12,500 metric tons; widths 54", 40½", 27"; black ink 452,902 pounds; color ink 74,369 pounds; single pages printed 17,396; average pages per issue 56(d); single plates used 69,200.
Equipment: EDITORIAL: Front-end hardware — AT/9000, Ap/Mac; Front-end software — AT, QPS. CLASSIFIED: Front-end hardware — AT/9000; Front-end software — AT. DISPLAY: Adv layout systems — SCS/Layout 8000; Front-end hardware — Dell/Sys 310; Front-end software — SCS/Layout 8000; Printers — HP/LaserJet. PRODUCTION: Typesetters — 3-Cx/Supersetter; Platemaking systems — Na; Plate exposers — 2-DP/Cold Light, 1-N; Plate processors — 2-N/Superstar, 2-Howson, DP; Scanners — 3-ECR/Autokon 1000; Production cameras — 1-C/Newspager, 1-C/Marathon; Automatic film processors — 4-DP, 1-SCREEN, 2-LE; Film transporters — 2-C; Color separation equipment (conventional) — 1-DS/737, 2-PixelCraft/7650, PixelCraft/4520 RS; Digital color separation equipment — 1-Lf/Leafscan 35.
PRESSROOM: Line 1 — 2-G/Mark I Headliner; Line 2 — 9-G/Urbanite; Folders — G/Offset 2:1, G/Letterpress; Pasters — G/Digital Predrive, Butler/Splicers; Reels and stands — G/Simplified Tension, Butler, Martin; Press control system — Hurletron, Fin. MAILROOM: Counter stackers — 6-Id/2000; Stuffers — 4-GMA/SLS-1000; Bundle tyer — 5-Power Strap; Wrapping singles — Manual; Addressing machine — 1-Ch. COMMUNICATIONS: Facsimile — 1-3M/VRC, 1-Konica, 2-Toshiba. WIRE SERVICES: News — AP Sports, KRT, Southstar Network; Stock tables — CP; Syndicates — TV Times; receiving dishes — size-6ft, CP. BUSINESS COMPUTERS: 1-DEC/VAX 8530, 1-DEC/Micro VAX 3100; Applications: Cobol: Adv billing/sales, Circ distribution/billing, Accts payable, Credit checking, Broadcasting, Payroll; PCs & micros networked; PCs & main system networked.

NIAGARA FALLS

'91 Census- 75,400; E&P '96 Est. 79,775
ABC-CZ (91): 75,399 (HH 28,280)

Niagara Falls Review

(e-mon to sat)

Niagara Falls Review, 4801 Valley Way; PO Box 270, Niagara Falls, ON L2E 6T6; tel (905) 358-5711; fax (905) 356-0785; web site http://www.niagara.com/niagnews/review/htm. Sterling Newspapers (Hollinger Inc.) group.
Circulation: 18,828(e); 18,828(e-sat); ABC Sept. 30, 1995.
Price: 75¢(d); $1.00(sat); $3.25/wk; $14.00/mo; $169.00/yr (carrier).
Advertising: Modular rate $0.86(e); $0.86(e-sat). **Representative:** Hollinger Inc.
News Service: CP. **Politics:** Independent. **Established:** 1879.
Advertising not accepted: At Publisher's Discretion.
Special Editions: Stylish Living (Jan); Car Care (Mar); Home Improvement (Apr); Home Improvement (Sept); Car Care, Stylish Living (Oct); John Law's Video Guide, Health File (quarterly).
Special Weekly Sections: Niagara-on-the-Lake (Zoned Edition) (tues); Port Erie (Zoned Edition) (wed); Home Finder (Real Estate) (thur); TV Scene (fri); Cover Story (Entertainment) (sat).

Ontario III-15

Magazines: Niagara-on-the-Lake Tourist Guide (annually-Apr); Niagara Family Fun (Niagara Falls Tourist Guide) (annually-May); Winter Festival of Lights Magazine (annually-Oct).

GENERAL MANAGEMENT
Publisher John Van Kooten
Payroll Clerk Vicki Douglas
Business Manager Rosemary Pelusi

ADVERTISING
Director Tony Bove
Supervisor-Classified Wendy Confiant
Sales Manager-Retail Bill Anderson

CIRCULATION
Manager Bob Thwaites

NEWS EXECUTIVE
Managing Editor Michael Brown

EDITORS AND MANAGERS
City Editor Stephen Fields
Editorial Writer Dave Claydon
Living Editor Leigh Williams
Sports Editor David Rigby

PRODUCTION
Director-Art Joanne Moreau
Foreman-Composing Harry Allan
Foreman-Pressroom Jim McMahon

Market Information: TMC; ADS.
Mechanical available: Offset; Black and 3 ROP colors; insert accepted — preprinted, product samples; non-newsprint publications; page cut-offs — 22¾".
Mechanical specifications: Type page 13" x 21½"; E - 6 cols, 2 1/16", ⅛" between; A - 6 cols, 2 1/16", ⅛" between; C - 9 cols, 1⅜", ⅛" between.
Commodity Consumption (estimated): Newsprint 118,927 kg; widths 25"; black ink 819 kg; single pages printed 847; average pages per issue 28(d), 36(sat); single plates used 1,098.
Equipment: EDITORIAL: Front-end hardware — Ap/Mac; Front-end software — QuarkXPress 3.31; CLASSIFIED: Front-end hardware — CD, Mk/Magician Plus, Mk/Page Magician; Front-end software — CD 3.1; PRODUCTION: Pagination software — CD 3.1; Typesetters — 2-COM/9400 Laser; Plate exposers — 1-N/Flip Top FT40LNS; Production cameras — 1-C/Spartan II 1244, ECR/Autokon 1000; Automatic film processors — Fuji/680A, LE/1200; Film transporters — 1-LE; Shrink lenses — 1-CK Optical.
PRESSROOM: Line 1 — 7-G/Urbanite; Press drives — 2-G/Motor; Folders — 1-G, 1-Quarter Folder; Reels and stands — 11 Reel Stands; Press control system — G; Press Registration Systems Manual. MAILROOM: Bundle tyer — 1-OVL. LIBRARY: Electronic — Ap/Mac, Apple-Search/Software. COMMUNICATIONS: Facsimile — Panasonic. WIRE SERVICES: News — CP; Photos — CP; receiving dishes — size-4ft. BUSINESS COMPUTERS: AT&T/Computer System; Applications: Payroll, Accts receivable. HP: Accounting. Epson: Circ. NEC: Administration.

NORTH BAY

'91 Census- 55,405; E&P '96 Est. 59,559
ABC-CZ (91): 55,405 (HH 20,615)

The North Bay Nugget
(e-mon to sat)

The North Bay Nugget, 259 Worthington St. West; PO Box 570, North Bay, ON P1B 8J6; tel (705) 472-3200; fax (705) 472-1438. Southam Newspapers group.
Circulation: 21,508(e); 21,508(e-sat); ABC Sept. 30, 1995.
Price: 75¢(d); $1.00(fri); $1.00(sat); $3.50/wk, $3.75/wk (motor route); $13.70/mo; $178.00/yr (carrier).
Advertising: Modular rate $1.624(e); $1.624 (e-sat). **Representative:** Southam Newspapers.
News Services: CP, SOU, Fin. Times, Can. Bus. Wire. **Politics:** Independent. **Established:** 1907.
Not Published: New Year; Good Friday; Victoria Day; Dominion Day; Aug Civic Holiday; Labor Day; Thanksgiving; Christmas.
Advertising not accepted: Sex Phone Lines.
Special Weekly Sections: Food (wed); Entertainment (thur); Real Estate (fri); Weekender (sat).
Magazines: Weekly TV Times Mini Tab (fri); Weekly Broadsheet (sat).

CORPORATE OFFICERS
President William Ardell
Vice Pres-Finance/Secretary John G Craig

GENERAL MANAGEMENT
Publisher Robert Hull
Business Manager Geof Rowell
Credit Manager Juli Lefebvre
Purchasing Agent Geof Rowell
Education Service Manager Richard Dinnes

ADVERTISING
Manager Richard Dinnes
Manager-Classified Ross Derry
Manager-Retail Andre LaLande
Manager-General Richard Dinnes

CIRCULATION
Manager R R Bean

NEWS EXECUTIVE
Editor David McLellan

EDITORS AND MANAGERS
City Editor Bruce Cowan
Columnist David McLellan
Columnist Jim Hutchison
Columnist Robert Hull
Columnist P J Wilson
Columnist Mike Umphrey
Editorial Writer Gary Hogg
Editorial Writer David McLellan
Editorial Writer P J Wilson
Editorial Writer Bruce Cowan
Education Carla Ammerata
Lifestyle Editor Marlene Horner
News Editor Randy Lucenti
Radio/Television Editor Dawn Clarke
Religion/Lifestyle Editor Dawn Clarke
Sports Editor Gerry Desormeau

PRODUCTION
Manager Paul Chapman
Superintendent Paul Chapman
Foreman-Pressroom Steve Hevenor
Foreman-Mailroom Paul Chapman
Foreman-Pre Press Richard Turcotte

Market Information: Zoned editions; TMC.
Mechanical available: Offset; Black and 3 ROP colors; insert accepted — product samples; page cut-offs — 22¾".
Mechanical specifications: Type page 11½" x 21⅜"; E - 6 cols, 2 1/16", ⅛" between; A - 10 cols, 1 1/16", ⅛" between; C - 9 cols, 1⅜", ⅛" between.
Commodity Consumption (estimated): Newsprint 2,200 metric tons; widths 27", 33½", 16¾"; 13½", 25¼"; single pages printed 9,069; average pages per issue 30(d), 36(sat).
Equipment: EDITORIAL: Front-end hardware — PC, IBM, Ap/Mac; Front-end software — CText, QuarkXPress; Printers — XIT/Laser Printer 11x17, LaserMaster/Prosetter 1800 18x24; Other equipment — Kk/Negscanner. CLASSIFIED: Front-end hardware — PC, Ap/Mac; Front-end software — CText; Printers — XIT/Laser Printer 11x17. DISPLAY: Adv layout systems — SCS/Layout 8000; Front-end hardware — DEC/VAX; Front-end software — SCS/Layout 8000; Printers — DEC/LG02. PRODUCTION: Pagination software — QuarkXPress 3.31; OCR software — Caere/Omni-Page, Ap/Mac, Adobe/Photoshop 2.5; Typesetters — XIT/Laser Printer 11x17; Platemaking systems — 3M/Pyrofax-, N/Plate Burner; Scanners — Ap/Mac; Production cameras — Dynagraf/Vertical; Automatic film processors — C/Powermatic 650; Color separation equipment (conventional) — Ap/Mac, Adobe/Photoshop 2.5; Digital color separation equipment — EPD, Ap/Mac.
PRESSROOM: Line 1 — 10-G/Community. MAILROOM: Counter stackers — BG/Count-O-Veyor 108, MM/285; Stuffers — KAN; Bundle tyer — MLN. WIRE SERVICES: News — CP; Syndicates — SOU; receiving dishes — CP. BUSINESS COMPUTERS: RSK/Tandy; Applications: WordPerfect Lotus/1-2-3; PCs & micros networked; PCs & main system networked.

ORILLIA

'91 Census- 25,925; E&P '96 Est. 27,709
ABC-CZ (91): 25,925 (HH 10,005)

The Packet & Times
(e-mon to sat)

The Packet & Times, 31 Colborne St. E., Orillia, ON L3V 1T4; tel (705) 325-1355. Sterling Newspapers (Hollinger Inc.) group.
Circulation: 10,068(e); 10,068(e-sat); ABC Sept. 30, 1995.
Price: 50¢(d); 50¢(sat); $3.10/wk; $155.00/yr (carrier).
Advertising: Modular rate $1.04(e); $1.04(e-sat). **Representative:** Thomson Newspapers.
News Service: CP. **Politics:** Independent. **Established:** 1867 (daily 1953).

GENERAL MANAGEMENT
Publisher/General Manager Colin J Bruce
Purchasing Agent Gail Kerr

ADVERTISING
Manager Peter Hinton

CIRCULATION
Manager Basil LaVoie

NEWS EXECUTIVE
Managing Editor Jeff Day

EDITORS AND MANAGERS
Auto Jeff Day
City Editor Randy Richmond
Editorial Page Editor Jeff Day
Farm Jeff Day
Food/Garden Mrs J Sidhu
News Editor Jeff Day
Radio/Television Jeff Day
Sports Dave Dawson
Teen Age Youth/Women's Mrs J Sidhu

PRODUCTION
Superintendent Ron Lawson
Foreman-Pressroom Jim Wallace

Market Information: TMC; ADS.
Mechanical available: Offset; Black and 3 ROP colors; insert accepted — preprinted; page cut-offs — 22¾".
Mechanical specifications: Type page 12 15/16"x 21½"; E - 6 cols, 2 1/16", ⅛" between; A - 6 cols, 2 1/16", ⅛" between; C - 9 cols, 1⅓", ⅛" between.
Commodity Consumption (estimated): Newsprint 410 metric tons; widths 27½"; average pages per issue 20(d).
Equipment: EDITORIAL: Front-end hardware — CD/Pagination; Other equipment — Ap/Mac Graphic. PRODUCTION: Plate exposers — F/plate-maker; Production cameras — 1-B/3000. MAILROOM: Bundle tyer — 1-Gd; Addressing machine — 1-El.

OTTAWA, ON-HULL, QC

'91 Census- 374,700 (Ottawa, ON 313,990; Hull, QC 60,710)(Metro Area 920,855); E&P '96 Est. 396,615 (Ottawa, ON 332,024; Hull, QC 64,591)(Metro Area 975,432)
Citizen
ABC-NDM (91): 920,857 (HH 349,255)
Le Droit
ABC-NDM (91): 726,610 (HH 284,235)
Sun
ABC-NDM (91): 625,479 (HH 242,812)

The Ottawa Citizen
(m-mon to fri; m-sat; S)

The Ottawa Citizen, 1101 Baxter Rd.; PO Box 5020, Ottawa, ON K2C 3M4; tel (613) 829-9100; fax (613) 596-8436; email ottawa-citizen@freenet.carleton.ca. Southam Newspapers group.
Circulation: 145,952(m); 202,892(m-sat); 134,017(S); ABC Sept. 30, 1995.
Price: 50¢(d); $1.50(sat); 50¢(S); $4.28/wk (GST included); $17.12/mo; $102.70/6 mos; $199.40/yr.
Advertising: Modular rate $7.97(m); $10.36 (m-sat); $7.97(S). **Representative:** Southam Newspapers.
News Services: CP, AP, UPI, SOU, LAT-WP, NYT, KRT, RN, SHNS. **Politics:** Independent. **Established:** 1845.
Note: Effective Feb. 1995, this publication changed its publishing plan from (all-day-mon to fri; m-sat; S) to (m-mon to fri; m-sat; S)
Not Published: Canadian statutory holidays.
Advertising not accepted: Tobacco.
Special Editions: Recreation & Culture, National Ski Week, Bridal Tab (Jan); Valentine's Restaurant Page, Discount Section, March Break, New Homes, Auto Show, Mutual Funds (Feb); Local Business Profile, High Technology, Spring Travel Directory (Mar); New Homes (Apr); Business Show, Spring Technology, Personal Computers, Summer Camps (May); Armed Forces, Canada Day, Summer Travel Directory (June); Discount Section (July); Back-to-School, Local Business Profile (Aug); Lively Arts, Kiwanis TV Auction, Fall Fashion, Insurance Review, Fall Travel Directory (Sept); City Wide Furniture, CHEO Review of a Lifetime, Investment Strategies (Oct); Winter Sun Vacations, Photo Contest, Ski Trails, Gift Pages (Nov); Sun 'n Ski, Baby Pages, Winter Travel Directory (Dec).
Magazines: TV-Times (sat); Ottawa Living (quarterly).

CORPORATE OFFICER
President William Ardell

GENERAL MANAGEMENT
Publisher Russ Mills
Vice Pres Marketing Jim Orban
Education Service Manager Don Hale

ADVERTISING
Vice Pres Kevin Bent
Key Account Manager Darrell Itterman
Sales Planning Manager Maurice Perron
Promotion Manager Marsha Skuce

TELECOMMUNICATIONS
Audiotex Manager Seymour Diener

CIRCULATION
Manager-City Harold Lundy
Manager-Single Copy Sales William Berry
Manager-Zone Andre Boileau
Manager-Office Phil Wong
Asst Manager-Office Robert Littlemore Jr
Manager-Traffic/Country Jacques Gouin

NEWS EXECUTIVES
Editor James Travers
Managing Editor Sharon Burnside
Asst Managing Editor Peter Robb
Asst Managing Editor Dave Guy
Asst Managing Editor Graham Parley

EDITORS AND MANAGERS
Action Line Tony Cote
Books Editor Charles Gordon
City Editor Tina Spencer
Columnist Tony Atherton
Columnist Charles Gordon
Columnist Dave Brown
Columnist Frank Howard
Columnist John Ibbitson
Columnist Roy MacGregor
Editorial Page Editor Peter Calamai
Editorial Writer Susan Riley
Editorial Writer Robert Reade
Editorial Writer April Lindgren
Farm Editor Roswitha Guggi
Fashion Editor Margo Roston
Film/Theater Editor Janice Kennedy
Food Editor Laura Robin
Lifestyles Editor Tina Spencer
Music/Dance Editor Norm Provencher
News Editor Graham Parley
News Editor Dave Guy
Photo Director Richard Starnes
Society Editor Tina Spencer
Sports Editor Tom Casey
Travel Editor Jane Defalco

MANAGEMENT INFORMATION SERVICES
Online Manager Ron Tysick
Data Processing Manager Mark Olesevich

PRODUCTION
Vice Pres Pat Brennan
Director-Purchasing Donna Brazeau
Security Director Don Edwards
Manager-Pre Press Jim McKnight
Manager-Pre Press (Night) Bruce Craig
Superintendent-Pressroom Steve Dale
Foreman-Pressroom Bruce Lennie
Foreman-Pressroom Bruce Daw
Superintendent-Mailroom George Gauthier
Foreman-Mailroom Garry Parks
Foreman-Mailroom Andy Gordon
Manager-Computer Information Services Mark Olesevich
Manager-Fleet Bill Nash

Market Information: Split Run; TMC; ADS; Operate database; Operate audiotex; Electronic edition.
Mechanical available: Offset; Black and 3 ROP colors; insert accepted — preprinted; page cut-offs — 23¾".
Mechanical specifications: Type page 11½" x 22⅛"; E - 6 cols, 2 1/16", ⅛" between; A - 10 cols, 1 1/16", ⅛" between; C - 10 cols, 1 1/16", ⅛" between.
Commodity Consumption (estimated): Newsprint 21,800 metric tons; widths 54", 40½", 27"; black ink 200,000 pounds; color ink 140,000 pounds; average pages per issue 68(d), 108(sat), 56(S); single plates used 130,000.
Equipment: EDITORIAL: Front-end hardware — PC/386, PC/486, Ap/Mac ci, Ap/Power Mac 6100-66, Ap/Mac PowerBook 150; Front-end software — DEC, QuarkXPress, QuarkDispatch, Quark Copydesk, QuickWire; Printers — AU/APS 6, VT/600, Ap/Mac LaserWriters, HP/LaserJet 4 PWS. CLASSIFIED: Front-end hardware — PCs; Front-end software — Cybergraphics; Other equipment — Sharp/610 scanner. AUDIOTEX: Hardware — PEP/Voice Print; Software — Unix 5.1; DISPLAY: Adv layout systems — SCS/Layout 8000; Front-end hardware — PC. PRODUCTION: Pagination software — QPS; Typesetters — 2-AU/APS-6-108C, 1-AU/APS-3850; Platemaking systems — 2-WL/Lith-X-Pozer 5; Plate exposers — 1-N/Flip Top FTUP; Plate processors — 2-W; Electronic picture desk — CD; Scanners — 3-Sharp/

III-16 Ontario

Flatbed, 4-Nikon/Negative Scanner, 1-ECR; Automatic film processors — 3-LE/2600, 1-LE/1800; Color separation equipment (conventional) — 6-Ap/Mac Quadra 8100.
PRESSROOM: Line 1 — 9-G/Metro Offset; Line 2 — 9-G/Metro Offset; Line 3 — 9-G/Metro Offset; Press drives — PPD; Folders — 3-G/3:2; Reels and stands — 24-G. MAILROOM: Counter stackers — 4-QWI/300, 2-SH/257; Stuffers — 2-Amerigraph/NP-630; Bundle tyer — 5-Power Strap/PSN-6. LIBRARY: Electronic — Infomart. WIRE SERVICES: News — CP; Syndicates — LAT-WP, NYT, RN, KRT, SHNS, Southam; receiving dishes — CP. BUSINESS COMPUTERS: IBM/386-40, IBM/486-33, IBM/486-66; Applications: Microsoft/Office.

Le Droit

(m-mon to fri; m-sat)

Le Droit, 47 Clarence St.; PO Box 8860, Ottawa, ON K1G 3J9; tel (613) 562-0111; fax (613) 562-6280 (Admin). UniMedia Inc. (Hollinger Inc.) group.
Circulation: 33,491(m); 40,637(m-sat); ABC Sept. 30, 1995.
Price: 65¢(d); $1.55(sat); $3.40/wk; $14.73/mo; $163.80/yr (carrier), $355.53/yr (mail).
Advertising: Modular rate $2.20(m); $2.25(m-sat). **Representative:** ProBec 5 LTD.
News Services: CP, AFP. **Politics:** Independent. **Established:** 1913.
Not Published: Jan 1; Apr 17; May 18; June 24; July 1; Aug 3; Sept 7; Oct 12; Dec 25.
Special Weekly Sections: Tendance Fashion (wed); Societe (Living) (thur); Weekend (entertainment) (fri); Habitation (homes) (sat).
Magazine: TV Guide (sat).

GENERAL MANAGEMENT
Publisher/General Manager Pierre Bergeron
Comptroller P Massie
Education Service Manager M Ouellette
ADVERTISING
Director M Ouellette
Manager-Classified Gilles Lamadeleine
MARKETING AND PROMOTION
Director M Ouellette
TELECOMMUNICATIONS
Audiotex Manager Jacques Blouin
CIRCULATION
Director Gilles Lamadeleine
NEWS EXECUTIVE
Managing Editor Francois Roy
EDITORS AND MANAGERS
Books Editor G Dallaire
Editorial Page Editor M Maltais
Editorial Writer M Maltais
Food Editor G Dallaire
Political Editor Michel Gauthier
Radio/Television Editor G Dallaire
Religion Editor G Dallaire
Society/Women's Editor G Dallaire
Sports Editor Michel Gauthier
MANAGEMENT INFORMATION SERVICES
Data Processing Manager Louis Simoneau
PRODUCTION
Computer Systems Manager Louis Simoneau
Manager Michel Normand

Market Information: TMC; Operate audiotex; Electronic edition.
Mechanical available: Offset; Black and 3 ROP colors; insert accepted — preprinted, subject to approval; page cut-offs — 15".
Mechanical specifications: Type page 10¼" x 14⅝"; E - 5 cols, 1⅞", 3/16" between; A - 5 cols, 1⅞", 3/16" between; C - 6 cols, 1 9/16", 3/16" between.
Commodity Consumption (estimated): Newsprint 2,700 short tons; 2,400 metric tons; widths 60", 45", 30"; black ink 90,000 pounds; color ink 20,000 pounds; single pages printed 20,175; average pages per issue 64(d); single plates used 29,500.
Equipment: EDITORIAL: Front-end hardware — 2-Compaq/386-33 Deskpro, 20-Teleray/Terminal, 10-Ap/Mac IIci; Front-end software — Sco Xenix, SCS/Editorial; Printers — 1-HP, 1-Ap/Mac LaserWriter Pro 630; Other equipment — 8-RSK/Tandy 100-102, 12-RSK/Tandy 1100 FD. CLASSIFIED: Front-end hardware — 2-Compaq/386-33 Deskpro; Front-end software — Sco Xenix, SCS/Classified; Printers — Fujitsu; Other equipment — 15-Teleray/Terminal. AUDIOTEX: Hardware — VMX; Software — Microsoft/Works 7.0; DISPLAY: Adv layout systems — SCS/Layout 8000 6.05 Compaq/386; Front-end hardware — 6-Ap/Mac IIci; Front-end software — Aldus/Freehand 4.0, QuarkXPress 3.31, Adobe/Illustrator 5.5; Printers — QMS/860, HP/LaserJet II. PRODUCTION: Pagination software — QuarkXPress 3.11, SCS/Linx 3.5.2; OCR software — STF/Auto OCR; Typesetters — 1-Linotype-Hell/300; Platemaking systems — N/Flip Top; Plate processors — Howtek; Electronic picture desk — CD/Newsline 2640, Ap/Mac IIci w/Adobe/Photoshop, CD/Newsline 2644; Scanners — 2-Nikon/L3500, 1-Howtek, 1-Kk, 1-Nikon/Cool Scan, 1-X, 1-Kk/2035, 1-AG/Horison; Production cameras — B; Automatic film processors — LE/Processor, LE; Digital color separation equipment — Ap/Power Mac 8100-100 w/Adobe/Photoshop.
PRESSROOM: Line 1 — 10-RKW/Creusoloire (2 ½ units; 3 Quad units); Folders — 2-UB30. MAILROOM: Counter stackers — MM/Wamack, MM; Stuffers — MM/II 4-in-1; Bundle tyer — Gd. LIBRARY: Electronic — Compaq/Deskpro; Combination — CD-Rom, Compaq/Deskpro, MicroFilm. WIRE SERVICES: News — CP; Photos — CP; Stock tables — CP; receiving dishes — size-2m, CP, API Graphiques. BUSINESS COMPUTERS: IBM/Sys 36, Sun; Applications: Accts, Circ, Inventory, Payroll; PCs & micros networked; PCs & main system networked.

The Ottawa Sun

(m-mon to fri; S)

The Ottawa Sun, 380 Hunt Club Rd.; PO Box 9729, Ottawa, ON K1G 5H7; tel (613) 739-7000; fax (613) 739-9383; email jpaton@sunpub.rogers.com (Pub), ottsun@ottawa.net (News). Toronto Sun Publishing Corp. group.
Circulation: 54,297(m); 61,540(S); ABC Sept. 30, 1995.
Price: 35¢(d); 75¢(S); $2.25/wk (carrier).
Advertising: Modular rate $2.47(m); $2.63(S); $2.25(m & S).
News Services: CP, UPI. **Established:** 1988.
Not Published: Jan 1; Apr 5; July1; Aug 5; Sept 2; Dec 25.
Special Edition: Welcome Home (Renovation Guide).
Special Weekly Sections: Car Market (thur); Home Style (S).
Magazines: TV Magazine (S); Modern Woman (Last S/month).

GENERAL MANAGEMENT
Publisher/CEO John Paton
ADVERTISING
Director-Sales Lise Desgroseilliers
Assoc Director Susan Dogg-Fulton
Sales Manager Steve Davis
MARKETING AND PROMOTION
Director-Promotion Don Creighton
CIRCULATION
Director Randy Hayley
NEWS EXECUTIVES
Editor in Chief Richard VanSickle
Editor Mark Bonokoski
Managing Editor Rob Paynter
Assoc Editor Rick Gibbons
MANAGEMENT INFORMATION SERVICES
Director-Computer Services Michael G Melnick
PRODUCTION
Director Charles Stapley
Director-Commercial Printing Claire-Anne Lalonde
Manager Tracie Legault
Superintendent-Pressroom Paul Valiquette

Mechanical available: Offset; Black and 3 ROP colors; insert accepted — preprinted, 11"x14 ½", single sheets must be folded; page cut-offs — 13½".
Mechanical specifications: Type page 10¼" x 12½"; E - 8 cols, 1.17", ⅛" between; A - 8 cols, 1.17", ⅛" between; C - 8 cols, 1.17", ⅛" between.
Commodity Consumption (estimated): Newsprint 6,700 metric tons; widths 23", 30", 33"; black ink 58,500 pounds; color ink 12,875 pounds; average pages per issue 64(d), 54(S).
Equipment: EDITORIAL: Front-end hardware — Ap/Mac Quadra, Ap/Power Mac, Ap/Mac Duo 230, Ap/Mac Duo 280; Front-end software — QuarkXPress, Adobe/Illustrator, QuarkXPress 3.3.1, Adobe/Illustrator 5.0, P.INK/Client, Aldus/Free Hand 4.0; Printers — QMS/860, Solo/Browser; Other equipment — Tektronix/Phaser 300. CLASSIFIED: Front-end hardware — Ap/Mac Quadra 700, PC; Front-end software — RSX/II 3.1, Multi-Ad 3.5.4, Aldus/FreeHand 4.0, Adobe/Illustrator 5.0; Printers — Tegra/Varityper, Am International. DISPLAY: Adv layout systems — Multi-Ad, Adobe/Illustrator, Aldus/FreeHand; Front-end hardware — Ap/Mac Quadra 700; Printers — QMS/860. PRODUCTION: Pagination software — Mk/Ad Director 1.5.2; Typesetters — QMS/860, III/3850, ECR/Newsrecorder; Plate exposers — 2-Burgess/Plate Burners; Plate processors — Azoplate/N263-A, Southern Technigraph/DN-85; Scanners — Kk/Neg Scanner; Production cameras — ECR/Autokon, Marathon/Horizontal; Automatic film processors — Luth/Superline 660, P/OL260, LE/1800; Film transporters — P/SC2050; Shrink lenses — Marathon/Camera; Digital color separation equipment — CD/200i, Howteck/Flatbet.
PRESSROOM: Line 1 — 10-G/Urbanite single width; Line 2 — 4-G/Urbanite single width; Press drives — Fin; Folders — 2-G/Urbanite 2:1; Pasters — 8-Enkel; Reels and stands — Enkel; Press control system — Fin. MAILROOM: Counter stackers — 3-Id; Stuffers — 3-MM/227, 1-HI/1372; Bundle tyer — 2-MLN, 1-Dynamic. LIBRARY: Electronic — DEC/VAX (Toronto); Combination — E-Mail, QuicKmail for Ap/Mac. COMMUNICATIONS: Digital ad delivery system — BBS on Ap/Power Mac 6100. WIRE SERVICES: News — CP, AP, Canwir; Photos — CP; Syndicates — CP, UPI, AP, RN, GNS, LATS; receiving dishes — size-7ft, CP. BUSINESS COMPUTERS: PC/286, PC/386, PC/486; Applications: Lotus WordPerfect; PCs & micros networked; PCs & main system networked.

OWEN SOUND

'91 Census- 21,675; E&P '96 Est. 23,300
ABC-CZ (91): 21,674 (HH 8,705)

The Sun Times

(e-mon to sat)

The Sun Times, 290 9th St. E.; PO Box 200, Owen Sound, ON N4K 5P2; tel (519) 376-2250; fax (519) 376-7190. Southam Newspapers group.
Circulation: 22,010(e); 22,010(e-sat); ABC Sept. 30, 1995.
Price: 75¢(d); 95 ¢(fri); 75¢(sat); $2.50/wk (carrier); $127.00/yr (carrier).
Advertising: Modular rate $1.453(e); $1.494(e-fri); $1.453(e-sat).
News Services: CP, Southam News. **Politics:** Independent. **Established:** 1853.
Not Published: New Year; Good Friday; Victoria Day; Canada Day; Civic Holiday; Labor Day; Thanksgiving; Christmas.
Special Editions: Brides (Jan); Industrial (Feb); Agriculture, Homes/Real Estate (Mar); Homes & Gardens (Apr); Summer Cookbook (May); Senior Scene, Restaurant Guide (June); ½ Price Sale (Aug); National Home Week (Sept); Fall Harvest Sale (Oct); X'mas Gift Guide (Nov); X'mas Greetings (Dec).
Special Weekly Sections: Seniors (tues); Food (wed); Auto (thur); Real Estate (fri).
Magazine: TV Times.

GENERAL MANAGEMENT
Publisher Ed Shultz
Business Manager Margaret A Eagle
ADVERTISING
Manager Robert Cannon-Sherlock
Manager-Classified Penny Morrison
Manager-Retail Warren Elder
MARKETING AND PROMOTION
Manager-Promotion Daniel J Patterson
CIRCULATION
Manager Daniel J Patterson
NEWS EXECUTIVE
Editor Jim Merriam
EDITORS AND MANAGERS
City Editor Dan Harrison
News Editor Karen Pridham
Photo Department Manager Willy Waterton
Sports Editor Heather Kehoe
PRODUCTION
Manager Ted Turner

Mechanical available: Offset; Black and 3 ROP colors; insert accepted — preprinted, envelopes, flyers; page cut-offs — 21¾".
Mechanical specifications: Type page 13" x 21¾"; E - 6 cols, 2 1/16", ⅛" between; A - 6 cols, 2 1/16", ⅛" between; C - 6 cols, 2 1/16", ⅛" between.
Commodity Consumption (estimated): Newsprint 2,425 metric tons; widths 17", 27½", 34"; single pages printed 7,015; average pages per issue 26(d); single plates used 20,000.
Equipment: EDITORIAL: Front-end hardware — 5-Ap/Mac Quadra 950, 26-RSK/Tandy 3000, QMS/850, 3-Ap/Mac LaserWriter; Front-end software — CText, QuarkXPress, Ventura; Printers — QMS/850, 3-Ap/Mac LaserWriter; Other equipment — Smith Corona/XDS 20. CLASSIFIED: Front-end hardware — 8-RSK/Tandy 3000; Front-end software — CText; Other equipment — 1-Ap/Mac LaserScanner. DISPLAY: Adv layout systems — 3-DVT/420; Front-end hardware — 1-Ap/Mac, 5-Ap/Mac fx, 1-Ap/Mac ci, 2-Ap/Mac SE; Front-end software — QuarkXPress, Adobe/Illustrator, Aldus/Free-Hand, Adobe/Photoshop; Printers — 3-Ap/Mac LaserPrinter; Other equipment — 2-Scan Maker/II, 2-Abaton, 1-Ap/Mac Scanner. PRODUCTION: Typesetters — ECR/Imagesetter; Plate exposers — N/Flip Top FT40UPNS; Plate processors — 1-Enco; Direct-to-plate imaging — 3M/Pyrofax; Scanners — AG/Repromaster-3000.
PRESSROOM: Line 1 — 5-G/Community(1 Community 4-high); Folders — 1-G/SC, 1-G/Suburban. MAILROOM: Counter stackers — 2-BG; Stuffers — MM/8-plus-1; Bundle tyer — MLN. COMMUNICATIONS: Facsimile — Sharp/FO-750, Konica/720. WIRE SERVICES: News — AP, CP, SOU; Photos — CP, AP; Stock tables — SOU; Syndicates — SOU, United Media; receiving dishes — size-6ft, CP. BUSINESS COMPUTERS: 1-Compaq/LTE 286, 1-IBM/PS2 Model 60, 2-IBM/PS2 Model 30; Applications: Lotus: Accts payable; PCs & main system networked.

PEMBROKE

'91 Census- 14,000; E&P '96 Est. 14,545
ABC-CZ (91): 15,758 (HH 6,315)

The Pembroke Daily News

(e-mon to sat)

Pembroke Daily News, 86 Pembroke St. W.; PO Box 10, Pembroke, ON K8A 6X1; tel (613) 735-3141; fax (613) 732-7214. Runge Newspapers group.
Circulation: 1,000(e); 18,000(e-wed), 8,000 (e-fri); 28,000(e-sat).
Price: 50¢(d); $1.50/wk; $74.95/yr.
Advertising: Modular rate 77¢(e); 87¢(e-wed), 83¢(e-fri); 97¢(e-sat). **Established:** 1992 (daily), 1934(weekly).
Note: Wednesday and Saturday distribution is free. This is a new listing. Circulation figures shown are estimates. Audit statement not available at presstime.

GENERAL MANAGEMENT
Publisher Jim Badgley
ADVERTISING
Manager Jim Badgley
CIRCULATION
Manager Elise Turcotte
NEWS EXECUTIVE
Editor Terry Myers

Market Information: TMC.
Mechanical available: Offset; Black and 3 ROP colors; insert accepted —
Mechanical specifications: Type page 10⅛" x 13¼"; E - 6 cols, 1⅝", ⅛" between; A - 6 cols, 1⅝", ⅛" between; C - 6 cols, 1⅝", ⅛" between.

Observer

(e-mon to fri; m-sat)

Observer, 186 Alexander St.; PO Box 190, Pembroke, ON K8A 4L9; tel (613) 732-3691; fax (613) 732-2645. Sterling Newspapers (Hollinger Inc.) group.
Circulation: 7,236(e); 7,236(m-sat); ABC Sept. 30, 1995.
Price: 60¢(d); 75¢(sat); $2.70/wk (carrier); $133.00/yr (carrier).
Advertising: Modular rate $1.07(e); $1.07(m-sat). **Representative:** Thomson Newspapers.
News Service: CP. **Politics:** Independent. **Established:** 1855 (daily 1957).
Advertising not accepted: Dubious Financial.

GENERAL MANAGEMENT
Publisher/General Manager Lois Hornby
Personnel Manager Pat Hahn
Purchasing Agent Pat Hahn
ADVERTISING
Manager Neal O'Donoghue
CIRCULATION
Manager Dave Bell
NEWS EXECUTIVE
Managing Editor Mike Walsh
EDITORS AND MANAGERS
City Editor Francis Baker
Sports Editor Adrian Brijbassi
Weekly Manager Jim Kwiatkowski

Ontario III-17

PRODUCTION

Superintendent Derrick Cracknell
Foreman-Pressroom Steve Turcotte

Market Information: TMC; ADS.
Mechanical available: Offset; Black and 3 ROP colors; insert accepted — preprinted, most; page cut-offs — 21½".
Mechanical specifications: Type page 13¾" x 21½"; E - 6 cols, 2¹⁄₁₆", ⅛" between; A - 6 cols, 2¹⁄₁₆", ⅛" between; C - 8 cols, 1½", ⅛" between.
Commodity Consumption (estimated): average pages per issue 8(d).
Equipment: EDITORIAL: Printers — 2-F. PRODUCTION: Typesetters — COM/II 316, COM/II 40348.
PRESSROOM: Line 1 — G/Community. MAILROOM: Bundle tyer — 1-Gd, TS/210; Addressing machine — Mail Rite.

PETERBOROUGH

'91 Census- 68,370; E&P '96 Est. 74,100
ABC-CZ (91): 68,371 (HH 26,605)

The Examiner

(e-mon to fri; m-sat; S)

The Examiner, 400 Water Street; PO Box 3890, Peterborough, ON K9J 8L4; tel (705) 745-4641; fax (705) 741-3217. Sterling Newspapers (Hollinger Inc.) group.
Circulation: 25,011(e); 25,011(m-sat); 22,993(S); ABC Sept. 30, 1995.
Price: 60¢(d); $1.00(sat); 75¢(S); $3.20/wk (carrier); $13.86/mo (pre-authorized payment); $161.20/yr (carrier), $245.00/yr (mail).
Advertising: Modular rate $1.75(e); $1.75(m-sat); $1.75(S). **Representative:** Hollinger Inc.
News Services: CP, AP, RN. **Established:** 1847.
Not Published: Statutory holidays.
Special Editions: Brides (Jan); Car Care, Progress Edition (Mar); Car Care, Home Improvement (May); Seniors Monthly (monthly); Cook Book (Spring); Cook Book (Christmas).
Special Weekly Section: Financial News Advertorial (2nd thur).
Magazines: TV Guide (sat); Seniors.

CORPORATE OFFICERS

President/Chief Operating Officer Jamie Milne
Chairman & CEO David Radler

GENERAL MANAGEMENT

Publisher Jamie Milne
General Manager Jamie Milne
Controller Catherine Trask-Elliott

ADVERTISING

Manager Bill Barthorpe

TELECOMMUNICATIONS

Audiotex Manager Bill Barthorpe

CIRCULATION

Manager Rick Smith

NEWS EXECUTIVE

Managing Editor Ed Arnold

EDITORS AND MANAGERS

City Editor Jim Hendry
Copy Editor Steve Wilkinson
District Editor Werner Bergen
Editorial Page Editor Ben Thompson
Features Editor Scott Whalen
Sports Editor Bob Feaver
Wire Editor Rob McCormick

PRODUCTION

Supervisor Larry Hogeboom
Foreman-Composing Terry Keating
Foreman-Pressroom John Amer

Market Information: TMC; ADS; Operate audiotex.
Mechanical available: Letterpress (direct); Black and 3 ROP colors; insert accepted — preprinted; page cut-offs — 23½".
Mechanical specifications: Type page 13" x 23.5"; E - 6 cols, 2¹⁄₁₆", ⅛" between; A - 6 cols, 2¹⁄₁₆", ⅛" between; C - 9 cols, 1⅓", ⅛" between.
Commodity Consumption (estimated): Newsprint 1,600 metric tons; widths 27½", 55"; single pages printed 10,900; average pages per issue 30(d), 28(S).
Equipment: EDITORIAL: Front-end hardware — Intel/486, Intel/386; Front-end software — CText, Microsoft/Windows 3.1, QuarkXPress 3.1, Microsoft/DOS 5.0; Printers — Ap/LaserWriter; Other equipment — 1-Ap/Mac IIcx, 2-Ap/Mac Quadra, 1-Ap/Mac Quadra 950, 1-Sharp/JX-610 flatbed scanner, 2-CD/Newsline 2644 Picture Desk, 2-Nikon/3500 Scanner, 2-AG/Arcus Flatbed Scanner. CLASSIFIED: Front-end hardware — Intel/386; Front-end software — CText/Classified Pagination Alps-OS2, CText/Adept (Ad building). AUDIOTEX: Hardware — 3-PC; Software — Ads on Call; Supplier name — The Computer Group. DISPLAY: Adv layout systems — SCS/Layout 8000; Front-end hardware — Intel/386; Front-end software — SCS/Layout 8000. PRODUCTION: Pagination software — QuarkXPress 3.1; Typesetters — 2-V/Series 6000 Imagesetter, 1-QMS/860 Print System; Platemaking systems — 1-He/Merigraph; Electronic picture desk — 2-CD/Newsline 2643 Picture Desk; Scanners — 2-Nikon/3500; Production cameras — 1-DS/Horizontal Page Camera C-260-D; Automatic film processors — 2-DS/220-QT, 1-Fuji/360F; Digital color separation equipment — CD/EPD.
PRESSROOM: Line 1 — 5-G/Headliner Letterpress; Folders — 1-G. MAILROOM: Bundle tyer — 2-OVL; Addressing machine — 1-El. LIBRARY: Electronic — SMS/Stauffer Gold; Combination — ATT. WIRE SERVICES: News — CP; Photos — CP; Stock tables — CP; receiving dishes — CP. BUSINESS COMPUTERS: ATT; Applications: Adv billing, Payroll, Circ billing; PCs & micros networked; PCs & main system networked.

PORT COLBORNE
See WELLAND

PORT HOPE

'91 Census- 11,505; E&P '96 Est. 12,466
ABC-CZ (91): 11,505 (HH 4,315)

Guide (e-mon to fri)

Guide, 121 C Toronto Rd.; PO Box 296, Port Hope, ON L1A 3W4; tel (905) 372-0131; fax (905) 885-7442. St. Catharines Standard Ltd. group.
Circulation: 3,176(e); ABC March 31, 1993.
Price: 60¢(d); 60¢(fri); $2.50/wk (carrier); $120.00/yr (carrier/mail).
Advertising: Modular rate 83¢(e). **Representative:** Bardal, Gosbee & Assoc. **Politics:** Independent. **Established:** 1852 (weekly), 1878 (daily).
Not Published: Statutory holidays.

CORPORATE OFFICER

President Henry B Burgoyne

GENERAL MANAGEMENT

Asst Publisher Cheryl McMenemy

ADVERTISING

Director Jim Bovaird

CIRCULATION

Manager Barbara Weightman

NEWS EXECUTIVE

Editor Jim T Grossmith

PRODUCTION

Director Bob Bell

Mechanical available: Offset; insert accepted — preprinted.
Mechanical specifications: Type page 13¾" x 21½"; E - 6 cols, 2¹⁄₁₆", ⅛" between.
Commodity Consumption (estimated): Newsprint 500 metric tons; widths 28", 34"; black ink 16,000 pounds; color ink 700 pounds; average pages per issue 30(d).

ST. CATHARINES

'91 Census- 129,300 (Metro Area 364,555); E&P '96 Est. 136,878 (Metro Area 388,042)
ABC-CZ (91): 138,741 (HH 53,570)

The Standard

(e-mon to sat)

The Standard, 17 Queen St., St. Catharines, ON L2R 5G5; tel (905) 684-7251; fax (905) 684-6670. St. Catharines Standard Ltd. group.
Circulation: 37,782(e); 46,771(e-sat); ABC Sept. 30, 1995.
Price: 55¢(d); $1.00(sat); $3.15/wk; $13.30/mo; $152.50/mo; $39.50/3 mo, $77.50/6 mo.
Advertising: Modular rate $2.29(e); $2.51(e-sat); $2.63 (mon & fri), 59¢ (wed only), $1.07 (sat only). **Representatives:** Publishers' Representatives of Florida; The Leonard Company.
News Service: CP. **Politics:** Independent. **Established:** 1891.
Special Editions: Baby Review, Spring Brides (Jan); Winter Sale, Financial Planning (Feb); Spring Fashion, Seniors (Mar); Home Builders, Car Care, Home Builders, Golf (Apr); Golf, Things are Looking Up (June); USA Tab, Summer Sale (July); Fall Fashion, Shopping Spree (Aug); USA Tab, Brides (Sept); Renovation, Fire Prevention, Car Care, At Home In Niagara (Oct); USA Tab, Gift Guide (Nov); Christmas Song Book, Year End Review, Baby of the Year (Dec).

CORPORATE OFFICERS

Chairman Henry B Burgoyne
Vice Pres/Secretary Dorothy J Doolittle
President C J Burke

GENERAL MANAGEMENT

Publisher J A Lehnen
General Manager G A Middleton
Comptroller B J Arnold
Credit Manager Donna Wing

ADVERTISING

Director E F Zwolak
Manager-Major Retail A M Bergemann
Manager-Retail B A Adams
Asst Manager-Retail T Kelcey
Coordinator-National N Kennedy
Manager-TV Times B Heit

CIRCULATION

Manager A J Muma

NEWS EXECUTIVES

Managing Editor Kevin Cavanagh
Asst Managing Editor Doug Herod

EDITORS AND MANAGERS

Assignment Editor Paul Harvey
Business Editor Paul Harvey
Assignment Editor Paul Harvey
Editorial Page Editor Tom Nevens
Education Paul Harvey
Environment Doug Draper
Family/Society Brian Collins
Fashion/Food Brian Collins
Music Sean Condon
News Editor Paul Harvey
Religion Steve Archer
Sports John Fedor
Travel Jim Blundell

MANAGEMENT INFORMATION SERVICES

Data Processing Manager Rick Brown

PRODUCTION

Foreman-Composing C Kletke
Foreman-Pressroom E Langelaan
Foreman-Plateroom E Langelaan

Market Information: TMC.
Mechanical available: Letterpress (direct); Black and 3 ROP colors; insert accepted — preprinted, roll-fed; page cut-offs — 22¼".
Mechanical specifications: Type page 13" x 22¼"; E - 6 cols, 2¹⁄₁₆", ⅛" between; A - 6 cols, 2¹⁄₁₆", ⅛" between; C - 6 cols, 2¹⁄₁₆", ⅛" between.
Commodity Consumption (estimated): Newsprint 3,200 metric tons; widths 55", 41¼", 27½"; black ink 110,000 pounds; color ink 15,000 pounds; single pages printed 13,000; average pages per issue 43(d); single plates used 21,500.
Equipment: EDITORIAL: Front-end hardware — 6-HL/8860, 4-HL/8900; Front-end software — HL/8300 6.0; Printers — Panasonic/24 P; Other equipment — Ap/Mac Centris 610, Microtek/600 DPI. CLASSIFIED: Front-end hardware — Ik/CPS-1030; Front-end software — Unitex; Printers — Panasonic/24 Pin, C.Itoh/24 Pin. DISPLAY: Adv layout systems — SCS/Layout 8000; Front-end hardware — Dell/486D, IBM/PC PS2 Model 60; Front-end software — SCS/Layout 8000; Printers — HP/LaserJet II, HP/LaserJet IV; Other equipment — US Robotics (V .32 Modem). PRODUCTION: Pagination software — HI 6.0, QuarkXPress 3.1; OCR software — Caere/OmniPage 2.12; Typesetters — 5-Linotron/202, 1-Ap/Mac LaserWriter IINTX, 2-ECR/Autokon 1000, 1-Tektronics/Color Quick Printer, 1-LaserMaster/Unity 1200 XL, 1-LaserMaster/Unity 1800 XL; Platemaking systems — Na; Electronic picture desk — CD; Scanners — 2-ECR/Autokon 1000DE, 2-Microtek/300 DPI, 1-Microtek/600 DPI, 1-Microtek/ScanMaker II; Production cameras — K; Automatic film processors — 1-LE/BQ24, 1-LE/24AR, 2-MOHRPRO/14, PC/1800; Film transporters — C/Newspager; Color separation equipment (conventional) — Ap/Mac IIfx, Adobe/Photoshop; Digital color separation equipment — Ap/Mac IIfx, Adobe/Photoshop.
PRESSROOM: Line 1 — 7-G/Headliner MKI; Press drives — 6-AC/Motor, 1-DC/Motor; Folders — 2-G/2:1; Reels and stands — 5-G/Reel, 2 Roll Stands; Press control system — CH. MAILROOM: Stuffers — 1-KAN/320 8 pocket, 1-KAN/480 8 pocket; Bundle tyer — 2-MLN/ML2EE, 1-MLN/Spirit, 2-MLN/MAG.90 II; Wrapping singles — 1-St/PM 720, 1-St/PM 510. LIBRARY: Combination — non-electronic. COMMUNICATIONS: Facsimile — Ricoh/3200L, Toshiba/TF 251. WIRE SERVICES: News — CP Dataspecials, CP Stocks, CP Newstream; Syndicates — Universal Press Syndicate, Canada Wide, LATS, Toronto Star; receiving dishes — size-6ft, CP. BUSINESS COMPUTERS: 1-IBM/Sys 38 Model 700, IBM/PS2, Epson/Printer, HP/LaserJet, QMS/Laser Printer, Gandalf/Modems, Hayes/Modems, RSK/Tandy Printer, IBM/Laser Printer; Applications: Microsoft/Windows: Data processing, Circ, Adv, Accounting, Payroll, Credit, Administration, Promotion; Microsoft/Windows Cobol Aldus/PageMaker Ventura PFS/Professional Ap/Mac Write CPF/Integrated Relational Database S/38 Performance Tools Lotus Microsoft/Excel Archetype/Corel Draw AllWays Parklane; PCs & micros networked.

ST. THOMAS

'91 Census- 29,990; E&P '96 Est. 31,666
ABC-CZ (91): 29,990 (HH 11,535)

St. Thomas Times-Journal

(e-mon to sat)

St. Thomas Times-Journal, 16 Hincks St., St. Thomas, ON N5R 5Z2; tel (519) 631-2790; fax (519) 631-5653. Bowes Publishers Limited (Toronto Sun Publishing) group.
Circulation: 8,930(e); 8,930(e-sat); ABC Sept. 30, 1995.
Price: 60¢(d); 60¢(sat); $2.60/wk; $11.27/mo; $124.80/yr (carrier).
Advertising: Modular rate $1.00(e); $1.00(e-sat).
News Services: CP, AP, RN. **Politics:** Independent. **Established:** 1882.
Not Published: New Year; Good Friday; Victoria Day; Labor Day; Thanksgiving; Christmas; Canada Day; Civic Holiday; Boxing Day.
Special Editions: All Aboard (Jan); Brides, Tour Elgin, Tourist Guide, Business & Industrial Review, Agricultural Section, Springtime in Elgin (Mar); Home & Garden Show, The Great Outdoors, It's Hot, Hot, Hot V.E Days, Coupon Daze, Burst of Colours (Apr); She's My Mom, Home & Garden (May); Women in Business (June); Spring into London, Sidewalk Sale, Best of Elgin (July); Family & Small Business, Our Farming Community, United Way (Sept); Iron Horse, City Directory, Car Care & Fall Home Improvement (Oct); Cookbook, Christmas Carol (Nov); Christmas Wishbook I, Christmas Wishbook II, Back-to-School (Dec).
Magazine: TV Tab (fri).

GENERAL MANAGEMENT

Publisher/General Manager Terry Carroll
Assoc Publisher Amber Ogilvie

ADVERTISING

Manager Amber Ogilvie

MARKETING AND PROMOTION

Manager-Marketing & Promotion Stew Royce

CIRCULATION

Manager Stew Royce

NEWS EXECUTIVE

Managing Editor Ross Porter

EDITOR AND MANAGER

Books Terry Carroll

PRODUCTION

Foreman-Pressroom Gilles LeBlanc
Foreman-Composing Richard Evans

Market Information: TMC.
Mechanical available: Offset; Black and 3 ROP colors; insert accepted — preprinted; page cut-offs — 17".
Mechanical specifications: Type page 10¼" x 16"; E - 5 cols, 1.9", ⅛" between; A - 5 cols, 1.9", ⅛" between; C - 7 cols, 1⅓", ⅛" between.
Commodity Consumption (estimated): Newsprint 300,900 kg short tons; widths 30"; black ink 2400 kg; single pages printed 4,380; average pages per issue 25(d), 24(sat); single plates used 3,600.
Equipment: EDITORIAL: Front-end hardware — Ap/Mac Quadra 610; Front-end software — QPS; Printers — Ap/Mac LaserWriter Pro 630; Other equipment — QMS/860 Print System. CLASSIFIED: Front-end hardware — Ap/Mac Quadra 610; Front-end software — Baseview; Printers — Ap/Mac LaserWriter Pro 630; Other equipment — QMS/86 Print System, QMS/Print System. DISPLAY: Front-end hardware — Ap/Mac; Front-end software — QuarkXPress, Multi-Ad; Printers — QMS/Laser Printers. PRODUCTION: OCR software — Caere/OmniPage; Typesetters — QMS/860 LaserWatler, Ap/Mac; Plate processors — Nat; Scanners — Umax/UC840; Production cameras — Acti; Automatic film processors — Screen/LD 220-QT.

PRESSROOM: Line 1 — 8-G/Community; Folders — 1-G/Quarter. MAILROOM: Counter stackers — BG/Count-O-Veyor; Bundle tyer — 2-Gd; Addressing machine — 1-El. COMMUNICATIONS: Satellite; Fiber Optic. WIRE SERVICES: News — CP; receiving dishes — CP. BUSINESS COMPUTERS: ATT/3B2-500.

SARNIA

'91 Census- 51,840; E&P '96 Est. 55,056
ABC-CZ (91): 79,900 (HH 30,264)

Observer

(e-mon to fri; m-sat)

Observer, 140 S. Front St., Sarnia, ON N7T 7M8; tel (519) 344-3641; fax (519) 332-2951. Thomson Newspapers group.

Circulation: 22,711(e); 22,711(m-sat); ABC Sept. 30, 1995.

Price: 50¢(d); 75¢(sat); $11.70/mo (carrier), $23.43/mo (mail); $135.20/yr (carrier), $281.15/yr (mail).

Advertising: Modular rate $1.50(e); $1.50(m-sat).

News Service: CP. **Politics:** Independent. **Established:** 1853.

Not Published: Statutory holidays.

Special Editions: Retirement Planning (Feb); Progress (Mar); Women's Club (June); Football (Aug); Fashion (Sept); Christmas Gift Guide (Nov).

GENERAL MANAGEMENT

Publisher	Daryl C Smith
Credit Manager/Purchasing Agent	Randy Racher

ADVERTISING

Manager	David Martieau
Manager-Classified	Barb McBride

CIRCULATION

Manager	Terry Pimlatt

NEWS EXECUTIVE

Managing Editor	Terry Shaw

EDITORS AND MANAGERS

Auto Editor	Terry Easterby
Business/Finance Editor	Bruce Langer
City Editor	Brian Bolt
Editorial Page Editor	Frank Raprik
Entertainment Editor	Bruce Langer
Fashion/Society Editor	Yvette Zandbergen
Picture Editor	Bruce Langer
Photo Department Manager	Glenn Ogilive
Radio/Television Editor	Bruce Langer
Sports Editor	Dave Borody
Travel Editor	Bruce Langer
Wire Editor	Bruce Langer

PRODUCTION

Foreman-Composing	George Morgan
Foreman-Pressroom	A Brazeau

Market Information: TMC; ADS.

Mechanical available: Letterpress (direct); Black and 3 ROP colors; insert accepted — preprinted; page cut-offs — 21½".

Mechanical specifications: Type page 13½" x 21$\frac{5}{16}$"; E - 6 cols, 2$\frac{1}{16}$", ⅛" between.

SAULT STE. MARIE

'91 Census- 81,475; E&P '96 Est. 85,109
ABC-CZ (91): 81,476 (HH 30,305)

The Sault Star (e-mon to sat)

The Sault Star, 145 Old Garden River Rd.; PO Box 460, Sault Ste. Marie, ON P6A 5M5; tel (705) 759-3030; fax (705) 942-8690. Southam Newspapers group.

Circulation: 23,382(e); 23,382(e-sat); ABC Sept. 30, 1995.

Price: 70¢(d); 79 ¢(fri); 79¢(sat); $3.50/wk; $15.00/mo; $165.00/yr (carrier).

Advertising: Modular rate $1.765(e); $1.765 (e-sat). **Representative:** Southam Newspapers.

News Services: CP, SNS. **Politics:** Independent. **Established:** 1912.

Not Published: New Year; Good Friday; Victoria Day; July 1; Civic Holiday; Labor Day; Thanksgiving; Christmas; Boxing Day.

Special Editions: Baby Tab, Money Matters, Brides '96 (Jan); Outlook '96, RRSP (Feb); Sportsman Show (C of C), Home Show, Car Care, Out Door Fun, Home & Garden, Spring Fashion, Earth Day, Gifts For Graduates (May); Side Walk Sale, Summer Cooking (June); Community Days, Station Mall Side Walk Sale, Graduation Tab (July); Twin Sault Student Guide, Back-to-School, Fall Fashion (Aug); Greyhounds, Sight & Sounds, Hunting & Fishing, Brides (Sept); Restaurant Month, Salute to Clubs, Cook Book, Travel Showcase, Women In Business, Station Mall, Birthday, Home Renovations (Oct); Queenstown Christmas, Technology in the Home (Nov); Gift Guide, Christmas Greetings, Songbook (Dec); Home Front, Mutual Funds (monthly).

Special Weekly Sections: Sports (mon); Classified (wed); District (sat).

Magazines: TV Times (fri); Features & Comics (sat).

GENERAL MANAGEMENT

Publisher	Robert Richardson
Credit Manager	Judie Soltys
Finance Manager/Manager-Human Resources	Fred Bright

ADVERTISING

Manager	Ian MacKenzie

MARKETING AND PROMOTION

Manager-Marketing & Promotion	Robert Richardson

TELECOMMUNICATIONS

Audiotex Manager	Gary Campbell

CIRCULATION

Manager-Reader Sales	Lou Malucci

NEWS EXECUTIVE

Editor	John Halucha

EDITORS AND MANAGERS

City/News Editor	Tom Mills
Editorial Page Editor	Fred Loader
Librarian	Joan Dorse
Local Columnist	Oliver Lehto
Photo Editor	Kenneth Dorse

MANAGEMENT INFORMATION SERVICES

Data Processing Manager	Robert Calderhead

PRODUCTION

Manager-Manufacturing	Bruno Vit
Foreman-Pressroom	Anthony Politano

Market Information: Split Run; TMC; ADS; Operate audiotex.

Mechanical available: Offset; Black and 3 ROP colors; insert accepted — preprinted; page cut-offs — 22¾".

Mechanical specifications: Type page 11.5" x 21½"; E - 5 cols, 2.18", ⅛" between; A - 10 cols, 1", ⅛" between; C - 10 cols, 1", ⅛" between.

Commodity Consumption (estimated): Newsprint 1,650 metric tons; widths 25", 12½"; black ink 15,000 kg; color ink 8,000 kg; single pages printed 10,100; average pages per issue 33(d), 28(sat).

Equipment: EDITORIAL: Front-end hardware — DEC/File servers, Ap/Mac, 20-RSK/Tandy 3000; Front-end software — UT/220, UT/102, CText, H/4000, Ap/Mac, QPS; Printers — DEC/LA-120, LP/25, QMS/860, Ap/LaserWriter NTX, Ap/LaserWriter IIg, LG02, AU/APS-108-12C. CLASSIFIED: Front-end hardware — DEC/File servers, RSK/Tandy 3000; Front-end software — CText; Printers — Ap/LaserWriter NTX. AUDIOTEX: Supplier name — Dial Source/PLUS. DISPLAY: Adv layout systems — SCS/Layout 8000; Front-end hardware — DEC/VT-102; Printers — LG02. PRODUCTION: Pagination software — QuarkXPress 3.1, Southam/Ad Tracking 2.9; OCR software — Caere/OmniPage; Typesetters — 2-M/202N, 4-Ap/Mac LaserPrinter, 2-AU/APS 108-12C; Platemaking systems — 1-3M/403-BZB-, Hoechst; Plate exposers — 1-N/Flip Top FT40UP; Plate processors — WL, Hoechst; Electronic picture desk — CD; Scanners — Ap/Mac, Ap/Mac Quadra 800; Production cameras — 1-C/Spartan III; Automatic film processors — 1-LE/LD24A, 1-COM/101; Digital color separation equipment — Pixel Craft, Adobe/Photoshop, Ap/Macs. PRESSROOM: Line 1 — 6-G/Urbanite; Folders — 1-G; Press control system — Fin. MAILROOM: Counter stackers — 1-SH; Stuffers — 1-KAN/320 4-station, 1-MM/Saddle Stitcher, MM/Quarter; Bundle tyer — 1-MLN/ML2EE, 6-Gd/Q; Addressing machine — 1-WM. LIBRARY: Combination — 2-Remington Rand/Lektreiver 9615-16X. COMMUNICATIONS: Facsimile — 1-AP/Laserphoto, 1-FAX, Ricoh/2700L, Ricoh/2500L, Fujitsu/Dex 740, Fast Fax. WIRE SERVICES: News — CP, SOU; Photos — CP; Stock tables — SOU; Syndicates — SOU; receiving dishes — CP, SOU. BUSINESS COMPUTERS: DEC/VAX; Applications: Adv billing, Accts receivable, Gen ledger, Payroll, Accts payable; PCs & micros networked; PCs & main system networked.

SIMCOE

'91 Census- 15,535; E&P '96 Est. 16,660
ABC-CZ (91): 15,539 (HH 5,875)

The Simcoe Reformer

(e-mon to fri; m-sat)

The Simcoe Reformer, 105 Donly Dr. S.; PO Box 370, Simcoe, ON N3Y 4L2; tel (519) 426-5710. Southwestern Ontario Publishing group.

Circulation: 9,462(e); 9,462(m-sat); ABC Sept. 30, 1995.

Price: 50¢(d); 60¢(fri); 50¢(sat); $2.25/wk; $56.25/mo; $117.00/yr (carrier), $208.00/yr (mail).

Advertising: Modular rate $1.02(e); $1.02(m-sat). **Representative:** Thomson Newspapers.

News Service: CP. **Politics:** Independent. **Established:** 1858.

Not Published: New Year; Good Friday; Victoria Day; Dominion Day; Civic Holiday; Labor Day; Thanksgiving; Christmas.

Special Editions: Tobacco; Brides; Spring Car Care; Great Outdoors; Vacationland; Friendship Weekend; Back-to-School; Home Builders; Fall Fair; Fall Car Care; Christmas Shopping; Christmas Greetings; New Year's Greetings; Cookbook.

GENERAL MANAGEMENT

Publisher	Mike Fredrick
Accountant	Paul Primmer

ADVERTISING

Manager	Simon O'Donovan

CIRCULATION

Manager	Steve Smithson

NEWS EXECUTIVE

Managing Editor	Kim Novak

EDITORS AND MANAGERS

Amusements/Books Editor	Kim Novak
Business/Finance Editor	Mike Bauslaugh
Editorial Page Editor	Kim Novak
Education	Pat Meiklejohn
Farm Editor	Ron Kowalsky
Fashion/Music Editor	Cheryl Bauslaugh
Food Editor	Cheryl Bauslaugh
Photo Department Manager	Bob Blakeley
Sports Editor	Jill Dennison
Women's/Society	Cheryl Bauslaugh

PRODUCTION

Manager	Eddie Hofland
Foreman-Composing	Eddie Hofland
Asst Foreman-Composing	Dan Lea
Foreman-Pressroom	Jack North

Market Information: Zoned editions; TMC.

Mechanical available: Offset; Black and 3 ROP colors; insert accepted — preprinted; page cut-offs — 21½".

Mechanical specifications: Type page 13" x 21½"; E - 6 cols, 2$\frac{1}{15}$", ⅛" between; A - 6 cols, 2$\frac{1}{15}$", ⅛" between; C - 9 cols, 1⅓", ⅛" between.

Commodity Consumption (estimated): Newsprint 19.508 short tons; 281 metric tons; widths 27"; single pages printed 4,524; average pages per issue 16(d); single plates used 5,676.

Equipment: EDITORIAL: Front-end hardware — Mk. CLASSIFIED: Front-end hardware — Mk. DISPLAY: Adv layout systems — Ap/Mac. PRODUCTION: Platemaking systems — 1-B; Production cameras — 2-R; Automatic film processors — 1-Fuji/360F. PRESSROOM: Line 1 — 6-G; Folders — 1-G/Quarter and Half fold. MAILROOM: Bundle tyer — 2-Bu, 2-Strapper; Addressing machine — ATT. LIBRARY: Combination — Microfilm, Microreader. COMMUNICATIONS: Satellite. WIRE SERVICES: News — CP; Syndicates — THO; receiving dishes — CP. BUSINESS COMPUTERS: ATT; PCs & micros networked; PCs & main system networked.

STRATFORD

'91 Census- 27,665; E&P '96 Est. 29,272
ABC-CZ (91): 27,666 (HH 11,050)

The Stratford Beacon-Herald (e-mon to sat)

The Stratford Beacon-Herald, 108 Ontario St.; PO Box 430, Stratford, ON N5A 6T6; tel (519) 271-2220.

Circulation: 12,888(e); 12,888(e-sat); ABC Sept. 30, 1995.

Price: 60¢(d); 60¢(sat); $2.80/wk (inc. GST); $39.05/3 mos (inc. GST); $139.66/yr (carrier) (inc. GST), $228.00/yr (mail).

Advertising: Modular rate $1.12(e); $1.12(e-sat).

News Service: CP. **Politics:** Independent. **Established:** 1854.

Not Published: New Year; Good Friday; Victoria Day; Dominion Day; Labor Day; Thanksgiving; Christmas; Boxing Day.

Special Edition: Festival (June).

Magazine: TV Week (fri).

CORPORATE OFFICERS

President	Stanford H Dingman
Vice Pres	Charles W Dingman
Secretary-Treasurer	Barry A Smith

GENERAL MANAGEMENT

Co-Publisher	Stanford H Dingman
Co-Publisher	Charles W Dingman
General Manager	Charles W Dingman
Purchasing Agent	Barry A Smith
Credit Manager	Barry A Smith
Education Service Manager	Carolyn Dingman

ADVERTISING

Manager	David B Nickel

MARKETING AND PROMOTION

Manager-Marketing & Promotion	Carolyn Dingman

CIRCULATION

Manager	Gerald G Doney

NEWS EXECUTIVES

Editor	Stanford H Dingman
Managing Editor	Ronald Carson

EDITOR AND MANAGER

Sports Editor	John Kastner

PRODUCTION

Manager	Lorne F Bolton

Market Information: TMC.

Mechanical available: Offset; Black and 3 ROP colors; insert accepted — preprinted; page cut-offs — 22¾".

Mechanical specifications: Type page 13" x 21¼"; E - 6 cols, 1$\frac{18}{16}$", ⅛" between; A - 6 cols, 1$\frac{13}{16}$", ⅛" between; C - 6 cols, 2$\frac{1}{16}$", 1$\frac{13}{16}$" between.

Commodity Consumption (estimated): Newsprint 551 metric tons; widths 25"; 27", 31", 34"; black ink 3,212 kg; color ink 1,078 kg; single pages printed 7,544; average pages per issue 25(d); single plates used 5,398.

Equipment: EDITORIAL: Front-end hardware — 18-COM/One System; Front-end software — COM/One System; Printers — 1-DEC/VT-600, 1-AG/DP3400, 2-XIT/Clipper, 1-Schooner. CLASSIFIED: Front-end hardware — COM/One System; Front-end software — COM/One System. DISPLAY: Front-end hardware — Ap/Mac; Front-end software — Multi-Ad, QuarkXPress, Adobe/Photoshop. PRODUCTION: OCR software — Caere/OmniPro; Plate processors — 1-Nat/A-250; Electronic picture desk — CD; Scanners — Ap/Mac, Microtek/1200; Production cameras — 1-Acti/204; Automatic film processors — Fuji/FG25 LSH Graphic Processor; Shrink lenses — 1-Kamarak; Color separation equipment (conventional) — Ap/Mac fx, Adobe/Photoshop; Digital color separation equipment — XIT/Schooner, Adobe/Photoshop. PRESSROOM: Line 1 — 8-SLN/Offset; Press control system — SLN. MAILROOM: Bundle tyer — 1-Nichiro Kogyo/TS-210; Wrapping singles — Beacon. WIRE SERVICES: News — CP; Photos — CP; receiving dishes — size-1m, CP. BUSINESS COMPUTERS: 1-DEC/1123; Applications: Circ, Adv, Invoicing; PCs & main system networked.

SUDBURY

'91 Census- 92,880 (Metro Area 157,610); E&P '96 Est. 98,310 (Metro Area 171,852)
ABC-CZ (91): 86,992 (HH 34,701)

The Sudbury Star

(e-mon to fri; m-sat; S)

The Sudbury Star, 33 Mackenzie St., Sudbury, ON P3C 4Y1; tel (705) 674-5271; fax (705) 674-0624. Thomson Newspapers group.

Circulation: 25,695(e); 25,695(m-sat); 23,737(S); ABC Sept. 30, 1995.

Price: 60¢(d); 75¢(sat); 75¢(S); $3.20/wk; $13.86/mo; $39.00/3 mos, $78.00/6 mos; $166.40/yr (carrier).

Advertising: Modular rate $1.70(e); $1.70(m-sat); $1.70(S). **Representative:** Thomson Newspapers.

News Service: CP. **Politics:** Independent. **Established:** 1909.

Not Published: New Year; Good Friday; Christmas.

Advertising not accepted: Those restricted by Provincial or Federal law.

Special Editions: Cook Book; Progress Review; Christmas Carols; Big Sale; Spring Car Care; Father's Day; Back-to-School; Boxing Day Sale; Frantic Friday Vacation Guide; Brides; Mining; Spring Home & Garden; Fall Home Improvement; Winter Car Care; Sudbury Wolves.

Ontario III-19

Special Weekly Sections: Motoring (thur); Travel (sat).
Magazines: Weekend Alive, Fine Home (Real Estate Guide) (fri); TV Scene; Trail Rider.

GENERAL MANAGEMENT
Publisher/General Manager Ken Seguin
Accountant Michael Bowen
ADVERTISING
Manager Paul Marcon
MARKETING AND PROMOTION
Director-Marketing & Promotion Keith Sabourin
CIRCULATION
Manager Dave Paquette
Manager-Regional Sergio Marione
NEWS EXECUTIVE
Managing Editor Boris Hrybinsky
EDITOR AND MANAGER
City Editor Roger Cazabon
PRODUCTION
Foreman-Composing M Smith
Foreman-Pressroom P Sarchiori

Market Information: Split Run; TMC; ADS.
Mechanical available: Letterpress; Black and 3 ROP colors; insert accepted — preprinted, all.
Mechanical specifications: Type page 13" x 22"; E - 6 cols, $2\frac{1}{16}$", $\frac{1}{8}$" between; A - 6 cols, $2\frac{1}{16}$", $\frac{1}{8}$" between; C - 6 cols, $2\frac{1}{16}$", $\frac{1}{8}$" between.
Commodity Consumption (estimated): Newsprint 1,450 metric tons; widths 139.7", 104.8", 69.9"; black ink 36,200 pounds; color ink 3,200 pounds; single pages printed 8,800; average pages per issue 28(d); single plates used 23,400.
Equipment: EDITORIAL: Front-end hardware — HAS; Front-end software — HAS. CLASSIFIED: Front-end software — HAS. PRODUCTION: Typesetters — 2-COM/8400; Plate processors — 2-He; Production cameras — B/3-in-1. MAILROOM: Bundle tyer — 3-Gd; Wrapping singles — Manual; Addressing machine — 1-Am. WIRE SERVICES: News — Syndicates — CP; receiving dishes — size-2ft. BUSINESS COMPUTERS: IBM/Sys 34; Applications: Circ, Accounting; PCs & main system networked.

THUNDER BAY

'91 Census- 113,950 (Metro Area 124,425); E&P '96 Est. 119,345 (Metro Area 127,330)
ABC-CZ (91): 113,946 (HH 43,455)

The Times-News
(m-mon to fri)
The Chronicle-Journal
(e-mon to fri)
The Times-News/The Chronicle-Journal
(m-sat; S)

The Times-News/The Chronicle-Journal, 75 S. Cumberland St., Thunder Bay, ON P7B 1A3; tel (807) 343-6200; fax (807) 345-5991. Thomson Newspapers group.
Circulation: 7,436(m); 26,561(e); 38,773(m-sat); 32,445(S); ABC Sept. 30, 1995.
Price: 75¢(d); $1.00(sat); $1.00(S); $3.65/wk (carrier); $189.80/yr (carrier), $665.00/yr (mail).
Advertising: Modular rate $1.98(m); $1.98(e); $1.98(m-sat); $1.98(S). **Representative:** Thomson Newspapers.
News Service: CP. **Politics:** Independent. **Established:** Times-Journal 1887, News-Chronicle 1903.
Special Editions: Business North; Independence (Super Saver Coupon Book); Annual Business & Industry Glossy Magazine (Apr); Angler & Hunter (Apr-Oct); North Western Trails (Sept-Feb).
Special Weekly Sections: Cover Story (thur); TV Scene (sat).
Magazine: Weekend (sat).
Cable TV: Operate leased cable TV in circulation area.

GENERAL MANAGEMENT
Publisher/General Manager Colin J Bruce
Business Manager Bert Maijala
ADVERTISING
Manager Gary Bruce
CIRCULATION
Manager Harry D P Brown
NEWS EXECUTIVE
Managing Editor Peter Haggert

Market Information: Zoned editions; TMC.
Mechanical available: Offset; Black and 3 ROP colors; insert accepted — preprinted; page cut-offs — $22\frac{3}{4}$".
Mechanical specifications: Type page 13" x $21\frac{1}{2}$"; E - 6 cols, $2\frac{1}{16}$", $\frac{1}{8}$" between; A - 6 cols, $2\frac{1}{16}$", $\frac{1}{8}$" between; C - 10 cols, $1\frac{1}{4}$", $\frac{1}{16}$" between.
Commodity Consumption (estimated): Newsprint 2,000 metric tons; widths $26\frac{1}{2}$", $30\frac{1}{2}$", 34"; average pages per issue 32(d).
Equipment: EDITORIAL: Front-end hardware — HAS. CLASSIFIED: Front-end hardware — HAS. PRODUCTION: Scanners — 3-HAS. PRESSROOM: Line 1 — 8-G/Urbanite; Folders — 1-G. MAILROOM: Counter stackers — Id; Bundle tyer — 2-Akibono; Addressing machine — ATT. WIRE SERVICES: News — CP; Stock tables — CP; Syndicates — THO, Toronto Star; receiving dishes — size-2, CP. BUSINESS COMPUTERS: 6-ATT.

TIMMINS

'91 Census- 47,460; E&P '96 Est. 49,745
ABC-CZ (91): 31,078 (HH 11,634)

The Daily Press
(m-mon to sat)

The Daily Press, 187 Cedar St. S., Timmins, ON P4N 2G9; tel (705) 268-5050; fax (705) 268-7373. Thomson Newspapers group.
Circulation: 10,818(m); 10,818(m-sat); ABC Sept. 30, 1995.
Price: 60¢(d); 60¢(sat); $3.10/wk; $12.50/mo; $135.00/yr.
Advertising: Modular rate $1.10(m); $1.10(m-sat). **Representative:** Thomson Newspapers.
News Service: CP. **Politics:** Independent. **Established:** 1934.
Not Published: New Year; Christmas Day.
Special Editions: Business & Industry North (monthly); Frontier Mining (quarterly).
Special Weekly Sections: TV Scene (fri); Cover Story (weekly).
Magazines: Progress (Mar); Mining (Apr).

GENERAL MANAGEMENT
Publisher/General Manager John A Farrington
ADVERTISING
Manager Sue Downs
CIRCULATION
Manager Tony Howell
NEWS EXECUTIVE
Managing Editor Dave McGee
EDITOR AND MANAGER
Editorial Page Editor Dave McGee
PRODUCTION
Manager-Creative Services Olaf Karls
Manager-Pressroom Joe Vodusek

Market Information: TMC.
Mechanical available: Offset; Black and 3 ROP colors; insert accepted — preprinted; page cut-offs — $22\frac{3}{4}$".
Mechanical specifications: Type page 13" x $21\frac{1}{2}$"; E - 6 cols, $2\frac{1}{16}$", $\frac{1}{8}$" between; A - 6 cols, $2\frac{1}{16}$", $\frac{1}{8}$" between; C - 9 cols, $1\frac{1}{3}$", $\frac{1}{8}$" between.
Commodity Consumption (estimated): widths 27", 33"; single pages printed 5,600; average pages per issue 12(d).
Equipment: EDITORIAL: Front-end hardware — CText. CLASSIFIED: Front-end hardware — CText. PRODUCTION: Electronic picture desk — CD; Direct-to-plate imaging — 3M/Pyrofax Imager 300; Production cameras — 1-N. PRESSROOM: Line 1 — 8-G/Community; Folders — 1-G. MAILROOM: Bundle tyer — 1-Gd; Other mailroom equipment — MM/Minuteman. LIBRARY: Electronic — 1-Preston/Micro Reader. WIRE SERVICES: News — CP.

TORONTO

'91 Census- 635,395 (Metro Area 3,893,045); E&P '96 Est. 670,511 (Metro Area 4,176,306)
ABC-NDM (91): 4,291,618 (HH 1,505,745)

The Globe and Mail
(m-mon to fri; m-sat)

The Globe and Mail (Canada's National Newspaper), 444 Front St. W., Toronto, ON M5V 2S9; tel (416) 585-5000; fax (416) 585-5085; web site http://www.theglobeandmail.com. Thomson Newspapers group.
Circulation: 306,260(m); 358,590(m-sat); December 31, 1994.
Price: 75¢(d); $1.00(sat); $4.70/wk; $20.37/mo; $244.44/yr.
Advertising: Modular rate $21.39(m); $21.39(m-sat). **Representative:** Thomson Newspapers.
News Services: CP, RN, NYT, DJ, SHNS, Economist, Telegraph. **Politics:** Independent. **Established:** The Globe-1844, The Mail-1872.
Note: The audited average circulation figures were not submitted by presstime. The figures presented by the newspaper are pre-audit numbers. Printing for The Globe and Mail is sub-contracted at six locations.
Not Published: Christmas.
Advertising not accepted: Tobacco.
Special Weekly Sections: Sports Weekend (mon); Travel (wed); Fashion & Design (thur); Travel, Focus (sat); Report on Mutual Funds (monthly).
Magazines: Report on Business Magazine (monthly); Broadcast Week (weekly); Real Estate Collection (2x/yr); Gusto, Fashion Design (4x/yr).

CORPORATE OFFICERS
Board Chairman Ken R Thomson
CEO Roger P Parkinson
GENERAL MANAGEMENT
Vice Pres/General Manager Grant Crosbie
Publisher Roger P Parkinson
Controller Ken Barnard
ADVERTISING
Vice Pres-Sales (acting) Grant Crosbie
CIRCULATION
Director Dimitri Chrus
Regional Manager-British Columbia Frank Wang
Regional Manager-Prairies Mike Volpe
Regional Manager-S.W. Ont. Miki Brem
Regional Manager-Toronto Glenn Lue
Regional Manager-E. Canada Joann Perrott
Branch Manager-Montreal Bob Laplante
Consumer Relations Maureen Enman
NEWS EXECUTIVES
Editor in Chief William Thorsell
Exec Editor Earle Gill
Assoc Editor Sarah Murdoch
Deputy Managing Editor Colin Mackenzie
Deputy Managing Editor John King
EDITORS AND MANAGERS
Editorial Arts Director Michael Gregg
Arts & Books Katherine Ashenburg
Business/Finance Editor Peggy Wente
Entertainment Editor James Adams
Fashion & Design Editor David Lasker
Librarian Amanda Valpy
Foreign Editor Patrick Martin
Picture Editor Dennis Robinson
Editor (Broadcast Week Mag) Trevor Cole
Editor (Report on Business Magazine) David Olive
National Editor (Bureaus) Sylvia Stead
National Editor (Beats) Cathrin Bradbury
Sports Editor David Langford
Travel Editor Les Buhasz
PRODUCTION
Building Manager-Facilities Gregory Dick

Market Information: Split Run; ADS; Operate database; Electronic edition.
Mechanical available: Offset; Black and 3 ROP colors; insert accepted — preprinted, magazines, product samples; page cut-offs — $22\frac{3}{4}$".
Mechanical specifications: Type page 13" x 22"; E - 6 cols, $2\frac{1}{16}$", $\frac{1}{8}$" between; A - 6 cols, $2\frac{1}{16}$", $\frac{1}{8}$" between; C - 6 cols, $2\frac{1}{16}$", $\frac{1}{8}$" between.
Commodity Consumption (estimated): Newsprint 36,000 metric tons; widths 27", $13\frac{1}{2}$"; black ink 1,000,000 pounds; color ink 48,000 pounds; single pages printed 19,968; average pages per issue 62(d), 78(sat); single plates used 109,200.
Equipment: EDITORIAL: Front-end hardware — AT, HI/8300 Pagination System; Front-end software — AT; Other equipment — Ap/Mac 630 (20MB RAM), Compaq/486 Presario (8MB RAM), Ethernet. CLASSIFIED: Front-end hardware — SyD/Text II; Printers — HP/7970. DISPLAY: Adv layout systems — HI/8300 Pagination System; Front-end software — HI; Other equipment — Ap/Mac. PRODUCTION: Typesetters — III/3850, Prosetter; Electronic picture desk — HI/Images Graphic Subsystem; Scanners — ECR/Autokon 2045, Sharp/600, Nikon. LIBRARY: Electronic — Info Globe; Combination — Power File. COMMUNICATIONS: Facsimile — 2-III/3750; Remote imagesetting — 10-III/3850 Colografix; Satellite. WIRE SERVICES: News — AP, CP, NYT, RN, DJ, Canada News Wire; Photos — AP, CP; Stock tables — Telerate, CP; Syndicates — WSJ, NYT, Economist; receiving dishes — size-1.5m, CP. BUSINESS COMPUTERS: Applications: Circ, Adv billing, Accts receivable, Gen ledger, Payroll, Accts payable; PCs & micros networked; PCs & main system networked.

The Toronto Star
(m-mon to fri; m-sat; S)

The Toronto Star, One Yonge St., Toronto, ON M5E 1E6; tel (416) 367-2000; fax (416) 869-4605; email info@scoop.torstar.comm. Torstar Corporation group.
Circulation: 491,411(m); 739,108(m-sat); 491,105(S); ABC Sept. 30, 1995.
Price: 60¢(d); $1.50(sat); 85¢(S).
Advertising: Modular rate $10.98(m); $13.50(m-sat); $8.62(S). **Representatives:** SY Kaplan Assoc.; Metro National Advertising Reps.
News Services: AP, CP, DJ, RN, UPI, LAT-WP. **Established:** 1892.
Not Published: Good Friday; Christmas.
Magazine: Starweek Magazine.

CORPORATE OFFICERS
Board Chairman John Evans
Vice Pres Burnett M Thall
GENERAL MANAGEMENT
Publisher John Honderich
Vice Pres-Operations Neil Clark
Vice Pres-Marketing & Development Victor Kruklis
Exec Director-Labor & Employee Relations Jagoda Pike
Director-Communications Fred Ross
Director-Corporate Systems Margaret McGrory
Director-Operations/Planning & Control Audrey Burke
Director-Production Glenn Simmonds
Director-Finance Joan Fairweather
Asst Controller Larry Miller
Manager-Customer Accounts Irene McNair
Manager-Data Centre Tom Eward
ADVERTISING
Vice Pres-Marketing & Development Victor Kruklis
Exec Director Andrew V Go
Director-Group James A McManus
Director-Group Frank J Bourjot
Director-Group Wayne Clifton
Manager-Marketing/Planning & Sales Development Judy E Master
Manager-National Travel Ian Bain
Manager-Classified/Real Estate Lisa Munroe
Manager-Marketing Research & Information Michael Trudeau
Manager-Syndicate Peter Taylor
TELECOMMUNICATIONS
Audiotex Manager Ken MacGray
CIRCULATION
Director Rupert Fry
Manager-Distribution Services Don O'Brien
Manager-Home Delivery Lou Macchiusi
Manager-Home Delivery Morris Greener
Manager-Single Copy Sales Robert Curphey
Manager-Sales Brian Master
Manager-Administration Bridget Jehle
Manager-Marketing Systems David Stewart
NEWS EXECUTIVES
Managing Editor Lou Clancy
Deputy Managing Editor-News Mary Deanne Shears
Deputy Managing Editor-Pre Press Brad Henderson
Ombudsman Don Sellar
EDITORS AND MANAGERS
Book Editor Judy Stoffman
Business/Finance Editor Fred Kuntz
City Editor Dave Ellis
Columnist Richard Gwyn
Columnist George Gamester
Columnist-Sports Jim Proudfoot
Columnist David Lewis Stein
Columnist-Life Linwood Barclay
Editorial Page Editor Haroon Siddiqui
Entertainment Editor Kathleen Kenna
Environment Writer Brian McAndrew
Fashion Editor Bernadette Morra
Fashion/Life Editor Carola Vyhnak
Food Editor Marion Kane
Foreign Editor Peter Goodspeed
Labor Writer Tony Van Alphen
Labor Writer Les Papp
Medicine Writer Lisa Priest
Music Writer William Littler
National Editor Alan Christie
Picture Editor Erin Combs
Radio/Television Writer Greg Quill
Star Week Editor Jim Atkins
Sports Editor Dave Perkins
Theater Writer Geoff Chapman
Travel Editor Mitch Smyth
Weekend Editor Joe Hall
MANAGEMENT INFORMATION SERVICES
Data Processing Manager Tom Edward

III-20 Ontario

PRODUCTION

Director-Press Center Glenn Simmonds
Asst Director Dean Zavarise
Manager-Photo Engraving Wayne MacMillan
Manager-Platemaking Larry Jenkins
Manager-Maintenance Planning Ken Dunn
Manager-Pre Press Barbara Clark
Manager-Press Centre (Night) Peter Hartley
Manager-Electrical Department George Donaldson
Superintendent-Composing Colin Booth
Superintendent-Pressroom Keith Cox
Superintendent-Mailing Doug Beatty
Chief Machinist Bill Ross
System Administrator Michael Renshaw

Market Information: Zoned editions; Split Run; TMC; Operate audiotex.
Mechanical available: Offset; Black and 3 ROP colors; insert accepted — preprinted; page cut-offs — 22".
Mechanical specifications: Type page 11.5" x 21.14"; E - 6 cols, $1\frac{3}{4}$", $\frac{1}{6}$" between; A - 10 cols, $1\frac{1}{16}$", $\frac{1}{12}$" between; C - 10 cols, $1\frac{1}{16}$", $\frac{1}{12}$" between.
Commodity Consumption (estimated): Newsprint 120,000 metric tons; widths 50", $37\frac{1}{2}$", 25"; black ink 4,320,00 pounds; color ink 628,200 pounds; single pages printed 35,120; average pages per issue 100(d), 180(sat), 84(S); single plates used 800,000.
Equipment: EDITORIAL: Front-end hardware — 210-SII/Coyote 22, 200-CMC/ST, 38-Ap/Mac, 10-IBM/PC; Front-end software — SII/Sys 55; Printers — 16-HP/LaserJet III, 2-Linotype-Hell/60. CLASSIFIED: Front-end hardware — Hitachi/Ex 80; Front-end software — CEES; Printers — IBM/3827, X/4045, X/4213, HP/3. AUDIOTEX: Hardware — Brite Voice Systems/Starphone, US Audiotext; Software — Brite Voice Systems. DISPLAY: Adv layout systems — TEDS; Front-end hardware — Sun/Micro Systems; Front-end software — TEDS; Printers — Ap/Mac Laser. PRODUCTION: Platemaking systems — 3-WL/10; Plate exposers — WL, 1-Litholite/Manual; Plate processors — WL; Scanners — 3-CD/Pager Fax; Automatic film processors — 3-P/26RA. PRESSROOM: Line 1 — 12-MAN/Colorman (50 printing couples); Line 2 — 12-MAN/Colorman (50 printing couples); Line 3 — 12-MAN/Colorman (50 printing couples); Line 4 — 12-MAN/Colorman (50 printing couples); Line 5 — 12-MAN/Colorman (50 printing couples); Line 6 — 12-MAN/Colorman (50 printing couples); Press drives — Harland Simon; Folders — MAN; Pasters — MAN/Automatic; Reels and stands — MAN; Press control system — Harland Simon; Press Registration Systems Harland Simon. MAILROOM: Counter stackers — 19-HL/II; Stuffers — 6-AMgraphics/630; Bundle tyer — 25-Power Strap, 18-Power Strap/inserting; Wrapping singles — 18-Power Strap/Three Quarter Wrap, 9-Power Strap/PSN 250; Addressing machine — 18-Domino/Inkjet, 12-Matthews/Inkjet inserting; Mailroom control system — 12-Labelling Technology/Skid labellers. Kinex/PCS. LIBRARY: Electronic — QL, Inmagic. COMMUNICATIONS: Facsimile — CD/Page fax; Fiber optic. WIRE SERVICES: News — AP, CP, RN, DJ, TV Data, SOU, Canada News Wire; Stock tables — Toronto Stock Exchange; Syndicates — Toronto Star Syndicate; receiving dishes — AP, CP. BUSINESS COMPUTERS: Hitachi/EX 80; Applications: MVS/XA; PCs & micros networked; PCs & main system networked.

The Toronto Sun

(m-mon to fri; m-sat; S)

The Toronto Sun, 333 King St. E., Toronto, ON M5A 3X5; tel (416) 947-2222. Toronto Sun Publishing Corp. group.
Circulation: 240,822(m); 187,259(m-sat); 413,665(S); ABC Sept. 30, 1995.
Price: 50¢(d); 50¢(sat); $1.25(S); $61.20/12 wks (m), $22.80/12 wks (S) (mail).
Advertising: Modular rate $6.40(m); $4.21(m-sat); $9.19(S).
News Service: CP. **Established:** 1971.
Not Published: Christmas.
Special Edition: Sun High (5x/yr).
Special Weekly Sections: New Homes, Showcase and Travel, Comments (S).
Magazines: Color Comics, TV Guide (S); Modern Woman, Marquee (monthly).

CORPORATE OFFICERS

Chairman Lionel H Schipper
President/CEO Paul V Godfrey
Vice Pres-Finance/Chief Financial Officer Bruce Jackson

GENERAL MANAGEMENT

Publisher Hartley Steward
Editor in Chief Peter O'Sullivan
Vice Pres-Corporate Affairs Trudy Eagan
Controller Jim McCormack
Credit Manager Peter Kotzer
Corporate Controller John Boots
Corporate Director-Human Resources Lynda Mitchell

ADVERTISING

Director Heather McKie
Manager-National Maureen Caruk
Manager-Retail Goff Wirth
Manager-Classified Ellen Cohen
Asst Manager-Classified Colin Campbell

MARKETING AND PROMOTION

Promotion Manager Lesley Annett
Director-Marketing Lynda Schwalm

CIRCULATION

Director Orest Melnyk
Asst Director Brian Martel
Manager-Home Delivery Robert Sproule

NEWS EXECUTIVES

Editor John Downing
Exec Entertainment Editor Bob Thompson
Managing Editor Mike Strobel
Asst Managing Editor Peter Brewster
Editor in Chief Peter O'Sullivan

EDITORS AND MANAGERS

Action Line Maryanna Lewyckyj
Books Editor Heather Mallick
Business/Finance Editor Linda Leatherdale
Corporate Art Director Andrew Donato
City Editor Bob McConachie
Entertainment Editor Kathy Brooks
Films Editor Bruce Kirkland
Food Editor Cynthia David
Librarian Julie Kirsh
Lifestyle Editor Marilyn Linton
Exec Entertainment Editor Bob Thompson
Sports Editor Scott Morrison
Corporate Sports Editor George Gross
Sunday Showcase Marco Passifume
Television Guide Gord Stimmel
Television Editor Claire Bickley
Theater Editor John Coulbourn
Travel Editor Jill Rigby
Wire Editor Phil Johnson

MANAGEMENT INFORMATION SERVICES

Corporate Director-Info Service David Blizzard
Director-Info Service Guy Huntingford

PRODUCTION

Director Lesley Annett
Asst Director Stu Patterson
Manager-Composing Paul Kelly
Supervisor-Maintenance Colin Robinson
Supervisor-Pressroom Bob Pulfer
Manager-Mailroom Peter Vendy

Mechanical available: Offset; Black and 3, 4 ROP colors; insert accepted — page cut-offs — 15".
Mechanical specifications: Type page $10\frac{1}{4}$" x $12\frac{9}{16}$"; E - 8 cols, $1\frac{3}{16}$", $\frac{1}{6}$" between; A - 8 cols, $1\frac{3}{16}$", $\frac{1}{6}$" between; C - 8 cols, $1\frac{3}{16}$", $\frac{1}{6}$" between.
Commodity Consumption (estimated): Newsprint 49,000 metric tons; widths 60", 30", 45", 55", 41", 27"; black ink 1,300,00 pounds; color ink 560,000 pounds; single pages printed 18,000,000; average pages per issue 121(d), 101(sat), 262(S); single plates used 280,000.
Equipment: EDITORIAL: Front-end hardware — CD, 3-DEC/PDP 11-84; Front-end software — CSI; Printers — Tegra/Varityper XP1000; Other equipment — Ap/Mac. CLASSIFIED: Front-end hardware — 3-DEC/PDP 11-84; Front-end software — CSI; Printers — Tegra/Varityper XP1000. DISPLAY: Adv layout systems — MES/Ad Director; Front-end hardware — Ap/Mac; Front-end software — Multi-Ad/Creator, QuarkXPress, Adobe/Illustrator; Printers — MON, Chelgraph, III/3850. PRODUCTION: Typesetters — Tegra/Varityper XP1000, Chelgraph, III/3850, ECR/Pelbox; Platemaking systems — WL/Aquamaster; Plate exposers — BKY, 2-WL, 1-Tasope; Plate processors — 4-WL, 3-Nugraphic/Plate Bender, 1-Air Foam/Auto Plate Bender; Electronic picture desk — CD/EPD; Scanners — 2-ECR/Autokon, HP/2-C; Production cameras — LE, 2-C/Spartan II; Automatic film processors — LE; Shrink lenses — ECR/Autokon; Color separation equipment (conventional) — CD, Howtek, Scitex, Ap/Mac, CD/646; Digital color separation equipment — Ap/Mac Quadra 950. PRESSROOM: Line 1 — 5-G/Metro, 2-G/Metro, 1-G/Metroliner; Line 2 — 5-G/Metro, 2-G/Metro, 1-G/Metroliner; Line 3 — 7-G/Metro, 1-G/Metroliner; Line 4 — 7-G/Metro, 1-G/Metroliner; Line 5 — 8-G/Metroliner; Press drives — Fin; Folders — 8-G/3:2; Pasters — G; Reels and stands — G; Press control system — G. MAILROOM: Counter stackers — 9-HL/Monitor, HL/Stackers, 7-Id/2000, 1-Id/2100; Stuffers — 2-Amerigraph/1372, 1-Amerigraph/2299; Bundle tyer — 4-Power Strap, 10-MLN, 3-News 90; Wrapping singles — 11-Id/Underwraps, 9-NJP/Underwraps; Addressing machine — 2-AVY/5209; Mailroom control system — Id/Tray Sys. DEC/VAX 3400. LIBRARY: Electronic — Vu/Text SAVE. COMMUNICATIONS: Facsimile — CD/K663 Page fax; Satellite. WIRE SERVICES: News — DJ, CP, Canada Corporate News, Fundata, AP, Toronto Sun, LATS, United Media Canada, TV Data, RN, Bloomberg Financial, Financial Times, Financial Post; Photos — RN, CP, AP, PressLink; Stock tables — Canada News Wire, TSE, CP Stock, IP Sharp, RN; receiving dishes — CP. BUSINESS COMPUTERS: DEC/VAX 8550, 2-DEC/VAX 6410, DEC/VAX 6510, DEC/VAX 4100; Applications: CJ/AIM Ross: Accts payable, Human resources; Lotus/1-2-3 Microsoft/DOS Microsoft/Windows Lotus/Organizer DEC/Pathworks; PCs & micros networked; PCs & main system networked.

WATERLOO

See KITCHENER

WELLAND-PORT COLBORNE

'91 Census- 66,685 (Welland 47,915; Port Colborne 18,770); E&P '96 Est. 70,728 (Welland 50,992; Port Colborne 19,736)
ABC-CZ (91): 47,914 (HH 18,245)

The Tribune

(m-mon to sat)

The Tribune, 228 E. Main St., Welland, ON L3B 3W8; tel (905) 732-2411; fax (905) 732-4883. Sterling Newspapers (Hollinger Inc.) group.
Circulation: 16,873(m); 16,873(m-sat); ABC Sept. 30, 1995.
Price: 50¢(d); 75¢(fri); 75¢(sat); $2.90/wk (carrier); $139.50/yr (carrier), $270.00/yr (mail).
Advertising: Modular rate $1.14(m); $1.14(m-sat). **Representative:** Thomson Newspapers.
News Services: CP, AP, RN. **Politics:** Independent. **Established:** 1863.
Not Published: New Year; Good Friday; Victoria Day; Labor Day; Thanksgiving; Christmas.
Special Editions: Progress (Feb); Fashion (July); Cookbook (Aug); Brides (monthly).

CORPORATE OFFICER

President Ken R Thomson

GENERAL MANAGEMENT

Publisher/General Manager David A Beattie

ADVERTISING

Manager Mark Holmes

CIRCULATION

Manager Karin Vanderzee

NEWS EXECUTIVE

Managing Editor Gary Manning

EDITORS AND MANAGERS

City Editor Joe Barkovich
Sports Editor Wayne Redshaw

PRODUCTION

Manager David Beattie
Supervisor-Pressroom Stan Frost

Market Information: TMC.
Mechanical available: Offset; Black and 3 ROP colors; insert accepted — preprinted; page cut-offs — $22\frac{3}{4}$".
Mechanical specifications: Type page 13" x $21\frac{1}{2}$"; E - 6 cols, $2\frac{1}{16}$", $\frac{1}{8}$" between; A - 6 cols, $2\frac{1}{16}$", $\frac{1}{8}$" between; C - 9 cols, $1\frac{3}{8}$", $\frac{1}{16}$" between.
Commodity Consumption (estimated): widths 27"; average pages per issue 28(d).
Equipment: EDITORIAL: Front-end hardware — HAS/System. PRODUCTION: Typesetters — 2-COM; Production cameras — 1-Liberator. PRESSROOM: Line 1 — 7-G/Urbanite; Folders — 2-G. MAILROOM: Bundle tyer — Gd, OVL; Addressing machine — Am. WIRE SERVICES: News — CP; Syndicates — NEA. BUSINESS COMPUTERS: PCs & micros networked.

WINDSOR

'91 Census- 191,435 (Metro Area 262,075); E&P '96 Est. 198,928 (Metro Area 269,418)
ABC-CZ (91): 217,536 (HH 82,781)

The Windsor Star

(e-mon to fri; m-sat)

The Windsor Star, 167 Ferry St., Windsor, ON N9A 4M5; tel (519) 255-5711; fax (519) 255-5778. Southam Newspapers group.
Circulation: 80,219(e); 92,743(m-sat); ABC Sept. 30, 1995.
Price: 65¢(d); $1.35(sat); $3.00/wk; $39.00/mo; $143.00/yr.
Advertising: Modular rate $2.41(e); $2.89(m-sat). **Representative:** Southam Newspapers.
News Services: AP, CP, Southam News, LAT-WP, SHNS. **Politics:** Independent. **Established:** 1918.
Not Published: New Year; Good Friday; Victoria Day; Canada Day; Civic Holiday; Labor Day; Thanksgiving; Christmas.
Special Editions: Shopping Spree, Financial Investment Review (Jan); Bridal Feature (Feb); Automotive Report, Spring Fashion, Boating/Leisure (Mar); Car Care, Spring Home Improvement (Apr); Physical Fitness, Garden Feature (May); Shopping Spree, Freedom Festival, Fun in the Sun, Bridal (June); Hockey, Symphony, Home Improvement, Fall Fashion, Bridal Feature (Sept); Automotive Report, Fall & Winter Leisure Guide (Oct); Home Entertainment, Senior Citizens Days, Festive Cookbook (Nov); Festive Fashion, Christmas Greetings, Baby Feature (Dec).
Special Weekly Sections: Express (thur); Mutual Fund.
Magazine: TV Times (sat).

GENERAL MANAGEMENT

Publisher-Interim James Bruce
Business Manager Kerrie Alexander
Personnel Manager Louise Veres

ADVERTISING

Director Lance Neale
Manager-Classified E Mosco
Manager-National Mark Jacques

CIRCULATION

Director Glen Ross
Community Relations Manager Linda Balga
Newspaper in Education Linda Balga

NEWS EXECUTIVES

Editor J Bruce
Assoc Editor Doug Firby
Managing Editor David Agnew

EDITORS AND MANAGERS

Administrative Asst Julie Dodson
Books Editor Marty Gervais
Columnist (Ottawa) Paul McKeague
Columnist-Auto Lauren Moore
Columnist-Sports Lloyd McLachlan
Columnist-Wine Brian Bannon
Editorial Page Editor John Coleman
Editorial Writer Karen Hall
Education Editor Dave Battagello
Entertainment Editor Doug Williamson
Features Saturday Marie Claire Simonetti
Labor Editor Gary Rennie
Metro Editor Bill Hickey
Asst Metro Editor M Frezell
Asst Metro Editor Tom McMahon
Asst Metro Editor Doug Williamson
Op Editorial Page Editor Lee Palser
Photo Editor Grant Black
Sports Editor Rob Van Nie

MANAGEMENT INFORMATION SERVICES

Data Processing Manager Gary Doran
Online Manager Kevin McIntosh

PRODUCTION

Manager-Data Systems Ted Markle
Foreman-Pressroom Thomas E Kulik
Foreman-Engraving Ken Ferrano
Foreman-Mailroom Roger Ellis
Manager-Plant Services & Data Processing Fred Gutz

Market Information: Zoned editions; Split Run; TMC; Operate database.
Mechanical available: Letterpress (direct); Black and 3 ROP colors; insert accepted — preprinted, hi-fi, partials, zones, catalogues; page cut-offs — $22\frac{3}{4}$".
Mechanical specifications: Type page 13" x $21\frac{1}{2}$"; E - 6 cols, $2\frac{1}{16}$", $\frac{1}{8}$" between; A - 6 cols, $2\frac{1}{16}$", $\frac{1}{8}$" between; C - 10 cols, $1\frac{7}{32}$", $\frac{1}{12}$" between.
Commodity Consumption (estimated): Newsprint 7,800 metric tons; widths 139.7cm, 104.6cm, 69.7cm; average pages per issue 56(d), 130(sat).

Equipment: EDITORIAL: Front-end hardware — Ap/Mac; Front-end software — QPS 1.1; Printers — HP, Ap. **CLASSIFIED:** Front-end hardware — HP; Front-end software — SyD, Cybergraphics; Printers — Graphic Enterprises. **AUDIOTEX:** Hardware — Telepublishing Inc.; Software — Telepublishing Inc.; Supplier name — Telepublishing Inc.. **DISPLAY:** Adv layout systems — SCS/Layout 8000, Southam/Ad Track; Front-end hardware — Ap/Mac; Front-end software — QuarkXPress, Adobe/Photoshop; Printers — Graphic Enterprises. **PRODUCTION:** Typesetters — AU/APS-6 108; Platemaking systems — Na; Plate exposers — Na/Titan; Plate processors — Na/NP-120; Electronic picture desk — CD, Adobe/Photoshop; Scanners — ECR; Production cameras — 1-C/Marathon, 1-C/Spartan; Automatic film processors — LE/On-line; Film transporters — C; Color separation equipment (conventional) — EPP, AU/APS-6-108 FC. **PRESSROOM:** Line 1 — 9-Cb; Line 2 — 6-Cb, 3-G; Line 3 — 11-Cb, 3-G/(2 7-unit press); Folders — 1-G/Single, 1-G/Double; Pasters — Cb; Reels and stands — Cb; Press control system — GE. **MAILROOM:** Counter stackers — MSI; Bundle tyer — Id/plastic wrap. **LIBRARY:** Electronic — Infomart. **WIRE SERVICES:** News — CP, SOU; Photos — CP, SOU; Stock tables — Michigan Wire, SOU; Syndicates — SOU; receiving dishes — CP. **BUSINESS COMPUTERS:** DEC/Micro VAX 3800, DEC/Micro VAX; Applications: Circ, Adv, Accts payable, Payroll; PCs & micros networked; PCs & main system networked.

WOODSTOCK-INGERSOLL

'91 Census—39,455 (Woodstock 30,075; Ingersoll 9,380); **E&P '96 Est.** 42,938 (Woodstock 32,804; Ingersoll 10,134)
ABC-CZ (91): 30,075 (HH 11,545)

The Daily Sentinel-Review
(e-mon to sat)

The Daily Sentinel-Review, 16-18 Brock St.; PO Box 1000, Woodstock, ON N4S 8A5; tel (519) 537-2341; fax (519) 537-3049. Southwestern Ontario Publishing group.
Circulation: 9,579(e); 9,579(e-sat); ABC Sept. 30, 1995.
Price: 60¢(d); 75¢(fri); 60¢(sat); $2.50/wk (carrier); $117.00/yr.
Advertising: Modular rate 97¢(e); 97¢(e-sat).
Representative: Thomson Media Sales.
News Services: UPI, THO. **Politics:** Independent. **Established:** 1854.
Not Published: New Year; Good Friday; Thanksgiving; Christmas; Canada Day; Labor Day; Civic Holiday.
Special Editions: Tourist Guide (May); Oxford Directory (Oct); Oxford Homes, Oxford Business (monthly); Home Improvement; Education Week; Progress; Outdoor Living; Canada Week; Brides; Fall Cook Book; Christmas Carols; Year-End Review.
Magazine: TV Scene (fri).

GENERAL MANAGEMENT
Publisher/General Manager — George Czerny
Credit Manager — Joan Brown
Purchasing Agent — Joan Brown
ADVERTISING
Manager — Kim Whitehead
MARKETING AND PROMOTION
Manager-Marketing & Promotion — George Czerny
CIRCULATION
Manager — Jim Douglas
NEWS EXECUTIVE
Managing Editor — George Czerny
EDITORS AND MANAGERS
Business/Finance Editor — Alison Downie
City Editor — Alison Downie
Editorial Page Editor — George Czerny
Fashion/Food Editor — Heather Buchanan
Home Furnishings — Heather Buchanan
News Editor — Alison Downie
Special Editions — Phyllis Coulter
Sports Editor — Mark Schadenberg
Travel Editor — Heather Buchanan
MANAGEMENT INFORMATION SERVICES
Data Processing Manager — Joan Brown
PRODUCTION
Foreman-Pressroom — Ed Lattimer
Foreman-Composing — Rick Vader

Market Information: TMC; ADS.

Mechanical available: Offset; Black and 3 ROP colors; insert accepted — preprinted; page cut-offs — 21½".

Mechanical specifications: Type page 12⅛" x 21¼"; E - 7 cols, 1⁹⁄₁₆", ⅛" between; A - 7 cols, 1⁹⁄₁₆", ⅛" between; C - 7 cols, 1⁹⁄₁₆", ⅛" between.

Commodity Consumption (estimated): Newsprint 330 metric tons; widths 26½"; black ink 5,000 pounds; color ink 1,800 pounds; single pages printed 5,700; average pages per issue 14(d); single plates used 4,000.

Equipment: EDITORIAL: Front-end hardware — 1-HI, 12-HAS; Other equipment — HAS/Pagination. **CLASSIFIED:** Front-end hardware — 1-HI, HAS. **DISPLAY:** Adv layout systems — Ap/Mac Graphics System; Front-end hardware — Ap/Mac; Printers — Ap/Mac. **PRODUCTION:** Typesetters — 2-COM/MCS 8400, 2-COM/9400 Laser; Plate exposers — N/Flip Top; Scanners — Microtek; Production cameras — B/2000; Automatic film processors — FU/61, FG/360F; Color separation equipment (conventional) — Adobe/Photoshop on Ap/Mac w/Viper; Digital color separation equipment — Adobe/Photoshop on Ap/Mac w/Viper. **PRESSROOM:** Line 1 — 8-G/Community. **MAILROOM:** Bundle tyer — Gd/Q 200A, Gd/RM 174 Strap; Addressing machine — ATT/Computer Print Out. **COMMUNICATIONS:** Facsimile — Sharp; Satellite. **WIRE SERVICES:** News — UPI; Syndicates — TN; receiving dishes — size-2m, UPI, CP. **BUSINESS COMPUTERS:** 5-ATT; Applications: Adv, Circ, Acct, Administation; PCs & micros networked; PCs & main system networked.

PRINCE EDWARD ISLAND

CHARLOTTETOWN
'91 Census— 15,395; **E&P '96 Est.** 16,528
ABC-CZ (91): 23,600 (HH 9,545)

The Guardian
(m-mon to sat)

The Guardian, 165 Prince St.; PO Box 760, Charlottetown, PEI C1A 4R7; tel (902) 629-6000; fax (902) 566-3808. Thomson Newspapers group.
Circulation: 22,352(m); 22,352(m-sat); ABC Sept. 30, 1995.
Price: 65¢(d); $1.00(sat); $3.10/wk; $161.20/yr.
Advertising: Modular rate $1.51(m); $1.51(m-sat). **Representative:** Thomson Newspapers.
News Services: AP, CP. **Politics:** Independent. **Established:** 1871.
Note: Effective June 9, 1995, the Evening Patriot (e-mon to sat) ceased publishing.
Not Published: New Year; Good Friday; Victoria Day; Dominion Day; Labor Day; Thanksgiving; Christmas.
Special Editions: Business; Farm; Cookbook; Vacation; Fall Fashion; RRSP; Auto Magazine; Harness Racing; Fisheries; Home Improvement.
Special Weekly Section: Island View.
Magazines: TV Scene (wed); Real Estate Guide (thur).

GENERAL MANAGEMENT
Publisher/General Manager — Don Brander
Controller — Bonnie Taylor
ADVERTISING
Manager — Mike Hancox
Manager-Promotion — Mike Hancox
CIRCULATION
Manager — Julie Murtha
NEWS EXECUTIVES
Managing Editor — Gary J MacDougall
Chief Editor — Jim Palmateer
EDITORS AND MANAGERS
Assignment Editor — Iris Phillips
Features Editor — Carolyn Drake
Sports Editor — Garth Hurley
PRODUCTION
Manager — Leo MacCarthy

Market Information: TMC; ADS.
Mechanical available: Offset; Black and 3 ROP colors; insert accepted — preprinted; page cut-offs — 22½".

Mechanical specifications: Type page 13" x 21½"; E - 6 cols, 2¹⁄₁₆", ⅛" between.

Commodity Consumption (estimated): Newsprint 400 short tons; widths 27½"; average pages per issue 16(d).

Equipment: EDITORIAL: Front-end hardware — 8-Ap/Mac Classic, 2-Ap/Mac IIci; Front-end software — QuarkXPress, Microsoft/Word; Printers — Ap/LaserWriter II; Other equipment — Ven-Tel/Modem(1200 baud). **CLASSIFIED:** Front-end hardware — Ap/Mac LC, Ap/Mac Classic; Front-end software — Claris/Filemakers Pro, QPS, Microsoft/Word; Printers — Ap/Stylewriter. **DISPLAY:** Adv layout systems — Ap/Mac; Front-end hardware — 2-Ap/Mac IIci; Front-end software — Multi-ad/Creator, QPS, Microsoft/Word, Adobe/Illustrator, Zedcor/Deskpaint, Adobe/Streamline; Printers — 2-Ap/LaserWriter II. **PRODUCTION:** Platemaking systems — 1-N; Production cameras — 1-B; Automatic film processors — 1-P/SQ24.

Mechanical specifications: Type page 13" x 21½"; E - 6 cols, 2¹⁄₁₆", ⅛" between; A - 9 cols, 2¹⁄₁₆", ⅛" between; C - 9 cols, 1³⁄₈", ⅛" between.
Commodity Consumption (estimated): average pages per issue 17(d).

Equipment: EDITORIAL: Front-end hardware — 28-HAS; Front-end software — HAS 2.5; Printers — Printronix, TI. **CLASSIFIED:** Front-end hardware — HAS; Front-end software — HAS 2.5; **DISPLAY:** Front-end hardware — Ap/Mac Quadra; Front-end software — QuarkXPress; Printers — HP/LaserJet. **PRODUCTION:** Typesetters — 2-COM/8400; Plate exposers — 1-N; Plate processors — 1-Nat; Electronic picture desk — 2-CD; Scanners — Microtek; Production cameras — 1-B, 1-SCREEN; Automatic film processors — 1-SCREEN; Film transporters — 1-B; Shrink lenses — 1-CK Optical; Color separation equipment (conventional) — ECR/Autokon.
PRESSROOM: Line 1 — G/Community (8 units; 1 stack unit); Press drives — Fin; Folders — G/SC; Press control system — Fin. **MAILROOM:** Addressing machine — 2-Am. **WIRE SERVICES:** News — CP; Photos — CP; Stock tables — CP; receiving dishes — size-6ft, CP. **BUSINESS COMPUTERS:** ATT.

SUMMERSIDE
'91 Census— 7,475; **E&P '96 Est.** 7,465
ABC-CZ (91): 13,164 (HH 4,720)

The Journal-Pioneer
(e-mon to sat)

The Journal-Pioneer, 4 Queen St.; PO Box 2480, Summerside, PEI C1N 4K5; tel (902) 436-2121; fax (902) 436-3027. Sterling Newspapers (Hollinger Inc.) group.
Circulation: 10,868(e); 10,868(e-sat); ABC Sept. 30, 1995.
Price: 50¢(d); 50¢(sat); $2.40/wk (carrier).
Advertising: Modular rate 92¢(e); 92¢(e-sat).
News Service: CP. **Politics:** Independent. **Established:** 1865.
Not Published: New Year; Good Friday; Victoria Day; Dominion Day; Labor Day; Thanksgiving; Christmas.
Advertising not accepted: Discriminatory; racist; obscene.
Special Editions: Harness Racing; Progress; Agriculture; Fisheries; Lobster Carnival; Car Care; Fashion; Tourist; Christmas; Home Improvement.
Magazine: Weekly TV-Guide (local, newsprint).

CORPORATE OFFICER
President — David R Radler
GENERAL MANAGEMENT
Publisher — Steen O Jorgensen
Accountant — Daphne Connolly
ADVERTISING
Manager — Bob McIntosh
CIRCULATION
Manager — Grant Gallont
NEWS EXECUTIVES
Managing Editor — Wayne Young
Asst Editor — Gertrude Deighan
EDITOR AND MANAGER
Sports Editor — Bill Semple

Mechanical available: Offset; Black and 3 ROP colors; insert accepted — preprinted; page cut-offs — 22¾".
Mechanical specifications: Type page 13" x 21½"; E - 6 cols, 2¹⁄₁₆", ⅛" between.

Quebec

PRESSROOM: Line 1 — 6-G/Community, 3-G/Community Color; Folders — 1-G. **MAILROOM:** Bundle tyer — 1-Pak/F16; Wrapping singles — Weld-Loc/Strapping; Addressing machine — 1-EI/3301. **COMMUNICATIONS:** Satellite. **WIRE SERVICES:** News — CP; receiving dishes — CP.

QUEBEC

CHICOUTIMI
'91 Census— 62,670 (Metro Area 160,925); **E&P '96 Est.** 66,503 (Metro Area 172,893)
Progres-Dimanche
ABC-CZ (91): 62,670 (HH 22,635)
Le Quotidien
ABC-CZ (91: 110,082 (HH 40,383)

Le Quotidien
(m-mon to sat)
Progres-Dimanche (S)

Le Quotidien, 1051 Talbot Blvd., Chicoutimi, QC G7H 5C1; tel (418) 545-4474; fax (418) 690-8806. UniMedia Inc. (Hollinger Inc.) group.
Circulation: 28,932(m); 28,932(m-sat); 46,190(S); ABC Sept. 30, 1995.
Price: 70¢(d); 70¢(sat); $1.40(S).
Advertising: Modular rate $2.01(m); $2.01(m-sat); $2.01(S). **Representative:** Probec 5.
News Service: CP. **Politics:** Independent. **Established:** 1973.
Magazine: TV Guide.

CORPORATE OFFICER
President & Editor — Claude Gagnon
GENERAL MANAGEMENT
General Manager — Claude Gagnon
ADVERTISING
Manager (Progres-Dimanche) — Jean Tremblay
Manager (Le Quotidien) — Yvon Girard
MARKETING AND PROMOTION
Manager Marketing & Promotion — Jean Tremblay
CIRCULATION
Manager — Jean-Louis Lavoie
EDITORS AND MANAGERS
Editorial Page Editor — Bertrand Genest
Editorial — Carol Neron
Features Editor — Gilles Lalaneette
PRODUCTION
Manager — Jean Simard

Market Information: Zoned editions; Split Run; TMC.
Mechanical available: Offset; Black and 3 ROP colors; insert accepted — preprinted, all inserts; page cut-offs — 21½".
Mechanical specifications: Type page 10¼" x 14¼"; E - 10 cols, ¹⁵⁄₁₆", ⅛" between; C - 5 cols, 1¹⁵⁄₁₆", ⅛" between.
Commodity Consumption (estimated): Newsprint 3,000 metric tons; widths 30"; black ink 170,000 pounds; color ink 80,000 pounds; average pages per issue 40(d), 160(S); single plates used 25,000.

Equipment: EDITORIAL: Front-end hardware — Cx, MI, Ap, Ik, Ap/Mac 475, Ap/Mac 6100; Front-end software — C, Cenotext 1.1.2; Printers — 7-M. **CLASSIFIED:** Front-end hardware — 4-Mk, Ap/Mac; Front-end software — Baseview/Class Manager. **DISPLAY:** Adv layout systems — Ap/Mac; Front-end hardware — Ap/Mac 650, Ap/Mac 800, Ap/Mac 950; Front-end software — Adobe/Illustrator, QPS, Adobe/Photoshop; Printers — Accuset/1000, Linotype-Hell/Lino 300, Linotype-Hell/Lino 200; Other equipment — QMS/860. **PRODUCTION:** Pagination systems — QPS; Typesetters — Canadian Linotype, Ik, Accuset/1000; Platemaking systems — Lp; Plate exposers — BKY; Electronic picture desk — CD; Scanners — Sharp/Flatbed, ECR, Cp; Production cameras — 1-B, 1-R; Automatic film processors — Kk; Color separation equipment (conventional) — BKY.
PRESSROOM: Line 1 — 9-G/Urbanite; Line 2 — HI; Press drives — Fin; Pasters — MM, 5-Martin/Automatic. **MAILROOM:** Counter stackers — MM; Stuffers — 1-HL; Bundle tyer — 1-MLN; Addressing machine — 1-Am. **WIRE SERVICES:** News — CP; Photos — CP, Photo

III-22 Quebec

Contractor; receiving dishes — AP, UPI. BUSINESS COMPUTERS: IBM/Sys 36 Model 5360, IBM/PC, Sun/Sparc; Applications: Accts payable, Circ, Accts receivable, Financial statement; PCs & main system networked.

GRANBY

'91 Census- 42,805; E&P '96 Est. 46,708
ABC-CZ (91): 59,227 (HH 22,960)

La Voix de l'Est

(m-mon to fri; m-sat)

La Voix de l'Est, 76 Dufferin St., Grandy, QC J2G 9L4; tel (514) 375-4555; fax (514) 777-4865. Les Journaux Trans-Canada/JTC group.
Circulation: 14,912(m); 18,692(m-sat); ABC Sept. 30, 1995.
Price: 50¢(d); $1.50(sat); $2.90/wk; $130.00/yr.
Advertising: Modular rate $1.52(m); $1.52(m-sat). **Representative:** Probec 5.
News Services: CP, AP, RN, AFP. **Politics:** Independent. **Established:** 1945 (d), 1935 (w).
Note: La Voix de l'Est is printed by La Tribune (Sherbrook, QC). For detailed advertising and production information, see the La Tribune listing. The La Voix de l'Est has a combination rate of $10.55 with the Montreal La Presse (mS).
Not Published: New Year; Jan 2; Easter Monday; Victoria Day; June 24; July 1; Labor Day; Thanksgiving; Christmas; Dec 26.
Advertising not accepted: No limitation, except for libel or good taste.
Special Editions: Agriculture (Mar); Fashion (Apr); Cars (May); Tourism (June); Agriculture (Sept); Travel (Oct); Winter Sports (Nov).
Magazines: TMC (wkly); TV schedule (sat).
Broadcast Affiliates: Radio CHEF (1450, MA Station).

CORPORATE OFFICER
President & Editor Pierre Gobeil

GENERAL MANAGEMENT
President & Editor Pierre Gobeil
Director-Finance & Administration Yvon Gauvin

ADVERTISING
Sales Manager Sylvain Denault

CIRCULATION
Director Jean-Nil Laplante

EDITORS AND MANAGERS
Business/Finance Editor Isabelle Ducas
Court House Richard Gosselin
Editorial Page Editor Valere Audy
Leisure/Sports Gaetan Roy
Newsroom Manager Dany Doucet
News Editor Dany Doucet
Sports Editor Andre Bilodeau

Mechanical available: Offset; Black and 3 ROP colors; insert accepted — preprinted; page cut-offs — 13¾".
Mechanical specifications: Type page 10¼" x 13¾"; E - 5 cols, 2", ⅛" between; A - 5 cols, 2", ⅛" between; C - 5 cols, 2", ⅛" between.
Commodity Consumption (estimated): widths 55"; average pages per issue 38(d), 72(sat).
Equipment: EDITORIAL: Front-end hardware — 1-HI/1730. CLASSIFIED: Front-end hardware — 1-HI/1730. MAILROOM: Bundle tyer — GD, OVL; Addressing machine — IBM/34. BUSINESS COMPUTERS: IBM/34; Applications: Circ, Accounting.

HULL

See OTTAWA, ON

MONTREAL

'91 Census- 1,017,665 (Metro Area 3,127,240); E&P '96 Est. 1,071,421 (Metro Area 3,293,945)
Le Devoir/La Presse/Le Journal de Montreal
ABC-NDM (91): 3,893,881 (HH 1,524,480)
Gazette
ABC-CZ (91): 2,469,615 (HH 1,014,385)

Le Devoir

(m-mon to fri; m-sat)

Le Devoir, 2050 de Bleury, 9th Fl., Montreal, QC H3A 3M9; tel (514) 985-3333; fax (514) 985-3360.
Circulation: 30,343(m); 38,962(m-sat); ABC Mar. 31, 1995.
Price: 65¢(d); $1.30(sat); $3.00/wk (carrier); $197.18/yr.
Advertising: Modular rate $3.55(m); $3.55(m-sat).
News Services: CP, AP, LE Monde, RN, AFP, CNW, Telbec. **Politics:** Independent. **Established:** 1910.
Note: All printing and distribution of Le Devoir Inc. is out sourced.
Not Published: New Year; Jan 2; Easter Monday; Victoria Day; St. Baptiste Day; Confederation Day; Labor Day; Thanksgiving; Christmas; Dec 26.

CORPORATE OFFICERS
President Marcel Couture
Secretary Gilles Carli

GENERAL MANAGEMENT
Publisher Lise Bissonnette
Business Manager Francois Thouin

ADVERTISING
Manager Lucie Pinsonneault

MARKETING AND PROMOTION
Director-Promotion Guy Renaud Kirouac

CIRCULATION
Manager Christianne Benjamin

NEWS EXECUTIVES
Director-Information Benoit Aubin
Editor in Chief Bernard Descoteaux
Asst Editor in Chief Jean-Robert Sansfacon

EDITORS AND MANAGERS
City Editor Roch Cote
City Editor Pierre Beaulieu
Cultural Pages Michel Belair
Economic Editor Gerard Berube
International Editor Francois Brousseau
Literary Pages Pierre Cayoutte

MANAGEMENT INFORMATION SERVICES
Director-Info Service Jean Lemay

PRODUCTION
Director Jean Lemay

Market Information: TMC.
Mechanical available: Offset; Black and 3 ROP colors; insert accepted — preprinted; page cut-offs — 21¾".
Mechanical specifications: Type page 13¾" x 21¾"; E - 6 cols, 2 1/16", ⅛" between; A - 6" cols, 2 1/16", ⅛" between; C - 9 cols, 1 5/16", ⅛" between.
Commodity Consumption (estimated): average pages per issue 16(d).
Equipment: EDITORIAL: Front-end hardware — Ap/Mac; Front-end software — Baseview/News Edit, QuarkXPress, Adobe/Photoshop; Printers — AG/Selectset 5000, AG/Selectset 7000, QMS/860, Ap/LaserWriter IIg, HP; Other equipment — Sharp/11x17 scanner, AG/Arcus, Nikon/3510AF, Radius/Vision Video Capture. CLASSIFIED: Front-end hardware — Novell/486 server; Front-end software — Informatel. DISPLAY: Adv layout systems — Ap/Macs; Front-end hardware — Ap/Macs; Front-end software — QuarkXPress, Aldus/FreeHand, Adobe/Illustrator, Adobe/Streamline, Adobe/Photoshop; Printers — QMS/860. PRODUCTION: Typesetters — AG/Selectset 5000, AG/Selectset 7000; Electronic picture desk — CD/2640; Scanners — AG/Arcus, Sharp, 2-Nikon/LS 3510AF. LIBRARY: Electronic — CD-Rom; Combination — Documentation Center. COMMUNICATIONS: Remote imagesetting — MagnaLink Bridge; Satellite. WIRE SERVICES: News — CP, AP, Le Monde, RN, AFP, CNW, Telbec; Photos — CP, AFP; Stock tables — CP; receiving dishes — size-3m, AFP, CP. BUSINESS COMPUTERS: PC/System; Applications: AccPac Informatel; PCs & micros networked; PCs & main system networked.

The Gazette

(m-mon to fri; m-sat; S)

The Gazette, 250 Rue St. Antoine W., Montreal, QC H2Y 3R7; tel (514) 987-2222; fax (514) 987-2270; web site http://www.vir.com/Gazette/index.html. Southam Newspapers group.
Circulation: 148,777(m); 217,055(m-sat); 137,983(S); ABC Sept. 30, 1995.
Price: 53¢(d); $1.54(sat); 53¢(S); $15.00/mo (carrier); $173.00/yr (carrier).
Advertising: Modular rate $6.83(m); $10.69 (m-sat); $6.83(S). **Representative:** Southam Newspapers.
News Services: AP, RN, NYT, LAT-WP, KRT, TSS, CP, NNS, DJ. **Politics:** Independent. **Established:** 1778.
Not Published: New Year; Good Friday; Victoria Day; St. Jean Baptiste; Canada Day; Labour Day; Thanksgiving; Christmas.
Advertising not accepted: Tobacco.
Special Weekly Sections: This Week In Business (mon); West Island (Community Edition), West End (Community Edition), South Shore (Community Edition) (thur); TV Times (sat).
Magazine: CHIC (Fashion & Beauty) (4x/yr).

GENERAL MANAGEMENT
Publisher Michael Goldbloom
Asst to the Publisher Rex Buckland
Director-Human Resources Jean-Pierre Tremblay
Purchasing Manager Tony DiStaulo
Education Service Manager Christine Tutt

ADVERTISING
Manager-National Elizabeth Austin
Manager-Retail Joyce Hammock
Manager-Classified Doris Bradley
Manager Special Sections and Promotion Marie Anne Colucci

MARKETING AND PROMOTION
Vice Pres Marketing Alan Allnutt
Marketing Manager Christine Tutt
Promotion Manager Nancy Diggins

TELECOMMUNICATIONS
Audiotex Manager Mark Stachiew

CIRCULATION
Vice Pres-Reader Sales & Service Cathy Hamilton Lambie
Manager-Reader Sales, Marketing & Service Jean Drolet

NEWS EXECUTIVES
Editor Joan Fraser
Managing Editor Raymond Brassard
Ombudsman Bob Walker
Asst Managing Editor Ashok Chandwani
Asst Managing Editor Marvin Zivitz
Asst Managing Editor Peter Cooney
Asst Managing Editor Jack Romanelli
Editorial Page Editor Jennifer Robinson

EDITORS AND MANAGERS
Books Editor Bryan Demchinsky
Senior Business Editor David Yates
City Editor Catherine Wallace
Columnist Don MacPherson
Columnist William Johnson
Columnist Jack Todd
Editorial Cartoonist Terry Mosher
Entertainment Editor Lucinda Chodan
Environment Reporter Graeme Hamilton
Fashion Editor Iona Monahan
Foreign Editor David Walker
Food Editor Julian Armstrong
Graphics Editor Ashok Chandwani
Living Editor Cecelia McGuire
National Brian Kappler
Photo Editor Barry Gray
Radio/Television Columnist Michael Boone
Religion Reporter Harvey Shepherd
Society Columnist Tom Schnurmacher
Sports Editor Dave Stubbs

MANAGEMENT INFORMATION SERVICES
Data Processing Manager Feli Varas
Editorial Systems Manager Peter Cooney

PRODUCTION
Director John Laurin
Asst Director Ron Haynes
Manager-Press Gordon Cumming
Manager-Pre Press Gretan Cote
Manager-Mailroom Maurice Seguin
Building Manager Richard Brown

Market Information: Zoned editions; Split Run; Operate audiotex; Electronic edition.
Mechanical available: Letterpress (direct); Black and 3 ROP colors; insert accepted — preprinted, product sampling; page cut-offs — 23 9/16".
Mechanical specifications: Type page 11.5" x 22⅛"; E - 5 cols, 2 1/16", ⅙" between; A - 10 cols, 1 1/12", 1/12" between; C - 10 cols, 1⅛", 1/24" between.
Commodity Consumption (estimated): Newsprint 22,000 metric tons; widths 50", 375", 25"; black ink 350,000 kg; color ink 71,000 kg; single pages printed 25,000; average pages per issue 60(d), 108(sat), 46(S); single plates used 122,000.
Equipment: EDITORIAL: Front-end hardware — 3-CSI/11-84, Ap/Power Mac, Ap/Mac Quadra, Ap/Mac Duo, Ap/Mac Power Book; Front-end software — MeD/112i, MeD/edit 90, MeD/112B, QPS, Adobe/Photoshop. CLASSIFIED: Front-end hardware — Cybergraphics, PC/386-SX; Front-end software — Sun. DISPLAY: Adv layout systems — SCS/Layout 8000; Front-end hardware — 30-Ap/Mac, 2-Sharp/JX 450 scanner, 4-Sharp/JX 320 scanner, 2-Ap/Mac scanner; Front-end software — Multi-Ad/Creator, Adobe/Photoshop, Adobe/Illustrator, QuarkXPress; Printers — 2-AU/LZR 2600. PRODUCTION: Typesetters — 2-AU/APS-6-108C, 1-AU/APS-3850, 2-AU/APS 800 PIPS, 4-AU/APS SOFPIP; Platemaking systems — Na; Plate exposers — 1-Na/Master, 2-Na/Titan; Plate processors — 2-C/120; Electronic picture desk — Lf/AP Leaf Picture Desk, CD; Production cameras — 2-C/Newspager; Automatic film processors — 4-LE; Film transporters — 2-LE/2600 System; Digital color separation equipment — Ap/Mac, Adobe/Photoshop. PRESSROOM: Line 1 — 9-G/MK II, 1-G/MK I; Line 2 — 24-G/MK I; Folders — 4-G; Pasters — G; Reels and stands — G; Press control system — G. MAILROOM: Counter stackers — 4-QWI/SJ191, 4-St/251; Stuffers — 3-Fg/6-into-1; Bundle tyer — 5-MLN/M-L, 7-Power Strap; Wrapping singles — 6-Monarch, 2-Id; Addressing machine — 6-DM. LIBRARY: Electronic — BASIS, DEC/VAX. WIRE SERVICES: News — CP, NNS, SHNS, AP, RN, NYT, LAT-WP, KRT, TSS, CNW, TelBec, CCN, DJ; Stock tables — CP. BUSINESS COMPUTERS: 2-DEC/VAX 4000-300; Applications: Financial applications, Circ; PCs & main system networked.

Le Journal de Montreal

(m-mon to fri; m-sat; S)

Le Journal de Montreal, 4545 Frontenac St., Montreal, QC H2H 2R7; tel (514) 521-4545; fax (514) 521-2173. Quebecor Inc. group.
Circulation: 270,607(m); 324,539(m-sat); 285,649(S); ABC Sept. 30, 1995.
Price: 60¢(d); $1.50(sat); 60¢(S); $4.25/wk (carrier); $221.00/yr.
Advertising: Modular rate $6.40(m); $6.40(m-sat); $6.40(S).
News Services: CP, Telbec, DJ, CNW, AFP. **Politics:** Independent. **Established:** 1964.
Special Weekly Section: Cahier Week-End (sat).

CORPORATE OFFICERS
Board Chairman Pierre Peladeau
Vice Pres Jacques Girard

GENERAL MANAGEMENT
Publisher Pierre Francoeur

ADVERTISING
Manager Claude A Dalpe
Manager-National Bernard Bigras

MARKETING AND PROMOTION
Manager Therese David

TELECOMMUNICATIONS
Audiotex Manager Pierre Lepine

CIRCULATION
Manager Christiane Benjamin

NEWS EXECUTIVE
Editor Jean-Philippe Decarie

EDITORS AND MANAGERS
News Editor Jean-Denis Lamoureux
Sports Editor Francois Leblond

MANAGEMENT INFORMATION SERVICES
Data Processing Manager Pierre Lepine

PRODUCTION
Manager Michel Dozois

Market Information: TMC; Operate audiotex.
Mechanical available: Offset; Black and 3 ROP colors; insert accepted — preprinted; page cut-offs — 22".
Mechanical specifications: Type page 10⅛" x 14¼"; E - 7 cols, 1⅓", ⅛" between; A - 7 cols, 1⅓", ⅛" between; C - 7 cols, 1⅓", 15/16" between.
Commodity Consumption (estimated): Newsprint 35,000 metric tons; widths 59 13/16", 44 13/16", 29 13/16"; black ink 335,000 kg; color ink 65,000 kg; single pages printed 38,000; average pages per issue 104(d), 88(S); single plates used 47,245.
Equipment: EDITORIAL: Front-end hardware — DEC/PDP 11-70, 50-DEC/VAX; Front-end software — TMS. CLASSIFIED: Front-end hardware — 2-Sun/Sparc 10-41, 42-PC; Front-end software — Unix/OS-2 Ver. 2.1, CText/Advision, CText/Alps; Printers — 2-QMS/860. AUDIOTEX: Hardware — PCs; Software — In-house. DISPLAY: Adv layout systems — SCS/Layout 8000; Front-end hardware — 15-Ap/Mac Quadra 800-840; Front-end software — QuarkXPress 3.1; Printers — Calcomp, Tek-

tronix, Data Products/LZR 2080, AU/APS 1560; Other equipment — 2-Sun/Sparc 10-51. PRODUCTION: Pagination software — QuarkXPress; Typesetters — 3-AU/F/08-C; Plate exposers — 4-N/Flip Top FT52NUPS; Plate processors — 1-WL/Litho Plate 38A, 2-WL/Litho Plate 38D; Electronic picture desk — CD/Picture Desk; Scanners — Eskofot/8200S, 4-X/7650, Chromograph/2000; Automatic film processors — 3-LE/Excel 26. PRESSROOM: Line 2 — 12-G/Cosmo; Line 3 — 18-G/Metro; Folders — 2-G/2:1, 3-G/3:2; Pasters — 10-G/Cosmo, 15-G/Metro. MAILROOM: Counter stackers — 6-RKW/40; Bundle tyer — 6-MLN/85495; Wrapping singles — 2-Ideal/7100. WIRE SERVICES: News — CP, Tel-horaire, CNW, Telbec; Photos — CD/Picture Desk; Stock tables — DJ; receiving dishes — CP. BUSINESS COMPUTERS: DEC/VAX/4000-300; Applications: Accts receivable, Accts payable, Billing, Gen ledger, Payroll; PCs & micros networked; PCs & main system networked.

La Presse

(m-mon to fri; m-sat; S)

La Presse, 7 Rue St. Jacques, Montreal, QC H2Y 1K9; tel (514) 285-7272. Les Journaux Trans-Canada/JTC group.

Circulation: 179,523(m); 302,178(m-sat); 184,842(S); ABC Sept. 30, 1995.

Price: 50¢(d); $1.50(sat); 50¢(S); $3.75/wk; $16.25/mo; $176.40/yr.

Advertising: Modular rate $9.14(m); $11.78 (m-sat); $9.14(S). **Representative:** North American Travel Publications.

News Services: AFP, CP, AP, UPI, DJ, RN. **Politics:** Independent. **Established:** 1884.

Note: The Montreal La Presse has a combination rate of $10.55 with Granby La Voix de l'Est (m); $11.46 with Sherbrook La Tribune (m); $11.59 with Trois-Rivieres Le Nouvelliste (m).

Not Published: New Year; Day after New Year; Good Friday; Easter Monday; Victoria Day; Canada Day; Labor Day; Thanksgiving; Christmas; Day after Christmas.

Special Editions: Travel; Entertainment; Real Estate; Lifestyle; Fashion; Food; Home Decoration; Automobile; Investments; PLUS Weekend Review.

Magazine: Tele-Presse TV-Radio Tab Magazine (sat).

CORPORATE OFFICERS

President Roger D Landry
Vice Pres Finance/Administration Daniel Rochon

GENERAL MANAGEMENT

Publisher Roger D Landry
Vice Pres/General Manager-J.T.C. Jean Sisto
Asst to President/Legal Counsel Philippe-Denis Richard
Controller Claude St. Gelais
Vice Pres-Marketing Mario Savard
Vice Pres-Personnel & Labor Relations Jacques Tousignant
Vice Pres/Asst Publisher Claude Masson

ADVERTISING

Director-Retail Denis Belanger
Director-National Fernand Lacourse
Manager-Retail Robert Aubin
Classified Real Laflamme

CIRCULATION

Director Serge Comtois

NEWS EXECUTIVES

Managing Editor Marcel Desgardins
Desk Editor (Day) Pierre Loignon
Desk Editor (Evening) Daniel Marsolais
Desk Editor (Evening) Yves Bellefleur
La Presse Plus Magazine Editor Andre Pratte
International Politics Andre Pratte
National & Provincial Politics Andre Pratte

EDITORS AND MANAGERS

Amusements Editor Alain De Repentigny
Art Director Julien Chung
Arts/Entertainment Editor Mario Roy
Business Editor Michel G Tremblay
Books Editor Reginald Martel
Cartoon Editor J P Girerd
Cinema Editor Serge Dussault
Cinema Editor Luc Perreault
City Editor Pierre Vincent
Editorial Writer Claudette Tougas
Editorial Writer Frederic Wagniere
Editorial Writer Pierre Gravel
Education Michele Ouimet
Fashion Editor Guy Pinard
Features Editor Guy Pinard
Finance Editor Michel G Tremblay
Food Editor Francoise Kayler
Librarian Gerard Monette
Metro Editor Marc Dore
Music Editor-Classical Claude Gingras
Music Editor-Pop Alain Brunet
News Editor Marcel Desgardins
Ottawa Bureau Philippe Dubuisson
Quebec Bureau Denis Lessard
Photography Editor Julien Chung
Radio/Television Editor Daniel Lemay
Real Estate Rudy Lecours
Religion Editor Jules Beliveau
Science/Technology Editor Carole Thibodeau
Sunday Editor Pierre Loignon
Technology Editor Guy Granger
Theatre Editor Jean Beaunoyer
Travel Editor Francois Trepanier
Women's Editor Guy Pinard

PRODUCTION

Vice Pres Jacques Vallee
Director Roland Cloutier
Administration Asst Francois Alin
Superintendent-Pre Press Marcel Roy
Superintendent-Pressroom Jean-Claude Decoste
Superintendent-Mailroom Roger Cholette

Market Information: Split Run; TMC.

Mechanical available: Letterpress - Napp Plates; Black and 3 ROP colors; insert accepted — preprinted; page cut-offs — $23\frac{9}{16}$".

Mechanical specifications: Type page $13\frac{1}{2}$" x $23\frac{9}{16}$"; E - 6 cols, $2\frac{1}{16}$", ¼" between; A - 6 cols, $2\frac{1}{16}$", $\frac{3}{16}$" between; C - 10 cols, $1\frac{3}{16}$", $\frac{3}{32}$" between.

Commodity Consumption (estimated): Newsprint 28,000 metric tons; widths 54", $40\frac{1}{2}$", 27"; black ink 1,150,000 pounds; color ink 180,000 pounds; single pages printed 28,000; average pages per issue 60(d), 150(S); single plates used 125,000.

Equipment: EDITORIAL: Front-end hardware — IBM/PS2-LAN, 85-IBM/PS2-30-286, COM/Ethernet; Front-end software — AT 3.6, AT/40; Other equipment — HI/Images Picture Desk 3, 2-Sun/Sparc, 3-HI/KM, 1-X/Scanner. CLASSIFIED: Front-end hardware — 2-Ap/Mac II. DISPLAY: Adv layout systems — SCS/Layout 8000; Front-end hardware — 8-HI/8300, 4-Zenith, 4-AT, 8-IBM/PS2-30-286. PRODUCTION: Typesetters — 2-AU/APS 6, 3-AU/APS Micro 5; Platemaking systems — Na; Plate exposers — 3-Na; Plate processors — 3-Na/Processor, 2-ECR/Autokon-1000; Scanners — 2-X/flatbed; Production cameras — 2-C/Marathon; Automatic film processors — 1-LO/24-AD, 1-LO/26 LVA, 1-Excel/26-10; Film transporters — 1-LO/281-Q, PC/310-1800; Digital color separation equipment — 1-Hel/38 DL. PRESSROOM: Line 1 — 36-G/Headliner; Folders — 4-G; Pasters — Automatic; Press control system — Beel Control. MAILROOM: Counter stackers — 7-HL; Stuffers — 1-S/48-P, 1-S/72-P; Bundle tyer — 7-Power Strap; Wrapping singles — 6-Mosca/(ACME). LIBRARY: Combination — CD-Rom. COMMUNICATIONS: Satellite. WIRE SERVICES: News — UPI, CP, AFP, PC, RN, AP; Photos — AP, CP, RN, AFP; receiving dishes — size-3ft, AP, AFP, RN. BUSINESS COMPUTERS: 2-IBM/4381; Applications: Prod, Accounting, Billing.

QUEBEC

'91 Census- 167,520 (Metro Area 667,300); E&P '96 Est. 177,288 (Metro Area 672,009)
ABC-NDM (91): 645,550 (HH 235,365)

Le Journal de Quebec

(m-mon to fri; m-sat; S)

Le Journal de Quebec, 450 Bechard Ave., Ville Vanier, QC G1M 2E9; tel (418) 683-1573. Quebecor Inc. group.

Circulation: 97,680(m); 114,471(m-sat); 96,000(S); ABC Sept. 30, 1995.

Price: 50¢(d); $1.00(sat); 50¢(S); $3.50/wk; $182.00/yr.

Advertising: Modular rate $3.20(m); $3.20(m-sat); $3.20(S). **Representative:** QUE.

News Services: PC, UPI, Canada News Wire, Telbec, AFP. **Established:** 1967.

Not Published: New Year; Day after New Year; Easter Monday; Victoria Day; St. John Baptiste Day; Confederation Day; Labor Day; Thanksgiving; Christmas; Day after Christmas.

Special Editions: Cashier 50%, Salon De La Marie'e, Voyage, Carnaval De Quebec, Resto St. Valentin (Jan); Ordinateur/Cellulaire, Salon De L'Auto (Feb); Paques Restauration (Mar); Fete Des Meres Resto (Apr); Automobile, Plein Air, Theatre D'Ete (May); Resto Pete Des Peres, Cashier 50% (June); La Rentree, Expo-Quebec, La Chasse, Jeunes Enterpreneurs (Aug); Rentree Spectaculaire, Ordinateur/Cellulaire, Decoration, Octobre Mois De La Restauration, Les Nordiques (Sept); Automobile, Ski (Oct); Enseignement Prive, Cadeaux (Nov); Resto Temps Des Fetes, Revue De L'Annee, Cashier 50% (Dec).

Special Weekly Sections: Automotive (mon); Fashion (tues); Consumer (wed); Home, Entertainment (sat).

Magazine: Tele-Horaire (TV Listings).

CORPORATE OFFICER

President Pierre Peladeau

GENERAL MANAGEMENT

Editor/General Manager Jean Claude L'Abbee
Controller Andre Berube

ADVERTISING

Manager Daniel Houde

MARKETING AND PROMOTION

Manager-Marketing & Promotion Jacques Lajeunesse

CIRCULATION

Manager Marc Couture

NEWS EXECUTIVE

Chief Editor Serge Cote

EDITORS AND MANAGERS

Auto/Books Editor Jocelyn Bourque
City Editor Michel Poirier
Entertainment Editor Jocelyn Bourque
Features Editor Serge Gosselin
Finance Editor Michel Poirier
Food Editor Jocelyn Bourque
Music Editor Jocelyn Bourque
News Editor Serge Gosselin
Political Editor Normand Girard
Political Editor Serge Gosselin
Radio/Television Editor Jocelyn Bourque
Real Estate Jocelyn Bourque
Religion Editor Michel Poirier
Science/Technology Editor Jocelyn Bourque
Sports Editor Claude Bedard
Women's Editor Jocelyn Bourque

MANAGEMENT INFORMATION SERVICES

Data Processing Manager Louis Chretien

PRODUCTION

Manager Nolin Richard

Market Information: Zoned editions.

Mechanical available: Offset; Black and 3 ROP colors; insert accepted — preprinted, all; page cut-offs — 22".

Mechanical specifications: Type page $10\frac{5}{16}$" x $14\frac{1}{4}$"; E - 7 cols, 1.34", .04" between; A - 7 cols, 1.34", .04" between; C - 7 cols, 1.34", .04" between.

Commodity Consumption (estimated): Newsprint 10,475 metric tons; widths 30", 15"; black ink 263,374 pounds; color ink 17,762 pounds; single pages printed 29,820; average pages per issue 88(d), 112(sat), 64(S); single plates used 31,134.

Equipment: EDITORIAL: Front-end hardware — TMS/V5-3, DEC/PDP 11-70, 37-DEC/VT-72; Other equipment — 26-RSK/TRS-80 Model 100, RSK. CLASSIFIED: Front-end hardware — 11-DEC/VT-173C; Front-end software — CMS 2.3, DEC/VT-173-C. DISPLAY: Adv layout systems — 9-AU/Raycomp-100. PRODUCTION: Typesetters — 2-AU/APS Micro 5; Platemaking systems — Wipe-on Plates; Plate exposers — 2-N; Plate processors — 2-WL; Production cameras — 1-Acti, 1-R, 1-Escofot; Automatic film processors — 2-P. PRESSROOM: Line 1 — 11-G/Urbanite 5000 Series; Line 2 — 11-G/Urbanite 5000 Series; Press drives — 2-Fin; Folders — 2-G/Urbanite; Pasters — 16-MEG/Flying DME Pasters. MAILROOM: Counter stackers — 2-FG; Bundle tyer — 3-Cyclops, 2-Power Strap; Wrapping singles — 2-RKW; Mailroom control system — 1-HL. LIBRARY: Electronic — DEC/VT 320, Photo Classification News Dep. COMMUNICATIONS: Facsimile — 1-Laser Photo/PC, 2-DEC/VAX 3200. WIRE SERVICES: News — UPI, Canada News Wire, Telbec, AFP, CP; Stock tables — On Line from CP. BUSINESS COMPUTERS: 1-DEC/PDP 11-70; Applications: Accounting; PCs & micros networked; PCs & main system networked.

Le Soleil

(m-mon to fri; m-sat; S)

Le Soleil, 925 Chemin; PO Box 1547 Succ. Terminus, St. Louis, QC G1K 7J6; tel (418) 686-3233. UniMedia Inc. (Hollinger Inc.) group.

Circulation: 90,780(m); 141,252(m-sat); 101,622(S); ABC Sept. 30, 1995.

Price: 60¢(d); $1.50(sat); 60¢(S); $4.00/wk (carrier).

Advertising: Modular rate $3.10(m); $3.47(m-sat); $3.10(S). **Representatives:** Probec 5; Landon Associates Inc.; Leonard Company.

News Services: CP, AFP, NYT, TELBEC, CN Wire, Reuter, AP. **Politics:** Independent. **Established:** 1896.

Not Published: New Year; Labor Day; Thanksgiving; Easter Monday; Dollar Day Christmas; Jan 2; June 24; July 1.

Special Weekly Sections: Automobile and Science, Entertainment (mon); Fashion (tues); Business (thur); Weekend Entertainment (fri); Entertainment, Home, Travel, Restaurants (sat); Entertainment (S).

Magazines: Tele-Magazine (mon); Mode Magazine (tues); Magazine (wed); Monde Magazine (thur); WEM (week-end magazine) (fri); Le Soleil Tele-Magazine (sat); Dimanche Magazine (S).

CORPORATE OFFICERS

Board Chairman/Editor Pierre Des Marais II
President Gilbert Lacasse

GENERAL MANAGEMENT

Publisher Gilbert Lacasse
General Manager Gilbert Lacasse
Data Processing Director Gilles Garneau

ADVERTISING

Retail-Group Head Andre Dumont
Manager-National Classified Jacques R Carrier
Manager-Telemarketing/Arts Jean Labranche

MARKETING AND PROMOTION

Director-Marketing Jasmin Gilbert
Manager-Promotion Celine Fournier

CIRCULATION

Manager Gilles Emond

NEWS EXECUTIVES

Managing Editor Gilbert Lavoie
Newsroom Director Andre Forgues

EDITORS AND MANAGERS

Arts Editor Jacques Samson
Auto Editor Marcel Collard
Cartoonist Roland Berthio
City Editor Berthold Landry
City Editor Gilles Ouellet
Consumer Interest Gilles Ouellet
Editorial Page Editor J Jacques Samson
Editorial Writer Raymond Giroux
Education Brigitte Breton
Features Editor Magella Soucy
Films/Theater Editor Normand Provencher
Librarian Andre Forgues
Music Editor Jacques Samson
News Editor Andre Forgues
Photo Department Manager Clement Thibault
Political Editor Andre Forgues
Real Estate Gilles Angers
Sports Editor Maurice Dumas
Teen-age/Youth Magella Soucy
Travel Editor Magella Soucy

MANAGEMENT INFORMATION SERVICES

Data Processing Manager Gilles Garneau

PRODUCTION

Director Gilles Garneau
Foreman-Composing Jean Marceau

Market Information: Zoned editions; ADS; Electronic edition.

Mechanical available: Letterpress (direct); Black and 3 ROP colors; insert accepted — preprinted; page cut-offs — $22\frac{3}{4}$".

Mechanical specifications: Type page $12\frac{1}{2}$" x 22"; E - 6 cols, $2\frac{1}{16}$", ⅛" between; A - 6 cols, $2\frac{1}{16}$", ⅛" between; C - 9 cols, $1\frac{1}{3}$", ⅛" between.

Commodity Consumption (estimated): Newsprint 10,000 metric tons; widths 41", $41\frac{1}{4}$", $27\frac{1}{2}$"; black ink 480,000 pounds; color ink 81,788 pounds; single pages printed 20,448; average pages per issue 58(d), 39(S); single plates used 55,682.

Equipment: EDITORIAL: Front-end hardware — 6-Ap/Mac IIvx, 2-Ap/Mac SE, 7-Ap/Power Mac 8100, 18-Ap/Power Mac 6100, 4-Ap/Mac Quadra 700, 1-Ap/Mac IIfx, 1-Ap/Mac Quadra

III-24 Quebec

800, 1-Ap/Mac IIx, 1-Ap/Mac SE 30, 3-Ap/Mac LC II, 10-Ap/Mac PowerBook, 13-LC/475; Front-end software — AT Ver. 4.5.1; Printers — Etherprint/3+, Ap/Mac ImageWriter, 1-Ap/Mac LaserWriter, 1-QMS/1660; Other equipment — 3-Ap/Mac LaserPrinter, 3-Ap. CLASSIFIED: Front-end hardware — AT; Front-end software — AT 4.4.5; Other equipment — Electronic Mail Box, TTS, Umax/300. AUDIOTEX: Hardware — Ap/Mac IIxx, Senior 450 Luxxon; Software — Adobe/Fetch 1.2; DISPLAY: Adv layout systems — Mk/Ad Director 5.2; Front-end hardware — Ap/Power Mac 7100-66; Front-end software — Service Bureau; Printers — 1-C.Itoh/5000, 2-Printronics, 5-Fuji/4500, Ap/Mac Pro; Other equipment — Ap/Mac LC 475. PRODUCTION: Pagination software — QuarkXPress 3.3; OCR software — 2-AG/Arcus II, 2-Kk/RFS 2035, 1-Howtek/Scanmaster 3+. Typesetters — AU. LIBRARY: Combination — CD-Rom. COMMUNICATIONS: Facsimile — AT&T; Fiber Optic. WIRE SERVICES: News — CP, AFP, CN Wire, Telbec, NYT; Photos — CP, AP, RN; Stock tables — CP; Syndicates — NYT; receiving dishes — size-10, CP. BUSINESS COMPUTERS: Sun/470, IBM/9370 Model 60; Applications: Circ, Finance, Adv; PCs & micros networked; PCs & main system networked.

SHERBROOKE

'91 Census- 76,425; E&P '96 Est. 81,118 Record
ABC-CZ (91): 114,815 (HH 46,639) La Tribune
ABC-NDM (91): 247,420 (HH 95,325)

The Record
(m-mon to fri)

The Record, 2850 Delorme, Sherbrooke, QC J1K 1A1; tel (819) 569-9526; fax (819) 569-3945. Quebecor Inc. group.
Circulation: 5,383(m); ABC Sept. 30, 1995.
Price: 50¢(d); 65¢(fri); $2.05/wk (carrier); $99.14/yr (mail), $106.60/yr (carrier).
Advertising: Modular rate $1.20(m). **Representatives:** Quebecor Media Sales (Toronto); Quebecor Ventes Media (Montreal).
News Services: CP, TELBEC. **Politics:** Independent. **Established:** 1897.
Not Published: Christmas; New Year; Jan 3; Thanksgiving; Dominion Day; Good Friday; Labor Day; Victoria Day; St. Jean Baptiste Day; Easter Monday.
Special Editions: Ski (Jan); Annual Review (Apr); Holiday (June); County Fairs (Summer); Fashions (Spring); Fashions (Fall); Blood Donor; Ski & Snow-Mobile & Winter Sports; Fishing; Gardening & Boating; Home Improvement.
Special Weekly Section: Townships Week (entertainment tab).

CORPORATE OFFICER
President — Pierre Pelodeau

GENERAL MANAGEMENT
Publisher/General Manager — Randy Kinnear

ADVERTISING
Director — Lloyd G Scheib

MARKETING AND PROMOTION
Manager-Marketing & Promotion — Lloyd G Scheib

CIRCULATION
Manager — Laurie Schoolcraft

EDITORS AND MANAGERS
Editorial Page Editor — Charles Bury
Sports Editor — Robert Matheson

PRODUCTION
Manager — Richard Lessard
Manager-Composing — Francine Thibault
Manager-Graphics — Joan Giroux

Market Information: TMC.
Mechanical available: Offset; Black and 3 ROP colors; insert accepted — preprinted; page cut-offs — 13 15/16".
Mechanical specifications: Type page 11½" x 14¾"; E - 5 cols, 1⅞", ⅛" between; A - 5 cols, 1⅞", ⅛" between; C - 5 cols, 1⅞", ⅛" between.
Commodity Consumption (estimated): average pages per issue 56(d).
Equipment: EDITORIAL: Printers — 3-COM/AKI. PRODUCTION: Typesetters — 1-COM/ACM 9000, 2-COM/2961 HS, 1-COM/7200, 1-COM/4961; Production cameras — 1-N. PRESSROOM: Line 1 — 4-G/Community 99921-7; Folders — 1-G. MAILROOM: Bundle tyer — 3-Bu; Addressing machine — 1-Am/1955B. WIRE SERVICES: News — AP, CP, RN; Syndicates — Telbec.

La Tribune
(m-mon to fri; m-sat)

La Tribune, 1950 Roy St., Sherbrooke, QC J1K 2X8; tel (819) 564-5450; fax (819) 564-5480. Les Journaux Trans-Canada/JTC group.
Circulation: 33,135(m); 41,499(m-sat); ABC Sept. 30, 1995.
Price: 55¢(d); $1.50(sat); $3.95/wk; $205.40/yr (incl. tax).
Advertising: Modular rate $3.99(m); $3.99(m-sat); comb with Montreal La Presse (mS) $11.46. **Representative:** Probec 5.
News Service: CP. **Politics:** Independent. **Established:** 1910.
Not Published: New Year; Day after New Year; St. Jean Baptist Day; Labor Day; Christmas; Day after Christmas.
Special Editions: Brides; Annual Business; Vacation; Automobiles; Scholar Entrance; Insurance; Living; Gifts; Agriculture; Winter Sports.
Magazine: Weekend Magazine (sat).

CORPORATE OFFICERS
Board Chairman — Paul G Des Marais
President — Raymond Tardif

GENERAL MANAGEMENT
Publisher/General Manager — Raymond Tardif
Controller — J G Farah

ADVERTISING
Manager — Francois Fouquet
Asst Manager — Alaiu LeClerc
Asst Manager — Jocelyn Godbout

CIRCULATION
Manager — Pierre Dubois

NEWS EXECUTIVE
Editor — Jacques Pronovost

EDITORS AND MANAGERS
Amusements/Books Editor — Pierrette Roy
Editorial Page Editor — Jacques Pronovost
Food Editor — Stephane Lavallee
Music Editor — Rachel Lussier
News Editor — Stephane Lavallee
Photo Department Manager — Jacques Pronovost
Radio/Television Editor — Pierrette Roy
Religion Editor — Stephane Lavallee
Society/Fashion Editor — Stephane Lavallee
Sports Editor — Mario Goupil
Women's Editor — Stephane Lavallee

PRODUCTION
Manager — Daniel Gauthier
Foreman-Composing — Guy Brosseau
Foreman-Engraving — Gaston Grenier
Foreman-Mailroom (Night) — Michel Doyon

Market Information: TMC.
Mechanical available: Offset; Black and 3 ROP colors; insert accepted — preprinted; page cut-offs — 22¾".
Mechanical specifications: Type page 13" x 21 9/16"; E - 6 cols, 2 1/16", ⅛" between; A - 6 cols, 2 1/16", ⅛" between; C - 10 cols, 1¼", 1/16" between.
Commodity Consumption (estimated): Newsprint 3,500 metric tons; widths 54", 40½", 27"; black ink 103,616 pounds; color ink 14,550 pounds; single pages printed 18,538; average pages per issue 40(d); single plates used 49,900.
Equipment: EDITORIAL: Front-end hardware — 2-HI/2560. CLASSIFIED: Front-end hardware — 2-HI/2560. DISPLAY: Adv layout systems — 3-HI/H-2200 (on-line); Front-end software — HI/H-2200 (on-line). PRODUCTION: Typesetters — 2-COM/8600 CRT; Plate exposers — 2-N, 1-BKY; Plate processors — 2-WL/30c; Production cameras — 1-C/Spartan II-2606, 1-C/Spartan III, 1-III/VGC-TC; Automatic film processors — 1-LE/LD-24; Film transporters — 1-C/1247. PRESSROOM: Line 1 — 6-G/Cosmo 3526 (Web Press Offset). MAILROOM: Counter stackers — 1-HL; Bundle tyer — 1-MLN/ML2EE, 1-MLN/MLL2A; Wrapping singles — 2-Gd/Q7070; Addressing machine — 1-Am/6400, 1-Am/2605. COMMUNICATIONS: Facsimile — 1-Nefax/(Bit one); Satellite. WIRE SERVICES: News — CP; Stock tables — CP; receiving dishes — size-10ft, CP. BUSINESS COMPUTERS: IBM/34; Applications: Accounting, Circ, Mailing Room Services; PCs & micros networked; PCs & main system networked.

TROIS-RIVIERES

'91 Census- 49,425 (Metro Area 136,305); E&P '96 Est. 51,756 (Metro Area 141,312)
ABC-NDM (91): 213,829 (HH 84,380)

Le Nouvelliste
(m-mon to sat)

Le Nouvelliste, 1920 Bellefeuille; PO Box 668, Trois-Rivieres, QC G9A 3Y2; tel (819) 376-2501; fax (819) 376-0946. Les Journaux Trans-Canada/JTC group.
Circulation: 46,484(m); 46,484(m-sat); ABC Sept. 30, 1995.
Price: 65¢(d); $1.50(sat); $3.95/wk; $192.00/yr.
Advertising: Modular rate $2.79(m); $2.79(m-sat); comb with Montreal La Presse (mS) $11.59. **Representative:** Target Media Inc.
News Services: CP, AP, AFP, RN, UPI, Telbec, Laserphoto. **Established:** 1920, 1982 (Le Nouvelliste).
Not Published: New Year; Day after New Year; Christmas; Day after Christmas.
Special Editions: Bride and Groom; Spring Fashion; Farming; Automoblie; Your Home; Tourist; Autumn Fashion; Winter Sports.
Magazine: Nouvelliste Plus (sat).

CORPORATE OFFICER
President/Editor — Gilbert Brunet

GENERAL MANAGEMENT
Manager-Personnel — Rene Ferron
Director-Finance — Lucien Daigle

ADVERTISING
Director — Ginette Panneton

MARKETING AND PROMOTION
Director — Justin Biron

CIRCULATION
Manager — Mario Poirier

NEWS EXECUTIVE
Chief Editor — Bernard Champoux

EDITORS AND MANAGERS
News Editor — Andre Poitras
News Editor-Night — Michel St. Amant

PRODUCTION
Manager — Marc Pronovost

Market Information: Split Run.
Mechanical available: Offset; Black and 3 ROP colors; insert accepted — preprinted, roll-fed; page cut-offs — 22¾".
Mechanical specifications: Type page 12" x 21⅜"; E - 10 cols, 1 1/16", 1/12" between; A - 10 cols, 1 1/16", 1/12" between; C - 10 cols, 1 1/16", 1/12" between.
Commodity Consumption (estimated): Newsprint 2,424 metric tons; widths 12.5"; black ink 26,665 kg; color ink 7,200 kg; single pages printed 11,234; average pages per issue 32(d), 64(sat); single plates used 30,000.
Equipment: EDITORIAL: Front-end hardware — 2-HI/XP-21; Front-end software — HI/PEN; Printers — AU/3850. CLASSIFIED: Front-end hardware — HI/Cash, 2-HI/XP-21; Printers — AU/3850. DISPLAY: Adv layout systems — HI/2100; Front-end hardware — HI/2100; Front-end software — HI; Printers — AU/3850. PRODUCTION: Pagination software — HI 2.1; Typesetters — 2-AU/3850; Platemaking systems — WL/Litho Plater; Plate exposers — 2-N/Flip Top; Plate processors — WL; Electronic picture desk — CD; Production cameras — 2-X/Scanner 7650, 2-X/8000; Automatic film processors — 2-P/24" On-line; Color separation equipment (conventional) — 2-X/Scanner 8000, 2-X/Power PC 8100; Digital color separation equipment — 2-Ap/Mac. PRESSROOM: Line 1 — 6-HI/1600; Line 2 — 8-HI/V-15; Pasters — 4-MEG, 4-Martin. MAILROOM: Counter stackers — 2-MM/C570; Bundle tyer — 3-Si; Addressing machine — 1-Head/R-4800-X, CH/Base 522. WIRE SERVICES: News — PC; Stock tables — PC; Syndicates — King Features, S.O.P.. BUSINESS COMPUTERS: IBM/AS-400; Applications: Circ, Adv billing, Accts receivable, Gen ledger, Payroll.

SASKATCHEWAN

MOOSE JAW

'91 Census- 33,595; E&P '96 Est. 34,507
ABC-CZ (91): 33,593 (HH 13,420)

The Moose Jaw Times-Herald (e-mon to sat)

The Moose Jaw Times-Herald, 44 Fairford St. W.; PO Box 3000, Moose Jaw, SK S6H 6E4; tel (306) 692-6441; fax (306) 692-2101. Sterling Newspapers (Hollinger Inc.) group.
Circulation: 10,136(e); 10,136(e-sat); ABC Sept. 30, 1995.
Price: 45¢(d); 45¢(sat); $2.00/wk; $8.66/mo; $104.00/yr (in Moose Jaw), $116.75/yr (in SK), $132.50/yr (in CN).
Advertising: Modular rate $1.18(e); $1.18(e-sat). **Representative:** Thomson Newspapers.
News Services: CP, AP, RN, THO. **Politics:** Independent. **Established:** 1889.
Not Published: New Year; Good Friday; Victoria Day; Canada Day; Labor Day; August 5; Civic Holiday; Thanksgiving; Remembrance Day; Christmas.
Special Editions: Cook Book; Progress; Kinsmen Band; Guide to Good Farming; Golden Years (Seniors-Spring & Fall); Vacation Guide; Hometown Heroes; Christmas Specials; Minor Hockey Special; Year-end Review.
Magazines: TV Scene (entertainment) (fri); Color Comics (sat).

GENERAL MANAGEMENT
Publisher/General Manager — Robert Calvert
Accountant — Johnna Abdou

ADVERTISING
Manager — Ab Calvert

CIRCULATION
Manager — Dave Mak

NEWS EXECUTIVE
Editor — Carl DeGurse

EDITOR AND MANAGER
City Editor — Leslie Shepherd

PRODUCTION
Manager — Doug Lix
Foreman-Composing — Jim Crozier
Foreman-Pressroom — Fraser Woreham

Market Information: TMC.
Mechanical available: Offset; Black and 3 ROP colors; insert accepted — preprinted; page cut-offs — 22¾".
Mechanical specifications: Type page 13¼" x 21½"; E - 6 cols, 2 1/16", ⅛" between; A - 6 cols, 2 1/16", ⅛" between; C - 9 cols, 1½", ⅛" between.
Commodity Consumption (estimated): average pages per issue 40(d).
Equipment: EDITORIAL: Front-end hardware — HAS; Front-end software — HAS, Ap/Mac. CLASSIFIED: Front-end hardware — HAS. DISPLAY: Front-end hardware — Ap/Mac Quadra, Ap/Power Mac PC; Front-end software — QuarkXPress 3.3, Adobe/Photoshop 2.5; Printers — QMS/860, ECR/News Recorder 1800. PRODUCTION: Typesetters — COM/8400; Plate processors — Graham; Electronic picture desk — CD; Scanners — Nikon, Imapro; Production cameras — ACI/125; Automatic film processors — P; Digital color separation equipment — ECR/Newsrecorder 1800, CD. PRESSROOM: Line 1 — G/Community (12 units); Press drives — Fin; Folders — 2-G/SC 818 Quarter. MAILROOM: Stuffers — Gd; Bundle tyer — 1-Gd. WIRE SERVICES: News — CP; receiving dishes — CP. BUSINESS COMPUTERS: ATT; Applications: Lotus/1-2-3; PCs & micros networked.

PRINCE ALBERT

'91 Census- 34,180; E&P '96 Est. 36,057
ABC-CZ (91): 34,181 (HH 12,410)

Prince Albert Daily Herald
(e-mon to sat)

Prince Albert Daily Herald, 30 10th St. E.; PO Box 550, Prince Albert, SK S6V 5R9; tel (306) 764-4276; fax (306) 763-3331. Sterling Newspapers (Hollinger Inc.) group.

Circulation: 9,594(e); 9,594(e-sat); ABC Sept. 30, 1995.
Price: 50¢(d); 50¢(sat); $2.25/wk (carrier); $29.25/3 mos, $117.00/yr.
Advertising: Modular rate $1.11(e); $1.11(e-sat). **Representative:** Thomson Newspapers.
News Services: CP, THO. **Politics:** Independent. **Established:** 1894.
Not Published: New Year; Good Friday; Victoria Day; Dominion Day; Labor Day; Thanksgiving; Armistice; Christmas.
Special Editions: Brides (Jan); Winter Festival (Feb); Progress, Tourist Guide (Mar); Cook Book (Nov); Car Care (Fall); Chamber of Commerce (quarterly).
Special Weekly Sections: Rural Roots (agriculture) (thur); Cover Story (entertainment) (fri).
Magazine: Entertainment Guide (local, newsprint) (fri).

GENERAL MANAGEMENT
Publisher/General Manager Robert W Gibb
ADVERTISING
Manager Verna Block
CIRCULATION
Manager Randy Emery
NEWS EXECUTIVE
Managing Editor Wayne Roznowsky
EDITORS AND MANAGERS
City Editor Ruth Griffiths
Editorial Page Editor Wayne Roznowsky
Rural Roots (Agriculture) Editor Barb Gustatson
PRODUCTION
Foreman-Composing David Sarchuk
Foreman-Pressroom Henry Mathers

Market Information: TMC; ADS.
Mechanical available: Offset; Black and 3 ROP colors; insert accepted — preprinted; page cut-offs — 22¾".
Mechanical specifications: Type page 14¼" x 21½"; E - 6 cols, 2 1/16", ⅛" between; A - 6 cols, 2 1/16", ⅛" between; C - 9 cols, 1⅜", 1/16" between.
Commodity Consumption (estimated): Newsprint 565 metric tons; widths 27½"; black ink 12,000 pounds; color ink 3,500 pounds; average pages per issue 18.1(d); single plates used 5,700.
Equipment: EDITORIAL: Front-end hardware — Mk; Printers — 3-COM. CLASSIFIED: Front-end hardware — Mk. PRODUCTION: Typesetters — 1-COM/Unisetter, 1-COM/2961, 1-COM/4961, 1-COM/7200; Platemaking systems — 1-N; Production cameras — 1-B; Automatic film processors — 1-Kk; Color separation equipment (conventional) — 1-WDS. PRESSROOM: Line 1 — 8-G/Community; Folders — 1-G. MAILROOM: Bundle tyer — 1-Gd/Q; Addressing machine — 1-El. WIRE SERVICES: News — CP, THO; receiving dishes — CP. BUSINESS COMPUTERS: PCs & main system networked.

REGINA

'91 Census- 179,180 (Metro Area 191,695); E&P '96 Est. 184,193 (Metro Area 196,799)
ABC-NDM (91): 307,811 (HH 115,765)

The Leader-Post

(e-mon to sat)

The Leader-Post, Victoria Ave. & Park St., Regina, SK S4P 3G4; tel (306) 565-8250; fax (306) 565-8350. Hollinger Inc. group.
Circulation: 62,216(e); 77,666(e-fri); 62,216(e-sat); ABC Sept. 30, 1995.
Price: 60¢(d); $1.00(fri); $1.00(sat); $2.65/wk.
Advertising: Modular rate $3.15(e); $3.40(e-fri); $3.40(e-sat).
News Services: CP, AP. **Politics:** Independent. **Established:** 1883.
Not Published: Statutory holidays.
Magazines: A-Section (News), Sports, Entertainment, Financial, Lifestyles, Classifieds, Careers (weekly); What's On (mon); Styles & Trends (tues); Food (wed); Driver's Seat (fri); Travel (sat); Weekender, Real Estate (S).

CORPORATE OFFICERS
President Michael G Sifton
Exec Vice Pres Bob Hughes
GENERAL MANAGEMENT
Human Resources Manager Janice Dockham
Controller Roger Hearn
Education Service Manager Wayne Kuss
ADVERTISING
Director Jim Ambrose
MARKETING AND PROMOTION
Marketing Services Manager Joe Laxdal
CIRCULATION
Manager Don Staples
NEWS EXECUTIVES
Editor John Swan
Managing Editor Marlon Marshall
EDITORS AND MANAGERS
City Editor Andy Cooper
Editorial Page Editor David Green
Finance Editor Bruce Johnstone
Librarian Eric Jenkins
Photo Department Manager Ian Caldwell
Sports Editor Greg Drinnan
PRODUCTION
Asst Manager-Pre Press/Sys Rick Fehler
Asst Manager-Distribution/Press Cec Harvey
Manager-Operations Ray Turgeon

Market Information: Zoned editions; TMC.
Mechanical available: Letterpress (offset); Black and 3 ROP colors; insert accepted — preprinted; page cut-offs — 22¾".
Mechanical specifications: Type page 13" x 21¾"; E - 6 cols, 1 13/16", ⅛" between; A - 6 cols, 1 13/16", ⅛" between; C - 6 cols, 1 13/16", ⅛" between.
Commodity Consumption (estimated): Newsprint 7,743 metric tons; widths 50", 37½", 12½"; black ink 40,000 pounds; color ink 14,000 pounds; single pages printed 17,400; average pages per issue 58(d); single plates used 40,000.
Equipment: EDITORIAL: Front-end hardware — 1-DEC/1170, 11-Ap/Mac; Front-end software — DEC/TMS; Printers — 1-DEC/LA 120, 2-DEC/LA 180; Other equipment — DEC/VT72, DEC/VT61. CLASSIFIED: Front-end hardware — 15-PC, Novell; Front-end software — CText; Printers — Okidata/OL-800. DISPLAY: Adv layout systems — SCS/Layout 8000; Front-end hardware — PC/486 DX2-66; Front-end software — WordPerfect, Oracle, Mk/Ad Director; Printers — HP/LaserJet 4; Other equipment — 12-Ap/Mac. PRODUCTION: Pagination software — QuarkXPress 3.31; Typesetters — 2-Ultra, 1-V/VT 5300E, 1-V/VT 6000, 1-V, Panther/Pro 486; Platemaking systems — 2-Howson-Algraphy; Plate exposers — 2-N/Printer, 1-Teak Tower; Plate processors — Howson-Algraphy; Electronic picture desk — CD; Scanners — Umax, Kk/Negscanner, AG/Arcus; Production cameras — 1-C/Newspager II; Automatic film processors — 1-LE/PC 1800, 1-LE/Maxim 26; Film transporters — 1-C/Newspager II. PRESSROOM: Line 1 — 8-G/Metroliners(4-black;4-color decked); Line 2 — 4-G/Community, 4-G/High Community; Press drives — Fin; Folders — 2-G/3:2, G/SSC, 5-G; Pasters — 8-Auto Pasters; Press control system — Manual. MAILROOM: Counter stackers — 4-KAN, 1-St/251; Stuffers — 1-MM/6 units, 2-MM/8-into-1; Bundle tyer — 3-MLN; Addressing machine — 2-Am/260. LIBRARY: Combination — 2-Recordak/RV-2, 1-Microseal/V-3, 1-Recordak/Reader. COMMUNICATIONS: Facsimile — 2-X/400, 6-X/410. WIRE SERVICES: News — CP; Photos — CP; Stock tables — CP; Syndicates — CP; receiving dishes — size-1m, CP. BUSINESS COMPUTERS: PBS/MediaPlus, DEC/486 DX2 66; Applications: SCS/Layout 8000: Accts payable, Accts receivable, Circ, Inventory, Personnel, Gen ledger; PCs & micros networked; PCs & main system networked.

SASKATOON

'91 Census- 186,060 (Metro Area 210,025); E&P '96 Est. 188,543 (Metro Area 216,964)
ABC-NDM. (91): 79,862 (HH 28,095)

The StarPhoenix

(m-mon to thur; m-fri; m-sat)

The StarPhoenix, 204 5th Ave. North, Saskatoon, SK S7K 2P1; tel (306) 652-9200; fax (306) 664-8208, (306) 664-0437; email dlacombe@eagle.wbm.ca; web site http://www.wbm.ca/star. Hollinger Inc. group.
Circulation: 57,402(m); 73,403(m-fri); 64,091(m-sat); ABC Sept. 30, 1995.
Price: 75¢(d); $1.25(fri); $1.25(sat); $11.25/mo (carrier); $415.80/yr (mail).
Advertising: Modular rate $3.09(m); $3.37(m-fri); $3.37(m-sat). **Representatives:** Canadian Media Connection; VJR.
News Services: CP, AP, NYT. **Politics:** Independent. **Established:** 1902.
Not Published: Statutory holidays.
Special Editions: Bridal (Jan); Super Sale, RRSP (Feb); Creative Adventure, Bridal, Spring Car Care (Mar); Auto Show & Sale, Spring Home Improvement (Apr); National Photo Week, Summer Fun, Adventure (May); It's Your Business (June); Dollar Power Days (July); Fall Yard & Garden, Fall Music & Dance (Aug); Fall Fashion, Your Home, National Furniture (Sept); Auto Showcase, Drive Into Winter, Consumer Electronics (Oct); Travel, Skiing, Recreation (Nov); Holiday Wish Book (Dec).
Special Weekly Section: Sports Monday (mon).

CORPORATE OFFICER
President Michael G Sifton
GENERAL MANAGEMENT
Publisher/Exec Vice Pres Lyle Sinkewicz
ADVERTISING
Director Greg McLean
MARKETING AND PROMOTION
Coordinator-Promotion Craig Peterson
TELECOMMUNICATIONS
Audiotex Manager Noreen Matthews
CIRCULATION
Manager Wayne Wohlberg
NEWS EXECUTIVES
Editor Steve Gibb
Assoc Editor Wilf Popoff
Managing Editor Cam Hutchinson
EDITORS AND MANAGERS
Books Editor Verne Clemence
Business Editor Ken Juba
City Editor Gord Struthers
Community Notes Editor Heather MacDonald
City Hall Bureau Chief Art Robinson
Editorial Page Editor Sarath Peiris
Entertainment Editor Pat Macsymic
Features Editor Ted Hainworth
Librarian Miriam Clemence
News Editor Donna Koolick
Outdoors Editor Tom Loran
Political Editor Randy Burton
TV Times Editor Brenda Valleau
Sports Editor Doug McConachie
Women's Editor Deanna Herman
MANAGEMENT INFORMATION SERVICES
Data Processing Manager Marvin Hydomako
PRODUCTION
Manager-Press Glen Houle
Manager-Pre Press Larry Funk
Systems Manager Marvin Hydomako
Manager-Distribution Darrell Drozd
Foreman-Pressroom Keith Coulter

Market Information: TMC; ADS; Operate audiotex; Electronic edition.
Mechanical available: Letterpress (direct); Black and 3 ROP colors; insert accepted — preprinted, catalogues, envelopes, flyers, sections, samples; page cut-offs — 23 9/16".
Mechanical specifications: Type page 12½" x 22⅛"; E - 6 cols, 2", ⅛" between; A - 6 cols, 2", ⅛" between; C - 6 cols, 2", ⅛" between.
Commodity Consumption (estimated): Newsprint 5,400 metric tons; widths 25", 37.5", 50"; black ink 220,000 pounds; color ink 60,000 pounds; single pages printed 15,800; average pages per issue 52(d), 72(sat); single plates used 33,000.
Equipment: EDITORIAL: Front-end hardware — 1-DEC/PDP 11/70, 27-DEC/VT72, 5-DEC/VT61, 1-DEC/Rainbow; Printers — 1-DEC/LA-180. CLASSIFIED: Front-end hardware — PC/386-25, Novell/Server; Front-end software — CText 5.2.03; Printers — Ap/NTX; Other equipment — PC/Clones. DISPLAY: Adv layout systems — SCS/Layout 8000; Front-end hardware — PC/486-66, Unix; Front-end software — SCS/Layout 8000; Printers — Microline; Other equipment — PC/Clones, DEC/VT320. PRODUCTION: Pagination software — QuarkXPress 3.3.1, CText/AIPS; Typesetters — 2-M/202, 1-Ultra, 1-AG/Accuset 1000, 2-COM/9400, 1-XIT/Clipper, 1-LaserMaster/11x17; Platemaking systems — Na; Plate exposers — 1-Na/Twin star, 1-Na/Starlite; Plate processors — 1-Na/Comet, 2-Na/Twin star; Electronic picture desk — CD/2643 (7.0); Scanners — 2-AG/Arcus Flatbed color, 1-AG/Focus color, 2-Microtek/Flatbed color, 1-HEL/300B drum color, 2-Umax/1280; Production cameras — 1-C/Spartan III, 1-C/Newspager; Automatic film processors — 2-LE/PC 18, 1-LE/BQ 24, 1-LE/LD 24A; Film transporters — 2-C; Digital color separation equipment — 1-Hcl/300B. PRESSROOM: Line 1 — 8-C; Folders — 2-G. MAILROOM: Counter stackers — 2-MM/231-U, 1-SH/251; Stuffers — 1-MM/227 6-into-1, 2-KAN/480 6-into-1; Bundle tyer — 2-Gd/415; Wrapping singles — 1-Samuels, 2-Gol. COMMUNICATIONS: Facsimile — 1-AP LaserPhoto. WIRE SERVICES: News — CP Datafile; Photos — CP NewLine; Stock tables — CP Dataspeed; Syndicates — CP Dataspecials; receiving dishes — size-10 ft, CP. BUSINESS COMPUTERS: PC/486-66, Unix; Applications: SCS/AR 8000: Adv billing, Accts receivable, Gen ledger, Accts payable, Circ, Transient & classified billing, Telemarketing; Oracle: Financial; PCs & micros networked.

YUKON TERRITORY

WHITEHORSE

'91 Census- 17,925; E&P '96 Est. 20,870
ABC-CZ (91): 17,925 (HH 6,195)

Whitehorse Star

(e-mon to thur; e-fri)

Whitehorse Star, 2149 2nd-Ave., Whitehorse, YT Y1A 1C5; tel (403) 668-2063; fax (403) 668-7130.
Circulation: 2,770(e); 4,030(e-fri); ABC Sept. 30, 1995.
Price: 75¢(d); $1.00(fri); $240.00/yr (mail-Canada), $400.00/yr (mail-U.S.).
Advertising: Modular rate $1.10(e); $1.10(e-fri).
News Service: CP. **Politics:** Independent. **Established:** 1900.
Not Published: Canadian Holidays.
Advertising not accepted: Anything libelous or against the law.
Special Editions: Rendezvous Quest (Feb); Visitor's Guide (May); X'mas Greetings (Dec).
Special Weekly Sections: Real Estate (wed-every 2 wks); Friday TV Guide (fri).

CORPORATE OFFICERS
President/Publisher Robert Erlam
Secretary Jackie Pierce
GENERAL MANAGEMENT
General Manager Jackie Pierce
ADVERTISING
Manager Jean Jobagy
CIRCULATION
Manager John Stuckey
NEWS EXECUTIVE
Editor in Chief Jim Butler

Market Information: Split Run; TMC.
Mechanical available: Offset Web; Black and 1 ROP color; insert accepted — preprinted; page cut-offs — 14½".
Mechanical specifications: Type page 10¼" x 14¼"; E - 5 cols, 1.85", ⅙" between; A - 5 cols, 1.85", ⅙" between; C - 6 cols, 1½", ⅙" between.
Commodity Consumption (estimated): Newsprint 200 short tons; single pages printed 8,736; average pages per issue 32(d).
Equipment: EDITORIAL: Front-end hardware — Mk/1100; Front-end software — Mk/1100. CLASSIFIED: Front-end hardware — Mk/1100; Front-end software — Mk/1100. PRODUCTION: Typesetters — XIT/Clipper 486; Scanners — Microtek, Ap/Mac; Production cameras — B/Horizontal; Automatic film processors — Kk/Eskofat; Color separation equipment (conventional) — Adobe/Photoshop. PRESSROOM: Line 1 — 6-G/Community. MAILROOM: Addressing machine — 1-PB. COMMUNICATIONS: Facsimile — 1-X; Satellite. WIRE SERVICES: News — CP; Photos — CP; Stock tables — CP; Syndicates — CP; receiving dishes — size-6, CP. BUSINESS COMPUTERS: Epson/Equity-PC II; Applications: Accounting, Sales, Receiving, Distribution; PCs & main system networked.

WEEKLY NEWSPAPERS PUBLISHED IN CANADA

ALBERTA

This directory covers weekly community newspapers of general interest published up to three times a week. The list is arranged alphabetically by provinces and within each province, by the principal community or neighborhood served by each paper.

Then follows, in light italic type, the exact name of the paper.

Following the dash appears the paper's address which may be in a different community from the area it serves. If only a postal code appears (in parenthesis) it may be assumed that the community's name heading the entry along with the postal code, forms a sufficient address.

The day or days of publication appear in abbreviated form. Circulations are shown as paid (pd) or free (fr), with the type of audit or report following: ABC - Audit Bureau of Circulation; CCAB - Canadian Circulation Audit Board; IAO - Independent Audit Organization; VAC - Verified Audit Circulation; VCC - Verified Circulation Control; VCP - Verified Circulations Paid; Sw - sworn statement of circulation; Est - estimate. Circulation figures are for September 30, 1995, where they were available.

The amount of cents/dollars is the national advertising rate for one agate line/one inch, respectively (the open line/inch rate); N/A indicates advertising is not sold in agate line/open inch units; a 'C' following the rate indicates that advertising is sold in combination with one or more weekly newspapers.

The names of the publisher, general manager, editor and managing editor follow the line rate where these were available.

Weekly papers of special interest (business or agricultural), limited circulation (military based) are not included in this section.

Airdrie: *Airdrie Echo* — 114 1st Ave. N.E.; Box 3820 (T4B 2B9); W; 3,231pd, 165fr (VCP); 76¢; C; publisher Bill McQuarrie; editor Paul Wells; tel (403) 948-7280; fax (403) 233-7226

Banff National Park: *Banff Crag & Canyon* — 225 Bear St.; Box 129, Banff (TOL 0CO); W; 4,112pd (VCP); 72¢; C; publisher Sandra Santa Lucia; editor David Rooney; tel (403) 762-2453; fax (403) 762-5274

Bashaw: *The Bashaw Star* — 50th Ave. & 51st St.; Box 188 (TOB OHO); Tu; 945pd, 22fr (VCP); 47¢; publisher Allan Willis; editor Darlene Adam; tel (403) 372-3608; fax (403) 372-4445

Bassano: *The Bassano Times* — 216 3rd St.; Box 780 (TOJ OBO); M; 734pd (VCP); 48¢; publisher & editor Mary Lou Brooks; tel (403) 641-3636; fax (403) 641-3952

Beaverlodge: *The Advertiser* — 920 1st Ave.; Box 300 (TOH OCO); W; 1,739pd (ABC); 40¢; publisher & editor Trevor P G Harris; tel (403) 354-2460; fax (403) 354-2460

Blairmore: *The Pass Herald Ltd.* — Crowsnest Mall; Box 960 (TOK OEO); Tu; 2,499pd, 251fr (Sw); $5.50; C; publisher Gail Sygutek; editor Trevor Slapak; tel (403) 562-2248; fax (403) 526-8379

Bonnyville: *Bonnyville Nouvelle* — 5304 50th Ave.; Box 8174 (T9N 2J5); Tu; 4,015pd, 1,840fr (VCP); 64¢; publisher Manfred Kronert; editor Darren Pinkoski; tel (403) 826-3876; fax (403) 826-7062

Bow Island: *The 40-Mile County Commentator* — 147 5th Ave. W.; Box 580 (TOK OGO); Tu; 4,454pd, 30fr (VCP); 54¢; publisher & editor Rob Schellenberg; publisher Tom Conquergood; tel (403) 545-2258; fax (403) 545-6886

Brooks: *The Brooks Bulletin* — Box 1450 (T1R 1C3); W; 5,549pd, 50fr (VCP); 58¢; publisher Jim L Nesbitt; editor Jim Nesbitt Jr; tel (403) 362-5571; fax (403) 362-5080

Calgary: *The Calgary Mirror* — 2080 39th Ave. N.E. (T2E 6P7); Sa; 152,000fr (Sw); 59¢; C; publisher Lyn LaFleche; editor Miles Durrie; tel (403) 777-2345; fax (403) 291-3028

Calgary: *Rural Times* — Box 3820, Airdrie (T4B 2B9); Tu; 90pd, 11,973fr (VCC); $1.10; C; publisher Keith Bennett; editor Ardith Finnegan; tel (403) 948-7280; fax (403) 932-3935

Camrose: *The Camrose Booster* — 4925 48th St. (T4V 1L7); Tu; 26pd, 12,157fr (Sw); 57¢; publisher W Blain Fowler; editor B H (Berdie) Fowler; tel (403) 672-3142; fax (403) 672-2518

Camrose: *The Camrose Canadian* — 4903 49th Ave. (T4V 0M9); W; 4,154pd, 90fr (VCP); $9.10; publisher Lynne Chernin; editor Douglas Stinson; tel (403) 672-4421; fax (403) 672-5323

Cardston: *Cardston Chronicle* — 56 3rd Ave. W.; Box 1800 (TOK OKO); Tu; 3,770pd (Est); 55¢; publisher & editor Marie Barr; tel (403) 653-2222; fax (403) 653-2240

Castor: *The Castor Advance* — Main St.; Box 120 (TOC OXO); Th; 1,017pd, 20fr (VCP); 47¢; publisher Alan R Willis; general manager Jacquie Charlton; tel (403) 882-4044; fax (403) 882-2010

Central Alberta: *Central Alberta Adviser* — 5929 48th Ave.; Bag 5023, Red Deer (T4N 6R4); Tu; 15pd, 25,118fr (Sw); $1.37; C; general manager Cal Dallas; editor Jim Claggett; tel (403) 346-3356; fax (403) 347-6620

Claresholm/Stavely/Granum: *Claresholm Local Press* — 4913 2nd St. W.; Box 520, Claresholm (TOL OTO); W; 2,000pd, 70fr (VCP); 46¢; publisher & editor Gordon Scott; tel (403) 625-4474; fax (403) 625-4278

Coaldale Co.: *Sunny South News* — 1802 20th Ave.; Box 30, Coaldale (T1M 1M2); Tu; 4,258pd, 101fr (VCP); 61¢; C; publisher Coleen Campbell; editor Harley Richards; tel (403) 345-3081; fax (403) 345-5408

Cochrane: *Cochrane This Week* — 315 1st St. E. (TOL OW1); Tu; 2,161pd, 125fr (VCP); 76¢; C; publisher Keith Bennett; editor Ardith Finnegan; tel (403) 932-3500; fax (403) 932-3935

Consort: *The Consort Enterprise* — Box 129 (TOC 1BO); W; 1,271pd (VCP); 34¢; publisher William J Readman; editor Mary K Readman; tel (403) 577-3611; fax (403) 577-3611

Coronation/Veteran/Brownfield: *Coronation Review* — 4923 Victoria Ave.; Box 70, Coronation (TOC 1CO); Tu; 1,368pd, 498fr (ABC); 42¢; publisher & editor Joyce Webster; tel (403) 578-4111; fax (403) 578-2088

Crowsnest Pass: *The Crowsnest Pass Promoter* — Main St.; Box 1019, Blairmore (TOK OEO); Tu; 1,699pd, 115fr (VCP); 56¢; publisher James Prentice; editor Ross Purnell; tel (403) 562-8884; fax (403) 562-2242

Didsbury: *The Didsbury Review* — 2017-19 Ave.; Box 760 (TOM OWO); Tu; 1,760pd, 23fr (VCP); 64¢; publisher Gene Hartmann; general manager Brad Hartmann; editor Janice Harrington; tel (403) 335-3301; fax (403) 335-8143

Drayton Valley: *Western Review* — 4905 52nd Ave.; Box 6960 (T7A 1S3); Tu; 4,655pd, 155fr (VCP); 62¢; publisher Kelly Stone; editor Mark Mellott; tel (403) 542-5380; fax (403) 542-9200

Drumheller: *Drumheller Mail* — 368 Centre St.; Box 1629 (TOJ OYO); W; 4,448pd, 359fr (VCP); 70¢; publisher & editor O R Sheddy; tel (403) 823-2580; fax (403) 823-3864

Eckville: *Eckville Examiner* — 4937 50th Ave.; Box 380, Rimbey (TOC 2J0); Tu; 559pd, 6fr (ABC); 44¢; publisher & editor John Roberts; tel (403) 746-3135; fax (403) 843-2990

Edson: *Edson Leader* — 4820 3rd Ave.; Box 6330 (T7E 1T8); M; 3,112pd, 84fr (VCP); $5.60; publisher Derek Pyne; editor John K White; tel (403) 723-3301; fax (403) 723-5171

Elk Point: *Elk Point Review* — 4809-50 Ave.; Box 309 (TOA 1AO); Tu; 641pd, 100fr (VCP); 39¢; C; publisher Guy Drouin; editor Vicki Brooker; tel (403) 724-4087; fax (403) 724-4211

Fairview: *Fairview Post* — 10118-110 St.; Box 1900 (TOH 1LO); Tu; 3,338pd, 30fr (ABC); 67¢; publisher Bob Doornenbal; editor Dennis Hegland; tel (403) 835-4925; fax (403) 835-4227

Fort Macleod: *The Macleod Gazette* — 310 24th St.; Box 720 (TOL OZO); W; 1,495pd, 16fr (VCP); 45¢; publisher & editor John H Murphy; tel (403) 553-3391; fax (403) 553-2961

Fort Saskatchewan: *The Record* — 9804 B 104th St. (T8L 2E6); Tu; 3,058pd, 7,442fr (Sw); $8.80; publisher & editor Andy Lorimer; tel (403) 998-7070; fax (403) 998-5515

Grande Cache: *Grande Cache Mountaineer* — 2702 Pine Plaza; Box 660 (TOE OYO); Tu; 1,401pd (VCP); 45¢; publisher Noel D Edey; editor Arthur B Veitch; tel (403) 827-3539; fax (403) 827-3530

High Level: *Echo* — Box 240 (TOH 1ZO); W; 1,352pd, 57fr (ABC); 48¢; C; publisher & editor Tom Mihaly; tel (403) 926-2000; fax (403) 926-2001

High Prairie: *South Peace News* — 4901 51st Ave.; Box 1000 (TOG 1EO); W; 1,932pd, 100fr (VCP); 63¢; publisher Jeff Burgar; editor Chris Clegg; tel (403) 523-4484; fax (403) 523-3039

High River: *The High River Times* — 618 Centre St. S. (T1V 1E9); Tu; 2,931pd, 199fr (Sw); 62¢; publisher Bill Holmes; editor Ann Holmes; tel (403) 652-2034; fax (403) 652-3962

Hinton: *The Parklander* — 104 MacLeod Ave. (T7V 2A9); M; 3,031pd, 28fr (VCP); 71¢; publisher John Prodan; editor Rod Kelly; tel (403) 865-3115; fax (403) 865-1252

Innisfail: *Innisfail Province* — 4733A 50th St. (T4G 1N7); M; 146pd, 8,071fr (VCC); 67¢; publisher & editor Jack Tennant; tel (403) 227-3612; fax (403) 227-1570

Innisfail District: *Innisfail Booster* — 4932 49th St., Innisfail (T4G 1N2); Tu; 18pd, 7,482fr (Sw); 65¢; C; publisher & editor Ray Brinson; tel (403) 227-3477; fax (403) 227-3330

Irricana/Crossfield: *5 Village Weekly* — 2nd St. & 2nd Ave.; Box 40, Irricana (TOM 1BO); Tu; 9,114pd (VCP); 73¢; publisher Dennis Taylor; editor Gladys Taylor; tel (403) 935-4221; fax (403) 935-4981

Jasper: *The Jasper Booster* — 622 Connaught St.; Box 940 (TOE 1EO); W; 1,502pd, 107fr (VCP); 65¢; editor David Berezowski; tel (403) 852-3620; fax (403) 852-3384

Lac La Biche: *Lac La Biche Post* — 10215 101st St.; Box 508 (TOA 2CO); Tu; 2,390pd (VCP); 53¢; publisher & editor Fisal Asiff; tel (403) 623-4221; fax (403) 623-4230

Lacombe: *Lacombe Globe* — 5022 50th St. (T4L 1W8); Tu; 3,467pd, 60fr (ABC); 64¢; publisher Ross Campbell; editor Bev Rudolfsen; tel (403) 782-3498; fax (403) 782-5850

Leduc: *Leduc Representative* — 4504-61 Ave.; Bag 220 (T9E 3Z1); W; 2,643pd, 5fr (VCP); $9.84; Su; 86pd, 10,481fr (VCP); $9.84; C; publisher Neil Sutcliffe; editor Susan Blackman; tel (403) 986-2271; fax (403) 986-6397

Lloydminster: *Lloydminster Meridian Booster* — 5714-44 St.; Box 830 (S9V 1C2); W; 98pd, 13,836fr (VCC); 75¢; Su; 98pd, 13,921fr (VCC); 75¢; C; publisher Brent Spilak; editor Lloyd Mack; tel (403) 875-3362; fax (403) 875-3423

Manning: *Banner Post* — Box 686 (TOH 2MO); W; 1,229pd, 74fr (ABC); 48¢; publisher & editor Jim Mihaly; tel (403) 836-3588; fax (403) 836-2820

Morinville: *Morinville & District Gazette* — 9920 103rd St.; Box 3095 (T8R 1R7); Tu; 28pd, 5,927fr (VCC); 58¢; publisher Duff Jamison; general manager Greg Foster; editor Will Gibson; tel (403) 939-7443; fax (403) 460-3964

Municipal District: *Smoky River Express* — 217 Main St. W.; Box 644, Falher (TOH 1MO); W; 2,392pd, 75fr (VCP); 61¢; publisher Jeff Burgar; editor Shari Maertens-Poole; tel (403) 837-2585; fax (403) 837-2102

Nanton: *The Nanton News* — 2129 20th St.; Box 429 (TOL 1RO); W; 1,333pd (VCP); 38¢; publisher & editor Frank McTighe; tel (403) 646-2023; fax (403) 646-2848

Okotoks: *Okotoks Western Wheel* — 9 McRae St.; Bag 9 (TOL 1TO); W; 7,171pd, 121fr (VCP); 58¢; publisher Paul W Rockley; editor Kathy Coutts; tel (403) 938-6397; fax (403) 938-2518

Olds/Mountain View Co.: *The Olds Gazette* — 5030 51st St.; Box 3870, Olds (T4H 1P6); W; 3,592pd, 208fr (Sw); 62¢; publisher Brian Leatherdale; editor Mary Jane Harper; tel (403) 556-3351; fax (403) 556-3464

Oyen: *Oyen Echo* — 109-6th Ave. E.; Box 420 (TOJ 2JO); W; 1,390pd (VCC); 50¢; C; publisher Ronald E Holmes; editors Diana Walker & Helen E Ball; tel (403) 664-3622; fax (403) 664-3622

Peace River: *The Record-Gazette* — 10009-100 Ave.; Box 6870 (T8S 1S6); W; 3,839pd, 108fr (VCP); 75¢; publisher Shaun Jessome; editor Irene Chomokovski; tel (403) 624-2591; fax (403) 624-8600

Pincher Creek: *Pincher Creek Echo* — 656 Main St.; Box 1000 (TOK 1WO); Tu; 2,273pd, 56fr (VCP); 48¢; C; publisher Bryce McGregor; editor Sherri Zickafoose; tel (403) 627-3252; fax (403) 627-3949

Ponoka: *The Ponoka Herald* — Bay 5, 5; Box 4308 (T4J 1R7); M; 6,100fr (VCP); 69¢; C; publisher Cal Dallas; editor Tara D Ennis-Reddick; tel (403) 783-3074; fax (403) 783-6106

Ponoka: *Ponoka News & Advertiser* — 5010 50th Ave.; Box 4217 (T4J 1R6); M; 6,100fr (VCC); 69¢; publisher Brian A Borle; editor George W Lee; tel (403) 783-3311; fax (403) 783-6300

Provost: *The Provost News* — 5111-50 St.; Box 180 (TOB 3SO); W; 2,059pd, 93fr (Est); $4.00; publisher & editor Richard C Holmes; tel (403) 753-2564; fax (403) 753-6117

Raymond/Warner: *The Raymond Review* — 89 Broadway N.; Box 315, Raymond (TOK 2SO); Tu; 3,601pd (Est); 55¢; publisher & editor Marie Barr; tel (403) 752-3111; fax (403) 752-3499

Red Deer: *Red Deer Adviser* — 5929 48th Ave. (T4N 6A1); Bag 5023 (T4N 6R4); Tu; 15pd, 25,118fr (Sw); $1.37; general manager Cal Dallas; editor Jim Claggett; tel (403) 346-3356; fax (403) 347-6620

Rimbey: *Rimbey Record* — 4937 50th Ave.; Box 380 (TOC 2JO); Tu; 2,099pd, 15fr (ABC); 58¢; publisher Ed Moller; editor John Roberts; tel (403) 843-2231; fax (403) 843-2990

Rocky Mountain House: *The Mountaineer* — 4814 49th St. (TOM 1T1); W; 4,796pd, 92fr (ABC); 56¢; publisher Lawrence O Mazza; editor Brian L Mazza; tel (403) 845-3334; fax (403) 845-5570

Rycroft/Spirit River: *Rycroft Central Peace Signal* — 4720 50th St.; Box 250, Rycroft (T0H 3A0); Tu; 2,552pd (ABC); 52¢; publisher Peter K Schierbeck; editor Dan Zahara; tel (403) 765-3604; fax (403) 765-2188

St. Albert: *St. Albert Gazette* — 25 Chisholm Ave.; Box 263 (T8N 1N3); W; 6,384pd, 361fr (VCP); 82¢; Sa; 132pd, 14,919fr (VCC); 82¢; publisher Duff Jamison; editor Sue Gawlak; tel (403) 460-5500; fax (403) 460-8220

St. Paul/Two Hills: *St. Paul Journal* — 4813 50th Ave.; Box 159, St. Paul (T0A 3A0); Tu; 4,999pd, 200fr (VCP); 73¢; C; publisher Guy Drouin; editor Rob Desjardins; tel (403) 645-3342; fax (403) 645-2346

Sherwood Park/Strathcona: *Sherwood Park News* — 168 Kaska Rd., Sherwood Park (T8A 4G7); W; 49pd, 20,700fr (Sw); 79¢; C; publisher John Prodar; editor Terri Kemball; tel (403) 464-0033; fax (403) 464-8512

Slave Lake: *Lakeside Leader* — 103 3rd Ave. N.E.; Box 849 (T0G 2A0); W; 1,861pd, 100fr (VCP); 61¢; publisher Jeff Burgar; editor Marilyn Partington-Richer; tel (403) 849-4380; fax (403) 849-3903

Slave Lake: *Scope* — Box 1130 (T0G 2A0); Su; 1,500pd (Est); $8.40; publisher & editor Bruce Thomas; tel (403) 849-4350; fax (403) 849-2433

Spruce Grove: *The Grove Examiner* — 323 McLeod Ave.; Box 4206 (T7X 3B4); Sa; 184pd, 4,907fr (VCC); 67¢; publisher Inez Scheideman; editor Rich Gossen; tel (403) 962-4257; fax (403) 962-0658

Stettler: *Stettler Independent* — 5006 50th Ave.; Box 310 (T0C 2L0); W; 4,229pd (ABC); 67¢; publishers Alan R Willis & R C Willis; editor Joy Zell; tel (403) 742-2395; fax (403) 742-8050

Stony Plain/Parkland: *The Stony Plain Reporter* — 5006 50th St.; Box 780, Stony Plain (T7Z 1T3); S; 7,835pd, 3,333fr (VCP); 67¢; publisher Inez Scheideman; editor Rich Gossen; tel (403) 963-2291; fax (403) 963-9716

Sundre: *Sundre Round-Up* — 103 2nd St. N.W.; Box 599 (T0M 1X0); W; 2,285pd (VCP); 60¢; publisher & editor Monica Leatherdale; publisher Neil Leatherdale; tel (403) 638-3577; fax (403) 638-3077

Swan Hills: *Grizzly Gazette* — 4924 Plaza Ave.; Box 1000 (T0G 2C0); Tu; 622pd, 51fr (Sw); 44¢; publisher & editor Carol Webster; tel (403) 333-2100; fax (403) 333-2111

Sylvan Lake: *Sylvan Lake News* — 5020-50A St. (T4S 1R2); W; 1,367pd, 17fr (ABC); $6.30; publisher Barry Hibbert; editor Mark Langen; tel (403) 887-2331; fax (403) 887-2081

Taber: *The Taber Times* — 5403 48th Ave. (T1G 1S6); W; 3,416pd, 84fr (VCP); 61¢; publisher Coleen Campbell; editor Harley Richards; tel (403) 223-2266; fax (403) 223-1408

Three Hills: *The Three Hills Capital* — 523 Main St.; Box 158 (T0M 2A0); W; 3,577pd, 39fr (ABC); 56¢; publisher & editor Timothy Shearlaw; tel (403) 443-5133; fax (403) 443-7331

Tofield: *Tofield Mercury* — 5312-50 St.; Box 150 (T0B 4J0); Tu; 2,207pd, 63fr (Sw); 45¢; C; publisher & editor Anne Francouer; tel (403) 662-4046; fax (403) 662-3735

Valleyview: *Valleyview Valley Views* — 4715 50th St.; Box 787 (T0H 3N0); W; 1,491pd, 47fr (Sw); 70¢; C; publisher & editor Joan Plaxton; tel (403) 524-3490; fax (403) 524-4545

Vauxhall: *Vauxhall Advance* — 516 2nd Ave. N.; Box 302 (T0K 2K0); Th; 775pd, 24fr (VCP); 45¢; publisher Coleen Campbell; editor Harley Richards; tel (403) 654-2122; fax (403) 654-4184

Vegreville: *Vegreville Observer* — 4910 50th St.; Box 160 (T9C 1R2); Tu; 755pd, 75fr (VCC); 45¢; publisher & editor Nancy McArthur; tel (403) 632-2353; fax (403) 632-3235

Vermilion/Mannville/Elk Point: *The Vermilion Standard* — 4917 50 Ave.; Box 750, Vermilion (T0B 4M0); Tu; 3,517pd (VCP); 58¢; publisher & editor Steven Dills; tel (403) 853-5344; fax (403) 853-5203

Vulcan: *Advocate* — 211 Centre St.; Box 389 (T0L 2B0); W; 2,391pd, 37fr (VCP); 52¢; publisher & editor Frank McTighe; tel (403) 485-2036; fax (403) 485-6938

Wainwright: *Star Chronicle* — 414 10th St. (T9W 1P5); W; 2,014pd, 50fr (VCP); 69¢; publisher & editor Roger Holmes; tel (403) 842-4465; fax (403) 842-2760

Westlock: *The Westlock News* — 9871 107th St.; Box 40 (T0G 2L0); M; 4,113pd, 247fr (VCP); 52¢; publisher Tyler Clements; editor Jim Veenbaaf; tel (403) 349-3033; fax (403) 349-3677

Wetaskiwin: *Times-Advertiser* — 5104 53rd Ave.; Box 6900 (T9A 2G5); M; 784pd, 11,196fr (Sw); 66¢; C; publisher Doug Hare; editor George Brown; tel (403) 352-2231; fax (403) 352-4333

Wheatland Co.: *Strathmore Standard* — 136 2nd Ave.; Box 2250, Strathmore (T1P 1K2); Tu; 3,367pd, 25fr (VCP); 67¢; publisher Lori Jorawsky; editor Jim Greer; tel (403) 934-3021; fax (403) 934-5011

Whitecourt: *The Whitecourt Star* — 4732-50th Ave.; Box 630 (T7S 1N7); W; 3,025pd, 27fr (Sw); 62¢; publisher Arni Stephenson; editor Gary Hickling; tel (403) 778-3977; fax (403) 778-6459

BRITISH COLUMBIA

100 Mile House: *100 Mile House Free Press* — 215 4th St.; Box 459 (V0K 2E0); W; 4,744pd, 189fr (VCP); $8.10; publisher Terry Gibbons; editor Steve Frasher; tel (604) 395-2219; fax (604) 395-3939

Aldergrove: *The Aldergrove Star* — 3089-272 St. (V4W 3R9); W; 6,500pd (Est); 52¢; publisher Central Fraser Valley Publishing Ltd.; editor Rudy Langmann; tel (604) 856-8303; fax (604) 856-5212

Armstrong: *Armstrong Advertiser* — Okanagan St.; Box 610 (V0E 1B0); W; 2,222pd (Sw); $8.48; publisher J H Jamieson; tel (604) 546-3121; fax (604) 546-3636

Ashcroft/Logan Lake: *The Ashcroft Journal* — Box 190, Ashcroft (V0K 1A0); Tu; 1,735pd, 1,819fr (Sw); $7.50; C; publisher Judy VanAllen; editor Barry Tait; tel (604) 453-2261

Barriere: *North Thompson Star/Journal* — 359 Brunswick Ave.; Box 1020 (V0E 1E0); M; 257pd, 4,143fr (Est); $7.10; publisher Tim Francis; editor Ann Piper; tel (604) 672-5611; fax (604) 672-9900

Burnaby: *Burnaby NOW* — 3430 Brighton Ave., Ste. 205A (V5A 3H4); W/Su; 47,245fr (CCAB); $21.74; C; publisher Brad Alden; editor Barry Gerding; tel (604) 444-3451; fax (604) 444-3460

Burnaby/New Westminster: *Burnaby and New Westminster News* — 6569 Kingsway, Burnaby (V5E 1E1); W/Su; 14,683pd, 49,013fr (Sw); $17.75; C; publisher Frank Kelly; editor David Beattie; tel (604) 438-6397; fax (604) 438-2815

Burns Lake: *Lakes District News* — 23-3rd Ave.; Box 309 (V0J 1E0); W; 1,821pd (Est); $9.10; C; publisher Jack Cusack; editor Mark Neilsen; tel (604) 692-7526

Campbell River: *The Campbell River Courier* — 1040 Ceder St.; Box 310 (V9W 5B5); Th; 8,274pd (Sw); 79¢; publisher James W Rice; tel (604) 287-7464; fax (604) 287-8891

Campbell River: *The Campbell River Mirror* — 104-250 Dogwood St. (V9W 2X9); W; 3,357pd, 10,671fr (VCC); 84¢; publisher Gerald E Soroka; editor Alistair Taylor; tel (604) 287-9227; fax (604) 287-3238

Campbell River: *The Campbell River Upper Islander* — 1040 Cedar St.; Box 310 (V9W 5B5); Tu; 7,026pd (Sw); 79¢; publisher James W Rice; tel (604) 287-7464

Castlegar: *Castlegar Sun* — 465 Columbia Ave. (V1N 1G8); W; 3,272pd, 160fr (VCC); $11.05; publisher Marilyn Stong; editor Derek Zeisman; tel (604) 365-5266; fax (604) 365-7762

Chetwynd/Hudson Hope: *The Chetwynd Echo* — Box 750, Chetwynd (V0C 1J0); Tu; 1,850pd, 50fr (Sw); $5.46; publisher & editor Margaret Movold; managing editor Rick Davison; tel (604) 788-2246; fax (604) 788-9988

Chilliwack: *Chilliwack Progress* — 45860 Spadina Ave. (V2P 6H9); W; 12,232pd, 2,040fr (CCAB); $15.30; publisher Julian Galbecka; editor Paul Bucci; tel (604) 792-1931; fax (604) 792-4936

Chilliwack: *Chilliwack Progress Weekender* — 45860 Spadina Ave. (V2P 6H9); F; 24,764fr (CCAB); $17.60; publisher Julian Galbecka; editor Paul Bucci; tel (604) 792-1931; fax (604) 792-4936

Chilliwack: *The Progress Community News* — 45860 Spadina Ave. (V2P 6H9); W; 9,027fr (CCAB); $2.30; publisher Julian Galbecka; editor Paul Bucci; tel (604) 792-1931; fax (604) 792-4936

Clearwater: *North Thompson Times* — R.R. 1, Box 1102 (V0E 1N0); Tu; 1,589pd, 1,859fr (VCC); 64¢; publisher Bruce Chappell; editor Nancy Chappell; tel (604) 674-3343; fax (604) 674-3777

Coquitlam/Port Moody: *The Sunday News* — 1405 Broadway St., Port Coquitlam (V3C 5W9); Su; 126,527fr (VCP); $2.46; publisher Bob Graham; editor Richard Dal Monte; tel (604) 525-6397; fax (604) 944-0703

Courtenay/Campbell River: *The North Island News* — 1625 Mephee Ave.; Box 3039, Courtenay (V9N 5N3); Su; 32,393fr (VCC); 96¢; publisher Lain McClymont; editor Jamie Bowman; tel (604) 334-4446; fax (604) 334-4983

Creston: *The Creston Valley Advance* — 115-10th Ave.; Box 1279 (V0B 1G0); M/Th; 4,086pd, 22fr (ABC); 76¢; publisher Helena White; tel (604) 428-2266; fax (604) 428-3320

Delta: *Delta Optimist* — 5485-48 Ave. (V4K 1X2); W; 50pd, 15,722fr (VCC); $15.40; Sa; 72pd, 16,197fr (VCC); $15.40; publisher Tom Siba; editor Ted Murphy; tel (604) 946-4451; fax (604) 946-5680

Duncan: *The Cowichan News Leader* — 2742 James St. (V9L 2X9); W; 60pd, 19,355fr (Sw); $1.06; publisher Manfred Tempelmayr; editor Brian LePine; tel (604) 746-4471; fax (604) 746-8529

Duncan: *The Pictorial* — 2742 James St. (V9L 2X9); Su; 15pd, 22,310fr (Sw); $1.06; publisher Manfred Tempelmayr; editor Brian LePine; tel (604) 746-4451; fax (604) 746-8529

East Vancouver: *Vancouver Echo* — 3355 Grandview Hwy., Vancouver (V5M 1Z5); W; 46,749fr (Sw); $24.78; publisher Jack Burch; general manager Mark Walker; managing editor Randy Shore; tel (604) 437-7030; fax (604) 439-3367

Elk Valley: *The Free Press* — 342 2nd Ave.; Bag 5000, Fernie (V0B 1M0); W/Su; 4,100pd (Est); 35¢; publisher Cindy Brunel; editor Jacqueline Waldorf; tel (604) 423-4666; fax (604) 423-3110

Enderby/Mabel Lake/Mara: *Enderby Commoner* — 908 Belvedere St.; Box 190, Enderby (V0E 1V0); W; 1,800pd (Sw); $6.00; publisher Andrew J K Yeates; editor Lisa McKnight-Yeates; tel (604) 838-7229; fax (604) 838-7801

Fort Nelson: *The Fort Nelson News* — Ste. 3 Sikanni Bldg., Liard St. N.; Box 600 (V0C 1R0); W; 2,409pd, 2,500fr (Sw); 57¢; publisher & editor Judith A Kenyon; tel (604) 774-2357; fax (604) 774-3612

Fort St. James: *Caledonia Courier* — Box 1298 (V0J 1P0); W; 1,170pd (Est); 64¢; publisher Mark Warner; editor Chris Miller; tel (604) 567-9258; fax (604) 567-2070

Fort St. John: *North Peace Express* — 9916 98th St. (V1J 3T8); Su; 10,300fr (Est); 82¢; publisher Bob Haugen; tel (604) 785-5631; fax (604) 785-3522

Fraser Valley (Central): *The News* — 34375 Cyril St., Abbotsford (V2S 2H5); W; 15,939pd, 3,750fr (ABC); $15.25; Sa; 40,775fr (ABC); $18.70; C; publisher Randall Blair; editor Gord Kurenoff; tel (604) 853-1144; fax (604) 850-5426

Gibsons: *Gibsons Coastlife* — #102-1064 Hwy. 101; Box 567 (V0N 1V0); M; 13,850fr (Est); $8.54; C; publisher Luba Arduin; editor Nancy Moote; tel (604) 886-7077; fax (604) 886-7141

Gibsons: *Gibsons Outlook* — #102-1064 Hwy. 101; Box 567 (V0N 1V0); M; 7,530fr (Est); $5.50; C; publisher Luba Arduin; editor Derek McNaughton; tel (604) 886-7077; fax (604) 886-7141

Golden: *Golden Star* — 419 B-9th Ave.; Box 149 (V0A 1H0); W; 2,269pd (Est); $5.50; publisher Holly Bentley; editor Joe Brewer; tel (604) 344-5251; fax (604) 344-5251

Grand Forks: *Gazette* — 7330 2nd St.; Box 700 (V0H 1H0); W; 3,615pd (Sw); 70¢; publisher John A Smith; editor Terry M Arseneau; tel (604) 442-2191; fax (604) 442-3336

Gulf Islands: *Gulf Islands Driftwood* — 328 Lower Ganges Rd., Salt Springs Island (V8K 2V3); W; 4,170pd, 223fr (VCP); 61¢; publisher Joyce Carlson; editor Tony Richards; tel (604) 537-9933; fax (604) 537-2613

Hope/Boston Bar/Yale: *Hope Standard Publications Ltd.* — 895 3rd Ave., Ste. 3; Box 1090, Hope (V0X 1L0); W; 2,800pd (Sw); $8.40; C; publisher Randall Blair; editor Neil Corbett; tel (604) 869-2421; fax (604) 869-7351

Houston: *Houston Today Newspaper* — Box 899 (V0J 1Z0); W; 1,250pd (Est); 26¢; publisher & editor M A Ruiter; tel (604) 845-2890

Invermere: *Valley Echo* — Box 70 (V0A 1K0); W; 3,347pd, 58fr (VCP); 65¢; publisher Keith T Bennett; editor Carol Maloney; tel (604) 342-9216; fax (604) 342-3930

Kelowna/Westbank/Peacucano/Winfield/Oyana/Okanagan Centre: *Kelowna Capital News* — 2495 Enterprise Way, Kelowna (V1X 7K2); W; 31pd, 46,371fr (CCAB); 75¢; F; 45pd, 41,125fr (CCAB); 75¢; Su; 24pd, 46,371fr (CCAB); 75¢; C; publisher Jim Clark; managing editor Bryden Winsby; tel (604) 763-3212; fax (604)763-8469

Kitimat: *News Advertiser* — 626 Enterprise Ave. (V8C 2E4); Sa; 34pd, 4,250fr (VCP); 51¢; publisher H T Mitchell; editor Carol Goddard; tel (604) 632-6144; fax (604) 639-9373

Kitimat/Terrace: *Northern Sentinel* — 626 Enterprise Ave., Kitimat (V8C 2E4); W; 2,374pd, 191fr (Sw); 38¢; publisher H T Mitchell; editor Carol Goddard; tel (604) 632-6144; fax (604) 639-9373

Ladysmith/Chemainus: *The Ladysmith-Chemainus Chronicle* — 23 High St.; Box 400, Ladysmith (V0R 2E0); Tu; 2,365pd (VCP); 45¢; publisher Manfred Tempelmayr; editor Eric Henderson; tel (604) 245-2277

Lake Cowichan: *The Lake News* — 75 S. Shore Rd.; Box 962 (V0R 2G0); W; 1,556pd, 240fr (VCC); $5.50; publisher & editor Ron Kenyon; publisher & general manager Sheila Kenyon; tel (604) 749-3143; fax (604) 749-3143

Langley: *Langley Advance* — 20488 Fraser Hwy.; Box 3310 (V3A 4R6); W/F; 35,000fr (Sw); $13.86; C; publisher Marilyn Boswyk; editor Bob Groeneveld; tel (604) 534-8641; fax (604) 534-3383

Langley: *Langley Times* — 20269 Fraser Hwy.; Box 3097 (V3A 4R3); W; 36,100fr (Sw); N/A; Sa; 36,100fr (Sw); 89¢; publisher Tanis Culley; editor Lance Peyerley; tel (604) 533-4157; fax (604) 533-0219

Lillooet: *Bridge River News* — 979 Main St.; Box 709 (V0K 1V0); W; 1,722pd, 804fr (VCP); 50¢; publisher & editor Jeff Den Biesen; tel (604) 256-4219; fax (604) 256-4210

Mackenzie: *The Times* — 128-403 Mackenzie Blvd.; Box 609 (V0J 2C0); W; 1,500pd (Est); 20¢; publisher & editor Jackie Benton; tel (604) 997-6675; fax (604) 997-4747

Maple Ridge/Pitt Meadows: *The Maple Ridge News* — 22328 119th Ave., Maple Ridge (V2X 2Z3); W/Su; 19,000fr (VCC); 94¢; C; publisher & editor Reg Romero; tel (604) 467-1122; fax (604) 463-4741

Maple Ridge/Pitt Meadows: *Maple Ridge/Pitt Meadow Times* — 22380 Lougheed Hwy., Maple Ridge (V2X 2T4); W/Su; 22,728fr (Sw); $13.02; publisher Lois Lee; editor Ken Goudswaard; tel (604) 463-2281; fax (604) 463-9943

Merritt: *Merritt Herald* — 1951 Garcia St.; Box 9 (V0K 2B0); W; 3,005pd (Est); 18¢; publisher Eric Cardwell; editor Susan Holmberg; tel (604) 378-4241; fax (604) 378-6818

Merritt: *Weekend News Advertiser* — 1951 Garcia Ave.; Box 9 (V0K 2B0); F; 4,000fr (Est); 20¢; publisher Eric Cardwell; editor Susan Holmberg; tel (604) 378-4241; fax (604) 378-6818

Mission: *Fraser Valley Record* — 33047 First Ave. (V2V 1G2); W; 4,941pd, 13fr (VCP); $10.90; publisher & editor Don Button; tel (604) 826-6221; fax (604) 826-8266

Nakusp: *Arrow Lakes News* — Box 10 (V0G 1R0); W; 2,373pd (Sw); 44¢; publisher & editor D Stanley; tel (604) 265-4215; fax (604) 265-3577

Nanaimo/Ladysmith: *Nanaimo Times Ltd.* — 296 Bastion St.; Box 486, Nanaimo (V9R 5L5); Tu/Th/Sa; 29,575fr (VCC); $15.47; publisher Roy Fisher; editor Steve Jenkinson; tel (604) 753-3277; fax (604) 753-9104

New Westminster: *Royal City Record/Now* — 418 6th St. (V3L 3B2); W/Sa; 14,818fr (CCAB); $14.56; C; publisher Steve Houston; editor Pat Tracy; tel (604) 525-6306; fax (604) 525-7360

Northwest Vancouver: *North Shore News* — 1139 Lonsdale Ave., North Vancouver (V7M 2H4); W/F/Su; 61,582fr (Sw); $36.26; publisher Peter Speck; editor Timothy Renshaw; tel (604) 985-2131; fax (604) 985-3227

Oak Bay: *Oak Bay News* — 219-2187 Oak Bay Ave., Victoria (V8T 3L8); W; 821pd, 8,381fr (VCC); $12.69; C; publisher & editor Anthony Kant; tel (604) 598-4123; fax (604) 598-1896

Oliver: *Oliver Chronicle* — 36083 97th St.; Box 880 (V0H 1T0); W; 3,249pd, 81fr (VCP); $5.25; publisher Michael Newman; editor Kathleen Connolly; tel (604) 498-3711; fax (604) 498-3966

Osoyoos: *Osoyoos Times* — 8712 76th Ave.; Box 359 (V0H 1V0); W; 2,567pd, 150fr (VCP); 50¢; publisher Chris Stodola; publisher & editor Patrick Turner; tel (604) 495-7225; fax (604) 495-6616

Parksville/Qualicum: *The News* — 4-154 Middleton Ave.; Box 1180, Parksville (V9P 2H2); Tu; 474pd, 15,349fr (VCC); $10.08; Th/Sa; 16,000fr (Est); $10.08; publisher Judi Thompson; editor Jeff Vircoe; tel (604) 248-4341; fax (604) 248-4655

Penticton/South Okanogan: *Penticton Western News* — 200 Front St., Penticton (V2A 1H4); W/F; 21,660fr (Sw); 85¢; publisher James (Pat) Duncan; editor Wayne Campbell; tel (604) 492-3636; fax (604) 492-8943

Pt. Coquitlam/Pt. Moody: *The Tri-City News* — 1405 Broadway St., Port Coquitlam (V3C 5W9); W/Su; 41,162fr (VCC); $1.24; C; publisher Bob Graham; editor Mark Hamilton; tel (604) 525-6397; fax (604) 944-0703

Port Hardy: *North Island Gazette* — Box 458 (V0N 2P0); W; 3,382pd, 101fr (Sw); 80¢; publisher Rodney Slugtett; editor Rob Giblak; tel (604) 949-6225; fax (604) 949-7655

Powell River: *Powell River News/Town Crier* — 7030 Alberni St. (V8A 2C3); M; 5,473pd, 186fr (ABC); 82¢; W; 5,473pd (ABC); 82¢; publisher Pam Krompocker; editor Terry Kruger; tel (604) 485-4255; fax (604) 485-5832

Princeton: *Princeton Similkameen Spotlight* — Box 340 (V0X 1W0); W; 2,083pd, 87fr (Est); 26¢; publisher & editor Fred Heck; tel (604) 295-3535; fax (604) 295-7322

Quesnel: *Quesnel Cariboo Observer* — 188 Carson Ave. (V2J 2A8); W; 5,200pd, 9,500fr (Sw); 93¢; Su; 5,200pd (Sw); 93¢; C; publisher & editor J F MacDonald; tel (604) 992-2121; fax (604) 992-5229

Revelstoke: *Revelstoke Times-Review* — Box 20 (V0E 2S0); W; 3,608pd, 44fr (ABC); 59¢; publisher Penny Graham; tel (604) 837-4667

Richmond: *Richmond News* — 5731 No.3 Rd. (V6X 2C9); W/Sa/Su; 422pd, 39,712fr (VCC); $1.44; publisher Frank Teskey; editor Rene McKnight; tel (604) 270-8031; fax (604) 270-2248

Richmond: *Richmond Review* — 120-5851 No.3 Rd. (V6X 2C9); W; 32pd, 41,852fr (CCAB); $1.69; Sa; 27pd, 42,337fr (CCAB); $1.69; publisher Dave McCullough; editor Carlyn Yandle; tel (604) 273-7744; fax (604) 273-5272

Salmon Arm: *Salmon Arm Observer/The Shwswap Market News* — 51 Hudson St. N.E.; Box 550 (V1E 4N7); W; 4,712pd, 226fr (Est); 76¢; Sa; 16,688fr (Est); 69¢; C; publisher Curt Duddy; editor Gordon Priestman; tel (604) 832-2131; fax (604) 832-5140

Sechelt/Gibsons: *Sechelt Press* — Box 519, Sechelt (V0N 3A0); M; 88pd, 8,935fr (Est); $5.50; C; publisher Luba Arduin; editor Nancy Moote; tel (604) 885-5121; fax (604) 885-5399

Sidney/Saanichton/Brentwood Bay: *The Peninsula News Review* — 9726 First St.; Box 2070, Sidney (V8L 3S5); W; 1,131pd, 11,866fr (Sw); $13.18; publisher Corrie Morozoff; editor Paul Wyke; tel (604) 656-1151; fax (604) 656-5526

Smithers: *The Interior News* — Box 2560 (V0J 2N0); W; 4,367pd, 57fr (VCC); 90¢; publisher Vic Swan; editor John Young; tel (604) 847-3266; fax (604) 847-2995

Sooke: *The Sooke Mirror* — Box 339 (V0S 1N0); W; 151pd, 4,809fr (VCC); $6.10; publisher Michael Turnpenny; editor Mitch Moneo; tel (604) 642-5752; fax (604) 642-4767

South Vancouver: *East Side* — 1736 E. 33rd Ave., Vancouver (V5N 3E2); Th; 5,600fr (Sw); $10.00; C; publisher & editor Rod Raglin; tel (604) 327-0221

Sparwood/Elkford/Fernie: *Elk Valley Miner* — Greenwood Mall; Box 820, Sparwood (V0B 2G0); Tu; 3,109pd (VCP); $6.80; C; publisher Fritz Brockel; editor Richard Collicut; tel (604) 425-6411/423-4222; fax (604) 425-6201

Summerland: *Summerland Review* — Victoria Rd.; Box 309 (V0H 1Z0); Th; 2,768pd, 175fr (VCP); $4.75; C; publisher Juanita Gibney; editor William Hodgson; tel (604) 494-5406; fax (604) 494-5453

Sunshine Coast: *The Sunshine Coast News* — Box 460, Gibsons (V0N 1V0); M/Th; 11,384fr (Est); $8.75; publisher Pat Tripp; editor Chuck Hart; tel (604) 886-2622; fax (604) 886-7725

Surrey/North Delta: *Surrey/North Delta Leader* — Box 276, Surrey (V3T 4W8); W/Su; 273pd, 78,500fr (Sw); $19.53; publisher Duane Geddes; editor Andrew Holdta; tel (604) 588-4313; fax (604) 588-1863

Surrey/North Delta: *Surrey/North Delta Now* — 201-7889 132nd St., Surrey (V3W 4N2); W/Sa; 72,460fr (CCAB); $20.87; publisher Frank Teskey; editor Jeff Beamist; tel (604) 572-0064; fax (604) 572-6438

Terrace: *The Terrace Standard* — 4647 Lazelle Ave. (V8G 1S8); W; 1,450pd, 6,391fr (Sw); $10.08; C; publisher & editor Rod Link; tel (604) 638-7283; fax (604) 638-8432

Tumbler Ridge: *Tumbler Ridge Weekly Record* — 202-235 Front St.; Box 1508 (V0C 2W0); Tu; 1,000pd (Sw); 57¢; publisher Randy Hill; editor Ruth Jorgerson; tel (604) 242-4789; fax (604) 242-4737

Valemount: *The Valley Sentinel* — Box 688 (V0E 2Z0); Tu; 1,183pd, 1,220fr (VCP); $5.25; publisher Bill Mahoney; editor Leann Torgulson; tel (604) 566-4425; fax (604) 566-4528

Vancouver: *Georgia Straight* — 1770 Burrard St., 2nd Fl. (V6J 3G7); F; 194pd, 95,800fr (VAC); $3.14; publisher & editor Dan McLeod; managing editor Charles Campbell; tel (604) 730-7000; fax (604) 730-7010

Vancouver: *Le Soleil de Colombie* — 1645 W. 5th Ave. (V6J 1N5); F; 3,000pd, 150fr (Est); 85¢; publisher Jacques Baillaut; editor Pierre Longnus; tel (604) 730-9575; fax (604) 683-9576

Vancouver: *L'Info* — 1956 W. Broadway; Bureau 208, Colombie-Britannique (V6J 1Z2); F; 6,000pd, 1,000fr (Est); 85¢; C; editor Pierre Honorat; managing editor Jacques Scala; tel (604) 685-9804

Vancouver: *The Vancouver Courier* — 1574 W. 6th Ave. (V6J 1R2); W; 46,217fr (CCAB); $33.88; Su; 101,793fr (CCAB); $47.60; publishers Peter Ballard & Phil Hager; general manager Jim Davis; editor Mick Maloney; tel (604) 738-1411; fax (604) 731-1474

Vancouver: *Vancouver Herald* — 3548 W. 38th Ave. (V6N 2Y1); F; 27,000fr (Est); 80¢; publisher Stephen Brown; editor Maureen Neal; tel (604) 263-5643

Vanderhoof: *Omineca Express* — 150 W. Columbia; Box 1007 (V0J 3A0); W; 1,829pd, 27fr (Sw); 68¢; publisher Mark Warner; editor Ken Furber; tel (604) 567-9258; fax (604) 567-2070

Vernon: *The Morning Star* — 4407 25th Ave. (V1T 1P5); W/F/Su; 78pd, 27,004fr (CCAB); $1.20; publisher Don Kendall; managing editor Glenn Mitchell; tel (604) 545-3322; fax (604) 542-1510

Victoria: *Victoria's Monday Magazine* — 1609 Blanshard St. (V8W 2J5); Th; 40,000fr (Sw); $1.54; publisher Andrew Lynch; general manager Alice Weins; editor Sid Tafler; tel (604) 382-6188; fax (604) 381-2662

Victoria/Western Commun.: *Goldstream News Gazette* — Box 7310 Depot D, Victoria (V9B 5B7); W; 1,509pd, 11,897fr (VCC); 96¢; publisher Terry Hamilton; editor Keith Norbury; tel (604) 478-9552; fax (604) 478-6545

Whistler: *The Whistler Question* — 307-4204 Village Sq. (V0N 1B4); M/Th; 4,626pd, 100fr (VCP); 85¢; C; publisher Claire MacDonald; editor Jacqueline Waldorf; tel (604) 932-5131; fax (604) 932-2862

White Rock/South Surrey: *The Peace Arch News* — 101-1440 George St.; Box 75149, White Rock (V4A 9M4); W/Sa; 162pd, 27,700fr (CCAB); 92¢; publisher Fred Gorman; editor Diane Strandberg; tel (604) 531-1711; fax (604) 531-7977

Williams Lake: *The Tribune* — 188 N. 1st Ave. (V2G 1Y8); Tu/Th; 6,130pd (VCC); 89¢; publisher Gary Crosina; editor Ken Alexander; tel (604) 392-2331; fax (604) 392-7253

MANITOBA

Altona: *The Red River Valley Echo* — Box 700 (R0G 0B0); Tu; 2,188pd, 932fr (VCP); 70¢; publisher & editor Liz Wieler; tel (204) 324-5001; fax (204) 324-1402

Baldur/Glenora/Belmont: *Gazette-News* — Box 280, Baldur (R0K 0B0); Tu; 1,184pd, 25fr (VCP); 40¢; publisher & editor Earl Johnson; tel (204) 535-2127; fax (204) 535-2350

Beausejour: *The Carillon* — 606 Park Ave.; Box 1148 (R0E 0C0); W; 12,000pd (Est); 58¢; C; publisher Derksen Printers; editor Peter Dyck; tel (204) 268-1155; fax (204) 268-1084

Birtle: *The Birtle Eye-Witness* — 353 Station Rd.; Box 160, Shoal Lake (R0J 1Z0); M; 1,047pd, 24fr (VCP); $6.30; publisher & editor Gregory Nesbitt; tel (204) 759-2644; fax (204) 759-2521

Boissevain: *The Recorder* — Box 220 (R0K 0E0); W; 1,624pd (Sw); $6.16; publisher & editor Miles G Phillips; tel (204) 534-6479; fax (204) 534-2977

Carberry: *Carberry News Express* — 34 Main St.; Box 220 (R0K 0H0); W; 1,309pd (VCP); $4.48; publisher & editor John W H Lupton; tel (204) 834-2153; fax (204) 834-2714

Carman/Elm Creek/Miami/Roland: *The Valley Leader* — 29 1st Ave. N.W.; Box 70, Carman (R0G 0J0); M; 463pd, 8,258fr (VCC); 86¢; publisher Melvin Farmer; editor Eugene Still; tel (204) 745-2051; fax (204) 745-3976

Cartwright: *Southern Manitoba Review* — 630 Bowles St.; Box 249 (R0K 0L0); Tu; 1,001pd, 24fr (VCP); 34¢; publisher & editor V M (Vicki) Hayward; tel (204) 529-2342; fax (204) 529-2029

Dauphin: *Dauphin Herald* — 120 1st Ave. N.E.; Box 548 (R7N 2V4); Tu; 6,367pd, 79fr (VCP); 99¢; publisher Brent Wright; editor Sheri Clegg; tel (204) 638-4420; fax (204) 638-8760

Deloraine: *The Deloraine Times and Star* — 122 Broadway N.; Box 407 (R0M 0M0); W; 1,212pd, 113fr (VCP); 38¢; publisher & editor Ben Kroeker; tel (204) 747-2249; fax (204) 747-2180

Glenboro: *Gazette* — 702 Railway; Box 10 (R0K 0X0); Tu; 1,003pd (VCP); 40¢; publishers & editors Mike Johnson & Travis Johnson; tel (204) 827-2343; fax (204) 827-2343

Grandview/Gilbert Plains: *Grandview Exponent* — 416 Main St.; Box 39, Grandview (R0L 0Y0); W; 1,563pd, 30fr (VCC); 38¢; publisher & editor Jim T Chaloner; tel (204) 546-2555; fax (204) 546-3081

Hamiota: *The Hamiota Echo* — 353 Station Rd.; Box 160, Shoal Lake (R0J 1Z0); M; 1,113pd (VCP); $6.30; publisher & editor Gregory Nesbitt; tel (204) 759-2644; fax (204) 759-2521

Killarney: *Killarney Guide* — 417 William Ave.; Box 670 (R0K 1G0); Tu; 1,621pd, 200fr (VCP); 41¢; publisher & editor Garry Struth; tel (204) 523-4611; fax (204) 523-4445

Lac du Bonnet: *Leader* — 83 3rd St.; Box 910 (R0E 1A0); Tu; 1,743pd, 23fr (VCP); 46¢; publisher & editor Russ Preston; tel (204) 345-8611; fax (204) 345-6344

Manitou: *The Western Canadian* — 424 Ellis Ave. E.; Box 190 (R0G 1G0); Tu; 1,793pd, 24fr (VCP); 40¢; publisher & editor B Klippenstein; tel (204) 242-2555; fax (204) 242-3137

Melita/Southwest Manitoba: *Melita New Era* — 149 Main St.; Box 820, Melita (R0M 1L0); Tu; 1,336pd, 83fr (VCP); 45¢; publisher Bruce Schwanke; general manager Marcia Snyder; tel (204) 522-3491; fax (204) 522-3648

Minnedosa/Erickson: *Minnedosa Tribune* — 14-3rd Ave. S.W.; Box 930, Minnedosa (R0J 1E0); Tu; 3,166pd (VAC); 56¢; publisher & editor Bob Mummery; tel (204) 867-3816; fax (204) 867-5171

Morris: *The Scratching River Post* — 143 Charles W.; Box 160 (R0G 1K0); Th; 343pd, 2,907fr (VCC); 73¢; publisher & editor Doug Penner; tel (204) 746-2868

Neepawa/McCreary: *The Neepawa Press* — 423 Mountain Ave.; Box 939, Neepawa (R0J 1H0); Tu; 2,777pd, 151fr (VCP); $8.26; publisher Ewan Pow; publisher & editor Jack Gibson; tel (204) 476-2309; fax (204) 476-5802

Pilot Mound/Crystal City: *The Sentinel-Courier* — 13 Railway St.; Box 179, Pilot Mound (R0G 1P0); Tu; 1,334pd, 25fr (VCP); $5.74; publisher Jeff Howell; editor S L Howell; tel (204) 825-2772; fax (204) 825-2772

Portage La Prairie: *Herald Leader Press* — 1941 Sask. Ave. W.; Box 130 (R1N 3B4); Tu; 479pd, 5,814fr (VCC); 73¢; publisher Tom Tenszen; editor Simon Blake; tel (204) 857-3427; fax (204) 239-1270

Reston: *The Reston Recorder* — 330 Main St. N.; Box 10 (R0M 1X0); Tu; 1,116pd, 60fr (VAC); 45¢; publisher & editor Bruce H Schwanke; tel (204) 877-3321; fax (204) 877-3331

Rivers/Rapid City/Oak River: *Rivers Banner* — 526 2nd Ave.; Box 70, Rivers (R0K 1X0); M; 193pd, 747fr (VCC); $4.00; C; publisher & editor Ken Waddell; general manager & managing editor Sheila Szapko; tel (204) 328-7494; fax (204) 328-5212

Roblin: *The Roblin Review* — 119 First Ave. N.W.; Box 938 (R0L 1P0); Tu; 1,986pd, 67fr (VCP); 52¢; publisher Brent Wright; editor Ed Doering; tel (204) 937-8377; fax (204) 937-8212

Rossburn: *The Rossburn Review* — 353 Station Rd.; Box 160, Shoal Lake (R0J 1Z0); M; 1,056pd (VCP); $6.30; publisher & editor Gregory Nesbitt; tel (204) 759-2644; fax (204) 759-2521

Russell: *Banner* — 310 Main St.; Box 100 (R0J 1W0); Tu; 1,960pd (VAC); 43¢; publisher & editor Clayton Chaloner; tel (204) 773-2069; fax (204) 773-2645

St. Boniface/French Manitoba: *La Liberte* — Box 190, St. Boniface (R2H 3B4); F; 4,300pd (Est); 45¢; publisher Jean-Francois Lacerte; editor Sylviane Lanthier; tel (204) 237-4823; fax (204) 231-1998

Selkirk/Oakbank/Dugald: *Selkirk Journal* — 410 Main St.; Box 190, Stonewall (R0C 2Z0); M; 125pd, 16,731fr (VCC); $1.08; publisher Mervin E Farmer; editor John Gluson; tel (204) 467-2421; fax (204) 467-5967

Shoal Lake: *The Shoal Lake Star* — 353 Station Rd.; Box 160 (R0J 1Z0); M; 1,113pd (VCP); $6.30; publisher & editor Gregory Nesbitt; tel (204) 759-2644; fax (204) 759-2521

Souris: *Souris Plaindealer* — 35 Crescent Ave. W.; Box 488 (R0K 2C0); M; 1,428pd, 25fr (VCP); 40¢; publisher & editor Shelley Ross; tel (204) 483-2070; fax (204) 483-3866

Steinbach/Grunthal: *The Carillon* — 377 Main St.; Box 1209, Steinbach (R0A 2A0); W; 12,232pd (ABC); $1.25; publisher Rick Derksen; editor Peter Dyck; tel (204) 326-3421; fax (204) 326-4860

Stonewall: *The Stonewall Argus/Teulon Times* — 410 Main St.; Box 190 (R0C 2Z0); M; 3,942pd, 640fr (VCP); $12.18; C; publisher Mervin E Farmer; editor Kelly Langerin; managing editor Lea Hilstrom; tel (204) 467-2421/8402; fax (204) 467-5967

Swan River: *Star & Times* — Box 670 (R0L 1Z0); W; 4,605pd, 28fr (VCP); 60¢; publisher Robert F Gilroy; editor Dean Pritchard; tel (204) 734-3858; fax (204) 734-4935

Thompson/N Manitoba: *Nickel Belt News* — 887 Thompson, Thompson (R8N 1N8); M; 7,082fr (VCP); 77¢; publisher Joan Wright; editor Grant Wright; tel (204) 677-4534; fax (204) 677-3681

Treherne: *The Times* — Broadway St.; Box 50 (R0G 2V0); M; 2,101pd, 802fr (VAC); 55¢; publisher & editor Gary Lodwick; tel (204) 723-2542; fax (204) 723-2754

Virden: *Virden Empire-Advance* — 300 Nelson St. W.; Box 250 (R0M 2C0); Tu; 2,876pd, 134fr (VCP); $4.25; publisher J H McLachlan; general manager K Riedel; editor B Griffith; tel (204) 748-3931; fax (204) 748-1816

Winkler: *Pembina Times* — 324 S. Railway; Box 1356 (R6W 4B3); M; 15pd, 7,437fr (VCC); 80¢; publisher Glen Friesen; editor Don Radford; tel (204) 325-4771; fax (204) 325-5059

Winnipeg/Northend: *The Times* — 1465 St. James St., Winnipeg (R3H 0W9); Tu; 23pd, 33,983fr (VCC); $1.58; C; publisher Gerald L Dorge; editor Brian Eastwood; tel (204) 949-6100; fax (204) 949-6122

Winnipeg/St. Boniface: *The Lance* — 1465 St. James St., Winnipeg (R3H 0W9); Tu; 23pd, 50,997fr (VCC); $2.05; C; publisher Gerald L Dorge; editor Brian Eastwood; tel (204) 949-6100; fax (204) 949-6122

Winnipeg/St. James: *The Metro* — 1465 St. James St., Winnipeg (R3H 0W9); Tu; 21pd, 53,312fr (VCC); $2.08; C; publisher Gerald L Dorge; editor Brian Eastwood; tel (204) 949-6100; fax (204) 949-6122

Winnipeg/Transcona: *The Herald* — 1465 St. James St., Winnipeg (R3H 0W9); Tu; 26pd, 39,022fr (VCC); $1.03; C; publisher Gerald L Dorge; editor Brian Eastwood; tel (204) 949-6100; fax (204) 949-6122

NEW BRUNSWICK

Andover: *Victoria County Record* — Box 990, Perth-Andover (E0J 1V0); W; 4,755pd (Est); 20¢; C; publisher David S Henley; editor Mark Rickard; tel (506) 273-2285; fax (506) 273-4441

Campbellton: *Journal L'Aviron* — 100 Water St.; Box 637 (E3N 3H1); W; 3,500pd (Est); 80¢; C; publisher Quebecor Inc.; editor Francois Fournier; tel (506) 753-7637; fax (506) 759-7738

Campbellton: *The Tribune* — 3 St. Louis Ave.; Box 486 (E3N 3G9); W; 6,102pd, 175fr (ABC); 80¢; C; publisher T J Raymond; editor Susan Shalala; tel (506) 753-4413; fax (506) 759-9595

Choleur Region: *The Northern Light* — 355 King Ave.; Box 416, Bathurst (E2A 3Z3); W; 8,124pd, 9fr (ABC); 95¢; publisher A J McCarthy; editor Greg Mulock; tel (506) 546-4491; fax (506) 546-1491

Edmundston: *Le Madawaska* — 20 rue St. Francois (E3V 1E3); W; 7,672pd, 215fr (ABC); 70¢; publisher & editor Jean Pierre Boucher; tel (506) 735-5575; fax (506) 735-8086

Grand Falls: *The Cataracte Weekly* — 208 Main St.; Box 2756 (E0J 1M0); W; 4,000pd (Est); 45¢; publisher David S Henley; editor Joan Weinman; tel (506) 473-3083; fax (506) 473-3105

Hartland: *Observer* — Box 330 (E0J 1N0); W; 5,400pd (Est); 20¢; publisher & editor Gordon Fairgrieve; tel (506) 375-4458; fax (506) 375-4281

Miramichi: *Miramichi Leader* — 65 Jane St.; Box 500, Newcastle (E1V 3M6); Tu; 8,204pd, 50fr (ABC); 77¢; publisher David Cadogan; editor Rick MacLean; tel (506) 622-2600; fax (506) 622-7422

Miramichi: *Miramichi Weekend* — 65 Jane St.; Box 500, Newcastle (E1V 3M6); F; 8,341pd, 33fr (ABC); 77¢; publisher David Cadogan; editor Rick MacLean; tel (506) 622-2600; fax (506) 622-7422

Oromocto: *The Oromocto Post-Gazette* — 101 Hersey St. (E2V 1J4); W; 4,000pd, 2,700fr (Est); 12¢; publisher Calvin McIntosh; editor John C Suart; tel (506) 357-9813; fax (506) 357-6440

Sackville: *The Sackville Tribune Post* — 21 W. Main St.; Box 1530 (E0A 3C0); W; 3,401pd, 22fr (ABC); 65¢; publisher Vince Arbing; editor Lourdes Richard; tel (506) 536-2500; fax (506) 536-4024

Saint John: *The New Freeman Catholic* — One Bayard Dr. (E2L 3L5); Sa; 6,950pd, 150fr (Sw); $7.50; publisher The New Freeman Ltd.; managing editor Bill Donovan; tel (506) 653-6806; fax (506) 653-6812

St. Stephen/Calais/Maine: *Saint Croix Courier* — 47 Milltown Blvd.; Box 250, St. Stephen (E3L 1G4); Tu; 6,312pd, 150fr (VCP); $6.30; C; publisher Courier Newspapers Ltd.; general manager Shelley McKeeman; editor Laura Haley; tel (506) 466-3220; fax (506) 466-9950

Sussex: *The Kings County Record* — 593 Main St.; Box 40 (E0E 1P9); Tu; 5,244pd, 125fr (ABC); 39¢; C; publisher David Cadogan; editor Jamie Roach; tel (506) 433-1070; fax (506) 432-3532

Woodstock: *The Bugle* — 110 Carleton St.; Box 130 (E0J 2B0); W; 6,892pd, 14fr (Sw); 72¢; publisher David S Henley; editor Deanna Bradley; tel (506) 328-8863; fax (506) 328-3208

NEWFOUNDLAND

Carbonear: *The Compass* — Box 760 (A0A 1T0); Tu; 7,296pd, 8fr (VCP); 75¢; C; publisher John Over; editor Heather May; tel (709) 786-7014; fax (709) 596-1700

Clarenville: *The Packet* — Box 339 (A0E 1J0); W; 6,831pd, 145fr (Est); 67¢; publisher Robinson-Blackmore Printing & Publishing; editor Barbara Dean-Simmons; tel (709) 466-2243; fax (709) 466-2717

Corner Brook: *The Humber Log* — Box 576 (A2H 6G1); W; 6,036pd, 69fr (VCP); 67¢; publisher Robinson-Blackmore Printing & Publishing; editor Carmel Turpin; tel (709) 639-9203; fax (709) 639-1125

Gander: *The Gander Beacon* — Box 420 (A1V 1W8); W; 6,898pd, 177fr (VCP); 63¢; publisher Robinson-Blackmore Printing & Publishing; editor Greg Seaward; tel (709) 256-4371; fax (709) 256-3826

Grand Falls/Windsor: *The Advertiser* — Box 129, Grand Falls (A2A 2J4); M/Th; 5,401pd, 265fr (VCP); 63¢; publisher Robinson-Blackmore Printing & Publishing; editor Kimberley Brett; tel (709) 489-2161; fax (709) 489-4817

Happy Valley/Goose Bay: *The Labradorian* — 174 Hamilton River Rd.; Box 39, Sta. B, Happy Valley (A0P 1E0); W; 2,400pd, 50fr (Est); 25¢; publisher Robinson-Blackmore Printing & Publishing; editor Bert Pomeroy; tel (709) 896-3341; fax (709) 896-8781

Labrador City/Wabush: *The Aurora* — 500 Vanier; Box 423, Labrador City (A2V 2K7); M; 2,952pd, 206fr (VCP); 46¢; publisher Robinson-Blackmore Printing & Publishing; editor Gordon Parsons; tel (709) 944-2957; fax (709) 944-2958

Lewisporte: *The Pilot* — Box 1210 (A0G 3A0); W; 5,051pd (VCP); 63¢; publisher Robinson-Blackmore Printing & Publishing; editor Kelley Bragg; tel (709) 535-6910; fax (709) 535-8640

Marystown: *The Southern Gazette* — Box 1116 (A0E 2M0); Tu; 5,544pd, 10fr (VCP); 75¢; C; publisher & editor George MacVicar; tel (709) 279-3188; fax (709) 279-2628

Port aux Basques: *The Gulf News* — Box 1090 (A0M 1C0); W; 3,823pd (VCP); 63¢; publisher Robinson-Blackmore Printing & Publishing; editor Jeff Ducharme; tel (709) 695-3671; fax (709) 695-7901

Springdale: *The Nor'Wester* — Main St.; Box 28 (A0J 1T0); W; 4,186pd, 200fr (VCP); $7.98; publisher Derek Hiscock; editor Randy Edison; managing editor Ron Ennis; tel (709) 673-3721; fax (709) 673-4171

St. Anthony: *The Northern Pen* — West St.; Box 520 (A0K 4S0); W; 6,186pd, 200fr (VCP); 45¢; publisher Bernard Bromley; editor Allan Bock; tel (709) 454-2191; fax (709) 454-3718

Stephenville: *The Georgian* — 60 West St.; Box 283 (A2N 2Z4); Tu; 2,262pd (Est); 67¢; publisher Robinson-Blackmore Printing & Publishing; editor Chisholm Pothier; tel (709) 643-4531; fax (709) 643-5041

NORTHWEST TERRITORIES

Canadian Eastern Arctic: *Nunatsiaq News* — Box 8, Iqaluit (X0A 0H0); F; 6,200pd, 1,100fr (Est); $2.44; publisher Steven Roberts; editor Todd Phillips; tel (819) 979-5357; fax (819) 979-4763

Fort Smith/Fort Chipewyan: *Slave River Journal* — 207 McDougal Rd.; Box 990, Fort Smith (X0E 0P0); Tu; 879pd, 1,229fr (Est); $1.78; publishers Don Jaque & Sandra Jaque; general manager Dixie Penner; editor James Carroll; tel (403) 872-2784; fax (403) 872-2754

Hay River: *The Hub* — Mackenzie Pl.; Box 1250 (X0E 0R0); Tu; 3,085pd (VCC); $1.25; publisher & editor Chris Brodeur; tel (403) 874-6577; fax (403) 874-2679

Yellowknife: *News/North* — 5108-50th St.; Box 2820 (X1A 2R1); M; 7,220pd, 2,311fr (VCP); $23.80; publisher & editor J W Sigvaldason; general manager Michael Scott; managing editor Bruce Valpy; tel (403) 873-4031; fax (403) 873-8507

Yellowknife: *Yellowknifer* — 5108-50th St.; Box 2820 (X1A 2R1); W/F; 5,028pd, 721fr (ABC); $1.68; publisher & editor J W Sigvaldason; tel (403) 873-4031; fax (403) 873-8507

NOVA SCOTIA

Amherst: *The Amherst Citizen* — Box 280 (B4H 3Z2); Sa; 6,491pd (Est); $9.24; publisher Earl J Gouchie; editor Jennifer Dempsey; tel (902) 667-5102; fax (902) 667-0419

Annapolis Royal: *The Spectator* — Sinclair Mews (B0S 1A0); Tu; 1,954pd, 100fr (VCP); 56¢; C; publisher Garnet Austen; editor Sandra Meers; tel (902) 532-2219; fax (902) 532-2246

Antigonish/E Nova Scotia: *The Casket* — 88 College St.; Box 1300, Antigonish (B2G 2LG); Tu; 7,140pd, 119fr (Sw); 42¢; publisher D L Gillis; editor Jackie Walsh; tel (902) 863-4370; fax (902) 863-1943

Berwick: *Register* — Box 640 (B0P 1E0); W; 2,659pd, 125fr (VCP); 61¢; C; publisher Garnet Austen; editor Fred Sgambati; tel (902) 538-3180; fax (902) 538-8583

Bridgetown: *Monitor* — Box 250 (B0S 1C0); Tu; 1,352pd, 80fr (VCP); 56¢; C; publisher Garnet Austen; editor Sandra Meers; tel (902) 665-4441; fax (902) 665-4014

Bridgewater: *The Bulletin* — 353 York St. (B4V 3K2); W; 11,612pd, 432fr (VCP); $11.06; C; publisher Lighthouse Publishing Ltd.; general manager Lynn Hennigar; editor Vernon Oickle; managing editor Margaret Hennigar; tel (902) 543-2457; fax (902) 543-2228

Cornwallis/Digby: *Ensign* — Box 280, CFB, Cornwallis (B0S 1H0); M; 800fr (Est); 41¢; C; publisher C F B Cornwallis; editor Anne M Wanstall; tel (902) 638-8536

Cumberland Co.: *The Citizen* — 10 Lawrence St.; Box 280, Amherst (B4H 3Z2); Sa; 6,255pd, 6fr (ABC); 71¢; publisher Earl J Gouchie; editor Jennifer Dempsey; tel (902) 667-5102; fax (902) 667-0419

Digby: *Courier* — Box 670 (B0V 1A0); W; 3,875pd, 150fr (VCP); 73¢; C; publisher Garnet Austen; editor John Demings; tel (902) 245-4715; fax (902) 245-1717

Greenwood: *The Aurora Newspaper* — Box 99 (B0P 1N0); M; 5,800fr (Est); 45¢; publisher Kentville Publishing Co. Ltd.; general manager Garnet Austen; editor Stephen R Boates; tel (902) 765-1494; fax (902) 765-1717

Kentville: *The Advertiser* — Box 430 (B4N 3G1); Tu; 8,221pd, 117fr (ABC); 87¢; F; 6,061pd, 40fr (ABC); 69¢; C; publisher Garnet Austen; editor Paul Sparks; tel (902) 681-2121; fax (902) 681-0830

Liverpool: *Advance* — 271 Main St.; Box 10 (B0T 1K0); W; 4,150pd (Est); 60¢; publisher G D MacLeod; editor Vernon Oickle; tel (902) 354-3441; fax (902) 354-2455

Lunenberg: *Progress Enterprise* — 353 York St., Bridgewater (B4V 3K2); W; 3,478pd, 205fr (Est); $8.12; C; publisher Lighthouse Publishing Ltd.; general manager Lynn Hennigar; editor Susan Corkum-Greek; managing editor Margaret Hennigar; tel (902) 634-8863; fax (902) 543-2228

Lunenberg Co.: *The Lighthouse Log* — 353 York St., Bridgewater (B4V 3K2); M; 19pd, 21,887fr (Est); $15.12; publisher Lighthouse Publishing Ltd.; general manager Lynn Hennigar; editor Margaret Hennigar; tel (902) 543-2457; fax (902) 543-2228

Middleton/Annapolis: *Mirror-Examiner* — 284 Main St.; Box 880, Middleton (B0S 1P0); W; 11,180pd, 432fr (VCP); 70¢; C; publisher Garnet Austen; editor Andy Gillis; tel (902) 825-3457; fax (902) 825-6707

Oxford/Springhill: *The Oxford Journal* — Rideau St.; Box 10, Oxford (B0M 1P0); W; 3,075pd, 103fr (VCP); $61.00; publisher Glenn Marchant; editor Ann Blake; tel (902) 447-2051

Pictou: *The Pictou Advocate* — 11 George St.; Box 1000 (B0K 1H0); W; 4,732pd, 185fr (VCP); 66¢; C; publisher George Bellefontaine; general manager Sean Murray; editor Gordon Stiles; tel (902) 485-8014; fax (902) 752-4816

Port Hawkesbury: *The Scotia Sun* — Box 599 (B0E 2V0); W; 5,877pd, 740fr (Est); 61¢; publisher Garnet Austen; editor Jude Ronayne; tel (902) 625-1900; fax (902) 625-2369

Shelburne Co.: *The Coast Guard* — Water St.; Box 100, Shelburne (B0T 1W0); Tu; 4,647pd (Est); 65¢; C; publisher South Shore Gazette Ltd.; editor Len Pace; tel (902) 875-3244; fax (902) 875-3454

Springhill: *Springhill & Parrsboro Record* — 55 Main St.; Box 670 (B0M 1X0); W; 4,290pd (Est); 34¢; publisher Kevin Cummings; editor Mark Rickard; tel (902) 597-3731; fax (902) 667-1402

Truro: *The Weekly Record* — 904 Prince St.; Box 946 (B2N 5G7); W; 3,488pd (Est); 35¢; C; publisher Tom MacLean; editor Peter Heckbert; tel (902) 895-7947

Windsor: *Hants Journal* — 73 Gerrish St.; Box 550 (B0N 2T0); W; 5,336pd, 105fr (Est); 58¢; C; publisher Kentville Publishing; editor Glen Parker; tel (902) 798-8371; fax (902) 798-5451

Yarmouth: *Le Courrier de la Nouvelle-Ecosse* — 4 Alma St.; Box 402 (B5A 4B3); F; 3,501fr (VCP); 84¢; publisher Dave LeBlanc; editor Claudia Collard; tel (902) 742-9119; fax (902) 942-9110

Yarmouth: *The Vanguard* — 2 Second St.; Box 128 (B5A 4B1); Tu; 8,105pd (ABC); 77¢; F; 4,895pd (ABC); 77¢; C; publisher Fundy Group Publications; editor Fred Hatfield; tel (902) 742-7111; fax (902) 742-2311

ONTARIO

Acton/Rockwood: *The Acton Tanner* — 12 Church St. E.; Box 150, Acton (L7J 2M3); W; 1,500pd, 7,100fr (Sw); $5.04; publisher & editor Paul Nolan; tel (519) 853-5100; fax (519) 853-5040

Ajax/Pickering: *Ajax/Whitby/Pickering News Advertiser* — 130 Commercial Ave., Ajax (L1S 2H5); W; 37,500pd (Est); 77¢; publisher Tim Whittaker; editor Greg Coates; tel (905) 683-5110; fax (905) 683-7363

Alliston: *The Herald* — 169 Dufferin St. S., Unit 22; Box 280 (L9R 1E6); W; 4,635pd (ABC); 80¢; publisher Jean Baker-Pearce; editor Catherine Haller; tel (705) 435-6228; fax (705) 435-3342

Almonte: *The Almonte Gazette* — 86 Mill St.; Box 130 (K0A 1A0); W; 2,783pd (ABC); 51¢; publisher Jeff Maguire; editor Ryland Coyne; tel (613) 256-1311; fax (613) 256-5168

Amherstburg: *Echo Community News* — 238 Dalhousie St. (N9V 2Z2); Su; 22pd, 10,551fr (VCC); $7.25; publisher Jack Kindred; editor E P Chant; tel (519) 736-2147; fax (519) 736-8384

Ancaster: *Ancaster News* — 311 Wilson St. E. (L9G 2B8); W; 8,116pd (VCC); 93¢; publisher John Young; editor Julie Hendricks; tel (905) 648-4464; fax (905) 648-7458

Arnprior/West Carleton: *The Arnprior Chronicle-Guide* — 116 John St. N., Arnprior (K7S 2N6); W; 4,455pd, 16fr (ABC); 40.5¢; publisher Marjory McBride-Cluff; general manager Fred Runge; editor Rita Racicot; tel (613) 623-6571; fax (613) 623-7518

Arthur: *Enterprise News* — Box 310 (N0G 1A0); W; 1,443pd, 103fr (VAC); 40¢; C; publisher & editor C B Williams; tel (519) 848-2410; fax (519) 848-3665

Atikokan: *Atikokan Progress* — 226 Burns St.; Box 220 (P0T 1C0); M; 1,715pd, 25fr (VCP); $5.25; publisher Eve Shine; editor Michael P McKinnon; tel (807) 597-2731; fax (807) 597-6103

Aylmer: *The Aylmer Express* — 390 Talbot St. E.; Box 160 (N5H 2R9); W; 4,201pd (ABC); 44¢; publisher Arthur Hueston; editor John Hueston; tel (519) 773-3126; fax (519) 773-3147

Copyright ©1996 by the Editor & Publisher Co.

III-30 **Ontario** *Canadian Weeklies*

Beeton/Schomberg: *Beeton-Schomberg Record Sentinel* — 34 Main St. W.; Box 310, Beeton (L0G 1A0); W; 960pd, 40fr (Sw); $9.24; C; publisher Bruce Haire; publisher & general manager John Archibald; editor Bruce R Haire; tel (905) 729-2287; fax (905) 729-2541

Belle River: *The North Essex News* — 419 Notre Dame St., Ste. 402; Box 429 (N0R 1A0); W; 1,542pd, 338fr (Sw); 51¢; publisher Gary Baxter; editor Gerry Harvieux; tel (519) 728-1082; fax (519) 728-4551

Belleville/Trenton: *The Belleville-Trenton Community Press* — Box 88, Stirling (K0K 3E0); W/Sa; 182pd, 11,066fr (VCC); $10.65; C; publisher John Seckar; editor Alan Coxwell; tel (613) 967-8467; fax (613) 395-2992

Blenheim: *Blenheim News-Tribune* — 62 Talbot St. W.; Box 160 (N0P 1A0); W; 2,579pd (ABC); 36¢; publisher & editor G S (Gord) Laurie; tel (519) 676-3321; fax (519) 676-3454

Bolton/Caledon: *Bolton Enterprise* — 2 Marconi Ct., Unit 13; Box 99, Bolton (L7E 5T1); Su; 60pd, 10,500fr (Sw); 82¢; publisher Bill Anderson; editor William Whitbread; tel (905) 857-3433; fax (905) 857-5002

Bothwell: *Bothwell Times* — 254 Main St.; Box 40 (N0P 1C0); W; 461pd, 200fr (VCP); 48¢; publisher Denise Thibeault; editor Peter Epp; tel (519) 683-4485; fax (519) 683-4355

Bowmanville: *The Bowmanville Canadian Statesman* — 62 Kings St. W.; Box 190 (L1C 3K9); W; 5,053pd (Est); 28¢; publisher Rick James; editor Peter Parrott; tel (905) 623-3303; fax (905) 623-6161

Bracebridge: *Bracebridge Examiner* — 16 Manitoba St.; Box 1049 (P1L 1S1); W; 4,547pd, 100fr (VCP); 72¢; C; publisher Edward Britton; editor Joe Fullerton; tel (705) 645-8771; fax (705) 645-1718

Bracebridge: *The Herald-Gazette* — 34 E.P. Lee Drive (P1L 1V6); W; 4,088pd, 510fr (ABC); 62¢; publisher Don Smith; editor Dave Opavsky; tel (705) 645-4463; fax (705) 645-3928

Bracebridge/Muskoka: *Muskoka Advance* — 34 E.P. Lee Dr.; Box 1600, Bracebridge (P1L 1V6); Su; 21,384fr (VCC); 80¢; publisher Don Smith; editor Dave Opavsky; tel (705) 645-4463; fax (705) 645-3928

Brampton: *Brampton Guardian* — 685 Queen St. W. (L6V 1A1); W; 900pd, 59,100fr (Sw); 42¢; F; 400pd, 59,600fr (Sw); 42¢; Su; 800pd, 59,200fr (Sw); 42¢; C; publisher Ken Nugent; editor Lorne Drury; managing editor John McGhie; tel (905) 454-4344; fax (905) 454-4385

Brantford/Brant Co.: *The Brant News* — 301-446 Grey St.; Box 2079, Brantford (N3T 5Y6); Tu; 41,500fr (Est); $1.35; publisher Diane Geerlinks; editor Ron Johnson; tel (519) 759-5550; fax (519) 759-8425

Brighton: *Brighton Independent* — 1 Young St.; Box 1030 (K0K 1H0); Tu; 2,144pd, 120fr (VCP); $11.20; publisher Stasha Conolly; editor Ernst Kuglin; tel (613) 475-0255; fax (613) 475-4546

Burks Falls/South River: *Burks Falls/Powassan/Almaguin News* — 183 Ontario St.; Box 518, Burks Falls (P0A 1C0); W; 5,252pd, 202fr (VCP); 65¢; publisher J Peter Barr; editor Allan Dennis; tel (705) 382-3843; fax (705) 382-3440

Burlington: *The Burlington Post* — 2321 Fairview St. (L7R 2E3); W; 900pd, 51,500fr (Sw); $2.27; F; 400pd, 52,000fr (Sw); $2.27; Su; 200pd, 52,200fr (Sw); $2.27; C; publisher Andrew Cook; editor Jill Davis; tel (905) 632-4444; fax (905) 632-6604

Caledon: *Caledon Citizen* — 25 Queen St. N., Bolton (L7E 1C1); W; 1,540pd, 5,860fr (Sw); 60¢; publisher Bruce Haire & Pamela A Claridge; editor Mark Pavilons; tel (905) 857-6626; fax (905) 857-6363

Caledonia: *The Grand River Sachem* — 3 Sutherland St. W. (N3W 1C1); Tu; 2,074pd, 107fr (VCP); 53¢; publishers Barbara Martindale; editor Andrea Lucas; tel (905) 765-4441; fax (905) 765-3651

Cambridge: *Cambridge Times* — 240 Holiday Inn Dr., Units B & C (N3C 3X4); W/Sa; 31,079fr (VCC); $16.24; C; publisher Ken Bosveld; editor Jeff Hurst; tel (519) 651-2390; fax (519) 651-2358

Campbellford: *Campbellford Herald* — 18 Bridge St.; Box 970 (K0L 1L0); Tu; 2,660pd (Est); 56¢; publisher Cheryl McMenemy; editor John Campbell; tel (705) 653-3684; fax (705) 653-5044

Campbellford/Havelock/Hastings/Norwood: *The Campbellford Community Press* — Box 88, Stirling (K0K 3E0); Sa; 56pd, 10,361fr (VCC); $6.86; C; publisher John Seckar; editor Alan Coxwell; tel (705) 653-5391; fax (613) 395-2992

Carleton Place: *The Carleton Place Canadian* — 53 Bridge St.; Box 430 (K7C 3P5); W; 3,653pd (ABC); 55¢; publisher Jeff Maguire; editor Ryland Coyne; tel (613) 257-1303; fax (613) 257-7373

Chapleau: *Sentinel* — 17 Young St.; Box 158 (P0M 1K0); Th; 1,300pd, 25fr (Sw); 39¢; publisher & editor Rene C Decosse; tel (705) 864-0640; fax (705) 864-2319

Chesley: *Enterprise* — 73 1st Ave. S.; Box 250 (N0G 1L0); W; 1,526pd, 28fr (ABC); 49¢; publisher William Twaddle; editor Mary Golem; tel (519) 363-2414; fax (519) 363-2726

Chesterville: *The Chesterville Record* — King St.; Box 368 (K0C 1H0); W; 2,397pd, 126fr (VCP); 48¢; C; publisher Robin R Morris; editor Elizabeth Moreau; tel (613) 448-2321; fax (613) 448-3260

Clinton: *Clinton News-Record* — 53 Albert St.; Box 39 (N0M 1L0); W; 3,149pd, 144fr (VCP); 60¢; publisher Tom Flynn; editor T David Emslie; tel (519) 482-3442; fax (519) 482-7341

Cobden: *The Cobden Sun* — 36 Crawford St.; Box 100 (K0J 1K0); W; 2,087pd, 8fr (VCP); 50¢; publishers Gerald J Tracey & Ron R Tracey; editor Marie Zettler; tel (613) 646-2380; fax (613) 628-3291

Cochrane: *Northland Post* — 142 Third St.; Box 10 (P0L 1C0); W; 2,400pd, 206fr (ABC); $5.46; C; publishers Daniel Brisson & Michael Palangio & William Cavell; general manager Lynne Parent; editor Janet Clermont; tel (705) 272-4363; fax (705) 272-2935

Colborne: *Colborne Chronicle* — 11 King St. E.; Box 208 (K0K 1F0); W; 1,700pd (Est); 56¢; publisher Cheryl McMenemy; editor Eileen Agryris; tel (905) 355-2843; fax (905) 355-1639

Collingwood/Creemore/Wagaga Beach/Stayner/Thornbury: *The Enterprise-Bulletin* — 77 St. Marie St.; Box 98, Collingwood (L9Y 3Z4); W/Sa; 5,051pd, 32fr (ABC); 82¢; C; publisher Michael Pearce; editor Ian Chadwick; tel (705) 445-4617; fax (705) 444-6477

Cornwall: *Le Journal de Cornwall* — 113 Montreal Rd. (K6H 1B2); Th; 2,073pd (ODC); 85¢; publisher & editor Roger Duplantie; tel (613) 938-1433; fax (613) 938-2798

Creemore: *The Creemore Star* — 3 Caroline St. W.; Box 70 (L0M 1G0); W; 1,450pd, 351fr (VCP); 54¢; C; publisher Gordon Badger; editor David Norris; tel (705) 322-1871; fax (705) 722-0846

Deep River: *The North Renfrew Times* — 25 A Champlain St.; Box 310 (K0J 1P0); W; 2,666pd, 102fr (VCP); 57¢; publisher Deep River Community Association; editor Kathy Hughes; tel (613) 584-4161; fax (613) 584-1062

Delhi: *Delhi News Record* — 222 Argyle Ave. (N4B 2Y2); W; 3,371pd, 729fr (Sw); 65¢; publisher Bart Crandon; editor Michael Jiggens; tel (519) 582-2510; fax (519) 582-4040

Dorchester: *The Signpost* — 15 Jane St. (N0L 1G2); W; 2,242pd (VCP); 55¢; publisher Fred Huxley; editor Meredith MacLeod; tel (519) 268-7337; fax (519) 268-3260

Drayton: *The Community News* — Wellington & Wood Sts.; Box 189 (N0G 1P0); W; 3,027pd (Est); 45¢; publisher William H Adsett; editor Cathy Bolger; tel (519) 638-3066; fax (519) 843-7607

Dresden: *North Kent Leader* — 254 Main St.; Box 490 (N0P 1M0); W; 1,929pd, 206fr (VCP); 58¢; publisher Denise Thibeault; editor Peter Epp; tel (519) 683-4485; fax (519) 683-4355

Dryden: *Dryden Observer* — Box 3009 (P8N 2Y9); Tu; 5,359pd, 147fr (ABC); 65¢; publisher Alex M Wilson; editor Sylvia Veal; tel (807) 223-2390; fax (807) 223-2907

Dundalk: *Herald* — 39 Proton St. N.; Box 280 (N0C 1B0); W; 549pd (Sw); 40¢; C; publisher Matthew Walls; editor Cathy Walls; tel (519) 923-2203; fax (519) 923-2747

Dundas: *Dundas Star* — 47 Cootes Dr. (L9H 1B5); W; 10,140fr (VCC); 97¢; publisher John Young; editor Debra Downey; tel (905) 628-6313; fax (905) 628-5485

Dunnville: *Dunnville Chronicle* — 131 Lock St. E.; Box 216 (N1A 2X5); W; 3,602pd, 3,712fr (ABC); 54¢; publisher David A Beattie; editor Angus Scott; tel (905) 774-5855; fax (905) 774-5744

Durham: *The Durham Chronicle* — 190 Elizabeth St. E.; Box 230 (N0G 1R0); W; 1,707pd, 43fr (ABC); 49¢; C; publisher Jim Merriam; editor Kris Svela; tel (519) 369-2504; fax (519) 369-3560

Dutton: *Dutton Advance* — 158 Main St.; Box 220 (N0L 1J0); W; 1,750pd (Est); 35¢; publisher Dan W Moore; editor Marlene Moore; tel (519) 762-2310

Eganville: *The Eganville Leader* — 154 John St.; Box 310 (K0J 1T0); W; 5,999pd, 2,500fr (Sw); 63¢; C; publishers Gerald J Tracey & Ron R Tracey; editor Ray Stamplecoski; tel (613) 628-2332; fax (613) 628-3291

Elliot Lake: *The Standard* — 14 Hillside Dr. S. (P5A 1M6); W; 5,323pd (Sw); 89¢; C; publisher Ray Ethelston; editor Bill Stevenson; tel (705) 848-7195; fax (705) 848-0249

Elmira: *The Elmira Independent* — 15 King St. (N3B 2R1); M; 5,531pd, 200fr (VCP); $11.65; C; publisher & editor Bob Verdun; general manager Hugh Weltz; tel (519) 669-5155; fax (519) 669-5928

Elmvale: *Elmvale Lance* — 3 Caroline St. W.; Box 70, Creemore (L0M 1G0); W; 1,450pd (Est); 35¢; C; publisher Gordon Badger; editor Joan Doyle; tel (705) 466-3431; fax (705) 466-3433

Erin/Hillsburgh: *The Erin Advocate* — 45 Main St.; Box 160, Erin (N0B 1T0); W; 1,800pd (Est); 57¢; C; publisher & editor Norman Philippsen; tel (519) 833-9603; fax (519) 833-9605

Espanola: *Mid-North Monitor* — 407 Centre St. (P5E 1J5); W; 3,274pd, 72fr (VCP); 40¢; publisher & editor Robert J Gordon; tel (705) 869-2860; fax (705) 869-5140

Essex: *Free Press* — 16 Centre St. (N8M 1N9); W; 4,400pd (Sw); 64¢; publisher & editor W R Brett; tel (519) 776-8511; fax (519) 776-4014

Etobicoke: *Etobicoke Guardian* — 252 Galaxy Blvd. (M9W 5R8); W/Sa; 2,500pd, 64,500fr (Sw); $2.34; C; publisher Betty Carr; editor Sal Bommarito; tel (416) 675-4390; fax (416) 675-9296

Exeter: *Times Advocate* — 424 Main St.; Box 850 (N0M 1S0); W; 4,511pd, 50fr (VCP); 68¢; publisher Jim Beckett; editor Adrian Harte; tel (519) 235-1331; fax (519) 235-0766

Fenelon Falls: *Fenelon Falls Gazette* — 45 Colborne St.; Box 340 (K0M 1N0); W; 1,590pd, 169fr (VAC); 13¢; C; publisher Andrea Douglas; editor Karen Hogg; tel (705) 887-2940; fax (705) 887-4531

Fergus: *The Wellington Advertiser* — 180 St. Andrew E.; Box 252 (N1M 2W8); M; 24,989fr (CCAB); 90¢; publisher William H Adsett; editor W H Adsett; tel (519) 843-5410; fax (519) 843-7607

Fergus/Elora: *The Fergus-Elora News Express* — 390 Tower St. N.; Box 130, Fergus (N1M 2W7); W; 3,476pd, 509fr (VCP); 65¢; publisher John Roberts; editor Lars Eedy; tel (519) 843-1310; fax (519) 843-1334

Flamborough: *The Flamborough Review* — 30 Main St. N.; Box 20, Waterdown (L0R 2H0); W; 3,862pd, 405fr (VCP); 63¢; publisher & editor Calvin Bosveld; tel (905) 689-4841; fax (905) 689-3110

Flesherton: *Advance* — 39 Proton St. N.; Box 280, Dundalk (N0C 1B0); Th; 172pd (Sw); 35¢; C; publisher Matthew Walls; editor Cathy Walls; tel (519) 923-2203; fax (519) 923-2747

Forest: *Forest Standard* — 1 King St. W.; Box 220 (N0N 1J0); W; 3,735pd, 41fr (VCP); 36¢; publisher & editor Jack Boyd; tel (519) 786-5242; fax (519) 786-4884

Fort Erie: *The Times-Review* — 450 Garrison Rd., Unit 5; Box 1219 (L2A 5Y2); Tu; 121pd, 11,044fr (VCC); 72¢; Sa; 112pd, 10,640fr (VCC); 72¢; C; publisher Earl Bateman; editor Gail Atkinson; tel (905) 871-3100/3106; fax (905) 871-5243

Fort Frances: *Fort Frances Times* — 116 First St.; Box 339 (P9A 3M7); W; 5,911pd, 207fr (ABC); $8.68; publisher J R Cumming; editor Michael Behan; tel (807) 274-5373; fax (807) 274-7286

Frankford: *Advertiser* — Box 270 (K0K 2C0); Th; 875pd, 174fr (Est); 12¢; publisher & editor Larry L Embury; tel (613) 398-8353

Gananoque: *The Reporter* — 79 King St. E. (K7G 1E8); W; 3,793pd (ABC); 67¢; publisher Paul G Scott; editor Mark King; tel (613) 382-2156; fax (613) 382-3010

Georgetown/Halton Hills: *Georgetown Independent/Acton Free Press* — 211 Armstrong Ave., Georgetown (L7G 4X5); W; 550pd, 16,450fr (Sw); $1.44; Su; 400pd, 16,600fr (Sw); $1.44; publisher Ken Nugent; editor Lorne Drury; tel (905) 873-0301; fax (905) 873-0398

Georgina: *Keswick Georgina Advocate* — 179 Simcoe Ave., Unit 4, Keswick (L4P 3S6); M; 247pd, 12,564fr (VCC); 83¢; publisher Mark Skelton; editor John Slykhuis; tel (905) 476-7753; fax (905) 476-5785

Geraldton/Longlac: *Geraldton-Longlac Times Star* — 401 Main St.; Box 490, Geraldton (P0T 1M0); W; 1,504pd, 39fr (VCP); 42¢; publisher & editor Douglas S Brydges; tel (807) 854-1919; fax (807) 854-1682

Glencoe: *Transcript & Free Press* — 243 Main St.; Box 400 (N0L 1M0); W; 2,856pd, 86fr (VCP); $6.16; publisher & editor Walter Vanderwaak; tel (519) 287-2615; fax (519) 287-2408

Glengarry County: *The Glengarry News Ltd.* — 3 Main St.; Box 10, Alexandria (K0C 1A0); W; 7,186pd (ABC); 70¢; publisher Joe Banks; editor Greg Kielec; tel (613) 525-2020; fax (613) 525-3824

Goderich: *The Goderich Signal-Star* — 120 Huckins St. Industrial Park; Box 220 (N7A 4B6); W; 5,288pd, 329fr (VCP); $50.54; C; publisher Tom Flynn; general manager Dave Sykes; tel (519) 524-2614; fax (519) 524-5145

Grand Bend/Zurich: *The Lakeshore Advance* — 27 Main St.; Box 190, Zurich (N0M 2T0); W; 2,812pd, 115fr (VCP); $6.72; C; publisher Tom Flynn; editor Patrick Raftis; tel (519) 236-4312; fax (519) 236-7558

Grand Valley: *Star & Vidette* — 14 Mill St., Orangeville (L9O 2M3); W; 1,100fr (Est); 23¢; publisher Pamela A Claridge; editor Wes Kellar; tel (519) 941-2230

Gravenhurst: *The Gravenhurst News* — 320 Muskoka Rd. N.; Box 609 (P1P 1T9); W; 2,015pd, 267fr (VCP); 69¢; publisher Gord Lomas; editor Dave Opavsky; tel (705) 687-2259; fax (705) 645-3928

Greater Kingston: *The Heritage* — 748 Bath Rd., Kingston (K7M 4Y2); Tu; 33pd, 29,567fr (Sw); 90¢; C; publisher Darryl Cembal; tel (613) 389-8884; fax (613) 389-1870

Grimsby: *The Grimsby Independent* — 19 Adelaide St.; Box 310 (L3M 4G5); W; 4,171pd, 202fr (VCP); 76¢; C; publisher Earl Bateman; editor Julie Hendricks; tel (905) 945-9264; fax (905) 945-0540

Guelph: *Guelph Tribune* — 650 Woodlawn Rd., Units 11 & 12 (N1K 1B8); W/Sa; 33,958fr (VCC); $1.49; C; publisher Ken Bosveld; editor Chris Clark; tel (519) 763-3333; fax (519) 763-4814

Haldimand: *Regional News This Week* — 345 Argyle St. S., Caledonia (N3W 1L8); W; 17,300fr (Sw); 59¢; publisher Kevan S Pickup; editor Chris Pickup; tel (905) 765-4210; fax (905) 765-3563

Haldimand: *The Haldimand Press* — 42 Talbot St. W.; Box 100, Cayuga (N0A 1E0); W; 4,332pd, 29fr (VCP); 50¢; publisher & editor Robert G Hall; tel (905) 768-3111; fax (905) 768-3340

Haliburton: *Haliburton County Echo* — York St.; Box 360 (K0M 1S0); Tu; 4,561pd, 126fr (VCP); 53¢; publisher Len Pizzey; editor Martha Perkins; tel (705) 457-1037; fax (705) 457-3275

Haliburton Co.: *The Times* — Bobcaygeon Rd. N.; Box 97, Minden (K0M 2K0); M; 4,129pd (Est); 48¢; publisher & editor Jack Brezina; tel (705) 286-1288; fax (705) 286-4768

Hamilton: *Hamilton Mountain News* — 333 Arvin Ave., Stoney Creek (L8E 2M6); W; 43,086fr (VCC); $1.57; C; publisher John Young; editor Diana Hutton; tel (905) 523-5800; fax (905) 523-4014

Hanover: *Hanover Post* — 413 18th Ave. (N4N 3S5); Tu; 4,707pd, 2fr (ABC); 76¢; C; publisher Marie David; editor Mike Turner; tel (519) 364-2001; fax (519) 364-6950

Harriston/Minto Twp: *The Harriston Review* — 44 Arthur St. E.; Box 370, Harriston (N0G 1Z0); Tu; 1,079pd (VCP); 40¢; C; publisher & editor Clive Williams; tel (519) 338-2341; fax (519) 338-3130

Harrow/South Colchester: *Harrow News* — 563 Queen St.; Box 310, Harrow (N0R 1G0); Tu; 1,392pd, 259fr (Sw); 37¢; publisher & editor Gary McKenzie; tel (519) 738-2542; fax (519) 738-3874

Hastings: *Hastings Star* — Box 250, Marmora (K0K 2M0); Tu; 52pd, 1,323fr (Sw); 65¢; C; publisher Joseph Cembal; editor Bill Freeman; tel (613) 472-2431; fax (613) 472-5026

Havelock: *Havelock Citizen* — Box 250, Marmora (K0K 2M0); Tu; 79pd, 2,146fr (Sw); 65¢; C; publisher Joseph Cembal; editor Nancy Powers; tel (613) 472-2431; fax (613) 472-5026

Hawkesbury: *Le Carillon* — 299 Principale St.; Box 1000 (K6A 3H1); W; 6,000pd, 4,000fr (Sw); 67¢; C; publisher & editor M A Paquette; tel (613) 632-4155; fax (613) 632-8601

Hawkesbury: *La Tribune-Express* — 176 Atlantique St.; Box 1000 (K6A 3H1); Sa; 22,700fr (Sw); 83¢; C; publisher La Cie D'Editon Ardre Paquette Inc.; general manager Bertrand Castonguay; editor Francois Legault; tel (613) 632-0191; fax (613) 632-6383

Hearst/Kapuskasing/Longlac/Geraldton/Hornepayne: *Le Nord* — 905 rue Georges; Box 2320, Hearst (P0L 1N0); W; 3,558pd, 95fr (Sw); $11.90; C; publisher & editor Omer Cantin; tel (705) 372-1233; fax (705) 362-5954

Hornepayne: *The Bear News* — 79 Front St.; Box 660 (P0M 1Z0); W; 500pd (Est); 38¢; publisher & editor Frank J Donney; tel (807) 868-2701; fax (807) 868-3337

Huntsville: *The Huntsville Forester* — 72 Main St. E.; Box 940 (P0A 1K0); W; 6,367pd, 105fr (ABC); $6.20; C; publisher Elizabeth Rice Aben; editor Ev Van Duuren; tel (705) 789-5541; fax (705) 789-9381

Huntsville: *The Huntsville Herald* — 59 Main St.; Box 789 (P1H 2B8); W; 216pd, 5,651fr (VCC); 18¢; publisher Don Smith; general manager Bill Allen; editor Heather Douglas; tel (705) 789-5578; fax (705) 789-1432

Ingersoll: *The Ingersoll Times* — 19 King St. W.; Box 38 (N5C 3K1); W; 3,252pd, 200fr (VCP); 56¢; editor Elizabeth Dadson; tel (519) 485-3631; fax (519) 485-6652

Innisfil Township: *Innisfil Scope* — Box 419, Stroud (L0L 2M0); W; 2,700pd, 150fr (Sw); 43¢; publisher Bruce R Haire; publisher John Archibald; editor Lorna Davis; tel (705) 458-4434; fax (705) 729-2541

Iroquois: *The Chieftain* — Shopping Plaza; Box 529 (K0E 1K0); W; 2,000fr (Sw); 47¢; publisher Brian Crawford; editor Shelley Cumberland; tel (613) 652-4395; fax (613) 652-2508

Iroquois Falls: *The Enterprise* — 231 Ambridge Dr.; Box 834 (P0K 1G0); W; 2,764pd, 115fr (ABC); $5.74; publisher William C Cavell; general manager Sherry Guillet; editor Frank Dagget; tel (705) 232-4081; fax (705) 232-4235

Kanata/Stittsville: *Kanata Kourier-Standard* — 3 Beaverbrook Rd., Kanata (K2K 1L2); F; 70pd, 19,339fr (CCAB); $9.80; C; publisher Angie Shepherd; general manager Fred Runge; managing editor Sally Gunther; tel (613) 591-3060; fax (613) 591-8503

Kapuskasing: *Northern Times* — 51 Riverside Dr. (P5N 1A7); W; 5,220pd, 46fr (Sw); 57¢; publisher Wayne Green; editor Wayne Major; tel (705) 335-2283; fax (705) 337-1222

Kemptville/Rideau Township: *The Weekly Advance* — 206 Prescott St.; Box 669, Kemptville (K0G 1J0); W; 4,950pd, 50fr (Sw); 59¢; publisher Garnet Crawford; editor Brian Crawford; tel (613) 258-3451; fax (613) 258-7734

Kincardine: *The Independent* — 840 Queen St.; Box 1240 (N2Z 2Z4); W; 2,848pd (VCP); $6.86; publisher & editor Eric Howald; tel (519) 396-3111; fax (519) 396-3899

Kincardine: *The Kincardine News* — 708 Queen St. (N2Z 2A3); W; 3,701pd, 188fr (VCP); 55¢; publisher Tom Flynn; editor Joy Manley; tel (519) 396-2963; fax (519) 396-3790

King Township/Vaughan: *The King Vaughan Weekly* — 237 Romina Dr., Unit 2, Concord (L4K 4V3); W; 76pd, 15,000fr (Est); $1.00; publisher Patrick Daley; editor Paul Russell; tel (905) 660-9556; fax (905) 660-9558

Kingsville: *The Kingsville Reporter* — 17 Chestnut St. (N9Y 1J9); Tu; 2,843pd, 120fr (VCP); 37¢; publisher Sims Publishing Inc.; editor Greg Sims; tel (519) 733-2211; fax (519) 733-6464

Kirkland Lake: *Kirkland Lake Gazette* — 101 Duncan Ave. N. (P2N 3N8); F; 7,375pd (Est); 49¢; publisher Dave Armstrong; editor Walter Franczyk; tel (705) 568-6397; fax (705) 568-4444

Lambeth: *News-Star* — 4287 Routledge St.; Box 490 (N0L 1S0); Th; 1,910pd (Est); 25¢; publisher & editor William A Seaton; tel (519) 652-3421; fax (519) 652-3421

Lanark: *Era* — 87 Clarence St. E.; Box 40 (K0G 1K0); Tu; 1,999pd (Est); 20¢; publisher & editor Wendy Vallillee; tel (613) 259-2220; fax (613) 259-3015

Leamington: *Leamington Post* — 27 Princess St.; Box 520 (N8H 3W5); W; 6,137pd, 222fr (Sw); $1.08; C; publisher Don Gage; editor Mike Thibodeau; tel (519) 326-4434; fax (519) 326-2171

Lincoln: *Lincoln Post-Express* — 4309 Central Ave.; Box 850, Beamsville (L0R 1B0); W; 2,568pd, 142fr (VCP); 69¢; publisher Earl Bateman; editor Julie Hendricks; tel (905) 563-5393; fax (905) 563-7977

Listowel: *The Listowel Banner* — 188 Wallace Ave. N.; Box 97 (N4W 3H2); W; 4,063pd, 87fr (VCP); 58¢; C; publisher Paul Teahen; editor Marion Duke; tel (519) 291-1660; fax (519) 291-3771

Lucknow: *The Lucknow Sentinel* — 619 Campbell St.; Box 400 (N0G 2H0); W; 1,950pd, 118fr (VCP); 45¢; publisher Tom Flynn; editor Pat Livingston; tel (519) 528-2822; fax (519) 528-3529

Madoc: *Madoc Review* — Box 250, Marmora (K0K 2M0); Tu; 102pd, 2,653fr (Sw); 65¢; C; publisher Joseph Cembal; editor Jeff Wilson; tel (613) 472-2431; fax (613) 472-5026

Manitoulin District: *Manitoulin Expositor* — Box 369, Little Current (P0P 1K0); W; 4,757pd, 307fr (ABC); 40¢; publisher R L McCutcheon; editor Ross Muir; tel (705) 368-2744; fax (705) 368-3822

Manitoulin Island: *Manitoulin Recorder* — Meredith St.; Box 235, Gore Bay (P0P 1H0); W; 4,128pd, 50fr (VCP); 53¢; publisher Margaret Sanderson; editor Theresa Noble; tel (705) 282-2003; fax (705) 282-2432

Manitouwadge: *The Echo* — 22 Manitou Rd.; Box 550 (P0T 2C0); W; 1,176pd, 33fr (Est); 46¢; publisher B J Schermann; managing editor Francine Levesque; tel (807) 826-3788

Marathon: *The Marathon Mercury* — 91 Peninsula Rd.; Box 369 (P0T 2E0); Tu; 1,950pd, 10fr (Sw); 56¢; publisher Garry R McInnes; editor P Douglas Gale; tel (805) 229-1520; fax (805) 229-1595

Markdale: *The Markdale Standard* — 13 Toronto St. N.; Box 465 (N0C 1H0); W; 1,338pd, 26fr (ABC); 49¢; publisher Jim Merriam; editor Mel Gateman; tel (519) 986-3151; fax (519) 986-4642

Markham: *Markham Economist & Sun* — 9 Heritage Rd. (L3P 1M3); W; 475pd, 32,644fr (Sw); $2.06; Sa; 475pd, 34,271fr (Sw); $2.00; publisher Patricia Pappas; editor Jo Ann Stevenson; tel (905) 294-2200; fax (905) 294-1538

Marmora: *Marmora Herald* — Box 250 (K0K 2M0); Tu; 129pd, 1,796fr (Sw); 65¢; C; publisher Joseph Cembal; editor Nancy Powers; tel (613) 472-2431; fax (613) 472-5026

Meaford: *Express* — 68 Sykes St. N. (N4L 1R2); W; 2,672pd, 20fr (ABC); 52¢; publisher Roderick (Rod) Brebner; editor Scott Woodhouse; tel (519) 538-1421; fax (519) 538-5028

Midland/Penetanguishene: *The Free Press* — 248 First St.; Box 37, Midland (L4R 4K6); W/F; 5,699pd (ABC); 82¢; publisher Wayne Campbell; editor Paul Welch; tel (705) 526-5431; fax (705) 526-1771

Mildmay/Hanover/Walkerton: *Town and Country Crier* — 100 Elora St.; Box 190, Mildmay (N0G 2J0); W; 1,800pd (Est); $4.00; publisher & editor John H Hafermehl; tel (519) 367-2681; fax (519) 367-5417

Milton: *The Canadian Champion* — 191 Main St.; Box 248 (L9T 1N7); W; 4,060pd, 9,740fr (Sw); $1.61; F; 11,500fr (Sw); $1.61; publisher Ian Oliver; editor Rob Kelly; tel (905) 878-2341; fax (905) 878-4943

Mississauga: *The Mississauga News* — 3145 Wolfedale Rd. (L5C 3A9); W; 2,427pd, 111,498fr (Sw); $3.13; F; 103pd, 103,525fr (Sw); $3.13; Su; 103pd, 103,936fr (Sw); $3.13; publisher Ron Lenyk; editor Judy Hughes; tel (905) 273-8111; fax (905) 273-4991

Mitchell: *The Mitchell Advocate* — 42 Montreal St.; Box 669 (N0K 1N0); W; 2,865pd, 180fr (VCP); 58¢; publisher Tom Flynn; editor Andy Bader; tel (519) 384-8431; fax (519) 348-8836

Morrisburg: *The Morrisburg Leader* — Hwy. 2, 31 Shopping Centre; Box 891 (K0C 1X0); W; 2,600pd, 250fr (Sw); 57¢; publisher & editor Art Laurin; tel (613) 543-2987; fax (613) 543-3643

Mount Forest: *Confederate* — 277 Main St. S.; Box 130 (N0G 2L0); W; 2,634pd, 50fr (VCP); 59¢; publisher J W Eedy Publications; editor Lynne Pinnegar; tel (519) 323-1550; fax (519) 323-4548

Napanee: *The Napanee Beaver* — 72 Dundas St. E. (K7R 1H9); W; 4,937pd, 174fr (VCP); 65¢; Su; 17,087fr (Sw); 65¢; C; publisher Jean M Morrison; editor Ross Lees; tel (613) 354-6641; fax (613) 354-2622

New Liskeard: *Temiskaming Speaker* — 18 Wellington St.; Box 580 (P0J 1P0); W; 7,303pd (Est); 64¢; C; publisher David Armstrong; editor Gordon Brock; tel (705) 647-6791; fax (705) 647-9669

Newmarket: *The Newmarket-Aurora Era-Banner* — 580 Steven Ct.; Box 236 (L3Y 4X1); Tu; 54,000pd (Sw); $34.16; Th; 44,000pd (Sw); $34.16; Su; 55,000pd (Sw); $34.16; C; publisher Bruce Annan; editor Brenda Larson; tel (905) 853-8888; fax (905) 853-4626

Niagara-on-the-Lake: *The Niagara Advance* — 1501 Hwy. 55; Box 430, Virgil (L0S 1T0); Tu; 5,600fr (VCC); 45¢; C; publisher G Earl Bateman; general manager Mark Dawson; editor Douglas Morton; tel (905) 468-3283; fax (905) 468-3137

Nipigon/Red Rock/Dorion: *Nipigon-Red Rock Gazette* — 145 Railway St.; Box 1057, Nipigon (P0T 2J0); Tu; 1,652pd (Est); 56¢; publisher Sandy Harbinson; editor Cindy Laundry; tel (807) 887-3583; fax (807) 887-3720

North Leeds: *The Rideau Review* — Main St.; Box 220, Elgin (K0G 1E0); F; 126pd, 9,101fr (VCC); 49¢; publisher & editor David Morris; tel (613) 359-5544; fax (613) 359-6123

North York: *North York Mirror* — 10 Tempo Ave., Willowdale (M2H 2N8); W/Su; 2,780pd, 101,220fr (Sw); $3.37; publisher Betty Carr; editor David Fuller; tel (416) 493-4400; fax (416) 493-4703

Northern Ontario: *Wawatay News* — 16 5th Ave.; Box 1180, Sioux Lookout (P8T 1B7); Th; 5,500pd (Est); $10.78; publisher Wawatay Communications Society; editor Bryan Phelan; tel (807) 737-2951; fax (807) 737-3224

Northumberland Co.: *East Northumberland* — 1 Young St.; Box 1030, Brighton (K0K 1H0); Tu; 2,144pd, 13,856fr (Sw); $12.60; publisher Stasha Conolly; editor Ernst Kuglin; tel (613) 475-0255; fax (613) 475-4546

Norwich: *The Norwich Gazette* — 46 Main St. W.; Box 459 (N0J 1P0); W; 1,585pd, 100fr (VCP); 53¢; editor Franklyn Smith; tel (519) 863-2334; fax (519) 863-3229

Norwood: *Norwood Register* — Box 250, Marmora (K0K 2M0); Tu; 74pd, 2,701fr (Sw); 65¢; C; publisher Joseph Cembal; editor Bill Freeman; tel (613) 472-2431; fax (613) 472-5026

Oakville: *Oakville Beaver* — 467 Speers Rd. (L6K 3S4); W; 20,120pd, 2,880fr (Sw); $1.91; F; 20,120pd, 10,880fr (Sw); $2.19; Su; 39,000fr (Sw); $2.33; publisher Ian Oliver; editor Norman Alexander; tel (905) 845-3824; fax (905) 845-3085

Oakville: *Oakville Free Press Journal* — 1158 S. Service Rd. W. (L6L 5T7); Tu; 37,000fr (Est); $1.85; publisher Arnold Huffman; editor Don Redmond; tel (905) 827-2244; fax (905) 827-2308

Orangeville: *Orangeville Citizen* — 14 Mill St. (L9W 2M3); W; 9,400fr (Est); 60¢; C; publisher Pamela A Claridge; editor Sheila Duncan; tel (519) 941-2230; fax (519) 941-9361

Orangeville: *The Orangeville Banner* — 37 Mill St. (N0J P0I); W/F; 6,276pd, 146fr (ABC); $11.90; publisher David J Mitchell; editor Steve Harron; tel (519) 941-1350; fax (519) 941-9600

Orono: *Weekly Times* — 5310 Main St.; Box 209 (L0B 1M0); W; 137pd, 908fr (VCC); 32¢; publisher & editor Troy Young; tel (519) 983-5301; fax (519) 983-5301

Oshawa/Whitby: *Oshawa Whitby This Week* — 865 Farewell Ave.; Box 481, Oshawa (L1H 7L5); W; 16,476pd, 70,524fr (Sw); $3.47; F; 16,476pd, 49,524fr (Sw); $3.23; Su; 16,476pd, 70,524fr (Sw); $3.61; publisher Timothy J Whittaker; editor Joanne Burghardt; tel (905) 579-4400; fax (905) 579-2238

Ottawa: *Hill Times* — 69 Sparks St. (K1P 5A5); Th; 11,320pd (Est); $2.22; publisher & editor Jim Creskey; publisher Ross Dickson; tel (613) 232-5925; fax (613) 232-9055

Ottawa: *Ottawa X Press* — 69 Sparks St. (K1P 5A5); W; 3pd, 28,813fr (VAC); $11.70; publisher & editor Jim Creskey; publisher Ross Dickson; managing editor Derek Raymaker; tel (613) 237-8226; fax (613) 232-9055

Ottawa/Nepean: *Nepean Clarion* — 25B Northside Rd.; Box 5166, Nepean (K2H 8S1); Tu; 50pd, 42,950fr (Sw); $1.40; publisher & editor Matin Khan; tel (613) 820-3126/3128; fax (613) 820-6147

Palmerston: *Palmerston Observer* — 295 Main St.; Box 757 (N0G 2P0); W; 1,417pd, 181fr (Sw); 41¢; publisher Laverne Long; editor Rob MacKenzie; tel (519) 343-2440; fax (519) 343-2267

Paris/Princeton/St. George: *Paris Star* — 59 Grand River St. N., Paris (N3L 2M3); W; 5,380fr (Est); 52¢; publisher Andrea DeMeer; editor Colleen Bissett; tel (519) 442-7866; fax (519) 442-3100

Parkhill: *The Parkhill Gazette* — 165 King St.; Box 400 (N0M 2K0); W; 1,848pd, 125fr (VCP); 40¢; publisher Carl Hayter; editor Gord Whitehead; tel (519) 294-6264; fax (519) 294-6391

Parry Sound: *North Star* — 67 James St.; Box 370 (P2A 2X4); W; 6,500pd (Est); 75¢; publisher Fred Heidman; editor Jim Hanna; tel (705) 746-2104; fax (705) 746-8369

Pelham: *Pelham Herald* — Pelham St.; Box 550, Fonthill (L0S 1E0); W; 7,546fr (VCC); 95¢; C; publisher Martha Cepuch; editor Carolyn Mullin; tel (905) 892-6022; fax (905) 892-0502

Perth: *The Perth Courier* — 30 Gore St. E.; Box 156 (K7H 3E3); W; 5,941pd (ABC); 65¢; publisher John Clement; editor Maureen Pegg; tel (613) 267-1100; fax (613) 267-3986

Peterborough: *Peterborough This Week* — 621 The Parkway; Box 2098 (K9J 7K2); Tu; 2,300pd, 1,900fr (Sw); $1.76; Th; 2,300pd, 34,200fr (Sw); $1.74; Su; 2,300pd, 40,200fr (Sw); $1.76; C; publisher John Sturrup; editor Harvey Spry; tel (705) 749-3383; fax (705) 749-0074

Petrolia: *Petrolia Topic* — 4182 Petrolia Line; Box 40 (N0N 1R0); W; 2,389pd (Est); 58¢; publisher Denise Thibeault; editor David Pattenaude; tel (519) 882-1770; fax (519) 882-3212

Pickering/Ajax/Whitey: *Pickering's Bay News* — 1730 McPherson Ct., Unit 18, Pickering (L1W 3E6); W; 4,000pd, 17,500fr (Est); $1.71; publisher Duncan Weir; editor Hal Baine; tel (905) 839-8087; fax (905) 839-8135

Picton: *Gazette* — 267 Main St.; Box 80 (K0K 2T0); Tu; 4,562pd, 135fr (VCP); 68¢; publisher Jean M Morrison; editor Kevin Wood; tel (613) 476-3201; fax (613) 476-3464

Port Colborne: *The Port Colborne News* — 21 Charlotte St. Upper; Box 130 (L3K 5V8); W; 60pd, 10,716fr (VCC); 68¢; C; publisher Sheila Littlewood; editor Paul Patterson; tel (905) 835-2411; fax (905) 835-2717

Port Dover: *Port Dover Maple Leaf* — 351 Main St.; Box 70 (N0A 1N0); W; 4,475pd, 500fr (Sw); $9.80; publisher Stan Morris; general manager Paul Morris; editor Andrew Bailey; tel (519) 583-0112; fax (519) 583-3200

Port Elgin: *Beacon Times* — 694 Goderich St.; Box 580 (N0H 2C0); W; 3,003pd, 36fr (ABC); 73¢; publisher Jim Merriam; editor Randy Derry; tel (519) 832-9001; fax (519) 389-4793

Port Hope/Cobourg: *Northumberland News* — 884 Division St., Bldg. 9, Unit 7, Cobourg (K9A 4J9); W; 1,177pd, 19,823fr (Sw); 58¢; Su; 1,177pd, 17,323fr (Sw); 63¢; publisher Tim Whittaker; editor Joanne Burghardt; tel (905) 373-7355; fax (905) 373-4719

Port Perry/Scugog Twp.: *The Port Perry Star* — 188 Mary St., Port Perry (L9L 1B7); Tu; 4,222pd, 158fr (VCP); 70¢; C; publisher J Peter Hvidsten; editor Scott Anderson; tel (905) 985-7383; fax (905) 985-3708

Prescott: *The Prescott Journal* — 231 King St. W.; Box 549 (K0E 1T0); W; 2,983pd (VCP); $20.56; C; publisher John Morris; editor Bruce Bonham; tel (613) 925-4265; fax (613) 925-3472

Rainy River: *Rainy River Record* — Box 188 (P0W 1L0); W; 1,500pd (VCC); $4.95; publisher Jim R Cumming; editor Ken Johnston; tel (807) 852-3366/3337; fax (807) 852-4434

Red Lake District: *The District News* — Box 328, Red Lake (P0V 2M0); Tu; 2,620pd (Est); 49¢; C; publishers & editors Bob Axford & Rick Smit; tel (807) 727-2618; fax (807) 727-3717

III-32 **Ontario** *Canadian Weeklies*

Renfrew: *The Renfrew Mercury* — Box 400 (K7V 4A8); W; 6,023pd, 113fr (ABC); $8.40; publisher Fred Runge; editor Elaine Dick; tel (613) 432-3655; fax (613) 432-6689

Richmond Hill: *The Richmond Hill/Thornill/ Vaughan Liberal* — 9350 Yonge St.; Box 390 (L4C 4Y6); W/Su; 64,000fr (Sw); $1.78; publisher Bruce Annan; editor Debora Kelly; tel (905) 881-3373; fax (905) 881-9924

Ridgetown: *Ridgetown Dominion* — 2 Main St. E.; Box 400 (N0P 2C0); W; 2,289pd, 200fr (VCP); 54¢; publisher Larry Koziana; editor Keith Knight; tel (519) 674-3232; fax (519) 674-5131

Rockland/Orleans/Gloucester/Cumberland: *The Star* — 1455 Youville Dr., Rm. 209, Orleans (K1C 4R1); W; 44,100fr (Sw); $1.73; publisher Publications Dumont; editor Regina Benhk; tel (613) 446-5196; fax (613) 830-1116

Rodney: *The Rodney Mercury* — 11 Ebenezer St. W.; Box 400, West Lorne (N0L 2C0); W; 644pd (Sw); 45¢; publisher Larry Koziana; editor Keith Knight; tel (800) 263-9726; fax (519) 768-2927

Russell Villager/Township: *Russell Villager* — Box 550, Russell (K4R 1E1); Th; 1,254pd, 36fr (VCP); 38¢; C; publisher Robin Morris; editor John Nelson; tel (613) 445-3805; fax (613) 445-3843

St. Marys: *Journal Argus* — 48-50 Water St. S.; Box 1030 (N4X 1B7); W; 3,454pd, 30fr (VCP); 66¢; publisher Lorne Eedy; editor Laura Santadrea; tel (519) 284-2440; fax (519) 284-3650

Sarnia/Lambton: *The Gazette* — 1383 Confederation St., Sarnia (N7T 5P1); Tu; 95pd, 21,405fr (CCAB); $1.02; publisher John Weese; editor Robert Browning; tel (519) 336-1100; fax (519) 336-1833

Scarborough: *The Scarborough Mirror* — 10 Tempo Ave., Willowdale (M2H 2N8); W/Su; 2,780pd, 101,220fr (Sw); $2.25; C; publisher Betty Carr; editor David Fuller; tel (416) 493-4400; fax (416) 493-6190

Seaforth: *The Huron Expositor* — 100 Main St. E.; Box 69 (N0K 1W0); W; 2,613pd, 156fr (VCP); 58¢; publisher Tom Flynn; editor Tim Cumming; tel (519) 527-0240; fax (519) 527-2858

Shelburne: *Free Press & Economist* — 167 Main St. W.; Box 100 (L0N 1S0); W; 3,400pd (Est); 39¢; publisher Thomas Claridge; editor Allan Claridge; tel (519) 925-2832; fax (519) 925-5500

Smiths Falls: *The Record News* — 65 Lorne St.; Box 158 (K7A 4T1); W; 4,213pd (ABC); 87¢; publisher Chuck Hudson; editor Michael Hayes; tel (613) 283-3182; fax (613) 283-7480

Southern Ontario: *The Woodbridge Advertiser Inc.* — R.R. 1, Palgrave (L0N 1P0); Tu; 6,500pd (Sw); 50¢; publisher & editor Karl Mallette; tel (905) 729-4501; fax (905) 729-3961

Stayner: *The Stayner Sun* — 250 Main St. E.; Box 80 (L0M 1S0); W; 1,088pd, 85fr (VCP); 55¢; publisher Fritz Schuller; editor Alicia Savage; tel (705) 428-2638; fax (705) 428-6909

Stirling: *Stirling News-Argus* — Box 250, Marmora (K0K 2M0); W; 9pd, 4,846fr (Sw); 65¢; C; publisher Joseph Cembal; editor Jeff Wilson; tel (613) 472-2431; fax (613) 472-5026

Stirling/Madoc/Marmora/Tweed: *The Stirling Community Press* — Box 88, Stirling (K0K 3E0); Sa; 182pd, 12,766fr (VCC); $7.56; C; publisher John Seckar; editor Alan Coxwell; tel (613) 395-3015; fax (613) 395-2992

Stittsville: *The Stittsville News* — 1488 Main St.; Box 610 (K2S 1A7); W; 3,647pd, 46fr (ABC); 50¢; publisher & editor John Curry; tel (613) 836-1357; fax (613) 836-1357

Stoney Creek: *Stoney Creek News* — 333 Arvin Ave. (L8E 2M6); W; 24,689fr (VCC); 81¢; publisher John Young; editor Stephen Beecroft; tel (905) 523-5800; fax (905) 523-4014

Stouffville/Uxbridge: *Stouffville/Uxbridge Tribune* — 6244 Main St., Stouffville (L4A 1E2); W; 480pd, 15,093fr (Sw); $1.42; Sa; 335pd, 12,371fr (Sw); $1.42; publisher Pat Pappas; editor JoAnn Stevenson; tel (905) 640-2100; fax (905) 640-5477

Strathroy: *The Age Dispatch* — 8 Front St. E. (N7G 1Y4); W; 4,938pd, 132fr (VCP); 57¢; C; publisher Steve Down; editor Dave Cameron; tel (519) 245-2370; fax (519) 245-1647

Sturgeon Falls: *The Tribune* — 162 King St.; Box 900 (P0H 2G0); Tu; 2,100pd (VCP); 60¢; publisher Len Barton; editor Suzanne Gammon; tel (705) 753-2930; fax (705) 753-5231

Sudbury: *Le Journal Le Voyageur* — 20 chemin Ste Anne (P3C 5N4); W; 3,619pd, 388fr (Sw); 91¢; publisher Guy Lemieux; editor Jacques des Becquets; tel (705) 673-3377; fax (705) 673-5854

Sudbury: *Northern Life* — 158 Elgin St. (P3E 3N5); W/F; 16,803pd, 27,702fr (CCAB); $1.62; Su; 16,926pd, 34,510fr (CCAB); $1.70; publisher John W Thompson; editor Carol Mulligan; tel (705) 673-5667; fax (705) 673-4652

Tavistock: *Gazette* — 119 Woodstock St. S.; Box 70 (N0B 2R0); W; 1,375pd (Est); 39¢; publisher & editor William J Gladding; tel (519) 655-2341; fax (519) 655-3070

Teeswater: *Teeswater News* — 13 Clinton St.; Box 250 (N0G 2S0); W; 1,546pd, 85fr (VCP); 43¢; publishers & editors Carol Helfenstein & Harry Helfenstein; tel (519) 392-6896; fax (519) 392-8345

Terrace Bay: *Terrace Bay Schreiber News* — 303 Scotia St.; Box 730 (P0T 2S0); Tu; 1,175pd (Est); 56¢; publisher Sandy Harbinson; editor Michael Scott; tel (807) 824-2021; fax (807) 824-2162

Thamesville: *Herald* — 65 London Rd.; Box 580 (N0P 2K0); W; 900pd (Sw); 25¢; publisher & editor Orval Schilbe; tel (519) 692-3825

Thornbury/Clarksburg: *Thornbury Courier-Herald* — 51 Bruce St. S.; Box 190, Thornbury (N0H 2P0); W; 1,400pd (Est); 52¢; publisher Roderick (Rod) Brebner; editor Rob Potter; tel (519) 599-3760; fax (709) 599-3214

Thorold/Allanburgh: *Thorold News* — 13 Front St. N., Thorold (L2V 3Y7); Tu; 1,994pd, 707fr (Est); 65¢; C; publisher Earl Bateman; editor Doug Todd; tel (416) 227-1141; fax (416) 227-0222

Thunder Bay: *Thunder Bay Post* — 1126 Roland St. (P7B 5M4); Tu; 49,000fr (Sw); $1.58; publisher Elizabeth Dougall; editor Simon Conolly; tel (807) 622-8588; fax (807) 622-2779

Tilbury: *The Tilbury Times* — 9 Prospect St.; Box 490 (N0P 2L0); W; 3,012pd, 288fr (Sw); 57¢; C; general manager Gary Baxter; tel (519) 682-0411; fax (519) 682-3633

Tillsonburg: *The Tillsonburg News* — 25 Townline Rd.; Box 190 (N4G 4H6); M; 5,344pd, 5,148fr (VCC); 47¢; W/F; 6,205pd, 549fr (VCC); 47¢; publisher Cam McKnight; editor Wendy Kudeba; tel (519) 688-6397; fax (519) 842-3511

Toronto: *L'Express* — 17 Carlaw Ave., 2nd Fl. (M4M 2R6); Tu; 5,000pd, 15,000fr (Est); $5.55; publisher Jean Mazare; editor Francois Bergeron; tel (905) 465-2107; fax (905) 465-3778

Toronto: *NOW* — 150 Danforth Ave. (M4K 1N1); Th; 1,817pd, 99,278fr (VAC); N/A; publisher Michael Hollett; general manager David Logan; editor Alice Klein; managing editors Ellie Kirzner & Glenn Wheeler; tel (416) 461-0871; fax (416) 461-2886

Tottenham: *Tottenham Times* — 34 Main St. W.; Box 310, Beeton (L0G 1A0); W; 2,275pd, 75fr (Sw); $9.24; C; publisher & editor Bruce Haire; publisher & general manager John Archibald; tel (905) 729-2287; fax (905) 729-2541

Trenton: *Contact* — Box 40, Astra (K0K 1B0); W; 4,000fr (Sw); $4.95; publisher Wing Commanders; editor Capt Charlene Fawcett; managing editor Jan Thistle; tel (613) 965-7248; fax (613) 965-7490

Trenton: *Trentonian & Tri-County News* — Quinte & Stewart St.; Box 130 (K8V 5R2); M/W/F; 8,020pd, 187fr (ABC); $14.42; C; publisher Garry Gordon; managing editor Barry Ellsworth; tel (613) 392-6501; fax (613) 392-0505

Tweed: *Tweed News* — 242 Victoria St. N.; Box 550 (K0K 3J0); W; 2,142pd, 15fr (VCP); 54¢; publisher & editor Ivy Hanna; tel (613) 478-2017; fax (613) 478-2749

Uxbridge: *Uxbridge Times-Journal* — 8 Church St.; Box 459 (L9P 1M9); W; 3,647pd, 264fr (VCC); 81¢; C; publisher Don MacLeod; managing editor Jim Belyea; tel (905) 852-9141; fax (905) 852-9341

Vankleek Hill: *The Review* — 41 High St.; Box 160 (K0B 1R0); W; 3,013pd, 669fr (VCP); 25¢; C; publisher & editor Louise Sproule; tel (613) 678-3327; fax (613) 678-2700

Walkerton: *Herald-Times* — 110 Durham St. E.; Box 190 (N0G 2V0); W; 3,287pd, 171fr (VCP); 60¢; publisher Tom Flynn; editor Ronald Wassink; tel (519) 881-1600; fax (519) 881-0276

Wallaceburg: *Courier Press* — 820 Dufferin Ave.; Box 410 (N8A 4X1); W; 11,367fr (VCC); 59¢; publisher John Weese; editor Gerry Harvieux; tel (519) 627-1488; fax (519) 627-0640

Wallaceburg/Dresden: *Wallaceburg News/ Weekender* — 222 Wellington St., Wallaceburg (N8A 4L5); W; 236pd, 8,222fr (VCC); 66¢; publisher Marjorie Fleming; editor Keith Knight; tel (519) 627-2243; fax (519) 627-6018

Warkworth: *Warkworth Journal* — 18 Bridge St. W.; Box 970, Campbellford (K0L 1L0); W; 800pd (Est); 50¢; publisher Cheryl McMenemy; editor John R Campbell; tel (705) 653-3684; fax (705) 653-5044

Waterloo: *Waterloo Chronicle* — 201-75 King St. S. (N2J 1P2); W; 96pd, 24,244fr (VCC); $1.13; C; publisher Rick Campbell; editor Melodee Martinuk; tel (519) 886-2830; fax (519) 886-9383

Waterloo/Brant/Oxford: *Ayr News* — 40 Piper St.; Box 40, Ayr (N0B 1E0); W; 4,250pd (Sw); 55¢; publisher James W Schmidt; editor John P Schmidt; tel (519) 632-7432; fax (519) 632-7743

Watford: *Watford Guide-Advocate* — 287 Main St.; Box 99 (N0M 2S0); W; 1,375pd, 70fr (VCP); 38¢; publisher & editor J H Aylesworth; tel (519) 876-2809; fax (519) 876-2322

Wawa: *The Algoma News Review* — 37 Ste. Marie St.; Box 528 (P0S 1K0); W; 1,850pd (Est); 40¢; publisher W R Avis; editor Gloria J Avis; tel (705) 856-2267; fax (705) 856-4952

West Lincoln Township: *West Lincoln Review* — 106 Griffin St. S.; Box 40, Smithville (L0R 2A0); W; 1,727pd, 200fr (VCP); 63¢; C; publisher Earl Bateman; editor Don Jackson; tel (905) 957-3315; fax (905) 957-0055

Westport/North Leeds Co.: *Rideau Valley Mirror* — 40 Main St.; Box 130, Westport (K0G 1X0); W; 2,511pd (Est); 48¢; publisher & editor Howie Crichton; tel (613) 273-8000; fax (613) 273-8001

Wheatley: *Wheatley Journal* — Box 10 (N0P 2P0); W; 1,360pd (Est); 28¢; publisher & editor R W Epplett; tel (519) 825-4541; fax (519) 825-4511

Whitby: *Whitby Free Press* — 131 Brock St. N.; Box 206 (L1N 5S1); W; 22pd, 27,057fr (VCP); $1.29; publisher Doug Anderson; editor Maurice Pifher; tel (905) 668-6111; fax (905) 668-0594

Wiarton: *The Wiarton Echo* — 573 Berford St.; Box 220 (N0H 2T0); W; 3,847pd, 90fr (ABC); 73¢; C; publisher William Twaddle; editor Keith Gilbert; tel (519) 534-1560; fax (519) 534-4616

Wilmot Township: *New Hamburg Independent* — 100 Huron St.; Box 670, New Hamburg (N0B 2G0); W; 3,145pd, 287fr (VCP); 71¢; publisher & editor Paul Knowles; tel (519) 662-1240; fax (519) 662-3521

Winchester: *Winchester Press* — 545 St. Lawrence; Box 399 (K0C 2K0); W; 4,372pd (VCP); 52¢; C; publisher J A H Morris; managing editor Allan Van Bridger; tel (613) 774-2524; fax (613) 774-3967

Windsor/Essex: *Le Rempart* — 7515 Forest Glade Dr., R.R. 2, Tecumseh (N8N 2M1); W; 1,685pd (ODC); 65¢; publisher & editor Jean Mongenais; tel (519) 948-4139

Wingham: *The Wingham Advance-Times* — 5 Diagonal Rd.; Box 390 (N0G 2W0); W; 1,869pd, 106fr (VCP); 58¢; C; publisher Hartley Coles; editor Cameron J Wood; tel (519) 357-2320; fax (519) 357-2900

PRINCE EDWARD ISLAND

Alberton: *West Prince Graphic* — Church St.; Box 339 (C0B 1B0); W; 2,135pd, 30fr (ABC); $9.66; C; publisher & editor Jim MacNeill; tel (902) 853-3320; fax (902) 853-3071

Montague: *The Eastern Graphic* — 9 Main St.; Box 790 (C0A 1R0); W; 5,508pd, 55fr (ABC); 80¢; C; publisher Jim MacNeill; editor Heather Moore; tel (902) 838-2515; fax (902) 838-4392

Summerside: *La Voix Acadienne* — 340 Court St.; Box 1420 (C1N 4K2); W; 1,100pd (Sw); 78¢; C; publisher & editor Marcia Enman; tel (902) 436-6005; fax (902) 888-3976

QUEBEC

Acton Vale: *La Penseede Bagot* — 962 St. Andre (J0H 1A0); Su; 12,350fr (Sw); 52¢; C; publisher & editor Michel DoRais; tel (514) 546-3271; fax (514) 546-3491

Ahuntsic: *Courrier-Ahuntsic* — 189 Ave. Laval, Laval (H7N 3V8); Su; 33,366fr (Est); 68¢; publisher Hebdos Transcontinental Inc.; editor Jacques Dion; tel (514) 667-4360; fax (514) 667-9498

Alma/Lac. St. Jean Co.: *Le Lac St. Jean* — 525 Ave. du Pont S.; Box 520, Alma (G8B 2T9); Su; 17,836fr (Est); 52¢; publisher Groupe Polyforme (1989) Inc.; editor Gaston Martin; tel (418) 668-4545; fax (418) 668-8522

Amqui: *L'Avant-Poste Gaspesien* — 73 St. Germain E.; Box 410, Rimouski (G5L 7C4); Su; 272pd, 8,323fr (Est); 56¢; publisher Groupe de Presse Bellavance; editor Claude Bellavance; tel (418) 723-4800; fax (418) 722-4078

Aylmer: *Le Regional d'Aylmer* — 79 Principale (J9H 3L6); W; 10,424fr (ODC); 48¢; C; publisher & editor Jacques Blais; tel (819) 684-0097; fax (819) 684-8634

Baie Comeau: *Le Nordic* — 896 Depuygalon (G5C 1N1); W; 10,500fr (Est); 48¢; C; publisher Paul Brisson; tel (418) 589-5900; fax (418) 589-8216

Baie Comeau: *Plein Jour sur Manicouagan* — 896 rue de Puyjaison (G5C 1W1); Sa; 12,600fr (Est); 52¢; publisher Paul Brisson; tel (418) 589-5900

Beloeil/St.-Hilaire: *L'Oeil Regional Inc.* — 393 Laurier Blvd., Beloeil (J3G 4H6); Sa; 27,000fr (ODC); 95¢; C; publisher & editor Guy Gilbert; tel (514) 467-1821; fax (514) 467-3087

Boucherville/Varennes: *La Releve* — 528 St. Charles St., Boucherville (J4B 3M5); Sa; 27,500fr (Sw); 67¢; publisher Charles Desmarteau; tel (514) 641-4844; fax (514) 641-4849

Buckingham/Gatineau: *The West-Quebec Post & Bulletin* — 585 James, Buckingham (J8L 2R7); W; 2,770pd, 214fr (VCC); 60¢; publishers Bob Phillips & Scott Stevenson; editor Katherine Aldred; tel (819) 986-8557; fax (819) 986-8167

Cap de la Madeleine: *Hebdo Journal* — 44 de La Fonderie (G8T 2E8); Su; 44,546fr (Sw); 92¢; publisher & editor Gilles Bechard; tel (819) 379-1490; fax (819) 379-0705

Cap de la Madeleine: *L'Hebdo Cap-de-La-Madeleine et Trois-Rivieres* — 44 de La Fonderie (G8T 2E8); M; 130pd, 35,876fr (ODC); 70¢; publisher Publi Hebdos Inc.; editor Claude Loranger; tel (819) 379-1490

Chibougamau/Chapais: *La Sentinelle de Chibouganau-chapais* — 329 3rd St.; Box 250, Chibougamau (G8P 2K7); Tu; 2,516pd, 50fr (ABC); 45¢; publisher Jacues Boivin; editor Guy Tremblay; tel (418) 748-6406

Chicoutimi: *Le Reveil a Chicoutimi* — 3388 Boul. St-Francois; Box 520, Jonquiere (G7X 7W4); Su; 30,702fr (Est); 68¢; publisher & editor Jacques Girard; tel (418) 695-2601; fax (418) 695-1391

Coaticook: *Le Progres de Coaticook* — 74 Child St.; Box 150 (J1A 259); Sa; 302pd, 7,281fr (Est); 41¢; publisher & editor Suzanne Jean-Marie; tel (819) 849-9846

Cowansville: *Le Guide de Cowansville* — 245 Rue Principale (J2K 1J4); Su; 16,000fr (Sw); 65¢; publisher & editor Andre DeGuire; tel (514) 263-5288/5488; fax (514) 263-9435

Dolbeau: *Le Point* — 1891 Sacre-Coeur (G8L 2A4); Su; 11,118fr (Est); 52¢; C; publisher & editor Jacques Girard; tel (418) 276-5110; fax (418) 276-5354

Dorion: *L'Echo* — Box 160 (J7V 5W1); Th; 22,500fr (Est); 70¢; publisher & editor Raymond LeFebvre; tel (514) 455-6111

Dorion: *L'Etoile de l'Outaouais-St-Lau* — 123 Dumont; Box 160 (J7V 5W1); Th; 30,000fr (Est); 56¢; publisher & editor Raymond Lefebvre; tel (514) 455-6111

Drummondville: *L'Express* — 1050, rue Cormier (J2C 2N6); Su; 38,600pd (Est); 85¢; publisher Hebdos Unimedia Inc.; editor Real Brodeur; tel (819) 478-8171; fax (819) 478-4306

Copyright ©1996 by the Editor & Publisher Co.

Drummondville: *La Parole* — 1050, rue Cormier (J2C 2N6); W; 28,800pd, 65fr (Est); 68¢; publisher Hebdos Unimedia Inc.; editor Real Brodeur; tel (819) 478-8171; fax (819) 478-4306

Farnham: *Journal des Rivieres* — 16 Riviere St., Bedford (J0J 1A0); M; 20,000fr (Est); 43¢; editor Denise Barrelet; tel (514) 248-3353

Farnham/Iberville: *L'Avenir de Brome Missisquoi* — 322 Rue Principale Est., Farnham (J2N 1L7); Sa; 8,726fr (Est); 47¢; publisher L'Avenir de Brome Missisquoi Inc.; tel (514) 293-3138; fax (514) 293-2093

Forestville: *Plein Jour Saguenay* — 896 rue de Puyjaion, Baie Comeau (G5C 1N1); M; 5,200pd (Est); 44¢; publisher Paul Brisson; tel (418) 589-5900

Gaspe: *Le Pharillon Voyageur* — 73 E. St. Germain; Box 410, Rimouski (G5L 7C4); Su; 257pd, 8,351fr (Est); 56¢; publisher Groupe Presse Bellavance; editor Claude Bellavance; tel (418) 368-3242; fax (418) 722-4078

Gaspe Coast: *Gaspe Peninsula SPEC* — 128 Main St.; Box 99, New Carlisle (G0C 1Z0); W; 3,200pd, 50fr (Sw); 65¢; C; publisher Sharon Farrell; general manager Joan Imhoff; editor Cynthia Dow; tel (418) 752-5400; fax (418) 752-6932

Gatineau: *La Revue de Gatineau* — 430 Boul. de L'Hopital, Ste. 106 (J8V 1T7); W; 35,811fr (Est); 85¢; C; publisher & editor Yves Blondin; tel (819) 568-7736; fax (819) 568-7038

Granby: *La Revue* — 45 Centre (J2G 5B4); Tu; 33,000fr (ODC); 73¢; C; publisher & editor Denis Lacasse; general manager & managing editor Louis Lamarre; tel (514) 372-3605; fax (514) 375-1249

Hudson: *Hudson Gazette* — Box 70 (J0P 1H0); W; 2,160pd (Sw); 60¢; publisher & editor Gregory B Jones; tel (514) 458-5482; fax (514) 458-3337

Hull: *Le Regional de Hull* — 141 Jean Proulx (J8Z 1T4); W; 26,352fr (Est); 70¢; C; publisher & editor Jacques Blais; tel (819) 776-1063; fax (819) 776-1668

Huntingdon: *Gleaner* — 66 Chateauguay St.; Box 130 (J0S 1H0); W; 4,495pd, 41fr (ABC); 60¢; publisher Roger H Daoust; editor Phil Norton; tel (514) 264-5364

Iles-de-la-Madeleine: *Le Radar* — 192 St. Germain E.; Box 580, Rinouski (G5L 7G7); W; 2,438pd, 71fr (ABC); 40¢; publisher & editor Achille Hubert; tel (418) 986-2345; fax (418) 986-6358

Joliette: *Joliette Journal* — 262 Boul L'Industrie (J6E 3Z1); W; 21,700fr (Sw); 53¢; publisher Raymond Coderre C A; editor Andre Nadeau; tel (514) 755-4747

Joliette: *L'Action* — 262 Boul L'Industrie (J6E 3Z1); Su; 44,000fr (Sw); $10.08; publisher & editor Raymond Coderre C A; tel (514) 759-3664; fax (514) 759-9828

Jonquiere: *Le Reveil a Jonquiere* — 3388 Blvd. Saint-Francois; Box 520 (G7X 7W4); Su; 69pd, 26,785fr (ODC); 68¢; publisher & editor Jacques Girard; tel (418) 695-2601; fax (418) 695-1391

La Baie: *Le Reveil A La Baie* — 3388 Boul. St. Francois; Box 520, Jonquiere (G7X 7W4); Su; 9,791fr (Est); 51¢; C; publisher & editor Jacques Girard; tel (418) 695-2601; fax (418) 695-1391

La Malbaie: *Plein Jour de Charlevoix* — 200 Book de Comporte (G0T 1J0); S; 12,015fr (Est); 56¢; C; publisher Paul Brisson; managing editor Charles Wamen; tel (418) 665-6121

La Tuque: *L'Echo de La Tuque* — 529 rue St. Louis; Box 310 (G9X 3P3); Su; 6,400fr (Est); 28¢; publisher Gaston Martin; editor Jeannot Boulianne; tel (819) 523-6141

Lac Etchemin: *La Voix du Sud* — 227-B-2nd Ave.; Box 789 (G0R 1S0); M; 12,800fr (Est); 44¢; C; publisher Les Grands Hebdos; editor M Leopold Bechette; tel (418) 625-7471; fax (418) 625-5200

Lac Megantic: *L'Echo de Frontenac* — 5040 Blvd. des Veterans, Lac Megantic, Cte. Megantic (G6B 2G5); M; 4,549pd, 4,124fr (ODC); 71¢; C; publisher & editor Gaetan Poulin; tel (819) 583-1630; fax (819) 583-1124

Lac St-Jean Quest: *Le Point de Dolbeau* — 3388 Boul. St-Francois; Box 520, Jonquiere (G7X 7W4); Su; 11,118fr (Est); 52¢; publisher & editor Jacques Girard; tel (418) 276-5110; fax (418) 695-1391

Lachine: *Lachine Messenger* — 1015 Notre Dame (H8S 2C3); W; 19,600fr (Sw); 35¢; publisher & editor Maurice LeBlanc; tel (514) 637-2381

Lachute/Brownsburg: *L'Argenteuil* — 52 Main St.; Box 220, Lachute (J8H 3A8); Su; 12,800fr (Sw); 68¢; publisher & editor Andre Paquette; general manager Bertrand Castonguay; managing editor Pierre Desrosiers; tel (514) 562-2494; fax (514) 562-1434

Lachute/Brownsburg: *Le Progres/The Watchman* — 52 Main St., Lachute (J8H 3X3); Sa; 10,800fr (Est); 68¢; general manager & editor Andre Paquette; managing editor Andre Bougie; tel (514) 562-8593; fax (514) 562-1434

Laprairie: *Le Reflet* — 54 Mairie Victorim, Delsom (G0R 1J0); W; 22,000fr (Est); 90¢; publisher Paul Blackburn; tel (514) 659-8881

Laval: *Courrier-Laval* — 189 Ave. Laval (H7N 3V8); Su; 90,955fr (Est); $1.50; publisher Telemedia Communicantions; editor Jacques Dion; tel (514) 667-4360; fax (514) 667-9498

Le Saguenay: *Le Reveil Jonquiere/Chicoutimi/La Baie* — 3388 Boul. St-Francois; Box 520, Jonquiere (G7X 7W4); Su; 67,532fr (Est); $1.17; publisher & editor Jacques Girard; tel (418) 695-2601; fax (418) 695-1391

Longueuil/Brossard/St. Hubert/St. Lambert/Lemoyne/Greenfiel: *Le Courrier du Sud/South Shore Courier* — 267 St. Charles W., Longueuil (J4H 1E3); Su; 117,500fr (Est); $1.80; publisher Lucie Masse; editor Jean-Paul Auclair; tel (514) 646-3333; fax (514) 674-0205

Lotbiniere Co.: *Peuple de Lotbiniere* — 1000 St-Joseph; Box 130, Laurier-Station (G0S 1N0); M; 562pd, 10,500fr (Est); 64¢; C; publisher Publications Le Peuple Inc.; general manager & editor Denys Simoneau; tel (418) 728-2131; fax (418) 728-4819

Louiseville: *L'Echo de Louiseville/Berthier* — 50 St. Aime St. (J5V 2Y7); W; 7,178pd, 48fr (ABC); 40¢; publisher & editor J Pierre Gagne; tel (819) 228-2766

Maniwaki: *La Gatineau* — 114 de la Ferme (J9E 3J9); Sa; 12,100fr (Est); 51¢; publisher Oneil Grondin; tel (819) 449-1725; fax (819) 449-5108

Maniwaki: *La Gazette de Maniwaki Inc.* — 93 Notre-Dame (J9E 2H5); Sa; 10,200fr (Sw); 51¢; publisher Denise Carriere; editor Georges LaFontaine; tel (819) 449-2233; fax (819) 449-7067

Matane: *La Voix Gaspesienne* — 305 de la Gare, Ste. 107 (G4W 3J2); Su; 5,343pd, 44fr (ABC); 47¢; publisher Hebcor Inc.; editor Jean-Guy Desjardins; tel (418) 562-4040; fax (418) 562-4607

Mirabel: *La Concorde* — 53 rue St-Eustache, St. Eustache (J7R 2L2); Su; 4,494pd (Est); 30¢; publisher Jocelyne Lamoureux; tel (514) 844-3131

Mont Joli: *L'Information* — 135 Doucet; Box 70 (G5H 1R6); Su; 12,000fr (Sw); 47¢; C; publisher Francis Desrosiers; editor Sonia Levesque; tel (418) 775-4381; fax (418) 775-7768

Montmagny: *Le Peuple de la Cote du Sud* — 4 Ruisseau; Box 430 (G5V 3S7); M; 16,250fr (ODC); 58¢; publisher Louise Laval Lee; tel (418) 248-0415; fax (418) 248-2377

Montreal: *Journal L'Avenir de l'Est* — 13307 Sherbrooke Est., Pointe-aux-Trembles (H1A 1C2); Tu/Su; 57,966fr (Est); 75¢; publisher Les Hebdos Transcontinental; editor Paul Sauve; tel (514) 644-8484; fax (514) 644-0666

Montreal: *Montreal Mirror* — 400 McGill St., Ste. 100 (H2Y 2G1); Th; 1,062pd, 75,938fr (ODC); $21.42; publishers Catherine Salisbury & Eyal Kattan; editor Peter Scowen; tel (514) 393-1010; fax (514) 393-3173

Montreal: *St. Henri La Voix Populaire* — 1735 Ave. de l'Eglise (H4E 1G6); M; 25,000fr (Est); 95¢; C; publisher Publications Dumont; editor Louis Mercier; tel (514) 768-4777; fax (514) 768-3306

Montreal: *The Monitor* — 5925 Monkland Ave. (H4A 1G7); W; 29,000fr (ODC); $1.44; C; publisher Robert Fisher; editor Leonard Gervais; tel (514) 481-7510; fax (514) 481-3492

Montreal: *The Suburban* — 8170 Wavell Rd., Cote St. Luc (H4W 1M3); W; 100,332fr (Sw); $2.79; C; general manager Doug Seip; editor Christy McCormick; tel (514) 484-1107; fax (514) 484-9616

Montreal/Cartierville: *Le Courrier Bordeaux/Cartierville* — 189 Ave. Laval, Laval (H7N 3V8); Su; 16,417fr (ODC); 62¢; publisher Hebdos Transcontinental; editor Jacques Dion; tel (514) 667-4360; fax (514) 667-9498

Montreal/Mount Royal: *The Town of Mount Royal Weekly Post/Le Post de Ville Mont* — 1255 Laird, Ste. 280, Mount Royal (H3P 2T1); Th; 7,000fr (Est); $15.12; publisher Robert Fisher; editor Marielle Bouchard; tel (514) 739-3302; fax (514) 739-3304

Montreal/Rosemont: *Hebdo Journal de Rosemont* — 5650 O'dberville; Bureau 303, Montreal (H2G 2B3); Tu; 36,200fr (Est); 96¢; publisher Les Hebdos Telemedia Inc.; editor Alain Vaillancourt; tel (514) 273-2525; fax (514) 273-1997

Montreal/St-Leonard: *Progres St-Leonard* — 6424 Jean-Talon Est., Ste. 202, St. Leonard (H1S 1M8); Tu; 34,668fr (ODC); $10.10; publisher Les Hebdos Transcontinental; editor Jean-Claude Picard; tel (514) 899-5888; fax (514) 899-5984

New Richmond: *Le Journal Chaleur* — 73 rue St. Germain E.; Box 410, Rimouski (G5L 7C4); Su; 103pd, 13,542fr (ODC); 53¢; publisher Bellavance Press Group; editor Claude Bellavance; tel (418) 723-4800; fax (418) 722-4078

Nicolet-Becancour: *Courrier-Sud* — 3255 Marie-Victorin; Box 1300, Nicolet (J3T 1X5); Su; 21,258fr (Est); 76¢; publisher Les Editions Du Lac St. Pierre Inc.; editor Jean Blanchette; tel (819) 293-4551; fax (819) 293-8758

Pierrefonds: *Cites Nouvelles/City News* — 15716 Gouin Blvd. W., Ste. Genevieve (H9H 1C4); Su; 57,000fr (Est); $1.20; publisher Publications Dumont Inc.; editor Marc Forget; tel (514) 620-0781; fax (514) 620-3705

Plessisville: *La Feuille d'Erable* — 1717 St-Calixte; Box 160 (G6L 2Y7); Tu; 4,281pd, 806fr (ABC); 55¢; publisher Publications Appalaches Ltee.; editor Andree Wright; tel (819) 362-7049; fax (819) 362-2216

Pontiac Co.: *The Equity* — Pontiac Printshop Ltd.; Box 430, Shawville (J0X 2Y0); W; 3,970pd, 60fr (ABC); 75¢; publishers Heather Dickson & Ross Dickson; editor Richard Wills; tel (819) 647-2204; fax (819) 647-2206

Repentigny: *L'Artisan* — 1004 Notre-Dame (J5Y 1S9); Tu; 43,130fr (ODC); 84¢; publisher Les Hebdos Transcontinental; editor Jacques Boulanger; tel (514) 581-5120

Rimouski: *Le Progres-Echo-Dimanche* — 73 rue St-Germain E.; Box 410 (G5L 7C4); Su; 27,742fr (ODC); 61¢; publisher & editor Claude Bellavance; tel (418) 723-4800; fax (418) 722-4078

Rimouski: *Le Rimouskois* — 156 Lepage; Box 410 (G5L 7C4); W; 96pd, 23,451fr (ODC); 58¢; publisher Les Editions Rimouskoises (1988) Inc.; editor Jean Morin; tel (418) 723-4800; fax (418) 723-4078

Riviere-du-Loup: *Le Saint-Laurent Echo du Grand-Po* — 16 Domaine (G5R 2P5); Sa; 367pd, 19,436fr (ODC); 48¢; publisher & managing editor Georges Fraser; tel (418) 862-1774; fax (418) 862-4387

Roberval/St-Felicien: *L'Etoile du Lac* — 376 Blvd Marcotte, Roberval (G8H 1Z6); Su; 148pd, 12,372fr (Est); 45¢; C; publisher Les Hebdos UniMedia, une division de Groupe UniMedia Inc.; editor Gaston Martin; tel (418) 275-2911; fax (418) 275-2834

Saint-Andre-Avellin: *La Petite Nation* — Box 240 (J0V 1W0); M; 8,008fr (ODC); 50¢; publisher Publication Dumont Inc.; editor Serge Lamarche; tel (819) 983-2725; fax (819) 983-6844

Saint-Eustache: *Courrier-Deux-Montagnes* — 189 ave. Laval, Laval (H7N 3V8); Su; 28,741fr (Est); 63¢; publisher Telemedia Communications Inc.; editor Jaques Dion; tel (514) 667-4360; fax (514) 667-9498

Saint-Georges-de-Beauce: *Beauce Nouvelle/L'Eclaireur-Progres* — 12625 1st Ave. E., Saint-Georges (G5Y 2E4); W/Sa; 195pd, 26,625fr (ODC); 68¢; publisher Editions Chaudet Inc.; editor Yvon Roy; tel (418) 228-8858; fax (418) 228-0268

Saint-Hyacinthe: *Le Clairon* — 655 St. Anne St.; Box 276 (J2S 7B6); W; 21,712fr (ODC); 80¢; publisher Guy Roy; editor Denis Lacasse; tel (514) 774-5375; fax (514) 773-3115

Saint-Hyacinthe: *Le Courrier de Saint-Hyacinthe* — 655 Sainte-Anne (J2S 5G4); Tu; 12,431pd, 572fr (ABC); 50¢; publisher Benoit Chartier; general manager Denis Lacasse; editor Pierre Bornais; tel (514) 773-6028; fax (514) 773-3115

Saint-Jean: *Le Canada Francais* — 84 rue Richelieu (J3B 6X3); W; 15,913pd, 313fr (ABC); 53¢; publisher Les Editions Le Canada Francais Ltee.; editor Robert Paradis; tel (514) 347-0323; fax (514) 347-4539

Saint-Jerome: *L'Echo du Nord* — 225 rue Du Palais (J7Z 1X7); W; 8,154pd, 336fr (ABC); $9.38; publisher Quebecor; editor Charles Michaud; tel (514) 436-5381; fax (514) 436-5904

Saint-Laurent: *Saint-Laurent News* — 1963 Pl. Thimens (H4R 1K8); Tu; 29,800fr (ODC); $1.00; publisher Jean H Mercer; editor Michel Jobin; tel (514) 339-1292; fax (514) 339-5304

Saint-Tite: *Le Dynamique de la Maurice* — 488 Frigon; Box 520 (G0X 3H0); Tu; 2,200pd (Est); 45¢; publisher Les Editions Dynamiques Inc.; editor Lise Leveille; tel (418) 365-6262

Sainte-Adele/Saint-Sauveur: *Le Journal des Pays D'en Haut* — 1012 Valiquette-Sainte-Adele; Box 1890, Sainte-Adele (J0R 1L0); W; 53pd, 18,794fr (ODC); 49¢; publisher Quebecor; general manager Michel Gareau; tel (514) 229-6664; fax (514) 229-6063

Sainte-Agathe-des-Monts: *Information Du Nord; Le Sommet* — 1107 Ouimet; Box 1480, Saint-Jovite (J0T 2H0); Sa; 106pd, 8,024fr (ODC); 40¢; C; general manager Luce St-Jean; tel (819) 326-1844

Sainte-Foy: *Quebec Chronicle Telegraph* — 3484 Chemin Ste-Foy, Ste-Foy (G1X 1S8); W; 2,265pd, 2,735fr (Est); 68¢; publisher & editor Karen MacDonald; general manager Mike Reshitnyk; tel (418) 650-1764; fax (418) 650-1764

Sainte-Foy/Sillery/Cap Rouge: *L'Appel* — 1380 Rene-Levesque Blvd. W., Quebec (G1S 1W6); Su; 27pd, 52,053fr (ODC); $17.50; C; publisher & editor M Leopold Bechette; managing editor Denis Fortin; tel (418) 681-3454; fax (418) 682-5910

Sainte-Therese: *Courrier-De Groulx* — 317 Montmorency, Laval (H7N 1X1); Su; 35,336fr (ODC); 70¢; publisher Hebdos Telemedia Inc.; editor Jacques Dion; tel (514) 667-4360; fax (514) 667-9498

Sainte-Therese: *Le Nord-Info* — 50 B rue Turgeon (J7E 3H4); Su; 43,500fr (Est); 81¢; C; publisher Jean Claude Langlois; editor Regean Goyette; tel (514) 435-6537; fax (514) 435-0588

Sainte-Therese/Blainville: *La Voix des Mille-Iles* — 50 B Turgeon, Sainte-Therese (J7E 3H4); Su; 43,600fr (Est); 81¢; publisher Editions Blainville Deux Montagues; editor Jean Claude Langlois; tel (514) 430-5111; fax (514) 435-0588

Sept-Isles: *Nordest/Nordest Plus* — 365 Boul. Laure (G4R 1X2); W/Su; 12,281fr (Est); 26¢; publisher & editor Martin Tino; tel (418) 962-9441

Shawinigan/Grand-Mere: *Hebdo du St. Maurice* — 2102 Champlain Ave.; Box 10, Shawinigan (G9N 2L4); Su; 28,277fr (ODC); $1.00; publisher & editor Michel Matteau; tel (819) 537-5111; fax (819) 537-5471

Stanstead Co.: *The Stanstead Journal* — 25 Dufferin; Box 30, Stanstead (J0B 3E0); W; 3,500pd, 300fr (Est); 55¢; publisher & editor Leonard Gervais; tel (819) 876-7514; fax (819) 876-7515

Terrebonne/Mascouche: *Courrier-des Moulins* — 189 ave. Laval, Laval (H7N 3V8); Su; 34,896fr (Est); 67¢; editor Jacques Dion; tel (514) 667-4360; fax (514) 667-9498

Terrebonne/Mascouche: *La Revue* — 231 Ste-Marie St., Terrebonne (J6W 3E4); Tu; 43,053fr (ODC); 74¢; publisher Marie-France Despatis; editor Aime Despatis; tel (514) 964-4444; fax (514) 471-1023

Val d'Or: *The Val d'Or Star* — Box 100 (J9P 4P2); W; 325pd, 35fr (ABC); 35¢; publisher Glenn Morton; editor Jacques Nadon; tel (819) 825-3755

Valleyfield/Chateauguay: *The St. Lawrence Sun* — 82 SaLa Berry Sud, Chateauguay (J6J 4J6); Sa; 300pd, 50,455fr (Sw); $1.05; publisher Michele Auclair; editor Jeanne D'Arc Germain; tel (514) 692-8552; fax (514) 692-3460

Vaudreuil/Soulauges: *L'Echo de Vaudreuil-Soulanges* — 123 Dumont, Dorion; Box 160, Vaudreuil (J7V 5W1); Sa; 30,000pd (Est); 56¢; publisher & editor Raymond Lefebvre; tel (514) 455-6111; fax (514) 455-0596

III-34 **Quebec** *Canadian Weeklies*

Verdun/Nuns Island: *Verdun Messenger* — 3650 Verdun Ave., Verdun (H4G 1K4); M; 31,000fr (Est); 80¢; publisher Maurice Duhamel; editor Pierre Lussier; tel (514) 768-2544

Victoriaville: *Journal L'Union, Inc.* — 43 Notre-Dame Est.; Box 130 (G6P 3Z4); W; 2,042pd, 23,108fr (ODC); 68¢; publisher Journal L'Union Inc.; general manager Michel Gauthier; managing editor Sylvie Cote; tel (819) 758-6211; fax (819) 758-2759

Victoriaville: *La Nouvelle* — 43 Notre Dame Est.; Box 504 (G6P 3Z4); Su; 38,000pd (Est); 76¢; publisher Michel Gauthier; editor Coty Sylvie; tel (819) 752-6718; fax (819) 752-2759

Ville-Marie: *Le Temiscamien* — Box 219 (J0Z 3W0); W; 295pd, 7,205fr (Est); 45¢; publisher & editor Lionel Lacasse; tel (819) 629-2618; fax (819) 629-2661

West Island: *The Chronicle* — 15 Cartier Ave., Pointe Claire (H9S 4R7); W; 19,151pd, 440fr (VCP); $17.50; C; publisher Gordon R Brewerton; editor Brenda O'Farrell; tel (514) 630-6688; fax (514) 694-7620

Westmount: *The Westmount Examiner* — 210 Victoria (H3Z 2M4); Th; 11,328fr (VCC); $16.10; publisher Bruce Stevenson; editor Bernie O'Neill; tel (514) 484-7523; fax (514) 484-6028

Windsor/Richmond: *L'Etincelle* — 193 rue St. Georges, Windsor (J1S 1J7); Sa; 2,400pd, 2,600fr (Est); 41¢; publisher Claude Frenette; editor Ginette Pouliri; tel (819) 845-2705

SASKATCHEWAN

Assiniboia: *Assiniboia Times* — 410 1st Ave. E.; Box 910 (S0H 0B0); Tu; 3,932pd, 39fr (ABC); 63¢; C; publisher Glen Hall; editor Delmar Davies; tel (306) 642-5901/5902; fax (306) 642-4519

Battlefords: *The Battlefords News-Optimist* — 1219 100th St.; Box 430, North Battleford (S9A 2Y5); W; 774pd, 60fr (Sw); 75¢; C; publisher Rod McDonald; editor Lorne Cooper; tel (306) 445-4401; fax (306) 445-1977

Bengough/Ogema: *Bengough-Ogema Star* — Box 370, Radville (S0C 2G0); F; 655pd, 560fr (ABC); 50¢; publisher George Hay; general manager Shauna Bourassa; editor Sue Stadnick; tel (306) 869-2202; fax (306) 869-2533

Biggar: *The Independent* — Box 40 (S0K 0M0); M; 2,350pd, 56fr (Est); 37¢; C; publisher Daryl Hasein; publisher & editor Margaret Hasein; tel (306) 948-3344; fax (306) 948-2133

Birch Hills: *The Birch Hills Gazette* — Main St.; Box 340, Kinistino (S0J 1H0); W; 972pd, 8fr (Est); 35¢; publisher Phillips Publishers Ltd.; editor Ron D Phillips; tel (306) 864-2266; fax (306) 752-5358

Broadview/Grayson: *Broadview Express* — Box 189, Grenfell (S0G 2B0); Tu; 718pd (VCP); $5.74; publisher R Dwayne Stone; editor Lisa Schmidt; tel (306) 697-2722; fax (306) 697-2689

Canora: *Canora Courier* — 123 1st Ave. E; Box 746 (S0A 0L0); W; 2,681pd, 57fr (Est); 25¢; publisher & editor Ken Sopkow; tel (306) 563-5131; fax (306) 563-6144

Carlyle/Manor/Wawota: *Carlyle Observer* — Box 160, Carlyle (S0C 0R0); Tu; 2,970pd, 25fr (Sw); 49¢; publisher E B O'Neill; editor E L O'Neill; tel (306) 453-2525; fax (306) 453-2938

Carnduff: *Gazette-Post News* — Box 220 (S0C 0S0); W; 1,283pd, 31fr (VCP); 44¢; publisher & editor Bill Grass; publisher Shirley Grass; tel (306) 482-3252; fax (306) 482-3373

Craik: *Weekly News* — 3rd St.; Box 360 (S0G 0V0); W; 1,501pd, 35fr (Est); 15¢; publisher & editor Harve Friedel; tel (306) 734-2313; fax (306) 734-2789

Cut Knife: *Highway 40 Courier* — 200 Steele St.; Box 400 (S0M 0N0); W; 662pd, 78fr (ABC); $5.32; publisher & editor Roger Manegre; managing editor Lorie Gibson; tel (306) 398-4901; fax (306) 398-4909

Davidson: *Davidson Leader* — 205 Washington St.; Box 786 (S0G 1A0); W; 1,793pd, 9fr (ABC); 33¢; publisher & editor V M Topping; tel (306) 567-2047; fax (306) 567-2900

Eastend: *Eastend Enterprise* — Box 729, Shaunavon (S0N 2M0); W; 3,535pd (Sw); 27¢; publisher Robert Irvine; editor Leslie Irvine; tel (306) 297-2711

Elrose/Kyle: *The Elrose/Kyle Review* — 112 Main St.; Box 787, Elrose (S0L 1A0); M; 936pd, 70fr (Est); 42¢; publisher & editor Verna D Thompson; tel (306) 962-3221; fax (306) 962-4445

Esterhazy: *The Potashville Miner-Journal* — 606 2nd Ave.; Box 1000 (S0A 0X0); W; 1,734pd, 214fr (VCP); 40¢; publisher & editor Robert Koskie; tel (306) 745-6669; fax (306) 745-2699

Estevan: *Mercury* — 814 4th St.; Box 730 (S4A 2A6); W; 4,928pd (Est); 22¢; publisher Peter Ng; editor Jonas Weinrauch; tel (306) 634-2654; fax (306) 634-3934

Eston: *The Eston Press* — Box 787 (S0L 1A0); M; 1,090pd, 58fr (Est); 30¢; publisher & editor Verna D Thompson; tel (306) 962-3221

Foam Lake: *Foam Lake Review* — Box 550 (S0A 1A0); M; 2,721pd (Est); 35¢; publisher & editor Carl A Johnson; tel (306) 272-3262; fax (306) 272-4521

Grenfell/Wolseley/Neudorf/Stoughton: *Sun* — Box 189, Grenfell (S0G 2B0); Tu; 1,727pd (VCP); $6.30; publisher R Dwayne Stone; editor Lisa Schmidt; tel (306) 697-2722; fax (306) 697-2689

Gull Lake: *Gull Lake Advance* — 1462 Conrad; Box 628 (S0N 1A0); Tu; 1,903pd (Est); 21¢; publisher & editor John Peters; tel (306) 672-3373

Hafford: *Riverbend Review* — 109 2nd Ave. E.; Box 309 (S0J 1A0); W; 595pd (Est); 18¢; publisher & editor Peter Kingsmill; tel (306) 549-2258; fax (306) 549-2304

Herbert: *The Herald* — 716 Herbert Ave.; Box 399 (S0H 2A0); Tu; 1,656pd, 20fr (VCP); 45¢; publisher Rhonda J Ens; editor Cynthia Firus; tel (306) 784-2422; fax (306) 784-3246

Hudson Bay: *Post-Review* — Box 10 (S0E 0Y0); Tu; 1,721pd, 20fr (ABC); 48¢; C; publisher Robert F Gilroy Jr; editor Bruce Paproski; tel (306) 865-2771; fax (306) 865-2340

Humboldt: *The Humboldt Journal* — 617 Main St.; Box 970 (S0K 2A0); Th; 3,990pd, 135fr (ABC); 70¢; C; publisher Chad Charbonneau; managing editor Sharon Domotor; tel (306) 682-2561; fax (306) 682-3322

Indian Head/Wolseley: *Indian Head-Wolseley News* — 510 Grand Ave.; Box 70, Indian Head (S0G 2K0); Tu; 2,281pd, 27fr (ABC); 20¢; publisher Wilson Publications Ltd.; editor Ken McCabe; tel (306) 695-3565

Ituna: *The Ituna News* — 306 Main St.; Box 413 (S0A 1N0); Th; 1,091pd (Est); 28¢; publisher Carl A Johnson; editor Susan Antonishyn; tel (306) 795-2412; fax (306) 795-3621

Kamsack: *The Kamsack Times* — 123 1st Ave. E.; Box 746, Canora (S0A 0L0); Th; 1,907pd, 45fr (Est); 19¢; publisher & editor Ken Sopkow; tel (306) 563-5131; fax (306) 563-6144

Kelvington: *The Kelvington Radio* — 102 1st St. N.E.; Box 667 (S0A 1W0); Th; 1,223pd, 49fr (ABC); $6.02; publisher & editor James R Headington; tel (306) 327-4656; fax (306) 338-2266

Kerrobert: *The Kerrobert Citizen* — 919 Main St.; Box 1150, Kindersley (S0L 1S0); W; 751pd, 57fr (ABC); $5.46; C; publisher & editor James F Crump; general manager Stewart Crump; tel (306) 463-4611; fax (306) 463-6505

Kindersley: *Clarion* — 919 Main St.; Box 1150 (S0L 1S0); W; 2,950pd, 97fr (ABC); $8.40; C; publisher James F Crump; general manager Stewart Crump; editor Tim Crump B A; tel (306) 463-4611; fax (306) 463-6505

Kindersley: *West Central Crossroads* — 919 Main St.; Box 1150 (S0L 1S0); W; 14,700pd (Sw); $8.40; C; publisher James F Crump; general manager Stewart Crump; editor Tim Crump B A; tel (306) 463-4611; fax (306) 463-6505

Kinistino/Birch Hills: *The Kinistino Birch Hills Post Gazette* — Box 1300, Melfort (S0E 1A0); Tu; 1,910pd, 25fr (VCP); 35¢; publisher Phillips Publishers Ltd.; editor Ron D Phillips; tel (306) 752-5737; fax (306) 752-5358

Kipling/Windthorst/Peebles/Glenavon/Corning/Kennedy/Langbank/Wawota: *The Citizen* — 521 Main St.; Box 329, Kipling (S0G 2S0); Su; 1,861pd, 50fr (VCP); 46¢; publisher South East Press Ltd.; general manager Scott Kearns; editor Thomas Kearns; managing editor Michael Kearns; tel (306) 736-2535; fax (306) 736-8445

La Ronge/Northern Saskatchewan: *The Northerner* — 715 La Ronge Ave.; Box 1350, La Ronge (S0J 1L0); Tu; 1,879pd, 45fr (ABC); 45¢; C; publisher & editor Scott Boyes; tel (306) 425-3344/3244; fax (306) 425-2827

Lampman/Arcola: *Prairie Progress* — 130 Main St.; Box 160, Carlyle (S0C 0R0); Tu; 1,405pd (Est); 12¢; publisher Ted O'Neill; editor E L O'Neill; tel (306) 453-2525; fax (306) 453-2938

Leader: *Leader News* — 919 Main St.; Box 1150, Kindersley (S0L 1S0); W; 1,008pd, 67fr (ABC); $5.60; C; publisher James F Crump; general manager Stewart Crump; editor Kim White; managing editor James Crump; tel (306) 463-4611; fax (306) 463-6505

Maidstone: *The Maidstone Mirror* — 311 Main St.; Box 308 (S0M 1M0); Th; 1,482pd, 12fr (VCP); $4.90; publisher Steve Dill; editor Jim Swettenham; tel (306) 893-2251; fax (306) 893-4707

Maple Creek: *The Maple Creek News* — Box 1360 (S0N 1N0); Tu; 3,478pd, 76fr (Est); $5.74; publisher & editor Duane Migowsky; tel (306) 662-2133; fax (306) 662-3092

Meadow Lake: *Meadow Lake Progress* — 311 Centre St.; Box 879 (S0M 1V0); Su; 3,366pd, 366fr (ABC); 38¢; publisher & editor Larry MacIntosh; tel (306) 236-5265

Melfort: *The Melfort Journal* — 310 Main St.; Box 1300 (S0E 1A0); Tu; 4,140pd, 116fr (VCP); 42¢; C; publisher Publishers Ltd.; editor Ron D Phillips; tel (306) 752-5737; fax (306) 752-5358

Melville: *The Melville Advance* — 218 3rd Ave. W.; Box 1420 (S0A 2P0); W; 3,196pd, 64fr (Sw); 58¢; publisher & editor Lin Orosz; publisher Mark Orosz; tel (306) 728-5448; fax (306) 728-4004

Moose Jaw: *Moose Jaw This Week* — 44 Fairford St. W. (S6H 6E4); Su; 21,062fr (Est); $1.18; publisher Bob Calvert; editor Ron Walter; tel (306) 692-2325; fax (306) 692-9166

Moosomin: *World-Spectator* — 624 Main St.; Box 250 (S0G 3N0); W; 3,294pd, 48fr (ABC); 50¢; publisher Bruce Penton; editor Kevin Weedmark; tel (306) 435-2445; fax (306) 435-3969

Nipawin: *Journal* — 218 Centre St.; Box 2014 (S0E 1E0); W; 4,948pd (Sw); 51¢; publisher & editor Ken M Nelson; tel (306) 862-4618; fax (306) 862-4566

Norquay: *The Norquay North Star* — 123 1st Ave. E.; Box 746, Canora (S0A 0L0); Th; 1,015pd, 25fr (Est); 22¢; publisher & editor Ken Sopkow; tel (306) 563-5131; fax (306) 563-6144

North Battleford: *The Battleford's Advertiser-Post* — 892-104 St.; Box 1029 (S9A 3E6); M; 19,229fr (Est); 74¢; publisher William R Warwick; editor Lois Walsh; tel (306) 445-7261; fax (306) 445-3223

North Battleford: *The Telegraph* — Box 1029 (S9A 3E6); W/F; 2,456pd, 25fr (Est); 47¢; publisher William R Warwick; editor Lois Walsh; tel (306) 445-7261; fax (306) 445-3223

Outlook: *The Outlook* — 108 Sask. Ave. E.; Box 399 (S0L 2N0); M; 2,677pd, 50fr (ABC); 55¢; publisher Roland Jenson; editor Debra Murphy; tel (306) 867-8262; fax (306) 867-9556

Oxbow: *Herald* — 219 Main St.; Box 420 (S0C 2B0); Tu; 1,511pd (Est); 17¢; publisher Mary Pedlar; editor J Ken Pedlar; tel (306) 483-2323; fax (306) 483-5258

Preeceville: *Preeceville Progress* — 123 1st Ave. E.; Box 746, Canora (S0A 0L0); Th; 1,812pd, 40fr (Est); 23¢; publisher & editor Ken Sopkow; tel (306) 563-5131; fax (306) 563-6144

Radville: *Radville Star* — Box 370 (S0C 2G0); Th; 1,031pd, 214fr (ABC); $4.00; publisher George Hay; general manager Shauna Bourassa; editor Sue Stadnick; tel (306) 869-2202; fax (306) 869-2533

Redvers: *The Optimist* — 10 Broadway St.; Box 490 (S0C 2H0); W; 1,870pd, 419fr (ABC); 26¢; publisher & editor James A Kadash; tel (306) 452-3363; fax (306) 452-3373

Rosetown: *The Rosetown Eagle* — 114 2nd Ave. W.; Box 130 (S0L 2V0); M; 2,637pd, 83fr (VCP); 46¢; publisher Rosetown Publishing Co. Ltd.; editor Dan Page; tel (306) 882-4202; fax (306) 882-4204

Rosthern: *Saskatchewan Valley News* — Box 10 (S0K 3R0); W; 3,934pd, 99fr (Est); 54¢; publisher Valley Printers Ltd.; editor Ewald Epp; tel (306) 232-4865; fax (306) 232-4694

Semans/Raymore: *Hi-Way 15 Gazette* — Box 10, Wynyard (S0A 4T0); M; 1,407pd, 60fr (Est); 35¢; publisher & editor Ray O Lachambre; tel (306) 554-2224; fax (306) 554-2099

Shaunavon: *The Shaunavon Standard* — 346 Centre St.; Box 729 (S0N 2M0); Tu; 3,059pd (Est); 37¢; publisher Robert Irvine; editor Leslie Irvine; tel (306) 297-2711; fax (306) 297-3357

Shellbrook: *Shellbrook Chronicle* — 44 Main St.; Box 10 (S0J 2E0); Tu; 2,902pd (ABC); $6.16; publisher C J Pepper; editor John Young; tel (306) 747-2442; fax (306) 747-3000

Spiritwood: *Spiritwood Herald* — 44 Main St.; Box 10, Shellbrook (S0J 2E0); W; 1,148pd, 5fr (ABC); $5.88; publisher C J Pepper; editor John Young; tel (306) 747-2442; fax (306) 747-3000

Stoughton: *Times* — 813 Desmond St.; Box 189, Grenfell (S0G 2B0); W; 758fr (Est); 12¢; publisher & editor Dwayne Stone; tel (306) 697-2722; fax (306) 697-2689

Strasbourg: *Last Mountain Times* — 103-1st Ave. W.; Box 340, Nokomis (S0G 3R0); M; 6,410pd (Sw); 42¢; publisher & editor Lyle Emmons; tel (306) 528-2020; fax (306) 528-2090

Swift Current: *Swift Current Sun* — 55-1st Ave. N.E.; Box 670 (S9H 3W7); W; 3,887pd, 60fr (ABC); 88¢; Su; 19,685fr (Sw); 88¢; publisher Mike Hertz; editor John Morran; tel (306) 773-3116; fax (306) 773-2653

Swift Current: *The Southwest Booster* — 30-4th Ave. N.W.; Box 1330 (S9H 3X4); M; 19,100fr (Sw); 88¢; publisher Bill Mann; editor Peter Godfrey; tel (306) 773-9321; fax (306) 773-9136

Tisdale: *The Tisdale Recorder* — Box 1660 (S0E 1T0); M; 2,869pd, 44fr (Est); 39¢; publisher & editor Larry Mitchell; tel (306) 873-4515; fax (306) 873-4912

Unity/Wilkie: *The Northwest Herald* — 304 Main St.; Box 309, Unity (S0K 4L0); W; 2,160pd (Est); 40¢; C; publisher Mikel L Hamm; editor Kevin T Hamm; tel (306) 228-2267; fax (306) 228-2767

Wadena: *The Wadena News* — 102 1st St. N.E.; Box 100 (S0A 4J0); W; 3,425pd, 119fr (ABC); $7.42; C; publisher & editor James R Headington; tel (306) 338-2231; fax (306) 338-2266

Wakaw: *The Wakaw Recorder* — Box 9 (S0K 4P0); W; 1,788pd, 85fr (Sw); 34¢; publisher & editor Dwayne Biccum; tel (306) 233-4325; fax (306) 233-4386

Watrous: *The Watrous Manitou* — 309 Main St.; Box 100 (S0K 4T0); M; 2,076pd, 36fr (Sw); 36¢; C; publisher & editor Frank W Wilson; tel (306) 946-3343; fax (306) 946-2026

Watson/Englefeld/LeRoy: *The Watson Witness* — 313 Railway Ave.; Box 129, Watson (S0K 4V0); W; 1,694pd, 39fr (VCP); 41¢; publisher Brian Hay; publisher & editor Maxine Hay; tel (306) 287-3245; fax (306) 287-4333

Weyburn: *Weyburn Review* — 904 East Ave.; Box 400 (S4H 2K4); W; 5,664pd, 20fr (ABC); $8.25; C; publisher Darryl Ward; editor Greg Nikkel; managing editor Patricia Ward; tel (306) 842-7487; fax (306) 842-0282

Whitewood: *Herald* — 708 Railway Ave.; Box 160 (S0G 5C0); Tu; 1,022pd, 45fr (Est); 16¢; publisher & editor Cliff Ashfield; tel (306) 735-2230; fax (306) 735-4458

Wilkie: *The Wilkie Press* — Box 309, Unity (S0K 4L0); W; 914pd, 61fr (ABC); 38¢; publisher Mikel L Hamm; editor Kevin T Hamm; tel (306) 228-2267; fax (306) 228-2767

Wynyard: *The Advance/Gazette* — Box 10 (S0A 4T0); M; 2,891pd, 60fr (Sw); 52¢; publisher & editor Ray O Lachambre; tel (306) 554-2224; fax (306) 554-3226

Yorkton: *Yorkton This Week & Enterprise* — 20 3rd Ave. N.; Box 1300 (S3N 2X3); W/Sa; 8,279pd, 81fr (ABC); $10.00; publisher Steve Gloster; editor G Hengen; tel (306) 782-2465; fax (306) 786-1898

YUKON TERRITORY

Whitehorse/Yukon Territory: *Yukon News* — 211 Wood St., Whitehorse (Y1A 2E4); W; 4,536pd, 2,544fr (CCAB); 23¢; F; 5,778pd, 2,540fr (CCAB); 23¢; publisher Doug Bell; general manager & managing editor Stephen Robertson; editor Peter Lesniak; tel (403) 667-6285; fax (403) 668-3755

PRINCIPAL ETHNIC NEWSPAPERS PUBLISHED IN CANADA

ARABIC

Toronto: *Akbar El-Arab El-Dawlah (Arab News International) (Est. 1978)* — 511 Queen St. E., Toronto, ON (M5A 1V1); Bi-wkly; 7,000pd (Est); $35.00; publisher S Allam; editor E El Masri; tel (416) 362-0304

Toronto: *Canada & Arab World (Est. 1975) (English)* — 511 Queen St. E., Toronto, ON (M5A 1V1); Bi-Wkly; 10,000pd (Est); $35.00; publisher S Allam; editor M Hegazy; tel (416) 362-0304

Toronto: *Dalil Al Arab (Arab Guide) (Est. 1979) (English)* — 511 Queen St. E., Toronto, ON (M5A 1V1); Bi-Wkly; 10,000pd (Est); $35.00; publisher & editor F Ahmed; publisher S Allam; tel (416) 362-0304; fax (416) 861-0238

Toronto: *Arc Arabic Journal* — 511 Queen St. E., Toronto, ON (M5A 1V1); Bi-Wkly; 7,000pd (Est); $35.00; publisher Emad Nafed; editor Emad Nafeh; tel (416) 362-0304; fax (416) 861-0238

CROAT/SERB/SLOVENIAN

London: *Trumpeter* — 260 Vancouver St., London, ON (N5W 4R8); Qrtly; 600pd (Est); 10¢; publisher Croatian Philatelic Society; editor Charles D Glavanic; tel (519) 685-2292

CZECH/SLOVAK/ENGLISH

Scarborough: *Novy Domov (New Homeland) (Est. 1948) (Czech/Slovak/English)* — 450 Scarborough Golf Club Rd., Scarborough, ON (M1G 1H1); Bi-Wkly; 2,700pd (Est); $1.25; C; publisher Masaryk Memorial Institute Inc.; general manager Jan J Travnicek; editor Vera M Roller; tel (416) 439-4646

Toronto: *Satellite 1416 (Est. 1991) (Czech/Slovak/English)* — PO Box 176, Station E, Toronto, ON (M6H 4E2); Bi-Wkly Th; 1,200fr (Est); $1.30; publisher & editor A Brezina; tel (416) 530-4222

DUTCH

Langley: *De Hollandse Krant (Est. 1969) (Dutch)* — #12 20505 Fraser Hwy., Langley, BC (V3A 4G3); Mthly; 7,446pd, 131fr (Sw); 78¢; publisher & editor Gerald Bonekamp; tel (604) 530-9446; fax (604) 530-9766

St. Catharines: *Christian Courier (Est. 1945) (English)* — 4-261 Martindale Rd., St. Catharines, ON (L2W 1A1); F; 5,000pd, 300fr (Est); $15.00; general manager Stan De Jong; editor Bert Witvoet; tel (905) 682-8311; fax (905) 682-8313

ESTONIAN

Toronto: *Meie Elu (Our Life) (Estonian)* — 958 Broadview Ave., Toronto, ON (M4K 2R6); Th; 2,500pd, 500fr (Est); $9.00; publisher Estonian Publishing Co. Ltd.; editor T Parming; tel (416) 466-0951; fax (416) 461-0448

FINNISH

Thunder Bay: *Canadan Uutiset (Est. 1915) (Finnish)* — 31 N. Court St., Thunder Bay, ON (P7A 4T4); W; 1,950pd, 50fr (Est); 77¢; publisher Finnews Ltd.; editor Sakri Viklund; managing editor Aarre Ertolahti; tel (807) 344-1611/2980; fax (807) 344-1879

GERMAN

Richmond: *Pazifische Rundschau (Pacific Review) (Est. 1965) (German)* — PO Box 88047 (Lansdowne), Richmond, BC (V6X 3T6); Sa; 12,390pd, 110fr (Sw); $3.50; publisher B Ackermann's Advtg. & News Service; editor Baldwin Ackermann; tel (604) 270-2923; fax (604) 273-9365

Steinbach: *Mennonitische Post (Est. 1977) (German)* — PO Box 1120, Steinbach, MB (R0A 2A0); Bi-Mthly; 5,225pd, 300fr (Est); 60¢; publisher Mennonite Central Committee; editor Isbran Hiebert; tel (204) 326-6790

Toronto: *Die Zeit (The Times) (Est. 1960) (German)* — 29 Coldwater Rd., Toronto, ON (M3B 1Y8); F; 9,500pd (Est); N/A; editor Dr Robert Leicht; tel (416) 391-4196

Winnipeg: *Kanada Kurier (8 editions) (Est. 1889) (German)* — 955 Alexander Ave., PO Box 1054, Winnipeg, MB (R3C 2X8); Th; 19,500pd (Est); $56.29; publisher Renee Topham; editor Dietrich E Wolf; tel (204) 774-1883

GREEK

Montreal: *Greek Canadian Tribune (Est. 1964)* — 897 Jean Talon W., Montreal, QC (H3N 1S7); Th; 15,000pd (Sw); $1.20; C; publisher & editor Christos Manikis; tel (514) 272-6873; fax (514) 272-3157

HUNGARIAN

Toronto: *Kanadai Magyarsag (Canadian Hungarians) (Est. 1950) (Hungarian)* — 74 Advance Rd., Etobicoke, ON (M8Z 2T7); Sa; 10,000pd (Est); $8.00; C; publisher & managing editor Irene Vorosvary; editor Csaba Gaal; tel (416) 233-3131; fax (416) 233-5984

Willowdale: *Magyar Elet (Hungarian Life) (Est. 1948) (Hungarian)* — 313 Shepherd Ave. E., Willowdale, ON (M2N 3B3); S; 7,846pd, 643fr (Est); $8.00; publisher Agnes Somorjai; editor Laszlo Bessenyei; tel (416) 221-6195; fax (416) 221-6358

ITALIAN

Montreal: *Corriere Italiano* — 6900 St. Denis St., Montreal, QC (H2S 2S2); W; 50,000pd (Est); $1.05; editor Alfred Gagliardi; tel (514) 279-4536

Montreal: *La Vace Degli (Italo Canadesi) (Italian/French/English)* — 6736 Monk Blvd., Montreal, QC (H4E 3J1); Semi-Mthly; 10,715pd, 181fr (Est); $1.25; publisher Carlo Gatti; editor Vicky Gatti; tel (514) 769-5711; fax (514) 366-4783

Ottawa: *L'Ora Di Ottawa (The Hour of Ottawa) (Est. 1968) (Italian)* — 203 Louisa St., Ottawa, ON (K1R 6Y9); Wkly; 2,400pd, 60fr (Sw); 51¢; publisher L'Ora Di Ottawa Ltd.; general manager Renalta Coppola; editor Elio Coppola; tel (613) 232-5689; fax (613) 563-2573

Quebec: *Insieme (Together) (Est. 1973) (Italian)* — 4358 Rue Charleroi, Montreal-North, QC (H1H 1T3); W; 16,100pd, 1,900fr (Sw); $1.16; publisher Enrico Morassut; editor Giuseppe De Rossi; tel (514) 328-2062; fax (514) 328-6562

Windsor: *La Gazzetta (Est. 1972) (English)* — 909 Howard Ave., Windsor, ON (N9A 1S3); F; 6,000pd (Est); 60¢; publisher & editor Walter Temelini; tel (519) 253-8883

JAPANESE

Toronto: *The Canada Times (Est. 1907) (Bilingual)* — 291 Dundas St. W., Ste. 206, Toronto, ON (M5T 1G1); Tu/F; 4,600pd, 400fr (Est); 65¢; publisher & editor Harry Taba; tel (416) 593-6953/2777; fax (416) 593-9769

Toronto: *New Canadian (Est. 1939) (Bilingual)* — 524 Front St. W., 2nd Fl., Toronto, ON (M5V 1B8); Th; 10,000pd (Est); N/A; publisher Shin Kawai; editor Sakura Torizuka; tel (416) 593-1583

JEWISH

Don Mills: *Canadian Jewish News (Est. 1971) (English/French)* — 10 Gateway Blvd., Ste. 420, Don Mills, ON (M3C 3A1); Th; 48,700pd (Sw); $2.39; C; general manager Gary Laforet; editor Mordechai Ben-Dat; tel (416) 422-2331; fax (416) 422-3790 (Advertising), (416) 424-1886 (Editorial)

Downsview: *Toronto Jewish Press (English)* — PO Box 428, Downsview, ON (M3M 3AB); Bi-Mthly; $1.50; publisher The Toronto Jewish Press; editor G Kissin; tel (416) 633-0202

Vancouver: *Jewish Bulletin (Est. 1930) (English)* — 203-873 Beatty St., Vancouver, BC (V6B 2M6); F; 3,000pd (Est); $22.00; C; publisher Andrew A Buerger; editor Ariela Friedman; tel (604) 689-1520; fax (604) 689-1525

Winnipeg: *Jewish Post & News (Est. 1925) (English)* — 117 Hutchings St., Winnipeg, MB (R2X 2V4); W; 3,467pd, 1,785fr (Est); 79¢; publisher The Jewish Post Ltd.; editor Matt Bellan; tel (204) 694-3332; fax (204) 694-3916

KOREAN

Toronto: *The Minjoong Shinmoon (The Korean-Canadian Community Paper (Est. 1979) (Korean)* — 802 Bloor St. W., Toronto, ON (M6G IL9); F; 3,800pd, 700fr (Est); 75¢; publisher Se-Yong Jeong; editor Hyun-Jae Yoon; tel (416) 537-3474; fax (416) 531-9624

LATVIAN

Toronto: *Latvija-Amerika (Latvian)* — 125 Broadview Ave., Toronto, ON (M4M 2E9); Sa; 5,000pd (Est); 50¢; publisher Latvija Amerika Publishing Ltd.; editor Ingida Viksna; tel (416) 465-7902

LITHUANIAN

Mississauga: *Teviskes Ziburiai (Lights of Homeland) (Est. 1949) (Lithuanian)* — 2185 Stavebank Rd., Mississauga, ON (L5C IT3); Tu; 5,300pd (Est); $7.00; publisher Lithuanian Canadian R C Society; editor Rev Dr Pranas Gaida; managing editor Ramune Jonaitis; tel (905) 275-4672; fax (905) 275-1336

MALAYALAM

Toronto: *Kerala Express (Est. 1979) (Malayalam)* — 1565 Jane St., PO Box 34556, Toronto, ON (M9N 2R3); W; 220pd, 1,710fr (Sw); 80¢; publisher J P George; editor V P George; tel (416) 654-0431

PAKISTANI

Willowdale: *Al-Hilal (Urdu Only) (Est. 1972)* — 338 Hollyberry Trl., Willowdale, ON (M2H 2P6); wkly; 1,200fr (Est); 85¢; publisher L Owaisi; editor Umm Ali; tel (416) 493-4374

POLISH

Toronto: *Glos Polski (Polish Voice) (Est. 1908) (Bilingual)* — 390 Roncesvalles Ave., Toronto, ON (M6R 2M9); Tu; 7,000pd, 2,000fr (Est); $8.00; publisher Polish National Union in Canada; editor Wieslaw Magiera; tel (416) 533-9469

Toronto: *Zwiazkowiec (Aliancer)* — 1638 Bloor St. W., Toronto, ON (M6P 4A8); Tu/Th; 8,000pd (Est); $8.00; publisher Polish Alliance Press Ltd.; editor Mr R Dlugoborski; tel (416) 531-2491

PORTUGUESE

Toronto: *Journal Acoriano (Azorean Newspaper) (Est. 1980)* — 803 Dundas St. W., Toronto, ON (M6J IV2); Mthly; 8,000pd (Est); $1.04; editor Fernando Raposo; tel (416) 868-6621

SERBIAN

Hamilton: *Kanadski Srbobran (The Canada Serbian) (Est. 1951) (Serbian/English)* — 335 Brittania Ave., Hamilton, ON (L8H 1Y4); Tu; 1,750pd, 250fr (Est); 45¢; publisher Serbian League of Canada; editor G Bajic; tel (905) 549-4079; fax (905) 549-8552

SLOVAK

Toronto: *Kanadsky Slovak (Canadian Slovak) (English/Slovak)* — 1736 Dundas St. W., Toronto, ON (M6K 1V5); Sa; 2,500pd, 100fr (Est); $2.00; publisher Slovak Canadian Publishing Inc.; editor Marian Jankovsky; tel (416) 531-2055

SPANISH

Toronto: *El Popular (Est. 1970) (Spanish)* — 2413 Dundas St. W., Toronto, ON (M6P 1X3); Daily; 10,000pd (Est); 88¢; C; publisher & managing editor Edvard Uruena; editor Walter Seminario; tel (416) 531-2495; fax (416) 531-7187

SWEDISH

Vancouver: *Swedish Press (NYA Svenska Pressen) (Est. 1929) (English/Swedish)* — 1294 W. 7th Ave., (PO Box 4302, Blaine, WA, US, 98231-4302), Vancouver, BC (V6H 1B6); Mthly; 8,000pd (Est); N/A; C; publisher Swedish Press Inc.; editor Anders Neumueller; tel (604) 731-6381; fax (604) 731-2292

UKRAINIAN

Etobicoke: *Svitlo (The Light) (Est. 1938) (Ukrainian)* — 265 Bering Ave., Etobicoke, ON (M8Z 3A5); Mthly; 2,500pd (Est); N/A; publisher Basilian Fathers; general manager D Weleschul; editor Rev V Cymbalisty; tel (416) 234-1212; fax (416) 234-1213

Toronto: *Homin Ukrainy (Ukrainian Echo) (Est. 1948)* — 140 Bathurst St., Toronto, ON (M5V 2R3); Th; 10,000pd (Est); $8.00; publisher W Okipniuk; editor O Romanyshyn; tel (416) 368-3443

Toronto: *Moloda Ukraina (Ukrainian)* — PO Box 40 Sta. M, Toronto, ON (M6S 4T2); Mthly; 750pd, 300fr (Est); 60¢; publisher Peter Rodak; editor Leonid Lishchyna; tel (416) 255-8604

Toronto: *Nowi Dni (New Days) (Est. 1950)* — PO Box 400 Sta. D, Toronto, ON (M6P 3J9); Mthly; 1,600pd (Est); $10.00; publisher Nowi DNI Co. Ltd.; editor M Dalney; tel (416) 767-4840

Winnipeg: *Ukrainsky Holos (Ukrainian Voice) (Est. 1910) (Ukrainian/English)* — 842 Main St., Winnipeg, MB (R2W 3N8); Mthly; 2,401pd, 42fr (Est); 58¢; C; publisher Trident Press Ltd.; general manager Nell Koropas; editor Ludmila Pavenski; editor & managing editor Nicholas Hryn; tel (204) 589-5871; fax (204) 586-3618

DAILY TABLOID NEWSPAPERS

ALBERTA
Calgary - Sun
Edmonton - Sun
Lethbridge - Herald *(Sunday Only)*

BRITISH COLUMBIA
Kamloops - News *(Saturday Only)*
Kelowna - Daily Courier *(Sunday Only)*
Vancouver - Province

MANITOBA
Flin Flon - Reminder
Winnipeg - Sun

NEW BRUNSWICK
Caraquet - L'Acadie Nouvelle

NOVA SCOTIA
Halifax - News

Truro - News *(Saturday only)*

ONTARIO
Fort Frances - Bulletin
Ottawa - Le Droit
Sun
Pembroke - News
St. Thomas - Times-Journal
Toronto - Sun

QUEBEC
Chicoutimi - Le Quotidien Du Saguenay
Montreal - Le Journal De Montreal
La Presse
Quebec - Le Journal De Quebec
Sherbrooke - Record

YUKON TERRITORY
Whitehorse - Star

Copyright ©1996 by the Editor & Publisher Co.

CANADIAN NEWSPAPER GROUPS

EDITOR'S NOTE: For the purpose of this listing, a group of daily newspapers is defined as two or more daily newspapers in different cities under the same principal ownership or control. In many groups each paper is a separate corporation, with little or no central direction of editorial policy.

Hollinger Inc. — 10 Toronto St., Toronto, ON M5C 2B7; tel (416) 363-8721; fax (416) 364-2088
President/CEO — F David Radler; Vice Pres.-Finance & Treasury — J A Boultbee.
Regina (SK) Leader-Post (e), Saskatoon (SK) StarPhoenix (m).
Sterling Newspapers: 1827 W. 5th Ave., Vancouver, BC V6J 1P5; tel (604) 732-4443; fax (604) 732-3961
Chairman — F David Radler; President — Jamie Milne; Vice Chairman — Bob Calvert; Vice President — Todd A Vogt; Vice Pres./CFO — Barry Tyner; Vice President — Mike Pearce.
Cranbrook (BC) Daily Townsman (e), Dawson Creek (BC) Peace River Block News (e), Fort St. John (BC) Alaska Highway News (e), Kimberley (BC) Bulletin (e), Nelson (BC) Daily News (e), Port Alberni (BC) Valley Times (e), Prince Rupert (BC) Daily News (e), Trail (BC) Times (e); Barrie (ON) Examiner (e), Belleville (ON) Intelligencer (eS), Cambridge (ON) Reporter (e), Guelph (ON) Mercury News (eS), Lindsay (ON) Daily Post (e), Niagara Falls (ON) Review (e), Orillia (ON) Packet & Times (e), Pembroke (ON) Observer (e), Peterborough (ON) Examiner (eS), Welland (ON) Tribune (m); Summerside (PEI) Journal-Pioneer (e); Moose Jaw (SK) Times-Herald (e); Prince Albert (SK) Daily Herald (e).
UniMedia Inc.: 600 Blvd. Maisonneuve W., Rm 3200, Montreal, QC H3A 3J2; tel (514) 284-2500; fax (514) 284-1129
Pres./CEO — Pierre Des Marais II; Vice Pres./Sec./Treas.— Pierre Richard; Pres./Editor (Ottawa) — Pierre Bergeron; Pres./Editor (Chicoutimi)— Claude Gagnon; Pres./Editor (Quebec City)—Gilbert Lacasse.
Ottawa (ON) Le Droit (m), Chicoutimi (QC) Le Quotidien du Saguenay (m), Quebec City (QC) Le Soleil (mS).
Hollinger Inc., through all subsidiaries, owns approximately 162 daily and 474 non-daily newspapers throughout Canada, the United States, the United Kingdom, Australia and Israel. Total circulation is approximately 14.8 million. These figures include Southam Inc., John Fairfax Holdings Limited (Australia) and the few other publications primarily owned but not controlled by Hollinger. The Sterling division operates 30 non-daily newspapers. All UniMedia Inc. properties (three daily, five non-daily, 12 free distribution newspapers) are French-language.

Les Journaux Trans-Canada (JTC) — 44 St. Antoine W., Montreal, QC H2Y 1J5; tel (514) 285-6918
Vice President — Jean Sisto.
Granby (QC) La Voix de L'Est (m), Montreal (QC) La Presse (m), Sherbrooke (QC) La Tribune (m), Trois-Rivieres (QC) La Nouvelliste (m).
JTC also owns seven weekly newspapers. All JTC publications are French-language.

New Brunswick Publishing Co. Ltd. — 210 Crown St., St. John, NB E2L 3V8; tel (506) 632-8888
GM/Exec. VP — Bruce Phinney.
St. John (NB) Telegraph-Journal (m), St. John (NB) Times-Globe (e).

Quebecor Group Inc. — 612 St. Jacques St., Montreal, QC H3C 4M8; tel (514) 877-9777
Pres./CEO — Pierre Peladeau; Exec. Vice Pres. — Raymond Lemay.
Winnipeg (MB) Sun (mS); Montreal (QC) Le Journal de Montreal (m), Quebec (QC) Le Journal de Quebec (mS), Sherbrooke (QC) Record (e).
Quebecor also owns over 40 regional weeklies, five business monthlies, two entertainment weeklies, and numerous magazines. In addition, Quebecor operates three book publishing houses and the second largest commercial printer in North America. It is also involved in forest products activities.

St. Catharines Standard Ltd. — 17 Queen St., St. Catharines, ON L2R 5G5; tel (905) 684-7251
Chairman — H B Burgoyne; President — C J Burke.
Cobourg (ON) Star (e), Port Hope (ON) Guide (e), St. Catharines (ON) Standard (e).
The Cobourg Star and the Port Hope Guide are grouped as Northumberland Publishers.

Southam Newspapers — 1450 Don Mills Road, Don Mills, ON M3B 2X7; tel (416) 445-6641; fax (416) 442-2077
Co-Chairman of the Board — Andre Desmarais; Co-Chairman of the Board — Conrad M Black; President/CEO (Southam Inc.) — William E Ardell; Exec. Vice Pres. — John G Craig; Sr. Vice Pres./CFO — Christian M Paupe; Vice Pres./CC — C G Jim Hewitt; Vice Pres./Gen. Counsel/Sec. — J Blair Mackenzie; Asst. Secretary — Elaine G Hills; Vice Pres.-Human Resources — John Minardi; Pres.-Southam City Newspapers & New Media — Andrew Prozes; Pres.-Southam New Media — Peter Irwin; Pres.-Southam Magazine & Information Group — William J Mann; Pres.-Southam Show Group (Southex Exhibitions) — Beverly A Morden.
Calgary (AB) Herald (m), Edmonton (AB) Journal (m), Medicine Hat (AB) News (e); Kamloops (BC) News (e), Prince George (BC) Citizen (e), Vancouver (BC) Province (mS), Vancouver (BC) Sun (m); Brantford (ON) Expositor (e), Hamilton (ON) Spectator (e), Kingston (ON) Whig-Standard (m), Kitchener-Waterloo (ON) Record (e), North Bay (ON) Nugget (e), Ottawa (ON) Citizen (mS), Owen Sound (ON) Sun Times (e), Sault Ste. Marie (ON) Sault Star (e), Windsor (ON) Star (e); Montreal (QC) Gazette (m).
A major, but non-controlling, interest in Southam Newspapers is held by Hollinger Inc. of Toronto. Southam also has three weekly newspaper groups: Barbant Newspapers (six); Fairway Group (eight); Gazette Press Ltd. (three).

Southwestern Ontario Publishing — 25 Townline Rd.; PO Box 190, Tillsonburg, ON N4G 4H6; tel (519) 688-6397; fax (519) 842-3511
President — Michael Fredericks; VP/Finance — Peter Muise.
Simcoe (ON) Reformer (e), Woodstock (ON) Sentinel-Review (e).
This group also owns five weekly papers and is a subsidiary of Newfoundland Capital Corp., which also owns the Halifax (NS) Daily News.

Summit Publishing — PO Box 3370, Fredericton, NB E3B 5A2; tel (506) 452-6671
President — Thomas Crowther.
Fredericton (NB) Daily Gleaner (e), Moncton (NB) Times-Transcript (e).

Thomson Newspapers — 65 Queen St. W., Ste. 2200, Toronto, ON M5H 2M8; tel (416) 864-1710; fax (416) 864-0109
Pres./CEO — Samuel E Hindman; Exec. Vice Pres./CEO Eastern Group — Ronald W Mitchell; Group Publisher-Central Group — Jon C Butler; Exec. Vice Pres./CEO Western Group — William Greenhalgh; Vice Pres./CFO — Thomas Hay; Vice Pres./Human Resources — Diane Barsoski.
Lethbridge (AB) Herald (e); Kelowna (BC) Daily Courier (e), Nanaimo (BC) Daily Free Press (e), Penticton (BC) Herald (e), Vernon (BC) Daily News (e), Victoria (BC) Times-Colonists (mS); Brandon (MB) Sun (e), Winnipeg (MB) Free Press (e); Corner Brook (NF) Western Star (e), St. John's (NF) Evening Telegram (eS); New Glasgow (NS) Evening News (e), Sydney (NS) Cape Breton Post (e), Truro (NS) Daily News (e); Chatham (ON) Daily News (e), Cornwall (ON) Standard-Freeholder (e), Kirkland Lake (ON) Northern Daily News (e), Sarnia (ON) Observer (e), Sudbury (ON) Star (e), Thunder Bay (ON) Times News (m), Thunder Bay (ON) Chronicle-Journal (e), Timmins (ON) Daily Press (e), Toronto (ON) Globe and Mail (m); Charlottetown (PEI) Guardian (m).
This group also owns eight non-daily newspapers. Advertising Sales Offices at 1117 St. Catherine St. W., Ste. 609, Montreal, QC H3B 1H9; tel (514) 843-7245 and at 1200 Burrard St., Ste. 900, Vancouver, BC V6Z 2C7; tel (604) 689-9811. See also Thomson Newspapers under U.S. newspaper group listing.

Toronto Sun Publishing Corp. — 333 Kings St. E., Toronto, ON M5A 3X5; tel (416) 947-2222; fax (416) 947-3228
President/CEO — Paul V Godfrey; Corp. Controller — John Boots; Vice Pres.-Comm Newspaper Div./Pres. & CEO (Bowes Pub. Ltd.) — William Dempsey; Vice Pres.-Corp. Affairs/Corp. Secretary — Trudy A Eagan; Washington Bureau Chief/Vice Pres. — Patrick A Harden; Vice Pres.-Finance/CFO — Bruce L Jackson; Publisher (Calgary Sun)/Vice Pres (Western Pub.) — Ken M King; Publisher (Financial Post) — Doug Knight; COB/President (Schipper Enterprises Inc.) — Lionel H Schipper; Publisher/CEO (Ottawa Sun)/Vice Pres — John Payton; Publisher (Toronto Sun) — Hartley Steward.
Calgary (AB) Sun (m), Edmonton (AB) Sun (m); Ottawa (ON) Sun (mS), Toronto (ON) Financial Post, Toronto (ON) Sun (mS).
Bowes Publishers Limited: 100-10471-178 Ave., Edmonton, AB T5A 1R5; tel (403) 451-1445; fax (403) 451-3320
Chairman — Bruce L Jackson; President/CEO — William R Dempsey; Exec. Vice Pres./COO — Donald J Sinclair.
Fort McMurray (AB) Today (e), Grand Prairie (AB) Daily Herald-Tribune (e); Portage La Prairie (MB) Daily Graphic (e); Kenora (ON) Daily Miner & News (e), St. Thomas (ON) Times Journal (e).
Toronto Sun also publishes 50 weekly newspapers and shoppers as well as eight magazine and specialty publications.

The #1 Newspaper Industry Database

Work Database Smart!

E&P's database is the most comprehensive newspaper industry resource available – important within the newspaper industry as well as in marketing and public relations areas. Reach the right people, find the right answers, make the right decisions. Rely on the industry's premier database.

For complete information and pricing, call Paul Arata at (212) 675-4380, ext. 509.

Copyright ©1996 by the Editor & Publisher Co.

SECTION IV

Newspapers Published in Foreign Countries

The British Press 1
Newspapers of the United Kingdom and Ireland 2-6
Newspapers of Europe 6-52
Newspapers of Africa 53-59
Newspapers of Asia and the Far East 59-84
Newspapers of the Caribbean Region 84-87
Newspapers of Central America and Mexico 87-100
Newspapers of the Middle East 101-104
Newspapers of South America 105-120
Newspapers of Australia and New Zealand 120-124
Newspapers of the Pacific Ocean Territories 124

THE BRITISH PRESS — 1995

By James Brennan

The weather remains the most common topic of conversation in the British Isles but the media, especially print journalism, runs a close second among the chattering classes. This year has seen the usual manifestations of the perennial media rat race, but this time spiced with changes of newspaper ownership, television franchises, subsequent wholesale sackings and bitter recriminations.

The breakup of the Thomson regional newspapers group, founded by Canadian Roy (later Baron) Thomson and continued by his son, Kenneth, and the takeover of the London *Independent* (both the daily and Sunday) by the Mirror Group, brought many changes, and more were threatened as the year ended. A brave new venture, the weekly *Yorkshire on Sunday*, was closed by Westminster Press in one of its well-known cost-cutting exercises. The cold fingers of dissolution had reached across the narrow Irish Sea in May, when the two dailies and the Sunday of the Irish Press Group in Dublin went into liquidation. The 600 employees among the group's 2,000 creditors were still hoping, as we went to press, that and abortive takeover by an American consortium would be revived.

You would have to live on the moon not to suspect that one of the world's biggest media tycoons, the Australian-American Rupert Murdoch, played a leading role in the cut-throat fight for advertising and circulation in Britain. His price-cutting formula of the previous year had succeeded in bringing the sales of his sensational tabloid, the *Sun*, back to the four million mark, and this was maintained against its strongest contender, the *Daily Mirror*, which slumped badly to under three million (Sept. ABC, see London figures listed below).

Evidently, Murdoch was prepared to lose a lot of cash on lowering the cover price in order to increase sales and thus hope to pull in more advertising. There are advertisers who do not allow considerations of taste to deter them from buying space in scandalous newspapers if they sell squillions of copies and the objective was accomplished. The price of the *Sun* was hiked up again, though kept twopence below that of the *Mirror*. The same tactic was employed in the quality field and the price of Murdoch's most prestigious property, the *Times*, was brought back up as it neared 700,000 — outstripping its nearest quality rival, the *Guardian*.

In Northern Ireland, where media ownership has long been held in mainland Britain, a successful rescue operation revitalized a remarkable daily, the Belfast *News Letter*. Claimed to be the oldest English-language newspaper in the world, it had losses of more than £2 million when it attracted the attention of a UK entrepreneur, Sir Ray Tindle, whose list of 70 publications lacked a single daily. In Belfast, where it is published, the *News Letter* is delivered free and has maintained a verified distribution of 66,000; as the *Ulster News Letter* it sells 33,000 to a wider audience. With the latest accounts, the Tindle Group reported a return to profitability, having installed a web-offset colour press and reduced the paper's burden of debt.

The Belfast *News Letter* traces its launching to 1737. It boasts a scoop over the rest of the world by being the first to publish outside the USA "the first news and full text" of the American Declaration of Independence — two months after the Declaration was signed. The second-oldest newspaper is the *Yorkshire Post*, founded in Leeds in 1754 and the claim for third place is shared by the *Chronicle Telegraph*, Quebec, and the *Hartford* (Conn.) *Courant*. When such historic treasures are in danger, there is a duty to rescue them, and the White Knight for the *News Letter* was Sir Ray Tindle.

The breaking up of the Thomson group, including the *News Letter*'s rival daily, the *Belfast Telegraph*, was the ending of a long-term process of withdrawal from Britain by Kenneth Thomson. It was nonetheless traumatic, so far as jobs were concerned. Trinity International, already owners of the Liverpool *Daily Post* and *Liverpool Echo* (and some North American publications) became Britain's biggest regional newspaper company with its takeover of Thomson's centres in England, Wales and Ulster. (Scotland was not part of the deal.)

Immediately after confirmation of the takeover, the editors and managers of Thomson's important Newcastle centre were ordered to cut costs by at least £1 million. The price of the group's Newcastle *Journal* went up by 2p and the *Sunday Sun* by 5p. All the managers of the Thomson publication centres in the UK were warned they would have to reapply for their own jobs when the new owners arrived at year's end. But it was a different story in Edinburgh, where the jewel of the Thomson crown, the *Scotsman*, was sold to David and Frederick Barclay, together with the Edinburgh *Evening News* and the group's weekly, *Scotland on Sunday*.

The Barclay brothers saved the international weekly, the *European*, after the death of its founder, Robert Maxwell, and have shown themselves to be positive and successful investors in staff, as well as machinery. They have been praised for their commitment to good journalism — and pay decent salaries. The complete redrawing of the newspaper map of Scotland, with the purchase of the two Aberdeen papers, the *Press & Journal* and the *Evening Express*, by Associated Newspapers (Daily Mail Group), awaited approval by the Monopolies & Mergers Commission.

The continued slide of Express Newspapers was highlighted in November by the sudden resignation of the popular editor of the London *Daily Express*, Sir Nicholas Lloyd. In spite of all his efforts, the circulation declined by 6% to 1,265,000. The *Sunday Express* fell by 8% to 1,379,000. The group's "pop", the *Daily Star*, fell to 739,000. The proprietor, Lord Stevens, was firmly refuting rumors that he was looking for a buyer. Operating profits from his national titles fell year-on-year by nearly 30% and an added problem was the £7.7 million cost of the 220 sackings ordered by Lord Stevens in midsummer.

Another high-profile editorial departure was that of former war correspondent, Max Hastings, from the chair of the high-Tory *Daily Telegraph*. The proprietor, Canadian Conrad Black, though preoccupied with a number of deals in Britain, North America and Australia, was gratified by the increased circulation of the daily by 2.45% to 1,064,700 and the *Sunday Telegraph* by 6.22% to 696,900.

But political differences between proprietor and editor over their attitude to the Major government led to the latter's sudden departure for the chair of his former employer, London's only evening paper, the *Evening Standard*. He had been wooed by Sir David English, right-hand man of the proprietor of Associated Newspapers, Lord Rothermere, who just happened to be preparing a farewell speech to the incumbent editor of the *Standard*, Stewart Steven, who is retiring after many years with the company.

Lord Rothermere had cause to be the happiest man in the pantheon of newspaper proprietors. His *Daily Mail* and *Mail on Sunday* have both registered considerable gains in recent years, while loftily ignoring the Murdoch-inspired price wars. The *Guardian* also refused to drop its price and suffered a slight loss to 392,200, while its old rival, the *Times*, recorded a massive 21% increase to 667,200. The wily Rupert Murdoch, whose *Sunday Times* had also put on sales, had triumphed again.

Copyright ©1996 by the Editor & Publisher Co.

NEWSPAPERS OF THE BRITISH ISLES
(CHANNEL ISLANDS, ENGLAND, NORTHERN IRELAND, REPUBLIC OF IRELAND, SCOTLAND & WALES)
Newspapers, personnel, circulation, advertising rates, etc.

CHANNEL ISLANDS
Pop. Est. 145,000

GUERNSEY
Pop. Est. 57,949

GUERNSEY EVENING PRESS (m) Est. 1897
Braye Rd., Vale; PO Box 57
Tel: (44-1481) 45866; Fax: (44-1481) 43421
Circ.—16,076 ABC
Prop.—Guernsey Press Co. Ltd.
Mng. Dir.—C R Sackett
Ed.—Graham Ingrouille
Ad. Mgr.—Steve Mauger
Ad.—£4.10 cm; £1,500 pg.

JERSEY
Pop. Est. 85,026

JERSEY EVENING POST (e) Est. 1890
Five Oaks, St. Saviour; PO Box 582
Tel: (44-1534) 73333
Circ.—23,736 ABC
Prop.—Jersey Evening Post Ltd.
Chmn.—J C Averty
Ed.—M J Bisson
Ad. Mgr.—David Edwards
Ad.—£6.60 cm; £1,495 pg.

ENGLAND
Pop. Est. 57,121,000

BARROW-IN-FURNESS
(Cumbria)
Pop. Est. 64,340

NORTH WESTERN EVENING MAIL (e) Est. 1898
Abbey Rd., LA14 5Q5
Tel: (44-1229) 821835; Fax: (44-1229) 832141
Circ.—21,780 ABC
Prop.—Furness Newspapers Ltd.
Mng. Dir.—Peter C Simpson
Ed.—Donald Martin
Ad. Dir.—Terry Hall
Ad.—£5.56 cm; £1,433 pg.

BASILDON
(Essex)
Pop. Est. 94,800

EVENING ECHO (e) Est. 1969
Chester Hall Lane, SS14 3BL
Tel: (44-1268) 522792; Fax: (44-1268) 532060
Circ.—51,200 ABC
Prop.—Westminster Press Ltd.
Mng. Dir.—V Lester
Ed.—Bob Dimond
Ad. Mgr.—R Blunt
Ad.—£7.15 cm; £2,187.90 pg.

BATH
(Avon)
Pop. Est. 84,740

BATH CHRONICLE (e) Est. 1760
33-34 Westgate St., BA1 1EW
Tel: (44-1225) 444044; Fax: (44-1225) 445969
Circ.—19,308 ABC
Prop.—Westminster Press Ltd.
Mng. Dir.—P J Harris
Ed.—David Gledhill
Ad. Mgr.—Avril Oliver
Ad.—£4.13 cm; £1,189.44 pg.

BIRMINGHAM
(West Midlands)
Pop. Est. 1,017,300

BIRMINGHAM EVENING MAIL (e) Est. 1870
28 Colmore Circus, Queensway; PO Box 18, BP 6AX
Tel: (44-121) 2363366; Fax: (44-121) 2332958
Circ.—201,476
Prop.—Midland Independent Newspapers Ltd.
Mng. Dir.—C Oakley
Ed.—Ian Dowell
Ad. Dir.—Patrick Sexton
Ad.—£20.00 cm; £7,269.60 pg.

THE BIRMINGHAM POST (m) Est. 1857
28 Colmore Circus, Queensway; PO Box 18, B4 6AX
Tel: (44-121) 2363366; Fax: (44-121) 2332958
Circ.—28,054 ABC
Prop.—Midland Independent Newspapers Ltd.
Mng. Dir.—C Oakley
Ed.—Nigel Hastilow
Ad. Dir.—Patrick Sexton
Ad.—£8.15 cm; £4,564 pg.

SUNDAY MERCURY (S) Est. 1918
28 Colmore Circus, Queensway; PO Box 60, B4 6AZ
Tel: (44-121) 2363366; Fax: (44-121) 2332958
Circ.—145,357
Prop.—Midland Independent Newspapers Ltd.
Mng. Dir.—C Oakley
Ed.—Peter Whitehouse
Ad. Dir.—Patrick Sexton
Ad.—£11.75 cm; £3,666 pg.

BLACKBURN
(Lancashire)
Pop. Est. 109,560

LANCASHIRE EVENING TELEGRAPH (e) Est. 1886
High Street, BB1 1HT
Tel: (44-1254) 678678; Fax: (44-1254) 682185
Circ.—47,929 ABC
Prop.—Reed Northern Newspapers
Mng. Dir.—Brenda T Rudge
Ed.—Peter R Butterfield
Ad. Mgr.—Bill Haworth
Ad.—£6.85 cm; £2,082 pg.

BLACKPOOL
(Lancashire)
Pop. Est. 149,970

WEST LANCASHIRE EVENING GAZETTE (e)
Preston New Rd.
Tel: (44-1253) 839999; Fax: (44-1253) 60352
Circ.—42,335 ABC
Prop.—United Newspapers
Mng. Dir.—R A Shaw
Ed.—David Upton
Ad. Mgr.—Brian Crawley
Ad.—£8.00 cm; £4,176 pg.

BOLTON
(Lancashire)
Pop. Est. 260,830

BOLTON EVENING NEWS (e) Est. 1867
Churchgate, BL1 1DE
Tel: (44-1204) 22345; Fax: (44-1204) 365068
Circ.—45,722 ABC
Prop.—Reed Northern Newspapers
Mng. Dir.—John Waters
Ed.—Andrew Smith
Ad. Mgr.—Susan Staff
Ad.—£6.80 cm; £2,100 pg.

BOURNEMOUTH
(Dorset)
Pop. Est. 148,820

EVENING ECHO (e) Est. 1900
Richmond Hill, BH2 6HH
Tel: (44-1202) 554601; Fax: (44-1202) 293676
Circ.—47,696 ABC
Prop.—Southern Newspapers Ltd.
Ch. Ex.—M W Stone
Ed.—Gareth Weekes
Ad. Mgr.—K Whiffin
Ad.—£5.35 cm; £1,700 pg.

BRADFORD
(West Yorkshire)
Pop. Est. 464,700

TELEGRAPH & ARGUS (e) Est. 1868
Hall Ings, BD1 1JR
Tel: (44-1274) 729511; Fax: (44-1274) 723634
Circ.—60,679 ABC
Prop.—Westminster Press Ltd.
Mng. Dir.—J P Banville
Ed.—Perry Austin-Clarke
Ad. Mgr.—Philip Walker
Ad.—£8.58 cm; £1,853.28 pg.

BRIGHTON
(East Sussex)
Pop. Est. 163,710

EVENING ARGUS (e) Est. 1980
Crowhurst Rd., BN1 8AR
Tel: (44-1273) 544544; Fax: (44-1273) 566114
Circ.—62,652 ABC
Prop.—Westminster Press Ltd.
Mng. Dir.—J A Holland
Ed.—Chris Fowler
Ad. Mgr.—S Russell
Ad.—£8.15 cm; £2,225 pg.

BRISTOL
(Avon)
Pop. Est. 413,860

WESTERN DAILY PRESS (m) Est. 1858
Temple Way, BS99 7HD
Tel: (44-117) 9260080; Fax: (44-117) 9279568
Circ.—62,692 ABC
Prop.—Bristol United Press Ltd.
Mng. Dir.—M J Gay
Ed.—Ian Beales
Ad. Mgr.—Nick Weston
Ad.—£6.87 cm; £1,876 pg.

EVENING POST (e) Est. 1932
Temple Way, BS99 7HD
Tel: (44-117) 9260080; Fax: (44-117) 9279568
Circ.—89,219 ABC
Prop.—Bristol United Press Ltd.
Mng. Dir.—M J Gay
Ed.—Adrian Faber
Ad. Mgr.—Nick Weston
Ad.—£10.32 cm; £2,818 pg.

BURTON-ON-TRENT
(Staffordshire)
Pop. Est. 50,250

BURTON MAIL (e) Est. 1898
65-68 High St., DE14 1LE
Tel: (44-1283) 512345; Fax: (44-1283) 510075
Circ.—20,414 ABC
Prop.—Yattendon Trust
Mng. Dir.—J Black
Ed.—B Vertigen
Ad. Mgr.—J P Knell
Ad.—£3.50 cm.; £860 pg.

CAMBRIDGE
(Cambridgeshire)
Pop. Est. 98,840

CAMBRIDGE EVENING NEWS (e) Est. 1888
51 Newmarket Rd., CB5 8EJ
Tel: (44-1223) 358877; Fax: (44-1223) 361720
Circ.—42,995 ABC
Prop.—Yattendon Trust
Mng. Dir.—Tony Steenson
Ed.—R Satchwell
Ad. Mgr.—Mike Carr
Ad.—£5.76 cm; £1,704.96 pg.

CARLISLE
(Cumbria)
Pop. Est. 71,440

EVENING NEWS & STAR (e-ex fri.) Est. 1914
Dalston Rd., CA2 5UA
Tel: (44-1228) 23488; Fax: (44-1228) 512828
Circ.—28,034 ABC
Prop.—Cumbrian Newspapers Ltd.
Mng. Dir.—R L F Burgess
Ed.—Keith Sutton
Ad.—£3.20 cm; £851.20 pg.

CHELTENHAM
(Gloucestershire)
Pop. Est. 75,560

GLOUCESTERSHIRE ECHO (e) Est. 1873
3 Clarence Parade, GL50 3NZ
Tel: (44-1242) 526261; Fax: (44-1242) 578394
Circ.—27,260 ABC
Prop.—Northcliffe Group
Mng. Dir.—T Sallis
Ed.—Anita Syvret
Ad.—£4.42 cm; £1,272.96 pg.

COLCHESTER
(Essex)
Pop. Est. 68,290

EVENING GAZETTE (e) Est. 1814/1970
43-44 North Hill, CO1 1TZ
Tel: (44-1206) 761212; Fax: (44-1206) 763033
Circ.—28,676 ABC
Prop.—Reed Group
Mng. Dir.—Colin Brannigan
Ed.—Martin McNeill
Ad. Mgr.—Bob Slowgrove
Ad.—£4.88 cm; £1,483.52 pg.

COVENTRY
(West Midlands)
Pop. Est. 314,124

COVENTRY EVENING TELEGRAPH (e) Est. 1891
Corporation St., CV1 1FP
Tel: (44-1203) 633633; Fax: (44-1203) 631736
Circ.—85,692 ABC
Prop.—Midland Independent Newspapers Ltd.
Mng. Dir.—F T Bunting
Ed.—Dan Mason
Ad. Mgr.—Pat Allen
Ad.—£10.55 cm; £3,291.60 pg.

DARLINGTON
(Durham)
Pop. Est. 85,890

THE NORTHERN ECHO (m) Est. 1870
Priestgate, DL1 1NF
Tel: (44-1325) 381313; Fax: (44-1325) 380539
Circ.—77,750 ABC
Prop.—Westminster Press Ltd.
Mng. Dir.—A Blood
Ed.—David Flintham
Ad. Mgr.—Lorraine Hutchinson
Ad.—£11.93 cm; £6,589 pg.

DERBY
(Derbyshire)
Pop. Est. 215,736

DERBY EVENING TELEGRAPH (e) Est. 1879
Meadow Rd., DE1 2DW
Tel: (44-1332) 291111; Fax: (44-1332) 290280
Circ.—66,798 ABC
Prop.—Northcliffe Group
Mng. Dir.—S Anderson-Dixon
Ed.—Mike Lowe
Ad. Mgr.—Clive Fidler
Ad.—£7.15 cm; £2,116.40 pg.

EXETER
(Devon)
Pop. Est. 94,180

EXPRESS & ECHO (e) Est. 1864
Heron Rd., EX2 7NF
Tel: (44-1392) 442211; Fax: (44-1392) 442297
Circ.—31,482 ABC
Prop.—Northcliffe Group
Mng. Dir.—M Gower

Copyright ©1996 by the Editor & Publisher Co.

Ed.—Rachel Campey
Ad. Mgr.—Gillian McHardy
Ad.—£4.50 cm; £1,314 pg.

GLOUCESTER
(Gloucestershire)
Pop. Est. 106,500

GLOUCESTERSHIRE CITIZEN (e) Est. 1876
St. John's Lane, GL1 2AY
Tel: (44-1452) 424442; Fax: (44-1452) 505597
Circ.—37,556 ABC
Prop.—Northcliffe Group
Mng. Dir.—K N Thompson
Ed.—Spencer Feeney
Ad. Mgr.—Trevor Sallis
Ad.—£4.47 cm; £1,287.36 pg.

GRIMSBY
(South Humberside)
Pop. Est. 95,150

GRIMSBY EVENING TELEGRAPH (e) Est. 1897
80 Cleethorpe Rd., DN31 3EH
Tel: (44-1472) 359232; Fax: (44-1472) 361093
Circ.—47,521 ABC
Prop.—Northcliffe Group
Mng. Dir.—T Knowles
Ed.—P Moore
Ad. Mgr.—Mark Webb
Ad.—£4.55 cm; £1,242.15 pg.

HALIFAX
(West Yorkshire)
Pop. Est. 90,320

EVENING COURIER (e) Est. 1882
King Cross St.; PO Box 19, HX1 2SF
Tel: (44-1422) 365711/(44-1422) 59151; Fax: (44-1422) 330021
Circ.—32,051 ABC
Prop.—Halifax Courier Holdings Ltd.
Mng. Dir.—E Wood
Dir./Ed.—E Riley
Ad. Mgr.—A Lax
Ad.—£4.30 cm; £2,167.20 pg.

HARTLEPOOL
(Cleveland)
Pop. Est. 97,160

THE MAIL (e) Est. 1877
Clarence Rd., TS24 8BU
Tel: (44-1429) 274441; Fax: (44-1429) 869024
Circ.—27,001 ABC
Prop.—Sunderland & Hartlepool Publishing & Printing Ltd.
Chmn.—C D Brims
Mng. Dir.—S D Bell
Ed.—Chris Cox
Ad. Mgr.—Chris Grieveson
Ad.—£3.92 cm; £995 pg.

HUDDERSFIELD
(West Yorkshire)
Pop. Est. 130,200

HUDDERSFIELD DAILY EXAMINER (e) Est. 1871
Queen St. South; PO Box A26, HD1 2TD
Tel: (44-1484) 430000; Fax: (44-1484) 423722
Circ.—38,480 ABC
Prop.—Huddersfield Newspapers Ltd.
Mng. Dir.—J E C Dicks
Ed.—Richard Mallinson
Ad. Dir.—Roger S Saunders
Ad.—£4.15 cm; £2,241 pg.

HULL
(North Humberside)
Pop. Est. 322,140

HULL DAILY MAIL (e) Est. 1885
Beverley Rd., Blundell's Corner, HU3 1XS
Tel: (44-1482) 327111; Fax: (44-1482) 584353
Circ.—92,693 ABC
Prop.—Northcliffe Group
Mng. Dir.—J J Brown
Ed.—Mike G Wood
Ad. Dir.—Steve Hollingsworth
Ad.—£9.20 cm; £2,732 pg.

IPSWICH
(Suffolk)
Pop. Est. 122,830

EAST ANGLIAN DAILY TIMES (m) Est. 1874
30 Lower Brook St., IP4 1AN
Tel: (44-1473) 230023; Fax: (44-1473) 232529

Circ.—49,217 ABC
Prop.—Eastern Counties N/PRS
Mng. Dir.—S M Garner
Ed.—Malcolm Pheby
Ad. Mgr.—Ian Turner
Ad.—£6.40 cm; £1,474.20 pg.

EVENING STAR (e) Est. 1885
30 Lower Brook St., IP4 1AN
Tel: (44-1473) 230023; Fax: (44-1473) 232529
Circ.—31,167 ABC
Prop.—Eastern Counties N/PRS
Mng. Dir.—S M Garner
Ed.—Terry Hunt
Ad. Mgr.—Ian Turner
Ad.—£5.25 cm; £1,260 pg.

KETTERING
(Northamptonshire)
Pop. Est. 43,350

NORTHAMPTONSHIRE EVENING TELEGRAPH (e) Est. 1897
Northfield Ave., NN16 9HU
Tel: (44-1536) 81111; Fax: (44-1536) 410101
Circ.—36,338
Prop.—EMAP Ltd.
Mng. Dir.—Anne Young
Ed.—Colin Grant
Ad. Dir.—Ian Duncan
Ad.—£6.22 cm; £1,791.36 pg.

LEEDS
(West Yorkshire)
Pop. Est. 716,100

YORKSHIRE EVENING POST (e) Est. 1890
Wellington St.; PO Box 168, LS1 1RF
Tel: (44-113) 2432701/(44-113) 2441234; Fax: (44-113) 2443430
Circ.—106,794 ABC
Prop.—United Newspapers
Mng. Dir.—G L Holbrook
Ed.—C H Bye
Ad. Mgr.—M Pennington
Ad.—£14.55 cm; £7,333.20 pg.

YORKSHIRE POST (m) Est. 1754
Wellington St., LS1 1RF
Tel: (44-113) 2432701/(44-113) 2441234
Circ.—79,094 ABC
Prop.—United Newspapers
Mng. Dir.—G L Holbrook
Ed.—A G Watson
Ad. Mgr.—Sally O'Neil
Ad.—£11.50 cm; £5,796 pg.

LEICESTER
(Leicestershire)
Pop. Est. 279,791

LEICESTER MERCURY (e) Est. 1874
St. George St., LE1 9FQ
Tel: (44-116) 2512512; Fax: (44-116) 2530654
Circ.—118,594 ABC
Prop.—Northcliffe Group
Mng. Dir.—J P Aldridge
Ed. in Ch.—Nick Carter
Ad. Dir.—Philip Brewin
Ad.—£10.90 cm; £3,400.80 pg.

SUNDAY SPORT Est. 1986
848 Melton Rd. Thurmaston, LE4 8BJ
Tel: (44-116) 2694892
Circ.—296,074 ABC
Prop.—Sport Newspapers Ltd.
Ed.—Tony Livesey
Ad. Dir.—Denize Smith
Ad.—£25 cm; £6,125 pg.

LINCOLN
(Lincolnshire)
Pop. Est. 73,810

LINCOLNSHIRE ECHO (e) Est. 1893
Brayford Wharf East, LN5 7AT
Tel: (44-1522) 525252; Fax: (44-1522) 545759
Circ.—31,366 ABC
Prop.—Northcliffe Group
Mng. Dir.—E Skaith
Ed.—Cliff Smith
Ad. Mgr.—D Leigh
Ad.—£3.80 cm; £1,061.90 pg.

LIVERPOOL
(Merseyside)
Pop. Est. 510,700

DAILY POST (m) Est. 1855
Old Hall St.; PO Box 48, L69 3EB
Tel: (44-151) 227200; Fax: (44-151) 236468

Circ.—73,691 ABC
Prop.—Liverpool Daily Post & Echo Ltd.
Mng. Dir.—C F Czilinsky
Ed.—Alastar Machray
Ad. Dir.—Heather Vasco
Ad.—£8.50 cm; £1,836 pg.

LIVERPOOL ECHO (e) Est. 1879
Old Hall St.; PO Box 48, L69 3EB
Tel: (44-151) 227200; Fax: (44-151) 236468
Circ.—168,748 ABC
Prop.—Liverpool Daily Post & Echo Ltd.
Mng. Dir.—C F Czilinsky
Dir./Ed.—J Griffith
Ad. Dir.—Heather Vasco
Ad.—£17.50 cm; £4,410 pg.

LONDON
Pop. Est. 6,765,100

DAILY EXPRESS (m) Est. 1900
Ludgate House, 245 Blackfriars Rd., SE1 9UX
Tel: (44-171) 9288000; Fax: (44-171) 6330244
Circ.—1,265,027 ABC
Prop.—United Newspapers
Adm. Dir.—A Bentley
Ed.—Sir Nicholas Lloyd
Ad. Dir.—Christine Costello
Ad.—£97 cm; £17,500 pg.

DAILY MAIL (m) Est. 1896
Northcliffe House, 2 Derry St., W8 5TT
Tel: (44-171) 9386000; Fax: (44-171) 9373251
Circ.—1,815,507 ABC
Prop.—Associated Newspapers Group Ltd.
Mng. Dir.—W J Pressey
Ed.—Paul Dacre
Ad. Dir.—Mike Ironside
Ad.—£90 cm; £30,240 pg.

DAILY MIRROR (m) Est. 1903
1 Canada Sq., Canary Wharf, E14 5AP
Tel: (44-171) 5103000; Fax: (44-171) 2933000
Circ.—2,568,957
Prop.—Mirror Group Newspapers Ltd. (1986)
Ch. Ex.—David Montgomery
Ed.—Colin Myler
Ad. Dir.—Mark Pritchett
Ad.—£100.00 cm; £25,900 pg.

DAILY STAR (m) Est. 1978
Ludgate House, 245 Blackfriars Rd., SE1 9UX
Tel: (44-171) 9288000; Fax: (44-171) 6330244
Circ.—739,210 ABC
Prop.—United Newspapers
Ed.—Philip Walker
Ad. Dir.—Christine Costello
Ad.—£44 cm; £12,000 pg.

DAILY TELEGRAPH (m) Est. 1855
1 Canada Sq., Canary Wharf, E14 5DT
Tel: (44-171) 5385000; Fax: (44-171) 5383810
Circ.—1,064,717 ABC
Prop.—The Telegraph plc.
Chmn.—Conrad Black
Ed.—Charles Moore
Ad. Dir.—Len Sanderson
Ad.—£83 cm; £36,500 pg.

THE EUROPEAN Est. 1990
200 Grays Inn Rd., WC1X 8NE
Tel: (44-171) 4187777; Fax: (44-171) 7131840
Circ.—204,110 ABC
Prop.—The European Ltd. (Barclay Brothers)
Ed.—Herbert Pearson
Ad. Dir.—Michael Moore
Ad.—£20 cm; £7,500 pg. (£11,250 pg. worldwide)

EVENING STANDARD Est. 1827
2 Derry St., W8 5EE
Tel: (44-171) 9386000; Fax: (44-171) 9373193
Circ.—456,126 ABC
Prop.—Associated Newspapers
Chmn.—H C Hardy
Ed.—Max Hastings
Ad. Dir.—Peter Gould
Ad.—£44 cm; £9,240 pg.

FINANCIAL TIMES (m) Est. 1888
1 Southwark Bridge, SE1 9HL
Tel: (44-171) 8733000; Fax: (44-171) 8733076
Circ.—291,198 ABC
Prop.—Financial Times (Pearson plc.)
Ch. Ex.—David Palmer

British Isles **England**

Ed.—Richard Lambert
Ad. Dir.—Tony Blin-Stoyle
Ad.—£69 cm; £30,902 pg.

THE GUARDIAN (m) Est. 1821
119 Farringdon Rd., EC1R 3ER
Tel: (44-171) 2782332; Fax: (44-171) 8372114
Circ.—392,222 ABC
Prop.—Guardian Media Group
Mng. Dir.—James Markwick
Ed.—Alan Rusbridger
Ad. Dir.—Carolyn McCall
Ad.—£36 cm; £15,500 pg.

THE INDEPENDENT (m) Est. 1986
1 Canada Sq., Canary Wharf, EC1Y 2DB
Tel: (44-171) 2531222; Fax: (44-171) 6081435
Circ.—296,171 ABC
Prop.—Newspaper Publishing Ltd.
Ed.—Ian Hargreaves
Ad. Dir.—Jeremy Reed
Ad.—£32 cm; £14,000 pg.

INDEPENDENT ON SUNDAY (e) Est. 1986
1 Canada Sq., Canary Wharf, EC1Y 2DB
Tel: (44-171) 2531212; Fax: (44-171) 9561435
Circ.—332,236
Prop.—Newspaper Publishing Ltd.
Ed.—Peter Wilby
Ad. Dir.—Jeremy Reed
Ad.—£32 cm; £14,000 pg.

MAIL ON SUNDAY Est. 1982
2 Derry St., W8 5EE
Tel: (44-171) 9386000; Fax: (44-171) 9373745
Circ.—2,004,994 ABC
Prop.—Associated Newspapers Ltd.
Mng. Dir.—Ian Pay
Ed.—Jonathan Holborow
Ad. Mgr.—Simon Barnes
Ad.—£107 cm; £28,300 pg.

NEWS OF THE WORLD (S) Est. 1843
Virginia St., E1 9XJ
Tel: (44-171) 7827000; Fax: (44-171) 5839504
Circ.—4,707,485 ABC
Prop.—News Group Newspapers Ltd.
Mng. Dir.—A A Fischer
Ed.—Piers Morgan
Ad. Dir.—C Milner
Ad.—£150 cm; £35,700 pg.

THE OBSERVER (S) Est. 1791
119 Farringdon Rd., EC1R 3ER
Tel: (44-171) 2982332; Fax: (44-171) 2781449
Circ.—455,027 ABC
Prop.—Guardian Media Group
Mng. Dir.—Jess Watts
Ed.—Andrew Jaspan
Ad. Dir.—Carolyn McCall
Ad.—£51 cm; £23,750 pg.

THE PEOPLE (S) Est. 1881
1 Canada Sq., E14 5AP
Tel: (44-171) 5103000; Fax: (44-171) 2933000
Circ.—2,074,417 ABC
Prop.—Mirror Group Newpapers Ltd. (1986)
Ed.—Bridget Rowe
Ad. Dir.—Mark Pritchett
Ad.—£83 cm; £21,750 pg.

THE SUN (m) Est. 1969
Virginia St., E1 9XJ
Tel: (44-171) 7827000; Fax: (44-171) 7825605
Circ.—4,023,548 ABC
Prop.—News Group Newspapers Ltd.
Mng. Dir.—A A Fischer
Ed.—Stuart Higgins
Ad. Dir.—Richard Webb
Ad.—£136 cm; £32,300 pg.

SUNDAY EXPRESS (S) Est. 1918
Ludgate House, 245 Blackfriars Rd., SE1 9UX
Tel: (44-171) 9288000; Fax: (44-171) 6330244
Circ.—1,379,825 ABC
Prop.—United Newspapers Ltd.
Ed.—Brian Hitchen
Ad. Dir.—Christine Costello
Ad.—£116 cm; £30,960 pg.

SUNDAY MIRROR (S) Est. 1963
1 Canada Sq., Canary Wharf, E14 5AP
Tel: (44-171) 5103000; Fax: (44-171) 2933000
Circ.—2,603,535 ABC
Prop.—Mirror Group Newspapers (1986) Ltd.
Ed.—Tessa Hilton
Ad. Dir.—Mark Pritchett
Ad.—£110 cm; £28,500 pg.

SUNDAY TELEGRAPH (S) Est. 1961
1 Canada Sq., Canary Wharf, E14 5DT
Tel: (44-171) 5385000; Fax: (44-171) 5381330
Circ.—696,964 ABC
Prop.—The Telegraph plc.
Ed.—Dominic Lawson
Ad. Dir.—Len Sanderson
Ad.—£60 cm; £27,000 pg.

SUNDAY TIMES
Virginia St., E1 9XT
Tel: (44-171) 78725000; Fax: (44-171) 7825658
Circ.—1,247,204 ABC
Prop.—News Group Newspapers Ltd.
Chmn.—Rupert Murdoch
Ed.—John Witherow
Ad. Mgr.—Trevor Pryer
Ad.—£105 cm; £47,000 pg.

THE TIMES (m) Est. 1785
Virginia St., E1 9XT
Tel: (44-171) 7825000; Fax: (44-171) 5839519
Circ.—667,238 ABC
Prop.—News UK Ltd.
Ed.—Peter Stothard
Ad. Dir.—Camilla Rhodes
Ad.—£39 cm; £17,000 pg.

MAIDSTONE
(Kent)
Pop. Est. 133,200

KENT TODAY (e) Est. 1968
New Hythe Lane, Larkfield, ME20 6SG
Tel: (44-1662) 717880; Fax: (44-1662) 719637
Circ.—26,317 ABC
Prop.—South Eastern Newspapers Ltd.
Mng. Ed.—W J Dorkell
Ed.—Charles Stewart
Ad. Mgr.—Paul Kerr
Ad.—£5.80 cm; £1,763.20 pg.

MANCHESTER
(Lancashire)
Pop. Est. 458,600

MANCHESTER EVENING NEWS (e) Est. 1868
164 Deansgate, M60 2RD
Tel: (44-161) 8327200; Fax: (44-161) 8325351
Circ.—193,952 ABC
Prop.—Guardian & Manchester Evening News Ltd.
Mng. Dir.—A J Boore
Ed.—M R Unger
Ad. Mgr.—Terry Blitcliffe
Ad.—£27.85 cm; £7,018.20 pg.

MIDDLESBROUGH
(Cleveland)
Pop. Est. 527,907

EVENING GAZETTE (e) Est. 1869
Borough Rd., TS1 3AZ
Tel: (44-1642) 245401; Fax: (44-1642) 210565
Circ.—68,450 ABC
Prop.—Thomson Corp.
Mng. Dir.—N J M Burnett
Ed.—Ranald Allan
Ad. Mgr.—Gary Fearon
Ad.—£9.45 cm; £4,915 pg.

NEWCASTLE-UPON-TYNE
(Tyne And Wear)
Pop. Est. 277,674

EVENING CHRONICLE (e) Est. 1885
Groat Market, NE1 1ED
Tel: (44-191) 2327500; Fax: (44-191) 2322256
Circ.—120,640 ABC
Prop.—Thomson Corp.
Mng. Dir.—A B Hill
Ed.—Neil Benson
Ad. Mgr.—Shaun Bowron
Ad.—£13.60 cm; £6,732 pg.

THE JOURNAL (m) Est. 1832
Groat Market, NE1 1ED
Tel: (44-191) 2327500; Fax: (44-191) 2322256
Circ.—57,677 ABC
Prop.—Thomson Corp.
Mng. Dir.—A B Hill

Ed.—Bill Bradshaw
Ad. Mgr.—Shaun Bowron
Ad.—£9.15 cm; £2,305 pg.

SUNDAY SUN (S) Est. 1919
Groat Market, NE1 1ED
Tel: (44-191) 2327500; Fax: (44-191) 2322256
Circ.—125,059 ABC
Prop.—Thomson Corp.
Mng. Dir.—A B Hill
Ed.—C Rushton
Ad. Mgr.—Shaun Bowron
Ad.—£10.60 cm; £2,673.72 pg.

NORTHAMPTON
(Northamptonshire)
Pop. Est. 154,170

CHRONICLE & ECHO (e) Est. 1880
Upper Mounts, NN1 3HR
Tel: (44-1604) 231122; Fax: (44-1604) 234000
Circ.—30,267 ABC
Prop.—EMAP Ltd.
Mng. Dir.—D E Wright
Dir./Ed.—C Hutchby
Ad. Mgr.—Christine Crossley
Ad.—£9.95 cm; £1,465.20 pg.

NORWICH
(Norfolk)
Pop. Est. 121,688

EASTERN DAILY PRESS (m) Est. 1870
Rouen Rd., NR1 1RE
Tel: (44-1603) 628311; Fax: (44-1603) 572930
Circ.—79,192 ABC
Prop.—Eastern Counties Newspapers Ltd.
Mng. Dir.—D L Bird
Ed.—Peter Franzen
Ad. Dir.—Richard Gasken
Ad.—£7.65 cm; £4,284.50 pg.

EVENING NEWS (e) Est. 1882
Rouen Rd., NR1 1RE
Tel: (44-1603) 628311
Circ.—41,563 ABC
Prop.—Eastern Counties Newspapers Ltd.
Mng. Dir.—D L Bird
Ed.—Claire Gillingwater
Ad. Dir.—Richard Gasken
Ad.—£5.32 cm; £1,532 pg.

NOTTINGHAM
(Nottinghamshire)
Pop. Est. 299,758

NOTTINGHAM EVENING POST (e) Est. 1878
Forman St., NG1 4AB
Tel: (44-114) 248200; Fax: (44-114) 2484753
Circ.—107,940
Prop.—Northcliffe Group
Mng. Dir.—Charles Wright
Ed.—Graham Glen
Ad. Mgr.—Kevan Weeds
Ad.—£10.10 cm; £7,495

NUNEATON
(Warwicks)
Pop. Est. 118,000

HEARTLAND EVENING NEWS (e) Est. 1992
11-15 Newtown Rd., CV11 4HR
Tel: (44-1203) 353534
Circ.—36,000
Prop.—Heartland Newspapers
Ed.—Tony Parrot
Ad. Mgr.—Linda Clark
Ad.—£3 cm; £840 pg.

OLDHAM
(Lancashire)
Pop. Est. 104,860

EVENING CHRONICLE (e) Est. 1880
172 Union St., OL1 1EQ
Tel: (44-161) 6332121; Fax: (44-161) 6270905
Circ.—36,009 ABC
Prop.—Hirst, Kidd & Rennie Ltd.
Mng. Dir.—H J Hirst
Ed.—Philip Hirst
Ad. Mgr.—Jim Whittingham
Ad.—£4.22 cm; £950 pg.

OXFORD
(Oxfordshire)
Pop. Est. 108,564

OXFORD MAIL (e) Est. 1928
Osney Mead, OX2 0EJ
Tel: (44-1865) 244988; Fax: (44-1865) 790423
Circ.—34,505 ABC
Prop.—Westminster Press Ltd.
Mng. Dir.—J G Hemsley
Ed.—Tim Blott
Ad. Mgr.—Sharon Wallace-Shanks
Ad.—£5.41 cm; £1,558.08 pg.

PETERBOROUGH
(Cambridgeshire)
Pop. Est. 70,630

PETERBOROUGH EVENING TELEGRAPH (e) Est. 1961
Telegraph House, Priestgate, PE1 1JW
Tel: (44-1733) 555111; Fax: (44-1733) 555188
Circ.—29,419 ABC
Prop.—EMAP Ltd.
Mng. Dir.—Barrie Holden
Ed.—Bob Crawley
Ad. Mgr.—Martyn Hammond
Ad.—£5.60 cm; £1,568 pg.

PLYMOUTH
(Devon)
Pop. Est. 243,895

SUNDAY INDEPENDENT (S) Est. 1808
Burrington Way, PL5 3LN
Tel: (44-1752) 777151; Fax: (44-1752) 780680
Circ.—40,351 ABC
Prop.—Yattendon Trust
Mng. Dir.—Brian Doel
Ed.—John Noble
Mktg. Mgr.—Tony Wilkins
Ad.—£5 cm; £1,000 pg.

WESTERN EVENING HERALD (e) Est. 1895
17 Brest Rd., PL6 5AA
Tel: (44-1752) 765500; Fax: (44-1752) 765543
Circ.—56,147 ABC
Prop.—Northcliffe Group
Mng. Dir.—J J Ramsden
Ed.—Alan Cooper
Ad.—£6.50 cm; £1,638 pg.

WESTERN MORNING NEWS (m) Est. 1860
17 Brest Rd., PL6 5AA
Tel: (44-1752) 765500; Fax: (44-1752) 765543
Circ.—52,123 ABC
Prop.—Northcliffe Group
Mng. Dir.—J J Ramsden
Ed.—Barry Williams
Ad.—£6.50 cm; £3,217.50 pg.

PORTSMOUTH
(Hampshire)
Pop. Est. 179,419

THE NEWS (e) Est. 1877
The News Centre, Hilsea, PO2 9SX
Tel: (44-1705) 664488; Fax: (44-1705) 692280
Circ.—78,633 ABC
Prop.—Portsmouth Publishing & Printing Ltd.
Mng. Dir.—Ben Stoneham
Ed.—Geoffrey Elliot
Ad. Dir.—D Middleton
Ad.—£8.70 cm; £2,253 pg.

PRESTON
(Lancashire)
Pop. Est. 95,450

LANCASHIRE EVENING POST (e) Est. 1886
Olivers Place, Fulwood, PR2 4ZA
Tel: (44-1772) 54841; Fax: (44-1772) 563288
Circ.—65,639 ABC
Prop.—United Newspapers
Mng. Dir.—W M West
Ed.—Philip Welsh
Ad. Mgr.—Jeanette Wilkinson
Ad.—£7.99 cm; £4,026.96 pg.

READING
(Berkshire)
Pop. Est. 194,700

EVENING POST (e) Est. 1965
8 Tessa Rd., RG1 8NS
Tel: (44-1734) 575833/(44-1734) 588588; Fax: (44-1734) 503592
Circ.—23,257 ABC

Prop.—Thomson Corp.
Mng. Dir.—S A Edwards
Ed.—Kim Chapman
Ad. Mgr.—Elaine Eva
Ad.—£6.88 cm; £2,229 pg.

SCARBOROUGH
(North Yorkshire)
Pop. Est. 43,080

SCARBOROUGH EVENING NEWS (e) Est. 1876
17-23 Aberdeen Walk, YO11 1BB
Tel: (44-1723) 363636; Fax: (44-1723) 354092
Circ.—16,966 ABC
Prop.—EMAP Ltd.
Mng. Dir.—D Fordham
Ed.—Neil Speight
Ad. Dir.—Ian Woodcock
Ad.—£4.13 cm; £1,189.44 pg.

SCUNTHORPE
(South Humberside)
Pop. Est. 59,600

SCUNTHORPE EVENING TELEGRAPH (e)
Doncaster Rd., DN15 7RE
Tel: (44-1724) 843421; Fax: (44-1724) 854395
Circ.—25,182
Prop.—Northcliffe Group
Dir./Gen. Mgr.—Ivor Bull
Ed.—Peter Moore
Ad. Mgr.—Maggie Fell
Ad.—£3.40 cm; £928.20 pg.

SHEFFIELD
(South Yorkshire)
Pop. Est. 545,800

THE STAR (e) Est. 1887
York St., S1 1PU
Tel: (44-114) 2767676
Circ.—92,388 ABC
Prop.—United Newspapers
Mng. Dir.—Chris Green
Ed.—Peter Charlton
Ad. Mgr.—Paul Bentham
Ad.—£14.35 cm; £3,343.90 pg.

SOUTH SHIELDS
(Tyne And Wear)
Pop. Est. 98,610

THE GAZETTE (e) Est. 1849
Chapter Row, NE33 1BL
Tel: (44-191) 4554661; Fax: (44-191) 4568270
Circ.—25,077 ABC
Prop.—The North-East Press Ltd.
Ed.—Ian Holland
Ad. Mgr.—G Ramsay
Ad.—£4.20 cm; £1,087 pg.

SOUTHAMPTON
(Hampshire)
Pop. Est. 204,406

SOUTHERN DAILY ECHO (e) Est. 1888
45 Above Bar, SO9 7BA
Tel: (44-1703) 634134; Fax: (44-1703) 630428
Circ.—61,567 ABC
Prop.—Southern Newspapers Ltd.
Gen. Mgr.—Gerald Bradley
Ed.—Pat Fleming
Ad. Mgr.—Pauline McArdle
Ad.—£7.10 cm; £1,924 pg.

STOKE-ON-TRENT
(Staffordshire)
Pop. Est. 252,351

EVENING SENTINEL (e) Est. 1873
Sentinel House, Etruria, ST1 5SS
Tel: (44-1782) 289800; Fax: (44-1782) 260516
Circ.—99,183 ABC
Prop.—Northcliffe Group
Mng. Dir.—P Keller
Ed.—Sean Dooley
Ad. Mgr.—Rudd Apsey
Ad.—£8 cm; £2,013 pg.

SUNDERLAND
(Tyne And Wear)
Pop. Est. 295,096

SUNDERLAND ECHO (e) Est. 1873
Pennywell, SR4 9ER
Tel: (44-191) 5343011; Fax: (44-191) 5343807/(44-191) 5345975
Circ.—60,060 ABC

Prop.—North-East Press Ltd.
Ed./Dir.—A G Hughes
Ad. Mgr.—J Wilson
Ad.—£7.90 cm; £2,046.10 pg.

SWINDON
(Wiltshire)
Pop. Est. 90,330

EVENING ADVERTISER (e) Est. 1898
100 Victoria Rd., SN1 3BE
Tel: (44-1793) 528144; Fax: (44-1793) 523883
Circ.—26,947 ABC
Prop.—Westminster Press Ltd.
Mng. Dir.—F G Higgs
Ed.—Geoff Tether
Ad. Mgr.—A Harris
Ad.—£4.12 cm; £2,266 pg.

TELFORD
(Shropshire)
Pop. Est. 39,622

SHROPSHIRE STAR (e) Est. 1964
Ketley, TF1 4HU
Tel: (44-1952) 242424; Fax: (44-1952) 254605
Circ.—95,047 ABC
Prop.—Shropshire Star Ltd.
Mng. Dir.—B A Jackson
Ed.—A Wright
Ad. Mgr.—A Harris
Ad.—£6.30 cm; £2,066.40 pg.

TORQUAY
(Devon)
Pop. Est. 106,400

HERALD EXPRESS (e) Est. 1925
Barton Hill Rd., TQ2 8JN
Tel: (44-1803) 213213; Fax: (44-1803) 313093
Circ.—29,722 ABC
Prop.—Northcliffe Group
Mng. Dir.—P Jameson
Ed.—J C Mitchell
Ad. Mgr.—Tony Aspinall
Ad.—£4 cm; £1,022 pg.

WEYMOUTH
(Dorset)
Pop. Est. 41,410

DORSET EVENING ECHO (e) Est. 1921
57 St. Thomas St., DT4 8EU
Tel: (44-1305) 784804; Fax: (44-1305) 761394
Circ.—22,188 ABC
Prop.—Southern Newspapers Ltd.
Gen. Mgr.—B Makepeace
Ed.—M Woods
Ad. Mgr.—D Johnston
Ad.—£2.85 cm; £775 pg.

WOLVERHAMPTON
(West Midlands)
Pop. Est. 263,500

EXPRESS & STAR (e) Est. 1874
51-53 Queen St., WV1 3BU
Tel: (44-1902) 313131; Fax: (44-1902) 21467
Circ.—212,739 ABC
Prop.—Express & Star Ltd.
Mng. Dir.—M Kersen
Ed.—W Wilson
Ad. Mgr.—M Wright
Ad.—£18 cm; £5,904 pg.

WORCESTER
(Worcestershire)
Pop. Est. 74,170

WORCESTER EVENING NEWS (e) Est. 1935
Hylton Rd., WR2 5JX
Tel: (44-1905) 748200; Fax: (44-1905) 429605
Circ.—24,387 ABC
Prop.—Reed Group
Pub./Dir.—Alan Josephson
Ed.—Malcolm Ward
Ad. Mgr.—Tina Hurley
Ad.—£5.05 cm; £1,535.20 pg.

YORK
(North Yorkshire)
Pop. Est. 123,120

YORKSHIRE EVENING PRESS (e) Est. 1882
76-86 Walmgate; PO Box 29, YO1 1YN
Tel: (44-1904) 653051; Fax: (44-1904) 611488
Circ.—46,642 ABC

Prop.—Westminster Press Ltd.
Ed.—David Nicholson
Ad. Mgr.—D James
Ad.—£7 cm; £3,024 pg.

NORTHERN IRELAND
Pop. Est. 1,575,000

BELFAST
(Antrim)
Pop. Est. 324,900

BELFAST TELEGRAPH (e) Est. 1870
124-144 Royal Ave., BT1 1EB
Tel: (44-1232) 321242; Fax: (44-1232) 242287
Circ.—136,714 ABC
Prop.—Thomson Corp.
Chmn./Mng. Dir.—R C Crane
Ed.—Edmund Curran
Ad. Mgr.—Ian Clarke
Ad.—£13.60 cm.; £7,616 pg.
IRISH NEWS (m) Est. 1855
113-117 Donegall St., BT1 2GE
Tel: (44-1232) 322226; Fax: (44-1232) 231282
Circ.—44,443 ABC
Prop.—Irish News Ltd.
Ed.—Tom Collins
Ad. Mgr.—Paddy Meehan
Ad.—£6.30 cm.; £2,990 pg.
NEWS LETTER (m) Est. 1989
46-56 Boucher Cres., BT12 2QY
Tel: (44-1232) 680000
Circ.—66,440 VDF
Prop.—Century Newspapers Ltd.
Ed.—Geoff Martin
Ad. Mgr.—Eva Mitchell
Ad.—£9.50 cm.; £2,460 pg.
SUNDAY LIFE (S) Est. 1988
124 Royal Ave., BT 12 2QY
Tel: (44-1232) 264300; Fax: (44-1232) 554507
Circ.—98,612 ABC
Prop.—Thomson Corp.
Mng. Dir.—R C Crane
Ed.—Martin Lindsay
Ad. Mgr.—Alastair Hunter
Ad.—£7.70 cm.; £1,994.30 pg.
ULSTER NEWS LETTER (m) Est. 1737
45-56 Boucher Cres., BT12 6QY
Tel: (44-1232) 680000
Circ.—33,233 ABC
Prop.—Century Newspapers Ltd.
Chmn.—O W J Henderson
Ed.—G Martin
Mktg. Dir.—H McWilliams
Ad.—£9.50 cm.; £2,460 pg.

REPUBLIC OF IRELAND
Pop. Est. 3,600,000

CORK
Pop. Est. (Metro Area) 282,790

CORK EVENING ECHO (e)
Academy St.; PO Box 21
Tel: (353-121) 272722
Circ.—24,647 ABC
Prop.—Thos. Crosbie & Co. Ltd.
Ed.—Nigel Omahony
Ad. Mgr.—F Hannigan
Ad.—£9.84 cm.; £2,450 pg.
CORK EXAMINER (m)
Academy St.; PO Box 21
Tel: (353-121) 272722
Circ.—52,084 ABC
Prop.—Thos. Crosbie & Co. Ltd.
Ed.—Brian Looney
Ad. Mgr.—F Hannigan
Ad.—IR£9.84 cm.; IR£2,450 pg.

DUBLIN
Pop. Est. 1,024,429

EVENING HERALD (e)
90 Middle Abbey St.
Tel: (353-11) 731666; Fax: (353-11) 722657
Circ.—90,384
Prop.—Independent Newspapers Ltd.
Mng. Dir.—B Pitcher
Ed.—Brian Quinn
Ad. Mgr.—Brendan McCabe
Ad.—£57.50 Sci; £5,000 pg.

IRISH INDEPENDENT (m)
90 Middle Abbey St.
Tel: (353-11) 8731666; Fax: (353-11) 8722657
Circ.—145,452 ABC
Prop.—Independent Newspapers Ltd.
Mng. Dir.—B P Pitcher
Ed.—Aiden Pender
Ad. Mgr.—Brendan McCabe
Ad.—£86.50 Sci.; £13,800 pg.
THE IRISH TIMES (m)
13 D'Olier St., 2
Tel: (353-11) 6792022; Fax: (353-11) 6793910
Circ.—93,678 ABC
Prop.—The Irish Times Ltd.
Mng. Dir.—Major T B McDowell
Ed.—R J D Gageby
Ad. Mgr.—Liam Holland
Ad.—£35.50 Scc.; £13,800 pg.
THE STAR (d)
62A Terenure Rd. North 6
Tel: (353-11) 4901228; Fax: (353-11) 4907425
Circ.—76,392 ABC
Prop.—The Independent Star Ltd.
Mng. Dir.—John Thomson
Ed.—Gerald O'Regan
Ad. Mgr.—Ken Grace
Ad.—£41 Sci.; £3,990 pg.
SUNDAY INDEPENDENT (S)
90 Middle Abbey St., 1
Tel: (353-11) 731666; Fax: (353-11) 731787
Circ.—258,291 ABC
Prop.—Independent Newspapers Ltd.
Mng. Dir.—B Pitcher
Ed.—Michael Hand
Ad. Mgr.—B McCabe
Ad.—£94.50 Sci.; £15,000 pg.
SUNDAY WORLD (S)
18 Rathfarnham Rd. North 6
Tel: (353-11) 4901980; Fax: (44-11) 4902177
Circ.—207,749 ABC
Prop.—Sunday Newspapers Ltd.
Mng. Dir.—Michael Brophy
Ed.—Colm McGinty
Ad. Dir.—M McCormack
Ad.—£85 Sci.; £8,000 pg.

SCOTLAND
Pop. Est. 5,200,000

ABERDEEN
(Grampian)
Pop. Est. 208,340

EVENING EXPRESS (e) Est. 1879
Lang Stracht, Mastrick, PO Box 43, AB9 8AF
Tel: (44-1224) 690222; Fax: (44-1224) 694613
Circ.—69,562 ABC
Prop.—Thomson Corp.
Mng. Dir.—A A Scott
Ed.—Dick Williamson
Ad. Mgr.—Janis Gallon Smith
Ad.—£13.50 cm.; £2,800 pg.
THE PRESS & JOURNAL (m) Est. 1748
Lang Stracht, Mastrick; PO Box 43
Tel: (44-1224) 690222; Fax: (44-1224) 694613
Circ.—107,965 ABC
Prop.—Thomson Group
Mng. Dir.—A A Scott
Ed.—Derek Tucker
Ad. Mgr.—Janis Gallon Smith
Ad.—£18 cm; £8,100 pg.

DUNDEE
(Tayside)
Pop. Est. 192,765

COURIER (m) Est. 1926
80 Kingsway East, DD4 8SL
Tel: (44-1382) 23131; Fax: (44-1382) 22214
Circ.—105,957 ABC
Prop.—D C Thomson & Co. Ltd.
Ed.—A Stewart
Ad. Mgr.—A McEwan
Ad.—£12.40 cm; £5,605 pg.

EVENING TELEGRAPH (m) Est. 1905
80 Kingsway East, DD4 8SL
Tel: (44-1382) 23131; Fax: (44-1382) 22214
Circ.—36,880 ABC
Prop.—D C Thomson & Co. Ltd.
Ed.—H B Pirie
Ad. Mgr.—A McEwan
Ad.—£4.60 cm.; £1,040 pg.
SUNDAY POST (S) Est. 1920
Albert Sq., DD1 9QJ
Tel: (44-1382) 23131; Fax: (44-1382) 22214
Circ.—940,349 ABC
Prop.—D C Thomson & Co. Ltd.
Ed.—R Reid
Ad. Mgr.—J I Foggie
Ad.—£43 cm; £9,735 pg.

EDINBURGH
(Lothian)
Pop. Est. 444,700

EVENING NEWS (e) Est. 1873
20 North Bridge, EH1 1YT
Tel: (44-131) 2252468; Fax: (44-131) 2257302
Circ.—88,780 ABC
Prop.—Barclay Brothers
Mng. Dir.—J A Logan
Ed.—Harry Roulston
Ad. Mgr.—Stuart Marritt
Ad.—£13.25 cm; £7,440 pg.
SCOTLAND ON SUNDAY (S) Est. 1988
20 North Bridge, EH1 1YT
Tel: (44-131) 2252468; Fax: (44-131) 2202443
Circ.—87,936 ABC
Prop.—Thomson Corp.
Mng. Dir.—Joe Logan
Ed.—Andrew Jaspan
Ad. Mgr.—Gordon Adam
Ad.—£18.20 cm; £7,725 pg.
THE SCOTSMAN (m) Est. 1817
20 North Bridge, EH1 1YT
Tel: (44-131) 2252468; Fax: (44-131) 2267420
Circ.—79,267 ABC
Prop.—Barclay Brothers
Mng. Dir.—J A Logan
Ed.—Jim Seaton
Ad. Mgr.—Gordon Adam
Ad.—£18.50 cm; £8,019 pg.

GLASGOW
(Strathclyde)
Pop. Est. 761,000

DAILY RECORD (m) Est. 1885
40 Anderston Quay, G3 8DA
Tel: (44-141) 2487000
Circ.—746,861 ABC
Prop.—Mirror Group Newspapers
Ed.—Terry Quinn
Ad. Dir.—Stephen Auty
Ad.—£38.95 cm; £10,200 pg.
EVENING TIMES (e) Est. 1876
195 Albion St., G1 1QP
Tel: (44-141) 5526255; Fax: (44-141) 5521344
Circ.—138,987 ABC
Prop.—Caledonian Newspapers
Mng. Dir.—I J Irvine
Ed.—George McKechnie
Ad. Dir.—Eric Farquharson
Ad.—£22 cm; £5,700 pg.
GLASGOW HERALD (m) Est. 1782
195 Albion St., G1 1QP
Tel: (44-141) 5526255; Fax: (44-141) 5521344
Circ.—108,165 ABC
Prop.—Caledonian Newspapers
Mng. Dir.—I J Irvine
Ed.—Arnold Kemp
Ad. Dir.—Eric Farquharson
Ad.—£22 cm; £10,700 pg.
SUNDAY MAIL (S) Est. 1919
40 Anderston Quay, G3 8DA
Tel: (44-141) 2487000
Circ.—884,279 ABC
Prop.—Mirror Group Newspapers
Ch. Ex.—V L Horwood
Ed.—James Cassidy
Ad. Dir.—David Bentley
Ad.—£41 cm; £10,745 pg.

Scotland — British Isles

GREENOCK
(Strathclyde)
Pop. Est. 69,171

GREENOCK TELEGRAPH (e) Est. 1857
2 Crawford St., PA15 1LH
Tel: (44-1475) 26511; Fax: (44-1475) 83734
Circ.—20,450 ABC
Prop.—Orr Pollock & Co. Ltd.
Mng. Dir.—Tom Welch
Ed.—Ian Wilson
Ad. Mgr.—Steve Povey
Ad.—£3.50 cm; £862 pg.

PAISLEY
(Strathclyde)
Pop. Est. 95,067

PAISLEY DAILY EXPRESS (m) Est. 1874
14 New St., Paisley, PA1 1XY
Tel: (44-141) 3312444; Fax: (44-141) 3324912
Circ.—8,464 ABC
Prop.—Scottish & Universal Newspapers (SUN)
Dir.—A W Lumsden
Ed.—Norman Macdonald
Ad. Mgr.—Liz Telford
Ad.—£4.55 cm; £1,200 pg.

WALES
Pop. Est. 2,836,000

CARDIFF
(South Glamorgan)
Pop. Est. 282,000

SOUTH WALES ECHO (e) Est. 1884
Thomson House, Havelock St., CF1 1WR
Tel: (44-1222) 223333; Fax: (44-1222) 239441/(44-1222) 237539
Circ.—79,844 ABC
Prop.—Thomson Corp.
Mng. Dir.—D Faulkner
Ed.—Keith Perch
Ad. Mgr.—Lynn Cardwell
Ad.—£12.95 cm; £3,626 pg.

WALES ON SUNDAY (S) Est. 1989
Thompson House, Havelock St., CF1 1WR
Tel: (44-1222) 223333; Fax: (44-1222) 224668
Circ.—63,341
Prop.—Western Mail & Echo Ltd.
Ed.—P Hollinson
Ad. Mgr.—Lawrence Winmill
Ad.—£7.20 cm; £2,016 pg.

WESTERN MAIL (m) Est. 1869
Thompson House, Havelock St., CF1 1WR
Tel: (44-1222) 583583; Fax: (44-1222) 583583/(44-1222) 237539
Circ.—64,602 ABC
Prop.—Thomson Corp.
Mng. Dir.—D Faulkner
Ed.—Neil Fowler
Ad. Mgr.—Lynn Cardwell
Ad.—£13.80 cm; £7,728 pg.

NEWPORT
(Gwent)
Pop. Est. 110,530

SOUTH WALES ARGUS (e) Est. 1892
Cardiff Rd., Maesglas, NP9 1QW
Tel: (44-1633) 810000; Fax: (44-1633) 810100
Circ.—35,644 ABC
Prop.—United Newspapers
Ed.—G Keighley

Ad. Dir.—Jane Thomas
Ad.—£5.22 cm; £2,871 pg.

SWANSEA
(West Glamorgan)
Pop. Est. 186,199

SOUTH WALES EVENING POST (e) Est. 1861
Adelaide St., SA1 1QT
Tel: (44-1792) 650841; Fax: (44-1792) 644008
Circ.—68,342 ABC
Prop.—Northcliffe Group
Ed.—H Berlyn
Ad. Mgr.—Les Morgan
Ad.—£6.50 cm; £1,872 pg.

WREXHAM
(Clwyd)
Pop. Est. 39,140

EVENING LEADER (e) Est. 1973
Wrexham Rd., Mold, CH7 1XY
Tel: (44-1352) 700022; Fax: (44-1352) 700048
Circ.—31,598 ABC
Prop.—North Wales Newspapers Ltd.
Mng. Dir.—P N Mansfield
Ed.—R Herbert
Ad. Mgr.—L Lommano
Ad.—£4.50 cm; £1,224 pg.

NEWSPAPERS OF EUROPE

ALBANIA, REPUBLIC OF
Pop. Est. 3,374,085

TIRANA
Pop. Est. 243,100

ALBANIAN NEWSPAPER (m) Italian
Rruga e Dibres
Tel: (355-42) 32646
Circ.—11,000
Prop.—EDISUD
Prop.—Viale Scipione l'Africano Bari/ITALY
Ed.—Carlo Bollino
BASHKIMI (Unity) Est. 1943
Blvd. Deshmoret e Kombit, 3rd. Floor
Tel: (355-42) 27768
Circ.—30,000
Prop.—Democratic Front
KOHA JONE (m)
Lagjia Misto Mame, Rr. Ferit Xhajko 29
Tel: (355-42) 33274; Fax: (355-42) 33274
Circ.—30,000
Pub.—Nikolle Lesi
Ed.—Aleksander Frangaj
REPUBLIKA Est. 1991
Blvd. Deshmoret e Kombit, No. 66
Tel: (355-42) 25988; Fax: (355-42) 25988
Prop.—Republican Party
Ed. in Ch.—Ylli Rakipi
RILINDJA DEMOKRATIKE (The Democratic Renaissance) (m) Est. 1991
Rr. Punetoret e Rilindjes, No. 16, ish godina e Hostenit
Tel: (355-42) 29609; Fax: (355-42) 32090
Circ.—10,000
Prop.—Democratic Party
Ed. in Ch.—Lorenc Ligori
ZERI I POPULLIT (People's Voice) (m) Est. 1942
Blvd. Deshmoret e Kombit
Tel: (355-42) 27045; Fax: (355-42) 27047
Circ.—35,000
Prop.—Socialist Party
Ed.—Thoma Gellci

ANDORRA
Pop. Est. 63,930

ANDORRA LA VELLA
Pop. Est. 17,163

CORREU ANDORRA
Ave. Meritxell, No. 112
Tel: (33-628) 22500/(33-628) 61794; Fax: (33-628) 22938
Mng. Dir.—Dr. Antoni Cornella

DIARI D'ANDORRA (Andorra Daily) (d)
Ave. B. Riberaygua, 39 4art
Tel: (33-628) 63700; Fax: (33-628) 63800
Prop.—Premsa Andorrana SA
Mng. Dir.—Dr. Gualbert Osorio
INDEPENDANT (d)
Ave. Meritxell, No.95
Tel: (33-628) 21056
INFORMACIONS (Information)
Calle de la Unio, No. 2
Tel: (33-628) 21134; Fax: (33-628) 60839
Mng. Dir.—Dr. Anna Ruíz
INFORMACIONS DIARI (Daily Information) (d)
Ave. Meritxell, No. 101 1r
Tel: (33-628) 63197/(33-628) 62942; Fax: (33-628) 63319/(33-628) 63193
Mng. Dir.—Franesc Ruiz
POBLE ANDORRA Catalan; Est. 1974
Carretera de la Comella
Tel: (33-628) 24557/(33-628) 22506; Fax: (33-628) 26696
Circ.—3,000
Prop.—Higini Cierco i Noguer
Mng. Dir.—Dr. Maria Carme Grau Ribot

ESCALDES-ENGORDANY

GUIA D'ANDORRA DIT & FET
Calle Pare Enric Graner, No. 2 1r, Ap. 135
Tel: (33-628) 28591/(33-628) 60533; Fax: (33-628) 61146
Mng. Dir.—Dr. Lluis Quintana

ARMENIA
Pop. Est. 3,521,517

EREVAN
(Yerevan)
Pop. Est. 1,168,000

GOLOS ARMENII Armenian
2, Prosp. Ordzhonokidze, 375023
Ed.—Boris M Mkrtchyan
Cir.—20,000

AUSTRIA
Pop. Est. 7,954,974

BREGENZ
Pop. Est. 105,345
Pop. Est. (Vorarlberg) 311,732

KURIER (Messenger) (d) Est. 1954
Heldendankstr. 40, 6900
Tel: (43-5574) 33560; Fax: (43-5574) 35349

Prop.—Kurier Zeitungsverlags
Pub.—Peter Rabl
Ed.—R Ströhle
NEUE VORARLBERGER TAGESZEITUNG (The New Vorarlberger Daily News) (d-ex mon.) Est. 1973
Arlbergstr. 117, 6900
Tel: (43-5574) 4090; Fax: (43-5574) 409300
Circ.—30,500 (tues.-S)
Prop.—Zeitung-und Verlagsgesellschaft mbH
Mng. Ed.—Bertram Burtscher
Ed. in Ch.—Arno Miller
Ad. Mgr.—Bernard Dürr
VORARLBERGER NACHRICHTEN (Vorarlberger News) (d-ex S) Est. 1945
Kirchstr. 35, 6901
Tel: (43-5574) 5123; Fax: (43-5574) 512227
Circ.—73,500 (mon.-fri.); 76,100 (sat.)
Prop.—Ruß GmbH
Pub./Ed. in Ch.—Eugen A Russ
Mng. Ed.—G Grabher
Ad. Mgr.—Bernhard Dürr

GRAZ
Pop. Est. 232,150
Pop. Est. (Styria) 1,182,599

KLEINE ZEITUNG (m-ex mon.) Est. 1904
Schoenaugasse 64, 8010
Tel: (43-316) 8063; Fax: (43-316) 816797
Circ.—264,000 (tues.;wed.;sat.); 264,000 (thurs.); 302,000 (fri.); 310,000 (S)
Prop.—Sytria Sterische Verlaganstalt
Ad. Mgr.—Dr. Herbert Wolny
NEUE ZEIT (The New Times) (m-ex mon.) Est. 1946
Ankerstr. 4, 8054
Tel: (43-316) 28080; Fax: (43-316) 2808325
Circ.—71,800 (tues.-thurs.; sat. & S); 75,950 (fri.)
Prop.—NZ Zeitungs-und Zeitschriften-Verlagsges mbH Co. KG
Pub./Ed. in Ch.—Josef Riedler
Ad. Dir.—Josef Wawrzyniak
STEIRERKRONE: NEUE KRONEN ZEITUNG (d)
Lendplatz 31, 8020
Tel: (43-316) 98400; Fax: (43-316) 913385
Circ.—156,500 (mon.-sat.); 204,800 (S)
Prop.—Krone-Verlag Gesellschaft mbH and Co.
Pub.—Hans Dichand
Mng. Ed.—K Herrmann
Ed. in Ch.—Markus Rutharde
Ad. Mgr.—Jorg Horstmann
Ad. Mgr.—Fritz Hintersonnleitner

INNSBRUCK
Pop. Est. 115,000
Pop. Est. (Tyrol) 605,774

KURIER (Messenger) (d) Est. 1954
Wilhelm-Greil-Str., 6020
Tel: (43-512) 59858; Fax: (43-512) 571021

Prop.—Kurier Zeitungsverlags
Pub.—Peter Rabl
Ed.—M Jäger
TIROLER TAGESZEITUNG (The Tiroler Daily News) (m-ex S) Est. 1946
Ing.-Etzel Str. 30, 6020
Tel: (43-512) 53540; Fax: (43-512) 575924
Circ.—94,965 (mon.-fri.); 109,715 (sat.)
Prop.—Schlüsselverlag J S Moser GesmbH and Co.
Mng. Ed.—Georg Nowakoski
Mng. Ed.—Walter Schrott
Ed. in Ch.—Dr. Bernhard Platzer
Ed. in Ch.—Rudolf Riener
Ad. Mgr.—Thomas Pupp
TIROLER UKRONE (d)
Schusterburgweg 86, 6020
Tel: (43-512) 23201; Fax: (43-512) 232210
Circ.—32,200 (mon.-sat.); 55,200 (S)
Prop.—Mediaprint Anzeigenges mbH & Co. KG
Pub.—Hans Dichand
Ed. in Ch.—Walter Prüller
Ad. Mgr.—Bernhard Kaiser
Ad. Mgr.—Jorg Horstmann

KLAGENFURT
Pop. Est. 85,000
Pop. Est. (Carinthia) 541,526

KÄRNTNER KRONE: NEUE KRONEN ZEITUNG (d)
Peter Str. 5, 9020
Tel: (43-463) 3815000; Fax: (43-463) 381400793
Circ.—78,200 (mon.-sat.); 99,700 (S)
Prop.—Krone-Verlag GesmbH & Co.
Pub.—Hans Dichand
Ed. in Ch.—Christoph Biro
Ad. Mgr.—Jörg Horstmann
KÄRNTNER TAGESZEITUNG (The Kaerntner Daily News) (d) Est. 1946
Viktringer Ring 28, 9020
Tel: (43-463) 58660; Fax: (43-463) 5866321
Circ.—54,100 (mon.; tues., sat. & S); 57,800 (wed.- fri.)
Prop.—Kärntner Druck & Verlagsges. mbH
Pub./Dir.—Helmut Fanzott
Mng. Ed.—Peter Weissensteiner
Ed. in Ch.—Dr. Hellwig Valentin
Bus. Mgr.—Helmut Fanzott
Ad. Mgr.—Jörg Horstmann
KLEINE ZEITUNG (d) Est. 1903
Funderstr. 1a, 9020
Tel: (43-463) 58000; Fax: (43-463) 56500
Circ.—269,655
Prop.—"Styria" Steirische Verlagsanstalt
Pub.—Dr. Hans Sassmann
Mng. Ed.—Siegfried Jost
Ed. in Ch.—Reinhold Dottolo
Bus. Mgr.—Dr. Hanns Sassmann
Ad. Mgr.—Johannes Schnaubelt

LINZ
Pop. Est. 203,000
Pop. Est. (Upper Austria) 1,290,497

KURIER (Messenger) (d)
Brucknerstr. 3; PF 368, 4021
Tel: (43-732) 603330; Fax: (43-732) 6033013
Prop.—Kurier Zeitungsverlags
Pub.—Peter Rabl
Ed.—P Affenzeller

NEUES VOLKSBLATT (d) Est. 1869
Hafenstr. 1, 4010
Tel: (43-732) 7819010; Fax: (43-732) 779242
Circ.—29,000 (mon.-thurs.; sat); 33,000 (fri.)
Prop.—Osterreichische Zeitungs-Verlags- und Vertriebsges. mbH
Pub./Bus. Mgr.—Josef Hartl
Ed. in Ch.—Peter Klar
Ad. Mg.—Dr. Herbert Fleischanderl

OBERÖSTERREICHISCHE NACHRICHTEN (d-ex S) Est. 1865
Anatasius Gruenstr. 6, 4010
Tel: (43-732) 28050; Fax: (43-732) 2805448
Circ.—124,000 (mon.-fri.); 160,000 (sat.)
Pub.—J Wimmer
Mng. Ed.—Prof. R Lehr
Ed.—R A Cuturi
Bus. Mgr.—Dr. Werner Schrotta
Ad. Dir.—Gernot Jachetti

OBERÖSTERREICHISCHE NEUE KRONEN ZEITUNG (d)
Industriezeile 56 b, 4020
Tel: (43-732) 78080; Fax: (43-732) 771290
Circ.—159,854 (mon.-sat.); 224,486 (S)
Prop.—Krone Verlag GesmbH Co.
Ed. in Ch.—Dr. Karl Drechsler
Ad. Dir.—Jörg Horstmann
Ad. Mgr.—Bernard Kaiser

OBERÖSTERREICHISCHE TAGBLATT (d-ex S)
Anatasius Gruenstr. 6, 410
Tel: (43-732) 665293
Circ.—68,750 (m-total); 26,800 (sat.)

OBERWART
KURIER (Messenger) (d) Est. 1954
Linkes Pinkaufer 28, 7400
Tel: (43-352) 8530; Fax: (43-352) 8529
Prop.—Kurier Zeitungsverlags
Pub.—Peter Rabl
Ed.—P Sitar

SALZBURG
Pop. Est. 144,000
Pop. Est. (Salzburg Land) 459,886

SALZBURG KRONE: NEUE KRONEN ZEITUNG (d)
Münchner Bundesstr. 160, 5020
Tel: (43-662) 335550; Fax: (43-662) 430388
Circ.—64,100 (mon.-sat.); 82,600 (S)
Prop.—Krone-Verlag GesmbH & Co. KG
Pub.—Hans Dichand
Ed. in Ch.—Hans-Peter Hasenorhl
Ad. Mgr.—Jörg Horstmann

SALZBURGER NACHRICHTEN (m-ex S) Est. 1946
Bergstr. 14, 5021
Tel: (43-662) 74571; Fax: (43-662) 880390
Circ.—88,423
Prop.—Salzburger Nachrichten Verlagsges mbH & Co. KG
Pub./Bus. Mgr.—Dr. Max Dasch
Mng. Ed.—Dr. Viktor Herrmann
Mng. Ed.—Dr. Gerhard Schwischei
Ed. in Ch.—Dr. Karl Heinz Ritschel
Bus. Mgr.—Ramon Torra
Ad. Mgr.—Fritz Gliederer

SVZ SALZBURGER VOLKSZEITUNG (d)
Elisabethkai 58/2; PF 302, 5021
Tel: (43-662) 8794910; Fax: (43-662) 879491/(43-662) 879413
Circ.—12,900
Prop.—Österreichische Volkspartei Landsorganization Salzburg
Ed. in Ch.—Prof. Willi Sauberer
Ad. Mgr.—G Neumann

VIENNA
Pop. Est. 1,600,000

KURIER (Messenger) (m&e) Est. 1954
Lindengasse 48-52, 1072
Tel: (43-1) 52111; Fax: (43-1) 521002263
Circ.—391,239 (mon.-sat.); 606,293 (S)
Prop.—Mediaprint Zeitungs & Zeitschriftenverlag GesmbH & Co.
Pub./Ed. in Ch.—Peter Rabl
Ed. in Ch.—Dr. Günther Wessig
Ed.—Hans Rauscher
Bus. Mgr.—Bernd Nacke
Ad. Mgr.—Franz J Ganser
U.S. Rep.—Publicitas
(Circulation is the total of all Kurier editions. See Bregenz Innsbruck, Linz and Oberwart.)

NEUE KRONENZEITUNG (d)
Muthgasse 2, 1190
Tel: (43-1) 521110; Fax: (43-1) 521102417
Circ.—1,000,480 (mon.; tues.; wed.; thurs.; sat); 1,413,765 (fri. & S)
Prop.—Krone-Verlag GesmbH & Co. KG
Pub./Ed. in Ch./Bus. Mgr.—Hans Dichand
Ad. Dir.—Jörg Horstmann

DER STANDARD (m) Est. 1988
Herrengasse 1, 1014
Tel: (43-1) 53170; Fax: (43-1) 53170
Circ.—83,738 (mon.-wed.); 101,070 (thurs. & fri.); 183,489 (sat.)
Prop.—Oscar Bronner GesmbH & Co.
Ed.—Oscar Bronner
Ad. Mgr.—Michael Sedivy

TÄGLICH ALLES (d) Est. 1988
Ignaz-Köck-Str. 17, 1210
Tel: (43-1) 291600; Fax: (43-1) 2916072
Circ.—496,000 (mon.-sat.); 847,000 (S)
Prop.—Familiapress Zeitungsges.
Pub./Bus. Mgr.—K Falk
Ed. in Ch.—M Grassl-Kosa
Bus. Mgr.—H-J Kleemann

WIENER ZEITUNG (d) Est. 1703
Rennweg 12 a, 1037
Tel: (43-1) 788535/(43-1) 787631; Fax: (43-1) 787631433
Circ.—30,000
Prop.—Republik Österreich Österreichscshe Staatsdruckerei
Gen. Dir.—Gerhard Gehmayr
Mng. Ed.—G Grossmaier
Ed. in Ch.—Heinz Fahnler
Bus. Mgr.—Dr. Aribert Schwarzmann
Ad. Mgr.—Ernst Tresh

AZERBAIJAN
Pop. Est. 7,684,456

BAKU
Pop. Est. 1,713,300

ADALAT (d)
Matbuat prospekti, Mahalla 529, 370146
Tel: (7-8922) 390057/(7-8922) 380550; Fax: (7-8922) 651064

AYDINLIG
Bulbul St. 20, 370014
Tel: (7-8922) 937131/(7-8922) 937586

AZERBAIJAN (d)
Matbuat prospekti, Mahalla 529, 4th Floor, 370140
Tel: (7-8922) 394323/(7-8922) 394491

AZERBAIJAN GANJRALI
Matbuat prospekti, Mahalla 529, 8th Floor, 370146
Tel: (7-8922) 321265

BAKU
Matbuat prospekti, Mahalla 529, 370146
Tel: (7-8922) 395039/(7-8922) 390074

ISTIGLAL
28th May St. 3, No. 11
Tel: (7-8922) 938148

MILLAT
Matbuat prospekti, Mahalla 529
Tel: (7-8922) 323082

MUKHALIFAT
Matbuat prospekti 24, 370146
Tel: (7-8922) 395427

RESPUBLIKA (Republic)
Matbuat prospekti, Mahalla 529, 7th Floor, 370146
Tel: (7-8922) 927541/(7-8922) 380114

SAHAR
Matbuat prospekti, Mahalla 529, 370146
Tel: (7-8922) 390002/(7-8922) 385173

BELARUS
Pop. Est. 10,404,862

MINSK
Pop. Est. 1,658,000

CHYRVONAYA ZMENA (Red Generation Rising)
Belarussian; Est. 1921
77 Leninski Prosp., 220041
Ed.—V Plyuskov

NARODNAYA GAZETA (People's Newspaper) (6x wk.) Belarussian & Russian; Est. 1990
10a B Khmyalnitskaha vul, 220013

NARODNAYA VOLYA (People's Freedom)
Belarussian & Russian; Est. 1995
10a B Khmyalnitskaha vul, 220013

RESPUBLIKA (Republic) (6x wk.) Belarussian & Russian; Est. 1991
10a B Khmyalnitskaha vul, 220013

SELYSKAYA GAZETA (Rural Gazette) (6x wk.)
Russian; Est. 1921
77 Leninski Prosp., 220041
Ed.—L K Tolkatch

SOVETSKAYA BELORUSSIA (Soviet Byelorussia) (6x wk.) Russian; Est. 1927
10a B Khmyalnitskaha vul, 220013
Ed.—A K Zinin

ZNAMYA YUNOSTI (Banner of Youth) Russian; Est. 1938
77 Leninski Prosp., 220041
Circ.—784,000
Ed.—A Solomakha

ZVYAZDA (Star) (6x wk.) Belarussian; Est. 1917
10a B Khmyalnitskaha vul, 220013
Ed.—I P Makalovitch

BELGIUM
Pop. Est. 10,062,836

ANTWERP
(Antwerp)
Pop. Est. 467,875

DE ANTWERPSE MORGEN (d) Dutch
Leopoldstraat 10, 2000
Tel: (32-3) 2331708; Fax: (32-3) 2333574
Circ.—52,000

DE FINANCIEEL EKONOMISCHE TIJD (m-5x wk.)
Dutch; Est. 1968
Uitgeversbedrijf Tijd, Posthoflei 3, PO Box 4, 2600
Tel: (32-3) 2860276; Fax: (32-3) 2860280
Circ.—40,309
Pub.—P Huybrechts
Ed. in Ch.—M H Maertens

GAZET VAN ANTWERPEN (d) Dutch; Est. 1891
Katwilgweg 2, 2050
Tel: (32-3) 2100210; Fax: (32-3) 2337480
Circ.—184,691
Prop.—De Vlijt NV
Pub.—Romain Van Tongerloo
Ed. in Ch.—Yos Huypens
Ad. Mgr.—Donald Cappelle

HET LAATSTE NIEUWS (d)
Leopoldstraat 10, 2000
Tel: (32-3) 2319680; Fax: (32-3) 2341666
Ed. in Ch.—R De Craecker

DE LLOYD/LE LLOYD (d-ex mon.) French, Dutch, & English; Est. 1858
Vleminckstraat 18, 2000
Tel: (32-3) 2340550; Fax: (32-3) 2342593
Circ.—10,600
Prop.—Antwerpen Lloyd NV
Dir.—G Dubois
Ed. in Ch.—J de Winter
Ed. in Ch.—B Van den Bossche

DE NIEUWE GAZET (d) Dutch; Est. 1897
Leopoldstraat 10, 2000
Tel: (32-3) 2319680; Fax: (32-3) 2341666
Circ.—298,882
Prop.—Uitgeverij J Hoste
Ed. in Ch.—L Van der Kelen
(Circulation figure combines with Het Laatste in Brussels.)

DE STANDAARD-HET NIEUWSBLAD (d) Dutch
De Keyserlei 58-60, 2018
Tel: (32-3) 2252544; Fax: (32-3) 2314229
Pub.—L van Loon

HET VOLK/DE NIEUWE GIDS (d)
Aalmoezenierstraat 14-16, 2000
Tel: (32-3) 2262590; Fax: (32-3) 2264529
Ed. in Ch.—Luc Martens

ARLON
(Luxemburg)
Pop. Est. 47,123

L'AVENIR DU LUXEMBOURG (d) French; Est. 1897
Rue des Desportes 38, 6700
Tel: (32-632) 20349; Fax: (32-632) 20516
Circ.—130,000
Prop.—La Presse Luxembourgeoise
Dir./Ed. in Ch.—J Mottet
(Circulation figure combines with L'Avenir Du Luxembourg in Marche-En-Famenne.)

LA MEUSE-LUXEMBOURG (d)
Place Leopold 5-6, 6700
Tel: (32-632) 20375; Fax: (32-632) 17754
Pub.—Michel Fromont
Ed. in Ch.—Wally Meurens

LE SOIR (d)
Rue Saint-Donat 30, 6700
Tel: (32-632) 23516; Fax: (32-632) 28275
Pub.—Annie Gaspard

BRUGES
(West Flanders)
Pop. Est. 117,100

GAZET VAN ANTWERPEN (d)
Geerwijnstratt 22, 8000
Tel: (32-50) 335253; Fax: (32-50) 335253

HET LAATSTE NIEUWS (d)
Vlamingstraat 62, 8000
Tel: (32-50) 336883; Fax: (32-50) 331721

HET VOLK (d)
Nievwstraat 7, 8000
Tel: (32-50) 337278; Fax: (32-50) 342226

BRUSSELS
(Brabant)
Pop. Est. 954,045

LE COURRIER DE LA BOURSE/ LA COTE LIBRE (d)
French; Est. 1896
Rue de Birmingham 131, 3rd Floor, 1070
Tel: (32-2) 5265666; Fax: (32-2) 5265660
Circ.—9,500
Prop.—Agefi Belgique SA
Dir./Ed. in Ch.—O de Beauffort

LA DERNIERE HEURE-LES SPORTS (d) French; Est. 1906
Blvd. Emile Jacqmain 127, 1000
Tel: (32-2) 2112888; Fax: (32-2) 2112870
Circ.—93,326
Prop.—Societe d`Imprimerie Commune
Ed. in Ch.—Daniel Van Wylick
Ch. of Info.—Raymond Arets

L'ECHO (d) French; Est. 1881
131 Rue de Birmingham 131, 1070
Tel: (32-2) 5265666; Fax: (32-2) 5265569
Circ.—27,948
Prop.—Nimify SA
Pub./Dir.—R Watson
Ed. in Ch.—Freddy Melaet
Ad. Mgr.—Francine Mirmovitch

DE FINANCIEEL EKONOMISCH TYJD (d) Dutch
Place Saint Lazare 2, bte 6, 1210
Tel: (32-2) 2172205; Fax: (32-2) 2170976

GAZET VON ANTWERPEN Dutch
Rue Joseph 11-20, 1040
Tel: (32-2) 2187802; Fax: (32-2) 2174104

HET BELANG VAN LIMBURG (d) Dutch
Avenue de Cortenbergh 79-81, 1040
Tel: (32-2) 7355767; Fax: (32-2) 7356549
Ed. in Ch.—Marc Platel

HET BELGISCH SLAATSBLAD (d) Dutch
Leiweseweg 40-42, 1000
Tel: (32-2) 5120026; Fax: (32-2) 5110184

HET VOLK Dutch
Rue Royale 105, 1000
Tel: (32-2) 2185605; Fax: (32-2) 2185906

LE JOURNAL ET INDEPENDENCE (d)
Blvd. Emile Jacqmain 79, 1000

HET LAATSTE NIEUWS (d) Dutch; Est. 1886
Brusselsesteenweg 347, Asse (Kobbegem), 1730
Tel: (32-2) 4542211; Fax: (32-2) 4542822
Circ.—298,882
Prop.—Uitgeverij J Hoste
Ed. in Ch.—Marcel Wilmet

LA LANTERNE (d) French; Est. 1944
Place de Louvain 21, 1000
Tel: (32-2) 2255600; Fax: (32-2) 2255913
Circ.—131,932
Prop.—Imprimerie et Journal La Meuse SA
Pub.—Michel Fromont
Ed. in Ch.—A Oger

LA LIBRE BELGIQUE (d) French; Est. 1884
Blvd. Emile Jacqmain 127, 1000
Tel: (32-2) 2112777; Fax: (32-2) 2112832
Circ.—82,834
Prop.—Societe d`Imprimerie Commune
Dir.—Jacques Franck
Ed. in Ch.—Jean-Paul Duchateau

LE LLOYD/DE LLOYD (d) French & Dutch
Rue de la Presse 4, 1000
Tel: (32-2) 2173199; Fax: (32-2) 2183141
Gen. Mgr.—Nele Brauers

LA MEUSE/LA LANTERNE/LA NOUVELLE GAZETTE (d)
Place de Louvain 21, 1000
Tel: (32-2) 2182100; Fax: (32-2) 2178149
Pub.—Michel Fromont
Ed. in Ch.—Benoît Degardin

LE MONITEUR BELGE (d)
Rue de Louvain 40-42, 1000
Tel: (32-2) 5120026; Fax: (32-2) 5110184
Dir.—B Van Damme

Belgium

DE MORGEN (d) Dutch
Rue Brogniez 54, 1070
Tel: (32-2) 5270030; Fax: (32-2) 5203515
Ed. in Ch.—Walter De Bock
DE NIEUWE GIDS (d) Dutch; Est. 1944
Rue Royale 105, 1000
Tel: (32-2) 2185605; Fax: (32-2) 2185906
Circ.—193,308
Prop.—Drukkerij Het Volk NV
(Circulation figure combines with De Antwerpse Gids in Antwerp.)
LE SOIR (d) French; Est. 1887
Place De Louvain 21, 1000
Tel: (32-2) 2555555; Fax: (32-2) 2255908
Circ.—467,800
Prop.—Regie Rossel & Cie SA
Ed.—Robert Hurbain
Ad. Mgr.—Rosette Van Rosse
U.S. Rep.—Publicitas
DE STANDAARD/HET NIEUWSBLAD/DE GENTENAAR (d) Dutch
Gossetlaan 30, Groot-Bijgaarden, 1720
Tel: (32-2) 4672211; Fax: (32-2) 4663093
Circ.—319,758
Prop.—VUM
Pub.—G Verdeyen
Ed. in Ch.—L De Clerck
Ed. in Ch.—D Achten
Ed. in Ch.—R Schoemans
WALL STREET JOURNAL EUROPE (d)
Blvd. de Waterloo 39, Hilton Tower, bte 7A, 1000
Tel: (32-2) 5139080; Fax: (32-2) 5137085
Circ.—47,821
Prop.—Dow Jones Publishing Co.

CHARLEROI
(Hainault)
Pop. Est. 209,395

LE JOURNAL ET INDEPENDENCE/LE PEUPLE
French; Est. 1837/1944
Rue du College 18, 6000
Tel: (32-71) 310190; Fax: (32-71) 331650
Circ.—19,483
Prop.—de Presse et d`Editions SA
Dir./Ed. in Ch.—Jean Guy
LA NOUVELLE GAZETTE (d) French; Est. 1878
Quai de Flandre 2, 6000
Tel: (32-71) 276411; Fax: (32-71) 276567
Circ.—92,802
Prop.—de Presse et d`Editions SA
Pub.—Patrick Hurbain
Dir.—Philippe Dautez
Ed. in Ch.—André Thioux
LE RAPPEL (d) French; Est. 1900
Rue de Montigny 24, 6000
Tel: (32-71) 312280; Fax: (32-71) 314361
Circ.—10,000
Prop.—Vers l`Avenir SA
Pub.—Carl Vandoorne
Ed. in Ch.—Christian De Bast
LE SOIR French
Blvd. Tirou 203, bte 9, 6000
Tel: (32-71) 327916/(32-71) 327962; Fax: (32-71) 320593
Adm.—Olivier Collot

EUPEN
(Liège)
Pop. Est. 16,869

GRENZ-ECHO (d-6x wk.) German; Est. 1927
Marktplatz 8, 4700
Tel: (32-87) 554705; Fax: (32-87) 743820
Circ.—13,500
Prop.—Grenz-Echo SC
Pub.—Alfred Küchenberg
Pub.—E Thommessen
Ed. in Ch.—Heinz Warny
Ad. Mgr.—O Verdin

GENT
(East Flanders)
Pop. Est. 230,246

DE GENTENAAR (d) Dutch; Est. 1879
Gouvernementstraat 30, 9000
Tel: (32-9) 2239530; Fax: (32-9) 2230956
Circ.—31,000
Prop.—Vlaamse Uitgeversmaatschappij NV
Dir.—G Verdeyen
HET LAASTSTE NIEUWS Dutch
Kouter 19-25, 9000
Tel: (32-9) 2256711; Fax: (32-9) 2240935
DE NIEUWE GIDS
Forelstraat 22, 9000
Tel: (32-9) 2656111; Fax: (32-9) 2252071

HET VOLK (d) Dutch; Est. 1891
Forelstraat 22, 9000
Tel: (32-9) 2655111; Fax: (32-9) 2236583
Circ.—164,795
Prop.—Dagblad Het Volk NV
Ad. Mgr.—Yannic Demeyer

GOSSELIES
(Hainault)

LE JOURNAL ET INDEPENDENCE (d)
Ave. des Etats Units 7, 6200

HASSELT
(Limburg)
Pop. Est. 359,324

HET BELANG VAN LIMBURG (d) Dutch; Est. 1879
Herckenrodesingel 10, 3500
Tel: (32-11) 878111; Fax: (32-11) 878204
Circ.—107,055
Prop.—Concentra NV
Ed.—Peter Baert
Ad. Mgr.—Louis Van Baelen
HET LAASTSE NIEUWS (d)
Koningin Astridlaan 7, 3500
Tel: (32-11) 221214; Fax: (32-11) 229983
Pub.—Theo Claes
HET VOLK (d) Dutch
Frans Massystraat 24, 3500
Tel: (32-11) 222934/(32-11) 222935; Fax: (32-11) 229054

HUY
(Liège)

LA MEUSE (d) French
Rue des Brasseurs 17, 4500
Tel: (32) 85211536; Fax: (32) 85235140
Pub.—Michel Fromont
Ed. in Ch.—Wally Meurens
VERS L'AVENIR (d) French
Rue des Rôtisseurs 4, 4500
Tel: (32) 85214911; Fax: (32) 85234808
Gen. Mgr.—Ch Dodet

KORTRIJK
(West Flanders)
Pop. Est. 76,216

GAZET VAN ANTWERPEN (d)
Louis Verweestraat 4, 8500
Tel: (32-56) 222054/(32-56) 211751; Fax: (32-56) 201580
HET LAATSTE NIEUWS (d) Dutch
Vlasmarkt 18, 8500
Tel: (32-56) 225369/(32-56) 215425; Fax: (32-56) 219942
HET VOLK (d) Dutch
Budastraat 17, 8500
Tel: (32-56) 224001; Fax: (32-56) 201664

LA LOUVIERE
(Hainault)
Pop. Est. 76,340

LA NOUVELLE GAZETTE (d) French
Rue Hamoir 65, 7100
Tel: (32-64) 223198/(32-64) 223197
Pub.—Patrick Hurbain
Dir.—Philippe Dautez
Ed. in Ch.—André Thioux

LIEGE
(Liège)
Pop. Est. 194,956

LA DERNIERE HEURE (d) French
Blvd. d`Avroy 26, 4000
Tel: (32-41) 221830/(32-41) 222058; Fax: (32-41) 231588
Gen. Mgr.—Edmond Finne
LA GAZETTE DE LIEGE (d) French; Est. 1840
Blvd. d`Avroy 26, 4000
Tel: (32-41) 231933; Fax: (32-41) 224126
Circ.—82,834
Prop.—Societe d`Imprimerie Commune
Dir.—Lily Portugaels
LA MEUSE (d) French; Est. 1855
Blvd. de la Sauveniere 8-12, 4000
Tel: (32-41) 200811; Fax: (32-41) 200839
Circ.—132,932
Prop.—Imprimerie et Journal La Meuse SA
Pub.—Michel Fromont
Ed. in Ch.—Wally Meurens
LE SOIR
Rue de Bex 15, 4000
Tel: (32-41) 224601/(32-41) 224697; Fax: (32-41) 235929
Gen. Mgr.—Guy Depas

VERS L'AVENIR
Blvd. d`Avroy 26, 4000
Tel: (32-41) 233626; Fax: (32-41) 233490
Ed. in Ch.—Yvon Lambert
LA WALLONIE (d) French; Est. 1919
Rue de la Regence 55, 4000
Tel: (32-41) 201811; Fax: (32-41) 233117
Circ.—50,000
Prop.—Societe d`Impression et d`Editions
Pub.—Rene Piron
Ed. in Ch.—Charles Rasir

MAASMECHELEN
(Limburg)

HET BELANG VAN LIMBURG-DE WEEKKRANT-JET MAGAZINE (d)
Rijksweg 404, 3630
Tel: (32-89) 764319; Fax: (32-89) 767032

MARCHE-EN-FAMENNE
(Luxemburg)

L'AVENIR DU LUXEMBOURG (d)
Place Roi Albert 9, 6900
Tel: (32-84) 311913; Fax: (32-84) 315439
Gen. Mgr.—J M Doucet
LA MEUSE LUXEMBOURG (d)
Rue de Luxembourg 54, 6900
Tel: (32-84) 311054/(32-84) 321232; Fax: (32-84) 316559

MECHELEN
(Antwerp)
Pop. Est. 293,050

GAZET VAN MECHELEN (d) Dutch; Est. 1896
Befferstraat 13, 2800
Tel: (32-15) 208383; Fax: (32-15) 206150
Circ.—189,811
Prop.—De Vlijt NV
Gen. Mgr.—Frans Teughels
(Circulation figure combines with Gazet Van Antwerpen in Antwerp.)
HET LAATSTE NIEUWS
Standonckstraat 2, 2800
Tel: (32-15) 205719/(32-15) 205752; Fax: (32-15) 208445
Gen. Mgr.—Leo De Nijn

MONS
(Hainault)
Pop. Est. 251,635

L'ECHO DU CENTRE French
Place du Marche aux Herbes 11-12, 7000
Tel: (32-65) 348304; Fax: (32-65) 347368
Dir./Ed. in Ch.—André Farine
LE JOURNAL DE MONS (d) Est. 1945
Place du Marche aux Herbes 11-12, 7000
Tel: (32-65) 348304; Fax: (32-65) 347368
Dir./Ed. in Ch.—André Farine
NORD-ECLAIR BELGE (d)
Place du Marché aux Herbes 11-12, 7000
Tel: (32-65) 348304; Fax: (32-65) 347368
Dir./Ed. in Ch.—André Farine
LA PROVINCE (The Province) (d) Est. 1910
Rue des Capucins 29, 7000
Tel: (32-65) 317151; Fax: (32-65) 338477
Pub.—Patrick Hurbain
Dir.—Philippe Dautez
Ed. in Ch.—André Thioux

MOUSCRON
(Hainault)
Pop. Est. 53,713

NORD-ECLAIR (d)
Grand' Place 32, 7700
Tel: (32-56) 341472; Fax: (32-56) 335476
Circ.—43,880
Dir./Ed. in Ch.—André Farine

NAMUR
(Namur)
Pop. Est. 263,917

LA LANTERNE/LA PROVINCE
Quai de Meuse 25, Jambes, 5100
Tel: (32-81) 308989; Fax: (32-81) 308832
Pub.—Michel Fromont
Dir./Ed. in Ch.—Jean-Pierre Vandermeuse
LA MEUSE French
Quai de Meuse 25, Jambes, 5100
Tel: (32-81) 309494; Fax: (32-81) 309468
Pub.—Michel Fromont
Ed. in Ch.—Wally Meurens
LA NOUVELLE GAZETTE (d) French
Quai de Meuse 25, Jambes, 5100
Tel: (32-81) 309292; Fax: (32-81) 309468
Pub.—Edith Heye
LE SOIR French
Rue Julie Billiart 21, bte 5, 5000
Tel: (32-81) 231736/(32-81) 231703; Fax: (32-81) 231768
Ch. of Info.—Pierre Hermans

DE STANDAARD (d)
Rue Lelièvre 8, 5000
Tel: (32-81) 224418; Fax: (32-81) 221872
VERS L'AVENIR (d) French; Est. 1918
Blvd. Ernest Melot 12, 5000
Tel: (32-81) 248811; Fax: (32-81) 226024
Circ.—64,327
Prop.—Vers l`Avenir SA
Ed. in Ch.—Yvon Lambert
LA WALLONE (d)
Rue J. B. de Marne 30, 5000
Tel: (32-81) 2600033/(32-81) 2600052; Fax: (32-81) 2600070
Pub.—Laurence Hottart

NIVELLES
(Brabant)

LA NOUVELLE GAZETTE (d) French
Rue de l'Evêché 12, 1400
Tel: (32-67) 220353; Fax: (32-67) 211070
Gen. Dir.—Patrick Hurbain
Dir.—Philippe Dautez
Ed. in Ch.—André Thioux
LE SOIR
Rue du Panier Vert 12, bte 24, 1400
Tel: (32-67) 215548; Fax: (32-67) 215548
Pub.—J Vandendries

OSTENDE
(West Flanders)
Pop. Est. 68,318

HET LAATSTE NIEUWS (d)
Ooststraat 42B, bte 7, 8400
Tel: (32-59) 503747; Fax: (32-59) 331721
Pub.—A Vollmacher

PHILIPPEVILLE
(Namur)

LA NOUVELLE GAZETTE (d) French
Rue du Corbeau, bte 91, 5600
Tel: (32-71) 667747; Fax: (32-71) 667427
Pub.—Patrick Hurbain
Dir.—Philippe Dautez
Ed. in Ch.—André Thioux
Ed.—Michel Fromont
VERS L'AVENIR E.S.M.
Place d'Armes 11, 5600
Tel: (32-71) 666949; Fax: (32-71) 668650
Pub.—Bruno Malter

ST. NICOLAS
(East Flanders)
Pop. Est. 68,082

GAZET VAN ANTWERPEN (d)
Mercatorstraat 75-77, 9100
Tel: (32-3) 7663636; Fax: (32-3) 7778417
Gen. Mgr.—Rita Van Meir

ST. VITH
(Liège)

GRENZ-ECHO (d) German
Haupstrasse 91, 4780
Tel: (32-80) 228676; Fax: (32-80) 226591
Prop.—Grenz-Echo Verlag SC

TOURNAI
(Hainault)
Pop. Est. 140,379

LE COURRIER DE L'ESCAUT (d) French; Est. 1829
Rue de Cure Notre-Dame 24, 7500
Tel: (32-69) 228143; Fax: (32-69) 232034
Circ.—25,000
Prop.—Vers l`Avenir SA
Dir.—M Lestienne
LA DERNIERE HEURE
Rue Bourdon-St.-Jacques 7, 7500
Tel: (32-69) 221093; Fax: (32-69) 221094
Ed.—A Desauvage
NORD-ECLAIR BELGE (d) French
Rue des Puits-l'Eau 10, 7500
Tel: (32-69) 228171; Fax: (32-69) 233392
Pub.—J P De Rouck

VERVIERS
(Liège)
Pop. Est. 247,810

LE JOUR-LE COURRIER (d) French; Est. 1838/1894
Rue du Brou 14, 4800
Tel: (32-87) 313200; Fax: (32-87) 316740
Circ.—15,000
Prop.—La Presse Vervietoise
Ed. in Ch.—Roger Monami
LA MEUSE
Rue Xhavee 26-28, 4800
Tel: (32-87) 333942; Fax: (32-87) 316987
Pub.—Michel Fromont
Ed. in Ch.—Wally Meurens

WAVRE
(Brabant)

LE SOIR French
Chaussée de Louvain 150, 1300
Tel: (32-10) 242942/(32-10) 242775;
Fax: (32-10) 242579
Ch. of Info.—Philippe Pierre
VERS L'AVENIR French
Rue du Chemin de Fer 41, 1300
Tel: (32-10) 228844; Fax: (32-10) 228852
Ed.—André-Marie Douillet

BULGARIA
Pop. Est. 8,799,986

BLAGOEVGRAD
Pop. Est. 74,236

PIRNSKO DELO (Pirin's Cause) (d)
19 Assen Khristov St.
Circ.—33,000
Prop.—"Pirinski Standart"
Ed. in Ch.—Todor Karastoyanov

BURGAS
(Bourgas)
Pop. Est. 211,580

CHERNOMORSKI FAR (Black Sea Beacon) (m-ex S) Est. 1958
9 Milin Kamack St., 8000
Tel: (359-56) 42248; Fax: (359-56) 40178
Circ.—60,000
Prop.—Publishing House "Chernomorski Far"
Ed.—Mladen Karpoulsky
Ad. Mgr.—Nadia Damianova

LOVECH
Pop. Est. 50,872

NAROLEN GLAS (Voice of the People) (d)
House of Political Education, 3rd Floor; PO Box 6, 5500
Circ.—50,000

PLOVDIV
Pop. Est. 379,112

MARITSA (d), 4000
Tel: (359-32) 268434; Fax: (359-32) 274760
Circ.—12,500
Prop.—Private
Ed. in Ch.—Stoyan Valvev
OTECHESTVEN GLAS (Voice of the Fatherland) (d)
9 Krakra St., 4000
Tel: (359-32) 226740
Circ.—100,000
Ed. in Ch.—Mihail Milchev

RAZGRAD
Pop. Est. 56,494

VAZKHOD (Progress) (d)
3 Dondukov St.
Circ.—45,000

SOFIA
Pop. Est. 1,140,800

BULGARSKA ARMIYA (Bulgarian Army) (d)
12 Ivan Vazov St., 1080
Tel: (359-2) 878116; Fax: (359-2) 874371
Circ.—25,000
Prop.—Ministry of Defense
Ed. in Ch.—Vladi Vladkov
24 CHASSA (24 Hours) (d) Est. 1991
Blvd. Stamboliiski 2A, 1000
Tel: (359-2) 43431; Fax: (359-2) 463254
Circ.—200,000
Prop.—168 Hours Ltd.
Ed. in Ch.—Valery Naidenov
DEMOCRATSIA (Democracy) (m) Est. 1990
134 Rakavski St., 1000
Tel: (359-2) 882501; Fax: (359-2) 390212
Circ.—190,000
Prop.—Union of Democratic Forces
Ed. in Ch.—Ivo Indjev
DOUMA (Word) (m)
47 Trakia Blvd., 1024
Tel: (359-2) 4631; Fax: (359-2) 446357
Circ.—400,000
Prop.—Bulgarian Socialist Party
Ed. in Ch.—Stefan Prodev
OTECHESTVEN VESTNIK (The Fatherland Gazette) (m) Est. 1942
47 Trakia Blvd., 1040
Tel: (359-2) 43431; Fax: (359-2) 463108
Circ.—300,000
Prop.—The Fatherland Alliance

PODKREPA (Support) (d)
37 Exarch Yossif St., 1000
Tel: (359-2) 657596; Fax: (359-2) 467374
Circ.—90,000
Prop.—Podkrepa Trade Union Confederation
Ed. in Ch.—Boyan Daskalov
TRUD (Labor) (m) Est. 1946
72 Dondukov Blvd., 1000
Tel: (359-2) 802344; Fax: (359-2) 802626
Circ.—260,000
Prop.—Confederation of Independent Trade Unions in Bulgaria
Ed. in Ch.—Tosho Toshev
VECHERNY NOVINI (Evening News) (e-ex S) Est. 1951
Blvd. Lenin 47, 1080
Tel: (359-2) 441469; Fax: (359-2) 465065
Circ.—122,000
Prop.—Vest Publishing House
Ed. in Ch.—Lyobomir Kolarov
ZEMEDELSKO ZNAME (Agrarian Banner) (m) Est. 1921
23 Yanko Zabunov St.
Tel: (359-2) 873851; Fax: (359-2) 874535
Circ.—178,000
Prop.—Bulgarian Agrarian People's Union (United)
Ed. in Ch.—Ilya Danov
ZEMYA (Earth) (d)
18 11th August St., 1000
Tel: (359-2) 835033; Fax: (359-2) 835227
Circ.—80,000
Prop.—Bulgarian Socialist Party
Ed. in Ch.—Kosta Andreev

VARNA
Pop. Est. 316,231

NARODNO DELO (People's Cause) (d) Est. 1944
3 Hristo Botev St., 9000
Tel: (359-52) 231178/(359-52) 231178;
Fax: (359-52) 231024
Prop.—The District Council
Mng. Dir.—Ilko Oucharov
Ed. in Ch.—Dimitar Kressimiov
Ed.—Dimitar Andreev
Ad. Mgr.—Marianne Vuchkova

CROATIA, REPUBLIC OF
Pop. Est. 4,697,614

OSIJEK
Pop. Est. 104,553

GLAS SLAVONIJE (d)
Prolaz Vitomira Sukica 2
Tel: (385-54) 126722; Fax: (385-54) 26751

RIJEKA
Pop. Est. 167,757

NOVI LIST (d)
Bulevar Marksa i Engelsa 20; PO Box 130
Tel: (385-51) 32122
LA VOCE DE POPOLO (d) Italian; Est. 1944
Bulevar Marksa i Engelsa 20

SPLIT
Pop. Est. 189,444

NEDJELJNA DOLMACIJA (d)
Splitskog Ordreda 4, 58000
Tel: (385-58) 513888

ZAGREB
Pop. Est. 930,753

SPORTSKE NOVOSTI (d)
Lj Gerovac br 1, 41000
Tel: (385-41) 515555
VECERNJI LIST (e)
Ave. Bratstva i Jedinstva 4, 41000
Tel: (385-41) 515555
Circ.—208,000
Prop.—Vercerndi List

CYPRUS, REPUBLIC OF
Pop. Est. 730,084

NICOSIA
Pop. Est. 181,000

AGON (Struggle) (m) Greek; Est. 1964
Makarios Ave. & Agapinoros St.; PO Box 1417
Tel: (357-2) 477181/(357-2) 477182;
Fax: (357-2) 457887

Europe — **Czech Republic** — IV-9

Circ.—5,000
Pub.—Nicos Koshis
Dir.—Leonidas Koshis
ALITHIA (Truth) Greek; Est. 1952
5 Pindaros & Androklis St.; PO Box 1695
Tel: (357-2) 463040; Fax: (357-2) 463945
Circ.—9,000
Prop.—Alithia Ekdotiki Eteria Ltd.
Dir.—Socrates Hasikos
Ch. Ed.—Alekos Constantinides
APOGEVMATINI (Afternoon) (e) Greek; Est. 1972
5 Aegaleo St., Strovolos; PO Box 5603
Tel: (357-2) 353603; Fax: (357-2) 353223
Circ.—9,000
Prop.—Dimosiographiki HLS Ltd.
Dir.—Efthymios Hadjiefthimiou
Dir.—Antonis Stavrides
Ch. Ed.—Alkis Andreou
BIRLIK (Unity) (m) Turkish; Est. 1980
43 Yediler St.
Tel: (357-2) 272959; Fax: (357-2) 282959
Circ.—4,500
Prop.—Ulus Matbaacilik Sti. Ltd.
Pub.—Günay Caymaz
Ed.—Lütfi Özter
THE CYPRUS FINANCIAL MIRROR English; Est. 1993
80B Thermopylon St., Acropolis; PO Box 4280
Tel: (357-2) 495790; Fax: (357-2) 495907
Circ.—3,000
Prop.—Harach Publications Ltd.
Dir./Ch. Ed.—Masis der Parthogh
CYPRUS MAIL (m) English; Est. 1945
24 Vassilios Voulgaroktonos St.; PO Box 1144
Tel: (357-2) 462074; Fax: (357-2) 366385
Circ.—3,800
Prop.—Cyprus Mail Co. Ltd.
Dir.—Kyriakos Iacovides
Ch. Ed.—Steve Myles
ELEFTHEROTYPIA (Free Press) (m) Greek; Est. 1979
50 Grivas Dighenis Ave.; PO Box 3821
Tel: (357-2) 454400; Fax: (357-2) 454413
Circ.—3,000
Prop.—Ekdoseis Provlimatismos-Elyftherotypia Ltd.
Dir.—Panos Englezos
Ch. Ed.—Andreas Constantinou
HALKIN SESI (People's Voice) (m) Turkish; Est. 1942
172 Kyrenia Ave.
Tel: (357-2) 520731/(357-2) 520741
Circ.—5,000
Prop.—Halkin Sesi Ltd.
Pub.—Hemhet Kügüek
Mgr.—Huseyin Cobanoglu
Ed.—Akay Cemal
HARAVGI (Dawn) (m) Greek; Est. 1956
6 Akamentos St.; PO Box 1556
Tel: (357-2) 476356; Fax: (357-2) 365154
Circ.—8,000
Prop.—Telegraphos Ltd.
Dir.—Nicos Katsourides
Ch. Ed.—Andreas Rousos
KIBRIS (Cyprus) Turkish; Est. 1988
Fazil Kucuk Bulvari, Yeni Sanayi Bolgesi
Tel: (357-2) 281922/(357-2) 281881;
Fax: (357-2) 281934/(357-2) 276176
Circ.—10,000
Prop.—A-N Graphics (KIBRIS) Ltd. adina
Pub./Dir.—Mehmet Ali Akpinar
Ed.—Suleyman Erguclu
MACHI (Battle) (m) Greek; Est. 1961
4 Danaes; PO Box 7628
Tel: (357-2) 477676; Fax: (357-2) 477701
Circ.—5,000
Prop.—Atrotos Ltd.
Dir.—Sotiris Samson
Ch. Ed.—Dimitris Savvides
ORTAM (Milieu) (m) Turkish; Est. 1980
Cengiz Han Sok, No. 7
Tel: (357-2) 274872/(357-2) 286993;
Fax: (357-2) 283784
Circ.—2,000
Prop.—Toplumcu Ltd.
Pub./Ed.—Resat Akaq
Dir.—Rifat Sertug
PARASKINIO (Behind the Scenes) Greek; Est. 1987
39 Kennedy Ave., Ste. 6
Tel: (357-2) 313334
Circ.—3,500
Prop.—Pararlama Ltd.
Dir./Ch. Ed.—Dinos Michael
PHILELEFTHEROS (Liberal) (m) Greek; Est. 1955
1 Dioghenous St., Engomi; PO Box 1094
Tel: (357-2) 463922; Fax: (357-2) 366122
Circ.—26,500

Pub./Dir.—Christoforos N Pattichis
Ch. Ed.—T Kounnafis
SIMERINI (Today) (m) Greek; Est. 1976
31 Archangelos Ave., Strovolos; PO Box 1836
Tel: (357-2) 353532; Fax: (357-2) 352298
Circ.—16,000
Prop.—Dias Publishing Co. Ltd.
Dir.—Costas Hajdicostis
Ch. Ed.—Savvas Iakovides
THARROS (Courage) Greek; Est. 1961
4 Danaes St.; PO Box 7628
Tel: (357-2) 477676; Fax: (357-2) 477701
Circ.—4,000
Prop.—Atrotos Ltd.
Dir.—Sotiris Samson
Ch. Ed.—Dimitris Savvides
VATAN (Homeland) Turkish; Est. 1990
Yediler Sokak
Tel: (357-2) 277557/(357-2) 287361;
Fax: (357-2) 277558
Circ.—500
Prop.—Yorum Yayincilik Ltd.
Dir.—Erten Kasimoglu
Ed.—Eren Noyan
VIMA TIS KYPROU (Cyprus Rostrum) (m) Greek; Est. 1994
176 Athalassa St.; PO Box 3356
Tel: (357-2) 496411; Fax: (357-2) 496790
Circ.—3,000
Prop.—Ekdoseis Epikinonia Ltd.
Dir.—George Eliades
Ch. Ed.—Costakis Antoniou
Ch. Ed.—Babis Vatis
YENI DEMOCRAT (New Democracy) Turkish; Est. 1994
Yeni Sanayi Bolgesi, 7-8 Sokak
Tel: (357-2) 281485; Fax: (357-2) 272558
Circ.—500
Prop.—Demokrat Matbacilik Ltd.
Dir./Ed.—Mustafa Okan
YENI DUZEN (New Order) (m) Turkish; Est. 1976
Organize Sanayi Bölgesi
Tel: (357-2) 286658/(357-2) 286659;
Fax: (357-2) 275240
Circ.—2,000
Prop.—Yeniduzen Ltd.
Pub.—Burhan Eraslan
Ed.—Sami Özuslu

CZECH REPUBLIC
Pop. Est. 10,408,280

BRNO
(Moravia)
Pop. Est. 387,986

BRNENSKY VECERNIK (Evening Daily) (e) Czech; Est. 1991
Jakubské nám 7, 65844
Tel: (42-5) 42216017/(42-5) 42321227;
Fax: (42-5) 4215150
Circ.—20,000
Prop.—Brnénsky Vecernik
Ed. in Ch.—Petr Hoskovec
ROVNOST (Equality) (d) Czech; Est. 1991
Moravské nám 13, 65822
Tel: (42-5) 749000; Fax: (42-5) 743882
Circ.—170,000 (total)
Prop.—Rovnost a.s.
Ed. in Ch.—Dr. Jiri Roupec
U.S. Rep.—Nielsen Communications

CESKE BUDELOVICE
(Bohemia)
Pop. Est. 97,283

JIHOCESKE LISTY (South Bohemia Daily) (d) Czech; Est. 1991
Vrbenská 23, 37045
Tel: (42-38) 22081; Fax: (42-38) 22061
Circ.—60,000
Prop.—Vltava Publishers
Ed. in Ch.—Vladimir Majer

HRADEC KRALOVE
(Bohemia)

HRADECKÉ NOVINY-DENK POCHODEN (d) Czech; Est. 1991
Skroupova 695, 50172
Tel: (42-49) 613511/(42-49) 613517;
Fax: (42-49) 615681
Circ.—30,000
Prop.—PN Press
Ed. in Ch.—Jaromir Fridrich

Czech Republic

OLOMOUC
(Moravia)
Pop. Est. 105,690

HANACKE NOVINY (d) Czech; Est. 1990
Michalská 4, 77186
Tel: (42-68) 23663; Fax: (42-68) 28723
Circ.—10,000
Pub.—Marcelo Zurkova
Ed. in Ch.—Ing Tomás Tichak

OSTRAVA
(Moravia)
Pop. Est. 327,553

GLOS LUDU (d-4x wk.) Polish; Est. 1945
Novinárská 3, 70907-1
Tel: (42-69) 5844111
Ed. in Ch.—Marian Siedlaczek
MORAVSKOSLEZSKY DEN (d) Czech; Est. 1990
Havlickovo nábr. 32, 72964-1
Tel: (42-69) 216281; Fax: (42-69) 216281
Circ.—110,000
Prop.—Moravskoslezsky Den
Ed.—Boleslav Navratil
SVOBODA (New Freedom) (m) Czech; Est. 1945
Novinárská 3, 70907-1
Tel: (42-69) 261682; Fax: (42-69) 262144
Circ.—220,000 (total)
Prop.—OSNA
Ed. in Ch.—Dr. Miroslav Mrkvica

PLIZEN
(Bohemia)
Pop. Est. 173,129

PLZENSKY DENIK (d) Czech
Husova trida 15, 30483
Tel: (42-19) 551320; Fax: (42-19) 551234
Prop.—Vltava
Ed. in Ch.—Ing Jan Pertl

PRAGUE
(Bohemia)
Pop. Est. 1,200,000

BLESK (d) Czech
Na Florenci 19, 11286-1
Tel: (42-2) 2822886
Circ.—420,000
Prop.—MUT
BOHEMIA DAILY STANDARD (d) English; Est. 1994
Senovázné nám. 21, 11000-1
Tel: (42-2) 24102300; Fax: (42-2) 24102324
Circ.—5000
Pub.—Erik Best
Mng. Ed.—Joe Cook
Ed.—Francis Harris
CESKY DENIK (d) Czech
Na Florenci 19, 11000-1
Tel: (42-2) 2326051/(42-2) 2823321;
Fax: (42-2) 24811416
Pub.—Josef Kudlacek
Ed.—Jan Patocka
HOSPODARSKE NOVINY (m-5x wk.)
Na Florenci 13, 11543-1
Tel: (42-2) 225742; Fax: (42-2) 2356868
Circ.—175,000
Prop.—Economia Ltd.
Pub.—Miroslav Pavel
Ed.—Jiri Sekera
Ad. Mgr.—Sylvio Smerakova
LIDOVA DEMOKRACIE (m-ex S) Czech; Est. 1945
Na Florenci 19, 11000-1
Tel: (42-2) 2823332; Fax: (42-2) 24226061
Cir.—230,000
Pro.—Pragoprint
Pub.—Fidelis Schlee
Ed.—Ivan Cervenka
Ad. Mgr.—Vana Vaneckova
LIDOVE NOVINY (m-ex S) Czech; Est. 1893
Melantrichova a5, 11000-1
Tel: (42-2) 2320924; Fax: (42-2) 2358919
Circ.—130,000
Prop.—Lidove Noviny
Ed.—Jaromir Stetina
Ad. Mgr.—Blahoslav Fort
METROPOLITNI TELEGRAF (d) Czech; Est. 1992
Na Florenci 19, 11286-1
Tel: (42-2) 2367487; Fax: (42-2) 267231
MLADA FRONTA DNES (Youth Front) (d) Czech; Est. 1945
Na porici 30, 11286-1
Tel: (42-2) 2321122/(42-2) 24225503;
Fax: (42-2) 24812709
Circ.—500,000
Prop.—Robert Hersant
Pub.—Karel Hvizdala
Ed. in Ch.—Libor Sevcik

OBCANSKY DENIKOF (Civic Daily News) (m-ex S); Est. 1989
Na Florenci 19, 11329-1
Tel: (42-2) 2326051; Fax: (42-2) 2320925
Circ.—109,000
Ed.—Jan Vavra
Ad. Mgr.—Oto Linhart
PRACE (Trade Union) (d-ex S) Czech; Est. 1945
Václavské nám. 15, 11258-1
Tel: (42-2) 266039; Fax: (42-2) 24226475
Circ.—350,000
Prop.—De Pra
Ed. in Ch.—Frantisek Conk
Ed.—Jan Chara
PRAGUE POST English
Na porici 12, 11530-1
Tel: (42-2) 24875000; Fax: (42-2) 24875000
Circ.—14,000
Prop.—Lion's Share Group
Gen. Mgr.—Lisa L Frankenberg
Ed. in Ch.—Alan Levy
Ed.—Martin Huckerby
Ad. Dir.—Kristin Spirkova
RUDE PRAVO (Red Right) (d) Czech; Est. 1920
Florenci 19, 11121-1
Tel: (42-2) 2822000/(42-2) 2822441;
Fax: (42-2) 24811607
Circ.—350,000
Prop.—Borgis
Ed. in Ch.—Zdenek Porybny
SVOBODNE SLOVO (Free Word) (d) Czech; Est. 1907
Václavské nám. 36, 11212-1
Tel: (42-2) 260341; Fax: (42-2) 266468
Circ.—442,000
Prop.—Melantrich
Ed. in Ch.—Jaromir Masek
Ed.—Jaroslav Bocek
TELEGRAF (d)
Václavské nám. 15, 11121-1
Tel: (42-2) 24217781/(42-2) 24217581;
Fax: (42-2) 24219186
VECERNIK PRAHA (Evening Daily) (e)
Na Florenci 19, 11000-1
Tel: (42-2) 2823332; Fax: (42-2) 24226061
Circ.—130,000
Prop.—Pragoprint

USTI NAD LABEM
(Bohemia)
Pop. Est. 99,739

SEVEROCESKY DENIK (d) Czech; Est. 1990
Belehradska 17, 40001
Tel: (42-47) 22244/(42-47) 22246; Fax: (42) 4723115
Prop.—Logos
Ed. in Ch.—Jaroslav Haidler

DENMARK
Pop. Est. 5,184,821

AABENRAA
(Jutland)
Pop. Est. 21,191

DER NORDSCHLESWIGER (m-6x wk.) German; Est. 1946
Skibbroen 4-6; PF 79, 6200
Tel: (45) 74623880; Fax: (45) 74629430
Circ.—2,901 ABC
Prop.—Deutscher Presseverein
Ed.—Siegfried Matlok
Ad. Mgr.—Jens Peter Hansen

AARHUS
(Jutland)
Pop. Est. 207,300

AARHUUS STIFTSTIDENDE (dS)
Olof Palmes Alle 39, 8200-N
Tel: (45) 86784000; Fax: (45) 86784401
Circ.—62,333 (d); 83,289 (S) ABC
Prop.—Aarhuus Stiftstidende AS
Ed. in Ch.—Aage Holm-Pedersen
Ed.—Aage Lundgaard

ALBORG
(Jutland)
Pop. Est. 115,200

ALBORG STIFTSTIDENDE (d)
Langagervej 1; PO Box 8000, 9220
Tel: (45) 99353535; Fax: (45) 99353565

Circ.—72,020 (d); 92,612 (S) ABC
Prop.—Alborg Stiftstidende AS
Ed. in Ch.—Erling Brondum
Ed.—Uffe Riis Sorensen

COPENHAGEN
(Sjaelland)
Pop. Est. 1,670,000
(Greater Copenhagen Area)

BERLINGSKE TIDENDE (mS) Est. 1749
Berlingske Annoncecenter, Pilestraede 34, 1147-K
Tel: (45) 33757500; Fax: (45) 33757575
Circ.—134,414 (d); 197,162 (S) ABC
Prop.—De Berlingske Dagblade AS
Ed. in Ch.—Hans Dam
Ed.—Erik Bistrup
B.T. (eS) Est. 1916
Berlingske Annoncecenter, Pilestraede 34, 1147-K
Tel: (45) 33757500; Fax: (45) 33752001
Circ.—163,984 (d); 192,675 (S) ABC
Prop.—Der Berlingske Dagblade AS
Ed. in Ch.—Peter Dall
Ed.—Henning Laessoe
BORSEN (m-5x wk.) Est. 1896
Montergade 19, 1140
Tel: (45) 33320102; Fax: (45) 33911050
Circ.—42,276 ABC
Prop.—Forlaget Borsen AS
Ed. in Ch.—Jan Cortzen
Ed. in Ch.—Leif Beck Fallesen
DET FRI AKTUELT (m-6x wk.) Est. 1872
Radhuspladsen 45-47, 1595-V
Tel: (45) 33324001; Fax: (45) 33134580
Circ.—40,075 ABC
Prop.—Pressen AS
Prop.—Fagbevaegelsens Presse
Ed. in Ch.—Lisbeth Knudsen
Ad. Mgr.—Torben Weissenborn
EKSTRA BLADET (dS) Est. 1904
Radhuspladsen 37, 1785-V
Tel: (45) 33111313; Fax: (45) 33121331
Circ.—176,928 (d); 192,852 (S) ABC
Prop.—Dagbladet Politiken AS
Ed. in Ch.—Sven Ove Gade
Ed. in Ch.—Bent Falbert
Ad. Mgr.—Jan Damgaard
ERHVERVS-BLADET (e-5x wk.)
Vesterbrogade 12, 1780-V
Tel: (45) 31213636; Fax: (45) 31218036
Circ.—109,210 ABC
Ed. in Ch.—Bertel Bernhard
INFORMATION (m-6x wk.) English
St. Kongensgade 40 C; PO Box 188, 1006-K
Tel: (45) 33141426; Fax: (45) 33145690
Circ.—23,796 ABC
Ed. in Ch.—Lasse Ellegaard
Ad. Mgr.—Georg Hutters
Ad. Mgr.—Henrik Schucher
KRISTELIGT DAGBLAD (m-6x wk.) Est. 1896
Fanogade 15, 2100-O
Tel: (45) 39271235; Fax: (45) 39271235
Circ.—14,193 ABC
Prop.—Kristeligt Dagblad AS
Pub.—Ib Nordland
Ed. in Ch.—Gunnar Rytgaard
Ad. Mgr.—Jytte Christensen
POLITIKEN (mS) Est. 1884
Annonceafdelingen, Radhuspladsen 37, 1785-V
Tel: (45) 33118511; Fax: (45) 33121331
Circ.—153,214 (m); 205,125 (S) ABC
Prop.—Dagbladet Politiken AS
Ed. in Ch.—Toger Seidenfaden
Ed. in Ch.—Agner Ahm
Ad. Mgr.—Alan Matthesen

ESBJERG
(Jutland)
Pop. Est. 81,843

JYDSKE VESTKYSTEN (mS)
Banegardspladsen, 6700
Tel: (45) 75124500; Fax: (45) 75132207
Circ.—95,370 (m); 109,417 (S) ABC
Prop.—Den Sydvestjdske Venstrepresse AS
Ed. in Ch.—Nils Thostrup
Ad. Mgr.—Hans Gunstrup

FJERRITSLEV
(Jutland)
Pop. Est. 8,308

FJERRITSLEV AVIS (e-6x wk.)
Ostergade 33-35, 9690
Tel: (45) 98211200; Fax: (45) 98213234
Circ.—3,848 ABC
Prop.—Fjerritslev Avis AS
Pub.—Einar Darnsgaard
Edit'l. Mgr.—Anne Marie Larsen
Ed.—Jens Darnsgaard

FLENSBORG
(Jutland)

FLENSBORG AVIS (d)
Wittenberger Weg 19; PO Box 2662, 2390
Tel: (45) 46158050; Fax: (45) 46159090
Circ.—7,108
Ed. in Ch.—Bjarne Lonborg

FREDERICIA
(Jutland)
Pop. Est. 46,617

FREDERICIA DAGBLAD (d)
Danmarksgade 28, 7000
Tel: (45) 75922600; Fax: (45) 75923355
Circ.—7,500
Ed. in Ch.—Hogens Sorensen

FREDERIKSHAVN
(Jutland)
Pop. Est. 35,524

FREDERIKSHAVNS AVIS (e-6x wk.)
Tordenskjoldsgade 2, 9900
Tel: (45) 99203333; Fax: (45) 99203333
Circ.—5,930 ABC
Ed.—Bent Eilertsen
Ad. Mgr.—Helmuth Fredriksen

GLOSTRUP
(Sjaelland)

LICITATIONEN (m-5x wk.)
Visholm Media a/s, Sydvestvej 49, 2600
Tel: (45) 43630222; Fax: (45) 43630121
Circ.—5,614 ABC
Prop.—Vishom Media AS

HELSINGOR
(Sjaelland)
Pop. Est. 56,794

HELSINGOR DAGBLAD (e-6x wk.)
Klostermosevej 101, 3000
Tel: (45) 42222110; Fax: (45) 42220650
Circ.—7,502 ABC
Prop.—Dansk Avis Tryk AS
Ed. in Ch.—John Bech
Ad. Mgr.—Asbjorn Ditevsen

HERNING
(Jutland)
Pop. Est. 56,195

HERNING FOLKEBLAD (e-6x wk.)
Ostergade 25, 7400
Tel: (45) 97123700; Fax: (45) 97223600
Circ.—15,681 ABC
Prop.—Herning Folkeblad AS
Pub.—Gorn Albrechtsen
Pub.—Flemming Larsen

HILLEROD
(Sjaelland)
Pop. Est. 33,628

FREDERIKSBORG AMTS AVIS (e-6x wk.)
Slotsgade 1, 3400
Tel: (45) 48244100; Fax: (45) 42254840
Circ.—31,281 ABC
Prop.—De Bergske Blade AS
Ed. in Ch.—Erik Jensen
Ad. Mgr.—Ib Andersen

HJORRING
(Jutland)
Pop. Est. 34,467

HJORRING (dS)
Frederikshavnsveg 79-81, 9800
Tel: (45) 98921700; Fax: (45) 98921700
Circ.—13,065 (d); 14,304 (S) ABC
VENDSYSSEL TIDENDE
Frederikshavnsjev 79-81, 9800
Tel: (45) 98921700; Fax: (45) 98921670
Circ.—81,339 ABC
Prop.—Vendsyssel Tidende AS
Pub.—L Juhl Andersen
Ed.—Claus Dindler
Ad. Dir.—O Bjerg Hansen

HOLBAEK
(Sjaelland)
Pop. Est. 30,821

HOLBAEK AMTS VENSTREBLAD (e-6x wk.)
Ahlgade 1, 4300
Tel: (45) 59480200; Fax: (45) 59442810
Circ.—20,410 ABC
Ed. in Ch.—Alfred Hansen
Ad. Mgr.—Allan Engberg

HOLSTEBRO
(Jutland)
Pop. Est. 37,992

DAGBLADET-HOLSTEBRO-STRUER (e-6x wk.)
Laegaardsvej 86, 7500
Tel: (45) 99128300; Fax: (45) 97410320
Circ.—12,815 ABC
Prop.—De Bergske Blade AS
Pub.—Peter Parbo
Ed. in Ch.—Erik Moller
Ad. Mgr./Sales Mgr.—Poul Erik Aagaard

HORSENS
(Jutland)
Pop. Est. 55,123

HORSENS FOLKEBLAD (m-6x wk.)
Sondergade 47, 8700
Tel: (45) 75624500; Fax: (45) 75615911
Circ.—22,162 ABC
Prop.—Horsens Folkeblad AS
Ed. in Ch.—Nogens Ahrenkiel
Ad. Mgr.—Jens Bebe

KALUNDBORG
(Sjaelland)
Pop. Est. 19,381

KALUNDBORG FOLKEBLAD (e-mon. to sat.)
Skibbrogade 40, 4400
Tel: (45) 53512460; Fax: (45) 53510233
Circ.—9,216 ABC
Prop.—Kalunborg Folkeblad AS
Pub./Ed.—Jorgen Jensen

KERTEMINDE
(Fyn)
Pop. Est. 10,168

KJERTEMINDE AVIS (e-6x wk.)
Nordre Ringvej 54, 5300
Tel: (45) 65321004; Fax: (45) 65322704
Circ.—1,612 ABC
Ed. in Ch.—Jorgen Wind-Hansen

KOLDING
(Jutland)
Pop. Est. 57,982

FOLKEBLADET-SYDJYLLAND (e-6x wk.)
Jernbanegade 35, 6000
Tel: (45) 75522000; Fax: (45) 75532144
Circ.—17,000
Prop.—De Bergske Blade AS
Ed. in Ch.—Tage Rasmussen
Ad. Mgr.—Tom Lykke

LOGSTOR
(Jutland)
Pop. Est. 10,804

LOGSTOR AVIS (d)
Torvegade 2, 9670
Tel: (45) 98671211; Fax: (45) 98671150
Circ.—2,697 ABC
Prop.—Logstor Avis AS
Ed. in Ch.—Ejnar Damsgaard

MIDDELFART
(Fyn)

MIDDELFART VENSTREBLAD (d)
Algade 48, 5500
Tel: (45) 64411303; Fax: (45) 64411307
Circ.—6,200
Ed. in Ch.—Lars Bech Nielsen

NAESTVED
(Sjaelland)
Pop. Est. 45,153

NAESTVED TIDENDE (e-6x wk.)
Ringstedgade 13, 4700
Tel: (45) 53724511; Fax: (45) 55773620
Circ.—34,291 ABC
Prop.—Naestved Tidende AS
Pub.—Poul Kristensen
Ed. in Ch.—Mogens Baden
Ed. in Ch.—Peter Glitten

NAKSKOV
(Lolland)
Pop. Est. 16,413

NY DAG (e-6x wk.)
Hojevej 15, 4900
Tel: (45) 53921400; Fax: (45) 53921109
Circ.—9,200
Prop.—A-Pressen AS
Prop.—Fagbevaegelsens Presse
Ed. in Ch.—Klaus Sivebaek

NYKOBING
(Llolland-Falster)
Pop. Est. 24,098

FOLKTIDENDE (e-6x wk.)
Tvaergade 14, 4800-F
Tel: (45) 54852066; Fax: (45) 54821175
Circ.—22,610 ABC
Ed. in Ch.—P Westergaard-Andersen
MORSO FOLKEBLAD (e-6x wk.)
Elsovej 105, 7900-M
Tel: (45) 97721000; Fax: (45) 97721010
Circ.—6,526 ABC
Prop.—Morso Folkeblad AS
Ed. in Ch.—Leif Kristiansen

ODENSE
(Fyn)
Pop. Est. 142,800

FYENS STIFTSTIDENDE (mS)
Postboks 428, 5220
Tel: (45) 66111111; Fax: (45) 65932583
Circ.—66,252 (m); 95,202 (S) ABC
Prop.—Fyens Stiftstidende AS
Ed. in Ch.—Bent A Koch
Ed. in Ch.—Egon Tottrup

PADBORG
(Jutland)
Pop. Est. 2,979

FLENSBORG AVIS (6x wk.)
PO Box 70, 6330
Tel: (45) 46150450
Circ.—7,184
Prop.—Flensborg Avis AS

RANDERS
(Jutland)
Pop. Est. 61,440

AMTS AVISEN (e-6x wk.) Est. 1810
Lille Voldgade 5, 8900
Tel: (45) 86427511; Fax: (45) 86418150
Circ.—27,824 ABC
Prop.—J M Elmenhoff & Son AS
Ed. in Ch.—Ole C Jorgensen
Ed. in Ch.—Ib Sleimann
Ad. Mgr.—Jorgen Dahlerup

RINGKOBING
(Jutland)
Pop. Est. 16,948

RINGKOBING AMTS DAGBLAD (m-6x wk.)
St. Blichersvej 9, 6950
Tel: (45) 99757300; Fax: (45) 97320546
Circ.—16,743 ABC
Prop.—De Bergske Blade AS
Pub.—C Korsgaard
Ed. in Ch.—Kristian Sand
Ad. Mgr.—Jacob Gade

RINGSTED
(Sjaelland)
Pop. Est. 28,559

DAGBLADET (e-6x wk.)
Sogade 4-12, 4100
Tel: (45) 53612500; Fax: (45) 57673113
Circ.—30,283 ABC
Ed. in Ch.—Torben Dalby Larsen

RONNE
(Bornholm)
Pop. Est. 15,236

BORNHOLMEREN (e-6x wk.)
Snellemark 26; PO Box 140, 3700
Tel: (45) 56952526; Fax: (45) 56958449
Circ.—6,000
Prop.—A-Pressen AS
Prop.—Fagbevaegelsens Presse
Ed. in Ch.—Bo Schriver
BORNHOLMS TIDENDE (e-6x wk.)
Norregade 11-19, 3700
Tel: (45) 56951400; Fax: (45) 56953119
Circ.—11,105 ABC
Dir.—Bjarne Pedersen
Ed. in Ch.—Jorgen Baungaard
Ad. Mgr.—Olaf Mikkelsen

ROSKILDE
(Sjaelland)
Pop. Est. 50,158

DAGBLADET/ROSKILDE TIDENDE (e-6x wk.)
Hersegade 22, 4000
Tel: (45) 42358500; Fax: (45) 42358040
Circ.—10,351 ABC

SILKEBORG
(Jutland)
Pop. Est. 47,890

MIDTJYLLANDS AVIS (e-6x wk.)
Vestergade 30; PO Box 317, 8600
Tel: (45) 86821300; Fax: (45) 86803655
Circ.—20,220 ABC
Prop.—Silkeborg Avis AS
Ed. in Ch.—Viggo Sorensen

SKAGEN
(Jutland)
Pop. Est. 13,919

SKAGENS AVIS (e-6x wk.)
Skolevej 8-12, 9990
Tel: (45) 98441155; Fax: (45) 98450570
Circ.—4,216 ABC
Pub./Ed. in Ch.—Johs Brunn-Bindslev
Ad. Mgr.—Flemming Stig

SKIVE
(Jutland)
Pop. Est. 26,774

SKIVE FOLKEBLAD (e-6x wk.)
Gemsevej 7-9, 7800
Tel: (45) 97513411; Fax: (45) 97511580
Circ.—13,915 ABC
Prop.—Garantselskabet Skive Folkeblad
Ed. in Ch.—Ole Dall
Ad. Mgr.—Anne Marie Sondergard

SLAGELSE
(Sjaelland)
Pop. Est. 33,935

SJAELLANDS TIDENDE (e-5x wk.)
Korsgade 4, 4200
Tel: (45) 53523700; Fax: (45) 53523497
Circ.—16,254
Prop.—Sjaellands Tidende AS
Ed. in Ch.—Peter Glitten
Ad. Mgr.—Jan Worm

SVENDBORG
(Fyn)
Pop. Est. 40,394

FYNS AMTS AVIS (m-5x wk.)
Sankt Nicolai Gade 3, 5700
Tel: (45) 62214621; Fax: (45) 62228949
Circ.—22,111 ABC
Prop.—Svendborg Avis AS
Ed. in Ch.—Arne Mariager
Ad. Mgr.—Poul Vig
Ad. Mgr.—Jens Rosenquist

THISTED
(Jutland)
Pop. Est. 29,848

THISTED DAGBLAD (e-6x wk.)
Jernbanegade 15-17, 7700
Tel: (45) 97923322; Fax: (45) 97910720
Circ.—10,446 ABC
Prop.—De Bergske Blade AS
Pub.—Tage Rasmussen
Ed. in Ch.—Hans Peter Kragh

VEJLE
(Jutland)
Pop. Est. 51,845

VEJLE AMTS FOLKEBLAD/FREDERICIA DAGBLAD
(d-5x wk.)
Bugattivej 8, 7100
Tel: (45) 75857788; Fax: (45) 75857274
Circ.—30,658 ABC
Prop.—Vejle Amts Folkeblad AS
Ed. in Ch.—Vagn Nygaard

VIBORG
(Jutland)
Pop. Est. 39,453

VIBORG STIFTS FOLKEBLAD (e-6x wk.)
Sct. Mathiasgade 7, 8800
Tel: (45) 89276300; Fax: (45) 86622220
Circ.—12,687 ABC
Prop.—De Bergske Blade AS
Ed. in Ch.—Per V Sunesen
Ad. Mgr.—Orla Vistisen

VIBY
(Jutland)

MORGENAVISEN JYLLANDS-POSTEN (eS)
Grondalsvej 3, 8260-J
Tel: (45) 87383838; Fax: (45) 87383489
Circ.—151,748 (d); 248,981 (S) ABC
Prop.—Jyllands-Posten AS
Ed. in Ch.—Jorgen Ejbol

ESTONIA
Pop. Est. 1,616,882

TALLINN
Pop. Est. 471,608

ESTONIYA (6x wk.) Estonian; Est. 1940
67a, Pyarnusskoe Shosse, 200090
Circ.—49,000
Ed.—S Tarakanov
MOLODEZH ESTONII (Youth of Estonia) (5x wk.)
Russian; Est. 1950
67a, Pyarnusskoe Shosse, 200090
Ed.—I Ristmyagi
NOORTE HAAL (The Voice of Youth) (6x wk.)
Estonian; Est. 1940
67a, Pyarnusskoe Shosse, 200090
Circ.—150,000
Ed.—T Tare
OHTULEHT (The Evening Paper) (e); Est. 1944
67a, Paarnu Maantee, 200090
Tel: (372-2) 681154; Fax: (372-2) 441924
PAEVALEHT (The Daily Paper) (d)
67a, Paarnu Maantee, PO Box 432, 200090
Tel: (372-2) 681235; Fax: (372-2) 442762
Ed. in Ch.—Margus Mets
RAHVA HAAL (The Voice of the People) (6x
wk.) Estonian; Est. 1940
67a, Paarnu Maantee, 200090
Circ.—175,000
Ed. in Ch.—Toomas Leito

TARTU

POSTIMEES (The Mailman) (d-ex S) Est. 1857
Gildi 1, 202400
Tel: (372-34) 433351; Fax: (372-2) 441446
Circ.—43,000
Prop.—Postmees Ltd.
Pub.—Mart Kadastik
Ed.—Vahur Kalmre
Ad. Mgr.—Tanel Joks

FAEROE ISLANDS
(Autonomous overseas part of Denmark)
Pop. Est. 48,427

ARGIR

FRIU FOROYAR Faeroese; Est. 1982
PO Box 255, 165
Tel: (298) 16444; Fax: (298) 18813
Circ.—1,400
Prop.—Frui Foroyar P/F
Ed.—Arnbjorn R Thomsen
SOSIALURIN (5x wk.) Faeroese; Est. 1927
Argjavegur 26; PO Box 76, 165
Tel: (298) 11820; Fax: (298) 14720
Circ.—6,400
Prop.—Sosialurin P/F
Ed.—Jan Muller

KLAKSVIK
Pop. Est. 5,403

NORDLYSID Faeroese; Est. 1915
PO Box 58, 700
Tel: (298) 56285; Fax: (298) 56498
Circ.—1,200
Prop.—Nordlysi P/F
Ed.—Oliver Joensen

TORSHAVN
Pop. Est. 14,767

DIMMALAETTING Faeroese & Danish; Est. 1877
PO Box 19, 110
Tel: (298) 11212; Fax: (298) 10941
Circ.—13,000
Prop.—Faero Amtstidende's Bogtrykkeri A/S
Ed.—Benny Samuelsen
FJURTANDI SEPTEMBER (September 14)
Faeroese; Est. 1976
PO Box 2069, 165
Tel: (298) 14412/(298) 14469; Fax:
(298) 19880
Circ.—3,000

Faeroe Islands

Prop.—Bladstarv, Vagsbotnur P/F
Ed.—Vilmund Jacobsen
OYGGJATIDINDI Faeroese; Est. 1976
PO Box 3312, 110
Tel: (298) 14411/(298) 16411; Fax: (298) 16410
Circ.—4,500
Prop.—Oyggjatdindi P/F
Ed.—Dan Klein

FINLAND
Pop. Est. 5,068,931

EKENAS
(Turku-Pori)
Pop. Est. 11,400

VÄSTRA NYLAND (m-6x wk.) Swedish
Genvägen 4; PO Box 26, 10600
Tel: (358-11) 2462800; Fax: (358-11) 2462812
Circ.—11,281
Ed. in Ch.—Karl-Olof Spring

FORSA

FORSSAN LEHTI (6x wk.)
Forssan Kirjapaino Oy, Esko Aaltosen Katu 2; PL 38, 30101
Tel: (358-916) 41551
Circ.—15,258

HAMEENLINNA
(Hame)
Pop. Est. 43,000

HAMEEN SANOMAT (d)
Vanajantie 7; PL 530, 13111
Tel: (358-17) 61511; Fax: (358-17) 6151390
Circ.—33,344
Ed. in Ch.—Esko Ojala

HANGÖ

HANGÖTIDNINGEN (m-6x wk.)
Hangö Tryckeri Ab, Bergg. 15-77; PO Box 2, 10901
Tel: (358-911) 84531; Fax: (358-911) 86431

HEINOLA

ITÄ-HÄME (6x wk.)
Esan Kirjapaino Oy, Kirjanpainajank-1; PL 10, 18101
Tel: (358-18) 158111; Fax: (358-18) 158117

HELSINKI
(Uusima)
Pop. Est. 497,542

DEMARI (e-5x wk.)
Kustannus Oy Demari, Paasivuorenkatu 3, 00530
Tel: (358-0) 701041; Fax: (358-0) 736796
Circ.—37,582
Mng. Ed.—Antti Marttinen
Mng. Ed.—Tapani Suominen
Ed. in Ch.—Jukka Halonen
HELSINGIN SANOMAT (mS) Est. 1889
Box 240, 00101
Tel: (358-0) 1221; Fax: (358-0) 1223229
Circ.—476,000 (m); 546,000 (S)
Prop.—Sanoma Corp.
Pub.—Seppo Kievari
Mng. Ed.—Pekka Kukkonen
Mng. Ed.—Jukka Ollila
Mng. Ed.—Heleena Savela
Ed. in Ch.—Janne Virkkunen
Ed.—Reetta Merilainen
Ed.—Keijo K Kulha
U.S. Rep.—Publicitas
HUFVUDSTADSBLADET (7x wk.) Swedish; Est. 1864
HBL; PO Box 217, 00101
Tel: (358-0) 12531; Fax: (358-0) 642269
Circ.—63,649
Mng. Ed.—Bo Finne
Ed. in Ch.—Rafael Paro
Ed. in Ch.—Bo Stenstrom
ILTALEHTI (6x wk.)
Kustannusakeyhtiö Iltalehti; PL 372, 00101
Tel: (358-0) 507721; Fax: (358-0) 533512
Circ.—116,036
Prop.—Uusi Suomi Co.
Mng. Ed.—Martti Backman
Ed. in Ch.—Veli-Antti Savolainen
Ed.—Anne Lyytikainen
Ed.—Ilkka Yrja
Ed.—Markku Virkkala
ILTA-SANOMAT (m-6x wk.) Est. 1932
Box 371, 00101
Tel: (358-0) 1221; Fax: (358-0) 1223665
Circ.—220,090
Prop.—Sanoma Corp.
Mng. Dir./Edit'l. Dir.—Vesa-Pekka Koljonen
Mng. Ed.—Erik Rissanen
Mng. Ed.—Kari Ylanne
Mng. Ed.—Antti-Pikka Pietila
Ed. in Ch.—Hannu Savola
U.S. Rep.—Publicitas
KANSAN UUTISET (4x wk.)
Kansan Uutiset Oy; PL 21, 00811
Tel: (358-0) 759601; Fax: (358-0) 75960301
Circ.—42,415
Prop.—Kansan Uutiset Oy
Ed. in Ch.—Yrjo Rautio
Ed.—Pertti Jokinen
KAUPPALEHTI (5x wk.)
Kustannus Oy Kauppalethi, Vetotie 3, 01610
Tel: (358-0) 5078648; Fax: (358-0) 5078641
Circ.—76,047
Prop.—Kustannus Oy Kauppalethi
Ex. Ed.—Lauri Helve
Ed. in Ch.—Hannu Olkinuora
Ed. in Ch.—Pekka Ritvos
UUSI SUOMI (m-7x wk.)
PL 139, 00101
Tel: (358-0) 50771; Fax: (358-0) 5078683
Circ.—73,284

HYRYLÄ

KESKI-UUSIMAA (m-7x wk.)
Keski-Uusimaa Oy, Klaavolantie 5; PL 52, 04301
Tel: (358) 255255; Fax: (358) 2731610

HYVINKAA
(Uusima)
Pop. Est. 38,843

HYVINKAAN SANOMAT (d-6x wk.)
Hyvinkään Sanomat Oy, Niinistönk 1; PL 106, 05801
Tel: (358-14) 485100; Fax: (358-14) 485112
Circ.—15,788
Prop.—Hyvinkaan Sanomat Oy
Mng. Ed.—Pekka Liukka
Ed. in Ch.—Pentti Kiiski

IISALMI
(Kuopio)
Pop. Est. 24,000

IISALMEN SANOMAT (m-7x wk.)
PL 11, 74101
Tel: (358-77) 15511; Fax: (358-77) 1551402
Circ.—19,986
Ed. in Ch.—Risto Ylitalo

IMATRA
(Kymi)
Pop. Est. 34,000

YLÄ-VUOKSI (m-6x wk.)
Ylä-Vuoksi Oy; PL 11, 55101
Tel: (358-54) 66066; Fax: (358-54) 67789
Circ.—15,504
Prop.—Yla-Vuoski Oy
Ed. in Ch.—Markku Soikkeli

JÄMSÄ

KOILLIS-HÄME (5x wk.)
Suomen Paikallissanomat Oy, Säterinitie 16, 42100
Tel: (358-82) 176200; Fax: (358-82) 222891
Circ.—9,613

JOENSUU
(Pohjois-Karjala)
Pop. Est. 48,182

KARJALAINEN (7x wk.)
Karjalainen; PL 99, 80141
Tel: (358-73) 1551; Fax: (358-73) 155427
Circ.—53,479
Ed. in Ch.—Pekka Sitari

JYVASKYLA
(Keski-Suomi)
Pop. Est. 67,026

KESKISUOMALAINEN (m-7x wk.)
Keskisuomalainen Oy; Box 159, 40101
Tel: (358-41) 622000; Fax: (358-41) 622380

Circ.—82,080
Prop.—Keskisuomalainen Oy
Ed. in Ch.—Erkki Laatkainen

KAJAANI
(Oulu)
Pop. Est. 36,000

KAINUUN SANOMAT (m-7x wk.) Est. 1918
Arja Kemppainen, PL 150, 87101
Tel: (358-86) 61661; Fax: (358-86) 623400
Circ.—26,230
Ed. in Ch.—Keijo Korhonen

KARLEBY

OESTERBOTTNINGEN (m-5x wk.)
Tel: (358-68) 8318888; Fax: (358-68) 8318110
Circ.—5,218

KEMI
(Lappi)
Pop. Est. 28,500

POHJOLAN SANOMAT (d)
Sairaalakatu 2, 94100
Tel: (358-698) 2911; Fax: (358-698) 291322
Circ.—42,105
Ed. in Ch.—Matti Lammi
Ed.—Reijo Alatormanen

KOKEMAKI
(Turku-Pori)
Pop. Est. 9,676

LALLI (5x wk.)
Tel: (358-39) 364855; Fax: (358-39) 364276
Circ.—10,431
Prop.—Keskustan Kustannus Oy
Ed. in Ch.—Seppo Keranen

KOKKOLA
(Vaasa)
Pop. Est. 35,000

KESKIPOHJANMAA (m-7x wk.)
Keski-Pohjanmaan Kirjapaino Oy; PL 45, 67101
Tel: (358-68) 8272000; Fax: (358-68) 8225039
Circ.—32,924
Prop.—Keski-Pohjanmaan Kirjapaino Oy
Ed. in Ch.—Lassi Jaakkola

KOTKA
Pop. Est. 56,515

KYMEN SANOMAT (m-6x wk.) Est. 1989
Kymen Sanomalehti Oy, Tornatorintie 3; PL 27, 48101
Tel: (358-52) 2100111; Fax: (358-52) 16382
Circ.—30,353
Prop.—Kymen Sanomalenti Oy
Ed. in Ch.—Jukka Vehkasalo

KOUVOLA
Pop. Est. 32,066

KOUVOLAN SANOMAT (d)
Lehtikkari 1 (45130); PL 40, 45101
Tel: (358-51) 28911; Fax: (358-51) 15335
Circ.—34,414
Ed. in Ch.—Juha Oksanen

KUOPIO
Pop. Est. 81,593

SAVON SANOMAT (d) Est. 1907
Vuorikatu 21-23, 70100
Tel: (358-71) 303111; Fax: (358-71) 303347
Circ.—83,061
Mng. Ed.—Risto Saesmaa
Ed. in Ch.—Tapani Lepola
Ed.—Raimo Ylinen

KUUSAMO

KOILLISSANOMAT (m-5x wk.)
Koillissanomat Oy, Kitkantie 31-33, 93600
Tel: (358-89) 853141; Fax: (358-89) 853147
Circ.—10,677

LAHTI
Pop. Est. 93,414

ETELA-SUOMEN SANOMAT (d) Est. 1900
Ilmarisentie 7; PL 80, 15101
Tel: (358-18) 57511; Fax: (358-18) 575466
Circ.—71,252
Ed. in Ch.—Kauko Maenpaa
Ed.—Pentti Vuorio
Ed. in Ch.—Olavi Kukkeenmaki

LAPPEENRANTA
(Villmanstrand)
Pop. Est. 55,358

ETELA-SAIMAA (7x wk.) Est. 1885
Postilokero 3, 53501
Tel: (358-53) 5591; Fax: (358-53) 4153292
Circ.—35,032
Ed. in Ch.—Kari Vaisanen

LOHJA

LÄNSI-UUSIMAA (m-6x wk.)
PL 60, 08101
Tel: (358-12) 1451; Fax: (358-12) 145357
Circ.—13,712

MARIEHAMN

ÅLAND (e-5x wk.)
Ålans Tidnings-Tryckeri AB; PB 50, 22101
Tel: (358-28) 26026
Circ.—11,502
NYA ÅLAND (m-4x wk.)
PB 21, 22101
Tel: (358-28) 23444; Fax: (358-28) 23450
Circ.—8,220

MIKKELI
Pop. Est. 32,000

LÄNSI-SAVO (m-7x wk.)
Länsi-Savo; PL 6, 50101
Tel: (358-55) 3501; Fax: (358-55) 350337
Circ.—29,194
Ed. in Ch.—Ilkka Juva
Ed. in Ch.—Seija Rasila

OULAINEN

PYHÄJOKISEUTU (e-4x wk.)
Pyhäjokiseudun Kustannus Oy, Sampsankatu 2; PL 1, 86301
Tel: (358-83) 4795111; Fax: (358-83) 4795125
Circ.—9,415

OULU
Pop. Est. 102,280

KALEVA (m-7x wk.) Est. 1899
PL 70, 90101
Tel: (358-81) 5377111; Fax: (358-81) 5377248
Circ.—87,615
Pub.—Martti Ursin
Mng. Ed.—Veikko Laulajainen
Mng. Ed.—Kaarina Helander
Ed. in Ch.—Teuvo Mallinen
KANSAN TAHTO (4x wk.)
Kustannus Oy Kansan Tahto; Box 61, 90101
Tel: (358-81) 371722; Fax: (358-81) 3116457
Circ.—11,198
LIITTO (m-6x wk.)
Osakeyhtiö Liito Lekatie; PL 52, 90101
Tel: (358-81) 5370011; Fax: (358-81) 5370229
Circ.—18,135
Ed. in Ch.—Samuli Pohjamo

PIEKSÄMAKI

PIEKSÄMÄEN LEHTI (5x wk.)
Hallipussi 2; PL 45, 76101
Tel: (358-58) 723456; Fax: (358-58) 7234369

PIETARSAARI
(Jakobstad)
Pop. Est. 20,284

JAKOBSTADS TIDNING (d) Swedish
Jakobsgatan 13 (68600); PL 22, 68601
Tel: (358-67) 7235555; Fax: (358-67) 7248277
Circ.—12,258
Prop.—Jakobstads Tryckeri och Tidnings AB
Ed.—Lars Hedman

PORI
Pop. Est. 76,432

SATAKUNNAN KANSA (m-7x wk.) Est. 1873
PO Box 58, 28101
Tel: (358-39) 6228111; Fax: (358-39) 6228169
Circ.—58,086
Ed.—Erkki Teikari

PORVOO
Pop. Est. 20,000

BORGABLADET (d) Swedish
Veckjarvigagen 3; PL 24, 06101
Tel: (358-15) 173333; Fax: (358-15) 173348
Circ.—11,097
Ed. in Ch.—Rolf Gabrielsson

UUSIMAA (5x wk.)
Uusimaa Oy, Teollisuustie 19; PL 15, 06151
Tel: (358-15) 66161
Circ.—13,032
Ed. in Ch.—Reijo Hirvonen

RAAHE

RAAHEN SEUTU (5x wk.)
Suomen Paikallossanomat Oy, Fellmaninpuistokatu 4; PL 61, 92101
Tel: (358-82) 222830; Fax: (358-82) 222830
Circ.—10,107

RAUMA
Pop. Est. 30,000

LÄNSI-SUOMI (7x wk.)
Oy Länsi Suomi, Kaivopuistontie 1, 26100
Tel: (358-38) 3361; Fax: (358-38) 240959
Circ.—20,207
Ed. in Ch.—Jyrki Niittyranta

ROVANIEMI
Pop. Est. 33,400

LAPIN KANSA (d)
Lapin Kansa Oy, Veitikantie 2, 96100
Tel: (358-60) 2911; Fax: (358-60) 291228
Circ.—43,759
Prop.—Lapin Kansa Oy
Ed. in Ch.—Heikki Tuomi-Nikula

SALO
Pop. Est. 20,629

SALON SEUDUN SANOMAT (m-7x wk.)
Salon Seudun Sanomalehti Osakeyhtiö, Örninkatu 14; PO Box 117, 24101
Tel: (358-24) 30021; Fax: (358-24) 3002222
Circ.—21,758
Prop.—Salon Seudun Sanomalehti Oy
Mng. Ed.—Kauko Mantyla
Ed. in Ch.—Jarmo Vasahilta
Ed. in Ch.—Seppo Suominen

SAVONLINNA
Pop. Est. 28,500

ITA-SAVO (mS)
Ita-Sav Oy, Savonlinnan Kirjapaino Oy; PL 35, 57101
Tel: (358-57) 57555; Fax: (358-57) 5755645/(358-57) 26511
Circ.—23,943 (m); 20,122 (S)
Ed. in Ch.—Esko Suikkanen

SEINAJOKI
Pop. Est. 28,000

ETELA-POHJANMAA (e-5x wk.)
Oy Seinäjoki, Koulukatu 10; PL 12, 60101
Tel: (358-64) 4142142; Fax: (358-64) 4148417
Circ.—11,921
Ed. in Ch.—Paula Hamalainen
ILKKA (e-7x wk.)
Itkka Oy; PL 60, 60101
Tel: (358-64) 44186555; Fax: (358-64) 44186600
Circ.—56,340
Ed.—Kari Hokkanen

TAMPERE
(Tammerfors)
Pop. Est. 173,797

AAMULEHTI (dS) Est. 1881
PO Box 327, 33101
Tel: (358-31) 666111; Fax: (358-31) 666470
Circ.—132,000 (d); 138,000 (S)
Prop.—Kustannus Oy Aamulehti
Mng. Ed.—Pentti Etu-Seppala
Mng. Ed.—Erkka Lehtola
Ed. in Ch.—Raimo Seppala

TURKU
(Åbo)
Pop. Est. 159,403

ÅBO UNDERRATTELSER (m-5x wk.) Swedish
Forlags AB Sydvästkusten Auragatan 1B; PB 211, 20101
Tel: (358-21) 333886; Fax: (358-21) 333964
Circ.—7,928
Ed. in Ch.—Torbjorn Kevin
TURUN PÄIVÄLEHTI (m-5x wk.)
PL 230, 20101
Tel: (358-21) 353900; Fax: (358-21) 357392
Circ.—10,958
Ed. in Ch.—Antti Vuorenrinne

TURUN SANOMAT (mS)
Kauppiaskatu 5, 20100
Tel: (358-21) 693311; Fax: (358-21) 693469
Circ.—115,000 (m); 127,000 (S)
Prop.—Oy Turun Sanomat
Ed. in Ch.—Ari Valjakka
Mng. Dir.—Keijo Ketonen

TUUSULA

KESKI-UUSIMAA (d)
Klaavolantie 5; PO Box 52, 04301
Tel: (358-0) 255255; Fax: (358-0) 255247
Circ.—24,715
Prop.—Keski-Uusimaa Oy
Ed. in Ch.—Auvo Kantola

VAASA
(Vasa)
Pop. Est. 53,764

KANSAN ÄÄNI
Pitkänlandenk 55, 65100
Tel: (358-61) 3122133; Fax: (358-61) 3120107
Circ.—10,988
POHJANMAAN DEMARI (5x wk.) Est. 1903
Kustannus Oy Demari, Klemetink 15; PL 18, 65101
Tel: (358-61) 174150
Circ.—10,054
Ed. in Ch.—Jaakko Elenius
VASABLADET (6x wk.) Swedish
VBL, Sandögatan 6, 65100
Tel: (358-61) 3121866; Fax: (358-61) 3121866
Circ.—27,485
Mng. Ed.—Birger Enges
Ed. in Ch.—Dennis Rundt

VALKEAKOSKI

VALKEAKOSKEN SANOMAT (m-5x wk.)
Kirjask. 1, 37600
Tel: (358-37) 7171
Circ.—8,627

VARKAUS

WARKAUDEN LEHTI (e-6x wk.)
Kampikuja 4; PL 161, 78201
Tel: (358-72) 5527111; Fax: (358-72) 5527139
Circ.—12,500

YLIVIESKA

KALAJOKILAAKSO (e-6x wk.)
PL 7, 84101
Tel: (358-83) 420421; Fax: (358-83) 420975
Circ.—9,777

FRANCE
Pop. Est. 57,840,445

AGEN
(Lot-et-Garonne)
Pop. Est. (Metro Area) 58,288

LE PETIT BLEU DU LOT-ET-GARONNE (d) Est. 1914
750 ave. de Colmar, F-4700
Tel: (33) 53981150; Fax: (33) 53965451
Circ.—12,827
Pub.—Jean-Marie Hellian
Dir.—Francis Milliard

AJACCIO
(Corsica)
Pop. Est. 54,089

JOURNAL DE LA CORSE (d) Est. 1815
1 rue du General-Campi; PO Box 255, 20179
Tel: (33) 95210184
Circ.—3,200
Pub./Ad. Mgr.—Catherine Fieschi-Livrelli

AMIENS
(Somme)
Pop. Est. (Metro Area) 156,694

LE COURRIER PICARD (d) Est. 1944
29 rue de la Republique, F-80010 (Cedex)
Tel: (33) 22826000; Fax: (33) 22826011
Circ.—78,410
Pub.—Jacques Benesse
Ed. in Ch.—Francois Perrier

ANGERS
(Maine-et-Loire)
Pop. Est. (Metro Area) 195,859

LE COURRIER DE L'OUEST (d) Est. 1944
blvd. Albert-Blanchoin; PO Box 728, 49005
Tel: (33) 140120777
Circ.—107,456
Pub.—Jean-Marie Desgrees du Lou
Ed. in Ch.—Etienne Charbonneau

ANGOULEME
(Charente)
Pop. Est. (Metro Area) 103,552

LA CHARENTE LIBRE (d)
No. 3, Zone Industrielle; PO Box 106, 16001 (Cedex)
Tel: (33) 45693333
Circ.—39,546
Pub.—Louis-Guy Gayan
Ed. in Ch.—Loic Hervouet

AUXERRE
(Yonne)
Pop. Est. (Metro Area) 42,126

YONNE REPUBLICAINE (d) Est. 1944
8-12 ave. Jean-Moulin; PO Box 399, 89006
Circ.—41,126
Pub.—Jean-Francois Comperat
Ed. in Ch.—Gilles Dauxerre

AVIGNON
(Vaucluse)
Pop. Est. (Metro Area) 174,264

LA MARSEILLAISE VAUCLUSE (d)
4 rue Agricol-Perdiguier, 84000
Tel: (33) 140120777
Ed. in Ch.—Marc Berrus
VAUCLUSE MATIN (d)
4 rue de la Republique; PO Box 134, 84000
Tel: (33) 90823280
Circ.—10,412 (d); 11,860 (S)
Ed.—Pierre Bail

BASTIA
(Corse)
Pop. Est. (Metro Area) 50,596

LE PETIT BASTIAIS (d) Est. 1875
2 rue Saint-Angelo, 20200
Tel: (33) 95310499
Circ.—1,200
Pub.—Catherine Fieschi-Livrelli
Pub.—Lois Rioni

BEAUVAIS
(Oise)
Pop. Est. (Metro Area) 55,817

OISE-MATIN (d)
7 rue Saint-Pierre, 60000
Ed.—Pascal Sellier

BORDEAUX
(Gironde)
Pop. Est. (Metro Area) 201,000

LA FRANCE-LA NOUVELLE REPUBLIQUE (d) Est. 1944
8 rue de Cheverus, F-33000
Circ.—8,210
Pub.—Jean-Michel Blanchy
SUD-OUEST/SUD-OUEST DIMANCHE (m) Est. 1944
8 rue de Cheverus, F-33000
Tel: (33-56) 909272
Circ.—349,283
Prop.—Sud Quest
Pub.—Jean-Francoise Lemoine
Ed. in Ch.—Joel Aubert
Ed. in Ch.—Pierre Veilietet
Ed. in Ch.—Pierre-Marie Cortella

BOULOGNE

CENTRE-PRESSE RODEZ (d)
83 rue du Chateau, 92513
Tel: (33) 146050506
Circ.—25,144

BOURGES
(Cher)
Pop. Est. (Metro Area) 87,205

LE BERRY REPUBLICAIN (d) Est. 1945
1-3 place du Berry; PO Box 141, F-18000
Tel: (33) 147123300; Fax: (33) 147122043
Circ.—40,000
Pub.—Guy Dugne
Ed. in Ch.—Serge Joffre

Europe **France** IV-13

CALAIS
(Pas-de-Calais)
Pop. Est. (Metro Area) 100,823

NORD-LITTORAL (d-ex mon.) Est. 1944
39 blvd. Jacquard; PO Box 108, 62100
Tel: (33) 147122300; Fax: (33) 147122043
Circ.—7,328
Pub./Ed. in Ch.—Pierre Maincent

CHALON-SUR-SAONE
(Saone-et-Loire)
Pop. Est. (Metro Area) 78,064

LE COURRIER DE SAONE-ET-LOIRE (d) Est. 1826
9 rue des Tonneliers, 71104
Circ.—45,079
Pub./Ed. in Ch.—Francois Pretet

CHARLEVILLE-MEZIERES
(Ardennes)
Pop. Est. (Metro Area) 67,694

L'ARDENNAIS (d) Est. 1944
36 cours Aristide-Briand; PO Box 220, F-08102
Tel: (33) 24339151; Fax: (33) 24330260
Circ.—27,477
Pub.—Pierre Didry
Ed. in Ch.—Pierre Delohen
Ad. Mgr.—Jean Glory

CHARTRES
(Eure-et-Loir)
Pop. Est. (Metro Area) 77,795

L'ECHO REPUBLICAIN (d) Est. 1829
39 rue de Chateaudun; PO Box 189, F-28004
Circ.—34,192
Pub.—Alain Gascon
Ed. in Ch.—Alain Bouzy

CHATEAUROUX
(Indre)
Pop. Est. (Metro Area) 66,851

LA MARSEILLAISE DU BERRY (d) Est. 1944
19 rue de la Poste; PO Box 152, 36000
Tel: (33) 54340015
Circ.—11,880

CHAUMONT
(Haute-Marne)
Pop. Est. (Metro Area) 28,383

LA HAUTE MARNE LIBEREE (d) Est. 1944
14 rue du Patronage-Laique, 52003
Tel: (33) 25321988
Circ.—14,651
Pub./Ed. in Ch.—Jean Bletner

CHERBOURG
(Manche)
Pop. Est. (Metro Area) 85,485

LA PRESSE DE LA MANCHE (d) Est. 1944
14 rue Gambetta, F-50104
Circ.—29,660
Pub.—Jeanne Giustiniani
Mng. Ed.—Daniel Jubert

CLERMONT-FERRAND
(Puy-de-Dome)
Pop. Est. (Metro Area) 253,244

LA MONTAGNE/LA MONTAGNE DIMANCHE (d) Est. 1919
28 rue Morel-Ladeuil, F-63003
Tel: (33) 73932291; Fax: (33) 73346985
Circ.—232,377
Prop.—Havas
Pub.—Rene Bonjean
Ed. in Ch.—Marcel Tourlonias

COMPIEGNE
(Oise)
Pop. Est. (Metro Area) 62,778

LE COURRIER DE L'OISE (d)
33 rue des Trois-Barbeaux, 60204
Circ.—14,671
Mgr.—Serge Donneux

DIJON
(Cote-d'Or)
Pop. Est. (Metro Area) 221,927

LE BIEN PUBLIC (d) Est. 1850
7 blvd. Chanoine-Kir; PO Box 550, 21015
Tel: (33) 80424242; Fax: (33) 80424232

Copyright ©1996 by the Editor & Publisher Co.

Circ.—52,387
Pub.—Arnould Thenard
Pub.—Louis de Broissia
Ed. in Ch.—Jean-Claude Aubry
LES DEPECHES DU CENTRE-EST (d)
5 rue Pierre-Palliot; PO Box 570, F-21015
Tel: (33) 80308310
Circ.—19,092
Prop.—Groupe Progress SA
Pub.—Denis Huertas
Ed.—Pierre Villez

EPINAL
(Vosges)
Pop. Est. (Metro Area) 51,495

LA LIBERTE DE L'EST/LA LIBERTE DE L'EST DIMANCHE (d) Est. 1945
40 quai des Bons-Enfants, F-88001
Tel: (33) 29829800; Fax: (33) 29823057
Circ.—32,235 (d); 30,783 (S)
Pub.—Serge Clement
Ed. in Ch.—Jacques Dalle

GRENOBLE
(Isere)
Pop. Est. (Metro Area) 392,021

LE DAUPHINE LIBERE/LE DAUPHINE LIBERE DIMANCHE (dS) Est. 1944
Les Iles Cordes, Veurey-Voroize, 38113
Circ.—408,000 (d); 506,847 (S)
Prop.—Le Dauphine Libre SA
Pub.—Guy Lescouer
Ed. in Ch.—Paul Blanc

LE HAVRE
(Seine-Maritime)
Pop. Est. (Metro Area) 254,595

HAVRE LIBRE (d) Est. 1944
37 rue Fontenelle; PO Box 1384, F-76066
Circ.—26,466
Pub.—Philippe Hersant
Ed. in Ch.—Roger Campion
Ed. in Ch.—Gerard Coucke
LE HAVRE PRESSE (d) Est. 1867
112 blvd. de Strasbourg, F-76600
Circ.—17,831
Prop.—Groupe Progress SA
Pub.—Michel Hersant
Ed. in Ch.—Roger Campion
Ed. in Ch.—Gerard Coucke

HEILLECOURT

L'EST REPUBLICAIN (d)
rue Theophraste-Renaudot, Houdemont, F-54180
Tel: (33) 83568054; Fax: (33) 83598013
Circ.—214,965
Prop.—L'Est Republicain

LENS
(Pas-de-Calais)
Pop. Est. (Metro Area) 327,383

NARODOWIEC (d) Polish; Est. 1909
99-101 rue Emile-Zola; PO Box 79, 62302 (Cedex)
Tel: (33) 21281821
Pub.—Michel-Alexandre Kwiatowski

LILLE
(Nord)
Pop. Est. (Metro Area) 936,295

LIBERTE (d) Est. 1944
113 rue de Lannoy; PO Box 571, F-59023
Tel: (33-20) 569350; Fax: (33-20) 046973
Circ.—93,000
Pub.—Albert Debosschere
Pub.—Jean-Raymond de Greve
Ed. in Ch.—Roger Delbarre
NORD-MATIN (d-ex mon.) Est. 1944
22-24 ave. Charles-Saint-Venant, 59023
Pub.—Roger Gruss
Ed. in Ch.—Pierre Pinson
LA VOIX DU NORD (m-ex mon.) Est. 1941
8 place du General-de Gaulle, 59023
Tel: (33) 784040; Fax: (33) 784244
Circ.—372,150
Prop.—La Voix Du Nord
Pub.—Rene Decock
Ed. in Ch.—Gerard Minart
Ad. Mgr.—Jacques Menard

LIMOGES
(Haute-Vienne)
Pop. Est. (Metro Area) 171,689

CENTRE FRANCE DIMANCHE
rue du General-Catroux; PO Box 54, 87011
L'ECHO DORDOYNE (d) Est. 1944
46 rue Turgot, F-87011
Tel: (33) 55344635
Circ.—11,041
L'ECHO DU CENTRE (d) Est. 1944
46-48 rue Turgot; PO Box 537, F-87000
Tel: (33) 55344635
Circ.—58,068
Pub.—Christian Audouin
Ed. in Ch.—Dominique Favier
LA MARSEILLAISE DU BERRY (d)
46 rue Turgot, F-87011
Tel: (33) 55343635
Circ.—11,880
LE POPULAIRE DU CENTRE (d) Est. 1905
rue du General-Catroux; PO Box 54, 87011
Circ.—55,565
Pub.—Rene Bonjean
Ed. in Ch.—Roger Queyroi

LORIENT
(Morbihan)
Pop. Est. (Metro Area) 104,025

LA LIBERTE DU MORBIHAN (d)
8 place de Clairambault, F-56101
Tel: (33) 97211018
Circ.—9,582
Pub./Ed. in Ch.—Herve Le Gouallac

LYONS
(Lyon)
(Rhone)
Pop. Est. (Metro Area) 1,220,844

LYON-FIGARO (d)
14 rue de la Charite, 69215
Pub./Ed. in Ch.—Alain Buhler
LYON-LIBERATION (d)
24 rue Childebert, F-69002
Tel: (33-7) 78420809; Fax: (33-7) 78422172
Circ.—11,934
Pub./Ed in Ch.—Michel Lepinay
LYON-MATIN/LYON-MATIN DIMANCHE (m)
14 rue de la Charite, 69002
Tel: (33-7) 72222525; Fax: (33-7) 72222560
Circ.—50,000 (d); 53,741 (S)
Prop.—Lyon Matin SA
Pub.—Bernard Saugey
Ed. in Ch.—Jean-Pierre Guillot
LE PROGRES/LE PROGRES DIMANCHE (d) Est. 1859
93 Chemin de Saint-Priest, Chassieu Cedex, 69680
Tel: (33-7) 78908118
Circ.—441,711
Prop.—Groupe Progres SA
Pub.—Denis Huertas
Ed. in Ch.—Jean-Louis Dousson

LE MANS
(Sarthe)
Pop. Est. (Metro Area) 191,080

LE MAINE LIBRE (d) Est. 1944
28-30 place de l'Eperon; PO Box 299, F-72007
Circ.—57,062
Pub.—Gerard Chol
Ed. in Ch.—Jean-Pierre Fouquet
Ad. Mgr.—P Berger

MARSEILLE
(Bouches-du-Rhone)
Pop. Est. (Metro Area) 1,110,511

L'ANTENNE (d)
17 rue Venture, 13221
Pub.—Edmund Olivia
LA MARSEILLAISE (d) Est. 1944
19 cours Honore-d'Estienne-d'Orves; PO Box 1862, F-13001
Tel: (33-91) 577500
Circ.—159,039
Pub.—Edmond Garcin
Ed. in Ch.—Alain Fabre
MEDIA SUD (d)
248 ave. Roger Salengro, F-13015
Tel: (33-91) 844545; Fax: (33-91) 844995
LE MERIDIONAL-LA FRANCE (d) Est. 1944
4 rue Cougit, 13015
Tel: (33-91) 844545
Circ.—67,996
Pub.—Roland Singer
Ed. in Ch.—Laurent Gilardino
LE PROVENCAL (m) Est. 1944
248 ave. Roger Salengro; PO Box 100, F-13015
Tel: (33-91) 844545; Fax: (33-91) 844995
Circ.—341,011
Prop.—Le Provencal
Pub.—Andre Poitevin
Ed. in Ch.—Jean-Louis Levreau
Ed. in Ch.—Claude Mattei
Ad. Dir.—Janine Dell
U.S. Rep.—Publicitas
LE SOIR (e)
248 ave. Roger Salengro, F-13015
Tel: (33-91) 844545; Fax: (33-91) 844995

MAZAMET
(Tarn)
Pop. Est. (Metro Area) 26,676

LA MONTAGNE NOIRE (d) Est. 1914
14 rue Mejanel, 81200
Circ.—2,000
Pub./Ed. in Ch.—Jacques Thiebault

METZ
(Moselle)
Pop. Est. (Metro Area) 186,437

LE REPUBLICAIN LORRAIN (d) Est. 1919
3 rue de Saint-Eloi; PO Box 89, F-57140
Tel: (33) 87332200
Circ.—183,755
Prop.—SMEI
Pub.—Marguerite Puhl-Demange
Ed. in Ch.—Jean-Charles Bourdier

MONTBELIARD
(Doubs)
Pop. Est. (Metro Area) 128,194

LE PAYS DE FRANCHE-COMTE (d)
21 place Denfert, 25000
Mgr.—Jacques Balthazard

MONTPELLIER
(Herault)
Pop. Est. (Metro Area) 221,307

MIDI LIBRE/MIDI LIBRE DIMANCHE (dS) Est. 1944
Le Mas de Grille, Saint-Jean-de-Vedas, 34063
Tel: (33-47) 122379; Fax: (33-47) 122043
Circ.—185,000 (d); 230,500 (S)
Prop.—Le Mas De Grille
Pub.—Christophe Marais-Laforgue
Ed.—Mekiou Arhap

MORLAIX
(Finistere)
Pop. Est. (Metro Area) 27,829

LE TELEGRAMME (d) Est. 1944
Voie d'acces au Port, F-29205
Tel: (33) 98621133; Fax: (33) 98634505
Circ.—180,260
Prop.—Independent
Pub.—Jean-Pierre Coudurier
Ad. Mgr.—Andre Herrou

MULHOUSE
(Haut-Rhin)
Pop. Est. (Metro Area) 220,613

L'ALSACE (FRENCH-ALSACE) (d-ex S) German; Est. 1944
25 ave. du President Kennedy; PO Box 1199, F-68053
Tel: (33) 89327000; Fax: (33) 89321126/(33) 881818
Circ.—117,200
Prop.—Societe Alsacienne de Publications
Pub.—Gilbert Klein
Mng. Ed.—Jean-Marie Haeffle

NANCY
(Meurthe-et-Moselle)
Pop. Est. 306,982

L'EST REPUBLICAIN/L'EST REPUBLICAIN DIMANCHE (d) Est. 1889
rue Theophraste-Renaudot, Houdemont, 54185
Pub.—Gerard Legnac
Ed. in Ch.—Roland Meval
Ad. Mgr.—Jacques Hommell

NANTES
(Loire-Atlantique)
Pop. Est. (Metro Area) 464,857

L'ECLAIR (d) Est. 1945
5 rue Santeuil, F-44010
Tel: (33) 40734445; Fax: (33) 40730588
Circ.—18,137
Pub.—Rolande Hersant

PRESSE-OCEAN (d) Est. 1945
7-8 allee Duguay-Trouin, F-44010
Tel: (33) 40442400
Circ.—80,586
Pub.—Christian Renet
Ed. in Ch.—Jean-Marie Gautier

NEVERS
(Nievre)
Pop. Est. (Metro Area) 59,274

JOURNAL DU CENTRE (d) Est. 1943
3 rue du Chemin-de-Fer; PO Box 14, F-58001
Tel: (33) 146409767
Circ.—37,376
Pub.—Rene Bonjean
Ed. in Ch.—Paul Berthelot

NICE
(Alpes-Maritimes)
Pop. Est. (Metro Area) 342,496

NICE-MATIN (mS) Est. 1944
214 rue de Grenoble; PO Box 23, F-06021
Tel: (33) 93217171
Circ.—253,100 (m); 242,850 (S)
Prop.—Nice Matin
Pub.—Michel Bavastro
Mng. Ed.—George Mars

ORLEANS
(Loiret)
Pop. Est. (Metro Area) 220,478

LA REPUBLIQUE DU CENTRE (d) Est. 1944
Rue de la Halte Saran; PO Box 35, F-45403
Tel: (33) 388637; Fax: (33) 38842149
Circ.—80,000
Pub.—Marc Carre
Ed. in Ch.—Jacques Camus

PARIS
(Ville-de-Paris)
Pop. Est. (Metro Area) 10,650,600

L'AGEFI (5x wk.) French; Est. 1911
48 rue Nortre-Dame des Victoires, 750023
Tel: (33-1) 44884646
Circ.—6,700
Prop.—Editeur l'agence economique et financiere AGEFI SA
Pub.—Jean-Louis Servan-Schreiber
Mng. Ed.—Jean-Michel Quatrepoint
Ed.—Henri Paul Vanel
Ad. Mgr.—Philippe Marquezy
Ad. Mgr.—Thierry Bollack
U.S. Rep.—AdMarket Int'l.
(This newspaper was formerly Agence Economique et Financiere.)
BULLETIN QUOTIDIEN (d)
13 ave. de l'Opera, 75001
Prop.—La Societe Generale de Presse
Pub.—Georges Berard-Quelin
Mng. Ed.—Etienne Lacour
CORRESPONDANCE DE LA PRESSE (d) Est. 1937
13 ave. de l'Opera, 75001
Prop.—La Societe Generale de Presse
Pub./Ed. in Ch.—Georges Berard-Quelin
Ed. in Ch.—Jacqueline Berard-Quelin
CORRESPONDANCE DE LA PUBLICITE (d) Est. 1953
13 ave. de l'Opera, 75001
Prop.—La Societe Generale de Presse
Pub./Ed. in Ch.—Georges Berard-Quelin
Ed. in Ch.—Jacqueline Berard-Quelin
CORRESPONDANCE ECONOMIQUE (d)
13 ave. de l'Opera, 75001
Prop.—La Societe Generale de Presse
Pub./Ed. in Ch.—Georges Berard-Quelin
Ed. in Ch.—Jacqueline Berard-Quelin
LA COTE DESFOSSES (d) Est. 1825
5-7 rue St. Augustine, 75002
Tel: (33-1) 42332130; Fax: (33-1) 42331236
Circ.—25,618
Prop.—D I Holding
Pub.—Jean Chamboulive
Mng. Ed.—Paul-Francois Trioux
LA CROIX L'EVENEMENT (e-ex S) Est. 1880
3-5 rue Bayard, 75393
Tel: (33-1) 44356718; Fax: (33-1) 44356003
Circ.—113,000
Pub.—Bernard Porte
Ed. in Ch.—Bruno Chenu
Ed. in Ch.—Christian Latu
LES ECHOS (d) Est. 1908
46 rue de la Boetie, F-75008
Tel: (33-1) 49536565; Fax: (33-1) 42254101
Circ.—120,960
Prop.—Group Les Echos
Pub.—Jacqueline Beytout
Ed.—Gilles Brochen
Ad. Mgr.—Eric Noblet
U.S. Rep.—Regent Advertising Sales
L'EQUIPE (d) Est. 1946
25 ave. Michlet, F-93400
Tel: (33-1) 40103030
Circ.—323,356
Prop.—Les Editions P Amaury

L'EQUIPE: LE QUOTIDIEN DU SPORT ET DE L'AUTOMOBILE (d) Est. 1946
4 rue Rouget de L'Isle, 92137
Circ.—239,632 (d); 311,196 (mon.)
Prop.—Societe Nouvelle De Publications Sportives et Industrielles
Pub.—Jean-Pierre Courcol
Mng. Ed.—Henri García
EUROPE JOURNAL (d) Chinese; Est. 1984
167 rue Lecourbe, 75015
Prop.—Orchi Media SARL
Pub./Ed. in Ch.—Nicolas Druz
EVENEMENTS ET PERSPECTIVES (d)
4 rue du Faubourg-Poissonniere, 75010
Pub./Ed. in Ch.—Gaston Gosselin
L'EXPANSION (The Expansion) (m) Est. 1987
Le Ponat, 25 rue LeBlanc, 75842
Tel: (33-1) 40604337; Fax: (33-1) 40604125
Circ.—60,890
Prop.—Group Expansion
LE FIGARO (m-ex S) Est. 1826
37 rue du Louvre, 75002
Tel: (33-1) 42216200
Circ.—376,310
Pub.—Robert Hersant
FINANCIAL TIMES (d) English; Est. 1988
168 rue de Rivoli, 75044
Tel: (33-1) 42972000; Fax: (33-1) 42970629
FRANCE-SOIR (d) Est. 1944
65 rue de Bercy, 75589
Tel: (33-1) 40018000; Fax: (33-1) 43414488
Circ.—191,558
Prop.—Presse Alliance
Pub.—Philippe Villin
Ed. in Ch.—Claude Lambert
Ed. in Ch.—Jean-Claude Nardonnet
HARATCH (d) Armenian; Est. 1925
83 rue d'Hauteville, 75010
Pub.—A Missakian
L'HUMANITE/L'HUMANITE DIMANCHE (d) Est. 1904/1948
rue Jean-Jaures, Boite Postal 229, 93523
Tel: (33-1) 49227438/(33-1) 49227445; Fax: (33-1) 49227448
Circ.—71,235
Prop.—Carrel
Pub.—Jean-Marc Ganille
Pub.—Christine Joaunne
Ed. in Ch.—Claude Cabanes
Ed. in Ch.—Francois Hilsum
Ad. Mgr.—Maurice Lewiner
Ad Mgr.—Albert Vilcot
INTERNATIONAL HERALD TRIBUNE (m-ex S) English; Est. 1887
181 ave. Charles-de-Gaulle, F-92200
Tel: (33-1) 46379300
Circ.—129,847
Prop.—International Herald Tribune SA
Pub.—Richard McClean
Ex. Ed.—John Vinocur
Ad. Dir.—James McLeod
LE JOURNAL OFFICIEL DE LA REPUBLIQUE FRANCAISE (d) Est. 1870
26 rue Desaix, F-75727
Tel: (33-1) 40587500; Fax: (33-1) 40587780
LIAISONS SOCIALES (d) Est. 1945
5 ave. de la Republique, 75541
Pub.—Patrice-Aristide Blank
Ed. in Ch.—Tristan de Carne
LIBERATION (d) Est. 1973
11 rue Beranger, 75154
Tel: (33-1) 42761789; Fax: (33-1) 42729493
Circ.—210,000
Prop.—La Societe Nouvelle de Presse et de Communication
Pub.—Serge July
Ed. in Ch.—Dominique Pouchin
MARCHES AGRICOLES-L'ECHO DES HALLES (d)
42 rue Olivier-Metra, 75020
Pub.—Rene-Charles Millet
Ed. in Ch.—Robert Raure
LE MATIN DE PARIS/LE MATIN DE DIMANCHE (d) Est. 1977
57 blvd. de la Villette, 75010
Circ.—178,352
Pub.—Didier Tourancheau
Ed. in Ch.—Pierre Feydel
U.S. Rep.—Northeast Media Group
LE MONDE/LE MONDE DIMANCHE (d) Est. 1944
1333 ave. Des Champs Elysees, 75409
Tel: (33-1) 44437639; Fax: (33-1) 44437728
Circ.—308,157
Prop.—Le Monde Publicite SA
Pub.—Jacques Lesourne
Ed. in Ch.—Bruno Frappat
Ed. in Ch.—Thomas Ferenczi
Ed. in Ch.—Phillippe Herreman
Ed. in Ch.—Jacques-Francois Simon
Ad. Mgr.—Catherine O'Kelly
PANORAMA DU MEDECIN (d) Est. 1975
15 bis rue de Marignan, 75008
Pub.—Dr. Gerard Dongradi
Ed. in Ch.—Alain Trebucq
Ed. in Ch.—Francois Chary
PARIS-TURF/DIMANCHE TURF (d)
100 rue Reaumur, 75002

Circ.—150,000
Pub.—Roger Alexandre
Mng. Ed.—Jean Fagu
LE PARISIEN (m-ex S) Est. 1944
25 ave. Michelet, 93408
Tel: (33-1) 40105300; Fax: (33-1) 40115800
Circ.—400,227
Prop.—Manchette Publicite
Pub.—Louis Gillet
Pub.—Richard Metzger
Mng. Ed.—Noel Couedal
Ed.—Christian Tribot
Ad. Mgr.—Jean-Claude Testaert
Mktg Dir.—Alix Imbert
LE QUOTIDIEN DU MAIRE (d)
122 ave. Charles-de-Gaulle, 92200
Mng. Ed.—Robert Toubon
LE QUOTIDIEN DU MEDECIN (d)
2 rue Ancelle, 92521
Circ.—56,500
Pub.—Marie-Claude Tesson-Millet
Mng. Ed.—Richard Liscia
Ad. Mgr.—Perrine Vincent
LE QUOTIDIEN DE PARIS (m-ex S) Est. 1979
140 rue Jules-Guesde, 92300
Tel: (33-1) 47307800; Fax: (33-1) 47307878
Circ.—64,000
Prop.—SEQP
Pub./Ed. in Ch.—Phillipe Tesson
Ad. Dir.—Patrice Gelobter
LE SPORT (d)
9-13 rue du Colonel Pierre Avia, F-75015
Tel: (33-1) 46622000
Pub.—Rene Teze
Ed. in Ch.—Patrick Blain
LA TRIBUNE DESFOSSÉS (d) Est. 1967
42 Notre-Dame des Victoires, 75002
Tel: (33-1) 40131313
Circ.—75,585
Prop.—Editeur l`Agence Economique et Financiere AGEFI SA
Pub.—Jean-Louis Servan-Schreiber
Ed.—Francois Roche

PAU
(Pyrenees-Atlantique)
Pop. Est. (Metro Area) 131,265

ECLAIR PYRENEES (d) Est. 1944
40 rue Emile Guichenne; PO Box 629, F-64006
Circ.—9,801
Pub.—Henri Loustalan
Ed.—Paul Guilhot
LA REPUBLIQUE DES PYRENEES (d)
40 rue Emile Guichenne, 64000
Circ.—29,984
Pub.—Dominique Videau

PERIGUEUX
(Dordogne)
Pop. Est. (Metro Area) 59,716

LA DORDOGNE LIBRE (d) Est. 1945
20 rue Gambetta, 24000
Tel: (33) 146409767
Circ.—3,860
Pub.—Richard Lavigne
L'ECHO DORDOGNE (d)
11 rue Antoine-Gadaud; PO Box 40, 24000
Tel: (33) 531444
Circ.—11,041

PERPIGNAN
(Pyrenees-Orientales)
Pop. Est. (Metro Area) 137,915

LE JOURNAL L'INDEPENDANT (d) Est. 1946
4 rue Emmanuel Brousse, F-66004
Tel: (33) 68355151
Circ.—84,743
Pub.—Jean-Dominique Pretet

POITIERS
(Vienne)
Pop. Est. (Metro Area) 103,204

CENTRE-PRESSE (d-ex S) Est. 1958
5 rue Victor Hugo, 86000
Tel: (33) 49411780; Fax: (33) 49559375
Circ.—23,126
Pub.—Cyrille Duval
Ed. in Ch.—Roland Barrat
U.S. Rep.—Nielsen Communications Ltd.

LE PUY
(Haute-Loire)
Pop. Est. (Metro Area) 42,382

L'EVEIL DE LA HAUTE-LOIRE/L'EVEIL DU DIMANCHE (d) Est. 1944
9 place Michelet; PO Box 24, F-43001
Tel: (33) 09321471; Fax: (33) 71029408
Circ.—13,367
Pub.—Louis Rabaste
Ed. in Ch.—Daniel Berger

REIMS
(Marne)
Pop. Est. (Metro Area) 199,388

L'UNION (d) Est. 1944
87-91 place Drouet-d'Erlon, F-51083
Tel: (33) 26478395
Circ.—108,556
Prop.—L'Union
Pub.—Philippe Hersant
Ed. in Ch.—Jacques Richard

RENNES
(Ille-et-Vilaine)
Pop. Est. (Metro Area) 234,418

OUEST-FRANCE (m-ex S) Est. 1944
rue de Breil; PO Box 586, F-35012
Tel: (33-99) 326000
Circ.—784,463
Prop.—Quest-France
Pub.—Francoise-Regis Hutin
Ed. in Ch.—Francois-Xavier Alix
Ad. Dir.—Emmanuel Doncelle
(Circulation figure combines with L'Eclair and Presse-Ocean in Nantes.)

RODEZ
(Aveyron)
Pop. Est. (Metro Area) 37,953

CENTRE PRESSE (d)
ave. de la Peyrinie, Bel Air; PO Box 137, 12001
Circ.—10,000
Pub.—Alain Almeras
Ed. in Ch.—Pierre Molier

ROUBAIX
(Nord within Lille Metro Area)
Pop. Est. 101,602

NORD-ECLAIR/NORD-MATIN (m-ex mon.) Est. 1944
15-21 rue du Caire, 59100
Tel: (33) 20759256
Circ.—99,000
Prop.—Nord Eclair Edition SA
Pub.—Michel Noziere
Ed. in Ch.—André Farine
Ad. Mgr.—Daniel Chabasse

ROUEN
(Seine-Maritime)
Pop. Est. (Metro Area) 379,879

PARIS-NORMANDIE (d) Est. 1945
19 place du General-de-Gaulle; PO Box 563, F-76004
Tel: (33) 35145656; Fax: (33) 35145615
Circ.—102,427
Prop.—Societe Normande de Presse Republicain
Pub.—Jean Allard
Ed. in Ch.—Herve Gueneron
Ed. in Ch.—Rene Collinet
Ed. in Ch.—Jean Boedec

SAINT-ETIENNE
(Loire)
Pop. Est. (Metro Area) 317,228

L'ESPOIR (d) Est. 1941
110 rue Bergson, 42000
Prop.—Groupe Progress SA
Ed.—Hubert Perrin
LOIRE-MATIN/LES DEPECHES (d) Est. 1944
16 place Drouet d'Erlon, 51052
Tel: (33) 77327997
Circ.—34,706 (d); 36,039 (S)
Ed.—Hubert Perrin
LA TRIBUNE-LE PROGRES (d)
110 rue Bergson, 42000
Prop.—Groupe Progess SA
Ed.—Hubert Perrin

STRASBOURG
(Bas-Rhin)
Pop. Est. (Metro Area) 252,000

LES DERNIERES NOUVELLES D'ALSACE (d-ex mon.) Est. 1877
17-21 rue de la Nuee-Bleu; PO Box 406, F-67000
Tel: (33-88) 233123
Circ.—223,200
Prop.—Dernières Nouvelles d'Alsace
Pub./Dir.—Jacques Puymartin
Ed. in Ch.—Alain Howiller
Ad. Mgr.—Andre Hodapp

TARBES
(Hautes-Pyrenees)
Pop. Est. (Metro Area) 78,056

LA NOUVELLE REPUBLIQUE DES PYRENEES (d) Est. 1944
48 ave. Bertrand-Barere, F-65001
Tel: (33) 62939090; Fax: (33) 62938143
Circ.—17,275
Pub./Ed. in Ch.—Claude Gaits

TOULON
(Var)
Pop. Est. (Metro Area) 410,393

VAR MATIN (d) Est. 1946
rue de la Seyne, a Ollioules, F-83190
Tel: (33) 94069191; Fax: (33) 94633449
Circ.—81,858
Pub.—Christian de Barbarin
Ed. in Ch.—Paul Mozzi
LE VAROIS-LA MARSEILLAISE (d)
11 rue Truguet; PO Box 946, 83050
Ed. in Ch.—Rene Fredon

TOULOUSE
(Haute-Garonne)
Pop. Est. (Metro Area) 359,000

LA DEPECHE DU MIDI (m) Est. 1870
ave. Jean-Baylet, F-31095
Tel: (33-61) 411149; Fax: (33-61) 447474
Circ.—233,350
Pub.—Evelyne-Jean Baylet
Ed. in Ch.—Fernand Cousteaux
Ed. in Ch.—Rene Mauries

TOURS
(Indre-et-Loire)
Pop. Est. (Metro Area) 262,786

LA NOUVELLE REPUBLIQUE DU CENTRE-OUEST (m-ex S) Est. 1944
232 ave. de Grammont, F-37048
Tel: (33-47) 317000; Fax: (33-47) 317148
Circ.—267,000
Prop.—La Nouvelle Republique
Ed. in Ch.—Guy Bonnet
Ad. Dir.—Jacques Medini

TROYES
(Aube)
Pop. Est. (Metro Area) 125,240

L'EST ECLAIR (d) Est. 1945
PO Box 532X, F-10081
Tel: (33) 25799010; Fax: (33) 25795854
Circ.—31,000
Ed. in Ch.—André Bruley
Ad. Mgr.—Yves Louys
LIBERATION CHAMPAGNE/LIBERATION CHAMPAGNE DU DIMANCHE (d)
126 rue du General-de-Gaulle; PO Box 713, F-10003
Circ.—16,470
Pub.—Francois le Saxhe
Ed.—Gilbert Boutsoque

GEORGIA
Pop. Est. 5,681,025

TBILISI
(Tiflis)
Pop. Est. 1,279,000

VESTNIK GRUZZI (6x wk.) Russian; Est. 1922
Ed.—A Ioseliani

GERMANY, FEDERAL REPUBLIC OF
Pop. Est. 81,087,506

AACHEN
Pop. Est. 239,200

AACHENER NACHRICHTEN (Aachen News) (6x wk.) Est. 1946
Dresdener Str. 3; PF 110, 52002
Tel: (49-241) 51010; Fax: (49-241) 5101397
Circ.—177,200 ABC

Germany, Federal Republic of — Europe

Prop.—Aachen Zeitungsverlag
Pub./Bus. Mgr.—U Cerfontaine
Mng. Ed.—W von Wilpert
Ed. in Ch.—D Mätschke
Bus. Mgr.—G Hildenbrandt
Bus. Mgr.—R Hofelich
Ad. Mgr.—H-W Ast
AACHENER VOLKSZEITUNG (6x wk.) Est. 1946
Dresden Str. 3; PF 110, 52068
Tel: (49-241) 51011; Fax: (49-241) 5101396
Circ.—177,200 ABC
Prop.—Zeitungsvig Aachen
Prop.—Aachener Verlagsges
Mng. Ed.—H Arnolds
Ed. in Ch.—O Braun
Ed. in Ch.—H Siemons
Ed. in Ch.—B Mathieu
Ad. Mgr.—H-W Ast

AALEN
Pop. Est. 63,300

SCHWÄBISCHE POST (Schwaben Post) (6x wk.) Est. 1948
Bahnhofstr. 65 (73430); PF 1680, 73406
Tel: (49-7361) 5940; Fax: (49-7361) 594125
Circ.—29,200 ABC
Prop.—Süddeutscher Zeitungdeinst
Pub.—Dr. J Binkowski
Pub.—K A Theiss
Mng. Ed./Ed. in Ch./Ed.—R Scheuber
Ed. in Ch.—E Hafner
Bus. Mgr.—E Looser
Ad. Mgr.—A Bopp
(This is an edition of the Südwest Presse Ulm in Ulm.)

AHLEN
Pop. Est. 51,900

AHLENER VOLKSZEITUNG (Ahlen People's News) (6x wk.) Est. 1898
Ostenmauer 1; PF 1151, 59201
Tel: (49-2382) 80880; Fax: (49-2382) 808848
Circ.—8,700 ABC
Prop.—Sommer
Bus. Mgr.—H Röer
Ad. Mgr.—Helga Sommer

ALFELD
Pop. Est. 22,500

ALFELDER ZEITUNG (6x wk.) Est. 1852
Ravenstr. 45; PF 1164, 31041
Tel: (49-5181) 80020; Fax: (49-5181) 800247
Circ.—11,300 ABC
Prop.—Alfelder Zeitung AZ
Pub.—P Dobler
Ed. in Ch.—R Grimm
Ed.—T Jahns
Bus. Mgr.—E Dobler
Ad. Mgr.—M Bombelka

ALSFELD
Pop. Est. 10,981

OBERHESSISCHE ZEITUNG (Upper Hessen News) (6x wk.) Est. 1833
Am Kreuz 10; PF 220, 36304
Tel: (49-6631) 7880; Fax: (49-6631) 78887
Circ.—8,200
Prop.—Ehrenklau
Pub.—F M Ehrenklau
Bus. Mgr.—G Vögele
Ad. Mgr.—H Valentin

ALTENA
Pop. Est. 22,100

ALTENAER KREISBLATT (6x wk.) Est. 1834
Lennstr. 48 (58742); PF 1661, 58746
Tel: (49-2352) 98710; Fax: (49-2352) 25584
Circ.—5,400 ABC
Prop.—Märkischer Zeitungsverlag
Ad. Mgr.—B Herzberger

ANSBACH
Pop. Est. 37,500

FRÄNKISHE LANDESZEITUNG (Franken District News) (6x wk.) Est. 1946
Nürnberger Str. 9 (91504); PF 1362, 91522
Tel: (49-981) 95000; Fax: (49-981) 13961
Circ.—54,200 ABC
Prop.—Fränkische Landeszeitung
Pub.—R Mehl
Pub.—K W Wiedfeld
Pub.—B Schnell
Ed. in Ch.—G Egetemayer
Ed. in Ch.—P M Szymanowski
Ad. Mgr.—H Messelhäusser

ASCHAFFENBURG
Pop. Est. 59,600

MAIN-ECHO (6x wk.) Est. 1945
Goldbacher Str. 25 (63739); PF 548, 63705
Tel: (49-6021) 3960; Fax: (49-6021) 39620641
Circ.—95,100 (total-all eds.) ABC
Prop.—Main-Echo
Pub.—Dr. W Engelhard
Mng. Ed./Ed. in Ch.—H Weiss
Ed. in Ch.—Dr. G Martin
Ed. in Ch.—Dr. H Teufel
Ed.—S Reis
Bus. Mgr.—K Eymann
Bus. Mgr.—R Golembiewski
Ad. Mgr.—R Fresaw
Ad. Mgr.—W Naumann

AUGSBURG
Pop. Est. 246,000

AUGSBURGER ALLGEMEINE (m-6x wk.) Est. 1945
Curt-Frenzel-Str. 2, 86133
Tel: (49-821) 7770; Fax: (49-821) 704471
Circ.—259,300 (total-all eds.) ABC
Prop.—Presse Druck & Verlag
Pub.—G Holland
Mng. Ed.—S Hilscher
Ed. in Ch.—R Bonhorst
Ed. in Ch.—W Striebel
Bus. Mgr.—W Mittermaier
Bus. Mgr.—Ellinor Holland
Bus. Mgr.—P Block
Ad. Mgr.—K Kammerer

AURICH
(Ostfriesland)
Pop. Est. 35,100

OSTFRIESISCHE NACHRICHTEN (The East Frisian News) (6x wk.) Est. 1864
Kirchstr. 8 (26603); PF 1540, 26585
Tel: (49-4941) 17080; Fax: (49-4941) 65254
Circ.—14,500 ABC
Prop.—Dunkmann
Ed. in Ch.—H W Theesfeld
Ed.—S Dunkmann
Bus. Mgr.—R Dreyer
Ad. Mgr.—K-H Rulfs

BACKNANG
Pop. Est. 29,700

BACKNANGER KREISZEITUNG (The Backnang District News) (6x wk.) Est. 1832
Postgasse 7 (71522); PF 1169, 71501
Tel: (49-7191) 8080; Fax: (49-7191) 80811
Circ.—19,100 ABC
Prop.—Stroh
Pub./Bus. Mgr./Ad. Mgr.—W Stroh
Pub.—L Stroh
Ed. in Ch.—R Fiedler

BADEN-BADEN
Pop. Est. 49,300

BADISCHES TAGBLATT (6x wk.) Est. 1840
Stefanienstr. 1 (76530); PF 120, 76481
Tel: (49-7221) 2150; Fax: (49-7221) 215290/(49-7221) 781158
Circ.—44,000 (total-all eds.) ABC
Prop.—H Badisches Tagblatt
Ed. in Ch.—H Besinger
Ed. in Ch.—V B Zanger
Ed.—M Scheibe
Ed.—G Hammes
Bus. Mgr.—W Bokelmann
Ad. Mgr.—W Hoffarth

BALINGEN
Pop. Est. 29,900

ZOLLERN-ALB KURIER (6x wk.) Est. 1850
Grünewaldstr. 15; PF 100264, 72302
Tel: (49-7433) 2660; Fax: (49-7433) 15000
Circ.—31,400 ABC
Prop.—Daniel
Ad. Mgr.—H Maier
(This is an edition of the Südwest Presse Ulm in Ulm.)

BAMBERG
Pop. Est. 69,600

FRÄNKISCHER TAG (The Frankish Daily) (6x wk.) Est. 1833
Gutenbergstr. 1, 96050
Tel: (49-951) 1880; Fax: (49-951) 188112
Circ.—81,800 (total-all eds.) ABC
Prop.—Fränkischer Tag
Pub.—B Wagner
Mng. Ed.—V Lindemann
Ed. in Ch.—S Hännl
Bus. Mgr.—M Grethe
Ad. Mgr.—F Schnurr

BARMSTEDT

BARMSTEDTER ZEITUNG (6x wk.) Est. 1879
Reichenstr. 17 (25355); PF 1162, 25349
Tel: (49-4123) 2031; Fax: (49-4123) 7077
Circ.—2,900
Prop.—Prange Verlag
Pub./Bus. Mgr./Ad. Mgr.—H-J Prange

BARSINGHAUSEN
Pop. Est. 32,500

DEISTER-LEINE-ZEITUNG (6x wk.) Est. 1885
Bahnhofstr. 5 (30890); PF 1262, 30882
Tel: (49-5105) 77070; Fax: (49-5105) 770733
Circ.—7,200 ABC
Prop.—Weinaug
Pub.—E Hillrichs Sr
Pub.—E Hillrichs Jr
Ad. Mgr.—E Hillrichs

BAYREUTH
Pop. Est. 72,300

NORDBAYERISCHER KURIER (The North Bavarian Messenger) (6x wk.) Est. 1968
Maxstr. 58 (95444); PF 100851, 95408
Tel: (49-921) 5000; Fax: (49-921) 500180
Circ.—45,500 (total-all eds.) ABC
Prop.—Nordbayerischer Kurier
Pub./Ed. in Ch.—W Ellwanger
Pub./Ed. in Ch.—Dr. L Fischer
Bus. Mgr.—K Dollinger
Ad. Mgr.—W Bücheler

BENDORF
Pop. Est. 14,270

BENDORFER ZEITUNG (d-5x wk.)
Bachstr. 55, 56170
Tel: (49-2622) 140556; Fax: (49-2622) 5193
Circ.—11,900
Prop.—Mittelrhein Verlag
Prop.—Rhine Zeiting
(This is an edition of the Koblenz Rhine-Zeitung in Koblenz.)

BENSHEIM
Pop. Est. 33,500

BA BERGSTRÄßER ANZEIGER (The Bergstrasser Messenger) (6x wk.) Est. 1833
Rodensteinstr. 6, 64625
Tel: (49-6251) 10080; Fax: (49-6251) 64272
Circ.—16,900 ABC
Prop.—Hess
Mng. Ed.—H Baumeister
Ed. in Ch.—J Bänker
Ed.—K J Bänker
Ed.—K H Schlitt
Bus. Mgr.—J Klück
Ad. Mgr.—W Essinger

BERCHTESGADEN
Pop. Est. 4,530

BERCHTESGADENER ANZEIGER (Berchtesgadener Advertiser) (5x wk.) Est. 1887
Griesstätterstr. 1 (83471); PF 1030, 83461
Tel: (49-8652) 61018; Fax: (49-8652) 61010
Circ.—6,900 ABC
Prop.—Berchtesgardener Anzeiger Verlag
Ed. in Ch.—H Esmarch
Ed.—Eva Bradner
Bus. Mgr.—W Krawehl
Bus. Mgr.—E Melcher

BERLIN
Pop. Est. 3,437,900

BERLINER KURIER (The Berlin Evening Messenger) (e-6x wk.) Est. 1949
Karl-Liebknecht-Str. 29; PF 102001, 10178
Tel: (49-30) 23276166; Fax: (49-30) 2513906
Circ.—259,100 ABC
Prop.—G & J Kaufenzeiten Verlages
Mng. Ed.—E Balfanz
Ed. in Ch.—W Sandmann
Ed. in Ch./Ed.—A K Schwaner
Bus. Mgr.—K Nagel
Ad. Mgr.—H Schlosser

BERLINER MORGENPOST (Berlin Morning Post) (m-6x wk.) Est. 1898
Kochstr. 50, Bln 11, 10969
Tel: (49-30) 25910; Fax: (49-30) 2516071
Circ.—201,700 ABC
Prop.—Ullstein Verlag Springer
Mng. Ed.—R Porsch
Ed. in Ch.—B Waltert
Ed.—U W Scholz
Ed.—J Stoltenberg
Ed.—W Furler
Bus. Mgr.—W Ludowig
Ad. Mgr.—N Wendt

BERLINER ZEITUNG (m-6x wk.) Est. 1945
Karl-Liebknecht Str. 29; GKP 10171, 10178
Tel: (49-30) 23279; Fax: (49-30) 23275533
Circ.—285,600 ABC
Prop.—G & J Berliner Zeitung Verlag
Mng. Ed.—H Kurtzbach
Ed. in Ch.—H Eggert
Ed.—Georgia Tornow
Ed.—H Kurtzbach
Bus. Mgr.—L Jarosch

B.Z. (m-5x wk.) Est. 1877
Kochstr. 50; PF 110303, 10969
Tel: (49-30) 25910; Fax: (49-30) 2516071
Circ.—285,600
Prop.—Ullstein
Pub.—W Pannier
Mng. Ed.—H P Buschheuer
Mng. Ed.—M Schierenbeck
Ed. in Ch.—W Kryszohn
Ed.—A Slominski
Ed.—G Knoll
Ed.—W Reith
Bus. Mgr.—H Reichardt
Ad. Mgr.—N Wendt

JUNGE WELT (Youth World) (m-6x wk.) Est. 1947
Am Treptower Park 28, 12435
Tel: (49-30) 68834301; Fax: (49-30) 68834397
Circ.—34,300 ABC
Prop.—Verlaganstatt in Berlin
Ed. in Ch.—O Tolmein
Ad. Mgr.—Renate Adolph
Bus. Mgr.—M Lattemann

NEUES DEUTSCHLAND (New Germany) (m-6x wk.) Est. 1946
Franz-Mehring-Platz 1; PF 400, 10243
Tel: (49-30) 58310; Fax: (49-30) 58312625
Circ.—86,500 ABC
Prop.—Neues Deutschland Druckerei Partei d. Demokrat Sozialismus
Mng. Ed./Ed. in Ch./Ed.—Brigitte Zimmermann
Mng. Ed./Ed. in Ch./Ed.—G Prokot
Ed. in Ch.—R Oschmann
Bus. Mgr.—Dr. W Spickermann
Ad. Mgr.—M Ibold

DER NORD-BERLINER (6x wk.) Est. 1949
Oraniendamm 48 (13469); PF 280380, 13443
Tel: (49-30) 419090; Fax: (49-30) 41909159
Circ.—37,000
Prop.—Der Nord-Berliner Verlag
Pub.—W Möller
Mng. Ed./Ed. in Ch./Ed.—D Puttins
Ed. in Ch.—L Lange
Bus. Mgr.—W-I Wengel

SPANDAUER VOLKSBLATT (d-ex mon.) Est. 1946
Breite Str. 52; PF 200260, 13597
Tel: (49-30) 3539060; Fax: (49-30) 35390640
Circ.—32,100 (d); 37,900 (S)
Prop.—Lezinsky
Pub.—Ingrid Below-Lezinsky
Ed. in Ch.—P Bolm
Bus. Mgr./Ad. Mgr.—G Dünnhaupt

DER TAGESSPIEGEL (The Daily Mirror) (m-6x wk.) Est. 1945
Potsdamer Str. 77 (10785); PF 304330, 10723
Tel: (49-30) 260090; Fax: (49-30) 26009332
Circ.—153,300
Prop.—Verlag Der Tagesspiegel
Pub.—D von Hoiltzbrink
Pub.—Dr. H Rudolph
Mng. Ed.—U Schüter
Mng. Ed.—H Zöllner
Ed. in Ch.—G Appenzeller
Ed.—Dr. W Stützle
Ed.—Dr. Monika Zimmermann
Bus. Mgr.—H Homrighausen
Ad. Mgr.—J Robotta
U.S. Rep.—Publicitas

DIE TAGESZEITUNG (m-6x wk.) Est. 1979
Kockstr. 18 (10969); PF 610229, 10923
Tel: (49-30) 259020; Fax: (49-30) 2515028
Circ.—82,300
Prop.—taz Verlagsgenossenschaft
Ed. in Ch.—M Sontheimer
Ad. Mgr.—G Thomas

BERNBURG

BERNBURGER ZEITUNG (6x wk.) Est. 1990
Hallesch Landstr. 111; PF 229, 06406
Tel: (49-3471) 71220; Fax: (49-3471) 7141

Circ.—10,400
Prop.—Hoffmann
Pub.—Renate Rumpeltin
Ed. in Ch.—D Lange
Ad. Mgr.—U Miethe
Bus. Mgr.—K Kahl

BIELEFELD
Pop. Est. 299,400

NEUE WESTFÄLISCHE (m-6x wk.) Est. 1967
Niedernstr. 21 (33602); PF 100225, 33502
Tel: (49-521) 5550; Fax: (49-521) 555348
Circ.—239,800
Prop.—Neue Westfälische Zeitungsverlag GmbH
Mng. Ed./Ed. in Ch./Ed.—J Juchtmann
Ed. in Ch.—R F Kirst
Ed. in Ch./Ed.—J Blum
Bus. Mgr.—W Dehne
Ad. Mgr.—W Geese
WESTFALEN-BLATT (m-6x wk.) Est. 1946
Südbrackstr. 14 (33611); PF 103171, 33531
Tel: (49-521) 5850; Fax: (49-521) 585230
Circ.—152,300 ABC
Prop.—Vereinigte Zeitungsverlage
Pub./Ed.in Ch.—C W Busse
Mng. Ed.—M Boge
Mng. Ed.—R Brockmann
Mng. Ed.—J Scheel
Ed. in Ch.—R-D Poch
Ed. in Ch.—R Dressler
Ad. Mgr.—Gabriele Förster

BIETIGHEIM-BISSINGEN
Pop. Est. 35,600

BIETIGHEIMER ZEITUNG (6x wk.) Est. 1874
Kronenbergstr. 10 (74321); PF 1164, 74301
Tel: (49-7142) 4030; Fax: (49-7142) 403128
Circ.—15,500 (total-all eds.) ABC
Prop.—Druck & Verlagsges Bietigheim
Pub.—M Gläser
Bus. Mgr.—P Scheufler
Ad. Mgr.—A Schmalzried

BOCHOLT
Pop. Est. 66,400

BOCHOLTER-BORKENER VOLKSBLATT (6x wk.)
Est. 1871
Europaplatz 26 (46399); PF 1254, 46362
Tel: (49-2871) 9550; Fax: (49-2871) 955119
Circ.—26,300 ABC
Prop.—Temming
Bus./Ad. Mgr.—U Deger

BOEBLINGEN
(BÖBLINGEN)

KREISZEITUNG (7x wk.) Est. 1825
Bahnhofstr. 27 (71034); PF 1560, 71005
Tel: (49-7031) 62000; Fax: (49-7031) 227443
Circ.—20,600 ABC
Prop.—Schlecht
Pub.—P Schlecht
Mng. Ed./Ed. in Ch.—W E A Heubach
Ed. in Ch./Bus. Mgr.—M Schlecht
Ad. Mgr.—G Schwenk

BONN
Pop. Est. 294,300

BONNER RUNDSCHAU (6x wk.) Est. 1945
Thomas-Mann-Str. 51 (53111); PF 1248, 53002
Tel: (49-228) 7210; Fax: (49-228) 721230
Circ.—67,100 ABC
Prop.—Heinen
Ad. Mgr.—H Litsch
GENERAL-ANZEIGER (The General Advertiser) (6x wk.) Est. 1725
Justus-von-Liebig Str. 15; GKP 53100, 53121
Tel: (49-228) 66880; Fax: (49-228) 6688170
Circ.—96,300 ABC
Prop.—Bonner Zeitungsdruckerei
Pub.—M Neusser
Pub.—H Neusser
Mng. Ed.—U Minne
Ed. in Ch.—Dr. H Herles
Ed. in Ch.—E Els
Bus. Mgr.—W Hundhausen
Ad. Mgr.—G T Berk

BORKEN
Pop. Est. 33,700

BORKENER ZEITUNG (6x wk.) Est. 1867
Bahnhofstr. 6 (46325); PF 1563, 46305
Tel: (49-2861) 80000; Fax: (49-2861) 800039
Circ.—17,900 ABC
Prop.—Mergelsberg
Bus. Mgr./Ad.Mgr.—H Damentgen

BORKUM

BORKUMER ZEITUNG und BADEZEITUNG (4x wk.) Est. 1882
Neue Str. 9 (26757); PF 2066, 26746
Tel: (49-4922) 1055; Fax: (49-4922) 3377
Circ.—1,700
Prop.—Specht
Pub./Mng. Ed./Ed. in Ch.—Wilke Specht

BRAUNSCHWEIG
(Brunswick)
Pop. Est. 247,800

BRAUNSCHWEIGER ZEITUNG (6x wk.) Est. 1946
Hamburger Str. 277 (38022); PF 3263, 38114
Tel: (49-531) 39000; Fax: (49-531) 3900610
Circ.—227,900 (total-all eds.) ABC
Prop.—Braunschweiger Zeitungsverlag
Pub.—H L Voigt
Mng. Ed./Ed. in Ch.—L Heydecke
Mng. Ed./Ed. in Ch.—E Schimf
Ed. in Ch.—Dr. A Rabbow
Bus. Mgr.—P J Lesemann
Ad. Mgr.—C Schilling
(Circulation is the total of all Braunschweiger Zeitung editions. See Wölfenbüttel.)

BREMEN
Pop. Est. 542,300

BREMER NACHRICHTEN (The Bremer News) (d) Est. 1743
Gerhard-Rohlfs-Str. 47, 28757
Tel: (49-421) 658450; Fax: (49-421) 6584544
Circ.—224,900
Prop.—Weser Zeitung
Ed. in Ch.—D Ide
WESER-KURIER (The Weser Messenger) (d) Est. 1945
Martinistr. 43 (28195); PF 107801, 28078
Tel: (49-421) 36710; Fax: (49-421) 328327
Circ.—224,900
Prop.—Bremer Tageszeitungen AG
Mng. Ed.—P Bauer
Ed. in Ch.—V Weise
Ed. in Ch.—J Bettmmann
Bus. Mgr.—H C Ordemann
Ad. Mgr.—A Vogel

BREMERHAVEN
Pop. Est. 132,200

NORDSEE-ZEITUNG (The North Sea News) (6x wk.) Est. 1895
Hafenstr. 140 (27576); PF 101228, 27512
Tel: (49-471) 5970; Fax: (49-471) 597555
Circ.—81,500 ABC
Prop.—Ditzen Verlag
Pub.—Dr. J Ditzen-Blanke
Bus. Mgr.—P Doll
Ad. Mgr.—U Katenkamp

BREMERVOERDE
(BREMERVÖRDE)
Pop. Est. 9,638

BREMERVÖRDER ZEITUNG (6x wk.) Est. 1854
Neue Str. 34 (27432); PF 1161, 27421
Tel: (49-4761) 9970; Fax: (49-4761) 86559
Circ.—8,600 ABC
Prop.—Borgardt
Ed. in Ch.—R Borgardt
Ed.—R Klöfkorn
Bus. Mgr.—J Borgardt
Bus. Mgr.—Detta Borgardt
Ad. Mgr.—N Ullrich

BUECKEBURG
(BÜCKEBURG)
Pop. Est. 20,400

SCHAUMBURG-LIPPISCHE LANDES-ZEITUNG (6x wk.) Est. 1889
Lange Str. 20 (36175); PF 1260, 31666
Tel: (49-5722) 4052; Fax: (49-5722) 4054
Circ.—3,300 ABC
Prop.—Grimme Verlag
Pub.—G Niemeyer
Pub.—H Niemeyer
Ad. Mgr.—W Plassmeier

BUERSTADT
(BÜRSTADT)
Pop. Est. 12,888

BÜRSTÄDTER ZEITUNG (6x wk.) Est. 1910
Mainstr. 13 (68642); PF 1160, 68636
Tel: (49-6206) 70660; Fax: (49-6206) 70635
Circ.—3,000 ABC
Prop.—Träger
Pub./Ed. in Ch./Bus. Mgr.—P J Träger

Europe — Germany, Federal Republic of — IV-17

BURG
(on Fehman Island)
Pop. Est. 6,041

FEHMARNSCHES TAGEBLATT (6x wk.) Est. 1856
Bahnhofstr. 1 (23769); PF 1169, 23763
Tel: (49-4371) 86750; Fax: (49-4371) 867550
Circ.—2,600 ABC
Prop.—Burg Verlag
Bus. Mgr.—D Schöningh

BUTZBACH
Pop. Est. 21,300

BUTZBACHER ZEITUNG (6x wk.) Est. 1843
Langgasse 18 (35510); PF 340, 35503
Tel: (49-6033) 96060; Fax: (49-6033) 960649
Circ.—7,800 ABC
Prop.—Gratzfeld Verlag
Ed. in Ch.—Christel Gratzfeld
Bus. Mgr.—H L Gratzfeld
Ad. Mgr.—Helga Mohr

BUXTEHUDE
Pop. Est. 32,500

BUXTEHUDER TAGEBLATT (6x wk.)
Ritterstr 16 (21614); PF 1162, 21601
Tel: (49-4161) 516730; Fax: (49-4161) 516792
Circ.—12,300 ABC
Prop.—Krause Zeitungsverlag
Ad. Mgr.—H Doehring

CALW
Pop. Est. 22,400

KREISNACHRICHTEN (6x wk.) Est. 1826
Lederstr. 23 (75365); PF 1162, 75351
Tel: (49-7051) 13080; Fax: (49-7051) 20077
Circ.—15,100 ABC
Prop.—Calw Zeitungsverlag GmbH
Ed. in Ch.—R Stöhr
Bus. Mgr.—H Krauss
Ad. Mgr.—W Katz

CELLE
Pop. Est. 70,200

CELLESCHE ZEITUNG (6x wk.) Est. 1817
Bahnhofstr. 1 (29221); PF 1502, 29205
Tel: (49-5141) 2790; Fax: (49-5141) 279191
Circ.—34,900 ABC
Prop.—Cellesche Zeitung
Pub.—E A Pfingsten
Mng. Ed./Ed. in Ch./Ed.—D Mehmke
Ed. in Ch.—M Rothfuchs
Bus. Mgr.—G Winkelmann
Ad. Mgr.—J Radünz

CHEMNITZ
Pop. Est. 294,244

FREIE PRESSE (The Free Press) (6x wk.) Est. 1962
Brückenstr. 15 (09111); PF 261, 09002
Tel: (49-371) 6560; Fax: (49-371) 643042
Circ.—529,800 ABC
Prop.—Chemnitzer Verlag & Druck
Mng. Ed.—G Sonntag
Ed. in Ch.—H Köhler
Ed.—D Geipel
Ed.—W Hub
Bus. Mgr.—R Bilz
Ad. Mgr.—R Beier

CLOPPENBURG
Pop. Est. 22,000

MÜNSTERLÄNDISCHE TAGESZEITUNG (6x wk.) Est. 1880
Lange Str. 9 (49661); PF 1420, 49644
Tel: (49-4471) 1780; Fax: (49-4471) 17830
Circ.—19,500 ABC
Prop.—Imsiecke
Ed. in Ch.—G Hafer
Ad. Mgr.—H Greiner

COBURG
Pop. Est. 44,400

COBURGER TAGEBLATT (6x wk.) Est. 1885
Hindenburgstr. 3a (96450); PF 1443, 96404
Tel: (49-9561) 8880; Fax: (49-9561) 888199
Circ.—17,800 ABC
Prop.—Coburger Tagblatt
Pub.—H Uhlemann
Mng. Ed.—N Karbach

Ed. in Ch.—Dr. Carolin Herrmann
Bus. Mgr.—H Mitzel
Ad. Mgr.—H Greiner
NEUE PRESSE (New Press) (6x wk.) Est. 1946
Friedrich-Rückert Str. 73 (96450); PF 2553, 96414
Tel: (49-9561) 8500; Fax: (49-9561) 850139
Circ.—35,800 ABC
Prop.—Duck & Verlagstanstalt Neue Presse
Mng. Ed.—M Fleischmann
Ed. in Ch.—L Hegenberg
Ed. in Ch./Ed.—W Braunschmidt
Bus. Mgr.—W Griego
Bus. Mgr.—P Leipold
Ad. Mgr.—T Platenberg

COESFELD
Pop. Est. 31,600

ALLGEMEINE ZEITUNG (6x wk.) Est. 1834
Rosenstr. 2 (48653); PF 1343, 48633
Tel: (49-2541) 9210; Fax: (49-2541) 92152
Circ.—18,800 (total-all eds.) ABC
Prop.—Fleissig
Pub./Bus. Mgr./Ad. Mgr.—H Fleissig

COLOGNE
(KÖLN)
Pop. Est. 955,500

EXPRESS (d-6x wk.) Est. 1963
Breite Str. 70 (50667); PF 101041, 50450
Tel: (49-221) 2240; Fax: (49-221) 2242700
Circ.—514,700 ABC
Prop.—DuMont Schauberg
Pub.—A N DuMont
Mng. Ed.—R Voss
Mng. Ed.—K Klammann
Ed. in Ch.—K Rottgen
Ed. in Ch.—R M Gefeller
Ed. in Ch.—B Müller
Bus. Mgr.—J Stöcker
Ad. Mgr.—Dr. B Almert
KÖLNER STADT-ANZEIGER (The Cologne City Advertiser) (m-5x wk.) Est. 1802
Breite Str. 70 (50667); GKP 101041, 50450
Tel: (49-221) 2240; Fax: (49-221) 2242524
Circ.—305,200 ABC
Prop.—DuMont Schauberg
Pub.—A N DuMont
Mng. Ed.—Dr. A Schiele
Ed. in Ch.—D Jepsen-Föge
Ed. in Ch.—Marie Hüllenkremer
Ed. in Ch.—T Meyer
Ad. Mgr.—Dr. B Almert
KÖLNISCHE RUNDSCHAU (6x wk.) Est. 1945
Stolkgasse 25 (50667); PF 102145, 50461
Tel: (49-221) 16320; Fax: (49-221) 1632491
Circ.—172,200 (total-all eds.) ABC
Prop.—Heinen-Verlag
Pub.—H Heinen
Ed. in Ch./Ed.—W Birkholz
Ed. in Ch./Ed.—E Gries
Ed. in Ch./Ed.—S A Casdorff
Ed. in Ch.—D Breuers
Bus. Mgr.—R Kleefisch
Ad. Mgr.—H Litsch
MAKEDONIA (5x wk.) Greek
Hildeboldplatz 13, 50672
Tel: (49-221) 134487/(49-221) 582213
Circ.—15,000
Prop.—Makedonia Verlag

COTTBUS
Pop. Est. 125,891

LAUSITZER RUNDSCHAU (6x wk.) Est. 1852
Str. der Jugend 54 (03050); PF 100279, 03002
Tel: (49-355) 4810; Fax: (49-355) 481293
Circ.—209,600 (total-all eds.) ABC
Prop.—L R Medienverlag
Mng. Ed.—T Klatt
Ed. in Ch.—W Nagorske
Ed. in Ch./Ed.—H-G Wackwitz
Bus. Mgr.—Evelin Sobottka
Bus. Mgr.—B Liske
Bus. Mgr.—B Hartmann
Ad. Mgr.—Monika Langenickel

CUXHAVEN
Pop. Est. 56,100

CUXHAVENER NACHRICHTEN (6x wk.) Est. 1976
Kammererplatz 2 (27472); PF 180, 27451
Tel: (49-4721) 5850; Fax: (49-4721) 5853229
Circ.—16,200 ABC
Prop.—Cuxhaven Verlagsges

Copyright ©1996 by the Editor & Publisher Co.

Germany, Federal Republic of

Ed. in Ch./Ed.—Ilse Cordes-Knape
Ed. in Ch.—H-C Winters
Bus. Mgr.—J P Jacobsen
Ad. Mgr.—J-P Knochen

DARMSTADT
Pop. Est. 133,600

DARMSTÄDTER ECHO (5x wk.) Est. 1945
Holzhofallee 25 (64295); PF 100155, 64201
Tel: (49-6151) 3871; Fax: (49-6151) 387307
Circ.—71,100 ABC
Prop.—Darmstädter Echo GmbH
Mng. Ed.—J Rierbartsch
Ed. in Ch./Ed.—J Diesner
Ed. in Ch.—R Hof
Bus./Ad. Mgr.—H Kreutzberger

THE STARS AND STRIPES (m-7x wk.) English; Est. 1942
Flughafenstr.; PF 111437, 64278
Tel: (49-6155) 601237; Fax: (49-6155) 601416
Circ.—93,000 ABC
Prop.—European Stars and Stripes
Mng. Ed.—B Walker
Ed. in Ch.—Bernard A Zovistoski
Ad. Mgr.—J Weisel
(Military Address within USA: APO New York 09211-4211. Local Military Address: APO 09211-5000.)

DELMENHORST
Pop. Est. 70,500

DELMENHORSTER KREISBLATT (6x wk.) Est. 1832
Lange Str. 122 (27749); PF 1244, 27732
Tel: (49-4221) 1560; Fax: (49-4221) 15625
Circ.—25,600 ABC
Prop.—Rieck
Pub./Bus. Mgr.—Anna-Louise Strathaus
Pub./Bus. Mgr.—D Schulte Strathaus
Ed. in Ch.—C Wetterman
Ed.—U Arlt
Ad. Mgr.—W Hollwedel

DETMOLD
Pop. Est. 66,700

LIPPISCHE LANDES-ZEITUNG (6x wk.) Est. 1767
Lagesche Str. 15 (32756); PF 2163, 32711
Tel: (49-5231) 9110; Fax: (49-5231) 911100
Circ.—46,800 ABC
Prop.—Lippischer Zeitungsverlag GmbH
Pub.—H Giesdorf
Mng. Ed.—T Trappmann
Bus. Mgr.—H Schmermund
Ad. Mgr.—J Hagemann
Ad. Mgr.—R Müller
(Gets editorial content from Neue Westfalishe.)

DILLENBURG
Pop. Est. 22,800

DILL-ZEITUNG (6x wk.) Est. 1839
Rathausstr. 1 (35683); PF 1262, 35662
Tel: (49-2771) 8740; Fax: (49-2771) 74261
Circ.—11,600 ABC
Prop.—Weidenbach
Pub./Bus. Mgr.—E Simon
Ed. in Ch./Ed.—F Sohnn
Ad. Mgr.—Elvira Schlaudraff

DINGOFING
Pop. Est. 10,548

DINGOLFINGER ANZEIGER (Dingolfinger Advertiser) (6x wk.)
Laaberstr. 2 (84130); PF 1360, 84124
Tel: (49-8731) 7030; Fax: (49-8731) 70333
Circ.—11,300 ABC
Prop.—Wälischmiller

DOBELN
(DÖBELN)

DÖBELNER ANZEIGER (Doebelner Advertiser) (6x wk.) Est. 1990
Bertholdstr. 1, 04720
Tel: (49-3431) 486544; Fax: (49-3431) 486583
Circ.—19,200 ABC
Prop.—Döbelner Anzeiger
Bus. Mgr.—W Graul
(Gets editorial content from Hellweger Anzeiger.)

DORTMUND
Pop. Est. 599,900

RUHR NACHRICHTEN (m-ex S) Est. 1949
Westenhellweg 86 (44137); PF 105051, 44047
Tel: (49-231) 90590; Fax: (49-231) 9059407
Circ.—249,300 (total-all eds.) ABC
Prop.—Ruhr-Nachrichten Verlag
Pub./Ed. in Ch/Bus. Mgr.—F Lensing-Wolff
Mng. Ed.—H Wagner
Ed. in Ch.—H Haffert
Ed. in Ch./Ed.—H E Hütt
Ad. Mgr.—Franz Pieper

WESTFÄLISCHE RUNDSCHAU (6x wk.) Est. 1946
Brüderweg 9 (44135); PF 105067, 44047
Tel: (49-231) 95730; Fax: (49-231) 95731202
Circ.—166,100
Prop.—Westfalen Zeitungsverlag
Pub.—G Hammer
Mng. Ed./Ed.—B Dagge
Ed. in Ch.—F Bünte
Ed.—K-H Evers
Ed.—J Westhoff
Bus. Mgr.—G Grotkamp
Bus. Mgr.—E Schumann
Ad. Mgr.—E Schillinger
Ad. Mgr.—W Sundermann (Essen)

DREIEICH

MILLIYET (7x wk.) Turkish
PF 102226, 63268
Circ.—26,000
Prop.—Türul Verlagsges

DRESDEN
Pop. Est. 490,571

DRESDNER NEUESTE NACHRICHTEN (6x wk.) Est. 1990
Hauptstr. 21 (01097); PF 100520, 01075
Tel: (49-351) 80750; Fax: (49-351) 8075112
Circ.—50,400 ABC
Prop.—Dresdner Nachrichten Verlag
Ed. in Ch./Ed.—Karla Tolksdorf
Ed. in Ch.—M G Stüting
Bus. Mgr.—W Saurin
Ad. Mgr.—A Stroeve

SÄCHSISCHE ZEITUNG (The Saxony News) (m-6x wk.) Est. 1952
Ostra-Allee 20, 01067
Tel: (49-351) 48640; Fax: (49-351) 4952143
Circ.—446,500 ABC
Prop.—Dresdner Druck & Verlagshaus
Mng. Ed.—H Ritter
Ed. in Ch.—K Gertoberens
Ed. in Ch.—J Marschner
Ed. in Ch.—O Kittel
Ed. in Ch.—R Schulze
Bus. Mgr.—Dr. M Frank

DUELMEN
(DÜLMEN)
Pop. Est. 40,100

DÜLMENER ZEITUNG (6x wk.) Est. 1874
Markstr. 25, 48249
Tel: (49-2594) 2961; Fax: (49-2594) 80216
Circ.—9,700 ABC
Prop.—Horstmann
Bus. Mgr.—H H Bednara

DUESSELDORF
(DÜSSELDORF)
Pop. Est. 576,700

DÜSSELDORF EXPRESS (6x wk.) Est. 1963
Königsallee 27 (40212); PF 101132, 40002
Tel: (49-211) 133010; Fax: (49-211) 324835
Circ.—146,400 ABC
Prop.—Düsseldorf Express Verlagsges

HANDELSBLATT (5x wk.) Est. 1946
Kasernenstr. 67 (40213); PF 102741, 40018
Tel: (49-211) 8870; Fax: (49-211) 329954
Circ.—167,300 ABC
Prop.—Verlagsgruppe Handelsblatt
Pub.—Dieter von Holzbrinck
Mng. Ed.—G Koop
Ed. in Ch.—R Nahrendorf
Ed. in Ch.—W Schäfer
Ad. Mgr.—H Brendt

RHEINISCHE POST (m-6x wk.) Est. 1946
Zülpicher Str. 10; GKP 40196, 40549
Tel: (49-211) 5050; Fax: (49-211) 5047562
Circ.—435,300 ABC
Prop.—Rheinisch-Bergische Druck & Verlagsges GmbH
Pub.—Dr. Esther Betz
Pub.—Dr. G Arnold

Mng. Ed.—M Hamerla
Mng. Ed.—K D Voss
Ed. in Ch./Ed.—H Zscherper
Ed. in Ch.—Dr. J Sobotta
Bus. Mgr.—C Bauer
Bus. Mgr.—D Reichel
Bus. Mgr.—Dr. H D Baumgart
Bus. Mgr.—Dr. A Mayer
Ad. Mgr.—L Schreiner
U.S. Rep.—Publicitas

WZ WESTDEUTSCHE ZEITUNG (6x wk.) Est. 1876
Königsallee 27 (40212); PF 101132, 40002
Tel: (49-211) 83820; Fax: (49-211) 8382392
Circ.—205,400 (total-all eds.) ABC
Prop.—Girardet
Pub.—Dr. M Girardet
Mng. Ed.—W Radau
Ed. in Ch./Ed.—M Hartmann
Ed. in Ch./Ed.—F Hänschen
Ed. in Ch.—P H Grupe
Bus. Mgr.—E G Winterhoff
Bus. Mgr.—W-D Drews
Bus. Mgr.—H Roth

EBERBACH
Pop. Est. 13,986

EBERBACHER ZEITUNG (6x wk.) Est. 1864
Friedrichsdorfer Landstr. 64 (69412); PF 1343, 69403
Tel: (49-6271) 2333; Fax: (49-6271) 1840
Circ.—4,100 ABC
Prop.—Krauth
Bus. Mgr.—R Göller

ECKERNFOERDE
(ECKERNFÖRDE)
Pop. Est. 24,500

ECKERNFÖRDER ZEITUNG (6x wk.) Est. 1851
Schulweg 7 (24340); PF 1169, 24331
Tel: (49-4351) 90080; Fax: (49-4351) 900891
Circ.—9,800 ABC
Prop.—Eckernförder Zeitung GmbH
Pub.—H Blencker
Pub.—Irmtraut Bleckner
Ed. in Ch.—G Kühl
Ed. in Ch.—J Griese

EINBECK
Pop. Est. 27,400

EINBECKER MORGENPOST (m-ex S) Est. 1810
Marktplatz 12 (37574); PF 1613, 37557
Tel: (49-5561) 4002; Fax: (49-5561) 73383
Circ.—10,600 ABC
Prop.—Rüttgerodt Verlag
Pub./Bus. Mgr.—J Rüttgerodt
Ed. in Ch.—Edith Kondziella
Ad. Mgr.—F Westerling

ELMSHORN
Pop. Est. 41,500

ELMSHORNER NACHRICHTEN (The Elmshorner News) (6x wk.) Est. 1851
Schulstr. 13; PF 340, 25303
Tel: (49-4121) 2970; Fax: (49-4121) 24105
Circ.—13,800 ABC
Prop.—Springer
Bus. Mgr.—V Koch
Ad. Mgr.—H Koch

EMDEN
Pop. Est. 49,600

EMDER ZEITUNG (6x wk.) Est. 1900
Zwischen beiden Märkten 2 (26721); PF 1453, 26694
Tel: (49-4921) 89000; Fax: (49-4921) 32440
Circ.—12,500 ABC
Prop.—Gerhard
Pub.—E Gerhard
Ed. in Ch./Ed.—K Fackert
Ed. in Ch.—H Kolbe
Ad. Mgr.—G Janssen

EMSDETTEN
Pop. Est. 31,100

EMSDETTENER TAGESBLATT (The Emsdettener Daily) (6x wk.)
Nordwalder Str. 4 (48282); PF 1531, 48273
Tel: (49-2572) 4018; Fax: (49-2572) 84521
Circ.—4,000 ABC
Prop.—Emsdettner Tageblatt Verlag
Ad. Mgr.—J Hoppe

EMSDETTENER VOLKSZEITUNG (The Emsdettener People's News) (6x wk.) Est. 1897
Mühlenstr. 23, 48282
Tel: (49-2572) 7021; Fax: (49-2572) 88686
Circ.—7,100 ABC
Prop.—Verlag Emsdettener Volkszeitung
Pub.—F Lensing-Wolff

ERBACH
Pop. Est. 6,858

ODENWÄLDER HEIMATZEITUNG (5x wk.)
Hauptstr. 59 (64295); PF 1355, 64703
Tel: (49-6062) 60100; Fax: (49-6062) 60124
Circ.—15,100 ABC
Prop.—Darmstädter Echo

ERFURT
Pop. Est. 208,989

THÜRINGER ALLGEMEINE (6x wk.) Est. 1946
Gottstedter Landstr. 6, 99092
Tel: (49-361) 2275101; Fax: (49-361) 2275107
Circ.—594,500 ABC
Prop.—Thüringer Allgemeine Verlag
Mng. Ed.—G Carl
Mng. Ed.—W Schilling
Ed. in Ch./Ed.—D Rave
Ed. in Ch./Ed.—W Lindenlaub

ERLANGEN
Pop. Est. 100,200

ERLANGER NACHRICHTEN (Erlangen News) (d-5x wk.) Est. 1859
Innere Brucker Str. 8 (91054), 91051
Tel: (49-9131) 80030; Fax: (49-9131) 800354
Circ.—42,300 ABC
Prop.—Junge & Sohn
Pub.—Anne Probst
Pub.—B Schnell
Ad. Mgr.—K Kreissel

ESCHWEGE
Pop. Est. 22,900

WERRA-RUNDSCHAU (7x wk.) Est. 1948
Vor dem Berge 2 (37269); PF 1680, 37256
Tel: (49-5651) 60024; Fax: (49-5651) 76592
Circ.—15,100 ABC
Prop.—Werra-Verlag
Pub./Bus. Mgr.—Dr. P Kluthe
Mng. Ed./Ed. in Ch./Ed.—C Cortis
Ed. in Ch.—K Kramer
Ad. Mgr.—O Schäfer
(Gets editorial content from Hessische/ Niedersächsische Allgemeine.)

ESSEN
Pop. Est. 626,100

NRZ (NEUE RHEIN-ZEITUNG and NEUE RUHR-ZEITUNG) (6x wk.) Est. 1947
Friedrichstr. 34; GKP 45123, 45128
Tel: (49-201) 8040; Fax: (49-201) 8042621
Circ.—1,332,800
Prop.—Niederrhein Zeitungsverlag
Pub.—Prof. Dr. D Oppenberg
Mng. Ed.—P Rosien
Ed. in Ch.—Dr. R Kiessler
Ed.—J Umbach
Bus. Mgr.—G Grotkamp
Bus. Mgr.—E Schumann
Ad. Mgr.—E Schillinger
Ad. Mgr.—W Sundermann
(Circulation figure combines with Westdeutche Allgemeine Waz.)

WESTDEUTSCHE ALLGEMEINE WAZ (6x wk.) Est. 1948
Friedrichstr. 34-38 (45128), PF 104161, 45041
Tel: (49-201) 80400; Fax: (49-201) 8042841
Circ.—1,313,400 ABC
Prop.—Westdeutsche Allgemeine Zeitungsverlagsges
Pub.—E Brost
Pub.—J Funke
Mng. Ed./Ed. in Ch.—B Zapp
Ed. in Ch.—R Lehmann
Ed. in Ch.—A Pieper
Ed. in Ch.—H-J Pöschke
Bus. Mgr.—G Grotkamp
Bus. Mgr.—E Schumann
Ad. Mgr.—M Kraemer
(Circulation figure combines with NRZ.)

ESSLINGEN am NECKAR
EßLINGEN am NECKAR
Pop. Est. 86,900

ESSLINGER ZEITUNG (6x wk.) Est. 1868
Zeppelinstr. 116 (73730); PF 569, 73706
Tel: (49-711) 93100; Fax: (49-711) 318174

Circ.—39,700 ABC
Prop.—Bechtle Verlag
Pub./Ed. in Ch.—O W Bechtle
Pub.—Dr. F Bechtle
Mng. Ed.—H-W Pradler
Ed. in Ch.—D-J Simmert
Bus. Mgr.—W Blumerski
Ad. Mgr.—N Kindler

EUTIN
Pop. Est. 17,596

OSTHOLSTEINER ANZEIGER (The East Holstein Advertiser) (6x wk.) Est. 1802
Schlossstr. 5 (23701); PF 320, 23693
Tel: (49-4521) 779170; Fax: (49-4521) 779190
Circ.—10,000 ABC
Prop.—Struve
Pub.—Dr. Gisela Wachholtz
Bus. Mgr.—R Bertheau
Ad. Mgr.—J Bebensee

FELLBACH
Pop. Est. 39,800

FELLBACHER ZEITUNG (6x wk.) Est. 1894
Vordere Str. 2 (70734); PF 1429, 70704
Tel: (49-711) 582126; Fax: (49-711) 581850
Circ.—6,900 ABC
Prop.—Stuttgarter Nachrichten
Ad. Mgr.—K Vogelreuter

FEUCHT
Pop. Est. 9,040

DER BOTE für NÜRNBERG-LAND (5x wk.) Est. 1852
Nürnberger Str. 5, 90537
Tel: (49-9128) 2055; Fax: (49-9128) 2056
Circ.—12,300 ABC
Prop.—Der Bote Verlag
Pub.—U Bollmann
Pub.—B Schnell
Ad. Mgr.—K Kreissel

FLENSBURG
Pop. Est. 85,700

FLENSBORG AVIS (6x wk.) Danish; Est. 1869
Wittenberger Weg 19 (24941), 24916
Tel: (49-461) 50450; Fax: (49-461) 59090
Circ.—8,000 ABC
Prop.—Flensborg Avis AG
Mng. Ed.—J L Hansen
Mng. Ed.—J Christensensen
Mng. Ed.—H Andresen
Ed. in Ch./Bus. Mgr.—B Lonborg
Ed. in Ch./Ed.—O Petersen
Ad. Mgr.—W Schneider
FLENSBURGER TAGEBLATT (d-6x wk.)
Nikolaistr. 7 (24937); PF 1553, 24905
Tel: (49-461) 8080; Fax: (49-461) 808348
Circ.—111,700 ABC
Prop.—Schleswig-Holsteinischer Zeitungsverlg
Mng. Ed.—T Schunck
Mng. Ed.—Barbara Post
Ed. in Ch.—S Lipsky
Ed. in Ch.—S Richter
Bus. Mgr.—K May
Bus. Mgr.—E F Lübcke
Ad. Mgr.—R Meyer

FRANKFURT am MAIN
Pop. Est. 647,200

BÖRSEN-ZEITUNG (5x wk.) Est. 1952
Düsseldorfer Str. 16 (60329); PF 110932, 60044
Tel: (49-69) 27320; Fax: (49-69) 232264
Prop.—Verlag Börsen-Zeitung
Mng. Ed.—M Lenius
Ed. in Ch.—H K Herdt
Ed.—D Hartwig
Bus. Mgr.—E Thomas
Ad. Mgr.—H Larsen
FINANCIAL TIMES (d-6x wk.) English
Nibelungenplatz 3, 60318
Tel: (49-69) 156850; Fax: (49-69) 5964542
Circ.—14,500
Prop.—The Financial Times (Europe)
Pub.—R Lambert
Ed. in Ch.—C Parkes
Ed. in Ch.—A Fisher
Bus. Mgr./Ad. Mgr.—E Hugo
FRANKFURTER ALLGEMEINE (m-5x wk.) Est. 1949
Hellerhofstr. 2, 60327
Tel: (49-69) 75910; Fax: (49-69) 75911743
Circ.—471,900 ABC
Prop.—Frankfurter Allgemeine Zeitung GmbH
Pub./Ed. in Ch.—J Jeske
Pub./Ed. in Ch.—Dr. H Müller-Vogg
Pub./Ed. in Ch.—Dr. R G Reissmüller
Pub./Ed. in Ch.—G Nonnenmacher
Pub./Ed. in Ch.—F Schirrmacher
Ad. Mgr.—W D Auerbach
Ad. Mgr.—D Dröll
U.S. Rep.—Publicitas
FRANKFURTER NEUE PRESSE (The Frankfurt New Press) (m-6x wk.) Est. 1946
Frankenallee 71 (60327); PF 100801, 60008
Tel: (49-69) 75010; Fax: (49-69) 7306965
Circ.—122,400 (total-all eds.) ABC
Prop.—Franfurter Societäts-Druckerei
Mng. Ed.—F W Kuck
Ed. in Ch.—P Fisher
Bus. Mgr.—V W Grams
Ad. Mgr.—J Mattutat
FRANKFURTER RUNDSCHAU (5x wk.) Est. 1945
Eschenheimer Str. 16; PF 100660, 60313
Tel: (49-69) 21991; Fax: (49-69) 2199421
Circ.—207,100 ABC
Prop.—Druck & Verlagshaus Frankfurt
Ed. in Ch.—C M Schöne
Ed. in Ch.—R Reifenrath
Ed. in Ch./Ed.—Dr. J Siemens
Bus. Mgr.—U Grimmer
Ad. Mgr.—P Schwalm

FRANKFURT an der ODER
Pop. Est. 86,131

MÄRKISCHE ODERZEITUNG (m-6x wk) Est. 1952
Kellenspring 6 (15230); PF 178, 15201
Tel: (49-335) 55300; Fax: (49-335) 5530538
Circ.—210,300 ABC
Prop.—Märkisches Verlags & Druckhaus
Pub.—C Detjen
Mng. Ed.—R Dröscher
Ed. in Ch.—H Kannenberg
Ed.—K Fischer
Ed.—R P Weise
Ad. Mgr.—W Noll

FREIBURG
Pop. Est. 186,200

BADISCHE ZEITUNG (m-6x wk.) Est. 1946
Basler Str. 88 (79115); PF 280, 79002
Tel: (49-761) 4960; Fax: (49-761) 41098
Circ.—208,100 ABC
Prop.—Badischer Verlag GmbH
Mng. Ed.—M Doelfs
Ed. in Ch.—Dr. A Fürst
Ed. in Ch./Ed.—H B Kienzle
Ad. Mgr.—K H Henze

FUESSEN
(FÜSSEN)
Pop. Est. 10,778

ALLGÄUER ZEITUNG (d-6x wk.)
Von-Freyberg-Str. 4, 87629
Tel: (49-8362) 507971; Fax: (49-8362) 507910
Circ.—11,900 ABC
Prop.—Holdenried
Pub.—G Holland
Pub.—G Fürst von Waldburg zu Zeil
Bus. Mgr.—G Blank

FULDA
Pop. Est. 54,100

FULDAER ZEITUNG (6x wk.) Est. 1874
Peterstor 18 (36037), 36004
Tel: (49-661) 2800; Fax: (49-661) 280279
Circ.—55,800 ABC
Prop.—Parzeller Verlag
Pub./Bus. Mgr.—Dr. T Schmitt
Mng. Ed./Ed. in Ch./Ed.—U B Herchen
Ed. in Ch.—H-J Konze
Ed.—C A Bradner
Ad. Mgr.—H Killian

GAILDORF
Pop. Est. 5,212

RUNDSCHAU für den SCHWÄBISCHEN WALD (d-6x wk.) Est. 1839
Grabenstr. 14 (74405); PF 130, 74402
Tel: (49-7971) 7088; Fax: (49-7971) 7076
Circ.—5,500
Prop.—Neue Kreis-Rundschau
Ed. in Ch.—K M Osswald
Bus./Ad. Mgr.—F S Horcher
(This is an edition of the Südwest Presse Ulm in Ulm.)

GANDERSHEIM, BAD
Pop. Est. 6,130

GANDERSHEIMER KREISBLATT (6x wk.) Est. 1833
Alte Gasse 19; PF 109, 37581
Tel: (49-5382) 98110; Fax: (49-5382) 6356
Circ.—5,900 ABC
Prop.—Gandersheimer Kreisblatt
Ed. in Ch./Bus.Mgr.—T Fischer
Ad. Mgr.—G Albrecht

GEISLINGEN an der STEIGE
Pop. Est. 26,200

GEISLINGER ZEITUNG (6x wk.) Est. 1884
Haupstr. 38 (73312); PF 1254, 73302
Tel: (49-7331) 2020; Fax: (49-7331) 20250
Circ.—16,800 ABC
Prop.—Geislinger Zeitung Verlagsges
Mng. Ed.—M Rahnefeld
Ed. in Ch.—R Schmauz
Bus. Mgr.—W Braig
Ad. Mgr.—Anke Grosse
(This is an edition of the Südwest Presse Ulm in Ulm.)

GELNHAEUSEN
(GELNHÄUSEN)
Pop. Est. 7,756

GELNHÄUSER NEUE ZEITUNG (6x wk.) German; Est. 1988
Barbarossastr. 5, 63571
Tel: (49-6051) 8240; Fax: (49-6051) 12468
Circ.—8,200 ABC
Prop.—Gelnhäuser Tageblatt Verlagsges
Pub.—K A Kalbfleisch
Ad. Mgr.—B Schneider
GELNHÄUSER TAGEBLATT (The Gelnhaeuser Daily Paper) (6x wk.) Est. 1832
Barbarossastr. 5, 63571
Tel: (49-6051) 8240; Fax: (49-6051) 12468
Circ.—17,000 ABC
Prop.—Gelnhäuser Tageblatt Verlag
Pub.—K A Kalbfleisch

GELSENKIRCHEN
Pop. Est. 283,600

BZ BUERSCHE ZEITUNG (6x wk.) Est. 1881
Hagenstr. 15 (45894); PF 200252, 45837
Tel: (49-209) 360010; Fax: (49-209) 3600111
Circ.—14,900 ABC
Prop.—Verlag Buersche Zeitung
Pub.—H Klöckner
Mng. Ed.—W Kämpfe
Bus. Mgr.—K Bauer
Ad. Mgr.—Monika Stramka

GERA
Pop. Est. 129,037

OSTTHÜRINGER ZEITUNG (6x wk.) Est. 1990
Alte Str. 1 (04626); PF 308, 07543
Tel: (49-3447) 524; Fax: (49-3447) 525914
Circ.—155,900
Prop.—OTZ Ostthüringer Zeitung Verlag
Mng. Ed.—W Hauser
Ed. in Ch.—U Erzigkeit
Ed.—K-H Kahnt
Bus. Mgr.—J Zaumsegel
Bus. Mgr.—H Fondermann
Bus. Mgr.—M Emmerich

GERABRONN
Pop. Est. 2,265

HOHENLOHER TAGBLATT (6x wk.) Est. 1838
Blaufeldener Str. 44 (74582); PF 80, 74580
Tel: (49-7952) 6020; Fax: (49-7952) 60244
Circ.—15,500 ABC
Prop.—Hohenloher Druck & Verlagshaus
Pub.—A Wankmüller
Mng. Ed./Ed. in Ch./Ed.—H Zigan
Ed. in Ch.—W Rupp
Bus. Mgr.—R Wankmüller
Ad. Mgr.—Carmen Höfler
(This is an edition of the Südwest Presse Ulm in Ulm.)

GEROLZHOFEN
Pop. Est. 6,083

DER STEIGERWALD-BOTE (6x wk.) Est. 1875
Weisse-Turm-Str. 18; PF 1240, 97442
Tel: (49-9382) 228; Fax: (49-9382) 4503

Europe **Germany, Federal Republic of** IV-19

Circ.—1,700 ABC
Prop.—Hampp & Partner
Bus. Mgr.—R Hampp
Ad. Mgr.—Helmtrude Pianski

GIESSEN
(GIEBEN)
Pop. Est. 71,000

GIEBENER ALLGEMEINE (6x wk.) Est. 1946
Marburger Str. 20 (35390); PF 100462, 35334
Tel: (49-641) 30030; Fax: (49-641) 32916
Circ.—71,700
Prop.—Mittelhessische Druck & Verlagses
Pub./Ed. in Ch./Bus. Mgr.—Dr. C Rempel
Ad. Mgr.—W Kämpf
GIEBENER ANZEIGER (The Giessener Advertiser) (6x wk.) Est. 1750
Am Urnenfeld 12, 35396
Tel: (49-641) 95040; Fax: (49-641) 9504200
Circ.—93,500 ABC
Prop.—Brühl
Pub.—H Wilhelm
Mng. Ed.—D T Hesse
Ed. in Ch.—Dr. W Maass
Ad. Mgr.—D Grah

GIFHORN
Pop. Est. 34,500

ALLER-ZEITUNG (6x wk.) Est. 1850
Steinweg 73 (38518); PF 1120, 38501
Tel: (49-5371) 8080; Fax: (49-5371) 808117
Circ.—29,300 ABC
Prop.—Enke
Pub.—H Enke
Pub.—F Göing
Pub.—Almuth Göing
Ed. in Ch.—K Hoffrichter
Ed.—K Alschner
Ad. Mgr.—W Kloss
Bus. Mgr.—W Gnieser

GOEPPINGEN
(GÖPPINGEN)
Pop. Est. 51,400

NWZ GÖPPINGER KREISNACHRICHTEN (The Goeppinger District News) (6x wk.) Est. 1946
Rosenstr. 24 (73033); PF 1469, 73014
Tel: (49-7161) 2040; Fax: (49-7161) 204152
Circ.—43,800 ABC
Prop.—Neue Presseges
Bus. Mgr./Ad. Mgr.—K H Grosse
(This is an edition of the Südwest Presse Ulm in Ulm.)

GOETTINGEN
(GÖTTINGEN)
Pop. Est. 133,800

GÖTTINGER TAGEBLATT (5x wk.) Est. 1889
Dransfelder Str. 1; GKP 37070, 37079
Tel: (49-551) 901320; Fax: (49-551) 901288
Circ.—53,000
Prop.—Göttinger Tageblatt Verlag
Mng. Ed.—Christine Jüttner
Ed.—H Hillebrecht
Bus. Mgr.—M Dallmann
Bus. Mgr.—H Flecken
Ad. Mgr.—M Fritzsche

GOSLAR
Pop. Est. 49,00

GOSLARSCHE ZEITUNG (6x wk.) Est. 1784
Bäckerstr. 31 (38640); PF 1580, 38605
Tel: (49-5321) 3330; Fax: (49-5321) 333399
Circ.—42,000 ABC
Prop.—Goslarsche Zeitung Verlag
Pub./Bus. Mgr.—Dr. Karl Krause
Pub./Bus. Mgr.—G Krause
Ed. in Ch./Ed.—H Krause
Mng. Ed.—H-H Schlottke
Ad. Mgr.—G Niehus

GRONAU
(Lower Saxony)

LEINE DEISTER ZEITUNG (d-6x wk.) Est. 1872
Junkerstr. 13 (31028); PF 1254, 31022
Tel: (49-5182) 5800; Fax: (49-5182) 58025
Circ.—5,600 ABC
Prop.—Wolff & Sohn Verlag
Ad./Bus. Mgr.—M Mäckeler

Germany, Federal Republic of — Europe

GROSS-GERAU
(GROß-GERAU)
Pop. Est. 21,500

HEIMAT ZEITUNG des KREISES GROß-GERAU (5x wk.) Est. 1884
Am Marktplatz 15; PF 1141, 64501
Tel: (49-6152) 81041; Fax: (49-6152) 83366
Circ.—20,500 ABC
Prop.—Darmstädter Echo & Darmstadt

GUNZENHAUSEN
Pop. Est. 9,586

ALTMÜHL-BOTE (6x wk.) Est. 1849
Kirchenplatz 3, 91710
Tel: (49-9831) 50080; Fax: (49-9831) 500840
Circ.—9,200 ABC
Prop.—Riedel
Pub.—B Schnell
Ad. Mgr.—K Kreissel
(Circulation figure combines with NZ Nordbayerische Zietung.)

HALLE
Pop. Est. 310,234

HALLER KREISBLATT (6x wk.) Est. 1882
Gutenbergstr. 2 (33790); PF 1452, 33779
Tel: (49-5201) 1501; Fax: (49-5201) 15166
Circ.—14,300 ABC
Prop.—Haller Kreisblatt Verlag
Bus. Mgr.—H Bratvogel
Bus./Ad. Mgr.—A Kaschub
MITTELDEUTSCHER EXPRESS (The Mid-German Express) (6x wk.) Est. 1990
Delitzscher Str. 65, 06112
Tel: (49-345) 5650; Fax: (49-345) 5655248
Circ.—104,100 ABC
Prop.—Mitteldt. Express GmbH.
Pub.—A Neven DuMont
Mng. Ed.—M Greiger
Ed. in Ch.—T Görger
Ed.—C Schims
Bus. Mgr.—D K Lerch
Ad. Mgr.—D Kötter
MITTELDEUTSCHER ZEITUNG (Mid-Germany News) (6x wk.) Est. 1990
Delitzscher Str. 65 (06112), 06101
Tel: (49-345) 5650; Fax: (49-345) 5654350
Circ.—437,100 ABC
Prop.—Mitteldt. Druck & Verlagshaus
Pub.—A Neven DeMont
Mng. Ed.—H Neuber
Mng. Ed.—Brigitte Kardelky
Ed. in Ch.—B von Hobe
Ed.—Dr. H Verfürth
Ed.—H-U Köhler
Ed.—F P Ewert
Bus. Mgr.—D K Lerch

HALVER
Pop. Est. 15,179

ALLGEMEINER ANZEIGER (The General Advertiser) (6x wk.) Est. 1901
Kirchstr. 5 (58553); PF 1154, 58541
Tel: (49-2353) 913450; Fax: (49-2353) 913434
Circ.—3,700 ABC
Prop.—Bell Verlag
Pub./Bus. Mgr.—P Bell
Ed. in Ch.—Ute Bornefeld
Ad. Mgr.—E Feick

HAMBURG
Pop. Est. 1,660,700

BERGEDORFER ZEITUNG (5x wk.) Est. 1882
Curslacker Neue Deich 50 (21029); PF 800340, 21003
Tel: (49-40) 725660; Fax: (49-40) 725660
Circ.—25,200 ABC
Prop.—Bergdorfer Buchdruckerei
Mng. Ed.—M Hardter
Ed. in Ch.—M Stachow
Bus. Mgr.—M Winter
Ad. Mgr.—K Radtke
BILD (m-6x wk.) Est. 1952
Axel-Springer Platz 1 (20355); PF 304630, 20315
Tel: (49-40) 34700; Fax: (49-40) 34722134
Circ.—5,567,100 ABC
Prop.—Springer
Pub.—H Fust
Ed. in Ch./Ed.—L Hagen
Ed. in Ch./Ed.—J F Hüls
Ed. in Ch./Ed.—N Körzdorfer
Ed. in Ch./Ed.—Dr. P C Martin
Ed. in Ch./Ed.—U Robel
Ed. in Ch./Ed.—K Dickmann
Ed. in Ch./Ed.—A Draxler
Ed. in Ch./Ed.—G Quandt
Ed. in Ch./Ed.—H Wolf
Ed. in Ch.—C Larass
Bus. Mgr.—C Delbrück
Ad. Mgr.—Hannelore Dietzsch
(Largest circulation in Europe; Circulation is the total of all Bild editions. Other editions include Berlin, Chemnitz, Dresden, Düsseldorf Erfurt, Frankfurt am Main, Hannover, Leipzig, Magdeburg, Munich (München), Rostock & Stuttgart.)
HAMBURGER ABENDBLATT (The Hamburg Evening Page) (e-5x wk.) Est. 1948
Axel-Springer Platz 1, 20355
Tel: (49-40) 34700; Fax: (49-40) 34726110
Circ.—324,800 ABC
Prop.—Springer
Mng. Ed.—K H Leinweber
Mng. Ed.—P Meyer
Mng. Ed.—G Meisling
Ed. in Ch.—P Kruse
Ed. in Ch.—O Frühauf
Ed. in Ch.—J Eckhardt
Ed. in Ch.—H Wessels
Ed. in Ch.—H-J Müller
Ed. in Ch.—K Kramer
Bus. Mgr.—Dr. V Blöte
Ad. Mgr.—Annette Budesheim
HAMBURGER MORGENPOST (Hamburger Morning-Post) (m-6x wk.) Est. 1949
Griegstr. 75 (22763); PF 501006, 22710
Tel: (49-40) 883030; Fax: (49-40) 88303237
Circ.—236,300 ABC
Prop.—Morgenpost Verlag
Pub.—H Dichand
Ed. in Ch.—M von Thein
Ed.—J Haarmeyer
Ed.—U Dulias
Bus. Mgr.—C Erhorn
Ad. Mgr.—H-J Eggers
HAMBURGER RUNDSCHAU Est. 1981
Lange Reihe 29, 20099
Tel: (49-40) 2801480; Fax: (49-40) 2803058
Circ.—10,000 ABC
Prop.—Neue Hamburger Rundschau
Pub./Ed. in Ch./Bus. Mgr.—Dr. J Müller
Mng. Ed./Ed. in Ch.—Petra Bäuerle
Ad. Mgr.—A Franken
HARBURGER ANZEIGEN und NACHRICHTEN (6x wk.) Est. 1844
Sand 20 (21073); PF 900453, 21044
Tel: (49-40) 766940; Fax: (49-40) 7650262
Circ.—30,900 ABC
Prop.—Lühmann
Mng. Ed.—P Hallauer
Ed. in Ch.—H-J Elwenspoek
Ed. in Ch.—L Krüger
Bus. Mgr.—H J Gangloff
Ad. Mgr.—K Leissner
DIE WELT (The World) (m-ex S) Est. 1946
Axel-Springer Platz 1; GKP 10888, 20355
Tel: (49-40) 34700; Fax: (49-40) 345514
Circ.—304,400 (mon.-fri.); 337,300 (sat.)
Prop.—Springer
Pub.—C Jacobi
Mng. Ed.—K J Fritzche
Ed. in Ch.—Dr. P Gillies
Ed. in Ch.—G Mumme
Ed.—W Baentsch
Ed.—H-W Einecke
Ed.—P Phillips
Ed.—H-J Schmahl
Bus. Mgr.—W Strum
Bus. Mgr.—D Rusche
Bus. Mgr.—J Degenhard
Ad. Mgr.—H Biehl
(This newspaper is nationally distributed.)

HAMELN
Pop. Est. 55,400

DEISTER-und WESERZEITUNG (5x wk.) Est. 1848
Baustr. 44; PF 101301, 31763
Tel: (49-5151) 2000; Fax: (49-5151) 200305
Circ.—77,100 ABC
Prop.—Niemeyer
Pub.—G Niemeyer
Pub.—H Niemeyer
Bus. Mgr.—B Gollan
Ad. Mgr.—H Körber

HAMM
Pop. Est. 166,000

WESTFÄLISCHER ANZEIGER (6x wk.) Est. 1821
Gutenbergstr. 1 (59065), PF 2727, 59017
Tel: (49-2381) 1050; Fax: (49-2381) 105239
Circ.—53,400
Prop.—Griebsch
Pub.—Dr. D Ippen
Ed. in Ch.—J Surholt
Ad./Bus. Mgr.—B Schmidt

HANAU
Pop. Est. 85,200

HANAUER ANZEIGER (The Hanauer Advertiser) (6x wk.) Est. 1725
Hammerstr. 9 (63450); PF 1945, 63409
Tel: (49-6181) 29030; Fax: (49-6181) 253999
Circ.—23,900 ABC
Prop.—Hanauer Anzeiger
Pub.—Dr. H Bauer
Mng. Ed.—H-H Schimpfermann
Ed. in Ch.—D Groos
Ad. Mgr.—Heidi Sickenberger

HANNOVER
Pop. Est. 514,400

HANNOVERSCHE ALLGEMEINE ZEITUNG (m-5x wk.) Est. 1949
Bemeroder Str. 58; GKP 30148, 30559
Tel: (49-511) 5180; Fax: (49-511) 513175
Circ.—249,600 ABC
Prop.—Madsack
Pub.—Luise Madsack
Mng. Ed./Ed. in Ch./Ed.—C von der Osten
Ed. in Ch./Ed.—U Neufert
Ed. in Ch.—Dr. W Mauersberg
Bus. Mgr.—V Jeuther
Ad. Mgr.—Helga Pieplow
NEUE PRESSE (The New Press) (d-6x wk.) Est. 1946
Bemeroder Str. 58, 30559
Tel: (49-511) 51031; Fax: (49-511) 5101275
Circ.—252,000 (mon.-fri.); 300,400 (sat.)
Prop.—Madsack
Mng. Ed.—U Rademacher
Ed. in Ch.—E Lutz
Ed.—R Mangold
Ad. Mgr./Bus. Mgr.—J Stern

HASSENFURT
(HAßENFURT)

HASSFURTER TAGEBLATT Est. 1868
Augsfelder Str. 19 (97437); PF 1313, 97430
Tel: (49-9521) 6990; Fax: (49-9521) 69911
Circ.—6,600
Prop.—Tageblatt-Druckerei
Pub.—J Gerhart
Ed. in Ch.—W Sandler
Bus. Mgr.—H Gerhart
Ad. Mgr.—P Zöller

HECHINGEN
Pop. Est. 10,600

HOHENZOLLERISCHE ZEITUNG (6x wk.) Est. 1945
Obertorplatz 19 (72379); PF 1264, 72372
Tel: (49-7471) 93150; Fax: (49-7471) 931550
Circ.—9,200 ABC
Prop.—Hohenzollerische Zeitung
Pub./Bus. Mgr.—Dr. E Konstanzer
Ed. in Ch.—E Wais
Ed.—E Klett
Ad. Mgr.—W Michler
(This is an edition of the Südwest Presse Ulm in Hechingen.)

HEIDE
Pop. Est. 20,700

DITHMARSCHER LANDESZEITUNG (6x wk.) Est. 1869
Wulf-Isebrand-Platz 1 (25746); PF 1880, 25738
Tel: (49-481) 6910; Fax: (49-481) 691261
Circ.—28,900 ABC
Prop.—Westholsteinische Verlagsanstalt
Pub.—U Boyens
Mng. Ed.—D Kienitz
Ed. in Ch.—K Kuppinger
Ed. in Ch.—G Wolf
Ad. Mgr.—K Böhlke

HEIDELBERG
Pop. Est. 136,200

RHEIN-NECKAR-ZEITUNG (6x wk.) Est. 1945
Hauptstr. 23 (69117); PF 104560, 69035
Tel: (49-6221) 5191; Fax: (49-6221) 519217
Circ.—114,400 ABC
Prop.—Rhein-Neckar-Zeitung GmbH
Mng. Ed.—Linde Fischer
Ed. in Ch./Bus. Mgr.—W Knorr
Ed. in Ch.—M Fritz
Ed. in Ch.—D Haas
Ad. Mgr.—W Siberzahn

HEIDENHEIM an der BRENZ
Pop. Est. 47,600

HEIDENHEIMER NEUE PRESSE (6x wk.) Est. 1962
Marienstr. 9 (89518); PF 1423, 89504
Tel: (49-7321) 3477; Fax: (49-7321) 347200
Circ.—9,000 ABC
Prop.—Heidenheimer Neue Presse
Pub.—K-H Wilhelm
Ed. in Ch.—Dr. M Allenhöfer
Bus. Mgr.—H-J Wilhelm
Ad. Mgr.—W Steinbuch
HEIDENHEIMER ZEITUNG (6x wk.) Est. 1849
Olgastr. 15; PF 1425, 89504
Tel: (49-7321) 3470; Fax: (49-7321) 347102
Circ.—36,600 ABC
Prop.—Heidenheimer Zeitung GmbH
Mng. Ed.—C Stäbler
Ed. in Ch.—N Pfisterer
Ed.—E Bachmann
Bus. Mgr.—H J Wilhelm
Ad. Mgr.—W Steinbuch
(This is an edition of the Südwest Press Ulm in Ulm.)

HEILBRONN
Pop. Est. 111,700

HEILBRONNER STIMME (The Heilbronner Voice) (6x wk.) Est. 1946
Allee 2 (74042); PF 2040, 74010
Tel: (49-7131) 6150; Fax: (49-7131) 615200
Circ.—106,500 ABC
Prop.—Heilbronner Stimme KG
Mng. Ed.—G Schwinghammer
Ed. in Ch.—U Jacobi
Ed. in Ch.—S Schilling
Ed.—W Bok
Bus. Mgr.—G Timmermann
Ad. Mgr.—H-J Klein

HEPPENHEIM
Pop. Est. 24,000

SÜDHESSISCHE POST (The South Hessen Post) (6x wk.) Est. 1858
Friedrichstr. 10 (64646); PF 1440, 64632
Tel: (49-6252) 1220; Fax: (49-6252) 122218
Circ.—9,999
Prop.—Südhessische Post
Bus. Mgr.—G Bucher
Bus. Mgr.—H Kreutzberger
Ad. Mgr.—P Wakter

HERFORD
Pop. Est. 59,500

HERFORDER KREISEBLATT (The Herforder District Paper) (6x wk.) Est. 1846
Brüderstr 30, 32052
Tel: (49-5221) 59080; Fax: (49-5221) 590816
Circ.—21,100 ABC
Prop.—Herforder Kreiseblatt

HERRENBERG
Pop. Est. 26,100

GÄUBOTE (6x wk.) Est. 1837
Horber Str. 42; PF 1161, 71070
Tel: (49-7032) 200494; Fax: (49-7032) 200459
Circ.—13,300 ABC
Prop.—Körner Verlag
Pub./Bus. Mgr./Ad. Mgr.—R Schöllkopf

HERSBRUCK
Pop. Est. 7,905

HERSBRUCKER ZEITUNG (6x wk.) Est. 1849
Nürnberger Str. 7 (91217), 91213
Tel: (49-9151) 73070; Fax: (49-9151) 2000
Circ.—9,000 ABC
Prop.—Pfeiffer
Pub.—E Pfeiffer
Pub.—B Schnell
Ad. Mgr.—K Kreissel

HERSFELD, BAD
Pop. Est. 27,200

HERSFELDER ZEITUNG (6x wk.) Est. 1763
Gutenbergstr. 1 (36251), 36247
Tel: (49-6621) 1610; Fax: (49-6621) 161157
Circ.—18,900 ABC
Prop.—Hoehl
Pub.—H-J Ott
Ed. in Ch.—P Lenz
Ed. in Ch.—A Zum Winkel
Bus. Mgr.—H F Otto
Ad. Mgr.—H Niemeyer

HERZBERG

HARZ KURIER (The Harz Messenger) (6x wk.) Est. 1969
Am Schlossbahnhof (37412); PF 1209, 37402
Tel: (49-5521) 8510; Fax: (49-5521) 85142
Circ.—22,100 ABC
Prop.—Jungfer Verlag
Ad. Mgr.—D Wege

HILDESHEIM
Pop. Est. 100,600

HILDESHEIMER ALLGEMEINE ZEITUNG (Hildesheim General News) (6x wk.) Est. 1705
Rathausstr 18 (31134); PF 100555, 31105
Tel: (49-5121) 1060; Fax: (49-5121) 106217
Circ.—52,500 ABC
Prop.—Gerstenberg
Pub.—Dr. B Gerstenberg
Mng. Ed.—P Hartmann
Ed. in Ch.—W Herbig
Ed. in Ch./Ed.—M Aden
Bus. Mgr.—G Uckrow
Ad. Mgr.—G von Holt

HOF
Pop. Est. 50,600

FRANKENPOST (6x wk.) Est. 1945
Poststr. 9 (95028), 95012
Tel: (49-9281) 8160; Fax: (49-9281) 816283
Circ.—117,600 ABC
Prop.—Frankenpost Verlag GmbH
Pub./Bus. Mgr.—H Wilhelms
Mng. Ed.—G Hossel
Ed. in Ch./Ed.—W Mergner
Ad. Mgr.—H Niederländer

HOLZMINDEN
Pop. Est. 21,100

TÄGLICHER ANZEIGER (The Daily Advertiser) (d-6x wk.) Est. 1777
Zeppelinstr. 10; PF 1453, 375603
Tel: (49-5531) 9340; Fax: (49-5531) 930441
Circ.—12,700 ABC
Prop.—Hupke & Sohn
Pub./Ed. in Ch.—K Mahnkopf
Pub.—Erna Hüpke
Pub.—Gerlinde Mahnkopf
Bus. Mgr./Ad. Mgr.—Constanze Mahnkopf

HONNEF, BAD
Pop. Est. 20,500

HONNEFER VOLKSZEITUNG (6x wk.) Est. 1881
Hauptstr. 38f (53604); PF 1360, 53583
Tel: (49-2224) 2075/(49-2224) 2722; Fax: (49-2224) 79494
Circ.—6,200
Prop.—Honnefer Volkszeitung Verlag
Pub./Bus. Mgr.—F J Kayser
Mng. Ed.—K Hoffstadt
Ed. in Ch./Ed.—Roswitha Oschmann
Ed. in Ch.—V Francke
Bus. Mgr.—P Böhmer

HOYERSWERDA

HOYERSWERDAER TAGEBLATT (6x wk.) German; Est. 1992
Friedrichsstr. 9, 02977
Tel: (49-3571) 48250; Fax: (49-3571) 8728
Prop.—Hoyerswerdaer Wochenblatt Verlag
Ed. in Ch.—F Treue
Bus. Mgr.—S Matsch

IBBENBUEREN
(IBBENBÜREN)
Pop. Est. 42,700

IBBENBÜRENER VOLKSZEITUNG (6x wk.) Est. 1898
Wilhelmstr. 240 (49479); PF 1363, 49463
Tel: (49-5451) 9330; Fax: (49-5451) 933192
Circ.—17,600 ABC
Prop.—Ibbenbürener Vereindruckerei
Bus. Mgr.—G Rieping
Ad. Mgr.—D Steinheimer

IMMENSTADT

ALLGÄUER ANZEIGEBLATT (6x wk.) Est. 1860
Kirchplatz 6, 87509
Tel: (49-8323) 8020; Fax: (49-8323) 802134
Circ.—21,400 ABC
Prop.—Eberl Verlag
Pub.—G Fürst von Waldburg zu Zeil
Pub./Bus. Mgr.—H Eberl
Pub.—G Holland
Ad. Mgr.—R Moser

INGOLSTADT
Pop. Est. 92,600

DONAUKURIER (The Danube Messenger) (6x wk.) Est. 1871
Stauffenbergstr. 2a (85051); PF 100259, 85002
Tel: (49-841) 96660; Fax: (49-841) 9666255
Circ.—88,300 ABC
Prop.—Donaukurier Verlagsges
Pub.—E Reissmüller
Mng. Ed.—H Ege
Ed. in Ch.—F Kraft
Bus. Mgr.—Dr. G Heyne
Ad. Mgr.—T Scherf-Clavel

ISERLOHN
Pop. Est. 89,500

ISERLOHNER KREISANZEIGER und ZEITUNG (6x wk.) Est. 1842
Theodor-Heuss-Ring 4 (58636); PF 1742, 58587
Tel: (49-2371) 82205; Fax: (49-2371) 8220
Circ.—34,100 ABC
Prop.—Iserlohn Zeitungsverlag
Pub.—Gertrud Wichelhoven
Ed. in Ch./Bus. Mgr.—K H Wichelhoven
Ad. Mgr.—L Plattes

ITZEHOE
Pop. Est. 31,700

NORDDEUTSCHE RUNDSCHAU (6x wk.) Est. 1817
Sandberg 18, 25524
Tel: (49-4821) 605140; Fax: (49-4821) 605144
Circ.—24,800 ABC
Prop.—Schleswig-Holsteinischer Zeitungsverlag

JEVER
Pop. Est. 10,094

JEVERSCHES WOCHENBLATT (6x wk.) Est. 1791
Wangerstr. 14 (26441); PF 120, 26435
Tel: (49-4461) 9440; Fax: (49-4461) 944119
Circ.—9,500 ABC
Prop.—Mettcker
Pub.—H Allmers
Pub.—Elisabeth Allmers
Ed. in Ch.—H Burlager
Ed.—K-D Heimann
Bus. Mgr.—H Loerts-Sabin
Ad. Mgr.—G Doden

KARLSRUHE
Pop. Est. 268,300

BADISCHE NEUESTE NACHRICHTEN (6x wk.) Est. 1946
Linkenheimer Landstr. 133 (76149); PF 311168, 76141
Tel: (49-721) 7890; Fax: (49-721) 789155/(49-721) 7825719
Circ.—177,400 ABC
Prop.—Badische Neueste Nachrichten
Pub.—H W Baur
Mng. Ed./Ed. in Ch.—W D Eberlein
Ed. in Ch.—H Gottmann
Ed. in Ch.—H Kopplestätter
Ed. in Ch.—Dr. G Capell
Bus. Mgr.—J Bauder
Ad. Mgr.—H Hinrichs

KASSEL
Pop. Est. 185,400

HNA HESSISCHE/NIEDERSACHSISCHE ALLGEMEINE (6x wk.) Est. 1945
Frankfurter Str. 168 (34121); PF 101009, 34010
Tel: (49-561) 20300; Fax: (49-561) 20306

Europe Germany, Federal Republic of IV-21

Circ.—300,700 ABC
Prop.—Dierichs
Pub./Bus. Mgr.—Dr. D Batz
Ed. in Ch.—L Orzechowski
Ad. Mgr.—H Prehm

KEMPTEN
(Allgau)
Pop. Est. 57,000

ALLGÄUER ZEITUNG (6x wk.) Est. 1968
Kotternerstr. 64 (87435); PF 1129, 87401
Tel: (49-831) 2060; Fax: (49-831) 29001
Circ.—121,800 ABC
Prop.—Allgäuer Zeitungsverlag
Pub.—G Fürst von Waldburg zu Zeil
Pub.—G Holland
Mng. Ed.—H Köning
Ed. in Ch.—H Hojer
Bus. Mgr.—M Brehm
Ad. Mgr.—M Müller

KIEL
Pop. Est. 243,600

KIELER NACHRICHTEN (The Kieler News) (6x wk.) Est. 1864
Fleethörn 1 (24103); PF 1111, 24100
Tel: (49-431) 9030; Fax: (49-431) 903935
Circ.—127,200 ABC
Prop.—Kieler Nachrichten
Mng. Ed./Ed. in Ch./Ed.—Dr. R-J Schröder
Ed. in Ch.—J Heinemann
Bus. Mgr.—C Heinrich
Bus. Mgr.—Dr. H Grote
Ad. Mgr.—R A Bumke

KIRCHHEIM UNTER TECK
Pop. Est. 34,000

DER TECKBOTE (6x wk.) Est. 1832
Alleenstr. 158 (73230); PF 1553, 73223
Tel: (49-7021) 97500; Fax: (49-7021) 975033
Circ.—18,000 ABC
Prop.—Gottlieb & Osswald
Pub./Ed. in Ch./Bus. Mgr.—Dr. C Gottlieb
Ed. in Ch./Ed.—Barbara Ibsch

KOBLENZ
Pop. Est. 110,300

RHEIN-ZEITUNG (m-6x wk.) Est. 1948
August-Horch. Str. 28 (56070); PF 1540, 56015
Tel: (49-261) 89200; Fax: (49-261) 892476
Circ.—257,900 ABC
Prop.—Mittlerhein- Verlag GmbH
Mng. Ed.—U Momber
Mng. Ed.—J Türk
Ed. in Ch./Ed.—K Forster
Ed. in Ch.—H Schilling
Bus. Mgr.—W Twer
Ad. Mgr.—K-H Muckelbauer

KOENIGSHOFEN, BAD
(KÖNIGSHOFEN, BAD)
Pop. Est. 3,549

BOTE vom GRABFELD (d) Est. 1880
Hindenburgstr. 28 (97631); PF 1329, 97628
Tel: (49-9761) 844; Fax: (49-9761) 6266
Circ.—3,400
Prop.—Schunk
Pub./Bus. Mgr.—R Schunk

KONSTANZ
Pop. Est. 70,500

SÜDKURIER (The Southern Messenger) (m-6x wk.) Est. 1945
Max-Stromeyer-Str. 178 (78467); PF 102001, 78420
Tel: (49-7531) 9990; Fax: (49-7531) 999485
Circ.—153,500 ABC
Prop.—Südkurier
Ed. in Ch./Ed.—D Wacker
Ed. in Ch.—W Schwarzwälder
Ad. Mgr.—A Schillinger

KORBACH
Pop. Est. 22,200

WALDECKISCHE LANDESZEITUNG (The Waldeckische District News) (6x wk.) Est. 1887
Lengefelder Str. 6 (34497); PF 1780, 34487
Tel: (49-5631) 56009; Fax: (49-5631) 6994
Circ.—30,100 ABC
Prop.—Bing

Pub./Ed. in Ch./Bus. Mgr.—Dr. W Bing
Pub.—Dr. H Bing
Ed. in Ch./Ed.—H-H Strippel
Ad. Mgr.—H Verlage

KORNWESTHEIM
Pop. Est. 27,000

KORNWESTHEIMER ZEITUNG (6x wk.) Est. 1907
Rechbergstr. 10 (70806); PF 1760, 70799
Tel: (49-7154) 13120; Fax: (49-7154) 131270
Circ.—6,200 ABC
Prop.—Reichert
Pub./Bus. Mgr.—H Reichert
Ed.—R Schuldt

KULMBACH
Pop. Est. 27,400

BAYERISCHE RUNDSCHAU (6x wk.) Est. 1902
E-C-Baumann-Str. 5 (95326); PF 1149, 95301
Tel: (49-9221) 9490; Fax: (49-9221) 949378
Circ.—18,100 ABC
Prop.—Baumann Verlag
Pub.—H Uhlemann
Ed. in Ch.—T Lange
Ed.—H-D Stutze
Bus. Mgr.—H O Korndörfer
Ad. Mgr.—H Schmidt

LAHR
Pop. Est. 34,600

LAHRER ZEITUNG (6x wk.) Est. 1794
Schillerstr. 14, 77933
Tel: (49-7821) 27830; Fax: (49-7821) 2783910
Circ.—16,100 ABC
Prop.—Lahrer Zeitung
Pub.—J Schauenburg
Ed. in Ch.—H Bosshammer
Ed. in Ch.—P Kürschner
Bus. Mgr.—C D Beck
Ad. Mgr.—O Kalt

LAMPERTHEIM
Pop. Est. 30,700

LAMPERTHEIMER ZEITUNG (6x wk.) Est. 1876
Ernst-Ludwig-Str. 5 (68623); PF 1260, 68602
Tel: (49-6206) 4041; Fax: (49-6206) 4043
Circ.—5,600 ABC
Prop.—Möck
Bus. Mgr.—E Möck

LANDSBERG am LECH
Pop. Est. 20,200

LANDSBERGER TAGBLATT (6x wk.)
Dominikus-Zimmermann-Str. 5, 86899
Tel: (49-8191) 3147; Fax: (49-8191) 3117
Circ.—16,400 ABC
Prop.—Presse-Druck GmbH

LANDSHUT
Pop. Est. 57,100

LANDSHUTER ZEITUNG (6x wk.) Est. 1849
Altstadt 89 (84028); PF 586, 84003
Tel: (49-871) 8500; Fax: (49-871) 850132
Circ.—58,800 ABC
Prop.—Thomann
Mng. Ed.—Dr. Gabriele Goderbauer
Bus. Mgr.—Dr. H Balle
Ad. Mgr.—A Mooser

LAUF an der PEGNITZ
Pop. Est. 22,200

PEGNITZ-ZEITUNG (5x wk.) Est. 1905
Nürnberger Str. 19 (91207), 91192
Tel: (49-9123) 1750; Fax: (49-9123) 3050
Circ.—14,200 ABC
Prop.—Fahner & Verlag Nürnberger Presse
Pub.—F Brandmüller
Pub.—L Herrmann
Pub.—B Schnell
Ad. Mgr.—K Kreissel

LAUTERBERG, BAD
Pop. Est. 10,129

BAD LAUTERBERGER TAGEBLATT (6x wk.) Est. 1854
Haupstr. 38 (37431); PF 1241, 37422
Tel: (49-5524) 85000; Fax: (49-5524) 850039

Germany, Federal Republic of — Europe

Circ.—3,800 ABC
Prop.—Kohlmann
Pub.—C Kohlmann
Bus. Mgr.—K Schmidt

LEER
(Ostfriesland)
Pop. Est. 30,100

OSTFRIESEN ZEITUNG (6x wk.) Est. 1945
Maiburger Str. 8; PF 1860, 26789
Tel: (49-491) 8040; Fax: (49-491) 804129
Circ.—46,400 ABC
Prop.—Ostfriesen Zeitung
Mng. Ed.—J Kaymer
Ed. in Ch.—B Fokken
Bus. Mgr.—H Hoppmann
Ad. Mgr.—H D Hoppen

LEIPZIG
Pop. Est. 507,800

LEIPZIGER VOLKSZEITUNG (m-6x wk.) Est. 1894
Petersstienweg 19, 04107
Tel: (49-341) 21810; Fax: (49-341) 311948
Circ.—393,800 ABC
Prop.—Leipziger Verlags & Druckereiges
Mng. Ed.—A Rentzch
Ed. in Ch./Ed.—P von Wilcke
Ed. in Ch.—H Hochstein
Bus. Mgr.—A H Wanke
Ad. Mgr.—A Müller

LEONBERG
Pop. Est. 40,200

LEONBERGER KREISZEITUNG (Leonberg District News) (6x wk.) Est. 1833
Stuttgarter Str. 7; PF 1562, 71205
Tel: (49-7152) 9370; Fax: (49-7152) 937202
Circ.—17,800 ABC
Prop.—Leonberger Kreiszeitung Verlag
Mng. Ed.—R Oldewemme
Ed. in Ch.—K Geibel
Ed. in Ch.—A Steinmann
Bus. Mgr.—H Krauss
Ad. Mgr.—H Pflüger

LEUTKIRCH

SCHWÄBISCHE ZEITUNG (dS) Est. 1945
Rudolph-Roth-Str. 18 (88299); PF 1145, 88291
Tel: (49-7561) 800; Fax: (49-7561) 80134
Circ.—205,000
Prop.—Schwäbischer Verlag
Bus. Mgr.—Dr. U Kolb
Bus. Mgr.—V Liebel
Ad. Mgr.—F J Wunden

LICHTENFELS
Pop. Est. 20,000

OBERMAIN-TAGBLATT (6x wk.) Est. 1857
Hirtenstr. 5; PF 1409, 96204
Tel: (49-9571) 7880; Fax: (49-9571) 70689
Circ.—14,200 ABC
Prop.—Meister
Ed.—Cornelia Herrmann
Ad. Mgr.—Christa Robisch

LIPPSTADT
Pop. Est. 60,100

DER PATRIOT (The Patriot) (6x wk.) Est. 1848
Hansastr. 2 (59557); PF 2350, 59533
Tel: (49-2941) 20100; Fax: (49-2941) 201285
Circ.—30,500 ABC
Prop.—Der Patriot Zietungsverlag
Pub.—Dr. R Laumanns
Pub.—Dr. M Laumanns
Ed. in Ch.—G Böer
Bus. Mgr.—W Bunsmann
Bus. Mgr.—K Jacobs
Ad. Mgr.—C Koteras

LOERRACH
(LÖRRACH)
Pop. Est. 41,200

OBERBADISCHES VOLKSBLATT (6x wk.) Est. 1885
Tumringer Str. 209; PF 2040, 79510
Tel: (49-7621) 40330; Fax: (49-7621) 13236
Circ.—22,500 ABC

Prop.—Oberbadisches Verlagshaus
Pub./Bus. Mgr.—Dr. H Jaumann
Ed. in Ch.—G Neidinger
Ad. Mgr.—M Zöbelin
(This is an edition of the Badische Zeitung in Freiburg.)

LOHR
Pop. Est. 11,322

LÖHRER ZEITUNG (d-6x wk.) Est. 1883
Farbergasse 19; PF 350, 97804
Tel: (49-9352) 2252; Fax: (49-9352) 6717
Circ.—1,500
Prop.—Keller Verlag
Pub.—Juliane Sommer
Ed.—K Anderlohr
Bus. Mgr.—H Wilczok
(This is an edition of the Main Post in Würzburg.)

LUDWIGSBURG
Pop. Est. 76,900

LUDWIGSBURGER KREISZEITUNG (The Ludwigsburg District News) (6x wk.) Est. 1818
Körnerstr. 14; PF 1040, 71634
Tel: (49-7141) 1300; Fax: (49-7141) 921426
Circ.—50,600 ABC
Prop.—Ungeheuer & Ulmer
Pub.—K Ulmer
Ed. in Ch./Ed.—H Spresser
Ed. in Ch.—W Simonis
Ad. Mgr.—J Merkle

LUDWIGSHAFEN am RHEIN
Pop. Est. 152,200

DIE RHEINPFALZ (m-6x wk.) Est. 1945
Amtsstr. 5 (67059); PF 211147, 67011
Tel: (49-621) 590201; Fax: (49-621) 5902297
Circ.—258,100 ABC
Prop.—Rheinpfalz Verlag
Pub.—Medien Union
Mng. Ed./Ed. in Ch./Ed.—G Krall
Ed. in Ch.—M Garthe
Bus. Mgr.—R Bilz
Ad. Mgr.—E Erbacher

LUEBECK
(LÜBECK)
Pop. Est. 209,200

LÜBECKER NACHRICHTEN/LÜBECKER NACHRICHTEN am SONNTAG (e-5x wk.) Est. 1946
Herrenholz 10; GKP 23543, 23556
Tel: (49-451) 1440; Fax: (49-451) 1441022
Circ.—134,100 ABC
Prop.—Lübecker Nachrichten
Pub./Ed.—J Wessel
Mng. Ed.—H S Müller
Ed. in Ch./Ed.—A Hauenschild
Ed. in Ch./Ed.—H-W Neubacher
Bus. Mgr.—Dr. G Semmerow
Bus. Mgr.—M Meyer-Böhm
Ad. Mgr.—J Rühmling

LUECHOW
(LÜCHOW)
Pop. Est. 5,942

ELBE-JEETZEL-ZEITUNG (6x wk.) Est. 1854
Wallstr. 22; PF 1163, 29431
Tel: (49-5841) 1270; Fax: (49-5841) 12750
Circ.—15,500 ABC
Prop.—Köhring
Mng. Ed.—J Feuerriegel
Ed. in Ch.—H-H Müller
Ed.—H Jung
Bus. Mgr.—W Köpper
Ad. Mgr.—G Böhme

LUEDENSCHEID
(LÜDENSCHEID)
Pop. Est. 73,400

LÜDENSCHEIDER NACHRICHTEN (The Luedenscheid News) (6x wk.) Est. 1854
Schillerstr. 20; GKP 58505, 58511
Tel: (49-2351) 1580; Fax: (49-2351) 158281
Circ.—21,300 ABC
Prop.—Märkischer Zeitungsverlag

Pub.—H Medernach
Ed. in Ch.—H-J Rittinghaus
Bus. Mgr./Ad. Mgr.—B Herzberger

LUENEBURG
(LÜNEBURG)
Pop. Est. 59,500

LANDESZEITUNG für die LÜNEBERGER HEIDE (5x wk.) Est. 1946
Am Sande 16 (21335); PF 2125, 21311
Tel: (49-4131) 7400; Fax: (49-4131) 740225
Circ.—36,900 ABC
Prop.—Landeszeitung für die Lüneburger Heide
Pub.—E Wiesemann
Pub.—A Bergmann
Pub.—T von Stern
Mng. Ed.—R Dubaschny
Ed. in Ch./Ed.—G Reiling
Ed. in Ch.—C Steiner
Ad. Mgr.—D Borchardt

NIEDERSÄCHSISCHES TAGEBLATT (5x wk.)
Am Sande 18; PF 2320, 21335
Tel: (49-4131) 44009; Fax: (49-4131) 46291
Circ.—151,900
Prop.—Niedersächsischer Zeitungsverlag
Ed. in Ch.—C Steiner

MAGDEBURG
Pop. Est. 278,807

MAGDEBURG ER VOLKSSTIMME (The Magdeburger People's Voice) (m-6x wk.) Est. 1890
Bahnhof Str. 17 (39104); PF 3469, 39011
Tel: (49-391) 59990; Fax: (49-391) 5999400
Circ.—335,300 ABC
Prop.—Madgeburger Verlags & Druckhaus
Pub.—H Bauer
Mng. Ed.—T Rauwald
Mng. Ed.—Dr. R Bartlit
Ed. in Ch.—Dr. H Oette
Ed.—Dr. W Kirkamm
Bus. Mgr.—K Lange
Bus. Mgr.—H von Pupka
Ad. Mgr.—U Levening

MAINBURG
Pop. Est. 6,319

HALLERTAUER ZEITUNG (6x wk.) Est. 1879
Gabelbergerstr. 13; PF 1320, 84044
Tel: (49-8751) 730; Fax: (49-8751) 7338
Circ.—6,100 ABC
Prop.—Pinsker
Pub.—H Pinsker
Ad. Mgr.—E Schott

MAINTAL
Pop. Est. 36,600

MAINTAL TAGESANZEIGER (The Maintal Daily Advertiser) (6x wk.) Est. 1978
Kennedystr. 44 (63477); PF 1269, 63462
Tel: (49-6181) 40900; Fax: (49-6181) 495988
Circ.—7,200
Pub.—Maintal Tagesanzeiger Verlag
Ed. in Ch.—U Trageser
Bus. Mgr.—R Brandl

MAINZ
Pop. Est. 189,000

ALLGEMEINE ZEITUNG (m-6x wk.) Est. 1850
Grosse Bleiche 44 (55116); PF 3120, 55021
Tel: (49-6131) 1440; Fax: (49-6131) 144577
Circ.—144,500 ABC
Prop.—Verlaggsgruppe Rhein Main
Mng. Ed.—K Nath
Ed. in Ch./Ed.—J Friedenberg
Ed. in Ch./Ed.—K Rhein
Ed. in Ch./Ed.—U Zink
Ed. in Ch.—K Beck
Bus. Mgr.—K Röthemeier
Bus. Mgr.—E Helfterich
Ad. Mgr.—W Dähn

MANNHEIM
Pop. Est. 294,600

MANNHEIMER MORGEN (Mannheimer Morning) (m-5x wk.) Est. 1946
R 1, 4; PF 121231, 68063
Tel: (49-621) 39201; Fax: (49-621) 3921376
Circ.—110,900 ABC
Prop.—Mannheimer Morgen
Pub.—Dr. K Ackermann
Pub.—R von Schilling
Mng. Ed.—H Reinhardt
Ed. in Ch.—S Heilmann
Ed. in Ch.—H D Schiele
Bus. Mgr.—M Bangerth
Ad. Mgr.—G Haeberle

MARBACH
Pop. Est. 10,402

MARBACHER ZEITUNG (6x wk.) Est. 1845
Charlottenstr. 4 (71672); PF 1118, 71666
Tel: (49-7144) 85000; Fax: (49-7144) 85000
Circ.—6,800 ABC
Prop.—Remppis
Pub./Bus. Mgr.—H Keller
Pub.—Brigitte Altehoefer
Mng. Ed.—H Schwarz
Ed. in Ch.—Elke Orth
Ad. Mgr.—R Demel

MARBURG
Pop. Est. 77,100

OBERHESSISCHE PRESSE (6x wk.) Est. 1866
Franz-Tuczek-Weg 1 (35039); PF 1829, 35007
Tel: (49-6421) 4090; Fax: (49-6421) 409302
Circ.—34,300 ABC
Prop.—Koch
Pub.—Dr. W Hitzeroth
Mng. Ed.—M Döringer
Ed. in Ch.—P-J Raue
Bus. Mgr.—R Sandmann
Ad. Mgr.—E Wilms

MARKTOBERDORF
Pop. Est. 10,086

ALLGÄUER ZEITUNG (The General News) (6x wk.)
Jahnstr. 7 (87616); PF 1352, 87611
Tel: (49-8342) 5011; Fax: (49-8342) 40273
Circ.—10,100 ABC
Prop.—Schnitzer
Pub.—G Fürst von Waldburg zu Zeil
Pub.—G Holland
Bus. Mgr./Ad. Mgr.—M Kraus

MARNE
Pop. Est. 5,270

MARNER ZEITUNG (6x wk.)
Norderstr. 9, 25709
Tel: (49-4851) 859417; Fax: (49-4851) 97999
Circ.—3,400
Prop.—Schleswig-Holsteinischer Zeitungsverlag
Ed.—H Maue
Ed.—F Buchholz

MEINERZHAGEN
Pop. Est. 17,198

MEINERZHAGENER ZEITUNG (6x wk.) Est. 1911
Haupstr. 42 (58540); PF 1462, 58530
Tel: (49-2354) 9270; Fax: (49-2354) 927126
Circ.—8,300 ABC
Prop.—Märkischer Zeitungverlag
Ad. Mgr.—B Herzberger

MELLRICHSTADT

RHÖN und STREUBOTE (6x wk.) Est. 1875
Friedenstr. 9 (97638); PF 26, 97634
Tel: (49-9776) 6687; Fax: (49-9776) 7138
Circ.—3,300 ABC
Prop.—Mack Verlag
Pub./Bus. Mgr.—R Mack
Ed. in Ch.—D Hilscher
Ed. in Ch.—B Stadtler
Ad. Mgr.—Frau I Mack

MEMMINGEN
Pop. Est. 37,300

MEMMINGER ZEITUNG (6x wk.)
Schrannenplatz 6 (87700); PF 1651, 87686
Tel: (49-8331) 109170; Fax: (49-8331) 109188
Circ.—23,800 ABC
Prop.—Memminger Zeitung
Pub./Bus. Mgr.—T Schuster
Ed. in Ch.—G Walcz
Ad. Mgr.—R Ebner

MENDEN
Pop. Est. 52,200

MENDENER ZEITUNG (6x wk.) Est. 1860
Kolpingstr. 35 (58706); PF 460, 58685
Tel: (49-2373) 1730; Fax: (49-2373) 17315
Circ.—6,600 ABC
Prop.—Riedel
Pub.—Dr. D Ippen
Bus. Mgr.—B Schmidt
Ad. Mgr.—O Dellmann

MERGENTHEIM, BAD
Pop. Est. 12,418

TAUBER-ZEITUNG (6x wk.) Est. 1791
Ledermarkt 8 (97980); PF 1804, 97968
Tel: (49-7931) 5960; Fax: (49-7931) 59644
Circ.—6,800 ABC
Prop.—Thomm
Pub.—Ellen Wahl
Ed. in Ch./Ed.—T Weller
Ed. in Ch.—C P Mühleck
Bus. Mgr.—M Wahl
Ad. Mgr.—Ariane Kolb
(This an edition of the Südwest Presse Ulm in Ulm.)

METZINGEN
Pop. Est. 13,641

SÜDWEST PRESSE (6x wk.) Est. 1830
Friedrichstr. 12 (72555); PF 1163, 72542
Tel: (49-7123) 42015; Fax: (49-7123) 42019
Circ.—13,700 ABC
Prop.—Hauser Verlag
Bus. Mgr.—Dr. G Hauser
Bus. Mgr.—Dr. T Hauser
Ad. Mgr.—A Weber
(This is an edition of the Südwest Presse Ulm in Ulm.)

MINDEN
Pop. Est. 75,400

MINDENER TAGEBLATT (6x wk.) Est. 1856
Obermarktr. 26 (32423); PF 2140, 32378
Tel: (49-571) 8820; Fax: (49-571) 882240
Circ.—40,000 ABC
Prop.—Bruns
Pub.—R Thomas
Ed. in Ch./Ed.—T Traue
Ed. in Ch.—C Pepper
Bus. Mgr./Ad. Mgr.—H Bornemann

MUEHLACKER
(MÜHLACKER)
Pop. Est. 23,800

MÜHLACKER TAGBLATT (6x wk.) Est. 1890
Kisslingweg 35; PF 1351, 75415
Tel: (49-7041) 8050; Fax: (49-7041) 80570
Circ.—9,800 ABC
Prop.—Elser Verlag
Pub./Bus. Mgr.—Brigitte Wetzel-Händle
Ad. Mgr.—H Mayer

MUENCHBERG
(MÜNCHBERG)
Pop. Est. 10,362

MÜNCHBERG-HELMBRECHSTER ZEITUNG FRANKENPOST (6x wk.) Est. 1838
Eibenstr. 15 (95213); PF 460, 95204
Tel: (49-9251) 450; Fax: (49-9251) 45100
Circ.—9,600 ABC
Prop.—Frankenpost & Münchberg-Helmbrechtser Zeitung Verlag
Pub.—Dr. Melitta Wirth
Ed. in Ch.—H L Wolfrum
Bus. Mgr.—W Herold
Ad. Mgr.—Angelika Wolfrum

MUENSINGEN
(MÜNSINGEN)
Pop. Est. 4,099

ALB BOTE (d-6x wk.) Est. 1839
Gutenbergstr. 1; PF 1150, 72521
Tel: (49-7381) 1870; Fax: (49-7381) 18735
Circ.—5,600 ABC
Prop.—Baader Neue Presseges
Ed. in Ch.—Susanne Leimstoll
Bus. Mgr.—Dr. H Schomaker
Ad. Mgr.—H Schepper
(This is an edition of the Südwest Presse Ulm in Ulm.)

MUENSTER
(MÜNSTER)
Pop. Est. 267,600

MÜNSTERSCHE ZEITUNG (6x wk.) Est. 1870
Neubrückenstr. 8 (48143); PF 5560, 48030
Tel: (49-251) 5920; Fax: (49-251) 592213
Circ.—74,600 ABC
Prop.—Lensing Wolff
Pub./Bus. Mgr.—F Lensing-Wolff
Mng. Ed./Ed. in Ch.—G Bothe
Ed. in Ch.—C J Spritzer
Ed. in Ch.—Dr. R R Koerner
Ad. Mgr.—K J Biele

WESTFÄLISCHE NACHRICHTEN/ZENO ZEITUNGEN (6x wk.) Est. 1946
Soester Str. 13, 48155
Tel: (49-251) 6900; Fax: (49-251) 690717
Circ.—241,100 ABC
Prop.—Aschendorff
Mng. Ed.—H Dieckmann
Ed. in Ch./Ed.—R Bage
Ed. in Ch.—J Springensguth
Ad. Mgr.—J Hoppe

MUNICH
(MÜNCHEN)
Pop. Est. 1,236,500

ABENDZEITUNG (The Evening News) (e-5x wk.) Est. 1948
Sendlingerstr. 10 (80002); PF 200202, 80265
Tel: (49-89) 23770; Fax: (49-89) 2377729
Circ.—256,900 ABC
Prop.—Die Abendzeitung Verlag
Pub.—H Anneliese
Pub.—Dr. J Friedmann
Mng. Ed.—A Rietzler
Mng. Ed.—D Kühnel
Ed. in Ch./Ed.—J Reiss
Ed. in Ch.—Dr. U Zimmer
Ed. in Ch.—F Mertgen
Bus. Mgr./Ad. Mgr.—F Mattes

MÜNCHNER MERKUR (5x wk.) Est. 1946
Paul-Heyse-Str. 2 (80336); PF 201401, 80014
Tel: (49-89) 53060; Fax: (49-89) 5306651
Circ.—210,000 ABC
Prop.—Münchener Zeitungsverlag
Pub.—B Kotting
Mng. Ed.—A Liegsalz
Ed. in Ch.—W Giers
Bus. Mgr.—Dr. F Meik
Ad. Mgr.—R Liebelt

SÜDDEUTSCHE ZEITUNG (m-5x wk.) Est. 1945
Sendlingerstr. 80, 80331
Tel: (49-89) 21830; Fax: (49-89) 2183787
Circ.—458,900 ABC
Prop.—Süddeutscher Verlag GmbH
Mng. Ed.—U Schulze
Ed. in Ch.—D Schröder
Ed. in Ch.—G Sittner
Bus. Mgr.—U Gehrhardt
Ad. Mgr.—H-J Grossmann

TZ (5x wk.) Est. 1968
Paul-Heyse-Str. 2-4 (80336); PF 201401, 80014
Tel: (49-89) 53060; Fax: (49-89) 5306552
Circ.—195,300 ABC
Prop.—Zeitungsverlag tz
Pub.—Dr. D Ippen
Mng. Ed.—J Schiessl
Ed. in Ch.—H Riehl
Ed. in Ch.—H Stegmann
Bus. Mgr.—Dr. F Meik
Ad. Mgr.—R Liebelt

MURRHARDT
Pop. Est. 11,071

MURRHARDTER ZEITUNG (The Murrhardter News) (6x wk.) Est. 1884
Grabenstr. 23; PF 1262, 71535
Tel: (49-7192) 8016; Fax: (49-7192) 8019
Circ.—3,900 ABC
Prop.—Murrhardter Zeitungsverlag
Ed. in Ch.—H Claus
Ed.—U Mayer
Bus. Mgr./Ad. Mgr.—F Mauser

NEU-ISENBURG
(Frankfurt Metro Area)
Pop. Est. 35,200

ÄRZTE ZEITUNG (5x wk.) Est. 1982
Am Forsthaus Gravenbruch 5; PF 101047, 63264
Tel: (49-6102) 5060; Fax: (49-6102) 506123/(49-6102) 58870
Circ.—48,600 ABC
Prop.—Ärzte Zeitungsverlag
Mng. Ed.—M Schürmann
Ed. in Ch.—H Rudolph
Ed.—K-F Erdmann
Ed.—H Laschet
Bus. Mgr.—G Kosaris
Bus. Mgr.—Dr. R Hennigs
Ad. Mgr.—Ute Krille
(This newspaper is nationally distributed.)

HÜRRIYET (7x wk.) Turkish
Admiral-Rosendahl-Str. 3a; PF 4014, 63263
Tel: (49-69) 697030; Fax: (49-69) 691075
Circ.—105,600 ABC
Prop.—Hürriyet Int'l. Verlag
Pub.—E Simavi
Ed.—N Akkutay
Ed.—E Erdogmus
Bus. Mgr.—T Cebeci

TERCÜMAN (7x wk.) Turkish
Admiral-Rosendahl-Str. 3b, 63263
Tel: (49-69) 6970010
Circ.—35,000
Prop.—Tercüman Internat

TÜRKIYE (7x wk.) Turkish
Dornhofstr. 38, 63263
Tel: (49-6102) 27024; Fax: (49-6102) 8941
Circ.—55,000
Ed. in Ch.—F Ergüm
Ad. Mgr.—M Z Koradays

NEUBRANDENBURG
Pop. Est. 89,284

NORDKURIER (The Northern Messenger) (6x wk.) Est. 1990
Flurstr. 2 (17034); PF 1528, 17005
Tel: (49-395) 1528; Fax: (49-395) 45750
Circ.—159,200 ABC
Prop.—Kurier Verlag
Mng. Ed.—W Stieglitz
Mng. Ed.—N Glamann
Ed. in Ch.—G Deckl
Ed.—J Spreemann
Ed.—D Granzow
Bus. Mgr.—R Lindner
Ad. Mgr.—A Pöller

NEUENBUERG
(NEUENBÜRG)

DER ENZTÄLER (6x wk.) Est. 1845
Bahnhofstr. 5 (75305); PF 1265, 75302
Tel: (49-7082) 60466; Fax: (49-7082) 20878
Circ.—5,300 ABC
Prop.—Neuenbürger Verlagsdruckerei
Pub./Bus. Mgr.—G Biesinger
Ad. Mgr.—P Kretschmer

NEUMUENSTER
(NEUMÜNSTER)
Pop. Est. 77,900

HOLSTEINISCHER COURIER (6x wk.) Est. 1871
Gänsemarkt 1, 24534
Tel: (49-4321) 94460; Fax: (49-4321) 946224
Circ.—20,100 ABC
Prop.—Wachholtz
Pub.—U Wachholtz
Pub.—Dr. Gisela Wachholtz
Ed. in Ch.—H Loose
Ed. in Ch.—K Lutter
Bus. Mgr.—W Kardel
Ad. Mgr.—J Kalkowski

NEUSS
Pop. Est. 143,800

NEUSS-GREVENBROICHER ZEITUNG (6x wk.) Est. 1874
Moselstr. 14 (41464); PF 101152, 41411
Tel: (49-2131) 40404; Fax: (49-2131) 404249
Circ.—52,600 ABC
Prop.—Neusser Zeitungsverlag
Ed. in Ch.—B Pütz
Ed.—L Baten
Ed.—Dr. H Brinkmann
Bus. Mgr.—A Kranz
Ad. Mgr.—S Rinnensland
(Circulation figure combines with Rheinische Post in Düsseldorf.)

NEUSTADT, BAD
Pop. Est. 8,783

RHÖN und SAALEPOST (6x wk.) Est. 1862
Industriestr. 8 (97616); PF 1560, 97605
Tel: (49-9771) 91930; Fax: (49-9771) 919355
Circ.—5,800 ABC
Prop.—Rötter
Pub./Bus. Mgr./Ed.—G Rötter

NIENBURG an der WESER
Pop. Est. 29,800

DIE HARKE (6x wk.) Est. 1821
An der Stadtgrenze 2 (31582); PF 1360, 31563
Tel: (49-5021) 9660; Fax: (49-5021) 966113
Circ.—24,500 ABC
Prop.—Hoffman
Pub.—Renate Rumpeltin
Ed. in Ch.—B Cichon
Ed. in Ch./Ed.—G Sommerfeld
Bus. Mgr.—K Kahl
Ad. Mgr.—U Kucharzik

NORDEN
Pop. Est. 23,600

OSTFRIESISCHER KURIER (The East Friesain Messenger) (6x wk.) Est. 1868
Stellmacherstr. 14; PF 450, 26494
Tel: (49-4931) 17080; Fax: (49-4931) 65254
Circ.—16,300
Prop.—SKN Druck
Pub.—C Basse
Mng. Ed.—J Rosendahl
Mng. Ed.—M Menssen
Ed. in Ch.—J Haddinga
Bus. Mgr.—H Hillebrenner
Ad. Mgr.—J-H Oltmanns

NORDENHAM
Pop. Est. 28,800

KREISZEITUNG WESERMARSCH (6x wk.) Est. 1876
Bahnhofstr. 36 (26954); PF 1155, 26941
Tel: (49-4731) 6031; Fax: (49-4731) 22048
Circ.—8,800 ABC
Prop.—Böning
Pub.—Dr. J Ditzen-Blanke
Bus. Mgr.—P Hartmann
Ad. Mgr.—T Hischke

NORDERNEY
Pop. Est. 9,589

NORDERNEYER BADEZEITUNG (6x wk.) Est. 1868
Lange Str. 6 (26548); PF 1465, 26536
Tel: (49-4932) 643; Fax: (49-4932) 821185
Circ.—2,200 ABC
Prop.—Soltau
Ad. Mgr.—G Barty

NORDHORN
Pop. Est. 48,000

GRAFSCHAFTER NACHRICHTEN (6x wk.) Est. 1874
Coesfelder Hof 2 (48527); PF 1449, 48504
Tel: (49-5921) 7070; Fax: (49-5921) 15166
Circ.—26,900 ABC
Prop.—Grafschafter Nachrichten
Pub.—Ursula Kip
Mng. Ed.—F Schulze
Ed. in Ch.—G Dörr
Ed.—R Masselink
Bus. Mgr.—J Wegmann
Ad. Mgr.—M Richter

NUERTINGEN
(NÜRTINGEN)
Pop. Est. 35,900

NÜRTINGER ZEITUNG (The Nuertinger News) (6x wk.) Est. 1831
Carl-Benz-Str. 1 (72622); PF 1849, 72608
Tel: (49-7022) 94640; Fax: (49-7022) 9464111
Circ.—25,000
Prop.—Senner
Pub./Bus. Mgr.—Trude Maier
Ed. in Ch./Ed.—J Gerrmann
Ed. in Ch.—G Schmitt
Ad. Mgr.—P Rhein

NUREMBERG
(NÜRNBERG)
Pop. Est. 467,400

NÜRNBERGER NACHRICHTEN (The Nuremberg News) (m-5x wk.) Est. 1945
Marienstr. 9; GKP 90327, 90402
Tel: (49-911) 2160; Fax: (49-911) 2162432
Circ.—352,500 ABC
Prop.—Nürnberger Presse Verlag
Pub./Bus. Mgr.—B Schnell
Ed. in Ch.—H-J Hauck
Ed. in Ch.—W Schmiegann
Ad. Mgr.—K Kreissel

NZ NÜRNBERGER ZEITUNG (m-ex S) Est. 1804
Marienstr. 9 (90402); PF 3347, 90016
Tel: (49-911) 23510; Fax: (49-911) 2418295
Circ.—12,400
Prop.—Nordbayerische Verlag
Mng. Ed./Ed. in Ch.—M Döbert
Ed. in Ch./Ed.—D Prell
Bus. Mgr.—D Puschmann
Ad. Mgr.—K Kreissel

Germany, Federal Republic of — Europe

OBERKIRCH
Pop. Est. 8,454

ACHER-RENCH-ZEITUNG (6x wk.)
Josef-Geldreich-Str. 2, 77704
Tel: (49-7802) 8040; Fax: (49-7802) 80441
Circ.—14,400 ABC
Prop.—Acher-Rench-Verlag
Pub.—G Sturn
Pub.—P Reiff
Bus. Mgr.—M Hammes
(Circulation figure figure combines with Offenburger Tageblatt.)

OBERNDORF
Pop. Est. 7,977

SCHWARZWÄLDER BOTE (6x wk.) Est. 1835
Kirchtorstr. 14 (78727); PF 1380, 78722
Tel: (49-7423) 780; Fax: (49-7423) 7873
Circ.—150,700 ABC
Prop.—Schwarzwälder Bote
Mng. Ed.—J Luz
Mng. Ed.—H-M Bihler
Ed. in ch.—K Siegmeier
Bus. Mgr./Ad. Mgr.—H-L Giebel

OCHTRUP

TAGEBLATT für den KREIS STEINFURT (6x wk.) Est. 1880
Bahnhofstr 18 (48607); PF 1245, 48601
Tel: (49-2553) 3005; Fax: (49-2553) 3000
Circ.—4,500 ABC
Prop.—Kirch Verlag
Pub./Bus. Mgr./Ad. Mgr.—H Werheid
Ed. in Ch.—R Menebröcker

OELDE
Pop. Est. 27,000

DIE GLOCKE (6x wk.) Est. 1880
Ruggestr. 27; PF 3240, 59281
Tel: (49-2522) 730; Fax: (49-2522) 73166
Circ.—69,000
Prop.—Holterdorf
Pub.—K F Gehring
Pub.—E Holterdorf
Mng. Ed.—R Geisenhanslüke
Ed. in Ch./Ed.—R Ummen
Ed. in Ch./Ed.—F H Loddenkemper
Ed. in Ch.—F Gehring
Bus. Mgr.—D Holterdorf
Ad. Mgr.—D Schönbeck

OFFENBACH am MAIN
Pop. Est. 107,100

OFFENBACH-POST (6x wk.) Est. 1773
Grosse Marktstr. 36 (63065); PF 100263, 63002
Tel: (49-69) 80630; Fax: (49-69) 8063386
Circ.—59,600
Prop.—Bintz
Mng. Ed./Ed. in Ch./Ed.—Dr. H J Seggewiss
Ed. in Ch.—U Jung
Ad. Mgr.—W Hüsemann

OFFENBURG
Pop. Est. 50,500

OFFENBURGER TAGEBLATT (6x wk.) Est. 1811
Marlener Str. 9 (77656); PF 2220, 77612
Tel: (49-781) 5040; Fax: (49-781) 504207
Circ.—76,100 ABC
Prop.—Reiff
Pub.—P Reiff
Pub.—T Arnold
Ad. Mgr.—K Hansmann

OLDENBURG
(Lower Saxony)
Pop. Est. 139,300

NORDWEST ZEITUNG (6x wk.) Est. 1945
Peterstr. 28 (26121); PF 2525, 26015
Tel: (49-441) 23901; Fax: (49-441) 239249
Circ.—349,500 ABC
Prop.—Nordwest Zeitung
Mng. Ed.—N Wahn
Ed. in Ch.—R Seelheim
Ed. in Ch.—O Ehlers
Bus. Mgr.—K J Ortmann
Ad. Mgr.—P Bremer

OLDESLOE, BAD
Pop. Est. 20,800

STORMARNER TAGEBLATT (6x wk.) Est. 1839
Hamburger Str. 5; PF 1229, 23843
Tel: (49-4531) 500630; Fax: (49-4531) 500642
Circ.—8,000 ABC
Prop.—Schleswig-Holsteinischer Zeitungsverlag

OSNABRUCK
Pop. Est. 153,800

NEUE OZ OSNABRUCKER ZEITUNG (m-6x wk.) Est. 1967
Grosse Str. 17 Breiter Gang 11; PF 4260, 49032
Tel: (49-541) 3250/(49-541) 3100; Fax: (49-541) 310234/(49-541) 325276
Circ.—328,900 ABC
Prop.—Neu Osnabrucker Zeitung
Pub./Bus. Mgr.—L V Fromm
Pub./Bus. Mgr.—H Elstermann
Mng. Ed.—M Brinkmann
Mng. Ed.—Dr. B Hamelmann
Ed. in Ch.—F Schmedt
Ad. Mgr.—F Henschen

OSTERODE am HARZ
Pop. Est. 27,000

OSTERODER KREIS-ANZEIGER (The Osteroder District Advertiser) (6x wk.) Est. 1820
Langer Krummer Bruch 32 (37520), 37505
Tel: (49-5522) 2018; Fax: (49-5522) 2755
Circ.—7,800 ABC
Prop.—Giebel & Oehlschägel
Pub.—H H Giebel
Bus. Mgr.—P J Lesemann
Ad. Mgr.—C Schilling

OTTERNDORF
Pop. Est. 6,424

NIEDERELBE-ZEITUNG (6x wk.) Est. 1955
Gutenbergstr. 1 (21762); PF 1153, 21758
Tel: (49-4751) 9010; Fax: (49-4751) 90149
Circ.—11,300 ABC
Prop.—Hottendorff
Pub./Bus. Mgr.—H Huster
Ed. in Ch.—H-H Kruse
Ed.—J C Montigny
Bus. Mgr./Ad. Mgr.—J Harms

PADERBORN
Pop. Est. 110,300

WESTFÄLISCHES VOLKSBLATT (6x wk.)
Rosenstr. 15, 33098
Tel: (49-5251) 1033; Fax: (49-5251) 103412
Circ.—49,400 ABC

PASSAU
Pop. Est. 52,700

PASSAUER NEUE PRESSE (The Passauer New Press) (m-5x wk.) Est. 1946
Medienstr. 5; PF 2040, 94036
Tel: (49-851) 8020; Fax: (49-851) 802256
Circ.—172,000 ABC
Prop.—Neue Presse Verlagsges GmbH
Mng. Ed.—K Kellerman
Ed. in Ch./Ed.—K Hermann
Ed. in Ch./Ed.—F Diederichs
Ed. in Ch./Ed.—Cornelia Wohlhüter
Ed. in Ch.—R Kollböck
Bus. Mgr.—F X Hirtreiter
Ad. Mgr.—W Lichtenegger

PEINE
Pop. Est. 45,600

PEINER ALLGEMEINE ZEITUNG (Piene General Newspaper) (6x wk.) Est. 1948
Werderstr. 49 (31224); PF 1660, 31206
Tel: (49-5171) 4060; Fax: (49-5171) 40627
Circ.—22,400
Prop.—Madsack
Pub.—Luise Madsack
Bus. Mgr.—W Gnieser
Ad. Mgr.—W Kloss

PFORZHEIM
Pop. Est. 104,500

PFORZHEIMER ZEITUNG (6x wk.) Est. 1794
Poststr. 5 (75172); PF 1360, 75113
Tel: (49-7231) 9330; Fax: (49-7231) 357405
Circ.—46,600 ABC
Prop.—Esslinger
Pub./Bus. Mgr./Ad. Mgr.—A Esslinger-Kiefer
Mng. Ed.—G Lache
Ed. in Ch.—H Piper

PINNEBERG
Pop. Est. 35,600

PINNEBERGER TAGEBLATT (6x wk.) Est. 1858
Damm 9, 25421
Tel: (49-4101) 20510; Fax: (49-4101) 2051290
Circ.—15,500 ABC
Prop.—Beig Verlag
Pub.—D Beig
Ed.in Ch.—K H Tang
Ed.—Sabine Skibbe
Bus. Mgr.—T Welkisch
Ad. Mgr.—M Faller

PIRMASENS
Pop. Est. 46,100

PZ PIRMASENSER ZEITUNG (6x wk.) Est. 1830
Gärtnerstr. 20 (66953), 66924
Tel: (49-6331) 80050; Fax: (49-6331) 800581
Circ.—17,500 ABC
Prop.—Deil
Pub./Bus. Mgr.—Hilde Becker-Baisch
Mng. Ed.—F-J Majer
Ed. in Ch./Bus. Mgr.—H F Baisch
Bus. Mgr./Ad. Mgr.—V Baisch

PLETTENBERG
Pop. Est. 27,600

SÜDERLÄNDER TAGEBLATT (6x wk.) Est. 1880
An der Lohmühle 7; PF 1609, 58840
Tel: (49-2391) 1767; Fax: (49-2391) 10904
Circ.—6,600 ABC
Prop.—Hundt
Pub./Bus. Mgr.—Valerie Hundt
Mng. Ed.—S Aschauer-Hundt
Ed. in Ch—H Hassel
Ad. Mgr.—F Bald

POTSDAM
Pop. Est. 139,794

MÄRKISCHE ALLGEMEINE (6x wk.) Est. 1946
Friedrich-Engles-Str. 24 (14473); PF 601153, 14411
Tel: (49-331) 28400; Fax: (49-331) 2840310
Circ.—259,800 ABC
Prop.—Märkische Verlags und Druckges mbH
Pub.—Dr. A Gauland
Mng. Ed.—A Rühl
Ed. in Ch.—Dr. H-U Conrad
Ed. in Ch.—P Mugay
Ed. in Ch./Ed.—P-J Nitsch
POTSDAMER NEUESTE NACHRICHTEN (m-6x wk.) Est. 1951
Lindenstr. 29 (14467); PF 601261, 14412
Tel: (49-331) 3760; Fax: (49-331) 2800850
Circ.—15,900 ABC
Prop.—Potsdamer Zeitungsverlagsges
Ad. Mgr.—N Mester

RECKLINGHAUSEN
Pop. Est. 117,600

RECKLINGHÄUSER ZEITUNG (6x wk.) Est. 1831
Breite Str. 4, 45657
Tel: (49-2361) 18050; Fax: (49-2361) 180555
Circ.—83,000
Prop.—Bauer
Mng. Ed.—W Poggenpohl
Ed. in Ch.—H Ruge
Ed. in Ch./Ed.—B Overwein
Ad. Mgr.—E Schilling

REGENSBURG
Pop. Est. 123,800

MITTELBAYERISCHE ZEITUNG (The Mid-Bavarian News) (6x wk.) Est. 1945
Margaretenstr. 4, 93047
Tel: (49-941) 2070; Fax: (49-941) 207437
Circ.—135,700 ABC
Prop.—Mittelbayerische Druckerei
Pub.—K H Esser
Mng. Ed.—H F Schmidt
Ed. in Ch.—K Hofner
Ed. in Ch.—G Otto
Bus. Mgr.—P Esser
Ad. Mgr.—R Kroiss

REICHENHALL, BAD
Pop. Est. 14,722

REICHENHALLER TAGBLATT (6x wk.) Est. 1840
Schachtstr. 4 (83435); PF 2109, 83423
Tel: (49-8651) 4051; Fax: (49-8651) 66860
Circ.—11,400 ABC
Prop.—Wiedemann
Mng. Ed./Ed. in Ch.—R Klingszot
Ed. in Ch.—P Auer
Ed. in Ch.—Gabi Hassinger
Bus. Mgr.—Frau D Thoma
Bus. Mgr.—L Wiedemann

REMSCHEID
Pop. Est. 121,000

REMSCHEIDER GENERAL-ANZEIGER (The Remscheider General-Advertiser) (6x wk.) Est. 1889
Konrad-Adenauer-Str. 2 (42853); PF 100761, 42807
Tel: (49-2191) 9090; Fax: (49-2191) 209180
Circ.—27,800 ABC
Prop.—Zeigler
Pub.—Dr. W Pütz
Ed. in Ch./Ed.—P Seringhaus
Ed. in Ch.—Susanne Kuczera
Ad. Mgr.—Gerlinde Karow

RENDSBURG
Pop. Est. 30,600

SCHLESWIG-HOLSTEINISCHE LANDESZEITUNG (The Schleswig Holstein District News) (6x wk.) Est. 1807
Stegen 1, 24768
Tel: (49-4331) 464153; Fax: (49-4331) 464103
Circ.—29,900 ABC
Prop.—Scleswig-Holsteinischer Landeszeitung
Ad. Mgr.—C Schilling

REUTLINGEN
Pop. Est. 97,900

REUTLINGER GENERAL-ANZEIGER (The Reutlinger General Advertiser) (6x wk.) Est. 1887
Burgstr. 1 (72764); PF 1642, 72706
Tel: (49-7121) 3020; Fax: (49-7121) 302677
Circ.—49,800 ABC
Prop.—Reutlinger General Anzeiger Zeitungsverlag
Pub.—V Lehari
Mng. Ed.—U Wilk
Ed. in Ch./Ed.—R Buchwald
Ad. Mgr.—W Frick
REUTLINGER NACHRICHTEN PFULLINGER ZEITUNG (6x wk.) Est. 1945
Burgplatz 1 (72764); PF 2454, 72714
Tel: (49-7121) 334661; Fax: (49-7121) 334663
Circ.—15,300 ABC
Prop.—Reutlinger Nachrichten GmbH
Bus. Mgr.—Dr. G Hauser
Bus. Mgr.—Dr. T Hauser
Ad. Mgr.—W Frick
(This is an edition of the Südwest Press Ulm in Ulm.)

RHAUDERFEHN

GENERAL-ANZEIGER (The General Advertiser) (6x wk.) Est. 1888
Untenende 21 (26817); PF 1165, 26811
Tel: (49-4952) 9270; Fax: (49-4952) 927157
Circ.—12,000 ABC
Prop.—Ostendorp
Pub./Ed. in Ch.—Klara Engelberg
Pub./Ed. in Ch.—Dr. G Engelberg
Mng. Ed.—C Merl
Bus. Mgr.—H Schreiber
Ad. Mgr.—L Groeneveld
Ad. Mgr.—C Birkhofer

RHEINE
Pop. Est. 70,400

MÜNSTERLÄNDISCHE VOLKSZEITUNG (6x wk.) Est. 1878
Bahnhofstr. 8, 48431
Tel: (49-5971) 4040; Fax: (49-5971) 40421
Circ.—19,100 ABC
Prop.—Altmeppen
Ad. Mgr.—Elisabeth Brügge

RINTELN
Pop. Est. 25,400

SCHAUMBURGER ZEITUNG (6x wk.) Est. 1761
Klosterstr. 32 (31737); PF 1240, 31722
Tel: (49-5751) 40000; Fax: (49-5751) 400077
Circ.—10,300 ABC
Prop.—Bösendahl
Pub.—C W Niemeyer
Ed.—H Weimann
Bus. Mgr./Ad. Mgr.—W Plassmeier

ROSENHEIM
Pop. Est. 53,200

OBERBAYERISCHES VOLKSBLATT (5x wk.) Est. 1854
Hafnerstr. 5, 83022
Tel: (49-8031) 1810; Fax: (49-8031) 181216
Circ.—80,400 ABC
Prop.—Oberbayerisches Volksblatt
Mng. Ed.—H Ainger
Ed. in Ch.—W Börsch
Bus. Mgr.—N Lauinger
Ad. Mgr.—M Breu

ROSTOCK
Pop. Est. 248,088

NORDDEUTSCHE NEUESTE NACHRICHTEN (m-6x wk.) Est. 1953
Bergstr. 10, 18057
Tel: (49-371) 4911611; Fax: (49-371) 4911621
Circ.—21,800
Prop.—Neueste Nachrichten Zeitungsverlag
Ed.—Dr. U B Vetter
Ad. Mgr.—J Kunze

OSTSEE-ZEITUNG (m-6x wk.) Est. 1951
Richard Wagner Str. 1a (18055); PF 101181, 18002
Tel: (49-381) 3650; Fax: (49-381) 365366
Circ.—240,200 ABC
Prop.—Ostsee-Zeitung
Pub.—H Reinke
Mng. Ed.—H Kröplin
Mng. Ed.—J Burnmeister
Ed. in Ch./Ed.—T Hoppe
Ed. in Ch.—G Spilker
Bus. Mgr.—M Feldenkirchen
Bus. Mgr.—Dr. K Sabathil
Bus. Mgr.—Dr. G Semmerow
Ad. Mgr.—M Schottmann

ROTENBURG

ROTENBURGER KREISZEITUNG (Rotenburger District News) (6x wk.) Est. 1867
Grosse Str. 37 (27356); PF 1580, 27345
Tel: (49-4261) 720; Fax: (49-4261) 7220
Circ.—12,500 ABC
Prop.—Sasse
Ed. in Ch.—W Palm
Ed.—W Bonath
Bus. Mgr.—G Richter
Ad. Mgr.—R D Goedecken

ROTH
Pop. Est. 24,100

ROTH-HILPOLTSTEINER VOLKSZEITUNG (6x wk.) Est. 1862
Allee 2 (91154), 91141
Tel: (49-9171) 970322; Fax: (49-9171) 970327
Circ.—12,800 ABC
Prop.—Müller
Pub.—B Schnell
Ed.—H-P Grasser
Ad. Mgr.—K Kreissel

ROTHENBURG
Pop. Est. 11,786

FRÄNKISCHER ANZEIGER (Franconian Advertiser) (6x wk.) Est. 1867
Erlbacher Str. 102 (91541), 91535
Tel: (49-9861) 4000; Fax: (49-9861) 40016
Circ.—6,700 ABC
Prop.—Schneider
Pub./Bus. Mgr.—W Schneider
Pub.—B Schnell
Ad. Mgr.—K Kreissel

RUESSELSHEIM
(RÜSSELSHEIM)
Pop. Est. 57,300

MAIN-SPITZE (6x wk.) Est. 1878
Franfurter Str. 2 2/10 (65428); PF 1662, 65406
Tel: (49-6142) 8550; Fax: (49-6142) 85533
Circ.—14,500 ABC
Prop.—Mainzer Verlagsanstalt
Ad. Mgr.—W Dähn

RÜSSELSHEIMER ECHO (6x wk.) Est. 1956
Frankurter Str. 2 (65428); PF 1861, 65408
Tel: (49-6142) 68096; Fax: (49-6142) 61200
Circ.—7,800
Prop.—Darmstädter Echo
Ad. Mgr.—Rosemarie Bruckner

SAARBRUECKEN
(SAARBRÜCKEN)
Pop. Est. 184,400

SAARBRÜCKER ZEITUNG (6x wk.) Est. 1761
Gutenbergerstr. 11, 66117
Tel: (49-681) 5020; Fax: (49-681) 502500
Circ.—206,900 ABC
Prop.—Saarbrücker Zeitung Verlag
Mng. Ed./Ed. in Ch.—R Müller
Ed. in Ch.—R Bernhard
Bus. Mgr.—U Jacobsen
Ad. Mgr.—M van Ackern

SALZWEDEL

ALTMARK ZEITUNG (The Altmark News) (6x wk.) Est. 1990
Vor dem Neuperver Tor 4 (29410); PF 89, 29402
Tel: (49-3901) 83140; Fax: (49-3901) 831483
Circ.—43,500 ABC
Prop.—Renner & Meineke
Mng. Ed.—T Schiefelbein
Ed. in Ch./Ed.—Ulrike Meineke
Ed. in Ch.—H-J Wicht
Ad. Mgr.—U Mertens

SCHIFFERSTADT

SCHIFFERSTADTER TAGBLATT (6x wk.) Est. 1905
Bahnhofstr. 70 (67105); PF 1163, 67099
Tel: (49-6235) 1091; Fax: (49-6235) 2044
Circ.—3,100 ABC
Prop.—Geier
Bus. Mgr.—E Geier

SCHONGAU
Pop. Est. 10,728

SCHONGAUER NACHRICHTEN (6x wk.) Est. 1876
Münzstr. 14 (86956); PF 1347, 86953
Tel: (49-8861) 920; Fax: (49-8861) 9815
Circ.—9,500 ABC
Prop.—Motz
Ed. in Ch.—J Jais

SCHORNDORF
Pop. Est. 34,700

SCHORNDORFER NACHRICHTEN (Schorndorfer News) (6x wk.)
Oberer Marktplatz 4 (73614); PF 1447, 73604
Tel: (49-7181) 20010; Fax: (49-7181) 200130
Circ.—18,600 ABC
Prop.—Zeitungsverlag GmbH & Co. Waiblingen KG
Ad. Mgr.—M Fessler

SCHWABACH
Pop. Est. 35,600

SCHWABACHER TAGBLATT (6x wk.) Est. 1802
Spitalberg 3, 91126
Tel: (49-9122) 15060; Fax: (49-9122) 150620
Circ.—17,400 ABC
Prop.—Buch & Offsetdruckerei Hermann Millizer
Pub.—M Schmitt
Pub.—B Schnell
Ad. Mgr.—K Kreissel

SCHWAEBISCH-GMUEND
(SCHÄBISCH-GMÜND)
Pop. Est. 56,100

GMÜNDER TAGESPOST (7x wk.) Est. 1959
Vordere Schmiedgasse 18 (73525); PF 1349, 73503
Tel: (49-7171) 60010; Fax: (49-7171) 600155
Circ.—13,000 ABC
Prop.—Gmünder Tagespost
Pub.—Prof. Dr. J Binkowski
Pub.—K A Theiss
Mng. Ed.—R Scheuber
Ed. in Ch.—Dr. R Grupp
Ed.—K Staudenmaier
Bus. Mgr.—Gertrud Theiss
Bus. Mgr.—E Looser
Ad. Mgr.—V Stroner
(This is an edition of the Südwest Presse Ulm in Ulm.)

REMS-ZEITUNG (6x wk.) Est. 1792
Paradiesstr. 12; PF 1749, 73507
Tel: (49-7171) 60060; Fax: (49-7171) 600658
Circ.—18,500 ABC
Prop.—Remsdruckerei, Sigg & Härtel
Mng. Ed./Ed. in Ch./Ed.—H Meier
Ed./Bus. Mgr.—M Sigg
Ad. Mgr.—E Berger

SCHWAEBISCH-HALL
(SCHÄBISCH-HALL)
Pop. Est. 30,900

HALLER TAGBLATT (6x wk.) Est. 1788
Schmollerstr. 31 (74523); PF 100340, 74503
Tel: (49-791) 4040; Fax: (49-791) 404411
Circ.—19,200 ABC
Prop.—Haller Tagblatt
Pub.—E Schwend
Pub.—M Schwend
Ed. in Ch.—R Hocher
Ad. Mgr.—R Bierlin
(This is an edition of the Südwest Presse Ulm in Ulm.)

SCHWERIN
Pop. Est. 127,447

SCHWERINER VOLKSZEITUNG (m-6x wk.) Est. 1946
Von-Strauffenberg-Str. 27, 19061
Tel: (49-385) 63780; Fax: (49-385) 375140
Circ.—184,900 ABC
Prop.—Landesverlags & Druckges
Pub.—H Markwort
Mng. Ed.—R Rump
Ed. in Ch.—C Hamm
Ed.—B Mackowiak
Ed.—W Schmidt
Bus. Mgr.—T Amann
Bus. Mgr.—E Aelker

SCHWETZINGEN
Pop. Est. 16,650

SCHWETZINGER ZEITUNG (6x wk.) Est. 1893
Scheffelstr. 55 (68723); PF 1820, 68708
Tel: (49-6202) 2050; Fax: (49-6202) 205206
Circ.—20,200 ABC
Prop.—Schwetzinger Verlagsdruckerei
Mng. Ed.—B Weinmann
Ed. in Ch./Bus. Mgr.—Dr. E Stemmle
Ad. Mgr.—A Moch

SEESEN
Pop. Est. 21,600

BEOBACHTER (The Observer) (6x wk.) Est. 1876
Lautenthaler Str. 3 (38723); PF 1252, 38712
Tel: (49-5381) 1025; Fax: (49-5381) 5755
Circ.—6,500 ABC
Prop.—Hofmann Verlag
Prop.—Secsener Beobachter
Ed. in Ch.—H J Poerschke
Bus. Mgr./Ad. Mgr.—B Wolter

SEGEBERG, BAD
Pop. Est. 12,527

SEGEBERGER ZEITUNG (6x wk.) Est. 1826
Hamburger Str. 26 (23795); PF 1533, 23785
Tel: (49-4551) 9040; Fax: (49-4551) 90449
Circ.—15,900 ABC
Prop.—Wäser
Pub.—H C Wulff
Mng. Ed./Ed. in Ch.—S Ures
Ad. Mgr.—H Broers

SELB
Pop. Est. 20,000

SELBER TAGBLATT FRANKENPOST (6x wk.) Est. 1875
Christoph-Krautheim Str. 98, 95100
Tel: (49-9287) 8520; Fax: (49-9287) 8533
Circ.—7,500 ABC
Prop.—Frankenpost Verlag
Ad. Mgr.—Marlene Berger

SIEGEN
Pop. Est. 107,300

SIEGENER ZEITUNG (6x wk.) Est. 1823
Obergraben 39 (57072); PF 101164, 57011
Tel: (49-271) 5941; Fax: (49-271) 594239
Circ.—65,500 ABC
Prop.—Siegener Zeitung
Ed. in Ch.—Dr. E Winterhager
Ed.—K-H Hof
Ad. Mgr.—U Knautz
Ad. Mgr.—C Plitsch

SIMMERN
Pop. Est. 5,567

HUNSRÜCKER ZEITUNG (6x wk.)
Koblenzer Str. 5, 55469
Tel: (49-6761) 2928; Fax: (49-6761) 12692
Circ.—9,400
Prop.—Mittelrhein Verlag

SINDELFINGEN
Pop. Est. 55,700

SINDELFINGER ZEITUNG (6x wk.) Est. 1890
Böblinger Str. 68; PF 280, 71060
Tel: (49-7031) 8620; Fax: (49-7031) 862201
Circ.—15,600 ABC
Prop.—Röhm
Pub.—Dr. W Röhm
Ad. Mgr.—S Klein

SOEST
Pop. Est. 42,000

SOESTER ANZEIGER (6x wk.) Est. 1848
Schloitweg 19 (59491); PF 1565, 59475
Tel: (49-2921) 6880; Fax: (49-2921) 68848
Circ.—33,200 ABC
Prop.—Jahn
Pub.—W Jahn
Ed. in Ch.—G Stoppe
Bus. Mgr.—B Schmidt
Ad. Mgr.—W Oberste-Schemmann

SOLINGEN
Pop. Est. 158,400

SOLINGER TAGEBLATT (6x wk.) Est. 1809
Mummstr. 9 (42651); PF 101256, 42612
Tel: (49-212) 2990; Fax: (49-212) 12343
Circ.—31,100 ABC
Prop.—Boll
Pub.—B Boll
Ed. in Ch./Ed.—P Getta
Ed. in Ch.—S M Kob
Bus. Mgr.—D Ramcke
Ad. Mgr.—R Hoebel

SOLTAU
Pop. Est. 15,013

BÖHME-ZEITUNG (6x wk.) Est. 1864
Harburgerstr. 63 (29614); PF 1344, 29603
Tel: (49-5191) 8080; Fax: (49-5191) 808165
Circ.—14,400 ABC
Prop.—Mundschenk
Pub./Bus. Mgr.—Dr. W-M Mundschenk
Ad. Mgr.—H H Rüdiger

SPRINGE
Pop. Est. 29,000

NEUE DEISTER ZEITUNG (6x wk.) Est. 1875
Bahnhofstr. 18 (31832); PF 100343, 31815
Tel: (49-5041) 7890; Fax: (49-5041) 78989
Circ.—7,300 ABC
Prop.—Erhardt
Pub./Ed. in Ch./Bus. Mgr.—K Schaper
Ad. Mgr.—B Schaper

STADE
Pop. Est. 43,000

STADER TAGEBLATT (6x wk.) Est. 1871
Glückstädter Str. 10; PF 2249, 21662
Tel: (49-4141) 9360; Fax: (49-4141) 936249
Circ.—28,400 ABC
Pub./Bus. Mgr.—H Gillen
Pub.—G Krause
Pub.—Dr. K Krause
Ad. Mgr.—G Schnabel

STADTHAGEN
Pop. Est. 22,300

GENERAL-ANZEIGER für den LANDKREIS SCHAUMBURG und UMGEBUNG (General Advertiser for the Schaumburg District and Region) (5x wk.) Est. 1871
Obernstr. 28, 31655
Tel: (49-5721) 97100; Fax: (49-5721) 72160
Circ.—2,600 ABC

Germany, Federal Republic of — Europe

Prop.—General-Anzeiger GmbH
Pub.—G Niemeyer
Pub.—H Niemeyer
Ed. in Ch.—K Poll
Bus. Mgr.—E Schienke
Ad. Mgr.—W Plassmeier
SCHAUMBURGER NACHRICHTEN (6x wk.)
Gerbergasse 2, 31655
Tel: (49-5721) 809230; Fax: (49-5721) 2007
Circ.—16,800 ABC
Prop.—Madsack
Ad. Mgr.—W W Braun

STRAUBING
Pop. Est. 41,600

STRAUBINGER TAGBLATT (6x wk.) Est. 1860
Ludwigsplatz 30 (94315); PF 354, 94303
Tel: (49-9421) 9400; Fax: (49-9421) 940206
Circ.—140,500 ABC
Prop.—Attenkofer
Mng. Ed.—H Guggeis
Ad. Mgr.—H Lauer

STUTTGART
Pop. Est. 583,700

CANNSTATTER ZEITUNG (6x wk.) Est. 1824
Wilhelmstr. 18 (70372); PF 500249, 70332
Tel: (49-711) 955680; Fax: (49-711) 9556833
Circ.—10,400 ABC
Prop.—Rotenberg Verlag
Pub.—O W Bechtle
Pub.—Dr. F Bechtle
Ed. in Ch.—S Baumann
Ed.—J Nauke
Ed.—A Wörner
Ad. Mgr.—H Kösling
FILDER-ZEITUNG (6x wk.) Est. 1872
Scharrstr. 13 (70563); PF 800960, 70509
Tel: (49-711) 737800; Fax: (49-711) 7378025
Circ.—10,300 ABC
Prop.—Scharr Verlag
Bus. Mgr.—G W Braun
Ad. Mgr.—C Urbas
NORD-STUTTGARTER RUNDSCHAU (6x wk.) Est. 1905
Bessemerstr. 7 (70435); PF 400360, 70403
Tel: (49-711) 820000; Fax: (49-711) 8200030
Circ.—5,600 ABC
Prop.—Heinz
Pub.—R Heinz
Pub./Bus. Mgr./Ad. Mgr.—H P Heinz
STUTTGARTER NACHRICHTEN (6x wk.) Est. 1946
Plieninger Str. 150 (70567); PF 104452, 70039
Tel: (49-711) 72050; Fax: (49-711) 7205747
Circ.—260,000
Prop.—Stuttgarter Nachrichten Verlagsges
Mng. Ed.—H Paeffgen
Ed. in Ch.—J Offenbach
Bus. Mgr.—Dr. H D Mössner
Ad. Mgr.—H J Kopp
STUTTGARTER ZEITUNG (The Stuttgarter News) (m-6x wk.) Est. 1945
Plieninger Str. 150 (70567); PF 106032, 70049
Tel: (49-711) 72050; Fax: (49-711) 7205516
Circ.—239,500 ABC
Prop.—Stuttgarter Zeitung Verlag
Mng. Ed.—H Paeffgen
Ad. Mgr.—M Scholl

SUHL
Pop. Est. 54,731

FREIES WORT (The Free Word) (m-6x wk.) Est. 1952
Friedrich-König-Str. 6 (98527); PF 210, 98501
Tel: (49-3681) 5130; Fax: (49-3681) 513211
Circ.—129,100
Prop.—Suhler Verlagsges
Mng. Ed.—G Weber
Ed. in Ch.—G Schwinger
Ed.—F Rauer
Bus. Mgr.—U Rendigs
Ad. Mgr.—M Eich
Ad. Mgr.—Dr. W Heise

SYKE
Pop. Est. 6,852

KREISZEITUNG fur die LANDKREISE DIEPHOLZ und VERDEN (The District News for the Districts Diepholz and Verden) (6x wk.) Est. 1860
Ristedter Weg 17 (28857); PF 1265, 28846
Tel: (49-4242) 580; Fax: (49-4242) 5837
Circ.—87,600 ABC
Prop.—Kreiszeitung Verlagsgesellschaft
Pub.—Dr. D Ippen
Pub.—K Schmidt
Pub.—W Schröder
Pub.—E Plenge
Ed. in Ch.—H-J Ziller
Bus. Mgr.—E J Wenske
Ad. Mgr.—A Wollschäger

TAUBERBISCHOFSHEIM
Pop. Est. 8,178

FRÄNKISCHE NACHRICHTEN (6x wk.) Est. 1946
Schmiederstr. 19 (97941); PF 1260, 97932
Tel: (49-9341) 830; Fax: (49-9341) 4764/(49-9341) 83146
Circ.—31,100 ABC
Prop.—Fränkische Nachrichten
Ed. in Ch.—T G Zügner
Bus. Mgr.—B H Holthaus
Ad. Mgr.—E Kramm

TITTMONING

SÜDOSTBAYERISCHE RUNDSCHAU (6x wk.) Est. 1949
Watzmannstr. 2a (84529); PF 1149, 84525
Tel: (49-8683) 955; Fax: (49-8683) 958
Circ.—5,800
Prop.—Erdl & Pustet Verlag
Mng. Ed./Ed. in Ch./Bus. Mgr.—W Pustet

TRAUNSTEIN
Pop. Est. 14,079

TRAUNSTEINER WOCHENBLATT (6x wk.) Est. 1855
Marienstr. 12; PF 1560, 83278
Tel: (49-861) 98770; Fax: (49-861) 8305
Circ.—16,400 ABC
Prop.—Miller
Pub./Bus. Mgr.—A Miller
Ed. in Ch./Ed.—K Oberkandler
Ed. in Ch.—M Miller

TRIER
Pop. Est. 93,100

TRIERISCHER VOLKSFREUND (The Trier's People's Friend) (6x wk.) Est. 1875
Nikolaus-Koch-Platz 1 (54290); PF 3770, 54227
Tel: (49-651) 71990; Fax: (49-651) 7199990
Circ.—104,600 ABC
Prop.—Volksfreund Druckerei
Ed. in Ch.—W W Weber
Ed.—Dr. H-L Schultze
Ed.—N A Sklorz
Bus. Mgr.—J Klasen
Bus. Mgr.—G Lehn
Bus. Mgr.—R Schlötzer
Ad. Mgr.—W Blass
Ad. Mgr.—H-D Fettes

TROSTBERG
Pop. Est. 7,200

TROSTBERGER TAGBLATT (6x wk.) Est. 1868
Gabelsbergerstr. 4, 83308
Tel: (49-8621) 8080; Fax: (49-8621) 80868
Circ.—20,700
Prop.—Erdl
Pub.—O Erdl
Pub.—W H Schacht
Ed. in Ch.—T Grabmüller

TUEBINGEN
(TÜBINGEN)
Pop. Est. 76,200

SÜDWEST PRESSE (SCHWÄBISCHES TAGBLATT) (6x wk.) Est. 1945
Schillerstr. 22; PF 1460, 72014
Tel: (49-7451) 900930; Fax: (49-7451) 900999
Circ.—46,700 ABC
Prop.—Schwäbisches Tagblatt Verlag
Ad. Mgr.—M Meyer
(This is an edition of the Südwest Presse Ulm in Ulm.)

UELZEN
Pop. Est. 35,100

ALLGEMEINE ZEITUNG der LUNEBURGER HEIDE (d-6x wk.) Est. 1849
Gr. Liederner Str. 45 (29525); PF 1161, 29501
Tel: (49-581) 8080; Fax: (49-581) 808157
Circ.—23,300 ABC
Prop.—Becker
Pub.—D Ippen
Ed. in Ch.—B Westerweg
Ed.—V Nolte
Bus. Mgr.—D Schmedt
Ad. Mgr.—U Mertens

UETERSEN
Pop. Est. 16,650

UETERSENER NACHRICHTEN (Uetersener News) (6x wk.) Est. 1864
Grosser Sand 3 (25436); PF 1161, 25429
Tel: (49-4122) 92500; Fax: (49-4122) 1858
Circ.—8,000 ABC
Prop.—Heydorn
Pub./Bus. Mgr.—L von Ziehlberg
Ad. Mgr.—P Salemke

ULM
Pop. Est. 100,700

SÜDWEST PRESSE (SCHWÄBISCHE DONAU ZEITUNG) (The Southwest Press (Schwabian Danube News) (6x wk.)
Frauenstr. 77, 89073
Tel: (49-731) 1560; Fax: (49-731) 156308
Circ.—70,000 ABC
Prop.—Neue Presseges
Ed. in Ch.—U Wildermuth
Bus. Mgr.—H Staiger
Bus. Mgr.—P Mattheis
(This is an edition of the Südwest Presse in Ulm.)
SÜDWEST PRESSE ULM (The Southwest Press) Est. 1945
Frauenstr. 77; GKP 89070, 89073
Tel: (49-731) 1560; Fax: (49-731) 156308
Circ.—382,400 (total-all eds.)
Prop.—Neue Presseges GmbH
Ed. in Ch.—U Wildermuth
Ad. Mgr.—Ms. Elke Philipsen
(Circulation is the total of all Südwest Presse editions. See Allen, Balingen, Gaildorf, Geislingen, Gerabrown, Göppinger, Hechingen, Heidenheim, Bad Mergentheim, Metzingen, Reutlingen, Schwäbisch Gmünd, Schwäbisch Hall, Tübingen, Ulm & Villingen-Schwenningen.)

UNNA
Pop. Est. 59,600

HELLWEGER ANZEIGER (Hellweger Advertiser) (6x wk.) Est. 1844
Wassenstr. 20 (59423), 59408
Tel: (49-2303) 2020; Fax: (49-2303) 202121
Circ.—27,500 ABC
Prop.—Graphische Betriebe Rubens
Pub.—G Rubens
Pub.—Dr. U Rubens-Laarmann
Ed. in Ch./Ed.—T Horschler
Ed. in Ch.—K Seifert
Bus. Mgr.—H Radermacher
Ad. Mgr./Ed.—Ursula Lindstedt

USINGEN
Pop. Est. 4,541

USINGER ANZEIGER (Usinger Advertiser) (6x wk.) Est. 1866
Am Riedborn 20 (61250); PF 1160, 61241
Tel: (49-6081) 1050; Fax: (49-6081) 105100
Circ.—7,300 ABC
Prop.—Taunus Verlag
Pub.—K Wagner
Bus. Mgr./Ad. Mgr.—W Tambornino

VAIHINGEN an der ENZ
Pop. Est. 22,900

VAIHINGER KREISZEITUNG (The Vaihingen District News) (6x wk.) Est. 1830
Marktplatz 15 (71655); PF 1140, 71654
Tel: (49-7042) 9190; Fax: (49-7042) 91959
Circ.—8,900 ABC
Prop.—Wimmershof
Ad. Mgr.—D Grossmann

VECHTA
Pop. Est. 24,200

OLDENBURGISCHE VOLKSZEITUNG (The Oldenburg People's News) (6x wk.) Est. 1835
Neuer Markt 2 (49377); PF 1464, 49363
Tel: (49-4441) 9400; Fax: (49-4441) 94030

Circ.—25,600 ABC
Prop.—Oldenburgische Volkszeitung
Mng. Ed./Ed. in Ch./Ed.—K Esslinger
Ed. in Ch.—C Riewerts
Bus. Mgr.—Dr. J H Uptmoor
Ad. Mgr.—G Beil

VIERNHEIM
Pop. Est. 29,100

VIERNHEIMER TAGEBLATT (6x wk.) Est. 1883
Rathausstr. 38a (68519); PF 1980, 68509
Tel: (49-6204) 96660; Fax: (49-6204) 5875
Circ.—6,300 ABC
Pub.—R Martin
Pub.—W Martin
Pub.—H Martin
Mng. Ed./Ed. in Ch.—W J Martin

VILLINGEN-SCHWENNINGEN
Pop. Est. 76,200

SÜDWEST PRESSE (DIE NECKARQUELLE) (The Southwest Press (The Neckar Source) (6x wk.) Est. 1880
Bert-Brecht Str. 15, 78054
Tel: (49-7720) 3940; Fax: (49-7720) 394222
Circ.—11,300 ABC
Prop.—Druck & Verlagshaus Hermann Kuhn
Pub.—H U Ziegler
Ed. in Ch.—H Noll
Ed.—R Wölfle
Ad. Mgr.—H Harre
Ad. Mgr.—W Lacher
(This is an edition of the Südwest Presse Ulm in Ulm.)

WAIBLINGEN
Pop. Est. 45,100

WAIBLINGER KREISZEITUNG (The Waiblinger District News) (6x wk.) Est. 1839
Siemensstr. 10 (71332); PF 1813, 71308
Tel: (49-7151) 5660; Fax: (49-7151) 566402
Circ.—19,600 ABC
Prop.—Waiblingen Zeitungsverlag
Bus. Mgr.—Dr. O Sanger
Bus. Mgr.—U Villinger
Ad. Mgr.—M Fessler

WALDSHUT-TIENGEN
Pop. Est. 21,900

ALB-BOTE (6x wk.) Est. 1880
Poststr. 4 (79761); PF 1945, 79746
Tel: (49-7751) 88010; Fax: (49-7751) 880125
Circ.—8,400 ABC
Prop.—Zimmermann
Ad. Mgr.—E Polster

WALSRODE
Pop. Est. 22,700

WALSRODER ZEITUNG (6x wk.) Est. 1867
Lange Str. 14; PF 1520, 29664
Tel: (49-5161) 60050; Fax: (49-5161) 600528
Circ.—13,900 ABC
Prop.—Gronemann Verlag
Pub.—Maria Muchka
Pub.—M Röhrbein
Ad. Mgr.—W Oermann

WEDEL
(Schleswig-Holstein)
Pop. Est. 30,500

WEDEL-SCHULAUER TAGEBLATT (6x wk.) Est. 1957
Bahnhofstr. 61, 22880
Tel: (49-4103) 82030; Fax: (49-4103) 83488
Circ.—4,700 ABC
Prop.—Beig Pinneberg Verlag
Ad. Mgr.—M Faller

WEENER
Pop. Est. 5,740

RHEIDERLAND (6x wk.) Est. 1860
Risiusstr. 6 (26826); PF 260, 26819
Tel: (49-4951) 3040; Fax: (49-4951) 30433
Circ.—6,400 ABC
Prop.—Risius Verlag
Ed. in Ch.—Dr. G Faupel
Ed.—B Lindemann
Bus. Mgr.—G Risius
Ad. Mgr.—M Dlubatz

WEIDEN in der OBERPFALZ
Pop. Est. 41,800

DER NEUE TAG (The New Day) (6x wk.) Est. 1946
 Weigelstr. 16 (92637); PF 1340, 92603
 Tel: (49-961) 850; Fax: (49-961) 44747
 Circ.—93,200 ABC
 Prop.—Der neue Tag
 Pub.—G Vogelsang
 Pub.—Barbel Panzer
 Pub.—Dr. Barbara Shananhan
 Mng. Ed./Ed. in Ch.—G Gruber
 Ed. in Ch.—H Klemm
 Ad. Mgr.—D Eckert
OBERPFÄLZER NACHRICHTEN (6x wk.) Est. 1949
 Hochstr. 21 (92637); PF 1825, 92608
 Tel: (49-961) 47110; Fax: (49-961) 7623
 Circ.—9,400 ABC
 Prop.—Spintler Verlag
 Pub./Bus.Mgr.—Dr. Renate Freuding-Spintler
 Ed. in Ch./Ed.—Dr. E Feneis
 Ed. in Ch.—Dr. E Freuding
 Ad. Mgr.—H Schosser

WEILER-SIMMERBERG
Pop. Est. 4,445

DER WESTALLGÄUER (6x wk.)
 Fridolin-Holzer-Str. 22, 88171
 Tel: (49-8387) 39929; Fax: (49-8387) 2729
 Circ.—9,000 ABC
 Prop.—Holzer
 Pub./Ad. Mgr.—Dr. E Holzer
 Ed. in Ch.—A Dorner

WEIMAR
Pop. Est. 60,326

THÜRINGISCHE LANDESZEITUNG (m) Est. 1945
 Marienstr. 14 (99432); PF 329, 99404
 Tel: (49-3643) 2063; Fax: (49-3643) 20642
 Circ.—68,000
 Prop.—Thüringische Landeszeitung Verlag
 Mng. Ed.—N Block
 Mng. Ed.—D Lücke
 Ed. in Ch./Ed.—O Werner
 Bus. Mgr.—W Felgentrebe

WEINHEIM
Pop. Est. 40,600

WEINHEIMER NACHRICHTEN (Weinheimer News) (6x wk.) Est. 1949
 Friedrichstr. 24 (69469); PF 100251, 69442
 Tel: (49-6201) 810; Fax: (49-6201) 81167
 Circ.—29,500 ABC
 Prop.—Diesbach
 Pub.—H Diesbach
 Ad. Mgr.—U Richter

WEISSENBURG
(WEIßENBURG)
Pop. Est. 13,818

WEISSENBURGER TAGBLATT (6x wk.)
 Wildbadstr. 16, 91781
 Tel: (49-9141) 4065; Fax: (49-9141) 4068
 Circ.—12,400 ABC
 Prop.—Braun & Elbel
 Pub.—L Braun
 Pub.—B Schnell
 Ad. Mgr.—K Kreissel

WELZHEIM

WELZHEIMER ZEITUNG (Wilzheimer News) (6x wk.) Est. 1866
 Wilhelmstr. 17 (73642); PF 1220, 73637
 Tel: (49-7182) 8802; Fax: (49-7182) 3377
 Circ.—3,900 ABC
 Prop.—Waiblinger Zeitungsverlag
 Ad. Mgr.—M Fessler

WERDOHL
Pop. Est. 20,300

SÜDERLÄNDER VOLKSFREUND (6x wk.) Est. 1888
 Freiheitstr. 30 (58791), 58772
 Tel: (49-2392) 50090; Fax: (49-2392) 500948
 Circ.—3,500 ABC
 Prop.—Flug Verlag
 Bus. Mgr.—P Flug
 Ad. Mgr.—R Scharmanske

WETZLAR
Pop. Est. 50,300

WETZLARER NEUE ZEITUNG (6x wk.) Est. 1946
 Elsa-Brandström-Str. 18; PF 2940, 35578
 Tel: (49-6441) 9590; Fax: (49-6441) 959292
 Circ.—79,200 ABC
 Prop.—Wetzlardruck
 Pub.—J Eifinger

 Ed. in Ch.—W Eigendorf
 Bus. Mgr.—W Kraus
 Bus. Mgr.—M Grude
 Ad. Mgr.—P Rother

WIESBADEN
Pop. Est. 266,500

WIESBADENER KURIER (Wiesbadener Messenger) (6x wk.) Est. 1945
 Langgasse 21 (65183); PF 6029, 65050
 Tel: (49-611) 3550; Fax: (49-611) 355377
 Circ.—94,600 ABC
 Prop.—Wiesbadener Kurier
 Mng. Ed./Ed. in Ch./Ed.—M Friedrich
 Ed. in Ch.—H Börsing
 Ad. Mgr.—R Vogt
WIESBADENER TAGBLATT (d-6x wk.) Est. 1852
 Michelsberg 3 (65183); PF 6009, 65050
 Tel: (49-611) 3490; Fax: (49-611) 34933
 Circ.—22,007
 Prop.—Wiesbadener Tagblatt
 Mng. Ed.—H-J Hauzel
 Ed. in Ch./Ed.—K Rein
 Ad. Mgr.—R Vogt

WILDESHAUSEN

WILDESHAUSER ZEITUNG (Wildeshauser News) (6x wk.) Est. 1859
 Bahnhofstr. 8, 27793
 Tel: (49-4431) 2527; Fax: (49-4431) 71120
 Circ.—1,300
 Prop.—Wildeshauser Zeitung

WILHELMSHAVEN
Pop. Est. 94,900

WILHELMSHAVENER ZEITUNG (Wilhelmshaven News) (e-6x wk.) Est. 1874
 Parkstr. 8 (26382); PF 1320, 26361
 Tel: (49-4421) 4880; Fax: (49-4421) 488259
 Circ.—32,600 ABC
 Prop.—Brune Verlag
 Pub.—M Adrian
 Pub.—W Brune
 Ed. in Ch.—J Westerhoff
 Ed.—J Peters
 Ad. Mgr.—W Ehlert

WILSTER
Pop. Est. 4,714

WILSTERSCHE ZEITUNG (6x wk.) Est. 1890
 Kolmarkt 12 (25554); PF 60, 25552
 Tel: (49-4823) 1661; Fax: (49-4823) 6191
 Circ.—2,600 ABC
 Prop.—Wilstersche Zeitung
 Pub./Bus. Mgr./Ad. Mgr.—J P Schwarck

WINDSHEIM, BAD
Pop. Est. 8,272

WINDSHEIMER ZEITUNG (The Wildsheim News) (6x wk.) Est. 1849
 Kegetstr. 11, 91438
 Tel: (49-9841) 9030; Fax: (49-9841) 90315
 Circ.—5,100 ABC
 Prop.—Delp
 Pub.—H Delp
 Pub.—B Schnell
 Ad. Mgr.—K Kreissel

WINNENDEN
Pop. Est. 23,100

WINNENDER ZEITUNG (The Winnender News) (6x wk.) Est. 1848
 Marktstr. 58 (71364); PF 148, 71349
 Tel: (49-7195) 690639; Fax: (49-7195) 690630
 Circ.—9,400 ABC
 Prop.—Zeitungsverlag Waiblingen
 Ed.—R Zeiffer
 Ad. Mgr.—M Fessler

WINSEN
(Lower Saxony)
Pop. Est. 27,400

WINSENER ANZEIGER (The Winsener Advertiser) (6x wk.)
 Schlossring 5 (21423); PF 1354, 21413
 Tel: (49-4171) 6580; Fax: (49-4171) 2953
 Circ.—11,500 ABC
 Prop.—Winsener Anzeiger
 Mng. Ed./Ed. in Ch./Ed.—N Braun
 Ed. in Ch./Bus. Mgr.—Dr. J P Ravens
 Bus. Mgr.—L Maack

WITTINGEN
Pop. Est. 5,219

ISENHAGENER KREISBLATT (6x wk.) Est. 1887
 Bahnhofstr. 48, 29378
 Tel: (49-5831) 29140; Fax: (49-5831) 291414

Europe   **Greece**

 Circ.—6,700 ABC
 Prop.—Beckers
 Ed. in Ch.—B Westerweg
 Ad. Mgr.—U Mertens

WITTMUND
Pop. Est. 6,371

ANZEIGER für HARLINGERLAND (6x wk.) Est. 1862
 Am Markt 18 (26409); PF 1352, 26400
 Tel: (49-4462) 8890; Fax: (49-4462) 88913
 Circ.—15,700 ABC
 Prop.—Mettcker
 Pub.—C L Mettcker
 Pub.—H Allmers
 Ed. in Ch.—W Malzahn
 Ed.—H Willms
 Bus. Mgr.—H Grönke
 Ad. Mgr.—N Peters

WUERZBURG
(WÜRZBURG)
Pop. Est. 127,100

MAIN POST (The Main Post) (6x wk.) Est. 1945
 Berner Str. 2 (97084); PF 6160, 97011
 Tel: (49-931) 60010; Fax: (49-931) 6001386
 Circ.—164,700 ABC
 Prop.—Mainpresse
 Pub.—L Glandt
 Pub.—J von Guttenberg
 Pub.—G Wiesemann
 Mng. Ed.—G-P Weirauch
 Ed. in Ch./Ed.—A Sahlender
 Ed. in Ch.—D Brandstätter
 Bus. Mgr.—E Aelker
 Ad. Mgr.—P Zoller
 (Circulation figure combines with Fränkische Volksblatt in Würzburg.)

ZEVEN
Pop. Est. 7,981

ZEVENER ZEITUNG (6x wk.) Est. 1889
 Gartenstr. 4 (27404); PF 1555, 27395
 Tel: (49-4281) 7190; Fax: (49-4281) 71966
 Circ.—10,300 ABC
 Prop.—Zeller
 Ed. in Ch.—U M Greiser
 Ad. Mgr.—H Ehlen

ZWEIBRUECKEN
(ZWEIBRÜCKEN)
Pop. Est. 32,700

PFÄLZISCHER MERKUR (6x wk.) Est. 1763
 Hauptstr. 66 (66482); PF 2064, 66470
 Tel: (49-6332) 92420; Fax: (49-6332) 924239
 Circ.—13,000 ABC
 Prop.—Zweibrücker Druckerei & Verlagsges
 Ed. in Ch.—E Steiger
 Bus. Mgr.—W Heller

ZWICKAU
Pop. Est. 114,600

ZWICKAUER TAGEBLATT (6x wk.) Est. 1990
 Schumannstr. 9 (08056); PF 115, 08002
 Tel: (49-375) 801127; Fax: (49-375) 25374
 Circ.—37,300 ABC
 Prop.—Westsachsen Verlag
 Ed. in Ch./Ed.—G Zielonka
 Ed. in Ch.—M Schissler
 Bus. Mgr.—C-H Kausche
 Ad. Mgr.—Barbara Bauer

GIBRALTAR
Pop. Est. 31,684

THE DEMOCRAT
 PO Box 156
 Tel: (350) 78363; Fax: (350) 78990
GIBRALTAR CHRONICLE (m) English; Est. 1801
 2 Library Gardens
 Tel: (350) 78589; Fax: (350) 79927
 Circ.—3,000
 Prop.—Gibralter Chronicle Ltd.
 Mng. Dir.—Jon Searle
 Ed.—F Cantos
THE GIBRALTAR ECHO (m) English & Spanish; Est. 1988
 56 Devil's Tower Rd.
 Pub.—Paul Campello
 Ed.—Eddie Campello

PANORAMA
 95 Irish Town
 Tel: (350) 79797; Fax: (350) 74664
THE PEOPLE
 Gibraltar Heights, Ste. 2
 Tel: (350) 71596
VOX
 40 Engineer Lane
 Tel: (350) 77414; Fax: (350) 72531

GREECE
Pop. Est. 10,564,630

AGIOS NICOLAOS
(Crete)

ANATOLI Est. 1932
 7 Polytechniou St., 72100
 Tel: (30) 84122242; Fax: (30) 84123843
 Pub.—E Koziris

AGRINION
(Aetolia & Acarnania)
(Central Greece)
Dept. Pop. Est. 219,764

PANAETOLIKI (d) Est. 1968
 25 Kakavia St., 30100
 Tel: (30) 64123411; Fax: (30) 64128232
 Prop.—Panaetoliki Etairia
 Ed.—G Stavropoulos

ALEXANDROUPOLI
(Thrace)
(Evros)
Dept. Pop. Est. 148,486

ELEFTHERI THRAKI (d) Est. 1945
 30 E. Venizelou St., 68100
 Tel: (30) 55126445; Fax: (30) 55124445
 Pub.—S Kondylis
EPARCHIAKOS TYPOS (d) Est. 1963
 71 E. Venizelou St., 68100
 Tel: (30) 55128008; Fax: (30) 55124077
 Pub.—Andrew Dagas
GNOMI (d) Est. 1984
 4 Moshonision St., 68100
 Tel: (30) 55124222
 Pub./Ed.—C Hatjopoulos

ARTA
(Epirus)
Dept. Pop. Est. 80,044

DEMOCRATIS (d) Est. 1974
 5 Koletti St., 47100
 Tel: (30) 68128008
 Pub.—A Agis
ICHO TIS ARTIS (d) Est. 1957
 2 Spirou Lambrou St., 47100
 Tel: (30) 68175100; Fax: (30) 68127940
 Pub.—K Tsaktsiras
MAHITIS (d) Est. 1983
 7 S. Matsou St., 47100
 Tel: (30) 68122779; Fax: (30) 68122779
 Pub.—D Spyrou
PARATIRITIS TIS ARTIS (d) Est. 1976
 5 Tzanetou St., 47100
 Tel: (30) 68125074
 Pub.—S Stasinou
PROINI (d) Est. 1989
 6 S. Labrou St., 47100
 Tel: (30) 68171888; Fax: (30) 68171888
 Pub.—K Getsis

ATHENS
(Central Greece)
Dept. Pop. Est. 3,027,331

ADESMEYTOS TYPOS
 36 Ionias St., 17456
 Tel: (30-1) 9958000; Fax: (30-1) 9958032/(30-1) 9958033
 Pub.—D Rizos
APOYEVMATINI (eS) Est. 1956
 12 Fidiou St., 10678
 Tel: (30-1) 36188115; Fax: (30-1) 3609876
 Circ.—72,904 (e); 73,178 (S)
 Prop.—Apogevmatini SA
 Ed.—Panos Karayiannis
 Ad. Mgr.—George Vitos
ATHENS NEWS (d) English
 3 Christou Lada St., 10237
 Tel: (30-1) 3250611/(30-1) 3250613; Fax: (30-1) 3228797

Greece

Circ.—10,000
Prop.—Dimosiographicos Organismos Lambraki SA
Pub.—C Lambrakis
ATHLITIKI ICHO (d) Est. 1950
11 Voulgari St., 10437
Tel: (30-1) 9233880; Fax: (30-1) 9233255
Circ.—24,117
Pub.—Athan Sembos
Pub.—G Georgalas A E
AVGHI (d) Est. 1952
12 Aghiou Konstantinou St., 10431
Tel: (30-1) 5231834; Fax: (30-1) 5231830
Circ.—9,053
Pub.—L Voutsas
Dir.—Grigoris Giannaros
AVRIANI (eS) Est. 1980
11Dimitros St., Tavros, 17778
Tel: (30-1) 3424090; Fax: (30-1) 3424090
Circ.—51,370 (e); 50,424 (S)
Prop.—George A Kouris SA
Ed.—John Gavrielatos
AZAT OR (d) Greek; Est. 1945
54 Sfigos St., 11745
Tel: (30-1) 9345237; Fax: (30-1) 9346229
Circ.—600
Prop.—Azator
Ed.—H Bazaziay
DIMOPRASSIAKA NEA O KOSMOS (d) Est. 1951
49 Didotou St., 10680
Tel: (30-1) 3639485
Pub.—P Konstandinis
ELEFTHERI ORA
32 Akadimias Ave., 10672
Tel: (30-1) 3644128
Pub.—Grigoris Michalopoulos
ELEFTHEROS (d) Est. 1986
18 Amerikis St., 10671
Tel: (30-1) 3630521; Fax: (30-1) 3619502
Pub.—Yola Michalopoulos
Ed. in Ch.—C Frigelis
ELEFTHEROS TYPOS/TYPOSS TIS KIPIAKIS (eS)
1 Mitropeleos St., 10557
Tel: (30-1) 3237671; Fax: (30-1) 9920980
Circ.—145,000 (e); 130,000 (S)
Pub.—Michael Sarris
Dir.—Cristos Passalaris
Ed.—Dimitris Pizos
Ad. Mgr.—Demetris Vourdouris
ELEFTHEROTYPIA (d) Est. 1974
8 Koloktroini, 10651
Tel: (30-1) 3242071; Fax: (30-1) 3242318
Circ.—1,858,316
Prop.—X K Tegopoulos Editions SA
Pub.—X K Tegopoulos
Dir.—S Fyntanidis
Ed. in Ch.—S Aperghis
ENIMEROSSI POLITIKI IKONOMIKI (d) Est. 1988
55-59 Deligiorgi St., 10437
Tel: (30-1) 5238525/(30-1) 5238526
Pub.—K Roubinetis
EPHIMERIS DIAKIRIXEON (d) Est. 1974
18 Ypsilantou St.
Tel: (30-1) 3214857
Pub.—T H Mallios
EPHIMERIS DIMOPRASION & PLEISTIRIASMON
(d) Est. 1929
3 Emmanuel Benaki St., 10564
Tel: (30-1) 3215692
Dir.—Zoi Lefkofrydi
Ed.—J Lefkofrydi
ESTIA (d) Est. 1898
7 Anthimou Gazi St., 10561
Tel: (30-1) 3230481/(30-1) 3230482; Fax: (30-1) 3243071
Circ.—92,646
Pub.—Adonis Kyrou
Ed. in Ch.—S Papageorghiou
ETHNOS (e) Est. 1982
Benaki St., Metamorfosi 15235
Tel: (30-1) 6380640; Fax: (30-1) 6391337
Circ.—76,000
Pub./Ed.—George Bobolas
Dir.—T H Kaloudis
Edit'l. Dir.—E Bartzinopoulos
Ed. in Ch.—John Amanatidis
Ad. Mgr.—Mazina Mantzari
EXORMISSI
13-15 Solomou St., 10682
Tel: (30-1) 3803311; Fax: (30-1) 3833326
Pub.—D Sapountzis
EXPRESS (m) Est. 1963
39 Halandriou St., 15125
Tel: (30-1) 6827582/(30-1) 68994007; Fax: (30-1) 6825858/(30-1) 6899422
Ed.—D Kalofolias
Ed.—S Galeos
Mgr.—E Maniatis
FILATHLOS (d) Est. 1982
11 Dimitrios St., 17778
Tel: (30-1) 3424090; Fax: (30-1) 3452190

Dir.—Nikos Karayannidis
Ed. in Ch.—Yannis Mathioudakis
FOS TON SPOR (d)
122 Athinon Ave., 10442
Tel: (30-1) 5245511
Ed.—T Nickolaids
GENIKI DIMOPRASION (d) Est. 1977
59 Arkadias St., 15234
Tel: (30-1) 6011097; Fax: (30-1) 5236927
Pub.—M Papanikolaou
ICHO TON DIMOPRASSION (d) Est. 1971
15 Amerikis St., 10672
Tel: (30-1) 3615917; Fax: (30-1) 3626073
Pub.—C Tzinis
KATHIMERINI (mS) Est. 1918
57 Socratous St., 10431
Tel: (30-1) 5231001; Fax: (30-1) 5228894
Circ.—17,622 (m); 67,884 (S)
Pub.—Themistoklis H A Alafouzos
Edit'l. Dir.—A Karkayiannis
Ed. in Ch.—A Stagos
Ed.—Panos Laukakos
KERDOS (d) Est. 1985
4 Vissarionos St., 15231
Tel: (30-1) 3646078; Fax: (30-1) 6477893
Pub.—D Liakounakos
Dir.—A Michaelidis
KINONIKI (d) Est. 1963
21 Alkminis St., 11854
Tel: (30-1) 4115225
Pub.—S T Karambezopolous
KYRIAKATIKI ELEFTHEROTYPIA (d)
10-16 Minoos St., 11743
Tel: (30-1) 9296001
LOGOS (m) Est. 1986
31 Demetros St., 17778
Tel: (30-1) 3424090; Fax: (30-1) 3452190
Pub.—Costas Gekoyikolos
Dir.—K Geronikolos
MALHITIKI FONI (d) Est. 1982
9 Ag. Georgiou St., 15234
Tel: (30-1) 6822555
Pub.—G Nikolopoulos
MESIMVRINI (Midday) (e-ex S)
10 Panepistimiou St., 10671
Tel: (30-1) 3646010; Fax: (30-1) 3631625
Cir.—30,756
Ed.—Ch Passalaris
NEA (d) Est. 1945
3 Christou Lada St., 10237
Tel: (30-1) 3250611/(30-1) 3250613; Fax: (30-1) 3228797
Prop.—Dimosiographicos Organisimos Lambraki SA
Pub.—C Lambrakis
Dir.—L Karapanayotis
Dir./Ed.—V Nikolopoulos
ORA GIA SPOR (d) Est. 1991
10 Spirou Donta St., 11743
Tel: (30-1) 9239659
Pub.—C Sebou
PARON (d) Est. 1974
24 Voulis St., 10563
Tel: (30-1) 3229688; Fax: (30-1) 3233263
Pub.—Panagis Koutoufas
PONTIKI (d) Est. 1974
10 Massalias St., 10680
Tel: (30-1) 3602361; Fax: (30-1) 3645406
Prop.—PONTIKI A E
RIZOSPASTIS (d) Est. 1974
145 Leoforos Irakliou Ave., 14231
Tel: (30-1) 2520247/(30-1) 2521352; Fax: (30-1) 2529480
Circ.—42,883
Pub.—G Tricalinos
Dir.—Takis Tsigas
Ed. in Ch.—T Karteros
SPORT TIME (d) Est. 1994
116 Kifisias & Davaki St., 11526
Tel: (30-1) 6490000; Fax: (30-1) 6229022
Pub.—Michalis Androulidakis
STAR (d) Est. 1993
31 Demetros St., 17778
Tel: (30-1) 3474700; Fax: (30-1) 3474945
TA NEA (d) Est. 1931
3 Christou-Lada St., 10237
Tel: (30-1) 3230221; Fax: (30-1) 3228797
Circ.—155,000
Prop.—Lambrakis Press SA
Ed. in Ch.—Cr Lambrakis
Ad. Mgr.—N Biliris

CHIOS
(Aegean Island)
Dept. Pop. Est. 49,865

ALITHIA (d) Est. 1987
1 Polihronopoulou St., 82100
Tel: (30) 27125838
Pub.—Yannis Tzoumas

CHIAKOS LAOS (d) Est. 1953
8 Rodokanaki St., 82100
Tel: (30) 27124329; Fax: (30) 27128596
Pub.—G Douvlis
DIMOKRATIKI (d) Est. 1988
36 Kountouriotou St., 82100
Tel: (30) 27122260; Fax: (30) 27123445
Pub.—E Tsouri
PROODOS (d) Est. 1927
44 Rodokanaki St., 82100
Tel: (30) 27123085; Fax: (30) 27126898
Pub.—N Frangoulis
Pub.—K Frangoulis

CORFU
(Ionian Islands)
Dept. Pop. Est. 99,477

ELEFTHERIA (d) Est. 1989
9 Delvinioti St., 49100
Tel: (30) 66122022
Pub./Dir.—I Tzevelikas
KERKYRAIKO VIMA (d) Est. 1976
11 Korinthion St., 49100
Tel: (30) 66137990; Fax: (30) 66124970
Pub./Dir.—K Balos
IDISSEIS TIS KERKIRAS (d)
Agios Elias St., 49100
Tel: (30) 66137986; Fax: (30) 66137986
Pub.—S T G Karvounis
SIMERINI Est. 1972
Palaiokastritsas National Rd., 49100
Tel: (30) 661361206
Dir.—E Vergis

DRAMA
(Macedonia)
Dept. Pop. Est. 94,772

DRAMINI (d)
2240 Ekklision St., 66100
Tel: (30) 52121333
Pub.—J Melidis
ICHO (d)
Stoa Gatzouli, 66100
Tel: (30) 52123444; Fax: (30) 52123444
Pub.—Thanassis Papadimitriou
PROINOS TYPOS (d)
3 G. Zervou St., 66100
Tel: (30) 52122364; Fax: (30) 52125611
Pub.—G Stavridis

EDESSA

PROINI (d) Est. 1981
21 L. Nikis St., 58200
Tel: (30) 25019; Fax: (30) 26333
Pub.—Soula St Vagourdi

FLORINA
(Macedonia)

POLITIS (d) Est. 1992
27 Kallergi St., 53100
Tel: (30) 23732/(30) 23920
Pub.—I Nikoltsannis

GIANNITSA
(Macedonia)

GIANNITSA (d) Est. 1994
113 E. Venizelou St.
Tel: (30) 38282333; Fax: (30) 38282333

GREVEMA
(Macedonia)

ENIMEROSSI (d) Est. 1987
11 Evagelistrias St., 51100
Tel: (30) 46224714
Pub.—Y Papadopoulos
IMMERISSIOS LOGOS (d) Est. 1992
2 Evagelistrias St., 51100
Tel: (30) 46224811
Pub.—Anastasia Migdani
PROINI (d)
3 Mitropoleas St., 51100
Tel: (30) 46223388
Pub.—Efth Tsaknakis

HALTIDA
(Central Greece)
(Evia)

EVOIKOS TYPOS (d) Est. 1992
3 Panidiu St., 34100
Tel: (30) 76686; Fax: (30) 87728
Pub.—N Smirnis

HANIA
(Crete)
Dept. Pop. Est. 125,856

AGONAS TIS KRITIS (d) Est. 1981
10 Peridou St., 73100
Tel: (30) 82153163
Pub.—D Agelakis

DIMOKRATIS TON HANION (d) Est. 1966
25 Peridou St., 73100
Tel: (30) 82123836; Fax: (30) 82158010
Pub.—I Malamadakis
HANIOTIKA NEA (d) Est. 1970
49 Karaiskaki St., 73100
Tel: (30) 82170563; Fax: (30) 82191900
Pub./Dir.—J Garedakis
HANIOTIKI ELEFTHEROTYPIA (d) Est. 1977
38 Ipsilanti St., 73100
Tel: (30) 82197174; Fax: (30) 82190400
Pub.—A Spanoudakis
Dir.—M Spanoudakis
KIRYX (d)
22 K. Hiotaki St., 73100
Tel: (30) 82198240; Fax: (30) 82194074
Prop.—Kiryx Corp.
Pub.—G Paradomenakis
Dir.—K Mitsotakis

IGOUMENITSA
(Epirus)
(Thesprotia)
Dept. Pop. Est. 41,278

ELEFTHERO VIMA (d) Est. 1966
19-23 Februaaiou St., 46100
Tel: (30) 66523767; Fax: (30) 66525451
Pub./Dir.—D Saloukas
THESPROTIKI (d) Est. 1969
15 Souliou St., 46100
Tel: (30) 66522493; Fax: (30) 66524355
Pub.—V Ntais

IOANNINA
(Epirus)
(Yanina)
Dept. Pop. Est. 147,304

ELEFTHERIA (d) Est. 1979
59-28 Octovriou St., 45444
Tel: (30) 65131602; Fax: (30) 65131602
Prop.—Ipirotikos Organismos Dimosiotitos
Pub.—K Kaltsis
ENIMEROSSI (d) Est. 1988
8 A. Spiridonos St., 45444
Tel: (30) 65173988; Fax: (30) 65131038
Pub.—D Kountourantzi
EPIROTIKOS AGON (d) Est. 1927
17 O. Poutetsi St., 45444
Tel: (30) 65125771; Fax: (30) 65134862
Pub.—Lucia Tzalla
NEOI AGONES EPIROU (d)
7 Dagli St., 45444
Tel: (30) 65177466; Fax: (30) 65137880
Pub.—Areti Malami-Anastasiadou
PROINA NEA (d) Est. 1964
A. Marinas & Katsari St., 45444
Tel: (30) 65126296; Fax: (30) 65120067
Pub./Dir.—P Christopoulos
PROINOS LOGOS (d) Est. 1957
11 Fotou Tzavella St., 45333
Tel: (30) 65133791
Prop.—Ekdotiki Ipirou Ltd.
Pub.—V Koutsoliontos
Dir.—I Zois

IRAKLION
(Crete)
(Iraklion)
Dept. Pop. Est. 243,622

ALLAGHI (d) Est. 1961
4 Kozani St., 71110
Tel: (30-81) 280022; Fax: (30-81) 243370
Pub.—Man Karellis
DEMOCRATIS (d) Est. 1951
17 Kantanoleon St., 71202
Tel: (30-81) 224225
Pub.—Anthousa E Papageorgiou
IRAKLIOTIKA NEA (d) Est. 1989
25 Komninon St., 71202
Tel: (30-81) 225466; Fax: (30-81) 242509
Pub.—D Petrakis
MESOGHIOS (d) Est. 1953
20 Handakos St., 71202
Tel: (30-81) 283138; Fax: (30-81) 282138
Pub.—C Grammatikakis
PATRIS (d) Est. 1950
7 Lappa St., 71305
Tel: (30-81) 282625; Fax: (30-81) 282138
Pub.—A Mykoniatis
TOLMI (d) Est. 1984
51 Dikeossinis St., 71202
Tel: (30-81) 221332
Pub.—N Vidakis

KALAMATA
(Peloponnese)
Dept. Pop. Est. 159,818

ELEFTHERIA (d) Est. 1981
13 Valaoritou, 24100
Tel: (30) 72121421; Fax: (30) 72121747
Pub./Dir.—N Plemmenos

SIMAEA (d) Est. 1916
  Plateia Mavromihali, 24100
  Tel: (30) 72122214; Fax: (30) 72123214
  Pub./Dir.—Roi Michalakea
THARROS (d) Est. 1899
  60 Stadiou St., 24100
  Tel: (30) 72122155
  Pub.—M Apostolakis
  Dir.—I Apostolakis

KARDITSA
(Thessaly)
Dept. Pop. Est. 124,930

MAHI (d) Est. 1983
  30 Valvi St., 43100
  Tel: (30) 44140200
  Pub./Dir.—A Foukalas
NEOS AGON (d) Est. 1935
  25 S. Lappa St., 43100
  Tel: (30) 44121544; Fax: (30) 44140344
  Pub./Dir.—F Alexiou
NEOI KEROI (d) Est. 1965
  34 Iezekiil St., 43100
  Tel: (30) 44171571; Fax: (30) 44120998
  Pub.—K H Bourlis
THESSALIKI ICHO (d)
  7 Kraterou St., 43100
  Tel: (30) 44121541
  Pub./Dir.—E Missas

KASTORIA
(Macedonia)

KATHIMERINI FONI (d) Est. 1992
  4-B Kolototroni St., 52100
  Tel: (30) 46727678; Fax: (30) 46726177
  Pub.—Sergios-Paraskevi Iatrou
OSIZONTESS (d) Est. 1989
  6 Dalipi St., 52100
  Tel: (30) 46724377; Fax: (30) 46724783
  Pub.—Agzata Zatta

KATERINI
(Pieria)
(Macedonia)

OLIMPIO VIMA (d) Est. 1975
  1 Gratsani St., 60100
  Tel: (30) 35124833
  Prop.—Ekdotiki Enimerotiki-Ikoromilos A E
PIERIKOI ANTILALOI Est. 1974
  5 Parodos Botsi St., 60100
  Tel: (30) 35125753; Fax: (30) 35125229
  Pub.—G Dermisis
PIEROFONIA (d) Est. 1988
  126 7th Merarhias St., 60100
  Tel: (30) 35135927
  Pub.—P Tzikas

KAVALA
(Macedonia)
Dept. Pop. Est. 135,218

EVDOMI (d) Est. 1981
  19 Filellinon St., 65403
  Tel: (30-51) 65403; Fax: (30-51) 834566
  Prop.—G Hzoros Sia A E
KAVALA (d) Est. 1977
  153 Omonia St., 65403
  Tel: (30-51) 221717
  Prop.—Ekdoseis Poseidon A E
PROINI (d) Est. 1951
  12 Kyprou St., 65403
  Tel: (30-51) 222288; Fax: (30-51) 223331
  Pub.—P Baklavas
  Dir.—M Genikopoulos
TAHIDROMOS (d) Est. 1931
  24 Pavlou Mela St., 65302
  Tel: (30-51) 223348; Fax: (30-51) 839263

KEFALONIA
(Ionian Island)

KATHE MERA (d)
  4 Vourvahi St.
  Tel: (30) 67125278; Fax: (30) 67125278
VRADINES ORES (d) Est. 1992
  4 Vourvahi St.
  Tel: (30) 67125278; Fax: (30) 67125278
  Pub.—M Georgatos

KILKIS
(Macedonia)

IMERISSIA Est. 1986
  179 21 Iouniou St., 61100
  Tel: (30) 34122900; Fax: (30) 34124100
  Pub.—S Orphanides

KOMOTINI
(Thrace)
(Rodopi)
Dept. Pop. Est. 107,957

AKRITIKI FONI (d) Est. 1992
  7 Miltiadou St., 69100
  Tel: (30) 53129223
  Pub.—D Gogou
ELEFTHERO VIMA (d) Est. 1982
  59 Fil. Eterias St., 69100
  Tel: (30) 53126444
  Prop.—Thrakikes Ekdoseis Co.
HRONOS Est. 1967
  22-24 N. Zoidou St., 69100
  Tel: (30) 53122791; Fax: (30) 53131302
  Dir.—A Fanfanis
PARATIRITIS TIS THRAKIS (d) Est. 1990
  1 Orfeos St., 69100
  Tel: (30) 53126027; Fax: (30) 53126027
  Prop.—Paratiritis E P E
PATRIDA (d) Est. 1977
  57 N. Zoidou St., 69100
  Tel: (30) 53131892; Fax: (30) 53127300
  Pub./Dir.—K E Tsetlakas

KORINTHOS
(Peloponnese)
Dept. Pop. Est. 1,096,390

IMERISSIA KORINTHOU (d) Est. 1935
  28 Adimadou St., 20100
  Tel: (30-741) 22810
  Pub.—M S Papasideris
KORINTHIAKA GEGONOTA (d) Est. 1992
  71 Kyprou St., 20100
  Tel: (30-741) 29444; Fax: (30-741) 72803
  Prop.—Ekdoseis Korinthiaka NEA
KORINTHIAKI IMERA (d) Est. 1983
  17 E. Antistaseos St., 20100
  Tel: (30-741) 22062
  Pub.—Chr Skoyteris

KOZANI
(Macedonia)
Dept. Pop. Est. 147,051

HRONOS (d) Est. 1980
  2 Ol. Georgaki St., 50100
  Tel: (30) 46125246; Fax: (30) 46141500
  Pub.—N Kostarellas
PROINOS LOGOS (d) Est. 1990
  2 I. Dragoumi St., 50100
  Tel: (30) 46140427; Fax: (30) 46140427
  Prop.—L Rigas J Sia O E
TAHIDROMOS (d) Est. 1985
  11 Evagelistrias St., 50100
  Tel: (30) 46128005; Fax: (30) 46128005
  Pub.—G Papadopoulos
THARROS (d) Est. 1985
  2 Tsontza St., 50100
  Tel: (30) 46138611; Fax: (30) 46134611

LAMIA
(Central Greece)
(Fthistida)
Dept. Pop. Est. 161,955

ENIMEROSI FTHIOTIKI (d) Est. 1992
  23 Diakou St., 35314
  Tel: (30) 23143580; Fax: (30) 23143500
  Pub.—P Dakoglou
EPIKEROS (d) Est. 1985
  6 Panourgia St., 35100
  Tel: (30) 23137583
  Pub.—Chr Karayannis
FOS (d) Est. 1963
  55 Ipsilantou St.
  Tel: (30) 23123303; Fax: (30) 23126970
  Dir.—D Papaefthimiou
LAMIAKOS TYPOS (d) Est. 1935
  42 Rozaki St., 35100
  Tel: (30) 23122360; Fax: (30) 23129331
  Pub./Dir.—D Rizos
PROINA NEA (d) Est. 1989
  31 Karaiskaki St., 35100
  Tel: (30) 23134666; Fax: (30) 23134244
  Pub.—F I Papalexis

LARISSA
(Thessaly)
Dept. Pop. Est. 254,295

ELEFTHERIA (d) Est. 1922
  6 Papastavrou St., 41000
  Tel: (30-41) 535784; Fax: (30-41) 535959
  Pub.—Pan Dimitrakopoulos
IMERISSIOS KYRIS (d) Est. 1929
  37 M. Alexandrou St., 41222
  Tel: (30-41) 252013; Fax: (30-41) 250762
  Pub.—A T H Zisopoulos

LEVADIA
(Central Greece)

NEA TIS VIOTIAS Est. 1986
  22 Athinon St., 32100
  Tel: (30) 26127180; Fax: (30) 26127423
  Pub.—Chr Kalintassis
VIOTIKI ORA (d) Est. 1979
  Pl Ethnikis Antistaseos
  Tel: (30) 26123175; Fax: (30) 26128489
  Pub.—P Houtzoumis

MEGARA
(Central Greece)
(Attiki)
Dept. Pop. Est. 342,093

MEGARIKOS TYPOS (d)
  52 28 Octobriou St.
  Pub./Dir.—M Papasideris

MESSOLONGHI
(Central Greece)
Dept. Pop. Est. 219,764

ETHNIKI ICHO (d) Est. 1969
  2-4 M. Makri St., 30200
  Tel: (30) 63124720/(30) 63128040
  Dir.—Irene K Riga

MYTILENE
(Aegean Islands)
(Lesvos)
Dept. Pop. Est. 104,620

EOLIKA NEA (d)
  3-B A. Irini St., 81100
  Tel: (30) 25142750; Fax: (30) 25143350
  Pub.—G Kondiloudis
LESBIAKOS KERIX (d) Est. 1959
  Stoa Grigoriou, 81100
  Tel: (30) 25128159
  Pub.—A Karvela

NOFPLIO
(Argolida)
(Peloponnese)

ARGOLIKI ENIMEROSSI (d) Est. 1994
  32 Asklipiou St., 21100
  Tel: (30) 75221014; Fax: (30) 75223037
  Pub.—P Dakoglou
EIDISSEIS Est. 1986
  2 Koleth St., 21100
  Tel: (30) 751276461/(30) 75125805;
  Fax: (30) 7512316
  Pub.—K Kalkanis

PATRAI
(Peloponnese)
(Achaias)
Dept. Pop. Est. 95,364

ALLAGHI (d) Est. 1981
  31 Maizonos St.
  Tel: (30-61) 31104; Fax: (30-61) 311322
  Pub./Dir.—G Alexopoulos
IMERA (m-ex mon.) Est. 1945
  45 Tsamadou St., 26222
  Tel: (30-61) 315010; Fax: (30-61) 344160
  Dir.—A Christopoulos
  Ed. in Ch.—A Babanevas
IMERISSIOS KERIX PATROM (d) Est. 1969
  27 Filopimenos St., 26221
  Tel: (30-61) 277384; Fax: (30-61) 271272
  Pub.—D Vris
  Ed.—Andreas A Vris
PELOPONISSOS (d) Est. 1886
  206 Mezonos St., 26225
  Tel: (30-61) 612530; Fax: (30-61) 612535
  Pub.—S Doukas

PIRAEUS
Dept. Pop. Est. 476,304

CHRONOGRAPHOS (d)
  58 Karaiskov St., 18532
  Tel: (30-1) 4178079; Fax: (30-1) 4178079
  Pub.—M Karayiannis
DEMOTIS (d) Est. 1954
  99 Ypsilantou St., 18532
  Tel: (30-1) 4120986; Fax: (30-1) 4120986
  Pub.—Christalia Raisi
FONI TOU PIREOS (d)
  77 Notara St., 18535
  Tel: (30-1) 4174233
  Pub.—P Petsas
NAFTEMBORIKI (d) Est. 1923
  3 Akti Miaouli, 18535
  Tel: (30-1) 4178691; Fax: (30-1) 4179030

  Pub.—N Athanassiades
  Edit'l. Dir.—N Saranthenas
NEOS LOGOS (d) Est. 1981
  5 A. Konstantinou St., 18531
  Tel: (30-1) 4175256
  Pub.—P Konstantinidis
NEI DROMI (d) Est. 1989
  99-101 Ypsilandou St., 18532
  Tel: (30-1) 4120986
  Pub.—K Raisi
PIRAIKO VIMA (d) Est. 1977
  58 Karaiskou St., 18531
  Tel: (30-1) 4177359
  Pub.—E Afara

PREVEZA
(Epirus)
Dept. Pop. Est. 55,915

ADESMEFTOS (d) Est. 1981
  97 P. Tsaldari St., 48100
  Tel: (30) 68222814
  Prop.—Ekdotki Enimerosi
  Dir.—Dimitrius Loupas
NEO VIMA (d) Est. 1987
  7 L. Virona St., 48100
  Tel: (30) 68222804
  Pub.—P E Baizis
TOPIKI FONI (d) Est. 1974
  28 E. Antistasseos St., 48100
  Tel: (30) 62827538
  Pub./Dir.—K Zervas
VIMA TIS PREVEZAS (d) Est. 1994
  85 E. Antistasseos St., 48100
  Tel: (30) 68229753; Fax: (30) 68229753
  Pub.—D Katsipanelis

PYRGOS
(Peloponnese)
Dept. Pop. Est. 160,305

PATRIS (d) Est. 1902
  13 Themistokleous St., 27100
  Tel: (30) 62122549
  Pub.—E Varouxis
PATRIS TIS KYRIAKIS (d) Est. 1989
  13 Themistokleous St., 27100
  Tel: (30) 62126683
  Pub.—E Varouxis
PROINI (d) Est. 1984
  37-28 Oktavriou St., 27100
  Tel: (30) 62126008; Fax: (30) 62131665

RETHYMNON
(Crete)
Dept. Pop. Est. 62,634

ELEFTHERI GNOMI (d)
  E. Venizelou Prokymaia
  Pub.—L G Sbokos
KRITIKI EPITHEORISSIS (d) Est. 1911
  138 L. Kountouriotou St., 74100
  Tel: (30) 83122867; Fax: (30) 83128258
  Pub.—S Kalaitzakis
RETHYMNIOTIKA NEA (d) Est. 1965
  7-9 I. Hatzigrigoraki St., 74100
  Tel: (30) 83127627; Fax: (30) 83121413
  Dir./Ed.—I Halkiadakis
VIMA (d)
  5 I. Melissinou St., 74100
  Tel: (30) 83122247
  Pub.—E Kafatos

RHODOS
(Dodekanisou)
Dept. Pop. Est. 145,071

DIMOKRATIKI TIS RODOU (d) Est. 1982
  13A Kladiou Peper St., 85100
  Tel: (30-241) 34722
  Pub./Dir.—V Athanasiou
PROODOS (d) Est. 1949
  21 M. Maliaraki St., 85100
  Tel: (30-241) 27356; Fax: (30-241) 20643
  Dir.—G Diamantides
RODIAKI (d) Est. 1915
  11 M. Maliaraki St., 85100
  Tel: (30-241) 24610; Fax: (30-241) 75641
  Pub.—S Tsopanakis

SERRES
(Macedonia)
Dept. Pop. Est. 196,247

AKRITIKI FONI (d) Est. 1989
  12 D. Solomou St., 62100
  Tel: (30) 32125621; Fax: (30) 32125621
  Pub.—M Vogiatzi
KATHIMERINOS PARATIRITIS (d) Est. 1980
  27 Spetson St., 62100
  Tel: (30) 32162600; Fax: (30) 32162345
  Pub./Dir.—I Nomidis

Greece

(continued)

NEA EPOHI (d) Est. 1988
7 P. Grigoriu St., 62100
Tel: (30) 32164600; Fax: (30) 32126191
Pub.—A Giannakou
PROODOS (d) Est. 1929
3 Tsimiski St., 62100
Tel: (30) 32122212
Pub.—K B Komitoudis
Pub.—A Kolokotronis
SERRAIKON THARROS (d) Est. 1974
177 E. Venizelou St., 62100
Tel: (30) 32122380; Fax: (30) 32125621
Pub./Dir.—E Arabadgis

SPARTA
(Peloponnese)

SPARTIATIKA NEA Est. 1936
116 Vrasidou St., 11252
Tel: (30) 73121103; Fax: (30) 73121103
Pub.—K Papadopoulos

SPARTI
(Peloponnese)

LAKONIKA KATHIMERINA NEA (d) Est. 1990
116 Vrassidou St., 23100
Tel: (30) 73121103; Fax: (30) 73121103
Pub.—T H Xeniotis

THESSALONIKI
(Macedonia)
Dept. Pop. Est. 871,580

AVRIANI VORIOU HELLADOS (d) Est. 1989
6 Karolou Dil St., 54623
Tel: (30-31) 276664; Fax: (30-31) 279282
Pub.—G Gavrielatos
BONUS (d) Est. 1994
153 Monastiriou St., 54627
Tel: (30-31) 252520; Fax: (30-31) 254980
Pub.—S Vlahopoulos
MACEDONIA (m-ex mon.) Est. 1911
77 Tsimiski St., 54622
Tel: (30-31) 521621; Fax: (30-31) 281033
Prop.—IK Vellis, Dimosiografkos Organismos Voriou Ellados AE
Pub.—Irene Athanassiadou
Ad. Mgr.—P Vassiliadis
PANELLINIA DIMOPRASION-DIAKIRIXEON (d) Est. 1993
2 Mitseon St., 54631
Tel: (30-31) 232536; Fax: (30-31) 243896
Pub.—I K Papadopoulos
SPOR TOU VORRA (d) Est. 1978
19 E. Antistasseos St., 54631
Tel: (30-31) 433602
Pub.—Z Simitzi
THESSALONIKI (e) Est. 1963
77 Tsimiski St., 54622
Tel: (30-31) 521621; Fax: (30-1) 281033
Cir.—108,738
Prop.—IK Vellis, Dimosiografkos Organismos Voriou Ellados AE
Ad. Mgr.—P Vassiliadis

TRIKALA
(Thessaly)
Dept. Pop. Est. 134,207

ENIMEROSI (d) Est. 1992
2 Koukoulari St., 42100
Tel: (30) 43123328; Fax: (30) 43128357
Pub.—K Tolis
EREVNA (d) Est. 1958
8 Kapodistriou St., 42100
Tel: (30) 43122055; Fax: (30) 43131892
Prop.—Ekdotiki Trikalon OE
Pub.—K Kiriakos
Pub.—G Katsiampas
Pub.—I Bakovasili
PROINOS LOGOS (d) Est. 1973
14 Kapodistriou St., 42100
Tel: (30) 43124230; Fax: (30) 43124953
Pub.—M Tsarouchas
Pub.—V Tsarouchas
TRIKALINA NEA (d) Est. 1963
5 Paparigopoulou St., 42100
Tel: (30) 43127519; Fax: (30) 43127519
Pub.—E Sabanikou

TRIPOLI
(Peloponnese)

KATHIMERINA NEA Est. 1985
69-71 Kalavriton St.
Tel: (30) 71223390; Fax: (30) 71231890
Pub.—E Karidis
PROINA NEA TIS ARKADIAS Est. 1993
13 Malliaropoulou St.
Tel: (30) 71227031; Fax: (30) 71239290
Pub.—D Spiliopoulou

VEROIA
(Macedonia)
Dept. Pop. Est. 133,750

IMERISIA (d) Est. 1984
270 Kentnikis, 59100
Tel: (30) 33166736
Pub.—A Stefanidis
LAOS (d) Est. 1965
10 Venizelou St.
Tel: (30) 33166913; Fax: (30) 33166979
Prop.—Patsikas Bros.
Pub.—M Patsikas
Dir.—C Patsikas

VOLOS
(Thessaly)
Dept. Pop. Est. 182,222

NEOS DROMOS (d) Est. 1993
36 Koutarelia St., 38221
Tel: (30) 42129367; Fax: (30) 42129368
Pub.—T H Popotas
TACHYDROMOS (d) Est. 1916
133 Angelopoulou St., 38221
Tel: (30) 42125463; Fax: (30) 42123683
Pub.—A Popotas
THESSALIA (m-ex mon.) Est. 1892
Lori & Iassonos Sts., 38221
Tel: (30) 42123303; Fax: (30) 42132828
Pub.—A Asvestas

XANTHI
(Thrace)
Dept. Pop. Est. 88,777

ADESMEFTI (d) Est. 1981
8 Hatzistavrou St., 67100
Tel: (30) 54128725
Pub./Dir.—P Papadopoulos
AGONAS (d) Est. 1983
3 Mecidania, 67100
Tel: (30) 54121717; Fax: (30) 54121155
Pub.—N Georgiadis
AKRITAS (d) Est. 1991
21-23 Venizelou St., 67100
Tel: (30) 54173333
Pub.—E Vasiliades
EMBROS (d) Est. 1977
31 Brokoumi St., 67100
Tel: (30) 54122950; Fax: (30) 54125608
Pub.—J Diafonidis
FONI TIS XANTHIS (d) Est. 1970
9 Velissariou St., 67100
Tel: (30) 54123262; Fax: (30) 54122549
Pub.—S Vlachopoulou

HUNGARY
Pop. Est. 10,319,113

BEKESCSABA
(Bekes)
Pop. Est. 67,266

BEKES MEGYEI HIRLAP Est. 1991
Munkacsy u. 4, 5601
Tel: (36) 66450450; Fax: (36) 66441020
Circ.—48,696
Ed. in Ch.—Dr. Zoltan Arpasi
NAPI DELKELET Est. 1992
Szigligetu u. 6, 5601
Tel: (36) 66324204/(36) 66323023; Fax: (36) 66322373
Prop.—Koropress
Pub.—Janos Kepenyes
Ed. in Ch.—Ilona Szatmari
Ed.—Sandor Seres
Ed.—Mihaly Tomka

BUDAPEST
(Pest)
Pop. Est. 2,018,000

BLIKK (d)
Robert Karoly krt. 61-65, 1134
Tel: (36-1) 2698587/(36-1) 2698588; Fax: (36-1) 2698589
Dir./Ed. in Ch.—Peter Toke
ESTI HIRLAP (Evening Journal) (e-ex S) Est. 1956
Blaha Lujza ter 3, 1085
Tel: (36-1) 1382399/(36-1) 1384300; Fax: (36-1) 1384550/(36-1) 1384058
Circ.—65,000
EXPRESSZ Est. 1984
Jozsef krt. 9, 1085
Tel: (36-1) 1338398/(36-1) 1341925
Circ.—75,000
Prop.—Hirlapkiado Vallalat
Pub.—Jozsef Horti
Ed.—Janos Mendel
Ed.—Istvanne Odor
Ed.—Janosne Sofalvi
KURIR Est. 1990
Koztarsasag ter 27 (1081); PF 614, 1425
Tel: (36-1) 2699269; Fax: (36-1) 2699340/(36-1) 2699341
Circ.—80,000
Ed. in Ch.—Gabor Szucs
Ed.—Tibor Muller
MAGYAR HIRLAP (Hungarian Journal) (d-ex S) Est. 1968
Kerepesi ut. 29/B, 1087
Tel: (36-1) 1330365/(36-1) 1334154; Fax: (36-1) 1334154
Circ.—80,000
Prop.—Pallas Lapes Konyvkiado Vallalat
Pub.—Magyar Hirlap
Pub.—Jozsef Kovalcsik
Ed. in Ch.—Peter Nemeth
U.S. Rep.—Nielsen Communications Ltd.
MAGYAR NEMZET (Hungarian Nation) (d-ex S) Est. 1938
Kinizsi u. 30-36, 1092
Tel: (36-1) 1343330; Fax: (36-1) 1344154
Circ.—390,000
Prop.—Pallas Lapes Konyvkiado Vallalat
Ed. in Ch.—Gabor Toth
U.S. Rep.—Nielsen Communications Ltd.
MAI NAP (The Sun) (d-ex sat.) Est. 1989
Konyves Kalman krt. 76, 1087
Tel: (36-1) 1343314/(36-1) 2100400; Fax: (36-1) 1339153
Circ.—130,000
Pub.—Peter Desi
Ed. in Ch.—Ferenc L Gazso
Ed.—Peter N Nagy
Ed.—Ferenc Pallagi
Ed.—Ferenc Szollosi
NAPI GAZDASAG Est. 1991
Csata u. 32 (1135); PF 534, 1397
Tel: (36-1) 1208062/(36-1) 1208217; Fax: (36-1) 1408111
Circ.—15,000
Pub.—Napi Gazdasag Kiado
Pub.—Janos Hont
Ed.—Adam Danko
NEMZETI SPORT (National Sport)
Visegradi u. 115, 1133
Tel: (36-1) 1384366; Fax: (36-1) 1384248
Circ.—170,000
Pub./Dir./Ed. in Ch.—Pal Borbely
NEPSPORT (People's Sport) (d-ex tues.) Est. 1944
Somogyi Bela ut. 6, 1085
Tel: (36-1) 1384366; Fax: (36-1) 1382463
Circ.—250,000
Prop.—Ifjusagi Lapes Konyvkiado Vallalat & Physical Training Council
Ed. in Ch.—Dr. Ferenc Kiraly
NEPSZAVA (Voice of the People) (m-ex mon.) Est. 1873
Torokvesz u. 30/a, 1022
Tel: (36-1) 2022988/(36-1) 2027788; Fax: (36-1) 2027798
Circ.—150,000
Prop.—Nepszava Kiado Vallalat & Trade Union Council
Pub.—Kalman Pyber
Ed. in Ch.—Dr. Andras Kereszty
NEPSZABADSAG (People's Freedom) (d-ex S) Est. 1942
Becsi ut. 122-124, 1960
Tel: (36-1) 2501680; Fax: (36-1) 2500250
Circ.—320,000
Prop.—Nepszabadsag
Pub.—Lengyel L Laszlo
Ed. in Ch.—Pal Eotvos
Ad. Mgr.—Fischer Andras
PESTI HIRLAP Est. 1992
Oktober 6 u. 8, 1051
Tel: (36-1) 2661006/(36-1) 2665503; Fax: (36-1) 1176029
Circ.—45,000
Pub./Dir./Ed. in Ch.—Andras Bencsik
PESTI MEGYEI HIRLAP (d-ex S) Est. 1956
Semogyi B., u. 6, 1446
Tel: (36-1) 1382399/(36-1) 1382539; Fax: (36-1) 1384416
Circ.—40,000
Prop.—Hirlapkiado Vallalat
Pub.—Jozsef Horti
Ed. in Ch.—Attila Vodros
PESTI RIPORT Est. 1991
Blaha Lujza ter 3, 1085
Tel: (36-1) 1382461; Fax: (36-1) 1384773
Circ.—50,000
Pub.—Szikra Lapnyomda
Pub.—Dr. Zoltan Csondes
Ed. in Ch.—Tibor Hamori
UJ MAGYARORSZAG Est. 1991
Blaha Lujza ter 3; PO Box 199, 1410
Tel: (36-1) 1185009; Fax: (36-1) 1222288
Circ.—60,000
Pub.—Zoltan E Horvath
Ed. in Ch.—Laszlo Fabian
UZLET NAPROL NAPRA
Bajcsy-Zsilinszky ut. 78, 1055
Tel: (36-1) 1117889/(36-1) 1317786
Ed. in Ch.—Istvan Ersek
VILAGGAZDASAG (d-ex S) Est. 1968
PO Box 3, 1426
Tel: (36-1) 1756722; Fax: (36-1) 1754191
Circ.—17,000
Pub./Ed.—Tamas Forro
Ed. in Ch.—Ilona Kocsi

DEBRECEN
(Hajdu-Bihar)
Pop. Est. 213,930

HAJDU-BIHARI NAPLO (Journal of Hajdu-Bihar County) (d-ex S) Est. 1944
Dosa Nador ter 10, 4024
Tel: (36-52) 312144; Fax: (36-52) 312326
Circ.—72,000
Prop.—Hajdu Megyei Lapkiado Vallalat
Pub.—Koch Thomas
Pub./Ed. in Ch.—Endre Bako

DUNAUJVAROS
(Fejer)

A HIRLAP (d)
Varoshaza ter 1, 2400
Tel: (36) 25310999
Ed. in Ch.—Dr. Csaba Kiss

EGER
(Heves)
Pop. Est. 61,283

HEVES MEGYEI HIRLAP Est. 1952
Barkoczy u. 7; Postfach 23, 3301
Tel: (36) 36413644; Fax: (36) 36412333
Circ.—33,000
Prop.—Axel Springer
Ed. in Ch.—Levente Kaposi

GYOR
(Gyor-Sopron)
Pop. Est. 129,600

KISALFOLD (Little Lowland) (d-ex S) Est. 1945
Szent Istvan ut. 51, 9022
Tel: (36-96) 315544; Fax: (36-96) 313042
Circ.—95,000
Prop.—Gyor Megyei Lapkiado Vallalat
Pub.—Kisalfold Kiado
Ed. in Ch.—Dr. Andor Kloss
NYUGATI HIRLAP Est. 1991
Kazinczy u. 16, 9021
Tel: (36-96) 11451; Fax: (36-96) 15374
Circ.—24,000
Pub.—Nyugat Kiado
Pub.—Sandor Nagy
Ed. in Ch.—Tibor N Magyar
UJ HIREK Est. 1991
Monus ut. 47-49, 9024
Tel: (36-96) 10277
Circ.—40,000
Pub.—Szo-Kep Kiadoi
Pub.—Denes Lukacsfly
Ed. in Ch.—Sandor Illes

KAPOSVAR
(Somogy)
Pop. Est. 72,330

SOMOGYI HIRLAP Est. 1990
Kontrassy u. 2/a; Postfach 31, 7401
Tel: (36-82) 311644; Fax: (36-82) 312315
Circ.—60,000
Pub.—Laszlo H Pordany
Ed. in Ch.—Dr. Imre Kercza
Ed.—Ferenc Biro
Ed.—Dr. Tibor Troszt

KECSKEMET
(Bacs-Kiskun)
Pop. Est. 91,929

PETOFI NEPE (Petofi's People) (d-ex S) Est. 1945
Szabadsag ter 1/a, 6001
Tel: (36) 76481391; Fax: (36) 76481434
Circ.—80,000
Prop.—Bacs Megyei Lapkiado Vallalat
Ed. in Ch.—Dr. Daniel Lovas

MISKOLC
(Borsod-Abauj-Zemplen)
Pop. Est. 194,000

DELI HIRLAP (d-ex S) Est. 1969
Bajcsy-Zsilinszky ut. 15, 3527
Tel: (36-46) 342694; Fax: (36-46) 342845
Circ.—15,600
Prop.—Borsod Megyei Lapkiado Vallalat
Pub.—Istvan Szanto
Ed. in Ch.—Laszlo Kiss

ESZAK-MAGYARORSZAG (Northern Hungary) (m) Est. 1948
Bajcsy-Zsilinszky ut. 15, 3527
Tel: (36-46) 341611; Fax: (36-46) 341630
Circ.—80,000
Prop.—Borsod Megyei Lapkiado Vallalat
Pub.—Eszak-Magyarorszag Lapkiado
Ed. in Ch.—Zoltan Nagy

NYIREGYHAZA
(Szabolcs-Szatmar)
Pop. Est. 108,156

KELET-MAGYARORSZAG (Eastern Hungary) (d-ex S) Est. 1944
Zrinyi Ilona u. 3-5, 4001
Tel: (36) 42311277; Fax: (36) 42315124
Circ.—81,000
Prop.—Szabolcs Megyei Lapkiado Vallalat
Pub.—Thomas Koch
Pub.—Esik Sandor
Ed. in Ch.—Dr. Sandor Angyal

UJ KELET (d)
Bercsenyi u. 8, 4400
Tel: (36) 42315678/(36) 42312903; Fax: (36) 42315532

PECS
(Baranya)
Pop. Est. 170,000

UJ DUNANTULI NAPLO (Hungarian Transdanubian Journal) (e) Est. 1943
Rakoczi ut. 34, 7623
Tel: (36) 72415000; Fax: (36) 72436345
Circ.—85,000
Prop.—Baranya Megyei Lapkiado Vallalat
Pub.—Gyorgy Molnar
Ed. in Ch.—Jeno Lombosi

SALGOTARJAN
(Nograd)
Pop. Est. 49,320

NOGRAD MEGYEI HIRLAP Est. 1992
Erzsebet ter 6, 3100
Tel: (36) 32316455; Fax: (36) 32312542
Circ.—21,000
Pub.—Jozsef Kulcsar
Ed. in Ch.—Dr. Ferenc Sztrapak

UJ NOGRAD (d-ex S) Est. 1949
Erzsebet ter 4, 3100
Tel: (36) 3210589/(36) 3216455
Circ.—28,000
Prop.—Nograd Megyei Lapkiado Vallalat
Ed. in Ch.—Laszlo Sulyok

SZEGED
(Csongrad)
Pop. Est. 176,100

CSONGRAD MEGYEI HIRLAP (Csongrad County Herald) (d-ex S) Est. 1943
Stefania ut. 10, 6740
Tel: (36) 62481281; Fax: (36) 481333
Circ.—67,000
Prop.—Csongrad Megyei Lapkiado Vallalat
Ed. in Ch.—Imre Dlusztus
Ed.—Istvan Sandi
Ed.—Istvan Szavay
Ed.—Lajos Tandi

DEL-MAGYARORSZAG (Southern Hungary) (d-ex S) Est. 1910
Stefania u. 10, 6740
Tel: (36) 62481281; Fax: (36) 62481333
Circ.—55,000
Prop.—Csongrad Megyei Lapkiado Vallalat & County Committee
Pub.—Theodore Christian
Pub./Ed. in Ch.—Imre Dlusztus
Ed.—Istvan Sandi
Ed.—Istvan Szavay
Ed.—Lajos Tandi

DELVILAG
Stefania u. 10, 6740
Tel: (36) 62423633/(36) 62313710
Circ.—18,000
Pub.—Theodore Christian
Pub./Ed. in Ch.—Imre Dlusztus
Ed.—Istvan Sandi
Ed.—Lajos Tandi

REGGELI DELVILAG
Stefania u. 10, 6740
Tel: (36) 62472872/(36) 62472769; Fax: (36) 62472244
Circ.—26,000
Pub.—Dr. Zsolt Szigeti
Ed. in Ch.—Dr. Istvan Nikolenyi

SZEKESFEHERVAR
(Fejer)
Pop. Est. 103,197

FEJER MEGYEI HIRLAP (Fejer County Herald) (d-ex S) Est. 1944
Honved u. 8, 8002
Tel: (36-22) 312450; Fax: (36-22) 312590
Circ.—52,360
Prop.—Fejer Megyei Lapkiando Vallalat
Ed. in Ch.—Pal Baranyi

SZEKSZARD
(Tolna)
Pop. Est. 34,592

TOLNAI NEPUJSAG (People's Paper) Est. 1990
Liszt Ferenc ter 3, 7100
Tel: (36) 74316211; Fax: (36) 74315508
Circ.—33,000
Ed. in Ch.—Gyorgyne Kamaras

SZOLNOK
(Szolnok)
Pop. Est. 77,000

UJ NEPLAP (d-ex S) Est. 1949
Kossuth ter 1, I. Irodahaz, 5001
Tel: (36-56) 424444; Fax: (36-56) 422853
Circ.—47,000
Prop.—Szolnok Megyei Lapkiado Vallalat Axel Springer
Ed. in Ch.—Jozsef Hajnal

SZOMBATHELY
(Vas)
Pop. Est. 82,830

VAS NEPE (People of Vas) (d-ex S) Est. 1957
Berzsenyi ter 2, 9701
Tel: (36) 94312232/(36) 94312895; Fax: (36) 94311524
Circ.—68,000
Prop.—Vas Megyei Lapkiado Vallalat & County Committee
Ed. in Ch.—Miklos Halmagyi

TATABANYA
(Komarom)
Pop. Est. 75,942

24 ORA (24 Hours) Est. 1990
Fo ter 4, 2801
Tel: (36) 34310811/(36) 34311991; Fax: (36) 34311010
Circ.—40,000
Pub.—Mihaly Vass
Ed. in Ch.—Gabor Gombkoto

VESZPREM
(Veszprem)
Pop. Est. 55,000

NAPLO (Journal) (d-ex S) Est. 1944
Szabadsag ter 15, 8201
Tel: (36-88) 327444; Fax: (36-88) 322915
Circ.—76,000
Prop.—Veszprem Megyei Lapkiado Vallalat
Ed. in Ch.—Elemer Balogh

ZALAEGERSZEG
(Zala)
Pop. Est. 39,671

ZALAI HIRLAP (d-ex S) Est. 1944
Ady Endre u. 62, 8901
Tel: (36-92) 312575; Fax: (36-92) 312581
Circ.—71,000
Prop.—Zala Megyei Lapkiado Vallalat
Pub.—Istvan Gyorffy
Ed. in Ch.—Hajnalka Magyar

ICELAND
Pop. Est. 263,599

AKUREYRI
Pop. Est. 14,436

DAGUR (Day)
Strandgata 31; PO Box 58, 600
Tel: (354-6) 24222; Fax: (354-6) 27639

KOPAVOGUR

PRESSAN
Nybylavegi 14-16, 200
Tel: (354-1) 681866
Circ.—25,000

REYKJAVIK
Pop. Est. 99,623

ALTHYDHUBLADID (Icelandic People's Paper) (d)
Hverfisgata 8-10, 101
Tel: (354-1) 625566; Fax: (354-1) 629244
Circ.—5,000
Prop.—Alprent Ltd.
Ed.—Sigurdur Tomas Bjoergvinsson

DAGBLADID/VISSIR (m-6x wk.) Est. 1910
Pall Steffansson & Ingolfur P Steinsson, Thverholt 11, 105
Tel: (354-1) 632700
Circ.—45,000
Prop.—Frajls Fjolmidlun Ltd.
Ed.—Jonas Kristiansson
Ed.—Elbert B Schram
Ad. Mgr.—Pall Stefansson
Ad. Mgr.—Ingolfur P Steinsson

MORGUNBLADID (Morning Paper) (m-6x wk.) Est. 1913
Kringlunni 1; PO Box 3040, 103
Tel: (354-1) 691100; Fax: (354-1) 691100
Circ.—52,000
Prop.—Arvakur Ltd.
Ed.—Matthias Johannessen
Ed.—Styrmir Gunnarsson
Ad. Mgr.—Gestur Einarsson

TIMINN (Times) (m-5x wk.) Est. 1917
Brautarholt 1, 105
Tel: (354-1) 5631600; Fax: (354-1) 5516270
Circ.—14,000
Prop.—The Progressive Party
Ed.—Jon Kristjansson
Ad. Mgr.—Steingrimur Gislason

ITALY
Pop. Est. 58,138,394

ANCONA
(Marche)
Pop. Est. 104,409

CORRIERE ADRIATICO (m) Est. 1860
Via Berti 20, 60100
Tel: (39-71) 42985; Fax: (39-71) 41898
Circ.—24,499 ABC
Prop.—Società Editrice Adriatica SpA
Dir.—Paolo Biagi
Vice Dir.—Sergio Roscani
Ed. in Ch.—Enzo Polverigiani

GAZZETTA ASTE E APPALTI PUBBLICI (d) Est. 1984
Via Valle Miano 13/h, 60125
Tel: (39-71) 897869; Fax: (39-71) 85627
Dir.—Fulvio Diamantini

LA GAZZETTA DI ANCONA (Ancona Gazette) (d) Est. 1986
Via Spadoni (Baraccola Ovest), 60100
Tel: (39-71) 8047111
Ed.—Paolo Farneti

AREZZO
(Toscana)
Pop. Est. 91,681

CORRIERE ARETINO (d)
Corso Italia 205, 52100
Tel: (39) 57524244
Mng. Ed.—Franco Franchini

LA GAZZETTA DI AREZZO (Arezzo Gazette) (d) Est. 1987
Via Cavour 119, 52100
Tel: (39) 575350881; Fax: (39) 575300320
Dir.—Paolo Farneti
Ed. in Ch.—Romano Salvi

ASCOLI PICENO

LA GAZZETTA DI ASCOLI PICENO (Ascoli Piceno Gazette) (d) Est. 1987
Via dei Guiderocchi 7, 63100
Tel: (39) 736255505; Fax: (39) 736255530
Dir.—Paolo Farneti

BARI
(Puglia)
Pop. Est. 363,597

LA GAZZETTA DEL MEZZOGIORNO (Mezzogiorno Gazette) (d) Est. 1922
Viale Scipione l'Africano 264, 70124
Tel: (39-80) 5470401; Fax: (39-80) 5470488
Circ.—76,357 ABC
Prop.—Edisud SpA
Chairman—Stefano Romanazzi
Ch. Dir.—Lino Patruno
Dir.—Franco Russo

PUGLIA (d) Est. 1979
Via Melo 195, Edipuglia, 70121
Tel: (39-80) 5210607; Fax: (39-80) 5213038
Dir.—Mario Gismondi

BENEVENTO

LA GAZZETTA DEL MATTINO (Mattino Gazette) (d)
Via Marraioli, Is. 1, 82030
Tel: (39) 824940018; Fax: (39) 284940029
Dir.—Ugo Ragozzino
Ed. in Ch.—Paolo Riceputi

BERGAMO
(Lombardia)
Pop. Est. 118,959

L'ECO DI BERGAMO (The Echo of Bergamo) (d) Est. 1880
Viale Papa Giovanni XXIII, 118, 24100
Tel: (39-35) 212344; Fax: (39-35) 225795
Circ.—59,264 ABC
Prop.—Società Editrice SS Alessandro Ambrogio Bassiano
Chairman—Arrigo Arrigoni
Vice Chairman—Aldo Nicoli
Dir.—Luigi Carrara
Vice Dir.—Giancarlo Zilio

IL GIORNALE DI BERGAMO OGGI (m) Est. 1981
Via Palazzolo 89, 24100
Tel: (39) 35247196
Circ.—10,000
Dir.—Andera Barberi

BOLOGNA
(Emilia-Romagna)
Pop. Est. 432,406

IL RESTO DEL CARLINO (m) Est. 1885
Via Enrico Mattei 106, 40138
Tel: (39-51) 536111; Fax: (39-51) 6570099
Circ.—228,027 ABC
Prop.—Poligrafici Editoriale SpA
Chairman—Attilio Monti
Vice Chairman—Giampiero Pesenti
Dir.—Marco Leonelli
Vice Dir.—Mauro Tedeschini
Vice Dir.—Giuseppe Castagnoli

BOLZANO
(Bozen)
(Trentino-Alto Adige)
Pop. Est. 101,515

ALTO ADIGE (d) Est. 1945
Via A. Volta 10, 39100
Tel: (39-471) 904111; Fax: (39-471) 904263
Circ.—42,909 ABC
Prop.—Seta SpA
Chairman—Giuliano Salvadori del Prato
Vice Chairman—Pietro Tosolini
Ch. Ex.—Carlo Cravero
Dir.—Franco De Battaglia
Ed. in Ch.—Franco Melchiori

DOLOMITEN (m-ex S) German; Est. 1923
Via del Vigneto 7; PF 417, 39100
Tel: (39-471) 925111; Fax: (39-471) 925440
Circ.—39,180 ABC
Prop.—Athesia SpA
Dir.—Joseph Rampold
Ed. in Ch.—Reinhold Marsoner

IL MATTINO DELL'ALTO ADIGE (d) Est. 1988
Via Dante 5, 39100
Tel: (39) 471990711; Fax: (39) 471990729
Dir.—Paolo Pagliaro
Ed. in Ch.—Franco Flippini

BRESCIA
(Lombardia)
Pop. Est. 199,286

BRESCIA OGGI (m) Est. 1974
Via Eritrea 20, 25126
Tel: (39-30) 22941; Fax: (39-30) 294229
Circ.—12,800
Dir.—Gianni Bonfadini
Ed. in Ch.—Giorgio Piglia

GIORNALE DI BRESCIA (d-ex mon.) Est. 1945
Via Solferino 22, 25121
Tel: (39-30) 37901; Fax: (39-30) 292226
Circ.—57,635 ABC
Prop.—Editoriale Bresciana SpA
Chairman—Giulio Togni
Dir.—Gian Battista Lanzani
Vice Dir.—Walter Semeraro

BRINDISI
(Puglia)
Pop. Est. 92,280

QUOTIDIANO DI BRINDISI (d) Est. 1979
Via Dalmazia 21/a, 72100
Tel: (39-831) 25455
Dir.—Vittorio Bruno Stamerra
Ed in Ch.—Oronzo Martucci

CAGLIARI
(Sardegna)
Pop. Est. 227,420

L'UNIONE SARDA (d-ex mon.) Est. 1889
Viale Regina Elena 12/14, 09124
Tel: (39-70) 60131; Fax: (39-70) 6013274
Circ.—75,469 ABC
Prop.—L'Unione Sarde SpA
Chairman—Giorgio Ribolini
Vice Chairman—Gianni Filippini
Ch. Ex.—Paolo Campana
Dir.—Antoangelo Liori
Vice Dir.—Mauro Manunza
Ed.—Alberto Rodríguez

CARPI
(Emilia-Romagna)
Pop. Est. 60,726

GAZZETTA DI CARPI (Carpi Gazette) (d)
Via Ciro Menotti 29, 41012
Circ.—10,405
Mng. Ed.—Pier Vittorio Marvasi
(Circulation figure combines with Il Gazzetta di Modena in Modena.)

CATANIA
(Sicilia)
Pop. Est. 372,486

ESPRESSO SERA-CORRIERE DI SICILIA (e-ex S)
Est. 1956
Viale Odorico da Pordenone 50, 95126
Tel: (39) 95333535; Fax: (39) 95336466
Dir.—Giusseppe Simili
Ed. in Ch.—Salvatore Barbagallo
LA SICILIA (The Sicilian) (m) Est. 1945
Viale Odorico da Pordenone 50, 95126
Tel: (39-95) 330544; Fax: (39-95) 337077
Circ.—64,873 ABC
Prop.—Domenico Sanfilippo Editore SpA
Dir.—Dr. Mario Ciancioi Sanfilippo

CATANZARO
(Calabria)
Pop. Est. 102,558

IL GIORNALE DI CALABRIA (Calabria Journal) (d)
Vico 1/a Filanda 1, 88100
Tel: (39) 96145552; Fax: (39) 96141031
Dir.—Giuseppe Soluri

CESENA

LA GAZZETTA DI CESENA (Cesena Gazette) (d)
Galleria Urtoteller 6, 47023
Tel: (39) 547610080; Fax: (39) 547610070
Dir.—Paolo Farneti
Ed. in Ch.—Elide Giordani

COMO
(Lombardia)
Pop. Est. 94,057

LA PROVINCIA DI COMO (The Province of Como) (m-ex mon.) Est. 1892
Via Anzani 52, 22100
Tel: (39-31) 3121; Fax: (39-31) 31281
Circ.—41,102 ABC
Prop.—Editoriale La Provincia di Como SpA
Chairman—Roberto Manfredi
Vice Chairman—Battista Somaini
Dir.—Vladimiro Dan

CREMONA
(Lombardia)
Pop. Est. 76,979

LA PROVINCIA DI CREMONA (The Province of Cremona) (m-ex mon.) Est. 1947
Via delle Industrie 2, 26100
Tel: (39-372) 462800; Fax: (39-372) 28487
Circ.—22,970 ABC
Prop.—Editoriale Cremonese SpA
Chairman—Mario Maestroni
Vice Chairman—Cesare Pasquali
Dir.—Roberto Gelmini
Vice. Dir.—Giuseppe Ghisani

FERRARA

LA GAZZETTA DI FERRARA (Ferrara Gazette) (d) Est. 1989
Via Ravenna 163, 44100
Tel: (39) 532740160; Fax: (39) 532740478
Dir.—Paolo Farneti
Ed. in Ch.—Angelo Frignani
LA NUOVA FERRARA (The New Ferrara) (d) Est. 1989
Viale Cavour 129, 44100
Tel: (39) 532200777; Fax: (39) 53247689
Dir.—Enrico Pirondini
Ed. in Ch.—Lucrezia Semenza

FIRENZE
(Florence)
(Toscana)
Pop. Est. 425,835

LA GAZZETTA DI FIRENZE (Firenze Gazette) (d-ex mon.) Est. 1980
Via Locchi 35/r, 50141
Tel: (39-55) 439811; Fax: (39-55) 416004
Dir.—Paolo Farneti
Ed. in Ch.—Ivo Brocchi
LA NAZIONE (The Nation) (m) Est. 1859
Via Ferdinando Paolieri 2, 50100
Tel: (39-55) 24851; Fax: (39-55) 2360307
Circ.—199,747 ABC
Prop.—Poligrafici Editoriale SpA
Dir.—Gabriele Canè
Vice Dir.—Umberto Cecchi
Ed. in Ch.—Sergio Di Battista

FOGGIA
(Puglia)
Pop. Est. 159,051

IL QUOTIDIANO DI FOGGIA (d) Est. 1985
Corso Roma 204/b, 71100
Tel: (39) 88186967; Fax: (39) 88177813
Dir.—Giuseppe Esposito
Ed. in Ch.—Giuseppe Cavotta

FORLI

LA GAZZETTA DI FORLI (Forli Gazette) (d)
Via Baldoni 17/23, 47100
Tel: (39) 54354654; Fax: (39) 54354907
Dir.—Paolo Farneti
Ed. in Ch.—Leonello Flamigni

FROSINONE

CIOCIARIA OGGI (d) Est. 1988
Via Lago Maggiore 42, 03100
Tel: (39) 775270551; Fax: (39) 775270608
Dir.—Michele Checchi

GENOVA
(Genoa)
(Liguria)
Pop. Est. 728,326

L'AVVISATORE MARITTIMO (d-ex mon.) Est. 1919
Via San Vincenzo 42, 16121
Tel: (39-10) 562929; Fax: (39-10) 566415
Dir.—Carlo Bellio
Ed. in Ch.—Alessandro Anelli
CORRIERE MERCANTILE (e) Est. 1824
Via Archimede 169 R
Tel: (39-10) 517851; Fax: (39-10) 504141
Circ.—15,000
Dir.—Mimmo Angeli
Vice Dir.—Alfredo Passadore
Ed. in Ch.—Alessandro Rocchi
IL LAVORO (m-ex mon.) Est. 1903
Via Donghi 38, Selpi, 16132
Tel: (39-10) 35331; Fax: (39-10) 3533263
Circ.—19,954
Dir.—Franco Manzitti
Ed. in Ch.—Luigi Gia
IL SECOLO XIX (m-ex mon.) Est. 1886
Via Varese 2, 16122
Tel: (39-10) 53881; Fax: (39-10) 5388560
Circ.—140,938 ABC
Prop.—Società Edizioni e Pubblicazioni SpA
Chairman—Carlo Perrone
Ch. Ex.—Cesare Brivio Sforza
Dir.—Mario Sconcerti
Vice Dir.—Gaetano Rizzuto
U.S. Rep.—Publicitas

LATINA

LATINA OGGI (d) Est. 1988
Via Malta 7, 04100
Tel: (39) 77123564; Fax: (39) 771858053
Dir.—Michele Checchi
Ed. in Ch.—Mauro Benedetti

LECCE
(Puglia)
Pop. Est. 100,981

QUOTIDIANO DI LECCE (d) Est. 1979
Viale degli Studenti-Palazzo Casto, 73100
Tel: (39-832) 338303; Fax: (39-832) 248592
Circ.—26,801
Prop.—Edisalento Srl
Chairman—Renato Minafra
Dir.—Dr. Vittorio Bruno Stamerra
Vice Dir.—Alessandro Barbano
Vice Dir.—Antonio Maglio
Ed. in Ch.—Antonio Muci

LECCO

LA PROVINCIA (The Province) (d)
Via delle Industrie 2, 26100
Tel: (39) 372411221; Fax: (39) 37228487
Dir.—Francesco Tartara
Ed. in Ch.—Sandro Valerio

LIVORNO
(Leghorn)
(Toscana)
Pop. Est. 174,065

IL TELEGRAFO (The Telegraph) (d)
Via Marradi 30, 57100
Tel: (39-586) 813211; Fax: (39-586) 854451
Dir.—Aurelio Seclba
Ed. in Ch.—Giuseppe Isozio
IL TIRRENO (m) Est. 1877
Viale Vittorio Alfieri 9, 57124
Tel: (39-586) 416511; Fax: (39-586) 402066
Circ.—93,809 ABC
Prop.—Editoriale Il Tirreno Srl
Chairman—Luigi Bianchi
Vice Chairman—Giuseppe Angella
Dir.—Ennio Simeone
Vice Dir.—Nino Sofia

LODI

IL CITTADINO (d) Est. 1890
Via Cavour 31, 20075
Tel: (39) 371420310; Fax: (39) 371422302
Dir.—Mario Ferrari
Vice Dir.—Ferruccio Pallavera

MACERATA

LA GAZETTA DI MACERATA (Macerata Gazette) (d) Est. 1986
Via Garibaldi 85, 62100
Tel: (39) 733231333; Fax: (39) 733232487
Dir.—Paolo Farneti
Ed. in Ch.—Giancarlo Padula

MANTOVA
(Mantua)
(Lombardia)
Pop. Est. 56,817

GAZETTA DI MANTOVA (Mantova Gazette) (d) Est. 1964
Via Fratelli Bandiera, 32, 46100
Tel: (39-376) 303270; Fax: (39-376) 303263
Circ.—36,742 ABC
Prop.—Finegil Editoriale SpA
Chairman—Carlo Caracciolo
Vice Chairman—Corrado Passera
Ch. Ex.—Marco Benedetto
Ch. Ex.—Mario Lenzi
Dir.—Sergio Baraldi

MESSINA
(Sicilia)
Pop. Est. 268,896

GAZETTA DEL SUD (South Gazette) (dS) Est. 1952
Via Uberto Bonino 15/C, 98100
Tel: (39-90) 2261; Fax: (39-90) 2936359
Circ.—90,225
Prop.—Editrice Siciliana SpA
Dir.—Nino Calarco
Vice Dir.—Biagio Belfiore

MILANO
(Milan)
(Lombardia)
Pop. Est. 1,511,717

AVVENIRE (d) Est. 1968
Via Mauro Macchi 81, 20124
Tel: (39-2) 67801; Fax: (39-2) 6780208
Circ.—91,350 ABC
Prop.—Nuova Editoriale Italiana SpA
Dir.—Dino Boffo
Ed. in Ch.—Marco Brizzi
CORRIERE DELLA SERA (eS) Est. 1876
Via Solferino 28, 20121
Tel: (39-2) 6339; Fax: (39-2) 29002847
Circ.—691,269 ABC
Prop.—Rcs Editoriale Quotidiani SpA
Dir.—Paolo Mieli
Vice Dir.—Guilio Giustiniani
Vice Dir.—Ferruccio Del Bortoli
Ed. in Ch.—Giulio Giustiniani
U.S. Rep.—Publicitas
LA GAZZETTA DELLO SPORT (mS) Est. 1896
Via Solferino 28, 20121
Tel: (39-2) 6339; Fax: (39-2) 29009668
Circ.—547,309
Prop.—Rcs Editoriale Quotidiani SpA
Chairman—Alberto Ronchey
Ch. Ex.—Alberto Donati
Dir.—Candido Cannavò
Vice Dir.—Roberto Milazzo
Vice Dir.—Alfio Caruso
Vice Dir.—Elio Trifari
Ed. in Ch.—Enzo Baroni
IL GIORNALE (The Journal) (mS) Est. 1974
Via Gaetano Negri 4, 20123
Tel: (39-2) 85661; Fax: (39-2) 72023859
Circ.—180,748 ABC
Prop.—Società Europea di Edizioni SpA
Chairman—Gina Galeazzo Biazzi Vergani
Dir.—Vittorio Feltri
Vice Dir.—Maurizio Belpietro
Vice Dir.—Luigi Cucchio
Vice Dir.—Paolo Granzotto
U.S. Rep.—Publicitas
IL GIORNO (mS) Est. 1956
Piazza Cavour 2, 20123
Tel: (39-2) 77681; Fax: (39-2) 76006656
Circ.—170,596 ABC
Prop.—Editrice Il Giorno
Dir.—Mario Padovani
L'INDIPENDENTE (The Independent) (d) Est. 1991
Via Valcava 6, 20155
Tel: (39-2) 330251; Fax: (39-2) 33025203
Circ.—82,118 ABC
Prop.—Editoriale L'Indipendente
Dir.—Vittorio Feltri
Vice. Dir.—Maurizio Belpietro
ITALIA OGGI (d)
Via Marco Burigozzo 5, 20122
Tel: (39-2) 582191; Fax: (39-2) 58317559/(39-2) 58317598
Circ.—32,704 ABC
Prop.—Errine Srl
Dir.—Pierluigi Magnaschi
Edit'l. Dir.—Paolo Panerai
LA NOTTE (The Note) (e) Est. 1952
Via Vitruvio 43, 20124
Tel: (39-2) 67171; Fax: (39-2) 6717210
Circ.—51,695 ABC
Prop.—Società Italiana Quotidiani SpA
Chairman—Angelo De Martini
Dir.—Massimo Donelli
Vice Dir.—Luigi Santambrogio
IL SOLE-24 ORE (m-ex mon.) Est. 1965
Via Paolo Lomazzo 52, 20154
Tel: (39-2) 31031; Fax: (39-2) 312055
Circ.—346,335 ABC
Prop.—Il Sole-24 Ore SpA
Chairman—Giancarlo Lombardi
Vice Chairman—Innocenzo Cipolletta
Vice Chairman—Gavino Manca
Ch. Ex.—Maurizio Galluzzo
Dir.—Salvatore Carrubba
Vice Dir.—Aldo Carboni
Vice Dir.—Gianfranco Fabi
Vice Dir.—Federico Rampini
Vice Dir.—Elia Zamboni
Vice Dir.—Pilade Del Buono
U.S. Rep.—Publicitas

MODENA
(Nuova)
Pop. Est. 176,880

NUOVA GAZZETTA DI MODENA (New Gazette of Modena) (d)
Via Taglio 22, 41100
Tel: (39-59) 223707; Fax: (39-59) 218903
Circ.—15,333
Prop.—Finegil Editoriale SpA
Chairman—Carlo Caracciolo
Vice Chairman—Corrado Passera
Ch. Ex.—Marco Benedetto
Ch. Ex.—Mario Lenzi
Dir.—Antonio Mascolo
(Circulation figure combines with Gazzetta di Carpi in Carpi.)

NAPOLI
(Naples)
(Campania)
Pop. Est. 1,204,929

IL GIORNALE DI NAPOLI (Napoli Journal) (e) Est. 1985
Via Diocleziano 109, 80125
Tel: (39-81) 7624300; Fax: (39-81) 7624544
Dir.—Lino Jannuzzi
Ed. in Ch.—Antonio Sasso

IL MATTINO (mS) Est. 1892
Via Chiatamone 65, 80121
Tel: (39-81) 7947111; Fax: (39-81) 7947288
Circ.—192,002
Prop.—Edime SpA
Chairman—Paolo De Palma
Dir.—Paolo Graldi

PADOVA
(Padua)
(Veneto)
Pop. Est. 225,769

IL MATTINO DI PADOVA (m) Est. 1978
Via Pelizzo 3, 35100
Tel: (39-49) 8292611; Fax: (39-49) 8070067
Circ.—32,353 ABC
Prop.—Finegil Editoriale SpA
Chairman—Carlo Caracciolo
Vice Chairman—Corrado Passera
Ch. Ex.—Mario Lenzi
Ch. Ex.—Marco Benedetto
Dir.—Claudio Giua
Vice Dir.—Valentino Pesci

PALERMO
(Sicilia)
Pop. Est. 724,642

GIORNALE DI SICILIA (Sicily Journal) (m) Est. 1860
Via Lincoln 21, 90133
Tel: (39-91) 6627111; Fax: (39-91) 277280
Circ.—66,051 ABC
Prop.—Editoriale Poligrafica SpA
Dir.—Dr. Antonio Ardizzone
Vice Dir.—Giovanni Pepi
Ed. in Ch.—Nonuccio Aselmo
L'ORA (e-ex S) Est. 1900
Piazza Napoli 5, 90141
Tel: (39-91) 581733; Fax: (39-91) 333439
Circ.—42,000
Dir.—Anselmo Calaciura
Ed. in Ch.—Guido Valdini

PARMA
(Emilia-Romagna)
Pop. Est. 174,368

GAZZETTA DI PARMA (Parma Gazette) (m) Est. 1735
Via Emilio Casa 5/A, 43100
Tel: (39-521) 2159; Fax: (39-521) 285515
Circ.—48,598 ABC
Prop.—Segea SpA
Dir.—Bruno Rossi
Vice Dir.—Pier Paolo Mendogni

PAVIA
(Lombardia)
Pop. Est. 82,065

LA PROVINCIA PAVESE (The Pavese Province) (m) Est. 1879
Via Canton Ticino 16/18, 27100
Tel: (39-382) 472101; Fax: (39-382) 473875
Circ.—27,248 ABC
Prop.—Editoriale Agenzie Giornali Srl
Chairman—Filippo Agusto Carbone
Vice Chairman—Mario Lenzi
Ch. Ex.—Carlo Arditi
Ch. Ex.—Delio Villani
Dir.—Luigi Carletti
Vice Dir.—Luigi Gia

PERUGIA
(Umbria)
Pop. Est. 146,713

CORRIERE DELL'UMBRIA (d) Est. 1983
Via Pievaiola Km. 5, 800, 06100
Tel: (39-75) 52731; Fax: (39-75) 5273259
Circ.—20,031 ABC
Prop.—Editoriale Quotidiani Srl
Dir.—Sergio Benincasa

PESARO

LA GAZZETTA DI FANO (Fano Gazette) (d) Est. 1986
Piazza Matteotti 22 A, 61100
Tel: (39-721) 69545; Fax: (39-721) 68065
Dir.—Paolo Farneti
Ed. in Ch.—Michele Romano
LA GAZZETTA DI PESARO (Pesaro Gazette) (d) Est. 1986
Piazza Matteotti 22 A, 61100
Tel: (39-721) 69545; Fax: (39-721) 68065
Dir.—Paolo Farneti
Ed. in Ch.—Michele Romano

PESCARA
(Abruzzi)
Pop. Est. 131,027

IL CENTRO (The Central) (d) Est. 1986
Corso Vittorio Emanuele 372, 65100
Tel: (39-85) 20521; Fax: (39-85) 4212460
Circ.—27,715 ABC
Prop.—Finegil Editoriale SpA
Chairman—Carlo Caracciolo
Vice Chairman—Corrado Passera
Dir.—Sergio Milani

PIACENZA
(Emilia-Romagna)
Pop. Est. 105,626

LIBERTA (Liberty) (m-ex mon.) Est. 1883
Via Benedettine 68, 29100
Tel: (39-523) 393939; Fax: (39-523) 39362
Circ.—33,762 ABC
Prop.—Stab. Tipografico Piacentino Sapa di E Prati & C.
Chairman—Donatella Ronconi
Dir.—Ernesto Leone

PORDENONE

CORRIERE DI PORDENONE (d)
Corso V. Emanuele 21/G, 33170
Tel: (39) 434521911; Fax: (39) 434366869
Dir.—Giorgio Zicari
Ed. in Ch.—Pietro Angelillo

PRATO

LA GAZZETTA DI PRATO (Prato Gazette) (d)
Via Piero della Francesca 2, 50047
Tel: (39) 574570830; Fax: (39) 574570547
Dir.—Paolo Franeti
Ed. in Ch.—Cristiano Draghi

REGGIO EMILIA
(Emilia-Romagna)
Pop. Est. 130,086

GAZZETTA DI REGGIO (Reggio Gazette) (d) Est. 1860
Via Sessi 1, 42100
Tel: (39-522) 453441; Fax: (39-522) 454279
Circ.—14,884 ABC
Prop.—Finegil Editoriale SpA
Chairman—Carlo Caracciolo
Vice Chairman—Corrado Passera
Ch. Ex.—Marco Benedetto
Ch. Ex.—Mario Lenzi
Dir.—Umberto Bonafini

RIMINI
(Emilia-Romagna)
Pop. Est. 130,210

LA GAZZETTA DI RIMINI (Rimini Gazette) (d) Est. 1987
Piazza tre Martiri 43/a, 47037
Tel: (39) 54151318; Fax: (39) 54152048
Dir.—Paolo Farneti
Ed. in Ch.—Federico Fioravanti

ROMA
(Rome)
(Lazio)
Pop. Est. 2,814,687

L'AGENZIA DI VIAGGI (d) Est. 1965
Via Rasella 155, 00187
Tel: (39-6) 4821539; Fax: (39-6) 4826721
Dir.—Marco Valerio Ambrosini
AVANTI (m-ex mon.) Est. 1896
Via Tomacelli 146, 00186
Tel: (39-6) 6878268
Circ.—83,000
Prop.—Italian Socialist Party
Dir.—Ugo Intini
Dir.—Roberto Villeti
Vice Dir.—Francesco Gozzano
Vice Dir.—Dario Beni
Ed. in Ch.—Vito Raponi
CORRIERE DELLO SPORT (m) Est. 1924
Piazza Indipendenza 11/b, 00185
Tel: (39-6) 49921; Fax: (39-6) 4992690
Circ.—381,216 ABC
Prop.—Corriere dello Sport Srl
Chairman—Roberto Amodei
Dir.—Italo Cucci
Vice Dir.—Guiseppe Pistilli
Vice Dir.—Andrea Girelli
Vice Dir.—Enrico Maida
DAILY AMERICAN (d) English; Est. 1945
Via S. Maria in Via 12, 00187
Prop.—New Daily American SPA
Dir.—Chantal Dubois
IL FIORINO (m-ex mon.) Est. 1969
Via Parigi 11, 00185
Tel: (39-6) 47490
Circ.—91,000
Dir.—Luigi D'Amato
IL GIORNALE D'ITALIA (The Journal of Italy) (d)
Via Parigi 11, 00185
Tel: (39-6) 474901; Fax: (39-6) 463435
Circ.—102,322

Dir.—Luigi D'Amato
Ed. in Ch.—Franco Rossi
Ed. in Ch.—Romano Tripodi
INFORMAZIONI PER IL COMMERCIO ESTERO (d)
Via Liszt 21, 00144
Tel: (39-6) 59921; Fax: (39-6) 4387030
Dir.—Marcello Inghilesi
INTERNATIONAL COURIER (d) English
Via di Ripetta 22
Gen. Dir.—Christopher Winner
Ed.—Roberto Scio
INTERNATIONAL DAILY NEWS (d) English
Via Barberini 3, 00186
Pub./Ed.—Robert H Cunningham Jr
Dir.—Giulio Carlo Riposio
IL MANIFESTO (The Manifest) (d) Est. 1971
Via Tomacelli 146, 00186
Tel: (39-6) 6878487; Fax: (39-6) 6892600
Circ.—56,608 ABC
Dir.—Luigi Pintor
Ed. in Ch.—Sandro Medici
IL MESSAGGERO (The Messenger) (m) Est. 1878
Via del Tritone 152, 00187
Tel: (39-6) 47201; Fax: (39-6) 472072
Circ.—267,259 ABC
Prop.—Editrice Il Messaggero SpA
Ch. Ex.—Alessandro Bonetti
Dir.—Giulio Anselmi
Vice Dir.—Paolo Bonaiuti
Vice Dir.—Paolo Gambescia
U.S. Rep.—Publicitas
ORE 12 (d) Est. 1960
Via Alfana 39, 00191
Tel: (39-6) 3331418; Fax: (39-6) 3331957
Dir.—Enzo Caretti
Ed. in Ch.—Mario Caretti
PAESE SERA (d)
Viale Francheschini 56, 00100
Tel: (39-6) 4072922
Circ.—130,988
Dir.—Arnaldo Agostini
Mng. Ed.—Silvano Rizza
IL POPOLO (m-ex S) Est. 1944
Piazza Cinque Lune 113, 00186
Tel: (39-6) 68551
Circ.—81,000
Prop.—Christian Democratic Party
Dir.—Sandro Fontana
Ed. in Ch.—Romano Bartoloni
LA REPUBBLICA (The Republic) (m-ex mon.) Est. 1976
Piazza Indipendenza 11/b, 00186
Tel: (39-6) 49821; Fax: (39-6) 49822923
Circ.—569,637 ABC
Prop.—Editoriale La Repubblica SpA
Chairman—Carlo Caracciolo
Vice Pres.—Corrado Passera
Dir.—Eugenio Scalfari
Ed. in Ch.—Franco Magannini
U.S. Rep.—Publicitas
SECOLO D'ITALIA (d) Est. 1952
Via della Mercede 33, 00187
Tel: (39-6) 6840290; Fax: (39-6) 6786522
Dir.—Aldo Giorleo
Ed. in Ch.—Gennaro Malgieri
IL TEMPO (m) Est. 1944
Piazza Colonna 366, 00187
Tel: (39-6) 675881; Fax: (39-6) 6758869
Circ.—106,561 ABC
Prop.—L'Editrice Romana Srl
Chairman—Andrea Riffeser
Dir.—Giovanni Mottola
Vice Dir.—Bruno Costi
Ed. in Ch.—Luigi Gambacorta
L'UMANITA (d) Est. 1947
Via degli Scialoja 6, 00196
Tel: (39-6) 3221546
Dir.—Gianni Piero Orsello
L'UNITA (d) Est. 1924
Via di due Macelli 23/13, 00187
Tel: (39-6) 699961; Fax: (39-6) 6783555
Circ.—143,506 ABC
Prop.—L'Arca Societa L'Unità SpA
Chairman—Antonio Bernardi
Dir.—Walter Veltroni
Vice Dir.—Giuseppe Caldarola
Edit'l. Dir.—Antonio Zollo
LA VOCE REPUBBLICANA (The Republican Voice) (d)
Piazza dei Caprettari 70
Tel: (39-6) 6544641; Fax: (39-6) 6542990
Dir.—Giorgio La Malfa
Ed. in Ch.—Luca Paci

SASSARI
(Sardegna)
Pop. Est. 121,067

LA NUOVA SARDEGNA (The New Sardegna) (m) Est. 1891
Via Porcellana 9, 07100
Tel: (39-79) 222400; Fax: (39-79) 236293

Circ.—65,684 ABC
Prop.—Editoriale la Nuova Sardegna SpA
Chairman—Carlo Caracciolo
Vice Chairman—Vittorio Cordella
Dir.—Livio Liuzzi
Vice Dir.—Giorgio Melis

SIENA
(Toscana)
Pop. Est. 59,712

LA GAZZETTA DI SIENA (The Siena Gazette) (d) Est. 1987
Via Tolomei 5, 53100
Tel: (39) 57750472
Dir.—Paolo Farneti
Ed. in Ch.—Stefano Bisi

SIRACUSA
(Syracuse)
(Sicilia)
Pop. Est. 122,534

IL DIARIO DI SIRACUSA (Siracusa Daily) (6x wk.) Est. 1976
Via M. Politi Laudien 7, 96100
Mng. Ed.—Enzo Bonifazi

TARANTO
(Puglia)
Pop. Est. 244,997

CORRIERE DEL GIORNO DI PUGLIA E LUCANIA (d) Est. 1947
Piazza Dante 5
Tel: (39) 993203; Fax: (39) 74100
Circ.—17,000
Dir.—Riccardo Catacchio
Vice Dir.—Clemente Salvaggio
Ed. in Ch.—Vincenzo Petrocelli
QUOTIDIANO DI TARANTO (d) Est. 1979
Via Acclavio 24, 74100
Tel: (39) 9926944
Dir.—Vittorio Bruno Stamerra
Vice Dir.—Antonio Maglio
Ed. in Ch.—Perangelo Putzolu

TORINO
(Turin)
(Piemonte)
Pop. Est. 1,024,952

LA STAMPA (m-ex mon.) Est. 1867
Via Carlo Marenco 32, 10126
Tel: (39-11) 6568; Fax: (39-11) 6568624
Circ.—428,689 ABC
Prop.—Editrice La Stampa SpA
Chairman—Giovanni Agnelli
Vice Chairman—Vittorio Caissotti di Chiusano
Vice Chairman—Umberto Cuttica
Dir.—Ezio Mauro
Vice Dir.—Lorenzo Mondo
Vice Dir.—Luigi La Spina
Vice Dir.—Gad Lerner
Vice Dir.—Marcello Sorgi
U.S. Rep.—Publicitas
STAMPA SERA (m&e) Est. 1867
Via Marenco 32, 10126
Tel: (39-11) 65681; Fax: (39-11) 655306
Circ.—26,006 (m); 405,358 (e)
Prop.—Editrice La Stampa SpA
Dir.—Luca Bernardelli
Vice Dir.—Carlo Bramardo
Ed. in Ch.—Ernesto Marenco
TUTTOSPORT (d) Est. 1945
Corso Svizzera 185, 10149
Tel: (39-11) 7773111; Fax: (39-11) 7773312
Circ.—116,446 ABC
Prop.—Società Editrice Sportiva SpA
Dir.—Franco Colombo
Vice Dir.—Ludovico Perricone

TRENTO
(Trent)
(Trentino-Alto Adige)
Pop. Est. 100,202

L'ADIGE (m-ex mon.) Est. 1946
Via Missioni Africane 17, 38100
Tel: (39-461) 886111; Fax: (39-461) 886262
Circ.—19,940 ABC
Prop.—Nuova Editrice Trentina Srl
Dir.—Giampaolo Visetti

TREVISO
(Veneto)
Pop. Est. 87,836

LA TRIBUNA DI TREVISO (Treviso Tribune) (d) Est. 1978
Corso del Popolo 42, 31100
Tel: (39-422) 410001; Fax: (39-422) 579212

Europe **Italy** IV-33

Italy

TRIESTE
(Friuli-Venezia Giulia)
Pop. Est. 239,031

IL PICCOLO (m) Est. 1881
Via Guido Reni 1, 34123
Tel: (39-40) 3733111; Fax: (39-40) 7797029
Circ.—51,807 ABC
Prop.—Org. Tipografica Editoriale SpA
Chairman—Carlo E Melzi
Vice Chairman—Guido Carignani
Vice Chairman—Luigino Rossi
Dir.—Mario Quaia
Vice Dir.—Leopoldo Petto
PRIMORSKI DNEVNIK (d) Slovene
Via Montecchi 6, 34137
Tel: (39-40) 7796644; Fax: (39-40) 772418
Dir.—Vpjimir Tavcar

UDINE
(Friuli-Venezia Giulia)
Pop. Est. 100,211

MESSAGGERO VENETO (Veneto Messenger) (m)
Est. 1946
Viale Palmanova 290, 33100
Tel: (39-432) 5271; Fax: (39-432) 523072
Circ.—52,106 ABC
Prop.—Società Veneta Editrice SpA
Dir.—Sergio Gervasutti
Vice Dir.—Giampaolo Nobili
Vice Dir.—Augusto Dell'Angelo

VARESE
(Lombardia)
Pop. Est. 88,353

LA PREALPINA (d) Est. 1888
Viale Tamagno 13, 21100
Tel: (39) 332286177
Circ.—25,000
Dir.—Mino Durand
Ed. in Ch.—Giorgio Minazzi

VENEZIA
(Venice)
(Veneto)
Pop. Est. 331,454

IL GAZZETTINO (d) Est. 1887
Via Torino 110, 30172
Tel: (39-41) 665111; Fax: (39-41) 665386/(39-41) 665387
Circ.—142,727 ABC
Prop.—Finanziara Editoriale S Marco SpA
Ch.—Luigino Rossi
Dir.—Giorgio Lago
Vice Dir.—Edoardo Pittalis
LA NUOVA VENEZIA (The New Venice) (d) Est. 1984
Campo S. Lio Castello 5620, 30100
Tel: (39-41) 5210300; Fax: (39-41) 5211007
Circ.—11,868 ABC
Prop.—Finegil Editoriale SpA
Chairman—Carlo Caracciolo
Vice Chairman—Corrado Passera
Ch. Ex.—Mario Lenzi
Ch. Ex.—Marco Benedetto
Dir.—Claudio Giua
Vice Dir.—Valentino Pesci

VERONA
(Veneto)
Pop. Est. 259,151

L'ARENA (The Arena) (d) Est. 1866
Viale del Lavoro 11, 37036
Tel: (39-45) 8094000; Fax: (39-45) 994527
Circ.—54,191 ABC
Prop.—Athesis SpA
Chairman—Luigi Righetti
Vice Chairman—Arrigo Armellini
Vice Chairman—Giuseppe Parolini
Dir.—Albino Longhi
Ed. in Ch.—Michelangelo Bellinetti

VICENZA
(Veneto)
Pop. Est. 110,449

IL GIORNALE DI VICENZA (Vicenza Journal) (d)
Est. 1943
Viale San Lazzaro 89, 36100
Tel: (39-444) 563211; Fax: (39-444) 570117
Circ.—45,128 ABC
Prop.—Athesis SpA
Chairman—Luigi Righetti
Vice Chairman—Arrigo Armellini
Vice Chairman—Giuseppe Parolini
Ch. Ex.—Alessandro Zelger
Dir.—Mino Allione

VITERBO

CORRIERE DI VITERBO (d) Est. 1989
Via del Gilgio 3, 01100
Tel: (39) 761344990; Fax: (39) 761344756
Circ.—42,696
Dir.—Sergio Benincasa

KAZAKHSTAN
Pop. Est. 17,267,554

ALMA-ATA
Pop. Est. 1,156,200

KAZAKHSTANSKAYA PRAVDA (Kazakhstan Truth) (5x wk.) Russian; Est. 1920
39 ul. Gogolya, 480044
Cir.—170,000
Ed.—F F Ignatov
LENINSHIL ZHAS (Leninist Youth) (5x wk.)
Kazakh; Est. 1921
50 ul. Gorykogo, 480044
Ed.—U Kalizhanov
LENINSKAYA SMENA (Leninist Rising Generation) (5x wk.) Russian; Est. 1922
50 ul. Gorykogo, 480044
Ed.—O Nikanov
SOTSIALIATIK KAZAKHSTAN (Socialist Kazakhstan) (6x wk.) Kazakh; Est. 1919
39 ul. Gogolya, 480044
Ed.—K Duiseev

KYRGYZSTAN
(Formerly Kirghizia SSR)
Pop. Est. 4,698,108

BISHKEK
(Formerly Frunze)
Pop. Est. 631,300

SLOVO KYRGYZSTANA (6x wk.) Russian; Est. 1925
193 ul. Kirova, 720013
Circ.—111,000
Ed.—V G Lukyashchenko
SOVETIK KYRZYSTAN (Soviet Kirghizia) (6x wk.) Est. 1924
193 ul. Kirova, 720013
Circ.—162,625
Ed.—T Ishemkulov

LATVIA
Pop. Est. 2,749,211

RIGA
Pop. Est. 897,078

SM-SEGODNYA (5x wk.) Russian; Est. 1945
3 Balasta Dambis, 226081
Circ.—205,400
Ed.—A Blinov
SOVIETSKAYA LATVIYA (Soviet Latvia) (6x wk.) Russian; Est. 1919
3 Balasta Dambis, 226081
Circ.—71,300
Ed.—A E Visilyonok

LIECHTENSTEIN
Pop. Est. 30,281

SCHAAN
Pop. Est. 5,083

LIECHTENSTEINER VOLKSBLATT (d-6x wk.)
German; Est. 1878
Feldkircherstrasse 5; PF 193, 9494
Tel: (41-75) 2375151; Fax: (41-75) 2375155
Circ.—9,040
Prop.—Liechtensteiner Volksblatt Publishing Co.
Ed.—Günther Meier
LIECHTENSTEINER WOCHE (The Liechtenstein Weekly) Est. 1993
Wiesengasse 17, 9494
Circ.—14,000
Owner—Hans Peter Rheinberger
Ed.—Ines Rampone-Wohlwend
Ad. Dir.—Ernst Matzeg

VADUZ
Pop. Est. 4,887

LIECHTENSTEINER VATERLAND (The Liechtensteiner Fatherland) (d-6x wk.)
German; Est. 1924
Fürst-Franz-Josef-Strasse 13, 9490
Tel: (41-75) 2361616; Fax: (41-75) 2361617
Circ.—9,778
Prop.—Liechtensteiner Vaterland Publishing Co.
Ed.—Günther Fritz

LITHUANIA
Pop. Est. 3,848,389

VILNIUS
(Vilna)
Pop. Est. 596,900

GOLOS LITVY (6x wk.) Lithuanian; Est. 1940
60 Prosp. Kosmonavtov, 232019
Circ.—76,000
Ed.—V K Emelyanov
LIETUVOS RYTAS (d)
Gedimino 12A, 2008
Tel: (370-2) 622680; Fax: (370-2) 221571
Circ.—240,000
Prop.—Lietuvos Rytas Co.
RESPUBLIKA (d) Russian; Est. 1989
A. Smetonos St. 2, 2600
Tel: (370-2) 223112; Fax: (370-2) 223538
Circ.—50,000
Prop.—Concern TTL
Ed.—Vitas Tomkus
Ad. Mgr.—Romas Bagdzius

LUXEMBOURG, GRAND DUCHY OF
Pop. Est. 401,900

LUXEMBOURG
Pop. Est. 75,662

LETZEBURGER JOURNAL (Liberal) (m) Est. 1880
123 rue allée Fischer; Boite Postal 2101, L-1021
Tel: (352) 493033; Fax: (352) 492065
Circ.—13,500
Ed. in Ch.—Rob Roemen
D'LETZEBURGER LAND (Liberal Independent)
62 rue de Strasbourg; Boite Postal 2083, L-1020
Tel: (352) 485757; Fax: (352) 496309
Circ.—6,500
Ed. in Ch.—M Jean-Paul Hoffman
LUXEMBOURG NEWS
31 allée Scheffer, 2520
Tel: (352) 4994501; Fax: (352) 470056
LUXEMBURGER WORT (m-ex S) German & French; Est. 1848
2 rue Ch. Plantil; PO Box 1908, 2988
Tel: (352) 49931; Fax (352) 402250
Circ.—87,727
Prop.—Imprimerie Saint-Paul SA
Ed.—Leon Zeches
Ad. Dir.—Joseph Colbach
LE REPUBLICAIN-LORRAIN (m) French; Est. 1961
7 rue d'Esch; Boite Postal 2211, L-1022
Tel: (352) 447744; Fax: (352) 442525
Circ.—24,000
Ed.—Jean-Marie Denninger
REVUE
1 rue J-P-Brasseur, L-1258
Tel: (352) 454151; Fax: (352) 458874
Circ.—29,078
Ed. in Ch.—Yolande Kieffer
TAGEBLATT (m-ex mon.) Est. 1927
44 rue du Canal; Boite Postal 147, L-4050
Tel: (352) 547131; Fax: (352) 547161
Circ.—27,544
Dir./Ed. in Ch.—M Alvin Sold
TELECRAN
13 rue Bourbon; Boite Postal 1008, L-1010
Tel: (352) 4994501; Fax: (352) 4994503
Circ.—40,358
Dir.—M l'Abbe Andre Heiderscheid
Ed. in Ch.—Fern Morbach
ZEITUNG VUM LETZEBURGER VOLLEK (d)
German; Est. 1946
16 rue Ch. Plantil; Boite Postal 2106, L-2339
Tel: (352) 4921012; Fax: (352) 496920
Circ.—8,000
Dir./Ed. in Ch.—Ali Ruckert

MALTA
(Maltese Islands)
Pop. Est. 366,767

G'MANGIA/PIETA
Pop. Est. 4,332

IL-MUMENT Maltese; Est. 1972
Herbert Ganado St.
Tel: (356) 243641/(356) 243642; Fax: (356) 242886
Circ.—24,000
Prop.—Independence Print
Ed.—Victor Camilleri
Ad. Mgr.—C Zammit Moore
IN-NAZZJON TAGHNA (d) Maltese; Est. 1970
Herbert Ganado St.
Tel: (356) 243641/(356) 243642; Fax: (356) 242886
Circ.—18,000
Prop.—Independence Print
Ed.—Mario Schiavone
Ad. Mgr.—C Zammit Moore

VALLETTA
Pop. Est. 9,199

THE MALTA INDEPENDENT English; Est. 1992
Airways House, High St.
Tel: (356) 345888; Fax: (356) 346062
Prop.—Standard Publications Ltd.
Ed.—Raymond Bugeja
L'ORIZZONT (m-ex mon.) Maltese; Est. 1962
Worker's Memorial Bldg., Old Bakery St.
Tel: (356) 241966/(356) 244451; Fax: (356) 243454
Circ.—15,856
Prop.—Union Press Publications (General Worker's Union)
Ed.—Felix Agius
Ad. Mgr.—Eddie Scicluna
THE SUNDAY TIMES English
341 St. Paul St.
Tel: (356) 241464/(356) 241121; Fax: (356) 237150
Circ.—28,000
Prop.—Allied Newspapers Ltd.
Ed.—Lawrence Grech
THE TIMES (d) English; Est. 1935
341 St. Paul St.
Tel: (356) 24146/(356) 241469; Fax: (356) 247901
Circ.—18,000
Prop.—Allied Newspapers Ltd.
Ed.—Ray Bugeja
IT-TORCA (The Torch) Maltese; Est. 1944
Worker's Memorial Bldg., Old Bakery St.
Tel: (356) 241966/(356) 244451; Fax: (356) 243454
Circ.—23,894
Prop.—Union Press Publications (General Worker's Union)
Ed.—Joey A Vella
Ad. Mgr.—Tony Ciappara

MOLDOVA
(Formerly Moldavia SSR)
Pop. Est. 4,473,033

KISHINEV
Pop. Est. 633,000

NEZAVISIMAYA MOLDOVA (6x wk.) Russian; Est. 1925
22 ul. Pushkina, 277612
Circ.—100,000
Ed.—I Panfilov

MONACO
Pop. Est. 31,278

MONACO-VILLE
Pop. Est. 29,972

NICE-MATIN (mS)
214 route de Grenoble, 06021

NETHERLANDS, THE
Pop. Est. 15,367,928

ALKMAAR
(North Holland)
Pop. Est. 92,962

NOORDHOLLANDS DAGBLAD (m&e)
PO Box 2, 1800 AA
Tel: (31-72) 196228; Fax: (31-72) 196186
Circ.—154,308
Prop.—nv Holdingmaatschappij De Telegraaf
Ed.—D P J van Reeuwijk

ALPHEN aan den RIJN
(South Holland)
Pop. Est. 66,143

RIJN EN GOUWE (m)
PO Box 1, 2400 AA
Tel: (31-1) 72087444; Fax: (31-1) 72087408
Circ.—36,922
Ed.—L M Heskes

AMERSFOORT
(Utrecht)
Pop. Est. 110,117

AMERSFOORTSE COURANT (e) Est. 1887
PO Box 3, 3800 AA
Tel: (31-33) 647911; Fax: (31-33) 647334
Circ.—42,051
Prop.—Wegener nv
Ed.—H Goessens

AMSTERDAM
(North Holland)
Pop. Est. 724,096

DE COURANT NIEUWS VAN DE DAG (e) Est. 1897
PO Box 376, 1000 EB
Tel: (31-20) 5859111; Fax: (31-20) 5852216
Circ.—56,600
Prop.—nv Holdingmaatschappij De Telegraaf
Ed.—P H H Wijnans
HET FINANCIEELE DAGBLAD (m-ex wknd.) Est. 1864
PO Box 216, 1000 AE
Tel: (31-20) 5928888; Fax: (31-20) 5928800
Circ.—41,555
Prop.—Het Financieele Dagblad bv
HET PAROOL (e) Est. 1940
PO Box 433, 1000 AK
Tel: (31-20) 5629333; Fax: (31-20) 5626283
Circ.—102,500
Prop.—Perscombinatie bv
Ed.—S van der Zee
DE TELEGRAAF (m) Est. 1897
PO Box 376, 1000 EB
Tel: (31-20) 5859111; Fax: (31-20) 5852216
Circ.—751,400
Prop.—nv Holdingmaatschappij De Telegraaf
Ed.—E Bos
TROUW (m) Est. 1943
PO Box 859, 1000 AW
Tel: (31-20) 5629444; Fax: (31-20) 6680389
Circ.—121,600
Prop.—Perscombinatie bv
Ed.—J Greven
DE VOLKSKRANT (m) Est. 1921
PO Box 1002, 1000 BA
Tel: (31-20) 5629222; Fax: (31-20) 5626289
Circ.—358,200
Prop.—Perscombinatie bv
Ed.—Dr. P I Broertjes

APELDOORN
(Gelderland)
Pop. Est. 149,449

APELDOORNSE COURANT (e) Est. 1903
PO Box 833, 7301 BB
Tel: (31-55) 766911; Fax: (31-55) 766305
Circ.—40,254
Prop.—Wegener Uitgeverij Gelderland bv
REFORMATORISCH DAGBLAD (e) Est. 1971
PO Box 670, 7300 AR
Tel: (31-55) 495222; Fax: (31-55) 424802

Circ.—55,575
Prop.—Reformatorisch Dagblad bv
Ed.—C S L Janse

ARNHEM
(Gelderland)
Pop. Est. 133,670

ARNHEMSE COURANT (e) Est. 1814
PO Box 9008, 6800 DK
Tel: (31-85) 757575; Fax: (31-85) 515451
Circ.—31,368
Prop.—Wegener nv
Ed.—G Dielessen

ASSEN
(Drenthe)
Pop. Est. 52,268

DRENTS GRONINGSE DAGBLADEN (e)
PO Box 36, 9400 AA
Tel: (31-5920) 29500; Fax: (31-5920) 20539
Circ.—209,062
Prop.—Noordelijke Dagblad Combinatie bv
Ed.—G J Laan

BARNEVELD
(Gelderland)
Pop. Est. 44,506

NEDERLANDS DAGBLAD (m)
PO Box 111, 3770 AC
Tel: (31-3420) 10720; Fax: (31-3420) 92619
Circ.—28,583
Prop.—Nederlands Dagblad/Gereformeerd Gezinsblad bv
Ed.—J P de Vries

BREDA
(North Brabant)
Pop. Est. 129,125

DE STEM (m) Est. 1860
PO Box 3229, 4800 MB
Tel: (31-76) 236911; Fax: (31-76) 236405
Circ.—110,120
Prop.—VNU Dagbladengroep bv
Ed.—H Coumans

DELFT

DELFTSCHE COURANT/WESTLANDSCHE COURANT
PO Box 18, 2600 AA
Tel: (31-15) 126700; Fax: (31-15) 135987
Circ.—17,452 (Delftsche ed.); 13,370 (Westlandsche ed.)

DEVENTER
(Overijssel)
Pop. Est. 69,079

DEVENTER DAGBLAD (e)
PO Box 18, 7400 AA
Tel: (31-5700) 48444; Fax: (41-5700) 21324
Circ.—34,849
Prop.—Wegener nv
Ed.—L Enthoven
GELDERS-OVERIJSSELSE COURANT/ZUTPHENS DAGBLAD
PO Box 18, 2600 AA
Tel: (31-5700) 48350/(31-5700) 48365
Circ.—20,725

DORDRECHT
(South Holland)
Pop. Est. 113,394

DE DORDTENAAR (m) Est. 1946
PO Box 54, 3300 AB
Tel: (31-78) 324711; Fax: (31-78) 324729
Circ.—38,759
Ed.—H Kerstiens

EINDHOVEN
(North Brabant)
Pop. Est. 196,130

EINDHOVENS DAGBLAD (m) Est. 1914
PO Box 534, 5600 AM
Tel: (31-40) 336336; Fax: (31-40) 445581
Circ.—132,655
Prop.—VNU Dagbladengroep bv
Ed.—J van der Hart

EMMEN

EMMER COURANT
PO Box 5, 7800 AA
Tel: (31-5910) 18600
Circ.—29,459

ENSCHEDE
(Overijssel)
Pop. Est. 147,624

DAGBLAD TUBANTIA/TWENTSCHE COURANT (e) Est. 1979
PO Box 28, 7500 AA
Tel: (31-53) 842842; Fax: (31-53) 842200

Circ.—152,583
Prop.—Wegener nv
Ed.—W P Timmers

GRONINGEN
(Groningen)
Pop. Est. 167,872

NIEUWSBLAD van het NOORDEN (e) Est. 1888
PO Box 60, 9700 MC
Tel: (31-50) 652222; Fax: (31-50) 125036
Circ.—140,729
Prop.—Nieuwsblad van het Noorden bv
Ed.—D T Dalmolen

HAARLEM
(North Holland)
Pop. Est. 150,213

HAARLEMS DAGBLAD (e) Est. 1656
PO Box 507, 2003 PA
Tel: (31-23) 150150; Fax: (31-23) 317337
Circ.—61,304
Prop.—nv Holdingmaatschappij De Telegraaf
Ed.—J G Majoor

THE HAGUE
(South Holland)
('S Gravenhage)
Pop. Est. 445,279

HET BINNENHOF (e) Est. 1945
PO Box 9, 2501 CA
Circ.—172,550
Prop.—Westerpers bv
Ed.—J J Hallewas
HAAGSCHE COURANT (e) Est. 1883
PO Box 16050, 2500 AA
Tel: (31-70) 3190911; Fax: (31-70) 3906447
Circ.—147,930
Prop.—Wegener nv
Ed.—J Schinkelshoek

HEERLEN
(Limburg)
Pop. Est. 95,794

LIMBURGS DAGBLAD (m) Est. 1917
PO Box 3100, 6401 DP
Tel: (31-45) 739911; Fax: (31-45) 739364
Circ.—79,810
Prop.—nv Holdingmaatschappij De Telegraaf
Ed.—R A M Brown

HENGELO
(Overijssel)
Pop. Est. 8,274

TWENTSCHE COURANT (e) Est. 1847
PO Box 125, 7550 AC
Tel: (31-74) 456789; Fax: (31-74) 913044
Circ.—49,100
Prop.—Drukkerij Twentsche Courant bv
Ed.—H H Morsink

HILVERSUM
(North Holland)
Pop. Est. 84,213

DE GOOI EN EEMLANDER (e) Est. 1871
PO Box 15, 1200 AA
Tel: (31-35) 257911; Fax: (31-35) 257227
Circ.—52,652
Prop.—Dagblad De Gooi-en Eemlander bv
Ed.—J H van Zenderen

HOUTEN
(Utrecht)
Pop. Est. 30,339

UTRECHTS NIEUWSBLAD (e) Est. 1893
PO Box 500, 3990 DM
Tel: (31-3403) 99911; Fax: (31-3403) 99226
Circ.—105,018
Prop.—Wegener nv
Ed.—G Selles

LEEUWARDEN
(Friesland)
Pop. Est. 87,464

FRIESCH DAGBLAD (e) Est. 1903
PO Box 412, 8901 BE
Tel: (31-58) 987654; Fax: (31-58) 987540
Circ.—22,147
Prop.—Provinciale Persevereniging voor Friesland
LEEUWARDER COURANT (e) Est. 1752
PO Box 394, 8901 BD
Tel: (31-58) 845845; Fax: (31-58) 845419

Circ.—111,341
Prop.—Noordelijke Dagblad Combinatie
Ed.—R Mulder

LEIDEN
(South Holland)
Pop. Est. 6,783

LEIDSCH DAGBLAD (e) Est. 1860
Haarlem; PO Box 54, 2300 PA
Tel: (31-71) 150150; Fax: (31-71) 317337
Circ.—50,227
Prop.—Uitgeversmaatschappij Leidesch Dagblad bv
Ed.—J G C Majoor
(Circulation figure combines with Alphens Dagblad.)
LEIDSE COURANT (e) Est. 1910
PO Box 11, 2300 AA
Tel: (31-71) 122244; Fax: (31-71) 134941
Circ.—9,967
Prop.—Westerpers bv
Ed.—J W C Leune

MAASTRICHT
(Limburg)
Pop. Est. 118,102

DE LIMBURGER (m) Est. 1845
PO Box 1056, 6201 MK
Tel: (31-43) 821234; Fax: (31-43) 619292
Circ.—144,746
Prop.—VNU Dagbladengroep bv
Ed.—G H Vogelaar

NIJMEGEN
(Gelderland)
Pop. Est. 147,018

DE GELDERLANDER/BARNEVELDSE KRANT (m&e) Est. 1849
PO Box 36, 6500 DA
Tel: (31-80) 650409; Fax: (31-80) 650402
Circ.—185,850
Prop.—VNU Dagbladengroep bv
Ed.—H J Kuyt

PURMEREND
(North Holland)
Pop. Est. 58,718

NIEUWE NOORDHOLLANDSE COURANT (e)
PO Box 14, 1440 AA
Tel: (31-2990) 32071; Fax: (31-2990) 30205
Circ.—10,986
Prop.—Uitgeversmaatschappij Midden-Noord-holland bv
Ed.—H Lansdaal

ROOSENDAAL en NISPEN
(North Brabant)
Pop. Est. 62,784

BRABANTS NIEUWSBLAD (m) Est. 1862
PO Box 1052, 4700 BB
Tel: (31-1650) 35970; Fax: (31-1650) 50035
Circ.—54,105
Prop.—VNU Dagbladengroep bv
Ed.—G Bielderman

ROTTERDAM
(South Holland)
Pop. Est. 598,521

ALGEMEEN DAGBLAD (m) Est. 1946
PO Box 8983, 3000 TC
Tel: (31-10) 4067211; Fax: (31-10) 4066966
Circ.—415,800
Ed.—Dr. P R van Dijk
NRC HANDELSBLAD (e) Est. 1971
PO Box 8987, 3009 TH
Tel: (31-10) 4066219; Fax: (31-10) 4066980
Circ.—268,250
Ed.—D P J van Reeuwijk
ROTTERDAMS DAGBLAD (e) Est. 1991
PO Box 1162, 3000 BD
Tel: (31-10) 4004200; Fax: (31-10) 4128509
Circ.—118,302
Ed.—J Prins
Ed.—L P Pronk
ROTTERDAMS NIEUWSBLAD (e) Est. 1878
PO Box 959, 3000 AZ
Tel: (31-10) 4067211; Fax: (31-10) 4066966
Prop.—Avonbladen Combinatie Rotterdam cv
Ed.—J Prins
Ed.—J R Soetenhorst
(For circulation figure please see Het Vrije Volk in Rotterdam.)

Netherlands, The — Europe

HET VRIJE VOLK (e) Est. 1900
PO Box 1162, 3000 BD
Circ.—153,615
Prop.—Avonbladen Combinatie Rotterdam cv
Ed.—G Krul
(Circulation figure combines with Rotterdam Nieuwsblad.)

S-HERTOGENBOSCH
(North Brabant)
Pop. Est. 95,448

BRABANTS DAGBLAD (m) Est. 1771
PO Box 235, 5201 HB
Tel: (31-73) 157157; Fax: (31-73) 143034
Circ.—153,615
Prop.—Avonbladen Combinatie Rotterdam cv
Ed.—G Krul
(Circulation figure combines with Rotterdam Nieuwsblad.)

TILBURG
(North Brabant)
Pop. Est. 156,421

HET NIEUWSBLAD, DAGBLAD VOOR MIDDEN-BRABANT (m) Est. 1913
Eersel, 5521 GD
Circ.—56,800
Prop.—Drukkerij Het Nieuwsblad bv
Ed.—J M P J Verstegen

VENLO
(Limburg)
Pop. Est. 65,367

DAGBLAD VOOR NOORD-LIMBURG (m) Est. 1945
PO Box 65, 5900 AB
Tel: (31-77) 551234; Fax: (31-77) 519533
Circ.—53,909
Prop.—VNU Dagbladengroep bv
Ed.—J L L Wijnen

VLISSINGEN
(Zeeland)
Pop. Est. 44,211

PROVINCIALE ZEEUWSE COURANT (m) Est. 1758
PO Box 18, 4380 AA
Tel: (31-1184) 84000; Fax: (31-1184) 70100
Circ.—62,398
Prop.—Uitgeverij Provinciale Zeeuwse Courant bv
Ed.—A Oosthoek

ZAANDAM
(North Holland)
Pop. Est. 65,551

DE TYPHOON DAGBLAD VOOR DE ZAANSTREEK (e)
PO Box 23, 1500 EA
Tel: (31-75) 813513; Fax: (31-75) 702367
Circ.—21,541
Prop.—Uitgeversmaatschappij Midden-Noord-holland bv
Ed.—P Wolfbergen

ZWOLLE
(Overijssel)
Pop. Est. 99,139

ZWOLSE COURANT (e)
PO Box 67, 8000 AB
Tel: (31-38) 275275; Fax: (31-38) 222062
Circ.—70,350
Prop.—Wegener bv
Ed.—J Bartelds

NORWAY
(Includes Svalbard)
Pop. Est. 4,314,604

ALESUND
Pop. Est. 35,563

SUNNOERSPOSTEN (m-6x wk.) Est. 1882
Boks 123, 6001
Tel: (47) 70120000; Fax: (47) 70129850
Circ.—36,751 ABC
Ed.—Roar Larsen
Ad. Mgr.—Odd Opshaug
Mng. Dir.—Roy P Jacobsen

ALTA

ALTAPOSTEN (6x wk.)
PO Box 1193, 9501
Tel: (47) 78435088; Fax: (47) 78436147
Circ.—5,198 ABC

ARENDAL
Pop. Est. 12,509

AGDERPOSTEN (m-6x wk.) Est. 1874
PO Box 8, 4801
Tel: (47) 04127000
Circ.—25,589
Mgr.—Endre Hoflandsal
Ed.—Thor Bjorn Seland
Sales Mgr.—Rolf Tallaksen

ASKIM

OEVRE SMAALENENE (5x wk.)
Oevre Smaalenene; Postboks 52, 1801
Tel: (47) 69881062; Fax: (47) 69886084
Circ.—8,890 ABC

BERGEN
Pop. Est. 209,320

BERGENS ARBEIDERBLAD (m-7x wk.) Est. 1927
Chr. Michelsensgate 4, 5001
Fax: (47) 65310486
Circ.—23,875
Mgr.—Olaw Terje Bergo
Ad. Mgr.—Astrid Osthus Sjursen
BERGENS TIDENDE (m-6x wk.)
Byåavdeling; PO Box 875, 5001
Tel: (47) 5214826; Fax: (47) 5312306
Circ.—95,455 ABC
Mng. Dir.—Liv Hatland
Ad. Mgr.—Helge Ovrebo
U.S. Rep.—Publicitas
BERGENSAVISEN (7x wk.) Est. 1927
PO Box 824, 5002
Tel: (47) 55235000; Fax: (47) 55310486
Circ.—27,398 ABC
Mgr./Ed.—Olav Terje Bergo
BILLINGSTAD (m-5x wk.)
PO Box 133, 1361
Tel: (47) 66986901; Fax: (47) 66980919
Circ.—31,720
DAGEN (e-6x wk.) Est. 1919
Postboks 76/77, 5001
Tel: (47) 05311755
Circ.—10,779
Mgr.—Inge Ree
Ad. Mgr.—Styrk Opheim
FISKAREN Est. 1923
PO Box 4053, 5023
Tel: (47) 65314300; Fax: (47) 65318201
Ed.—Nils Torsvik
Mgr.—Jan L Larsen
GULA TIDEND Est. 1904
PO Box 250, 5001
Tel: (47) 65230330; Fax: (47) 65902436
Circ.—4,111
Ed.—Gunnar Wiederstrom

BODOE
Pop. Est. 35,377

NORDLANDS FRAMTID (m-6x wk.) Est. 1910
Ann. Avd.-Framtid Reklame Storgt. 9; PO Box 313, 8001
Tel: (47) 08120160; Fax: (47) 08128811
Circ.—20,238 ABC
Mgr.—Kurt Borgen
Ad. Mgr.—Odd Lorentzen
NORDLANDSPOSTEN (m-6x wk.) Est. 1910
PO Box 44, 8001
Tel: (47) 08127200; Fax: (47) 08127222
Circ.—20,238
Mgr.—Iver Hammeren
Mktg. Mgr.—Turid Anderson

BRANDBU
Pop. Est. 12,545

HADELAND (m-4x wk.) Est. 1918
Hadeland; Postboks 85, 2760
Tel: (47) 06334120; Fax: (47) 61260960
Circ.—7,694
Ed.—Marit Ascheoug
Mgr.—Ole Hamstad
Ad. Mgr.—Torgeir Sater

BROENNOEYSUND

BROENNOEYSUND AVIS (5x wk.)
Storgaten 32, 8901
Tel: (47) 75020022; Fax: (47) 75021827
Circ.—4,900 ABC

DRAMMEN
Pop. Est. 50,700

DE FIRE NESTE (6x wk.)
Postboks 7032, 3007
Tel: (47) 32826190; Fax: (47) 32204210
Circ.—442,000
DRAMMENS TIDENDE og BUSKERUDS BLAD A/S (m-6x wk.) Est. 1832
Boks 7033, 3007
Tel: (47) 3204000; Fax: (47) 32204210
Circ.—43,611 ABC
Mng. Dir.—Finn Grindt
Mktg. Dir.—Roar Odd Haust
FREMTIDEN (m-6x wk.) Est. 1905
PO Box 7031, 3007
Tel: (47) 03823580; Fax: (47) 03823600
Circ.—19,300
Ed.—Knut S Evensen
Mgr.—Terje Ledahal
Mktg. Mgr.—Svein-Inge Nilsenn

DROEBAK

AKERSHUS AMTSTIDENDE (e-5x wk.) Est. 1873
PO Box 12, 1441
Tel: (47) 64930660; Fax: (47) 64933744
Circ.—7,366 ABC
Prop.—Akershus Amstidende
Ed.—Terje Lundefaret
Mgr.—Finn Lund
Mng. Dir.—Oivind Taugboi
Sales Mgr.—Hilde Kallard Sem

EIDSVOLL
Pop. Est. 16,242

EIDSVOLD BLAD/ULLENSAKER BLAD Est. 1901
AS Eidsvold Blad; Postboks 130, 2081
Tel: (47) 63964910; Fax: (47) 63965630
Circ.—8,574 ABC
Prop.—Eidsvold Blad AS
Ed.—Bjorn Terje Kaspersen
Mgr.—Oddvar Oyangen

ELVERUM
Pop. Est. 17,224

OESTLENDINGEN/HAMAR/OESTLENDINGEN SOLER-ODAL (m-6x wk.) Est. 1901
Gamle Trysilvei 6, 2401
Tel: (47) 62410144; Fax: (47) 62411590
Circ.—26,652 ABC
Mng. Dir./Adm. Dir.—Bjorn Fjellmosveen
Mktg. Dir.—Kjetil Grambo

FAGERNES
Pop. Est. 6,565

VALDRES (m-4x wk.) Est. 1903
Postboks 54, 2901
Tel: (47) 61360300; Fax: (47) 61361506
Circ.—10,142 ABC
Prop.—Valdres & Valdres Trykkeri AS
Ed.—Geir Beitrusten
Ad. Mgr.—Tom O Martinsen
Mng. Dir.—H Pedersen

FARSUND
Pop. Est. 9,431

FARSUNDS AVIS (m-6x wk.) Est. 1889
Postboks 23, 4551
Tel: (47) 38390444; Fax: (47) 38392086
Circ.—5,936 ABC
Ed.—Gunvald A Justnaes
Mgr.—Steinar Spielkaviknej
Ad. Mgr.—Paul Iddeland

FINNSNES
Pop. Est. 26,558

TROMS FOLKEBLAD Est. 1965
PO Box 308, 9301
Tel: (47) 08940511; Fax: (47) 08941809
Circ.—4,300
Mgr./Ed.—Rolf A Erstad
Mktg. Mgr.—Egil A Moxness

FLOROE
Pop. Est. 9,592

FIRDAPOSTEN Est. 1948
PO Box 38, 6901
Tel: (47) 05741144; Fax: (47) 05714313
Circ.—5,960
Mgr./Ed.—Erik Stephansen
Ad. Mgr.—Malvin Horne

FOERDE
Pop. Est. 8,143

FIRDA (5x wk.) Est. 1917
PO Box 160, 6801
Tel: (47) 05729500; Fax: (47) 05720404

Circ.—13,166
Mgr.—Dag Solheim
Ad. Mgr.—Bjarte Nordeide

FREDRIKSTAD
Pop. Est. 27,618

FREDRIKSTAD AVISA DEMOKRATEN (e-6x wk.) Est. 1906
PO Box 83, 1601
Tel: (47) 09319999
Circ.—11,285
Mgr.—Oyvind Tveter
FREDRIKSSTAD BLAD (6x wk.) Est. 1889
PO Box 143, 1601
Tel: (47) 09319000
Circ.—17,810
Ed.—Truls Velgaard
Mktg. Mgr.—Alx-Petter Halvorsen
Mng. Dir.—Per H Karlsrud

GJOEVIK
Pop. Est. 25,972

OPPLAND ARBEIDERBLAD (m-6x wk.) Est. 1924
Postboks 24, 2801
Tel: (47) 06189300; Fax: (47) 06170725
Circ.—27,666 ABC
Ed.—Leif Sveen
Ad. Mgr.—Oystein Brekke
Mgr.—Asmund Oppenid
SAMHOLD (m-6x wk.) Est. 1860
PO Box 22, 2801
Tel: (47) 06170000; Fax: (47) 06177451
Circ.—6,700
Mktg. Mgr.—Tom Torkehagen

HALDEN
Pop. Est. 25,848

HALDEN ARBEIDERBLAD (m-6x wk.) Est. 1929
Torggt 2, 1751
Tel: (47) 09180033; Fax: (47) 09180033
Circ.—10,500 ABC
Ed.—Bjorn Ystrom
Mgr.—Kjell Lovhaug
Sales Mgr.—Odd Olestad

HAMAR
Pop. Est. 15,775

HAMAR ARBEIDERBLAD (m-6x wk.) Est. 1925
Groennegate 64; Boks 262, 2301
Tel: (47) 62527540; Fax: (47) 62523324
Circ.—27,946 ABC
Ed.—Magne Bjornrud
Mgr.—Roger Bjurling
Sales Mgr.—Britt Dahl
HEDMARK/OPPLAND SAMKJOERINGEN (m-6x wk.)
Postboks 443, 2301
Tel: (47) 62532211; Fax: (47) 06533609
Circ.—91,191

HAMMERFEST
Pop. Est. 7,208

FINNMARK DAGBLAD (m-6x wk.) Est. 1913
Kirkegaten 8, 9601
Tel: (47) 78411422; Fax: (47) 78413436
Circ.—11,750 ABC
Ed.—Knut Erik Olsen
Mgr.—Bjornar Nilsen
Ad. Mgr.—Kjell Kristoffersen

HARSTAD
Pop. Est. 22,277

HARSTAD TIDENDE (m-6x wk.) Est. 1887
Storgatan 11; Postboks 85, 9401
Tel: (47) 77018000; Fax: (47) 77018007
Circ.—16,418 ABC
Ed.—Odd Rikard Olsen
Mgr.—Ivar Iversen
Ad. Mgr.—Stein Fossen

HAUGESUND
Pop. Est. 26,947

HAUGESUNDS AVIS (m-6x wk.) Est. 1895
Box 2024, 5501
Tel: (47) 52719595; Fax: (47) 52719440
Circ.—36,586 ABC
Ed.—Rune Halheim
Mng. Dir.—Inge Sundjor
Ad. Mgr.—Odd S Kringeland
Mktg. Mgr.—Gislaug Rydland

HOENEFOSS
Pop. Est. 33,711

RINGERIKES BLAD (m-6x wk.) Est. 1845
Postboks 68, 3501
Tel: (47) 32128000; Fax: (47) 32121774
Circ.—13,453 ABC
Ed.—Trond Hjerpseth

Mng. Dir.—Bjorn Larssen
Sales Mgr.—Ragnar Enerhaugeu

HOEYANGER
Pop. Est. 4,967

SOGN DAGBLAD (m-6x wk.) Est. 1938
PO Box 129, 5901
Tel: (47) 05712933; Fax: (47) 05712917
Circ.—5,476
Ed.—Norvald Stedje
Mgr.—Jarle Oren
Ad. Mgr.—Odd Rune Forsund

HORTEN
Pop. Est. 12,917

GJENGANGEREN (m-6x wk.) Est. 1851
PO Box 85, 3191
Tel: (47) 03342404/(47) 03342901; Fax: (47) 03345549
Circ.—5,842
Mgr./Ed.—Dag N Kristoffersen
Mktg. Mgr.—Gaute Bjornoy

KONGSBERG
Pop. Est. 21,262

LAAGENDALSPOSTEN (m-5x wk.) Est. 1903
Bekkedokk 3; Postboks 480, 3601
Tel: (47) 32731044; Fax: (47) 32735930
Circ.—10,410 ABC
Ed.—Odd Einar Andersen
Mgr.—Tor R Jensen
Mktg. Mgr.—Ingunn Evensen

KONGSVINGER
Pop. Est. 17,425

GLAMDALEN (m-6x wk.) Est. 1926
Postuttak, 2201
Tel: (47) 62815016; Fax: (47) 62815516
Circ.—22,623 ABC
Mgr.—Bengt Haakerud
Mktg. Mgr.—Leix Bongsund

KRAGEROE
Pop. Est. 10,870

KRAGEROE BLAD Est. 1844
Karl Fredd Kristensen; PO Box 55, 3771
Tel: (47) 03981100; Fax: (47) 03983236
Circ.—4,200
Ed.—Willy Nilsen
Mgr.—Hans R Naper
VESTMAR
PO Box 85, 3771
Tel: (47) 03981241; Fax: (47) 03980983
Mgr.—Hans Ch Paus-Knudsen

KRISTIANSUND
Pop. Est. 17,516

FAEDRELANDSVEIEN (m-6x wk.) Est. 1875
Boks 369, 4601
Tel: (47) 38013000; Fax: (47) 38013710
Circ.—46,520 ABC
Ed.—Egil Remi Jensen
Ed.—Jens Vetland
Mng. Dir.—Kare Weshund
Sales Mgr.—Fan A Elden
TIDENS KRAV (6x wk.) Est. 1906
Tidens Krav; Postboks 8, 6501
Tel: (47) 07377811
Circ.—14,289
Mgr.—Rolx G Nergaard
Sales Mgr.—Fan Grasto

LARVIK
Pop. Est. 8,152

OSTLANDS-POSTEN (e-6x wk.) Est. 1881
PO Box 2000, 3251-18
Tel: (47) 03484000; Fax: (47) 034183425
Circ.—14,087
Mng. Ed.—Fan C Nass
Ad. Mgr.—Svein Andrisen
Adm. Dir.—Tor R Jensen

LEIKANGER

SOGN AVIS (m-5x wk.), 5842
Tel: (47) 57653022; Fax: (47) 57653543
Circ.—11,900 ABC

LILLEHAMMER
Pop. Est. 22,310

DAGNINGEN (m-6x wk.) Est. 1924
Postboks 952, 2601
Tel: (47) 61255000; Fax: (47) 61263405
Circ.—12,441 ABC
Mgr.—O Dissen
Sales Mgr.—Steinar Brubakk
GUDBRANDSDOELEN LILLEHAMMER TILSKUER
(m-6x wk.) Est. 1894
Postboks 952, 2601
Tel: (47) 61289833; Fax: (47) 61260960

Circ.—22,433 ABC
Mktg. Dir.—Erling Nustad
Ad. Mgr.—Odd Fostervoll
Adm. Dir.—Asbjorn Ringen

LILLESTROM
Pop. Est. 32,347

AKERSHUS/ROMERIKES BLAD (eS) Est. 1913/1902
NCC Service A/S; Postboks 235, 2001
Tel: (47) 63819090; Fax: (47) 63803719/(47) 63813719
Circ.—39,263 (e); 38,782 (S) ABC
Prop.—Akershus Arbeiderpresse AS
Adm. Dir.—Oivind Taugboel
ROMERIKES BLAD (e-6x wk.) Est. 1902
Akershus Arbeiderpresse A/L; Postboks 235, 2001
Tel: (47) 63819090; Fax: (47) 63803719
Circ.—12,390 ABC
Prop.—Akershus Arbeiderpresse AS
Mng. Dir.—Oivind Taugbol
Ad. Mgr.—Joern Staale Tufte

LYSAKER

FINANSAVISEN (5x wk.)
Postboks 31, 1324
Tel: (47) 02583990; Fax: (47) 02583980
Circ.—20,000 ABC

MANDAL
Pop. Est. 12,384

LINDESNES (m-6x wk.) Est. 1889
Lindesnes; Postboks 41, 4501
Tel: (47) 38263333; Fax: (47) 38263433
Circ.—6,680 ABC
Ed.—Odd Nygaard
Ed.—Kjell Gase Nygaard
Ad. Mgr.—O Pettersen

MELHUS

TROENDERBLADET
Boks 160, 7084
Tel: (47) 87870055; Fax: (47) 87871233

MO
Pop. Est. 34,411

RANA BLAD (m-6x wk.) Est. 1902
Boks 55, 8601
Tel: (47) 75125500; Fax: (47) 75125570
Circ.—11,358 ABC
Ed.—Svein Meyer Svendsen
Mgr.—Ole Ingar Lindsith
Ad. Mgr.—Leif Kallestad

MOLDE
Pop. Est. 21,784

FYLKET Est. 1926
PO Box 2012, 6401
Tel: (47) 07251088; Fax: (47) 07251442
Mgr./Ed.—Lars Steinar Anses
ROMSDALS BUDSTIKKE (m-6x wk.) Est. 1843
Romsdalsgt. 15; Postboks 55, 6401
Tel: (47) 72150000; Fax: (47) 71250011
Circ.—18,308 ABC
Prop.—Romsdals Budstikke
Ed.—Odd Reider Solem
Mgr.—S Solstad
Mktg. Mgr.—Nils Petter Heggem
Sales Mgr.—Kare Endresplass

MOSJOEEN
Pop. Est. 16,689

HELGELAND ARBEIDERBLAD (m-6x wk.) Est. 1929
PO Box 336, 8651
Tel: (47) 08770411; Fax: (47) 08770495
Circ.—9,741
Ed.—Are Andersen
Mgr.—Olav Fensen
Ad. Mgr.—Paul Rugeldal
Mktg. Mgr.—Ewe Rostin Enge

MOSS
Pop. Est. 24,747

MOSS AVIS (m-6x wk.) Est. 1876
Moss Avis A/S; Postboks 248, 1501
Tel: (47) 69253040; Fax: (47) 69250685
Circ.—14,342 ABC
Prop.—Moss Avis AS
Mng. Dir.—Bjornar Berger
Ad. Mgr.—Per O Mordre
MOSS DAGBLAD (m-6x wk.) Est. 1912
Postboks 248/250, 1501
Tel: (47) 09256070; Fax: (47) 09254770
Circ.—7,080 ABC
Ed.—Geir Lilleberg
Mgr.—Oyvind Tveter
Dir.—Ole Egeland

NAMSOS
Pop. Est. 11,805

NAMDAL ARBEIDERBLAD (m-6x wk.) Est. 1917
Namdal Arbeiderblads Trykkeri; Postboks 158, 7801
Tel: (47) 07771795
Circ.—11,296 ABC
Prop.—Namdal Arbeiderblads Trykkeri
Ed.—Morten Nordmeland
Mgr.—Arne Varem
Mktg. Mgr.—Torfinn Flak
NORDTROENDEREN OG NAMDALEN (m-6x wk.) Est. 1882
Havnegaten 12; Postboks 10, 7801
Tel: (47) 07772955
Circ.—3,500 ABC
Prop.—Namdalpresse AS
Mgr.—Arnt Farbu
Ad. Mgr.—Bjoern Hyrrold

NARVIK
Pop. Est. 18,470

FREMOVER (m-6x wk.) Est. 1903
Boks 324, 8501
Tel: (47) 76950000; Fax: (47) 76950030
Circ.—10,921
Mgr.—Henry Arnee Hansen
Mktg. Mgr.—Magne Johansen
NORSK LYSINGSBLAD
Postboks 177, 8501
Tel: (47) 76950550; Fax: (47) 76950580
Circ.—12,000 ABC
OFOTENS TIDENDE Est. 1899
PO Box 283, 8501
Tel: (47) 08241526; Fax: (47) 08245360

ORKANGER
Pop. Est. 9,988

SOER-TROENDELAG (m-5x wk.) Est. 1908
Boks 55, 7301
Tel: (47) 72480222; Fax: (47) 72482270
Circ.—7,390 ABC
Ed.—Finn Nielsen
Mgr.—Sein Eilertsen
Mktg. Mgr.—Stein A Kirkaune

OSLO
Pop. Est. 452,415

A-MAGASINET Est. 1860
PO Box 1178, 0107
Tel: (47) 22863000; Fax: (47) 22421593
AFTENNUMMER (e-5x wk.) Est. 1767
Akersgt. 510180
Tel: (47) 22863119; Fax: (47) 22420893
Circ.—267,809
Mng. Dir.—Gunnar Gran
Dir.—Hanoslav Holmoy
Adm. Dir.—Kaare Frydenberg
U.S. Rep.—Publicitas
AFTENPOSTEN (e-5x wk.)
Postboks 178, Sentrum, 0107
Tel: (47) 22863000; Fax: (47) 22421593
Circ.—189,000 ABC
AFTENPOSTEN (m-7x wk.)
Postboks 1178, Sentrum, 0107
Tel: (47) 22863000; Fax: (47) 22426325
Circ.—280,000
AFTENPOSTEN (S)
Postboks 1178, Sentrum, 0107
Tel: (47) 22863000; Fax: (47) 22426325
Circ.—217,000
ARBEIDBLADET (m-6x wk.) Est. 1884
PO Box 1183, Sentrum, 0107
Tel: (47) 22726000; Fax: (47) 22649282
Circ.—51,786
Mng. Dir.—Hans Raqstad
Sales Mgr.—Jan Rummelhoff
DAGBLADET (m-7x wk.) Est. 1869
A/S Dagbladet; PO Box 1184, 0107
Tel: (47) 22310600; Fax: (47) 22362461
Circ.—227,000
Prop.—Dagbladet AS
Mng. Dir.—Arne Jorgensen
Mktg. Dir.—Anne Fonurkjor
Ad. Dir.—Claus Andersen
Adm. Dir.—Dagfinn Bakken
DAGBLADET (wknd.)
A/S Dagbladet; Postboks 1184, 0107
Tel: (47) 22310600; Fax: (47) 22310501
Circ.—305,000 (sat.); 120,000 (S) ABC
DAGENS NAERINGSLIV (m-5x wk.) Est. 1890
Grev Wedels plass 9; Postboks 1182, 0107
Tel: (47) 22001000; Fax: (47) 22001070
Circ.—49,000
Prop.—Dagens Naeringsliv AS
Ad. Dir.—Kare Valebrokk
U.S. Rep.—Publicitas

Europe **Norway** IV-37

FOLKET Est. 1919
Moellergst. 38, 0179
Tel: (47) 22115510; Fax: (47) 22114375
Mgr./Ed.—Inge Groesland
FOLKLETS FRAMTID Est. 1946
Ovre Slottsgate 18/20, 0157
Tel: (47) 22411430; Fax: (47) 22336250
Circ.—8,615
Ed.—Odd Hagen
Mgr.—Kjell Mathiesen
KLASSEKAMPEN (e-6x wk.)
KLASSEKAMPEN; Postboks 83, 0611
Tel: (47) 02649320; Fax: (47) 02630579
Circ.—10,042
NATIONEN (m-6x wk.) Est. 1918
PO Box 447, Sentrum, 0104
Tel: (47) 22425050
Circ.—20,691
Mng. Dir.—Tone Flaa
Mktg. Mgr.—Bjorn Morken
Adm. Dir.—Tora Flaa
NY TID Est. 1975
Gronland; PO Box 9316, 0135
Tel: (47) 22173110; Fax: (47) 22175211
Mgr./Ed.—Gunnar Ringheim
VART LAND (m-6x wk.)
Tveita; Postboks 68, 0617
Tel: (47) 22264000; Fax: (47) 22269082
Circ.—27,014 ABC
Mng. Dir./Adm. Dir.—Helge Simonnes
Mktg. Mgr.—Bjorn Markussen
Ad. Mgr.—Halvor Stensnid
VERDENS GANG (mS) Est. 1945
Postboks 1185, Sentrum, 0107
Tel: (47) 22000000; Fax: (47) 22425811
Circ.—381,224 (m); 264,526 (S) ABC
Prop.—Verdens Gang AS
Mng. Dir.—Aslak Ona
Ad. Mgr.—Tore Berg

RJUKAN
Pop. Est. 11,008

RJUKAN ARBEIDERBLAD (d-5x wk.) Est. 1923
PO Box 63, 3661
Tel: (47) 03691366; Fax: (47) 03691038
Circ.—2,614
Ed.—Kjell Gunnar Dahle
Mgr.—Terje Paulsen

SANDEFJORD
Pop. Est. 35,549

SANDEFJORDS BLAD (m-6x wk.) Est. 1861
Postboks 2042, 3201
Tel: (47) 33460000; Fax: (47) 33462155
Circ.—15,018 ABC
Mng. Dir.—Roar Larsen
Mktg. Mgr.—Arne Lindstrom
Adm. Dir.—Leif Magne Flemmen
Ad. Mgr.—Stein F Hoel Enksen

SANDVIKA
Pop. Est. 81,294

ASKER OG BAERUMS BUDSTIKKE (e-5x wk.) Est. 1898
PO Box 133, 1361
Tel: (47) 02980901; Fax: (47) 0298099
Circ.—31,672
Mng. Dir./Adm. Dir.—Odd A Brevik
Mktg. Mgr.—Fan-Tore Fohnsen

SARPSBORG
Pop. Est. 11,757

SARPSBORG ARBEIDERBLAD (e-6x wk.) Est. 1929
PO Box 87, 1701
Tel: (47) 09155000; Fax: (47) 09155536
Circ.—17,195
Ad. Mgr.—Oivind Tveter
Ad. Mgr.—K Soensteby

SKI
Pop. Est. 21,979

OESTLANDETS BLAD (e-5x wk.) Est. 1908
PO Box 113, 1401
Tel: (47) 09875060; Fax: (47) 09875787
Circ.—18,217
Ed.—Tom Ullsgard
Mng. Dir.—Andreas Gjolme
Mktg. Mgr.—Olav T Skogseth
Adm. Dir.—Oyvin Norborg

SKIEN
Pop. Est. 47,531

TELEMARK ARBEIDERBLAD (m-6x wk.) Est. 1921
Postboks 625, 3703
Tel: (47) 35585500; Fax: (47) 35530590

Copyright ©1996 by the Editor & Publisher Co.

Norway / Europe

Circ.—21,000 ABC
Mgr.—Martin Skov
Ad. Mgr.—Asb J Skarholt
Adm. Dir.—Leif Aage Eilertsen
VARDEN (m-6x wk.) Est. 1874
Prinsessegate 8; Postboks 8, 3701
Tel: (47) 03521066; Fax: (47) 03528323
Circ.—31,144 ABC
Mng. Dir.—Tom Forgensen
Ed.—Bjorn Jacobsen
Mktg. Mgr.—Terje Andersen
Ad. Mgr.—Svein Pedersen

SORTLAND
Pop. Est. 8,214

BLADET VESTERÅLEN (m-4x wk.) Est. 1921
Vesterålen, K. Nordahl A/S; Boks 33, 8401
Tel: (47) 76121622; Fax: (47) 76121295
Circ.—10,050 ABC
Prop.—Vesteralen K Nordahl AS
Mgr./Ed.—Karl Glad Nordahl
VESTERÅLEN (m-4x wk.)
Boks 33, 8401
Tel: (47) 76121622; Fax: (47) 76124253
Circ.—10,334 ABC

STAVANGER
Pop. Est. 97,716

ROGALANDS AVIS (m-6x wk.) Est. 1899
Boks 233, 4001
Tel: (47) 04585060; Fax: (47) 04582970
Circ.—18,897
Mgr.—Norulv Oevrebotten
STAVANGER AFTENBLAD (m-6x wk.) Est. 1893
Boks 229, 4001
Tel: (47) 51500000; Fax: (47) 51893225
Circ.—71,771 ABC
Mng. Dir.—Svein Kverneland
Adm. Dir./Ed.—Thor Bjarne Bore
Mktg. Mgr.—Oddvar Bjorkvik
Ad. Mgr.—Rolf Nordin

STEINKJER
Pop. Est. 20,658

TROENDER-AVISA (m-6x wk.)
Postboks 2520, 7701
Tel: (47) 74163000
Circ.—23,243 ABC
Mgr.—Arnt Farbu
Ad. Mgr.—Bjorn Saether

STORD

SUNNHORDLAND
PO Box 100, 5401
Tel: (47) 05410488; Fax: (47) 05414330

SVOLVAER
Pop. Est. 9,571

LOFOTPOSTEN (m-6x wk.) Est. 1896
PO Box 85, 8301
Tel: (47) 08870011; Fax: (47) 08870009
Circ.—12,400
Mgr.—Bjoern Paulsen
Mktg. Mgr.—Normann L Fohansen
Ad. Mgr.—Harald Karlsen

TONSBERG

TONSBERG (m-6x wk.)
Postboks 2003, 3103
Tel: (47) 33310000; Fax: (47) 33333858
Circ.—32,641 ABC
Prop.—Tonsberg Blad AS

TROMSOE
Pop. Est. 49,459

NORDLYS (6x wk.)
PO Box 656, 9001
Tel: (47) 08323500
Circ.—32,300
TROMSOE (m-6x wk.) Est. 1902
Postboks 1028, 9001
Tel: (47) 08356600; Fax: (47) 08355117
Circ.—9,497 ABC
Ed.—Per Eliassen
Mgr.—Dag Nowang
Mktg. Mgr.—Rolf Olsen
Ad. Mgr.—Gunnar Wonun

TRONDHEIM
Pop. Est. 135,010

ADRESSEAVISEN (m-6x wk.) Est. 1767
Postboks 6070, 7003
Tel: (47) 72500000; Fax: (47) 72501754
Circ.—90,158 ABC
Mng. Dir./Adm. Dir.—Jon Aass
Mktg. Mgr.—Odd Einar Drilsvik
U.S. Rep.—Publicitas
ARBEIDER-AVISA (6x wk.) Est. 1924
PO Box 5440, 7002
Tel: (47) 07921122; Fax: (47) 07921410
Circ.—15,300
Mgr.—Randi Rasmussen
AVISA TRONDHEIM (e-6x wk.)
Prinsens gt. 39, 7005
Tel: (47) 73898700; Fax: (47) 73898701
Circ.—13,766 ABC

VADSOE
Pop. Est. 5,894

FINNMARKEN (m-6x wk.) Est. 1899
Postboks 6, 9801
Tel: (47) 8553555; Fax: (47) 8552106
Circ.—8,327
Mgr.—I Karlsen
Ed.—Bjoru Hidonell

POLAND, REPUBLIC OF
Pop. Est. 38,654,561

BIALYSTOK
Pop. Est. 295,600

GAZETA WSPOLCZESNA (Contemporary Gazette) (m) Est. 1951
ul. Suraska 1, 15-950
Tel: (48-85) 22710; Fax (48-85) 23245
Circ.—50,000
Prop.—Kresy Ltd.
Ex. Ed.—Tomasz Kalinowski
Ed.—Adam Jerzy Socha
Ed. in Ch.—Wojciech Jarmolowicz
KURIER PODLASKI (Podlasie Courier) (m) Est. 1983
ul. Suraska 4, 15-950
Tel: (48-85) 436715; Fax: (48-85) 28152
Circ.—30,000
Prop.—Spoldzielnia Pracy
Ed. in Ch.—Andrzej Rozalski
KURIER PORANNY (m) Est. 1989
ul. Lipowa 19/21, 15-424
Tel: (48-85) 21493
Circ.—20,000
Prop.—Agencja Wydawniczo-Handlowa
Ex. Ed.—Jan Oniszczuk
Ed. in Ch.—Wojciech Potocki

BIELSKO BIALA

DZIENNIK BESKIDZKI (d) Est. 1992
3 Maja 1, 43-300
Tel: (48-52) 22617; Fax: (48-52) 27287
Circ.—30,000
Prop.—Fibak-Norma-Press SA
Ed. in Ch.—Andrzej Otczyk

BYDGOSZCZ
Pop. Est. 372,600

DZIENNIK WIECZORNY (Evening Daily) Est. 1959
ul. Dworcowa 110, 80-010
Tel: (48-52) 224600; Fax: (48-52) 227117
Circ.—30,000
Prop.—Wydawnictwo "Nowy Dziennik Wieczorny" Pol Tech Sp. zo.o
Ex. Ed.—Jerzy Derenda
Ed. in Ch.—Andrzej Bialoszycki
EXPRESS BYDGOSKI (d) Est. 1989
ul. Warszawska 1, 85-058
Tel: (48-52) 222614/(48-52) 222615; Fax: (48-52) 222615
Circ.—16,000
Prop.—Wydawnictwo "Express"
Ed. in Ch.—Marek Zagorski
GAZETA POMORSKA (Pomerian Gazette) (m-ex S) Est. 1948
ul. Sniadeckich 1, 85-011
Tel: (48-52) 222623; Fax: (48-52) 221542
Circ.—100,000
Prop.—Spoldzielnia Pracy Dziennikary i Wydawcow
Ex. Ed.—Ryszard Buczek
Ed. in Ch.—Maciej Kaminski
ILUSTOWANY KURIER POLSKI (Illustrated Polish Courier) (e) Est. 1945
ul. Marszalka Focha 20
Circ.—82,000
Prop.—Przedsiebiorstwo Wielobranzowe, IKP
Ex. Ed.—Bogdan Zielinski
Ex. Ed.—Pawel Anton Kiewick
Ed. in Ch.—Marek Fasciczewski

CZESTOCHOWA

DZIENNIK CZESTOCHOWSK-24 GODZINY (d) Est. 1989
Czestochewa 17, 42-200
Tel: (48) 49975/(48) 44686; Fax: (48) 49681
Circ.—10,000
Pub.—Spotka Drogowiec
Ex. Ed.—Emilia Zapata
Ed. in Ch.—Marian Piotr Rawinis
ZYCIE CZESTOCHOWY (d) Est. 1947
ul. Kilinskiego 40, 42-200
Tel: (48) 42245/(48) 45966; Fax: (48) 42278
Prop.—Zycie Press Sp. zo.o
Ex. Ed.—Dariusz Fiuty
Ed. in Ch.—Wojciech Skrodzki

GDANSK
Pop. Est. 404,600

DZIENNIK BALTYCKI (Economic Maritime) (m) Est. 1945
ul. Targ Drzewny 3/7, Gdansk skr.; poczt. 419, 80-886
Tel: (48-58) 313560; Fax: (48-58) 313560
Circ.—330,000 (total)
Prop.—Prasa Galanska Ltd.
Ed. in Ch.—Jan Jakubowski
GAZETA GDANSKA (d) Est. 1990
ul. Targ Drzewny 3/7, 80-886
Tel: (48-58) 311864/(48-58) 311474; Fax: (48-58) 310971
Circ.—30,000
Prop.—Wydawnictwo "Gazeta Gdanska"
Ex. Ed.—Dariusz Chabior
Ed. in Ch.—Marek Formela
GLOS WYBRZEZA (Seashore Voice) (d) Est. 1948
ul. Targ Drzewny 3/7, 80-886
Circ.—50,000
Prop.—Wydawnictwo Prywatne
Ex. Ed.—Jaroslaw Tuminowski
Ed. in Ch.—Zbigniew Zukowski
WIECZOR WYBRZEZA (Seashore Evening) (e) Est. 1957
ul. Targ Drzewny 3/7, 80-958
Tel: (48-58) 311124/(48-58) 314250
Circ.—220,000 (total)
Prop.—Prasa Wybrzeza Sp. zo. o. Adresjv
Ed. in Ch.—Edmund Szczeslak

KATOWICE
Pop. Est. 368,600

DZIENNIK ZACHODNI (Western Daily) (m) Est. 1945
ul. Mlynska 1, 40-925
Tel: (48-3) 2537241; Fax: (48-3) 2538196
Circ.—750,000 (total)
Prop.—"Prasa Slaska" Sp. zo. o.
Ex. Ed.—Wojciech Mszyca
Ed. in Ch.—Wlodzimierz Pazniewski
GAZETA KATOWICKA (Katowicka Gazette) (d)
Plac Oddz. Mlodziezy Powstanczej 1, 46-061
Tel: (48-3) 2512225/(48-3) 2512130; Fax: (48-3) 2517084
KURIER ZACHODNI (d) Est. 1990
ul. Opolska 1/6, 40-084
Tel: (48-3) 2539314
Circ.—25,000
SPORT (d) Est. 1945
ul. Mlynsksa 1, 40-953
Tel: (48-3) 539995; Fax: (48-3) 537138
Circ.—100,000
Prop.—Fibak Norma Press
Ex. Ed.—Lidia Nowakowa
Ed. in Ch.—Adam Barteczka
TRYBUNA SLASKA (Worker's Tribune) (m-ex S) Est. 1945
ul. Mlynska 1, 40-098
Tel: (48-3) 2537241/(48-3) 2537997; Fax: (48-3) 2537997
Circ.—180,000
Prop.—National Organization of the People's United Worker's Party
Ex. Ed.—Andrzej Klimek
Ed. in Ch.—Tadeusz Bledzki
WIECZOR (e) Est. 1946
ul. Rynek 13, 40-953
Tel: (48-3) 2539901; Fax: (48-3) 2538333
Circ.—35,000
Prop.—AKAPIT Sp. zo.o.
Ex. Ed.—Beata Netz
Ed. in Ch.—Krzysztof Kuzniewski

KIELCE
Pop. Est. 208,100

ECHO DNIA (d) Est. 1971
ul. Targowa 18, 25-511; skr. poczt. 12
Circ.—20,000
Prop.—Agencja Handlui Marketingu "Acumen" Sp. zo.o
Ex. Ed.—Anderzej Orliev
Ed. in Ch.—Waldemar Pactawski

GAZETA KIELECKA-24 GODZINY (d) Est. 1989
ul. Zlota 3, 25-015, 40-098
Tel: (48) 57248/(48) 46689; Fax: (48) 56197
Circ.—30,000
Prop.—"Drogowiec" Sp. z.o.o.
Ex. Ed.—Maria Modrek
Ex. Ed.—Andrzej Mackowski
Ed. in Ch.—Anna Krawiecka
SLOWO LUDU (Word of the People) (m-ex S) Est. 1949
ul. Targowa 18/12; skr. poczt. 171, 25-953
Circ.—114,400
Prop.—Eksud 13 Sp. zo.o. adresjv
Ex. Ed.—Grzegorz Sciwiarski
Ed. in Ch.—Krzysztof Falkiewicz

KOSZALIN
Pop. Est. 104,700

GLOS KOSZALINSKI (d) Est. 1991
ul. Pitsudskiego 43, 75-502
Tel: (48) 24058/(48) 25916; Fax: (48) 24058
Circ.—30,000
Prop.—Dziennikarska Oficyna Wydawnicza "Rondo"
Ex. Ed.—Jozef Narkowiczk
Ed. in Ch.—Miroslaw Marek Kromer
GLOS POMORZA (Voice of Pomerania) (m) Est. 1952
ul. Zwyciestwa 137/139, 75-604
Circ.—57,000
Prop.—Koncern Wydawniczy Forum
Ex. Ed.—Roman Wojcieszak
Ed. in Ch.—Jaroslaw Przybylak
GONIEC POMORSKI (d) Est. 1989
ul. Grun Waldzka 8/10, 75-24
Tel: (48) 24760/(48) 26807; Fax: (48) 26792
Circ.—35,000
Prop.—Agencja Wydawniczo-Reklamowa LGH
Ex. Ed.—Katarzyna Rychiewicz
Ex. Ed.—Pawel Nikiel
Ed. in Ch.—Jerzy Banasiak

KRAKOW
Pop. Est. 748,400

CZAS KRAKOWSKI (d) Est. 1990
ul. Rynek Kleparski 4, 31-150
Tel: (48-12) 225355; Fax: (48-12) 217502
Circ.—55,000
Prop.—Arka Press SA
Ex. Ed.—Wachaw Krupinski
Ed. in Ch.—Jan Polkowski
DZIENNIK POLSKI (Polish Daily) (m-ex mon.) Est. 1945
ul. Wielopol 1, 31-072
Tel: (48-12) 226304; Fax: (48-12) 228249
Circ.—140,000
Prop.—Wydawnictwo "Jagiellonia" SA
Ex. Ed.—Kazimierz Starowicz
Ex. Ed.—Andrzej Koziol
Ed. in Ch.—Czestaw T Niemczynski
ECHO KRAKOWA (Krakow Echo) (e) Est. 1946
ul. Wielopole 1; skr. poczt. 64, 31-072
Tel: (48-12) 227588
Circ.—55,000
Prop.—Echo Krakowa Sp. zo.o
Ed. in Ch.—Witold Grzybowski
GAZETA KRAKOWSKA (Krakow Gazette) (d) Est. 1949
ul. Wielopole 1, 31-072
Tel: (48-12) 227588; Fax: (48-12) 221563
Circ.—82,000
Prop.—Wydawnictwo "Gazeta Krakowska" Sp. zo.o
Ex. Ed.—Beata Sliwinska
Ed. in Ch.—Jerzy Sadecki
GAZETA W KRAKOWIE (d)
ul. Rynek Glowny, 30-010
Tel: (48-12) 218271/(48-12) 219636; Fax: (48-12) 219906
TEMPO (The Rate) (d) Est. 1948
ul. Wielopole 1, 31-072
Tel: (48-12) 222960; Fax: (48-12) 222960
Circ.—140,000 (total)
Prop.—Sport-Press Sp. zo.o. adresjv
Ed. in Ch.—Ryszard Niemec

LESZNO

DZIENNIK INFORMACYJNY (Information Daily) (d) Est. 1990
ul. Slowianska 63, 64-100
Tel: (48) 206142/(48) 207061; Fax: (48) 208055
Circ.—18,000
Prop.—Leszczynska Oficyna Wydawnicza
Ex. Ed.—Halina Siecinska
Ed. in Ch.—Antoni Neczynski

LODZ
Pop. Est. 851,700

DZIENNIK LODZKI (Lodz Daily) (m) Est. 1945
ul. Sienkiewicza 9, 90-113
Tel: (48-42) 320289; Fax: (48-42) 886138

Circ.—190,000
Prop.—"Polskapress" Sp. zo.o.
Ex. Ed.—Jerzy Barski
Ed. in Ch.—Zdzislaw Szczepaniak
U.S. Rep.—Nielsen Communications
EXPRESS ILUSTROWANY (Illustrated Express) (e) Est. 1923
ul. Sienkiewicza 3/5, 90-113
Tel: (48-42) 330962; Fax: (48-42) 320637
Circ.—370,000 (total)
Prop.—"Polskapress" Sp. zo.o.
Ed. in Ch.—Julian Beck
U.S. Rep.—Nielsen Communications
GAZETA LODZKA (d)
ul. Piotrkowska 45, 90-410
Tel: (48-42) 321970/(48-42) 321935; Fax: (48-42) 337320
GLOS PORANNY (d) Est. 1945
ul. Sienkiewicza 3/5, lub. 90-950; skr. poczt. 12, 90-113
Tel: (48-42) 366785; Fax: (48-42) 334171
Circ.—52,000
Prop.—Lodzkie Wydawnictwo Prasowe
Ex. Ed.—Jadwiga Rybicka-Dzikowi
Ed. in Ch.—Gustaw Romanowski
GLOS ROBOTNICZY (Worker's Voice) (d) Est. 1945
ul. Piotrkowska 95, 90-103
Tel: (48-42) 366785
Circ.—144,000
Prop.—People's United Worker's Party
Ed. in Ch.—Krzysztof Pogorzelec
WIADOMOMOSCI DNIA (d)
ul. Piotrkowska 175, 90-447
Tel: (48-42) 374688; Fax: (48-42) 361153
Circ.—150,000
Prop.—Spolka Akeyjna "LUS" adresjw
Ex. Ed.—Elzbieta Sokolowska
Ed. in Ch.—Ewa Kluczkowska

LUBLIN
Pop. Est. 333,000

DZIENNIK LUBELSKI (d) Est. 1990
ul. Zana 38C; skr. poczt. 178, 6th Floor 20-601
Tel: (48-81) 558000; Fax: (48-81) 558010
Circ.—80,000
Prop.—"Kadex-Edytor" Sp. Cyw.
Ex. Ed.—Zbigniew Miazga
Ex. Ed.—Henryk Kwiatkowski
Ed. in Ch.—Alojzy Leszek Gzella
GAZETA W LUBLINIE (d)
ul. Gorma 4A, 20-005
Tel: (48-81) 22127/(48-81) 22844; Fax: (48-81) 52541
KURIER LUBELSKI (Lublin Courier) (d) Est. 1957
ul. Armii Wojska Polskiego 5, 20-950
Tel: (48-81) 26634; Fax: (48-81) 26835
Circ.—40,000
Prop.—Multico Sp. zo.o.
Ed. in Ch.—Wlodzimierz Wojcikowski
A-STOP (d) Est. 1992
Al. Krolewska 15, 20-109
Tel: (48-81) 28160
Prop.—"Kadex Edytor" Sp. Cyw.
Ed. in Ch.—Tomasz Orlowski
SZTANDAR LUDU (People's Banner) (m) Est. 1945
Al. Raclawickie 1, 20-059
Tel: (48-81) 23234
Circ.—114,000
Prop.—People's United Worker's Party
Ed. in Ch.—Tadeuz Fita

OLSZTYN
Pop. Est. 154,900

DZIENNIK POJEZIERZA (Pojezierze Daily) (d) Est. 1983
Al. 1 Marszalka Jozefa Pilsudskiego 54a, 10-557
Tel: (48-89) 336140; Fax: (48-89) 333751
Circ.—30,000
Prop.—"Polskapress" Sp. zo.o.
Ed. in Ch.—Pawel Krupa
GAZETA OLSZTYNSKA (Olsztyn Gazette) (d) Est. 1886
ul. Towarowa 2, 10-417
Tel: (48-89) 330277; Fax: (48-89) 332691
Circ.—48,000
Prop.—"Edytor" Sp. zo.o.
Ex. Ed.—Marek Baranski
Ex. Ed.—Adam Bartnikowski
Ed. in Ch.—Tomasz Srutkowski

OPOLE
Pop. Est. 128,200

TRYBUNA OPOLSKA (Opole Tribune) (m) Est. 1952
ul. Powstancow Sl. 9, 45-086
Tel: (48) 37241; Fax: (48) 38822
Circ.—80,000
Prop.—"OPOLPRESS" Sp. zo.o.
Ex. Ed.—Piotr Jankowski
Ed. in Ch.—Marian Szczurek

POZNAN
Pop. Est. 588,700

DZIENNIK POZNANSKI (d) Est. 1859
ul. Mlynska 5, 61-729
Tel: (48) 523681; Fax: (48) 525879
Circ.—40,000
Prop.—"Express-Polfost"
Ex. Ed.—Zdzislaw Narbuntowicz
Ex. Ed.—Marek Nowak
Ed. in Ch.—Konrad Napierala
EXPRESS POZNANSKI (Poznan Express) (e) Est. 1946
ul. Grunwaldzka 19, 60-959
Tel: (48-61) 666041; Fax: (48-61) 665848
Circ.—50,000
Prop.—Wydawnictwo "Express Poznanski" Sp. zo.o.
Ex. Ed.—Jan Zatubski
Ex. Ed.—Bogdan Kisiel
Ex. Ed.—Kazimierz Orlewicz
Ed. in Ch.—Darusz Nowaczyk
GAZETA POZNANSKA (Poznan Gazette) (m) Est. 1948
ul. Grunwaldzka 19, 60-782
Tel: (48-61) 665568; Fax: (48-61) 665638
Circ.—100,000
Prop.—Fibak Investment Group SA
Ex. Ed.—Andrzej Niczyperowicz
Ed. in Ch.—Przemyslaw Nowicki
GAZETA WIELKOPOLSKA (d)
ul. Jezycka 43, 66-864
Tel: (48-61) 483472; Fax: (48-61) 484871
GLOS WIELKOPOLSKI (Voice of Wielkopolska) (d) Est. 1945
ul. Grunwaldzka 19, 60-959
Tel: (48-61) 666041; Fax: (48-61) 43073
Circ.—100,000
Prop.—Oficyna Wydawnicza
Ex. Ed.—Tomasz Tokarczyk
Ed. in Ch.—Marian Marek Przybylski

RADOM

DZIENNIK RADOMSKI-24 GODZINY (d) Est. 1991
ul. Stowackiego 1, 26-600
Tel: (48-48) 27995; Fax: (48-48) 29091
Circ.—12,000
Ed. in Ch.—Marek Oleszuk

RZESZOW
Pop. Est. 147,300

A-Z DZIENNIK OBYWATELSKI (d) Est. 1990
Pl. Wolnosci 2, 35-061
Tel: (48) 39491/(48) 36831; Fax: (48) 33749
Circ.—30,000
Prop.—Wydawenictwa i Kolportaz "A-Z", Sp. zo.o.
Ex. Ed.—Marek Wojcik
Ex. Ed.—Danuta Majko
Ed. in Ch.—Andrzej Potocki
NOWINY (News) (m) Est. 1949
Unii Lubelskiej 9, 35-959
Tel: (48) 34775; Fax: (48) 33836
Circ.—80,000 (m); 180,000 (wknd.)
Prop.—R-Press Sp. zo.o.
Pub.—Zbigniew Sieczkes
Ex. Ed.—Wladyslaw Boczar
Ex. Ed.—Jan Filipowicz
Ex. Ed.—Wojciech Furman
Ed. in Ch.—Jan A Stepek
Ad. Mgr.—Leonia Zubel
NOWINY WIECZORNE (d) Est. 1991
ul. Lisa Kuli 19, 35-959
Tel: (48) 37143/(48) 33836
Circ.—15,000
Ex. Ed.—Jan Filipowicz
Ed. in Ch.—Jan Stepek

SLUPSK

GLOS SLUPSKI (d) Est. 1991
ul. Jednosci Narodowej 4/5, 76-200
Tel: (48) 25418; Fax: (48) 27112
Circ.—30,000
Prop.—Dziennikarska Oficyna Wydawnieza "Rondo"
Ex. Ed.—Jozef Narkowicz
Ed. in Ch.—Miroslaw Marek Kromer
Ed. in Ch.—Lucyna Lubiniecka

SZCZECIN
Pop. Est. 412,100

GAZETA NA POMORZU (d)
Al. Wojska Polskiego 52, 71-477
Tel: (48-91) 533068/(48-91) 533004; Fax: (48-91) 38028
GLOS SZCZECINSKI (Voice of Szczecin) (d) Est. 1947
Pl. Holdu Pruskiego 8, 70-550
Tel: (48-91) 34864; Fax: (48-91) 34864
Circ.—60,000
Prop.—Wydawnictwo "Glos" Sp. zo.o.
Ex. Ed.—Krzysztof Zaborowki
Ed. in Ch.—Micczyslaw Kaczynowski

KURIER SZCZECINSKI (Szczecin Courier) (e) Est. 1945
Pl. Holdu Pruskiego 8 skr. poczt., 70-550
Tel: (48-91) 43021
Circ.—40,000
Ex. Ed.—Bernard Ziolkiewicz
Ed. in Ch.—Anna Wieckowska-Machay

TORUN
Pop. Est. 197,000

NOWOSCI (Novelties) (d) Est. 1967
ul. Szosa Lubicka 2/18, 87-100
Tel: (48-56) 21222/(48-56) 21221; Fax: (48-56) 27286
Circ.—55,000
Prop.—Spoldzielnia Dziennikarsko-Wydawnica
Ex. Ed.—Stanislaw Frankowski
Ex. Ed.—Przemyslaw Luczak
Ed. in Ch.—Andrzej Szmak

WALBRZYCH

EXPRESS SUDECKI (d) Est. 1991
Pl. Magistracki 3, 58-300
Tel: (48) 26721/(48) 26925
Circ.—25,000
Prop.—Spoldzielna "Wieczor Wroclawia"
Ex. Ed.—Iwona Rubin
Ed. in Ch.—Wojciech Romanowski

WARSZAWA
(Warsaw)
Pop. Est. 1,655,100

DZIENNIK LUDOWY (People's Daily) (d) Est. 1945
ul. Grzybowska 4-8, 00-139
Tel: (48-22) 200251
Circ.—152,000
Prop.—United People's Party
Ed. in Ch.—Janusz Tarniewski
EXPRESS WIECZORNY (Evening Express) (e-5x wk.) Est. 1946
Al. Jerozolimskie 1/27; skr. poczt. 125, 02-017
Tel: (48-22) 285327; Fax: (48-22) 284929
Circ.—480,000 (total)
Prop.—Wydawnictwo Fundacji Prasowej "Solidarnosci"
Ex. Ed.—Remigiusz Kosciuscko
Ed. in Ch.—Krzysztof Czabanski
GAZETA MLODYCH (Youth Gazette) (d) Est. 1982
ul. Nowy Zjazd 1, 00-304
Circ.—49,000
Prop.—RSW Prasa-Ksiazka-Ruch
Ed. in Ch.—Witold Wisniewski
GAZETA WYBORCZA (d) Est. 1989
ul. Czerska 8/10, 00-732
Tel: (48-22) 415513; Fax: (48-22) 416920
Circ.—500,000
Prop.—Agora
Prop.—Gazeta Ltd.
Ed. in Ch.—Adam Michnik
Ad. Mgr.—Jacek Fronczak
GLOB 24 (d) Est. 1991
ul. Konstrukurska 3A, 02-673
Tel: (48-22) 435001; Fax: (48-22) 488254
Circ.—100,000
Prop.—"Vega" SA
Ex. Ed.—Krzyszlof Rozum
Ed. in Ch.—Dobrochna Kedzierska
KURIER POLSKI (Democratic Party) (e-5x wk.) Est. 1729
ul. Zgoda 11, 00-018
Tel: (48-22) 278081; Fax: (48-22) 270552
Circ.—470,000 (total)
Prop.—Kurier Polski Sp. zo.o.
Ex. Ed.—Kama Szlachowicz
Ed. in Ch.—Andrzej Nierychlo
NOWA EUROPA (d) Est. 1991
ul. Miedziana 11, 00-958
Tel: (48-22) 206161; Fax: (48-22) 206161
Circ.—40,000
Prop.—Nowa Europa
Ed. in Ch.—Wifold Gadomski
NOWY SWIAT (PISMO CODZIENNE DLA WSZYSTKICH SFER) (d) Est. 1991
ul. Bialobrzeska 53, 02-325
Tel: (48-22) 6583230; Fax: (48-22) 6583171
Cir.—120,000
Prop.—Niezalezny Instytut Wydawniczy Sp. zo.
Ex. Ed.—Antoni Bartkiewicz
Ed. in Ch.—Andrzej Karnkowski
OBSERWATOR CODZIENNY (d) Est. 1991
ul. Solec 22, 00-410
Tel: (48-22) 6253525/(48-22) 6253101; Fax: (48-22) 6250068
Circ.—120,000
Prop.—Przedsiebiorstwo Zagraniczne Batax
Ex. Ed.—Jan Cywinski
Ed. in Ch.—Damian Kolbarczyk

POLSKA ZBROJNA (d) Est. 1990
ul. Grzybowska 77; skr. poczt. 29, 00-950
Tel: (48-22) 204293; Fax: (48-22) 202127
Circ.—50,000
Prop.—Czasopisma Wojskowe
Ex. Ed.—Jacek Niespodziany
Ed. in Ch.—Antoni Bartkiewicz
PRZEGLAD SPORTOWY (Sports Review) (5x wk.) Est. 1921
Al. Jerozolimskie 125/127; PO Box 181 02-017
Tel: (48-22) 289116; Fax: (48-22) 218697
Circ.—265,000 (total)
Prop.—Spoldzielnia Pracy Dziennikarzy
Ex. Ed.—Janusz Nowozeniuk
Ex. Ed.—Tomasz Wolfe
Ex. Ed.—Krzysztof Zorski
Ed. in Ch.—Maciej Polkowski
RYNKI ZAGRANICZNE (d) Est. 1957
Trebacka 4, 00-074
Tel: (48-22) 260042; Fax: (48-22) 260042
Circ.—10,000
Ed. in Ch.—Andrzej Zielinski
RZECZPOSPOLITA (Republic) (d) Est. 1982
Krucza 36, 00-921
Tel: (48-22) 280493; Fax: (48-22) 6280588
Circ.—250,000
Prop.—Presspublika Sp. zo.o.
Ex. Ed.—Jerzy Paciorkowski
Ex. Ed.—Robert Lutomski
Ex. Ed.—Krzysztof Ziewiec
Ed. in Ch.—Dariusz Fikus
SLOWO POWSZECHNE (Catholic) (d) Est. 1947
ul. Mokotowska 43, 00-551
Tel: (48-22) 297767; Fax: (48-22) 6286739
Circ.—157,000 (total)
Prop.—Inco-Veritas Sp. zo.o.
Prop.—Zespot Prasy & Wydawnictwo PAX
Ed. in Ch.—Anna Borowska
SUPER EXPRESS (d) Est. 1991
ul. Miedziana 11; skr. poczt. p-19, 09-953
Tel: (48-22) 6253221; Fax: (48-22) 6251400
Circ.—70,000
Prop.—"ZPR-Express" Sp. zo.o.
Ex. Ed.—Andrzej Czerski
Ed. in Ch.—Jan Stachurski
SWIAT MLODYCH (d) Est. 1949
Mokotowska 24, 00-561
Tel: (48-22) 6285618; Fax: (48-22) 292142
Circ.—62,000
Prop.—Smat Mlodych SA
Ed. in Ch.—Jaroslaw Machowiak
SZTANDAR MLODYCH (Youth Banner) (m) Est. 1950
ul. Wspolna 61, 00-687
Tel: (48-22) 6284853; Fax: (48-22) 6282049
Circ.—110,000
Prop.—"SM-MEDIA" Sp. zo.o.
Ex. Ed.—Pawet Sybicz
Ex. Ed.—Marek Kluczek
Ed. in Ch.—Grazyna Minkowska
TELEGAZETA (d) Est. 1989
ul. J P Woronicza 17, 00-950
Tel: (48-22) 476561/(48-22) 476705; Fax: (48-22) 435774
Prop.—Polskie Radio i Telewizja
Ed. in Ch.—Czeslaw Berenda
TRYBUNA (e-ex S) Est. 1991
Al. St. Zjednoczonych 53, 04-029
Tel: (48-22) 132040; Fax: (48-22) 100592
Circ.—143,000 (mon.-fri.); 265,000 (sat.)
Prop.—"Ad Novum" Sp. zo.o.
Ex. Ed.—Jozef Szewczyk
Ex. Ed.—Marek Siwiec
TRYBUNA LUDU (United Worker's Party) (m) Est. 1948
Pl. Starynkiewicza 7, 02-015
Tel: (48-22) 216119
Circ.—439,500
Prop.—People's United Worker's Party
Ed. in Ch.—Jerzy Majka
ZOLNIERZ WOLNOSCI (Soldier of Freedom) (m) Est. 1943
ul. Grzybowska 77, 00-950
Tel: (48-22) 201227
Circ.—123,000
Prop.—Wydawnictwo Czasopisma Wojskowe
Ed. in Ch.—Col. Zdzislaw Janos
ZYCIE WARSZAWY (Warsaw Life) (m&e) Est. 1944
Armii Ludowej 3/5, 00-624
Tel: (48-22) 626686; Fax: (48-22) 6522426
Circ.—208,000 (mon.-fri.); 330,000 (sat.)
Prop.—Zycie Press Zo.o.
Ex. Ed.—Joanna Lubieniecka
Ed. in Ch.—Kazimierz Woycicki

Poland, Republic of

WROCLAW
Pop. Est. 642,300

GAZETA DOLNOSLASKA (d)
ul. Krupnicza 13
Tel: (48) 38489/(48) 38126; Fax: (48) 448450
GAZETA ROBOTNICZA (Worker's Gazette) (d) Est. 1948
ul. Podwale 62, 50-010
Tel: (48) 441281/(48) 442325; Fax: (48) 447080/(48) 357356
Circ.—105,000
Prop.—Spoldzielnia Pracy Dziennikarzy i Wydawcow
Ed. in Ch.—Andrzej Bulat
SLOWO POLSKIE (Polish Word) (m-ex mon.) Est. 1948
ul. Podwale 62, 50-010
Circ.—90,000
Prop.—Slowo-Media Ltd.
Ex. Ed.—Cezary Zeromski
Ed. in Ch.—Andrzej Karminski
WIECZOR WROCLAWIA (Wroclaw Evening) (e) Est. 1966
ul. Podwale 62; skr. poczt. 1003, 50-010
Circ.—30,000
Prop.—RSW Prasa-Ksiazka-Ruch
Ex. Ed.—Jadwiga Jakubek
Ed. in Ch.—Roman Rubin

ZIELONA GORA
Pop. Est. 134,300

GAZETA LUBUSKA (Lubuska Gazette) (d) Est. 1952
ul. Niepodleglosci 25, 65-042
Circ.—135,400
Prop.—People's United Worker's Party
Ed. in Ch.—Miroslaw Rataj

PORTUGAL, REPUBLIC OF
(Includes Azores and Madeira)
Pop. Est. 10,524,210

AMADORA
Pop. Est. 66,189

O DIARIO (Daily) (d)
Rua Joao de Deus 24, Venda Nova, 2700
Circ.—5,666,915
Pub.—Antonio Albuto Borja
Pub./Ed.—Caminho Sarl

ANGRA DO HEROISMO
(Azores)
Pop. Est. 78,207

DIARIO INSULAR (Insular Daily) (m) Est. 1946
Rua das Minhas Terras, 1721
Circ.—684,143
Prop.—Sociedade Terceirense de Publicidade Lda.
Dir.—Dr. Antonio Fantasia
(Circulation figure is of total annual estimation.)
A UNIAO (e) Est. 1893
Rua Padre Antonio Cordeiro, 1321
Circ.—298,833
Prop.—Diocese
Dir.—Manuel Coelho de Sousa
(Circulation figure is of total annual estimation.)

BEJA
Pop. Est. 186,907

DIARIO DO ALENTEJO (Alentejo Daily) (d)
Praca da Republica 43
Circ.—15,000
Prop.—Associacao dos Municipios do Distrito de Beja
Pub.—Dr. Joao Paulo Marcelo Vélez
JORNAL DO ALENTEJO (Alentejo Journal) (e)
Avda. Miguel Fernandes 23, 7800
Prop.—Cooperative Editorial de Cultura Jornal do Aleutejo
Pub.—Louis Asilio Caeito

BRAGA
Pop. Est. 712,350

CORREIO DO MINHO (m)
Palacio de Exposicoes e Desportos; Apdo. Postal 290, 4703
Tel: (351-53) 22353
Circ.—1,500
Prop.—Editora Correiro do Minho Servicos Municipalizados
Dir.—José Ferreira Salgado
DIARIO DO MINHO (Minho Daily) (m) Est. 1918
Rua de Santa Margarida 4A, 4719
Tel: (351-53) 22014
Circ.—2,500
Prop.—Empressa do Diario do Minho Lda. Sucessora
Dir.—P Domingos Araujo

COIMBRA
Pop. Est. 435,631

CORREIO DE COIMBRA (d)
Blvd. S. José 2, 30-49
Pub.—Antonio Duarte Almeida
DIARIO DE COIMBRA (Coimbra Daily) (m) Est. 1930
Rua da Sofia 179; Apdo. Postal 144, 3000
Tel: (351-39) 33895/(351-39) 32546
Circ.—8,000
Prop.—Beiras Lda.
Pub./Ed.—Adriano Lucas
Pub.—Lino A Vinhal

EVORA
Pop. Est. 177,414

DIARIO DO SUL (m) Est. 1969
Travessa de Santo Andre 6-8; Apdo. Postal 37, 7001
Tel: (351-66) 741252
Circ.—2,800
Pub./Dir.—Manuel Madeirra Picarra
NOTICIAS DE EVORA (Evora News) (m) Est. 1900
Rua do Raimundo 41-3, 7000
Tel: (351-66) 22348
Circ.—2,041
Prop.—Carlos María Pinto Pedrosa Herdeiros Ltd.
Dir.—Carlos Pedrosa Reis

FUNCHAL
Pop. Est. 263,710

DIARIO DE NOTICIAS DO FUNCHAL (Daily News of Funchal) (m)
Rua da Alfandega 8
Circ.—8,427
Prop.—Empresa Diario de Noticias Lda.
Dir.—Silvio Silvia
ECO DO FUNCHAL (Funchal Echo) (d)
Travessa dos Freitos 10-14
Prop.—Rodríguez & Caldeira Ltd.
Pub.—Rogerio Margues Caldeira
O JORNAL DA MADEIRA (Madeira Journal) (m) Est. 1927
Rua Dr. Ferrao Ornelas 35 r/c
Circ.—8,000
Prop.—Empresa do Jornal da Madeira Lda.
Dir.—P Manuel Tome Veloso

GUARDA

DIARIO DA GUARDA (Guarda Daily) (d)
Fica na Avda. Cidade de Waterbury B.R/ch, Povoa do Mileu
Tel: (351-71) 25533

HORTA
(Faial)
(Azores)
Pop. Est. 36,153

CORREIO DA HORTA (e) Est. 1930
Rua Ernesto Rebelo 5
Circ.—1,020
Prop.—Empresa do Correio da Horta Lda.
Dir.—Fernando Faria Ribeiro
O TELEGRAFO (Telegraph) (m)
Rua Conselheiro Medeiros 30
Circ.—1,850
Prop.—Empresa do Jornal O Telegrafo Lda.
Dir.—Rogerio da Silva Goncalves

LEIRO

DIARIO DE LEIRIA (d)
Avda. Herois de Angola 76-3-C, 2400
Tel: (351-39) 33881; Fax: (351-39) 24606

LISBON
Pop. Est. 677,790

A CAPITAL (e) Est. 1968
Travessa Poco da Cidade 26, Lisboa Codex, 1124
Tel: (351-1) 3468593/(351-1) 3468595; Fax: (351-1) 3463497
Circ.—37,000
Prop.—Sojornal Sociedade Jornalistica Editorial Saral
Dir.—José Sarabando
Ed. in Ch.—Joao Vaz
Mktg. Mgr.—Arlindo Barreiros
CORREIO DA MANHA (m)
Rua Mouzinho Silveira 27-7, 1200
Tel: (351-1) 527636; Fax: (351-1) 533726
Circ.—81,000
Prop.—Presselivre-Impresna Livre SARL
Dir.—Vitor Direito
DIARIO DE NOTICIAS (Daily News) (mS)
Apdo. Postal 2346
Tel: (351-1) 3558436
Circ.—70,000 (m); 80,000 (S)
Prop.—EPNC (Empresa Publica dos Jornais Noticias e Capital)
Pres.—Antonio Veigz Anjos
Ed.—Dinis de Abren
Ad. Mgr.—Alberto Rosario
U.S. Rep.—Publicitas
DIARIO POPULAR (Popular Daily) (e-ex S) Est. 1942
Rua Luz Soriano 67, 1200
Tel: (351-1) 3476281
Circ.—62,000
Prop.—Sociedade Editora Record
Dir.—D Rodolfo Iriarte
Ed. in Ch.—Carlos Morgado
O DIA (Day) (d) Est. 1988
Campo Pequeño 74, Porta 3r/c, 1000
Tel: (351-1) 35817130/(351-1) 27863421
Circ.—49,300
Pub./Dir.—Vera Lagoa
O DIARIO (Daily) (d) Est. 1976
Rua de S Bernardo 14-2, 1200
Tel: (351-1) 605534/(351-1) 670194; Fax: (351-1) 668793
Circ.—29,000
Prop.—Editorial Caminho SARL
Pub.—Antonio Alberto Alves Pereira Borja
O PUBLICO (Public) (d)
Rua Amilcar Cabral, Lote Quinta do Lambert, 1700
Tel: (351-1) 7599523/(351-1) 7599247; Fax: (351-1) 7587138
Circ.—70,000
Prop.—Publico Comunicacao Social
Dir.—Vicente Jorge Silva

OPORTO
(Porto)
Pop. Est. 350,000

O COMERCIO DO PORTO (mS) Est. 1854
Avda. dos Aliados 107; Apdo. Postal 490, 4008
Tel: (351-2) 321021; Fax: (351-2) 380576
Circ.—24,237
Prop.—Empresa de O Comercio do Porto SARL
Dir.—Dr. Manuel Pinto Teixeira
Ed.—Alberto Carvalho
DIARIO INFORMADOR (d)
Rua Elisio Melo 28
JORNAL DE NOTICIAS (News Journal) (m) Est. 1888
Rua Goncalo Cristovao 195-219, 4000
Tel: (351-2) 381331; Fax: (351-2) 382617
Circ.—85,000
Prop.—Empresa do Jornal de Noticias
Dir.—Sergio de Andrade
Ed. in Ch.—Pinto García
Ed. in Ch.—José Luís de Abreu
Mktg. Mgr.—Alvaro Cardinal
O PRIMEIRO DE JANEIRO (m) Est. 1868
Rua de Santa Catarina 326, 4000
Tel: (351-2) 2008401; Fax: (351-2) 315840
Circ.—32,101
Prop.—Empresa de O Primeiro de Janeiro
Dir.—José Manuel Barroso
Ed. in Ch.—Carlos Moura

PONTA DEL GADA
(Azores)
Pop. Est. 147,744

ACORIANO ORIENTAL (m) Est. 1835
Rua Dr. Bruno T. Carreiro 36
Circ.—5,000
Prop.—Impracor Sociedade de Imprensae Publicidade SARL
Dir.—Gustavo Moura
CORREIO DOS ACORES Est. 1920
Rua da Misericordia 42
Circ.—2,700
Prop.—Grafiea Acoriana Ltd.
Dir.—Jorge do Nascimento Cabral
DIARIO DOS ACORES (e) Est. 1870
Rua do Diario dos Acores 11
Circ.—2,020
Dir.—Costa Silva Jr

VISEU

DIARIO VISEU (Viseu Daily) (d)
Gavete das Avenidas José Relvas e Alfeces Maldonado 1, 3502
Tel: (351-32) 24062; Fax: (351-32) 25817

ROMANIA, REPUBLIC OF
Pop. Est. 23,181,415

ALBA IULIA

ARDEALUL (d)
29 Piata Iuliu Maniu
Tel: (40-68) 13026
Ed. in Ch.—Ioan Maier
UNIREA (The Union) (d-ex mon.) Est. 1968
27 Decebal St.
Tel: (40-68) 11420
Circ.—32,000
Ed. in Ch.—Horea Sandu

ARAD

ADEVARUL (d)
81 Revolutiei Blvd.
Tel: (40-66) 13302
Ed. in Ch.—Dumitru Toma
JELEN (d) Hungarian
81 B-dul Revolutiei St.
Tel: (40-66) 12141
Ed. in Ch.—Janos Irhazi
Ad. Mgr.—Janos Boros

ARGES

ARGESUL LIBER (d)
7A Dija St., Apt. 1
Tel: (40) 7630490/(40) 7636419
Ed. in Ch.—Marin Manolache

BACAU

DESTEPTAREA (d)
63 Alecsandri Vasile St.
Tel: (40-34) 25456
Ed. in Ch.—Ion Enache

BIHOR

BIHARI NAPLO (d) Hungarian
3 Romana St.
Tel: (40-91) 12727
Ed. in Ch.—Tompa Z Mihaly
CRISANA (d)
3 Romana St.
Tel: (40-91) 17421/(40-91) 13606
Ed. in Ch.—Ioan Cretu
ERDELYI NAPLO (d) Hungarian
16 Baritiu Gh. St.
Tel: (40) 9131267
Ed. in Ch.—Stanih Istvan
MAJOMSZIGET (d) Hungarian
27 Leontin Salajan St.
Tel: (40) 9111737 ext. 122
Ed. in Ch.—Magdas Attila

BISTRITA

RASUNETUL (d)
6 Bistricioarei St.
Tel: (40-90) 11684/(40-90) 17546
Ed. in Ch.—Vasile Tabara

BOTOSANI

GAZETA DE BOTOSANI (Botosani Gazette) (d)
91 Eminescu Blvd.
Tel: (40) 851106
Ed. in Ch.—Gheorghe Zanea

BRASOV
Pop. Est. 323,835

GAZETA DE TRANSILVANIA (Transilvania Gazette) (d)
3 Sadoveanu M St.
Tel: (40-68) 42029/(40-68) 42512
Dir.—George Barit
Ed. in Ch.—Eduard Huidan
INCOTRO BRASOVUL (d)
58 Calea Calarasilor
Tel: (40-68) 94631740/(40-68) 94631741
Ed. in Ch.—Chinea Mitrea
LIBERTATRA (Liberty) (d)
1 Piata Independentei
Tel: (40-68) 94635946/(40-68) 94635943
Dir./Ed. in Ch.—Rodica Oana

BUCURESTI
(Bucharest)
Pop. Est. 2,351,000

ADEVARUL (d)
1 Piata Presei Libere
Tel: (40-0) 6182030/(40-0) 6176010; Fax: (40-0) 175540
Dir.—Dumitru Tinu
Dir.—Sergiu Anton
Dir.—Viorei Salagean

Dir.—Cristian Popescu Tudor
Dir.—Constantin Pavel
AZI (d)
  Section 1, 39 A Calea Vicotreie
  Tel: (40-0) 6133147
  Ed. in Ch.—Octavian Sireteanu
COTIDIANUL (d)
  Calea-Plevnei 114, 6734
  Tel: (40-0) 6377195; Fax: (40-0) 6376892
  Owner—Ion Retiu
  Mgr.—Tiberiu Rubnicu
CURIERUL NATIONAL (d)
  2-4 Ministerului St.
  Tel: (40-0) 6142437/(40-0) 6159512;
  Fax: (40-0) 139483
  Dir.—Horia Alexandrescu
  Ed. in Ch.—Constantin Dragomir
DIMINEATA (d)
  48 Roma St., Section 1
  Tel: (40-0) 6177622/(40-0) 6793692
  Dir.—Alexandru Piru
GAZETA SPORTURILOR (d)
  16 Conta Vasile St.
  Tel: (40-0) 6116033; Fax: (40-0) 6113459
  Ed. in Ch.—Constantin Macovei
LIBERTATEA (d)
  23-25 Brezoianu St.
  Tel: (40-0) 6132777
  Circ.—150,000
  Ed. in Ch.—Octavian Andronic
NEUER WEG (New Way) (d-ex mon.) German;
  Est. 1949
  1 Piata Presei Libere
  Tel: (40-0) 6181723/(40-0) 6181830;
  Fax: (40-0) 6183758
  Ed. in Ch.—Emmerich Reichrath
REALITATEA ROMANEASCA (d)
  1 Piata Presei Libere
  Tel: (40-0) 6183935/(40-0) 6183407
  Dir.—Corneliu Piloff
  Ed.—Gheorghe Pantazi
  Ed.—Ion Parhon
ROMANIA LIBERA (Free Romania) (dS) Est. 1943
  1 Piata Presei Libere, 71341
  Tel: (40-0) 6176010 ext. 1683; Fax: (40-0) 174205
  Circ.—100,000
  Prop.—Romania Libera
  Dir.—Octavian Paler
  Dir.—Peter Mihai Bacanu
  Dir.—Mihai Creanga
  Dir.—Florica Ichim
  Dir.—Tia Serbanescu
  Dir.—Theodor Serbanescu
  Dir.—Anton Uncu
  Dir.—Corneliu Vlad
  Ed. in Ch.—Mihai Creanga
ROMANIAI MAGYAR SZO (d) Hungarian
  1 Piata Presei Libere
  Tel: (40-0) 6180302
  Ed. in Ch.—Gyarmath Janos
TINERETUL LIBER (d)
  1 Piata Presei Libere
  Tel: (40-0) 6176010
  Ed. in Ch.—Stefan Mitroi
VIITORUL (d)
  21 Balcescu Blvd.
  Tel: (40-0) 6147555/(40-0) 6155192;
  Fax: (40-0) 6155055
  Dir.—Alexandru Dinca
  Ed.—Eugen Iordache
  Ed.—Horia Florin Popescu
  Ed.—Adina Silvia Fandeanu

BUZAU

BRIGADA 24 (d)
  28 Garii Blvd.
  Tel: (40) 7436045
  Dir.—Constantin Niculescu
  Ed. in Ch.—Ion Nicolae
OPINIA (d)
  3 Chiristigii St.
  Tel: (40) 7412764
  Dir.—Mihai Bizu
  Ed. in Ch.—Corneliu Stefan

CARAS-SEVERIN

TIMPUL (d)
  7 Piata Republicii St.
  Tel: (40) 6412739/(40) 6411901
  Ed. in Ch.—George Jurma

CLUJ-NAPOCA
Pop. Est. 328,008

ADEVARUL DE CLUJ (d)
  16 Napoca St.
  Tel: (40-64) 11032
  Circ.—200,000
  Prop.—Casa De Editura
  Ed. in Ch.—Ilie Calin
ADEVARUL IN LIBERTATE (d)
  16 Napoca St.
  Tel: (40-64) 11032/(40-64) 17507
  Ed. in Ch.—Ilie Calin

MESAGERUL TRANSILVANEAN (d)
  58 22 Decembrie Blvd.
  Tel: (40-64) 16416
  Ed. in Ch.—Ion Istrate
SZABADSAG (d) Hungarian
  16 Napoca St.
  Tel: (40-64) 16213
  Ed. in Ch.—Tibor Szabo Lajos

CONSTANTA
Pop. Est. 350,476

CUGET LIBER (d)
  5 Bratianu IC Blvd.
  Tel: (40-41) 65605; Fax: (40-41) 65606
  Dir.—Arcadi Strahilevici

COVASNA

CUVINTUL NOU (d)
  8A Pietei St.
  Tel: (40) 2311388/(40) 2311210
  Ed. in Ch.—Dumitru Manolachescu
HOROMSZEK (d) Hungarian
  8A Presei St.
  Tel: (40) 2311504
  Ed. in Ch.—Magyari Lajos

DOLJ

CUVINTUL LIBER (d)
  8 Oltet St.
  Tel: (40) 4112457
  Ed. in Ch.—Dan Lupescu
INDEPENDENTUL (d)
  17 Kogalniceanu St.
  Tel: (40) 4132367
  Dir.—I P Surdu

GALATI
Pop. Est. 325,788

VIATA NOUA (New Life) (d-ex mon.) Est. 1944
  48 Domneasca St.
  Tel: (40-36) 14620/(40-36) 11772
  Dir.—Radu Macovel

GORJ

DIMINEATA GORJULUI (d)
  24 Eroilor St.
  Tel: (40) 12017
  Ed. in Ch.—E Popoescu
GORJEANUL (d)
  15 Constantin Brincusi
  Tel: (40) 17464/(40) 12072
  Ed. in Ch.—Brinzaru Nicolae

HARGHITA

ADEVARUL HARGHITEI (d)
  45 Leticeni St.
  Tel: (40) 5813019
  Ed. in Ch.—Mihai Groza
UJ SPORT (d) Hungarian
  1 Lenin St.
  Tel: (40) 5815940
  Ed. in Ch.—Peter Laszlo

HUNEDOARA

CUVINTUL LIBER (d)
  35 1 Decembrie St.
  Tel: (40) 5611275/(40) 5611585
  Ed. in Ch.—Nicolae Tircob
HARGHITA NEPE (d)
  45 Sinzienei St.
  Tel: (40) 5615507
  Ed. in Ch.—Borhely Laszlo

IASI
(Lasi)
Pop. Est. 342,994

24 ORE (24 Hours) (d)
  25 Elena Doamna St.
  Tel: (40-32) 17440/(40-32) 17427; Fax: (40-32) 13101
  Ed. in Ch.—Adi Cristi
  Ed. in Ch.—Leib Rosentzveig
EVENIMENTUL (d)
  4 Stefan cel Mare St.
  Tel: (40-32) 12023/(40-32) 12027; Fax: (40-32) 12025
  Ed. in Ch.—Constantin Paladuta
OPINIA (d)
  8 V. Alecsandri St.
  Tel: (40-32) 452105/(40-32) 417494
  Ed. in Ch.—Vasile Filip

MARAMURES

RAIUL MARAMURESULUI (d)
  25 Bucuresti Blvd.
  Tel: (40) 9431035/(40) 9431734
  Ed. in Ch.—Augustin Cozmuta

MEHEDINTI

DATINA (d)
  89 Traian St.
  Tel: (40) 119950 ext. 152/(40) 112216 ext. 152
  Ed. in Ch.—Gheorghe Buretea

MURES

CUVINTUL LIBER (d)
  9 Gheorghe St.
  Tel: (40) 5436636
  Ed. in Ch.—Lazar Ladariu
NEPUJSAG (d) Hungarian
  9 Gh. Doja St.
  Tel: (40) 5436881
  Ed. in Ch.—Makkai Janos

NEAMT

CEAHLAUL (d)
  14 Aleea Tiparului
  Tel: (40) 3625282 ext. 153/(40) 3612890 ext. 290
  Ed. in Ch.—Viorel Tudose

OLT

GLASUL ADEVARULUI (d)
  5 Filimon St.
  Tel: (40) 4422131/(40) 4422222

PRAHOVA

PRAHOVA (d)
  2 Republicii Blvd.
  Tel: (40) 45691

SALAJ

GRAIUL SALAJULUI (d)
  7 Piata Unirii
  Tel: (40) 9614120 ext. 216
  Ed. in Ch.—Ioan Lupa

SATU-MARE

UNIVERS SATMAREAN (d)
  1 Piata 25 Octombrie
  Tel: (40-97) 13692 ext. 106

SIBIU

DIMINEATA (d)
  2 Samuel Brukenthal
  Tel: (40-69) 18103/(40-69) 18181
  Ed. in Ch.—Traian Suciu
RADICAL (d)
  2 Samuel Brukenthal
  Tel: (40-69) 92418108/(40-69) 92415998
  Ed. in Ch.—Traian Suciu
TRIBUNA (Tribune) (d)
  7 Dr. I. Ratiu
  Tel: (40-69) 92413833/(40-69) 92412810; Fax: (40-69) 92412026
  Dir.—Emil David
  Ed. in Ch.—Octavian Rusu

SUCEAVA

CRAI NOU (d)
  36 Stefan cel Mare
  Tel: (40) 8714723
  Ed. in Ch.—Ion Paranici

TELEORMAN

TELEORMANUL LIBER (d)
  178 Dunarii St.
  Tel: (40) 11950
  Ed. in Ch.—Gheorghe Filip

TIMISOARA
Pop. Est. 334,278

AGENDA (d)
  1 CP 184
  Dir.—Zoltan Kovacs
CURIER SPORTIV BANATEAN
  2 Intrarea Zinelor
DELTA (d)
  4 Spitalului St.
  Tel: (40-56) 12406; Fax: (40-56) 52235
  Ed. in Ch.—Nicolai Amihulesei
NEUE BANATER ZEITUNG (d) German
  8 Revolutiei Blvd., 1989
  Tel: (40-56) 15586/(40-56) 15317
  Ed. in Ch.—Gerhard Binder
RENASTEREA BANATEANA (d)
  8-16 Decembrie St.
  Tel: (40-56) 19176

VALCEA

ACTUALITATEA VRANCEANA (d)
  7-9 Tudor Vladimirescu
  Tel: (40) 479471126
  Dir.—Petre Ungureanu
  Ed. in Ch.—Dan Manolache
CURIERUL DE VILCEA (d)
  127 Calea Iui Traian
  Tel: (40) 4794711265/(40) 4794711394
  Dir.—Silviu Popescu
  Ed. in Ch.—Gheorghe Sempreanu
EVENIMENTUL (d)
  7-9 Tudor Vladimirescu
  Tel: (40) 4711006/(40) 4713373
  Ed. in Ch.—Lucian Pavel

RUSSIA
(Formerly Russian Soviet Federated Socialist Republic)
Pop. Est. 149,608,953

MOSCOW
Pop. Est. 8,747,000

GUDOK (Whistle) (d-ex mon.) Est. 1917
  Gertsena ul., 8 Khlynovsky Tupik, 103858
  Circ.—500,000
  Prop.—Ministry of Post & Telecommunications Railway and Transport Construction Worker's Union
  Ed.—G I Laptev
IZVESTIA (News) (d-ex S) Est. 1917
  5 Pushkinskaja ul., 103791
  Tel: (7-095) 2093674; Fax: (7-095) 2302303
  Circ.—1,600,000
  Prop.—Employee's Group
  Ed.—I N Golembiovsky
  (Official national newspaper. Printed daily in two editions with Moscow evening edition dating from 1960. Authoritative source for foreign affairs and workings of local politics.)
KRASNAYA ZVEZDA (Red Star) (d-ex mon.) Est. 1924
  38 Khoroshevskoye Shosse, 123826
  Tel: (7-095) 9412158/(7-095) 9412120
  Circ.—650,650
  Prop.—Defense Ministry
  Ed.—I M Panov
  (This newspaper is nationally distributed for the armed forces.)
KURANTY (d-5x wk.)
  12 ul. Stankevicha
  Tel: (7-095) 2030610; Fax: (7-095) 2925515
  Circ.—300,000
  Prop.—Employee's Group
  Ed.—A S Pankov
LESNAYA GAZETA (d) Est. 1991
  25 Oktyabrya GSP, 103645
  Tel: (7-095) 9211260
LZ-NARODNAYA GAZETA (d-ex mon.) Est. 1918
  7 ul. 1905 Goda, 123847
  (This newspaper is a local publication.)
MOSKOVSKAYA PRAVDA (Moskow Truth) (d-ex mon.) Est. 1918
  7 ul. 1905 Goda, 123846
  Tel: (7-095) 2598233
  Circ.—500,000
  Ed.—Sh S Muladzanov
MOSKOVSKI KOMSOMOLYETS (Moskow Communist Youth) (d-ex mon.) Est. 1919
  7 ul. 1905 Goda, 123846
  Circ.—1,200,000
  Prop.—Moskow City District Committees
  (This newspaper is a local Moscow area youth publication.)
NEZARISIMAYA GAZETA (5x wk.)
  13-10 ul. Miasnitskaja, 10100
  Tel: (7-095) 9253888; Fax: (7-095) 9252161
  Cir.—1,500,000
  Prop. Moskow City Deputies
  Pub.—Cynthia Neu
  Ed.—V T Tretyakov
  U.S. Rep.—The Cal Hart Co.
PRAVDA (The Truth) (d-ex S) Est. 1912
  GSP 24 ul. Pravdy, 125867
  Tel: (7-095) 2573272; Fax: (7-095) 2002291
  Circ.—1,385,000
  Prop.—Employee's Group
  Ed.—G N Seleznev
  (Printed nationwide with most of its circulation outside Moscow. Published daily in two editions; Glasnost being a supplement.)

Russia

RABOCHAYA TRIBUNA (Worker's Tribune) (d-ex mon.) Est. 1969
24 ul. Pravdy, 125869
Tel: (7-095) 2572751
Circ.—1,451,000
Ed.—A A Baranov
(National newspaper for rural areas; printed and published nationwide in two editions.)
ROSSIYSKAYA GAZETA (d-ex S)
24 ul. Pravdy, 125866
Tel: (7-095) 2701185; Fax: (7-095) 2572892
Circ.—1,000,000
Prop.—Supreme Soviet
Ed.—V A Logunov
SELSKAYA ZHIZN (Rural Life) (d-ex mon.) Est. 1918
24 ul. Pravdy, 125886
Tel: (7-095) 2572457
Circ.—9,000,000
Prop.—Employee's Group
Ed.—A A Baranov
(National newspaper for rural areas; printed nationwide in two editions.)
SOVETSKAYA ROSSIA (Soviet Russia) (d-ex mon.) Est. 1956
24 ul. Pravdy, 125866
Tel: (7-095) 2572772
Circ.—1,000,000
Ed.—V V Chikin
(Newspaper for the Commonwealth of Independent States.)
SOVIETSKI SPORT (Soviet Sport) (d-ex mon.) Est. 1924
8 ul. Arkhipova, 101913
Tel: (7-095) 9247428
Circ.—495,000
Prop.—C I S Committee of Physical Culture and Sports
Ed.—V G Kudryavtsev
STROITELNAYA GAZETA (6x wk.) Est. 1924
24 ul. Mariny Raskovoi, 125885
Circ.—360,000
Prop.—Editorial Board
(National newspaper for the Construction Industry.)
TRUD (Labor) (d-5x wk.) Est. 1921
4 Natasyinsky per., 103792
Tel: (7-095) 2993906/(7-095) 2994200
Circ.—13,520,000
Prop.—Publimedia
Ed.—A S Petapov
(Working-class newspaper with an emphasis on union affairs. This newspaper is printed nationwide.)
VECHERNAYA MOSKVA (Moskow Evening News) (d-5x wk.)
7 ul. 1905 Goda GSP, 123849
Tel: (7-095) 2590526
Circ.—620,000
Prop.—Publimedia
Ed.—A I Lissin

ST. PETERSBURG
(Formerly Leningrad)
Pop. Est. 4,437,000

NEVSKOYE VREMYA (The Times of Neva) Est. 1991
St. Petersburg ul. Bol. Morskaya 47, 190000
Tel: (7-812) 3124040/(7-812) 3155050;
Fax: (7-812) 3122078
Circ.—100,000
Prop.—St. Petersburg City Council (Soviet)
Ed. in Ch.—V Chichin
SANKT-PETERBURGSKIE VEDOMOSTI Est. 1918
D-23 Fontanka 29, 191023
Circ.—273,500
Prop.—Staff of the Newspaper
Prop.—St. Petersburg City Mayoralty
Ed. in Ch.—Oleg S Kuzin
SMENA (Shift) Est. 1919
D-23 Fontanka 59, 191023
Tel: (7-812) 2108052/(7-812) 2108013;
Fax: (7-812) 3110957
Circ.—100,285
Prop.—Staff of the Newspaper
Ed. in Ch.—Aleksei Razorionov
VECHERNIY PETERSBURG (Evening St. Petersburg) (e) Est. 1917
Fontana 59, 121023
Tel: (7-812) 3118875/(7-812) 3118988;
Fax: (7-812) 3143105
Circ.—135,628
Prop.—St. Petersburg City Council
Ed. in Ch.—V V Mayorov

VLADIVOSTOK
Pop. Est. 615,000

KRASNOYE ZNAMYE (The Red Banner) (d) Est. 1917
Leninskaya 43
Ed.—V G Chukhlantsev

SAN MARINO
Pop. Est. 24,091

SAN MARINO
Pop. Est. 4,500

NOTIZIARIO (d)
Segreteria Esteri-Contrada Omerelli
Ed. in Ch.—Pier Roberto De Biagi
IL NUOVO TITANO (d) Est. 1902
Via Gino Giacomini
Circ.—1,300
Pub.—Augusto Zonzini
RISCOSSA SOCIALISTA (d) Est. 1955
Via Della Tana 117
Pub.—Mauro Busignani
SAN MARINO (d)
Piazzetta Bramante
Ed. in Ch.—Carlo Franciosi
LA SCINTILIA (d) Est. 1944
Via Sentier Rosso, 1
Pub.—Georges Santi

SLOVAK REPUBLIC
Pop. Est. 5,403,505

BANSKA BYSTRICA
Pop. Est. 79,520

SMER DNES (d) Slovak
Cs. armády 10, 97543
Tel: (42-88) 25478; Fax: (42-88) 25506
Circ.—25,000 (d); 65,000 (sat.)
Prop.—BeBe-Press a.s.
Ed. in Ch.—Ivan Baca

BRATISLAVA
Pop. Est. 441,453

HLAS LUDU (Voice of the People) (d) Slovak; Est. 1949
Sliacska 1; PO Box 70, 83008
Tel: (42-7) 251383; Fax: (42-7) 251268
Circ.—28,800
Prop.—Press Business Inc. spol. sro
Ed. in Ch.—Pavol Dinka
MERIDIAN (d) Slovak
Stúrova 4, 81580
Tel: (42-7) 53087; Fax: (42-7) 50531/(42-7) 55154
Circ.—5,000
Prop.—DANUBIAPRINT sp
Ed. in Ch.—Miroslav Jaslovsky
NARODNA OBRODA (m-ex S) Slovak; Est. 1990
Trnavská cesta 112; PO Box 63, 83000
Tel: (42-7) 5220433; Fax: (42-7) 5220594
Circ.—88,000
Prop.—NOFRA
Ed. in Ch.—Juraj Veres
Ad. Mgr.—Roman Frastacky
NOVY CAS (d) Slovak
Gorkého 5, 81278
Tel: (42-7) 59070; Fax: (42-7) 59104
Circ.—250,000
Prop.—CAS a.s.
Ed. in Ch.—Jozef Bielik
NOVY SLOVAK (d) Slovak
Teslova 26; PO Box 254, 81499
Tel: (42-7) 67239; Fax: (42-7) 67042
Circ.—18,000
Prop.—AVIZO concept team s.r.o.
Ed. in Ch.—Peter Skultéty
PRACA (Trade Unions) (d) Slovak; Est. 1946
Odborárske nam. 3, 81271
Tel: (42-7) 65060; Fax: (42-7) 212985
Circ.—127,810
Prop.—The Trade-Union Confederation of the Slovak Republic
Ed. in Ch.—Milos Nemecek
PRAVDA (m) Slovak
Pribinova 25, 81011
Tel: (42-7) 323760; Fax: (42-7) 2104798
Circ.—235,000
Prop.—PEREX a.s.
Ed. in Ch.—Peter Sitányi
REPUBLIKA (Republic) (d) Slovak
Pribinova 21, 80000
Circ.—50,000
Prop.—Press Agency of the Slovak Republic
Ed. in Ch.—Smolec Jan
ROLNICKE NOVINY (Farmer's News) (d) Slovak; Est. 1946
Dobrovicova 12, 81378
Tel: (42-7) 55515; Fax: (42-7) 51282
Circ.—27,000
Prop.—RONO PRESS a.s.
Ed. in Ch.—Juraj Seják
SLOVENSKY DENNIK (d) Slovak
Martanovicova 25, 81932
Tel: (42-7) 50545; Fax: (42-7) 53061
Circ.—27,000
Prop.—Interslovakia s.r.o.
Ed. in Ch.—Anton Balaz
SMENA (Shift Journal-Youth) (d) Slovak; Est. 1947
Dostojevske-ho rad 1, 81924
Tel: (42-7) 490255; Fax: (42-7) 58655
Circ.—80,000
Prop.—Dennik SMENA a.s.
Ed. in Ch.—Gabriela Baranovicova
SME NA (d) Slovak
Pribinova 25, 81913
Tel: (42-7) 2104566; Fax: (42-7) 55058
Circ.—70,000
Prop.—JUVENTUS s.r.o.
Ed. in Ch.—Karol Jezík
SPORT (d) Slovak; Est. 1947
Svätoplukova 2, 81923
Tel: (42-7) 60053; Fax: (42-7) 211380
Circ.—60,000
Prop.—SPORT PRESS spol. s.r.o.
Ed. in Ch.—Zdeno Simonides
SZABAD UJSAG (d) Hungarian
Pribinova 25, 81911
Tel: (42-7) 2103998; Fax: (42-7) 2103992
Circ.—10,000
Prop.—Madach-Posonium Kfl
Ed. in Ch.—Ján Meszáros
UJ SZO (d) Hungarian
Pribinova 25, 81915
Tel: (42-7) 53220; Fax: (42-7) 50529
Circ.—60,000
Prop.—Vox Nova a.s.
Ed. in Ch.—Jozef Szilvássy
U.S. Rep.—Nielsen Communications
ECERNIK (d) Slovak
Pribinova 25, 81916
Tel: (42-7) 2104517; Fax: (42-7) 2104521
Circ.—42,000
Prop.—GAPress a.s.
Ed. in Ch.—Rudolf Machala

KOSICE
Pop. Est. 234,840

KOSICKY VECER (d) Slovak
Trieda SNP 24, 04297
Tel: (42-95) 420021; Fax: (42-95) 421214
Circ.—22,400
Prop.—CASSOVIA PRESS a.s.
Ed. in Ch.—Mikulás Jesensky
LUC (d) Slovak
B. Nemcovej 32, 04262
Tel: (42-95) 34538; Fax: (42-95) 359090
Circ.—15,000
Prop.—LUC a.s.
Ed. in Ch.—Imrich Steliar
SLOVENSKY VYCHOD (d) Slovak
Letná 45, 04266
Tel: (42-95) 53979; Fax: (42-95) 53950
Circ.—56,000
Prop.—SLOVENSKY VYCHOD a.s.
Ed. in Ch.—Dusan Klinger

PRESOV

PRESOVSKY VECERNIK (d) Slovak
Jarkova 4, 08001
Tel: (42-91) 24563; Fax: (42-91) 23398
Circ.—13,000
Prop.—PRIVATPRESS
Ed. in Ch.—Peter Licák

SLOVENIA, REPUBLIC OF
Pop. Est. 1,972,227

LJUBLJANA
Pop. Est. 276,153

DELO (d) Est. 1959
Dunajska 5, 61000
Tel: (386-61) 118255/(386-61) 115315;
Fax: (386-61) 311871/(386-61) 302339
Mng. Ed.—Tit Dobersek
DNEVNIK (m-ex S) Est. 1951
Kopitarjeva 2-4, 61000
Tel: (386-61) 131511; Fax: (386-61) 317954
Cir.—64,000
Mng. Ed.—Zlatko Setinc
Ad. Mgr.—Tereza Gomilsek
SLOVENEC (m-ex S) Est. 1991
Dunajska 9; PO Box 59, 61000
Tel: (386-61) 320841; Fax: (386-61) 319751
Mng. Ed.—Joze Mlakar
SLOVENSKE NOVICE (d)
Dunajska 5, 61000
Tel: (386-61) 115315; Fax: (386-61) 318193
Mng. Ed.—Marjan Bauer

MARIBOR
Pop. Est. 108,122

VECER (d) Est. 1949
E. Svetozarevska St. 14, 62101
Tel: (386-62) 224221; Fax: (386-62) 227736

SPAIN
(Including Canary and Balearic Islands)
Pop. Est. 39,302,665

ALBACETE
Pop. Est. 339,373

LA TRIBUNA DE ALBACETE (Albacete Tribune) (d)
Salamanca, 17, 02001
Tel: (34-67) 210121; Fax: (34-67) 211275
Prop.—Publicaciones Albacete SA
Dir.—Carlos Zuloaga López
Ed. in Ch.—Adolfo Jiménez Martínez-Falero
LA VERDAD DE ALBACETE (The Truth of Albacete) (d)
Teodoro Camino 19, entlo., 02002
Tel: (34-67) 219311/(34-67) 219350;
Fax: (34-67) 210781
Dir.—Adolfo Roldán Fernández
Adm.—Alejandro López Arce

ALCALA DE HENARES

DIARIO DE ALCALA (Alcala Daily)
Diego de Torres, 3, 28801
Tel: (34-1) 8894162/(34-1) 8894761;
Fax: (34-1) 8895115
Gen. Dir.—Antonio Alféraz Callejón
Dir.—José Manuel Serrano Alvarez
Ed. in Ch.—Antonio R Naranjo

ALCOBENDAS
(Madrid)

YA (d) Est. 1935
Valportillo Primera, 11, 28100
Tel: (34-1) 6234100; Fax: (34-1) 6234171
Circ.—75,441
Dir.—Rogelio Rodríguez Blanco
Ed. in Ch.—José Vilamor
Ed. in Ch.—Carlos López de Francisco
Ed. in Ch.—Juan Balboa
Ed. in Ch.—Leopoldo Gómez
Ed. in Ch.—Miguel Angel Bautista

ALCOY

CIUDAD DE ALCOY (City of Alcoy) (d)
San Lorenzo, 33, 03801
Tel: (34-6) 5544111/(34-6) 5541564;
Fax: (34-6) 5544287
Prop.—Graficas Ciudad SA
Dir.—José Vicente Botella Cantó
Ed. in Ch.—Ramón Climent Vaello
Ad. Mgr.—José Luís Lozano Tolsá

ALGECIRAS

EUROPA SUR (Southern Europe) (d)
José Antonio, 9, 3.o. Edificio Los Gálvez, 11201
Tel: (34-56) 666811; Fax: (34-56) 631167
Dir.—José Téllez Rubio
Ed. in Ch.—José Luís Tobalina Cuerda
Ed. in Ch.—Luís Romero Bartumeus

ALICANTE
Pop. Est. 1,149,181

ABC (d)
Mayor, 22, 03002
Tel: (34-6) 5140765; Fax: (34-6) 5210319
Ed. in Ch.—Enrique de Diego Villagrán
INFORMACION (Information) (m-ex mon.) Est. 1941
Avda. Doctor Rico 17; Apdo. Postal 214, 03005
Tel: (34-6) 5921611/(34-6) 5921758;
Fax: (34-6) 5227527/(34-6) 5921611
Circ.—34,197
Gen. Dir.—Jesús Prado Sánchez
Dir.—Francisco Esquivel Morales

Ed. in Ch.—Fernando Pachón
Ed. in Ch.—Carlos Esteve
Ed. in Ch.—Fernando Ramón
Ed. in Ch.—Juan Ramón Gil
Ed. in Ch.—Alberto Olaizola
Ed. in Ch.—Rafael Torres
Ed. in Ch.—José María Perea Soro
Ed. in Ch.—Javier Llopis Arques
LA VERDAD DE ALICANTE (The Truth of Alicante) (d)
Avda. Oscar Esplá, 2, bajo 5, 03003
Tel: (34-6) 5921950; Fax: (34-6) 5922488
Dir.—Adolfo Roldán Fernández
Ed. in Ch.—Ramón Gómez Carrión

ALMERIA
Pop. Est. 410,831

LA CRONICA del SUR (The Chronicle of the South) (d)
Andalucia 8; Apdo. Postal 555, 04007
Tel: (34-50) 276511; Fax: (34-50) 243863/(34-50) 271683
Prop.—Aimeria de Comunicaciones SA
Dir.—Joaquín Abad Rodríguez
Ed. in Ch.—Francisco Venegas Alonso
LA VOZ DE ALMERIA (The Voice of Almeria) (m-ex mon.) Est. 1939
Avda. de Montserrat, 50, 04006
Tel: (34-50) 250888/(34-50) 250682;
Fax: (34-50) 256458/(34-50) 268903
Circ.—5,264
Dir.—Pedro Manuel de la Cruz Alonso
Ed. in Ch.—Angel Iturbide Elizondo

ANDOAIN
(Guipizcoa)

EUSKALDUNON EGUNKARIA
Gudarien Etorbidea, z/g., 20140
Dir.—Martxelo Otamendi
Ed. in Ch.—Imanol Murua

ARRECIFE LANZAROTE
(Las Palmas)

LA VOZ DIARIO DE LANZAROTE (Daily Voice of Lanzarote)
Plaza de la Constitución, 2, 2.o., 35500
Tel: (34-28) 803949/(34-28) 800303;
Fax: (34-28) 814225
Dir.—Augustín D Acosta Hernández
Ed. in ch.—Manuel García Deniz

ASTORGA
Pop. Est. 11,794

EL FARO ASTORGANO (d)
Prensa Astorgana 2; Apdo. Postal 13, 24700
Tel: (34-87) 617012; Fax: (34-87) 617025
Circ.—2,747
Prop.—Edicaciones y Publicaciones Astroganas SA
Dir.—Paulino Sutil Juan
Ed. in Ch.—Isidro Martínez Rodríguez

AVILA
Pop. Est. 183,586

EL DIARIO DE AVILA (Avila Daily) (e) Est. 1898
Carretera de Valladolid, Km. 0,800, 05004
Tel: (34-20) 252052; Fax: (34-20) 251406
Circ.—6,000
Prop.—El Diario de Avila SA
Dir.—José Manuel Serrano Alvarez
Ed. in Ch.—Fernando Alda Sánchez
Ed. in Ch.—José Ramón Alonso Trigueros

AVILES
(Asturias)
Pop. Est. 19,992

LA VOZ DE AVILES (The Voice of Aviles) (m-ex mon.)
Avda. de Gijón, 70; Apdo. Postal 59, 33400
Tel: (34-8) 5540000/(34-8) 5540244;
Fax: (34-8) 5544340
Circ.—17,092
Prop.—La Voz de Aviles SA
Dir.—Juan Manuel Wes López
Ed. in Ch.—José María Urbano García

BADAJOZ
Pop. Est. 114,361

HOY-DIARIO DE EXTREMADURA (m-ex mon.) Est. 1933
Carretera de Madrid-Lisboa, 22, 06008
Tel: (34-24) 252511/(34-24) 252600;
Fax: (34-24) 243004/(34-24) 245359
Circ.—18,015
Prop.—Corporacion de Medios de Badajoz SA
Dir.—Teresiano Rodríguez Núñez

BADALONA
(Barcelona)

EL PUNT-EDICIO BARCELONES
Conquesta, 60, 08912
Tel: (34-3) 4601010
Dir.—Jordi Graui Ramió

BARCELONA
Pop. Est. 1,707,286

ABC (d)
Valencia, 84-86, 08015
Tel: (34-3) 2263750/(34-3) 2263805;
Fax: (34-3) 2263518
Ed. in Ch.—José Alejandro Vara Sotelo
AVUI (d) Est. 1976
Consell de Cent, 425, 6.a. planta, 08009
Tel: (34-3) 2656000; Fax: (34-3) 2658251/(34-3) 2318010
Circ.—38,890
Prop.—Prensa Catalana SA
Dir.—Vicenç Villatoro i Lamolla
Ed. in Ch.—Angel A Castillo i Marco
Ed. in Ch.—Pere Tió i Sauleda
Ed. in Ch.—David Catillo i Büils
Ed. in Ch.—Richard Fité i Labaila
Ed. in Ch.—Pere Prats i Sobrepere
Ed. in Ch.—Richard Sánchez Velázquez
Ed. in Ch.—Andreu Catellet i Homet
BOLENTIN DE BOLSA 16 BARCELONA (d)
San Gervasio, 8, entlo., 08022
Tel: (34-3) 4184779; Fax: (34-3) 4184251
Dir.—Rafael Rubio Gómez-Caminero
DIARI DE BARCELONA (Barcelona Daily) (d) Est. 1792
Carretera de Tamarit, 155, 08015
Tel: (34-3) 3294446; Fax: (34-3) 3290227
Prop.—Publicaciones De Barcelona SA
Dir.—Carles Reves i Escale
DIARI QUATRE GATS (d)
Portal Nou, 24, bajos, 08003
Tel: (34-3) 3150225; Fax: (34-3) 2684873
Dir.—Rubén Adrián Valenzuela
DIARIO MARITIMAS
Paseo de Colón, 24, 08002
Tel: (34-3) 3015516; Fax: (34-3) 3186645
Dir.—Juan Cardona Delclós
NOU DIARI BARCELONA
Tamarit, 155, 08015
Tel: (34-3) 5424200; Fax: (34-3) 5424201
Dir.—Pasqual Llongueras Arola
EL OBSERVADOR (The Observer) (d) Est. 1990
Sector C. Calle D. Polígono Industrial Zona Franca, 08040
Tel: (34-3) 2630304; Fax: (34-3) 2631679
Circ.—76,000
Prop.—Promotora Editorial Europea SA
Dir.—Enric Canals
EL PAIS (The Country) (d)
Zona Franca, Sector B. Calle D, 08040
Tel: (34-3) 4010500; Fax: (34-3) 3353925
Ed. in Ch.—Agustí Fancelli Pardo
Ed. in Ch.—Juan Manuel Perdigó Serra
EL PERIODICO DE CATALUNYA (Catalunya Newspaper) (d) Est. 1978
Consell de Cent, 425-427, 08009
Tel: (34-3) 2655353; Fax: (34-3) 4846513
Circ.—153,735
Prop.—Ediciones Primera Plana SA (Grupo Zeta)
Dir.—Antonio Franco Estadella
Ed. in Ch.—José L Martínez Ibáñez
LA VANGUARDIA (The Vanguard) (d)
Pelayo, 28, 08001
Tel: (34-3) 3015454; Fax: (34-3) 3185587
Dir.—Juan Tapia
EL VIGIA (d)
Plaza Duque de Medinaceli, 5, 1.o., 08002
Tel: (34-3) 3180286; Fax: (34-3) 3022954
Prop.—Publicaciones El Vigia SA
Dir.—Angel Joaniquet Ortega
Ed. in Ch.—Gloria Bescós Guijarro

BILBAO
(Vizcaya)
Pop. Est. 457,655

EL CORREO ESPAÑOL/EL PUEBLO VASCO (The Spanish Mail/Vasco Town) (m)
Pintor Losada, 7, 48004
Tel: (34-4) 4120100/(34-4) 4120521;
Fax: (34-4) 4125377/(34-4) 4126272
Circ.—123,123
Prop.—Bilbao Editorial SA
Dir.—José Antonio Zarzalejos Nieto
Ed. in Ch.—Mikel Iturralde Lázaro
Ed. in Ch.—José Miguel Santamaría
Ed. in Ch.—José Luis Peñalva Abrisqueta
Ed. in Ch.—César Coca García
Ed. in Ch.—Pedro Ontoso Soto
Ed. in Ch.—Juan Angel Marugán
Ed. in Ch.—Pedro Briongos Velasco
Ed. in Ch.—Ignacio Irízar Villar

DEIA (d)
Carretera Bilbao Galdácano, 8, 48004
Tel: (34-4) 4120211/(34-4) 4125306;
Fax: (34-4) 4125307
Circ.—50,018
Prop.—Editorial Iparraguire SA
Dir.—Antón Eguía Cuadra
Ed. in Ch.—Félix Macua Zugasti
Ed. in Ch.—María Jesús Gandariasbeítia de la Torre
Ed. in Ch.—Angel Ruiz de Azúa
EL MUNDO DEL PAIS VASCO (The World of Vasco Country) (d)
Carretera de Bilbao a Galdácano, 20, 48004
Tel: (34-4) 4739100; Fax: (34-4) 4730208
Dir.—Melchor Miralles Sangro

BURGOS
Pop. Est. 156,449

DIARIO 16 BURGOS (Burgos Daily 16) (d)
Maese Calvo, 1, bajo, 09002
Tel: (34-47) 204616; Fax: (34-47) 201618
Prop.—Publicaciones y Prensa de Burgos SA
DIARIO DE BURGOS (Burgos Daily) (dS) Est. 1981
San Pedro de Cardeña, 34, 09002
Tel: (34-47) 267280/(34-47) 268375;
Fax: (34-47) 268003
Circ.—12,244
Prop.—Diario de Burgos SA
Dir.—Vicente Ruíz de Mencía
Ed. in Ch.—Antonio José Mencía Gullón

CACERES
Pop. Est. 71,852

EL PERIODICO EXTREMADURA (m) Est. 1923
Camino Llano, 9, 10002
Tel: (34-27) 210661; Fax: (34-27) 210372
Circ.—4,723
Prop.—Editorial Extremadura SA
Dir.—José Higuero Manzano
Ed. in Ch.—Félix Pinero Sánchez
Ed. in Ch.—Manuel Hernández Carracedo

CADIZ
Pop. Est. 157,766

DIARIO DE CADIZ (Cadiz Daily) (dS) Est. 1867
Ceballos, 1, 11003
Tel: (34-56) 226705/(34-56) 211603;
Fax: (34-56) 211601/(34-56) 224883
Circ.—28,112
Prop.—Federico Joly y Cia SA
Dir.—José Joly Palomino
Ed. in Ch.—Antonio Rivera Ruiz
Ed. in Ch.—José María Otero Bada
Ed. in Ch.—María Eulalia González Santiago
Ed. in Ch.—Francisco Perea Márquez
Ed. in Ch.—Ignacio de la Varga Pérez
Ed. in Ch.—Juan José Téllez Rubio
INFORMACION CADIZ (Cadiz Information) (d)
Plaza Esquivel 1, entresuelo Z, 11010
Tel: (34-56) 264900/(34-26) 264906;
Fax: (34-26) 289505
Ed. in Ch.—Juan León Moriche

CARTAGENA
(Murcia)

LA VERDAD DE CARTAGENA (The Truth of Cartagena) (d)
Jara, 34, 4.o. B, 30201
Tel: (34-68) 504400; Fax: (34-68) 528616
Dir.—Adolfo Roldán Fernández

CASTELLON
Pop. Est. 126,464

CASTELLON DIARIO (Castellon Daily) (d)
Carretera Valencia-Barcelona, km. 68:700;
Apdo. Postal 505, 12080
Tel: (34-64) 209599/(34-64) 209598;
Fax: (34-64) 243650/(34-64) 209193
Circ.—4,230
Prop.—Castellon Editorial SA
Dir.—Juan Enrique Más Molina
Ed. in Ch.—Christina Rodríguez Schillhofer
MEDITERRANEO (Mediterranean) (d) Est. 1938
Carretera de Almazora, s/n, 12005
Tel: (34-64) 349500; Fax: (34-64) 349505
Circ.—6,662
Prop.—Promociones y Edicaciones Culturales SA (Pesa)
Dir.—Jesús Montesinos Cervera
Ed. in Ch.—Jesús López Flor
Ed. in Ch.—José Vicente Felip

Europe **Spain** IV-43

CASTILLA-LA-MANCHA

ABC (d)
Alfonso XII, 7, bajo A, Toledo, 45002
Tel: (34-25) 212206; Fax: (34-25) 212820
EL DIA DE TOLEDO (The Day of Toledo) (d)
Plaza Zocodover, 7, 3.o. Toledo, 45001
Tel: (34-25) 221170/(34-25) 221400;
Fax: (34-25) 214065
Dir.—Santiago Mateo Sahuquillo
LA VOZ DEL TAJO (The Voice of Tajo) (d)
Marques de Mirasol, 19, Talavera De La Reina, Toledo, 45600
Tel: (34-25) 812400; Fax: (34-25) 812454
Dir.—Segundo Marino Vasquez
LANZA
Alferez Provisional, 1, Toledo, 45001
Tel: (34-25) 254713; Fax: (34-25) 254391
Dir.—José Antonio Casado Corrales
YA (Enough) (d)
Nuncio Viejo, 3, 2.o. A, Toledo, 45002
Tel: (34-25) 211154; Fax: (34-25) 211351

CEUTA
Pop. Est. 78,182

EL FARO DE CEUTA (m-ex mon.)
Sargento Mena, 8, 11701
Tel: (34-56) 513649/(34-56) 511024;
Fax: (34-56) 517603
Prop.—Joaquin Ferrer y Cía. SA
Dir.—Germinal Castillo Aguilar

CIUDAD REAL
Pop. Est. 41,708

LANZA-CIUDAD REAL (m-ex S) Est. 1943
Ronda del Carmen, s/n, 13003
Tel: (34-26) 220339/(34-26) 220910;
Fax: (34-26) 222977
Dir.—José Antonio Casado Corrales
Ed. in Ch.—Pedro Pintado
LA TRIBUNA DE CIUDAD REAL (Real City Tribune) (d)
Plaza del Pilar, 7, 13001
Tel: (34-26) 215301; Fax: (34-26) 215306
Dir.—Manuel López Camarena
Ed. in Ch.—Carlos Muñoz de Luna

CORDOBA
Pop. Est. 284,737

CORDOBA (d) Est. 1941
Ingeniero Juan de la Cierva, 18, Polígono Industrial, La Torrecilla, 14013
Tel: (34-57) 291711; Fax: (34-57) 204648/(34-57) 295531
Circ.—10,738
Prop.—Diario Cordoba SA
Dir.—Antonio Ramos Espejo
Ed. in Ch.—Manuel Fernández Fernández
Ed. in Ch.—Antonio Galán Ortíz

LA CORUÑA
Pop. Est. 232,356

LA VOZ DE GALICIA (The Voice of Galicia) (m-ex mon.) Est. 1882
Concepción Arenal, 11-13, 15006
Tel: (34-81) 180180; Fax: (34-81) 295918/(34-81) 295365
Circ.—77,078
Dir.—Juan Ramón Díaz García
Ed. in Ch.—Arturo Lezcano Fernández
Ed. in Ch.—Francisco Ríos Alvarez

CUENCA
Pop. Est. 41,791

EL DIA DE CUENCA (The Day of Cuenca) (6x wk.) Est. 1984
Polígono El Cantorral, 13, 16004
Tel: (34-69) 212291; Fax: (34-69) 213200
Prop.—El Dia De Cuenca SA
Pres./Dir.—Santiago Mateo Sahuquillo
Ed. in Ch.—José María Dávila
NUEVO DIARIO (New Daily) (d)
Calderon de la Barca, 14, 16001
Tel: (34-66) 230404; Fax: (34-66) 222304
Prop.—Nuevo Diario del Jucar SA
Dir.—Inmaculada Cruz Salcedo

EL PUERTO DE SANTA MARIA
(Cadiz)

INFORMACION EL PUERTO (El Puerto Information) (d)
Aurora, 11, 1.o. local 7, 11500
Tel: (34-56) 540688; Fax: (34-56) 540683

Spain

ELCHE
(Alicante)

HOY DE LA PROVINCIA DE ALICANTE (Today From Alicante Province)
Polígono Industrial Altabix, Elda, 35, 03203
Tel: (34-6) 54565861/(34-6) 5456875;
Fax: (34-6) 5456519
Dir.—Vicente Marco Valladolid
Ed. in Ch.—María José March García
LA VERDAD DE ELCHE (The Truth of Elche) (d)
Maestro Albéniz, 10, 03200
Tel: (34-6) 5452443/(34-6) 5452849;
Fax: (34-6) 5420548
Dir.—Adolfo Roldán Fernández

GERONA
Pop. Est. 87,648

DIARI DE GIRONA (Gerona Daily) (d)
Comerç, s/n, 17458
Tel: (34-72) 476277; Fax: (34-72) 476240
Circ.—7,392
Dir.—Narcís Planas i Gifreu
Ed. in Ch.—Alfons Petit
NOU DIARI GIRANA (d)
Ultònia, 10-12, 17002
Tel: (34-72) 409300; Fax: (34-72) 409301
Dir.—Josep Gil Franquesa
Ed. in Ch.—Josep Mir Hurtado
EL PUNT-EDICIO DE GERONA (m-ex mon.)
Figuerola, 28, Bajos, 17001
Tel: (34-72) 221010; Fax: (34-72) 218630
Circ.—12,390
Prop.—Ediciones Periodigues de les Comarques SA
Ed. in Ch.—Angel Madriá i Roura
Ed. in Ch.—Enric Serra i Amat

GIJON
(Asturias)
Pop. Est. 255,969

EL COMERCIO (The Commercial) (dS)
Ferrocarril, 1, 33207
Tel: (34-8) 5351946; Fax: (34-8) 5342226
Circ.—21,005
Prop.—El Comercio SA
Dir.—Francisco Carantoña Dubert
Ed. in Ch.—Marcelino González Menéndez
Ed. in Ch.—Rubén Espiniella Castro

GRANADA
Pop. Est. 262,182

IDEAL (dS) Est. 1932
Cádiz, s/n. Polígono Industrial "La Unidad" de Asegra, 18210
Tel: (34-58) 405161; Fax: (34-58) 405072/(34-58) 402420
Circ.—25,561
Dir.—Melchor Sáiz-Pardo Rubio

HERNANI

EGIN (d)
Polígono Eciago, 10B, 20120
Tel: (34-43) 554712; Fax: (34-43) 551207/(34-43) 553494
Dir.—Jabier Salutregi Mentxaka
Ed. in Ch.—Mertxe Aizpurua
Ed. in Ch.—Iñaki Iriondo
Ed. in Ch.—Juan Carlos Elorza
Ed. in Ch.—Martín Garitano
Ed. in Ch.—Fermín Munarriz

HUARTE
(Navarra)

DIARIO DE NOTICIAS (Daily News) (d)
Polígono Areta Huarte, s/n, 31620
Tel: (34-48) 332533; Fax: (34-48) 332518
Dir.—Fernando Múgica Goñi
Ed. in Ch.—Paloma Sánchez Bargos
Ed. in Ch.—Javier Errea Múgica
NAVARRA HOY (Navarra Today) (d)
Polígono Areta Huarte, s/n, 31620
Tel: (34-48) 332533; Fax: (34-48) 332518
Circ.—8,810
Prop.—Navarra De Prensa y Comunicaciones SA
Dir.—Ramón Mur Gimeno

HUELVA
Pop. Est. 127,806

ABC (d)
Martín Alonso Pinzón, 24, 21003
Tel: (34-59) 262032; Fax: (34-59) 261022
Ed. in Ch.—José Cejudo Hidalgo

HUELVA INFORMACION (Huelva Information) (d) Est. 1983
Plaza San Pedro, 7, 21004
Tel: (34-59) 284375/(34-59) 285113;
Fax: (34-59) 260608
Circ.—6,270
Prop.—Huelva Informacion SA
Dir.—Fernando María Merchán Alvarez
Ed. in Ch.—Antonio Peinazo Pleguezuelos
Ed. in Ch.—Rafael Pérez Unquiles
Ed. in Ch.—Victoriano Ruizgómez Domínguez

HUESCA

DIARIO DEL ALTOARAGON (Altoaragon Daily) (d)
La Palma 9; Apdo. Postal 21, 22001
Tel: (34-74) 223993; Fax: (34-74) 245444
Circ.—4,518
Dir.—Antonio Angulo Araguás
Ed. in Ch.—Javier García Antón
HERALDO DE HUESCA (Huesca Herald) (d)
Coso Bajo, 28, 22001
Tel: (34-74) 226774; Fax: (34-74) 240510
Dir.—Antonio Bruned Mompeón

IBIZA
(Balearic Islands)
Pop. Est. 16,943

DIARIO DE IBIZA (Ibiza Daily) (m-ex mon.)
Fray Vicente Nicolás, 27, 07800
Tel: (34-71) 190000; Fax: (34-71) 190322/(34-71) 190321
Circ.—4,386
Dir.—Joan Serra Tur
Ed. in Ch.—Bartomeu Planells Planells

JAEN
Pop. Est. 96,429

JAEN (d)
Torredonjimeno, 1, Polígono Los Olivares, 23009
Tel: (34-53) 221881/(34-53) 221345;
Fax: (34-53) 221877/(34-53) 260207
Circ.—3,635
Prop.—Raymex SA
Dir.—José Luís Moreno Codina
Ed. in Ch.—Juan Espejo González

JEREZ DE LA FRONTERA
(Cadiz)

ABC
Hornos, 3, 11403
Tel: (34-56) 340007; Fax: (34-56) 345832
Ed. in Ch.—Antonio Castro Caro
DIARIO DE JEREZ (Jerez Daily) (d)
Patricio Garvey, s/n, 1.o, 11402
Tel: (34-56) 321411; Fax: (34-56) 320011/(34-56) 349904
Circ.—6,754
Prop.—Federico Joly y Cia SA
Dir.—Manuel de la Peña Muñoz
Ed. in Ch.—Juan Pedro Simó Marra-López
Ed. in Ch.—Manuel Barea Alvarez
INFORMACION JEREZ (Jerez Information) (d)
Córdoba, 16, 11405
Tel: (34-56) 302511; Fax: (34-56) 307912/(34-56) 183421
Dir.—Alejandro Ramírez Fernández
EL PERIODICO DEL GUADALETE (Guadalete Newspapers) (d)
Córdoba, 16, 11405
Tel: (34-56) 302511; Fax: (34-56) 307912/(34-56) 183421
Dir.—Fernando Merchán Alvarez
Ed. in Ch.—Manuel Hernández Carracedo
Ed. in Ch.—Juan Manuel Muñoz Gómez-Landero

LA LAGUNA

LA GACETA DE CANARIAS (Canarias Gazette) (d)
Fernando Díaz Cutillas, s/n, Polígono Industrial, 38108
Tel: (34-22) 655216/(34-22) 655555;
Fax: (34-22) 654460
Dir.—Jorge Bethencourt González
Ed. in Ch.—Juan Carlos Castañeda

LEON
Pop. Est. 131,132

LA CRONICA 16 DE LEON (d)
Paseo de la Facultad, 16, bajo, 24004
Tel: (34-87) 212024; Fax: (34-87) 213152
Prop.—Promociones Periodisticas Leonesas SA (Propelesa)
Dir.—Oscar Campillo Madrigal
DIARIO DE LEON (Leon Daily) (d)
Carretera de León-Astorga, Km. 4,6.
Trobajo del Camino, 24010

Tel: (34-87) 802411/(34-87) 800400;
Fax: (34-87) 800514/(34-87) 802614
Circ.—13,328
Gen. Dir.—José Gabriel González Arias
Dir.—Francisco J Martínez Carrión
Ed. in Ch.—Susana Vergara
Ed. in Ch.—Vicente Pueyo
Ed. in Ch.—Camino Gallego

LA LINEA DE LA CONCEPCION

AREA CAMPO DE GIBRALTAR Y COSTA DEL SOL (Area Camp of Gilbraltar and Coast of the Sun) (d)
Gibraltar, 13-15, 11300
Tel: (34-56) 101476/(34-56) 101477;
Fax: (34-56) 763050
Prop.—Diario del Campo de Gibraltar
Dir.—José Antonio Gómez Amado

LLEIDA

NOU DIARI LLEIDA (d) Est. 1885
Pallars, 4, 25004
Tel: (34-73) 700500; Fax: (34-73) 700501/(34-73) 700507
Circ.—14,000
Prop.—Publicaciones Catolicas
Dir.—Ramón Badía Vidal
Ed. in Ch.—Joan Tort
LA MAÑANA-DIARI DE PONENT (d) Est. 1938
Polígono Industrial El Segre, Parcela 118;
Apdo. Postal 11, 25080
Tel: (34-73) 204600; Fax: (34-73) 201646
Circ.—5,063
Prop.—Diario La Mañana SA
Dir.—Jordi Pérez Ansótegui
Ed. in Ch.—Jesús Bometón
SEGRE (dS)
Calle del Riu, 6, 25007
Tel: (34-73) 248000; Fax: (34-73) 246031
Circ.—7,195
Prop.—Prensa Leridana SA
Ex. Dir.—Juan Cal Sánchez
Ch. Dir.—Santiago Costa Miranda
Ed. in Ch.—Gloria Farré Lorente
Ed. in Ch.—Joan Miras i Muntadas
Ed. in Ch.—Anna Gómez i Marsol

LOGROÑO
(La Rioja)
Pop. Est. 84,000

LA VOZ DE LA RIOJA (The Voice of the Rioja) (m-ex mon.) Est. 1938
Avda. de Portugal, 2; Apdo. Postal 28, 26001
Tel: (34-41) 211000/(34-41) 211119;
Fax: (34-41) 211166
Circ.—12,305
Prop.—Nueva Rioja SA
Dir.—José María Esteban Ibáñez

LUGO
Pop. Est. 73,986

EL PROGRESO (The Progress) (m) Est. 1908
Progreso, 12, 27001
Tel: (34-82) 298100; Fax: (34-82) 298101/(34-82) 298102
Circ.—10,916
Prop.—El Progreso DeLugo, SL
Dir.—Fernando Salgado García
Ed. in Ch.—Angel Martínez Fernández de la Vega
Ed. in Ch.—Juan Soto Gutiérrez

LUGONES-SIERO

EL PERIODICO-LA VOZ DE ASTURIAS (Newspaper-The Voice of Asturias) (d)
Polígono Puente Nora, 33420
Tel: (34-8) 5101500; Fax: (34-8) 5101512/(34-8) 5101505
Dir.—Faustino Fernández Alvarez

MADRID
Pop. Est. 3,120,732

ABC (d) Est. 1905
Avda. de América, 124, 28027
Tel: (34-1) 3399000; Fax: (34-1) 3203620/(34-1) 3203555
Circ.—247,225
Prop.—Prensa Española SA
Dir.—Luis María Ansón Oliart
Ed. in Ch.—Angel Antonio González Pérez
Ed. in Ch.—Rodrigo Gutiérrez del Berrio
Ed. in Ch.—Vicente Angel Pérez López
AS (dS) Est. 1967
Cuesta de San Vicente, 26, 28008
Tel: (34-1) 2472300; Fax: (34-1) 2486121
Circ.—156,534
Prop.—Semana SA
Dir.—Rafael Rienzi Gómez Redondo
EL BOLETIN DE LA TARDE (The Afternoon Bulletin) (d)
Lagasca, 71, 28001
Tel: (34-1) 4316102; Fax: (34-1) 5777367
Dir.—Carlos Humanes

DELEGACION MADRID (Madrid Delegation) (d)
Zorrilla, 21, 2.o. C., 28014
Tel: (34-1) 5212768; Fax: (34-1) 5212937
DIARIO 16 (dS) Est. 1976
Basauri, 17, 28023
Tel: (34-1) 5589896; Fax: (34-1) 5589897/(34-1) 3044971
Circ.—136,099
Dir.—José Luís Gutiérrez
Ed. in Ch.—Alberto Otaño Zubiri
IBERIAN DAILY SUN (d) English
Zurbano, 74, 28010
Tel: (34-1) 4427700/(34-1) 4427689;
Fax: (34-1) 4427854
Circ.—5,134
Dir.—Pedro Serra Bauzá
LA INFORMACION DE MADRID (The Information of Madrid) (d)
Francisco Sancha, 4, 28034
Tel: (34-1) 3346100/(34-1) 3346116;
Fax: (34-1) 3346148
Dir.—Manuel Marlasca
MARCA (Mark) (d)
Paseo de Recoletos 14, 1.o., 28801
Tel: (34-1) 4319701
Circ.—143,821
Dir.—Luís Infante Bravo
EL MUNDO DEL SIGLO VEINTIUNO (d)
Pradillo, 42, 28002
Tel: (34-1) 5864800/(34-1) 5864700;
Fax: (34-1) 5864848
Circ.—104,000
Dir.—Pedro J Ramírez Codina
Ed. in Ch.—Angel Ibáñez
EL PAIS (The Country) (dS)
Miguel Yuste, 40, 28037
Tel: (34-1) 3378200; Fax: (34-1) 3048766
Circ.—372,741
Prop.—Promotora De Información SA
Dir.—Jesús Ceberio Galardi
Ed. in Ch.—Lorenzo Romero
LA REGION INTERNACIONAL (The International Region) (d)
O'Donnell, 14, Oficina 4 (Torre Valencia), 28009
Tel: (34-1) 5756739; Fax: (34-1) 5752053
Dir.—Alfonso Sánchez Izquierdo
Gen. Dir.—Marcelo Carbone

MAHON
(Balearic Islands)
Pop. Est. 36,547

MENORCA (m-ex S) Est. 1941
Avda. Central, 5, 07714
Tel: (34-71) 351600; Fax: (34-71) 351983
Circ.—4,200
Prop.—Editorial Menorca SA
Dir.—Joan Bosco Marqués Bosch
Ed. in Ch.—Juan Carlos Ortego Elvira

MALAGA
Pop. Est. 503,251

DIARIO 16 MALAGA (Malaga Daily 16) (d)
Faro, 4, 29016
Tel: (34-5) 2227301/(34-5) 2210440;
Fax: (34-5) 2210448/(34-5) 2227199
Dir.—Juan de Dios Mellado Morales
Ed. in Ch.—Tomás Mayoral
DIARIO MALAGA-COSTA DEL SOL (Malaga Daily-Coast of the Sun) (d)
Avda. García Morato, 50, 29004
Tel: (34-5) 2244353/(34-5) 2244354;
Fax: (34-5) 2245540
Dir.—Julián Romaguera Mena
Ed. in Ch.—José A Hierrezuelo
LA GACETA DE MALAGA (Malaga Gazette) (d)
Puerta del Mar, 5-7, 1A y 2A, 29005
Tel: (34-52) 218858; Fax: (34-52) 218819
EL SOL DEL MEDITERRANEO (The Mediterranean Sun) (d)
Carretera de Azucarera-Intelhorce, 24, 29004
Tel: (34-52) 233500; Fax: (34-52) 239911
Dir.—Antonio Sanchez Morillaa
SUR (m-ex mon.) Est. 1937
Avda. Doctor Marañón, 48, 29009
Tel: (34-5) 2393900/(34-5) 2282950;
Fax: (34-5) 2279504/(34-5) 2279508
Circ.—27,087
Prop.—Prensa Malagueña SA
Dir.—Joaquín Marín Alarcón
Ed. in Ch.—Pedro Luís Gómez Carmona
Ed. in Ch.—Leopoldo Canivell Salas
Ed. in Ch.—Manuel Castillo Caserneiro
Ed. in Ch.—José Castro
LA VOZ DE MELILLA (The Voice of Melilla) (d)
Cervantes, 2, 1.o., 29801
Tel: (34-52) 670688/(34-52) 670690;
Fax: (34-52) 670689
Dir.—José M Navarro Gil

Copyright ©1996 by the Editor & Publisher Co.

MANRESA
(Barcelona)

REGIO 7 INFORMATIVO INTERCOMARCAL (d)
Catalan
Santa Antoni María Claret, 32, 08240
Tel: (34-3) 8746454; Fax: (34-3) 8740352
Circ.—5,342
Prop.—Edicaciones Intercomareals SA
Dir.—Goncal Manzcuñán Boix
Ed. in Ch.—Salvador Redó Martí
Ed. in Ch.—Marc Marcé Casaponsa
Ed. in Ch.—Domènec Orrit Pujol

MELILLA
(Malaga)

MELILLA HOY (Melilla Today) (d)
General Mola, 30, 29804
Tel: (34-5) 2681092/(34-5) 2684026;
Fax: (34-5) 2685326
Dir.—Irene Flores Sáez
Ed. in Ch.—María Angeles Jiménez Padilla
EL TELEGRAMA DE MELILLA (The Melilla Telegram) (d)
Muelle Ribera (Antigua Lonja Pesquera), 29801
Tel: (34-5) 2685555/(34-5) 2685613;
Fax: (34-5) 2684814
Dir.—Juan José Medina Roldán
Ed. in Ch.—Ignacio Gaztelumendi Doejo

MESOIRO

EL IDEAL GALLEGO (The Gallego Ideal) (m-ex mon.) Est. 1917
Polígono de Pocomaco, Parcela C-12, 15190
Tel: (34-81) 299000; Fax: (34-81) 299327
Circ.—10,508
Dir.—Valentín Alejandro Martínez Fernández

MURCIA
Pop. Est. 288,631

DIARIO 16 DE MURCIA (Murcia Daily 16) (d)
Cartagena, 4, 30002
Tel: (34-68) 220911/(34-68) 220542;
Fax: (34-68) 221926/(34-68) 221914
Gen. Dir.—José Alfonso Orrico Martínez
Dir.—Jesús Pozo Gómez
Ed. in Ch.—José Antonio Montesinos Agulló
LA OPINION DE MURCIA (The Opinion of Murcia) (d)
Plaza Condestable, 3, 30009
Tel: (34-68) 281888/(34-68) 281890;
Fax: (34-68) 281417
Dir.—Paloma Reverte de Luis
Ed. in Ch.—Javier Soto Andrados
LA VERDAD DE MURCIA (The Truth of Murcia) (dS) Est. 1903
Camino Viejo de Monteagudo, s/n, 30160
Tel: (34-68) 369100; Fax: (34-68) 852255/(34-68) 852510
Circ.—43,271
Prop.—Corporación de Medios de Murcia SA
Dir.—Adolfo Roldán Fernández
Ed. in Ch.—Joaquín García Cruz
Ed. in Ch.—Gregorio Bustamente Herráiz
Ed. in Ch.—Juan Antonio Calvo Carazo
Ed. in Ch.—Pedro Soler Gómez

ORENSE
Pop. Est. 96,085

LA REGION (The Region) (m-ex mon.) Est. 1910
Polígono San Cibrán de Viñas, Calle 4, 32091
Tel: (34-88) 222211; Fax: (34-88) 256633/(34-88) 244449
Circ.—11,380
Prop.—La Region SA
Dir.—Alfonso Sánchez Izquierdo
Ed. in Ch.—Miguel Sánchez López

OVIEDO
(Asturias)
Pop. Est. 154,117

LA NUEVA ESPAÑA (The New Spain) (d) Est. 1937
Calvo Sotelo, 7, 33007
Tel: (34-8) 5279700; Fax: (34-8) 5279711/(34-8) 5279704
Circ.—36,013 (d); 86,846 (wknd.)
Prop.—Editorial Prensa Asturiana SA
Dir.—Melchor Fernández Díaz
Ed. in Ch.—Evelio González Palacios
Ed. in Ch.—Isidoro Nicieza
Ed. in Ch.—Alberto Menéndez

PALENCIA
Pop. Est. 74,080

ALERTA DE PALENCIA (Palencia Alert) (d)
Valentín Calderón, 4, 34001
Tel: (34-79) 750700; Fax: (34-79) 750666
Dir.—Juan Luís Fernández Vega
Ed. in Ch.—Gonzalo Romero de la Villa

EL DIARIO PALENTINO/EL DIA DE PALENCIA (The Daily Palentino/The Day of Palencia) (d) Est. 1882
Mayor, 67, 34001
Tel: (34-79) 744822; Fax: (34-79) 743360
Circ.—10,000
Prop.—El Diario Palentino
Prop.—El Dia de Palencia SL
Dir.—Mariano Gutiérrez Carlón
Ed. in Ch.—Gonzalo Ortega Aragón

PALMA DE MALLORCA
(Balearic Islands)
Pop. Est. 234,098

BALEARES (e-ex mon.) Est. 1939
Paseo de Mallorca, 9A, 07011
Tel: (34-71) 788322; Fax: (34-71) 455740
Circ.—10,557
Dir.—Miguel Serra Magraner
Ed. in Ch.—Amaya Michelena Alberdi
EL DIA DEL MUNDO DE BALEARES (The Day of Baleares World) (d)
Gremio de Herreros, 42, Polígono Son Castelló, 07009
Tel: (34-71) 767600; Fax: (34-71) 767656
Dir.—Basilio Baltasar Cifre
Ed. in Ch.—Macia Riera Llinás
DIARIO 16 BALEARES (d)
Unió, 2A, 2.o., 07001
Tel: (34-71) 717333/(34-71) 717444;
Fax: (34-71) 717146
Circ.—14,156
DIARIO DE MALLORCA (Mallorca Daily) (m-ex mon.) Est. 1953
Puerto Rico, 15, Polígono de Levante, 07007
Tel: (34-71) 170300; Fax: (34-71) 170301/(34-71) 170307
Circ.—21,716
Prop.—Editora Balaer SA
Dir.—Pedro Pablo Alonso García
Ed. in Ch.—Juan Riera Munar
Ed. in Ch.—Antonio Ruíz Pomar
Ed. in Ch.—José María Frau Gayá
MAJORCA DAILY BULLETIN (m-ex mon.)
English; Est. 1962
Paseo Mallorca, 9A, 07011
Tel: (34-71) 788400; Fax: (34-71) 719706
Circ.—4,888
Prop.—Majorca Daily Bulletin SA
Dir.—Miguel Serra Magraner
Ed. in Ch.—Irene Taylor
ULTIMA HORA (The Last Hour) (e-ex S) Est. 1893
Paseo Mallorca, 9A, 07011
Tel: (34-71) 788333; Fax: (34-71) 454190
Circ.—25,048
Prop.—Hora Nova SA
Dir.—Pedro Comás Barceló
Ed. in Ch.—Lourdes Terrasa Messuti

LAS PALMAS DE GRAN CANARIA
(Canary Islands)
Pop. Est. 287,038

CANARIAS 7 (d)
Profesor Lozano, 7, Urbanización "El Cebadal", 35008
Tel: (34-28) 466000/(34-28) 467120;
Fax: (34-28) 468435
Circ.—12,194
Prop.—Información Canarias SA
Dir.—José Luis Torró Micó
Ed. in Ch.—Vicente Llorca Linares
Ed. in Ch.—Martín J Marrero Pérez
Ed. in Ch.—Dolores Santana Alonso
DIARIO DE LAS PALMAS (Las Palmas Daily) (e-ex S) Est. 1893
Alcade Ramírez Bethencourt, 8, 35003
Tel: (34-28) 479448; Fax: (34-28) 479421
Circ.—11,545
Prop.—Editorial Prensa Canaria SA
Dir.—Santiago Betancor Brito
Ed. in Ch.—Cristóbal Rodríguez Rodríguez
Ed. in Ch.—Rafael González Morera
LA PROVINCIA (The Province) (m) Est. 1911
Alcade Ramírez Bethencourt, 8, 35003
Tel: (34-28) 479410; Fax: (34-28) 479401
Circ.—38,537
Prop.—Editorial Prensa Canaria SA
Dir.—Diego Talavera Alemán
Ed. in Ch.—Antonio Cruz Domínguez

PAMPLONA
(Navarra)
Pop. Est. 147,158

DIARIO DE NAVARRA (Navarra Daily) (dS) Est. 1903
Zapatería, 49, 31001
Tel: (34-48) 236050; Fax: (34-48) 237940/(34-48) 150484
Circ.—43,374 (d); 53,582 (S)
Prop.—La Información SA

Europe

Dir.—Julio Martínez Torres
Ed. in Ch.—Miguel Angel Riezu Boj
Ed. in Ch.—Inés Artajo Ayesa
Ed. in Ch.—Luís Castiella Muruzabal
Ed. in Ch.—José Javier Testaut Atozqui

ONTEVEDRA
Pop. Est. 65,137

DIARIO DE PONTEVEDRA (Pontevedra Daily) (d)
Secundino Esperón, 5, 36002
Tel: (34-86) 866550/(34-86) 856554;
Fax: (34-86) 863275
Prop.—Cooperativa De Produccion Diario
Dir.—Pedro Antonio Rivas Fontenla

REUS

NOU DIARI REUS (d)
Roser, 4, 43201
Tel: (34-77) 759800; Fax: (34-77) 759801
Dir.—Xavier Abelló Tomás

SABADELL

DIARI DE SABADELL (Sabadell Daily) (5x wk.)
San Quirze, 37-41, 2.o., 08201
Tel: (34-3) 7261100; Fax: (34-3) 7270865
Circ.—6,448
Prop.—Vallencana De Publicaciones SA
Dir.—Ramón Rodríguez Zorrilla
Ed. in Ch.—Maties Serracant Clermont
Ed. in Ch.—Joaquín Fité Borguñó

SALAMANCA
Pop. Est. 167,131

EL ADELANTO (d) Est. 1883
Gran Vía, 56, 37001
Tel: (34-23) 216595/(34-23) 138846;
Fax: (34-23) 219435/(34-23) 138071
Circ.—7,610
Prop.—Publicaciones Regionales SA
Dir.—Carlos del Pueyo Pérez
Ed. in Ch.—Carlos Alonso Argaiz
LA GACETA REGIONAL DE SALAMANCA (The Regional Gazette of Salamanca) (m-ex mon.)
Peña Primera, 18-24, 37002
Tel: (34-23) 218607/(34-23) 218609;
Fax: (34-23) 213929
Circ.—8,380
Dir.—Iñigo Domínguez de Calatayud
TRIBUNA DE SALMANCA (Salamanca Tribune) (d)
Avda. de Salamanca, 270, 37004
Tel: (34-23) 121010; Fax: (34-23) 235101
Dir.—Carlos B Pérez Díaz

SAN FERNANDO
(Cadiz)

INFORMACION SAN FERNANDO (San Fernando Information) (d)
San Nicolás, 34, 11100
Tel: (34-56) 888591; Fax: (34-56) 590096

SAN SEBASTIAN
(Guipuzcoa)
Pop. Est. 165,829

EL DIARIO VASCO (The Vasco Daily) (d)
Camino de Portuetxe, 2, Barrio Ibaeta, 20009
Tel: (34-43) 410700; Fax: (34-43) 410813/(34-43) 410816
Circ.—80,714
Prop.—Sociedad Vascongada De Publicaciones SA
Dir.—Salvador Pérez-Puig y Sanchís
Ed. in Ch.—Javier Peña Albizu
Ed. in Ch.—Julio Díaz de Alda
Ed. in Ch.—Pedro Gabilondo Pujol
Ed. in Ch.—Sebastián Valencia Abete
Ed. in Ch.—Iñigo Beltrán de Heredia

SANTA CRUZ DE TENERIFE
(Canary Islands)
Pop. Est. 151,361

EL DIA (The Day) (m-ex mon.) Est. 1910
Avda. Buenos Aires, 71, 38005
Tel: (34-22) 211000; Fax: (34-22) 214247/(34-22) 213834
Circ.—25,779
Prop.—Herederos De Leoncio Rodríguez
Dir.—José Rodríguez Ramírez
Ed. in Ch.—José Moreno García
Ed. in Ch.—Juan Carlos Ramos Martín
Ed. in Ch.—Julio Rodríguez de la Plata

Spain **IV-45**

DIARIO DE AVISOS (m-ex mon.) Est. 1890
Salamanca, 5, 38006
Tel: (34-22) 272350/(34-22) 272354;
Fax: (34-22) 241039/(34-22) 272757
Circ.—9,721
Prop.—Canaria De Avisos SA
Dir.—Leopoldo Fernández Cabeza de Vaca
Ed. in Ch.—Carmen Ruano
JORNADA DEPORTIVA (d)
Avda. Buenos Aires, 71, 38005
Tel: (34-22) 211000/(34-22) 201057;
Fax: (34-22) 213834/(34-22) 200229
Dir.—José Rodríguez Ramírez
Ed. in Ch.—Juan Sánchez Quintana
Ed. in Ch.—Yolanda Arenas
Ed. in Ch.—Ventura González

SANTANDER
(Cantabria)
Pop. Est. 149,704

ALERTA DE CANTABRIA (Cantabria Alert) (m-ex mon.) Est. 1937
1.o. de Mayo, s/n, Barrio San Martín, Peñacastillo, 39011
Tel: (34-42) 320033; Fax: (34-42) 322046
Circ.—22,404
Prop.—Cantabrico de Prensa SA
Dir.—Juan Luis Fernández Vega
Ed. in Ch.—José Ramón Díaz Rivas
Ed. in Ch.—José Luis Valdezate Paul
EL DIARIO MONTAÑES (The Montañés Daily) (d)
Canda Landa, s/n, La Albericia, 39012
Tel: (34-42) 346622; Fax: (34-42) 341007/(34-42) 341806
Circ.—25,899 (d); 62,044 (wknd.)
Prop.—Editorial Cantabria SA
Dir.—Manuel Angel Castañeda Pérez
Ed. in Ch.—José Ramón San Juan Jiménez
Ed. in Ch.—José Antonio González Casares
Ed. in Ch.—Pepa Talenti Alvargonzalez
EL NORTE (The North) (d)
Fernández de Isla 28, 39008
Tel: (34-42) 230000; Fax: (34-42) 231017
Dir.—Víctor Giján Peñas
Ed. in Ch.—Pablo Quevedo Lázaro
Ed. in Ch.—Marcos Bermejo Gil
Ed. in Ch.—Eva Postigo Días

SANTIAGO DE COMPOSTELA

EL CORREO GALLEGO (The Gallego Mail) (m-ex mon.)
Preguntoiro, 29, 15704
Tel: (34-81) 582600; Fax: (34-81) 562395/(34-81) 571335
Prop.—Editorial Compostela SA
Dir.—José Manuel Rey Nóvoa
Ed. in Ch.—Víctor Tobío Barreira
Ed. in Ch.—José A Pérez Docampo
Ed. in Ch.—Luis Pérez Fernández

SEGOVIA
Pop. Est. 53,237

EL ADELANTADO DE SEGOVIA (e-ex S) Est. 1901
San Agustín, 3, 40001
Tel: (34-21) 437261; Fax: (34-21) 442432
Circ.—7,923
Dir.—Fernando Ganuza Laita

SEVILLE
(SEVILLA)
Pop. Est. 678,218

ABC (m-ex mon.) Est. 1929
Cardenal Iluindaín, 9, 41013
Tel: (34-5) 4616200; Fax: (34-5) 4627106
Circ.—56,692
Prop.—Prensa Espanola SA
Dir.—Francisco Giménez Alemán
Ed. in Ch.—Carlos Bernal Merino
Ed. in Ch.—Benito Fernández Pérez
Ed. in Ch.—Manuel Jesús Florencio Caro
Ed. in Ch.—Angel Luís Pérez Guerra
Ed. in Ch.—Antonio de la Torre Simó
Ed. in Ch.—Alvaro Ybarra Pacheco
Ed. in Ch.—Clara Guzmán Esteban
DIARIO 16 ANDALUCIA (Andalucia Daily 16) (d)
Polígono Calonge, Calle B, 13, 41007
Tel: (34-5) 4431561; Fax: (34-5) 4361058
Dir.—José Aguilar Villagrán
Ed. in Ch.—Ramón Ramos Torres
EL CORREO DE ANDALUCIA (m-ex mon.) Est. 1899
Avda. de la Prensa, 1, Polígono Industrial, Carretera Amarilla, 41007
Tel: (34-5) 4517142/(34-5) 4517911;
Fax: (34-5) 4517635
Circ.—10,292

Spain *Europe*

Dir.—Manuel Gómez Cardeña
Ed. in Ch.—Rafael Guerrero Moreno
Ed. in Ch.—Antonio Avendaño Ródenas
Ed. in Ch.—Sebastián García Casado

SORIA

DIARIO DE SORIA (Soria Daily) (d)
Morales Contreras, 2, 42003
Tel: (34-75) 212063/(34-75) 212008;
Fax: (34-75) 221504
Dir.—José Manuel Serrano Alvarez
Ed. in Ch.—Jesús Angel García García

TALAVERA DE LA REINA
(Toledo)

LA VOZ DE TAJO (The Voice of Tajo) (d)
Banderas de Castilla, 2 (entreplanta), 45600
Tel: (34-25) 812400; Fax: (34-25) 812454
Dir.—Joaquín Menéndez del Río

TARRAGONA
Pop. Est. 80,710

DIARI DE TARRAGONA (Tarragona Daily) (m-ex mon.) Est. 1939
Doménech Guansé, 2; Apdo. Postal 38, 43005
Tel: (34-77) 299700; Fax: (34-77) 223013
Circ.—7,940
Dir.—Antonio Coll i Gilabert
Ed. in Ch.—Carlos Abelló Alfonso
NOU DIARI TARRAGONA (New Tarragona Daily) (d)
Rambla Nova, 110, bajos, 43001
Tel: (34-77) 214200; Fax: (34-77) 214633
Dir.—Xavier Abelló Tomás
Dir.—Xavier Cassadó Garriga

TERRASSA
(Barcelona)

DIARI DE TERRASSA (Terrassa Daily) (5x wk.)
Galileo, 347, 08224
Tel: (34-3) 7886166/(34-3) 7886712;
Fax: (34-3) 7887458
Circ.—5,315
Pub.—Julian Sanz Soria
Dir.—Ana Muñoz Núñez
Ed. in Ch.—Ricard Rivera Aymerich
Ed. in Ch.—Pedro Millán Reyes

TERUEL
Pop. Est. 28,225

DIARIO DE TERUEL (Teruel Daily) (e-ex S) Est. 1936
Avda. de Sagunto, 27, 44002
Tel: (34-78) 601662; Fax: (34-78) 600682
Dir.—Carlos Hernández Salvador
Ed. in Ch.—Juan José Francisco Valero

TOLEDO

ABC (d)
Trinidad 5, 1.o. A, 45002
Tel: (34-25) 252923; Fax: (34-25) 252920
Ed. in Ch.—César García Serrano
EL DIA DE TOLEDO (The Day of Toledo) (d) Est. 1987
Plaza Zocodover, 7, 3.o., 45001
Tel: (34-25) 221170/(34-25) 221400;
Fax: (34-25) 214065
Pres./Dir.—Santiago Mateo Sahuquillo
DIARIO 16 (Daily 16) (d)
Pasaje de Mayoral, 2 (Multicines María Cristina), 45003
Tel: (34-25) 228100; Fax: (34-25) 228114
Ed. in Ch.—Joaquín Menéndez del Río
YA (Enough) (d)
Nuncio Viejo, 3, 2.o. A, 45002
Tel: (34-25) 211150/(34-25) 211154;
Fax: (34-25) 211351
Ed. in Ch.—Miguel Angel Larriba Terrell

VALENCIA
Pop. Est. 758,738

ABC (d)
Plaza del Ayuntamiento, 19, 46002
Tel: (34-6) 3513142; Fax: (34-6) 3513769
Ed. in Ch.—Ignacio Zaragüeta Barrachina
DIARIO 16 VALENCIA (Valencia Daily 16) (d)
Avda. Reino de Valencia, 58, 1.o., Puerta 3, 46005
Tel: (34-6) 3736911; Fax: (34-6) 3736971
Dir.—Jesús Pozo Gómez
Ed. in Ch.—Francisco Romero Pérez
LEVANTE-EL MERCANTIL VALENCIANO (d) Est. 1939
Traginers, 7, 46014
Tel: (34-6) 3790800; Fax: (34-6) 3502542/(34-6) 3791676

Circ.—27,384 (m); 87,000 (S)
Prop.—Editorial Prensa Valenciana SA
Dir.—Ferrán Belda Pérez
MINI DIARIO VALENCIA (Valencia Mini Daily) (d)
Artes Gráficas, 5, entlo., 46010
Tel: (34-6) 3606662; Fax: (34-6) 3602695
Dir.—Ignacio Nebot Beltrán
LAS PROVINCIAS (The Provinces) (dS) Est. 1865
Polígono Industrial Vara de Quart, Calle Gremis, 4, 46014
Tel: (34-6) 3502211; Fax: (34-6) 3598288
Circ.—56,498 (d); 78,711 (S)
Prop.—Federico Domenech SA
Dir.—Maria Consuelo Reyna Domenech
Ed. in Ch.—Vicente Furió
Ed. in Ch.—Ricardo Bellveser Icardo
Ed. in Ch.—Baltasar Bueno Tárrega
VALENCIA MARITIMA (d)
Doctor J. J. Dómine, 5, 1.0. 1.a., 46011
Tel: (34-6) 3670721/(34-6) 3678555;
Fax: (34-6) 3563191
Dir.—Antonio Martínez Fernández

VALLADOLID
Pop. Est. 330,242

ABC (d)
Santiago, 13, 1.o. D., 47001
Tel: (34-83) 373211; Fax: (34-83) 374090
Ed. in Ch.—Manuel Erice
EL MUNDO DE VALLADOLID (The World of Valladolid) (d)
Esgueva, 13, 47003
Tel: (34-83) 421700; Fax: (34-83) 421715/(34-83) 421717
Dir.—Félix Lázaro Lázaro
EL NORTE DE CASTILLA (North of Castilla) (dS) Est. 1854
Montero Calvo, 7, 47001
Tel: (34-83) 300877/(34-83) 300955;
Fax: (34-83) 205347
Circ.—24,335 (d); 36,520 (S)
Prop.—Norte de Castilla SA
Dir.—José Jiménez Lozano
Ed. in Ch.—José Antonio Antón Reglero
Ed. in Ch.—Fernando de la Torre de la Orden
Ed. in Ch.—Isabel Barbadillo
Ed. in Ch.—Carmen Díez Gutiérrez
Ed. in Ch.—Fernando Bravo Santos

VIGO
(Pontevedra)
Pop. Est. 197,144

ATLANTICO DIARIO (Atlantic Daily) (d)
Avda. García Barbón, 106, 1.a. planta, 36201
Tel: (34-86) 227878/(34-86) 228069;
Fax: (34-86) 226941/(34-86) 226923
Dir.—Manuel Orio Avila
Ed. in Ch.—María José Blanco Tobio
DIARIO 16 DE GALICIA (Galicia Daily 16) (d)
Alcalde Lavadores, 124, 36214
Tel: (34-86) 375500/(34-86) 375200;
Fax: (34-86) 375631
Dir.—Alberto Alonso Gallego
FARO DE VIGO (d)
Colón, 30, 36201
Tel: (34-86) 453000; Fax: (34-86) 452005
Dir.—Ceferino de Blas García
Ed. in Ch.—Jesús Portela Medraño
Ed. in Ch.—José Angel Xesteria Pazos

ZAMORA
Pop. Est. 59,734

LA OPINION-EL CORREO DE ZAMORA (The Opinion-The Zamora Mail) (d)
Rúa de los Francos, 20, 49001
Tel: (34-80) 534759/(34-80) 534760;
Fax: (34-80) 523552/(34-80) 532514
Dir.—Juan Jesús Rodero Ares
Ed. in Ch.—Vicente Díez
Ed. in Ch.—Dalmiro Gavilán

ZARAGOZA
Pop. Est. 590,750

ABC (d)
San Jorge, 10, 50001
Tel: (34-76) 290061/(34-76) 290240;
Fax: (34-76) 290037
Ed. in Ch.—Alfredo Aycart Muro
EL DIA (The Day) (d)
Polígono El Portazgo, Km. 2400, Nave 24, 50011
Tel: (34-76) 703500; Fax: (34-76) 319006
DIARIO 16 ARAGON (Aragon Daily 16) (d)
Avda. Cataluña, 17, 50014
Tel: (34-76) 396767; Fax: (34-76) 294069
EL EBRO ECONOMICO (d)
Polígono Arguelas, s/n, 50012
Dir.—José Luís Andres Lacasa

HERALDO DE ARAGON (Aragon Herald) (d) Est. 1895
Paseo de la Independencia, 29, 50001
Tel: (34-76) 221858; Fax: (34-76) 238888
Circ.—49,274
Dir.—Antonio Bruned Mompeón
Ed. in Ch.—Encarna Samitier Laín
Ed. in Ch.—Alejandro Lucea Labuena
Ed. in Ch.—Luís García Bandrés
Ed. in Ch.—Joaquín Aranda Herrera
Ed. in Ch.—José Carlos Arnal Losilla
EL NUEVO DIA DE ARAGON (The New Day of Aragon) (d)
Poligono Arguelas, s/n, 50012
Tel: (34-76) 703500; Fax: (34-76) 319006
Prop.—Ediciones Del Valle SA
Dir.—Manuel Gracia Alonso
EL PERIODICO DE ARAGON (Aragon Newspaper) (d)
Polígono Pamplona, 12-14, 50004
Tel: (34-76) 700400; Fax: (34-76) 700458
Dir.—Miguel Angel Liso Tejada
Ed. in Ch.—Lola Esther Uzven
Ed. in Ch.—Juan Carlos García de Frutos

SWEDEN
Pop. Est. 8,778,461

ÄNGELHOLM
Pop. Est. 34,149

NORDVÄSTRA SKÅNES TIDNINGAR (m-7x wk.) Est. 1847
Metallgatan 8 (26283); Box 1102, 26222
Tel: (46-431) 84000; Fax: (46-431) 84400
Circ.—45,863 ABC
Prop.—Nya Wemlands-Tidningens AB
Mng. Dir./Ch. Ed.—Bennie Ohlsson

BOLLNÄS
Pop. Est. 28,094

LJUSNAN (m-6x wk.) Est. 1912
Stationsgatan 8; Box 1059, 82112
Tel: (46-278) 27500; Fax: (46-278) 27517
Circ.—15,000 ABC
Prop.—Gefle Dagblads AB
Mng. Dir.—Jan Cahling
Ch. Ed.—Börje Timerdal

BORLÄNGE
Pop. Est. 45,990

BORLÄNGE TIDNING (d-6x wk.) Est. 1885
Borgänsvägen 37; Box 29, 78121
Tel: (46-243) 64400; Fax: (46-243) 228065
Circ.—9,900 ABC
Prop.—Dalarnes Tidningar AB
Mng. Dir.—Lennart Bengtsson

BORÅS
Pop. Est. 101,766

BORÅS TIDNING (m-7x wk.) Est. 1826
Allégatan 67; Box 224, 50104
Tel: (46-33) 178000; Fax: (46-33) 178253
Circ.—59,410 ABC
Prop.—Borås Tidning AB
Mng. Dir.—Leif Hedelin
Ed.—Jan Öjmertz

EKSJÖ
Pop. Est. 18,121

SMÅLANDS-TIDNINGEN (6x wk.) Est. 1899
Stor Torget 4; Box 261, 57523
Tel: (46-381) 13200; Fax: (46-381) 12215
Circ.—36,700
Prop.—Herenco AB
Mng. Dir./Ch. Ed.—Bengt Wendle

ENKÖPING

ENKÖPINGS-POSTEN (6x wk.) Est. 1880
Vastra Ringgatan 12; Box 918, 74515
Tel: (46-171) 33200; Fax: (46-171) 34307
Circ.—12,616 ABC
Prop.—Nya Wemlands-Tidningens AB
Mng. Ed.—Sven Danielsson
Ch. Ed.—Rolf Matthies

ESKILSTUNA
Pop. Est. 88,568

ESKILSTUNA-KURIREN med STRENGNÄS TIDNING (6x wk.) Est. 1890
Rademachergatan 16; Box 120, 63102
Tel: (46-16) 156000; Fax: (46-16) 5116304/(46-16) 123906

Circ.—34,100 ABC
Prop.—Eskilstuna Kurirens Stiftelse
Mng. Dir.—Dan Lannerö
Ch. Ed.—Jerker Norin
FOLKET (m-6x wk.) Est. 1905
Rademachergatan 29; Box 368, 63105
Tel: (46-16) 127800; Fax: (46-16) 125790
Circ.—12,409 ABC
Prop.—Tidningen Folket AB
Mng. Dir.—Roland Selinder
Ch. Ed.—Rolf Svensson

FALKENBERG
Pop. Est. 37,622

HALLANDS NYHETER (6x wk.) Est. 1905
Storgatan 22, 31181
Tel: (46-346) 29000/(46-346) 29123;
Fax: (46-346) 29120
Circ.—31,100 ABC
Prop.—Centertidningar AB
Mng. Dir.—Sture Lagerberg
Ch. Ed.—Doris Gunnarsson

FALKÖPING
Pop. Est. 31,994

FALKÖPINGS TIDNING (4x wk.) Est. 1857
Landbogatan 4, 52182
Tel: (46-515) 81200; Fax: (46-515) 81815
Circ.—13,700
Prop.—Herenco AB
Mng. Dir.—Sven Wedell
Ch. Ed.—Bo Johansson

FALUN
Pop. Est. 53,748

DALA-DEMOKRATEN (6x wk.) Est. 1917
Stigaregatan 17; Box 825, 79129
Tel: (46-23) 47500; Fax: (46-23) 29115/(46-23) 29116
Circ.—27,400 ABC
Prop.—Lokala Ägare
Mng. Dir.—Leif Lundin
Ch. Ed.—Villy Bergström
FALU KURIREN (m-6x wk.) Est. 1894
Engelbrektsgatan 25; Box 265, 79126
Tel: (46-23) 93500; Fax: (46-23) 21800
Circ.—30,800 ABC
Prop.—Dalarnas Tidningar AB
Mng. Dir.—Lennart Bengtsson

GÄVLE
Pop. Est. 88,568

ARBETARBLADET (m-6x wk.) Est. 1902
Hattmakargatan 12; Box 287, 80104
Tel: (46-26) 159300; Fax: (46-26) 187521
Circ.—29,600 ABC
Prop.—Lokala Arbetarerörelsens i Gästrikland och norra Uppland
Mng. Dir.—Björn Jacobsson
Ch. Ed.—Kennet Lutti
GEFLE DAGBLAD (6x wk.) Est. 1895
Hattmakargatan 14; Box 367, 80105
Tel: (46-26) 159500; Fax: (46-26) 159710
Circ.—34,061 ABC
Prop.—Gefle Dagblads AB
Mng. Dir.—Jan Cahling
Ch. Ed.—Robert Rosén

GÖTEBORG
Pop. Est. 710,894

ARBETET NYHETERNA (6x wk.) Est. 1992
Järntorget 8; Box 66, 40121
Tel: (46-31) 609000; Fax: (46-31) 110708
Prop.—Nya Arbetet AB
Mng. Dir.—Per Bergknut
Ch. Ed.—Bertil Johansson
GÖTEBORGS-POSTEN (mS) Est. 1858
Polhemsplatsen 5, 40502
Tel: (46-31) 624000; Fax: (46-31) 157918
Circ.—276,000 (m); 312,000 (S) ABC
Prop.—Tidnings AB Stampen
Pub./Ch. Ed—Peter Hjörne
Mng. Dir.—Torgny Karlsson
U.S. Rep.—Publicitas
IDAG (7x wk.) Est. 1990
Exportgatan 2-4; Box 417, 40126
Tel: (46-31) 639000; Fax: (46-31) 528350
Circ.—172,800 (mon.-sat.); 238,500 (S) ABC
Mng. Dir.—Tommy Carlsson
Ed.—Bengt Hansson
Ad. Mgr.—Torbjoern Wittstroem
U.S. Rep.—Publicitas

HALMSTAD
Pop. Est. 80,061

HALLANDSPOSTEN AB (m-6x wk.) Est. 1850
Fiskaregatan 21; Box 144, 30181
Tel: (46-35) 147500; Fax: (46-35) 213714/(46-35) 109742

Europe **Sweden** **IV-47**

Circ.—32,900 ABC
Prop.—Liberal Press Invest
Mng. Dir.—Göran Johansson
Ch. Ed.—Sverker Emanuelsson

HÄRNÖSAND
Pop. Est. 27,446

NYA NORRLAND (6x wk.) Est. 1907
Strandgatan 4; Box 120, 87123
Tel: (46-611) 88800; Fax: (46-611) 88840
Circ.—20,932 ABC
Prop.—Västernorrlands Press AB
Mng. Dir.—Bertil Astby
Ch. Ed.—Per Åhlstrom
VÄSTERNORRLANDS ALLEHANDA (m-6x wk.)
Est. 1874
Nybrogatan 13; Box 208, 87124
Tel: (46-611) 15000; Fax: (46-611) 15142/(46-611) 15498
Circ.—15,800 ABC
Prop.—Högerns Förlagsshftelse
Mng. Dir.—Per Fahlquist
Ed.—Bo Östman

HÄSSLEHOLM
Pop. Est. 49,106

NORRA SKANE (m-6x wk.) Est. 1899
Väpnarestigen 6, 28181
Tel: (46-451) 14200; Fax: (46-451) 12622
Circ.—26,107 ABC
Prop.—Kristianstad läns lantmäns tryckeriförening
Mng. Dir.—Bengt-Åke Adolfsson
Ch. Ed.—Yngve Sunesson

HEDEMORA

SÖDRA DALARNES TIDNING (6x wk.) Est. 1882
Fredsgatan 5; Box 42, 77621
Tel: (46-225) 12100; Fax: (46-225) 10190
Circ.—6,300 ABC
Prop.—Dalarnes Tidningar AB
Mng. Dir.—Lennart Bengtsson

HELSINGBORG
Pop. Est. 109,267

HELSINGBORGS DAGBLAD (mS) Est. 1867
Vasatorpsvägen 1; Box 822, 25108
Tel: (46-42) 175000; Fax: (46-42) 175195
Circ.—51,600 (m); 51,600 (S) ABC
Prop.—Helsingborgs Dagblad AB
Mng. Dir.—Lars Svensson
Ch. Ed.—Sven-Åke Olofsson

HUDIKSVALL
Pop. Est. 38,328

HUDIKSVALLS TIDNING (med HÄLSINGLANDS TIDNING) (m-6x wk.) Est. 1909
Västra Tullgatan 18-20; Box 1201, 82415
Tel: (46-650) 15400; Fax: (46-650) 15610
Circ.—19,000 ABC
Prop.—Centertidningar AB
Mng. Dir.—Bengt Ekelund
Ch. Ed.—Jörgen Bengtson

JÖNKÖPING
Pop. Est. 111,486

JÖNKÖPING-POSTEN/SMALANDS ALLEHANDA (6x wk.) Est. 1865
Skolgatan 24, 55180
Tel: (46-36) 304050; Fax: (46-36) 122715
Circ.—44,700
Prop.—Herenco AB
Mng. Dir./Ch. Ed.—Stig Fredriksson

KALMAR
Pop. Est. 56,206

BAROMETERN och OSKARSHAMNS-TIDNINGEN (6x wk.) Est. 1841
PO Box 620, 39237
Tel: (46-480) 59100; Fax: (46-480) 24406/(46-480) 29763
Circ.—51,340 ABC
Prop.—Stift Barometern/Sydostpress AB
Pub./Ch. Ed.—Anders Wendelberg
Mng. Dir.—Tomas Arvidsson
ÖSTRA SMÅLAND/NYHETERNA (6x wk.) Est. 1928/1860
Amerikavägen 1; Box 612, 39126
Tel: (46-480) 61300; Fax: (46-480) 87545
Circ.—13,000 (Östra); 6,600 (Nyheterna) ABC
Prop.—Avisa AB
Prop.—Soms ägs av Rospress AB
Mng. Dir.—Thomas Karlsson
Ch. Ed.—Thore Arnström
Ch. Ed.—Jan G Andersson

KARLSKOGA
Pop. Est. 33,869

KARLSKOGA TIDNING (6x wk.) Est. 1883
Anders Ersgatan 3; Box 407, 69127
Tel: (46-586) 36400; Fax: (46-586) 36405
Circ.—10,500 ABC
Prop.—NWT-Koncernen
Ch. Ed.—Hans Jansson

KARLSKRONA
Pop. Est. 59,054

BLEKINGE LÄNS TIDNING (m-6x wk.) Est. 1869
Landbrogatan 15, 37189
Tel: (46-455) 77000; Fax: (46-455) 13765
Circ.—33,000 ABC
Prop.—Stiftelsen Barometern
Mng. Dir.—Pär Fagerström
Ch. Ed.—Lennart Hjelmstedt
SYDÖSTRAN SYDÖSTRA SVERIGES DAGBLAD (m-6x wk.) Est. 1903
Landbrogatan 17, 37188
Tel: (46-455) 19000; Fax: (46-455) 12403/(46-455) 12596
Circ.—23,600 ABC
Prop.—Avisa AB
Mng. Dir.—Ulf Hellberg
Ch. Ed.—Häkan Quisth

KARLSTAD
Pop. Est. 76,467

NYA WERMLANDS-TIDNINGEN (m-6x wk.) Est. 1907
Herrgårdsgatan 13-15; Box 28, 65102
Tel: (46-54) 199000; Fax: (46-54) 199100
Circ.—72,100 ABC
Prop.—Nya Wermlands-Tidningens AB
Mng. Dir.—Lars G Ander
Ch. Ed.—Staffan E Ander
VÄRMLANDS FOLKBLAD (m- 6x wk.) Est. 1918
Säterivägen 7; Box 67, 65103
Tel: (46-54) 190500; Fax: (46-54) 190110/(46-54) 187931
Circ.—27,600
Prop.—Varmlands Tidningsintressenters AB
Mng. Dir.—Sune Lundh
Ch. Ed.—Rolf H Jansson

KATRINEHOLM
Pop. Est. 32,764

KATRINEHOLMS-KURIREN (m-6x wk.) Est. 1917
Köpmangatan 2; Box 111, 64122
Tel: (46-150) 72800; Fax: (46-150) 53500/(46-150) 53900
Circ.—13,300 ABC
Prop.—Katrineholms-Kurirens Stiftelse
Mng. Dir.—Dan Lannerö
Ed.—Lorentz Hedman

KÖPING
Pop. Est. 26,444

BÄRGSLAGSBLADET/ARBOGA TIDNING (d-5x wk.) Est. 1890
Västra Länggatan 11; Box 120, 73123
Tel: (46-221) 18400; Fax: (46-221) 10214/(46-221) 15406
Circ.—15,500
Prop.—Vestmanlands läns tidning
Mng. Dir./Ch. Ed.—Kent Karlsson

KRISTIANSTAD
Pop. Est. 71,750

KRISTIANSTADSBLADET (6x wk.) Est. 1856
Västra Vallgatan 2; Box 537, 29125
Tel: (46-44) 185500; Fax: (46-44) 126276
Circ.—32,300
Prop.—Kristianstadsbladets Tryckeri AB
Mng. Dir.—Nils Erik Larsson

LAHOLM
Pop. Est. 22,661

LAHOLMS TIDNING (m-6x wk.) Est. 1931
Hästtorget 5; Box 70, 31221
Tel: (46-430) 10300/(46-430) 11111; Fax: (46-430) 13532
Circ.—4,900 ABC
Prop.—Föreningen Laholms Tidning upa
Mng. Dir.—Karl-Olof Rosengren

LINDESBERG
Pop. Est. 24,663

BERGSLAGSPOSTEN (6x wk.) Est. 1892
Järnvägsgatan 8, 71181
Tel: (46-581) 84400; Fax: (46-581) 84441
Circ.—11,200
Prop.—Nerikes Allehanda AB
Mng. Dir.—Lennart Ohlsson-Leijon
Ch. Ed.—Ingemar Anderson

LINKÖPING
Pop. Est. 122,268

ÖSTGÖTA CORRESPONDENTEN (m-6x wk.) Est. 1838
Badhusgatan 5, 58189
Tel: (46-13) 280000; Fax: (46-13) 115715
Circ.—66,400 ABC
Prop.—Släkten Ridderstad
Mng. Dir.—Jan Åndell
Ed.—Ernst Klein
ÖSTGÖTEN (6x wk.) Est. 1872
Kungsgatan 41 A; Box 330, 58103
Tel: (46-13) 249400; Fax: (46-13) 141194
Circ.—5,800 ABC
Prop.—Nya Östgöten i Linköping AB
Mng. Dir.—Janne Berglund
Ch. Ed.—Mark Olson

LJUNGBY
Pop. Est. 27,490

SMÅLÄNNINGEN (5x wk.) Est. 1921
Storgatan 32; Box 304, 34126
Tel: (46-372) 12430; Fax: (46-372) 80022/(46-372) 82168
Circ.—14,623 ABC
Prop.—Herenco AB
Mng. Dir.—Sven Durango

LJUSDAL
Pop. Est. 21,163

LJUSDALS-POSTEN (e-4x wk.) Est. 1914
Södra Järnvägsgatan 52B; Box 707, 82725
Tel: (46-651) 13360; Fax: (46-651) 11090/(46-651) 14815
Circ.—8,500 ABC
Prop.—Ljusdals-Posten AB
Mng. Dir.—Lars Svender
Ch. Ed.—Tage Ohlsson

LUDVIKA

NYA LUDVIKA TIDNING (m-6x wk.) Est. 1993
Carlavägen 14; Box 223, 77125
Tel: (46-240) 88200; Fax: (46-240) 88220
Circ.—10,400 ABC
Prop.—Dalarnes Tidningar AB
Prop.—Nerikes Allehanda
Ch. Ed.—Karin Rosencrantz Bergdahl

LULEA
Pop. Est. 68,412

NORRBOTTENS-KURIREN (6x wk.) Est. 1861
Stationsgatan 36, 97181
Tel: (46-920) 37500; Fax: (46-920) 37600
Circ.—31,700 ABC
Prop.—Luleå Boktryckeri AB
Mng. Dir.—Stellan Minnhagen
Ch. Ed.—PeO Wärring
NORRLÄNDSKA SOCIALDEMOKRATEN (m-6x wk.) Est. 1919
Robertsviksgatan 5, 97183
Tel: (46-920) 36000/(46-920) 69810; Fax: (46-920) 89210
Circ.—42,800 ABC
Prop.—Valrossen AB
Mng. Dir.—Christer Lindfors
Ch. Ed.—Lennart Håkansson

LYSEKIL
Pop. Est. 15,197

LYSEKILSPOSTEN (e-4x wk.) Est. 1905
Rosviksgatan 9, 45300
Tel: (46-523) 14050; Fax: (46-523) 14978
Circ.—4,000 ABC
Prop.—Lysekils Nya Tryckeri AB
Mng. Dir./Ch. Ed.—Helge Gustafzon

MALMÖ
Pop. Est. 475,224

ARBETET (mS) Est. 1887
Bergsgatan 20; Box 125, 20121
Tel: (46-40) 205000; Fax: (46-40) 72265
Circ.—114,677 (m); 104,653 (S) ABC
Prop.—Official Journal of the Labour Party
Ch. Ed.—Anders Ferm
Ad. Mgr.—Magnus Stahl
IDAG GT KVALLSPOSTEN (eS) Est. 1948
Tel: (46-40) 281600; Fax: (46-40) 939567
Circ.—82,200 (e); 109,800 (S)
Prop.—Kvallspostens AB
Ed.—Bengt Hansson
IDAG SYG (eS)
Idag AB, 20526
Tel: (46-40) 281732; Fax: (46-40) 939567
Circ.—86,800 (e); 113,700 (S)

SKÅNSKA DAGBLADET (e-7x wk.) Est. 1888
Östergatan 11; Box 165, 20121
Tel: (46-40) 73800; Fax: (46-40) 70445
Circ.—30,000 (mon.-sat.); 30,000 (S)
Prop.—Skånska Dagbladet AB
Mng. Dir.—Richard Kling
Ch. Ed.—Jan A Johansson
SYDSVENSKA DAGBLADET SNAELLPOSTEN (mS) Est. 1848
PO Box 145, 20121
Tel: (46-40) 281200; Fax: (46-40) 281460
Circ.—121,000 (m); 140,900 (S)
Ad. Mgr.—Imge Gyllin
U.S. Rep.—Publicitas
SYDSVENSKAN (mS) Est. 1848
Krusegaten 19, 20505
Tel: (46-40) 281200; Fax: (46-40) 935476
Circ.—121,000 (m); 140,900 (S) ABC
Prop.—Sydsvenska Dagbladets AB
Mng. Dir.—Håkan Sechlstedt
Ch. Ed.—Jan Wifstrand
Ed.—Per T Ohlsson

MARIESTAD
Pop. Est. 24,682

MARIESTADS-TIDNINGEN (m-5x wk.) Est. 1817
Stockholmsvägen 21; Box 242, 54223
Tel: (46-501) 68700; Fax: (46-501) 16700/(46-501) 77558
Circ.—14,300 ABC
Prop.—Tidning för Skaraborgs Lan AB
Mng. Dir.—Hans Andersson
Ch. Ed.—Olle Karlsson

MOTALA
Pop. Est. 41,994

MOTALA TIDNING med VADSTENA TIDNING (m-6x wk.) Est. 1926
Industrigatan 9; Box 945, 59129
Tel: (46-141) 16390; Fax: (46-141) 58868
Circ.—13,000 ABC
Prop.—Liberela Tidningar Kommanditbolag
Mng. Dir.—Lennart Ohlsson-Leijon
Ed.—Sven Slotter

NORRKÖPING
Pop. Est. 120,522

FOLKBLADET i NORRKÖPING (6x wk.) Est. 1905
Idrottsgaten 12, 60184
Tel: (46-11) 186420; Fax: (46-11) 124841
Circ.—12,500 ABC
Prop.—Nya Folkbladet Östgöten AB
Mng. Dir.—Janne Berglund
NORRKÖPINGS TIDNINGAR (6x wk.) Est. 1758
Stohagsgatan 2; Box 402, 60183
Tel: (46-11) 200000; Fax: (46-11) 200140
Circ.—50,100
Prop.—Erik och Asta Sundins Stiftelse
Mng. Dir.—Sven H Ericson
Ed.—Karl-Ake Bredenberg

NORRTÄLJE
Pop. Est. 46,165

NORRTÄLJE TIDNING (5x wk.) Est. 1800
Tibeliusgatan 1, 76184
Tel: (46-176) 79500; Fax: (46-176) 10008/(46-176) 11287
Circ.—14,100 ABC
Prop.—Centertidningar AB
Mng. Dir.—Sören Karlsson
Ch. Ed.—Carl-Erik Nilsson

NYKÖPING
Pop. Est. 65,908

SÖDERMANLANDS NYHETER (6x wk.) Est. 1893
S:t Annegatan 3, 61129
Tel: (46-155) 76700; Fax: (46-155) 268801
Circ.—24,500 ABC
Prop.—Centertidningar AB
Mng. Dir.—Tommy Ljung
Ch. Ed.—Lars J Erikkson

ÖREBRO
Pop. Est. 120,944

NERIKES ALLEHANDA (m-ex S) Est. 1843
Norra Strandgatan 5; Box 1603, 70116
Tel: (46-19) 155000; Fax: (46-19) 115485
Circ.—70,880 ABC
Prop.—Liberala Tidningar KB
Ed.—Olle Goldkuhl
Ad. Dir.—Gosta Goldkuhl
ÖREBRO-KURIREN, KARLSKOGA-KURIREN (6x wk.) Est. 1902
Hagmarksgatan 56; Box 1703, 70117
Tel: (46-19) 305300; Fax: (46-19) 305360

Circ.—12,600 ABC
Prop.—Örebro Press AB
Mng. Dir.—Jerry Wiklund
Ch. Ed.—Helle Klein

ÖRNSKÖLDSVIK
Pop. Est. 59,379

ÖRNSKÖLDSVIKS ALLEHANDA (m-6x wk.) Est. 1894
Centralgatan 18; Box 110, 89123
Tel: (46-660) 10060; Fax: (46-660) 14585
Circ.—22,200 ABC
Prop.—Sundvalls Tidning AB
Mng. Dir.—Erik Anund Hallin
Ch. Ed.—Jerry Erixon

ÖSTERSUND
Pop. Est. 58,317

LÄNSTIDNINGEN, ÖSTERSUND (m-6x wk.) Est. 1924
Rådhusgatan 37, 83189
Tel: (46-63) 155500; Fax: (46-63) 102060/(46-63) 155595
Circ.—29,300 ABC
Prop.—Näringslivet SAP
Prop.—Jämtpubliktioner AB
Mng. Dir.—Lars Tengqvist
Ch. Ed.—Christer Sjöstrom
Ch. Ed.—Peter Swedenmark
ÖSTERSUNDS-POSTEN (m-6x wk.) Est. 1877
Kyrkgatan 52; Box 720, 83128
Tel: (46-63) 161600; Fax: (46-63) 111100
Circ.—29,400
Prop.—Centertidningar AB
Mng. Dir.—Jesper Kärrbrink
Ch. Ed.—Håkan Larsson

PITEÅ
Pop. Est. 40,034

PITEÅ-TIDNINGEN (m-6x wk.) Est. 1915
Hamnplan 5; Box 193, 94124
Tel: (46-911) 64500; Fax: (46-911) 64640
Circ.—19,000 ABC
Prop.—Piteå-Tidningens AB
Mng. Dir.—Anna-Stina Nordmark Nilsson
Ch. Ed.—Lennart Lindgren

SALA
Pop. Est. 21,820

SALA ALLEHANDA-ÖSTRA LÄNSTIDNINGEN (6x wk.) Est. 1879
Aquéligatan 9; Box 303, 73325
Tel: (46-224) 13330; Fax: (46-224) 14417
Circ.—10,700
Prop.—Vestmanlands Läns Tidnings AB
Mng. Dir./Ch. Ed.—Kent Karlsson

SKARA
Pop. Est. 18,689

SKARABORGS LÄNS TIDNING (m-6x wk.) Est. 1884
Skaraborgsgatan 17; Box 214, 53223
Tel: (46-511) 13010; Fax: (46-511) 13702/(46-511) 17402
Circ.—19,000 ABC
Prop.—Herenco AB
Mng. Dir.—Sven Wedell
Ch. Ed.—Hans Menzing

SKELLEFTEÅ
Pop. Est. 75,258

NORRA VÄSTERBOTTEN (6x wk.) Est. 1910
Kanalgatan 59; Box 58, 93121
Tel: (46-910) 14000; Fax: (46-910) 56513/(46-910) 56543
Circ.—33,593 ABC
Prop.—Stiftelsen Skellefteapress
Mng. Dir.—Cal Wikström
Ed.—Stig Ericsson

SKÖVDE
Pop. Est. 47,259

SKARABORG LÄNS ALLEHANDA (m-6x wk.) Est. 1884
Garpastigen 3; Box 407, 54128
Tel: (46-500) 467500; Fax: (46-500) 480582
Circ.—24,263 ABC
Prop.—Nya Wermlands-Tidningens AB
Mng. Dir.—Hans Andersson
Ch. Ed.—Måns Johnson
SKÖVDE NYHETER (m-6x wk.) Est. 1906
Torggatan 16; Box 409, 54128
Tel: (46-500) 485000; Fax: (46-500) 483848/(46-500) 484611

Circ.—9,600 ABC
Prop.—Skövde Nyheter HB
Mng. Dir.—Hans Mörée
Ch. Ed.—Christer Svensson

SÖDERHAMN
Pop. Est. 29,624

HÄLSINGE KURIREN (6x wk.) Est. 1895
Brädgårdsgatan 6; Box 514, 82627
Tel: (46-270) 74000; Fax: (46-270) 10325/(46-270) 12807
Circ.—11,600 ABC
Prop.—Halsinge-Kuriren AB
Mng. Dir.—Kent Lundquist
Ed.—Soren Thunell

SODERTALJE
Pop. Est. 81,786

LANSTIDNINGEN (6x wk.) Est. 1861
Bergviksgatan 16-18; Box 226, 15123
Tel: (46-8) 55092100; Fax: (46-8) 55087772
Circ.—18,700 ABC
Prop.—Centertidningar AB
Mng. Dir.—Bo Andersson
Ch. Ed.—Torsten Carlsson

STENUNGSUND

STENUNGSUNDS-POSTEN med ORUST-TJÖRN (4x wk.) Est. 1978
Norra vägen 6; Box 198, 44423
Tel: (46-303) 81919; Fax: (46-303) 81919
Circ.—2,200 ABC
Mng. Dir./Ch. Ed.—Helge Gustafzon

STOCKHOLM
Pop. Est. 1,491,726

AFTONBLADET (eS) Est. 1830
Vattngatan 12, 10518
Tel: (46-8) 7252000; Fax: (46-8) 600182
Circ.—371,000 (e); 458,000 (S) ABC
Prop.—Aftonbladet Hierta AB
Ed.—Rolf Alsing
Ed.—Thorbjörn Larsson
Ad. Mgr.—Mart Nurle
DAGEN (The Daily News) (m-5x wk.) Est. 1945
Gammelgårdsvägen 38, 10536
Tel: (46-8) 6192400; Fax: (46-8) 6566051/(46-8) 6567852
Circ.—22,163 ABC
Prop.—Dagen-gruppen AB
Ed.—Olle Nordahl
Ch. Ed.—Olof Djurfeldt
DAGENS INDUSTRI (Industry Today) (m-6x wk.) Est. 1976
Holländargatan 13; Box 3177, 10363
Tel: (46-8) 7365000; Fax: (46-8) 7898867
Circ.—90,100 ABC
Prop.—Dagens Industri AB
Ed. in Ch.—Hasse Olsson
Ad. Mgr.—Soren Summo
U.S. Rep.—Nielsen Communications
DAGENS NYHETER (mS) Est. 1864
Rålambsvägen 17, 10515
Tel: (46-8) 7381000; Fax: (46-8) 6190790
Circ.—389,904 (m); 446,675 (S)
Prop.—Dagens Nyheters AB
Ed.—Christina Jutterstrom
Ad. Mgr.—Lars-Gosta Julin
U.S. Rep.—Publicitas
EXPRESSEN (eS) Est. 1944
Gjörwellsgatan 30, 10516
Tel: (46-8) 7383000; Fax: (46-8) 6190050
Circ.—491,400 (e); 646,300 (S) ABC
Prop.—Kvällstidningen Expressen AB
Ed.—Erik Maansson
Ad. Mgr.—Stefan Sebo
U.S. Rep.—Publicitas
FINANS TIDNINGEN (Financial Times) (5x wk.) Est. 1989
Kungsgatan 18; Box 70347, 10723
Tel: (46-8) 6774500/(46-8) 6774580; Fax: (46-8) 6774581
Circ.—8,800 ABC
Prop.—Sveriges Finansnyheter AB
Mng. Dir.—Raoul Grünthal
POST-OCH INRIKES TIDNINGAR (5x wk.) Est. 1645
Barnängsgatan 21; Box 4731, 11692
Tel: (46-8) 7028050; Fax: (46-8) 6427345
Circ.—3,000 ABC
Prop.—Norstedts Tryckeri AB
Mng. Dir.—Rolf Bäcklund
Ch. Ed.—Hans Holm
SVENSKA DAGBLADET (mS) Est. 1884
Gjörwellsgatan 28, 10517
Tel: (46-8) 135000; Fax: (46-8) 135730

Circ.—227,446 (m); 239,520 (S) ABC
Prop.—Svenska Dagbladets AB & Co.
Mng. Dir.—Sven Höök
Ch. Ed.—Mats Svegfors

SUNDSVALL
Pop. Est. 93,808

DAGBLADET/NYA SAMHÄLLET (6x wk.) Est. 1900
Köpmangatan 1; Box 446, 85106
Tel: (46-60) 157570; Fax: (46-60) 611150
Circ.—11,300 ABC
Prop.—Västernorrlands Press AB
Mng. Dir.—Bertil Astby
Ch. Ed.—Per Åhlström
SUNDSVALLS TIDNING (m-7x wk.) Est. 1841
Träsgårdsgatan 27-29, 85172
Tel: (46-60) 197000; Fax: (46-60) 122217
Circ.—40,600 (mon.-sat.); 44,300 (S) ABC
Prop.—Sundsvalls Tidnings AB
Mng. Dir.—Rolf Jonsson
Ch. Ed.—Kjell Carnbro
Ad. Mgr.—Bernt Nystrom

TIDAHOLM
Pop. Est. 13,283

VÄSTGÖTA-BLADET (4x wk.) Est. 1905
Villagatan 1; Box 302, 52226
Tel: (46-502) 10001/(46-502) 15010; Fax: (46-502) 10122
Circ.—5,300 ABC
Prop.—Herenco AB
Mng. Dir.—Sven Wedell
Ed.—Per-Erik Vrang

TRANÅS
Pop. Est. 17,806

TRÅNAS-POSTEN (m-6x wk.) Est. 1918
Kanalgatan 3; Box 1020, 57328
Tel: (46-140) 53020; Fax: (46-140) 12111
Circ.—900
Prop.—Gamla TP AB
Pub./Ed.—Jan Justegard

TRELLEBORG
Pop. Est. 35,997

TRELLEBORGS ALLEHANDA (m-6x wk.) Est. 1876
Algatan 27; Box 73, 23121
Tel: (46-410) 54500; Fax: (46-410) 17410/(46-410) 17100
Circ.—10,500 ABC
Prop.—Allehandagruppen
Mng. Dir.—Håkan Swärd
Ch. Ed.—Mats Wickström

TROLLHATTAN
Pop. Est. 51,047

TROLLHÄTTANS TIDNING och LILLA EDET POSTEN (m-5x wk.) Est. 1906
Staveredsgatan 18; Box 54, 46122
Tel: (46-520) 12670; Fax: (46-520) 10439
Circ.—17,600 ABC
Prop.—Vestmanlands Läns Tidning AB
Mng. Dir.—Björn Öhlin
Ch. Ed.—Torbjörn Håkansson

UDDEVALLA
Pop. Est. 47,345

BOHUSLÄNINGEN/DALS DAGBLAD (m-6x wk.) Est. 1878
Norra Drottninggatan 19-21, 45183
Tel: (46-552) 99200; Fax: (46-522) 19634/(46-522) 19644
Circ.—36,200 ABC
Prop.—Bohusläningens AB
Mng. Dir.—Bo Andréasson
Ch. Ed.—Ulf Johansson

UMEÅ
Pop. Est. 91,258

VÄSTERBOTTENS FOLKBLAD (m-6x wk.) Est. 1917
Formvägen 16; Box 6104, 90604
Tel: (46-90) 170000; Fax: (46-90) 170250
Circ.—20,600 ABC
Prop.—Nya Västerbottens Folkblad AB
Mng. Dir.—Hans Boström
Ch. Ed.—Lennart Andersson
VÄSTERBOTTENS-KURIREN (m-6x wk.) Est. 1900
Förrådsvägen 9, 90170
Tel: (46-90) 151000; Fax: (46-90) 114647
Circ.—45,500 ABC
Prop.—Stiftelsen VK-press
Mng. Dir.—Bert-Åke Hällberg
Ch. Ed.—Olof Kleberg
Ch. Ed.—Lars Westerlund

UPPSALA
Pop. Est. 167,508

UPSALA NYA TIDNING (m-ex S) Est. 1890
Danmarksgatan 28; Box 36, 75103
Tel: (46-18) 170000; Fax: (46-18) 129507
Circ.—65,400 ABC
Prop.—Uppsala Nya Tidning AB
Pub.—Svante Thorell
Ch. Ed.—Jörgen Ullenhag
Ad. Mgr.—Soren Axelsson

VÄNERSBORG

ELFSBORGS LÄNS ALLEHANDA (5x wk.) Est. 1885
Kyrkogatan 10; Box 111, 46222
Tel: (46-521) 13940; Fax: (46-521) 62833
Circ.—14,300 ABC
Prop.—Tvastads Tidnings AB
Mng. Dir.—Björn Öhlin
Ch. Ed.—Torbjörn Håakansson

VÄRNAMO
Pop. Est. 31,315

VÄRNAMO NYHETER (m-4x wk.) Est. 1930
Storgatsbacken 13, 33184
Tel: (46-370) 301950; Fax: (46-370) 18251/(46-370) 19110
Circ.—25,300 ABC
Prop.—Herenco AB
Mng. Dir./Ch. Ed.—Sven Lindström

VÄSTERÅS
Pop. Est. 119,761

VESTMANLANDS LÄNS TIDNING (m-6x wk.) Est. 1831
Slottsgatan 27; Box 3, 72103
Tel: (46-21) 199000; Fax: (46-21) 199226/(46-21) 415641
Circ.—50,400 ABC
Prop.—Vestmanlands Läns Tidnings AB
Mng. Dir./Ch. Ed.—Anders Harald Pers

VÄSTERVIK
Pop. Est. 39,908

VÄSTERVIKS-TIDNINGEN (m-6x wk.) Est. 1834
Timmergatan 6, 59382
Tel: (46-490) 66600; Fax: (46-490) 66699
Circ.—13,300 ABC
Prop.—Erik och Asta Sundins Stiftelse
Mng. Dir.—Sven H Ericson
Ch. Ed.—Bertil Andersson

VÄXJÖ
Pop. Est. 69,547

SMÅLANDSPOSTEN (m-6x wk.) Est. 1866
Storgatan 1 (35170); Box 63, 35103
Tel: (46-470) 770500; Fax: (46-470) 48425
Circ.—42,400 ABC
Prop.—Stiftelsen Barometern genom Sydostpress AB
Mng. Dir.—Björn-Fredrick Tollin
Ed.—Kjell Svensson

VIMMERBY
Pop. Est. 15,867

VIMMERBY TIDNING/KINDA-POSTEN (m-6x wk.) Est. 1865
Stångågatan 46, 59880
Tel: (46-492) 16000; Fax: (46-492) 10102/(46-492) 14102
Circ.—11,600 ABC
Prop.—Vimmerby Tidnings och Tryckeri för Tryckeriforening upa
Mng. Dir./Ch. Ed.—Bengt Ingemarsson

VISBY (Gotland)
Pop. Est. (Gotland) 57,108

GOTLANDS ALLEHANDA (6x wk.) Est. 1872
Brovåg 21; Box 1284, 62123
Tel: (46-498) 202500; Fax: (46-498) 217997
Circ.—12,300 ABC
Prop.—Högens Förlagsstiftelse och Stiftelsen Gotlandspressen
Mng. Dir.—Lars Herlin
Ch. Ed.—Göran Mattsson
GOTLANDS TIDNINGAR (m-6x wk.) Est. 1983
Brovåg 10; Box 1223, 62123
Tel: (46-498) 215230; Fax: (46-498) 215080
Circ.—13,100 ABC
Prop.—Gotlands Tidningar AB
Mng. Dir.—Gunnar Öberg
Ch. Ed.—Hans E Andersson
Ch. Ed.—Håkan Ericsson

YSTAD
Pop. Est. 24,999

YSTADS ALLEHANDA (m-6x wk.) Est. 1873
Lilla Norregatan 9, 27181

Tel: (46-411) 64500; Fax: (46-411) 13955/(46-411) 16085
Circ.—24,600 ABC
Prop.—Allehanda Syd AB
Mng. Dir.—Håkan Swärd
Ch. Ed.—Staffan Björnberg

SWITZERLAND
Pop. Est. 7,040,119

AARAU
(Aargau)
Pop. Est. 504,547

AARGAUER TAGBLATT (6x wk.) German; Est. 1846
Bahnhofstrasse 39; Postfach 2103, 5001
Tel: (41-64) 266161; Fax: (41-64) 266376/(41-64) 266398
Circ.—57,338
Prop.—Aargauer Tagblatt AG
Pub.—Walter Widmer
Ch. Ed.—Dr. Franz Straub
Ch. Ed.—Hermann Rauber

FREIER AARGAUER (5x wk.) German; Est. 1846
Bahnhofstrasse 35, 5001
Circ.—4,800
Prop.—Sozialdemokratische Presseunion des Kantons Aarau

ALTDORF

URNER ZEITUNG (6x wk.) German
Herrengasse 2, 6460
Tel: (41-44) 20114; Fax: (41-44) 21059
Ed. in Ch.—Bruno Arnold

ALTSTAETTEN
(St. Gallen)
Pop. Est. 9,556

RHEINTALISCHE VOLKSZEITUNG (The Rhein Valley People's News) (6x wk.) German; Est. 1854
Kesselbachstrasse 40; PF 9450
Tel: (41-71) 751291; Fax: (41-71) 756062
Circ.—5,679
Prop.—Rheintalische Volkszeitung AG
Ed. in Ch.—Thomas Schwizer

ARBON
(Thurgau)
Pop. Est. 12,293

SCHWEIZERISCHE BODENSEE ZEITUNG (6x wk.) German; Est. 1849
Romanshornerstrasse 36, 9320
Tel: (41-71) 465121; Fax: (41-71) 465126
Circ.—15,874
Prop.—A Hug & Co. AG
Prop.—Schweizerische Bodensee-Zeitung AG
Dir.—G Hug
Ch. Ed.—Patrick Hug

BADEN
(Aargau)
Pop. Est. 14,058

AARGAUER VOLKSBLATT (d-6x wk.) German; Est. 1911
Stadtturmstrasse 19, 5401
Tel: (41-56) 225507; Fax: (41-56) 228152
Circ.—9,240
Prop.—Buchdruckerei Baden AG
Ed.—Othmar Mueller

BADENER TAGBLATT German; Est. 1849
Stadtturmstrasse 19, 5401
Tel: (41-56) 216161; Fax: (41-56) 222390
Circ.—103,288
Prop.—Velag Druckerei Wanner AG
Pub.—Dr. Otto Wanner
Pub.—Peter Wanner
Ch. Ed.—Hans Fahrlander

BASEL
(Basel-Stadt)
Pop. Est. 193,512

BASLER AZ/ABENDZEITUNG AZ (Basler AZ/The Evening News) (e-6x wk.) German
Hochbergerstrasse 15, 4002
Tel: (41-61) 6391111; Fax: (41-61) 6311582
Circ.—117,417

Prop.—Volksdruckerei Basel
Ch. Ed.—Hans-Peter Platz

BASLER ZEITUNG (The Basel News) (6x wk.) German; Est. 1842
Hochbergerstrasse 15, 4002
Tel: (41-61) 6391111; Fax: (41-61) 6311582
Circ.—117,000
Prop.—National-Zeitung/Basler Nachrichten AG
Pub.—Martin Hicklin
Ed. in Ch.—Hans-Peter Platz
U.S. Rep.—Publicitas

BASLERSTAB (6x wk.)
Schlüsselberg 4, 4001
Tel: (41-61) 2616161; Fax: (41-61) 2616786
Circ.—105,000
Prop.—Verlag Inserateunion AG
Ch. Ed.—Susanna Grüninger-Horber

NORDSCHWEIZ/BASLER VOLKSBLATT (6x wk.) German; Est. 1873
Petersgasse 34, 4001
Tel: (41-61) 2618166; Fax: (41-61) 2610481
Circ.—32,727
Prop.—Cratander AG
Pub.—M Thurlemann
Die.—O Amrein
Ed. in Ch.—Klaus Kocher

BASSERSDORF
(Zurich)
Pop. Est. 4,241

ZÜRCHER UNTERLÄNDER (d-6x wk.) German; Est. 1948
Tel: (41-1) 8366555; Fax: (41-1) 8364285
Circ.—18,255
Prop.—H Akeret Druck/Verlag AG
Ed. in Ch.—Christine Fivian

BELLINZONA
(Ticini)
Pop. Est. 16,886

IL DOVERE (6x wk.) Italian; Est. 1878
Ghiringhelli 9, 6501
Tel: (41-92) 262252; Fax: (41-92) 262713
Circ.—20,578
Prop.—Arti Grafiche SA
Dir.—Giuseppe Buffi

POPOLO E LIBERTA (6x wk.) Italian; Est. 1901
via GM Bouzanigo 6, 6500
Circ.—4,900
Prop.—Tipografia La Buona Stampa
Ed. in Ch.—Saverio Snider

LA REGIONE (The Region) (d-6x wk.) Italian
via Ghiringhelli, 6500
Tel: (41-92) 262252; Fax: (41-92) 263461/ (41-92) 263462
Circ.—33,578
Dir.—Monica Piffaretti
(Circulation figure combines with Il Dovere & Echo di Locarno.)

BERNE
Pop. Est. 952,595

BERNER TAGWACHT/SEELANDER VOLKSZEITUNG (6x wk.) German; Est. 1894
Monbijoustrasse 61; PF 5436, 3001
Tel: (41-31) 3716658; Fax: (41-31) 3715738
Circ.—10,029
Prop.—Berner Tagwacht AG
Pub./Ed. in Ch.—Richard Mueller

BERNER ZEITUNG BZ (6x wk.) German; Est. 1844
Dammweg 9, 3001
Tel: (41-31) 3303111; Fax: (41-31) 3327724
Circ.—128,333
Ch. Ed.—Beat Hurni

DER BUND (6x wk.) German; Est. 1850
Bubenbergplatz 8, 3001
Tel: (41-31) 3851111; Fax: (41-31) 3851112
Circ.—60,916
Prop.—Der Bund Verlag und Druckerei AG
Ch. Ed.—Dr. Peter Ziegler
U.S. Rep.—Publicitas

JOURNAL DU JURA (6x wk.) French
135 Chemin du Long-Champ, 2501
Tel: (41-32) 428111; Fax: (41-32) 428332
Circ.—16,000
Ed. in Ch.—Mario Sessa
Ed.—Pierre-Alain Brenzikofer
Ed.—Catherine Favre
Ed.—Aldo Rustichelli

Europe **Switzerland** **IV-49**

Ed.—Rene Villars
Ed.—Jean-Francois Krähenbühl
Ed.—Oliviėr Odiet
Ed.—Daniel Bachmann

SCHWEIZERISCHES HANDELSAMTSBLATT (6x wk.) German, French & Italian; Est. 1883
Effingerstrasse 1, 3001
Tel: (41-31) 612221; Fax: (41-31) 253207
Circ.—21,000
Prop.—Der Bund Verlag AG

TW-BERNER TAGWACHT (d)
Monbijoustrasse 61, 3001
Tel: (41-31) 457270; Fax: (41-31) 455738
Circ.—10,000

BIEL
(Bienne/Bern)
Pop. Est. 51,341

BIELER TAGBLATT (6x wk.) German; Est. 1850
Längfeldweg 135, 2501
Tel: (41-32) 428333; Fax: (41-32) 428335
Circ.—35,800
Prop.—W Gassman AG
Ch. Ed.—Thomas Dähler

JOURNAL DU JURA/TRIBUNE JURASSIENNE (6x wk.) French; Est. 1864
Freiestrasse 11-13; Postfach 455, 2501
Tel: (41-32) 216111; Fax: (41-32) 428332
Circ.—13,610
Pub.—W Gassman
Ed. in Ch.—Bernard Eggler

BISCHOFSZELL
(Thurgau)

BISCHOFSZELLER NACHRICHTEN (The Bischofszeller News) (6x wk.) German; Est. 1908
Bahnhofstrasse 1, 9220
Tel: (41-71) 812533; Fax: (41-71) 812344
Circ.—1,095
Prop.—Vereinsbuchdruckerei of Frauenfeld
Ch. Ed.—Esther Simon

BISCHOFSZELLER ZEITUNG (6x wk.) German
Grabenstrasse 1, 9220
Tel: (41-71) 811988; Fax: (41-71) 811988
Circ.—3,790
Ch. Ed.—Dr. Peter Forster

BRIG
(Valais/Wallis)
Pop. Est. (Brig-Glis Area) 10,402

WALLISER BOTE (mit WALLISER SPIEGEL) (6x wk.) German
Furkastrasse 21; Postfach 720, 3900
Tel: (41-28) 243131; Fax: (41-28) 238468
Circ.—26,905
Prop.—Tscherring AG
Ch. Ed.—Pius Rieder

BRUGG

BRUGGER TAGBLATT (6x wk.)
Schulthess-Allee 7, 5200
Tel: (41-56) 414050; Fax: (41-56) 419767
Circ.—15,000
Prop.—Aargauer Tagblatt AG
Ch. Ed.—Christoph Mühläuser

BUCHS
(St. Gallen)
Pop. Est. 9,077

WERDENBERGER UND OBERTOGGENBURGER (5x wk.) German; Est. 1869
Tel: (41-81) 7500200; Fax: (41-81) 7562960
Circ.—10,471
Ch. Ed.—Hans Jakob Reich
Ed.—Heini Schwendener
Ed.—Reto Neurauter
Ed.—Marc Meschenmoser
Ed.—Hansruedi Rohrer

BUELACH
(BÜLACH)
(Zurich)
Pop. Est. 13,292

NEUES BÜLACHER TAGBLATT (6x wk.) German
Bahnhofstrasse 44, 8180
Tel: (41-1) 8601414; Fax: (41-1) 8605114

Circ.—6,442
Prop.—Druckerei Graf AG
Ch. Ed.—Dr. Hans Ulrich Graf

BURGDORF
(Bern)
Pop. Est. 15,072

BURGDORFER TAGBLATT (5x wk.) German; Est. 1831
Friedeggstrasse 4; Postfach 496, 3400
Tel: (41-34) 222256; Fax: (41-34) 234801
Circ.—3,486
Prop.—Haller & Jenzer AG
Ch. Ed.—Werner Zuber

CHAUX-DE-FONDS
(Neuchatel)
Pop. Est. 35,726

L'IMPARTIAL (6x wk.) French; Est. 1880
rue Neuve 14, 2301
Tel: (41-39) 210210; Fax: (41-39) 210360
Circ.—28,143
Prop.—Journal L'Impartial SA
Ed. in Ch.—Gil Baillod

CHUR
(Graubuenden/Grisons)
Pop. Est. 30,740

BÜNDNER TAGBLATT (6x wk.) German; Est. 1852
Hartberstrasse 7, 7001
Tel: (41-81) 221423; Fax: (41-81) 222309
Circ.—11,451
Prop.—Bündner Tagblatt Verlags AG
Ch. Ed.—Dr. Claudio Willi
Ed.—Franz Bamert
Ed.—Fredy Bühler
Ed.—Mario Candreia
Ed.—Karin Huber
Ed.—Sebastian Kirsch
Ed.—Jürg Sigel

BÜNDNER ZEITUNG (6x wk.) German; Est. 1876
Kasernstasse 95; Postfach 102, 7007
Tel: (41-81) 2555050; Fax: (41-81) 2555102
Circ.—42,908
Prop.—Gasser AG
Ch. Ed.—Andrea Masüger

DELEMONT
(Jura)
Pop. Est. 11,298

LE QUOTIDIAN JURASSIEN (6x wk.) French; Est. 1877
Route de Courroux 6, 2800
Tel: (41-66) 221751; Fax: (41-66) 226821
Circ.—25,000
Prop.—Imprimerie du Democrate SA
Ch. Ed.—Pierre-André Chapatt

DIETIKON

LIMMATTALER TAGBLATT (5x wk.) German
Kirchstrasse 21; Postfach 504, 8953
Tel: (41-1) 7414900; Fax: (41-1) 7408205
Circ.—10,412
Ed. in Ch.—Dr. Alfred Borter
Ed. in Ch.—Markus Hegglin

EINSIEDELN
(Schwyz)
Pop. Est. 9,900

NEUE EINSIEDLER ZEITUNG (The New Einsiedler News) (6x wk.) German; Est. 1908
Muchlestrasse 9, 8842
Circ.—2,977
Prop.—Marcel Kuerz AG
Ed. in Ch.—Oskar Hiestand

FLAWIL
(St. Gallen)
Pop. Est. 8,424

DER VOLKSFREUND/WILER ZEITUNG/GOSSAUER ZEITUNG (People's Friend/The Wiler News/The Gossauer News) (6x wk.) German
Burgauerstrasse 50, 9230
Tel: (41-71) 849696; Fax: (41-71) 836639
Circ.—12,514
Ch. Ed.—Johannes Rutz

Switzerland

FRAUENFELD
(Thurgau)
Pop. Est. 18,944

THURGAUER VOLKSZEITUNG (The Thurgauer People's News) (6x wk.) German; Est. 1844
Zürcherstrasse 179, 8500
Tel: (41-54) 275555; Fax: (41-54) 222268
Circ.—3,249
Ch. Ed.—Andreas Anderegg

THURGAUER ZEITUNG (The Thurgauer News) (6x wk.) German; Est. 1798
Promenadenstrasse 16, 8501
Tel: (41-54) 235757; Fax: (41-54) 210002
Circ.—31,311
Ch. Ed.—Dr. Peter Forster

FRIBOURG
(Freiburg)
Pop. Est. 33,935

FREIBURGER NACHRICHTEN (The Freiburger News) (6x wk.) German; Est. 1863
Perolles-Strasse 42; Postfach 1045, 1701
Tel: (41-37) 864747; Fax: (41-37) 864740
Circ.—18,871
Prop.—Freiburger Nachrichten AG
Ch. Ed.—Walter Buchs

LA LIBERTÉ (The Liberty) (6x wk.) French; Est. 1871
Blvd. Pérolles 42; Case Postale 1056, 1705
Tel: (41-37) 864411; Fax: (41-37) 864400
Circ.—35,418
Prop.—Imprimerie St. Paul SA
Pub.—Charles Bays
Ed. in Ch.—José Ribeaud

GENEVA
(GENÈVE)
Pop. Est. 378,849

AGENCE ECONOMIQUE ET FINANCIERE (AGEFI) (d)
Postfach 113, 1211-26
Circ.—5,900

LE COURRIER (The Courier) (6x wk.) French; Est. 1867
Rue de la Truite 3; Case Postale 238, 1211-4
Tel: (41-22) 3282280; Fax: (41-22) 3294274
Circ.—6,000
Ed. in Ch.—Patrice Mugny

GENEVA POST (5x wk.) English
28 Boulevard Pont d-arve, 1211
Tel: (41-22) 7080101; Fax: (41-22) 7080110
Circ.—15,000
Ch. Ed.—Harvey Morris

JOURNAL DE GENÈVE ET GAZETTE DE LAUSANNE (6x wk.) French; Est. 1826
rue Hesse 12; Case Postale 5160, 1211-11
Tel: (41-22) 8198888; Fax: (41-22) 8198989
Circ.—32,500
Pub./Dir.—Marian Stepczynski
Ed. in Ch.—Antoine Maurice
U.S. Rep.—Publicitas

LA SUISSE (6x wk.) French; Est. 1898
rue des Savoises 15, 1211-11
Tel: (41-22) 7085050; Fax: (41-22) 7085204
Circ.—58,188 (mon.-fri.); 112,365 (S)
Prop.—Sonor SA
Pub.—Charles Baudinat
Ed. in Ch.—Jean-Pierre Gattoni
Ed.—Daniel Hagler
U.S. Rep.—Publicitas

TRIBUNE DE GENÈVE (6x wk.) French; Est. 1879
42 rue de Stand; Case Postale 5115, 1211-11
Tel: (41-22) 3224000; Fax: (41-22) 7810107
Circ.—60,212
Prop.—Tribune de Geneve SA
Pub.—Gerald Sapey
Ch. Ed.—Guy Mettan
U.S. Rep.—Publicitas

GLARUS
Pop. Est. 38,114

GLARNER NACHRICHTEN (The Glarner News) (6x wk.) German; Est. 1875
Zwinglistrasse 6, 8750
Tel: (41-58) 611921; Fax: (41-58) 616440
Circ.—10,576
Prop.—Tschudi Druck & Verlag AG
Ch. Ed.—Ruedi Hertach

GLATTBRUGG

NEUES SONNTAGS BLATT (S) German; Est. 1986
Industriestrasse 54, 8152
Circ.—440,000
Prop.—Sonntagsblatt Verlags AG

HALLAU
(Schaffhausen)
Pop. Est. 1,966

KLETTGAUER ZEITUNG/SCHAFFHAUSERLAND German
Tel: (41-53) 613129; Fax: (41-53) 614006
Circ.—2,908
Prop.—Grüninger, Auer & Co.
Ed.—Fritz Grüninger

HEERBRUGG
(St. Gallen)
Pop. Est. 8,292

DER RHEINTALER (6x wk.) German
Tel: (41-71) 723503; Fax: (41-71) 723527
Circ.—11,445
Prop.—Rheintaler Druckerei & Verlag Ag
Ch. Ed.—Hanspeter Thurnherr
Ed.—Hans Andres
Ed.—Regina Schwendener
Ed.—Renê Schneider
Ed.—Renê Jann
Ed.—Sandro Küng
Ed.—Claudia Hutter
Ed.—Andrea Kobelt

HERISAU
(Aargau)
Pop. Est. 14,947

APPENZELLER ZEITUNG (Appenzeller News) (6x wk.) German; Est. 1828
Kassernenstrasse 64, 9100
Tel: (41-71) 513132; Fax: (41-71) 521422
Circ.—15,044
Prop.—Schlapfer & Co. AG
Pub.—Peter Schläpfer
Ed. in Ch.—Marcel Steiner

INTERLAKEN
(Bern)
Pop. Est. 4,738

OBERLÄNDISCHES VOLKSBLATT (6x wk.) German; Est. 1863
Aarmühlestrasse 8, 3800
Tel: (41-36) 232370; Fax: (41-36) 224041
Circ.—10,038
Prop.—Schlaefli AG
Ch. Ed.—Ueli Flück
Ed.—Peter Schmid
Ed.—Sandro Hügli

KREUZLINGEN
(Thurgau)
Pop. Est. 16,149

TAGESSPIEGEL (The Daily Mirror) (6x wk.) German
Tel: (41-72) 745363; Fax: (41-72) 751332
Circ.—29,102
Ed.—Markus Rutishauser
Ed.—Ralf Baumann
Ed.—Thomas Werner

THURGAUER VOLKSFREUND MIT TAGESSPIEGEL (The Thurgauer People's Friend with the Daily Mirror) (6x wk.) German; Est. 1882
Zelgstrasse 1, 8280
Tel: (41-72) 745353; Fax: (41-72) 751332
Circ.—9,004
Prop.—Bodan AG
Ed. in Ch.—Martin Bächer

Ed. in Ch.—Andy Theler
Ed.—Kurt Peter
Ed.—Markus Rustishauser
Ed.—Carmelina Seeman-Castellino
Ed.—Thomas Werner

LACHEN

MARCH-ANZEIGER (6x wk.)
Mittlere Bahnhofstrasse 6, 8853
Tel: (41-55) 612828; Fax: (41-55) 612829
Circ.—9,180
Ch. Ed.—Peter Wirz
Ed.—Alois Schwyter
Ed.—Katja Marty
Ed.—Conny Walder
Ed.—Vincenzo Capodici

LANGENTHAL
(Bern)
Pop. Est. 13,868

BERNER RUNDSCHAU/LANGENTHALER TAGBLATT (6x wk.) German; Est. 1964
Marktgasse 3, 4900
Tel: (41-63) 231414; Fax: (41-63) 229390
Circ.—8,314
Prop.—Vogt Schild Ag
Ed.—Jürg Nussbaum

LAUFEN
(Bern)
Pop. Est. 4,565

NORDSCHWEIZ (North Switzerland) (d-ex S) German
Hauptstrasse 5, 4242
Circ.—4,635

LAUSANNE
(Vaud)
Pop. Est. 124,206

GAZETTE de LAUSANNE et JOURNAL SUISSE et JOURNAL DE GENEVE (m-ex S) French; Est. 1798
rue St. Martin 7; Case Postale 765, 1001
Tel: (41-21) 206161; Fax: (41-21) 232380
Circ.—10,173
Mng. Ed.—Jean-Claude Poulin
Ed. in Ch.—Jasmine Audemars

LE MATIN (d) French; Est. 1865
Ave. de la Gare 33; Case Postale 1095, 1001
Tel: (41-21) 3494949; Fax: (41-21) 3494929
Circ.—58,642 (mon.-fri.); 179,349 (S)
Prop.—Le Matin
Pub.—Marc Lamuniere
Ed. in Ch.—Antoine Exchaquet
Mktg. Dir.—Juan Carlos Sánchez

NOUVELLE REVUE de LAUSANNE (d) French
Ave. Ruchonnat 15; Case Postale 885, 1001
Tel: (41-21) 201371; Fax: (41-21) 201374
Circ.—10,202
Prop.—Societe de la Nouvelle Revue de Lausanne
Prop.—Imprimerie Vaudoisse SA
Dir.—Michel Jaccard
Mng. Ed.—Philippe Bendel
Mng. Ed.—Simone Collet
Mng. Ed.—Jean-Pierre Thevoz
Ed. in Ch.—Jean-Jacques Mauler

LE NOUVEAU QUOTIDIEN (5x wk.) French
78 chemin de Montelly, 1007
Tel: (41-21) 6262524; Fax: (41-21) 6262523
Circ.—37,000
Ed. in Ch.—Jacques Pilet

24 HEURES (24 Hours) (6x wk.) French; Est. 1762
Ave. de la Gare 33; Case Postale 585, 1001
Tel: (41-21) 3494444; Fax: (41-21) 3494110
Circ.—91,137
Prop.—24 Heures Societe d'Edition SA
Pub.—Marc Lamuniere
Dir.—Giam Pozzi
Ed. in Ch.—Jean-Marie Vodoz
Mktg. Dir—Marielle Stamm
U.S. Rep.—Publicitas

LIESTAL
(Baselland)
Pop. Est. 12,161

BASELLANDSCHAFTLICHE ZEITUNG (6x wk.) German; Est. 1832
Schützenstrasse 2-6, 4410

Tel: (41-61) 9212211; Fax: (41-61) 9212268
Circ.—71,000
Prop.—Verlag Ludin AG
Ch. Ed.—Franz C Widmer

LUCERNE
(Luzern)
Pop. Est. 59,904

LUZERNER NEUSTE NACHRICHTEN (Luzerner Newest News) (5x wk.) German; Est. 1897
Zürichstrasse 5, 6002
Tel: (41-41) 391212/(41-41) 391515; Fax: (41-41) 391472/(41-41) 391525
Circ.—116,263
Prop.—C J Bucher AG
Dir.—Karl Bühlmann
Ch. Ed.—Sacha Wigdorovits

LUZERNER TAGBLATT/NIDWALDNER TAGBLATT (m-ex S) German; Est. 1852
Baselstrasse 11-13, 6602
Tel: (41-41) 281111; Fax: (41-41) 222253
Circ.—26,012
Prop.—Keller & Co. AG
Pub.—W Iten
Ed. in Ch.—Rolf Siegrist
Ad. Mgr.—Elmar Elmiger

LUZERNER ZEITUNG (The Luzerner News) (6x wk.) German
Maihofstrasse 76, 6002
Tel: (41-41) 395151; Fax: (41-41) 395181
Circ.—84,053
Prop.—Vaterland Druckerei Maihof AG
Ch. Ed.—Thomas Bornhauser

LUGANO
(Ticino)
Pop. Est. 27,462

CORRIERE DEL TICINO (6x wk.) Italian; Est. 1891
Corso Elvezia 33, 6091
Tel: (41-91) 232471; Fax: (41-91) 228588
Circ.—35,000
Prop.—Soc. Editrice Corriere del Ticino SA
Dir.—Dr. Sergio Caratti
Ed. in Ch.—Mauro Maestrini
Ed. in Ch.—Carlo Manzoni
U.S. Rep.—Publicitas

GAZZETTA TICINESE (6x wk.) Italian; Est. 1801
Via Peri 18, 6900
Circ.—5,025
Prop.—Tipografia La Buona Stampa
Dir.—Giovanni Caserla

GIORNALE DEL POPOLO (6x wk.) Italian; Est. 1926
Via San Gottardo 50; Case Postale 233, 6903
Tel: (41-91) 23227175; Fax: (41-91) 232805
Circ.—24,832
Prop.—Tipografia La Buona Stampa
Pub.—D Leber
Gen. Mgr.—Filippo Lombardi
Ed.—Alfonso Pezzati

LIBERA STAMPA (6x wk.) Italian; Est. 1913
Case Postale 2962, 6901
Tel: (41-91) 228075/(41-91) 228076; Fax: (41-91) 228201
Circ.—6,363
Prop.—SCOE Lugano
Ed. in Ch.—Silvano Ballinari

MELS
(St. Gallen)
Pop. Est. 5,254

SARGANSERLÄNDER (5x wk.) German
Tel: (41-81) 7253232; Fax: (41-81) 7253230
Circ.—10,295
Ch. Ed.—Thomas Schwizer
Ed.—Helen Baur-Rigendinger
Ed.—Flums Hochwiese

MONTREUX
(Vaud)
Pop. Est. 18,970

LA PRESSE RIVIERA/CHABLATS (6x wk.) French
22 Ave. des Planches, 1820
Tel: (41-21) 9634141; Fax: (41-21) 963385
Circ.—22,200
Prop.—Imprimerie Corbaz SA
Ed. in Ch.—Pierre-Alain Luginbuhl

NEUCHATEL
Pop. Est. 162,458

L'EXPRESS (6x wk.)
rue Pierre-à-vazel 39; Case Postale 561, 2001
Tel: (41-38) 256501; Fax: (41-38) 250039
Circ.—33,428
Ed. in Ch.—Jean-Luc Vautravers
FEUILLE D'AVIS DE NEUCHATEL-L'EXPRESS (6x wk.) French; Est. 1738
39 rue de la Pierre a Mazel, 2001
Tel: (41-38) 256501; Fax: (41-38) 250039
Circ.—33,428
Prop.—Feuille d'Avis de Neuchatel
Ed. in Ch.—Jean-Luc Vautravers

NYON
(Vaud)

LE QUOTIDIEN DE LA COTE (5x wk.) French
12 rue de la Colombière; Case Postale 155, 1260
Tel: (41-22) 3613951; Fax: (41-22) 3621308
Circ.—12,500
Ed. in Ch.—Gilles Vallat
Ed.—Anne-Lise Calame
Ed.—Elisabeth Guyot-Noth
Ed.—Pierre Härtel
Ed.—Céline Jaquinet
Ed.—Michel Jotterand
Ed.—Claire Leresche
Ed.—Francoise Menetrey

OLTEN
(Solothurn)
Pop. Est. 17,800

OLTNER TAGBLATT (6x wk.) German; Est. 1878
Ziegelfeldstrasse 60, 4601
Tel: (41-62) 324141; Fax: (41-62) 322154
Circ.—19,510
Prop.—Dietschi AG
Ch. Ed.—Kurt Schibler
SOLOTHURNER NACHRICHTEN (6x wk.)
German; Est. 1961
Ziegelfeldstrasse 60, 4601
Tel: (41-62) 324141; Fax: (41-62) 322154
Circ.—3,461
Prop.—Maihof Druck AG
Ch. Ed.—Kurt Schibler

PORRENTRUY
(Jura)
Pop. Est. 7,300

LE PAYS (6x wk.) French; Est. 1873
Allee des Soupirs 3-7; Case Postale 315, 2900
Circ.—12,500
Prop.—Le Pays SA
Dir./Ed. in Ch.—Pierre-Andre Chapatte

RAPPERSWIL

LINTH ZEITUNG (4x wk.)
Merkurstrasse 41; Postfach 1473, 8640
Tel: (41-55) 210031; Fax: (41-55) 210021

RORSCHACH
(St. Gallen)
Pop. Est. 9,927

OSTSCHWEIZER TAGBLATT (6x wk.) German; Est. 1845
Signalstrasse 8, 9400
Circ.—7,729
Prop.—Zollikofer AG
Pub.—Urs Lanz
RORSCHACHER ZEITUNG (The Rorschacher News) (6x wk.) German; Est. 1899
Circ.—4,284
Prop.—Ostschweiz Druck & Verlag AG
Ex. Ed.—Dr. Roland Mattes
Ed. in Ch.—Edgar Oehler

SARGANS
(St. Gallen)

OBERLÄNDER TAGBLATT (6x wk.) German
Schwefelbadplatz, 7320
Circ.—1,572
Prop.—Gasser AG (Chur)
Ed. in Ch.—Stefan Buehler

SCHAFFHAUSEN
Pop. Est. 74,454

SCHAFFHAUSER AZ (6x wk.) German; Est. 1918
Webergasse 39, 8201
Tel: (41-53) 251186; Fax: (41-53) 243471
Circ.—3,500

SCHAFFHAUSER NACHRICHTEN (The Schaffhauser News) (6x wk.) German; Est. 1861
Vordergasse 58, 8201
Tel: (41-53) 833111; Fax: (41-53) 833401
Circ.—3,901
Prop.—Meier & Cie AG
Pub.—J W Reiff
Ch. Ed.—Norbert Neininger
Ch. Ed.—Karl Hotz
Ch. Ed.—Martin Schweizer

SCHWYZ
Pop. Est. 112,986

BOTE DER URSCHWEIZ German
Schniedgasse 7, 6430
Tel: (41-43) 211037; Fax: (41-43) 217037
Circ.—15,230
Ed.—Jürg Aufdermaur
SCHWYZER ZEITUNG (The Swiss News) (6x wk.) German
Bahnofstrasse 14; PF 563, 6430
Tel: (41-43) 213333; Fax: (41-43) 217428
Circ.—3,600
Ed.—Josias Clavadetscher
Ed.—Kurt Rühle

SIEBEN

DER AUSSERSCHWYZER (6x wk.) German
Glanerstrasse 5, 8854
Tel: (41-55) 644372; Fax: (41-55) 643302
Circ.—4,555
Ed.—Frans-Xaver Risi
Ed.—Andreas Knobel
Ed.—Alois Schwyter
Ed.—Aldo Lombardi

SION
(Valais)
Pop. Est. 23,504

NOUVELLISTE (6x wk.) French
rue de l'Industrie 13, 1950
Tel: (41-27) 297511; Fax: (41-27) 297565
Circ.—44,500
Prop.—Imprimerie Moderne de Sion SA

SOLOTHURN
Pop. Est. 230,068

SOLOTHURNER ZEITUNG (Solothurner News) (6x wk.) German; Est. 1907
Zuchwilerstrasse 21; Postfach 716, 4501
Tel: (41-65) 247267; Fax: (41-65) 247249
Circ.—47,389
Prop.—Vogt-Schild AG
Ch. Ed.—Werner Hunziker

SPIEZ
(Bern)
Pop. Est. 10,197

BERNER OBERLÄNDER (6x wk.) German; Est. 1898
Seestrasse 42, 3700
Tel: (41-33) 544444; Fax: (41-33) 547894
Circ.—22,057
Ch. Ed.—Arthur Wüthrich

ST. GALLEN
Pop. Est. 426,689

DIE OSTSCHWEIZ (6x wk.) German; Est. 1873
Obererer Graben 8, 9001
Tel: (41-71) 208580; Fax: (41-71) 233844
Circ.—30,068
Prop.—Ostschweiz Druck & Verlag Ag
Ch. Ed.—Marco Volken
OSTSCHWEIZER AZ (5x wk.) German; Est. 1905
Langgasse 148; Postfach 221, 9008
Tel: (41-71) 257777; Fax: (41-71) 247701
Circ.—3,550
Prop.—Druckerei & Verlag AG
Ed.—Jürg Bareiss
Ed.—Michael Walther
ST. GALLER TAGBLATT (6x wk.) German; Est. 1839
Fürstenlandstrasse 122, 9001
Tel: (41-71) 297711; Fax: (41-71) 297476
Circ.—72,129
Prop.—Zollikofer AG
Pub.—H Zollikofer
Ch. Ed.—Gottlieb F Höpli

Europe **Switzerland** IV-51

STAFA
(Zurich)
Pop. Est. 10,404

ZÜRICHSEE-ZEITUNG (The Lake Zurich News) (5x wk.) German; Est. 1845
Seestrasse 86; Postfach 382, 8712
Tel: (41-1) 9285111; Fax: (41-1) 9285200
Circ.—29,482
Prop.—Zürichsee Medien AG
Pub./Ad. Mgr.—Armin Zuckschwerdt
Ed. in Ch.—Dr. Ulrich E Gut

STANS
(Nidwalden)

NIDWALDNER ZEITUNG (6x wk.) German
Stansstaderstrasse 10, 6370
Tel: (41-41) 616313; Fax: (41-41) 616510
Circ.—8,254
Prop.—Druckerei Maihof AG
Ch. Ed.—Thomas Bornhauser

SULGEN

THURGAUER ANZEIGER (Thurgauer Advertiser) (6x wk.) German
Tel: (41-72) 421414; Fax: (41-72) 424179
Circ.—2,500
Ed.—Roman Salzmann

TEUFEN
(Aargau)

APPENZELLER TAGBLATT (6x wk.) German
Circ.—5,240
Prop.—Zolliker AG (in St. Gallen)
Pub.—H Zollikofer
Ed. in Ch.—Jürg Tobler

THUN
(Bern)
Pop. Est. 37,074

THUNER TAGBLATT (6x wk.) German; Est. 1876
Rampenstrasse 1, 3602
Tel: (41-33) 228833; Fax: (41-33) 234867
Circ.—18,723
Prop.—Schaer Thun AG
Ch. Ed.—René E Gygax

USTER
(Zurich)
Pop. Est. 25,227

DIE REGIONALZEITUNG
Imkerstrasse 4, 8610
Tel: (41-1) 9415115; Fax: (41-1) 9402883
Circ.—11,516
Ch. Ed.—Beat Schertenleib
URNER ZEITUNG (d-6x wk.) German
Herrengasse 2, 6460
Tel: (41-44) 20114; Fax: (41-44) 21059
Circ.—3,500
Ed.—Martin Übelhart
Ed.—Gregor Poletti
Ed.—Erhard Gick
ANZEIGER VON USTER (The Advertiser from Uster) (6x wk.) German; Est. 1846
Imkerstrasse 4, 8610
Tel: (41-1) 9404747; Fax: (41-1) 9402883
Circ.—11,516
Prop.—Eugen Weilenmann AG
Ed. in Ch.—Peter Wirz

UZNACH

GASTERLÄNDER/LINTH PRESSE (6x wk.)
Obergasse 4, 8730
Tel: (41-55) 726777; Fax: (41-55) 726787
Circ.—3,715
Ch. Ed.—Franz-Xaver Risi

VEVEY
(Vaud)
Pop. Est. 15,021

JOURNAL ET FEUILLE D'AVIS DE VEVEY-RIVIERA (6x wk.) French
29 Ave. Nestle, 1800
Circ.—8,462
Prop.—Sauberlin & Pfeiffer SA
Ed. in Ch.—Jean-Louis Rebetez

WAEDENSWIL
(Zurich)
Pop. Est. 19,084

ALLGEMEINER ANZEIGER VOM ZÜRICHSEE (The General Advertiser of Lake Zurich) (5x wk.) German
Postfach 48, 8820
Circ.—8,500
Ch. Ed.—Recco Däppeler

WEINFELDEN
(Thurgau)
Pop. Est. 6,954

THURGAUER TAGBLATT mit TAGESSPIEGEL (6x wk.) German
Schützenstrasse 15, 8570
Tel: (41-72) 224648; Fax: (41-72) 225730
Circ.—7,439
Prop.—Thurgauer Tagblatt AG
Ch. Ed.—Rolf Müller

WETZIKON
(Zurich)
Pop. Est. 16,549

DER ZÜRCHER OBERLÄNDER (6x wk.) German; Est. 1852
Tel: (41-1) 9333333; Fax: (41-1) 9323232
Circ.—35,156
Prop.—Druckerei Wetzikon AG
Pub.—H Sigrist
Ch. Ed.—Dr. Oscar Fritschi

WIL
(St. Gallen)
Pop. Est. 16,124

NEUES WILER TAGBLATT (6x wk.) German; Est. 1872
Zürcherstrasse 17, 9500
Tel: (41-73) 225307; Fax: (41-73) 226343
Circ.—3,113
Prop.—Vereinsbuchdruckerei of Frauenfeld
Ch. Ed.—Matthias Unseld

WINTERTHUR
(Zurich)
Pop. Est. 84,548

DER LANDBOTE (m-6x wk.) German; Est. 1836
Garnmarkt 1; Postfach 778, 8401
Tel: (41-52) 2134051; Fax: (41-52) 2127518
Circ.—42,143
Prop.—Geschwister Ziegler & Co.
Ch. Ed.—Dr. Rudolf Gerber
WEINLÄNDER TAGBLATT (6x wk.) German
PF 8401
Circ.—24,116
Prop.—Verlag Weinlaender Tagblatt
Pub./Ed. in Ch.—Dr. Erwin Akeret
Dir.—Myrtha Akeret
WINTERTHURER AZ (6x wk.) German; Est. 1897
Technikumstrasse 90; Postfach 1254, 8401
Tel: (41-52) 2126121; Fax: (41-52) 2127507
Circ.—4,057
Ed.—Käther Bänziger
Ed.—Tanja Polli
Ed.—Helen Hürlimann

YVERDON
(Vaud)
Pop. Est. 21,004

JOURNAL DU NORD VAUDOIS (6x wk.) French; Est. 1773
Ave. Haldimand 4, 1401
Tel: (41-24) 231151; Fax: (41-24) 210996
Circ.—11,329
Prop.—Ste. du Journal d'Yverdon
Pub.—Roger Juillerat
Ed. in Ch.—Jacques-Antoine Lombard

ZOFINGEN
(Aargau)
Pop. Est. 8,643

ZOFINGER TAGBLATT (6x wk.) German; Est. 1873
Henzmanstrasse 18, 4800
Tel: (41-62) 511734; Fax: (41-62) 512952
Circ.—16,806
Prop.—Zofinger Tagblatt AG
Pub.—B Imfeld
Ed. in Ch.—Paul Ehinger

Copyright ©1996 by the Editor & Publisher Co.

Switzerland

ZUG
(Zaug)
Pop. Est. 21,569

ZUGER NACHRICHTEN (The Zug News) (6x wk.)
German
Gotthardstrasse 14; Postfach 364, 6301
Tel: (41-42) 211626; Fax: (41-42) 212137
Circ.—26,905
Ch. Ed.—Dieter Mittler

ZUGER ZEITUNG (d-6x wk.) German
Gotthardstrasse 14, 6301
Tel: (41-42) 214051; Fax: (41-42) 221664
Circ.—8,014
Ed. in Ch.—Werner Steinmann
Ed.—Niklaus Zeier
Ed.—Ronald Schenkel
Ed.—Annemarie Setz

ZURICH
Pop. Est. 1,159,000

BLICK (6x wk.) German; Est. 1959
Dufourstrasse 23, 8021
Tel: (41-1) 2596262; Fax: (41-1) 2622953
Circ.—365,520
Prop.—fur Presseerzeugnisse
Ch. Ed.—Fridolin Luchsinger

DAZ (d-5x wk.) German
Postfach 926, 8021
Tel: (41-1) 2959252; Fax: (41-1) 2912224
Circ.—5,200
Ed.—Matthias Ersinger
Ed.—Koni Loepfe
Ed.—Susanna Hübscher
Ed.—Detlev Bruggmann
Ed.—Judith Anna Stofer

NEUE ZÜRCHER NACHRICHTEN (6x wk.)
German; Est. 1896
Birmensdorferstrasse 52, 8004
Circ.—8,500
Prop.—Ostschweiz Druck
Prop.—Verlag AG of St. Gallen
Ad. Mgr.—F Monego

NEUE ZÜRCHER ZEITUNG (6x wk.) German; Est. 1780
Falkenstrasse 11, 8021
Tel: (41-1) 2581111; Fax: (41-1) 2521329
Circ.—151,660
Prop.—für die Neue Zürcher Zeitung AZ
Ed. in Ch.—Hugo Bütler
U.S. Rep.—Publicitas

SONNTAGSBLICK (S) German
Dufourstrasse 23, 8008
Circ.—375,120
Pub.—H J Kloeti
Ad. Mgr.—H Raeber

TAGBLATT DER STADT ZÜRICH (6x wk.) German
Werdstrasse 21, 8021
Tel: (41-1) 2484190; Fax: (41-1) 2485006
Circ.—197,028
Prop.—Berichthaus Verlag
Ch. Ed.—Markus Hegglin

TAGES-ANZEIGER (The Daily Advertiser) (6x wk.) German; Est. 1893
Werdstrasse 21, 8021
Tel: (41-1) 2484411; Fax: (41-1) 2484471
Circ.—279,805
Prop.—Tages-Anzeiger
Pub.—J Pepe Wiss
Ch. Ed.—Roger de Weck
U.S. Rep.—Publicitas

TAGES ANZEIGER SONNTAGS-ZEITUNG (S)
German; Est. 1987
Werdstrasse 21, 8021
Circ.—250,000
Prop.—Tages-Anzeiger
Pub.—J Pepe Wiss
Ad. Mgr.—Daniel C Nadelhofer

VOLKSRECHT (5x wk.) German; Est. 1898
Postfach 512, 8021
Tel: (41-1) 2426622; Fax: (41-1) 2912224
Circ.—5,200
Prop.—Zurich City
Prop.—Canton Social Democratic Party Organization
Pub./Ad. Mgr.—R Stockler

ZÜRCHER UNTERLÄNDER (6x wk.) German
Schulstrasse 12; Postfach 311, 8157
Tel: (41-1) 8548282; Fax: (41-1) 8548233
Circ.—18,166
Ch. Ed.—Christina Fivian

ZÜRICHSEE-ZEITUNG (6x wk.)
Seestrasse 86; Postfach 382, 8712
Tel: (41-1) 9285555; Fax: (41-1) 9285200
Circ.—29,482
Ch. Ed.—Dr. Ulrich E Gut
Ed.—Urs Köche
Ed.—Sebastian Leicht
Ed.—Peter Hasler
Ed.—Robert Hangartner
Ed.—Christian Dietz
Ed.—Bernd Beck
Ed.—Adrian Müller
Ed.—Elisabeth Tschiemer
Ed.—Michael Kaspar
Ed.—Ev Schroeder-Baviera
Ed.—Marionne Wagensteiner

TAJIKISTAN
(Formerly Tadzhikistan SSR)
Pop. Est. 5,995,469

DUSHANBE
Pop. Est. 582,000

NARODNAYA GAZETA (6x wk.) Russian; Est. 1925
37, Prosp. Lenina, 734025
Ed.—V P Naumov

TURKMENSKAYA ISKRA (6x wk.)
20, ul. Atabaeva, 744604
Circ.—62,946
Ed.—V V Slushny

UKRAINE
Pop. Est. 51,846,958

CRIMEA
Pop. Est. 2,700,000

KRYMSKAYA PRAVDA (4x wk.) Russian; Est. 1918
44 Gen. Vasyliev St., Simferopol
Tel: (7-0652) 445838
Circ.—125,000

DONETSK
Pop. Est. 1,121,000

DONBASS (5x wk.) Russian; Est. 1917
48 Kievskky Prospect, 118, 340118
Tel: (7-0622) 553305
Circ.—102,000

KHARKIV
Pop. Est. 1,622,000

SLOBODSKIY KRAY Ukrainian; Est. 1917
247 Moskovskki Prospect, 310302
Tel: (7-0572) 924309
Circ.—102,000
Prop.—Kharkiv Regional Council

KIEV
Pop. Est. 2,637,000

DEMOKRATYCHNA UKRAINA (Democratic Ukraine) (5x wk.) Ukranian
50, Prosp. Peremohy, 252047
Tel: (7-044) 4418333
Cir.—210,000
Prop.—Ukrainy Publishing House
Ed. in Ch.—V Stadnichenko

HOLOS UKRAINY (Voice of Ukraine) (5x wk.)
Ukranian & Russian; Est. 1990
4, Nesterov St., 252047
Tel: (7-044) 4469211; Fax: (7-044) 2247254
Circ.—768,000
Ed. in Ch.—S Pravdenko

KIEVSKIE VEDOMOSTI (7x wk.) Russian; Est. 1992
31 Degtyarska St., 252057
Tel: (7-044) 2168095; Fax: (7-044) 2162476
Circ.—361,000
Prop.—"Dovira"
Ed.—S Kichigin

NEZAVISIMOST (Independence) Russian; Est. 1938
50, Prosp. Peremohy
Tel: (7-044) 4418233; Fax: (7-044) 4468411
Circ.—228,000
Ed.—V Kuleba

PRAVDA UKRAINY (5x wk.) Russian
50, Prosp. Premohy, 252047
Tel: (7-044) 4418534; Fax: (7-044) 4469421
Circ.—300,000
Ed. in Ch.—A Agorobets

PROFAPILKOVA HAZETA (Trade Union Gazette)
2, Maidan Nezaleznhosti, 252001
Tel: (7-044) 2280162/(7-044) 2281392

RABOCHAYA GAZETA (e-5x wk.) Russian; Est. 1957
50 Peremoga Ave., 252047
Tel: (7-044) 44181657; Fax: (7-044) 4460298
Circ.—160,673
Prop.—Pressa Ukrainy
Ed.—Evelina V Babanko-Pivtoradni
Ad. Mgr.—Alexander Phomin

ROBITNYCHA GAZETA (Worker's Gazette) (5x wk.) Ukrainian & Russian
50, Prosp. Peremohy, 252047
Tel: (7-044) 4418656
Circ.—155,000
Prop.—Cabinet of Ministers
Ed.—N Shibik

UKRAINA-BIZNES (Ukraine Business)
26g Lenin St.
Tel: (7-044) 2253260

URYADOVIVY KUR'ER (Government Courier) (4x wk.) Ukrainian; Est. 1990
1 Sadova St., 252008
Tel: (7-044) 2930440; Fax: (7-044) 2262447
Circ.—120,000
Ed.—M Sorokka

VECHIRNIY KYIV (Evening Kiev) (d) Russian & Ukrainian
13, Marshal Hrechko St., 252136
Tel: (7-044) 4436581; Fax: (7-044) 4439609

LUGANSK
Pop. Est. 504,000

LUGANSKAJA PRAVDA Russian; Est. 1917
1-B Lermontov St., 348022
Tel: (7-0642) 536130
Circ.—190,000

LVIV
Pop. Est. 803,000

VYSOLIY ZAMOK (5x wk.) Ukrainian & Russian, Est. 1992
2 Volodimira Velykoho St., 26, 290026
Tel: (7-0322) 433263
Circ.—90,000
Prop.—Lviv Regional Council

ODESSA
Pop. Est. 1,104,000

ODESKI VISTI (Odessa News) (4x wk.)
Ukrainian & Russian; Est. 1992
83 Sverdlov St., 270107
Tel: (7-0482) 284367
Prop.—Odessa Regional Council

UZBEKISTAN
Pop. Est. 23,000,000

TASHKENT
Pop. Est. 2,200,300

KHALQ SOZI (5x wk.) Est. 1992
19 Matbuotchilar St., 700000
Tel: (7-3712) 331522; Fax: (7-3712) 362721
Circ.—52,000
Ed.—Anvar Juraboev

NARODNOE SLOVO (5x wk.) Russian; Est. 1992
19 Matbuotchilar St., 700000
Tel: (7-3712) 337107; Fax: (7-3712) 362721
Circ.—21,000
Ed.—Anvar Juraboev

PRAVDA VOSTOKA (Eastern Truth) (5x wk.)
Russian; Est. 1917
32 Matbuotchilar Str., 700083
Circ.—35,000
Ed.—Ruben Safarov

SOVET UZBEKISTONI (Soviet Uzbekistan) (6x wk.) Uzbekistanian
32 ul. Leningradskaja, 700083
Ed.—L Kayumov

VATICAN CITY
Pop. Est. 821

L'OSSERVATORE ROMANO (d-ex mon.) Italian; Est. 1861
Via del Pellegrino, 00120
Tel: (39-6) 6983461; Fax: (39-6) 6983675
Circ.—70,000
Prop.—Tipografie Vaticane
Pub.—Mario Agnes
Adm. Dir.—Giacomo Bonassoli

YUGOSLAVIA
(Serbia And Montenegro)
Pop. Est. 10,500,000

BELGRADE
(Beograde)
Pop. Est. 5,753,825

BORBA (m-ex S) Est. 1922
RG Nicole Pasica 7, 11000
Tel: (381-11) 345361; Fax: (381-11) 344413
Circ.—85,000
Prop.—Socialist Alliance of the Working People of Yugoslavia
Dir.—Milan Rakas
Ed. in Ch.—Stanislav Marikovic
Ad. Mgr.—Zoran Vuckovic
(This newspaper is nationally distributed. An edition is printed in both the Cyrillic and Roman Alphabet.)

POLITIKA (Politics) (e) Est. 1904
Makedonska 29, 11000
Tel: (38-11) 324191
Circ.—200,000
Dir./Ed. in Ch.—Zivorad Minovic

POLITIKA EKSPRES (Political Express) (e)
Makedonska 29, (XII XI sprat), 11000
Tel: (38-11) 326982
Circ.—250,000
Prop.—Politika Press Publishing House
Ed. in Ch.—Bozidar Bogdanovic

PRIVREDNI PREGLED (Belgrade Economic Review) (m) Est. 1950
Marsala Birjuzova 3-5, 11000
Tel: (38-11) 182888
Circ.—15,000
Dir.—Radovan Markovic
Ed. in Ch.—Miodrag Rakic

VECERNJE NOVOSTI (Evening News) (e) Est. 1953
Trg Marska i Engelsa 7
Tel: (381-11) 344531
Circ.—35,000
Prop.—Socialist Alliance of the Working People of Yugoslavia
Ed. in Ch.—Tomislav Milinovic
Ad. Mgr.—Zivorad Zivkovic

NOVI SAD
(Vojvodina)
Pop. Est. 257,685

DNEVNIK (Vojvodina Socialist) (m) Est. 1942
Bulevar 23, oktobra 31
Tel: (38-21) 621555
Circ.—30,325
Prop.—Socialist Alliance of the Working People of Vojvodina
Dir.—Jovan Vilovac
Ed. in Ch.—Jovan Smederevac

MAGYAR SZO (Hungarian Word) (m)
Hungarian; Est. 1944
Vojvode Misica 1
Tel: (38-21) 611300
Circ.—25,590
Prop.—Socialist Alliance of the Working People of Vojvodina
Ed. in Ch.—Karoly Erdelyi

PODGORICA
Pop. Est. 616,327

POBJEDA (m) Est. 1945
Bulevar revolucije 11
Tel: (38-81) 45955
Circ.—19,424
Prop.—Socialist Alliance of the Working People of Montenegro
Ed. in Ch.—Petar Boskovic

PRISTINA
Pop. Est. 210,040

JEDINSTVO (m)
Marsala Tita 49
Tel: (38-38) 29090
Circ.—6,090
Ed. in Ch.—Milenko Jevtovic

NEWSPAPERS OF AFRICA

ALGERIA
Pop. Est. 27,895,068

ALGIERS
(El Djazair)
Pop. Est. 2,500,000

ALGERIE-ACTUALITES (d) French
2, rue de La Liberte, 16000
Tel: (213) 2637030
Circ.—150,000
Dir.—B Ramdani
ECH-CHAAB (d) Arabic; Est. 1962
1 Place Maurice Audin
Tel: (213) 2595211/(213) 2596333
Circ.—80,000
Prop.—ANEP-1-Avenue Pasteur
Pub.—Mohamed Bouarroudj
Ad. Mgr.—L Hadri
HORIZONS (d) French; Est. 1965
2, rue de La Liberte
Tel: (213) 2637030
Circ.—280,000
Dir.—B Ramdani
EL MASSA (d) Arabic
2, rue de La Liberte
Tel: (213) 2637030
Circ.—10,000
Dir.—B Ramdani
EL-MOUDJAHID (d) Arabic & French; Est. 1965
2, rue de la Liberte
Tel: (213) 2637030
Circ.—440,000
Prop.—ANEP-1-Avenue Pasteur
Dir.—B Ramdani

CONSTANTINE
Pop. Est. 500,000

AN-NASR (d) Arabic; Est. 1963
Zone Industrielle, La Palma; Boite Postal 388
Tel: (213) 4939216
Circ.—340,000
Prop.—ANEP-Cite Fadila Saadane
Ed.—Kamel Ayache
Ad. Mgr.—L Hadri

ORAN
Pop. Est. 600,000

AL-JOUMHOURIA (d) Arabic; Est. 1963
6, rue Benjenouci Hamida
Circ.—70,000
Prop.—ANEP-1-Avenue Pasteur
Pub.—Aissa Adjina
Ad. Mgr.—L Hadri
LA REPUBLIQUE (The Republic) (d) French
6, rue ben Senoussi Hamida
Circ.—70,000
Prop.—ANEP-1-Avenue Pasteur
Ad. Mgr.—L Hadri

ANGOLA
Pop. Est. 9,803,576

LUANDA
Pop. Est. 1,100,000

ABC DIARIO DE ANGOLA (ABC Angola Daily) (e) Portuguese
Estrada de Catete
Circ.—8,500
Ad. Mgr.—M Oliveira
DIARIO DA LUANDA (Luanda Daily) (m)
Rua Serpa Pinto; Box CP 1290
Circ.—18,000
Ad. Mgr.—Filipe Amado
DIARIO DA REPUBLICA (Republic Daily) (d) Portuguese
Caixa Postal 1306
JORNAL DE ANGOLA (Angola Journal) (m-ex mon.) Portuguese; Est. 1923
18/24 rua Rainha Ginga; Caixa Postal 1312
Tel: (244-2) 331619/(244-2) 333466;
Fax: (244-2) 337224
Circ.—60,000
Prop.—Empresa Grafica de Angola
Dir.—José Cardoso
Ed.—David Maestre
Ad. Mgr.—Marques da Silva
PROVINCIA DE ANGOLA (Angola Province) (d) Portuguese; Est. 1923
18/24, rua Salvador Correia
Circ.—35,000
Ad. Mgr.—R C de Freitas

BENIN, PEOPLE'S REPUBLIC OF
Pop. Est. 5,341,710

COTONOU
Pop. Est. 500,000

EHUZU (d)
Gov't. Information Service; Boite Postal 1210
Tel: (229) 313681
Circ.—12,000
Pub./Dir.—Maurice Chabi
LE FORUM (The Forum)
Tel: (229) 300340; Fax: (229) 305391
LA GAZETTE DU GOLFE
Boite Postal 03-1624
Tel: (229) 314865/(229) 313558; Fax: (229) 315053
L'OPINION (The Opinion)
Boite Postal 1268
Tel: (229) 331385
TAM-TAM EXPRESS
Boite Postal 2302
Tel: (229) 300011; Fax: (229) 305324

BOTSWANA
Pop. Est. 1,359,352

GABORONE
Pop. Est. 133,791

BOTSWANA ADVERTISER
5647 Nakedi Rd., Broadhurst; PO Box 130
Tel: (267-31) 312844
BOTSWANA DAILY NEWS/DIKGANG TSA GOMPIENO (d) English & Setswana
Private Postbag 00600
Tel: (267-31) 352541
Circ.—35,000
Prop.—Dept. of Printing & Publishing Services
BOTSWANA GUARDIAN English
688 Botswana Rd.; PO Box 1641
Tel: (267-31) 314937; Fax: (267-31) 374381
Circ.—14,734
Prop.—Pula Printing & Publishing (Pty.) Ltd.
Pub.—William Jones
Ed.—Joel Sebionego
Ad. Mgr.—Disney Meloyo
THE GAZETTE English
PO Box 1605
MMEGI WA DIKMANG English & Setswana
PO Box 20906
Prop.—Mgemi Publishing Trust
Ed.—Metlhaitsile Leepile

BURKINA FASO
Pop. Est. 10,134,661

OUAGADOUGOU
Pop. Est. 500,000

BULLETIN QUOTIDIEN D'INFORMATION (m)
French; Est. 1959
Boite Postal 507
Circ.—1,500
Prop.—La Presse Ecrite (Ministry of Information)
Dir.—Hubert Bazie
Ed.—Pierre-Clavier Tassembedo
CAREFOUR AFRICAIN Est. 1959
5, rue du Marche; Boite Postal 507
Prop.—This newspaper is owned by the government.
DUNIA (d)
Boite Postale 3013
NOTRE COMBAT (d)
Boite Postale 507
L'OBSERVATEUR (The Observer) (m) Est. 1991
Boite Postale 810
Circ.—8,000
SIDWAYA (d-ex S) Est. 1984
5 rue du Marche 01; Boite Postale 507
Tel: (226) 306307
Circ.—3,500
Prop.—This newspaper is owned by the government.

BURUNDI
Pop. Est. 6,124,747

BUJUMBURA
Pop. Est. (Metro Area) 272,600

BURUNDI CHRETIEN French
Boite Postal 232
LE RENOUVEAU DU BURUNDI (d-ex mon.) French; Est. 1978
Boite Postal 2870
Circ.—20,000
Prop.—Ministry of Information
Dir.—Jean Nzeyimana
UBUMWE (KIRUNDI) French
Boite Postal 1400
Tel: (257-2) 23929

CAMEROON, REPUBLIC OF
Pop. Est. 13,132,191

DOUALA
Pop. Est. 908,000

CHALLENGE HEBDO French
PO Box 1388
Tel: (237) 400329; Fax: (237) 402608/ (237) 409846
Circ.—50,000
Prop.—Journal d'Information Generales
Pub.—Pius N Njawe
Gen. Mgr.—Benjamin Zebaze
LE COMBATTANT French
PO Box 7117
Gen. Mgr.—Joseph Benyimbe
LA DETENTE French
PO Box 8373
Circ.—20,000
Gen. Mgr.—Samuel Eleme
THE GAZETTE French; Est. 1974
PO Box 5485
Circ.—35,000
Gen. Mgr.—Abobel Karimou
THE HERALD English
PO Box 4995
Tel: (237) 315522; Fax: (237) 318161
Circ.—10,000
Gen. Mgr.—Boniface Forbin
LE MESSAGER (The Messenger) French & English
PO Box 5925
Circ.—40,000
Gen. Mgr.—Pius N Njawe
LE MONT-CAMEROUN French & English
PO Box 3979
Pub.—Issac-Desire Boundja
LA NOUVELLE EXPRESSION French
PO Box 15333
Tel: (237) 432227; Fax: (237) 432669
Circ.—35,000
Gen. Mgr.—Severin Tchounkeu
LE TEMPS French; Est. 1980
PO Box 12931
Tel: (237) 433119
Circ.—15,000
Gen. Mgr.—Benjamin Malake
LA VISION (The Vision) French
PO Box 8454
Tel: (237) 430839; Fax: (237) 430265
Circ.—20,000
Gen. Mgr.—Edouard Kingue

YAOUNDE
Pop. Est. (Metro Area) 700,000

AFRIQUE EN DOSSIER (d)
PO Box 1715
CAMEROON TRIBUNE (d-ex S) French & English; Est. 1974
PO Box 1218
Tel: (237) 222700
Circ.—66,000 (French ed.); 25,000 (English ed.)
Pub.—Joseph Charles Doumba
(The government of Cameroon publishes a French edition daily and an English edition on Wednesday.)

CAPE VERDE
Pop. Est. 423,120

PRAIA
Pop. Est. 50,000

BOLETIM INFORMATIVO Portuguese
Sao Tiago; Caixa Postal 126
BOLETIM OFICIAL Portuguese
Sao Tiago; Caixa Postal 113

CENTRAL AFRICAN REPUBLIC (CAR)
Pop. Est. 3,142,182

BANGUI
Pop. Est. 596,000

BANGUI CENTRAFRIC PRESS (d)
Boite Postal 1290

CHAD REPUBLIC
Pop. Est. 5,466,771

N'DJAMENA
Pop. Est. (Metro Area) 600,000

N'DJAMENA HEBDO
N 5164 Ave. Ch. de Gaulle-Moursal; Boite Postal 760
Tel: (235-51) 5314; Fax: (235-51) 5800
Circ.—9,500
Prop.—Media-Pub.
Pub.—Hondo Ben Mala
Dir.—Y Begoto Oulatar
Ed. in Ch.—D Ben Djonabaye
INFO-TCHAD (d) French
ATP; Boite Postale 670
Tel: (235-51) 5867
Circ.—1,500
Prop.—Ministry of Information
Dir.—Khamis Togo
(Daily News bulletin of the Chad Press Agency.)
TCHAD ET CULTURE
Boite Postal 907
Tel: (235-51) 5432/(235-51) 4142
Dir./Pub.—Jean Geli
Ed. in Ch.—Sabine Laplane

CONGO, REPUBLIC OF
Pop. Est. 2,446,902

BRAZZAVILLE
Pop. Est. (Metro Area) 595,102

ACI (Daily News Bulletin)
Boite Postal 2144
Tel: (242) 810591
COURRIER D'AFRIQUE (African Courier) (d) French
Boite Postal 2027

Copyright ©1996 by the Editor & Publisher Co.

Congo, Republic of

ETUMBA
Boite Postal 23
Tel: (242) 811389
Circ.—8,000
JOURNAL DE BRAZZAVILLE (Brazzaville Journal)
(d) French
Boite Postal 132
Pub.—M J Devoue
JOURNAL OFFICIAL DE LA REPUBLIQUE DU CONGO (Official Journal of the Republic of Congo) (d) French
Boite Postal 58
MWETI (d) French
Boite Postal 991
Tel: (242) 811087
Circ.—8,000
Dir.—Claude Bivoua

POINTE-NOIRE
Pop. Est. (Metro Area) 297,000

L'EVEIL DE POINTE-NOIRE (d)
Boite Postal 66

COTE D'IVOIRE, REPUBLIC OF
(IVORY COAST)
Pop. Est. 14,295,501

ABIDJAN
Pop. Est. 1,850,000

ABIDJAN 7 JOURS
Boite Postal 1965
Tel: (225) 353939
FRATERNITE-MATIN (m-ex S) French; Est. 1964
Blvd. General de Gaulle; Boite Postal 1807
Tel: (225) 212727
Circ.—80,000
Prop.—Societe de Presse de la Cote d'Ivoire
Pub.—Amadou Thiam
Ed.—Auguste Miremont
Ad. Mgr.—Michael Dubius
IVOIRE DIMANCHE French; Est. 1971
Blvd. General de Gaulle; Boite Postal 1807
Circ.—75,000
Ad. Mgr.—Hughes Perinel
IVOIR'SOIR (e-5x wk.)
Blvd. General de Gaulle; Boite Postal 1807
Tel: (225) 371667; (225) 372545
Circ.—60,000
Ed.—Auguste Miremont
Ad. Mgr.—Michael Dubius
U.S. Rep.—AdMarket Int'l.

DJIBOUTI, REPUBLIC OF
Pop. Est. 412,599

DJIBOUTI
(Capital City)
Pop. Est. 395,000

LA NATION DE DJIBOUTI (Djibouti Nation)
French
Place du 27 Junin; Boite Postal 32
Tel: (253) 352201

EGYPT, ARAB REPUBLIC OF
Pop. Est. 60,765,028

ALEXANDRIA
Pop. Est. 3,183,000

BARID EL CHARIKAT (e) Arabic
PO Box 813
AL ITTIHAD EL MISRI (e) Arabic
13 Sharia Sidi Abdel Razzak
LE JOURNAL D'ALEXANDRIE (Alexandria Journal) (e) French
1 Sharia Rolo
LA REFORME (The Reform) (d) French
8 Passage Sherif
AL SAFEER (e) Arabic
4 El Sahafa St.
TACHYDROMOS EGYPTOS (d) Greek; Est. 1880
4 Sharia Zangarol
Tel: (20-3) 35650
Circ.—2,000
Ed.—Dinos Coutsoumis
Ad. Mgr.—Penny Coutsoumis

CAIRO
Pop. Est. 12,560,000

AL AHALI (d) Arabic
23 Abdal Khalek, Tharwat
Tel: (20-2) 759114
AL AHRAM (m-5x wk.) Arabic; Est. 1875
Sharia al-Galaa, Post No. 11511
Tel: (20-2) 758333; Fax: (20-2) 745888
Circ.—2,117,599
Prop.—Al Ahram Establishment
Pub./Ed. in Ch.—Ibrahim Nafie
Ed.—Aly Hamdy El-Gamma
Ad. Mgr.—Adel Afifi
U.S. Rep.—Publicitas
AL AKHBAR (m-ex sat.) Arabic; Est. 1944
6 Sharia al-Sahafa St.
Tel: (20-2) 758888
Circ.—789,268
Dir.—Atta Abdel Maged
Ed.—Ibrahim Saada
AKHBAR EL YOM/AL AKHBAR Arabic; Est. 1944
6 Sharia al-Sahafa St.
Tel: (20-2) 758888
Circ.—1,159,339
Prop.—Akhbar El-Yom Publishing House
Pub.—Talaat El Zouhri
Ed.—Abdel Hamid Abdel Ghani
Ad. Mgr.—Osman El Abd
AREV (e) Armenian
3 Sharia Soliman Halaby
EGYPTIAN GAZETTE (m) English; Est. 1879
24-26 Sharia Zakaria Ahmed St., Al Tahir
Tel: (20-2) 751511
Circ.—35,000
Ad. Dir.—Mahmoud Rasheed
EGYPTIAN MAIL English
24-26 Sharia Zakaria Ahmed St., Al Tahrir
Tel: (20-2) 751511
AL GOUMHOURYIA (m-5x wk.) Arabic; Est. 1953
24-26 Sharia Zakaria Ahmed St.
Tel: (20-2) 751711
Circ.—650,000
Prop.—Al Tahrir Publishing House
Ad. Dir.—Mahmoud Rasheed
AL HAYAT (d)
1 Latin America St., Garden City
Tel: (20-2) 3546646; Fax: (20-2) 3546646
LE JOURNAL D'EGYPTE (Egyptian Journal) (mS) French; Est. 1940
1 Borsa El Guedida St.
Circ.—25,000
Pub.—Lita Gallad
Ed.—Mohamed Rashad
AL KORA WAL MALACEB Arabic; Est. 1976
24-26 Zakaria Ahmed St.
Circ.—95,000
Mng. Dir.—Abdel Hamid Hamrouch
Ed.—Hamdi El Nahas
AL MISSA (e) Arabic; Est. 1956
24-26 Sharia Zakaria Ahmed St.
Tel: (20-2) 751511
Circ.—105,000
Ad. Dir.—Mahmoud Rasheed
PHOS (d) Greek
14 Sharia Zakaria Ahmed
LE PROGRES EGYPTIEN/LE PROGRES DIMANCHE (mS) French; Est. 1897
24-26 Sharia Zacharia Ahmed St.
Tel: (20-2) 741611
Circ.—21,000
Ad. Dir.—Mahmoud Rasheed

EQUATORIAL GUINEA, REPUBLIC OF
Pop. Est. 409,550

BATA
Pop. Est. 27,024

EGYPTIAN MAIL English
24-26 Sharia Zakaria Ahmed St., Al Tahrir
Tel: (240-8) 7441/(240-8) 7466
POTO POTO (d) Fang & Spanish
Apdo. Postal 236
Pub.—Francisco de Anta Franco

ETHIOPIA
Pop. Est. 54,927,108

ADDIS ABABA
(Shewa)
Pop. Est. 3,000,000

ADDIS ZEMEN (m-ex mon.) Amharic; Est. 1941
Victory Sq.; PO Box 30145
Circ.—37,000
Prop.—Ministry of Information & Nat'l. Guidance
Ed.—Merid Bekele
ETHIOPIAN HERALD (m) English; Est. 1943
Victory Sq.; PO Box 30701
Tel: (251-1) 119050
Circ.—15,000
Prop.—Ministry of Information & Nat'l. Guidance
Ed.—Kiflom Adgoi
Ad. Mgr.—Hiruy Mitiku
YEZARIETU ETHIOPIA (Ethiopia Today)
Amharic & English
Victory Sq.; PO Box 30232
Circ.—25,000
Ed.—Shiferaw Mengeshaw

ASMARA
(Eritrea)
Pop. Est. 275,385

ASMARA HEBRET/AL WADHA (d) Tigrinya & Arabic
PO Box 247
Circ.—4,000
Prop.—Ministry of Information & Nat'l. Guidance
Ed. in Ch.—Gurgia Tesfaselassie
QUOTIDIANO ERITREO (d) Italian
PO Box 247

GABON REPUBLIC
Pop. Est. 1,139,006

LIBREVILLE
Pop. Est. (Metro Area) 352,000

GABON D'AUJOURD'HUI
Boite Postal 750
Prop.—Ministry of Information
GABON-MATIN (m) French
Boite Postal 168
Prop.—Agence Gabonaise de Presse
L'UNION (The Union) (d) French
Boite Postal 3849
Circ.—15,000

GAMBIA
Pop. Est. 959,300

BANJUL
Pop. Est. 40,000

THE DAILY OBSERVER
New Town-Sait Matty Junction, Bakau; PO Box 131
Pub.—A A Barry
THE FOROYAA
Bundungkakunda; PO Box 2306
Pub.—Sam Sarr
THE GAMBIA ONWARD
46 Grant St.
Pub.—R S Allen
THE GAMBIA TIMES
21 Leman St.; PO Box 698
Prop.—People's Progressive Party
Pub./Ed.—Jay Saidy
THE GAMBIA WEEKLY English
14 Hagan St.
Prop.—Ministry of Information and Broadcasting
Prop.—The Gambia Information Services
THE GAMBIAN
60 Lancaster St.
Pub.—Ngiang Thomas
THE NATION
2 Box Bar Rd., Campama
Pub.—W Dixon Colley
THE POINT
1A Hagan St.
Prop.—Joint Publishers
THE WORKER (d) Est. 1974
6 Albion Pl.; PO Box 508
Circ.—1,000
Prop.—The Gambia Labour Congress
Ed.—M M Ceesey
Ad. Mgr.—B B Kebbeh

GHANA
Pop. Est. 17,225,185

ACCRA
Pop. Est. 1,000,000

DAILY TELEGRAPH (m-ex S)
PO Box 742
Tel: (223-21) 228911
Circ.—10,000
Prop.—Graphic Corp.
Ad. Mgr.—W J Cooke
ECHO
PO Box 5288
Circ.—40,000
THE GHANAIAN CHRONICLE English
PO Box 16369
Tel: (233-21) 27789; Fax: (233-21) 226573
Circ.—60,000
Prop.—Ghanaian Chronicle
Ed.—Nana Kofi Coomson
Ad. Mgr.—Elizabeth Torto
GHANAIAN TIMES (m-ex S) English; Est. 1958
PO Box 2638
Tel: (233-21) 228282
Circ.—40,000
Prop.—New Times Corp.
Pub.—Christian Aggrey
Ad. Mgr.—F S Lassey
GRAPHIC SPORTS English
PO Box 742
Tel: (233-21) 228911
Circ.—60,000
Prop.—Graphic Corp.
THE MIRROR English
PO Box 742
Tel: (233-21) 228911; Fax: (233-21) 669886
Circ.—70,000
Prop.—Graphic Corp.
Ed.—E M O Provencal
Ad. Mgr.—Nana Baiden
PEOPLE'S DAILY GRAPHIC (d) English
PO Box 742
Tel: (233-21) 228911; Fax: (233-21) 669886
Circ.—100,000
Prop.—Graphic Corp.
Ed.—Elvis Aryeh
Ad. Mgr.—E K Baiden
PEOPLE'S EVENING NEWS (e) English
PO Box 7505
Tel: (233-21) 229416/(233-21) 229461
Circ.—60,000
Ed.—Osei Poku
WEEKLY SPECTATOR English
PO Box 2638
Tel: (233-21) 228282
Circ.—165,000
Prop.—New Times Corp.
Ed.—Willie Donkor
Ad. Mgr.—W K Amponsah

KUMASI
Pop. Est. 450,900

THE PIONEER (m-ex S) English; Est. 1939
PO Box 325
Tel: (233-51) 552204
Circ.—100,000
Prop.—Abura Printing Works Ltd.
Ed.—T W Ewousi-Brookman
Ad. Mgr.—Alan B Atubanansah

GUINEA, REPUBLIC OF
Pop. Est. 6,391,536

CONAKRY
Pop. Est. 705,000

FONIKE (Sports)
Boite Postal 341
HOROYA (Dignity) French
Boite Postal 191
Circ.—20,000
Prop.—PDG (Party-State)
Pub.—Mamadi Keita
Ed. in Ch.—Mamadou Saliou Balde
Ed. in Ch.—Fassiri Camara

GUINEA-BISSAU
Pop. Est. 1,098,231

BISSAU
Pop. Est. 110,000

VOZ DA GUINE (d) Portuguese
Circ.—6,000
Prop.—Sociedade Editora de Guinea SARL

KENYA, REPUBLIC OF
Pop. Est. 28,240,658

NAIROBI
Pop. Est. 1,200,000

CHEMSHA BONGO Kiswahili
PO Box 57657
DAILY NATION/SUNDAY EDITION (m) English; Est. 1960
PO Box 49010
Tel: (254-2) 337691
Circ.—204,160
Prop.—Nation Newspapers
Pub.—Albert Ekirapa
Ed.—George Mbuggus
Ad. Mgr.—Solomon Mukuna
KENYA LEO (d) Swahili
PO Box 30958
Tel: (254-2) 337798; Fax: (254-2) 340695
Prop.—Kenya Media Trust
Ed.—Job Mubungi
Ad. Mgr.—John Thande
KENYA TIMES (m) Est. 1983
PO Box 30958
Tel: (254-2) 24251; Fax: (254-2) 340695
Circ.—75,000
Ed.—A Andere
Ad. Mgr.—John Thande
THE STANDARD (m-ex S) English; Est. 1902
Likoni Rd.; PO Box 30080
Tel: (254-2) 540280; Fax: (254-2) 553939
Circ.—60,000 ABC
Prop.—The Standard Ltd.
Pub.—C Robinson
Ed.—Paul Odonde
Ad. Mgr.—Ali Mohamed
SUNDAY NATION Est. 1960
PO Box 49010
Tel: (254-2) 337691
Circ.—210,000
Prop.—Nation Newspapers
Ed. in Ch.—Bernard Nderitu
SUNDAY STANDARD (S)
Likoni Rd.; PO Box 30080
Tel: (254-2) 540280; Fax: (254-2) 553939
Circ.—54,340
Ad. Mgr.—F Githui
SUNDAY TIMES OF KENYA (S)
PO Box 30958
Tel: (254-2) 24251
TAIFA LEO (m-ex S) Swahili; Est. 1960
Tom Mboya St.; PO Box 40910
Tel: (254-2) 337691
Circ.—62,981 ABC
Prop.—National Newspapers Ltd.
Ed.—George Mbuggus
Ad. Mgr.—Solomon Mukuna

LESOTHO
Pop. Est. 1,944,493

MASERU
Pop. Est. 356,500

LENTSOE LA BASOTHO Sesotho; Est. 1974
PO Box 353
Tel: (266) 323561; Fax: (266) 310003
Circ.—10,000
Prop.—Dept. of Information
Ed.—Khahliso Lesenya
Ad. Mgr.—Ms. Teboho Lethoba
LESOTHO TODAY English; Est. 1977
PO Box 353
Tel: (266) 323561; Fax: (266) 310003
Circ.—5,000
Prop.—Dept. of Information
Ed.—Kubutu Makhakhe
Ad. Mgr.—Ms. Teboho Lethoba
MAKATOLLE Sesotho; Est. 1963
PO Box 111
Circ.—20,000
Prop.—Makatolle Newspapers
Ed.—Mohaila Mohale
Ad. Mgr.—Zacharia R Motaung
THE MIRROR English; Est. 1988
PO Box 903
Tel: (266) 315602
Circ.—4,000
Prop.—Mirror Newspapers
Ed./Ad. Mgr.—T Mlungoange
MOAFRIKA Sesotho; Est. 1990
PO Box 7234
Circ.—3,500
Pub./Ad. Mgr.—Thabang Khalieli
MOHLANKA Sesotho; Est. 1992
PO Box 124
Circ.—6,000
Prop.—Mohlanka Newspapers
Ed./Ad. Mgr.—C S Maboloka
MPHATLALATSANE Sesotho; Est. 1991
PO Box 7066
Circ.—4,000
Prop.—Mphatlalatsane Publishers
Ed./Ad. Mgr.—Ms. Mamello Morrison

MAZENOD

MOELETSI OA BASOTHO Sesotho; Est. 1993
PO Box 18
Tel: (266) 350224
Circ.—20,000
Prop.—Roman Catholic Church
Ed.—Rev. M Khutlang
Ad. Mgr.—Mrs. M Moeletsi

MORIJA

LESELINYANA LA LESOTHO Est. 1886
PO Box 7
Circ.—15,000
Prop.—Lesotho Evangelical Church
Ed./Ad. Mgr.—Aaron B Thoahlane

LIBERIA
Pop. Est. 2,972,766

MONROVIA
(Montserrado County)
Pop. Est. 425,000

DAILY LISTENER (m-ex wknd.) English
Johnson & Carey Sts.; PO Box 35
Circ.—3,500
Ad. Mgr.—Charles C Dennis Sr
DAILY OBSERVER (mS) English
117 Broad St., Crown Hill; PO Box 1858
Tel: (231) 223545
Circ.—12,000
Mng. Dir.—Kenneth Y Best
FOOTPRINTS TODAY (dS) English
PO Box 3496
LIBERIAN AGE (m)
Carey St.; PO Box 9031
Circ.—4,000
LIBERIAN STAR (m) Est. 1954
PO Box 691
Circ.—3,500
Prop.—Republic Press Inc.
Ed.—Henry B Cole
MIRROR (d) English
Logan Town; PO Box 891
NEW LIBERIAN (d-ex wed.)
Capitol Hill; PO Box 9021
Prop.—Ministry of Information
Ed. in Ch.—J Emmanuel Zehkpehge Bowier
(This publication is an official newspaper of the Liberian government.)
SUN TIMES (d)
33 Gurley St.; PO Box 2475

LIBYA
Pop. Est. 5,057,392

TRIPOLI
Pop. Est. 591,000

AL FAJR AL-JADEED (New Dawn) (d) Arabic; Est. 1972
PO Box 2303
Tel: (218-21) 37106
Circ.—40,000
Prop.—Jamahiriyah News Agency
Ed.—Ali Mahmaud Mariya
AL-JIHAD (d) Arabic
2 Sharia Jama Syala
Prop.—General Press Corporation
Ed.—Ali Al-Mahdi

LIBYAN PRESS REVIEW (d) English
PO Box 2461
Tel: (218-21) 42781
AL ZAHF AL-AKHDAR (d) Arabic
PO Box 15246
Tel: (218-21) 602418

MADAGASCAR
Pop. Est. 13,427,758

ANTANANARIVO
Pop. Est. 700,000

ATRIKA (d) French & Malagasy
rue Ratsimilaho, Antaninarenina; Boite Postal 271
Tel: (261-2) 22220
Circ.—13,000
Prop.—Ministry of Information
IMONGO VAOVAO (d) Malagasy
11-k, 4 Bis, Andravoahangy; Boite Postal 7041
Tel: (261-2) 21045
Circ.—10,000
Pub.—Clement Ramamonjisoa
MADAGASCAR TRIBUNE (m) French & Malagasy; Est. 1972
Rue Ravoninahitriniarivo, Ankorodrano, Antananarivo 101
Tel: (261-2) 22635; Fax: (261-2) 34753
Circ.—10,000
Prop.—Immenble SME
Pub.—Rahaga Ramaholimihaso
Ed.—Franck Raharison
(This newspaper was formerly Madagascar-Matin.)
MARASAKA (d) Malagasy; Est. 1953
12 Lalana Dr. Ratsimba Rajohn, Antananarivo
Tel: (261-2) 23568
Circ.—5,000
Ed.—M Rabefananina
MIDI-MADAGASCAR (d) French
Ialana Ravoninahitriniarivo; Boite Postal 1414
Tel: (261-2) 30038
Circ.—16,500
Pub.—Aline Ralainarvio
SAHY (d) Malagasy
Ambanidia Lot V.D. 42
Tel: (261-2) 22715
Circ.—2,500
Prop.—La Typo-Expredd Ambanidia
Ed.—Aline Rakoto

MALAWI
Pop. Est. 9,732,409

BLANTYRE
Pop. Est. 331,588

COMPUTER MONITOR (d)
PO Box 2521
Tel: (265) 623863; Fax: (265) 623289
Prop.—Commercial Development Ltd.
Owner—Richard Stambuli
DAILY TIMES (m-5x wk.) English; Est. 1895
Scott Rd.; PO Box 39
Tel: (265) 671566; Fax: (265) 671114
Circ.—22,000
Prop.—Blantyre Printing & Publishing Co.
Ed. in Ch.—Ken Lipanje
Ad. Mgr.—Elvis Somanje
THE INDEPENDENT (d)
PO Box 2094
Tel: (265) 674314
Prop.—New Publications Ltd.
Owner—Zeenat Karim
Ed. in Ch.—Janet Z Karim
MALAWI NEWS English & Chichewa; Est. 1956
Scott Rd.; Private Bag 39
Tel: (265) 671566; Fax: (265) 671114
Circ.—30,000
Prop.—Blantyre Printing & Publishing Co.
Ed.—Dr. K Lipenga
Ad. Mgr.—Elvis Somanje
MICHIRU SUN (d)
PO Box 90143
Tel: (265) 641671; Fax: (265) 645095
Prop.—G E Publications Ltd.

Owner/Mng. Ed.—Edward Chitsulo
Owner—Gray Mang'Anda
THE NATION (d)
PO Box 30403
Tel: (265) 674208/(265) 674419; Fax: (265) 674343
Prop.—Nation Publications Ltd.
THE NEW EXPRESS (d)
PO Box 30717
Tel: (265) 624168
Owner/Mng. Ed.—Willie Zingani
U.D.F. NEWS (d)
PO Box 3052
Tel: (265) 673043/(265) 643245
Prop.—United Democratic Front

BVUMBWE

THE ENQUIRER (d)
PO Box 110
Tel: (265) 675229
Prop.—Midas Publications

MALI, REPUBLIC OF
Pop. Est. 9,112,950

BAMAKO
Pop. Est. (Metro Area) 746,000

BULLETIN QUOTIDIEN (m) French; Est. 1936
Boite Postal 46
Prop.—Chambre de Commerce et d'Industrie du Mali
L'ESSOR-LA VOIX DU PEUPLE (d) Est. 1949
Boite Postal 141
Tel: (223) 223683/(223) 222647
Circ.—4,000
Prop.—Le Ministere de la Communication
Ed.—S Drabo
JOURNAL OFFICIEL DE LA REPUBLIQUE DU MALI
(Official Journal of the Republic of Mali)
French
Boite Postal 1463
Prop.—President of the Republic of Mali
Prop.—Secretary General of the Gov't.

MAURITANIA
Pop. Est. 2,192,777

NOUAKCHOTT
Pop. Est. 400,000

ACH-CHABB (d) Arabic & French
Boite Postal 371-618

MAURITIUS
Pop. Est. 1,116,923

PORT LOUIS
Pop. Est. 155,000

ADVANCE (d-ex S) English & French; Est. 1930
5 Dumat St.
Circ.—10,000
Prop.—Mauritius Free Press Co. Ltd.
Ad. Mgr.—Roger Merven
CHINA TIMES (e) Chinese; Est. 1953
34 La Rempe St.; PO Box 324
Tel: (230) 223067
Circ.—3,000
Pub./Ed./Ad. Mgr.—L S Ah Keng
CHINESE DAILY NEWS (e) Chinese; Est. 1932
32 Remy Ollier; PO Box 8440
Circ.—5,000
Pub./Ed.—Li Kwong In
Ad. Mgr.—L K Ah Keng
L'EXPRESS (The Express) (dS) French & English; Est. 1963
Brown Sequard St.; PO Box 247
Tel: (230) 21827
Circ.—20,000
Prop.—La Sentinelle Ltd.
Pub.—Edgar Adolphe
Ed.—Yvan Martial
Ad. Mgr.—Marie Noelle

Mauritius

LE MAURICIEN (The Mauritian) (e-ex S) French & English; Est. 1906
8 George St.; PO Box 7
Tel: (230) 23248
Circ.—15,000
Prop.—Le Mauricien Ltd.
Pub.—Jacques Rivet
Ed.—Lindsay Riviere
Ad. Mgr.—Fritz Too-Him
LE NOUVEAU MILITANT (d) French & English; Est. 1980
21 Poudriere St.
Circ.—5,000
Pub./Ed.—Jean-Claude de L'Estrac
NEW CHINESE COMMERCIAL PAPER (d)
Chinese, English & French
12 Arsenal St.
THE NEW NATION (m) French & English; Est. 1985
31 Edith Cavell St.; PO Box 647
Circ.—15,000
Prop.—Independent Publications Ltd.
Pub./Ed.—Jugdish Joypaul
Ad. Mgr.—Raveen Kreshwan Singh
LE SOCIALISTE (The Socialist) (d) French & English; Est. 1981
Brabant St.
Tel: (230) 20329
Circ.—5,000
Pub.—Peter Craig
Ed.—Vedi Ballah
SUN (d) English & French
31 Edith Cavell St.

MAYOTTE ISLAND
(Dependency of France)
Pop. Est. 93,468

MAMOUDZOU

LE JOURNAL de MAYOTTE (Mayotte Journal) French; Est. 1983
Boite Postal 181, 97600
Circ.—1,200
Prop.—Association pour Le Developement de la Culture et de La Communication a Mayotte (ADCCM)
Pub.—Dr. Martial Henry
Ad. Mgr.—Brigitte Kern

MOROCCO, KINGDOM OF
Pop. Est. 28,558,635

CASABLANCA
Pop. Est. 3,500,000

AL BAYANE (d) Arabic & French
62, rue de la Gironde
Tel: (212-2) 307882/(212-2) 308080
Circ.—5,000
Pub.—Ali Yata
BAYANE AL YOUM
62, rue La Gironde
Tel: (212-2) 307666
Dir.—Ali Yata
AL ITTIHID AL ICHTILAQI (Socialist Union) (d)
33, rue Al Amir abdelkader
Tel: (212-2) 407380/(212-2) 407385
Circ.—75,000
Pub.—Mohamed El Brini
LIBERATION
33, rue Emir abdelkader
Tel: (212-2) 310062
Dir.—Med Elyazhi
MAROC-SOIR (e) French; Est. 1908
34, rue Mohamed Smiha
Tel: (212-2) 301271
Circ.—27,000
Pub.—Driss El Alami
Ed. in Ch.—Hassan Kacimi Alaoui
AL MASSIRA AL KHADRA (d) Arabic
33, rue Mohamed Smiha
Tel: (212-2) 75043
LE MATIN DU SAHARA ET DU MAGHREB (m) French; Est. 1971
34, rue Mohamed Smiha
Tel: (212-2) 301271; Fax: (212-2) 271473
Circ.—100,000
Pub.—Abdellatif Bennis
Ed. in Ch.—Ahmed Chahid
Ad. Mgr.—Abderrazak Bennis
RISSALAT AL OUMMA (d)
158 Ave. des Forces Armees Royales, 361354
Tel: (212-2) 361384
Circ.—7,000
Dir.—Mohamed Alaoui M'hammedi

RABAT
Pop. Est. 1,000,000

AL ALAM (The Flag) (d) Arabic; Est. 1946
11, rue Allal Ben Abdallah; PO Box 141
Tel: (212-7) 732419
Circ.—45,000
Dir./Ed.—Messari Mohamed Larbi
AL ANBAA (Information) (d) Arabic; Est. 1970
11, rue Patrice Lumumba
Tel: (212-7) 724367
Circ.—15,000
Prop.—Ministry of Information
Pub.—El Ahmed Yaakoubi
ANNIDAL ADDIMOQRATI (d)
13, rue Tunis
Tel: (212-7) 732127
Dir.—Arsalane El Jadidi
ANOUAL
5, Bis., Ave. Hassan
Tel: (212-7) 726733
Dir.—Abdellatif Aouad
AL HARAKA
8, Place Alaouiyne
Tel: (212-7) 704493
Dir.—Ali Alaoui
AL ITTIHAD AL ICHTIRAKI (Socialist Unity) (d) Arabic; Est. 1977
17, rue Oued Souss, Agdal
Tel: (212-7) 773903
Circ.—25,000
Prop.—Editions Maghrebines
Pub.—Hassan Moutahir
Ed.—Mohamed El Yarini
AL MAGHRIB (d) French; Est. 1977
6, rue Laos
Tel: (212-7) 722708
Pub.—Mustapha Iznasni
AL MITAKH AL WATANI (d) Arabic; Est. 1977
6, rue du Laos
Tel: (212-7) 722709
Circ.—15,000
Pub.—Mohammed Oujjar
L'OPINION (The Opinion) (m) Arabic; Est. 1946
11, rue Allal ben Abdallah; Boite Postal 10
Tel: (212-7) 727812; Fax: (212-7) 732182
Circ.—60,000
Prop.—Arrissala
Pub.—Mohamed Idrissi Kaituni
Ed. in Ch.—Khalid Jamai
Ad. Mgr.—Mouhid Simane
LA TRIBUNE POPULAIRE (The Popular Tribune)
12, rue Al Mariniyine
Tel: (212-7) 730808
Dir.—Soulahi Bouzekri

MOZAMBIQUE
Pop. Est. 17,346,280

BEIRA
Pop. Est. 291,604

DIARIO DE MOZAMBIQUE (Mozambique Daily) (d) Portuguese
rue D. Joao de Mascarenhas; PO Box 81
Circ.—16,000
Ed.—Ezequiel Ambrosio

MAPUTO
Pop. Est. 1,000,000

DESAFIO Portuguese
55, rua Joaquim de Lapa; PO Box 327
Tel: (258-1) 431026; Fax: (258-1) 431726
Circ.—40,000
Prop.—Sociedad Noticias SARL
Ed.—Jorge Matine
DOMINGO Portuguese
55, rua Joaquim de Lapa; PO Box 327
Tel: (258-1) 424081
Circ.—50,000
Prop.—Sociedad Noticias SARL
Ed.—Jorge Matine
NOTICIAS (News) (mS) Portuguese; Est. 1926
55, rua Joaquim de Lapa; PO Box 327
Tel: (258-1) 420119; Fax: (258-1) 431726
Circ.—65,000
Prop.—Sociedad Noticias SARL
Ed.—Bernado Mavanga
Ad. Mgr.—Nathaniel Mabasso
SAVAN (d) Portuguese
1049, Ave. Amilcar Cabral; PO Box 73
Tel: (258-1) 430106/(258-1) 430108; Fax: (258-1) 430721
Prop.—Mediacoop
Prop.—Jornalistas Associados srf
Dir.—Kok Nam
Ed.—Salomao Moiana
Ed.—Lourenco Jossias

NAMIBIA
Pop. Est. 1,595,567

WINDHOEK
Pop. Est. 180,000

ALLGEMEINE ZEITUNG (The General News) (e-5x wk.) German; Est. 1916
Stübelstr. 49; PO Box 56, 9000
Tel: (264-61) 225411; Fax: (264-61) 224843
Circ.—5,000 (per day)
Prop.—John Meinert (Pty.) Ltd.
Prop.—Democratic Media Holdings
Ed.—Hans Feddersen
Ad. Mgr.—H Roggengalk
DIE REPUBLIKEIN (The Republican) (d) Afrikaans, English & German
PO Box 3436
Tel: (264-61) 230331; Fax: (264-61) 35674/(264-61) 223721
Circ.—11,500 (mon-wed.); 12,500 (thurs. & fri.; per day)
Prop.—Die Republiken Beperk
Prop.—Democratic Media Holdings
Ed.—Chris Jacobie
Ad. Mgr.—Glenda Manthe
NAMIB TIMES Afrikaans & English; Est. 1958
Walvis Bay; PO Box 706
Tel: (264-61) 6425854; Fax: (264-61) 6424813
Circ.—4,500 (tues. & fri.)
Pub./Owner/Ed.—Paul Vincent
THE NAMIBIAN (d) English
PO Box 20783
Tel: (264-61) 36970; Fax: (264-61) 33980
Circ.—9,000 (mon.-thurs.; per day); 10,000 (fri.; per day)
Prop.—Free Press of Namibia
Ed.—Gwen Lister
TEMPO (S) Afrikaans, English & German; Est. 1992
PO Box 1794
Tel: (264-61) 230331; Fax: (264-61) 22110
Circ.—11,500 (per wk.)
Prop.—Democratic Media Holdings
Ed.—Gerritt Lloete
Ad. Mgr.—Glenda Mantne
THE WINDHOEK ADVERTISER (e) English
PO Box 2255
Tel: (264-61) 225464; Fax: (264-61) 221737
Circ.—1,800 (mon.-thurs.; per day); 10,000 (sat.; per wk.)
Prop.—John Meinert (Pty.) Ltd.
Owner/Ed.—Hannes Smith

NIGER REPUBLIC
Pop. Est. 8,971,605

NIAMEY
Pop. Est. 350,000

ANFANI
PO Box 2096
Tel: (227) 740880
Pub.—Grmah Boucar
LE DEMOCRATE (The Democrat)
PO Box 11066
Tel: (227) 735762
AL FAZAR
rue du Paon
Tel: (227) 733054; Fax: (227) 760023
Circ.—1,500
Pub.—Djibo Karama
HAOKE (d)
PO Box 297
Tel: (227) 741844
Pub.—Ibrahim Cheick Diop
LE PAON AFRICAIN
PO Box 10381
Tel: (227) 733054
LE REPUBLICAIN (The Republican) (d) French
PO Box 12015
Tel: (227) 734798
Circ.—3,000
Pub.—Maman Abou
Ed.—Abdoulaye M Massalatchi
LE SAHEL (d) French; Est. 1960
PO Box 368
Tel: (227) 722020
Circ.—5,000
Prop.—Gov't. Information Service
Pub.—Kamed Abdoulaye
Ed.—Mahamat Sile
LE SAHEL DIMANCHE
PO Box 368
Tel: (227) 722020
Circ.—3,000
Prop.—Gov't. Information Service
Pub.—Kamed Abdoulaye
Ed.—Mahamat Sile
LE SAHEL HEBDO French
PO Box 368
Tel: (227) 722020
Circ.—3,500
Ed. in Ch.—Adamou Garba
LE TRIBUNE du PEUPLE (d) French
PO Box 2624
Circ.—3,000
Pub.—Ibrahim Hamidou

NIGERIA, FEDERAL REPUBLIC OF
Pop. Est. 98,091,097

BENIN CITY
(Edo & Delta)

NIGERIAN OBSERVER (m) English; Est. 1968
18 Airport Rd.; PO Box 1334
Tel: (234) 240050
Prop.—Bendel Newspapers Corp.
Ed.—Sam Equaron
(This newspaper is nationally distributed.)

CALABAR
(Cross-River)

NIGERIAN CHRONICLE (m) Est. 1974
Barracks Rd.; PO Box 1074
Prop.—Cross River State Newspaper Corp.
Pub.—Patrick A Okon
Ad. Mgr.—John Egbelo

ENUGU
(Anambra & Enugu)
Pop. Est. 2,159,848

DAILY STAR/EVENING STAR (m&e) English; Est. 1970
9 Works Rd.; PO Box 1139
Tel: (234) 253561
Prop.—Star Printing & Publishing
Ed.—Josef Bel-Molokwu
SATELLITE (d) English
PO Box 9429

IBADAN
(Oyo)
Pop. Est. 1,172,000

DAILY SKETCH/EVENING SKETCH/SUNDAY SKETCH (mS) Est. 1964
OBA, Adebimpe Rd.; PO Box 5067
Tel: (234-22) 414851/(234-22) 414893
Circ.—64,000 (m); 125,000 (S)
Prop.—Western State Government
Ed.—Ademola Idowi
Ad. Mgr.—O Olalere
IMOLE OWURO (d)
Yemetu Aladorin; PO Box 5239
Prop.—People's Star Press Ltd.
NIGERIAN TRIBUNE (mS) English; Est. 1980
Imalefalafia St., Oke-Ado; PO Box 78
Tel: (234-22) 310886
Circ.—109,000
Prop.—African Newspapers of Nigeria Ltd.
Pub.—Oluwole Awolowo
Ed.—Felix A Adenaike
Ad. Mgr.—P J Faduka
(This newspaper is nationally distributed.)
PMB INDEPENDENT (d)
PO Box 5109

ILORIN
(Kwara & Kogo)
Pop. Est. 1,566,469

NIGERIAN HERALD (m) Est. 1973
Offa Rd.; PO Box 1369
Tel: (234) 12436
Circ.—20,000
Prop.—Kwara State Gov't.
Ed.—Ahmed Hameed
(This newspaper is nationally distributed.)

Copyright ©1996 by the Editor & Publisher Co.

JOS
(Plateau)
Pop. Est. 3,283,704

NIGERIAN STANDARD/SUNDAY STANDARD (mS) English; Est. 1972
5 Joseph Gornwalic Rd.; PO Box 2112
Circ.—100,000
Prop.—Plateau State Gov't.
Ed.—Sale Iliya
Ad. Mgr.—Paul Wakkias

KADUNA
(Kaduna)
Pop. Est. 3,969,252

GASKIYA TAFI KWABO (d) Hausa
Ed.—Babanzara Hassan
(This newspaper is of local dialect.)
NEW DEMOCRAT (d) English; Est. 1983
9 Ahmed Talib Ave.; PO Box 4457
Circ.—70,000
Prop.—New Africa Holding Co.
Ed.—Kanmi Ademiluyi
Ad. Mgr.—Dennis Ajufo
NEW NIGERIAN (m) English; Est. 1966
Ahmadu Bello Way; PO Box 254
Tel: (234-62) 201420
Circ.—80,000
Prop.—New Nigerian Newspapers Ltd.
Pub.—Inuwa Jibirin
Ed.—Ms. Bilkisu Tusuf
(This newspaper is nationally distributed.)
THE REPORTER (d) English
Kaduna South
Mng. Dir.—Muhammed Sulaiman

KANO
(Kano)
Pop. Est. 5,632,040

TRIUMPH (d) English
Sa'ad Zungur House
Ed.—Garba Shehy
(This newspaper is nationally distributed.)

LAGOS
(Lagos)
Pop. Est. 5,685,781

AMANA (d) Hausa
Ikeja; PO Box 4483
Tel: (234-1) 713595335
DAILY CHAMPION/SUNDAY CHAMPION (m) Est. 1988
PO Box 2276
Tel: (234-1) 524421; Fax: (234-1) 525796
Circ.—150,000
Prop.—Champion Newspapers Ltd.
Ed.—Emma Agu
Ad. Mgr.—Ejike Okeagu
DAILY EXPRESS (d) Est. 1938
5-11 Apongbon St.; PO Box 163
Prop.—Commercial Amalgamated Printers
(This newspaper is nationally distributed.)
DAILY TIMES/SUNDAY TIMES/EVENING TIMES (m) English; Est. 1925
New Isheri Rd., Agidingbi, Ikeja; PO Box 21340, Ikeja
Tel: (234-1) 9008509
Circ.—400,000
Prop.—Daily Times of Nigeria Ltd.
Ed.—Onyema Yugochkuj
Ad. Mgr.—Ola Yasuff
(This newspaper is nationally distributed.)
THE GUARDIAN (d) English; Est. 1983
Rutam House, Isolo Expressway; PO Box 1217
Tel: (234-1) 5241111; Fax: (234-1) 522027
Circ.—80,000
NATIONAL CONCORD (m) Est. 1980
Concord House, 4 Concord Way, Ikeja; PO Box 4483
Tel: (234-1) 9010109
Circ.—200,000
Prop.—Concord Printing of Nigeria Ltd.
Pub.—Chief M K O Abiola
Ed.—Ben Onyeachonam
NEW NIGERIAN (Kaduna) (d) English
PO Box 254
Circ.—80,000
(This newspaper is nationally distributed.)
THE PUNCH (dS) Est. 1977
Kudeti St., Onipetesi, Ikeja; PO Box 21204
Tel: (234-1) 963580
Circ.—150,000
Prop.—Skyway Press
Ed.—Demola Oshinubi
(This newspaper is nationally distributed.)
UDORAN (d) Ibo
Prop.—Concord Newspaper

OWERRI
(Imo)
Pop. Est. 2,485,499

DAILY NATION (m)
43 Okigwe Rd., Aba
Ed.—Gab Okafor
NIGERIAN STATESMAN/SUNDAY STATESMAN (dS) Est. 1978
Owerri/Egbo Rd.; PO Box 1095
Tel: (234) 3230099
Prop.—Imo Newspapers
Pub.—Chike Okonkwo
Ed.—Ebube Wadibia
(This newspaper is nationally distributed.)

PORT HARCOURT
(Rivers)
Pop. Est. 3,983,857

NIGERIAN STAR (d) English
97 Aggrey Rd.; PO Box 73
NIGERIAN TIDE/SUNDAY TIDE (mS) English; Est. 1971
4 Ikwerre Rd.; PO Box 5072
Circ.—30,000
Prop.—River State Press
Ed.—Augustine Njoagwuani
(This newspaper is nationally distributed.)

REUNION ISLAND
Pop. Est. 652,857

SAINT-DENIS
Pop. Est. 207,158

LE JOURNAL DE L'ILE DE LA REUNION (e) French; Est. 1950
42, rue Alexis-de-Villeneuve; Boite Postal 98, 97463
Tel: (262) 213264; Fax: (262) 410977
Circ.—26,000
Prop.—Cazal SA, Baloukjy G, Baloukjy Ph., et Societe France Antilles & Co.
Pub.—Philippe Baloukjy
Ed. in Ch.—Jacques Tillier
Ed.—Michel Szkaradek
Ad. Mgr.—Alex Eyquem
LE QUOTIDIEN DE LA REUNION (d) French; Est. 1973
Boite Postal 303, 97467
Tel: (262) 291010; Fax: (262) 282528
Circ.—23,000
Pub.—Maximin Chane Ki-Chune
Ed. in Ch.—Jean-Louis Rabou
Ad. Mgr.—Daniele Arrighi
LE REUNIONNAIS
190, rue des Deux-Canons, 97490
Tel: (262) 287777; Fax: (262) 282816
Prop.—Armand Apavou
Ed. in Ch.—Jean Noel Fortier
TEMOIGNAGES (d) French; Est. 1944
21 bis., rue de l'Est; Boite Postal 192, 97465
Tel: (262) 211307
Circ.—6,000
Prop.—Imprimerie Cazal
Pub.—Jean-Marcel Courteaud
Ed.—Elie Hoarau

RWANDA
Pop. Est. 8,373,963

KIGALI
Pop. Est. 300,000

ARP (d) French; Est. 1976
Rwandese Press Agency; PO Box 83
Circ.—100,000
Prop.—Office Rwandais d'Information (ORINFOR)
DIALOGUE French; Est. 1970
PO Box 442
Circ.—10,000
Prop.—Eglise Catholique (The Catholic Church)
IMVAHO (The Truth) Kinyarwanda; Est. 1960
PO Box 83
Tel: (250) 5724
Circ.—60,000
Prop.—Office Rwandais d'Information (ORINFOR)
LE RELEVE (Raising Up) French; Est. 1974
PO Box 83

Africa

Circ.—2,000 ABC
Prop.—Office Rwandais d'Information (ORINFOR)

SENEGAL
Pop. Est. 8,730,508

DAKAR
Pop. Est. 1,300,000

LE SOLEIL (The Sun) (m) French
Route du service Geographique; Boite Postal 92
Tel: (221) 214692
Circ.—50,000
Prop.—Societe Senegalaise de Presse et de Publication
Pub.—Alioune Drame

SEYCHELLES
Pop. Est. 72,113

VICTORIA
(Mahe)
Pop. Est. 23,000

THE SEYCHELLES NATION (d-ex S) Creole, English & French
PO Box 321
Tel: (248) 224161; Fax: (248) 221006
Circ.—3,200
Prop.—Ministry of Finance, Defense, Info. & Telecommunications Division
Ed.—Denis Rose
(This newspaper is nationally distributed.)

SIERRA LEONE
Pop. Est. 4,630,037

FREETOWN
Pop. Est. 500,000

DAILY MAIL (m) English; Est. 1931
29-31 Rawdon St.; PO Box 53
Tel: (232-22) 23191/(232-22) 22197
Circ.—20,000
Prop.—Sierra Leone Daily Mail
Pub.—J M Johnson
Ed.—Arika Awuta-Coker
Ad. Mgr.—Ted King
NEW SHAFT
60 Old Railway Line, Brookfields
Tel: (232-22) 41093
WEEKEND SPARK
7 Lamina Sankoh St.
Tel: (232-22) 22397
WE YONE English; Est. 1961
89 Fort St.
Ed.—Sam Metzeger

SOMALIA
Pop. Est. 6,666,873

MOGADISHU
Pop. Est. 700,000

HEEGAN English
PO Box 1178
Prop.—Ministry of Information & National Guidance
HORSEED Arabic & Italian
Prop.—Ministry of Information & National Guidance
XIDDIGTA OBKTOBAR (October Star) (d) Somali
PO Box 1178
Prop.—Ministry of Information & National Guidance

South Africa, Republic of   IV-57

SOUTH AFRICA, REPUBLIC OF
Pop. Est. 43,930,631

BLOEMFONTEIN
(Orange Free State)
Pop. Est. 311,150

DIE VOLKSBLAD (e&sat.) Afrikaans; Est. 1917
79 Voortrekker St.; PO Box 267, 9300
Tel: (27-51) 473351; Fax: (27-51) 477363
Circ.—28,699 (e); 23,164 (sat.)
Prop.—National Media Ltd.
Pub.—J M Meintjies
Ed.—J De Wet
Ad. Mgr.—A E Murray
WEEKLY MAIL E GUARDIAN English
PO Box 32362, 2017
Tel: (27-51) 4037111; Fax: (27-51) 4031025
Circ.—28,968
Prop.—MEG Media (Pty.) Ltd.
Ed.—A Harber

CAPE TOWN
(KAAPSTAD)
(Western Cape)
Pop. Est. 2,350,157

THE ARGUS (e) English; Est. 1857
122 St. George's St.; PO Box 56, 8000
Tel: (27-21) 4884911; Fax: (27-21) 4884151
Circ.—110,000
Prop.—Argus Printing & Publishing Co. Ltd.
Gen. Mgr.—F J Collings
Ed.—Andrew Drysdale
Ad. Mgr.—John Lloyd
DIE BURGER (d-ex S) Afrikaans; Est. 1915
Nasionale Koerante Beperk; PO Box 692, 8000
Tel: (27-21) 4884911; Fax: (27-21) 4884110
Circ.—92,855 (m); 102,247 (sat.) ABC
Prop.—National Media Ltd.
Mng. Dir.—J Prins
Mng. Dir.—J H Naude
Ed.—E Dommisse
Ad. Mgr.—Innes Van Eeden
THE CAPE TIMES (m-ex S) English; Est. 1876
122 St. Georges St.; PO Box 56, 8000
Tel: (27-21) 4884911; Fax: (27-21) 4884762
Circ.—59,030 (m); 54,005 (sat.) ABC
Prop.—Times Media Ltd.
Pub.—F J Collings
Ed.—J C Viviers
Ad. Mgr.—Malcolm Dean-Smith

DURBAN
(Kwazulu & Natal)
Pop. Est. 1,137,378

THE DAILY NEWS (e-ex S) English; Est. 1878
85 Field St., Greyville; PO Box 47549, 4023
Tel: (27-31) 3082911; Fax: (27-31) 3082333
Circ.—94,467 (e); 110,000 (sat.) ABC
Prop.—Natal Newspapers (Pty.) Ltd.
Pub.—E L Booth
Ed. in Ch.—Mostert Van Schoor
Ad. Mgr.—F L Card
ILANGA English & Zulu; Est. 1903
128 Umgeni Rd.; PO Box 2159, 4000
Tel: (27-31) 3094350; Fax: (27-31) 3093489
Circ.—130,699
Prop.—Mandla Matla Publishing (Pty.) Ltd.
Ed.—O Kunene
Ed.—T Mthembu
THE NATAL MERCURY (m) English; Est. 1852
12 Devonshire Place; PO Box 47549, 4023
Tel: (27-31) 3082911; Fax: (27-31) 3082333
Circ.—60,692 ABC
Prop.—Natal Newspapers (Pty.) Ltd.
Pub.—E L Booth
Ed.—J Patton
Ad. Mgr.—A P Hiles
POST NATAL (S) English
PO Box 733, 4000
Tel: (27-31) 3082400; Fax: (27-31) 3082427
Circ.—52,509
Ed.—B Ramguthee
SUNDAY TRIBUNE (S) English; Est. 1937
85 Field St., Greyville; PO Box 47549, 4000
Tel: (27-31) 308401; Fax: (27-31) 3082430
Circ.—126,503 ABC
Prop.—Natal Newspapers (Pty.) Ltd.
Pub.—E L Booth
Ed.—David Wightman
Ad. Mgr.—A P Hiles

South Africa, Republic of — Africa

UMAFRIKA
Marianhill; PO Box 11002, 3601
Tel: (27-31) 7004600; **Fax:** (27-31) 7003707
Circ.—37,248
Prop.—Marianhill Mission Institute
Ed.—B Shoba

EAST LONDON
(Eastern Cape)
Pop. Est. 102,325

DAILY DISPATCH (m) English; Est. 1872
31 Caxton St.
Tel: (27-431) 430010; **Fax:** (27-431) 435159
Circ.—37,083 ABC
Prop.—Dispatch Media (Pty.) Ltd.
Pub.—Terry Briceland
Ed.—J G Williams
Ad. Mgr.—A Robinson

JOHANNESBURG
(PWV)
Pop. Est. 1,916,063

BEELD (m) Afrikaans; Est. 1974
32 Miller St., Ellis Park; PO Box 5425, 2001
Tel: (27-11) 4021460; **Fax:** (27-11) 4020523
Circ.—113,315 ABC
Prop.—National Media Ltd.
Mgr.—F L Wiese
Ed.—W Kühn
Ad. Mgr.—D J de Bruin
BUSINESS DAY (d) English; Est. 1986
11 Diagonal St.; PO Box 1090, 2001
Tel: (27-11) 4972560; **Fax:** (27-11) 4972279
Circ.—34,943
Prop.—Times Media Ltd.
Ed.—Jim Jones
Ad. Mgr.—Vana Wassenaar
THE CITIZEN (d-ex S) English
PO Box 7712
Tel: (27-11) 4026313; **Fax:** (27-11) 4027538
Circ.—140,000 (d); 102,000 (sat.)
Prop.—The Citizen (Pty.) Ltd.
Ed. in Ch.—M A Johnson
Ad. Mgr.—M Tame
CITY PRESS English
PO Box 3413, 2000
Tel: (27-11) 4021632; **Fax:** (27-11) 4026501
Circ.—263,917
Ed.—K Sibiya
FINANCIAL MAIL
PO Box 9959, 2000
Tel: (27-11) 492711; **Fax:** (27-11) 8341686
Circ.—31,263
Prop.—Times Media Ltd.
Ed.—N Bruce
THE NEW NATION
PO Box 10674, 2001
Tel: (27-11) 3332721/(27-11) 3332722;
Fax: (27-11) 3332733
Circ.—29,660
Prop.—New Nation Publishing Co.
Ed.—G Tugwana
RAPPORT (S) Afrikaans; Est. 1970
PO Box 8422, 2000
Tel: (27-11) 4022620; **Fax:** (27-11) 4027275
Circ.—403,120 ABC
Prop.—Rapport Uitgewers Beperk
Ed.—I de Villiers
Ad. Mgr.—H W Groenewald
(This newspaper is nationally distributed.)
THE SOWETAN (m-ex wknd.) English; Est. 1981
61 Commando Rd., Industria W; PO Box 6663, 2000
Tel: (27-11) 4740128; **Fax:** (27-11) 4743810
Circ.—213,897 ABC
Prop.—Argus Printing & Pub. Co. Ltd.
Ed.—Z A Klaaste
Ad. Mgr.—D P Wills
(The Sowetan is a Black newspaper.)
THE STAR/WEEKEND STAR (e-7x wk.) English; Est. 1887/1985
47 Sauer St.; PO Box 1014, 2000
Tel: (27-11) 6339111; **Fax:** (27-11) 8383019/(27-11) 8342960
Circ.—206,219 (e); 258,272 (wknd.) ABC
Prop.—Argus Printing & Pub. Co. Ltd.
Pub.—J Nuttall
Ed. in Ch.—Richard Steyn
Ad. Mgr.—Ross Montgomery
SUNDAY TIMES (S) English; Est. 1906
171 Main St.; PO Box 1090, 2000
Tel: (27-11) 4972711; **Fax:** (27-11) 8341686
Circ.—567,934 ABC
Prop.—Times Media Ltd.
Ed.—Ken Owen
Ad. Mgr.—Robin Parker

KIMBERLEY
(Northern Cape)
Pop. Est. 167,060

DIAMOND FIELDS ADVERTISER (m) English; Est. 1878
PO Box 610, 8300
Tel: (27-531) 23161; **Fax:** (27-531) 22581
Circ.—6,546
Prop.—Argus Printing & Pub. Co. Ltd.
Pub.—L J van Gerve
Ed.—K Ritchie
Ad. Mgr.—J J Rohlandt

KING WILLIAMSTOWN
(Eastern Cape)
Pop. Est. 167,802

IMVO ZABANTSUNDU English & Xhosa
PO Box 190, 5600
Tel: (27-433) 23550
Circ.—53,965
Prop.—Perskorporasie van Beperk SA
Ed.—D du Plessis

PIETERMARITZBURG
(Kwazulu & Natal)
Pop. Est. 228,549

THE NATAL WITNESS (m) English; Est. 1846
244 Longmarket St., PO Box 362, 3200
Tel: (27-331) 942011; **Fax:** (27-331) 940468
Circ.—28,590
Prop.—The Natal Witness (Pty.) Ltd.
Pub.—S A White
Ed.—D Willers
Ad. Mgr.—J Deare

PORT ELIZABETH
(Eastern Cape)
Pop. Est. 853,204

EASTERN PROVINCE HERALD (m-ex S) English; Est. 1845
PO Box 1141, 6000
Tel: (27-41) 5047911; **Fax:** (27-41) 563315
Circ.—29,660 (m); 24,531 (sat.) ABC
Prop.—Times Media Ltd.
Pub.—Derek Smith
Ed.—Rick Wilson
Ad. Mgr.—Dave Grey
EVENING POST/WEEKEND POST (e-7x wk.) English; Est. 1950/1948
PO Box 1117, 6000
Tel: (27-41) 5047911; **Fax:** (27-41) 563315
Circ.—17,763 (e); 35,430 (wknd.) ABC
Prop.—Times Media Ltd.
Pub.—Derek Smith
Ed.—Neville M Woudberg
Ad. Mgr.—Dave Grey

PRETORIA
(PWV)
Pop. Est. 1,080,187

THE PRETORIA NEWS (m-ex S) English; Est. 1898
216 Vermeulen St.; PO Box 439, 0001
Tel: (27-12) 3255382; **Fax:** (27-12) 3257300
Circ.—26,279 (m); 15,495 (sat.) ABC
Prop.—Pretoria News (Pty.) Ltd.
Pub.—E Bottenberg
Ed.—Deon du Plessis
Ad. Mgr.—C A Humphris

TROYEVILLE

FINANSIES EN TEGNIEK
PO Box 53171, 2139
Tel: (27-11) 4026372; **Fax:** (27-11) 4041701
Circ.—21,117
Ed.—G Marais

ST. HELENA
(Dependency of U.K. in S. Atlantic)
Pop. Est. 6,741

JAMESTOWN
Pop. Est. 1,330

ST. HELENA NEWS English
Broadway House
Circ.—1,500
Prop.—Government of St. Helena
Ed.—John Cranfield

SUDAN
Pop. Est. 29,419,798

KHARTOUM
Pop. Est. 476,000

AL AYAM (d-ex sat.) Arabic; Est. 1953
UN Square, Aboul Ela Bldg.; PO Box 303
Circ.—200,000
Pub.—Dar Al Ayam
Pub.—Beshir M Said
Ed.—Mahagoub Mohmed Salih
AL KHARTOUM (d-ex fri.) Arabic; Est. 1988
PO Box 3981
Circ.—25,000
Pub.—Dar El Khartoum
Ed.—Fadalla Mohmed
AL SIASA (d-ex S) Arabic; Est. 1986
PO Box 3130
Circ.—60,000
Pub.—Dar El Siasa
Pub.—Dr. Khalio Farah
SUDAN STANDARD (d) English
PO Box 2651
Prop.—Ministry of Culture & Information
AL SUDANI (d-ex fri.) Arabic; Est. 1985
Circ.—305,000
Prop.—Dar El Sudani Khrt.
Ed.—Mahagoub M Elhassan Irwa

SWAZILAND
Pop. Est. 936,369

MBABANE
Pop. Est. 45,000

SWAZILAND OBSERVER (d) English; Est. 1982
Swazi Plaza; PO Box A385
Tel: (268) 44436/(268) 45190
TIKHATSI TEMASWATI (d) Siswati
PO Box 156
Tel: (268) 42211
TIMES OF SWAZILAND (d) English; Est. 1896
Allister Miller St.; PO Box 156
Tel: (268) 42520
Circ.—8,000
Prop.—African Echo (Pty.) Ltd.
Ed.—Patrick P Nxumalo
Ad. Mgr.—Alberto Samuels

TANZANIA
Pop. Est. 27,985,660

DAR ES SALAAM
Pop. Est. 1,260,850

DAILY NEWS (dS) English; Est. 1930
Maktaba St.; PO Box 9033
Tel: (255-51) 29881; **Fax:** (255-51) 46227
Circ.—314,413 ABC
Prop.—Tanzania Standard (Newspapers) Ltd.
Ed.—Charles Rajaby
Ad. Mgr.—Anthony Baretto
UHURU/MZALENDO (m) Swahili; Est. 1961
PO Box 9221
Tel: (255-51) 35121; **Fax:** (255-51) 35116
Circ.—50,000
Prop.—National Printing Co.
Ed. in Ch.—Yahya Buzaragi
Ad. Mgr.—Edward S Lema

ZANZIBAR
Pop. Est. 157,634

KIPANGA (d) Swahili
PO Box 199

TOGO, REPUBLIC OF
Pop. Est. 4,255,090

LOME
Pop. Est. 350,000

JOURNAL OFFICIEL DE LA REPUBLIQUE DU TOGO
(Official Journal of the Republic of Togo) (d)
Boite Postal 891
TOGO-PRESSE Ewe & French; Est. 1961
Boite Postal 891
Tel: (228) 213718; **Fax:** (228) 221489
Circ.—10,000
Prop.—La Société Nationale des Editions du Togo
Dir.—Prosper Kokou
Dir.—Wolah Amabley
Ed. in Ch.—Kokou Edina Logo

TUNISIA
Pop. Est. 8,726,562

TUNIS
Pop. Est. 1,000,000

ACH-CHOUROUK (d) Arabic
10, rue Esh-Sham, 1002
Tel: (216-1) 289357; **Fax:** (216-1) 289375
Gen. Dir.—Slaheddine Amri
Ch. Dir.—Hassan Hamada
L'ACTION (The Action) (m-ex mon.) French; Est. 1932
Dar al Amal, rue 2 Mars 1934
Tel: (216-1) 264899
Circ.—50,000
U.S. Rep.—Int'l. Media Service
AL AMAL (d) Arabic; Est. 1934
Dar al Amal, rue 2 Mars 1934
Tel: (216-1) 264899
Circ.—50,000
U.S. Rep.—Int'l. Media Service
AS-SAHAFA (d) Arabic
6, rue Ali Bach-Hambra
Tel: (216-1) 341066; **Fax:** (216-1) 341468
Dir.—Mohamed Mahfoudh
Ch. Ed.—Jamel Karmaoui
ASSABAH (d) Arabic
Ave. du 7 Novembre, El Menzah; Boite Postal 441, 1004
Tel: (216-1) 717222/(216-1) 352839; **Fax:** (216-1) 717481
Circ.—50,000
Dir.—Moncef Cheikh Rouhou
Ch. Ed.—Abdessalem Haj Kassem
ERRAI EL-AM (d) Arabic
10, rue IBW Khaldoun, 1001
Tel: (216-1) 334688; **Fax:** (216-1) 337048
Dir.—Abdejelil Dammak
Ch. Ed.—Salah Hajja
LA PRESSE (m-ex mon.) French; Est. 1936
55, ave. du 7 Novembre
Tel: (216-1) 341066; **Fax:** (216-1) 341066/(216-1) 349720
Circ.—50,000
Ad. Mgr.—Abdelhakim Belkiria
LE RENOUVEAU (m) French
8, rue de Rome, 1000
Tel: (216-1) 345828/(216-1) 352255; **Fax:** (216-1) 351927
Circ.—23,000
Dir.—Zouhaier Dhaouadi
Ch. Ed.—Tahar Nefzi
LE TEMPS (m-ex mon.) French; Est. 1975
4, rue Ali Bach-Hambra; Boite Postal 441, 1004
Tel: (216-1) 340222
Circ.—42,000
Pub.—Dar as Sabah
Dir.—Moncef Cheikh Rouhou
Ch. Dir.—Mustapha Khammari

UGANDA
Pop. Est. 19,121,934

KAMPALA
Pop. Est. 774,241

THE MINITOR
3 Dewinton Rd.; PO Box 12141
Tel: (256-41) 236939
MUNNO (d) Luganda
PO Box 4027
Tel: (256-41) 233571
Circ.—15,000
Prop.—Munno Publications Ltd.
NEW VISION (m-ex mon.) English; Est. 1986
PO Box 9815
Tel: (256-41) 235209/(256-41) 235846; **Fax:** (256-41) 235221
Circ.—30,000
Prop.—New Vision Printing & Publishing Corp.
Ed. in Ch.—William Pike
Ad. Mgr.—Henry Akankwasa

ZAIRE, REPUBLIC OF
Pop. Est. 42,684,091

BUKAVU

CENTRE-AFRIQUE (e)
67 Ave. du Prince Regent; Boite Postal 379
Prop.—Centre Afrique SPRL
Ad. Mgr.—M van Leeuwan

KINSHASA
Pop. Est. 3,000,000

COURRIER D'AFRIQUE (m-ex S)
Boite Postal 4826
Circ.—15,000
Prop.—Publicongo
Ad. Mgr.—G Makosso
ELIMA (d)
1 Ave. de la Revolution, Limite; Boite Postal 11498
SALONGO (d)
143 10eme rue, Limite; Boite Postal 601
Tel: (243-12) 77367

KISANGANI
Pop. Est. 450,000

BOYOMA (d)
31 Ave. Mobutu, Kinshasa Haute-Zaire
LE STANLEYVILLOIS (e) French
PO Box 6
Pub.—Georges Hensenne

LUBUMBASHI-SHABA
Pop. Est. 525,000

LA DEPECHE (d) French
PO Box 2474
Circ.—20,000
Prop.—La Presse Congolaise
Ad. Mgr.—A Tumba
L'ESSOR DU ZAIRE (m)
490 Ave. President Mobutu; PO Box 525
Circ.—10,000
Ed.—Mikola Jack
Ad. Mgr.—Jacques Kote Tshilembe
MJUMBE (d)
Boite Postal 2474
Tel: (243-22) 225348
TAIFA
536 Ave. Lubumba
Ed.—Lwambwa Milambo

ZAMBIA
Pop. Est. 9,188,190

LUSAKA
Pop. Est. 1,300,000

DAILY MAIL (m-ex S) English
Longolongo Rd., PO Box 31421
Tel: (260-1) 211722/(260-1) 225131;
Fax: (260-1) 225881
Circ.—34,356
Prop.—Zambia Publishing Co. Ltd.
Prop.—National Media Corp.
Ed.—Emmanuel Nyirenda
Ad. Mgr.—Margaret Heptinstall
TIMES OF ZAMBIA/SUNDAY TIMES OF ZAMBIA (mS) English; Est. 1943
PO Box 30394
Tel: (260-1) 229076; Fax: (260-2) 222880
Circ.—32,093 (m); 44,253 (S) ABC
Prop.—Times Newspapers Zambia Ltd.
Ed.—K Kachinga
Ad. Mgr.—R Mpundu
ZAMBIA DAILY MAIL (m-ex S) English; Est. 1968
PO Box 31421, 10101
Tel: (260-1) 211722; Fax: (260-1) 225881
Circ.—40,000
Prop.—Official Journal of the Gov't.
Ed.—Kevin Muyunda Mutumwenu
Ad. Mgr.—Brain Nkamba

ZIMBABWE
Pop. Est. 10,975,078

BULAWAYO
Pop. Est. (Metro Area) 429,000

THE CHRONICLE (m-ex S) English; Est. 1894
Ninth Ave.; PO Box 585
Tel: (263-9) 65471; Fax: (263-9) 75522
Circ.—57,000 ABC
Prop.—Mass Media Trust
Pub.—Davidson Sadza
Ed.—Steve Mpofu
Ad. Mgr.—Livingstone Kusano
SUNDAY NEWS (S) English; Est. 1930
Ninth Ave.; PO Box 585
Tel: (263-9) 65471; Fax: (263-9) 71349
Circ.—55,065 ABC
Prop.—Zimbabwe Newspapers Ltd.
Pub.—Oscar Phiri
Ed.—L Chikuwira
Ad. Mgr.—Livingstone Kusano

HARARE
Pop. Est. (Metro Area) 730,000

THE HERALD/THE SUNDAY HERALD (m) English; Est. 1891
2nd St., Causeway; PO Box 396
Tel: (263-4) 795771; Fax: (263-4) 791311
Circ.—135,000 ABC
Prop.—Zimbabwe Newspapers Ltd.
Pub.—E Tachiona
Ed.—T A Sithole
Ad. Mgr.—F Samupindi
ZIMBABWE GOVERNMENT GAZETTE
Gordon Ave.; PO Box 8062
Tel: (263-4) 724215

NEWSPAPERS OF ASIA AND THE FAR EAST

AFGHANISTAN
Pop. Est. 16,903,400

BAGHLAN
Pop. Est. 29,000

ETTEHADI-BAGHLAN (Unity) (d) Dari & Pushtu; Est. 1922
Circ.—1,200

BOST

HELMAND (m) Dari & Pushtu; Est. 1953
Circ.—1,700

FAIZABAD
Pop. Est. 25,000

BADAKHSHAN (m) Dari & Pushtu; Est. 1945
Circ.—3,000

FARAH
Pop. Est. 10,000

SIESTAN (d) Dari & Pushtu; Est. 1947
Circ.—1,800

GHAZNI
Pop. Est. 24,000

SANAI (d) Dari & Pushtu; Est. 1953
Circ.—2,000

HERAT
Pop. Est. 157,000

ITTIFAK ISLAM (Islam Unity) (m) Dari & Pushtu; Est. 1919
Circ.—2,500

JALALABAD
Pop. Est. 58,000

NANGAHOR (d) Pushtu; Est. 1918
Circ.—1,500

KABUL
Pop. Est. 2,000,000

ANIS (Friendship) (e) Dari & Pushtu; Est. 1927
Circ.—25,000
Prop.—Ministry of the State Press
Ed.—Syyed Khal
HAQIQAT-E-ENQELAB-E-SAUR (National Front) (d) Dari; Est. 1980
Hizbi-Watan; PO Box 1949
Circ.—50,000
HEWAD (d) Dari & Pushtu
Circ.—12,200
NEW KABUL TIMES (m) English; Est. 1962
Ansari Wat; PO Box 983
Tel: 9361847
Circ.—10,000
Prop.—State Press
Ad. Mgr.—M Faramoze
PAYAM (d) Est. 1980
Circ.—100,000
Prop.—State Press
Ed.—Bariq Shafiee

KANDAHAR
Pop. Est. 209,000

TULU-I-AFGHAN (Afghan Rise) (d) Pushtu; Est. 1924
Circ.—1,500

MAZAR-I-SHARIF
Pop. Est. 97,000

BEDAR (m) Dari & Pushtu; Est. 1920
Circ.—2,500

PAKTIA

WOLANGA (d) Pushtu
Circ.—1,500

BANGLADESH, PEOPLE'S REPUBLIC OF
Pop. Est. 125,149,469

CHITTAGONG
Pop. Est. (Metro Area) 1,400,000

AZADI (m) Bengali; Est. 1960
9 CDA, Momin Rd., 4000
Tel: (880-31) 231920
Circ.—30,200
Prop.—Kohinoor Electric Press
Pub.—Abdul Malek
Ed.—M A Khaled
Ad.—100(Tk.)
DAILY BURBOKONE (d) Bengali; Est. 1986
Book Society Bldg., Jubli Rd., 4000
Tel: (880-31) 226057/(880-31) 212476
Circ.—28,875
Pub.—MD Yusuf Chowdhury
Ed.—Taslim Uddin Chowdhury
Ad.—100(Tk.)
DAILY LIFE (m) English; Est. 1977
27 Sadarghat Rd., 100 E. Nasirabad
Tel: (880-31) 651111/(880-31) 211044;
Fax: (880-31) 650150
Circ.—16,065
Pub./Ed.—Arife Islam
Ad.—89(Tk.)
DAINIK NAYA BANGLA (d) Bengali; Est. 1978
101 Momin Rd., 4000
Tel: (880-31) 202816/(880-31) 228122
Circ.—16,605
Pub./Ed.—Ziauddin M Anyetullah Heru
Ad. Mgr.—Nurul Afser
Ad.—90(Tk.)
PEOPLE'S VIEW (d) English; Est. 1969
129 Panchlaish Residential Area
Tel: (880-31) 204993/(880-31) 227403
Circ.—4,018
Pub./Ed.—Sabbir Islam
Ad.—78(Tk.)
PURBA TARA (d) Bengali; Est. 1970
390 Sirajuddohla Rd.
Tel: (880-31) 226356
Circ.—4,003
Pub./Ed.—M M Afzal Matin Siddique
Ad.—78(Tk.)
ZAMANA (d) Bengali
Razar Dewry, 2nd Lane

DHAKA (DACCA)
Pop. Est. (Metro Area) 3,400,000

BANGLADESH OBSERVER (m) English; Est. 1949
33 Toyenbi Circular Rd., Motijheel, 1000
Tel: (880-2) 235105; Fax: (880-2) 833565
Circ.—42,830
Pub.—Manzoor A Chowdhury
Ed.—K M A Munim
Ad. Mgr.—Abdul Quddus
Ad.—109/50(Tk.)
BANGLADESH TIMES (m) English; Est. 1974
1 DIT Ave., Motijheel, 2, 1000
Tel: (880-2) 258840/(880-2) 237215
Circ.—35,150
Pub./Ed.—Mahbub Anam
Ad.—105(Tk.)
BANGLAR BANI (d) Bengali; Est. 1972
81 Motijheel, 1000
Tel: (880-2) 237548; Fax: (880-2) 861772
Circ.—124,240
Prop.—Bani Group of Publications
Ed.—Sheikh Fazlul Karim Selim
Ad.—139/20(Tk.)
DAILY SHAKTI (d) Bengali; Est. 1982
165/1, DIT Extension Rd., 1203
Tel: (880-2) 415170
Circ.—16,510
Pub./Ed.—A Q M Zainul Abedin
Ad. Mgr.—M D Liaquat Ali
Ad.—90(Tk.)
DAILY STAR (d) English; Est. 1991
28/1 Toyenbi Circular Rd.; PO Box 3257, 1205
Tel: (880-2) 863036/(880-2) 500091;
Fax: (880-2) 863035
Circ.—30,010
Pub.—A S Mahmud
Ed.—Mahfuz Anam
Ad.—103(Tk.)
DAINIK BANGLA (m) Bengali; Est. 1964
1 DIT Ave., 1000
Tel: (880-2) 234304/(880-2) 232112;
Fax: (880-2) 867328
Circ.—69,550
Pub./Ed.—Ahmed Humayun
Ad. Mgr.—Shapan Debonath
Ad.—121(Tk.)
DAINIK DINKAL (d) Bengali; Est. 1987
13, Naya Paltan, 1000
Tel: (880-2) 865151/(880-2) 248779;
Fax: (880-2) 245084
Circ.—40,300
Prop.—Jatiatabadi Prokashona LTD.
Pub.—Prof. Mazidul Islam
Ed.—Sanaullah Nuri
Ad.—108(Tk.)
DAINIK INQILAB (d) Bengali; Est. 1986
2/1 R.K. Mission Rd., 1203
Tel: (880-2) 240147/(880-2) 862783;
Fax: (880-2) 833122/(880-2) 232881
Circ.—180,140
Prop.—Inqilab Enterprise
Pub.—A S M Bakibillah
Ed.—A M M Bahauddin
Ad. Mgr.—Shamsul Islam
Ad.—156(Tk.)
DAINIK JANATA (d) Bengali; Est. 1984
24, Aminbagh, Shantinagar, 1217
Tel: (880-2) 400498/(880-2) 416383
Circ.—20,090
Pub./Ed.—Dr. MD Asadur Rahman
Ad.—93(Tk.)
DAINIK KHABAR (d) Bengali; Est. 1985
260/C, Tejgaon Industrial Area, 1208
Tel: (880-2) 882720/(880-2) 605444;
Fax: (880-2) 883925/(880-2) 870271
Circ.—24,535

Copyright ©1996 by the Editor & Publisher Co.

Bangladesh, People's Republic of

Pub./Ed.—Mizanur Rahman Mizan
Ad. Mgr.—Mesbahul Islam
Ad.—98(Tk.)
DAINIK KISHAN (d) Bengali; Est. 1976
309 Outer Circular Rd., 1217
Tel: (880-2) 600360; Fax: (880-2) 883543
Circ.—6,030
Pub./Ed.—Kazi A Qader
Ad. Mgr.—Abdur Razzak
Ad.—80(Tk.)
DAINIK PATRIKA (d) Bengali; Est. 1986
85 Elephant Rd., 1217
Tel: (880-2) 415057
Circ.—6,260
Pub./Ch. Ed.—Miah Musha Hossain
Ad. Mgr.—Sushil Kumar Das
Ad.—80(Tk.)
DAINIK SANGRAM (d) Bengali; Est. 1977
423 Elephant Rd., 1217
Tel: (880-2) 414450; Fax: (880-2) 831250
Circ.—50,980
Prop.—Bangladesh Publications Ltd.
Pub.—MD Yunus
Ed.—Abdul Asad
Ad. Mgr.—Abdul Khair Chowdhury
Ad.—113/40(Tk.)
ITTEFAQ (m) Bengali; Est. 1955
1 Ramkrishna Mission Rd., 1203
Tel: (880-2) 245011; Fax: (880-2) 865776
Circ.—215,900
Prop.—New Nation Printing Press
Pub./Ed.—Anwar Hussain
Ad.—160(Tk.)
MORNING SUN (d) English; Est. 1990
15/1 South Kamalapur, 1000
Tel: (880-2) 400907/(880-2) 401198;
Fax: (880-2) 831618
Circ.—18,125
Pub.—Leena Islam
Pub.—Atiqul Islam
Ad.—91(Tk.)
NEW NATION (d) English; Est. 1981
1 Ramkrishna Mission Rd., 1203
Tel: (880-2) 252037/(880-2) 245011;
Fax: (880-2) 245536
Circ.—10,920
Pub.—Mainul Hosein
Ed.—Alamgir Mohiuddin
Ad. Mgr.—Altef Hossain
Ad.—84(Tk.)
SANGBAD (m) Bengali; Est. 1951
36 Purana Paltan, 1000
Tel: (880-2) 238148/(880-2) 238147;
Fax: (880-2) 865159
Circ.—49,300
Prop.—The Sangbad Ltd.
Pub./Ed.—Ahmedul Kabir
Ad. Mgr.—A Halim
Ad.—112/50(Tk.)
SANGRAM (d) Bengali
423 Bara Maghbazar, Elephant Rd.

DINAJPUR
Pop. Est. (Metro Area) 96,718

DAINIK UTTARA (d) Bengali; Est. 1974
Bahadur Bazar
Tel: (880) 415911/(880) 0531
Circ.—6,705
Pub./Ed.—MD Mohsin
Ad. Mgr.—Komol Sen
Ad.—78(Tk.)

JESSORE
Pop. Est. (Metro Area) 148,927

RUNNER (d) Bengali; Est. 1980
Pyari Mohan Das Rd., Bejpura
Tel: (880) 26943
Circ.—3,150
Pub.—Rabeya Khatun
Ed.—R M Saiful Alam Mukul
Ad.—75(Tk.)
SPHULINGA (d) Bengali; Est. 1976
Amin Villa, P-5 Housing Estate
Tel: (880) 86433
Circ.—3,050
Pub./Ed.—Mia A Sattar
Ad.—75(Tk.)
THINKANA (d) Bengali; Est. 1976
1/1 W Goal Chamet
Tel: (880) 0621/(880) 3086
Circ.—3,150
Pub./Ed.—Abdul Hussain Mir
Ad.—75(Tk.)

KHULNA
Pop. Est. (Metro Area) 646,000

DAILY JANABARTA (d) Bengali; Est. 1976
5 Babul Khan Rd.
Tel: (880-41) 21075

Circ.—3,175
Pub./Ed.—Syed Shohorab Hussain
Ad.—75(Tk.)
DAILY PURBANCHAL (d) Bengali
38 Iqbal Nagaran Rd.
Tel: (880-41) 21944; Fax: (880-41) 21432/(880-41) 21013
Circ.—10,310
Pub.—Liaquat Ali
Ed.—Ferdausi Ali
Ad. Mgr.—Zakir Hossain
Ad.—81(Tk.)
DAINIK PROBAHA (d) Bengali; Est. 1977
2 Raypara Cross Rd.
Tel: (880-41) 23650/(880-41) 22552
Circ.—10,505
Pub./Ed.—Ashraful Haque
Ad.—82(Tk.)
JANA BARTA (d) Bengali; Est. 1974
Khanjahan Rd.
Circ.—5,000
Ed.—Syed Sohrab Hussain
PURBACHAL (d) Bengali; Est. 1974
31 Iqbal Nagar Mosque Rd.
Tel: (880-41) 21944
Circ.—3,000
Pub.—Liaquat Ali
TRIBUNE (d) English; Est. 1978
38 Iqbal Nagar Mosque Rd.
Tel: (880-41) 21944; Fax: (880-41) 21432/(880-41) 21013
Circ.—8,060
Pub.—Liaquat Ali
Ed.—Ferdaus Ali
Ad. Mgr.—Zakir Hossain
Ad.—79(Tk.)

RAJSHAHI
Pop. Est. (Metro Area) 253,740

DAINIK BARTA (m) Bengali; Est. 1976
Natori Rd., Razi Villa, Rani Bazar, 6100
Tel: (880) 2699/(880) 4799
Circ.—3,000
Pub.—Advocate Kamrul Monir
Ed.—Mir Mahbub Ali
Ad.—75(Tk.)
RAJSHAHI BARTA (d) Bengali; Est. 1961
Natore Rd., Shaheib Bazar
Tel: (880) 0721/(880) 5778
Circ.—1,120
Pub./Ed.—MD Abdus Shamed
Ad.—52(Tk.)
(This newspaper is of regional government.)

BHUTAN

THIMPHU
Pop. Est. 30,000

KUENSEL Dzongkha, English & Nepalese
PO Box 204
Circ.—10,500
Prop.—Department of Information & Broadcasting
Ed.—Mr. Kinley Dorji

BRUNEI DARUSSALAM
Pop. Est. 284,653

BANDAR SERI BEGAWAN
Pop. Est. 64,000

PELITA BRUNEI Malay
Old Airport Complex, 2041
Tel: (673-2) 240400/(673-2) 240401;
Fax: (673-2) 244104/(673-2) 225942
Circ.—45,000
Prop.—Information Department (Prime Minister's Office)

KUALA BELAIT

BORNEO BULLETIN (d) English & Malay
72 Jalan Sungal; PO Box 69, 6000
Tel: (673-3) 334344; Fax: (673-3) 334346
Circ.—20,000 (mon.-fri.); 25,000 (wknd.)
Prop.—QAF Holding Ltd.
Gen. Mgr.—Mr. Reggie See
Ad.—$5.75 casual rate

CHINA, PEOPLE'S REPUBLIC OF
Pop. Est. 1,190,431,106

AMOY

XIAMEN RIBAO (d)
46 Sentian Rd.
Circ.—100,000

BEIJING
(PEKING)
Pop. Est. 9,600,000

BEIJING RIBAO (d) Est. 1952
34 Xibiaobei Hutong, Dongdan, 100734
Tel: (86-1) 553431
Circ.—510,000
BEIJING WANBAO (Beijing Evening News) (e)
34 Xibiaobei Hutong, Dongdan, 100734
Tel: (86-1) 553431
Circ.—50,000
(This newspaper is nationally distributed.)
CANKAO (Big Reference) (d)
20 Guo Hui Jie
CHINA DAILY (m) English; Est. 1981
2 Jintai Xilu
Tel: (86-1) 581958; Fax: (86-1) 593963
Circ.—70,000
Ed.—Feng Xi-Liang
Ad. Mgr.—Hu Xian Xin
ECONOMIC DAILY (d) Est. 1983
277 Wangfujing St., 100746
Tel: (86-1) 5232854; Fax: (86-1) 5125015
Circ.—1,500,000
GONGREN RIBAO (Worker's Daily) (d) Est. 1949
Liupukeng, Andingmen Wai
Tel: (86-1) 4211561; Fax: (86-1) 4214890
Circ.—150,000
Prop.—All-China Federation of Trade Unions
(This newspaper is nationally distributed.)
GUANGMING RIBAO (Guangming Daily) (d) Est. 1949
106 Yong-an Lu
Tel: (86-1) 338561
Circ.—1,500,000
Ed.—Yao Xihua
Ad. Mgr.—Yang Rui
(This newspaper is nationally distributed.)
JIEFANGJUN RIBAO (Liberation Army Daily) (d) Est. 1949
Circ.—100,000
(This newspaper is circulated mainly in Shanghai.)
NONGMIN RIBAO (Peasant's Daily) (d)
61 Fuxing Lu
Tel: (861-1) 812565
RENMIN RIBAO (People's Daily) Est. 1948
2 Jintai Xi Lu
Tel: (86-1) 5092121; Fax: (86-1) 5939
Circ.—2,740,000
Dir.—Gao Di
Ed. in Ch.—Shao Huaze
U.S. Rep.—TLI Int'l. Corp.
(This newspaper is nationally distributed. Also, it is the official organization of the Communist Party.)
ZHONGGUO QINGNIAN BAO (Youth Daily) (d)
2 Haiyuncang, Dongzhimen Nei
Tel: (861-1) 446581

CHANGCHUN
(Jilin)

JILIN RIBAO (Kirin Daily) (d) Est. 1948
68 Stalin St.
Circ.—500,000

CHANGSHA
(Hunan)

XIN HUNAN RIBAO (New Hunan Daily) (d)
55 Zhongshan Lu, Nanjing

CHENGDU
(Szechuan)

CHONGQING RIBAO (Chungking Daily) (d)
19 South Quing Yung St.
Circ.—500,000
(This newspaper is circulated mainly in Szechuan.)
SICHUAN RIBAO (Szechuan Daily) (d)
287 Hongxing Lu
Circ.—1,350,000

FUJIAN
(Fu Kien)

FUJIAN RIBAO (Fujian Daily) (d) Est. 1949
Hualin Rd.
Tel: (86) 33482
Circ.—600,000
U.S. Rep.—TLI Int'l. Corp.

GUANGZHOU
(CANTON)
(Guangdong)

GUANGDONG NONGMIN RIBAO (Peasant's Daily News) (d)
Circ.—20,000
GUANGXI RIBAO (d)
Minzhu Rd.
Circ.—650,000
GUANGZHOU RIBAO (Canton Daily) (d)
10 Tongle Lu, 510121
Tel: (86-20) 8883088
Circ.—600,000
Ed.—Huang Yong-Zhan
Ad. Mgr.—Xing Zhen
(Rep.-Shanghai Ad. Corp., 97 Yuen Ming Yuen Rd., Shanghai)
NANFANG RIBAO (South China Daily) (d) Est. 1949
729 Dong Feng Rd. 5
Tel: (86-20) 77022
Circ.—880,000
U.S. Rep.—TLI Int'l. Corp.
SHENZHEN SPECIAL ZONE HERALD
1 Shen South Blvd.
YANGCHENG EVENING NEWS (e)
733 Dongfeng Donglu
Tel: (86-20) 776211
Circ.—1,900,000
U.S. Rep.—TLI Int'l. Corp.

GUIYANG
(Guiyang)

GUIZHOU RIBAO (Kweichow Daily) (d)
Circ.—300,000

HANGZHOU
(Zhejiang)

HANGZHOU RIBAO (Hangzhou Daily) (d) Est. 1955
4 Guohuo Rd.
Tel: (86) 213166/(86) 218868
Circ.—200,000
(Rep.-Shanghai Ad. Corp., 97 Yuen Ming Yuen Rd., Shanghai)
ZHEJIANG RIBAO (The Zhejiang Daily) (d)
Circ.—700,000
(This newspaper is nationally distributed.)

HARBIN
(Heilongjiang)
Pop. Est. 3,730,000

HEILONGJAING RIBAO (Heilungkiang Daily) (d)
Circ.—500,000
(This newspaper is circulated mainly in Jilin.)

JINAN
(Shandong)

DAZHONG RIBAO (Public Daily) (d)
41 Lishan Rd.
Circ.—800,000
(This newspaper is circulated mainly in Shandong.)

KUMMING
(Hunan)

HUNAN RIBAO (d)
Circ.—300,000
(This newspaper is circulated mainly in Hunan.)

NANJING
(Jiangsu)
Pop. Est. 4,560,000

XIN HUA RIBAO (New China Daily) (d)
55 Zhongshan Lu
Tel: (86) 42638
Circ.—900,000
(This newspaper is circulated mainly in Jiangsu.)

NANNING
(Jiangsu)

GUANGXI RIBAO (Kwangsi Daily) (d) Est. 1949
Minzhu Rd.
Circ.—400,000
(This newspaper is circulated mainly in Guangxi.)

SHANGHAI
Pop. Est. 11,940,000

JIEFANG RIBAO (Liberation Daily) (d) Est. 1949
74 Hankou Lu
Tel: (86-21) 3221300
Circ.—1,000,000
Ed. in Ch.—Ding Ximan
(This newspaper is nationally distributed.)

WEN HUI BAO DAILY (d) Est. 1938
50 Huqiu Lu, 20020
Tel: (86-21) 3290235
Circ.—1,300,000
Pub.—H S Yu
Ed. in Ch.—Ma Da
U.S. Rep.—Dow Jones Int'l. Marketing Service
(This newspaper is nationally distributed. Also, it is the official orginization of the Communist Party.)

XIN MIN WAN BAO (Shanghai Evening News) (e) Est. 1903
Juijian Lu 41
Tel: (86-21) 217307
Pub.—Le Shengli

SHENGYANG
(Liaoning)

LIAONING RIBAO (The Liaoning Daily) (d)
1 Er Sangjing St.
Tel: (86) 472746
Circ.—600,000
(This newspaper is circulated mainly in Liaoning.)

TIANJIN
(Formerly Tientsin)

TIANJIN RIBAO (Tianjin Daily) (d) Est. 1949
54 Ansham Dao
Tel: (86) 701024; Fax: (86) 707915
Circ.—1,000,000
(Rep.-Tianjin Ad. Corp., 128 Ma Chang Rd.)

WUHAN
(Hubei)
Pop. Est. 5,940,000

HUBEI RIBAO (The Hubei Daily) (d)
Wu Luo Lu
Circ.—700,000
(This newspaper is circulated mainly in Hubei.)

XI'AN
(Shaanxi)

SHAANXI RIBAO (Shansi Daily) (d)
Circ.—500,000
(This newspaper is circulated mainly in Shaanxi.)

ZHENGZHOU
(Hainan)

HAINAN RIBAO (Hainan Daily) (d)
Circ.—100,000
(This newspaper is circulated mainly in Hainan.)

HONG KONG
Pop. Est. 5,548,754

ASAHI SHIMBUN
1 King's Rd., 27/F, Apartment E, Park Tower, Tower II
Tel: (852) 8062126/(852) 8062144; Fax: (852) 8062079

ASIAN WALL STREET JOURNAL (d) English; Est. 1976
AIA Bldg., 2/F, 1 Stubbs Rd.; GPO Box 9825
Tel: (852) 5737121; Fax: (852) 8345291
Circ.—45,957
Prop.—Dow Jones Publishing Co.
Pub.—Fred Zimmerman
Mng. Dir.—William P Adamopulos
Mng. Ed.—Steven Jones
Ed.—Urban C Lehner
Ad. Dir.—Robert Stone
Ad. Mgr.—Michael Wilson
(See Wall Street Journal, New York, New York.)

THE AUSTRALIAN English
15 New Eastern Terrace, 3/F, Causeway Bay
Tel: (852) 8879492; Fax: (852) 5714320

BOSTON GLOBE English
88 Kennedy Rd., Flat A2, 1/F, Wanchai
Tel: (852) 5916786; Fax: (852) 5916790

CHINA DAILY NEWS
1118 King's Rd., 20C, Block 5, Kornhill Garden, Quarry Bay
Tel: (852) 8858609; Fax: (852) 8861933

CHING PAO DAILY (m) Est. 1956
141 Queen's Rd. East
Tel: (852) 5273836
Circ.—100,000
Prop.—Ching Po Daily Ltd.
Ed.—Mok Kwong
Ad. Mgr.—So Shui Hung

CHIU YIN PAO (m)
458-460 Lockhart Rd.
Tel: (852) 8919361
Circ.—30,000
Ed.—Kwong Lai

CHOSUN DAILY
Sing Ho Finance Bldg., 166-168 Gloucester Rd., 5B, Wanchai
Tel: (852) 5910150; Fax: (852) 5910569

CHUNICHI SHIMBUN & TOKYO SHIMBUN
Fortress MTR Tower, 238 King's Rd., Flat 1804, Block B, North Point
Tel: (852) 5107907; Fax: (852) 5033057

DAILY COMMODITY QUOTATIONS (m) English & Chinese; Est. 1948
2 Moon St., "F", Ground Floor
Circ.—12,000
Prop.—O K Printing Press
Ed.—Edward Ip

DAILY TELEGRAPH English
Evergreen Villa, 43 Stubbs Rd., D1, 4th Fl.
Tel: (852) 5732800; Fax: (852) 5733004

EASTERN EXPRESS (m)
Oriental Press Centre, 7 Wang Tai Rd., Kowloon Bay, Kowloon
Tel: (852) 7071111; Fax: (852) 7071122
Ch. Ed.—Michael Chugani
Mng. Ed.—Jack Beattle

DIENA Latvian
31 Perth St., Apartment 2C, Homantin, Kowloon
Tel: (852) 7610890; Fax: (852) 7610890

THE DONG-A ILBO
Korea Centre, 119-120 Connaught Rd., Rm. 1704
Tel: (852) 5444652; Fax: (852) 5415381

EVENING STANDARD English
23 Plantation Rd., 1/F, The Peak
Tel: (852) 8494800; Fax: (852) 8494811

EXPRESS NEWS (FAI PAO) (m) Est. 1963
Aik San Factory Bldg., 14 Westlands Rd., Quarry Bay
Tel: (852) 5653555; Fax: (852) 5658716
Circ.—62,746
Prop.—The Express News Ltd.
Pub.—Woo Chark Kwun
Ex. Ch. Ed.—Ping-hang Lam
Ad. Mgr.—Fung Kam Chung

GOLDEN PAO (m) Est. 1975
N Point Industrial Bldg., 499 King's Rd., 13/F, Flat B
Circ.—60,000
Pub./Ed.—Wong Chun Lung

THE GUAURDIAN
Kingsfield Tower, 73 Bonham Rd., Flat A1, 25/F
Tel: (852) 8573431; Fax: (852) 5170258

HELSINGIN SANOMAT
8B Ying Yin Mansion, 50-52 Western St.
Tel: (852) 5481435; Fax: (852) 5481358

HONG KONG COMMERCIAL DAILY (m)
499 King's Rd., 20/F, North Point
Tel: (852) 5640768; Fax: (852) 5655456
Circ.—70,000
Pub.—N G Sui-Sang
Pres.—Cho-jat Lee
Vice Pres./Ch. Ed.—Lik Ma
Ex. Ch. Ed.—Tan Chan
Ad. Mgr.—Tong Hoi Wan

HONG KONG DAILY NEWS (m) Est. 1959
Hong Kong Industrial Bldg., 17/F, 444-452 Des Voeux Rd. West
Tel: (852) 8160261; Fax: (852) 8198717
Circ.—121,542 ABC
Prop.—Hong Kong Daily News Group
Ed.—K C Lung
Ad. Mgr.—Vincent Wang

HONG KONG ECONOMIC JOURNAL (SHUN PO) (m)
North Point Industrial Bldg., 22/F, 499 King's Rd., North Point
Tel: (852) 8567567; Fax: (852) 8111070
Circ.—42,000
Pub.—Shan-muk Lam
Ex. Dir.—Mrs. Sally Lam
Gen. Mgr.—Shefield Kwok
Ch. Ed.—Dr. George Shen

HONG KONG ECONOMIC TIMES (m)
Kodak House II, 5/F, 321 Jawa Rd., North Point
Tel: (852) 8802888; Fax: (852) 5651278
Pres./Pub./Ch. Ed.—Lawrence Siu-por Fung
Ad. Mgr.—Peter Man

HONG KONG PEOPLE'S DAILY (m)
Aik San Industrial Bldg., 1/F, Block B, 14 Westlands Rd., Quarry Bay
Tel: (852) 8111763; Fax: (852) 8112196
Ex. Ch. Ed.—Kam-hung Ng
Ch. Ed.—Winston Chou

HONG KONG POST (d) Japanese
Washington Plaza, 230-230A Wanchai Rd., 12/F
Tel: (852) 8339021; Fax: (852) 5725315
Sales Mgr.—T Sano

HONG KONG STANDARD (m) English; Est. 1949
Sing Tao Bldg., 4/F, 1 Wang Kwong Rd., Kowloon Bay, Kowloon
Tel: (852) 8339021; Fax: (852) 5725315
Circ.—26,000
Prop.—Hong Kong Standard Newspapers Ltd.
Ch. Ed.—David Wong
Ed.—Ikegaya Naohito
Ad. Dir.—Bryan Robinson

HONG KONG TIMES (m) Est. 1949
64-66 Gloucester Rd.
Tel: (852) 5279321; Fax: (852) 5295480
Circ.—60,000
Prop.—Hong Kong Times Ltd.
Pub.—Ta-kai King
Ch. Ed.—Yuk-ting Ng
Mng. Ed.—Kam Tung
Ad. Mgr.—Timothy Mak

HUANAN JINGJI JOURNAL (m)
Culturecom Centre, 8/F, 47 Hung To Rd., Kwun Tong
Tel: (852) 9508700; Fax: (852) 3451966
Ch. Ed.—Shing To
Ed.—Joe Law

HUNG LOOK DAILY NEWS (d)
30-32 D'Aguilar St., 10th Floor
Circ.—50,000
Ed.—Yam Tat-Nin

THE INDEPENDENT
Sceneway Gardens, Flat 2A, Block 12, Lam Tin, Kowloon
Tel: (852) 3488381; Fax: (852) 3488381

INTERNATIONAL HERALD TRIBUNE (m-ex S) English; Est. 1982
Malaysia Bldg., 50 Gloucester Rd., 7/F
Tel: (852) 92221188; Fax: (852) 92221190

JOCKEY DAILY NEWS (d)
2 Hok Yuen St. East, Hung Hom Kowloon, Ste. 5, Hilder Ctr.
Circ.—80,000
Ed.—Kenneth Liang
Ad. Sales Mgr.—McVicar Wong

JOURNAL OF COMMERCE
Universal Trade Centre, 3-5 Arbuthnot Rd., Rm. 2404, Central
Tel: (852) 8100056; Fax: (852) 5371652

KAM YEH PAO (m)
6-16 Tin Lok Lane, Block B, 1st Floor
Ed.—Allan Fong

THE KOREA ECONOMIC DAILY
27A Tsui Kung Mansion
Tel: (852) 8851677; Fax: (852) 5670741

LIANHE ZAOBAO
Century Square, 1-13 D'Aguilar St., 18/F
Tel: (852) 5246191; Fax: (852) 5247394

LIBERATION
Pioneer Court, 17 Ventris Rd., Flat 12B, Happy Valley
Tel: (852) 8080489; Fax: (852) 8080549

LLOYD'S OF LONDON PRESS
1101 Hollywood Centre, 233 Hollywood Rd.
Tel: (852) 8543222; Fax: (852) 8541538

LOS ANGELES TIMES
66 MacDonnell Rd., Flat 8B
Tel: (852) 5251795; Fax: (852) 5216015

MAINICHI SHIMBUN
Mainichi Bureau, 6 Gleneaiy, Flat 6A, Central
Tel: (852) 5245646

EL MERCURIO Spanish
First Pacific Bank Centre, 51-57 Gloucester Rd., 24/F, Wanchai
Tel: (852) 5270777; Fax: (852) 5271607

MINAMI-NIPPON SHIMBUN
1 King's Rd., Flat A, 34/F, Tower II, Park Tower
Tel: (852) 5701303; Fax: (852) 8060892

MING PAO DAILY NEWS (m) Est. 1959
Ming Pao Industrial Centre, 16/F, Block A, 18 Ka Yip St., Chai Wan
Tel: (852) 5953121; Fax: (852) 8983282
Circ.—114,873
Prop.—Ming Pao Daily News
Pub.—Yang-ping Cheng
Ch. Ex. Ed.—Kin-bor Cheung
Ad. Mgr.—Tai Mou Sang

MING TANG YAT PAO (m)
196 Tsat Tse Mui Rd., 3rd Floor
Circ.—45,000
Ed.—Fong Leung

THE MORNING NEWS (m)
Aik San Factory Bldg., 14/C, 14 Westland Rd., Quarry Bay
Tel: (852) 5640131; Fax: (852) 5655408
Pub./Ch. Ed.—Kin-bong Wai

MORGENAVISEN JYLLANDS-POSTEN
41 Barker Rd., Flat 1B
Tel: (852) 8496430; Fax: (852) 8496408

NEW EVENING POST (e) Est. 1950
342 Hennessy Rd., Wan Chai
Tel: (852) 8919872; Fax: (852) 8382307
Circ.—100,000
Prop.—New Evening Post Ltd.
Pub.—Fei Yi Ming
Ch. Ed.—Zuo-xing Li
Ad. Mgr.—B L Lam

THE OBSERVER
Beverly Court, 6D, Shiu Fai Terrace, 2C
Tel: (852) 5731994; Fax: (852) 5732533

ORIENTAL DAILY NEWS (m) Est. 1969
Oriental Press Centre, 7 Wang Tai Rd., Kowloon Bay, Kowloon
Tel: (852) 7951111; Fax: (852) 7952299
Circ.—600,000
Prop.—Oriental Daily News Ltd.
Pub.—Shun-choi Lam
Ch. Ed.—Chung-pak Ma
Ad. Mgr.—Danny Siu

THE PEOPLE"S DAILY
387 Queen's Rd. East
Tel: (852) 8314271/(852) 8314333; Fax: (852) 8382027

POPULAR DAILY (m)
Kingston Bldg., 6/F, Block 4, 2-4 Kingston St., Causeway Bay
Tel: (852) 8901763; Fax: (852) 5770737
Pub.—Ji Kon
Ch. Ed.—Leung Fong
Ed.—Chi-chun Chan

SANG PO (m) Est. 1975
N Point Industrial Bldg., 13/F, King's Rd., Block 4
Circ.—10,000
Pub./Ed.—Wong Chun Lung

THE SANKEI SHIMBUN
Dragon Court, 6 Dragon Terrace, Flat 4, 8/F, Block B
Tel: (852) 5786062; Fax: (852) 8879600

SENG WENG EVENING NEWS (e) Est. 1960
198 Tsat Tsz Mui Rd., 5/F
Tel: (852) 5644367; Fax: (852) 5655987
Circ.—80,000
Prop.—Seng Weng Evening News Ltd.
Ch. Ed.—Kok-sang Chow
Ed.—Chai-ku Yu
Ad. Mgr.—Cheng Wing Cheong

SHENZHEN HONG KONG ECONOMIC TIMES (m)
Sing Tao Bldg., 5/B, 1 Wang Kwong Rd., Kowloon Bay, Kowloon
Tel: (852) 7075701; Fax: (852) 3181764
Ex. Ed. in Ch.—Kai-woon Lee

SING PAO DAILY NEWS (m) Est. 1939
Sing Pao Bldg., 101 King's Rd.
Tel: (852) 5702201; Fax: (852) 8870348
Circ.—215,000
Pub.—Man-fat Ho
Ch. Ed.—Chung-suen Hon
Ad. Mgr.—Ho Kwok Ying

SING TAO DAILY (m)
Sing Tao Bldg., 3/F, Block A, 1 Wang Kwong Rd., Kowloon Bay, Kowloon
Tel: (852) 7982323; Fax: (852) 7953007
Circ.—120,000
Ed. in Ch.—Dick Ho Ting Man

SING TAO EVENING POST (e)
Sing Tao Bldg., 3/F, Block A, 1 Wang Kwong Rd., Kowloon Bay, Kowloon
Tel: (852) 7982323; Fax: (852) 7953007
Ch. Ed.—Ms. Irene Shuk-wai Sung
Mng. Ed.—Yick-Kwan Tang
U.S. Rep.—Publicitas

SING TAO JIH PAO (m&e) Est. 1938
Sing Tao Bldg., 3/F, Block A, 1 Wang Kwong Rd., Kowloon Bay, Kowloon
Tel: (852) 7982898; Fax: (852) 7953017
Circ.—61,224 (m); 79,05

SING TAO WAN PAO (e) Est. 1938
Sing Tao Bldg., 3/F, Block A, 1 Wang Kwong Rd., Kowloon Bay, Kowloon
Tel: (852) 7982556; Fax: (852) 7953022
Circ.—125,000
Prop.—Sing Tao Newspapers Ltd.
Dir.—Aw Sian
Ed.—Kam-hung Lee
Ad. Mgr.—Roddy Yu
U.S. Rep.—Publicitas

Copyright ©1996 by the Editor & Publisher Co.

Hong Kong

SOUTH CHINA MORNING POST (m) English; Est. 1903
GPO Box 47
Tel: (852) 5652435; Fax: (852) 5655380
Circ.—101,058
Prop.—South China Morning Post Ltd.
Ed.—David Armstrong
Ad. Dir.—Sally Chow
U.S. Rep.—Dow Jones Int'l. Marketing Services; The N DeFilippes Corp.
SUNDAY HONG KONG STANDARD (S)
Sing Tao Bldg., 4/F, 1 Wang Kwong Rd., Kowloon Bay, Kowloon
Tel: (852) 7982801; Fax: (852) 7953009
Ed. in Ch.—David Wong
STRAITS TIMES
Century Square, 1-13 D'Aguilar St., 18/F, Central
Tel: (852) 5237675; Fax: (852) 8459934
SUNDAY MORNING POST (S)
South China Morning Post Bldg., Tong Chong St., Quarry Bay
Tel: (852) 5652254; Fax: (852) 5651423
Ed.—Mrs. Ann Quon
SYDNEY MORNING HERALD
Citicorp Centre, 18 Whitfield Rd., 25/F
Tel: (852) 5084384; Fax: (852) 8179187
TA KUNG PAO (m) Est. 1948
342 Hennessy Rd.
Tel: (852) 5757181; Fax: (852) 8346631/(852) 8381171
Circ.—134,500
Ch. Ed.—Tak-sing Tsang
Ad. Mgr.—Kerry K T Pang
(This newspaper publishes a weekly edition in English.)
TAIWAN SHIN WEN PAO
Kornhill Garden, 1118 Quarry Bay, 20C, Block 5
Tel: (852) 8858609; Fax: (852) 8988023
TARGET FINANCIAL SERVICE (5x wk.) English
Wah Tas Bldg., 4th Floor, 42 Wood Rd., Wanchai
Circ.—100,000
Prop.—Target Newspaper Ltd.
THE TIMES
2 Old Peak Rd., Flat 23B
Tel: (852) 5302949; Fax: (852) 5302944
TIMES OF INDIA
Peak Rd., G-5, Black A, 3E
Tel: (852) 9811204
TIN FUNG DAILY NEWS (m)
265-267 Queen's Rd. East, 1st Floor, Block B
Ed.—Chan Chi-shing
TIN TIN DAILY NEWS (m)
Culturecom Centre, 10/F, 47 Hung To Rd.
Tel: (852) 9507307; Fax: (852) 3452285
Pub.—Sai-chu Ho
Ex. Ch. Ed.—King-bun Louie
TIN TIN YAT PO (m) Est. 1960
28 Tong Chong St., Quarry Bay
Tel: (852) 5652663; Fax: (852) 5658036
Circ.—173,659
Prop.—Tin Tin Publ. Development Ltd.
Dir.—Ho Shi Chu
Ch. Ed.—Cheung Wan Fung
Ad. Mgr.—James Lee
TIN WONG EVENING NEWS (e)
25-33 Johnston Rd., 15/F., Flat C
Tel: (852) 5293577; Fax: (852) 8657452
Pub.—Chi-mou Yui
Gen. Mgr.—Pui-ying Hue
TODAY NEWS (d)
657 King's Rd., North Point
Circ.—12,000
Pub.—Won Chun Hing
TORONTO STAR
21 Headland Dr., Discovery Bay
Tel: (852) 9874348; Fax: (852) 9874317
TRUTH DAILY (e)
29 Gage St., 1st Floor
Ed.—Luk Koon-Cheung
TSAO PAO (m)
657 King's Rd., 1st Floor, Flat C, North Point
Circ.—28,000
Ed.—Chun-Keung Wong
VANCOUVER SUN
76 Kennedy Rd., Flat 3101
Tel: (852) 5720146; Fax: (852) 8360955
LA VANGUARDIA Spanish
41E Seabird Lane, Discovery Bay
Tel: (852) 9878340; Fax: (852) 9879208
VILLA VERDE POST (m) Est. 1974
123 Hennessy Rd., Causeway Bay
Circ.—25,000
Prop.—Ville Verde Post Ltd.

Pub.—Cheng Fei Hong
Ed.—Kam-Pei Fung
WAH KIU MAN PO (e) Est. 1945
Morning Post Bldg., 28 Tong Chong St., 6/F, Quarry Bay
Tel: (852) 5654810/(852) 5654812; Fax: (852) 5611774
Circ.—58,000
Prop.—Overseas Chinese Daily News Ltd.
Ed.—Shiu-chiu Chan
Ad. Dir. Shum Wai
WAH KIU YAT PO (m) Est. 1925
110 Hollywood Rd.
Tel: (852) 5491181; Fax: (852) 5590406
Circ.—125,000
Prop.—Overseas Chinese Daily News Ltd.
Pub.—Choi-sang Shum
Ch. Ed.—N G Kwok-kai
Ad. Mgr.—Ta Kam-sang
WALL STREET JOURNAL
c/o Asian Wall Street Journal, AIA Bldg., 1 Stubbs Rd., 2/F
Tel: (852) 5737121; Fax: (852) 8345291
WEN WEI PO (m) Est. 1948
197-199 Wanchai Rd.
Tel: (852) 5722211; Fax: (852) 8382827
Circ.—170,000
Prop.—Wen Wei Po Ltd.
Pub.—Y Chau
Ed. in Ch.—Zai-ming Liu
Ad. Mgr.—Chow Jor Keung
U.S. Rep.—Dow Jones Int'l. Marketing Services
WORLD DAILY NEWS (m)
North Point Industrial Bldg., 4/F, Block B, 499 King's Rd.
Tel: (852) 5635141; Fax: (852) 5659675
Circ.—40,000
Pub./Ch. Ed.—Ho-keung Lo
YEDIOT ACHARONOT
Hong Kong University of Science & Technology, Tower 1, Senior Staff Quarters, Clear Water Bay Rd.
Tel: (852) 3588262
YOMIURI SHIMBUN
Windsor House, 311 Gloucester Rd., Rm. 3506
Tel: (852) 8821392; Fax: (852) 5765236

INDIA
Pop. Est. 919,903,056

AGARTALA
(Tripura)
Pop. Est. 131,513

DAINIK GANADOOT (d) Bengali; Est. 1968
Palace Compound, 799-001
Tel: (91) 5018/(91) 4157
Circ.—10,075
Ed.—Sushil Chaudhuri
DAINIK SAMBAD (d) Bengali; Est. 1966
11 Jagannathbari Rd.; PO Box 2, 799-001, West Tripura
Tel: (91) 5336/(91) 4792
Circ.—13,201
Prop.—Bhupendra Chandra Dutta Bhaumik
Pub.—Smt Malina Das
Ad. Mgr.—Sri Dutta Majumder

AGRA
(Uttar Pradesh)
Pop. Est. 770,352

AMAR UJALA (dS) Hindi; Est. 1948
Sikandara Rd., 282-007
Tel: (91) 72408
Circ.—119,335 (total-all eds.); 71,464 (Agra ed.)
Prop.—Amar Ujala Publications
Pub.—Rajual Maheshwari
Ed.—P D Khandelwal
Ad. Mgr.—Anil Kumar Agarwal
(Circulation figure is the total of all Amar Ujala editions. See Barcilly.)
SAINIK (d) Hindi; Est. 1925
4-A John's Bungalow, Jeoni Mandi, 282-004
Tel: (91) 72996
Circ.—14,817
Prop.—Sainik Publications
Mng. Ed.—D D Paliwal
Ad. Mgr.—R L Sharma

VIKAS SHEEL BHARAT (d) Hindi; Est. 1982
Transport Nagar
Tel: (91) 63929/(91) 72944
Circ.—25,076
Pub.—M R Aggarwal

AHMEDABAD
(Gujarat)
Pop. Est. 2,872,865

GUJARAT SAMACHAR (m) Gujarati; Est. 1932
Khanpur; PO Box 254, 380-001
Tel: (91-79) 22821
Circ.—387,000
Prop.—Lok Prakashan Ltd.
Pub.—Sheyans S Shah
Ed.—Shantilal S Shal
Ad. Mgr.—P D'costa
HINDU (m) Sindhi; Est. 1948
Naroda Rd., Anant Industrial Estate
Circ.—35,790
Pub./Ed.—Kishan Varyani
Ad. Mgr.—Assan Varyani
INDIAN EXPRESS (mS) English; Est. 1968
Janasatta Bhaven, Mirzapur Rd., 380-001
Circ.—17,251
Prop.—Indian Express Newspapers Bombay (Pvt.) Ltd.
Pub.—V Ranganathan
Ed.—B G Verghese
Ad. Mgr.—R C Sheopuri
Ad. Mgr.—Ralph Pais
JAI HIND (m) Gujarati; Est. 1948
Ashram Rd.; PO Box 4100
Tel: (91-79) 4070/(91-79) 5154
Circ.—11,364
Prop.—Jai-Hind Publications
Mng. Ed.—Y N Shah
LOKASATTA-JANASATTA (mS) Gujarati; Est. 1953
Mirzapur Rd., 380-001
Tel: (91-79) 26300/(91-79) 26306
Circ.—108,379 (total-all eds.); 33,845 (Ahmedabad ed.)
Prop.—Traders (Pvt.) Ltd.
Pub./Ed.—Sri Devendra J Joshi
Ad. Mgr.—Sri A S Ramakrishnan
PRABHAT (m) Gujarati; Est. 1935
Dr. Tankaria Rd.; PO Box 121, 380-001
Tel: (91-79) 22195/(91-79) 22196
Circ.—47,000
Prop.—New Prabhat Publicity Company
Pub./Ed.—R K Kothari
Ad. Mgr.—R R Kothari
SANDESH (m) Gujarati; Est. 1923
Sandesh Bhavan, Gheekanta, 380-001
Tel: (91-79) 24241/(91-79) 24243
Circ.—225,443
Prop.—Sandesh Ltd.
Dir.—F C Patel
Ed.—Chimanbhai Somabhai Patel
Ad. Mgr.—Umashankar Singh
THE TIMES OF INDIA (mS) English; Est. 1968
139 Ashram Rd.; PO Box 4046, 380-009
Tel: (91-79) 402151
Circ.—50,774
Prop.—Bennet, Coleman & Co. Ltd.
Mng. Dir.—Dr. Ram S Tarneja
Ed.—Girilal Jain
Ad. Mgr.—G R Warrier
WESTERN TIMES (d) Gujarati; Est. 1967
Gujarat Samachar Bhavan, Khanpur, 380-001
Tel: (91-79) 380006
Circ.—27,962
Prop.—The Western Times Publication (Pvt.) Ltd.
Mng. Ed.—Nikunj R Patel

AHMEDNAGAR
(Maharashtra)
Pop. Est. 181,239

KESARI (m) Marathi; Est. 1987
Circ.—11,654
Prop.—Kesari Mahratta Trust

AJMER
(Rajasthan)
Pop. Est. 374,350

ADHUNIK RAJASTHAN (d) Hindi; Est. 1979
PO Box 101, 305-001
Tel: (91) 21669/(91) 24707
Circ.—144,762
Pub./Ed.—Dilip Jain
Ad. Mgr.—N K Jain
HINDU (d) Sindhi; Est. 1948
Khari Kui; PO Box 83, 305-001
Tel: (91) 21430/(91) 21019
Pub./Ed.—Kishan Varyani

NAVAJYOTI (m) Hindi; Est. 1936
Kaisarganj; PO Box 72
Circ.—108,000
Pub./Ed.—Durga Prasad Chaudhary
Ad. Mgr.—Arvind Agarwal
NYAYA (m) Hindi; Est. 1953
Babu Mohalla; PO Box 150
Tel: (91) 21632
Circ.—170,164
Pub./Ed.—V D Sharma
Ad. Mgr.—V K Sharma

AKOLA
(Maharashtra)
Pop. Est. 225,402

MATRIBHUMI (m) Marathi; Est. 1931
Gorakshan Rd.; PO Box 32, 444-001
Tel: (91) 3839
Circ.—9,673
Prop.—Padm Pratisthan
Pub./Ed.—Kamal K Biyani

ALIGARH
(Uttar Pradesh)
Pop. Est. 319,981

JANTAYUG (m) Hindi; Est. 1959
Gandhi Marg
Circ.—21,000
Pub./Ed.—Gauri Shankar
Ad. Mgr.—S C Kulshrestha

ALLAHABAD
(Uttar Pradesh)
Pop. Est. 642,420

AJ (mS) Hindi; Est. 1984
Circ.—29,612
Prop.—Jnanamandal Ltd.
AMRITA PRABHAT (m) Hindi; Est. 1977
10 Edmonstone Rd., 211-001
Tel: (91) 52620/(91) 52665
Circ.—19,043
Prop.—Allahabad Patrika (Pvt.) Ltd.
Ed.—K B Mathur
Ad. Mgr.—Kalipada Banerjee
BHARAT (m) Hindi; Est. 1928
3 Leader Rd., 211-001
Circ.—15,000
Pub./Ed.—Santosh Tiwari
Ad. Mgr.—L M Tipathi
MAYA (d) Hindi; Est. 1929
281 Muthiganj, 211-003
Tel: (91) 51042/(91) 53681
Circ.—237,366
Prop.—Mitra Prakashan (Pvt.) Ltd.
Ed. in Ch.—Aloke Mitra
Ad. Mgr.—Priya Raj
NORTHERN INDIA PATRIKA (m) English; Est. 1950
10 Edmonstone Rd., 211-001
Circ.—49,268
Prop.—Allahabad Patrika (Pvt.) Ltd.
Mng. Dir.—Tamal Kanti Ghosh
Ed.—Tishar Kanti Ghosh

AMRAVATI
(Maharashtra)
Pop. Est. 261,387

MATRIBHUMI (m) Marathi; Est. 1964
Circ.—3,212
Prop.—Padm Pratisthan

ANAND
(Gujarat)

NAYA PADKAR (d) Gujarati; Est. 1985
Station Rd., Sathi Estate, 388-001
Tel: (91) 4199/(91) 4210
Circ.—16,787
Prop.—Gujarat Sathi Prakashan (Pvt.) Ltd.
Mng. Ed.—D C Patel

AURANGABAD
(Maharashtra)
Pop. Est. 316,244

DAINIK LOKMAT (dS) Marathi; Est. 1982
Lokmat Bhavan, MIDC Jalna Rd., 431-010
Circ.—72,064
Prop.—Prithvi Prakashan (Pvt.) Ltd.
MARATHWADA (mS) Marathi; Est. 1948
PO Box 22, Sanmitra Colony, 431-001
Tel: (91) 3475/(91) 4845
Circ.—13,679
Prop.—Marathwada Trust
Gen. Mgr.—K S Deshpande
Ed.—A K Bhalerao
Ad. Mgr.—V S Apsingekar

BANGALORE
(Karnataka)
Pop. Est. 3,900,000

ANDHRA PRABHA (mS) Telugu; Est. 1966
1 Queen's Rd., 560-001
Circ.—15,989
Prop.—Andhra Prabha (Pvt.) Ltd.
Mng. Dir.—Mrs. Saroj Goenka
Ad. Mgr.—M Nagarajan
DAILY SALAR (d) Urdu; Est. 1964
103 St. John's Church Rd., 560-005
Tel: (91-80) 571059/(91-80) 572325
Prop.—Salar Publications Trust
Mng. Ed.—I K Khan
Ad. Mgr.—B A Nagaraju
DAILY THANTHI (mS) Tamil; Est. 1942
Circ.—23,492
Prop.—The Thanthi Trust
DECCAN HERALD (m) English; Est. 1948
75 Mahatma Gandhi Rd., 560-001
Tel: (91-80) 573291
Circ.—140,151 (m); 142,864 (S)
Prop.—The Printers (Mysore) Ltd.
Pub.—Anantha Ramu
Pub.—K N Hari Kumar
Ed.—M P Yashwanth Kumar
Mktg. Mgr./Ad. Mgr.—P N Devaya
DINA SUDAR (d) Tamil; Est. 1964
11/2 Queen's Rd., 560-052
Tel: (91-80) 566260/(91-80) 566213
Prop.—B S Mani
Gen. Mgr.—B T Amudhan
Ad. Mgr.—V Gandhi
THE ECONOMIC TIMES (mS) English; Est. 1985
S & B Towers, 2nd Floor, 88 MG Rd., 560-001
Tel: (91-80) 562520
Circ.—9,562
Prop.—Bennett, Coleman & Co. Ltd.
Mgr.—Sunil Rajshekhar
THE HINDU (mS) English
5 Infantry Rd.
Circ.—53,052
Prop.—Kasturi & Sons Ltd.
INDIAN EXPRESS (mS) English; Est. 1965
1 Queen's Rd.
Tel: (91-80) 76894
Circ.—315,751
Prop.—Indian Express (Madurai) (Pvt.) Ltd.
Pub.—K Sankaran
Ad. Mgr.—T V R Rao
JANAVANI (e) Kannada; Est. 1934
25 Sheshadri Rd., Gandhi Nagar
Circ.—63,000
Pub./Ed.—M D Nataraj
Ad. Mgr.—M Mallikarjun
KANNADA PRABHA (mS) Kannada; Est. 1967
1 Queen's Rd., 560-001
Tel: (91-80) 76893
Circ.—96,533
Prop.—Indian Express (Madurai) (Pvt.) Ltd.
Mng. Dir.—Mrs. Saroj Goenka
Ed.—Khadri Shamanna
Ad. Mgr.—C V Raman
PRAJAVANI (mS) Kannada; Est. 1948
66 Mahatma Gandhi Rd.; PO Box 5331, 560-001
Tel: (91-80) 573291
Circ.—202,211 (m); 210,377 (S)
Prop.—The Printers (Mysore) Ltd.
Pub.—A Ramu
Ed.—M B Singh
Ad. Mgr.—T K Rajagopal
SANJEVANI (s) Kannada; Est. 1982
11/2 Queen's Rd., 560-052
Tel: (91-80) 568882
Prop.—Karnataka News Publication (Pvt.) Ltd.
Ed.—M S Nivas
Ad. Mgr.—N Madhusudhan
THE TIMES OF INDIA (m) English; Est. 1985
Circ.—12,784
Prop.—Bennett, Coleman & Co. Ltd.

BAREILLY
(Uttar Pradesh)
Pop. Est. 437,801

AMAR UJALA (d) Hindi; Est. 1969
19 Civil Lines
Tel: (91) 72408
Circ.—48,250
Prop.—Amar Ujala Prakashan

BARODA
(Gujarat)
Pop. Est. 744,043

GUJARAT SAMACHAR (m) Gujarati; Est. 1987
Circ.—47,835
Prop.—Lok Prakashan Ltd.
LOKASATTA-JANASATTA (mS) Gujarati; Est. 1951
Lokasatta Karyala, Nagarwada, 390-001
Tel: (91-265) 556221/(91-265) 556222
Circ.—41,240
Prop.—Traders (Pvt.) Ltd.
Pub.—Reginald Hurry
Ed.—Jayanti Shukia
Ad. Mgr.—Navinchandra Shah

BELGAUM
(Karnataka)
Pop. Est. 300,290

KANNADAMMA (d) Kannada; Est. 1974
2003 Ganapati Galli, 590-002
Tel: (91) 28850
Ad. Mgr.—Shri M S Suldhal
TARUN BHARAT (d) Marathi; Est. 1928
3524, Narvekar St., 590-002
Tel: (91) 20732/(91) 23804
Circ.—20,162
Prop.—Kiran D Thakur & Partners
Pub.—Kiran D Thakur
Ad. Mgr.—Mrs. Roma Thakur

BHAVNAGAR
(Gujarat)
Pop. Est. 308,194

SAURASHTRA SAMACHAR (m) Gujarati; Est. 1961
Balwantrai Mehta Rd., 364-001
Tel: (91) 24801/(91) 25815
Circ.—28,562
Prop.—Saurashtra Samachar (Pvt.) Ltd.
Ed.—M K Maniar
Ad. Mgr.—T C Shah

BHOPAL
(Madhya Pradesh)
Pop. Est. 672,329

DAILY JAGRAN (m) Hindi; Est. 1953
33 Muharana Pratap Nagar, 462-001
Tel: (91-755) 67429/(91-755) 64739
Circ.—61,191
Prop.—Jagran Publication
Pub./Ed.—Rajiv Mohan Gupta
Ad. Dir.—Hari Mohan Gupta
DAINIK ALOK (d) Hindi; Est. 1952
Alok Bhawan, Tallaiya, 462-001
Tel: (91-755) 73564/(91-755) 75264
Circ.—13,391
Pub.—Sanjay Sharma
Ad. Mgr.—P N Premi
DAINIK BHASKAR (m) Hindi; Est. 1958
6 Dwarka Sadan, Press Complex, Maharana Pratap Nagar, Habibganj
Circ.—35,903
Prop.—Writers & Publishers Ltd.
Mng. Dir.—L N Varma
Ed. in Ch.—Ramesh Chandra Agarwal
Ad. Mgr.—S A Siddiqui
DAINIK MADHYADESH (m) Hindi; Est. 1966
462 Madhya Marg
Circ.—20,000
Pub.—Inder Narain Dube
Ed.—V N Sharma
THE HITAVADA (d) English; Est. 1911
Gangotri Complex, Central T.T. Nagar, 462-003
Tel: (91-755) 24820
Circ.—16,993
Prop.—Progressive Writers & Publishers Society
Mng. Dir./Ed.—Beni Madhav Tiwari
MADHYA PRADESH CHRONICLE (m) English; Est. 1957
Nava Bharat Prakashan
Tel: (91-755) 64175
Circ.—172,979
Pub./Ed.—P K Maheshwari
NAVA BHARAT (m) Hindi; Est. 1956
3 Indira Complex, Maharana Pratap Nagar, 462-003
Circ.—25,389
Prop.—Nava Bharat Press
Pub.—R G Maheswari

BHUBANESWAR
(Orissa)
Pop. Est. 219,419

DHARITRI (d) Oriya; Est. 1974
B-26 Industrial Estate, 751-010
Tel: (91) 51243/(91) 50784
Circ.—30,430
Prop.—Samjavadi Society
Ed.—Tathaga Satpathy
Mgr.—Indramani Sahoo
DINALIPI (d) Oriya; Est. 1981
A/69 Industrial Area, Unit-III, 751-001
Circ.—24,170
Prop.—Surya Media Pvt. Ltd.
Ed.—Satya Mohapatra
PRAGATIVADI (m) Oriya; Est. 1973
2130 Vivekananda Marg, 751-002
Circ.—36,859
Prop.—Pragatividi Publishers
Pub.—Rabi Das
Ed.—Pradyumna Bal
Ad. Mgr.—Smt Saswati Bal
SAMBAD (d) Oriya; Est. 1984
A/62 Nayapalli, 751-003
Tel: (91) 55345/(91) 55346
Circ.—59,962
Pub.—B K Patnaik
Ed.—S R Patnaik
SWARAJYA (m) Oriya; Est. 1966
561 Shaeed Nagar Rd., 751-007
Circ.—11,000
Pub.—R N Behara
Ed.—B C Mohanty
Ad. Mgr.—N P Khilar

BHUJ
(Gujarat)

KUTCH MITRA (mS) Gujarati; Est. 1945
Kutchmitra Karyalaya Kutch
Tel: (91) 60447
Circ.—22,756
Prop.—Saurashtra Trust
Pub.—Suresh G Shah
Ed.—Kirti Khatri

BIJNOR
(Uttar Pradesh)
Pop. Est. 43,000

BINJNOR TIMES (d) Hindi; Est. 1963
Bijnor Times Rd., 246-701
Circ.—22,000
Pub./Ed.—Babu Singh Chauhan
Bus. Mgr.—S D Sharma
Ad. Mgr.—S M Raghuwanshi
UTTAR BHARAT TIMES (d) Hindi; Est. 1981
Court Rd., 246-701
Tel: (91) 864364
Pub.—Paresh Kumar Kashyap
Ed.—R P S Kashyap
Ad. Mgr.—S Devi

BIKANER
(Rajasthan)
Pop. Est. 280,366

RAJASTHAN PATRIKA (mS) Est. 1987
Circ.—14,489
Prop.—Rajasthan Patrika (Pvt.) Ltd.

BILASPUR
(Madhya Pradesh)
Pop. Est. 186,885

NAVA BHARAT (m) Hindi; Est. 1984
Circ.—21,293
Prop.—Nava Bharat Press
Pub.—P R Maheshwari

BOMBAY
(Maharashtra)
Pop. Est. 8,700,000

THE AFTERNOON DISPATCH & COURIER (d) English; Est. 1985
Sassoon Bldg., 143 MG Rd., Fert, 400-023
Tel: (91-22) 275343/(91-22) 274850
Prop.—Courier Publications (Pvt.) Ltd.
Ed.—Behram Contractor
Gen. Mgr.—P J Dastur
BOMBAY SAMACHAR (m) Gujarati; Est. 1822
PO Box 676, 400-001
Tel: (91-22) 2045531/(91-22) 2046642
Circ.—129,600 ABC
Prop.—Bombay Samachar (Pvt.) Ltd.
Ed.—Jehanbux D Daruwala
Ad. Mgr.—V S Deshpande
DAILY (d) English; Est. 1981
87 West View, Nathalal Parekh Marg, Colaba, 400-005
Tel: (91-22) 216355/(91-22) 216831
Prop.—Daily Enterprise (Pvt.) Ltd.
Ed.—J D Singh
Gen. Mgr.—S Vaidyanathan
DAILY SAKAL/SUNDAY SAKAL (mS) Marathi; Est. 1970
Dr. N B Parvlekar Marg, 400-025
Circ.—18,039 (m); 30,437 (S)
Prop.—Sakal Papers (Pvt.) Ltd.
THE ECONOMIC TIMES (m) English; Est. 1961
The Times of India Bldg., Dr. Dadabhai Naoroji Rd.; PO Box 213, 400-001
Tel: (91-22) 2620085; Fax: (91-22) 2659248
Circ.—363,000 ABC
Prop.—Bennett, Coleman & Co. Ltd.
Pub.—K N Amaria
Ed.—Kiron Kasbekar
Ad. Dir.—Pradeep Guha
U.S. Rep.—AdMarket Int'l.
(Circulation is the total of all The Economic Times editions. See Bangalore, Calcutta & Delhi/New Delhi.)
EVENING NEWS OF INDIA (e) English; Est. 1923
Dr. Dadabhai Naoroji Rd.; PO Box 213, 400-001
Circ.—12,923
Mng. Dir.—Dr. Ram S Tarneja
Ed.—Girilal Jain
Ad. Dir.—G R Warrier
FINANCIAL EXPRESS (m) English; Est. 1961
PO Box 867, 400-021
Tel: (91-22) 2022627; Fax: (91-22) 2044654
Circ.—39,784 ABC
Prop.—Indian Express Newspapers (Bombay) (Pvt.) Ltd.
Ed.—J Jaganathan
Ad. Mgr.—R S Sheopuri
U.S. Rep.—Conover Brown Inc.
FREE PRESS BULLETIN (e) English; Est. 1947
Free Press House, 225 Free Press Journal Rd., 400-021
Tel: (91-22) 2874566
Circ.—15,818
Prop.—The Indian National Press (Bombay) Ltd.
Mng. Dir.—Jai Kumar Karnani
Ed.—Arun Sadhu
FREE PRESS JOURNAL (mS) English; Est. 1930
Free Press House, 225 Free Press Journal Rd., 400-021
Tel: (91-22) 2874566
Circ.—40,000
Prop.—Indian National Press (Bombay) Ltd.
Pub.—G L Lakhotia
Ed.—Arun Sadhu
GUJARAT SAMACHAR (m) Guharati; Est. 1985
Circ.—5,742
Prop.—Lok Prakashan Ltd.
HINDUSTAN (m) Sindhi; Est. 1916
19-21 Ambalal Doshi Marg, Fort, 400-023
Tel: (91-22) 273014/(91-22) 273043
Circ.—8,054
Prop.—The Bombay Printers Ltd.
Ed.—Tirath G Sabhani
Ad. Mgr.—R H Advani
INDIAN EXPRESS (m) English; Est. 1940
Express Towers, Nariman Point, 400-021
Tel: (91-22) 2022627; Fax: (91-22) 2022139
Circ.—576,200 (total-all eds.); 284,900 (m-Bombay ed.)
Prop.—Indian Express Newspapers Bombay (Pvt.) Ltd.
Pub.—V Ranganthan
Ed.—Prabhu Chawla
Ad. Mgr.—Santosh Goenka
(Circulation figure is the total of all Indian Express editions. See Ahmedabad, Bangalore, Bombay, Chandigarh, Cochin, Delhi/New Delhi, Hyderabad, Madras, Madurai, Pune, Vijaywada & Vizianagram.)
INQUILAB (m) Urdu; Est. 1938
156 D. J. Dadajee Rd., 400-034
Tel: (91-22) 4942586
Circ.—24,656
Prop.—Middy Publications (Pvt.) Ltd.
Pub.—Dawood Y Sayed
Ed.—Riyaz A Khan
JAM-E-JAMSHED (m) Gujarati & English; Est. 1832
Ballard House, Adi Marzban Path, Ballard Estate, 400-038
Tel: (91-22) 262571
Circ.—10,000
Prop.—J B Marzban & Co. (Pvt.) Ltd.
Pub.—Rusi Adi Dhondy
Ad. Mgr.—Vera A Dhondy
JANMABHOOMI (m) Gujarati; Est. 1934
Janmabhoomi Bhavan, Janmabhoomi Marg, Fort, 400-001
Tel: (91-22) 2870831
Circ.—33,892
Prop.—Saurashtra Trust
Pub.—Dhirubhai Desai
Ed.—Harindra Dave
Ad. Mgr.—J B Oza
JANMABHOOMI-PARVASI (dS) Gujarati; Est. 1979
24 Ghoga St., Janmabhoomi Bhavan, Fort, 400-001
Circ.—37,265 (d); 94,830 (S)
Prop.—Saurashtra Trust

India — Asia

LOKASATTA (mS) Marathi; Est. 1948
Express Towers, Nariman Point, 400-001
Tel: (91-22) 2022627
Circ.—258,087 (m); 379,194 (S)
Prop.—Indian Express Newspapers Bombay (Pvt.) Ltd.
Pub.—V Ranganathan
Ed.—Madhav Gadkari
Ad. Mgr.—R C Sheopuri

MADHYANTAR (d) Gujarati
Salva Chambers, 40 Cawasji Patel St., Fort, 400-023
Tel: (91-22) 2044171/(91-22) 2044381
Circ.—17,027
Prop.—Warsha Publications (Pvt.) Ltd.
Pub./Ed.—R M Bhutta
Ad. Mgr.—S Chandrashekhar

MAHARASHTRA TIMES (mS) Marathi; Est. 1962
Dr. Dadabhai Naoroji Rd.; PO Box 213, 400-001
Tel: (91-22) 4150271
Circ.—163,643
Prop.—Bennett, Coleman & Co. Ltd.
Pub./Dir.—Pritish Nandy
Mng. Dir.—Dr. Ram S Tarneja
Ed.—G S Talwalkar

MID-DAY/SUNDAY MID-DAY (dS) English; Est. 1979
156 D. J. Dadajee Rd., 400-034
Tel: (91-22) 4942586/(91-22) 4942589
Circ.—45,441
Prop.—Mid-Day Publications (Pvt.) Ltd.
Pub.—Sanjeeva K Salian
Ed. in Ch.—Anil Dharkar
Ad. Mgr.—Kishwar Ara Hussain

MUMBAI SAKAL (dS) Marathi; Est. 1970
Dr. N. B. Parulekar Marg, 400-025
Tel: (91-22) 4304387
Circ.—21,829 (d); 38,215 (S)
Prop.—Sakal Paper (Pvt.) Ltd.
Ed.—Shri Atmaram K Sawant
Mgr.—Shri Deshpande SA

MUMBAI TARUN BHARAT (d) Marathi; Est. 1980
A/36 Shriram Industrial Estate, G.D. Ambekar Marg, Wadala, 400-031
Tel: (91-22) 4127288
Prop.—Bharatiya Vichar Darshan
Ed.—Sudhir M Jogalekar
Ad. Mgr.—R V Mulye

NAVAKAL (m) Marathi; Est. 1923
13, Shenviwadi, Khadilkar Rd., 400-004
Circ.—52,350
Prop.—N Y Khadilkar & Partners
Pub./Ed./Ad. Mgr.—N Y Khadilkar

NAVBHARAT TIMES (mS) Hindi; Est. 1950
Dr. Dadabhai Naoroji Rd.; PO Box 213, 400-001
Tel: (91-22) 4150271
Circ.—450,000
Prop.—Bennett, Coleman & Co. Ltd.
Dir.—Dr. Ram S Tarneja
Ed.—Rajendra Mathur
Ad. Mgr.—Pradeep Guha

NAVSHAKTI (mS) Marathi; Est. 1932
215 Nariman Point, 400-021
Tel: (91-22) 2874566
Circ.—27,720
Pub.—G L Lakhotia
Ed.—T S Kokji

PRAVASI (d) Gujarati; Est. 1979
Ghoga St., Janmabhoomi Bhavan, Fort, 400-001
Tel: (91-22) 2870831
Circ.—38,110
Gen. Mgr.—V S Narayan
Ed.—Harindra Dave
Ad. Mgr.—J B Oza

QUAMI AWAZ (mS) Urdu; Est. 1945
35 Jolly Maker Chamber II, 225 Nariman Point, 400-021
Ed.—Ishrat Ali Siddiqui
Ad. Mgr.—P S K Singh

SAMAKALEEN (d) Gujarati; Est. 1984
Express Towers, Nariman Point, 400-021
Circ.—48,224
Prop.—Indian Express Newspapers (Bombay) Ltd.

SANJ TARUN BHARAT (d) Marathi; Est. 1980
160 Dr. Dadabhai Naoroji Rd., 1st Floor, Fort, 400-001
Ed.—Chittaranjan D Pandit
Ad. Mgr.—R V Mulye

SUNDAY OBSERVER (S) English
121-127 MG Rd.
Tel: (91-22) 270621
Ed. in Ch.—Rahul Singh

THE TIMES OF INDIA (m) English; Est. 1838
The Times of India, Dr. Dadabhai Naoroji Rd.; PO Box 213, 400-001
Tel: (91-22) 2620085; Fax: (91-22) 2659248
Circ.—813,300 ABC
Prop.—Bennett, Coleman & Co. Ltd.
Pub.—K N Amaria
Ed.—Gautam Adhikari
Ad. Dir.—Pradeep Guha
U.S. Rep.—AdMarket Int'l.

CALCUTTA
(West Bengal)
Pop. Est. (Metro Area) 9,900,000

AAJKAAL (mS) Bengali; Est. 1981
96 Raja Rammohan Sarani, 700-009
Tel: (91-33) 353671/(91-33) 355484
Circ.—162,097 (m); 186,832 (S)
Prop.—Aajkaal Publishers (Pvt.) Ltd.
Pub.—Pratap K Roy
Ed.—Asoke Dasgupta

AKKAS DAILY (d) Urdu; Est. 1966
1/A Khetradass Lane; PO Box 7825, 700-012
Tel: (91-33) 263298/(91-33) 277051
Circ.—15,221
Prop.—Karim Raza Monghyri
Ad. Mgr.—Ranjit Naskar

AMRITA BAZAR PATRIKA (m) English; Est. 1868
41/A Acharya J. C. Bose Rd., 700-017
Tel: (91-33) 296055
Circ.—128,101
Prop.—Amrita Bazar Patrika (Pvt.) Ltd.
Pub.—Tulsi Kanti De Biswas
Ed.—Tushar Kanti Ghosh
Ad. Mgr.—P K Sen

ANANDA BAZAR PATRIKA (m) Bengali; Est. 1922
Bappaditya Ray, 6 Prafulla Sarkar St., 700-001
Tel: (91-33) 274880; Fax: (91-33) 270995
Circ.—393,400 ABC
Prop.—Ananda Bazar Patrika Ltd.
Pub.—Bappaditya Roy
Ed.—Asoke Kumar Sakar
Ad. Mgr.—C B Sen
(This newspaper is nationally distributed.)

AWAZ (d) Hindi; Est. 1947
138 Biplabi Rash Bihari Basu Rd.
Tel: (91-33) 250073
Prop.—Awaz Prakashan (Pvt.) Ltd.
Pub.—D N Singh
Ed.—Brahmdeo S Sharma

AZAD HIND (d) Urdu; Est. 1948
25 Eden Hospital Rd., 700
Circ.—16,000
Pub./Ed.—Ahmad Said Malihabadi
Ad. Mgr.—Anwar Saeed

BARTAMAN (d) Bengali; Est. 1984
76-A Acharya Jagadish Chandra Bose Rd., 700-014
Circ.—105,424
Prop.—Bartaman Printers & Publishers Ltd.
Pub.—Arun Sinah
Ed.—Barun Sengupta

BHARAT KATHA (d) Bengali; Est. 1986
83 B.K. Paul Ave., 700-005
Circ.—18,978
Prop.—Bharatkatha Publications (Pvt.) Ltd.
Ed.—Narayan Basu

BUSINESS STANDARD (mS) English; Est. 1975
6 Prafulla Sarkar St., 700-001
Tel: (91-33) 274880/(91-33) 278000
Circ.—21,144
Prop.—Ananda Bazar Patrika Ltd.
Ed.—Aveek Sarkar
Ad. Mgr.—Udayan Bhattacharya
(This newspaper is nationally distributed.)

DAINIK BASUMATI (m) Bengali; Est. 1914
166 Bepin Behari Ganguly St., 700-012
Tel: (91-33) 359462
Circ.—27,273
Prop.—Basumati Co. Ltd.
Ed.—Buddhadeb Ghosh
Ad. Mgr.—Binoy Chakrabarti

DAINIK CHHAPTE-CHHAPTE (d) Hindi; Est. 1972
24C Rabindra Sarani, 700-073
Tel: (91-33) 271488
Circ.—35,133
Pub./Ed.—Bishambhar Newar
Ad. Mgr.—Shyam S Goswami

THE ECONOMIC TIMES (mS) English; Est. 1976
105/7A S. N. Banerjee Rd., 700-014
Tel: (91-33) 294400
Circ.—17,675
Prop.—Bennett, Coleman & Co. Ltd.
Mgr.—Bhaskar Das

HINDUSTAN STANDARD (e) English; Est. 1937
6 Prafulla Sarkar St.; PO Box 2536, 700-001
Tel: (91-33) 274880/(91-33) 270995
Circ.—6,000 ABC
Prop.—Ananda Bazar Patrika Ltd.
Ed.—Aveek Sarkar

JUGANTAR (m) Bengali; Est. 1937
72/1 Baghbazar St., 700-003
Tel: (91-33) 296055
Circ.—302,000 ABC
Prop.—The Jugantar Ltd.
Ad. Mgr.—Ramen Guha

KALANTAR (d) Bengali; Est. 1966
30/6 Jhautala Rd., 700
Circ.—23,000
Pub./Ed.—Probhat Das Gupta
Ad. Mgr.—Tapan Some

NAVI PARBHAT (m) Punjabi; Est. 1952
264 M. Bepin Behari Ganguly St., 700-012
Circ.—12,000
Pub./Ed./Ad. Mgr.—S R S Dharni

PAIGAM (d) Bengali; Est. 1948
26/1 Market St., 700-087
Tel: (91-33) 246040
Circ.—14,151
Pub.—Morzina Tarafdar
Pub.—Momarzad Ali

RAVIVAR Hindi; Est. 1977
6 Prafulla Sarkar St., 700-001
Circ.—36,411
Prop.—Ananda Bazar Patrika Ltd.
(This newspaper is nationally distributed.)

ROOPLEKHA (m) Hindi; Est. 1953
9 Lenin Sarani St., 700-013
Circ.—36,783
Pub.—B K Shah
Ed.—B L Shah

ROZANA HIND (m) Urdu; Est. 1929
17 Sagar Dutta Lane, 700-073
Circ.—17,500
Prop.—Rozana Hind Workers Trust
Pub.—Q H Sabuwala
Ed.—R Faridi
Ad. Mgr.—Saleh Bhai

SANMARG (m) Hindi; Est. 1948
160/C Chittaranjan Ave., 700-007
Tel: (91-33) 315301
Circ.—69,140
Prop.—Sanmarg (Pvt.) Ltd.
Pub.—Ramesh Kumar Khaitan
Ed.—Ramawater Gupta
Ad. Mgr.—A S Roy

SATYAJUG (m) Bengali; Est. 1972
13 Prafulla Sarkar St., 700-072
Circ.—38,000
Prop.—Satyajug Publications Ltd.
Pub./Ed.—Shri Jibanlal Banerjee
Ad. Mgr.—Animesh Gaswami

THE STATESMAN (m) English; Est. 1875
4 Chowringhee Square, 700-001
Tel: (91-33) 3882/(91-33) 3884; Fax: (91-33) 270118
Circ.—148,382
Prop.—The Statesman Ltd.
Pub.—Basudev Ray
Ed. in Ch.—C R Irani
Ad. Mgr.—Sarbajit Ray

SUNDAY English; Est. 1975
6 Prafulla Sarkar St., 700-001
Circ.—127,506
Prop.—Amanda Bazar Patrika Ltd.
(This newspaper is nationally distributed.)

THE TELEGRAPH (d) English; Est. 1982
629 Prafulla Sarkar St., 700-001
Tel: (91-33) 274880/(91-33) 278000; Fax: (91-33) 270995/(91-33) 271139
Circ.—129,000
Prop.—Ananda Bazar Patrika Ltd.
Ed.—M J Akbar
(This newspaper is nationally distributed.)

VISHWAMITRA (d) Hindi; Est. 1917
74 Lenin Sarani, 700-013
Tel: (91-33) 249567/(91-33) 241139
Circ.—83,000
Prop.—Vishwamitra Karyalaya
Pub.—K Chandra
Ed./Ad. Mgr.—K C Agrawalla

CALICUT
(Kozhikode)
(Kerala)
Pop. Est. 546,060

CALICUT TIMES (d) Malayalam; Est. 1982
Emciyem Bldg., Kammathi Lane, 673-002
Pub.—M Joy Verghese
Ed.—Jacob Roy
Mgr.—K V Kunhammea

CHANDRIKA DAILY (d) Malayalam; Est. 1935
Y.M.C.A. Rd.; PO Box 64, 673-001
Tel: (91) 76021/(91) 76022
Circ.—31,735
Prop.—The Muslim Printing & Pub. Co. Ltd.
Ed.—C Kunhutty
Ad. Mgr.—T Moideen Koya

DESHABHIMANI (m) Malayalam; Est. 1946
Convent Rd.; PO Box 56, 673-032
Tel: (91) 72078/(91) 77286
Circ.—61,595

Pub.—E M S Namboodirpadu
Pub.—P Kannan Nair
Ed. in Ch.—S R Pillai

KERALA KAUMUDI (dS) Malayalam; Est. 1984
Pub.—The Kerala Kaumudi (Pvt.) Ltd.

MALAYALA MANORAMA (mS) Malayalam; Est. 1966
Nadakkave; PO Box 187, 673-011
Circ.—202,357 (m); 204,196 (S)
Prop.—Malayala Manorama Co. Ltd.

THE MATHRUBHUMI (mS) Malayalam; Est. 1923
Mathrubhumi Bldg., Robinson Rd.; PO Box 46, 673-001
Tel: (91) 63651/(91) 63756
Circ.—454,351 (total-all eds.); 304,084 (Calicut ed.)
Prop.—The Mathrubhumi Printing & Pub. Co. Ltd.
Pub.—P V Chandran
Ed.—M D Nalapat
Ad. Mgr.—T Srikumar
(Circulation is the total of all Mathrubhumi editions. See Cochin & Trivandrum.)

CHANDIGARH
(Chandigarh Union Territory)
Pop. Est. 450,061

DAINIK TRIBUNE (m) Hindi; Est. 1978
Sector 29-C, 160-020
Circ.—33,797
Prop.—The Tribune Trust
Pub.—O P Lamba
Ed. in Ch.—Prem Bhatia
Ad. Mgr.—S Paul

INDIAN EXPRESS (mS) English; Est. 1977
186-B Industrial Area; PO Box 623
Tel: (91-172) 31871/(91-172) 31875
Circ.—53,128 (m); 60,477 (S)
Prop.—Indian Express Newspapers (Bombay) (Pvt.) Ltd.
Ed.—Arun Shourie
Mgr.—Santosh Kumar

PUNJABI TRIBUNE (d) Punjabi; Est. 1978
Sector 29-C, 160-020
Circ.—42,211
Prop.—The Tribune Trust
Ed. in Ch.—Prem Bhatia
Ad. Mgr.—S Paul

THE TRIBUNE (m) English, Hindu & Punjabi; Est. 1881
Sector 29-C, 160-020
Tel: (91-172) 41035
Circ.—159,600 (English); 53,000 (Hindru); 60,000 (Punjabi)
Prop.—The Tribune Press
Pub.—O P Lamba
Ed.—V N Narganan
Ad. Mgr.—S Paul

COCHIN
(Kerala)
Pop. Est. 685,686

DESHABHIMANI (m) Malayalam; Est. 1968
Tel: (91) 360346/(91) 360747
Mgr.—P Kannan Nair

INDIAN EXPRESS (m) English; Est. 1973
Aspinwal Bldg., Calvetty, 682-001
Circ.—71,897
Prop.—Indian Express Newspapers (Madurai) (Pvt.) Ltd.
Pub.—P Krishnaswami
Ed. in Ch.—B G Verghese
Ad. Mgr.—K Damodaran

JANMABHUMI (d) Malayalam; Est. 1966
50/47-A Perandur Rd., Elamakkara, 682-026
Tel: (91) 360824
Prop.—Mathruka Pracharanalayam Ltd.
Dir.—P Sundaram
Mgr.—P Narayanan

KERALA TIMES (d) Malayalam; Est. 1957
Banerji Rd., Ernakulam; PO Box 1929, 682-018
Tel: (91) 352696/(91) 355167
Circ.—20,739
Prop.—The Kerala Cultural Society Ltd.
Pub.—K V Joseph
Ed.—P M Jussay

MALAYALA MANORAMA (mS) Malayalam; Est. 1977
Panampily Nagar; PO Box 2314, 682-016
Circ.—147,940 (m); 148,429 (S)
Prop.—Malayala Manorama Co. Ltd.

THE MATHRUBHUMI (mS) Malayalam; Est. 1962
Kaloor, 682-017
Circ.—155,159
Prop.—The Mathrubhumi Printing & Pub. Co. Ltd.
Pub.—V Bhaskara Menon

Asia   India   IV-65

VEEKSHANAM (m) Malayalam; Est. 1976
Kaloor Cross Rd., 682-017
Tel: (91) 354747/(91) 367926
Circ.—33,000
Pub.—A C Jose
Ed.—C P Sreedharan
Ad. Mgr.—V Ramachandran
THE WEEK (S) English; Est. 1982
Manorama Bldg., Panampilly Nagar
Ernakulam, 682-016
Circ.—63,662
Prop.—Malayala Manorama Co. Ltd.
(This paper is nationally distributed.)

COIMBATORE
(Tamil Nadu)
Pop. Est. 917,155

DAILY THANTHI (mS) Tamil; Est. 1942
Circ.—43,043
Prop.—The Thanthi Trust
THE HINDU (mS) English
6/48 Avanashi Rd.
Circ.—64,146 (m)
Prop.—Kasturi & Sons Ltd.

CUDDALORE
(Tamil Nadu)
Pop. Est. 127,569

DAILY THANTHI (mS) Tamil; Est. 1942
Circ.—19,813
Prop.—The Thanthi Trust

CUTTACK
(Orissa)
Pop. Est. 326,463

NEWS OF THE WORLD (d) English; Est. 1975
Kaligali, 753
Circ.—19,000
Pub.—Kala o Sahitya Bikash
Ed.—N K Mohapatra
Ad. Mgr.—T Mohapatra
PRAJATANTRA (e) Oriya; Est. 1947
Prajatantra Bldg., Behari Baug, 753-002
Tel: (91) 23590/(91) 21362
Circ.—78,321
Prop.—Prajatantra Prachar Samiti
Ed.—Bharekrushna Mahtab
Ad. Mgr.—A Swim
THE SAMAJ (eS) Oriya; Est. 1919
Gopabandhu Bhavan, Baxibazar, 753-001
Tel: (91) 20994/(91) 20183
Circ.—109,270
Prop.—The Servants of the People Society
Pub.—Ananda ku Pani
Ed.—Radhanath Rath
Ad. Mgr.—Upendra Mahapatra

DELHI/NEW DELHI
Pop. Est. (total) 7,200,000

DAILY JATHE DAR (m) Punjabi
14 Shidipura St., New Delhi, 110-002
Circ.—13,000
Ed.—Bir Inder Singh
Ad. Mgr.—S J Singh
DAILY MILAP (mS) Urdu; Est. 1923
8-A Bahadurshah Zafar Marg, New Delhi, 110-002
Tel: (91-11) 3317737
Circ.—21,391
Prop.—The Daily Milap (Pvt.) Ltd.
Pub.—Punam Suri
Ed.—Navin Suri
DAILY PRATAP (d) Urdu; Est. 1919
5 Bahadur Shah Zafar Marg, New Delhi, 110-002
Tel: (91-11) 3317938
Circ.—27,470
Pub.—Anil Narenda
Ed.—K Narenda
Ad. Mgr.—Parwana Rudaulvi
THE ECONOMIC TIMES (mS) English; Est. 1974
7 Bahadurshah Zafar Marg, New Delhi, 110-002
Tel: (91-11) 61337/(91-11) 61338
Circ.—26,559
Prop.—Bennett, Coleman & Co. Ltd.
Gen. Mgr.—Nandita Jain
FINANCIAL EXPRESS (m) English; Est. 1974
9-10 Bahadurshah Zafar Marg, New Delhi; PO Box 7126, 110-002
Tel: (91-11) 3311111/(91-11) 3311062
Circ.—12,182
Prop.—Indian Express Newspapers (Bombay) (Pvt.) Ltd.
THE HINDU (mS) English
Circ.—16,886
Prop.—Kasturi & Sons Ltd.
HINDUSTAN (mS) Hindi; Est. 1936
18/20 Kasturba Gandhi Marg, New Delhi, 110-001
Tel: (91-11) 3318201; Fax: (91-11) 3321189

Circ.—141,813
Prop.—The Hindustan Times Ltd.
Pub.—Rajendra Prasad
Ed.—Hari Narain Nigam
Ad. Mgr.—Ved Prakash
THE HINDUSTAN TIMES (m) English; Est. 1924
Hindustan Times House, 18/20 Kasturba Gandhi Marg, New Delhi, 110-001
Tel: (91-11) 3318201; Fax: (91-11) 3321189
Circ.—345,892 ABC
Prop.—The Hindustan Times Ltd.
Pub.—Rajendra Prasda
Ed.—V N Narayanan
Ad. Mgr.—R S Awasthy
(This newspaper is nationally distributed.)
HINDUSTAN TIMES EVENING NEWS (e-ex S) English; Est. 1944
Hindustan Times House, 18/20 Kasturba Gandhi Marg, New Delhi, 110-001
Tel: (91-11) 3318201; Fax: (91-11) 3321189
Circ.—5,628
Prop.—The Hindustan Times Ltd.
Pub.—Rajendra Prasad
Ed.—K Sriram
Ad. Mgr.—Ved Prakash
INDIAN EXPRESS (m) English; Est. 1953
9-10 Bahadurshah Zafar Marg, New Delhi; PO Box 7126, 110-002
Tel: (91-11) 3311111
Circ.—155,698
Prop.—Indian Express Newspapers (Bombay) (Pvt.) Ltd.
Pub.—S K Kohli
Ed.—Arun Shourie
AL JAMIAT (d) Urdu; Est. 1925
1502 Jamiat Bldg., Qasim Jan St., Delhi, 110-006
Pub.—Maulana Asraul
Ad. Mgr.—Mohammad Hassain
JANASATTA (dS) Hindi; Est. 1983
9-10 Bahadurshah Zafar Marg, New Delhi; PO Box 1126, 110-002
Tel: (91-11) 331111
Circ.—103,268
Prop.—Indian Express Newspapers (Bombay) (Pvt.) Ltd.
Pub.—S K Kohli
JANYUG (d) Hindi; Est. 1973
5E Rani Jhansi Rd., New Delhi, 110-055
Circ.—14,000
Pub.—Mukhtar Ahmed Khan
Ed.—H K Vyas
Ad. Mgr.—OM A Khan
NATIONAL HERALD (mS) English; Est. 1938
Herald House, 5A Bahadurshah Zafar Marg, New Delhi, 110-002
Tel: (91-11) 3319014
Circ.—36,160
NAVBHARAT TIMES (mS) Hindi; Est. 1950
7 Bahadurshah Zafar Marg, New Delhi, 110-002
Tel: (91-11) 3312277
Circ.—399,887
Prop.—Bennett, Coleman & Co. Ltd.
Pub./Ed.—P K Maheshwari
PATRIOT (mS) English; Est. 1963
Link House, Bahadurshah Zafar Marg; PO Box 727, 110-002
Tel: (91-11) 3311056
Circ.—33,000
Prop.—United India Periodicals (Pvt.) Ltd.
Pub.—A K Painuli
Ed.—R K Misra
Ad. Mgr.—Suven Mukherjee
PIONEER
Link House, Bahadurshah Zafar Marg, New Delhi, 110-002
Tel: (91-11) 3717505/(91-11) 3755271;
Fax: (91-11) 3711497
PUNJAB KESARI (dS) Hindi; Est. 1983
A-68/3 G. T. Karnal Rd., Industrial Area, Delhi, 110-003
Circ.—173,385 (d); 248,654 (S)
Prop.—The Hind Samachar Ltd.
QUAMI AWAZ (mS) Urdu; Est. 1945
Herald House, Bahadurshah Zafar Marg, New Delhi, 110-002
Prop.—Associated Journals Ltd.
Dir.—K C Khanna
Ed.—I A Siddiqui
Ad. Mgr.—M S Dutta
SANDHYA TIMES (d-ex S) Hindi; Est. 1979
7 Bahadurshah Zafar Marg, New Delhi, 110-002
Circ.—49,878
Prop.—Bennett, Coleman & Co. Ltd.
Pub.—Ramesh Chandra
Ed.—Anand Jain
Ad. Mgr.—S D Pillai
SARITA (mS) Hindi; Est. 1945
E3 Jhandewala Estate, Rani Jhansi Rd., 110-055
Tel: (91-11) 526311

Circ.—260,577
Prop.—Delhi Press Patra Prakashan (Pvt.) Ltd.
Pub./Ed.—Vishwa Nath
THE STATESMAN (mS) English; Est. 1931
Connaught Circus, 110-001
Tel: (91-11) 3315911
Circ.—201,906
Prop.—The Statesman Ltd.
Pub.—D J Gooptu
Ed.—S Sahay
Ad. Mgr.—S K Basu
TEJ (mS) Urdu; Est. 1923
8B Bahadurshah Zafar Marg, New Delhi, 110-002
Circ.—10,000
Mng. Dir./Ed.—Vishwa Bandhi Gupta
Ad. Mgr.—Jai Prakash Gupta
THE TIMES OF INDIA (mS) English; Est. 1950
7 Bahadurshah Zafar Marg, New Delhi, 110-002
Tel: (91-11) 3312277
Circ.—194,160
Prop.—Bennett, Coleman & Co Ltd.
Pub.—Ramesh Chandra
VIRARJUN (m) Hindi; Est. 1954
5 Mathura Rd., New Delhi, 110-002
Circ.—27,000
Pub.—Anil Narendra
Ed.—K Narendra
VYAPAR BHARATI (d) English; Est. 1972
15 Transport Centre, Rohtak Rd., 110-035
Tel: (91-11) 5437741
Circ.—12,134
Pub.—K C Gupta
Ad. Mgr.—V K Jain

DHANBAD
(Bihar)

AWAZ (m) Hindi; Est. 1947
Hari Mandir Rd., 826-001
Circ.—88,136
Prop.—Awaz Prakashan (Pvt.) Ltd.
Pub.—D N Singh
Ed.—Brahmdeo S Sharma
Ad. Mgr.—S Keskar

ERODE
(Tamil Nadu)
Pop. Est. 275,103

DINAMALAR (mS) Tamil; Est. 1984
10-11 Norris Colony, Birds Rd.
Circ.—68,925 (fri.); 41,007 (S)
Prop.—T V Ramasubba Iyer & Sons

GORAKHPUR
(Uttar Pradesh)
Pop. Est. 306,399

AJ (mS) Hindi; Est. 1980
Circ.—41,522
Prop.—Jnanamandal Ltd.
DAILY JAGRAN (m) Hindi; Est. 1975
23 Civil Lines, Gorakhpur-1
Circ.—44,572
Prop.—Jagran Prakashan (Pvt.) Ltd.
SWATANTRA CHETNA (d) Hindi; Est. 1986
Shahmaroof, 273-001
Circ.—10,341
Prop.—DA Chetna Prakashan (Pvt.) Ltd.
Ed.—A Misra

GUWAHATI
(Assam)
Pop. Est. 200,377

ASSAM EXPRESS (m) Est. 1971
Uzan Bazar, Bhuban Rd., 781-001
Circ.—8,000
Prop.—Assam Express Ltd.
Pub.—S Bijoy Singh
Ed.—Jiba Kanta Gogoi
Ad. Mgr.—Biren Sarma
ASSAM TRIBUNE (m) English; Est. 1939
Tribune Bldg., 781-003
Tel: (91) 40063
Circ.—39,800
Prop.—T G Baruah & Partners
Pub.—Kunjalal Thapa
Ed.—R N Barooah
Ad. Mgr.—S Banarjee
DAINIK ASAM (m) Assamese; Est. 1965
Tribune Bldg., 781-003
Circ.—46,401
Prop.—T G Baruah & Partners
Pub.—Mohan Tamuli
Ed.—K N Hazarika
Ad. Mgr.—Pabitra Kumar Deka

GWALIOR
(Madhya Pradesh)
Pop. Est. 559,776

AACHARAN (d) Hindi; Est. 1970
Aacharan Bhavan, Jinsi Rd., 474-001
Tel: (91) 21927/(91) 28436
Circ.—21,209
Prop.—Aacharan Printers (Pvt.) Ltd.
Mng. Dir.—A H Qureshi
Ed.—Ram Vidrohi
Gen. Mgr.—Santosh Sharma
DAINIK BHASKAR GWALIOR (m) Hindi; Est. 1967
Bhaskar Lane, Jayendraganj, 474-009
Circ.—16,793
Prop.—Bhaskar Publications & Allied Industries (Pvt.) Ltd.
Ed.—D K Tiwari
Ed. in Ch.—R C Agarwal
DAINIK NIRANJAN (m) Hindi; Est. 1964
Jinsi Nala, No. 1, 474-001
Tel: (91) 22237
Circ.—16,142
Pub./Ed.—Smt. Ram Sumarini Saxena
Ad. Mgr.—P V Khirwadkar
NAV PRABHAT (d) Hindi; Est. 1948
Shree Bhawan, Sarafa Rd., 474-001
Circ.—16,000
Prop.—Hindustan Journal (Pvt.) Ltd.
Ed.—C M Nagory
Ad. Mgr.—Uttam Kumar Dubey
SWADESH (m) Hindi; Est. 1971
53 Jayendraganj, 474-009
Tel: (91) 24370/(91) 23330
Circ.—20,960
Prop.—Swadesh Prakashan Gwalior (Pvt.) Ltd.
Ed.—Shri Rajendra Sharma

HUBLI-DHARWAR
(Karnataka)
Pop. Est. 526,493

SAMYUKTA KARNATAKA (mS) Kannada; Est. 1933
Koppikar Rd.; PO Box 30, 580-020
Tel: (91) 64858/(91) 64305
Circ.—62,286 (m); 75,951 (S)
Prop.—L S T Hubli Bangalore
Pub.—V G Vaidye

HYDERABAD
(Andhra Pradesh)
Pop. Est. 2,800,000

ANDHRA PATRIKA (m) Telugu; Est. 1975
Hill Fort Palace Annex, 500
Circ.—22,486
Prop.—Editions Vijayawada
Pub.—S Nageswara Rao
Mng. Dir.—S Radhakrishna
Ad. Mgr.—K Rama Chandraiah
ANDHRA PRABHA (m) Telugu; Est. 1977
Express Centre, Valmiki Nagar, Domalguda, 500-029
Circ.—24,992
Prop.—Andhra Prabha (Pvt.) Ltd.
Pub.—K Pattabhiraman
Ad. Mgr.—C Kuppuswamy
CITIZEN'S EVENING (e) English; Est. 1984
365-A-Bakaram, 500-002
Circ.—23,735
Prop.—Citizen Press
Mng. Ed.—S Ramesh
DEECAN CHRONICLE (d) English; Est. 1938
36 Sarojini Devi Rd., 500-003
Tel: (91-40) 72126
Circ.—63,700
EENADU (mS) Telugu; Est. 1975
Eenadu Compound, Somajiguda, 500-082
Tel: (91-40) 223422; Fax: (91-40) 228787
Circ.—289,900 (total-all eds.)
Prop.—Ushodaya Enterprise (Pvt.) Ltd.
Ed.—Ramoji Rao
Ad. Mgr.—I Venkat
(Circulation is the total of all Eenadu editions. See Tirupathi, Vijayawada & Vishakhaptnam.)
THE HINDU (mS) English
6-3-879 & 879-B Begumpet Public Rd.
Circ.—73,949
Prop.—Kasturi & Sons Ltd.
Ed.—G Kasturbi
INDIAN EXPRESS (mS) English; Est. 1977
Express Centre, Valmiki Nagar, Domalguda, 500-029
Circ.—33,022

India — Asia

Prop.—Indian Express (Madurai) (Pvt.) Ltd.
Pub.—A C Venkgtakrisnan
Ad. Mgr.—C Kuppuswamy
MUNSIF (d) Urdu; Est. 1977
Nampally Station Rd.; PO Box 363, 500-001
Tel: (91-40) 43204
Circ.—10,582
Pub./Ed.—Mahmood Ansari
Ad. Mgr.—Sheikh Ibrahim
NEWSTIME (d) English
6-3-570 Somajiguda, 500-084
Tel: (91-40) 223422
Circ.—60,000
RAHNUMA-E-DECCAN (m) Urdu; Est. 1949
5-3-831, Shankar Bagh, 500-012
Tel: (91-40) 43210
Circ.—23,000
Pub./Ed.—Syed Vicaruddin
Ad. Mgr.—S M Hassan
SIASAT (mS) Urdu; Est. 1949
Jawaharlal Nehru Rd.; PO Box 197, 500-001
Tel: (91-40) 44180/(91-40) 44188
Circ.—40,626
Prop.—Abid Ali Khan & Partners
Pub./Ed.—Abi Ali Khan
Ad. Mgr.—M A Siddigui
TARAKA PRABHA (d) Est. 1984
1-2-593/37 Gangamahal Colony, 500-029
Prop.—Taraka Prabna Pubs. Ltd.
Pub.—K Ramakrishna Prasad
UDAYAM (d) Telugu; Est. 1983
7/1 Azamabad Industrial Area, 500-020
Tel: (91-40) 68802/(91-40) 68262
Circ.—45,825
Ed. in Ch.—D N Rao
Ad. Mgr.—K R P Reddy

INDORE
(Madhya Pradesh)
Pop. Est. 827,071

DAINIK BHASKAR (m) Hindi; Est. 1983
4/54 Press Complex, Agra Bombay Rd., 452-008
Circ.—58,173
Prop.—Bhaskar Graphic & Printing Arts Ltd.
FREE PRESS (dS) English; Est. 1983
3/54 Press Complex, Bombay-Agra Rd., 452-008
Tel: (91-731) 21981/(91-731) 21982
Circ.—10,085
Prop.—The Indian National Press (Indore) Ltd.
Pub.—S G Porwal
Ed.—Arun Shadu
INDORE SAMACHAR (m) Hindi; Est. 1946
17 New Dewas Rd.; PO Box 228, 452-003
Circ.—7,000
Prop.—Associated Printers & Publishers
Pub.—Suresh Sheth
Ed.—Sohan Mehra
Ad. Mgr.—R P Rathore
JAGRAN (m) Hindi; Est. 1950
Kadavghat Main Rd., 452
Circ.—13,000
Ed.—I C Jain
NAI DUNIA (m) Hindi; Est. 1947
60/1 Babu Labhchand Chhajlani Marg, 452-009
Tel: (91-731) 62061; Fax: (91-731) 65770
Circ.—141,270
Prop.—Basantilal Sethia & Partners
Pub.—Basantilal Sethia
Ed.—Abhay Chhajlani
Ad. Mgr.—V B Tilwanka
NAVA BHARAT (m) Hindi; Est. 1956
3 Indira Press Complex, Mah. Pra. Nagar, 3/5 Manoramaganj
Tel: (91-731) 22848
Circ.—10,068
Pub.—P K Maheshwari
Ed. in Ch.—R G Maheshwari
SWADESH (m) Hindi; Est. 1966
123 Tilak Path; PO Box 86, 452-004
Tel: (91-731) 33277
Circ.—20,000
Prop.—Shri Rewa Prakashan Ltd.
Pub.—Prakash Bohra
Ad. Mgr.—Vinayak Raut

JABALPUR
(Madhya Pradesh)
Pop. Est. 757,726

DAINIK BHASKAR (m) Hindi; Est. 1986
581 South Civil Lines, 482
Tel: (91) 29352/(91) 29353
Circ.—25,142
Prop.—Partnership Concern
Pub.—B D Agarwal
DESH BANDHU (m) Hindi; Est. 1971
625 Gandhi Marg, 482-002
Circ.—6,000
Pub./Ed.—M R Surjan
Ad. Mgr.—H K Misra
NAVA BHARAT (m) Hindi; Est. 1950
Napier Town; PO Box 67
Tel: (91) 21252
Circ.—171,920
Pub.—P K Maheshwari
NAVEEN DUNIA (m) Hindi; Est. 1959
2566 Wright Town, 482-002
Tel: (91) 24103/(91) 24703
Circ.—22,421
Prop.—Naveen Duniya Kohinoor Tobacco Co.
Pub.—S K Patel
Ed.—Brij Vilas Shukla
Ad. Mgr.—V S Bele Gutamganj
YUGADHARMA (d) Hindi; Est. 1956
Shrinath Ki Talaiya, 482-002
Tel: (91) 23385/(91) 26486
Circ.—6,558
Prop.—Vindhyachal Prakashan
Pub.—Shri M T Pingle
Ed.—R P Tiwari

JAIPUR
(Rajasthan)
Pop. Est. 1,004,669

ADHIKAR (d) Hindi
Laxminagar, Hatwada Marg, Ajmer Rd., 302-006
Tel: (91-141) 62604
Circ.—48,779
Pub.—Vishnu Sharma
NAVAJYOTI (m) Hindi; Est. 1960
Jobner Baug, Station Rd.; PO Box 132, 302-006
Pub./Ed.—Durga Prasad Chaudhary
Ad. Mgr.—Arvind Agauwal
RAJASTHAN PATRIKA (m) Hindi; Est. 1956
Kesargarh, Jawaharlal Lal Nehru Marg, 302-004
Tel: (91-141) 561582; Fax: (91-141) 566011
Circ.—206,688 (total-all eds.); 194,777 (Jaipur ed.)
Prop.—Rajasthan Patrika (Pvt.) Ltd.
Pub.—Jai Singh Kothari
Ch. Ed.—R K Mohla
Ed.—Milap Kothari
(Circulation is the total of all Rajasthan Patrika editions. See Bikaner, Jodhpur, Kota & Udaipur.)
RAJASTHAN PATRIKA (d) English; Est. 1984
Kesargarh, Jawaharlal Lal Nehru Marg, 302-004
Tel: (91-141) 61321
Circ.—3,958
Prop.—Rajasthan Patrika (Pvt.) Ltd.
Ed.—Milap Kothari
(There are editions of Rajasthan Patrika in Bikaner, Jodphur, Kota & Udaipur.)
RASHTRADOOT (m) Hindi; Est. 1951
Sundharma; PO Box 30, 302-001
Tel: (91-141) 72634
Circ.—124,958
Pub.—Hazari Lal Sharma
Ed.—Rajesh Sharma
Ad. Mgr.—K C Sharma

JALGAON
(Maharashtra)
Pop. Est. 145,254

JANASHAKTI (d) Marathi; Est. 1956
Janashakti Karyalayla, 200, Navipeth, 425-001
Tel: (91) 3842
Prop.—Dainik Nanashakti Trust
Pub./Ed.—Bhuta Patil
Ad. Mgr.—W W Kulkarni
LOKMAT (m) Marathi; Est. 1977
Lokmat Bhavan, C-19, Addl. MIDC Area; PO Box 73, 425-003
Tel: (91) 6696/(91) 6697
Circ.—28,694
Prop.—Lokmat Newspapers (Pvt.) Ltd.
Mng. Ed.—Vijay Darda

JAMSHEDPUR
(Bihar)
Pop. Est. 669,984

AMRITA BAZAR PATRIKA (m) English; Est. 1985
Ulyan Kadma
Circ.—15,772
Prop.—Amrita Bazar Patrika (Pvt.) Ltd.
UDITVANI (d) Hindi; Est. 1980
Jugsalai, 831-006
Tel: (91) 28198/(91) 27387
Pub./Ed.—Radhe Shyam Agrawal
Ad. Mgr.—S Dass

JHANSI
(Uttar Pradesh)
Pop. Est. 281,332

DAILY JAGRAN (mS) Hindi; Est. 1942
Jagran Bhavan, 362, Civil Lines
Circ.—26,512
Prop.—Daily Jagran Jhansi
Pub.—Rajendra Gupta
DAINIK VISHWA PARIWAR (d) Hindi; Est. 1978
34 Chandra Sekhar Azad, 284-002
Circ.—14,425
Prop.—P K Jain
Pub.—K C Jain
Ed.—J K Jain

JODPHUR
(Rajasthan)
Pop. Est. 493,609

JALTE DEEP (m) Hindi; Est. 1969
Jalori Gate, 342-003
Tel: (91) 22896
Circ.—38,000
Pub.—Manak Prakashan
Pub./Ed.—Padam Mehta
Ad. Mgr.—P L Arya
JANGAN (m) Hindi; Est. 1971
Near Anand Cinema, 342-001
Tel: (91) 20429/(91) 28216
Circ.—10,075
Pub./Ed. in Ch./Ad. Mgr.—Manak M Chopra
RAJASTHAN PATRIKA (m) Hindi; Est. 1979
Shyamgarh ki Haveli, Udai Mandir Marg, 342-006
Tel: (91) 20830
Prop.—Rajasthan Patrika (Pvt.) Ltd.
Pub.—Prashant Kothari
Ed.—Vijay Bhandari
Ad. Mgr.—Gulab Kothari

JORHAT
(Assam)

DAINIK JANAMBHUMI (m) Assamese; Est. 1972
Nehru Park Rd.; PO Box 1, 785-001
Tel: (91) 20033/(91) 21693
Circ.—34,610
Pub.—Arun Chandra Sharma
Pub./Ed.—Kanak Chandra Sharma

JULLUNDUR
(Punjab)
Pop. Est. 405,700

AJIT (m) Punjabi; Est. 1955
Ajit Bhavan, Nehru Garden Rd., 144-001
Tel: (91-181) 75961
Circ.—98,323
Prop.—Sadhu Singh Hamdard Trust
AKALI PATRIKA (m) Punjabi; Est. 1920
26 Chahar Bagh, 144-001
Circ.—35,000
Prop.—The Sikh Newspapers Ltd.
Pub.—R S Sodhi
Ed.—S Niranjan Singh Mithra
DAILY MILAP (dS) Urdu; Est. 1923
Milap Rd.
Circ.—24,039
Pub.—Punam Suri
Ed. in Ch.—Navin Suri
HIND SAMACHAR (mS) Urdu; Est. 1949
Pucca Bagh, 144-001
Circ.—62,633 (m); 77,688 (S)
Prop.—Hind Samachar Ltd.
Pub./Ed.—Vijaya Kumar Chopra
Ad. Mgr.—Arvind Chopra
JAG BANI (dS) Punjabi; Est. 1978
Pucca Bagh, 144-001
Circ.—94,175 (d); 115,556 (S)
Prop.—Hind Samachar Ltd.
Pub./Ed.—Vijay Kumar Chopra
Ad. Mgr.—Arvind Chopra
PRATAP DAILY (m) Urdu; Est. 1912
Nehru Garden Rd., 144-001
Circ.—9,669
Pub.—Chander Mohan
PUNJAB KESARI (m) Hindi; Est. 1965
Pucca Bagh, 144-001
Tel: (91-181) 75951
Circ.—519,298 (total-all eds.); 701,870 (S); 345,913 (d-Jullundur ed.); 453,216 (S)
Dir./Ad. Mgr.—Vijay Kumar Chopra
Ad. Mgr.—Arvind Chopra
(Circulation is the total of all Punjab Kesari editions. See Delhi/New Delhi.)
VIR PRATAP (m) Urdu; Est. 1955
Pratap Bhavan, Nehru Garden Rd., 144-001
Circ.—34,000
Dir./Ad. Mgr.—Chandar Mohan
Ed.—Lalit Mohan

KANPUR
(Uttar Pradesh)
Pop. Est. 1,688,242

AJ (dS) Hindi; Est. 1979
79/75 Bans Mandi, Kanpur, 208-001
Tel: (91-512) 60686/(91-512) 60695
Circ.—53,624
Prop.—AJ Prakashan Ltd.
Dir.—Poonam Gupta
Ed.—S V Gupta
DAILY JAGRAN (mS) Hindi; Est. 1947
2 Sarvodaya Nagar, 208-005
Tel: (91-512) 216161; Fax: (91-512) 216972
Circ.—409,477
Prop.—Jagran Prakashan (Pvt.) Ltd.
Pub./Ed.—Narendra Mohan
Ad. Dir.—Y M Gupta
GANESH (d) Hindi; Est. 1971
117 Pandu Nagar, 208
Circ.—14,000
Pub.—K N Tripathi
Ad. Mgr.—Sharad Avasthi
LOK BHARTI (d) Hindi; Est. 1983
White House, Yasoda Nagar
Tel: (91-512) 71237
Circ.—14,657
Pub.—Rama Kant Pandey
Mgr.—Anam Pandey
Ad. Mgr.—Rama Kant Mishra
SIYASIT JADID (m) Urdu; Est. 1953
Siyasat Bldg., Siyasat Akhbar Rd., Chamnganj; PO Box 418, 208-001
Circ.—11,000
Pub.—M Ishaq Ilmi
Ed.—Khan Ghufran Zahidi
VISHWAMITRA (m) Hindi; Est. 1948
128 Mahatma Gandhi Rd., 208-001
Pub./Ed.—Kanak Chandra Agrawalla
Ad. Mgr.—P Chandra Agrawalla
VYAPAR SANDESH (d) Hindi; Est. 1958
26/104, Birhana Rd.; PO Box 121, 208-001
Tel: (91-512) 68842/(91-512) 64757
Circ.—17,000
Ed.—Hari Shankar Sharma
Ad. Mgr.—Suresh Sharma

KOLHAPUR
(Maharashtra)
Pop. Est. 351,073

PUDHARI (mS) Marathi; Est. 1939
2318 C. Ward, Bhausinghji Rd., 416-002
Tel: (91) 26252/(91) 26254
Circ.—44,549
Pub./Ed.—P G Jadhav
Ad. Mgr.—D A Munshi Palkan
SAKAL/SUNDAY SAKAL (mS) Marathi; Est. 1980
413-1-1A, Mudshingi, Gandhinagar, 416-119
Circ.—24,920 (m); 27,154 (S)
Prop.—Sakal Newspapers (Pvt.) Ltd.
Dir.—Shri S V Nagarkar
Ed.—Shri S K Kulkami
SATYAWADI (m) Marathi; Est. 1926
Bhawan, Laxmipuri, 416
Circ.—23,000
Pub./Ad. Mgr.—Shri Suresh B Patil

KOTA
(Rajasthan)

JANNAYAK (d) Hindi; Est. 1973
Jannayak Bhawan Rd., 327-001
Tel: (91) 25244/(91) 27344
Circ.—28,585
Pub./Ed.—Bhanwar Sharma Atal
Ad. Mgr.—Omvir Sharma
RAJASTHAN PATRIKA (mS) Hindi; Est. 1986
Circ.—21,280
Prop.—Rajasthan Patrika (Pvt.) Ltd.

KOTTAYAM
(Kerala)
Pop. Est. 59,714

DEEPIKA (mS) Malayalam; Est. 1887
Deepika Bldg., College Rd.; PO Box 7, 686-001
Circ.—50,785
Prop.—Deepika Printers
Pub./Ed.—Thomas A Aykara
Ad. Mgr.—Sebastian Kochupura
MALAYALA MANORAMA (mS) Malayalam; Est. 1888
Manorama Bldg., K. K. Rd.; PO Box 26, 686-001
Tel: (91-481) 563646
Circ.—630,068 (m-total); 635,732 (S); 192,134 (m-Kottayam ed.); 192,515 (S)

Prop.—Malayala Manorama Co. Ltd.
Pub.—Mammen Varghese
Ed.—Mammen Mathew
Mktg. Mgr.—T M Mathews

LUCKNOW
(Uttar Pradesh)
Pop. Est. 1,006,538

AMRITA PRABHAT (m) Hindi; Est. 1979
 Circ.—25,754
 Prop.—Allahabad Patrika (Pvt.) Ltd.
DAILY JAGRAN (mS) Hindi
 75 Hazratganj, 226-001
NATIONAL HERALD (m) English; Est. 1938
 1 Biheshwar Nath Rd.; PO Box 122, 226-001
 Tel: (91) 49832
 Circ.—73,419
 Prop.—Associated Journals Ltd.
 Pub./Mng. Ed.—K G Sikka
 Ed.—Anser Kidwai
 Ad. Mgr.—P K Gupta
NAVJIVAN (m) Hindi; Est. 1947
 1 Bisheshwar Nath Rd.; PO Box 122, 226-001
 Circ.—11,326
 Chmn./Ed.—Yashpal Kapoor
NORTHERN INDIA PATRIKA (mS) English; Est. 1979
 25 Ashok Marg, 226-001
 Tel: (91) 47647/(91) 36451
 Circ.—59,212
 Prop.—Allahabad Patrika (Pvt.) Ltd.
 Pub.—Shibendra Kumar De Biswas
 Pub.—D K Gupta
 Ed.—Sunil Bose
THE PIONEER (m) English; Est. 1865
 20 Vidhan Sabha Marg, 226-001
 Tel: (91) 36516/(91) 36519
 Circ.—96,750
 Pub.—G K Daruka
 Ed.—S N Sapru
QUAMI AWAZ (m) Urdu; Est. 1945
 1 Bisheswar Nath Rd., 226-001
 Prop.—Associated Journals Ltd.
 Mgr.—D B Tandon
 Ed.—Ishrat Ali Siddiqui
 Ad. Mgr.—P S K Singh
SWATANTRA BHARAT (m) Hindi; Est. 1947
 20 Vidhan Sabha Marg, 226-001
 Tel: (91) 36516/(91) 36519
 Circ.—121,650
 Prop.—The Pioneer Ltd.
 Ed.—Raj Nath Singh
 Ad. Mgr.—Ashok K Ohri

LUDHIANA
(Punjab)
Pop. Est. 606,250

DAILY ROHJAN (d) Urdu; Est. 1984
 Deepak Cinema Rd., 141-008
 Tel: (91) 20622
 Circ.—11,270
 Prop.—K Sharma
 Pub./Ed.—Shri Sunil Sharma
TARJMAN (e) Punjabi; Est. 1952
 47/49 Kailash Cinema Market, Civil Lines
 Tel: (91) 20372/(91) 22764
 Circ.—17,525
 Prop.—Amardass Bhatia & Sons
 Pub.—Amardass Bhatia
 Gen. Mgr.—Ashwari Kumar

MADRAS
(Tamil Nadu)
Pop. Est. 4,900,000

ALAI OSAI (m) Tamil; Est. 1971
 A-84, 3rd St., Anna Nagar, 600-102
 Circ.—37,000
 Pub.—Velur D Narayanan
 Ed.—S Sambathi
 Ad. Mgr.—K S Srinivasan
ANDHRA PRABHA (mS) Telugu; Est. 1988
 Circ.—3,615
 Prop.—Andhra Prabha (Pvt.) Ltd.
ANNA (e) Tamil; Est. 1976
 62 Officers Colony, 4th Cross St., 600-029
 Tel: (91-44) 420212/(91-44) 429074
 Circ.—54,694
 Prop.—Thangamani Publications
 Pub./Ed.—K Ravindram
 Ad. Mgr.—A P Padmanabhan
DAILY THANTHI (mS) Tamil; Est. 1942
 PO Box 467, 600-007
 Tel: (91-44) 587731
 Circ.—313,624 (total-all eds.); 93,491 (Madras ed.)
 Prop.—The Thanthi Trust
 Pub.—R Somasundarum
 Ed.—Sri D Thiruvadi
 Ad. Mgr.—Sri D Rajaiah
 (Circulation is the total of all Daily Thanthi editions. See Bangalore, Coimbatore, Cuddalore, Madurai, Salem, Tiruchirapallu, Tirunelveli & Vellore.)
DINAKARAN (d) Tamil; Est. 1977
 106-107, Kutchery Rd., Mylapore, 600-004
 Tel: (91-44) 71006/(91-44) 71007
 Circ.—155,756
 Prop.—Kumar Publications Trust
 Ed.—K Kesavan
 Ad. Mgr.—G Gurunthan
DINAMALAR (mS) Tamil; Est. 1979
 Madurai, Tamilnadu
 Tel: (91-44) 811495/(91-44) 88715
 Circ.—129,235 (m); 138,888 (fri.); 167,549 (S)
 Prop.—T V Ramasubbaier & Sons
 Ed.—R Krishnamurthy
 Ad. Mgr.—G Sathiamurthy
DINAMANI (mS) Tamil; Est. 1934
 Express Estate, Mount Rd., 600-002
 Tel: (91-44) 810551
 Circ.—178,232
 Prop.—Indian Express (Madurai) (Pvt.) Ltd.
 Pub.—M K Sonthalia
 Ed.—I Mahadevan
 Ad. Mgr.—K Krishnan
DINASARI (d) Tamil; Est. 1984
 29 Police Commissioners Office Rd., Egmore, 600-008
 Tel: (91-44) 562738
 Circ.—65,739
 Prop.—Coromandel Publications Ltd.
 Pub.—S James Fredrick
FINANCIAL EXPRESS (m) English; Est. 1980
 Express Estate, Mount Rd., 600-002
 Tel: (91-44) 846517/(91-44) 846818
 Circ.—6,446
 Prop.—Indian Express Newspapers (Bombay) (Pvt.) Ltd.
THE HINDU (m) English; Est. 1878
 Kasturi Bldg., 859-860, Mount Rd., 600-002
 Tel: (91-44) 566567; Fax: (91-44) 83525
 Circ.—424,100 ABC (total-all eds.)
 Prop.—Kasturi & Sons Ltd.
 Pub.—S Rangarajan
 Ed.—G Kasturi
 Ad. Mgr.—V Chakrapani
 (Circulation is the total of all The Hindu editions. See Ahmedabad, Bangalore, Coimbatore, Delhi/New Delhi, Hyderabad & Madurai.)
INDIAN EXPRESS (mS) English; Est. 1959
 Express Estate, Mount Rd., 600-002
 Tel: (91-44) 810551
 Circ.—301,558
 Prop.—Indian Express (Madurai) (Pvt.) Ltd.
 Pub.—M K Sonthalia
 Ed.—Arun Shourie
 Ad. Mgr.—C V Raman
MAIL (e) English; Est. 1868
 Mail Bldg., 210 Mount Rd., 600-002
 Circ.—10,000
 Pub.—R K Anantharaman
 Ed.—V P V Rajan
MAKKAL KURAL (e) Tamil; Est. 1973
 1 Main Rd., United India Colony, 600-0024
 Circ.—39,000
 Pub./Ed.—M Shanmugavel
 Ad. Mgr.—K Sitharanjan
MALAI MURASU (e) Tamil; Est. 1961
 712 Anna Salai, Thousand Lights, 600-006
 Tel: (91-44) 869211/(91-44) 869222
 Circ.—21,668
 Pub./Ed.—V Ramasamy
 Ad. Mgr.—R Swaminathan
MURASOLI (m) Tamil; Est. 1960
 93 Kodambakkam High Rd., 600-034
 Tel: (91-44) 470044/(91-44) 470140
 Circ.—54,000
 Prop.—Anjugam Pathipagam
 Ed.—Murasoli Maron
 Ad. Mgr.—A L Manickam
SWADESMITRAN (d) Tamil; Est. 1880
 2 Vembuliamman Koli St., Virugambakkam, 600-092
 Tel: (91-44) 420504
 Circ.—3,529
 Prop.—The Swadesamitran Ltd.
 Ed.—Sri K Porko
THANTHI (d) Tamil; Est. 1942
 46 E. V. K. Sampath Rd., 600-007
 Tel: (91-44) 31331
 Circ.—297,797
 Prop.—Thanthi Trust
 Pub./Ed.—R Thiruvadi

MADURAI
(Tamil Nadu)
Pop. Est. 904,362

ATHIRSTAM (d) Tamil; Est. 1984
 32 Palam Station Rd., Sellur, 625-002
 Circ.—30,020
 Pub./Ed.—S Manimaran
 Ad. Mgr.—M Elango

Asia   India   IV-67

DAILY THANTHI (d) Tamil; Est. 1942
 1 Central Bus Stand Rd., 625-001
 Circ.—31,175
 Prop.—The Thanthi Trust
 Pub./Ed.—R S Rathanam
DINAKARAN (d) Tamil
 182 Kamarajar Salai, 625-009
 Pub./Ed.—S Jayapandian
 Ad. Mgr.—G Gurunathan
DINAMALAR (mS) Tamil; Est. 1980
 Circ.—31,476 (m); 37,153 (fri.); 42,906 (S)
 Prop.—T V Ramasubba Iyer & Sons
DINAMANI (mS) Tamil; Est. 1959
 Pankajam Gardens, 137, Ramnad Rd., 625-009
 Tel: (91-44) 23221
 Circ.—191,924 (total-all eds.); 101,655 (Madurai ed.)
 Prop.—Indian Express (Madurai) (Pvt.) Ltd.
 Pub.—P Krishnaswami
 Ad. Mgr.—S Krishnan
THE HINDU (mS) English
 Circ.—56,498
 Prop.—Kasturi & Sons Ltd.
INDIAN EXPRESS (mS) English; Est. 1959
 Pankajam Gardens, 137 Ramnad Rd., 625-009
 Circ.—272,670
 Prop.—Indian Express (Madurai) (Pvt.) Ltd.
 Pub.—N R Swaminathan
 Ed.—Suman Dubey
 Ad. Mgr.—K Parthasarathy

MANGALORE
(Karnataka)
Pop. Est. 305,513

MUNGARU (d) Kannada; Est. 1984
 J. V. Bldg., Hampankatta, 575-001
 Tel: (91) 32411
 Circ.—31,530
 Prop.—Mungaru Prakashan Ltd.
 Ed.—V Raghurama Shetty
NAVABHARATH (m) Kannada; Est. 1941
 Kodialbali; PO Box 706, 575-003
 Circ.—12,000
 Pub./Ed.—Sanjiv V Kudva
 Ad. Mgr.—F Fakeer

MANIPAL
(Karataka)

UDAYAVANI (mS) Kannada; Est. 1970
 Udayavani Bldg., Press Corner, Manipal-19
 Circ.—77,891 (m); 84,315 (S)
 Prop.—Manipal Printers & Publishers Ltd.
 Pub./Ed.—Tonse Satish Upendra Pai
 Ad. Mgr.—V Shankar

NAGPUR
(Maharashtra)
Pop. Est. 930,459

DAINIK MAHASAGAR (d) Marathi; Est. 1971
 Tekdi Rd., Sitabuldi, 440-012
 Tel: (91) 25501/(91) 49501
 Pub./Ed.—Shrikrishna Chandak
 Ad. Mgr.—Kishor Inamdar
HITAVADA (mS) English; Est. 1911
 Wardha Rd.; PO Box 210, 440-012
 Tel: (91) 23155/(91) 23447
 Circ.—27,525
 Prop.—Purohit & Co. Publications Division
 Pub.—Rajenda Purohit
 Ed.—M Y Bodhankar
 Ad. Mgr.—Vinay Paonaskar
LOKMAT (mS) Marathi; Est. 1971
 Lokmat Bhavan, Wardha Rd.; PO Box 216, 440-012
 Tel: (91) 23527/(91) 23528
 Circ.—102,867 (Nagpur ed.)
 Prop.—Lokmat Newspapers (Pvt.) Ltd.
 Pub.—Baburao Khumkar
 Mng. Ed.—Vijay Darda
 Ad. Mgr.—Ashok Jain
MAHAVIDRABHA (e) Marathi; Est. 1973
 Kamgar Bhavan, Kamgar Sq., 440-003
 Tel: (91) 44547/(91) 46071
 Circ.—12,512
 Ed.—Kesheorao R Nalamwar
NAGPUR PATRIKA (d) Marathi; Est. 1978
 37 Farmland, Ramdspeth, 440-010
 Tel: (91) 22935/(91) 34780
 Circ.—20,398
 Prop.—Nava Samaj Ltd.
 Ed.—Chandra Shekhar Phadnis

NAGPUR TIMES (mS) English; Est. 1933
 37 Farmland, Ramdaspeth, 440-010
 Tel: (91) 34780/(91) 22450
 Circ.—15,343
 Prop.—Nava Samaj Ltd.
 Pub.—S R Shrode
 Ed.—Naresh Gadre
 Ad. Mgr.—W T Kashhedikar
NAVA BHARAT (m) Hindi; Est. 1937
 Nava Bharat Bhavan, Cotton Market, 440-003
 Circ.—185,777 (total-all eds.); 142,000 (Nagpur ed.)
 Prop.—Nava Bharat Press
 Pub./Ad. Mgr.—V K Maheshwari
 Ed.—R G Maheshwari
 (Circulation is the total of all Nava Bharat editions. See Bhopal, Bilaspur, Indore, Jabalpur & Raipur.)
TARUN BHARAT (mS) Marathi; Est. 1944
 28 Farmland, Ramdas Peth; PO Box 296, 440-010
 Tel: (91) 26440/(91) 31758
 Circ.—72,891 (total-all eds.); 46,206 (Nagpur ed.)
 Prop.—Shri Narkesari Prakashan Ltd.
 Pub.—L T Joshi
 Mng. Dir.—G K Athawale
 (Circulation is the total of all Tarun Bharat editions. See Pune.)
YUGADHARMA (m) Hindi; Est. 1951
 28 Farmland, Ramdas Peth, 440-010
 Circ.—31,000
 Pub.—Rarnlal Pandey
 Ed.—D S Potnis

NASIK
(Maharashtra)
Pop. Est. 428,778

DESHDOOT/SUNDAY DESHDOOT (dS) Marathi; Est. 1970
 New Congress House, MG Rd.
 Tel: (91) 77444/(91) 75716
 Circ.—13,393 (d); 21,208 (S)
 Prop.—Shrirang Prakashan (Pvt.) Ltd.
 Pub./Ed.—Shri N S Avadhoot
GAVAKARI (mS) Marathi; Est. 1938
 Gavakali Karyalaya, 430/H, Tilak Path Nashik, 422-001
 Tel: (91) 72945/(91) 74546
 Circ.—30,720
 Prop.—Gavakari Prakashan
 Pub./Ed.—D S Potnis
SARWAMAT (d) Marathi; Est. 1976
 New Congress House, MG Rd., 422-001
 Tel: (91) 75716/(91) 72400
 Circ.—10,905
 Prop.—Shrirang Prakashan (Pvt.) Ltd.
 Pub.—V R Deshmukh

ORAI
(Uttar Pradesh)
Pop. Est. 42,513

DAINIK KARMYUG PRAKASH (d) Hindi; Est. 1971
 76 Gopal Ganj, 285-001
 Circ.—17,300
 Pub./Ed.—R C Gupta
KARMYUG PRAKASH (m) Hindi; Est. 1971
 76 Gopalganj, 285-001
 Circ.—20,000
 Pub./Ed.—R C Gupta
 Ad. Mgr.—D U Gupta

PANAJI
(Panjim)
(Territory of Daman, Diu & Goa)
Pop. Est. 59,258

GOMANTAK (m) Marathi; Est. 1962
 Gomantak Bhavan, St. Inez; PO Box 41, 403-001
 Circ.—15,194
 Prop.—Gomantak (Pvt.) Ltd.
 Pub./Ed.—Narayan G Athawalay
NAVHIND TIMES (m) English; Est. 1963
 Dempo House, Campal
 Circ.—14,000
 Prop.—Navhind Papers & Pubs. (Pvt.) Ltd.
 Pub./Ad. Mgr.—Vilas V Sardessai
 Ed.—M M Mudiliar
RASHTRAMAT (mS) Marathi; Est. 1963
 Margao, Goa; PO Box 109, 403-601
 Circ.—8,400
 Pub.—Nav-Gaomant Prakashan
 Mng. Dir.—S P Madkaiker
 Ed.—Chandrakant S Keni

India — Asia

PATNA
(Bihar)
Pop. Est. 916,102

AATMA KATHA (d) Hindi; Est. 1970
Sandesh Bhavan, Sinha Library Rd., 800-001
Circ.—21,450
Prop.—Sakhareshwari Publications (Pvt.) Ltd.
Pub.—Arun Kumar
Ad. Dir.—Maheshwar Jha
AJ (mS) Hindi; Est. 1979
Aj Bhawan, Frazer Rd., 800-001
Circ.—90,607
Prop.—Shashwat Printers (Pvt.) Ltd.
Pub.—Amitav Chakravorty
Ed.—Shardul Vikram Gupta
Ad. Mgr.—Shudhanshu Shekhar
ARYAVARTA (m) Hindi; Est. 1940
Mazharul Haque Path, 800-001
Tel: (91) 22130/(91) 22351
Circ.—43,940
Prop.—The Newspaper & Publications Ltd.
Pub./Ed. in Ch.—S N Jha
Ad. Mgr.—U B Singh
INDIAN NATION (m) English; Est. 1930
Mazharul Haque Path, 800-001
Tel: (91) 22130
Circ.—16,673
Prop.—The Newspapers & Publications Ltd.
Ed. in Ch.—S N Jha
Ad. Mgr.—Mahadeva Mishra
JANASHAKTI (d) Hindi; Est. 1975
Amarnath Rd., PO Box 124, 800-001
Circ.—41,212
Pub.—Navchetan Samiti
Pub.—Shyam Nandan Prasad Singh
Ed.—Upendra Nath Mishra
Ad. Mgr.—Narendra K Singh
PRADEEP (m) Hindi; Est. 1947
Buddha Marg; PO Box 43, 800-001
Tel: (91) 23413
Circ.—33,110
Pub.—B P Jhunjhunwala
Ed.—Paras Nath Singh
Ad. Mgr.—A S Raghunath
QUAMI AWAZ (m) Urdu; Est. 1945
Shyam Sadan Annexe, Exhibition Rd.
Mgr.—J N Jha
THE SEARCHLIGHT (m) English; Est. 1918
Buddha Marg; PO Box 43, 800-001
Circ.—22,741
Pub.—B P Jhunjhunwala
Ed.—R K Mukker
VISHWABANDHU (m) Hindi; Est. 1967
Braj Kishore, 800-001
Circ.—14,000
Pub.—Raghunandan Singh
Ed.—Avadh Kishore Singh

PUNE
(Maharashtra)
Pop. Est. 4,164,470

AAJ KA ANAND (d) Hindi; Est. 1979
303 Narayan Path, 411-030
Tel: (91) 420383
Circ.—14,993
Pub./Ed.—Shyam G Agarwal
Mgr.—Ram Agarwal
INDIAN EXPRESS (mS) English; Est. 1987
Circ.—22,754 (m); 25,762 (S)
Prop.—Indian Express Newspapers (Bombay) (Pvt.) Ltd.
KESARI (mS) Marathi; Est. 1981
568 Narayan Peth, 411-030
Tel: (91) 449250/(91) 449051
Circ.—84,573 (total-all eds.); 47,917 (Pune ed.)
Prop.—Kesari Mahratta Trust
Pub.—D J Tilak
Ed.—S D Gokhale
Ad. Mgr.—R H Deshmukh
MAHARASHTRA HERALD (d) Hindi; Est. 1963
2 General Thimayya Rd., 411-001
Tel: (91) 65592/(91) 65572
Circ.—19,150
Prop.—Poona Herald (Pvt.) Ltd.
Mng. Dir.—Nalini K Gera
Ed.—S D Wagh
PRABHAT (dS) Marathi; Est. 1932
303 Narayan Peth, 411-030
Tel: (91) 444841/(91) 445631
Circ.—27,618
Prop.—Daily Prabhat
Prop.—Poona Daily News Ltd.
Ed.—M G Khandkar

SAKAL/SUNDAY SAKAL (mS) Marathi; Est. 1932/1936
595 Budhwar Peth, 411-002
Tel: (91) 448403
Circ.—145,082; 151,616 (S)
Prop.—Sakal Papers (Pvt.) Ltd.
Pub.—Madame S G P Parulekar
Ed.—Shri S K Kulkarni
TARUN BHARAT (mS) Marathi; Est. 1957
1360 Shukrawar Peth; PO Box 598, 411-030
Tel: (91) 441750/(91) 441752
Circ.—53,446
Prop.—Rashtriya Vichar Prasarak Mandal
Pub.—L D Kane
Ed.—M R Kulkarni
Ad. Mgr.—V V Atre
VISHAL SAHYADRI (m) Marathi; Est. 1958
Sahyadri Sadan, Tilak Rd., 411-030
Circ.—20,000
Prop.—Vishal Sahyadri Trust
Ed.—A V Patel
Ad. Mgr.—M G Ranadive

RAIPUR
(Madhya Pradesh)
Pop. Est. 338,973

AMRIT SANDESH (d) Hindi; Est. 1984
Jawaharlal Nehru Marg; PO Box 18, 492-001
Circ.—26,232
Prop.—Pragati Prakashan (Pvt.) Ltd.
Ed. in Ch.—Govindlal Vora
Mgr.—Vitthal Das Ojha
DESH BANDHU (mS) Hindi; Est. 1959
Desh Bandhu Complex, Ramsagarpara Layout, 492-001
Tel: (91) 28008/(91) 28009
Circ.—38,230 (Raipur ed.)
Prop.—Patrakar Prakashan (Pvt.) Ltd.
Ed.—Maya Ram Surjan
Mng. Ed.—Lalit Surjan
Ad. Mgr.—Palash Surjan
NAVA BHARAT (m) Hindi; Est. 1959
Subhash Marg, Bilaspur
Tel: (91) 29166
Circ.—171,920 (total-all eds.)
Pub.—P R Maheshwari
Ed.—R G Maheshwari
(Circulation is the total of all Nava Bharat editions. See Bhopal, Bilaspur, Indore, Jabalpur & Nagpur.)
YUGADHARMA (m) Hindi; Est. 1951
Civil Lines, City Station, 492-001
Tel: (91) 25361
Circ.—6,500
Prop.—Shreedeep Prakashan
Ed.—Shri K M Jain

RAJKOT
(Gujarat)
Pop. Est. 444,156

JAI HIND (m) Gujarati; Est. 1948
Opp. Sharda Baug, 360-001
Circ.—51,694 (total-all eds.); 40,330 (Rajkot ed.)
Prop.—Jai-Hind Publications
Pub./Ed.—N L Shah
Ad. Mgr.—B B Shah
LOKASATTA-JANASATTA (mS) Gujarati; Est. 1967
Sadar, 300-001
Circ.—19,538
Prop.—Traders (Pvt.) Ltd.
PHULCHHAB (mS) Gujarati; Est. 1921
Mahatma Gandhi Rd.; PO Box 118, 360-001
Tel: (91) 44611
Circ.—93,365
Prop.—Saurashtra Trust
Pub.—Manshkh C Joshi
Ed.—Harsukh Sanghani
SANJ SAMACHAR (d-ex S) Gujarati; Est. 1986
Opp. Sharda Baug, 360-001
Circ.—38,906
Prop.—Jai-Hind Publications
SHRI NUTAN SAURASHTRA (m) Gujarati; Est. 1948
Ram Nivas, Sadar Bazar; PO Box 85, 360-001
Tel: (91) 47047
Circ.—13,000
Pub.—K J Rawal
Ed.—H J Rawal
Ad. Mgr.—N J Rawal

RANCHI
(Bihar)
Pop. Est. 500,593

AJ (mS) Hindi; Est. 1984
Circ.—39,830
Prop.—Shashwat Printers (Pvt.) Ltd.
(There are editions of AJ in Allahabad, Gorakhpur, Kanpur, Patna & Varanasi.)
RANCHI EXPRESS (dS) Hindi; Est. 1963
55 Baralal St.; PO Box 110, 834-001
Tel: (91) 22111
Circ.—51,287
Prop.—Ranchi Prakashan (Pvt.) Ltd.
Ed.—Balbir Dutt
Ad. Mgr.—Pawan Kumar

REWA
(Madhya Pradesh)
Pop. Est. 100,519

BANDHAVIYA SAMACHAR (m) Hindi; Est. 1971
Surya Kiran, Kalamandir Rd.
Circ.—9,000
Pub.—Rakesh Prasad Mishra
Ed.—Madhava Prasad Mishra
Ad. Mgr.—H Prasad Mishra

SALEM
(Tamil Nadu)
Pop. Est. 515,021

DAILY THANTHI (mS) Tamil; Est. 1942
Circ.—20,560
Prop.—The Thanthi Trust

SANGLI
(Maharashtra)
Pop. Est. 268,962

KESARI (mS) Marathi; Est. 1986
Circ.—14,240
Prop.—Kesari Mahratta Trust

SATNA
(Madhya Pradesh)

DESH BANDHU (mS) Hindi; Est. 1985
Khermai Rd.
Circ.—15,750
Prop.—Patrakar Prakashan (Pvt.) Ltd.

SECUNDERABAD
(Andhra Pradesh)
Pop. Est. 345,052

ANDHRA BHOOMI (mS) Telugu; Est. 1960
36 Sarojini Devi Rd., 500-003
Tel: (91) 72126
Circ.—6,917
Pub.—T Venkatram Reddy
Ed.—G Malla Reddy
Ad. Mgr.—P Seshagiri Rao
DECCAN CHRONICLE (mS) English; Est. 1938
36 Sarojini Devi Rd., 500-003
Tel: (91) 72126
Circ.—51,068
Pub./Ed.—T Venkatram Reddy
Ad. Mgr.—P Seshagiri Rao

SHOLAPUR
(Maharashtra)
Pop. Est. 514,461

KESARI (mS) Marathi; Est. 1984
Circ.—19,257
Prop.—Kesari Mahratta Trust
SANCHAR (m) Marathi; Est. 1961
Industrial Estate, Hotgi Rd., 413-003
Circ.—17,852
Prop.—Sangam Paper Corp.
Pub./Ed.—R M Vaidya
Ad. Mgr.—M M Kadadi

SHRIRAMPUR
Maharashtra

SARWAMAT (dS) Marathi; Est. 1976
3366 Somani Bldg., Ward No. 7
Circ.—13,165
Prop.—Shrirang Prakashan (Pvt.) Ltd.

SURAT
(Gujarat)
Pop. Est. 912,568

GUJARAT SAMACHAR (m) Gujarati; Est. 1975
Circ.—54,841
Prop.—Lok Prakashan Ltd.
GUJARATMITRA & GUJARATDARPAN (mS) Gujarat; Est. 1863
Near Old Civil Hospital, Sonifalia; PO Box 297, 395-003
Tel: (91-261) 23283/(91-261) 23284

Circ.—79,529
Prop.—Gujaratmitra (Pvt.) Ltd.
Pub./Ed.—B P Reshamwala
PRATAP (dS) Gujarati; Est. 1926
Nanavat; PO Box 242, 395-003
Tel: (91-261) 23251/(91-261) 23252
Circ.—13,010
Prop.—Saurashtra Trust
Pub./Ed.—Jagdish Shah
Ad. Mgr.—K D Shukla

TIRUCHIRAPALLI
(Tamil Nadu)
Pop. Est. 607,815

DAILY THANTHI (mS) Tamil; Est. 1942
Circ.—36,998
Prop.—The Thanthi Trust
DINAMALAR (mS) Tamil; Est. 1951
10/11 Norris Colony, Bird Rd.; PO Box 43
Circ.—324,921 (total-all eds.); 55,453 (Tiruchirapalli ed.); 200,312 (S-total-all eds.); 34,500 (S-Tiruchirapalli ed.)
Prop.—T V Ramasubba Iyer & Sons

TIRUNELVELI
(Tamil Nadu)

DAILY THANTHI (mS) Tamil; Est. 1942
5-C Madurai Rd., 627-001
Circ.—24,496
Prop.—The Thanthi Trust
Pub./Ed.—R S Rathnamm
DINAMALAR (mS) Tamil; Est. 1951
Madurai Rd.; PO Box 43, 627-001
Circ.—40,666 (m); 46,648 (fri.); 50,590 (S)
Prop.—TV Ramasubba Iyer & Sons
Ed.—R Krishnamurthy
Ad. Mgr.—R Lakshmipathy

TIRUPATI
(Andhra Pradesh)

EENADU (mS) Telugu; Est. 1982
Circ.—39,144
Prop.—Ushodaya Enterprises (Pvt.) Ltd.

TRICHUR
(Kerala)
Pop. Est. 170,093

DEEPIKA (mS) Malayalam; Est. 1887
Broadway Lodge Bldg., 2nd Floor, Round South, 680-001
Circ.—50,785
Prop.—Deepika Printers
(There is an edition of Deepika in Kottayam.)
THE EXPRESS (m) Malayalam; Est. 1944
PO Box 15
Tel: (91) 24640/(91) 28130
Circ.—51,083
Pub./Ed.—K Balakrishnan

TRIVANDRUM
(Kerala)
Pop. Est. 519,766

KERALA KAUMUDI (d) Malayalam; Est. 1911
Pettah; PO Box 77, 695-924
Tel: (91-495) 56555; Fax: (91-495) 56656
Circ.—1,720,000 (total-all eds.)
Prop.—The Kerala Kaumudi (Pvt.) Ltd.
Pub.—M S Ravi
Ed.—M S Mani
Ad. Mgr.—Ng Subramaniam
(Circulation is the total of all Kerala Kaumudi editions. See Calicut.)
KERALA PATHRIKA (d) Malayalam; Est. 1975
Vavanjalikulam Rd., 695-001
Circ.—37,181
Prop.—Kerala Pathrika (Pvt.) Ltd.
Mng. Ed.—P Balakrishna Pillai
Ed.—K P Vasudevan Nair
MALAYALA MANORAMA (mS) Malayalam; Est. 1987
Circ.—90,100 (m); 90,592 (S)
Prop.—Malayala Manorama Co. Ltd.
THE MATHRUBHUMI (mS) Malayalam; Est. 1980
TC 36/411, Perumthanni, 695-008
Circ.—108,330
Prop.—The Mathrubhumi Printing & Publishing Co. Ltd.
Pub.—K Kumoran Nair
Ed.—M D Nalapat

UDAIPUR
(Rajasthan)
Pop. Est. 229,762

JAI RAJASTHAN (d) Hindi; Est. 1972
Gandhi Marg, I/S Hathipole

Tel: (91) 24917
Circ.—22,554
Prop.—Shri Chandresh Vyash
RAJASTHAN PATRIKA (mS) Hindi; Est. 1981
Sunderwas, 313-001
Tel: (91) 25756
Circ.—196,267 (total-all eds.)
Prop.—Rajasthan Patrika (Pvt.) Ltd.
Ed.—V Bhandari
(Circulation is the total of all Rajasthan Patrika editions. See Bikaner, Jaipur, Jodhpur & Kota.)

VARANASI
(Benares)
(Uttar Pradesh)
Pop. Est. 793,542

AJ (mS) Hindi
Sant Kabir Rd.; PO Box 1007, 221-001
Tel: (91) 62061/(91) 62065
Circ.—285,401 (total-all eds.); 84,219 (Varanasi ed.)
Prop.—Jnanamandal Ltd.
Ed./Mng. Dir.—Shardul Vikrain Gupta
Ad. Mgr.—Satish Narain Dhawan
(Circulation is the total of all AJ editions. See Allahabad, Gorakhpur, Kanpur, Patna & Ranchi.)
DAILY JAGRAN (mS) Hindi; Est. 1981
Andhra Pull, 221-002
Tel: (91) 43300/(91) 43301
Circ.—409,477 (total-all eds.)
Prop.—Jagran Prakashan
Ed.—Narendra Mohan
(Circulation is the total of all Daily Jagran editions. See Gorakhpur, Jhansi, Kanpur & Lucknow.)
GANDIVA (e) Hindi; Est. 1950
Aas Bhairo; PO Box 1143, 221-001
Tel: (91) 56333/(91) 54545
Circ.—10,454
Pub.—Dr. Bhagwan Dass Arora
Pub./Ed.—Rajeeva Arora
JANAVARTA (d) Hindi; Est. 1972
52/82, Shakari Bhawan Nadesar, 221-002
Tel: (91) 42844
Circ.—15,000
Prop.—Janavarta Prakashav (Pvt.) Ltd.
Ed.—Ishwar D Mishra
SANMARG (e) Hindi; Est. 1946
Tulsi Mandir, Bhadaini, 221-001
Circ.—11,500
Pub.—Veer Bhadra Mishra
Ed.—S N Saraswati

VELLORE
(Tamil Nadu)
Pop. Est. 246,937

DAILY THANTHI (mS) Tamil; Est. 1942
Circ.—16,445
Prop.—The Thanthi Trust

VIJAYAWADA
(Andhra Pradesh)
Pop. Est. 544,958

ANDHRA JYOTI (dS) Telugu; Est. 1960
Andhra Jyoti Bldg.; PO Box 712, 520-010
Tel: (91) 74532/(91) 74533
Circ.—64,556
Prop.—Andhra Printers Ltd.
Pub./Ed.—K Jagdish Prasad
Ed.—Nanduri R Rao
ANDHRA PATRIKA (d) Telugu; Est. 1914
Gandhinagar; PO Box 534, 520-003
Tel: (91) 61247/(91) 61248
Circ.—22,486
Prop.—Nageswara Rao Estates (Pvt.) Ltd.
Pub.—S Nageswara Rao
Ed.—S Radhakrishna
Ad. Mgr.—K Ramachandraiah
ANDHRA PRABHA (mS) Telugu; Est. 1946
16-1-28, Kolandareddy Rd., Poornanadampet, 520-016
Tel: (91) 61351
Circ.—83,210 (total-all eds.); 29,199 (Vijayawada ed.)
Prop.—Andhra Prabha (Pvt.) Ltd.
Dir.—M K Sonthalia
Ed.—P V Rao
Ad. Mgr.—C V Raman
(Circulation is the total of all Andhra Prabha editions. See Bangalore, Hyderabad, Madras & Vizianagaram.)
EENADU (mS) Telugu; Est. 1978
Patamatalanka, 520-006
Circ.—91,735
Prop.—Ushodaya Enterprises (Pvt.) Ltd.
INDIAN EXPRESS (mS) English; Est. 1959
16-1-28, Kolandareddy Rd., Poornanadampet, 520-003

Circ.—315,751
Prop.—Indian Express (Madurai) (Pvt.) Ltd.
Pub.—A C Venatakrishnan
Ad. Mgr.—B S Rajaram
VISALAANDHRA (dS) Telugu; Est. 1952
Visalaandhra Bldg., 520-004
Tel: (91) 75301/(91) 75301
Pub.—Visalaandhra Vignana Samiti
Pub.—T Venkateswara Rao
Ed.—C Raghavachari

VISHAKAPATNAM
(Andhra Pradesh)
Pop. Est. 594,259

EENADU (mS) Telugu; Est. 1974
Circ.—39,754
Prop.—Ushodaya Enterprises (Pvt.) Ltd.
(There are editions of Eenadu in Hyderabad, Tirupati & Vijayawada.)

VIZIANAGARAM
(Andhra Pradesh)
Pop. Est. 115,209

ANDHRA PRABHA (mS) Telugu; Est. 1985
Circ.—7,870
Prop.—Andhra Prabha (Pvt.) Ltd.
(There are editions of Andhra Prabha in Bangalore, Hyderabad,) Madras & Vijayawada.
INDIAN EXPRESS (mS) English; Est. 1985
Circ.—16,130
Prop.—Indian Express (Madurai) (Pvt.) Ltd.

INDONESIA
Pop. Est. 200,409,741

BALIKPAPAN
(East Kalimantan)
Pop. Est. 1,863,059

HARIAN PAGI MANUNTUNG (d)
Jl. Jenderal Sudirman, RI XVI/82
Tel: (62-542) 32158
Circ.—12,000
Ch. Ed.—Rizal Effendi

BANDA ACEH
(Aceh)
Pop. Est. 3,407,198

ACEH POST (m) Est. 1960
Jl. Perdagangan, No. 11
Circ.—18,000
Prop.—Yayasan Pancacita Press
Ed.—Syamsul Kahar
Ed.—Tia Husphia

BANDJARMASIN
(South Kalimantan)
Pop. Est. 2,507,523

BANJARMASIN POST (m) Est. 1971
Jl. Letjen MT Haryono 54
Tel: (62-511) 3266
Circ.—20,000
Pub./Ed.—H J Djok Mentaya
GAWI MANUNTUNG (d) Est. 1967
Jl. Pangeran Samudra, No. 97
Tel: (62-511) 2701
Mgr.—Ali Sri Inderadjaja
Dir.—Hr. Gawi Manuntung
MEDIA MASYARAKAT HARIAN (m) Est. 1971
Jl. Pangeran Samudera, No. 99-Jl. Baamang Tengah II/170
Tel: (62-511) 3701
Circ.—15,000
Prop.—Yayasan Enam Enam Press
Ed.—Syahran R Anang Adenansi

BANDUNG
(West Java)
Pop. Est. 34,433,935

BANDUNG POST (d) Est. 1969
Jl. Lodaya, No. 38A
Tel: (62-22) 302881
Dir.—Rachat Soelaeman
BERITA HARIAN Est. 1980
Jl. Terusan Rajawali, No. 160
GALA MEDIA (d) Est. 1968
Jl. Asia-Afrika, 84 Atas
Tel: (62-22) 445936
Circ.—25,000
Prop.—P T Galamedia
Dir.—H Syamsuyar Adnan
Ed.—Aria Pandji

GALURA KORAN SUNDA (d)
Jl. Asia-Afrika, No. 77
Tel: (62-22) 444269
MANDALA (d) Est. 1969
Jend. Gatot Subroto, No. 42
Prop.—P T Satya Mandala Raya
Pub.—Krisna Harahap
PIKIRAN RAKJAT (m) Est. 1966
Jl. Asia-Afrika, No. 77; PO Box 219
Circ.—135,000
Prop.—P T Granesia
Dir.—Soeharmono Tjitroseowarno
Ed.—Bram Mucharam Darmapranira
Mktg. Dir.—Dalius Achyar Supriyadi

DENPASAR
(Bali)
Pop. Est. 2,811,475

BALI POST (m) Est. 1948
Jl. Kepundung, No. 67A, 80232
Tel: (62-361) 25764; Fax: (62-361) 27418
Circ.—50,000
Prop.—P T Bali Post
Pub./Ed.—K Nadha
Ad. Mgr.—Kariawan Kariadi
NUSA TENGGARA (d) Est. 1968
Jl. Hayam Wuruk, No. 110
Tel: (62-361) 25249
Circ.—13,000
Edit'l. Dir.—Jimmy Z Zaputan

JAKARTA
(Java)
Pop. Est. 9,406,477

ANGKATAN BERSENJATA (m) Est. 1965
CTC Bldg., Jl. Kramat Raya, No. 94, 3rd Floor
Tel: (62-21) 46071
Circ.—52,000
Prop.—HAB (Jamaker)
Pub.—Emir H Mungaweang
Ed.—M Hilmy Naustion
(This newspaper is published for the armed forces.)
BERITA BUANA (m) Est. 1970
Jl. Tanah Abang Dua, No. 33/35, 10110
Tel: (62-21) 40011; Fax: (62-21) 5491555
Circ.—123,525
Prop.—P T Yudha Gama
Pub.—H Darajad
Pub.—M Soewignyo
Ed.—Sukarno H Wibowo
Ad. Mgr.—Nurul Iman
BERITA JAYAKARTA (d) Est. 1985
Jl. Otto Iskandarinata, III/30
Prop.—P T Dipaguna Press
BERITA YUDHA (d) Est. 1965
Wisma Bis. Indo., 5th & 26th Floor, Jl. Letjen, S Parman, Kav. 11-13
Tel: (62-21) 5304016
Circ.—80,000
Prop.—Yayasan Parikesit
Dir.—Bagyo Purwantho
Ed.—Sugeng Widjala
Ad. Mgr.—Bobby Monka Jr
BISNIS INDONESIA (d) Est. 1985
Jl. Karamat, No. V/8, 10430
Tel: (62-21) 342191/(62-21) 3844642
Circ.—30,000
Mng. Dir.—Eric Samola SH
Ed.—Amir Daud
Ed.—Shirato Syafei
INDONESIA OBSERVER (m) English; Est. 1950
PO Box 2211, 10130
Tel: (62-21) 3845355; Fax: (62-21) 363660
Circ.—35,000
Prop.—The Indonesian Observer Ltd.
Pub.—Herawati Diah
Ad. Mgr.—Muslich Aliehoesin
INDONESIA TIMES (m) English; Est. 1974
31C Jl. Bak, 10012
Tel: (62-21) 3488170; Fax: (62-21) 375012
Circ.—41,000
Prop.—P T Wiwara Jaya
Dir.—Djamal Ali
Ed.—Tribuana Said
JAKARTA POST (d) English; Est. 1983
Jl. Palmerah Selatan, 15 B/c; PO Box 85, 10270
Tel: (62-21) 5483948; Fax: (62-21) 5492685
Circ.—21,500

Prop.—P T Bina Media Tenggara
Pub.—Mohammed Chudori
Ed.—Susanto Pudjomartono
Ad. Mgr.—Daisy Taniredja
KOMPAS MORNING DAILY (m) Est. 1965
Jl. Gajah Mada, No. 104, 10270
Tel: (62-21) 6297809; Fax: (62-21) 6297742
Circ.—550,000
Prop.—Kompas Media Nusantara PT
Pub./Ed.—Jakob Oetama
Ad. Mgr.—Daisy Taniredja
LENSA GENERASI (d)
AKA Bldg., Jl. Bangka, No. 11/2
Dir.—Aggi Tjetje
MERDEKA (m) Est. 1945
Jl. A.M. Sangaji, No. 11
Tel: (62-21) 364858; Fax: (62-21) 363660
Circ.—120,000
Prop.—P T Merdeka Press
Dir.—Soepano Sumardjo
Ed. in Ch.—B M Diah
Ad. Mgr.—Arda Kaitupan
PELITA (m) Est. 1979
Jl. Diponegoro, No. 60
Tel: (62-21) 332558
Circ.—20,000
Dir.—Dr. Abdul Gafur
(This newspaper is a Muslim religion-oriented paper.)
POS KOTA (d) Est. 1970
Jl. Gajah Mada, No. 63
Tel: (62-21) 6290874/(62-21) 6292026
Circ.—250,000
Prop.—P T Metro Pos
Pres.—H Tahar
Ad. Mgr.—H M Imam Subardy
SINAR HARAPAN (eS) Est. 1961
Jl. Dewi Sartika 136-D
Tel: (62-21) 8093208; Fax: (62-21) 8096129
Circ.—285,000 (e); 295,000 (S)
Prop.—PT Sinar Kasih
Ed.—Setiadi Tryman
Ad. Mgr.—S H Iskandar Widjaja
SINAR PAGI (m) Est. 1970
Jl. Letjen Haryono, No. 22, Selatan
Tel: (62-21) 8294140/(62-21) 8281044
Circ.—15,000
Prop.—Golden Web
Dir.—Jimmy Juneato
Ed.—Charly T Siahaan
SUARA RAKYAT MEMBANGUN (d) Est. 1976
Jl. Bangka Raya, No. 11/2, Kebayoran Baru
Circ.—100,000
Prop.—P T Suara Rakyat Membangun
Ed.—Sjamsul Basri
Ad. Mgr.—Imran Sidik
SUARA PEMBARUAN (e) Est. 1987
Jl. Gajah Mada 16, 10130
Tel: (62-21) 375476; Fax: (62-21) 8091652
Circ.—250,000
Prop.—P T Media Interaksi Utama
Dir.—Albert Hasibuan
Ad. Mgr.—Iskandar Widjaya

JAYAPURA
(Irian Jaya)
Pop. Est. 1,600,390

CENDERAWASIH (d) Est. 1962
Jl. Irian, No. 11
Dir.—J M Simatupang
Dir.—T Seriwa

JOGJAKARTA
(Java)
Pop. Est. 3,171,695

KEDAULATAN RAKYAT (m) Est. 1945
Jl. P. Mangkubumi, No. 40/42
Tel: (62-274) 65685
Circ.—72,000
Prop.—P T Badan Penebit Kedaulatan Rakyat
Mgr.—Soemadi M Wononito
Ed.—Iman Soetrisno
BERITA NASIONAL (m) Est. 1965
M T Haryono, No. 15
Tel: (62-274) 62643
Circ.—15,000
Prop.—Yayasan Mercu Suar
Ed.—Mustafa W Hasjim

Indonesia — Asia

LAMPUNG
(Sumatra)
Pop. Est. 7,585,487

LAMPUNG POS (d)
Jl. Paughal Pinang, No. 46
Dir.—H Sofian Achmad

MEDAN
(North Sumatra)
Pop. Est. 10,541,224

ANALISA (m) Est. 1972
Jl. Jenderal A. Yani, No. 37-43; PO Box 482
Circ.—80,000
Pub.—Percetakaen Kumango
Dir.—Januar Junaedi
Ed.—M Soffyan
Ad. Mgr.—Joeli Salim
BUKIT BARISAN (d)
Jl. Lahat, No. 11
Circ.—10,000
MIMBAR UMUM (m) Est. 1947
Jl. Riau, No. 79
Tel: (62-61) 517807
Circ.—15,000
Prop.—Firma Hasmar
Pub./Ed.—H Fauzi Lubis
SINAR INDONESIA BARU (d) Est. 1970
Jl. Brigjen Katamso, No. 54, ABCD
Tel: (62-61) 24950/(62-61) 26930
Circ.—75,000
Pub./Ed.—G M Panggabean
Ad. Mgr.—Amrul Umar
SINAR PEMBANGUNAN HARIAN UMUM (m) Est. 1956
Jl. Mayjen Sutoyo, Siswomiharjo, No. 107-109
Circ.—10,000
Prop.—Yayasan Berdikari
Ed.—Ibrahim Sinik

MENADO
(North Sulawesi)
Pop. Est. 2,509,107

CAHAYA SIANG
Jl. Sam Ratulangi, No. 390, Wanea
Tel: (62-431) 60095
Circ.—12,000
Ed.—Lanny Politan
MANADO POST (d) Est. 1961
Jl. Balaikota, No. 18
Tel: (62-431) 64812
Circ.—22,000
Prop.—Yayasan Suluh Merdeka
Dir.—W J Engka
Ed.—Simon N Sangkay
Ad. Mgr.—M L Tuju

PADANG
(West Sumatra)
Pop. Est. 3,947,390

HALUAN (d) Est. 1949
Jl. Damar, No. 59CDEF
Tel: (62-751) 31660
Circ.—20,000
Prop.—P T Badan Penerbit Huluan
Pub.—Kasoema Bim R Hoesin
Ed.—Rival Mariaut
SINGGALANG (m) Est. 1968
Jl. Veteran, No. 17
Tel: (62-751) 25001
Circ.—20,000
Pub./Ed.—Basril Djabar

PALANGKARAYA
(Central Kalimantan)
Pop. Est. 1,312,678

PALANGKARAYA POS (d) Est. 1971
Jl. Jend A. Yani, Blok C
Tel: (62-751) 21055
Dir.—D A Dharmo
Dir.—Siun Ihil

PALEMBANG
(South Sumatra)
Pop. Est. 6,243,176

BERITA EXPRESS (d)
Jend Sudirman, No. 24
Tel: (62-711) 27258
Prop.—Yayasan Berita Express

GARUDA POST (d) Est. 1969
Jl. Jenderal Sudirman Rgr. Mesjid Agung, No. 46
Pub.—H Rivolis
SUARA RAKYAT SEMESTA (d)
Jl. Indra, No. 6
Tel: (62-711) 22956
Circ.—4,000
Pub.—Yayasun Suara Rakyat
Pub./Ed.—D Abdullah

PONTIANAK
(West Kalimantan)
Pop. Est. 3,227,804

AKCAYA (m) Est. 1967
Nusa Indah BI, No. B-62
Tel: (62-561) 34595
Circ.—10,000
Prop.—Yayasan Akaya Press
Pub./Ed.—Yacob Mochsin

SEMARANG
(Central Java)
Pop. Est. 29,016,675

BAHARI MINGGUAN UMUM (d) Est. 1969
Jl. Sekayu Raya, No. 261
Tel: (62-24) 289515
Pub.—Yulistyo Suyatno
KARTIKA (m) Est. 1965
Jl. Pemuda, No. 145
Tel: (62-24) 23991
Circ.—10,000
Prop.—Yayasan Penerbit Diponegoro
Ed.—M Soebagio
SUARA MERDEKA (m) Est. 1950
Jl. Raya Kaligawe, Km. 5
Tel: (62-24) 515621
Circ.—125,000
Prop.—Suara Merdeka Press Ltd.
Pub.—Ir Budi Santoso
Ed.—S H Soewarno

SURABAYA
(East Java)
Pop. Est. 33,205,843

HARIAN PAGI MEMORANDUM (d)
Jl. Pahlawan 116
Tel: (62-31) 7204915; **Fax:** (62-31) 7204803/(62-31) 7398500
Circ.—190,000
Prop.—P T Jawa Postt
Ad. Mgr.—Zaman Syah
JAWA POS (d) Est. 1949
Karah Agung 45
Tel: (62-31) 833950; **Fax:** (62-31) 830996
Circ.—35,000
Prop.—P T Jawa Postt
Pub.—Eric Samola
Ed.—Dahian Iskan
Ad. Mgr.—Ratna Dewi
KARYA DARMA (d)
Jemursari Selatan IV, Kav. 20-22
Tel: (62-31) 832993
Circ.—30,000
Prop.—P T Ali & Son
Pub.—Agil H Ali
SUARA INDONESIA (d) Est. 1976
Jl. Roden Saleh, No. 8
Tel: (62-31) 46566
Circ.—8,000
Dir.—Aco Manafe
SURABAJA POST (e) Est. 1953
Jl. Taman AIS Nasution I
Tel: (62-31) 520863
Circ.—105,000
Prop.—Surabaya Post CV
Ed.—Tuti Aziz
Ad. Mgr.—Indrajaya Aziz

TELUKBETUNG
(Sumatra)

TAMTAMA (d)
Jl. Veteran, No. 154A
Dir.—J Koesri
Dir.—Bachtiar Jalil

UJUNG PANDANG
(South Sulawesi)
Pop. Est. 7,082,118

GEMA (d) Est. 1966
Jl. Jend A. Yani, No. 13 (Atas)
Dir.—H A Zaiyani

Dir.—Henky Jonas
Dir.—M N Sam
PEDOMAN RAKYAT (m) Est. 1947
Jl. Azief Rate, No. 28
Tel: (62) 83344
Circ.—25,000
Pub.—Fa Perak
Dir.—L E Manahua
Ed.—M Basir
UJUNG PANDANG POST
Circ.—8,000
Ed.—Alwi Hamid

JAPAN
Pop. Est. 125,106,937

AKITA
(Tohoku)
Pop. Est. 302,362

THE AKITA SAKIGAKE SHIMPO (m&e) Est. 1874
1-1, San-norin-kai-cho, 010
Tel: (81-188) 881800
Circ.—257,301 (m); 257,301 (e) ABC
Prop.—The Akita Sakigake Shimpo
Pres.—Zenjiro Hayashi
Ex. Dir./Ed./Ch. Edit'l. Wr.—Joji Fujikawa
Mng. Dir./Sales Mgr./Ad. Mgr.—Jisaku Nimura
Dir./Mng. Ed.—Tsuyoshi Ito
Dir./Ad. Mgr.—Hiroshi Sugibuchi
Sales Mgr.—Masayasu Kamiya

AOMORI
(Tohoku)
Pop. Est. 287,808

TO-O NIPPO (m&e) Est. 1888
78, Kanbayashi, Yatsuyaku, 030-01
Tel: (81-177) 391111
Circ.—255,879 (m); 251,592 (e) ABC
Prop.—The To-o Nippo Press Co. Ltd.
Pres.—Yoshihiro Iwabuchi
Ex. Dir./Ad./Sales—Takao Sasaki
Dir./Mng. Ed.—Shun-ichi Kobayashi
Dir./Ch. Edit'l. Wr.—Mitsuro Wada
Ad. Mgr.—Isami Takeuchi
Sales Mgr.—Chuichi Hanada
Bus. Mgr.—Syoji Shiraki

ASAHIKAWA CITY
(Hokkaido)
Pop. Est. 359,071

HOKKAIDO SHIMBUN (m&e)
10, Shijo-dori, 070-91
Tel: (81-166) 232111
Circ.—253,360 (m); 138,839 (e) ABC
Prop.—The Hokkaido Shimbun Press
Asahikawa Headofficer—Fumio Tohara
(There are editions of Hokkaido Shimbun in Hakodate, Kushiro & Sapporo.)
HOKKAI TIMES (m) Est. 1046
13, 6-jo, 070
Tel: (81-166) 234171
Circ.—67,520
Prop.—The Hokkai Times Press Co Ltd.
Asahikawa Headofficer—Tadao Aoba
(There is an edition of the Hokkai Times in Sapporo.)

CHIBA
(Kanto)
Pop. Est. 829,455

CHIBA NIPPO (m) Est. 1957
4-14-10, Chuo, Chuo-ku, 260
Tel: (81-43) 2229211
Circ.—59,698
Prop.—Chiba Nippo Press Co. Ltd.
Ch.—Hideo Tsuruoka
Pres.—Kiyoshi Tsuruoka
Vice Pres.—Miyuki Yamamoto
Ex. Dir./Ed.—Hachiro Nakijima
Dir./Mng. Ed.—Noburo Hayashi
Dir./Bus. Mgr.—Tsutomu Abe
Dir./Ad. Mgr.—Tadao Hayashi
Dir./Sales Mgr.—Takao Kusumi

FUKUI
(Hokuriku)
Pop. Est. 252,743

FUKUI SHIMBUN (m) Est. 1899
1-1-14, Haruyama, 910
Tel: (81-776) 235111
Circ.—184,591 ABC
Prop.—The Fukui Shimbun
Pres.—Kousuke Yoshida
Ex. Dir./Ed.—Fumio Yamada

Ex. Dir./Ad. Mgr./Bus.—Munemitsu Sasaki
Dir./Ch. Edit'l. Wr.—Midori Matsushima
Dir./Sales Mgr.—Bun-yu Tatara
Mng. Ed.—Yusuke Iwanaga
Bus. Mgr.—Tsunehiro Nakamura
NIKKAN KENMIN FUKUI (m) Est. 1977
3-1-8, Ohte, 920
Tel: (81-776) 220950
Circ.—61,315
Prop.—Nikkan Fukui
Headofficer—Bungo Shirai

FUKUOKA
(Kyushu)
Pop. Est. 1,750,000

DEMPA SHIMBUN (m) Est. 1977
2-13-23, Hakata-eki-mae, Haka-ta-ku, 812
Tel: (81-92) 4317411
Prop.—Dempa Publications Inc. (Dempa Shim-bun-sha)
Pres.—Kazuya Nishida
(There is an edition of Dempa Shimbun in Tokyo.)
FUKUNICHI (m) Est. 1946
2-22-40, Higashi-Naka, Hakata-ku, 816
Tel: (81-92) 4733520
Prop.—Fukunichi Press
Pres.—Tatsukuni Touyama
Mng. Ed.—Seiji Iwasaki
Ch. Edit'l. Wr.—Hideharu Uchikawa
Bus. Mgr.—Hironori Yasuhiro
Ad. Mgr.—Toshiaki Urata
Sales Mgr.—Kazuaki Koga
KYUSHU SPORTS (m) Est. 1966
Fukuoka Tenjin Center Bldg., 2-14-8, Tenjin-cho, Chuo-ku, 810
Tel: (81-92) 7817401
Prop.—Tokyo Sports Press
Kyushu Headofficer—Teruo Okamiya
NIHON KEIZAI SHIMBUN (m&e) Est. 1964
2-16-1, Hakata-eki-Higashi, Hakata-ku, 812
Tel: (81-92) 4733300
Circ.—194,273 (m); 70,380 (e) ABC
Prop.—Nihon Keizai Shimbun Inc.
Dir./Seibu Headofficer—Gen Tanaka
(There are editions of Nihon Keizai Shimbun in Osaka & Tokyo.)
NISHI NIPPON SHIMBUN (m&e) Est. 1877
1-4-1, Tenjin, Chuo-ku, 810
Tel: (81-92) 7115555
Circ.—821,756 (m); 201,192 (e) ABC
Prop.—Nishi Nippon Shimbun
Pres.—Shigeru Aoki
Ex. Dir./Bus. Mgr.—Katsumi Yamada
Ex. Dir./Sales Mgr.—Hiroo Shimada
Dir./Mng. Ed.—Kenji Ishizaki
Dir./Ad. Mgr.—Takeo Matsumura
Ch. Edit'l. Wr.—Kenjiro Nishi
Bus. Mgr.—Tadao Kuwahara
NISHI NIPPON SPORTS (m) Est. 1954
1-4-1, Tenijin, Chuo-ku, 810
Prop.—Nishi Nippon Shimbun-sha

FUKUSHIMA
(Tohoku)
Pop. Est. 277,528

FUKUSHIMA MIMPO (m&e) Est. 1892
13-17, Ohta-machi, 960
Tel: (81-245) 314111
Circ.—293,516 (m); 10,500 (e) ABC
Prop.—Press Fukushima Mimpo
Honorary Ch.—Teijou Tobishima
Pres.—Yoshio Kobari
Vice Pres.—Katsuji Yamada
Mng. Dir./Ed.—Noriyuki Saito
Mng. Dir./Ad.—Shin-ichi Suzuki
Dir./Mng. Ed.—Seiichi Watanabe
Dir./Ch. Edit'l. Wr.—Takashiro Yamazaki
Dir./Ad. Mgr.—Hidenori Watanabe
Dir./Sales/Bus.—Yoshiyuki Sato
Sales Mgr.—Yukio Anzai
Bus. Mgr.—Masahiko Sugawara
FUKUSHIMA MINYU (m&e) Est. 1895
4-29, Yanagimachi, 960
Tel: (81-245) 231191
Circ.—193,896 (m); 7,074 (e) ABC
Prop.—Fukushima Minyu Shimbun
Ch.—Yosoji Kobayashi
Pres./Ed. in Ch.—Takashi Kinoshita
Vice Pres.—Tsuneo Muramatsu
Ex. Dir./Sales/Bus.—Susumu Imai
Dir./Mng. Ed.—Hiroyuki Tarui
Dir./Ad. Mgr.—Sadao Okatsu
Ch. Edit'l. Wr.—Gouichi Moriai
Sales Mgr.—Morio Saito

GIFU
(Chubu)
Pop. Est. 410,324

GIFU SHIMBUN (m&e) Est. 1879
9, Imakomachi, 500
Tel: (81-582) 641151

Circ.—157,522 (m); 31,654 (e) ABC
Prop.—Gifu Shimbun Co. Ltd.
Pres.—Mikio Sugiyama
Ex. Dir./Ed.—Kiminori Muto
Mng. Dir./Ad./Sales—Nagatoshi Sawaki
Dir./Mng. Ed.—Yutaka Sawafuji
Dir./Bus. Mgr.—Shigeru Sunahara
Dir./Ad. Mgr.—Syodo Tanaka
Dir./Sales Mgr.—Hidefumi Imao
Ch. Edit'l. Wr.—Hiromichi Miwa

HACHINOHE
(Tohoku)
Pop. Est. 241,057

DAILY TOHOKU (1945) Est. 1945
1-3-12, Jyoka, Hachinoche, 031
Tel: (81-178) 445111
Circ.—103,401 ABC
Prop.—Daily Tohoku Shimbun-sha
Ch.—Hiroaki Niiyama
Ex. Dir./Ad. Mgr.—Yoshihisa Kato
Mng. Dir./Ed.—Etsuro Kumano
Dir./Mng. Ed.—Isamu Honda
Sales Mgr.—Kouzo Kanahama

HAKODATE
(Hokkaido)
Pop. Est. 307,249

HOKKAIDO SHIMBUN (m&e) Est. 1942
31-3, Goryokaku-machi, 040-91
Tel: (81-138) 532111
Circ.—141,684 (m); 117,569 (e) ABC
Prop.—The Hokkaido Shimbun Press
Hakodate Headofficer—Kouji Sakata
(There are editions of Hokkaido Shimbun in Asahikawa City, Kushiro & Sapporo.)

HAMAMATSU CITY
(Chubu)
Pop. Est. 534,620

CHUNICHI SHIMBUN (m&e) Est. 1981
45, Yakushin-machi, 435
Tel: (81-53) 4217711
Prop.—The Chunichi Shimbun (Hamamatsu)
Ex. Dir./Tokai Headofficer/Mng. Ed.—Kazuo Narita
Bus. Mgr.—Naotake Murata
(There is an edition of Chunichi Shimbun in Nagoya.)

HIROSAKI
(Tohoku)
Pop. Est. 133,800

MUTSU SHIMPO (m) Est. 1946
2-1, Shimo-shirogane-cho, 036
Tel: (81-172) 343111
Prop.—Mutsu Shimpo
Pres.—Tokuhiro Shimoyama
Mng. Dir./Bus./Ad.—Misao Honma
Bus. Mgr.—Takashi Tsushrima
Sales Mgr.—Toshiaki Abo

HIROSHIMA
(Chugoku)
Pop. Est. 1,085,705

CHUGOKU SHIMBUN (m&e) Est. 1892
7-1, Dobashi-cho, Naka-ku, 730
Tel: (81-82) 2362111
Circ.—709,925 (m); 100,581 (e) ABC
Prop.—Chugoku Shimbun
Ch.—Akira Yamammoto
Pres.—Jiro Yamamoto
Ex. Dir./Ch. Edit'l. Wr.—Takumi Usui
Ex. Dir./Bus.—Kazutaka Yamamoto
Dir./Mng. Ed.—Wataru Imanaka
Dir./Ad. Mgr.—Akira Yamanaka
Dir./Sales Mgr.—Hirohiko Murakami
Bus. Mgr.—Shohei Kawamoto

ICHINOSEKI CITY
(Tohoku)
Pop. Est. 50,100

IWATE NICHI-NICHI SHIMBUN (m) Est. 1923
60, Minami-shin-machi, 021
Tel: (81-191) 265111
Circ.—41,671
Prop.—Iwate Nichi-Nichi Shimbun-sha
Pres./Ed. in Ch.—Takeshi Yamagishi
Ex. Dir./Ad.—Tsuneo Sato
Ex. Dir./Bus.—Choichiro Onodera
Dir./Sales Mgr.—Kazumi Sato

ISHIGAKI
(Kyushu)

YAEYAMA MAINICHI SHIMBUN (m) Est. 1950
258, Ishigaki, Ishigaki-shi, 907
Tel: (81-9808) 22121
Circ.—13,000
Prop.—Yaeyama Mainichi Shimbun-sha
Pres.—Choyu Itosu
Ex. Dir./Bus.—Hirokichi Ohama
Dir./Mng. Ed.—Yushio Uechi
Ad. Mgr.—Kiyotaka Nakama

ISHINOMAKI CITY
(Tohoku)
Pop. Est. 121,976

ISHINOMAKI SHIMBUN (e) Est. 1946
2-1-28, Sumiyoshi-machi, 986
Tel: (81-225) 223201
Circ.—13,120
Prop.—Ishinomaki Press
Pres.—Motomi Wada
Mng. Ed.—Shigeru Nogami
Bus. Mgr.—Minoru Wada
Ad. Mgr.—Kou Motoki

IZUMO
(Chugoku)
Pop. Est. 69,600

SHIMANE NICNI-NICHI SHIMBUN (e) Est. 1980
545, Sato-gata-cho, 693
Tel: (81-853) 236760
Circ.—20,585
Owner/Mng. Ed.—Kosuke Kikuchi
Pres.—Emiko Kikuchi
Ed. in Ch.—Toyomi Hino
Ed. in Ch.—Shinji Horii
Bus. Mgr.—Jyoji Yamada
Ad. Mgr.—Keiichi Kanda
Sales Mgr.—Kokichi Mishima

KAGOSHIMA
(Kyushu)
Pop. Est. 536,752

KAGOSHIMA SHIMPO (m) Est. 1959
7-28, Jonan-cho, 892
Tel: (81-992) 262100
Circ.—45,800 ABC
Prop.—Kagoshima Shimpo Daily Press
Pres.—Akira Hano
Dir./Mng. Ed.—Junsuke Kinoshita
Dir./Edit'l. Wr.—Takeo Fukumitsu
Dir./Ad. Mgr.—Masaru Sakoya
Dir./Sales Mgr.—Satoru Nakamura
Ch. Edit'l. Wr.—Koryu Horinouchi
MINAMI NIPPON SHIMBUN (m&e) Est. 1881
1-2, Yasui-cho, 892
Tel: (81-992) 264111
Circ.—387,972 (m); 28,136 (e) ABC
Prop.—Minami Nippon Shimbun Co. Ltd.
Pres.—Umashi Hidaka
Ex. Dir./Bus./Ad.—Hiroshi Hurukawa
Ex. Dir./Sales—Yoshio Irita
Mng. Dir./Ed.—Ryoichi Hirota
Mng. Ed.—Hiroaki Toyokawa
Ch. Edit'l. Wr.—Ryuichi Otsuji
Ad. Mgr.—Osami Hukano
Sales Mgr.—Takakuni Kojima
Bus. Mgr.—Toshiaki Kamizono

KANAZAWA CITY
(Hokuriku)
Pop. Est. 442,868

HOKKOKU SHIMBUN (m&e) Est. 1893
2-5-1, Kohrinbo, 920
Circ.—332,306 (m-total); 111,316 (e) ABC
Prop.—Hokkoku Shimbun
(Circulation is the total of all Hokkoku Shimbun editions. See Kanazawa & Toyama.)
HOKKOKU SHIMBUN (m&e) Est. 1893
2-5-1, Kohrinbo, 920
Tel: (81-762) 632111
Circ.—285,249 (m); 111,316 (e) ABC
Prop.—The Hokkoku Shimbun
Ch.—Naotsuyo Okada
Pres./Ed. in Ch.—Hidekazu Tobita
Ex. Dir.—Yukinobu Maekawa
Mng. Dir./Ed./Ch. Edit'l. Wr.—Takeshi Matsumura
Mng. Dir./Bus.—Minoru Kita
Mng. Dir./Sales—Tsutomu Yoshida
Mng. Ed.—Masayuki Ohnishi
HOKURIKU CHUNICHI SHIMBUN (m&e) Est. 1960
2-7-15, Kohrinbo, 920
Tel: (81-762) 613111
Circ.—113,389 (m); 15,048 (e)
Prop.—The Hokuriku Chunichi Shimbun
Dir./Hokuriku Headofficer—Ken Oyaizu
Mng. Ed.—Tadashi Numa
Bus. Mgr.—Kousuke Maki
(There is an edition of Chunichi Shimbun in Nagoya.)

Asia Japan IV-71

KITAKYUSHU
(Kyushu)
Pop. Est. 1,026,455

ASAHI SHIMBUN (m&e) Est. 1935
1-12-1, Sunatsu, Kokurakita-ku, 802
Tel: (81-93) 5311131
Circ.—821,861 (m); 178,352 (e) ABC
Prop.—Asahi Shimbun Publishing Co.
Ex. Dir./Seibu Headofficer—Kouichi Okuo
Mng. Ed.—Kiyomasa Habara
Sales Mgr.—Nabuo Nakazawa
(There are editions of Asahi Shimbun in Nagoya, Osaka, Sapporo & Tokyo.)
MAINICHI SHIMBUN (m&e) Est. 1935
13-1, Kon-ya-machi, Kokura-Kita-ku, 802
Tel: (81-93) 5413131
Circ.—657,562 (m); 140,346 (e) ABC
Prop.—The Mainichi Newspapers
Ex. Dir./Seibu Headofficer—Kunio Shirane
Mng. Ed.—Ken-ichi Katayama
Ad. Mgr.—Tsunao Imai
Sales Mgr.—Kenji Tanaka
(There are editions of Mainichi Shimbun in Nagoya, Osaka, Sapporo & Tokyo.)
YOMIURI SHIMBUN (m&e) Est. 1964
1-11, Meiwa-machi, Kokurakita-ku, 820
Tel: (81-93) 5315131
Circ.—964,246 (m); 123,209 (e) ABC
Prop.—The Yomiuri Shimbun Seibu
Pres.—Tsuneo Watanabe
Vice Pres./Seibu Headofficer—Yoshinori Fukaya
Mng. Ed.—Yuuji Adachi
Ad. Mgr.—Akio Sugai
Sales Mgr.—Michio Yasuhara
(There are editions of Yomiuri Shimbun in Osaka, Sapporo, Takaoka City & Tokyo.)

KOBE
(Kinki)
Pop. Est. 1,477,410

DAILY SPORTS (m&e) Est. 1948
1-2-5, Murotani, Nish-ku, 651-22
Tel: (81-78) 9934100
Prop.—The Daily Sports
Pres.—Katsuro Arakawa
Ex. Dir./Ad./Bus.—Shinzaburo Ohta
Ex. Dir./Sales Mgr.—Minoru Inoue
Dir./Tokyo Headofficer—Hirokazu Toyoda
Ad./Bus. Mgr.—Yoshihiko Shimomura
(There are editions of Daily Sports in Osaka & Tokyo.)
KOBE SHIMBUN (m&e) Est. 1898
1-2-5, Murotani, Mishi-ku, 651-22
Tel: (81-78) 9934100
Circ.—523,028 (m); 276,969 (e) ABC
Prop.—The Kobe Shimbun
Pres.—Katsuro Arakawa
Ex. Dir./Mng. Ed.—Hideo Yamane
Ex. Dir./Ad.—Akeshi Iwamoto
Ex. Dir./Sales Mgr.—Tadao Tanaka
Dir./Ch. Edit'l. Wr.—Yasuhiro Miki
Dir./Bus. Mgr.—Hiroshi Yamada
Dir./Ad. Mgr.—Masaaki Kurata

KOCHI
(Shikoku)
Pop. Est. 317,069

KOCHI SHIMBUN (m&e) Est. 1904
3-2-15, Hon-cho, 780
Tel: (81-888) 222111
Circ.—225,582 (m); 140,010 (e) ABC
Prop.—The Kochi Shimbun Co. Ltd.
Pres.—Shoroku Hashii
Ex. Dir./Sales Mgr.—Yasuyuki Kuwao
Mng. Dir./Ad.—Toshihiko Kakemizu
Dir./Mng. Ed.—Toshio Iwai
Dir./Ch. Edit'l. Wr.—Hiroshi Kamimura
Ad. Mgr.—Yoshiaki Matsuda

KOFU CITY
(Chubu)
Pop. Est. 200,626

YAMANASHI NICHI-NICHI SHIMBUN (m) Est. 1872
2-6-10, Kitaguchi, 400
Tel: (81-552) 313000
Circ.—188,148 ABC
Prop.—Yamanashi Nichi-Nichi Newspaper Co.
Honorary Ch.—Kayo Noguchi
Ch.—Shigeru Kobayashi
Vice Ch.—Kineo Sasamoto
Pres.—Nagamasa Mitsui
Dir./Mng. Ed.—Osamu Ueda

Dir./Ch. Edit'l. Wr.—Takehisa Nakagomi
Ad. Mgr.—Minoru Ohki
Sales Mgr.—Matsuo Morimoto

KUMAMOTO
(Kyushu)
Pop. Est. 579,306

KUMAMOTO NICHI-NICHI SHIMBUN (m&e) Est. 1942
2-33, Kamidori-machi, 860
Tel: (81-96) 3273111
Circ.—379,335 (m); 98,530 (e) ABC
Prop.—Kumamoto Nichi-Nichi Shimbun
Pres.—Mitsuya Nagano
Ex. Dir./Ed.—Kenjiro Hirayama
Ex. Dir./Ad./Bus.—Syozaburo Ban
Dir./Ch. Edit'l. Wr.—Keisuke Hisano
Dir./Sales—Jun-ichiro Tomioka
Auditor/Mng. Ed.—Kazunari Nishimura
Auditor/Sales Mgr.—Toshiki Hashimoto
Ad. Mgr.—Yasuhiro Harada
Bus. Mgr.—Katsuhiko Sakaguchi

KUSHIRO
(Hokkaido)
Pop. Est. 205,639

HOKKAIDO SHIMBUN (m&e) Est. 1942
11-5, Kurogane-cho, 085-91
Tel: (81-154) 222121
Circ.—148,551 (m); 117,197 (e) ABC
Prop.—The Hokkaido Shimbun Press
Kushiro Headofficer—Kouichi Watanabe
(There are editions of Hokkaido Shimbun in Asahikawa City, Hakodate & Sapporo.)
KUSHIRO SHIMBUN (m) Est. 1955
7-3, Kurogane-cho, 085
Tel: (81-154) 221111
Circ.—56,575
Prop.—Kushiro Press
Ch.—Mutsuzo Katayama
Pres.—Gouki Hirakawa
Ex. Dir./Mng. Ed.—Kazuo Yokozawa

KYOTO
(Kinki)
Pop. Est. 1,461,103

KYOTO SHIMBUN (m&e) Est. 1879
239, Shoshoi-machi, Ebisugawa-Kitairu, Karasuma-dori, Nakagyo-ku, 604
Tel: (81-75) 2222111
Circ.—479,223 (m); 334,241 (e) ABC
Prop.—The Kyoto Shimbun Newspaper Co. Ltd.
Ch.—Yukio Shiraishi
Pres./Ed. in Ch.—Morio Sakagami
Vice Pres.—Eitaro Nomura
Ex. Dir./Bus.—Syozo Masuda
Mng. Dir./Ed.—Mamouru Utsumi
Dir./Shiga Headofficer—Kunitsugu Takahashi
Dir./Tokyo Headofficer—Yoshio Sugimoto
Dir./Osaka Headofficer—Kozaburo Nakanishi
Dir./Mng. Ed.—Hiroshi Horino
Dir./Sales Mgr.—Kanji Yoshida
Dir./Ad.—Yoshihisa Nishimoto
Nanbu Headofficer—Takeshi Fujii
Ch. Edit'l. Wr.—Osamu Yamashita
Ad. Mgr.—Kenzo Matsunaga
Bus. Mgr.—Hiroshi Kishino

MAEBASHI
(Kanto)
Pop. Est. 286,261

JOMO SHIMBUN (m) Est. 1887
1-50-21, Furuichi-machi, 371
Tel: (81-272) 514341
Circ.—281,948
Prop.—Jomo Newspaper Co. Ltd.
Ch.—Shun-ichi Satori
Pres.—Tatsuo Satori
Vice Pres.—Masayuki Higuchi
Mng. Dir./Sales—Toshio Miyauchi
Dir./Ed. in Ch.—Akio Shimada
Dir./Ad.—Kouzo Takahashi
Dir./Ch. Edit'l. Wr.—Isao Araki
Mng. Ed.—Tsutomu Shibasaki
Ad. Mgr.—Yoshitoki Koseki
Sales Mgr.—Saburo Nagasawa

MATSUE
(Chugoku)
Pop. Est. 142,956

SAN-IN-CHUO SHIMPO (m) Est. 1942
383, Tomo-machi, 690
Tel: (81-852) 214491

Japan — Asia

Circ.—160,924
Prop.—The San-in Chuo Shimpo Newspaper Co.
Ch.—Seiichi Mataga
Pres.—Shusuke Kowata
Mng. Dir.—Seigo Kawabe
Dir./Tottori Headofficer—Mitsuaki Kamemoto
Dir./Seibu Headofficer—Hisanori Shibutani
Dir./Ed.—Yuzuru Moriwaki
Dir./Ad. Mgr.—Noboru Okamoto
Mng. Ed.—Yasushi Obara
Ch. Edit'l. Wr.—Makato Nagano
Sales Mgr.—Hiroshi Hara

MATSUMOTO
(Chubu)
Pop. Est. 200,715

SHINANO MAINICHI SHIMBUN (m&e) Est. 1950
2-10, Miyata, 399
Tel: (81-263) 255080
Circ.—193,526 (m); 19,608 (e) ABC
Prop.—Shinano Mainichi Shimbun
Mng. Dir./Matsumoto Headofficer—Kiyoharu Muto

MATSUYAMA
(Shikoku)
Pop. Est. 443,322

EHIME SHIMBUN (m) Est. 1941
1-12-1, Ohte-machi, 790
Tel: (81-899) 352111
Circ.—308,512 (m) ABC
Prop.—The Ehime Shimbun Co. Ltd.
Ch.—Isao Matsushita
Pres.—Rurio Imai
Ex. Dir./Sales—Saburo Tsuchiya
Dir./Mng. Ed.—Isao Nitta
Dir./Ch. Edit'l. Wr.—Yasuhiko Hori
Dir./Ad. Mgr.—Takafumi Makino
Dir./Sales Mgr.—Seizo Fujita

MITO
(Kanto)
Pop. Est. 234,968

IBARAKI SHIMBUN (m) Est. 1891
2-15, Kitami-machi, 310
Tel: (81-292) 213121
Circ.—133,002
Prop.—The Ibaraki Shimbun
Ch.—Takeichiro Goto
Pres.—Sadao Ohkuma
Ex. Dir./Ad./Bus.—Yoshirou Noguchi
Mng. Dir./Ch. Edit'l. Wr.—Isamu Murofushi
Dir./Mng. Ed.—Masao Mitomi
Dir./Ad. Mgr./Bus. Mgr.—Kunio Suzuki
Dir./Sales Mgr.—Masao Mitomi

MIYAZAKI
(Kyushu)
Pop. Est. 237,352

MIYAZAKI NICHI-NICHI SHIMBUN (m) Est. 1940
1-1-33, Takachiho-dori, 880
Tel: (81-985) 269315
Circ.—222,480 ABC
Prop.—The Miyanichi
Pres.—Shujiro Hirashima
Ex. Dir./Ad. Mgr.—Kantaro Nagatomo
Dir./Sales Mgr.—Chikashi Hidaka
Dir./Ch. Edit'l. Wr.—Ryoji Tanaka
Mng. Ed.—Riichiro Miyake

MORIOKA CITY
(Tohoku)
Pop. Est. 235,434

IWATE NIPPO (m&e) Est. 1928
3-7, Uchimaru, 020
Tel: (81-196) 534111
Circ.—227,176 (m); 227,176 (e)
Prop.—The Iwate Nippo Co. Ltd.
Pres.—Kichinoemon Kuji
Ex. Dir./Mng. Ed.—Gen-ichiro Murata
Ex. Dir./Ch. Edit'l. Wr.—Eiichiro Uchikawa
Ex. Dir./Ad./Bus.—Mitsuo Moriya
Ex. Dir./Sales Mgr.—Satoshi Ohshida
Mng. Dir.—Sueki Toujima
Dir./Ad. Mgr.—Kohjiro Takaizumi
Dir./Sales Mgr.—Ryuji Sasaki
Dir./Bus. Mgr.—Hiroshi Fujiwara

MURORAN
(Hokkaido)
Pop. Est. 117,855

MURORAN MIMPO (m&e) Est. 1945
1-3-16, Hon-cho, 051
Tel: (81-143) 225121
Circ.—59,905 (m); 52,630 (e)
Prop.—Muroran Mimpo-sha
Pres.—Toyonobu Ichinohe
Ex. Dir./Sales Mgr.—Tomizo Murakami
Dir./Ad. Mgr.—Yoshimi Kikuchi
Dir./Bus. Mgr.—Takeo Sumitomo
Mng. Ed.—Hiroshi Shinpo
Ch. Edit'l. Wr.—Saichiro Tanaka

NAGANO
(Chubu)
Pop. Est. 347,026

SHINANO MAINICHI SHIMBUN (m&e) Est. 1873
657, Minamiagata-cho, 380
Circ.—446,147 (m); 57,762 (e) ABC
Prop.—Shinano Mainichi Shimbun
SHINANO MAINICHI SHIMBUN (m&e) Est. 1873
657, Minamiagata-cho, 380
Tel: (81-262) 363000
Circ.—252,621 (m); 38,154 (e) ABC
Prop.—The Shinano Mainichi Shimbun
Pres.—Kensuke Kosaka
Ex. Dir./Ch. Edit'l. Wr.—Kazue Komiyama
Ex. Dir./Bus. Mgr.—Takao Ikeuchi
Dir./Mng. Ed.—Kiyoshi Segi
Sales Mgr.—Hiromu Iwamoto
Ad. Mgr.—Hisatada Tateiwa
Bus. Mgr.—Tamotsu Sakurai

NAGASAKI
(Kyushu)
Pop. Est. 444,599

NAGASAKI SHIMBUN (m) Est. 1889
3-1, Mori-machi, 852
Tel: (81-958) 442111
Circ.—189,124 (m)
Prop.—Nagasaki Shimbun-sha Co. Ltd.
Pres.—Yuichiro Ogawa
Dir./Mng. Ed.—Akio Tomonaga
Dir./Ad. Mgr.—Hideyuki Katsumoto
Dir./Sales Mgr.—Satoshi Honda
Ch. Edit'l. Wr.—Koji Umehara
Bus. Mgr.—Shigemitsu Sato

NAGOYA
(Chubu)
Pop. Est. 2,154,793

ASAHI SHIMBUN (m&e) Est. 1935
1-3-3, Sakae-Naka-ku, 460-88
Tel: (81-52) 2318131
Circ.—489,898 (m); 207,438 (e) ABC
Prop.—Asahi Shimbun Publishing Co.
Nagoya Headofficer—Hideo Ichiriki
Mng. Ed.—Masao Kimiwaba
Bus. Mgr.—Katsuhiko Kaigo
(There are editions of Asahi Shimbun in Kitakyushu, Osaka, Sapporo & Tokyo.)
CHUBU KEIZAI SHIMBUN (m) Est. 1946
4-4-12, Meieki, Nakamura-ku, 450
Tel: (81-52) 5615215
Circ.—94,632
Prop.—The Mid-Japan Economist
Pres.—Hakaru Yoshida
Dir./Ed./Ch. Edit'l. Wr.—Takayoshi Nakamura
Dir./Sales Mgr.—Hiromu Matsuoka
Dir./Bus.—Fukuyuki Hayashi
Mng. Ed.—Tatsuokii Kato
Bus. Mgr.—Takako Mizuno
CHUKYO SPORTS (e) Est. 1968
Sakae-miyashita Bldg., 1-15-6, Nakamura-ku, Sakae, 3rd Floor, 460
Tel: (81-52) 2121451
Circ.—99,500
Prop.—Tokyo Sports Press
Chukyo Headofficer—Katsuhisa Higuchi
CHUNICHI SHIMBUN (m&e) Est. 1942
1-6-1, San-no-maru, Naka-ku, 460
Circ.—3,075,320 (m-total); 1,247,822 (e)
Prop.—The Chunichi Shimbun
Ch.—Miichiro Kato
Pres.—Hirohiko Ohshima
Vice Pres.—Masahiko Iwai
Ex. Dir./Ed.—Tsuyoshi Sato
Ex. Dir./Sales—Hisashi Kushida
Dir./Ad.—Isamu Koyama
Dir./Ch. Edit'l. Wr.—Shinsuke Yoshimura
Dir./Bus.—Kanzo Sako
Dir./Bus.—Juro Natsume
(Circulation is the total of all Chunichi Shimbun editions. See Hamamatsu & Nagoya.)
CHUNICHI SHIMBUN (m&e) Est. 1942
1-6-1, San-no-maru, Naka-ku, 460
Tel: (81-52) 2018811
Circ.—2,261,345 (m); 795,633 (e)
Prop.—The Chunichi Shimbun
Mng. Dir./Nagoya Headofficer—Bungo Shirai
Dir./Mng. Ed.—Tadashi Yokouchi
Ch. Edit'l. Wr.—Shinji Tamura
Ad. Mgr.—Yoshitaka Enomoto
Sales Mgr.—Mitsuo Saito
Bus. Mgr.—Kanzo Sako
(There is an edition of the Chunichi Shimbun in Hamamatsu.)
CHUNICHI SPORTS (e) Est. 1954
1-6-1, San-no-maru, Naka-ku, 460
Tel: (81-52) 2018811
Prop.—The Chunichi Sports
Chunichi Sports Headofficer—Takao Watanabe
MAINICHI SHIMBUN (m&e) Est. 1935
4-7-35, Meieki, Nakamura-ku, 450
Tel: (81-52) 5612211
Circ.—199,032 (m); 75,132 (e) ABC
Prop.—The Mainichi Newspapers
Chubu Headofficer/Bus. Mgr.—Jun-ichi Yoshida
Mng. Ed.—Hiroshi Matsutani
(There are editions of Mainchi Shimbun in Kitakyushu, Osaka, Sapporo & Tokyo.)
NAGOYA TIMES (e) Est. 1946
1-3-10, Marunouchi, Naka-ku, 460
Tel: (81-52) 2311331
Circ.—96,270 ABC
Prop.—The Nagoya Times
Pres./Ed. in Ch.—Toshio Taniguchi
Ex. Dir./Ad.—Takahiro Sumiyasu
Dir./Sales Mgr.—Hideo Nakayama
Mng. Ed.—Osamu Kato
Ad. Mgr.—Sueo Ishida
NIHON KEIZAI SHIMBUN (m&e) Est. 1980
2-3-1, Masaki, Naka-ku, 460
Tel: (81-52) 3222561
Circ.—183,669 (m); 139,681 (e) ABC
Prop.—Nihon Keizai Shimbun Inc.
Ex. Dir./Nagoya Headofficer—Sadahiko Sugaya
(There is an edition of Nihon Keizai Shimbun in Tokyo.)
YOMIURI SHIMBUN (m) Est. 1975
1-17-6, Sakae, Naka-ku, 460
Tel: (81-52) 2111201
Circ.—197,053 ABC
Prop.—The Yomiuri Shimbun Chubu Head Office
Pres.—Tsuneo Watanabe
Vice Pres./Chubu Headofficer/Bus. Mgr.—Mikio Ishisone
Mng. Ed.—Masao Nakane

NAHA
(Kyushu)
(Okinawa)
Pop. Est. (Naha) 304,836
Pop. Est. (Okinawa) 1,105,852

OKINAWA TIMES (m&e) Est. 1948
2-2-2, Kumoji, 900
Tel: (81-98) 8673111
Circ.—186,924 (m); 186,924 (e)
Prop.—The Okinawa Times Co. Ltd.
Ch.—Akira Arakawa
Pres./Ed. in Ch.—Ryoichi Toyohira
Ex. Dir./Sales Mgr./Ad./Bus.—Akira Makiya
Ex. Dir./Ad. Mgr.—Seikyu Arakaki
Ex. Dir./Sales—Nakahiro Yufuso
Dir./Mng. Ed.—Tetsu Ohyama
Dir./Ad. Mgr.—Yasuji Miyagi
Dir./Sales Mgr.—Anki Moromizato
Ch. Edit'l. Wr.—Kiyotsune Hanashiro
RYUKYU SHIMPO (m&e) Est. 1893
1-10-3, Izumisaki, 900
Tel: (81-98) 8655111
Circ.—184,984 (m); 184,984 (e) ABC
Prop.—Ryukyu Shimpo
Pres.—Ichiro Oyadomari
Ex. Dir./Sales Mgr./Ad./Bus.—Akira Makiya
Mng. Dir.—Akiya Miyazato
Dir./Mng. Ed.—Takeshi Miki
Dir./Ad. Mgr.—Tatsuhiro Higa
Dir./Sales Mgr.—Tomio Kamiyama
Ch. Edit'l. Wr.—Yasumi Yoshida
Bus. Mgr.—Takahiro Tomori

NARA
(Kinki)
Pop. Est. 349,349

NARA SHIMBUN (m) Est. 1946
606, Sanjo-machi, 630
Tel: (81-742) 261331
Circ.—107,824
Prop.—The Nara Shimbun
Owner—Kinji Nishijima
Pres./Ch. Edit'l. Wr.—Tadao Watanabe
Vice Pres.—Hisami Sakamoto
Dir./Mng. Ed.—Haruo Amari

Dir./Bus. Mgr.—Toshimi Yakai
Dir./Tokyo Headofficer—Toshimi Yakai
Dir./Osaka Headofficer—Tadayoshi Tsurui
Ad. Mgr.—Tatsuo Ueda
Sales Mgr.—Jun-ichi Fujiyama

NAZE
(Amami)
(Kyushu)
Pop. Est. 46,306

NANKAI NICHI-NICHI SHIMBUN (m) Est. 1946
10-3, Nagahama-cho, 894
Tel: (81-997) 532121
Circ.—25,500 ABC
Prop.—The Nankai Nichi-Nichi Shimbun Co. Ltd.
Ch.—Kuniie Murayama
Pres.—Michio Murayama
Dir./Ch. Edit'l. Wr.—Tominori Kuni
Mng. Ed.—Terumi Matsui
Bus. Mgr.—Takuro Nitta

NIIGATA
(Hokuriku)
Pop. Est. 486,097

NIIGATA NIPPO (m&e) Est. 1942
258-24 Sanban-cho, Nishi-bori-dori, Niigata, 951
Tel: (81-25) 3789111
Circ.—475,966 (m); 76,256 (e) ABC
Prop.—The Niigata Nippo
Pres.—Sachio Igarashi
Mng. Dir./Ed.—Sachio Igarashi
Mng. Dir./Sales/Bus.—Shinji Harada
Dir./Mng. Ed.—Kenji Aizawa
Ch. Edit'l. Wr.—Shizuka Ojima
Sales Mgr.—Saburo Onozuka
Bus. Mgr.—Sho Komatsu

NOSHIRO
(Tohoku)
Pop. Est. 47,800

HOKUU SHIMPO (m) Est. 1895
3-2, Nishi-dori-machi, 016
Tel: (81-185) 543150
Circ.—26,900
Prop.—Hokuu Shimpo
Pres.—Kouichi Yamaki

OBIHIRO
(Hokkaido)
Pop. Est. 167,384

TOKACHI MAINICHI SHIMBUN (e) Est. 1919
8-2, Minami, Higashi-Ichijo, 080
Tel: (81-155) 222121
Circ.—79,477 ABC
Prop.—Tokachi Mainichi Newspaper
Pres./Ed. in Ch.—Mitsushige Hayashi
Ex. Dir./Bus. Mgr.—Masahiro Hayashi
Dir./Mng. Ed.—Mutsuhisa Terai
Dir./Ad. Mgr.—Kenji Fukui
Dir./Sales Mgr.—Ichiro Kawasaki

OITA
(Kyushu)
Pop. Est. 408,501

OITA GODO SHIMBUN (m&e) Est. 1886
3-9-15, Fudai-cho, 870
Tel: (81-975) 362121
Circ.—227,810 (m); 227,799 (e) ABC
Prop.—Oita Godo Shimbun
Pres.—Takeshi Nagano
Ex. Dir./Bus. Mgr.—Yoshimi Eto
Mng. Dir.—Atsushi Nagano
Dir./Ed. in Ch.—Shunsaku Nanri
Dir./Mng. Ed.—Maskatsu Tanabe
Dir./Ch. Edit'l. Wr.—Hidenori Umeki
Dir./Sales Mgr.—Nobuyuki Goto

OKAYAMA
(Chugoku)
Pop. Est. 593,730

OKAYAMA-NICHI-NICHI-SHIMBUN (e) Est. 1946
6-30, Hon-cho, 700
Tel: (81-86) 2314211
Circ.—20,698
Prop.—Okayama Daily Newspaper Co. Ltd.
Ch.—Katsumi Nozu
Pres.—Takashi Nozu
Vice Pres.—Hirokazu Kakihara
Ex. Dir./Ch. Edit'l. Wr./Mng. Ed.—Takashi Ando
Ex. Dir./Sales/Ad.—Izumi Ishimura
Ad. Mgr.—Yuzo Fuji
SANYO SHIMBUN (m&e) Est. 1879
2-1-23, Yanagi-cho, 700
Tel: (81-86) 2312210

Circ.—428,180 (m); 72,279 (e)
Prop.—The Sanyo Press
Pres.—Katsumi Sasaki
Ex. Dir./Sales Mgr.—Isamu Ujibashi
Ex. Dir./Ad. Mgr.—Hiroaki Fujioka
Dir./Mng. Ed.—Satoshi Kodera
Dir./Bus. Mgr.—Yoshiki Moritaka
Sales Mgr.—Nobutoshi Tanaka

OSAKA
(Osaka)
Pop. Est. (Metro Area) 16,900,000

ASAHI SHIMBUN (m&e) Est. 1879
3-2-4, Nakanoshima, Kita-ku, 530-11
Tel: (81-6) 2310131
Circ.—2,293,041 (m); 1,390,311 (e) ABC
Prop.—Asahi Shimbun Publishing Co.
Ex. Dir./Osaka Headofficer—Michisada Hirose
Mng. Ed.—Chiaki Hasegawa
Ad. Mgr.—Hideki Nakao
Sales Mgr.—Yoshio Nakae
(There are editions of Asahi Shimbun in Kitakyushu, Nagoya, Sapporo & Tokyo.)
DAILY SPORTS (m&e) Est. 1948
1-18-11, Edobori, Nishi-ku, 550
Tel: (81-6) 4430421
Prop.—The Daily Sports
Mng. Ed.—Tsutomu Kishida
Sales Mgr.—Minoru Inoue
(There are editions of Daily Sports in Kobe & Tokyo.)
DEMPA SHIMBUN (m) Est. 1965
3-2-4, Nakanoshima, Kita-Ku, 530
Tel: (81-6) 3023361
Prop.—Dempa Publications Inc. (Dempa Shimbun-sha)
Pres.—Masaaki Yoshida
(There are editions of the Dempa Shimbun in Fukuoka & Tokyo.)
HOCHI SHIMBUN (m) Est. 1964
2-22-17, Honjo-Nishi, Kita-ku, 531
Tel: (81-6) 3742311
Circ.—403,877
Prop.—The Hochi Shimbun
Mng. Dir./Osaka Headofficer—Eiji Tomita
Dir./Mng. Ed.—Akira Yamamoto
Dir./Ad. Mgr.—Munesuke Seki
Sales Mgr.—Toshio Tsuruta
(There is an edition of the Hochi Shimbun in Tokyo.)
THE MAINICHI DAILY NEWS (m) English; Est. 1922
3-4-5, Umeda, Kita-ku, 530-51
Tel: (81-6) 3451551
Prop.—The Mainichi Newspapers
Mng. Ed.—Haruo Nishimura
(There is an edition of Mainichi Daily News in Tokyo.)
MAINICHI SHIMBUN (m&e) Est. 1882
3-4-5, Umeda, Kita-ku, 530-51
Tel: (81-6) 3451551
Circ.—1,434,928 (m); 935,436 (e) ABC
Prop.—The Mainichi Newspapers
Mng. Dir./Osaka Headofficer—Futoshi Sakoda
Mng. Ed.—Atsumu Kido
Ad. Mgr.—Keiji Miyawaki
Sales Mgr.—Yasumasa Hashimoto
(There are editions of Mainichi Shimbun in Kitakyushu, Nagoya, Sapporo & Tokyo.)
NIHON KEIZAI SHIMBUN (m&e) Est. 1950
1-1-1, Ohtemae, Chuo-ku, 540
Tel: (81-6) 9437111
Circ.—771,358 (m); 488,849 (e) ABC
Prop.—Nihon Keizai Shimbun Inc.
Ex Dir./Osaka Headofficer—Ippei Yamagishi
Mng. Ed.—Kenjiro Horikawa
Ad. Mgr.—Susumu Kinoshita
Dir./Sales Mgr.—Takashige Banda
(There are editions of Nihon Keizai Shimbun in Fukuoka & Tokyo.)
NIHON KOGYO SHIMBUN (m)
2-4-9, Umeda, Kita-ku, 530
Tel: (81-6) 3431221
Prop.—The Japan Industrial Journal
Dir./Osaka Headofficer—Hirofumi Iwami
(There is an edition of Nihon Kogyo Shimbun in Tokyo.)
NIKKAN SPORTS (m) Est. 1950
5-92-1, Hattori-Kotobuki-cho, Toyonaka, 561
Tel: (81-6) 8668713
Prop.—The Nikkan Sports Press
Pres.—Moriaki Matsunami
Mng. Dir./Ad.—Nobuo Iizuka
Dir./Ed.—Reiki Fujimelu
Mng. Ed.—Shigeo Wada
Ad. Mgr.—Shigeharu Saishin
Sales Mgr.—Yasushige Kamiki
(There are editions of Nikkan Sports in Sapporo & Tokyo.)

OSAKA NICHI-NICHI SHIMBUN (e) Est. 1946
3-6-17, Tateuribori Nishi-Ku, 530-78
Tel: (81-6) 3468500
Prop.—The Daily Osaka Nichi-Nichi Co. Ltd.
Owner—Mamoru Kitamura
Pres.—Masuo Kato
Dir./Bus. Mgr./Ad.—Hajime Kisaku
Mng. Ed.—Satoshi Takahashi
Ad. Mgr.—Norifumi Fukuda
Sales Mgr.—Shiro Matsuoka
OSAKA SHIMBUN (e) Est. 1922
2-4-9, Umeda, Kita-ku, 530
Tel: (81-6) 3431221
Prop.—Osaka Shimbun sha
Pres.—Shunji Nakane
Dir./Mng. Ed.—Minoru Morimoto
Dir./Bus. Mgr.—Takuo Masuda
Bus. Mgr.—Masayoshi Mizoguchi
Tokyo Headofficer—Tsutomu Norose
OSAKA SPORTS (e) Est. 1968
Osaka-ekimae Daiichi Bldg., 4th Floor, 1-3-400, Umeda, Kita-ku, 530
Tel: (81-6) 3457657
Prop.—Tokyo Sports Press
Osaka Headofficer—Sen Asano
SANKEI SHIMBUN (m&e) Est. 1933
2-4-9, Umeda, Kita-ku, 530
Tel: (81-6) 3431221
Circ.—1,134,807 (m); 667,255 (e) ABC
Prop.—Sankei Shimbun Co. Ltd.
Vice Pres./Osaka Headofficer—Akiyoshi Sawa
Dir./Mng. Ed.—Shinji Yamada
Ad. Mgr.—Hiroyuki Goto
Sales Mgr.—Masakazu Hamano
Bus. Mgr.—Tadashi Minohara
(There is an edition of Sankei Shimbun in Tokyo.)
SANKEI SPORTS (m) Est. 1955
2-4-9, Umeda, Kita-ku, 530
Circ.—547,802
Osaka Headofficer/Bus. Mgr.—Hiroyuki Katsumi
Bus. Mgr.—Michiyuki Nishide
(There is an edition of Sankei Sports in Tokyo.)
SHIN OSAKA (e) Est. 1946
1-4-28, Kawaguchi, Nishi-ku, 550
Tel: (81-6) 5845005
Prop.—Shin Osaka Shimbun-sha
Pres.—Jinshin Enomoto
Vice Pres./Sales—Yasuhito Enomoto
Dir./Mng. Ed.—Masayuki Okamura
Dir./Tokyo Headofficer—Yoshihito Enomoto
SPORTS NIPPON (m) Est. 1949
3-4-5, Umeda, Kita-ku, 530-78
Tel: (81-6) 3468500
Prop.—The Sports Nippon
Pres.—Michio Kouzuma
Dir./Ed./Bus. Mgr.—Jiro Tanaka
Dir./Ad. Mgr.—Akira Maeda
Dir./Sales Mgr.—Masanao Aono
Mng. Ed.—Yoshimitsu Ohnishi
(There is an edition of Sports Nippon in Tokyo.)
YOMIURI SHIMBUN (m&e) Est. 1952
5-9, Nozaki-cho, Kita-ku, 530
Tel: (81-6) 3611111
Circ.—2,502,335 (m); 1,427,229 (e) ABC
Prop.—The Yomiuri Shimbun Osaka
Pres.—Ken-ya Mizukami
Ex. Dir./Ad. Mgr.—Toshio Yoshimura
Mng. Dir./Sales Mgr.—Kazufumi Imai
Mng. Ed.—Akira Nakaho
Ch. Edit'l. Wr.—Nobukatsu Tsukada
Bus. Mgr.—Syodo Ichikawa
(There are editions of Yomiuri Shimbun in Kitakyushu, Sapporo & Takao City.)
YUKAN FUJI (m) Est. 1969
Circ.—275,847
Vice Pres./Headofficer—Shun-ichiro Kondo
Mng. Ed.—Tomio Saito
Bus. Mgr.—Takeshi Miyazaki

SAGA
(Kyushu)
Pop. Est. 169,963

SAGA SHIMBUN (m) Est. 1884
3-2-23, Tenjin, 840
Tel: (81-952) 282111
Circ.—132,639 ABC
Prop.—Saga Shimbun
Pres.—Seiichiro Nakao
Vice Pres./Ed. in Ch.—Shigeo Nishimura
Ex. Dir./Ad. Mgr.—Shigeo Inada
Dir./Mng. Ed.—Norichika Yoshino
Dir./Sales Mgr.—Hiromi Uchikawa
Ch. Edit'l. Wr.—Hirofumi Kawahara
Bus. Mgr.—Kenji Tsuruta

Asia Japan IV-73

SAPPORO
(Hokkaido)
Pop. Est. 1,671,742

ASAHI SHIMBUN (m&e) Est. 1959
1-1-1, Nishi, Kita-nijo, Chuo-ku
Tel: (81-11) 2812131
Circ.—174,862 (m); 87,878 (e) ABC
Prop.—Asahi Shimbun Publishing Co.
Hokkaido Headofficer—Tadashi Nakai
(There are editions of the Asahi Shimbun in Kitakyushu, Nagoya, Osaka & Tokyo.)
DOSHIN SPORTS (m) Est. 1982
3-6, Ohdori-Nishi, Chuo-ku, 060
Tel: (81-11) 2411230
Circ.—99,014
Prop.—The Doshin Sports Press
Pres.—Yoshiaki Kodama
Ex. Dir./Bus. Mgr.—Susumu Tanaka
Dir./Mng. Ed.—Keisaku Machida
HOCHI SHIMBUN (m) Est. 1973
4-1, Nishi, Kita-yojo, Chuo-ku, 060
Tel: (81-11) 2513671
Prop.—The Hochi Shimbun
Vice Pres./Hokkaido Headofficer—Tsutomu Ikeda
HOKKAI TIMES (m) Est. 1946
10-6, Nishi, Minami, Ichijo, 060
Circ.—180,170
Prop.—The Hokkai Times Press
Owner—Yukio Takahashi
HOKKAI TIMES (m) Est. 1946
10-6, Nishi, Minami-Ichijo, Chuo-ku, 060
Tel: (81-11) 2310131
Circ.—112,650
Prop.—The Hokkai Times Press Co. Ltd.
Ch.—Yukio Takahashi
Pres.—Kouichi Fujino
Ex. Dir./Sales—Wataru Kawamura
Dir./Ed.—Ryoji Kikuchi
Dir./Ad.—Masanori Kazuyori
Mng. Ed.—Noboru Muraki
Ch. Edit'l. Wr.—Hideaki Matsuka
Ad. Mgr.—Kouki Ito
Sales Mgr.—Tadaharu Nakasendo
HOKKAIDO SHIMBUN (m&e) Est. 1942
3-6, Ohdori-Nishi, Chuo-ku, 060
Circ.—1,191,028 (m-total); 773,746 (e)
Prop.—Hokkaido Shimbun
(Circulation is the total of all Hokkaido Shimbun editions. See Asahikawa City, Hakodate, Kushiro & Sapporo.)
HOKKAIDO SHIMBUN (m&e) Est. 1942
3-6, Ohdori-Nishi, Chuo-ku, 060
Tel: (81-11) 2212111
Circ.—648,433 (m); 400,141 (e) ABC
Prop.—The Hokkaido Shimbun Press
Ch.—Hideji Kitagawa
Pres.—Akira Sakanoue
Ex. Dir./Ed.—Matsuo Yoshida
Ex. Dir./Sales/Ad.—Yoshiichi Kinashi
Ad. Mgr.—Tadashi Kishimoto
Sales Mgr.—Masaichi Kusakabe
(There are editions of the Hokkaido Shimbun in Asahikawa City, Hakodate & Kushiro.)
MAINICHI SHIMBUN (m&e) Est. 1959
6-1, Nishi, Kita-4ojo, Chuo-ku, 060
Tel: (81-11) 2214141
Circ.—92,972 (m); 29,834 (e)
Prop.—The Mainichi Newspapers
Hokkaido Headofficer—Yasuo Yoshikawa
(There are editions of the Mainichi Shimbun in Kitakyushu, Nagoya, Osaka & Tokyo.)
NIHON KEIZAI SHIMBUN (m) Est. 1970
7-3, Nishi, Kita-Ichijo, Chuo-ku, 060
Tel: (81-11) 2813211
Circ.—54,942 ABC
Prop.—Nihon Keizai Shimbun Inc.
Hokkaido Headofficer—Takenori Yomoda
(There are editions of the Nihon Keizai Shimbun in Fukuoko, Osaka & Tokyo.)
NIKKAN SPORTS (m) Est. 1962
3-1-30, Higashi, Kita-3jo, Chuo-ku, 060
Tel: (81-11) 2423900
Circ.—40,568
Prop.—Nikkan Sports Hokkaido
Pres.—Shizuo Hasegawa
Mng. Ed.—Masanori Hanawa
Ad. Mgr.—Toshio Ushijima
(There are editions of Nikkan Sports in Osaka & Tokyo.)
YOMIURI SHIMBUN (m&e) Est. 1959
4-1, Nishi, Kita-4jo, Chuo-ku, 060
Tel: (81-11) 2423111
Circ.—256,146 (m); 95,346 (e) ABC
Prop.—The Yomiuri Shimbun
Hokkaido Headofficer—Mitsuo Miyamura
(There are editions of Yomiuri Shimbun in Kitakyushu, Osaka, Takaoka City & Tokyo.)

SENDAI CITY
(Tohoku)
Pop. Est. 918,398

KAHOKU SHIMPO (m&e) Est. 1897
1-2-28, Itsutsu-bashi, Aoba-ku, 980
Tel: (81-22) 2111111
Circ.—480,853 (m); 155,592 (e) ABC
Prop.—Kahoku Shimpo Publishing Co.
Owner/Ch.—Kazuo Ichiriki
Ex. Dir./Bus.—Zenjiro Shiraishi
Dir./Ed.—Yuichiro Aizawa
Dir./Ad. Mgr.—Makoto Takao
Dir./Sales Mgr.—Hiroaki Hanzawa
Dir./Sales Mgr.—Keiichi Koizumi
Ch. Edit'l. Wr.—Shigeyuki Atsumi
Mng. Ed.—Masakazu Ono
Bus. Mgr.—Ken-ichiro Sasaki
Ad. Mgr.—Tohru Suginome

SHIMONOSEKI
(Chugoku)
Pop. Est. 262,635

YAMAGUCHI SHIMBUN (m) Est. 1946
1-1-7, Higashi-Yamato-cho, 750
Tel: (81-832) 663211
Prop.—Yamaguchi
Pres.—Kazuyuki Ogawa
Mng. Ed.—Syoichi Sasaki
Bus. Mgr.—Masahiro Akimoto

SHIZUOKA
(Chubu)
Pop. Est. 472,196

SHIZUOKA SHIMBUN (m&e) Est. 1941
3-1-1, Toro, 422
Tel: (81-54) 2821111
Circ.—710,701 (m); 710,384 (e) ABC
Prop.—The Shizuoka Shimbun
Pres.—Masumitsu Oh-ishi
Ex. Dir./Bus./Ad.—Sanae Akita
Dir./Mng. Ed.—Takahiro Oyaizu
Dir./Ad. Mgr.—Yasuhiro Miyagishima
Dir./Bus. Mgr.—Shuji Kawanishi
Sales Mgr.—Ginpei Oda

SUWA
(Chubu)
Pop. Est. 52,464

NAGANO NIPPO (m) Est. 1901
3-1323-1, Takashima, 392
Tel: (81-266) 522000
Circ.—47,170
Prop.—Nagano Nippo Co. Ltd.
Pres.—Harukazu Ueda
Ex. Dir.—Megumi Yoshida
Mng. Dir.—Shigeru Takayama
Mng. Ed.—Kenjirou Banzai
Ch. Edit'l. Wr.—Hirokazu Hara
Ad. Mgr.—Fujio Hayashi
Sales Mgr./Bus.—Hideyuki Sato

TAKAMATSU CITY
(Shikoku)
Pop. Est. 329,684

SHIKOKU SHIMBUN (m) Est. 1889
15-1, Nakano-machi, 760
Tel: (81-878) 331111
Circ.—212,278 ABC
Prop.—The Shikoku Shimbun
Owner—Takushi Hirai
Mng. Dir.—Seisuke Iwata
Dir./Mng. Ed.—Shigeki Mori
Dir./Ad. Mgr.—Kiyoshi Nagao
Dir./Sales Mgr.—Keio Imamura
Dir./Bus. Mgr.—Akira Tsumori
Ch. Edit'l. Wr.—Kazuhiro Nonaka

TAKAOKA CITY
(Hokuriku)
Pop. Est. 175,466

YOMIURI SHIMBUN (m&e) Est. 1961
4-5, Shomonoseki-machi, 933
Tel: (81-766) 266812
Circ.—137,395 (m); 8,197 (e) ABC
Prop.—The Yomiuri Shimbun
Hokuriku Headofficer—Takashi Syoriki
(There are editions of Yomuri Shimbun in Kitakyushu, Osaka, Sapporo & Tokyo.)

TANABE CITY
(Kinki)
Pop. Est. 59,100

KII MIMPO (e) Est. 1911
100, Akitsu-machi, 646
Tel: (81-739) 227171
Circ.—35,860 ABC
Prop.—Kii Mimpo
Ch.—Shujiro Koyama
Pres.—Yohachiro Koyama
Vice Pres./Mng. Ed.—Soh-ichi Tanikawa
Ch. Edit'l. Wr.—Yotaro Komori
Bus. Mgr.—Keiji Ui
Ad. Mgr.—Etsuo Tamai
Sales Mgr.—Masayuki Nose

TOKUSHIMA CITY
(Shikoku)
Pop. Est. 263,356

TOKUSHIMA SHIMBUN (m&e) Est. 1941
2-5-2, Naka-Tokushima-cho, 770
Tel: (81-886) 557373
Circ.—238,154 (m); 50,508 (e) ABC
Prop.—Tokushima Press
Ch.—Yoshimi Ibata
Pres.—Yuko Sakata
Dir./Mng. Ed.—Yuji Tada
Dir./Ch. Edit'l. Wr.—Tetsuro Noguchi
Dir./Ad. Mgr.—Hiromi Ogawa
Sales Mgr.—Isao Takeda
Bus. Mgr.—Tadashi Miyakoshi

TOKYO
Pop. Est. (Metro Area) 30,300,000

ASAHI EVENING NEWS (e) English; Est. 1954
5-3-2 Tsukiji, Chuo-ku, 104-11
Tel: (81-3) 55407641
Circ.—38,800
Prop.—Asahi Shimbun Publishing Co.
Ex. Ed.—Yasunori Asai
Mng. Ed.—Makoto Uchiyama
Mng. Ed.—Tateo Tsunemi
Bus. Mgr.—Takao Satake

ASAHI SHIMBUN (m&e) Est. 1888
5-3-2, Tsukiji, Chuo-ku, 104-11
Circ.—8,258,739 (m-total); 4,439,159 (e) ABC
Prop.—Asahi Shimbun Publishing Co.
Owner—Michiko Murayama
Owner—Jun-ichi Ueno
Pres.—Toshitada Nakae
Ex. Dir./Bus.—Takayoshi Murayama
Ex. Dir./Sales—Michio Hisatomi
Mng. Dir./Ed.—Muneyuki Matsushita
Ch. Edit'l. Wr.—Chuma Kiyohoku
(Circulation is the total of all Asahi Shimbun editions. See Kitakyushu, Nagoya, Osaka, Sapporo & Tokyo.)

ASAHI SHIMBUN (m&e) Est. 1888
5-3-2, Tsukiji, Chuo-ku, 104-11
Tel: (81-3) 35450131
Circ.—4,479,077 (m); 2,575,180 (e) ABC
Prop.—Asahi Shimbun Publishing Co.
Ex. Dir./Tokyo Headofficer—Syojiro Wada
Mng. Ed.—Akihiro Kamitsuka
Ad. Mgr.—Isao Ohno
Sales Mgr.—Yasuto Miyazawa
(There are editions of Asahi Shimbun in Kitakyushu, Nagoya, Osaka & Sapporo.)

DAILY SPORTS (m&e) Est. 1948
1-5-11, Osaki, Shinagawa-ku, 141
Tel: (81-3) 54341752
Circ.—50,000
Prop.—The Daily Sports
Tokyo Headofficer—Hirokazu Toyoda
(There are editions of Daily Sports in Kobe & Osaka.)

THE DAILY YOMIURI (m) English; Est. 1955
1-7-1, Ohte-machi, Chiyodo-ku, 100
Tel: (81-3) 32421111
Circ.—51,498 ABC
Prop.—The Yomiuri Shimbun
Mng. Ed.—Ryuji Nakazono

DEMPA SHIMBUN (m) Est. 1950
1-11-15, Higashi Gotanda, Shinagawa-ku, 141
Tel: (81-3) 34456111
Prop.—Dempa Publications Inc. (Dempa Shimbun-sha)
Pres.—Tetsuo Hirayama
Ex. Dir./Mng. Ed.—Toshio Kasuya
Dir./Sales Mgr.—Hajime Ninomiya
Dir./Ch. Edit'l. Wr.—Hidesuna Sasaki
Sales Mgr.—Seijiro Katsuki
(There is an edition of Dempa Shimbun in Fukuoka.)

HOCHI SHIMBUN (m) Est. 1872
4-6-9, Konan Minato-ku, 108
Tel: (81-3) 54791111
Circ.—678,006 ABC
Prop.—The Hochi Shimbun
Pres.—Hiroshi Yamakita
Vice Pres./Bus.—Noboru Sugibayashi
Mng. Dir./Ed.—Takashi Kageyama
Dir./Ad. Mgr.—Takashi Tokunaga
Mng. Ed.—Shingo Ito
Sales Mgr.—Akira Osada
(There is an edition of Hochi Shimbun in Osaka.)

JAPAN TIMES (m) English; Est. 1897
4-5-4, Shibaura, Minato-ku, 108
Tel: (81-3) 34535312
Circ.—65,596 ABC
Prop.—The Japan Times Ltd.
Owner/Ch./Pres.—Toshiaki Ogasawara
Ex. Dir./Bus.—Yoshihisa Ohta
Dir./Ed. in Ch.—Jun-ichiro Suzuki
Dir./Ed.—Shigeo Shimada
Dir./Mng. Ed.—Yoshikazu Ishizuka
Dir./Ch. Edit'l. Wr.—Yutaka Mataebara
Osaka Headofficer—Toshiaki Ogasawara
Ad. Mgr.—Toshirou Tatsuma
Sales Mgr.—Toyohiko Sakurai
U.S. Rep.—Publicitas

THE MAINICHI DAILY NEWS (m) English; Est. 1922
1-1-1, Hitotsubashi, Chiyoda-ku, 100-51
Tel: (81-3) 32120321
Circ.—46,000
Prop.—The Mainichi Newspapers
Dir./Headofficer—Yoshimasa Furuno
Mng. Ed.—Michio Takimoto
(There is an edition of Mainichi Daily News in Osaka.)

MAINICHI SHIMBUN (m&e) Est. 1872
1-1-1, Hitotsubashi, Chiyoda-ku, 100
Circ.—4,010,231 (m-total); 1,937,102 (e) ABC
Prop.—The Mainichi Newspapers
Pres.—Tadao Koike
Ex. Dir./Ed. in Ch.—Akira Saito
Dir./Ad.—Kuninori Ishii
Dir./Sales—Akira Nakata
Ch. Edit'l. Wr.—Mikio Shimizu
Ch. Edit'l. Wr.—Mikio Shimizu
(Circulation is the total of all Mainichi Shimbun editions. See Kitakyushu, Nagoya, Osaka & Sapporo.)

MAINICHI SHIMBUN (m&e) Est. 1982
1-1-1, Hitotsubashi, Chiyoda-ku, 100-51
Tel: (81-3) 32120321
Circ.—1,625,737 (m); 756,354 (e) ABC
Prop.—The Mainichi Newspapers
Ex. Dir./Tokyo Headofficer—Tetsu Akiyama
Ex. Dir./Mng. Ed.—Akira Saito
Ad. Mgr.—Kuninori Ishii
Sales Mgr.—Akira Nakata
(There are editions of the Mainichi Shimbun in Kitakyushu, Nagoya, Osaka & Sapporo.)

NAIGAI TIMES (e) Est. 1949
2-4-20 Shiohama, Koto-ku, 135
Tel: (81-3) 56834405
Prop.—Naigai Times
Pres.—Kazuhiro Nagoya
Mng. Ed.—Masahiro Morita
Ed. in Ch.—Toru Yoshikawa
Ad./Bus. Mgr.—Shozo Yashinari

NIHON KAIJI SHIMBUN (m) Est. 1942
5-13-4, Shimbashi, Minato-ku, 105
Tel: (81-3) 34363221
Circ.—50,000
Prop.—The Japan Maritime Daily
Pres.—Takaaki Ohyama
Dir./Ed. in Ch.—Osami Endo
Dir./Mng. Ed.—Minoru Takashimizu
Dir./Bus. Mgr.—Hideo Sakon

NIHON KEIZAI SHIMBUN (m&e) Est. 1876
1-9-5, Ohte-machi, Chiyoda-ku, 100-66
Circ.—2,882,479 (m-total); 1,654,082 (e) ABC
Prop.—Nihon Keizai Shimbun Inc.
CEO/Pres.—Takuhiko Tsuruta
Mng. Dir./Ed. in Ch.—Ryoki Sugita
U.S. Rep.—Dow Jones Int'l. Marketing Services
(This are editions of the Nihon Keizai Shimbun in Fukuoka, Osaka & Sapporo.)

NIHON KEIZAI SHIMBUN (m&e) Est. 1876
1-9-5, Ohte-machi, Chiyoda-ku, 100-66
Tel: (81-3) 32700251
Circ.—1,678,237 (m); 955,172 (e) ABC
Prop.—Nihon Keizai Shimbun Inc.
Ch.—Akira Arai
Pres.—Takuhiko Tsuruta
Vice Pres.—Tsuneyoshi Natsumeda
Ex. Dir./Ad.—Toshiharu Sakuma
Ex. Dir./Sales—Fumio Aimono
Dir./Mng. Ed.—Jun-ichi Arai
Dir./Ch. Edit'l. Wr.—Yoichiro Ichioka
Dir./Ad. Mgr.—Masanobu Chiba
Sales Mgr.—Koichiro Akashi
(There are editions of Nihon Keizai Shimbun in Fukuoka, Osaka & Sapporo.)

NIHON KOGYO SHIMBUN (m) Est. 1933
1-7-2, Ohte-machi, Chiyoda-ku, 100
Tel: (81-3) 32317111
Prop.—The Nihon Kogyo Shimbun Co. Ltd.
Pres.—Youichi Hosoya
Ex. Dir./Ed.—Akira Yaginuma
Dir./Bus. Mgr.—Yasuo Inoue
Mng. Ed.—Hidetatsu Furuta
Ch. Edit'l. Wr.—Okitsugu Yoshida
Sales Mgr.—Yoshizo Kamiya
Bus. Mgr.—Hideo Okada

NIHON NOGYO SHIMBUN (Agriculture) (m) Est. 1928
2-3, Akihabara, Taito-ku, 110
Tel: (81-3) 52957411
Circ.—469,828 ABC
Prop.—The Japan Agricultural News
Ch.—Yuuichi Kurihara
Vice Ch.—Tsuchio Yamaguchi
Ex. Dir./Ed.—Masao Oku
Dir./Bus./Sales—Kazuaki Kobayashi
Mng. Ed.—Keiichiro Shimada
Ch. Edit'l. Wr.—Yuichi Suda
Bus. Mgr.—Eigo Chitose
Ad. Mgr.—Kuniyuki Murakami

NIHON SEN-I SHIMBUN (Fabric) (m) Est. 1943
1-13-12, Nihonbashi-muromachi, Chuo-ku, 103
Tel: (81-3) 32701661
Prop.—Nihon Sen-i Shimbun-sha
Ch.—Fukuo Ashikawa
Pres.—Masayoshi Tokoro
Mng. Ed.—Kiyoshige Seiryu
Ad. Mgr.—Kazushi Ikeda

NIKKAN KOGYO SHIMBUN (m) Est. 1917
1-8-10, Kudan-Kita, Chiyoda-ku, 102
Tel: (81-3) 32227111
Circ.—548,180
Prop.—The Business & Technology Daily News
Pres.—Toshio Fujiyoshi
Mng. Dir./Ed.—Isao Mizoguchi
Dir./Ad. Mgr.—Naotoshi Miyasaka
Dir./Sales Mgr.—Kouzo Ogawa
Mng. Ed.—Nobukatsu Okumura
Ch. Edit'l. Wr.—Isamu Nemoto

NIKKAN SPORTS (m) Est. 1946
3-5-10, Tsukiji, Chuo-ku, 104-55
Tel: (81-3) 55508888
Circ.—923,717
Prop.—The Nikkan Sports News Co. Ltd.
Ch.—Hiroyoshi Kawata
Pres.—Syu Hayashi
Ex. Dir./Ad. Mgr.—Yoshitsugu Tamura
Ex. Dir./Sales—Akira Kado
Mng. Ed.—Takashi Magakura
Sales Mgr.—Satoshi Kato
(There is an edition of Nikkon Sports in Sapporo.)

NOZEI TSUSHIN (Tax's News Service) Est. 1948
3-8-4, Minami-Ikebukuro, To-shima-ku, 171
Tel: (81-3) 39710111
Prop.—NP Tsushin-sha
Ch.—Akemi Aida
Pres.—Shiro Yoshida
Ex. Dir./Mng. Ed.—Youji Aida
Ex. Dir./Bus. Mgr.—Nobuya Aida

SANKEI SHIMBUN (m&e) Est. 1933
1-7-2, Ohte-machi, Chiyoda-ku, 100-77
Circ.—1,916,412 (m-total); 965,840 (e-total) ABC
Prop.—Sankei Shimbun Co. Ltd.
Pres.—Shigeaki Hazama
Vice Pres.—Syun-ichiro Kondo
Vice Pres.—Akiyoshi Sawa
Ex. Dir./Bus./Ad.—Yukihide Yamashita
Ex. Dir./Sales Mgr.—Takatoshi Suzuki
Mng. Dir./Ed.—Takehiko Kiyohara
Mng. Ed.—Nagayoshi Sumida
Ch. Edit'l. Wr.—Nobuyuki Yoshida
(Circulation is the total of all Sankei Shimbun editions. See Osaka & Tokyo.)

SANKEI SHIMBUN (m&e) Est. 1950
1-7-2, Ohte-machi, Chiyoda-ku, 100-77
Tel: (81-3) 32317111
Circ.—781,605 (m); 298,585 (e) ABC
Prop.—Sankei Shimbun Co. Ltd.
Vice Pres.—Syun-ichiro Kondo
Mng. Ed.—Nagayoshi Sumida
Ch. Edit'l. Wr.—Nobuyuki Yoshida
Ad. Mgr.—Toyoo Kagawa
Bus. Mgr.—Eiji Ito
Sales Mgr.—Seiki Tamura
(There is an edition of Sankei Shimbun in Tokyo.)

SANKEI SPORTS (m) Est. 1963
1-7-2, Ohte-machi, Chiyoda-ku, 100-77
Circ.—809,166
Vice Pres./Dir./Headofficer—Syun-ichiro Kondo
Dir./Mng. Ed.—Masahiko Kobayashi
Bus. Mgr.—Chiaki Anzai
(There is an edition of Sankei Sports in Osaka.)

SPORTS NIPPON (m) Est. 1949
2-1-30, Ecchujima, Koto-ku, 135
Tel: (81-3) 38200700
Circ.—980,821 ABC
Prop.—The Sports Nippon Newspapers
Ch.—Setsuo Makiuchi
Pres.—Kouichi Mori
Ex. Dir./Ad.—Ryotaro Konishi
Dir./Mng. Ed.—Kazuo Hagiwara
Dir./Bus. Mgr.—Seiichi Ogawa
Dir./Sales—Nobuo Katada
Hokkaido Headofficer—Kazuo Mito
Ad. Mgr.—Nobuyoshi Ide
Sales Mgr.—Kaiya Fujimoto
(There is an edition of Sports Nippon in Osaka.)

STARS AND STRIPES (d) English; Est. 1947
23-17, Roppongi, 7-chrome, Minato-ku, 106
Tel: (81-3) 2254505/(81-3) 2254506
(This newspaper is published for the armed forces.)

SUISAN KEIZAI SHIMBUN (m) Est. 1948
6-8-19, Roppongi, Minato-ku, 106
Tel: (81-3) 34046531
Prop.—The Suisan Keizai
Ch.—Kazuko Yamaguchi
Pres.—Nagiko Yasunari
Ex. Dir./Bus./Ad.—Sadayoshi Sasago
Dir./Mng. Ed.—Koushi Torinoumi
Dir./Sales Mgr.—Kinzo Nakanishi

TOKYO CHUNICHI SPORTS (e) Est. 1956
2-3-13, Kohnan, Minato-ku, 108
Tel: (81-3) 34712211
Prop.—The Tokyo Chunichi Sports
Tokyo Chunichi Headofficer—Nobuyuki Kato

TOKYO SHIMBUN (m&e) Est. 1942
2-3-13, Konan, Minato-ku, 108
Tel: (81-3) 34712211
Circ.—700,586 (m); 437,141 (e)
Prop.—The Tokyo Shimbun
Mng. Ed.—Tsuyoshi Sato
Ch. Edit'l. Wr.—Shinsuke Yoshimura
Tokyo Headofficer—Masahiko Iwai
Ad. Mgr.—Torao Oshima
Sales Mgr.—Hisashi Koshida
Bus. Mgr.—Juro Natsume

TOKYO SPORTS (m&e) Est. 1959
2-1-30, Ecchujima, Koto-ku, 135
Tel: (81-3) 38200801
Circ.—556,500
Prop.—Tokyo Sports Press
Dir./Mng. Ed.—Yasuo Sakurai
Dir./Ad. Mgr.—Kunii Makino
Dir./Sales Mgr.—Katsuhisa Higuchi

YOMIURI SHIMBUN (m&e) Est. 1874
1-7-1, Ohte-machi, Chiyoda-ku, 100-55
Circ.—10,115,811 (m-total); 4,458,177 (e) ABC
Prop.—The Yomiuri Shimbun
(Circulation is the total of all Yomiuri Shimbun editions. See Kitakyushu, Osaka, Sapporo, Takaoka City & Tokyo.)

YOMIURI SHIMBUN (m&e) Est. 1874
1-7-1, Ohte-machi, Chiyoda-ku, 100-55
Tel: (81-3) 32421111
Circ.—6,058,636 (m); 2,804,196 (e) ABC
Prop.—The Yomiuri Shimbun
Owner—Tohru Shoriki
Ch.—Yosoji Kobayashi
Pres./Ed. in Ch.—Tsuneo Watanabe
Vice Pres./Ed.—Ken-ya Mizukami
Vice Pres./Bus.—Hirohisa Kato
Mng. Dir./Sales—Syoji Fukushima
Dir./Sales Mgr.—Haruo Takano
Mng. Ed.—Yoshinori Horikawa
Ch. Edit'l. Wr.—Naoki Ogino
Ad. Mgr.—Yoshio Matsui
Bus. Mgr.—Fumio Goto
(There are editions of Yomiuri Shimbun in Kitakyushu, Osaka, Sapporo & Takaoka City.)

TOMAKOMAI
(Hokkaido)
Pop. Est. 160,118

TOMAKOMAI MIMPO (e) Est. 1950
3-1-8, Wakakusa-cho, 053
Tel: (81-144) 325311
Circ.—60,676

Prop.—Daily News Tomakomai Mimpo Co. Ltd.
Pres./Ed. in Ch.—Keiji Nakazawa
Mng. Dir./Mng. Ed.—Katsutoshi Tsuda
Dir./Ad. Mgr.—Tokuho Mitsui
Dir./Sales Mgr.—Katsuhiko Tsunoka
Dir./Chitose Headofficer—Nobuo Kaketa

TOTTORI
(Chugoku)
Pop. Est. 132,310

NIHONKAI SHIMBUN (m) Est. 1976
2-137, Tomiyasu, 680
Tel: (81-857) 212888
Circ.—71,389 ABC
Prop.—Shin-Nihonkai Shimbun Co. Ltd.
Owner/Pres.—Toshikata Yoshioka
Vice Pres.—Takaaki Honda
Ex. Dir./Ch. Edit'l. Wr./Mng. Ed.—Hisahiro Tanaka
Mng. Dir./Chubu Headofficer—Mitsuya Sakiyama
Mng. Dir./Mng. Ed.—Takashi Shiraiwa
Dir./Ad. Mgr.—Akira Takahashi
Dir./Ad. Mgr.—Ken-ichi Hayashi
Sales Mgr.—Yoshioka Nishitani
Bus. Mgr.—Kouichi Katsuhara

TOYAMA
(Hokuriku)
Pop. Est. 321,254

KITANIPPON SHIMBUN (m&e) Est. 1940
2-14, Yasuzumi-cho, 930
Tel: (81-763) 453300
Circ.—211,897 (m); 30,640 (e) ABC
Prop.—The Kitanippon Press
Pres.—Ryuzo Ueno
Ex. Dir./Mng. Ed.—Seiji Ishiguro
Mng. Dir.—Katsumi Kaneko
Dir./Sales Mgr.—Akihiro Shouji
Dir./Sales—Nobuo Matsuura
Ch. Edit'l. Wr.—Shiko Akashi
Ad. Mgr.—Hiroto Mori
Bus. Mgr.—Yoshiyuki Nakamura

TOYAMA SHIMBUN (m) Est. 1923
5-1, Ohte-machi, 930
Tel: (81-764) 918111
Circ.—47,057 ABC
Prop.—The Toyama Shimbun
Toyama Headofficer/Mng. Ed.—Hisatsugu Aikawa
Bus. Mgr.—Hajime Murahama

TOYOHASHI CITY
(Chubu)
Pop. Est. 337,982

HIGASHI-AICHI SHIMBUN (m) Est. 1957
62, Torinawate, Shinsakae-machi, 440
Tel: (81-532) 323111
Circ.—22,792
Prop.—The Higashi-Aichi Press
Pres.—Keigo Fujimura
Mng. Ed.—Motoyuki Muramatsu
Tokyo Headofficer—Miyoshi Fujitake
Bus. Mgr.—Kanehiko Umemura
Ad. Mgr.—Takashi Mitsube

TSU
(Kinki)
Pop. Est. 157,177

ISE SHIMBUN (m) Est. 1878
34-6, Hon-cho, 514
Tel: (81-592) 240003
Prop.—Ise Shimbun
Pres./Mng. Ed.—Masao Kobayashi
Ed. in Ch.—Fujio Yamamoto
Ch. Edit'l. Wr.—Hajime Shimizu
Bus. Mgr.—Toshiaki Fukuyama

TSUCHIURA
(Kanto)
Pop. Est. 127,471

JYOYO SHIMBUN (m) Est. 1948
2-7-6, Manabe, 300
Tel: (81-298) 211780
Circ.—23,500
Prop.—Jyoyo Shimbun Press
Ch.—Shinobu Nozawa
Pres./Ed. in Ch.—Mineo Iwanami
Mng. Ed.—Tsuneo Mikawa
Ad. Mgr.—Nobuo Obata
Sales Mgr.—Reiji Nakamoto

TSURUOKA
(Tohoku)
Pop. Est. 99,889

SHONAI NIPPO (m) Est. 1946
8-29, Baba-cho, 997
Tel: (81-235) 221480

Circ.—19,941
Prop.—The Shonai Nippo
Pres.—Taichiro Akiyama
Ex. Dir./Ch. Edit'l. Wr.—Masatoshi Matsunoki
Ex. Dir./Bus.—Takao Sato
Mng. Dir./Sales—Shunji Shouji
Bus. Mgr.—Shigeo Shouji
Sales Mgr.—Hitoshi Tagashi

UBE
(Chugoku)
Pop. Est. 175,053

UBE JIHO (e) Est. 1912
3-6-1, Kotobuki-chi, 755
Tel: (81-836) 311511
Circ.—43,168
Prop.—Ube Jiho-sha
Pres.—Fumio Tokuda
Ex. Dir./Mng. Ed./Ch. Edit'l. Wr.—Kazuya Waki
Dir./Bus. Mgr.—Hiromi Uchida

URAWA CITY
(Kanto)
Pop. Est. 418,271

SAITAMA SHIMBUN (m) Est. 1944
6-12-11, Kishi-machi, 336
Tel: (81-48) 8623371
Circ.—153,976
Prop.—The Saitama Shimbun
Ch.—Hiroshi Takei
Pres.—Ichiro Takahashi
Ex. Dir./Bus. Mgr.—Yoshimasa Takayama
Mng. Dir./Ad. Mgr.—Akira Maruyama
Mng. Dir./Sales Mgr.—Kisao Sekiguchi
Mng. Ed.—Yotaro Numata
Ed. in Ch./Ch. Edit'l. Wr.—Mizuki Fukuoka
Tokyo Headofficer—Shigeaki Kobayashi

UTSUNOMIYA
(Kanto)
Pop. Est. 426,795

SHIMOTSUKE SHIMBUN (m) Est. 1884
1-8-11, Showa, 320
Tel: (81-268) 251111
Circ.—282,073 ABC
Prop.—Shimotsuke Newspapers
Ch.—Hiroshi Eguchi
Pres.—Niro Hayakawa
Dir./Ed. in Ch./Ch. Edit'l. Wr.—Hideyuki Satoyoshi
Dir./Mng. Ed.—Eisuke Toda
Dir./Sales Mgr./Ad. Mgr.—Isao Sawamura
Sales Mgr.—Hironobu Sekine
Bus. Mgr.—Mitsuo Fukuda

YAMAGATA
(Tohoku)
Pop. Est. 249,487

YAMAGATA SHIMBUN (m&e) Est. 1876
2-5-12, Hatago-cho, 990
Tel: (81-236) 225271
Circ.—217,105 (m); 217,105 (e)
Prop.—The Yamagata Shimbun
Owner—Tsuneo Hattori
Ch.—Kyoichi Okazaki
Pres./Ed. in Ch.—Ken-ichi Sohma
Ex. Dir./Ad. Mgr.—Teruaki Hirano
Dir./Mng. Ed.—Yousuke Kurosawa
Dir./Ch. Edit'l. Wr.—Yuuji Shibuya
Dir./Sales Mgr.—Shohzaburo Matsuya

YOKOHAMA CITY
(Kanto)
Pop. Est. 3,220,331

KANAGAWA SHIMBUN (m) Est. 1942
2-23, Ohta-machi, Naka-ku, 231
Tel: (81-45) 2010831
Circ.—233,025 ABC
Prop.—The Kanagawa Shimbun
Pres.—Toshio Morimoto
Dir./Ch. Edit'l. Wr.—Tadashi Ito
Dir./Sales Mgr.—Ryouhei Makiuchi
Mng. Ed.—Susumu Hosomizu
Ad. Mgr.—Susumu Fukui

YONEZAWA CITY
(Tohoku)
Pop. Est. 94,760

YONEZAWA SHIMBUN (m) Est. 1879
3-3-7, Monto-cho, 992
Tel: (81-238) 224411
Circ.—13,973
Prop.—Yonezawa Newspaper Co. Ltd.
Pres.—Yukio Seino
Ex. Dir./Ed. in Ch.—Makoto Sato
Dir./Bus. Mgr.—Akira Murayama

KOREA, NORTH
Pop. Est. 23,066,573

PYONGYANG
Pop. Est. 2,355,000

JOSON INMINGUN (People's Army) (d)
RODON CHANGNYON (Youth) (d)
RODONG SHINMUN (Labor Daily)
Circ.—1,000,000

KOREA, REPUBLIC OF SOUTH
Pop. Est. 45,082,880

ANSAN
(Kyonggi)
Province Pop. Est. 6,243,330

KYUNGIN MAEIL SHINMUN (m) Est. 1989
102-8, Sonpu-Dong
Tel: (82-345) 863411
Pres.—Yon-Sok Shin
Mng. Ed.—Han-Sik Kang
Ad. Mgr.—Song-Kyun O

CHANGWON
(Kyongsang)
Province Pop. Est. 3,767,196

KYUNGNAM DAILY NEWS (e) Est. 1946
100-5, Shinwol-dong
Tel: (82) 832211
Circ.—159,728
Pres.—Tong-Kyu Kimg
Ed. in Ch.—Song-Kwan Pak
Ad. Mgr.—Kyong-Hun Lee

CHEJU
Pop. Est. 496,119

CHE MIN ILBO (e) Est. 1990
290-64, Yon-Dong
Tel: (82-6) 4413111
Pres.—Myong-Pyo Hong
Mng. Ed.—Chong-Hung Kang
Ad. Mgr.—Tok-Nam Kim
CHEJU SHINMOON (m) Est. 1945
203-6, Yon-dong
Tel: (82-6) 4406114
Circ.—32,150
Pres.—Tae-Song Kim
Mng. Ed.—Pyong-Hui Kang
Ad. Mgr.—Chang-Po Pyon
HALLA ILBO (e) Est. 1989
568-1, Samdo 1-dong
Tel: (82-6) 4502114
Pres.—Chang-Un Pyon
Mng. Ed.—Sun-Man Hong
Ad. Mgr.—Chong-Chang Kim

CHINJU
(Kyongsang)
Province Pop. Est. 3,767,196

SHIN KYUNGNAM ILBO (m) Est. 1909
237-4, Sangpyong-dong
Tel: (82-591) 7511000
Pres.—Hung-Chi Kim
Ch. Edit'l. Wr.—Nak-Ryul Song
Mng. Ed.—Yong-Jin Park

CHONGJU
(Chungchong)
Province Pop. Est. 1,882,306

CHUNGCHONG DAILY NEWS (e) Est. 1946
30-4, Sachang-dong
Tel: (82-431) 2795114
Circ.—38,020
Pres.—Chae-Hwi Kim
Mng. Ed.—Chae-Chon Lee
JOONG-BU MAEIL (m) Est. 1990
150-1, Shinpong-Dong, Hungtok-gu
Tel: (82-431) 2752001
Pres.—Sung-Chae Lee
Mng. Ed.—Yong-Hoe Kim

CHONJU
(Cholla)
Province Pop. Est. 2,348,303

CHOLLA ILBO (m) Est. 1988
748-3, 3-ga, Ua-dong, Tokchin-gy
Tel: (82-652) 537111
Pres.—On-Song Hwang
Mng. Ed.—Chong-Kyu Chong
CHONBUK DOMIN ILBO (m) Est. 1988
207-10, 2-GA, Tokchin-dong, Tokchingu
Tel: (82-652) 2517114
Chmn.—Chae-Ho Kim
Mng. Ed.—Chae-Suk Yang
CHUNBOK ILBO (e) Est. 1973
710-5, Kumam 1-dong, Tokchin-gu
Tel: (82-652) 741001
Pres.—Chong-Sang So
Mng. Ed.—Kwang-Yong Lee
Ad. Mgr.—Chong-Ryang Kim

CHUNEHON
(Kangwon)
Province Pop. Est. 1,549,062

KANGWEON ILBO (e) Est. 1945
53, 1-GA, Chungangno
Tel: (82-361) 524881
Circ.—58,381
Pres.—Hyong-Pae Kim
Mng. Ed.—Tong-Ju Kim

INCHON
Pop. Est. 2,056,833

INCHON ILBO (e) Est. 1988
18-1, 4-ga, Hang-dong, Chung-gu
Tel: (82-32) 7638811
Pres.—Chae-Chun Chang
Mng. Ed.—Kwang-Chol Oh
Ad. Mgr.—Chong-Won Oh
KIHO ILBO (e) Est. 1988
1, 1-ga, Chungang-dong, Chung-gu
Tel: (82-32) 7610001
Pres.—Kang-Hun So
Mng. Ed.—Nak-Chun Kim

KWANGJU
(Gwangju)
Pop. Est. 1,214,662

CHONNAM ILBO (e) Est. 1989
700-5, Chunghung-dong, Puk-gu
Tel: (82-62) 5270015
Pres.—Chong-Il Lee
Ed. in Ch.—Sun-Tae Mun
Mng. Ed.—Chang-Yol Yang
CHONNAM MAEIL SHINMUN (e) Est. 1989
183-2, 5ga, Kumnam-No, Tong-Gu
Tel: (82-62) 5282041
Pres.—U-Chun Kim
Mng. Ed.—Hui-Taek Choe
KWANGJU DAILY NEWS (e) Est. 1980
1-1, Kumnamno, Tong-go
Tel: (82-62) 2228111
Pres.—Sung-Ho Choe
Mng. Ed.—I-Song Kong
Ad. Mgr.—Yong-Ho Lee
MOODEUNG ILBO
699-2, Chunghung-Dong, Puk-Gu
Tel: (82-62) 5271112
Pres.—Yong-Ho Shin
Ch. Ed.—Chae-II So

MASAN
(Kyongsang)
Province Pop. Est. 3,767,196

DONGNAM ILBO (d)
2-3, 3-ga, Chungang-dong, Happo-gu
Tel: (82-551) 211300
Pres.—In-Tae Kim
Ch. Ed.—Chi-Sok Kim
KYUNGNAM DAILY NEWS (e) Est. 1988
100-5, Shinwol-Dong, Changwon
Tel: (82-551) 832211
Pres.—Tong-Kyu Kim
Mng. Ed.—Pu-Hui Nam

PUCHON
(Kyonggi)
Province Pop. Est. 6,243,330

SOODOKWON ILBO (d)
1029-21, Kokye, 1-Dong, Tongan-Gu
Tel: (82-34) 3589060
Pres.—Chae-Chung Kim
Ch. Ed.—Yong-Ho Son

Korea, Republic of South — Asia

PUSAN
Pop. Est. 3,841,746

HAHNGDO ILBO (m) Est. 1989
1637-1, Yonsan 2-dong, Tongrae-gu
Tel: (82-51) 8630071
 Pres.—In-Su Kim
 Ad. Mgr.—Ki-To Nam
KOOKJE SHINMUN (e) Est. 1947
76-2, Koje-Dong, Yonje-Gu
Tel: (82-51) 5005114
 Pres.—Chong-Shik Nam
 Mng. Ed.—Kyu-Tae Kim
 Ad. Mgr.—Pyonmg-Kyu O
PUSAN ILBO (e) Est. 1946
1-10, Sujong-dong, Tong-gu, 601-738
Tel: (82-51) 4639193/(82-51) 7347642;
Fax: (82-51) 4638880
 Circ.—700,000
 Pub.—Jung-Jea Song
 Ed.—Kee-Sul Lee
 Ad. Mgr.—Yung-Hwan Roh
PUSAN MAEIL SHINMUN (d)
1637-1, Yonsan-2-dong, Tongrae-gu
Tel: (82-51) 8630071
 Pres.—In-Hyong Lee
 Ch. Ed.—Chae-Kun Song

SEOUL
Pop. Est. 10,904,527

CHOSUN ILBO (m) Est. 1920
61, 1-ga, Taepyung-ro, Chung-gu; PO Box 199, 100-756
Tel: (82-2) 7245114; Fax: (82-2) 7245109
 Circ.—2,225,000
 Prop.—The Chosun Ilbo Ltd.
 Pub.—Sang-Hoon Bang
 Ed.—Bo-Kil Ihn
 Ad. Dir.—Mok-Song Hyung
 U.S. Rep.—AdMarket Int'l.
DAILY INDUSTRIAL NEWS (d)
1, 2-ga, Myong-dong, Chung-gu
Tel: (82-2) 7740091
DAILY TRADE NEWS (d)
159-1, Samsong-dong, Kangnam-gu
Tel: (82-2) 5510114
 Pub.—Tok-U Nam
 Ed.—Sang-Chick Lee
DONG-A ILBO (The Oriental Daily News) (m) Est. 1920
139, 3-ga, Chungchong-No, Seodaemun-Gu, 110
Tel: (82-2) 3610777; Fax: (82-2) 3610440
 Circ.—2,150,000
 Pub.—Byung-Kwan Kim
 Pres.—O-Ki Kwon
 Ad. Mgr.—Tae-Sun Kim
FINANCIAL & SECURITIES DAILY (d)
86-4, Songsan-dong, Mapo-gu
Tel: (82-2) 3388833
HAN-JOONG DAILY NEWS (m) Chinese; Est. 1953
91-1, 2-ga, Myong-dong, Chung-gu
Tel: (82-2) 7762801
 Circ.—5,000
 Pres.—Su-Tong Kang
 Mng. Dir.—Chung-Son Lee
 Mng. Ed.—Chun-Saeng Im
HANKOOK ILBO (m) Est. 1954
14, Chunghak-dong, Chongno-gu
Tel: (82-2) 7242114
 Circ.—1,156,000
 Chmn.—Chae-Kuk Chang
 Mng. Ed.—Song-U Kim
 Ad. Mgr.—SonIt-Chun Lee
HANKYOREH SHINMUN (m) Est. 1988
116-25, Kongtok-dong, Mapo-gu
Tel: (82-2) 7100114
 Chmn.—Kun-Sul Kwon
 Pres.—Tu-Sik Kim
 Mng. Ed.—Han-Pyo Sung
JEIL ECONOMIC DAILY (d)
40-1, 3-ga, Hangang-no, Yongsan-gu
Tel: (82-2) 7921133
JOONG-ANG DAILY NEWS (e) Est. 1965
7, Sunhwa-dong, Chung-Ku, 100-759
Tel: (82-2) 7515114; Fax: (82-2) 7515521
 Circ.—1,550,000
 Chmn.—Kon-Hui Lee
 Pres./Pub.—Sok-Hyun Hong
 Mng. Ed.—Sang-Sun Shin
 Ad. Mgr.—In-Bae Lee
KOOK-MIN ILBO (e) Est. 1988
371-16, Shinsu-dong, Mapo-gu
Tel: (82-2) 7054114

 Pres.—Kong-Yong Lee
 Ed. in Ch.—Song-Hwan Hong
 Dir./Mng. Ed.—Chan-Kyun Shin
KOREA DAILY (d) English
55-1, 2-ga, Chongno, Chongno-gu
Tel: (82-2) 2796621
KOREA ECONOMIC DAILY (m) Est. 1964
441, Chungnim-dong, Chung-gu; PO Box 960
Tel: (82-2) 3135511; Fax: (82-2) 3126610
 Circ.—520,000
 Pres.—Yong-Chong Pak
 Ed.—Yung-Jin Ho
 Ad. Dir.—Hwa-Seun Hong
KOREA HERALD (m) English; Est. 1956
1-12, 3-ga, Hoehyon-dong, Chung-gu
Tel: (82-2) 7567711
 Circ.—44,103
 Pres.—Jin-Ok Kim
 Mng. Ed.—Ki-Sok Min
 Ad. Mgr.—Chang-Son Chon
KOREA TIMES (m-ex mon.) English; Est. 1950
14, Chunghak-dong, Chongno-gu, 110-792
Tel: (82-2) 7346872/(82-2) 7346873; Fax: (82-2) 3243827/(82-2) 3248328
 Circ.—200,000
 Prop.—The Hankook Ilbo Co. Ltd.
 Pub.—Jae-Kook Chang
 Ed.—Kon-Ju Han
 Ad. Dir.—Wan-Ho Lee
KYUNG-HYANG DAILY NEWS (e) Est. 1946
22, Chong-dong, Chung-gu, 100-702
Tel: (82-2) 7305151/(82-2) 7306151; Fax: (82-2) 7376362
 Circ.—1,478,537
 Ed.—Sang-Ki Sim
 Ad. Mgr.—Sung-Ho Lee
MAEIL KYUNGIE SHINMUN (The Economic Daily) (e) Est. 1966
51, 1-ga, Pil-dong, Jung-ku, 100-271
Tel: (82-2) 2626322/(82-2) 2626632; Fax: (82-2) 2776445/(82-2) 2641534
 Circ.—250,000
 Pub.—Dae-Hwan Jang
 Pres.—Tae-Hwan Chang
 Ed.—Chang-Jang Byung
MINJU DAILY NEWS (m) Est. 1989
44-37, Youido-dong, Yongdungpo-gu
Tel: (82-2) 6321981
 Pres./Ad. Mgr.—Yong-Su Kim
NAEWAY ECONOMIC DAILY (d) Est. 1973
1-12, 3-ga, Hoehyon-dong, Chung-gu
Tel: (82-2) 7567711
 Pres.—Jin-Ok Kim
 Ed. in Ch.—Song-Won So
SEGYE TIMES (m) Est. 1989
63-1, 3-ga, Hangangno, Yongsan-gu
Tel: (82-2) 7994114
 Pres.—Hwan-Chae Hwang
 Mng. Ed.—Baek-Jin Song
 Ad. Mgr.—Kwang-Se Kwon
SEOUL KYUNGJE SHINMUN (d) Est. 1969
19, Chunghak-dong, Chongno-gu
Tel: (82-2) 7324151; Fax: (82-2) 7395928
 Circ.—500,000
 Prop.—The Hangkook Ilbo Co. Ltd.
 Ed.—Pyong-Yung Pak
SEOUL SHINMUN (m) Est. 1945
25, 1-ga, Taepyongno, Chung-gu; PO Box 152
Tel: (82-2) 7357711; Fax: (82-2) 7345240/(82-2) 7202909
 Circ.—900,000
 Pub.—Woo-Shik Shin
SPORTS CHOSUN (m) Est. 1990
61, 1-ga, Taepyongno, Chung-gu
Tel: (82-2) 7246114
 Pres.—Tong-Ho Shin
 Mng. Ed.—Yong-Ho Lee
 Ad. Mgr.—Shil-On Ma

SUWON
(Kyonggi)
Province Pop. Est. 6,243,330

JOONG BOO ILBO (d)
1036-2, Ingye-dong, Paltal-gu
Tel: (82-331) 302114
 Pres.—Wan-Su Im
 Ed. in Ch.—Chin-Yong Lee
KYEONGGI ILBO (e) Est. 1988
452-1, Songjuk-dong, Changan-gu
Tel: (82-331) 473333
 Pres.—Ki-Hon Hong
 Mng. Ed.—Sun-Man Im
 Ad. Mgr.—Yong-Su Lee
KYEONGIN ILBO (e) Est. 1973
1122-11, Ingye-dong, Paltal-Gu
Tel: (82-331) 315114

 Circ.—127,900
 Pres.—Chin-Ki Chong
 Mng. Ed.—Yong-Jun Chong
 Ad. Mgr.—Chon-U Lee

TAEGU
(Daegu)
Pop. Est. 2,229,000

DAEGU ILBO (m) Est. 1989
271-31, 3-ga, Tonin-dong, Chung-gu
Tel: (82-53) 4218001
 Pres.—Kwon-Hum Pak
 Mng. Ed.—Chae-In Yun
KYUNG BUK ILBO (e) Est. 1988
286-2, Hyomok-dong, Tong-gu
Tel: (82-53) 7412222
 Pres.—Hong-Sok Ko
 Mng. Ed.—Chong-Hwa Yu
 Ad.. Mgr.—Chu-Yong Pak
MAEIL SHINMUN (e) Est. 1946
71, 2-ga, Kyesan-dong, Chung-gu
Tel: (82-53) 2555001
 Circ.—204,900
 Pres.—Pu-Ki Kim
 Mng. Ed.—Shi-Hon Ryu
 Ad. Mgr.—Kim-Un Shik
TAEGU ILBO (d)
271-31, 3-ga, Tongin, Chung-gu
Tel: (82-53) 4218001
 Pres.—Kwon-Hum Pak
 Mng. Ed.—Chae-In Yun
YEONG NAM ILBO (e) Est. 1945
111, Shinchon-Dong, Tong-gu
Tel: (82-53) 7568001
 Pres.—Myong-Hwan Han
 Mng. Ed.—Yong-Kyu Pak
 Ad. Mgr.—Sok-Su Yun

TAEJON
Pop. Est. 1,050,000

DAEJON MAEIL SHINMUN (e) Est. 1990
32-23, Kajang-dong, So-gu
Tel: (82-42) 5215511
 Circ.—90,087
 Pres.—Chi-Yong Lee
 Mng. Dir.—Chae-Ok Song
 Mng. Ed.—Han-Shin Lee
JOONGDO ILBO (e) Est. 1951
274-7, Kalma-dong, So-gu
Tel: (82-42) 5304114
 Pres.—Ki-Chang Lee
 Mng. Ed./Ad. Mgr.—Han-Chol Shin
KYEONGIN ILBO (e) Est. 1973
136, Kyo-dong, Kwonson-gu
 Circ.—127,900
 Pres.—Sang-Kyu Im
 Mng. Ed.—Chae-Chan U
 Ad. Mgr.—Chon-U Lee
TAEJON ILBO (e) Est. 1950
1-135, Munhwa-dong, Chung-gu
Tel: (82-42) 2513311
 Pres.—Chun-Won So
 Mng. Dir.—Tae-Yon Kwak
 Mng. Ed.—Yun-Won Lee

ULSAN
(Kyongsang)
Province Pop. Est. 3,767,196

KYUNGSANG ILBO (e) Est. 1989
299-10, Mugo-dong, Nam-gu
Tel: (82-522) 481001
 Pres.—Nam-Chul Hong
 Mng. Ed.—Pyong-Kil Kim

YOCHON
(Cholla)
Province Pop. Est. 2,348,303

HANNAM DAILY NEWS (e) Est. 1990
44-3, Hak-dong
Tel: (82) 65843501
 Pres.—Chong-Kyun Chong
 Mng. Ed.—Chung-Hong Yun
 Ad. Mgr.—Chang-Hyon Kim

LAOS
Pop. Est. 4,701,654

VIENTIANE
Pop. Est. 250,000

KHAO SAN PATHET LAO (Laos Newsletter) French & English; Est. 1968
80 Sethathirat; PO Box 3770
Tel: (856-21) 215402; Fax: (856-21) 212446
 Cir.—1,200
 Prop.—Lao People's Democratic Republic
PAXAXON (The People) Est. 1950
66 Sethathirat; Boite Postal 1110
Tel: (856-21) 212466
 Circ.—12,000
 Prop.—Lao People's Revolutionary Party (This publication is an official government newspaper.)
VIENTIANE MAI (New Vientiane) (m) Est. 1975
36 Sethathirati, PO Box 989
Tel: (856-21) 212623
 Circ.—4,700
 Prop.—Voice of Vientiane Municipality

MACAO
Pop. Est. 484,557

BOLETIM DIARIO DE INFORMACAO (d)
Rua da Praia Grande 31
 Ed.—Rogerio Beltrao Coelho
CHENG POU Chinese; Est. 1978
Travessa da Caldeira 11
 Ed.—Kung Su Kan
O CLARIM Portuguese; Est. 1947
26-A, Rua Central
Tel: (853) 573860
 Ed.—Pe Albino Bento Pais
COMERCIO DE MACAU Portuguese
9-4-D, Rua da Praia Grande
Tel: (853) 310428
DIARIO DE MACAU (d) Portuguese; Est. 1979
37 Ave. Infante D. Henrique
 Ed.—Leonel Borralho
EXPRESSO DO ORIENTE Portuguese
6-8, Rua do Chunambeiro, Ed. Keng Fai, 60C
Tel: (853) 71950/(853) 566395
GAZETA MACAENSE (Macao Gazette) (d) Portuguese
Rua de S. Clara, Ed. Ribeiro
Tel: (853) 575626/(853) 573318
JORNAL DE MACAU (d) Portuguese; Est. 1982
6 Calcada de Treneo Velhe
Tel: (853) 573277
 Ed.—Joao Fernandes
JORNAL VA KIO (d) Chinese
7-9, Rua da Alfandega
Tel: (853) 572251
 Circ.—35,000
OU MUN LAT POU (Macao Daily News) (d) Chinese; Est. 1958
37, Rua do Pedro Nolasco da Silva
Tel: (853) 71688
 Dir.—K W Leung
 Ed.—Lei Seng Chong
SENG POU (Star) (d) Chinese; Est. 1963
11 Travessa da Caldeira
Tel: (853) 84023
 Ed.—Kuok Kam Seng
SI MAN POU (d) Chinese; Est. 1944
Jornal do Cidadao, 45-3 Rua dos Mercadores
Tel: (853) 77808
 Circ.—7,500
 Ed.—Im Heng Kei
TAI CHUNG POU (d) Chinese & Portuguese; Est. 1933
136-2, Rua dos Mercadores
Tel: (853) 578378
 Circ.—16,000
 Ed.—Choi Hak Meng
 Ad. Mgr.—Chan Tai Pak
TRIBUNA Portuguese; Est. 1982
33, Rua de Praia Grande
Tel: (853) 381278
 Ed.—Pedro Correia
WAK'IO POU (Journal Va K'io) (d) Chinese; Est. 1937
7, Rua da Alfandega
 Ed.—Chiu Lu Nang

MALAYSIA
(Malaysia includes Malaya, Sabah and Sarawak)
Pop. Est. 19,283,157

KOTA KINABALU
(Sabah)
Pop. Est. 55,997

ASIA TIMES (d) Chinese
126, Wisma Sabah; PO Box 11280, 88814

Tel: (60-88) 420901/(60-88) 54085; Fax: (60-88) 429159/(60-88) 426155
Circ.—14,278 ABC
Ed.—Lai Su Chon

BORNEO MAIL (d) Malay
Beg Berkunci 139, 88999
Tel: (60-88) 711595; Fax: (60-88) 711633
Circ.—16,217 ABC
Ed. in Ch.—George Kanavathi
Ed.—Amin Muin
Ed.—Frankie Inoh

DAILY EXPRESS (d) English & Malay; Est. 1963
75, Gaya St.; PO Box 10139, 88801
Tel: (60-88) 56422/(60-88) 56080; Fax: (60-88) 52551/(60-88) 211033
Circ.—26,344 ABC
Pub.—Tan Sri Yeh Pau Tzu
Ch. Ed.—Eddy Lok Aun Kheng
Ed.—Surya Irawan
Ed.—James Mudi
Ad. Mgr.—Ngui Boon Ngee

NEW STRAIT TIMES (d) English
Tingkat 1, Lot 27, Block E, SEDCO Complex
Tel: (60-88) 213552/(60-88) 219771;
Fax: (60-88) 224916

OVERSEAS CHINESE DAILY NEWS (d)
16, Jalan Pasar Baru (88000 Kg. Air); PO Box 10139, 88801
Tel: (60-88) 238666/(60-88) 238711;
Fax: (60-88) 238611
Circ.—16,548 ABC
Pub.—Tan Sri Yeh Pau Tzu
Ed.—Hii Yuk Seng

SABAH SHI PAO/WAN PAO (d) Chinese
207, Tingkat 2, Gaya Centre; PO Box 11500, 88816
Tel: (60-88) 244313/(60-88) 54484; Fax: (60-88) 249666/(60-88) 246401
Circ.—8,000
Ch. Ed.—Siva Kumar
Ch. Ed.—Liaw Thien Loi

SABAH TIMES (m) English, Malay & Kadazan; Est. 1968
Syarikat Sabah Times Sdn. Bhd., Peti Surat 10525, 88805
Tel: (60-88) 249333/(60-88) 249111;
Fax: (60-88) 249222
Circ.—15,000
Pub.—Michael Wong Mon Wai
Ch. Ed.—Kan Yaw Chong
Ed.—Christopher Bubud
Ed.—Lokman Sunggim

SEH HWA DAILY NEWS (d) Chinese
PO Box 14210, 88848
Tel: (60-88) 421717; Fax: (60-88) 421716
Ed. in Ch.—Toh Chee Kong

SIN JEW JIT PHO (d) Chinese
Tingkat 7, Wisma KTS; PO Box 14192, 88842
Tel: (60-88) 242491; Fax: (60-88) 242491

KUALA LUMPUR
Pop. Est. 1,200,000

BERITA HARIAN/SND BHD (mS) Malay
31, Jalan Riong, 59100
Tel: (60-3) 2822323; Fax: (60-3) 2822425
Circ.—322,808 ABC
Prop.—New Straits Times
(This newspaper is nationally distributed.)

BUSINESS TIMES (m) English; Est. 1976
31, Jalan Riong, 59100
Tel: (60-3) 2822628; Fax: (60-3) 2825424
Circ.—13,000
Prop.—New Straits Times
Ed.—Hardev Kaur

CHINA PRESS (m) Chinese
40, Jalan Lima, Off Jalan Chan Sow Lin, 55200
Tel: (60-3) 2214255/(60-3) 2213555;
Fax: (60-3) 2214310/(60-3) 2228382
Circ.—133,209 ABC
Mng. Ed.—Puah Yoo Lai
Ex. Ed.—Wong Siew Peng
Ed.—Lim Wai Kiong

HARAKAN (d) Malay
28A, Jalan Pahang Barat, Off Jalan Pahang, 53000
Tel: (60-3) 4213343/(60-3) 4213425;
Fax: (60-3) 4212422
Ed. in Ch.—Hj Abdul Halim Arshat
Ed.—Taufek Yahya

KUMPULAN AKHBAR WATAN SDN BHD (d) Malay
No. 35-1, Jalan 11/55A, Taman Setiawangsa, 54200
Tel: (60-3) 4523040; Fax: (60-3) 4523043
Ed.—Zahari B Affandi

KUMPULAN KARANGKRAF SDN BHD (d) Malay
50-54, Lorong Rahim Kajai 14, Taman Tun Dr. Ismail, 60000
Tel: (60-3) 7192111; Fax: (60-3) 7172880
Pub./Ed. in Ch.—Hishamuddin B Hj Yaacub

MALAY MAIL (e) English; Est. 1869
31, Jalan Riong, PO Box 250, 59100
Tel: (60-3) 2823322; Fax: (60-3) 2821434
Circ.—65,543 ABC
Prop.—New Straits Times Press (m) Bhd.
Ed.—Mohd Fauzi Omar
Ad. Mgr.—Stanley Wong

MALAYSIAN NANBAN Tamil
11, Jalan Murai Dua, Batu Kompeks, Batu 3, Jalan Ipoh, 51200
Tel: (60-3) 6215981/(60-3) 6215984;
Fax: (60-3) 6215986
Circ.—192,820 ABC
Mng. Ed.—Athi Kumanan

NANYANG SIANG PAU (mS) Chinese; Est. 1923
No. 1, Jalan 557/2, 47301 Petaling Jaya; PO Box 10631, 59100
Tel: (60-3) 7776000; Fax: (60-3) 7776855/(60-3) 7776858
Circ.—180,000 (m); 200,000 (s)
Ed. in Ch.—Fong Siling
Ed.—Chang Chew Teh

NEW STRAITS TIMES & NEW SUNDAY TIMES (mS) English; Est. 1845
31, Jalan Riong, 59100
Tel: (60-3) 2823322; Fax: (60-3) 2821434
Circ.—178,463 (d); 225,000 (S) ABC
Prop.—New Straits Times Press (M) Bhd.
Ed. (New Sunday Times)—Sheila Natarajan
Ed. (New Sunday Times)—Nursheila Abdullah
Ed. (New Straits Times)—Tony Francis

SHIN MIN DAILY NEWS (mS) Chinese; Est. 1967
31, Jalan Riong, 59100
Tel: (60-3) 2826363
Circ.—68,000 (m); 82,000 (S)
Prop.—Shin Min Daily News (M) Bhd.
Ed. in Ch.—Cheng Song Huat
Ad. Mgr.—Margaret Teh

SUNDAY MAIL (S) English
31, Jalan Riong; PO Box 250, 59100
Tel: (60-3) 2823322; Fax: (60-3) 2821434
Circ.—85,835 ABC
Prop.—The New Straits Times Press (M) Bhd.
Ed.—Joachim Ng Bye Pink

TAMIL NESAN (m) Tamil; Est. 1924
28, Jalan Yew, Melalui Pasar Pudu, 55100
Tel: (60-3) 2216411/(60-3) 2216495;
Fax: (60-3) 2210448
Circ.—30,000 (d); 65,000 (S)
Prop.—Tamil Nesan (M) Sdn. Bhd.
Ed.—V Vivekanandan

UTUSAN MALAYSIA (m) Est. 1965
46M, Jalan Lima, Melalui Jalan Chan Son Lin; PO Box 671, 55200
Tel: (60-3) 2217055/(60-3) 2217151;
Fax: (60-3) 2227876
Circ.—255,184 ABC
Prop.—Utusan Melayu Malaysia Bhd.
Ed.—H J Suhaimi B Mokhtar
Ad. Dir.—Abd Latif Nordin

UTUSAN MELAYU (mS) Malay; Est. 1939
46M, Jalan Lima, Melalui Jalan Chan Son Lin, 55200
Tel: (60-3) 2217055/(60-3) 2217559;
Fax: (60-3) 2227876/(60-3) 2220911
Circ.—13,964 (Utusan Melayu); 14,432 (Utusan Zaman) ABC
Prop.—Utusan Melayu & Malaysia Bhd.

KUCHING
(Sarawak)
Pop. Est. 368,386

BERITA PETANG SARAWAK (e) Chinese; Est. 1972
13, Jalan Gedung, Pending Industrial Estate, 93450
Tel: (60-82) 480771; Fax: (60-82) 489006
Circ.—7,668
Prop.—Berita Petang Sarawak Sdn. Bhd.

BORNEO BULLETIN (d)
Lot 250, Tingkat 1, Jalan Haji Taha, 93400
Tel: (60-82) 426309; Fax: (60-82) 419069
Ch. Ed.—Ketua Penyunting

Asia Malaysia IV-77

CHINESE DAILY NEWS (dS) Chinese; Est. 1945
Lot 164, Jalan Sungai Padungan, 93754
Tel: (60-82) 233399; Fax: (60-82) 421476
Circ.—6,540
Prop.—Sarawak Press Sdn. Bhd.
Ed. in Ch.—Yong Kim Seng
Ed.—Vong Chit Siong

INTERNATIONAL TIMES (m) Chinese; Est. 1968
Lot 7778, Jalan Tun Abdul Razak, 93450
Tel: (60-82) 487779/(60-82) 487616;
Fax: (60-82) 480996
Circ.—21,215
Prop.—Borneo Publications Sdn. Bhd.
Ed. in Ch.—Lee Fook Onn

THE NEW STRAITS TIMES
Lot 267, Lorong 9, Jalan Satok, 93400
Tel: (60-82) 259329/(60-82) 429876;
Fax: (60-82) 256598

THE PEOPLE'S MIRROR (d) Malay
Lot 357, Tabuan Laru Commercial Centre, Beg Berkunci 3025, 93990
Tel: (60-82) 365649; Fax: (60-82) 363278
Circ.—22,312
Ed.—Mohammad B Kasim

THE SARAWAK TRIBUNE/SUNDAY TRIBUNE (mS) English; Est. 1945
Lot 231, Jalan Nipah; PO Box 138, 93700
Tel: (60-82) 424411/(60-82) 241710;
Fax: (60-82) 428330
Circ.—22,163 ABC
Prop.—Sarawak Press Sdn. Bhd.
Ex. Ed.—Awang Asfia

UTUSAN SARAWAK (d) Malay
Jalan Nipah; PO Box 138, 93700
Tel: (60-82) 252036/(60-82) 424411;
Fax: (60-82) 420358
Prop.—Warta Distribution Sdn. Bhd.

MIRI
(Sarawak)
Pop. Est. 100,000

THE MIRI DAILY NEWS (m) Chinese; Est. 1957
Jalan Piasau; PO Box 377, 98007
Tel: (60-85) 418448/(60-85) 666666;
Fax: (60-85) 418333/(60-85) 655655
Circ.—20,834 ABC
Pub.—Wong Keh Huang

SEE HUA DAILY NEWS/BERHAD Chinese; Est. 1957
Lot 433, Sg. Merah Town District, Sg Antu Industrial Estate, 96000
Circ.—48,809 ABC
Prop.—Sin Hua Daily News Sdn. Bhd.
Pub.—Wong Keh Huong
Ch. Ed.—Ho Bu Tin

PENANG
(Georgetown)
Pop. Est. 300,000

KWONG WAH YIT POH (mS) Chinese; Est. 1910
19, Lebuh Presgrave, 10300
Tel: (60-4) 612312; Fax: (60-4) 611432
Circ.—62,707 (m); 71,524 (S)
Prop.—Kwong Wah Yit Poh Press Bhd.
Mng. Dir.—Oon Choo Khye
Ed. in Ch.—Sze Toh Tgam
Ad. Mgr.—Lau Hong Chong

PETALING JAYA
(Selangor)
Pop. Est. 351,179

CHINA PRESS (d) Chinese
40, Jalan Lima, Melalui Jalan Chan San Lein, 5520
Tel: (60-3) 2214386/(60-3) 2214323;
Fax: (60-3) 2214310
Circ.—106,000
Ed.—Lein Kewong
Gen. Mgr.—Jeremy Gah

MALAYAN THUNG (PAU TONG BAO) (d) Chinese; Est. 1959
13, Jalan 13/6, 46200
Tel: (60-3) 57911; Fax: (60-3) 7577798
Circ.—62,000
Prop.—Star Publications Bhd.
Pub.—Stephen Tan
Ed. in Ch.—Ng Ho Peng
Gen. Mgr.—Goh Tuch Hai
Ad. Mgr.—Chin Kon Wen

NEW LIFE POST (m) Chinese; Est. 1972
2A, Jalan 19/1, 46890
Tel: (60-3) 7556814/(60-3) 7562929;
Fax: (60-3) 7552836

Circ.—130,433 ABC
Prop.—Life Publishers Sdn. Bhd.
Pub.—Erik Chow
Gen. Mgr.—Chew Poh Onn
Ed. in Ch.—Chin Boon Lit
Ad. Mgr.—Jeremy Goh

SIN CHEW JIT POH (m) Chinese; Est. 1929
19, Jalan Semangat, 46200
Tel: (60-3) 7587777/(60-3) 7582888;
Fax: (60-3) 7556881/(60-3) 7570627
Circ.—210,593 ABC
Prop.—Sin Poh (Star News) Amal Sdn. Bhd.
Pub.—Lim Goek Lan
Ed.—Pook Ah Lek
Ed. in Ch.—Liew Chen Chuan

THE STAR (mS) English; Est. 1971
13, Jalan 13/6, 46200
Tel: (60-3) 7581188; Fax: (60-3) 7554039/(60-3) 7552959
Circ.—195,117 (m); 179,115 (S)
Prop.—Star Publications Bhd.
Pub.—Stephen Tan
Mng. Ed.—Michael Aeria

THINA MARASU Tamil
123, Batu 1, Jalan Ipoh, 51200
Tel: (60-3) 4439291; Fax: (60-3) 4435292
Circ.—25,000

PULAU PINANG

GUANG MING DAILY (d) Chinese
75, Lebuh Katz, 10300
Tel: (60-4) 622111; Fax: (60-4) 631253/(60-4) 620225
Ex. Ed.—Low Hon Leong
Ed. in Ch.—Liew Chen Chuan
Ed.—Yong Yeow Khoon

SANDAKAN
(Sabah)
Pop. Est. 50,000

MERDEKA DAILY NEWS (m) Chinese; Est. 1968
Lot 56, Taman BDC, Batu 1 1/2, Jalan Labuk; PO Box 332, 90007
Tel: (60-89) 214517/(60-89) 214610;
Fax: (60-89) 666537
Circ.—6,295 ABC
Pub./Mng. Dir.—Khoo Thau Chiang
Ed. in Ch.—Kwan Kuh Hang

SANDAKAN JIH PAO (d) Chinese
Lot 12, Hook Seng Industrial Estate, Mile 3, North Rd.; PO Box 337, 90007
Tel: (60-89) 212569/(60-89) 212566;
Fax: (60-89) 212570
Circ.—4,971 ABC
Ed. in Ch.—Lim Yee Boo

TAWAU MORNING POST (d) Chinese
PO Box 102, 91007
Tel: (60-89) 775160/(60-89) 777708;
Fax: (60-89) 771741
Circ.—7,261
Prop.—HFR Publications Sdn. Bhd
Ed.—Steven Lai

SIBU
(Sarawak)
Pop. Est. 45,100

THE BORNEO POST (m) English; Est. 1978
Lot 433, Sg Merah Town District, Sg Antu Industrial Estate, 96000
Tel: (60-84) 332055/(60-84) 831714;
Fax: (60-84) 310702/(60-84) 321255
Circ.—29,919 ABC
Mng. Dir.—Lau Hui Siong
Ed. in Ch.—Joe Ang Ban Seng
Gen. Mgr.—Philip L H Lau

MALAYSIA DAILY NEWS (m) Chinese; Est. 1966
7, Jalan Island, 96000
Tel: (60-84) 330211; Fax: (60-84) 339019
Circ.—21,056 ABC
Pub./Ed.—Wong Seng Kwong
Ad. Mgr.—Soo Yee Ming

SARAWAK SIANG PAO (m) Chinese; Est. 1966
4 Ole St., SAR
Circ.—5,000

SEE HAU DAILY NEWS BERHAD (d)
Lot 433, Sungai Meran Town District, Sungai Antu, IE; PO Box 96007, 96000
Tel: (60-84) 332055; Fax: (60-84) 321255
Ch. Ed.—Ho Bu Tin

Copyright ©1996 by the Editor & Publisher Co.

MALDIVES, REPUBLIC OF
Pop. Est. 252,077

MALE
Pop. Est. 46,344

AAFATHIS (m) Divehi & English; Est. 1979
Sunlight Press, M. Manadhooge
Circ.—550
Prop.—Sunlight Press
Owner—Abbas Ibrahim
Ed.—Abdul Satter
HAVEERU DAILY (e) Divehi & English; Est. 1978
PO Box 20103
Tel: (960) 325671/(960) 323685; Fax: (960) 323103
Circ.—2,300
Prop.—Island Printers
Owner/Pub.—Mohamed Zahir Hussain
Ed.—Ali Rafeeq
Ad. Mgr.—Mohamed Sageer

MONGOLIA, PEOPLE'S REPUBLIC OF
Pop. Est. 2,429,762

ULAN BATOR
Pop. Est. 488,000

NOVOSTI MONGOLII (News From Mongolia) (d) Russian; Est. 1942
15 Suhbaataryn Talbay
Circ.—37,000
Prop.—Montsame (Mongolian News Agency)
UNEN (Truth) (d) Est. 1920
24 Nayramdlyn Gudamzh
Circ.—170,000
Prop.—Central Committee of the Mongolian People's Revolutionary Party
(This newspaper is an official party publication.)

MYANMAR, UNION OF
(Formerly Burma)
Pop. Est. 45,400,000

MANDALAY
Pop. Est. 532,895

THE HANTHAWADDY (m) Burmese
96 Aung San St.; PO Box 1025
Circ.—23,000
Ed.—U Win Tin

YANGON
(Formerly Rangoon)
Pop. Est. 4,500,000

BOTAHTAYUNG (The Vanguard) (m) Burmese; Est. 1958
PO Box 539
Tel: (95-1) 74310
Circ.—96,000
Prop.—News & Periodicals Corp.
KYEMON (The Mirror) Burmese; Est. 1951
77 52nd St., Pazundaung; PO Box 819
Tel: (95-1) 82777
Circ.—100,000
Prop.—News & Periodicals Corp.
LOKTHA PYITHU NAYZIN (m) Burmese & English; Est. 1963
PO Box 40
Tel: (95-1) 73182
Circ.—160,000 (Burmese ed.); 24,000 (English ed.)
Prop.—News & Periodicals Corp.
Ed.—Itla Myaing
MYANMA ALIN (The New Light of Myanmar) Burmese
212 Theinbyu Rd., Botahtaung; PO Box 40
Tel: (95-1) 173206
Circ.—160,000
Prop.—News & Periodicals Enterprise
Ed.—Itla Myaing
THE NEW LIGHT OF MYANMAR (d) English
No. 22/30 Strand Rd.
Tel: (95-1) 173202
Prop.—News & Periodicals Enterprise
WORKING PEOPLE'S DAILY PRESS (m) English; Est. 1964
PO Box 43
Tel: (95-1) 76220
Circ.—24,000
Prop.—News & Periodicals Corp.
Ed.—U Ko Ko Lay
Ad. Mgr.—U Kyaw Yin

NEPAL
Pop. Est. 21,041,527

BHAIRAWA

DAINIK NIRNAYS (d) Nepali
Ed.—Pratap Kumar Bhattachan

BIRATNAGAR
(Kosi Anchal)
Pop. Est. 33,292

GHATNA (d) Nepali
Ed.—Keshav Prasad Aacharya
JANAVART (d) Nepali
Ed.—Kosh Raj Regmi
NIRMAN (d) Nepali
Ed.—Suresh Kumar Adhikari

KATMANDU
Pop. Est. (Metro Area) 422,000

THE COMMONER (m) English; Est. 1952
Naradevi Netapacho; PO Box 203
Circ.—7,000
Prop.—Commoner Alliance Press Ltd.
Ed.—Gopal Das Shrestha
DAILY NEWS (e) Nepali & English
Balkhu; GPO Box 285, 9900
Tel: (977-1) 221147; Fax: (977-1) 225544
Circ.—18,000
Pub.—Subha Luxmi Sakya
Ed.—Manju Ratna Sakya
Ad. Mgr.—Bhai Ram Maharjan
DAINIK NEPAL (d) Nepali; Est. 1957
Anu Printing Press, 5/82 Jhochhen
Circ.—1,000
Pub./Ed.—Indra Kant Mishra
DAINIK NIRNAYA (d) Nepali
Bhairawa
Ed.—Pratap Kumar Bhattachar
GLIMPSE (d) English
Dilli Bazar
Ed.—Madan Raj Subedi
THE GORKHAPATRA (d) Nepali; Est. 1900
Dharma Path
Circ.—50,000
Prop.—Gorkhapatra Corp.
Pub.—Purushottam Basnet
Pub./Ed.—Balmokunda Der Pandley
HIMALI BELA (m) English; Est. 1973
Bhawani Printing Press, Tripureshor
Circ.—2,000
Prop.—Himali Bela Private Ltd.
Ed.—S S Rajbhandari
JAN JIVAN (e) Nepali; Est. 1968
Rani Pokhari
Circ.—1,000
Prop.—Gorakha Printers
Pub./Ed.—Sitaram Bhandari
JANADOOT (e) Nepali; Est. 1970
Kamalokhar
Tel: (977-1) 412501
Circ.—6,500
Prop.—Matribhumi Press
Pub./Ed.—Govinda Biyogi
Ad. Mgr.—Jyoti Vaidya
KANTIPUR DAILY Nepali; Est. 1992
PO Box 5320
Tel: (977-1) 214083; Fax: (977-1) 226513
Circ.—8000
Prop.—Goenka Prakashan Ltd.
THE KATMANDU POST (d) English; Est. 1992
PO Box 5320
Tel: (977-1) 216014; Fax: (977-1) 226513
Circ.—3,000
Prop.—Goenka Prakashan (Pvt.) Ltd

Ed.—Yogesh Upadhyaya
THE MOTHER LAND (d) English; Est. 1955
New Baneshwar; GPO Box 1184
Circ.—5,000
Prop.—Monika Press
Pub./Ed.—Mahendra Raj Pandey
NABIN KHABAR Nepali; Est. 1970
Gokhale
Circ.—3,000
Prop.—Anu Printing Press
NAYA NEPAL (d) Nepali; Est. 1972
Kilagal Tole
Circ.—3,000
Ed.—Gowinda Pradhan
NAYA SANDESH (d) Nepali & English; Est. 1959
Maitideri
Circ.—8,000
Prop.—Sasang Press
Pub./Ed.—Ramesh Nath Pandey
NEPAL BHASA PATRIKA (d) Newari
Kel Tole
Circ.—850
Ed.—Malla K Sunder
NEPAL SAMACHAR (e) Nepali; Est. 1945
Ramshah Path
Circ.—1,000
Prop.—Sagarmatha Press
Pub.—Dhandevi Sharma
Ed.—Narendra Bilas Pandey
NEPAL TIMES (m) Nepali; Est. 1966
Maruhiti
Circ.—3,000
Prop.—Ashok Press
Pub./Ed.—Chandra Lal Jha
THE NEPALI HINDI DAILY (d) Hindi; Est. 1958
Ward 32, Maitidevi
Tel: (977-1) 411374; Fax: (977-1) 419148
Circ.—41,500
Pub.—Uma Kant Das
Ed.—V K Das
Ad. Mgr.—A K Das
THE NEW HERALD (m) English; Est. 1971
Maitidevi
Circ.—4,000
Prop.—Sasang Press
Pub./Ed.—Ramesh Nath Pandev
THE RISING NEPAL (d) English; Est. 1965
Dharma Path
Tel: (977-1) 222252
Circ.—12,000
Prop.—Gorkhapatra Corp.
Ed.—Shyam Bahader KC
SAHI AAWAZ (e) Nepali; Est. 1970
Bhotebahal
Circ.—500
Pub./Ed.—Surya Lal Pidit
SAMAJ (e) Nepali; Est. 1954
Dilli Bazar
Circ.—5,000
Prop.—National Printing Press
Pub./Ed.—Maniraj Upadhyahya
SAMALOCHANA
Kalimati; PO Box 4910
SAMAYA (e) Nepali; Est. 1962
Ramshah Path
Circ.—18,000
Prop.—Kamal Press
Pub./Ed.—Manik Lal Shrestha
SWATANTRA SAMACHAR (d) Nepali; Est. 1957
Chhetrapati
Circ.—2,000
Prop.—Vina Bhandranalya
Pub.—Chandrakala Deri
Ed.—Madan Dev Sharma

PAKISTAN
Pop. Est. 128,855,965

ABBOTTABAD

FUTURE (d) English
Kawai House, Mansehra
Ed.—Ghulan Jan Khan
Ed.—Tahir Khaili
MUSTAQBAL (d) Urdu
Kawai House, Mansehra
Ed.—Ghulam Jan Khan
Ed.—Tahir Khaili

BAHAWALPUR
(Bahawalpur)
Pop. Est. 204,000

AFTAB-E-MASHRIQ (d) Urdu
Mohalla Kajal Pura, Punjab
Ed.—Arshad Hayay

DASTOOR (d) Urdu
4-A, 796-R Zanana Hospital Rd., Punjab
Ed.—Mumtaz Zaman
KAINAT (d) Urdu
Near Eidgah Rd., Punjab
Prop.—Daily Kainat House
Ed.—Waliullah Ohad
KARWAN (d) Urdu
Ahmed Nagar, Punjab
Ed.—Syed Ali Ahmed
MAGHRABI PAKISTAN (d) Urdu
16 McLeod Rd., Punjab
Ed.—Sh M Shafaat
Ad. Mgr.—Syed Jobal Bukhar
MASHAL (d) Urdu
Mohallah Dinpura, Victoria Hospital, Punjab
Ed.—Majeeb Hashmi
NAWA-E-NORAZ (d) Urdu
Setellete Town, Punjab
Ed.—Sufia Sultan
NIDA-E-WAQT (d) Urdu
Mohallah Shah Fatah Khan, Punjab
Ed.—Zafar Khan
PARA (d) Urdu
Circular Rd., Punjab
Ed.—Qamar Malik
REHBAR (d) Urdu
17-B East Trust Colony, Durrani Manzil, Punjab
Circ.—10,000
Pub.—Chah Fatehkhan
Ed.—Mian Najeebuddin Awasi
SADA-E-PAKISTAN (d) Urdu & Punjab
Ed.—Rana Abdul Saleem
SAYADAT (d) Urdu
H 719 Islampur, Punjab
Ed.—Muhammed Humayun
SUTLEJ (d) Urdu
Zanana Hospital Rd., Punjab
Ed.—Fazal Hameed Ahmed
TABEER (d) Urdu
Bahawalpur, Punjab
Ed.—Khalid Zamir

FAISALABAD
(Faisalabad)
Pop. Est. 1,920,000

AMAN (d) Urdu
Council House, Kutchery Bazar, Punjab
Ed.—Arshad Khalid
ASIA TIMES (d) Urdu
Wakinanwali Gali, Chiniot Bazar, Office Daily Ailan, Punjab
Ed.—Anayat-ullah Qadir
AWAM (d) Urdu; Est. 1947
Tawakal Bldg., Kutchery Bazar, Punjab
Ed./Ad. Mgr.—Zaheer Qureshi
AYYAM (d) Urdu
Council House, Kutchery Bazar, Punjab
Ed.—Adbul Sattar Javed
BUSINESS REPORT (d) Urdu
Railway Rd., Punjab; PO Box 6
Tel: (92-441) 22131
Ed.—Abdul Rashid Ghazil
CHENAB (d) Urdu
Bismillah Market, Wakilen St., Punjab
Ed.—Mustafa Malik
COMMERCE (d) Urdu
Railway Rd., Punjab
Ed.—Javaid Iqbal
COMMERCIAL NEWS (d) Urdu
Railway Rd., Punjab; PO Box 316
Ed.—Arshad Anami
DAILY NEWS (d) Urdu
Medicine Market, Chiniot Bazar, Punjab
Ed.—Munir A Pervaiz
DAILY REPORT (d) Urdu
Aminpura Bazar, Punjab
Ed.—Dr. Nazir Ahmed
FARHAN (d) Urdu
A1-Khayam Hotel Bldg., Punjab
Ed.—Ramzan Pervaiz
FOOTPATH (d) Urdu
Rehman Bldg., Kutchery Bazar, Punjab
Ed.—Malik Ehsanul Haq
GHAREEB (d) Urdu
Kutchery Bazar, Punjab
Ed.—Tanveer Shaukat
AL-KHABAR (d) Urdu
Akbar Manzil, Amin Pura Bazar, Punjab
Ed.—Younas Rana
LIAQUAT (d) Urdu
Kotwali Rd., Punjab
Ed.—Haji Abdul Ghani
MILLAT (d) Urdu
F-159 B. Circular Rd., Punjab
Ed.—Sajid Aleem
MUBASSAR (d) Urdu
Kutchery Bazar, Punjab
Tel: (92-441) 23819
Ed.—Ijaz Batalvi

Asia — Pakistan

AL-NAQEEB (d) Urdu
6-Kutchery Bazar, Punjab
Ed.—Asghar Ali Jahangir
NASEER (d) Urdu
Ayub Plaza, Kutchery Bazar, Punjab
Ed.—Sh Naseer
PAIGHAM (d) Urdu
Kutchery Bazar, Punjab
Tel: (92-441) 50151
Circ.—20,000
Ed.—Syed Muhammad Munir
PUNJABI NEWS (d) Urdu
Kutchery Bazar, Punjab; PO Box 419
Tel: (92-441) 50151
Ed.—Muhammad Abbas
SAADAT (d) Urdu; Est. 1937
Railway Rd., Punjab
Tel: (92-441) 2220
Pub.—Khaliq-ur-Rehman Saifi
Ed.—Akhtar Sadedi
Ad. Mgr.—Atiq-ur Rehman
SHAHKAR (d) Urdu
Awaz Market, Wakeelan St., No. 7 Choniot Bazar, Punjab
Ed.—Raies Ahmed Khalid
SORTEHAL (d) Urdu
Chirag Bldg., Chiniot Bazar, Punjab
Ed.—Khalid Mahmood
TARJUMAN (d) Urdu
Kutchery Bazar, Punjab
Ed.—Shahbaz Chaudhry
TIJARATI REHBAR (d) Urdu
Kutchery Bazar, Punjab
Ed.—Atiq-ur Rehman

GUJRANWALA
Pop. Est. 360,419

TIJARAT (d) Urdu
Sahrai Market, Railway Rd., Punjab
Ed.—Jamil Athar
TOHFA (d) Urdu
Gondwala Rd., Punjab
Ed.—M Sarwar Chaudhary

HYDERABAD
(Hyderabad)
Pop. Est. 795,000

AFTAB (d) Sindhi
Circular Bldg., Sind
Tel: (92-221) 24358
Ed.—Sheikh Ali Mohammad
BASHARAT (d) Urdu
Sharah-e-Quaid-e-Azam, Sind
Tel: (92-221) 23791
Ed.—Syed Musharaf Razajafri
THE DAILY JOURNAL (d) Sindhi & Urdu
Near New Famous Printers, Holmstead Hall Charni, Sind
Ed.—Muhammad Akhlaque
FATEH ISLAM (d) Urdu
Tilak Incline, Sind
Tel: (92-221) 23625
Ed.—Akhtar Hussain Kamal
IBRAT (d) Sindhi; Est. 1941
Daily Ibrat, Gari Khata, Sind
Tel: (92-221) 26393
Ed.—Khair Muhammad Khokhar
INDUS TRIBUNE (d) English; Est. Urdu
Ibrat Bldg., Gari Khata, Sind
Ed.—Kazi Asad Abid
KAWISH (d) Sindhi
Sindh Printing & Publishing House, Gari Khata, Sind
Ed.—Amjad Abid
KHADIM-E-WATAN (d) Sindhi; Est. 1954
11-A Latifabad, Sind
Tel: (92-221) 83622
Ed.—Syed Wajahat Ali Shah
MEHRAN (d) Sindhi
Kingiri Press, Habib Ave., Sind
Tel: (92-221) 24788
Ed.—Mahmood Yousuf Ali
PASBAN (d) Urdu
Pasban Press, Gari Khata, Sind
Ed.—Akhtar Ali Shah
THE SAFEER (d) Urdu
Sind Printing & Publishing House, Gari Khata, Sind
Ed.—Qazi Muhammad Ali
SIND OBSERVER (d) English
Sindh Printing & Publishing House, Gari Khata, Sind
Tel: (92-221) 27302
Ed.—Asalm Akbar Qazi
SINDH NEWS (d) Sindh; Est. 1976
Sindh Printing & Publishing House, Gari Khata, Sind
Tel: (92-221) 25840
Circ.—10,000
Ed.—Qazi Saeed Akbar

SINDH TODAY (d) English
49-Circular Bldg., Sind
Ed.—Muhammad A Hassan
ZAMIN (d) Urdu
152/8-E Latifabad, Sind
Ed.—Muhammad Ali Khalid

ISLAMABAD
Pop. Est. 150,000

CENTRE (d) English
Buland Markaz, 33 Blue Area
Ed.—Khurshid Ahmed
DEYANAT (d) Urdu
Flat No. 1, Plot No. 16, Zeshan Plaza
INQILAB (d) Urdu
Ali Akbar House, G-8
Ed.—Zahid Malik
ISLAMABAD OBSERVER (d) English
H St., No. 20, G-6/2
Ed.—Habib Hayat
JIHAD (d) Urdu & Pashto
H St., No. 398, St. No. 4.3, G-9/1
Ed.—Sharif Farooq
MARKAZ (d) Urdu
Buland Markaz, 33-Blue Area
Ed.—Khurshid Ahmed Khan
THE MUSLIM (d) English; Est. 1979
9-Hameed Chambers, Aabpara
Tel: (92-51) 810296
Circ.—22,000
Pub.—S Tahir Hussain Nashhadi
Ed.—Farhad Zaidi
THE NATION (d) English
The Nation Publications, G-8 Markaz
Ed.—Majid Nizami
NAWA-I-PAKISTAN (d) Urdu
H St., No. 15, St. No. 22, F-8/2
Ed.—Shabaz Ali
PAKISTAN (d) English & Urdu
Civic Centre
Ed.—Abdul Rashid
PAKISTAN OBSERVER (e) English
Ali Akbar House, G-8 Markaz
Prop.—Pakistan Times Press
Ed.—Zahid Malik
PAKISTAN TIMES (d) English
Pakistan Times Press, Zero Point
Ed.—Maqbool A Sharif
PUKAR (d) Urdu
10-Shan Plaza, Blue Area East
Ed.—Shorish Malik
SHAM (d) Urdu
Bldg. No. 1, Bazar No. 7, I-10/2
Ed.—Imtiaz Ali

JACCOBABAD
Pop. Est. 35,278

NAWA-E-SINDH (d) Sindhi
Nawa-e-Sindh Press, Old Municipality, Sind
Ed.—Mumtaz Ali Mangrid
SARANG (d) Sindhi
Quaid-e-Azam Rd., Sind
Ed.—Tariq Latif
SHAHADAT (d) Sindhi & Urdu
Shah Bhitai Bazar, Sind
Ed.—Syed Nazar Abbas Bukhari
SITARA-E-SINDH (d) Sindhi
Old Municipal Bldg., Sind
Ed.—Ali Sher Afridi

JHANG

UROOJ (d) Urdu
Shaheed Rd., Punjab
Tel: (92) 2118
Ed.—Khalid Mahmood

KARACHI
Pop. Est. 5,208,100

ACTION (d) Urdu
Central B-2, A North Nazimabad
Tel: (92-21) 210902/(92-21) 214608
Ed.—Mushtaq Ahmed Qureshi
ADVANTAGE (d) English, Sindhi & Urdu
447-4th Floor, Sunny Plaza, Hasrat Mohani Rd., Sind
Ed.—Najamuddin Shaikh
AGHAZ (e) Urdu
11-Preedy St., Saddar, Japan Mansions, 74400, Sind
Tel: (92-21) 721688/(92-21) 722125
Circ.—39,500
Ed.—Muhammad Anwar Farooqui
AILAN (d) Urdu
303-Rainbow Centre, Saddar, Sind
Tel: (92-21) 714636
Ed.—Dr. Muhammad Nawaz Khan
AKHBAR-E-NAU (d) Urdu
9-E-553, Orangi Town, Sind
Ed.—Syed Jamil Ragbhi

AKHBAR-E-WATAN (d) Urdu
Noor Muhammad Lodge, 444 Dr. Ziauddin Ahmed Rd., Sind
Tel: (92-21) 2172313
Ed.—Munir Hussain
AMN (d) Urdu
Akhbar Manzil, Elender Rd., Sind
Tel: (92-21) 212315/(92-21) 212525
Ed.—Afzal Siddiqui
BHUTTO TIMES (d) Urdu
C/2-II, Ayaz Town, Gulshan-e-Iqbal, Sind
Ed.—Shahzada Alamgir
BUSINESS RECORDER (d) English; Est. 1966
Business Recorder Rd., Sind, 74800
Tel: (92-21) 710311/(92-21) 718001
Circ.—18,000
Ed.—M A Zuberi
Ad. Mgr.—Yousuf Muhammadi
DAHAISAR (d) English & Urdu
F-1/13-B, C-3/iv, Gulshan-e-Iqbal, Sind
Ed.—Shah Muhammad Sheikh
THE DAILY MALL (d) English
24/1 Khayabane Shaheen Phase IV, Defence Housing Soc., Sind
Ed.—Anwer Hassan Mooraj
DAILY NEWS (e) English; Est. 1962
Jang Bldg., I.I. Chundrigar Rd., Sind; PO Box 2
Tel: (92-51) 210711; Fax: (92-51) 736066
Circ.—50,000 ABC
Ed.—Mohammad Jami
Ad. Dir.—Shahrukh Hasan
DAWN (m) English; Est. 1947
Dr. Ziauddin Ahmed Rd., Karachi Sind, 520080
Tel: (92-51) 520080; Fax: (92-51) 5683801
Circ.—70,000
Prop.—Pakistan Herald Publications (Pvt.) Ltd.
Pub.—Ziauddin T Kissat
Ed.—Ahmed Ali Khan
Ad. Dir.—Masood Hamid
U.S. Rep.—Publicitas
DAWN GUJRATI (m) Gujrati; Est. 1947
Haroon House, Dr. Ziauddin Ahmed Rd.
Tel: (92-51) 520080; Fax: (92-51) 5683801
Circ.—13,500 ABC
Prop.—Pakistan Herald Publications (Pvt.) Ltd.
Pub.—G A Mirza
Ed.—Ibrahim Shabaz
Ad. Mgr.—Masood Hamid
U.S. Rep.—Publicitas
DEYANAT (d) Urdu
74/3 Roheel Khund, Housing Society
Tel: (92-21) 419547/(92-21) 210344
Ed.—Shahbuddin Shaikh
EILAN (e) Urdu
303 Rainbow Centre, Saddar, Sind
Ed.—Muhammad Akhtar Shad
EVENING NEWS (d) Urdu
23, Azra Bldg., Symagoga St., Ranchore Line, Sind
Ed.—Khalid Shakeel
FRONTIER POST (d) English
706 Panorama Centre, Sind
Ed.—Shukat Javeed
GHAREEB AWAM (d) Urdu
36/3 Masood Chambers, M.A. Jinnah Rd., Sind
Ed.—Farrukh Kamal Hussain
GUARDIAN (d) English
Falak (Pvt.) Ltd. Press, 191 Altaf Hussain Rd., Sind
Ed.—Pirzada Syed
Ed.—Inquilab Matri
HILAL-E-PAKISTAN (d) Sindhi; Est. 1972
Court View Bldg., M.A. Jinnah Rd., Sind
Tel: (92-21) 215384/(92-21) 211317
Circ.—15,000
Prop.—Sheik Sultan Trust
Ed.—Iqbal Dal
Ad. Mgr.—Ghaffer Memon
HOT NEWS (d) English
C-3 Darakshan-Villa, Defence IV, Clifton, Sind
Ed.—Shahnaz Tariq
HURRIYET (m) Urdu
Haroon House, Dr. Ziauddin Ahmad Rd., 4, Sind; PO Box 3926
Tel: (92-21) 520080; Fax: (92-21) 5683801
Circ.—600,000
Prop.—Pakistan Herald (Pvt.) Publications
Ed.—Sajjad Mir
Ad. Dir.—Ziauddin T Kisat

INQILAB (d) Urdu
Grand Hotel Bldg., I.I. Chundrigar Rd., Sind
Tel: (92-21) 219337
Circ.—10,000
Ed.—Syed Majid Ali
JAMHOOR (d) Urdu
Central-55, Yousuf Plaza, F.B. Area, Sind
Ed.—Kabir Ahmed Pirzada
JANG (mS) Urdu; Est. 1937
Jang Bldg., I.I. Chundrigar Rd., Sind; PO Box 52
Tel: (92-21) 26371119; Fax: (92-21) 2636066/(92-21) 2634395
Circ.—820,000 ABC
Prop.—Independent Newspapers Corp.
Pub./Ed.—Mir Javed-ur-Rehman
Ex. Dir.—Zlauddin T Kisat
Ed. in Ch.—Mir Shakil-ur-Rahman
Ad. Dir.—Shahrukh Hasan
JANG KARACHI (m) Urdu
PO Box 52
Tel: (92-21) 26371119; Fax: (92-21) 2636066/(82-21) 2634395
Circ.—307,000 ABC
Ed.—Mir Khalil-ur-Rahman
Ad. Dir.—Shahrukh Hasan
JASARAT (m) Urdu; Est. 1970
Eveready Chambers, Muhammad Bin Qasim Rd., I. I. Chundrigar Rd., Sind
Tel: (92-21) 210391/(92-21) 211964
Circ.—50,000
Prop.—Azad Papers Ltd.
Ed.—Mahmood Aslam
KAMRAN (d) Urdu
Ms. Printers, 84-85 Hockey Stadium, Sind
Ed.—Muhammad Ishaq Khan
KHYBER POST (d) Urdu
706 Panorama Centre, Sind
Ed.—Shukat Javeed
THE LEADER (e) English
Millat Press, Altaf Hussain Rd., New Challi, Sind
Tel: (92-21) 221515
Circ.—11,000
Ed.—Syed Mazarul Hassan
MASHRIQ (d) Urdu; Est. 1954
42-B, Block 6-PECHS, Sind
Tel: (92-21) 4310715
Prop.—National Press Trust
Ed.—Irshad Ahmad Kahn
MASHRIQ EVENING SPECIAL (e) Urdu
42-B, Block 6-PECHS, Sind
Tel: (92-21) 4310715
Ed.—Irshad Ahmed Khan
MAZDOOR (d) Urdu
Garden East, Business Recorder Rd.
Ed.—M Anwar Bin Abbas
MILLAT GUJRATI (d) Gujrati; Est. 1946
191-South Napier Rd., New Challi, Sind
Tel: (92-21) 222517
Circ.—28,500
Prop.—Leader Publishing
Ed.—Inqilab Matri
Ad. Mgr.—Jafer Mansoor
MORNING NEWS (mS) English; Est. 1942
PO Box 2804
Tel: (92-21) 2103948/(92-21) 2103949
Circ.—25,000 (m); 30,000 (S)
Prop.—National News Publications Ltd.
Ed.—Amanullah Hussain
Ad. Mgr.—Rai Faroog Azal
MUSAWAT (d) Sindhi & Urdu
People's House, Shireen Jinnah Colony, Sind
Ed.—Achchi Memon Kasbati
Ed.—Syed Badruddin
THE MUSLIM (d) English
Spencer's Bldg., 1st Floor, I.I. Chundrigar, Sind
Ed.—Ali Hasan Khan
NAI ROSHNI (d) Urdu
546, A-5, Gulshan-e-Iqbal, Sind
Ed.—Syed Mehboob Ali
NATIONAL TIMES (d) English
A-3, Kahkashan APTS. Block-7, Clifton, Sind
Ed.—H B Khokhar
NAWA-E-WAQT (d) Urdu
Office Nawa-e-Waqt, M.A. Jinnah Rd., Opp. Quaid-e-Azam Mazar
Tel: (92-21) 719356/(92-21) 7188925
Ed.—Nayyar Alvi
NEWS (d) English
Jang Group of Publications, Jang I.I. Chundrigar Rd., Sind
Tel: (92-21) 2107115/(92-21) 211230
Ed.—Wajid Shamsul Hassan
NEWS EXPRESS (d) Urdu
5-F, 16-Orangi Town, Sind
Ed.—Noor Ahmed Anjum

Pakistan

NEWS & NEWS (d) English
C-3, Darakshan Villas, Phase 1V, Defence Cliftion, Sind
Ed.—Shahnaz Tariq

NEWS TIMES (d) Urdu
1710-Muhammadabad, Gulbahar, Sind
Tel: (92-21) 218566
Ed.—Samiullah Alias Sami Jawed

THE OBSERVER (d) Urdu
21 Sector-14/b, Sind
Ed.—Ghulam Rabbani

PAKISTAN EXPRESS (d) Urdu
A-81, Block No. 9-PECHS, Sind
Ed.—Mijan Mujibur Rahman

THE PAKISTAN PEOPLE'S DAILY (d) Urdu
706-Panorama Centre, Saddar, Sind
Ed.—Tariq Ishaq Mirza

THE PARLIAMENT (d) English
Apex Int'l., 1013, Qasimabad, Liaquatabad, Sind
Ed.—S F H Zaidi

THE PEOPLE (d) English
People's House, Shireen Jinnah Colony, Sind
Ed.—Syed Badruddin

PEOPLE'S TIMES (d) Urdu
14-Abuzar Square, Block-N, North Nazimabad, Sind
Ed.—Muhammad Munzir Jafri

QAUMI AKHBAR (d) Urdu
11-Gopal St., Lee Market, Sind
Tel: (92-21) 211712/(92-21) 215244
Ed.—Muhammad Akhtar Shad

QUMI MILAP (d) Urdu
14/6, 5-C, Paposhnagar, Nazimabad No. 5, Sind
Ed.—Muhammad Akhtar Shad

QURBANI (d) Sindhi
Lakhi Gate Shikarpur, Sind
Ed.—Ghulam Rasool Memon

RIYASAT (d) Urdu
191-Altaf Hussain Rd., New Challi, Sind
Prop.—Falak Press (Pvt.) Ltd.
Ed.—Pirzada Syed
Ed.—Inquilab Matri

SAVERA (d) Urdu
108-Adam Arcade, Shaheed-e-Millat Rd.
Tel: (92-21) 2196168
Ed.—Rukhsana Suham Mirza

THE STAR (d) English
Haroon House, Dr. Ziauddin Ahmed Rd., Sind
Tel: (92-21) 520080; Fax: (92-21) 5683801
Circ.—38,000
Prop.—Pakistan Herald (Pvt.) Publications
Pub.—G A Mirza
Ed.—I H Burney
Ad. Mgr.—Masood Hamid
U.S. Rep.—Publicitas

SUB-KA-AKHBAR (d) Urdu
C-3, Darkshan Villa, Phase IV, Defence Housing Auth., Sind
Ed.—Shehnaz Tarif

SURAT (d) Urdu
46/A, Yousuf Plaza, F.B. Area, Sind
Ed.—Syed Wajahat Ali

TODAY (d) English
B-7, Gulshan-e-Zubeda, Block-E-North, Nazimabad, Sind
Ed.—Syed Mazahir Hussain

TODAY SPECIAL (d) Urdu
35 M.A. Jinnah Rd., 2nd Floor, Aurangzeb Market, Sind
Ed.—Muhammad Babar Faisal

THE TRIBUNE (d) English
Camp Office 502-Kashif Centre, Sind
Ed.—Agha Saddaruddin Ismaili

THE WATAN (e-ex fri.) Gujrati; Est. 1942
Haroon House, Dr. Ziauddin Ahmed Rd., Sind
Tel: (92-21) 520080; Fax: (92-21) 5683801
Circ.—15,000 ABC
Prop.—Pakistan Herald (Pvt.) Publications
Pub.—G A Mirza
Ed.—Ilyas Gadit
Ad. Mgr.—Masood Hamid
U.S. Rep.—Publicitas

WOMEN DAILY (d) English
Recorder House, 351-Business Recorder Rd., Sind
Ed.—Muhammad Ahmed Zuberi

LAHORE
(Lahore)
Pop. Est. 2,952,700

AAJ KA AKHBAR (d) Urdu
H No. 1, St. 10, Tajpura, Punjab
Ed.—Mohammad Abbas Athar

AAJ KAL (d) Urdu
118-A, Garden Town, Punjab
Ed.—Muhammad Qavi Khan

AFTAB (d) Urdu
3-Nisbat Rd., Punjab
Tel: (92-42) 52353
Ed.—Mumtaz Tahir

AFAQ (d) Urdu
22-Abbot Rd., Punjab
Ed.—Shaukat H Shaukat

AILAN (d) Urdu
Office Daily Ailan

AILAN-E-JNG (d) Urdu
77-Nisbat Rd., Punjab
Ed.—Shahzada Alamgir

ALAM GIR (d) Punjabi
Shah Din Bldg., Punjab
Ed.—Tahir Javaid

AWAZ-E-JEHAN (d) Urdu
Mian Market, Gulberg, Punjab
Ed.—Abdul Qadir Hassan

AZADI Urdu
29-Railway Rd., Punjab
Tel: (92-42) 56725
Ed.—Sh Riazuddin

BALAGHAT (d) Urdu
57-Badami Bagh, Punjab
Ed.—Syed Munawar Hussain

BHUTTO TIMES (d) Urdu
77-Nisbat Rd., Punjab
Ed.—Shahzada Alamgir

BUSINESS VOICE (d) English
8-Abbot Rd., Punjab
Ed.—Siddiq Azher

CHONAN (d) Punjabi
7-Nadirabad, Punjab
Ed.—Muhammad Ikram

JANG DAILY (d) Urdu & English; Est. 1937
13-Davis Rd., Punjab
Tel: (92-42) 6267480; Fax: (92-42) 6365185
Circ.—1,200,000 ABC
Prop.—Independent Newspapers Corp.
Pub.—Dr. Arshad Islam
Ed. in Ch.—Mir Shakil-ur-Rahman
Ad. Mgr.—Yunus Arain

JANG LAHORE (m) Urdu; Est. 1939
13 Sir Agha Khan Rd. (Davis Rd.); PO Box 609
Tel: (92-42) 305820; Fax: (92-42) 305785
Circ.—1,200,000
Prop.—Jang Publications Ltd.
ED.—Mir Khalil-ur-Rahman

DASTAK (d) Urdu
14-D Manzoor Plaza, Blue Area
Ed.—Afzal Shahid

EXPRESS (d) Urdu
43/16-Main Gulberg, Punjab
Ed.—Mir Javaid Rehman

FINANCIAL TIMES (d) English
16-Temple Rd., Punjab
Ed.—Tariq Majid Ch

HAJUM (d) Urdu
H No. 4, St. 1, Sanda Rd., Punjab
Ed.—Khalique Ahmed

HAYAT NAU (d) Urdu
416-Jahanzeb Block, Allama Iqbal Town, Punjab
Ed.—Israrul Haq

IMROZE (m) Urdu; Est. 1947
Rattan Chand Rd., Punjab
Tel: (92-42) 64241
Circ.—120,000
Prop.—Progressive Papers Ltd.
Ed.—Haider Ali

ISHARA (d) Urdu
Degree College, Chowk Near Asghar Mall, Punjab
Ed.—Muhammad Noor Tahir

JAHAN NUMA (d) Urdu
18-Beadon Rd., Punjab
Ed.—Tariq Farooq

JUBLEE (d) Urdu
91/K Zafarul Haq Rd., Punjab
Ed.—Syed Qaisara Sherazi

KARKUN (d) Urdu
Crown Arcade, Crown Cemina, Ghari Shahoo, Punjab
Ed.—Ayyub Sarwar Khan

MADAM (d) Urdu
29-Main Rd., Samnabad, Punjab
Ed.—Anwar Ul Haq

MAGHRABI PAKISTAN (d) Urdu
16 McLeod Rd., Punjab
Circ.—3,000
Ed.—Sh M Shafaat
Ad. Mgr.—S I Bukhazi

MASHRIQ (m) Urdu; Est. 1954
7 Mehmood Gaznavi Rd., Punjab
Tel: (92-42) 226691
Circ.—175,000
Pub.—Iftikhar Ahmed Malik
Ed.—Rashid Ahmed Siddiqui
Ad. Mgr.—M A Latif

MEDIA NEWS (d) Urdu
Ferozepur Rd., Punjab
Ed.—S A Khan Durrani

MUSAWAAT (d) Urdu
15-Montgomery Rd., Punjab
Ed.—Zaheer Kashmiri

NATION (d) English
Nipco Homes, 4-Shahrah-e-Fatima Jinnah Rd., Punjab, 54000
Tel: (92-42) 6304495/(92-42) 6367579; Fax: (92-42) 6367005
Circ.—92,621 ABC
Prop.—Nations Publications (Pvt.) Ltd.
Pub.—Majid Nizami
Ed.—Arif Nizami
Ad. Mgr.—Rai Farooz Afzal

NATIONAL VOICE (d) English
336-Rehmanpura, Punjab
Ed.—Syed Azhar-ul-Hasan

NAWA-E-SEHAR (d) Urdu
15-Anarkali, Punjab
Ed.—H M Hassan

NAWA-E-WAQT (m) Urdu; Est. 1940
Nipco Homes, 4-Shahrah-e-Fatima Jinnah Rd., Punjab, 54000
Tel: (92-42) 6302050/(92-42) 6367551; Fax: (92-42) 63675838/(92-42) 6367616
Circ.—573,921 ABC
Pub./Ed.—Majid Nizami
Ad. Mgr.—M S Warsi

NEWS (d) English
13-Davis Rd., Punjab
Ed.—Hussain Naqi

NEWS SPECIAL (d) Urdu
139-Islamia St., McLeod Rd., Punjab
Ed. Saifuddin

NIDA-E-SADAQAT (d) Urdu
16 Ratigun Rd., Punjab
Ed.—Syed Abbas Anwar

PAKISTAN (d) Urdu
41 Jail Rd., Punjab
Ed.—Zia Shahid

PAKISTAN TIMES (d) English; Est. 1947
Rattan Chand Rd., Punjab; PO Box 223
Tel: (92-42) 226271
Circ.—75,000
Prop.—Gov't. Press
Ed.—Nasim Ahmed
Ad. Mgr.—Shamin Ahmed

PUNJAB CHRONICLE (d)
107/2 Allama Iqbal Rd., Punjab
Ed.—Zia ul-Islam

SAADAT (d) Urdu; Est. 1937
Fazal Bldg., Cooper Rd., Punjab
Circ.—40,000
Ed.—Kahlil ur-Rehman

SACHCHAI (d) Urdu
19 Akbar St., Punjab
Ed.—Muhammad Khalil

SADAQAT (d) Urdu
7/45 Beadon Rd., Punjab
Ed.—Naveed Iqbal Qureshi

SAKAB (d) Urdu
15 Shahrah-e-Quaid-e-Azam, Punjab
Ed.—Farid Haqe Zaidi

SALAB (d) Urdu
15 The Mall, Punjab
Ed.—Farid Haq

SEERAT (d) Urdu
Ujala Press, Athurtan Rd., Punjab
Ed.—Mian M Ismael

SHER-E-PAKISTAN (d) Urdu
6/C Data Darbar Market, Punjab
Ed.—Mir Israr Chouhan

SIYASAT (d) Urdu
Cooper Rd., Punjab
Ed.—Asar Chohan

TIJARAT (d) Urdu
14 Abbot Rd., Punjab
Ed.—Jamil Athar

THE TRIBUNE (d) English
8-A Sharif Colony, Gulberg, Punjab
Ed.—Sikandar Shaheen

URDU TIMES (d) Urdu
Shahzeb Market, Cooper Rd., Punjab
Ed.—Bashir A Sheikh

WAQT (d) Urdu
2-B Shah Alam Market, Punjab
Ed.—Khawaja Nazir Butt

WIFAQ (d) Urdu
6-A Waris Rd., Punjab
Tel: (92-42) 60506
Ed.—Wiqar Mustafa

WORLD TODAY (d)
43/16 Main Gulberg, Punjab
Ed.—Mir Javid

ZAMAN (d) Urdu

LARKANA

AGWAN (d) Sindh
Office Daily Agwan, Sind

LASBELLA

INTEKHAB (d) Urdu
Lasbella, Balochistan
Ed.—Anwar Sajidi

MANSEHRA

FUTURE (d) English
Kawai House, Mansehra
Ed.—Ghulam Jankhan Tahir Khaili

MASTUNG

HIMMAT (d)
Ed.—Kausar Hussain

MULTAN CITY
(Multan)
Pop. Est. 742,000

ADAL (d) Urdu
Tipu Sultan Colony, Punjab; PO Box 124
Ed.—Jalal Rabbani

AFTAB (d) Urdu
Near Pul-Shahwala, Punjab
Ed.—Aziz Anjum

AILAN HAQ (d) Urdu
Pul Shahwala Baher Gate, Punjab
Ed.—Muhtammad Ali

AKHBAR-E-MILLAT (d) Urdu
Abdali Rd., Punjab
Tel: (92-61) 73766
Ed.—Rana Muhammad Aslam

ELAN (d) Urdu
1902/W-7 Mohni Buri Babar St., Purana Dangal, Punjab
Ed.—Abdul Rehman Malik

HAQ (d) Urdu
28 Hassan, Parwana Colony, Punjab
Ed.—Qaisar Malik

HARAFAT (d) Urdu
131/A Purana Bahawalpur Rd., 1st Floor, Punjab
Ed.—Nazir Ahmed

HIJRAT (d) Urdu
Mahlem Press Bldg.
Ed.—Khalil Bhatti

IMROZE (d) Urdu
Hasan Parwana Rd., Punjab
Tel: (92-61) 2570
Ed.—Syed Sultan Ahmed

NAWA-E-MULTAN (d) Urdu
Near Beef Market, Opp. Haram Gate, Punjab
Ed.—Khalil Bhatti

NAWA-E-WAQT (d) Urdu
Waqt Bldg., Guldin Colony, Punjab
Ed.—Riaz Pervaiz

QUAMI AWAZ (d) Urdu
Hassan Parwana Rd., Punjab
Ed.—Eisar Raee

SUNG-E-MEEL (d) Urdu
Hassan Parwana Rd., Punjab
Ed.—M R Roohani

PESHAWAR
(Peshawar)
Pop. Est. 555,000

AIHAQ (d) Urdu
Islamia Club Bldg., Khyber Bazar
Tel: (92-521) 2131
Ed.—Bashir Tabasum

AKHBAR (d) Urdu
Bazar Kalan Tehsil
Tel: (92-521) 213076
Ed.—Khurshid Amed

ALFALAH (d) Urdu; Est. 1939
Saddar Rd.
Tel: (92-521) 73783
Circ.—8,000
Pub.—Iltaf Hussain
Ed.—S Mohammad Seddiq Shah
Ad. Mgr.—Zulaqar Ali Shah

ALJAMIAT-E-SARHAD (d) Urdu; Est. 1941
Chakagali
Ed.—S Muhammad Hussain Gilani
Ad. Mgr.—S M Niwaz Gilani

ANJAM (d) Urdu
Islamia College Bldg.
Ed.—Mustafa Qureshi

AWAZ (d) Urdu
Cantonment Plaza, Arbab Rd.
Ed.—Martaza Malik

AZME NAU (d) Urdu
Kuku Bldg., Ginta Ghar
Tel: (92-521) 21493
Ed.—Khawaja Imran

BAGRAM (d) Urdu
Bazar Kalan Tehsil
Tel: (92-521) 213076
Ed.—Khurshid Ahmed
DAWN (d) English
Haroon Mansion
Tel: (92-521) 64443
FRONTIER POST (d) English
2 Sir Syed Rd.; PO Box 1161
Tel: (92-521) 79175
Ed.—Rehmat Shah Afridi
HAMARA PAKISTAN (e) Urdu; Est. 1947
Mohammed Ali Johar Rd.
Ed.—Ghulam Ghaus Sehrai
Ad. Mgr.—Mohammad Ali Tariq
HAQEEQAT (d) Urdu
20 Islamia Club Bldg.
Tel: (92-521) 213141
Ed.—Hasamuddin
INQILAB (d) Urdu
Bazar Kalan
Ed.—Khurshid Ahmad
IRRUM (d) Urdu
20 Islamia Club Bldg.
Tel: (92-521) 213141
JEHAD (m) Urdu; Est. 1975
20 Islamia Club Bldg., Khyber Bazar
Circ.—8,000
Ed.—Sharif Farooq
JIDDAT (d) Urdu
Rehman Baba Colony
Tel: (92-521) 211921
Ed.—Qaser Rizvi
KHYBER MAIL (d) English; Est. 1932
95-A Saddar Rd.
Circ.—6,500
Ed.—Sheikh Zakaullah
Ad. Mgr.—S Inayatullah
MASHRIQ (d) Urdu
2 Railway Rd.
Tel: (92-521) 211150
Ed.—A W Yousfi
NISHAN-I-HAIDER (d) Urdu
Rehman Baba Colony
Tel: (92-521) 211921
Ed.—Qasir Rizvi
QUAID (d) Urdu
20 Islamia Club Bldg.
Tel: (92-521) 210574
Ed.—Naeem Sarhadi
RAHAT (d) Urdu
Chowk Yadgar
Ed.—Zabuir Kazmir
SANG (d) Urdu
Fancy Market Bazar Kalan
Tel: (92-521) 213735
Ed.—S Nazli
SARHAD (d) Urdu
Asad Anwar Colony
Tel: (92-521) 63743
Ed.—Hafeez Ulfat
SHAHBAZ (d) Urdu
Nazar Bagh Flats
Tel: (92-521) 61188
Ed.—Begum Naseem
Ed.—Wali Khan
TARJUMAN-E-AFGHAN (d) Urdu
Azmat Bldg., Chowk Yadgar
Ed.—Javed Akhtar
Ad. Mgr.—Abdul Hamid Mufti
WAHDAT (d) Pushto
20 Islamia Club Bldg., Khyber Bazar
Ed.—Pir Syed Safaid Shah
WATTAN (d) Urdu
10 Nazar Bagh Flats
Ed.—Bari Malik

QUETTA
(Quetta)
Pop. Est. 285,000

BALOCHISTAN TIMES (d) English
Adalat Rd.
Tel: (92-81) 71217/(92-81) 71148
Prop.—National Press Trust
Ed.—Syed Faseih Iqbal
BOLAN-E-JADEED (d) Urdu
Near Bohra Thana Rd.
Tel: (92-81) 73340
Ed.—Nusrat Hussain
EITEMAD (d) Urdu
Jinnah Rd.
Tel: (92-81) 71124
Ed.—Javed Ahmed
JANG (d) Urdu; Est. 1954
Jamiat Rai Rd.
Tel: (92-81) 70515/(92-81) 73064
Pub.—Mir Javed-ur-Rahman
Ed.—Habibur Rehman
JANG QUETTA (m) Urdu; Est. 1972
Jamiat Rai Rd.
Tel: (92-81) 70921; Fax: (92-81) 70515
Circ.—21,000
Prop.—Independent Newspaper Corp.
Ed.—Majeud Asghat

MASHRIQ (d) Urdu
Dr. Shar Mahammad Rd.
Tel: (92-81) 72086
Prop.—National Press Trust
Ed.—Maqbool Rana
MEEZAN (d) Urdu
Meezan Chambers Mecongi Rd.
Ed.—Jamilur Rehman
NARA-E-HAQ (d) Urdu
Mecongi Rd.
Ed.—Iftikhar Yousaf
SHAZ (d) Urdu
Al-Syed Bldg., Jinnah Rd.
Ed.—Abdul Haque
TAMEER-E-BALOCHISTAN (d) Urdu
Al-Syed Bldg., Jinnah Rd.
Ed.—M Noor Ahmed Baloch
ZAMANA (d) Urdu
Adalat Rd.
Tel: (92-81) 73023/(92-81) 71217
Circ.—5,000
Ed.—Imdad Nizami

RAHIMYAR KHAN
Pop. Est. 130,000

IBADAT (d) Urdu
Shah Jahan Bldg., Rahim Yar Khan
Railway Rd., Punjab
Ed.—Muhammad Aslam Khan
ISRAR Urdu
8/P Gulran Usmania, Punjab
Ed.—Muhammad Israrul Haqe
SHAHADAT (d) Urdu
Shahi Rd., Punjab
Ed.—Zia-ullah Khan
TAKMEEL-E-PAKISTAN (d) Urdu
Rahim Yar Khan
Ed.—Munawar Naqvi
WIFAQ (d) Urdu
112 Bano Bazar, Punjab
Prop.—Abasin Press
Ed.—Wiqar Mustafa

RAWALPINDI
(Rawalpindi)
Pop. Est. 920,000

HAIDER (d) Urdu
1901-M Murree Rd., Punjab
Ed.—Ijaz Butt
JANG (m) Urdu; Est. 1937
Rehman Plaza, Murree Rd., Punjab
Tel: (92-51) 7022327
Circ.—65,000
Ed.—Mir Javed-ur-Rehman
JANG RAWALPINDI (m) Urdu; Est. 1950
Al-Rahman Bldg., Murree Rd.; PO Box 30
Tel: (92-51) 556233/(92-51) 556232;
Fax: (92-51) 552711
Circ.—128,000 ABC
Ed.—Mir Javed-ur-Rahman
Ad. Dir.—Raja Aziz
JURAT (d) Urdu
125-N Circular Rd., Punjab
Ed.—Jamil Athar
MILLAT NEWS (d) English
J-259 Liaquat Chowk, Murree Rd., Punjab
Ed.—Asar Ali Chauhan
NADA-I-HAQ (d) Urdu
52-B Satellite Town, Punjab
Ed.—Habib Wahabul Khairi
NAWA-E-WAQT (m) Urdu
Al-Mir Bldg., Bank Rd., Punjab
Tel: (92-51) 67677
Circ.—3,000
Prop.—Niadi-Millat Ltd.
Pub.—Majid Nizami
Ed.—Tariq Warsi
TAMEER (d) Urdu; Est. 1949
A-1-Abbas Market, Punjab
Circ.—15,000
Ed.—Bashir-ul-Islam Usmani
Ad. Mgr.—S Nasim Humayun
WIFAQ (d) Urdu
406 Murree Rd., Mohallah Waris Khan, Punjab
Ed.—Wiqar Mustafa

SAHIWAL
Pop. Est. 152,000

JAMHOORISTAN (d) Urdu
Stadium Chowk, Railway Rd., Punjab
Ed.—Pervaiz Ahmed Kharal
PAIGHAM (d) Urdu
120 Civil Line Rd., Punjab
Ed.—Syed Muhammad Wakeel

SARGODHA
(Rawalpindi)
Pop. Est. 294,000

AZADI Urdu
Block 14, Kutchery Bazar, Punjab
Ed.—Ashiq Jafri

Asia

NIZAM-E-NAU (d) Urdu
Kutchery Bazar, Punjab
Ed.—Mukhtar Younas
SHOLA (d) Urdu
9-Jauhar Colony, Punjab
Tel: (92-451) 2982
Ed.—Mir Khalid Mahmood
TIJARAT (d) Urdu
Kutchery Bazar, Punjab
Ed.—Malik Aamer Afzal
WIFAQ (d) Urdu
Aminpur Bazar, Punjab
Ed.—Moazam Tauseef

SUKKUR
(Khairpur)
Pop. Est. 103,216

BAYAN (d) Urdu
C-488/1 Wallice Rd., Sind
Tel: (92-71) 83269/(92-71) 83289
Ed.—Attaullah Khan
DEYANAT (d) Urdu
Supper Queens Rd., Sind
Tel: (92-71) 84254
Ed.—Najmuddin Shaikh
KALEEM (d) Urdu; Est. 1918
Iqal Manzil, Wallice Rd., Sind; PO Box 88
Tel: (92-71) 82086/(92-71) 85988
Ed.—Shahid Mehar Shamsi
Ad. Mgr.—Javed Mehar Shamsi
MAGHRABI PAKISTAN (d) Urdu
Mehran Market, Sind
Tel: (92-71) 85642
Ed.—Ch Fazul-ul-Din Naseem
Ad. Mgr.—Syed I Bukhari
NAWA-E-INQILAB (d) Sindhi
Queens Rd., Sind
Tel: (92-71) 4783
Ed.—Inamur Rehman
NIJAAT (d) Sindhi
Golimar Rd., Sind; PO Box 70
Ed.—Mukhdoom Muhammad Rafiqu
YADGAR (d) Urdu
Office Daily Yadgar, Mehran Centre, Sind
Tel: (92-71) 84238
Ed.—Javed Ashfaq

PHILIPPINES
Pop. Est. 69,808,930

CEBU CITY
Pop. Est. 552,200

CEBU ADVOCATE (m) English; Est. 1964
158 Padilla St.
Tel: (63-32) 93737
Circ.—4,000
Pub.—Danny Gonzales
Ed.—Elma C Avellanosa
CEBU DAILY TIMES
F. Gonzales St.
Pub.—Edgardo Mongaya
Ed.—Wilfredo Veloso
THE FREEMAN (m) English & Visayan
107-109 V. Gulles St.
Circ.—6,500
Prop.—JS Publications
Ed.—Pachico A Seares
MORNING TIMES (d-ex mon.) English & Visayan; Est. 1942
Zulueta St.; PO Box 51
Tel: (63-32) 77032
Circ.—4,000
Pub./Ed.—Pedro D Calomarde
REPUBLICAN NEWS (d-ex mon.)
57-59 Colon St.
Circ.—12,175
Pub.—Dioscoro B Lazaro
Ed.—José G Logarte
SUN-STAR DAILY
Osmena Blvd.
Prop.—Sun-Star Publishing Inc.

DAVAO CITY
Pop. Est. 625,000

DAVAO STAR
230 Solas, Aquarius St.
Pub.—José M Santes
DIGOS TIMES
Digos, Davao del Sur
Ed.—Bievenida Sacada

Philippines

MINDANAO DAILY MIRROR (d)
270 R. Magsaysay Ave.
Circ.—10,000
Pub.—Anita Flaviano
MINDANAO INQUIRER
153 Pichon St.
Pub.—Doreta A Flaviano
MINDANAO MAIL English & Visayan
Lozano Bldg., Rm. 183, C.M. Recto Ave.
Ed.—Angelo M Abarico
MINDANAO MIRROR BULLETIN
278 Magsaysay Ave.
Pub.—Teresita F Basilio
MINDANAO TIMES (m) English & Tagalog; Est. 1946
C.M. Recto Ave.
Circ.—10,000
Prop.—Mindanao Publishing Co.
Pub.—Serafin Ledesma-Regional
Ed.—Jesús Durez
Ad. Mgr.—José Angliongto
PEOPLE'S FORM
153 Pichon St.
Pub.—Rogelio J Flaviano
SAN PEDRO EXPRESS
Covern Trade Bldg., Gen. Luna St.
Pub.—Leoniloa G Claudio
VOICE OF ISLAM
PO Box 407
Pub.—Muhammad Al Rashid

MANILA
Pop. Est. 4,221,485

ABANTE (d) English & Pilipino
268 Atlanta
Tel: (63-2) 472575
Circ.—320,000
Prop.—Monica Publishing Corp.
Mng. Ed.—Nicholas Quijano
Ad. Mgr.—Ron Tamayo
ANG PAHAYAGANG MALAYA (Freedom Newspaper) (d) English
70 Serrano Laktaw
Circ.—165,000
ANG PILIPINO NGAYON (Philippines Today) (m-ex S) Pilipino
202 Railroad & 13th St., Port Area
Tel: (63-2) 401871/(63-2) 401873; Fax: (63-2) 5224998
Circ.—286,452
Prop.—Daily Star Publications
Pub.—Antonio V Roces
Mng. Ed.—Pat S Sigue
BALITA (News) (m) Pilipino; Est. 1972
2249 Pasong Tamo, Makati, Rizal (Metro Manila)
Tel: (63-2) 8193101; Fax: (63-2) 8175167
Circ.—181,415
Prop.—Liwayway Publishing Inc.
Pres./Gen. Mgr.—Buenaventura M Gonda
Ed. in Ch.—Marcelo Lagmay
Ad. Mgr.—Florencio Seville
BUSINESS STAR (5x wk.) English; Est. 1987
202 Railroad St. & 13th St., Port Area
Pub./Ed.—Gabriel V Manalac
BUSINESS WORLD NEWSPAPER (5x wk.) English; Est. 1987
Diamond Motor Bldg., 4/F, Ortigas Ave.
Tel: (63-2) 799291/(63-2) 799292; Fax: (63-2) 7226214
Circ.—52,000
Prop.—Businessworld Publishing Corp.
Pres./Pub.—Raúl L Locsin
Mng. Ed.—Leticia M Locsin
Ad. Mgr.—Danilo Ocampo
CHINA TOWN NEWS (m) Chinese
429 Nueva St., Binondo
Circ.—20,000
Prop.—A&A Company Inc.
Pub.—Bangong Dina
Ed. in Ch.—José Locsin
CHINESE COMMERCIAL NEWS (m) Chinese
652 St. Tomas St., Intramuros
Tel: (63-2) 482742
Prop.—Yutituting Communications Inc.
Ed. in Ch.—Rizal Yutitung
DAILY GLOBE (d) English
17 Shaw Blvd., Pasig (Metro Manila)
Tel: (63-2) 6730496/(63-2) 6730499
Circ.—93,342
DAILY TRIBUNE (d) English & Pilipino
1 Ponte St., Marie de la Paz Village, Makati (Metro Manila)
Circ.—35,000
EVENING POST (e) English
20th St. & Bonifacio Dr., Port Area
Tel: (63-2) 481234
Circ.—90,000

Philippines

EVENING STAR (e-ex S) English; Est. 1987
202 Railroad & 13th St., Port Area
Pub.—Betty Go-Belmonte
Ed. in Ch.—Luís D Beltran
FINANCIAL TIMES OF MANILA (d)
Times Journal Bldg., Railroad & 19th St., Port Area
HEADLINE (d) English & Tagalog
Railroad & Chicago Sts.
Tel: (63-2) 478661; Fax: (63-2) 478668
Circ.—105,000
Pub.—Juan Dayang
HERALD TRIBUNE (d) English
140 Amorsolo St., Legaspi Village, Makati (Metro Manila)
Tel: (63-2) 853711
THE JOURNAL (d) English; Est. 1972
Times Journal Bldg., Railroad & 19th St.
Pub.—Manuel C Villa-Real Jr
Ed. in Ch.—Feliciano H Magno
THE MAKATI BUSINESS DAILY (d) English
429 Mueva St.
Pub./Ed.—Veronica T Velosoyap
MALAYA (Freedom) (mS) English; Est. 1981
C.C. Castro Bldg., Tomog Ave.
Tel: (63-2) 98327176
Circ.—140,066
Prop.—People's Independent Media Inc.
Pub.—Amado P Macasaet
Pub./Ex. Ed.—Luís R Maurico
MANILA BULLETIN (d) English; Est. 1900
Corner of Muralla & Recoletos, Intramuros; PO Box 769
Tel: (63-2) 473621
Circ.—300,000 (m); 275,000 (S)
Prop.—Bulletin Publishing Corp.
Ex. Vice Pres.—Augusto T Africa
Pub.—Napoleon O Rama
Ed. in Ch.—Ben Rodríguez
U.S. Rep.—Northeast Media Group; Int'l. Media Group
MANILA CHRONICLE (m) English; Est. 1945
371 Bonifacio Dr., Port Area
Tel: (63-2) 478261/(63-2) 478269; Fax: (63-2) 476909/(63-2) 476948
Circ.—95,000
Prop.—Manila Chronicle Publishing Corp.
Chmn.—Roberto T Villanueva
Ed. in Ch.—Amando Doronila
Ad. Mgr.—Antonette G Ca
MANILA EVENING POST (e) English
20th St., Port Area
Tel: (63-2) 481234
Circ.—90,000
Prop.—Orient Media Inc.
MANILA STANDARD (m) English; Est. 1986
Elizalde Bldg., Ayalda Ave, 4th Floor
Tel: (63-2) 163893
Prop.—Standard Publication Ltd.
Pub.—Rodolfo T Reyes
Ed. in Ch.—Alejandro del Rosario
THE MANILA TIMES (d) English
30 Pioneer St. on the corner of EDSA, Mandaluyong
Tel: (63-2) 472786
NEWS TODAY (m) English
FEMI Bldg., Aduana St., Intramuros; PO Box 4245
Circ.—35,000
Prop.—New Publishing Co.
Ed. in Ch.—Augusta B Villanueva
OBSERVER (d) English & Pilipino
Times Journal Bldg., Railroad & 19th St., Port Area
Circ.—60,000
ORIENT NEWS (d) English & Chinese
Times Journal Bldg., Railroad & 13th St., Port Area
Tel: (63-2) 472694
Circ.—26,000
PEOPLE'S BAGONG TALIBA (m)
Times Journal Bldg., Railroad & 19th St., Port Area
Tel: (63-2) 487511
Circ.—508,000
Pub.—Manuel C Villa-Real Jr
Ed. in Ch.—Ben Esquival
PEOPLE'S JOURNAL (m) English; Est. 1978
Times Journal Bldg., Railroad & 19th St., Port Area
Tel: (63-2) 287511
Circ.—383,300
Prop.—Philippines Journalists Inc.
Pub.—Alfredo Marquez
Pub.—Zacarios Nuguid Jr
Ed.—Alex Alan
Ad. Mgr.—Domingo Flores
PEOPLE'S TONIGHT (d) English; Est. 1978
Times Journal Bldg., Railroad & 19th St., Port Area
Tel: (63-2) 287511

Circ.—179,358
Prop.—Philippines Journalists Inc.
Pub.—Zacarios Nuguid
Mng. Ed.—Alfredo Márquez
Ad. Mgr.—Roger Banta
PHILIPPINE DAILY GLOBE (m) English; Est. 1978
Rundgen Bldg., 2nd Floor, I & II, Shaw Blvd. & Meralco Ave.
Pub.—Benjamin C Ramos
Ex. Ed.—Neal H Cruz
PHILIPPINE DAILY INQUIRER (mS) English; Est. 1985
YIC Bldg., No. 1006, Romualdez St., UN Ave.
Tel: (63-2) 508061
Circ.—250,000
Pub.—Isagani Tambot
Ex. Ed.—Federico D Pasqual Jr
U.S. Rep.—Northeast Media Group; Int'l. Media Service
PHILIPPINE STAR (m) English; Est. 1986
202 Railroad & 13th St., Port Area
Tel: (63-2) 401871; Fax: (63-2) 5224998
Circ.—200,000
Prop.—Philippines Today Inc.
Pub./Chmn.-of-the-Board—Maxim V Soliven
Ad. Mgr.—Lydia M Santos
U.S. Rep.—Northeast Media Group; Int'l. Media Service
PHILIPPINE TIMES JOURNAL (m) English; Est. 1972
Times Journal Bldg., Railroad & 19th St., Port Area
Tel: (63-2) 487511; Fax: (63-2) 483891
Circ.—111,457
Prop.—Philippine Journalists Inc.
Pub.—Guillermo H A Sontos
Ed.—Manolo B Sontos
Ad. Mgr.—Romulo D de Dios
TALIBA (The Newspapers) (d) Pilipino
Times Journal Bldg., Railroad & 19th St., Port Area
Tel: (63-2) 48751126
Circ.—206,348
TEMPO (m) English
Recoletos & Muralla St., Intramuros
Tel: (63-2) 47155155
Circ.—180,000
Prop.—Bulletin Publishing Corp.
Pub.—Napoleon Rama
Ed. in Ch.—Ben Rodríguez
UNITED DAILY NEWS (m) English & Chinese; Est. 1973
812 Benavides St., Binondo
Tel: (63-2) 219806
Circ.—24,000
Prop.—United Daily News Inc.
Ed. in Ch.—Sy Unchow
UNIVERSAL DAILY NEWS (m) Chinese
Traders Bldg., 275 Juan Luna St., 2nd Floor
Circ.—5,000
Ed.—Eddie Lee
Ad. Mgr.—Henry Sy
WORLD NEWS (d) Chinese
549 T. Pinpin St., Binondo
Tel: (63-2) 402650/(63-2) 402751
Circ.—35,000
Prop.—World News Publishing Corp.
Pub.—Florencio Mallare
Ed. in Ch.—Go Eng Guan
Ad. Mgr.—Joseph Ong

QUEZON CITY
Pop. Est. 2,265,865

THE MANILA TIMES (dS) English; Est. 1945
Scout Santiago St.
Tel: (63) 2964448/(63) 2994354
Circ.—157,105
Pub.—Ramón Roces
Ex. Ed.—Federico Agcagili
Ad. Mgr.—Romulo G de Dios

SINGAPORE, REPUBLIC OF
Pop. Est. 2,859,142

BERITA HARIAN (m-ex S) Malay & English; Est. 1957
News Centre, 82 Genting Lane
Tel: (65) 7438800; Fax: (65) 7484144

Circ.—44,693
Prop.—The Straits Times Press Ltd.
Dir.—Denis Tay Koom Tek
Ed.—Guntor Sadali
Ad. Mgr.—Lawrence Loh
BUSINESS TIMES (m-ex S) English, Chinese & Malay; Est. 1976
News Centre, 82 Genting Lane
Tel: (65) 7438800; Fax: (65) 7484144
Circ.—23,205
Prop.—Times Business Publications
Gen. Mgr.—Roy Mackie
Ed.—Mano Sabnani
Ad. Mgr.—Lawrence Loh
U.S. Rep.—Dow Jones Int'l. Marketing Services
LIANHE WANBAO (eS) Chinese & English; Est. 1984
News Centre, 82 Genting Lane, 1334
Tel: (65) 7438800; Fax: (65) 7432437
Circ.—85,000
Prop.—Lianhe Bao Ltd.
Ch. Ed.—Chen Cheng
Ad. Mgr.—Lee Cheok Yew
U.S. Rep.—Dow Jones Int'l. Marketing Services
LIANHE ZAOBAO (m) Chinese; Est. 1984
News Centre, 82 Genting Lane, 1334
Tel: (65) 7438800; Fax: (65) 7482652
Circ.—185,037
Prop.—Lianhe Bao Ltd.
Ed.—Loy Teck Juan
Ad. Mgr.—Lawrence Loh
U.S. Rep.—Dow Jones Int'l. Marketing Services
NANYANG XINGZHOU/LIANHE ZAOBAO (United Morning Daily/United Evening Daily) (m&e) Chinese & English; Est. 1923
307 Alexandra Rd., 0315
Tel: (65) 635555
Circ.—195,000 (Zaobao); 70,000 (Wanbao)
Prop.—Singapore Press Holdings
Ed.—Loy Teck Juan
Ed. (Zaobao)—Mok Lee Zwang
Ed. (Wanbao)—Chen Cheng
Ad. Mgr.—Teo Hankim
Mktg. Mgr.—Lee Cheok Yew
THE NEW PAPER (e-ex S) English; Est. 1988
News Centre, 82 Genting Lane
Tel: (65) 7438800; Fax: (65) 7484144
Circ.—65,818
Prop.—The Straits Times Press Ltd.
Ed.—P N Baliji
Ad. Mgr.—Lawrence Loh
SHIN MIN DAILY NEWS (m) Chinese; Est. 1967
News Centre, 82 Genting Lane
Tel: (65) 7438800; Fax: (65) 7484144
Circ.—104,314
Prop.—The Straits Times Press
Mng. Dir.—Denis Tay Koon Tek
Ed.—Seng Han Thong
Ad. Mgr.—Lawrence Loh
STRAITS TIMES (m-ex S) Chinese, English, Malay & Tamil; Est. 1945
News Centre, 82 Genting Lane, 0923
Tel: (65) 7370071; Fax: (65) 7484144/(65) 7320131
Circ.—313,588 ABC
Prop.—The Straits Times Press Ltd.
Ed.—Leslie Fong
Ad. Mgr.—Lawrence Loh
U.S. Rep.—Dow Jones Int'l. Marketing Services
SUNDAY TIMES (S) Chinese, English, Malay & Tamil; Est. 1931
News Centre, 82 Genting Lane
Tel: (65) 7438800; Fax: (65) 7484144
Circ.—354,501 ABC
Prop.—The Straits Times Press Ltd.
Dir.—Denis Tay Koon Tek
Ed.—Leslie Fong
Ad. Mgr.—Lawrence Loh
TAMIL MURASU & SUN (mS) Tamil; Est. 1935
139-141 Lavender St.; PO Box 621, 1233
Tel: (65) 2980249; Fax: (65) 2932941
Circ.—8,500 (m); 10,000 (S)
Pub./Gen. Mgr.—Balaram Sarangapany
Ed.—V T Arasu
USA TODAY (d) English
7500A Beach Rd., 0719
Tel: (65) 2972933; Fax: (65) 2965446
Prop.—USA Today Int'l. Corp.
U.S. Rep.—Gannett Publishing Group

SRI LANKA, DEMOCRATIC SOCIALIST REPUBLIC OF
Pop. Est. 18,129,850

COLOMBO
Pop. Est. 1,200,000

CEYLON OBSERVER (eS) English; Est. 1834
PO Box 248
Tel: (94-1) 545433; Fax: (94-1) 449069
Circ.—14,000 (e); 120,000 (S)
Prop.—Associated Newspapers of Ceylon Ltd.
Ed.—Harold Peiris
Ad. Mgr.—Charles Tissera
DAILY LANKADEEPA (d) Sinhala; Est. 1976
10 Hunupitiya Cross Rd.
Tel: (94-1) 438039/(94-1) 438037; Fax: (94-1) 449504
Circ.—259,172
Prop.—Wijeya Newspapers Ltd.
Ed.—Siri Ransinghe
Ad. Mgr.—C U Matugama
CEYLON DAILY NEWS (m-ex S) English; Est. 1918
PO Box 248
Tel: (94-1) 545433; Fax: (94-1) 449069
Circ.—65,000
Prop.—Associated Newspapers of Ceylon Ltd.
Ed.—Manik De Silva
Ad. Mgr.—Waruna H Mallawacrachchi
DINAMINA (m-ex S) Sinhala; Est. 1909
PO Box 248
Tel: (94-1) 421181
Circ.—140,000
Prop.—Associated Newspapers of Ceylon Ltd.
Ed.—G S Perera
Ad. Mgr.—Waruna H Mallawacrachchi
DIVAINA (d) Sinhala; Est. 1982
223 Bloemendhal Rd., Colombo 13; PO Box 1942
Tel: (94-1) 24001
Circ.—100,000
Prop.—Upali Newspapers Ltd.
Ed.—Edmund Ranasinghe
THE ISLAND/THE ISLAND SUNDAY EDITION (dS) English; Est. 1981
223 Bloemendhal Rd., Colombo 13; PO Box 1942
Tel: (94-1) 24001
Circ.—33,000 (d); 87,000 (S)
Prop.—Upali Newspapers Ltd.
Ed.—Gamini Weerakoon
JANATHA (e-5x wk.) Sinhala; Est. 1953
Lake House, D.R. Wijewardena Mawatha, Colombo 10; PO Box 248
Tel: (94-1) 21181
Circ.—9,400
Prop.—Associated Newspapers of Ceylon Ltd.
Ed.—M N Pinto
MITHRAN (m) Tamil; Est. 1966
185 Grandpass Rd., Colombo 14
Tel: (94-1) 20881
Circ.—21,100
Prop.—Express Newspapers Ltd.
Ed.—A Sivanesaselvan
SILUMINA Sinhala; Est. 1930
Lake House, D.R. Wijewardena Mawatha, Colombo 10; PO Box 248
Tel: (94-1) 21181
Circ.—380,100
Prop.—Associated Newspapers of Ceylon Ltd.
Ed.—D C Karunaratne
THINAKARAN (mS) Tamil; Est. 1932
Lake House, D.R. Wijewardena Mawatha, Colombo 10; PO Box 248
Tel: (94-1) 21181
Circ.—18,500 (m); 22,430 (S)
Prop.—Associated Newspapers of Ceylon Ltd.
Ed.—R Sivagurunathan
VIRAKESARI (mS) Tamil; Est. 1930
185 Grandpass Rd., Colombo 14; PO Box 160
Tel: (94-1) 20881
Circ.—24,300 (m)
Prop.—Express Newspapers Ltd.
Ed.—A Sivanesaselvan

JAFFNA
Pop. Est. 270,000

EELAMURASU (d) Tamil; Est. 1984
140 Navalar Rd.
Tel: (94-21) 22389
Pub.—M Amirthalingam
EELANADU (m) Tamil; Est. 1958
165 Sivan Kovil West Rd.; PO Box 49
Tel: (94-21) 22389
Circ.—21,000
Prop.—Eelanadu Ltd.
Ed.—N Sabaratnam
Ad. Mgr.—A Sivamoorthy

TAIWAN
(Republic Of China)
Pop. Est. 21,298,930

HUALIEN
Pop. Est. 352,233

KENG SHENG DAILY NEWS (m) Est. 1947
36 Wuchuan St.
Tel: (886-3) 8340131; Fax: (886-3) 8329664
Circ.—5,000
Pub.—Ying-Yi Hseieh
Ed.—Chen Hsing

KAOHSIUNG
Pop. Est. (Metro Area) 1,405,860

CHINA DAILY
1366 Chunghua 5th Rd.
Tel: (886-7) 3332203; Fax: (886-7) 3349557
Pub.—H H Liu
Ch.—Wen-Hsia Lee
CHINA EVENING NEWS Est. 1956
71 Linhai St., Fengshan
Tel: (886-7) 8122525; Fax: (886-7) 8416565
Circ.—60,000
Ch.—Jung-Tsen Lai
Pub.—Chun-Hsien Liu
THE COMMONS DAIRY (m) Est. 1950
180 Minchuan 2nd. Rd.
Tel: (886-7) 3363131; Fax: (886-7) 3363604
Circ.—30,000
Pub.—Jui-Paio Lee
Ed.—Hwang Yeh
MIN CHUNG DAILY NEWS
180 Minchuan 2nd. Rd.
Tel: (886-7) 3363131; Fax: (886-7) 3363604/(886-7) 3363605
Ch./Pub.—J P Lee
PACIFIC DAILY NEWS (m) Est. 1988
13 Yencheng St.
Tel: (886-7) 5316131; Fax: (886-7) 5215993
Ch.—C C Chen
Pub.—K P Cheng
TAIWAN SHIN WEN DAILY NEWS (m) Est. 1949
249 Chungcheng 4th Rd.
Tel: (886-7) 2135129/(886-7) 2135137; Fax: (886-7) 2412491/(886-7) 2412492
Pub./Dir.—Wey-Ping Wang
Ed.—Yen-Li Yeh
TAIWAN TIMES (m) Est. 1971
110 Chungshan 1st Rd.
Tel: (886-7) 2155666; Fax: (886-7) 2150264
Circ.—100,000
Ch.—Y F Wang
Pub.—Yu-Chen Wang
Ed.—Hsin-Chang Tsai

KINMEN
(Quemoy)
Pop. Est. 44,515

KINMEN DAILY (m) Est. 1965
1 Chengkung Village, Chinhu Township
Tel: (886-8) 2332440
Circ.—5,00
Pub.—Wei-Sung Huang
Ed.—Hsien-Min Hsai

MATSU
Pop. Est. 5,855

MATSU DAILY NEWS (m) Est. 1957
1 Jenai Village, Mankan Hsiang
Tel: (886-1) 0822087
Pub.—Huai-Tsu Kao
Ed.—Keng-Hsing Liao

PENGHU
(Pescadores)
Pop. Est. 95,932

CHIEN KUO DAILY NEWS (m) Est. 1949
36 Minsheng Rd., Makung City
Tel: (886-6) 9272341; Fax: (886-6) 9273618
Circ.—15,000
Pub.—Kuo Chung
Ed.—Lien-Chen Wang

TAICHUNG
Pop. Est. 799,640

CHUNG KUO DAILY NEWS
147-10 Chungching Rd.
Tel: (886-4) 2922108
DAILY FREE PRESS (e) Est. 1978
402-12 Peitun Rd.
Circ.—20,000
Pub.—E-M Wu
Ed.—Hsin-Chang Tsai
TAIWAN DAILY NEWS (m) Est. 1974
7F, 361 Wen-Chin Rd., Section 3
Tel: (886-4) 2958366; Fax: (886-4) 2958427
Circ.—300,000
Prop.—Taiwan Newspaper Corp.
Gen. Mgr.—Tu-Hung Chen
Ad. Dir.—Yin-Yuan Liao

TAINAN
Pop. Est. (Metro Area) 694,878

CHINA DAILY NEWS (m)
57 Hsihua St.
Tel: (806-6) 2202691; Fax: (806-6) 5069105
Circ.—670,000
Ch.—Yu-Lung Kan
Pub.—Tien-Shing Chan
Ed.—Chi-Lin Chiang

TAIPEI
Pop. Est. (Metro Area) 2,686,974

CENTRAL DAILY NEWS (m) Est. 1928
260 Pateh Rd., Section 2
Tel: (886-2) 7213710; Fax: (886-2) 7775835
Circ.—600,000
Ch.—Hwai-I Juang
Pub.—Yung-Kuei Shih
Ed. in Ch.—Tse-Din Sheh
CHAO JAN TIMES (m) Est. 1988
139 Nanchang Rd., 2nd Floor, Section 2
Pub.—Pao-Hai Yuan
Ed.—Ho-Chien Li
THE CHILDREN'S DAILY NEWS (m) Est. 1988
6F, 38 Fuhsing North Rd.
Tel: (886-2) 7716622; Fax: (886-2) 7755769
Pub.—Hung-Tien Lin
Ed.—Hua-Jung Wang
CHINA DAILY NEWS (m) Est. 1946
10/F, 109-1, Tung Hsing St.
Tel: (886-2) 7686002; Fax: (886-2) 7686773
Circ.—100,000
Prop.—China News Co. Ltd.
Pub.—Simone Wei
Gen. Mgr./Ad.—Ada Ong
Ed.—Ong Hock Chuan
CHINA MORNING NEWS (m) Est. 1988
16 Nanking East Rd., 7th Floor-5, Section 1
Tel: (886-2) 5231545
Pub./Ed.—Hung Te-Jung
THE CHINA NEWS (m) English; Est. 1949
10F, 109-1 Tung Hsing St.
Tel: (886-2) 7686002; Fax: (886-2) 7686773/(886-2) 7686908
Circ.—50,000
Ch./Pub.—Simone Wei
Ed.—C H Wang
THE CHINA POST (mS) English; Est. 1952
8 Fushun St., 10453
Tel: (886-2) 5969971; Fax: (886-2) 5957962
Circ.—150,000
Pres./Pub.—Jack C Huang
Ad. Dir.—Heidi Chen
CHINA TIMES (mS) Est. 1950
42 Chung Hwa Rd., Sec 1, ROC 100
Tel: (886-2) 2818720; Fax: (886-2) 3310590
Circ.—1,270,000
Vice Pres.—Sheng-Yuan Chou
Ad. Mgr.—K S Chang
CHINA TIMES EXPRESS (e) Est. 1988
132 Tali St.
Tel: (886-2) 3087111; Fax: (886-2) 3810659
Ch.—Chi-Chung Yu
Pub.—Fan-Ying Yu
Ed.—Hung-Jen Hu
CHUNG CHENG PAO (m) Est. 1948
34/2 Twelve Chang Rd.
Circ.—50,000
Pub.—Hsing-Hua Tsao
Ed.—Chi-Tung Liang
COMMERCIAL TIMES (m) Est. 1978
132 Da Li St.
Tel: (886-2) 3087111; Faxz: (886-2) 3048138
Circ.—250,000

Asia — Philippines

Ch.—Ching-Chih Chu
Pub.—Fan-Ying Yu
Ed. in Ch.—Chen Iou
U.S. Rep.—Publicitas
DA-MIN NEWS
5F, 18, Alley 1, Lane 768, Paleh Rd., Section 4
Tel: (886-2) 7885570; Fax: (886-2) 7864782
Pub.—Pal-Hsun Liu
Ch.—Tsai-Wang Lan
ECONOMIC DAILY NEWS (mS) Est. 1967
555 Chunghsiao East Rd., Section 4, 10156
Tel: (886-2) 7638095; Fax: (886-2) 7634124/(886-2) 7567994
Circ.—325,000
Ch.—Pi-Cheng Wang
Pub.—Pi-Ly Wang
Ed.—Shyh Shyuang Lu
U.S. Rep.—AdMarket Int'l.; World Journal
LES ECHOS DE LA REPUBLIQUE DE CHINE (The Echoes of the Republic of China)
2 Tientsin St.
Tel: (886-2) 3228718; Fax: (886-2) 3568233
Pub.—Jason C Hu
FINANCE AND ECONOMIC TIMES (m) Est. 1988
7F, 61 Roosevelt Rd., 7th Floor, Section 1
Tel: (886-2) 3221772; Fax: (886-2) 3221776
Pub.—Hsi-Kuang Yuan
Ed.—Tien-Ming Yuan
FORTUNE DAILY NEWS
6F, 20, Alley 1, Lane 768, Pateh Rd., Section 4
Tel: (886-2) 7820005; Fax: (886-2) 7820426
Pub./Dir.—C T Hsu
THE FREE CHINA JOURNAL English
2 Tientsin St.
Tel: (886-2) 3970180; Fax: (886-2) 3568233
Pub.—Jason C Hu
THE GREAT NEWS
216 Chengteh Rd., Section 3
Tel: (866-2) 5973111; Fax: (886-2) 5963689
Ch.—Yao Shun
Pub.—Deng-Fei Liu
GYOYEU RYHBAW
2-10, Fuchow St.
Tel: (886-2) 3921133; Fax: (886-2) 3410203
Pub./Dir.—Lin Liang
THE HERALD NEWS (m) Est. 1988
203 Chunghsiao West Rd., 3rd Floor, Section 1
Tel: (886-2) 3112951
Pub./Ed.—C C Lee
THE INDEPENDENCE EVENING POST (e) Est. 1947
15 Chinan Rd., Section 2
Tel: (886-2) 3519621; Fax: (886-2) 3419054/(886-2) 3964541
Circ.—330,510
Pres.—Frank Wu Feng-Shan
Pub.—Dr. Shuh-Min Wu
THE INDEPENDENCE MORNING POST (m)
15 Chinan Rd., Section 2
Tel: (886-2) 3519621; Fax: (886-2) 3215211
Pub./Ed.—Cheng-Chao Kuo
KING LIGHT (m) Est. 1988
10 Chungking South Rd., B Floor-1, Section 1
Pub./Ed.—Owen Zou
LIBERTY TIMES (e) Est. 1988
137 Nanking East Rd., 11th Floor, Section 2
Tel: (886-2) 5042828; Fax: (886-2) 5042846
Pres./Pub.—Ah-Meng Wu
Ed.—Chien-Lien Lin
MANDARIN DAILY NEWS (m) Est. 1948
10 Foochow St.
Tel: (886-2) 3921133; Fax: (886-2) 3410203
Pub.—Ju-Te Yang
Ed.—Lin Liang
MANDARIN TIMES
38 Nan King Rd., 9th Floor, Rm. G, Section 2
Tel: (866-2) 5611592
Pub.—C C Lee
MIN SHENG DAILY (d) Est. 1978
555 Chunghsaio East Rd., Section 4
Tel: (886-2) 7681234; Fax: (886-2) 7616519

IV-83

Circ.—467,125
Pub.—Hsiao-Lan Wang
Ed.—Shih Min
MIN SHEN PAO
555 Chunghsiao East Rd., Section 4
Tel: (886-2) 7681234; Fax: (886-2) 7560955
Ch.—Pi-Cheng Wang
Pub.—Shaw-lan Wang
TAIWAN LIH PAO (m) Est. 1988
1 Lane 17, Mueha Rd., Section 1
Ch.—Ming-Hsun Yeh
Pub./Dir.—Lu-Hsi Cheng
TAIWAN SHIN SHENG DAILY NEWS (m) Est. 1945
12F, 110 Yenping South Rd., 12th Floor
Tel: (886-2) 3110873; Fax: (886-2) 3115319
Circ.—460,000
Ch.—Sen-Iung Lo
Pub./Dir.—Yu-Chen Su
Ed.—Hsu Chang
TATUNG TIMES (m) Est. 1988
45 Antung St., 10th Floor-7
Pub./Ed.—Li-Ping Cheng
TRADERS EXPRESS
8F, 333 Keelung Rd., 8th Floor, Section 1
Tel: (886-2) 7255200
Pub./Ed.—Yen-Tsu Liu
UNIFICATION DAILY (m) Est. 1989
70 Nanchang Rd., 9th Floor-1, Section 2
Pub./Ed.—Hsai-Chou Peng
UNITED DAILY NEWS (mS) Est. 1951
555 Chunghsaio East Rd., Section 4, 10516
Tel: (886-2) 7681234; Fax: (886-2) 7672169
Circ.—1,300,000
Prop.—United Daily News Publishing Co.
Ch.—Pi-Cheng Wang
Pub.—Shaw-Lan Wang
Ed.—Li-Tung Chang
UNITED EVENING NEWS (e) Est. 1988
555 Chunghsaio East Rd., Section 4
Tel: (886-2) 7681234; Fax: (886-2) 7569074
Ch.—Pi-Cheng Wang
Pub.—Pi-Ly Wang
Ed.—Huang Kuan
WEALTH NEWS
11F, 52 Nanking East Rd., 7th Floor, Section 1
Tel: (866-2) 5512561; Fax: (866-2) 5316438/(866-2) 5415273
Dir.—W H Sun
Pres./Pub.—Y H Chiu
WORLD TRIBUNE (m) Est. 1988
342 Keeling Rd., 9th Floor, Section 1
Tel: (886-2) 7231791
Pub./Ed.—Huai-Hsuan Chung
YOUTH DAILY NEWS (m) Est. 1984
3 Hsinyi Rd., Section 1
Tel: (886-2) 3222722; Fax: (886-2) 3222456
Dir.—Chen Chi
Pub.—Cho-Chun Lo
Ed.—Chen-Yu Nien

TOUNAN

TAIWAN JUSTICE DAILY NEWS
1 Kunglun Rd.
Tel: (886-5) 5960626
Ch.—Hsiao-Tien Wu
Pub.—Wu-Sheng Hsu

THAILAND
Pop. Est. 59,510,471

BANGKOK
Pop. Est. 5,876,000

BAN MUANG (m) Thai; Est. 1972
1 Soi Pluemmanee, Vibhavadi Rangsit Rd., 10900
Tel: (66-2) 5133101/(66-2) 5130230; Fax: (66-2) 5133106/(66-2) 5133103
Circ.—70,000
Prop.—National City Press Co. Ltd.
Pub./Ed.—Mana Praephan
Ad. Mgr.—Vijan Pukphibulya

Thailand

BANGKOK POST (m) English; Est. 1948
136 Na Ranong Rd., off Sunthorn Kosa Rd., 10110
Tel: (66-2) 2403700; Fax: (66-2) 2403790/(66-2) 2403791
Circ.—50,172 ABC
Prop.—Post Publishing Co. Ltd.
Dir.—Ian Fawcett
Ed.—Paisal Sricharutchanya
Mktg. Dir.—Prasit Maekwatana
Ad. Mgr.—Laddaval Ratanawongse
U.S. Rep.—Trade Media Int'l.

BANGKOK WORLD (e) English; Est. 1958
U-Chuliang Foundation Bldg., 968 Rama IV Rd., 3rd Floor
Circ.—12,000
Prop.—World Press Co. Ltd.
Ed.—Anussorn Thavisin
Mktg. Dir.—Prasit Maekwatana

DAILY MIRROR (e) Thai; Est. 1978
15/8 Lardprao, 501124
Tel: (66-2) 5380220; Fax: (66-2) 5301826
Circ.—60,000
Prop.—Daily Mirror Co. Ltd.
Pub./Ed.—Yingpan Manasikavn

DAILY NEWS (m) Thai; Est. 1964
1/4 Vibhavadi Rangsit
Tel: (66-2) 5790010
Circ.—450,000
Prop.—Si-Phya Publishing Co.
Dir.—Prasit Hetrakul
Ed.—Pracha Hetrakul
Ad. Mgr.—Prapa Srinulhad

DAILY TIMES (m) Est. 1974
60 Sukumvit Soi 42, Kluey Nam Thai
Tel: (66-2) 3925021
Circ.—10,000
Prop.—The Ihichai Co. Ltd.
Pub./Ed.—Chote Maneenoi
Ad. Mgr.—Van Chalerm

DAO SIAM (m) Est. 1974
60 Mansion 4, Rajadumnoenklang Ave.
Tel: (66-2) 2226129
Circ.—140,000
Prop.—Sakorn Siam Co. Ltd.
Dir.—Sompojana Kyayatanakij
Pub./Ed.—Santi Ontrakran

KHAO PANICH (Daily Trade News) (d) Thai
22/27 Ratchadapisek Rd.
Tel: (66-2) 5115066
Circ.—30,000
Prop.—Department of Communication Relations
Prop.—Ministry of Commerce
Pub./Ed.—Somsak Rakansuk

KHOA SOD DAILY NEWSPAPER (d)
12 Tethsaban-naremern Rd., Prachanivate 1, 10900
Tel: (66-2) 5800021; Fax: (66-2) 5899112
Circ.—120,000
Prop.—Koam Kome Co. Ltd.

KIATTIYOS (m)
25 Prachathiprathai Rd.
Circ.—5,000
Pub./Ed.—Phajon Pinthuyothin

KROHLEK (e)
499/9 Petchburi Rd., Ratchthevi, Phyathai, 4

Circ.—8,000
Pub./Ed.—Sangwian Soodrak

KRUNGTHEB VICHARN (m)
1111-2 Soi Thinnakorn, Phyathai Rd.
Circ.—1,500
Pub./Ed.—Kongkiat Na Ranong

MATICHON DAILY NEWSPAPER (m) Est. 1978
12 Thedsaban Naruban Rd., Prachanivej 1, Bangkhen, 10900
Tel: (66-2) 5800021; Fax: (66-2) 5899112
Circ.—280,000
Prop.—Matichon Co. Ltd.
Pub.—Ruengchai Supniran
Ed.—Wipa Sukit
Ad. Mgr.—Narong Joonjuasuparerk

MORNING EXPRESS (m) English
242 Ammuay Songkram Rd.
Circ.—10,000
Prop.—The Press Express Co. Ltd.
Dir./Ed.—Usum Nimmanhemindra

NAEW NA (d) Thai
96 Mooh 7, Vibhavadi Rangsit Rd., 2, 10210
Tel: (66-2) 5214647/(66-2) 5215121; Fax: (66-2) 5523880
Circ.—250,000
Prop.—Naewna Newspaper Co. Ltd.
Ed.—Saner Thanadsorn
Ad. Mgr.—Jariya Pulserivong

THE NATION (m) English; Est. 1971
44 Moo 10, Bangna-Trat Rd., Km. 4.5, 10260
Tel: (66-2) 3170420; Fax: (66-2) 3171384
Circ.—58,000
Prop.—Nation Publishing Group
Pub.—Thanachai Tuanglaktham
Ed.—Thepchai Yong
Ad. Mgr.—Sutee Poonsriratt
U.S. Rep.—AdMarket Int'l.

NEW CHINESE DAILY NEWS (m) Chinese; Est. 1974
1022-30 Charoen Krung Rd., Talad Noi
Tel: (66-2) 2340684
Circ.—72,000
Prop.—Talad-Noi Co. Ltd.
Dir.—Kriet Leephone
Ed.—Niyom Pracharkamol
Ad. Mgr.—Phanem Than-Thonr

PALANG CHON (m)
275 Krungthep-Nonth
Tel: (66-2) 5859852
Circ.—2,000
Prop.—Upparaoh Vachareeboon
Pub./Ed.—Phoomchai Inthapanti

PHAYA CRUT (m) Est. 1976
72 Soi Woranpong Samsen Rd.
Circ.—100,000
Pub.—Wandee Thongprapa
Ed.—Wason Thonvisud

PIMTHAI (m) Est. 1978
163/54 Phrapinklao
Tel: (66-2) 4335997
Circ.—10,000
Prop.—Tana Sakdi Panit Co.
Pub./Ed.—Chamnong Khumpairoj

PRACHA CHANG DAILY NEWS (d)
861 New Rd., 10100

Prop.—Prachachang Press
Pub.—Preeda Hetrakool

SAI KLANG (e)
163 Phrapinklao
Tel: (66-2) 4337787
Circ.—10,000
Pub./Ed.—Suvit Phadermchit

SIAM POST (m) Est. 1992
13 Na Ranong Rd., 10110
Tel: (66-2) 2403700; Fax: (66-2) 2403790/(66-2) 2403791
Circ.—60,000 ABC
Prop.—The Post Publishing Co. Ltd.
Ed.—Paisal Sricharutchanya
Ad. Mgr.—Laddaval Ratanwongse
U.S. Rep.—Trade Media Int'l. Corp.

SIAM RATH (e) Est. 1950
6/F 12 Rajdamnern Ave.
Tel: (66-2) 2219593; Fax: (66-2) 2241982
Circ.—85,000
Prop.—Siam Rath Co. Ltd.
Dir.—Rayoon Chindasilpa
Ed.—Sambat Pookarn
Ad. Mgr.—Narong Pumee

SIAM TIMES (m) Thai
192/8-9 Soi Voraphong, Visuthikasat Rd.
Tel: (66-2) 2817422
Circ.—5,000
Pub.—Nerong Charusophon

SIANG PUANG CHON (Voice of the People) (m)
52/3-8 Banpanthom Lane, Prasumen
Tel: (66-2) 2811076
Circ.—93,000
Prop.—Kampol Piriyalert
Dir./Ed.—Ruang-nan Ruang-Vooth

SING SIAN YIT PAO DAILY NEWS (m) Chinese; Est. 1950
267 New Rd., 10100
Tel: (66-2) 2250070; Fax: (66-2) 2254663
Circ.—80,000
Prop.—Sin Poh (Thailand) Ltd.
Pub.—Lee Santipongchai
Ed.—Tawee Yodpetch
Ad. Mgr.—Niramol Ditamrungkul

SIRINAKORN (m) Chinese; Est. 1969
108 Suapa Rd.
Tel: (66-2) 2214182; Fax: (66-2) 2254073
Circ.—80,000
Prop.—Sirinakorn Co. Ltd.
Dir.—Prasert Areeves
Ed.—Prasil Sirivareeves

TAWAN SIAM (m) Est. 1976
72 Soi Worapong, Samsen Rd.
Circ.—97,000
Dir.—Wandee Thongprapa
Ed.—Charlerm Siboonrveng

TEP SIAM (m)
120 Charoen Krung Rd.
Circ.—2,000
Pub./Ed.—Angun Saardsaengthong

THAI (m) Thai
423-425 Chao Khamrop Rd.
Tel: (66-2) 2233175
Circ.—4,000
Pub./Ed.—Kris Leemakkadej

THAI CHONG DAILY NEWS (m) Chinese
970/31 Charoen Krung, Talad Noi
Circ.—10,000
Prop.—New Tiger Mass Media Co. Ltd.
Pub./Ed.—Arunee Ammarjbundit

THAI RATH (m) Thai; Est. 1958
1 Vibhavadi Rangsit Rd., 10900
Tel: (66-2) 2710217; Fax: (66-2) 2797988/(66-2) 2797989
Circ.—700,000
Prop.—Vacharaphol Co. Ltd.
Ed.—Paitoon Soontorn
Ad. Dir.—Yinglak Vacharaphol

THAI SHANG YIG PAO (e) Chinese
877-879 Charoen Krung Rd., 10100
Tel: (66-2) 2369172/(66-2) 2369176; Fax: (66-2) 2385286
Circ.—85,000
Ed.—Chart Payonitikarn
Ad. Mgr.—Samnuk Kyayatanokij

TONG HUA DAILY NEWS (m) Chinese
877-9 New Rd.
Tel: (66-2) 2360144
Circ.—50,000
Dir.—Sakorn Kyavatanaki
Ed.—Chart Payonitikarn

UNIVERSAL DAILY NEWS (m) Chinese; Est. 1955
21/1 New Rd.
Tel: (66-2) 2264849/(66-2) 2213411; Fax: (66-2) 2244745/(66-2) 2255352
Circ.—25,000
Prop.—United Daily News Group
Ed.—Lin Wen In
Mktg. Dir.—H C Yang

VISNEWS (d) Thai
72 Soi Vorapong, Samson Rd.
Tel: (66-2) 2820643

VIETNAM
Pop. Est. 73,103,898

HANOI
Pop. Est. (Metro Area) 4,000,000

HANOI MOI (New Hanoi) (d) French; Est. 1976
44 Le Thai To Ave.
Tel: (84-4) 255880
Prop.—Hanoi Committee of the Communist Party
Ed.—Hong Linh

NHAN DAN (The People) (d) Est. 1951
71 Hang Trong St.
Tel: (84-4) 255673
Circ.—300,000
Prop.—The Communist Party
Ed.—Hoang Tung

QUAN DOI NHAN DAN (People's Army) (d) Est. 1950
7 Phan Dinh Phung St.
Tel: (84-4) 254788
Circ.—150,000
Prop.—Army of Vietnam

HO CHI MINH CITY

GIAI PHONG (Liberation) (d) Est. 1975
432 Xo Viet Nghe Tink St.
Tel: (84-8) 325351
Circ.—45,000
Prop.—National Front
Ed.—Nguyen Tuat Viet

NEWSPAPERS OF THE CARIBBEAN REGION

ANGUILLA, B.W.I.
(Dependency of United Kingdom)
Pop. Est. 7,052

THE VALLEY
Pop. Est. 1,042

THE VANTAGE NEWSPAPER English; Est. 1987
PO Box 72
Prop.—Union Communications Network Ltd.
Ed./Ad. Mgr.—James Fleming
(This newspaper is also distributed in St. Thomas & U.S. Virgin Islands.)

ANTIGUA AND BARBUDA
Pop. Est. 64,762

ST. JOHN'S
Pop. Est. 36,000

THE NATION
Cnr. Factory Road & Carnival Gardens
Tel: (809) 4620010
Prop.—Government of Antigua (Information Dept.)
Ed.—George Joseph

OUTLET Est. 1968
McKinnons; PO Box 493
Tel: (809) 4624453; Fax: (809) 4620438
Cir.—5,000

Prop.—Outlet Publishers
Ed.—Tim Hector
Ad. Mgr.—Cicely James
U.S. Rep.—AdMarket Int'l.; Charney/Palacios & Co. Inc.

SENTINEL
Saint Mary St.; PO Box 270
Tel: (809) 4625000; Fax: (809) 4624211/(809) 4624084
Prop.—Sentinel Printing & Publishing Ltd.
Ed.—Norman (Gus) Thomas

WHAT'S HAPPENING
Lower Redcliffe St.; PO Box 1477
Tel: (809) 4621918
Prop.—BB & B International

THE WORKER'S VOICE
46 North St.; PO Box 670
Tel: (809) 4620090
Circ.—2,000
Prop.—Antigua Trades & Labour Union
Ed.—Hyacinth Walter

ARUBA
Pop. Est. 65,545

ORANJESTAD
Pop. Est. 17,210

AMIGOE (Friend) (6x wk.) Dutch
Caya Gilberto; PO Box 323
Tel: (297-8) 24333; Fax: (297-8) 22368
Circ.—13,000
Prop.—Uitgeverij Amigoe Aruba NV
Ed.—Jos van der Schoot
(There is an edition of Amigoe in Willemstad, Netherlands Antilles.)

THE ARUBA GAZETTE (6x wk.) English
Dakota Shopping Paradise Fergusonstraat

Circ.—3,000
Pub.—Edvin Irausquin
ARUBA TODAY/BON DIA ARUBA (6x wk.) English & Papiamento
Weststratt 22
Tel: (297-8) 27800; Fax: (297-8) 27044/ (297-8) 27093
Circ.—10,000
Prop.—Caribbean Speed Printing
BEURS EN NIEUSBERICHT (6x wk.) Dutch
PO Box 566
Tel: (297-8) 9624681
Circ.—1,100
Prop.—CDUM
Ed.—E Lacle
EL DIARIO (The Daily) (d-ex S) Papiamento; Est. 1976
Engelandstratt 29; PO Box 577
Tel: (297-8) 26747; Fax: (297-8) 28551
Circ.—17,000
Ed.—Jossy Mansur
Ad. Mgr.—Aureen Werleman
U.S. Rep.—Charney/Palacios & Co. Inc.
EXTRA (6x wk.) Papiamento
Margrietstraat, No. 3
Prop.—Extra Productions-Curacao
Ed.—Victor Winklaar
MATUTINO CORANT (Morning Courant) (6x wk.) Papiamento
Newtonstraat, No. 14
Circ.—4,000
Pub.—Albertico Arends
Ed.—Stanley Arends
MATUTINO DI NOS (6x wk.) Papiamento
J. G. Emanstraat, No. 68
Circ.—3,000
Pub./Ed.—Jacobo Arends
MERIDIANO (Meridian) (6x wk.) Papiamento
Wilhelminastraat, No. 88
Circ.—3,600
Pub.—Jossy Mansur
Ed.—Jubi Naar
THE NEWS (5x wk.) English; Est. 1951
Italiestraat, No. 5; PO Box 300
Tel: (297-8) 24725; Fax: (297-8) 26125
Circ.—10,000
Pub.—Sir Gerry J Schouten
Ed.—B Blanchard
U.S. Rep.—AdMarket Int'l.; Charney/Palacios & Co. Inc.
LA PRENSA (The Press) (6x wk.) Papiamento
Bachstraat, No. 6
Tel: (297-8) 962486
Circ.—4,500
Prop.—Uitgeverij de Pers NV
Ed.—Tom Pietersz
Ed.—Harold Faro
ULTIMO NOTICIA (Last News) (6x wk.)
Papiamento
Dominicanessenstraat, No. 17
Tel: (297-8) 96244
Circ.—2,000
Prop.—Aruba Independent Press Service
Ed.—Norma Erasmus

POS CKIKITO
Pop. Est. 400

NOBO ARUBA (6x wk.) Papiamento
Pos Chikito, No. 3-D
Tel: (297-8) 9673500
Circ.—1,500
Prop.—ABC Informa NV
Ed.—Meredith Carrion-Koolman

BAHAMAS
Pop. Est. 273,055

FREEPORT
Pop. Est. 41,035

THE FREEPORT NEWS (e-5x wk.) Est. 1961
Grand Bahama; PO Box F-7
Tel: (809) 3528321; Fax: (809) 3528324
Circ.—6,000
Gen. Mgr.—Debra S Dames
Ed.—Oswald T Brown
Ad. Mgr.—Joseph Major
U.S. Rep.—The Nassau Guardian Ltd.

NASSAU
Pop. Est. 171,502

THE INTERNATIONAL TRIBUNE (tues.-sat.) Est. 1993
Shirley St.; PO Box N-3207
Tel: (809) 3221986; Fax: (809) 3282398
Circ.—15,000
Prop.—The Tribune Ltd.
Pub./Ed.—Eileen Dupuch Carron
U.S. Rep.—The Cal Hart Co.

THE NASSAU GUARDIAN (m-ex S) Est. 1844
Oakesfield; PO Box N-3011
Tel: (809) 3235654; Fax: (809) 3253379
Circ.—16,500
Prop.—The Nassau Guardian Ltd.
Pub.—Kenneth N Francis
Ed.—Christopher Symonette
Ad. Mgr.—Frederick C Sturrup
U.S. Rep.—AdMarket Int'l.; The N DeFilippes Corp.
THE NASSAU TRIBUNE (e-ex S) Est. 1903
Shirley St.; PO Box N-3207
Tel: (809) 3221986; Fax: (809) 3282398
Circ.—13,500
Pub./Ed.—Eileen Dupuch Carron
Gen. Mgr.—Robert Carron

BARBADOS
Pop. Est. 255,827

BRIDGETOWN
Pop. Est. 90,000

BARBADOS ADVOCATE/SUNDAY ADVOCATE-NEWS (mS) Est. 1895
Fontabelle, St. Michael; PO Box 230
Tel: (809) 4261210; Fax: (809) 4297045
Circ.—15,000 (m); 21,000 (S) ABC
Prop.—The Advocate Co. Ltd.
Ed.—E Smith
Ad. Mgr.—Sandra Clarke
U.S. Rep.—AdMarket Int'l.
THE DAILY NATION/THE WEEKEND NATION/THE SUNDAY SUN (m) Est. 1973
Nation House, Fontabelle, St. Michael
Tel: (809) 4366240; Fax: (809) 4276968
Circ.—32,000 (m); 41,000 (fri.); 52,000 (S) ABC
Prop.—The Nation Publishing Co.
Pub.—Harold Hoyte
Ed.-(Sun)—Roxanne Gibbs
Ad. Dir.—Wilfred Field
U.S. Rep.—Charney/Palacios & Co. Inc.

BERMUDA
Pop. Est. 61,158

HAMILTON
Pop. Est. 2,000

BERMUDA SUN Est. 1964
41 Victoria St.; PO Box HM 1241
Tel: (809) 2953902; Fax: (809) 2925597
Circ.—12,500 ABC
Prop.—Bermuda Sun Ltd.
Pub./Ad. Mgr.—Randolph French
Ed.—Tom Vesey
U.S. Rep.—AdMarket Int'l.
BERMUDA TIMES Est. 1987
Arcade Bldg., 9 Burnaby St.; PO Box HM 12
Tel: (809) 2922596
Circ.—6,000
Prop.—Bermuda Times Ltd.
Pub.—Ewart F Brown
Ed.—K Murray Brown
Ad. Mgr.—Rennie Rowling
ROYAL GAZETTE/MID OCEAN NEWS (m) Est. 1828/1925
2-Par-La-Ville Rd.; PO Box 1025
Tel: (809) 2955881/(809) 2956666; Fax: (809) 2959813
Circ.—18,800 (Gazette); 13,000 (News) ABC
Prop.—Bermuda Press (Holdings) Ltd.
Pub.—Keith R Jensen
Ed.-(Gazette)—David L White
Ed.-(News)—Tim Hoogson
Ad. Mgr./Ad. Dir.—Gary L Ritchie
U.S. Rep.—Charney/Palacios & Co. Inc.

CAYMAN ISLANDS
(Dependency of the United Kingdom)
Pop. Est. 31,790

GEORGE TOWN
(Grand Cayman)
Pop. Est. 10,000
Pop. Est. (Grand Cayman) 27,500

CAYMANIAN COMPASS (m-5x wk.) Est. 1965
Grand Cayman; PO Box 1365
Tel: (809) 9495111; Fax: (809) 9497033

Circ.—8,500
Prop.—Cayman Free Press Ltd.
Pub.—Brian Uzzell
Ed.—Ursula Gill
Ad. Mgr.—Betty Smith

CUBA
Pop. Est. 11,064,344

BAYAMO

LA DEMAJAGUA (d)
Amado Estévez y Calle 10, Reparto Roberto Reyes
Tel: 42720/43635
Circ.—10,000
Dir.—Pedro Mora Estrada

CAMAGUEY
Pop. Est. 260,782

ADELANTE (Forward) (m-ex mon.) Est. 1959
Avda. A. Repart Ayama
Tel: 71313/71114
Circ.—26,000
Dir.—Armando Boudet Gómez

CIEGO DE AVILA

EL INVASOR (d)
Avda. de Los Deportes s/n Plaza Ubel Santamaría
Tel: 28525/25125
Circ.—7,000
Dir.—Migdalia Utrera Peña

CIENFUEGOS

CINCO DE SEPTIEMBRE (5th of September)
Poligráfico Calle 63 y Circunvalación, Reparto Pueblo, Fraffo
Tel: 22636
Circ.—15,000
Dir.—Francisco Valdés Petitón

GUANTANAMO

VENCEREMOS (d)
Avda. Regine Botti, No. 715, N. López y J. del Sol
Tel: 34040
Circ.—10,000
Dir.—Carlos Manuel Barruecos Ríos

HAVANA
Pop. Est. 2,013,746

GRANMA (mS) Est. 1965
Avda. General Suarez y Calle Territorial, Plaza de la Revolución, José Marti, 6260
Tel: 813333; Fax: 53733
Circ.—675,000
Prop.—Official Organization of the Communist Party of Cuba
Dir.—Frank Agüero
(This newspaper is nationally distributed.)
LOS TRABAJADORES (The Workers) (d)
Territorial Esquina a General Suárez, Plaza de la Revolución, 10698
Tel: 7790819
Circ.—120,000
Prop.—Sindicatos de Cuba
Dir.—Jorge Luis Canela Aurana
TRIBUNA (Tribune) (d)
Avda. General Suárez y Calle Territorial, Plaza de la Revolución
Tel: 7790050
Circ.—60,000

HOLGUIN
Pop. Est. 194,728

AHORA (Now) (d)
Carretera San Germán y Circunvalación, Zona de Desarrollo Industrial
Tel: 442466/425707
Circ.—22,000
Dir.—Rodobaldo Martinez Pérez

ISLA DE LA JUVENTUD

VICTORIA (Victory) (d)
Piligráfico Carretera La Fey, Km. 1 1/2, Nueva Gerona
Tel: 24868/24879

Circ.—9,000
Dir.—Pedro Gerardo Casanova Hernández

MATANZAS

GIRON (d)
Avda. Camilo Cienfuegos, 10505 Pueblo Nuevo
Tel: 5657/5442
Circ.—25,000
Dir.—Othoniel González Quevedo

PINAR DEL RIO

GUERRILLERO (d)
Avda. Colon Delicias, 4 Adela Azcuy
Tel: 5516/2623
Circ.—21,000
Dir.—Olga Crespo Porben

SANCTI SPIRITUS

ESCAMBRAY (d)
Avda. del Castillo, No. 10, Avda. de los Mártires y Tello Sánchez
Tel: 23047
Circ.—10,000
Dir.—Cristóbal Alamo Pérez

SANTA CLARA
Pop. Est. 178,278

VANGUARDIA (Vanguard) (d)
Calle Céspedes, No. 6, Placido y Maceo
Tel: 27103
Circ.—24,000
Dir.—Alberto Lázaro Peña Gareia

SANTIAGO DE CUBA
Pop. Est. 358,764

SIERRA MAESTRA (d)
Combinado Poligráfico, Plaza de la Revolución Antonio Maceo
Tel: 22504
Circ.—25,000
Dir.—Arnaldo Clavel Carmenaty

TUNAS

VEINTISEIS (Twenty Six) (d)
Avda. Carlos J. Finlay s/n Las Tunas
Tel: 42950/43573
Circ.—6,400
Dir.—Ramiro Segura García

DOMINICA
Pop. Est. 87,696

ROSEAU
Pop. Est. 20,000

DOMINICA OFFICIAL GAZETTE English
Prop.—Gov't. Printing
THE NEW CHRONICLE English; Est. 1909
Queen Mary St.; PO Box 124
Tel: (809) 4482121
Circ.—4,500

DOMINICAN REPUBLIC
Pop. Est. 7,826,075

SAN PEDRO de MACORIS
Pop. Est. 111,517

EL DIARIO de MACORIS (Macoris Daily) Est. 1922
Pub.—Nestor Febles

SANTIAGO DE LOS CABALLEROS
Pop. Est. 500,000

LA INFORMACION (The Information) (e) Est. 1915
Carretera Licey Km. 3, Santiago de Los Caballeros
Tel: (809) 5811915; Fax: (809) 5817770
Circ.—15,000
Prop.—Impresora del Yagua
Pub.—L Enrique Franco
U.S. Rep.—AdMarket Int'l.; The N DeFilippes Corp.

Dominican Republic — Caribbean

SANTO DOMINGO
Pop. Est. 2,200,000

EL CARIBE (The Caribbean) (m-ex S) Est. 1948
Autopista Duarte, Km. 7 1/2; Apdo. Postal 416
Tel: (809) 5668161; Fax: (809) 5444003
Circ.—75,300
Prop.—Editoria del Caribe, C por A
Dir.—German E Ornes
Ch. Ed.—Antonio Gil
Ad. Mgr.—Virgilio Ortiz Bush
U.S. Rep.—Charney/Palacios & Co. Inc.; AdMarket Int'l.

DIARIO LAS AMERICAS (American Daily) (d)
Avda. Tiradentes
Tel: (809) 5664577

HOY (Today) (m-ex S) Est. 1981
Avda. San Martin, No. 236
Tel: (809) 5416779; Fax: (809) 5675915
Circ.—54,000
Prop.—Editora Hoy, C por A
Dir./Ed.—Mario Alvarez Dugan
U.S. Rep.—Charney/Palacios & Co. Inc.

LA INFORMACION (The Information)
Maximo Gómez, No. 16-18
Tel: (809) 5837281

LISTIN DIARIO (mS) Est. 1889
Apartado 1455
Tel: (809) 6866688; Fax: (809) 6823237
Circ.—68,000 (m); 68,000 (S)
Prop.—Editora Listin Diario, C por A
Dir.—Francisco Comarazamy
Gen. Mgr.—Pedro Gañan
Ed.—Rafael Herrera
U.S. Rep.—Charney/Palacios & Co. Inc.; The N DeFilippes Corp.

EL NACIONAL (The National) (m) Est. 1966
Avda. San Martin; Apdo. Postal 1402
Tel: (809) 5655581; Fax: (809) 5175915
Circ.—56,000
Prop.—Publicaciones Ahora Sepora
Dir.—Radhames Gómez Pepin
Ad. Mgr.—Rafael A Reyes Bisono
U.S. Rep.—AdMarket International; Charney/Palacios & Co. Inc.; The N DeFilippes Corp.

LA NOTICIA (The News) (eS) Est. 1973
Calle Julio Verne, Nos. 14 y 16
Tel: (809) 6873131
Circ.—15,000
Prop.—Editora La Razón
Dir.—Dr. Miguel Angel Prestol
Ch. Ed.—José Rafael Vargas
Ad. Mgr.—B Bueno Torres

EL NUEVO DIARIO (The New Daily) (d) Est. 1981
Avda. Francia, No. 41
Circ.—10,000
Pub.—Persio Caro
Ed.—Pedro Caro

SANTO DOMINGO NEWS
Zona 2; Apdo. Postal 106
Tel: (809) 5321333

EL SIGLO (The Sign) (d-5x wk.) Est. 1989
Calle San Anton, No. 2, Zona Industrial de Herrera
Tel: (809) 5441000; Fax: (809) 5474797
Prop.—Editorial Golfo
Dir.—Bienvenido Alvarez Vega
Ed. in Ch.—Alejandro Paniagua
Ad. Mgr.—Manuel Fco Santana

EL SOL (The Sun) (m) Est. 1971
Carretera Sánchez, Km. 6 1/2
Tel: (809) 5329511
Circ.—16,000
Prop.—Editora El Pais, C por A
Gen. Dir.—Miguel Angel Cedeno
Ch. Ed.—Manuel Figueroa

ULTIMA HORA (Last Hour) (e) Est. 1970
Paseo de Los Periodístas, No. 52; Apdo. Postal 1455
Tel: (809) 6883361; Fax: (809) 6866594
Circ.—50,000
Prop.—Editora Ultima Hora, C por A
Pub.—Rogelio Arpuro Pellerano R
Dir.—Ruddy Gonzalez
Gen. Mgr.—Pedro Gañan
Ad. Mgr.—Natividad Goyco
U.S. Rep.—AdMarket Int'l.; Charney/Palacios & Co. Inc.

GRENADA
Pop. Est. 94,109

ST. GEORGE'S
Pop. Est. 6,000

GOVERNMENT GAZETTE English
Prime Minister's Office

THE GRENADIAN VOICE English; Est. 1982
PO Box 3; Tel: (809) 1498
Prop.—Spice Island Printers
Ed.—Leslie Pierre

THE INFORMER English; Est. 1984
Market Hill, St. George's
Tel: (809) 1530
Ed.—Carla Briggs

GUADELOUPE
(Overseas Department of France)
Pop. Est. 428,947

POINTE-A-PITRE
(On Grande Terre Island)
Pop. Est. 157,000

FRANCE-ANTILLES (d) French
Rue Paul Lacave; Boite Postal 658, 97169
Tel: (590) 902525; Fax: (590) 917831
Circ.—65,000 (total-all eds.); 35,000 (Guadeloupe ed.)
Dir.—Philippe Hersant
(Circulation is the total of all France-Antilles editions. See Martinique.)

HAITI
Pop. Est. 6,491,450

PORT-AU-PRINCE
Pop. Est. 790,000

LE MATIN (m-ex mon.) French; Est. 1907
33, rue du Quai; PO Box 367
Tel: (509) 122040
Circ.—30,000
Pub.—Clement Magloire
Ad. Mgr.—Frank Magloire

LE NOUVELLISTE (e) French; Est. 1896
198, rue du Centre; PO Box 1013
Tel: (509) 122114
Circ.—5,500
Pub.—Max Chauvet
Ad. Mgr.—Mrs. Max Chauvet

L' UNION (d)
Ave. Pie, No. XII
Circ.—7,000
Dir.—Pierre Clitandre

PANORAMA (6x wk.) Est. 1956
27 rue du Peuple
Circ.—1,500
Pub./Ed.—Paul Blanchet

JAMAICA
Pop. Est. 2,500,064

KINGSTON
Pop. Est. (Metro Area) 850,000

DAILY GLEANER/SUNDAY GLEANER (mS) Est. 1834
7 North St.; PO Box 40
Tel: (809) 9227727; Fax: (809) 9222058
Circ.—50,000 (m); 100,000 (S)
Prop.—The Gleaner Co. Ltd.
Mng. Dir.—Oliver F Clarke
Ed.—Ken Allen
Ad. Mgr.—Leon Mitchell
U.S. Rep.—AdMarket Int'l.; Charney/Palacios & Co. Inc.

THE JAMAICA HERALD (d)
29 Molynes Rd.
Tel: (809) 9687723; Fax: (809) 9687722
Chmn.—Neville Blythe
Mng. Ed.—Franklyn McKnight

THE DAILY STAR/THE THURSDAY STAR (e) Est. 1951
7 North St.; PO Box 40
Tel: (809) 9225375; Fax: (809) 9222058
Circ.—45,000 (mon.; tues.; wed. & sat.); 60,000 (thurs.)
Prop.—The Gleaner Co. Ltd.
Mng. Dir.—Oliver F Clarke
Ed.—Dudley Stokes
Ad. Mgr.—Leon Mitchell

MARTINIQUE
(Overseas Department of France)
Pop. Est. 392,362

FORT-DE-FRANCE
Pop. Est. 101,540

AUJOURD'HUI DIMANCHE French
Ave. Frantz Fanon, Presbytere de Bellevue, 97200
Circ.—6,000
Dir.—Fr. Pere Gauthier

FRANCE-ANTILLES (d) French
Place de Stalingrad; Boite Postal 577, 97200
Circ.—30,000
Dir.—Philippe Hersant
Ed. in Ch.—Henry Mangatalle
(There is an edition of France-Antilles in Guadeloupe.)

MONTSERRAT, B.W.I.
(Dependency of United Kingdom)
Pop. Est. 12,701

PLYMOUTH
Pop. Est. 1,110

MONTSERRAT NEWS English; Est. 1991
PO Box 888
Tel: (809) 4918888
Circ.—1,500
Owner/Ed.—J D Fenton

MONTSERRAT REPORTER English; Est. 1985
Parliament St., N.D.P. Headquarters; PO Box 215
Tel: (809) 4913600
Circ.—1,200
Prop.—National Development Party
Ed.—Dave Fenton

NETHERLANDS ANTILLES
Pop. Est. 185,790

ST. MAARTEN

THE CHRONICLE (m) English; Est. 1985
Groundove Rd., Point Blanch; PO Box 488
Circ.—3,000
Prop.—A&R Publishing Co. NV
Pub.—Roger F Snow
Ed.—Mary J Hellmund
Ad. Mgr.—Irene Morris
(This newspaper is distributed in several countries of the northeastern Caribbean.)

THE NEWS (m-5x wk.) English; Est. 1951
Italiestraat, No. 5
Circ.—7,500
Prop.—Oranjestad Printing
Pub.—G J Schouten
Ed.—B Bennett
(Circulation figure combines with Amigoe Di Curacao in Willemstad.)

WILLEMSTAD
(Curacao)
Pop. Est. (Curacao) 160,000

AMIGOE DI CURACAO (Friend of Curacao) (e)
Papiamento; Est. 1884
Schepenheuvel ZN; PO Box 577
Tel: (599-9) 672000
Circ.—7,500
Prop.—Uitgeverij Amigoe NV
Dir.—F H Oduber
Ed. in Ch.—Frans Heiligers
Ad. Mgr.—Ingrid de Maayer
(There is an edition of Amigoe in Oranjestad, Aruba. Also, circulation figure combines with the News in St. Maarten.)

BEURS & NIEUWSBERICHTEN (e) Dutch; Est. 1934
W.I. Compagniestraat, No. 41; PO Box 215
Tel: (599-9) 626333; Fax: (599-9) 628411
Circ.—10,000
Prop.—Uitgeverij Druckerij Curacao NV
Ed.—Lauren Setenk
Ad. Mgr.—Ronny Zalm
U.S. Rep.—Charney/Palacios & Co. Inc.

EXTRA (d-ex S) Papiamento
W.I. Compagniestraat, No. 41; PO Box 3011
Circ.—23,000
U.S. Rep.—Extra Productions NV

NOBO (d-ex S) Papiamento
PO Box 323
Tel: (599-9) 673500
Circ.—12,000
Prop.—Rotoprint NV
Pub.—Carlos Daantje
Ad. Mgr.—Madeline Van Eps
U.S. Rep.—AdMarket Int'l.

LA PRENSA (m-ex S) Papiamento; Est. 1928
W.I. Compagniestraat, No. 41
Tel: (599-9) 623850; Fax: (599-9) 625983
Circ.—14,000
Prop.—Uitgeverij De Pers NV
Pub.—R Irausquin
Ed.—August Jonckheer
Ad. Mgr.—K Irausquin

PUERTO RICO
Pop. Est. 3,801,977

SAN JUAN
Pop. Est. 437,745

EL NUEVO DIA (The New Day) (mS) Est. 1909
PO Box 297, 00902-0297
Tel: (809) 7937070; Fax: (809) 7938850
Circ.—220,000 (m); 231,000 (S)
Prop.—El Dia Inc.
Pres.—Antonio Luís Ferre
Vice Pres.—Luis G Gonzales Esteves
Dir./Ed.—Jesus (Chu) García
Ad. Mgr.—Manuel González
U.S. Rep.—AdMarket Int'l.; Charney/Palacios & Co. Inc.

PERIODICO CLARIDAD (Clarity Newspaper)
1899 Avda. Ponce De Leon, Santurce, 00909
Tel: (809) 7265221
Dir.—Manolo Coss

THE SAN JUAN STAR (m) Est. 1959
GPO Box 4187, 00936-4187
Tel: (809) 7824200; Fax: (809) 7835788
Circ.—46,000 (m); 58,000 (thurs.)
Prop.—Scripps-Howard
Pub.—Adolfo Comos-Baccardi
Dir./Gen. Mgr.—John A Zebre Jr
Ed.—Andrew Viglucci
Ad. Dir.—Tony Martinez
U.S. Rep.—Charney/Palacios & Co. Inc.

EL VOCERO DE PUERTO RICO (The Voice of Puerto Rico) (m-ex S) Est. 1974
Old San Juan; PO Box 3831, 00902-3831
Tel: (809) 7212300; Fax: (809) 7232845
Circ.—262,000 ABC
Prop.—Caribbean International News Corp.
Pub./Ed.—Gasper Roca
Vice Pres.—Alfredo Arias
Ed. in Ch.—Cruz Roque Vicens
U.S. Rep.—AdMarket Int'l.; The N DeFilippes Corp.

ST. KITTS AND NEVIS
Pop. Est. 40,671

BASSETERRE
(St. Kitts)
Pop. Est. 18,500

DEMOCRAT Est. 1948
Canyon St.; PO Box 30
Circ.—3,500
Ed.—FitzRoy P Jones
U.S. Rep.—AdMarket Int'l.; Charney/Palacios & Co. Inc.

THE LABOUR SPOKESMAN Est. 1957
PO Box 239
Tel: (809) 4652229; Fax: (809) 4655519
Circ.—6,000
Prop.—St. Kitts-Nevis Trades & Labour Union
Ed.—Dawud Modada
Ad. Mgr.—Walfor Gumbs

ST. LUCIA
Pop. Est. 145,090

CASTRIES
Pop. Est. 72,878

CRUSADER Est. 1970
19 St. Louis St.
Tel: (809) 22203
Circ.—4,000
Ed.—George Odlum
ST. LUCIA STAR English; Est. 1987
PO Box 1146
Circ.—6,000
Prop.—The Star Publishing Co. Ltd.
Owner/Pub./Ed.—Rick Wayne
Owner/Mng. Dir.—Mae Sabbagh
U.S. Rep.—AdMarket Int'l.
VOICE OF SAINT LUCIA English; Est. 1882
Odessa Bldg., Darling Rd.; PO Box 104
Tel: (809) 4522590; Fax: (809) 4531453
Circ.—15,000
Ed.—Guy Ellis
Ad. Mgr.—Simone Gustave
U.S. Rep.—AdMarket Int'l.;
Charney/Palacios & Co. Inc.

ST. PIERRE & MIQUELON
(Overseas Department of France, near Canada)
Pop. Est. 6,704

SAINT-PIERRE
Pop. Est. 5,415

L'ECHO des CAPS French
Mairie de Saint-Pierre
Circ.—1,850
Dir.—Albert Pen
Dir—Nadege LeSenechal
Ed.—Didier Gil

TRINIDAD AND TOBAGO
Pop. Est. 1,344,639

BARATARIA

SUNDAY PUNCH
9th Ave. & 9th St.
Tel: (809) 6741692; Fax: (809) 6743228
Circ.—44,000
Prop.—T&T Newspaper Publishing Group
Pub.—Daniel Chookolingo
Ed.—R Shah
Ad. Mgr.—W Carpenter
TNT MIRROR Est. 1982
9th Ave. & 9th St.
Tel: (809) 6741692; Fax: (809) 6743228
Circ.—73,000 (total)
Prop.—T&T Newspaper Publishing Group
Pub.—Daniel Chookolingo
Ed.—Sherperd Ali
Ad. Mgr.—W Carpenter

CUREPE

THE BOMB
Southern Main Rd. & Clifford St.
THE WEEKEND HEAT
Southern Main Rd. & Clifford St.

PORT-OF-SPAIN

EVENING NEWS (e-5x wk.) Est. 1917
PO Box 122
Tel: (809) 6238870/(809) 6238879; Fax: (809) 6257211
Circ.—33,739
Prop.—Trinidad Publishing Co. Ltd.
Ed.—Lenn Chongsing
Ad. Mgr.—Dennis Cumming
U.S. Rep.—Charney/Palacios & Co. Inc.
NEWSDAY (d) Est. 1993
19-21 Chacon St.
Tel: (809) 6234929; Fax: (809) 6258362
Circ.—25,000
Prop.—Daily News Ltd.
TRINIDAD EXPRESS/SUNDAY EXPRESS (mS)
English; Est. 1967
35 Independence Sq.; PO Box 1252
Tel: (809) 6231711; Fax: (809) 6271451
Circ.—51,000 (m); 56,000 (S)
Prop.—Caribbean Communications Network
Pub.—Kenneth Gordon
Ed.—Keith Smith
Ad. Mgr.—James Persaud
TRINIDAD GUARDIAN/SUNDAY GUARDIAN (mS)
English; Est. 1917
22 Saint Vincent St.; PO Box 122
Tel: (809) 6238870; Fax: (809) 6257211

Central America **Costa Rica** IV-87

Circ.—46,764 (m); 60,042 (S)
Prop.—Trinidad Publishing Co. Ltd.
Pub.—Mark A Conyers
Ed.—Jones P Madeira
Ad. Mgr.—Dennis Cumming
U.S. Rep.—AdMarket Int'l.; Charney/Palacios & Co. Inc.

SAN JUAN

THE BLAST
Hingoo Lands
Prop.—Blast Publishing Co. Ltd.

TURKS & CAICOS ISLANDS
(Dependency of United Kingdom)
Pop. Est. 13,552

GRAND TURK
(Grand Turk Islands)
Pop. Est. 3,146

TURKS and CAICOS NEWS English; Est. 1982
Central Square, Providenciales; PO Box 52
Circ.—5,000
Ad. Mgr.—Blythe Dunacason
U.S. Rep.—Charney/Palacios & Co. Inc.

VIRGIN ISLANDS (BRITISH)
Pop. Est. 12,000

ROAD TOWN
(Tortola Island)
Pop. Est. 2,479

THE BVI BEACON Est. 1984
Porters & Russell Hill Roads; PO Box 3030
Tel: (809) 4943767; Fax: (809) 4946267
Circ.—1,577
Prop.—Beacon BVI Ltd.
Owner/Ed/Ad. Mgr.—Linnell M Abbott
Ad. Mgr.—Brittny Sessions
U.S. Rep.—AdMarket Int'l.

THE ISLAND SUN Est. 1962
Main St.; PO Box 21
Tel: (809) 4942476; Fax: (809) 4944540
Circ.—2,000
Prop.—Sun Enterprises (BVI) Ltd.
Ed.—Vernon Pickering
Ad. Mgr.—Delseita (Peggy) Carney

VIRGIN ISLANDS (U.S.)
Pop. Est. 97,564

ST. CROIX
Pop. Est. 50,139
CHRISTIANSTED
Pop. Est. 2,555

DAILY NEWS
Vitraco Mall, Golden Rock, 00820
Fax: (809) 7731621
Circ.—18,500
Pub.—Ariel Melchior Jr
Ed.—Penny Feuerzeig
Ad. Dir.—Roger Reynolds
ST. CROIX AVIS (m) English; Est. 1844
PO Box 750, 00821
Tel: (809) 7732300; Fax: (809) 7735511
Circ.—8,000
Prop.—Brodhurst Printeries Inc.
Owner/Pub.—Rena Brodhurst-Knight
Ed.—Wynn Brant
Ad. Mgr.—Lesa Fisher
U.S. Rep.—AdMarket Int'l.;
Charney/Palacios & Co. Inc.; The N DeFilippes Corp.

ST. THOMAS
Pop. Est. 46,531
CHARLOTTE AMALIE
Pop. Est. 12,331

VIRGIN ISLANDS DAILY NEWS (m) English; Est. 1930
Estate Thomas, Parcel 49 & 52A; PO Box 7760, 00801
Tel: (809) 7748772; Fax: (809) 7760740
Circ.—15,560
Prop.—Daily News of Virgin Islands
CEO—Ronald E Dillman
Pub.—Ariel Melchoir
Ex. Ed.—Penny Feuerzeig
Ad. Dir.—Roger W Reynolds
U.S. Rep.—AdMarket Int'l.; The N DeFilippes Corp.

NEWSPAPERS OF CENTRAL AMERICA & MEXICO

BELIZE
Pop. Est. 208,904

BELIZE CITY
Pop. Est. 47,000

AMANDALA (Black Power) English
3304 Partridge St.; PO Box 15
Tel: (501-2) 72391/(501-2) 77276; Fax: (501-2) 75934
Circ.—9,500
Ed.—Evan X Hyde
U.S. Rep.—The Cal Hart Co.
THE BELIZE TIMES English
3 Queen St.; PO Box 506
Tel: (501-2) 45757; Fax: (501-2) 31940
Circ.—7,000
Prop.—The Belize Times Press Ltd.
Ed.—Polo Velásquez
THE PEOPLE'S PULSE English
19 King St.
Ed.—Silas Cayetano
THE REPORTER (S) English; Est. 1946
63 Cemetry Rd.; PO Box 707
Tel: (501-2) 72503; Fax: (501-2) 78118
Circ.—7,000
Prop.—The Industrial Press Ltd.
Ad. Mgr.—Harry Lawrence

COSTA RICA
Pop. Est. 3,342,154

SAN JOSÉ
Pop. Est. 1,175,651

AL DIA (Per Day) (m) Est. 1992
Del Cruce de Llorente de Tibás, 400 metros este; Apdo. Postal 7-0270-1000, 874666
Tel: (506) 2474647; Fax: (506) 2474665
Prop.—Editorial Los Olivos SA
Pres.—Fernán Vargas Rohrmoser
Ex. Dir.—Manuel Francisco Jiménez Echeverria
Gen. Mgr.—Auxiliadora Protti
Dir.—Guillermo Fernández Rojas
Ch. of Info.—Armando González Quesada
EXTRA (m) Est. 1978
Avda. 4, Calle 4
Tel: (506) 2239505/(506) 2337018; Fax: (506) 2236101
Circ.—95,000
Prop.—Sociedad Periodística Extra Ltda.
Pub.—Marcos P Valverde
Pres./Dir.—William Gómez Vargas
Mgr.—Dunia Ugalde Cordero
Ed. in Ch.—Rocio Péroz
EL HERALDO (The Herald) (m) Est. 1994
Del INS 400 metros este, Barrio Aranjuez, Paseo de los Estudiantes; Apdo. Postal 1500-1002
Tel: (506) 2223035/(506) 2218292; Fax: (506) 2223039
Prop.—El Heraldo
Pres.—Manuel Polini
Dir.—Erwin Knohr
Gen. Mgr.—Monroe Poyser
Ed. in Ch.—Francisco Gamboa
Ch. of Info.—Elodia Mora
LA NACION (The Nation) (m) Est. 1946
Del Cruce de Llorente de Tibás; Apdo. Postal 10138-1000
Tel: (506) 2474747; Fax: (506) 2406480/(506) 2406485
Circ.—107,000
Prop.—La Nación SA
Pres.—Fernán Vargas Rohrmoser
Ex. Dir.—Manuel Francisco Jiménez Echeverria
Gen. Mgr.—Fernando Leñero Testart
Dir.—Eduardo Ulibarri
Ed. in Ch.—Marcela Angulo Grillo
Ch. of Info.—Juan Fernando Cordero
Ch. of Info.—Carlos Cortés
Ch. of Info.—Bosco Valverde
Ch. of Info.—Edgar Fonseca
Ch. of Info.—Víctor H Murillo
Ad. Dir.—Luís Amon
U.S. Rep.—Charney/Palacios & Co. Inc.
LA PRENSA LIBRE (The Free Press) (e) Est. 1889
Calle 4, Avda. 4
Tel: (506) 2236666; Fax: (506) 2234671
Circ.—63,000
Prop.—La Prensa Libre
Pres./Dir.—Andrés Borrasé Sanou
Vice Pres.—Carlos Borrasé Taylor
Gen. Mgr.—William Gómez Vargas
Ed. in Ch.—Joaquín Cerdas
Ad. Mgr.—Ligia Carvajal
LA REPUBLICA (The Republic) (m) Est. 1950
Barrio Tournón, 100 norte y 150 este del Kamakiri; Apdo. Postal 2130-1000
Tel: (506) 2230266; Fax: (506) 2553950
Circ.—67,500
Prop.—Editorial La Razón SA
Pres.—Alvaro Chaves Gómez
Gen. Mgr.—Martin Robles Robles
Dir.—Yehudi Monestel
Ed. in Ch.—Jesús Mora
Ch. of Info.—Mariana Lev Schtirbu
Ch. of Info.—Jesús Mora Rodríguez
Ch. of Info.—Ramón A Soto Sanabria
Ad. Mgr.—Johnny Chacón
U.S. Rep.—Charney/Palacios & Co. Inc.

Copyright ©1996 by the Editor & Publisher Co.

IV-88   El Salvador   *Central America*

EL SALVADOR
Pop. Est. 5,752,511

SAN SALVADOR
Pop. Est. 1,500,000

DIARIO de HOY (Today's Daily) (m) Est. 1936
11 Calle, Oriente, No. 271; Apdo. Postal 495
Tel: (503) 2710100/(503) 2710122; Fax: (503) 2712040
Circ.—78,000
Prop.—Editorial Altamirano Madriz SA
Pres./Ed.—Enrique Altamirano Madriz
Ex. Dir.—Fabricio Altamirano Basil
Ed. in Ch.—Rolando Monterrosa Gutiérrez
Sales Mgr.—José Regalado
Ad. Mgr.—Valentin Arrieta
U.S. Rep.—Charney/Palacios & Co. Inc.

DIARIO LATINO (Latin Daily) (e) Est. 1890
23 Avda. Sur., No. 225
Tel: (503) 2710671/(503) 2711303; Fax: (503) 2710971
Circ.—30,000
Prop.—Editora Salvadoreña SA
Dir.—Francisco Elías Valencia
Ed. in Ch.—Jorge Armando Contreras
Ch. of Info.—Nelson Ernesto López

EL MUNDO (The World) (e) Est. 1967
2 Avda. Norte, No. 211
Tel: (503) 2714400; Fax: (503) 2714342
Circ.—40,000
Prop.—Editora El Mundo SA
Pres.—Juan José Borja Nathan
Dir.—Cristóbal Iglesias
Ed. in Ch.—Rodolfo Vásquez
Gen. Mgr.—Arturo Argüello Oertel
U.S. Rep.—Latin America Inc.

LA NOTICIA (The News) (e) Est. 1986
Avda. España, Edificio España, No. 321
Tel: (503) 2227906/(503) 2227927; Fax: (503) 2221934
Circ.—30,000
Prop.—Editora del Pacifico SA de CV
Pres.—José Alfredo Dutriz
Dir.—Narciso Castillo
Gen. Mgr.—Francisco Imendia
Ed. in Ch.—Luis Mario Pérez
Ch. of Info.—Carlos Benjamín Alvarenga

LA PRENSA GRAFICA (The Graphic Press) (mS) Est. 1915
3 Calle Poniente, No. 130; Apdo. Postal 06-202
Tel: (503) 2713333/(503) 2813333; Fax: (503) 2711808
Circ.—95,000
Prop.—Dutriz Hermanos SA de CV
Pres—Alex Dutriz
Dir.—Rodolfo Dutriz
Gen. Mgr.—José Alfredo Dutriz
Ch. Ed.—Eduardo Torres
Ch. of Info.—Ricardo Chacón

GUATEMALA
Pop. Est. 10,721,387

GUATEMALA CITY
Pop. Est. 1,900,452

DIARIO de CENTRO AMERICA (Central America Daily) (m-5x wk.) Est. 1880
Anexo Edificio, Tipografia Nacional, 18 Calle, No. 6-72, Zona 1
Tel: (502-2) 24417/(502-2) 24418
Circ.—8,000
Prop.—El Gobierno de Guatemala
Pub./Ed.—Oscar Marroquín Rojas
Dir.—Héctor Cifuentes Aguirre
Ed. in Ch.—Tono Ortiz
Ed.—Rafael Matta Retana
Ad. Mgr.—Marvin Salionas
Adm.—Alma Liliana García

EL GRAFICO (The Graphic) (mS) Est. 1963
14 Avda., No. 4-33, Zona 1
Tel: (502-2) 510021/(502-2) 510001; Fax: (502-2) 21832/(502-2) 510014
Circ.—60,000
Prop.—Compañía Editora El Gráfico
Founder—Jorge Carpio Nicolle (QEPD)
Pres.—Marta Arrivilla de Carpio
Gen. Dir.—Rodrigo Carpio Arrivillaga
Gen. Mgr.—Jorge Carpio Arrivillaga
Ed. in Ch.—Eduardo Gómez
Ch. of Info.—Arnoldo Cruz
Ad. Mgr.—Rodolfo Aragon-Ordonez
U.S. Rep.—Charney/Palacios & Co. Inc.

LA HORA (The Hour) (e) Est. 1944
9 Calle "A", No. 1-56, Zona 1; Apdo. Postal 1593
Tel: (502-2) 21903/(502-2) 25919; Fax: (502-2) 517084
Circ.—22,000
Prop.—Diario La Hora
Gen. Dir.—Oscar Marroquín Rojas
Dir.—Oscar Clemente Marroquín G
Ch. of Info.—Carlos González
Sales Mgr.—Marvin Giovanni Salinas

PRENSA LIBRE (Free Press) (m) Est. 1951
13 Calle, No. 9-31, Zona 1
Tel: (502-2) 80052/(502-2) 510368; Fax: (502-2) 518768/(502-2) 28888
Circ.—100,000
Prop.—Empresa Editora Prensa Libre SA
Pres.—Pedro Julio García
Vice Pres.—Alvaro Contreras Vélez
Dir.—José Eduardo Zarco Bolaños
Gen. Mgr.—Edgar Contreras Molina
Ed. in Ch.—German Duarte Castaneda
Ch. of Info.—Jaime Córdova Palacios
U.S. Rep.—Charney/Palacios & Co. Inc.

LA REPUBLICA (The Republic) (m) Est. 1993
13 Calle, No. 8-41, Zona 10
Tel: (502-2) 343843/(502-2) 343844; Fax: (502-2) 343740/(502-2) 343844
Prop.—Grupo de Prensa Total
Ex. Dir.—Luís Marroquín Godoy
Gen. Dir.—Gonzalo Marroquín Godoy
Ed. in Ch.—Mario Recinos Lima
Ch. of Info.—Mario R Sierra
Sales Mgr.—Manuel Juárez Montenegro

SIGLO VEINTIUNO (Century Twenty One) (m) Est. 1990
7 Avda., No. 11-63, Zona 9, Edificio Galerías España, nivel, 6
Tel: (502-2) 346216/(502-2) 346217; Fax: (502-2) 319145
Circ.—50,000
Prop.—Corporación de Noticias SA
Pres.—José Rubén Zamora
Ex. Dir.—Jorge Yee
Gen. Dir.—Mauricio Barrera
Gen. Mgr.—Edgar Díaz Alonzo
Ed. in Ch.—Tulio Juárez

HONDURAS
Pop. Est. 5,314,794

SAN PEDRO SULA
Pop. Est. 450,000

LA NACION (The Nation) (m) Est. 1993
Edificio San Miguel, Calle Los Horcones, 1359
Tel: (504) 511961; Fax: (504) 510511
Prop.—Editorial La Nación
Ed. in Ch.—Armando Cerrato Cortés
Gen. Mgr.—Juan José Aguirre

LA PRENSA (The Press) (mS) Est. 1964
3a. Avda. N.O., No. 143, 6 y 7 Calle
Tel: (504) 533104; Fax: (504) 530778/(503) 534020
Circ.—42,000
Prop.—Organización Publicitaria SA
Pub.—Gen. Adolfo Hung
Pres.—Jorge Canahuati Larach
Ex. Dir.—Nelson Fernández
Ed. in Ch.—María Antonia Martínez M
U.S. Rep.—Charney/Palacios & Co. Inc.

TIEMPO (Time) (m) Est. 1970
1 Calle, 5a. Avda., No. 102; Apdo. Postal 450
Tel: (504) 533388/(504) 534590; Fax: (504) 534590
Circ.—36,000
Prop.—Editorial Honduras SA de CU
Pres.—Jaime Rosenthal Oliva
Ex. Dir.—Manuel Gamero
Gen. Mgr.—Ricardo Hidalgo
Adm. Dir.—Yani Rosenthal
Ed. in Ch.—Germán Quintanilla
Ad. Mgr.—María Rubio de Medina
U.S. Rep.—Charney/Palacios & Co. Inc.

TEGUCIGALPA
(Central District)
Pop. Est. 521,000

EL HERALDO (The Herald) (m) Est. 1979
Bo. San Felipe, frente a oficinas del PANI; Apdo. Postal 1938
Tel: (504) 366000; Fax: (504) 326284
Circ.—31,000
Prop.—Publicaciones y Noticias SA
Pres.—Jorge Canahuati
Ex. Dir.—Francisco Morales
Ed. in Ch.—Julio César Marín
Ch. of Info.—Paulino Medina

EL PERIODICO (The Newspaper) (m) Est. 1993
Carretera Al Batallón, Barrio al Benque, 5a. Calle, entre 7a. y 8a. Avda.
Tel: (504) 343086/(504) 343087; Fax: (504) 343090
Prop.—Medios Publicitarios del Caribe SA
Ex. Dir.—Adolfo Hernández
Gen. Dir.—Armando Boquín
Dir.—Herman Allan Padget
Gen. Mgr.—Suyapa Meléndez de Salmerón
Ed. in Ch.—Oscar Armando Martínez
Ch. of Info.—Marcio Moya

LA TRIBUNA (The Tribune) (m) Est. 1976
Carretera 1er. Batallón, Col. Santa Bárbara; Apdo. Postal 1501
Tel: (504) 331283/(504) 331293; Fax: (504) 343050/(504) 331188
Circ.—40,000
Prop.—Periódicos y Revistas SA de CV
Pres.—Carlos Roberto Flores
Dir.—Adán Elvir Flores
Gen. Mgr.—Manuel Acosta Medina
Ed. in Ch.—Winston Cálix
Ad. Mgr.—Adriana de Lago
U.S. Rep.—Charney/Palacios & Co. Inc.

MEXICO
Pop. Est. 92,202,199

ACAPONETA
(Nayarit)

EL ECO DE NAYARIT (The Echo of Nayarit) (d)
Allende 12, Poniente
Tel: (52-325) 20015/(52-325) 20286
Mng. Dir.—Antonio Saizar Quintero

ACAPULCO
(Guerrero)
Pop. Est. 593,212

AVANCE (Advance) (d) Est. 1967
Avda. Costera Miguel Alemán, No. 187
Tel: (52-74) 821097
Pub.—Fernando Alcala Pérez
Ad. Mgr.—Emilia Montero V

DIARIO DE ACAPULCO (Acapulco Daily) (d) Est. 1952
J. Ruiz de Alarcon, No. 2
Tel: (52-74) 822908
Circ.—6,500
Pub.—Alfredo G Lobato Castro

DIARIO DIECISIETE (Seventeen Daily) (m) Est. 1989
Calzada Pie de la Cuesta, No. 90, Esquina Calle Revolución, Col. Miguel Aleman, 39580
Tel: (52-74) 824601/(52-74) 824738; Fax: (52-74) 831387/(52-74) 837802
Circ.—27,000
Prop.—Impulsora Editorial de Guerrero SA de CV
Dir.—Prof. Victor Manuel García García
Ad.—$12.50

DIARIO DEL PACIFICO (Pacific Daily) (m) Est. 1970
Progreso 17
Tel: (52-74) 826922/(52-74) 822375
Circ.—8,000
Dir.—Arturo Caballero Velaz
Ed.—Ernesto Caballero Velaz
Ad. Mgr.—Francisco Cabellero Velaz

EL GRAFICO (The Graphic) (m) Est. 1960
Nicolas Bravo y E. Mendoza Local 1
Tel: (52-74) 821916/(52-74) 830210
Circ.—15,000
Dir.—José M Severiano Gómez

NOVEDADES DE ACAPULCO (m) Est. 1969
Avda. Costera Miguel Alemán, No. 258, Fraccionamiento, 39300
Tel: (52-74) 851155; Fax: (52-74) 854881
Circ.—40,000
Prop.—Novedades de Acapulco SA de CV
Pres./Gen. Dir.—Romulo O'Farrill Jr

Mgr.—Francisco Pineda Pineda
Ad. Mgr.—Francisco Javier Pérez Arellano
Ad.—$15.00

LA OPINION (The Opinion) (m)
Nicolas Bravo, No. 4-8
Tel: (52-74) 837112
Circ.—4,000
Pub.—Juan López García

PRENSA LIBRE (Free Press) (e) Est. 1960
Nicolas Bravo y E. Mendoza
Tel: (52-74) 821916/(52-74) 830210
Circ.—15,000
Gen. Dir.—José M Severiano Gómez

REVOLUCION (Revolution) (m) Est. 1956
Comonfort 3
Tel: (52-74) 822177/(52-74) 834780
Circ.—15,000
Dir.—Rodrigo Huerta Pegueros

EL SOL DE ACAPULCO (The Acapulco Sun) (m) Est. 1978
Avda. Costera Miguel Alemán, No. 250, Francccionamiento, Hornos Insurgentes, 39350
Tel: (52-74) 854314/(52-74) 853958; Fax: (52-74) 856867/(52-74) 858748
Circ.—17,000
Prop.—Cía. Periodística del Sol De Acapulco SA
Pres./Gen. Dir.—Mario Vázquez Raña
Ad.—$12.00

EL SOL DE GUERRERO (The Guerrero Sun) (d-ex mon.) Est. 1961
Chinacos, No. 4
Tel: (52-74) 821250; Fax: (52-74) 822550
Circ.—19,000
Prop.—Prensa Nacional Asociada
Pub./Gen. Dir.—Donato Valdez Ortega
Ad. Mgr.—Blanca P de Valdez

TRIBUNA (Tribune) (e) Est. 1978
J. Ruiz de Alarcon, No. 2
Pub.—Alfredo G Lobato Castro

TROPICO (Tropical) (m) Est. 1939
Nicolas Bravo, No. 17, Centro
Tel: (52-74) 822674
Circ.—16,000
Dir.—Andrez Pérez García

ULTIMA HORA (Last Hour) (m) Est. 1977
Redacción y Talleres Calle Progreso, No. 17
Tel: (52-74) 826922
Circ.—8,000
Pub.—Ernesto Cabellero Vela

ULTIMAS NOTICIAS (Last News) (m) Est. 1964
Nicolas Bravo, No. 25
Tel: (52-74) 834497
Circ.—12,000
Pub.—Reemberto Valdez Ortega
Ad. Mgr.—Blanca P de Valdez

LA VERDAD DE GUERRERO (The Truth of Guerrero) (d)
5 de Mayo, No. 73-H
Tel: (52-74) 820610
Dir.—Reynol Gómez Escalera

AGUA PRIETA
(Sonora)
Pop. Est. 20,754

EL SOL DE AGUA PRIETA (The Black Water Sun) (d)
Prop.—Organización Editora Mexicana

LA VERDAD DE AGUA PRIETA (The Truth of Black Water) (d)
Calle 8 y Avda. 30
Tel: (52-633) 81012
Gen. Dir.—Antonio Palomares Niebla

AGUASCALIENTES
(Aguascalientes)
Pop. Est. 506,272

EL HERALDO (The Herald) (mS) Est. 1954
Blvd. José María Chávez, No. 120, Col. Centro; Apdo. Postal 18, 20000
Tel: (52-491) 53223/(52-491) 53231; Fax: (52-491) 82220
Circ.—7,000 (m); 10,200 (S)
Prop.—El Heraldo
Ed.—Wilbert Patron
Ad.—$10.20 (m); $11.70 (S)

HIDROCALIDO (Hidrocalido) (d) Est. 1981
5a. Avda. y Ecuador, Col. Las Americas, 20230
Tel: (52-491) 68100/(52-491) 72728
Circ.—30,000
Pres./Gen. Dir.—Agustín Morales Padilla
Ad.—$6.50

OPINION DE AGUASCALIENTES (Aguascalientes Opinion) (d) Est. 1978
Juan de Montoro y Cosio
Tel: (52-491) 63411
Circ.—20,000
Pub.—Gustavo A Lomelin Guerra
Ad. Mgr.—Salvador Noriega M

Copyright ©1996 by the Editor & Publisher Co.

Central America **Mexico** IV-89

EL SOL DEL CENTRO (The Central Sun) (m) Est. 1954
Avda. Madero, No. 460; Apdo. Postal 88, 20000
Tel: (52-491) 53005/(59-491) 53476;
Fax: (52-491) 82239
Circ.—22,000
Prop.—Cía. Periodística del Sol de Aguascalientes
Pres./Gen. Dir.—Mario Vázquez Raña
Gen. Dir.—Francisco Gamboa López
Ad.—$7.50

APATZINGAN
(Michoacan)
Pop. Est. 100,926

EL DIARIO (The Daily) (m) Est. 1968
Pedro José Bermeo, No. 10
Tel: (52-453) 40493
Circ.—10,000
Pub.—Carlos Urena
MOMENTO DE MICHOACAN (Michoacan Moment) (d)
Manuel Doblado, No. 174
Tel: (52-453) 40812
Dir.—Eleazar Carillo Quezada
NUEVO DIA (New Day) (m) Est. 1972
Avda. Constitución, No. 85, Sur
Tel: (52-453) 41695
Circ.—10,000
Pub.—Herminio Angeles Magallon
Ad. Mgr.—Alejandro T Angeles Fernandez
LA OPINION DE APATZINGAN (m) Est. 1994
Estéban Vaca Calderón, No. 170, 60600
Tel: (52-453) 41289/(52-453) 40082
Circ.—10,000
Prop.—La Opinion de Apatzingan
Ex. Dir.—Carlos Antonio Huerta Pérez
Ad.—$14.38
TIEMPO DE APATZINGAN (Apatzingan Time) (d-ex mon.) Est. 1952
Avda. 22 de Octubre 870 y Allende, 60600
Tel: (52-453) 40239/(52-453) 40491
Circ.—10,000
Gen. Dir.—Felipe Arturo Ibañez Torres
Ad.—$7.81

APIZACO
(Tlaxcala)

LA VOZ DE APIZACO (The Voice of Apizaco) (d)
Josefa Ortiz de Dominguez, No. 711, Sur
Tel: (52-241) 23937
Gen. Dir.—Roman Sánchez Araoz

AUTLAN
(Jalisco)
Pop. Est. 46,747

NUEVA EPOCA (New Epic)
Guadalupe Victoria, No. 173
Tel: (52) 21540

CABORCA
(Sonora)

NORTE DE CABORCA (North of Caborca) (d)
Calle 12 s/n
Tel: (52-637) 21606
Gen. Dir.—Francisco Moreno Bustamante

CAMPECHE
(Campeche)
Pop. Est. 173,645

CRONICA (Chronic) (m)
Privada de Montecristo, No. 5, Col. Barrio de San Román, 24040
Tel: (52-981) 11414
Circ.—30,000
Prop.—Ediciones de Campeche SA de CV
Gen. Dir.—Virgilio S Soberanis Rodríguez
DIARIO DE CAMPECHE (Campeche Daily) (m)
Niebla, No. 4, Fraccionamiento 2000
Circ.—10,000
Pub.—José Luís Ilovera Baranda
EDICIONES DE CAMPECHE (Editions of Campeche)
Tel: (52-981) 11414
Dir.—Virgilio Soberanis Rodríguez
NOVEDADES DE CAMPECHE (d) Est. 1973
Avda. Ruiz Cortines y 49-B, Area Ah-Kim-Pech, Col. Centro, 24030
Tel: (52-981) 64286; Fax: (52-981) 64294
Circ.—40,000
Prop.—Novedades de Campeche SA de CV
Pres.—Rómulo O'Farrill Jr
Ex. Vice Pres.—Rolando Carrillo Fajardo
Gen. Dir.—Andrés García Gamboa
Gen. Mgr.—Abraham Rodas Lecona
Ed. in Ch.—Marcelo Alamilla
Ed.—Ricardo Calderón Puerto
Ad.—$9.90

EL SUR (The South) (m) Est. 1994
Calle 10, No. 397, Col. San Román, 24040
Tel: (52-981) 61345; Fax: (52-981) 63176
Circ.—10,000
Prop.—Compañía Editorial de Golfo SA de CV
Gen. Dir.—José Luis Llovera Baranda
Ad.—$9.90
TRIBUNA (Tribune) (m) Est. 1975
Talieresi, Calle Tamaulipas 15-B, entre Nicaragua y Zacatecas, Col. Santa Ana, 24050
Tel: (52-981) 67287; Fax: (52-981) 66658/(52-981) 68482
Circ.—20,000
Prop.—Organización Editorial del Sureste SA de CV
Pub.—Jorge González Valdez
Gen. Mgr.—Irma Carmona De Sánchez
Ad.—$12.50

CANANEA
(Sonora)

NORTE DE CANANEA (North of Cananea) (d)
Avda. Obregon, No. 92
Tel: (52-622) 20432
Gen. Dir.—Francisco Moreno Bustamante

CANCUN
(Quintana Roo)
Pop. Est. 176,765

CANCUN NEWS (d) English; Est. 1991
Calle 10, s/n SM 64 Manzana, 12 Lote, 18 Esquina, Andador 9, Col. Super Manzana 64, 77500
Tel: (52-98) 840639/(52-98) 840944; Fax: (52-98) 840833
Circ.—12,000
Prop.—Multigrafica Cancún SA de CV
Founder—Dr. Othón Arróniz Báez
Gen. Dir.—Clementina de la Huerta de Arróniz
Ad. Mgr.—Marisol Arróniz de Márquez
Ad.—$15.14
CARIBBEAN REPORT (m) English & Spanish; Est. 1982
Avda. Chichen-Itza, No. 51, Retorno 7 Ceibo
Circ.—5,000
Pub.—Victor Hugo de la Cadena
Ed.—Rogelio Rodríguez González
DIARIO DEL CARIBE (Caribbean Daily) (mS) Est. 1969
Avda. Xel-Ha, No. 67
Tel: (52-98) 830007
Circ.—14,000
Pub.—Federico de León
Ad. Mgr.—Vicente López Torres
EL MUNDO DE CANCUN (The World of Cancun) (d)
Calle 10, s/n SM Manzana, 12 Lote, 18 Esquina, Andador 9, Col. Super Manzana, 77500
Tel: (52-98) 840639/(52-98) 840944; Fax: (52-98) 840833
Circ.—10,000
Prop.—Multigrafica Cancún SA de CV
Gen. Dir.—Clementina de la Huerta de Arroniz
Adm. Dir.—Mónica Almudena Arróniz
Ed.—Auricela Castro Garcia
NOVEDADES DE QUINTANA ROO (d) Est. 1974
Calle Pecari, No. 2, Retorno 3, Supermanzana 20, Manzana 6, 77500
Tel: (52-98) 841700/(52-98) 841735
Circ.—25,000
Prop.—Novedades de Quintana Roo SA de CV
Pres.—Rómulo O'Farrill Jr
Gen. Dir.—Andrés García Lavín
Gen. Mgr.—Angel J Dupinet Thomas
Edit'l. Dir.—Fidel Interian Baeza
Ad.—$14.40
POR ESTO! (For This!) (m)
Venado, No. 69, Supermanzana 20, 77500
Tel: (52-98) 844931/(52-98) 847396; Fax: (52-98) 844775
Gen. Dir.—Mario Renato Menéndez Rodríguez
Dir.—Leopoldo Creoglio

CELAYA
(Guanajuato)
Pop. Est. 113,723

AM CELAYA (m) Est. 1978
Blvd. Adolfo López Mateos, No. 1239, Oeste, 38080
Tel: (52-461) 23492/(52-461) 26377; Fax: (52-461) 28553
Circ.—19,000
Prop.—AM de Celaya SA de CV
Gen. Dir.—Enrique Gómez Orozco
Ad.—$6.00

EL SOL DEL BAJIO (The Bajio Sun) (mS) Est. 1949
Guadalupe, No. 221; Apdo. Postal 132, 38000
Tel: (52-461) 20505/(52-461) 20700
Circ.—21,840
Prop.—Organización Editorial Mexicana SA de CV
Pres./Pub./Gen. Dir.—Mario Vázquez Raña
Gen. Dir.—Miguel Angel Chico Herrera
Ad.—$4.25

CERRADA
(Distrito Federal)

UNO MAS UNO (One Plus One) (m) Est. 1977
Retorno de Corregio 12
Circ.—70,000
Pub.—Manuel Becerea Acosta
Ad. Mgr.—José Bermudez Gómez

CHETUMAL
(Quintana Roo)
Pop. Est. 172,563

DIARIO DE QUINTANA ROO (Quintana Roo Daily) Est. 1985
Avda. Universidad, No. 615, Esquina Ignacio Comonfort; Apdo. Postal 135, 77000
Tel: (52-983) 45200; Fax: (52-983) 22168
Circ.—20,000
Prop.—Cía. Editoria de Quintana Roo SA de CV
Pres.—John N Baroudi Estéfano
Gen. Dir.—Abraham Farah Wejebe
Gen. Mgr.—María Brillante Farah Villanueva
Edit'l. Dir.—David Romero Vara
Ad.—$10.94
NOVEDADES (m) Est. 1974
Carmen Ochoa de Merino, Esquina Heroes
Tel: (52-983) 20075
Circ.—16,000
Prop.—Novedades Editores
Pub.—Rómulo O'Farrill
Ad. Mgr.—Wilberth Boeta

CHIHUAHUA
(Chihuahua)
Pop. Est. 530,783

DIARIO DE CHIHUAHUA (Chihuahua Daily) (m) Est. 1985
Avda. Universidad, No. 1502, 31320
Tel: (52-14) 134161/(52-14) 143705
Circ.—50,000
Prop.—Editora Paso del Norte SA de CV
Gen. Dir.—Francisco J Pizarro Chávez
Gen. Mgr.—Héctor Santillanes Lugo
Ad.—$10.80
EL HERALDO DE CHIHUAHUA (Chihuahua Herald) (mS) Est. 1927
Avda. Universidad, No. 2507; Apdo. Postal 1515, 31240
Tel: (52-14) 139339; Fax: (52-14) 135625/(52-14) 131034
Circ.—68,000
Prop.—Organización Editorial Mexicana SA de CV
Pres./Gen. Dir.—Mario Vázquez Raña
Dir.—Javier Contreras O'
Gen. Mgr.—Raúl Ramírez González
Ad.—$14.00
EL HERALDO DE LA TARDE (The Afternoon Herald) (e-ex S) Est. 1955
Avda. Universidad, No. 2507; Apdo. Postal 1515, 31240
Tel: (52-14) 131086; Fax: (52-14) 135625/(52-14) 131034
Circ.—20,700
Prop.—Cía. Periodística del Sol de Chihuahua SA de CV
Pres./Gen. Dir.—Mario Vázquez Raña
Gen. Mgr.—Raúl Ramírez González
Dir.—Javier Contreras O'
INDICE (e) Est. 1976
Avda. Aldama, No. 413
Tel: (52-14) 24535
Circ.—17,000
Pub.—Rosalba Torres de Gallardo
Ad. Mgr.—Lauro Gómez Arteaga
NORTE (North) (m) Est. 1954
Avda. Juarez, No. 1103; Apdo. Postal 1103
Tel: (52-14) 161222/(52-14) 129455; Fax: (52-14) 162821
Circ.—40,000
Prop.—Editorial Ltd.
Dir.—Oscar A Cantú
Gen. Mgr.—Alberto Riva Palacio
NOVEDADES DE CHIHUAHUA (d) Est. 1980
Avda. Revolución, No. 501
Tel: (58-14) 163333/(58-14) 163385

Circ.—32,000
Prop.—Novedades Editores
Dir./Ed.—Gerardo Santoyo
Dir.—Rodolfo Javier Figueroa Cardona

CHILPANCINGO
(Guerrero)
Pop. Est. 136,164

AVANCE (Advance) (d) Est. 1970
Cuauhtemoc y Corregidora
Tel: (52-747) 22553
Pub.—Fernando Alcala Pérez
DIARIO DE GUERRERO (Guerrero Daily) (d-ex mon.) Est. 1947
17 de Febrero, No. 5, Col. Juárez
Tel: (52-747) 22888
Circ.—12,000
Prop.—Ediciones Diario de Guerrero
Gen. Dir.—Héctor García Alvarez
Gen. Mgr.—Héctor García Cantú
Ad.—$6.00
DIARIO DE ZIHUATANEJO (Zihuatanejo Daily) (d)
17 de Febrero, No. 5, Col. Juárez
Tel: (52-747) 22887/(52-747) 22888
Dir.—Héctor García Alvarez
ECOS DE GUERRERO (Echoes of Guerrero) (d)
Avda. Insurgentes, 66 Privada, Insurgentes 2
Tel: (52-747) 25607
Dir.—Raúl Arriaga Rodríguez
EXPRESION POPULAR (Popular Expression) (d)
Emiliano Zapata, No. 25
Tel: (52-747) 29248
Mgr.—Javier Cordero Muñoz
PUEBLO (Town) (d)
Plazuela de San Francisco, No. 19-C
Tel: (52-747) 28070; Fax: (52-747) 29094
Dir.—José Gómez Sandoval
EL REPORTERO (The Reporter) (m)
Juan Ruiz de Alarcón, No. 9, Col. Centro, 39000
Tel: (52-747) 27020; Fax: (52-747) 27020
Prop.—Editorial Tiempos del Sur SA de CV
Ed.—Andrés Campuzano
EL SOL DE CHILPANCINGO (The Chilpancingo Sun) (m) Est. 1954
Avda. Alvarez, No. 48, 39000
Tel: (52-747) 22865; Fax: (52-747) 27418
Circ.—15,000
Prop.—Organización Editorial Mexicana
Founder—Reemberto Valdez Ortega
Mng. Dir.—Pedro Julio Valdez Vilchis
Dir.—Enrique Vargas Orozco
Ad.—$5.40
EL SOL DE GUERRERO (The Guerrero Sun) (d)
Chinacos, No. 4
Tel: (52-747) 22550/(52-747) 21250
Gen. Dir.—Alejandro Valdaz Pineiro
LA TARDE (The Afternoon) (d)
Alvarez Norte, No. 48
Tel: (52-747) 22865/(52-747) 27418
Dir.—Reemberto Valdez Ortega
VERTICE (d)
Morelos, No. 10
Tel: (52-747) 25747/(52-747) 25494
Dir.—Miguel Angel Alfonzo Castorena

CINTALAPA
(Chiapas)

ECOS DEL VALLE (Echoes of Valle) (d)
1a. Avda., Poniente, Sur No. 30-A
Tel: (52-966) 42071
Gen. Dir.—Jorge Gonzalez Lara

CIUDAD ACUNA
(Coahuila)
Pop. Est. 43,297

EL COAHUILENSE (The Coahuilense) (m)
2 de Abril, No. 755
Circ.—8,000
Pub.—Rogelio Castaneda Guerrero
EL ECO (The Echo) (m) Est. 1959
Allende Norte, No. 250
Tel: (52-877) 21250/(52-877) 22933; Fax: (52-887) 21250
Circ.—8,500
Gen. Dir.—Enrique V Castaneda
ZOCALO (m) Est. 1975
Bravo y Emiliano Zapata, 26200
Tel: (52-877) 25304/(52-877) 25705; Fax: (52-877) 25939
Circ.—22,000
Dir.—Francisco Juaristi
Gen. Mgr.—Emilio Del Olmo Vallejo
Ad.—$4.76

Copyright ©1996 by the Editor & Publisher Co.

CIUDAD ALTAMIRANO
(Guerrero)
Pop. Est. 46,710

EL CALENTANO (m)
Independencia Oriente, No. 14, 40660
Tel: (52-464) 22946; Fax: (52-464) 22946
Circ.—8,000
Gen. Dir.—Urbano Delgado Castañeda
Dir.—Ernesto Castro Sagardez
Mgr.—Jorge Jaimes Salgado
Ed.—Gerardo Delgado Castañeda
Ad.—$5.00

CIUDAD CUAUHTEMOC
(Chihuahua)

DIARIO DE CUAUHTEMOC (d)
Calle 3a, No. 273
Tel: (52-158) 24451/(52-158) 26965
Dir.—Elias Montañez Alvarado
EL HERALDO DE CUAUHTEMOC (The Cuauhtemoc Herald) (m) Est. 1983
Calle Morelos y Octava, No. 630, 31500
Tel: (52-158) 23248; Fax: (52-158) 24511
Circ.—10,000
Prop.—Cía. Periodística del Sol de Chihuahua SA
Pres./Gen. Dir.—Mario Vásquez Raña
Dir.—Rafael Salas García
Ad.—$2.80
NOVEDADES DE CUAUHTEMOC (d)
Morelos y Calle 17, Altos
Tel: (52-158) 22447
Dir.—Rodolfo Javier Figueroa Cardona

CIUDAD DEL CARMEN
(Campeche)
Pop. Est. 179,795

TRIBUNA del CARMEN (Carmen Tribune) (m) Est. 1985
Calle 31 por 32 Altos
Tel: (52-981) 22338/(52-981) 22394; Fax: (52-981) 21368
Circ.—50,000
Prop.—Organización Editorial del Sureste SA de CV
Gen. Dir.—Jorge Luís González Valdez
Dir.—Sixto Sosa Barrera
Gen. Mgr.—Irma Carmona de Sánchez
Ad. Mgr.—León Humberto Aillaud R

CIUDAD HIDALGO
(Michoacan)

EL CLARIN
Leandro Valle, No. 12
Tel: (52-725) 40421/(52-725) 41289
Dir.—Héctor Edmundo Tinajero

CIUDAD JUAREZ
(Chihuahua)
Pop. Est. 798,499

CORREO (Mail) (m) Est. 1959
20 de Noviembre y Saltillo
Circ.—18,000
Pub.—A Q Gutiérrez
Ad. Mgr.—Arturo Rivera Olivas
DIARIO de JUAREZ (Juarez Daily) (m) Est. 1976
Paseo Triunfo de la República, No. 3505 y Anillo Envolvente, 32310
Tel: (52-16) 291900; Fax: (52-16) 291990/(52-16) 112191
Circ.—60,000
Prop.—Editora Paso del Norte
Gen. Dir.—Marco Antonio Torres Moreno
Ad. Mgr.—Federico González Acuña
Ad.—$18.30
DIARIO de la MAÑANA (The Morning Daily) (m) Est. 1970
Justo Sierra, No. 485, Norte; Apdo. Postal 16
Circ.—27,500
Pub.—Salvador Holguin Gutiérrez
Ad. Mgr.—Gloria Leticia Escarcega
EL FRONTERIZO (The Frontier) (mS) Est. 1943
Col. Ramón Corona y H. Galeana, No. 301, Centro, 32230
Tel: (52-16) 121980/(52-16) 121981
Circ.—24,060
Prop.—Organización Editorial Mexicana SA de CV
Pres./Gen. Dir.—Mario Vázquez Raña
Dir.—Alma Leticia Landavazo Carrillo
Mgr.—Jaíme Gutiérrez Melchor
Ad. Mgr.—Carla Sánchez Chávez
EL MEXICANO (The Mexican) (e-ex S) Est. 1947
Col. Ramón Corona y H. Galeana, No. 301, Centro, 32230
Circ.—15,000
Prop.—Chihuahua SA de CV "Sucursa l-Juarez"
Pres./Gen. Dir.—Mario Vázquez Raña
Dir.—Alma Leticia Landavazo Carrillo
Mgr.—Jaíme Gutiérrez Melchor
Ad.—$3.50
EL NORTE DE CIUDAD JUAREZ (The North of Juarez City) (m) Est. 1990
Avda. Valle Juarez, No. 6689, 32320
Tel: (52-16) 170044/(52-16) 170250
Circ.—26,000
Prop.—Norte de Ciudad Juárez
Pres.—Oscar A Cantú
Gen. Dir.—Marco Antonio Torres
U.S. Rep.—CWO&O
Ad.—$14.00

CIUDAD MANTE
(Tamaulipas)
Pop. Est. 76,799

EL DIARIO DE CIUDAD MANTE (Mante City Daily) (d)
Canales y Anahuac
Tel: (52-123) 23431
Dir.—Paulino Ramírez Juárez
ECO DEL MANTE (Echoes of Mante) (e) Est. 1939
Galeana, No. 212, Sur; Apdo. Postal 105
Circ.—6,000
Prop.—Editorial El Mante
Pub.—Cesar Arturo Cervantes Gómez
LA EXTRA (Extra) (d)
Canales, No. 307, Poniente
MATUTINO (Morning) (m) Est. 1964
M. Gonzalez, No. 106, Sur; Apdo. Postal 105, 89800
Tel: (52-123) 20475; Fax: (52-123) 24435
Circ.—12,000
Prop.—Publicaciones Coronado SA de CV
Pres./Gen. Dir.—Marco A Coronado
Ad.—$3.75
EL TIEMPO DE CIUDAD MANTE (Mante City Time) (m) Est. 1972
Galeana, No. 109, Norte, 89800
Tel: (52-123) 20143/(52-123) 21555
Circ.—30,000
Pres./Gen. Dir.—Gabriel Puga Tovar
Dir.—Alfredo Olvera Reséndiz
Ad.—$16.25

CIUDAD MIGUEL ALEMAN
(Tamaulipas)
Pop. Est. 17,030

EL TIEMPO DE CIUDAD MIGUEL ALEMAN (The Time of Miguel Aleman City) (d-ex mon.) Est. 1969
Insurgentes, No. 170, 88300
Tel: (52-827) 20754; Fax: (52-827) 20482
Circ.—12,000
Prop.—Editorial El Tiempo
Dir.—Mariano Bueno Gil
Ad.—$5.50

CIUDAD NEZAHUALCOYOTL
(México)

LAS NOTICIAS DE ULTIMA HORA (News of the Last Hour) (d)
Calle 9, No. 86, Col. Las Aguilas
Tel: (52-79) 75718/(52-79) 36624; Fax: (52-79) 36624
Gen. Dir.—Federico Zavalza Ramírez
Dir./Ed.—Ignacio del Castillo Díaz

CIUDAD OBREGON
(Sonora)
Pop. Est. 311,443

DIARIO DEL YAQUI (Yaqui Daily) (m) Est. 1942
Calle Sinaloa, No. 418; Apdo. Postal 196, 85000
Tel: (52-641) 43232/(52-641) 45990
Circ.—25,000
Prop.—Editorial Diario del Yaqui SA
Founder/Pres.—Jesús Corral Ruiz
Dir.—Gilberto Márquez Trujillo
Gen. Mgr.—Jesús Javier Ruiz García
Ad.—$14.63
EXTRA DE LA TARDE (Afternoon Extra) (e) Est. 1974
Chihuahua, No. 534, Sur
Circ.—12,000
Pub.—Heriberto León Peña
Ad. Mgr.—Lilia Torres Morgan
TRIBUNA DEL YAQUI (Yaqui Tribune) (m) Est. 1965
Avda. Rodolfo E. Calles y Durango; Apdo. Postal 769, 85160
Tel: (52-641) 61500; Fax: (52-641) 63511
Circ.—35,000
Prop.—Periódicos Sonorenses SA de CV
Dir.—Salomón Hamed García
Ed.—Gilberto Félix Escalante
Ad.—Gabriel Roberto Monteverde Cañez
Ad.—$13.20

CIUDAD SATELITE
(Mexico)

OBJECTIVO (Objective) (sat.) Est. 1975
Lago Como, No. 124, Anáhuac, 11320
Tel: (52) 2503088; Fax: (52) 2503949
Prop.—Grupo Editorial Objectivo SA de CV
Founder/Gen. Dir.—Benigno Vázquez Olazo

CIUDAD VALLES
(San Luis Potosi)
Pop. Est. 130,939

CRONICA (Chronic) (m) Est. 1992
Calle Las Damas, Esquina Malí, Fraccionamiento Valle Alto, 79020
Tel: (52-138) 24925/(52-138) 11877
Circ.—10,000
Prop.—Producciones Hornos de Ciudad Valles SA de CV
Gen. Dir.—Dr. Alfonso Cruz Sahagún
Ad.—$6.10
DIARIO DE LAS HUASTECAS (Huastecas Daily) (d)
Prof. Porfirio Diaz, No. 41, altos
Tel: (52-138) 21655
Gen. Dir.—Esteban Lopre Cardenas
DIARIO DE VALLES (Valles Daily) (m) Est. 1968
Taninul, No. 5, Fraccionamiento Las Lomas
Tel: (52-138) 21558
Circ.—4,000
Gen. Dir.—José Angel de la Garza González
LA EXTRA (Extra) (d)
Acapulco y Ferrocarril; Apdo. Postal 166
Tel: (52-138) 21764
Dir.—Ricardo Figueroa Sánchez
EL MAÑANA (Tomorrow) (m) Est. 1975
Carretera Valles-Rio Verde y Guerrero, 79000
Tel: (52-138) 21867/(52-138) 22363; Fax: (52-138) 23108
Circ.—18,000
Pub./Dir.—Pascual Oyarvide Sánchez
Gen. Mgr.—Ernesto Escárcega Savignon
Ad.—$23.75
OPINION (m)
Venustiano Carretera, No. 433
Circ.—10,000
Pub.—Ignacio A Rosillo
EL SOL DE LA HUASTECA (Huasteca Sun) (m) Est. 1979
Avda. Juarez y Pedro A. Santos
Circ.—10,000
Prop.—Organización Editorial Mexicana
Pub.—Florencio Ruiz de la Peña
LA VOZ DE LA HUASTECA (d)
Clavel 10, Col. Doraceli
Tel: (52) 13820561
Dir.—David Flores Guzman

CIUDAD VICTORIA
(Tamaulipas)
Pop. Est. 194,996

EL DIARIO DE CIUDAD VICTORIA (Victoria City Daily) (m) Est. 1955
Allende y 20 de Noviembre, No. 316, 87000
Tel: (52-131) 20685/(52-131) 24238; Fax: (52-131) 29817
Circ.—39,000
Prop.—El Diario de Victoria SA
Gen. Dir.—Francisco Filizola González
Ad. Mgr.—Raúl Tizoc Tovar Leal
Ad.—$7.00
EL EDITOR (The Editor) (e) Est. 1976
13 Hidalgo y Morelos
Circ.—4,000
Pub.—Gildo R Garza
LA EXTRA (Extra) (d) Est. 1978
Matamoros, No. 301, Otemán
Circ.—8,000
Pub.—José Villarreal Caballero
EL GRAFICO (The Graphic) (d) Est. 1970
Zaragoza 2 y 3, No. 1525
Tel: (52-131) 22364; Fax: (52-131) 24564
Circ.—8,500
Gen. Dir.—José Guadalupe Díaz Jr
EL MERCURIO (The Mercury) (m) Est. 1974
Matamoros, No. 301, Oriente, 87000
Tel: (52-131) 22143; Fax: (52-131) 23828
Circ.—42,000
Prop.—Editora El Mercurio SCL
Gen. Dir.—José Villarreal Caballero
Ad.—$6.30
NUEVAS NOTICIAS DE TAMAULIPAS (New News of Tamaulipas) (d) Est. 1994
Calle Hidalgo 21 y 22, No. 561, 87000
Tel: (52-131) 22143/(52-131) 25118; Fax: (52-131) 25232
Circ.—30,000
Prop.—Sociedad Cooperativa de Producción y Editora de Tamaulipas SCL
Gen. Dir.—Antonio Villarreal Saldívar
Dir.—Ricardo González De La Viña
Ad. Mgr.—Jorge Othón Rocha
Ad.—$5.00
LA VERDAD DE TAMAULIPAS (The Truth of Tamaulipas) (d) Est. 1984
Calle Hidalgo 21 y 22, No. 543, 87000
Tel: (52-131) 25645; Fax: (52-131) 25232
Circ.—30,000
Prop.—Sociedad Cooperativa de Producción y Editora de Tamaulipas
Gen. Dir.—Eduardo Pérez Castañedo
Adm. Dir.—Ricardo Villarreal Rodríguez
Edit'l Dir.—Luís M Díez Cuan

COATZACOALCOS
(Veracruz)
Pop. Est. 233,115

DIARIO DEL ISTMO (Istmo Daily) (m) Est. 1982
Avda. Hidalgo, No. 1115, Col. Centro, 96400
Tel: (52-921) 48800/(52-921) 48802; Fax: (52-921) 48514
Circ.—64,600
Prop.—Editora La Voz del Istmo SA de CV
Gen. Dir.—José Pablo Robles Martínez
Dir.—Héctor Robles Barajas
Gen. Mgr.—Rafael Vega Robles
Ad.—$9.10
DIARIO DE SOTAVENTO (Sotavento Daily) (m) Est. 1958
La Llave, No. 103
Tel: (52-921) 20318
Circ.—15,000
Pub.—Alfonso Grajales G
Ad. Mgr.—Hilda Lara Alvarez
EL LIBERAL DE COATZACOALCOS (Coatzacoalcos Liberal) (m) Est. 1992
Lázaro Cárdenas, No. 801, Esquina Aldama, 96400
Tel: (52-921) 26040/(52-921) 26644; Fax: (52-921) 21670
Circ.—16,000
Prop.—Editoriales del Sur SA de CV
Gen. Dir.—Jorge Díaz Mirón Benitez
Ad.—$9.75
NOTICIAS (News) (d)
Avda. Hidalgo, No. 1115, 96400
Tel: (52-921) 48802
Circ.—30,000
Dir.—Héctor Zaragoza López
Ed. in Ch.—Natalio Bernal Amador

COLIMA
(Colima)
Pop. Est. 116,505

EL COMENTARIO (The Commentary) (m-ex S) Est. 1974
Gildardo Gómez, No. 66, 28000
Tel: (52-331) 22440/(52-331) 25740; Fax: (52-331) 22440/(52-331) 25750
Circ.—1,500
Gen. Dir.—Roberto M Guzmán Benítez
Ad.—$4.50
EL DIARIO DE COLIMA (Colima Daily) (m) Est. 1953
Gabino Barreda, No. 119, Col. Centro, 28000
Tel: (52-331) 20111/(52-331) 20777
Circ.—25,000
Prop.—Editora Diario de Colima
Gen. Dir.—Héctor Sánchez De La Madrid
Gen. Mgr.—Angel Pérez Fuentes
Sales Mgr.—Gloria Cabrera
Ad.—$9.23
ECOS DE LA COSTA (Echoes of the Coast) (m) Est. 1927
Gabino Barreda, No. 452, 28000
Tel: (52-331) 28040/(52-331) 42840; Fax: (52-331) 28040/(52-331) 42840
Circ.—22,000
Prop.—Editorial Ecos de la Costa
Dir.—Armando Martínez De La Rosa
Ad.—$6.50
EL IMPARCIAL (The Impartial) (d-ex S) Est. 1952
G. Torres Quintero, No. 113, 28000
Tel: (52-331) 22749/(52-331) 21239
Circ.—20,000
Gen. Dir.—Carlos Manuel Zepeda Rosas
Ad.—$3.90

EL INDEPENDIENTE DE COLIMA (Independence of Colima) (d) Est. 1990
Libertad, No. 264, 28000
Tel: (52-331) 40149/(52-331) 40150; Fax: (52-331) 40201
Circ.—28,000
Prop.—Grupo Editorial Colimense
Gen. Dir.—Gabriel Macías Becerril
Adm.—Leonel C Lozano Baltazar
EL MUNDO DESDE COLIMA (The World From Colima) (m)
Independencia, No. 133, 28000
Tel: (52-331) 25700; Fax: (52-331) 23353
Circ.—25,000
Prop.—Editora Colimense SA
Pres.—Manuel Sánchez De la Madrid
Ad.—$12.50
EL NOTICIERO DE COLIMA (The News of Colima) (m) Est. 1973
Avda. Rey de Colimá, No. 225, Col. Centro, 28000
Tel: (52-331) 23395/(52-331) 23070; Fax: (52-331) 23140
Circ.—20,000
Prop.—El Noticiero de Colima
Pub./Gen. Dir.—Carlos Valdez Ramírez
Ad.—$7.30
PANORAMA (m) Est. 1966
Ocampo, No. 67, 28000
Tel: (52-331) 21815; Fax: (52-331) 43740
Circ.—16,000
Dir.—Luis Arvizu Negrete
Ad.—$4.50

CORDOBA
(Veracruz)
Pop. Est. 150,454

ABC CORDOBA (d) Est. 1985
Avda. 3, No. 1504, Col. Centro, 94500
Tel: (52-271) 43551
Circ.—10,000
Prop.—Editores Vera Cruzanos ABC
Gen. Dir.—Alfredo Ríos Hernández
DIARIO 2001 (Daily 2001) (d)
Calle 9, No. 311
EL MUNDO DE CORDOBA (The World of Córdoba) (m) Est. 1960
Calle 43 s/n, Zona Industrial, 94690
Tel: (52-271) 24402; Fax: (52-271) 26777
Circ.—35,000
Founder—Dr. Othón Arróniz Báez
Gen. Dir.—Clementina de la Huerta de Arróniz
Ad. Mgr.—María Sol Arróniz de Márquez
Ad.—$7.50
EL SOL DE ORIZABA (The Orizaba Sun) (d)
Sur 5, entre 2 Ote y 4, 94500
Tel: (52-271) 59631/(52-271) 55680
Circ.—12,000
EL SOL DE LA TARDE (The Afternoon Sun) (e-ex S) Est. 1974
Calle 9, No. 31, 94500
Tel: (52-271) 22115/(52-271) 22750; Fax: (52-271) 20389/(52-271) 40377
Circ.—10,000
Pub—Eduardo G Valdez
EL SOL DEL CENTRO (The Central Sun) (m) Est. 1975
Calle 9, No. 311, 94500
Tel: (52-271) 21115/(52-271) 25212
Circ.—14,000
Prop.—Organización Editorial Mexicana
Pres./Gen. Dir.—Mario Vázquez Raña
Dir.—Adolfo Antonio Rico González
Ad.—$3.50

CUAUTLA
(Morelos)
Pop. Est. 120,315

POLIGRAFO (Polygraph) (d) Est. 1949
2 de Mayo, No. 25
Circ.—8,000
Pub.—Enrique Romano Hernandez
Ad. Mgr.—Faustino Romano
EL SOL DE CUAUTLA (The Cuaulta Sun) (mS) Est. 1978
Francisco I. Madero, No. 157, Col. Emiliano Zapata, 62744
Tel: (52-735) 34573/(52-735) 34633
Circ.—12,000
Prop.—Cía. Periodística del Sol de Cuautla SA
Pres./Gen. Dir.—Mario Vázquez Raña
Gen. Dir.—Enrique Gutiérrez Ortega
Dir.—Miguel Angel Maldonado
Mgr.—Anselmo de Jesús Ruiz Zavala
Ad.—$10.50

CUERNAVACA
(Morelos)
Pop. Est. 281,294

AVANCE (Advance) (d) Est. 1965
Galeana, No. 2213
Tel: (52-73) 122238
Circ.—10,000
Pub.—Alfonso García B
DIARIO DE MORELOS (Morelos Daily) (m)
Avda. Morelos, Sur, No. 817, 62000
Tel: (52-73) 142660/(52-73) 185086
Circ.—47,000
Prop.—Editoriales de México
Gen. Dir.—Federico Bracamontes
Gen. Mgr.—Augustín Arana M
Ad.—$15.90
EL FINANCIERO (The Financer) (m-ex wknd.)
Avda. A. López Mateos, No. 102-A, Col. El Vergel, 62400
Tel: (52-73) 183594
Circ.—8,000
Dir.—Rogelio Cárdenas Sarmiento
Ad.—$15.00
EL MUNDO (The World) (d)
Degollado 104
Tel: (52-73) 180388/(52-73) 180336
Dir.—Andres Alberdi Aburto
OPINION (d)
Jardin Juarez, No. 7-104, Edificio Bellavista
Dir.—Sergio Parra Roman
EL REGIONAL DEL SUR (The Regional Sun) (d) Est. 1988
Avda. Lázaro Cárdenas, No. 494, Col. Jiquilpan, 62170
Tel: (52-73) 174779; Fax: (52-73) 174056
Circ.—12,000
Gen. Dir.—Efraín E Pacheco Cedillo
Gen. Mgr.—Bonifacio Pacheco Cedillo
Ad.—$17.50
EL RENOVADOR (The Renovator) (d)
Rayon 2-1
Tel: (52-731) 84914/(52-731) 84908
Dir.—Rodolfo Barrera Gutiérrez
EL SOL DE CUERNAVACA (Cuernavaca Sun) (mS) Est. 1978
Galeana, No. 507, Col. Centro, 62000
Tel: (52-73) 142122/(52-73) 142733; Fax: (52-73) 124692
Circ.—14,000
Prop.—Cía. Periodística del Sol de Cuernavaca SA
Pres./Gen. Dir.—Mario Vázquez Raña
Dir.—Miguel Angel Maldonado
Mgr.—Anselmo de Jesús Ruíz Zavala
Ad.—$10.50
LA UNION DE MORELOS (The Union of Morelos) (m) Est. 1992
Avda. Vicente Guerrero, No. 777, Col. Tezontepec, 62250
Tel: (52-73) 114631
Circ.—45,000
Prop.—Periódico Diario de Información
Prop.—General Ecos de Morelos
Pres./Gen. Dir.—Mario Estrada Elizondo
Gen. Mgr.—Prof. Emilio Benítez Gutiérrez
Ad.—$18.80
LA VOZ (The Voice) (m) Est. 1948
Salazar, No. 107
Tel: (52-73) 120120
Circ.—7,000
Gen. Dir.—José Gutiérrez Sandoval

CULIACAN
(Sinaloa)
Pop. Est. 601,123

EL DEBATE DE CULIACAN (The Culiacán Debate) (mS) Est. 1972
Madero, No. 556, Poniente, 80000
Tel: (52-67) 166353; Fax: (52-67) 157131
Circ.—27,636 (m); 27,487 (S)
Prop.—Cía. Editorial El Debate de Culiacán SA de CV
Mng. Dir.—José Isabel Ramos Santos
Ad. Dir.—Armando X López Angulo
Ad.—$10.00
EL DIARIO DE CULIACAN (The Culiacán Daily) (m) Est. 1949
Rosales, No. 167, Oriente; Apdo. Postales 234 y 269, 80000
Tel: (52-67) 130947
Circ.—25,000
Pub.—Gonzalo R A Valdez
EL DIARIO DE SINALOA (The Sinaloa Daily) (m)
Rosales, No. 167, Oriente; Apdo. Postales 234 y 269, 80000
Tel: (52-67) 130947; Fax: (52-67) 154600
Circ.—46,000
Prop.—Sociedad Cooperativa El Diario de Sinaloa SCL
Gen. Dir.—Miguel Valle Campos
Ad.—$8.00
LA HORA DE SINALOA (The Sinaloa Time) (m) Est. 1992
Blvd. Francisco I. Madero, No. 490-B, Poniente, 80000
Tel: (52-67) 168840
Circ.—8,000
Prop.—Editorial Paralelo 39
Pres./Gen. Dir.—Silvino Silva Lozano
Ad.—$8.00
NORESTE CULIACAN (mS) Est. 1973
Angel Flores, No. 282, Oriente, Col. Centro; Apdo. Postal 90, 80000
Tel: (52-67) 132100/(52-67) 132358; Fax: (52-67) 128006/(52-67) 162259
Circ.—50,000
Prop.—Editorial Culiacán
Edit'l. Dir.—Jesús Cantú Escalante
Ex. Dir.—Julio Gaytán Martínez
Ad. Mgr.—Ana Cecilia Castro Castro
Ad.—$12.50
EL SOL DE CULIACAN (The Culiacán Sun) (e-ex S) Est. 1965
Blvd. Leyva Solano y Corona; Apdo. Postal 412, 80000
Tel: (52-67) 131320/(52-67) 131621; Fax: (52-67) 136590
Circ.—10,750
Prop.—Cía. Periodística del Sol de Culiacán SA de CV
Pres./Gen. Dir.—Mario Vázquez Raña
Dir.—Jorge Luis Téllaz Salazar
EL SOL DE SINALOA (The Sinaloa Sun) (m) Est. 1956
Blvd. Leyva Solano y Corona; Apdo. Postal 412, 80000
Tel: (52-67) 131621/(52-67) 131597
Circ.—30,000
Prop.—Organización Editorial Mexicana SA de CV
Pres./Gen. Mgr.—Mario Vázquez Raña
Mng. Dir./Mgr.—José Carlos Rodríguez Terrón
Dir.—Jorge Luís Téllaz Salazar

DELICIAS
(Chihuahua)
Pop. Est. 104,014

DIARIO DE DELICIAS (Delicias Daily) (m) Est. 1990
Avda. 6ta. y Calle 4ta., Sur
Tel: (52-14) 720003; Fax: (52-14) 728233
Circ.—6,000
Prop.—Editora Paso del Norte
Dir.—Rubén Valles Mata
Ad.—$5.50
EL HERALDO DE DELICIAS (The Delicias Herald) (m) Est. 1989
Avda. Río Chuviscar, Oriente, No. 201, Esquina Avda. 1a., 33000
Tel: (52-14) 723787; Fax: (52-14) 725626
Circ.—5,000
Prop.—Cía. Periodística del Sol de Chihuahua
Pres./Gen. Dir.—Mario Vázquez Raña
Dir.—Javier Contreras O'
Ad.—$4.00

DURANGO
(Durango)
Pop. Est. 413,835

DIARIO DE DURANGO (Durango Daily) (e-ex S) Est. 1975
Negrete, No. 901, Poniente, 34000
Tel: (52-181) 12100/(52-181) 12220; Fax: (52-181) 15742
Circ.—23,000
Prop.—Cía. Periodística del Sol de Durango SA de CV
Pres./Gen. Dir.—Mario Vázquez Raña
Ad.—$3.50
IMPULSO (Impulse) (d)
Excampo Deportivo, No. 3
Tel: (52-181) 20962
Dir.—Jesús Asef Rodríguez
MERIDIANO (Meridian) (e-ex S) Est. 1979
Juarez, No. 110, Sur
Circ.—10,000
Pub.—Salvador Nava Rodríguez
NORTE (North) (m)
Hidalgo, No. 117, Sur
Circ.—28,000
Prop.—Cía. Periodística Norte
Dir.—Alfonso Bautista
PROVINCIA (Province) (d)
Rebote, No. 929
Tel: (52-181) 23541; Fax: (52-181) 18895
Dir.—Agapito Salazar
SATURNO (Saturn) (d) Est. 1981
Constitución, No. 415, Norte
Circ.—13,000
Pub.—Oscar Hiram Herrera Muñoz
EL SIGLO DE DURANGO (The Durango Century) (m)
Hildalgo, No. 419, Sur, 34000
Tel: (52-181) 25050/(52-181) 25058

Prop.—Editora De La Laguna SA de CV
Founder—Antonio De Juambelz y Bracho
Mng. Dir.—Didier Bracho Soto
Gen. Mgr.—Miguel Angel Ruelas T
Ad.—$6.70
EL SOL DE DURANGO (The Durango Sun) (m) Est. 1947
Zaragoza, No. 202, Sur, 34000
Tel: (52-181) 12220/(52-181) 12100; Fax: (52-181) 15742
Circ.—36,000
Prop.—Cía. Periodística del Sol de Durango SA de CV
Pres./Gen. Dir.—Mario Vázquez Raña
EL SOL DE LA LAGUNA (The Laguna Sun) (m) Est. 1980
Zaragoza, No. 202, Sur; Apdo. Postal 184
Tel: (52-181) 42845
Circ.—15,000
Prop.—Organización Editora Mexicana
Pub./Gen. Dir.—Daniel Ramos Nava
Ed. in Ch.—Joaquín Maldonado
Ed. in Ch.—Gómez Palacio
Ad. Mgr.—Angel Gómez Silva
VICTORIA DE DURANGO (Victory of Durango) (e-ex S)
Pino Suárez, No. 801, Oriente, 24000
Tel: (52-181) 170330/(52-181) 170450; Fax: (52-181) 178838/(52-181) 179210
Circ.—5,000
Prop.—Durango Hoy SA de CV
Gen. Dir.—Victor Manuel Garza Ayala
Ad. Mgr.—Liia Rojas Unzueta
Ad.—$6.00
LA VOZ DE DURANGO (The Durango Voice) (mS) Est. 1956
Calle Juarez, No. 110, 34000
Tel: (52-181) 29947
Circ.—36,000
Pub./Founder/Dir.—Salvador Nava Rodríguez
Dir.—Rosa María Nava de Cisneros
Ad.—$6.40

ENSENADA
(Baja California Norte)
Pop. Est. 171,513

ABC (m) Est. 1980
Blancarte, No. 369-4
Tel: (52-667) 40318; Fax: (52-667) 81010/(52-667) 81277
Pub./Gen. Mgr.—Francisco Guerrero
Dir.—Ernesto Paredes Villegas

FRESNILLO
(Zacatecas)
Pop. Est. 160,181

LA VOZ DE FRESNILLO (The Fresnillo Voice) (m-ex S) Est. 1952
García Salinas, No. 208, 99000
Tel: (52) 20013/(52) 26771
Circ.—10,000
Prop.—Editora de Periodicos, Libros y Revistas de Fresnillo
Founder—Andrés A Frías C
Gen. Dir.—Fernando Frias Salcedo
Gen. Mgr.—María de los Angeles Fernández
Ad.—$11.00

GOMEZ PALACIO
(Durango)
Pop. Est. 107,318

LA EPOCA (The Epoch) (m) Est. 1954
Blvd. Alemán y Calle Santiago Papasquiaro ZI, Gomez Palacio
Tel: (52-171) 29180; Fax: (52-171) 27944
Circ.—10,000
Gen. Dir.—José Gonzalez Cantú

GUADALAJARA
(Jalisco)
Pop. Est. 3,000,000

EL DIARIO DE GUADALAJARA (The Guadalajara Daily) (m) Est. 1969
López Mateos, Norte, No. 249, Esquina Avda. Mexico, 44940
Tel: (52-3) 6162150/(52-3) 6162278
Circ.—60,000
Prop.—Editorial Hispano Mexicana SA de CV
Pres./Gen. Dir.—Luís A González Becerra
EL FINANCIERO (The Financer) (m-ex wknd.) Est. 1981
Zaragoza, No. 376, Sector Hidalgo, Col. Artesanos, 44290
Tel: (52-3) 6137830/(52-3) 6148534; Fax: (52-3) 6581798

Circ.—9,500
Dir.—Rogelio Cárdenas Sarmiento
Ad.—$33.00
EL INFORMADOR (The Informer) (mS) Est. 1917
Calle Independencia, No. 300; Apdo.
Postal 3 Bis, 44100
Tel: (52-3) 6146340/(52-3) 6147070;
Fax: (52-3) 6144653
Circ.—68,000
Prop.—Unión Editorial SA de CV
Ed.—Jorge Alvarez del Castillo Zuloaga
EL JALISCIENSE (The Jalisciense) (m) Est. 1981
Avda. Rio Nilo, No. 2003, Lomas del
Paradero Sector Reforma, 44840
Tel: (52-3) 6394445; Fax: (52-3) 6393675
Circ.—30,000
Prop.—Editora La Voz de Jalisco SA de CV
Gen. Dir.—Alfredo Pérez Díaz
LET'S ENJOY English
Avda. Nino Obrero, No. 706, Chapalita CP
Tel: (52-3) 6215201
EL OCCIDENTAL (mS) Est. 1942
Calzada Independencia, No. 324, Sur;
Apdo. Postal 1-669, 44100
Tel: (52-3) 6130690; Fax: (52-3) 6136796
Circ.—49,400
Prop.—Cía. Periodística del Sol de
Guadalajara SA de CV
Pres./Gen. Dir.—Mario Vázquez Raña
Mng. Dir.—Ricardo Del Valle Del Paral
Ad.—$18.26
OCHO COLUMNAS (Eight Columns) (d)
Avda. Patria, No. 1201, Col. Lomas del
Valle, 45129
Tel: (52-3) 6410309/(52-3) 6415051;
Fax: (52-3) 6422691
Circ.—48,000
Prop.—CECUN
Pres./Gen. Dir.—Gonzalo Leaño Reyes
Dir./Ed.—Rafael Rodríguez López
Ad.—$14.55
SIGLO 21 (Century 21) (m) Est. 1991
Avda. Washington, No. 250-A, Col.
Ferrocarril, 44440
Tel: (52-3) 6500561; Fax: (52-3) 6500433
Circ.—34,646
Prop.—Alda Editores SA de CV
Pres.—Alfonso Dau
Dir.—Dr. Jorge Zepeda
EL SOL DE GUADALAJARA (The Guadalajara
Sun) (e-ex S) Est. 1948
Calzada Independencia, No. 324, Sur;
Apdo. Postal 1-699, 44100
Tel: (52-3) 6130690; Fax: (52-3) 6136796
Prop.—Cía. Periodística del Sol de
Guadalajara SA de CV
Pres./Gen. Dir.—Mario Vázquez Raña
Mng. Dir.—Ricardo Del Valle Del Peral
Ad.—$7.39
TABLOIDE (Tabloid) (d)
Tamaulipas, No. 1293
Tel: (52-3) 6241637/(52-3) 6241313
Dir.—Miguel Ochoa de la Mora
TIEMPO DE JALISCO (Jalisco Time) (m&e) Est. 1976
Cerro Viejo, No. 1200, Col. Lomas de
Independencia, Sector Libertad
Tel: (52-3) 6378990/(52-3) 6378981
Circ.—15,000 (m); 8,000 (e)

GUAMUCHIL
(Sinaloa)
Pop. Est. 66,659

EL AVANCE DE GUAMUCHIL (The Guamuchil
Advance) (m) Est. 1980
Benito Juarez, No. 64, Norte
Tel: (52-673) 20426
Circ.—9,000
Pub.—Aureliano Pérez
Ed.—Romano Lanciani
EL DEBATE DE GUAMUCHIL (The Guamuchil
Debate) (mS) Est. 1980
Silverio Trueba y 22 de Diciembre, 84000
Tel: (52-67) 25150; Fax: (52-67) 25154
Circ.—3,083 (m); 2,786 (S)
Prop.—El Debate de Culiacán SA
Mng. Dir.—José Isabel Ramos Santos
Ad.—$10.00
EL INFORMADOR (The Informer) (d) Est. 1961
Mina 239 Sur
Circ.—12,000
Pub.—José Betancourt Gómez
NOROESTE (m)
Agustín Ramírez, No. 66, Sur, 81400
Tel: (52-673) 20220; Fax: (52-673) 24085
Circ.—20,000
Prop.—Editorial Noroeste SA de CV
Ex. Dir.—Julio Gaytán Martínez
Edit'l. Dir.—Jesús Cantú Martínez

Mgr.—Ahmed Montes Leyva
Ed.—Armando Ojeda
Ad.—$12.50

GUANAJUATO
(Guanajuato)
Pop. Est. 119,170

AM GUANAJUATO (m) Est. 1990
Pasaje Manuel M. Leal, Local C, 36000
Tel: (52-473) 27727; Fax: (52-473) 27727
Gen. Dir.—Enrique Gómez Orozco
Edit'l. Dir.—Miguel Barrágan T
Ad.—$6.00
CONTACTO (Contact)
Plaza de Guanajuato, No. 49, 1er. Piso, 36000
DIARIO DE GUANAJUATO (Guanajuato Daily)
(m) Est. 1981
Hotel Castillo
Circ.—15,000
Pub.—Carlos Loret de Mola
Ad. Mgr.—Arturo Joel Padilla
EL NACIONAL (The National) (m) Est. 1987
Carretera Guanajuato-Juventud Rosas, Km.
9.5; Apdo. Postal 32
Tel: (52-473) 26665/(52-473) 31266;
Fax: (52-473) 31288
Circ.—60,000
Prop.—El Nacional de Guanajuato SA de CV
Gen. Dir.—Arnoldo Cuéllar Ornelas
Ad.—$22.50

GUASAVE
(Sinaloa)
Pop. Est. 258,130

EL DEBATE (The Debate) (mS) Est. 1984
Calle Cuauhtémoc, No. 52, Entre Zaragoza
y Zapata, 81000
Tel: (52-687) 23200; Fax: (52-687) 21530
Circ.—4,076 (m); 3,623 (S)
Prop.—El Debate SA
Mng. Dir.—José Isabel Ramos Santos
Ad. Dir.—Verónica Angulo Sánchez
Ad.—$10.00
EL GUASAVENSE (The Guasavense) (d-ex
mon.) Est. 1976
Vicente Guerrero, No. 110, 81000
Tel: (52-687) 22350; Fax: (52-687) 22350
Circ.—32,000
Gen. Dir.—Francisco Echavarría Salazar
Gen. Mgr.—Martín García Araujo
Ad.—$8.50
LA OPINION DEL VALLE (The Valle Opinion) (e)
Est. 1971
Colon, No. 673 Bis
Tel: (52-687) 20039
Circ.—13,000
Pub.—Ramón Hernández Rubio
EL REGIONAL (The Regional) (d)
Cesar Aguilar López, s/n, Col. Angel Flores;
Apdo. Postal 7
Tel: (52-687) 720591/(52-687) 22976;
Fax: (52-687) 20970
Gen. Dir.—Romualdo Ruiz

GUAYMAS
(Sonora)
Pop. Est. 129,092

EL DIARIO (The Daily) (e-ex S) Est. 1934
Calle 18 y Avda. Adolfo de la Huerta;
Apdo. Postal 27
Tel: (52-62) 220028
Circ.—4,500
Prop.—Talleres Linotipograficos El Diario
Pub.—Alejandro Ramírez Cisneros
Ad. Mgr.—Bernardo Gastelum
EL ECO (The Echo) (m)
Blvd. García López, s/n
Circ.—13,000
Pub.—José G Rodríguez
EL FINANCIERO (The Financer) (m-ex wknd.)
Privada Inalámbrica, No. 26, Col. San
Benito, 83190
Tel: (52-62) 101963; Fax: (52-62) 101962
Circ.—10,000
Dir.—Rogelio Cárdenas Sarmiento
LA GACETA (The Gazette) (fri.)
Avda. A. L. Rodríguez y Calle 16; Apdo.
Postal 82, 85460
Tel: (52-66) 21355/(52-66) 27879
Dir.—Miguel Escobar Valdez
EL INDEPENDIENTE (The Independent) (m)
Blvd. Luís Encinas y Royal,
Fraccionamiento Los Naranjos, 83060
Tel: (52-62) 135757/(52-62) 136028
Prop.—Editora La Voz de Sonora
Pres./Gen. Dir.—Juan Francisco Ealy Ortiz

Dir.—Roberto Gutiérrez Torres
Mgr.—José Luis Cornejo
Ad. Mgr.—Javier Rascón
LA VOZ DEL PUERTO (The Puerto Voice) (m)
Calle 10, No. 142, 85400
Tel: (52-62) 242183/(52-62) 242184;
Fax: (52-62) 224117
Circ.—35,000
Prop.—Periódicos Sonorenses SA de CV
Dir.—José Luís Bórquez Rivas
Ad. Mgr.—Enrique Rodríguez L
Mgr.—Víctor M Blanco
Ad.—$10.80

HERMOSILLO
(Sonora)
Pop. Est. 448,966

CAMBIO (Change) (m)
Morelia, No. 37, 83000
Tel: (52-62) 132676; Fax: (52-62) 173409
Circ.—20,000
Prop.—Diario La Expresión SA de CV
Pres.—Editorial La Voz del Sur de Jalisco
Vice Pres.—F Javier Sánchez Campuzano
Dir.—Rodolfo Barraza González
Ad.—$17.20
EL FINANCIERO (The Financer) (m-ex wknd.)
Privada Inalámbrica, No. 26, Col. San
Benito, 83190
Tel: (52-62) 101963; Fax: (52-62) 101962
Circ.—10,000
Dir.—Rogelio Cárdenas Sarmiento
EL HERALDO (The Herald) (d)
Pino Suarez y Felipe Salido
HERMOSILLO FLASH (d)
Blvd. Rodríguez, No. 26-B
Tel: (52-62) 127065/(52-62) 127067
Dir.—Eduardo Gómez Torres
EL IMPARCIAL (The Impartial) (mS) Est. 1937
Mina y Sufragio Efectivo, No. 71; Apdo.
Postal 66, 83000
Tel: (52-62) 174700; Fax: (52-62) 174483
Circ.—35,562 (m); 35,504 (S)
Prop.—Impresora y Editorial SA de CV
Pres./Gen. Dir.—José Alberto Healy Noriega
Ad.—$15.00
EL INDEPENDIENTE (The Independent) (m)
Blvd. Luis Encinas y Royal,
Fraccionamiento Los Naranjos, 83060
Tel: (52-62) 135757/(52-62) 136028
Pres./Gen. Dir.—Juan Francisco Ealy Ortiz
Dir.—Roberto Gutiérrez Torres
Mgr.—Julio Cesar Campa Campa
Ad. Mgr.—Nora Vianey Sotelo
INFORMACION DE HERMOSILLO (Hermosillo
Information) (d) Est. 1972
Colima, No. 52
Tel: (52-62) 134800
Circ.—15,000
Pub.—Abelardo Casanova Labrada
Ad. Mgr.—Myrna Gamez
EL NACIONAL (The National) (d)
Morelia 10 y Manuel Gonzalez
Tel: (52-62) 134153/(52-62) 132676
Dir.—José Angel Calderon Trujillo
OPINION (Opinion) (m) Est. 1986
Rama Blanca, No. 32-By Periférico,
Oriente, 83010
Tel: (52-62) 158700; Fax: (52-62) 158567
Circ.—15,000
Prop.—Editorial Latinoamericana
Gen. Dir.—José Luis Hernández Salas
Gen. Mgr.—Joel Valdez Campos
Ad.—$9.95
PRIMERA PLANA (First Plan) (d)
Revolución, No. 14, Norte
Tel: (52-62) 145600
Circ.—10,000
Gen. Dir.—Francisco Javier Ruíz Quirrin
EL SONORENSE (m) Est. 1963
Blvd. Transversal y Royal Fraccionamiento
Col. Los Naranjos, 83060
Tel: (52-62) 135757/(52-62) 125310
Circ.—40,000
Gen. Dir.—Fortino Léon Ahumada

HUIXTLA
(Chiapas)
Pop. Est. 44,496

EL INFORMADOR (The Informer) (d-ex mon.)
Avda. Juarez, No. 3, Sur, 30640
Tel: (52) 20873
Gen. Dir.—Guillermo Soto de la Cruz

IGUALA
(Guerrero)
Pop. Est. 101,067

EL CORREO (The Mail) (d-ex mon.) Est. 1961
Matamoros, No. 114, 40000
Tel: (52-733) 22777/(52-733) 20679

Circ.—8,000
Pub.—Ismael Velasco Vázquez
Dir.—Raul Velasco Vázquez
Ad.—$7.00
DIARIO 21 (Daily 21) (d) Est. 1991
Morelos, No. 74, 40000
Tel: (52-733) 20400; Fax: (52-733) 20054
Circ.—8,000
Dir.—Prof. Jorge Albarrán Jaramillo
Gen. Mgr.—Arturo Domínguez Rodríguez
Ad.—$4.50
VANGUARDIA (Vanguard) (m) Est. 1986
Periférico Norte, 40020
Tel: (52-733) 29330/(52-733) 29332
Dir.—Mario Delgado Castañeda
Ed.—Gerardo Delgado Casteñeda
Ad.—$5.00

IRAPUATO
(Guanajuato)
Pop. Est. 362,915

EL CENTRO DE IRAPUATO (The Center of
Irapuato) (mS) Est. 1981
Blvd. Diaz Ordaz, No. 132, Sur, 36500
Tel: (52-462) 73896/(52-462) 64415;
Fax: (52-462) 70831
Circ.—30,000
Prop.—Corporación Editorial Guanajuato
SA de CV
Gen. Dir.—Reynaldo González Alvarez del
Castillo
Ad. Mgr.—Dr. María Elena Alarcón Castro
EL DIARIO DE LA TARDE (The Afternoon Daily)
(d)
Reforma, No. 432
Tel: (52-462) 62139
Mng. Dir.—Eugenio Albo Moreno
GUANAJUATO (d) Est. 1932
Donato Guerra, No. 249
Tel: (52-462) 61917
Circ.—4,000
Pub.—Armando Calderón
EL HERALDO DE IRAPUATO (The Irapuato Daily)
(mS) Est. 1966
Blvd. Díaz Ordaz, No. 666, 36500
Tel: (52-462) 61114/(52-462) 61132
Circ.—6,800 (m); 5,300 (S)
Prop.—Cía. Periodística del Sol de Irapuato
Gen. Dir.—Mauricio Bercún Melnic
Mgr.—Carlos Enrique Andrade González
Ad.—$12.10 (m); $13.90 (S)
EL SOL DE IRAPUATO (The Irapuato Sun) (mS)
Est. 1954
Avda. de la Reforma, No. 432, Poniente,
Apdo. Postal 144, 36650
Tel: (52-462) 42139/(52-462) 42366
Circ.—34,000
Prop.—Periodística del Sol de Irapuato
Pres./Gen. Dir.—Eugenio Albo Moreno
Ad.—$5.50
EL SOL DE LA TARDE (The Afternoon Sun) (e)
Est. 1978
Avda. de la Reforma, No. 432, Poniente;
Apdo. Postal 144, 36650
Tel: (52-462) 62139
Circ.—15,000

JACONA
(Michoacan)

EL HERALDO MICHOACANO (The Michoacano
Herald) (d)
Morelos, No. 93
Tel: (52-351) 26829
Dir.—Epifanio Torres Padilla

JALAPA
(Veracruz)
Pop. Est. 275,725

DIARIO DE XALAPA (Xalapa Daily) (mS) Est.
1943
Avda. Avila Camacho, No. 3, 91000
Tel: (52-28) 183000; Fax: (52-28) 177100
Circ.—40,000
Prop.—Editorial Pabello Acosta
Dir.—Rubén Pabello Acosta
Ad. Mgr.—Vincente Zurutuza Bonilla
Ad.—$8.00
GRAFICO DE XALAPA (Xalapa Graphic) (m) Est.
1971
Ursulo Galván, No. 31 y 45, 91000
Tel: (52-28) 170248/(52-28) 183119;
Fax: (52-28) 180831/(52-28) 183028
Circ.—35,000
Gen. Dir.—José Luis Poceros Dominguez
Ad. Mgr.—Jesús Mejía Trejo
Ad.—$5.56
MUNDO DE XALAPA (The World of Xalapa) (m)
Est. 1967
Dr. R. Lucio, No. 22
Tel: (52-28) 175652
Circ.—12,000
Pub.—Ernesto Rizzo Murrieta

POLITICA (Political) (d)
Avda. Revolución, No. 11-202
Tel: (52-28) 189191/(52-28) 189391
Gen. Dir.—Leodegario Gutiérrez
PUNTO y APARTE (Point and Apart) (d)
Juarez, No. 79
Tel: (52-28) 170387/(52-28) 178228;
Fax: (52-28) 187115
Dir.—Froylan López Cancela
EL SOL VERACRUZANO (The Veracruzano Sun) (m) Est. 1985
Avda. de Las Américas, No. 169, 91030
Tel: (52-28) 154999/(52-28) 154977;
Fax: (52-28) 159457
Circ.—12,000
Prop.—Cía. Periodística del Sol de Jalapa SA
Pres./Gen. Dir.—Mario Vázquez Raña
Mng. Dir.—Nicolás Rico Bañuelos
Ad. Mgr.—Virginia Benítez García
Ad.—$5.00

JIQUILPAN
(Michoacán)

EL VIGIA DE LA CIENEGA DE CHAPALA (d)
Cuauhtemoc, No. 80
Tel: (52-353) 20156/(52-353) 20606
Gen. Dir.—José Luís Arceo Galvez

JUCHITAN DE ZARAGOZA
(Oaxaca)

ENLACE DE OAXACA (d)
Doctor Roque Robles 6 Barrio Lima
Gen. Dir.—Armando Santibanez Olivera

LA PAZ
(Baja California Sur)
Pop. Est. 160,970

AVANTE (d) Est. 1973
Editorial Avante Abasalo y Cuauhtemoc, No. 471
Tel: (52-682) 29221; Fax: (52-682) 20949
Circ.—9,000
Prop.—Editorial Avante
Dir.—José María Tapia Ruiz
DIARIO PENINSULA (Peninsula Daily) (m) Est. 1990
Reforma, No. 1355, Col. Guerrero; Apdo. Postal 813, 23000
Tel: (52-682) 21675; Fax: (52-682) 28715
Circ.—17,000
Prop.—Cía. Editora Calínico SA de CV
Gen. Dir.—Carlos Bucheli y Derat
Edit'l. Dir.—Benedicto Hernández Zepeda
Adm. Dir.—Salvador Estrada P
Ad.—$26.88
LA EXTRA (Extra) (d-ex mon.) Est. 1979
Josefa Ortiz de Dominguez y Heroes de la Independencia, Col. Centro de la Ciudad, 23000
Tel: (52-682) 25386/(52-682) 28386;
Fax: (52-682) 54828
Circ.—6,000
Prop.—Editorial de Baja California Sur SA de CV
Gen. Dir.—Daniel Roldán Zimbron
Ed.—Angel Roldan Gomez
Ad.—$10.94
SUDCALIFORNIANO (Southern Californian) (m)
Constitución, No. 706, entre Altamirano y Gómez Farías, Cent, 23000
Tel: (52-682) 20144/(52-682) 20044;
Fax: (52-682) 54041
Circ.—19,000
Pres./Gen. Dir.—Mario Vázquez Raña
Mgr.—Vicente Marín Hernández
Ad.—$6.25
EL TIEMPO DE LA PAZ (A Time of Peace) (m)
Heroes de Independencia, No. 954, N
Tel: (52-682) 22163
Circ.—13,000
Prop.—Editorial Aristos
Pub.—Octavio Hernández
ULTIMAS NOTICIAS (Last News) (m-ex mon.) Est. 1953
Belisario Domínguez, No. 291, 23000
Tel: (52-682) 20775
Circ.—10,000
Dir./Gen. Mgr.—Arturo Sotelo y Canett
Mgr.—Arturo Sotelo Salgado
Ad.—$3.50
LA VOZ (The Voice) (d)
Márquez de León, entre Carranza y Olachea
Tel: (52-682) 54505; Fax: (52-682) 54505
Dir.—Adán García Gónzalez

LA PIEDAD
(Michoacan)
Pop. Est. 81,162

AM LA PIEDAD (m) Est. 1990
Centro Comercial Plaza, Local 37
Tel: (52-352) 29560
Gen. Dir.—Enrique Gómez Orozco
Edit'l. Dir.—Miguel Barragán T
Ad.—$6.60
EL CRUZADO DE LA PIEDAD (The Crossing of La Piedad) (d)
Hidalgo, No. 190
Tel: (52-352) 22088/(52-352) 23434
Dir.—Roberto Murillo Lara
DESPERTAR (Awaken) (d) Est. 1974
Reforma, Eso. Pino Suarez, 59300
Tel: (52-352) 20377/(52-352) 20032;
Fax: (52-352) 23662
Circ.—10,000
Prop.—Reforma Lemus
Gen. Dir.—Marco Antonio Avina Martínez
VIDA DE LA PIEDAD (La Piedad Life) (m) Est. 1948
Matamoros, No. 100
Tel: (52-352) 21242
Circ.—12,000
Prop.—Editorial Vida
Pub.—Rafael Rodríguez Salgado
Ed.—Salvador Plascencia R
Ad. Mgr.—Crescencio Abarca Melgoza

LAGOS DE MORENO
(Jalisco)

PROVINCIA (Province) (d)
Lic. Primo de Vedad 133-13
Tel: (52-474) 20888/(52) 47421174
Dir.—Alfredo Hernández Martin del Campo

LAZARO CARDENAS
(Michoacan)
Pop. Est. 134,969

EL DIARIO DE LAZARO CARDENAS (Lazaro Cardenas Daily) (m) Est. 1991
Avda. Melchor Ocampo, No. 58-C, 60950
Tel: (52-743) 71681; Fax: (52-743) 71681
Circ.—12,000
Dir.—Rogelio Rodríguez González
EL QUIJOTE (d)
Autonomia Universitaria, No. 41-C
Tel: (52-743) 27722
Dir.—Raúl Macias Reyes

LEON
(Guanajuato)
Pop. Est. 867,920

AM DE LEON (AM Leon) (mS) Est. 1978
Blvd. A. López Mateos, No. 3601, Oeste;
Apdo. Postal E-72, 37530
Tel: (52-47) 115050; Fax: (52-47) 114535/(52-47) 110401
Circ.—25,224 (m); 19,110 (S)
Prop.—Cía. Periodística Meridiano SA
Gen. Dir.—Enrique Gómez Orozco
Edit'l. Dir.—Miguel Barragán T
Ad.—$12.00
COMPAÑIA PERIODISTICA MERIDIANO
Blvd. A. López Mateos, No. 3601, Oeste 37530
Tel: (52-47) 115051; Fax: (52-47) 114535
CONTACTO DE GUANAJUATO (Guanajuato Contact) (d)
Blvd. Cerrito de Jerez, No. 103 y Blvd. A. López Mateos, Oriente
Tel: (52-47) 140004/(52-47) 162757;
Fax: (52-47) 169600
Pres.—Luís Torres Martínez
Gen. Dir.—Juan I Morales Castaneda
CONTACTO DE LEON (Leon Contact) (d)
Blvd. Cerrito de Jerez, No. 103 y Blvd. A. López Mateos, Oriente
Tel: (52-47) 140004/(52-47) 162757;
Fax: (52-47) 169600
Pres.—Luís Torres Martínez
Gen. Dir.—Juan I Morales Castaneda
EL HERALDO DE LEON (The Leon Herald) (mS) Est. 1957
Hermanos Aldama, No. 222, Col. Zona Centro; Apdo. Postal 299, 37530
Tel: (52-47) 131194/(52-47) 133528;
Fax: (52-47) 155411/(52-47) 143464
Circ.—20,285
Prop.—El Heraldo de León Cía. Editorial SA de CV
Gen. Dir.—Mauricio Bercún Melnic
Mgr.—Juana Pérez de Orozco
NOTICIAS VESPERTINAS (Evening News) (e-ex S) Est. 1961
Francisco I. Madera, No. 312, 37000
Tel: (52-47) 168290/(52-47) 140955
Circ.—15,000
Prop.—Cía. Periodística del Sol de León SA de CV
Pres./Gen. Dir.—Mario Vázquez Raña
Dir.—Carlos Martínez Inda
Ad.—$8.00
OPINION DE LEON (Opinion of Leon) (m)
Miguel Cervantes Saavedra, No. 201
Tel: (52-47) 162566
Circ.—20,000
Prop.—Editorial Libros y Periodicos SCL
Pub.—Gustavo A Leomelin Guerra
EL SOL DE LEON (The Leon Sun) (mS) Est. 1946
Francisco I. Madera, No. 312, 37000
Tel: (52-47) 133354; Fax: (52-47) 168290/(52-47) 140955
Circ.—36,000
Prop.—Cía. Periodística del Sol de León SA de CV
Pres./Gen. Dir.—Mario Vázquez Raña
Dir.—Carlos Martínez Inda
Ad.—$10.00

LOS MOCHIS
(Sinaloa)
Pop. Est. 303,558

ASI ES LA POLITICA (This is Politics) (d)
Avda. 10 de Mayo, No. 577, Poniente, Col. Jiquilpan
Tel: (52-681) 57310
Dir.—Ramiro Valenzuela Medina
EL DEBATE DE LOS MOCHIS (Los Mochis Debate) (mS) Est. 1941
Obregón, No. 8, Poniente, 81200
Tel: (52-681) 58040; Fax: (52-681) 57454
Circ.—16,133 (m); 15,984 (S)
Prop.—El Debate
Gen. Dir.—José Isabel Ramos Santos
Ed. in Ch.—Jaime Pérez Rocha
Ad. Dir.—Raúl Aguilar Valdez
LAS NOTICIAS (The News) (m) Est. 1979
Guillermo Prieto y G. Victoria, 81200
Tel: (52-681) 20749
Gen. Mgr.—J Elias Chávez
LA OPINION DEL PACIFICO (The Pacific Opinion) (d)
Avda. Gabriel Leyva y Callejon Rubi
Tel: (52-681) 80262/(52-681) 80264;
Fax: (52-681) 80263
Circ.—36,000
EL SOL DE LOS MOCHIS (Los Mochis Sun) (m) Est. 1992
Prof. Marcial Ordoñez, No. 118, Poniente, Col. Centro, 81200
Tel: (52-681) 80265
Circ.—6,000
Prop.—Compañía Periodística Del Sol de Los Mochis SA de CV
Pres./Gen. Dir.—Mario Vázquez Raña
Dir.—Lorenzo Valdez López
Mgr.—Raúl Rivera Haro
Ad.—$7.50
TRIBUNA DE SINALOA (Sinaloa Tribune) (d)
Blvd. Rosales y Juarez
Tel: (52-681) 50001/(52-681) 29034
Dir.—Melchor Angulo Castro

LOS REYES
(Michoacan)

PRESENCIA (Presence) (d)
Rayon, No. 74
Tel: (52-354) 20760/(52-354) 20001
Dir.—Jesús Chávez Andrade

MANZANILLO
(Colima)
Pop. Est. 92,863

EL CORREO DE MANZANILLO (The Manzanillo Mail) (m) Est. 1982
Avda. Juarez, No. 143, Locales 6 y 8 (Pasaje Oscarana), 28200
Tel: (52-333) 24779/(52-333) 25705;
Fax: (52-333) 25705/(52-333) 24779
Circ.—15,500
Prop.—Editorial Ecos de La Costa
Dir.—Miguel De la Mora Anguiano
Ad.—$7.00

MATAMOROS
(Tamaulipas)
Pop. Est. 303,293

EL BRAVO (Bravo) (m) Est. 1951
Morelos y Primera, No. 129; Apdo. Postal 483, 87300
Tel: (52-891) 60100/(52-891) 60518;
Fax: (52-891) 62007
Circ.—60,000
Pres./Gen. Dir.—José Carretero Balboa
Edit'l. Dir.—Roberto Gutiérrez Turrubiartes
Dir.—Isauro Rodríguez Garza
Ad.—$14.00
EXPRESION (Expression) (d)
Calle 3a. y Novedades, No. 1, Col. Periodístas, 87300
Tel: (52-891) 25248
Circ.—50,000
Gen. Dir.—José Nativatiny Alemán González

Central America   **Mexico**   IV-93

EL GRAFICO (The Graphic) (d) Est. 1964
Abasolo 4 y 5, No. 58
Tel: (52-891) 21792
Circ.—10,000
Pub.—Victor Manuel González Rubio
EL MAÑANA (The Morning) (m) Est. 1971
Gonzalez y Segunda
Tel: (52-88) 20749
Circ.—20,000
Pub.—Orlando Deandar Martínez
LA OPINION DE MATAMOROS (The Opinion of Matamoros) (d) Est. 1971
Blvd. Lauro Villar, No. 200; Apdo. Postal 486, 87400
Tel: (52-88) 123141/(52-88) 123544;
Fax: (52-88) 122132
Circ.—50,000
Prop.—Cía. Editora La Opinión de Tamaulipas
Pres.—Juan B García Aguayo
Gen. Dir.—Juan B García Gómez
Gen. Mgr.—Emiliano Escobedo Segura
Ad.—$19.00
PM DE EL BRAVO (PM Bravo) (e) Est. 1984
Morelos y Primera, No. 129; Apdo. Postal 483, 87300
Tel: (52-891) 60100/(52-891) 60518;
Fax: (52-891) 63848
Circ.—40,000
Prop.—Cía. Periodística del Bravo SA
Pres./Gen. Dir.—José Carretero Balboa
Edit'l. Dir.—Roberto Gutiérrez Turrubiartes
Dir.—Rafael Romero Contreras
Ad.—$11.50
PRENSA LIBRE (Free Press) (d)
Gonzalez 1 y 1, No. 29
Tel: (52-891) 22446/(52-891) 39091
Dir.—Ruben Herrera Ramos
PRENSA DE MATAMOROS (Matamoros Press) (m) Est. 1973
Guerrero, No. 71-A
Tel: (52-88) 20775
Circ.—10,000
Pub.—Antonio Manzur Maron
EL VESPERTINO (The Evening) (d)
Calle 12, No. 17

MATEHUALA
(San Luis Potosi)
Pop. Est. 25,000

MOMENTO (Moment) (mS) Est. 1981
Zenon Fernandez y Leandro Valle
Circ.—15,000
Pub.—Alejandro Leal Tovias
Ad. Mgr.—Mateo Seguro León

MAZATLAN
(Sinaloa)
Pop. Est. 314,345

ACUACULTURA INTERNACIONAL (International Agriculture)
Apdo. Postal 343
Tel: (52-69) 841668; Fax: (52-69) 836711
EL DEMOCRATA SINALOENSE (The Sinaloense Democrat) (m) Est. 1919
Gaviotas, No. 610, Fraccionamiento Lomas del Mar Mazatlán
Tel: (52-69) 854209; Fax: (52-69) 815608
Circ.—8,500
Prop.—Publicaciones y Ediciones del Pacifico SA
Dir.—Quirino Ordaz Coppel
Ad.—$5.00
NOTICIAS DEL SOL (News of The Sun) (e-ex S) Est. 1954
Avda. Miguel Alemán y Benito Juarez, 82000
Tel: (52-69) 890222/(52-69) 890244;
Fax: (52-69) 821998/(52-69) 812243
Circ.—17,000
Prop.—Cía. Periodística del Sol de Mazatlan SA de CV
Pres./Gen. Dir.—Mario Vázquez Raña
Dir.—José Angel Sánchez López
Mgr.—Idelfonso Manuel Avilés Montoya
Ad.—$3.00
NOROESTE DE MAZATLAN (mS) Est. 1979
Avda. Ejército Mexicano, No. 2004-PB, Local Principal, Edificio Central, Col. Insurgentes, 82010
Tel: (52-69) 865286; Fax: (52-69) 865297
Circ.—40,000
Prop.—Editorial Noroeste SA de CV
Edit'l. Dir.—Jesús Cantú Escalante
Ex. Dir.—Manuel Becerra González
Ad. Mgr.—Patricia Murua Beltrán
Gen. Ed.—Joel Díaz Fonseca
EL SINALOENSE (The Sinaloense) (m) Est. 1936
Carnaval y Playa Rosarito, s/n
Fraccionamiento Playa Sur; Apdo. Postal 260
Tel: (52-69) 813073/(52-69) 826799;
Fax: (52-69) 826768

Circ.—12,000
Prop.—Editora Playa Sur SA de CV
Founder—Blas Rojo Lira
Gen. Dir.—José Nilo Rojo Robles
Ad.—$7.00
EL SOL DEL PACIFICO (The Pacific Sun) (mS)
Est. 1947
Avda. Miguel Alemán y Benito Juarez, No. 312, Col. Playa Sur, 82040
Tel: (52-69) 820922/(52-69) 820944;
Fax: (52-69) 821998/(52-69) 812243
Circ.—36,000
Prop.—Cía. Periodística del Sol de Mazatlan SA de CV
Pres./Gen. Dir.—Mario Vázquez Raña
Dir.—José Angel Sánchez López
Mgr.—Idelfonso Manuel Avilés Montoya
Ad.—$8.00

MERIDA
(Yucatan)
Pop. Est. 555,819

DIARIO DEL SURESTE (Sureste Daily) (mS) Est. 1931
Calle 60, No. 532, 97000
Tel: (52-99) 281087/(52-99) 237393;
Fax: (52-99) 237393
Circ.—29,000 (m); 32,000 (S)
Prop.—Tallares Gráficos del Sudeste SA de CV
Gen. Dir.—Gaspar Villanueva
Ed. in Ch.—Marcos Heredia Pérez
Ad.—$13.50
DIARIO DE YUCATAN (Yucatán Daily) (mS) Est. 1925
Calle 60, No. 521; Apdo. Postal 64, 97000
Tel: (52-99) 288444; Fax: (52-99) 282850
Prop.—Cía. Tipográfica Yucateca SA de CV
Founder—Carlos R Menéndez
Ed. in Ch.—José Luís Tejeda Muñoz
Mng. Dir.—Carlos R Menéndez Navarrete
Ad.—$13.64
EL FINANCIERO (The Financer)
Km. 9, Carretera Mérida-Umán Ampliación, Col. Industrial, 97288
Tel: (52-99) 462222/(52-99) 462224
Dir.—Rogelio Cárdenas Sarmiento
Ad.—$25.00
NOVEDADES DE YUCATAN (mS) Est. 1964
Calle 62, No. 514-A, 97000
Tel: (52-99) 239933; Fax: (52-99) 247080
Circ.—35,000
Prop.—Novedades de Mérida SA de CV
Pres.—Rómulo O' Farrill Jr
Ex. Dir./Gen. Mgr.—Gerardo García Gamboa
Edit'l. Dir.—Juan Antonio Arenas de la Rosa
Ad.—$12.50
POR ESTO (For This) (m) Est. 1991
Calle 60, No. 576, entre 73 y 71, Centro, 97000
Tel: (52-99) 286514; Fax: (52-99) 286514
Circ.—40,000
Prop.—Editorial Nuestra América SA
Gen. Dir.—Mario R Menéndez Rodríguez
Gen. Mgr.—Hernán R Menéndez Rodríguez
Ad.—$17.50
TRIBUNA DE YUCATAN (Yucatán Tribune) (m) Est. 1987
Calle 61, No. 524-2, 97000
Tel: (52-99) 236459; Fax: (52-99) 238010
Prop.—Organización Editorial del Sureste SA
Dir.—Jorge González Valdez
Ed.—Alfredo Gil Gómez
Gen. Mgr.—Irma Carmona de Sánchez
Ad.—$10.63

MEXICALI
(Baja California Norte)
Pop. Est. 601,938

ABC de MEXICALI (ABC Mexicali) (d)
Plaza Cholula, No. 1095-D Centro, Civico
Tel: (52-65) 571544/(52-65) 571123
Dir.—Franti E Canales
LA CRONICA (m)
Avda. Héroes de la Patria, No. 952, Centro Civico, 21000
Tel: (52-65) 574801; Fax: (52-65) 570424
Circ.—30,000
Prop.—Editorial de Baja California SA
Pres./Ed.—Jóse Alberto Healy N
Ex. Dir.—Adolfo Healy R
Gen. Dir.—Jóse Santiago Healy L
Ad. Mgr.—Jorge Ricardo Carrillo Chávez
Ad.—$7.92
EL CENTINELA (The Sentinel) (e) Est. 1976
Avda. Cristóbal Colón, No. 1512; Apdo. Postal 946, 21100
Tel: (52-65) 534545/(52-65) 536912

Circ.—17,000
Prop.—Editora del Colorado SA
Pres./Gen. Dir.—Mario Vázquez Raña
Gen. Mgr.—Mario Valdez Hernández
Dir.—Felipe de Jesús López
Ad. Mgr.—Carlos Calderón De La Barca C
Adm—Antonio López Espinoza
Ad.—$4.15
NOVEDADES DE BAJA CALIFORNIA (d)
Avda. Patria, No. 952 Centro Civico
Tel: (52-65) 574801
Circ.—45,000
Prop.—Organización Editorial Prigresso
Gen. Dir.—Adolfo Sanchéz Rodríguez
LA VOZ DE LA FRONTERA (The Voice of the Frontier) (mS) Est. 1964
Avda. Madero, No. 1545; Apdo. Postal 946, 21100
Tel: (52-65) 534545; Fax: (52-65) 536912
Circ.—67,000
Prop.—Editora América Latina SA
Pres./Gen. Dir.—Mario Vázquez Raña
Gen. Mgr.—Mario Valdéz Hernández
Ad. Mgr.—Carlos Calderón De la Barca
Ad.—$15.00

MEXICO CITY
(Distrito Federal)
(CIUDAD de MEXICO)
Pop. Est. 12,900,000

LA AFICION (mS) Est. 1930
Ignacio Mariscal, No. 23, Col. Tabacalera;
Apdo. Postal 64-Bis, 06030
Tel: (52-5) 464780
Circ.—150,000
Prop.—Cía. Periodística La Afición
Pres./Gen. Dir.—Juan Francisco Ealy Ortiz
Dir.—Franco Carreño
Ad. Mgr.—Héctor Polo Bernal
Ad.—$4.20
CINE MUNDIAL (World Mundial) (d) Est. 1953
Avda. Cuauhtémoc, No. 16-4o. piso, Col. Doctores, 06720
Tel: (52-5) 5880426/(52-5) 5785244
Circ.—50,000
Prop.—Editora Mundial
Dir.—Antonio Alvarez Jiménez
Ad. Mgr.—Melitón López García
Ad.—$7.00
CUESTION (Question) (e-ex S) Est. 1980
Laguna de Mayran, No. 410, Col. Anáhuac, 11320
Tel: (52-5) 2600499/(52-5) 2603645;
Fax: (52-5) 2604562
Circ.—37,000
Prop.—Editorial Hara SA
Gen. Dir.—Alberto González Parra
Mgr.—Sergio Ramírez
Ad. Mgr.—Luís Casas Acevedo
Ad.—$5.00
EL DIA (The Day) (mS) Est. 1962
Avda. Insurgentes, Norte, No. 1210, Col. Capultitlán, 07370
Tel: (52-5) 7592155/(52-5) 5374825;
Fax: (52-5) 5376629/(52-5) 5375283
Circ.—35,000
Prop.—Sociedad Cooperativa Publicaciones Mexicanas SCL
Gen. Dir.—José Luis Camacho López
Ad.—$9.00
DIARIO DE MEXICO (Mexico Daily) (m) Est. 1948
Chimalpopoca, No. 38, Col. Obrera, 06800
Tel: (52-5) 5789437
Circ.—76,000
Prop.—Editoriales de Mexico SA de CV
Gen. Mgr.—Agustín Arana M
Dir.—Rafael Lizardí Durán
Ad.—$7.20
EL ECONOMISTA (The Economist) (d-ex wknd.) Est. 1988
Avda. Coyoacán, No. 515, Col. Del Valle, 03100
Tel: (52-5) 3265454; Fax: (52-5) 2370774/(52-2) 6829060
Circ.—28,000
Prop.—Periódico El Economista SA de CV
Gen. Dir.—Luis Enrique Mercado Sánchez
Ad. Mgr.—Manuel Hinojosa
Ad.—$13.50
ESTO (This) (m) Est. 1941
Guillermo Prieto, No. 9-1er. Piso, 06470
Tel: (52-5) 5352722/(52-5) 5464345;
Fax: (52-5) 5352687
Circ.—242,383 (tues.-S); 253,575 (mon.)
Prop.—Cía. Periodística ESTO SA de CV
Pres./Gen. Dir.—Mario Vázquez Raña
Ad. Mgr.—Arnulfo García Ramírez
Ad.—$4.73 (m); $4.20 (S)

EXCELSIOR (m) Est. 1917
Reforma, No. 18; Apdo. Postal 120 Bis, 06600
Tel: (52-5) 5356552/(52-5) 5467076;
Fax: (52-5) 5460787
Circ.—200,000
Prop.—Cía. Editorial SCL
Gen. Dir.—Regino Díaz Redondo
Gen. Mgr.—Juventino Olivera López
Ad. Mgr.—Gabriel Manzanilla Aragón
U.S. Rep.—Latin America Inc.
Ad.—$11.15
EL FINANCIERO (The Financer) (m) Est. 1981
Lago Bolsena, No. 176, Col. Anáhuac entre Lago Peypus y, Lago Onega, 11320
Tel: (52-5) 2277600; Fax: (52-5) 2551881
Circ.—135,000
Prop.—Grupo Editorial SEFI
Prop.—El Financiero SA
Pub.—Alejandro Ramos
Dir.—Rogelio Cárdenas Sarmiento
Ad.—$15.00
EL HERALDO DE MEXICO (Mexico Herald) (mS) Est. 1965
Dr. Lucio y Dr. Velasco, Col. Doctores, 06720
Tel: (52-5) 5787022; Fax: (52-5) 5789824/(52-5) 5786467
Circ.—373,600
Prop.—El Heraldo de Mexico SA
Pres./Gen. Dir.—Gabriel Alarcón Velázquez
Ad. Mgr.—Maurilio Zertuche
LA JORNADA (The Journal) (m) Est. 1985
Balderas, No. 68, Centro, 06050
Tel: (52-5) 7282900; Fax: (52-5) 5183952
Circ.—75,000
Prop.—DEMOS, Desarrollo de Medios SA de CV
Gen. Dir.—Carlos Payán Velver
MEDIODIA (Afternoon) (d-ex S) Est. 1965
Guillermo Prieto, No. 7, Col. San Rafael, 06470
Circ.—45,000
Prop.—Cía. Periodística del Sol de Mexico SA de CV
Pres./Gen. Dir.—Mario Vázquez Raña
(This is the afternoon edition of El Sol de Mexico in Mexico City.)
EL NACIONAL (The National) (mS) Est. 1929
Ignacio Mariscal, No. 25; Apdo. Postal 446, 06030
Tel: (52-5) 5353074/(52-5) 5354624
Circ.—210,000
Prop.—El Nacional
Gen. Dir.—Guillermo Ibarrá Ramírez
Ad.—$16.40
THE NEWS (m) English; Est. 1950
Balderas, No. 87, Esquina Morelos Centro, 06040
Tel: (52-5) 5185481
Circ.—35,000
Prop.—Novedades Editores SA de CV
Pres./Gen. Dir.—Rómulo O' Farrill Jr
Ad.—$12.90
NOVEDADES (mS) Est. 1936
Balderas, No. 87, Esquina Morelos, Centro, 06040
Tel: (52-5) 5185481
Circ.—80,000 (tues.-sat.); 110,000 (mon. & S)
Prop.—Novedades Editores SA de CV
Pres./Gen. Dir.—Rómulo O'Farrill Jr
Ad.—$3.50
OVACIONES (Ovations) (m&e) Est. 1957
Lago Zirahuén, No. 279, 2o. Piso, Col. Anahuac, 11320
Tel: (52-5) 3280700
Circ.—130,000 (m); 100,000 (e)
Prop.—Editorial Televisa SA de CV
Pres.—Jacobo Zabludovsky
Edit'l. Dir.—Fernando Alcalá
Ad. Mgr.—Carlos Gómez Balmorí
Ad.—$6.50 (m-mon.); $6.00 (m-tues.-S); $8.00 (e)
LA PRENSA (The Press) (m) Est. 1928
Basilio Vadillo, No. 40, Col. Tabacalera, 06030
Tel: (52-5) 5120799; Fax: (52-5) 2288947
Circ.—208,147 (mon.-sat.); 172,465 (S)
Prop.—Editora La Prensa SA de CV
Honorary Pres.—Mario Santaella De La Cajiga
Pres.—Carlos Abedrop Dávila
Gen. Dir.—Manuel Alonso Muñoz
Gen. Mgr.—Manuel de Polanco Moreno
Ed. in Ch.—Antonio Pérez Vieytez
Ad. Mgr.—Alejandro Guerrero Molina
REFORMA (Reform) (m) Est. 1993
Avda. Mexico Coyoacán, No. 40, Col. Santa Cruz Atoyac, 03310
Tel: (52-5) 6787878; Fax: (52-5) 6287511
Circ.—98,000
Prop.—Consorcio Interamericano de Comunicación

Pres./Gen. Dir.—Alejandro Junco De La Vega
Ex. Dir.—Rodolfo Junco De La Vega
Edit'l. Dir.—Ramón Alberto Garza
Edit'l. Dir.—Lazaro Ríos
EL SOL DE MEXICO (Mexican Sun) (m) Est. 1965
Guillermo Prieto, No. 7, Col. San Rafael, 06470
Tel: (52-5) 5662866/(52-5) 5661511 ext. 423
Circ.—45,000
Prop.—Periodística del Sol de México
Pres./Gen. Dir.—Mario Vázquez Raña
Dir.—Pilar Ferreira Garcia
Ad.—$6.06
TRIBUNA (Tribune) (m) Est. 1989
Bahia de San Hipólito, No. 56-401, Col. Verónica Anzures, 11300
Tel: (52-5) 2607841/(52-5) 2601543;
Fax: (52-5) 2600695
Circ.—41,800
Prop.—Corporación Editorial y Periodística Latinoamerica SA de CV
Pres.—Miguel Angel Morales
ULTIMAS NOTICIAS de EXCELSIOR (Last News of Excelsior) (e) Est. 1936
Reforma 18; Apdo. Postal 120-Bis, 06600
Tel: (52-5) 5467087
Circ.—54,000
Prop.—Organización Editorial Mexicana
Pub.—Regino Díaz Redondo
Ad. Mgr.—G A Manzanilla
Ad.—$2.30
EL UNIVERSAL (The Universe) (mS) Est. 1916
Bucareli, No. 8, Centro, 06040
Tel: (52-5) 7091313; Fax: (52-5) 5218080
Circ.—150,855 (m); 165,629 (S)
Prop.—El Universal Compañia Periodística Nacional SA de CV
Pres./Gen. Dir.—Juan Francisco Ealy Ortiz
Gen. Mgr.—Daniel López Barroso
Ad.—$12.35
EL UNIVERSAL GRAFICO (The Graphic Universe) (e-ex S) Est. 1922
Bucareli, No. 8, Centro, 06040
Tel: (52-5) 7091313
Circ.—85,000
Prop.—Cía. Periodística Nacional
Pres./Gen. Dir.—Juan Francisco Ealy Ortiz
Gen. Mgr.—Daniel López Barroso
UNO MAS UNO (One Plus One) (m) Est. 1977
Retorno de Correggio, No. 12, 07320
Tel: (52-5) 5639911
Circ.—60,000
Prop.—Editorial Uno SA de CV
Gen. Dir.—Luís Gutiérrez Rodríguez
Ed.—Carlos Vásquez García
Mgr.—José Gómez Robledo

MINATITLAN
(Veracruz)
Pop. Est. 195,523

LA OPINION (The Opinion) (mS) Est. 1934
Hidalgo, No. 94; Apdo. Postal 34, 96700
Tel: (52-922) 40032/(52-922) 48432;
Fax: (52-922) 40998
Circ.—15,000
Prop.—Editorial La Opinión SA
Dir.—Hiram Rodríguez Jara
Ad.—Trinidad De la Rosa
Ad.—Silvia Anota José
Ad.—$8.40

MONCLOVA
(Coahuila)
Pop. Est. 178,606

EL DIA (The Day) (m) Est. 1954
Avda. Venustiano Carranza, No. 224, Oriente
Tel: (52-863) 33542
Circ.—6,000
Pub.—Jorge Zertuche Tenorio
LA OPINION (The Opinion) (m) Est. 1973
Allende y Guatemala; Apdo. Postal 242
Tel: (52-863) 33253
Circ.—15,000
Prop.—Editora de Coahuila
Pub.—Mario Garay
EL TIEMPO (The Time) (m) Est. 1964
Col. Calle de la Ermita, 25700
Tel: (52-863) 20620/(52-863) 20067
Circ.—46,000
Founder—Manuel E Martínez
Gen. Dir.—Raúl E Martínez Ramón
Ad.—$7.00
VANGUARDIA (Vanguard) (m) Est. 1978
Francisco I. Madero, No. 611, Col. Guadalupe, 25750
Tel: (52-863) 52060/(52-863) 53060
Prop.—Cía. Editora Coahuilense SA
Pres./Gen. Dir.—Armando Castilla Sánchez
Ad.—$6.00

Central America **Mexico** IV-95

LA VOZ DE COAHUILA (The Voice of Coahuila) (d)
Allende y Guatemala; Apdo. Postal 242
Tel: (52-863) 52060; Fax: (52-863) 52311
Circ.—15,000
Gen. Dir.—German Kamar
Ed./Dir.—Victor Garza

LA VOZ DE MONCLOVA (The Voice of Monclova) (m) Est. 1986
Guatemala y Allende, Col. Guadalupe; Apdo. Postal 242, 25750
Tel: (52-863) 33253/(52-863) 33254
Circ.—20,000
Prop.—Editorial de Monclova SA de CV
Gen. Dir.—José Luis de Luna Abrego
Edit'l. Dir.—Fidel Ortiz Morales
Ad.—$5.00

MONTERREY
(Nuevo Leon)
Pop. Est. 1,069,238

ABC (mS) Est. 1985
Platón Sánchez, No. 411, Sur, 64000
Tel: (52-8) 3444480/(52-8) 3442510
Circ.—75,000
Pres./Gen. Dir.—Gonzalo Estrada Cruz
Edit'l. Dir.—Gonzalo Estrada Torres
Ad.—$17.00 (m); $20.00 (S)

CAMBIO (Change) (m) Est. 1986
15 de Mayo, No. 455, Poniente
Tel: (52-83) 3454410; Fax: (52-8) 3455642
Circ.—20,000
Pres.—F Javier Sánchez Campuzano
Gen. Dir.—Guillermo Salinas Treviño
Ad.—$17.20

EL DIARIO DE MONTERREY (Monterrey Daily) (m) Est. 1974
Eugenio Garza Sada, No. 2245, Sur, Col. Roma; Apdo. Postal 3128, 64700
Tel: (52-8) 3592525
Circ.—80,000
Prop.—Periódico El Diario de Monterrey SA de CV
Founder/Pres.—Jesús D González
Pres.—Francisco A González
Gen. Dir.—Jorge Villegas Nuñez
Ad.—$25.000

EXTRA (e-ex S) Est. 1975
Eugenio Garza Sada, No. 2245, Sur, Col. Roma; Apdo. Postal 3128, 64700
Tel: (52-8) 3592525
Circ.—55,000
Prop.—Editorial Estrellas de Oro
Founder/Pres.—Jesús D González
Pres.—Francisco A González
Gen. Dir.—Jorge Villegas Nuñez
Ad.—$10.00

EXTRA/MAS NOTICIAS/MAS DEPORTES (Extra/More News/More Sports) (mS) Est. 1965
Eugenio Garza Sada, No. 2245, Sur, Col. Roma; Apdo. Postal 3128, 64700
Tel: (52-8) 3592525
Circ.—75,000
Prop.—Periódico El Diario de Monterrey
Prop.—Editora Cronos
Founder/Pres.—Jesús D González
Pres.—Francisco A González
Gen. Dir.—Jorge Villegas
Ad.—$12.00

EL FINANCIERO (The Financer) (m-ex wknd.)
Río Pánuco, No. 1942, Col. Roma Monterrey
Tel: (52-8) 3589931/(52-8) 3580090; Fax: (52-8) 3589932
Circ.—12,000
Dir.—Rogelio Cárdenas Sarmiento
Ad.—$33.00

METRO (m) Est. 1988
Washington, No. 629, Oriente; Apdo. Postal 186, 64000
Tel: (52-8) 3453388; Fax: (52-8) 3188300
Circ.—43,903
Founder—Rodolfo Junco de la Vega Sr
Ex. Dir.—Rodolfo Junco de la Vega
Edit'l. Dir.—Ramón Alberto Campos M
Gen. Dir.—Alejandro Junco de la Vega
Ad.—$24.00

LA MONEDA (d-5x wk.)
Zaragoza, No. 844, Sur, Centro, 64000
Tel: (52-8) 3442607/(52-8) 3436834; Fax: (52-8) 3442622
Circ.—10,000
Prop.—Editora Regiomontana
Gen. Dir.—Archibaldo Rullán

EL MUNDO DE LAS ESTRELLAS (The World of the Stars) (d)
Eugenio Garza, No. 2245, Sur, Col. Roma
Tel: (52-8) 3592525
Gen. Dir.—Francisco A Gonzalez Sánchez

EL NORTE (The North) (mS) Est. 1938
Washington, No. 629, Oriente; Apdo. Postal 186, 64000
Tel: (52-8) 3453388/(52-8) 3188300; Fax: (52-8) 3432476
Circ.—133,872 (m); 154,951 (S)
Prop.—Editora El Sol SA de CV
Founder—Rodolfo Junco de la Vega Sr
Ex. Dir.—Rodolfo Junco de la Vega
Gen. Dir.—Alejandro Junco de la Vega
Edit'l. Dir.—Ramón Alberto Campos M

EL PORVENIR (mS) Est. 1919
Galeana, No. 344; Sur, Apdo. Postal 218, 64000
Tel: (52-8) 3454080; Fax: (52-8) 3457795
Circ.—75,000
Prop.—Editorial El Porvenir SA de CV
Gen. Dir.—Jesús Gerardo Cantú Escalante
Edit'l. Dir.—Rogelio Cantú Escalente
Ad.—$23.00

LA RAZON (The Reason) (m) Est. 1978
José María Rojo, No. 440, 64000
Tel: (52-8) 3429697/(52-8) 3435404; Fax: (52-8) 3429698
Circ.—34,693
Prop.—Cía. Editorial
Gen. Dir.—Francisco Tijerina González
Ad.—$15.63

EL SOL (The Sun) (e-ex S) Est. 1922
Washington, No. 629; Apdo. Postal 186, 64000
Tel: (52-8) 3453388/(52-8) 3188300; Fax: (52-8) 3432476
Circ.—34,693
Prop.—Editora El Sol SA
Founder—Rodolfo Junco de la Vega Sr
Gen. Dir.—Alejandro Junco de la Vega
Ex. Dir.—Rodolfo Junco de la Vega
Edit'l. Dir.—Ramón Alberto Garza
Ad.—$14.00

EL SOL VESPERTINO (The Evening Sun) (d)
Washington, No. 629, Oriente; Apdo. Postal 186, 64000
Tel: (52-8) 3188300/(52-8) 3453388; Fax: (52-8) 3432476
Prop.—Editora El Sol
Founder/Ex. Dir.—Rodolfo Junco de la Vega
Edit'l. Dir—Ramón Alberto Garza

EL TIEMPO (The Time) (e) Est. 1936
Avda. Colon, No. 101, Poniente; Apdo. Postal 804
Tel: (52-8) 3750226
Circ.—20,000
Prop.—Editora Cronos
Pub.—Alberto Escamilla González
Ed.—Eduardo Martínez Celis

TRIBUNA DE MONTERREY (Monterrey Tribune) (m) Est. 1968
Isaac Garza, No. 200, Oriente, 64000
Tel: (52-8) 3757300/(52-8) 3755576; Fax: (52-8) 3744467
Circ.—23,000
Prop.—Cía. Periodística del Sol de Monterrey SA de CV
Pres./Gen. Dir.—Mario Vázquez Raña
Dir.—Francisco Cerda Muñoz
Mgr.—José Saúl Homero Hernández Ayala

MORELIA
(Michoacan)
Pop. Est. 287,511

CAMBIO DE MICHOACAN (Michoacan Change) (m) Est. 1992
20 de Noviembre, No. 263, Esquina Belisario Domínguez, Cent, 58000
Tel: (52-451) 38414
Circ.—40,000
Prop.—Sociedad Editora de Michoacán SA de CV
Mgr.—Luis Nahum Pedraza Arriaga
Ad. Mgr.—Eleazar Zizumbo Herrera
Ed. in Ch.—Francisco Hernández Rodríguez
Ad.—$4.06

CRONICA (d)
Privada Teniente Aleman, No. 96, Col. Chapultepec, Sur
Tel: (52-451) 52851
Dir.—Enrique Ibarra Carreón

DIARIO DE MORELIA (Morelia Daily) (m) Est. 1947
Abasolo, No. 355
Tel: (52-451) 20850
Circ.—12,000
Prop.—Editorial Diario de Morelia
Pub.—Miguel Sánchez Vargas

HERALDO MICHOACANO (Michoacan Herald) (e) Est. 1938
Avda. del Periodismo, No. 2001, 58000
Circ.—23,000
Pub.—Humberto Hernández Pimentel

NOTICIAS DE MORELIA (Morelia News) (m-ex S) Est. 1962
Avda. del Periodismo, No. 2001, 58000
Circ.—37,000
Gen. Dir.—Humberto Hernández Pimentel
Ad.—$7.80

PRESENCIA DE MICHOACAN (Michoacan Presence) (d)
Andador Bernardo Arreola, No. 92
Tel: (52-451) 31130; Fax: (52-451) 32605
Dir.—Javier Lozano Solís

REFORMA (Reform) (d)
Caltzontzin, No. 184, Fraccionamiento, Rancho del Charro
Tel: (52-451) 41767
Dir.—Gilberto Chávez Valencia

EL SOL DE MORELIA (Morelia Sun) (mS) Est. 1978
Madero, No. 783, Oriente, 58000
Tel: (52-45) 132568/(52-45) 127773; Fax: (52-45) 132408
Circ.—40,000
Prop.—Cía. Periodística del Sol de Morelia SA de CV
Pres./Gen. Dir.—Mario Vázquez Raña
Mng. Dir.—Armando Palomino Morales
Ad. Mgr.—Octavio Ramírez Cendejas
Ad.—$10.50

TIEMPO DE MORELIA (Morelia Time) (d)
Corregidora, No. 610
Tel: (52-451) 39071
Dir.—Francisco Javier González Pizano

LA VOZ DE MICHOACAN (Michoacan Voice) (mS) Est. 1948
Blvd. del Periodismo, No. 1270; Apdo. Postal 121, 58190
Tel: (52-45) 161730/(52-45) 160624; Fax: (52-45) 161151
Circ.—50,000
Prop.—La Voz de Michoacán SA de CV
Gen. Dir.—Miguel Medina Robles
Gen. Mgr.—Miguel Medina González
Ad.—$17.10

MOROLEON
(Guanajuato)

EL INFORMADOR (The Informer) (d)
Pipila, No. 154
Tel: (52-466) 70446
Gen. Dir.—José G González

NAUCALPAN DE JUAREZ
(Mexico)
Pop. Est. 786,551

EL SOL DEL VALLE DE MEXICO (Mexico Valley Sun) (mS) Est. 1978
Urbina, No. 65
Circ.—28,000
Prop.—Organización Editorial Mexicana
Pub.—Luís Jasso

NAVOJOA
(Sonora)
Pop. Est. 122,061

EL INFORMADOR DEL MAYO (The May Informer) (m) Est. 1957
Rayón y Jesús Salido, 85800
Tel: (52-642) 20997/(52-642) 20983; Fax: (52-642) 20587
Circ.—35,000
Prop.—El Informador del Mayo SA de CV
Dir.—Gerardo Armenta Balderrama
Mgr.—Jesús García Pérez
Ad.—$10.80

NUESTRO TIEMPO (Our Time) (m) Est. 1991
Morelos, No. 711, Poniente, 85800
Tel: (52-642) 20309/(52-642) 22195; Fax: (52-642) 21464
Circ.—25,000
Prop.—Editorial Navojoa Nuestro Tiempo SA de CV
Pres./Ed.—Alejandro González Izábal
Gen. Dir.—Sergio R Padilla Solano
Ad.—$12.50

LA VOZ DEL PUEBLO (The Town Voice) (d)
Rincon, No. 504, Norte
Tel: (52-642) 21777
Dir.—Rogelio Altamirano Sánchez

NOGALES
(Sonora)
Pop. Est. 107,939

ACCION (Action) (e) Est. 1937
Ingenieros, No. 30
Tel: (52-631) 22287
Circ.—5,000
Pub.—José Ramón Velasco Beruben

EL CENTINELA (The Sentinel) (e) Est. 1970
Calzada de los Alamos, No. 249
Tel: (52-631) 26340
Circ.—8,000
Pub.—Jesús Orozco Morales
Ad. Mgr.—Maricruz Quijada Chavarin

DIARIO DE LA FRONTERA (Frontier Daily) (m) Est. 1991
Avda. Tecnológico, No. 564, Esquina Navojoa, 84000
Tel: (52-631) 46820/(52-631) 46820
Circ.—15,000
Prop.—Editorial Diario de la Frontera SA de CV
Gen. Dir.—Luís Orduño González

DIARIO DE NOGALES (Nogales Daily) (d) Est. 1972
Avda. Obregon, No. 1199, Altos
Tel: (52-631) 23100
Circ.—10,000
Pub.—Carlos de la Isla Ortiz
Ad. Mgr.—Ramón Quijada

LA VOZ DEL NORTE (The Northern Voice) (m) Est. 1979
Periferico Norte, s/n; Apdo. Postal 776, 84000
Tel: (52-631) 23100/(52-631) 27171; Fax: (52-631) 25900
Circ.—20,000
Prop.—Editora La Voz del Norte
Pres.—Arnoldo Ahumada Barrera
Dir.—Hugo Penoc Rico

NUEVA ROSITA
(Coahuila)
Pop. Est. 34,706

EL DEMOCRATA (The Democrat) (d)
Reforma, No. 125
Circ.—12,000
Pub.—Francisco Baltazaar García

NUEVO LAREDO
(Tamaulipas)
Pop. Est. 219,456

EL CORREO (The Mail) (e-ex S)
Gonzalez, No. 2409, 88000
Tel: (52-87) 128444; Fax: (52-87) 128221
Circ.—17,337
Prop.—Editorial Villamar SA
Dir.—Ricardo David Villarreal Marroquín
Mgr.—Gloria G de Morales
Ed.—Ruperto Villarreal Marroquín
Ad.—$7.80

EL DIARIO DE NUEVO LAREDO (New Laredo Daily) (mS) Est. 1948
Gonzalez, No. 2409; Apdo. Postal 101, 88000
Tel: (52-87) 128444; Fax: (52-87) 128221
Circ.—68,130 (m); 73,495 (S)
Prop.—Editorial Villamar SA de CV
Dir.—Luís F Villarreal Marroquín
Gen. Mgr.—Marco G Villareal Marroquín
Ed.—Ruperto Villarreal Montemayor
Ad.—$19.50

EL MAÑANA DE NUEVO LAREDO (The Morning of New Laredo) (mS) Est. 1932
Juárez y Perú; Apdo. Postal 90, 88000
Tel: (52-87) 148219; Fax: (52-87) 150405
Prop.—Editora Argos SA de CV
Founder—Heriberto Deandár Amador
Dir.—Heriberto Cantú Deandar

EL SOL DE NUEVO LAREDO (New Laredo Sun) (e) Est. 1972
Guatemala, No. 1737
Circ.—10,000
Prop.—Organización Editorial Mexicana
Pub.—Raúl Cuellar García
Ad. Mgr.—José González Rodríguez

OAXACA
(Oaxaca)
Pop. Est. 213,985

DIARIO EXTRA (Extra Daily)
Abasolo, No. 119, 68000
Tel: (52-951) 65579/(52-951) 60221; Fax: (52-951) 64590
Prop.—Publi-Editorial Scorpio SA de CV

EL EXTRA (Extra) (m) Est. 1980
Abasolo, No. 119, 68000
Tel: (52-951) 65579/(52-951) 60221; Fax: (52-951) 64500
Circ.—15,000
Prop.—Publi-Editorial Scorpio SA de CV

Copyright ©1996 by the Editor & Publisher Co.

Mexico — Central America

Gen. Dir.—Héctor Puega Ramírez Leyva
Mgr.—Pablo Ramírez Puga
Ad.—$4.80
EL IMPARCIAL (The Impartial) (m) Est. 1951
Armenta y López, No. 312; Apdo. Postal 322, 68000
Tel: (52-951) 62812
Circ.—30,000
Prop.—Publicaciones Fernández Pichardo
Gen. Dir.—Benjamín Fernández Pichardo
Ad.—$14.00
NOTICIAS (News) (m) Est. 1976
Libres, No. 407, 68000
Tel: (52-951) 54690/(52-951) 54989
Circ.—30,000
Prop.—Editorial Taller SA de CV
Gen. Dir.—José Martínez Bastida
Dir./Ed.—Ericel Gómez Nucamendi
Edit'l. Dir.—Ismael Sanmartín
Gen. Mgr.—Luís Lagunas Aragón
Ad.—$14.00
EL NUEVO INFORMADOR (The New Informer) (m) Est. 1970
Guerrero, No. 1001
Tel: (52-951) 65705/(52-951) 67114
Circ.—20,000
Gen. Dir.—Evaristo Martínez López
EL OBSERVADOR (The Observer) Est. 1988
Guerrero, No. 607, 68000
Tel: (52-951) 60035
LA OPINION (The Opinion) (m) Est. 1979
Privida de Morelos, No. 4-A
Tel: (52-951) 67079
Circ.—15,000
Pub.—Manuel Humberto Siordia
EL SOL DE OAXACA (Oaxaca Sun) (d) Est. 1981
Avda. Independencia, No. 1405-A, 68000
Tel: (52-951) 54847; Fax: (52-951) 60925
Circ.—18,500
Prop.—Editorial Chimall
Gen. Dir.—Ana Gloria Villicana Jiménez
EL SUR (The South) (m)
Emilio Carranza, No. 820, Col. Reforma, 68050
Tel: (52-951) 34577/(52-951) 34541; Fax: (52-951) 52688
Circ.—35,000
Prop.—Comunicación de Oaxaca SA de CV
Ed.—Narciso Reyes
Ed.—Evaristo Martínez López
Ed.—Alfredo Martínez De Aguilar
Ed.—Patricia Alvarez
Ad.—$14.75

ORIZABA
(Veracruz)
Pop. Est. 114,216

EL MUNDO DE ORIZABA (The World of Orizaba) (m) Est. 1963
Oriente 6, No. 126, 94000
Tel: (52-272) 53897; Fax: (52-272) 51445
Circ.—25,000
Prop.—El Sociedad Editora del Mundo de Orizaba S de RL de CV
Founder—Othón Arróniz Báez
Gen. Dir.—Clementina de la Huerta de Arróniz
Edit'l. Dir.—Auricela Castro García
Ad. Mgr.—Marisol Arróniz de Marquez
Ad.—$7.50
EL SOL DE ORIZABA (Orizaba Sun) (m)
Avda. Colon, No. 303, Altos Orizaba
Tel: (52-272) 55646
Circ.—12,000
Prop.—Periodística del Sol de Córdoba SA
Pres./Gen. Dir.—Mario Vázquez Raña
Dir.—Adolfo Antonio Rico González
Ad.—$3.50

PACHUCA
(Hidalgo)
Pop. Est. 180,630

AVANZANDO (Advancing) (d)
Avda. Juarez, No. 106
Tel: (52-771) 55970/(52-771) 45863
Gen. Dir.—Gabriela Rodríguez Torres
EL HIDALGUENSE (d)
Avda. Heroico Colegio Militar, No. 51-3
Tel: (52-771) 23707
EL NUEVO DIA (A New Day) (d)
Avda. Revolución, No. 1109
Tel: (52-771) 31991
Gen. Dir.—Marco Antonio González Pineda

NUEVO GRAFICO (New Graphic) (d)
Guerrero, No. 1106-7
Tel: (52-771) 22933/(52-771) 51018
Gen. Dir.—Consuelo Rodríguez Gálvez
Dir.—Julio José Gálvez Méndez
NUEVO HIDALGO (New Hidalgo) (d)
Arista, No. 207
Tel: (52-771) 50058
Gen. Dir.—Maria Thalia Sánchez Richardos
EL SOL DE HIDALGO (Hidalgo Sun) (m) Est. 1949
Matamoros, No. 508, 42000
Tel: (52-771) 50027/(52-771) 50047
Circ.—39,000
Prop.—Cía Periodística del Sol de Pachuca SA de CV
Pres./Gen. Dir.—Mario Vázquez Raña
Dir.—Fausto Marín Tamayo
Ad.—$5.50

PARRAL
(Chihuahua)
Pop. Est. 90,647

EL CORREO (The Mail) (e) Est. 1922
Avda. 20 de Noviembre, No. 7
Circ.—10,000
Pub.—Rubén Rocha Chávez
EL MONITOR (The Monitor) (m) Est. 1960
Calle del Cerre, No. 34; Apdo. Postal 200, 33800
Tel: (52-152) 20979; Fax: (52-152) 27640
Circ.—20,000
Dir.—Luís Salayandia Saenz
EL SOL DE PARRAL (Parral Sun) (m) Est. 1980
Colegio, No. 20, 33800
Tel: (52-152) 25250
Circ.—7,500
Prop.—Periodística del Sol de Parral SA de CV
Pres./Gen. Dir.—Mario Vázquez Raña
Pub./Dir.—Isabel Gutiérrez Estrada
Ed.—Lorenzo Guillen Ruiz
Ad. Mgr.—María Guadalupe Horta Martínez
Ad.—$3.52

PATZCUARO
(Michoacan)

AVANCE (Advance) (d)
Serrato, No. 32
Tel: (52-454) 22140/(52-454) 21933
Dir.—Susana Alcala Dominguez
CRITICA REGIONAL (Critical Region) (d)
San Juan de Dios, No. 6
Tel: (52-454) 21978/(52-454) 20432
Dir.—Lucio Herrera Alonso

PIEDRAS NEGRAS
(Coahuila)
Pop. Est. 98,185

EL DIARIO DE PIEDRAS NEGRAS (Black Rock Daily) (m) Est. 1963
Edificio El Diario, 1er. Piso, Avda. Carranza y Hermosillo; Apdo. Postal 169, 26000
Tel: (52-878) 20910/(52-878) 20379; Fax: (52-878) 20538
Circ.—44,000
Prop.—Cía. Editora El Diario SA
Gen. Dir.—Hugo H Martínez Tijerina
Ad.—$8.00
LA EXTRA DE ZOCALO (Zocalo Extra) (e) Est. 1976
Cuauhtemoc, No. 714, Norte; Apdo. Postal 320
Tel: (52-878) 21090/(52-878) 23990
Circ.—11,500
Prop.—Editorial Piedras Negras
Dir.—Francisco Juaristi Septien
Ed. in Ch.—Paul Garza
Ad. Mgr.—José Luís Rosales
LA VOZ DEL NORTE (The Voice of the North) (m) Est. 1949
E. Carranza, No. 1300, Edificio 21
Circ.—25,000
Prop.—Cía. Editora El Bravo
Pub.—Juan Antonio Guajardo Coss
Ad. Mgr.—Isidro Pena Guajardo
ZOCALO (m) Est. 1965
Avda. Cuauhtemoc, No. 714, Norte; Apdo. Postal 148, 26000
Tel: (52-878) 21090/(52-878) 20990
Circ.—48,300
Prop.—Editorial Piedras Negras

Gen. Dir.—Francisco Juaristi Juaristi
Mng. Dir.—Francisco Juaristi Septién
Ad.—$8.25

POZA RICA
(Veracruz)
Pop. Est. 151,739

EL DIARIO NORTE DE POZA RICA (Poza Rica Northern Daily) (d) Est. 1989
Avda. Juarez, No. 103, Col. Tajin, 93320
Tel: (52-782) 29190/(52-782) 37750; Fax: (52-782) 27729
Circ.—8,000
Prop.—El Norte del Estado SA de CV
Founder—Dr. Othón Arróniz Baez
Gen. Dir.—Clementina de la Huerta de Arróniz
Dir.—Raúl Arróniz de la Huerta
Ad. Mgr.—Marisol Arróniz de Márquez
Ad.—$5.40
DOCE HORAS (Twelve Hours) (e) Est. 1956
Blvd. Adolfo Ruiz Cortinez, No. 613
Circ.—18,000
Pub.—Federico Hernández León
Ed. in Ch.—Juan García Sánchez
HOY EN POZA RICA (Today in Poza Rica) Est. 1988
5 de Mayo, No. 200, Col. Tajin, 93330
Tel: (52-782) 26296
Circ.—10,000
Prop.—Editorial Arenas
Dir./Gen. Mgr.—Juan Arenas Ramírez
Ad.—$4.21
EL MUNDO DE POZA RICA (The World of Poza Rica) (m) Est. 1973
Avda. 6, No. 40, Norte, 93200
Tel: (52-782) 20017
Circ.—27,000
Prop.—Publicaciones Provincia SA
Gen. Dir.—Antonio Manzur Marón
Ad.—$8.25
LA OPINION (The Opinion) (m) Est. 1953
M. Arista, No. 209; Apdo. Postal 303, 95330
Tel: (52-782) 20196/(52-782) 20241; Fax: (52-782) 33542/(52-782) 42124
Circ.—32,000
Prop.—Editorial Gibb SA de CV
Gen. Dir.—Raúl Gibb Guerrero
Gen. Mgr.—Silvia Gibb Guerrero
Ad.—$13.13

PUEBLA
(Puebla)
Pop. Est. 1,057,454

ABC (d)
Calzada Manantiales, No. 14, Carretera Federal Mexico-Puebla
Tel: (52-22) 472905/(52-22) 472816
Dir.—Angel García López
CAMBIO (Change) (m-ex S) Est. 1978
2 Sur, No. 509, altos 10, Col. Centro, 72000
Tel: (52-22) 329305; Fax: (52-22) 469392
Circ.—15,000
Prop.—Editora Chignautelli
Dir.—Gabriel Sánchez Andraca
Mgr.—Jesús Francisco Zavala Vázquez
DIARIO DE PUEBLA (Puebla Daily) (d)
4 Norte, No. 208
Tel: (52-22) 414424
Gen. Dir.—Gilberto Cruz Flores
EL FINANCIERO (The Financer) (m-ex wknd.)
11 Poniente, No. 1303
Tel: (52-22) 461442/(52-22) 461347; Fax: (52-22) 420548
Circ.—11,000
Dir.—Rogelio Cárdenas Sarmiento
Ad.—$2.70
EL HERALDO DE MEXICO EN PUEBLA (The Mexican Herald in Puebla) (m) Est. 1966
Calle 8, Oriente, No. 216, 72000
Tel: (52-22) 461840/(52-22) 461854; Fax: (52-22) 463949
Circ.—46,000
Prop.—El Heraldo de Mexico
Pres./Gen. Dir.—Gabriel Alarcón V
Dir.—Sergio Reguero
Ad. Mgr.—Maurilio Zertuche
Ad.—$1.20
MOMENTO (Moment) (d)
7 Oriente, No. 406
Tel: (52-22) 429853/(52-22) 428570
Gen. Dir.—Baraquiel Alatriste Montoto
Dir.—Mario González Rivera
LA OPINION (The Opinion) (d-ex S) Est. 1924
3 Oriente, No. 1207; Apdo. Postal D-238, 72000
Tel: (52-22) 464358/(52-22) 464362; Fax: (52-22) 327772
Circ.—15,000

Prop.—La Opinión Editora Periodística SA de CV
Dir.—Oscar López Morales
Ad.—$7.81
LA OPINION DE PUEBLA (The Opinion of Puebla) (d) Est. 1976
Avda. Lic. Luís Sánchez Ponton, No. 414, Col. Zona Dorada, 72530
Tel: (52-22) 400776/(52-22) 432631; Fax: (52-22) 400976
Gen. Dir.—Manuel Sánchez Pontón
Ad.—$8.33
EL SOL DE PUEBLA (The Puebla Sun) (mS) Est. 1944
Avda. 3, Oriente, No. 201; Apdo. Postal 190
Tel: (52-22) 424560/(52-22) 320622; Fax: (52-22) 420869
Circ.—67,000
Prop.—Cía. Periodística del Sol de Puebla
Pres./Gen. Dir.—Mario Vázquez Raña
Mng. Dir.—Rodolfo Sierra Sánchez
Ad.—$8.00
LA VOZ DE PUEBLA (The Voice of Puebla) (e-ex S) Est. 1953
Avda. 3, Oriente, No. 201; Apdo. Postal 190, 72000
Tel: (52-22) 424560/(52-22) 320622; Fax: (52-22) 460869
Circ.—17,000
Prop.—Cía. Periodística del Sol de Puebla SA de CV
Pres./Gen. Dir.—Mario Vázquez Raña
Dir.—Jerónimo Morales Hernández
Ad. Mgr.—Juan Silva Zepeda

PUERTO VALLARTA
(Jalisco)
Pop. Est. 111,457

MERCURIO (Mercury) (m) Est. 1989
Avda. Las Torres, No. 120, Fraccionamiento Los Sauces, 48320
Tel: (52-322) 40266/(52-322) 45125; Fax: (52-322) 40356
Circ.—9,000
Prop.—Editorial Peñas SA de CV
Pres./Gen. Dir.—Juan de Dios De la Torre Valencia
Ad.—$11.00
MERIDIANO (Meridian) (m)
Morelos, No. 800, Esquina Pípila
Tel: (52-322) 32975; Fax: (52-322) 32976
Circ.—30,000
Prop.—Cía. Editorial Alpesor S de RL
Dir.—Jose Antonio Aguilar Bibeni
Ad.—$13.75
NOTICIAS DEL PUERTO (Puerto News) (d)
Juarez, No. 144
Tel: (52-322) 21151/(52-322) 21890
Gen. Dir.—Rafael de la Cruz Corona
TRIBUNA DE LA BAHIA (Bahia Tribune) (m) Est. 1989
Basilio Badillo, No. 430, Col. Emiliano Zapata, 48380
Tel: (52-322) 30585/(52-322) 31302; Fax: (52-322) 24361
Circ.—7,000
Prop.—Ediciones y Publicaciones Siete de Junio SA de CV
Gen. Dir.—Próccoro Hernández Oropeza
Ed.—Francisco Quezeda Hernández
Ch. of Info.—Gerardo Sandoval Ortiz
Ad.—$9.35
VALLARTA OPINA (Vallarta's Opinion) (m) Est. 1978
Merida, No. 118, Col. Versalles, 48310
Tel: (52-322) 22928/(52-322) 22407; Fax: (52-322) 21186
Circ.—25,000
Prop.—Editora de la Costa
Gen. Dir.—Luís Reyes Brambila

QUERETARO
(Queretaro)
Pop. Est. 456,458

DIARIO DE QUERETARO (Queretaro Daily) (mS) Est. 1963
General Escobedo, No. 65; Apdo. Postal 266, 76000
Tel: (52-42) 21300
Circ.—35,000
Prop.—Cía. Periodística del Sol de Querétaro SA de CV
Pres./Gen. Dir.—Mario Vázquez Raña
Mng. Dir.—Luís R Amieva
Ad.—$6.00
(This is the morning edition of El Sol De Queretaro.)

EL FINANCIERO (The Financer) (m-ex wknd.)
Luis M. Vega, No. 106, Col. Cimatario
Tel: (52-42) 143981; Fax: (52-42) 122832
Circ.—9,000
Dir.—Rogelio Cárdenas Sarmiento
Ad.—$15.00
NOTICIAS (News) (m)
Ezequiel Montes, No. 14, Norte
Tel: (52-42) 125888; Fax: (52-42) 143821
Circ.—23,000
Prop.—Editora Offset Color SA de CV
Pres./Dir.—Rogelio Garfias Ruíz
EL SOL DE QUERETARO (Queretaro Sun) (e) Est. 1980
Escobedo, No. 65; Apdo. Postal 266
Tel: (52-42) 121300; Fax: (52-42) 130355
Circ.—8,000
Prop.—Cía. Periodística del Sol de Queretaro
Pres./Gen. Dir.—Mario Vázquez Raña
Mng. Dir.—Luís R Amieva
(This is the evening edition of Diario de Queretaro.)

RAMOS ARIZPE
(Coahuila)

VANGUARDIA (Vanguard) (m) Est. 1980
Calle Ocampo, esquina Calle Juárez
Circ.—6,000
Prop.—Editora Coahuilense
Pub.—Armando Castilla Sánchez
Ad. Mgr.—Angel Vela Rios

REYNOSA
(Tamaulipas)
Pop. Est. 282,667

EL MAÑANA DE REYNOSA (The Morning of Reynosa) (m) Est. 1949
Lauro Aguirre con Matias Canales; Apdo. Postal 14, 88620
Tel: (52-892) 36415/(52-892) 36311; Fax: (52-892) 36662/(52-892) 30198
Circ.—65,000
Prop.—Editora Demar SA de CV
Gen. Dir.—Heriberto Deandar Martínez
Ad.—$16.43
NOTICIAS (News) (m) Est. 1958
Mina, No. 1125 y Zaragoza, Col. Longoria, 88500
Tel: (52-892) 30090
Circ.—36,000
Mng. Dir.—Mario Lucio Martínez García
PRENSA DE REYNOSA (Reynosa Press) (m) Est. 1963
Matamoros y González Ortega, 88500
Tel: (52-892) 23515/(52-892) 23349; Fax: (52-892) 23823
Circ.—60,000
Mng. Dir.—Félix Mario Garza Elizondo
Ad.—$18.00
LA TARDE (The Afternoon) (e)
Prof. Lauro Aguirre con Mantias Canales
Tel: (52-892) 36662/(52-892) 36311
Circ.—30,000
Prop.—Editora Demar SA de CV
Gen. Dir.—Orlando Deandar Martínez
Ad.—$8.22
ULTIMA HORA (Last Hour) (e)
Avda. Aguascalientes, No. 680, Sur, Esquina Nuevo León, Col. Rodríguez, 88630
Tel: (52-892) 234111/(52-892) 234112
Prop.—Editorial Ultima Hora
Gen. Dir.—Isauro Rodríguez Garza
Edit'l. Dir.—Angel Virgen Alvarado
Ed.—Waldo Rodríguez Valenzuela
VALLE DE NORTE (Reynosa Time) (m-ex S) Est. 1960
E. Carranza y Rio Sabinas, Col. Longoria
Tel: (52-892) 38800/(52-892) 38355; Fax: (52-892) 38572
Circ.—10,000
Prop.—Editora de Periódicos y Revistas Valle del Norte
Gen. Dir.—Fernando J De Luna Leal
Ad.—$8.25

RIO VERDE
(San Luis Potosi)
Pop. Est. 88,165

LA OPINION (The Opinion) (m) Est. 1978
Venustiano Carranza, No. 433
Circ.—20,000
Pub.—Ignacio A Rosillo
EL SOL DEL RIO VERDE (Green River Sun) (mS) Est. 1978
Calle Dr. Gallardo, No. 2-B
Tel: (52) 21111
Circ.—3,000
Prop.—Organización Editorial Mexicana
Pub.—Florencio Ruíz de la Peña

SABINAS
(Coahuila)
Pop. Est. 47,030

PRESENTE (Present) (m) Est. 1968
Labradores, No. 416; Apdo. Postal 140
Tel: (52-861) 21057
Circ.—10,000
Pub.—Enrique V Castaneda
VANGUARDIA DE SABINAS (Sabinas Vanguard) (d)
Farias, No. 1405, Col. Residencial San Luis
Tel: (52-861) 30957
Gen. Dir.—Rubén Mena
Dir.—Natalia M de Mena
LA VOZ DE SABINAS (The Voice of Sabinas) (m)
Madero, No. 442, 26700
Tel: (52-861) 22301
Circ.—10,000
Prop.—Editorial de Monclova SA de CV
Gen. Dir.—José Luís de Luna Abrego
Edit'l. Dir.—Fidel Ortiz Morales
Ad.—$5.00

SAHUAYO
(Michoacan)

PROVINCIA (Province) (d)
Allende, No. 145
Tel: (52-353) 20400
Dir.—Luís Amerzcua Arceo

SALAMANCA
(Guanajuato)
Pop. Est. 204,311

EL SOL DE SALAMANCA (Salamanca Sun) (mS) Est. 1958
Sánchez Torrado, No. 202, Esquina Morelos, 36700
Tel: (52-464) 72624/(52-464) 70144
Circ.—15,800
Prop.—Cía. Periodística del Sol de Irapuato SA de CV
Pres./Gen. Dir.—Mario Vázquez Raña
Dir.—Eugenio Albo Moreno
Ad.—$3.85
EL SOL DE LA TARDE (The Afternoon Sun) (e) Est. 1978
Sánchez Torrado, No. 202, Esquina Morelos, 36700
Tel: (52-464) 82428; Fax: (52-464) 80064
Circ.—9,000
Dir.—Eugenio Albo Moreno
TRIBUNA (Tribune) (m) Est. 1959
Morelos, No. 327, 36700
Tel: (52-464) 83922; Fax: (52-464) 83922
Circ.—10,000
Pres./Gen. Dir.—Ramón López Díaz

SALINA CRUZ
(Oaxaca)
Pop. Est. 65,707

EL IMPARCIAL DEL ISTMO (The Impartial of Istmo) (m) Est. 1972
Avda. Tampico, No. 22, Esquina Manzanillo, Edificio "A", 1er. Piso, Local 4, 70610
Tel: (52-464) 40513
Circ.—25,000
Prop.—Publicaciones Fernández Pichardo SA
Gen. Dir.—Benjamin Fernández Pichardo
Dir.—Guillermo Soto Bejarano

SALTILLO
(Coahuila)
Pop. Est. 440,920

EL DIARIO DE COAHUILA (Coahuila Daily) (m) Est. 1986
Othón Mendizábal, Esquina Universidad, 25000
Tel: (52-841) 58555/(52-841) 55959; Fax: (52-841) 55839
Circ.—25,000
Prop.—Compañía Periodística Criterios
Gen. Dir.—Luís Horacio Salinas Aguilera
Ad.—$15.00
EXTRA! DIARIO DE LA TARDE (Extra! Evening Daily) (e-ex S) Est. 1976
Blvd. Venustiano Carranza y Chiapas, No. 1918; Apdo. Postal 500, 25280
Tel: (52-841) 53381
Circ.—15,212
Prop.—Cía. Editora Coahuilense SA
Pres./Gen. Dir.—Armando Castilla Sánchez
Ad.—$5.00

EL HERALDO DE SALTILLO (Saltillo Herald) (d) Est. 1963
Avda. Abasolo, No. 228, Norte, Col. Centro, 25000
Tel: (52-841) 24201; Fax: (52-841) 48874
Circ.—10,000
Prop.—Cía. Editora de Coahuila SA
Dir.—Francisco J de la Peña D
Ed. in Ch.—Martín A Salazar
Ed.—Eduardo De La Peña
EL INDEPENDIENTE (The Independent) (m) Est. 1970
Xicotencatl Norte, No. 1100
Circ.—10,000
Prop.—Editora Independiente
Gen. Dir.—Jorge A Estrada García
EL SOL DEL NORTE (The North Sun) (m) Est. 1955
Cuauhtémoc, No. 349, Sur, 25000
Tel: (52-841) 22694/(52-841) 22692; Fax: (52-841) 21101
Circ.—12,000
Prop.—Cía. Periodística del Sol de Saltillo
Pres./Gen. Dir.—Mario Vázquez Raña
Dir.—José Concepción Hernández
Mgr.—Alfonso Garza Becerra
Ad.—$7.00
EL SOL DE SALTILLO (Saltillo Sun) (d)
Cuauhtemoc, No. 349, Sur
Tel: (52-841) 22694/(52-841) 22692; Fax: (52-841) 21101
Gen. Dir.—David Brondo García
VANGUARDIA (Vanguard) (mS) Est. 1975
Blvd. Venustiano Carranza y Chiapas, 25280
Tel: (52-841) 53381; Fax: (52-841) 53821
Circ.—16,543 (m); 16,143 (S)
Prop.—Cía. Editora Coahuilense
Pres./Gen. Dir.—Armando Castilla Sánchez
Edit'l. Dir.—Oscar Medrano Sánchez
Ad.—$13.00

SALVATIERRA
(Guanajuato)
Pop. Est. 97,599

EL SOL DEL SUR DEL BAJIO (The Southern Sun of Bajio) (m) Est. 1978
Guillermo Prieto, No. 328-B, 38900
Tel: (52-466) 20505/(52-466) 21569
Circ.—8,000
Prop.—Periodística del Sol de Celaya
Pres./Gen. Dir.—Mario Vázquez Raña
Mng. Dir.—Miguel Angel Chico Herrera

SAN ANDRES TUXTLA
(Veracruz)
Pop. Est. 98,559

EL DIARIO DE LOS TUXTLAS (The Tuxtlas Daily) (mS) Est. 1944
Avda. Tampico, No. 22, Esquina Manzanillo, Edificio "A", 1er. Piso, Local 4, 70610
Tel: (52-294) 40513
Circ.—25,000
Gen. Dir.—Benjamín Fernández Pichardo
Dir.—Guillermo Soto Bejarano
Ad.—$7.15

SAN FRANCISCO DEL RINCON
(Guanajuato)
Pop. Est. 83,601

AM DE SAN FRANCISCO (m) Est. 1985
Carranza, No. 126, Oriente
Tel: (52-464) 30336; Fax: (52-464) 30336
Gen. Dir.—Enrique Gómez Orozco
Edit'l. Dir.—Miguel Barragán T
Ad.—$6.60

SAN JUAN DEL RIO
(Queretaro)
Pop. Est. 126,555

EL SOL DE SAN JUAN DEL RIO (San Juan Del Rio Sun) (m) Est. 1980
Avda. Juarez, No. 50-109, Poniente
Tel: (52-467) 20556
Circ.—9,000
Prop.—Cía. Periodística del Sol de Querétaro SA de CV
Pres./Gen. Dir.—Mario Vázquez Raña
Mng. Dir.—Luís R Amieva
Ad.—$3.75

SAN LUIS POTOSI
(San Luis Potosi)
Pop. Est. 525,733

EL HERALDO (The Herald) (mS) Est. 1942
Villerias, No. 305, 78000
Tel: (52-48) 123312/(52-48) 123657; Fax: (52-48) 122081
Circ.—60,620
Prop.—El Heraldo Cía. Editorial SA
Gen. Dir.—Alejandro Villasana Mena
Dir.—Vicente Villasana Mena
Gen. Mgr.—Rodrigo Villasana Mena
Gen. Adm.—Armando Tostado Vázquez
Ad.—$12.50
MOMENTO (Moment) (m) Est. 1975
Zenón Fernandez y Leandro Valle, 78280
Tel: (52-48) 123312; Fax: (52-48) 120216/(52-48) 122020
Circ.—40,000
Prop.—Editora Regional del Centro SA de CV
Gen. Dir.—Ramón Pedroza Langarcia
Gen. Mgr.—J Armando Flores Navarro
Ad.—$9.15
LA OPINION (The Opinion) (d) Est. 1978
Venustiano Carranza, No. 433
Tel: (52-48) 120049
Circ.—25,000
Pub.—Ignacio A Rosillo
PULSO (Pulse) (m)
Galeana, No. 485, 78000
Tel: (52-48) 127575/(52-48) 127512; Fax: (52-48) 123525
Circ.—60,000
Prop.—Editora Mival SA
Gen. Dir.—Miguel Valladares García
Edit'l. Dir.—Florencio Ruíz De la Peña
Ad. Mgr.—Rogelio Cataño Barrera
Ad.—$8.75
SAN LUIS HOY (San Luis Today) (m) Est. 1993
Independencia, No. 1205, Centro; Apdo. Postal 421, 78000
Tel: (52-48) 124412; Fax: (52-48) 100100
Circ.—25,000
Prop.—Editora de Medios Impresos SA de CV
Pub.—Alejandro Leal Toviás
Gen. Mgr.—Jesús E Martens Rodríguez
Edit'l. Dir.—Ernesto Guajardo Wong
Ad.—$9.00
EL SOL DE SAN LUIS (San Luis Sun) (mS) Est. 1952
Avda. Universidad, No. 565; Apdo. Postal 342, 78000
Tel: (52-48) 124412
Circ.—60,000
Prop.—Cía. Periodística del Sol de San Luis Potosi SA de CV
Pres./Gen. Dir.—Mario Vázquez Raña
Dir.—José Angel Martínez Limón
Mgr.—Francisco López Espinosa
Ad.—$6.25

SAN LUIS RIO COLORADO
(Sonora)
Pop. Est. 110,530

EL HERALDO (The Herald) (m)
Callejon Obregon y Cinco A
Tel: (52-635) 41025
Pub.—Jesús Pedro Campa H
TRIBUNA DE SAN LUIS (San Luis Tribune) (d) Est. 1974
Calle Sexta y Avda. Juarez, No. 609, Col. Commercial, 83449
Tel: (52-653) 41999; Fax: (52-653) 42542
Circ.—10,000
Prop.—Editora Sonora Baja California SA
Pres./Gen. Dir.—Mario Vázquez Raña
Dir.—Miguel Angel Moreno Cota
Gen. Mgr.—Mario Valdés H
Ad. Mgr.—Carlos Calderón De la Barca Ceballos
Ad.—$3.05

TACAMBARO
(Michoacan)

AVANZADA (Advancer) (d)
Fray Alonso de la Veracruz, No. 58
Tel: (52-454) 60027
Dir.—Servio Tulio Gutiérrez Venegas
PIONERO (Pioneer) (d)
Agustin Lara, No. 24
Dir.—Margarita Tapia Quintana

TAMPICO
(Tamaulipas)
Pop. Est. 272,690

EL CORREO (The Mail) (d)
Ejercito Nacional, No. 201
Pub.—Antonio M Marón
EL DIARIO DE TAMPICO (Tampico Daily) Est. 1990
Altamira, No. 800, Poniente, Esquina
Avda. Hidalgo; Apdo. Postal 708, 89000
Tel: (52-12) 190395; Fax: (52-12) 123304
Circ.—35,000
Prop.—Periodíco El Diario de Tampico SA de CV
Founder/Pres.—Jesús D González
Gen. Dir.—Francisco A González
Edit'l. Dir.—Jorge Villegas
Dir.—María Eugenia González
Ad.—$13.00
EXTRA DIARIO DE TAMPICO (Extra Tampico Daily) (e-ex S) Est. 1991
Altamira, No. 800, Poniente, Esquina
Avda. Hidalgo; Apdo. Postal 708, 89000
Tel: (52-12) 190395; Fax: (52-12) 123304
Circ.—15,000
Prop.—El Diario De Tampico SA de CV
Founder/Pres.—Jesús D González
Gen. Dir.—Francisco A González
Ad.—$7.00
EL HERALDO DE TAMPICO (Tampico Herald) (mS) Est. 1976
Venustiano Carranza, No. 801, Poniente
Tel: (52-12) 128260
Circ.—95,000
Pub.—Mauricio Bercun
Ad. Mgr.—Faustino Paredes
EL MUNDO (The World) (mS) Est. 1918
Ejército Nacional, No. 201, Col. Guadalupe, 89120
Tel: (52-12) 134570/(52-12) 134084
Circ.—54,000
Prop.—Editora Tamaulipas del Golfo SA
Gen. Dir.—Antonio Manzur Marón
Mgr.—Jesús L Hernández Pérez
Ad.—$9.00
EL SOL DE TAMPICO (Tampico Sun) (mS) Est. 1950
Altamira, No. 311, Poniente, Apdo. Postal 434, 89000
Tel: (52-12) 123061/(59-12) 123566; Fax: (52-12) 126821/(52-12) 120170
Circ.—77,000
Prop.—Cía. Periodística de Tampico SA de CV
Pres./Gen. Dir.—Mario Vázquez Raña
Mng. Dir.—Rubén Diaz de la Garza
Ad.—$6.00
(This is the morning edition of El Sol De La Tarde.)
EL SOL DE LA TARDE (Afternoon Sun) (e-ex S) Est. 1955
Altamira, No. 311, Poniente; Apdo. Postal 434, 89000
Tel: (52-12) 123061/(52-12) 123566; Fax: (52-12) 126821/(52-12) 120170
Circ.—37,000
Prop.—Cía. Periodística del Sol de Tampico SA de CV
Pres./Gen. Dir.—Mario Vázquez Raña
Mng. Dir.—Rubén Díaz de la Garza
Sub. Mgr.—Alberto González Enríquez
(This is the evening edition of El Sol de Tampico in Tampico.)

TAPACHULA
(Chiapas)
Pop. Est. 222,405

DIARIO DEL SUR (South Daily) (m-ex mon.) Est. 1947
2a. Poniente, No. 4, 30700
Tel: (52-962) 61132; Fax: (52-962) 64301
Circ.—10,000
Prop.—Cía. Editorial
Founder—Juan Abarca Pérez
Gen. Dir.—Luís Guízar Oceguera
Ad.—$6.00
NOTICIAS DE CHIAPAS (Chiapas News) (m-ex mon.) Est. 1983
3a. Norte, No. 8, 30700
Tel: (52-962) 62335; Fax: (52-962) 68310
Circ.—15,000
Gen. Dir.—Carlos Correa Leo
Ad.—$5.00

EL SOL DEL SOCONUSCO (Soconusco Sun) (m) Est. 1952
2a. Avda. Sur, No. 23-B
Tel: (52-962) 64360
Circ.—8,000
Prop.—Organización Editora Mexicana
Dir.—Nahum Gómez Grajales
SUR DE MEXICO (South of Mexico) (d-ex mon.)
Centro Poniente, No. 36, 30700
Tel: (52-962) 65306/(52-962) 50591
Circ.—10,000
Dir.—Augusto Enrique Villareal Quezada
Ad.—$19.36
SURESTE (m) Est. 1994
10a. Avda., No. 162, Sur, Col. Hortalizas Japonesas, 30799
Tel: (52-962) 61814/(52-962) 68406
Circ.—30,000
Edit'l. Dir.—Sergio Gutiérrez Vargas
Adm. Dir.—José M Piña González

TAXCO
(Guerrero)
Pop. Est. 86,864

DIARIO DE TAXCO (Taxco Daily) (m) Est. 1991
Morelos, No. 37, Int. 5, 40200
Tel: (52-733) 23950
Circ.—15,000
Gen. Dir.—Urbano Delgado Castañeda
Dir.—Agustín Mazón Barrera
Mgr.—Alfredo Desentis Ruíz
Ed.—Urbano Delgado Castaneda

TECOMAN
(Colima)

MONITOR DE COLIMA (Colima Monitor) (d)
Antonio Montes, No. 27, Sur
Tel: (52-332) 42350
Dir.—Tranquilino Contreras Renteria

TEHUACAN
(Puebla)
Pop. Est. 155,563

LA ESCOBA (The Broom) (m) Est. 1932
1 Norte, No. 212; Apdo. Postal 87
Tel: (52-238) 21233/(52-238) 21044
Circ.—10,000
Prop.—Organización de Periodícos La Escoba
Gen. Dir.—Daniel Gamez Andrade
EL MUNDO DE TEHUACAN (The World of Tehuacan) (m) Est. 1981
Avda. Reforma, No. 100, Norte Altos 1, Col. Centro, 75700
Tel: (52-238) 23903/(52-238) 22691; Fax: (52-238) 22629
Circ.—10,000
Prop.—Sociedad Editora Arróniz SA
Founder—Dr. Othón Arróniz Báez
Gen. Dir.—Clementina de la Huerta de Arróniz
Dir.—José Manuel Castillo Zárate
Ad. Mgr.—Marisol Arróniz de Márquez
Ad.—$7.50
EL SOL DE TEHUACAN (Tehuacan Sun) (m) Est. 1944
Avda. Independencia, No. 101, 72000
Tel: (52-238) 23204
Circ.—9,000
Prop.—Cía. Periodística del Sol de Puebla SA de CV
Pres./Gen. Dir.—Mario Vázquez Raña
Dir.—Angel Torres García
Mgr.—Rodolfo Sierra Sánchez
Ad.—$1.30

TEPIC
(Nayarit)
Pop. Est. 241,463

DIARIO DEL PACIFICO (Pacific Daily) (d)
Avda. Mexico, No. 189, Sur
Tel: (52-321) 31899
Gen. Mgr.—Emilio Valdéz Hernández
EXPRESS (d)
Ejido, No. 251, Norte y Amado Nervo
Tel: (52-321) 26731
Gen. Mgr.—Edgar Arellano Ontiveros
MERIDIANO (Meridian) (m) Est. 1942
Emiliano Zapata, No. 73, Poniente; Apdo. Postal 65, 63000
Tel: (52-321) 20145/(52-321) 29418; Fax: (52-321) 26630
Circ.—60,000
Prop.—Cía. Editorial Alpesor
Dir.—Dr. José Luís David Alfaro
Ad.—$13.75

NOVEDADES (d)
Avda. Insurgentes, No. 170, Poniente
Prop.—Novedades Editores
EL OBSERVADOR (The Observer) (m)
Querétaro, No. 246, Sur, 2o. Piso, 63000
Tel: (52-321) 46262; Fax: (52-321) 46363
Circ.—50,000
Prop.—Editorial Hispano Mexicano
Pres./Gen. Dir.—Luís Arturo González Becerra
Mng. Dir.—Fernando Gutiérrez Pinedo
Mgr.—José Iñiguez Nuñez
Ad. Mgr.—Francisco Ortiz
Ad.—$18.00
PRENSA LIBRE (Free Press) (d) Est. 1932
Morelos, No. 120, Poniente
Pub.—José González Reyna
Ad. Mgr.—Ignacia López Ramírez
EL PUEBLO (The Town) (d)
13 de Septiembre, No. 33
REALIDADES (Realities) (m) Est. 1981
Avda. Juarez, No. 408, Oriente, 63000
Tel: (52-321) 34651; Fax: (52-321) 40657
Gen. Dir.—Hugo Rodríguez Jiménez
Ad.—$12.00
EL SOL DE TEPIC (Tepic Sun) (m-ex S) Est. 1951
Zacatecas, Sur, No. 148, Altos; Apdo. Postal 112
Tel: (52-321) 36996/(52-321) 36581
Circ.—10,000
Prop.—Editorial Sol de Nayarit
Gen. Dir.—Prof. Guillermo E Rodríguez Jiménez
Ed. in Ch.—Oziel Rosas Nuñez
Ad.—$5.80
EL TIEMPO DE NAYARIT (The Time of Nayarit) (m) Est. 1955
Avda. Insurgentes, No. 278, Poniente
Tel: (52-321) 35333
Circ.—10,000
Gen. Dir.—Ramón Audelo Landazuri
Dir.—Antonio García Hernández
ULTIMAS NOTICIAS DE NAYARIT (Last News of Nayarit) (d)
Hidalgo, No. 240, Poniente
Tel: (52-321) 21634
Gen. Dir.—César A Renteria Velázquez
LA VOZ DE NAYARIT (The Voice of Nayarit) (d)
Zacatecas, No. 224, Norte
Tel: (52-321) 20503
Gen. Dir.—Marco Antonio Casillas

TIJUANA
(Baja California Norte)
Pop. Est. 747,381

ABC (e) Est. 1977
Aguas Caliente, No. 2700, Col. Cacho, 22150
Tel: (52-66) 841644/(52-66) 840971
Circ.—50,000
Gen. Mgr.—Rafael A Martínez
BAJA CALIFORNIA (m) Est. 1947
Calle 1, Poniente, No. 109-A, Ciudad Industrial, 22450
Tel: (52-66) 235022; Fax: (52-66) 235030
Circ.—55,000
Prop.—Cía. Periodística Bajacaliforniana SA
Gen. Dir.—Marco Antonio Blásquez Salinas
Ad.—$19.50
DIARIO 29 (Daily 29) (m) Est. 1992
Paseo de los Heroes y Mina, Central Tijuana, Locales 6 y 7, Col. Zona Rio, 22320
Tel: (52-66) 340084/(52-66) 340083; Fax: (52-66) 340083
Circ.—40,000
Gen. Dir.—Virgilio Muñoz
Edit'l. Dir.—Rogelio Lozoya Godoy
EL HERALDO DE BAJA CALIFORNIA (Baja California Herald) (m) Est. 1941
Rio Colorado, No. 315, Col. Marrón; Apdo. Postal 1226, 22400
Tel: (52-66) 864314; Fax: (52-66) 864365
Circ.—20,000
Prop.—El Heraldo SA
Gen. Dir.—Francisco Ramírez Guerrero
Ad.—$11.00
EL MEXICANO (The Mexican) (m) Est. 1959
Carretera al Aeropuerto, s/n
Fraccionamiento Alamar; Apdo. Postal 2333, 22540
Tel: (52-66) 261602; Fax: (52-66) 212944
Circ.—80,000
Pres./Gen. Dir.—Eligio Valencia Roque
Ad. Mgr.—Salvador Rueda Badillo
Ad.—$8.70
SEGUNDA EDICION (Second Edition) (e-ex S)
Carretera al Aeropuerto, s/n
Fraccionamiento, Alamar La Mesa
Tel: (52-66) 213400; Fax: (52-66) 212944
Circ.—45,000
Pres./Gen. Dir.—Eligio Valencia Roque
Dir.—Francisco Juarez López
Ad. Dir.—Salvador Rueda Badillo
Ad.—$5.10

EL SOL DE TIJUANA (Tijuana Sun) (m) Est. 1989
Rufino Tamayo, No. 4, Zona Rio, 22320
Tel: (52-66) 343232; Fax: (52-66) 343211
Circ.—50,000
Prop.—Cía. Periodística del Sol de Tijuana SA
Dir.—Mario Vázquez Raña
Dir.—Rubén Téllez Fuentes
Mgr.—Moisés Velasco Murillo
Ad. Mgr.—Teresa Rodríguez
ULTIMAS NOTICIAS (Last News) (e)
Carretera al Aeropuerto Alamar; Apdo. Postal 2333
Tel: (52-66) 868001
Circ.—45,000
Pub.—José de Jesús Rios
Ad. Mgr.—Salvador Rueda Badillo

TLANEPANTLA
(Mexico)
Pop. Est. 915,178

AVANCE (Advance) (dS) Est. 1970
Juarez, No. 23-6
Tel: (52-56) 58125
Circ.—20,000
Pub.—José O'Farrill Larranaga

TLAXCALA
(Tlaxcala)
Pop. Est. 50,492

EL SOL DE TLAXCALA (Tlaxcala Sun) (m) Est. 1955
Calle 3, No. 815, Col. Xicoténcatl, 90070
Tel: (52-246) 25742/(52-246) 25743; Fax: (52-246) 26233
Circ.—15,000
Prop.—Cía. Periodística Del Sol de Tlaxcala SA
Pub.—Mario Vázquez Raña
Mng. Dir.—Vicente Morales Galaviz
Adm.—Serafín Salazar Arellano
Ad. Mgr.—Antonia Pérez Pérez
Ad.—$3.70

TOLUCA
(Mexico)
Pop. Est. 487,612

ABC (m) Est. 1984
Avda. Hidalgo, No. 1339, Oriente, 50000
Tel: (52-72) 179880/(52-72) 179640
Circ.—65,000
Prop.—Editores ABC del Estado de México SA de CV
Pres./Ed.—Miled Libien Kaui
Gen. Dir.—Miled Libien Santiago
Dir.—Guillermo Padilla Cruz
Gen. Mgr.—Gabriela Libien Santiago
Ad. Mgr.—Francisco Rodríguez
Ad.—$6.00
AMANECER (Sunrise) (d)
Paseo Tollocan, No. 802, Poniente
Tel: (52-72) 179100/(52-72) 172885; Fax: (52-72) 179547
Dir.—Juan López Cruz
Mng. Ed.—Naim Libien Kaul
ATARDECER (Sunset) (d)
Paseo Tollocan, No. 802, Poniente
Tel: (52-72) 179100/(52-72) 172885; Fax: (52-72) 179547
Dir.—Juan López Cruz
Mng. Ed.—Naim Libien Kaul
EL DIARIO (The Daily) (mS) Est. 1980
Allende, No. 207, Sur, 50000
Tel: (52-72) 142403/(52-72) 141658; Fax: (52-72) 141523
Circ.—22,000
Prop.—Corporación Editorial MAC SA de CV
Pub.—Luís Maccise Uribe
Vice Pres.—Anuar Maccise Uribe
Mng. Dir.—Jorge Ortiz Arrieta
Ed.—Victor Yanez
Ad.—$6.80
EXTRA DEL SOL (Sun Extra) (e-ex S) Est. 1957
Santos Degollado, No. 105; Apdo. Postal 54, 50050
Tel: (52-72) 150340/(52-72) 153881; Fax: (52-72) 150340/(52-72) 147441
Circ.—17,000
Prop.—Cía. Periodística del Sol de Toluca SA de CV
Pres./Gen. Dir.—Mario Vázquez Raña
Dir.—Rafael Vilchis Gil De Arévalo
Mgr.—Napoleon Galván Tellez
Ad. Mgr.—Emilio Díaz Hernández
Ad.—$3.00
EL FINANCIERO (The Financer) (m-ex wknd.)
Matamoros, Sur, No. 117, Bis. Centro
Tel: (52-72) 147053; Fax: (52-72) 134532
Circ.—6,000
Dir.—Rogelio Cárdenas Sarmiento
Ad.—$17.50

EL HERALDO DE TOLUCA (Toluca Herald) (m)
Salvador Díaz Mirón, No. 700, Col.
Sanchez Colin, 50150
Tel: (52-72) 174913/(52-72) 173542;
Fax: (52-72) 122535
Circ.—90,000
Prop.—Editora Tolotzin
Ex. Ed.—Alberto Barraza Sánchez A
Ad.—$7.46
EL MAÑANA (Tomorrow) (m) Est. 1986
Avda. Hidalgo, No. 1339, Oriente
Tel: (52-72) 179880/(52-72) 179640
Circ.—65,000
Pres./Ed.—Miled Libien Kaui
Gen. Dir.—Miled Libien Santiago
Dir.—Prof. Santos Sánchez Albarrán
Dir.—Guillermo Padilla Cruz
Gen. Mgr.—Gabriela Libien Santiago
Ad.—$4.00
EL NOTICIERO (e) Est. 1993
Allende Sur, No. 205, 50000
Tel: (52-72) 142403; Fax: (52-72) 141523
Circ.—10,000
Prop.—Editora Lithomex
Vice Pres.—Anuar Macisse Uribe
Mng. Dir.—Jorge Ortiz Arrieta
Gen. Dir.—Luis Macisse Uribe
Ed.—Anuar Macisse Dib
Ad.—$6.80
RUMBO (mS) Est. 1969
Allende, Sur, No. 205
Tel: (52-72) 142403/(52-72) 141658;
Fax: (52-72) 141523
Circ.—10,800
Prop.—Corporación Editorial MAC SA de CV
Vice Pres.—Anuar Maccise Uribe
Gen. Dir.—Luís Maccise Uribe
Dir.—Antonio García Rojas
Ed.—Anuar Maccise Dib
Mng. Dir.—Jorge Ortiz Arrieta
Ad.—$6.80
EL SOL DE TOLUCA (Toluca Sun) (mS) Est. 1947
Santos Degollado, No. 105; Apdo. Postal 54, 50050
Tel: (52-72) 150340/(52-72) 153881;
Fax: (52-72) 150340/(52-72) 147441
Circ.—42,000
Prop.—Cía. Periodística del Sol de Toluca SA de CV
Pres./Gen. Dir.—Mario Vázquez Raña
Dir.—Rafael Vilchis Gil De Arévalo
Mgr.—Napoleón Galván Téllez
Ad. Mgr.—Emilio Díaz Hernández
Ad.—$6.00
EL VESPERTINO (The Evening) (e-ex S) Est. 1985
Avda. Hidalgo, No. 1339, Oriente
Tel: (52-72) 179880/(52-72) 179640
Circ.—25,000
Pres./Ed.—Miled Libien Kaui
Gen. Dir.—Miled Libien Santiago
Gen. Mgr.—Gabriela Libien Santiago
Ad. Mgr.—Francisco Rodríguez
Ad.—$3.00

TORREON
(Coahuila)
Pop. Est. 464,825

NOTICIAS DEL SOL DE LA LAGUNA (News of the Laguna Sun) (m) Est. 1975
Blvd. Constitución y Javier Mina, s/n, 27350
Tel: (52-17) 164040; Fax: (52-17) 161717/(52-17) 164503
Circ.—17,000
Prop.—Editorial Noticias
Pres./Gen. Dir.—Mario Vázquez Raña
Mng. Dir.—Régulo Esquivel Gámez
Ad. Mgr.—Guillermina Ulloa Ugarte
Ad.—$6.50
LA OPINION (The Opinion) (m) Est. 1917
Blvd. Independencia, No. 1492, Oriente;
Apdo. Postal 86, 27010
Tel: (52-17) 138777; Fax: (52-17) 138164/(52-17) 189030
Circ.—40,000
Prop.—Editorial La Opinión SA
Pres.—Francisco A González
Gen. Dir.—Jorge Villegas
Ad.—$13.00
LA OPINION DE LA TARDE (The Opinion of the Afternoon) (e-ex S) Est. 1955
Blvd. Independencia, No. 1492, Oriente;
Apdo. Postal 86, 27010
Tel: (52-17) 173434; Fax: (52-17) 138164
Circ.—20,000
Prop.—Editorial La Opinión SA
Pres.—Francisco A González
Pub.—V M Guillermo Jaramillo
Gen. Dir.—Jorge Villegas
Ad.—$7.00
(This is the evening edition of La Opinion in Torreon.)

EL SIGLO DE TORREON (The Torreon Century) (mS) Est. 1922
Avda. Matamoros, No. 1056, Poniente;
Apdo. Postal 19, 27000
Tel: (52-17) 124800/(52-17) 124500
Circ.—38,611 (m); 38,526 (S)
Prop.—Cía. Editora de la Laguna SA de CV
Gen. Mgr.—Miguel Angel Ruelas Talamantes
Ad.—$14.00
VANGUARDIA LAGUNA (Laguna Vanguard) (m) Est. 1980
Matamoros, No. 1018, Poniente
Circ.—40,000
Pub.—Oscar Medrano Sánchez
Ad. Mgr.—Gustavo Valdéz Ramírez

TULA
(Hidalgo)
Pop. Est. 53,213

LA REGION (The Region) (d) Est. 1951
Leandro Valle, No. 118
Tel: (52) 20324
Circ.—6,000
Pub.—Francisco Tovar Pérez

TULANCINGO
(Hidalgo)
Pop. Est. 92,570

EL SOL DE TULANCINGO (The Tulancingo Sun) (mS) Est. 1976
Periodístas, Esquina M. F. Soto, 43600
Tel: (52-775) 35800
Circ.—12,000
Prop.—Cía. Periodística del Sol de Pachuca SA de CV
Pres./Gen. Dir.—Mario Vázquez Raña
Dir.—Fausto Marín Tamayo
Ad.—$3.80

TUXPAM
(Veracruz)
Pop. Est. 118,520

DIARIO DE TUXPAM (Tuxpam Daily) (m)
Avda. Juarez, No. 44-202, Centro, 92800
Tel: (52-783) 46248; Fax: (52-783) 46247
Circ.—16,000
Prop.—Editoriales del Norte de Veracruz SA de CV
Founder.—Dr. Othón Arróniz Báez
Gen. Dir.—Clementina de la Huerta de Arróniz
Edit'l. Dir.—Miguel Angel Cristiani G
Ad. Mgr.—Marisol Arróniz de Márquez
Ad.—$7.81
LA TRIBUNA (The Tribune) (m) Est. 1940
Garizurieta, No. 5
Circ.—11,000
Pub.—Carlos Rodríguez R
LA VOZ DE LA HUAXTECA (The Voice of Huaxteca) (m-ex S) Est. 1980
Garizurieta, No. 25, 92800
Tel: (52-783) 41160; Fax: (52-783) 46438/(52-783) 41160
Circ.—24,000
Gen. Dir.—Calixto Almazán Ferrer
Ad.—$12.50

TUXPAN
(Nayarit)

CORREO DEL PACIFICO (Pacific Mail) (d)
Juarez y Lerdo
Tel: (52-323) 20300
Gen. Dir.—Arturo Flores Mejia

TUXTLA GUTIERREZ
(Chiapas)
Pop. Est. 295,608

AMBAR (d)
3a. Poniente, No. 170, Sur
Tel: (52-961) 33163/(52-961) 35376
Gen. Dir.—Juan Balboa Cuesta
CHIAPAS LIBRE (Free Chiapas) (d)
Avda. Pino Suarez, No. 164, Col. Juárez
Tel: (52-961) 10676
Gen. Dir.—Julio Barrera Gordillo
CUARTO PODER (Fourth Might) (m)
3a. Norte, No. 141, Norte, 14013
Tel: (52-961) 14013; Fax: (52-961) 25242
Circ.—30,000
Gen. Dir.—Conrado De la cruz Jiménez
Ad.—$15.00
EL DIA (The Day) (m) Est. 1979
Carretera Miraflores
Circ.—15,000
Pub.—Enrique Toledo Esponda

Central America **Mexico**

ES! DIARIO POPULAR (Is! Popular Daily) (m-ex mon.) Est. 1948
1a. Avda., No. 611, Sur, Oriente, Centro, 29000
Tel: (52-961) 20595; Fax: (52-961) 20595
Circ.—28,000
Founder.—Gervasio Macias Grajales Gómez
Dir.—Alfonso Macías Grajales Burguete
Ad.—$17.50
LA EXTRA (The Extra) (d)
4a. Poniente y 1a. Norte; Apdo. Postal 87
Tel: (52-961) 20219
Gen. Dir.—Francisco Nuñez López
Ad. Dir.—Gonzalo Nuñez de León
EL HERALDO DE CHIAPAS (Chiapas Herald) (d) Est. 1947
1a. Calle Norte, No. 721, Poniente
Tel: (52-961) 21682
Circ.—18,000
Gen. Dir.—Mario Maturana López
Dir.—Hubert Ochoa Ramírez
NOVEDADES DE CHIAPAS (m) Est. 1968
4a. Avda. Sur, No. 414, Oriente, 29000
Tel: (52-961) 22115; Fax: (52-961) 22115
Circ.—12,000
Founder/Ed.—Fernando H Arévalo Juárez
Mgr.—Julio César Arévalo Zavaleta
Ad.—$12.00
NUMERO UNO (Number One) (m-ex mon.) Est. 1981
1a. Avda. Norte, y 2a. Calle, Oriente
Tel: (52-961) 11285/(52-961) 11324;
Fax: (52-961) 28136
Circ.—15,000
Prop.—Organización Editorial de Chiapas
Pres./Gen. Dir.—Jaíme Fernández Armendariz
EL OBSERVADOR DE LA FRONTERA SUR (The Observer of the Southern Frontier) (d)
9a. Sur, No. 2203, Oriente
Tel: (52-961) 29067; Fax: (52-961) 37431
Gen. Dir.—Francisco J Ramírez Solís
EL PERIODICO CUARTO PODER DE CHIAPAS (The Fourth Might Newspaper of Chiapas) (m) Est. 1974
3a. Parte, No. 141, Norte, Col. Centro, 29000
Tel: (52-961) 24353
Pub.—Conrado de la Cruz Jimengo
Ad. Mgr.—Conrado de la Cruz Morales
Ad.—$4.00
EL PLANETA DE CHIAPAS (The Planet of Chiapas) (d-ex mon.) Est. 1974
1a. Avda., No. 1036, Sur, Poniente; Apdo. Postal 28, 29000
Tel: (52-961) 23829; Fax: (52-961) 11344
Circ.—17,000
Dir.—Rafael Revueltas Marín
Ad.—$5.50
LA REPUBLICA EN CHIAPAS (The Republic of Chiapas) (m) Est. 1976
Carretera Panamericana, Km. 1088
Tel: (52-961) 21759/(52-961) 35050;
Fax: (52-961) 28729
Circ.—12,000
Gen. Dir.—José Juan Mendoza Hernández
EL SOL DE CHIAPAS (Chiapas Sun) (dS) Est. 1957
4a. Calle Poniente, No. 221, Norte; Apdo. Postal 87
Tel: (52-961) 20219
Circ.—15,000
Mng. Dir.—Francisco Nuñez López
EL SOL DE TUXTLA GUTIERREZ (Tuxtla Gutierrez Sun) (dS) Est. 1957
4a. Calle Poniente, No. 221, Norte; Apdo. Postal 87
Circ.—15,000
Pub.—Francisco Nuñez López
LA TRIBUNA (The Tribune) (m-ex mon.) Est. 1958
Avda. Central, Poniente, No. 1013
Tel: (52-961) 20614/(52-961) 22206
Circ.—10,000
Prop.—Ediciones La Tribuna Diario de Chiapas
Gen. Dir.—José Luís Cancino Guillén
Ad.—$3.50
LA VERSION (The Version) (d)
2a. Oriente Sur, No. 350
Tel: (52-961) 31506/(52-961) 23204
Gen. Dir.—Ciro Antonio Jimenez Rodríguez
Dir.—Luís Castillo Peralta
LA VOZ DEL SURESTE (The Voice of Sureste) (m-ex mon.) Est. 1948
5a. Norte, Poniente, No. 1412, 29000
Tel: (52-961) 25742/(52-961) 32921

Circ.—12,000
Gen. Dir.—Roberto Coello Trego
Ad.—$7.00

URUAPAN
(Michoacan)
Pop. Est. 217,068

EL CRUZADO (4x wk.) Est. 1961
Privada Lerdo de Tejada, No. 26; Apdo. Postal 233, 60040
Tel: (52-453) 34488/(52-453) 35293
Prop.—Editorial El Cruzado
Gen. Dir.—Roberto Murillo Rocha
Ad.—$7.80
DIARIO DE MICHOACAN (Michoacan Daily) (m-ex mon.) Est. 1971
Filomeno Mata, No. 468, Col. El Periodista, 60120
Tel: (52-452) 40072/(52-452) 37303;
Fax: (52-452) 40072
Circ.—13,000
Prop.—Ediciones Diario de Michoacán
Gen. Dir.—Felipe Arturo Ibañez Torres
Gen. Mgr.—Ulises Ibañez Torres
Ad.—$4.00
LA OPINION DE MICHOACAN (m) Est. 1968
Calzada Benito Juárez, No. 178-A, 60000
Tel: (52-452) 30200; Fax: (52-452) 38989
Circ.—18,000
Prop.—La Opinión de Uruapan SA de CV
Gen. Dir.—Carlos Andrade Ríncón
Ad.—$10.00

VERACRUZ
(Veracruz)
Pop. Est. 328,607

DIARIO DE VERACRUZ (Veracruz Daily) (d) Est. 1979
Zaragoza, No. 236
Tel: (52-29) 51055
Circ.—20,000
Pub.—Rubén Pabello Acosta
EL DICTAMEN (mS) Est. 1898
16 de Septiembre y Arista, 91700
Tel: (52-29) 311745; Fax: (52-29) 315804/(52-29) 313380
Circ.—38,000 (m); 39,000 (S)
Prop.—Editorial Sotavento de Veracruz S de RL de CV
Ex. Vice Pres.—Abel Malpica Martínez
Edit'l. Dir.—Juan Malpica Mimendi
Ad.—$10.00
HOY LA NACION (Today The Nation) (m) Est. 1963
Victimas del 25 de Junio, No. 222, 91700
Tel: (52-29) 315424/(52-29) 315624
Circ.—30,000
Gen. Dir.—Fernando De La Miyar Barrios
Ad.—$6.00
LA NOTICIA (The News) (m) Est. 1966
Holtzunger, No. 76, 91700
Tel: (52-29) 344398
Circ.—18,500
Gen. Dir.—Apolonio Gamboa González
NOTIVER (m)
Francisco Canal y Gómez Farias, s/n, 96999
Tel: (52-29) 360649/(52-29) 310013;
Fax: (52-29) 316146
Circ.—38,000
Prop.—Notiver
Dir.—Alfonso Salces Fernández
Ad.—$12.50
EL SOL DE VERACRUZ (Veracruz Sun) (mS) Est. 1978
Cinco de Mayo, No. 1045
Tel: (52-29) 45520
Circ.—21,000
Prop.—Organización Editorial Mexicana
Pub.—Wilbur Patron O
Ad. Mgr.—Héctor Noguera Trujillo
SUR (South) (m) Est. 1990
Avda. Lerdo, No. 116, Esquina Hidalgo, Col. Centro, 91700
Tel: (52-29) 314531
Circ.—40,000
Prop.—Editora La Voz del Istmo SA de CV
Gen. Dir.—José P Robles Martínez
Dir.—Luís Velázquez Rivera
Gen. Mgr.—Rafael Vega Robles
Ad.—$9.41
LA TARDE (The Afternoon) (e) Est. 1944
16 de Septiembre y Arista
Tel: (52-29) 60011
Circ.—26,000
Gen. Dir.—Juan Malpica Mimendi

Mexico

LA VOZ DE VERACRUZ (The Voice of Veracruz) (m) Est. 1978
Gomez Farias, No. 313
Circ.—35,000
Pub.—Manuel Bravo Malpica

VILLAFLORES
(Chiapas)

EL FRAYLESCANO (d)
Belisario Dominguez, No. 198, Col. Bienestar Social
Tel: (52-961) 34220/(52-961) 29919
Dir.—Julio Archila Gómez

VILLAHERMOSA
(Tabasco)
Pop. Est. 386,779

AVANCE (Advance) (m) Est. 1971
Avda. Mexico, No. 6, Col. El Bosque, 86160
Tel: (52-93) 514400/(52-93) 514401; **Fax:** (52-93) 510311
Circ.—28,000
Prop.—Editora e Impresora del Sureste SA de CV
Pres./Gen. Dir.—Ignacio Cobo González
Gen. Mgr.—Alfonso Valdivia Martínez
Ad. Mgr.—José Luís García Gaspar
Ad.—$14.00

DIARIO DE TABASCO (Tabasco Daily) (m) Est. 1959
Calle Nueva, No. 132, Col. 10 de Mayo
Tel: (52-931) 121715
Circ.—5,000
Pub.—Erwin Macario Rodríguez

NOVEDADES DE TABASCO (m) Est. 1983
Adolfo Ruiz Cortines y Paseo Tabasco, 86030
Tel: (52-93) 158303/(52-93) 158304; **Fax:** (52-93) 155638
Circ.—32,000
Prop.—Novedades de Tabasco SA de CV
Gen. Dir.—Gerardo Gaudiano Peralta
Gen. Mgr.—José Fabián Mondaca Castro
Ad. Mgr.—Lila del Carmen García Faces
Ad.—$9.00

PRESENTE (Present) (m) Est. 1959
José Pagés Llergo s/n, Esquina Sánchez Magallanes, Col. Nueva Villahermosa, 86040
Tel: (52-93) 121755/(52-93) 121775; **Fax:** (52-93) 143493
Pub./Mng. Dir.—Jorge Fausto Calles Broca
Ad.—$19.13

PRESENTE DE LA CHONTALPA (m)
José Pagés Llergo s/n, Esquina Sánchez Magallanes, Col. Nueva Villahermosa, 86040
Tel: (52-93) 121775/(52-93) 121755; **Fax:** (52-93) 143493
Pub./Mng. Dir.—Jorge Fausto Calles Broca
Ad.—$19.13

EL SURESTE DE TABASCO (m)
Avda. Ruiz Cortines, No. 1203, Fraccionamiento, Oropeza, 86035
Tel: (52-93) 154041/(52-93) 154018
Circ.—35,000
Prop.—Ediciones Empresariales del Sureste SA de CV
Edit'l. Dir.—César Velázquez De León
Adm. Dir.—Carlos Madrazo Cardena
Ad.—$8.20

TABASCO HOY (Tabasco Today) (m) Est. 1987
Avda. de los Rios, No. 206, 86035
Tel: (52-93) 162136/(52-93) 160320
Circ.—50,000
Gen. Dir.—Miguel Cantón Zetina
Gen. Mgr.—Antonio Pando Marino
Ad. Mgr.—Norberto López Zetina
Ad.—$14.00

EL VESPERTINO DE PRESENTE (The Present Evening) (e)
José Pagés Llergo s/n, Esquina Sánchez Magallanes, Col. Nueva Villahermosa, 86040
Tel: (52-93) 121775/(52-93) 121755; **Fax:** (52-93) 143493
Pub./Mng. Dir.—Jorge Fausto Calles Broca
Ad.—$19.13

XALISCO
(Nayarit)

DIARIO 13 (d)
Avda. Mexico 21
Gen. Dir.—Andrés González Reyna

ZACAPU
(Michoacan)

REALIDAD (Reality) (d)
Felix Acosta, No. 25
Tel: (52-456) 31383
Dir.—Arturo Velásquez Rivera

ZACAPU EN MARCHA (Zacapu Marching) (d)
Felix Acosta, No. 23
Tel: (52-456) 31383
Dir.—Arturo Velásquez Rivera

ZACATECAS
(Zacatecas)
Pop. Est. 108,556

EL HERALDO (The Herald) (m) Est. 1954
Enrique Estrada, No. 104, Int. 1, Centro, 98000
Tel: (52-492) 24719
Circ.—16,000
Gen. Dir.—Rodrigo Villasana López
Mgr.—Alejandro Villasana Mena
Ad. Mgr.—Jesús Cardona Vega
Ad.—$5.00

IMAGEN (Imagine) (m) Est. 1991
Miguel Auza, No. 312, 98000
Tel: (52-492) 28664/(52-492) 21593
Circ.—60,000
Prop.—Universo Editorial SA de CV
Ex. Dir.—Francisco Javier Llamas Félix
Ex. Dir.—Francisco Javier Llamas Alba
Gen. Mgr.—Edmundo Llamas Félix
Ad.—$15.63

MOMENTO (Moment) (m) Est. 1975
Interior Alameda, No. 440, 98000
Tel: (52-492) 23425/(52-492) 26160; **Fax:** (52-492) 29011
Circ.—40,000
Prop.—Editora Regional del Centro SA de CV
Gen. Dir.—Ramón Pedroza Langarcia
Dir.—Francisco Javier Santillan Medina
Gen. Mgr.—J Armando Flores Navarro
Ad.—$12.25

OPINION DE ZACATECAS (Opinion of Zacatecas) (m)
Avda. González Ortega, No. 101
Tel: (52-492) 25032
Circ.—20,000
Prop.—Editorial Libros y Periodicos
Pub.—Gustavo A Lomelin Guerra
Ad. Mgr.—Salvador Noriega M

EL SOL DE ZACATECAS (mS) Est. 1964
Avda. Quebradilla, No. 602, Col. Caminera, 98000
Tel: (52-492) 26583/(52-492) 26585; **Fax:** (52-492) 23267
Circ.—45,800
Prop.—Cía. Periodística del Sol de Zacatecas SA
Pres./Gen. Dir.—Mario Vázquez Raña
Mng. Dir.—Juan Gómez Hernández
Ad.—$10.00

LA VOZ DEL PUEBLO (The Voice of the Town) (e) Est. 1948
Jardin Hidalgo, No. 606
Circ.—10,000
Pub.—R de Jesús Luna Martínez
Ad. Mgr.—Rafaela Miranda Moreno

ZAMORA
(Michoacan)
Pop. Est. 144,899

EL DIARIO DE ZAMORA (Zamora Daily) (m-ex mon.) Est. 1966
Olivo, No. 430; Apdo. Postal 51, 59600
Tel: (52-351) 20926/(52-351) 26467
Circ.—10,000
Dir.—Jaíme Ochoa Ceja
Ad.—$14.38

EL HERALDO DE ZAMORA (Zamora Herald) (m) Est. 1952
Colon, No. 49, Poniente, 59600
Tel: (52-351) 21939; **Fax:** (52-351) 28756
Circ.—21,000
Prop.—El Heraldo de Zamora SA de CV
Mng. Dir.—José Guadalupe Segura Salazar
Dir.—Efraín González Núñez
Ad.—$9.00

EL SOL DE ZAMORA (Zamora Sun) (m) Est. 1981
Morelos, No. 353, Sur, 59600
Tel: (52-351) 24187; **Fax:** (52-351) 53360
Circ.—16,000
Prop.—Cía. Periodística del Sol de Zamora SA de CV
Pres./Gen. Dir.—Mario Vázquez Raña
Dir.—Armando Palomino Morales
Mgr.—Antonio Ortega Medina
Ed. in Ch.—Miguel Monge Monge
Ad. Mgr.—Antonio Duarte Ruíz
Ad.—$7.00

LA VOZ DE ZAMORA (Zamora Voice) (d) Est. 1958
Jardin del Teco, No. 91
Tel: (52-351) 21560

Circ.—12,000
Pub.—Miguel Valencia Mora

Z DE ZAMORA (Z of Zamora) (d-ex mon.)
Privada 5 de Mayo, No. 2-101
Tel: (52-351) 54489
Mng. Dir.—David Niño Zayala
Ad.—$7.90

ZIHUATANEJO

EL DIARIO DE ZIHUATANEJO (Zihuatanejo Daily) (m-ex mon.) Est. 1971
Domicilio Conocido en Agua de Correa Zihuatanejo
Tel: (52-753) 43246
Circ.—5,000
Prop.—Ediciones Diario de Zihuatanejo
Gen. Dir.—Héctor García Cantú
Gen. Mgr.—Héctor García Alvarez
Ad.—$6.00

ZITACUARO
(Michoacan)
Pop. Est. 107,475

LA VERDAD (The Truth) (d-ex mon.) Est. 1961
Avda. Revolución, No. 23, Norte, Esquina Cuauhtemoc, 61500
Tel: (52-725) 31310
Circ.—10,000
Prop.—Editora de la Verdad de Michoacán
Gen. Dir.—Juan Rueda Juárez
Dir.—Blanca Estela Rueda Cazares
Ad.—$8.40

Central America

NICARAGUA
Pop. Est. 4,096,689

MANAGUA
Pop. Est. 992,020

BARRICADA (Barricade) (m) Est. 1979
Detrás del Bolerama, Camino de Oriente
Tel: (505-2) 674727/(505-2) 674885; **Fax:** (502-2) 673941
Circ.—35,000
Prop.—Editorial El Amanecer
Pres.—Bayardo Arce Castaño
Dir.—Lumberto Campbell Hoocker
Gen. Mgr.—Ronaldo Gómez R
Ch. Ed.—William Grigsby Vado
Ed. in Ch.—Roberto Fonseca
Ed.—Juan Ramón Huerta
Sales Mgr.—Medardo Mendoza

EL NUEVO DIARIO (The New Daily) (m) Est. 1980
Pista Pedro Joaquín Chamorro, Km. 4 Carretera Norte; Apdo. Postal 4591
Tel: (505-2) 491190/(505-2) 42153; **Fax:** (505-2) 490700
Circ.—50,000
Prop.—El Nuevo Diario SA
Pres./Gen. Mgr./Dir.—Xavier Chamorro Cordenal
Ed.—Francisco Chamorro García
Ed.—Mario Fulvio Espinoza
Ed.—Carlos Martínez
Ch. of Info.—Ernesto Aburto

LA PRENSA (The Press) (e) Est. 1926
Pista Pedro Joaquín Chamorro, Km. 4 1/2; Apdo. Postal 192
Tel: (505-2) 490322/(505-2) 493569; **Fax:** (505-2) 496926/(505-2) 496928
Circ.—45,000
Prop.—Editorial La Prensa
Pres.—Jaime Chamorro Cardenal
Ex. Dir.—Horacio Ruíz Solís
Gen. Dir.—Pablo Antonio Cuadra
Gen. Mgr.—Horacio Vivas Downing
Ed. in Ch.—Fidelina Suárez
Ed.—Iván Cisneros
Ed.—José Davila
Ed.—Carlos Ramírez M
Ed.—Ana María Ruíz
Ed.—Pedro Xavier Solís
Ed.—Edwin Yllescas
U.S. Rep.—Charney/Palacios & Co. Inc.

LA TRIBUNA (The Tribune) (m) Est. 1993
Detrás del Banco Mercantil Plaza España
Tel: (505-2) 667581/(505-2) 667585; **Fax:** (505-2) 667588/(505-2) 669089
Prop.—Publicaciones La Tribuna SA
Pres./Gen. Dir.—Haroldo J Montealegre L
Vice Pres.—Roberto Sansón
Gen. Mgr.—Armando Castillo
Mgr.—Adolfo Vivas
Ed.—Oswaldo Bonilla Henríquez
Ed.—María Eugenia de Castillo
Ed.—Eduardo Estrada
Ed.—Juan Navarro

PANAMA
Pop. Est. 2,063,000

PANAMA CITY
Pop. Est. 1,072,127

CRITICA LIBRE (Free Critic) (m) Est. 1958
Vía Ricardo J. Alfaro; Apdo. Postal B-4, 9-A
Tel: (507) 301666; **Fax:** (507) 300165
Circ.—35,000
Prop.—Editora Panamá América SA
Pres./Owner—Rosario Arias de Galindo
Vice Pres.—Francisco Arias
Gen. Mgr.—Ignacio Mallol
Ch. Ed.—Eduardo Soto
Dir./Ed.—Antonio Díaz
Edit'l. Dir.—Octavio Amat
Ed. in Ch.—Luís Quintero
Ad. Dir.—Marcos Cordoba

LA ESTRELLA DE PANAMA (The Panama Star) (mS) Est. 1853
Calle Alejandro Duque G; Apdo. Postal Q-4
Tel: (507) 270555/(507) 270559; **Fax:** (507) 270734/(507) 270723
Circ.—21,000
Prop.—The Star & Herald Co.
Pres./Dir.—Tomás Gabriel Altamirano Duque
Gen. Mgr.—Ricardo Morcillo
Ed. in Ch.—Juan Carlos Duque Mc
Ad. Dir.—Juan Antonio González
Ed.—Carlos Ozores
Ed.—Victor Raúl Vásquez
U.S. Rep.—Charney/Palacios & Co. Inc.; AdMarket Int'l.

EL EXPRESSO (The Express) (d) Chinese; Est. 1992
Local 14, Edificio Via Veneto Plaza al lado del Hotel Panama
Tel: (507) 237304/(507) 237313; **Fax:** (507) 691026
Circ.—1,500
Dir.—Marcel Ho
Ed.—Liu Gan

HOY (Today) (m) Est. 1993
Condominio Anayansi, Avda. Chile y Calle 38, Local No. 1; Apdo. Postal 87-0289
Tel: (507) 251666; **Fax:** (507) 270740
Circ.—12,000
Pres./Dir./Ed.—Eduardo Vallarino
Gen. Mgr.—Sergio A Rodríguez Montes de Oca
Ed. in Ch.—Euclides M Corro R
Ch. of Info.—Austreberta T de Navarro
Adm. Mgr.—Mayre de Calvo

EL PANAMA AMERICA (Panama America) (d) Est. 1925
Vía Ricardo J. Alfaro; Apdo. Postal B-4, 9-A
Tel: (507) 301666; **Fax:** (507) 300165
Circ.—25,000
Prop.—Editora Panamá América SA
Pres.—Rosario Arias de Galindo
Vice Pres.—Francisco Arias
Gen. Mgr.—Ignacio Mallol
Dir.—Carlos A Mendoza
Ed. in Ch.—Mari-Carmen Sarsanedas
Ch. of Info.—Migdalia Fuentes de Pineda
Ad. Dir.—Marcos Cordoba

LA PRENSA (The Press) (d) Est. 1980
Avda. 12 de Octubre y Calle C, Hato Pintado; Apdo. Postal 6-4586, El Dorado
Tel: (507) 217222/(507) 217537; **Fax:** (507) 217328
Circ.—38,000
Prop.—Corporación La Prensa SA
Owner—Roberto Eisenmann
Pres./Dir.—I Roberto Eisenmann Jr
Gen. Mgr.—Juan Luís Correra E
Ad. Dir.—Adela Mendoza
Ed. in Ch.—Nubia Aparicio de Zamorano
Ex. Ed.—Nicolás Gonzalez
U.S. Rep.—Charney/Palacios & Co. Inc.

EL SIGLO (The Century) (m) Est. 1985
Urbana Obarrio, Calle 58, No. 12; Apdo. Postal W-4
Tel: (507) 693311/(507) 644126; **Fax:** (507) 696954/(507) 635383
Circ.—27,000
Prop.—Corporación Universal de Información
Pres.—Jaime Padilla Béliz
Gen. Mgr.—Manolis I Padilla
Dir.—Aneldo Arosemana
Ed. in Ch./Ed.—Rigoberto Caballero
Ad. Dir.—Tatiana Padilla
Ch. of Info.—Agustín Jurado

NEWSPAPERS OF THE MIDDLE EAST

BAHRAIN
Pop. Est. 585,683

MANAMA
Pop. Est. 82,700

AL ADHWAA Arabic
PO Box 250
Tel: (973) 245251/(973) 258552
Circ.—16,000
Prop.—Arab Printing & Publishing House
AL AYAM (m) Arabic; Est. 1989
PO Box 3232
Tel: (973) 727111; Fax: (973) 729009
Circ.—21,565 ABC
Prop.—Al Ayam Press, Publishing & Distribution
Ed.—Nabeel Al Hamar
Ad. Mgr.—Younis Faraj
AKHBAR AL BAHRAIN (d) Arabic
PO Box 253
Prop.—The Ministry of Information
AKHBAR AL KHALEEJ (d) Arabic
PO Box 5300
Tel: (973) 620111; Fax: (973) 621566/(973) 624325
Circ.—30,000
Prop.—Dar Akhbar Al-Khaleej Press
Pub.—Anwar M Abdulraham
Ed.—Ahmed Salman Kamal
Ad. Mgr.—Philip Jacob
U.S. Rep.—AdMarket Int'l.
AL BAHRAIN Arabic
PO Box 253
Tel: (973) 681555
Circ.—4,000
Prop.—Ministry of Information
GULF DAILY NEWS (mS) English; Est. 1978
PO Box 5244
Tel: (973) 293131; Fax: (973) 293400
Circ.—10,000
Prop.—Al Hilah Publishing & Marketing Group
Pub.—Dar Akbar Al Khaleej
AL JARIDA AL RASMIYA (Official Gazette) Arabic
PO Box 253
Prop.—Ministry of Information
SADA AL USBOU (Political) Arabic
PO Box 549
Tel: (973) 253543
Circ.—5,000

IRAN
Pop. Est. 65,615,474

ESFAHAN
(Isfahan)
Pop. Est. 1,422,308

RAHNEJAT (d)
Darvazeh Dowlat
Pub.—N Rahnejat

GILAN

AZAD (d)
Khayaban Shahnaz

KERMAN

ANDESHA (d)
PO Box 77

MASHHAD
(Khorasan)
Pop. Est. 1,463,508

KHORASSAN (d) Est. 1948
14 Zohre St., Mobarezan Ave.
Circ.—40,000
Pub.—M S Tehrnian

SHIRAZ
(Fars)
Pop. Est. 848,000

BAHARI IRAN (d)
Khayaban Khayam
Tel: (98-71) 33738

TEHERAN
Pop. Est. 6,042,584

ABRAR (Rightly Guided) (d) Farsi
Apadan Ave. 198, Abbasabad
Tel: (98-21) 859971
Circ.—75,000
ALIK (e) Armenian; Est. 1931
Jomhouri Islami Ave., Allik Alley; PO Box 11365-953
Tel: (98-21) 676671
Circ.—3,400
Pub.—A Ajemian
ETTELA'AT (Information) (e) Farsi; Est. 1925
Khayyam St.
Tel: (98-21) 311071; Fax: (98-21) 311223
Circ.—350,000
Dir.—Seyyed Mahmud Do'a'i
Ed.—M Shirani
JOURNAL DE TEHERAN
Khayyam Ave.
Circ.—8,000
KAYHAN (e-ex fri.) Farsi; Est. 1941
Ferdowsi Ave.
Tel: (98-21) 310251; Fax: (98-21) 314228
Circ.—350,000
Prop.—Mostazafin Foundation
Dir.—Muhammad Khatami
Ed.—Reza Tehrani
Gen. Mgr.—M Farsa
KAYHAN INTERNATIONAL (m-ex fri.) English; Est. 1959
Ferdowsi Ave.
Tel: (98-21) 310251; Fax: (98-21) 212467
Prop.—Mostazafin Foundation
Gen. Mgr.—M Farsa
KHORASSAN (d)
14 Zohre St., Mobarezan Ave.
Circ.—1,948
TEHERAN TIMES (d) English; Est. 1979
Nejatullahi Ave., 32 Kouche Bimch
Tel: (98-21) 839900
Circ.—7,700
Ed.—M Ansari

IRAQ
Pop. Est. 19,889,666

BAGHDAD
Pop. Est. (Metro Area) 3,400,000

BABIL Arabic
PO Box 5922
Tel: (964-1) 8862008
Pub./Ed.—Udai Saddam Hussein
BAGHDAD OBSERVER (m-ex fri.) English
Dar Al-Ma'mum; PO Box 624
Tel: (964-1) 4169341
Circ.—22,000
Prop.—Dar al-Manum for Translation and Publishing
Ed.—Naji al-Hadithi
AL-BAGTH AL-RIYADI Arabic
PO Box 5922
Tel: (964-1) 8862008
Prop.—Iraqi International Olympic Committee
Ed.—Salman Ali
HAWKARI Kurdish
Kurdish Cultural and Publishing House
Tel: (964-1) 4251846
Ed.—Badr Khan al-Sindi
AL-IRAQ (d) Arabic
PO Box 5717
Tel: (964-1) 7186580; Fax: (964-1) 7186583
Circ.—110,000
Prop.—Dar al-Iraq for Press & Publishing
Ed.—Nasralla al-Dawoodi
AL-JUMHURIYA (d) Arabic; Est. 1958
Waziriya, Al Sarafia; PO Box 491
Tel: (964-1) 4169341; Fax: (964-1) 4161875
Circ.—25,000
Prop.—Al-Jamaheer Press House
Ed.—Sami Mahdi

AL-QADISSIYA Arabic
Hai Al-Tashri
Tel: (964-1) 7765191
Prop.—Ministry of Information
AL-THAWRA (The Revolution) (m) Arabic
Aqaba bin Nafis Sq.; PO Box 2009
Tel: (964-1) 7196161; Fax: (964-1) 7196818
Circ.—250,000
Prop.—Dar Ath Thawra for Publishing
Ed.—Taha al-Basri

ISRAEL
Pop. Est. 5,050,850

HAIFA
Pop. Est. 251,000

AL-ITICHIYAD (d) Arabic
PO Box 104
Tel: (972-4) 511296; Fax: (972-4) 511297

JERUSALEM
Pop. Est. 544,200

AL-ALMUWAKAF
PO Box 21592
Tel: (972-2) 851176
AL ANBA (The News) (m) Arabic; Est. 1968
37 Hillel St.; PO Box 428
Circ.—14,000
Ed. in Ch.—Ovadia Danon
BAHAMANE
Army Post 01013, IDF
Tel: (972-2) 4211364; Fax: (972-2) 4211363
AL-BAIDER AL-SIASI
3 Al-Rashid
Tel: (972-2) 851176
EREV SHABBAT
PO Box 81
Tel: (972-2) 551620; Fax: (972-2) 537527
AL-FAJR (Dawn) (d) Arabic
PO Box 19315-20517
Tel: (972-2) 283336
Ed.—Hana Siniora
HAMACHANE HAHAREDI
PO Box 5783
Tel: (972-2) 380407; Fax: (972-2) 385582
HAMODI'A (The Informer) (m) Hebrew
5 Yehuda HaMalach Jerusalem
Tel: (972-2) 389255; Fax: (972-2) 389108
Circ.—7,000 (S-thurs.); 8,000 (fri.)
Prop.—Agudat Yisrael (Orthodox Jewish Religious Party)
Ed.—Y Levin
JERUSALEM POST (mS) English; Est. 1932
The Jerusalem Post Bldg.; PO Box 81, 91000
Tel: (972-2) 315606; Fax: (972-2) 315631
Circ.—30,000 (m); 51,000 (fri.)
Prop.—Jerusalem Post Pub. Ltd.
Pub.—Yehuda Levy
Ed.—David Bar-Ilan
AL-NA'AR
PO Box 19243
Tel: (972-2) 288260
AL-QUDS (m) Arabic; Est. 1952
PO Box 19788
Tel: (972-2) 282475/(972-2) 284061
Circ.—40,000
Ed.—M Abu-Zuluf
LA SEMANA (The Week) (d) Spanish
PO Box 2427
Tel: (972-2) 664637; Fax: (972-2) 290774
AL-SHA'AB (People) (d) Arabic
Salehadin; PO Box 19154
Tel: (972-2) 289881

NAZARETH

AL-SINARA
PO Box 148
Tel: (972-6) 555750; Fax: (972-6) 578092

TEL-AVIV
Pop. Est. 353,200

A'AOURORA (d) Spanish
PO Box 18066
Tel: (972-3) 5462785; Fax: (972-3) 5469977
CHADSHOT HASPORT (m) Hebrew; Est. 1954
2 Tushia St.; PO Box 20011, 61200
Circ.—27,000
DAVAR (m-ex sat.) Hebrew; Est. 1925
PO Box 199
Tel: (972-3) 286141; Fax: (972-3) 294783
Circ.—30,000 (m); 51,000 (fri.)
Prop.—Histadrut (Labour Federation) Davar Ltd.
Ad. Dir.—Nissan Gan-Mor
GLOBES (d) Hebrew; Est. 1983
127 Igal Alon St., 67443
Tel: (972-3) 210333
Circ.—29,000
Ed.—Matti Golan
HA'ARETZ (The Land) (m-ex sat.) Hebrew; Est. 1918
21 Zalman Shoken St.; PO Box 233, 67770
Tel: (972-3) 5121212; Fax: (972-3) 6815857
Circ.—60,000 (S-thurs.); 110,000 (fri.)
Prop.—Haaretz Daily Newspaper Ltd.
Pub.—Schocken Amos
Ad. Mgr.—Segal Eitan
U.S. Rep.—Israel Communications Inc.; Publicitas
HADASHOT (The News) (m-ex sat.) Hebrew; Est. 1984
103 Yigal Alon St., 67801
Tel: (972-3) 5623084/(972-3) 5611354; Fax: (972-3) 5624257
Circ.—55,000 (S-thurs.); 9,000 (fri.)
Prop.—Hadashot Daily Newspaper Ltd.
Pub./Dir.—Roni Aran
Ed.—Yoel Esteron
Ad. Dir.—Samuel Segal
HADASHOT ISRAEL (d) German
4 HaNeget St.; PO Box 28284
Tel: (972-3) 377111
AL HAMISHMAR (The Guardian) (m) Hebrew; Est. 1943
2 Homa Migdal, 61999
Tel: (972-3) 378833; Fax: (972-3) 5370037
Circ.—26,000
Prop.—Worker's Party
Ed. in Ch.—Sever Ploczker
HAMODIA (d)
5 Yehuda HaMalach
HAOLAM HAZEH (This World) (e) Hebrew
2 Chomah U'migdal
Tel: (972-3) 5376844; Fax: (972-3) 5376811
HATZOFEH (The Watchman) (m) Hebrew
66 Hamasger
Tel: (972-3) 5622951; Fax: (972-3) 5621502
Circ.—16,000
Prop.—National Religious Front
Ed.—M Ishon
ISRAELSKI FAR TRIBUNA (m) Bulgarian; Est. 1952
113 Givat Herzl St.
Tel: (972-3) 370011
Circ.—4,000 (S-thurs.); 6,000 (fri.)
Ed.—D Amarillo
LE JOURNAL D'ISRAEL (The Journal of Israel) (m) French; Est. 1971
26 Agra St.; PO Box 28330
Circ.—10,000
Ed.—Y Rabin
LATZA NEISS (d) Yiddish
52 Harakevet St.
Tel: (972-3) 370011; Fax: (972-3) 5371921
LETZTE NYESS (m) Yiddish; Est. 1949
52 Harakevet St.; PO Box 28034
Tel: (972-3) 35815/(972-3) 35816
Circ.—16,000 (S-thurs.); 20,000 (fri.)
Prop.—Idpars Ltd.
Ed. in Ch.—S Himmelfarb
MA'ARIV EVENING (e-ex sat.) Hebrew; Est. 1948
2 Carlebach St.; PO Box 20010, 61200
Tel: (972-3) 5632111; Fax: (972-3) 5610614
Circ.—130,000 ABC
Prop.—Modin Publishing House Ltd.
Pub.—Offer Nimrodi
Ed.—Ya'acoc Erez

Copyright ©1996 by the Editor & Publisher Co.

Israel Middle East

Ad. Dir.—Yaakov Kedmi
U.S. Rep.—Israel Communications Inc.; Publicitas
MA'ARIV VREMIA
2 Cartebach, 67132
Tel: (972-3) 5632417; Fax: (972-3) 5632029
MABAT LEKALKALA VE-HEVRA Hebrew
Shefa Tal St.
Tel: (972-3) 5627711
NASHA STRANA (m) Russian; Est. 1968
52 Harakevet St., 67770
Tel: (972-3) 370011; Fax: (972-3) 5371921
Circ.—35,000
Ed.—S Himmelfarb
NOWINY KURIER (m) Polish; Est. 1958
52 Harakevet St.
Circ.—12,000 (S-thurs.); 16,000 (fri.)
Pub.—Chadshot Hayom Ltd.
Ed.—S Himmelfarb
SHA'AR (m) Hebrew; Est. 1964
52 Harakevet St., 64284
Tel: (972-3) 5286141
Ed.—Y Kena'an
SHE'ARIM (The Gates) (m) Hebrew; Est. 1951
64 Frisham St.; PO Box 11044
Tel: (972-3) 5230689
Circ.—5,000
Prop.—Poalei Agudat Irael (Labor Branch of Agudat Israel)
TRIBUNA (Tribune) (m) Russian; Est. 1971
113 Givat Herzl
Circ.—4,500
UJ KELET (m) Hungarian; Est. 1918
52 Haeakevet Sy.; PO Box 831
Tel: (972-3) 370011
Circ.—20,000
Ed.—S Himmelfarb
(Uj Kelet is an independent publication.)
VIATA-NOASTRA-LUMEA-NOASTRA (m)
Romanian; Est. 1950
52 Harakevet St.; PO Box 14022
Tel: (972-3) 37801/(972-3) 37805
Circ.—30,000
Prop.—Mapai Party
Pub.—S Himmelfarb
Ed. in Ch.—A Zacharino
YATED NEEMAN
16 Aaronovich, Bnei Brak
Tel: (972-3) 5709171; Fax: (972-3) 5709181
YEDIOT AHRANOT (Latest News) (m-ex sat.) Hebrew; Est. 1939
2 Rehov Mozez St.; PO Box 109, 61000
Tel: (972-3) 212212; Fax: (972-3) 6953950
Circ.—300,000 (m); 600,000 (fri.)
Prop.—Yedioth Ahronoth Ltd.
Dir.—Oded Mozes
Dir.—Arnon Mozes
Ed.—Moshe Vardi
Ad. Mgr.—Israe Sorek
YIDDISCHE ZEITUNG (d) Yiddish
52 Harakevet St.
Tel: (972-3) 370011; Fax: (972-3) 5371921
YOM-YOM (m) Hebrew; Est. 1961
34-36 Itzchak Sadeh St.; PO Box 1194
Circ.—2,500
Prop.—Maba Publishers Ltd.
Ed.—Nachman Pavian

JORDAN
Pop. Est. 4,000,000

AMMAN
Pop. Est. 1,047,870

AD DUSTOUR (Constitution) (m) Arabic; Est. 1967
University St.; PO Box 591
Tel: (962-6) 664153/(962-6) 686121; Fax: (962-6) 667170/(962-6) 685810
Circ.—85,000
Prop.—Jordan Press & Publishing Co.
Pub.—Salah Al Zu'bi
Ed.—Dr. Musa Kilani
Ad. Mgr.—Yousif Ammari
JORDAN TIMES (d) English
University Rd.; PO Box 6710
Tel: (962-6) 667171; Fax: (962-6) 661242
Circ.—12,000
Prop.—Jordan Press Foundation
Ed. in Ch.—George Hawatmeh
Ad. Mgr.—Nader Horani
U.S. Rep.—AdMarket Int'l.; The N DeFilippes Corp.
AL RA'I (Opinion) (d) Arabic; Est. 1971
PO Box 6710
Tel: (962-6) 667171; Fax: (962-6) 661242
Circ.—90,000
Prop.—Jordan Press Foundation
Ed. in Ch.—Mahmoud Al Kayed
Ad. Mgr.—Nader Horani
U.S. Rep.—AdMarket Int'l.; The N DeFilippes Corp.
SAWT AL-SHAAB (m) Est. 1983
Al-Jaminah St.; PO Box 3037-925155
Tel: (962-6) 667199; Fax: (962-6) 667993/(962-6) 687373
Circ.—30,000
Prop.—Dal Al Shaab Press
Ed.—Hashim Khraisat
Ad. Mgr.—Ahmad Mahashel

KUWAIT
Pop. Est. 1,819,322

AL-KUWAIT
Pop. Est. (Metro Area) 633,153

AL ANBA'A (The News) (d) Arabic; Est. 1974
Sahafa St.; PO Box 23915, 13100 Safat
Tel: (965) 4831082/(965) 4831168; Fax: (965) 4831043
Circ.—121,000 ABC
Prop.—Kuwait Press House SAK
Ed. in Ch.—Waleed Khaled Al-Marzooq
U.S. Rep.—AdMarket Int'l.
ARAB TIMES (DAR AL-SEYASSAH) (m) English; Est. 1977
PO Box 2270, 13023
Tel: (965) 4813566; Fax: (965) 4813566
Circ.—70,000
Prop.—Dar Al-Seyassah Press
AL JAMEHEER (d) Arabic
Sahafa St.; PO Box 21162, Safat
Circ.—83,000
Prop.—Al-Jamaheer Newspaper
KUWAIT TIMES (d) English; Est. 1961
PO Box 1301, 13014
Tel: (965) 4835616/(965) 4835617; Fax: (965) 4835620
Circ.—32,000
Prop.—Kuwait Times Publishing House
Pub.—Yousef S Alyan
Ed.—Masud Ulla Khan
Ad. Mgr.—Malek G Azzam
AL-QABAS (Firebrand) (d) Arabic; Est. 1972
PO Box 21800, Safat, 13078
Tel: (965) 4812822; Fax: (965) 4834355
Circ.—115,972
Prop.—Al Qabas Ltd.
Dir.—Z Kobeissi
Ed.—Jassim Ahmad Al-Nusuf
Ad. Mgr.—Saber Amin
Al-RAI AL-AAM (Voice of the People) (m) Arabic; Est. 1961
PO Box 695
Tel: (965) 813133
Circ.—84,700
Prop.—Dar Al-Rai El Aam Press
Ad. Mgr.—Mohammed Ayyoub
AL RESALA (d) Arabic
PO Box 2490
AL SEYASSAH (Policy) (d) Arabic; Est. 1965
PO Box 2270, Safat, 13023
Tel: (965) 4813566/(965) 4818267; Fax: (965) 4813566
Circ.—90,000
Prop.—Dar Al Seyassah Press
Pub./Ed.—Ahmed S Al-Jarallah
Ad. Mgr.—Twafig Mansour
U.S. Rep.—Publicitas
AL-WATAN (Homeland) (m) Arabic; Est. 1974
PO Box 1142, Safat, 13012
Tel: (965) 4840950; Fax: (965) 4840950
Circ.—75,000
Prop.—Dar Al Watan Printing & Publishing
Dir.—Abdullah Bin Hindi
Ed.—Jassim M Al-Mutawa
Ad. Mgr.—Ahmad Al-Hodrup
U.S. Rep.—Marston Webb & Associates

SHUWAIKH

AL RAI AL AAM Arabic
Kuwait Showaikh, Sahafa St.; PO Box 595, 13007
Fax: (965) 4831462
Circ.—88,740

LEBANON
Pop. Est. 3,620,395

BEIRUT
Pop. Est. 1,100,000

AL-AHRAR (d) Arabic
Al-Jeitaoui Al-Marsad St.; PO Box 165600
Tel: (961-1) 333899
Circ.—15,000
Prop.—Dar Al-Bouhous
AL-AMAL (Phalangist) (m) Arabic; Est. 1939
PO Box 959
Tel: (961-1) 382992
Circ.—30,000
Prop.—Dar Al-Amal for Publishing
Gen. Mgr.—Georges Oumayra
AL-ANWAR (m) Arabic; Est. 1959
PO Box 1038
Tel: (961-1) 450933
Circ.—58,675
Prop.—Dar Assayad SAL
Pub.—Bassam Freihai
Ed.—Said Frayha
Ad. Mgr.—Anwar Aswad
AYK (d) English
PO Box 2623
AL-BAYRAK (d) Est. 1928
PO Box 165612
Pub./Ed.—Melhem Karanz
AL-BILAL (d)
PO Box 113-5554
Prop.—Dar Al Bilal
Pub.—Afif Chams
DAILY STAR (d) English
Gargarian Bldg., Emile Edde St., Hamra; PO Box 11-987
AL HAYAT Arabic
Tel: (961-1) 809282; Fax: (961-1) 866177
AL-LIWAA (d) Arabic; Est. 1940
Independence St.; PO Box 11-2402
Tel: (961-1) 364626
Circ.—10,000
Pub.—Abdel Rani Salam
Ed.—Abdel Goui Salam
AN-NAHAR (mS) Arabic; Est. 1933
rue Banque Central du Liban; PO Box 110226
Tel: (961-1) 340960
Circ.—65,000
Prop.—Trans Arab Media & Mgmt. SAL
Gen. Mgr.—Georges Oumayra
Ed.—Ghassan Tueni
Ad. Mgr.—Jamale Rassi
U.S. Rep.—AdMarket Int'l.
AL-NIDAA (d)
PO Box 4744
Pub.—Ibrahim Kaiss
L'ORIENT/LE JOUR (m) French; Est. 1924
Media Center; PO Box 166495
Tel: (961-1) 340560
Circ.—18,450
Prop.—Societe Generale de Presse
Dir.—Amine Abou-Khaled
Ed.—Issa Goraleb
Ad. Mgr.—Jamale Rassi
LE REVEIL (m) French; Est. 1977
Sin El-Fil Blvd.; PO Box 11-8383
Tel: (961-1) 890700
Circ.—10,000
Pub.—Raymond Daou
AL-SHARQ (d) Est. 1926
Center Anis Assaf
Circ.—36,000
Pub.—Albert Freiha
Pub.—Aouni El-Kaake
Ed.—Nouriddin Madoud
LE SOIR (e) French; Est. 1947
rue de Syrie; PO Box 1470
Circ.—13,000
Ad. Mgr.—Elie Msaboungi

OMAN
Pop. Est. 1,701,470

CAPITAL AREA
(Includes Muscat, Muttrah, Qurm & Ruwi)
Pop. Est. 250,000

AL ADWAA Arabic
PO Box 580, Ruwi, Muscat
Tel: (968) 704353
Circ.—10,000
AKHBAR OMAN (d) English
PO Box 5884
Circ.—8,000
Prop.—International Printing Press
AL NAHDA (Renaissance-illus) Arabic
PO Box 979, Muscat
Tel: (968) 713934
Circ.—11,000
Prop.—Al-Nahda Publications
OMAN (d) Arabic
PO Box 6002, Ruwi
Tel: (968) 701555
Circ.—21,500
Prop.—Oman Newspaper House
Prop.—Ministry of Information
Ed. in Ch.—Habib Muhammad Nasib
(This newspaper is nationally distributed.)
OMAN DAILY OBSERVER (d-ex fri.) English; Est. 1981
Ruwi; PO Box 6002
Tel: (968) 701555
Circ.—15,000
Prop.—Oman Newspaper House (Ministry of Information)
Ed.—Ian Cummins
(This newspaper is nationally distributed.)
TIMES OF OMAN English
PO Box 3770, Ruwi, Muscat
Tel: (968) 701953; Fax: (968) 799153
Circ.—15,000
Prop.—Al-Essa Printing & Publishing House
Ed. in Ch.—Anees Essa
AL-WATAN (d) Arabic; Est. 1971
PO Box 463, Muscat
Tel: (968) 561554
Circ.—18,000
Prop.—Omani Establishment for Printing & Publishing
(This newspaper is nationally distributed.)

QATAR
Pop. Est. 512,779

DOHA
Pop. Est. 250,000

AL ARAB (d)
PO Box 3464
Tel: (974) 325874; Fax: (974) 325874
Circ.—25,000
Prop.—Dar Al Ourouba Press & Publishing House
Pub.—Abdulla Hussain Naama
Ed.—Khaled Abdallah Naame
Ad. Mgr.—Gopal Nair
ARRAYAH (d)
Gulf Rd.; PO Box 3464
Tel: (974) 810450; Fax: (974) 810450
Circ.—18,000
Prop.—Gulf Publishing & Printing Organization
Ed.—Ahmed Ali
Ad. Mgr.—Bashar Da Doush
U.S. Rep.—The N DeFilippes Corp.
DAILY NEWS BULLETIN (d) English & Arabic
PO Box 3299
Tel: (974) 322725
Prop.—Qatar News Agency
DAILY GULF TIMES & WEEKLY GULF TIMES (m) English
PO Box 2888
Tel: (974) 329424; Fax: (974) 601808
Circ.—10,000
Prop.—Gulf Publishing & Printing Organization
Pub./Ed.—Abdul Rahman Saif Al Madhadi
Ed.—Brian Nichols
Ad. Mgr.—Osama El Shafie
AL-SHARQ
PO Box 3488
Tel: (974) 662444/(974) 662462
Ed.—Nasser Mohamed Al-Othman

SAUDI ARABIA
Pop. Est. 18,196,783

DAMMAM
Pop. Est. 350,000

AL-YOUM (Today) (m-ex fri.) Arabic; Est. 1960
PO Box 565, 31421
Tel: (966-3) 8331906; Fax: (966-3) 340677
Circ.—100,000
Prop.—Dar Al-Yaum Publishing
Pub.—Al Ghani Al Rahman Mohammad
Ed.—Sultan Al Bazzie

JEDDAH
Pop. Est. 2,500,000

ARAB NEWS (m-ex S) English; Est. 1975
Arab News Bldg.; PO Box 4556, 21412
Tel: (966-2) 6691888; Fax: (966-2) 6671650
Circ.—59,066 ABC
Prop.—Saudi Research & Marketing Co.
Ed.—Abdul Qader Tash
Ad. Mgr.—Tatal A Hafiz
U.S. Rep.—Attache Inc.
(This newspaper is nationally distributed.)
AL-ASHARQ AL-AWSAT (The Middle East) (m)
Arabic; Est. 1978
Arab News Bldg., Medina Rd.; PO Box 4556, 21412
Tel: (966-2) 6691888; Fax: (966-2) 6671650
Circ.—224,992 ABC
Prop.—Saudi Research & Marketing Co.
Ed.—Othman Al-Omeir
Ad. Mgr.—Mohammad Fal
U.S. Rep.—Attache Inc.
AL-BILAD (The Country) (m) Arabic; Est. 1934
PO Box 6340, 21442
Tel: (966-2) 6711000; Fax: (966-2) 6732000
Circ.—67,738 ABC
Prop.—Al-Bilad Publishing Organization
Pub.—Mohamed Hasan Fagi
Gen. Mgr.—Mohammad Ibrahim Massoud
Ed.—A Al-Nahari
Ad. Mgr.—H Al-Zahrani
AL-HAYAT (Life) (d) Arabic
PO Box 13676, 21414
Tel: (966-2) 6607517/(966-2) 6607529;
Fax: (966-2) 6607537
Prop.—Al Hayat Publishing Co. Ltd.
AL-MADINA NEWSPAPER (Medina City) (m)
Arabic
PO Box 807, 21421
Tel: (966-2) 6712100; Fax: (966-2) 6720011
Circ.—80,000 ABC
Prop.—Al Madina Press Co.
Ed.—Ovsama Sabal
Ad. Mgr.—Fouad Kamal
U.S. Rep.—Marston Webb & Associates
AL-MANAWARA (d) Arabic; Est. 1937
PO Box 807, 21421
Tel: (966-2) 6880344
Circ.—47,143
Prop.—Al Madina Publishing House
Dir.—Othman Ibrehim al-Fradl
Ed.—Ghalib Hamza Abu al-Faraj
OKAZ (m) Arabic; Est. 1965
PO Box 1508, 21441
Tel: (966-2) 6722630; Fax: (966-2) 6724277
Circ.—147,000
Prop.—Okaz Organization for Press & Publication
Pub.—Komal Alsalous
Ed.—Hashim Abdo Hashim
Ad. Mgr.—Mohd Abu El-Eash
SAUDI GAZETTE (m) English; Est. 1975
PO Box 1508, 21441
Tel: (966-2) 6722630/(966-2) 6721354;
Fax: (966-2) 6724277
Circ.—30,347 ABC
Prop.—Okaz Organization for Press & Publication
Dir.—Iyad A Madani
Ed.—Rida M Larry
Ad. Mgr.—Mohd Abu El-Eash
U.S. Rep.—AdMarket Int'l.; Marston Webb & Associates; The N DeFilippes Corp.
URDU NEWS (d) Urdu
Arab News Bldg.; PO Box 4556, 21412
Tel: (966-2) 6691888; Fax: (966-2) 6611273
Circ.—30,000
Prop.—Saudi Research & Publishing Co.
Ed.—Othman Al-Omeir

MAKKAH
(Mecca)
Pop. Est. 550,000

AL-NADWA (The Symposium) (d) Arabic; Est. 1958
PO Box 5803
Tel: (966-2) 5200111; Fax: (966-2) 5203055
Circ.—35,000
Prop.—Mecca Establishment for Printings
Pub.—Dr. Hamid Harasani
Ed.—Saleh Mohammed-Jamal

RIYADH
Pop. Est. 3,000,000

AL-JAZIRA (The Peninsula) (e) Arabic
Nassiria Rd.; PO Box 354, 11411
Tel: (966-2) 4021440; Fax: (966-1) 4021795
Circ.—84,240
Prop.—Al-Jazeerah Corp.
Pub.—Saleh Al Ajroush
Ed.—Mohammed Bin Abbas
AL-MASSAIYAH (The Evening) (d)
PO Box 354, 11411
Tel: (966-1) 4021440; Fax: (966-1) 4021795
AL-RIYADH (m) Arabic; Est. 1965
PO Box 851, 11421
Tel: (966-1) 4778440; Fax: (966-1) 478598
Circ.—150,000
Prop.—Al-Yamama Press Establishment
Pub.—Ahmed Al-Houshan
Gen. Mgr.—Abdullah Hamad Al-Qarawi
Ed.—Turki Al-Sedury
RIYADH DAILY (m) English
PO Box 2943, 11476
Tel: (966-1) 4783039; Fax: (966-1) 4777203
Circ.—50,000
Ed. in Ch.—Talaat Wafa
U.S. Rep.—The N DeFilippes Corp.

SYRIA
Pop. Est. 14,886,672

ALEPPO
Pop. Est. 1,308,000

BARQ AL SHIMAL (d) Arabic
rue Aziziyah
AL SHABAB (d) Arabic
rue Al Tawil

DAMASCUS
Pop. Est. (Metro Area) 1,361,000

AL BAATH (Renaissance) (m) Arabic
PO Box 9389
Tel: (963-11) 664600
Circ.—75,000
Prop.—Organization of the Ba'ath Arab Socialist Party
Dir.—Taurkii Sakker
Ed.—Saber Falhoot
AL JAMAHEER AL ARABIA (m) Arabic
PO Box 2448
Tel: (963-11) 225219
Circ.—10,000
Prop.—Al-Wihdat Press
SYRIA TIMES (d) English
Dar Al Tichrin; PO Box 5452
Tel: (963-11) 886904
Prop.—Tishreen Foundation
AL THAWRAH (Revolution) (m) Arabic
PO Box 2448
Tel: (963-11) 232018
Circ.—75,000
Prop.—Al-Wihdat Press
Dir.—A H Kassab
TICHRIN (d) Arabic
Baghdad St.; PO Box 5452
Tel: (963-11) 886904
Circ.—75,000
Prop.—Tishreen Foundation
Pub.—Jamal Rahme

HAMA
Pop. Est. 229,000

AL FIDAA (d) Arabic
PO Box 2448
Tel: (963) 225219
Circ.—4,000
Prop.—Al-Wihdat Press
Ed.—A Aulwani

HOMS
Pop. Est. 464,000

ARAVELK (d) Armenian
Aleppo, Damascus
BARQ AL SHIMAL (d) Arabic
Rue Aziziyah, Aleppo, Damascus
AL OUROUBA (d) Arabic
PO Box 2448
Tel: (963-31) 225219
Circ.—10,000
Prop.—Al-Wihdat Press

TURKEY
Pop. Est. 62,153,898

ADANA
Pop. Est. 916,150

BUGUN (d) Est. 1989
Sun Sinemasi Sokagi
Pub.—Onay Bilgin
CUMHURIYET (d) Est. 1924
Inonu, Caddesi 119, Sokak No. 1/1
Prop.—Cumhuriyet Matbaacilik Ve Gaz. A/S
Pub.—Nadir Nadi
FOTOSPOR (d) Est. 1989
Ceyhan Yolu 5-Km. Yuregir
Pub.—Birol Nadir
GUNAYDIN (d) Est. 1968
Ceydan Yolu 5-Km.
Pub.—Asil Nadir
GUNES (d) Est. 1982
Ceyhan Yelu S. Km. Cumhuriyet Mah.
Prop.—Guclu Gazetecilik A/S
Pub.—Asil Nadir
HURRIYET (d) Est. 1948
Ceyhan Karayolu 5-Km.
Prop.—Hurriyet Holdings A/A
Pub.—Erol Simavi
MILLIYET (d) Est. 1950
Ataturk Caddesi Toren Apt., Kat:3
Prop.—Milliyet Gazetecilik A/S
Pub.—Aydin Dogan
SABAH (d) Est. 1985
Cinarli Mah. 126, Sokak No. 4
Prop.—Sabah Gazetecilik A/S
Pub.—Dinc Bilgin
TERCUMAN (d) Est. 1961
Istiklal Mah. 190, Sokak No. 27
Prop.—Tercuman Gazetecilik A/S
Pub.—Kemal Ilicak
TURKIYE (d) Est. 1970
C. Gursel Caddesi, No. 21
Pub.—Enver Oren
ZAMAN (d) Est. 1986
Saydam, Caddesi 46-1, Sokak No. 2
Pub.—Alaeddin Kaya

ANKARA
Pop. Est. 2,559,471

BUGUN (d) Est. 1989
Karum is Merkezi; Kat:6, Kavaklidere
Tel: (90-312) 4685050; Fax: (90-312) 4685060
Pub.—Onay Bilgin
CUMHURIYET (m) Est. 1924
Ataturk Bulvari, No. 125, Kat:4, Bakalikar
Tel: (90-312) 4195020; Fax: (90-312) 4195027
Prop.—Cumhuriyet Matbaacilik Ve Gaz. A/S
Pub.—Nadir Nadi
DUNYA (d) Est. 1953
Karanfil Sokak 43/6 Kizilay
Tel: (90-312) 4258369; Fax: (90-312) 4186424
Pub.—Nezih Demirkent
FOTOSPOR (d) Est. 1989
Ruzgarli, Sokak No. 34/1, Ulus
Tel: (90-312) 3091015; Fax: (90-312) 3091021/(90-312) 3091022
Pub.—Birol Nadir
GUNAYDIN-TAN (d) Est. 1968
Ruzgarli Gayret, Sokak No. 2, Ulus
Tel: (90-312) 3091080/(90-312) 3126222; Fax: (90-312) 3116055
Prop.—Veb Ofset Ileri Mat.
Pub.—Asil Nadir
GUNES (d) Est. 1982
Ruzgarli Gayret, Sokak No. 4, Ulus
Tel: (90-312) 3102000; Fax: (90-312) 3125212
Prop.—Guclu Gazetecilik A/S
Pub.—Asil Nadir
HURRIYET (d) Est. 1948
Cinnah, Caddesi 8, Kavaklider, 06690
Tel: (90-312) 4670020
Pub.—Erol Simavi
MEYDAN (d) Est. 1990
Nevzat Tandogan Caddesi 8, Asagi Ayranci, 06540
Tel: (90-312) 472100; Fax: (90-312) 475500
MILLI GAZETE (d) Est. 1973
Ziya Bey, Caddesi 9, Sokak 10/2-4, Balgat
Tel: (90-312) 2873345
Pub.—Hazim Oktay Baser
MILLIYET (d) Est. 1950
Neyzat Tandogan, Caddesi 8, Asagi Ayranci
Tel: (90-312) 4191400; Fax: (90-312) 4173878
Prop.—Milliyet Gazetecilik A/S
Pub.—Aydin Dogan
ORTADOGU Est. 1964
2 Izmir, Caddesi No. 55/13, Kizilay
Tel: (90-312) 4182860/(90-312) 4186824; Fax: (90-312) 4188925
SABAH (d) Est. 1985
Iran Caddesi Karum is Merkez, Kat:6, Kavaklidere
Tel: (90-312) 4685050; Fax: (90-312) 4685060/(90-312) 4266365
Prop.—Sabah Gazetecilik A/S
Pub./Owner—Dinc Bilgin
TAN (d) Est. 1983
Istanbul, Caddesi Gayret Sokak No. 2, Ulus
Pub.—Asil Nadir
TERCUMAN (d) Est. 1961
Tunus, Caddesi 9/12-15, Bakanliklar
Tel: (90-312) 4195262; Fax: (90-312) 4195260/(90-312) 4195261
TURKISH DAILY NEWS (d) English; Est. 1961
Tunus, Caddesi 50/A-7, Kavaklider, 06680
Tel: (90-312) 4282956/(90-312) 4282957; Fax: (90-312) 4278890
Prop.—Gazetecilik ve Matbaacilile A/S
Pub.—Ilhan Cevik
Ed. in Ch.—Ilnur Cevik
TURKIYE (d) Est. 1970
Ataturk Bul. Ata Han 117/22, Bakanliklar
Tel: (90-312) 4185488/(90-312) 418488; Fax: (90-312) 4185310
Pub./Owner—Dr. Enver Oren
ULUS Est. 1986
Ruzgarli Gazret, Sokak No. 2, Ulus
Tel: (90-312) 3103731/(90-312) 2125353
Owner—Omer Erdal Yilmaz
Ed. in Ch.—Sedat Yazicioglu
YENI ASIR (d) Est. 1895
Iran Caddesi, Karum Ismerkezi, Kat:6, KavaklIdene
Tel: (90-312) 3532585/(90-312) 3532900; Fax: (90-312) 3532908/(90-312) 3532909
Pub.—Dinc Bilgrin
YENI NESIL (d) Est. 1970
Ataturk Bul. Atahan, No. 117/31, Bakanliklar
Tel: (90-312) 4415000; Fax: (90-312) 252200/(90-312) 199290
Pub.—Bekir Berk
ZAMAN (d) Est. 1986
Samsun Devlet, Kanayolv, No. 106, Siteler
Tel: (90-312) 3104925; Fax: (90-312) 3101448
Circ.—61,000
Pub.—Alaattin Kaya

BURSA
Pop. Est. 834,576

DUNYA Est. 1953
Unlu Caddesi Bilbay Apt., Kat:1
Pub.—Nezih Demirkent
ZAMAN Est. 1986
Ataturk Caddesi Koruyucu Ishani, Kat:5
Pub.—Alaeddin Kaya

DIYARBAKIR
Pop. Est. 1,086,290

MILLIYET Est. 1950
Feray Apt., Kat:1
Pub.—Aydin Dogan

ERZURUM
Pop. Est. 848,840

HURRIYET (d) Est. 1948
Gezkoy Cikisi Organize Sanayi Bolgesi
Prop.—Hurriyet Holdings A/S
Pub.—Erol Simavi
MILLIYET Est. 1950
Muratpasa Mah. ismet pasa, Caddesi No. 4/3
Prop.—Milliyet Gazetecilik A/S
Pub.—Aydin Dogan
TURKIYE Est. 1970
Cumhuriyey Caddesi Ozel Idare Ticaret Sitesi, Kat:2
Pub.—Enver Oren

ISTANBUL
Pop. Est. 6,620,241

AYDINLIK Est. 1921
Yol. Sokak Polat Celil Aga Ishani; Kat:S, Mecidiyekoy
Tel: (90-212) 2667634/(90-212) 2757413; Fax: (90-212) 2884805/(90-212) 2883732
Pub.—Mehmet Sabuncu
BUGUN (d) Est. 1989
Medya Plaza Basin Ekspres Yolu, Gunesli, 34540
Tel: (90-212) 5504900; Fax: (90-212) 5023340
Circ.—179,188
Owner/Pub.—Onay Bilgrin
Ed.—Orhan Vural

Turkey

CUMHURIYET (Republic) (m) Est. 1924
Turkocagi, Caddesi No. 39/41; PK 246
Tel: (90-212) 5120505; Fax: (90-212) 5138595
Circ.—120,000
Pub.—Berin Nadi
Ed. in Ch.—Ozgen Acar

DUNYA (The World) (d) Est. 1953
Narlibahce, Sokak No. 15, Cagaloglu, 34440
Tel: (90-212) 5120190; Fax: (90-212) 5140687/(90-212) 5191474
Circ.—19,000
Pub.—Nezih Demirkent
Ed. in Ch.—Alp Orcun

FOTOMAC
Medya Plaza Basin Ekspress Yolu, Gunesli, 34540
Tel: (90-212) 5504890
Owner—Busah Bilgin

FOTOSPOR (d) Est. 1989
Ekspress Basin Yolu Kavsagi, Matbaacilar Sitsei, Gunesli
Tel: (90-212) 6525094; Fax: (90-212) 6524224
Circ.—215,000
Owner/Pub.—Birol Nadir
Ed. in Ch.—Ersan Celik

GUN Est. 1993
Medya Plaza, Gunesli 34540
Tel: (90-212) 5504810; Fax: (90-212) 5028340
Owner—Ali Karacan
Ed. in Ch.—Selahattin Duman

GUNAYDIN-TAN (d) Est. 1968
Alaykoksu, Caddesi Erylmaz Sokak No. 13, Cagaloglu
Tel: (90-212) 5120050; Fax: (90-212) 5260823/(90-212) 5265013
Circ.—386,000
Prop.—Veb Ofset Ileri Mat.
Pub.—Asil Nadir
Ed. in Ch.—Seckin Turesay

GUNES (d) Est. 1982
Turanli, Sokak No. 20, Beyazit
Tel: (90-212) 5166600; Fax: (90-212) 5171990/(90-212) 5171992
Circ.—84,000
Prop.—Guclu Gazetecilik A/S
Pub.—Asil Nadir
Ed. in Ch.—Ertugrul Ozkok

HURRIYET (d) Est. 1948
Guneslikoy, 34540 Bakirkoy, Babiali Caddesi 15-17, Cagaloglu, 34360
Tel: (90-212) 5120000/(90-212) 5550050; Fax: (90-212) 5156705
Circ.—615,579
Prop.—Hurriyet Holdings A/S
Pub.—Erol Simavi
Pres.—Sedat Simavi
Ed. in Ch.—Ertugrul Ozkok
(Wash., D.C. Rep.-Sedat Ergin Office: 3440 39th St. NW, # B-692, Washington, D.C. 20016.)

MEYDAN (d) Est. 1990
Yuzyil Mahallesi, Mahmutbey Viyadugü Alti, Ikitelli, Cagaloglu, 34410
Tel: (90-212) 5056111; Fax: (90-212) 5056436/(90-212) 5056437
Owner—Refik Aras
Ed. in Ch.—Rahmi Turan

MILLI GAZETE (d) Est. 1973
Cayhane Sokak 1, Topkapi, 34020
Tel: (90-212) 5674775; Fax: (90-212) 5674024
Circ.—40,000
Pub.—Milsan Basin Sanazi
Pub.—Hazim Oktay Baser
Ed. in Ch.—Ekrek Iziltas

MILLIYET (Nationalism) (d) Est. 1950
Yuzyil, Mahmutbey Viyadugu Alti Ikitelli
Tel: (90-212) 5056111; Fax: (90-212) 5056280
Circ.—394,598
Prop.—Milliyet Gazetecilik A/S
Pub./Owner—Aydin Dogan
Ed. in Ch.—Umur Talu

ORTADOGU Est. 1964
Namik Kemal Caddesi, No. 107, Yenikapi, 34300
Tel: (90-212) 5304537/(90-212) 5301014; Fax: (90-212) 5307292
Pub.—Zeki Saracogiu

SABAH (d) Est. 1985
Medya Plaza Basin Ekspres Yolu, Gunesli, 34540
Tel: (90-212) 5504900/(90-212) 5504810; Fax: (90-212) 5028990/(90-212) 5028641

Circ.—722,950
Prop.—Sabah Gazetecilik A/S
Pub./Owner—Dinc Bilgin
Ed. in Ch.—Zafer Mutlu
(Wash., D.C. Rep.-Savas Suzal Office: 5432 Midship Court, Burke, VA 22015.)

TAN (d) Est. 1983
Alaykosku, Caddesi Eryilmaz, Sokak No. 13, Cagaloglu
Tel: (90-212) 5120050; Fax: (90-212) 5265013
Circ.—170,000
Pub.—Asil Nadir
Ed. in Ch.—Fikret Ercan

TERCUMAN (d) Est. 1961
Sercelale, Sokak No. 4, Topaki, 34370
Tel: (90-212) 5016263/(90-212) 5017505; Fax: (90-212) 5446562/(90-212) 6120658
Circ.—66,000
Prop.—Tercuman Gazetecilik A/S
Owner/Pub.—Sedat Colak
Ed. in Ch.—Nazif Okumus

TURKISH DAILY NEWS (d) English; Est. 1961
Istiklal, Caddesi No. 79, Mim Han 4-29, Beyoglu
Tel: (90-212) 1454730; Fax: (90-212) 1454730
Pub.—Ilhan Cevik

TURKIYE (d) Est. 1970
Catalcesme, Sokak No. 17, Cagaloglu, 34410
Tel: (90-212) 5139900; Fax: (90-212) 5138973
Circ.—312,771
Owner/Pub.—Enver Oren
Ed. in Ch.—Kenan Akin

YENI ASIR (New Century) (d) Est. 1895
Atakan, Sokak No. 14, Mecidiyekoy
Pub.—Dinc Bilgin

YENI NESIL (New Generation) (d) Est. 1970
Yenibosna Sanayi Caddesi Selvi, Sokak No. 5, Bakirkoy
Tel: (90-212) 5846261; Fax: (90-212) 5567289
Circ.—80,000
Prop.—Nesil Matbaacilik A/S
Pub.—Bekir Berk
Ed. in Ch.—Umit Simsek

ZAMAN (d) Est. 1986
Cobancesme Kalander, Sokak No. 21, Yenibosna, 34530
Tel: (90-212) 6523350/(90-212) 5512822; Fax: (90-212) 6522423/(90-212) 6525512
Circ.—122,457
Pub.—Alaeddin Kaya
Ed.—Adem Kalac

IZMIR
Pop. Est. 1,757,414

BUGUN (d) Est. 1989
Gaziosmanpasa Bul. No. 5
Pub.—Onay Bilgin

CUMHURIYET (d) Est. 1924
Halit Ziya Bul. 1352, Sokak No. 2/3
Prop.—Cumhuriyet Matbaacilik ve Gaz. A/S
Pub.—Nadir Nadi

DUNYA (d) Est. 1953
Cumhuriyet Bul. Elcin Ishani, No. 118, Kat:2
Pub.—Nezih Demirkent

FOTOSPOR (d) Est. 1989
Vali Kazim Dirik Caddesi, No. 13
Pub.—Birol Nadir

GUNAYDIN (d) Est. 1968
Murselpasa Bul., No. 161
Prop.—Veb Ofset Ileri Mat.
Pub.—Asil Nadir

GUNES (d) Est. 1982
Murselpasa Bul., No. 161
Prop.—Guclu Gazetecilik A/S
Pub.—Asil Nadir

HURRIYET (d) Est. 1948
Sehit Fethi Bey Caddesi, No. 53
Prop.—Hurriyet Holdings A/S
Pub.—Erol Simavi

MILLIYET (d) Est. 1950
Sehit Fethi Bey Caddesi, No. 79/A
Prop.—Milliyet Gazetecilik A/S
Pub.—Aydin Dogan

SABAH (d) Est. 1985
Gazi Osman Pasa Bulvari, No. 5, Cankaya
Prop.—Sabah Gazetecilik A/S
Pub.—Dinc Bilgin

TAN (d) Est. 1983
Murselpasa Bul., No. 61
Pub.—Asil Nadir

TERCUMAN (d) Est. 1961
1371, Sokak No. 5/2, Cankaya
Prop.—Tercuman Gazetecilik A/S
Pub.—Kemal Ilicak

TURKISH DAILY NEWS (d) English; Est. 1961
1379, Sokak No. 59, Guven Ishani, Kat:3, No. 301
Pub.—Ilhan Cevik

TURKIYE (d) Est. 1970
1479, Sokak No. 9, Alsancak
Pub.—Enver Oren

YENI ASIR (d) Est. 1895
Gazismanasa Bulvari, 5 Cankaya
Tel: (90-51) 441500; Fax: (90-51) 199290
Circ.—43,000
Pub./Owner—Dinc Bilgin
Ed. in Ch.—Cemil Devrim

ZAMAN (d) Est. 1986
Gaziler Caddesi 1271, Sokak No. 1, Kat:1-2, Kocana Ishani
Pub.—Alaeddin Kaya

KAYSERI
Pop. Est. 421,362

MILLIYET (d) Est. 1950
Istasyan Caddesi Tapinc Han, Kat:3
Pub.—Aydin Dogan

KOCAELI
Pop. Est. 931,000

MILLI GAZETE (d) Est. 1973
Fethiye Caddesi Bilim Pas., Kat:1, No. 6
Pub.—Hazim Oktay Baser

SAMSUN
Pop. Est. 1,177,000

MILLIYET (d) Est. 1950
19 Mayis Mah. Hurriyet, Sokak No. 8, Kat:3
Pub.—Aydin Dogan

UNITED ARAB EMIRATES
Pop. Est. 2,791,141

ABU DHABI
Pop. Est. 363,432

EMIRATES NEWS (mS) English; Est. 1970
PO Box 791
Tel: (971-2) 451600; Fax: (971-2) 451801
Circ.—21,000
Prop.—Al-Ittihad Press & Publishing Corp.
Ad. Mgr.—Mahmood Najar
U.S. Rep.—AdMarket Int'l.

AL FAJR (d) Arabic
PO Box 505
Tel: (971-2) 478300; Fax: (971-2) 478436
Circ.—20,700
Prop.—Dar Al-Fajr Press
Pub./Ed.—Obaid Al Mazroie

GULF NEWS
PO Box 7441
Tel: (971-2) 211388; Fax: (971-2) 213662

AL-ITTIHAD (d) Est. 1969
PO Box 17
Tel: (971-2) 461600; Fax: (971-2) 462206
Circ.—60,000
Prop.—Al-Ittihad Press & Publishing Corp.
Mng. Ed.—Mohammad Yousef
Ad. Mgr.—Mahmood Najar
U.S. Rep.—Marston Webb & Associates

KHALEEJ TIMES
PO Box 3082
Tel: (971-2) 336000; Fax: (971-2) 336424

AL-WADA
PO Box 2488
Tel: (971-2) 478400; Fax: (971-2) 478937

DUBAI
Pop. Est. 318,000

AL-BAYAN (m) Arabic; Est. 1979
PO Box 2710
Tel: (971-4) 444400; Fax: (971-4) 445257
Circ.—32,651 ABC
Prop.—Al-Bayan Press
Pub.—Sheikh Hasher Al Maktoum

Ed.—Saif Al Marri
Ad. Mgr.—Adib Baki

AL FAJR (d) Arabic
Port Said Arga; PO Box 10422
Tel: (971-4) 667577
Circ.—22,000

GULF NEWS (d) English
PO Box 6519
Tel: (971-4) 211388/(971-4) 447100; Fax: (971-4) 441627
Circ.—50,000
Prop.—Almsr Publishing
Pub.—Obaid Hamaid Al Tayer
Ed.—Bikram Vohra
Ad. Mgr.—Dilip George

AL-ITTIHAD
PO Box 3446
Tel: (971-4) 666611; Fax: (971-4) 692669

KHALEEJ TIMES (d) English; Est. 1978
PO Box 11243
Tel: (971-4) 382400; Fax: (971-4) 382238
Circ.—48,047
Prop.—Galadari Printing & Publishing Establishment
Pub.—Muzammil Ahmed
Ed. in Ch.—Abdul Latif E Galadari
Ad. Mgr.—Robert Nocholas

MATHRUBHUMI (d) Malayalam
PO Box 11243
Prop.—Galdari Printing & Publishing

AL WAHDA (d) Arabic
PO Box 2488
Tel: (971-4) 474121
Circ.—10,000
Pub.—Dar Al-Wahda
Ed.—Rashed Aweidha

SHARJAH
Pop. Est. 190,000

AL KHALEEJ (d) Arabic
PO Box 30
Tel: (971-6) 598777; Fax: (971-6) 598547
Circ.—85,000
Prop.—Dar Al Khaleej Publishing
Pub.—Taryam Omran
Ed.—Ghassan Tahboub
Ad. Mgr.—Faraj Yassine

AL-ITTIHAD
PO Box 1777
Tel: (971-6) 377555; Fax: (971-6) 525654

YEMEN, REPUBLIC OF
Pop. Est. 11,105,202

ADEN
Pop. Est. 365,000

ADEN NEWS BULLETINS Arabic & English
PO Box 1166, Tawahi

AR-RABI ASHAR MIN UKTUBAR (14th October) (m) Arabic; Est. 1968
PO Box 4227, Crater
Circ.—20,000
Ed.—Mohamed Hussein Mohamed

SANA
Pop. Est. 427,000

AL SHURA
PO Box 15114
Tel: (967-1) 213584; Fax: (967-1) 213468
Circ.—15,000
Ed.—Abdullah Sa'ad

AL THAWRA (26th September) (d)
PO Box 2195
Tel: (967-1) 262626/(967-1) 232281; Fax: (967-1) 274139/(967-1) 251505
Circ.—110,000
Prop.—Ministry of Information
Ed.—Mohamed Alzorkah

YEMEN TIMES English
PO Box 2579
Tel: (967-1) 268661; Fax: (967-1) 268663
Circ.—20,000
Pub.—Abdulaziz Al-Saqqaf

TAIZ
Pop. Est. 278,043

AL JUMHURIYA (d) Arabic
Taiz Information Office
Tel: (967-4) 216748
Circ.—100,000
Prop.—Information Office

NEWSPAPERS OF SOUTH AMERICA

ARGENTINA
Pop. Est. 33,912,994

ARRECIFES
(Buenos Aires)

ACCION (Action) (d) Est. 1945
Santiago H. Pérez 664, 2740
Dir.—Rubén Luís Blanco
ARRECIFES (d)
R. Gutiérrez 631, 2740
Dir.—Horacio A Bancalari
EL PROGRESO (The Progress) (m) Est. 1936
Vincente López y Planes 62, 2740
Dir.—Tomás Jauregui
TRIBUNA CHAQUENA (Chaquena Tribune) (d) Est. 1934
Calle Saavedra 462, Presidencia RS
Circ.—4,500
Pub.—Rubén Germinal Váldez

AVELLANEDA
(Buenos Aires)
Pop. Est. 337,538

LA CALLE (The Street) (d)
Monseror Piaggio 136, 1870
Dir.—Nestor Luís Santos
LA CIUDAD (The City) (m) Est. 1959
La Madrid 117/125, 1870
Prop.—La Ciudad SRL
Dir.—Roberto Persico
DIARIO POPULAR (Popular Daily) (m) Est. 1974
Inte. Bequerestain 182, 1870
Circ.—100,000
Prop.—Impreba SA
Pub.—Jorge Fascetto
Ad. Mgr.—Nestor Dutiil

AZUL
(Buenos Aires)
Pop. Est. 36,023

PREGON (e-ex S) Est. 1953
Necochea 545, 7300
Dir.—Mary L M de Gonta
EL TIEMPO (The Time) (m) Est. 1933
Calles Burgos y Belgrano, 7300
Circ.—8,500
Dir.—Alfred C Ronchetti

BAHIA BLANCA
(Buenos Aires)
Pop. Est. 200,000

LA NUEVA PROVINCIA (The New Province) (mS) Est. 1989
Sarmiento 54/64, 8000
Tel: (54-91) 20201
Circ.—36,000 (m); 55,000 (S)
Prop.—Diario La Nueva Provincia SRL
Dir.—Diana Julio de Massot
Ed.—Frederico C Massot
Ad. Mgr.—Osvaldo Manrique

BALCARCE
(Buenos Aires)
Pop. Est. 26,461

EL LIBERAL (The Liberal) (m) Est. 1921
Mitre 672, 7620
Circ.—4,500
Dir.—José Raúl Pollio
Dir.—Enrique Andrés Serres

BOLIVAR
(Buenos Aires)
Pop. Est. 23,366

LA MAÑANA (The Morning) (m) Est. 1953
Venezuela 159, 6550
Circ.—4,300
Dir.—Oscar C Cabreros
NOTICIAS (News) Est. 1952
Casilla de Correro, 6550
Dir.—Adela A Asin

BRAGADO
(Buenos Aires)
Pop. Est. 23,366

EL CENSOR (m) Est. 1909
Avda. General Paz 1269, 6440
Circ.—6,00
Dir.—Juan J O Devenutto
LA VOZ DE BRAGADO (The Voice of Bragado) (m) Est. 1962
Rivadavia 1330, 6640
Circ.—4,800
Dir.—Hugo Oscar Soto

CAMPANA
(Buenos Aires)

LA DEFENSA POPULAR (The Popular Defense) (m-ex mon.) Est. 1909
Becerra 834, 2804

CANADA de GOMEZ
(Santa Fe)

ESTRELLA (Star) (m-5x wk.) Est. 1954
Lavalle 1140, 2500
Pub.—José Antonio Ramacciotti

CARLOS CASARES
(Buenos Aires)

EL ARGENTINO (The Argentinian) (d-ex mon.) Est. 1887
Colon 146, 6530
Pub.—Darío E Cuence
EL CRONISTA (m-ex mon.) Est. 1950
Moreno y Cramer, 6530
Pub.—Hugo Perojo
EL IMPARCIAL (The Impartial) Est. 1944
Libres del Sur 98, 6530
Pub.—Fernando R Pieske

CHIVILCOY
(Buenos Aires)
Pop. Est. 37,190

LA CAMPANA DE CHIVILCOY (The Bell of Chivilcoy) (d)
Alvear 62, 6620
Dir.—José María Grange
Dir.—Gaspar Astarita
LA RAZON (The Reason) (d) Est. 1910
Avda. Cevallos 98, 6620
Circ.—7,000
Dir.—Carlos Sergio Pérez

CITY of BUENOS AIRES
Pop. Est. 10,500,000

ACCION (Action) (d) Est. 1966
Rivadavia, 1944
Pub.—Robert Gómez
AMBITO FINANCIERO (5x wk.) Est. 1976
Pasaje Carabelas 241-009, Piso 8
Tel: (54-1) 3315516/(54-1) 3315519; Fax: (54-1) 3311404
Circ.—125,000
Pub./Ad. Mgr.—Eduardo Ribas Somar
Ed.—Julio A Ramos
U.S. Rep.—Charney/Palacios & Co. Inc.; The N DeFilippes Corp.
ARGENTINISCHES TAGEBLATT (d) German; Est. 1889
25 de Mayo 626, 1002
Tel: (54-1) 3119561; Fax: (54-1) 3115798
Circ.—20,000
Prop.—Alemann S R I
ARMENIA (d) Est. 1931
El Salvador, 4627
Circ.—3,000
Pub.—José Oghoulian
BOLETIN OFICIAL DE LA REPUBLICA ARGENTINA (Official Bulletin of the Argentinian Republic) (m) Est. 1893
Suipacha 767, Capital Federal, 1008
Tel: (54-1) 3224164
Pub.—Dr. Eduardo A Maschwitz
BUENOS AIRES HERALD (mS) English; Est. 1876
Azopardo 455, Capital Federal, 1107
Tel: (54-1) 348476; Fax: (54-1) 3347917
Circ.—10,000 (m); 20,000 (S)
Prop.—Buenos Aires Herald Ltda. SA
Ed.—Michael Soltye
Ed.—Nicholas Tozer
Ad. Mgr.—Federico Guillermo Aubone
U.S. Rep.—AdMarket Int'l.; The N DeFilippes Corp.

EL CENSOR DEL OESTE (d)
Bolivar, 2782
Pub.—Ricardo D Victorero
EL CIVISMO (d) Est. 1916
Dr. Muñiz, 654
Pub.—María M Márquez de Gigante
CLARIN DAILY (mS) Est. 1945
Calle Piedras 1743, Capital Federal, 1140
Tel: (54-1) 270061/(54-1) 270079; Fax: (54-1) 265308/(54-1) 275254
Circ.—670,000 (d); 1,015,000 (S)
Ad. Dir.—Humberto Danucio
Ad. Mgr.—Rodolfo L Grattoni
Ad.—Alberto Pazos
U.S. Rep.—Charney/Palacios & Co. Inc.; The N DeFilippes Corp.
CONVICCION (Conviction) (m) Est. 1978
Red. Luzuriaga 1700
Pub.—Hugo Ezequiel Lezama
CRONICA (Chronicle) (m) Est. 1963
Avda. Juan de Garay 124/30, Capital Federal, 1063
Circ.—330,000 (d); 450,000 (S)
Prop.—Editorial Sarmiento
Pub.—Americo Barrios
EL CRONISTA COMERCIAL (m-ex S) Est. 1908
Honduras 5673, Capital Federal, 1414
Tel: (54-1) 333015; Fax: (54-1) 7750531
Circ.—32,000
Prop.—Sociedad Anonoma de Ediciones e Impresiones
Pub.—A Borrini
Ed.—Juan Carlos de Pabio
Ad. Mgr.—José María Guitart
U.S. Rep.—AdMarket Int'l.; Martin Media Communications; The N DeFilippes Corp.
DIARIO POPULAR (Popular Daily) (m) Est. 1974
Beguerestain 182, 1870
Tel: (54-1) 2046056
Circ.—145,000
Prop.—Publiexito SA
Pub.—Alberto S Albertengo
Ad. Dir.—Nestor Dutil
FREIE PRESSE (Free Press) (mS) German; Est. 1945
Viamonte 369, 1053
Circ.—5,000
Pub.—Ricardo L Bach Cano
GIORNALE D'ITALIA (Italian Journal) (d) Italian; Est. 1906; Tres Sargentas 457, 1003
Circ.—5,000
Pub.—Eduardo Castella
MERCADO (Market)
Peru 263, p2, 1067
Tel: (54-1) 346713
LA NACION (The Nation) (mS) Est. 1870
Bouchard 557, 1106
Tel: (54-1) 3133003; Fax: (54-1) 3131277
Circ.—630,000 (m); 835,000 (S)
Prop.—SA La Nación
Pub.—Dr. Bartolome Mitre
Ad. Mgr.—Daniel Goyeneche
U.S. Rep.—AdMarket Int'l.; Charney/Palacios & Co. Inc.; The N DeFilippes Corp.
PAGINA (Page)
Belgrano 671/7, Capital Federal, 1067
Tel: (54-1) 3342322/(54-1) 3342324; Fax: (54-1) 3131299/(54-1) 3342330
PRENSA ECONOMICA (Economic Press)
Rivadavia 926, p5, 1002
Tel: (54-1) 374410/(54-1) 376020
LA PRENSA (The Press) (mS) Est. 1869
Avda. de Mayo 567, Capital Federal, 1319
Tel: (54-1) 3311001; Fax: (54-1) 3311545
Circ.—70,000
Prop.—La Prensa SA
Pub.—Maximo Gainza
Ad. Mgr.—José Carlos Iglesias
LA PRENSA ISRAELITA (The Israeli Press) (m)
Hebrew; Est. 1918
Castelli 330
Pub.—Adela Fruchter
LA PRENSITA (The Press) (d) Est. 1963
Avda. Hipolito Yrigoyen 677
Pub.—Andres M Pocchiola
LA PROVINCIA (The Province) (d)
San Maria de Oro 889
Pub.—Juan R Salomon
LA RAZON (The Reason) (e) Est. 1905
General Hornes 690, 1272
Tel: (54-1) 269051
Circ.—315,000
Prop.—La Razon SA
Pub.—Patricio Peralta Ramos
Ed.—Jacabo Timmerman
Ad. Mgr.—Maros Peralta Ramos

TIEMPO ARGENTINO (Argentinian Time) (d)
Est. 1982
Lafayette 1910, 1286
Tel: (54-1) 281929
Circ.—75,000
Prop.—Tiempo Argentino SA
Pub.—Rául Horacio Burzaco
Ed.—Ricardo Camara
LA VOX (d)
Tabare 1641, 1437
Tel: (54-1) 9223800
Pub.—Vincente Leonides Saadi

COLON
(Buenos Aires)

LA VOZ DE COLON (The Voice of Colon) (e) Est. 1922
Calle 18, No. 713
Pub.—Jaime Juan Orpella

COMODORO RIVADAVIA
(Chubut)
Pop. Est. 101,016

ACCION (Action) (d)
Rivadavia 1275
Prop.—Instituto de Cultura
Pub.—Silvia S de Pereda
CRONICA (Chronicle) (m) Est. 1962
Namuncura 122, 9900
Tel: (54) 26015
Circ.—10,000
Prop.—Impresora Patagonica SA
Pub.—Diego J Zamit
Ad. Mgr.—Robert A Zamit
EL PATAGONICO (m) Est. 1967
Sarmiento 625
Prop.—El Chenque SA
Pub.—Dr. Roque González

CONCEPCION DEL URUGUAY
(Entre Rios)

LA CALLE (The Street) (e) Est. 1944
Mariano Moreno 139, 3260
Dir.—Ricardo Saenz Valiente

CONCORDIA
(Entre Rios)
Pop. Est. 110,000

CONCORDIA (Concord) (m) Est. 1980
San Martín 119, 3200
Dir.—F J Garay
EL HERALDO (The Herald) (d) Est. 1915
Quintana 46, 3200
Tel: (54-45) 215304; Fax: (54-45) 213554
Circ.—10,000
Dir.—Dr. Carlos Lieberman
Dir.—Gracieta Lieberman
EL SOL (The Sun) (m) Est. 1964
Entre Rios 414
Pub.—José E Morelli

CORDOBA
(Cordoba)
Pop. Est. 1,000,000

COMERCIO Y JUSTICIA (d) Est. 1939
Mariano Moreno 378, 5000
Tel: (54-51) 33788
Circ.—10,000
Prop.—Comercio y Justicia Egula & Cía.
Pub.—Dr. Jorge R Egula
Ad. Mgr.—Julio C Basualdo
CORDOBA (e) Est. 1928
Santa Rosa 677, 5000
Tel: (54-51) 22072
Circ.—25,000
Prop.—Sociedad Ed. Cordoba SA
Ad. Mgr.—José María López Bravo
LOS PRINCIPIOS (The Principles) (m) Est. 1894
Rodriguez Peña 460
Circ.—16,000
Prop.—Los Principios SA
Pub.—Orlando A Segovia
TIEMPO DE CORDOBA (Cordoba Time) (m) Est. 1978
Avda. General Paz 410
Pub.—Carlos Novillo Corvalan
LA VOZ DEL INTERIOR (The Interior Voice) (m) Est. 1904
Avda. 1651, 5000
Tel: (54-51) 729535
Circ.—87,000
Prop.—La Voz del Interior SA
Dir.—Luís Eduardo Remonda

Copyright ©1996 by the Editor & Publisher Co.

Argentina — South America

CORONEL BORREGO
(Buenos Aires)

LA VOZ (The Voice) (d) Est. 1944
Avda. San Martín 619
Pub.—Roberto A Vecchi

CORONEL PRINGLES
(Buenos Aires)
Pop. Est. 16,228

EL ORDEN (The Order) (d) Est. 1915
Leandro N. Alem 1025, 7530
Circ.—2,400
Pub.—Raúl Héctor Cejas

CORONEL SUAREZ
(Buenos Aires)
Pop. Est. 14,570

EL IMPARCIAL (The Impartial) (d) Est. 1921
Sarmiento 275, 7540
Circ.—3,000
Prop.—Editorial El Imparcial
Pub.—Pablo A García Plandolit

CORRIENTES
(Corrientes)
Pop. Est. 136,924

EPOCA (Epoch) (m) Est. 1973
Avda. Hipolito Yrigoyen 835, 3400
Dir.—Manuel F Seoane Riera
EL LIBERAL (The Liberal) (e) Est. 1909
Avda. 25 de Mayo 345
Tel: (54-783) 22069
Circ.—4,000
Prop.—Juan Francisco Torrent y Hermanos
Pub./Ed.—Juan Francisco Torrent
EL LITORAL (The Literal) (d) Est. 1960
Avda. Hipolito Yrigoyen 990, 3400
Tel: (54-783) 22264
Circ.—25,000
Dir.—Gabriel Ferris

CRESPO
(Buenos Aires)

LAR (d) Est. 1965
San Martín y Moreno
Pub.—Antonio Luís de Casas

DOLORES
(Buenos Aires)
Pop. Est. 17,414

EL NACIONAL (The National) (d) Est. 1902
Rico y Avda. del Valle, 7100
Circ.—3,200
Dir.—Dr. Gustavo M Conti
EL TRIBUNO (The Tribune) (e) Est. 1926
Avda. del Valle 296, 7100
Circ.—2,000
Dir.—María O E de Conti

ESQUEL
(Chubut)
Pop. Est. 13,771

ESQUEL (m) Est. 1925
Rivadavia 979, 9200
Circ.—3,200
Pub.—Carlos Juan Azparen

FORMOSA
(Formosa)
Pop. Est. 61,071

EL DIARIO (The Daily) (m) Est. 1966
Pederna 1212
Pub.—H M Pérez
LA MAÑANA (The Morning) Est. 1961
Dean Funes 950, 3600
Circ.—2,000
Prop.—La Manana SA
Dir./Ed.—Enrique H Read
NUEVO DIARIO (New Daily) (d)
Salta 164, 3600
Pres.—Julio A Micilio
LA OPINION (The Opinion) (e-ex S) Est. 1913
San Martín 682
Circ.—3,000
Pub.—E R Saa
LA VICTORIA (The Victory) (d)
Entre Rios 8
Pub.—Jorge A Castro

GARIN
(Buenos Aires)

SU ZONA EN LA NOTICIA (Your Zone in the News) (d) Est. 1972
Cabo 1 of Sullings 782, 1619
Circ.—13,000 (tues.-sat.); 18,000 (S)
Founder/Pub.—Margarita María Fernandez

GENERAL BELGRANO
(Buenos Aires)

EL MANGRULLO (d)
Guido 650, 7223
Dir.—Héctor A Carricaburu Carou

GENERAL PAZ
(Buenos Aires)

LA PALABRA (The Word) (d) Est. 1931
Vivot y Ceijas, 1987
Pub.—Héctor A Carricaburu Carou

GENERAL PICO
(La Pampa)
Pop. Est. 21,897

LA REFORMA (The Refomer) (d) Est. 1923
Belgrano 627, 6360
Circ.—6,000
Dir.—Juan Carlos Matilla

GENERAL SARMIENTO
(Buenos Aires)

LA VOZ DE GENERAL SARMIENTO (The Voice of General Sarmiento) (m) Est. 1960
Misiones 698, 1663
Pub.—Roberto Campos

GOYA
(Corrientes)
Pop. Est. 20,800

PRIMERA HORA (First Hour) (m) Est. 1972
Alvear 391, 3450
Circ.—3,100
Dir.—Abelardo Palisa

GUALEGUAY
(Entre Rios)
Pop. Est. 20,401

EL DEBATE-PREGON (dS) Est. 1945
Islas Malvinas 170, 2840
Dir.—Alberto M Lagrenade
Dir.—Arturo J Etchevehere
EL SUPREMO (The Supreme) (m) Est. 1980
Avda. 25 de Mayo 569, 2840
Dir.—Miguel A Nefia
Dir.—Roberto Martínez

GUALEGUAYCHU
(Entre Rios)
Pop. Est. 40,661

EL ARGENTINO (The Argentinian) (m) Est. 1911
9 de Julio 45, 2820
Circ.—7,200
Prop.—Diario El Argentino
Dir.—Nestor Cardoro Bachini
NOTICIAS (News) (m) Est. 1970
Avda. 25 de Mayo 740, 2820
Pub.—Julian Majul

JOSE INGENIEROS
(Buenos Aires)

JOSE INGENIEROS (d)
Rotarismo Argentino 1992, 1778
Pub.—Alba Gómez
EL MANGRULLO (d)
Pub.—Héctor A Carricaburu Carou

JUAREZ
(Buenos Aires)

TRIBUNA (Tribune) (e) Est. 1927
Brown 50-D, 7020
Circ.—4,000
Pub.—Héctor R Bonini

JUNIN
(Buenos Aires)
Pop. Est. 59,020

DEMOCRACIA (Democracy) (e) Est. 1931
Rivadavia 436, 6000
Circ.—7,000
Pub.—Dora de Lebensohn
Ad. Mgr.—An La Panizza de Dana

LA VERDAD
(The Truth) (m) Est. 1917
Roque Saenz Peña 167, 6000
Circ.—10,000 (m); 10,500 (S)
Prop.—Junta Parroquial Accion Catolica
Pub.—Domingo Cancelleri
Ed.—Anibal R Sánchez
Ad. Mgr.—Marcos B Julia

LA LUCILA
(Buenos Aires)

EL PARQUE (The Park) (d) Est. 1964
J. M. Estrada 3608, 1636
Dir.—Héctor Rostro

LA PLATA
(Buenos Aires)
Pop. Est. 450,000

EL DIA (The Day) (mS) Est. 1884
No. 817/21, 1900
Tel: (54-21) 210101; **Fax:** (54-21) 24550
Circ.—55,000
Prop.—El Dia SACIF
Pub.—Raúl Kraiselburd
Ad. Mgr.—Luís Americo Fauci
LA GACETA DE LA TARDE (The Afternoon Gazette) (e) Est. 1964
Calle 46, No. 423, 1900
Circ.—12,875
Prop.—Sociedad Impresora Platense SA Comercial e Ind.
Pub.—Juan Carlos Mohamed
PREGON (d) Est. 1942
Avda. 13, No. 857
Dir.—Hernando Navas

LA RIOJA
(La Rioja)
Pop. Est. 46,090

EL INDEPENDIENTE (The Independent) (m) Est. 1959
9 de Julio 223, 5300
Circ.—6,000
Dir.—Leandro López Alcaraz
EL SOL (The Sun) (e) Est. 1972
Avda. 25 de Mayo 76, 5300
Dir.—Tomás N Alvarez Saavedra

LANUS
(Buenos Aires)

PREGON (d) Est. 1941
Ituzaingo 1066, 1824
Circ.—10,000
Pub.—Gustavo Roberto Herrera
VIDA DE LANUS (Lanus Life) (d) Est. 1927
29 de Septiembre 1830, 1824
Pub.—J José Ibanez

LAS FLORES
(Buenos Aires)
Pop. Est. 10,000

PROGRESO (Progress) (d) Est. 1969
Pueyrredon 443, 7200
Circ.—4,000
Pub.—Ricardo H Caputo

LINCOLN
(Buenos Aires)

LA VOZ DE LINCOLN (The Voice of Lincoln) (d) Est. 1970
Urquiza 81, 6070
Dir.—María Teresa Ruíz

LOBERIA
(Buenos Aires)

NUESTRA CIUDAD (Our City) (m) Est. 1961
Belgrano 139
Dir.—Luís Raúl Armandelli

LOMAS DE ZAMORA
(Buenos Aires)
Pop. Est. 410,806

LA UNION (The Union) (mS) Est. 1897
Avda. Hipolito Yrigoyen 8867, 1832
Circ.—12,000
Dir.—Juan Antonio Gritta

LOMAS DEL MIRADOR
(Buenos Aires)

EL CENSOR DEL OESTE (d)
Bolivar
Pub.—Ricardo D Victorero

MAR del PLATA
(Buenos Aires)
Pop. Est. 302,282

EL ATLANTICO (The Atlantic) (m) Est. 1938
Bolivar 2975, 7600
Tel: (54-23) 35462
Circ.—20,000

Dir.—Oscar Alberto Gastiarena
Ad. Mgr.—Jorge Oscar Linari
LA CAPITAL (The Capital) (d) Est. 1905
Avda. Champagnat 2551, 7600
Tel: (54-23) 771164
Circ.—32,000
Prop.—Editorial La Capital SA
Pub.—Dr. Ernesto Llan de Rosos
Ad. Mgr.—Pedro Ventura

MENDOZA
(Mendoza)
Pop. Est. 118,568
Pop. Est. (Metro Area) 470,896

LOS ANDES (The Andes) (mS) Est. 1882
San Martín 1049, 5500
Tel: (54-61) 244500
Circ.—60,000
Prop.—Sociedad Diario Los Andes (Hnos. Calle)
Pub.—Elcira Videla de S de Azevedo
EL ANDINO (e) Est. 1968
San Martín 1049, 5500
Circ.—2,128
Pub.—Elcira Videla de S de Azevedo
MENDOZA (m) Est. 1969
San Martín 947, 5500
Tel: (54-61) 241064
Circ.—23,000
Prop.—Prensa del Oeste
Dir.—José Llopart
LA VICTORIA (The Victory) (d)
Entre Rios 78
Pub.—Jorge A Castro

MERCEDES
(Buenos Aires)
Pop. Est. 39,760

LA HORA (The Hour) (m) Est. 1932
Calle 18, No. 905, 6600
Circ.—4,000
Dir.—Juan M Spalla
Dir.—E Pardos
Dir.—B Ponce
IMPULSO (Impulse) (d) Est. 1958
Avda. Mitre 538, 6600
Pub.—Eduardo L Estrada Dubor
EL OESTE (m) Est. 1924
Calle 33, 6600
Circ.—2,500
Dir.—Teobaldo Bustos Barrando
Dir.—Marcelo Bustos Barrando

MONTE GRANDE
(Buenos Aires)

LA VOZ DEL PUEBLO (The Town Voice) (m) Est. 1944
Vincente López 14, 1842
Dir.—Marcelo E Bachman

MORENO
(Buenos Aires)

LA OPINION (The Opinion) (m) Est. 1976
Independencia 977, 1744
Dir.—Juan Carlos Lacusta

NAVARRO
(Buenos Aires)

AMANECER (Awaken) (d) Est. 1962
Bartolome Mitre 500
Dir.—Jorge H Clavellino

NECOCHEA
(Buenos Aires)
Pop. Est. 39,868

ECOS DIARIOS (Daily Echos) (mS) Est. 1921
Calle 62, No. 2470, 7630
Circ.—3,600
Prop.—Sociedad Anonima Editora, Comercial e Imobiliaria
Dir.—Saol Ignacio
Ad. Mgr.—Rubén Carlos Leys

NOGOYA
(Entre Rios)

ACCION (Action) (m) Est. 1912
Caseros 989, 3150
Dir.—Gustavo J Etchevehere
NOGOYA (e) Est. 1974
San Martín 911
Pub.—César Jaroslavsky
LA TARDE (The Afternoon) (d) Est. 1956
Junin 469, 3150
Dir.—Salvador Solorzano

NUEVE DE JULIO
(Buenos Aires)

EL 9 DE JULIO (The Ninth of July) (e) Est. 1909
Avda. Vadia 362, 6500
Dir.—Antonio Alta

IV-106

Copyright ©1996 by the Editor & Publisher Co.

South America — Argentina

EL ORDEN (The Order) (m) Est. 1920
Mendoza 351, 6500
Pub.—Abel Rodríguez

OLAVARRIA
(Buenos Aires)
Pop. Est. 90,000

EL POPULAR (Popular) (m) Est. 1919
Vicente López 2626, 7400
Circ.—12,000
Dir.—Julio M Pagano
TRIBUNA (Tribune) (e) Est. 1955
Vicente López 2437
Circ.—5,500
Pub.—Juan G Becker

PARANA
(Entre Ríos)
Pop. Est. 127,635

EL DIARIO (The Daily) (m) Est. 1914
Urquiza y Buenos Aires
Tel: (54-43) 210082
Circ.—20,000
Prop.—El Diario Sociedad Anonima
Pub.—Dr. Arturo J Etchevehere
Mgr.—Dr. Luis F Etchevehere

PEHUAJO
(Buenos Aires)
Pop. Est. 21,078

NOTICIAS (News) (m) Est. 1949
Avda. Rivera Indarte 370, 6450
Circ.—8,500
Prop.—Indugraf SA
Dir.—Robert E Rossi

PERGAMINO
(Buenos Aires)
Pop. Est. 56,078

LA OPINION (The Opinion) (m) Est. 1917
9 de Julio 568, 2700
Circ.—6,400
Dir.—Julio Venini

POSADAS
(Misiones)
Pop. Est. 97,514

EL TERRITORIO (The Territory) (mS) Est. 1925
Avda. Quaranta, 4307
Tel: (54-752) 37112
Circ.—22,000 (m); 28,000 (S)
Dir.—Humberto A Perez
Ad. Mgr.—Santos Miguel García

PUERTO DESEADO
(Buenos Aires)

EL ORDEN (The Order) (d)
Don Bosco 1055
Pub.—José A Rodríguez

QUILMES
(Buenos Aires)
Pop. Est. 354,976

EL SOL (The Sun) (d) Est. 1927
Avda. Hipolito Yrigoyen 122
Tel: (54) 2533320; Fax: (54) 458714
Circ.—25,000
Dir.—José M Ghisani
Ed.—Rodolfo Alberto Imperiali

RAFAELA
(Santa Fe)
Pop. Est. 43,695

LA OPINION (The Opinion) (e) Est. 1921
Lavalle 171
Circ.—7,000
Pub.—Emilio J Grande

RAMOS MEJIA
(Buenos Aires)

NUEVA IDEA (New Idea) (d) Est. 1943
Almirante Brown 1041, 1704
Dir.—Marta Irene G de Falcon

RAUCH
(Buenos Aires)

EL MUNICIPIO (The Municipal) (m) Est. 1932
Alem 83, 7203
Dir.—Julio Gonzalez

RESISTENCIA
(Chaco)
Pop. Est. (Metro Area) 200,000

NORTE (North) Est. 1968
Pirovano 311
Circ.—13,000
Prop.—Editorial Chaco SA
Pub.—Miguel A Fernandez
Bus. Mgr.—Armando Sosa Mena
EL TERRITORIO (The Territory) Est. 1919
Casilla Correo 320
Circ.—15,000
Pub.—Raúl Andrés Aguirre
Ed. in Ch.—Reynaldo A Martínez

RIO CUARTO
(Cordoba)
Pop. Est. 88,852

LA CALLE (The Street) (m) Est. 1953
Sobremonte 743
Circ.—6,000
Pub.—Francisco Savino
EL PUEBLO (The Town) (m) Est. 1912
San Martín 160
Circ.—3,000
Pub.—Luciano Subirachs
PUNTAL
Rivadavia 180
Circ.—11,000
Prop.—Editorial Fundamento
Pub.—Jorge Molineusco
Ed.—Daniel Placci
Ad. Mgr.—Raúl Ontivero

RIO GALLEGOS
(Santa Cruz)
Pop. Est. 27,833

LA OPINION AUSTRAL (m) Est. 1959
Zapiola 35, 9400
Circ.—4,000
Dir.—Alberto Raúl Segovia

RIO GRANDE
(Santa Cruz)

LA CIUDAD NUEVA (The New City) (d)
Ameghino 626
Pub.—Leonor María Pinero

RIO TERCERO
(Cordoba)

CRONICA (Chronicle) (S)
Sgto. Cabral 142, 5850
Pub.—José María Lioy

ROJAS
(Buenos Aires)
Pop. Est. 10,074

LA VOZ DE ROJAS (The Voice of Rojas) (d) Est. 1944
Leandro N. Alem 472, 2705
Circ.—2,000
Dir.—Carlos A Rodríguez

ROSARIO
(Santa Fe)
Pop. Est. 750,455

LA CAPITAL (The Capital) (mS) Est. 1867
Sarmiento 763; Casilla Correo 320, 2000
Tel: (54-41) 3922193
Circ.—94,000 (m); 115,700 (S)
Prop.—Family Lagos
Pub./Ed.—Carlos Lagos
Ad. Mgr.—Orlando Prendes
LA TRIBUNA (The Tribune) (e) Est. 1950
Santa Fe 966, 2000
Circ.—30,000
Prop.—Publicitaria Rosarina
Pub.—Raúl N Gardelli

RUFINO
(Santa Fe)

NOTICIAS (News) (d) Est. 1952
Avda. Hipolito Yrigoyen 333, 6100
Pub.—María R de Sosa Covian

SALTA
(Salta)
Pop. Est. 275,300

CRONICA DEL NOA (Noa Chronicle) (d)
España 478
EL TRIBUNO (The Tribune) (d) Est. 1949
Ruta 68, Km. 1592, 4400
Tel: (54) 241382; Fax: (54) 240877
Circ.—41,215
Prop.—Horizontas SA
Dir.—Robert Romero

SALTO
(Buenos Aires)
Pop. Est. 7,771

EL NORTE (The North) (d) Est. 1953
Buenos Aires 636, 2741
Pub.—Jorge Nahara

SAN CARLOS DE BARILOCHE
(Rio Negro)

DIARIO LA ULTIMA (The Ultimate Daily) (m) Est. 1980
Pje. Gutiérrez 101
Pub.—José Antoni Jalil
RIO NEGRO (Black River) (m) Est. 1912
9 de Julio 733, 8400
Circ.—32,374
Pub.—Fernando Rajineri
Ed./Mng. Dir.—Dr. Julio Raúl Raineri

SAN FRANCISCO
(Cordoba)
Pop. Est. 48,896

LA VOZ DE SAN JUSTO (The Voice of San Justo) (d) Est. 1914
Blvd. 9 de Julio 2001, 2400
Circ.—7,000
Prop.—La Voz De San Justo SRL
Pub.—Joaquín Gregorio Martínez

SAN FRANCISCO del VALLE de CATAMARCA
(Catamarca)
Pop. Est. 57,228

EL SOL (The Sun) (m) Est. 1973
Esq. 551, 4700
Pub.—T Alvarez Saavedra
LA UNION (The Union) (m) Est. 1920
San Martín 671, 4700
Circ.—5,000
Prop.—Bishopric of Catamarca
Dir.—Benedicto Dardo Soria

SAN ISIDRO
(Buenos Aires)

SOL DEL PLATA (d) Est. 1940
Garibaldi 527, 1642
Dir.—Eve Lila del Valle Di Carlo

SAN JUAN
(San Juan)
Pop. Est. 165,000
Pop. Est. (Metro Area) 320,000

DIARIO DE CUYO (Cuyo Daily) (d) Est. 1947
Mendoza 380, 5400
Tel: (54-61) 29680
Circ.—25,000
Prop.—Francisco S Montes SA
Dir.—Francisco S Montes
TRIBUNA DE LA TARDE (The Afternoon Tribune) (d) Est. 1931
Mitre 85 Oeste, 5400
Tel: (54-61) 400923
Circ.—9,000
Pub.—Cristóbal Carbajal
Mng. Dir.—Dr. Armando Guevara

SAN JUSTO
(Buenos Aires)

EL INFORMATIVO (The Informer) (m)
Dr. 1, Arieta 2789, 1754
Pub.—Ana María Policastro

SAN LUIS
(San Luis)
Pop. Est. 50,771

EL DIARIO DE SAN LUIS (San Luis Daily) (d) Est. 1966
Pedemera 1212, 5700
Dir.—Edgardo L Cordera
LA OPINION (The Opinion) (e) Est. 1913
Aysoucho 1257, 5700
Circ.—3,000
Dir.—Eduardo Rodríguez Saa

SAN MARTIN
(Buenos Aires)

EL MUNICIPIO (The Municipal) (m) Est. 1938
Pueyrredon 414, 1650
Dir.—Diego R Gómez
LA RECONQUISTA (d) Est. 1928
Calle 93, No. 1841, 1650
Dir.—Manuel G Morillo

SAN MIGUEL de TUCUMAN
(Tecuman)
Pop. Est. 321,567
Pop. Est. (Metro Area) 366,392

LA GAZETA (The Gazette) (mS) Est. 1912
Mendoza 654, 4000
Circ.—84,000
Prop.—Sociedad Editora La Gazeta SA
Pub.—Eduardo García Hamilton
Ad. Dir.—Julio Paz
PREGON (mS) Est. 1956
Belgrano 563
Circ.—17,000
Pub.—Jorge Annuar
LA TARDE (The Afternoon) Est. 1961
Mendoza 654, 4000
Tel: (54) 219260
Dir.—Daniel Alberto Dessein
EL TRIBUNO (The Tribune) (m) Est. 1980
Belgrano 645
Pub.—Emma Barcena de Gronda

SAN NICOLAS
(Buenos Aires)
Pop. Est. 64,730

HOY (Today) (d)
1.o. de Mayo 2820, 3000
Circ.—30,000
EL LITORAL (The Literal) (d)
San Martín 2651-59, 3000
Tel: (54-41) 20101
Circ.—40,000
EL NORTE (The North) (d) Est. 1926
Francia 64, 2900
Circ.—30,000
Pub.—Haroldo Zeulgary

SAN RAFAEL
(Mendoza)
Pop. Est. 58,237

LA CAPITAL (The Capital) (d-ex S) Est. 1916
Bdo. de Irigoyen 236
Pub.—Raúl A Morales
EL COMERCIO (m) Est. 1920
Avda. Mitre 327
Pub.—Manuel E Butti

SAN SALVADOR de JUJUY
(Jujuy)
Pop. Est. 82,637

PREGON (d) Est. 1965
Belgrano 563, 4600
EL TRIBUNO (The Tribune) (d) Est. 1980
Belgrano 306, 4600
Dir.—Miguel Angel Armatta

SANTA FE
(Santa Fe)
Pop. Est. 224,655

EDICION (Edition) (d) Est. 1974
9 de Julio 889
Pub.—Emilio Cesar Adobato
HOY (Today) (d)
1.o. de Mayo 2820, 3000
Circ.—30,000
EL IMPARCIAL (The Impartial) (mS) Est. 1914
Avda. General Paz 6301, 3000
Circ.—10,000
Dir.—Dr. Raúl S Capoccetti
EL LITORAL (The Literal) (d) Est. 1918
San Martín 2651/59, 3000
Tel: (54-41) 20101
Circ.—40,000
Prop.—El Litoral SRL
Pub.—Riobo Caputto

SANTA ROSA
(La Pampa)
Pop. Est. 33,649

LA ARENA (The Arena) (d) Est. 1933
Avda. 25 de Mayo 336
Circ.—11,000
Pres.—Antonio Mario D'Atri
LA CAPITAL (The Capital) (m) Est. 1893
Pellegrini 126, 6300
Pub.—Angel Ortiz

SANTIAGO DEL ESTERO
(Buenos Aires)

EL LIBERAL (The Liberal) (d)
Libertad 263, 4200
Tel: (54-84) 224400
Circ.—30,000

SANTOS LUGARES
(Buenos Aires)

EL MATUTINO (The Morning) (m) Est. 1977
Pablo Giorello 1688, 1676
Dir.—Remagio M Amaya

Copyright ©1996 by the Editor & Publisher Co.

Argentina — South America

TANDIL
(Buenos Aires)
Pop. Est. 65,876

EL ECO DE TANDIL (The Echo of Tandil) (d) Est. 1882
Avda. Hipolito Yrigoyen 560, 7000
Circ.—7,500
Dir.—Rogelio A Rotonda
NUEVA ERA (New Era) (e) Est. 1919
General Rodríguez 445, 7000
Circ.—6,000
Prop.—Editorial Nueva Era SECPA
Dir.—Aribal Fillipini
Ad. Mgr.—Jorge Oliver
EL PAIS (The Country) (d)
Prop.—Editora Independencia

TIGRE
(Buenos Aires)

FOMENTO (mS)
Avda. Hipolito Yrigoyen 707, 1648
Pub.—Enrique Innocensi

TRELEW
(Chubut)

EL CHUBUT (m) Est. 1975
Avda. 9 de Julio 324, 9100
Pub.—José María Saez
JORNADA (Journey) (d) Est. 1954
Avda. Hipolito Yrigoyen 577, 9100
Pub.—Bernardo A Feldman

TRENQUE LAUQUEN
(Buenos Aires)
Pop. Est. 18,169

LA OPINION (The Opinion) (m) Est. 1919
Avda. General Roca 752, 6400
Circ.—7,000
Pub.—Juan R Nazar

TRES ARROYOS
(Buenos Aires)
Pop. Est. 55,068

LA VOZ DEL PUEBLO (Town Voice) (m) Est. 1902
Colon 29/33, 7500
Circ.—7,500
Prop.—Maciel Hermanos SAECI
Dir.—Antonio Maciel
Ad. Mgr.—Lindor Sanguinetti

VEINTICINCO DE MAYO
(Buenos Aires)

LA MAÑANA (The Morning) (d) Est. 1962
Calle 28, No. 1141, 6600
Dir.—Alberto Eduardo Rocha

VICENTE LOPEZ
(Buenos Aires)

LA RIBERA (d) Est. 1925
Lisandro de la Torre 222; PO Box "A", 1638
Ed.—Alejandro Vincente Chiodi

VICTORIA
(Corrientes)
Pop. Est. 17,406

CRISOL (d) Est. 1947
Las Piedras 63, 3153
Dir.—Dr. Arturo J Etchevehere
LA MAÑANA (The Morning) (m) Est. 1933
Italia 566
Dir.—César Jaroslavsky

VILLA DOLORES
(Cordoba)

DEMOCRACIA (Democracy) (d) Est. 1925
Lib. Urquiza 101, 5870
Dir.—Oscar A Tello

VILLA MARIA
(Cordoba)
Pop. Est. 30,500

NOTICIAS (News) (m) Est. 1970
Sante Fe 1025, 5900
Pub.—Héctor Oscar Bernaus

VILLA MERCEDES
(San Luis)

IMPULSO (Impulse) (m) Est. 1980
Avda. Mitre 538, 5730
Circ.—9,500
Pub.—Dr. Eduardo Luís Estrada Dubor

LA VOZ DEL SUD (The Voice of the South) (m)
Belgrano 200, 5730
Dir.—Isaura Martín de Curchod

VILLAGUAY
(Entre Rios)
Pop. Est. 15,591

EL PUEBLO (The Town) (e) Est. 1926
San Martín 362/366, 3240
Circ.—3,700
Dir.—Juan Carlos Surre

ZAPALA
(Misiones)
Pop. Est. 11,385

ECOS CORDILLERANOS (d) Est. 1956
Ivorquis 120
Circ.—4,200
Pub.—Manuel Vega

ZARATE
(Buenos Aires)
Pop. Est. 54,772

EL DEBATE (The Debate) (d) Est. 1900
Alte. Brown 44, 2800
Circ.—4,000
Dir.—Alfredo Della Casa
Ad. Mgr.—Armando Correa
EL PUEBLO (The Town) (e) Est. 1949
Castelli 900, 2800
Circ.—4,000
Pub.—Ruque F de Paolo
Ad. Mgr.—Jorge de Paolo

BOLIVIA, REPUBLIC OF
Pop. Est. 7,719,445

COCHABAMBA
Pop. Est. 1,093,625

OPINION (d)
Casilla Correo 287
Tel: (591-42) 24080
Pub.—Edwin Tapia Frontanilla
LOS TIEMPOS (The Times) (d) Est. 1943
Calle Santivanez, No. 2110; Casilla Correo 525
Tel: (591-42) 28286/(591-42) 28228; Fax: (591-42) 25811
Circ.—18,000
Pub.—Carlos Canelas

LA PAZ
Pop. Est. 1,883,122

EL DIARIO (The Daily) (mS) Est. 1904
Calle Loayza, No. 1118; Casilla Correo 5
Tel: (591-2) 356835; Fax: (591-2) 363846
Circ.—90,000 (m); 115,000 (S)
Prop.—Empresa Editora El Diario SA
Pub.—Jorge Carrasco Jr
U.S. Rep.—Charney/Palacios & Co. Inc.
HOY (Today) (m) Est. 1968
Avda. 6 de Agosto, No. 2170; Casilla Correo 477
Tel: (591-2) 320311; Fax: (591-2) 370564
Circ.—25,000
Prop.—Empresa Editora Siglo
Pub.—Gonzalo Serrate
Ed.—Carlow Serrate Reich
Ad. Mgr.—Ana Maria de Sandoval
JORNADA (Journal) (e) Est. 1964
Calle Junin, No. 608; Casilla Correo 1628
Tel: (591-2) 356213
Circ.—11,500
Pub.—Jaime Rios Chacón
PRESENCIA (Presence) (mS) Est. 1952
Avda. Mariscal Santa Cruz, No. 1295; Casilla Correo 3276
Tel: (591-2) 372344; Fax: (591-2) 391040
Circ.—68,000 (m); 78,000 (S)
Prop.—Editora Pregencia Ltd.
Mng. Dir.—Armando María V
Ed.—Huascar Cajias K
U.S. Rep.—Charney/Palacios & Co. Inc.
LA RAZON (The Reason) Est. 1989
Calle Jorge Saenz, No. 1330
Tel: (591-2) 342615/(591-2) 352633
Prop.—Comunicaciones El Pais SA
Mng. Dir.—Jorge Canelas Saenz
ULTIMA HORA (Last Hour) (e) Est. 1929
Avda. Camacho, No. 1372; Casilla Correo 5920
Tel: (591-2) 370262

Circ.—35,000
Pub.—Lupe Andrade
Ad. Mgr.—Hugo Ortiz
VOZ DEL PUEBLO (Town Voice) (e)
Ayachuso, No. 208; Casilla Correo 525
Circ.—10,000
Pub.—Roberto Zapata Cusicanqui

POTOSI
Pop. Est. 645,817

EL SIGLO (The Century) (m) Est. 1975
Calle Linares, No. 99; Casilla Correo 389
Circ.—1,500
Ad. Mgr.—Guido Romay

SANTA CRUZ DE LA SIERRA
Pop. Est. 1,351,191

EL DEBER (The Will) (m) Est. 1965
Casilla Correo 2144
Tel: (591-33) 324139/(591-33) 343345
Circ.—8,000
Prop.—Editorial Oriente
Pub.—Pedro Rivero Mercado
EL MUNDO (The World) (d)
Florida, No. 593
Tel: (591-33) 334770; Fax: (591-33) 3325057
Circ.—20,000

BRAZIL
Pop. Est. 158,739,257

AMAMBAI
(Mato Grosso do Sul)

A NOTICIA (News)
Avda. Pedro Manvailer, No. 1177, 79990

AMERICANA
(Sao Paulo)
Pop. Est. 156,800

DIARIO DE AMERICANA (American Daily)
Rua Alvaro Ribeiro, No. 610, 13470
O LIBERAL (Liberal) (d) Est. 1952
Rua Padre Manoel da Nobrega, No. 154, 13470
Circ.—7,000
Prop.—Empresa Editora O Liberal Ltda.
Pub.—Jessyr Bianco

ANDRADINA
(Sao Paulo)
Pop. Est. 45,934

EDITORA O JORNAL DA REGIAO LTDA. (d) Est. 1963
Rua Ceara, No. 771, 16900
Circ.—7,000
Pub.—Isael Soares Fernandes

APUCARANA
(Parana)
Pop. Est. 95,251

TRIBUNA DA CIDADE (City Tribune) (d)
Rua Nagib Daher, No. 467, 86800
Prop.—Empresa Jornalistica Atualidade Ltd.

ARACAJU
(Sergipe)
Pop. Est. 361,544

DIARIO OFICIAL DO ESTADO DE SERGIPE (Official Daily of Sergipe State)
Rua Propia, No. 227, 49000
EMPRESSA GRAFICA JORNAL DA CIDADE LTDA.
Antonio Cabral, No. 1069, 49000
GAZETA DE SERGIPE
Avda. Rio Branco, No. 298, 49000
INDUSTRIA GRAFICA TRIBUNA DE ARACAJU LTD.
Travesa Basilio Rocha, No. 49, 49000
JORNAL DA CIDADE (City Journal) (d)
Avda. Rio Branco 40
JORNAL RESUMO DA SEMANA (d)
Rua Divina Pastor 450

ARACATUBA
(Sao Paulo)
Pop. Est. 142,308

FOLHA DA REGIAO (d) Est. 1972
Rua Afonso Peña, No. 632, 16100
Circ.—15,000
Prop.—Editora Folha da Regiao da Aracatuba Ltd.
Pub.—Genilson Senche
JORNAL A COMARCA (d) Est. 1924
Rua Marechal Deodora, No. 433, 16100
Circ.—9,000
Prop.—Editora Grafica Jornal A Comerca Ltd.
Pub.—Paulo Alcides Jorge

ARARAQUARA
(Sao Paulo)
Pop. Est. 145,430

O DIARIO (Daily) (d) Est. 1965
Rua 9 de Julho, No. 504, 14800
Circ.—5,000
Prop.—Diario da Araraquarense
Pub.—Roberto Barbieri
FOLHA DA CIDADE
Rua Italia, No. 1416, 14800
O IMPARCIAL (d) Est. 1931
Avda. José Bonifacio, No. 715, 14800
Circ.—8,000
Prop.—Empresa O Imparcial Ltda.
Pub.—Paulo de Arruda Correada Silva

ARIQUEMES
(Rondonia)

EMPRESSA JORNALISTICA O PARCELEIRO LTDA.
Avda. Pres. Jusoelino, No. 2302, 78920

ASSIS
(Sao Paulo)
Pop. Est. 74,149

A GAZETA DE ASSIS (Assis Gazette) (d) Est. 1954
Rua Rangel Pestana, No. 2, 19800
Circ.—2,000
Prop.—Empresa Editora de Jornais Regional Ltda.
Pub.—Nelson de Souza
VOZ DA TERRA (Voice of Terra) (d) Est. 1963
Avda. Rui Barbosa, No. 1291, 19800
Circ.—6,500
Prop.—Empresa Jornalistica Voz de Terra Ltda.
Pub.—Egidio Coelho da Silva

AVARE
(Sao Paulo)

O AVARE
Largo Sao Joao, No. 144, 18700

BAGE
(Rio Grande do Sul)
Pop. Est. 106,294

CORREIO DO SUL (m) Est. 1914
Avda. 7 de Setembro, No. 664, 96400
Circ.—3,500
Prop.—Empresa Grafica do Correio do Sul Ltda.
Pub.—Mario Nogueira Lópes

BARRA MANSA
(Rio de Janeiro)
Pop. Est. 187,891

A VOZ DA CIDADE (City Voice) (d) Est. 1970
Avda. Dario Aragao, No. 837, 27400
Circ.—8,000
Prop.—MAPA Publicidade Ltda.
Pub.—Geraldo Almeida Pancardes

BARRETOS
(Sao Paulo)
Pop. Est. 80,107

O DIARIO (The Daily) (d)
Avda. Dezessete, No. 753, 14780
Circ.—2,000
Pub.—Joao Monteiro de Barros Filho

BAURU
(Sao Paulo)
Pop. Est. 220,871

DIARIO DE BAURU (Bauru Daily) (d) Est. 1946
Praca D. Pedro II, No. 2-77, 17015
Circ.—10,000
Prop.—Empresa Grafica e Editora Bauru
Pub.—Zarcillo R Barbosa
JORNAL DA CIDADE (d) Est. 1967
Rua Xingu, No. 4-44, 17013
Circ.—15,000
Prop.—Jornal da Cidade de Bauru Ltda.
Pub.—Nilson Ferreira Costa

BELEM
(Para)
Pop. Est. 1,120,777

DIARIO OFICIAL DO ESTADO (Official State Daily)
Travesa do Chaco, No. S/N, 66000
DIARIO OFICIAL DO MUNICIPIO (Official Municipal Daily)
Praca D. Pedro II, No. S/N, 66000
DIARIO DO PARA (Para Daily) (d) Est. 1911
Rua Gaspar Viana, No. 773, 66000
Circ.—24,000

Prop.—Editora O Estado do Para
Pub.—Avertano Barreto da Rocha
Ed.—Walmir Botelho
JORNAL O LIBERAL (Liberal Journal) (d)
Rua Gaspar Viana, No. 253, 66000
Circ.—110,000
Prop.—Delta Publicidade SA
Pub.—Reginaldo Ferreira
A PROVINCIA DO PARA (Para Province) (d) Est. 1876
Travesa Campos Sales, No. 210, 66000
Circ.—28,000
Prop.—Empresa A Provincia do Para Ltda.
Pub.—Milton Blanco de Abrunhosa Trinidade

BELO HORIZONTE
(Minas Gerais)
Pop. Est. 2,122,073

COMUNICADO AGROMETEOROLOGICO
Avda. Amazonas, No. 115, 30188
DIARIO DO COMERCIO EMPRESA JORNALIT LTDA.
Rua Padre Rolim, No. 652, 30130
DIARIO DE MINAS (Minas Daily) (e) Est. 1949
Praca Raúl Soares, No. 339, 3000
Tel: (55-31) 2127107
Circ.—35,000
Prop.—Diario de Minas SA
Pub.—Maurilio Machado Brandao Fernandes
DIARIO DA TARDE (Afternoon Daily) (e) Est. 1936
Rua Goitacazes, No. 71, 30190
Tel: (55-31) 2262322; Fax: (55-31) 2732322
Circ.—36,000
Prop.—Estado de Minas SA
Ed.—Fabio Proenca Doyle
ESTADO DE MINAS (Minas State) (mS) Est. 1929
Rua Goitacazes, No. 36; Caixa Postal 140, 3000
Tel: (55-31) 2732322; Fax: (55-31) 2268070/(55-31) 2734400
Circ.—75,000 (m); 175,000 (S)
Prop.—Estado de Minas SA
Pub.—Roberto Elisio de Castro e Silva
Ed.—Joeo B Martin Sales
Ad. Mgr.—Edison Zenobio
JORNAL DE MINAS (Minas Journal) (e) Est. 1935
Avda. Francisco Sales, No. 536, 30150
Prop.—Jornal de Minas SA
Pub.—Alfonso Araujo Paulino
MINAS GERAIS
Avda. Augusto da Lima, No. 270, 30190
REVISTA SOM
Rua da Bahia, No. 1148, 30160
TEMPOS E MOVIMENTOS
Rua Aimores, No. 1451, 30000

BIRIGUI
(Sao Paulo)
Pop. Est. 63,858

DIARIO DE BIRIGUI (Birigui Daily) (d) Est. 1974
Rua Saudades, No. 1395, 16200
Circ.—2,000
Prop.—Jornal Diario de Birigui Ltda.
Pub.—Geraldo Silvero
O NOROESTINO LTDA. (d) Est. 1967
Rua Santos Dumont, No. 74, 16200
Circ.—1,000
Pub.—Leonardo Sabioni

BLUMENAU
(Santa Catarina)
Pop. Est. 192,871

DIARIO DA NOITE (d)
Rua Republica Argentina, No. 653, 89050
JORNAL DE SANTA CATARINA (Santa Catarina Journal) (d) Est. 1971
Sao Paulo, No. 1120, 89100
Circ.—25,000
Prop.—Empresa Editora Jornal de Santa Catarina Ltda.
Pub.—Flavio José de Almeida Coelho
Ed.—Luís Antonio Soares
Ad. Mgr.—Telvio Maestrini

BOA VISTA
(Roraima)

DIARIO OFICIAL (Official Daily)
Rua Coronel Pinto, No. 84, 69300
FOLHA DE BOA VISTA
Avda. Santos Dumont, No. 1736, 69300
JORNAL O RORAIMA
Avda. Getulio Vargas, No. 1883, 69300

BRAGANCA PAULISTA
(Sao Paulo)
Pop. Est. 105,462

BRAGANCA JORNAL DIARIO (Braganca Daily Journal) (d) Est. 1927
Praca José Bonifacio, No. 61, 12900
Circ.—4,200
Pub.—Oomair Fagundes de Oliveira

BRASILIA
(Federal District)
Pop. Est. 1,470,300

COPY DESK
SCS Ed Bern Sayao, No. S/N
CORREIO BRASILIENSE (mS) Est. 1960
SIG Quandra 2 Lotes, No. 340, 70610
Tel: (55-61) 3211314; Fax: (55-61) 3212856
Circ.—40,000
Prop.—SA Correio Brasiliense
Dir.—Mauricio Dinepi
U.S. Rep.—The N DeFilippes Corp.
DF REPORTER
SIG Quandra 8 Lotes 2286/2296, No. 15, 70610
DIARIO DE BRASILIA (Brasilia Daily) (d) Est. 1972
Avda. W-3, Quadro 503
Circ.—18,000
Pub.—Dyrno Pires Ferreira
DIARIO DO CONGRESSO NACIONAL (National Congress Journal)
Praca Dos Tres Poderes, No. S/N, 7016
DIARIO OFICIAL (Official Daily)
Setor de Industrias Graficas, No. S/N, 70604
DIARIO OFICIAL DO DISTRITO FEDERAL (Official Federal District Daily)
Praca do Burito Anex, No. 1, 70075
GAZETA MERCANTIL
SCS Ed Oscar Niemeyer, No. 401/3, 70316
JORNAL DE BRASILIA (Brasilia Journal) (d) Est. 1971
SIG Lotes 585/645, 70610
Tel: (55-61) 2252515
Circ.—50,000
Prop.—Jaime Camara e Irmaos SA
Pub.—Jaime Camara
Mng. Dir.—Jorge Olavo Degraza Barbosa
U.S. Rep.—Charney/Palacios & Co. Inc.
ULTIMA HORA DE BRASILIA (Last Hour of Brasilia) (d)
1 A/Sul Quadra 3 Lotes, 1645/55, No. S/N, 71200

CACERES
(Mato Grosso)
Pop. Est. 78,825

CORREIO CACERENSE (d)
Rua General Osorio, No. 363, 78700
Circ.—2,000
Pub.—Alvisio Coelho Barros
FOLHA DO POVO
Rua Sao Jorge, No. 93, 78700

CAMPINA GRANDE
(Paraiba)
Pop. Est. 280,665

DIARIO DA BORBOREMA (Borborema Daily) (d) Est. 1957
Rua Venacio Neiva, No. 198, 58100
Circ.—7,000
Prop.—Diario da Borborema SA
Pub.—Nereu Gusmao Bastos
JORNAL DA PARAIBA (Paraiba Journal) (d) Est. 1971
Rua Major Juvino do O, No. 81, 58100
Circ.—12,000
Prop.—Editora Jornal da Paraiba SA
Pub.—José Carlos da Silva

CAMPINAS
(Sao Paulo)
Pop. Est. 845,057

CORREIO POPULAR (d) Est. 1927
Rua Cinceicao, No. 124, 13100
Tel: (55-19) 328588
Circ.—30,000
Prop.—Correio Popular SA
Pub.—Carmela de Vita Godoy
DIARIO DO POVO (Povo Daily) (d) Est. 1912
Rua Cezar Bierrenbach, No. 67, 13015
Circ.—25,000
Prop.—Empresa Jornalistica Editora Regional Ltda.
Pub.—María Beatriz C de Carvalho Moreira
DIARIO OFICIAL DO MUNICIPIO (Official Municipal Daily)
Avda. Anchieta, No. 200, 13100
INFORMATIVO CATI
Avda. Brasil, No. 2340, 13020

CAMPO GRANDE
(Mato Grosso)
Pop. Est. 386,520

CORREIO DO ESTADO (d)
Avda. Calogeras, No. 356, 79100
DIARIO OFICIAL O ESTADO MS (Official Daily of Mato Grosso State)
Parque dos Poderos, No. S/N, 79100
DIARIO DA SERRA (Serra Daily) (d) Est. 1968
Rua Engenheiro Roberto Marge, No. 849, 79100
Circ.—6,000
Prop.—Diario da Serra SA
Pub.—César Quintas Guimaraes
JORNAL DA MANHA (Manha Journal) (d) Est. 1973
Avda. Afonso Peña, No. 1408, 79100
Circ.—6,000
Pub.—Francisco Pedro Godoy
PATROPI-JORNAL DA ZONA OESTE
Rua Aurelio de Figueiredo 115, Grupo 210
Tel: (55) 3944450; Fax: (55) 3944450

CAMPOS
(Rio de Janeiro)
Pop. Est. 367,134

A CIDADE (City)
Rua dos Andradas, No. 128, 28100
FOLHA DA MANHA (d)
Rua Carlos de Lacerda, No. 75, 28100
Prop.—Plena Editora Grafica Ltda.
Pub.—Dr. Aluysio dos Santos Abreu
MONITOR CAMPISTA (dS) Est. 1834
Rua Joao Pessoa, No. 202, 28100
Circ.—5,000
Prop.—Monitor Campista SA
Pub.—Everaldo Lima
A NOTICIA (News) (d) Est. 1916
Avda. 7 de Setembro, 28100
Circ.—7,000
Pub.—Herve Salgado Rodrígues

CARAZINHO
(Rio Grande do Sul)
Pop. Est. 62,141

DIARIO DA MANHA (Manha Daily)
Avda. Flores da Cunha, No. 1504, 99500
Prop.—Jornalistica Diario da Manha

CASCAVEL
(Parana)
Pop. Est. 201,475

O PARANA (d) Est. 1976
Rua Pernambuco, No. 1592, 85800
Circ.—12,000
Prop.—Editora O Parana Ltda.
Pub.—J M Scanagatta

CATANDUVA
(Sao Paulo)
Pop. Est. 80,214

A CIDADE (City) (d) Est. 1930
Rua 13 de Maio, No. 248, 15800
Circ.—6,000
Pub.—Nair de Frietas
JORNAL OPINIAO (Opinion Journal)
Rua Mato Grosso, No. 393, 15800
O REGIONAL (Region) (d) Est. 1971
Rua Para, No. 147, 15800
Circ.—3,000
Prop.—Empresa de Publicidade Catanduva Ltda.
Pub.—José Gerson de Camargo Gabas

CAXIAS DO SUL
(Rio Grande do Sul)
Pop. Est. 267,869

O PIONEIRO (Pioneer) (d)
Rua Jacob Lucchesi, No. 2374, 90530
Circ.—19,000
Prop.—Empresa Jornalistica Pioneiro SA

CHAPECO
(Santa Catarina)
Pop. Est. 101,230

DIARIO DA MANHA (Manha Daily) (d)
Avda. Getulio Vargas, No. 3125
Circ.—4,000
Prop.—Empresa Jornalistica Diario da Manha Ltda.

CORUMBA
(Mato Grosso)
Pop. Est. 80,656

DIARIO DA MANHA (Manha Daily)
Rua Cabrah, No. 1121, 79300
JORNAL DIARIO DE CORUMBA (Daily Journal of Corumba)
Rua Antonio Joao, No. 381, 79300
JORNAL O MOMENTO (Moment Journal) (d) Est. 1944
Rua Delamare, No. 1380, 79300
Circ.—6,000
Pub.—Nelson Dias de Rosa

CRUZ ALTA
(Rio Grande do Sul)
Pop. Est. 71,853

DIARIO SERRANO (Serrano Daily) (d) Est. 1939
Avda. Pres. Vargas, No. 892, 98100
Circ.—5,000
Prop.—Empresa Jornalistica Planalto Medio Ltda.
Pub.—Riograndino Portes Abreu

CRUZEIRO
(Sao Paulo)

JORNAL DA CIDADE (City Journal)
Rua Capitao Avelino Bastos, No. 47, 12700

CUIABA
(Mato Grosso)
Pop. Est. 283,075

DIARIO DE CUIABA (Cuiaba Daily) (d) Est. 1968
Avda. XV de Novembro, No. 207, 7800
Circ.—3,500 (d); 4,500 (S)
Prop.—Imprensa Oficial
Pub.—Iris Capile de Oliveira
DIARIO DA JUSTICA DO ESTADO DE MT (Daily Justice of Mato Grosso State)
Rua 13 de Junho, No. 431, 78000
DIARIO OFICIAL DO ESTADO DE MATO GROSSO (Official Daily of Mato Grosso State) (d) Est. 1890
Rua 13 de Junho, No. 431, 78000
Circ.—120,000
Prop.—Imprensa Ribeiro
Pub.—Emanuel Ribeiro Daubian
O ESTADO DE MATO GROSSO (Mato Grosso State) (d) Est. 1939
Rua Cursino do Amarante, No. 881, 78000
Circ.—8,000
Prop.—Editora Cuiaba Ltda.
Pub.—Pedro Rocha Juca
JORNAL DO DIA (Journal of the Day)
Rua Pontes Elacerda Q 98, No. 98, 78100

CURITIBA
(Parana)
Pop. Est. 1,285,027

ANAIS DA ASSEMBLEIA
Rua Schiller, No. 1305, 80000
BOLETIM BOLSA DE VALORES DO PARANA
Rua Mar Deodora, No. 344, 80000
BOLETIM INFORMATIVO DIARIO SIMA (Informative Bulletin of Sima Daily)
Rua dos Funcionarios, No. 1559, 80000
DIARIO E ANAIS DA ASSEMBLIA
Rua Schiller, No. 1305, 80000
DIARIO OFICIAL DO ESTADO (Official State Daily)
Rua dos Funcionarios, No. 1645, 80000
DIARIO OFICIAL DA JUSTICA (Official Justice Daily)
Rua 115 de Novembro, 1190, 80000
DIARIO POPULAR (Popular Daily) (d) Est. 1963
Rua XV de Novembro, No. 1190, 80000
Tel: (55-41) 237139/(55-41) 248776
Circ.—15,000
Prop.—Editora Diario Popular Ltda.
Pub.—Abdo Aref Kudri
O ESTADO DO PARANA (Parana State) (m) Est. 1951
Rua Joao Tscharnell, No. 800, 80000
Tel: (55-41) 2338811; Fax: (55-41) 2336983
Circ.—25,000
Prop.—Editora O Estado de Parana Ltda.
Pub.—Paulo Cruz Pimentel
FOLHA DE CURITIBA
Rua Joao Negrao, No. 558, 80000
GAZETA DO POVO (Povo Gazette) (d)
PCA Carlos Gomes, No. 4, 80000
Tel: (55-41) 2240522
Circ.—45,000
Prop.—Editora Gazeta do Povo Ltda.
Pub.—Francisco da Cunha Pereira Filho
JORNAL DO ESTADO (State Journal) (d)
Rua Dr. Roberto Barroso, 22, 80520
Prop.—Editora Jornal do Estado Ltda.
Pub.—Roberto Barrozo Filho
JORNAL INDUSTRIA E COMERCIO DO PARANA (Industry and Commercial Parana Journal)
Travesa Itare, No. 52, 80000
A TRIBUNA DO PARANA (Parana Tribune) (d) Est. 1951
Rua Joao Tschannel, No. 869, 80000
Tel: (55-41) 2338811; Fax: (55-41) 2336983

DIVINOPOLIS
(Minas Gerais)

JORNAL AGORA (Agora Journal)
Avda. 1 de Junho, No. 708, 35500

DOURADOS
(Mato Grosso do Sul)
Pop. Est. 124,241

FOLHA DE DOURADOS (d) Est. 1968
Rua Honofre Pereira de Matas, No. 2176, 79800
Circ.—5,000
Prop.—Folha de Dourados Ltda.
Pub.—Theodorico Luiz Viegas
O PANORAMA
Rua Piaul, No. 1738, 79800
O PROGRESSO (Progress) (d) Est. 1951
Avda. Presidente Vargas, No. 439, 79800
Circ.—5,400
Pub.—Vlademiro Muller do Amaral

DUQUE de CAXIAS
(Rio de Janeiro)
Pop. Est. 575,533

FOLHA DA CIDADE
Rua Sorocaba, No. 1053, 25000

FEIRA DE SANTANA
(Bahia)
Pop. Est. 356,660

JORNAL FEIRA HOJE
Rua Macario Cerqueira, No. 313, 44100

FERNANDOPOLIS
(Sao Paulo)
Pop. Est. 51,735

GAZETA DA REGIAO (d) Est. 1969
Rua Rio de Janeiro, No. 417, 15600
Circ.—2,600
Prop.—Editora Freitas Ferreira Ltda.
Pub.—José de Freitas
NA HORA
Avda. Angelo Miotto, No. 121, 15600

FERRAZ DE VASCONCELOS
(Sao Paulo)

DIARIO 4 CIDADES (Four Cities Daily)
Rua Luciano Poleti, No. 87, 08500

FLORIANOPOLIS
(Santa Catarina)
Pop. Est. 218,853

DIARIO DA JUSTICA (Justice Daily)
Rua Duque do Caxias, No. 33, 88045
DIARIO OFICIAL (Official Daily)
Rua Duque do Caxias, No. 33, 88045
O ESTADO (State) (d) Est. 1915
Rodovia SC-401, Km. 3, 88030
Tel: (55) 482335555
Circ.—20,000
Prop.—Empresa Editora O Estado Ltda.
Pub.—José Matusalem Comelli
A GAZETA (Gazette) (d)
Rua Conselheiro Mafra, No. 51, 88010
Tel: (55) 482225592
Circ.—4,000
Pub.—J M Fereira

FORTALEZA
(Ceara)
Pop. Est. 1,588,709

DIARIO DO NORDESTE
Praca da Imprensa, No. S/N, 60170
Circ.—35,000
Prop.—Editora Verdes Mares Ltda.
DIARIO OFICIAL DO ESTADO CEARA
Washington Soares, No. 1300, 60810
DIARIO OFICIAL DO MUNICIPIO (Official Municipal Daily)
Avda. Francisco SA, No. 2041, 60000
JORNAL O ESTADO (State Journal) (d)
Avda. Santos Dumont, No. 1840, 60150
Circ.—18,000
Prop.—Rede Independente de Jornais do Nordeste
O POVO (e) Est. 1928
Avda. Aquanambi, No. 282; Caixa Postal D-50, 60055
Tel: (55-85) 2119666
Circ.—40,000
Prop.—Empresa Jornalistica O Povo Ltda.
Pub.—Albanisa Rocha Sarasate
TRIBUNA DO CEARA (Ceara Tribune) (d) Est. 1957
Avda. Desembargador Moreira, No. 2470, 60170
Tel: (55-85) 2473066
Circ.—12,000
Pub.—José Afonso Sancho
VD COURAGEM DE DIZER
Rua Carlos Camara, No. 1048, 60020

FRANCA
(Sao Paulo)
Pop. Est. 183,595

COMERCIO DA FRANCA (Franca Commercial) (d) Est. 1915
Rua Ouvidor Freire, No. 1986, 14400
Circ.—10,000
Prop.—Empresa Franca Editora de Jornais Revistas Ltda.
Pub.—José Correra Neves
DIARIO DA FRANCA (Franca Daily)
Rua Tiradentes, No. 1517, 14400

GOIANIA
(Goias)
Pop. Est. 928,046

DIARIO DA ASSEMBLEIA
Alameda dos Buritas, No. 231, 74110
DIARIO DA JUSTICA DO ESTADO DE GOIAS (Daily Justice of Goias State)
Avda. Pres. Costa E. Silva, No. S/N, 74510
DIARIO OFICIAL DO ESTADO DE GOIAS (Official Daily of Goias State)
Avda. Pres. Costa E. Silva, No. S/N, 74510
O POPULAR (Popular) (d) Est. 1938
Avda. Thomaz Edson-7, No. S/N, 74000
Tel: (55-62) 2415533
Circ.—23,000
Prop.—Jaime Camara e Irmaos SA
Pub.—Jaime Camara

GOVERNADOR VALADARES
(Minas Gerais)
Pop. Est. 217,434

DIARIO DO RIO DOCE (Rio Doce Daily) (d) Est. 1958
Rua Barbara Heliodoro, No. 231, 35010
Circ.—5,000
Prop.—Equsa Editora e Grafica Uniao SA
Pub.—Oswaldo Alcantara

GUAJARA-MIRIM
(Rondonia)

JORNAL O IMPARCIAL (Impartial Journal)
Avda. Costa Marques, No. S/N, 78980

GUARULHOS
(Sao Paulo)
Pop. Est. 717,723

O DIARIO DE GUARULHOS (Guarulhos Daily) (d) Est. 1961
Rua Basilio Castanho Oliveira, No. 13, 70000
Circ.—4,000
Prop.—Empresa Jornalistica Nove de Julho Ltda.
FOLHA METROPOLITANA (d) Est. 1972
Praca Tereza Cristina, No. 21, 70000
Circ.—8,000
Prop.—Empresa Jornalistica Folha Metropolitana SA
Pub.—Paschoal Thomeu

ILHEUS
(Bahia)
Pop. Est. 146,139

DIARIO DA TARDE (Afternoon Daily) (e)
Rua Marques de Paranaqua, No. 9, 45660
Prop.—Editora Diario da Manha Ltda.
Pub.—Eduardo José Nascimento Cardoso
JORNAL DA MANHA (Manha Journal) (d) Est. 1976
Rua Maria Quiteria, No. 75, 45660
Circ.—2,000
Prop.—Editora Diario da Manha Ltda.
Pub.—Diamentino Correra da Cruz

IMPERATRIZ
(Maranhao)
Pop. Est. 236,957

O JORNAL DE IMPERATIZ (Imperatiz Journal)
Rua Godofredo Viana, No. 568, 65900
O PROGRESSO (Progress) (d)
Rua Cel Manoel Bandeira, No. 1690, 65900
Circ.—2,000
Prop.—Editora O Progresso Ltda.

IPATINGA
(Minas Gerais)
Pop. Est. 214,358

DIARIO DO ACO LTDA.
Rua Ponte Nova, No. 40, 35160
Circ.—5,000
Prop.—Editora e Grafica Diario do Aco Ltda.
DIARIO DOS BAIRROS
Avda. Macapa, No. 335, 35160
DIARIO DA MANHA (Manha Daily) (d) Est. 1969
Rua Diamantia, No. 160, 35160
Circ.—3,000
Prop.—Editora Diario da Manha Ltda.
Pub.—José Rodrigues do Amaral

ITABUNA
(Bahia)
Pop. Est. 178,733

DIARIO DO CACAO (Cacao Daily)
Avda. Juracy Magachaes, No. 343, 45600
DIARIO DE ITABUNA (Itabuna Daily) (d) Est. 1957
Praca José Bastos, No. 2, 45600
Circ.—6,000
Prop.—Editora Diario de Itabuna Ltda.
Pub.—José Oduque Teixeria
TRIBUNA DO CACAU (Cacau Tribune) (d) Est. 1964
Avda. Princeza Izabel, No. S/N, 45600
Circ.—5,000
Prop.—Empresa de Divulgacao Sulbahiano SA
Pub.—Paulo Simoes Machada

ITAJAI
(Santa Catarina)
Pop. Est. 104,473

DIARIO DO LITORAL (Literal Daily) (d)
Avda. Marcos Jonder, No. 1, 88300
Circ.—2,000
Prop.—Sociedad Publiticidad Editora Catarinense

ITAPETININGA
(Sao Paulo)
Pop. Est. 105,878

FOLHA DE ITAPETININGA
Rua Campos Sales, No. 393, 18200

ITAPEVA
(Sao Paulo)
Pop. Est. 82,245

TRIBUNA SUL PAULISTA (d)
Rua Prof. Rivadavia M. Junior, No. 103, 18400
Circ.—4,000
Pub.—Jandir Abreu Gonzaga

ITATINGA
(Sao Paulo)

JORNAL DE ITATIBA (Itatiba Journal)
Rua Cel Camilo Pires, No. 372, 13250

ITUIUTABA
(Minas Gerais)
Pop. Est. 85,716

CIDADE DE ITUIUTABA (Ituiutaba Daily) (d) Est. 1965; Rua 18, No. 923, 38300
Circ.—5,000
Prop.—Jornal Cidade de Ituiutaba Ltda.
Pub.—Jargas T Gómes

JACAREI
(Sao Paulo)
Pop. Est. 149,824

DIARIO DE JACAREI (Jacarei Daily) (d)
Rua Antonio Afonso, No. 178, 12300
Circ.—3,000
Prop.—Empresa Jornalistica Diario de Jacarei

JAU
(Sao Paulo)
Pop. Est. 92,867

COMERCIO DO JAHU
Rua Marechal Bitencourt, No. 346, 17200

JOAO PESSOA
(Paraiba)
Pop. Est. 397,715

CORREIO
Avda. Dom Pedro II, No. 623, 58020
Prop.—Jornal Correio da Paraiba Ltda.
O NORTE (North) (dS) Est. 1907
Avda. Dom Pedro II, No. 889, 58000
Circ.—7,000
Pub.—Nereu Gusmao Bastos

A UNIAIO (d) Est. 1892
EST BR 101, Km. 03, District Industrial, 58070
Circ.—5,000
Prop.—Uniao Cia. Editora
Pub.—Aluysio Moura

JOINVILLE
(Santa Catarina)
Pop. Est. 304,414

EXTRA O DIARIO DA REGIAO NORTE
Rua Otto Boehm, No. 108, 89200
A NOTICIA (News) (d) Est. 1923
Rua Cacador, No. 112, 89200
Circ.—21,000
Prop.—A Noticia SA
Pub.—Empresa Jornalistica
Pub.—Romeu Bohn Mendes

JUIZ DE FORA
(Minas Gerais)
Pop. Est. 350,687

CORREIO DA MATA LTDA.
Avda. Rio Branco, No. 2067, 36013
TRIBUNA DE MINAS (Minas Tribune) (d)
Rua Halfield, No. 1179, 36015
Circ.—15,000
Prop.—Esdeva Empresa Grafica Ltda.

JUNDIAI
(Sao Paulo)
Pop. Est. 314,909

JORNAL DA CIDADE (City Journal) (d) Est. 1969
Rua Coronel Leme da Fonseca, No. 344, 13200
Circ.—13,000
Prop.—Editora Panorama Ltda.
Pub.—Gustavo Leopoldo Maryssael de Campos
JORNAL DE JUNDIAI REGIONAL (Journal of Jundial Region) (d) Est. 1965
Rua Barao de Jundiai, No. 374, 13200
Circ.—14,500
Prop.—Editora Jundiai Ltda.
Pub.—Tobias Muzaiel

LAGES
(Santa Catarina)
Pop. Est. 193,558

CORREIO LAGEANO (d)
Rua Coronel Cordova, No. 84, 88500
Circ.—5,000
Prop.—Correio Lageano Ltda.
Pub.—José P Baggio

LAJEADO
(Rio Grande do Sul)

O INFORMATIVO DO VALE (d)
Avda. Benjamin Constant, No. 2197, 95900
Circ.—6,000
Prop.—Oswaldo Carlos van Leeuwen

LIMEIRA
(Sao Paulo)
Pop. Est. 187,820

GAZETA DE LIMEIRA (Limeira Gazette) (d) Est. 1972
Rua Senador Vergueiro, No. 136, 13480
Circ.—6,000
Pub.—Sebastiao Ferraz

LINS
(Sao Paulo)
Pop. Est. 56,185

CORREIO DE LINS DIARIO DA CIDADE
Rua Vol Vitoriano Borges, No. 33, 16400
JORNAL DE LINS (Lins Journal)
Rua Vol Vitoriano Borges, No. 430, 16400

LONDRINA
(Parana)
Pop. Est. 347,707

BOLETIM NOTICIA (Bulletin News)
Campus Universitario, No. S/N, 86051
FOLHA DE LONDRINA (d) Est. 1948
Rua Piaui, No. 241, 86100
Tel: (55) 432223636
Circ.—40,000
Prop.—Empresa Jornalistica Folha de Londrina Ltda.
Pub.—Antonio Carlos Macarini

MACAPA
(Amapa)

DIARIO OFICIAL (Official Daily)
Rua Cadido Mendes, 68900

MACEIO
(Alagoas)
Pop. Est. 484,094

DIARIO OFICIAL DO ESTADO DE ALAGOAS
(Official Daily of Alagoas State)
Avda. Duraval de Goes Mostiero, No. 7, 57000
JORNAL DE ALAGOAS (Alagoas Journal) (dS)
R. Cons. Lourenco de Albuquerque, No. 115, 57000
Circ.—6,000 (d); 8,000 (S)
Pub.—Aecio Diniz Almeida
JORNAL GAZETA DE ALAGOAS (Alagoas Journal Gazette) (d) Est. 1934
Avda. Durval de Goes Monteiro, 57000
Circ.—12,000
Prop.—Jornal Gazeta de Alagoas Ltda.
Pub.—Fernando Collor de Mello
JORNAL DE HOJE (Hoje Journal) (d) Est. 1961
Rua Barao de Alagoas, No. 160, 57000
Circ.—5,000
Prop.—K P Assuncao Jornal de Hoje
Pub.—Dauntenorio de Oliveira

MANAUS
(Amazonas)
Pop. Est. 834,541

A CRITICA (Critic) (mS) Est. 1949
Rua Lobo Dalmada, No. 278, 69007
Tel: (55) 922321400
Circ.—90,000 (m); 120,000 (S)
Prop.—Empresa de Jornais Calderaro
Ed.—Carlos Martins
U.S. Rep.—Charney/Palacios & Co. Inc.
IMPRENSA OFICIAL
Rua Leonardo Malcher, No. 1189, 69000
JORNAL DIARIO DO AMAZONAS (Amazonas Daily Journal) (d) Est. 1985
Avda. Djalma Batista, No. 2010, 69000
Circ.—10,000
Prop.—Editora Ana Cassia Ltda.
Pub.—Cassiano Cirilo Anuniacato
Ed.—Pilinio Valerio
Ad. Mgr.—Cassiano Filho
JORNAL DO COMERCIO (m) Est. 1904
Avda. Santa Cruz Mackado, No. 170A, 69000
Tel: (55) 922373218
Circ.—5,000
Prop.—Empresa de Jornal do Comercio Ltda.
Pub.—Selma Bonfim Silva
Ed.—Guilherme Gadelha
A NOTICIA (News) (d) Est. 1969
Estrada do Contorno, No. S/N, 69000
Circ.—12,000
Prop.—Editora García Ltda.
Pub.—Francisco García Rodrígues
Ed.—Raimundo Nonato Cardosa

MARILIA
(Sao Paulo)
Pop. Est. 136,518

JORNAL DO COMERCIO (Commercial Journal) (d) Est. 1975
Rua 9 de Julho, No. 1440, 17500
Circ.—6,000
Pub.—Irigino Camargo
JORNAL CORREIO DE MARILIA
Rua Bahia, No. 374, 17500
JORNAL DA MANHA (Manha Journal)
Rua Castro Alves, No. 185, 17500

MARINGA
(Parana)
Pop. Est. 197,527

O DIARIO DO NORTE DO PARANA (North Parana Daily) (d) Est. 1974
Avda. Maua, No. 1988, 87050
Circ.—8,000
Prop.—Editora Central Ltda.
Pub.—Franklin Vierira da Silva
O JORNAL DE MARINGA (Maringa Journal) (d) Est. 1953
Avda. Bento Munhoz da Rocha Netto, No. 1318, 87030
Circ.—10,000
Prop.—Editora Edimar Ltda.
Pub.—Dr. Jerdellicio Barbosa

MOGI DAS CRUZES
(Sao Paulo)
Pop. Est. 234,937

DIARIO DE MOGI (Mogi Daily) (d) Est. 1957
Rua Ricardo Vilela, No. 586, 8700
Circ.—15,000
Prop.—Diario de Mogi Empresa Jornalistica SA
Pub.—Tirreno Dasambiagio

MOGI-MIRIM
(Minas Gerais)

A COMARCA
Rua Paissandu, No. 272, 13800

MONTES CLAROS
(Minas Gerais)
Pop. Est. 215,323

DIARIO DE MONTES CLAROS (Montes Claros Daily)
Rua Messias Pimenta, No. 328, 39400
O JORNAL DE MONTES CLAROS (Montes Claros Journal) (d) Est. 1951
Avda. Dulce Sarmento, No. 397, 39400
Circ.—15,000
Prop.—Grafica Jornal de Montes Claros Ltda.
Pub.—Oswaldo Alves Antunes
Ed.—Waldyr de Senna Batista
JORNAL DO NORTE (Northern Journal)
Avda. Magalhaes Pinto, No. 4317, 39400

MOSSORO
(Rio Grande do Norte)

GAZETA DO OESTE
Avda. Cunha da Mota, No. 96, 59600
O MOSSOROENSE
RO Mossroense, No. 42, 59600

NATAL
(Rio Grande do Norte)
Pop. Est. 512,241

DIARIO DE NATAL (Natal Daily) (dS) Est. 1939
Avda. Deodoro, No. 245, 59000
Circ.—11,000 (d); 14,000 (S)
Prop.—Editora O Diario SA
Pub.—Luiz María Alves
DIARIO OFICIAL DO ESTADO (Official State Daily) (d) Est. 1929
Avda. Junqueira Aires, No. 355
Tel: (55) 8423748
Circ.—1,500
Prop.—Imprensa Oficial
Pub.—Marcelo Fernandes de Oliveira
A REPUBLICA (Republic) (d) Est. 1889
Avda. Junqueira Aires, No. 355, 59000
Circ.—2,000
Prop.—Companhia Editora do Rio Grande do Norte
Pub.—Marcelo Fernandes de Oliveira
TRIBUNA DO NORTE (North Tribune) (m) Est. 1950
Travesa Nizia Floresta, No. 100, 59000
Circ.—20,000
Prop.—Empresa Jornalistica Tribuna do Norte SA
Pub.—Aluizio Alves
Ed.—Dorian Jorge Freire

NAZARE
(Bahia)

TRIBUNA DA BAHIA (Bahia Tribune)
Djalma Dutra, No. 121, 40000

NITEROI
(Rio de Janeiro)
Pop. Est. 442,706

O FLUMINENSE (m) Est. 1878
Visconde de Itoborai, No. 184, 24030
Tel: (55-21) 7193311
Circ.—62,000
Prop.—Editora Fluminese Ltda.
Pub.—Alberto Francisco Torres
A TRIBUNA (Tribune) (d) Est. 1936
Rua Barao do Amazonas, No. 31, 24030
Tel: (55-21) 7191886
Circ.—18,000
Prop.—Editora Esquena Ltda.
Pub.—Jourdan Amora

NOVA IGUACU
(Rio de Janeiro)
Pop. Est. 1,324,639

JORNAL DE HOJE (Hoje Journal) (d) Est. 1971
Rua Kennedy, No. 101, 26260
Circ.—80,000
Prop.—Grafica e Editora Jornalistica de Hoje Ltda.
Pub.—Walcir Alemeida
O PONTUAL
Rua Getulic Vargas, No. 130, 26255

NOVO HAMBURGO
(Rio Grande do Sul)
Pop. Est. 168,460

JORNAL NH (d)
Avda. Coronel Federico Linck, No. 71, 93330
Circ.—22,000
Prop.—Grupo Editorial Sinos SA
Pub.—Mario A de Paula Gusmao

OSASCO
(Sao Paulo)
Pop. Est. 594,249

A REGIAO GRAFICA E EDITORA LTDA.
Rua Pedro Fioreyyi, No. 225, 06010

OURINHOS
(Sao Paulo)
Pop. Est. 65,762

JORNAL DA DIVISA (Divisa Journal) (d) Est. 1964
Rua Euclides da Cunha, No. 80, 19900
Circ.—4,600
Prop.—Empresa Editora Jornais de Ourinhos Ltda.
Pub.—Benedito da Silva Ecoy

PARAIBA DO SUL
(Rio de Janeiro)

JORNAL DE PARAIBA DO SUL (Paraiba Do Sul Journal)
Rua Dr. Saturino Braga, No. 104, 25850

PARANAGUA
(Parana)
Pop. Est. 97,300

DIARIO DO COMERCIO (Commercial Journal) (d) Est. 1912
Rua Mar Alberto de Abreu, No. 140, 83200
Circ.—1,000
Prop.—Anastacio e Anastacio
Pub.—N Miguel Anastacio Netto
DIARIO POPULAR (Popular Daily)
Rua XV de Novembro, 1190

PARANAVAI
(Parana)

DIARIO NOROESTE (d) Est. 1955
Avda. Rio Grande do Norte, No. 1451, 87700
Circ.—5,000
Pub.—Euclides Bogoni

PASSO FUNDO
(Rio Grande do Sul)
Pop. Est. 138,226

DIARIO DA MANHA (Manha Daily) (d) Est. 1935
Avda. 7 de Septembre, No. 909, 99100
Circ.—5,500
Prop.—Empresa Jornalistica Diario da Manha Ltda.
Pub.—Dyogenes Auildo Martins Pinto
O EXPRESSO JORNAL (Express Journal)
Avda. Brasil Oeste, No. 1226, 99100
O NACIONAL (National) (e) Est. 1925
Rua Sete de Setembro, No. 481, 99100
Circ.—6,000
Pub.—Mucio de Castro

PELOTAS
(Rio Grande do Sul)
Pop. Est. 278,427

DIARIO DA MANHA (Manha Daily) (d)
Andrade Neves, No. 214, 96020
Circ.—8,000
Prop.—Empresa Jornalistica Diario da Manha Ltda.
DIARIO POPULAR (Popular Daily) (d) Est. 1890
Rua 15 de Novembro, No. 718, 96015
Tel: (55-532) 255566
Circ.—6,000
Prop.—Grafica Diario Popular Ltda.
Pub.—Ruy Faria de Queiroz
Dir.—Clayr Lobo Rochefort

PENAPOLIS
(Sao Paulo)
Pop. Est. 44,399

INTERIOR (d)
Rua Dr. Mario Sabino, No. 72, 16300
Circ.—270,723
Prop.—Penapolis Grafica e Editora Ltda.

PETROPOLIS
(Rio de Janeiro)
Pop. Est. 275,076

CORREIO PETROPOLITANO (d)
Rua General Osorio, No. 41, 25620
DIARIO DE PETROPOLIS (Petropolis Daily) (d) Est. 1954
Rua Epitacio Pessoa, No. 84, 25610
Circ.—4,000
Pub.—José Carneiro Dias

JORNAL DE PETROPOLIS (Petropolis Journal) (d)
Rua do Imperador, No. 1004, 25600
Circ.—4,000
Prop.—Editora Jornal de Petropolis Ltda.
PETROPOLIS POST
Rua do Imperador, No. 1006, 25620
TRIBUNA DE PETROPOLIS (Petropolis Tribune) (d)
Rua Alencar Lima, No. 26, 25620
Circ.—15,000
Prop.—Tribuna de Petropolis Ltda.

PINDAMONHANGABA
(Sao Paulo)

JORNAL DA DIVISA (Divisa Journal)
Rua Euclides da Cunha, No. 80, 19900

PIRACICABA
(Sao Paulo)
Pop. Est. 193,716

O DIARIO (Daily) (d) Est. 1935
Rua Sao Jose, No. 844, 13400
Circ.—8,000
Prop.—Empresa O Diario Ltda.
Pub.—Cecilio Elias Netto
DIARIO OFICIAL DO MUNICIPIO (Official Municipal Daily)
Rua Prudente de Moraes, No. 930, 13400
JORNAL DE PIRACICABA (Piracicaba Journal) (d) Est. 1900
Rua Moraes Barros, No. 825, 13400
Circ.—15,000
Prop.—Jornal de Piracicaba Ltda.
Pub.—Fortunato Losso Netto
TRIBUNA PIRACICABANA (Piracicaba Tribune) (d) Est. 1974
Rua Rangel Pestana, No. 94, 13400
Circ.—1,500
Prop.—Tribuna Piracicabana Jornal e Grafica Ltda.
Pub.—Evaldo A Vincente

POCOS DE CALDAS
(Minas Gerais)
Pop. Est. 100,414

DIARIO DE POCOS DE CALDAS (Pocos de Caldas Daily) (d) Est. 1944
Rua Santa Catarina, No. 715, 37700
Circ.—1,600
Pub.—Trajano Barroco
JORNAL CIDADE LIVRE (Livre City Journal)
Avda. Joao Pinheiro, No. 143, 37700
JORNAL DA MANTIQUEIRA (Mantiqueira Journal) (d) Est. 1974
Avda. Joao Pineheiro, No. 177, 37700
Circ.—3,000
Prop.—Empresa Jornalistica Pocos De Caldas Ltda.
Pub.—Cedio Alves de Morais

PONTA GROSSA
(Parana)
Pop. Est. 223,989

DIARIO DOS CAMPOS (Dos Campos Daily) (d)
Rua Santos Dumont, No. 747, 84100
Circ.—725,000
Prop.—Impressora Campos Gerais Ltda.
JORNAL DA MANHA (Manha Journal) (d) Est. 1954
Rua Santos Dumont, No. 1039, 84100
Circ.—8,000
Pub.—Gustavo Horst

PORTA PORA
(Mato Grosso)

JORNAL DA PRACA (Praca Journal)
Rua Rio Branco, No. 279, 79900

PORTO ALEGRE
(Rio Grande do Sul)
Pop. Est. 2,631,465

CORREIO DO POVO (dS) Est. 1895
Avda. Caldas Junior, No. 219, 90000
Tel: (55-51) 2244555
Circ.—80,000 (d); 150,000 (S)
Prop.—Empresa Jornalistica Caldas Junior Ltda.
Dir.—Breno Caldas
Ad. Mgr.—Francisco A Caldas
DIARIO DA ASSEMBLEIA (Assembleia Daily)
Praca Mal Deodoro, No. S/N, 90010
Circ.—23,000
DIARIO OFICIAL DO ESTADO DO RS (Official Daily of Rio Grande do Sul State) (d) Est. 1973
Rua Cel. Aparicip Borges, No. 2199, 90630

Circ.—5,000
Prop.—Imprensa Oficial
Pub.—Antonio Setembrino de Mesquita
JORNAL DO COMERCIO (Commercial Journal) (d) Est. 1933
Avda. Joao Pessoa, No. 1282, 90040
Circ.—30,000
Prop.—Cia. Jornalistica
Pub.—J C Jarros
Pres.—Zaida Jayme Jarros
Edit'l. Dir.—Homero Guerreiro
Ad. Dir.—Sepe Tiaraju Matzenbacher
ZERO HORA (Zero Hour) (dS) Est. 1960
Avda. Ipiranga, No. 1075, 90000
Tel: (55-51) 2234266
Circ.—727,188 (total-d); 237,282 (S)
Prop.—Zero Hora Editora Jornalistica SA
Pres.—Jayme Sirotsky
Ed. Dir.—Lauro Schirmer
Ad. Dir.—Alceu Gandini
U.S. Rep.—The N DeFilippes Corp.

PORTO VELHO
(Rondonia)
Pop. Est. 202,011

ALTO MADEIRA (d) Est. 1917
Avda. Costa E. Silva, No. S/N, 78900
Circ.—3,000
Prop.—Empresa Alto Madeira
Pub.—Epaminondas Barahuna
DIARIO OFICIAL DO ESTADO DE RONDONIA (Official Daily of Rondonia State)
Avda. Farquar, No. S/N, 78900
DIARIO OFICIAL DO MUNICIPIO DE PORTO VELHO (Official Municipal Daily of Porto Velho)
Praca Pe Joao Nicoletti, No. 826, 78900
JORNAL O ESTADO (State Journal) (d)
Avda. Duque de Caxias, No. 1523, 78900
Circ.—12,000
Pub.—Mario Calixto Filho
A TRIBUNA (Tribune)
Avda. Sete de Setembro, No. 02689, 78900

PRESIDENTE PRUDENTE
(Sao Paulo)
Pop. Est. 156,319

CORREIO DA SOROCABANA (d)
Rua Espiritu Santo, No. 20, 19100
O IMPARCIAL (Impartial) (d) Est. 1939
Rua Siqueira Campos, No. 600, 19100
Circ.—13,000
Prop.—Editora Imprensa Ltda.
Pub.—Dr. Deodato da Silva

RECIFE
(Pernambuco)
Pop. Est. 2,300,000

DIARIO DA MANHA (Manha Daily) (d) Est. 1927
Rua do Imerador Dom Pedro II, No. 227, 50000
Circ.—12,000
Prop.—Grafica Editora do Recife SA
Pub.—Benita Fernandes de Gouveia
DIARIO DE PERNAMBUCO (Pernambuco Daily) (d) Est. 1825
PCA da Independencia, No. 12, 50018
Tel: (55-81) 2316222
Circ.—36,000
Prop.—Diario de Pernambuco SA
Pub.—Antonio Camelo da Costa
DIARIO OFICIAL DO ESTADO DE PERNAMBUCO (Official Daily of Pernambuco State)
Rua Coelho Leite, No. 530, 50000
JORNAL DO COMERCIO (m) Est. 1929
Rua do Imperador, Dom. Pedro II, No. 346
Tel: (55-81) 2316222
Circ.—25,000
Prop.—Empresa Jornal do Comercio SA
Pub.—Cleber Domingos

RESENDE
(Rio de Janeiro)

O ALAMBARI
Rod Pres. Dutra, Km. 305, No. S/N, 27500
BOLETIM INTERNO DO HOSP. DE CONV. DE ITATIAIA
Praca Mariana Rocha Lead, No. 20, 27540

RIBEIRAO PRETO
(Sao Paulo)
Pop. Est. 384,604

A CIDADE (City) (d) Est. 1905
Rua Sao Sebastiao, No. 610, 14015
Circ.—12,000
Pub.—Orestes Lópes Camargo
O DIARIO (Daily) (d) Est. 1955
Rua Americo Brasiliense, No. 140, 14010
Circ.—15,000
Prop.—Editora Costabile Romano Ltda.
Pub.—Marcelino Romano Machado
DIARIO DA MANHA (Manha Daily)
Rua Duque de Caxias, No. 179, 14015
Tel: (55) 166340909
Circ.—17,000
DIARIO OFICIAL DO MUNDO DE RIBEIRAO PRETO (Official Daily of Ribeirao Preto World)
Rua Alvares Cabral, No. 629, 14010

RIO BRANCO
(Acre)
Pop. Est. 145,948

DIARIO OFICIAL DO ESTADO DO ACRE (Official Daily of Acre State)
Avda. Ceara, No. 1364, 69900
FOLHA DO ACRE
Boulevard Augusto Montiero, No. 1357, 69900
GAZETA DO ACRE (Acre Gazette)
Travesa Guapore, No. 280, 69900
O RIO BRANCO (d) Est. 1969
Rua Cel. Joao Donato, No. 1312, 69900
Circ.—2,000
Prop.—Empresa O Rio Branco Ltda.
Pub.—José Chalub Leite

RIO CLARO
(Sao Paulo)
Pop. Est. 130,309

DIARIO DO RIO CLARO LTDA. (Rio Claro Daily Ltd.) (d) Est. 1806
Avda. Dois, No. 1068, 13500
Circ.—7,500
Prop.—Diario do Rio Claro Ltda.
Pub.—Geraldo Zanello
JORNAL CIDADE DE RIO CLARO (Rio Claro City Journal) (d) Est. 1934
Avda. Quatro, No. 522, 13500
Circ.—4,500
Pub.—José Marcos Pires de Oliveira
JORNAL DE RIO CLARO (Rio Claro Journal)
Rua 3, No. 802, 13500

RIO DE JANEIRO
Pop. Est. 5,615,149

BOLETIM INFORMATIVO DIARIO (Informative Bulletin Daily)
Avda. General Justo, No. 307, 20022
DIARIO COMERCIAL (Commercial Daily)
Sacadura Cabral, No. 229, 20221
DIARIO DAS CONCORRENCIAS
Rua Leandro Martins, No. 20, 20080
DIARIO ECONOMICO FINANCEIRO (Economic Financial Daily)
Laderia do Russel, No. 57
GAZETA MERCANTIL (m-5x wk.) Est. 1920
Circ.—82,312
(There is an edition of Gazeta Mercantil in Sao Paulo.)
GAZETA DE NOTICIAS (News Gazette)
Rua Leandro Martins, No. 72, 20080
O GLOBO (Globe) (mS) Est. 1925
Rua Irineu Marinho, 35; Caixa Postal 1090, 20233-900
Tel: (55-21) 2722000; Fax: (55-21) 2227882
Circ.—266,546 (d); 518,147 (S)
Pub.—Roberto Marinho
Ed.—Evandro Carlos de Andrade
Ad. Mgr.—Luiz Eduardo Vasconcelos
U.S. Rep.—The N DeFilippes Corp.
INFORME DINAMICO (Dynamic Information)
Rua Sete de Setembro, No. 92, 20050
JORNAL DO BRASIL (Brasil Journal) (mS) Est. 1891
Avda. Brasil, No. 500, 20949
Tel: (55-21) 5854422; Fax: (55-21) 5854428
Circ.—140,826 (m); 212,744 (S)
Ed.—Marcos Sa Correa
Ad. Mgr.—Sergio do Rego Moneiro
JORNAL DO COMERCIO (Commercial Journal) (d) Est. 1827
Rua do Livramento, No. 189, 20011
Tel: (55-21) 2536675
Circ.—31,000
Pub.—Joao Medeiros Calmon
JORNAL O DIA (Day Journal) (mS) Est. 1951
Rua Riachuelo, No. 359
Circ.—180,000
Prop.—Editora e Impressora de Jornais e Revistas SA
Pub.—Paschoal Marchetti
JORNAL DOS SPORTS (Sports Journal) (m) Est. 1931
Rua Tenente Possolo, No. 15/25, 20230
Tel: (55-21) 2328010
Circ.—70,000
Prop.—Jornal do Sports SA
Pub.—Fernando Horacio
JORNAL ULTIMA HORA (Last Hour Journal) (m)
Rua Riachuelo, No. 359
LATIN AMERICAN DAILY POST (mS) English; Est. 1979
Rua do Resende, 65
Circ.—28,600
Prop.—Sao Marcelo de Publicacoes Ltda.
Pub.—Giberto Huber
Ed.—Mauro Salles
SIMA BOLETIM INFORMATIVO DIARIO
Avda. Brasil, No. 19001
TRIBUNA DA IMPRENSA (Press Tribune) (e) Est. 1949
Rua do Lavradio, No. 98, 20230
Tel: (55-21) 2526040
Circ.—12,000
Prop.—Editora Tribuna do Imprensa SA
Pub.—Nice Lourdes García Brant

RIO GRANDE
(Rio Grande do Sul)
Pop. Est. 164,636

JORNAL AGORA (Agora Journal) (d)
Rua Aquidabam, No. 695, 96200
Circ.—2,500
Prop.—Organizacoes Risul
Pub.—Germano Torales Leite
JORNAL RIO GRANDE (Rio Grande Journal) (m)
Rua General Bacellar, No. 210, 96200

SALVADOR
(Bahia)
Pop. Est. 1,811,367

CORREIO DA BAHIA (d)
Avda. Luiz Viana Filho, No. S/N, 40000
Prop.—Empresa Saiana de Jornalistica
Pub.—Armando Goncalves
DIARIO OFICIAL DO ESTADO DA BAHIA (Official Daily of Bahia State)
Rua Melo Morais Filho, No. 189, 40000
INFORME DO EMPRESARIO
Rua Portugal, No. 11, 40000
JORNAL A TARDE (Afternoon Journal) (mS) Est. 1912
Avda. Prof. Magalhaes Neto, No. S/N, 40000
Circ.—75,000 (m); 123,000 (S)
Prop.—Empresa Editora A Tarde SA
Pub.—Regina Helena Simoes de Mello Lettao
Ed.—Jorge Calmon
Ad. Dir.—Bentto Rocha
JORNAL DA BAHIA (Bahia Journal) (mS) Est. 1958
Rua Djalma Dutra, No. 121, 40000
Circ.—39,000
Pub.—Joao da Costa Falcao
Ed. in Ch.—Sergio Toniello
A TARDE (Afternoon)
Avda. Magalhaes Neto S/N
Tel: (55-71) 2310077; Fax: (55-71) 2311064
Pres.—Renato Simoes

SANTA BARBARA D'OESTE
(Sao Paulo)

EDICAO BARBARENSE
Rua General Osorio, No. 35, 13450

SANTA MARIA
(Rio Grande do Sul)
Pop. Est. 197,177

JORNAL A RAZAO (Razao Journal) (d) Est. 1934
Rua Serafim Valandro, No. 1284, 97100
Circ.—3,000
Pub.—Estado Duarte Santiago Ramos

SANTANA DO LIVRAMENTO
(Rio Grande do Sul)
Pop. Est. 70,322

FOLHA POPULAR (d) Est. 1937
Vasco Alves, No. 423, 97570
Prop.—Editora Folha Popular SA
Pub.—José Getulio M Pereira
JORNAL A PLATEIA (d)
Rua 13 de Maio, No. 715, 97570

SANTO ANDRE
(Sao Paulo)
Pop. Est. 3,000,000

DIARIO DO GRANDE ABC (ABC Big Daily) (dS) Est. 1958
Rua Catequese, No. 562, SP, CEP, 09090
Circ.—46,000 (d); 79,000 (S)
Prop.—Diario do Grande ABC SA
Pub.—Edson Danillo Dotto

SANTOS
(Sao Paulo)
Pop. Est. 461,096

BOLETIM INFORMATIVO (Informative Bulletin)
Rua XV de Novembro, No. 111, 11010
CIDADE DE SANTOS (Santos City) (d) Est. 1967
Rua do Comercio, No. 32, 11100
Circ.—40,000
Prop.—Empresa Folha da Manha Ltda.
Pub.—Octavio Frias de Oliveira
DIARIO OFICIAL DO MUNICIPIO (Official Municipal Daily)
Rua Assis Correa, No. 20, 11055
A TRIBUNA (Tribune) (mS) Est. 1894
Rua General Camara, No. 90, 11100
Circ.—40,000
Prop.—A Tribuna de Santos Jornal e Editora
Pub.—Giusfredo Santin

SAO CARLOS
(Sao Paulo)
Pop. Est. 140,860

O DIARIO (Daily) (d) Est. 1969
Rua Dona Alexandria, No. 1090, 13560
Circ.—3,000
Prop.—Empresa Jornalistica Decisao Ltda.
Pub.—J Sigueira
Pub.—P E D Duarte
Pub.—Rubens Betting
A FOLHA (d) Est. 1962
Avda. Dr. José Pereira Lópes, No. 188, 13560
Circ.—7,000
Prop.—Empresa O Imperial Ltda.
Pub.—Paulo de Arruda Correra da Silva
A TRIBUNA (Tribune) (d) Est. 1972
Rua Conde do Pinhal, No. 2443, 13560
Circ.—6,000
Pub.—Celso Luíz Guimeres Keppe

SAO GONCALO
(Rio de Janeiro)
Pop. Est. 731,061

O SAO GONCALO (d) Est. 1931
Rua Feliciano Sodre, No. 223, 24400
Circ.—5,000
Pub.—Irene de Mattos Monteiro

SAO JOAO DEL REI
(Minas Gerais)

JORNAL DO POSTE
Avda. General Ozorio, No. 477, 36300
JORNAL DO POVAO
Rua do Carmo, No. 11, 36300

SAO JOSÉ DO RIO PRETO
(Sao Paulo)
Pop. Est. 230,151

DIARIO DA REGIAO (d) Est. 1950
Rua Delegado Pinto de Toledo, No. 2844, 15100
Circ.—12,000
Pub.—Norberto Bizzini
FOLHA DE RIO PRETO (d) Est. 1966
Rua Coronel Spindola Castro, No. 3562, 15100
Circ.—6,000
Pub.—José Barbar Cury
A NOTICIA (News) (d) Est. 1924
Rua General Glicerio, No. 2023, 15100
Circ.—8,000
Pub.—Fausto Gómes

SAO JOSÉ DOS CAMPOS
(Sao Paulo)
Pop. Est. 374,526

AGORA (d) Est. 1969
Rua Sao Paulo, No. 217, 12215
Circ.—9,600
Prop.—JAC Editora Ltda.
Pub.—José Cristovao Ribeiro Cursino
JORNAL O VALEPARAIBANO LTDA.
Estrada Velha Rio Sao Paulo, No. 3755, 12200
O VALEPARAIBANO (dS) Est. 1971
Estrada Velha Rio Sao Paulo, 3755
Circ.—50,000
Pub.—Ferdinando Salerno

SAO JOSÉ DOS PINHAIS
(Parana)

FOLHA DE SAO JOSÉ
Rua Mota Junior, No. 1342, 83100

SAO LEOPOLDO
(Rio Grande do Sul)

JORNAL VALE DOS SINOS
Avda. Joac Correa, No. 1017, 93000

SAO LUIS
(Maranhao)
Pop. Est. 564,434

O DEBATE (Debate)
Rua Da Manga, No. 250, 65000
DIARIO OFICIAL (Official Daily)
Rua Sao Joao, No. 505, 65000
O ESTADO DE MARANHAO (Maranhao State) (d)
Avda. Ana Jansen, 65000
Circ.—5,000
Prop.—Grafica Escolar SA
Ed.—Antonio Carlos Lima
Ad. Mgr.—Evilson Almeida
O IMPARCIAL (Impartial) (d) Est. 1926
Rua Afonso Peña, No. 46, 65000
Circ.—5,000
Prop.—Empresa Pacotilha Ltda.
JORNAL DE HOJE (Hoje Journal) (d)
Rua dos Crioulas, No. 480, 65000
Circ.—12,000
Prop.—Grupo Editorial Cordeiro Filho Ltda.
JORNAL PEQUEÑO (Small Journal) (d)
Rua Formosa, No. 171, 65000
Circ.—6,000
Pub.—J M Ferreira

SAO PAULO
(Sao Paulo)
Pop. Est. 12,600,000

BOLETIM DIARIO DE INFORMACOES (Daily Bulletin Informations)
Rua Alvares Penteado, No. 151, 01012
BOLETIM DIARIO DE PRECOS
Avda. Miguel Esfano, No. 3900, 04301
BOLETIM GERAL
Avda. Cruzeiro do Sul, No. 260, 03033
BOLETIM INFORMATIVO DIARIO (Informative Bulletin Daily)
Avda. Dr. Gastao Vidigal, No. 1946, 05316
BOLETIM SERVICO REGIONAL IAPAS S. PAULO
Viaduto Sta. Ifigenia, No. 266
BRASILTURIS JORNAL
Avda. Pacaembu 1400
Tel: (55-11) 8856811
BRAZIL-POST (d) German; Est. 1950
Avda. Sen. Casemiro da Rocha, 701; Caixa Postal 6401, 01064-970
Tel: (59-12) 5792917; Fax: (59-12) 5811442
Prop.—Editora Braizil-Post
Pub.—Ursula Dormien
Ad. Mgr.—K D Dormien
O DIA DE SAO PAULO (Sao Paulo Daily)
Rua Verguero, No. 218, 01404
DIARIO DO COMERCIO (Commercial Daily) (m) Est. 1924
Rua Boa Vista, No. 51, 10140
Circ.—25,000
Prop.—Associacao Comercial de Sao Paulo
Pub.—Guilherme Afif Domingos
Ed.—Angelo Darubbi Neto
DIARIO COMERCIO & INDUSTRIA (Commercial & Industry Daily) (d) Est. 1933
Rua Alvaro de Carvalho, No. 354, 01050-070
Tel: (55-11) 2565011; Fax: (55-11) 2581919
Circ.—58,000
Prop.—DCI-Editora Jornalistica SA
Pub.—Walter Nori
Ed.—José Paulo Kupfer
Ad. Dir.—Eduardo Aidar Netto
DIARIO NIPPAK (Nippak Daily)
Rua da Glorio, No. 332, 01510
DIARIO OFICIAL EXECUTIVO (Official Executive Daily)
Rua da Mooca, No. 1921, 03103
DIARIO OFICIAL INEDITORIAL
Rua da Mooca, No. 1921, 03103
DIARIO OFICIAL JUSTICA (Official Justice Daily)
Rua da Mooca, No. 1921, 03103
DIARIO POPULAR (Popular Daily) (e) Est. 1884
Rua Mayor Quendinho, No. 28, 03103
Tel: (55-11) 2582133; Fax: (55-11) 2581683
Circ.—160,000
Prop.—Empresa Jornalistica Diario Popular SA
Pub.—Rodrigo Soares Jr
EMPRESA JORNALISTICA DIARIO POPULAR LTDA.
Rua Major Quedinho, No. 28
Tel: (55-11) 7131973
O ESTADO DE SAO PAULO (Sao Paulo State) (mS) Est. 1875
41 Avda. Engenheiro Caetano Alvares, 55, 2OM, 02598
Tel: (55-11) 8562122; Fax: (55-11) 2658022
Circ.—1,230,160 (m-total); 410,615 (S)
Prop.—O Estado de Sao Paulo SA
Pub.—José Vieira de Carvalho Mesquita
U.S. Rep.—The N DeFilippes Corp.
FOLHA BANCARIA
Rua Sao Bento, No. 365, 01011
FOLHA DE MANHA (d-ex mon.)
Al. Barao de Limeira 425, 01202
Tel: (55-11) 2200011
Circ.—50,000 (tues.-sat.); 60,000 (S)
Prop.—Cía. Paulista Editora de Jornais
Gen. Mgr.—Renato Castanhari
U.S. Rep.—Charney/Palacios & Co. Inc.
FOLHA DE SAO PAULO (mS) Est. 1921
Al. Barao de Limeira, No. 425, 01290
Tel: (55-11) 2243129; Fax: (55-11) 2243712
Circ.—286,000 (m); 466,000 (S)
Ed. in Ch.—Otávio Frias Filho
FOLHA DA TARDE (e) Est. 1949
Al. Barao de Limeira, No. 425, 01290
Circ.—90,000
Prop.—Empresa Folha de Manha SA
Ed. in Ch.—Antonio Aggio Jr
GAZETA MERCANTIL (m) Est. 1920
Rua Major Quedinho, No. 90, 01050
Tel: (55-11) 2583137; Fax: (55-11) 2586334
Circ.—104,000
Prop.—Gazeta Mercantil SA
Pub.—Luís Fernando Ferreira Levy
Gen. Dir.—Dirceu Brisola
Ed.—Matias Molina
Ad. Mgr.—Maria Humberg
U.S. Rep.—AdMarket Int'l.; Charney/Palacios & Co. Inc.; Dow Jones Int'l. Marketing Services; The N DeFilippes Corp.
O IMPARCIAL-CONSORCIO
Rua Senador Feijo-6o. andar
JORNAL DA MANHA (Manha Journal) (d) Est. 1975
Avda. Ipiranga, No. 1251, 1039
Circ.—40,000
Pub.—Severino Souta Maior
JORNAL PAULISTA (Paulista Journal) (d)
Avda. Ipiranga 1251-9, 01039
Prop.—Jornal Paulista Ltda.
JORNAL DA TARDE (Afternoon Journal) (e-ex S) Est. 1966
41 Avda. Eugenheiro Caetano Alvares, No. 55, 20M; Caixa Postal 8005, 8005
Tel: (55-11) 8587788; Fax: (55-11) 2656203
Circ.—709,793 (total)
Prop.—O Estado de Sao Paulo SA
Pub.—Julio de Mesquita Netto
U.S. Rep.—The N DeFilippes Corp.
LATIN AMERICA DAILY POST (d)
Alameda Barao de Limeira, No. 458, 01202
NOTICIAS POPULARES (Popular News) (m) Est. 1963
Al. Barao de Limeira, No. 425, 01290
Tel: (55-11) 8742222
Circ.—140,000
Prop.—Noticias Populares SA
Ed. in Ch.—Ebrahim Ramadan
OBSERVADO DE MERCADOS ED DIARIA
Avda. Senador Queiroz, No. 611, 01206
POPULAR DA TARDE (Popular Afternoon) (e) Est. 1968
Rua Major Quedinho, No. 28, 01050
Circ.—110,000
Pub.—Rodrigo Soares Jr
SAO PAULO SHIMBUN (d) Japanese
Rua Tomas de Lima, No. 573, 01513
SINDILUTA
Rua Tamandare, No. 348, 01525
VISAO/REVISTA
Rua Alfonso Celso 143
Tel: (55-11) 2394533

SOROCABA
(Sao Paulo)
Pop. Est. 328,787

CRUZEIRO DO SUL (d) Est. 1903
Avda. Eng. Carlos Reinaldo Mendes, No. 2800, 18100
Circ.—20,000
Pub.—F S de Oliveira Camargo
DIARIO SOROCABA (Sorocaba Daily) (d) Est. 1958
Rua da Penha, No. 609, 18010
Circ.—17,000
Prop.—Jornal e Editora Ltda.
Pub.—Fernando de Lucas Neto

SUMARE
(Sao Paulo)

COMUNICACAO JORNAL
Avda. Reboucas, No. 2350, 13170
EMPRESA JORNALISTICA JORNAL SUMARE SC LT
Rua Barbara Blumer, No. 123, 13170

TAQUARITINGA
(Sao Paulo)
Pop. Est. 45,082

CIDADE DE TAQUARITINGA (d) Est. 1930
Rua Marechal Deodoro, No. 1131, 15900
Circ.—4,000
Pub.—Joao Atello

TAUBATE
(Sao Paulo)
Pop. Est. 205,941

DIARIO DE TAUBATE (Taubate Daily)
Rua Dr. Souza, No. 844, 12020
A VOZ DO VALE DO PARIABO (d)
Rua Dr. Emilio Winther, No. 79, 12030
Circ.—5,000
Pub.—Waldemar Duarte

TERESINA
(Piaui)
Pop. Est. 476,102

DIARIO OFICIAL DO PIAUI (Official Piaui Daily)
Praca Marechal Deodoro, No. 774, 64000
JORNAL CORREIO DO PIAUI
Rua 19 de Novembro, No. 126, 64000
JORNAL O DIA (Day Journal) (d) Est. 1951
Rua Governador Arturo de Vasconcelos, No. 131, 64000
Circ.—10,000
Pub.—Otávio Miranda
JORNAL O ESTADO (State Journal)
Avda. Centenario, No. 1200, 64000
JORNAL DA MANHA (Manha Journal) (m)
Rua Lisandro Nogueira, No. 870, 64000
Circ.—3,000
Prop.—Editora Grafica Rijora Ltda.
Pub.—José Ribomar Oliveira
JORNAL DO PIAUI (Piaui Daily)
Rua 24 de Janeiro, No. 505, 64000

TERESOPOLIS
(Rio de Janeiro)

GAZETA DE TERESOPOLIS (Teresopolis Gazette)
Rua Darcy Menezes de Aragao, No. 51, 25950

TOLEDO
(Parana)

JORNAL DO OESTE (Oeste Journal)
Avda. Parigot de Souza, No. 1710, 859500

TRES RIOS
(Rio de Janeiro)

O DIARIO (Daily)
Rua Dr. Oswaldo Cruz, No. 172, 25800
ENTRE RIOS JORNAL (Entre Rios Journal)
Rua 15 de Novembro, No. 173, 25800

TUPA
(Sao Paulo)
Pop. Est. 62,293

FOLHA DO POVO (m) Est. 1967
Rua Caetes, No. 587, 17600
Circ.—4,000
Pub.—Sylvio Antonio Brigantini
JORNAL DA REGIAO
Avda. Tamoios, No. 1299, 17600
JORNAL SUPERIOR (Superior Journal)
Rua Caingangs, No. 432, 17600

UBERABA
(Minas Gerais)
Pop. Est. 245,921

JORNAL DA MANHA (Manha Journal) (d) Est. 1972
Avda. Dr. Fidelis Reis, No. 820, 38100
Circ.—5,000
Pub.—Joaquim dos Santos Martíns
LAVOURA E COMERCIO
Rua Vigario Silva, No. 9, 38100

UBERLANDIA
(Minas Gerais)
Pop. Est. 313,651

CORREIO DE UBERLANDIA Est. 1937
PCA Clarimundo Carneiro, No. 149, 38400
Circ.—3,000
Pub.—Agenor Alves García
PRIMEIRA HORA (First Hour)
Avda. Vitalino Rezende Carmo, No. 77, 38400
O TRIANGULO Est. 1928
Rua Vigario Dantas, No. 325, 38400
Circ.—6,000
Pub.—Alberto Herculano Rodrígues Naves

UMUARAMA
(Parana)

A TRIBUNA DO POVO (Povo Tribune)
Avda. Pres. Castelo Branco, No. 3715, 87500
UMUARAMA ILUSTRADO (Umuarama Illustrated)
Rua Antonio Ostrenski, No. 3954, 87500

VARGINHA
(Minas Gerais)
Pop. Est. 74,936

CORREIO DO SUL (d) Est. 1945
Avda. Francisco Navarra, No. 300, 37100
Circ.—10,000
Pub.—Mariano Tarcisco Campos
Ed.—Antonio Carlos Medes Campos
GAZETA DE VARGINHA (Varginha Gazette)
Praca Mateus Tavares, No. 156, 37100

VITORIA
(Espirito Santo)
Pop. Est. 254,448

DEPARTAMENTO DE IMPRENSA OFICIAL
Avda. Mal Mascarenhas de Morais, No. 2375, 29000
A GAZETA (Gazette) (d) Est. 1928
Rua Chafic Murad, No. 902, 29000
Tel: (55-27) 2228338
Prop.—A Gazeta SA
Pub.—Carlos Lindenberg Filho
JORNAL DE CIDADE (City Journal) (d) Est. 1968
Avda. Cezar Hilal 905, Ed. Caribe
Tel: (55-27) 2259155/(55-27) 2253826
Circ.—10,000
Pub.—Djalma Juárez Magalhaes

VITORIA DA CONQUISTA
(Bahia)
Pop. Est. 148,966

TRIBUNA DO CAFE (Cafe Tribune) (d) Est. 1974
Ernesto Dantas, No. 170, 45100
Circ.—5,000
Pub.—Isnard Vasconcelos

VOTUPORANGA
(Sao Paulo)

A CIDADE (City)
Rua Ponta Pora, No. 818, 15500
DIARIO DE VOTUPORANGA (Votuporanga Daily)
Praco dos Expedicionarios, No. 44, 15500

CHILE
Pop. Est. 13,950,557

ANGOL
Pop. Est. 22,957

RENACER DE CHILE (Chile Reborn) (d)
Avda. Prat, No. 442; PO Box 7
Tel: (56-45) 711105; Fax: (56-45) 711105
Pub.—Napoleon Rubilar Pérez

ANTOFAGASTA
Pop. Est. 219,291

LA ESTRELLA DEL NORTE (The North Star) (e) Est. 1966
Calle Manuel Antonio Matta, No. 2112, 222847
Tel: (56-55) 222847/(56-55) 264835; Fax: (56-55) 257710
Circ.—10,000
Prop.—Sociedad Chilena de Publicaciones y Comercio SA
Pub.—Roberto Retamal Pacheco
Ad. Mgr.—Jaime Mayol
EL MERCURIO (The Mercury) (d) Est. 1906
Calle Manuel Antonio Matta, No. 2112; PO Box F, 222847
Tel: (56-55) 223406/(56-55) 264787
Circ.—20,000
Prop.—Sociedad Chilena de Publicaciones y Comercio SA
Ad. Mgr.—Rodolfo Garces Guzman
Ad. Mgr.—Jaime Mayol

ARAUCO

CELARAUCO (m)
Pedro de Valdivia, No. 80
Dir.—Adalia Valencia Fuentealba

ARICA
Pop. Est. 66,224

ARICA EN MARCHA (Arica in Marching) (m)
Avda. 7 de Junio, No. 188
Dir.—Nelson Torres Otarola
LA DEFENSA (The Defense) (d)
Avda. 18 de Septiembre, No. 470
Dir.—Juan Carlos Poli Iglesias

Chile — South America

LA ESTRELLA DE ARICA (The Arica Star) (m)
Est. 1976
San Marcos, No. 580; PO Box 606
Tel: (56-58) 225024; Fax: (56-58) 252890
Circ.—12,000
Prop.—Empresa Periodística El Norte SA
Pub.—Darío Canut Debon Urrutia
Ad. Mgr.—Héctor Orrego

BULNES

LA OPINION (The Opinion) (m)
Federico Errazuriz, No. 92
Dir.—Juan Luís Ramírez A

CALAMA

LA ESTRELLA DEL LOA (The Loa Star) (mS)
Abaroa, No. 1929
Tel: (56-55) 212535/(56-55) 342535;
Fax: (56-55) 342078
Circ.—4,000 (m); 7,000 (S)
Dir.—Reinaldo Neira
EL MERCURIO DE CALAMA (The Calama Mercury) (d)
Abaroa, No. 1929
Tel: (56-55) 341604; Fax: (56-55) 341604
Dir.—Roberto Retamal Pacheco

CAUQUENES

EL INDEPENDIENTE (The Independent) (m)
Antonio Varas, No. 150
Dir.—Luís Bascur

CHILLAN
Pop. Est. 83,117

LA COMUNA (The Commune) (d)
Municipalidad de Chillan
Dir.—Carlos Bastias Fuentes
LA DISCUSION DE CHILLAN (The Discussion of Chillan) (d) Est. 1870
18 de Septiembre, No. 721; PO Box 479
Tel: (56-42) 222651/(56-42) 212650;
Fax: (56-42) 213578
Circ.—8,500
Prop.—Universidad de Concepción
Dir.—Tito Castillo Peralta

CONCEPCION
Pop. Est. 307,626

CRONICA (Chronicle) (e)
Calle Freire, No. 799; Casilla 8-C
EL SUR (The South) (mS) Est. 1882
Calle Freire, No. 799; Casilla 8-C
Tel: (56-41) 235825; Fax: (56-41) 235825
Circ.—50,000 (m); 80,000 (S)
Prop.—Diario El Sur SA
Gen. Mgr.—Aurelio Maira
U.S. Rep.—AdMarket Int'l.

CONSTITUCION

EL MAULE (d)
Freire, No. 792
Dir.—Orlando Ilufi Coloma
NUEVA BILBAO DEL MAULE (m)
Zanartu S/No.

COPIAPO
Pop. Est. 40,378

ATACAMA (d)
Manuel Rodríguez, No. 740
Tel: (56) 2255
Circ.—6,500
Dir.—Samuel Salgado Godoy
PANORAMA UDA (m)
Avda. Kennedy, No. 485
Dir.—Juan Iglesias Díaz
VISION DE ATACAMA (Atacama Vision) (m)
Edificio Alboreda, Los Carrera S/No., 1er. Piso
Dir.—Felipe Berstein Jiménez

COYHAIQUE

EL DIARIO DE AYSEN (Aysen Daily) (m)
21 de Mayo, No. 410
Tel: (56-67) 232318; Fax: (56-67) 232318
Dir.—Aldo Marchesse

CURICO
Pop. Est. 42,290

CURICO AVANZA (m)
Carmen S/No.
Dir.—Sergio Correa de la Cerda
LA PRENSA (The Press) (d) Est. 1898
Merced 373; Casilla 6-D
Tel: (56-75) 310132/(56-75) 310453;
Fax: (56-75) 311924
Circ.—4,000
Prop.—Empresa Periodística Curico Ltda.
Dir.—Manuel Massa Mautino

EL SALVADOR

ANDINO (m)
Avda. El Tofo, No. 531
Dir.—Pedro Serazzi Ahumada

GRANEROS

EL ESFUERZO (The Struggle) (m)
Riquelme, No. 559, Corvi Norte
Dir.—Sergio Faundez Faundez Gaete

ILLAPEL

LA OPINION DEL NORTE (The Opinion of the North) (m)
Avda. Ignacio Silva, No. 124; Casilla 365
Dir.—Katarina Fauda Vega
LA VOZ DE CHOAPA (The Choapa Voice) (d)
Constitición, No. 371
Dir.—Humberto Villarroel

IQUIQUE
Pop. Est. 65,953

LA ESTRELLA DE IQUIQUE (The Iquique Star) (e) Est. 1966
Luis Uribe, No. 452; Casilla 58-A
Tel: (56-57) 411379; Fax: (56-57) 427975
Circ.—10,000
Prop.—Empresa Periodística El Norte SA
Dir.—Arcadio Castillo Ortiz
Ad. Mgr.—Héctor Orrego
EL PAMPINO (m)
Baquedano, No. 898
Dir.—Héctor Rojas Cabrera
EL TARAPACA (d)
Casilla, No. 557

LA LIGUA

LA RAZON (The Reason) (m)
Uno Poniente, No. 17
Dir.—Carmen Pinonez Tapia

LA SERENA
Pop. Est. 99,908

EL DIA (The Day) (d)
Brasil, No. 431; Casilla 556
Tel: (56-51) 222844; Fax: (56-51) 222844
Circ.—11,000
Dir.—Antonio Puga Rodríguez

LINARES
Pop. Est. 34,166

EL HERALDO (The Herald) (d)
Independencia, No. 109
Tel: (56-73) 210069
Dir.—Enrique Gutiérrez Muñoz
MI PROVINCIA (My Province) (m)
Gobernación Provincial
Dir.—Sergio Hernández Carrasco

LOS ANDES
Pop. Est. 24,909

EL ANDINO (d)
Santa Rosa, No. 442
Dir.—Luís Rios Muñoz

LOS ANGELES
Pop. Est. 44,955

LA TRIBUNA (The Tribune) (d)
Calle Colo-Colo, No. 464; Casilla 15-D
Tel: (56) 313315; Fax: (56) 311040
Circ.—10,000
Dir.—Cirilo Guzman de la Fuente

MOLINA
Pop. Est. 10,000

EL LONTUE (m)
Quecherreguas, No. 1644
Dir.—Mercedes Reyes G
LA RAZON (The Reason) (d)
Quecherreguas, No. 1631
Dir.—Augusto Trivino Trivino Díaz

OSORNO
Pop. Est. 190,857

EL DIARIO AUSTRAL (m) Est. 1982
Bernardo O'Higgins, No. 870
Tel: (56-64) 235191/(56-64) 235192;
Fax: (56-64) 234163
Circ.—6,500
Prop.—Sociedad Periodísta Araucania SA
Dir.—Carlos Nollia
Ed.—German Carmona

DIARIO 24 HORAS (24 Hours Daily) (d)
Ramírez, No. 951
Tel: (56) 2300

OVALLE
Pop. Est. 31,591

LA PROVINCIA (The Province) (d) Est. 1936
Libertad, No. 435
Circ.—5,000
Prop.—Sociedad Periodísta La Provincia
Dir.—Mario Banic Illanes

PARRAL
Pop. Est. 14,610

LA PRENSA (The Press) (d)
Anibal Pinto, No. 615
Dir.—Alfonso Candia Barras

PEUMO
Pop. Est. 5,000

EL PROGRESO DE CACHAPOAL (The Progress of Cachapoal) (d)
Carlos Walker Martínez, No. 464
Dir.—Gustavo Fuentes Miranda

PICHILEMU

EL PICHILEMO (m)
Casilla, No. 37
Dir.—Washington Saldias

PUERTO MONTT
Pop. Est. 119,059

AUSTRAL (d)
San Felipe, No. 129
Prop.—Sociedad Periodísta Araucania
Dir.—Edmundo Espinoza Aparico
EL LLANQUIHUE (d) Est. 1936
Antonio Varas, No. 167
Tel: (56) 2578
Circ.—6,000
Prop.—Sociedad Periodísta del Sur
Dir.—Miguel Veyl Betanzo
Ad. Mgr.—Luís Brand

PUERTO VARAS

EL HERALDO AUSTRAL (d)
Del Salvador, No. 560
Prop.—Sociedad Periodísta Araucania
Dir.—Rosendo Alvarez Araneda

PUNTA ARENAS
Pop. Est. 110,000

EL MAGALLANES (e) Est. 1894
Waldo Seguel, No. 636; Casilla 9-D
Tel: (56) 221976
Circ.—6,000
Prop.—Empresa Publicidad de La Prensa Austral Ltda.
Dir.—Pablo Cruz Nocetti
Ad. Mgr.—Estanislao Karelovic
LA PRENSA AUSTRAL (m) Est. 1941
Waldo Seguel, No. 636; Casilla 9-D
Tel: (56) 221976
Circ.—10,000
Prop.—Empresa Publicidad de La Prensa Austral Ltda.
Dir.—Pablo Cruz Nocetti
Ad. Mgr.—Estanislao Karelovic

QUILLOTA
Pop. Est. 39,086

EL OBSERVADOR (The Observer) (d)
Empresa Periodística, La Concepción, No. 277; Casilla 1-D
Tel: (56-33) 312096/(56-33) 311417;
Fax: (56-33) 311417
Dir.—Roberta Silva Bijit

RANCAGUA
Pop. Est. 180,000

EL HERALDO (The Herald) (d) Est. 1968
Avda. Los Proceres
Dir.—Francisco Morales
EL RANCAGUINO (d)
O'Carroll, No. 518; Casilla 50
Tel: (56-72) 230358; Fax: (56-72) 221483
Circ.—10,000
Dir.—Héctor González Valenzuela
EL TENIENTE (d)
Millan, No. 240
Dir.—José Aranguiz Fuenzalida

RENGO
Pop. Est. 15,000

EL RENGUINO (d)
Pasaje Fresia No. 145, Pob. 2
Dir.—Hugo Peña
Dir.—Lillo Valenzuela

SAN ANTONIO

OASIS (m)
Pedro Montt, No. 40
Dir.—Franco Belmonte
PROA REGIONAL (d)
Barros Luco, No. 1697
Dir.—Edmund Guerra Galaz

SAN CARLOS

EL COMERCIO (m)
Serrano, No. 424
Dir.—Mirthala Navarro R

SAN FELIPE
Pop. Est. 23,293

EL TRABAJO (The Work) (d)
Salinas, No. 569
Dir.—Miguel Yuri Yuri

SAN FERNANDO
Pop. Est. 26,820

EL COLCHAGUINO (d)
Manuel Rodríguez, No. 917
Dir.—Enrique Fuentes Fuentes
LA REGION (The Region) (d)
Bernardo O' Higgins, No. 564
Dir.—Emilio Avila Aguilera

SAN JAVIER

LA TRIBUNA (The Tribune) (d)
Sargento Aldea, No. 2568
Dir.—Gustavo Prado Santos

SAN VINCENTE DE TAGUA-TAGUA
Pop. Est. 10,000

LA LIBERTAD (The Liberty) (d)
Carlos Walker Martínez, No. 128
Dir.—Octavio Castro Ruíz
LA REGION (The Region) (m)
Carmen Gallegos, No. 174
Dir.—Juan Carlos Ramírez Paredes

SANTA CRUZ
Pop. Est. 10,000

EL CONDOR (d)
R. Casanova, No. 186
Dir.—Aguiles de la Fuente

SANTIAGO
Pop. Est. 5,236,361

AMERICA ECONOMIA (American Economy)
Galvarino Gallardo, No. 1670; Casilla 113, Correo 35
Tel: (56-2) 2358090/(56-2) 2573990;
Fax: (56-2) 2352498
Ed.—Ricardo Zisis
LA CUARTA (The Fourth) (m)
Avda. Vicuna Mackenna, No. 1842; Casilla 2795, Correo Central
Tel: (56-2) 5550034; Fax: (56-2) 5561017/(56-2) 5568727
Circ.—120,000
Owner—Alvaro Saieh
Dir.—Diozel Pérez Vergara
EL DIARIO (The Daily) (d-ex S)
Suecia 659; Casilla 9893
Tel: (56-2) 6951242; Fax: (56-2) 6951324
Circ.—12,000
Prop.—Ediciones Financieras SA
Ed.—Roberto Meza Antognoni
Ad. Mgr.—Rodrigo Guzman G
U.S. Rep.—AdMarket Int'l.; The N DeFilippes Corp.
DIARIO OFICIAL DE LA REPUBLICA DE CHILE (Official Daily of the Republic of Chile) (d)
Agustinas, No. 1269; Casilla 81-D
Tel: (56-2) 6982222/(56-2) 6983969;
Fax: (56-2) 6982222 Ext. 187
Circ.—15,000
Dir.—Florencio Ceballos
LA EPOCHA (The Epoch) (m)
Serrano, No. 240; Casilla 50360
Tel: (56-2) 6384444/(56-2) 6380221;
Fax: (56-2) 6381105/(56-2) 6968051
Circ.—50,000
Dir.—Ascanio Cavallo
ESTRATEGIA (Strategy)
Rafael Canas 114; Casilla 16485, Correo 9
Tel: (56-2) 2359331/(56-2) 2359153;
Fax: (56-2) 2745494/(56-2) 2361114
Dir.—Victor Manuel Ojeda
EL MERCURIO (The Mercury) (mS) Est. 1827
Avda. Santa María 5542, Las Condes;
Casilla 13-D, Correo Central
Tel: (56-2) 3301213; Fax: (56-2) 2289289
Circ.—150,000 (m); 180,000 (sat.);
300,000 (S)

Prop.—Sociedad Chilena de Publicaciones y Comercio
Dir.—Augustin Edwards Eastman
Ad. Mgr.—Alejandro Arze
Ad. Mgr.—Eolo Cifre
U.S. Rep.—AdMarket Int'l.; Charney/Palacios & Co. Inc.; The N DeFilippes Corp.
LA NACION (The Nation) (mS) Est. 1917
Augustinas, No. 1269; Casilla 81-D
Tel: (56-2) 6982222; Fax: (56-2) 6981059
Circ.—50,000 (m); 60,000 (S)
Prop.—Empresa Periodística La Nación SA
Ed.—Abraham Santibanez
U.S. Rep.—AdMarket Int'l.
NEGRO EN EL BLANCO (Black in the White) (m)
San Ignacio, No. 89
Dir.—Gilberto Puentes K
LA PRENSA AUSTRAL
Dr. Sotero del Rio, No. 326/8 piso
Tel: (56-2) 721446; Fax: (56-2) 6966922
LA SEGUNDA (The Second) (e-ex S) Est. 1931
Avda. Santa María, No. 5542, Las Condes; Casilla 13-D
Tel: (56-2) 2287048; Fax: (56-2) 2289568
Circ.—75,000
Prop.—Empresa El Mercurio SAP
Dir.—Cristian Zegers Ariztia
Ad. Mgr.—Alejandro Arze
U.S. Rep.—Charney/Palacios & Co. Inc.; AdMarket Int'l.
LA TERCERA (The Third) (mS) Est. 1950
Vicuna Mackenna, No. 1870; Casilla 9-D
Tel: (56-2) 5517067/(56-2) 5510034; Fax: (56-2) 5561017
Circ.—210,000 (d); 277,000 (S)
Prop.—Consorcio Periodística de Chile
Ad. Mgr.—Gustavo Aldunate Silva
Dir.—Hector Olave
LAS ULTIMAS NOTICIAS (The Last News) (m-ex mon.) Est. 1902
Avda. Santa María, No. 5542, Las Condes; Casilla 13-D
Tel: (56-2) 2287048; Fax: (56-2) 2289568
Circ.—180,000 (m); 130,000 (S)
Prop.—El Mercurio SA
Dir.—Fernando Diaz P
Ad. Mgr.—Alejandro Arze
U.S. Rep.—AdMarket Int'l.; Charney/Palacios & Co. Inc.

TALCA
Pop. Est. 136,160

LA MAÑANA DE TALCA (The Morning of Talca) (d) Est. 1906
4 Sur 1016
Tel: (56-71) 237199/(56-71) 237200; Fax: (56-71) 237199
Circ.—10,000
Dir.—Juan Bravo Ramos

TEMUCO
Pop. Est. 245,757

EL DIARIO AUSTRAL (m) Est. 1916
Antonio Varas 945; Casilla 1-D
Tel: (56-45) 212575
Circ.—26,000
Prop.—Sociedad Periodística Araucania SA
Dir.—Marco Antonio Pinto Zepeda
Ed.—German Carmona

TOCOPILLA
Pop. Est. 24,414

LA PRENSA (The Press) (m) Est. 1924
Bolivar, No. 1252
Tel: (56-55) 813036; Fax: (56-55) 813180
Circ.—8,000 (d); 12,000 (sat.)
Prop.—Sociedad Chilena de Publicaciones
Prop.—Alfonso Castagneto y Comercio SA
Ad. Mgr.—Enrique Schroeder

TRAIGUEN

EL COLONO (d)
Lagos, No. 733
Dir.—Javier Alberto Brito Munita

VALDIVIA CITY
Pop. Est. 115,500

EL CORREO DE VALDIVIA (Valdivia Mail) (d)
Yungay, No. 758; Casilla 15-D
Circ.—12,000

VALPARAISO
Pop. Est. 266,428

LA ESTRELLA (The Star) (e) Est. 1921
Esmeralda, No. 1002; Casilla 57-V
Tel: (56-32) 258011; Fax: (56-32) 250497
Circ.—30,000 (e); 40,000 (sat.)
Prop.—Empresa El Mercurio SAP
Dir.—Alfonso Castagneto Rodríguez
Ed.—Julio Hurtado

EL MERCURIO DE VALPARAISO (Valparaiso Mercury) (m) Est. 1827
Esmeralda, No. 1002; Casilla 57-V
Tel: (56-32) 258011; Fax: (56-32) 218287
Circ.—10,000
Ad. Mgr.—Enrique Schroeder
U.S. Rep.—AdMarket Int'l.; Charney/Palacios & Co. Inc.

VICTORIA
Pop. Est. 19,000

LAS NOTICIAS (The News) (d)
Conferación Suiza, No. 895; Casilla 92
Circ.—8,000
Dir.—Transito Bustamente Molina

VILLA ALEMANA

EL VILLALEMANINO (d)
Santiago, No. 655, Oficina 5-A
Dir.—Juan Guillermo Casanova Carrillo

YUMBEL

LA PRENSA (The Press) (d)
Bernardo O'Higgins, No. 725
Dir.—Mario Rocha Osses

COLOMBIA
Pop. Est. 35,577,556

ARMENIA

DIARIO DEL QUINDIO (Quindio Daily) (d)
Carrera 13-26-14
Tel: (57-67) 411111
Pub.—Hernan Barberi Cano

BARRANQUILLA
(Atlantico)
Pop. Est. 1,120,000

EL HERALDO (The Herald) (m-ex S) Est. 1933
Calle 53B, No. 46-25; Apdo. Aero 157
Tel: (57-58) 416066; Fax: (57-58) 410342
Circ.—48,000
Prop.—El Heraldo Ltda.
Gen. Dir.—Juan B Fernandez Renowitsky
U.S. Rep.—Charney/Palacios & Co. Inc.
LA LIBERTAD (The Liberty) (d) Est. 1979
Carrera 53, No. 55-166
Tel: (57-58) 320898
Prop.—Esper Editores SA
Pub.—Luís E Vásquez
Ed.—Roberto Espet R

BOGOTA
(Colombia)
Pop. Est. 5,500,000

DIARIO 5 P.M. (5 P.M. Daily)
Carrera 40, No. 16-24
Tel: (57-1) 2692111
Dir.—Luís Guillermo Velez Trujillo
EL ESPACIO (The Space) (4x wk.) Est. 1965
Carrera 61, No. 45-35; Apdo. Aereo 80111
Tel: (57-1) 2636666; Fax: (57-1) 2958512
Circ.—92,047
Mgr.—Hernando Reyes-D
EL ESPECTADOR (The Spectator) (mS) Est. 1887
Carrera 68, No. 22-71; Apdo. Aereo 3441
Tel: (57-1) 2945555; Fax: (57-1) 2606648
Circ.—632,030 (m); 234,780 (S)
Prop.—El Espectador (Cano Izaza y Cía.)
Dir.—Guillermo Cano
Ad. Mgr.—Vicente Castillo
U.S. Rep.—AdMarket Int'l.; Charney/Palacios & Co. Inc.; The N DeFilippes Corp.
LA PRENSA (The Press) (m) Est. 1988
Carrera 23, No. 20-46; Apdo. Aereo 9390
Tel: (57-1) 2320827; Fax: (57-1) 2854541
Circ.—38,000
Prop.—Editora Supernova
Pub./Ed.—Juan Carlos Pastrana Arango
Gen. Mgr.—Jaime Pastrana
EL SIGLO (The Sign) (mS) Est. 1936
Avda. El Dorado, No. 96-50; Apdo. Aereo 5452
Tel: (57-1) 4139200; Fax: (57-1) 4138547
Circ.—65,000
Pub.—Gabriel Melo Guevara
Ed.—Guillermo Gómez Moncayo
EL TIEMPO (The Time) (mS) Est. 1911
Avda. El Dorado, No. 57-90; Apdo. Aereo 3633
Tel: (57-1) 4109555; Fax: (57-1) 4105088
Circ.—350,000 (d); 425,000 (S)
Prop.—Editorial El Tiempo Ltd.
Pub.—Hernando Santos Castillo
Ed.—Enrique Santos Castillo
Ad. Mgr.—Felipe Santos

South America **Colombia** IV-115

EL VESPERTINO (The Evening) (e)
Avda. 68, No. 22 A-71
Prop.—Cano Isaza y Cía.
Pub.—Guillermo Cano

BUCARAMANGA
(Santander)
Pop. Est. 545,000

DIARIO EL FRENTE (Forward Daily) (m) Est. 1942
Calle 35, No. 12-26; Apdo. Aereo 665
Tel: (57-76) 425369; Fax: (57-76) 434541
Circ.—13,000
Pub.—Rafael Ortiz González
EL DEBER (The Might) (m) Est. 1923
Carrera 12, No. 30-35; Apdo. Aereo 698
Prop.—Sociedad Editorial El Deber
Pub.—Sr. Jorge Gutiérrez Reyes
LA VANGUARDIA LIBERAL (The Liberal Vanguard) (mS) Est. 1919
Calle 34, No. 13-42
Tel: (57-76) 334000; Fax: (57-76) 422366
Circ.—42,000 (m); 36,867 (S)
Pub.—Alejandro Galvis Ramírez

CALI
(Valle)
Pop. Est. 1,654,000

EL CALENO (d) Est. 1977
Calle 25, No. 3-20
Tel: (57-23) 893500
Pub.—Mauricio Montejo
Ed.—Oscar Hincape
EL CRISOL (m)
Carrera 1, No. 31-A-45
Tel: (57-23) 438404
Circ.—45,000
OCCIDENTE (m) Est. 1961
Calle 12, No. 5-22; Apdo. Aereo 5252
Tel: (57-23) 807102; Fax: (57-23) 836097
Circ.—57,000
Pub.—Alvaro H Caicedo
Ad. Mgr.—Fabio Rubio
EL PAIS (The Country) (mS) Est. 1949
Carrera 2, No. 24-26; Apdo. Aereo 1608
Tel: (57-23) 831181; Fax: (57-23) 835014
Circ.—72,500 (d); 110,000 (S)
Prop.—El Pais Ltda.
Pub.—Alvaro José Lloreda Caicedo
Ad. Mgr.—J Guillermo Sanche
LA REPUBLICA (The Republic) (mS) Est. 1954
Avda. de las Americas, No. 26BN-33
Tel: (57-23) 688345
Circ.—20,000
Prop.—Mercedes Rincón
Pub.—Rodrigo Ospina Hernández
Ed.—Claudio Ochoa Moreno

CARTAGENA
(Bolivar)
Pop. Est. 530,000

EL UNIVERSAL (The Universe) (dS) Est. 1948
Calle San Juan de Dios, No. 3-81
Tel: (57-59) 653078; Fax: (57-59) 646333
Circ.—23,000 (d); 12,664 (S)
Prop.—Editora del Mar SA
Pub.—Gerardo Araujo Perdomo
Dir.—Dr. Gonzalo Zúñiga
Ad. Mgr.—Gloria Sanint

CUCUTA
(Santander Del Norte)
Pop. Est. 270,000

DIARIO DE LA FRONTERA (Frontier Daily) (d) Est. 1950
Calle 14, No. 3-44; Apdo. Aereo 711
Tel: (57-70) 710589
Circ.—15,000
Pub.—Luís Parra Bolivar
LA OPINION (The Opinion) (d)
Avda. 4, No. 16-12
Tel: (57-70) 719999
Circ.—6,000
Pub.—Ciceron Florez Moya

GIRADOT

EL DIARIO (The Daily) (d)
Calle 14, No. 11-48
Pub.—José J Nino

IBAGUE
(Tolima)
Pop. Est. 200,000

EL CRONISTA (d-ex mon.) Est. 1911
Carrera 4A, No. 9-33

Circ.—20,000
Pub.—Dr. Diego Castilla Duran

MANIZALES
(Caldas)
Pop. Est. 230,000

LA PATRIA (The Patriot) (m) Est. 1921
Carrera 20, No. 21-51; Apdo. Aereo 70
Tel: (57-69) 842460; Fax: (57-69) 842460
Circ.—33,000
Prop.—Editorial La Patria
Pub.—Luís José Restrepo N

MEDELLIN
(Antioquia)
Pop. Est. 2,069,000

EL COLOMBIANO (The Colombian) (mS) Est. 1912
Carrera 48, No. 30-Sur-119; Apdo. Aereo 80636
Tel: (57-4) 3315252; Fax: (57-4) 3314848
Circ.—120,000 (d); 140,000 (S) ABC
Prop.—Empresa El Colombiano Ltda.
Ed.—Jorge Hernandez
Ad. Mgr.—Luis Miguel de Bedout
U.S. Rep.—Charney/Palacios & Co. Inc.; The N DeFilippes Corp.
EL MUNDO (The World) (d) Est. 1979
Calle 53, No. 74-50
Tel: (57-4) 2642800
Circ.—50,000
Prop.—Editorial Promotora de Edi. y Com.
Pub.—Pablo Emilio Becerra Rico
Ed.—Piedad Correra Z

NEIVA

DIARIO DEL HUILA (Huila Daily) (d) Est. 1966
Calle 8, No. 6-30
Tel: (57-80) 712459
Pub.—María Mercedes Rengifo de Duque

PASTO
(Narino)
Pop. Est. 125,000

EL DERECHO (The Right) (m) Est. 1928
Carrera 22, No. 20-59
Tel: (57) 230385
Circ.—5,000
Pub.—Dr. Rogerio Bolanos
EL RADIO (The Radio) (m) Est. 1933
Circ.—5,000
Pub.—Dr. Carlos C Puyana

PEREIRA
(Quindio)
Pop. Est. 210,000

EL DIARIO DEL OTUN (Otun Daily) (e) Est. 1929
Carrera 8A, No. 26-69; Apdo. Aereo 2533
Tel: (57-61) 351313
Circ.—10,000
Prop.—Editorial El Diario Ltda.
Pub.—Alfonso Jaramillo Orrego
LA TARDE (The Afternoon) (d) Est. 1982
Carrera 9A, No. 20-54, 43013
Tel: (57-61) 354666
Circ.—10,000
Pub.—Fabio Alfonso

POPAYAN
(Cauca)
Pop. Est. 94,000

EL LIBERAL (The Liberal) (m) Est. 1938
Carrera 3, No. 2-60; Apdo. Aereo 538
Tel: (57-28) 231937
Circ.—4,500
Pub.—Gerardo Fernandez Cifuentes

SANTA MARTA
(Magdalena)
Pop. Est. 140,000

EL INFORMADOR (The Informer) (d) Est. 1921
Avda. Libertados, No. 12A37
Tel: (57-56) 234771
Circ.—9,000
Pub.—José B Vives Campos

TUNJA
(Boyaca)
Pop. Est. 75,000

DIARIO BOYACA (Boyaca Daily) (d)
Calle 19, No. 11-31, Of. 203
Tel: (57-87) 422233
Circ.—3,000
Pub.—Dr. Carlos H Mojica

Copyright ©1996 by the Editor & Publisher Co.

Colombia   South America

EL ORIENTE (d)
Calle 19, No. 9-35, Of. 1007
Tel: (57-87) 423360
Pub.—Luís Rodríguez López

ECUADOR
Pop. Est. 10,677,067

AMBATO
Pop. Est. 76,833

EL HERALDO (The Herald) (d)
Calle Sucre, No. 209
Circ.—10,000
Pub.—Obispado de Ambato
Pub.—Luís Torres

BAHIA
Pop. Est. 33,622

EL GLOBO (The Globe) (d) Est. 1911
Circ.—6,000
Pub.—Alberto Palan Jr

CUENCA
Pop. Est. 201,490

EL MERCURIO (The Mercury) (mS) Est. 1924
Avda. De Las Americas, Diagonal a Indurumud
Tel: (593-7) 811726/(593-7) 811809; **Fax:** (593-7) 811766
Circ.—13,000
Pub.—Marina Merchan Luco de Zamora
Ed.—Nicador Merchan Luco
EL TIEMPO (The Time) (d) Est. 1944
PO Box 4909
Tel: (593-7) 311366; **Fax:** (593-7) 832117
Circ.—10,000
Pub.—Hunberto Toral Leon

GUAYAQUIL
Pop. Est. 1,600,000

EXTRA (d)
9 de Octubre y Chimborazo; Casilla 5890
Tel: (593-4) 329042/(593-4) 327473
Circ.—70,000
Pub.—Nicolas Ulloa Figuera
GACETA TRIBUTARIA (Tributary Gazette) (d)
Calle P. Moncayo 222 y M. Galecio
Prop.—Angel E Tamayo
HOY (Today)
9 de Octubre, No. 2202
Tel: (593-4) 287891; **Fax:** (593-4) 288348
Prop.—Editores y Impresores SA
EL MERIDIANO (The Meridian) (d)
Apdo. Postal 10996
Circ.—30,000
Prop.—Eq-Editorial SA
Pub.—Dr. Gustavo Ibañez Ruíz
LA RAZON (The Reason) (e) Est. 1964
Avda. 9 de Octubre, No. 427
Tel: (593-4) 327473/(593-4) 329042
Circ.—40,000
Pub.—Ramón Yulle Taysing
EL TELEGRAFO (The Telegraph) (mS) Est. 1884
Avda. 10 de Agosto 601 y Boyaca; Apdo. Postal 415
Tel: (593-4) 325172/(593-4) 327950; **Fax:** (593-4) 323265
Circ.—15,000
Pub.—Eduardo Arosemena Gómez
U.S. Rep.—Latin America Inc.
EL UNIVERSO (The Universe) (mS) Est. 1921
Escobedo y 9 de Octubre; Apdo. Postal 531
Tel: (593-4) 324630; **Fax:** (593-4) 321565
Circ.—190,000 (m); 210,000 (S)
Ed.—Carlos Pérez Perasso

IBARRA
Pop. Est. 70,000

LA VERDAD (The Truth) (d) Est. 1944
Avda. Flores, No. 545
Circ.—3,000
Pub.—Jaime Vásquez Jativa

LOJA
Pop. Est. 47,219

EL MUNDO (The World) (d) Est. 1975
Avda. Colon S/N
Circ.—10,000
Prop.—El Mundo SA
Pub.—Luciano Laza

MACHALA
Pop. Est. 67,321

EL CORREO (The Mail) (d)
Junin, No. 104
Circ.—5,000
Pub.—Enrique Valle Lozano
EL NACIONAL (The National) (d) Est. 1964
Calle Sucre, No. 209
Circ.—6,000
Pub.—Alfonso Veintimilla

MANTA
Pop. Est. 95,000

EL MERCURIO (The Mercury) (m) Est. 1925
Avda. 6, No. 12-37
Circ.—6,000
Pub.—Gil Ricardo Delgado Aray
Ad. Mgr.—Patricio Reese R

PORTOVIEJO
Pop. Est. 106,825

DIARIO MANABITA (Manabita Daily) (mS) Est. 1934
Apdo. Postal 50
Circ.—15,000
Pub.—Pedro Zambrano
Ad. Mgr.—Angela López
LA PROVINCIA (The Province) (d) Est. 1928
Circ.—1,500
Pub.—Saul Morales

QUITO
Pop. Est. 1,200,000

EL COMERCIO (mS) Est. 1906
Chile 1347; Apdo. Postal 57
Tel: (593-2) 610999; **Fax:** (593-2) 614923
Circ.—140,000 (d); 175,000 (S)
Prop.—C.A. El Comercio
Pub.—Guadalupe Mantilla
Ad. Mgr.—Marcelo Landivar
LA HORA (The Time) (d)
Casilla, No. 11243
Tel: (593-2) 475723; **Fax:** (593-2) 476085
Circ.—15,000
HOY (Today) (d)
Apdo. Postal 9069
Tel: (593-2) 539888
Circ.—41,000
Prop.—Edimpres SA
Pub.—Jaime Mantilla
Ed.—Benjamin Ortiz Brennan
ULTIMAS NOTICIAS (Last News) (e-ex S) Est. 1903
Chile, No. 1345
Tel: (593-2) 610999; **Fax:** (593-2) 614923
Circ.—80,000 (d); 100,000 (sat.)
Prop.—El Commercio CA
Ed.—Carlos Jaramillo

RIOBAMBA
Pop. Est. 57,443

EL ESPECTADOR (The Spectator) (d) Est. 1972
Avda. 10 de Agosto, 2334
Circ.—1,200
Pub.—L F Vallejo
EL PAIS (The Country) (d) Est. 1957
Calle Espejo
Circ.—2,000
Pub.—Medardo Proano B

FRENCH GUIANA
Pop. Est. 139,299

CAYENNE
Pop. Est. 38,091

l'AUTRE VERSION DE LA GUYANE
54, rue F Arago, 97300
CAYENNE HEBDO
CSCG-Rd., Point Mirza, 97300
CORRESPONDENT DU MONDE
9, rue du 14 Juillet, 97300
FRANCE-GUYANE
88, Ave. de Gaulle, 97300
Circ.—4,000
LA PRESSE DE GUYANE (d)
Boite Postal 5021, 97305
Circ.—16,000
Dir.—Fabien Roubaud
LA SEMAINE GUYANAISE
3, rue Cne. Bernard, 97300

GUYANA
Pop. Est. 729,425

GEORGETOWN
Pop. Est. 200,000

CATHOLIC STANDARD English
293 Oronoque St., Queenstown; PO Box 10720
Tel: (592-2) 61540
Circ.—10,000
GUYANA CHRONICLE (m-ex mon.) English; Est. 1881
10 Lama Ave., Bel Air Park; PO Box 11
Tel: (592-2) 54475; **Fax:** (592-2) 53108
Circ.—18,600 (tues.-sat.); 39,600 (S)
Prop.—Guyana National Newspapers Ltd.
Ed.—Shariet Khan
Ad. Mgr.—Vernon Hinds
U.S. Rep.—AdMarket Int'l.; Charney/Palacios & Co. Inc.
MIRROR (eS) English; Est. 1944
Lot 8, Ruimveldt Industrial Estate; PO Box 101088
Tel: (592-2) 62471
Circ.—20,000
Prop.—People's Progressive Party
NEW NATION English
Sophia Exhibition Site
Tel: (592-2) 68520
Circ.—26,000
Prop.—Guyana National Newspapers Ltd.
THE OFFICIAL GAZETTE English
18-20 Brickdam
Prop.—Ministry of Information
STABROEK NEWS English
45-46 Robb St., Lalcytown
Tel: (592-2) 57473/(592-2) 68981

PARAGUAY
Pop. Est. 5,213,772

ASUNCION
Pop. Est. 700,000

ABC COLOR (mS) Est. 1967
Yegros 745
Tel: (595-21) 491160; **Fax:** (595-21) 493059
Circ.—56,000 (m); 92,000 (S)
Prop.—Editorial AZETA SA
Ed.—Aldo Zuccolillo
Ad. Mgr.—Miguel A Dibello
U.S. Rep.—Charney/Palacios & Co. Inc.
EL DIARIO/NOTICIAS (The Daily/News) (mS) Est. 1984
Avda's. Artigas & Brasilia
Tel: (595-21) 292721; **Fax:** (595-21) 292840
Circ.—35,000 (m); 45,000 (S)
Prop.—Editorial Continental SA
Pub.—Nicolas Bo
Dir.—Hassel Aquilar Sosa
(This newspaper is nationally distributed.)
HOY (Today) (dS) Est. 1978
Avda. Mariscal López 2948
Tel: (595-21) 660383; **Fax:** (595-21) 660385
Circ.—50,000
Prop.—Editora Hoy SA
Ed.—Vicente Sarubbi
Ad. Mgr.—Hugo Aranda
U.S. Rep.—Charney/Palacios & Co. Inc.
PATRIA/UNION (Patriot/Union) (m) Est. 1946
Calle Tacuari 443
Tel: (595-21) 92011
Circ.—8,000
Pub.—Junta Gobierno
(Organization of the Colorado Party.)
ULTIMA HORA (Last Hour) (e-ex S) Est. 1973
Avda. Benjamin Constant 658
Tel: (595-21) 492261; **Fax:** (595-21) 447071
Circ.—45,000
Prop.—Editorial El Pais SA
Ad. Mgr.—Antonio Breglia

PERU
Pop. Est. 23,650,671

ABANCAY
(Apurimac)
Pop. Est. 53,848

LA PATRIA (The Patriot) (d) Est. 1938
Pub.—Guillermo Viladegut

AREQUIPA
Pop. Est. 634,500

CORREO (Mail) (d) Est. 1963
Calle Bolivar, No. 204
Tel: (51-54) 235150
Circ.—12,000
Prop.—Empresa Periodística Nacional
Dir.—Antenor del Pozo
Ad. Mgr.—Mercedes de Guinassi
U.S. Rep.—The N DeFilippes Corp.
NOTICIAS (News) (m) Est. 1927
Avda. Bolivar, No. 204
Circ.—5,000
Prop.—Empresa Periodística Nacional
Pub.—Gaston Aquirre Morales
EL PUEBLO (The Town) (m) Est. 1905
Sucre, No. 208; Apdo. Postal 35
Circ.—70,000
Prop.—Editorial Coroffset SA
Pub.—Felipe Quintanilla
Ed.—E Hegarra Ballon
Ad. Mgr.—Luís A Weis

AYACUCHO
(Cangallo)
Pop. Est. 69,862

FRATERNIDAD (d) Est. 1942
Pub.—Mauro Escobar A
PALADIN (d)
Calle Manoc Capac, No. 245
Circ.—3,000
Pub.—Propero Nuñez Bedrinana

CAJABAMBA
(Cajamarca)
Pop. Est. 60,739

FRAGUA (d) Est. 1953
Pub.—Juan Antonio Mendoza Magno

CALLAO
Pop. Est. 589,000

EL CALLAO (d) Est. 1883
Pedro Ruíz, No. 141
Prop.—Editora Argu SA
Pub.—Miguel Cavero Egusquiza
Ed.—Walter Ramírez Belaunde

CAMANA
(Arequipa)
Pop. Est. 23,717

LA VOZ DE CAMANA (The Voice of Camana) (d) Est. 1952
Pub.—Luzmila Justo de Ochea

CARAZ
(Ancash)
Pop. Est. 38,450

LA VOZ DE CARAZ (The Voice of Caraz) (d) Est. 1952
Pub.—Jaul Meneses

CERRO DE PASCO
Pop. Est. 101,533

EL MINERO (The Mineral) (e) Est. 1896
Circ.—3,600
Pub.—Pedro Caballero y Lira

CHICLAYO
(Lambayeque)
Pop. Est. 426,300

EL CICLON (The Cyclone) (d)
Calle Balta 910, 3er. piso
Circ.—50,000
LA INDUSTRIA (The Industry) (d)
Tacna, No. 610
Tel: (51-74) 427757/(51-74) 427761
Circ.—80,000
Pub.—Maria Ofelia Cerro
IL TIEMPO (Time) (d)
Apdo. Casilla 66

CHIMBOTE
(Ancash)
Pop. Est. 208,434

EL CENTINELA (d) Est. 1957
Pub.—Alberto Romero Legula
EL FARO (d) Est. 1954
Avda. Manuel Ruis, No. 585
Circ.—1,000
Pub.—Luís Baca Gonzáles
EL SANTA (mS) Est. 1928
Avda. Alfonso Ugarte, No. 441
Circ.—30,000
Pub.—Nicholas Arias Olivera
Ed.—Eleodoro Cordova G

ULTIMAS NOTICIAS (Last News) (d)
Avda. Alfonso Ugarte, No. 425
Circ.—3,000
Pub.—Dionicio Rodríguez

CHINCHA
Pop. Est. 96,152

LA VERDAD DE CHINCHA (Chincha Truth) (d)
Circ.—2,000
Pub.—Marcos Chumbiauca R
Ed.—Juan E Ortiz

CUZCO
Pop. Est. 150,000

EL COMERCIO (e) Est. 1896
Casilla 70
Circ.—60,000
Pub.—César Lomelini Carenzi
Ed.—Caliyto Coanqui Quispe
EL SOL (The Sun) (d) Est. 1901
Meson de la Estrella, No. 172
Pub.—Claudio Zuniga Carrasco
Ed. in Ch.—Efrain Paliza Nava

HUACHO
(Lima)
Pop. Est. 251,155

EL IMPARCIAL (The Impartial) (d) Est. 1891
Circ.—1,000
Pub.—Juan Jesús García
LA VERDAD (The Truth) (d) Est. 1930
Pub.—José Carbajal Manrique

HUANCAYO
(Junin)
Pop. Est. 256,156

CORREO (Mail) (d)
Jiron Cusco, No. 337
Circ.—9,000
Prop.—Empresa Periodística Nacional SA
Pub.—Ordonez Berrospi
LA OPINION POPULAR (The Popular Opinion) (d)
Huancas, No. 251
Tel: (51-64) 8231149
LA VOZ DE HUANCAYO (The Voice of Huancayo) (m) Est. 1912
Calle Real, No. 342
Circ.—5,000
Prop.—Empresa Ed. Huancayo SA
Pub.—César Arauco Aliago

HUANUCO
Pop. Est. 114,832

LA DEFENSA (The Defense) (d) Est. 1935
Circ.—500
Pub.—Manuel Jauregui Cornejo

HUARAZ
(Ancash)
Pop. Est. 82,948

EL DEPARTMENTO (The Department) (d)
Avda. Raymondi, No. 350
Circ.—500
Pub.—Francisco Jaramillo Molina
LA HORA (The Hour) (d) Est. 1954
Pub.—Fortunato Flores G

ICA
Pop. Est. 142,789

LA OPINION (The Opinion) (e)
Calle 176; Apdo. Postal, No. 19
Circ.—500
LA VOZ DE ICA (The Voice of Ica) (d) Est. 1918
Castrovirreyna, No. 193
Tel: (51-34) 232112
Circ.—5,000
Pub.—Octavio Niani

IQUITOS
(Loreto)
Pop. Est. 203,448

EL ECO (The Echo) (d) Est. 1924
Jiron Lima 100-108; Apdo. Postal 170
Circ.—6,000
Pub.—Eduardo Reategui Alvarez
EL MATUTINO (The Morning) (d)
Casilla Correo 788
Tel: (51-94) 235256
Pub.—Venancio Perea B
EL ORIENTE (e) Est. 1905
Calle Morona 153; Casilla 161
Circ.—7,000
Pub.—Ernesto Fernández Nuñez

JAUJA
(Junin)
Pop. Est. 99,155

EL PORVENIR (d) Est. 1908
Circ.—500
Pub.—Ernesto F Sanguinetti

JUNIN
Pop. Est. 29,439

EL VOCERO ANTIGUO (d) Est. 1952
Pub.—Jaime Loyola Martínez

LIMA
Pop. Est. 5,826,000

CARETAS (Faces)
Camana, No. 615, Oficina 308; Casilla 737
Tel: (51-14) 318324/(51-14) 289490;
Fax: (51-14) 332524
EL COMERCIO (mS) Est. 1839
Jiron Antonio Miro Queseda, No. 300
Tel: (51-14) 275800; Fax: (51-14) 285352
Circ.—185,000 (m); 200,000 (S)
Prop.—Empresa El Comercio SA
Ed.—Eduardo Carbajal
Ad. Dir.—Alvaro Ruiz de Somocurcio
U.S. Rep.—Charney/Palacios & Co. Inc.;
The N DeFilippes Corp.
CORREO (Mail) (mS) Est. 1963
Avda. Inca Garcilazo de la Vega, No. 1249
Tel: (51-14) 414065
Circ.—80,000
Pub.—Enrique Agois
Ad. Mgr.—Rafael Documet Vásquez
Ed.—Luís Agois Banchero
LA CRONICA/LA NEUVA CRONICA (m) Est. 1912
Jiron Andahuayla, No. 1472; Apdo. Postal 928
Circ.—208,000
Pub.—Rodolfo Orozco M
Ed.—Agusto Razuri
DEBATE (Debate)
Gonzales Larranaga, No. 265
Tel: (51-14) 467070/(51-14) 455237;
Fax: (51-14) 455946
EL DIARIO (The Daily) (d)
Camilo Carrillo, No. 465
Circ.—40,000
Dir.—Jorge Flores Lamas
DIARIO DE CALLAO (Callao Daily) (d)
Pub.—Carlos Arteaga
EDITORA LA REPUBLICA
Jiron Camana 320
Tel: (51-14) 310527; Fax: (51-14) 323053
EXPRESO (Express) (mS) Est. 1961
Jiron Ica 646; PO Box 4826
Tel: (51-14) 287470; Fax: (51-14) 318314
Circ.—70,000 (m); 85,000 (S)
Ad. Mgr.—Oscar Saettone
U.S. Rep.—The N DeFilippes Corp.
EXTRA (Extra) (e) Est. 1964
Jiron Ica 646
Tel: (51-14) 287470
Circ.—92,000
Pub.—Guillermo Cortes Nuñez
Ed. in Ch.—Juan Gargurevich Regal
(This newspaper is nationally distributed.)
GESTION (mS)
Calle General Salaverry, No. 152-156, Milaflores
Tel: (51-14) 476919; Fax: (51-14) 476569
Circ.—25,000
Prop.—Empresa Editora Gestion SA
Ad. Mgr.—Ada M Ulloa Schiantarelli
HOY (Today) (m) Est. 1983
Avda. Aramburu 830, Surquillo
Circ.—80,000
Prop.—Editora Futura SA
Pub.—Eduardo Gordillo
Ed.—Max Obregon Rossi
Ad. Mgr.—Javier Garrues
EL OBSERVADOR (The Observer) (d)
Avda. Sánchez Carrion, No. 601 Jesús María
Circ.—180,000
OJO (Eye) (m)
Avda. Garcilazo de la Vega, No. 1249
Circ.—180,000
Pub.—Augustín Figueroa Benza
EL PERUANO (The Perurian) (m) Est. 1825
Jiron Quilca, No. 556; Apdo. Postal 303
Circ.—75,000
Prop.—Perruvian Government
Pub.—Jesús Mimbela Pérez
Ad. Mgr.—Ernesto A Benavent Serrano
(This is an official government newspaper.)
LA PRENSA (The Press) (d)
Jiron Union, No. 745
LA REPUBLICA (The Republic) (e) Est. 1981
Jiron Camana 320a 446, 4th Floor
Circ.—110,000
Prop.—Editora la Republica SA
Pub.—Gustavo Mohme
Ed.—Guillermo Thorndike
REVISTA GENTE
Eduardo de Habich, No. 170, Miraflores
Tel: (51-14) 451747; Fax: (51-14) 461173
LA TERCERA (The Third) (d)
Jiron Andahuaylas, No. 1472; Apdo. Postal 928
Circ.—70,000
Prop.—Empresa Ed. La Cronica y Variedades
Dir.—Augusto Tamayo Vargas

LA TRIBUNA (The Tribune) (d)
Jiron Andahuaylas, No. 1472; Apdo. Postal 928
ULTIMA HORA (Last Hour) (d)
Jiron Union, No. 745

NAZCA
(Ica)
Pop. Est. 46,141

NOTICIAS (News) (d) Est. 1926
Circ.—2,000
Pub.—Alejandro Bocanegray Meija

PACASMAYO
(La Libertad)
Pop. Est. 90,719

ULTIMAS NOTICIAS (Last News) (e)
2 de Mayo, No. 27-29
Circ.—3,000
LA UNION (The Union) (d) Est. 1913
Circ.—3,000
Pub.—Manuel Pasto Rios

PISCO
(Ica)
Pop. Est. 63,946

LA INDEPENDENCIA (The Independency) (d) Est. 1940
Pub.—Alfredo Pérez Figueroa
ULTIMAS NOTICIAS (Last News) (d)
Avda. 2 de Mayo, No. 33
Circ.—1,500
Pub.—Alberto Ballena Sánchez

PIURA
Pop. Est. 283,580

CORREO (Mail) (d)
Jiron Ica, No. 782
Circ.—12,000
Prop.—Empresa Perodistíca Nacional
Pub.—Renan Estrad Tavara
Ad. Mgr.—Juan Zuñiga Sanudo
ECOS Y NOTICIAS (Echoes and News) (e)
Libertadad 902 y Ayacucho 307; Casilla Postal 110
Circ.—4,000
EL NORTE (The North) (d)
Avda. Bolivar, No. 300
Circ.—1,500
Pub.—Eleodoro Teran y Moya
EL TIEMPO (The Time) (dS) Est. 1916
Ayacucho, No. 751
Tel: (51-74) 323671
Circ.—30,000
Pub.—Victor Helguero

PUCALLPA
(Ucaya Li)

IMPETU (d)
Avda. 9 de Diciembre, No. 699
Circ.—2,000
Pub.—Fernando Vela Sánchez

PUNO
Pop. Est. 24,500

LOS ANDES (The Andes) (d)
Lima, No. 775; Casillo Postal 110
Tel: (51) 352142
Circ.—7,000
Pub.—Samuel Frisancho Pineda

TACNA
Pop. Est. 30,000

CORREO (Mail) (d)
Jiron Hipolito Unanue, No. 605
Circ.—8,000
Prop.—Empresa Periodistica Nacional
Pub.—Julio Zereceda Macedo
LA VOZ DE TACNA (The Voice of Tacna) (d)
Jiron Lima, No. 1202
Circ.—50,000
Pub.—Segundo Morales Villagra

TRUJILLO
(La Libertad)
Pop. Est. 532,000

LA INDUSTRIA (The Industry) (d)
Gamarra, No. 443
Circ.—19,000
Pub.—Isabel C de Burga
LA NACION (The Nation) (d)
Francisco Pizarro; Apdo. Postal 33
Circ.—7,000

SATELITE
Calle Gamarra, No. 443
Circ.—19,000
Pub.—Lorenzo Kcomt Kooseng

SURINAME
Pop. Est. 422,840

PARAMARIBO
Pop. Est. 180,000

OMHOOG Dutch
21 Gravenstraat; PO Box 1802
Tel: (597) 72521
ONZE TIJD
60 Wagenwegstraat
SURINAME (d)
120 Gravenstraat
DE WARE TIJD (m) Dutch; Est. 1957
Malebatrumstraat 11; PO Box 1200
Tel: (597) 72823
Circ.—10,000
Pub.—C Tjong Akiet
Ed.—L Mopurgo
Ad. Mgr.—A H Sardjoe Mishre
(This is an independent and liberal newspaper.)
DE WEST (e) Dutch; Est. 1909
Dr. J. C. de Mirandastraat 2-6; PO Box 176
Tel: (597) 73338
Circ.—15,000
Ed.—G R H Ferrier
(This is a liberal newspaper.)

URUGUAY
Pop. Est. 3,198,910

CANELONES
Pop. Est. 15,938

EL NOTICIOSO (d)
José E. Rodoy y F. Sánchez
Circ.—1,000
Pub.—Héctor A Montserrat
NUEVOS RUMBOS (d-ex S)
José E. Rodoy, No. 478
Circ.—500
Pub.—Santiago O Torterolo
EL PUEBLO (The Town) (d)
Rivera, No. 713; Apdo. Postal 17
Pub.—Juan C Lanus

COLONIA

LA COLONIA (The Colony) (d)
Gen Flores, No. 2317

FLORIDA
(Florida)
Pop. Est. 25,030

EL HERALDO (The Herald) (e) Est. 1919
Independencia, No. 824
Circ.—2,000
Prop.—El Heraldo SC
Pub.—Alberto Riva Buglio

MALDONADO
(Maldonado)
Pop. Est. 22,159

PUNTA DEL ESTE (d)
Avda. Florida, No. 864
Circ.—3,000
Pub.—David R Borges

MELO
Pop. Est. 38,260

EL DEBER CIVICO (The Civil Will) (d)
Calle José P. Varela, No. 610

MERCEDES
(Soriano)
Pop. Est. 34,667

ACCION (Action) (d) Est. 1935
Avda. Eusebio Jimenez 683
Circ.—6,000
Pub.—Fernando Fernandez
Ed.—T Balarini

Uruguay — South America

MINAS
(Lavalleja)
Pop. Est. 35,433

LA UNION (The Union) (e)
Florencio Sánchez, No. 569
Tel: (598-442) 2065
Circ.—3,000
Pub.—Edgar Martínez Lucero

MONTEVIDEO
Pop. Est. 1,500,000

EL DIA (The Day) (m) Est. 1886
Avda. 18 de Julio, No. 1297
Tel: (598-2) 905261/(598-2) 920310
Circ.—15,000
Dir.—Dr. Enrique Tarigo
EL DIARIO (The Daily) (e) Est. 1923
Bartolome Mitre, No. 1275
Tel: (598-2) 1178
Circ.—170,000
Ed.—Antonio Mercader
EL DIARIO ESPANOL (The Spanish Daily) (m) Est. 1906
Cerrito, No. 551-555; Apdo. Postal 899
Tel: (598-2) 959545/(598-2) 959481
Circ.—20,000
Pub.—Carlos M Reinante
DIARIO OFICIAL (Official Daily) (d)
Florida, No. 1178
DIARIO EL PAIS (Country Daily) (mS) Est. 1918
Plaza Cagancha, No. 1168
Tel: (598-2) 920464
Circ.—60,000 (mon.-fri.); 80,000 (sat.); 120,000 (S)
Pub.—Caniel Scheck
Ad. Mgr.—Martin Aguirre
DIARIO LA REPUBLICA (Republic Daily) (d)
Garibaldi, No. 2579
Tel: (598-2) 473565; Fax: (598-2) 472419
LA GACETA COMERCIAL (The Commercial Gazette) (d)
Plaza Independencia, No. 717, 11000
Tel: (598-2) 900459
HOY (Today) (d)
Rincon, No. 541
Prop.—Impresora Polo
Pub.—Danilo Arbilla
LA JUSTICIA URUGUAY (Uruguay Justice) (d)
25 de Mayo, No. 555, 11000
Tel: (598-2) 959721
LA MAÑANA Y EL DIARIO (The Morning and The Daily) (mS) Est. 1917
Rio Negro, No. 1028, 11100
Tel: (598-2) 920348/(598-2) 917373
Circ.—40,000
Ed. in Ch.—Daniel Alvarez
Ed.—Andres Falca
MUNDO COLOR (Color World) (e) Est. 1976
Cuareim, No. 1287
Circ.—60,000
Ed. in Ch.—Daniel Herrera Lussich
(This newspaper is owned by the government.)
EL PAIS (The Country) (mS) Est. 1918
Plaza Cagancha 1162
Tel: (598-2) 983230; Fax: (598-2) 984102
Circ.—100,000 (m); 120,000 (S)
Ad. Dir.—Carlos E Scheck
U.S. Rep.—Charney/Palacios & Co. Inc.
LA PLATA (d)
Plaza Libertad, No. 1164
ULTIMAS NOTICIAS (Last News) (d)
Paysandu, No. 1179
Tel: (598-2) 920452
Circ.—19,000
Prop.—Impresora Polo Ltda.
Pub.—Julian Safi
Ed.—Omar Piva
Ad. Mgr.—Hugo Piva
VIDA MARITIMA (e)
Colon, No. 1580

PAYSANDU
(Paysandu)
Pop. Est. 62,412

EL TELEGRAFO (The Telegraph) (d) Est. 1910
18 de Julio, No. 1027
Circ.—10,000
Pub.—Fernando Miguel Baccaro

RIVERA
Pop. Est. 49,013

NORTE (North) (d)
Avda. General San Martín, No. 715
Circ.—2,200
Pub.—Rik J Araujo

ROCHA
(Rocha)
Pop. Est. 21,612

ECOS DEL ESTE (The Eastern Echo) (d-ex S)
Florencio Sanchez, 94A
Circ.—500
Pub.—Angel M Pereyra
LA GACETA (The Gazette) (d)
Calle Treinta y Tres, No. 130
Circ.—1,200
Pub.—Elio T Sánchez
LA PALABRA (The Word) (d)
19 de April, No. 70
Pub.—Carlos N Rocha

SALTO
(Salto)
Pop. Est. 74,881

LA PRENSA (The Press) (e) Est. 1942
Calle Amorim, No. 56
Circ.—1,000
Prop.—Empresa Por la Prensa
Pub.—Alfonso Cardoza
Ad. Mgr.—María Martínez
EL PUEBLO (The Town) (d)
Avda. 18 de Julio, No. 151
Circ.—2,300
Pub.—Enrique A Cesio
TRIBUNA SALTENA (The Salton Tribune) (mS) Est. 1906
Joaquín Suarez, No. 7
Circ.—2,300
Pub.—Modesto Llantada

SAN JOSE DE MAYO
(San Jose)
Pop. Est. 28,427

AQUI ESTA (Here It Is) (d) Est. 1952
Calle Sarandi, No. 746
Circ.—1,000
Pub.—Ariel Chabalgoity
LA MAÑANA Y EL DIARIO (The Morning and the Daily)
Rio Negro, No. 1028
Tel: (598) 920348/(598) 987047

VENEZUELA
Pop. Est. 20,562,405

ACARIGUA
(Portuguesa)
Pop. Est. 116,551

ULTIMA HORA (Last Hour) (d)
Regeneracion a Guayabal, Puente Hierro Torre, Mezzanina, Oficina "B"
Tel: (58) 5542746/(58) 5542966; Fax: (58) 55212353
Prop.—Lalano Adentro
Pub.—Rubico Ramírez

ANACO
(Anzoategui)
Pop. Est. 61,386

EL ANAQUENSE
Avda. San Martín, Angelitos a Jesús, Edificio La Palma, Piso 1, Oficina 104
Tel: (58) 8222063
LA NOTICIA DE ORIENTE (d)
Peligro a Puente Repúblca, La Candelaria, Edificio Ormonde, Local 5
Tel: (58) 8221856/(58) 8222253

ARAURE
(Portuguesa)
Pop. Est. 55,299

EL REGIONAL (The Region) (d)
Avda. Francisco de Miranda, Chacao Edificio Galerias, Miranda, Piso 3, Oficina 309
Tel: (58) 5546037; Fax: (58) 5544977

BARCELONA
(Anzoategui)
Pop. Est. 221,792

DIARIO METROPOLITANO (Metropolitan Daily) (d)
Puente Victoria a No Pastor, La Candelaria, Centro Parque, Carabobo, Torre B, Piso 16, Oficina 11
Tel: (58-81) 779644/(58-81) 779466; Fax: (58-81) 779277

BARINAS
(Barinas)
Pop. Est. 153,630

DIARIO DE FRENTE (d)
Parque Central, Edificio Mohedano Mezzanina, Oficina OM3
Tel: (58) 7329095/(58) 7328369; Fax: (58) 7328366
EL ESPACIO (The Space) (d)
Avda. San Martín, Angelitos a Jesús, Edificio La Palma, Piso 1, Oficina 107
Tel: (58-73) 29983/(58-73) 29973; Fax: (58-73) 27224
LA PRENSA (The Press) (d)
Regeneracion a Guayabal, Puente Hierro Torre Mezzanina, Oficina "B"
Tel: (58) 7326835/(58) 7326840; Fax: (58) 7328020

BARQUISIMETO
(Lara)
Pop. Est. 625,450

EL IMPULSO (Impulse) (m) Est. 1904
PO Box 602
Tel: (58-51) 313011/(58-51) 313155; Fax: (58-51) 313011
Circ.—40,000
Pub.—Gustavo A Carmona
Ed.—Juan Carmona
Ad. Mgr.—Carlos Carmona
U.S. Rep.—Charney/Palacios & Co. Inc.
EL INFORMADOR (The Informer) (d) Est. 1972
Avda. Mohedamo, c/c Avda. Las Chaguaramas/Urb. La Castellana, Centro Generencial Mohedano, Piso 5, Oficina 5-B
Tel: (58-51) 311811; Fax: (58-51) 310624
Circ.—35,000
Pub.—Edecio González
PRONTO (Fast) (d)
Avda. Venezuela, No. 19-89
Prop.—Publicaciones Obelisco CA
Pub.—Anselmo Reyes Navarro
Ed. in Ch.—Lazaro Aranguren

CABIMAS
(Zulia)
Pop. Est. 165,755

EL CIERRE (m) Est. 1974
Edificio Brion, Avda. Mexico
Circ.—5,000
Prop.—Ediciones El Cierre CA
Pres.—Gustavo Rodríguez
Ed.—Guillermo Alvarez Bajares
Bus. Mgr.—Simon Barela
EL INFORMADOR (The Informer) (d) Est. 1972
Avda. Modedano, Urb. La Castellana, Centro Generencial, Mohedano, Piso 5, Oficina 5-B
Tel: (58-64) 311811; Fax: (58-64) 310624
Circ.—35,000
Pub.—Edecio González
EL REGIONAL DEL ZULIA (Zulia Region) (d)
Calle El Recreo, Sabana Grande, Edificio Estoril, Piso-Oficina 12
Tel: (58-64) 711096/(58-64) 716336; Fax: (58-64) 714969

CARACAS
Pop. Est. 1,822,465

THE DAILY JOURNAL (mS) English; Est. 1941
Avda. Fuerzas Armadas, No. 65; Apdo. Postal 1408, 1010
Tel: (58-2) 5621122; Fax: (58-2) 5626752
Circ.—15,300 (m); 17,200 (S)
Prop.—The Daily Journal CA
Pub.—Jules L Walman
Ed.—Nigel Cumberbatch
Ad. Mgr.—José Feijoo
U.S. Rep.—AdMarket Int'l.; Lee & Steel Inc.; The N DeFilippes Corp.
DIARIO 2001 (dS) Est. 1973
Final Avda. San Martín, Edificio Bloque DeArmas; Apdo. Postal 575, 1020
Tel: (58-2) 4431575; Fax: (58-2) 4438692
Circ.—160,000 (d); 130,000 (S)
Dir.—Federico Fautes
EL DIARIO DE CARACAS (The Caracas Daily) (dS) Est. 1979
Avda. Principal de Boleita, Norte Frente a Montaña Gráfica; Apdo. Postal 76478, 1070
Tel: (58-2) 2391722; Fax: (58-2) 349196
Circ.—90,000 (d); 110,000 (S)
Prop.—El Diario de Caracas CA
Pub.—Carlos A Ball
Ed.—Marcel Granier
Ad. Mgr.—Rodolfo Schmidt
U.S. Rep.—Charney/Palacios & Co. Inc.
EL DIARIO DE LA COSTA ORIENTAL (Oriental Coast Daily) (d)
Segunda Avda., Urb. Campos Alegre, Torre Credival, Planta Baja, Local C-1
Tel: (58-2) 2637103/(58-2) 2639350; Fax: (58-2) 2636255/(58-2) 2634840
DIARIO EL GLOBO (Globe Daily) (d)
Avda. Principal de Maripérez, Transversal Colon con Avda., Libertador
Tel: (58-2) 5764111; Fax: (58-2) 5744353
ECONOMIA HOY (Economy Today) (d)
Alcabala a Urapal, La Candelaria, Edificio Di Mase, Planta Baja
Tel: (58-2) 5111518; Fax: (58-2) 5115110
Circ.—35,000
Ad. Mgr.—Antonia Martin
U.S. Rep.—Charney/Palacios & Co. Inc.; The N DeFilippes Corp.
EL GLOBO (The Globe) (d)
Avda. Principal, Urb. Maripérez, Transversal Colon, Avda.'s La Sinagaga & Libertador
Tel: (58-2) 5764111/(58-2) 5773648; Fax: (58-2) 5744353
MERIDIANO (Meridian) (dS) Est. 1969
Final Avda. San Martín, Edificio Bloque DeArmas, 1020
Tel: (58-2) 4431066; Fax: (58-2) 4438692
Circ.—300,000
Prop.—Bloque de Armas Publicaciones
Ad. Dir.—Federico Fantes
(This newspaper is nationally distributed.)
GRUPO EDITORIAL PRODUCTO (Editorial Product Group) (d)
Edificio ACO, Piso 7; Apdo. Postal 88578
Tel: (58-2) 7519746/(58-2) 7519846; Fax: (58-2) 7519635
EL MUNDO (The World) (e-ex S) Est. 1958
Torre de La Prensa, Piso 4, Plaza del Panteón; Apdo. Postal 1192
Tel: (58-2) 814931
Circ.—270,315
Pub.—José Vásquez Losada
Ad. Dir.—Gilberto Roman
U.S. Rep.—The N DeFilippes Corp.
EL NACIONAL (The National) (mS) Est. 1943
Avda. La Salle, Torre Impreabogado Plaza Venezuela
Tel: (58-2) 408325; Fax: (58-2) 4834174/(58-2) 4083181
Circ.—340,000 (mon.-fri.); 185,000 (sat.); 250,000 (S) ABC
Prop.—Editora El Nacional SA
Pub.—Dr. Oscar Palacios Herrera
Ed.—Alberto Quiroz Corradi
Ad. Mgr.—Evelyn Goliz
U.S. Rep.—AdMarket Int'l.; Charney/Palacios & Co. Inc.; The N DeFilippes Corp.
EL NUEVO PAIS (The New Country) (d)
Pinto a Santa Rosalia, No. 44
Tel: (58-2) 5415211; Fax: (58-2) 5459675
PUNTO (Point) (m) Est. 1973
Edificio San Marcos, Avda. San Martín
Prop.—Equipo Editor
Pub.—Pompeyo Márquez
LA RELIGION (The Religion) (d)
Torre a Madrices, Edificio Juan XXIII
Tel: (58-2) 5630600/(58-2) 5630800; Fax: (58-2) 5635583
ULTIMAS NOTICIAS (Last News) (e) Est. 1941
Torre de La Prensa, Piso 3, Plaza del Panteón; Apdo. Postal 1192
Tel: (58-2) 832399; Fax: (58-2) 838835
Circ.—352,479
Prop.—Publicaciones Capriles
Pub.—Miguel Angel Capriles
Ed.—Nelson Luis Martinez
Ad. Mgr.—José Vazquez Losada
U.S. Rep.—The N DeFilippes Corp.; Charney/Palacios & Co. Inc.
EL UNIVERSAL (The Universe) (mS) Est. 1909
Avda. Urdaneta, Esquina de Animas, La Candelaria; Apdo. Postal 1909
Tel: (58-2) 5617511; Fax: (58-2) 5613393
Circ.—159,000 (m); 242,000 (S)
Prop.—Editorial Ambos Mundos CA
Pub.—Luís Teofilo Nuñez
Ed.—Luís Alfredo Chávez
Ad. Mgr.—P Perez Sanchez
U.S. Rep.—AdMarket Int'l.; Charney/Palacios & Co. Inc.; The N DeFilippes Corp. Inc.; Lee & Steel Inc.

CARORA
(Lara)
Pop. Est. 70,715

EL DIARIO (The Daily) (m) Est. 1919
Avda. Universidad, Trapasas a Charro, Centro Empresarial, Piso 7
Tel: (58) 5231017/(58) 5232379
Circ.—16,000
Pub.—Lila de Herrera Oropeza
Ed.—Jesús Antonio Herrera
Ad. Mgr.—Pedro Claver Herrera

CARUPANO
(Sucre)
Pop. Est. 92,333

DIARIO DE SUCRE (Sucre Daily) (d)
Avda. Francisco de Miranda, Chacao, Edificio Galerias, Miranda, Piso 2, Oficina 204
Tel: (58) 311676/(58) 310336

CIUDAD BOLIVAR
(Bolivar)
Pop. Est. 225,340

EL BOLIVARENSE (d) Est. 1957
Alcabala a Peligro, La Candelaria Torre Alcabala, Entrada A, Pisa 5, Oficina 53
Tel: (58-85) 24034/(58-85) 26602
Circ.—10,000
Pres.—Alvaro Natera Febres
EL EXPRESO (The Express) (d) Est. 1969
Calle Vidal con Urbina; Apdo. Postal 208
Tel: (58-85) 23936
Circ.—20,000
Pub.—J M Guzman Gómez
Ad. Mgr.—J M Guzman Gómez Jr
EL LUCHADOR (The Fighter) (e) Est. 1905
Edificio Bolivar, Calle Cumana cruce con 28 de Octobre; Apdo. Postal 65
Tel: (58-85) 20779
Circ.—12,000
Prop.—J Suegart & Cia.
Pub.—G Suegart
Ed.—J A Brito
Ad. Mgr.—Andres Bello

CIUDAD GUAYANA
(Bolivar)
Pop. Est. 453,047

DIARIO DE LA TARDE (Afternoon Daily)
Avda. Calle Democracia Frente La Plaza Centurian
EL GUAYANES (d)
Avda. Francisco de Miranda, Chacao, Galerias Miranda, Piso 2, Oficina 204
NOTIDIARIO (d)
Avda. Guaicaipuro, Urb. El Rosa, Torre Hener Mezzanina, Oficina M-2
Fax: (58) 86224076

CORO
(Falcon)
Pop. Est. 150,000

EL FALCONIANO (d)
Avda. Panteón, San Gabriel a Palo Negro, Edificio Or, Piso 3; Apdo. Postal 74
Tel: (58-68) 516278/(58-68) 517543;
Fax: (58-68) 512275
LA MAÑANA (The Morning) (d)
Mijares a Mercedes, Residencia La Avelena, Piso 1, Oficina 11-A
Tel: (58-68) 518667; Fax: (58-68) 515314
Circ.—5,000
Pub.—Atilio Yanez Esis
LA PRENSA (The Press)
Avda. San Martín, Angelitos a Jesús, Edificio La Palma, Piso 1, Oficina 104
Tel: (58-68) 513862/(58-68) 519241;
Fax: (58-68) 518918

CUMANA
(Sucre)
Pop. Est. 212,432

DIARIO REGION (Region Daily) (d)
Calle Bompland, Edificio Regio
Tel: (58-93) 911778
PROVINCIA (Province)
Angelitos a Jesús, Avda. San Martín, Edificio La Palma, Piso 1; Apdo. Postal 104
Tel: (58-93) 23540/(58-93) 23381
Pub.—Ramón Yanez
REGION (Region) (d)
Avda. Andrés Bello, Urb. Los Palos Grandes, Edificio Atlantico, Piso 4, Oficina 2
Tel: (58-93) 25463
Pub.—Lois Marcan Barrios
SIGLO 21 (Twenty First Sign) (d)
Avda. Francisco de Miranda, Chacao, Edificio Galerías Miranda, Piso 3, Oficina 309-310
Tel: (58-93) 662059

EL TIGRE
(Anzoategui)
Pop. Est. 93,229

ANTORCHA (d) Est. 1954
Alcabala a Peligro, La Candelaria, Torre Alcabala, Entrada "A", Piso 5, Oficina 53
Tel: (58) 83352383/(58) 83352384
Circ.—20,000
Pub.—Edmundo Barrios
LA NOTICIA DE ORIENTE (d) English; Est. 1984
Avda. Fernandez Padilla-6-69

Prop.—Repuestos Petroleros SA
Pub.—Jacinto Romero Luna
Ed.—Aquiles L Marcano

GUANARE
(Portuguesa)
Pop. Est. 84,904

EL PERIODICO DE OCCIDENTE (d)
Avda. Lecuna, Parque Central, Edificio Catuche, Piso 1; Apdo. 1-D
Tel: (58) 5755926/(58) 5755973; Fax: (58) 5755926/(58) 5771184

GUARENAS
(Miranda)
Pop. Est. 134,158

LA VOZ (The Voice) (d)
Centro Comercial Guarenas, Trapichito-Sector 2
Tel: (58-36) 220851/(58-36) 228817;
Fax: (58-36) 22093

LOS TEQUES
(Miranda)
Pop. Est. 140,617

DIARIO AVANCE (Advance Daily) (d)
Avda. Francisco de Miranda, Boleita Edificio Seguros La Paz, Piso 5, Oficina E-51
Tel: (58-32) 46982; Fax: (58-32) 47545
LA REGION (The Region) (d)
Calle Ribas c/c Calle Guaicaipuro, Edificio Dioce, Piso 2
Tel: (58-32) 311008/(58-32) 311737;
Fax: (58-32) 211035

MARACAIBO
(Zulia)
Pop. Est. 1,249,670

CRITICA (Critical) (m) Est. 1966
Torre De La Prensa Zuliana, Calle 92, 3; Apdo. Postal 480
Tel: (58-61) 28748; Fax: (58-61) 211552
Circ.—77,000
Prop.—La Prensa Zuliana
Dir.—Samir Makarem Urdaneta
U.S. Rep.—The N DeFilippes Corp. Inc.
DIARIO LA COLUMNA (Column Daily) (m) Est. 1925
Avda. Urdaneta, Esquina Animas, Edificio Iberia, Piso 3, Oficina 3-C
Tel: (58-61) 223884/(58-61) 255955;
Fax: (58-61) 227921
Circ.—20,000
Prop.—Tipografia La Columna CA
Pub.—Omar Soto Lugo
Ed.—Pedro Hernández H
PANORAMA (mS) Est. 1914
Avda. 15; Apdo. Postal 425
Tel: (58-61) 2110006; Fax: (58-61) 223678
Circ.—125,000 (m); 123,000 (S) ABC
Prop.—Diario Panorama C.A.
Pub./Ed.—Esteban R Pineda Belloso
Ad. Mgr.—Len Nava
U.S. Rep.—Charney/Palacios & Co. Inc.
EL REGIONAL DE ZULIA (Zulia Region) (d)
Carretera "N", Avda. Pal-Zona Industrial Galpon 9
Tel: (58-61) 29019; Fax: (58-61) 920632

MARACAY
(Aragua)
Pop. Est. 354,196

EL ARAGUENO (d)
Santa Teresa a Cipreses Centro Profesional Cipreses, Piso 1, Oficina 103
Tel: (58-43) 21606/(58-43) 21607; Fax: (58-43) 451886/(58-43) 5458142
Circ.—8,000
Pub.—Martín Villaroel
EL IMPARCIAL (The Impartial) (d)
Calle Cristóbal Rojas, Urb. Las Mercedes, Sector Los Naranjos, Residencia Independencia; Apdo. Postal 4
Tel: (58-43) 336178/(58-43) 336189;
Fax: (58-43) 336178
EL PERIODICO (The Newspaper) (d)
Avda. Francisco de Miranda, Chacao, Edificio Galerías Miranda, Piso 3, Oficina 309
Tel: (58-43) 335209/(58-43) 336987;
Fax: (58-43) 335709
EL SIGLO (The Sign) (d)
Esquina de Luneta, Parroquina Altagracia, Edificio Centre Valores, Piso 6, Oficina 3
Tel: (58-43) 544867/(58-43) 549265
Circ.—65,000
Prop.—Publicaciones Capriles
Pub.—Manuel Capriles H

South America Venezuela IV-119

MATURIN
(Monagas)
Pop. Est. 206,654

EL DIARIO (The Daily) (d)
Peligro a Puente República, La Candelaria, Edificio Ormonde Mezzanina, Local 5
Tel: (58-91) 22250
Pub.—J Saragoza
EL ORIENTAL (d)
Avda. Francisco de Miranda, Urb. Altamira, Edificio Seguros Adriatica, Oficina 83
Tel: (58-91) 23657; Fax: (58-91) 413856
Pub.—Gustavo Urbina
EL SOL DE MATURIN (The Maturin Sun) (d)
Avda. Francisco Solano López, Chacaito Residencia Sans Souci, Edificio El Samán, Piso 7; Apdo. Postal 71
Tel: (58-91) 22632; Fax: (58-91) 27994
Pub.—Luís Guevara Monosalva

MERIDA
(Merida)
Pop. Est. 170,902

CORREO DE LOS ANDES (d)
Avda. Mohedano c/c Calle Blandin, Quinta No. 10, Urb. La, Castellana
Tel: (58-74) 632270
FRONTERA (Frontier) (d)
Avda. Lecura, Parque Centro, Edificio Mohedano Mezzanina, Oficina OM2
Tel: (58-74) 93963/(58-74) 93957; Fax: (58-74) 93929
EL VIGILANTE (The Vigilante) (m) Est. 1923
Blvd. de Sabana Grande, Edificio Albernia, Piso 4, Oficina, 42
Tel: (58-74) 525510; Fax: (58-74) 521839
Circ.—3,000
Prop.—Empresa El Vigilante
Pub.—Ecio Rojo Paredes
Ad. Mgr.—R Rodríguez A

PORLAMAR
(Nueva Esparta)
Pop. Est. 62,739

EL CARIBE (The Caribbean) (d)
Avda. Urdaneta, Esquina Punceres, Edificio Marciales, Piso 4, Oficina 46
Tel: (58) 9522855
DIARIO INSULAR (d)
Avda. Principal, Urb. Colinas de Bello Monte, Centro Comercial Caracas, Piso 1, Oficina 9
Tel: (58) 9523101/(58) 95614343; Fax: (58) 95614487
EL SOL DE MARGARITA (The Magarita Sun) (d)
Avda. Francisco de Miranda, Chacao, Edificio Galerías, Piso 3, Oficinas 309 y 310
Tel: (58) 9523845/(58) 9523615

PUERTO LA CRUZ
(Anzoategui)
Pop. Est. 155,731

DIARIO DE ORIENTE (d)
Avda. Casanove c/c Avda. Las Acacias, Sabana Grande, Torre Banhoriet, Planta Baja
Tel: (58) 81665913/(58) 81665915
Prop.—Corporiente SA
EL NORTE (The North) (d)
Calle Bolivar, Chacao, Edificio Don David, Piso 5, Oficina 52
Tel: (58) 81763753/(58) 81762351; Fax: (58) 81763753
EL TIEMPO (The Time) (dS) Est. 1958
Avda. Urdaneta, Ibarras a Pelota, Edificio Caoma, Piso 2, Oficina 214
Tel: (58-81) 665422/(58-81) 665219;
Fax: (58-81) 665092
Circ.—20,000
Prop.—Editores Orientales
Pub.—Dr. Jesús Alvarado

PUERTO ORDAZ
(Bolivar)
Pop. Est. 453,047

CORREO DEL CARONI (d) Est. 1977
Alcabala Peligro, La Candelaria, Torre Alcabala, Entrada "A", Piso 5, Oficina 53
Tel: (58) 86225465/(58) 86225468
Circ.—70,000
Prop.—Editorial Roderick
Pub.—David Natera Febres
Ad. Mgr.—Luís Natera Febres

PUNTO FIJO
(Falcon)
Pop. Est. 88,681

MEDANO (d)
Peligro a Puente República, La Canelaria, Edificio Ormonde, Local 5
Tel: (58) 69451484/(58) 69450654
Circ.—8,000
Pub.—Rafael Martínez Hidalgo

SAN CARLOS
Pop. Est. 50,708

LAS NOTICIAS DE COJEDES (Cojedes News) (d)
Regeneración a Guayacal, Torre Puente de Hierro, Mezzanina, Oficina B
Tel: (58) 58330394; Fax: (58) 58331129

SAN CRISTOBAL
(Tachira)
Pop. Est. 494,000

DIARIO CATOLICO (Catholic Daily) (d) Est. 1924
Miguelachoa a Misericordia, La Candeleria, Edificio Doramil, Piso 1
Tel: (58-76) 432015/(58-76) 432819
Circ.—25,000
Prop.—Diocese of San Cristobal
Pub.—Mons. Nelson Arellano Roa
Ed.—Elida Marina Rivas Ostos
DIARIO DE LA NACION (Daily Nation) (mS) Est. 1968
Calle 4, Esquina Carrera 6
Tel: (58-76) 410403
Circ.—27,084 (m); 28,624 (S)
Pres.—José Rafael Cortes
Ed.—Miguel E Nuñez
LA NACION (The Nation) (mS) Est. 1968
Calle 500, Quinta Crespo, Edificio Lirio, Local B
Tel: (58-76) 26401/(58-76) 26402; Fax: (58-76) 465051
Circ.—32,000
Pub.—Gloria Nino de Cortes
Ed.—José Rafael Cortes
PUEBLO (Town) (d)
Avda. Andrés Bello, Urb. Los Palos Grandes, Edificio Atlántico, Piso 4, Oficina 2
Tel: (58-76) 445111/(58-76) 445227
VANGUARDIA (Vanguard) (d)
Avda. Andrés Bello, Urb. San Bernardino, Edificio Normandie, Piso 25, Oficina 251
Tel: (58-76) 435555
Circ.—4,000
Pub.—Ricardo Proano

SAN FELIPE
(Yaracuy)
Pop. Est. 65,509

POR QUE (Why) (d)
Avda. 8, Calle 7
Circ.—2,000
Pub.—Ricardo Proano
YARACUY AL DIA (Yaracuy Per Day) (d) Est. 1973
Puente Victoria a No Pastor, La Candelaria, Centro Parque, Carabobo, Torre "A", Piso 4, Oficina 406
Tel: (58) 5439764/(58) 5443108; Fax: (58) 5441155
Circ.—5,000
Pub.—Carlos José Pinto Dominguez

SAN FERNANDO DE APURE
(Apure)
Pop. Est. 72,716

DIARIO ABC DE APURE (ABC Daily of Apure) (d)
Avda. San Martín, Angelitos a Jesús, Edificio La Palma, Oficina 103

SAN JUAN DE LOS MORROS
Pop. Est. 67,791

EL NACIONALISTA (The Nationalist) (d)
Avda. Francisco de Miranda, Chacao, Edificio Galerías Miranda, Piso 3, Oficina 309
Tel: (58) 64314437/(58) 64312562
LA PRENSA DEL LLANO (The Llano Press) (d)
Avda. San Martín, Angelitos a Jesús, Edificio La Palma, Oficina 104
Tel: (58) 64315289; Fax: (58) 64310254

Copyright ©1996 by the Editor & Publisher Co.

Venezuela — South America

VALENCIA
(Carabobo)
Pop. Est. 903,621

ABORIGEN (d)
Peligro a Puente República, La Candelaria, Edificio Ormonde, Local 5
Tel: (58-41) 58810/(58-41) 84243
DIARIO LA CALLE (Street Daily) (d)
Plaza Venezuela, Torre Capriles, Piso 2, Oficina 208
Tel: (58-41) 574225/(58-41) 579794;
Fax: (58-41) 589794
EL ESPECTADOR (The Spectator)
Centro Comercial Concresa, Nivel TD, Oficina 2-D, Redoma de Prados del Este.
Tel: (58-41) 210709/(58-41) 219112;
Fax: (58-41) 226309
HORA CERO (Zero Hour) (d) Est. 1973
Santa Teresa y Cipreses
Circ.—5,000
Prop.—Publicaciones Anton CA
Pub.—Guillermo Anton Santana
Ed.—Jesús Muchacho Matheus
NOTI-TARDE (e)
Avda. Montes de Oca, No. 105-60
Tel: (58-41) 574411; Fax: (58-41) 574192
Prop.—Fondo Editorial del Central
Pub.—Miguel Jiménez Márquez
Ed. in Ch.—Francisco Silvino
EL REGIONAL (d)
Avda. Urdaneta
Ed.—Aracelis Molina

VALERA
(Trujillo)
Pop. Est. 97,012

DIARIO DE LOS ANDES (Andes Daily) (d)
Avda. Libertador, Edificio Araguaney, Piso 5, Oficina 5-B
Tel: (58) 7159505/(58) 7158294
Pub.—Eladio Muchacho Unda
EL TIEMPO (The Time) (d)
Avda. Lecuna, Parque Centro, Edificio Catuche, Piso 1, Apdo. 1-D
Tel: (58) 7153656/(58) 7153657;
Fax: (58) 7158677
Pub.—Luís Mazzari

NEWSPAPERS OF AUSTRALIA AND NEW ZEALAND

AUSTRALIA
Pop. Est. 18,077,419

ADELAIDE
(South Australia)
Pop. Est. (Metro Area) 1,023,597

THE ADELAIDE ADVERTISER (m-mon. to sat.) Est. 1858
121 King William St., (5000); GPO Box 339, 5001
Tel: (61-8) 2062000; Fax: (61-8) 2063669
Circ.—205,965 (mon.-fri.); 263,735 (sat.) ABC
Prop.—Advertiser Newspapers Ltd.
Mng. Dir.—Peter Wylie
Gen. Mgr.—John Sanders
Edit'l. Mgr.—Andrew Hall
Ed.—Peter Blunden
Ad. Mgr.—Tony Adams
Ad. Mgr.—John Gordon
Mktg. Mgr.—R John
Ad.—$20.25 casual rate (mon.-fri.); $24.95 casual rate (sat.)
THE ADELAIDE NEWS (e-mon. to fri.) Est. 1923
11-15 Waymouth St., (5000); GPO Box 1771, 5001
Tel: (61-8) 2062000; Fax: (61-8) 2063688
Circ.—143,418
Prop.—The News (Pty.) Ltd.
Mng. Ed.—Roger G Holden
Ad. Mgr.—Jennifer Kenney
THE AUSTRALIAN (e-mon. to sat.) Est. 1964
11 Waymouth St., 5000
Prop.—Nationwide News (Pty.) Ltd.
SUNDAY MAIL (S) Est. 1912
121 King William St., (5000); GPO Box 339, 5001
Tel: (61-8) 2062000; Fax: (61-8) 2063646
Circ.—323,615 ABC
Prop.—Advertiser-News Weekend Publishing Co. (Pty.) Ltd.
Ed.—Kerry Sullivan
Ad. Mgr.—John Turner
Ad.—$28.05 casual rate

ALBURY
(New South Wales)
Pop. Est. (Metro Area) 72,871

THE BORDER MORNING MAIL (mon. to sat.) Est. 1903
Swift & Kiewa Sts.; PO Box 346, 2640
Tel: (61-60) 211555; Fax: (61-60) 216781
Circ.—26,024 ABC
Prop.—Border Morning Mail (Pty.) Ltd.
Gen. Mgr.—Gordon R Beavan
Ed.—Jeff Stephenson
Ad. Mgr.—John Sutherland
Ad.—$8.00 casual rate (mon.-fri.); $8.20 casual rate (sat.)

BALLARAT
(Victoria)
Pop. Est. (Metro Area) 78,342

THE BALLARAT COURIER (m-mon. to sat.) Est. 1867
110 Creswick Rd., 3353
Tel: (61-53) 311211; Fax: (61-53) 331651
Circ.—21,210 ABC
Prop.—The Ballarat Courier (Pty.) Ltd.
Pub.—Doug Cowles
Gen. Mgr.—Tom O'Meara
Ed.—Ken McGregor
Ad. Mgr.—Stephen Humphrey
Ad.—$6.95 casual rate (mon.-fri.); $7.65 casual rate (sat.)

BATHURST
(New South Wales)
Pop. Est. 19,640

WESTERN ADVOCATE (m-mon. to fri.) Est. 1963
208 Browning St.; PO Box 11, 2795
Tel: (61-63) 324614; Fax: (61-63) 324614
Circ.—5,084 ABC
Prop.—Western Advocate Ltd.
Pub.—L A Shehade
Ed.—Kevin Stafford
Ad. Mgr.—Sue Parkes
Ad.—$5.29 casual rate

BENDIGO
(Victoria)
Pop. Est. 67,315

BENDIGO ADVERTISER (m-mon. to sat.) Est. 1853
96-98 Pall Mall; PO Box 61, 3550
Tel: (61-54) 436333; Fax: (61-54) 413808
Circ.—15,231 ABC
Prop.—Independent Newspapers
Gen. Mgr.—Bruce Baskett
Ed.—Wayne Gregson
Ad. Mgr.—Ashley Cooper
Ad.—$5.95 casual rate

BRISBANE
(Queensland)
Pop. Est. (Metro Area) 1,334,017

THE AUSTRALIAN (m-mon. to sat.) Est. 1964
Newspaper House, 289 Queen St., 6th Floor; GPO Box 2145, 4001
Prop.—Nationwide News (Pty.) Ltd.
THE COURIER MAIL (m-mon. to sat.) Est. 1933
41 Campbell St., (Bowen Hills, 4006); GPO Box 130, 4001
Tel: (61-7) 2526011; Fax: (61-7) 2526696
Circ.—225,019 (mon.-fri.); 330,634 (sat.) ABC
Prop.—Queensland Newspapers (Pty.) Ltd.
Gen. Mgr.—Lachlan Murdoch
Ed. in Ch.—Jack Lunn
Ed.—Des Houghton
Ad. Dir.—Evan Davies
Ad. Mgr.—John Banks
Ad.—$41.50 casual rate (mon.-fri.)
THE DAILY SUN (e-mon. to fri.)
Brunswick & McLachlan Sts., (4006); GPO Box 222, 4001
Tel: (61-7) 2533333; Fax: (61-7) 2533103
Circ.—121,872
Prop.—Sun Newspapers (Pty.) Ltd.
Pub.—F Moore
Ed.—Mike Quirk
Ad. Mgr.—Bill Stephens
THE SUNDAY MAIL (S) Est. 1933
41 Campbell St., (Bowen Hills, 4006); GPO Box 130, 4001
Tel: (61-7) 2526011; Fax: (61-7) 2526692
Circ.—579,578 ABC
Prop.—Queensland Newspapers (Pty.) Ltd.
Mng. Ed.—R Richards
Ed.—Alan Revell
Ad. Mgr.—Hesper Chainey
Ad.—$41.50 casual rate
SUNDAY SUN (S) Est. 1901
Brunswick & McLachlan Sts., (4006); GPO Box 222, 4001
Tel: (61-7) 2533333; Fax: (61-7) 2533103
Circ.—352,115
Prop.—Sun Newspapers (Pty.) Ltd.
Pub.—F Moore
Ad. Mgr.—B Stephens

BROKEN HILL
(New South Wales)
Pop. Est. (Broken Hill Area) 26,913

BARRIER DAILY TRUTH (m-mon. to sat.) Est. 1908
179 Blende St.; PO Box 463, 2880
Tel: (61-80) 872354; Fax: (61-80) 885066
Circ.—7,563 ABC
Prop.—Barrier Daily Truth
Gen. Mgr.—Chris Faulkner
Ed.—John Hudswell
Ad. Mgr.—Peter R Keenan
Ad.—$6.00 casual rate

BUNDABERG
(Queensland)
Pop. Est. (Metro Area) 32,560

NEWS-MAIL (m-mon. to sat.) Est. 1907
22/24 Targo St.; PO Box 539, 4670
Tel: (61-71) 538555; Fax: (61-71) 531028
Circ.—12,842 ABC
Prop.—Bundaberg Newspaper Co. (Pty.) Ltd.
Ed.—John Schalch
Ad. Mgr.—Michael Randall
Ad.—$7.90 casual rate

BURNIE
(Tasmania)
Pop. Est. (Burnie-Somerset Area) 20,368

THE ADVOCATE (m-mon. to sat.) Est. 1890
56 Mount St.; PO Box 63, 7320
Tel: (61-4) 301409; Fax: (61-4) 301461
Circ.—25,867 ABC
Prop.—The Advocate Newspaper (Pty.) Ltd.
Mng. Dir.—Paul Harris
Gen. Mgr.—Nigel Harris
Edit'l. Mgr.—Tony Southwell
Ed.—Henry Catchpole
Ad. Mgr.—Peter Sproule
Ad.—$7.85 casual rate
THE WEEKENDER Est. 1968
54-56 Mount St.; PO Box 63, 7320
Circ.—13,671
Prop.—The Advocate Newspaper (Pty.) Ltd.
Ed.—D J Cherry
Ad. Mgr.—P Sproule

CABRAMATTA
(New South Wales)
(Part of the City of Fairfield in suburban Sydney)
Pop. Est. (City of Fairfield) 129,557

CHIEU DUONG (Sunrise) (tues. to sat.)
Vietnamese
PO Box 64, 2166
Circ.—55,000
Ed. in Ch.—Mr. Nhat Giang

CAIRNS
(Queensland)
Pop. Est. (Cairns Area) 48,557

CAIRNS POST (m-mon. to sat.) Est. 1882
22-24 Abbott St.; PO Box 126, 4870
Tel: (61-70) 526666; Fax: (61-70) 526632
Circ.—30,609 ABC
Prop.—The Cairns Post (Pty.) Ltd.
Gen. Mgr.—David Maguire
Ed.—Don Iedema
Ad. Mgr.—John Kelly
Ad.—$7.20 casual rate (mon.-fri.); $7.92 casual rate (sat.)
F.N.Q. SUNDAY (S) Est. 1986
22 Abbott St.; PO Box 126, 4870
Circ.—28,500
Prop.—The Cairns Post (Pty.) Ltd.

CANBERRA
(Australian Capital Territory)
(Metro Area includes City of Queanbeyan in N.S.W.)
Pop. Est. (Metro Area) 303,846

THE AUSTRALIAN (m) Est. 1964
42 Mort St., Braddon, 2601
Tel: (61-6) 2707000; Fax: (61-6) 2707070
Prop.—Nationwide News (Pty.) Ltd.
THE CANBERRA TIMES (mS) Est. 1926
9 Pirie St., (2609); GPO Box 7115, 2610
Tel: (61-6) 2802122; Fax: (61-6) 2802282
Circ.—41,258 (mon.-fri.); 68,600 (sat.); 37,642 (S) ABC
Prop.—Federal Capital Press of Australia (Pty.) Ltd.
Mng. Dir.—Ian Meikle
Ed.—Michelle Grattan
Ad. Mgr.—Wayne Geale
Ad.—$11.30 base rate (mon.-fri.); $13.85 base rate (sat.); $10.15 base rate (S)

COFFS HARBOUR
(New South Wales)
Pop. Est. 51,520

THE ADVOCATE (m-tues. to sat.) Est. 1907
53 Moonee St.; PO Box 534, 2450
Tel: (61-66) 522522; Fax: (61-66) 514492
Circ.—20,000 (tues.; thur.; fri.); 28,000 (wed.); 24,500 (sat.)
Prop.—North Coast News (Pty.) Ltd.
Ed.—Howard Spencer
Ad. Mgr.—R Habgood
Ad.—$7.05 casual rate

DARWIN
(Northern Territory)
Pop. Est. (Northern Territory) 74,800
Pop. Est. (Darwin Metro Area) 70,072

NORTHERN TERRITORY NEWS Est. 1952
6-8 McMinn St., (0800); GPO Box 1300, 0801
Tel: (61-89) 449900; Fax: (61-89) 816045
Circ.—22,020 (mon.-fri.); 28,113 (sat.) ABC
Prop.—News (Pty.) Ltd.
Gen. Mgr.—Don Kennedy
Ed.—Bill Murray
Ad. Mgr.—Cecilia Queck
Ad. Mgr.—David Jackson
Mktg. Mgr.—Kevin Smith
SUNDAY TERRITORIAN (S) Est. 1984
6-8 McMinn St., (0800); GPO Box 1300, 0801
Tel: (61-89) 449900; Fax: (61-89) 818392
Circ.—24,957 ABC
Prop.—News Ltd.
Gen. Mgr.—Don Kennedy
Ed.—Nigel Adam
Ad. Mgr.—Cecilia Quek
Ad. Mgr.—David Jackson
Mktg. Mgr.—Kevin Smith

DUBBO
(New South Wales)
Pop. Est. 23,986

DAILY LIBERAL (m-mon. to sat.) Est. 1874
216 Macquarie St.; PO Box 311, 2830
Tel: (61-68) 832900; Fax: (61-68) 825898
Circ.—6,307 ABC
Prop.—Macquarie Publications (Pty.) Ltd.
Pub./Ed.—Richard Lawson
Ad. Mgr.—Pamela Simmons
Ad.—$7.00 casual rate

GEELONG
(Victoria)
Pop. Est. (Metro Area) 145,325

THE ECHO (d)
PO Box 91
Ed.—Gavin Whyte
GEELONG ADVERTISER (m-mon. to sat.) Est. 1840
191-197 Ryrie St.; PO Box 91, 3220
Tel: (61-52) 274300; Fax: (61-52) 274330
Circ.—30,625 ABC
Prop.—Geelong Advertiser (Pty.) Ltd.
Gen. Mgr.—Dale Jennings
Ed. in Ch.—Daryl McLure
Ed.—Graeme Vincent
Sales Mgr.—Bob MacKinnon
Ad.—$8.10 casual rate
GEELONG NEWS (d)
PO Box 91, 3220
Ed.—Gavin Whyte

GERALDTON
(Western Australia)
Pop. Est. 20,895

GERALDTON GUARDIAN (e-tues. to fri.) Est. 1906
PO Box 128, 6530
Tel: (61) 211795
Circ.—5,954
Prop.—Geraldton Newspapers Ltd.
Pub./Mgr.—V W O'Dea
Ed.—Tony Whitbread
Ad. Mgr.—Steve Boylan

GLADSTONE
(Queensland)
Pop. Est. 22,083

THE GLADSTONE OBSERVER (m-tues. to sat.) Est. 1868
27-29 Goondoon St.; PO Box 351, 4680
Tel: (61-79) 721022; Fax: (61-79) 723740
Circ.—7,512 ABC
Prop.—Gladstone Newspaper Co. (Pty.) Ltd.
Gen. Mgr.—Ken Steinke
Ad. Mgr.—Liz Rye
Ad.—$5.00 casual rate

GOULBURN
(New South Wales)
Pop. Est. 21,755

GOULBURN POST (m-mon. to sat.) Est. 1870
199 Auburn St.; PO Box 152, 2580
Tel: (61-48) 273500; Fax: (61-48) 221609
Circ.—4,181 ABC
Prop.—Western Newspapers Ltd.
Ed.—John Thistleton
Ad. Mgr.—Simon Green
Ad.—$7.60 casual rate

GRAFTON
(New South Wales)
Pop. Est. 17,005

THE DAILY EXAMINER (m-mon. to sat.) Est. 1859
81-83 Victoria St.; PO Box 271, 2460
Tel: (61-66) 421366; Fax: (61-66) 427156
Circ.—7,751 ABC
Prop.—The Daily Examiner (Pty.) Ltd.
Gen. Mgr.—Trevor Lee
Ed.—Robert Milne
Ad. Mgr.—Warren Lentfer
Ad.—$6.25 casual rate

GRIFFITH
(New South Wales)
Pop. Est. 13,187

THE AREA NEWS
Ulong St.; PO Box 1004, 2680
Tel: (61-69) 621733; Fax: (61-69) 625740
Circ.—3,545
Prop.—Riverina Newspapers Griffith (Pty.) Ltd.
Ed.—Chris Dobson
Ad. Mgr.—Max Roberts

GYMPIE
(Queensland)
Pop. Est. 10,768

THE GYMPIE TIMES (m-tues. to sat.) Est. 1868
197 Mary St., PO Box 394, 4570
Tel: (61-74) 821011; Fax: (61-74) 826969
Circ.—5,501 ABC
Prop.—The Gympie Times (Pty.) Ltd.
Mng. Ed.—Michael Roser
Ed.—Kev Pearce
Ad. Mgr.—Tracey McKean
Ad.—$6.70 casual rate

HOBART
(Tasmania)
Pop. Est. (Metro Area) 181,832

THE AUSTRALIAN (m-6x wk.) Est. 1964
49 Salamanca Place, Battery Point, 7000
Tel: (61-02) 238176; Fax: (61-02) 238861
Prop.—Nationwide News (Pty.) Ltd.
U.S. Rep.—Chris Barry; The Media Centre (Pty.) Ltd.
THE MERCURY (m-mon. to sat.) Est. 1854
91-93 Macquarie St., (7000); GPO Box 334D, 7001
Tel: (61-02) 300622; Fax: (61-02) 300711
Circ.—50,865 (mon.-fri.); 63,069 (sat.) ABC
Prop.—Davies Brothers Ltd.
Pub.—D R Flynn
Mng. Dir.—Rex Gardner
Ed.—Ian McCausland
Ad. Mgr.—Ken Ashlin
Ad. Mgr.—Eric Gordon
Ad. Mgr.—Gail Tubb
Ad.—$10.60 casual rate (mon.-fri.); $11.90 casual rate (sat.)
THE SUNDAY TASMANIAN (S) Est. 1984
91-93 Macquarie St., (7000); GPO Box 334D, 7001
Tel: (61-02) 300622; Fax: (61-02) 300711
Circ.—54,240 ABC
Prop.—Davies Brothers Ltd.
Mng. Dir.—Rex Gardner
Ed.—Ian McCausland
Ad. Mgr.—Rod Archer
Ad.—$9.55 casual rate

IPSWICH
(Queensland)
Pop. Est. 73,299

THE QUEENSLAND TIMES (m-mon. to sat.) Est. 1859
260 Brisbane St.; PO Box 260, 4305
Tel: (61-07) 2811300; Fax: (61-07) 2022790/(61-07) 2024922
Circ.—16,297 ABC
Prop.—The Queensland Times (Pty.) Ltd.
Ed.—Mark Hinchliffe
Ad. Mgr.—Don Hunt
Ad.—$7.65 casual rate

KALGOORLIE
(Western Australia)
Pop. Est. (Kalgoorlie-Boulder Area) 19,848

KALGOORLIE MINER (m-mon. to sat.) Est. 1895
127 Hannan St., PO Box 120, 6430
Tel: (61-90) 220555; Fax: (61-90) 218355
Circ.—8,049 ABC
Prop.—Hocking & Co. (Pty.) Ltd.
Pub.—R Booth
Mgr.—Jeffrey A Gibb
Ed.—Peter Jones
Ad.—$3.65 casual rate

LAUNCESTON
(Tasmania)
Pop. Est. 93,581

THE EXAMINER (mS) Est. 1842
71-75 Paterson St.; PO Box 99A, 7250
Tel: (61-03) 315111; Fax: (61-03) 347327
Circ.—37,873 ABC
Prop.—The Examiner Newspaper (Pty.) Ltd.
Ch. Ex.—Peter Cooper
Ed.—Rod Scott
Ad. Mgr.—Gilbert Sellars
Ad. Mgr.—Sally Roper
Ad. Mgr.—Ken Nichols
Ad.—$10.00 casual rate (mon.-fri.); $11.00 casual rate (sat.)
THE SUNDAY EXAMINER (S) Est. 1984
71-75 Paterson St.; PO Box 99A, 7250
Tel: (61-03) 315111; Fax: (61-03) 347327
Circ.—42,058 ABC
Prop.—Examiner Newspaper (Pty.) Ltd.
Ed.—Bruce Morgan
Ad. Mgr.—Gilbert Sellars
Ad. Mgr.—Ken Nichols
Ad. Mgr.—Sally Roper
Ad.—$10.00 casual rate

LEICHHARDT
(New South Wales)
(Municipality in suburban Sydney)
Pop. Est. (Municipality of Leichhardt) 58,484

GREEK HERALD (m-mon. to fri.)
1-9 Glebe Point Rd., (Broadway, 2037); PO Box 146, 2007
Circ.—23,328 ABC
Prop.—Foreign Language Publications (Pty.) Ltd.
Pub.—Theo Skalkos
Ed.—Michael Mystakidis

LISMORE
(New South Wales)
Pop. Est. 24,033

THE NORTHERN STAR (m-mon. to sat.) Est. 1876
83 Keen St.; PO Box 423, 2480
Circ.—20,968 ABC
Prop.—Northern Star Ltd.
Ed.—Richard Jones
Ad. Mgr.—Phil Calnan
Ad.—$7.55 casual rate

MACKAY
(Queensland)
Pop. Est. 53,934

THE DAILY MERCURY (m-mon. to sat.) Est. 1866
38-40 Wellington St., (4740), Mail Centre; PO Box 5666, 4741
Tel: (61-79) 570444; Fax: (61-79) 514007
Circ.—18,039 ABC
Prop.—The Mackay Printing & Publishing Co. (Pty.) Ltd.
Gen. Mgr.—Martin Simons
Ed.—Rod J Manning
Ad. Mgr.—Diana Stowes
Ad.—$7.55 casual rate

MAITLAND
(New South Wales)
Pop. Est. 38,865

MAITLAND MERCURY (e-mon. to fri.) Est. 1843
258 High St.; PO Box 222, 2320
Tel: (61-49) 336633; Fax: (61-49) 341334
Circ.—5,505 ABC
Prop.—Regional Publishers (Pty.) Ltd.
Mng. Ed.—Andrew Meenahan
Ad. Mgr.—Colin Merrick
Ad.—$7.45 casual rate

MAROOCHYDORE
(Queensland)
Pop. Est. (Maroochydore-Mooloolaba Area) 17,460

SUNSHINE COAST DAILY (m-mon. to sat.) Est. 1980
Dalton Dr.; PO Box 56, 4558
Tel: (61-74) 308000; Fax: (61-74) 435150
Circ.—21,186 ABC
Prop.—Sunshine Coast Newspaper Co. (Pty.) Ltd.
Ed.—Peter Owen
Ad. Mgr.—Murray Jones

MARYBOROUGH
(Queensland)
Pop. Est. 20,111

CHRONICLE (m-mon. to sat.) Est. 1860
131-135 Bazaar St.; PO Box 216, 4650
Tel: (61-71) 222222; Fax: (61-71) 224734
Circ.—9,186 ABC
Prop.—The Maryborough Newspaper Co. (Pty.) Ltd.
Gen. Mgr.—Terry Kirkland
Ed.—Nancy Bates
Ad. Mgr.—P Begley
Ad.—$7.82 casual rate

MELBOURNE
(Victoria)
Pop. Est. (Metro Area) 3,189,200

THE AGE (m-mon. to sat.) Est. 1854
250 Spencer St., (3000); GPO Box 257C, 3001
Tel: (61-3) 6004211; Fax: (61-3) 6707514
Circ.—204,948 (mon.-fri.); 361,204 (sat.) ABC
Prop.—David Syme & Co. Ltd.
Mng. Dir.—Stuart Simson
Ed.—Alan Kohler
Ad. Mgr.—Ray J Tebbutt
Ad. Mgr.—Tony Hatton
Ad.—$32.20 casual rate (mon.-fri.); $45.00 casual rate (sat.)
THE AUSTRALIAN (m-mon. to sat.) Est. 1964
26 Flinders St.,
Tel: (61-3) 6522888; Fax: (61-3) 2707070
Prop.—Nationwide News (Pty.) Ltd.
THE AUSTRALIAN CHINESE DAILY (mon. to sat.)
270a Russell St., 3000
Tel: (61-3) 6638046; Fax: (61-3) 6392645
Circ.—20,000
Prop.—Australian Chinese Newspaper (Pty.) Ltd.
Adm. Mgr.—Charles Ng
Ad.—$3.00 casual rate (mon.-fri.); $3.70 casual rate (sat.)
THE HERALD SUN (mon. to sat.) Est. 1840
44-74 Flinders St., (3000); GPO Box 751F, 3001
Tel: (61-3) 6521111; Fax: (61-3) 6522112
Circ.—568,945 (mon.-fri.); 529,341 (sat.) ABC
Prop.—The Herald & Weekly Times Ltd.
Mng. Dir.—Julian Clarke
Gen. Mgr.—Reg Cordina
Ed. in Ch.—Steve Harris
Ed.—Alan Oakley
Ad. Dir.—Ray Atkinson
Ad. Mgr.—Mark Elgood
Ad.—$70.50 casual rate (mon-fri.); $63.00 casual rate (sat.)
THE SUN NEWS-PICTORIAL (m-mon. to sat.) Est. 1922
44-74 Flinders St., 3000
Circ.—557,803
Prop.—The Herald & Weekly Times Ltd.
Ed.—Colin Duck
Ad. Mgr.—Ian Rose
SUNDAY AGE (S) Est. 1989
250 Spencer St., (3000); GPO Box 257C, 3001
Tel: (61-3) 6004211; Fax: (61-3) 6021856
Circ.—188,640
Prop.—David Syme & Co. Ltd.
Pub.—Stuart Simson
Ed.—Bruce Guthrie
Ad. Mgr.—Terry Plowman
Ad.—$24.50 casual rate
THE SUNDAY HERALD SUN (S)
44-74 Flinders St., (3000); PO Box 244B, 3001
Tel: (61-03) 6521111; Fax: (61-03) 6522080
Circ.—491,149 ABC
Prop.—The Herald & Weekly Times Ltd.
Ed.—Alan Howe
Ad.—$47.50 casual rate
SUNDAY OBSERVER (S) Est. 1971
45-50 Porter St., Prahran, 3181
Tel: (61-3) 525555
Circ.—91,545
Prop.—Peter Isaacson Publications (Pty.) Ltd.
Pub.—Leigh Garwood
Ed.—Jim Lawrence

MILDURA
(Victoria)
Pop. Est. 15,763

SUNRAYSIA DAILY (m-mon. to sat.) Est. 1920
22 Deakin Ave., (3500); PO Box 1400, 3502
Tel: (61-50) 230211; Fax: (61-50) 234817
Circ.—8,197 ABC
Prop.—Sunraysia Pub. Co. (Pty.) Ltd.
Pub.—W R Lanyon
Gen. Mgr.—Des Morris
Ed.—Kevin Boyle
Ad. Mgr.—Malcolm J Goodieson
Ad.—$4.55 casual rate

MOUNT GAMBIER
(South Australia)
Pop. Est. 19,880

BORDER WATCH (e-ex wed.) Est. 1861
81 Commercial St. E; PO Box 309, 5290
Tel: (61-87) 257333; Fax: (61-87) 258431
Circ.—8,164
Prop.—The Border Watch (Pty.) Ltd.
Pub.—G J Gilbertson
Gen. Mgr.—Gary Trotter
Ad. Mgr.—Pam Rogers
Ad.—$4.25 casual rate

MOUNT ISA
(Queensland)
Pop. Est. 23,679

THE NORTH WEST STAR (m-mon. to fri.) Est. 1966
112 Camooweal St.; PO Box 777, 4825
Tel: (61-77) 433355; Fax: (61-77) 432459
Circ.—4,183 ABC
Prop.—Carpentaria Newspapers (Pty.) Ltd.
Pub./Gen. Mgr.—Kel J Fairbairn
Ed.—Liz Corbett
Ad. Mgr.—Max Hardwicke
Ad.—$6.44 casual rate

MURWILLUMBAH
(New South Wales)
Pop. Est. 7,807
Gold Coast Metro Area
(Queensland/New South Wales)
Pop. Est. 219,200

DAILY NEWS (m-mon. to sat.)
13-17 Rivendell Estate, South Tweed Heads; PO Box 6336, 2486
Tel: (61-75) 246400; Fax: (61-75) 246333

Australia — South Pacific

Circ.—7,204 ABC
Prop.—Tweed Newspaper Co. (Pty.) Ltd.
Ed.—Steve Gibbons
Ad.—$4.95 casual rate

NEWCASTLE
(New South Wales)
Pop. Est. (Metro Area) 427,824

THE NEWCASTLE HERALD (m.-mon. to sat.) Est. 1858
28-30 Bolton St., 2300
Tel: (61-49) 263222
Circ.—50,972
Prop.—Newcastle Newspapers (Pty.) Ltd.
Ed.—Brad Pomfrett
Ad. Mgr.—Craig Andrew

NOWRA
(New South Wales)

SOUTH COAST (mon. to fri.)
122 Kinghorne St.; PO Box 106, 2541
Tel: (61-44) 212999; Fax: (61-44) 218160
Circ.—45,600
Prop.—South Coast Register (Pty.) Ltd.
Ed./Ad. Mgr.—John Rankin
Ad.—$5.45 casual rate

ORANGE
(New South Wales)
Pop. Est. 27,626

CENTRAL WESTERN DAILY (m.-mon. to sat.) Est. 1945
132 Kite St.; PO Box 321, 2800
Tel: (61-63) 912900; Fax: (61-63) 629679
Circ.—5,863 ABC
Prop.—Western Newspapers Ltd.
Gen. Mgr.—Jill Jiear
Ed.—Steve Gosch
Ad. Mgr.—Janine Melville
Ad.—$5.65 casual rate

PERTH
(Western Australia)
Pop. Est. (Metro Area) 1,143,249

THE AUSTRALIAN (m.-mon. to sat.) Est. 1964
34-42 Stirling St., 6000
Tel: (61-9) 3268297; Fax: (61-9) 3268370
Prop.—Nationwide News (Pty.) Ltd.
SUNDAY TIMES (S) Est. 1897
34 Stirling St., (6000); GPO Box D174, 6001
Tel: (61-9) 3268326; Fax: (61-9) 2211121
Circ.—345,672 ABC
Prop.—News Corp.
Pub.—Denis Thompson
Gen. Mgr.—Bill Repard
Mng. Ed.—Don Smith
Ad. Mgr.—Liz Molyneux
Ad.—$31.60 casual rate
THE WEST AUSTRALIAN (m.-mon. to sat.) Est. 1833
219 St. George's Terrace, (6000); GPO Box D162, 6001
Tel: (61-9) 4823111; Fax: (61-9) 3241416
Circ.—239,087 (mon.-fri.); 379,526 (sat.) ABC
Prop.—West Australian Newspapers Ltd.
Ed. in Ch.—Robert Cronin
Ed.—Paul Murray
Ad. Mgr.—Peter Stevens
Ad.—$22.80 casual rate (mon.-fri.); $31.50 casual rate (sat.)

ROCKHAMPTON
(Queensland)
Pop. Est. 62,797

THE MORNING BULLETIN (m.-mon. to sat.) Est. 1861
162-164 Quay St.; PO Box 397, 4700
Tel: (61-79) 304222; Fax: (61-79) 304360
Circ.—21,808 ABC
Prop.—Capricornia Newspapers (Pty.) Ltd.
Gen. Mgr.—Claude Olive
Ed.—Glenis Green
Ad. Mgr.—Ron Reedman
Ad.—$8.00 casual rate

SHEPPARTON
(Victoria)
Pop. Est. 25,820

THE SHEPPARTON NEWS (m.-mon. to fri.) Est. 1877
Melbourne Rd.; PO Box 204, 3630
Tel: (61-58) 312312; Fax: (61-58) 312059
Circ.—10,156 ABC
Prop.—Shepparton Newspapers (Pty.) Ltd.
Pub.—C R McPherson
Ed.—Robert McLean
Ad. Mgr.—Trevor Dainton
Ad.—$5.70 casual rate

SOUTHPORT
(Queensland)
Pop. Est. (City of Gold Coast) 116,540
(Gold Coast Metro Area)
(Queensland/New South Wales)
Pop. Est. 219,200

GOLD COAST BULLETIN (e.-mon. to sat.) Est. 1885
385 Nerang Rd., (Molendinar, 4214); PO Box 1, 4215
Tel: (61-75) 392522; Fax: (61-75) 393950
Circ.—38,411 ABC
Prop.—Gold Coast Publications (Pty.) Ltd.
Mng. Dir.—Ian L Jeffers
Gen. Mgr./Ad. Dir.—Neil Cooper
Mng. Ed.—Greg Chamberlin
Ed.—John Burton
Ad. Mgr.—Alan Flower
Ad.—$8.45 casual rate (mon.-fri.); $9.10 casual rate (sat.)

SYDNEY
(New South Wales)
Pop. Est. (Metro Area) 3,538,749

THE AUSTRALIAN (m.-mon. to sat.) Est. 1964
2 Holt St., (Surry Hills, 2010); PO Box 4245, 2001
Tel: (61-2) 2883000; Fax: (61-2) 2882370
Circ.—113,654 (mon.-fri.); 313,360 (sat.) ABC
Prop.—News Ltd.
Pub.—G Paton
Ed. in Ch.—Paul Kelly
Ed.—Chris Mitchell
Ad. Mgr.—Jerry Harris
Ad.—$29.90 casual rate (mon.-fri.); $56.00 casual rate (sat.)
AUSTRALIAN FINANCIAL REVIEW (m.-mon. to fri.) Est. 1951
235 Jones St., (Broadway, 2007); PO Box 506, 2001
Tel: (61-2) 2822822; Fax: (61-2) 2821640
Circ.—82,004 ABC
Prop.—John Fairfax Group
Pub.—Gerard Noonan
Mng. Ed.—Doreen Wildon
Ed. in Ch.—John Alexander
Ed.—Gregory Hywood
Ad. Mgr.—Peter Ryall
Ad.—$34.25 casual rate
CHINESE HERALD (mon. to sat.)
752 George St., Level 3, (Sydney, 2000); GPO Box K65, 2001
Tel: (61-2) 2812966; Fax: (61-2) 2818328
Circ.—20,000
Prop.—Chinese Herald (Pty.) Ltd.
Pub.—Roger Huang
Ch. Ed.—Raymond Deng
Ad. Mgr.—Almon Tong
DAILY COMMERCIAL NEWS (m.-mon. to fri.)
2 Elizabeth Plaza, Level 1, (2060); GPO Box 1552, 2001
Tel: (61-2) 2114055; Fax: (61-2) 2811763
Prop.—Peter Isaacson (Pty.) Ltd.
Pub.—Peter Ryall
Ed.—Dale Crisp
Adm. Mgr.—Shirley Fyander
Ad.—$11.90 casual rate
DAILY TELEGRAPH MIRROR (mon. to sat.) Est. 1879
2 Holt St., (Surry Hills, 2010); GPO Box 4245, 2001
Tel: (61-2) 2883000; Fax: (61-2) 2882300
Circ.—445,022 (mon.-fri.); 331,666 (sat.) ABC
Prop.—Nationwide News (Pty.) Ltd.
Ed. in Ch.—John Hartigan
Ed.—Colin Allan
Ad. Dir.—Peter Miller
Ad. Mgr.—Martin O'Loughlin
Ad.—$59.28 casual rate (mon.-fri.); $48.03 casual rate (sat.)
THE INDEPENDENCE DAILY (mon. to sat.)
141 Broadway, 2007
Tel: (61-2) 2114611; Fax: (61-2) 2122451
Circ.—15,000
Prop.—The Independence Daily (Pty.) Ltd.
Ed.—Mr. Yuan-hui Hu
Ad. Mgr.—Michael Pun
Ad.—$6.00 casual rate
THE MANLY DAILY (tues. to sat.)
26 Sydney Rd., (Manly, 2095); PO Box 286, 2095
Tel: (61-2) 9773333; Fax: (61-2) 9772831
Circ.—87,000 CAB
Prop.—Cumberland Newspaper Group
Ad. Mgr.—Jennifer Skokeld
Ad.—$9.65 casual rate
SING TAO JIH PAO (mon. to sat.) Chinese
545 Kent St., Level 1; PO Box K351, 2000
Tel: (61-2) 2642273; Fax: (61-2) 2671474
Circ.—25,000 (mon.-fri.); 28,000 (sat.)
Prop.—Sing Tao Newspapers (Pty.) Ltd.
Dir.—Sally Aw Sian
Dir.—Gordon Channing
Ed.—Patrick Poon
Ad. Mgr.—Sukkie Lau
THE SUN HERALD (S) Est. 1953
201 Sussex St., Level 24, (2000); GPO Box 506, 2001
Tel: (61-2) 2822822; Fax: (61-2) 2821640
Circ.—571,525 ABC
Prop.—John Fairfax Group (Pty.) Ltd.
Pub.—Peter Gaunt
Mng. Dir.—Doreen Wilson
Ed.—Andrew Clark
Ad. Mgr.—Paul Ryan
Ad.—$68.90 casual rate
SUNDAY TELEGRAPH (S) Est. 1939
2 Holt St., (Surry Hills, 2010); GPO Box 4245, 2001
Tel: (61-2) 2883000; Fax: (61-2) 2882300
Circ.—663,502 ABC
Prop.—News (Pty.) Ltd.
Mng. Dir.—Ken Cowley
Gen. Mgr.—Malcolm Noad
Ed. in Ch.—John Hartigan
Ed.—Roy Miller
Ad. Dir.—Peter Miller
Ad. Mgr.—Martin O'Loughlin
Ad.—$75.00 casual rate
THE SYDNEY MORNING HERALD (m.-mon. to sat.) Est. 1831
235 Jones St., (Broadway, 2007); PO Box 506, 2001
Tel: (61-2) 2822822; Fax: (61-2) 2821640
Circ.—254,290 (mon.-fri.); 385,669 (sat.) ABC
Prop.—John Fairfax Group (Pty.) Ltd.
Pub.—Peter Gaunt
Mng. Dir.—Doreen Wilson
Ed. in Ch.—John Alexander
Ad./Sales Mgr.—Denis Ford
Ad.—$45.00 casual rate (mon.-fri.); $54.40 casual rate (sat.)

TAMWORTH
(New South Wales)
Pop. Est. 29,657

THE NORTHERN DAILY LEADER (m.-mon. to sat.) Est. 1872
92 Brisbane St.; PO Box 525, 2340
Tel: (61-67) 667294; Fax: (61-67) 667631
Circ.—10,453 ABC
Prop.—Regional Publishers (Pty.) Ltd.
Ed.—Graham Fuller
Ad. Mgr.—Barry Harley
Ad.—$7.70 casual rate

TOOWOOMBA
(Queensland)
Pop. Est. 81,043

THE CHRONICLE (m.-mon. to fri.) Est. 1861
618 Ruthven St.; PO Box 40, 4350
Tel: (61-76) 909300; Fax: (61-76) 909302
Circ.—30,632 ABC
Prop.—Toowoomba Newspapers (Pty.) Ltd.
Pub.—B Manning
Ed.—Bruce Hinchliffe
Ad. Mgr.—Mark Jamieson
Ad.—$8.25 casual rate

TOWNSVILLE
(Queensland)
Pop. Est. (Metro Area) 101,398

TOWNSVILLE BULLETIN (m.-mon. to sat.) Est. 1881
198-238 Ogden St.; PO Box 587, 4810
Tel: (61-77) 224400; Fax: (61-77) 211410
Circ.—26,086 ABC
Prop.—The North Queensland Newspaper Co. Ltd.
Pub.—J E Hogan
Ed.—Warwick Wockner
Ad. Mgr.—Tony Yianni
Ad.—$7.05 casual rate

WAGGA WAGGA
(New South Wales)
Pop. Est. 53,447

THE DAILY ADVERTISER (m.-mon. to sat.) Est. 1868
48 Trail St.; PO Box 35, 2650
Tel: (61) 69212021; Fax: (61) 69216950
Circ.—14,406
Prop.—The Wagga Daily Advertiser (Pty.) Ltd.
Pub.—J C Jackson
Ed.—Graham Gorrel
Ad. Mgr.—Peter McAlister

WARRNAMBOOL
(Victoria)
Pop. Est. 32,398

THE STANDARD (m.-mon. to sat.) Est. 1872
170-176 Koroit St.; PO Box 419, 3280
Tel: (61-55) 614000;. Fax: (61-55) 620389
Circ.—13,234 ABC
Prop.—The Warrnambool Standard (Pty.) Ltd.
Pub.—Cheryl Fleming
Mng. Ed.—Ted Cavey
Ed.—Ian Pech
Ad. Mgr.—Geoff Rollinson
Ad. Mgr.—Wayne Cashion
Ad.—$5.70 casual rate

WARWICK
(Queensland)
Pop. Est. 8,853

DAILY NEWS (m.-mon. to sat.) Est. 1864
50 Albion St.; PO Box 358, 4370
Tel: (61-76) 619191
Circ.—5,456 ABC
Prop.—The Warwick Newspaper (Pty.) Ltd.
Gen. Mgr.—James Irwin
Ed.—Donna Lomas
Ad. Mgr.—Andrew Smith
Ad.—$6.95 casual rate

WOLLONGONG
(New South Wales)
Pop. Est. (Metro Area) 235,966

ILLAWARRA MERCURY (m.-mon. to sat.) Est. 1855
282 Keira St.; PO Box 1215, 2500
Tel: (61-42) 212333; Fax: (61-42) 297899
Circ.—35,474 ABC
Prop.—Illawarra Newspapers Holdings (Pty.) Ltd.
Ed.—Peter Cullen
Ad. Mgr.—Allan Parks
Mktg. Mgr.—Glenys Holby
Ad.—$3.69 casual rate

NEW ZEALAND
Pop. Est. 3,388,737

ASHBURTON
Pop. Est. 15,172

ASHBURTON GUARDIAN (e) Est. 1880
PO Box 77
Circ.—6,360
Prop.—Ashburton Guardian Co.
Pub.—J M Bell
Ed.—Sue Newman
Ad. Mgr.—Nancye Pitt

AUCKLAND CITY
Pop. Est. 855,571

AUCKLAND CITY HARBOUR NEWS
St. Luke's; Private Bag 41906
Ed.—Isabell Speck
BAYS AND REMUERA TIMES
Howick; PO Box 38-189
Tel: (64-9) 5346889; Fax: (64-9) 5354123
Ed.—Barbara Weil
CENTRAL LEADER
St. Luke's; Private Bag 41906
Ed.—Isabell Speck
DRIVETIMES
Symonds St.; PO Box 8970
Ed.—Ray Willmott
EAST AND BAYS COURIER
Penrose; Private Bag 92815
Tel: (64-9) 5251133; Fax: (64-9) 5276628
Ed.—Laura Basham
EASTERN COURIER
Howick; PO Box 38-312
Ed.—Duncan Pardon
FLASH
PO Box 1327
Ed.—Bob Lovett
FRANKLIN COUNTY NEWS
Pukekohe; PO Box 14
Tel: (64-9) 2384179; Fax: (64-9) 2389744
Ed.—Rex Warwood
HOWICK AND PAKURANGA
Howick; PO Box 38-189
Tel: (64-9) 5346889; Fax: (64-9) 5354123
Ed.—Mike Smith
MANUKAU COURIER
PO Box 76-400
Ed.—Peter Tiffany
NATIONAL BUSINESS REVIEW (5x wk.)
PO Box 1734
Tel: (64-9) 3071629; Fax: (64-9) 3097879
Circ.—12,565 ABC
Prop.—Fourth Estate Holdings Ltd.
Pub.—Barry Coleman

Ed.—Frances O'Sullivan
Ad. Mgr.—Cushla Martini
U.S. Rep.—Marston Webb & Associates
THE NEW ZEALAND HERALD (m) Est. 1863
PO Box 32
Tel: (64-9) 3070646; Fax: (64-9) 3795050
Circ.—248,430
Prop.—Wilson & Hortan Ltd.
Pub.—H M Horton
Ed.—Peter J Scherer
Ad. Mgr.—Noel Townsend
U.S. Rep.—Publicitas
THE NEW ZEALAND LISTENER
PO Box 7
Circ.—210,216
Ed.—Geoff Baylis
NORTH HARBOUR NEWS
Albany; PO Box 494
Tel: (64-9) 4157430; Fax: (64-9) 4157431
Ed.—Elizabeth Mahoney
NORWEST NEWSBRIEF
Kumeu; PO Box 46
Tel: (64-9) 4128589; Fax: (64-9) 4127806
Ed.—Geoff Dobson
PAPAKURA COURIER
PO Box 76-400
Ed.—Peter Tiffany
SUNDAY NEWS (S)
Auckland; PO Box 1327
Tel: (64-9) 3797626/(64-9) 3660095
Circ.—135,229 ABC
Prop.—News Media
Pub.—Wayne Rolls
Ed.—Suzanne Chetwin
SUNDAY STAR TIMES (e)
Auckland; PO Box 1409
Tel: (64-9) 3797626; Fax: (64-9) 3660095
Circ.—187,277 ABC
Ed.—Michael Prain
Ad. Mgr.—Maggie Maxwell
U.S. Rep.—Lee & Steel Inc.
WESTERN LEADER
PO Box 21-167
Ed.—Wally Thomas

BLENHEIM
Pop. Est. 23,800

MARLBOROUGH EXPRESS (e-5x wk.) Est. 1866
PO Box 242
Circ.—10,327
Prop.—Marlborough Express Newspaper Co.
Pub.—R G Rose
Ed.—Reg Spowart
Ad. Mgr.—Grant Davidson

CHRISTCHURCH CITY
Pop. Est. 307,179

THE PRESS (m-ex mon.) Est. 1861
Private Bag 4722
Tel: (64-3) 790940; Fax: (64-3) 791531
Circ.—102,200 ABC
Prop.—Christchurch Press Co. Ltd.
Pub.—R A Barker
Ed.—David Wilson
Ad. Mgr.—M D Pope
THE STAR (e) Est. 1868
PO Box 1467
Tel: (64-3) 3797100; Fax: (64-3) 3660180
Circ.—121,213
Prop.—Wilson & Hortan Ltd.
Pub./Ed.—M Fletcher
Ad. Mgr.—Paul Yaxley

DANNEVIRKE
Pop. Est. 5,900

EVENING NEWS (e) Est. 1909
PO Box 92
Circ.—2,800
Prop.—Dannevirke Publishing Co.
Pub.—Carl Grant
Ed.—Sue Emeny
Ad. Mgr.—John Schluze

DARGAVILLE
Pop. Est. 4,880

NORTHLAND TIMES (e) Est. 1905
PO Box 96
Circ.—3,040
Prop.—North Auckland Times Co. Ltd.
Pub.—R Maxed
Ed.—Colin Johnson
Ad. Mgr.—Sue Maxed

DUNEDIN CITY
Pop. Est. 116,577

DUNEDIN STAR WEEKENDER (S)
PO Box 517
Circ.—43,000
Ed.—Richard Stedman
THE NEW ZEALAND TABLET
PO Box 1285
Circ.—8,495
Ed.—Kevin Molloy

OTAGO DAILY TIMES (m) Est. 1861
PO Box 181
Tel: (64-3) 4774760; Fax: (64-3) 4771313
Circ.—50,260
Prop.—Allied Press Ltd.
Pub.—J C S Smith
Ed.—Geoff Adams
Ad. Mgr.—Peter Braam

GISBORNE CITY
Pop. Est. 31,400

GISBORNE HERALD (e) Est. 1874
PO Box 1143
Circ.—10,006
Prop.—Gisborne Herald Co. Ltd.
Pub.—M C Muir
Ed.—Iain Gillies
Ad. Mgr.—S Lawrence

GORE
Pop. Est. 11,000

THE ENSIGN (e) Est. 1878
PO Box 182
Circ.—3,171
Prop.—The Gore Publication Co. Ltd.
Pub./Ed.—W Kornet
Ad. Mgr.—Graham Avery

GREYMOUTH
Pop. Est. 10,500

THE GREYMOUTH EVENING STAR (e) Est. 1866
PO Box 3
Circ.—5,663
Prop.—Greymouth Evening Star Co.
Pub.—A W Negri
Ed.—Frank A Neate
Ad. Mgr.—T Dixon

HAMILTON CITY
Pop. Est. 148,625

WAIKATO TIMES (e) Est. 1872
Private Bag 3086
Tel: (64-7) 8496180; Fax: (64-7) 8499554
Circ.—40,774
Prop.—Independent Newspapers Ltd.
Pub.—Peter Henson
Ed.—Tim Parkhurst
Ad. Mgr.—Delwyn Knight

HASTINGS CITY
Pop. Est. 57,748

HAWKE'S BAY HERALD-TRIBUNE (e) Est. 1857
PO Box 180
Tel: (64-6) 8785155; Fax: (64-6) 8785668
Circ.—20,773
Prop.—Wilson & Hortan Ltd.
Pub.—Ron Hall
Ed.—James Morgan
Ad. Mgr.—Max Bothefway

HAWERA
Pop. Est. 11,200

HAWERA STAR (e)
PO Box 428
Circ.—13,452
Ed.—Mary Davis

INVERCARGILL CITY
Pop. Est. 56,148

THE MIRROR
PO Box 805
Ed.—Catherine Ladbrook
NEWSLINK
PO Box 805
Ed.—Catherine Ladbrook
SOUTHLAND TIMES (m) Est. 1862
PO Box 805
Tel: (64-3) 2181909; Fax: (64-3) 2149905
Circ.—32,974
Prop.—Independent Newspapers Ltd.
Pub.—Robin Watson
Ed.—Clive A Lind
Ad. Mgr.—A Bob Wills

KAIKOHE

THE NEWS
PO Box 1
Ed.—Mike Barrington

LEVIN
Pop. Est. 19,050

THE CHRONICLE (e)
PO Box 547
Circ.—6,463
Prop.—Kerslake, Billens & Humphrey Ltd.
Pub.—M H McCaul
Ed.—Dave Sounders
Ad. Mgr.—Cliff MacKay

South Pacific **New Zealand** IV-123

LOWER HUTT
Pop. Est. 94,540

HUTT NEWS
Lower Hutt; PO Box 30-029
Tel: (64-4) 5663125; Fax: (64-4) 5665485
Prop.—Independent Newspapers Ltd.
Pub.—Trevor Howes
Ed.—Simon Edwards
KAPI MANA NEWS/NORWESTER
Porirua; PO Box 50-012
Tel: (64-4) 2378118; Fax: (64-4) 2378552
Ed.—R Olsen
KAPITI NEWSPAPER
Paraparaumu; PO Box 110
Tel: (64-4) 2972996; Fax: (64-4) 2982073
Ed.—Richard Woodd
UPPER HUTT LEADER
Upper Hutt; PO Box 40-001
Tel: (64-4) 5289654; Fax: (64-4) 5283021
Ed.—Rosemary McLennan
WAIRARAPA NEWS
Carterton; PO Box 18
Tel: (64-6) 3798039; Fax: (64-6) 3796481
Ed.—Colin Wheeler

MASTERTON
Pop. Est. 20,100

WAIRARAPA TIMES-AGE (e) Est. 1938
PO Box 445
Circ.—9,197
Prop.—Wairarapa Times-Age Newspaper Co. Ltd.
Pub.—T Mck Kerse
Ed.—Andrew G Wyatt
Ad. Mgr.—Matthew Sherry

MORRINSVILLE

PIAKO POST
Morrinsville; PO Box 125
Tel: (64-7) 8897099; Fax: (64-7) 8896572
Ed.—Ian Harrop

NAPIER CITY
Pop. Est. 51,645

DAILY TELEGRAPH (e) Est. 1871
PO Box 343
Tel: (64-6) 8354488; Fax: (64-6) 8351129
Prop.—Wilson & Hortan Ltd.
Pub.—J Silvester
Ed.—Ken Hawker
Ad. Mgr.—G D Gardiner

NELSON CITY
Pop. Est. 47,800

NELSON EVENING MAIL (e) Est. 1866
PO Box 244
Tel: (64-3) 5487079; Fax: (64-3) 5462802
Circ.—19,549
Prop.—Independent Newspapers Ltd.
Pub.—Nigel Watt
Ed.—David Mitchell
Ad. Mgr.—Bernie Milroy

NEW PLYMOUTH CITY
Pop. Est. 48,200

THE DAILY NEWS (m) Est. 1857
PO Box 444
Tel: (64-6) 580559; Fax: (64-6) 586849
Circ.—29,451
Prop.—Independent Newspapers Ltd.
Ed.—Murray Goston
Ad. Mgr.—R Pryce
NORTH TARANAKI MIDWEEK/WEEKENDER
PO Box 444
Ed.—Carol Lucas

OAMARU
Pop. Est. 13,750

OAMARU MAIL (e)
PO Box 343
Circ.—3,811
Prop.—Wilson & Hortan Ltd.
Pub.—Rod Bidois
Ed.—Roni Lauren
Ad. Mgr.—Kathy Hobbs

PALMERSTON NORTH CITY
Pop. Est. 70,951

THE EVENING STANDARD (e) Est. 1880
PO Box 3
Tel: (64-6) 3569009
Circ.—25,855

Prop.—Independent Newspapers Ltd.
Pub.—Adrian Broad
Ed.—John R Harvey
Ad. Mgr.—Dan Kilkelly
FIELDING HERALD
PO Box 3
Ed.—Ann Kilduff
MANAWATU HERALD
PO Box 3
Ed.—Ann Kilduff
RANGITIKEI MAIL
PO Box 3
Ed.—Ann Kilduff
THE TRIBUNE
PO Box 3
Ed.—Ann Kilduff

PUKEKOHE

PUKEKOHE WEEKEND
PO Box 14
Tel: (64-9) 2384179; Fax: (64-9) 2389744
Ed.—H Danes

ROTORUA
Pop. Est. 53,702

DAILY POST (e) Est. 1886
PO Box 1442
Tel: (64-7) 3486199; Fax: (64-7) 3460153
Circ.—13,399
Prop.—Wilson & Hortan Ltd.
Pub.—R F Smith
Ed.—Robin Mayston
Ad. Mgr.—W Jones
ROTORUA REVIEW
PO Box 2344
Ed.—Rod Hall
RURAL REVIEW
PO Box 2344
Ed.—Rod Hall

TAUPO

TAUPO TIMES
PO Box 205
Tel: (64-7) 3789060; Fax: (64-7) 3780247
Ed.—Helen Faville

TAURANGA CITY
Pop. Est. 70,803

BAY OF PLENTY TIMES (e) Est. 1872
Tel: (64-7) 5783059; Fax: (64-7) 5780047
Circ.—20,658
Pub.—W Pomona
Ed.—Glen Pettit
Ad. Mgr.—P G Cooper
HAURAKI HERALD
Thames; PO Box 363
Ed.—Eric Toplis

TE PUKE

TE PUKE TIMES
PO Box 260
Tel: (64-7) 5737078; Fax: (64-7) 5736012
Ed.—John McMenamin

TIMARU CITY
Pop. Est. 27,100

TIMARU HERALD (m) Est. 1864
PO Box 46
Tel: (64-3) 6844129; Fax: (64-3) 6881024
Circ.—15,254
Prop.—Independent Newspapers Ltd.
Pub.—Chris Jagusch
Ed.—Barry Appleby
Ad. Mgr.—N Taylor

TOKOROA

SOUTH WAIKATO NEWS
Tokoroa; PO Box 89
Tel: (64-7) 8869159; Fax: (64-7) 8865347
Ed.—Allan Winter

WANGANUI CITY
Pop. Est. 41,400

WANGANUI CHRONICLE (m) Est. 1856
PO Box 433
Tel: (64-6) 3453919; Fax: (64-6) 3453232
Circ.—15,861
Prop.—Wison & Hortan Ltd.
Pub.—R A Jardan
Ed.—Jim McLees
Ad. Mgr.—Mike Moughan

IV-124   New Zealand   South Pacific

WELLINGTON CITY
Pop. Est. 375,000

CONTACT
PO Box 3740
Ed.—Judy Bradwell
THE DOMINION (m-ex S) Est. 1907
PO Box 3740
Tel: (64-4) 4740222; Fax: (64-4) 4740490
Circ.—66,987 ABC
Prop.—Independent Newspapers Ltd.
Ed.—Richard Long
Ad. Mgr.—Ty Dallas
EVENING POST (e) Est. 1865
PO Box 3740
Tel: (64-4) 4740222; Fax: (64-4) 4740490/
(64-4) 4740237
Circ.—72,710
Prop.—Independent Newspapers Ltd.
Ed.—S L Carty
Ad. Mgr.—Ty Dallas

WESTPORT
Pop. Est. 4,660

THE WESTPORT NEWS (e-ex sat.)
PO Box 249
Circ.—2,375
Prop.—Westport News Ltd.

Ed.—Colin Warren
Ad. Mgr.—Norma Smith

WHANGAREI CITY
Pop. Est. 44,183

NORTHERN ADVOCATE (e)
PO Box 210
Tel: (64-9) 4382399; Fax: (64-9) 4381673
Circ.—16,654
Prop.—Northern Publishing Co.
Pub.—W K Crawford
Ed.—Graeme Barrow
Ad. Mgr.—K H Crawford

NEWSPAPERS OF THE PACIFIC OCEAN TERRITORIES

AMERICAN SAMOA
Pop. Est. 55,223

PAGO PAGO
Pop. Est. 10,000

SAMOA JOURNAL & ADVERTISER English & Samoan; Est. 1983
PO Box 3986
Circ.—2,000
Pub./Ad. Mgr.—Rowena King
SAMOA NEWS (5x wk.) English & Samoan; Est. 1965
PO Box 909
Circ.—2,800
Pub./Ed.—Lewis Wolman
Ad. Mgr.—Patty Page

COOK ISLANDS
(Dependency of New Zealand)
Pop. Est. 19,124

RAROTONGA ISLAND
Pop. Est. 9,678

COOK ISLANDS DAILY NEWS (m-6x wk.) English & Maori; Est. 1944
PO Box 126
Circ.—2,000
Prop.—Cook Islands Broadcasting & Newspaper Corp.
Pub.—Arthur Taripo
Ed.—Alexander Sword

FIJI, REPUBLIC OF
Pop. Est. 764,382

SUVA
Pop. Est. 69,000

FIJI TIMES (m-ex S) English; Est. 1869
177 Victoria Parade; PO Box 1167
Tel: (679) 304111; Fax: (679) 302633
Circ.—40,000
Prop.—Pacifique Press Communications
Owner—Rupert Murdoch
Pub.—Brian O'Flaherty
Ed. in Ch.—Vijendra Kumar
Ed.—Jale Moala
Ad. Mgr.—Lionel Heffernan

FRENCH POLYNESIA
(Includes Moorea & Tahiti)
Pop. Est. 215,129

PAPEETE
Pop. Est. 30,000

LA DEPECHE DE TAHITI (d) French; Est. 1964
Boite Postal 50
Tel: (689) 424343
Circ.—15,000
Prop.—Societe Oceanienne de Communication
Pub.—Phillippe Mazellier
Mng. Ed.—Michel Anglade

LE JOURNAL DE TAHITI (d) French
Boite Postal 6000
LES NOUVELLES DE TAHITI (d) French; Est. 1960
Boite Postal 629 & 1767
Tel: (689) 429556
Circ.—5,000
Mng. Ed.—Louis Bresson
TAHITI BULLETIN (d) English & French
Boite Postal 912

GUAM
Pop. Est. 149,620

AGANA
Pop. Est. 135,000

PACIFIC DAILY NEWS/SUNDAY NEWS (mS) Est. 1970
PO Box DN, 96910
Tel: (671) 4779711/(671) 4770359
Circ.—28,000 (m); 25,000 (S)
Prop.—Gannett Publications
Pub.—Lee P Webber
Mng. Ed.—Margaret Sizemore
Ad. Dir.—David Schajatovic
U.S. Rep.—Gannett Nat'l. Newspaper

MARSHALL ISLANDS
(Independent Republic)
Pop. Est. 54,031

MAJURO
Pop. Est. 24,000

THE MARSHALL ISLANDS GAZETTE English & Marshallese
PO Box 2, 96960
Prop.—Ministry of Foreign Affairs
THE MARSHALL ISLANDS JOURNAL English & Marshallese; Est. 1970
PO Box 14, 96960
Circ.—10,000
Prop.—Micronitor News & Printing Co.
Pub.—Joe Murphy
Ed.—Giff Johnson
Ad. Mgr.—Brit Schellhase

NEW CALEDONIA
Pop. Est. 181,309

NOUMEA
Pop. Est. 60,112

LA FRANCE AUSTRALE (d)
5 rue de la Somme; Boite Postal 25
Tel: (687) 274444
LES NOUVELLES CALEDONIENNES (d) French; Est. 1917
41-43 Blvd. de Sebastopol; Boite Postal 179
Tel: (687) 272584; Fax: (687) 281627
Circ.—18,000
Pub.—Jean-Henri Morni
Ed. in Ch.—Henri Perron
LA PRESSE CALEDONIENNE (d)
14, rue Sebastopol; Boite Postal 4034
Tel: (687) 285055

NIUE
(Dependency of New Zealand)
Pop. Est. 1,906

ALOFI

TOHI TALA NIUE Niuean & English
PO Box 67
Prop.—Media Services
Prop.—Niue Office of Community Affairs
Sub. Ed.—Patrick Lino

NORFOLK ISLAND
(Dependency of Australia)
Pop. Est. 2,710

THE NORFOLK ISLANDER English; Est. 1965
Greenways Press; PO Box 150
Circ.—1,200
Owner/Ed.—Tim Lloyd
Owner/Ed./Pub./Ad. Mgr.—Tom Lloyd

NORTHERN MARIANA ISLANDS
(U.S. Commonwealth)
Pop. Est. 49,799

SAIPAN ISLAND
Pop. Est. 14,585

THE MARIANAS REVIEW English; Est. 1985
PO Box 1074, MP 96950
Circ.—2,000
Owner/Pub.—Luis C Benavente
Ed.—Ruth L Tighe

PAPUA NEW GUINEA
Pop. Est. 4,196,806

BOROKO

NIUGINI NIUS & WEEKENDER (5x wk.) Est. 1979
PO Box 1982
Circ.—31,000
Ed.—Sinclaire Solomon

PORT MORESBY
Pop. Est. (Metro Area) 200,000

PAPUA NEW GUINEA POST-COURIER (m)
English; Est. 1969
PO Box 85
Tel: (675) 212577
Circ.—33,960
Prop.—The Herald & Weekly Times Co. of Australia
Ed.—Luke Sela
Ad. Mgr.—K Head

SOLOMON ISLANDS
Pop. Est. 385,811

HONIARA
(Guadalcanal)
Pop. Est. 30,000

SOLOMON NIUS English; Est. 1987
PO Box 718
Circ.—3,000
Prop.—Government Information Service
Ed.—William Houmac-Lome
SOLOMONS STAR English; Est. 1982
PO Box 255
Tel: (677) 22913
Circ.—3,000
Prop.—Solomon Star Ltd.
Ed.—John Lamani
SOLOMONS VOICE English; Est. 1977
PO Box 599
Circ.—3,000
Prop.—Solomons Voice
Ed.—John Asipara

TONGA
Pop. Est. 104,778

NUKU'ALOFA
Pop. Est. 29,000

TONGA CHRONICLE (d) English & Tongan; Est. 1964
PO Box 197
Tel: (676) 21300
Circ.—7,000
Prop.—Gov't of Tongan
Ed.—Paua Manuatu

TUVALU
Pop. Est. 9,831

FUNAFUTI
Pop. Est. 2,500

TUVALU ECHOES English; Est. 1984
Broadcasting & Information Office of Tuvalu
Circ.—250
Prop.—Broadcasting & Information Office of Tuvalu
Ed.—Ms. Vaiatoa Uale

VANUATU, REPUBLIC OF
Pop. Est. 169,776

PORT VILA
Pop. Est. 23,600

TAM TAM
PO Box 637
Ch. Ed./Ad. Dir.—Marc Lowen
VANUASCOPE
PO Box 711
Circ.—1,500
Ch. Ed./Ad. Dir.—Patrick Decloitre
VANUATU WEEKLY Bislama, English & French; Est. 1980
Private Bag 049; PO Box 927
Tel: (678) 2999
Circ.—2,500
Prop.—Vanuatu Information Dept.
Ch. Ed./Ad. Dir.—Kaltan Ayong

Copyright ©1996 by the Editor & Publisher Co.

SECTION V

News, Picture and Syndicate Services

News, picture and syndicate services 1-11
Comic section groups and networks 12-13
Newspaper distributed magazine sections 13-16
Syndicated TMC publications 16

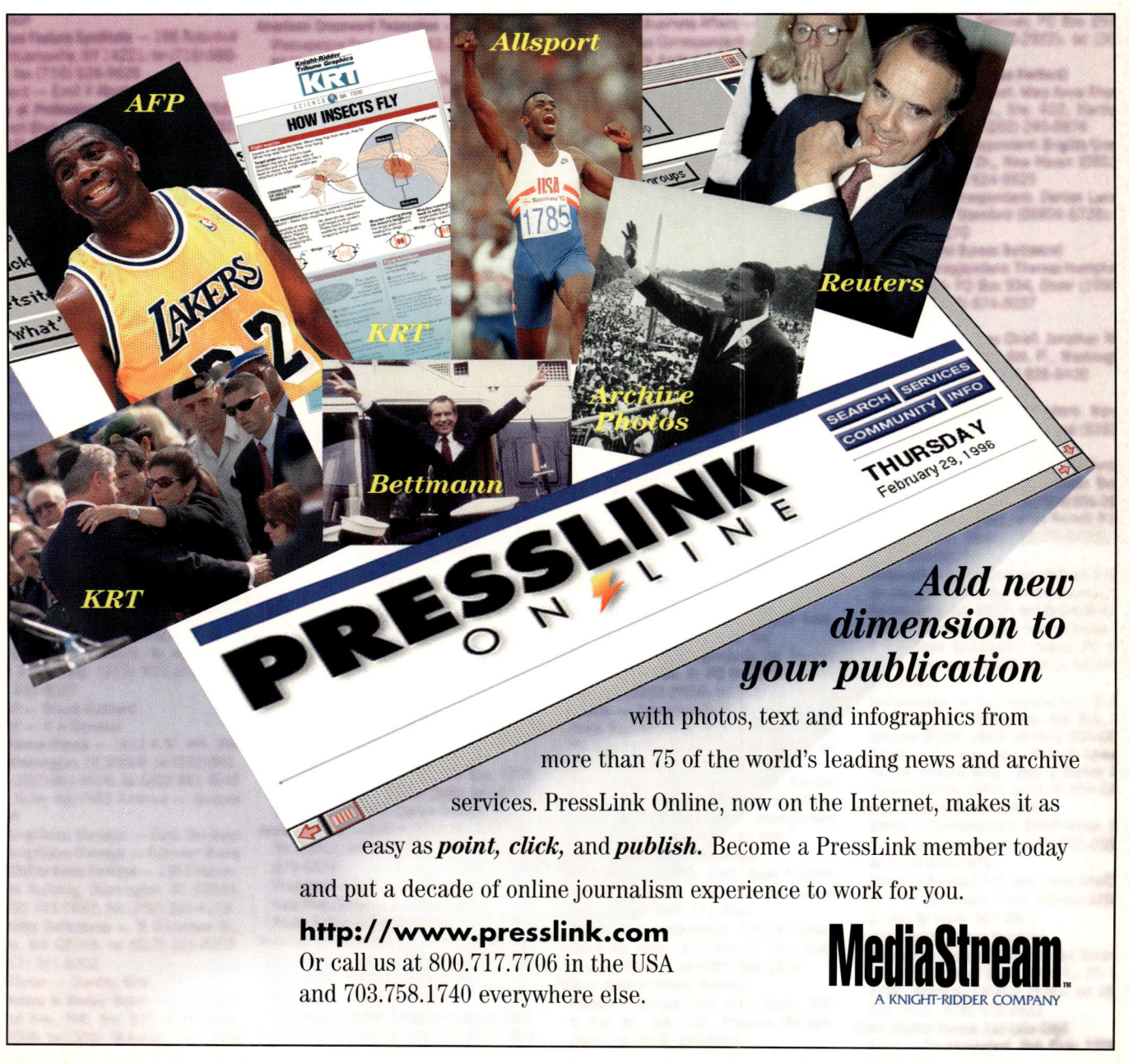

NEWS, PICTURE & SYNDICATE SERVICES

A

A & A — PO Box 330008, Ft. Worth, TX 76163-0008; tel (817) 292-1855; fax (817) 292-1855
President — Elaine Sandra Abramson
Senior Vice President — Stan Abramson
VP/Marketing & Sales — Mitchell Lee
VP/Special Projects — Deborah Abramson

Abrahamian Feature Syndicate — 198 Robinhill Dr., Williamsville, NY 14221; tel (716) 688-0902; fax (716) 689-3030
President — Emil V. Abrahamian

Academy of Professional Umpiring — 12885 Research Blvd., Ste. 107, Austin, TX 78750; tel (512) 335-5959; fax (512) 335-5411
Self-Syndicated — Jim Evans

AccuWeather Inc. — 619 W. College Ave., State College, PA 16801; tel (814) 234-9601 ext. 400; fax (814) 238-1339
President — Dr. Joel N. Myers
Exec. Vice President — Barry Lee Myers
Sr. Vice President — Elliot Abrams
Sr. Vice President — Joseph P. Sobel
Sr. Vice President — Evan A. Myers
Sr. Vice President — Michael A. Steinberg
Dir. of Sales — Sheldon Levine
Mgr. of Sales & Marketing — Andrew Hoover

Acme Features Syndicate — 147 N.E. Yamhill, Sheridan, OR 97378; tel (503) 843-4555; fax (503) 843-4001
Exec. Dir./Editorial Dir. — Sondra Gatewood

Adventure Feature Syndicate — 329 Harvey Dr., Ste. 400, Glendale, CA 91206; tel (818) 551-0077; fax (818) 551-0077
Managing Editor — William H. Barry
Business Manager — D.J. Chamberlain

Advertising Workshop — College of Communications, 111 Carnegie Bldg., Penn State University, University Park, PA 16802; tel (814) 865-6597; fax (814) 863-8044
Self-Syndicated — Jim Avery

Advisor Group, The — 86 Colonial Rd., Grosse Pointe Shores, MI 48236; tel (313) 882-8641; fax (313) 882-8641
Contact — Bruce Hubbard
Contact — Holly A. Olmsted

Africa Information Afrique — 777 United Nations Plz., New York, NY 10017; tel (212) 286-0123; fax (212) 818-9249; e-mail ipsgin@igc.apc.org
Director — Lisa Vives

Agence France-Presse — 1015 15th St. NW, Ste. 500, Washington, DC 20005; tel (202) 414-0535/(202) 414-0536; fax (202) 414-0634
Marketing/Sales Manager — Carol DeHaven
Marketing/Sales Manager — Kathleen Burke

Agencia Efe/Efe News Services — 1262 National Press Bldg., Washington, DC 20045; tel (202) 745-7692; fax (202) 393-4119
Contact — Fernando Pajares

Ahle, Dorothy Caricatures — 8 Grimshaw St., Malden, MA 02148; tel (617) 321-8302; fax (617) 321-8302

AIM (Accuracy in Media) Report — 4455 Connecticut Ave. NW, Ste. 330, Washington, DC 20008; tel (202) 364-4401; fax (202) 364-4098
Chairman — Reed J. Irvine
Dir. of Media Analysis — Joseph C. Goulden
Director of Communications — Bernard Yoh
Executive Secretary — Donald K. Irvine
Public Affairs Director — Deborah Lambert

Alburn Bureau, The — PO Box 2345, Tucson, AZ 85702; tel (520) 325-9501
Contact — Leo Sonderegger

All-Sports Publications — 72 Harvard Dr., Carmel, NY 10512; tel (914) 225-7735; fax (914) 278-9403
VP/Senior Editor — George D'Alessandro
VP of Marketing — Marilyn Schnitter
VP/Photo Editor — G. S. D'Alessandro

Allsport Photography USA — 17383 Sunset Blvd., Ste. 300, Pacific Palisades, CA 90272; tel (310) 230-3400/(212) 979-0903 (New York Office)/(800) 927-3638; fax (310) 573-7600
President — Steve Powell
Chief Executive Officer — Adrian Murrell
Vice President — Greg Walker
Senior Managing Editor — Simon P. Barnett
Director of Photography — Mike Powell
Darkroom Manager — Scott Ridgway
Systems Administrator — Matthew Schoen
New York Representative — Darrell Ingham
Business Mgr. (New York) — Peter Orlowsky
Director of Sales & Marketing — Sue Baldus
Overseas Manager — Markus Boesch
Photo Editor — Glenn Cratty
Picture Desk Editor — Tim Curlee
Account Representative — Matthew Venegas
Amateur Sports Editor — Rebecca Butala
Track & Field Editor — Gervaise McGraw
Account Representative — Suzy Schaffer
Sr. Manager/HR — Margaret Weiner

Alsop, Jonathon — 336 Washington St., Brookline, MA 02146; tel (617) 731-3593; fax (617) 731-4880; e-mail jalsop@world.std.com

American Crossword Federation — PO Box 69, Massapequa Park, NY 11762; tel (516) 795-8823
President/Editor — Stanley Newman
Vice Pres./Dir. of Sales — Joseph Vallely
Vice Pres./Senior Editor — David A. Rosen
Vice Pres./Senior Editor — Jon Delfin

American Federation of Teachers — 555 New Jersey Ave. NW, Washington, DC 20001; tel (800) 238-1133/(202) 879-4596; fax (202) 879-4545
President — Albert Shanker
Secretary/Treasurer — Edward J. McElroy

American International Syndicate — 1324 N. 3rd St., St. Joseph, MO 64501; tel (816) 279-9315
Pres./Cartoon Editor — Gerald A. Bennett
Vice President/Art Director — Wes Clark
Exec. Vice President — Linda Bennett
Marketing Director — Joyce Clark

American Way Features, The — 128 Lighthouse Dr., Jupiter, FL 33469; tel (305) 746-7815
Publisher — Thomas J. Anderson
Circulation Manager — Linda Parton

Ampersand Communications — 2311 S. Bayshore Dr., Miami, FL 33133; tel (305) 285-2200; fax on request
Editor — George Leposky
Marketing Director — Rosalie Leposky

And Sew On — PO Box 71, Martinsville, NJ 08836; tel (908) 722-5676
President/Author — Alida Macor

Another Way — 1251 Virginia Ave., Harrisonburg, VA 22801-2497; tel (800) 999-3534/(540) 434-6701; fax (540) 434-5556
Self-Syndicated — Melodie M. Davis

Antique Detective Syndicate — 4794 N.E. 17th Ave., Ft. Lauderdale, FL 33334-5610; tel (305) 491-5368; fax (305) 491-8481
President/Writer — Anne Gilbert

AP/Wide World Photos — 50 Rockefeller Plaza, New York, NY 10020; tel (212) 621-1930; fax (212) 621-1955
Director — Patricia Lantis

Aquino Productions — PO Box 15760, Stamford, CT 06901-0760; tel (203) 967-9952/(203) 353-9841 BBS; fax (203) 353-9661
Owner — Andres Aquino

Arcadia Feature Syndicate — PO Box 1205, Galesburg, IL 61402; tel (309) 341-0737
Managing Editor — Clarice Anders

Archive Photos — 530 W. 25th St., New York, NY 10001; tel (212) 675-0115; fax (212) 675-0379
President — Patrick Montgomery
Vice Pres./Sales — Eric Rachlis
Photo Editor — Carole Moore

Arms & The World — PO Box 32221, Washington, DC 20007; tel (202) 337-1560; fax (202) 625-1999
Author — Russell Warren Howe

Arrigoni Travel Syndication — 15 Rockridge Rd. (94930); PO Box 1004, Fairfax, CA 94978; tel (415) 454-0876; fax (415) 456-2697
President — Patricia Arrigoni

Arthur's International — 2613 High Range Dr., Las Vegas, NV 89134; tel (702) 228-3731
President — Marvin C. Arthur

Artists and Writers Syndicate — PO Box 60688, Washington, DC 20039-0688; tel (202) 882-8882; fax (202) 829-9283
President/Executive Editor — Philip Steitz
Managing Editor — Marjorie Steitz

Ascher Features Syndicate — 214 Boston Ave., Egg Harbor Twp., NJ 08234-6923; tel (609) 927-1842
President — Sidney Ascher
Secretary/Treasurer — Evelyn Ascher

Ashleigh Brilliant — 117 W. Valerio St., Santa Barbara, CA 93101; tel (805) 682-0531
President — Ashleigh Brilliant
Vice President — Dorothy Brilliant

Ask Pippa — 550 Carlaw Ave., Toronto, ON M4K 3J7 Canada; tel (416) 463-0257/(416) 596-6098
Science and Childrens Writer — Pippa B. Wysong

Associated Features Inc. — PO Box 7099, Fairfax Station, VA 22039; tel (703) 764-0496; fax (703) 764-9131
Pres./Editor/Gen. Mgr. — Douglas A. Cohn
Washington Correspondent — Warren Rogers
Richmond Correspondent — Robert Holland
Denver and L.A. Correspondent — B. Trefny
National Correspondent — Jack Kemp
Consumer & Business Affairs — Ralph Nader
Dallas & Texas Correspondent — Lee Cullum
Editor — Jack Anderson

Associated Press, AP Newsfeatures — 50 Rockefeller Plz., New York, NY 10020; tel (212) 621-1821; voice mail (212) 621-1820
Dir./APN Special Projects — Norm Goldstein

Associated Press, The — 50 Rockefeller Plz., New York, NY 10020; tel (212) 621-1500
President/CEO — Louis D. Boccardi
VP/CFO/Dir. of Bus. Development — Patrick T. O'Brien
VP/Exec. Editor — William E. Ahearn
VP/Sec./Dir. of Human Resources — James M. Donna
VP/Dir. of World Srvs. — Claude E. Erbsen
VP/Dir. of Communications & Technology — John W. Reid
VP/Dir. of Newspaper Membership — Wick Temple
VP/Dir. of Broadcast Srvs.— James R. Williams
Executive Photo Editor — Vincent Alabiso
Asst. to the Pres. for Electronic Darkroom & PhotoStream — Harold G. Buell
Managing Editor — Darrell L. Christian
Assistant to the Pres. — Kelly Smith Tunney
Dir. of Strategic Planning — Thomas E. Slaughter
Dir. of State News — Martin C. Thompson
Dir. of Corporate Comm. — Susan S. Welch

Alabama (Control Bureau Atlanta, GA)
Birmingham — Correspondent: Jay Reeves; 2200 Fourth Ave. N.; PO Box 2553, Birmingham, AL 35202-2553; tel (205) 251-4221
Mobile — Correspondent: Garry Mitchell; Press Register Bldg., 304 Government St.; PO Box 2488, Mobile, AL 36652-2488; tel (334) 433-7269
Montgomery — Correspondent: Kendal Weaver; The Associated Press, 116 S. McDonough St.; PO Box 1000, Montgomery, AL 36101-1000; tel (334) 262-5947

Alaska (Control Bureau Anchorage)
Anchorage — Bureau Chief: Dean Fosdick; 750 W. 2nd Ave., Ste. 102, Anchorage, AK 99501; tel (907) 272-7549
Juneau — Correspondent: David Germain; Court Plz. Bldg., 240 Main St., Ste. 602, Juneau, AK 99801; tel (907) 586-1515

Arizona (Control Bureau Phoenix)
Phoenix — Bureau Chief: Kevin Walsh; 500 N. 3rd St., Ste. 120, Phoenix, AZ 85004-3904; tel (602) 258-8934
Tucson — Correspondent: Arthur H. Rotstcin; Tucson Newspapers Inc., 4850 S. Park Ave.; PO Box 26807, Phoenix, AZ 85726-6807; tel (520) 294-1400
Little Rock, AR — Bureau Chief: Bill Simmons; 10802 Executive Center Dr., Benton Bldg., Ste. 100, Little Rock AR, 72211-4377; tel (501) 225-3668

California (Control Bureau Los Angeles)
Los Angeles — Bureau Chief: Andy Lippman; 211 S. Figueroa, 3rd Fl., Los Angeles, CA 90012-2501; tel (213) 626-1200/(213) 626-2500 (Photos)
San Diego — Correspondent: Amanda Covarrubias; Union-Tribune Bldg., 350 Camino de la Reina; PO Box 191, San Diego, CA 92112-4106; tel (619) 231-3587

California (Control Bureau San Francisco)
Berkeley — Correspondent: Michelle Locke; 101 Sproul Hall, Public Affairs UCB, Berkeley, CA 94720-4202; tel (510) 643-1458
Fresno — Correspondent: Joseph A. Bigham; 1755 E St., Rm. 109, Fresno, CA 93706-2022; tel (209) 264-3000/(209) 264-3009
San Francisco — Bureau Chief: Daniel Day; 1390 Market St., Ste. 318, San Francisco, CA 94102-5405; tel (415) 621-7432
San Jose — Correspondent: Catalina Ortiz; 1735 Technology Dr., Ste. 320, San Jose, CA 95110-1352; tel (408) 453-0354
Sacramento — Correspondent: Nick Geranios; 925 L St., Ste. 320, Sacramento, CA 95814-3773; tel (916) 448-9555

Colorado (Control Bureau Denver)
Denver — Bureau Chief: Joe McGowan Jr.; 1444 Wazee St., Ste. 130, Denver, CO 80202-1395; tel (303) 825-0123
Grand Junction — Correspondent: Robert Weller; Daily Sentinel; PO Box 2922, Grand Junction, CO 81502-2922; tel (970) 241-6083

Connecticut (Control Bureau Hartford)
Hartford — Bureau Chief: Mary Anne Rhyne; 55 Farmington Ave., Ste. 402, Hartford, CT 06105-3711; tel (860) 246-6876
New Haven — Correspondent: Brigitte Greenberg; 40 Sargent Dr., New Haven, CT 06511-5939; tel (203) 624-9825
Stamford — Correspondent: Denise Lavoie; PO Box 6728, Stamford, CT 06904-6728; tel (203) 964-9270

Delaware (Control Bureau Baltimore)
Dover — Correspondent: Theresa Humphrey; State Capitol; PO Box 934, Dover, DE 19903-0934; tel (302) 674-3037
Washington, DC — Bureau Chief: Jonathan Wolman; 2021 K St. NW, 6th Fl., Washington, DC 20006-1082; tel (202) 776-9400

Florida (Control Bureau Miami)
Cape Canaveral — Correspondent: Marcia Dunn; PO Box 327, Cape Canaveral, FL 32920-0327; tel (407) 639-8801
Jacksonville — Correspondent: Ron Word; Florida Times-Union Bldg., 1 Riverside Ave., Jacksonville, FL 32202-4984; tel (904) 356-2829
Miami — Bureau Chief: James Reindl; 9100 N.W. 36th St., Miami, FL 33178-2420; tel (305) 594-5825
Pensacola — Correspondent: William S. Kaczor; News Journal Bldg., 1 News Journal Plz., Pensacola, FL 32501-5607; tel (904) 438-4951
Orlando — Correspondent: Isaac M. Flores; 47 E. Robinson St.(32801-1630); PO Box 2831, Orlando, FL 32802-2831; tel (407) 425-4547
Tallahassee — Correspondent: Brent Kallestad; 336 E. College Ave., Ste. 301, Tallahassee, FL 32301-1560; tel (904) 224-1211
Tampa — Correspondent: Lisa Holewa; Tampa Tribune Bldg., 202 S. Parker St., Tampa, FL 33606-2395; tel (813) 254-6316

Georgia (Control Bureau Atlanta)
Albany — Correspondent: Elliott Minor; 126 N. Washington St., Albany, GA 31701-2552; tel (912) 435-7473
Atlanta — Bureau Chief: Gary Clark; One CNN Ctr., Ste. 500, South Tower, Atlanta, GA 30303-2705; tel (404) 522-8971

Hawaii (Control Bureau Honolulu)
Honolulu — Bureau Chief: Gordon Sakamoto; 605 Kapiolani Blvd., 2nd Fl.; PO Box 2956, Honolulu, HI 96802-2956; tel (808) 536-5510

Idaho (Control Bureau Salt Lake City)
Boise — Correspondent: Bob Fick; Statehouse, 700 S. Jefferson (83720-0001); PO Box 1187, Boise, ID 83701-1187; tel (208) 343-1894

Illinois (Control Bureau Chicago)
Champaign — Correspondent: Matt Kelley; Champaign News-Gazette Bldg., 15 Main St., Champaign, IL 61820-3641; tel (217) 351-4094
Chicago — Bureau Chief: James Wilson; 230 N. Michigan Ave., Chicago, IL 60601-5960; tel (312) 781-0500
Peoria — Correspondent: Christopher Wills; Journal Star Bldg., 1 News Plz., Peoria, IL 61643-0002; tel (309) 682-0141
Springfield — Correspondent: Sandra Skowron; State Capitol, Press Room, Springfield, IL 62704-0001; tel (217) 789-2700
Carbondale — Correspondent: Frank Fisher; Carbondale Southern Illinoisan; 710 N. Illinois Ave., Carbondale, IL 62901-1283; tel (618) 529-2538

Indiana (Control Bureau Indianapolis)
Evansville — Correspondent: Ted Bridis; 300 E. Walnut (47713-1985); PO Box 1010, Evansville, IN 47706-1010; tel (812) 423-8136
Indianapolis — Bureau Chief: Robert Shaw; Star-News Bldg., 307 N. Pennsylvania St., Rm. 315; PO Box 1950, Indianapolis, IN 46206-1950; tel (317) 639-5501

Copyright ©1996 by the Editor & Publisher Co.

South Bend — Correspondent: Nancy Armour; 223 W. Colfax, South Bend, IN 46626-1001; tel (219) 288-1649

Iowa (Control Bureau Des Moines)

Des Moines — Bureau Chief: Kristi Umbreit; 505 Fifth Ave., Ste. 1000, Des Moines, IA 50309-2315; tel (515) 243-3281

Iowa City — Correspondent: Greg Smith; 103 E. College, Ste. 208, Iowa City, IA 52240-4014; tel (319) 337-5615

Kansas (Control Bureau Kansas City)

Topeka — Correspondent: Lewis L. Ferguson; Capital-Journal Bldg., 616 S.E. Jefferson St., Topeka, KS 66607-1120; tel (913) 234-5654

Wichita — Correspondent: Michael Bates; Wichita Eagle-Beacon, 825 E. Douglas; PO Box 820, Wichita, KS 67201-0820; tel (316) 263-4601

Kentucky (Control Bureau Louisville)

Frankfort — Correspondent: Mark Chellgren; State Capitol, Rm. 243, Frankfort, KY 40601-3490; tel (502) 223-3222

Lexington — Correspondent: Michael D. Embry; Herald-Leader Bldg., 100 Midland Ave., Lexington, KY 40508-1999; tel (606) 254-2070

Louisville — Bureau Chief: Howard E. (Ed) Staats; Courier-Journal Bldg., 525 W. Broadway, Louisville, KY 40202-2137; tel (502) 583-7718

Pikeville — Correspondent: Allen G. Breed; 201 Caroline Ave.; PO Box 131, Pikeville, KY 41501-0131; tel (606) 432-4965

Louisiana (Control Bureau New Orleans)

Baton Rouge — Correspondent: E. Guy Coates; State Capitol Bldg., Press Room, Ground Fl.; PO Box 44395, Baton Rouge, LA 70804-4395; tel (304) 343-1325

New Orleans — Bureau Chief: Charlotte Porter; 1001 Howard Ave., Ste. 200-A, New Orleans, LA 70113-2077; tel (504) 523-3931

Maine (Control Bureau Concord, NH)

Augusta — Correspondent: Peter Jackson; State House, Media Ctr.; PO Box 349, Augusta, ME 04330-0349; tel (207) 622-3018

Portland — Correspondent: Elizabeth Edwardsen; 75 Market St., Ste. 402 (04104); PO Box 15008, Portland, ME 04112-5008; tel (207) 772-4157

Maryland (Control Bureau Baltimore)

Annapolis — Correspondent: Tom C. Stuckey; State House, State Cir.; PO Box 2450, Annapolis, MD 21404-1471; tel (301) 269-0196

Baltimore — Bureau Chief: Linda Stowell; 222 St. Paul Pl., Ste. 400, Baltimore, MD 21202-2066; tel (301) 539-3524

Hagerstown — Correspondent: Debra Riechmann; Herald-Mail Bldg., 100 Summit Ave.; PO Box 648, Hagerstown, MD 21741-0648; tel (301) 791-5246

Massachusetts (Control Bureau Boston)

Boston — Bureau Chief: Michael Short; 184 High St., Boston, MA 02110; tel (617) 357-8100

Springfield — Correspondent: Jeff Donn; 1537 Main St., Springfield, MA 01103; tel (413) 781-0217

Michigan (Control Bureau Detroit)

Detroit — Bureau Chief: Charles Hill; 300 River Pl., Ste. 2400, Detroit, MI 48207; tel (313) 259-0650

Grand Rapids — Correspondent: Ed White; Press Bldg., 155 Michigan Ave., Grand Rapids, MI 49503-2353

Lansing — Correspondent: Kathy Barks Hoffman; 200 N. Capitol Ave., Ste. 450, Lansing, MI 48933; tel (517) 482-8011

Traverse City — Correspondent: John Flesher; 120 W. Front St., Traverse City, MI 49684; tel (616) 929-4180

Minnesota (Control Bureau Minneapolis)

Minneapolis — Bureau Chief: Dave Pyle; 511 11th Ave. S., Business & Technical Ctr., Ste. 404, Minneapolis, MN 55415; tel (612) 332-2727

St. Paul — Correspondent: Josh Lemieux; State Capitol Bldg., 75 Constitution Ave., Rm. B-28, St. Paul, MN 55155; tel (612) 222-4821

Mississippi (Control Bureau New Orleans, LA)

Jackson — Correspondent: Robert Naylor Jr.; 125 S. Congress, Ste. L-170, Capitol Towers, Jackson, MS 39201-3301; tel (601) 948-5897

Missouri (Control Bureau Kansas City)

Jefferson City — Correspondent: Scott Charton; Capitol Press Room, Rm. 118-B (65101-1556); PO Box 272, Jefferson City, MO 65102-0272; tel (314) 636-9415

Kansas City — Bureau Chief: Paul Stevens; 215 W. Pershing Rd., Kansas City, MO 61408-4300; tel (816) 421-4844

St. Louis — Correspondent: Lori Dodge Rose; Post-Dispatch Bldg., 900 N. Tucker Blvd., St. Louis, MO 63101-1098; tel (314) 241-2496

Springfield — Correspondent: Jerry Nachtigal; 651 Boonville, Springfield, MO 65806-1005; tel (417) 831-3158

Montana (Control Bureau Helena)

Helena — Bureau Chief: John Kuglin; 1300 Cedar St., West Bldg., Rm. C (59601-0909); PO Box 5810, Helena, MT 59604-5810; tel (406) 442-7440

Nebraska (Control Bureau Omaha)

Lincoln — Correspondent: Edward W. Howard; Journal-Star Bldg., 926 P St. (68508-3615); PO Box 82061, Lincoln, NE 68501-2061; tel (402) 476-2525

Omaha — Bureau Chief: Paul Simon; 232 World Herald Bldg., Omaha, NE 68102-1122; tel (402) 341-4963

Nevada (Control Bureau San Francisco)

Carson City — Correspondent: Brendan Riley; State Capitol, Press Room, Rm. 32, Carson City, NV 89710-0001; tel (702) 687-4190

Nevada (Control Bureau Los Angeles)

Las Vegas — Correspondent: Robert Macy; Review-Journal Bldg., 1111 W. Bonanza (89106-3545); PO Box 70, Las Vegas, NV 89125-0070; tel (702) 382-7440

Nevada (Control Bureau San Francisco)

Reno — Correspondent: Thomas D. Gardner III; Gazette-Journal Bldg. (89502-1160); PO Box 22000, Reno, NV 89520-2000; tel (702) 322-3639

New Hampshire (Control Bureau Concord)

Concord — Bureau Chief: Larry Laughlin; 5 Blake St. (03301); PO Box 1200, Concord, NH 03302-1200; tel (603) 224-3327

New Jersey (Control Bureau Trenton)

Pleasantville — Correspondent: John Curran; The Press, Devins Ln., Pleasantville, NJ 08232-4199; tel (609) 645-2063

Cranbury — Plant Manager: Rudy Bakker; Cranbury Technical Ctr.; 19 Commerce Ctr. W., Cranbury, NJ 08512-9416; tel (609) 860-6900

Newark — Correspondent: Arthur Allen; Rte. 1 & 9 S., Hemisphere Ctr., Newark, NJ 07114; tel (201) 642-0151

Trenton — Bureau Chief: Mark Mittelstadt; 50 W. State St., Ste. 1114, Trenton, NJ 08608; tel (609) 392-3622

Trenton — Correspondent: Thomas Martello; State House, CN 021, Trenton, NJ 08625; tel (609) 292-5172

Woodbury — Correspondent: Melanie L. Burney; Gloucester County Times, 309 S. Broad St., Woodbury, NJ 08096; tel (609) 853-6134

New Mexico (Control Bureau Albuquerque)

Albuquerque — Bureau Chief: Dan Even; The Journal Ctr., 7777 Jefferson N.E., Ste. 303 (87109-4360); PO Box 1845, Albuquerque, NM 87103-1845; tel (505) 822-9022

Santa Fe — Correspondent: Barry Massey; Journal N. Bldg., 328 Galisteo, Santa Fe, NM 87501-2642; tel (505) 982-1012

New York (Control Bureau Albany)

Albany — Bureau Chief: Lew Wheaton; 645 Albany-Shaker Rd.; PO Box 11010, Albany, NY 12211-0010; tel (518) 458-7821

Albany — Correspondent: Marc A. Humbert; Capital Station; PO Box 7165, Albany, NY 12224; tel (518) 449-7131

Buffalo — Correspondent: John Affleck; Buffalo Evening News, 1 News Plz., Buffalo, NY 14240; tel (716) 852-1051

Rochester — Correspondent: Ben Dobbin; 55 Exchange St., Rochester, NY 14614; tel (716) 232-2219

Syracuse — Correspondent: William J. Kates Jr.; The Syracuse Bldg., 224 Harrison St., Syracuse, NY 13202; tel (315) 471-6471

New York (Control Bureau New York City)

Mineola — Correspondent: Pat Milton; State Supreme Ct. Bldg., 100 Supreme Ct. Dr., Rm. 137, Mineola, NY 11501; tel (516) 746-3484

New York City — Chief of Bureau: Sam Boyle; 50 Rockefeller Plz., New York, NY 10020; tel (212) 621-1670

Jersey City, NJ — Managing Editor: John Hitchcock; AP-Dow Jones, Harborside Financial Ctr., 600 Plaza Two, 8th Fl., Jersey City, NJ 07311; tel (201) 938-4370

White Plains — Correspondent: Marlene Aig; County Bldg., Press Room 148 Martine Ave., White Plains, NY 10601-3378; tel (914) 946-8841

North Carolina (Control Bureau Raleigh)

Charlotte — Correspondent: Paul Nowell; 500 E. Morehead St., Ste. 316, Charlotte, NC 28202; tel (704) 334-4624

Raleigh — Chief of Bureau: Ambrose Dudley; 4020 WestChase Blvd., Raleigh, NC 27607-3933; tel (919) 833-8687

North Dakota (Control Bureau Sioux Falls, SD)

Bismarck — Correspondent: Phyllis Mensing; 707 E. Front Ave.; PO Box 1018 (58502-1018), Bismarck, ND 58504-5646; tel (701) 223-8450

North Dakota (Control Bureau Fargo)

Fargo — Correspondent: Marilynn Wheeler; Forum Building, 101 5th St. N., Fargo, ND 58102-2020; tel (701) 235-1908

Ohio (Control Bureau Columbus)

Cincinnati — Correspondent: John Nolan; The Cincinnati Enquirer, 312 Elm St., Cincinnati, OH 45202; tel (513) 241-2386

Cleveland — Correspondent: Rich Harris; Superior Bldg., 815 Superior Ave., Ste. 1203, Cleveland, OH 44114; tel (216) 771-2172

Columbus — Chief of Bureau: Jake Booher; 1103 Schrock Rd., Ste. 300, Columbus, OH 43229; tel (614) 885-2727

Dayton — Correspondent: Jim Hannah; Dayton News & Journal Herald Bldg., 37 S. Ludlow St., 5th Fl., Dayton, OH 45402; tel (513) 225-2269

Toledo — Correspondent: Mitch Weiss; The Blade Bldg., 541 N. Superior St., Toledo, OH 43660; tel (419) 255-7113

Oklahoma (Control Bureau Oklahoma City)

Oklahoma City — Bureau Chief: Lindel G. Hutson; 525 Central Park Dr., Ste. 202, Oklahoma City, OK 73105; tel (405) 525-2121

Tulsa — Correspondent: Doug Ferguson; 315 S. Boulder (74103); PO Box 1770, Tulsa, OK 74102; tel (918) 584-4346

Oregon (Control Bureau Portland)

Grants Pass — Correspondent: Jeff Barnard; The Courier, 409 S.E. Seventh; PO Box 1468, Grants Pass, OR 97526; tel (503) 476-1722

Portland — Bureau Chief: Eva Parziale; Chief of Communications: Robert Young; 121 S.W. Salmon St., Ste. 1450, Portland, OR 97204-2924; tel (503) 228-2169

Salem — Correspondent: Brad Cain; State Office Bldg., Press Room, Salem, OR 97310; tel (503) 363-0010

Pennsylvania (Control Bureau Philadelphia)

Harrisburg — Correspondent: Rich Kirkpatrick; Main Capitol, E Fl., Rm. 526 (17120); PO Box 10630, Harrisburg, PA 17105-0630; tel (717) 238-9413

Philadelphia — Bureau Chief: George Zucker; 1 Franklin Plz., Ste. 250, Philadelphia, PA 19102; tel (215) 561-1133/(215) 561-1144 (Photos)

Pittsburgh — Correspondent: Tara Bradley-Steck; 6 Gateway Ctr., Ste. 222, Pittsburgh, PA 15222-1312; tel (412) 281-3747

State College — Correspondent: Mike Giarrusso; 3400 E. College Ave.; PO Box 89, State College, PA 16804; tel (814) 238-3649

Rhode Island (Control Bureau Boston, MA)

Providence — Correspondent: Frank Baker; 10 Dorrance St., Providence, RI 02903-2084; tel (401) 274-2270

South Carolina (Control Bureau Columbia)

Charleston — Correspondent: Bruce M. Smith; 92 Broad St., Ste. 303, Charleston, SC 29401; tel (803) 722-1660

Columbia — Bureau Chief: John Shurr; 1311 Marion St., Columbia, SC 29201; tel (803) 799-6418/(803) 799-5510 (Photos)

South Dakota (Control Bureau Sioux Falls)

Pierre — Correspondent: Chet Brokaw; 124 S. Euclid, Ste. 104; PO Box 368, Pierre, SD 57501-0368; tel (605) 224-7811

Sioux Falls — Bureau Chief: Tena Haraldson; 330 N. Main Ave., Ste. 303 (57102); PO Box 1125, Sioux Falls, SD 57101-1125; tel (605) 332-2111

Tennessee (Control Bureau Nashville)

Chattanooga — Correspondent: Michelle Williams; 400 E. 11th St., Chattanooga, TN 37402; tel (423) 266-4600

Johnson City — Correspondent: Leslie Lloyd; 207 N. Boone, Rm. 500, Johnson City, TN 37601; tel (423) 929-9091

Knoxville — Correspondent: Duncan Mansfield; 204 W. Church St., Knoxville, TN 37902-1674; tel (423) 522-3936

Memphis — Correspondent: Woodrow Baird; Commercial Appeal Bldg., 495 Union Ave., Memphis, TN 38101; tel (901) 525-1972

Nashville — Bureau Chief: Kent Flanagan; Banner-Tennessean Bldg., 1100 Broadway (37203); PO Box 22990, Nashville, TN 37202-2990; tel (615) 244-2205

Texas (Control Bureau Dallas)

Austin — Correspondent: Mike Holmes; 1005 Congress Ave., Ste. 995, Austin, TX 78701; tel (512) 472-4004

Dallas — Bureau Chief: John Lumpkin; 4581 LBJ Fwy., Ste. 300, Dallas, TX 75244-6002; tel (214) 991-2100

El Paso — Correspondent: Ed Montes; El Paso Times, 300 N. Campbell Ave., El Paso, TX 79991-1402; tel (915) 532-1939

Fort Worth — Correspondent: Mike Cochran; Fort Worth Star-Telegram Bldg., 7th & Taylor, Fort Worth, TX 76101; tel (817) 336-9271

Harlingen — Correspondent: Pauline Arrillaga; 9201 W. Expy. 83, (Mail: KGBT-TV), Harlingen, TX 78552; tel (210) 423-7790

Houston — Correspondent: Michael L. Graczyk; 16945 Northchase Dr., Ste. 2110, Houston, TX 77060; tel (713) 872-8900

Lubbock — Correspondent: Jean Pagel; Lubbock Avalanche-Journal, 710 Ave. J, Lubbock, TX 79401-1895; tel (806) 765-0394

San Antonio — Correspondent: Kelly Shannon; Express-News, 423 4th St., San Antonio, TX 78205; tel (210) 222-2713

Utah (Control Bureau Salt Lake City)

Salt Lake City — Bureau Chief: William Beecham; 161 S. Regent St., Mezz., Salt Lake City, UT 84111-1903; tel (801) 322-3405

Vermont (Control Bureau Concord, NH)

Montpelier — Correspondent: Christopher L. Graff; Thrush Tavern, 107 State St., 2nd Fl. (05602-2837); PO Box 866, Montpelier, VT 05602-0866; tel (802) 229-0577

Virginia (Control Bureau Richmond)

Norfolk — Correspondent: Joseph Taylor; 150 W. Brambleton Ave., Norfolk, VA 23510; tel (804) 625-2047

Richmond — Bureau Chief: Dorothy Abernathy; 700 E. Main St., Ste. 1380, Richmond, VA 23219-2684; tel (804) 643-6646

Roanoke — Correspondent: David J. Reed; 145 Campbell Ave., Ste. 520, Roanoke, VA 24011; tel (703) 344-5860

Springfield — Correspondent: Anne Gearan; 7600-D Boston Blvd., Rm. 158, Springfield, VA 22153; tel (703) 913-1183

Washington (Control Bureau Seattle)

Olympia — Correspondent: John E. White; 1417-19 S. Columbia; PO Box 607, Olympia, WA 98507-0607; tel (360) 753-7222

Seattle — Bureau Chief: Dale Leach; 201 Boren Ave. N., Seattle, WA 98109; tel (206) 682-1812

Spokane — Correspondent: John Wiley; Review Tower, W. 999 Riverside, Rm. 502; PO Box 2173, Spokane, WA 99210-2173; tel (509) 624-1258

Yakima — Correspondent: Aviva Brandt; Yakima Herald Republic, 114 N. Fourth St. (98909); PO Box 1349, Yakima, WA 98907; tel (509) 453-1951

West Virginia (Control Bureau Charleston)

Charleston — Bureau Chief: Peter Mattiace; Charleston Newspapers Bldg., 1001 Virginia St. E., Rm. 206, Charleston, WV 25301-2895; tel (304) 346-0897

Huntington — Correspondent: Martha Bryson Hodel; Huntington Publishing Co. 946 Fifth Ave., Huntington, WV 25701-2004; tel (304) 523-8721

Morgantown — Correspondent: David Wilkison; Dominion-Post, Greer Bldg. 1251 Earl L. Core Rd., Morgantown, WV 26505-5896; tel (304) 291-6161

Wisconsin (Control Bureau Milwaukee)

Madison — Correspondent: Arthur L. Srb; 1901 Fish Hatchery Rd., Madison, WI 53713; tel (608) 258-9235

Milwaukee — Bureau Chief: T. Lee Hughes; 918 N. 4th St., Milwaukee, WI 53203-1596; tel (414) 225-3580

Wausau — Correspondent: Robert Imrie; Wausau Daily Herald Bldg., 800 Scott St.; PO Box 1286, Wausau, WI 54401-4949; tel (715) 842-2728

Wyoming (Control Bureau Denver, CO)

Cheyenne — Correspondent: Jim Angell; 320 W. 25th St., Ste. 310, Cheyenne, WY 82001-3005; tel (307) 632-9351

Asterisk Features — Mallard Rd., RR #2, Box 9, Nanoose Bay, BC V0R 2R0 Canada; tel (604) 468-7584; fax (604) 468-7520
President — John R. Somerville

Atlanta Bureau, The — 417 4th St. N.E., Atlanta, GA 30308-2006; tel (404) 875-6572; fax (404) 875-6503
Managing Editor — Jerry Schwartz
Asst. Managing Editor — Paulette Inabinet
Technology Editor — Ron Hosek

Atlantic Feature Syndicate — 16 Slayton Rd., Melrose, MA 02176; tel (617) 665-4442
Contact — Mark Parisi
Contact — Lynn Reznick

Australian Broadcasting Corp. — 630 5th Ave., Ste. 2260, New York, NY 10111; tel (212) 332-2540; fax (212) 332-2546

Auto Digest — 12377 Paiute Ct., (Powell Butte, 97753); PO Box 459, Prineville, OR 97754-0459; tel (503) 923-3936; fax (503) 923-3936
Contact — Bill Schaffer
Contact — Barbara Schaffer

Auto Page Syndicate — 980 Macungie Ave., Emmaus, PA 18049; tel (610) 965-4257; fax (610) 965-4257 (call first)
President — John Heilig

Avanti NewsFeatures — 29106 Palomino Dr., Warren, MI 48093-3505; tel (810) 573-2755; fax (810) 573-2755; internet avanti1054@aol.com
Senior Managing Editor — Hawke Fracassa
Senior Editor/Automotive — Anne Fracassa
Technology & Computer Ed. — Craig Oldani
Politics Editor — Michael Raveane
Parenting Columnist — Tracey Lee-Petri
Car Care Editor — Dave Menard
Country Music Editor — Bob Gramer
Arts Editor — Anthony W. Guerrero
Food Editor — Francesca Fracassa
Medical Editor — Becca Fracassa
Arts & Crafts Editor — Karen Oldani
Tools Editor — Tony Oldani
Travel Editor — Filip Fracassa
Sports Editor — Jeff Lee
Lifestyle Editor — Bev Harvey

B

Barbara Burtoff Syndicated Features — 4201 Cathedral Ave. NW, Ste. 614-W, Washington, DC 20016-4963; tel (202) 966-6570
Editor/Publisher — Barbara Burtoff

Basch, Buddy Feature Syndicate — 771 West End Ave., New York, NY 10025-5572; tel (212) 666-2300
Publisher — Buddy Basch
Assistant to the Publisher/Women's Editor — Frances Scott
Reporter — Murri Barber
Reporter — Charles J. Brand
Research — Peter Mallon
Photographer — Michael Flaster
Attorney — G. Godfrey, Esq.

Basic Chess Features — PO Box 1138, New York, NY 10025; tel (212) 586-3700; fax (212) 943-2300
President — Shelby Lyman

Bernthal, Ron — PO Drawer 259, Hurleyville, NY 12747; tel (919) 434-1529; fax (914) 434-4806

Better Homes & Gardens Features Syndicate — 1716 Locust St., Des Moines, IA 50309-3023; tel (800) 678-8135; fax (800) 678-5994
Director — Dale Schenkelberg
Vice Pres.-Publishing Group — Jerry Ward
West Coast Rep. — Dennis Christensen
Southeast Rep. — Michael Thompson

Bettmann Archive/Bettman Newsphotos — 902 Broadway, New York, NY 10010; tel (212) 777-6200; fax (212) 533-4034
Director — Herbert Gstalder
Associate Director — Anne Rudden
Research Manager — Darby Harper
Marketing Director — Dann Pierce

Birthday Game, The — New Haven Register, 40 Sargent Dr., New Haven, CT 06511; tel (203) 789-5205
Administration — Ann Marie Brennan

Black Press Service Inc. — 166 Madison Ave., New York, NY 10016; tel (212) 686-6850; fax (212) 686-7308
President — Jay R. Levy
Editor — Roy Thompson
Associate Editor — Bill Baldwin
Sales Manager — Peter Knight

Black Star Pub. Co. Inc. — 116 E. 27th St., New York, NY 10016; tel (212) 679-3288
President — Ben Chapnick
Exec. Vice President — John P. Chapnick

Bloomberg Business News — 499 Park Ave., New York, NY 10022; tel (212) 318-2300; fax (212) 980-2480
Editor-In-Chief — Matt Winkler
New York Bureau Chief — David Wilson

BONAT's Diversified — 255 N. El Cielo, Ste. 688, Palm Springs, CA 92262; tel (619) 324-1503; fax (714) 660-8551
President — Natalie Carlton
Vice Pres./Secretary — Teresa Carlton

Bootstraps Syndications — 249 W. 21st St., New York, NY 10011; tel (212) 989-3105
Editor — William Neal

Boston Features Syndicate — 42 Eugenie St., Randolph, MA 02368; tel (617) 963-5073
President — Harry Privette
Director — Martin Hanna

BPI Entertainment News Wire — 100 Boylston St., Ste. 210, Boston, MA 02116; tel (617) 482-9447; fax (617) 482-9562
VP/News & Photo Services — John Morgan

Brenfeatures — PO Box 233, Needham, MA 02192-2820; tel (617) 444-8244/(800) 830-4014; fax (800) 830-4014
President/Editor — John Brennan
VP/Associate Editor — Alice F. Brennan

Briargate Media — PO Box 998, Colorado Springs, CO 80901; tel (719) 531-3304; fax (719) 531-3302
Contact — Becky Blair
Author — James C. Dobson Ph.D.

Broadcast News Limited — 36 King St. E., Toronto, ON M5C 2L9 Canada; tel (416) 364-3172; fax (416) 364-8896
Chairman — Roger D. Landry-Montreal
Chief Executive/President — Keith Kincaid
Treasurer — Donald Jarrett
Vice Pres./Broadcasting — Wayne Waldroff
Sales/Marketing Manager — Jerry Fairbridge
Business Manager — Michelle Poulin
General News Director — Mike Omelus
General Exec.-Client Liaison — Terry Scott
Satellite Services Mgr. — Rina Steverman

Quebec National Assembly, Quebec City — Peter Ray; 1050 rue St. Augustin, Ste. 207, Quebec City, QC G1R 5A4; tel (418) 646-7100; fax (418) 523-9686

Parliament Hill Bureau — News Editor: Malcolm Bernard Dan Dugas; 1 O'Connor St., Ottawa, ON K1P 5M3; tel (613) 236-4571; fax (613) 232-5163

Ontario Legislature — Terry Pedwell; Queen's Park, Toronto, ON; tel (416) 325-7846

Saskatchewan Legislature — Jay Branch; Rm. 335, Press Gallery, Regina, SK S4S 0B3; tel (306) 585-1024; fax (306) 585-1027

Alberta Legislature — John Cotter, Edmonton, AB; tel (403) 427-2773

British Columbia Legislature — Scott Sutherland; Radio Rm. 012-F, BC Legislature, Parliament Bldg., Victoria, BC V8V 1X4; tel (604) 386-2552; fax (604) 356-9597

New Brunswick Legislature — Steve Fairbairn; The Press Gallery, Box 6000, Queen St., Fredericton, NB E3B 5H1; tel (506) 457-0746; fax (506) 457-9708

Nova Scotia Legislature — Barbara Pike, Halifax, NS; tel (902) 423-5152

Service in French-Nouvelles Tele-Radio:

Montreal, QC — News Director: Serge Cossette; Director-Manager: Pierre Durivage; 245 St. Jacques W., Place d'Armes; PO Box 998, Montreal, QC H2Y 3J6; tel (514) 849-8008; fax (514) 282-6915

Regional Offices:

Edmonton, AB — Chris Vaughan-Johnston; 305 Corner Pt. Bldg.; Box 10179, 105th St., Edmonton, AB T5J 3N1; tel (403) 428-6490; fax (403) 428-0663

Halifax, NS — John Valorzi; 2021 Brunswick St.; Box 37, Sta. M, Halifax, NS B3J 2L4; tel (902) 422-9284; fax (902) 425-2675

Toronto, ON — General News Director: Mike Omelus; Deputy News Director: Keith Leslie; 36 King St. E., Toronto, ON M5C 2L9; tel (416) 364-3172; fax (416) 364-1325

Winnipeg, MB — 386 Broadway Ave., Ste. 101, Winnipeg, MB R3C 3R5; tel (204) 942-8188; fax (204) 942-4788

Vancouver, BC — Stephen Ward; 840 Howe St., Ste. 250, Vancouver, BC V6Z 2L2; tel (604) 687-2464; fax (604) 687-5040

Calgary, AB — Anna Geddes; 100 4th Ave. S.W., Ste. 507, Calgary, AB T2P 3N2; tel (403) 233-7004; fax (403) 262-7520

London, England — Helen Branswell; Associated Press House, 12 Norwich St., London, EC4A 1EJ England; tel (011) 171-353-6366; fax (011) 171-583-4238

Washington, DC — Brian Kennedy; 1825 K St. NW, Ste. 615, Washington, DC 20006-1253; tel (202) 223-8813; fax (202) 728-0348

Brock, Steve Book Reviews On The Internet — 2323 Mapleton, Boulder, CO 80304; tel (303) 786-7375; e-mail sbrock@ucsub.colorado.edu

Business Features Syndicate — PO Box A, North Stratford, NH 03590; tel (603) 922-8338; fax (603) 922-8339
Editor — Dana K. Cassell

Business Newsfeatures — 20630 Harper Ave., Ste. 103, Harper Woods, MI 48225; tel (313) 886-2331
Operations/Marketing — Robert H. Meyering
Marketing — Steven F. Lacey

Business Wire — 44 Montgomery St., 39th Fl., San Francisco, CA 94104; tel (415) 986-4422/NY Office (212) 575-8822; fax (415) 788-5335
President — Lorry I. Lokey
Senior V. Pres. — Cathy Baron Tamraz
Vice President-Operations — Terry Vitorelo
Vice President-Marketing & Creative Services — Michael Lissauer
Corporate Secretary — Ann L. Lokey

Eastern Division:

New York, NY — VP/Northeast Region: Gregg Castano; VP/Eastern Division: Cathy Baron-Tamraz; New York Regional Manager-Phyllis Dantuono; 1185 Ave. of the Americas, New York, NY 10036; tel (212) 575-8822/(800) 221-2462; fax (212) 575-1854

Atlanta, GA — Regional Manager: Neal Wells, Atlanta, GA; tel (770) 953-6555; fax (770) 953-6355

Boston, MA — New England Region Manager: Mary Lou Hubbert; 101 Huntington Ave., 21st Fl., Boston, MA 02199; tel (617) 330-5322; fax (617) 236-7740

Charlotte, NC — Regional Manager: Greg Valenstein; 128 S. Tryon St., Ste. 1565, Charlotte, NC 28202; tel (704) 377-0151; fax (704) 331-9760

Cleveland, OH — Midwest Region Manager: Suzanne Moore; 1300 E. 9th St., Ste. 601, Cleveland, OH 44114; tel (216) 781-0220/(800) 769-0220; fax (216) 781-0237/(800) 827-0237

Hollywood, FL — Regional Manager: Laura Sturaitis; 3440 Hollywood Blvd., Ste. 417, Hollywood, FL 33021; tel (305) 961-3888; fax (305) 961-9611

Minneapolis, MN — Regional Manager: Bernadette McCormick; 100 N. 6th St., Ste. 750B, Minneapolis, MN 55403; tel (612) 376-7979; fax (612) 376-9080

Nashville, TN — Southeast Region Manager: Tom Mulgrew; 222 2nd Ave. N., Ste. 420, Nashville, TN 37201; tel (615) 242-3696

Philadelphia, PA — Regional Manager: Lee Marshall; 201 N. Presidential Blvd., Ste. 102, Philadelphia, PA 19004; tel (610) 617-9560/(800) 999-1178; fax (610) 617-9723

Western Division:

San Francisco, CA — Vice Pres./Operations: Theresa Vitorelo; Vice Pres./Regional Sales: Janet Lynn; Sales Manager-Ann Lokey; 44 Montgomery St., 39th Fl., San Francisco, CA 94104; tel (415) 986-4422/(800) 227-0845; fax (415) 788-5335

Denver, CO — Account Executive: Konr Beetch; 1660 Lincoln St., Ste. 2510, Denver, CO 80264; tel (303) 861-8833/(800) 308-0166; fax (303) 830-2442

Los Angeles, CA — Regional Manager: Amy Thompson; 1990 S. Bundy Dr., Ste. 580, Los Angeles, CA 90025; tel (310) 820-9473/(800) 237-8212; fax (310) 820-7363

Newport Beach, CA — Regional Manager: Tom Becktold; 4100 Newport Pl., Ste. 820, Newport Beach, CA 92660; tel (714) 757-1021; fax (714) 757-1019

Phoenix, AZ — Regional Manager: Tony Brancanovich; 6991 E. Camelback Rd., Ste. B-210, Scottsdale, AZ 85251; tel (602) 990-9942; fax (602) 990-9948

San Diego, CA — District Manager: Michael Ziskin; 591 Camino de la Reina, Ste. 408, San Diego, CA 92108; tel (619) 686-8650; fax (619) 686-8659

Seattle, WA — Regional Manager: Tony Perucca; 1200 6th Ave., Ste. 1501, Seattle, WA 98101-1128; tel (206) 622-1632; fax (206) 467-7847

Silicon Valley, CA — District Manager: Carole Holmes; 5201 Great America Pkwy., Ste. 526, Santa Clara, CA 95054; tel (408) 970-4550; fax (408) 970-4560

C

California Features International Inc. — PO Box 58, Beverly Hills, CA 90213; tel (310) 441-0565; fax (310) 441-4544
President — Brad Elterman
Vice President — Stann Findelle, Esq.

Canada Wide Feature Service Ltd. — PO Box 345, Sta. A, Toronto, ON M5W 1C2 Canada; tel (416) 947-2191/(416) 947-2450
General Manager — Joe Marino
Sales Rep./Miller Features Syndicate Inc. — Richard Vroom
Photo Sales — Wanda Goodwin

Canadian Press & Broadcast News, The — 36 King St. E., Toronto, ON M5C 2L9 Canada; tel (416) 364-0321; fax (416) 364-0207
Chairman — Rodger D. Landry
President — Keith Kincaid
VP/Fin. & Adm. — Donald Jarrett
VP/Editorial — Jim Poling
VP/Broadcasting — Wayne Waldroff
VP/French Services — Denis Tremblay
VP/Mktg. & Comm. — Joe Freeman
Gen. Sports Editor — Neil Davidson
Chief of Ontario Service — Paul Woods

Edmonton, AB — Bureau Chief: Chris Vaughan-Johnston; Cornerpoint, 10179 105 St., Ste. 305, Edmonton, AB T5J 3N1; tel (403) 428-6107; fax (403) 428-0663

Halifax, NS — Bureau Chief: John Valorzi; 2021 Brunswick St.; PO Box 37, Sta. M, Halifax, NS B3J 2L4; tel (902) 422-8496; fax (902) 425-2675

London, England — Bureau Chief: Helen Branswell; 12 Norwich St., London, EC4A 1EJ England; tel (011) 171-353-6366; fax (011) 171-583-4238

Montreal, QC — Vice President/French Services: Dennis Tremblay; 245 St. James St. W., Montreal, QC H2Y 3J6; tel (514) 849-3212; fax (514) 282-6915

Ottawa, ON — Bureau Chief: Gerry Arnold; Deputy Bureau Chief: Heather Boyd; 140 Wellington St.; PO Box 595, Sta. B (Letters), Ottawa, ON K1P 5P7; tel (613) 238-4142; fax (613) 238-4452

Quebec City, QC — Bureau Chief: Maurice Girard; 1050 rue St. Augustin, Quebec City, QC G1R 5A4; tel (418) 523-0445; fax (418) 523-9686

Vancouver, BC — Bureau Chief: Stephen Ward; 840 Howe St., Ste. 250, Vancouver, BC V6Z 2L2; tel (604) 731-3191; fax (604) 687-5040

Washington, DC — Bureau Chief: Christine Morris; 1825 K St. NW, Ste. 615, Washington, DC 20006; tel (202) 828-9669; fax (202) 728-0348

Staff Correspondents:

Calgary, AB — Correspondent: Steve Ewart; 100 4th Ave. S.W., Ste. 507, Calgary, AB T2P 3N2; tel (403) 233-7004; fax (403) 262-7520

Fredericton, NB — Correspondent: Judith Monchuk; Press Gallery, Legis. Bldg.; PO Box 600, Fredericton, NB E3B 5H1; tel (506) 455-9493; fax (506) 457-9708

Regina, SK — Correspondent: Sandra Cordon; Legis. Bldg., Press Gallery, Rm. 335, Regina, SK S4S 0B3; tel (306) 585-1011; fax (306) 585-1027

St. John's, NF — Correspondent: Ian Bailey; Battery Hotel Media Ctr., St. John's, NF A1C 5X4; tel (709) 576-0687; fax (709) 576-0049

Toronto, ON — Chief of Picture Service: Ron Poling; CP Picture Service, 36 King St. E., Toronto, ON M5C 2L9; tel (416) 364-0321; fax (416) 594-2168

Victoria, BC — Correspondent: Mike Smyth; Press Gallery, Victoria, BC V8V 1X4; tel (604) 384-4912; fax (604) 356-9597

Winnipeg, MB — Correspondent: Nelle Oosterom; 386 Broadway Ave., Ste. 101, Winnipeg, MB R3C 3R6; tel (204) 942-8188; fax (204) 942-4788

Service in French:

Montreal — Deputy Bureau Chief: Claude Papineau; 245 St. James St. W.; Box 998, Place d'Armes (Letters), Montreal, QC H2Y 3J6; tel (514) 849-3212; fax (514) 282-6915

Cannery Row Creations — 69 Paso Hondo, Carmel Valley, CA 93924; tel (408) 659-1845; fax (408) 659-1399
Self-Syndicated/Owner — Yavor Bachev

Capital Connections — 1698 32nd St. NW, Washington, DC 20007; tel (202) 337-2044; fax (202) 338-4750; e-mail btwm32a@prodigy.com
Columnist — Karen Feld

Capitol Auto Reporting Service — 5783 Yellowrose Ct., Columbia, MD 21045; tel (301) 854-9074; fax (301) 854-9074
Editor — Mark Tapscott

Capitol News Service — 1713 J St., Ste. 202, Sacramento, CA 95814; tel (916) 445-6336
Executive Editor — David A. Kline

Carberry Columns — 1349 Douglas Ave., Flossmoor, IL 60422; tel (708) 799-6360
Author/Owner — Mary Margaret Carberry

Career Source/Column — PO Box 65754, Washington, DC 20035-5754; tel (202) 334-5353/(703) 284-4566
Owner/Author — Sheryl Silver

Carlinsky Features — 301 E. 78th St., New York, NY 10021; tel (212) 861-2526
Director — Dan Carlinsky

Carter, Tim — 3166 N. Farmcrest Dr., Cincinnati, OH 45213-1112; tel (513) 531-9229; fax (513) 531-9094; e-mail tmcarter@tso.cin.ix.net

Cartoon Comedy Club — 560 Lakeforest, Cleveland, OH 44140; tel (216) 871-5449
Cartoon Editor — John Shepherd
Business Manager — Harriet Barker

Copyright ©1996 by the Editor & Publisher Co.

Cartoonews Inc. — 9 Mountain Laurel Dr., Greenwich, CT 06831; tel (203) 622-1547; fax (203) 622-1648
President — T.R. Fletcher
VP In Charge of Sales — L. Raymond
Dir. of Administration — Elaine A. Aquino
Graphic Assistant — Steve Lefkowitz
Accountant/CPA — John Schmidt

Cartoonists & Writers Syndicate — 67 Riverside Dr., Ste. 1-D, New York, NY 10024; tel (212) 362-9256/(212) CARTOON; fax (212) 595-4218
Pres./Editorial Director — Jerry Robinson
Vice Pres./Editor — Jens Robinson
Assoc. Ed.-Feature Sales — Peter Hultberg
Assoc. Ed.-Special Sales — Susan Monagan
Assist. Editor-Production — David Sung
Assist. Editor-Business — Patricia Gregory

Caruba Organization, The — 9 Brookside Rd.; PO Box 40, Maplewood, NJ 07040-0040; tel (201) 763-6392; fax (201) 763-4287
President — Alan Caruba

Catholic News Services — 3211 4th St. NE, Washington, DC 20017-1100; tel (202) 541-3250; fax (202) 541-3255
Dir./Editor-In-Chief — Thomas N. Lorsung
General News Editor — James Lackey
Features Editor — David Gibson

Central News Agency Inc. — 2 Penn Plz., 18th Fl., c/o UPI, New York, NY 10001; tel (212) 643-9332
NY Bureau Chief — David Yin-Chi Wang

Central Press Features of London — 400 Madison Ave., Ste. 1704, New York, NY 10017; tel (212) 832-2839
U.S. Editor — Jeffrey Blyth

Centre Ice Communications — 43 1/2 Sentinel Rd., Lake Placid, NY 12946; tel (518) 523-4289; fax (518) 523-4289

Chesstours — PO Box 1182, Reno, NV 89504; tel (702) 786-3178
Author/Owner — Larry Evans

Chicago Sun-Times Features Inc. — 401 N. Wabash Ave., Ste. 532-A, Chicago, IL 60611; tel (312) 321-2890; fax (312) 321-2336
President — Andrew B. Davis
Syndicate Mgr. — Elizabeth Owens-Schiele

Chicago Tribune Press Service Inc. — 220 E. 42nd St., Rm. 1402, New York, NY 10017; tel (212) 986-0970/(212) 210-5983; fax (212) 210-5988
Bureau Chief — Lisa Anderson

Child Life — 2212 The Circle, Raleigh, NC 27608; tel (919) 834-0105
Author — Beverly Mills

Children's Express — 1440 New York Ave. NW, Ste. 510, Washington, DC 20005; tel (202) 737-7377; fax (202) 737-0193
President & Publisher — Robert H. Clampitt
VP/Marketing & Comm. — Lee Wood
VP/Development — Judith Fiske Moak

Chronicle Features — 870 Market St., San Francisco, CA 94102; tel (415) 777-7212
Editor/General Manager — Stuart Dodds
Office Manager — Rennie Kirby
Associate Editor — Susan Peters
Production Manager — Harley Colbert

Cineman Syndicate — PO Box 4433, Middletown, NY 10940-8301; tel (914) 692-4572; fax (914) 692-8311; internet 213-9111@mcimail.com
Editor — Jay A. Brown
Associate Editor — Don Casciato
Associate Editor — Robert Edelstein

City News Bureau of Chicago — 35 E. Wacker Dr., Ste. 792, Chicago, IL 60601; tel (312) 782-8100
Editor/Gen. Manager — Joseph Reilly
Managing Editor — Paul Zimbrakos
City Editor (night) — Dan Haar
News Editor — Kim Kishbaugh
Chief Copy Editor — Woody Hoffman
Broadcast Editor — Susan Stevens
Overnight Editor — Wally Tokarz

City News Service Inc. — 6255 Sunset Blvd., Ste. 1905, Los Angeles, CA 90028; tel (213) 465-8792; fax (213) 465-7236
Business Manager — Chris Armellini

Clear Creek Features — PO Box 3303, Grass Valley, CA 95945; tel (916) 272-7176
Author/Self-Syndicated — Mike Drummond

Collector Watch Ltd. — PO Box 25615, Washington, DC 20007; tel (202) 333-3007; fax (202) 333-3007
President/White House Correspondent/Critic — L. Clayton Willis

Collins Communications — 11 Madison Ave., Westwood, NJ 07675; tel (201) 358-2929/Home (201) 652-4263; fax (201) 358-2824
Contact — Chaunce Hayden

Colombian Comics Syndicate — 1450 Coral Way, Ste. 7, Miami, FL 33145; tel (305) 858-9613; fax (305) 858-7547
Director — Jorge Grosso
Assistant Director — Carmelo Vergara
Repres. for U.S. & Canada — William Grosso

Columbia Features — PO Box 1957, New Smyrna Beach, FL 32170; tel (904) 428-0447
Editor — Robert Ferguson
President — Edward Funkhauser
Associate Editor — Anne Ferguson

Comic Art Therapy Services — PO Box 7981 C.A.T.S., Corpus Christi, TX 78415; tel (512) 850-2930; fax (512) 857-2424
Art Director — Pedro Moreno
Advertising Manager — Liz Fernandez
Comic Editor — James Rodriguez
Secretary — Christina Moreno
Secretary — Daniela Moreno

Common Communications Inc. — 162 Rockland St., Portsmouth, NH 03801; tel (603) 433-5596

Communication International/National News — 1423 N. Orange Grove Ave.; PO Box 46-181, Los Angeles, CA 90046; tel (213) 876-1668; fax (213) 876-1404
President — Hillary Bekins
Editor — S. Allengham
Lead Columnist — Bonnie Churchild

Community Press Service — 117 W. 2nd St.; PO Box 639, Frankfort, KY 40602; tel (502) 223-1736; fax (502) 223-2679
Owner — Heritage Printing
Contact — Phyllis Cornett
Contact — Rick Calvert

Compass Syndicate — PO Box 395, Carmel, IN 46032; tel (317) 844-1188
Owner/Editor — Peggy Gisler
Owner/Editor — Marge Eberts

ComputerUser — 220 S. Sixth St., Ste. 500, Minneapolis, MN 55402-4507; tel (612) 339-7571 (office)/(612) 336-9279 (direct); e-mail 310.3179@MCIMail.com
Editor-In-Chief — Steve Deyo
Managing Editor — Krista Hauenstein

Congressional Quarterly Service — 1414 22nd St. NW, Washington, DC 20037; tel (202) 887-8500
Publisher & President — Neil Skene
Exec. Editor & Vice President — Robert Merry
Dir. Sales & Mktg. — Ed Hauck
Dir. Marketing Programs — Kevin Donoghue
Media Market Mgr. — Jeanne Jennings

Consumer News Systems, Ltd. — 6045 N. Scottsdale Rd., Ste. 206, Scottsdale, AZ 88253; tel (800) 267-8525/(602) 905-8000; fax (602) 905-8190
Vice President — Mark Perkins

Continental Features/Continental News Service — 341 W. Broadway, Ste. 265, San Diego, CA 92101; tel (619) 492-8696/(202) 452-7453
Syndicate Editor — Gary P. Salamone

Cook, A.J. — 6785 Slash Pine, Memphis, TN 38119; tel (901) 754-8925

Copley News Service — 123 Camino de la Reina, Ste. E-250 (92108); PO Box 190, San Diego, CA 92112; tel (619) 293-1818/(800) 238-6196; fax (619) 297-0537
President — David C. Copley
Exec. VP/Editor — Robert M. Witty
VP/Business Mng. — Patricia E. Gonzales
Sales Manager — Gabriel Bradford
Editorial Manager — Glenda Winders
Los Angeles, CA — Bureau Chief: Paul M. Pringle; 485-A Hall of Administration, 500 W. Temple St., Los Angeles, CA 90012; tel (213) 974-8975; fax (213) 628-1935
Sacramento, CA — Bureau Chief: James P. Sweeney; Park Executive Bldg., 925 L St., Ste. 1190, Sacramento, CA 95814; tel (916) 445-6655; fax (916) 443-1912
Washington, DC — Vice President/Bureau Chief: George E. Condon; National Press Bldg., 529 14th St. NW, Rm. 1100, Washington, DC; tel (202) 737-6960; fax (202) 393-3643
Springfield, IL — Bureau Chief: Ray Serati; State Capitol, Pressroom, Springfield, IL 62706; tel (217) 544-3666; fax (217) 544-9611
Chicago, IL — Bureau Chief: Roderick Kelly; Chicago Regional Bureau, 1430 Branding Ln., Ste. 119, Downers Grove, IL 60515; tel (708) 964-8990; fax (708) 964-9382
Mexico City, Mexico — Bureau Chief: S. Lynne Walker; Mexico City Bureau, Tres Cruces, No. 11, Colonia Coyoacan, DF 04000 Mexico; tel (011) 525-554-1658; fax (011) 525-554-7240

Cox Enterprises Inc. — PO Box 105357, Atlanta, GA 30348; tel (404) 843-5000
President/COO — David Easterly

Cox Newspapers Washington Bureau — 2000 Pennsylvania Ave. NW, Ste. 10000, Washington, DC 20006-1894; tel (202) 331-0900; fax (202) 331-1055
Bureau Chief — Andrew J. Glass
Deputy Bureau Chief — Andrew Alexander

Coyote Inc. — 207 Norland Ave., New Orleans, LA 70131; tel (504) 391-3385; fax (504) 394-3377
Owner/Author — Marie Gould

Craft Patterns Inc. — 3545 Stern Ave., St. Charles, IL 60174; tel (708) 584-3334; fax (708) 584-3418; (800) 747-1429
Editor — Brian Woodley Smith
Marketing Service Mgr. — Marsha Sidmore

Crain News Service — 220 E. 42nd St., New York, NY 60611-2590; tel (212) 254-0890; fax (212) 254-7646
Sales Manager — Joseph Hanley
Chicago, IL — Editor: Henry Bernstein; Administrative Assistant: Melanie Glover; 740 E. Rush St.; PO Box 105357, Chicago IL 60611-2590; tel (312) 649-5464; fax (312) 649-5228

Creative Comic Syndicate — 1608 South Dakota Ave., Sioux Falls, SD 57105; tel (605) 336-9434
Owner/Manager — Ken Alvine

Creative Syndication Services — PO Box 40, Eureka, MO 63025; tel (314) 938-9116
Publisher — Edward A. Baldwin

Creators Syndicate — 5777 W. Century Blvd., Ste. 700, Los Angeles, CA 90045; tel (310) 337-7003; fax (310) 337-7625
President/CEO — Richard S. Newcombe
Executive Vice President — Anita Tobias
Executive Vice President — Mike Santiago
VP/Editorial Director — Katherine Searcy
Sales Executive — Peter Alcan
Sales Executive — Mary Ann Veldman
Sales Administrator — Jennifer Turner
Sales Executive — Margo Sugrue
Sales Executive — Tony Rossi

Cricket Communications Inc. — PO Box 527, Ardmore, PA 19003; tel (215) 747-6684; fax (215) 747-7082
President/Publisher — Edwin Marks
Editor — Mark E. Battersby

Critic's Choice Reviews — 8166 Montgomery Rd., Ste. 422, Cincinnati, OH 45236; tel (513) 761-1188; fax (513) 761-9011; e-mail critic@aol.com
Communications Director — Lori Pearson
Editor-In-Chief — Aris Christofides
Executive Editor — Don Prues
Managing Editor — Robin Gee
Senior Critic — Dan Amrich
Senior Critic — Susan Conner
Senior Critic — Ken Hughes
Senior Critic — Dan O'Keeffe
Senior Critic — Rick Anderson
Senior Critic — Craig Boldman
Senior Critic — Lori Christofides
Senior Critic — Teressa L. Elliott
Contributing Critic — Wade R. Gossett
Contributing Critic — Brandon MacGoohan
Contributing Critic — A.T. Pearson
Contributing Critic — George Schatzman
Contributing Critic — Elton De Stephano

Cromley News-Features — 1912 Martha's Rd., 46989 Washington DC (20050-6989), Alexandria, VA 22307; tel (703) 765-4184/(703) 695-5118; fax (703) 693-7206
President — Ray Cromley

Cronin Feature Syndicating Inc. — 1000 Parkview Dr., Ste. 631, Hallandale, FL 33009; tel (305) 376-6057
Vice President/Author — Sylvia Cronin
Sales Manager — Edward Wallace Dresner

Crowe, J.D. — 2400 Kettner Blvd., Studio 214, San Diego, CA 92101; tel (619) 582-2769/(619) 234-3405

Crown Syndicate Inc. — 3817 W. Parkmont Pl.; PO Box 99126, Seattle, WA 98199; tel (206) 285-1888
President — L.M. Boyd
Vice President — Patricia Boyd

D

Dail Advertising Service — PO Box 10278, Goldsboro, NC 27532; tel (919) 736-0447/(800) 326-3615; fax (919) 736-0483
National Representative — Bobby Dail

Daily Telegraph, The — One Canada Sq., Canary Wharf, London E14 5DT, England tel (800) 367-8313
Bureau Chief — Charles Laurence
Correspondent — Hugh Davies
Financial Correspondent — Kate Rankine

DANY News Service — 22 Lesley Dr., Syosset, NY 11791; tel (516) 921-4611
President — David Nydick
Editor — Robert Manhemer

Davy Associates Media Features — 215 Avenida Del Mar, San Clemente, CA 92672; tel (714) 498-0833; fax (714) 498-6573
Owner — James L. Davy

Demko Publishing — 21946 Pine Trace, Boca Raton, FL 33428; tel (305) 237-4159/(407) 482-6271; e-mail AgeAmerNet@aol.com, Web site http://home.aol.com/AgeAmerNet
Editor-in-Chief, Aging American News Net — David J. Demko Ph.D.
Author-Health Care & Housing — Marie Mentzer
Author-Arts & Entert. — Elizabeth Rupich
Author-Education — Dorothy Harris
Author-Legislation — Harold Correll

Deutsche Presse-Agentur (dpa) — 969 National Press Bldg. NW, Washington, DC 20045; tel (202) 783-5097; fax (202) 783-4116
Bureau Chief — Herbert Winkler
Deputy Bureau Chief — Hanns-Jochen Kaffsack
Ankara, Turkey — Bestekar Sokak 80/4; Kavaklidere-Ankara, Ankara, Turkey; tel (90-312) 4677398/(90-312) 4677399; fax (90-4) 4674436
Asuncion, Paraguay — Alberdi 733, piso 3, Edif. Ypacarar, ofc. 10, Asuncion, Paraguay; tel (595-21) 495451; fax (595-21) 448116
Athens, Greece — Miniati 1, Athens, GR 11636, Greece; tel (30-1) 9247774; fax (30-1) 9222185
Beijing, China — San Li Tun, Ban Gong Lou, 1-31, Beijing, China; tel (86-1) 5321473; fax (86-1) 5321615; telex 22297 dpapk cn
Bogota, Columbia — Carrera 7 No. 17-01, Oficina 909, Apartado 044245, Bogota, Columbia; tel (57-1) 2420941/(57-1) 2847481; fax (57-1) 2818065
Brussels, Belgium — Boulevard Charlemagne 1, Bte. 17, International Press Centre, Brussels 1041, Belgium; tel (322) 2380937/(322) 2303691/(322) 2380934/(322) 2380938; fax (322) 2309696
Buenos Aires, Argentina — Bouchard 557, 5th Fl., Buenos Aires 1106, Argentina; tel (00541) 315 05 45; fax (00541) 311 53 11
Cairo, Egypt — 1125 Corniche el Nil, 14th Fl.; PO Box 368 Mhd Farid, Maspero-Cairo, Egypt; tel (20-2) 5780351/(20-2) 5780353/(20-2) 5780355 (Sales); fax (20-2) 5780354/(20-2) 5780356 (Sales); telex 92054 dpa un
Caracas, Venezuela — Av. Fco. de Miranda, Centro Plaza, Torre D, 11th Fl.; of. B. Los Palos Grandes, Caracas, Venezuela; tel (58-2) 5751235; fax (58-2) 5736331
Copenhagen, Denmark — Mikkel Bryggers Gade 5, Copenhagen K DK 1460, Denmark; tel (45) 33142219; fax (45) 33146672
Geneva, Switzerland — 10 Palais des Nations, Ste. 84, Geneva 1211, Switzerland; tel (41-22) 7315117/(41-22) 4412373; fax (41-22) 7332706
Guatemala City, Guatemala — 5a calle 4-30, Zona 1; Apartado postal 2333, Ciudad de Guatemala, Guatemala; tel (502-2) 517505/(502-2) 23444; fax (502-2) 517505; telex 5227
Hamburg, Germany — Mittelweg 38 D-20148, Germany; tel (49) 40 41130; fax (49) 40 4113351; telex 272888
Havana, Cuba — Edificio Focsa, Apt. 2-K, Calle 17 y M Vedado, Havana, Cuba; tel 333501; fax 333501
Islamabad, Pakistan — Nazimuddin Rd., F 6/1, Islamabad 40, Pakistan; tel (92-51) 821925
Johannesburg, South Africa — 96 Jorrisen St., Nedbank Corner Bldg., Rm. 201; PO Box 32521, Johannesburg-Braamfontein 2017, South Africa; tel (27-11) 3391148; fax (27-11) 3396679
Kiev, Ukraine — Kreschtschalik 29, Kiev 252001, Ukraine; tel (7-044) 2255760/(7-044) 2302569; fax (7-044) 2255760/(7-044) 2302569
La Paz, Bolivia — Piso 9, ofc. 3, La Paz Dr.; Mariscal Santa Cruz 2150, Enricio Experanze, Casilla 13885 La Paz; tel (591-2) 352684; fax (591-2) 392488
Lima, Peru — Schell 343 Ofc. 707, Apartado 18-1362, Lima 18, Miraflores, Peru; tel (51-14) 443775/(51-14) 441437
London, England — 30 Old Queen St., London SW1H 9HP, England; tel (44-71) 2332888; fax (44-71) 2333534
Madrid, Spain — Espronceda 32, 5th Fl., Madrid 28003, Spain; tel (34-1) 4416484/(34-1) 4412373; fax (34-1) 4427706; telex 22480
Managua, Nicaragua — Apartado Postal 2095, Managua, D N, Nicaragua; tel (505-2) 74361/(505-2) 781862; fax (505-2) 781863
Manama, Bahrain — Mahooz, Apt. 2, Bldg. 1464, Rd. 3435; Area 334; PO Box 26995, Manama, Bahrain; tel (973) 727523; fax (973) 725440; telex 9542 dpa bn

Copyright ©1996 by the Editor & Publisher Co.

Manila, Philippines — Physician's Tower Bldg., PH; United Nations Ave., 1000 Ermila, Manila, Philippines; tel (63-2) 591321/(63-2) 591334; telex 23476
Mexico City, Mexico — Avenida Cuauhtemoc 16, Colonia Doctores, Mexico City Distrito Federal 06720, Mexico; tel (52-5) 5784829/(52-5) 7612435; fax (52-5) 7610762
Mona Vale, Australia — 36 Heath St., Mona Vale NSW 2103, Australia; tel (61-2) 9798253; fax (61-2) 9773154
Montevideo, Uruguay — Av. 18 de Julio 994, 4th Fl., Ofc. A, Montevideo, Uruguay; tel (598-2) 906201; fax (598-2) 922662
Moscow, Russia — Wohnung 210, Kutusowski Prospekt 7/4, Moscow, Russia; tel (7-502) 2241131 (Sat.)/(7-502) 2439790/(7-502) 2302563; fax (7-095) 2302543; telex 413122
Nairobi, Kenya — Chester House, 1st Fl., Koinange St.; PO Box 48546, Nairobi, Kenya; tel (254-2) 330274; fax (254-2) 221902; telex 22330
New Delhi, India — 39 Golf Links, New Delhi 110003, India; tel (91-11) 4617792/(91-11) 4627120; fax (91-11) 4625772; telex 3174031
New York, U.S. — Bureau Chief: Helmut Rather; United Nations, Rm. S-352, New York NY 10017; tel (212) 319-6626/ (212) 355-0318; fax (212) 753-6168
Ottawa, Canada — 702 National Press Bldg., 150 Wellington, Ottawa ON K1P 5A4 Canada; tel (613) 234-6024
Panama City, Panama — Apartado 1550, Panama City 1, Panama; tel (507) 330396; fax (507) 335393
Paris, France — 30 rue St. Augustin, Paris 75002, France; tel (33) 147429502; fax (33) 147425175
Prague, Czech Republic — Petrske namesli 1/1186, Prague 1 110 00, Czech Republic; tel (42-2) 2311810/(42-2) 2315230; fax (42-2) 2315196
Quito, Ecuador — Edificio Atrium, ofc. S-7; Gonzales Suarez 894, Quito, Ecuador; tel (593-2) 506450/(593-2) 568986; fax (593-2) 505632
Rio de Janeiro, Brazil — Rua Abade Ramos, 65, Rio de Janeiro 22,641, Brazil; tel (55-21) 26659.7/(55-21) 2862800; fax (55-21) 2860349
Rome, Italy — Via della Mercede 55 Int. 15, Rome 100187, Italy; tel (39-6) 6789810/(39-6) 6789176; fax (39-6) 69941598
San Jose, Costa Rica — Edificio 152, tercer piso; Avenida 1 y 3, Apartado 7156, San Jose Calle 11, Costa Rica; tel (506) 330604; fax (506) 330604
San Juan, Puerto Rico — Calle Lopez Landron 1509, Santurce; American Airlines Office Bldg., Ofc. 900, San Juan 00911-1936, Puerto Rico; tel (809) 722-4870; fax (809) 722-2935
San Salvador, El Salvador — 2a planta, ofc. 1/Apartado Postal 150; Avenida Espana 225, Edificio Quan, San Salvador, El Salvador; tel (503) 222640; fax (503) 222640
Santiago, Chile — San Antonio 427, Santiago, Chile; tel (56-2) 6326818/(56-2) 6326817; fax (56-2) 6393633
Seoul, South Korea — Hae-Yung Bldg., 10th Fl.; 148 Angug-Dong, Jongro-Ku, Seoul 110, South Korea; tel (82-2) 7383808; fax (82-2) 7386040
Singapore — 2 Vanda Crescent, Singapore 1128, Singapore; tel (65) 4695935; fax (65) 4626591
Tegucigalpa, Honduras — 48 calle y 5a avenida, No. 405, efficine 203; Edificio Jimenez Castro, Apartado postal 3522, Tegucigalpa, Honduras; tel (504) 378570; fax (504) 378570
Tel Aviv, Israel — 3-D Ibn Gvirol, Tel Aviv 61161, Israel; tel (972-3) 6954268/(972-3) 6959007; fax (972-3) 6963594
The Hague, The Netherlands — Eisenhoweriaan 128, The Hague 2517 KM, Netherlands; tel (31-70) 3561468; fax (31-70) 3521637
Tokyo, Japan — Nippon Press Center Bldg., Ste. 3-F; Chiyoda-ku, Tokyo 100, Japan; tel (81-3) 35806829/(81-3) 35805577; fax (81-3) 35937888
Vienna, Austria — Gunoldstrasse 14, IPZ, Vienna A-1199, Austria; tel (43-1) 362158/(43-1) 362159; fax (43-1) 3698549; telex 114633
Warsaw, Poland — Saska 7 a, Warsaw UI 03-908, Poland; tel (48-22) 6171058; fax (48-22) 6178481; telex 813374 pl
Zagreb, Croatia/Yugoslavia — c/o HINA, Marulicev Irg 16, Zagreb 4100, Croatia; tel (385-41) 427102; fax (385-41) 426124

Di Prieto, Sylvia — 55 W. 14th St., New York, NY 10011; tel (212) 255-4059; fax (212) 255-4059

Didato Associates — 175 Seton Dr., New Rochelle, NY 10804; tel (914) 636-0807; fax (914) 636-0807 (call first)

Distinguising Features Ltd — 1530 Locust, Ste. 205, Philadelphia, PA 19102
Self-Syndicated — David Wallace

Diversified News Service — 5249 E. 82nd St., Indianapolis, IN 46250; tel (317) 849-0526
President/Editor — Alex Hatton
VP/Bureau Chief — Orbrey Phipps
Publisher/Secretary — Kathi Gasaway
Treasurer — Nan Woods
Advertising Director — Susan Phipps

Dorsey Communications — 9239 Doheny Rd., Los Angeles, CA 90069; tel (310) 273-2245; fax (310) 273-6967
Chief Executive Officer — Helen Dorsey

Dow Jones Financial News Services — 200 Liberty St., 14th Fl., New York, NY 10281; tel (212) 416-2414/(800) 223-2274
Director — Craig O. Allsopp
Director of Administration — Bob Williams
Managing Editor — Robert Prinsky
Deputy Managing Editor — Neal Lipschutz
Nat'l. Director of Sales — Darrell W. Gunter
New York, NY — Managing Editor: Jim Furlong; Deputy Managing Editor: John Hitchcock, (212) 416-2321; Asst. News Editor: Marcus Wright, (212) 416-2316; Asst. News Editor: Hammad Jawdat, (212) 416-2316; Asst. News Editor: Bob Kozrna, (212) 416-2403; 200 Liberty St., 12th Fl., New York, NY 10281; tel (212) 416-2313
London, England — Chief European Correspondent: Arjen Bongard; 10 Fleet Pl., Limeburner Ln., London, EC4M 7RB England; tel (44-71) 832-9105; fax (44-71) 832-9101
Amsterdam, The Netherlands — Correspondent: Art Mooradian; Postbus 1016, 1000 BA, Amsterdam, Netherlands
Manana, Bahrain — c/o The Associated Press Bahrain Tourism Co. Building; PO Box 11022 Diplomatic Area, Manana, Bahrain; tel (97-3) 530-758; fax (97-3) 530-249
Bangkok, Thailand — Correspondent: Alwyn Scott; Charn Issara Tower, 14th Fl., 942/51 Rama IV Rd.; Mail To: PO Box 775, Bangkok 10501, Bangkok 10500, Thailand; tel (662) 235-0490; fax (662) 238-2661
Bonn, Germany — Correspondent: Andrew Jonus; Bonn Ctr. A, 11-412, Bonn 1 53113, Germany; tel (49-228) 215-717; fax (49-228) 216-746
Brussels, Belgium — Correspondent: Peter Greiff; 1 Blvd. Charlemagne, International Press Centre, Brussels 1041, Belgium; tel (32-2) 230-5997; fax (32-2) 230-7226
Buenos Aires, Argentina — Correspondent: Michelle Wallin; Casilla de Correo 1296, Buenos Aires, Argentina; tel (54-1) 315-1690; fax (54-1) 311-0083
Canberra, Australia — Correspondent: Ray Brindal; Parliament House, Ste. 90, Canberra A.C.T. 2600, Australia; tel (616) 273-1993; fax (616) 273-4073
Caracas, Venezuela — Correspondent: Richard Sanders; Apartado de Correo 1015, Caracas, Carmelita 1010, Venezuela; tel (58-2) 481-1785; fax (58-2) 483-5623
Copenhagen, Denmark — Correspondent: Xueling Lin; DK-1069 Copenhagen K, Bremerholm 1, Copenhagen, Denmark; tel (45-33) 111-524; fax (45-33) 938-420
Frankfurt, Germany — Correspondent: Silvia Astarelli; Mendelssohnstrasse 53, Frankfurt 60325, Germany; tel (49-69) 740-906; fax (49-69) 752-624
Geneva, Switzerland — Correspondent: Bhushan Bahree; 1211 Geneva, Palaise Des Nations, Bureau C-12, Geneva, Switzerland; tel (41-22) 732-4927; fax (41-22) 733-1337
Hong Kong — Correspondent: James Areddy; 1282 Telecom House, 3 Gloucester Rd., Hong Kong; tel (85-2) 802-4888
Jakarta, Indonesia — Correspondent: Peter Halesworth; PO Box 2056, Jakarta 10110, Indonesia; tel (62-21) 386-1344
Johannesburg, South Africa — Correspondent: Nancy Koates; PO Box 880, Aukland Park, Johannesburg 2006, South Africa; tel (27-11) 726-7903; fax (27-11) 726-7855
Kuala Lumpur, Malaysia — Correspondent: Matthew Geiger; Wisma Bernama, Ground Fl. No. 28, Rd. 1/65 A off Jalan Tun; Tun Razak, Malaysia, Kuala Lumpur; tel (60-3) 292-5254; fax (60-3) 292-9272
Madrid, Spain — c/o The Associated Press; PO Box 844, Madrid 28041, Spain; tel (34-1) 442-9856/0065; fax (34-1) 399-1930
Manila, Philippines — Correspondent: Lilian Karununean; PO Box 2274, Manila, Philippines; tel (63-2) 574-616/617/618; fax (63-2) 521-2430
Mexico City, Mexico — Correspondent: Peter R. Fritsch; c/o The Associated Press, Apartado Postal 1181, Mexico City, Mexico; tel (525) 592-1651/566-3488; fax (525) 703-3028
Milan, Italy — Correspondent: Debra Marks; Plz. Cavour 2, Milan 20121, Italy; tel (39-2) 7601-5386; fax (39-2) 783-284
Moscow, Russia (U.S. Office) — Correspondent: Gregory White; Associated Press/ Moscow Bureau, 50 Rockefeller Plz., New York, NY 10020; tel (7-095) 243-5153/5692; fax (7-095) 974-8026
Paris, France — Correspondent: David Pearson; 162, rue du Faubourg, Saint Honore, Paris 75008, France; tel (33-14) 256-0972; fax (33-14) 225-8736
Sao Paulo, Brazil — Correspondent: John Wright; Rua Major Quendinho 111 Sala 707, Sao Paulo 01050, Brazil; tel (55-11) 256-0520/(55-11) 256-4135
Seoul, Korea — Correspondent: Soo-mi Kim; Yonhap Agency Bldg., Ste. 85-1, Susongdong, Chongno-gu, Seoul, Korea; tel (82-2) 737-7048; fax (886-2) 500-7133
Singapore — Correspondent: Lim Mui Khi; 6 Battery Rd. #26-06 0104, Singapore; tel (65) 222-9213/221-8604; fax (65) 323-6673
Stockholm, Sweden — Correspondent: Robert Flint; Sveavagen 17; Box 1726, Stockholm, Sweden; tel (46-8) 118-440/(46-8) 791-7202
Sydney, Australia — Correspondent: Anthony Patrick; Level 6, 309 Kent St., Sydney NSW 2000, Australia; tel (61-2) 262-2622; fax (61-2) 262-2655
Taipei, Taiwan — Correspondent: Shirley Lai; Central News Agency Bldg., 209 Sung Kiang Rd., 6th Fl., Taipei, Taiwan; tel (886-2) 502-2557; fax (886-2) 500-7133
Tokyo, Japan — Correspondent: Akihiro Sato; New ATT Bldg., 13th Fl., 2-11-7 Akasaka, Minatu-Ku, Tokyo 107, Japan; tel (81-3) 3505-5901 thru 5905; fax (81-3) 3505-5950
Zurich, Switzerland — Correspondent: Dennis Baker; 59 Lowenstrasse, Zurich CH-8023, Switzerland; tel (41-1) 211-7014; fax (41-1) 211-7014
Washington, DC — Correspondent: William Murray; 1025 Connecticut Ave. NW, Ste. 800, Washington, DC 20036; tel (202) 862-9272; fax (202) 223-8039
Wellington, New Zealand — Correspondent: Mark Reynolds; PO Box 1504, Wellington, New Zealand; tel (64-4) 471-1902; fax (64-4) 471-0075
Dow Jones News Service utilizes all the news bureau staff of The Wall Street Journal throughout the U.S.-New York, Atlanta, Boston, Chicago, Cleveland, Dallas, Detroit, Los Angeles, Philadelphia, Pittsburgh, St. Louis, San Francisco, Washington DC.

Downtown — 155 1st Ave., New York, NY 10003; tel (212) 529-2255; fax (212) 529-2269
Publisher — Jane Resenbrink
Manager — Mary Hyatt
Columnist — Larry Litt

Dunkel Sports Research Service — 94 Ormond Pkwy.; PO Box 2167, Ormond Beach, FL 32176; tel (904) 677-6100
Author/Owner — Dick Dunkel

E

Editor's Copy Syndicate — 3803 Pin Oaks St., Sarasota, FL 34232; tel (941) 366-2169/(704) 628-1994
Editor/Publisher — Edward H. Sims
Business Manager — Bente Christensen
Circulation Manager — L.M. Hughes

Editorial Consultant Service — PO Box 524, West Hempstead, NY 11552; tel (516) 481-5487
Vice President — Richard Kiley
Editorial Director — Arthur A. Ingoglia

Editors Press Service Inc. — 330 W. 42nd St., 15th Fl., New York, NY 10036; tel (212) 563-2252; fax (212) 563-2517
Chairman — John F. Klem
Vice President/CEO — Mario Lorenzo
Vice President/Sales — Kerry Slagle

Edman Co., The — 390 Woodstock Ave.; PO Box 666, Putnam, CT 06260-0666; tel (203) 928-3500
Author/Owner — Louis S. Edman

EH Communications — PO Box 1452, Indianapolis, IN 46206; tel (317) 926-0204
Author — Erik Hromadka

Emerson, James B. — PO Box 14604, San Francisco, CA 94114-9991

Engberg, Karen M., M.D. — 2329 Oak Park Ln., Santa Barbara, CA 93105; tel (805) 682-8844; fax (805) 682-6499

Entertainment News Calendar — 250 W. 57th St., Ste. 1517-132, New York, NY 10107; tel (212) 421-1370; fax (212) 563-3488
Bureau Chief — Evelyn Heyward

Entertainment News Syndicate — PO Box 20481, D.H.C.C., New York, NY 10017; tel (212) 223-1821; fax (212) 223-3737
Editor — Lee Canaan
Sports Editor — Jed Canaan
Fashion/Beauty Editor — Barbara Marsten
Hospitality Editor — Marilyn Kirk
Music Film Editor — Robert Michaels
Contact — Jed Baron

Environment Cartoon Features — 3508 W. 151 St., Cleveland, OH 44111-2105; tel (216) 251-1389
Artist/Owner — Dean Norman

ESPN/SportsTicker — Harborside Financial Ctr., 600 Plaza Two, Jersey City, NJ 07311-3992; tel (201) 309-1200; fax (201) 860-9742
Vice President — Rick Alessandri
Managing Editor — Joe Carnicelli
General Manager — John Mastrobernardino
Dir./Marketing Services — Lou Monaco
Mgr./National Accounts — N. Ray Bledsoe
Manager/Media Sales — Vincent Bagnaturo

Europa Press News Service — Darlo Urzua, No. 152, Clasificador No. 5, Tajamar, Providencia, Santiago, Chile; tel (56) 2-235-2902/(56) 2-235-1584; fax (56) 2-235-1731
Director — Jose J Rios Vial
General Manager — Renato Campodonico
Editor — Maria Marta Raggio; Providencia, Tajamar; Clasificador No. 5
Manager — Mariana Tomasi
Executive Director — Pedro Erramouspe; Calle Lerma No. 482, Buenos Aires CP 1414, Argentina; tel (56 2) 777-7588

Evening News Broadcasting & Willis News Service — PO Box 25615, Washington, DC 20007; tel (202) 333-3007
President/White House Correspondent/Photojournalist — L. Clayton Willis
Blue Ridge Summit, PA — Camp David Bureau, 12374 Monterey Ln., Blue Ridge Summit PA 17214

Exhibitor Relations Co. — 116 N. Robertson Blvd., Ste. 606, Los Angeles, CA 90048; tel (310) 657-2005; fax (310) 657-7283
President — John Krier
Executive Vice Pres. — Paul Dergarabedian

Extra Newspaper Features — 18 First Ave. S.E.; PO Box 6118, Rochester, MN 55903-6118; tel (507) 285-7671; fax (507) 285-7666
Editor/Director — Kelly J. Boldan

F

F.A.C.—P.A.C. Inc. — Advisory Counsel, 5909 N.W. Expwy., Ste. 230, Oklahoma City, OK 73132-5102; tel (405) 728-8000/(800) 322-6080
President — Larry W. Beavers
Vice President — David M. Bailey
Secretary/Treasurer — J. June Bailey

Family Features Editorial Services Inc. — 8309 Melrose Dr., Shawnee Mission, KS 66214; tel (913) 888-3800; fax (913) 888-3503
President — Dianne S. Hogerty
Director of Marketing — Nancy A. Parsons

Family Matters Publications — 10422 Weddington St.; PO Box 650 (91603), North Hollywood, CA 91601; tel (818) 762-1707; fax (310) 478-1949
Contact — Mike Brown
Contact — Carol Wanzek

Farmer, W.D. Residence Designer Inc. — 2007 Montreal Rd. (Tucker, 30084); PO Box 450025, Atlanta, GA 31145; tel (770) 934-7380; fax (770) 934-1700

Fashion Sense — 445 E. 80th St., New York, NY 10021; tel (212) 861-3779
President — Lila Nadell

Feature Photo Service Inc. — 62 W. 45th St., New York, NY 10036; tel (212) 944-7744; fax (212) 944-9536
President — Bob Goldberg
Vice President — Richard Horwitz

Feature Service Syndicate — 855 Moulin Ave., Madison Heights, MI 48071-0654; tel (810) 544-0470
President — William R. Hatch
Exec. VP/Senior Editor — Glenn E. Dibble
Sales Manager — Alex Cedc

Features International of London — 400 Madison Ave., Ste. 1704, New York, NY 10017; tel (212) 832-2839
U.S. Editor — Jeffrey Blyth

The 5th Wave — 16 Rowe Pt., Rockport, MA 01966; tel (508) 546-2448; fax (508) 546-7747
Cartoonist — Rich Tennant
Assistant — Debbie Clarke

Financial Times — 1 Southwark Bridge, London, SE1 9HL England; tel (44-0171) 873-3000; fax (44-0171) 873-3082
Chief Executive — David Bell

FNA News — PO Box 11999, Salt Lake City, UT 84147; tel (801) 355-3336/(801) 355-1901
Managing Editor — Richard Goldberger
Washington Bureau Chief — Francine Modderno
Society Editor — Pamela Teplick
Health Editor/Acting Bureau Chief-Los Angeles — Connie Terry
Environmental Editor — Colleen Kellem
Legal Affairs Editor — M.F. Heyrend
Technology Editor — Marlon U. Stones
Business and Finance Ed. — Roger Comfort
Energy Editor/Acting Bureau Chief-Houston — K. Rossi

Fog City Features — 1585 Beach St., Ste. 203, San Francisco, CA 94123; tel (415) 921-6076

Food Nutrition Health News Service — 1712 Taylor St. NW, Washington, DC 20011; tel (202) 723-2477; fax (202) 882-9335
Author/Owner — Goody L. Solomon

Fotopress Independent News Service Int'l. — Box 1268, Sta. Q, Toronto, ON M4T 2P4 Canada; tel (416) 445-3594; fax (416) 445-4953
Operations Director — John M. Kubik
Accounts Administrator — Steven Brown
United Kingdom — Gordon Irving
Europe — Tore Eide Svenning
Europe — Wes Jonasson
Middle East — Michael Weiss
Africa — Andrew Mwansa
Africa — Obafimi Oredein
Indochina — David Dickinson
Japan — Shotaro Kotake
South America — Hugo Fernandez
South America — Alfonso Tobar
Central America — Vincent Delgado
Southern Europe & Middle East — Bruno Pavan

Fotos International — 4230 Ben Ave., Studio City, CA 91604-2021; tel (818) 508-6400; fax (310) 836-0200; e-mail entertainment@earthlink.net
Publisher — Max B. Miller
Editor — Frank Edwards
Manager — Alexandra Horvathova

Four Geez Press — 1911 Douglas Blvd., Ste. 85, Roseville, CA 95661; tel (916) 781-3440; fax (916) 781-6837

Franklin Features — 203 Lohmann St., Boerne, TX 78006-2031; tel (210) 816-9668/(210) 816-2177
Editor/Publisher — Robert Clark

From The Ground Up — 4621 Congress Dr., Midland, MI 48642; tel (517) 631-2333; fax (517) 631-2359
Author/Owner — Edward Hutchison

Future Features Syndicate — 1923 N. Wickham Rd., Ste. 117, Melbourne, FL 32935; tel (407) 259-3822; fax (407) 259-1471; e-mail futrfeat@iu.net; web site http://www.spindata.com/futrfeat/
President — Ada Lewis Forney
Creative Director — Jerome L. Forney

G

Gadget Guru, The — 95 White Bridge Rd., Ste. 212, Nashville, TN 37205; tel (615) 356-9595; fax (615) 356-9596
President — Andy Pargh

Gambill Arts & Graphix Syndicate — 66435 Pierson Blvd., Desert Hot Springs, CA 92240; tel (619) 251-2401; fax (619) 251-2401
Creator/Owner/Artist — George (Buzz) Gambill
Feature Editor — Suzanne Gambill

Gamma-Liaison Inc. — 11 E. 26th St., 17th Fl., New York, NY 10010; tel (212) 779-6300; fax (212) 779-6334
President — Michel G. Bernard
Exec. Vice President — Jennifer B. Coley

Gannett News Service — 1000 Wilson Blvd., 10th Fl., Arlington, VA 22229-0001; tel (703) 276-5800; fax (703) 558-3813
Editor — Robert W. Ritter
Man. Editor/Features/Graphics & Photography — J. Ford Huffman
National & Regional Ed. — Jefferey Stinson
National Editor — Ron Cohen
Regional Editor/West — Judi Austin
Regional Editor/East — Phil Pruitt
Sports Editor — Jerry Langdon
Copy Desk Chief — Emilie Davis
Business Editor — Craig Schwed
Albany, NY — Bureau Chief: Jay Gallagher; 150 State St., Albany, NY 12207; tel (518) 436-9781; fax (518) 436-0130
Baton Rouge, LA — Bureau Chief: John Hill; PO Box 44337, Capital Sta., Baton Rouge, LA 70804; tel (504) 387-6506; fax (504) 342-7333
Columbus, OH — Bureau Chief: Sandy Theis; 16 E. Broad St., Ste. 1001, Columbus, OH 43215; tel (614) 224-4640; fax (614) 221-0781
Harrisburg, PA — Bureau Chief: Brad Bumstead; State Capital, News Room, Harrisburg, PA 17105; tel (717) 783-3763; fax (717) 787-3941
Indianapolis, IN — 150 W. Market St., Ste. 400, Indianapolis, IN 46204; tel (317) 634-9751; fax (317) 634-0674
Olympia, WA — Bureau Chief: Bob Partlow; 1417 S. Columbia St., 2nd Fl., Olympia, WA 98504; tel (206) 753-1688; fax (206) 745-5408
San Francisco, CA — Nat'l. West Coast Correspondent: Ellan Hale; 1928 Pierce St., San Francisco, CA 94115; tel (415) 885-01324; fax (415) 885-0132
Sacramento, CA — Bureau Chief: Jake Henshaw; 925 L St., Ste. 110, Sacramento, CA 95814; tel (916) 446-1036; fax (916) 446-7326
Springfield, IL — Bureau Chief: Spencer Hunt; State Capital Bldg., Press Room-Mezzanine, Springfield, IL 62706; tel (217) 782-2959; fax (217) 782-2529
Tallahassee, FL — Bureau Chief: Keith Goldschmidt; 336 E. College Ave., Tallahassee, FL 32301; tel (904) 222-8384; fax (904) 222-7851

Gayles, Yolonda & Associates — PO Box 19616, Chicago, IL 60619; tel (312) 783-3333

Gelman Feature Syndicate, The — 826 E. 14th St., Brooklyn, NY 11230; tel (718) 434-6050
Owner/Editor — Bernard Gelman

Gemini News Service — 400 Madison Ave., Ste. 1704, New York, NY 10017; tel (212) 832-2839
U.S. Editor — Jeffrey Blyth

German Press Agency — 405 E. 42nd St., United Nations, Rm. S-352, New York, NY 10017; tel (212) 319-6626; fax (212) 753-6168
Chief Correspondent — Helmut Raether

Glasserfield Directory — 10240 Camarillo St., Ste. 210, Toluca Lake, CA 91602; tel (818) 769-4774
President/Editor — Selma Glasser

Glenmoor Enterprise Media Group — 733 S. Main St., Ste. 173, Willits, CA 95490; tel (707) 459-6027; fax (707) 459-6027
General Manager — Ron C. Moorhead

Global Horizons — 1330 New Hampshire Ave. NW, Ste. 609, Washington, DC 20036; tel (202) 659-1921
President — Edward Flattau
Editor — Pam Ebert

Globe Photos Inc. — 275 7th Ave., New York, NY 10001; tel (212) 689-1340
President — Mary Beth Whelan
Vice President — Raymond D. Whelan
Bureau Chief — Dick Denuet
Assignment Editor — Raymond F. Whelan

Globe Syndicate — 499 Richardson Rd., Strasburg, VA 22657-9502; tel (540) 635-3229 (Editorial Offices & Inquiries); fax (703) 519-8275; (703) 549-2322 (Production & Inquiries), e-mail bourjfam@delphi.com
Editor/Publisher — Monte Bourjaily Jr.
Editor/Assoc. Pub. — M.F. Bourjaily III; 218 S. Fairfax St., Alexandria, VA 22314

Golf Publishing Syndicate — 2743 Saxon St., Allentown, PA 18103; tel (610) 437-4982; fax (610) 866-3967
President — Karl D. Gilbert

Goodwin, Dave & Associates — PO Drawer 54-6661, Surfside, FL 33154; tel (305) 531-0071; fax (305) 531-5490
Author/Owner — Dave Goodwin

Graham News Syndicate — 2770 W. 5th St., Ste. G-20, Brooklyn, NY 11224; tel (718) 372-1920
Pres./Editor-in-Chief — Paula Royce Graham
Correspondent — Lane W. Hall
Correspondent — Liz Clifton

Grammar Gremlins — PO Box 2121, Knoxville, TN 37901; tel (615) 688-3400
Author — Don K. Ferguson

Graphics Syndicate — 1000 Gerrard St. E.; PO Box 98098, Toronto, ON M4M 3L9 Canada; tel (416) 463-3824; fax (416) 463-7854
General Manager — Michael Lea
Editorial Manager — Catherine Farley
Syndication Representative — Cindy Vautour

Green Grass Syndicated Features — 2972 115th St., Toledo, OH 43611-2838; tel (419) 726-1037; fax (419) 726-8868; e-mail 73437.1730@compuserve.com
Editor/Publisher — Marcia King

Green Thumb, The — Ingleside Rd.; PO Box 579, Naples, NY 14512; tel (716) 374-5400
Editor — George Abraham
Assistant Editor — Katherine Abraham

Griffith News Feature Service Worldwide — 234 5th Ave., New York, NY 10001; tel (212) 779-3492/(212) 686-0001
Editor-In-Chief — Bill Griffith
Picture Editor — James Griffith

Gulbranson Communications Group — 1121 Birnam Woods Dr., Virginia Beach, VA 23464; tel (804) 366-5224; fax (804) 366-0661

H

Harmon Football Forecast — PO Box 994, Long Beach, NY 11561; tel (516) 432-6376
Editor/Publisher — James M. Harmon

Health Promotion Features & Training Consultants — PO Box 920, Verdi, NV 89439; tel (702) 852-0754; fax (702) 852-OSKI
Editor & Director — John Yacenda
Associate Editor — Benita Crocco

Hearst News Service — 1701 Pennsylvania Ave. NW, Washington, DC 20006; tel (202) 298-6920; fax (202) 333-1184
Washington Bureau Chief — Charles J. Lewis
Asst. Bureau Chief/News Ed. — Susanna McBee
Office Manager — Katie Harrison

Hearst Newspapers — 1701 Pennsylvania Ave. NW, Washington, DC 20006; tel (202) 298-6920
Paris Bureau Chief — Bernard Kaplan; 8, rue Picot, Paris 75116, France

HFM Literary Enterprises — 3283 Casorso Rd., Ste. 104, Kelowna, BC V1W 3L6 Canada; tel (604) 868-8603
Author — Dr. Frank MacInnis

Hinders, Peggy — PO Box 6294, Chesterfield, MO 63017; tel (314) 537-2582

Hollywood Inside Syndicate — Los Angeles, CA; tel (909) 672-8459; fax (909) 672-8459;
Director — John Austin
Please call for delivery address.

Hollywood News Calendar — 14755 Ventura Blvd., Ste. 1562, Sherman Oaks, CA 91403; tel (818) 986-8168; fax (818) 789-8047
Editor-In-Chief — Carolyn Fox
Editor — Susan Fox-Davis

Home Improvement Time Inc. — 7425 Steubenville Pike, Oakdale, PA 15071; tel (412) 787-2881
Contact — James A. Stewart Jr.

HomeStyles Publishing and Marketing Inc. — 275 Market St., Ste. 521, Minneapolis, MN 55405; tel (612) 338-8155/(800) 547-5570; fax (612) 338-5866
Publisher — Roger Heegaard
President — Jeff Heegaard
Marketing Director — Wendy Schroeder

Hometown Flavor — 1504 S. Marengo Ave., Pasadena, CA 91106-4230; tel (818) 799-0467
Editor/Manager — Kerwin Hoover

Hopkins Syndicate Inc., The — 802 S. Washington St., Bloomington, IN 47401-4644; tel (812) 331-7753
General Manager — S.L. Abram
Sales Manager — Matthew J. Ross

Horowitz, Rick — 4014 N. Morris Blvd., Shorewood, WI 53211; tel (414) 963-9333

Hubbard, Janice — 1560 E. Garfield Ave., Salt Lake City, UT 84105; tel (801) 467-2117

Humor Books Syndicate — 28 Clare Street, Stafford, VA 22554; tel (703) 720-6300; fax (703) 720-6877
Cartoonist/Columnist — Al Brooks

Humornet — 313 E. 6th St., 2nd Fl., New York, NY 10003; tel (212) 614-1591; fax (212) 614-9563
Editor — Larry Litt

I

Imagination's Edge — PO Box 9864, Berkeley, CA 94709-0864; tel (510) 849-3541
Self-Syndicated — Michael Berry

Impact Visuals Photo & Graphics Inc. — 24 W. 25th St., 12th Fl., New York, NY 10010; tel (212) 807-6622; fax (212) 807-6644
General Manager — Robert Fox
Managing Editor — Marcia Dover Hoffman
Picture Editor — Karen Berman
Sales Manager — Jane Welna
Comptroller — Peter Davis
Billing & Returns — Larry Reilly

In A Nutshell — 119 Washington Ave., Staten Island, NY 10314; tel (718) 698-6979; fax (718) 698-3535
Author/Owner — Barbara Naness

Incremona, Frank — 3660 Round Meadow Ln., Hatboro, PA 19040; tel (215) 675-1753; fax (215) 675-1753

Independence Feature Syndicate — 14142 Denver W. Pkwy., Ste. 185, Golden, CO 80401-3134; tel (303) 279-6536; fax (303) 279-4176
Editor — David Kopel

Independent Cartoonist Freelance — 2007 Surf Ave., Apt. 10-B, Brooklyn, NY 11224; tel (718) 946-4949/(718) 266-6321
Columnist — Irving Robertson

Inman News Features — 5335 College Ave., Ste. 25, Oakland, CA 94618; tel (510) 658-9252
Owner — Bradley Inman

INSIGHT News — 17 St. Joseph St., Ste. 309, Toronto, ON M4Y 1J8 Canada; tel (416) 413-4900; fax (416) 413-4887
Executive Editor — W. Richard Reynolds

Inter Press Service (Distributed by Global Info. Network) — 777 United Nations Plz., New York, NY 10017; tel (212) 286-0123; fax (212) 818-9249; e-mail ipsgin@igc.apc.org
Director — Lisa Vives
Spanish Division Director — Patricia Corrige
News Editor — Andrew Whitehead
Technical Engineer — Chris Agee

Interior Design Teacher — 74 Chestnut St., Lakewood, NJ 08701; tel (908) 370-1441
Author — Michael Guarini

International Business Information Service — PO Box 4082, Irvine, CA 92716; tel (714) 552-8494

International BusinessMan News Bureau — 535 5th Ave., 33rd Fl.; PO Box 5595, New York, NY 10185; tel (212) 476-0802; fax (212) 663-1663; e-mail 3418747@mcimail.com, cable NEWSBUREAU NEW YORK
Chairman/CEO/Editor-In-Chief — J.J. Edwards
President — Ellen M. Vahidi
VP/Bureau Chief — E.J. Edwards
VP/Food Ed., Test Kitchen — C.P. Hennessy
Software Review Editor — T.O. Edwards
New York, NY — Test Kitchen: 241 W. 97th St., Ste. 7-N, New York, NY 10025; tel (212) 476-0802; fax (212) 663-1663

International News Agency — 2445 Pine Tree Dr., Ste. 20, Miami Beach, FL 33140-4611; tel (305) 674-9746; fax (305) 674-1939
Bureau Chief — C.H. Garvey
Executive Editor — R.J. Sherker
Assistant Editor — T.M. Mosberg
Managing Editor — Larry Lowis
Arts Department — Donna Shaw
Business Department — Ed Dever
Charity Department — Ed Hayden
Food — Roz Sholin
Sports — Pat Simpson
Travel — Judy Putnam

International Photo News — 193 Sanpiper Ave., West Palm Beach, FL 33411-2937; tel (407) 793-3424
Bureau Chief — Elliott S. Kravetz
Assistant Bureau Chief — Jay N. Kravetz

International Press Syndicate — 50, ave. des Champs-Elysees, Paris, 75008; France; tel (45) 633344/(45) 633399; fax (45) 633388
President — George J. Gendelman
Chairman — Paul O. Gendelman

International Puzzle Features — 740 Van Rensselaer Ave., Niagara Falls, NY 14305; tel (716) 285-6105
President — Pat Battaglia

International/New England Motorsports Syndication — 84 Smith Ave., Stoughton, MA 02072; tel (617) 446-5448/(617) 344-2837
Author — Lou Modestino

Interpress of London and New York — 400 Madison Ave., Ste. 1704, New York, NY 10017; tel (212) 832-2839
Chief Editor — Jeffrey Blyth

Interstate News Services — 237 S. Clark Ave., St. Louis, MO 63135; tel (314) 522-1300/(800) 522-1300; fax (314) 522-1999
Pres./Managing Editor — Michael J. Olds
Secretary/Treasurer — Ellen M. Olds
Asst. Managing Editor — Diane Ross
Little Rock, AR — Arkansas Capitol Bldg. Press Room, Little Rock, AR 72201; tel (800) 522-1301; fax (314) 521-1016
Springfield, IL — Bureau Chief: Diane Ross; ILCA Press Room, West Mezzanine; Statehouse, Springfield, IL 62706; tel (217) 785-7231

Ironwood Publications — PO Box 974, Charleston, IL 61920; tel (217) 581-2719; (217) 345-6812
Self-Syndicated — Allen W. Smith

J

James, Gary — 111 Shearin Ave., East Syracuse, NY 13057; tel (315) 463-8348

Jamieson Associates — 61 S. Main St., Ste. 101, West Hartford, CT 06107-2403; tel (203) 521-2373; fax (203) 521-5477
Principal — Lee Jamieson

Jandon Features — 53961 222nd St., Glenwood, IA 51534; tel (712) 527-9517; fax (712) 527-5063; e-mail driggenbach@mci-mail.com
Manager — Don Riggenbach

Copyright ©1996 by the Editor & Publisher Co.

Jerusalem Post Foreign Service, The — 211 E. 43rd St., New York, NY 10017; tel (212) 599-3666; fax (212) 599-4743
Information Officer — Nina Keren-David
Manager/North America — Daphne Raz
New York Correspondent — Marylyn Henry
Washington DC Corres. — Filley Kuttler

Jewish Telegraphic Agency Inc. — 330 7th Ave., 11th Fl., New York, NY 10001-5010; tel (212) 643-1890; fax (212) 643-8498; e-mail jtany@aol.com
Executive Editor/Publisher — Mark Joffe
President — Caryn Rosen Adelman
Editor — Lisa Hostein
Managing Editor — Kenneth Bandler

Jiji Press America Ltd. — 120 W. 45th St., Ste. 1401, New York, NY 10036; tel (212) 575-5830; fax (212) 764-3950
President — Supuru Sasaki
Managing Editor — Kuniji Oguro

Jill, Jodi Features — 1705 14th St., Ste. 321, Boulder, CO 80302; tel (303) 575-1319
President — Jodi Jill
Vice President — J.J. Wishmore
Assistant Vice President — Iarvin Coolman
Editor — Carol Handz
Editorial Director — Pete Brownston
Circulation Director — Bub Wellington
International Director — Louise Furston-Ball
Graphics Coordinator — Ted C. Sparks
Sales Manager — Hal Cells
Assistant Sales — A.J. (Spot) Feal
Mailroom Manager — Cleo Housely
Assistant Graphic Coord. — Kimber Parman
Technical Specialist — Belle Trujillo
Assistant Editor — Michael Tipes
Writer's Block Solver — Robert Colonfyse
Promotions Director — Shelia Hutson
Public Relations — Allen Kniese
ECO/Coordinator — Jim Simon

Journal Press Syndicate — PO Box 931, Grand Central Sta., New York, NY 10163-0931; tel (212) 580-8559; fax (212) 769-4384
Director — Donald Finck
Editor — Eugene R. Smith
Managing Editor — John Lynker
Art Director — William Kresse

K

Kahn, A.D. Inc. — 24901 Northwestern Hwy., Ste. 316-B, Southfield, MI 48075-2207; tel (810) 355-4100; fax (810) 356-4344

Keister-Williams Newspaper Services — PO Box 8005, Charlottesville, VA 22906; tel (804) 293-4709/(800) 293-4709; fax (804) 293-4884
Author — Jean Lindsay
Marketing Director — Meta L. Nay
Sales Vice-President — Ky Lindsay

Kentoons — 3 Kelsey Dr., Rossville, GA 30741; tel (706) 801-3346/(706) 277-2777

Keystone Press Agency Inc. — 202 E. 42nd St., 4th Fl., New York, NY 10017; tel (212) 924-8123; fax (212) 924-8123
Managing Editor — Brian F. Alpert

Kids Today — 1000 Wilson Blvd., Arlington, VA 22229-0002; tel (800) 368-3553 Ext. 3796; fax (703) 558-3814
Editor — Anita Sama
Associate Editor — Nicole Carroll
Editorial Assistant — Leslie Anderson
Graphic Designer — Eve Billig
Graphic Designer — Scott Gormley

KidSmarts — PO Box 333, Whitehouse Station, NJ 08889; tel (908) 534-1793; fax (908) 534-9881
Author — Maureen B. LaMarca
Author — Daria Price Bowman

King Features Syndicate Inc. — 235 E. 45th St., New York, NY 10017; tel (212) 455-4000/(800) 526-5464
President — Joseph F. D'Angelo
Exec. VP & Gen. Mgr. — Lawrence T. Olsen
Dir. of Ad. & P. R. — Ted Hannah
Comics Editor — Jay Kennedy
Director of Operations — Paul G. Eberhart
Managing Editor — Maria Carmicino
Director of Sales — Richard Heimlich
Assist. Sales Mgr./Midwest Sales — John Killian
Southwest Sales — Dick Lafave
Southeast Sales — John Perry
Northeast Sales — George Haeberlein
Telemarketing Sales Mgr. — Dennis Danko
Telemarketing Sales Rep. — Chris Monahan
Color Comics Manager — James F. Nolan
Director of Print Sales — Jack Walsh
Wkly. Svr. Nat. Sales Dir. — Richard Wilson
Weekly Service Man. Ed. — Diane Eckert
Weekly Service Sales Mgr. — Bradley Elson
Administrative Assist. — Charlotte Bruckner
Sr Dir. of Domestic Licensing — Ita Golzman
Domestic Licensing Mgr. — Irene Ackerman
Dir. of Int'l. Licensing — Cathleen Titus
Assist. Int'l. Sales Mgr. — Mary Anne Miller
Mgr. of Prod. and Shipping — Pete Gibilaro
Mgr. of Wire Transmissions — Venetta Smith

KMM Inc. — 14 High St., Locust Valley, NY 11560; tel (516) 759-9709
President — Keith M. Manzella

Knight-Ridder Financial News — 740 National Press Bldg., Washington, DC 20045; tel (202) 383-6150
Man. Dir./Exec. Editor — Angus Robertson
News Development Mgr. — Mark Leheney
Washington Bureau Chief — Bruce Harmon
Chicago, IL — Associate Editor: Robert R. Bogda; 30 S. Wacker, Ste. 1200, Chicago, IL 60606; tel (312) 454-3450
Kansas City, KS — Bureau Chief: Linda Ewing; 2020 W. 89th St.; PO Box 6053, Leawood, KS 66206; tel (913) 642-7373
London, England — Editor-Europe: Barry Schneider; 72/78 Fleet St., London, EC4Y 1HY England; tel (071) 842-4000
New York, NY — Editorial Director: Sally Heinemann; 75 Wall St., New York, NY 10005; tel (212) 269-1110
Tokyo, Japan — Editor-Asia: Atsushi Yuzawa; 3-12 Kioicho Bldg., Chiyoda-Ku, Tokyo 102, Japan; tel (01) 8133-230-1155
Additional bureaus in various national and international cities.

Knight-Ridder/Tribune Information Services — 790 National Press Bldg., Washington, DC 20045; tel (202) 383-6080; fax (202) 393-2460
Editor — Jane Scholz
Sales Director — Walter Mahoney; 435 N. Michigan Ave., Ste. 1500, Chicago, IL 60611; tel (312) 222-4695
Managing Editor/News Service and KRT Kids — Mike Duggan; tel (202) 383-6081
Director/Photo Service — Charles Borst; tel (202) 383-6169
Director/Graphic Service and News in Motion — George Rorick; tel (202) 383-6069
Director/Business News — Robert Harris; tel (202) 383-6134
Additional offices in various national and international cities.

Kolkman, Richard — PO Box 68256, Indianapolis, IN 46268; tel (317) 858-0630; e-mail BIGFLATCIT@aol.com

Koopersmith's Kreative Kingdom & Kalendar — 1437 W. Rosemont, Ste. 1-W, Chicago, IL 60660-1319; tel (312) 743-5341
Founder/CEO — Adrienne Sioux Kooper Smith

Krebbs Cycle Productions — 3940 Hilyard St., Eugene, OR 97405; tel (503) 344-3416; fax (503) 344-3057
Author/Owner — Yuri Samer

Kruza Kaleidoscopix Inc. — PO Box 389, Franklin, MA 02038-0389; tel (508) 528-6211
Photo News Writer — J.A. Kruza
Auto News Writer — David M. Ward

Kyodo News Service — 50 Rockefeller Plaza, Ste. 816, New York, NY 10020; tel (212) 603-6600; fax (212) 603-6621
NY Bureau Chief — Kunihiko Suzuki
Deputy Bureau Chief — Akihiro Onoda
Deputy Bureau Chief — Masaru Imai
Correspondent — Shintaro Nishiyama
Correspondent — Toru Maruyama
Correspondent — Hitoshi Kawahara
Correspondent — Hiroki Sugita
Correspondent — Yasuki Matsumoto
Correspondent — Miho Tabuchi
Correspondent — Hajime Miyagawa
Correspondent — Eiji Yamazaki

L

Landmark Designs Inc. — 630 S. Bertelsen; PO Box 2307, Eugene, OR 97402-0380; tel (800) 562-1041/(503) 345-3429; fax (503) 343-8525
President — J.E. McAlexander
Treasurer — M.J. McAlexander
Project Coordinator — W.S. McAlexander

Larsen, Ted Media — 96 Columbus Ave., Salem, MA 01970; tel (508) 741-3916

Law Education Institute — 281 Tampico Dr., Walnut Creek, CA 94598-2914; tel (510) 944-1344
Editor/Co-owner — Martin J. Ross
Director/Co-owner — Diane Ross
Assistant Editor — Jeffrey S. Ross
Secretary — Elizabeth G. Ross

Le Figaro — 8, rue Pierre Brossolette, Levallois-Perret, 92300 France; tel (33-1) 4087-4245; fax (33-1) 4087-4246
Editor-in-Chief — Franz Olivier Gesbert
Copyrights Manager — Michel Godmer

Leaning Tree Features — 3922 Alsace Pl., Indianapolis, IN 46226; tel (317) 898-3728
Contact Person — Charles Coffey

Learning and Loving It — 3889 Christopher; PO Box 1147, Brighton, MI 48116; tel (810) 227-7866
Author — Mary Tomczyk

Legal Briefs — 6100 W. Suburban Dr. (33156); PO Box 414253, Miami, FL 33141; tel (305) 372-0933; fax (305) 372-0836
President/Writer — John Ritter

Legi-Slate — 777 N. Capitol St., Washington, DC 20002; tel (202) 898-2300/(800) 733-1131; fax (202) 898-3030
President — Mark L. Capaldini
Dir. & Managing Editor — Nancy Schwerzler

Lester Syndicate — PO Box 1183, Cupertino, CA 95015; tel (408) 257-9567
Publisher — Mary Lester
Executive Editor — William Lester

Levin Represents — PO Box 5575, Santa Monica, CA 90409; tel (310) 392-5146; fax (310) 392-3856
President — Deborah Levin

Levine, Samuel P. — 42367 Cosmic Dr., Temecula, CA 92592; tel (909) 676-3976

Liaison International — 11 E. 26th St., 17th Fl., New York, NY 10010; tel (212) 779-6300; fax (212) 779-6334
President — Michel G. Bernard
Sales & Marketing Director — John Clarke
Corporate Director — Pat Hugg

Liberty Features Syndicate — PO Box 1436, Lewistown, NY 14092; tel (800) 388-1356; fax (416) 834-1683
President — Richard Vroom

Listening Inc. — 8716 Pine Ave., Gary, IN 46403; tel (219) 938-6962
President — Richard Bennett
Vice President — Patricia Bennett

Little, Lew Enterprises Inc. — 42-C Spring Canyon; PO Box 47, Bisbee, AZ 85603-0047; tel (520) 432-8003; fax (520) 432-8004
Managing Editor — Mary Ellen Corbett
Editor — Lewis A. Little

Long, Jerry — 2101 S. Boston, Ste. 10, Tulsa, OK 74114; tel (918) 582-9257

Los Angeles Features Syndicate — 16032 Sherman Way, Ste. 112, Van Nuys, CA 91406; tel (800) 959-9977/(708) 446-4082; fax (708) 446-4804
President — A.V. Licht
Managing Editor — Alice O'Neill

Los Angeles Times Syndicate — 218 S. Spring St., Los Angeles, CA 90012; tel (213) 237-5485; fax (213) 237-3698
President/CEO — Jesse E. Levine
VP/General Manager — Steven Christensen
Sales Executive/Ohio — Jim Lomenzo
Dir. of Acct. Relations & Article Sales — Beth Barber
Sales Exec./West & South — Tom Griffiths
Reprints and Permissions — Lupe Salazar
V.P./Dir. of Sales-LATSI — Gary Neeleman
Sales Executive/Midwest & Southwest — Grant Armendariz
Promotion Manager — Cathryn Irvine

Los Angeles Times Syndicate International — 2 Park Ave., Ste. 1802, New York, NY 10016; tel (212) 447-1450; fax (212) 447-1454/(212) 447-1455
President/CEO — Beth Barber
VP/Director of Sales — Gary Neeleman
Dir. Acct. Relations/Article Sales — Beth Barber
Contact — Charles Curmi
Contact — Maryann Grau; Tribune Bldg., 143 Main St., 8th Fl.; PO Box 8005, Salt Lake City, UT 84111; tel (801) 363-4934; fax (801) 363-4941

Los Angeles Times-Washington Post News Service — 1150 15th St. NW, Washington, DC 20071; tel (202) 334-6173; fax (202) 334-5096
President/Editorial Director — Al Leeds
V. Pres./General Manager — John W. Payne
VP/Comm. Director — Dick Preston
Treasurer — Bao N. Dang
Man. Ed./Washington — John Cullicott
Marketing Manager — Robert S. Cleland
Man. Ed./Los Angeles — Michael J. Kaeser

Lynn, Richard Enterprises — 3741 N. 400 E, Lagro, IN 46941; tel (219) 782-2345

M

M.C.E. Media Syndicate — 3252 N. Seminary, Chicago, IL 60657; tel (312) 665-1231; fax (312) 665-1288; e-mail mcoast@ix.netcom.com
President — John F. Woldenberg

Magnum Photos Inc. — 151 W. 25th St., 5th Fl., New York, NY 10012; tel (212) 929-6000
Director of New Media Projects — Tom Keller

Main Street Features — 4725 Dorsey Hall Dr., Ste. A-500, Ellicott City, MD 21043; tel (410) 740-8890
Man. Ed./Columnist — Larry E. Sturgill
Assoc. Ed./Columnist — Cynthia R. Sparrow
Assoc. Ed./Special Feature — J.D. Sparrow

Making It Productions — 1147 Manhattan Ave.; PO Box 10007-64, Manhattan Beach, CA 90266; tel (310) 379-5337; fax (310) 379-4345; e-mail makingit@netcom.com
Cartoonist/Owner — Keith Robinson

Mark-Morgan Inc. — 14 E. Washington St. (30263); PO Box 995, Newnan, GA 30264; tel (404) 253-5355
President — R. David Boyd
Secretary/Treasurer — Rosalyn M. Boyd

Market News Service — 100 William St., 3rd Fl., New York, NY 10038-3284; tel (212) 509-4444; fax (212) 509-5520
Managing Editor — Tony Mace
Washington Bureau Chief — Denis Gulino
London Bureau Chief — Jon Hurdle
European Editor — John Carter

MarketPlace Project, The — 566 Fairfield Rd. (East Windsor, 08520); PO Box 7231, Princeton, NJ 08543; tel (609) 443-4012; fax (609) 443-9841
Author — Lawrence H. Zisman
Author — Anabel Kligerman

Markgraf, Richard — 1830 Avenida del Mundo, Coronado, CA 92118; tel (619) 435-2514
Self Sydicator — Richard Markgraf

Marks & Frederick Associates Inc. — 7 Broadway, New York, NY 10004; tel (718) 783-0083; fax (718) 399-6557
President — Ted Marks; 135 Eastern Pkwy., Brooklyn, NY 11238

Masterfile (Stock Color Photo Library) — 175 Bloor St. E., South Tower, 2nd Fl., Toronto, ON M4W 3R8 Canada; tel (800) 387-9010; fax (416) 929-2104
Pres./Gen. Mgr. — Steve Pigeon

Mature Life Features — PO Box 9720, San Diego, CA 92169; tel (619) 483-3412; fax available on request
Travel Editor — Igor Lobanov
Nat'l. Affairs/Health Ed. — James B. Gaffney
Editor-In-Chief/Financial Ed. — Cecil Scaglione

Mature Market Editorial Services — 10 Town Plz., Ste. 313, Durango, CO 81301; tel (970) 385-6999; e-mail 75474.141@compuserve.com, e-mail LENHANSEN@aol.com
Columnist/Editor — Leonard J. Hansen

Mature Traveler, The — PO Box 50820, Reno, NV 89513-0820; tel (702) 786-7419
Editor & Publisher — Gene Malott
Editor & Publisher — Adele Malott

Maturity News Service — 1101 Connecticut Ave. NW, Ste. 310, Washington, DC 20036; tel (202) 785-6629; fax (202) 466-8661
Managing Editor — Rick Bowers

MDA Management Co. Inc. — 16 Dumond Pl., Coram, NY 11727; tel (516) 736-7973; fax (516) 736-1617
Managing Editor — Annette Diano

Mead, Jerry D. Enterprises — PO Box 2796, Carson City, NV 89702; tel (702) 884-2648; fax (702) 884-2484

Media Maven, The — PO Box 191087, Atlanta, GA 31119-1087; tel (404) 264-9380
Self-Syndicated — Howard Hopwood

Medical Center News — 962 Wildwood Rd., Oradell, NJ 07649; tel (201) 261-6713; fax (201) 261-6717

Medical Insurance Claims Inc. — Kinnelon Professional Complex, 170 Kinnelon Rd., Ste. 10, Kinnelon, NJ 07405; tel (201) 492-2828; fax (201) 492-9068
Author — Irene C. Card

Megalo Media — PO Box 678, Syosset, NY 11791; tel (212) 535-6811
President — J. Baxter Newgate
Editor/Vice President — Sandy Applegreen
Associate Editor — Paul Merenbloom

Meilach, Dona Z. Features — 2018 Saliente Way, Carlsbad, CA 92009; tel (619) 436-4395; fax (619) 436-1402; e-mail dmeilach@mcimail.com

Merrell Enterprises — 2610 Garfield St. NW, Washington, DC 20008-4104; tel (202) 265-1925; fax (202) 265-8721
President — Jesse H. Merrell
Exec. VP — Margaret R. Miller

Metropolitan Press Syndicate, The — 648 Onondaga Ln., Stratford, CT 06497; tel (203)377-5525
President — Milton Rockmore
General Manager — Sylvia Rockmore
Secretary/Treasurer — S.M. Moss

Michaels News — Rte. 5, Box 367, Black River Falls, WI 54615-9160; tel (715) 284-5638
President & Editor — Marion Michaels

Midwest Features — PO Box 9907, Madison, WI 53715-0907; tel (608) 274-8925
Founder/Editor — Mary Bergin

Midwest Journal, The — 28441 El Dorado Pl., Lathrup Village, MI 48076; tel (810) 443-1753; fax (810) 443-0014
Self-Syndicated — Michael Gauf

Miko's Pacific News Service — PO Box 1312, New York, NY 10018; tel (203) 378-2803
Editor — Robert J. Miko

Military Update — PO Box 1230, Centreville, VA 22020; tel (703) 830-6863
Self Syndicator — Tom Philpott

Miller Features Syndicate Inc. — 180 Bloor St. W., Ste. 1100, Toronto, ON M5S 2V6 Canada; tel (416) 924-9588; fax (416) 924-1683
President — Richard Vroom

Milligan Syndicate — 981 Longmeadow Ct., Barrington, IL 60010; tel (708) 382-1593
Editor — Molly Milligan
Assistant Editor — Annie Milligan

Minority Features Syndicate Inc. — PO Box 421, Farrel, PA 16121; tel (412) 342-5300; fax (412) 342-6244
President — Bill Murray
Managing Editor — Merry Frable

Moeller, Jan & Bill — 4912 Hickory St., Omaha, NE 68106; tel (402) 553-3654

Moneywatch — PO Box 4092, Beverly Hills, CA 90213-4092; tel (310) 858-5160; fax (310) 858-5112
Editor — Jay Goldinger

Morris News Service — 229 Peachtree St. N.E., Ste. 202, Atlanta, GA 30303; tel (404) 522-8424/(404) 589-8424; fax (404) 589-8429
Bureau Chief — Frank LoMonte
Austin, TX — Bureau Chief: Mary Alice Robbins; 1122 Colorado St., Ste. 111-A, Austin TX 78701; tel (512) 482-9429; fax (512) 495-9685

Mortgage Market Information Services — 53 E. St. Charles Rd., Villa Park, IL 60181; tel (800) 509-INFO/(708) 834-7555; fax (708) 834-7283
Writer/President — James R. DeBoth

Mortgage News Company — 1810 E. 17th St., Ste. 100, Santa Ana, CA 92701; tel (714) 836-1177
President/Author — Earl Peattie

Moskowitz, Gary — 73-05 150th St., Ste. 3-D, Flushing, NY 11367; tel (718) 263-8234; fax (718) 263-0234

Motor Matters — 4635 Bailey Dr., Wilmington, DE 19808; tel (302) 998-1650
General Manager — Bill McCormick

Mountain Media — PO Box 4422, Las Vegas, NV 89127-4422; tel (702) 870-3515; e-mail vin@terminus.intermind.net,
President — Vin Suprynowicz

Mullich Communications — 908 W. Marshall St., Norristown, PA 19401; tel (610) 279-5473; fax (610) 239-0843
Owner/Writer — Joe Mullich
Business Manager — John Breckenridge

Munsey News Service — PO Box 573, Pompano Beach, FL 33061-0573
Editor — Al LaPresto

Musick Toons — PO Box 1215, Bucyrus, OH 44820-4215; tel (419) 562-4778; fax (419) 562-4778
Managing Editor — Earl T. Musick

N

Name Game Co. Inc., The — 401 S.W. 54th Ave., Plantation, FL 33317; tel (800) 583-6056/(954) 321-0032; fax (954) 321-8617
President — Melodye Hecht Icart
VP-Sales & Development — Mitchell J. Free
Executive Director — Gary Zehner

Nasco Products Co. — 23600 Cloverlawn, Oak Park, MI 48237; tel (810) 547-7056
President — Norma Schonwetter

National Cartoonists Society — PO Box 20267, Columbus Cir. Sta., New York, NY 10023; tel (212) 627-1550/(212) NCS-1550
President — Frank Springer
1st Vice President — Jack Caprio
2nd Vice President — Daryl Cagyl
3rd Vice President — Jose Delbo
Secretary — Robb Armstrong
Membership Chair & Info. Contact — Joe Duffy
Chapter Representative — George Breisacher

National Features Syndicate — 2359 Jefferson Dr. S.E.; PO Box 1390, Grand Rapids, MI 49507; tel (616) 243-0082/(616) 243-0888; fax (616) 243-2144
President — Robert Gill Ph.D.

National Financial News Service, The — 1210 Ashbridge Rd., Ste. 3, West Chester, PA 19380; tel (800) 939-6367/(610) 344-7380; fax (610) 696-1184
CEO — Ronald S. Shur
Director of Marketing — Bruce A. Myers

National News Bureau — PO Box 43039, Philadelphia, PA 19129; tel (215) 546-8088
Publisher — Harry Jay Katz
Vice President — Andy Edelman

National Newspaper Syndicate — 3502 Hillvale Rd., Louisville, KY 40241; tel (502) 339-0334; fax (502) 339-0823
Editor/Columnist — Gary Klott

National Press Syndicate — 401 E. 74th St., Ste. 15-M, New York, NY 10021; fax (212) 744-4623
Publisher — Paulette Cooper

Neilan, Edward — CPO Box 554, Tokyo, 100-91 Japan; tel 81-3-33 063858; fax 81-3-33 063858

Nelson, Ray & Jane — 117 Cottage Ave., Cashmere, WA 98815; tel (509) 782-2644

New Consumer Institute — PO Box 51, Wauconda, IL 60084; tel (708) 526-0522
Columnist — John Wasik

New England News Service Inc. — 66 Alexander Rd., Newton, MA 02161; tel (617) 969-4102
President/CEO — Eleanor Gun
Bureau Chief — Milton Gun

New Wave Syndication — PO Box 232, North Quincy, MA 02171; tel (617) 471-8733

New York Press Photographers Association — 225 E. 36th St., New York, NY 10016; tel (212) 889-6633; fax (212) 889-3099
President — Arty Pomerantz

New York Times News Service — 229 W. 43rd St., Rm. 943, New York, NY 10036; tel (212) 556-1927
Executive Editor — Peggy Walsh
Associate Editor — Jim Robison
Director Graphics/Photos — Peter Trigg
Dir. Consumer Mrkg. — Barbara Mancuso

New York Times Syndication Sales Corp. — 122 E. 42nd St., 14th Fl., New York, NY 10168; tel (212) 499-3300; fax (212) 499-3382
President/Editor-In-Chief — John Brewer
Pres./International — Karl Horwitz
VP/Central & South America — Paul Finch
VP/Exec. Ed. — Gloria Brown Anderson
Sales Exec./North America — Bob Farnell
Sales Exec./North America — Connie White
Director of Special Projects — Patrick Vance

Newhouse News Service — 1101 Connecticut Ave. NW, Washington, DC 20036; tel (202) 383-7800
Washington Bureau Chief/Ed. — Deborah Howell
National Editor/Deputy Bureau Chief — Robert Hodierne
Office Manager — Hope Horman

News USA Inc. — 8300 Boone Blvd., Ste. 810, Vienna, VA 22182; tel (800) 355-9500/(703) 827-5800; fax (703) 827-5814; e-mail vpmedia@newsusa.com; http://www.newsusa.com;
Chairman & CEO — Richard D. Smith
President & COO — Chris Petersen
VP/Media Services — William H. Watson
Managing Editor — Denny Townsend
Ass't. Managing Editor — John Pitts
Production Manager — Macky Hall
Media Relations — Victoria Jancek

Newsfinder — 330 E. Kilbourn Ave., Ste. 200, Milwaukee, WI 53202-3166; tel (800) 922-4655/(414) 283-4386; fax (414) 283-4357
Manager — Sandy Hamm

Newslink Africa Ltd. — 7-11 Kensington High St., London, W8 5NP; England; tel (0171) 411-3111; fax (0171) 938-4168
Managing Editor — Shamlal Puri
Deputy Editor — Manju Dhiri
Deputy Editor — Sid Kumar

Newspaper Enterprise Association — 200 Madison Ave., New York, NY 10016; tel (212) 293-8500/(800) 221-4816; fax (212) 293-8760/(212) 293-8600
President/CEO — Douglas R. Stern
Sr. Vice President/Gen. Manager Syndication — Sidney Goldberg
VP and Editorial Director — Diana B. Loevy
VP/Sales and Marketing — Lisa Klem Wilson
Dir. Int'l. Syndication — Eduardo Kaplan
Exec. Editor/UFS and NEA — Robert Levy
Managing Editor/Comic Art — Amy Lago
Promotion Manager — Mary Anne Grimes

Newspaper Features Council Inc. — 37 Arch St., Greenwich, CT 06830; tel (203) 661-3386; fax (203) 661-3386
President — Ron Patel
1st Vice President — Richard S. Newcombe
2nd Vice President — Jane Amari
Secretary/Treasurer — Steven Christensen

Newsportraits Syndicate — PO Box 564, Hackensack, NJ 07602-0564; tel (201) 342-2985
Executive Editor — Y.L. Tiajcliff
Business Manager — Martin Sager

North America Syndicate — 216 E. 45th St., New York, NY 10017; tel (212) 455-4000/(800) 526-5464
President — Joseph F. D'Angelo
Exec. Vice President & General Manager — Lawrence T. Olsen
Dir. of Ad. & P. R. — Ted Hannah
Comics Editor — Jay Kennedy
Director of Operations — Paul G. Eberhart
Managing Editor — Maria Carmicino
Director of Sales — Richard P. Heimlich
Assist. Sales Mgr./Midwest Sales — John Killian
Southwest Sales — Dick Lafave
Southeast Sales — John Perry
Northeast Sales — George Haeberlein
Telemarketing Sales Mgr. — Dennis Danko
Telemarketing Sales Rep. — Chris Monahan
Color Comics Manager — James F. Nolan
Director of Print Sales — Jack Walsh
Wkly. Srv. Nat. Sales Dir. — Richard Wilson
Weekly Service Man. Ed. — Diane Eckert
Weekly Service Sales Mgr. — Bradley Elson
Administrative Assist. — Charlotte Bruckner
Sr. Dir. of Domestic Licensing — Ita Golzman
Domestic Licensing Mgr. — Irene Ackerman
Dir. of Int'l. Licensing — Cathleen Titus
Assist. Int'.l Sales Mgr. — Mary Anne Miller

North American Auto Writers Syndicate — 8680 Louetta Rd., Spring, TX 77379; tel (800) 227-6229
General Manager/Editor — J. Todd Hayes

North American Precis Syndicate Inc., The — 201 E. 42nd St., New York, NY 10017; tel (800) 222-5551/(212) 867-9000; fax (212) 983-0970
Service Manager — Steve Seeman
Editor-In-Chief — Candace Lieberman
Pres. & Executive Editor — Ronald N. Levy

NYT Graphics — 229 W. 43rd St., Rm. 943, New York, NY 10036; tel (212) 556-4204
Director — Peter Trigg
Asst. Director — Deborah Marchand

NYT Photo Service — 229 W. 43rd St., Rm. 943, New York, NY 10036; tel (212) 556-4204
Director Photo/Graphics — Peter Trigg
Asst. Director — Deborah Marchand
Dir. Consumer Mktg. — Barbara Mancuso

O

O'Connor, Lona — 21114 White Oak Ave., Boca Raton, FL 33428-1715; tel (407) 487-5104
Author — Lona O'Connor

O'Neil, Patrick M. — PO Box 891, Sullivan's Island, SC 29482
President — Patrick M. O'Neil

Oceanic Press Service — 1030 Calle Cordillera, Unit 105, Seaview Business Park, San Clemente, CA 92673; tel (714) 498-7227; fax (714) 498-2162
Manager — Helen Lee
Editorial Manager — Janis Hawkridge

Olshan's, Mort Sports Features — 9255 Sunset Blvd., Ste. 523, Los Angeles, CA 90069; tel (310) 274-0848 Ext. 213; fax (310) 273-5932
Editor/Publisher — Mort Olshan
Managing Editor — Carl Giordano

Onion Features Syndicate — 33 University Sq. Ste 270, Madison, WI 53715; tel (800) 695-4376; fax (608) 256-2525
Managing Editor — Scott Dikkers
Assistant Managing Editor — Ben Karlin

Online USA — PO Box 75, Beverly Hills, CA 90213-0075; tel (310) 587-0025; fax (310) 587-0027; modem (310) 587-0028, ISDN (310) 587-0099
Contact — Brad Elterman

OPECNA (Distributed by Global Information Network) — 777 United Nations Plz., New York, NY 10017; tel (212) 286-0123; fax (212) 818-9249; e-mail ipsgin@igc.apc.org
Director — Lisa Vives

Ottaway News Service — 1025 Connecticut Ave. NW, Ste. 310, Washington, DC 20036; tel (202) 828-3390
Bureau Chief — William F. Schmick III

P

P/K Associates Inc. — 3006 Gregory St., Madison, WI 53711-1847; tel (608) 231-1003/(800) 260-1120; compuserve 73220,117
President — Judi K-Turkel
Director — Franklynn Peterson

Pacheco Automotive News Service — PO Box 6691, Concord, CA 94524; tel (510) 228-7821; fax (510) 228-1410
Pres./General Manager — Lawrence R. Hagin

Pacific News Service — 450 Mission St., Ste. 204, San Francisco, CA 94105-2526; tel (415) 243-4364
Executive Editor — Sandy Close
Associate Editor — Franz Schurmann
Associate Editor — Richard Rodriguez
Associate Editor — Andrew Lam
Publications Manager — Kris Schell
Youth Outlook Editor — Nell Bernstein

Pacific Rim News Service Inc. — 2400 E. Roy St., Seattle, WA 98112; tel (206) 329-9242; fax (206) 329-5509
Contact — Gordon Burridge

Pen Tip International Features — PO Box 3789, Portland, ME 04104-3789; tel (207) 775-4211; fax (207) 775-4280
President — Paul Kolsti

Phillip Jewell Illustration — 235 E. 51st St., Ste. 3-A, New York, NY 10022; tel (212) 758-1816; http://www.interport.net/~pjewell

Photo Communications Co. Inc. — 26 Broadway, Ste. 400, New York, NY 10004; tel (212) 758-1816

Photo International/Photo Associates News Service — 3421 M St. NW, Ste. 1636, Washington, DC 20007; tel (202) 965-4428; fax (202) 337-1969/(703) 765-6756; voice mail/pager (800) 915-6353
Bureau Manager — Peter Heimsath

Photopress Washington — National Press Bldg., Ste. 2105, Washington, DC 20045; tel (202) 234-8787; fax (703) 237-0554
Dir. of Photography — Robert Visser
Office Manager — Kathleen Bryan
Falls Church, VA — 120 S. Spring St., Falls Church, VA 22046

Photosource International — Pine Lake Farm, 1910 35th, Osceola, WI 54020; tel (715) 248-3800; fax (715) 248-7394
Director — Rohn Engh

Piercy & Barclay Designers Inc. — 7080 S.W. Fir Loop, Ste. 100, Tigard, OR 97223; tel (503) 620-4551; fax (503) 684-7032
Self Syndicator — Janet Piercy

Plain Label Press — 7529 Forsyth, 3rd Fl., Clayton, MO 63105; tel (314) 727-0530; fax (314) 727-8710
Managing Editor — Ed Chermoore
Director of Comic — Richard Kalina
Director of Sales/Promotion (Business Director) — Laura Meyer

PLN Syndicate — 508 Whitingham Dr., Silver Spring, MD 20904; tel (301) 622-0195; fax (301) 622-0195
Columnist — Deborah Leigh Nelson

Posner, Jack Syndicate — 216 Ellesmere E., Deerfield, FL 33442; tel (305) 427-8068

POSRO Comics — 1139 E. Jersey St., Ste. 403, Elizabeth, NJ 07201; tel (908) 289-3700; fax (908) 289-0020

Post/Dispatch Features — 703 Ridgemark Dr., Hollister, CA 95023; tel (408) 637-9795; fax (408) 636-1225
President — George Crenshaw
Managing Editor — Van Masters
Sales Promotion — Al Otis

PR Newswire — 810 7th Ave., 35th Fl., New York, NY 10019; tel (800) 832-5522; http://www.prnewswire.com
President — Ian Capps
Senior Vice President — John Williams
Editorial Director — Ken Dowell
Features Coordinator — Fred Ferguson
Atlanta, Georgia — 950 E. Paces Ferry Rd., Ste. 2155, Atlanta, GA 30326-1144; tel (404) 231-1814/(800) 232-3998; fax (404) 231-2045
Boston, MA — 111 Devonshire St., Ste. 720, Boston, MA 02109-5412; tel (617) 482-5355; fax (617) 423-4157
Charlotte, NC — 212 S. Tyron St., Ste. 1060, Charlotte, NC 28281-0001; tel (704) 338-9366/(800) 998-9806; fax (704) 338-9566
Cleveland, OH — 1375 E. 9th St., Ste. 2730, Cleveland, OH 44114; tel (216) 566-7777/(800) 826-3133; fax (216) 566-1234
Coral Gables, FL — One Columbus Ctr., Ialhambra Plz., Ste. 610, Coral Gables, FL 33134; tel (305) 461-8666/(800) 683-6397; fax (305) 461-8670
Denver, CO — 370 17th St., Ste. 2270, Denver, CO 80202-5622; tel (303) 592-5077/(800) 843-2495; fax (303) 592-5078
Los Angeles, CA — 865 S. Figueroa St., Ste. 2310, Los Angeles, CA 90017-2565; tel (213) 626-5500/(800) 321-8169; fax (213) 488-1152
Minneapolis, MN — 970 E. Hennepin Ave., Minneapolis, MN 55414; tel (612) 331-7800; fax (612) 331-3700
Orange County, CA — 4600 Campus Dr., Ste. 102, Newport Beach, CA 92660-1802; tel (714) 251-6993; fax (714) 474-7737
Orlando, FL — 111 N. Orange Ave., Ste. 1409, Orlando, FL 32801-2388; tel (407) 649-4795; fax (407) 649-4948

Copyright ©1996 by the Editor & Publisher Co.

News, picture & syndicate services V-9

Philadelphia, PA — One Penn Ctr., 1617 JFK Blvd., Ste. 1150, Philadelphia, PA 19103-1811; tel (215) 568-6300/(800) 523-4424; fax (215) 568-0898
Pittsburgh, PA — 300 6th Ave., Ste. 606, Pittsburgh, PA 15222-2511; tel (412) 232-3050; fax (412) 232-3053
Salt Lake City, UT — 5 Triad Ctr., Ste. 600, Salt Lake City, UT 84180; tel (801) 350-9402/(801) 350-9252; fax (801) 350-9403/(800) 473-5152
San Diego, CA — 450 B St., Ste. 1850, San Diego, CA 92101-8004; tel (619) 232-4497; fax (619) 232-9304
San Francisco, CA — 71 Stevenson St., Ste. 1615, San Francisco, CA 94105-2938; tel (415) 543-7800/(800) 334-6692; fax (415) 543-3555
San Jose, CA — 150 Almaden Blvd., Ste. 1350, San Jose, CA 95113-2009; tel (408) 295-3600/(800) 423-3445; fax (408) 295-3322
Seattle, WA — 1001 4th Ave., Ste. 2138, Seattle, WA 98154-1101; tel (206) 624-2414/(800) 367-8555; fax (206) 624-2343
Southfield, MI — 26555 Evergreen Rd., Ste. 1710, Southfield, MI 48076-4206; tel (810) 352-5200/(800) 697-9712; fax (810) 352-3540
Washington, DC — The Homer Building, 601 13th St. NW, Ste. 560, Washington, DC 20005-1794; tel (202) 347-5155; fax (202) 347-6606
Prensa Latina — UN Secretariat Bldg., Rm. 450, New York, NY 10017; tel (212) 753-5572; fax (212) 753-5572; (212) 963-7151
Chief Correspondent — Roberto Molina
Press Associates Inc. — 806 15th St. NW, Ste. 632, Washington, DC 20005; tel (202) 638-0444; fax (202) 638-0955
Editor — Mark J. Gruenberg
Executive Editor — Robert B. Cooney
Editor — Henry S. Kenyon
Press Features International — 292 Hardenburgh Ave., PO Box 107, Demarest, NJ 07627; tel (201) 767-7667; fax (201) 767-3450; telex 426068
Managing Editor — George Simor
Press News Ltd. — 36 King St. E., Toronto, ON M5C 2L9 Canada; tel (416) 364-0321; fax (416) 594-2163
Chief Executive — Keith Kincaid
Chairman — Roger D. Landry
Press News Syndicate — 2073 Gerritsen Ave., Brooklyn, NY 11229; tel (718) 339-1417
Director — Martin Pine
Press Photo Service — 79-14 Parsons Blvd., Flushing, NY 11366; tel (718) 526-9069
President/Editor — Harris Sutter
Vice President — Mike Weber
General Manager — Charles Phillips
Entertainment/Sports Ed. — Jeff Hollander
PressLink Inc. — 11800 Sunrise Valley Dr., Ste. 1130, Reston, VA 22091; tel (703) 758-1740; fax (703) 758-8368
President — Rich Cates
CFO — Jeff Jackson
Director-Sales & Mktg. — Mike Martucci
Technical Operating Mgr. — Tom Priddy
Print Marketing Concepts — 10590 Westoffice Dr., Ste. 250, Houston, TX 77042; tel (713) 780-7055; fax (713) 780-9731
President — Charles Dye
VP National Sales — Robin L. Good
Controller — Nancy Kissman
New York, NY — 1120 Ave. of the Americas, 4th Fl., New York, NY 10036; tel (212) 626-6801; fax (212) 626-6804
Pro-Am Sports Service/Mile Square Publisher — PO Box 24072, Indianapolis, IN 46224; tel (317) 632-1984; fax (317) 634-2969
Editor & Publisher — David C. Sassman
Professional Communications Group — 250 Miller Pl., Hicksville, NY 11801; tel (516) 997-7000; fax (516) 393-9259
President — William Trimble
Sales Manager — Sal Citrano
Public Education Monthly — PO Box 1561, Hillsbourgh, NC 27278; tel (919) 933-8883/(800) 407-9444; fax (800) 407-9444; e-mail 71613.2314@compuserve.com
Editor & Publisher — Jean Bolduc
Punch In Travel & Entertainment News Syndicate — 400 E. 59th St., Ste. 9-F, New York, NY 10022; tel (212) 755-4363; fax (212) 755-4365; e-mail punchin@punchin.com
President — J. Walman
Managing Editor — Jerry Preiser
Managing Editor — Nancy Preiser
Contributing Writer — Laurie Lawson
Contributing Writer — Tom Weston
Contributing Writer — Norma Tormey
Contributing Writer — Donna Shore
Contributing Writer — Frank Gariky
Contributing Writer — William Murray
Contributing Writer — John Edwards
Puzzle Features Syndicate — 29971 Pebble Beach Dr., Sun City, CA 92586; tel (800) 292-4308; fax (909) 672-2594
Editor — Jackie Mathews
Editor — Calvin R. Mathews
Puzzles By Shanta — 566 Westchester Ave., Rye Brook, NY 10573; tel (914) 939-2111; fax (914) 939-5138
President — Shane Tabatch
Editorial Director — Bree Altamn
Research — Kathy Cocciara

Q

Quaternary Features — PO Box 72, New York, NY 10021; tel (212) 744-1867
Manager — Ken Fisher
Quiz Features — 4007 Connecticut Ave. NW, Washington, DC 20008; tel (202) 966-0025; fax (202) 966-0025
Author — Donald Saltz
Research Director — Mozelle Saltz

R

Raia, James — 2301 J St., Ste. 205, Sacramento, CA 96816; tel (916) 448-5122; fax (916) 448-0205; e-mail RaiaRuns@aol.com
RDR Books — 4456 Piedmont Ave., Oakland, CA 94611; tel (510) 595-0595; fax (510) 595-0598
Chairman — Roger Rapoport
Real Estate Matters Syndicate — 395 Dundee Rd., Glencoe, IL 60022; tel (708) 835-3450; fax (708) 835-3451; e-mail IlyceGlink@aol.com
President — Ilyce R. Glink
Real Estate News Group — 8306 Wilshire Blvd., Ste. 7078, Beverly Hills, CA 90211; tel (310) 657-4626; fax (310) 657-5391
Author/Associate — Ron Galperin
Religion News Service — 1101 Connecticut Ave. NW, Ste. 350, Washington, DC 20036; tel (202) 463-8777; fax (202) 463-0033
Publisher — Dale Hanson Bourke
Editor — Joan Connell
News Editor — Tom Billitteri
National Correspondent — Ira Rifkin
National Correspondent — David Anderson
National Correspondent — Adelle Banks
Religious Drawings Inc. — 6624 Golf Hill Dr., Dallas, TX 75232; tel (214) 371-3986
Artist/Director — Jack Hamm
Secretary — D.A. Alexander
Renberg, Werner — 6 Sabina Rd., Chappaqua, NY 10514; tel (914) 241-2038; fax (914) 242-0470
Retail News Bureau (Div. of Retail Reporting Corp.) — 302 5th Ave., New York, NY 10001; tel (212) 279-7000; fax (212) 279-7014
Publisher — Larry Fuersich
Reuters — 1333 H St. NW, Washington, DC 20005; tel (202) 898-8300; fax (202) 898-8383
Editor-Reuters America/Sr. VP-News & TV — Stephen Jukes
News Editor — Bob Basler
Washington Bureau Chief — Rob Doherty
Sr. VP-Sales & Mktg. — Andrew Nibley
Atlanta, GA — 1355 Peachtree St., Atlanta, GA 30309; tel (404) 870-7340; fax (404) 870-7339
Boston, MA — Exchange Pl., 53 State St., Boston, MA; tel (617) 367-4106; fax (617) 248-9563
Chicago, IL — 311 S. Wacker Dr., Ste. 1200, Chicago, IL 60606; tel (312) 408-8700; fax (312) 922-6657
Denver, CO — 410 17th St., Ste. 1105, Denver, CO 80202; tel (303) 820-3900; fax (303) 820-3905
Detroit, MI — 31500 Northwestern Hwy., Ste. 220, Farmington Hills, MI 48018; tel (810) 737-2525; fax (810) 637-4540
Hartford, CT — One Commercial Plz., 23rd Fl., 280 Trumbull St., Hartford, CT 06103; tel (203) 727-0224; fax (203) 727-8608
Kansas City, MO — 4900 Main St., Ste. 713, Kansas City, MO 64112; tel (816) 561-8671; fax (816) 931-4291
Los Angeles, CA — 445 S. Figueroa, Ste. 2100, Los Angeles, CA 90071; tel (213) 380-2014; fax (213) 622-0056
Miami, FL — 1001 S. Bayshore Dr., Ste. 1601, Miami, FL 33131; tel (305) 374-5014; fax (305) 358-6317
Palo Alto, CA — Correspondent: Susan Moran, Palo Alto, CA; tel (415) 462-2610; fax (415) 324-8531
San Francisco, CA — 153 Kearney St., Ste. 301, San Francisco, CA 94108; tel (415) 677-2541; fax (415) 986-5147
Washington, DC — 1333 H St. NW, Ste. 400, Washington, DC; tel (202) 898-8300 (general news/Reuters TV)/(202) 898-8333 (photo desk)/(800) 949-4976 (sales and marketing)
Reuters TV Bureau, New York — 747 3rd Ave., New York, NY 10009; tel (212) 833-9300; fax (212) 207-8743
New York, NY — PO Box 20; Grand Central Sta., New York, NY 10163
United Nations Bureau, New York — United Nations, Rm. C-316, New York, NY 10017; tel (212) 355-7424; (212) 355-0143
US Courthouse Bureau, New York — 40 Centre St., Rm. 508-A, New York, NY 10007; tel (212) 385-2466
Charlotte, NC — 212 S. Tryong, Charlotte, NC 28281; tel (704) 358-0266
Dallas, TX — 1999 Bryan St., Ste. 1516, Dallas, TX 75201; tel (214) 953-0744
Houston, TX — Summit Tower, 11 Greenway Plz., Ste. 1200, Houston, TX 77046; tel (713) 850-1677
Philadelphia, PA — 1835 Market St., 11 Penn Ctr., Ste. 501, Philadelphia, PA 19103; tel (215) 972-0618
Pittsburgh, PA — Liberty Ctr., 1001 Liberty Ave., Ste. 501, Pittsburgh, PA 15222; tel (412) 471-7008
Seattle, WA — Columbia Ctr., 701 Fifth Ave., Ste. 6770, Seattle, WA 98104; tel (206) 386-4848
Calgary, AB — Scotia Ctr., 700 Second St. S.W., Ste. 2340, Calgary, AB T2P 2W2 Canada; tel (403) 531-1624
Montreal, QC — 231 St. Jacques St., Ste. 880, Montreal, QC H2Y 1M6 Canada; tel (514) 985-2434
Ottawa, ON — Booth Bldg., 165 Sparks St., Ste. 500, Ottawa, ON K1P 5B9 Canada; tel (613) 235-6745
Toronto, ON — Standard Life Ctr., 121 King St. W., Ste. 2000, Toronto, ON M5H 3T9 Canada; tel (416) 941-8100
Vancouver, BC — 700 W. Pender St., Ste. 1405, Vancouver, BC V6C 1G8 Canada; tel (604) 684-9784
Reuters America Inc. — 1333 H St. NW, Ste. 400, Washington, DC 20005; tel (800) 949-4976 (sales & marketing)/(202) 898-8409 (sales & marketing); fax (202) 898-8448
VP/Sales and Mktg. — Jeanette McClennan
Mktg. Mgr./Media News — A. Mitchell Koppelman
Rexford Group, The — PO Box 50377, St. Louis, MO 63105; tel (314) 727-5850; fax (314) 727-5819
President — Peter Rexford
RMS Syndication — 14713 Pleasant Hill Rd., Charlotte, NC 28278-7927; tel (704) 588-2453
President — David A. Butler
Roberts, H. Armstrong — 1178 Broadway, 4th Fl., New York, NY 10001; tel (800) 786-6300; fax (800) 786-1920
Philadelphia, PA (Home Office) — 4203 Locust St., Philadelphia, PA 19104; tel (800) 786-6300; fax (800) 786-1920
Chicago, IL — 233 E. Wacker Dr., Rm. 4305, Chicago, IL 60601; tel (800) 786-6300; fax (800) 786-1920
Roll Call Report Syndicate (Thomas Reports Inc.) — 1257-B National Press Bldg., Washington, DC 20045; tel (202) 737-1888
Editor & Publisher — Richard G. Thomas
Assistant Editor — Cora Hoopes
Rothco Cartoons — 1463 44th St., Brooklyn, NY 11219; tel (718) 853-5435
President — Steven Weiss
Royal Features — PO Box 58174, Houston, TX 77258-8174; tel (713) 532-2145
Executive Director — Fay W. Henry

S

Salmon Syndication — PO Box 4272, Vallejo, CA 94590-9991; tel (707) 552-1699; fax (707) 644-2680
Author — Ray Salmon
Editor/Promotion — Donna Salmon
Production — Stephen Salmon
Sam Mantics Enterprise — PO Box 7727, Menlo Park, CA 94026; tel (415) 854-3132; fax (415) 854-9698; e-mail corrcook@syndicate.com
President/Cartoon Editor — Carey Orr Cook
Internet/WWW Editor — Kylie Cook
SATCO Marketing & Promotional Printing — 1100 Ponce de Leon Blvd., Coral Gables, FL 33134; tel (305) 441-2526/(800) 535-5844; fax (305) 443-2176
President — Scott Thompson
Schleier, Curt Reviews — 646 Jones Rd., River Vale, NJ 07675; tel (201) 391-7135; fax (201) 391-7135; e-mail 72760.2013@compuserve.com
President — Curt Schleier
Schmidt Services Inc. — 720 Creek Rd., Attica, NY 14011; tel (716) 591-3010
President — Stephen P. Schmidt
Schwadron Cartoon & Illustration Service — PO Box 1347, Ann Arbor, MI 48106; tel (313) 426-8433; fax (313) 426-8433
Editor — Harley Schwadron
Secretary — Sally Booth
Schwartz, Gary — 931 4th St., Mukilteo, WA 98275; tel (206) 348-5598; fax (206) 290-5842
Self-Syndicated — Gary Schwartz
Partner — Debbie Hansen
Science Communications — 5318 Stirling Ct., Newark, CA 94650-1352; tel (510) 794-1446
Writer/Editor — Pat Kite
Science Features Service — 8758 Sophia Ave., North Hills, CA 91343; tel (818) 892-9433
Managing Editor — Chuck Gordon
Editor — Steve Russell
Scoop News Service — 307 E. 37th St., Ste. 3, New York, NY 10016; tel (212) 867-2025; fax (212) 867-2048
Scrambl-Gram Inc. — 1772 State Rd., Cuyahoga Falls, OH 44223; tel (216) 923-2397; fax (216) 923-4346
President — Charles R. Elum
General Manager — Scott Bowers
Sales Director — Mary Elum
Sales Development — R.A. (Rube) Faloon
Screening Room — PO Box 2236, Pittsfield, MA 01202-2236; tel (413) 442-1256; fax (413) 443-2445
Self-Syndicator — Jonathan Levine
Scripps Howard News Service — 1090 Vermont Ave. NW, Ste. 1000, Washington, DC 20005; tel (212) 293-8612 (sales/information)
Bureau Chief/Editor — Dan Thomasson
Managing Editor — Marvin West
Asst. Man. Editor-Features — Walter Veazey
Editorial Development — Sid Goldberg
General Executive — Irwin Breslauer
Sports Editor — Thomas O'Toole
Semple Comics Features — 725 Coronation Blvd., Cambridge, ON N1R 7S9 Canada; tel (519) 622-1520; fax (519) 622-9954
Editor/Publisher — Richard Comely
Senior Wire News Service — 2377 Elm St., Denver, CO 80207; tel (303) 355-3882; fax (303) 355-2720; e-mail 72370.3520@compuserve.com
Publisher & Editor — Allison St. Claire
Sharpnack, Joe — PO Box 3325, Iowa City, IA 52244; tel (319) 337-4726
Shetland Productions — 4679 Goodland Park Rd., Madison, WI 53711; tel (608) 222-5522
Business Manager — Robert Kovalic
Editor — Eleanor Williams
Office Manager — Alexander Schiller
Assoc. Editor — Bob Smithson
Sho-Ban News, The — Pima Dr.; PO Box 900, Fort Hall, ID 83203; tel (208) 238-3888; fax (208) 238-3702
News Editor — Roy Ivey
Sidebar News International — PO Box 612, Scotch Plains, NJ 07076-0612; tel (908) 322-8343; fax (908) 322-8902
Editorial Director — Charles Horner
Silver Bird Travel Features — Gate 6 1/2, Berth 4, Sausalito, CA 94965; tel (415) 331-7700
Author — Kevin Keating
Simini, Joseph Peter — PO Box 31420, San Francisco, CA 94131-0420; tel (415) 282-1950
Singer Media Corp. — SeaView Business Park, 1030 Calle Cordillera, Unit 106, San Clemente, CA 92673; tel (714) 498-7227; fax (714) 498-2162
President — Kurt Singer
Executive Vice President — Katherine Han
Treasurer — Helen J. Lee
Assistant to the President — Janis Hawkridge
Sipa News Service — 59 E. 54th St., New York, NY 10022; tel (212) 759-5571; fax (212) 593-5194
Chairman/Editor-In-Chief — Henry O. Dormann
President/Executive Editor — Darrell Brown
Sisters Syndicate — 177 Sound Beach Ave., Ste. 6, Old Greenwich, CT 06870; tel (203) 637-1233
President — Christine Negroni
Vice President — Andrea Lee Negroni
Skintalk — 32905 W. 12 Mile Rd., Ste. 330, Farmington Hills, MI 48334; tel (810) 553-2900
President — Jon H. Blum M.D.
Skoglund Features — HC 35, Box 249, St. George, ME 04857; tel (207) 372-8052; fax (207) 372-8052
Columnist — Robert Skoglund

Copyright ©1996 by the Editor & Publisher Co.

Slightly Off — 1168 Sagebrush Trail, Cary, IL 60013; tel (708) 639-1232
Author/Owner — Deb Di Sandro
Humor/Lifestyle

Small Talk — 45 Commonwealth Ave., Boston, MA 02116; tel (617) 267-1396
Creative Director — Allan H. Kelly Jr.

Smith, Al Feature Service Inc. — 6048 Skipper Ln., Zephyrhills, FL 33541; tel (813) 788-1998
Owner/Gen, Mgr. — Dorothea J. Coates
Owner — Marie Schiller

Smith, Jack H. — 3045 Buena Vida Cir., Las Cruces, NM 88001; tel (505) 522-1277

Sola, Mike — 701 S. Mt. Vernon Ave., San Bernadino, CA 92410; tel (714) 888-6511 Ext. 1466; fax (909) 862-3569

Southam Syndicate — 151 Sparks St., Ste. 512, Ottawa, ON K1P 5E3 Canada; tel (613) 236-0491; fax (613) 236-1788
Manager — Beth Burgess
Editorial Coordinator — Dan Smythe

Southern California Focus — 1720 Oak St., Santa Monica, CA 90405; tel (213) 452-3918/(213) 452-3101
Author — Thomas Elias

Sovfoto-Eastfoto Agency Inc. — 48 W. 21st St., 11th Fl., New York, NY 10010; tel (212) 727-8170; fax (212) 727-8228
Director — Victoria Edwards

Speaking of Soaps Inc. — 331 Boyle Ave., Totowa, NJ 07512; tel (201) 790-1582; fax (201) 790-1936
Writer — Mary Ann Cooper

Specialty Features Syndicate — 17255 Redford Ave., Detroit, MI 48219; tel (313) 533-1846
Manager/Managing Editor — L.E. Crandall
Food Editor — Verdice Kordel
Business Editor — Louis Kaye

Spectrum Features — Bloomsburg University, BCH 106, Bloomsburg, PA 17815; tel (717) 389-4825/(717) 389-4565
Executive Editor — Jen Buscin
Associate Editor — John Michaels
Business Manager — Angela Elliott

Spectrum Syndicate — 2017 Greenwood Dr., Woodstock, Il 60098; tel (815) 338-5096; fax (815) 338-9992
Marketing Director — Pat DiPrima

Sports Adviser Features — 1323 S. 6th St.; PO Box 891, St. Charles, IL 60174; tel (708) 377-6676
Author/Owner/President — P. Andrew Andersen, Ph.D.

Sports Biofile & Bio-Toons — 71 Dockerty Hollow Rd., West Milford, NJ 07480; tel (201) 728-0591
Editor — Mark Malinowski
Artist — Bud Boccone

Sports by Voort — 255 Main St. Ste. C-2, Madison, NJ 07940; tel (908) 862-2416; fax (908) 862-2416

Sports Network, The (Div. of Computer Info. Network) — 701 Mason's Mill Business Park, Huntington Valley, PA 19006; tel (215) 947-2400; fax (215) 938-8466
President — Mickey Charles
Vice Pres./Sales — Ken Zajac
Dir. Technical Operations — Bruce Michaels
Dir of Marketing — Stacy B. Tucker
Media Sales — Kevin Spiegel

Sportsbuff Features — PO Box 197, Hamilton, MA 01936; tel (508) 468-2632
Editor — Steve Ollove
Associate Editor — Ken Wagner

Springer Foreign News Service — 565 5th Ave., 8th Fl., New York, NY 10017; tel (212) 983-1983; fax (212) 983-2464
Bureau Chief — Irmintraud Jost

Stadium Circle Features — 335 Court St., Ste. 85, Brooklyn, NY 11231-4331; tel (718) 797-0210; fax (718) 797-0210; e-mail 373-1994@mcimail.com, America Online NewYorkBob, Compuserve 72407,3343, GEnie R.Anthony4, Prodigy KTPM03A
Editor & Columnist — Robert S. Anthony

Stamping Grounds — 25 E. Penn St.; PO Box 632, Long Beach, NY 11561; tel (516) 431-6697
Author/Owner — Joseph Zollman

Star Reporter News/Features — 847-A 2nd Ave., Ste. 171, New York, NY 10017; tel (212) 631-3520
Editor/Owner — Laurie Sue Brockway

Starcott Media Services — 6906 Royalgreen Dr., Cincinnati, OH 45244; tel (513) 231-6034; fax (513) 231-6180
President — James T. Dulley

States News Service (NY Times Subscriber Service) — 1333 F St. NW, Ste. 400, Washington, DC 20004; tel (202) 628-3100
Editor — Leland Schwartz
Deputy Managing Editor — Laura Hamburg

Stevens Features/Mark Stevens & Co. — 709 Westchester Ave., Ste. L-9, White Plains, NY 10604; tel (914) 428-6200; fax (914) 428-6902
President — Mark Stevens
Vice President — Carol Stevens

Stevens, Gary Associates — 235 W. 56th St., Ste. 11-B, New York, NY 10019; tel (212) 265-8054; fax (212) 582-3152
President — Gary Stevens
Vice President — Jacqueline Gonzalez

Style International — PO Box 330063, San Francisco, CA 94133-0063; tel (415) 457-7141; fax (415) 457-7141 (must call before faxing)
President — Nancy Steidtmann
Managing Editor — Christina Tom
Pacific Rim Report — K. Okada

Sun Features Inc. — 45 Kennedy Pkwy.; PO Box 45, Cardiff, CA 92007; tel (619) 431-1660; fax (619) 431-1669
President — Joyce Lain Kennedy
Vice President — Tim K. Horrell

Suzerain Group — 3223 Aldrich Ave. N., Minneapolis, MN 55412; tel (612) 522-4183
President — David Watkins
Secretary — Amy Lahner

Swedish Information Service (Consulate General of Sweden) — One Dag Hammarskjold Plz., 45th Fl., New York, NY 10017-2201; tel (212) 751-5900; fax (212) 752-4789
Editor — Kjersti Board

Sylvia Syndicate — 1440 N. Dayton, Chicago, IL 60622; tel (312) 943-4862
President — Nicole Hollander

Syndicate X — 310 Elm St., Ste. 4-L, Northampton, MA 01060; tel (800) 584-6758; e-mail SYNDCTX@aol.com
President — Lou Cove

Syndicated Automotive News — 131 Norlyn Dr., Walnut Creek, CA 94596-4257; tel (510) 935-0809; fax (510) 935-0809
Editor — Bill Russ
Assistant Editor — Carey Russ

Syndicated News Service — 232 Post Ave., Rochester, NY 14619-1398; tel (716) 328-2144; fax (716) 328-7018; voice mail (800) 306-1277; e-mail SNS3@aol.com, 72662.2077@compuserve.com, SNS@rochgte.fidonet.org; http://pages.prodigy.com/NY/sns/sns.html
Editor/Publisher — Frank Judge
Assoc. Publisher/Art Dir. — Mary Whitney
Executive Assistant — Bryan Campbell
Associate Editor — Sid Rosenzweig
Associate Editor — Ken O'Brien
Assistant Editor — Paul Ferguson
Features Editor — David Williams
Features Editor — Peter Heinrich
Chicago, IL — Bureau Chief: Aljay Randall; 7312 S. Eberhart, Chicago, IL 60619
New York, NY — Bureau Chief: Lemington Ridley; 235 E. 83rd St., Ste. 2-G, New York, NY 10028-2859; tel (212) 734-6289
Toronto, ON — Bureau Chief: Lana McKenzie; 6 Washington Ave., Toronto, ON M5S 1L2; tel (416) 596-1188; fax (416) 596-1074

Syndication Associates Inc. — 2502 E. 71st, Ste. A (Tulsa, 74136); PO Box 400, Jenks, OK 74037; tel (918) 481-6050; fax (918) 481-6380
Marketing — Ann M. Wayland

T

T.A.S. Syndicate, The — PO Box 1773, Dept. E, Sonoma, CA 95476-1773; tel (707) 585-0328
President — Tom Silberkleit

Taipei Economic & Cultural Office, Information Division — 1230 Ave. of the Americas, 2nd Fl., New York, NY 10020-1513; tel (212) 373-1800; fax (212) 373-1866
Senior Information Officer — T.K. Lee
Atlanta, GA — Peachtree Center, Harris Tower 233 Peachtree St. N.E., Ste. 201, Atlanta, GA 30303; tel (404) 522-0482; fax (404) 523-4035
Boston, MA — 99 Summer St., Ste. 801, Boston, MA 02110; tel (617) 737-2057; fax (617) 737-2061
Chicago, IL — 180 N. Stetson Ave., 2 Prudential Plaza, 57th Fl., Ste. 5702, Chicago, IL 60601; tel (312) 263-4669/(312) 616-6716; fax (312) 616-1497
Houston, TX — 5 Greenway Plz., Ste. 270, Houston, TX 77046-0585; tel (713) 961-9465; fax (713) 961-1365
Los Angeles, CA — 6300 Wilshire Blvd., Ste. 1510, Los Angeles, CA 90048; tel (213) 782-8765; fax (213) 782-8761
San Francisco, CA — 555 Montgomery St., Ste. 504, San Francisco, CA 94111; tel (415) 362-7680; fax (415) 362-5304
Washington, DC — 4201 Wisconsin Ave. NW, Washington, DC 20016-2137; tel (202) 895-1800; fax (202) 362-6144

Taming The Workplace — 3003 14th Ave. W., Ste. 201, Seattle, WA 98119; tel (206) 284-9566; fax (206) 282-5183; internet MrScribe@aol.com
Columnist — Eric L. Zoeckler

Tel-Aire Publications Inc. — 3105 E. Carpenter Fwy. (Irving, 75062); PO Box 561467, Dallas, TX 75356-1467; tel (800) 749-1841; fax (214) 579-7483; (214) 438-4111
President — David A. McGee
National Sales Manager — Richard Stein

Thanks A Million Inc. — 5151 Edina Industrial Blvd., 2nd Fl., Minneapolis, MN 55439; tel (612) 835-2400; fax (612) 835-2403; (800) 328-6300
President — Percy Ross

This Modern World — 1424-C 2nd Ave. (94122); PO Box 170515, San Francisco, CA 94117; tel (415) 750-9784; fax (415) 664-7223; e-mail Tomorrow@Well.com
Creator/Syndicator — Dan Perkins

This Side of 60 — PO Box 332, North Newton, KS 67117; tel (316) 283-2309; fax (316) 284-0500
Self-Syndicated — Marie Snider

Thomson News Service — 1331 Pennsylvania Ave. NW, Ste. 524, Washington, DC 20004; tel (202) 628-2157; fax (202) 347-5017
Bureau Chief — Bill Sterberg

tidbits — 5800 Fairhaven Ave., Woodland Hills, CA 91367; tel (818) 884-7137
Self-Syndicator — Susan Shelley

Tilton, David V. — PO Box 3516, North Fort Myers, FL 33918-3516; tel (941) 656-0225; fax (941) 656-5177; voice mail (813) 338-5756; BBS (941)

Tim's Features — BLYTSVEJ 7, 1th., 2000 FRB., Denmark; tel (011) 45 31 863092; fax (011) 45 31 863092
Self-Syndicator — Tim Newlin

Time Data Syndicate — PO Box 717, Manchester, NH 03105-0717; tel (800) 322-5101
Director — Larry White
Treasurer — Marcia White

Times Newspapers of London — 1 Pennington St., London, El 9XN England; tel (44 171) 782-5000/(44 171) 782-6240; fax (44 171) 782-6244; telex 94014385 News G
Syndicate Manager/Times Newspapers — Ralph Nodder
Editorial/Syndications Mgr. — Lisa Chookasezian; 1211 Ave of the Americas, 4th Fl., New York, NY 10036; tel (212) 852-7600
The Times Newspapers of London have an agreement with the Los Angeles Times Syndicate to syndicate its news service in the North American market.

Toronto Star Syndicate — 1 Yonge St., Toronto, ON M5E 1E6 Canada; tel (416) 869-4991/(416) 869-4989; fax (416) 869-4587
Manager — Peter W. Taylor
Sales — Robin Graham
Sales — Dolores Johnstone
Sales — Ted Cowan

Trade News Service (Published by Parmax Inc.) — 3701 Rte. 21 S., Canandaigua, NY 14424-9020; tel (716) 396-0027; fax (716) 396-3057
Senior Editor — Dennis C. Maxfield

Trade Service Corp. — 10996 Torreyana Rd., San Diego, CA 92121; tel (619) 457-5920; fax (619) 457-4923
Chairman/CEO — James A. Simpson
Vice President — Tony Patterson
Market Development Mgr. — Kent N. Dial
Managing Editor — Bonnie J. Dudley

Travel & Leisure Features — 66 Alexander Rd., Newton, MA 02161; tel (617) 969-4102
CEO/President — E.J. Gun
Vice President — Eleanor Margolis
Publisher/Editor — Milton J. Gun

Trends Research Institute — 330 Salisbury Tpk., Rhinebeck, NY 12572; tel (914) 876-6700; fax (914) 758-5252; e-mail 73441.3516@compuserve.com
VP-Professional Srv. — Mary Ann Martinsons

Tribune Media Services Inc. — 435 N. Michigan Ave., Ste. 1500, Chicago, IL 60611; tel (800) 245-6536/(312) 222-4444; fax (312) 222-8620
President/CEO — David D. Williams
Vice President Sales/Syndicate and KRT Products — Walter F. Mahoney
Vice President of Data Base and Advertising — Barbara Needleman
VP/Editorial and Bus. Dev. — Michael A. Silver
Man. Editor/News & Features — Mark Mathes
Dir. of Database Products — John Kelleher
Sales Mgr./TMS TV Listings TMS Stocks and TMS Weather Serv. — Thomas J. Beatty
Gen. Mgr./Elect. Info. Services — Jay Fehnel
Licensing Director — Elyce Small Goldstein

Tribune Media Services-Television Listings — County Line Rd.; PO Box 900, Glens Falls, NY 12801-0900; tel (800) 424-4747; fax (800) 541-7676
Operations Manager — George A. Ferone
Sales Manager — Thomas J. Beatty
Regional Accounts Mgr. — David Blackwood
Regional Accounts Mgr. — Dan Burson
Regional Accounts Mgr. — James Donahue
Managing Editor — Michael Cushing
Technical Operations Manager — Gary Carter
Systems Manager — Gary Evans
Desktop Publishing Manager — Wade Lapan
Database Operations Manager — Julia Young
Features Editor — Jay Bobbin
Features Editor — Kate O'Hare
Sports Editor — Matt Meachem
Production Manager — Brenda Sweet
Telemarketing Sales Rep. — Roark VanDien
Telemarketing Sales Rep. — Juanita Delgado
Customer Support Mgr. — Vicki Reynolds

Tuttle Comics — 3972 Barranca Pkwy., Ste. 102, Irvine, CA 92714; tel (310) 453-0304; fax (310) 458-3990
Artist/Author — Gregg Kaminsky

TV Data — Northway Plz., Queensbury, NY 12804; tel (518) 792-9914/(800) 338-TVDT; fax (518) 761-6820; e-mail tvdata@tvdata.com
Pres./Chief Exec. Officer — Arthur Bassin
Vice President/Sales — Kathleen F. Wern
Assistant VP/Sales — Bill Callahan
VP/Marketing & Product Development — Michael Laddin
VP/Business Development — Kenneth Carter
VP/Operations and Exec. Ed. — Roger K. Moore
VP/Info. Systems — James McCormick
Director of Newspaper Sales & Interactive Services — John T. Dodds
Regional Sales Director — Tom Counce
Regional Sales Director — Mike Pearson
Regional Sales Director — Cameron Yung
Regional Sales Director — Martin Siniawski
National Accounts Dir. — Robyn DiPhillips
Dir. of Client and Tech. Srvs. — Brenda Wheatley
Managing Editor — Amy Mann
Editor/Entertainment Features Syndicate — Deborah Flack
Asst. Managing Ed./Ent. Features Syndicate — Brett Bobo
Ombudsman — Michael Bennett
Interac. & Online Srvs. Prod. Mgr. — Kevin Joyce
Pagination Product Mgr. — Andrew Heinz
TransEdit Product Manager — Rich Young
TV Book Editor — Ann Babcock

Twenty First Century Family Syndicate — 64 Plainfield St., Newton, MA 02168; tel (617) 527-1549
President — Victor Capoccia Ph.D.
Chief Exec. Officer — Janet Sumperer

U

U-Bild Newspaper Features — PO Box 2383, Van Nuys, CA 91409; tel (800) 828-2453
President — Lyn Carothers
General Manager — Helen Perry
Features Editor — Kevin Taylor

United Feature Syndicate — 200 Madison Ave., New York, NY 10016; tel (212) 293-8500/(800) 221-4816; fax (212) 293-8760/(212) 293-8600
President/CEO — Douglas R. Stern
Sr. Vice President/General Manager Syndication — Sidney Goldberg
VP/Editorial Director — Diana B. Loevy
VP/Sales and Mktg. — Lisa Klem Wilson
Dir. Int'l. Syndication — Eduardo Kaplan
Exec. Editor/UFS and NEA — Robert Levy
Managing Editor/Comic Art — Amy Lago
Promotion Manager — Mary Anne Grimes

United Media — 200 Madison Ave., New York, NY 10016; tel (212) 293-8500/(800) 221-4816; fax (212) 293-8760/(212) 293-8600
President/CEO — Douglas R. Stern
Sr. VP Fin. and Adminis. — Kevin Ryan
Sr. VP/Gen. Mgr./Syndication — Sidney Goldberg
Sr. Vice Pres./U.S. Licensing — Diane Shaib
VP/Editorial Director — Diana B. Loevy
Vice President/Sales and Marketing — Lisa Klem Wilson
Dir. of Int'l. Syndication — Eduardo Kaplan
Exec. Editor/UFS and NEA — Robert Levy
Managing Editor of Comic Art — Amy Lago
Director of Communications — Diane Iselin
Promotion Mgr. — Mary Anne Grimes

United Press International — World Headquarters, 1400 I St. NW, Washington, DC 20005; tel (202) 898-8200; fax (202) 898-8057
CEO — L. Brewster Jackson
Vice Pres. of Operations — Peter Leach
Vice Pres./Sales & Mktg. — Ron MacIntyre

Copyright ©1996 by the Editor & Publisher Co.

CFO — Roger Kohl
Man. Editor/International — Robert Martin
Man. Editor/North America — Tobin Beck
Executive Editor — Raphael Calis
Washington Bureau Mgr. — Kathleen Silvassy
UPI White House Bureau Mgr. — Helen Thomas
Dir. of Human Resources — Annette Chapin
Director of Marketing — Ryon Packer
Business Editor — Jerry Kronenberg
Science Editor — Larry Schuster
Sports Editor — Ian Love
Entertainment Editor — Valerie Kuklenski

Austin, TX — 1005 Congress Ave., Ste. B-45, Austin, TX 78701; tel (512) 472-2471
Cambridge, MA — 215 First St., Cambridge, MA 02142; tel (617) 542-2967
Cape Canaveral, FL — Kennedy Space Ctr.; PO Box 466, Cape Canaveral, FL 32920; tel (407) 639-3733
Chicago, IL — 203 N. Wabash Ave., Ste. 600, Chicago, IL 60601; tel (312) 781-1600
Columbus, OH — 50 W. Broad St., Ste. 1325, Columbus, OH 43215; tel (614) 221-2015
Coral Gables, FL — Douglas Entrance Executive Tower, 800 Douglas Rd., Ste. 570, Coral Gables, FL 33145; tel (305) 445-1750
Dallas, TX — 750 N. St. Paul St., Ste. 830, Dallas, TX 75201; tel (214) 880-0444
Harrisburg, PA — Capitol Newsroom, Rm. 524, E Fl., Harrisburg, PA 17101; tel (717) 234-2842
Houston, TX — 808 Travis St., Houston, TX 77002; tel (713) 227-2121
Lansing, MI — House Press Rm., State Capitol Bldg., Lansing, MI 48904; tel (517) 482-1923
Los Angeles, CA — 201 N. Figueroa St., Los Angeles, CA 90012; tel (213) 580-9880
Madison, WI — State Capitol Press Room, Rm. 217 S.W., Madison, WI 53702; tel (608) 251-2686
New York, NY — 2 Penn Plz., 18th Fl., New York, NY 10001; tel (212) 560-1100
Philadelphia, PA — Penn Towers Bldg., Ste. 301, 1819 JFK Blvd., Philadelphia, PA 15222; tel (215) 563-6008
Pittsburgh, PA — 7 Wood St., 5th Fl., Pittsburgh, PA 19103; tel (412) 553-5300
Sacramento, CA — 925 L St., Ste. 325-A, Sacramento, CA 95814; tel (916) 445-7755
San Francisco, CA — 451 Hays St., San Francisco, CA 94102; tel (415) 552-5900
Seattle, WA — 110 Cherry St., Ste. 200, Seattle, WA 98104; tel (206) 283-3262
Springfield, IL — State Capitol Press Rm., Springfield, IL 62706; tel (217) 525-2327
Toronto, ON — 144 Front St. W., Ste. 432, Toronto, ON M5J 2L7; tel (416) 340-7276

Caribbean Division:
San Juan, PR — Stop 18 Sta.; PO Box 9655, Santurce, PR 00908; tel (809) 725-4460

Mexico-Central America-Panama Division:
Avenida, Panama — 20-G Norte 4-H, Altos de Miraflores/Apartado 393, Panama 9A, RP; tel (011) 507-61-9613 (Office)
Managua, Panama — Reparto Serranto 1166, Managua, Nicaragua; tel (011) 505-2-24-192
Mexico City, Mexico — Apartado Postal 32-680, Mexico City, DF 06030, Mexico; tel (905) 761-5365
San Salvador, El Salvador — Aconcagua 12 Poligono U, San Salvador, El Salvador; tel (011) 503-25-28-85

South America Division:
Bogota, Colombia — Aereo 57570, Bogato 2, Bogato, Colombia; tel (011) 571-211-9106
Brasilia, D.F., Brazil — Edificio Gilberto Salomao, Sala 813, Sector Commercial Sul, Brasilia, Brazil; tel (011) 55-61-224-4213
Buenos Aires, Argentina — Casilla de Correo 796, Correo Central, Buenos Aires 1000, Argentina; tel (011) 54-1-34-5501
Caracas, Venezuela — Avenida Urdaneta, Animas a Plaza España, Oficina 4, Caracas, Venezuela; tel (011) 58-2-561-6731
La Paz, Bolivia — Casilla 1219, La Paz, Bolivia; tel (591-2)371278
Lima, Peru — Jiron Puno 271, Oficina 601, Casilla 153, Lima, Peru; tel (011) 54-14-27-4827
Montevideo, Uruguay — Avenida 18 de Julio 1224, 2 Piso, Montevideo, Uruguay; tel (011) 598-2-900-122
Quito, Ecuador — Numero 18-11 Y Alpallana, Torre 2, Apt. 108, Quito, Ecuador; tel (593-2) 560-519
Rio De Janeiro, Brazil — Vice President: Luiz Menezes; Chief Correspondent for Brazil: Brian Nicholson; Rua Uruguaiana 94, 18 Andar, Centro, Rio De Janeiro 20050, Brazil; tel (55-21) 224-4194
Sao Paulo, Brazil — Rua Sete de Abril 230 Bloco A, Andar 8, Salas 816,817 Centro, Sao Paulo, CEP 01044, Brazil; tel (55-11) 258-6866

Europe-Middle East-Africa Division:
Beirut, Lebanon — Correspondent: Riad Kaaj; The An-Nahar Bldg., 4th Fl., Hamra St., Beirut, Lebanon; tel (961) 800905
Bonn, Germany — Heuss Allee 2-10 Pressehaus 2, Zimmer 224, 5300 Bonn 1, Bonn, Germany; tel (49-228) 215031
Belgrade, Yugoslavia (Serbia & Montenegro) — Generala Zdanova 19, Belgrade 11000, Yugoslavia; tel (38-11) 342-490
Brussels, Belgium — 17, rue Philipe le Bon B-1040, Brussels, Belgium; tel (322) 230-4330; fax Telex: 26997
Cairo, Egypt — 4 Eloui St., Abdine, Cairo, Egypt; tel (202) 3924-000 (238); fax Telex: 92217
Geneva, Switzerland — UPI, Rm. 76, Palais des Nations, Geneva 1211, Switzerland; tel (4122) 734-1740; fax Telex: 22300
Jerusalem, Israel — Beit Agron, 37 Hillel St., Jerusalem, Israel; tel (9722) 252-131; fax Telex: 26415
Johannesburg, South Africa — PO Box 32661, Braamfontein Johannesburg 2017, South Africa; tel (2711) 403-3910
London, England — 2 Greenwich View Pl., London E14 9NN, England; tel (4471) 333-0990; fax 28829; 8811443
Moscow, Russia — Kutuzovsky Prospekt 7/4, Apt. 68, Moscow, Russia; tel (7095) 230-2515; fax Telex: 413-424
Paris, France — 8, rue de Choiseul, Paris 75002, France; tel (331) 4260-3087
Rome, Italy — Via Della Mercede 55, Rome 00187, Italy; tel 396-679-3525/4463/5747
Vienna, Austria — UPI International Pressezentrum, Gunoldstrasse 14, Vienna 1199, Austria; tel (431) 369-1258; fax (431) 367341
Warsaw, Poland — Piekna St. 68, Rm. 306, 00-672, Warsaw, Poland; tel (4822) 216-795

Asia/Pacific Division:
Bangkok, Thailand — U Chuliang Bldg., 968 Rama IV Rd., 2nd Fl., Bangkok 10500, Thailand; tel (662) 238-5244
Beijing, China — 7-1-11 Qi Jia Yuan, Beijing, China; tel (861) 532-3456
Hong Kong — 1260 Telecom House, 3 Gloucester Rd., Wanchai, Hong Kong; tel (852) 802-0221; fax (852) 802-4972
Islamabad, Pakistan — Al-Shafig 39th St. 27, F-6/2, Islamabad, Pakistan; tel (9251) 821-472
Kuala Lumpur, Malaysia — 28 Jalan 1/65A Off Jalau Tun, Rm. 1, Kuala Lumpur 50400, Malaysia; tel (603) 293-3393/3362
Manila, Philippines — Pavilion Hotel Manila, United Nations Ave., Rm. 205, Ermita, Manila 1000, Philippines; tel (632) 521-2074
New Delhi, India — Ambassador Hotel, Ste. 202/204, Sujan Singh Park, New Delhi 110003, India; tel (9111) 698-705-991
Singapore — 420 N. Bridge Rd., Ste. 06-32 Ctr., Singapore 0718; tel (65) 337-3715/337-3824; fax (65) 338-9867
Sydney, Australia — No. 1 Newland St., Bendi Junction, Level 507, 5th Level, Sydney 2022, Australia; tel (612)387-5478
Taipei, Taiwan — 6/F Chih Ching Bldg., 209 Sunkiang Rd., Taipei, Taiwan; tel (8862) 505-2549/502-4311
Tokyo, Japan — Palaceside Bldg., 111 Hitotsubashi, Chiyoda-Ku, Tokyo 100, Japan; tel (813) 32127-911

Universal Press Syndicate — 4900 Main St., 9th Fl., Kansas City, MO 64112; tel (816) 932-6600/(800) 255-6734
President/CEO — John McMeel
VP/Co-Chairman — Kathleen Andrews
Vice President — Thomas Thornton
Vice Pres./Editorial Director — Lee Salem
Vice President/Finance — Elena Fallon
Vice President/Sales — Robert Duffy
VP/Contributing Editor — Donna Martin
Vice President/Creative — George Diggs
VP/Editorial Special Srvs. — Harriet Choice
Asst. VP/Managing Editor — Alan McDermott
Asst. VP/Sales Manager — Dan Dalton
Asst. Managing Editor — Sue Roush
Associate Editor — Jake Morrissey
Associate Editor — Elizabeth Andersen
Assistant Editor — Lisa Tarry
Assistant Editor — Darrell Coleman
Editorial Services Manager — Scott Shorter
Man. Director/International — John Klem
Dir. International — Henry Hartzenbusch
Sales Administrator/Int'l. — Anne Whittaker
Mgr./Mktg. Administration — Denise Clark
Asst. VP/Sales Mgr./Southwest Div. — Brendt DeMetrotion
Sales Manager/Northeast Div. — Tom Smith
Sales Administrator — Jan Flemington
Sales Manager/Western Div. — William Weir
Sales Administrator — Sally Hile
Sales Manager/Southeast Div. — Jack Prahl
Sales Administrator — Carrie Hicks
Sales Manager/Midwest Div. — John Vivona
Sales Administrator — Marcia Graves
Special Sales/Telemaktg. — Debra Weydert
Promotions Director — Ann Hall
Permissions Director — Mary Suggett

US Newswire — 1272 National Press Bldg., Washington, DC 20045; tel (202) 347-2770; fax (202) 347-2767
Contact — Mark Bagley

Usual Suspects, The/Mystery Fiction Lineup — Box 3308 Merchandise Mart, Chicago, IL 60654-0308; tel (708) 965-2388

V

Vektor/Synsat Ltd. — PO Box 7110, Pittsburgh, PA 15213; tel (412) 683-2532; fax (412) 683-8477
Marketing Director — John Uldrich

Vintage Notes — 103 Louise Dr., Nederland, TX 77627; tel (409) 727-0393
Owner/Author — Bruce A. Van Boskirk

VIP Medical Grapevine — 161 Nasa Cir., Round Lake, IL 60073; tel (708) 546-6557; fax (708) 546-9228
Author/Owner — Ruth Nathan Anderson

Voter News Service — 225 W. 34th St., Ste. 310, New York, NY 10122; tel (212) 947-7280; fax (212) 947-7756
Managing Director — R. Flaherty

W

Wagner International Photos Inc. — 62 W. 45th St., 8th Fl., New York, NY 10036-4208; tel (212) 944-7744
President — Larry Lettera
Chief Photographer — Patrick Callahan

Washington Monthly Co., The — 1611 Connecticut Ave. NW, Washington, DC 20009; tel (202) 462-0128; fax (202) 332-8413
Publisher — Casandra Tate
Editor-In-Chief — Charles Peters
Editor — Amy Waldman

Washington Post Writers Group, The — 1150 15th St. NW, Washington, DC 20071-9200; tel (202) 334-6375/(800) 879-9794
Editorial Dir./Gen. Mge.r — Alan Shearer
Associate Editor — Anna Karavangelos
Sales Manager/Int'l. — Mary Fleming
Sales Manager/North America — Grace Hill
Oper. Mgr./Comics Ed. — Suzanne Whelton

Wedig, Tony — PO Box 243, McQueeney, TX 78123; tel (210) 557-5039; fax (210) 557-6426

West Coast Syndicate — 320 Vista Linda Dr., Mill Valley, CA 94941; tel (415) 388-2024
Pres./Executive Editor — Carol Townsend

Western Producer Newsfeature Service, The — 2310 Millar Ave.; PO Box 2500, Saskatoon, SK S7K 2C4 Canada; tel (306) 665-9605; fax (306) 934-2401
Manager — Michael Gillgannon
Editorial Services — R. Bruce Dyck

What's Brewing — 160 Dexter Ave., Meriden, CT 06450; tel (203) 235-1758; e-mail jimzbrewer@aol.com

What's New In Medicine — 1143 Chamberlain Hwy., Kensington, CT 06037; tel (203) 828-5016
Author/Owner — L.A. Chotkowski, M.D.

White Castle Communications — PO Box 295, Morris, CT 06763; tel (203) 567-5336
Owner/Editor — William Clifford

White, Leo Productions — 168 Strasser Ave., Westwood, MA 02090; tel (617) 326-9240
President — Leo White
Editor — Mary V. White
Sales Manager — Mary Arrigo

Whitegate Features Syndicate — 71 Faunce Dr., Ste. 1, Providence, RI 02906; tel (401) 274-2149
President — Ed Isaac
VP/General Manager — Steve Corey
Office Manager — Mari Howard
Talent Mgr./Special Sales — Eve Green

Whiting, Jim Cartoons — 773 S. Nardo, Ste. M-10, Solana Beach, CA 92075-2338; tel (619) 755-7449; fax (619) 755-2356

Wide Angle Humor — PO Box 962, Northampton, MA 01061; tel (413) 586-2634; fax (413) 585-0407

Wideworld News Service — PO Box 20056, St. Louis, MO 63144; tel (314) 962-6362; fax (314) 962-6362
Editor — Paul Sievers
Business Manager — David Knickers
Feature Writer — Al Saffa

Wieck Photo DataBase Inc. — 13500 Midway Rd., Ste 500 (75244); PO Box 59408, Dallas, TX 75229; tel (214) 392-0888; fax (214) 934-8848
Chairman/CEO — Travis Hughs
President/COO — Jim Wieck
Vice President-Systems — Tim Roberts
Vice President-Sales — Marge Boatright
Director of Marketing — Jere Cox

Williams Syndications Inc. — PO Box 3993, Holiday, FL 34690; tel (800) 760-3100/(813) 844-0405; fax (813) 848-8877
President — James L. Williams Jr.
Secretary/Treasurer — Nancy Ann Rawlings
Motor Sports Ed./Orlando — Jzonn Cureton
Features Editor/Orlando — Dick Jackson
Features Editor/Chicago — James Llewellyn
Features Editor/Chicago — John Theodore
Features Ed./Los Angeles — Daniel T. Luse
Medicare & S.S. Ed./Tampa — Jean Taylor
Cartoonist/Everett, WA — Andrew Wahl

Wilson, Ray — 406 N.W. 68th Ave., Ste. 311, Plantation, FL 33317; tel (305) 862-2953

Witzzle Co., The — 1323 Columbia Dr., Ste. 307; PO Box 831853, Richardson, TX 75083-1853; tel (214) 234-6161; fax (214) 234-5626
Owner/President — Louis Y. Sher

Women's Feature Service/USA — 20 W. 20th St., Ste. 1103, New York, NY 10011; tel (212) 807-9192; fax (212) 807-9331
Executive Director — Rebecca Foster
Marketing Director — Margaret Bald

Woodson, Charles — PO Box 11883, Berkeley, CA 94712-2883; tel (510) 643-6614; fax (510) 642-3555; e-mail Woodson@soe.berkeley.edu

World Features Syndicate — 3162 Morning Way, La Jolla, CA 92037; tel (609) 468-1099; fax (619) 558-1293
President — Ronald A. Sataloff
Associate Editor — Karl A. Van Asselt

World Images News Service — 6520 China Grove Ct., Alexandria, VA 22310; tel (703) 922-1756; fax (703) 631-4693
CEO/Chief Photographer — Jack W. Sykes
Photo Editor — Donna L. Southard
News Editor — Robert H. Williams

World News Syndicate Ltd. — PO Box 419, Hollywood, CA 90078; tel (213) 469-2333; fax (213) 469-2333
Publisher — Bill Lane
General Manager — William P. Jenkins
Managing Editor — Laurie A. Williams

World Press — 1811 Monroe, Dearborn, MI 48124; tel (313) 563-0360; fax (313) 563-0360
Editor — Stephen R. Castor

World Press Review — 200 Madison Ave., Ste. 2104, New York, NY 10016; tel (212) 889-5155; fax (212) 889-5634
Editor — Larry Martz
Managing Editor — Gail Robinson
Senior Editor — B.J. Kowalski
Senior Editor — Barry Shelby
Assistant Editor — Caroline Nath
Editorial Administrator — Joanna G. Lowenstein

World Union Press — Rm. 373, Press Section, United Nations, New York, NY 10017; tel (212) 963-7154/(212) 688-7557; fax (212) 688-7557
Editor — David Horowitz
Staff — Raymond Reuven Solomon
Staff — Gregg Sitrin

World Watch/Foreign Affairs Syndicate — 144-21 Charter Rd., Ste. 5-C, Kew Garden Hills, NY 11435; tel (718) 591-7246
Editor — John J. Metzler

Writers Clearinghouse — PO Box 607, Quinebaug, CT 06262; tel (203) 923-9925; fax (508) 764-2774
Managing Director — Richard D. Carreno

Y

Yossarian Universal News Service — PO Box 236, Millbrae, CA 94030; tel (415) 588-5990
Managing Editor — Pamela Meuser
Editorial Director — Katherine Daly
Executive Editor — Charlie Chase
Associate Editor — Bruce Pryor
Editor — Paul Fericano

Z

Zondervan Press Syndicate — 5300 Patterson Ave. S.E., Grand Rapids, MI 49530; tel (616) 698-3209; fax (616) 698-3223; (612) 339-6973 (on line)
Managing Editor — Judy Waggoner

NEWSPAPER COMICS SECTION GROUPS AND NETWORKS
United States and Canadian independent as well as syndicated comics sections in which advertising may be scheduled for entire groups with one order

ARKANSAS-TEXAS COMIC GROUP — 315 Pine St., Texarkana, TX 75501; tel (903) 794-3311; fax (903) 792-7183
Pres./Editor — Walter E Hussman Jr
Adv. Dir. — Kirk Blair
Asst. Adv. Dir. — Rick Meredith
Gen. Mgr. — Buddy King
Representative — Papert Companies
A three-newspaper combination or any two of three newspapers listed:
El Dorado (AR) News Times
Hot Springs (AR) Sentinel-Record
Texarkana (AR-TX) Gazette
Circ.—32,790 (mon to sat); 36,697 (S); ABC

LE DROIT (published in French) — 47 Clarence St., Ste. 222, PO Box 8860, Ottawa, ON K1G 3J9 Canada; tel (613) 562-0111
Publisher — Pierre Bergeron
Mktg. Director — Marc Ouellette
Ottawa Le Droit

METRO-PUCK COMICS NETWORK — 260 Madison Ave., New York, NY 10016; tel (212) 689-8200
Pres./CEO — Carmen Willix
Exec. VP — Phyllis Cavaliere
Chicago, IL — 75 E. Wacker Dr., Chicago, IL 60601; tel (312) 372-9310
Manager — Ken Tarzon
Detroit, MI — 15450 E. Jefferson Ave., Ste. 100, Grosse Point Park, MI 48230
Manager — Don Jumisco
Los Angeles, CA — 4601 Wilshire Blvd., Los Angeles, CA 90010; tel (213) 933-5623
President — Norman Branchflower
San Francisco, CA — 101 California St., Ste. 930, San Francisco, CA 94111; tel (415) 421-7946; Manager — Ron DeCook
Included in the following newspapers:
Akron (OH) Beacon Journal
Alameda (CA) Metro Group
Albany (NY) Times Union
Albuquerque (NM) Journal/Tribune
Allentown (PA) Morning Call
Amarillo (TX) News-Globe
Ann Arbor (MI) News
Appleton-Neenah (WI) Post Crescent
Asbury Park (NJ) Press
Ashland (KY) Independent
Atlanta (GA) Journal & Constitution
Augusta (GA) Chronicle Herald
Austin (TX) American Statesman
Bakersfield (CA) Californian
Baltimore (MD) Sun
Bangor (ME) News
Battle Creek (MI) Enquirer
Bay City (MI) Times
Beaumont (TX) Enterprise
Bergen County (NJ) Record
Biloxi-Gulfport (MS) Sun Herald
Birmingham (AL) News
Bloomington-Bedford (IN) Herald Times
Boston (MA) Globe
Boston (MA) Herald
Brockton (MA) Enterprise
Buffalo (NY) News
Camden (NJ) Courier Post
Canton (OH) Repository
Cedar Rapids (IA) Gazette
Charleston (WV) Gazette Mail
Charleston (SC) Post & Courier
Charlotte (NC) Observer
Chattanooga (TN) News-Free Press
Chicago (IL) Sun-Times
Chicago (IL) Tribune
Cleveland (OH) Plain Dealer
Colorado Springs (CO) Gazette Telegraph
Columbia (SC) State
Columbus (GA) Ledger Enquirer
Contra Costa County (CA) Group
Copley (Torrance, CA) Newspapers
Corpus Christi (TX) Caller
Corsicana (TX) Sun
Dallas (TX) Morning News
Danbury (CT) News Times
Davenport (IA) Quad City Times
Dayton (OH) News
Daytona Beach (FL) News Journal
Del Rio (TX) News Herald
Denison (TX) Herald
Denver (CO) Post
Denver (CO) Rocky Mountain News
Des Moines (IA) Register
Detroit (MI) News & Free Press
Durham (NC) Herald
Easton (PA) Express
El Paso (TX) Times
Elmira (NY) Star Gazette
Erie (PA) Times News
Evansville (IN) Courier & Press
Fargo (ND) Forum
Flint (MI) Journal
Fort Lauderdale (FL) Sun Sentinel
Fort Myers (FL) News Press
Fort Wayne (IN) Journal-Gazette
Fort Worth (TX) Star-Telegram
Fresno (CA) Bee
Gary (IN) Post Tribune
Grand Rapids (MI) Press
Great Falls (MT) Tribune
Greater Philadelphia (PA) Newspaper
Green Bay (WI) Press Gazette
Greensboro (NC) News Record
Greensburg (PA) Tribune-Review
Greenville (SC) News-Piedmont
Greenwich (CT) Time
Harrisburg (PA) Patriot News
Hartford (CT) Courant
Honolulu (HI) Star Bulletin & Advertiser
Houston (TX) Chronicle
Huntsville (AL) Times
Hyannis (MA) Cape Cod Times
Indianapolis-Muncie (IN) Star
Jackson (MI) Citizen Patriot
Kalamazoo (MI) Gazette
Kansas City (MO) Star
Lakeland (FL) Ledger
Lansing-E Lansing (MI) State Journal
Las Vegas (NV) Review Journal
Lawrence (KA) Eagle Journal
Lewiston (ME) Sunday Sun-Journal
Lexington (KY) Herald Leader
Lincoln (NE) Journal Star
Little Rock (AR) Democrat Gazette
Long Beach (CA) Press Telegram
Long Island (NY) Newsday
Longview (TX) News-Journal
Los Angeles (CA) Daily News
Los Angeles (CA) Times
Louisville (KY) Courier Journal
Lowell (MA) Sun
Lubbock (TX) Avalanche Journal
Macon (GA) Telegraph & News
Madison (WI) State Journal
Mansfield (OH) News-Journal
Marion (IN) Chronicle Tribune
Memphis (TN) Commercial Appeal
Miami (FL) Herald
Middlesex County (NJ) Home News
Middletown (NY) Times Herald Record
Midland (TX) Reporter-Telegram
Milwaukee (WI) Journal Sentinel
Minneapolis (MN) Star and Tribune
Mobile (AL) Press Reigister
Moline (IL) Dispatch/Rock Island (IL) Argus
Monterey (CA) County Herald
Montgomery (AL) Advertiser-Journal
Munster-Hammond (IN) Times
Muskegon (MI) Chronicle
Myrtle Beach (SC) News
Nashville (TN) Tennessean
New Bedford (MA) Standard Times
New Brunswick (NJ) Home News
New Haven (CT) Register
New Orleans (LA) Times Picayune
New York (NY) Daily News
Newark (NJ) Star-Ledger
Newport News-Hampton (VA) Press
Norfolk (VA) Virginian-Pilot
Odessa (TX) American
Oklahoma City (OK) Sunday Oklahoman
Ontario (CA) Inland Valley Daily Bulletin
Orlando (FL) Sentinel
Parkersburg (WV) News
Passaic-Clifton (NJ) North Jersey Herald & News
Pensacola (FL) News Journal
Peoria (IL) Journal Star
Philadelphia (PA) Inquirer
Pittsburgh (PA) Post Gazette
Plattsburgh (NY) Press-Republican
Port Arthur (TX) News
Port Huron (MI) Times Herald
Portland (ME) Telegram
Portland (OR) Oregonian
Poughkeepsie (NY) Journal
Providence (RI) Journal
Pueblo (CO) Chieftain
Raleigh (NC) News & Observer
Reading (PA) Eagle
Reno (NV) Gazette Journal
Richmond (VA) Times Dispatch
Riverside (CA) Press Enterprise
Rochester (NY) Democrat & Chronicle
Sacramento-Modesto (CA) Bee
Saginaw (MI) News
Salem (OR) Statesman-Journal
Salt Lake (UT) Trib/Deseret News
San Antonio (TX) Express News
San Diego (CA) Union
San Francisco (CA) Examiner & Chronicle
San Gabriel Valley (CA) Newspapers
San Jose (CA) Mercury News
Santa Ana (CA) Orange County Register
Santa Barbara (CA) News Press
Santa Rosa (CA) Press Democrat
Sarasota (FL) Herald Tribune
Savannah (GA) News Press
Scranton (PA) Sunday Times
Shreveport (LA) Times
Sioux Falls (SD) Argus Leader
South Bend (IN) Tribune
Springfield (IL) State Journal Register
Springfield (MA) Union-News/Republican
St. Petersburg (FL) Times
Stamford (CT) Advocate
Staten Island (NY) Advance
Stockton (CA) Record
Stroudsburg-Pocono (PA) Record
Syracuse (NY) Herald American
Tacoma (WA) News Tribune
Tallahassee (FL) Democrat
Tampa (FL) Tribune and Times
Toledo (OH) Blade
Topeka (KS) Capital Journal
Trenton (NJ) Times
Troy (NY) Sunday Record
Tulsa (OK) World
Vallejo (CA) Times-Herald
Ventura (CA) County Star
Victorville (CA) Daily Press
Waco (TX) Tribune Herald
Washington (DC) Post
Waterbury (CT) Republican
West Palm Beach (FL) Post
Westchester (NY) Rockland Newspapers
Wheeling (WV) Register
Wichita (KS) Eagle Beacon
Wilkes-Barre (PA) Times Leader
Wilmington (DE) News Journal
Winston-Salem (NC) Journal
Woodbridge (NJ) News Tribune
Worcester (MA) Telegram
Yakima (WA) Vindicator
Youngstown (OH) Vindicator
Circ.—43,800,237; Sworn Mar. 31, 1994

MONTANA NEWSPAPER GROUP — 401 N. Broadway; PO Box 36300 (59107), Billings, MT 59101; tel (406) 657-1200
Publisher — Wayne Schile
Editor — Dick Wesnick
Adv. Dir. — David Payson
Nat'l. Adv. Coord. — Diana Russiff
Representative — Landon Associates
Newspapers Distributing:
Billings (MT) Gazette
Butte-Anaconda (MT) Montana Standard
Great Falls (MT) Tribune
Helena (MT) Independent-Record
Missoula (MT) Missoulian
Circ.—146,963 (mon to sat); 170,807 (S); ABC Mar. 31, 1994

RIO GRANDE VALLEY GROUP — 1310 S. Commerce St., Harlingen, TX 78551; tel (210) 423-5511/(210) 430-6211; fax (210) 430-6274
Publisher — Lyle DeBolt
Publisher — Ray M Stafford
Publisher — Douglas Hardie
Gen. Adv. Mgr. — Marcia Bleier
Included in the following newspapers:
Brownsville (TX) Herald
Harlingen (TX) Valley Morning Star
McAllen (TX) Monitor
Circ.—86,342 (mon to sat); 98,452 (S); ABC Mar. 31, 1995

SOUTHAM COMIC GROUP — 1450 Don Mills Rd., Don Mills, ON M3B 2X7, Canada; tel (416) 442-3444; fax (416) 442-2088
Dir. of Sales — David Titcombe
Distributed on Saturday by:
Brantford (ON) Expositor
Calgary (AB) Herald
Edmonton (AB) Journal
Hamilton (ON) Spectator
Kingston (ON) Whig-Standard
Kitchener-Waterloo (ON) Record
London (ON) Free Press
Medicine Hat (AB) News
Monction (NB) Times Transcript
Montreal (QC) Gazette
North Bay (ON) Nugget
Ottawa (ON) Citizen
Owen Sound (ON) Sun-Times
Regina (SK) Leader Post
St. Catherines (ON) Standard
Saint John (NF) Telegraph Journal
Saskatoon (SK) Star-Phoenix
Sault Ste. Marie (ON) Star
Vancouver (BC) Province
Vancouver (BC) Sun
Windsor (ON) Star
Circ.—See individual newspapers

TEXAS SUNDAY COMIC SECTION INC. — 400 N. St. Paul St., Ste. 1300, Dallas, TX 75201; tel (214) 969-0000
Chairman — S W Papert Jr
President — S W Papert III
Secretary — Michael Lovell
Included in the following newspapers:
Altus (OK) Times
Amarillo (TX) Globe News
Bartlesville (OK) Examiner-Enterprise
Blackwell (OK) Journal-Tribune
Borger (TX) News-Herald
Brownsville (TX) Herald
Brownwood (TX) Bulletin
Chickasha (OK) Express
Claremore (OK) Daily Progress
Columbia (TN) Herald
Duncan (OK) Banner
Durant (OK) Democrat
El Dorado (AR) News
Fort Smith (AR) Southwest Times Record
Gainesville (TX) Register
Guymon (OK) Herald
Harlington (TX) Star
Hobbs (NM) News-Sun
Hot Springs (AR) Sentinel-Record
Independence (KS) Reporter
Lubbock (TX) Avalanche Journal
McAllen (TX) Monitor
Moberly (MO) Monitor-Index & Democrat
Mount Pleasant (TX) Tribune
Norman (OK) Transcript
Odessa (TX) American
Okmulgee (OK) Daily Times
Pampa (TX) News
Paragould (AR) Press
Pine Bluff (AR) Commercial
Rogers (AR) Northwest Arkansas News
Sherman (TX) Democrat
Springdale (AR) News
Stillwater (OK) News-Press
Temple (TX) Telegram
Texarkana (TX) Gazette-News
Waxahachie (TX) Light
Circ.—832,000; ABC Mar. 31, 1993

THOMSON COMICS GROUP — 65 Queen St. W., Toronto, ON M5H 2M8 Canada; tel (416) 864-1710; fax (416) 864-1697
Media Sales Mgr. — Bruce Seater
Published in the following newspapers:
Brandon (MB) Sun
Charlottetown (PEI) Evening Patriot
Manitoba Brandon Sun
Lethbridge (AB) Herald
Okanagan (BC) Saturday
Prince Albert (SK) Daily Herald
St. John's (NF) Telegram
Sudbury (ON) Star
Thunder Bay (ON) Times-News/Chronicle Journal
Timmins (ON) Daily Press
Victoria (BC) Times-Colonist
Winnipeg (MB) Free Press
Circ.—See individual newspapers

THOMSON NEWSPAPERS COMIC GROUP — 3150 Des Plaines Ave., Des Plaines, IL 60018; tel (708) 299-5544
Sr. Vice Pres./COO — Michael Sheppard
Representative — Thomson Newspapers Inc.
Distributed Sunday with the following newspapers:
Ada (OK) News
Albert Lea (MN) Tribune
Appleton-Neenah-Menasha (WI) Post Crescent
Ashtabula-Conneaut-Chardon (OH) N.E. Ohio Newspapers
Atchison (KS) Times
Austin (MN) Herald
Beckley (WV) Register Herald
Big Spring (TX) Herald
Blue Field (WV) Daily Telegraph
Bridgeport (CT) Post-Telegram
Canton (OH) Repository
Charleston (WV) Mail Gazette

Copyright ©1996 by the Editor & Publisher Co.

Coshocton (OH) Tribune
Council Bluffs (IA) Nonpareil
Cumberland (MD) News/Times
Dalton (GA) Daily Citizen News
Del Rio (TX) News-Herald
Dickinson (ND) Press
Dothan (AL) Eagle
Easton (PA) Express
Elizabeth City (NC) Advance
Enid (OK) News-Eagle
Enterprise (AL) Ledger
Eureka (CA) Times Standard
Fairmont (WV) Times & West Virginian
Fayetteville (AR) Northwest Arkansas Times
Fitchburg (MA) Sentinel-Enterprise
Florence (SC) News
Fond du Lac (WI) Reporter
Hamilton (OH) Journal-News

Hanover (PA) Sun
Huntsville (TX) Item
Jacksonville (IL) Courier-Journal
Key West (FL) Citizen
Kokomo (IN) Tribune
Lafayette (LA) Advertiser
Lancaster (OH) Eagle-Gazette
Leavenworth (KS) Times
Lebanon (PA) News Pennsylvanian
Manitowoc (WI) Herald Times Reporter
Marianna (FL) Jackson County Floridian
Marion (OH) Star
Marshall (TX) News Messenger
Middletown (OH) Journal
Mitchell (SD) Republic
Monroe (NC) Enquirer-Journal
New Albany (IN) Tribune/Ledger
Newark (OH) Advocate

Distributed magazine sections V-13

Newburgh (NY) News
Opelika-Auburn (AL) News
Oxnard (CA) Press-Courier
Petersburg (VA) Progress-Index
Portsmouth (NH) Herald
Rocky Mount (NC) Telegram
St. George (UT) Spectrum
Salisbury (MD) Times
San Gabriel Valley (CA) Tribune News
Sedalia (MO) Democrat
Sikeston (MO) Standard
St. George (UT) Spectrum
Valdosta (GA) Times

Waukesha (WI) Freeman
Zanesville (OH) Times-Recorder
WYOMING COLOR COMIC GROUP — 702 W. Lincolnway, Cheyenne, WY 82001; tel (307) 634-3361
Advert. Dir. — Scott Walker
Representative — Papert Companies
Standard & Tabloid Size Section included in the following newspapers:
Cheyenne (WY) Wyoming Sunday Tribune-Eagle
Laramie (WY) Boomerang
Rawlins (WY) Times
Circ.—See individual newspapers

NEWSPAPER DISTRIBUTED MAGAZINE SECTIONS

ACTIVETIMES PUBLICATIONS INC. — 417 Main St., Carbondale, CO 81613; tel (970) 963-8252; fax (970) 963-8271
Publisher — Albert Myers
President — James Rathell
Dir. Newspaper Relations — Peter Sinding
Editor — Chris Kelly
Distributed by the following newspapers:
Ada (OK) News
Albert Lea (MN) Tribune
Alton (IL) Telegraph
Anderson (IN) Herald-Bulletin
Athens (TX) Daily Review
Austin (MN) Daily Herald
Bad Axe (MI) Huron Daily Tribune
Bakersfield (CA) Californian
Belleville (IL) News Democrat
Bentonville (AR) Benton County Daily Record
Bismarck (ND) Tribune
Canon City (CO) Daily Record
Carbondale (IL) Southern Illinoisan
Chicago (IL) Sun-Times
Cleburne (TX) Times-Review
Clinton (IA) Herald
Cottonwood (AZ) Verdi Independent
Dallas (TX) Morning News
Decatur (AL) Daily
Denver (CO) Post
Doylestown (PA) Intelligencer/Record
Duluth (MN) News Tribune
Eau Claire (WI) Leader-Telegram
Elyria (OH) Chronicle-Telegram
Eugene (OR) Register Guard
Fergus Falls (MN) Daily Journal
Fort Pierce (FL) Tribune
Fort Walton (FL) Northwest Florida Daily News
Fort Wayne (IN) Newspapers
Frankfort (KY) State Journal
Georgetown (KY) News-Graphic
Grand Rapids (MI) Press
Greenville (SC) News/Piedmont
Hannibal (MO) Courier-Post
Harrisburg (PA) Patriot News
Hays (KS) Daily News
Henderson (KY) Gleaner
Huntsville (AL) Times
Jacksonville (TX) Daily Progress
Johnstown (PA) Tribune-Democrat
Kansas City (MO) Star
Kilgore (TX) News Herald
Lubbock (TX) Avalanche Journal
Minneapolis (MN) Star Tribune
Midland (TX) Reporter Telegram
Montgomery (AL) Advertiser
Munster (IN) Times
New Philadelphia (OH) Times-Reporter
Ocala (FL) Star-Banner
Omaha (NE) World Herald
Orlando (FL) Sentinel
Pauls Valley (OK) Daily Democrat
Peoria (IL) Journal Star
Plainview (TX) Herald
Raleigh (NC) Extra
San Diego (CA) Union-Tribune
Santa Barbara (CA) News-Press
Santa Cruz (CA) Sentinel
Sonoma (CA) Index-Tribune
Spokane (WA) Advertiser
Springfield (IL) State Journal-Register
State College (PA) Centre Daily Times
Stuart (FL) News
Temple (TX) Daily Telegram
Ventura (CA) County Star
Victorville (CA) Daily Press
Weatherford (TX) Democrat
Wilkes-Barre (PA) Times-Leader
York (PA) Dispatch Record News

BLOOMBERG PERSONAL — 499 Park Ave., New York, NY 10022; tel (212) 318-2000; fax (212) 940-1930
Publisher — Michael Bloomberg
Editor-in-Chief — Matthew Winkler
Editor — William Inman
Sr. Editor — Ellen Cannon
Sr. Editor — Steven Gittelson
Sr. Editor — Christine Miles
Sr. Editor — Elizabeth Ungar
Sales Director — Lou Eccleston
Sales Manager — George Geyer
Nat'l. Magazine Sales — Timothy Kelly
Distributed by the following newspapers:
Alameda (CA) Group
Baltimore (MD) Sun
Bergen (NJ) Record
Boston (MA) Herald
Chicago (IL) Star Newspapers
Chicago (IL) Sun-Times
Cincinnati (OH) Enquirer
Contra Costa (CA) Group
Dallas (TX) Morning News
Denver (CO) Post
Detroit (MI) News
Gannett (NY) Suburban Newspapers
Hartford (CT) Courant
Houston (TX) Chronicle
New York (NY) Daily News
Phoenix (AZ) Arizona Republic
Pittsburg (PA) Post-Gazette
Raleigh (NC) Post-Gazette
St. Petersburg (FL) Times
Santa Ana (CA) Orange County Register
Washington (DC) Post
Circ.—6,701,926; ABC October 1995
FAMILY TIMES MAGAZINE — 417 Main St., Carbondale, CO 81623; tel (970) 963-8252; fax (970) 963-8271
Publisher — Albert Myers
President — James Rathell
Dir. Newspaper Relations — Peter Sinding
Editor — Chris Kelly
Distributed by the following newspapers:
Montgomery (AL) Advertiser
Bentonville (AR) Benton County Daily Record
Bakersfield (CA) Californian
Victorville (CA) Daily Press
Clinton (IA) Herald
Chicago (IL) Sun-Times
Rockford (IL) Register Star
Springfield (IL) State Journal-Register
Wilkes-Barre (PA) Times-Leader
Midland (TX) Reporter Telegram
Plainview (TX) The Herald
KIDS TODAY — 1000 Wilson Blvd., Arlington, VA 22229-0002; tel (703) 276-3796; fax (703) 558-3814
Editor — Anita Sama
Assoc. Editor — Nicole Carroll
Distributed by the following newspapers:
Battle Creek (MI) Enquirer
Boise (ID) Statesman
Camden (NJ) Courier-Post
Elkhart (IN) Truth
El Paso (TX) Times
Fort Collins (CO) Coloradoan
Fort Myers (FL) News Press
Frederick (MD) News Post
Gannett Rochester Newspapers
Guam Pacific Daily News
Hagerstown (MD) Herald Mail
Hattiesburg (MS) American
Holland (MI) Sentinel
Honolulu (HI) Advertiser
Landsdale (PA) Reporter
Lansing (MI) State Journal

Louisville (KY) Courier-Journal
Marion (IN) Chronicle-Tribune
Melbourne (FL) Florida Today
Monroe (LA) News Star
Nashville (TN) Tennessean
Niagara (NY) Gazette
North Hills (PA) News Register
Pennsburg (PA) Town and Country
Pensacola (FL) News Journal
Port Huron (MI) Times Herald
Richmond (IN) Palladium Item
Reno (NV) Gazette Journal
Rockford (IL) Register Star
St. Cloud (MN) Daily Times
Saratoga Springs (NY) Saratogian
Shreveport (LA) Times
Sioux Falls (SD) Argus Leader
Springfield (MO) News-Leader
Tulsa (OK) World
Wausau (WI) Daily Herald
Westchester (NY) Rockland Newspapers
Wilmington (DE) News Journal
Circ.—2,000,000; Sworn and Audited
MOLINE/ROCK ISLAND/QUAD CITY METRO UNIT MAGAZINES — 1720 5th Ave., Moline, IL 61265; tel (309) 797-0318; fax (309) 797-0321
Representative — TV Week Network
Distributed on Sunday by:
Moline (IL) Dispatch/TV Week
Rock Island (IL) Argus/TV Week
Circ.—51,927; ABC Mar. 31, 1995
PARADE PUBLICATIONS INC. — 711 3rd Ave., New York, NY 10017; tel (212) 450-7000
Chairman/Publisher — Carlo Vittorini
Sr. Vice President — Milt Lieberman
Editor — Walter Anderson
VP/Dir. Newspaper Rel. — Frederick H Johnson
VP/Western Region Mgr./Newspaper Rel. — Ron O'Neal
VP/Midwest Mgr./Newspaper Rel. — John Meyer
NW Mgr./Newspaper Rel. — Michael J Perry
SE Mgr./Newspaper Rel. — William Shiver
SW Mgr./Newspaper Rel. — Howard E Hoffman
Newspaper Rel. Prom. Mgr. — Liz Manigan
VP/Manufacturing — John Garvey
Distributed by the following newspapers:
Akron (OH) Beacon Journal
Alamogordo (NM) Daily News
Albany (NY) Times Union
Albert Lea (MN) Tribune
Albuquerque (NM) Journal
Allentown (PA) Morning Call
Amarillo (TX) Sunday News-Globe
Ann Arbor (MI) News
Anchorage (AK) Daily News
Asheville (NC) Citizen-Times
Ashland (KY) Sunday Independent
Athens (GA) Daily News/Banner-Herald
Atlanta (GA) Journal and Constitution
Auburn (NY) Citizen
Augusta (GA) Chronicle
Austin (TX) American-Statesman
Austin (MN) Daily Herald
Bakersfield (CA) Californian
Baltimore (MD) Sun
Barre-Montpelier (VT) Sunday Times-Argus
Bartlesville (OK) Examiner-Enterprise
Baton Rouge (LA) Sunday Advocate
Bay City (MI) Times
Beaumont (TX) Enterprise
Belleville (IL) News Democrat
Bend (OR) Bulletin
Bentonville (AR) Benton County Daily Record
Bergen County (NJ) Sunday Record
Billings (MT) Gazette
Biloxi-Gulfport (MS) Sun Herald
Birmingham (AL) News

Bismark (ND) Tribune
Bloomington (IN) Sunday Herald-Times
Boston (MA) Sunday Globe
Bowling Green (KY) Daily News
Bozeman (MT) Daily Chronicle
Brainerd (MN) Daily Dispatch
Branson (MO) Tri-Lakes Daily News
Bristol (VA) Herald Courier
Burlington (NC) Daily Times-News
Butte (MT) Montana Standard
Canandaigua (NY) Sunday Messenger
Canton (OH) Repository
Cape Cod (MA) Sunday Times
Carbondale (IL) Southern Illinoisan
Carson City (NV) Nevada Appeal
Casper (WY) Sunday Star-Tribune
Cedar Rapids (IA) Gazette
Centralia (IL) Sentinel
Chandler (AZ) Arizonan-Tribune
Charleston (SC) Post & Courier
Charleston (WV) Sunday Gazette-Mail
Charlotte (NC) Observer
Chattanooga (TN) Free Press
Chicago (IL) Tribune
Clarksburg (WV) Sunday Exponent-Telegram
Clarksville (TN) Leaf-Chronicle
Colorado Springs (CO) Gazette Telegraph
Columbia (TN) Daily Herald
Columbia (SC) State
Columbus (GA) Ledger-Enquirer
Columbus (MS) Commercial Dispatch
Cookeville (TN) Herald-Citizen
Corning (NY) Sunday Leader
Corpus Christi (TX) Caller-Times
Corvallis (OR) Gazette-Times
Dallas (TX) Morning News
Danbury (CT) News-Times
Davenport (IA) Quad City Times
Dayton (OH) Daily News
Daytona Beach (FL) Sunday News-Journal
Decatur (IL) Herald and Review
Del Rio (TX) News-Herald
Denver (CO) Rocky Mountain News
Dothan (AL) Eagle
Dover (DE) Delaware State News
Doylestown (PA) Daily Intelligencer/Record
Du Bois (PA) Tri-County Sunday
Duluth (MN) News Tribune
Elyria (OH) Chronicle-Telegram
Erie (PA) Times-News
Eugene (OR) Register-Guard
Eureka (CA) Times-Standard
Evansville (IN) Sunday Courier
Fairbanks (AK) Daily News Miner
Fairfield County (CT) Connecticut Post
Fairmont (WV) Times-West Virginian
Fargo (ND) Forum
Faribault (MN) Daily News
Farmington (NM) Daily Times
Fayetteville (AR) Northwest Arkansas Times
Fayetteville (NC) Observer-Times
Flint (MI) Journal
Florence-Sheffield (AL) Times Daily
Florence (SC) Morning News
Fort Dodge (IA) Messenger
Fort Pierce (FL) Tribune
Fort Walton Beach (FL) Northwest Florida Daily News
Fort Wayne (IN) Journal-Gazette
Fort Worth (TX) Star-Telegram
Fresno (CA) Bee
Gadsden (AL) Times
Gainesville (FL) Sun
Gary (IN) Post Tribune
Geneva (NY) Finger Lakes Times
Grand Island (NE) Independent
Grand Junction (CO) Daily Sentinel

Copyright ©1996 by the Editor & Publisher Co.

V-14 Distributed magazine sections

Grand Rapids (MI) Press
Greensboro (NC) News and Record
Greenville (NC) Daily Reflector
Greenville (SC) News
Greenwich (CT) Times
Greenwood (MS) Commonwealth
Hagerstown (MD) Herald Mail
Hamilton (OH) Journal-News
Harlingen (TX) Valley Morning Star
Harrisburg (PA) Sunday Patriot-News
Hartford (CT) Courant
Helena (MT) Independent Record
Henderson (NC) Daily Dispatch
Hendersonville (NC) Times-News
Hobbs (NM) News-Sun
Houma (LA) Daily Courier
Houston (TX) Chronicle
Huntsville (AL) Times
Huron (SD) Daily Plainsman
Idaho Falls (ID) Post-Register
Indianapolis (IN) Star
Jackson (MI) Citizen Patriot
Jacksonville (FL) Florida Times-Union
Jacksonville (NC) Daily News
Jefferson City (MO) Sunday News Tribune
Johnson City (TN) Press
Johnstown (PA) Sunday Tribune-Democrat
Jonesboro (AR) Sun
Joplin (MO) Globe
Juneau (AK) Empire
Kalamazoo (MI) Gazette
Kansas City (MO) Star
Kenosha (WI) Sunday News
Kerrville (TX) Daily Times
Kilgore (TX) News Herald
Kingman (AZ) Daily Miner
Kingsport (TN) Times-News
Knoxville (TN) News-Sentinel
LaCrosse (WI) Tribune
Lafayette (LA) Daily Advertiser
Lake Charles (LA) American Press
Lake County-East Chicago (IL) Times
Lake Havasu (AZ) Today's News-Herald
Lakeland (FL) Ledger
Lancaster (PA) Sunday News
Las Cruces (NM) Sun-News
Laurel (MS) Leader-Call
Leesburg (FL) Daily Commercial
Levittown (PA) Bucks County Courier Times
Lewiston-Clarkston (ID) Tribune
Lexington (KY) Herald-Leader
Lincoln (NE) Journal-Star
Little Rock (AR) Arkansas Democrat-Gazette
Logan (UT) Herald Journal
Long Beach (CA) Press-Telegram
Lubbock (TX) Avalanche Journal
Lufkin (TX) Daily News
Macon (GA) Telegraph
Madison (WI) Wisconsin State Journal
Manchester (NH) Sunday News
Mankato (MN) Free Press
Marquette (MI) Mining Journal
Marshall (TX) News Messenger
Marshaltown (IA) Times-Republican
Martinsburg (WV) Sunday Journal
Martinsville (VA) Bulletin
Mason City (IA) Sunday Globe
McComb (MS) Enterprise-Journal
Medford (OR) Mail Tribune
Memphis (TN) Commercial Appeal
Mesa (AZ) Tribune
Miami (FL) Herald
Middletown (OH) Journal
Middletown (NY) Sunday Record
Milwaukee (WI) Journal Sentinel
Minot (ND) Daily News
Missoula (MT) Missoulian
Mobile (AL) Press Register
Modesto (CA) Bee
Monroe (MI) Sunday News
Monterey (CA) Herald
Montgomery (AL) Sunday Advertiser
Morgantown (WV) Dominion-Post
Morristown (TN) Citizen Tribune
Muncie (IN) Star
Murfreesboro (TN) Daily News Journal
Muskegon (MI) Chronicle
Myrtle Beach (SC) Sun News
Nacogdoches (TX) Daily Sentinel
Nampa-Caldwell (ID) Idaho Press-Tribune
Naples (FL) Daily News
New Albany (IN) Ledger Tribune
New Bedford (MA) Sunday Standard-Times
New London (CT) Day
New Orleans (LA) Times-Picayune
New Ulm (MN) Journal
Newark (NJ) Star-Ledger
Newport News-Hampton (VA) Daily Press
Norfolk (VA) Virginian-Pilot
Oakland (CA) Tribune
Ocala (FL) Star-Banner
Oceanside (CA) Blade Citizen

Odessa (TX) American
Ogden (UT) Standard-Examiner
Oklahoma City (OK) Sunday Oklahoman
Omaha (NE) World-Herald
Opelika-Auburn (AL) News
Oshkosh (WI) Northwestern
Owensboro (KY) Messenger-Inquirer
Owatonna (MN) People's Press
Parkersburg (WV) News
Pascagoula (MS) Mississippi Press
Pasco (WA) Tri-City Herald
Peoria (IL) Journal-Star
Petersburg (VA) Progress-Index
Phoenix (AZ) Arizona Republic
Pine Bluff (AR) Commercial
Pittsburg (KS) Morning Sun
Pittsburgh (PA) Post-Gazette
Pittsfield (MA) Berkshire Eagle
Plattsburgh (NY) Press-Republican
Pocatello (ID) Idaho State Journal
Pontiac (MI) Oakland Press
Poplar Bluff (MO) Daily American Republic
Portland (ME) Maine Sunday Telegram
Portland (OR) Sunday Oregonian
Portsmouth (NH) Herald Sunday
Prescott (AZ) Courier
Providence (RI) Sunday Journal
Pueblo (CO) Sunday Chieftain
Quincy (IL) Herald-Whig
Racine (WI) Journal Times
Raleigh (NC) News & Observer
Rapid City (SD) Journal
Reading (PA) Eagle
Redding (CA) Record Searchlight
Redlands (CA) Daily Facts
Richmond (VA) Times-Dispatch
Riverside (CA) Press-Enterprise
Roanoke (VA) Times & World News
Rocky Mount (NC) Sunday Telegram
Roseburg (OR) News-Review
Rutland (VT) Sunday Herald
Sacramento (CA) Bee
Saginaw (MI) News
St. George (UT) Daily Spectrum
St. Joseph (MO) News-Press
St. Louis (MO) Post-Dispatch
St. Paul (MN) Pioneer Press
St. Petersburg (FL) Times
Salem (NY) Today's Sunbeam
Salisbury (MD) Daily Times
Salt Lake City (UT) Tribune
San Antonio (TX) Express News
San Diego (CA) Union-Tribune
San Francisco (CA) Examiner & Chronicle
San Gabriel Valley (CA) Newspapers
San Jose (CA) Mercury-News
Santa Ana (CA) Orange County Register
Santa Barbara (CA) News-Press
Santa Rosa (CA) Press-Democrat
Sarasota (FL) Herald-Tribune
Savannah (GA) Morning News
Scranton (PA) Sunday Times/The Scrantonian
Seattle (WA) Times/Post-Intelligencer
Sedalia (MO) Democrat
Sherman (TX) Democrat
Simi Valley (CA) Star
Sioux City (IA) Sunday Journal
South Bend (IN) Tribune
Sparks (NV) Tribune Sunday
Spartanburg (SC) Herald Journal
Spokane (WA) Spokesman-Review
Springfield (OH) News-Sun
Springfield (MA) Republican
Springfield (IL) State Journal-Register
Stamford (CT) Advocate
State College (PA) Centre Daily Times
Staten Island (NY) Sunday Advance
Staunton (VA) Sunday News Leader
Sterling (IL) Sauk Valley Sunday
Steubenville (OH) Herald Star
Stockton (CA) Record
Stroudsburg (PA) Pocono Record
Stuart (FL) News
Sumter (SC) Daily Item
Sunbury (PA) Daily Item
Syracuse (NY) Herald American
Tallahassee (FL) Democrat
Tampa (FL) Tribune and Times
Tempe (AZ) Daily News-Tribune
Toledo (OH) Blade
Topeka (KS) Capital-Journal
Torrance (CA) Daily Breeze
Towanda (PA) Sunday Review
Traverse City (MI) Record-Eagle
Trenton (NJ) Times
Troy (OH) Miami Valley Sunday News
Tucson (AZ) Arizona Daily Star
Tuscaloosa (AL) News
Twin Falls (ID) Times-News
Uniontown (PA) Herald-Standard
Valdosta (GA) Daily Times
Vallejo (CA) Times-Herald

Ventura (CA) County Star
Vero Beach (FL) Press Journal
Vicksburg (MS) Sunday Post
Victorville (CA) Victor Valley Daily Press
Waco (TX) Tribune-Herald
Wailuku (HI) Maui News
Washington (DC) Post
Waterbury (CT) Sunday Republican
Waterloo (IA) Courier
West Palm Beach (FL) Post
Wheeling (WV) News-Register
Wichita (KS) Eagle
Wichita Falls (TX) Times-Record News
Williamsport (PA) Sun-Gazette
Willingboro (NJ) Burlington County Times
Wilmington (NC) Sunday Star-News
Winona (MN) Daily News
Winston-Salem (NC) Journal
Woodbury (NJ) Gloucester County Times
Worcester (MA) Sunday Telegram
Yakima (WA) Herald-Republic
York (PA) Sunday News
Youngstown (OH) Vindicator
Yuma (AZ) Daily Sun
Circ.—37,166,000; Based on Jan. 7, 1996

PRINT MARKETING CONCEPTS — 1120 Ave. of the Americas, New York, NY 10036; tel (212) 626-6801; fax (212) 626-6804
President — Charles Dye
VP/National Sales — Robin L Good
VP/Newspaper Relations — Ed Bryant
Director of Finance — Nancy Kissman
Houston, TX — 10590 Westoffice Dr., Ste. 250, Houston, TX 77042; tel (713) 780-7055; fax (713) 780-9731
Print Marketing Concepts distributes TV Update Magazine to 141 newspapers nationwide.

REACT — 711 3rd Ave., New York, NY 10017; tel (212) 450-7000
Chairman/Publisher — Carlo Vittorini
Sr. Vice President — Milt Lieberman
Editor — Lee Kravitz
VP/Dir. Newspaper Rel. — Frederick H Johnson
VP/Western Region Mgr./Newspaper Rel. — Ron O'Neal
VP/Midwest Mgr./Newspaper Rel. — John Meyer
NW Mgr./Newspaper Rel. — Michael J Perry
SE Mgr./Newspaper Rel. — William Shiver
SW Mgr./Newspaper Rel. — Howard E Hoffman
Newspaper Rel. Prom. Mgr. — Liz Manigan
VP/Manufacturing — John Garvey
Distributed by the following newspapers:
Albany (NY) Times-Union
Ann Arbor (MI) News
Bay City (MI) Times
Clarksville (TN) Leaf-Chronicle
Colorado Springs (CO) Gazette-Telegraph
Dallas Morning News
Denver Rocky Mountain News
Fargo (ND) Forum
Flint (MI) Journal
Gainesville (FL) Sun
Grand Rapids (MI) Press
Greenville (SC) News
Hagerstown (MD) Herald Mail
Harlingen (TX) Valley Morning News
Huntsville (AL) Times
Jackson (MI) Citizen Patriot
Jonesboro (AR) Sun
Johnstown (PA) Tribune-Democrat
Joplin (MO) Globe
Kalamazoo (MI) Gazette
Lakeland (FL) Ledger
Levittown (PA) Bucks County Courier Times
Lincoln (NE) Journal & Star
Manchester (NH) Union Leader
Milwaukee Journal Sentinel
Mobile (AL) Press Register
Modesto (CA) Bee
Muskegon (MI) Chronicle
Newark (NJ) Star Ledger
New Orleans (LA) Times-Picayune
Ocala (FL) Star-Banner
Oklahoma City Oklahoman
Oshkosh (WI) Northwestern
Owensboro (KY) Messenger-Inquirer
Pascagoula (MS) Mississippi Press Register
Phoenix Arizona Republic
Portland Oregonian
Riverside (CA) Press-Enterprise
Saginaw (MI) News
St. Petersburg (FL) Times
Santa Ana (CA) Orange County Register
South Bend (IN) Tribune
Spokane (WA) Spokesman-Review
Springfield (MA) Union-News
Staten Island (NY) Advance
Sumter (SC) Item
Syracuse (NY) Herald-American
Traverse City (MI) Record-Eagle
Trenton (NJ) Times
Troy (OH) Daily News
Tucson (AZ) Arizona Daily Star
Ventura (CA) Newspaper Group
Victorville (CA) Daily Press
Wilkes-Barre (PA) Leader

SOUTHAM TV TIMES — 1450 Don Mills Rd., Don Mills, ON M3B 2X7, Canada; tel (416) 442-3444; fax (416) 442-2088
Sales Director — David Titcombe

SUNDAY MAGAZINE NETWORK — 260 Madison Ave., New York, NY 10016; tel (212) 689-8200
President/CEO — Carmen Willix
Executive VP — Phyllis Cavaliere
New York Manager — Francis Bee
Chicago, IL — 75 E. Wacker Dr., Chicago, IL 60601; tel (312) 372-9310
Manager — Ken Tarzon
Detroit, MI — 15450 E. Jefferson Ave., Ste. 100, Grosse Pointe Park, MI 48230; tel (313) 331-4300
Manager — Don Jumisco
Los Angeles, CA — 4601 Wilshire Blvd., Los Angeles, CA 90010; tel (213) 933-5623
Western Associate — Norman Branchflower
San Francisco, CA — 101 California St., Ste. 930, San Francisco, CA 94111; tel (415) 421-7946
Western Associate — Ron DeCook
Member Newspapers:
Akron (OH) Beacon Journal
Baltimore (MD) Sun
Boston (MA) Globe
Boston (MA) Herald
Buffalo (NY) News
Chicago (IL) Tribune
Cleveland (OH) Plain Dealer
Dallas (TX) Morning News
Detroit (MI) News & Free Press
Fort Lauderdale (FL) Sun Sentinel
Hartford (CT) Courant
Houston (TX) Chronicle
Kansas City (MO) Star
Miami (FL) Herald
Milwaukee (WI) Journal Sentinel
New York (NY) Daily News
Orlando (FL) Sentinel
Philadelphia (PA) Inquirer
Pittsburgh (PA) Post-Gazette
Providence (RI) Journal
St. Louis (MO) Post-Dispatch
San Antonio (TX) Express-News
San Jose (CA) Mercury-News
Tulsa (OK) World
Washington (DC) Post
Circ.—14,801,491; ABC Mar. 31, 1993

TRIBUNE TV LOG — 435 N. Michigan, Ste. 1500, Chicago, IL 60601; tel (312) 222-5968; fax (312) 222-8620
Pres./CEO — David D Williams
Vice Pres. — Barbara Needleman
Sales Rep. — Jan Guszynski
Sales Rep. — Anne Mathieson
New York, NY — 136 E. 57th St., New York, NY 10022; tel (212) 687-0660
Los Angeles, CA — 4601 Wilshire Blvd., Ste. 112, Los Angeles, CA 90010; tel (213) 931-1583
Distributed by:
Abilene (TX) Reporter News
Akron (OH) Beacon Journal
Albany (NY) Times Union
Albuquerque (NM) Journal
Allentown (PA) Morning Call
Altoona (PA) Mirror
Amarillo (TX) News-Globe
Anderson (SC) Independent-Mail
Appleton (WI) Post-Crescent
Asbury Park (NJ) Press
Athens (GA) Daily News & Banner Herald
Atlanta (GA) Journal & Constitution
Atlantic City (NJ) Press
Augusta (GA) Chronicle
Austin (TX) American Statesman
Bakersfield (CA) Californian
Baltimore (MD) Sun
Bangor (ME) News
Battle Creek (MI) Enquirer & News
Beaumont (TX) Enterprise Journal
Beaver (PA) County Times
Belleville (IL) News-Democrat
Bellevue (WA) Journal American
Bergen County (NJ) Record
Biloxi-Gulfport (MS) Sun
Binghamton (NY) Press & Sun-Bulletin
Birmingham (AL) News
Boca Raton (FL) News
Boise (ID) Idaho Statesman
Boston (MA) Globe
Boston (MA) Herald
Boulder (CO) Daily Camera
Bridgeport (CT) Post-Telegram
Bridgewater (NJ) Courier News
Buffalo (NY) News
Burlington (VT) Free Press
Camden (NJ) Courier-Post
Canton (OH) Repository
Cedar Rapids (IA) Gazette
Champaign (IL) News Gazette
Charleston (WV) Mail
Charlotte (NC) Observer
Chicago (IL) Arlington Heights Daily Herald

Copyright ©1996 by the Editor & Publisher Co.

Distributed magazine sections   V-15

TV WEEK NETWORK — 435 N. Michigan Ave., Ste. 1500, Chicago, IL 60611; tel (800) 245-6536/(312) 222-4444
President — David D Williams
USA WEEKEND — 535 Madison Ave., 21st Fl., New York, NY 10022; tel (212) 715-2100
Publisher — Brette Popper
Managing Editor — Amy Eisman
Editor — Marcia Bullard
Exec. VP — Charles Gabrielson
VP/Newspaper Comm. — Sue Agresta
VP/Advertising — Beth Lawrence
VP/Production — Thomas Meisel
VP/New Bus. Develop. — Carol Kerner-Odgis
VP/Finance — Tobey Lyden
Advertising Dir./East Coast — Jim Hackett
West Coast Manager — Shari Cohen-Kairey
Director/Midwest Sales — Jodi Vevoda
Director/Agency Relations — Jim Powers
Dir./Newspaper Relations — Dave Barber
Personnel — Carol Gottlieb
Advertising Offices:
Chicago, IL — 444 N. Michigan Ave., Chicago, IL 60611; tel (312) 467-0510
Troy, MI — 340 E. Big Beaver Rd., Ste. 150, Troy, MI 48083; tel (313) 680-1220
Los Angeles, CA — 11111 Santa Monica Blvd., Ste. 2100, Los Angeles, CA 90025; tel (310) 444-2140
Distributed by the following 452 newspapers:

Aberdeen (SD) American News
Aberdeen (WA) World
Abilene (TX) Reporter-News
Adrian (MI) Telegram
Aiken (SC) Standard
Alameda (CA) Times Star
Albany (GA) Herald
Albany (OR) Democrat-Herald
Alexandria (LA) Town Talk
Alexandria (VA) Journal
Alpena (MI) News
Alton (IL) Telegraph
Altoona (PA) Mirror
Anderson (IN) Herald Bulletin
Anderson (SC) Independent-Mail
Annapolis (MD) Capital
Anniston (AL) Star
Antioch (CA) Ledger
Appleton (WI) Post-Crescent
Arlington (VA) Journal
Asheboro (NC) Courier-Tribune
Ashtabula-Conneaut (OH) Star Beacon
Athens (OH) Messenger
Atlantic City (NJ) Press
Attleboro (MA) Sun Chronicle
Auburn (IN) Evening Star
Auburn (CA) Journal
Augusta (ME) Kennebec Journal
Aurora (IL) Beacon-News
Bad Axe (MI) Huron Tribune
Bangor (ME) News
Battle Creek (MI) Enquirer
Baytown (TX) Sun
Beatrice (NE) Sun
Beaufort (SC) Gazette
Beaver (PA) County Times
Beaver Dam (WI) Citizen
Beckley (WV) Register-Herald
Bellevue (WA) Journal American
Bellingham (WA) Herald
Benton (IL) Evening News
Benton Harbor (MI) Herald-Palladium
Beverly (MA) Times
Biddeford (ME) Journal-Tribune
Binghamton (NY) Press & Sun Bulletin
Bloomington (IL) Pantagraph
Bloomsburg (PA) Press Enterprise
Bluefield (WV) Daily Telegraph
Bluffton (IN) News Banner
Blytheville (AR) Courier-News
Boca Raton (FL) News
Bogalusa (LA) News
Boise (ID) Idaho Statesman
Boston (MA) Herald
Bradenton (FL) Herald
Bradford (PA) Era
Bremerton (WA) Sun
Bridgewater (NJ) Courier-News
Bristol (CT) Press
Brockton (MA) Enterprise
Brownsville (TX) Herald
Bryan-College Station (TX) Eagle
Bucyrus (OH) Telegraph-Forum
Buffalo (NY) News
Burlington (IA) Hawk Eye
Burlington (VT) Free Press
Butler (PA) Eagle
Cape Girardeau (MO) Southeast Missourian
Carlsbad (NM) Current-Argus
Carmi (IL) Times
Carrolton (GA) Times Georgian

Carterville (GA) Tribune-News
Casa Grande (AZ) Dispatch
Chambersburg (PA) Public Opinion
Champaign-Urbana (IL) News-Gazette
Charlotte Harbor (FL) Sun-Herald
Charlottesville (VA) Progress
Cherry Hill-Camden (NJ) Courier Post
Chester (PA) Delaware County Times
Chicago (IL) Daily Herald
Chicago (IL) Daily Southtown
Chicago (IL) Sun Times
Chico (CA) Enterprise-Record
Chillicothe (OH) Gazette
Cincinnati (OH) Enquirer
Clearfield (PA) Progress
Cleveland (TN) Banner
Clovis (NM) News Journal
Clute (TX) Brazosport Facts
Coeur D'Alene (ID) North Idaho Sunday
Columbia (MO) Tribune
Columbia City (IN) Post & Mail
Columbus (IN) Republic
Concord (NH) Monitor
Concord (NC) Tribune
Conroe (TX) Courier
Conyers (GA) Rockdale Citizen
Coos Bay-North Bend (OR) World
Corsicana (TX) Sun
Coshocton (OH) Tribune
Council Bluffs (IA) Nonpareil
Crawfordsville (IN) Journal Review
Crystal Lake (IL) Northwest Herald
Crystal River (FL) Citrus County Chronicle
Culpeper (VA) Star-Exponent
Cumberland (MD) Times-News
Dalton (GA) Daily Citizen-News
Danville (IL) Commercial News
Danville (VA) Register & Bee
Davis (CA) Enterprise
De Kalb (IL) News-Chronicle
De Ridder (LA) Beauregard Daily News
Decatur (AL) Daily
Decatur (IN) Daily Democrat
Defiance (OH) Crescent-News
Denton (TX) Record-Chronicle
Denver (CO) Post
Des Moines (IA) Register
Detroit (MI) News and Free Press
Dixon (IL) Telegraph
Douglasville (GA) Douglas County Sentinel
Dover (NH) Foster's Democrat
Dover-New Philadelphia (OH) Times-Reporter
Du Quoin (IL) Evening Call
Dublin (GA) Courier-Herald
Dubuque (IA) Telegraph Herald
Dunkirk (NY) Observer
Durango (CO) Herald
Durham (NC) Herald-Sun
Dyersburg (TN) State Gazette
East Brunswick (NJ) Home News
Easton (MD) Star-Democrat
Easton (PA) Express-Times
El Cajon (CA) Californian
El Dorado (IL) Daily Journal
El Dorado (AR) News-Times
El Paso (TX) Times
Elgin (IL) Courier-News
Elizabeth City (NC) Advance
Elizabethtown (KY) News-Enterprise
Elkhart (IN) Truth
Elkins (WV) Inter-Mountain
Elmira (NY) Star-Gazette
Enid (OK) News & Eagle
Escondido (CA) Times-Advocate
Everett (WA) Herald
Fairfax (VA) Journal
Fairfield (CA) Daily Republic
Fall River (MA) Herald News
Findlay (OH) Courier
Fitchburg (MA) Sentinel & Enterprise
Flagstaff (AZ) Arizona Daily Sun
Flora (IL) Daily County Advocate Press
Fond Du Lac (WI) Reporter
Ft. Collins (CO) Coloradoan
Ft. Myers (FL) News-Press
Ft. Smith (AR) Southwest Times Record
Framingham (MA) Middlesex News
Franklin (IN) Journal
Fredericksburg (VA) Free Lance-Star
Fremont (CA) Argus
Fremont (OH) News-Messenger
Gainsville (GA) Times
Gallup (NM) Independent
Galveston (TX) News
Gastonia (NC) Gaston Gazette
Glendale (CA) News-Press
Gloucester (MA) Times
Goldsboro (NC) News-Argus
Grand Forks (ND) Herald
Great Falls (MT) Tribune
Green Bay (WI) Press-Gazette

Chicago (IL) Southtown
Chicago (IL) Tribune
Cincinnati (OH) Enquirer
Cincinnati (OH) Post
Clarion (MS) Ledger
Cleveland (OH) Plain Dealer
Clute (TX) Brazosport Facts
Coatesville (PA) Record
Colorado Springs (CO) Gazette Telegraph
Columbia (SC) State
Contra Costa (CA) Times
Columbus (OH) Dispatch
Davenport (IA) Quad City Times
Dayton (OH) News
Daytona Beach (FL) News-Journal
Decatur (IL) Herald Review
Denver (CO) Post
Denver (CO) Rocky Mountain News
Des Moines (IA) Register
Detroit (MI) Free Press
Detroit (MI) News
Doylestown (PA) Intelligencer
Duluth (MN) News Tribune & Herald
Durham (NC) Sun
Easton (PA) Express-Times
El Paso (TX) Herald Post
El Paso (TX) Times
Elizabeth (NJ) Journal
Elgin (IL) Courier News
Elmira (NY) Telegram
Erie (PA) Weekender
Escondido (CA) Times Advocate
Evansville (IN) Courier & Press
Everett (WA) Herald
Fargo (ND) Forum
Fayetteville (NC) Observer & Times
Florida (FL) Today
Flint (MI) Journal
Fort Myers (FL) News Press
Franklin (IN) Daily Journal
Fresno (CA) Bee
Gainesville (FL) Sun
Galveston (TX) Daily News
Gannett Suburban (NY) Newspapers
Gary (IN) Post-Tribune
Glens Falls (NY) Post Star
Grand Forks (ND) Herald
Grand Rapids (MI) Press
Green Bay (WI) Press-Gazette
Greensboro (NC) News & Record
Greensburg (PA) Tribune Review
Greenville (SC) News-Piedmont
Greenwich (CT) Time
Harrisburg (PA) Patriot-News
Hartford (CT) Courant
Holyoke (MA) Transcript-Telegram
Houston (TX) Chronicle
Hutchinson (KS) News
Indianapolis (IN) News
Indianapolis (IN) Star
Ithaca (NY) Journal
Jacksonville (FL) Times-Union
Jersey City (NJ) Jersey Journal
Johnson City (TN) Press Chronicle
Johnstown (PA) Tribune-Democrat
Kalamazoo (MI) Gazette
Kansas City (MO) Star
Kenosha (WI) News
Kent (WA) Valley Newspaper
Kingsport (TN) Times News
Lafayette (IN) Journal & Courier
Lakeland (FL) Ledger
Lansing (MI) State Journal
Las Vegas (NV) Review Journal
Las Vegas (NV) Showbiz Magazine
Lawrence (KS) Journal-World
Lewiston (ME) Journal
Levittown (PA) Bucks County Courier Times
Lexington (KY) Herald Leader
Lincoln (NE) Star & Journal
Little Rock (AR) Arkansas Democrat/Gazette
Long Beach (CA) Press-Telegram
Lorain (OH) Journal
Los Angeles (CA) Daily Breeze
Los Angeles (CA) News
Los Angeles (CA) Times
Lynchburg (VA) Advance
Lowell (MA) Sun
Madison (WI) Capitol Times/Wis. State Journal
Manchester (NH) New Hampshire News
Melbourne (FL) Florida Today
Mesa (AZ) Tribune
Miami (FL) Herald
Milwaukee (WI) Journal Sentinel
Minneapolis (MN) Star Tribune
Modesto (CA) Bee
Moline (IL) Dispatch
Monroe (LA) News-Star-World
Montgomery (AL) Advertiser-Journal
Morristown (NH) Record
Muskegon (MI) Chronicle
Myrtle Beach (SC) Sun News
Nampa (ID) Press Tribune
Nashville (TN) Banner
Nashville (TN) Tennessean
Nashua (NH) Telegraph
New Haven (CT) Register

New York (NY) Daily News
New York (NY) El Diario-La Prensa
New York (NY) Post
Newark (NJ) Star Ledger
Newport News (VA) Times-Herald
Newport News (VA) Daily Press
Niagara Falls (NY) Gazette
Oklahoma City (OK) Oklahoman & Times
Omaha (NE) World-Herald
Orlando (FL) Sentinel-Star
Palm Springs (LA) Desert Sun
Pasadena (CA) Star News
Passaic (NJ) North Jersey Herald & News
Pekin (IL) Daily Times
Pensacola (FL) News-Journal
Philadelphia (PA) Daily News
Philadelphia (PA) Inquirer
Phoenix (AZ) Arizona Republic
Phoenix (AZ) Gazette
Pittsburgh (PA) Post-Gazette
Port Arthur (TX) News
Port Huron (MI) Times Herald
Portland (OR) Oregonian
Portland (ME) Press-Herald
Pueblo (CO) Chieftain & Star Journal
Raleigh (NC) News & Observer
Quincy (MA) Patroit Leader
Racine (WI) Journal Times
Reading (PA) Eagle
Racine (WI) Journal Times
Richmond (VA) News Leader/Times-Dispatch
Richmond (IN) Palladium-Item
Riverside (CA) Press
Roanoke (VA) Times & World News
Rochester (NY) Democrat & Chronicle
Rochester (NY) Times-Union
Rockford (IL) Register Star Herald
Rome (GA) News Tribune
Sacramento (CA) Bee
Saginaw (MI) News
St. Augustine (FL) Record
St. Joseph (MO) News-Press
St. Louis (MO) Post-Dispatch
St. Paul (MN) Pioneer-Press
St. Petersburg (FL) Times
Salem (OR) Statesman-Journal
Salinas (CA) Californian
Salt Lake City (UT) Tribune & Deseret News
San Angelo (TX) Standard Times
San Antonio (TX) Express-News
San Diego (CA) Union-Tribune
San Francisco (CA) Chronicle-Examiner
San Gabriel (CA) Valley Tribune
San Jose (CA) Mercury-News
San Rafael (CA) Marin County Independent Journal
Santa Ana (CA) Orange County Register
Saratoga Springs (NY) Saratogian
Savannah (GA) News
Savannah (GA) Press
Scranton (PA) Scrantonian
Scranton (PA) Times
Shreveport (LA) Journal
Shreveport (LA) Times
Spartanburg (SC) Herald-Journal
Spokane (WA) Spokesman/Review
Springfield (IL) Journal Register
Springfield (MO) News & Leader
Springfield (MA) Union-News
Springfield (MO) Republican
Springfield (MO) News-Leader
Springfield (OH) New Sun
Stamford (CT) Advocate
Syracuse (NY) Herald Journal
Tacoma (WA) News Tribune
Tonawanda (NY) News
Topeka (KS) Capital Journal
Torrance (CA) Daily Breeze
Trenton (NJ) Times
Troy (NY) Times Record
Tucson (AZ) Arizona Star
Tucson (AZ) Daily Citizen
Tulsa (OK) World
Uniontown (PA) Herald Standard
Waterbury (CT) American
Visalia (CA) Times Delta
Waco (TX) Tribune Herald
Walnut Creek (CA) Contra Costa Times
Washington (DC) Post
Washington (DC) Times
Waterbury (CT) Republican-American
Waterloo (IA) Courier
West Palm Beach (FL) Post
Wilkes Barre (PA) Times-Leader
Willingboro (NJ) Burlington County Times
Wilmington (DE) News Journal
Winston-Salem (NC) Journal
Woodbridge (NJ) News Tribune
Woodbury (NJ) Gloucester County Times
Worcester (MA) Telegram & Gazette
Yakima (WA) Herald-Republic
York (PA) Daily Record
Youngstown (OH) Vindicator
Yuma (AZ) Sun
Circ.—79,274,741; Rate Base effective June 27, 1993

Copyright ©1996 by the Editor & Publisher Co.

V-16　Distributed magazine sections

Greencastle (IN) Banner Graphic
Greenfield (IN) Daily Reporter
Greenfield (MA) Recorder
Greensburg (PA) Tribune-Review
Greenville (MS) Delta Democrat-Times
Greenville (TX) Herald-Banner
Griffin (GA) News
Hammond (LA) Daily Star
Hanford (CA) Sentinel
Hanover (PA) Sun
Harrisburg (IL) Daily Register
Harrison (AZ) Daily Times
Hattiesburg (MS) American
Haverhill (MA) Gazette
Hays (KS) News
Hayward (CA) Review
Hazleton (PA) Standard-Speaker
Hemet (CA) News
Henderson (KY) Gleaner
Hibbing (MN) Tribune
Hickory (NC) Daily Record
High Point (NC) Enterprise
Hilo (HI) Tribune-Herald
Hilton Head (SC) Island Packet
Holland (MI) Sentinel
Honolulu (HI) Star Bulletin & Advertiser
Hot Springs (AR) Sentinel-Record
Huntington (WV) Herald-Dispatch
Hutchinson (KS) News
Independence-Blue Springs (MO) Examiner
Indiana (PA) Gazette
Iowa City (IA) Press-Citizen
Ironton (OH) Tribune
Ithaca (NY) Journal
Jackson (MS) Clarion-Ledger
Jackson (TN) Sun
Jacksonville (IL) Journal Courier
Jamestown (NY) Post-Journal
Janesville (WI) Gazette
Jersey City (NJ) Jersey Journal
Joliet (IL) Herald-News
Jonesboro (GA) Clayton News/Daily
Junction City (KS) Union
Kailua-Kona (HI) West Hawaii Today
Kankakee (IL) Journal
Kannapolis (NC) Independent
Kansas City (KS) Kansan
Keene (NH) Sentinel
Kendallville (IN) News Sun
Kent-Ravenna (OH) Record-Courier
Kent-Renton-Auburn (WA) Valley News
Key West (FL) Citizen
Killeen (TX) Herald
Kingston (NY) Freeman
Kinston (NC) Free Press
Klamath Falls (OR) Herald & News
Kokomo (IN) Tribune
La Salle (IN) News Tribune
Lafayette-West Lafayette (IN) Journal & Courier
Lakeport (CA) Lake County Record Bee
Lancaster (OH) Eagle-Gazette
Lanham (MD) Prince George's Journal
Lansdale (PA) Reporter
Lansing (MI) State Journal
Laramie (WY) Boomerang
Laredo (TX) Times
Las Vegas (NV) Review-Journal
Lawrence (MA) Eagle-Tribune
Lawrence (KS) Journal-World
Lawton (OK) Sunday Constitution
Leavenworth (KS) Times
Lebanon (PA) News
Lebanon-Hanover (NH) Valley News
Leesville (LA) Leader
Lenoir (NC) News-Topic
Lewiston-Auburn (ME) Sun Journal/Sunday
Lima (OH) News
Lisbon (OH) Journal
Logansport (IN) Pharos-Tribune
Lompoc (CA) Record
Longview (TX) News Journal
Lorain (OH) Journal
Los Angeles (CA) Daily News
Louisville (KY) Courier-Journal
Lowell (MA) Sun
Lumberton (NC) Robesonian
Madera (CA) Tribune
Madisonville (KY) Messenger
Mamaroneck (NY) Times
Manchester (CT) Journal Inquirer
Manitowoc (WI) Herald Times Reporter
Mansfield (OH) News Journal
Marietta (GA) Journal
Marietta (OH) Times
Marin County (CA) Independent Journal
Marion (IN) Chronicle Tribune
Marion (IL) Republican
Marion (OH) Star
Marshfield (WI) News-Herald
Martinez (CA) News Gazette
Martins Ferry (OH) Times Leader

Martinsville (IN) Reporter
Marysville (CA) Appeal Democrat
Maryville-Alcoa (TN) Times
Massillon (OH) Independent
McAlester (OK) News-Capital & Democrat
McKeesport (PA) News
Meadville (PA) Tribune
Melbourne (FL) Florida Today
Merced (CA) Sun-Star
Meriden (CT) Record-Journal
Meridian (MS) Star
Michigan City (IN) News Dispatch
Middletown (CT) Press
Midland (MI) News
Midland (TX) Telegram
Milford (MA) News
Milledgeville (GA) Union Recorder
Minneapolis (MN) Star Tribune
Moline (IL) Dispattch
Monroe (NC) Enquirer-Journal
Monroe (LA) News-Star
Morganton (NC) News-Herald
Morristown (NJ) Record
Mount Airy (NC) News
Mount Pleasant-Alma (MI) Sun
Mount Vernon (NY) Argus
Mountain Home (AR) Baxter Bulletin
Muskogee (OK) Phoenix & Times Democrat
Napa (CA) Register
Nashua (NH) Telegraph
Nashville (TN) Tennessean
Natchez (MS) Democrat
Neptune (NJ) Asbury Park Press
New Bern (NC) Sun-Journal
New Britain (CT) Herald
New Castle (PA) News
New Haven (CT) Register
New Iberia (LA) Iberian
New Kensington (PA) Valley News Dispatch
New Rochelle (NY) Standard-Star
New York (NY) Daily News
Newark (OH) Advocate
Newburyport (MA) News
Newport (RI) News
Niagara Falls (NY) Gazette
Noblesville (IN) Ledger
Norman (OK) Transcript
Norristown (PA) Times Herald
North Platte (NE) Telegraph
Northampton (MA) Hampshire Gazette
Norwalk (CT) Hour
Norwich (CT) Bulletin
Nyack (NY) Rockland Journal-News
Oak Ridge (TN) Oak Ridger
Olathe (KS) News
Olean (NY) Times-Herald
Olney (IL) Mail
Olympia (WA) Olympian
Ontario (CA) Inland Valley Bulletin
Orange (TX) Leader
Oroville (CA) Mercury Register
Ossining (NY) Citizen-Register
Oswego (NY) Palladium-Times
Owosso (MI) Argus-Press
Paducah (KY) Sun
Palm Springs (CA) Desert Sun
Palmdale (CA) Antelope Valley Press
Panama City (FL) News-Herald
Paragould (AR) Daily Press
Passaic (NJ) Herald & News
Pawtucket (RI) Times
Peabody (MA) Times
Peekskill (NY) Star
Pensacola (FL) News-Journal
Phoenixville (PA) Phoenix
Plainview (TX) Herald
Plano (TX) Star Courier
Pleasanton (CA) Tri-Valley Herald
Pleasanton (CA) Valley Times
Port Angeles (WA) Peninsula News
Port Arthur (TX) News
Port Chester (NY) Item
Port Clinton (OH) News Herald
Port Huron (MI) Times Herald
Porterville (CA) Recorder
Portsmouth (OH) Times
Pottstown (PA) Mercury
Pottsville (PA) Republican
Poughkeepsie (NY) Journal
Provo (UT) Herald
Quincy (MA) Patriot-Ledger
Reno (NV) Gazette-Journal
Richmond (IN) Palladium-Item
Richmond (Pinole, CA) West County Times
Roanoke Rapids (NC) Daily Herald
Rochester (MN) Post-Bulletin
Rochester (NY) Democrat & Chronicle
Rock Hill (SC) Herald
Rock Island (IL) Argus
Rock Springs (WY) Rocket-Miner
Rockford (IL) Register Star

Rockville (MD) Montgomery Journal
Rome (GA) News-Tribune
Roswell (NM) Record
Russellville (AR) Courier
Salem (MA) News
Salem (OR) Statesman-Journal
Salina (KS) Journal
Salinas (CA) Californian
Salisbury (NC) Post
San Angelo (TX) Standard-Times
San Bernardino (CA) Sun
San Luis Obispo (CA) Telegram-Tribune
San Mateo (CA) Times
Sandusky-Norwalk (OH) Register
Santa Cruz (CA) Sentinel
Santa Fe (NM) New Mexican
Santa Maria (CA) Times
Santa Monica (CA) Outlook
Saratoga Springs (NY) Gazette
Sault Ste. Marie (MI) Evening News
Schenectady (NY) Gazette
Scottsbluff (NE) Star-Herald
Scottsdale (AZ) Progress Tribune
Searcy (AR) Daily Citizen
Selma (AL) Times-Journal
Sevierville (TN) Mountain Press
Seymour (IN) Tribune
Sharon (PA) Herald
Sheboygan (WI) Press
Shelby (NC) Star
Shelbyville (IN) News
Shreveport (LA) Journal Times
Sikeston (MO) Standard Democrat
Sioux Falls (SD) Argus Leader
Somerset (PA) American
Southbridge (MA) News
Springdale (AR) Morning News of Northwest Arkansas
Springfield (MO) News-Leader
St. Augustine (FL) Record
St. Cloud (MN) Times
Statesville (NC) Record & Landmark
Steubenville (OH) Herald-Star
Suffolk (VA) News-Herald
Sulphur (LA) Southwest Daily News
Sun City (AZ) News-Sun
Superior (WI) Telegram
Tacoma (WA) News Tribune
Tarrytown (NY) News
Taunton (MA) Gazette
Temecula (CA) Californian
Terre Haute (IN) Tribune Star
Texarkana (TX) Gazette
Texas City (TX) Sun
Thomasville (GA) Times-Enterprise
Tiffin (OH) Advertiser-Tribune
Torrington (CT) Register Citizen
Trenton (NJ) Trentonian
Troy (NY) Record
Tucson (AZ) Citizen
Tulare (CA) Advance Register
Tulsa (OK) World
Turlock (CA) Journal
Ukiah (CA) Journal
Utica (NY) Observer-Dispatch
Vancouver (WA) Columbian
Victoria (TX) Advocate
Virginia (MN) Mesabi News
Visalia (CA) Times Delta
Walla Walla (WA) Union-Bulletin
Walnut Creek (CA) Contra Costa Times
Warner Robins (GA) Sun
Warren (OH) Tribune Chronicle
Warren (PA) Times-Observer
Warrendale (PA) North Hills News Record
Washington (DC) Times
Washington (NC) News
Washington (PA) Observer-Reporter
Watertown (NY) Times

Watertown (WI) Times
Waterville (ME) Central Sentinel
Watsonville (CA) Register-Pajaronian
Waukegan (IL) News-Sun
Waukesha (WI) Freeman
Wausau (WI) Herald
Wenatchee (WA) World
West Bend (WI) News
West Chester (PA) Local News
West Frankfort (IL) Daily American
West Warwick (RI) Kent County Times
Westerly (RI) Sun
Westminster (MD) Carroll County Times
White Plains (NY) Reporter-Dispatch
Wilkes Barre (PA) Citizens' Voice
Willoughby (OH) News-Herald
Wilmington (DE) News Journal
Winchester (VA) Star
Winter Haven (FL) News Chief
Wisconsin Rapids (WI) Tribune
Woodbridge (NJ) News Tribune
Woodbridge (VA) Potomac News
Woodland (CA) Democrat
Woonsocket (RI) Call
Wooster (OH) Record
Yonkers (NY) Herald Statesman
Zanesville (OH) Times Recorder
Circ.—19,100,000; Rate Base effective Oct 1, 1995

VISTA - THE HISPANIC MAGAZINE — 999 Ponce de Leon Blvd., Ste. 600, Coral Gables, FL 33134; tel (305) 442-2462; fax (305) 443-7650
Publisher — Gustavo Godoy
Assoc. Pub. — Coleman Travelstead
Editor — Julio Lobaco
Mktg. Services Coord. — Angela Kim
Advertising Offices:
New York, NY — 51 E. 25th St., New York, NY 10010; tel (212) 683-2288; Acct. Manager —Lauri Blinder
Los Angeles, CA — 8491 Sunset Blvd., Ste. 571, Los Angeles, CA 90069; tel (213) 650-8161; Acct. Manager —Ivan Pichardo
Chicago, IL — 717 S. Gunderson Ave., Oak Park, IL 60304; tel (708) 383-8582; fax (708) 383-8589; Acct. Manager —Raul Chavarria
Detroit, MI — 6050 Whethersfield Ln., Ste. B, Bloomfield Hills, MI 48301; tel (810) 647-6520; Acct. Manager —Larry Finn
Miami, FL — 2850 Flamingo Dr., Miami Beach, FL 33140; tel (305) 672-0071 Acct. Manager —Leslie Russell
Distributed by the following newspapers:
Albuquerque (NM) Tribune
Austin (TX) American Statesman
Brownsville (TX) Herald
Dallas (TX) Morning News
El Paso (TX) Times
Hanford (CA) Sentinel
Harlingen (TX) Valley Star
Laredo (TX) Times
Madera (CA) Tribune
McAllen (TX) Monitor
Merced (CA) Sun Star
Miami (FL) El Nuevo Herald
Phoenix (AZ) Gazette
Porterville (CA) Recorder
San Antonio (TX) Express-News
San Pedro (CA) News-Pilot
Santa Fe (NM) New Mexican
Tampa (FL) Tribune
Tulare (CA) Advance Register
Ventura (TX) County Star
Watsonville (CA) Register-Pajaronian
Circ.—1,100,000; Rate Base effective Jan. 1, 1994

SYNDICATED TOTAL MARKET COVERAGE PUBLICATIONS

CoverStory — 3150 Des Plaines Ave., Ste. 115, Des Plaines, IL 60018; tel (847) 299-9500; fax (847) 299-9509
Publisher — Paul A Camp
Marketing Director — Jenn Champion
Sales Manager — Anthony George
SpotLight — PO Box 3159, Winston-Salem, NC 27101; tel (910) 727-7406; fax (910) 727-4096
Exec. Ed./Business Manager — Alan Cronk
Editor — Katherine White
Sales Agent — Jim Hollis; (803) 655-5619
Star Watch — PO Box 3159, Winston-Salem, NC 27101; tel (910) 727-7406; fax (910) 727-4096
Exec. Ed./Business Manager — Alan Cronk
Editor — Ken Winter
Sales Agent — Jim Hollis; (803) 655-5619

US/Express — 435 N. Michigan Ave., Chicago, IL 60611; tel (800) 245-6536/(312) 222-8697; fax (312) 222-2581
Gen. Mgr.-Sentinel Publ. — Bethany Mott
Man. Ed.-Sentinel Publ. — Allan Smith
Paginated Products Manager — Deborah Dreyfuss-Tuchman
Prod./Graphics Mgr. — Ken Paskman
Editor — John Terry
Special Sections Editor — Chuck McClung
Production Designer — Dawn Douglass
Customer Service Coord. — Carol Nelson
Sentinel Publishing
75 E. Amelia St., Orlando, FL 32801; tel (407) 420-5680; fax (407) 420-5759
Syndicated by Tribune Media Services
Published by Sentinel Publishing
Circ.—6,045,000

SECTION VI

Equipment/Interactive Products and Services

Equipment, supplies and services
    Directory of company names 1-22
    Type of business directory 23-44
Interactive products and services
    Directory of company names 45-61
    Type of business directory 61-63
Mechanical forces pay scales 64-66
Top and starting minimum scales 67-68

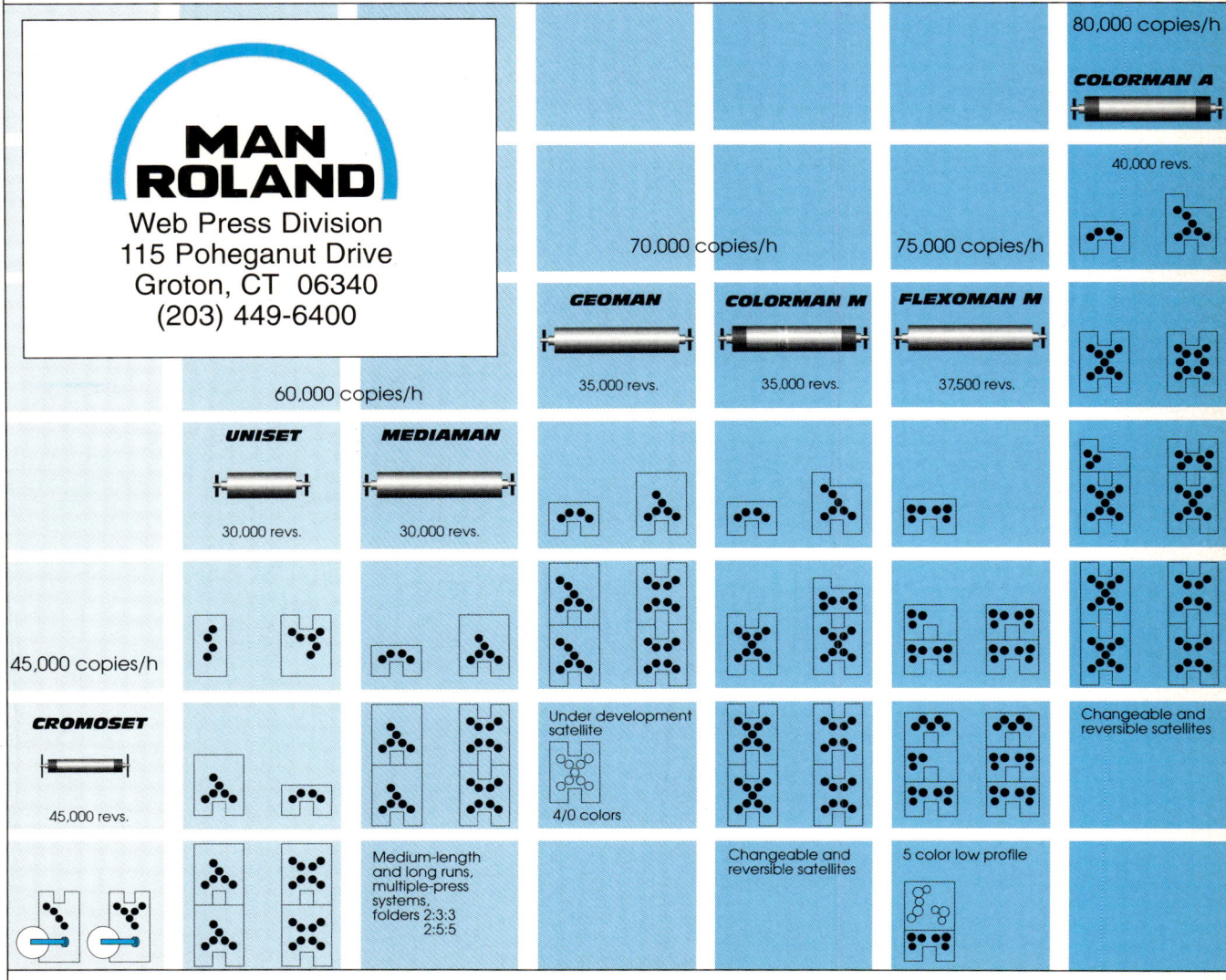

METRO USERS

Please consider updating your press units with the very latest in inking and electronic control technology.

After seven years of dedicated engineering development, we are proud to introduce an inking system that provides excellent print quality and capital savings in newsprint & other press consumables.

Available in one or more of the following configurations:

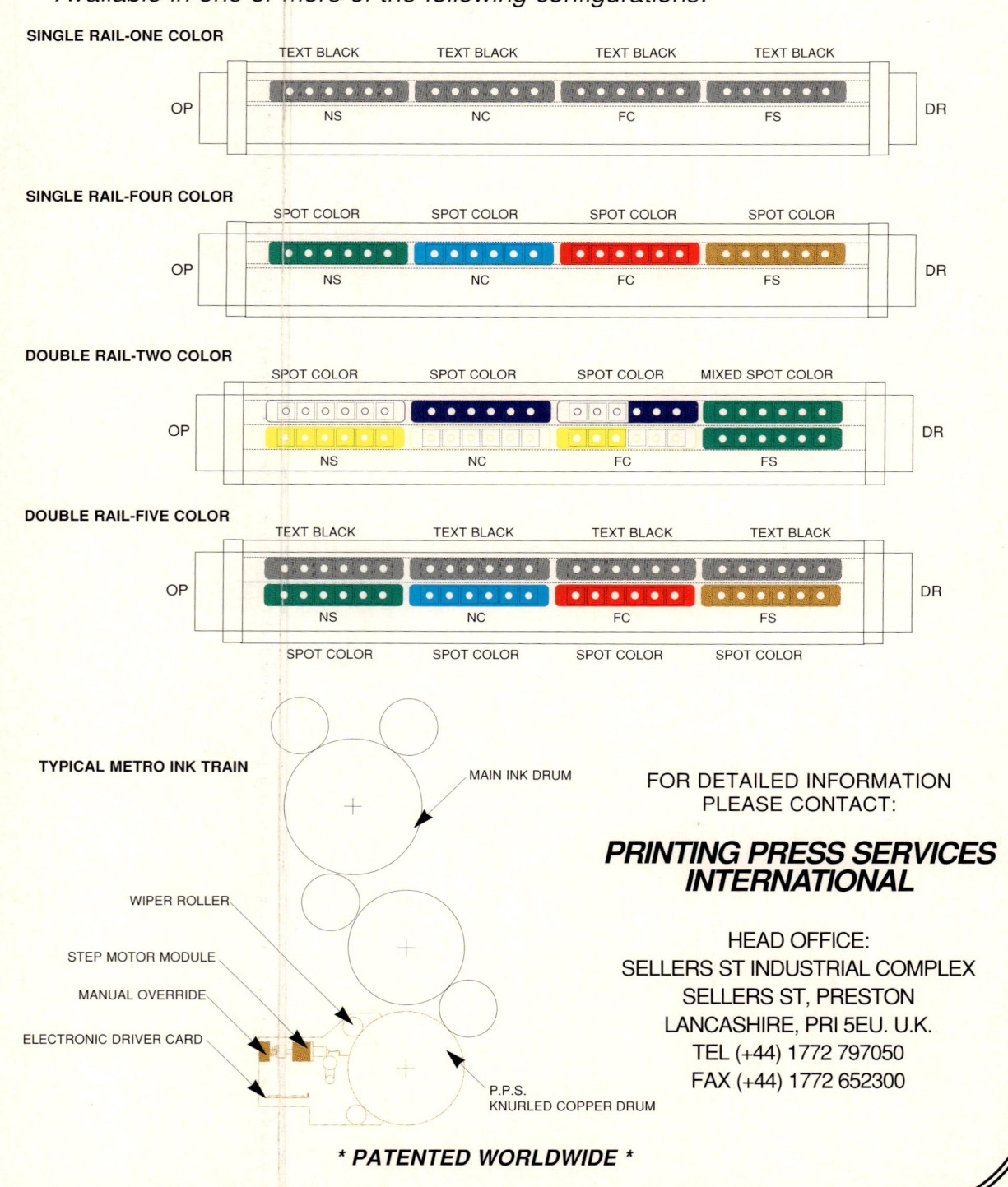

FOR DETAILED INFORMATION
PLEASE CONTACT:

PRINTING PRESS SERVICES INTERNATIONAL

HEAD OFFICE:
SELLERS ST INDUSTRIAL COMPLEX
SELLERS ST, PRESTON
LANCASHIRE, PR1 5EU. U.K.
TEL (+44) 1772 797050
FAX (+44) 1772 652300

* PATENTED WORLDWIDE *

EQUIPMENT, SUPPLIES AND SERVICES COMPANIES SERVING THE NEWSPAPER INDUSTRY

A

A & A Research
690 Sunset Blvd.
Kalispell, MT 59901
tel (406) 752-7857
President — Judith Doonan
Research Dir. — E.B. Eiselein, Ph.D.
Sales Dir. — Neil Blum

Aaro Roller Corp.
4338 11th St.
Rockford, IL 61109
tel (815) 398-7655; fax (815) 398-7669
President — Rick Wilson

ABB Process Automation Inc.(Printing Systems Div.)
2300 N. Barrington Rd., Ste. 400
Hoffman Estates, IL 60195
tel (708) 490-5310
VP/GM-ABB Industrial Systems-Printing Div. — John C. Jellovitz

ABDEX Inc.
15-1 Warwick Rd.; PO Box 55
Winchester, NH 03470
tel (603) 239-7500
President — Richard Abdoo

Abelson Communications Inc.
43D Rocklyn Ave.
Lynbrook, NY 11563
tel (516) 596-9610; fax (516) 596-9618
President — Glenn R. Abelson
Vice Pres. — Susan K. Abelson

Abitibi-Price Sales Corp.
4 Manhanttenville Rd.
Purchase, NY 10577
tel (914) 696-6900
Pres.-Int'l. Div. — D.L. Loretto
Pres.-N. American Pub. Div. — C.D. Martin
VP-Reg'l. Mgr.-Eastern Div.-N. American Publishing Div. — Joseph M. Barry

Able Printing Co.
7045 Central Hwy.
Pennsauken, NJ 08109
tel (609) 663-8181; fax (609) 663-8139
Pressroom Mgr. — Frank Oliveti

Abodia Lighted Slide Storage
PO Box 3201
Charleston, WV 25332
tel (304) 344-2335
Mktg. Mgr. — Ted Elden

Accelerated VOICE
25 Stillman St., Ste. 200
San Francisco, CA 94107
tel (415) 543-2773; fax (415) 543-6398
Sales Manager — Ted Glenwright

Accurate Step & Repeat System Inc.
860 Sussex Blvd.; PO Box 577
Broomall, PA 19008
tel (215) 544-6451; fax (215) 544-1564
President — Edward Capkovic

Acme Design Technology Co.
1000 Allview Dr.; PO Box 427
Crozet, VA 22932
tel (804) 823-4351; fax (804) 823-1625
President — Thomas D. Hall
VP-Strategic & Product Planning — Deanna L. Hall
Vice Pres./Controller — Massie E. Hughes
Admn. Asst. — Alberta H. Dodson

Action Management Inc.
58 W. Valley Ave.; PO Box 276
Elysburg, PA 17824
tel (717) 672-9732; fax (717) 672-9922
President — Harry A. Strausser Jr.

Ad Express Inc.
400 TechneCenter Dr., Ste. 101
Milford, OH 45150
tel (513) 248-8110; fax (513) 248-8102
Vice President-National Sales Manager — Thomas C. Plunkett

Ad Vantage Computer Systems Inc.
1509 Michigan St.
Des Moines, IA 50314
tel (515) 288-2600; fax (515) 288-6161
President — Dennis Hays

AD/SAT (A Div. of Skylight Inc.)
527 W. 34th St.
New York, NY 10001
tel (212) 330-0678; fax (212) 330-0683/(212) 330-0670
Dir.-Cus. Svc. — Wanda Roldan
VP-Tech. Oper. — Christopher D. Wood
Product Dev. — Jim Jenkins
VP/Controller — Jack Langstine
Sales Mgr. — Diana Moore

Ad-Star/Publishing Technologies
11755 Wilshire Blvd., Ste. 1670
Los Angeles, CA 90025
tel (310) 479-5458; fax (310) 479-1076
President — Leslie Bernhard
Exec. Vice Pres. — Eli Rousso
Vice Pres. — Jeffrey Diamond

Adhesives Research Inc.
PO Box 100
Glen Rock, PA 17327
tel (717) 235-7979; fax (717) 235-8320
President — Edward Daisey
Vice Pres.-Tech. — C. Fox
Vice Pres.-Mktg. Dev. — G. Cramer
Vice Pres.-Fin. — Al Haley
Vice Pres.-Mgr. — C. Lanius
VP-Splicing Tape Div. — Tracy Pleet
Purchasing — T. Heiland
Q.A. Manager — T. Coggeshall
Marketing — Kate Green

Adobe Systems Inc.
1585 Charleston Rd.; PO Box 7900
Mountain View, CA 94043-7900
tel (415) 961-4400/(800) 833-6687 (Sales); fax (415) 961-3769
e-mail http://www.adobe.com
President/COO — Charles M. Geschke
Chairman/CEO — John E. Warnock
CFO — M. Bruce Nakao
Office of CEO — Stephen A. MacDonald
Office of CEO — David B. Pratt
VP/Gen. Counsel & Sec. — Colleen M. Pouliot
Dir.-Corp. Comm. — Carol Sacks

Adtrack Inc.
9125 Philips Hwy.
Jacksonville, FL 32256
tel (904) 363-0016; fax (904) 363-8384
President — Bill Jones

Advance Graphics Equipment of York Inc.
1390 Roosevelt Ave.
York, PA 17404
tel (717) 848-6221; fax (717) 845-5591
VP-Sales & Mktg. — (William) Bill Stober

Advanced Graphic Systems (KAIM)
19324 Iron Mountain Dr.
Grass Valley, CA 95949
tel (916) 268-3291
President — Earl T. Price
Vice Pres.-Eng. — Andy Bacigalupo

Advanced Publishing Technology
826 S. Victory Blvd.
Burbank, CA 91502-2446
tel (818) 557-3035; fax (818) 557-1281
e-mail 74541.3353@compuserve.com
President — David Kraai
Vice Pres. — Jeff Sie

Advanced Technical Solutions
873 Tpke. St., Ste. 204
North Andover, MA 01845
tel (508) 689-9161; fax (508) 682-0709
President — Raymond F. Toothaker
Vice Pres./Treas. — William Page

Advanced Telecom Services
996 Old Eagle School Rd.
Wayne, PA 19087-1806
tel (610) 688-6000; fax (610) 964-9117
President — Tom Coffey

Sr. Vice Pres. — Bob Bentz
CFO — Bret Dunlap
Sales Manager — Alan Turner
Newspaper Svc. Product Mgr. — David Sawyer

Advantex Marketing International, Inc.
491 Eglinton Ave. W., 3rd Fl.
Toronto, ON M5N 1A8 Canada
tel (416) 481-5657; fax (416) 481-5692
Director-Promotions — Barbara Walker
Sr. Program Mgr. — Cindy Bergman
Asst. Promotion Mgr. — Cathie Peters

Advertisers Exchange Inc.
36 Forest Rd.; PO Box 74
Tranquility, NJ 07879
tel (908) 852-2186; fax (908) 852-8863
Mktg. Dir. — Malcolm G. Smith

Advertising Checking Bureau Inc.
221 W. 41st St.
New York, NY 10036
tel (212) 921-0080; fax (212) 840-7638
President/CEO — Edward C. Davis
Sr. Vice Pres. — Bill Panczak
Exec. VP/Dir.-Mktg. — Brian T. McShane

AG Industries Inc.
One American Rd.
Cleveland, OH 44144
tel (216) 252-6737; fax (216) 252-6773
Marketing Manager — Mike Andrey
Nat'l Acct. Mgr. — John Watson

Agfa Division, Bayer Inc.
200 Ballardvale St.
Wilmington, MA 01887
tel (508) 658-5600; fax (508) 658-6285
Dir.-Mktg. Comm./Electronic Prepress Systems — Peter Broderick
U.S. — Mark Sullivan
Europe — Marc Verbiest

Agfa Div./Miles Inc./Graphic Systems
100 Challenger Rd.
Ridgefield Park, NJ 07660
tel (201) 440-2500
Sr. VP-Graphic Sys. — Dr. Juergen Stolt
Vice Pres. Mktg.-Electronic & Photographic Prepress Products — Christian Aumond
Mktg. Comms. Mgr. — Mark Sullivan
Trade Shows Events PR Mgr. — Holly Hokrein

Airloc Products
5 Fisher St.; PO Box 269
Franklin, MA 02038
tel (508) 528-0022; fax (508) 528-7555
Vice Pres.-Sales — Robert A. Geromini

Air Systems International Inc.
5244 Brighton Ave., S.E.
Montrose, MN 55363
tel (612) 972-3420; fax (612) 972-2085
President — David Norton
Vice Pres. — James Whittenberg
Sales Mgr. — E.M. (Rheis) Asbury

AirSystems Inc.
16528 Westgrove
Dallas, TX 75248
tel (214) 931-0711; fax (214) 250-2034
President — Milton Lemaster

Alan Graphic Systems Inc.
1000 N. Division St.; PO Box 628
Peekskill, NY 10566
tel (914) 737-7600; fax (914) 737-2167
e-mail twistedper@aol.com
Gen. Mgr. — Per Hallingberg
Sales Mgr. — Greg Nygard

Alar Engineering Corp.
9651 W. 196th St.
Mokena, IL 60448
tel (708) 479-6100; fax (708) 479-9059
Mktg. & Adv. Dir. — Terry Henschel

Alaska Information Marketing (AIM)
2142 Forest Park
Anchorage, AK 99517
tel (907) 277-9996; fax (907) 272-0010
President — Kevin Tubbs

Albar Labs & Industrial Supplies Inc.
103 Lee St.
Ft. Worth, TX 76140
tel (817) 551-6181; fax (817) 551-6184
Owner/President — Albert Stein

Alden Electronics Inc.
40 Washington St.; PO Box 500
Westborough, MA 01581-0500
tel (508) 366-8851; fax (508) 898-2427
e-mail bessomj@alden.com
Product Mgr. — Jeff Bessom
Adv. Mgr. — John P. Carlson

All Systems Color Inc.
8775 Gander Creek Dr.
Miamisburg, OH 45342
tel (513) 433-5054; fax (513) 433-8992
President — Geeter Kyrazis
CEO — Richard I. Castaneda
Midwest & Southern Regional Sales Rep. — Tom Kiser

Alliance Rubber Co.
PO Box 599
Franklin, KY 42134
tel (502) 586-3218; fax (502) 586-5738
Vice Pres.-Sales & Mktg. — Bonnie Swayze
Vice Pres.-Sales — Tom Zeka

Allpress Equipment Inc.
4524 Curry Ford Rd., Ste. 533
Orlando, FL 32812
tel (407) 281-0111; fax (407) 281-0111
Contact — Jennie M. Schofield

Allstates Litho Plate Corp.
PO Box 337
Scottsdale, AZ 85252
tel (602) 945-2925; fax (602) 945-3093
e-mail 102124.2750@compuserve
Gen. Mgr. — Benjamin Kaufman

Allsystems Go
8A Industrial Way
Salem, NH 03079
tel (603) 890-6800; fax (603) 893-2623
President — Rich Pape

ALLTEL Supply Inc.
6625 The Corners Pkwy.
Norcross, GA 30092
tel (770) 448-5210; fax (770) 446-0420
President — Ray Gunti
Dir.-Eastern Sales — Tom Davis
Dir.-Westen Sales — Dave Hadley

Alpha-Omega Color Graphics Inc.
7 E. Center St.
Mt. Morris, IL 61054
tel (815) 734-6066; fax (815) 734-6078
Owner — Gary R. Mennenga
Owner — Ronald A. Blumeyer

ALTA Graphics Inc.
530 Saddle Creek Cir.
Roswell, GA 30076-1034
tel (770) 552-1528; fax (770) 552-2669
President — Albert A. Taber
Director — Albert A. Taber Jr.
Director — Bill Kanipe

Alteneder, Theo & Sons
439 Main St.
Darby, PA 19023
tel (215) 522-9444; fax (215) 522-9446
President — David T. Alteneder
Secretary — Susan Alteneder
Treasurer — Emily Alteneder

Alternate Postal Delivery
1 Ionia S.W., Ste. 300
Grand Rapids, MI 49503
tel (616) 235-0698; fax (616) 235-3405
Vice Pres.-Newspapers Sales — Warren Smith

AMECRM, See ECRM

Amergraph Corp.
Rte. 15; PO Box 905
Sparta, NJ 07871
tel (201) 383-8700; fax (201) 383-9225
President — Robert Lesko

Copyright ©1996 by the Editor & Publisher Co.

VI-2   Equipment, supplies, services

America's Interactive Production Network
1515 Locust St., 8th Fl.
Philadelphia, PA 19102
tel (215) 545-1212/(609) 486-1200
fax (215) 545-2233
e-mail aipn@netaxs.com
President — Bruce Billow

The American Assn. of Independent News Distributors
16 Santa Ana Pl.
Walnut Creek, CA 94598
tel (510) 935-2026; fax (510) 906-0922
President — Joe Grassi
Vice Pres. — Tom Mader
Treas./Sec. — Judy Fisher
Exec. Dir. — Deborah Dobbs

American Consulting Services
1405 S.E. 164th. Ave., Ste. 201
Vancouver, WA 98684
tel (800) 597-9798; fax (360) 254-0189
President — Mark Rood

American Data Voice Systems
155 E. Ohio St.
Chicago, IL 60611
tel (312) 951-5553; fax (312) 951-2533
President — Robert Ashbrook

American Fidelity
2000 Classen Blvd.
Oklahoma City, OK 73106
tel (405) 523-2000; fax (405) 523-5645

American Graphics L.P.
16232 Filbert St.
Sylmar, CA 91342
tel (818) 362-9483; fax (818) 367-5105
Sales — Jack Thomsen
Sales — Bill Nicol

American Graphic Arts Inc.
150 Broadway; PO Box 240
Elizabeth, NJ 07206
tel (908) 351-6906; fax (908) 351-7156
Vice President — John Jacobson

American Ink Jet Corp.
13 Alexander Rd.
Billerica, MA 01821
tel (508) 670-9200; fax (508) 670-5637
Sales & Mktg. Mgr. — Peter Kimten

American International Communications Inc.
5595 E. 7th St., Ste. 110
Long Beach, CA 90804
tel (310) 433-8818; fax (310) 434-6085
Pres./CEO — Paul Keever

American Litho Inc.
4155 Danvers Ct. S.E.
Grand Rapids, MI 49512
tel (616) 957-2650; fax (616) 957-0509
Chairman — J.C. Huizenga
President — Steve Klotz
Vice Pres. — Mary Joe McCory

American Message Centers
18341 Sherman Way, Ste. 200
Reseda, CA 91335
tel (818) 757-8800; fax (818) 757-8803
Sales Mgr. — Ron Tilton

American Newspaper Representatives
1000 Shelard Pkwy., Ste. 360
Minneapolis, MN 55426
tel (612) 545-1116; fax (612) 545-1481

American Opinion Research
707 State Rd., Ste. 102
Princeton, NJ 08540
tel (609) 683-4860; fax (609) 683-8398
President — Tony Casale
Vice Pres. — Lois Kaufman

American Printer
29 N. Wacker Dr.
Chicago, IL 60606-3298
tel (312) 726-2802; fax (312) 726-2574
Publisher — John Favat
Vice President — John Skeels
Vice Pres.-Circulation — Nick Cavnar
Marketing Mgr. — Pam Martin

American Roller Co.
2223 Lakeside Dr.
Bannockburn, IL 60015
tel (708) 295-6750; fax (708) 295-2796
President — Robert Ditzler
Vice Pres.-Financial — L. Michael Vogus

Vice Pres.-Nat'l. Accts. — Pat Carney
Director-Mfg. — Peter Ditzler
Tech. Director — Ron Buono
Nat'l. Sales Mgr. — Richard Wilson

Ampersand/New Media Division of E&P
11 W. 19th St.
New York, NY 10011
tel (212) 675-4380; fax (212) 929-1894
Managing Director/Board of Directors — D. Colin Phillips
Vice Pres.-Operations — Dennis O'Neill
Vice Pres.-Bus. Dev. — Martin Radelfinger

Amplas Inc.
PO Box 13397
Greenbay, WI 54307-3397
tel (414) 496-0525; fax (414) 496-0560
Gen. Sales Mgr. — Gary Sargin
Sales Secretary — Barb Bernetzke

Anchor (Imaging Products Division)
50 Industrial Loop N.
Orange Park, FL 32073
tel (904) 264-3500; fax (904) 269-8932/(904) 269-3841
Director-New Products & Marketing — John Stephens

R C Anderson Associates Inc.
1 Grove St.; PO Box 300
Pittsford, NY 14534
tel (716) 248-5385; fax (716) 248-9551
President — Ronald C. Anderson
Vice Pres. — Catherine M. Anderson
Mktg. Mgr. — Karen Cavacos

ANI Promotions/DBA
1110 Van Houten Ave.
Clifton, NJ 07013
tel (201) 473-0022; fax (201) 473-5368
Sales Mgr. — Paul Procacci
Vice Pres. — Robin Honig

Anitec
1200 E. Ridgewood Ave.
Ridgewood, NJ 07450
tel (201) 670-7900; fax (201) 670-7095
Anitec Bus. Unity/GM — Anthony P. Crupi
Mgr.-Digital Imaging — Richard A. Mazur

Anitec Printing Plates
383 Dwight St.
Holyoke, MA 01040
tel (413) 538-9624; fax (413) 532-3937
Bus. Unit Mgr. — Carlton Mappin
Dir.-Mktg. — Robert H. Johnson
Mktg. Svc. Mgr. — Jeannie Sharkey
Gen. Sales Mgr. — Stephen F. Montanino

Anocoil Corp. (Plate Div.)
60 E. Main St.; PO Box 1318
Rockville, CT 06066
tel (203) 871-1200; fax (203) 872-0534
President — H.A. Fromson
Vice Pres.-Mktg. & Sales — C.G. Knorr Jr.
Vice Pres.-Oper. — Michael Fromson
VP-Commercial Sales — Timothy A. Fromson

Aon/WNIC Special Markets
123 N. Wacker Dr., 16th Fl.
Chicago, IL 60606
tel (312) 701-1687; fax (312) 701-4123

Apex Machine Co.
3000 N.E. 12th Ter.
Fort Lauderdale, FL 33334-4497
tel (305) 565-APEX (2739)
fax (305) 563-2844
President — A. Robert Coningsby
Vice Pres.-Sales & Mktg. — Bob Coningsby

Apple Computer Inc.
1 Infinity Loop
Cupertino, CA 95014
tel (408) 996-1010/(800) 776-2333
(Customer Service); fax (408) 862-0040/(408) 974-9994 (Customer Service)
e-mail apple computer inc./via/spock.austin.apple.com
VP-World Wide Mktg. Sales — Mike Dion

Application Engineering Corp.
801 AEC Dr.
Wood Dale, IL 60191
tel (708) 595-1060; fax (708) 595-6641
Mktg. Mgr. — Rich Achor
Comms. Coord. — David Pugh

Applied Learning Corp.
1376 Glen Hardie Rd.
Wayne, PA 19087
tel (610) 688-6866; fax (610) 688-6866
President — James J. Barrett

Applied Segmentation Technology
1624 Market St., Ste. 300A
Denver, CO 80202
tel (303) 446-2525; fax (303) 446-2901
President — Tom Ratkovich

APS
1275 Bloomfield Ave.; PO Box 712
Fairfield, NJ 07004
tel (201) 575-1040; fax (201) 575-6540
Vice Pres.-Sales — Eric Verbeke
Dir.-Sales — Henry Verbeke

APS Development
112 E. Sixth St.; PO Box 1120
Gaylord, MI 49735
tel (517) 732-2081; fax (517) 732-8300
Gen. Mgr./Mktg. Mgr. — Ken Bradstreet

ARC/Doyle Machinery Corp.
9307 Monroe Rd.; PO Box 17049
Charlotte, NC 28270-0099
tel (704) 845-1540; fax (704) 845-1539
President — Jim McDonald

Arc International
3900 Rose Lake Dr.
Charlotte, NC 28217
tel (704) 398-2266; fax (704) 399-8314
VP-Sales & Mktg. — Mike Tagliaferri
Newspaper Flexo Sales — Mike Foran

Archetype Inc.
100 5th Ave.
Waltham, MA 02154
tel (617) 890-7544; fax (617) 890-3661
e-mail janice@atype.com
Pres./CEO — Paul Trevithick
Exec. Vice Pres. — Sue Robertson
Mktg. Mgr. — Janice Justice

Arco Engineering Inc. (Newspaper Div.)
3135 S. Preston St.
Louisville, KY 40213
tel (502) 635-2603; fax (502) 635-2641
President — Steve Watson

Arpac L.P.
9511 W. River St.
Schiller Park, IL 60176
tel (708) 678-9034; fax (708) 671-7006
Mktg. Mgr. — Luis L. Cortez

Arri Systems Inc.
PO Box 7166
Capistrano Beach, CA 92624
tel (714) 459-8898; fax (714) 459-8819
President — Bruce G. Popko

Arrow Printing Co.
115 W. Woodland; PO Box 2898
Salina, KS 67402
tel (913) 825-8124; fax (913) 826-0784
Advg. Mgr. — Dennis Swelter

Artbeats
2611 S. Myrtle Rd.; PO Box 709
Myrtle Creek, OR 97457
tel (541) 863-4429; fax (541) 863-4547
President — Phil Bates
Mktg. Dir. — Lenie Kissell

Ashcraft Consulting
PO Box 430209
Pontiac, MI 48343
tel (810) 334-4329; fax (810) 334-2226
Mktg. Dir. — Sheila Ashcraft

AT&S/Voice Magic
3402 Fernandina Rd., Ste. C
Columbia, SC 29210
tel (803) 750-7279; fax (803) 798-0351
Vice Pres.-Mktg. — Steve Rogers

AT & T Business Marketing
55 Corporate Dr.
Bridgewater, NJ 08807
tel (908) 658-6528
National Mktg. Mgr. — Bob Markowitz

AT & T Information Systems (GCBS)
1 Speedwell Ave., Rm. 88-543E
Morristown, NJ 07960
tel (800) 247-7000
District Mgr. — Maryann Seduski

Atlantic Packaging Products Ltd.
111 Progress Ave.
Scarborough, ON M1P 2Y9 Canada
tel (416) 298-8101; fax (416) 297-2218
Mktg. Mgr. — Roger Keeley

Atlas Specialty Lighting
7304 N. Florida Ave.
Tampa, FL 33604
tel (813) 238-6481; fax (813) 238-6656
Mktg. Dir. — Troy Jones

AudioFAX Inc.
2000 Powers Ferry Rd., Ste. 200
Marietta, GA 30067
tel (404) 933-7600; fax (404) 933-7606
CFO — Mark Noyd

Audit Bureau of Circulations
900 N. Meacham Rd.
Schaumburg, IL 60173-4968
tel (708) 605-0909; fax (708) 605-0483
Mgr.-Newspaper Mktg. — Mark Stoecklin

Auditec Computing Services Inc.
Corporate Hill 2; 1633 Des Peres Rd.
St. Louis, MO 63131
tel (314) 984-8400; fax (314) 984-8233
Media Svc. Mgr. — Pete Kazlauskas

The Austin Co.
3650 Mayfield Rd.
Cleveland, OH 44121-1791
tel (216) 382-6600; fax (216) 291-6684
Dir.-Eng./Newspapers — G.V. Brister
Mgr.-PR & Advertising — Joan M. Krause

Auto-Grafica Corp.
58A Hobart St.
Hackensack, NJ 07601
tel (201) 343-8585; fax (201) 343-0711
e-mail autografica@eworld.com
President — Ruth C. Hall
Gen. Mgr. — Frank DiAmbrosio
Exec. VP-Sales — Panayotis Jerominides
Vice Pres. — Wendy Hall Putignano

The Autographix Systems
7 Main Ave.
Passaic, NJ 07055
tel (201) 471-7322; fax (201) 773-7304
Vice Pres. — Harvey Furman

Autologic Inc. (Subsidiary of Volt Info. Svc.)
1050 Rancho Conejo Blvd.
Thousand Oaks, CA 91320-1794
tel (805) 498-9611; fax (805) 499-1167
e-mail rmedina@autologic.com
President — Dennis D. Doolittle
Mgr. Mkt. Svc. — Ruta Medina
Vice Pres.-Domestic Sales — Al Brunner
Vice Pres.-Cust. Svc. — Robert A. Oster
Vice Pres.-Eng. — Reza Pourzia
Vice Pres.-Mktg. — James C. Hanger

Autologic Information International Inc.
5757 W. Century Blvd., Ste. 2000
Los Angeles, CA 90045-6400
tel (310) 417-8400; fax (310) 258-2101
e-mail rtg@triplei.com
COB — Ralph S. Roth
President — Al Edwards
Sr. VP-Cust. Support — Harry M. Dahl
Vice Pres.-Fin. — Manuel Morrero
VP-Mktg. Planning — Richard Ritterbush
Dir.-Eng. — Ron Travar

Automated Mailing Systems Corp.
10730 Spangler Rd.
Dallas, TX 75220-7120
tel (800) 527-1668; fax (214) 869-2735
Mktg. Mgr. — Russell L. Helsley

Automated News Vending Systems
6110 Rittiman Rd.
San Antonio, TX 78218
tel (800) 600-2687; fax (210) 662-9293
President — Greg Gomm
Dir.-Mktg. & Sales — Gary Gomm

Automated Newsstand
6 S. Parker Dr.
Monsey, NY 10952
tel (201) 473-0022; fax (201) 473-5368

Avenor America Inc.
1 N. Broadway
White Plains, NY 10601
tel (914) 761-5454; fax (914) 761-9427
Pres.Newsprint Mktg. Div. — Edmund Hughs
VP-Nat'l. Accts. — George H. Murphy Jr.
VP-Commercial Div. — Norman J. Gennarelli
Asst. Comptroller & Corp. Sec. — Alan R. Blackstock

Avenor Inc.
1250 Rene-Levesque Blvd. W.
Montreal, QC H3B 4Y3 Canada
tel (514) 846-4811; fax (514) 846-4850

Copyright ©1996 by the Editor & Publisher Co.

Equipment, supplies, services — VI-3

COB — Michel Belanger
President/CEO — Paul E. Gagne
Pres.-Newsprint Group — Jerry P. Soderberg
President-Pacific Forest Products — Sandy M. Fulton
Pres.-White Paper Group — David G. Toole
Pres.-Pulp Group — David J. Steuart
Sr. VP/Gen. Counsel — Marc Regnier
Vice Pres./CFO — Denis Aubin
VP-Mktg.-White Paper — Denis Auclair
VP-Comm. & Govt. Affairs — Emmanuelle Collin
Vice Pres.-MIS — Gaudry Delisle
Vice Pres./Comptroller — Robert Sartor
VP-Corp. Dev. & Logistics — Norman W. Lord
VP-Mktg. Newsprint Group — John H. Sim
VP-Environment — Wallace M. Vrooman
Secretary — Jacques Beauchamp
Internal Auditor — Anthony Iasenza
Co-ord./Public Affairs & Comm. — Meredith Royds

Aviel Vending Machines Ltd.
4020 Payne Ave.
Cleveland, OH 44103
tel (800) 838-1924; fax (800) 249-1855
President/Owner — Aviel Dafna

Axelrod, Norman N., Assoc./Optical, Laser & Vision Systems
445 E. 86th St.
New York, NY 10028
tel (212) 228-0900
President — Norman N. Axelrod
Vice Pres. — V.A. Grant
Mgr.-Software Dev. — R. Rolle
Mgr.-Electronics — F. Bosso
Mgr.-Optical Sensing — A. Bryan
Dir.-Systems Integrator/Mgr.-Image Processing — N. Axelrod

Ayers/Johanek Publication Design
4750 Rolling Hills Dr.
Bozeman, MT 59715
tel (406) 585-8826; fax (406) 585-8837
e-mail johanek@aol.com
Partner — John Johanek
Partner — Robert Ayers

B

B & T Press Supplies (Affiliated with Canadian Web)
34 Attridge Dr.
Aurora, ON L4G 6J3 Canada
tel (905) 727-0215; fax (905) 727-2513
President — Michele Belanger
Vice Pres. — Stephen Tweddle

Baird Manufacturing Inc.
Hwy. 79 E.; PO Box 338
Clarendon, AR 72029
tel (800) 682-2278; fax (501) 747-3743
President — James W. Baird
Regional Sales Mgr. — Richard N. Baird
Vice Pres.-Sales — Buzzie Samuels
Engineering Mgr. — Earl Jackson

Baldor Electric Co.
PO Box 2400
Fort Smith, AR 72902
tel (501) 646-4711; fax (501) 648-5792
Chairman — R.S. Boreham Jr.
President/CEO — R.L. Qualls
Vice Pres.-Sales — John McFarland
Vice Pres.-Mktg. — Jerry Peerbolte

Baldwin Dampening Systems (Div. of Baldwin Graphic Systems)
141 Sheridan Dr.
Naugatuck, CT 06770
tel (203) 729-4455; fax (203) 723-2908
VP/GM — Raymond L. Gauvin
Dir.-Engineering — Robert MacDonald
Cust. Serv. — Liz Woodin

Baldwin Graphics Products (Div. of Baldwin Technology)
401 Shippan Ave.; PO Box 9314
Stamford, CT 06904
tel (203) 325-3581/(800) 654-4999
fax (203) 359-8631
President — Peter E. Anselmo
Mktg. Mgr. Svc. — Lucille Sabia
VP-Sales & Mktg. — Shaun J. Kilfoyle
Tech. Svc. Mgr. — Rich Rubin
Newspaper & Directory Mgr. — Joseph Collins
Dir.-Cus. Oper. — Jim DeCarlo
Dir.-Engineering — Robert Gasparrini

Baldwin Stobb (Div. of Baldwin Technology)
1351 E. Riverview Dr.
San Bernardino, CA 92408
tel (909) 799-9950; fax (909) 796-8297
President — John St. John

Baldwin Web Controls (Div./Subsidiary Baldwin Technology)
1051-B N. Main St.
Lombard, IL 60148-1375
tel (708) 261-9180; fax (708) 261-9186
Vice Pres./Gen. Mgr. — Ron Callan
Vice Pres.-Sales & Mktg. — Shaun Kilfoyle
Newspaper & Directory Mgr. — Joseph Collins

Base-Line Inc.
PO Box 1658
Auburn, WA 98071-1658
tel (206) 852-6681; fax (206) 852-6796
President — Grant Beck
Gen. Mgr. — Dick Rice
Accounting Mgr. — Eric Scott
Dir.-Nat'l. Sales & Mktg. — Buzz Leonard
Operations Dir. — Bill Zieske
Mktg. Mgr. — Angela Anderson

Baseview Products Inc.
333 Jackson Plz. (48103); PO Box 1198
Ann Arbor, MI 48106
tel (313) 662-5800; fax (313) 662-5204
e-mail marketing@baseview.com
President — Don Rogers
Vice President — Jim Meyer
Vice President — Dave Luther
Marketing Director — Robert Yoder
Sales Director — Al Geist
Domestic Sales/Co-ordinator — Vickie Bair

BASF Corp.
3000 Continental Dr., N.
Mt. Olive, NJ 07828
tel (201) 426-2600; fax (201) 426-2837
Dir.-Services — Terrence O'Conner

Baton Lock & Hardware Co. Inc.
14275 Commerce Dr.
Garden Grove, CA 92643
tel (800) 395-8880/(714) 265-3636
fax (714) 265-3630
President — Peace Hsu

Baumfolder Corp.
1660 Campbell Rd.
Sidney, OH 45365
tel (513) 492-1281; fax (513) 492-7280
President — Michael Grauel
Vice Pres.-Fin. — Carl Fullenkamp
Marketing — Larry Galinski
Parts — Mike Scott
Service — Jerry Trisler
Personnel — Janice Benanzer
Engineering — Bob Kinson
Operations — Sam Pryor

Beach Manufacturing Corp., See K & F Co.

Charles Beck Machine Corp.
400 W. Church Rd.
King of Prussia, PA 19406-3185
tel (610) 265-0500; fax (610) 265-5627
Vice Pres.-Mktg. — C. Arthur Beck

Beckart Environmental Inc.
6900 46th St.
Kenosha, WI 53144
tel (414) 656-7680; fax (414) 656-7699
Vice Pres. — Thomas M. Fedrigon

Beckerman Associates Inc.
14001 Miramar Ave.
Madeira Beach, FL 33708
tel (813) 391-2824; fax (813) 391-2824
Pres./Co-Owner — Bernice S. Beckerman
Co-Owner — Milton B. Beckerman

Behrens International Ltd.
567 San Nicholas Dr., Ste. 304
Newport Beach, CA 92660-6201
tel (714) 644-2661; fax (714) 644-0283
Chairman — Stanley Behrens

B E & K Inc.
PO Box 2332
Birmingham, AL 35201-2332
tel (205) 972-6000; fax (205) 972-6651
Chairman — T.C. Kennedy
President — T.M. Goodrich
Sr. Vice Pres. — S.C. Harlin
Projects Manager — Juergen H. Matt
Vice Pres.-Sales & Mktg. — Tom Freeland

Belden Associates
3102 Oak Lawn Ave., Ste. 500
Dallas, TX 75219
tel (214) 522-8630; fax (214) 522-0926
President — Deanne L. Termini
Sr. Vice Pres. — Suzanne Phillips
Vice Pres. — Muriel E. Carter

Bell & Howell
5215 Old Orchard Rd.
Skokie, IL 60077
tel (708) 470-7100; fax (708) 470-9825
President — James Roemer
Vice Pres.-Adm. — Henry D'Ambrosio

Bell & Howell/Phillipsburg Co.
795 Roble Rd.; PO Box 25079
Lehigh Valley, PA 18002-5079
tel (610) 264-4510/(800) 220-3030
fax (610) 266-4603
President — Ben L. McSwiney
Vice Pres.-Nat'l. Sales — Ron Nabors
Vice Pres.-Svc. — Michael Littleton
Vice Pres.-Mfg. — William Grove
Dir.-Communciations — Carro Ford
Vice Pres.-Fin. — James Bearrows
Vice Pres.-Mktg. — Robert Bassett

Bell & Howell Publication Systems Co.
5700 Lombardo Ctr.
Seven Hills, OH 44131
tel (216) 642-9060; fax (216) 642-4308
President/CEO — Robert A. Nero

Bruce Bell & Associates
425 Main St., Ste. 10
Canon City, CO 81212
tel (800) 359-7738; fax (719) 275-1664
CEO — Bruce Bell
President — Jim Parnau

Bell Camp Inc.
170 Kinnelon Rd., Ste. 17
Kinnelon, NJ 07405
tel (201) 492-8877; fax (201) 492-9777
President — Gustavo Izurieta

Bellatrix Systems Inc.
1015 S.W. Emkay
Bend, OR 97702
tel (503) 382-2208; fax (503) 385-3277
President — Bill Hemingway
CEO — Tom Ellsberg
Sr. VP-Sales & Mktg. — Steve Morris
Vice Pres.-Bus. Dev. — William Raven

Bellatrix Systems INC.
10917 Savona Rd.
Los Angeles, CA 90077
tel (310) 476-7375; fax (310) 476-4180
e-mail smorris@aol.com
Sr. VP-Sales & Mktg. — Steve Morris

Belt Corporation of America
3455 Hutchinson Rd.
Cumming, GA 30130
tel (770) 887-9725/(800) 235-0947
fax (770) 887-4138
President — William C. Levensalor

Belting Industries Co. Inc.
20 Boright Ave.; PO Box 310
Kenilworth, NJ 07033-0310
tel (908) 272-8591; fax (908) 272-3825
Chairman — Webb A. Cooper
President — Scott Cooper
Manufacturing Manager — Kurt Malkus
Sales Manager — Gene Hobson
General Manager — Joseph F. Abramczyk
Comptroller — Paul West

Bender Machine Inc.
2150 E. 37th St.
Vernon, CA 90058
tel (213) 232-2371; fax (213) 232-1790
Mktg. Mgr. — Gene Oldham

Berkshire/Westwood Graphics Group Inc.
20 Hadley Mills Rd.; PO Box 1399
Holyoke, MA 01041
tel (413) 532-1735; fax (413) 532-6508
President — Mike Sullivan

Berlee Vacuum Systems
54 Winter St.; PO Box 351
Holyoke, MA 01041
tel (413) 538-8341; fax (413) 533-2709
President — Bernard L. Adams

Berting Communications
6330 Woburn Dr.
Indianapolis, IN 46250
tel (800) 536-5408; fax (317) 849-5408
President — Bob Berting

BESCO Graphic Systems Corp.
35 E. Wacker, Ste. 3500
Chicago, IL 60601
tel (312) 220-0042; fax (312) 220-0091

COB — Daniel Z. Tropp
President — Lawrence B. Tropp
Exec. Vice Pres. — Pete Walsh
Exec. Vice Pres.-Oper. — Dee Morse
Exec. Vice Pres. — Ron Smith
Exec. Vice Pres. — James Penney

Beta Screen Corp.
707 Commercial Ave.
Carlstadt, NJ 07072
tel (201) 939-2400; fax (201) 939-7656
President-Sales — Arnold Serchuk

Bidco Manufacturing Corp.
PO Box 757
Plainview, NY 11803-0757
tel (516) 433-0740; fax (516) 433-0745
President — Harvey Bidner
Controller — P.D. Reinfurt

Bio-Safe Industries
2280 S. Xanadu Way, Ste. 250
Aurora, CO 80014
tel (303) 745-9245; fax (303) 745-9246
President — Richard (Dick) H. Olson

Birmy Graphics Corp.
250 East Dr., Ste. H
Melbourne, FL 32904
tel (407) 768-6766; fax (407) 768-9669
Vice Pres. — Ted Birmingham

Bitstream Inc.
215 First St.
Cambridge, MA 02142-1270
tel (617) 497-6222/(800) 522-FONT
fax (617) 868-0784
e-mail bitstream.com
Mgr.-Public Relations — Stefan Wennik

Black Hills Publishers Inc.
2352 Fulton St.
Sturgis, SD 57785
tel (605) 347-2440; fax (605) 343-7678
CEO — Morris Hallock

Blevins Harding Group (Western Office)
2060 Broadway, Ste. One
Boulder, CO 80302
tel (303) 443-2535; fax (303) 443-2289
President — Kenneth A. Harding
CEO — Chuck Blevins

Blower Application Co. Inc.
N114 W19125 Clinton Dr.; PO Box 279
Germantown, WI 53022
tel (414) 255-5580; fax (414) 255-3446
President — Lawrence A. Brenner
Vice Pres.-Mfg. — John Stanislowski
Vice Pres.-Eng. — Michael J. Young

BMF Newspaper Accounting Systems
18 S. Main #511 (76501); PO Box 1590
Temple, TX 76503
tel (817) 778-8918; fax (817) 778-1832
Owner — Bill Frank
Manager — Marilyn Frank

Bobst Group Inc.
146 Harrison Ave.
Roseland, NJ 07068
tel (201) 226-8000; fax (201) 226-8625
President — Harvey S. Share
Sales & Mktg. Dir. — William B. Seymour

Boles, Morgan & Canino Inc.
102 S. Court St., Ste. 505
Florence, AL 35630
tel (205) 740-8234; fax (205) 740-8203
e-mail keysectr@attmail.com
President — Harold Van Morgan Jr.
Vice Pres. — Durelle Boles

BOLITHO-CRIBB & Associates
1 Annette Park Dr.; PO Box 3008
Bozeman, MT 59715
tel (406) 586-6621; fax (406) 586-6774
e-mail jcribb@imt.net
President — John Cribb

Borden Inc.
180 E. Broad St.
Columbus, OH 43215
tel (614) 225-4000; fax (614) 225-3410
Mktg. Mgr. — Rick Witt

R.W. Borrowdale Co. (RWB Enterprises Div.)
250 W. 83rd St.
Chicago, IL 60620-1798
tel (312) 723-7100; fax (312) 723-7113
Marketing Dir. — Linda L. Pentecost

Copyright ©1996 by the Editor & Publisher Co.

VI-4   Equipment, supplies, services

Bottcher America Corp.
4600 Mercedes Dr.; PO Box 480
Belcamp, MD 21017
tel (410) 273-7000; fax (410) 273-7174
President — Larry Lowe

Bottom Line Industries
9556 Cozycroft Ave. (91311)
PO Box 2144
Chatsworth, CA 91313
tel (800) 334-6044/(800) 337-6044
fax (818) 700-8232
Mktg. Mgr. — Lisa Reichman

Bowater-Great Northern Paper Inc.
1 Katahdin Ave.
Millinocket, ME 04462
tel (207) 723-5131; fax (207) 723-2529
President/Gen. Mgr. — Don McNeil
Mgr. Public Relations — Gordon Manuel

Bowater Inc.
55 E. Camperdown Way (29601)
PO Box 1028
Greenville, SC 29602
tel (803) 271-7733; fax (803) 282-9482
Chairman — A.P. Gammie
President/CEO — Arnold M. Nemriow
Sr. Vice Pres./CFO — David G. Maffucci
Vice Pres.-Corp. Dev. — D.J. D'Antuono
VP-Pulp & Paper Sales — C. Randy Ellington
Vice Pres.-Fin. — David G. Maffucci
Vice Pres.-Corp. Relations — R.D. Leahy
Treasurer — D.G. Maffucci
Mgr.-Internal Comms. — Michele C. Day
Sales Division:
President — C. Randy Ellington
VP-Newsprint Sales — Owen F. Cardell
Vice Pres.-Pulp Sales — Ben L. Pelton

Bowater Inc. (Coated Paper & Market Pulp Division)
5300 Cureton Ferry Rd.; PO Box 7
Catawba, SC 29704
tel (803) 981-8000; fax (803) 329-2949
e-mail jlc2@aol.com
President — Pat Duffy
Vice Pres.-Mill Mgr. — Alvin Humphrey
Pres./Gen. Mgr. — E.F. Walker
Asst. Gen. Mgr. — Barre R. Mitchell
Controller — Rob A. Rozee
VP-Coated Paper Sales — Steve Naman
VP-Market Pulp Sales — Ben Pelton
VP-Admin. & Planning — Craig Stevens
VP-Newsprint Sales Domestic — Randy Ellington

Bowater Mersey Paper Co. Ltd.
134 Brooklyn Hwy.; PO Box 1150
Liverpool, NS B0T 1K0 Canada
tel (902) 354-3411; fax (902) 354-2271
Chairman — A.P. Gammie
Pres./Gen. Mgr. — J.H. Dunlop
Mill Mgr. — B.S. Anthony
Woodlands Mgr. — J.M. Porter
Sec./Dir. PR — Mary Kingston
Controller — E.D. Cross
Sales Mgr. — D.L. Lohnes
Purchasing & Stores Mgr. — R.M. Sturge
Mgr.-Human Resources — D.L. Veinot
Quality Dev. Mgr. — F.S. Giffin

Bowater Newsprint (Div. of Bowater Inc.)
5020 Hwy. 11 S.
Calhoun, TN 37309-5249
tel (617) 336-7215; fax (617) 336-7950
VP- Oper. & Resident Mgr — R. Donald Newman
VP-Wood Products — Richard K. Hamilton
Mill Manager — Howard G. Johnson
Human Resource Mgr. — Darrell E. Douglas

Allen Bradley Co. (Motion Control Div.)
6400 W. Enterprise Dr.; PO Box 760
Mequon, WI 53092
tel (414) 242-8200; fax (414) 242-8579
http://www.ab.com
Product Mktg. Mgr. — Tim Clague
Mktg. Comm. Specialist — MichaelFaas Sr.
Graphic Sys. Mgr. — Donald Schroeder

Brady & Paul Communications
63 Hillside Ave.
Melrose, MA 02176
tel (617) 665-4941; fax (617) 662-4356
President — John Brady

Brainworks Inc.
1461 Old Country Rd.; PO Box 167
Riverhead, NY 11901
tel (800) 886-6434; fax (516) 369-5930
Mktg. Dir. — Mike Lynch
Mktg. Dir. — Cheryl Heather

Richard Briggs & Associates
206 Turner St.; PO Box 579
Landrum, SC 29356
tel (803) 457-3846; fax (803) 457-3847
e-mail 75712.2565@compuserve.com
President/Owner — Richard Briggs

Brilliant Ideas For Publishers
PO Box 32
Clam Lake, WI 54517
tel (715) 794-2186
President — Naomi K. Shapiro

R.J. Brimo Enterprises Ltd.
31 Viger
Kirkland, QC H9J 2E6 Canada
tel (514) 695-7172
President — Rene J. Brimo

Brite
7309 E. 21st St. N.
Wichita, KS 67206
tel (316) 652-6500; fax (316) 631-3400
VP/GM-Media Newspaper Products & Service Div. — Bud Calvert
Sr. Product Mgr. — Dan Weatherford
Product Mgr. — Kyle Rogg
Sales Rep. — Norton Jackson
Sales Rep. — Tad Snarenberger
Sales Rep. — Darrell Stewart
Sales Rep. — Steve Coffman
Sales Rep. — Hank Schichtle
Nat'l Sale Specialist — Dan Weatherford

The Douglas Britt Co.
1503 Shoreline Dr.
St. Charles, IL 60174
tel (800) 325-0559; fax (708) 377-0199
Mktg. Dir. — Darla Temple

Brodie System Inc.
1539 W. Elizabeth Ave.
Linden, NJ 07036
tel (908) 862-8620; fax (908) 862-8632
President — Thomas W. Nielsen
Plant Mgr. — Paul J. Kamage
Asst. Plant Mgr. — James F. Vatalano

Sara Brown & Associates
6651 Sunset Dr.
Miami, FL 33143
tel (305) 669-9202/(503) 797-2801
(Portland, OR); fax (305) 662-8765
President — Sara Brown

Brown & Sharpe Mfg. Co.
200 French Town Rd.
North Kingstown, RI 02852
tel (401) 886-2000/(800) 766-4673
fax (401) 886-2762/(800) 933-2937
Advg. Mgr. — Terry Sweeny
Int'l. Sales — John R. Larimer
Dir. Mktg. — Micheal Mariani
Dir.-Advg./PR & Comm. — David Genest

Len Brown & Sons Inc.
520 N. Washington; PO Box 326
Mexico, MO 65265
tel (314) 581-7278
Contact — Gena Brown Sr.
Contact — L.G. Brown Jr.

Bruno Unger USA
5606 W. 90th St. Ter.
Overland Park, KS 66207
tel (913) 648-8497; fax (913) 642-4237
Owner — Al Elton

Russell J. Bryant Co.
1206 Manor Rd.
Havertown, PA 19083
Marketing Director — Russell J. Bryant

Buffalo Inc.
2805 19th St. S.E.
Salem, OR 97302-1520
tel (503) 585-3414; fax (503) 585-4505
e-mail buffinc@teleport.com
President — Rick Stanczak

Bulbtronics
45 Banfi Plz.; PO Box 306
Farmingdale, NY 11735
tel (516) 249-2272; fax (516) 249-6066

President — Frances Thaw
Vice Pres.-Oper. — Susan Winters
Vice Pres.-Mktg. — Diana Jacobson
Vice Pres.-Sales — Elaine Gray
Marketing Manager — John Roberts

B.H. Bunn Co.
2730 Drane Field Rd.
Lakeland, FL 33811
tel (813) 647-1555; fax (813) 686-2866
President — Richard B. Bunn
Vice Pres. — Pamela L. Maxwell
Corporate Secretary — Harriet Bunn

Burgess Industries Inc.
2700 Campus Dr.
Plymouth, MN 55441
tel (800) 233-2589/(612) 553-7800
fax (612) 553-9289
Pres./CEO — Dennis Burgess
Mktg. Specialist — Molly Burgess

M.W. Burke & Associates Inc.
177 Front St., Ste. L
Danville, CA 94526
tel (510) 838-9070; fax (510) 838-4695
Chairman — M.W. (Maury) Burke
President — Mike DeNardo

Busch Inc.
516 Viking Dr.
Virginia Beach, VA 23452
tel (804) 463-7800; fax (804) 463-7407
President — Paul G. Swank
Sec./Treas. — Michael Junge
Mktg. Specialist — Kate Ernst

The Business Scribe Inc.
105 Randolph's Green
Williamsburg, VA 23185
tel (804) 229-7752; fax (804) 229-7752
e-mail hal@wmbg.com
President — Hal Gieseking

Butler SMC.
480 Neponset St.
Canton, MA 02021
tel (617) 828-5450; fax (617) 828-2715
President — Andrew P. Butler
Vice Pres.-Marketing — Carl E. Miller
CFO/Treasurer — Paul Cleary

ByChrome Co.
PO Box 1085
Columbus, OH 43216-1085
tel (614) 875-1000; fax (614) 875-5005
Exec. Vice Pres. — James R. Byrum

Byers Industries Inc.
6800 N.E. 59th Pl.
Portland, OR 97218
tel (503) 281-0069; fax (503) 281-1669
Chairman — Edwin J. Fackler
Dir.-Sales & Mktg. — Laurin Larsen

C

Cable Classified Advertising Network (CCAN)
9815 E. Crestline Cir.
Englewood, CO 80111
tel (303) 694-1637
President — Michael G. Golden
VP-Sales & Mktg. — Stephen T. Lindberg

CalComp
2411 W. La Palma Ave.
Anaheim, CA 92801
tel (714) 821-2000; fax (714) 821-2005
Dir.-Product Mktg. — Gene Ornstead

Canadian Pacific Forest Products Inc.
311 S. Wacker Dr., Ste. 2625
Chicago, IL 60606-6604
tel (312) 554-0661/(800) 326-6689
fax (312) 554-0648
Vice Pres. — George H. Murphy
Vice Pres. — Alexander L. West
Mgr.-Newsprint Mktg. (Midwest) — John I. Marshall

Canadian Web Consultants Ltd.
34 Attridge Dr.
Aurora, ON L4G 6J3 Canada
tel (905) 841-8523; fax (905) 727-2513
President — Stephen Tweddle
Vice Pres. — Michele Belanger
Office Manager — Linda Clark

Cannon Equipment
324 W. Washington
Cannon Falls, MN 55009
tel (507) 263-4231; fax (507) 263-4010
President/CEO — Ron Rosa
Exec. VP-Sales & Mktg. — Scott Rosa
Dir.-Engineering — Hugh Myer

Dir.-Newspaper Handling Systems — Pat Geraghty
Vice Pres.-Sales — Bob Grimm
Design Eng. Mgr. — Mark Sickman

Canoga-Perkins Corp.
21012 Lassen St.
Chatsworth, CA 91311
tel (818) 718-6300; fax (818) 718-6312
Director-Sales — Paul Stennes

Canon USA Inc.
1 Canon Plz.
Lake Success, NY 11042
tel (516) 488-6700
President — Haruo Murase
Sr. Vice Pres./GM — David F.E. Farr

Capco Machinery Systems Inc.
4535 EastPark Dr. (24019)
PO Box 11945
Roanoke, VA 24022
tel (540) 977-0404; fax (540) 977-2781
President — Edward E. West

Capital Track Co.
424 W. Town St.
Columbus, OH 43215
tel (614) 221-4110; fax (614) 341-6990
President — Richard Vrenna

Caprock Developments Inc.
475 Speedwell Ave.; PO Box 95
Morris Plains, NJ 07950
tel (201) 267-9292; fax (201) 292-0614
President — Alan Schwartz
Gen. Mgr.-Sales — S. Schwartz

Carborundum Abrasives Co.
6600 Walmore Rd.
Niagara Falls, NY 14304
tel (716) 731-7777; fax (716) 731-2467
President — Carl Rapp
Mktg. Comm. Mgr. — Robert Bender

Cariweb Products
PO Box 1349
Harlingen, TX 78551
tel (210) 423-5766; fax (210) 748-3417
Mktg. Mgr. — John David Guevara

Carlson Design/Construct Corp.
3 Speen St., Ste. 410
Framingham, MA 01701
tel (617) 969-1200; fax (508) 626-2390
President — Daniel Hunter
Exec. Vice Pres. — Bill Johnson
Mechnical Mgr. — Joe Hale

Carter & Associates
PO Box 2144
El Cajon, CA 92021
tel (619) 588-5339; fax (619) 588-7306
President — David Carter
Vice Pres. — Russ Hunsaker

Cary Design Inc., See Jardis Industries Inc.

Cascade Corp.
2201 N.E. 201st (Troutdale, 97060)
PO Box 20187
Portland, OR 97294-0187
tel (800) 227-2233/(503) 669-6300
fax (503) 669-6367
Chairman/CEO — Joseph Barclay
President/COO — Robert Warren
President/CEO — Larry Maunder
Vice Pres.-Manufacturing — Terry Cathey
Vice Pres.-Eng. — Zouhdi Derhalli
VP-Human Resources — Greg Anderson
Vice Pres.-Finance — Gerald Bitz
Mgr.-Cust. Support Center — Dave Geurts
US Sales Mgr. — Bob Mott

Cass Communications Inc.
1800 Sherman Pl.
Evanston, IL 60201-3769
tel (708) 475-8800; fax (708) 475-8807
Chairman — Alan M. Weisman
Pub./Nat'l. Sales Mgr. — Robert M. Roen
Vice Pres.-Central Region Sales Mgr. — Gary Thomas
Mktg. & Research Coord. — Tracy Anderson

CCI Europe
Oster Parkvej 9
Hojbjerg, DK-8270 Denmark
tel (45) 86295588; fax (45) 86299430

CE Engineering
3121 Swetzer Rd., Ste. F
Loomis, CA 95650
tel (916) 652-5263; fax (916) 652-5264
President — Robert Waterhouse
CEO — Chris Ellsworth

Copyright ©1996 by the Editor & Publisher Co.

Equipment, supplies, services

Cemco Inc.
1120 N. Peoria St.
Tulsa, OK 74106
tel (918) 585-8216; fax (918) 585-8274
President — Rick Holsted

Central Graphics
1302 Enterprise Dr.
Romeoville, IL 60446
tel (708) 759-1696; fax (708) 759-1792
Marketing Manager — Annette Narell
Sales Manager — Rick Arold

Cerutti North America
211 RIDC Park W. Dr.
Pittsburgh, PA 15275
tel (412) 788-1750; fax (412) 928-0515
President-Italy — Dr. Giancarlo Cerutti
Vice President — Bob Mrak
Vice Pres.-Sales & Admin. — Paul Cappa
Vice Pres.-Sales Italy — Riccardo Berrone

Gene Chamberlin Newspaper Consultants
1809 3rd St.
Brookings, SD 57006
tel (605) 692-6826; fax (605) 692-7132
Owner — Gene Chamberlin

Champion International Corp.
One Championship Plz.
Stamford, CT 06921
tel (203) 358-7000; fax (203) 358-7603

Chapel Hill Manufacturing Co.
1807 Walnut Ave.; PO Box 208
Oreland, PA 19075
tel (215) 884-3614; fax (215) 884-3617
Pres./Vice Pres.-Mktg. — John Seeburger
Vice Pres. — Norma Seeburger
Vice Pres.-Sales — J. Robert Seeburger

Chemetron
4251 Seminole Trail; PO Box 7146
Charlottesville, VA 22911
tel (804) 973-4361
President — Michael Dempsey
Vice Pres.-Sales — Bob Lodi

Chemetron/Badger Fire Systems
1000 Governors Hwy.
University Park, IL 60466
tel (708) 534-1000; fax (708) 534-1011
Manager — Steve Dmitrovich

Chemical Management Technology Inc.
329-7 Parkridge Ave.
Orange Park, FL 32065
tel (904) 276-3737; fax (904) 272-7751
President — Chuck Freeman
Vice Pres. — John Grisell
Vice Pres.-Sales — Ben Bryant

CHI/COR Information Management Inc.
300 S. Wacker Dr., Ste. 1800
Chicago, IL 60606
tel (312) 322-0150; fax (312) 322-0161
Mktg. Mgr. — Heidi Ewell

Chinon America Inc.
615 Hawaii Ave.
Torrance, CA 90503-9747
tel (310) 533-0274; fax (310) 533-1727

Chismark & Co.
901 Northpoint Pkwy. #102
West Palm Beach, FL 33407
tel (407) 688-9099; fax (407) 688-9092
President — George Chismark
Vice President — Kathy Chismark

Chronicle-Tribune (Gannet Color Div.)
610 South Adams
Marion, IN 46952
tel (800) 955-7888; fax (317) 664-0335
Director-Marketing — Sherry French

Church Rickards, Whitlock & Co. Inc.
10001 Roosevelt Rd.
Westchester, IL 60154
tel (708) 345-7500; fax (708) 345-1166
President — E.H. Powell
Vice Pres. — Dan Marcquenski
Vice Pres./Gen. Mgr. — Fred Hohnke

Circulation Development Inc. (CDI)
118 Centre on the Lake
Lake St. Louis, MO 63367
tel (314) 625-2315; fax (314) 625-2306
Chairman — Bill Wesa
President — Jim Oden

Circulation Solutions
1327 Loftin Dr.
Auburn, AL 36830
tel (334) 821-8373
President — Van Dozier

Circulation III Telemarketing Services
2619 Electronics Ln., Ste. 202
Dallas, TX 75220
tel (214) 352-1123; fax (214) 358-0987
President — John Dinan

Circulation Verification Council
PO Box 31523
St. Louis, MO 63131-0523
tel (800) 262-6392; fax (314) 230-8878
e-mail cucaudit@aol.com
President — Tim A. Bingaman
Audit Manager — David J. Little
Member Services — Susan M. Ries

Citiplate Inc.
275 Warner Ave.
Roslyn Heights, NY 11577
tel (516) 484-2000; fax (516)484-9778
President — Charles Cusumano
Mktg. Mgr. — Charles Cusumano Jr.
Exec. Asst. — Joan Combs

CK Optical Co. Inc.
631 Mary Ann Dr.; PO Box 1067
Redondo Beach, CA 90278
tel (310) 372-0372; fax (310) 372-7966
President — Herbert W Carlbom
Vice Pres. — Nigel Miller

Claritas
1525 Wilson Blvd., Ste. 1000
Arlington, VA 22209
tel (703) 812-2700/(800) 284-4868
fax (703) 812-2701
COO — Nancy Deck
Vice Pres.-Print Media — Soraya Chemaly
VP-Agency & Media Mktg. — Terry Pittman

Clark-Cutler-McDermoth Co. (Airloc Div.)
5 Fisher St.; PO Box 269
Franklin, MA 02038
tel (508) 528-0022; fax (508) 528-7555
Gen. Mgr. — Benny J. Sgaggero
Vice Pres. — Robert A. Geromini

Clark Material Handling Co.
749 W. Short St.
Lexington, KY 40508
tel (606) 288-1200; fax (606) 288-1226
Dir.-Mktg. — Frank Sanchez

Clayton/Curtis/Cottrell
2020 Pearl St.
Boulder, CO 80302
tel (303) 444-2381; fax (303) 444-2303
President — Robert Cottrell

Clipper Belt Lacer Co.
1995 Oak Industrial Dr., N.E.
Grand Rapids, MI 49505
tel (616) 459-3196; fax (616) 459-4176
General Manager — Richard E. Kelly
Mktg. Mgr. — John H. Meulenberg
Treasurer — Deb Gancarz
Prod. Mktg. — Beth Miller

CM Publishing Co.
141 Pineview Dr.; PO Box 545
King, NC 27201
tel (919) 983-3109; fax (919) 983-8203
President — T.J. Tergilafera

CNI Corp.
50 Old Temple Rd.; PO Box 247
Lyndeboro, NH 03082
tel (603) 654-5990; fax (603) 654-5992
e-mail 70302.2544@compuserve
President — Mike Gold
Vice Pres. — Scott Rozansky

Co Operative Printing Solutions
5950 Live Oak Pkwy., Ste. 175
Norcross, GA 30093
tel (770) 840-0810; fax (770) 448-7821
e-mail sales@copstalk.com
President — Guy Mariande
Account Mgr. — Joe Huber

Coddbarrett Associates Inc.
24 Bosworth St.
Barrington, RI 02806
tel (401) 247-2171
President/CEO — Mary Codd

Cole Machine-Applied Design Inc.
3420 Hickory Rdg.
Edmond, OK 73013
tel (405) 672-2222; fax (405) 672-2272
President — R. Gilson

Coleman Advertising
6000 S. Padre Island Dr., Ste. 202
PO Box 271316
Corpus Christi, TX 78427
tel (512) 992-6499
Owner — Zack Coleman

Coleman/Caskey Architects
100 Pacifica, Ste. 300
Irvine, CA 92718
tel (714) 727-4400; fax (714) 727-4401
Vice Pres. — Paul Guiso

Color y Autoedicion Nitida - S.A. de C.V.
Ave. Alfonso Reyes 4520-2,
Col. Villa Del Rio
Monterrey, Neuvo Leon 64850 Mexico
tel (011-52) 83 49 3668

The Color Partnership
2002 Jimmy Durant Blvd., Ste. 303
Del Mar, CA 92014
tel (619) 259-8688; fax (619) 259-8709
e-mail sara@colorpar.com
Dir.-Product Marketing — Sara Akerman

Colortran Inc.
1015 Chestnut St.
Burbank, CA 91506
tel (818) 843-1200; fax (818) 972-5599
President — Robert F. Sherman
Vice Pres.-Sales — John Fuller
Sr. VP-Fin. & Admn. — Bernard Wong

Communications Management Service Inc.
720 Barnum Ave. Cutoff
Stratford, CT 06497
tel (800) 233-7785; fax (203) 377-2632
President — John F. Roy
Vice Pres. — Daniel F. Rindos

Communications Service Co.
PO Box 2956
Naples, FL 33939
tel (708) 395-7358; fax (708) 395-7312
President — John A. Mehaffey

Community Papers Verification Services
6120 University Ave., Ste. 201
Middleton, WI 53562
tel (608) 238-5011; fax (608) 235-5013
President — James Pearson

Competitive Media Reporting
11 W. 42nd St., 11th Fl.
New York, NY 10036
tel (212) 789-1400; fax (212) 789-3640
Sr. Vice Pres. — Rick Spicer

Computer Devices Inc.
34 Linnell Cir.
Nutting Lake, MA 01865
tel (508) 663-4980; fax (508) 667-8561
President — Robert J. Moore
Vice Pres.-Sales — Robert J. Moore Jr.
Mktg. Administrative Mgr. — Cheryl Mayr

Computer Services Group Inc.
5515 Cherokee Rd.
Alexandria, VA 22312
tel (703) 642-2800; fax (703) 642-3746
President — Bruce M. Waldack

Computer Talk Technology Inc.
225 E. Beaver Crk.
Richmond Hill, ON L4B 3P4 Canada
tel (905) 882-5000; fax (905) 882-5501
President/CEO — Mandle Cheung
Mktg. Mgr. — Lindsay Aitken
Sales-Director — Jennie Cooper

Computer Tree
1880 Healy Dr.
Winston-Salem, NC 27103
tel (910) 760-9820; fax (910) 760-3309
Contact — Joseph Young

Computerease Software Inc.
654 Metacom Ave.; PO Box 170
Warren, RI 02885
tel (401) 245-1523; fax (401) 245-1850
President — Carl Berg
Vice Pres. — Carol Berg

ComputerUser
220 S. 6th St., Ste. 500
Minneapolis, MN 55402-4507
tel (612) 339-7571; fax (612) 339-5806
e-mail msp@mcimail.com
Editor-In-Chief — Steve Deyo

CompuText Inc.
16866 Royal Crest Dr.
Houston, TX 77058
tel (713) 480-3494; fax (713) 480-3559
President — Jimmy W. Connell
Sales Dir. — Nicholas Koriakin
Dir.-Operations — Molly Heitmann

Comtel Instruments Co.
PO Box 43259
Cleveland, OH 44143
tel (216) 442-8080; fax (216) 442-6009
President — Donald Colosimo
Sales Manager — Bruce Johnson

Concept Publishing Systems
809 Park Ave.
Beaver Dam, WI 53916
tel (414) 887-3731; fax (414) 887-0439
President — Jim Conley
Programming Mgr. — Dan Kirk

Connexperts
13355 Noel Rd., Ste. 1600
Dallas, TX 75240
tel (214) 358-4800; fax (214) 239-6490
President — Tim Wilde
Sales Mgr. — Jeff Heath
Int'l. Sales Mgr. — Jerry Mecca

Consolidated International Corp.
4501 S. Western Blvd.
Chicago, IL 60609
tel (312) 376-5600; fax (312) 376-5835
Chairman — Benjamin Sugarman
President — C.J. Meyers
Exec. Vice Pres. — John C. Grieder

Continental Inks
1565 Integrity Dr. E.
Columbus, OH 43209
tel (614) 444-7843; fax (614) 444-7846
President — Y. Pete Jacob
Plant Manager — Sharon Cash

Continental Printing Machinery
11104 Walrond St.
Kansas City, MO 64137
tel (816) 761-4749; fax (816) 765-0992
President — Kenneth W. Langley

Continental Products
2000 West Blvd.; PO Box 760
Mexico, MO 65265
tel (314) 581-4128; fax (314) 581-4461
Outside Sales Mgr. — Barry Garrett
Mktg. Asst. — Emily Woodward
Inside Sales & Customer Service Mgr. —
Vince Fuemmeler II

Control Engineering Co.
8212 Harbor Springs Rd.
Harbor Springs, MI 49740
tel (616) 347-3931; fax (616) 348-7201
Sales Mgr. — Earl Raynal Jr.
Mktg. Coord.-Sales — Thomas J. Burke
Vice Pres./Gen. Mgr. — A.R. Vokes
Controller — Rick Bowen
Sales Engineer — Bruce Lindsay
Operations Mgr. — Jim Schoemaker Jr.

Controls Group Inc.
3370 Forrest View Rd.
Rockford, IL 61109
tel (815) 227-0027; fax (815) 227-0025
President — Richard Atwater
Vice Pres. — Mike Hatlak

Copley Computer Services
7701 Herschel Ave.; PO Box 1530
La Jolla, CA 92037
tel (619) 551-2200; fax (619) 456-2854
Gen. Mgr. — Sam Hunt
Mgr. Tech. Svc. — Charles V. Wagner

Core-Concepts
PO Box 2013
Naples, FL 33939
tel (941) 261-5303
President — Charles C. Knudson
Vice Pres. — Gerald Critchfield

CPS Corp.
3257 Middle Rd.
Dunkirk, NY 14048
tel (716) 366-6010; fax (716) 366-4962
President — Frank Moravec
Vice Pres. — George Polasik
Vice Pres.-Sales — Frank Kuhn
Product Mgr. — Paul Barnstorf

CPS Technologies Inc.
350 Rte. 46 W. Ste. 1J; PO Box 648
Rockaway, NJ 07866
tel (201) 625-7900; fax (201) 586-9478
e-mail cpstech@ios.com
President — John Attas
Chairperson — Patricia Hoover
Vice Pres.-Operations — Brian Attas
Vice Pres.-Marketing — Walter Tertan

Copyright ©1996 by the Editor & Publisher Co.

VI-6   Equipment, supplies, services

Craftsmen Machinery Co./Graphic Export Corp.
840 Main St.; PO Box 38
Millis, MA 02054
tel (508) 376-2001; fax (508) 376-2003
CEO — S.J. Marks

Craig Cold Type Supply Inc.
1409 Veterans Dr.
Fairfield, OH 45014
tel (513) 829-7724; fax (513) 829-6354
President — Joe Craig
Vice Pres. — John Craig

Creative Brilliance Advertising/Marketing & Public Relations
PO Box 44237
Madison, WI 53744-4237
tel (608) 233-2669
Contact — Naomi K. Shapiro

Creative House Print Media Consultants
227 Ninth St.; PO Box 160
Sheldon, IA 51201
tel (712) 324-5347; fax (712) 324-2345
President — Peter W. Wagner
Vice Pres. — Connie Wagner
Sec./Treas. — Jeff Wagner

Creative Specialty Products Inc.
3250 Corporate Way
Hollywood, FL 33025
tel (305) 949-5380; fax (954) 430-7401
Nat'l. Sales Mgr. — Steve Raymond
Mktg. Mgr. — Donna Raymond

Creative Strategies
60 E. 42nd St.
New York, NY 10165
tel (212) 682-2977; fax (212) 682-0373
e-mail 73160.1124@compuserve.com
President — Robert F. Kaufman

Cribb Media Service
1 Annette Park Dr.
Bozeman, MT 59715
tel (406) 586-6621
President — John T. Cribb

Crosfield Electronic Ltd.
3 Cherry Tree Ln.; Hemel Hempsteap
Herts, HP2 7RH England
tel (800) 538-7668 (US Sales)
All sales in U.S. done through DuPont for info call Don Synder (302) 992-5326

CText Inc.
1428 E. Ellsworth Rd.
Ann Arbor, MI 48108
tel (313) 677-4700; fax (313) 677-4747
e-mail Individuals at CText have interest in e-mail addresses
CEO/Pres. — Larry Moore
Vice Pres.-Group Newspaper Dev. — Jimmie Garner
Vice Pres.-Product Dev. — Eugene Kiel
Vice Pres.-Tech. Oper. — Wade Harris
Vice Pres.-Sales & Support Svc. — Edward Rowden
Dir.-Sales/Support Svc. — Paul Mrozinski
Vice Pres.-Admn. — Lynne Dodd
Dir.-Engineering — Dave LeRoy

Cutler-Hammer
200 Westinghouse Cr.
Horseheads, NY 14845
tel (607) 796-3361; fax (607) 796-3364
Plant Mgr. — J. Kevin McLean

Cybergraphic Inc.
200 Wheeler Rd.
Burlington, MA 01803
tel (617) 221-0077; fax (617) 221-0070
Chairman — Bernard Grinberg
Gen. Mgr. — Donald Hollands
Sales Mgr. — Brian Trombley
Mktg. Mgr. — Wendy Bruce

D

D & R Engineering (Graybar Int'l.)
12629 Crenshaw Blvd.
Hawthorne, CA 90250
tel (310) 676-4896; fax (310) 676-3420
Owner — Daws Waffer

DAC Systems
60 Todd Rd., Ste. 1B
Shelton, CT 06484
tel (203) 924-7000; fax (203) 944-1618
President — Mark Nickson

Dahlgren USA Inc.
1725 Sandy Lake Rd. #102 (75006)
PO Box 115140
Carrollton, TX 75011-5140
tel (214) 245-0035; fax (214) 245-0768
President — Brian Bargenquest
Sales Manager — James E. Taylor

Daige Products Inc.
1 Albertson Ave.; PO Box 223
Albertson, NY 11507
tel (800) 645-3323; fax (516) 621-1916
Advg. Mgr. — Ike Harris

Dail Advertising Service
808 E. Ash St. (27530); PO Box 10278
Goldsboro, NC 27532
tel (919) 736-0447; fax (919) 736-0483
Mktg. Mgr. — Bobby Dail

Daishowa Forest Products Ltd.
181 Bay St., Ste. 1540
Toronto, ON M5J 2S1 Canada
tel (416) 862-5000; fax (416) 862-7051
Vice Pres.-Mktg. & Dist. — Daniel McKinnon
Dir.-Export Sales — Ian Michaud
Dir.-Tech. Sales & Service — Archie Flora
Exec. Sec. — Sheryl Irwin

Dampening Systems Inc.
141 S. Main St.; PO Box 16
Beacon Falls, CT 06403
tel (203) 723-4082; fax (203) 729-8592
Mktg. Mgr. — Jack Merancy

Dan-Bar Electric Inc.
PO Box 193
Clarcona, FL 32710
tel (407) 293-4985; fax (407) 578-1156
President — Kathleen M. Baratta
Vice Pres. — Daniel J. Baratta

Danagraf North America
2635 Hampton Ave.
St. Louis, MO 63139
tel (314) 645-0230; fax (314) 645-7476
President — Jack Strobel
Vice Pres. — Cathy Strobel

Daniel, Mann, Johnson & Mendenhall (DMJM)
300 W. Clarendon Ave., Ste. 400
Phoenix, AZ 85013-3499
tel (602) 264-0217; fax (602) 285-1984
Division Mgr.- A/E — Robert Schill
Div. Mgr.-Engineer — Doyle Wiste
Planning Manager — Robert Eubanks

Danka Omnifax
8700 Bellanca Ave.
Los Angeles, CA 90045
tel (800) 221-8330
Vice Pres.-Sales — Frank May

Dario Designs Inc.
1 Elda Rd.
Framingham, MA 01701
tel (508) 877-4444; fax (508) 877-4474
President — Dario Dimare, AIA
Vice President — David Mogan, AIA

Data Sciences Inc.
2150 Industrial Pkwy.
Silver Spring, MD 20904
tel (301) 622-6770; fax (301) 622-7954
President — Mark J. Ganslaw
Vice Pres. — Sally Shahbazian
VP-Sales & Mktg. — Daniel C. Martini

DataEase International Inc.
7 Cambridge Dr.
Trumbull, CT 06611
tel (800) 243-5123; fax (203) 365-2317
President/CEO — Stephen Page
Dir.-Marketing — Massimo Picchi

Datafest Technologies Inc.
1751 W. Alexander St., Ste. 100
PO Box 27916
Salt Lake City, UT 84119
tel (801) 975-0409; fax (801) 975-0906
President — Scott A. Clawson

Datalogics
441 W. Huron St.
Chicago, IL 60610
tel (312) 266-4444; fax (312) 266-4473
President — Steve Brown
Vice Pres-Sales & Sys. Dev. — Claude Finn
VP-Composition Sys. — Chuck Myers

Dataproducts
1757 Tapo Canyon Rd.
Simi Valley, CA 93063
tel (805) 579-4000; fax (805) 578-4001
Dir.-Human Resources — George Litterini

DataTimes Corp.
14000 Quail Springs Pkwy., Ste. 450
Oklahoma City, OK 73134
tel (405) 751-6400; fax (405) 755-8028
Chairman — E.L. Gaylord
President — Allen W. Paschal
Vice Pres. — John Paschal

Dauphin Graphic Machines Inc.
PO Box 573
Elizabethville, PA 17023
tel (800) 346-6119; fax (717) 362-4165
Sales Manager — Jack Little

David M. Co.
201 Valentine Way
Longwood, FL 32750
tel (800) 327-2204; fax (407) 323-8167
President — E.G. Mills
Nat'l. Sales Mgr. — Bob Hasinbiller
Dir.-Tech./R&D — H.V. Mycroft
Tech. Svc. Mgr. — Charlie Edwards
Group Mktg. Dir. — Kathryn Marx

Day International Inc.
333 W. First St. (45402); PO Box 338
Dayton, OH 45401-0338
tel (513) 224-4000; fax (513) 226-1855
President — Dennis R. Wolters
Product Mgr. — Wayne Rentz
Dir.-Sales — Julio Vela
Dir.-Sales — Bill Smals
Vice Pres.-Sales — Gordon Edwards

Day-Glo Color Corp. (Subsidiary of RPM Corp.)
4515 St. Clair Ave.
Cleveland, OH 44103
tel (216) 391-7070; fax (216) 391-7751
President — Michael J. Cavanaugh
Vice Pres.-Mktg. — Lawrence A. Caughlin
Vice Pres.-Sales — Ed Rudolph
Vice Pres.-R&D — Charles E. Moore

DayStar Digital Inc.
5556 Atlanta Hwy.
Flowery Branch, GA 30542
tel (404) 967-2077; fax (404) 967-3018
Mktg. Mgr. — Gary Dailey

Deadline Data Systems Inc.
31 Rowley Rd.
Topsfield, MA 01983-1029
tel (508) 887-3547; fax (508) 887-7357
President — Peter G. Marsh

Dean Machinery International Inc.
5380 Peachtree Industrial Blvd., Ste. 100
Norcross, GA 30071
tel (770) 448-5284; fax (770) 263-0047
Sales Administrator — Daisy Martinez

DeltaPoint Inc.
2 Harris Ct., Ste. B1
Monterey, CA 93940
tel (408) 648-4000; fax (408) 648-4020
Sales Director — John Hoskin

DemoSource Inc.
8502 E. Via de Ventura, Ste. 220
Scottsdale, AZ 85258
tel (800) 283-4759/(602) 922-5500
fax (610) 922-5572
President — Brian L. Berman

Denex Inc.
211 Overlook Dr.
Sewickley, PA 15143
tel (412) 749-0970; fax (412) 749-0977
President — Gary J. Carroll
Nat'l. Sale & Mktg. Dir. — Jeffrey Gelfand

Derus Media Service Inc./Editorial Pace
500 N. Dearborn St., Ste. 516
Chicago, IL 60610
tel (312) 644-4360; fax (312) 644-9192
President — Pat Derus
Exec. Vice Pres. — Matt McGann
Production Mgr. — Mike Vinikour

Design Science
4028 Broadway
Long Beach, CA 90803
tel (310) 433-0685; fax (310) 433-6969
President — Paul Topping
Office Mgr. — Donna Hamlin

Dewar Information Systems Corp.
Woodlands Ct. 3, 3050 Finley Rd.
Downer's Grove, IL 60515
tel (708) 241-3500/(800) USA-DEWAR
(Sales); fax (708) 241-3503
e-mail dewar.com@compuserve.com
President/COO — Clive Segal
Director-Operations — Adrian Warner

Dial Tech International
211 W. 2nd St.
East Greenville, PA 18041
tel (215) 679-0443; fax (215) 679-0717
Nat'l. Sales Mgr. — Homer Stewart

Diamond Roller Corp.
36 Mascolo Rd.
South Windsor, CT 06074
tel (203) 289-7748; fax (203) 291-9177
Vice Pres. — Charlie Stavola

Diamond Roller Corp.
150 Mar Ave.
Marietta, GA 30060
tel (404) 795-8556; fax (404) 795-8943
Controller Assist — Diane Goodman
Sales Mgr. — Bill Sheridan

A.B. Dick Co.
5700 W. Touhy Ave.
Niles, IL 60714
tel (312) 763-4455
President/CEO — Ronald Peterson
VP-Sales & Svc. — Richard Peterson
Vice Pres.-Oper. — Dennis Mahoney
VP/Gen. Counsel Sec. — Harris Walker
Vice Pres. Int'l. — Bill Pesch
Vice Pres.-Fin. — Richard Cleys

A.B. Dick Co. (Itek Graphix Div.)
811 Jefferson Rd.
Rochester, NY 14623-3211
tel (716) 475-9050; fax (716) 475-1271
Vice Pres./Gen. Mgr. — Lubomir Szmigel

Dick Mailer Co.
11812 Mt. Batten
Raleigh, NC 27613
tel (919) 676-0032
Sales Mgr. — N.W. Metke II

Didde Web Press
1200 Graphic Arts Rd.
Emporia, KS 66801
tel (316) 342-4740; fax (316) 342-7383
Advg. & Sales Prom. Mgr. — Lee Clifford

Digital Collections Inc.
1301 Marina Vlg. Pkwy.
Alameda, CA 94501
tel (510) 814-7200; fax (510) 814-6100
e-mail dcinc.applelink.apple.com
Vice Pres.-Product Dev. & Mktg. — Katherine Pfaff

Digital Design Inc.
4650 Kenny Rd.
Columbus, OH 43220
tel (614) 538-9222; fax (614) 538-1119
Office Mgr. — Judy Godsey

Digital Equipment Corp.
Digital Dr., MKO-1K32
Merrimack, NH 03054
tel (603) 884-0549; fax (603) 884-2740
e-mail farquhar@mkotsa.enet.dec.com
Interactive Publishing Mgr. — Jim Bovay
Vice President — Bob Farquhar
Newspaper Industry Mktg. Mgr. — Bob Farquhar

Digital Information Group
PO Box 110235
Stamford, CT 06911-0235
tel (203) 348-2751; fax (203) 977-8310
Publisher — Jeff Silverstein

Digital Technology International
500 W. 1200 S.
Orem, UT 84058
tel (801) 226-2984; fax (801) 221-9254
e-mail kathy-bray@powertalk.dtint.com
applelink d1067/
President — JoAnn Froelich
CEO — Don Oldham
Training Manager — Joel Kjar
Technical Manager — Jeff Carpenter
Marketing Director — Garth Despain

The Directory Center
117 W. Harrison St., Ste. 500
Chicago, IL 60605-1709
tel (312) 939-2602; fax (312) 939-2520
President — Diedre Wood
Marketing Manager — Tom Marin

Direct Reproduction Corp.
34 Macquesten Pkwy. S.
Mt. Vernon, NY 10550-1704
tel (914) 665-6515; fax (914) 665-6518
President — Ronald L. Russo

Equipment, supplies, services

Dispensa-Matic Label Dispensers
725 N. 23rd. St.
St. Louis, MO 63103
tel (314) 231-6006/(800) 325-7303
fax (314) 621-1602
Sales Mgr. — Richard Laycob

DK & A Inc.
1010 Turquoise St., Ste. 300
San Diego, CA 92109
tel (619) 488-8118; fax (619) 488-4021
COO/Vice Pres.-Mktg. — Robert Kline

Domino Amjet Inc.
1290 Lakeside Dr.
Gurnee, IL 60031-2400
tel (708) 244-2501; fax (708) 244-1421
President — Kris Bierbaum
Mgr. Corp. Comm. — Anna M. Amoresano

Domtar Inc.
395 de Maisonneuve Blvd. W.
Montreal, QC H3A 1L6 Canada
tel (514) 848-5400; fax (514) 848-5400
Chairman — Paul Gobeil
VP-Comm. & Gov't Rel. — Denis Coture

RR Donnelley & Sons Co.
77 W. Wacker Dr.
Chicago, IL 60601
tel (312) 326-8000; fax (312) 326-8262
Contact — Steve Bono

Donohue Inc.
801 chemin St-Louis
Quebec, QC G1S 4W3 Canada
tel (418) 684-7700; fax (418) 684-7727
COB — C.A. Poissant
CEO/Pres./Dir. — Michel Desbiens
Exec. VP-Pulp & Paper — Denis Jean
Vice Pres./CFO — Claude Helie
Vice President/Sec./Gen. Counsel — Claude Vadboncoeur
Vice Pres.-Pulp Sales — Roger Quesnel
Vice President-Environment & Energy — Jacques Angers
Vice PresLegislation & Gov't. Relations — Wilbrod Gauthier
Vice President-Mktg. & Sales-Paper — Gaston Bouffard
Treasurer — Marlene Kandalaft
Asst. Treasurer — Luc Dufour
Corp. Controller — Yvan Gingras
Asst. Sec. — Maureen Gurrie

Douthitt Corp.
245 Adair St.
Detroit, MI 48207-4287
tel (800) DOUTHITT; fax (313) 259-6806
Contact — Mark W. Diehl

The Dow Chemical Co.
2030 Dow Ctr.
Midland, MI 48674
tel (517) 636-1000; fax (517) 636-3518
Chairman — Frank Popoff
VP-HR — Larry J. Washington
Grp. Mgr.-Performance Products — Jean Aukerman

DPS Typecraft (Acorn House)
Great Oaks
Basildon, Essex SS14 1AH England
tel (44-2) 68523471; fax (44-2) 68281090
Managing Director — Richard Kemm
Sales Director — Richard Hall
Financial Director — Geoffrey Walker

Dragon Systems Inc.
320 Nevada St.
Newton, MA 02160
tel (617) 965-5200; fax (617) 527-0372
Mgr.-Corp. Comm. — Chris Gardner

Drake Communications Inc.
2435 Squire Pl., Ste. 400
Dallas, TX 75234
tel (214) 243-2500; fax (214) 243-2500
President — Cecil Drake
Vice Pres. — L.G. Drake

Frank Drazan
3526 Raymond Ave.
Brookfield, IL 60513
tel (708) 485-6973; fax (708) 485-1019
Mktg. Mgr. — Frank Drazan

Drew Products
1717 Fourth St.
Berkeley, CA 94710
tel (510) 527-7100; fax (510) 527-7817
Contact — Mike Drew

DS America, See Screen (USA)

DTK Computer Inc.
18501 E. Gale Ave., Ste. 150
City of Industry, Los Angeles, CA 91748
tel (818) 810-8880; fax (818) 810-5233
Mgr. Mktg. — Michelle Nguyen
Accounting — Joe Shen

Du-Pont Printing & Publishing
65 Harristown Rd.
Glen Rock, NJ 07452
tel (201) 447-5800; fax (201) 612-5933
President — Ed Wollard
Regional Sales Mgr. — Dennis Griff

Duarte Register Systems Inc.
990 San Antonio Rd.
Palo Alto, CA 94303
tel (415) 493-0174/(800) 345-6445
fax (415) 493-0178
President — Martin A. Peters
Vice Pres.-Mktg. Mgr. — Karilyn R. Duarte
Gen. Mgr. — Kevin Klass

Dunhill International List Co. Inc.
1951 N.W. 19th St.
Boca Raton, FL 33431
tel (407) 347-0200/(800) 386-4455
fax (407) 347-0400
President — Robert Dunhill
Vice Pres. — Cindy Dunhill
Vice Pres. — Andy Dunhill
Vice Pres. — Candy Dunhill

William Dunkerley Publishing Consultant
275 Batterson Dr.
New Britain, CT 06053
tel (203) 827-8896; fax (203) 224-9094
e-mail 0002088305@mcimail.com
Consultant — William Dunkerley

Dunn Technology Inc.
1855 E. Vista Way
Vista, CA 92084
tel (619) 758-9460; fax (619) 758-5401
President — Patrice Dunn

Duostat Co. (Affiliated with VGC Corp.)
3 Luger Rd.
Denville, NJ 07834
tel (800) 524-2140; fax (201) 586-2585
President — Mike Ostroff
Treasurer — Ray Domis

DuPont Co.
PO Box 80010
Wilmington, DE 19880
tel (302) 774-1000/(800) 5 Dupont (538-7669) (Sales)
Contact — Donna Snyder

Durbin Associates
3711 Southwood Dr.
Easton, PA 18045
tel (610) 252-6331; fax (610) 559-0195
President — Harold C. Durbin
Secretary — Frances Bailey

DYC Supply Co./Dynaric Inc.
500 Frank W. Burr Blvd.
Teaneck, NJ 07666
tel (201) 692-7700; fax (201) 692-7757
e-mail joem@interport.net
President — Joseph Martinez

Dynalith Inc.
114 N. Washington St.; PO Box 440
Easton, MD 21601
tel (410) 822-4400/(800) 368-2524
fax (410) 820-8649
Sales Mgr. — Lila Simmons
Newspaper Sales — Connie Coughenour
Comptroller — Christy Brinsfield

Dynamic Graphics Inc.
6000 N. Forest Park Dr.
Peoria, IL 61614
tel (309) 688-8800/(800) 255-8800
fax (309) 688-5873
Chairman — John L. Rush
President — Jayme Mueller
Exec. Vice Pres. — Nancy Ruenzel
Vice Pres.-Mktg. & Sales — Peter Force

Dynamo International Inc.
PO Box 173
Wheaton, IL 60189
tel (708) 665-0060; fax (708) 665-0879
Mktg. Mgr. — Arnold DeLuca, Ph.D.

E

E-FAX Communications Inc.
1611 Telegraph Ave., Ste. 555
Oakland, CA 94612
tel (510) 836-6000; fax (510) 836-8935

President — Joseph Karwat
Vice Pres.-Mktg. — William S. Perell
Vice Pres.-Tech. Dev. — Eric Karlson

EAM-Mosca Corp.
675 Jaycee Dr., Valmont Industrial Park
West Hazleton, PA 18201
tel (717) 459-3426; fax (717) 455-2442
Sales Manager — Bob Leighton
Applications Engineer — C. David Jackson

Earmark
1125 Dixwell Ave.
Hamden, CT 06514
tel (203) 777-2130; fax (203) 777-2886
President — Gerald Bloom

Eastman Kodak/Professional Printing & Publishing Imaging
343 State St.
Rochester, NY 14650
tel (716) 724-4000
Exhibits Coord. — Ron Shurgot
Dir.-Newspapers — Debra Hogan
Pro. Imaging Photo Journalism — Paul Curtis

EB Metal Industries
PO Box 149
Whitehall, NY 12887
tel (518) 499-1222; fax (518) 499-2220
President — Howard Shames

Ebway Industries Inc. (Div. of Jardis Industries Inc.)
1215 Karl Rt. #201; PO Box 369
Wauconda, IL 60084
tel (708) 526-7757; fax (708) 526-7813
President — Alan W. Jardis
Dir.-Sales & Mktg. — Gary Klawinski
South American Sales — Mike Anderson

Eclectic Co. Inc.
2571 Timber Ln.
Dayton, OH 45414
tel (513) 277-7410; fax (513) 277-8395
President — Ronald M. Wantz
Vice Pres./Treas. — Mary A. Wantz
Sales Eng. — Judd McCreary
Project Mgr. — Douglas Wantz

Eclipse Services (Div. of Quadrivium Inc.)
34 Copley Rd.
Upper Darby, PA 19082
tel (610) 352-6800; fax (610) 352-6857
President — Jenette MacNeille

ECRM
554 Clark Rd.
Tewksbury, MA 01876
tel (508) 851-0207; fax (508) 851-7016
e-mail ecrm.sales@applelink.apple.com
President/CEO — William R. Givens
Exec. VP-COO — Gerald L. Governile
Sr. Vice Pres. — Philip G. Rowlinson
Sr. Vice Pres.-Mktg. — G. Paul Markham
Vice Pres.-Tech. & Bus. Dev. — W. Thomas Boston
Vice Pres.-Finance — Rudy Bunde
VP-Product Mgt. — Edward Neylon
Mgr. Advertising Sales — Irvin Press

EDCO Services
4107 Gunn Hwy.
Tampa, FL 33624
tel (813) 962-7800; fax (813) 960-2356
e-mail edco@gate.net
Mktg. Mgr. — Ed Cohen

Edgil Associates Inc.
15 Tyngsboro Rd.
North Chelmsford, MA 01863
tel (508) 251-9932; fax (508) 251-9970
President — Ed Hopey
Vice Pres. — Gilbert Wolsky
Dir.-Sales & Mktg. — Linda Gagnon
Mktg. Coord. — Jeff Kosiorek

Editor & Publisher
11 W. 19th St.
New York, NY 10011-4234
tel (212) 675-4380; fax (212) 929-1259 (Advertising)/(212) 691-6939 (Circulation)/(212) 691-7287 (Editorial)
e-mail edpub@mediainfo.com
Co-Publisher — D. Colin Phillips
Co-Publisher — Christopher Phillips
Advertising Dir. — Steve Townsley

E & P Research Inc.
7615 Brigham Dr.
Atlanta, GA 30350
tel (404) 391-0224; fax (404) 391-0319
Co-Publisher — D. Colin Phillips
Co-Publisher — Christopher Phillips
President — Frederic B. Farrar
Research Dir. — Francisco Vasquez

Editorial Consultant Service
268 Garden Pl./W. Hempstead
New York, NY 11552
tel (516) 481-5487
Vice Pres. — James Thorpe
Sr. Columnist — Ray Hite

Editorial Management Strategies
795 E. 19th St.
Brooklyn, NY 11230
tel (718) 434-1100
President — Rita Stollman

Editorial System Engineering Co. (ESE)
3 Preston Ct.
Bedford, MA 01730
tel (617) 276-9400; fax (617) 275-5782
President — Ignacio Magias
Vice Pres. — David Francoeur

EdiWise/A Div. of Abitibi-Price
2240 Speakman Dr.
Mississauga, ON L5K 1A9 Canada
tel (905) 855-7855; fax (905) 855-2475
Mktg. Dir. — Ijen Huang

Egenolf Machine Inc. (Egenolf Contracting & Rigging)
2916 Bluff Rd.
Indianapolis, IN 46225
tel (317) 787-5301/(317) 782-2722
fax (317) 787-5018
President — James Egenolf
Exec. Vice Pres. — Joe Egenolf

EGS Americas Inc.
18200 Yorba Linda
Yorba Linda, CA 92686
tel (708) 823-6650; fax (708) 823-5589
President — Jeffrey Rex
Vice Pres. — Jose Martinez
Vice Pres.-Sales — Dennis Pearson

Ehrenreich Photo-Optical, See Nikon Inc.

Eighty/20 Software
8 S. 1st Ave.
Yakima, WA 98902
tel (509) 248-8309
CEO — Robert Guchee

The Electric Tachometer Corp.
68th & Upland Sts.
Philadelphia, PA 19142
tel (215) 726-7723; fax (215) 724-3682
President — T.J. Porter
Vice Pres.-Sales Mgr. — F.M. Porter
Secretary — A.J. Karpinski

Electronic Specialists Inc.
171 S. Main St.; PO Box 389
Natick, MA 01760-0389
tel (508) 655-1532; fax (508) 653-0268
President — F.J. Stifter

Electronic Systems Engineering Co.
1 Eseco Rd.
Cushing, OK 74023
tel (800) 331-5904; fax (918) 225-1284
President — A.A. Kaminshine
Vice Pres.-Eng. — Steve Holley
Vice Pres.-Training. Dir. — V.A. Smith

Electronic Tele-Communications Inc.
1915 MacArthur Rd.
Waukesha, WI 53188
tel (414) 542-5600; fax (414) 542-1524
Advg./PR Mgr. — Anne Finn
Vice Pres.-Sales — Johnny Johns
Dir.-Mktg. — Connie Crabb-Velez

Electronics For Imaging Inc.
6600 Silacci
Gilroy, CA 95020
tel (800) 285-4565; fax (408) 848-5784
President — Jim Chapman

Employers Reinsurance Corp.-Communications Liability Depart.
5200 Metcalf Ave.; PO Box 2991
Overland Park, KS 66201-1391
tel (913) 676-5200

Copyright ©1996 by the Editor & Publisher Co.

VI-8 Equipment, supplies, services

Human Resources — Martha Phillips
Mgr. Comm. Liability Dept. — Suzanne Shank

Engage Communication Inc.
9053 Soquel Dr.
Aptos, CA 95003-4034
tel (408) 688-1021; fax (408) 688-1421
President — Mark Doyle
Reg. Sales Mgr. — Michael Graham
Mktg. Project Mgr. — Mark Worden
Dir.-Operations — Thomas Ver Ploeg

Engelhard
12 Thompson Rd.; PO Box 570
East Windsor, CT 06088-0570
tel (203) 623-9901; fax (203) 623-4657
VP/GM-Suface Tech. Specialty Products Group — Daniel W. Parker
Commercial Dir.-Surface Tech. — Anthony J. Rotolico
Chief Engineer-Surface Tech. — Garald L. Kutner

Engineering Products Co.
3051 Southstate St. (60441); PO Box 66
Lockport, IL 60441
tel (815) 726-8640; fax (815) 726-3253
Vice Pres.-Sale — Robert Herman
Gen Mgr. — Sharon Fazil

Enkel Corp.
(A Baldwin Technology Co.)
8155 Burden Rd.; PO Box 2902
Rockford, IL 61132-2902
tel (815) 654-9355; fax (815) 654-3331
President — Chester Moore
Vice Pres. — Raymond Cornell
Vice Pres.-Int'l. Sales — Fred Hertz
Vice Pres. — Robert Page Olmsted

Equipto
225 S. Highland Ave.
Aurora, IL 60506
tel (708) 859-1000; fax (708) 859-3255
President — Thomas Matyas

Ergotron Inc.
1181 Trapp Rd.
St. Paul, MN 55121
tel (612) 452-8135; fax (612) 452-8346
Sales — Carole Wilson

Eskofot Canada Ltd.
6250 Kestrel Rd.
Mississauga, ON L5T 1Y9 Canada
tel (905) 670-7860; fax (905) 670-7720
President — Arne Nordtorp

Essex Products Group
30 Industrial Park Rd.; PO Box 307
Centerbrook, CT 06409
tel (860) 767-7130; fax (860) 767-9137
Sales Manager — Peter Alfano
Marketing — John F. Moriarty

Ewert America Electronics Ltd.
869 Pickens Industrial Dr. N.E., Ste. 12
Marietta, GA 30062
tel (770) 421-0774; fax (770) 421-0731
President — Richard Ewert
Exec. Vice Pres. — Chris Eickhoff

Executive Resource Group
29 Oakhurst Rd.
Cape Elizabeth, ME 04107
tel (207) 767-1320; fax (207) 799-8624
e-mail sibphae@aol.com
President — Sibyl Masquelier

Extratec Corp.
5930 Muncaster Mill Rd.
Rockville, MD 20855
tel (301) 924-5150; fax (301) 924-5151
President — Regis E. Finn

F

F & F Printing Ink Corp.
14-16 Delaware Dr.
Salem, NH 03079
tel (800) 824-4030; fax (603) 894-4384
Comptroller — Kevin Price

Falco Data Products Inc.
440 Potrero Ave.
Sunnyvale, CA 94086
tel (408) 745-7123; fax (408) 745-7860
Dir.-Sales — Chris Perry

FAR Systems Inc.
7898 High Ridge Rd.
Fort Atkinson, WI 53538
tel (414) 563-2221; fax (414) 563-1865
Gen. Mgr. — Helen M. Rose

FELINS Inc.
8304 W. Parkland Ct.
Milwaukee, WI 53223
tel (414) 355-7747; fax (414) 355-7559
President — James Chisholm
Vice Pres./Gen. Mgr. — Tim Wainscott

Ferag Inc.
190 Rittenhouse Cir.; PO Box 137
Bristol, PA 19007-0137
tel (215) 788-0892; fax (215) 785-0604
President — Martin Roark
Sr. Exec. Vice Pres. — Walter Wild
VP-Mid Atlantic — Herman A. Hazen
VP-Northeast — Andrew J. Leszczynski
Vice Pres.-South — Joe Ondras
Vice Pres.-Midwest — William Shuler
Vice Pres.-West — Paul Amelung
Dir.-Public Relations — Herman A . Hazen

FFC International Inc.
530 Saddle Creek Cir.
Roswell, GA 30076-1034
tel (770) 552-1528; fax (770) 552-2669
President — Ken Fidler
Vice Pres. — Albert (Al) A. Taber

Fincor/Electronics Div. Inc.
3750 E. Market St.
York, PA 17402
tel (717) 751-4200; fax (717) 751-4272
Sales Mgr.-Printing Industry Products — Jim Young
Assoc. Sales Mgr. — Lee Hanicey

The Findlay Group
12575 Broadmoor
Overland Park, KS 66209
tel (913) 491-4353
e-mail tfindlay@unicom.net
President — Ted Findlay

Fleming Enterprises
928 Blue Mound Rd.
Fort Worth, TX 76131
tel (817) 485-0448
Owner — Jeff M. Fleming
Office Admn. — D.E. Fleming Sr.
Service Rep. — Mark Fleming
Service Rep. — Pete Fleming

Fletcher Challenge Paper Co.
650 California St., 24th Fl.
San Francisco, CA 94108
tel (415) 693-1400; fax (415) 989-4301
President — Thomas H. Pitts
Mgr. Mktg. Svc. — Ginny Hanger

Flexo Printing Equipment Corp.
1298 Helmo Ave. N.
Oakdale, MN 55128
tel (612) 731-9499; fax (612) 731-0525
Pres./Mktg. Mgr. — E.W. Lidell

Flint Ink Corp.
25111 Glendale Ave.
Detroit, MI 48239
tel (313) 538-6800; fax (313) 538-3538
Chmn./CEO — H. Howard Flint II
Pres./COO — Leonard D. Frescoln
Vice Pres.-Quality — Joseph B. Price
Exec. Vice Pres. — David B. Flint
Group Vice Pres.-Publication Inks — Gregory M. Lawson
VP-Research & Dev. — Robert G. Savageau
Vice Pres.-NewsInk — Roy T. Beagle
Group Mktg. Dir. — Kathy Prochnow Marx

Florida Printing Equipment and Supply
PO Box 150669
Altamonte Springs, FL 32717
tel (407) 834-7716; fax (407) 834-7811
President — Milton Mercado

Fluorographic Services Inc.
622 Olive St.
Santa Barbara, CA 93101
tel (805) 962-7615; fax (805) 564-7829
Gen. Mgr. — Sandra N. Stites
Tech. Rep. — Charles P. Collier

Flying Color Graphics
1001 W. North St.
Pontiac, IL 61764
tel (800) 892-2853; fax (815) 844-1044
e-mail fcg@fcg.net
Managing Dir. — Vicki Glennon

Flynn Burner Corp.
425 Fifth Ave.
New Rochelle, NY 10802
tel (914) 636-1320; fax (914) 636-3751
President — Edward S. Flynn
Vice Pres.-Fin. Admin. Mgr. — John Hunt
Vice Pres. — Julian Modzeleski
Chief Eng. — Jim Pezzuto

FMC Corp. (Material Handling Systems Div.)
400 Highpoint Dr.
Chalfont, PA 18914
tel (215) 822-4300; fax (215) 822-4342
Area Sales Mgr. Unit Handling — Henry Strawn
Sales & Mktg. Marketing — John Harper

Focus/Graphics
8380 Olive Blvd.
St. Louis, MO 63132-2814
tel (314) 991-1698; fax (314) 997-1898
President — Charles L. Klotzer
Vice Pres. — Rose F. Klotzer

Foley, Torregiani & Associates, Inc.
9 Twin Isles Rd.
Londonderry, NH 03053
tel (603) 434-5100; fax (603) 437-9132
e-mail billfta@aol.com
President — James Torregiani
Treasurer — William Foley

FontBank Inc.
2620 Central St.
Evanston, IL 60201
tel (708) 328-7370; fax (708) 328-7491
e-mail fontbank@aol.com
President — Jerry Saperstein

Forrest Consulting
121 W. Wesley St., Ste. 100
Wheaton, IL 60187
tel (708) 871-2565; fax (708) 653-1333
e-mail leepublish@aol.com
President — Lee Crumbaugh

Fortec Inc.
W226 N825 Eastmound Dr.
Waukesha, WI 53186
tel (414) 544-4300; fax (414) 544-9272
President — Jack Olson
Vice Pres.-Admn. — Joe Schnorr

Foster Mfg. Co.
414 N. 13th St.
Philadelphia, PA 19108
tel (215) 625-0500; fax (215) 625-0196
President — Ted W. Borowsky
Customer Service — Margot Bucak
Customer Service — Sheree Robinson
Sales — Will Cartagena

Foundation of Flexographic Technical Association
900 Marconi Ave.
Ronkonkoma, NY 11779
tel (516) 737-6020; fax (516) 737-6813

John Foust Advertising/Training
PO Box 10861
Raleigh, NC 27605
tel (919) 834-2056
Owner — John Foust

Fox Bay Industries Inc.
4150 B Pl., N.W. #101
Auburn, WA 98001
tel (206) 941-9155; fax (206) 941-9197
President — Wayne E. Walker
Vice Pres. — Grant A. Walker
Treasurer — Ladele Walker
Secretary — Teri Yuskoff

Jimmy R. Fox, Mail Room Consultant
9222 Elizabeth Rd.
Houston, TX 77055
tel (713) 468-5827
Mailroom Consultant — Jimmy R. Fox
Co-Owner — Veronica L. Fox

Frame Technology Corp.
333 W. San Carlos St.
San Jose, CA 95110
tel (408) 975-6000; fax (408) 975-6799
e-mail comments@frame.com
PR Specialist — Carol Kaplan

Franklin Wire Works Inc.
3615 Newburg Rd.
Belvidere, IL 61008
tel (815) 544-5300; fax (815) 544-2363
Sales Mgr. — Robert Mutert
Outside Sales Mgr. — Bo Boger

Frankton Press Inc.
Corner of Washington & Plum Sts.
PO Box 278
Frankton, IN 46044
tel (317) 754-7920; fax (317) 754-8180
President — Paul Lennon
Secretary — Elaine Lennon

Freedom System Integrators
405 S. Holland St.
Wichita, KS 67209
tel (316) 722-8100; fax (316) 722-8708
CFO — Rick Firner
Vice Pres./Gen. Mgr. — Terry Borchers
Mktg. Dir. — Deanna Brgoch

Barry French
Ashlawn Rd.
Assonet, MA 02702
tel (508) 644-5772
Mktg. Dir. — Barry French

Freudenberg Building Systems Inc.
94 Glenn St.
Lawrence, MA 01843
tel (800) 332-6672; fax (508) 975-0110
President — Volker Siems
Vice Pres.-Sales — William Blasek
Vice Pres.-Fin. — Louis Gebala
Exec. Mktg. Asst. — Carol Fudge

Fry Communications
800 W. Church Rd.
Mechanicsburg, PA 17055
tel (717) 766-0211; fax (717) 691-0341
Vice Pres.-Sales — Gary Shughart

FSC Paper Co.
13101 S. Pulaski Rd.
Alsip, IL 60658
tel (708) 389-8520; fax (708) 389-8237/(708) 389-8567 (Sales)
President — Stanly B. Tamkin
Mktg. Mgr. — John McDonough

EAE • Design • Manufacturing • Installation • Retrofit • Service • Spare Parts

EWERT AMERICA ELECTRONICS, LTD.
869 Pickens Industrial Drive NE #12
Marietta, GA 30062
Telephone (770) 421-0774 • FAX (770) 421-0731

Copyright ©1996 by the Editor & Publisher Co.

Equipment, supplies, services

Fuji Photo Film USA/Graphic Arts Products Div.
1285 Hamilton Pkwy.
Itasca, IL 60143
tel (708) 773-7200; fax (708) 773-2457
Gen. Mgr. Graphic Arts Product — Stanley E. Freimuth
Nat'l. Sales Mgr.-Film — Larry Warter
National. Sales Manager.-PS-Plates — Robert L. Riley
Mgr. Product Dev.-PS-Plates — David H. Gullett
Mgr. Product Dev.-Film — Timothy Combs
Nat'l. Svc. Mgr.-Graphic Arts Products Div. — Gary Rohrbaugh
Mktg. Comm. Mgr. — Philip Laskowsky
Product Dev. Mgr.-Color Proofing — Lonny Martin

Fuji Photo Film USA (Distribution Ctr.)
400 Commerce Blvd.
Carlstadt, NJ 07072
tel (201) 507-2500; fax (201) 804-3345
Mgr.-Human Resources — Robert Adler

Fulco Inc.
30 Broad St.
Denville, NJ 07834
tel (201) 627-2427; fax (201) 627-5872
President — Bob Boyken
Vice Pres. — Jim Duffy

Fulfillment Corp. of America (FCA)
205 W. Ctr. St.
Marion, OH 43302-3707
tel (614) 383-5231; fax (614) 383-2875
Mktg. Mgr. — Sherry Hall
Dir.-Sales — Sharon Jerome

Ralph Fusco Inc.
30 Fern Dr.
Commack, NY 11725-4104
tel (516) 864-1352
President — Ralph Fusco

G

Gammerler (US) Corp.
930 Muirfield Dr.
Hanover Park, IL 60103-5457
tel (708) 439-8882; fax (708) 582-7770
e-mail gamm@interaccess.com
President — Gunter Gammerler
Vice Pres.-Sales & Mktg. — Mark Legac

Garden State Paper Co. Inc.
River Drive Ctr. 2
Elmwood Park, NJ 07407
tel (201) 796-0600; fax (201) 796-8470
VP-Sales & Mktg. — Richard Franklin

GB Techniques Ltd.
Glenburn House Glenburn Rd.
Prestwick, Ayrshire KA9 2NS Scotland

Geac/Vision Shift
3707 W. Cherry St.
Tampa, FL 33607
tel (813) 872-9990; fax (813) 876-8786
Gen. Mgr. — Warren Fletcher
Nat'l. Sales Mgr. — Richard A. Kitzmiller
Vice Pres.-R&D — James E. Douglas

Geiss-America Inc.
4821 W. Main St.
Skokie, IL 60077
tel (708) 674-5800; fax (708) 674-5854
President — LeRoy Cohen

General Binding Corp.
1 GBC Plz.
Northbrook, IL 60062
tel (708) 272-3700; fax (708) 272-7087
President — Govi Reddy
CFO — Ed McNulty
Vice Pres.-Sales — Robert Zanchelli
Project Coord. — Cindy Andreoli
Dir.-Mktg. & Comm. — Sally Folkes

General DataComm Inc.
1579 Straits Tpke.; PO Box 1299
Middlebury, CT 06762-1299
tel (203) 574-1118; fax (203) 758-8507
e-mail http://www.gdc.com
Advg. Mgr. — Arthur Sorrentino

Georgia-Pacific Corp.
7000 Central Pkwy., Ste. 860
Atlanta, GA 30328
tel (404) 698-8040; fax (404) 551-6017
Manager — John Walker

GeoRack Inc.
2691 Coolidge Hwy.
Berkley, MI 48072
tel (810) 544-2340; fax (810) 399-2431
Gen. Sales Mgr. — Norman L. Schmitt

Gerber Systems Corp.
83 Gerber Rd. W.
South Windsor, CT 06074
tel (203) 644-1551; fax (203) 649-7157
CEO — H.J. Gerber
Mgr.-Mktg. Svc. — Robert W. Layton

Gerrard Ovalstrapping
5330 S. Service Rd.
Burlington, ON L7L 5L1 Canada
tel (905) 632-3662; fax (905) 639-2290
President/Gen. Mgr. — Jack E. White
Admn. Asst. — Maureen Oldfield

Gilbane Building Co.
7 Jackson Walkway
Providence, RI 02940
tel (401) 456-5800; fax (401) 456-5936
COB — William Gilbane Sr.
President — Paul J. Choquette Jr.
Exec. Vice Pres. — Thomas F. Gilbane Jr.
Vice Pres.-Mktg. — Alfred K. Potter II
VP-Reg. Mgr.-New England — William Gilbane Jr.
VP-Reg. Mgr.-Northeast — Walter Mckelvey
VP-Reg. Mgr.-Midwest — Joseph Clare
VP-Reg. Mgr.-Southwest — David Chapman
VP-Reg. Mgr.-Mid Atlantic — Albert Jaggears

Ginsberg, William Associates
114 E. 32nd St.
New York, NY 10016
tel (212) 686-6661; fax (212) 481-5425
President — R.K. Ginsberg

Global Graphics Inc.
11640 W. 90th St.
Overland Park, KS 66214
tel (913) 541-8886; fax (913) 541-8960
President — John F. Velilla

Global Press Sales Inc.
270 Davidson Ave., Ste. 100
Somerset, NJ 08873
tel (908) 560-9364; fax (908) 560-9422
President — Edward R. Padilla
Vice Pres.-Sales & Mktg. — John A. Pascarella
Sales Manager — Edward J. Uchrin
Engineering Mgr. — David Lukas

Global Turnkey Systems Inc.
20 Waterview Blvd., 3rd Fl.
Parsippany, NJ 07054
tel (201) 331-1010; fax (201) 331-0042
President/CEO — Robert E. Farina
Vice Pres.-Software — Stephen V. Langer
Vice Pres.-Finance — Michael R. Winer
Vice Pres.-Cus. Svc. — Christine Campbell
Sales & Mktg. — Michael Fitzgerald

GMA Inc.
2980 Ave. B
Bethlehem, PA 18017
tel (610) 694-9494; fax (610) 694-0776
President/CEO — Randy R. Seidel
Dir.-Customer Service — Frank Berry

Exec. VP-Sales & Mktg. — Richard M. Connor
Vice Pres.-Specific Projects — Walter Hatt
Vice Pres.-Operations — Ron Karpovich
Vice Pres.Fin. Admn. — Charles Spierto
Director-Mktg. Svc. — Carl Bahn
Contoller — Clayton Henke
Regional Sales Director — Skip Connors
Regional Sales Director — Robert Mongold
Regional Sales Director — Tom Stuart
Regional Sales Director — John Jakopin
Regional Sales Mgr. — Terry Connors
Regional Sales Mgr. — Keith Hockenbery
Regional Sales Mgr. — Hamed Seyedi

GMTI-Gannett Media Technical International
151 W. 4th St., 2nd Fl.
Cincinnati, OH 45202
tel (513) 665-7777; fax (513) 241-7219
e-mail dzito@gmti.gannett.com
President/CEO — Daniel Zito

Rene Gnam Consultation Corp.
3 Response Rd.
Tarpon Springs, FL 34689-8500
tel (813) 938-1555; fax (813) 934-0416
Client Services — Lisa Hart

Go Plastics Inc.
79 Shoemaker St.
Kitchener, ON N2E 3B5 Canada
tel (519) 894-9498; fax (519) 894-9966
Mktg. Mgr. — Brian Bauman

M. Golda Engineering
433 Soland Dr.
Benicia, CA 94510
tel (707) 745-6073; fax (707) 745-6073
Mktg. Mgr. — Robert W. Johnson

Gomm & Co. Inc.
27025 Smithson Valley
San Antonio, TX 78261
tel (210) 366-9366; fax (210) 366-1600
Pres./Vice Pres. — R. Gary Gomm
Consultant — Haney Wolmack

Gowe Printing Co.
620 E. Smith Rd.
Medina, OH 44256
tel (216) 725-4161; fax (216) 225-4531
Vice Pres./Gen. Mgr. — Jim Hoch

GP Plastics Corp.
904 Regal Row (75247); PO Box 560584
Dallas, TX 75356
tel (800) 527-9459; fax (214) 689-3920
Sales Mgr. — Pamela Hauserman

Grace Tec/W.R. Grace & Co.
830 Prosper Rd.; PO Box 30
Depere, WI 54115
tel (414) 336-5715; fax (414) 336-3404

President — Alan Fiers
Sales Dir. — Lawrence M. Miller

Grafica Worldwide Inc.
50 Main St., 10th Fl.
White Plains, NY 10606
tel (914) 761-6360; fax (914) 761-0597
President — Hank F. Damhuis

Grafitek International
3620-21 Netaji Subhash Marg
New Delhi, 110 002 India
tel (91-11) 32 66055
fax (91-11) 32 73136
Managing Director — Anil Raghbeer
Technical Director — Arun Jain
GM-Export — Taposh Chatterjee

Graham Co.
8800 W. Bradley Rd.; PO Box 23880
Milwaukee, WI 53223
tel (414) 355-8800
fax (414) 355-6117
Exec. Vice Pres. — Chuck Manv
Mktg. Mgr. — Roger Maves

Graph X Inc.
444 E. Susquehanna St.
Allentown, PA 18103
tel (610) 797-5515; fax (610) 797-8740
e-mail graphxinc@aol.com
President — Douglas S. Turner
Vice Pres.-Systems — James B. Pfeiffer

Graphic Arts Monthly
249 W. 17th St.
New York, NY 10011
tel (212) 463-6834; fax (212) 463-6530
Publisher — Ron Andriani
Promotion Mgr. — Dorian Torregrossa

Graphic Arts Technical & Consulting Services
867 Astoria Blvd.
Long Island City, NY 11102
tel (718) 721-3737; fax (718) 721-3998
President — Albert S. Canale
Research Dir. — Bernard Cohn

Graphic Enterprises
PO Box 5507
Weirs Beach, NH 03247-5507
tel (603) 293-4715; fax (603) 293-2855
President — Alfred F. Jagusch Jr.

Graphic Enterprises of Ohio Inc.
3874 Higland Park N.W.; PO Box 3080
North Canton, OH 44720-8080
tel (216) 494-9694/(800) 321-9874
fax (216) 494-5481
CFO — Daryl Miller
President/CEO — Rich Jusseaume
Corp. VP-Sales & Mktg. — Les Beyeler
Sys. Integration Mgr. — Bob Behringer
Public Relations — Deborah L. Combs

A DONALD G. MUTERT COMPANY

FRANKLIN WIRE WORKS, INC.

Franklin Wire Works, Inc. is dedicated and committed to providing the best newspaper rack in the business.

- QUALITY POINT OF PURCHASE DISPLAYS
- STOCKING PROGRAMS
- CUSTOM DISPLAY DESIGNS AVAILABLE
- MANUFACTURER DIRECT
- WIRE AND TUBING SPECIALISTS
- MIDWEST LOCATION

1-800-399-8680
F.W.W.

20 Years Experience In The Newspaper Industry.

Copyright ©1996 by the Editor & Publisher Co.

VI-10   Equipment, supplies, services

Graphic Instruments Inc.
9804 Main St.; PO Box 353
Hebron, IL 60034
tel (815) 648-4611; fax (815) 648-2856
President — James Anzelmo

Graphic Printing Roller Ltd.
343 Rodick Rd., #6
Markham, ON L6G 1B1 Canada
tel (800) 265-7418; fax (905) 475-3421
General Manager — Brian Venis

Graphic Publishing Systems Inc.
200 Jefferson St.; PO Box 1216
Clinton, MS 39056
tel (601) 924-0405; fax (601) 924-4769
Gen. Mgr. — Bob Gilmore

Graphic System Services
120 E. Railroad Ave.
Bensenville, IL 60106
tel (708) 860-5959; fax (708) 860-6515
Co-Owner — Allan Jardis
Co-Owner — Michael Szczesniak
Co-Owner — Michael Anderson

Graphics Microsystems Inc.
1284 Forgewood Ave.
Sunnyvale, CA 94089-2215
tel (408) 745-7745/(800) 336-1464
fax (408) 747-0222
VP-Mkt. & Sales — Frederick A. Barnes Jr.
Mgr.-Mktg. Comm. & Sales — Patricia Johnson

Graphline
5701 N.W. 94th Ave.
Tamarac, FL 33321
tel (305) 722-3000; fax (305) 724-2299
Mktg. Dir. — Pat Yonker
Mktg. Dir. APP — Tom Brancato

GraphLine Inc.
5701 N.W. 94th Ave.
Tamarac, FL 33321
tel (305) 722-3000; fax (305) 724-2330
President — Mike Ostroff
Exec. Vice Pres./CFO — Ray Domis
VP-Finance & Operations — Ralph Theile

Great Southern Corp. (Sirco Div.)
PO Box 18710
Memphis, TN 38181
tel (901) 365-1611; fax (901) 365-4498
President/Manager — Scott Vaught
Vice Pres. — Steve Vaught

Greenwood Partnership, The (A Professional Corp.)
901 Main St.; PO Box 617
Lynchburg, VA 24505
tel (804) 847-3400; fax (804) 845-7938
Man. Partner/PE — William C. Greenwood
Partner/PE — Donald P. Manning
Partner/CPA — Michael E. Watson
Partner/PE — B. Gordon Watkins
Partner/PE — David A. Kincaid

Greerco Corp.
2 Wentworth Dr.; PO Box 187
Hudson, NH 03051
tel (603) 883-5517; fax (603) 882-6025
President — William C. Howes
Vice Pres.-Oper. — Paul V. Hunt II
Engineering Mgr. — Joseph Ciarcia
Inside Sales Mgr. — Charlene Chevalier
Sales Consultant — Charles Miller

W B Grimes & Co. Inc.
PO Box 442
Clarksburg, MD 20871
tel (301) 540-0636; fax (301) 540-0636
President — Larry Grimes
Founder — Walter Grimes
Southern Region — Wren Barnett
Midwest — Dane Claussen
Canada — Bruce Lantz
Canada — Ron Holla
New England — Tom Sexton

Group 1 Software Inc.
4200 Parliament Pl., Ste. 600
Lanham, MD 20706-1844
tel (800) 368-5806/(301) 731-2300
fax (301) 731-0360
Mgr.-PR — Suzanne Porter-Kuchay
Dir.-Mktg. — Ann Jurczyk
Senior Management:
Chmn./CEO — Robert S. Bowen
Pres./COO/Acting VP-Sales — Ronald F. Friedman
Exec. Vice Pres. — Alan P. Slater

Vice Pres.-Fin. — Charles A. Crew
Regional VP-Sales — Max Carnecchia
Regional Vice Pres.-Sales — Steve Bebee
Vice Pres.-Tech Svc. — Sally Campbell
Vice Pres.-Product Dev. — B. Scott Miller

GSP Inc.
4 Broadway Ext.; PO Box 305
Mystic, CT 06355
tel (860) 572-8951/(860) 572-8507
fax (860) 536-3961
President — Erik H. Ljungberg
Vice Pres. — Jens E. Ljungberg
Tech. Dir. — Maurice G. Blanchet
Treasurer — Maija L. Ljungberg

GTI Graphic Technology Inc.
211 Dupont Ave.; Box 3138
Newburgh, NY 12550
tel (914) 562-7066; fax (914) 562-2543
VP-Sales & Mktg. — Robert McCurdy

Gulf Coast System Design Co.
2025 Cattlemen Rd.; PO Box 1746
Sarasota, FL 34230
tel (941) 371-3231; fax (941) 377-6112
President — D.G.B. Lindsay

Norman X Guttman Inc.
3904 10th Ave.
Brooklyn, NY 11219
tel (718) 438-6663; fax (718) 438-5678
President — Daniel Guttman

H

H&M Paster Sales & Service Inc.
PO Box 3135
Kirkland, WA 98083-3135
tel (206) 883-4451; fax (206) 867-9483
President — Steven Bjorklund
Office Mgr. — Heather Lane

Hadronics
4570 Steel Pl.
Cincinnati, OH 45209
tel (513) 321-9350; fax (513) 321-9377
President — Fred Harding
Exec. Vice Pres. — Ken Green
Vice Pres.-Oper. — Mike Green
Vice Pres.-Sales & Mktg. — Eric Harding
Sales Rep. — Jeffrey H. McCarty

George R Hall Inc.
33530 Pin Oak Pkwy.
Avon Lake, OH 44012-2320
tel (216) 933-4100; fax (216) 933-7070
CEO — Graham Hall
President — Richard A. Taylor
Sec./Treas. — Dennis E. Bushman
Asst. Sec. — Richard W. Portmanm
Mgr. Installation Svc. — Arthur Jarrell
Mgr. Installation Svc. — Donald Bish

Hall Processing Systems
2633 N. 37th Ave., Ste. 3
Phoenix, AZ 85009
tel (602) 272-2005; fax (602) 278-2373
President/CEO — Michael Williams

Hamada of America Inc.
110 Arovista Cir.
Brea, CA 92621
tel (714) 990-1999; fax (714) 990-1930
President — T. Tom

Hamilton Circulation Supplies Co.
(Newspaper Mailroom Supplies)
522 Gould; PO Box 398
Beecher, IL 60401
tel (708) 946-2208; fax (708) 946-3733
President — George Hamilton
Vice Pres. — Joseph Beaudry

Hammermill Papers (Div. of International Papers)
6400 Poplar Ave.
Memphis, TN 38197
tel (901) 763-7800; fax (901) 763-6396
Mktg. Dir. — Ken Walsh

Hare Associates Inc.
62 Black Walnut Dr.
Rochester, NY 14615
tel (716) 621-6873
President — Richard L. Hare

Harper Corp. of America (Anilox Roll Supplier)
11625 Steele Creek Rd.; PO Box 410369
Charlotte, NC 28241-0369
tel (704) 588-3371; fax (704) 588-3819

Chairman — Ron Harper
President — Katherine Harper
Vice Pres./Gen. Mgr. — Jim Harper
Vice Pres.-Sales — Dale Patterson
Int'l. Sales & Svc. Coord. — Carlos Carrillo
Dir.-Marketing — Georgia H. Ehrenberg

Harris Corp. (Corporate Headquaters)
1025 W. Nasa Blvd.
Melbourne, FL 32919
tel (407) 727-9100
Chmn./CEO — Phillip W. Farmer
Sr. Vice Pres./Pres./CFO — Bryan R. Roub
VP-Human Resources — Nick E. Heldreth
Pres.-Lanier Worldwide — Wesley E. Cantrell
Pres.-Semiconductor Sector — John Garrett
Pres.-Comm. Sector — Guy W. Numann
VP-Corp. Relations — W. Peter Carney
Vice Pres.-Treas. — Robert W. Fay
VP-Info. Management — Herbert N. McCauley
Vice Pres.-Taxes — David S. Wasserman
VP-Gen. Counsel & Sec. — Richard L. Ballantyne

Harris Publishing Systems Corp.
505 John Rodes Blvd., Bldg. 1
Melbourne, FL 32934-9196
tel (407) 242-5000/(407) 242-5320
fax (407) 242-4074
e-mail tcarnoha@harris.com
Vice Pres.-Sales — Tony Peri
Sales Director — Bill Coates
Mgr.-Nat'l. Accts. — Mike Connell
Mktg. Director — Ron Jones
Dir.-Int'l. Sales — Darlene Schmitt
Mktg. Specialist — Jennifer L. Kennedy
Sales Reps.:
Melbourne Beach, FL — Judson F. Edwards
Riverside, CA — Donald L. Haddix
Cresskill, NJ — Gregory P. Hagopian
Lenexa, KS — David L. Huston
Roseland, NJ — Gerald S. Levitz
Groton, CT — Rodney J. St. Pierre
Englewood, CO — Gary L. Schwartzkopf

Hart Industries
43 Doran St.
East Haven, CT 06512
tel (203) 469-6344; fax (203) 469-6592
President — Steve Mancuso

Hartcid Industry Inc.
590 Belleville Tpke., Bldg. 5B
Kearny, NJ 07032
tel (201) 955-9191; fax (201) 955-9189
President — Peter J. Harteveld
Vice Pres. — Louis Cid
Office Mgr. — Edward Wilson

Faye Harvey
PO Box 588
Lebanon, MO 65536
tel (417) 532-4506
President — Faye Harvey

The Haskell Co.
Haskell Bldg., 111 Riverside Ave.
Jacksonville, FL 32231-4100
tel (904) 791-4500; fax (904) 791-4699
Sr. Vice Pres. — Michael M. Pusich, AIA

Hasselblad USA Inc. (Electronic Imaging)
10 Madison Rd.
Fairfield, NJ 07004
tel (201) 227-7320; fax (201) 227-3249
Mgr.-Elec. Imaging — Rudolph J. Guttosch

Heidelberg Harris Inc.
121 Broadway
Dover, NH 03820-3290
tel (603) 743-5610; fax (603) 749-3301
Chairman — Wolfgang Pfizenmaier
President — Robert A. Brown
Mktg. Mgr. — David S. Noel
Vice Pres.-Eng. — Richard L. McKrell
Vice Pres.-Cus. Svc. — Spencer Mieras
Vice Pres.-Fin. — A. James Garde
Vice Pres.-Mktg. — John M. Hobby
Vice Pres.-Sales — Mark J. Levin

Heidelberg USA
1000 Gutenberg Dr.
Kennesaw, GA 30144
tel (770) 419-6641; fax (770) 419-6625
Advg. Dir. — Joe Niehueser

Heidelberg USA
250 E. Grand Ave., Ste. 35
South San Francisco, CA 94080
tel (415) 873-0490; fax (415) 873-2054
Regional Mgr. — Charles Bloom

Heitz Service Corp.
34-11 62nd St.; PO Box 427
Woodside, NY 11377
tel (718) 565-0004; fax (718) 565-2582
President — Karl Heitz
Vice Pres. — Loretta Rosas

Herco Graphic Products
1215 Karl Ct., Ste. 201; PO Box 369
Wauconda, IL 60084
tel (708) 526-1300; fax (708) 526-7813
President — Gary Klawinski
Dir.-Sales — Christine Sanko

Hercules Inc.
1313 N. Market St., Hercules Plz.
Wilmington, DE 19894-0001
tel (800) 247-4372
COB/CEO — Thomas L. Gossage
Sr. Vice Pres.-Admn. — Robert J.A. Fraser
Sr. Vice Pres./CFO — R. Keith Elliott
Group Vice Pres. — Vincent J. Corbo
Group Vice Pres. — C. Doyle Miller
Group Vice Pres. — Thomas G. Tepas
Vice Pres. — James D. Beach

Hewlett Packard Co.
3000 Hannover St.
Palo Alto, CA 94304-1181
tel (415) 857-1501/ (415) 813-3137
(PR Line)

HFW Industries
196 Philadelphia St.
Buffalo, NY 14207
tel (716) 875-3380; fax (716) 875-3385
Vice Pres.-Sales — Robert Kelley

Hobart Brothers Co.
600 W. Main St.
Troy, OH 45373
tel (513) 332-4000; fax (513) 332-4336
President — Frank Anderson
Vice Pres.-Mktg. & Sales — Ray Shook

Hoechst Printing Products North America
50 Meister Ave.; PO Box 3700
Somerville, NJ 08876
tel (800) 2-HERKST/(908) 231-5000
fax (908) 231-5209
Vice Pres./Gen. Mgr. — Perry Premdas
Dir.-Sales & Mktg. — Thomas Saggiomo
Communications — Diane J. Cielo

Honeywell Information Systems
2701 4th Ave. S.
Minneapolis, MN 55408
tel (612) 951-1000/(612) 951-1707
(Response Center)
Vice Pres. CIS — Bill Sanders

Horizon Software Inc.
4764 Norrisville Rd.
White Hall, MD 21161
tel (410) 557-8350
President — James E. Natale

Horizons Inc.
18531 S. Miles Rd.
Cleveland, OH 44128
tel (216) 475-0555; fax (216) 475-6507
Vice Pres.-Mktg. — Rod Richards
Vice Pres.-Mktg — Wayne Duignan

The House of Grids
PO Box 424
Tallmadge, OH 44278
tel (216) 794-9751; fax (216) 794-1434
Sales Mgr. — Don Martin

Howtek
21 Park Ave.
Hudson, NH 03051
tel (603) 882-5200; fax (603) 880-3843
CEO — David Bothwell
COO — Russell Leonard
Chairman — Robert Howard
Vice Pres.-Sales — Robert Dusseault

Hughes Network Systems Inc.
11717 Exploration Ln.
Germantown, MD 20876
tel (301) 428-5500; fax (301) 428-1868
e-mail hns.com
Dir.-Mktg. Comm. — Judy Blake

Hurletron Inc.
1938 E. Fairchild St.
Danville, IL 61832
tel (217) 446-6500; fax (217) 446-3286
Dir.-Mktg. & Sales — Darryl Bergmann
Gen. Mgr. — M. Klein

Hyphen Inc.
16 Upton Dr.
Wilmington, MA 01887
tel (508) 988-0880; fax (508) 988-0879
Exec. VP/GM — Richard Steensma

Copyright ©1996 by the Editor & Publisher Co.

Equipment, supplies, services

I

IBC/Integrated Business Computers
2685 Park Center Dr.
Simi, CA 93063
tel (805) 527-8792; fax (805) 527-6362
e-mail randyj@ibc.com
President — Randall Huddleston
Vice Pres.-Mktg. — Randy Johnson
Sales Mgr. — Arun Vaishampayan

IBM Corp.
Old Orchard Rd.
Armonk, NY 10504
tel (617) 895-2222
CEO — Lewis Gerstner
VP-Worldwide Sales & Services — Neb Lautenbach
Vice Pres.-Mktg. — Abby Kohnstamm
Mgr.-Media Industry — Bernard Bailey

IC Systems Solutions
270 Broadway
Hillsdale, NJ 07642
tel (201) 666-1122
Vice Pres. — Philip K. Nolan
Sr. Acct. Mgr. — Douglas K. Nolan

Icanon Associates Inc.
275 Commerce Dr., Ste. 214
Ft. Washington, PA 19034
tel (215) 653-0754; fax (215) 653-0829
Contact — Joe Lewinski

IdeaFisher Systems Inc.
2222 Martin St., Ste. 110
Irvine, CA 92715
tel (714) 474-8111; fax (714) 757-2896
CEO — Marsh Fisher

Ideal Equipment (of America) Inc.
4701 Rivard St.
Montreal, QC H2J 2N5 Canada
tel (514) 845-9291; fax (514) 845-2652
Vice Pres.-Sales — Alan Pollock

Illumination Industries, See UVP Inc.

ImagiTex Inc.
75 Northeastern Blvd.
Nashua, NH 03062
tel (603) 889-6600; fax (603) 889-0088
President — Gary Moore
Finance Mgr. — Dick Lacasse
Dir.-Bus. Development — Nick Haddon
Dir.-Mktg. — Ray Vermokowitz

Imaje Ink Jet Printing
1650 Airport Rd.
Kennesaw, GA 30144
tel (770) 421-7700; fax (770) 421-7702
Show Mgr. — Eileen Wildt

Imapro Corp.
2400 St. Laurent Blvd.
Ottawa, ON K1G 5A4 Canada
tel (613) 738-3000/(613) 738-3000 ext. 281 (Sales); fax (613) 738-5038
President — Goffredo (Fred) Andreone
Sales & Mktg. Spec. — Peter Beninger
Secretary — Karen Lo

Imo Industries Inc. (Fincor Electrics Div.)
3750 E. Market St.
York, PA 17402
tel (717) 751-4200; fax (717) 751-4372
Mktg. Mgr. — Ron Eichelberger

Imperial Metal & Chemical Co. (Div. of Dupont)
2050 Byberry Rd.
Philadelphia, PA 19116-3016
tel (215) 671-1200; fax (215) 677-1979
COO — Harry J. Moroz Jr.

IMSI
1895 Francisco Blvd. E.
San Rafael, CA 94901
tel (415) 257-3000; fax (415) 257-3565
e-mail http://www.imsisoft.com
VP-Sales & Int'l. Mktg. — Robert Mayer
Dir.-Mktg. — Rob Halligan
Mktg. Mgr. — Karen Davies

The Inco Company
PO Box 110636-M
Cleveland, OH 44111
tel (216) 281-2252; fax (216) 281-6865
President — Clark Craven

Industrial Acoustics Co.
1160 Commerce Ave.
Bronx, NY 10462
tel (718) 931-8000; fax (718) 863-1138
Dir.-Comm. — Zachary Jaquett

Industrial Noise Control Inc.
1411 Jeffrey Dr.
Addison, IL 60101
tel (800) 954-1998; fax (800) 420-4928
Mktg. Dir. — Kathy Bauer

Infocom Systems
1209 Central Ave. S., Ste. 140
Kent, WA 98032
tel (206) 859-0700; fax (206) 852-4713
CEO — Bob Lewis

INFO-CONNECT (J.H. Zerby Newspapers Inc.)
111 Mohantongo St.
Pottsville, PA 17901
tel (717) 628-6076; fax (717) 621-3308
e-mail sesmith@ricnet.pottsville.com
Director — Jim D. Bie
Director-Sales & Marketing — Sharon E. Smith

Information Engineering
3 Preston Ct.
Bedford, MA 01730
tel (617) 275-3870; fax (617) 276-9402
e-mail mikem@sdc.tiac.net
President — Michael McKenna

Ingenuity Inc.
2506 W. 6th St.
Amarillo, TX 79106
tel (806) 373-5050; fax (806) 371-8358
President/CEI — Dale P. Roush
Exec. Admn. — Beverley Mahan
Gen. Mgr. — Bennie Garcia
Parts Mgr. — Ron Mastick

Ingersoll-Rand-Aro Fluid Product Div.
1 Aro Ctr.
Bryan, OH 43506
tel (419) 636-4242; fax (419) 636-2115
Sales Prom. Mgr. — Russ Davies

Ingersoll-Rand Corp./Power Tool & Hoist Div.
PO Box 1776
Liberty Corner, NJ 07938
tel (908) 647-6000; fax (908) 647-6007
Vice Pres./Gen. Mgr. — Joseph Kiah

The Ink Co.
1115 Shore St.
West Sacramento, CA 95691
tel (916) 372-2452; fax (916) 372-1860
President — George Tholke
Dir.-Corp. Svcs. — Bob Throckmorton

Inland Graphics International L.C.
9990 S.W. 77th Ave., Ste. 315
Miami, FL 33156
tel (305) 271-6118; fax (305) 271-0841
President — Beau Campbell
Int'l. Sales Dir. — Charles Kuryla
Mktg. Dir. — Thomas Jacobson

Inland Newspaper Machinery Corp.
14500 W. 105th St.; PO Box 15999
Lenexa, KS 66215
tel (913) 492-9050/(800) 255-6746
fax (913) 492-6217
President — Beau Campbell
Sales Mgr. — Jim Allison
Sales Rep. — Jim Arensberg

Inland Press Association Inc.
777 Busse Hwy.
Park Ridge, IL 60068
tel (708) 696-1140; fax (708) 696-2463
e-mail inlander 1 e@aol.com
Exec. Dir. — Ray Carlsen

Innovative Systems Design Inc.
16025A Pierrefonds Blvd.
Pierrefonds, QC H9H 3X6 Canada
tel (514) 696-8377; fax (514) 696-9016
Sales Manager — Jeff Tierney
Sales Rep. — Dave Dorman

Insurance Specialties Services Inc.
3503 York Rd., Buckingham Commons; PO Box 515
Furlong, PA 18925
tel (800) 533-4579; fax (215) 794-8537
President — Kenneth P. Smith

Integrated Newspaper Systems Inc.
50 W. State St., Ste. 1202
Trenton, NJ 08608-1298
tel (609) 393-9293; fax (609) 393-9491
Mktg. Spec. — Georgine Maciolek
Exec. Vice Pres. — Jean B. Clifton
Vice Pres. — Allen J. Mailman

Intelligence Technology Corp.
16526 Westgrove
Dallas, TX 75248
tel (214) 265-8344
President — Walker Morris

Inter-Continental Web Inc.
11640 W. 90th St.
Overland Park, KS 66214
tel (913) 438-5800; fax (913) 438-5801
President — John F. Velilla
Sales Coordinator — Judith E. Wenzel

Interlake (Power Strap Div.)
6843 Santa Fe Dr.
Hodgkins, IL 60525
tel (800) 346-4600; fax (708) 482-9562
Vice Pres.-Sales & Mktg. — Tom Gould

Interlake Packaging Corp.
6843 Santa Fe Dr.
Hodgkins, IL 60525
tel (800) 323-4424; fax (708) 482-9562
Vice Pres.-Sales & Mktg. — Tom Gould

Interlink
PO Box 207
Berrien Springs, MI 49103
tel (616) 473-3103; fax (616) 473-1190
e-mail interfun1@aol.com
Pres.-Sales — William E. Garber

International Memory Products of Illinois Inc.
225 Larkin Dr.
Wheeling, IL 60090
tel (708) 537-8000/(800) 323-6322
fax (708) 537-1414
President — Robert Rosenfeld
Sales Rep. — Kelly Schneider

International Paper Box Machine
90 Northeastern Blvd.; PO Box 787
Nashua, NH 03061-0787
tel (603) 889-6651; fax (603) 882-2865
President — Louis C. Chagnon
Vice Pres./CFO — Donald Millek
Mktg. Dir. — Michael A. Sutcliffe
Sales & Mktg Mgr. — Jeffery Watts

The International School For Pressroom Management
3526 Raymond Ave.
Brookfield, IL 60513
tel (708) 485-6973; fax (708) 485-1019
President — Frank Drazan

International Trademark Association
1133 Ave. of the Americas
New York, NY 10036
tel (212) 768-9887; fax (212) 768-7796
Exec. Dir. — Robin Rolfe

Inx International Ink Co.
5501 W. Mill Rd.
Milwaukee, WI 53218
tel (414) 438-4383; fax (414) 438-4390
Chairman — M. Matsuzawa
President — Frank Moravec
Vice Pres.-Mktg. Dir. — G. Stromberg

IRIS Graphics Inc. (Marketed By Scitex America)
6 Crosby Dr.
Bedford, MA 01730
tel (617) 275-8777; fax (617) 275-8590
Vice Pres.-Sales — Robert Dusseault
Mktg. Dir. — Alan Renda

Irving Forest Products Inc.
120 White Plains Rd.
Tarrytown, NY 06836-2535
tel (914) 332-8850; fax (914) 332-9182
Office Mgr. — Bonnie D. Munro
Vice Pres.-Sales — Jorge Santelli
Regional Sales Mgr.-Specialty Papers — Gerry Benavides
Oper. Tech. Support — Greg Sampson
Vice Pres.-Tech. Dir. — J. Kirk

Isomet Corp.
5263 Port Royal Rd.
Springfield, VA 22151
tel (703) 321-8301; fax (703) 321-8546
Dir.-Sales & Mktg Systems — Phill Solow

J

James River Corp.
300 Lakeside Dr., Rm. 1493
Oakland, CA 94612-3592
tel (510) 874-3400; fax (510) 874-3497
VP-Converting & Specialty Papers — Bob Morgan
Bus. Mgr.-Groundwood Specialities — Gary Haskett
Mktg. Communications — Mary Plimpton

Jardis Industries Inc. (Cary Equipment Div.)
120 Railroad Ave.
Bensenville, IL 60106
tel (708) 860-5959; fax (708) 860-6515
President — Alan W. Jardis
Chief Eng. — Robert LaBarre
Controller — David D. Hansen
Director-Sales — Gary M. Klawinski
South American Sales — Mike Anderson

Jaye Communications
550 Interstate N. Pkwy., Ste. 150
Atlanta, GA 30339
tel (770) 984-9444; fax (770) 933-9072/(770) 612-0780
Vice Pres.-Mktg. — Alexis Caldwell

John Juliano Computer Services Co.
215 Church St., Ste. 205
Decatur, GA 30030
tel (404) 377-9450; fax (404) 377-9931
e-mail jjcs@jjcs.com
President — John Juliano
Acct. Exec. — Tor Hansen

Johnstone Engineering & Machine Co.
315 1st Ave. & S. Gay St.
Parkesburg, PA 19365
tel (215) 857-5511; fax (215) 857-1425
Sales Mgr. — C.J. Lauletta

Jomac Inc.
863 Easton Rd.
Warrington, PA 18976
tel (215) 343-0800; fax (215) 343-0912
Chairman/Pres. — William S. Colehower

Just Normlicht Inc.
1504 Grundy's Ln.
Bristol, PA 19007
tel (215) 860-5878; fax (215) 860-6229
Nat'l. Sales Mgr. — Joseph Murray
Sales Mgr. — Mary Ellen Riederer
Sales Mgr. — Cyndi Rauch

K

K & F/Printing Systems International
12633 Industrial Park Dr.; PO Box 340
Granger, IN 46530
tel (219) 272-9950/(800) 348-5070
fax (219) 277-6566
N. American Mktg. Dir. — Joseph A. Bella
Int'l. Mktg. Dir. — Terry Kelly

K-Jack Engineering Co. Inc.
1522 W. 134th St.; PO Box 47090
Gardena, CA 90249
tel (310) 327-8389/(800) 77K-JACK
fax (310) 769-6999
President — Jack S. Chalabian
VP — Jacqueline Chalabian-Jernigan
Exec. Asst. — Harlene Chalabian

Kaim & Associates Int'l. Marketing Inc.
W10980 Lakeview Dr.
Lodi, WI 53555
tel (608) 592-7404/North America (800) 729-9327; fax (608) 592-7504
President — Wayne Kaim

Kevin Brian Kamen & Co.
2355 Pershing Blvd., Ste. 301
Baldwin, New York 11510
tel (516) 379-2797/(813) 786-5930
President — Kevin Brian Kamen

Kanaly Financial Health Club
4550 Post Oak Pl., Ste. 139
Houston, TX 77027
tel (800) 882-8723; fax (713) 877-8744
Mktg. Mgr. — Beth Woehler

Kansa Corp. (Baldwin Technology Co.)
3700 Oakes Dr.; PO Box 668
Emporia, KS 66801
tel (316) 343-6700; fax (316) 343-2108
President — Jerry Waddell
Vice Pres./Dir.-Mktg. — Ron Swint
Nat'l. Sales Mgr. — Steve Spencer
Service Mgr. — Joe Zumbrum

Kaspar Wire Works Inc./Sho-Rack
1127 Sho Rack Dr.; PO Box 667
Shiner, TX 77984
tel (512) 594-2911/(800) 527-1134
fax (512) 594-4264
Vice Pres.-Sales — David C. Kaspar
Gen. Sales Mgr. — Cliff Long

Copyright ©1996 by the Editor & Publisher Co.

VI-12 Equipment, supplies, services

Cust. Svc. Mgr. — Chris Stlucka
Sys. Analyst — Jenette Berkovsky
Sales Consultant — Don Wallace
Sales — Vincent Savickas
Sales — Bill Dempsey
Sales — Gordon Fales
Sales — Dick Bailey
Sales — Bruce Tischer
Sales — Gary Grosz
Sales — Barry Schopp
Sales — Bill Alexander
Sales — Kevin Grady
Sales — Mike Kaczmarek
Sales — Donnie Saxon
Sales — Bob Sanders
Sales — George Welsey
Sales — Darrel Clements

KBA-Motter Corp. (Koenig & Bauer-Albert Group)
3900 E. Market St.; PO Box 1562
York, PA 17405
tel (717) 755-1071; fax (717) 755-2327
President/CEO — Scott R. Smith
Vice. Pres./CFO — Gerrit Zwergel
Vice Pres.-K&B Sales — Heinz Schmid
Dir.-Newspaper Sales — Gary Owen
Nat'l. Accts. Mgr. — Bruce Richardson

The Keenan Group Inc.
208 Ren-Mar Dr.; PO Box 458
Pleasantview, TN 37146-0458
tel (800) 229-0922/(615) 746-2443
fax (615) 746-2270
President — Robert P. Keenan Sr.
Vice Pres.-Sales, Advg. & Mktg. — Debra B. Keenan
Bookkeeping — Lisa Emord
Sales Dir. — Joe D. Moore
Sales-Newspaper Div. — Greg Bolden
Sales-Newspaper Div. — John Knowles
Cus. Svc. Rep. — Julie Lewendowski
Cus. Svc. Rep. — Suzette Chavez
Prod. Coord.-Printing — Lindsey Doris
Graphic Designer — Joe Walton

Keene Technology Inc. (KTI)
14357 Commercial Pkwy.
South Beloit, IL 61080
tel (815) 624-8989; fax (815) 624-4223
President — John Keene
Sales Mgr. — Darrel D. Spors

Kidder Inc.
270 Main St.
Agawam, MA 01001
tel (413) 786-8692; fax (413) 786-8785
President — Charles Rae

King Corp., See Solna Web USA Inc.

King Press Corp.
13th & Maiden Ln.; PO Box 21
Joplin, MO 64802-0021
tel (800) 781-0914; fax (417) 781-4002
COB — Evans Kostas
Vice Pres.-Eng. — Cliff Eighmy
Vice Pres.-Fin. — Terry Riley
Vice Pres.-Int'l Sales — Lou Patoto
Vice Pres.-Cus. Svc. — Julius Rosewicz
Vice Pres.-Manuf. — Chuck Winscott
Contract Admin. — Neina Bellm
Mgr.-Contract Admin. — Roger Kaughman
Reg. Mgr. — Geoff Symanek
Reg. Mgr. — John Peck

Kirk-Rudy Inc.
2700 Due W. Dr.
Kennesaw, GA 30144
tel (404) 427-4203; fax (404) 427-4036
President — Melvin R. Collins

Knight-Ridder Information Inc.
2440 El Camino Real
Mountain View, CA 94040
tel (415) 254-7000; fax (415) 254-8000
Mktg. Mgr. — Susan Higgins

Knowledge Unlimited
PO Box 52
Madison, WI 53701
tel (800) 356-2303; fax (608) 831-1570
Mktg. Mgr. — Nancy Ketterhagan

Knox Accounts Service
912 Main St.; PO Box 892
Vincennes, IN 47591
tel (812) 882-0909; fax (812) 882-6171
Mktg. Mgr. — Terry Grimes

Koenig & Bauer- Albert AG (KBA)
Postfach 6060
Wuerzburg, D 97010 Germany
tel (49-931) 9090; fax (49-931) 9094101
President — Reinhart Siewert
Vice Pres.-Sales — Burkard Roos
Mktg. Mgr. — Klaus Schmidt

Komori America Corp.
5520 Meadowbrook Industrial Ct.
Rolling Meadows, IL 60008
tel (708) 806-9000; fax (708) 806-9038
President — Hiro Abe
Exec. Vice Pres. — Harry McMillan
Vice Pres. — John W. Goodell
Vice Pres. — James E. Scott
Vice Pres. — David Maret

Konica Imaging USA Inc.
71 Charles St.
Glen Cove, NY 11542
tel (516) 674-2500; fax (516) 676-4124
e-mail rhf@ix.netcom.com
President — Hideaki Iwama
Vice Pres.-Mktg. — Robert Feldberg
Sr. Vice Pres.-Fin. — John Orlando
Sr. VP-Mktg.,Sales & Svc. — Steve Schuster

Kreonite Inc.
715 E. 10th St.; PO Box 2099
Wichita, KS 67201-2099
tel (316) 263-1111/(800) 835-1032
fax (316) 263-6829
President/Mktg. Dir. — Carl Best
Vice Pres.-Graphic Arts — Bob Irving

Krohm International
4216 S. Hocker Dr., Ste. 200
Smith Independence, MO 64055-4766
tel (816) 373-7828; fax (816) 373-8990
Mktg. Mgr. — Gary Krohm

Kruger Pulp & Paper Sales Inc.
489 Fifth Ave.
New York, NY 10017
tel (212) 697-9700; fax (212) 972-4680
Mgr.-Admn. — George Monk

Krypton Systems
5-2100 Thurston Dr., Ste. 100
Ottawa, ON K1G 4K8 Canada
tel (613) 738-3175; fax (613) 738-3176
President — Gautam Subra
Vice Pres. — Nizar Hammad

Kye International Corp.
2605 E. Cedar St.; PO Box 51474
Ontario, CA 91761
tel (909) 923-3510; fax (909) 923-5494

L

Lamb-Grays Harbor Co.
Blaine and Firman Sts.; PO Box 359
Hoquiam, WA 98550
tel (360) 532-1000; fax (360) 533-2549
Mgr.-Contracts — Ernie Howard
Mgr.-Engineering — Hal Arnold

Laser Products Technologies
N5554 Abbey Rd.
Onalaska, WI 54650
tel (608) 781-1606; fax (608) 781-1626
Mktg. Mgr. — Bob King

LaserMaster Corp.
6900 Shady Oak Rd.
Eden Prairie, MN 55344
tel (612) 944-9457; fax (612) 943-3469
Editor — Tony Shen

Layton Marketing Group Inc.
1212 Red Fox Rd.
St. Paul, MN 55112
tel (612) 490-5000; fax (612) 490-9409
CEO — Les Layton
COO — Joe Brunner

Lazer-fare Media Services Ltd.
916 Grosvenor Ave.
Winnipeg, MB R3B ON4 Canada
tel (204) 452-5023; fax (204) 452-5061

Le Cotton & Co.
5711 Florin-Perkins Rd., Ste. H
Sacramento, CA 95828
tel (916) 387-1440; fax (916) 387-1619
Owner — Ada Wright

Leadership Advertising Development Co.
25 Azalea Dr.
Syosset, NY 11791
tel (516) 921-5079
President — Daniel Lionel

Leaf Systems Inc.
8 Technology Dr.
Westboro, MA 01581
tel (508) 836-5500/(508) 836-5588
(Tech & Sales); fax (508) 836-5599
Vice Pres.-Mktg. — Susan Willerd

Learning Tree International
1805 Library St.
Reston, VA 22090
tel (800) 843-8733; fax (800) 709-6405
e-mail uscourses@learningtree.com
www.learningtree.com
Mgr.-Educational Services — Linda Trude

Leber Ink (US Ink)
17300 W. Valley Hwy. (Tukwila, 98188);
PO Box 88700
Seattle, WA 98138
tel (206) 251-8700; fax (206) 226-8774
Sales Mgr. — Vern Bates

Peter A. Lendrum Architects
4350 E. Camelback Rd., Ste. C200
Phoenix, AZ 85018
tel (602) 952-2800; fax (602) 952-8300
President — Peter A. Lendrum

Levien Instruments Co.
PO Box 31
McDowell, VA 24458
tel (703) 396-3345
Sales — J R Levien

LEXIS-NEXIS
9443 Springboro Pike; PO Box 933
Dayton, OH 45401
tel (800) 227-9597
e-mail elizabeth.ashton@lexis-nexis.com
Pres./CEO — Ira Siegel
Product Mgr.-Newview Solution — Betsy Ashton

LiftSafe Systems Inc.
PO Box 1241
Westfield, MA 01086-1241
tel (413) 568-9646; fax (413) 568-9646
President — Chuck Jasa
Vice Pres. — Orinda Jerue
Reg. Sales Mgr. — Bob Wensley

Lincoln Industrial
1 Lincoln Way
St. Louis, MO 63120-1578
tel (314) 679-4200; fax (314) 679-4433
President — John Little
VP-Product Eng. & Quality — Pete Laucis
Vice Pres.-Sales & Mktg. — Jim Grove
Vice Pres. Oper. — Steve Hager
Mgr.-Mktg. Svc. — Jerry O'Brien

Linde-Baker Material Handling Corp.
2450 W. 5th North St.; PO Box 2400
Summerville, SC 29484
tel (803) 875-8000; fax (803) 875-8380
President — Mitch Milovich
VP-Sales & Mktg. — Nelson C. Henry
Mktg. Dir. — S. Craig Plank

Linotype-Hell Co.
145 Pinelawn Rd.
Melville, NY 11747
tel (516) 434-2000; fax (516) 434-2748
President — Edward LaGraice
Vice Pres.-Sales — Scott Rimmer
Mgr.-Newspaper Sales & Mktg. — Bob Larsen
Mktg. Mgr. — Jon Guerringue

Litco International Inc.
One Litco Dr.
Vienna, OH 44473
tel (216) 539-5433; fax (216) 539-5388
President — Lionel F. Trebilcock
Vice Pres. — Gary L. Trebilcock
Gen. Sales Mgr.-Molded Wood Products Group — Gary A. Sharon
Controller — Thomas Paskert

Lockwood Greene Engineers Inc.
PO Box 491
Spartanburg, SC 29304
tel (803) 578-2000/(800) 845-3302
fax (803) 599-0436
Pres./Chmn./CEO — Donald R. Luger
Dir.-Newpaper Div. — Mike Luciano
Group Mgr.-Corp. Bus. Dev. — Owen Olson
VP-Corp. Bus. Dev. & Mktg. — Steve Dickman
Mktg. Coord. — Charis D. Jolliffe

LogEtronics Corp.
7001 Loisdale Rd.
Springfield, VA 22150
tel (703) 971-1400; fax (703) 971-9325
President — Raymond Luca
Vice Pres.-Oper. — Al Royston
Dir.-Dealer Sales-West — Roger Taylor
Dir.-Dealer Sales-East — Gary Aheimer
Dir.-OEM Sales — Frank Kensek
Dir.-Int'l. Sales — Richard Kavesh

The Loki Group Inc.
2720 W. Jerome
Chicago, IL 60645
tel (312) 761-4654; fax (312) 761-4825
e-mail dave@loki.com
President — David Rose
Vice Pres. — Stephanie C. Harding
Vice Pres. — Edward A. Heinrich

London Litho Aluminum Co. Inc.
7100 N. Lawndale Ave.
Lincolnwood, IL 60645
tel (708) 679-4600; fax (708) 679-6453
President — Eric London
Chairman — Melvyn London

James Lorenzen & Associates
2100 Lee Rd., Ste. E.
Winter Park, FL 32789
tel (407) 740-8865/(800) 257-6659
fax (407) 740-5519
Owner — James Lorenzen

Loudon Plastics
787 Watervliet-Shaker Rd.
Latham, NY 12110
tel (518) 783-7776/(800) 833-3800
fax (518) 783-0004
President — Dom DeMichelle
Vice Pres. — Bob Reiuik

Lubriplate Div./Fiske Bros. Refining Co.
129 Lockwood St.
Newark, NJ 07105
tel (201) 589-9150; fax (201) 589-4432
President — F.J. Snyder Jr.
Vice Pres./Gen. Mgr. — James Girard
Vice Pres./Treas. — Richard T. McCluskey

Lumisys
238 Santa Anna Ct.
Sunnyvale, CA 94086
tel (408) 733-6565
President — Gregory E. Johnson
Worldwide Sales Mgr. — Greg Colston
Worldwide Sales Mgr. — John Calderwood
Marketing Director — Grace Hes

Luwa Bahnson Inc.
PO Box 10458
Winston-Salem, NC 27108
tel (910) 760-3111; fax (910) 760-1548
President — Tim Whitener

Luwa HVAC Filters
10415 Westlake Dr.; PO Box 7263
Charlotte, NC 28241
tel (704) 588-5220; fax (704) 588-5721
Sales Eng. — William P. Kinken
Personnel Asst. — Lisa Roe

M

Macbeth, Div. of Kollmorgen Inst. Corp.
405 Little Britain Rd.
New Windsor, NY 12553-6148
tel (914) 565-7660; fax (914) 561-0390
President — Steve Reber
Advertising — Kristine Schrull
Supervisor Prom. Services — Elaine Tito

The MacDonald Classified Service
14 N. 2nd St.
Lafayette, IN 47901-1204
tel (800) 237-9075; fax (317) 742-2843
Sales Mgr. — Michael Kiser

Machine Design Service Inc.
3535 Larimer St.
Denver, CO 80205
tel (303) 294-0275; fax (303) 294-0634
Pres./Vice Pres. — Peter Nemeth
Marketing — Greg Greenan
East Coast Rep. — Pete Medina

James MacLaren Industries Inc.
2 Monteral Rd., Massom Angers
PO Box 2400
Buckingham, QC J8M 1K6 Canada
tel (819) 986-3345; fax (819) 986-1726
Vice Pres.-Newsprint Sales — Jock Coulson
Great Lakes Div.-Reg'l. Mgr. Newsprint Sales — Donanld C. Westphal
New England Div.-Reg'l. Mgr. Newsprint Sales — William Raby
Regional Sales Mgr. — John P. Doelman
Regional Sales Mgr. — Richard Rumble

Copyright ©1996 by the Editor & Publisher Co.

Equipment, supplies, services — VI-13

MacMillan Bloedel
925 W. Georgia St.
Vancouver, BC U6C 362 Canada
tel (604) 661-8000; fax (604) 683-1702
Vice Pres.-Paper Mktg. — A.N. Small

Macromedia Corp.
600 Townsend St.
San Francisco, CA 94103
tel (415) 252-2000/(800) 888-9335/(800) 288-4797 (Sales)
fax (415) 626-0554
e-mail http://www.macromedia.com
President — John (Bud) C. Colligane
VP-World Wide Sales — Susan Gordon Bird
Manager-PR — Mary Leong

MacSolutions
2441 NW 93rd Ave., Ste. 102
Miami, FL 33172
tel (305) 477-8885; fax (305) 477-7409
e-mail reiner@shadow.net
Gen. Mgr. — Salvador Romero

The Madden Corp.
9 Rockefeller Plz.
New York, NY 10020
tel (212) 246-9373; fax (212) 765-0869
President — Raimo E. Waltasaari
Sr. Vice Pres. — Marcus J. Lindh
Sr. Vice Pres. — Peter Littley
Vice Pres. — Frank A. Torcia
Vice Pres. — Warren Cohen
Treasurer — Joseph E. Rolston

Magnacraft, See McCain Manufacturing Corp.

MAH Machine Co. Inc.
3301 S. Central Ave.
Cicero, IL 60650
tel (708) 656-1826; fax (708) 656-4152
President — Martin Hozjan
Engineer — Peter Bui

Mail Advertising Supply Co.
1450 S. West Ave.; PO Box 363
Waukesha, WI 53187
tel (800) 558-2126/(800) 242-1739

Mailers Equipment Co. Inc. (Mircofilm Products)
20 Squadron Blvd.
New City, NY 11956
tel (914) 634-7676; fax (914) 634-6101
President — Herbert I. Moelis
Vice Pres. — Gary Moelis

Mailing Machine Systems
PO Box 668
Emporia, KS 66801
tel (316) 343-6700; fax (316) 343-2108

Malow Corp.
1835 S. Nordic Rd.
Mt. Prospect, IL 60056
tel (847) 956-0200; fax (847) 956-0935
Mktg. Dir. — Neal Malow

MAN Roland Inc. (Web Press Div.)
115 Pohegaunt Dr.
Groton, CT 06340
tel (860) 499-6400; fax (860) 449-6690
CEO — Hans Schmidt-Liermann
Dir.-Tech. Svc. & Commercial Sales — Joe Abbott
Dir.-Newspaper Sales — Vincent Lapinski

MAN Roland/Aston Div.
81A Brunswick Blvd./DDO
Dollard des Ormeaux, QC H9B 2J5 Canada
tel (514) 335-1942; fax (514) 421-7087
President — R.C. Holliday

Managing Editor Software Inc.
Jenkintown Plz./101 Greenwood Ave.
Ste. 550
Jenkintown, PA 19046
tel (215) 886-5662; fax (215) 886-5681
President — Dennis McGuire
Sales Mgr. — Dana Baseom

Manassy Precision Corp.
37-26 27th St.
Long Island City, NY 11101
tel (718) 392-6800; fax (718) 361-9286
President — Joel Marcus

Manistique Papers Inc.
453 S. Mackinac
Manistique, MI 49854
tel (906) 341-2175; fax (906) 341-5635

Mannschreck
920 S. 6th St.; PO Box 7
St. Joseph, MO 64502
tel (816) 279-0855; fax (816) 279-4105
President — Steve Pitluck

Mantis Computer Parts Inc.
8 Rebel Rd., Unit 2
Hudson, NH 03051
tel (603) 595-5210; fax (603) 595-5209
President — John P. Marshall
Mktg. Mgr. — Dennis A. Doscher

Market Opinion Research/Pace
31700 Middlebelt Rd.
Farmington Hills, MI 48334
tel (810) 737-5300; fax (810) 737-5326
VP-Media Studies Div. — James Buckley
Analyst — Jeffrey Leiman
Librarian — Pat Allmen

Marketing Research Associates Inc.
4901 W. 77th St., Ste. 125
Minneapolis, MN 55435
tel (800) 524-6466
Mktg. Dir. — Adam Scott Day

Marketing Strategies Inc.
10 Forbes Rd.
Braintree, MA 02184
tel (617) 356-5090; fax (617) 356-5948
President — Lloyd F. Thompsom

Marks & Frederick Associates Inc.
135 Eastern Pkwy., 10K
Brooklyn, NY 11238
tel (718) 783-0083; fax (718) 399-6557
e-mail tmarks@pipeline.com
President — Ted Marks

Martin Automatic Inc.
1661 Northrock Ct.
Rockford, IL 61103
tel (815) 654-4800
Comm. Coord. — Jan Crawford
Vice Pres.-Sales — David A. Wright
Contract Admn. — Gavin Rittmeyer
Contract Admn. — Rob Cunningham

James Martin & Associates
3061 Cranston Dr.; PO Box 798
Dublin, OH 43017
tel (614) 889-9747; fax (614) 889-2659
e-mail frfj70d@prodigy.com
President — James Martin
CFO — A.M. Martin

Martin Yale Inc.
251 Wedcor Ave.
Wabash, IN 46992
tel (219) 563-0641; fax (219) 563-4575
President — Bill Reed
Vice Pres.-Eng. — Humbergo Rodriguez
Vice Pres.-Mfg. — Tom Rhoten
Dir.-M.I.S. — Ron Ruper
Dir.-Sales — Dan Wilson
Controller — Rick Grey
Marketing Manager — Ralp Graver

Master Flo Technology
579 Country Rd. 190
Emporia, KS 66801
tel (316) 343-1255; fax (316) 343-1316
Vice Pres.-Sales — Robert Doudican

The Master Group
30 Mathers Rd.
Ambler, PA 19002
tel (215) 643-0060; fax (215) 643-1702
President — Rodney S. Guenst
Gen. Mgr. Oper. — Stephen C. Guenst
Eng. Mgr. — Frank Di Nunzio
Mfg. Mgr. — Andre Pace

Masthead International Inc.
PO Box 1952
Albuquerque, NM 87103
tel (505) 842-1357; fax (505) 243-6058
Vice Pres. — Harry L. Andersen

Wayne Matthews Corp.
PO Box 54
Safety Harbor, FL 34695
tel (813) 726-8431; fax (813) 725-5186

MBG Associates Ltd.
370 Lexington Ave., Ste. 2008
New York, NY 10017
tel (212) 687-8580; fax (212) 557-1348
Contact — Joyce Lenzillo

MBM Corp.
3134 Industry Dr.; PO Box 40249
North Charleston, SC 29418
tel (803) 552-2700; fax (803) 552-2974
President — William Golde
Vice Pres./Sales Mgr. — Thomas Gallagher
Advg. Mgr. — Holly H. Wilson

McCain Manufacturing Corp.
6200 W. 60th St.
Chicago, IL 60638
tel (312) 586-6200; fax (312) 586-6210
President — Tom Carroll
Vice Pres.-Eng. — Ron Weller
Vice Pres.-Sales & Mktg. — Vic Krzyzanski

McCain Printing Co.
PO Box 3443
Danville, VA 24543
tel (804) 792-1331; fax (804) 703-5473
Owner — Eugene Sounders

McClier Corp.
401 E. Illinois St., Ste. 625
Chicago, IL 60611
tel (312) 836-7700; fax (312) 836-7710
Pres.-Newspaper Group — Alan Stromberg
VP-Newspaper Grp. — Frederick K. Rogers

McClure Media Marketing Motivation Co.
19 E. Snapper Pt. Dr.
Key Largo, FL 33037
tel (305) 367-2589; fax (305) 367-3549
President — J. Warren McClure

J. Thomas McHugh Co. Inc.
12931 Ford Dr.
Fishers, IN 46038
tel (800) 543-2750/(317) 577-2121
fax (317) 577-2125
Chairman — Thomas J. Bryant
Vice Pres./Gen. Mgr. — Bill Vincent

MCI
1650 Tyson Blvd.
McLean, VA 22102
tel (800) 888-0800
fax (703) 506-6000/(703) 506-6636

Meadows Co.
2296 John Henry Ln.
Myrtle Beach, SC 29577
tel (800) 344-9001; fax (800) 887-2654
President — Ralph C. Meadows Jr.

Media Advertising Credit Services
238 Chestnut Ave.; PO Box 1011
Vineland, NJ 08360
tel (800) 257-8243/(609) 692-0555
fax (609) 692-0102
President — David Melamed

Media Consultants & Associates
Rural Rte. 1, Box 36
Tunbridge, VT 05077
tel (802) 889-5600; fax (802) 889-5627
Mng. Partner — C. Peter Jorgensen

Media Cybernetics L.P.
8484 Georgia Ave., Ste. 200
Silver Spring, MD 20910
tel (301) 495-3305; fax (301) 495-5964
e-mail sales@mediaci.com
President — Michael Galvin
CFO — Gerard Fleury
Engineering Dir. — Jean-Paul Martin
Chief Tech. Officer — John Schmitz
Mktg. Admn. — Caroline Cho

Media Marketing Inc.
5749 Arapahoe Ave.
Boulder, CO 80303
tel (303) 440-7855; fax (303) 440-8035
Pres./CEO/R&D — James Theall
VP-Mktg. & Sales — Charles Mauldin
VP-Cus. Support & Training — Chris Browne
Bus. Mgr. — Bruce Becker

Media Monitors Inc.
2511 E. 46th St., Ste. L; PO Box 55592
Indianapolis, IN 46205
tel (800) 676-3342; fax (317) 549-0331
e-mail jselig@mediamonitor.com
President — John L. Selig
Regional Sales Manager — Robert D. Gould

Media Professional Insurance
2 Pershing Sq., 2300 Main St., Ste. 800
Kansas City, MO 64108-2404
tel (816) 471-6118; fax (816) 471-6119
Sr. VP-Underwriting — Dennis Brenton
Marketing Manager — Scott May

M E G (US) Inc.
401 Central Ave.
East Rutherford, NJ 07073
tel (201) 939-6600; fax (201) 939-0135
President — John Dangelmaier
Vice Pres. — Donald Dionne
Nat'l. Svc. Mgr. — Sam Ramlogun
Oper. Mgr. — Stephen McAuley
Fin. Mgr. — Bob Wirth
Nat'l. Sales & Mktg. Mgr. — Ralph Casale

Megadata Computer & Communications Corp.
35 Orville Dr.
Bohemia, NY 11716-2598
tel (516) 589-6800; fax (516) 589-6858
CEO — Ari Bachana

Megasys International Inc.
45H Industrial Rd. W.
Tolland, CT 06084
tel (203) 871-8713; fax (203) 871-8710

Louis Melind Co.
7631 N. Austin Ave.
Skokie, IL 60076
tel (708) 581-2500; fax (708) 581-2530
President — David B. Sterrett
Vice Pres.-Mktg. — Donald M. Dowd
Vice Pres.-Production — Gene Griffiths
Customer Svc. Mgr. — Donna Wagner

Melita International Corp.
5051 Peachtree Corners Cir.
Norcross, GA 30092
tel (404) 446-7800; fax (404) 409-4444
Chairman/CEO — Aleksander Szlam
President — J. Neil Smith

Merix Chemical Co. (Dept. TR)
2234 E. 75th St.
Chicago, IL 60649
tel (312) 221-8242; fax (312) 221-3047
President — Eric O. Sonneman
Dir.-Pub. & Adv. — Z. Blount

Merrimac Associates
RR 1, Box 161
Center Harbor, NH 03226-9720
tel (603) 253-4245; fax (603) 253-4365
Mktg. Mgr. — Gayle Wheeler

Metafix Inc.
1925 46th Ave.
Montreal, QC H8T 2P1 Canada
tel (514) 633-8663; fax (514) 633-1678
President — John La Riviere

Metafix Silver Recovery Systems
C/O Hart Industries; 43 Doran St.
East Haven, CT 06512
tel (203) 469-6344; fax (203) 469-6592
President — Steve Mancuso

Metro Creative Graphics Inc.
33 W. 34th St.
New York, NY 10001
tel (212) 947-5100; fax (212) 967-4602
President — Robert Zimmerman

Metroland Printing/Publishing & Distributing Ltd.
10 Tempo Ave.
Willowdale, ON M2H 2N8 Canada
tel (416) 493-1300; fax (416) 493-0623
Dir.-Human Resources — Brenda Biller

Metromail Corp.
360 E. 22nd St.
Lombard, IL 60148
tel (708) 620-3300; fax (708) 620-2961
President — Susan Henricks

MFB Corp.
106 Kennedy St.
River Falls, WI 54022
tel (715) 425-5818
Vice Pres.-Sales — Bob Baldwin

MGD Graphic Systems Div., See Rockwell Graphic Systems

MGI International Inc.
1800 Chapman Ave.
Rockville, MD 20852
tel (301) 881-4242; fax (301) 881-9121
President — Arthur Hamlin
Mgr.-Sales & Svc. Oper. — John Gramates

Micom Communications Corp.
4100 Los Angeles Ave.
Simi Valley, CA 93063
tel (805) 583-8600; fax (805) 583-1997
Customer Support — Art Stewart
Chairman/CEO — Barry Phelps
Vice Pres.-Corp. Strategy — Ken Guy

Micro Systems Specialists Inc. (MSSI)
Franklin Ave.; PO Box 347
Millbrook, NY 12545-0347
tel (914) 677-6150; fax (914) 677-6620
President-Mktg. — Catherine M. Culkin
Vice Pres.-Mktg. — Dawn M. Roeller
Treasurer — Eileen F. Sunderland
Secretary — Judy M. Bruning

Copyright ©1996 by the Editor & Publisher Co.

VI-14   Equipment, supplies, services

Microfax Inc.
7041 Saulsbury St.
Arvada, CO 80003
tel (303) 467-1207; fax (303) 467-1364
Owner/Pres. — Jill R. Nagrodsky
Vice Pres. — George Nagrodsky

Microtech Computer Systems (MSC)
81 The East Mall
Toronto, ON M8Z 5W4 Canada
tel (416) 253-6611; fax (416) 253-6780
Mktg. Dir. — Alec Lorentiu

Microtek
3715 Doolittle Dr.
Redondo Beach, CA 90278-1226
tel (310) 297-5000; fax (310) 297-5050
Dir.-Mktg. — Mary Ann Whitlock

Mid-America Graphics Inc.
1501 Vine St.; PO Box 466
Harrisonville, MO 64701
tel (816) 887-2414/(800) 356-4886
fax (816) 887-2762
Exec. Vice Pres. — William David George
Gen. Mgr. — Chris George

Mid Atlantic Lighting
1830 S. 19th St.; PO Box 2206
Harrisburg, PA 17105-2206
tel (717) 986-9358; fax (717) 939-6527/(717) 986-9316
Sales Assoc. — Justin Litz

MidLantic Equipment Co. Inc.
368 Oakwood Dr.
Wyckoff, NJ 07481
tel (201) 891-4888; fax (201) 891-6165
Mktg. Mgr. — Arlene Vanderweert

Midwest Independent Postal
7837 Sprinkle Rd.
Kalamazoo, MI 49001
tel (616) 324-1003; fax (616) 324-1005
Gen. Mgr. — Kurt Post
Sales — Tim Neal

Midwest Publishers Supply Co.
4640 N. Olcott Ave.
Chicago, IL 60656
tel (800) 621-1507; fax (800) 832-3189
President — James Rezabek
Vice Pres. — Michael A. Carfagnini

Simon Miller Sales Co.
1218 Chestnut St.
Philadelphia, PA 19107
tel (215) 923-3600; fax (215) 923-1173
President — Joseph Levit
Vice Pres. — Henri C. Levit

Mimic Inc.
PO Box 705
Islington, MA 02090-0705
tel (617) 329-9593
Mktg. Mgr. — S.H. Thurston

Minnesota Opinion Research Inc. (MORI)
Three Paramount Plz., 7831 Glenroy Rd., Ste. 100
Minneapolis, MN 55439-9737
tel (612) 835-3050; fax (612) 835-3385
President — Kristin McGrath
Research Systems Dir. — Brent Stahl
Account Mgr. — Jay Furnald
Account Mgr. — Katherine Harter
Admn. Asst. — Cindy Jones

Mirachem Corp.
1045 S. Edward Dr. (85281)
PO Box 27608
Tempe, AZ 85285
tel (602) 966-3030; fax (602) 966-0890
Vice Pres.-Sales — Don Lee

Miracle Industries Inc.
259 Great Hill Rd.
Naugatuck, CT 06770
tel (203) 723-0928; fax (203) 723-0394
President — John Chabot
Sales — David Fitzmorris

Mission Critical Technologies
150 Baker Ave.
Concord, MA 01742
tel (508) 287-0018 ext. 110
fax (508) 287-0021
Director-Marketing — Pat Sorn

Missouri Press Service Inc.
802 Locust St.
Columbia, MO 65201
tel (314) 449-4167; fax (314) 874-5894
Exec. Dir. — Doug Crews
Adv. Dir. — Mike Sell

Mitchell's Newspaper Delivery Service
28 Royalston Ln.
Centereach, NY 11720
tel (212) 594-6426; fax (212) 594-7262
Mktg. Dir. — Mitchell Newman

Mitchell's World Finest Paper Delivery
Jaf Station-PO Box 2431
New York, NY 10116-2431
tel (212) 594-6397; fax (212) 594-7262
President — Roy Newman

Mitsubishi Electronics America
5665 Plaza Dr.
Cypress, CA 90630
tel (714) 236-6183

Mitsubishi Heavy Industries Ltd. (MLP USA Inc.)
600 Barclay Blvd.
Lincolnshire, IL 60069
tel (708) 634-9100; fax (708) 634-9109
Dir.-Newspapers — Roy Yokovchi
Sales Mgr. — Ron Ehrhardt

Mitsubishi Lithographic Presses USA Inc.
600 Barclay Blvd.
Lincolnshire, IL 60069
tel (708) 634-9100; fax (708) 634-5504
Dir.-Newspaper Sales — Roy Yokoushi
Sales Mgr. — Ronald Ehrhardt Jr
Admn. Asst.-Newspaper Press — Vicki Miller

Mobile Reclamation System (MRS) Div. of Marpax
1115 Shore St.
West Sacramento, CA 95691
tel (800) 824-0065; fax (713) 621-1878
Division President — Greg Pope

Mohr Enterprise (Div. of Mohr Lino-Saw Co.)
65 E. Palatine Rd., Ste. 103
Prospect Heights, IL 60070
tel (708) 465-0048; fax (708) 465-0044
President — G. Robert Jackson
Service Manager — Jerry Clements
Marketing Director — Jim Jackson

Mo-Money Associates Inc.
PO Box 12591
Pensacola, FL 32574
tel (904) 432-6301/(800) 874-7681
fax (904) 434-5645
Mktg. Mgr. — Tom McVoy

Monotype Systems Inc.
2100 Golf Rd., Ste. 220
Rolling Meadows, IL 60008
tel (708) 427-8800; fax (708) 427-8860
President — Dennis E. Nierman
Vice Pres.-Sales — John Lally
Dir.-Support Oper. — Keith Roeske
Dir.-Admn. — Pamela Alioto
Nat'l. Sales Mgr. — Randy Johnson
Controller — Steve Farkas
Cus. Svc. Mgr. — Brian Sundquist
Mktg. Coord. — Danelle Fanshier

Monotype Typography Inc.
150 S. Wacker Dr., Ste. 2630
Chicago, IL 60606
tel (312) 855-1440; fax (312) 855-9475
Sales & Mktg. Mgr. — Steve Kuhlman

The Morrison Group/Morrison Ink
4801 W. 160th St.
Cleveland, OH 44135
tel (216) 267-8820; fax (216) 267-5490
Chairman/CEO — Donald B. Morrison
President — D. Scott Morrison
Exec. Vice Pres. — John C. Hoffman
Sec./Treas. — John C. Hoffman

Mortgage Market Information Services
53 E. St. Charles Rd.
Villa Park, IL 60181
tel (800) 509-INFO/(708) 834-7555
fax (708) 834-7283
President — James R. De Both
Mktg. Dir. — Keith J. Kubik

Mountain States Inc.
5260 E. Canada St.
Tucson, AZ 85706
tel (520) 574-0031; fax (520) 574-0477
President — Ernie Phillips

Mouser Institute School of Advertising
124 E. Carolina Ave.; PO Box 87
Crewe, VA 23930
tel (804) 645-8200; fax (804) 645-8232

MTL Systems Inc.
3481 Dayton-Xenia Rd.
Dayton, OH 45432
tel (513) 426-3111; fax (513) 426-8301
President — Arnold Fife

Muller Martini Corp.
PO Box 3360
Smithtown, NY 11787-0811
tel (516) 582-4343; fax (516) 348-1961
Mktg. Mgr. — William Milkofsky

Multi Ad Services Inc.
1720 W. Detweiller Dr.; PO Box 786
Peoria, IL 61615
tel (309) 692-1530; fax (309) 693-1648
e-mail multi.ad@applelink.apple.com
Mktg. Mgr. — Marc Radosevic
Sales Mgr. — Doug Gregory
Vice Pres.-Media Div. — Dennis Mullen

Mumford Micro Systems
3933 Antone Rd.
Santa Barbara, CA 93110
tel (805) 687-5116
Mktg. Dir. — Susan Haville

Mustek Inc.
1702 McGaw Ave.
Irvine, CA 92714
tel (714) 250-8855; fax (714) 250-3372
Mktg. Dir. — David Hsieh
Office Mgr. — Edith Fisher

Mutual Insurance Co. Ltd.
PO Box 3212
Hamilton, HM NX Bermuda
tel (809) 292-7633; fax (809) 295-7562
Manager — B.P. Kelly

N

N/S Corp.
235 W. Florence Ave.
Inglewood, CA 90301
tel (800) 782-1582; fax (310) 673-0276
Pres./Vice Pres. — Thomas G. Ennis
Advg. Mgr. — James E. Soucck Jr.
Controller — Mike Bahmer

N & L Enterprises Inc.
2950 Drake Ave.; PO Box 2128
Huntsville, AL 35804
tel (205) 883-8700/(800) 633-7240
fax (205) 880-8800
President — Nick Lioce
Vice Pres. — Louise Lioce
Sales Rep. — Glynda Cooper

Naft International Ltd.
611 Broadway, Ste. 415
New York, NY 10012-2608
tel (212) 982-0800; fax (212) 979-2999
Sales Rep. — Stephen Grassotti

Nama Graphics Inc.
1200 Roosevelt Rd., Ste. 200
Glen Ellyn, IL 60137
tel (708) 627-5285; fax (708) 627-5245
Contact — John M. Gavelda

Napp Systems Inc.
360 S. Pacific St.
San Marcos, CA 92069
tel (619) 744-4387; fax (619) 489-1853
President — Kai Wenk-Wolff
Vice Pres. — G.O. Miller
Dir.-Sales & New Bus. — Howard W. Helmbrecht

Nasco Products Co.
23600 Cloverlawn
Oak Park, MI 48237
tel (810) 547-7056
President — Norma Schonwetter

National Graphic Sales Inc.
181 S. Bloomingdale Rd., Ste. 102
Bloomingdale, IL 60108
tel (708) 894-3333; fax (708) 894-4233
Marketing Manager — Tom Cooper

National Graphic Supply Corp.
226 N. Allen St.
Albany, NY 12206
tel (518) 438-8411; fax (518) 438-0940
CEO — Alfred Landess
President — Stuart Kletter
Vice Pres.-Nat'l. Acct. & Oper. — Roberta Berkowitz
Vice Pres.-Sales — Jerry Campana

National Machine
861 Expressview Dr.; PO Box 2127
Mansfield, OH 44905
tel (419) 589-6134; fax (419) 589-8317
President — Robert Buckler
Vice Pres. — Marianni Buckler-Bates

National Research
2 Boars Head Pl., Ste. 120
Charlottesville, VA 22902
tel (804) 295-3927; fax (804) 296-5412
President — Samuel Yount Jr.
Vice Pres. — Elizabeth Payne

National Research Bureau
200 N. 4th St.; PO Box 1
Burlington, IA 52601-0001
tel (319) 752-5415; fax (319) 752-3421
Directors — Michael & Diane Darnall

National Soy Ink Info. Center
1025 Ashworth Rd. #310
West Des Moines, IA 50265
tel (515) 223-1423; fax (515) 223-4331
e-mail jpatte01@interserv.com
Soy Ink Coordinator — Jo Patterson

National Utility Service Inc.
One Maynard Dr.; PO Box 712
Park Ridge, NJ 07656-0712
tel (201) 391-4300; fax (201) 391-8158
Vice Pres.-Mktg. & PR — Peter Bedrosian

NB Finishing Inc.
1845 S. 55th Ave.
Cicero, IL 60650
tel (708) 863-8892
Oper. Mgr. — Dave Nichols

NCS Inc.
112 Kings Hwy.
Landing, NJ 07850-1055
tel (201) 770-0800; fax (201) 770-0808
President — Fred Fazzio
Vice Pres.-Mktg. — Tim Cooper

Neasi-Weber International
8550 Balboa Blvd., Ste. 100
Northridge, CA 91325
tel (818) 895-6900; fax (818) 895-9915
President — Jim S. Weber
CEO — Dennis J. Neasi
Sr. VP-Sales & Mktg. — Michael Brier
CFO — John F. Reid
Exec. Asst. — Debi Byrnes

NENSCO
50 Railroad Ave.; PO Box 348
Millbury, MA 01590
tel (508) 865-0800; fax (508) 865-0811
President — Brad Beaton
Exec. Vice Pres. — Larry Erwin
Vice Pres.-Oper. — Dan Mahoney
Bus. Mgr.-Pre-Press Prod. — David Vito
Bus. Mgr.-Press Room Prod. — Bob Rooney
Mktg.-Post-Press Prod. — Yvonne Okerberg
Treasurer — Maurice Crouteau

Network Industrial Services Inc.
PO Box 504
Lake Zurich, IL 60047-0504
tel (708) 487-1160; fax (708) 487-4001
e-mail jhhahny@aol.com
President — James Hajny

Network Newspaper Advertising Inc.
23811 Chagrin Blvd., #110
Cleveland, OH 44122
tel (216) 595-3990; fax (216) 595-3992
President — Charles Hickman
Vice Pres. — Charles E. Briggs

The Networks Inc.
20 W. Market St.
York, PA 17401
tel (717) 849-0600; fax (717) 849-0620
e-mail http://www.net-works.net
President — David Dreyer
Dir.-Admin. & Cust. Svc. — Patricia Chadderdon

New Seagull Photographic Paper
3701 W. Moore Ave.
Santa Ana, CA 92704
tel (714) 432-7070; fax (714) 432-7102
Vice Pres. — Carmen Pacella

Newer Technology
7803 E. Osie St., #105
Wichita, KS 67201
tel (316) 685-4904; fax (316) 685-9368
e-mail sales@newertech.com
Mktg. Dir. — Gene Hilldebrandt

Copyright ©1996 by the Editor & Publisher Co.

Equipment, supplies, services   VI-15

Newman International
4210 Johnson Dr., Ste. 37
Mission, KS 66205
tel (913) 362-8888; fax (913) 362-8901
President — John T. Newman
Vice Pres. — Mary C. Newman
Office Mgr. — Mary Lopez

News-Type Service
1506 Gardena Ave.
Glendale, CA 91204
tel (818) 247-7821; fax (818) 247-9331
President — Ernest A. Lindner

Newspaper Association of America (EDI)
11600 Sunrise Valley Dr.
Reston, VA 22091
tel (703) 648-1000/(703) 648-1224
Dir.-Membership Svc. — Kimberly Lysik
Chief Mktg. Officer — Nick Cannistraro
Dir.-Advanced Computer Science — John W. Iobst, Ph.D.
CEO — Cathie Black
CFO — Mary Anne Kanter
Sr. Vice Pres.-Comms. — Debra Shriver

Newspaper Computer Systems
PO Box 1518
Victoria, TX 77902
tel (512) 575-1451; fax (512) 572-4884
Mktg. Mgr. — Jim Blankenshit

Newspaper Electronics Corp.
510 E. 28th St.
Kansas City, MO 64108-3101
tel (816) 474-1441/(800) 821-5442
fax (816) 474-1221
President — Kelvin W. Perry
Vice Pres. — Jon L. Montgomery
Office Mgr. — A. Michele Rushing
Special Markets Dir. — Vincent P. Sacks Sr.

Newspaper Space Bank
405 Lexington Ave., 14th Fl.
New York, NY 10174-0203
tel (212) 286-9656; fax (212) 808-0622
Sr. Vice Pres. — Frank Savino
Vice Pres. — Thomas Cabeen

Newspaper Systems Group Inc.
5631 Palmer Way, Ste. E
Carlsbad, CA 92008-7243
tel (619) 929-2190; fax (619) 929-1885
President — George Sugar

Newspapers & Technology
1623 Blake St., #444
Denver, CO 80202
tel (303) 575-9595; fax (303) 575-9555
e-mail ntmvm@aol.com
Publisher — Mary L. Van Meter
Editor — Brad Moritz

Newsprint Sales
80 Field Pt. Rd.
Greenwich, CT 06830
tel (203) 661-3344; fax (203) 661-3349
President — Peter M Brant
Exec. Vice Pres. — Joseph Allen
Vice Pres.-Fin. — Edward Sherrick
Vice Pres.-Sales & Mktg. — Thomas Armstrong

Newsprint South Inc.
460 Briarwood Dr., Ste. 505
Jackson, MS 39206
tel (601) 982-0900; fax (601) 957-6182
President/CEO — Don W. Westfall
Sr. Vice Pres.-Sales — Bob Reynolds
Sr. Vice Pres./GM — Stewart Thomas
Vice Pres.-Finance — Tony Bond

Newstar Communications Inc.(dba Newspaper Satellite Network)
18333 Preston Rd., Ste. 410, LB6
Dallas, TX 75252
tel (214) 931-9858; fax (214) 931-0069
Sales & Service — Diana Edwards
Production — Dawn Van Breeman-Wilks
Aministrative — Keli A. Hardwick

Newstech Co. (Div. of Rovinter Inc.)
1775 Opa Locka Blvd.
Miami, FL 33054
tel (305) 688-1407; fax (305) 688-2109
President — Oscar Rovito
Vice Pres. — Rey Vergara
Vice Pres. — Diego A. Rovito

NGCP/Laser Concepts
1000 Johnson Ferry Rd., Ste. F-145
Marietta, GA 30068
tel (770) 386-4297

Nikka Corp.
1720 Sleepy Hollow Dr.
Southlake, TX 76092
tel (817) 421-8747; fax (817) 488-9569
Vice Pres.-Sales — Lloyd Tompkins

Nikon Inc./Electronic Imaging Department
1300 Walt Whitman Rd.
Melville, NY 11747
tel (516) 547-4355; fax (516) 547-0305
Nat'l. Sales Mgr. — Joe Carfora
Mktg. Dev. Mgr. — John Harcourt

Niles & Nelson Inc.
19 Rector St.
New York, NY 10006
tel (212) 269-2625
President — E.F. Smith

Nisus Software Inc.
107 S. Cedros Ave.; PO Box 1300
Solana Beach, CA 92075-1900
tel (619) 481-1477; fax (619) 481-6154
e-mail info@nisus-soft.com, www.nisus-soft.com/~nisus
Contact — Trineka Greer

Noise Monitoring & Control Inc.
PO Box 43067
Philadelphia, PA 19129
tel (215) 438-1800; fax (215) 438-7110
President — D.D. Meisel PE
Exec. Vice Pres. — Walter M. Stein
Vice Pres. — Gary L. Meisel
Treas./Sec. — Marcia A. Price

Nomads Inc.
8031 W. Central Rd., Ste. 324
Omaha, NE 68124
tel (402) 391-3110; fax (800) 831-5830
Marketing — Jim Catania

Nortec Imaging
2500 Niagra Ln.
Plymouth, MN 55447
tel (612) 404-0226; fax (612) 404-0227
Vice Pres.-Sales & Mktg. — Joel Llyod

Nortec Industries
PO Box 698
Ogdensburg, NY 13669
tel (315) 425-1255; fax (613) 822-7964
Gen. Mgr. — Urs Schenk
Vice Pres.-Sales & Mktg. — Gary Berlin
Mktg. & Sales. — Mike Hurley

North Atlantic Publishing Systems Inc.
9 Acton Rd., Ste. 13
Chelmsford, MA 01824
tel (508) 250-8080; fax (508) 250-8179
President — Peter J. Baumgartner

North Shore Consultants Inc.
4910 N. Monitor Ave.
Chicago, IL 60630
tel (312) 286-7245; fax (312) 286-1974
Prod. Mgr. — Dennis B. Wojtecki

Northeast Industries Inc.
121 North Ave. 60
Los Angeles, CA 90042
tel (213) 256-4791; fax (213) 256-7607
President — Sam W. Boyles
Vice Pres. — Louis J. Timar
Gen. Mgr. — Norm Bartlett

Northern Graphic Supply
155 Glendale Ave., Unit 11/12
Sparks, NV 89431
tel (702) 359-6466; fax (702) 359-6966
President — Tom Gouldston

Northwest Publishers Inc.
710 Lake St.; PO Box 275
Spirit Lake, IA 51360-0275
tel (712) 336-2805; fax (712) 336-0611
President — John E. van der Linden
Secretary — Marjorie W. van der Linden

Norwood Paper
6547 N. Avondale Ave., #303
Chicago, IL 60631
tel (312) 792-0677; fax (312) 792-3094
Marketing Director — Robert Zeman

NRD Inc.
2937 Alt Blvd.
Grand Island, NY 14072
tel (716) 773-7634; fax (716) 773-7744
Product Mgr. — Kelly J. Walck
Vice Pres.-Sales — Larry Keating

NuArc Co. Inc.
6200 W. Howard St.
Niles, IL 60714
tel (708) 967-4400; fax (708) 967-9664

President — Don Cims
Exec. Vice Pres. — Joseph M. Dixler
Exec. Vice Pres. — Barbara Morgenstern
S.E. Div. Sales Mgr. — Ed Moehring
Vice Pres.-Eng. — Chuck Leonhart
Controller — Ruth Stulik

Nutek Inc.
3182 MacArthur Dr.
Northbrook, IL 60062
tel (708) 564-3070; fax (708) 564-7725
Vice Pres.-Sales — Barry Ades
Vice Pres.-Eng. — Tom Jacobs
Sales Manager — Jim Tybov
Sales — Paul Hasimoto
Sales — Bruce Norikane

O

Occupational and Environmental Health Analysts Inc.
100 S. Jersey Ave., #32
Setauket, NY 11733
tel (516) 689-1405; fax (516) 689-1406
Mktg. Dir. — Otto White

Offset Web Sales Inc.
73 N. Sunset Dr.
Camano Island, WA 98292
tel (360) 387-0097; fax (360) 387-9090
President — Tim M. York
Sec./Treas. — Ruth E. York

Olin Electronic Chemicals
2873 N. Nevada St.
Chandler, AZ 85225-1213
tel (602) 926-2020/(800) 553-6546
(Customer Service)/(800) 222-4868
(Customer Support); fax (602) 497-0848
President — Mike Campbell
Vice Pres. — Jack Murphy
Vice Pres.-Int'l Mktg. — Jim LaCasse
Dir.-Sales — Mario Stanghellini

Olivetti Office USA
765 US Hwy. 202; PO Box 6945
Bridgewater, NJ 08807-0945
tel (908) 526-8200; fax (908) 526-8405
e-mail msetar@royalnet.com
President — Salomon Suwalsky
Vice Pres.-Sales — William Lubrano
Mktg. Comms. Mgr. — Monica Setar

Olympus America Inc.
145 Crossways Park
Woodbury, NY 11797
tel (516) 844-5000; fax (516) 677-1699
Advg. Dir. — Christine E. Moossmann

Omni Industry (Div. of Global Turnkey Systems Inc.)
1801 Broadway, Ste. 450
Denver, CO 80202
tel (303) 293-2666; fax (303) 293-8340
President/CEO — Robert E. Farina
VP-Sales & Mktg. — Mike Fitzergald
Vice Pres.-Software — Stephen U. Langer
VP-Field Svc. & Mfg. — Michael Urban
Vice Pres.-Fin. — Michael R. Winer

ONE Corp.
455 E. Paces Ferry Rd., Ste. 350, N.E.
Atlanta, GA 30305
tel (404) 842-0111; fax (404) 842-0525
President — Durelle Boles
Sales Assoc. — Angela Culpepper

Optronics/An Intergraph Corp. Div.
7 Stuart Rd.
Chelmsford, MA 01824
tel (508) 256-4511; fax (508) 256-1872
e-mail marketing@optron.ingr.com
Gen. Mgr. — Jamie Jacobs
Dir.-Bus. Dev./Mktg. Comm. Mgr. — Ed Chrusciel

Ottaway Newspaper
Rt. 416; PO Box 401
Campbell Hall, NY 10916
tel (914) 294-8181; fax (914) 294-1659
Contact — Chester Warzynski

Ovalstrapping Inc.
PO Box 738
Hoquaim, WA 98550
tel (360) 532-9101; fax (360) 532-1792
Manager — Larry Lock

Ovalstrapping Inc.
120 55th St. N.E.
Fort Payne, AL 35967
tel (205) 845-1914; fax (205) 845-1493
Mgr. Sales & Mktg. — Morgan Stout

Overland Data Inc.
8975 Balboa Ave.
San Diego, CA 92123-1499
tel (619) 571-5555; fax (619) 571-0982
e-mail BBS (619) 571-3651
Sales Mgr. — Rebecca Amroian

Oxy-Dry Corp.
26C Worlds Fair Dr.
Somerset, NJ 08873
tel (908) 560-8880; fax (908) 560-1848
President — Edward T. McLoughlin
Corp. Mktg. Dir. — Mary Ellen Cahill

P

P*Ink Software Engineering GMBH & Co.
Rothenbaumchaussee 5
Hamburg, 20148 Germany
tel (49-40) 4117090; fax (49-40) 41170910
e-mail apple link ger.xse 0006
Public Relations/Press — Andrea Stiens

P & E Inc.
7482 President's Dr.
Orlando, FL 32809
tel (407) 857-3888; fax (407) 857-9444
CFO — Sue Bell

Pacesetter Graphic Service Corp.
2672 Hickory Grove Rd.; PO Box 499
Acworth, GA 30101
tel (770) 974-0297/(800) 241-7970
fax (770) 975-3511
President — Robert Allen
Exec. Vice Pres. — Jeri Hammond
Direct Sales — June Evans
Dealer Sales — Jim Fidanza

Pacific Newspaper Services Inc.
1020-F N. Batavia St.
Orange, CA 92667
tel (800) 201-7500/(714) 289-7576
fax (714) 289-1312
President — Tom Mastin

PAGE
998 Old Eagle School Rd., Ste. 1202
Wayne, PA 19087
tel (610) 687-3778; fax (610) 687-2147
e-mail pagewayne@aol.com
Gen. Mgr. — H. Charles Berkey

Abbott E Paine (Newspaper Broker Services)
PO Box 6267
Orange, CA 92613-6267
tel (714) 921-0769; fax (714) 998-1091
Owner — Abbott E. Paine

Pako Corp.
2440 Fernbrook Ln. N.
Plymouth, MN 55447
tel (612) 559-7600; fax (612) 559-8787
President — Richard Reedy
Controller — Barry Heimbuch
Dir.-Nat'l. Accounts — Darrell Watson Jr.

Pamarco Inc.
235 E. 11th Ave.
Roselle, NJ 07203
tel (908) 241-1200; fax (908) 241-4237
President — Maurice Buckley
Vice Pres.-Sales & Mktg. — Brian Jacob

Pan American Papers Inc.
5105 N.W. 37th Ave.
Miami, FL 33142
tel (305) 635-2534; fax (305) 635-2538
Marketing Director — Jesus A. Roca

Pantone Inc.
590 Commerce Blvd.
Carlstadt, NJ 07072
tel (201) 935-5500; fax (201) 896-0242
Dir.-Sales Support — J. de Sibour

Paragon Publishing Systems
5 Pine Tree Pl., 360-801 Rte. 101
Bedford, NH 03110
tel (603) 471-0077; fax (603) 471-0501
Oper. Mgr. — Gary Grindle

Copyright ©1996 by the Editor & Publisher Co.

VI-16 Equipment, supplies, services

Parascan Technologies Inc.
93 Glen Karrn Cr.
Sparks, NV 89431
tel (702) 385-6446/(800) 259-5778
(Service); fax (702) 358-6769
Sales Manager — Roger Pyle
Office Manager — Colleen Badgley

Parsons Main Inc.
Prudential Ctr., 101 Huntington Ave.
Boston, MA 02199
tel (617) 262-3200; fax (617) 859-2107
President — James T. Callahan
Managing Dir.-Bus. Dev.-Printing & Publishing — William Whooley
Oper. Mgr. — Nicolas Mariani

Paste-Up Supply
2616 Stingle Ave.
Rosemead, CA 91770
tel (213) 283-4610; fax (818) 288-0258
Owner — Pat Treanor

P.D.I. Plastics
5037 Pine Creek Dr.
Westerville, OH 43081
tel (800) 634-0017; fax (614) 890-0467
Mktg. Mgr. — Tracy Moody

PDQ Recruiters
PO Box 1641
Media, PA 19063
tel (610) 353-4722; fax (610) 353-2207
President — Pat Quinn

Pearce Inc.
12026 Zelis Rd.
Cleveland, OH 44135
tel (216) 252-0550; fax (216) 252-0551
President — G. Myatt

Penco Products
Brower Ave.; PO Box 378
Oaks, PA 19456
tel (610) 666-0500/(800) 562-1000
fax (610) 666-7561
President — Arthur H. Muti
Vice Pres.-Mktg. — William H. Epp
Mgr.-Mktg. Svc. — Philip H. Krugler

Penske Truck Leasing
3000 Expressway Dr. S.
Central Islip, NY 11722-1407
tel (516) 348-1271; fax (516) 348-1373
Sr. Vice Pres.-Sales — Jim Molinaro
Marketing — Jim Feenstra

Penske Truck Leasing
Rte. 10, Green Hills; PO Box 563
Reading, PA 19603-0563
tel (610) 775-6000; fax (610) 775-8342
Marketing Director — Jim Feenstra

Penta Software Inc.
107 Lakefront Dr.
Hunt Valley, MD 21030
tel (410) 771-8973; fax (410) 771-4020
e-mail salex@penta.com
Chairman — Charles Lanford
President — Frederick Ayers
Vice Pres. Sales & Mktg. — David Lewis

Periphonics Corp.
4000 Veterans Hwy.
Bohemia, NY 11716
tel (516) 467-0500; fax (516) 981-2689
President — Peter J. Cohen
Marketing Manager — Karen L. Ferraro
Sr. Vice Pres.-Sales — Richard A. Daniels
Vice Pres.-Marketing — Terry Meehan
Vice Pres.-R&D — Jay Patel
Vice Pres.-Tech. Svc. — Richard Giannotti
Vice Pres.-Financial — Kevin O'Brien
Vice Pres.-Major Accts. — George W. Cole

Perma-Fix Environmental Services
104 E. 5th St.
Kansas City, MO 64106
tel (800) 966-0059; fax (816) 221-8180
Tech. Services — Fran Jackson

Perretta Graphics Corp.
40 Violet Ave.
Poughkeepsie, NY 12601
tel (914) 473-0550; fax (914) 454-7507
President — Lawrence Perretta
East Reg'l. Mgr. — Andrew J. Kosky
Western Reg'l. Mgr. — Denise Reily
Nat'l. Sales Mgr. — Bruce L. Quilliam

Petco Roller Co.
28041 Bradley Rd.
Lake Forest, IL 60045
tel (708) 362-1820; fax (708) 362-1833
Marketing Manager — Dale Glenn

Phoenetix Corp.
2 E. Beaver Creek, Bldg. # 2
Richmond, ON L4B 2N3 Canada
tel (905) 707-1777; fax (905) 707-1015
Contact — Mirek Vesely

Photo Systems Inc.
7200 Huron River Dr.
Dexter, MI 48130
tel (313) 426-4646; fax (313) 426-3780
President — Alan Fischer
Sales Coord. — Marc J. Freund

PhotoSource International
Pine Lake Farm
Osceola, WI 54020
tel (715) 248-3800; fax (715) 248-7394
Publisher — Rohn Engh
Editor — Lori Johnson

Pitman Co.
721 Union Blvd.
Totowa, NJ 07512-2207
tel (201) 812-0400; fax (201) 812-1630
Chairman/President — John W. Dreyer
Exec. VP/COO — Gerald R. Knueven
Sr. Vice Pres./Sec. — Robert P. Schmidt

Pitman Photo Supply
8650 S.W. 132nd St.
Miami, FL 33156-6507
tel (800) 252-3008; fax (800) 835-3995
President — Michael Werner
Vice Pres.-Sales Mgr. — Lowell H. Elsea

Pitney Bowes Business Systems
One Elmcroft Rd.
Stamford, CT 06926-0700
tel (203) 243-7650; fax (203) 351-6303
Pres.-Sales & Oper. — Michael J. Quigley

PixelCraft Inc.
PO Box 14467
Oakland, CA 94614
tel (510) 562-2480; fax (510) 562-6451
President/CEO — Jeffrey Tung
Vice Pres. — Bruce Mills
Vice Pres. — Aldo Alesini

PixoArts Corp.
2570 W. El Camino Real, Ste. 105
Mountain View, CA 94040
tel (415) 949-2578; fax (415) 949-1359
Mktg. Sales — Cliv Liu

Plumtree Inc.
PO Box 13098
Savannah, GA 31416
tel (912) 354-0045; fax (912) 354-1375
President — Tim Cooper
Sales — Lou Poole

Polaroid Corp.
575 Technology Sq.
Cambridge, MA 02139
tel (617) 386-2000
Fin. Mgr. — George Brouder

Polaroid Graphics Imaging Inc.
103 Fourth Ave.
Waltham, MA 02154
tel (617) 386-2400; fax (617) 386-2481
Mktg. Mgr. — George Gray

Polychrome Corp.
222 Bridge Plz. S.
Fort Lee, NJ 07024
tel (201) 224-4600; fax (201) 224-4392
President/CEO — Thomas Bittner
VP-Worldwide Film Oper. — Burton H. Waxman
VP-Mktg. & Oper. — Michael Adelman
Vice Pres.-Sales & Mktg. — Noel Stegner

Polyfibron Technologies Inc.
900 Middlesex Turnpike Bldg. 2
Billerica, MA 01821
tel (508) 439-2000; fax (508) 439-2015
Print Tech./LETTERFLEX SYSTEMS:
Nat'l. Svc. Mgr. — David E. Vincent
Mktg. Sales Mgr. — H. Theodore Miller Jr.
Reg'l Acct. Mgr. — Francis J. Rendulic
Reg'l Acct. Mgr. — James R. Guenard
Print Tech/PRINTING BLANKETS:
Sales Mgr. — G. Peter Healey
Cus. Svc. Mgr. — Karen A. O'Connell
Gen. Sales Mgr. — H. Theodore Miller Jr.

Poolside Lithographic Supply Inc.
14060 Gannet St., #103
Santa Fe Springs, CA 90670
tel (310) 921-5545; fax (310) 921-6238
Pres./Sales Mgr. — Robert P. Pursel
Vice Pres. — Howard W. Britton
CFO — Leora J. Pursel

Portage Newspaper Supply Co.
1868 Akron Peninsula Rd.; PO Box 5500
Akron, OH 44334-0500
tel (800) 321-2183/(216) 929-4454
fax (216) 922-0506
President — Robert Belter
Vice Pres. — Carolyn Belter

Portfolios Unlimited Inc.
205 W. End Ave., #9P
New York, NY 10023
tel (212) 877-2622; fax (212) 724-3824
e-mail dpstorch@aol.com
Vice Pres. — Patricia Storch
Mktg. Mgr. — Dennis Storch

PostPress Equipment Co.
PO Box 16355
Savannah, GA 31416
tel (912) 354-0009; fax (912) 354-1375
President — Tim Cooper
Vice Pres.-Sales — Roman Krywopusk

Power Strap
6843 Sante Fe Dr.
Hodgkins, IL 60525
tel (800) 346-4600; fax (708) 482-9562
Vice Pres.-Sales & Mktg. — Tom Gould

PPI (UK) Ltd.
84A High St.; Stony Stratford
Milton Keynes, MK11 1AH United Kingdom
tel (44-1487) 830329; fax (44-1487) 832097
Sales Director — Brain Freeman

Praxair
39 Old Ridgeberry Rd.
Danbury, CT 06810
tel (203) 837-2000; fax (203) 837-2513
Chmn./CEO — H.W. Lichtenberger
President — Edgar Hotard
CFO — John A. Clerico
Vice Pres.-Comm. — Nigel Muir

Praxair Surface Technologies Inc.
12401 S. Kedvale Ave.
Alsip, IL 60658
tel (708) 389-8227; fax (708) 371-4566
Business Manager — K.H. Riekemann
Nat'l. Sales Mgr. — S.W. Liezert

Pre-Press Technologies Inc.
2443 Impala Dr. (Carlsbad, 92008)
PO Box 231045
Encinitas, CA 92023-01#45
tel (619) 931-2695; fax (619) 931-2698
Mktg. Dir. — Joe Mintz

PrePRESS DIRECT
11 Mount Pleasant Ave.
East Hannover, NJ 07936
tel (800) 443-6600/(201) 887-8000 (Sales); fax (201) 887-4300
e-mail catalog@prepress.pps.com,
http://www.prepress.pps.com
Vice Pres. — Marc Daniell

PrePRESS SOLUTIONS
11 Mount Pleasant Ave.
East Hannover, NJ 07936
tel (201) 887-8000/(800) 631-8134
fax (201) 884-6210
e-mail info@prepress.pps.com,
http://www.prepress.pps.com
President — Robert Trenkamp
Dir.-Newspaper Operations — Jay Roberts
Vice Pres.-Sales — Mike Dillon

PrePRESS SUPPORT
11 Mount Pleasant Ave.
East Hannover, NJ 07936
tel (201) 887-8000; fax (201) 884-6210
e-mail http://www.prepress.pps.com
VP-Support Services — Irene Schrader

Press-Enterprise Color Graphics
3185 Lackawanna Ave.
Bloomsburg, PA 17815
tel (800) 228-3483; fax (717) 784-9226
Color Graphics Mgr. — Robert Braun
Sys. Supervisor — Brent DeFranco
Stripping & Camera Supvr. — Jim Seybert

Press-Tec Inc.
320 8th. St. S.E.; PO Box 129
Altoona, IA 50009
tel (515) 967-5092; fax (515) 967-2847
President — Jack E. Alsted

Press and Bindery Systems Inc.
2852 N.W. 63rd St.
Oklahoma City, OK 73116
tel (405) 842-6034; fax (405) 842-8513
President — Robert Orner
Vice Pres. — Ron Hendricks

Press Rubber Co. Inc.
10925 Stephen Ct.
Mokena, IL 60448
tel (708) 479-1810; fax (708) 479-7712
President — Boyd A. Wagenaar
Chairwoman — Carolyn R. Wagenaar

Pressroom Products Inc.
3835 Industrial Ave.
Rolling Meadows, IL 60008-1038
tel (708) 398-6570; fax (708) 398-7570
President — Ross A. Hart
Controller — Jordana Hart
VP-Sales & Mktg. — Paul W. Geralds

Presstime (Newspaper Association of America)
11600 Sunrise Valley Dr.
Reston, VA 22091
tel (703) 648-1000; fax (703) 620-4557
Editor — Terry Poltrack
Managing Editor — Nancy Davis
Art Director — Charlene Gridley
Associate Editor — Margaret G. Carter

Price Waterhouse Valuation Services
200 E. Randolph Dr.
Chicago, IL 60601
tel (312) 540-2690; fax (312) 565-1458
Nat'l. Dir. — Stephen M. Carr

Prim Hall Enterprises Inc.
11 Spellman Rd.
Plattsburgh, NY 12901
tel (518) 561-7408; fax (518) 563-1472
President — John E. Prim
Vice Pres. — David E. Hall
Mid Atlantic Sales Rep. — Mike Dodds
NE Sales Rep. — Randy Trombly
SE Sales Rep. — Scott Renkes
Mid West Sales Rep. — C. Larsen
West Sales Rep. — J.T. Schwalm

Primark Tool Group
1350 S. 15th St.
Louisville, KY 40210
tel (502) 635-8100
President — Ralph Cox
Sales Mgr. — Fred Garms
Mfg. Mgr. — Rich Pund

Print Marketing Concepts
10590 Westoffice Dr., Ste. 250
Houston, TX 77042
tel (713) 780-7055; fax (713) 780-9731
President — Charles L. Dye
VP-Newspaper Relations — Ed Bryant
Southern Newspaper Relations — Zac Creech
Midwest Newspaper Relations — Paul Morgan
NE Newspaper Relations — Cheryl Pavell
VP-National TV Network — Robin Good

Printers Hot Line
15400 Knoll Trail Rd., Ste. 500
Dallas, TX 75248
tel (214) 233-5131/(800) 950-7746
fax (214) 239-3173
Gen. Mgr. — George Sparkman
Sales Mgr. — Jeanine Smith

Printers' Service
26 Blanchard St.
Newark, NJ 07105
tel (201) 589-7800; fax (201) 589-3225
President — Richard B. Liroff
CFO — Mark Wininger
Exec. Vice Pres. — Barry Kronman
VP-Research & Tech. — David Gerson
Mktg. Dir. — Bruce Learoff
Solvent & Safety Dir. — Robert Reck
Operations Director — Joe Schleck
Sales Mgr. — Jeff Matusow
Tech. Rep. — Bob Feldman
Tech. Rep. — Jerry Shikora

Printex Products Corp.
4150 Belden Village St., Ste. 507
Canton, OH 44718
tel (216) 493-8383; fax (216) 493-8388
President — Ron Whatling

Copyright ©1996 by the Editor & Publisher Co.

Equipment, supplies, services VI-17

Printing Equipment Specialists Inc.
1060 E. Addison Ct.
Arlington Heights, IL 60005
tel (708) 640-8700; fax (708) 956-7074
Sales — Robert Schwermer
Sales — Dennis Clark

Printing Press Services Inc.
Seller's St. Factory
Preston Lanc's, PR1 5EU England
tel (44-772) 797050; fax (44-772) 797611
President — Joe McManamon
Managing Dir. — David McManamon
USA Agent — Dave Evans

Printmark
28 Elm St.; PO Box 36
Montpelier, VT 05601
tel (802) 229-9743; fax (802) 229-9746
Production Dir. — Alex Brown

Printronix
PO Box 19559
Irvine, CA 92713
tel (714) 863-1900; fax (714) 660-8682
Mktg. Dir. — Hank Schmidt

Printware
1270 Eagan Industrial Rd.
St. Paul, MN 55121
tel (612) 456-1400; fax (612) 454-3684
e-mail sales@printwareinc.com
President — Daniel Baker Ph.D.
Dir.-Sales & Mktg. — Tim Murphy
Mktg. Specialist — Roberta Wilson

Pro Systems Inc.
3000 France Ave. S.
St. Louis Park, MN 55416
tel (612) 926-2496; fax (612) 926-9814
Mktg. Dir. — George H. West
Fin. Dir. — Theodore Politis

PROMO STAR Systems (See Bruce Bell & Associates)

PromoFax
1335 Dublin Rd., Ste. 200A
Columbus, OH 43215
tel (800) MORE-ADS; fax (614) 548-0397
Mktg. Mgr. — Lee Smith

Promotion Sources
6114 La Salle Ave., Ste. 601
Oakland, CA 94611
tel (800) 788-1849; fax (800) 788-1849
Owner — Michael Robert Miller

Provan Associates Inc.
6265 Old Hickory Pt., N.W.
Atlanta, GA 30328
tel (404) 252-0402; fax (404) 255-7706
President — Norm Provan
Sec./Treas. — LaVerne R. Provan
Corp. Counsel — Michael J. Provan

PSC Flo-Turn Inc.
111 Long Ave.
Hillside, NJ 07205
tel (201) 923-3110; fax (201) 923-0816
President — Rod Chrysler

Publishers' Auxiliary National Newspaper Association
1525 Wilson Blvd., Ste. 550
Arlington, VA 22209
tel (703) 907-7900/(800) 829-4NNA
fax (703) 907-7901
Mgr.-Sales & Mktg. — Mark Daly
Managing Editor — Chuck Holahan
News Editor — Stan Schwartz
Graphic Editor — Val Padron

Publishers Equipment Corp.
16660 Dallas Pkwy., Ste. 1100
Dallas, TX 75248
tel (214) 931-2312; fax (214) 931-2399
COB — Evans Kostas
Vice Pres.-Finance — Roger Baier

Publishers Idea Exchange
228 E. 1st St.; Box 191
Monticello, IA 52310
tel (319) 465-5300/(800) 383-8491
fax (319) 465-9908
Owner — Roger W. Bryant

Publishing Business Systems Inc.
1350 E. Touhy Ave., Ste. 150 W.
Des Plaines, IL 60018
tel (708) 699-5727; fax (708) 699-8989
President — Stephen R. Smith
COO — Bud DePietto
CFO — Ike Barfield
Vice Pres.-Mktg. — Dale Eskra
VP-Strategic Bus. Dev. — David Lipsey
VP-Eastern Region — Spencer Rutledge
Vice Pres.-Western Region — Bob Larson
Vice Pres.-Client Svc. — Joe Cardosi

Publishing Partners International
670 N. Commercial St.
Manchester, NH 03101
tel (603) 644-3339; fax (603) 623-6170
Marketing Dir. — Samuel List

Pulse Research Inc.
PO Box 23035
Portland, OR 97281
tel (503) 292-2718; fax (503) 292-3498
e-mail marling@pulse-research.com
CEO — John W. Marling
Vice Pres. — Denice Nichols
Admn. Mgr. — Anna Todd

Q

QMS Inc.
1 Magnum Pass
Mobile, AL 36618
tel (800) 523-2696; fax (334) 633-4866
Vice Pres.-Mktg. — Richard Bowles

Quad/Tech Int'l.
N64 W23110 Main St.
Sussex, WI 53089
tel (414) 246-7500; fax (414) 246-5170/(414) 246-5160
President — Tom Quadracci
VP-Sales & Mktg. — Randy Freeman
Dir.-Worldwide Sales — Karl Fritchen

Quality Components Corp.
31 W. 331 Schoger Dr.
Naperville, IL 60565
tel (708) 851-9909; fax (708) 851-9731
President — Wally Stoneham

Quark Inc.
1800 Grant St.
Denver, CO 80203
tel (303) 894-8888; fax (303) 894-3399
Dir.-Corp. Comm. — Cheryl Gordon
Trade Show Mgr. — LeeAnn Ryan

Quebecor Printing Providence
99 W. River St.
Providence, RI 02904
tel (401) 331-1771; fax (401) 331-5020
Exec. Vice Pres.-Sales — Robert Russell
Vice Pres./Gen. Mgr. — William Mahoney
Vice Pres.-Mktg. — Dennis Meyer
Purchasing Mgr. — Charles E. Hyson
Mktg. Mgr. — Judy Dorff

Quebecor Printing USA Corp.
1999 Shepard Rd.
St. Paul, MN 55116
tel (612) 690-7576; fax (612) 690-7438
Mktg. Dir. — Mark Anderson

Quickwire
44 Frid St.
Hamilton, ON L8N 3G3 Canada
tel (905) 526-3217; fax (905) 526-0147
e-mail quickwire@aol.com
Product Mgr. — Bill Muir

Quipp System Inc.
4800 N.W. 157th St.
Miami, FL 33014
tel (305) 623-8700; fax (305) 623-0980
President — Louis D. Kipp
VP-Mktg. & Int'l Sales — John F. Green
USA Sales Dir. — Angel Arrabal
Exec. Vice Pres. — Christer Stogren

QUNO Corp.
80 King St.
St. Catharines, ON L2R 7G1 Canada
tel (905) 688-5030; fax (905) 688-6005
Vice Pres.-Mktg. & Sales — M.L. Bundy

R

R & K Communications
5186 Jaycox Rd.
North Ridgeville, OH 44039
tel (216) 327-5398; fax (216) 327-4552
e-mail rpleban@aol.com
President — Ron Pleban

Radius
1710 Fortune Dr.
San Jose, CA 95131
tel (408) 434-1010; fax (408) 434-0770
e-mail www.radius.com
Marketing Dir. — Dee Cravens

Rainy River Forest Products Inc.
145 3rd St. W.
Fort Frances, ON P9A 3N2 Canada
tel (807) 274-5311; fax (807) 274-6596
Manager — Ian Murray

Ramsey Technology Inc.
501 90th Ave., N.W.
Minneapolis, MN 55433
tel (612) 783-2500; fax (612) 780-2315
Mktg. Comm. Mgr. — Don Bina

Random Access
62 Birdsall St.
Greene, NY 13778
tel (607) 656-7584
Mktg. Mgr. — William Marsland

RapidTec Inc.
9126 Industrial Blvd.
Covington, GA 30209
tel (800) 252-6538/(770) 787-5080
fax (770) 787-4589
President — Kenneth Holmes
Vice Pres.-Finance — Alan Taylor
Cus. Svc. Mgr. — Rita Harper

Rapistan Demag Corp.
507 Plymouth Ave., N.E.
Grand Rapids, MI 49505
tel (616) 451-6525; fax (616) 451-6425
President — P.J. Metros
Vice Pres.-Marketing — J. Raab
Vice Pres.-Field Sales — J.C. Brouckman
Vice Pres.-Finance — W. Marchido
Purchasing Manager — R. Klaasen
Mktg. Support Spec. — Esther M. Land

Rasterops
2500 Walsh Ave.
Santa Clara, CA 95051
tel (408) 562-4200; fax (408) 562-4065
Dir.-Product Mktg. — Carl Calabria

Bob Ray & Associates Inc.
41 Walter Ct.
Algonquin, IL 60102
tel (708) 658-1984; fax (708) 658-3397
President — Robert E. Ray
Vice Pres. — William R. Markham
Vice Pres.-Sales — John R. Steker

Moss Reck & Associates Inc.
15 W. 700 N. Frontage Rd., #116
Hinsdale, IL 60521
tel (800) 326-1357/(800) 826-1357
(Western US)/fax (708) 655-9890
President- U.S. — Moss Reck

Reeves Brothers Inc.
PO Box 1531
Spartanburg, SC 29304-1531
tel (803) 576-9210; fax (803) 595-2166
Gen. Sales Mgr. — John Kirsey

Rein Tech Inc. (Printing Systems Technology)
1226 Arthur Rd.
Naperville, IL 60540
tel (708) 357-8903; fax (708) 357-8903
President — Ray Reinertson

Rendic International
10700 Carribean, Ste. 204
Miami, FL 33189
tel (305) 567-1913; fax (305) 567-1918
President — Jerko E. Rendic
Regional Sales Mgr.-Brasil/S. Africa/Middle East — Paul Chmielewicz
Regional Sales Mgr.-Australia/New Zealand/Far East — Raymond Achen
Regional Sales Mgr.-South America — Fernando Tavara
Regional Sales Mgr.-Central America/Caribbean — Nestor Porto
Technical Service Mgr. — Al Miller

Renfro-Franklin Co.
525 W. Brooks St.
Ontario, CA 91762
tel (909) 984-5500/(800) 334-0937
fax (909) 984-2322
President — Thomas G. Turner
Gen. Mgr. — Ronald L. Grassette
Office Mgr. — Joyce Oley
Sales Mgr. — Donald Kemby
Sec./Treas. — Inge E. Turner

Republic Roller Corp.
1233 Millard St.; PO Box 330
Three Rivers, MI 49093-0330
tel (800) Rollers; fax (800) 273-ROLL
President — G.L. Umphrey

Republic Service Co.
415 S. Lively Blvd.
Elk Grove Village, IL 60007
tel (708) 830-8280/(708) 640-7586
Mktg. Mgr. — Roy Zemack

Research USA Inc.
645 N. Michigan Ave., Ste. 640
Chicago, IL 60611
tel (312) 337-1992; fax (312) 337-5079
Vice Pres.-Mktg. — Chris Mink

Resource Net International
7848 Barton
Lenexa, KS 66214
tel (913) 631-8700; fax (913) 631-3036
Vice Pres. — Don Trytten

Results Media
26 Jericho Tpke.
Jericho, NY 11753
tel (516) 997-7000; fax (516) 334-4055

Retail Solutions Group
100 Matsonford Rd., Bldg. 5, Ste. 375
Radnor, PA 19087
tel (610) 293-7100; fax (610) 293-7117
Managing Director — Bruce Sholes

Revere Graphics Worldwide
5 Boundary St.
Plymouth, MA 02360
tel (508) 746-1000; fax (508) 747-4589
President — Warren Kohnke
Mktg. Dir. — Ann Casey

Richard Mfg. Co. Inc.
206 State Rd., 200; PO Box 1080
Fernandina Beach, FL 32034
tel (904) 261-4075; fax (904) 261-9736
President — J. Carroll Fletcher
Sales Mgr. — J. Carter Fletcher

Richmond/Graphic Products Inc.
51 Worthington Rd.
Cranston, RI 02920
tel (401) 941-4144; fax (401) 467-1825
President — Hugh C. Neville
Vice Pres.-Mfg. — Dana N. Neville
Controller — P.J. Griffee

Ricoh Corp.
5 Dedrick Pl.
West Caldwell, NJ 07006
tel (201) 882-2000; fax (201) 882-5840
Chairman — H. Kubo
Vice Chairman — Hisao Yuasa

Roadshow International Inc.
8300 Greensboro Dr., Ste. 400
McLean, VA 22102
tel (703) 790-8300; fax (703) 790-8333
Vice Pres.-Sales — Vince Polentes

Robertson Press Machinery Co. Inc.
1502 S. Madison
Webb City, MO 64870
tel (417) 673-1929; fax (417) 673-4628
President — Bob Robertson
Mktg. Mgr. — Scheryl Lallemant

Rochester Institute of Technology
1 Lomb Memorial Dr.; PO Box 9887
Rochester, NY 14623-0887
tel (716) 475-2633; fax (716) 475-7029
e-mail rghppr@rit
Prof. — Dr. Robert G. Hacker
Tech. Svc. Coord. — John M. Marciniak

Rock-Built
1885 Main St.
Pittsburgh, PA 15215
tel (412) 784-1520; fax (412) 782-5267
President — Rock A. Ferrone
Vice Pres. — Bruce A. Barna

Rockwell Computer Solutions
810 N. Missouri Ave.
Corning, AR 72422-0128
tel (501) 857-3531/(800) 874-1490
fax (501) 857-5204
Sales — Diane McCullough

Rockwell Graphic Systems
108 Corporate Park, Ste. 200
White Plains, NY 10604
tel (914) 697-4200; fax (914) 697-4224
Vice Pres.-Sales — William Boston
Controller — Bernard Strache

Rockwell Graphic Systems
700 Oakmont Ln.
Westmont, IL 60559-5546
tel (708) 850-5600; fax (708) 850-6310
President — Robert L. Swift
Vice Pres.-Goss Newspaper Products — P.M. Kienzle
Contact — Wayne Perk

Roconex Corp.
20 Mary Bill Dr.
Troy, OH 45373
tel (513) 339-2616; fax (513) 339-1470
President — Tyrone Spear
Nat'l Sales Mgr. — Tom Snow

Copyright ©1996 by the Editor & Publisher Co.

VI-18   Equipment, supplies, services

Rogersal Inc.
5538 Northnorthwest Hwy.
Chicago, IL 60630
tel (312) 735-5100; fax (312) 775-9414
Owner — Charles Palmer
President — Norman Nichol
Director-Marketing — Kip Koran

Roggen Management Consultants Inc.
425 E. 63rd St.
New York, NY 10021
tel (212) 888-6269/(800) 676-4436
fax (212) 888-6270
President — Mark N. Roggen

Roll-Crafters/Custom Rubber Products
3902 E. 16th St.
Indianapolis, IN 46201
tel (317) 359-2776/(800) 428-9180
fax (317) 359-3983
President — Dwayne Henry
Division Manger — James Bredlow

Rollem Corp. of America
43 Polk Ave.
Hempstead, NY 11550
tel (516) 485-6655; fax (516) 485-5936
Vice Pres. — Richard Nigro

George Romano Ltd.
6165 N. Via de La Tortola
Tucson, AZ 85718
tel (520) 299-5292
President — George Romano

Roosevelt Paper
7601 State Rd.
Philadelphia, PA 19136
tel (215) 331-5000/(800) 523-3470
fax (215) 338-1199
President — Ted Kosloff

Rosback Co.
125 Hawthorne Ave.
St. Joseph, MI 49085
tel (616) 983-2582; fax (616) 983-2516
President — L.R. Bowman
Vice Pres.-Sales — R.F. Bowman

Rotation Dynamics Corp.
15 Salt Creek Ln., Ste. 309
Hinsdale, IL 60521
tel (708) 325-1460; fax (708) 325-0745
VP-Sales & Mktg. — John A. Costello

Rothesay Newsprint Sales Inc., See Irving Forest Products

Rotoflex International
420 Ambassador Dr.
Mississayga, ON L5T 2R5 Canada
tel (905) 670-8700; fax (905) 670-3402
President — Reinhard Muhs
Vice Pres. — Harald Muhs
Finance Manager — Rod Allen
Director-Manufacturing — Gordon Draper
GM/VP-Sales & Mktg. — Val Rimas

H.B. Rouse & Co.
1101 W. Diggins St.
Harvard, IL 60033
tel (815) 943-4426; fax (815) 943-7156
President — John H. Knoll

Rowlett Advertising Service Inc.
PO Box 50
Goodlettsville, TN 37070-0050
tel (615) 859-6609; fax (615) 851-7187
President — Richard Rowlett
Sec./Treas. — Mary Belcher

Royal Press Parts Inc.
1502 S. Madison
Webb City, MO 64870
tel (417) 673-4627; fax (417) 673-4628
President — Bob Robertson
Mktg. Mgr. — Scheryl Lallemant

RRA, INC. & Associates
13 Blutt Head Rd.
Sharon, MA 02067
tel (617) 784-7501; fax (617) 784-5451
Pres — Richard S. Rowse
VP — Dwight L. Rogers

R T P Technical Specialists
1210 Pinar Dr.
Orlando, FL 32825
tel (407) 273-9379/1 (500) 673-9379
Owner — William C. Spells

RTR Computer Consulting Inc.
49 Range Rd., Rte. 111 (03087)
PO Box 4010
Windham, NH 03087-4010
tel (603) 894-5166; fax (603) 894-5168
President — Tom Drane

Bill Rudder & Associates Inc.
122-B Stroupe Rd.
Gastonia, NC 28056-8652
tel (704) 824-7865; fax (704) 824-2043
President — Bill Rudder

Rummel Engineering
39 Green St.
Waltham, MA 02154
tel (617) 736-7959; fax (617) 736-7975
Vice Pres.-Mktg. — Rosanna Garcia

Ryco Graphic Manufacturing Inc.
2181 S. Foster Ave.
Wheeling, IL 60090
tel (708) 259-3330; fax (708) 259-3422
Chairman — A.J. Magro
Eng. & Production Dir. — R. Nelson
Reg. Sales. Mgr. — Steven J. Brown
Director — Thomas J. Carbery
Ryco Technology (A Subsidiary of Ryco)
President — Thomas G. Switall
Secretary — Barbara Miller
Eng. Mgr. — Gregory Stewart

Rycoline Products Inc.
5540 N.W. Hwy.
Chicago, IL 60630
tel (312) 775-6755/(800) 621-1003
fax (312) 775-7414
President — Norman J. Nichol
Dir.-Special Mkts. — Donald D. Geralds

Ryder System Inc.
3600 N.W. 82nd. Ave.; PO Box 020816
Miami, FL 33166
tel (305) 593-3726; fax (305) 593-3203
Chairman/Pres./CEO — Anthony M. Burns
Exec. Vice Pres.-Mktg. — J. Ernie Riddle

S

S & P ComStock
600 Mamaroneck Ave.
Harrison, NY 10528
tel (914) 381-7000; fax (914) 381-7021
Mktg. Mgr. — Jennifer Mello

Safety-Kleen Corp.
1000 N. Randall Rd.
Elgin, IL 60123-7857
tel (708) 697-8460; fax (708) 468-8515
Chairman — Donald W. Brinckman
President/CEO — John G. Johnson
Sr. Vice Pres.-Mktg. — Michael Carney
Coordinator — Annette Wilson

The Safetyloid Reclaiming Co. Inc.
125 Glenn St.
Lawrence, MA 01843
tel (800) 942-5337; fax (508) 688-8416
President — Dean A. Quinlan
Vice Pres./Treas. — Thomas Quinlan
Oper. Mgr. — Gene Mullen

Sakata Inx USA Corp.
651 Bonnie Ln.
Elk Grove Village, IL 60007
tel (708) 593-3211; fax (708) 364-5290
Branch Mgr. — George Suemasa

Sales Development Services
1335 Dublin Rd., Ste. 200A
Columbus, OH 43215
tel (614) 481-3530/(800) MORE-ADS
fax (614) 548-0397
President — C. Lee Smith

Sales Training Consultants Inc.
10312 Panama St.
Hollywood, FL 33026
tel (305) 436-3096/(800) 940-1230
President — Alice Kemper
Sales & Mktg. Mgr. — Michelle Barton
Consultant/Trainer — Jacqueline Tezyk

Saxe Inc.
6070 Greenwood Plz. Blvd.
Englewood, CO 80111
tel (303) 770-3300; fax (303) 220-8822
e-mail pdeltoro@saxe.com
Owner — Andrew Saxe
Dir.-Strategic Mktg. — Paul DelToro

Saxmayer Corp.
318 W. Adrian; PO Box 10
Blissfield, MI 49228
tel (517) 486-2164; fax (517) 486-2055
CEO — Maria Vennekotter
Pres. — Bret M. Veldhoff
Sr. Acct. Exec. — Ruth Rodesiler
Sec./Treas. — Phyllis Mallory

SCA Promotions Inc.
8300 Douglas Ave., Ste. 625
Dallas, TX 75225
tel (214) 363-8744/(800) 527-5409
fax (214) 691-3071
President — Robert D. Hamman
Vice Pres. — Susan Singer
Vice Pres./Gen. Mgr. — Barry Schaffer
Mktg. Coordinator — Susan Wingo

Scandinavian PC Systems Inc.
PO Box 3156
Baton Rouge, LA 70821-3156
tel (504) 338-9580; fax (504) 338-9670
e-mail spcsinc@intersurf.com
http://www.intersurf.com/~spcsinc/
President — Mark W. McBride

Scantronix
14311 Cerise, Ste. 108
Hawthorne, CA 90250
tel (310) 644-8585; fax (310) 644-6027
Mktg. Mgr. — Stephen Dulley

Scarborough Associates
3102 Oak Lawn Ave.
Dallas, TX 75219
tel (214) 520-0270; fax (214) 522-4739
President — Robert L. Cohen
Sr. Vice Pres. — Gary Seidner

Ernest Schaefer Inc.
731 Lehigh Ave.
Union, NJ 07083
tel (908) 964-1280; fax (908) 964-6787
Sales Mgr. — Ernest Schaefer Jr.

Schaefer Machine Co. Inc.
200 Commercial Dr.
Deep River, CT 06417
tel (860) 526-4000; fax (860) 526-4654
President — Bob Gammons
Vice Pres. — Virginia Gammons

Schuler Sales/A Kolbus Group Subsidiary
25 Whitney Rd.
Mahwah, NJ 07430
tel (201) 848-8600; fax (201) 848-0368
Exec. Vice Pres. — Al Katz
Vice Pres.-Sales — Tom Roche
Gen. Mgr. — Bob Reynolds
Advg. Mktg. Mgr. — Sam Troiano
Controller — John Sloane

Scitex America Corp.
8 Oak Park Dr.
Bedford, MA 01730
tel (617) 275-5150; fax (617) 275-3430
e-mail ..scitex.com
President/CEO — Shimon Alone
Vice Pres./Gen. Mgr. — Ray Wilson
Vice Pres.-Sales — Charlie Noonan
Vice Pres.-Cust. Support — Bill Davidson
Vice Pres.-Finance — Sue Rogers
VP-Human Resources — Jack Whelan

SCREEN (USA)
5110 Tollview Dr.
Rolling Meadows, IL 60008
tel (708) 870-7400; fax (708) 870-0149
President/CEO — Kenneth Newton
Vice Pres.-Finance — Hiro Matsuo
Vice Pres.-Oper. — Tryhisa Kosaka
Mgr.-Product Mktg. — Dave Mitchell

SeeColor Corp.
PO Box 3148
Federal Way, WA 98063
tel (206) 946-1948; fax (206) 946-2739
President — Ron LaForge
Dir.-OEM Sales — Dale Lehn
Vice Pres.-Sales — Karen Barr

SEG
126 A Main St.
Watertown, MA 02172
tel (617) 924-6664; fax (617) 924-3402
President — Andrew Agoos

Selling Dynamics Inc.
1723 Dooley Ln.; PO Box 5186
Lakeland, FL 33813
tel (813) 644-4412; fax (813) 648-1279
Mktg. Mgr. — Lou Del Castillo

Semler Industries Inc. (Graphic Arts Products Div.)
3800 N. Carnation St.
Franklin Park, IL 60131-1295
tel (708) 671-5650; fax (708) 671-7686
President — Loren H. Semler
Dir.-Product Bus. Dev. — Alan M. Scheufler
Sales Dir. — William E. Schulz

Seybold Publications Inc.
428 E. Baltimore Ave.; PO Box 644
Media, PA 19063
tel (610) 565-2480; fax (610) 565-4659
e-mail sedwards@sbexpos.com
Publisher — Jonathan Seybold
Editor — Stephen Edwards
Assoc. Editor — Peter Dyson

Shaffstall Corp.
7901 E. 88th St.
Indianapolis, IN 46256-1293
tel (317) 842-2077; fax (317) 842-8294
President — Everett L. Shaffstall
Applications Mgr. — J. Olin
Vice Pres.-Sales — A.L. Shaffstall

Sheridan Systems
4900 Webster St.
Dayton, OH 45414
tel (513) 278-2651; fax (513) 274-5719
President — Richard J. Bonnie
Sr. Vice Pres.-Sales — Peter J. Gettings
Vice Pres.-Sales — M. Doug Gibson
Mgr.-Mktg. & Admn. — David C. Slauter

H. Sherr Engravers Inc.
54 W. 21st St., Ste. 706
New York, NY 10010
tel (212) 242-8630
President — Henry Sherr

Shreve Systems
1200 Marshall St.
Shreveport, LA 71101
tel (318) 424-9777; fax (318) 424-9771
Sales Mgr. — Jesse Steel

David A. Shulda Enterprises Inc.
307 Avenida Adobe
San Clemente, CA 92672
tel (714) 964-6661
Consultant — David A. Shulda

Shuttleworth Inc.
10 Commercial Rd.
Huntington, IN 46750
tel (219) 356-8500; fax (219) 356-1315
Chairman — James J. Shuttleworth
Dir.-Sales & Mktg. — John C. Jepsen
Mgr.-Tech. Oper. — Steve Hart

SI Handling Systems Inc.
600 Kuebler Rd.; PO Box 70
Easton, PA 18040
tel (610) 252-7321; fax (610) 250-9677
Chairman — Edward J. Fahey
President/CEO — Leonard S. Yurkovic
Mktg. Mgr. — Thomas J. Meyers
Vice Pres.-Sales — William J. Casey
Vice Pres.-Oper. — James L. Thatcher

Siebert Inc.
8134 W. 47th. St.
Lyons, IL 60534
tel (708) 442-2010; fax (708) 447-9353
President — J.P. Mulcahy
Secretary — Mrs. P. Mulcahy

Siemens Rolm Communications Inc.
4900 Old Ironsides Dr.; PO Box 58075
Santa Clara, CA 95054
tel (408) 492-2000; fax (408) 492-2160
President/CEO — Karl Geng
Exec. Vice Pres./CFO — Gebhard Doermer
Sr. Vice Pres.-Svc. — Dean Beckwith
Sr. Vice Pres.-Dev. — Hans Schwarz
Sr. Vice Pres.-Mfg. — Glenn BeFort
Sr. Vice Pres.-Mktg. — Richard Mattern
Mgr.-Media & Gov't. Relations — Carter Cromwell

Sifco Selective Plating (Div. of Sifco Industries Inc.)
5708 Schaaf Rd.
Cleveland, OH 44131-1394
tel (216) 524-0099; fax (216) 524-6331
President — Carter A. Graff
Mktg. Mgr. — Mike Moskowitz

Signode Corp.
3610 W. Lake Ave.
Glenview, IL 60025
tel (708) 724-6100; fax (708) 724-5910
President — R. Flaum
Graphic Arts Mgr. — Bill Sullivan
Dir.-Mktg. Comms. — Jim Fallon

Copyright ©1996 by the Editor & Publisher Co.

Equipment, supplies, services VI-19

Silverman Newspaper Management Consultants
143 Rosemont Ct.
Walnut Creek, CA 94596
tel (510) 939-3030; fax (510) 937-6143
Owner — Herman Silverman

Silver Treatment Systems Inc.
20 Aegean Dr.
Methuen, MA 01844
tel (508) 682-6407; fax (508) 682-1396
President — Gerson Rosenfield

Simco Co. Inc.
2257 N. Penn Rd.
Hatfield, PA 19440
tel (215) 822-2171; fax (215) 822-3795
President/GM — Gary Swink
Vice Pres.-Finance — Michael Oldt
Vice Pres.-Operations — Bob McGuire
Vice Pres.-Engineering — Chuck Noll
Sales Director — Jay Perry
Sales Manager — Bob Heacock
Mktg. Manager — John Begley

Sinclair Imaging Inc.
871 Mountain Ave.
Springfield, NJ 07081
tel (201) 376-1272; fax (201) 376-0903
President — George A. Sinclair

SITMA USA Inc.
45 Empire Dr.
St. Paul, MN 55103-1856
tel (612) 222-2324/(800) 728-1254
fax (612) 222-4652
Managing Dir. — Pete Butikis

SKO Brenner American
196 Merrick Rd.
Oceanside, NY 11572
tel (516) 764-4400; fax (516) 764-4490
CEO — Stuart Brenner
COO — Jon R. Lunn

H.R. Slater Co. Inc.
2050 W. 18th St.
Chicago, IL 60608
tel (312) 666-1855; fax (312) 666-1856
Office Mgr. — William C. St. Hilaire
Sales Mgr. — Robert Kurzka

Lee Smith Industries
4602 Bittersweet Rd.
Louisville, KY 40218
tel (502) 966-3669; fax (502) 964-2928
Owner — Lee Smith
Office Mgr. — Tina Becker

Smith RPM Corp.
9040 Cody St.
Overland Park, KS 66214
tel (913) 888-0695; fax (913) 888-0699
President — Vicky F. Smith

Smurfit Newsprint Corp.
427 Main St.
Oregon City, OR 97045
tel (503) 650-4211
President — Truman L. Sturdevant
Mgr.-Sales & Mktg. — Jon E. Melkerson
Director-Operations — Jay D Lamb
VP-Sales & Mktg. — James R. Tisdale
Reg. Sales Mgr. — Ronald A Osberg.

Snow Graphics
285 Mooselodge Rd.
Griffin, GA 30223
tel (404) 228-5596
President — Virgil Snow

Software Consulting Services
3162 Bath Pike
Nazareth, PA 18064
tel (215) 837-8484; fax (215) 837-8080
President — Richard J. Cichelli
Vice Pres. — Martha J. Cichelli
Vice Pres.-Sales — Edward J. Houcek
Dir.-Oper. — Curtis Jackson

The Software Development Group Inc.
49 Berwyn Pl.
Fair Lawn, NJ 07410
tel (201) 703-0243; fax (201) 791-0497
President — Ronald Berg

Solna Web USA Inc.
14500 W. 105th St.; PO Box 15066
Lenexa, KS 66285-5066
tel (913) 492-9925; fax (913) 492-0170
President — Rich Kerns
Dir.-Sales & Mktg. — Travis D. Ferguson
Sales Eng. — Roger Bare

Sonic Systems
225 Santa Monica Blvd., Ste. 312
Santa Monica, CA 90401
tel (310) 458-9999; fax (310) 394-4645
Nat'l. Sales Mgr. — Shawn Isaacson

Sonoco Products Co.
1 N. 2nd St.
Hartsville, SC 29550
tel (803) 383-7000; fax (803) 339-6011
Global IPD Mktg. Mgr./PMC — Scott Pleune
Product Mgr.-PMC/NA — Linwood Roper

Sony Electronics Inc.
1 Sony Dr.
Park Ridge, NJ 07656-8003
tel (201) 930-6121; fax (201) 358-4942
Chmn./CEO — Michael Shulof
President/COO — Carl Yankowski
VP-Mktg. Consumer Products — Y. Nozoe
Vice Pres.-Corp. Comm. — Jason Sarrow
Dir.-Consumer Advg. — Richard Johnson

Source Data Systems
950 Ridgemont Dr., N.E.
Cedar Rapids, IA 52402
tel (319) 393-3343; fax (319) 393-8553
Vice Pres.-Sales & Mktg. — Jeff Kenjar

Southeast Paper Newsprint Sales
1800 Parkway Pl., Ste. 1020
Marietta, GA 30067
tel (770) 919-7502; fax (770) 919-7523
President — G.B. DeLashmet
Sales Mgr. — Mark S. Klimko
Mgr.-Tech. Sales — John D. Freeman
Mgr.-Cus. Svc. — John M. Fletcher

Southern Lithoplate Inc.
105 Jeffrey Way; PO Box 9400
Wake Forest, NC 27587
tel (919) 556-9400/(800) 638-7990
fax (919) 554-0786
VP-Sales & Mktg. — Steve Mattingly

Southwest Alabama Radio Resources Bureau
2665 Pleasant Valley Rd.
Mobile, AL 36606
tel (334) 473-3946
Associate Editor — Roy E. Kadel

SPECTRUM Human Resource Systems Corp.
1625 Broadway, Ste. 2700
Denver, CO 80202-4718
tel (303) 534-8813/(800) 334-5660
fax (303) 592-3227
President — James E. Spoor
Vice Pres.-Mktg. — Nancy E. Spoor
Mktg. Svc. Mgr. — Pam Oberly

William C. Spells (RTP Technical Specialists)
1210 Pinar Dr.
Orlando, FL 32825-7820
tel (407) 273-9379
Tech. Spec. — William C. Spells

Springfield Silver Service
10815 State Rte. 161; PO Box 89
Mechanicsburg, OH 43044
tel (513) 834-2293; fax (513) 834-2164
Sales Mgr. — Terry Ransbottom

Spruce Falls Inc.
2 Carlton St., Ste. 605
Toronto, ON M5B 1J9 Canada
tel (800) 565-3021; fax (416) 977-4780
President/CEO — F.A. Dottori
Vice Pres.-Mktg. — D.J. Schalk
Vice Pres.-Corp. Dev. — M.R. Hicks
Vice Pres.- Finance — M.J. Dumas
VP/GM-Newsprint Oper. — D.A. Turcotte
VP/GM-Forest Products Div. — D.R. Goss
VP-Eng. & Purchasing — L.N. Parent

SRDS (Standard Rate & Data Service)
1700 Higgens Rd.
Des Plaines, IL 60018
tel (708) 375-5000; fax (708) 375-5001
Publisher — Kathleen Geary
Director-Mktg. — Edward R. Padin

Standard Electric and Engineering Co.
930 Linden Ave.
South San Francisco, CA 94080
tel (415) 952-6500; fax (415) 952-0102
President — E.C. (Bud) Torr
Vice Pres. — Gary Thompson
Mgr. Mfg. — Mike Vitalie
Mgr. Installation — Bob Hansen

Standlee and Associates Inc.
7609 Pine Hollow Ct.
Orlando, FL 32822
tel (407) 273-5218; fax (407) 273-9011
President — James L. Standlee
Office Mgr. — Deborah L. Standlee
Sales — Fred S. Foster

Stanford Div./MAN Roland Inc.
Rte. 50 W.; PO Box 578
Salem, IL 62881
tel (618) 548-2600; fax (618) 548-6782

Marketing Director — Larry Boyles
Gen. Mgr. — R. Sherman
Customer Service Mgr. — Tim Andrews
Parts Manager — Deann Sager

Star International Corp.
601 Oakmont Ln., Ste. 450
Westmont, IL 60559
tel (708) 850-4333; fax (708) 850-8787
President — A.W. Hospel
Marketing Mgr. — Annette Lesieutre

Starlite Software Corp.
Port Hadlock
Seattle, WA 98339
tel (360) 385-7125; fax (360) 385-7136
e-mail starlite@daka.com
President — Gordon Wanner
Head Tech. — Mike Butler

Stauffer Media Systems
3316 E. 32nd St.; PO Box 1330
Joplin, MO 64802
tel (417) 782-0280; fax (417) 782-1282
Sales Mgr. — Keith Wood
Sales Rep. — Kim Sexton
Sales Rep. — Mike Forman

Steel City Corp./Motor Route Supplies
PO Box 1227
Youngstown, OH 44501
tel (800) 321-0350; fax (216) 792-7951
President — C. Kenneth Fibus
Vice Pres.-Sales — Lee Rouse

Stepper Inc.
PO Box 1126
Olathe, KS 66051-1126
tel (913) 782-2580; fax (913) 782-2441
Vice Pres. — Charles Hannon
Mktg. Mgr. — Dave Hannon

Sterling Packaging Systems
25800 1st St.
Westlake, OH 44145
tel (216) 899-2626; fax (216) 899-2622
GM — Carl Hansen

Sterling Type Foundry
7830 Ridgeland Dr.; Box 50234
Indianapolis, IN 46250
tel (317) 849-5665; fax (317) 849-1616
Works Mgr. — David C. Churchman
Asst. Mgr. — David W. Peat

Stewart Glapat Corp.
1639 Moxahala Ave.; PO Box 2486
Zanesville, OH 43702-2486
tel (614) 452-3601; fax (614) 452-9140
Sales Mgr. — C. Dutch Lewis

STI - Separation Technologies Inc.
4000 E. Leaverton Ct.
Anaheim, CA 92807
tel (714) 632-1306; fax (714) 632-3269
President — H. Leonard

Herman H. Sticht Co. Inc.
57 Front St.
Brooklyn, NY 11201
tel (718) 852-7602; fax (718) 852-7915
President — Paul H. Plotkin

STM Wireless Inc.
1 Mauchly
Irvine, CA 92718
tel (714) 753-7864; fax (714) 753-1122
Vice Chairman/Exec. VP — Frank Connors

Walter Stobb Associates Inc.
1515 Murex Dr.
Naples, FL 33940
tel (941) 262-8400; fax (941) 262-8400
President — Walter J. Stobb
Sec./Treas. — J.M. Stobb

Stoesser Register Systems
2440 Leghorn St.; PO Box 7231
Mountain View, CA 94043
tel (800) 877-1283/(415) 969-3252
fax (415) 967-5963
President — Bill J. Stoesser
CFO — Michael Rogers
Mktg. & Comm. Mgr. — Sheri Dunn

Stone Consolidated
2 Soundview Dr.
Greenwich, CT 06836
tel (203) 861-0300; fax (203) 869-5353
President — David A. Schirmer
VP-Uncoated Groundwood Papers — Hugh McCloskey
Vice Pres.-Publisher Sales — Eli Babcock

Stone-Consolidated Corp.
800 Rene-Levesque Blvd., W.
Montreal, QC H3B 1Y9 Canada
tel (514) 875-2160; fax (514) 875-6284
Chairman — Roger W. Stone
President/CEO — James Doughan
Pres./Stone-Consolidated Paper Sales Corp. — D.A. Schirmer
PR/Comm. Mgr. — Denise Dallaire

Stone-Consolidated Newsprint Inc.
555 Fifth Ave., Seventh Fl.
New York, NY 10017
tel (212) 687-1200
President — David A. Schirmer

Lester A. Stone Inc.
PO Box 590
Holyoke, MA 01041
tel (413) 532-7207
President — Lillian C. Stone

Stonier Trucking Co. Inc.
2315 Beach Blvd., Ste. 201
Jacksonville Beach, FL 32250
tel (904) 249-0604/(800) 242-8548
fax (904) 249-7299
President — Deane Stonier
Vice Pres. — David Stonier
Treas./Sec. — Keith Kelley
Bookkeeping — Karen Smith
Bookkeeping — Lorah Barber
Bookkeeping — Gene Wood
Dispatcher — Traci Jones
Dispatcher — Lorrie Chauncey
Dispatcher — Brian Dick
Dispatcher — Nancy Hillier

Stowe Woodward Co. (Div. BTR Paper Group)
333 Turnpike Rd.
Southborough, MA 01772
tel (508) 460-9600; fax (508) 481-5392
President — N.N. August
Vice Pres.-Sales — Ron C. Westgate

Strapex Corp.
PO Box 7526
Charlotte, NC 28241-7526
tel (704) 588-2510; fax (704) 588-8795
Mktg. Admn. — Annette Barnett
Dir.-Nat'l. Accts. — Mike Mingle

Strategic Telemedia
Box 1162, Old Chelsea Sta.
New York, NY 10011
tel (212) 366-0895; fax (212) 366-0897
Mktg. Research & Consultant — Mark Plakias

Summerville Press Inc.
1733 King St.
Alexandria, VA 22314
tel (703) 838-2820; fax (703) 838-2826
President — Margaret Byrne Heimbold
Circulation Mgr. — Gregory L. Watson

Sun Graphic Inc.
1820 N.W. 21st St.
Pompano Beach, FL 33069
tel (305) 974-0217; fax (305) 974-0304
Chairman/Owner — Charles Palmer
President — Norman Nichol

SunShine Paper Co.
12601 E. 33rd Ave.
Aurora, CO 80011-1839
tel (303) 341-2990; fax (303) 341-2995
President — John Ankerman
Plant Mgr. — James Morland
Vice Pres.-Mktg. — Alison Ankerman
Customer Service — Sarah Jones

Superior Lithoplate of Indiana Inc.
Strawberry Rd.; PO Box 192
Rockville, IN 47872
tel (317) 569-2094; fax (317) 569-2096
President — Robert T. Blane
Accounts Manager — Tracy Nickle

Support Products Inc.
309 W. Professional Park Ave.; PO Box 1185
Effingham, IL 62401
tel (217) 347-0711; fax (217) 536-6828
CEO — Jim Calhoon
Pres./Vice Pres.-Sales — Ina Schlechte
Vice Pres.-Sales Mgr. — Bob McWilliams

Support Systems International Corp.
150 S. 2nd St.
Richmond, CA 94804
tel (510) 234-9090; fax (510) 233-8888
President — Ben Parsons
Vice Pres.-Mktg. — Richard St. John

Copyright ©1996 by the Editor & Publisher Co.

VI-20 Equipment, supplies, services

Synaptic Micro Solutions
1075 S. Van Dyke Rd.
Appleton, WI 54915-8844
tel (800) 526-6547/(414) 734-6535;
fax (414) 734-8003
e-mail moreinfo@smsc.com
President — Elwin Coats
Sales Mgr. — Jim O'Neill
Eastern Sales — Steve Kuckuk
Western Sales — Bruce Kuechmann

Syntactics
PO Box 50036
Palo Alto, CA 94303-0036
tel (408) 727-6400; fax (408) 727-0309
Sales Mgr. — Erwin Morton

Syntellect Inc.
15810 N. 28th Ave.
Phoenix, AZ 85023
tel (602) 789-2800; fax (602) 789-2899
President — Steve Nussrallah
Mktg. Dir. — Tricia Lester

Sysdeco U.S.
15 Crosby Dr.
Bedford, MA 01730-1418
tel (617) 275-2323; fax (617) 276-1253
COO — Clive Segal

CFO — Debra Belanger
Dir.-Sales — Jerome Riley

System Facilities Inc.
500 E. Westfield Rd.; PO Box 7079
Charlottesville, VA 22906
tel (804) 978-4409; fax (804) 974-1752
President — John Badoud
Bus. Mgr. — Tori Walker

System Guides
31 Sandpiper Strand
Coronado, CA 92118
tel (619) 575-6974
Mktg. Dir. — James Root

Systems Oasis (Div. of Graphic Enterprises of Ohio Inc.)
439 Market Ave. N.
Canton, OH 44702
tel (216) 452-2033;fax (216) 452-8417
Dir.-Bus. Dev/ — Donald Frank
Vice Pres. — Les Beyeler

T

T/Maker Co.
1390 Villa St.
Mountain View, CA 94041
tel (415) 962-0195; fax (415) 962-0201
Public Relations Mgr. — Michelle Mecham

T/One Inc.
Batterymarch Park I
Quincy, MA 02169
tel (617) 328-6645; fax (617) 328-9845
President — David M. Tenenbaum

Tab Newspapers
1254 Chestnut St.
Newton, MA 02164-9113
tel (617) 964-2400; fax (617) 964-2476
Sales Dir. — Cris Warren

Taft Contracting Co. (not affiliated w/Taft Equipment. Co.)
5525 W. Roosevelt Rd.
Chicago, IL 60650
tel (708) 656-7500; fax (708) 656-8945
Chairman/Pres. — Richard J. Walsh
Vice Pres.-Sales — Michael Walsh
Vice Pres.-Oper. — John Bianchi
Graphic Sales Mgr. — John Medigovich

TALX Corp.
1850 Borman Ct.
St. Louis, MO 63146
tel (314) 434-0046; fax (314) 434-9205
e-mail moreinfo@talx.com
Mktg. Specialist — Tracy Baunach

Tasope Co.
1051 E. Church St.; PO Box 111
Aurora, MO 65605
tel (417) 678-4193
President — C.R. Hillhouse
Secretary — D.L. Hillhouse
Vice Pres. — Raelynn Hillhouse

Tech-Energy Co.
1111 Schneider Dr.
Cibolo, TX 78108
tel (210) 658-0614; fax (210) 658-0653
President — John E. Pickard
Vice Pres. — Beth Benke
Int'l. Sales Mgr. — Rachel Bell
Nat'l. Sales Mgr. — Louis Benke
Secretary — Phyllis Pickard
Treasurer — Teresa Moeller

Technidyne Corp.
100 Quality Ave.
New Albany, IN 47150-2272
tel (812) 948-2884; fax (812) 945-6847
e-mail 74734.1131@compuserve.com
President — S. Jerry Popson
Exec. Vice Pres — David D. Malthouse
Expert Sales Mgr. — Paul M. Crawford

The Technology Group
36 S. Charles St., Ste. 2200
Baltimore, MD 21201
tel (410) 576-2040; fax (410) 576-1968

Techtron Imaging Center
160 E. Illinois
Chicago, IL 60611
tel (312) 644-4999; fax (312) 337-3727
Gen. Mgr. — Neal Schecter
Vice Pres.-Sales — Robert Harley
Vice Pres./Dir.-Oper. — Wally Pabst

Tecnavia SA/Press Div.
Via Cadepiano 28
6917 Barbengo Lugano, Switzerland
tel (41-91) 552121; fax (41-91) 552223
General Manager — Dona Vanoni
Sales — Bruno Rimoldi
Tech. Dir. — Giancarlo Vanoni

Tecnigraph T.G.I. International Inc.
289 3rd Ave., CP 400
Lac Etchemin, QC G0R 1S0 Canada
tel (418) 625-4801; fax (418) 625-4801
President — Michel Begin

Tel-Aire Publications Inc.
PO Box 561467
Dallas, TX 75356-1467
tel (800) 749-1841; fax (214) 579-7483
Mktg. Dir. — Richard Stein

Tel-Management Inc.
2337 Lemoine Ave.
Fort Lee, NJ 07024
tel (201) 224-6510; fax (201) 224-6510 ext.123
Reg. Mgr. — Dave Tirpak

Tele-Publishing Inc.
126 Brookline Ave.
Boston, MA 02215
tel (617) 536-2340; fax (617) 536-7977
President — Andrew B. Sutcliffe
Vice Pres. — David M. Dinnage
Dir.-Development — Peter J. Brennan

Nat'l. Sales Dir. — David Miller
Mktg. Dir. — Nancilee Franklyn
Dir.-New Media — Scott Herzog

Tele-Sales Systems Inc.
2720 E. Thomas Rd., Ste. B-200
Phoenix, AZ 85016
tel (602) 954-7717; fax (602) 954-7730
President — Salvatore C. Terzo

Telecorp Systems Inc.
1000 Holcomb Woods Pkwy., Ste. 410A
Roswell, GA 30076
tel (404) 587-0700; fax (404) 587-0589
CEO — Larry Bradner

TeleDirect International Inc.
5510 Utica Ridge Rd.
Davenport, IA 52807
tel (319) 355-6440; fax (319) 355-4890
e-mail teledirect@netins.net
President — Kathleen Kelly
Vice Pres.-Sales & Mktg. — Thomas Miller
Sales Mgr.-East — Laura Blong
Sales Mgr.-Midwest — Jeff Kinning

Telephone Response Technologies
1624 Santa Clara Dr., Ste. 200
Roseville, CA 95661
tel (916) 784-7777; fax (916) 784-7781
President — Chris Bajorek
Sales Director — Mark Stadler
Dir-Operations — Kim Lane

Telesonic Packaging Corp.
108 Comstock Hill Rd.
Norwalk, CT 06851
tel (203) 847-2454; fax (203) 847-3618
President — Bernard Katz

TeleSystems Marketing Inc.
11320 Random Hills Rd., Ste. 200
Fairfax, VA 22030
tel (703) 385-1212; fax (703) 385-2091
Regional Accts. Mgr. — Dan Krantz
Regional Accts. Mgr. — Guy Williams

TeleTypesetting Co.
311 Harvard St.
Brookline, MA 02146
tel (617) 734-9700; fax (617) 734-3974
e-mail info@teletype.com
Mktg. Mgr. — Marlene Winer
Mktg. Mgr. — Edward Freeman

Ternes Register System
2361 W. Hwy. 36
St. Paul, MN 55113
tel (612) 633-2361; fax (612) 633-2373
President — Clifford L. Allen
Sales Mgr. — Robert Rotter
Director-Bus. Dev. — David Martin

Texas Instruments Inc.
13510 N. Central Expwy.; PO Box 655012
Dallas, TX 75265
tel (800) 336-5236

Thompson Cabinet Co.
510 E. Lake St.; PO Box 607
Ludington, MI 49431
tel (616) 843-7000; fax (616) 843-4200
VP-Sales Mgr. — Edward Thompson Jr.

Three Sigma
1329 Santa Cruz Dr.
Minden, NV 89423
tel (702) 267-5760; fax (702) 267-2360
President — Ann Tisue

3M Printing & Publishing Systems Div.
3M Ctr., Bldg. 223-2N-01
St. Paul, MN 55144-1000
tel (612) 733-0483; fax (612) 737-4771
Mktg. Comm. Mgr. — William Schultz

Tidland Corp.
2305 S.E. 8th Ave.; PO Box 1008
Camas, WA 98607
tel (800) 426-1000/(360) 834-2345
fax (360) 834-5865
President — Boren Biswas
Vice Pres.-Fin. — Alan R. Deming
Int'l./Nat'l. Sales Mgr. — Bill Leistritz
Mktg. Mgr. — Laurie Winton

Tilt-Lock Inc.
3800 5th St. N.E.
Columbia Heights, MN 55421
tel (612) 781-5095; fax (612) 781-5194
Sales Mgr. — Joe Burns

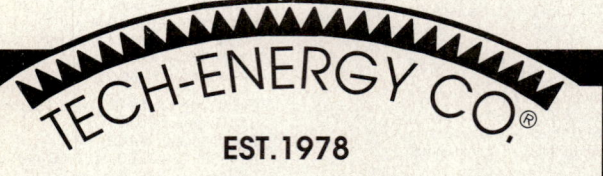

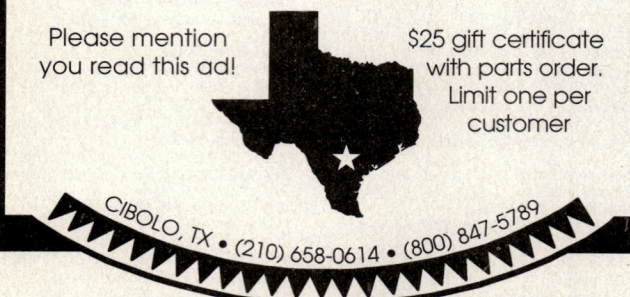

TECH-ENERGY CO. ® EST. 1978

"WHY SETTLE FOR ACCEPTABLE, WHEN YOU CAN HAVE EXCEPTIONAL!"

Replacement Press Parts • Service

★

Double Width Cutdown

★

Segmented Ink Fountain Blade

★

Hydraulic Roll Lifter

★

Running Circumferential

★

Save!
• Paper • Ink • Time • Money

Please mention you read this ad!

$25 gift certificate with parts order. Limit one per customer

CIBOLO, TX • (210) 658-0614 • (800) 847-5789

Copyright ©1996 by the Editor & Publisher Co.

Equipment, supplies, services

Tingue Brown & Co.
535 N. Midland Ave.
Saddle Brook, NJ 07663-5521
tel (201) 796-4490; fax (201) 796-5820
President — William J. Tingue

TKS (USA) Inc.
1201 Commerce Dr.
Richardson, TX 75081
tel (214) 437-4466; fax (214) 437-5858
Exec. Vice Pres.-Sales — John Hall
Sr. Sales Mgr. — Jesse M. Strong
Exec. Vice Pres. Eng. — Iwao Fukui
Sr. Mgr.-Cus. Svc. — Gary James
Dir.-R&D/Sys. Eng. — Charles (Chuck) Taylor
Sales & Installation Mgr. — Rick Palmer
Press Parts Sales — Robert Tovar

Tobias Associates Inc.
50 Industrial Dr.; PO Box 2699
Ivyland, PA 18974-0347
tel (215) 322-1500/(800) 877-3367
fax (215) 322-1504
President — Philip E. Tobias
Vice Pres. — Charlotte Tobias
Advg. Mgr. — Robin Crowley

Todd Machinery
10665 N.W. 42nd Dr.
Coral Springs, FL 33065
tel (305) 755-1777; fax (305) 755-1637
President — Todd Puntolillo
Vice Pres. — Kathryn Puntolillo

Tolerans-Ingol Inc.
1750 Brielle Ave., Unit B-2
Wanamassa, NJ 07712
tel (908) 918-8700; fax (908) 918-8701
Gen. Mgr. — Sterling Caudill

Toltech Systems
Carolina 98 Ste. 401
Mexico City, D F 03710 Mexico
tel (52-5) 615-2222; fax (52-5) 598-1352
e-mail toltechmail.internet.com.mx
Gen. Dir. — Timothy J. Tolman
Mktg. Dir. — Marti Gallagher

Toshiba Machine Co. America
755 Greenleaf Ave.
Elk Grove Village, IL 60007
tel (708) 593-1616; fax (708) 640-6197
Vice Pres.-Sales & Svc. — Robert F. Kinzel

Total Image Corp.
66 Willow Ave., Ste. 208
Staten Island, NY 10305-1237
tel (718) 720-9266; fax (718) 720-5715

Total Systems Engineering Inc.
990 E. Breckinridge St.
Louisville, KY 40204
tel (502) 587-0575; fax (502) 587-0484
President — Richard J. Masters
VP-Sales & Mktg. — Mark B. Thompson
Dir.-Operations — Martin Whelan
Business Manager — Robert Masters

Tower Products Inc.
2703 Freemansburg Ave.; PO Box 3070
Palmer, PA 18043
tel (800) 527-8626; fax (610) 258-9695
President — R.J. Principato

Transportation Consultants Inc.
5605 Glenridge Dr., Ste. 950
Atlanta, GA 30342
tel (404) 250-0100; fax (404) 250-0253
President — Paul Gold

Trauner Consulting Services Inc.
1500 Walnut St., Ste. 800
Philadelphia, PA 19102
tel (215) 546-0288; fax (215) 546-0285
Principal — Theodore J. Trauner Jr.
Vice Pres.-Bus. Dev. — Tracy M. Doyle
Mgr.-Bus. Dev. — Kathleen A. Morris
Mktg. Asst. — Patricia E. Power

Trendsetters Ltd.
30 Woods Grove Rd.
Westport, CT 06880
tel (203) 221-0221
President — James A Dye

Tribune Solutions
505 C St.; Box 957
Lewiston, ID 83501
tel (208) 743-9411; fax (208) 746-3741
e-mail gc@lmtribune.com
Gen. Mgr. — Wayne Hollingshead
Mgr.-Tribune Solutions — Glenn Cruickshank

TRUMATCH Inc.
25 W. 43rd St., Ste. 817
New York, NY 10036-7406
tel (212) 302-9100 (Metro NY)/(800) TRU-9100 (U.S. & Canada); fax (212) 302-0890/(212) 517-2237
e-mail 71333.3620@compuserve.com
President — Steven J. Abramson
Vice Pres. — Jane E. Nichols
Office Mgr. — Joan Dalessandro

Truproof Ltd.
31 Cunliffe Dr. Kettering
Northamptonshire, NN16 8LD England
tel (44-604) 414544; fax (44-604) 414483
Managing Director — G.M. Walden

Trutone Co.
3615 Goodlett Rd. S, Bldg. 108
Memphis, TN 38118
tel (800) 727-0979; fax (901) 362-8603
Office Mgr. — Sherry Davis

TSA
2040 W. Sam Houston Parkway N.
Houston, TX 77043
tel (800) 442-4872; fax (713) 935-1500/(713) 935-1555
e-mail claym@tsa.com
Sales — Clay Moore

TSI International
45 Danbury Rd.
Wilton, CT 06897
tel (203) 761-8600; fax (203) 762-9677
President — Connie Galley
Mktg. Dir. — Robert Bouton

TV Data Technologies
Northway Plz.
Queensbury, NY 12804
tel (518) 792-9914/(800) 338-TVDT (8838); fax (518) 761-7118
e-mail tvdata@tvdata.com
President/CEO — Arthur J. Bassin
VP/Oper./Exec. Editor — Roger Moore
Vice Pres.-Sales — Kathleen Wern
VP-Mktg.& Product Dev. — Michael Laddin
VP-Info. Systems — James McCormick
CFO/VP-New Bus. Dev. — Kenneth Carter
Nat'l. Accts. Dir. — Robyn DiPhillips
Asst. Vice Pres.-Sales — Bill Callahan
Reg'l. Sales Dir. — Tom Counce
Dir.-Newspaper Sales & Interactive Svc. — John Dodds
Reg'l. Sales Dir. — Mike Pearson
Reg'l Sales Dir. — Martin Siniawski
Reg'l. Sales Dir. — Cameron Yung
Dir.-Client & Tech. Svc. — Brenda Wheatley
Managing Editor — Amy Mann
Mgr.-Pagination Prod. — Andrew Heinz
Mgr.-Transedit Product — Rich Young
Mgr.-Online Product — Kevin Joyce
Ed.-Features Syndicate — Deborah Flack

U

Ultra Corp.
2441 N.W. 93rd Ave., Ste. 108
Miami, FL 33172
tel (305) 599-5268; fax (305) 599-8576
e-mail ultr@netrunner.net
Vice Pres. — Nadja Pardo
Director — Antonio Pardo

ULTRE (Div. of Linotype-Hell Co.)
145 Pinelawn Rd.
Melville, NY 11747
tel (516) 753-4800; fax (516) 753-4801
Vice Pres./GM — David Green
Dir.-Sales/Mktg. — James D. Martin
Mktg. & Sales Admn. — Debbie Rampulla

UMAX Technologies Inc.
3353 Gateway Blvd.
Fremont, CA 94538
tel (510) 651-8883; fax (510) 651-8834
e-mail http.www.umax.com
Mktg. Supervisor — Bobby Chao

UMI
1981 S.W. Biltmore St.
Port St. Lucie, FL 34984-3417
tel (407) 340-1666; fax (407) 340-0580
President — Bob MacKenzie

Unicom
5450 A St.
Anchorage, AK 99518
tel (907) 561-1674; fax (907) 563-3185
Mgr.-Voice Appl. — Kathleen Johnson

Union Rubber Inc.
PO Box 1040
Trenton, NJ 08606
tel (609) 396-9328/(800) 334-3120
fax (609) 396-3587
President — Paul Neiber
Plant Mgr. — Robert Hoch

Unique Photo
451 S. Jefferson St.
Orange, NJ 07050
tel (201) 673-0100; fax (201) 676-7577
Manager — Mary Robertson

U.S. Petrolon Industrial
4906 N. 95th St.
Omaha, NE 68134
tel (402) 572-7272/(800) 727-1577
fax (402) 572-5266
Reg. Dist. — Al Harrell

U.S. Postal Service
475 L'Enfant Plz.
Washington, DC 20260-3000
tel (202) 268-2163; fax (202) 268-2175
Info. Sys. Coord. — Charles Slocum

U.S. Pulp & Newsprint (Div. of Kimberly-Clark)
17589 Plant Rd.
Coosa Pines, AL 35044
tel (205) 378-5541; fax (205) 378-2150
Pres.-Pulp & Newsprint Sector — S.T. Erwin
VP-Oper.-Pulp & Newsprint Sector — L.D. Grimm
VP-Mktg. & Sales, U.S. Pulp & Newsprint — L.W. Howell
Mill Mgr.-U.S. Pulp & Newsprint — Mark Kerstetter

US Ink Corp.
651 Garden St.
Carlstadt, NJ 07072
tel (201) 935-8666; fax (201) 933-3728
President — Ronald C. Baker
Vice Pres.-Mktg. — Michael W. Mylett
VP-Operations — Lawrence J. Lepore
Technical Director — Peter I. Ford

USG
1000 Central Pkwy N., Ste. 235
San Antonio, TX 78232
tel (210) 494-3433; fax (210) 494-3476
CEO — Ron Landreth
Dir.-Marketing — Jim Chapman

Utilimaster
PO Box 585
Wakarusa, IN 46573
tel (219) 862-4561; fax (219) 862-4517
Mktg. Mgr. — Gregg Kinkade

UVP Inc.
2066 W. 11th St.
Upland, CA 91786
tel (909) 946-3197; fax (909) 946-3597
President — Paul Warren
Mktg. Dir. — Alex Waluszko
Comm. Mktg. Svc. — Kathy Luna

V

Valco Sales Inc.
3491 Delaware Ave., Ste. 210
Buffalo, NY 14217
tel (716) 873-2266; fax (716) 873-8970
President — Barbara Vanyo

Valley Remanufacturing Co.
777 E. Fairmont St.
Allentown, PA 18103
tel (610) 820-9669; fax (610) 820-0738
Mktg. Mgr. — Bruce L. Seidel

Value Checks
15880 S.W. Barnard Ct.
Beaverton, OR 97007
tel (503) 643-1827; fax (503) 641-0900
Pres./Mktg. Mgr. — David Luman

Van Son Holland Ink Corp. of America
92 Union St.
Mineola, NY 11501
tel (516) 294-8811; fax (516) 294-8608
President — Joseph Bendowski

Vapo Systems Co.
132 W. Home Ave.
Villa Park, IL 60181
tel (708) 832-7678; fax (708) 832-3613
Gen. Mgr. — Herbert Pfisterer

Varn International
8 Allerman Rd.
Oakland, NJ 07436
tel (201) 337-3600; fax (201) 337-2034
President — Joseph Von Zwehl
Exec. Vice Pres. — Vincent Von Zwehl
VP-Nat'l. Sales Mgr. — David Pheatt
Advg. Mgr. — John G. Yelle
Canadian Sales Mgr. — Barry Neal
Varn Mktg. Mgr. — Dennis J Ryan
Western Sales Mgr. — Archie Doyle
Kompac Mktg. Mgr. — James Trisuzzi
Midwestern Sales Mgr. — Carroll Long

Vendors International Inc.
10825 Walnut St., N.E.
St. Petersburg, FL 33716
tel (813) 596-6952; fax (813) 595-1759
President — Mark A. Okopny

Vendors International Ltd.
2245 Wyecroft Rd., Unit #2
Oakville, ON L6L 5L7 Canada
tel (905) 847-3302; fax (905) 847-6457
General Manager — Morris Okopny

Ver-A-Fast Corp.
20545 Ctr. Ridge Rd., 3rd Fl., Ste. 300
Rocky River, OH 44116
tel (800) 327-8463; fax (216) 331-2701
President — Robert M. Bensman
Vice Pres.-Mktg. & Dev. — Nanette Kubera
Mgr. Mkt. Dev. — James L. Tanner

Veratec Div.
100 Elm St.
Walpole, MA 02081
tel (508) 660-3300; fax (508) 668-8473
Prod. Mgr. — R.A. Chiricosta
Prod. Mgr. — Kevin Dill
Mktg. Mgr. — S. Thress

Verity Inc.
1550 Plymouth St.
Mountain View, CA 94043
tel (415) 960-7600; fax (415) 960-7698
e-mail info@verity.com
President/CEO — Philippe Courtot
Vice Pres./CFO — Don McCauley

Vidar Systems Corp.
460 Spring Park Pl.
Herndon, VA 22070
tel (703) 471-7070; fax (703) 471-1165
Dir.-Mktg. Comm. — Mary Jefferson

Videojet Systems International Inc.
1500 Mittel Blvd.
Wood Dale, IL 60191-1073
tel (708) 860-7300; fax (708) 616-3623
President — H.J. Bode
Exec. Vice Pres. — Craig E. Bauer
Vice Pres.-Finance — Joe McLaughlin
Mgr.-Mktg. Comm. — Harlene Henry

VirtualColor (Screaming Technology Inc.)
125 N. Prospect Ave.
Itasca, IL 60143
tel (708) 250-9500; fax (708) 250-8729
Vice Pres.-Mktg. — Carl Aiello

Vision Data Equipment Corp.
1377 Third St.
Rensselaer, NY 12144
tel (518) 434-2193; fax (518) 434-3457
President — Thomas Dempsey

VNU Business Information Services
11 W. 42nd St.
New York, NY 10036-8088
tel (212) 789-3680; fax (212) 789-3650
Sr. VP-Newspaper Svc. — James Robertson

VoCal Telecommunications
77 W. Las Tunas Dr. 202
Arcadia, CA 91007
tel (818) 447-9425; fax (818) 447-2115
e-mail CompuServe 73142, 2547
President — Ron Emerling

Voice Connexion
17971 SkyPark Cir., Ste. F
Irvine, CA 92714
tel (714) 261-2366; fax (714) 261-8563
Vice Pres.-Sales & Mktg. — Shirlee Dworak

VoiceSmart Corp.
2160 N. Central Rd.
Fort Lee, NJ 07024
tel (201) 592-0505; fax (201) 592-6962
e-mail sheila@voicesmart.com
President — Alex Mashinsky
Dir.-Int'l. Sales & Mktg. — Sheila Peterson

The Von Entress Group
1544 Clyde Dr.
Naperville, IL 60565
tel (708) 717-5554; fax (708) 717-5554
CEO — Albert E. Von Entress

Copyright ©1996 by the Editor & Publisher Co.

Equipment, supplies, services

VU/TEXT Library Services Inc.
1 Commerce Sq., 2005 Market St.
Ste. 1010
Philadelphia, PA 19103
tel (215) 587-4410; fax (215) 587-2148
Vice Pres./Gen. Mgr. — Joseph DiMarino
Mgr.-Tech. Support — Alan Crawford
Mgr.-Product Dev. — Robert Kennedy
Mgr.-Acct. Svc. — Mary Lou Whitman

W

Gordon Wahls Co./Executive Search Consultants
601 E. Baltimore Pike; PO Box 905
Media, PA 19063
tel (610) 565-0800/(800) 523-7112
fax (610) 565-1698
President — Thomas F. Glancey Jr.
Publishing Dir. — Walter Lynn

Walterry Insurance
7411 Old Branch Ave.; PO Box 128
Clinton, MD 20735
tel (301) 868-7200; fax (301) 868-2611
Mktg. Dir. — Walter J. Coady Jr.

Warner Color Corp. (Therm-O-Scan Div.)
3375 S.W. Temple
Salt Lake City, UT 84115-4303
tel (801) 485-7885; fax (801) 487-4983
President — Glen Warner
Inventor — Gordon (Doc) Warner
Technician — Paul Warner

S.D. Warren
225 Franklin St.
Boston, MA 02110
tel (617) 423-7300; fax (617) 423-5494
Vice Pres.-Mktg. — Henry Mollenhauer

WeatherData Inc.
245 N. Waco St., Ste. 310
Wichita, KS 67202
tel (316) 265-9127; fax (316) 265-1949
President — Mike Smith
Dir.-Sales — Kristi Francis

Weatherline Inc.
12119 St. Charles Rock Rd.
St. Louis, MO 63044
tel (314) 291-1000; fax (314) 291-3226
President — Richard H. Friedman
Sr. Vice Pres. — Nancy J. Friedman
Exec. Vice Pres. — Michelle Parent
Vice Pres. — Joan Maniscalco
Vice Pres. — Martha Murphy
Vice Pres. — Stephen L. Smith

Web Press Corp.
22023-68th Ave. S.
Kent, WA 98032
tel (206) 395-3343; fax (206) 395-4492
President — Wayne R. Marcouiller
Vice Pres.-Sales — Charles A. Gath
Sales Sec. — Jo Bunger

Web Printing Controls/WPC Machinery Corp.
23872 N. Kelsey Rd.
Barrington, IL 60010
tel (708) 382-7970; fax (708) 382-2348
President — Herman Gnuechtel
Vice Pres. — Bruce Fetherling
Int'l. Sales Mgr. — Gerry Ferron
Dist. Sales Mgr. — James Tasch

Web Tapes Inc.
3690 Lexington Dr.
Hoffman Estates, IL 60195
tel (708) 358-5185
President — Jim Stirtz

Jervis B. Webb Co.
World Headquarters/34375 W. Twelve Mile Rd.
Farmington Hills, MI 48331
tel (810) 553-1220; fax (810) 553-1300
President/CEO — George H. Webb
Prod./Media Mgr. — John M. Rankin

Webeq International Inc.
15 E. Palatine Rd.
Prospect Heights, IL 60070
tel (708) 459-9700; fax (708) 459-9707
President — Jerome Kosoglad

Bob Weber Inc.
23580 Commerce Park Rd.
Cleveland, OH 44122
tel (216) 831-0480/(800) 399-4BWI (4294); fax (216) 831-1628/(800) 837-TYPE (8973)
e-mail linotek@aol.com, 73752.2356@compuserve.com
President — Robert J. Weber

Vice Pres. — Betty Weber
Production Mgr. — Steve Fondriest
Tele-Sales Rep. — Jennifer Klett
Mgr.-Mgt. Info. Sys/Sys. Integ. — Shaolin Hu
Graphic Sys. Specialist — Lance Little
Data Entry — Elaine Brown
Field Service Technician — Jim Moore
Refurb. Technician — Ron Feeney
Advertising — Leslie Schmidt
Refurb Technician — Anthony Kopij
Auditor & A/R Collections — Jennifer Weber
Accountant (Pt.-Time) — Bob Wittine

Wedge Computer Systems
9714 N. Kings Hwy.
Myrtle Beach, SC 29572
tel (803) 449-8372; fax (803) 449-1276
Mktg. Mgr. — Eliot Godfrey

Deane Weinberg Insurance Agency Inc.
1754 Westwood Blvd.
Los Angeles, CA 90024
tel (800) 732-3227; fax (310) 474-0802
President — Deane Weinberg

J.N. Wells & Co. Inc.
21 W. 075 Monticello Rd.
Lombard, IL 60148
tel (708) 916-6491; fax (708) 627-1233
President — Joe N. Wells

We're Your Type!
201 Varick St.; PO Box 45
New York, NY 10014
tel (212) 929-2278
e-mail okayannie@aol.com
President — Diane Fisher

Wesco Graphics
2034 Research Dr.
Livermore, CA 94550
tel (510) 443-2400; fax (510) 443-0452
President — Jim Estes
Mktg. Mgr. — Waverly Bailey

West Coast Computer Systems/Newspaper Technologies
211 E. Walnut
Stockton, CA 95204
tel (209) 948-5499; fax (209) 948-4508
Owner — Ed Kobrin

West-Mor Mailroom Services
427-3 Amherst St., Ste. 258
Nashua, NH 03063
tel (603) 889-6293; fax (603) 883-0490
Mktg. Dir. — Glenn Aborn
Partner — Norma Moreau
Partner — Arlene West Aborn

Western Automation
1700 N. 55th St.
Boulder, CO 80301
tel (303) 449-6400; fax (303) 939-8844
Mktg. Mgr. — John Kranz

Western LithoTech
3433 Tree Ct. Industrial Blvd.
St. Louis, MO 63122
tel (314) 225-5031/(800) 325-3310
fax (314) 825-4681
President/CEO — William Streeter
Sr. Vice Pres. — Wesley K. Gass
Sr. VP-Sales & Mktg. — Lane Palmer
Vice Pres.-Machinery Div. — John Powers
Newspaper Product Mgr. — Keith Walker
Vice Pres.-Admn. — Hugh McGaughty
Int'l. Sales Mgr. — Ed Eisenberg
Mktg. Mgr.-U.S. & Int'l. — Kathryn May
Nat'l. Sales Mgr.-Newspapers — Todd Socia

Western Lithotech
2625 N. Neergard
Springfield, MO 65803
tel (800) 421-0051; fax (417) 831-0142
Dir.-Machinery Sales — Edward R. Barnett

Western Printing Machinery
9229 Ivanhoe St.
Schiller Park, IL 60176
tel (708) 678-1740; fax (708) 678-6176
President/Chairman — R.D. Musgrave
Sales Mgr. — Bill Layman
Sales Mgr. — Walt Powley
Sales Mgr. — Brad Brown
Controller — Michael Musgrave

Western Quartz Products Inc.
2432 Spring St.
Paso Robles, CA 93446
tel (805) 238-3524; fax (805) 238-6811
Sales Mgr. — Kathryn E. Wetterstrand

Western Roller Corp.
63393 Nels Anderson Rd.
Bend, OR 97701
tel (503) 382-5643; fax (503) 382-0159
Product Sales & Mktg. Eng. — Doug Collver
Newsprint Sales — James Anderson

Western Web Sales
PO Box 611
Atwood, CA 92601
tel (714) 970-9036; fax (714) 970-9388
President — Ted O'Toole

Wifag
640 Gundy Rd.
Marietta, GA 30067
tel (770) 850-8511; fax (770) 850-8550
VP-N. American Sales — Joe Ondras

Will-Pemco Inc.
3333 Crocker Ave.
Sheboygan, WI 53081
tel (414) 458-2500; fax (414) 458-1265
President/CEO — Klaus Haasamann
Sales Coordinator — Martha A Baker

Keister Williams Newspaper Services
PO Box 8005
Charlottesville, VA 22906
tel (804) 293-4709; fax (804) 293-4884
Mktg. Mgr. — Meta L. Nay

Willow Bend Communications Inc.
16479 Dallas Pkwy., #770
Dallas, TX 75379-7485
tel (214) 248-0451; fax (214) 732-8807
President/CEO — Stephen L. Thompson
Exec. Vice Pres./COO — Darryl E. White
Secretary — Sam L. Moffett
Asst. Sec. — Joseph Guerin
Asst. Sec. — C. Diane Thompson

Willow Six Technologies
647 Camino De Los Mares, Ste. 108
San Clemente, CA 92673
tel (714) 492-1060; fax (714) 492-1060
e-mail willowsix@aol.com
Contact — Mike Ellis

Wilson Gregory Agency
2309 Market St.; PO Box 8
Camp Hill, PA 17001-0008
tel (717) 730-9777; fax (717) 730-9328
President — Ted Gregory

Windmoeller and Hoelscher Corp./Flexo Newspaper Press Group
23 New England Way
Lincoln, RI 02865
tel (401) 333-2770; fax (401) 333-6491
President — James Feeney
Sr. Vice Pres. — Hans Deamer
Project Mgr. — Manfred Gutte

Chauncey Wing's Sons Inc.
78 Pierce St., Dept. P; Box 351
Greenfield, MA 01302
tel (413) 772-6611; fax (800) 654-0430
Mktg. Mgr. — Anne C. Wing

Winton Engineering Co.
2303 W. 18th St.
Chicago, IL 60608
tel (312) 733-5200; fax (312) 733-0446
Sales Mgr. — Richard Ponx

Witte Energy Management
PO Box 10566
Midland, TX 79702
tel (915) 685-1878; fax (915) 686-0852
President — Richard Witte

Wolk Advertising Inc. (Retail Carpet Ad Service)
346 Park St.
Birmingham, MI 48009
tel (810) 540-5980; fax (810) 540-5981
President — Erv Wolk

Word Mark International Corp.
101 Park Center Plz. Ste. 1111
San Jose, CA 95113
tel (408) 975-1100; fax (408) 975-1111
e-mail wordmarc@netcom.com
Vice Pres.-Mktg. — Jeff Jakus

World Net & Associates Inc.
1140 Heards Ferry Rd.
Atlanta, GA 30328
tel (770) 953-4683; fax (770) 953-4683
Contact — Ron Erhardt

WPC Machinery Corp.
2700 Wisconsin Ave.
Downers Grove, IL 60515-4226
tel (708) 960-1032; fax (708) 960-9055
Sales-Eng. — Bert McGready
Dir.-Oper. — Phil Gurgone
Nat'l. Sales Mgr. — William Burke
Sales Sec. — Lynn A. Loetz

Wrubel Communications
12-32 River Rd.
Fair Lawn, NJ 07410
tel (201) 796-8621; fax (201) 796-5083
President — Charles Wrubel

X

X-Rite Inc.
3100 44th St., S.W.
Grandville, MI 49418
tel (616) 534-7663; fax (616) 534-0723/(616) 534-8960
President — Bruce Jorgensen
COO — Ted Thompson
CFO — D. Kluting
Director-Operations — Jeff Smolinski
Director-Engineering — Bernie Berg
Product Manager — Ian Pike
Tech. Consultant — David Hinson
Sales Manager — Kelly VandenBosch

Xerox (Corp. HQ)
800 Long Ridge Rd.; PO Box 1600
Stamford, CT 06904-1600
tel (800) TEAM XRX (269-6979)
(716) 423-4436
President/CEO — Paul Allaire
Exec. Vice Pres.-Oper. Xerox Corp. — A. Berry Rand
Exec. Vice Press-Oper. Xerox Corp. — Peter van Cuylenburg

Xerox Corp.
Xerox Sq.-05C
Rochester, NY 14644
tel (800) 275-9376/(800) 832-6979
COB/CEO — Paul A. Allaire
Coordinator-Public Info. Center — Nancy L. Dempsey
Exec. Vice Pres./CFO — Barry D. Romeril
Exec. Vice Pres.-Oper. — A. Barry Rand
Exec. VP-Oper. — Peter van Cuylenburg
Exec. VP/Chmn./CEO/Xerox Fin. Svc. Inc. — Stuart B. Ross
Sr. Vice Pres. /Chief Staff Officer — William F. Buehler
Sr. Vice Pres. /Corp. Strategic Svc. — Allan E. Dugan
Sr. VP-Systems Strategy & Bus. Dev. — Julius I. Marcus
Sr. VP/Corp. Res.& Tech. — Mark B. Myers
Sr. Vice Pres. -Corp. Bus. Strategy — David R. Myerscough

Xerox Corp.-Desktop Document Systems
Xerox Corp.; 3400 Hillview Ave.
Palo Alto, CA 94303
tel (415) 813-6800
President — Paul A. Ricci
Vice Pres.-Mktg. & Sales — Michael Tivnan

Xerox Corp.-Xerox Engineering Systems
Xerox Sq.; 100 Clinton Ave. S.
Rochester, NY 14644
tel (716) 427-5400; fax (716) 383-7450
Pres.-Xerox Eng. Sys. — Patricia C. Barron
Coordinator-PR Svc. — Nancy L. Dempsey
Dir.-Int'l. Oper. — Kaz Herchold

Xitron Inc.
3768 Plz. Dr.
Ann Arbor, MI 48108
tel (313) 913-8080; fax (313) 913-8088
Vice Pres.-Mktg. — Mark Fioravanti

XSoft (Division of Xerox Corp.)
3400 Hillview Ave.; PO Box 10034
Palo Alto, CA 94303-0816
tel (415) 424-0111
President — Dennis W. Andrews

XYonicz
6754 Martin St.
Rome, NY 13440
tel (315) 334-4214; fax (315) 336-3177
Mktg. Mgr. — Ed Zionc

Y

Yale Materials Handling Corp.
15 Junction Rd.
Flemington, NJ 08822-9499
tel (800) 233-YALE; (908) 788-3386
President — Colin Wilson
Sr. Vice Pres.-Mktg. — David Coward
VP-Parts Svc. Mktg. — Lawrence M. LoMonico

Z

Zeos
1301 Industrial Blvd.
Minneapolis, MN 55413
tel (612) 633-4591; fax (612) 633-0110
Vice Pres.-Sales — Justin Morris

Copyright ©1996 by the Editor & Publisher Co.

CATEGORIES OF EQUIPMENT, SUPPLIES AND SERVICES
(M) Manufacturer; (D) Distributor; (S) Service Organization

Abrasives
Borden Inc. (M)
Carborundum Abrasives Co. (M,D)
Newstech Co. (Div. of Rovinter Inc.) (D)
Deane Weinberg Insurance Agency Inc. (S)

Acid Dispensing Systems
The Master Group (M)
Newstech Co. (Div. of Rovinter Inc.) (D)
Tasope Co. (M)

Addressing Machines
Automated Mailing Systems Corp. (D)
Dick Mailer Co. (M)
Dispensa-Matic Label Dispensers (M)
Domino Amjet Inc. (M,D,S)
GSP Inc. (M)
Kansa Corp. (Baldwin Technology Co.) (M,D)
Kirk-Rudy Inc. (M)
Mailers Equipment Co. Inc. (Mircofilm Products) (D)
Megasys International Inc. (D)
Newstech Co. (Div. of Rovinter Inc.) (D)
Quipp System Inc. (D)
Scandinavian PC Systems Inc. (M,D)
SITMA USA Inc. (M)
Stepper Inc. (M)
Videojet Systems International Inc. (M)
Chauncey Wing's Sons Inc. (M)

Adhesive Wax Coaters
Allpress Equipment Inc. (D)
Craig Cold Type Supply Inc. (D)
Daige Products Inc. (M)
Duostat Co. (Affiliated with VGC Corp.) (D)
Midwest Publishers Supply Co. (D)
National Graphic Supply Corp. (D)
NENSCO (D)
Newstech Co. (Div. of Rovinter Inc.) (D)
Paste-Up Supply (M)
Poolside Lithographic Supply Inc. (D)
Portage Newspaper Supply Co. (M)
Republic Roller Corp. (S)
Schaefer Machine Co. Inc. (M)
Support Products Inc. (D)

Adhesives
Adhesives Research Inc. (M)
BESCO Graphic Systems Corp. (D)
Craig Cold Type Supply Inc. (D)
Daige Products Inc. (M)
Duostat Co. (Affiliated with VGC Corp.) (D)
H&M Paster Sales & Service Inc. (D)
Hamilton Circulation Supplies Co. (Newspaper Mailroom Supplies) (D)
Hercules Inc. (M)
Horizons Inc. (D)
Manassy Precision Corp. (D)
Midwest Publishers Supply Co. (D)
National Graphic Supply Corp. (D)
NENSCO (D)
Newstech Co. (Div. of Rovinter Inc.) (D)
North Shore Consultants Inc. (M)
Portage Newspaper Supply Co. (D)
Republic Roller Corp. (S)
Rosback Co. (D)
Ernest Schaefer Inc. (D)
Schaefer Machine Co. Inc. (M)
Support Products Inc. (D)
Tech-Energy Co. (D,S)
UMI (D)
Union Rubber Inc. (M)
Chauncey Wing's Sons Inc. (M)

Architects/Engineers
Application Engineering Corp. (M)
The Austin Co. (S)
B E & K Inc. (S)
Blevins Harding Group (Western Office) (S)
Carlson Design/Construct Corp. (S)
Coleman/Caskey Architects (S)
Daniel, Mann, Johnson & Mendenhall (DMJM) (S)
Dario Designs Inc. (M,D,S)
Ralph Fusco Inc. (S)
Gilbane Building Co. (S)
Ginsberg, William Associates (S)
Graphic System Services (D,S)
Greenwood Partnership, The (A Professional Corp.) (S)
The Haskell Co. (S)
Industrial Noise Control Inc. (M)
Peter A. Lendrum Architects (S)

Lockwood Greene Engineers Inc. (S)
Luwa Bahnson Inc. (S)
MAH Machine Co. Inc. (M,S)
Mannschreck (D)
McClier Corp. (S)
MGI International Inc. (M,D)
Midwest Publishers Supply Co. (S)
Pacific Newspaper Services Inc. (M,D,S)
Parsons Main Inc. (S)
RRA Inc. & Associates
William C. Spells (RTP Technical Specialists) (S)
Standard Electric and Engineering Co. (M,S)
Trauner Consulting Services Inc. (S)
Xerox Corp.-Xerox Engineering Systems (M)

Archiving Systems
Baseview Products Inc. (M,D)
Computer Tree (D)
Foster Mfg. Co. (M)
Freedom System Integrators (D)
GMTI-Gannett Media Technical International (S)
Newstech Co. (Div. of Rovinter Inc.) (D)
Total Image Corp. (M)
Tribune Solutions (M,D,Photo Archiving,M,S)

Art & Layout Equipment and Services (See also Layout Tables)
Agfa Division, Bayer Inc. (M,D)
Allsystems Go (D)
Arrow Printing Co. (S)
Auto-Grafica Corp. (D)
Automated Newsstand (D)
Ayers/Johanek Publication Design (S)
Beta Screen Corp. (S)
R.W. Borrowdale Co. (RWB Enterprises Div.) (M)
Computer Tree (D)
Consolidated International Corp. (M)
Derus Media Service Inc./Editorial Pace (S)
A.B. Dick Co. (D)
Duostat Co. (Affiliated with VGC Corp.) (D)
Dynamic Graphics Inc. (M)
Foster Mfg. Co. (M)
Harris Publishing Systems Corp. (M)
The House of Grids (M,D)
Megasys International Inc. (D)
Midwest Publishers Supply Co. (M,D)
National Graphic Supply Corp. (M)
National Research Bureau (D)
NENSCO (D)
Newstech Co. (Div. of Rovinter Inc.) (D)
NuArc Co. Inc. (M)
Poolside Lithographic Supply Inc. (D)
Portage Newspaper Supply Co. (M,D)
Printers' Service (M)
Richmond/Graphic Products Inc. (M)
Stoesser Register Systems (M)

T/Maker Co. (M,D)
Techtron Imaging Center (S)
Ternes Register System (M)
VirtualColor (Screaming Technology Inc.) (S)
Wolk Advertising Inc. (Retail Carpet Ad Service) (S)

Automatic Film Processors
Agfa Division, Bayer Inc. (M,D)
Allpress Equipment Inc. (D)
Allsystems Go (D)
Auto-Grafica Corp. (D)
Berkshire/Westwood Graphics Group Inc. (D)
BESCO Graphic Systems Corp. (D)
Duostat Co. (Affiliated with VGC Corp.) (D)
Fuji Photo Film USA/Graphic Arts Products Div. (M)
GraphLine Inc. (D)
Konica Imaging USA Inc. (D)
Kreonite Inc. (M)
Linotype-Hell Co. (D,S)
Mohr Enterprise (Div. of Mohr Lino-Saw Co.) (D)
Monotype Systems Inc. (D)
National Graphic Supply Corp. (D)
NENSCO (D)
Newstech Co. (Div. of Rovinter Inc.) (D)
Pako Corp. (M)
Printing Equipment Specialists Inc. (S)
Richmond/Graphic Products Inc. (M)
SCREEN (USA) (M)
Tech-Energy Co. (D,S)
Techtron Imaging Center (S)
Bob Weber Inc. (D)

Automatic Plastic Bagging Equipment
Amplas Inc. (M,D,S)
Stepper Inc. (M)
Telesonic Packaging Corp. (M)

Automatic Press Wash-Ups
Allpress Equipment Inc. (D)
Baldwin Graphics Products (Div. of Baldwin Technology) (M)
Heidelberg Harris Inc. (D)
National Graphic Sales Inc. (S)
Nikka Corp. (M,D)
Printing Equipment Specialists Inc. (S)
Ryco Graphic Manufacturing Inc. (M)
Tech-Energy Co. (D,S)
Tower Products Inc. (M)

Baling Machines
Craftsmen Machinery Co./ Graphic Export Corp. (D)
Gerrard Ovalstrapping (D)
Kaim & Associates Int'l. Marketing Inc. (D)

Machine Design Service Inc. (M)
Megasys International Inc. (D)
Mid-America Graphics Inc. (S)
Midwest Publishers Supply Co. (D)
Ovalstrapping Inc. (M)
Printing Equipment Specialists Inc. (S)

Belts, Belting, V-Belts
Allpress Equipment Inc. (D)
Arco Engineering Inc. (Newspaper Div.) (D)
Baumfolder Corp. (M,D)
Belt Corporation of America (M)
Belting Industries Co. Inc. (M,D)
BESCO Graphic Systems Corp. (D)
Central Graphics (D)
Clipper Belt Lacer Co. (M)
Manassy Precision Corp. (D)
Mid-America Graphics Inc. (S)
Newstech Co. (Div. of Rovinter Inc.) (D)
Moss Reck & Associates Inc. (D)
Tech-Energy Co. (D,S)
Tingue Brown & Co. (D)
UMI (D)
WPC Machinery Corp. (D)

Binding Machines
General Binding Corp. (M,D)

Blanket Cleaner/Washer (Automatic)
Allpress Equipment Inc. (D)
Berkshire/Westwood Graphics Group Inc. (D)
GraphLine Inc. (D)
Midwest Publishers Supply Co. (D)
Newstech Co. (Div. of Rovinter Inc.) (D)
Oxy-Dry Corp. (M)
Rogersal Inc. (M,D)

Blanket Mounting and Bars
Allstates Litho Plate Corp. (D)
Apex Machine Co. (M)
BESCO Graphic Systems Corp. (D)
Russell J. Bryant Co. (D)
CPS Corp. (D)
Day International Inc. (M)
Duostat Co. (Affiliated with VGC Corp.) (D)
Heidelberg Harris Inc. (D)
London Litho Aluminum Co. Inc. (D)
J. Thomas McHugh Co. Inc. (D)
Midwest Publishers Supply Co. (D)
The Morrison Group/Morrison Ink (M,D)
NENSCO (D)
Newstech Co. (Div. of Rovinter Inc.) (D)
Niles & Nelson Inc. (D)
Pacesetter Graphic Service Corp. (D)
Pitman Co. (S)
Polyfibron Technologies Inc. (M)
Quality Components Corp. (M)

I believe if we make our decisions based on what is in the best interest of our clients, it will prove to be in our best interest in the long run. Dario D. D. DiMare, AIA

NEWSPAPER FACILITY DESIGN

ARCHITECTURE
PROGRAMMING
MASTER PLANNING
FEASIBILITY STUDIES
OPERATIONAL COST STUDIES
EQUIPMENT MANNING STUDIES

DARIO DESIGNS INC.
1 ELDA ROAD
FRAMINGHAM, MA 01701
508-877-4444
FAX 877-4474

Copyright ©1996 by the Editor & Publisher Co.

VI-24 Equipment, supplies, services

RapidTec Inc. (M)
Reeves Brothers Inc. (M)
Rotation Dynamics Corp. (M,D)
Sun Graphic Inc. (M,D)
Tech-Energy Co. (D,S)
Tingue Brown & Co. (D)
UMI (D)

Blankets
Allpress Equipment Inc. (D)
Berkshire/Westwood Graphics Group Inc. (D)
David M. Co. (M,D)
DYC Supply Co./Dynaric Inc. (M,D)
Flint Ink Corp. (D)
GraphLine Inc. (D)
GSP Inc. (D)
J. Thomas McHugh Co. Inc. (D)
Midwest Publishers Supply Co. (D)
National Graphic Supply Corp. (D)
Newstech Co. (Div. of Rovinter Inc.) (D)
Pacesetter Graphic Service Corp. (D)
Rendic International (D)
Rotation Dynamics Corp. (M,D)
Rycoline Products Inc. (M)

Blue Line Grids
Midwest Publishers Supply Co. (M)
National Graphic Supply Corp. (D)
Newstech Co. (Div. of Rovinter Inc.) (D)

Bonding Material
Tech-Energy Co. (D,S)

Brokers & Appraisers
ALTA Graphics Inc. (S)
Beckerman Associates Inc. (S)
BOLITHO-CRIBB & Associates (S)
Circulation Verification Council (S)
Cribb Media Service (M,D,S)
Barry French (S)
Gomm & Co. Inc. (S)
W B Grimes & Co. Inc. (S)
Kevin Brian Kamen & Co. (S)
James Martin & Associates (S)
Media Consultants & Associates (M,D,S)
Northwest Publishers Inc. (S)
ONE Corp. (S)
Abbott E Paine (Newspaper Broker Services) (S)
Press and Bindery Systems Inc. (D)
Printing Equipment Specialists Inc. (S)
George Romano Ltd. (S)
Todd Machinery (S)
Bob Weber Inc. (S)
J.N. Wells & Co. Inc. (S)
World Net & Associates Inc. (S)

Bundling and Tying Machines
ALTA Graphics Inc. (S)
Automated Mailing Systems Corp. (D)
Baldwin Stobb (Div. of Baldwin Technology) (M,D,S)
B.H. Bunn Co. (M)
Craftsmen Machinery Co./Graphic Export Corp. (D)
DYC Supply Co./Dynaric Inc. (M,D)
FELINS Inc. (D)
Ferag Inc. (M)
Florida Printing Equipment and Supply (D)
Gerrard Ovalstrapping (M)
GMA Inc. (M,D)
Heidelberg Harris Inc. (D)

Interlake Packaging Corp. (M)
Machine Design Service Inc. (M)
Mailers Equipment Co. Inc. (Mircofilm Products) (D)
Malow Corp. (D)
Megasys International Inc. (D)
Mid-America Graphics Inc. (D)
Midwest Publishers Supply Co. (D)
National Research Bureau (D)
Newstech Co. (Div. of Rovinter Inc.) (D)
Ovalstrapping Inc. (M)
Parsons Main Inc. (S)
Power Strap (M)
Printing Equipment Specialists Inc. (S)
Quipp System Inc. (D)
Saxmayer Corp. (M)
Sheridan Systems (M)
Signode Corp. (M,D)
SITMA USA Inc. (M)
Sterling Packaging Systems (M)
Strapex Corp. (M)
Telesonic Packaging Corp. (M)
West-Mor Mailroom Services (D,S)

Business Computers
Advanced Publishing Technology (M)
Advanced Technical Solutions (S)
American Data Voice Systems (D,S)
AT & T Business Marketing (M,D)
Auto-Grafica Corp. (D)
BESCO Graphic Systems Corp. (D)
Computer Devices Inc. (D)
Computer Services Group Inc. (S)
CPS Technologies Inc. (D)
Danagraf North America (D)
DemoSource Inc. (D)
Digital Design Inc. (D)
Electronic Specialists Inc. (M)
Falco Data Products Inc. (M)
Geac/Vision Shift (D)
GMTI-Gannett Media Technical International (D)
Gulf Coast System Design Co. (D,S)
Harris Corp. (Corporate Headquaters) (M,D)
Horizon Software Inc. (D)
IBM Corp. (M,D,S)
IC Systems Solutions (M,D,S)
Icanon Associates Inc. (M)
Integrated Newspaper Systems Inc. (D)
International Memory Products of Illinois Inc. (D)
Krypton Systems (S)
Micro Systems Specialists Inc. (MSSI) (D)
Midwest Publishers Supply Co. (D)
National Research Bureau (D)
The Networks Inc. (D,S)
Newspaper Electronics Corp. (D,S)
Newstech Co. (Div. of Rovinter Inc.) (D)
Omni Industry (Div. of Global Turnkey Systems Inc.) (M,D,S)
Stauffer Media Systems (D,S)
Support Systems International Corp. (M)
Synaptic Micro Solutions (M,D)
Telecorp Systems Inc. (M,D,S)
Vision Data Equipment Corp. (M)

Cabinets
Acme Design Technology Co. (M)
BESCO Graphic Systems Corp. (D)
Control Engineering Co. (M)
Craig Cold Type Supply Inc. (D)
Douthitt Corp. (M,D)

Duostat Co. (Affiliated with VGC Corp.) (D)
Equipto (M)
Foster Mfg. Co. (M)
Kreonite (M)
Midwest Publishers Supply Co. (M,D)
Newstech Co. (Div. of Rovinter Inc.) (D)
Penco Products (M)
Roconex Corp. (M)
Thompson Cabinet Co. (M)
Western LithoTech (M)

Calibration Software/Hardware
Baton Lock & Hardware Co. Inc. (M)
Beta Screen Corp. (D)
Computer Tree (D)
Midwest Publishers Supply Co. (D)
Newstech Co. (Div. of Rovinter Inc.) (D)
PrePRESS DIRECT (D)
Willow Six Technologies (M)

Cameras & Accessories (See also Lenses [Camera])
Agfa Division, Bayer Inc. (M)
Alan Graphic Systems Inc. (M,D)
Allpress Equipment Inc. (D)
BESCO Graphic Systems Corp. (D)
R.W. Borrowdale Co. (RWB Enterprises Div.) (M)
Bulbtronics (D)
Canon USA Inc. (S)
Caprock Developments Inc. (M,D)
CK Optical Co. Inc. (M,D)
Consolidated International Corp. (M)
A.B. Dick Co. (M)
A.B. Dick Co. (Itek Graphix Div.) (M)
Durbin Associates (S)
Eastman Kodak/Professional Printing & Publishing Imaging (M)
Florida Printing Equipment and Supply (D)
Fuji Photo Film USA (Distribution Ctr.) (M)
Geiss-America Inc. (D)
Hasselblad USA Inc. (Electronic Imaging) (D)
Heitz Service Corp. (D)
Konica Imaging USA Inc. (M)
Mid Atlantic Lighting (D)
Midwest Publishers Supply Co. (D)
National Graphic Supply Corp. (D)
NENSCO (D)
Newstech Co. (Div. of Rovinter Inc.) (D)
Nikon Inc./Electronic Imaging Department (M,D)
NuArc Co. Inc. (M)
Nutek Inc. (D)
Olympus America Inc. (M)
Parsons Main Inc. (S)
Polaroid Corp. (M,D,S)
Printing Equipment Specialists Inc. (S)
Ricoh Corp. (M,D)
Rochester Institute of Technology (S)
SCREEN (USA) (M)
Sony Electronics Inc. (M)
Unique Photo (M)

Chemicals: Chuck (Paper Roll)
Allpress Equipment Inc. (D)
Anchor (Imaging Products Division) (M)
Central Graphics (M,D)
NENSCO (D)
Quality Components Corp. (D)
Support Products Inc. (D)
Tech-Energy Co. (M,D,S)
Tidland Corp. (M,D)
Tilt-Lock Inc. (M)
Will-Pemco Inc. (M)

Chemicals: Photographic
Allstates Litho Plate Corp. (D)
Anitec (M)
Auto-Grafica Corp. (D)

Berkshire/Westwood Graphics Group Inc. (D)
BESCO Graphic Systems Corp. (D)
ByChrome Co. (M)
A.B. Dick Co. (Itek Graphix Div.) (M)
Duostat Co. (Affiliated with VGC Corp.) (D)
Florida Printing Equipment and Supply (D)
Fuji Photo Film USA/Graphic Arts Products Div. (M)
GraphLine Inc. (D)
Horizons Inc. (M)
Konica Imaging USA Inc. (M)
Merix Chemical Co. (Dept. TR) (M)
Mohr Enterprise (Div. of Mohr Lino-Saw Co.) (M)
National Graphic Supply Corp. (D)
NENSCO (D)
New Seagull Photographic Paper (D)
Newstech Co. (Div. of Rovinter Inc.) (D)
Parsons Main Inc. (S)
Photo Systems Inc. (M,D)
Pitman Photo Supply (D)
Portage Newspaper Supply Co. (M)
Ricoh Corp. (M,D)
Techtron Imaging Center (S)
3M Printing & Publishing Systems Div. (M)
Unique Photo (M)
Bob Weber Inc. (D)

Chemicals: Plate Processing
Allpress Equipment Inc. (D)
Allstates Litho Plate Corp. (D)
American Litho Inc. (D)
Anitec
Anitec Printing Plates (M)
Auto-Grafica Corp. (D)
Berkshire/Westwood Graphics Group Inc. (D)
BESCO Graphic Systems Corp. (D)
Citiplate Inc. (M)
A.B. Dick Co. (D)
Duostat Co. (Affiliated with VGC Corp.) (D)
Dynalith Inc. (M)
Florida Printing Equipment and Supply (D)
Fuji Photo Film USA/Graphic Arts Products Div. (M)
Graphic Arts Technical & Consulting Services (M)
GraphLine Inc. (D)
Imperial Metal & Chemical Co. (Div. of Dupont) (M,D)
London Litho Aluminum Co. Inc. (D)
Martin Yale Inc. (D)
Mid Atlantic Lighting (D)
National Graphic Supply Corp. (D)
NENSCO (D)
Newstech Co. (Div. of Rovinter Inc.) (D)
Parsons Main Inc. (S)
Pitman Co. (S)
Polychrome Corp. (M)
Poolside Lithographic Supply Inc. (D)
Printers' Service (M)
Rendic International (D)
Rycoline Products Inc. (M)
Southern Lithoplate Inc. (M)
Star International Corp. (D)
Superior Lithoplate of Indiana Inc. (D)
3M Printing & Publishing Systems Div. (M)
Unique Photo (D)
Varn International (M)
Western LithoTech (M)

Chemicals: Pressroom
Allpress Equipment Inc. (D)
Allstates Litho Plate Corp. (D)
American Litho Inc. (D)
Anchor (Imaging Products Division) (M)
Auto-Grafica Corp. (D)
B & T Press Supplies (Affiliated with Canadian Web) (D)
Berkshire/Westwood Graphics Group Inc. (D)
BESCO Graphic Systems Corp. (D)
CPS Corp. (M)
Duostat Co. (Affiliated with VGC Corp.) (D)
Engelhard (M)
Florida Printing Equipment and Supply (D)
Graphic Arts Technical & Consulting Services (M)
GraphLine Inc. (D)
Imperial Metal & Chemical Co. (Div. of Dupont) (M,D)
The Inco Company (M)
Inx International Ink Co. (D)
Jomac Inc. (M)
London Litho Aluminum Co. Inc. (D)
J. Thomas McHugh Co. Inc. (D)
Mid Atlantic Lighting (D)
Midwest Publishers Supply Co. (D)
The Morrison Group/Morrison Ink (M,D)
National Graphic Supply Corp. (D)
National Research Bureau (D)
NENSCO (M)
Newstech Co. (Div. of Rovinter Inc.) (D)
Parsons Main Inc. (S)
Pitman Co. (S)
Poolside Lithographic Supply Inc. (D)

RICHARD S. ROWSE

DWIGHT L. ROGERS

RRA, INC. & ASSOCIATES
customized consulting services for the printing and publishing industry

• master planning • process layout
• architecture • engineering • facility upgrading
• project and construction management
617-784-7501

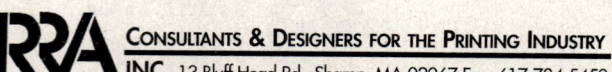 CONSULTANTS & DESIGNERS FOR THE PRINTING INDUSTRY
INC. 13 Bluff Head Rd., Sharon, MA 02067 Fax: 617-784-5450

Copyright ©1996 by the Editor & Publisher Co.

Equipment, supplies, services VI-25

Printers' Service (M)
Printex Products Corp. (M,D)
Rendic International (D)
Rycoline Products Inc. (M)
Southern Lithoplate Inc. (M)
Superior Lithoplate of Indiana Inc. (D)
Tech-Energy Co. (D,S)
Tower Products Inc. (M)
Unique Photo (D)
Varn International (M)
Western LithoTech (M)
Western Roller Corp. (M)
Winton Engineering Co. (M)
World Net & Associates Inc. (D)

Chemicals: Roller Cleaning
Allpress Equipment Inc. (D)
Allstates Litho Plate Corp. (D)
Anchor (Imaging Products Division) (M)
Auto-Grafica Corp. (D)
B & T Press Supplies (Affiliated with Canadian Web) (D)
Berkshire/Westwood Graphics Group Inc. (D)
BESCO Graphic Systems Corp. (D)
Bio-Safe Industries (M,D)
Duostat Co. (Affiliated with VGC Corp.) (D)
Flint Ink Corp. (M)
Graphic Arts Technical & Consulting Services (M)
The Inco Company (M)
Midwest Publishers Supply Co. (D)
The Morrison Group/Morrison Ink (M,D)
National Graphic Supply Corp. (M)
NENSCO (M)
Newstech Co. (Div. of Rovinter Inc.) (D)
Pitman Co. (S)
Printers' Service (M)
Rendic International (D)
Rogersal Inc. (M,D)
Rycoline Products Inc. (M)
Siebert Inc. (M)
Support Products Inc. (D)
Tech-Energy Co. (D,S)
Tower Products Inc. (M)
UMI (D)
Unique Photo (D)
Varn International (M)
Western LithoTech (M)
Winton Engineering Co. (M)

Circulation Equipment & Supplies
Alliance Rubber Co. (M)
American International Communications Inc. (M,D)
R C Anderson Associates Inc. (S)
ANI Promotions/DBA (D)
Baldwin Dampening Systems (Div. of Baldwin Graphic Systems) (M)
Bellatrix Systems Inc. (M,D)
Certified Audit of Circulations Inc. (S)
Circulation Verification Council (M)
Communications Management Service Inc. (S)
Franklin Wire Works Inc. (M,D)
GeoRack Inc. (M)
Go Plastics Inc. (V)
GP Plastics Corp. (M)
Great Southern Corp. (Sirco Div.) (D)
Hamilton Circulation Supplies Co. (Newspaper Mailroom Supplies) (D)
Imaje Ink Jet Printing (M)
K-Jack Engineering Co. Inc. (M)
Konica Imaging USA Inc. (M)
Master Flo Technology (M)
Meadows Co. (D)
Midwest Independent Postal (M)
NENSCO (D)
Newstech Co. (Div. of Rovinter Inc.) (D)
Quipp System Inc. (M,D)
Rycoline Products Inc. (M)
Scandinavian PC Systems Inc. (M,D)
Sheridan Systems (M)
Steel City Corp./Motor Route Supplies (M)
Vendors International Inc. (M,D)
Vendors International Ltd. (M)
Deane Weinberg Insurance Agency Inc. (S)
West-Mor Mailroom Services (D,S)

Cleaners & Solvents
Albar Labs & Industrial Supplies Inc. (M)
Auto-Grafica Corp. (D)
B & T Press Supplies (Affiliated with Canadian Web) (D)
Berkshire/Westwood Graphics Group Inc. (D)
BESCO Graphic Systems Corp. (D)
Bio-Safe Industries (M,D)
Continental Inks (D)
A.B. Dick Co. (M)
The Dow Chemical Co. (M)
Graphic Arts Technical & Consulting Services (M)
GraphLine Inc. (D)
The Inco Company (M)
Inx International Ink Co. (D)
Master Flo Technology (M)
Louis Melind Co. (M)

Merix Chemical Co. (Dept. TR) (M)
Midwest Publishers Supply Co. (D)
Mirachem Corp. (M,D)
The Morrison Group/Morrison Ink (M,D)
NENSCO (M)
Newstech Co. (Div. of Rovinter Inc.) (D)
Poolside Lithographic Supply Inc. (D)
Printers' Service (M)
Rogersal Inc. (M,D)
Rycoline Products Inc. (M)
Siebert Inc. (M)
TechEnergy Co. (D,S)
Tower Products Inc. (M)
UMI (D)
Varn International (M)
Veratec Div. (M)

Cleaning Sheet
Midwest Publishers Supply Co. (D)

Collating Equipment
ALTA Graphics Inc. (S)
Baumfolder Corp. (M,D)
A.B. Dick Co. (M)
Duostat Co. (Affiliated with VGC Corp.) (D)
Hartcid Industry Inc. (S)
MBM Corp. (D)
Newstech Co. (Div. of Rovinter Inc.) (D)
Pitney Bowes Business Systems (M,D)

Printing Equipment Specialists Inc. (S)
Quipp System Inc. (M)
Rosback Co. (D)
Rummel Engineering (M)
Sheridan Systems (M)
SITMA USA Inc. (M)
Stepper Inc. (M)
Todd Machinery (S)

Color Analyzers
BESCO Graphic Systems Corp. (D)
Caprock Developments Inc. (M,D)

Equipment, supplies, services

Computer Tree (D)
Crosfield Electronic Ltd. (M)
DuPont Co. (D)
Electronic Systems Engineering Co. (M)
Macbeth, Div. of Kollmorgen Inst. Corp. (M)
Midwest Publishers Supply Co. (D)
Newstech Co. (Div. of Rovinter Inc.) (D)
Nutek Inc. (D)
Pantone Inc. (M)
Pitman Photo Supply (D)
Scantronix

Color Printing Frames
Amergraph Corp. (M)
Computer Devices Inc. (D)
Consolidated International Corp. (M)
Duostat Co. (Affiliated with VGC Corp.) (D)
Midwest Publishers Supply Co. (D)
NENSCO (D)
Newstech Co. (Div. of Rovinter Inc.) (D)
SCREEN (USA) (M)

Color Proofing
All Systems Color Inc. (D)
Allsystems Go (D)
Anitec (M)
Auto-Grafica Corp. (D)
Berkshire/Westwood Graphics Group Inc. (D)
BESCO Graphic Systems Corp. (D)
Beta Screen Corp. (M)
Burgess Industries Inc. (M)
ByChrome Co. (M)
The Color Partnership (D)
Computer Tree (D)
CPS Technologies Inc. (D)
Crosfield Electronic Ltd. (M)
Direct Reproduction Corp. (M)
Duostat Co. (Affiliated with VGC Corp.) (D)
DuPont Co. (D)
Eastman Kodak/Professional Printing & Publishing Imaging (M)
Fuji Photo Film USA/Graphic Arts Products Div. (M)
GraphLine Inc. (D)

Harris Publishing Systems Corp. (S)
Hoechst Printing Products North America (M)
The Inco Company (M)
IRIS Graphics Inc. (Marketed By Scitex America) (M)
Konica Imaging USA Inc. (M)
Levien Instruments Co. (M,D)
LogEtronics Corp. (M,D)
London Litho Aluminum Co. Inc. (D)
Macbeth, Div. of Kollmorgen Inst. Corp. (M)
Midwest Publishers Supply Co. (D)
National Graphic Supply Corp. (D)
NENSCO (D)
Newstech Co. (Div. of Rovinter Inc.) (D)
NuArc Co. Inc. (M)
Nutek Inc. (D)
Pitman Co. (S)
Polychrome Corp. (D)
PrePRESS DIRECT (D)
Press-Enterprise Color Graphics (M,S)
Printing Equipment Specialists Inc. (S)
Scitex America Corp. (M,D)
SCREEN (USA) (M)
Techtron Imaging Center (S)
3M Printing & Publishing Systems Div. (M)
Truproof Ltd. (M)
Bob Weber Inc. (D)
Western LithoTech (M)
Willow Six Technologies (M)

Color Registration
Advanced Technical Solutions (S)
Allsystems Go (D)
Baldwin Web Controls (Div./Subsidiary Baldwin Technology) (M)
BESCO Graphic Systems Corp. (D)
Burgess Industries Inc. (M)
ByChrome Co. (M)
Caprock Developments Inc. (M,D)
Crosfield Electronic Ltd. (M)
Direct Reproduction Corp. (M)
Duarte Register Systems Inc. (M)
Duostat Co. (Affiliated with VGC Corp.) (D)
DuPont Co. (D)

Florida Printing Equipment and Supply (D)
Hurletron Inc. (M)
K & F/Printing Systems International (M)
Kaim & Associates Int'l. Marketing Inc. (D)
Konica Imaging USA Inc. (D)
Levien Instruments Co. (M,D)
Midwest Publishers Supply Co. (D)
National Graphic Supply Corp. (D)
NENSCO (D)
Newstech Co. (Div. of Rovinter Inc.) (D)
Perretta Graphics Corp. (M)
Pitman Co. (S)
Quad/Tech Int'l. (M)
Robertson Press Machinery Co. Inc. (D)
R T P Technical Specialists (S)
William C. Spells (RTP Technical Specialists) (S)
Stoesser Register Systems (M)
Tech-Energy Co. (M,D,S)
Techtron Imaging Center (S)
Ternes Register System (M)
Western LithoTech (M)
Western Lithotech (M)

Color Separation Enlargers
Allpress Equipment Inc. (D)
Auto-Grafica Corp. (D)
BESCO Graphic Systems Corp. (D)
Consolidated International Corp. (M)
Duostat Co. (Affiliated with VGC Corp.) (D)
Levien Instruments Co. (M,D)
Midwest Publishers Supply Co. (D)
Newstech Co. (Div. of Rovinter Inc.) (D)
Printing Equipment Specialists Inc. (S)
SCREEN (USA) (M)
VirtualColor (Screaming Technology Inc.) (S)

Color Separation Guides
Auto-Grafica Corp. (D)
BESCO Graphic Systems Corp. (D)
Levien Instruments Co. (M,D)
Midwest Publishers Supply Co. (D)
Newstech Co. (Div. of Rovinter Inc.) (D)
TRUMATCH Inc. (M)

Color Separation Scanners
All Systems Color Inc. (D)
Allsystems Go (D)
Auto-Grafica Corp. (D)
Autologic Inc. (Subsidiary of Volt Info. Svc.) (M)
BESCO Graphic Systems Corp. (D)
Birmy Graphics Corp. (D)
CNI Corp. (D)
Computer Tree (D)
CPS Technologies Inc. (D)
Crosfield Electronic Ltd. (M)
Danagraf North America (D)
A.B. Dick Co. (D)
A.B. Dick Co. (Itek Graphix Div.) (M)
Duostat Co. (Affiliated with VGC Corp.) (D)
DuPont Co. (D)
Durbin Associates (S)
Graphic Publishing Systems Inc. (D)
GraphLine Inc. (D)
Howtek (M)
ImagiTex Inc. (M,D,S)
Imapro Corp. (M)
International Memory Products of Illinois Inc. (D)
Konica Imaging USA Inc. (D)
Levien Instruments Co. (M,D)
Linotype-Hell Co. (M,D,S)
Microtek (M)
Midwest Publishers Supply Co. (D)
Monotype Systems Inc. (D)
National Graphic Supply Corp. (D)
Newstech Co. (Div. of Rovinter Inc.) (D)
Pitman Co. (S)
Pitman Photo Supply (D)
PrePRESS DIRECT (D)
Printing Equipment Specialists Inc. (S)
Scantronix (D)
Scitex America Corp. (M,D)
SCREEN (USA) (M)
Sinclair Imaging Inc. (S)
Techtron Imaging Center (S)
Truproof Ltd. (M)
UMAX Technologies Inc. (M)
Bob Weber Inc. (D)

Color Separations, Positives
All Systems Color Inc. (D)
Allsystems Go (D)
BESCO Graphic Systems Corp. (D)
Chronicle-Tribune (Gannett Color Div.) (S)
Levien Instruments Co. (M,D)
Newstech Co. (Div. of Rovinter Inc.) (D)
Press-Enterprise Color Graphics (M,S)
TV Data Technologies (M)

Color Viewing Equipment
Auto-Grafica Corp. (D)
Baldwin Web Controls (Div./Subsidiary Baldwin Technology) (M)

BESCO Graphic Systems Corp. (D)
Beta Screen Corp. (M)
Caprock Developments Inc. (M,D)
Consolidated International Corp. (M)
Crosfield Electronic Ltd. (M)
Duostat Co. (Affiliated with VGC Corp.) (D)
DuPont Co. (D)
GTI Graphic Technology Inc. (M)
Konica Imaging USA Inc. (D)
Levien Instruments Co. (M,D)
Macbeth, Div. of Kollmorgen Inst. Corp. (M)
Midwest Publishers Supply Co. (D)
National Graphic Supply Corp. (D)
NENSCO (D)
Newstech Co. (Div. of Rovinter Inc.) (D)
Pantone Inc. (M)
Pitman Co. (S)
Techtron Imaging Center (S)
Truproof Ltd. (D)

Composing Room Equipment & Supplies
Agfa Division, Bayer Inc. (M,D)
Allsystems Go (D)
Alteneder, Theo & Sons (M)
B & T Press Supplies (Affiliated with Canadian Web) (D)
Berkshire/Westwood Graphics Group Inc. (D)
BESCO Graphic Systems Corp. (D)
Beta Screen Corp. (M)
Consolidated International Corp. (M)
CPS Technologies Inc. (M,D)
Craig Cold Type Supply Inc. (M,D)
DPS Typecraft (Acorn House) (M)
Duostat Co. (Affiliated with VGC Corp.) (D)
Dynalith Inc. (D)
Foley, Torregiani & Associates, Inc. (D)
Harris Publishing Systems Corp. (S)
IBM Corp. (M,D,S)
Kreonite Inc. (M)
Megasys International (S)
Midwest Publishers Supply Co. (M,D)
N & L Enterprises Inc. (D)
National Graphic Supply Corp. (D)
NENSCO (D)
Newstech Co. (Div. of Rovinter Inc.) (D)
PAGE (D)
Parsons Main Inc. (S)
Poolside Lithographic Supply Inc. (D)
H. Sherr Engravers Inc. (M,D)
Stoesser Register Systems (M)
Support Products Inc. (D)
Thompson Cabinet Co. (M)
Veratec Div. (M)
Western Lithotech (M)

Computers: Hardware & Software Integrators
ABDEX Inc. (M,D)
Abelson Communications Inc. (S)
Ad Vantage Computer Systems Inc. (S)
Advanced Technical Solutions (M)
Allsystems Go (D)
The American Assn. of Independent News Distributors (D)
Applied Segmentation Technology (D,S)
Arri Systems Inc. (M,D)
Auto-Grafica Corp. (D)
Autologic Inc. (Subsidiary of Volt Info. Svc.) (M)
Baseview Products Inc. (M,D)
Bottom Line Industries (D,S)
Buffalo Inc. (M)
CE Engineering (M)
Computer Tree (D)
CompuText Inc. (M)
Copley Computer Services (S)
Core-Concepts (D,S)
CPS Technologies Inc. (D)
Cybergraphic Inc. (D,S)
Data Sciences Inc. (D)
DayStar Digital Inc. (M)
DTK Computer Inc. (M,D)
Duostat Co. (Affiliated with VGC Corp.) (D)
Foley, Torregiani & Associates, Inc. (D)
Freedom System Integrators (S)
General DataComm Inc. (M)
Global Turnkey Systems Inc. (S)
GMTI-Gannett Media Technical International (M)
Graphic Publishing Systems Inc. (D)
GraphLine Inc. (D)
Harris Publishing Systems Corp. (M)
IBC/Integrated Business Computers (M)
Icanon Associates Inc. (D)
Imaje Ink Jet Printing (M)
Imapro Corp. (M)
Kye International Corp. (M)
Lazer-fare Media Services Ltd. (D,S)
London Litho Aluminum Co. Inc. (D)
Mantis Computer Parts Inc. (D)
Monotype Systems Inc. (D)
Mustek Inc. (M)
Naft International Ltd. (D)
Newer Technology (M)
Newspaper Electronics Corp. (M,D,S)
Newspaper Systems Group Inc. (D)

BULBTRONICS
An International Company

Replacement Bulbs for THE GRAPHIC ARTS

Applications: Scanners, Color Separators, Platemakers, Cameras, Curing, Exposure Units, WEB Presses, Light Boxes, Paper Cutters.

Bulb Types: Xenon, Mercury, Halogen, Lasers, Metal Halide, Diazo, Photopolymer, Fluorescent, Grids, Quartz.

Replacement Lamps For: Berkey, Heidelberg, Nuarc, Theimer, Itek, Burgess, Riston, Violux, Colight, 3M, A.B. Dick, Addalux, Brown, Bruning, Royal Zenith, Crossfield.

East
Farmingdale, NY
516-249-2272

For Information Please Call:
800-654-8542

West
Hollywood, CA
213-461-6262

Equipment, supplies, services VI-27

Newstech Co. (Div. of Rovinter Inc.) (D)
Paragon Publishing Systems (D)
Photo Systems Inc. (D)
PPI (UK) Ltd. (S)
PrePRESS SUPPORT (M)
Printronix (M)
Publishing Business Systems Inc. (D)
Publishing Partners International (S)
Retail Solutions Group (M)
Roadshow International Inc. (M,D)
Saxe Inc. (M,D)
Scitex America Corp. (M,D)
Shreve Systems (D)
Software Consulting Services (M,D)
Solna Web USA Inc. (M)
Source Data Systems (D)
Stauffer Media Systems (D,S)
Synaptic Micro Solutions (M)
Sysdeco U.S. (M,D,S)
System Guides (M)
Systems Oasis (Div. of Graphic Enterprises of Ohio Inc.) (M,D)
Telephone Response Technologies (M)
Toltech Systems (M)
Total Image Corp. (D)
Total Systems Engineering Inc. (D)
Trutone Co. (D)
TSA (D)
Ultra Corp. (D)
VoCal Telecommunications (M)
Voice Connexion (M)
Bob Weber Inc. (D)
Wedge Computer Systems (S)
Western Automation (M)
Willow Bend Communications Inc. (M)
Xerox Corp.-Xerox Engineering Systems (M)
Zeos (M,D,S)

Computers: Laptop & Portable
Abelson Communications Inc. (S)
Ad Vantage Computer Systems Inc. (S)
Allsystems Go (D)
Auto-Grafica Corp. (D)
Baseview Products Inc. (D)
Computerease Software Inc. (D)
CompuText Inc. (D)
Core-Concepts (D,S)
CPS Technologies Inc. (D)
DTK Computer Inc. (M,D)
Freedom System Integrators (D)
GMTI-Gannett Media Technical International (D)
GraphLine Inc. (D)
Lazer-fare Media Services Ltd. (D,S)
London Litho Aluminum Co. Inc. (D)
Mantis Computer Parts Inc. (D)
Media Marketing Inc. (M,D,S)
Midwest Publishers Supply Co. (D)
Naft International Ltd. (D)
Newer Technology (M)
Newspaper Electronics Corp. (D,S)
Newspaper Systems Group Inc. (D)
Newstech Co. (Div. of Rovinter Inc.) (D)
Photo Systems Inc. (D)
Stauffer Media Systems (D,S)
Sysdeco U.S. (D)
Trutone Co. (D)
Voice Connexion (M)
Wedge Computer Systems (S)

Computers: Local Area Networks (LANS)
Abelson Communications Inc. (S)
Ad Vantage Computer Systems Inc. (S)
Advanced Graphic Systems (KAIM) (M)
Advanced Technical Solutions (S)
Allsystems Go (D)
Auto-Grafica Corp. (D)
Baseview Products Inc. (D)
Buffalo Inc. (M)
Computer Tree (D)
Computerease Software Inc. (D)
CompuText Inc. (D)
Connexperts (M)
Copley Computer Services (S)
Core-Concepts (S)
CPS Technologies Inc. (D)
Data Sciences Inc. (D)
DTK Computer Inc. (M,D)
Engage Communication Inc. (M,D)
Freedom System Integrators (D)
GMTI-Gannett Media Technical International (M)
Graphic Publishing Systems Inc. (D)
GraphLine Inc. (D)
Harris Publishing Systems Corp. (S)
Icanon Associates Inc. (D)
Imapro Corp. (M)
Kye International Corp. (M)
Lazer-fare Media Services Ltd. (S)
London Litho Aluminum Co. Inc. (D)
Mantis Computer Parts Inc. (D)
Micro Systems Specialists Inc. (MSSI) (D)
Monotype Systems Inc. (D)

Naft International Ltd. (D)
Newer Technology (M)
Newspaper Electronics Corp. (M,D,S)
Newstech Co. (Div. of Rovinter Inc.) (D)
Paragon Publishing Systems (D)
PrePRESS DIRECT (D)
Stauffer Media Systems (D,S)
Synaptic Micro Solutions (D)
Sysdeco U.S. (D)
Total Systems Engineering Inc. (S)
Ultra Corp. (D)
Bob Weber Inc. (S)
Wedge Computer Systems (S)
Word Mark International Corp. (M,D)

Computers: Pagination/Layout
Editorial System Engineering Co. (ESE) (M,D)
Ewert America Electronics Ltd. (M)

Computers: Storage Devices
Abelson Communications Inc. (S)
Ad Vantage Computer Systems Inc. (S)
Allsystems Go (D)
Auto-Grafica Corp. (D)
Bell & Howell Publication Systems Co. (M)
Buffalo Inc. (M)
Computer Tree (D)
Core-Concepts (S)
CPS Technologies Inc. (D)
DTK Computer Inc. (M,D)
DYC Supply Co./Dynaric Inc. (M,D)
Equipto (M)
Ergotron Inc. (M,D)
Freedom System Integrators (D)
GraphLine Inc. (D)
Lazer-fare Media Services Ltd. (D)
London Litho Aluminum Co. Inc. (D)
Mantis Computer Parts Inc. (D)
Midwest Publishers Supply Co. (D)
Monotype Systems Inc. (D)
Naft International Ltd. (D)
Newspaper Electronics Corp. (D,S)
Newspaper Systems Group Inc. (D)
Newstech Co. (Div. of Rovinter Inc.) (D)
Overland Data Inc. (M,D,S)
PrePRESS DIRECT (D)
Software Consulting Services (D)
Stauffer Media Systems (D,S)
Sysdeco U.S. (D)
Tecnavia S A/Press Div. (M)
Thompson Cabinet Co. (M)
Total Systems Engineering Inc. (D)
Trutone Co. (D)
Wedge Computer Systems (S)
Western LithoTech (M,D)

Consulting Services: Advertising
Abelson Communications Inc. (S)
Adtrack Inc. (S)
Advertisers Exchange Inc. (S)
Allsystems Go (S)
America's Interactive Production Network (S)
American Consulting Services (S)
American Newspaper Representatives (S)
American Opinion Research (S)
Applied Segmentation Technology (S)
Arrow Printing Co. (S)
Auto-Grafica Corp. (S)
Baseview Products Inc. (S)
Berting Communications (S)
Brilliant Ideas For Publishers (S)
Brite (S)
The Douglas Britt Co. (S)
M.W. Burke & Associates Inc. (S)
Cable Classified Advertising Network (CCAN) (S)
Cass Communications Inc. (S)
Gene Chamberlin Newspaper Consultants (S)
Chismark & Co. (S)
Coleman Advertising (S)
Competitive Media Reporting (S)
CompuText Inc. (S)
Copley Computer Services (S)
Creative Brilliance Advertising/Marketing & Public Relations (S)
Creative House Print Media Consultants (S)
Creative Strategies (S)
Cybergraphic Inc. (S)
Dail Advertising Service (S)
Data Sciences Inc. (S)
William Dunkerley Publishing Consultant (S)
Dynamo International Inc. (S)
Forrest Consulting (S)
John Foust Advertising/Training (S)
Geac/Vision Shift (S)
Rene Gnam Consultation Corp. (S)
W B Grimes & Co. Inc. (S)
Hare Associates Inc. (S)
Icanon Associates Inc. (S)
INFO-CONNECT (J.H. Zerby Newspapers Inc.) (S)
Integrated Newspaper Systems Inc. (S)
Kevin Brian Kamen & Co. (S)
The Keenan Group Inc. (S)
Lazer-fare Media Services Ltd. (S)
Leadership Advertising Development Co. (S)
The Loki Group Inc. (S)
The MacDonald Classified Service (S)
Marketing Research Associates Inc. (S)
Marketing Strategies Inc. (S)
Marks & Frederick Associates Inc. (S)
Media Marketing Inc. (S)
Media Monitors Inc. (S)
Minnesota Opinion Research Inc. (MORI) (S)
Missouri Press Service Inc. (S)
Mortgage Market Information Services (S)
Multi Ad Services Inc. (S)
National Research Bureau (S)
Network Newspaper Advertising Inc. (S)
Newspaper Space Bank (S)
Northwest Publishers Inc. (S)
Print Marketing Concepts (S)
PromoFax (S)
Publishing Business Systems Inc. (S)
Pulse Research Inc. (S)
Rowlett Advertising Service Inc. (S)
Sales Development Services (S)
Sales Training Consultants Inc. (S)
Selling Dynamics Inc. (S)
Silverman Newspaper Management Consultants (S)
Software Consulting Services (S)
Summerville Press Inc. (S)
Sysdeco U.S. (S)
Weatherline Inc. (S)
Wedge Computer Systems (S)
Keister Williams Newspaper Services (S)
Willow Bend Communications Inc. (S)
Wolk Advertising Inc. (Retail Carpet Ad Service) (S)
Wrubel Communications (S)

Consulting Services: Circulation
Abelson Communications Inc. (S)
Allsystems Go (S)
Alternate Postal Delivery (S)
The American Assn. of Independent News Distributors (S)
American International Communications Inc. (S)
American Opinion Research (S)
R C Anderson Associates Inc. (S)
Applied Segmentation Technology (S)
APS Development (S)
Ashcraft Consulting (S)
Baseview Products Inc. (S)
Blevins Harding Group (Western Office) (S)
M.W. Burke & Associates Inc. (S)
Cable Classified Advertising Network (CCAN) (S)
Carlson Design/Construct Corp. (S)
Gene Chamberlin Newspaper Consultants (S)
Church Rickards, Whitlock & Co. Inc. (S)
Circulation Development Inc. (CDI) (S)
Circulation Solutions (S)
Circulation III Telemarketing Services (S)
Circulation Verification Council (S)
Communications Management Service Inc. (S)
Communications Co. (S)
Community Papers Verification Services (S)
Copley Computer Services (S)
Creative House Print Media Consultants (S)
Creative Strategies (S)
Data Sciences Inc. (S)
DemoSource Inc. (S)
Forrest Consulting (S)
Geac/Vision Shift (S)
Rene Gnam Consultation Corp. (S)
Icanon Associates Inc. (S)
Inland Press Association Inc. (S)
Integrated Newspaper Systems Inc. (S)
Kevin Brian Kamen & Co. (S)
The Keenan Group Inc. (S)
Knox Accounts Service (S)
Layton Marketing Group Inc. (S)
Lazer-fare Media Services Ltd. (S)
Marketing Research Associates Inc. (S)
Marks & Frederick Associates Inc. (S)
Wayne Matthews Corp. (S)
Metromail Corp. (S)
Midwest Independent Postal (S)
Minnesota Opinion Research Inc. (MORI) (S)
Parsons Main Inc. (S)
Publishing Business Systems Inc. (S)
Pulse Research Inc. (S)

STAUFFER GOLD

Computer Systems for Newspapers Like Yours

Quality Doesn't Have to Cost Extra

Stauffer Gold products continue the tradition of efficient and economical computer systems for your newspaper. New products for '95 include updated and expanded audiotext features, and database solutions for business software. Created by newspaper people for newspaper people, Stauffer Gold provides easy solutions to complex problems, without sacrificing your budget. Let us show you how Stauffer Gold can work for you.

FRONT-END SYSTEMS
BUSINESS SYSTEMS
LIBRARY SYSTEMS
AUDIOTEXT SYSTEMS

« Affordable »
« Efficient »
« Easy to Use »

For more information call Keith Wood, sales mgr.
1-800-777-7171

Stauffer Media Systems P. O. Box 1330 Joplin, MO 64802

Copyright ©1996 by the Editor & Publisher Co.

VI-28 Equipment, supplies, services

Roggen Management Consultants Inc. (S)
Sales Training Consultants Inc. (S)
Saxe Inc. (S)
Selling Dynamics Inc. (S)
Silverman Newspaper Management Consultants (S)
Software Consulting Services (S)
Summerville Press Inc. (S)
Syntellect Inc. (S)
Sysdeco U.S. (S)
Tele-Sales Systems Inc. (S)
Transportation Consultants Inc. (S)
Ver-A-Fast Corp. (S)
The Von Entress Group (S)
Willow Bend Communications Inc. (S)
Wrubel Communications (S)

Consulting Services: Computer
Abelson Communications Inc. (S)
Ad Vantage Computer Systems Inc. (S)
Allsystems Go (S)
Applied Segmentation Technology (S)
Ashcraft Consulting (S)
Auto-Grafica Corp. (S)
Baseview Products Inc. (S)
The Business Scribe Inc. (S)
CE Engineering (S)
Gene Chamberlin Newspaper Consultants (S)
Computer Tree (S)
CompuText Inc. (S)
Copley Computer Services (S)
Core-Concepts (S)
Creative House Print Media Consultants (S)
Data Sciences Inc. (S)
Deadline Data Systems Inc. (S)
Digital Information Group (S)
Dunn Technology Inc. (S)
Eclipse Services (Div. of Quadrivium Inc.) (S)
Engage Communication Inc. (S)
Global Turnkey Systems Inc. (S)
Gulf Coast System Design Co. (S)
Icanon Associates Inc. (S)
Information Engineering (S)
Lazer-fare Media Services Ltd. (S)
Midwest Publishers Supply Co. (S)
Newspaper Electronics Corp. (S)
Newspaper Systems Group Inc. (S)
North Atlantic Publishing Systems Inc. (S)
Photo Systems Inc. (S)
PrePRESS SUPPORT (S)
Publishing Business Systems Inc. (S)
Random Access (S)
RTR Computer Consulting Inc. (S)
Sales Development Services (S)
Software Consulting Services (S)
Summerville Press Inc. (S)
Sysdeco U.S. (S)
Total Image Corp. (S)
Total Systems Engineering Inc. (S)
Bob Weber Inc. (S)
Wedge Computer Systems (S)
Willow Bend Communications Inc. (S)

Consulting Services: Editorial
Abelson Communications Inc. (S)
Ad Vantage Computer Systems Inc. (S)
Allsystems Go (S)
American Opinion Research (S)
Ashcraft Consulting (S)
Auto-Grafica Corp. (S)
Ayers/Johanek Publication Design (S)
Baseview Products Inc. (S)
Brady & Paul Communications (S)
Brilliant Ideas For Publishers (S)
Sara Brown & Associates (S)
The Business Scribe Inc. (S)
Carter & Associates (S)
CE Engineering (S)
Gene Chamberlin Newspaper Consultants (S)
CompuText Inc. (S)
Copley Computer Services (S)
CPS Technologies Inc. (S)
Creative Brilliance Advertising/Marketing & Public Relations (S)
Creative House Print Media Consultants (S)
Creative Strategies (S)
Cybergraphic Inc. (S)
William Dunkerley Publishing Consultant (S)
Editorial Consultant Service (S)
Editorial Management Strategies (S)
Editorial System Engineering Co. (ESE) (S)
Executive Resource Group (S)
The Findlay Group (S)
W B Grimes & Co. Inc. (S)
Hare Associates Inc. (S)
INFO-CONNECT (J.H. Zerby Newspapers Inc.) (S)
Information Engineering (S)
Lazer-fare Media Services Ltd. (S)
The Loki Group Inc. (S)
Marks & Frederick Associates Inc. (S)
Minnesota Opinion Research Inc. (MORI) (S)

Mortgage Market Information Services (S)
Nasco Products Co. (S)
National Research Bureau (S)
North Atlantic Publishing Systems Inc. (S)
Northwest Publishers Inc. (S)
RTR Computer Consulting Inc. (S)
Silverman Newspaper Management Consultants (S)
Software Consulting Services (S)
Summerville Press Inc. (S)
Sysdeco U.S. (S)
TV Data Information Services (M)
WeatherData Inc. (S)
Willow Six Technologies (S)
Wrubel Communications (S)

Consulting Services: Equipment
Abelson Communications Inc. (S)
Ad Vantage Computer Systems Inc. (S)
Advanced Technical Solutions (S)
Allsystems Go (S)
ALTA Graphics Inc. (S)
Apex Machine Co. (S)
The Austin Co. (S)
Auto-Grafica Corp. (S)
Axelrod, Norman N., Assoc./Optical, Laser & Vision Systems (S)
Baseview Products Inc. (S)
Blevins Harding Group (Western Office) (S)
Boles, Morgan & Canino (S)
Canadian Web Consultants Ltd. (S)
CE Engineering (S)
Central Graphics (S)
Gene Chamberlin Newspaper Consultants (S)
Computer Tree (S)
CompuText Inc. (S)
Core-Concepts (S)
CPS Technologies Inc. (S)
Dario Designs Inc. (S)
Data Sciences Inc. (S)
Equipto (S)
Jimmy R. Fox, Mail Room Consultant (S)
Ralph Fusco Inc. (S)
Ginsberg, William Associates (S)
Graphic System Services (S)
The Haskell Co. (S)
The International School For Pressroom Management (S)
The Keenan Group Inc. (S)
Lazer-fare Media Services Ltd. (S)
Midwest Publishers Supply Co. (S)
Nama Graphics Inc. (S)
Network Industrial Services Inc. (S)
Newstech Co. (Div. of Rovinter Inc.) (S)
Pacific Newspaper Services Inc. (S)
R T P Technical Specialists (S)
Sheridan Systems (S)
Software Consulting Services (S)
Solna Web USA Inc. (S)
Standard Electric and Engineering Co. (S)
Standlee and Associates Inc. (S)
Walter Stobb Associates Inc. (S)
Sysdeco U.S. (S)
Tech-Energy Co. (S)
Ternes Register System (S)
Three Sigma (S)
Tidland Corp. (S)
TKS (USA) Inc. (S)
Todd Machinery (S)
Wedge Computer Systems (S)
World Net & Associates Inc. (S)

Consulting Services: Ergonomics
Allsystems Go (S)
Applied Learning Corp. (S)
Blevins Harding Group (Western Office) (S)
Dario Designs Inc. (S)
Equipto (S)
Fox Bay Industries Inc. (S)
The International School For Pressroom Management (S)
Lazer-fare Media Services Ltd. (S)
Midwest Publishers Supply Co. (S)
Sysdeco U.S. (S)

Consulting Services: Financial
Ashcraft Consulting (S)
Boles, Morgan & Canino (S)
BOLITHO-CRIBB & Associates (S)
Gene Chamberlin Newspaper Consultants (S)
Communications Service Co. (S)
CompuText Inc. (S)
Creative House Print Media Consultants (S)
Data Sciences Inc. (S)
Digital Information Group (S)
William Dunkerley Publishing Consultant (S)
Forrest Consulting (S)
Barry French (S)
W B Grimes & Co. Inc. (S)
Hare Associates Inc. (S)
Inland Press Association Inc. (S)

Integrated Newspaper Systems Inc. (S)
The International School For Pressroom Management (S)
Kevin Brian Kamen & Co. (S)
Kanaly Financial Health Club (S)
James Lorenzen & Associates (S)
Marks & Frederick Associates Inc. (S)
James Martin & Associates (S)
Media Advertising Credit Services (S)
Mortgage Market Information Services (S)
Parsons Main Inc. (S)
Price Waterhouse Valuation Services (S)
Publishing Business Systems Inc. (S)
Roggen Management Consultants Inc. (S)
Silverman Newspaper Management Consultants (S)
Software Consulting Services (S)
Source Data Systems (S)
Summerville Press Inc. (S)
Sysdeco U.S. (S)
Walterry Insurance (S)
J.N. Wells & Co. Inc. (S)
Wrubel Communications (S)

Consulting Services: Marketing
Allsystems Go (S)
Alternate Postal Delivery (S)
America's Interactive Production Network (S)
American Opinion Research (S)
Applied Segmentation Technology (S)
Arrow Printing Co. (S)
Auditec Computing Services Inc. (S)
Belden Associates (S)
Berting Communications (S)
Richard Briggs & Associates (S)
Brilliant Ideas For Publishers (S)
The Business Scribe Inc. (S)
Cable Classified Advertising Network (CCAN) (S)
Gene Chamberlin Newspaper Consultants (S)
Claritas (S)
Communications Management Service Inc. (S)
Communications Service Co. (S)
Computer Services Group Inc. (S)
Creative Brilliance Advertising/Marketing & Public Relations (S)
Creative House Print Media Consultants (S)
Creative Strategies (S)
Cybergraphic Inc. (S)
Data Sciences Inc. (S)
William Dunkerley Publishing Consultant (S)
Dynamo International Inc. (S)
Forrest Consulting (S)
Rene Gnam Consultation Corp. (S)
W B Grimes & Co. Inc. (S)
Hare Associates Inc. (S)
Information Engineering (S)
Inland Press Association Inc. (S)
Inx International Ink Co. (S)
Kevin Brian Kamen & Co. (S)
The Keenan Group Inc. (S)
Layton Marketing Group Inc. (S)
Market Opinion Research/Pace (S)
Marketing Research Associates Inc. (S)
Marketing Strategies Inc. (S)
Marks & Frederick Associates Inc. (S)
McClure Media Marketing Motivation Co. (S)
Media Consultants & Associates (S)
Louis Melind Co. (S)
Metromail Corp. (S)
Minnesota Opinion Research Inc. (MORI) (S)
Mo-Money Associates Inc. (S)
Mortgage Market Information Services (S)
Multi Ad Services Inc. (S)
Nasco Products Co. (S)
National Research Bureau (S)
PromoFax (S)
Publishing Business Systems Inc. (S)
Pulse Research Inc. (S)
Research USA Inc. (S)
Roggen Management Consultants Inc. (S)
Sales Development Services (S)
Selling Dynamics Inc. (S)
Silverman Newspaper Management Consultants (S)
Sinclair Imaging Inc. (S)
Software Consulting Services (S)
Strategic Telemedia (S)
Summerville Press Inc. (S)
Sysdeco U.S. (S)
Valco Sales Inc. (S)
Ver-A-Fast Corp. (S)
Keister Williams Newspaper Services (S)
Willow Bend Communications Inc. (S)
World Net & Associates Inc. (S)
Wrubel Communications (S)

Consulting Services: Production
Ad Vantage Computer Systems Inc. (S)
Allsystems Go (S)
ALTA Graphics Inc. (S)
Arrow Printing Co. (S)
The Austin Co. (S)
Baseview Products Inc. (S)
Blevins Harding Group (Western Office) (S)
Boles, Morgan & Canino Inc. (S)
M.W. Burke & Associates (S)

Canadian Web Consultants Ltd. (S)
Carlson Design/Construct Corp. (S)
Gene Chamberlin Newspaper Consultants (S)
CNI Corp. (S)
Computer Services Group Inc. (S)
Computer Tree (S)
CompuText Inc. (S)
Copley Computer Services (S)
Core-Concepts (S)
Creative House Print Media Consultants (S)
Cybergraphic Inc. (S)
Dario Designs Inc. (S)
Deadline Data Systems Inc. (S)
The Directory Center (S)
Durbin Associates (S)
Focus/Graphics (S)
Foley, Torregiani & Associates, Inc. (S)
Jimmy R. Fox, Mail Room Consultant (S)
Ralph Fusco Inc. (S)
Ginsberg, William Associates (S)
Global Press Sales Inc. (S)
GMA Inc. (S)
The International School For Pressroom Management (S)
The Keenan Group Inc. (S)
Lazer-fare Media Services Ltd. (S)
The Loki Group Inc. (S)
Midwest Publishers Supply Co. (S)
NCS Inc. (S)
Newstech Co. (Div. of Rovinter Inc.) (S)
ONE Corp. (S)
Pacific Newspaper Services Inc. (S)
Parsons Main Inc. (S)
Printmark (S)
Quebecor Printing Providence (S)
Quipp System Inc. (S)
Rein Tech Inc. (Printing Systems Technology)(S)
R T P Technical Specialists (S)
RTR Computer Consulting Inc. (S)
Selling Dynamics Inc. (S)
Sheridan Systems (S)
Software Consulting Services (S)
The Software Development Group Inc. (S)
William C. Spells (RTP Technical Specialists) (S)
Standard Electric and Engineering Co. (S)
Standlee and Associates Inc. (S)
Summerville Press Inc. (S)
Sysdeco U.S. (S)
Tech-Energy Co. (S)
TKS (USA) Inc. (S)
Willow Six Technologies (S)
World Net & Associates Inc. (S)

Controllers-Press
AirSystems Inc. (M,D)
Arco Engineering Inc. (Newspaper Div.) (M,D)
Baldwin Web Controls (Div./Subsidiary Baldwin Technology) (M)
Allen Bradley Co. (Motion Control Div.) (M)
Fincor/Electronics Div. Inc. (M)
Fleming Enterprises (M)
Imo Industries Inc. (Fincor Electrics Div.) (M,D,S)
The International School For Pressroom Management (M)
MAH Machine Co. Inc. (M,S)
Newstech Co. (Div. of Rovinter Inc.) (D)
R T P Technical Specialists (S)
William C. Spells (RTP Technical Specialists) (D,S)
Standard Electric and Engineering Co. (M,D,S)
Tech-Energy Co. (D,S)
TKS (USA) Inc. (M,D)
World Net & Associates Inc. (S)
WPC Machinery Corp. (S)

Controls: Exposure
Amergraph Corp. (M)
R.W. Borrowdale Co.(RWB Enterprises Div.) (M)
Burgess Industries Inc. (M)
Douthitt Corp. (M,D)
Duostat Co. (Affiliated with VGC Corp.) (D)
Newstech Co. (Div. of Rovinter Inc.) (D)
NuArc Co. Inc. (M)
Portage Newspaper Supply Co. (M)
Stoesser Register Systems (M)
Western LithoTech (M)

Controls: Photoelectric
Advanced Graphic Systems (KAIM) (M)
Baldwin Web Controls (Div./Subsidiary Baldwin Technology) (M)
Newstech Co. (Div. of Rovinter Inc.) (D)
William C. Spells (RTP Technical Specialists) (D,S)

Controls: Register
Allpress Equipment Inc. (D)
Baldwin Web Controls (Div./Subsidiary Baldwin Technology) (M)
Burgess Industries Inc. (M)
Crosfield Electronic Ltd. (M)
Duostat Co. (Affiliated with VGC Corp.) (D)
DuPont Co. (M)
Kaim & Associates Int'l. Marketing Inc. (D)
London Litho Aluminum Co. Inc. (D)
National Graphic Sales Inc. (S)
National Graphic Supply Corp. (D)

Copyright ©1996 by the Editor & Publisher Co.

Equipment, supplies, services VI-29

Newstech Co. (Div. of Rovinter Inc.) (D)
Quad/Tech Int'l. (M)
R T P Technical Specialists (S)
William C. Spells (RTP Technical Specialists) (D,S)
Stoesser Register Systems (M)
Tech-Energy Co. (M,D,S)
Ternes Register System (M)
Western LithoTech (M)

Conversion Equipment
Advance Graphics Equipment of York Inc. (M,D)
Charles Beck Machine Corp. (M)
Enkel Corp. (A Baldwin Technology Co.) (M)
Hartcid Industry Inc. (D,S)
International Paper Box Machine (M)
Kaim & Associates Int'l. Marketing Inc. (D)
KBA-Motter Corp. (Koenig & Bauer-Albert Group) (M)
MAH Machine Co. Inc. (S)
Pressroom Products Inc. (D)
Printing Equipment Specialists Inc. (S)
Printing Press Services Inc. (M,D)
Republic Roller Corp. (S)
Rotoflex International (M)
R T P Technical Specialists (S)
Ryco Graphic Manufacturing Inc. (M)
William C. Spells (RTP Technical Specialists) (D,S)
Standard Electric and Engineering Co. (M,D,S)
Tech-Energy Co. (M,D,S)
Tecnigraph T.G.I. International Inc. (M)
Telesonic Packaging Corp. (M)
Tidland Corp. (M,D)
TKS (USA) Inc. (M,D)
Web Tapes Inc. (S)
Will-Pemco Inc. (M)

Conveyors
Allpress Equipment Inc. (D)
ALTA Graphics Inc. (S)
Arco Engineering Inc. (Newspaper Div.) (S)
Butler SMC. (M)
Control Engineering Co. (M)
Engineering Products Co. (D,S)
Ferag Inc. (M)
Florida Printing Equipment and Supply (D)
FMC Corp. (Material Handling Systems Div.) (M)
Jimmy R. Fox, Mail Room Consultant (S)
Gammerler (US) Corp. (M,D)
Gerrard Ovalstrapping (M,D)
GMA Inc. (M)
Hall Processing Systems (M)
Hartcid Industry Inc. (D,S)
Heidelberg Harris Inc. (M)
Interlake Packaging Corp. (M)
Kansa Corp. (Baldwin Technology Co.) (M,D)
Lamb-Grays Harbor Co. (M)
Machine Design Service Inc. (M)
MAH Machine Co. Inc. (S)
Manassy Precision Corp. (M)
The Master Group (M)
N/S Corp. (M)
National Graphic Sales Inc. (S)
Network Industrial Services Inc. (S)
Newstech Co. (Div. of Rovinter Inc.) (D)
Ovalstrapping Inc. (M)
Pako Corp. (M)
Parsons Main Inc. (S)
Power Strap (M)
Press-Tec Inc. (S)
PSC Flo-Turn Inc. (M)
Quipp System Inc. (M)
Rapistan Demag Corp. (M)
Sheridan Systems (M)
Shuttleworth Inc. (M)
SI Handling Systems Inc. (M)
SITMA USA Inc. (M)
Standard Electric and Engineering Co. (M,D,S)
Standlee and Associates Inc. (M,D,S)
Star International Corp. (D)
Tech-Energy Co. (M,D,S)
Valley Remanufacturing Co. (M)
Jervis B. Webb Co. (M)
West-Mor Mailroom Services (D,S)
Western LithoTech (M)
Will-Pemco Inc. (M)
World Net & Associates Inc. (D)

Copper Plating Drums
Aaro Roller Corp. (M)
Brodie System Inc. (S)
Central Graphics (D)
Hadronics (M,S)
Hartcid Industry Inc. (S)
MAH Machine Co. Inc. (M)
Moss Reck & Associates Inc. (D)
Rotation Dynamics Corp. (M)
Tech-Energy Co. (M,D,S)
UMI (M)

Core Cutters, Restorers, Rounders
Craftsmen Machinery Co./Graphic Export Corp. (D)
Tech-Energy Co. (D,S)
Tidland Corp. (M,D)

Core Strippers & Separators
Graphic Enterprises (M,D,S)
National Graphic Sales Inc. (S)

Counting, Stacking, Bundling Machines
Allpress Equipment Inc. (D)
ALTA Graphics Inc. (S)
American Graphics L.P. (M,D)
Baldwin Stobb (Div. of Baldwin Technology) (M,D,S)
Baumfolder Corp. (M,D)
Butler SMC. (M)
Central Graphics (D)
D & R Engineering (Graybar Int'l.) (M,D)
Ferag Inc. (M)
Florida Printing Equipment and Supply (D)
Gerrard Ovalstrapping (M,D)
Global Graphics Inc. (D)
GMA Inc. (M,D)
Heidelberg Harris Inc. (D)
IC Systems Solutions (S)
Kaim & Associates Int'l. Marketing Inc. (D)
Kansa Corp. (Baldwin Technology Co.) (M,D)
Machine Design Service Inc. (M)
Muller Martini Corp. (M)
National Graphic Sales Inc. (S)
National Research Bureau (D)
NCS Inc. (M)
Network Industrial Services Inc. (S)
Newstech Co. (Div. of Rovinter Inc.) (D)
Offset Web Sales Inc. (D)
Parsons Main Inc. (S)
Printing Equipment Specialists Inc. (S)
Quipp System Inc. (M)
Schuler Sales/A Kolbus Group Subsidiary (M)
Sheridan Systems (M)
SITMA USA Inc. (M)
Solna Web USA Inc. (D)
Standlee and Associates Inc. (D,S)
Tech-Energy Co. (D,S)
Valley Remanufacturing Co. (M)
West-Mor Mailroom Services (M,D,S)

Credit & Collections
Media Advertising Credit Services (S)
SKO Brenner American (M,D,S)

Cutters & Trimmers
Advance Graphics Equipment of York Inc. (M,D)
ALTA Graphics Inc. (S)
Baumfolder Corp. (M,D)
BESCO Graphic Systems Corp. (D)
Butler SMC. (M)
Consolidated International Corp. (M)
Duostat Co. (Affiliated with VGC Corp.) (D)
Gammerler (US) Corp. (D)
Heidelberg USA (D)
Martin Yale Inc. (M)
MBM Corp. (D)
Midwest Publishers Supply Co. (M)
Muller Martini Corp. (M)
National Graphic Sales Inc. (S)
National Graphic Supply Corp. (D)
Newstech Co. (Div. of Rovinter Inc.) (D)
Portage Newspaper Supply Co. (D)
Press Rubber Co. Inc. (M,D)
Primark Tool Group (M)

handling systems for newspapers...
of any size

Every newspaper, regardless of circulation, shares a common goal: deliver a quality product, on time, in good condition. Machine Design Service, Inc., has assisted newspapers worldwide in achieving this goal since 1976. We provide...
- roll handling
- mailroom
- bundle distribution
- waste handling
- custom designed equipment

...for newspapers of any size. Call today for a free newspaper handling check-up and a free video highlighting many of our current systems.

  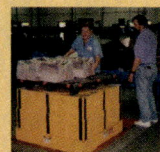

Roll Handling *Waste Handling* *Custom Equipment*

Machine Design Service, Inc.
3535 Larimer Street • Denver, Colorado 80205 • (303) 294-0275 ext 126 • FAX: (303) 294-0634

Copyright ©1996 by the Editor & Publisher Co.

VI-30 Equipment, supplies, services

Printing Equipment Specialists Inc. (S)
Resource Net International (D)
Schuler Sales/A Kolbus
　Group Subsidiary (M)
Tech-Energy Co. (M,D,S)
Ternes Register System (D)
Tidland Corp. (M)
Todd Machinery (S)
UMI
Western Printing Machinery (M)
Will-Pemco Inc. (M)

Cutting & Creasing Presses
Consolidated International Corp. (M)
Newstech Co. (Div. of Rovinter Inc.) (D)
Press Rubber Co. Inc. (M,D)
Printing Equipment Specialists Inc. (S)
Tech-Energy Co. (M,D,S)

Cutting Tools
BESCO Graphic Systems Corp. (D)
Duostat Co. (Affiliated with VGC Corp.) (D)
Newstech Co. (Div. of Rovinter Inc.) (D)
Press Rubber Co. Inc. (M,D)
Primark Tool Group (M)
Tidland Corp. (M,D)
UMI (M)

Cylinder Repair
Allpress Equipment Inc. (D)
Brodie System Inc. (M)
Len Brown & Sons Inc. (M)
Central Graphics (M)
Duostat Co. (Affiliated with VGC Corp.) (D)
Florida Printing Equipment
　and Supply (D)
Hadronics (M,S)
Kaim & Associates Int'l. Marketing Inc. (D)
MAH Machine Co. Inc. (M,S)
Mountain States Inc. (M,S)
Newstech Co. (Div. of Rovinter Inc.) (D)
Quality Components Corp. (M)
Moss Reck & Associates Inc. (D)
Sifco Selective Plating (Div. of Sifco
　Industries Inc.) (M)
Tech-Energy Co. (M,D,S)
TKS (USA) Inc. (M)
UMI (M)
West-Mor Mailroom Services (D,S)
Wesco Graphics (S)

Dampening Systems
Arrow Printing Co. (S)
Baldwin Dampening Systems (Div. of Baldwin
　Graphic Systems) (M)
BESCO Graphic Systems Corp. (D)
Chapel Hill Manufacturing Co. (M)
Clark-Cutler-McDermoth Co. (Airloc Div.) (M,D)
Dahlgren USA Inc. (M)
Dampening Systems Inc. (M)
A.B. Dick Co. (D,M)
Duostat Co. (Affiliated
　with VGC Corp.) (D)
Graphic Instruments Inc. (M)
Hadronics (M,S)
Heidelberg Harris Inc. (M)
Jomac Inc. (M)
Master Flo Technology (M)
M E G (US) Inc. (M)
National Graphic Sales Inc. (S)

National Graphic Supply Corp. (D)
Newstech Co. (Div. of Rovinter Inc.) (D)
Pitman Co. (S)
Pressroom Products Inc. (M,D,S)
Printers' Service (M)
Printing Equipment Specialists Inc. (S)
Moss Reck & Associates Inc. (D)
Republic Roller Corp. (S)
Robertson Press Machinery Co. Inc. (D)
R T P Technical Specialists (S)
Ryco Graphic Manufacturing Inc. (M)
Rycoline Products Inc. (M)
Semler Industries Inc. (Graphic Arts Products
　Div.) (M)
Smith RPM Corp. (M)
Solna Web USA Inc. (M)
William C. Spells (RTP Technical Specialists)
　(D,S)
Star International Corp. (D)
Tech-Energy Co. (M,D,S)
Varn International (M)
Veratec Div. (M)

Dark Room Equipment
Allpress Equipment Inc. (D)
Allstates Litho Plate Corp. (S)
Berkshire/Westwood Graphics Group Inc. (D)
BESCO Graphic Systems Corp. (D)
Beta Screen Corp. (M)
R.W. Borrowdale Co. (RWB Enterprises Div.) (M)
Caprock Developments Inc. (M,D)
Consolidated International Corp. (M)
Douthitt Corp. (M)
Duostat Co. (Affiliated with VGC Corp.) (D)
Electronic Systems Engineering Co. (M)
GraphLine Inc. (D)
Hart Industries (D)
Konica Imaging USA Inc. (D)
Kreonite Inc. (M)
LogEtronics Corp. (M,D)
Mid Atlantic Lighting (D)
Midwest Publishers Supply Co. (D)
National Graphic Supply Corp. (D)
National Research Bureau (D)
New Seagull Photographic Paper (D)
Newstech Co. (Div. of Rovinter Inc.) (D)
NuArc Co. Inc. (M)
Nutek Inc. (D)
Pacific Newspaper Services Inc. (D,S)
Parsons Main Inc. (S)
Photo Systems Inc. (D)
Pitman Co. (S)
Pitman Photo Supply (D)
Portage Newspaper Supply Co. (M,D)
Printing Equipment Specialists Inc. (S)
Richard Mfg. Co. Inc. (M)
SCREEN (USA) (M)
Sinclair Imaging Inc. (M)
Stoesser Register Systems (M)
Support Products Inc. (D)
Ternes Register System (M)

Data Communication
Ad-Star/Publishing Technologies (M,D)
Advanced Technical Solutions (S)
Alden Electronics Inc. (M)
AT & T Business Marketing (M,D)
AT & T Information Systems (GCBS) (D)
AudioFAX Inc. (M)
Auto-Grafica Corp. (D)

Bellatrix Systems INC. (M,Newspapers
　Dispensers (Mechanical/Electronic),M)
BESCO Graphic Systems Corp. (D)
Canoga-Perkins Corp. (M)
CNI Corp. (D)
Computer Devices Inc. (M)
Copley Computer Services (S)
CPS Technologies Inc. (D)
Crosfield Electronic Ltd. (M)
DataEase International Inc. (S)
Datalogics (M,D)
Digital Design Inc. (D)
Duostat Co. (Affiliated with VGC Corp.) (D)
DuPont Co. (D)
Foley, Torregiani & Associates, Inc. (D)
Harris Corp. (Corporate Headquaters) (D)
Intelligence Technology Corp. (M)
International Memory Products of Illinois Inc. (D)
Master Flo Technology (M)
MCI (S)
Megadata Computer & Communications Corp.(S)
Micom Communications Corp. (M)
Midwest Publishers Supply Co. (D)
The Networks Inc. (D,S)
Newspaper Systems Group Inc. (S)
Newstech Co. (Div. of Rovinter Inc.) (D)
Sinclair Imaging Inc. (M)
STM Wireless Inc. (M)
Sysdeco U.S. (D)
Three Sigma (S)
Toltech Systems (M)

Delivery Equipment
Baird Manufacturing Inc. (M)
Baumfolder Corp. (M,D)
Duostat Co. (Affiliated with VGC Corp.) (D)
Hamilton Circulation Supplies Co.
　(Newspaper Mailroom Supplies) (D)
Imaje Ink Jet Printing (D)
Kansa Corp. (Baldwin Technology Co.) (M,D)
Machine Design Service Inc. (M)
Master Flo Technology (M)
Quipp System Inc. (M)
Sheridan Systems (M)
H.R. Slater Co. Inc. (M)
Standlee and Associates Inc. (M,D,S)
Stepper Inc. (M)
Utilimaster (M)
West-Mor Mailroom Services (D,S)
Western Roller Corp. (M)

Densitometers
Allpress Equipment Inc. (D)
Auto-Grafica Corp. (D)
B & T Press Supplies (Affiliated with
　Canadian Web) (D)
Berkshire/Westwood Graphics Group Inc. (D)
BESCO Graphic Systems Corp. (D)
Beta Screen Corp. (M)
A.B. Dick Co. (D)
Duostat Co. (Affiliated with VGC Corp.) (D)
Electronic Systems Engineering Co. (M)
Graphics Microsystems Inc. (M)
GraphLine Inc. (D)
Konica Imaging USA Inc. (D)
Levien Instruments Co. (D)
London Litho Aluminum Co. Inc. (D)
Macbeth, Div. of Kollmorgen Inst. Corp. (M)
Mid Atlantic Lighting (D)
Midwest Publishers Supply Co. (D)
National Graphic Supply Corp. (D)
Newstech Co. (Div. of Rovinter Inc.) (D)
Perretta Graphics Corp. (M)
Pitman Co. (S)
Portage Newspaper Supply Co. (M)

PrePRESS DIRECT (D)
SCREEN (USA) (M)
Star International Corp. (D)
Tobias Associates Inc. (M)
Truproof Ltd. (D)
Bob Weber Inc. (M)
X-Rite Inc. (M)

Developing and Processing
Agfa Division, Bayer Inc. (M,D)
Bell & Howell Publication Systems Co. (M)
Berkshire/Westwood Graphics Group Inc. (D)
BESCO Graphic Systems Corp. (D)
Fuji Photo Film USA/Graphic Arts
　Products Div. (M)
GraphLine Inc. (D)
Konica Imaging USA Inc. (D)
National Machine (M)
Newstech Co. (Div. of Rovinter Inc.) (D)
Richard Mfg. Co. Inc. (M)
Western LithoTech (M)

Dies (Perforating and Slitting)
Newstech Co. (Div. of Rovinter Inc.) (D)

Diffusion Transfer Processors
Berkshire/Westwood Graphics Group Inc. (D)
BESCO Graphic Systems Corp. (D)
Craftsmen Machinery Co./Graphic Export
　Corp. (M)
Duostat Co. (Affiliated with VGC Corp.) (D)
Dynalith Inc. (D)
GraphLine Inc. (D)
Konica Imaging USA Inc. (D)
National Graphic Supply Corp. (D)
Newstech Co. (Div. of Rovinter Inc.) (D)
NuArc Co. Inc. (M)
Pitman Co. (S)

DiLitho Press Conversion
Brainworks Inc. (M)
Duostat Co. (Affiliated with VGC Corp.) (D)
Hartcid Industry Inc. (S)
Pacific Newspaper Services Inc. (S)
Pressroom Products Inc. (D,S)

Disk Drive Sales/Repair
Auto-Grafica Corp. (D)
Duostat Co. (Affiliated with VGC Corp.) (D)
Freedom System Integrators (S)
Imapro Corp. (M)
Mantis Computer Parts Inc. (D)
Midwest Publishers Supply Co. (D)
Monotype Systems Inc. (D)
Newspaper Systems Group Inc. (D)
Newstech Co. (Div. of Rovinter Inc.) (D)
PrePRESS DIRECT (D)
Sysdeco U.S. (D,S)
Bob Weber Inc. (S)

Distortion Cameras
Alan Graphic Systems Inc. (M,D)
Midwest Publishers Supply Co. (D)
Newstech Co. (Div. of Rovinter Inc.) (D)
Roconex Corp. (M)

Drives & Controls
ABB Process Automation Inc.(Printing
　Systems Div.) (D,S)
Baldor Electric Co. (M)
Allen Bradley Co. (Motion Control Div.) (M)
Len Brown & Sons Inc. (D)
Ewert America Electronics Ltd. (M)
Fincor/Electronics Div. Inc. (M)
Fleming Enterprises (M)
Global Graphics Inc. (D)
M. Golda Engineering (S)
Graham Co. (M)
Heidelberg Harris Inc. (D)
Inland Graphics International L.C. (D)
International Memory Products of
　Illinois Inc. (D)
Kaim & Associates Int'l. Marketing Inc. (D)
KBA-Motter Corp. (Koenig & Bauer-
　Albert Group) (M)
MAH Machine Co. Inc. (S)
Masthead International Inc. (S)
Newstech Co. (Div. of Rovinter Inc.) (D)
Northeast Industries Inc. (D)
ONE Corp. (D)
Moss Reck & Associates Inc. (D)
Robertson Press Machinery Co. Inc. (D)
R T P Technical Specialists (S)
Standard Electric and Engineering Co. (M,D,S)
Star International Corp. (D)
Tech-Energy Co. (D,S)
TKS (USA) Inc. (M)
Web Tapes Inc. (S)
World Net & Associates Inc. (D)

Dryers: Film & Paper
Agfa Division, Bayer Inc. (M,D)
Allpress Equipment Inc. (D)
BESCO Graphic Systems Corp. (D)

Before you decide on a web change...
STOP!
Contact the proven industry leader..."Bob Ray"
Various Makes/Models of Equipment • Competitive Pricing
Professional Engineering Evaluation • 54, 54/50 and 50 Inch Formats

Bob Ray & Associates, Inc.
THE WEB WIDTH REDUCTION PROFESSIONALS

41 Walter Court
Algonquin, IL 60102
1-800-522-5343
FAX 708-658-3397

Copyright ©1996 by the Editor & Publisher Co.

Equipment, supplies, services VI-31

Duostat Co. (Affiliated with VGC Corp.) (D)
Fleming Enterprises (S)
Grace Tec/W.R. Grace & Co. (M)
GraphLine Inc. (M)
Imapro Corp. (M)
The Inco Company (M)
Jardis Industries Inc. (Cary Equipment Div.) (D)
Kreonite Inc. (M)
M E G (US) Inc. (M)
Midwest Publishers Supply Co. (D)
National Graphic Sales Inc. (S)
National Graphic Supply Corp. (D)
Newstech Co. (Div. of Rovinter Inc.) (D)
Nutek Inc. (D)
Photo Systems Inc. (D)
Pitman Photo Supply (D)
Unique Photo (D)
Bob Weber Inc. (D)

Drying Systems
Apex Machine Co. (M)
BESCO Graphic Systems Corp. (D)
Dahlgren USA Inc. (M)
Fleming Enterprises (S)
GraphLine Inc. (D)
M E G (US) Inc. (M)
Mid Atlantic Lighting (D)
N/S Corp. (M)
National Graphic Sales Inc. (S)
Newstech Co. (Div. of Rovinter Inc.) (D)
Oxy-Dry Corp. (M)
Ver-A-Fast Corp. (S)
WPC Machinery Corp. (S)

Electronic Ad Delivery
America's Interactive Production Network (S)
Cable Classified Advertising Network (CCAN) (D)
National Graphic Supply Corp. (D)
Newspaper Space Bank (D)
Sysdeco U.S. (D)

Electronic Pre-Scan Systems
Action Management Inc. (S)
BESCO Graphic Systems Corp. (D)
Computer Tree (D)
DayStar Digital Inc. (M)
Fleming Enterprises (S)
International Memory Products of Illinois Inc. (D)
Levien Instruments Inc. (D)
Mantis Computer Parts Inc. (D)
Metroland Printing/Publishing & Distributing Ltd. (D)
National Graphic Supply Corp. (D)
Press-Enterprise Color Graphics (S)
Sinclair Imaging Inc. (D)

Enlargers (Photographic)
Allpress Equipment Inc. (D)
BESCO Graphic Systems Corp. (D)
Consolidated International Corp. (M)
A.B. Dick Co. (Itek Graphix Div.) (M)
GraphLine Inc. (D)
Levien Instruments Inc. (D)
National Graphic Supply Corp. (D)
Newstech Co. (Div. of Rovinter Inc.) (D)
Nutek Inc. (D)
Photo Systems Inc. (D)
Pitman Photo Supply (D)
SCREEN (USA) (M)
T/One Inc. (M,D)

Environmental Control System
Action Management Inc. (S)
Alar Engineering Corp. (M)
Baldwin Dampening Systems (Div. of Baldwin Graphic Systems) (M)
BESCO Graphic Systems Corp. (D)
R.J. Brimo Enterprises Ltd. (M)
Byers Industries Inc. (M)
Dynalith Inc. (D)
Eastman Kodak/Professional Printing & Publishing Imaging (M)
Eclectic Co. Inc. (M,D,S)
Extratec Corp. (D)
Industrial Acoustics Co. (M)
Kaim & Associates Int'l. Marketing Inc. (D)
Kidder Inc. (M)
Konica Imaging USA Inc. (D)
LogEtronics Corp. (M,D)
Luwa Bahnson Inc. (S)
Master Flo Technology (M)
Metafix Inc. (D)
Metafix Silver Recovery Systems (D)
Metroland Printing/Publishing & Distributing Ltd. (D)
MGI International Inc. (M,D)
N/S Corp. (M)
Parsons Main Inc. (S)
Perma-Fix Environmental Services (D)
The Safetyloid Reclaiming Co. Inc. (M,D)
David A. Shulda Enterprises Inc. (M)

STI - Separation Technologies Inc. (M)
Voice Connexion (M)
Western LithoTech (M)

Equipment Dealers (New)
Ad Vantage Computer Systems Inc. (S)
Advanced Technical Solutions (S)
Arco Engineering Inc. (Newspaper Div.) (M,D)
Auto-Grafica Corp. (D)
Automated Mailing Systems Corp. (D)
Berkshire/Westwood Graphics Group Inc. (D)
BESCO Graphic Systems Corp. (D)
Brown & Sharpe Mfg. Co. (M)
Consolidated International Corp. (M)
CPS Technologies Inc. (D)
Digital Design Inc. (D)
Duostat Co. (Affiliated with VGC Corp.) (D)
Dynalith Inc. (D)
Enkel Corp. (A Baldwin Technology Co.) (M)
Florida Printing Equipment and Supply (D)
Foley, Torregiani & Associates, Inc. (D)
George R Hall Inc. (S)
Heidelberg USA (M)
Inland Graphics International L.C. (D)
Konica Imaging USA Inc. (M)
Linotype-Hell Co. (M,D,S)
LogEtronics Corp. (M)
London Litho Aluminum Co. Inc. (D)
MAH Machine Co. Inc. (S)
Mailers Equipment Co. Inc. (Mircofilm Products) (D)
Mantis Computer Parts Inc. (D)
Megasys International Inc. (D)
Mid-America Graphics Inc. (M)
Midwest Publishers Supply Co. (S)
Monotype Systems Inc. (M,D,S)
N & L Enterprises Inc. (D)
Newstech Co. (Div. of Rovinter Inc.) (D)
Pacific Newspaper Services Inc. (M,D)
Pitman Co. (D)
Pressroom Products Inc. (D)
Prim Hall Enterprises Inc. (M,D)
Printing Equipment Specialists Inc. (S)
Printing Press Services Inc. (M)
Republic Roller Corp. (S)
Republic Service Co. (D)
Robertson Press Machinery Co. Inc. (D)
Rockwell Graphic Systems (M)
The Safetyloid Reclaiming Co. Inc. (M,D)
Solna Web USA Inc. (D)
William C. Spells (RTP Technical Specialists) (D,S)
Standlee and Associates Inc. (M,D,S)
Stepper Inc. (M)
Tech-Energy Co. (M,D,S)
Telesonic Packaging Corp. (M)
TSA (D)
Valley Remanufacturing Co. (M)
Web Tapes Inc. (S)
Bob Weber Inc. (D)
West Coast Computer Systems/Newspaper Technologies (D)
West-Mor Mailroom Services (M,D,S)
World Net & Associates Inc. (M)
XYonicz (M)

Equipment Dealers (Used)
Advanced Technical Solutions (S)
Allpress Equipment Inc. (D)
ALTA Graphics Inc. (S)
American Graphic Arts Inc. (S)
Arco Engineering Inc. (Newspaper Div.) (M,D)
Auto-Grafica Corp. (D)
Automated Mailing Systems Corp. (D)
Bell Camp Inc. (S)

Berkshire/Westwood Graphics Group Inc. (D)
BESCO Graphic Systems Corp. (D)
Len Brown & Sons Inc. (D)
Central Graphics (S)
Computer Tree (D)
CPS Technologies Inc. (D)
Digital Design Inc. (D)
Duostat Co. (Affiliated with VGC Corp.) (D)
EGS Americas Inc. (S)
Fleming Enterprises (S)
Florida Printing Equipment and Supply (D)
Jimmy R. Fox, Mail Room Consultant (S)
Global Graphics Inc. (D)
Global Press Sales Inc. (D)
George R Hall Inc. (D)
Heidelberg Harris Inc. (S)
Inland Graphics International L.C. (D)
Inland Newspaper Machinery Corp. (S)
Linotype-Hell Co. (M,D,S)
MAH Machine Co. Inc. (M,S)
Mailers Equipment Co. Inc. (Mircofilm Products) (D)
Mantis Computer Parts Inc. (D)
Megasys International Inc. (D)
Microfax Inc. (M)
Mid-America Graphics Inc. (M)
Midwest Publishers Supply Co. (D)
Monotype Systems Inc. (D,S)
N & L Enterprises Inc. (D)
Newstech Co. (Div. of Rovinter Inc.) (D)
Northeast Industries Inc. (D)
Offset Web Sales Inc. (D)
ONE Corp. (D)
Pacific Newspaper Services Inc. (D)
Plumtree (D)
PostPress Equipment Co. (S)
Press and Bindery Systems Inc. (D)
Pressroom Products Inc. (D)
Prim Hall Enterprises Inc. (M,D)
Printing Press Services Inc. (M,D)
Republic Roller Corp. (S)
Republic Service Co. (D)
Rockwell Graphic Systems (M)
R T P Technical Specialists (S)
Sheridan Systems (M)
Solna Web USA Inc. (D)
William C. Spells (RTP Technical Specialists) (D,S)
Standlee and Associates Inc. (D,S)
Tech-Energy Co. (M,D,S)
Todd Machinery (D)
TSA (D)
Valley Remanufacturing Co. (M)
Web Tapes Inc. (S)
Webeq International Inc. (S)
Bob Weber Inc. (D)
Wesco Graphics (S)
West Coast Computer Systems/Newspaper Technologies (D)
West-Mor Mailroom Services (M,D,S)
World Net & Associates Inc. (M)

Erectors & Riggers
Len Brown & Sons Inc. (D)
Canadian Web Consultants Ltd. (S)
Central Graphics (S)
Dan-Bar Electric Inc. (S)
Fleming Enterprises (S)
Jimmy R. Fox, Mail Room Consultant (S)
Global Graphics Inc. (D)

George R Hall Inc. (S)
Hartcid Industry Inc. (S)
Heidelberg Harris Inc. (S)
Kaim & Associates Int'l. Marketing Inc. (D)
MAH Machine Co. Inc. (S)
Masthead International Inc. (S)
Mountain States Inc. (D)
Offset Web Sales Inc. (M)
Press-Tec Inc. (S)
Printing Press Services Inc. (M)
Bob Ray & Associates Inc. (M,D,S)
Robertson Press Machinery Co. Inc. (S)
R T P Technical Specialists (S)
Sheridan Systems (M)
Solna Web USA Inc. (D)
Wesco Graphics (S)
William C. Spells (RTP Technical Specialists) (D,S)
Tech-Energy Co. (M,D,S)
UMI (M)

Etching Machinery
BESCO Graphic Systems Corp. (D)
The Master Group (M)
Newstech Co. (Div. of Rovinter Inc.) (D)
Revere Graphics Worldwide (D)
Sifco Selective Plating (Div. of Sifco Industries Inc.) (M)

Exposure Lamps
Allpress Equipment Inc. (D)
Amergraph Corp. (M)
Bulbtronics (D)
Mid Atlantic Lighting (D)
Midwest Publishers Supply Co. (D)
NENSCO (D)
Newstech Co. (Div. of Rovinter Inc.) (D)
Printing Equipment Specialists Inc. (S)
Richmond/Graphic Products Inc. (M)
UVP Inc. (M)
Western Quartz Products Inc. (M)

Facsimile Transmission Systems
Alden Electronics Inc. (M)
AT & T Business Marketing (M,D)
AudioFAX Inc. (M)
Autologic Inc. (Subsidiary of Volt Info. Svc.) (M)
Autologic Information International Inc. (M)
Canon USA Inc. (S)
Communications Management Service Inc. (S)
Craftsmen Machinery Co./Graphic Export Corp. (D)
Crosfield Electronic Ltd. (M)
Cybergraphic Inc. (D)
DAC Systems (M,D)
Danka Omnifax (M)
DuPont Co. (S)
E-FAX Communications Inc. (M,D,S)
Electronic Specialists Inc. (S)
FAR Systems Inc. (M)
Harris Corp. (Corporate Headquaters) (D)
Microfax Inc. (D)
Monotype Systems Inc. (D,S)
N & L Enterprises Inc. (D)
National Graphic Supply Corp. (D)
National Research Bureau (D)
The Networks Inc. (D)
Newstech Co. (Div. of Rovinter Inc.) (D)
Olivetti Office USA (M)
Pitney Bowes Business Systems (M,D)

Thanks To Our Many Friends For
Allowing Us To Provide...

25 Years of Service

• Turnkey Press Installations • Web Width Reductions
• Press Drive Control Repower and Upgrades

MASTHEAD INTERNATIONAL, INC.
P.O. Box 1952
Albuquerque, NM 87103

(800) 545-6908   (505) 842-1357

Copyright ©1996 by the Editor & Publisher Co.

VI-32 Equipment, supplies, services

Ricoh Corp. (M,D)
Sinclair Imaging Inc. (M)
STM Wireless Inc. (M)
Three Sigma (S)
Xerox Corp. (M,D)

Feeder, Press
Fleming Enterprises (S)
Jardis Industries Inc. (Cary Equipment Div.) (M)
Newstech Co. (Div. of Rovinter Inc.) (D)
Printing Equipment Specialists Inc. (S)

Feeding, Folding, Delivery Equipment
Advance Graphics Equipment of York Inc. (M,D)
ALTA Graphics Inc. (S)
American Graphics L.P. (M)
Arco Engineering Inc. (Newspaper Div.) (S)
Baumfolder Corp. (M,D)
Brodie System Inc. (S)
Duostat Co. (Affiliated with VGC Corp.) (D)
Fleming Enterprises (S)
Jardis Industries Inc. (Cary Equipment Div.) (M)
Kansa Corp. (Baldwin Technology Co.) (M,D)
Machine Design Service Inc. (M)
Master Flo Technology (M)
Mid-America Graphics Inc. (S)
National Graphic Sales Inc. (S)
National Research Bureau (D)
Republic Roller Corp. (S)
Rock-Built (M)
SITMA USA Inc. (M)
Solna Web USA Inc. (M)
Standlee and Associates Inc. (D,S)
Stepper Inc. (M)
Tech-Energy Co. (M,D,S)
World Net & Associates Inc. (M)
XYonicz (M)

Files, Storage
Acme Design Technology Co. (M)
Auto-Grafica Corp. (D)
BESCO Graphic Systems Corp. (D)
Canon USA Inc. (S)
Duostat Co. (Affiliated with VGC Corp.) (D)
Equipto (M)
Foster Mfg. Co. (M)
Lazer-fare Media Services Ltd. (D,S)
Midwest Publishers Supply Co. (M,D)
National Graphic Supply Corp. (D)
The Networks Inc. (D)
Newstech Co. (Div. of Rovinter Inc.) (D)
Roconex Corp. (M)
H.B. Rouse & Co. (M)
The Safetyloid Reclaiming Co. Inc. (M,D)

Film & Paper: Contact
Berkshire/Westwood Graphics Group Inc. (D)
ByChrome Co. (D)
Eastman Kodak/Professional Printing & Publishing Imaging (M)
Fuji Photo Film USA/Graphic Arts Products Div. (M)
Fuji Photo Film USA (Distribution Ctr.) (M)
GraphLine Co. (D)
National Graphic Supply Corp. (D)
Newstech Co. (Div. of Rovinter Inc.) (D)
PAGE (S)
Pitman Co. (S)
Techtron Imaging Center (S)

Film & Paper: Duplicating
Anitec (M)
Berkshire/Westwood Graphics Group Inc. (D)
ByChrome Co. (D)
Canon USA Inc. (S)
A.B. Dick Co. (D)
Duostat Co. (Affiliated with VGC Corp.) (D)
Eastman Kodak/Professional Printing & Publishing Imaging (M)
Fuji Photo Film USA/Graphic Arts Products Div. (M)
Fuji Photo Film USA (Distribution Ctr.) (M)
GraphLine Co. (D)
Ingenuity Inc. (M,D)
Konica Imaging USA Inc. (M)
London Litho Aluminum Co. Inc. (D)
Megasys International Inc. (D)
National Graphic Supply Corp. (D)
NENSCO (D)
Newstech Co. (Div. of Rovinter Inc.) (D)
PAGE (S)
Pitman Co. (S)
Printing Equipment Specialists Inc. (S)
Techtron Imaging Center (S)
3M Printing & Publishing Systems Div. (M)
Xerox Corp. (M,D)

Film & Paper: Film Processing Machines
Berkshire/Westwood Graphics Group Inc. (D)
BESCO Graphic Systems Corp. (D)
Byers Industries Inc. (M)
Danagraf North America (M)
A.B. Dick Co. (Itek Graphix Div.) (M)
Duostat Co. (Affiliated with VGC Corp.) (D)
Durbin Associates (S)
Electronic Systems Engineering Co. (M)
Florida Printing Equipment and Supply (D)
Frankton Press Inc. (S)
Fuji Photo Film USA/Graphic Arts Products Div. (M)
Fuji Photo Film USA (Distribution Ctr.) (M)
Graphic Publishing Systems Inc. (D)
GraphLine Inc. (D)
Konica Imaging USA Inc. (D)
Kreonite Inc. (D)
Linotype-Hell Co. (D,S)
LogEtronics Corp. (M,D)
National Graphic Supply Corp. (D)
NENSCO (D)
Newstech Co. (Div. of Rovinter Inc.) (D)
PAGE (S)
Pako Corp. (M)
PrePRESS DIRECT (D)
Printing Equipment Specialists Inc. (S)
Richmond/Graphic Products Inc. (M)
SCREEN (USA) (M)
Techtron Imaging Center (S)

Film & Paper: Film Roll Dispensers
BESCO Graphic Systems Corp. (D)
Beta Screen Corp. (D)
Duostat Co. (Affiliated with VGC Corp.) (D)
Fuji Photo Film USA (Distribution Ctr.) (M)
GraphLine Inc. (D)
Kreonite Inc. (D)
National Graphic Supply Corp. (D)
NENSCO (D)
Newstech Co. (Div. of Rovinter Inc.) (D)
PAGE (S)
Roconex Corp. (M)

Film & Paper: Filters (Photographic)
Allpress Equipment Inc. (D)
Berkshire/Westwood Graphics Group Inc. (D)
BESCO Graphic Systems Corp. (D)
Fuji Photo Film USA (Distribution Ctr.) (M)
GraphLine Inc. (D)
National Graphic Supply Corp. (D)
NENSCO (D)
Newstech Co. (Div. of Rovinter Inc.) (D)
PAGE (S)
Pitman Photo Supply (D)
Polaroid Corp. (M,D,S)
Portage Newspaper Supply Co. (D)
Semler Industries Inc. (Graphic Arts Products Div.) (D)
David A. Shulda Enterprises Inc. (S)
Unique Photo (D)

Film & Paper: Photographic
Allstates Litho Plate Corp. (D)
Alpha-Omega Color Graphics Inc. (M)
Anitec (M)
Berkshire/Westwood Graphics Group Inc. (D)
A.B. Dick Co. (Itek Graphix Div.) (M)
Duostat Co. (Affiliated with VGC Corp.) (D)
Dynalith Inc. (D)
Eastman Kodak/Professional Printing & Publishing Imaging (M)
Florida Printing Equipment and Supply (D)
Fuji Photo Film USA/Graphic Arts Products Div. (M)
Fuji Photo Film USA (Distribution Ctr.) (M)
GraphLine Inc. (D)
Konica Imaging USA Inc. (D)
National Graphic Supply Corp. (D)
NENSCO (D)
New Seagull Photographic Paper (D)
Newstech Co. (Div. of Rovinter Inc.) (D)
PAGE (S)
Photo Systems Inc. (D)
Pitman Photo Supply (D)
Portage Newspaper Supply Co. (D)
Techtron Imaging Center (S)
3M Printing & Publishing Systems Div. (M)
Unique Photo (D)

Film & Paper: Phototypesetting
Allstates Litho Plate Corp. (D)
Anitec (M)
Auto-Grafica Corp. (D)
Berkshire/Westwood Graphics Group Inc. (D)
ByChrome Co. (D)
A.B. Dick Co. (Itek Graphix Div.) (M)
Duostat Co. (Affiliated with VGC Corp.) (D)
Dynalith Inc. (D)
Eastman Kodak/Professional Printing & Publishing Imaging (M)
Frankton Press Inc. (S)
Fuji Photo Film USA/Graphic Arts Products Div. (M)
Graphic Arts Technical & Consulting Services (D)
Graphic Enterprises of Ohio Inc. (M)
Graphic Publishing Systems Inc. (D)
GraphLine Inc. (D)
Hyphen Inc. (D)
Konica Imaging USA Inc. (M)
London Litho Aluminum Co. Inc. (D)
National Graphic Supply Corp. (D)
NENSCO (D)
Newstech Co. (Div. of Rovinter Inc.) (D)
PAGE (S)
Pitman Co. (S)
Pitman Photo Supply (D)
PrePRESS DIRECT (D)
Techtron Imaging Center (S)
Bob Weber Inc. (D)

Fire Protection
Chemetron (M,D,S)
Chemetron/Badger Fire Systems (M)
Dario Designs Inc. (S)
Pacific Newspaper Services Inc. (D,S)

Fixing & Stop Baths
Duostat Co. (Affiliated with VGC Corp.) (D)
GraphLine Inc. (D)
Konica Imaging USA Inc. (M)
Louis Melind Co. (D)
National Graphic Supply Corp. (D)
Newstech Co. (Div. of Rovinter Inc.) (D)
Pitman Photo Supply (D)
3M Printing & Publishing Systems Div. (M)
Unique Photo (D)

Flexographic Press Conversion
Borden Inc. (S)
Duostat Co. (Affiliated with VGC Corp.) (D)
Hartcid Industry Inc. (S)
KBA-Motter Corp. (Koenig & Bauer-Albert Group) (M)
Kidder Inc. (M)
Koenig & Bauer- Albert AG (KBA) (M)
MAH Machine Co. Inc. (S)
Pacific Newspaper Services Inc. (D,S)
Printing Equipment Specialists Inc. (S)
Republic Roller Corp. (S)
R T P Technical Specialists (S)

Flooring
Freudenberg Building Systems Inc. (M,D)
Gerrard Ovalstrapping (M,D)
Mannschreck (D)
Newstech Co. (Div. of Rovinter Inc.) (D)

Fluid Handling: Pressroom
Graphic System Services (D,S)
The International School For Pressroom Management (S)
Pressroom Products Inc. (M)
Ryco Graphic Manufacturing Inc. (M,D)

Flying Pasters
Advanced Graphic Systems (KAIM) (M)
ALTA Graphics Inc. (S)
Butler SMC. (M)
Cerutti North America (M)
Controls Group Inc. (M)
Ebway Industries Inc. (Div. of Jardis Industries Inc.) (M)
Enkel Corp. (A Baldwin Technology Co.) (M)
Florida Printing Equipment and Supply (D)
Graphic System Services (M,D,S)
George R Hall Inc. (D)
Heidelberg Harris Inc. (D)
Jardis Industries Inc. (Cary Equipment Div.) (M)
Kaim & Associates Int'l. Marketing Inc. (M)
Koenig & Bauer- Albert AG (KBA) (M)
MAH Machine Co. Inc. (S)
Martin Automatic Inc. (M)
M E G (US) Inc. (M)
Mitsubishi Heavy Industries Ltd. (MLP USA Inc.) (M)
Newstech Co. (Div. of Rovinter Inc.) (D)
North Shore Consultants Inc. (D)
Northeast Industries Inc. (D)
ONE Corp. (D)
Portage Newspaper Supply Co. (D)
Printing Equipment Specialists Inc. (S)
Printing Press Services Inc. (M,D)
R T P Technical Specialists (S)
Solna Web USA Inc. (M)
William C. Spells (RTP Technical Specialists) (D,S)
UMI (D)
Web Tapes Inc. (S)
World Net & Associates Inc. (D)

Folder Knives
Allpress Equipment Inc. (D)
Baumfolder Corp. (M)
Bruno Unger USA (M,D)
Central Graphics (D)
Manassy Precision Corp. (M)
NENSCO (D)
Newstech Co. (Div. of Rovinter Inc.) (D)
Press Rubber Co. Inc. (D)
Quality Components Corp. (D)
Moss Reck & Associates Inc. (D)
Star International Corp. (D)
Tech-Energy Co. (D,S)
UMI (D)

Folding Machines
ALTA Graphics Inc. (S)
ARC/Doyle Machinery Corp. (M)
Arco Engineering Inc. (Newspaper Div.) (S)
Arrow Printing Co. (S)
Baumfolder Corp. (M,D)
BESCO Graphic Systems Corp. (D)
Brodie System Inc. (S)
Cerutti North America (M)
Cole Machine-Applied Design Inc. (M,D)
A.B. Dick Co. (M)
Duostat Co. (Affiliated with VGC Corp.) (D)
Fleming Enterprises (S)
Florida Printing Equipment and Supply (D)
Heidelberg USA (D)
Kansa Corp. (Baldwin Technology Co.) (M,D)
Mailers Equipment Co. Inc. (Mircofilm Products) (D)
Martin Yale Inc. (M)
Megasys International Inc. (D)
National Graphic Sales Inc. (S)
National Research Bureau (D)
Newstech Co. (Div. of Rovinter Inc.) (D)
Northeast Industries Inc. (D)
Pitney Bowes Business Systems (M,D)
Printing Equipment Specialists Inc. (S)
SITMA USA Inc. (M)
Solna Web USA Inc. (M)
Stepper Inc. (M)
Tech-Energy Co. (D,S)
Todd Machinery (S)
World Net & Associates Inc. (D)

Front-End Systems
Concept Publishing Systems (M)
Three Sigma (S)

Gauges, Measuring
Arco Engineering Inc. (Newspaper Div.) (D,S)
Axelrod, Norman N., Assoc./Optical, Laser & Vision Systems (M,S)
B & T Press Supplies (Affiliated with Canadian Web) (D)
BESCO Graphic Systems Corp. (D)
Beta Screen Corp. (D)
Brown & Sharpe Mfg. Co. (M,D)
Caprock Developments Inc. (D)
Cemco Inc. (M)
Manassy Precision Corp. (M)
Midwest Publishers Supply Co. (D)
Newstech Co. (Div. of Rovinter Inc.) (D)
Roconex Corp. (M)
H.R. Slater Co. Inc. (M)
SunShine Paper Co. (D)

Gluing Systems
Graphic Enterprises (M,D,S)
H&M Paster Sales & Service Inc. (M)
Newstech Co. (Div. of Rovinter Inc.) (D)
Pressroom Products Inc. (M)
Moss Reck & Associates Inc. (M)
Schaefer Machine Co. Inc. (M)
Western Printing Machinery (M,D)

Grater Wrap-Roller Covering
Allpress Equipment Inc. (D)
B & T Press Supplies (Affiliated with Canadian Web) (D)

Humidifiers
Luwa Bahnson Inc. (S)
M E G (US) Inc. (M)
Newstech Co. (Div. of Rovinter Inc.) (D)
Nortec Industries (M)
Pacific Newspaper Services Inc. (D,S)
Parsons Main Inc. (S)
PrePRESS DIRECT (D)
PrePRESS SOLUTIONS (M)
SCREEN (USA) (M)
Software Consulting Services (D)
The Software Development Group Inc. (S)
Total Systems Engineering Inc. (S)
Bob Weber Inc. (D,S)
Wedge Computer Systems (S)
Xitron (M)

In-Line Trimming Systems
Advance Graphics Equipment of York Inc. (M,D)
ALTA Graphics Inc. (S)

Copyright ©1996 by the Editor & Publisher Co.

Equipment, supplies, services VI-33

Ferag Inc. (M)
MGI International Inc. (M,D,S)
Midwest Publishers Supply Co. (D)
Muller Martini Corp. (M)
World Net & Associates Inc. (D)

Infeed Stackers
ALTA Graphics Inc. (S)
GMA Inc. (M)
Jardis Industries Inc. (Cary Equipment Div.) (M)
Kansa Corp. (Baldwin Technology Co.) (M,D)
M E G (US) Inc. (M)
Quipp System Inc. (M)
Tech-Energy Co. (D,S)
West-Mor Mailroom Services (M,D,S)

Ink Blending Equipment
Continental Inks (M,D)
Ingersoll-Rand-Aro Fluid Product Div. (M)
Inx International Ink Co. (D)
MGI International Inc. (M,D)
Newstech Co. (Div. of Rovinter Inc.) (D)
Parsons Main Inc. (S)
Semler Industries Inc. (Graphic Arts Products Div.) (M)

Ink Controls, Computerized
ABB Process Automation Inc.(Printing Systems Div.) (D,S)
Arco Engineering Inc. (Newspaper Div.) (M,D)
BESCO Graphic Systems Corp. (D)
Controls Group Inc. (M)
Essex Products Group (M)
Fincor/Electronics Div. Inc. (M)
M. Golda Engineering (S)
Graphics Microsystems Inc. (M)
Macbeth, Div. of Kollmorgen Inst. Corp. (M)
MAH Machine Co. Inc. (S)
Master Flo Technology (M)
MGI International Inc. (M,D)
Newstech Co. (Div. of Rovinter Inc.) (D)
Pacific Newspaper Services Inc. (M,D,S)
Parsons Main Inc. (S)
Perretta Graphics Corp. (M)
Printing Press Services Inc. (M)
TKS (USA) Inc. (M,D)

Ink Controls, Computerized
George R Hall Inc. (D)
Printing Press Services Inc. (M)

Ink De-Misting Systems
Arco Engineering Inc. (Newspaper Div.) (M)
BESCO Graphic Systems Corp. (D)
Carlson Design/Construct Corp. (S)
Eclectic Co. Inc. (M,D,S)
Luwa HVAC Filters (M)
Manassy Precision Corp. (M)
MGI International Inc. (M,D)
Parsons Main Inc. (S)

Ink Fountains & Accessories
Allpress Equipment Inc. (D)
Arrow Printing Co. (D)
BESCO Graphic Systems Corp. (D)
Brodie System Inc. (S)
Capco Machinery Systems Inc. (M)
Controls Group Inc. (M)
Graphic Printing Roller Ltd. (M)
GraphLine Inc. (D)
Hadronics (M,S)
The Inco Company (M,D)
Inx International Ink Co. (D)
Manassy Precision Corp. (M)
Master Flo Technology (M)
MGI International Inc. (M,D,S)
National Graphic Supply Corp. (D)
Newstech Co. (Div. of Rovinter Inc.) (D)
Offset Web Sales Inc. (S)
Pacific Newspaper Services Inc. (D,S)
Perretta Graphics Corp. (M)
Moss Reck & Associates Inc. (D)
David A. Shulda Enterprises Inc. (M)
Solna Web USA Inc. (M)
Support Products Inc. (M)
Tech-Energy Co. (M,D,S)
WPC Machinery Corp. (M)

Ink Page Pac Reconditioning
George R Hall Inc. (D)

Ink Pumping Systems
Allpress Equipment Inc. (D)
ARC/Doyle Machinery Corp. (M)
Arco Engineering Inc. (Newspaper Div.) (M,D)
Baldwin Graphics Products (Div. of Baldwin Technology) (M)
BESCO Graphic Systems Corp. (D)
Carlson Design/Construct Corp. (S)
Controls Group Inc. (M)
Flint Ink Corp. (M)
Florida Printing Equipment and Supply (D)
M. Golda Engineering (S)

Graphic System Services (D,S)
Ingersoll-Rand-Aro Fluid Product Div. (M)
The Ink Co. (S)
Inx International Ink Co. (D)
Manassy Precision Corp. (M)
Master Flo Technology (M)
The Morrison Group/Morrison Ink (D)
Newstech Co. (Div. of Rovinter Inc.) (D)
Pacific Newspaper Services Inc. (M,D,S)
Parsons Main Inc. (S)
Printing Press Services Inc. (M)
Rendic International (D)
Semler Industries Inc. (Graphic Arts Products Div.) (D,M)
Star International Corp. (D)
STI - Separation Technologies Inc. (M)
Tech-Energy Co. (D,S)
TKS (USA) Inc. (M,D)
Varn International (M)

Ink Recovery Systems
BESCO Graphic Systems Corp. (D)
Eclectic Co. Inc. (M,D,S)
Flint Ink Corp. (D)
M. Golda Engineering (S)
The Ink Co. (S)
Kaim & Associates Int'l. Marketing Inc. (D)
MGI International Inc. (M,D)
Mobile Reclamation System (MRS) Div. of Marpax (S)
NENSCO (D)
Newstech Co. (Div. of Rovinter Inc.) (D)
Pacific Newspaper Services Inc. (D,S)
Parsons Main Inc. (S)
Rendic International (D)
Semler Industries Inc. (Graphic Arts Products Div.) (M)
David A. Shulda Enterprises Inc. (M)
Star International Corp. (D)
STI - Separation Technologies Inc. (M)
Tech-Energy Co. (D,S)

Ink Storage Tanks
BESCO Graphic Systems Corp. (D)
Carlson Design/Construct Corp. (S)
Cemco Inc. (M)
The Ink Co. (S)
Inx International Ink Co. (D)
Newstech Co. (Div. of Rovinter Inc.) (D)
Pacific Newspaper Services Inc. (D,S)
Parsons Main Inc. (S)
Pressroom Products Inc. (M,D)
Quality Components Corp. (D)
David A. Shulda Enterprises Inc. (M)
STI - Separation Technologies Inc. (M)
Tech-Energy Co. (D,S)

Ink Tank Monitors
MGI International Inc. (M,D,S)
Pacific Newspaper Services Inc. (D,S)
STI - Separation Technologies Inc. (M)

Inks
AirSystems Inc. (M,D)
American Ink Jet Corp. (M)
Apex Machine Co. (D)
BESCO Graphic Systems Corp. (D)
Borden Inc. (M)
Continental Inks (M)
CPS Corp. (D)
Day-Glo Color Corp. (Subsidiary of RPM Corp.) (M)
A.B. Dick Co. (M)
Duostat Co. (Affiliated with VGC Corp.) (D)
F & F Printing Ink Corp. (M)
Flint Ink Corp. (M,D)
Frankton Press Inc. (S)
GraphLine Inc. (D)
Norman X Guttman Inc. (M,D)
The Inco Company (M)
The Ink Co. (S)
Inland Graphics International L.C. (D)
Inx International Ink Co. (D)
Leber Ink (US Ink) (M,D)
Louis Melind Co. (M)
Midwest Publishers Supply Co. (D)
The Morrison Group/Morrison Ink (M)
National Soy Ink Info. Center (S)
Newstech Co. (Div. of Rovinter Inc.) (D)
PAGE (S)
Pamarco Inc. (M,D)
Pantone Inc. (S)
Rendic International (M,D)
Sakata Inx USA Corp. (D)
Southern Lithoplate Inc. (D)
Star International Corp. (D)
Tech-Energy Co. (D,S)
US Ink Corp. (M)
UVP Inc. (M)
Van Son Holland Ink Corp. of America (M)
Videojet Systems International Inc. (M)

Input & Editing Systems
Ad Vantage Computer Systems Inc. (S)
Advanced Publishing Technology (M)
Advanced Technical Solutions (M)
Agfa Division, Bayer Inc. (M,D)
America's Interactive Production Network (S)
American Data Voice Systems (M,S)
Auto-Grafica Corp. (M)
Autologic Information International Inc. (M)
CNI Corporation (M)
Computer Services Group Inc. (S)
Computerease Software Inc. (M)
CompuText Inc. (M)
CPS Technologies Inc. (M,D)
Crosfield Electronic Ltd. (M)
Cybergraphic Inc. (M,D)
Danagraf North America (D)
Datalogics (M,D)
Design Science (M)
Dewar Information Systems Corp. (S)
Digital Equipment Corp. (M)
Digital Technology International (M)
Duostat Co. (Affiliated with VGC Corp.) (D)
DuPont Co. (D)
Durbin Associates (S)
Foley, Torregiani & Associates, Inc. (D)
Graphic Publishing Systems Inc. (D)
Harris Corp. (Corporate Headquaters) (D)
Harris Publishing Systems Corp. (M)
Horizons Inc. (M)
Hyphen Inc. (D)
International Memory Products of Illinois Inc. (D)
Krypton Systems (S)
Linotype-Hell Co. (M,D,S)
Mantis Computer Parts Inc. (D)
Megadata Computer & Communications Corp. (S)
Mimic Inc. (M)
The Networks Inc. (D,S)
Newspaper Systems Group Inc. (D)
Newstech Co. (Div. of Rovinter Inc.) (D)
NGCP/Laser Concepts (D)
Nikon Inc./Electronic Imaging Department (M,D)
Penta Software Inc. (S)
PrePRESS DIRECT (D)
Press-Enterprise Color Graphics (S)
Quebecor Printing Providence (S)
Quickwire (M,D)
Rasterops (M)
Scandinavian PC Systems Inc. (M,D)
Shaffstall Corp. (M)
Software Consulting Services (M)
The Software Development Group Inc. (M)
Stauffer Media Systems (D,S)
Syntactics (M)
T/One Inc. (M,D)
Tecnavia S A/Press Div. (M)
Telecorp Systems Inc. (M,D)
Bob Weber Inc. (D,S)
West Coast Computer Systems/Newspaper Technologies (M,D)

Inserting Equipment (Includes Stuffing Machines)
Advance Graphics Equipment of York Inc. (M,D)
Allpress Equipment Inc. (D)
ALTA Graphics Inc. (S)
Automated Mailing Systems Corp. (D)

Baumfolder Corp. (M,D)
Dario Designs Inc. (S)
Ferag Inc. (M)
Florida Printing Equipment and Supply (D)
Jimmy R. Fox, Mail Room Consultant (S)
GMA Inc. (M)
Hartcid Industry Inc. (S)
Kansa Corp. (Baldwin Technology Co.) (M,D)
Kirk-Rudy Inc. (M)
Manassy Precision Corp. (M)
Master Flo Technology (M)
McCain Manufacturing Corp. (M)
Newstech Co. (Div. of Rovinter Inc.) (D)
Offset Web Sales Inc. (S)
ONE Corp. (D)
Pacific Newspaper Services Inc. (S)
Pitney Bowes Business Systems (M,D)
PostPress Equipment Co. (S)
Printing Equipment Specialists Inc. (S)
Sheridan Systems (M)
SITMA USA Inc. (M)
Standlee and Associates Inc. (S)
Star International Corp. (D)
Stepper Inc. (M)
Tech-Energy Co. (D,S)
Valley Remanufacturing Co. (M)
Wesco Graphics (S)

Insurance
Aon/WNIC Special Markets (S)
Church Rickards, Whitlock & Co. Inc. (D)
Employers Reinsurance Corp.- Communications Liability Depart. (S)
Insurance Specialties Services Inc. (D)
Media Professional Insurance (S)
Mutual Insurance Co. Ltd. (S)
Newstech Co. (Div. of Rovinter Inc.) (D)
PAGE (S)
SCA Promotions Inc. (D)
Deane Weinberg Insurance Agency Inc. (S)
Wilson Gregory Agency (S)

Integrated Fax Servers
CompuText Inc. (M)
DAC Systems (M,D)
FAR Systems Inc. (M)
Newstech Co. (Div. of Rovinter Inc.) (D)
Telephone Response Technologies (M)

Integrated Logistics
Foley, Torregiani & Associates, Inc. (D)
Sysdeco U.S. (M,D,S)

Interfaces
Ad-Star/Publishing Technologies (M,D)
Advanced Technical Solutions (M)
Auto-Grafica Corp. (D)
Autologic Inc. (Subsidiary of Volt Info. Svc.) (M)
Brite (M)
Computer Devices Inc. (D)
CompuText Inc. (M)
Connexperts (M)
CPS Technologies Inc. (M,D)
Crosfield Electronic Ltd. (M)
Cybergraphic Inc. (M,D)
Digital Technology International (M)
DuPont Co. (D)
Durbin Associates (S)
Foley, Torregiani & Associates, Inc. (D)
Freedom System Integrators (M)

DEANE WEINBERG INSURANCE AGENCY, INC.

The company that created carrier accident insurance and bonding for newspapers.

800·200·4340

1550 Sorrento Drive
Pacific Palisades, CA 90272-2747

Copyright ©1996 by the Editor & Publisher Co.

Equipment, supplies, services

M. Golda Engineering (S)
Hyphen Inc. (D)
Mimic Inc. (M)
Monotype Systems Inc. (M,D,S)
Newstech Co. (Div. of Rovinter Inc.) (D)
Scantronix
Shaffstall Corp. (M)
STM Wireless Inc. (M)
Support Systems International Corp. (M)
Sysdeco U.S. (M)

Keyless Inking Conversions & Add-ons
KBA-Motter Corp. (Koenig & Bauer-Albert Group) (M)
Koenig & Bauer- Albert AG (KBA) (M)
Ryco Graphic Manufacturing Inc. (M)
Solna Web USA Inc. (M)
Tech-Energy Co. (D,S)
World Net & Associates Inc. (D)

Label Printing Machines
ALTA Graphics Inc. (S)
Arrow Printing Co. (S)
Craftsmen Machinery Co./Graphic Export Corp. (D)
Domino Amjet Inc. (M,D,S)
Florida Printing Equipment and Supply (D)
Horizons Inc. (M)
Malow Corp. (D)
Martin Yale Inc. (M)
Megasys International Inc. (D)
Press and Bindery Systems Inc. (D)
Printing Equipment Specialists Inc. (S)
Quipp System Inc. (D)
Scandinavian PC Systems Inc. (M,D)
Videojet Systems International Inc. (M)

Laser Printers
Arrow Printing Co. (S)
Autologic Inc. (Subsidiary of Volt Info. Svc.) (M)
CompuText Inc. (D)
Creative Specialty Products Inc. (D,S)
Dataproducts (M,D)
Domino Amjet Inc. (M,D,S)
Duostat Co. (Affiliated with VGC Corp.) (D)
Freedom System Integrators (D)
Graphic Enterprises of Ohio Inc. (M)
Graphic Publishing Systems Inc. (M)
GraphLine Inc. (D)
Hewlett Packard Co. (M,D)
Mantis Computer Parts Inc. (M)
Megasys International Inc. (D)
Midwest Publishers Supply Co. (D)
Monotype Systems Inc. (D,S)
National Research Bureau (D)
Olivetti Office USA (M)
PrePRESS DIRECT (D)
PrePRESS SOLUTIONS (M)
Quipp System Inc. (D)
System Facilities Inc. (D)
Texas Instruments Inc. (M)
Three Sigma (S)
Truproof Ltd. (D)
Bob Weber Inc. (D,S)
Xerox Corp.-Xerox Engineering Systems (M)

Layout Tables, Light Tables & Workstations (See also Tables)
Allpress Equipment Inc. (D)
Arrow Printing Co. (S)
Auto-Grafica Corp. (D)
Berkshire/Westwood Graphics Group Inc. (D)
BESCO Graphic Systems Corp. (D)
Beta Screen Corp. (D)
Consolidated International Corp. (M)
Craig Cold Type Supply Inc. (D)
Douthitt Corp. (M)
Duostat Co. (Affiliated with VGC Corp.) (D)
Dynalith Inc. (D)
Foster Mfg. Co. (M)
GTI Graphic Technology Inc. (M)
Kreonite Inc. (M)
London Litho Aluminum Co. Inc. (D)
Midwest Publishers Supply Co. (M,D)
National Graphic Supply Corp. (D)
National Research Bureau (D)
NENSCO (M)
Newstech Co. (Div. of Rovinter Inc.) (D)
NuArc Co. Inc. (M)
Pitman Co. (D)
Poolside Lithographic Supply Inc. (D)
Pro Systems Inc. (M)
Richmond/Graphic Products Inc. (M)
Roconex Corp. (M)
SCREEN (USA) (M)
Support Products Inc. (D)
Truproof Ltd. (D)
Western LithoTech (M)

Lenses (Camera) (See also Cameras & Accessories)
Alan Graphic Systems Inc. (M,D)
Allpress Equipment Inc. (D)
BESCO Graphic Systems Corp. (D)
R.W. Borrowdale Co. (RWB Enterprises Div.) (M)
Caprock Developments Inc. (D)
CK Optical Co. Inc. (M,D)
Consolidated International Corp. (M)
Duostat Co. (Affiliated with VGC Corp.) (D)
Heitz Service Corp. (D)
Mantis Computer Parts Inc. (D)
Midwest Publishers Supply Co. (D)
National Graphic Supply Corp. (D)
National Research Bureau
Newstech Co. (Div. of Rovinter Inc.) (D)
Nikon Inc./Electronic Imaging Department (M,D)
Pitman Photo Supply (D)
Polaroid Corp. (M,D,S)

Letterpress Conversion
Apex Machine Co. (M)
MAH Machine Co. Inc. (S)
Pacific Newspaper Services Inc. (D,S)
Pressroom Products Inc. (D)
R T P Technical Specialists (S)
William C. Spells (RTP Technical Specialists) (D,S)
Tech-Energy Co. (M,D,S)
Tecnigraph T.G.I. International Inc. (M)
TKS (USA) Inc. (M,D)
World Net & Associates Inc. (D)

Library Retrieval Systems
Advanced Technical Solutions (S)
Advertising Checking Bureau Inc. (S)
Auto-Grafica Corp. (D)
Baseview Products Inc. (M,D)
Computer Tree (D)
CompuText Inc. (D)
DataTimes Corp. (D)
Digital Equipment Corp. (M,D)
Digital Technology International (M)
Harris Publishing Systems Corp. (M)
Lazer-fare Media Services Ltd. (D,S)
LEXIS-NEXIS (D)
The Networks Inc. (D,S)
Newstech Co. (Div. of Rovinter Inc.) (D)
Scandinavian PC Systems Inc. (M,D)
Stauffer Media Systems (M,D)
Sysdeco U.S. (D,S)
T/One Inc. (M,D)
Verity Inc. (D)
VU/TEXT Library Services Inc. (M,D)
Western Automation (M)

Lift Trucks
Berlee Vacuum Systems (M,D,S)
Cascade Corp. (M)
Clark Material Handling Co. (M)
Linde-Baker Material Handling Corp. (M)
Machine Design Service Inc. (M)
Midwest Publishers Supply Co. (D)
National Graphic Supply Corp. (D)
Newstech Co. (Div. of Rovinter Inc.) (D)
Penske Truck Leasing (S)
Penske Truck Leasing (S)
Printing Equipment Specialists Inc. (S)
Republic Service Co. (S)
Ryder System Inc. (S)
Tech-Energy Co. (D,S)
Wesco Graphics
Yale Materials Handling Corp. (M)

Light Integrators
Amergraph Corp. (M)
Axelrod, Norman N., Assoc./Optical, Laser & Vision Systems (M,S)
BESCO Graphic Systems Corp. (D)
Burgess Industries Inc. (M)
Consolidated International Corp. (M)
Douthitt Corp. (M,D)
Konica Imaging USA Inc. (D)
National Graphic Supply Corp. (D)
Newstech Co. (Div. of Rovinter Inc.) (D)
NuArc Co. Inc. (M)
Richmond/Graphic Products Inc. (M)
Roconex Corp. (D)
Western LithoTech (D)

Lighting Equipment
Atlas Specialty Lighting (M)
BESCO Graphic Systems Corp. (D)
Burgess Industries Inc. (M)
Caprock Developments Inc. (D)
Colortran Inc. (M)
Consolidated International Corp. (M)
Douthitt Corp. (M,D)
GTI Graphic Technology Inc. (M)
George R Hall Inc. (M)
Just Normlicht Inc. (M)
Macbeth, Div. of Kollmorgen Inst. Corp. (M)
Midwest Publishers Supply Co. (D)
National Graphic Supply Corp. (D)
Newstech Co. (Div. of Rovinter Inc.) (D)
NuArc Co. (M)
Tingue Brown & Co. (D)

Lubricants
Albar Labs & Industrial Supplies Inc. (D)
Baumfolder Corp. (M,D)
BESCO Graphic Systems Corp. (D)
Hercules Inc. (M)
Lincoln Industrial (M)
Lubriplate Div./Fiske Bros. Refining Co. (M)
Newstech Co. (Div. of Rovinter Inc.) (D)
Tech-Energy Co. (D,S)

Mailing List Compiler
Arrow Printing Co. (S)
Baseview Products Inc. (M)
Dunhill International List Co. Inc. (M)
Layton Marketing Group Inc. (S)

Mailroom Systems & Equipment (Includes Software)
ALTA Graphics Inc. (S)
Arco Engineering Inc. (Newspaper Div.) (S)
Automated Mailing Systems Corp. (D)
Baird Manufacturing Inc. (M)
Baseview Products Inc. (M)
Bell & Howell (M,D,S)
Bell & Howell/Phillipsburg Co. (M)
Bobst Group Inc. (M,D)
Cannon Equipment (M)
Carlson Design/Construct Corp. (S)
Dean Machinery International Inc. (M)
Derus Media Service Inc./Editorial Pace (S)
Dispensa-Matic Label Dispensers (M)
EAM-Mosca Corp. (M,D)
FELINS Inc. (M)
Ferag Inc. (M)
Florida Printing Equipment and Supply (D)
Jimmy R. Fox, Mail Room Consultant (S)
Gerrard Ovalstrapping (M,D)
Ginsberg, William Associates (S)
GMA Inc. (M)
Group 1 Software Inc. (M)
GSP Inc. (M)
Hall Processing Systems (M)
Hartcid Industry Inc. (S)
Ideal Equipment (of America) Inc. (M)
Imaje Ink Jet Printing (M)
Interlake Packaging Corp. (M)
Kansa Corp. (Baldwin Technology Co.) (M,D)
Kirk-Rudy Inc. (M)
Machine Design Service Inc. (M)
MAH Machine Co. Inc. (S)
Martin Yale Inc. (M)
McCain Manufacturing Corp. (M)
Meadows Co. (S)
Megasys International Inc. (D)
National Research Bureau (D)
Neasi-Weber International (M,D,S)
Northeast Industries Inc. (M,D)
ONE Corp. (D)
Ovalstrapping Inc. (M)
Parsons Main Inc. (S)
Pitney Bowes Business Systems (M,D)
Power Strap (M)
Press-Tec Inc. (S)
Prim Hall Enterprises Inc. (M,D)
Printing Equipment Specialists Inc. (S)
Quipp System Inc. (M,D)
Scandinavian PC Systems Inc. (M,D)
Sheridan Systems (M)
SI Handling Systems Inc. (M)
Signode Corp. (M,D)
SITMA USA Inc. (M)
H.R. Slater Co. Inc. (M)
Standlee and Associates Inc. (M,D,S)
Stepper Inc. (M)
Sterling Packaging Systems (M)
Strapex Corp. (M)
U.S. Postal Service (S)
Valley Remanufacturing Co. (M)
Videojet Systems International Inc. (M)
Jervis B. Webb Co. (M)
West-Mor Mailroom Services (M,D,S)
Western Roller Corp. (M)
Chauncey Wing's Sons Inc. (M)
World Net & Associates Inc. (D)
XYonicz (M)

Maintenance, Plant & Equipment
Advanced Technical Solutions (S)
Core-Concepts (D,S)
Eclectic Co. Inc. (M,D,S)
George R Hall Inc. (M)
Manassy Precision Corp. (M,D)
Master Flo Technology (M)
Mid Atlantic Lighting (D)
Pacific Newspaper Services Inc. (D,S)
Republic Service Co. (S)
R T P Technical Specialists (S)
Standlee and Associates Inc. (M)
Tech-Energy Co. (M,D,S)
TKS (USA) Inc. (M)
Witte Energy Management (S)

Market Research
A & A Research (S)
Advertising Checking Bureau Inc. (S)
Arrow Printing Co. (S)
Auditec Computing Services Inc. (M,D)
Axelrod, Norman N., Assoc./Optical, Laser & Vision Systems (S)
Richard Briggs & Associates (S)
Circulation Verification Council (S)
Claritas (M,D)
Clayton/Curtis/Cottrell (S)
Community Papers Verification Services (S)
Derus Media Service Inc./Editorial Pace (S)
William Dunkerley Publishing Consultant (M)
W B Grimes & Co. Inc. (S)
Kevin Brian Kamen & Co. (S)
Layton Marketing Group Inc. (S)
Market Opinion Research/Pace (S)
Metromail Corp. (M)
Mid Atlantic Lighting (D)
National Research Bureau (D)
PAGE (S)
Silverman Newspaper Management Consultants (S)
Strategic Telemedia (S)
Valco Sales Inc. (S)
VNU Business Information Services (M,D,S)

Marketing Database Design and Implementation
CompuText Inc. (M)
Sysdeco U.S. (M,D,S)
World Net & Associates Inc. (S)

Masking Materials (See also Offset Negative Masking Paper)
Allstates Litho Plate Corp. (D)
Base-Line Inc. (M)

THE BEST INFORMATION ON ACQUIRING . . .
USED PRESS MAILROOM BINDERY EQUIPMENT
AL TABER
BILL KANIPE
ALTA GRAPHICS INC
PHONE (770) 552-1528
FAX (770) 552-2669
PHONE (770) 428-5817
FAX (770) 590-7267

Equipment, supplies, services — VI-35

Berkshire/Westwood Graphics Group Inc. (D)
BESCO Graphic Systems Corp. (D)
Craig Cold Type Supply Inc. (S)
Direct Reproduction Corp. (M)
Duostat Co. (Affiliated with VGC Corp.) (D)
Fluorographic Services Inc. (M,D)
Konica Imaging USA Inc. (M)
Midwest Publishers Supply Co. (D)
National Graphic Supply Corp. (D)
NENSCO (D)
Poolside Lithographic Supply Inc. (D)
Support Products Inc. (D)

Masking Systems
Fluorographic Services Inc. (M,D)
Midwest Publishers Supply Co. (D)

Material Handling Equipment: Automatic Guided Vehicles
Control Engineering Co. (M)
FMC Corp. (Material Handling Systems Div.) (M)
Ginsberg, William Associates (S)
Heidelberg Harris Inc. (D)
Lamb-Grays Harbor Co. (M)
National Graphic Sales Inc. (S)
Rapistan Demag Corp. (M)
SI Handling Systems Inc. (M)
Jervis B. Webb Co. (M)

Material Handling Equipment: Palletizing Machines
Butler SMC. (M)
Ferag Inc. (M)
Ginsberg, William Associates (S)
Heidelberg Harris Inc. (D)
Kidder Inc. (M)
Machine Design Service Inc. (M)
National Graphic Sales Inc. (S)
Quipp System Inc. (D)
Schuler Sales/A Kolbus Group Subsidiary (M)

Material Handling Equipment: Pallets & Palletizers
Ginsberg, William Associates (S)
Hamilton Circulation Supplies Co. (Newspaper Mailroom Supplies) (D)
Litco International Inc. (M,D)
Machine Design Service Inc. (M)
Master Flo Technology (M)
National Research Bureau (D)
NENSCO (D)
Quipp System Inc. (D)

Material Handling Equipment: Truck Loaders
ALTA Graphics Inc. (S)
Ginsberg, William Associates (S)
Lamb-Grays Harbor Co. (M)
Machine Design Service Inc. (M)
Quipp System Inc. (D)
Rapistan Demag Corp. (M)
Standlee and Associates Inc. (D,S)
Star International Corp. (D)
Stewart Glapat Corp. (M)
Wesco Graphics
West-Mor Mailroom Services (M,D,S)

Material Handling Equipment: Vehicle Loading
Kansa Corp. (Baldwin Technology Co.) (M,D)
Lamb-Grays Harbor Co. (M)
Machine Design Service Inc. (M)
M E G (US) Inc. (M)
Quipp System Inc. (D)
Standlee and Associates Inc. (M,D,S)

Microfilming
Eastman Kodak/Professional Printing & Publishing Imaging (M)
Newstech Co. (Div. of Rovinter Inc.) (D)

Motors
Allpress Equipment Inc. (D)
Arco Engineering Inc. (Newspaper Div.) (S)
Baldor Electric Co. (M)
Fincor/Electronics Div. Inc. (M)
Graham Co. (M)
Hobart Brothers Co. (M,D,S)
Ingersoll-Rand Corp./Power Tool & Hoist Div. (M)
Kaim & Associates Int'l. Marketing Inc. (D)
Miracle Industries Inc. (M)
Mountain States Inc. (S)
Offset Web Sales Inc. (S)
Robertson Press Machinery Co. Inc. (D)
Star International Corp. (D)
Tech-Energy Co. (D,S)
West-Mor Mailroom Services (D,S)
WPC Machinery Corp. (D)

Multiplexers/Routers
Autologic Inc. (Subsidiary of Volt Info. Svc.) (M)
Automated Newsstand (D)
Graphic Enterprises of Ohio Inc. (M)
Newstech Co. (Div. of Rovinter Inc.) (D)
PrePRESS DIRECT (D)

Newpaper Counter
Pressroom Products Inc. (M)

News Wire Capture System
Automated Newsstand (D)
Baseview Products Inc. (M)
Computer Tree (D)
Freedom System Integrators (M)
Lazer-fare Media Services Ltd. (D,S)
Sysdeco U.S. (M)

Newspaper Bags
ANI Promotions/DBA (D)
Automated Newsstand (D)
Continental Products (M)
Hamilton Circulation Supplies Co. (Newspaper Mailroom Supplies) (D)
The Keenan Group Inc. (D)
Le Cotton & Co. (M)
Malow Corp. (D)
Meadows Co. (D)
National Research Bureau (D)
NENSCO (D)
P.D.I. Plastics (M)
SITMA USA Inc. (M)

Newspaper Counter
Allpress Equipment Inc. (D)
Automated Newsstand (D)
Machine Design Service Inc. (M)
Newstech Co. (Div. of Rovinter Inc.) (D)
Provan Associates Inc. (S)
Ramsey Technology Inc. (M)

Newspaper Dispensers (Mechanical/Electronic)
AG Industries Inc. (M,D)
ANI Promotions/DBA (D)
Automated News Vending Systems (M,D)
Automated Newsstand (D)
EB Metal Industries (M)
Fortec Inc. (M)
GeoRack Inc. (M)
Go Plastics Inc. (M)
Hamilton Circulation Supplies Co. (Newspaper Mailroom Supplies) (D)
Kaspar Wire Works Inc./Sho-Rack (M,D)
The Keenan Group Inc. (D)
National Research Bureau (D)
Renfro-Franklin Co. (M)
Vendors International Inc. (M,D)

Newspaper Marketing
Ad-Star/Publishing Technologies (M,D)
The American Assn. of Independent News Distributors (D)
Baseview Products Inc. (M)
Cable Classified Advertising Network (CCAN) (S)
Claritas (M,D)
CM Publishing Co. (S)
Communications Management Service Inc. (S)
Hamilton Circulation Supplies Co. (Newspaper Mailroom Supplies) (D)
Kevin Brian Kamen & Co. (S)
The Keenan Group Inc. (S)
Layton Marketing Group Inc. (S)
Newspaper Association of America (EDI) (S)
Newspaper Computer Systems (S)
Northern Graphic Supply (S)
SCA Promotions Inc. (D)
Scandinavian PC Systems Inc. (M,D)
Ver-A-Fast Corp. (S)
VNU Business Information Services (S)

Newsprint (See also Paper)
Abitibi-Price Sales Corp. (M)
Avenor America Inc. (M)
Avenor Inc. (M)
Behrens International Ltd. (D,S)
Bender Machine Inc. (S)
Bowater-Great Northern Paper Inc. (M)
Bowater Inc. (M)
Bowater Inc. (Coated Paper & Market Pulp Division) (M)
Bowater Mersey Paper Co. Ltd. (M)
Bowater Newsprint (Div. of Bowater Inc.) (M,D)
Canadian Pacific Forest Products Inc. (D)
Champion International Corp. (M,D)
Core-Concepts (S)
Daishowa Forest Products Ltd. (M)
Donohue Inc. (M)
Fletcher Challenge Paper Co. (M,D)
FSC Paper Co. (M,D)
Garden State Paper Co. Inc. (M)
Irving Forest Products Inc. (M,D)
Kruger Pulp & Paper Sales Inc. (M)
James MacLaren Industries Inc. (M,D,S)
MacMillan Bloedel (M)
The Madden Corp. (D)
Manistique Papers Inc. (M)
Simon Miller Sales Co. (D)
National Research Bureau (D)
Newsprint Sales (M,D,S)
Newsprint South Inc. (M)
PAGE (S)
Parsons Main Inc. (S)
QUNO Corp. (M)
Roosevelt Paper (D)
Smurfit Newsprint Corp. (M)
Southeast Paper Newsprint Sales (M,D)
Spruce Falls Inc. (M)
Stone Consolidated (S)
Stone-Consolidated Corp. (M)

Stone-Consolidated Newsprint Inc. (M,D)
U.S. Pulp & Newsprint (Div. of Kimberly-Clark) (M)
Wesco Graphics (M)

Newsprint Handling Equipment
Bender Machine Inc. (S)
Carlson Design/Construct Corp. (S)
Cascade Inc. (M)
Dario Designs Inc. (S)
Ebway Industries Inc. (Div. of Jardis Industries Inc.) (M)
Enkel Corp. (A Baldwin Technology Co.) (M)
Florida Printing Equipment and Supply (D)
FMC Corp. (Material Handling Systems Div.) (M)
Ginsberg, William Associates (S)
M. Golda Engineering (S)
Greerco Corp. (M)
Kansa Corp. (Baldwin Technology Co.) (M,D)
LiftSafe Systems Inc. (M,D)
Machine Design Service Inc. (M)
National Research Bureau (D)
Parsons Main Inc. (S)
Prim Hall Enterprises Inc. (M,D)
Quality Components Corp. (M)
Republic Service Co. (M)
Rosback Co. (M)
H.R. Slater Co. Inc. (M)
TKS (USA) Inc. (M,D)
Jervis B. Webb Co. (M)
World Net & Associates Inc. (D)
XYonicz (M)

Noise Control
Airloc Products (M)
Arco Engineering Inc. (Newspaper Div.) (M)
Eclectic Co. Inc. (M,D,S)
Ginsberg, William Associates (S)
Industrial Noise Control Inc. (M)
Noise Monitoring & Control Inc. (S)
Parsons Main Inc. (S)

Numbering Machines
Advance Graphics Equipment of York Inc. (M,D)
Arrow Printing Co. (S)
Craftsmen Machinery Co./Graphic Export Corp. (D)
A.B. Dick Co. (M,D)
Domino Amjet Inc. (M,D,S)
General Binding Corp. (M,D)
Imaje Ink Jet Printing (M)
Kaim & Associates Int'l. Marketing Inc. (D)
Martin Yale Inc. (M)
Louis Melind Co. (M)
National Graphic Supply Corp. (D)
Newstech Co. (Div. of Rovinter Inc.) (D)
Rollem Corp. of America (D)
Web Printing Controls/WPC Machinery Corp. (M)
Western Printing Machinery (M)

Offset Blanket Thickness Gauge
Allpress Equipment Inc. (D)
Allstates Litho Plate Corp. (D)
B & T Press Supplies (Affiliated with Canadian Web) (D)
BESCO Graphic Systems Corp. (D)
Central Graphics (D)
Midwest Publishers Supply Co. (D)

MID AMERICA GRAPHICS INC.

Mid-America Graphics offers the highest quality new and refurbished mail and press room equipment from manufacturers such as:

- Muller Martini®
- Cole®
- Kansa®
- Custom Bilt®
- IDAB®
- Chesire®
- Quipp®
- Hall®
- Baldwin®
- Harris Sheridan®
- McCain®
- Signode®

and many others

SERVING THE PRINTING INDUSTRY WITH QUALITY REFURBISHED AND NEW GRAPHIC ARTS EQUIPMENT

Featuring our Counterstacker

1501 Vine, Harrisonville, MO 64701

800-356-4886
816-887-2414
FAX 816-887-2762

Copyright ©1996 by the Editor & Publisher Co.

VI-36 Equipment, supplies, services

The Morrison Group/Morrison Ink (D)
National Graphic Supply Corp. (D)
NENSCO (D)
Newstech Co. (Div. of Rovinter Inc.) (D)
Printers' Service (M)
Moss Reck & Associates Inc. (D)
Bill Rudder & Associates Inc. (M)
Star International Corp. (D)
SunShine Paper Co. (D)
Support Products Inc. (M)
Tech-Energy Co. (D,S)

Offset Blankets, Blanket Wash
Allpress Equipment Inc. (D)
Allstates Litho Plate Corp. (D)
B & T Press Supplies (Affiliated with Canadian Web) (D)
Berkshire/Westwood Graphics Group Inc. (D)
BESCO Graphic Systems Corp. (D)
Bruno Unger USA (D)
A.B. Dick Co. (M)
DYC Supply Co./Dynaric Inc. (M,D)
FFC International Inc. (M)
Florida Printing Equipment and Supply (D)
Global Graphics Inc. (D)
Graphic Arts Technical & Consulting Services (M)
GraphLine Inc. (D)
The Inco Company (M)
Midwest Publishers Supply Co. (D)
The Morrison Group/Morrison Ink (M,D)
National Graphic Supply Corp. (D)
NENSCO (D)
Newstech Co. (Div. of Rovinter Inc.) (D)
Poolside Lithographic Supply Inc. (D)
Printers' Service (M)
Rycoline Products Inc. (M)
Star International Corp. (D)
Sun Graphic Inc. (M,D)
SunShine Paper Co. (D)
Tech-Energy Co. (D,S)
UMI (M)

Offset Camera, Darkroom Equipment
Alan Graphic Systems Inc. (D)
Allpress Equipment Inc. (D)
Arrow Printing Co. (S)
Berkshire/Westwood Graphics Group Inc. (D)
BESCO Graphic Systems Corp. (D)
R.W. Borrowdale Co. (RWB Enterprises Div.) (D)
CK Optical Co. Inc. (M,D)
Consolidated International Corp. (M)
Florida Printing Equipment and Supply (D)
GraphLine Inc. (D)
LogEtronics Corp. (M,D)
Midwest Publishers Supply Co. (D)
National Graphic Supply Corp. (D)
NENSCO (D)
Newstech Co. (Div. of Rovinter Inc.) (D)
SCREEN (USA) (M)
Support Products Inc. (D)

Offset Chemicals & Supplies
Allpress Equipment Inc. (D)
Allstates Litho Plate Corp. (D)
American Litho Inc. (D)
Anitec (M)
Arrow Printing Co. (S)
Berkshire/Westwood Graphics Group Inc. (D)
BESCO Graphic Systems Corp. (D)
Citiplate Inc. (M)
A.B. Dick Co. (M)
Dynalith Inc. (D)
FFC International Inc. (M)
Florida Printing Equipment and Supply (D)
Graphic Arts Technical & Consulting Services (M)
GraphLine Inc. (D)
The Inco Company (M)
London Litho Aluminum Co. Inc. (D)
Master Flo Technology (M)
Midwest Publishers Supply Co. (D)
The Morrison Group/Morrison Ink (M,D)
National Graphic Supply Corp. (D)
NENSCO (D)
Newstech Co. (Div. of Rovinter Inc.) (D)
Poolside Lithographic Supply Inc. (D)
Printers' Service (M)
Superior Lithoplate of Indiana Inc. (D)
Tech-Energy Co. (D,S)
3M Printing & Publishing Systems Div. (M)
Varn International (M)
Veratec Div. (M)
Western LithoTech (M)
Winton Engineering Co. (M)

Offset Film
Allstates Litho Plate Corp. (D)
Anitec (M)
Arrow Printing Co. (S)
Berkshire/Westwood Graphics Group Inc. (D)
BESCO Graphic Systems Corp. (D)
Dynalith Inc. (D)
Eastman Kodak/Professional Printing & Publishing Imaging (M)
Florida Printing Equipment and Supply (D)
GraphLine Inc. (D)
London Litho Aluminum Co. Inc. (D)
National Graphic Supply Corp. (D)
Newstech Co. (Div. of Rovinter Inc.) (D)
Pitman Photo Supply (D)
3M Printing & Publishing Systems Div. (M)

Offset Fountain Controls
American Graphics L.P. (M,D)
Arrow Printing Co. (S)
BESCO Graphic Systems Corp. (D)
Dahlgren USA Inc. (M)
GraphLine Inc. (D)
Heidelberg Harris Inc. (M)
The Inco Company (M)
Master Flo Technology (M)
Newstech Co. (Div. of Rovinter Inc.) (D)
Perretta Graphics Corp. (M)
Pressroom Products Inc. (M)
Printers' Service (M)
Ryco Graphic Manufacturing Inc. (M)
Rycoline Products Inc. (M)
Solna Web USA Inc. (M)
Tech-Energy Co. (D,S)

Offset Fountain Solutions
Allpress Equipment Inc. (D)
Allstates Litho Plate Corp. (D)
ALTA Graphics Inc. (S)
American Litho Inc. (D)
Arrow Printing Co. (S)
Berkshire/Westwood Graphics Group Inc. (D)
BESCO Graphic Systems Corp. (D)
A.B. Dick Co. (M)
FFC International Inc. (M)
Graphic Arts Technical & Consulting Services (M)
GraphLine Inc. (D)
The Inco Company (M)
London Litho Aluminum Co. Inc. (D)
Master Flo Technology (M)
Midwest Publishers Supply Co. (D)
The Morrison Group/Morrison Ink (M,D)
National Graphic Supply Corp. (D)
NENSCO (M)
Newstech Co. (Div. of Rovinter Inc.) (D)
Poolside Lithographic Supply Inc. (D)
Printers' Service (M)
Rycoline Products Inc. (M)
Star International Corp. (D)
Tech-Energy Co. (D,S)

3M Printing & Publishing Systems Div. (M)
Varn International (M)
Western LithoTech (M)

Offset Negative Masking Paper
Allstates Litho Plate Corp. (D)
Arrow Printing Co. (S)
Berkshire/Westwood Graphics Group Inc. (D)
BESCO Graphic Systems Corp. (D)
A.B. Dick Co. (M)
Direct Reproduction Corp. (M)
Midwest Publishers Supply Co. (D)
National Graphic Supply Corp. (D)
NENSCO (D)
Newstech Co. (Div. of Rovinter Inc.) (D)
Poolside Lithographic Supply Inc. (D)

Offset Plate Erasers
Berkshire/Westwood Graphics Group Inc. (D)
BESCO Graphic Systems Corp. (D)
A.B. Dick Co. (M)
GraphLine Inc. (D)
Midwest Publishers Supply Co. (D)
National Graphic Supply Corp. (D)
NENSCO (D)
Newstech Co. (Div. of Rovinter Inc.) (D)
Poolside Lithographic Supply Inc. (D)
Western LithoTech (M)

Offset Plate Files
Arrow Printing Co. (S)
BESCO Graphic Systems Corp. (D)
Dynalith Inc. (D)
Midwest Publishers Supply Co. (D)
National Graphic Supply Corp. (D)
NENSCO (D)
Newstech Co. (Div. of Rovinter Inc.) (D)
Roconex Corp. (M)

Offset Plate Holders
Arrow Printing Co. (S)
BESCO Graphic Systems Corp. (D)
Midwest Publishers Supply Co. (D)
NENSCO (D)
Newstech Co. (Div. of Rovinter Inc.) (D)
Tech-Energy Co. (D,S)

Offset Plate-Making Service & Equipment
Amergraph Corp. (M)
American Litho Inc. (D)
Anitec (M)
Arrow Printing Co. (S)
BESCO Graphic Systems Corp. (D)
Carlson Design/Construct Corp. (S)
Consolidated International Corp. (M)
A.B. Dick Co. (M)
Douthitt Corp. (M)
Eastman Kodak/Professional Printing & Publishing Imaging (M)
GraphLine Inc. (D)
Hercules Inc. (M)
K & F/Printing Systems International (M)
LogEtronics Corp. (M,D)
The Master Group (M)
Newstech Co. (Div. of Rovinter Inc.) (D)
NuArc Co. Inc. (M)
Poolside Lithographic Supply Inc. (D)
Printing Equipment Specialists Inc. (S)
Printware (M,D)
Richmond/Graphic Products Inc. (M)
SCREEN (USA) (M)
Star International Corp. (D)
Tasope Co. (M)
Tech-Energy Co. (D,S)
Ternes Register System (M)
3M Printing & Publishing Systems Div. (M)
Veratec Div. (M)
Western LithoTech (M)
Western Lithotech (M)

Offset Prevention-Materials & Equipment
Arrow Printing Co. (S)
BESCO Graphic Systems Corp. (D)
SunShine Paper Co. (D)
Tech-Energy Co. (D,S)
Varn International (M)
Winton Engineering Co. (M)

Optical Character Recognition (OCR)
CNI Corp. (D)
CPS Technologies Inc. (D)
Graphic Publishing Systems Inc. (D)
IC Systems Solutions (M,D,S)
International Memory Products of Illinois Inc. (D)
Krypton Systems (S)
Mantis Computer Parts Inc. (D)
Media Cybernetics L.P. (M)
Newstech Co. (Div. of Rovinter Inc.) (D)
NGCP/Laser Concepts (D)
VoCal Telecommunications (M)
Xerox Corp. (M)
Xerox Corp.-Desktop Document Systems (M)

QUIET PRESS ZONE

Designing and building state-of-the-art quiet zones in newspaper production facilities has been our business for over twenty years. Our newspaper clients realize improved safety, productivity and quality and our O.E.M. clients enhance their offerings to their customers.

Let us show you how to achieve these benefits as part of your construction, modernization or expansion projects. Contact us for a free copy of our brochure *Noise Control for Newspaper Printing Facilities.*

- Pressroom Quiet Rooms
- Press Noise Control Systems
- Mailroom Control Rooms
- Production Offices
- Acoustic Treatments
- Ancillary Equipment Rooms

® Specialists in noise control products and services

industrial noise control, inc.

1411 Jeffrey Dr., Addison, IL 60101

(800)954-1998
fax (800)420-4928

Copyright ©1996 by the Editor & Publisher Co.

Equipment, supplies, services VI-37

Optical Products
Alan Graphic Systems Inc. (M)
Axelrod, Norman N., Assoc./Optical, Laser & Vision Systems (M,S)
Beta Screen Corp. (M)
Caprock Developments Inc. (M,D)
Chinon America Inc. (M)
Computer Devices Inc. (D)
Computer Services Group Inc. (D)
CPS Technologies Inc. (D)
Crosfield Electronic Ltd. (M)
DuPont Co. (D)
DYC Supply Co./Dynaric Inc. (M)
IC Systems Solutions (D,S)
International Memory Products of Illinois Inc. (D)
Newstech Co. (Div. of Rovinter Inc.) (D)
Perretta Graphics Corp. (M)
Technidyne Corp. (M)
Three Sigma (M)
Western LithoTech (D)
X-Rite Inc. (M)

Output Management and Preflight Software
Autologic Inc. (Subsidiary of Volt Info. Svc.) (M)
Computer Tree (D)
Graphic Enterprises of Ohio Inc. (M)
Newstech Co. (Div. of Rovinter Inc.) (D)
PrePRESS DIRECT (D)
PrePRESS SOLUTIONS (M)

Pagination Systems
Advanced Technical Solutions (M)
Auto-Grafica Corp. (D)
Autologic Information International Inc. (M)
CNI Corp. (M,D)
Computer Tree (D)
CompuText Inc. (M)
Concept Publishing Systems (M)
CPS Technologies Inc. (M,D)
Creative House Print Media Consultants (S)
Crosfield Electronic Ltd. (M)
Cybergraphic Inc. (M,D)
Datalogics (M,D)
Deadline Data Systems Inc. (D)
Dewar Information Systems Corp. (S)
Digital Technology International (M)
DuPont Co. (D)
Durbin Associates (S)
Foley, Torregiani & Associates, Inc. (D)
Freedom System Integrators (M)
Graphic Publishing Systems Inc. (D)
Harris Corp. (Corporate Headquaters) (M)
Harris Publishing Systems Corp. (M)
Konica Imaging USA Inc. (M)
Lazer-fare Media Services Ltd. (D,S)
Levien Instruments Co. (M,D)
Linotype-Hell Co. (M)
Newstech Co. (Div. of Rovinter Inc.) (D)
NGCP/Laser Concepts (D)
Penta Software Inc. (S)
PrePRESS DIRECT (D)
Sinclair Imaging Inc. (D)
Sysdeco (M,D,S)
West Coast Computer Systems/Newspaper Technologies (D)

Papaer Testing Instruments
Newstech Co. (Div. of Rovinter Inc.) (D)

Paper Cleaners
BESCO Graphic Systems Corp. (D)
Hercules Inc. (M)
Newstech Co. (Div. of Rovinter Inc.) (D)

Paper Handling Equipment
Carlson Design/Construct Corp. (S)
Dario Designs Inc. (S)
Ebway Industries Inc. (Div. of Jardis Industries Inc.) (M)
Enkel Corp. (A Baldwin Technology Co.) (M)
FMC Corp. (Material Handling Systems Div.) (M)
Ginsberg, William Associates (S)
M. Golda Engineering (S)
Greerco Corp. (M)
Jardis Industries Inc. (Cary Equipment Div.) (M)
Kansa Corp. (Baldwin Technology Co.) (M,D)
Keene Technology Inc. (KTI) (M)
LiftSafe Systems Inc. (M,D)
Martin Yale Inc. (M)
National Research Bureau (D)
Parsons Main Inc. (S)
Prim Hall Enterprises Inc. (M,D)
Resource Net International (D)
Rosback Co. (M)
H.R. Slater Co. Inc. (M)
Star International Corp. (D)
Tech-Energy Co. (M,D,S)
Jervis B. Webb Co. (M)

Paper Shredders
BESCO Graphic Systems Corp. (D)
Blower Application Co. Inc. (M)
General Binding Corp. (M,D)
Kaim & Associates Int'l. Marketing Inc. (D)
Martin Yale Inc. (M)
Megasys International Inc. (M)
National Graphic Supply Corp. (D)
Newstech Co. (Div. of Rovinter Inc.) (D)

Paper Testing Instruments
Axelrod, Norman N., Assoc./Optical, Laser & Vision Systems (M,S)
Midwest Publishers Supply Co. (D)
SunShine Paper Co. (D)
Technidyne Corp. (M)

Paper: Coated Groundwood Offset
Bowater-Great Northern Paper Inc. (M)
Bowater Inc. (Coated Paper & Market Pulp Division) (M)
Hammermill Papers (Div. of International Papers) (M,D)
Simon Miller Sales Co. (D)
Norwood Paper (D,S)
Roosevelt Paper (D)
S.D. Warren (M)

Paper: Groundwood Specialties
Bowater-Great Northern Paper Inc. (M)
Hammermill Papers (Div. of International Papers) (M,D)
James River Corp. (M)
MacMillan Bloedel (M)
Manistique Papers Inc. (M)
Norwood Paper (D,S)
Roosevelt Paper (D)
Spruce Falls Inc. (M)
Stone-Consolidated Corp. (M)
U.S. Pulp & Newsprint (Div. of Kimberly-Clark) (M)
S.D. Warren (M)

Paper: Specialty Printing Paper
Bowater-Great Northern Paper Inc. (M)
Domtar Inc. (M)
FSC Paper Co. (M,D)
Hammermill Papers (Div. of International Papers) (M,D)
Midwest Publishers Supply Co. (D)
Simon Miller Sales Co. (D)
Norwood Paper (D,S)
Roosevelt Paper (D)
S.D. Warren (M)

Pasters (See also Flying Pasters)
Allpress Equipment Inc. (D)
ALTA Graphics Inc. (S)
Arco Engineering Inc. (Newspaper Div.) (M,S)
Butler SMC. (M)
Cariweb Products (M)
Controls Group Inc. (M)
Ebway Industries Inc. (Div. of Jardis Industries Inc.) (M)
Enkel Corp. (A Baldwin Technology Co.) (M)
Graphic System Services (M,D,S)
H&M Paster Sales & Service Inc. (M)
Kaim & Associates Int'l. Marketing Inc. (D)
MAH Machine Co. Inc. (S)
M E G (US) Inc. (M)
National Graphic Sales Inc. (S)
Newstech Co. (Div. of Rovinter Inc.) (D)
Portage Newspaper Supply Co. (D)
R T P Technical Specialists (S)
William C. Spells (RTP Technical Specialists) (D,S)
Veratec Div. (M)
Web Tapes Inc. (S)

Photo Archiving
Baseview Products Inc. (M,D)
Computer Tree (D)
CompuText Inc. (M)
Lazer-fare Media Services Ltd. (D,S)
National Graphic Supply Corp. (D)
Newstech Co. (Div. of Rovinter Inc.) (D)
Sysdeco U.S. (M,D,S)

Photo Proofing Papers
Arrow Printing Co. (S)
BESCO Graphic Systems Corp. (D)
Computer Tree (D)
Danagraf North America (D)
Eastman Kodak/Professional Printing & Publishing Imaging (M)
Konica Imaging USA Inc. (M)
Mantis Computer Parts Inc. (D)
National Graphic Supply Corp. (D)
Newstech Co. (Div. of Rovinter Inc.) (D)
NGCP/Laser Concepts (D)

Photo Proofing Systems
Arrow Printing Co. (S)
Auto-Grafica Corp. (D)
BESCO Graphic Systems Corp. (D)
Computer Tree (D)
Danagraf North America (D)
Eastman Kodak/Professional Printing & Publishing Imaging (M)
Konica Imaging USA Inc. (M)
Macbeth, Div. of Kollmorgen Inst. Corp. (M)
Mantis Computer Parts Inc. (D)
Midwest Publishers Supply Co. (D)
National Graphic Supply Corp. (D)
Newstech Co. (Div. of Rovinter Inc.) (D)
Nikon Inc./Electronic Imaging Department (M,D)
NuArc Co. Inc. (M)
Nutek Inc. (D)
Sinclair Imaging Inc. (D)
Western LithoTech (M)

Photography: Digital/Electronic Cameras
Ad Vantage Computer Systems Inc. (S)
Arrow Printing Co. (S)
Auto-Grafica Corp. (D)
Computer Tree (D)
DayStar Digital Inc. (M)
LogEtronics Corp. (M,D)
Mantis Computer Parts Inc. (D)
Midwest Publishers Supply Co. (D)
National Graphic Supply Corp. (D)
Newstech Co. (Div. of Rovinter Inc.) (D)
Nikon Inc./Electronic Imaging Department (M,D)
Photo Systems Inc. (D)
Pitman Photo Supply (D)
PrePRESS DIRECT (D)
Scantronix (D)
SCREEN (USA) (M)
T/One Inc. (M,D)

Photostat: Chemicals
Allstates Litho Plate Corp. (D)
Anitec (M)
BESCO Graphic Systems Corp. (D)
A.B. Dick Co. (M)
A.B. Dick Co. (Itek Graphix Div.) (M)
Eastman Kodak/Professional Printing & Publishing Imaging (M)
GraphLine Inc. (D)
National Graphic Supply Corp. (D)
Newstech Co. (Div. of Rovinter Inc.) (D)

Photostat: Machines
BESCO Graphic Systems Corp. (D)
Creative Specialty Products Inc. (D,S)
A.B. Dick Co. (M)
A.B. Dick Co. (Itek Graphix Div.) (M)
Megasys International Inc. (M)
National Graphic Supply Corp. (D)
Newstech Co. (Div. of Rovinter Inc.) (D)

Photostat: Paper
Allstates Litho Plate Corp. (D)
Anitec (M)
Avenor Inc. (M)
BESCO Graphic Systems Corp. (D)
A.B. Dick Co. (M)
A.B. Dick Co. (Itek Graphix Div.) (M)
Georgia-Pacific Corp. (M)
GraphLine Inc. (D)
Mitchell's World Finest Paper Delivery (S)
National Graphic Supply Corp. (D)
Newstech Co. (Div. of Rovinter Inc.) (D)
Rainy River Forest Products Inc. (M)
S.D. Warren (M)
Will-Pemco Inc. (M)

Phototypesetting Computer Programs
Advanced Technical Solutions (D)
Arrow Printing Co. (S)
Auto-Grafica Corp. (D)
Autologic Information International Inc. (M)
Computer Tree (D)
Concept Publishing Systems (M)
CPS Technologies Inc. (M,D)
Durbin Associates (S)
Foley, Torregiani & Associates, Inc. (D)
Lazer-fare Media Services Ltd. (D,S)
Monotype Systems Inc. (M,D,S)
Newstech Co. (Div. of Rovinter Inc.) (D)
NGCP/Laser Concepts (D)
Penta Software Inc. (S)
Bob Weber Inc. (S)

Phototypesetting Fonts
Agfa Division, Bayer Inc. (M,D)
Arrow Printing Co. (S)
Auto-Grafica Corp. (D)
Autologic Inc. (Subsidiary of Volt Info. Svc.) (M)
CPS Technologies Inc. (D)
A.B. Dick Co. (Itek Graphix Div.) (M)
GraphLine Inc. (D)
Lazer-fare Media Services Ltd. (D,S)
Linotype-Hell Co. (M)
Newstech Co. (Div. of Rovinter Inc.) (D)
NGCP/Laser Concepts (D)
PrePRESS DIRECT (D)
System Facilities Inc. (D)
ULTRE (Div. of Linotype-Hell Co.) (M,D,S)
Bob Weber Inc. (D)

Phototypesetting Interface Equipment (See also Interfaces)
Advanced Technical Solutions (D)
Agfa Division, Bayer Inc. (M,D)
Arrow Printing Co. (S)
Auto-Grafica Corp. (D)
Autologic Information International Inc. (M,D)
CompuText Inc. (M)
CPS Technologies Inc. (M,D)
Crosfield Electronic Ltd. (M)
DuPont Co. (D)
Durbin Associates (S)
Foley, Torregiani & Associates, Inc. (D)
Harris Publishing Systems Corp. (S)
Hyphen Inc. (D)
Lazer-fare Media Services Ltd. (D,S)
Monotype Systems Inc. (M,D,S)
Newstech Co. (Div. of Rovinter Inc.) (D)
Penta Software Inc. (S)
ULTRE (Div. of Linotype-Hell Co.) (M,D,S)
Bob Weber Inc. (D)
Xitron Inc. (S)

Picture Scalers
Midwest Publishers Supply Co. (D)

Pin Register Systems
Accurate Step & Repeat System Inc. (M)
Allpress Equipment Inc. (D)
ARC/Doyle Machinery Corp. (M)
ByChrome Co. (M)

Pitman Photo Supply
THE PHOTOGRAPHIC WAREHOUSE

- Specializing in Serving the Needs of the Newspaper and Wire Service Industry
- Nationwide supplier
- Rush and Overnight Delivery Our Specialty
- Competitive Prices

NATIONAL 1-800-252-3008
FAX 1-800-835-3995
MIAMI 305-256-9558

8650 S.W. 132nd Street • Miami, FL 33156-6507

Copyright ©1996 by the Editor & Publisher Co.

VI-38 Equipment, supplies, services

Central Graphics (D)
Duarte Register Systems Inc. (M)
Florida Printing Equipment and Supply (D)
K & F/Printing Systems International (M)
Konica Imaging USA Inc. (M)
Midwest Publishers Supply Co. (D)
National Graphic Supply Co. (D)
Newstech Co. (Div. of Rovinter Inc.) (D)
Poolside Lithographic Supply Inc. (D)
SCREEN (USA) (D)
Solna Web USA Inc. (D)
Stoesser Register Systems (M)
Ternes Register System (M)
Western LithoTech (M)

Plastic Folders
Automated Newsstand (D)
Midwest Publishers Supply Co. (D)
National Graphic Supply Corp. (D)
P & E Inc. (M)

Plastic Plate-Making Systems
Apex Machine Co. (M)
The Master Group (M)
Napp Systems Inc. (M)
P & E Inc. (M)

Plate Bending Systems
Allpress Equipment Inc. (D)
Burgess Industries Inc. (M)
K & F/Printing Systems International (M)
National Graphic Supply Corp. (D)
Newstech Co. (Div. of Rovinter Inc.) (D)
Solna Web USA Inc. (D)
Tasope Co. (M)
Western LithoTech (M)
World Net & Associates Inc. (D)

Plate Cleaners
Allstates Litho Plate Corp. (D)
Apex Machine Co. (D)
Berkshire/Westwood Graphics Group Inc. (M)
BESCO Graphic Systems Corp. (D)
Dynalith Inc. (S)
Graphic Arts Technical & Consulting Services (M)
GraphLine Inc. (D)
Midwest Publishers Supply Co. (D)
National Graphic Supply Corp. (D)
Newstech Co. (Div. of Rovinter Inc.) (D)
Superior Lithoplate of Indiana Inc. (D)
Support Products Inc. (D)
Varn International (M)
Western LithoTech (M)

Plate Coating Machines
Allpress Equipment Inc. (D)
Allstates Litho Plate Corp. (D)
American Litho Inc. (D)
BESCO Graphic Systems Corp. (D)
Florida Printing Equipment and Supply (D)
National Machine (M)
Newstech Co. (Div. of Rovinter Inc.) (D)
Star International Corp. (D)
Tasope Co. (M)
Western LithoTech (M)
Western Lithotech (M)

Plate Curvers
Apex Machine Co. (M)
Newstech Co. (Div. of Rovinter Inc.) (D)
Stoesser Register Systems (M)
Ternes Register System (M)
Western Lithotech (M)

Plate Exposure Units
Allpress Equipment Inc. (D)
Amergraph Corp. (M)
BASF Corp. (M,D)
Berkshire/Westwood Graphics Group Inc. (D)
BESCO Graphic Systems Corp. (D)
Douthitt Corp. (M)
Dynalith Inc. (D)
Gerber Systems Corp. (M)
GraphLine Inc. (D)
Konica Imaging USA Inc. (D)
Martin Yale Inc. (M)
Louis Melind Co. (M)
Napp Systems Inc. (M)
National Graphic Supply Co. (D)
National Machine (M)
Newstech Co. (Div. of Rovinter Inc.) (D)
NuArc Co. Inc. (M)
Pitman Co. (D)
Poolside Lithographic Supply Inc. (D)
Roconex Corp. (M)
Star International Corp. (D)
Stoesser Register Systems (M)

Tasope Co. (M)
Three Sigma (S)
Western LithoTech (M)

Plate Finishing
Allstates Litho Plate Corp. (D)
BASF Corp. (M,D)
BESCO Graphic Systems Corp. (D)
Graphic Arts Technical & Consulting Services (M)
Newstech Co. (Div. of Rovinter Inc.) (D)
Steel City Corp./Motor Route Supplies (M)
Western LithoTech (M)

Plate Mounting & Register Systems
Apex Machine Co. (D)
Arrow Printing Co. (S)
BASF Corp. (M,D)
BESCO Graphic Systems Corp. (D)
Burgess Industries Inc. (M)
A.B. Dick Co. (M)
Duostat Co. (Affiliated with VGC Corp.) (D)
National Graphic Supply Corp. (D)
Newstech Co. (Div. of Rovinter Inc.) (D)
Robertson Press Machinery Co. Inc. (D)
Stoesser Register Systems (M)
Tech-Energy Co. (M,D,S)
Ternes Register System (M)
Western LithoTech (M)
Western Lithotech (M)
World Net & Associates Inc. (D)

Plate Processors
Allpress Equipment Inc. (D)
Allstates Litho Plate Corp. (D)
American Litho Inc. (D)
Anitec (M)
Anitec Printing Plates (M)
Auto-Grafica Corp. (D)
BASF Corp. (M,D)
Berkshire/Westwood Graphics Group Inc. (M,D)
BESCO Graphic Systems Corp. (D)
Citiplate Inc. (M)
A.B. Dick Co. (M)
Dynalith Inc. (M,D)
Eastman Kodak/Professional Printing & Publishing Imaging (M)
Florida Printing Equipment and Supply (D)
GraphLine Inc. (D)
Hercules Inc. (M)
Hoechst Printing Products North America (M)
K & F/Printing Systems International (M)
Napp Systems Inc. (M)
National Graphic Supply Corp. (D)
National Machine (M)
NB Finishing Inc. (S)
Newstech Co. (Div. of Rovinter Inc.) (D)
Pitman Co. (D)
Poolside Lithographic Supply Inc. (D)
Printware (M,D)
Richmond/Graphic Products Inc. (M)
Roconex Corp. (M)
Southern Lithoplate Inc. (M)
Star International Corp. (D)
Tasope Co. (M)
3M Printing & Publishing Systems Div. (M)
Warner Color Corp. (Therm-O-Scan Div.) (M)
Western LithoTech (M)

Plate Scanning Systems
Tobias Associates Inc. (M)

Platemakers: Direct
Advanced Technical Solutions (S)
Allsystems Go (D)
Apex Machine Co. (M)
Auto-Grafica Corp. (D)
BESCO Graphic Systems Corp. (D)
A.B. Dick Co. (M)
A.B. Dick Co. (Itek Graphix Div.) (M)
Donohue Inc. (M)
GraphLine Inc. (D)
The Master Group (M)
Newstech Co. (Div. of Rovinter Inc.) (D)
Polyfibron Technologies Inc. (M)
PrePRESS DIRECT (D)
PrePRESS SOLUTIONS (M)
Western LithoTech (M)

Platemakers: Flexographic
Amergraph Corp. (M)
Apex Machine Co. (M)
BASF Corp. (M,D)
Douthitt Corp. (M)
The Master Group (M)
Louis Melind Co. (M)
Napp Systems Inc. (M)

National Machine (M)
Polyfibron Technologies Inc. (M)

Platemakers: Laser (Includes Laser Plate Systems)
Autologic Inc. (Subsidiary of Volt Info. Svc.) (M)
Axelrod, Norman N., Assoc./Optical, Laser & Vision Systems (S)
Computer Tree (D)
CPS Technologies Inc. (D)
Crosfield Electronic Ltd. (M)
DuPont Co. (D)
Gerber Systems Corp. (M)
Graphic Enterprises of Ohio Inc. (M)
Graphic Publishing Systems Inc. (M)
GraphLine Inc. (D)
Monotype Systems Inc. (M,D,S)
Newstech Co. (Div. of Rovinter Inc.) (D)
NGCP/Laser Concepts (M)
PrePRESS DIRECT (D)
PrePRESS SOLUTIONS (M)
Printware (M,D)
Three Sigma (S)
Wedge Computer Systems (S)
Western LithoTech (D)

Platemakers: Letterpress
Amergraph Corp. (M)
Apex Machine Co. (M)
Arrow Printing Co. (S)
BASF Corp. (M,D)
Citiplate Inc. (M)
A.B. Dick Co. (M)
Duostat Co. (Affiliated with VGC Corp.) (D)
Hercules Inc. (M)
The Master Group (M)
Napp Systems Inc. (M)
National Machine (M)
Polyfibron Technologies Inc. (M)
Printing Equipment Specialists Inc. (S)
Sterling Type Foundry (M)

Platemakers: Offset
Allpress Equipment Inc. (D)
Arrow Printing Co. (S)
Berkshire/Westwood Graphics Group Inc. (D)
Douthitt Corp. (M)
Duostat Co. (Affiliated with VGC Corp.) (D)
Dynalith Inc. (D)
Graphic Arts Technical & Consulting Services (D)
GraphLine Inc. (D)
Ingenuity Inc. (M,D)
K & F/Printing Systems International (M)
Louis Melind Co. (M)
National Graphic Supply Corp. (D)
NENSCO (M)
Newstech Co. (Div. of Rovinter Inc.) (D)
Poolside Lithographic Supply Inc. (D)
PrePRESS DIRECT (D)
Printware (M)
Roconex Corp. (M)
SCREEN (USA) (M)
Solna Web USA Inc. (M)
Star International Corp. (D)
Tasope Co. (M)
Tech-Energy Co. (D,S)
Western LithoTech (M)

Plates: Flexographic
Anitec (M)
Apex Machine Co. (M)
BASF Corp. (M,D)
Duostat Co. (Affiliated with VGC Corp.) (D)
The Master Group (M)
Louis Melind Co. (M)
Napp Systems Inc. (M)
Pitman Co. (D)
Polyfibron Technologies Inc. (M)
Printing Equipment Specialists Inc. (S)

Plates: Letterpress
Apex Machine Co. (M)
Arrow Printing Co. (S)
BASF Corp. (M,D)
BESCO Graphic Systems Corp. (D)
Citiplate Inc. (M)
Duostat Co. (Affiliated with VGC Corp.) (D)
Hercules Inc. (M)
The Master Group (M)
Napp Systems Inc. (M)
Pitman Co. (D)
Polychrome Corp. (M)
Polyfibron Technologies Inc. (M)

Plates: Offset
Allstates Litho Plate Corp. (D)
American Litho Inc. (M)
Anitec (M)
Anitec Printing Plates (M)
Apex Machine Co. (M)
Arrow Printing Co. (S)

Berkshire/Westwood Graphics Group Inc. (D)
BESCO Graphic Systems Corp. (D)
ByChrome Co. (D)
Citiplate Inc. (M)
A.B. Dick Co. (M,D)
A.B. Dick Co. (Itek Graphix Div.) (M)
Dynalith Inc. (D)
Eastman Kodak/Professional Printing & Publishing Imaging (M)
Florida Printing Equipment and Supply (D)
Global Graphics Inc. (D)
Graphic Arts Technical & Consulting Services (D)
GraphLine Inc. (D)
GSP Inc. (D)
Hoechst Printing Products North America (M)
Imperial Metal & Chemical Co. (Div. of Dupont) (M,D)
London Litho Aluminum Co. Inc. (D)
The Master Group (M)
National Graphic Supply Corp. (D)
NENSCO (M)
Newstech Co. (Div. of Rovinter Inc.) (D)
PAGE (S)
Pitman Co. (D)
Polychrome Corp. (M)
Poolside Lithographic Supply Inc. (D)
Printing Equipment Specialists Inc. (S)
Printware (M,D)
Rendic International (M)
Southern Lithoplate Inc. (M)
Star International Corp. (D)
Superior Lithoplate of Indiana Inc. (M)
Tech-Energy Co. (D,S)
3M Printing & Publishing Systems Div. (M)
Western LithoTech (M)

Portable Terminals
Ad-Star/Publishing Technologies (M,D)
American Data Voice Systems (D,S)
Computer Devices Inc. (D)
CompuText Inc. (D)
CPS Technologies Inc. (D)
Duostat Co. (Affiliated with VGC Corp.) (D)
Freedom System Integrators (D)
M. Golda Engineering (S)
Harris Corp. (Corporate Headquaters) (D)
IC Systems Solutions (D,S)
Linotype-Hell Co. (D,S)
Midwest Publishers Supply Co. (D)
Newstech Co. (Div. of Rovinter Inc.) (D)

Postscript Fonts
Computer Tree (D)
Freedom System Integrators (D)
GraphLine Inc. (D)
Newstech Co. (Div. of Rovinter Inc.) (D)
PrePRESS DIRECT (D)
PrePRESS SOLUTIONS (M)

Prepress Color Proofing Systems (See also Color Proofing)
All Systems Color Inc. (D)
ARC/Doyle Machinery Corp. (M)
Arrow Printing Co. (S)
Auto-Grafica Corp. (D)
BESCO Graphic Systems Corp. (D)
M.W. Burke & Associates Inc. (S)
Caprock Developments Inc. (M,D)
CCI Europe (M)
CNI Corp. (D)
Computer Tree (D)
Consolidated International Corp. (M)
Crosfield Electronic Ltd. (M)
Direct Reproduction Corp. (M)
Duostat Co. (Affiliated with VGC Corp.) (D)
DuPont Co. (D)
Eastman Kodak/Professional Printing & Publishing Imaging (M)
GraphLine Inc. (D)
Hoechst Printing Products North America (M)
International Memory Products of Illinois Inc. (D)
Midwest Publishers Supply Co. (D)
National Graphic Supply Corp. (D)
Newstech Co. (Div. of Rovinter Inc.) (D)
NuArc Co. Inc. (M)
Nutek Inc. (D)
Pantone Inc. (S)
Polychrome Corp. (D)
PrePRESS DIRECT (D)
PrePRESS SOLUTIONS (M)
Sinclair Imaging Inc. (D)
3M Printing & Publishing Systems Div. (M)
Total Systems Engineering Inc. (S)
Truproof Ltd. (D)
Western LithoTech (M)
Western Lithotech (M)

Preprint, Service & Production
Arrow Printing Co. (S)
The Directory Center (S)
RR Donnelley & Sons Co. (M)

Copyright ©1996 by the Editor & Publisher Co.

Equipment, supplies, services VI-39

Duostat Co. (Affiliated with VGC Corp.) (D)
Newstech Co. (Div. of Rovinter Inc.) (D)
Quebecor Printing Providence (M)
Tel-Aire Publications Inc. (M)
Total Systems Engineering Inc. (S)

Press Accessories, Parts & Supplies
Aaro Roller Corp. (M)
Allpress Equipment Inc. (D)
ALTA Graphics Inc. (S)
Application Engineering Corp. (M)
Bruno Unger USA (D)
Central Graphics (M)
Dauphin Graphic Machines Inc. (M,D,S)
Diamond Roller Corp. (M,D,S)
Global Graphics Inc. (D)
Graphic Printing Roller Ltd. (M)
Graphic System Services (M,D,S)
GTI Graphic Technology Inc. (M)
Inland Graphics International L.C. (D)
Martin Automatic Inc. (M)
Master Flo Technology (M)
Mid Atlantic Lighting (M)
Midwest Publishers Supply Co. (D)
Miracle Industries Inc. (M)
NENSCO (D)
Newstech Co. (Div. of Rovinter Inc.) (D)
Oxy-Dry Corp. (M)
PAGE (S)
Quality Components Corp. (M)
Moss Reck & Associates Inc. (M)
Rockwell Graphic Systems (M)
R T P Technical Specialists (S)
Solna Web USA Inc. (M)
Star International Corp. (D)
Tech-Energy Co. (D,S)
Ternes Register System (M)
Varn International (M)
Veratec Div. (M)
Web Tapes Inc. (S)
Western Printing Machinery (M)

Press Control Systems
ABB Process Automation Inc.(Printing Systems Div.) (D,S)
Arco Engineering Inc. (Newspaper Div.) (M,D,S)
Axelrod, Norman N., Assoc./Optical, Laser & Vision Systems (S)
Baldwin Web Controls (Div./Subsidiary Baldwin Technology) (M)
Allen Bradley Co. (Motion Control Div.) (M)
Controls Group Inc. (M)
Core-Concepts (S)
Crosfield Electronic Ltd. (M)
Duostat Co. (Affiliated with VGC Corp.) (D)
DuPont Co. (D)
The Electric Tachometer Corp. (M,D)
Global Graphics Inc. (D)
George R Hall Inc. (D)
Harris Corp. (Corporate Headquaters) (M,D)
Heidelberg Harris Inc. (M)
Kaim & Associates Int'l. Marketing Inc. (D)
Koenig & Bauer- Albert AG (KBA) (M)
MAH Machine Co. Inc. (S)
Miracle Industries Inc. (M)
National Graphic Sales Inc. (M)
NCS Inc. (M)
Parsons Main Inc. (S)
Perretta Graphics Corp. (M)
Robertson Press Machinery Co. Inc. (D)
Rockwell Graphic Systems (M)
R T P Technical Specialists (S)
Solna Web USA Inc. (M)
William C. Spells (RTP Technical Specialists) (D,S)
Standard Electric and Engineering Co. (M,D,S)
Support Systems International Corp. (M)
Tech-Energy Co. (D,S)
Web Printing Controls/WPC Machinery Corp. (M)
Web Tapes Inc. (S)
Wesco Graphics (S)
World Net & Associates Inc. (S)
WPC Machinery Corp. (D)

Press Data Accumulators
Controls Group Inc. (M)
The Electric Tachometer Corp. (M,D)
Pressroom Products Inc. (M)
Solna Web USA Inc. (M)

Press Engineers
ALTA Graphics Inc. (S)
Arrow Printing Co. (S)
Carlson Design/Construct Corp. (S)
Continental Printing Machinery (S)
Duostat Co. (Affiliated with VGC Corp.) (D)
George R Hall Inc. (D)
Heidelberg Harris Inc. (M)
Kaim & Associates Int'l. Marketing Inc. (D)

MAH Machine Co. Inc. (M,S)
Miracle Industries Inc. (M)
Mountain States Inc. (S)
Network Industrial Services Inc. (D)
Robertson Press Machinery Co. Inc. (D)
Royal Press Parts Inc. (M)
R T P Technical Specialists (S)
William C. Spells (RTP Technical Specialists) (D,S)
Tech-Energy Co. (S)
Web Tapes Inc. (S)
Wesco Graphics (S)
World Net & Associates Inc. (S)
WPC Machinery Corp. (M,S)

Press Rebuilding
Allpress Equipment Inc. (D)
ALTA Graphics Inc. (S)
Len Brown & Sons Inc. (M)
Egenolf Machine Inc. (Egenolf Contracting & Rigging) (S)
Global Graphics Inc. (D)
George R Hall Inc. (M)
Inland Newspaper Machinery Corp. (S)
King Press Corp. (M)
Network Industrial Services Inc. (D)
Rockwell Graphic Systems (M)
Royal Press Parts Inc. (M)
R T P Technical Specialists (S)
Solna Web USA Inc. (M)
World Net & Associates Inc. (S)

Press Repairs
Allpress Equipment Inc. (D)
Len Brown & Sons Inc. (M)
Egenolf Machine Inc. (Egenolf Contracting & Rigging) (S)
Global Graphics Inc. (D)
George R Hall Inc. (M)
King Press Corp. (M)
Network Industrial Services Inc. (D)
Rockwell Graphic Systems (M)
MAH Machine Co. Inc. (S)
Royal Press Parts Inc. (M)
R T P Technical Specialists (S)
World Net & Associates Inc. (S)

Presses: DiLitho
Global Press Sales Inc. (D)
Graphic Enterprises (S)
Northeast Industries Inc. (D)
Pacific Newspaper Services Inc. (S)
Press-Tec Inc. (S)
Press and Bindery Systems Inc. (D)
R T P Technical Specialists (S)

Presses: Flexographic
ALTA Graphics Inc. (S)
Apex Machine Co. (M)
Cerutti North America (M)
Flexo Printing Equipment Corp. (D)
Global Press Sales Inc. (D)
Graphic Enterprises (S)
KBA-Motter Corp. (Koenig & Bauer-Albert Group) (M)
Kidder Inc. (M)
Koenig & Bauer- Albert AG (KBA) (M)
MAH Machine Co. Inc. (S)
MAN Roland Inc. (Web Press Div.) (M)
Manassy Precision Corp. (M)
Northeast Industries Inc. (S)
Pacific Newspaper Services Inc. (S)
Press-Tec Inc. (S)
Press and Bindery Systems Inc. (D)
Publishers Equipment Corp. (M)
Rockwell Graphic Systems (M)
R T P Technical Specialists (S)
William C. Spells (RTP Technical Specialists) (S)
Toshiba Machine Co. America (M)
Windmoeller and Hoelscher Corp./Flexo Newspaper Press Group (M)

Presses: Letterpress
ALTA Graphics Inc. (S)
Apex Machine Co. (M)
Arrow Printing Co. (S)
Bell Camp Inc. (S)
Global Press Sales Inc. (D)
Graphic Enterprises (S)
MAH Machine Co. Inc. (S)
Manassy Precision Corp. (M)
Northeast Industries Inc. (D)
Pacific Newspaper Services Inc. (S)
Pearce Inc. (M)
Press-Tec Inc. (S)
Printing Equipment Specialists Inc. (S)
Rockwell Graphic Systems (M)
R T P Technical Specialists (S)
William C. Spells (RTP Technical Specialists) (D,S)
Sterling Type Foundry (S)
Tech-Energy Co. (D,S)
Todd Machinery (S)

Presses: Offset
Allpress Equipment Inc. (D)
ALTA Graphics Inc. (S)
American Graphics L.P. (M,D)
Apex Machine Co. (M)
Arrow Printing Co. (S)
Bell Camp Inc. (S)
Len Brown & Sons Inc. (D)
Central Graphics (D)
Consolidated International Corp. (M)
Dauphin Graphic Machines Inc. (M,D,S)
Diamond Roller Corp. (M,D,S)
A.B. Dick Co. (M,D)
Didde Web Press (M)
Durbin Associates (S)
EGS Americas Inc. (M)
Florida Printing Equipment and Supply (D)
Frankton Press Inc. (S)
Global Graphics Inc. (D)
Global Press Sales Inc. (D)
Gowe Printing Co. (S)
Grafica Worldwide Inc. (S)
Grafitek International (M)
Graphic Enterprises (S)
GSP Inc. (D)
Hamada of America Inc. (M)
Heidelberg Harris Inc. (M)
Heidelberg USA (D,S)
Inland Graphics International L.C. (D)
Inland Newspaper Machinery Corp. (S)
Inter-Continental Web Inc. (D)
KBA-Motter Corp. (Koenig & Bauer-Albert Group) (M)
King Press Corp. (M)
Koenig & Bauer- Albert AG (KBA) (M)
Komori America Corp. (M)
MAH Machine Co. Inc. (S)
MAN Roland Inc. (Web Press Div.) (M)
Manassy Precision Corp. (M)
Miracle Industries Inc. (M)
Mitsubishi Heavy Industries Ltd. (MLP USA Inc.) (M)
Mitsubishi Lithographic Presses USA Inc. (M)
Mountain States Inc. (S)
Network Industrial Services Inc. (D)
Newman International (D)
Newstech Co. (Div. of Rovinter Inc.) (D)
Northeast Industries Inc. (D)
Offset Web Sales Inc. (D,S)
ONE Corp. (D)
Pacific Newspaper Services Inc. (S)
Press-Tec Inc. (S)
Press and Bindery Systems Inc. (D)
Printing Press Services Inc. (M,S)
Provan Associates Inc. (S)
Publishers Equipment Corp. (M)
Rendic International (D)
Resource Net International (D)
Rockwell Graphic Systems (M)
Rockwell Graphic Systems (M)
R T P Technical Specialists (S)
Lee Smith Industries (D)
Solna Web USA Inc. (M)
William C. Spells (RTP Technical Specialists) (D,S)
Tech-Energy Co. (D,S)
Tecnigraph T.G.I. International Inc. (M)
TKS (USA) Inc. (M,D)
Todd Machinery (S)
Toshiba Machine Co. America (M)
Web Press Corp. (M)
Webeq International Inc. (S)
Wesco Graphics (S)
Western Web Sales (D)
Wifag (D)
World Net & Associates Inc. (M)

Presses: Rotogravure
Apex Machine Co. (M)
Bell Camp Inc. (S)
Cerutti North America (M)
Continental Printing Machinery (S)
Durbin Associates (S)
EGS Americas Inc. (M)
Grafitek International (M)
Graphic Enterprises (S)
Heidelberg USA (D)
KBA-Motter Corp. (Koenig & Bauer-Albert Group) (M)
Kidder Inc. (S)
Koenig & Bauer- Albert AG (KBA) (M)
MAH Machine Co. Inc. (S)
MAN Roland Inc. (Web Press Div.) (M)
MAN Roland/Aston Div. (M)
Manassy Precision Corp. (M)
Mountain States Inc. (S)
News-Type Service (S)
Offset Web Sales Inc. (S)

Press-Tec Inc. (S)
Press and Bindery Systems Inc. (D)
Printing Equipment Specialists Inc. (S)
Quebecor Printing Providence (M)
Robertson Press Machinery Co. Inc. (D)
William C. Spells (RTP Technical Specialists) (D,S)
Toshiba Machine Co. America (M)
Webeq International Inc. (S)
Windmoeller and Hoelscher Corp./Flexo Newspaper Press Group (M)

Processors: Diffusion Transfer
Allpress Equipment Inc. (D)
Allstates Litho Plate Corp. (D)
Berkshire/Westwood Graphics Group Inc. (D)
BESCO Graphic Systems Corp. (D)
Craftsmen Machinery Co./Graphic Export Corp. (D)
Durbin Associates (S)
Konica Imaging USA Inc. (D)
LogEtronics Corp. (M,D)
Midwest Publishers Supply Co. (D)
National Graphic Supply Corp. (D)
NENSCO (D)
Newstech Co. (Div. of Rovinter Inc.) (D)
NuArc Co. Inc. (D)
PAGE (S)
PrePRESS DIRECT (D)
Richmond/Graphic Products Inc. (D)

Processors: Film & Paper
Agfa Division, Bayer Inc. (M,D)
Allpress Equipment Inc. (D)
Allstates Litho Plate Corp. (D)
American Ink Jet Corp. (M)
Arrow Printing Co. (S)
Auto-Grafica Corp. (D)
Bender Machine Inc. (S)
Berkshire/Westwood Graphics Group Inc. (D)
BESCO Graphic Systems Corp. (D)
Byers Industries Inc. (M)
Durbin Associates (S)
Eastman Kodak/Professional Printing & Publishing Imaging (M)
Florida Printing Equipment and Supply (D)
Frankton Press Inc. (S)
Hercules Inc. (M)
Konica Imaging USA Inc. (D)
Kreonite Inc. (M)
Linotype-Hell Co. (D)
LogEtronics Corp. (M,D)
London Litho Aluminum Co. Inc. (D)
Mohr Enterprise (Div. of Mohr Lino-Saw Co.) (D)
Monotype Systems Inc. (D,S)
National Graphic Supply Corp. (D)
NENSCO (D)
Newstech Co. (Div. of Rovinter Inc.) (D)
Nutek Inc. (D)
PAGE (S)
Portage Newspaper Supply Co. (M)
Portfolios Unlimited Inc. (D,S)
PrePRESS DIRECT (D)
Richmond/Graphic Products Inc. (M)
SCREEN (USA) (M)
Tasope Co. (M)
Total Systems Engineering Inc. (S)
Bob Weber Inc. (D)

Production Control Systems (See also Press Control Systems)
ABB Process Automation Inc.(Printing Systems Div.) (D,S)
Advanced Technical Solutions (M)
Axelrod, Norman N., Assoc./Optical, Laser & Vision Systems (M,S)
Carlson Design/Construct Corp. (S)
Denex Inc. (M,D)
Fleming Enterprises (M)
GMA Inc. (M)
Master Flo Technology (M)
NCS Inc. (M)
Newstech Co. (Div. of Rovinter Inc.) (D)
Parsons Main Inc. (S)
Quipp System Inc. (S)
R T P Technical Specialists (S)
William C. Spells (RTP Technical Specialists) (D,S)
Standard Electric and Engineering Co. (M,D,S)
Standlee and Associates Inc. (M,D,S)
Support Systems International Corp. (M)

Promotion Services
ANI Promotions/DBA (D)
Arrow Printing Co. (S)
Brite (M)

VI-40 Equipment, supplies, services

Derus Media Service Inc./Editorial Pace (D)
Kevin Brian Kamen & Co. (S)
McClure Media Marketing Motivation Co. (S)
Mo-Money Associates Inc. (M,D,S)
National Research Bureau (S)
Promotion Sources (S)
SCA Promotions Inc. (S)
Tel-Aire Publications Inc. (M,D)
Tele-Publishing Inc. (S)
Value Checks (S)

Proofing Systems
Ad Vantage Computer Systems Inc. (S)
Advanced Technical Solutions (S)
ARC/Doyle Machinery Corp. (M)
Arrow Printing Co. (S)
Auto-Grafica Corp. (D)
BESCO Graphic Systems Corp. (S)
Birmy Graphics Corp. (D)
Burgess Industries Inc. (M)
Computer Tree (D)
Douthitt Corp. (M)
Eastman Kodak/Professional Printing & Publishing Imaging (M)
Graphic Enterprises of Ohio Inc. (M)
Konica Imaging USA Inc. (M)
London Litho Aluminum Co. Inc. (D)
Macbeth, Div. of Kollmorgen Inst. Corp. (M)
Midwest Publishers Supply Co. (D)
Monotype Systems Inc. (D,S)
N & L Enterprises Inc. (D)
National Graphic Supply Corp. (D)
National Research Bureau (D)
NENSCO (D)
Newstech Co. (Div. of Rovinter Inc.) (D)
NGCP/Laser Concepts (D)
NuArc Co. Inc. (D)
Pantone Inc. (S)
Scandinavian PC Systems Inc. (M,D)
SCREEN (USA) (M)
Bob Weber Inc. (D)
Western LithoTech (M)
Willow Six Technologies (M)

Publishing Systems (See also Software)
Ad-Star/Publishing Technologies (M,D)
Advanced Technical Solutions (S)
Agfa Division, Bayer Inc. (M)
Auto-Grafica Corp. (D)
Autologic Inc. (Subsidiary of Volt Info. Svc.) (M)
Autologic Information International Inc. (M)
Bell & Howell (M,D,S)
Black Hills Publishers Inc. (S)
CNI Corp. (M,D)
Computer Tree (D)
Computerease Software Inc. (M)
CompuText Inc. (D)
Concept Publishing Systems (M)
Copley Computer Services (S)
Crosfield Electronic Ltd. (D)
Dewar Information Systems Corp. (S)
Digital Technology International (M)
DuPont Co. (D)
Durbin Associates (S)
Flying Color Graphics (M)
Freedom System Integrators (M)
Fry Communications (M)
Harris Corp. (Corporate Headquaters) (D)
Harris Publishing Systems Corp. (M)
Hyphen Inc. (D)
International Memory Products of Illinois Inc. (D)
Linotype-Hell Co. (M)
National Research Bureau (D)
Newstech Co. (Div. of Rovinter Inc.) (D)
NGCP/Laser Concepts (D)
Omni Industry (Div. of Global Turnkey Systems Inc.) (M,D,S)
Ottaway Newspaper (S)
Penta Software Inc. (S)
Quickwire (M,D)
Scandinavian PC Systems Inc. (M,D)
Stauffer Media Systems (D,S)
Sysdeco U.S. (M,D,S)
TeleTypesetting Co. (S)
Vision Data Equipment Corp. (M)
West Coast Computer Systems/Newspaper Technologies (M,D)

Pumps (Air, Ink, Vacuum)
ALTA Graphics Inc. (S)
Baumfolder Corp. (M)
BESCO Graphic Systems Corp. (D)
Busch Inc. (M)
Carlson Design/Construct Corp. (S)
Douthitt Corp. (M,D)
Florida Printing Equipment and Supply (D)
Jimmy R. Fox, Mail Room Consultant (S)
Graphic System Services (D,S)
Ingersoll-Rand-Aro Fluid Product Div. (M)
Ingersoll-Rand Corp./Power Tool & Hoist Div. (M)
LiftSafe Systems Inc. (M,D)
Lincoln Industrial (M)
Master Flo Technology (M)
The Morrison Group/Morrison Ink (D)
Pacific Newspaper Services Inc. (D,S)
Parsons Main Inc. (S)
Ryco Graphic Manufacturing Inc. (M,D)
Semler Industries Inc. (Graphic Arts Products Div.) (D)
Tech-Energy Co. (D)

Punching Equipment
Arrow Printing Co. (S)
BESCO Graphic Systems Corp. (D)
A.B. Dick Co. (M)
Duostat Co. (Affiliated with VGC Corp.) (D)
Monotype Systems Inc. (D,S)
Newstech Co. (Div. of Rovinter Inc.) (D)
Rosback Co. (M,D)
SCREEN (USA) (M)
Stoesser Register Systems (M)
Tech-Energy Co. (D)
Western LithoTech (M)
Western Lithotech (M)
Western Printing Machinery (M)

Rack Display Cards
Automated Newsstand (D)

Raster Image Processors
Arri Systems Inc. (D)
Auto-Grafica Corp. (D)
Autologic Inc. (Subsidiary of Volt Info. Svc.) (M)
Autologic Information International Inc. (M,D)
Berkshire/Westwood Graphics Group Inc. (D)
Duostat Co. (Affiliated with VGC Corp.) (D)
Graphic Enterprises of Ohio Inc. (M)
Graphic Publishing Systems Inc. (M)
GraphLine Inc. (M)
Konica Imaging USA Inc. (D)
Lazer-fare Media Services Ltd. (M)
Monotype Systems Inc. (M,D)
National Graphic Supply Corp. (D)
Newstech Co. (Div. of Rovinter Inc.) (D)
PrePRESS DIRECT (M)
PrePRESS SOLUTIONS (M)
SCREEN (USA) (M)
Three Sigma (S)
Total Systems Engineering Inc. (S)
Bob Weber Inc. (D,S)
Xitron Inc. (D)

Recirculators
Application Engineering Corp. (M)
Byers Industries Inc. (M)
Duostat Co. (Affiliated with VGC Corp.) (D)
Konica Imaging USA Inc. (D)
Master Flo Technology (M)
Network Industrial Services Inc. (M)
Pressroom Products Inc. (M)
Printers' Service (M)
Ryco Graphic Manufacturing Inc. (M,D)
Tech-Energy Co. (D,S)
Bob Weber Inc. (D,S)
Wesco Graphics (S)

Recycling Newsprint
Atlantic Packaging Products Ltd. (S)

Reel & Tensions (See also Web Guides)
Advanced Graphic Systems (KAIM) (M)
ALTA Graphics Inc. (S)
Arco Engineering Inc. (Newspaper Div.) (M,D,S)
Controls Group Inc. (M)
Duostat Co. (Affiliated with VGC Corp.) (D)
Ebway Industries Inc. (Div. of Jardis Industries Inc.) (M)
Enkel Corp. (A Baldwin Technology Co.) (M)
Graphic System Services (M,D,S)
George R Hall Inc. (M)
Jardis Industries Inc. (Cary Equipment Div.) (M)
Johnstone Engineering & Machine Co. (M)
Kaim & Associates Int'l. Marketing Inc. (D)
Koenig & Bauer- Albert AG (KBA) (M)
MAH Machine Co. Inc. (S)
Manassy Precision Corp. (M)
M E G (US) Inc. (M)
Mitsubishi Heavy Industries Ltd. (MLP USA Inc.) (M)
Robertson Press Machinery Co. Inc. (M)
R T P Technical Specialists (S)
William C. Spells (RTP Technical Specialists) (M,D,S)
Tech-Energy Co. (D)
Tidland Corp. (M)
Web Tapes Inc. (S)
Wesco Graphics (S)
Will-Pemco Inc. (M)
World Net & Associates Inc. (D)
WPC Machinery Corp. (D)

Reels (Includes Paper Reels)
Advanced Graphic Systems (KAIM) (M)
ALTA Graphics Inc. (S)
Arco Engineering Inc. (Newspaper Div.) (S)
Controls Group Inc. (M)
Duostat Co. (Affiliated with VGC Corp.) (D)
Ebway Industries Inc. (Div. of Jardis Industries Inc.) (M)
Enkel Corp. (A Baldwin Technology Co.) (M)
George R Hall Inc. (M)
Jardis Industries Inc. (Cary Equipment Div.) (M)
Johnstone Engineering & Machine Co. (M)
MAH Machine Co. Inc. (S)
National Graphic Supply Co. (D)
R T P Technical Specialists (S)
William C. Spells (RTP Technical Specialists) (D,S)
Tech-Energy Co. (D)
Tidland Corp. (M)
Web Tapes Inc. (S)
Will-Pemco Inc. (M)
Wesco Graphics (S)
World Net & Associates Inc. (D)

Remanufactured Equipment
Allpress Equipment Inc. (D)
ALTA Graphics Inc. (S)
GMA Inc. (M)
Graphic Enterprises (D,S)
Graphic System Services (M,D,S)
George R Hall Inc. (D)
HFW Industries (M)
Ingenuity Inc. (M,D)
Network Industrial Services Inc. (D)
Newstech Co. (Div. of Rovinter Inc.) (D)
R T P Technical Specialists (S)
Wesco Graphics (S)
World Net & Associates Inc. (D)

Reproportioning Equipment (Photomechanical & Electronic)
CK Optical Co. Inc. (M,D)
Newstech Co. (Div. of Rovinter Inc.) (D)
NuArc Co. Inc. (M)
Pro Systems Inc. (M)
Roconex Corp. (M)

Research Studies
Advertising Checking Bureau (S)
Axelrod, Norman N., Assoc./Optical, Laser & Vision Systems (M,S)
Belden Associates (M)
Duostat Co. (Affiliated with VGC Corp.) (D)
Kevin Brian Kamen & Co. (S)
Market Opinion Research/Pace (M)
MTL Systems Inc. (S)
National Research Bureau (D)
Scarborough Associates (M)
Southwest Alabama Radio Resources Bureau (M,S)
Sysdeco U.S. (M,D,S)
VNU Business Information Services (M,D,S)
Gordon Wahls Co./Executive Search Consultants (S)

Rewinders
Ebway Industries Inc. (Div. of Jardis Industries Inc.) (M)
Enkel Corp. (A Baldwin Technology Co.) (M)
Florida Printing Equipment and Supply (D)
Johnstone Engineering & Machine Co. (M)
Keene Technology Inc. (KTI) (M)
Kidder Inc. (M)
Martin Automatic Inc. (M)
Quality Components Corp. (D)
Moss Reck & Associates Inc. (D)
Robertson Press Machinery Co. Inc. (M)
Rotoflex International (M)
Bill Rudder & Associates Inc. (M)
Stanford Div./MAN Roland Inc. (M)
Tech-Energy Co. (M,D)
Telesonic Packaging Corp. (M)
World Net & Associates Inc. (D)

Roll Cleaning Equipment
Duostat Co. (Affiliated with VGC Corp.) (D)
Kaim & Associates Int'l. Marketing Inc. (D)
Midwest Publishers Supply Co. (D)
Newstech Co. (Div. of Rovinter Inc.) (D)
Ryco Graphic Manufacturing Inc. (M)
Tech-Energy Co. (D)

Roll Converters
Norman X Guttman Inc. (M,D)
SunShine Paper Co. (M)

Roll Coverings
American Roller Co. (M)
Herco Graphic Products (D,Rollers,D)
Midwest Publishers Supply Co. (D)
Rotation Dynamics Corp. (M)
Stowe Woodward Co. (Div. BTR Paper Group) (M)

Roll Handling Equipment
Butler SMC. (M)
Capital Track Co. (M,D)
Carlson Design/Construct Corp. (S)
Cascade Corp. (M)
Dario Designs Inc. (S)
Ebway Industries Inc. (Div. of Jardis Industries Inc.) (M)
Enkel Corp. (A Baldwin Technology Co.) (M)
Fleming Enterprises (S)
Gerrard Ovalstrapping (M,D)
Greerco Corp. (M)
Jardis Industries Inc. (Cary Equipment Div.) (M)
Johnstone Engineering & Machine Co. (M)
Keene Technology Inc. (KTI) (M)
Koenig & Bauer- Albert AG (KBA) (M)
Lamb-Grays Harbor Co. (M)
Newstech Co. (Div. of Rovinter Inc.) (D)
Parsons Main Inc. (S)
Portage Newspaper Supply Co. (D)
Quality Components Corp. (M)
Republic Service Co. (D)
H.R. Slater Co. Inc. (M)
Tech-Energy Co. (M,D)
Tilt-Lock Inc. (M)
Jervis B. Webb Co. (M)
Wesco Graphics (S)
Will-Pemco Inc. (S)
XYonicz (M)

Roll Preparation Equipment
Koenig & Bauer- Albert AG (KBA) (M)
Mitsubishi Heavy Industries Ltd. (MLP USA Inc.) (M)
Newstech Co. (Div. of Rovinter Inc.) (D)

Roll Grinders
Bender Machine Inc. (S)
Capco Machinery Systems Inc. (M)
Fleming Enterprises (S)
Graphic Printing Roller Ltd. (M)
Mountain States Inc. (M)
Printing Press Services Inc. (M)
Tech-Energy Co. (D)

Roller Grinding Services
Aaro Roller Corp. (M)
Bender Machine Inc. (S)
Brodie System Inc. (M)
Len Brown & Sons Inc. (M)
Capco Machinery Systems Inc. (M)
Central Graphics (M)
Graphic Printing Roller Ltd. (M)
Norman X Guttman Inc. (M,D)
Hadronics (M,S)
MAH Machine Co. Inc. (S)
Miracle Industries Inc. (M)
Mountain States Inc. (M)
NB Finishing Inc. (S)
NENSCO (M)
Moss Reck & Associates Inc. (D)
Roll-Crafters/Custom Rubber Products (S)
Stowe Woodward Co. (Div. BTR Paper Group) (M)
Tech-Energy Co. (M,D)
WPC Machinery Corp. (D)

Rollers
Aaro Roller Corp. (M)
Allpress Equipment Inc. (D)
American Roller Co. (M)
Arco Engineering Inc. (Newspaper Div.) (S)
BESCO Graphic Systems Corp. (D)
Bottcher America Corp. (M,D)
Brodie System Inc. (M)
Central Graphics (M)
Diamond Roller Corp. (M,D,S)
Florida Printing Equipment and Supply (D)
Graphic Printing Roller Ltd. (M)
Norman X Guttman Inc. (M,D)
Hadronics (M,S)
Harper Corp. of America (Anilox Roll Supplier) (M)
Heidelberg Harris Inc. (M,D)
Kaim & Associates Int'l. Marketing Inc. (D)
MAH Machine Co. Inc. (M,S)
Manassy Precision Corp. (M)
Master Flo Technology (M)
Mountain States Inc. (M)

Copyright ©1996 by the Editor & Publisher Co.

Equipment, supplies, services VI-41

NENSCO (M)
Niles & Nelson Inc. (D)
Pacesetter Graphic Service Corp. (M)
Petco Roller Co. (M)
Praxair (M)
Praxair Surface Technologies Inc. (M)
Quality Components Corp. (M)
Moss Reck & Associates Inc. (M)
Roll-Crafters/Custom Rubber Products (M)
Rotation Dynamics Corp. (M,D)
Stowe Woodward Co. (Div. BTR Paper Group) (M)
Tech-Energy Co. (M,D)
Telesonic Packaging Corp. (M)
Wesco Graphics (S)
WPC Machinery Corp. (M)

Rollers: Dampening
Aaro Roller Corp. (M)
American Roller Co. (M)
BESCO Graphic Systems Corp. (D)
Brodie System Inc. (M)
Central Graphics (M)
Dahlgren USA Inc. (M)
Diamond Roller Corp. (M)
Duostat Co. (Affiliated with VGC Corp.) (M)
Graphic Printing Roller Ltd. (M)
Greerco Corp. (M)
Norman X Guttman Inc. (M,D)
Hadronics (M,S)
MAH Machine Co. Inc. (M,S)
Mountain States Inc. (M,S)
Nama Graphics Inc. (M,D)
National Graphic Supply Corp. (M)
NENSCO (M)
Newstech Co. (Div. of Rovinter Inc.) (D)
Pacesetter Graphic Service Corp. (M)
Petco Roller Co. (M)
Pitman Co. (D)
Praxair Surface Technologies Inc. (M)
Pressroom Products Inc. (D)
Quality Components Corp. (M)
Moss Reck & Associates Inc. (D)
Rotation Dynamics Corp. (M,D)
Ryco Graphic Manufacturing Inc. (M)
Tech-Energy Co. (M,D)
Varn International (M)
Veratec Div. (M)

Rules
Alteneder, Theo & Sons (M)
Midwest Publishers Supply Co. (D)
NENSCO (D)
Newstech Co. (Div. of Rovinter Inc.) (D)
Support Products Inc. (D)

Saddles
K & F/Printing Systems International (M)
Tech-Energy Co. (M,D)
Western LithoTech (M)
Western Lithotech (M)

Satellite Communication Services
AD/SAT (A Div. of Skylight Inc.) (S)
Engage Communication Inc. (M,D)
Hughes Network Systems Inc. (M)
Mantis Computer Parts Inc. (D)
Newspaper Space Bank (D)
Newstech Co. (Div. of Rovinter Inc.) (D)

Scanners: Color, B&W, Plates, Web
Arco Engineering Inc. (Newspaper Div.) (M)
Arri Systems Inc. (M,D)
Arrow Printing Co. (S)
Auto-Grafica Corp. (D)
Autologic Inc. (Subsidiary of Volt Info. Svc.) (M)
Autologic Information International Inc. (M,D)
Berkshire/Westwood Graphics Group Inc. (D)
BESCO Graphic Systems Corp. (D)
Computer Devices Inc. (D)
Computer Tree (D)
CPS Technologies Inc. (D)
Danagraf North America (D)
A.B. Dick Co. (M)
A.B. Dick Co. (Itek Graphix Div.) (M)
Duostat Co. (Affiliated with VGC Corp.) (D)
Durbin Associates (S)
ECRM (M)
Eskofot Canada Ltd. (D,S)
Florida Printing Equipment and Supply (D)
Freedom System Integrators (M)
GraphLine Inc. (D)
Heidelberg Harris Inc. (M)
Howtek (M)
ImagiTex Inc. (M,D,S)
Imapro Corp. (M)
Isomet Corp. (M)
Konica Imaging USA Inc. (D)
Krypton Systems (M)
Kye International Corp. (M)
Lazer-fare Media Services Ltd. (D,S)
Leaf Systems Inc. (M,D,S)
Linotype-Hell Co. (M)
Lumisys (M)
Mantis Computer Parts Inc. (D)
Microtek (M)
Midwest Publishers Supply Co. (D)
Monotype Systems Inc. (D,S)
Mustek Inc. (M)
National Graphic Supply Corp. (D)
Newstech Co. (Div. of Rovinter Inc.) (D)
NGCP/Laser Concepts (M)
Nikon Inc./Electronic Imaging Department (M,D)
Optronics/An Intergraph Corp. Div. (D)
Photo Systems Inc. (D)
Pitman Co. (D)
PixelCraft Inc. (M,D,S)
Polaroid Corp. (M,D,S)
Portfolios Unlimited Inc. (D,S)
PrePRESS DIRECT (D)
Printing Equipment Specialists Inc. (S)
SCREEN (USA) (M)
Sinclair Imaging Inc. (D)
System Facilities Inc. (D)
Three Sigma (M,S)
TKS (USA) Inc. (M,D)
UMAX Technologies Inc. (M)
Vidar Systems Corp. (M)
Bob Weber Inc. (S)
Xerox (Corp. HQ) (M)

Sensitized Metal
Allstates Litho Plate Corp. (D)
BESCO Graphic Systems Corp. (D)
A.B. Dick Co. (M)
GraphLine Inc. (D)
Imperial Metal & Chemical Co. (Div. of Dupont) (D)
Western LithoTech (M)

Shrink Wrapping Equipment
ALTA Graphics Inc. (S)
APS (M)
Arpac L.P. (M)
Duostat Co. (Affiliated with VGC Corp.) (D)
Malow Corp. (M)
Midwest Publishers Supply Co. (D)
National Graphic Supply Corp. (D)
National Research Bureau (D)
Quipp System Inc. (D)
Signode Corp. (M,D)
SITMA USA Inc. (M)
Tech-Energy Co. (D,S)
Telesonic Packaging Corp. (M)
UMI (D)
X-Rite Inc. (M)

Silver Recovery
BESCO Graphic Systems Corp. (D)
R.J. Brimo Enterprises Ltd. (M)
Byers Industries Inc. (M)
Danagraf North America (D)
Drew Products (M,D,S)
Duostat Co. (Affiliated with VGC Corp.) (D)
Dynalith Inc. (S)
Hart Industries (D)
Konica Imaging USA Inc. (D)
Metafix Inc. (D)
Metafix Silver Recovery Systems (M,D)
Midwest Publishers Supply Co. (D)
National Graphic Supply Corp. (D)
NENSCO (D)
Newstech Co. (Div. of Rovinter Inc.) (D)
Pacific Newspaper Services Inc. (D,S)
Parsons Main Inc. (S)
Photo Systems Inc. (D)
Pitman Co. (D)
Silver Treatment Systems Inc. (M)
Springfield Silver Service (M,D,S)
Bob Weber Inc. (S)
X-Rite Inc. (M)

Sinks
Allpress Equipment Inc. (D)
BESCO Graphic Systems Corp. (D)
Duostat Co. (Affiliated with VGC Corp.) (D)
National Graphic Supply Corp. (D)
National Research Bureau (D)
Newstech Co. (Div. of Rovinter Inc.) (D)

Software: Advertising
Ad Vantage Computer Systems Inc. (S)
Advanced Publishing Technology (M)
Advanced Technical Solutions (M)
Allsystems Go (D)
Autologic Information International Inc. (M)
Baseview Products Inc. (M,D,Software: Circulation,M)
Bruce Bell & Associates (M,D)
BMF Newspaper Accounting Systems (M,D)
Brainworks Inc. (M)
Cable Classified Advertising Network (CCAN) (S)
CE Engineering (M)
Computer Tree (D)
Computerease Software Inc. (M)
CompuText Inc. (M)
Concept Publishing Systems (M)
Copley Computer Services (S)
CPS Technologies Inc. (D)
CText Inc. (M)
Cybergraphic Inc. (M,D)
Data Sciences Inc. (S)
Datafest Technologies Inc. (M)
Digital Technology International (M)
Duostat Co. (Affiliated with VGC Corp.) (D)
Eclipse Services (Div. of Quadrivium Inc.) (S)
Edgil Associates Inc. (M)
Freedom System Integrators (M)
Geac/Vision Shift (M)
GMTI-Gannett Media Technical International (M)
Graph X Inc. (M)
Harris Publishing Systems Corp. (M)
Icanon Associates Inc. (M)
IdeaFisher Systems Inc. (M)
Innovative Systems Design Inc. (M)
Interlink (M)
Lazer-fare Media Services Ltd. (D,S)
The Loki Group Inc. (M)
Managing Editor Software Inc. (M,D)
Media Marketing Inc. (M,D,S)
Merrimac Associates (D,S)
Micro Systems Specialists Inc. (MSSI) (M,D)
Multi Ad Services Inc. (M,D)
National Research Bureau (D)
Neasi-Weber International (M,D,S)
Newspaper Space Bank (D)
Newstech Co. (Div. of Rovinter Inc.) (D)
P*Ink Software Engineering GMBH & Co. (M)
PPI (UK) Ltd. (M,D)
PrePRESS DIRECT (D)
PROMO STAR Systems (See Bruce Bell & Associates) (M,D)
PromoFax (S)
Publishing Business Systems Inc. (M,D)
Publishing Partners International (M)
Retail Solutions Group (M)
Sales Development Services (M)
Selling Dynamics Inc. (S)
Software Consulting Services (M,D)
Sysdeco U.S. (M,D,S)
Willow Bend Communications Inc. (M)

Software: Circulation
Bellatrix Systems INC. (M)
BMF Newspaper Accounting Systems (M,D)
Circulation Verification Council
Data Sciences Inc. (S)
Edgil Associates Inc. (M)
Geac/Vision Shift (M)
Icanon Associates Inc. (M)
Innovative Systems Design Inc. (M)
Interlink (M)
Lazer-fare Media Services Ltd. (D,S)
Merrimac Associates (D,S)
Micro Systems Specialists Inc. (MSSI) (M,D)
Neasi-Weber International (M,D,S)
Publishing Business Systems Inc. (M,D)
Sysdeco U.S. (D,S)
USG (M)
Vision Data Equipment Corp. (M)

Software: Design/Graphics
Ad Vantage Computer Systems Inc. (S)
Adobe Systems Inc. (M,D)
Advanced Technical Solutions (M)
Allsystems Go (D)
Arri Systems Inc. (M,D)
Artbeats (S)
Auto-Grafica Corp. (D)
Baseview Products Inc. (D)
CalComp (M,D)
Co Operative Printing Solutions (M,D)
The Color Partnership (D)
Computer Tree (D)
CompuText Inc. (M)
Concept Publishing Systems (M)
CPS Technologies Inc. (D)
Cybergraphic Inc. (M,D)
DayStar Digital Inc. (M)
DeltaPoint (S)
Digital Technology International (M)
DK & A Inc. (M)
Du-Pont Printing & Publishing (S)
Duostat Co. (Affiliated with VGC Corp.) (D)
Electronics For Imaging Inc. (D)
Flying Color Graphics (M)
Freedom System Integrators (D)
GMTI-Gannett Media Technical International (S)
GraphLine Inc. (D)
Harris Publishing Systems Corp. (M)
IMSI (M,D)
Lazer-fare Media Services Ltd. (D,S)
Macromedia Corp. (M)
Managing Editor Software Inc. (M,D)
Mantis Computer Parts Inc. (D)
MBG Associates Ltd. (M)
Metro Creative Graphics Inc. (S)
Midwest Publishers Supply Co. (D)
Multi Ad Services Inc. (M,D)
National Research Bureau (D)
Newstech Co. (Div. of Rovinter Inc.) (D)
Nikon Inc./Electronic Imaging Department (D)
Pantone Inc. (M)
PrePRESS DIRECT (D)
SCREEN (USA) (M)
SeeColor Corp. (M,D)
SEG (M)
Software Consulting Services (D)
Synaptic Micro Solutions (D)
Sysdeco U.S. (M,D,S)
T/Maker Co. (M)
Total Systems Engineering Inc. (S)
TV Data Technologies (M)

Software: Editorial
ABDEX Inc. (M)
Ad Vantage Computer Systems Inc. (S)
Adobe Systems Inc. (M,D)
Advanced Publishing Technology (M)
Advanced Technical Solutions (M)
Allsystems Go (D)
Auto-Grafica (D)
Autologic Information International Inc. (M)
Baseview Products Inc. (M)
CE Engineering (M)
Computer Tree (D)
Computerease Software Inc. (M)
CompuText Inc. (M)
Concept Publishing Systems (M)
CPS Technologies Inc. (D)
CText Inc. (M)
Cybergraphic Inc. (M,D)
Digital Technology International (M)
Du-Pont Printing & Publishing (S)
Duostat Co. (Affiliated with VGC Corp.) (D)
Edgil Associates Inc. (M)
Editorial System Engineering Co. (ESE) (M,D)
Eighty/20 Software (M,D)
Freedom System Integrators (M)
Harris Publishing Systems Corp. (M)
Lazer-fare Media Services Ltd. (D,S)
The Loki Group Inc. (M)
MacSolutions (D)
Managing Editor Software Inc. (M,D)
National Research Bureau (D)
Newspaper Systems Group Inc. (D)
Newstech Co. (Div. of Rovinter Inc.) (D)
North Atlantic Publishing Systems Inc. (M)
P*Ink Software Engineering GMBH & Co. (M)
Paragon Publishing Systems (M)
PPI (UK) Ltd. (M)
PrePRESS DIRECT (D)
Publishing Partners International (D)
Quickwire (M,D)
Rockwell Computer Solutions (D)
Starlite Software Corp. (M)
Stauffer Media Systems (D,S)
Synaptic Micro Solutions (D)
Sysdeco U.S. (M,D,S)
T/One Inc. (M,D)
The Technology Group (M)
TV Data Technologies (M)
Ultra Corp. (D)
We're Your Type! (M,D)
XSoft (Division of Xerox Corp.) (M,D)

Software: Electronic Data Interchange
Ad Express Inc. (S)
Advanced Technical Solutions (M)
Agfa Division, Bayer Inc. (M,D)
Allsystems Go (D)
Archetype Inc. (M,D)
Auto-Grafica Corp. (D)
Autologic Inc. (Subsidiary of Volt Info. Svc.) (M)
Baseview Products Inc. (D)
CE Engineering (M)
Coddbarrett Associates Inc. (M)
The Color Partnership (D)
Computer Talk Technology Inc. (S)
Computer Tree (D)
Computerease Software Inc. (M)
CompuText Inc. (M)
Copley Computer Services (S)
CPS Technologies Inc. (D)
Cybergraphic Inc. (M,D)

Copyright ©1996 by the Editor & Publisher Co.

VI-42 Equipment, supplies, services

DayStar Digital Inc. (M)
Digital Collections (M)
Duostat Co. (Affiliated with VGC Corp.) (D)
Editorial System Engineering Co. (ESE) (M,D)
Foley, Torregiani & Associates, Inc. (M)
GMTI-Gannett Media Technical International (M)
Harris Publishing Systems Corp. (M)
Icanon Associates Inc. (M)
IMSI (M,D)
Lazer-fare Media Services Ltd. (D,S)
The Loki Group Inc. (M)
North Atlantic Publishing Systems Inc. (M)
Shaffstall Corp. (M)
Source Data Systems (M)
Systems Oasis (Div. of Graphic Enterprises of Ohio Inc.) (M,D)
Toltech Systems (M)
TSI International (M,D,S)
Verity Inc. (M)
XSoft (Division of Xerox Corp.) (M,D)

Software: Pagination/Layout
Ad Vantage Computer Systems Inc. (S)
Adobe Systems Inc. (M,D)
Advanced Publishing Technology (M)
Advanced Technical Solutions (M)
Allsystems Go (D)
Auto-Grafica Corp. (D)
Autologic Information International Inc. (M)
Baseview Products Inc. (M,D)
Brainworks Inc. (D)
CE Engineering
Computer Tree (D)
Computerease Software Inc. (M,D)
CompuText Inc. (D)
Concept Publishing Systems (M)
CPS Technologies Inc. (D)
CText Inc. (M)
Cybergraphic Inc. (M,D)
Deadline Data Systems Inc. (S)
Digital Technology International (M)
DK & A Inc. (M,D)
Duostat Co. (Affiliated with VGC Corp.) (D)
EDCO Services (M,D)
Foley, Torregiani & Associates, Inc. (D)
Freedom System Integrators (M)
GMTI-Gannett Media Technical International (M)
GraphLine Inc. (D)
Harris Publishing Systems Corp. (M)
Imapro Corp. (M)
IMSI (M)
John Juliano Computer Services Co. (M)
Lazer-fare Media Services Ltd. (D,S)
London Litho Aluminum Co. Inc. (D)
MacSolutions (M)
Managing Editor Software Inc. (M,D)
Media Cybernetics L.P. (M)
Monotype Systems Inc. (M,D,S)
National Research Bureau (M)
Newstech Co. (Div. of Rovinter Inc.) (D)
P*Ink Software Engineering GMBH & Co. (M)
Paragon Publishing Systems (M)
PPI (UK) Ltd. (D)
PrePRESS DIRECT (D)
Publishing Partners International (D)
Quark Inc. (M,D,S)
Quickwire (M,D)
Retail Solutions Group (D)
SCREEN (USA) (M)
Stauffer Media Systems (D,S)
Synaptic Micro Solutions (M)
Sysdeco U.S. (M,D,S)
Total Image Corp. (M)
Total Systems Engineering Inc. (S)
TV Data Technologies (M)
Ultra Corp. (D)
Wedge Computer Systems (S)

Solvent Recovery Systems
Allpress Equipment Inc. (D)
Baldwin Dampening Systems (Div. of Baldwin Graphic Systems) (M)
BESCO Graphic Systems Corp. (D)
R.J. Brimo Enterprises Ltd. (M)
Carlson Design/Construct Corp. (M)
Chemical Management Technology Inc. (M)
Dynalith Inc. (S)
Eclectic Co. Inc. (M,D,S)
Graphic Enterprises (M,D,S)
Master Flo Technology (M)
Newstech Co. (Div. of Rovinter Inc.) (D)
Oxy-Dry Corp. (M)
Pacific Newspaper Services Inc. (D,S)
Parsons Main Inc. (S)
Safety-Kleen Corp. (S)

Speech Recognition
ABDEX Inc. (M)
DAC Systems (M,D)
Dragon Systems Inc. (M,D,S)
FAR Systems Inc. (M)
System Guides (M)
TALX Corp. (S)
Voice Connexion (M)

Splicers, Automatic
Allpress Equipment Inc. (D)
ALTA Graphics Inc. (S)
American Graphics L.P. (M,D)
Butler SMC. (M)
Enkel Corp. (A Baldwin Technology Co.) (M)
Florida Printing Equipment and Supply (D)
Grafitek International (M)
Graphic System Services (D,S)
Keene Technology Inc. (KTI) (M)
MAH Machine Co. Inc. (M)
Martin Automatic Inc. (M)
M E G (US) Inc. (M)
North Shore Consultants Inc. (S)
Offset Web Sales Inc. (S)
ONE Corp. (M)
Press and Bindery Systems Inc. (D)
Printing Equipment Specialists Inc. (S)
R T P Technical Specialists (S)
Solna Web USA Inc. (M)
William C. Spells (RTP Technical Specialists) (D,S)
UMI (M)
Veratec Div. (M)
Web Tapes Inc. (M)
Will-Pemco Inc. (M)

Static Eliminators
Baldwin Graphics Products (Div. of Baldwin Technology) (M)
BESCO Graphic Systems Corp. (D)
Beta Screen Corp. (D)
Burgess Industries Inc. (D)
Craig Cold Type Supply Inc. (D)
Duostat Co. (Affiliated with VGC Corp.) (D)
Hurletron Inc. (M)
The Inco Company (M,D)
Martin Yale Inc. (M)
Midwest Publishers Supply Co. (D)
The Morrison Group/Morrison Ink (D)
National Graphic Sales Inc. (S)
National Research Bureau (D)
NRD Inc. (M)
Pressroom Products Inc. (M)
Simco Co. Inc. (M)
Herman B. Sticht Co. Inc. (M)
Support Products Inc. (D)
Varn International (M)

Step & Repeat Systems
Alan Graphic Systems Inc. (M,D)
BESCO Graphic Systems Corp. (D)
Consolidated International Corp. (M)
Douthitt Corp. (M)
Duarte Register Systems Inc. (M)
Newstech Co. (Div. of Rovinter Inc.) (D)
Printing Equipment Specialists Inc. (S)
Pro Systems Inc. (D)
SCREEN (USA) (M)
Stoesser Register Systems (M)

Stitchers (Including In-Line)
Allpress Equipment Inc. (D)
ALTA Graphics Inc. (S)
Newstech Co. (Div. of Rovinter Inc.) (D)
Sheridan Systems (M)
Tolerans-Ingol Inc. (M,D)

Storage/Retrieval Systems
Acme Design Technology Co. (M)
Computer Tree (D)
CompuText Inc. (D)
Core-Concepts (D,S)
Dario Designs Inc. (S)
GMA Inc. (M)
GMTI-Gannett Media Technical International (M)
Newstech Co. (Div. of Rovinter Inc.) (D)
Penco Products (M)
Verity Inc. (M)
Jervis B. Webb Co. (M)
Western LithoTech (D)

Strapping Machines
ALTA Graphics Inc. (S)
B.H. Bunn Co. (D)
DYC Supply Co./Dynaric Inc. (M,D)
EAM-Mosca Corp. (M)
FELINS Inc. (M)
Ferag Inc. (M)
Florida Printing Equipment and Supply (D)
Gerrard Ovalstrapping (M,D)
Interlake (Power Strap Div.)
Interlake Packaging Corp. (M)
Malow Inc. (M)
Megasys International Inc. (D)
Network Industrial Services Inc. (D)
Newstech Co. (Div. of Rovinter Inc.) (D)
Ovalstrapping Inc. (M)
Ovalstrapping Inc. (M)
Power Strap (M)
Quipp System Inc. (D)
Sheridan Systems (M)
Signode Corp. (M,D)
Standlee and Associates Inc. (M,D,S)
Star International Corp. (D)
Sterling Packaging Systems (M)
Strapex Corp. (M,D)
West-Mor Mailroom Services (D,S)

Stripping Film
Allstates Litho Plate Corp. (D)
Base-Line Inc. (M)
Berkshire/Westwood Graphics Group Inc. (D)
BESCO Graphic Systems Corp. (D)
Craig Cold Type Supply Inc. (S)
Duostat Co. (Affiliated with VGC Corp.) (D)
GraphLine Inc. (D)
Newstech Co. (Div. of Rovinter Inc.) (D)

Subscription Fulfillment Systems
Data Sciences Inc. (S)
Fulco Inc. (S)
Fulfillment Corp. of America (FCA) (S)
Geac/Vision Shift (M)
Global Turnkey Systems Inc. (M)
Grafica Worldwide Inc. (D)
MFB Corp. (M,D)
National Research Bureau (D)
Synaptic Micro Solutions (M)
Syntellect Inc. (M)

System Installations
Advanced Technical Solutions (M)
Baseview Products Inc. (M)
CE Engineering (M)
Computer Tree (D)
CompuText Inc. (M)
Core-Concepts (D,S)
CText Inc. (S)
Cybergraphic Inc. (M,D)
Editorial System Engineering Co. (ESE) (M,D)
Freedom System Integrators (S)
GMTI-Gannett Media Technical International (S)
Graphic Enterprises of Ohio Inc. (M)
Harris Publishing Systems Corp. (M)
Lazer-fare Media Services Ltd. (D,S)
Monotype Systems Inc. (M,D,S)
Newspaper Systems Group Inc. (S)
Newstech Co. (Div. of Rovinter Inc.) (D)
Pacific Newspaper Services Inc. (M,D,S)
PrePRESS DIRECT (D)
PrePRESS SOLUTIONS (M)
PrePRESS SUPPORT (M)
R T P Technical Specialists (S)
Sheridan Systems (M)
Source Data Systems (M)
Synaptic Micro Solutions (M)
Sysdeco U.S. (M,D,S)

System Integration Services
Advanced Technical Solutions (M)
Autologic Inc. (Subsidiary of Volt Info. Svc.) (M)
Axelrod, Norman N., Assoc./Optical, Laser & Vision Systems (M,S)
Baseview Products Inc. (M)
CE Engineering (M)
Computer Talk Technology Inc. (S)
Computer Tree (D)
CompuText Inc. (M)
Core-Concepts (D,S)
CText Inc. (S)
Eclipse Services (Div. of Quadrivium Inc.) (S)
Editorial System Engineering Co. (ESE) (M,D)
Foley, Torregiani & Associates, Inc. (D)
Freedom System Integrators (S)
GMA Inc. (M)
Icanon Associates Inc. (M)
Infocom Systems (S)
Lazer-fare Media Services Ltd. (D,S)
Microtech Computer Systems (MSC) (S)
Newstech Co. (Div. of Rovinter Inc.) (D)
PPI (UK) Ltd. (S)
PrePRESS DIRECT (D)
PrePRESS SOLUTIONS (M)
PrePRESS SUPPORT (M)
Publishing Business Systems Inc. (M)
Publishing Partners International (S)
Random Access (S)
R T P Technical Specialists (D)
Source Data Systems (M)
Sysdeco U.S. (M,D,S)

Tables (Dot, Etch, Opaquing, Register, Retouching, Stripping)(See also Layout Tables)
Auto-Grafica Corp. (D)
BESCO Graphic Systems Corp. (D)
Beta Screen Corp. (D)
Consolidated International Corp. (M)
Douthitt Corp. (M)
Duostat Co. (Affiliated with VGC Corp.) (D)
Foster Mfg. Co. (M)
Midwest Publishers Supply Co. (M,D)
National Graphic Supply Corp. (M)
Newstech Co. (Div. of Rovinter Inc.) (D)
NuArc Co. Inc. (M)
Richmond/Graphic Products Inc. (M)
Roconex Corp. (M)
SCREEN (USA) (M)
Thompson Cabinet Co. (M)
Western LithoTech (M)

Tape (Typesetters)
Duostat Co. (Affiliated with VGC Corp.) (D)
Microfax Inc. (D)
National Graphic Supply Corp. (D)

Tape Perforators
Western Printing Machinery (M)

Tape Splicing Equipment
North Shore Consultants Inc. (S)
UMI (M)
Veratec Div. (M)

Telecommunications
Advanced Graphic Systems (KAIM) (M)
Advanced Telecom Services (S)
ALLTEL Supply Inc. (M,D,S)
American Message Centers (M,S)
Ampersand/New Media Division of E&P (S)
AT&S/Voice Magic (S)
Auto-Grafica Corp. (M)
Baseview Products Inc. (M,D)
Brite (M)
Cable Classified Advertising Network (CCAN) (M)
Computerease Software Inc. (M)
Copley Computer Services (S)
DAC Systems (M,D)
DemoSource Inc. (M,D)
Drake Communications Inc. (S)
Earmark (M)
Electronic Tele-Communications Inc. (M)
FAR Systems Inc. (M)
General DataComm Inc. (M)
Lazer-fare Media Services Ltd. (S)
Mantis Computer Parts Inc. (S)
MBG Associates Ltd. (M)
Monotype Systems Inc. (D,S)
National Utility Service Inc. (S)
Newstech Co. (Div. of Rovinter Inc.) (D)
Periphonics Corp. (M)
Phoenetix Corp. (D)
Siemens Rolm Communications Inc. (M,D)
Sonic Systems (M,D)
Syntellect Inc. (M)
Sysdeco U.S. (M,D,S)
System Guides (M)
Tecnavia S A/Press Div. (M)
TeleDirect International Inc. (M)
Telephone Response Technologies (M)
Toltech Systems (M)
Unicom (S)
VoiceSmart Corp. (M)

Tension & Web Controls (See also Reel & Tensions)
Advanced Graphic Systems (KAIM) (M)
ARC/Doyle Machinery Corp. (M)
Arco Engineering Inc. (Newspaper Div.) (M,D,S)
B & T Press Supplies (Affiliated with Canadian Web) (D)
Baldwin Web Controls (Div./Subsidiary Baldwin Technology) (M)
Butler SMC. (M)
Ebway Industries Inc. (Div. of Jardis Industries Inc.) (M)
Enkel Corp. (A Baldwin Technology Co.) (M)
Fleming Enterprises (M)
Graphic System Services (M,D,S)
Norman X Guttman Inc. (M)
Kaim & Associates Int'l. Marketing Inc. (M)
Keene Technology Inc. (KTI) (M)
MAH Machine Co. Inc. (M)
Martin Automatic Inc. (M)
Newstech Co. (Div. of Rovinter Inc.) (D)
Offset Web Sales Inc. (S)
Printing Press Services Inc. (M,D,S)
Robertson Press Machinery Co. Inc. (D)
R T P Technical Specialists (S)

Source Data Systems (M)
Sysdeco U.S. (M,D,S)

Equipment, supplies, services VI-43

Bill Rudder & Associates Inc. (M)
Solna Web USA Inc. (M)
William C. Spells (RTP Technical Specialists) (M,D,S)
Tidland Corp. (M,D)
TKS (USA) Inc. (M,D)
UMI (D)
Web Printing Controls/WPC Machinery Corp. (M)
Web Tapes Inc. (S)
Will-Pemco Inc. (M)
WPC Machinery Corp. (M,D)

Testing Instruments
Advanced Graphic Systems (KAIM) (M)
Axelrod, Norman N., Assoc./Optical, Laser & Vision Systems (M,S)
The Electric Tachometer Corp. (M,D)
M. Golda Engineering (S)
Graphic Enterprises (M,D,S)
Macbeth, Div. of Kollmorgen Inst. Corp. (M)
The Morrison Group/Morrison Ink (D)
Newstech Co. (Div. of Rovinter Inc.) (D)
Occupational and Environmental Health Analysts Inc. (S)
Technidyne Corp. (M)
TKS (USA) Inc. (M,D)

Three Knife Trimmer
Advance Graphics Equipment of York Inc. (M,D)
ALTA Graphics Inc. (S)
Crosfield Electronic Ltd. (M)
DuPont Co. (D)
Midwest Publishers Supply Co. (D)
Network Industrial Services Inc. (D)
Newstech Co. (Div. of Rovinter Inc.) (D)
Rosback Co. (M)
Sheridan Systems (D)
Wesco Graphics (S)
World Net & Associates Inc. (D)

Totalizing Systems
Denex Inc. (M,D)
The Electric Tachometer Corp. (M,D)
GMA Inc. (M)
IC Systems Solutions (M,D,S)
Machine Design Service Inc. (M)
NCS Inc. (M)

Newstech Co. (Div. of Rovinter Inc.) (D)
Plumtree Co. (M)
PostPress Equipment Co. (S)
Quipp System Inc. (M)
R & K Communications (S)
Sheridan Systems (M)
Standlee and Associates Inc. (M,D,S)
TKS (USA) Inc. (M,D)
Jervis B. Webb Co. (M)
Western Lithotech (M)

Trade Publications
The American Assn. of Independent News Distributors (D)
American Printer (M)
R C Anderson Associates Inc. (M,D)
ComputerUser (M)
The Directory Center (S)
Editor & Publisher (S)
Foundation of Flexographic Technical Association (S)
Fry Communications (M)
Graphic Arts Monthly (S)
The International School For Pressroom Management (M,D,S)
Jaye Communications (S)
Mouser Institute School of Advertising (S)
National Research Bureau (D)
Newspapers & Technology (M,D,S)
PhotoSource International (M)
Presstime (Newspaper Association of America) (M)
Printers Hot Line (M,D,S)
Publishers' Auxiliary National Newspaper Association (M,D,S)
Publishers Idea Exchange (S)
Quebecor Printing USA Corp. (M)
Seybold Publications Inc. (M,D)
Tel-Aire Publications Inc. (M)
Willow Bend Communications Inc. (M)

Training (Press Operation and Maintenance)
Frank Drazan (M,D,S)
Inland Newspaper Machinery Corp. (S)
Network Industrial Services Inc. (D)
R T P Technical Specialists (M,D,S)
Silverman Newspaper Management Consultants (S)
Wesco Graphics (S)

Training Services (Includes Keyboard Operator Training)
Applied Learning Corp. (M,D)
Autologic Inc. (Subsidiary of Volt Info. Svc.) (M)
Blevins Harding Group (Western Office) (S)
CNI Corp. (D,S)
Computer Services Group Inc. (S)
Computer Tree (D)
CompuText Inc. (M)
CText Inc. (S)
Frank Drazan (M,D,S)
Foley, Torregiani & Associates, Inc. (D)
Freedom System Integrators (S)
IC Systems Solutions (M,D,S)
The International School For Pressroom Management (M,D,S)
Lazer-fare Media Services Ltd. (M,D,S)
Learning Tree International (M,D)
Linotype-Hell Co. (M)
Monotype Systems Inc. (D,S)
Multi Ad Services Inc. (M,D)
Newstar Communications Inc.(dba Newspaper Satellite Network) (S)
Newstech Co. (Div. of Rovinter Inc.) (D)
NGCP/Laser Concepts (D)
Pacific Newspaper Services Inc. (M)
Paragon Publishing Systems (M)
Parsons Main Inc. (S)
PrePRESS DIRECT (D)
PrePRESS SUPPORT (S)
R T P Technical Specialists (M,D,S)
Scandinavian PC Systems Inc. (M,D)
Selling Dynamics Inc. (S)
Silverman Newspaper Management Consultants (S)
William C. Spells (RTP Technical Specialists) (M,D,S)
Synaptic Micro Solutions (M)
Sysdeco U.S. (M,D,S)
Trauner Consulting Services Inc. (S)

Tubes, Racks (Includes Racks; Motor Route Tubes)
Continental Products (M)

Fortec Inc. (M)
GeoRack Inc. (M)
Hamilton Circulation Supplies Co. (Newspaper Mailroom Supplies) (D)
Kaspar Wire Works Inc./Sho-Rack (M,D)
Newstech Co. (Div. of Rovinter Inc.) (D)
PAGE (S)
Vendors International Inc. (M,D)

Type, Fonts (See also Phototypesetting Fonts)
Agfa Division, Bayer Inc. (M,D)
Autologic Inc. (Subsidiary of Volt Info. Svc.) (M)
Bitstream Inc. (M)
CPS Technologies Inc. (D)
Derus Media Service Inc./Editorial Pace (S)
Design Science (M)
GMTI-Gannett Media Technical International (S)
GraphLine Inc. (D)
Linotype-Hell Co. (M)
Mantis Computer Parts Inc. (D)
Monotype Typography Inc. (M)
Newstech Co. (Div. of Rovinter Inc.) (D)
NGCP/Laser Concepts (D)
Ernest Schaefer Inc. (M)
Software Consulting Services (D)
Sterling Type Foundry (M)
ULTRE (Div. of Linotype-Hell Co.) (M,D,S)
Bob Weber Inc. (D)

Typesetters: Direct Impression
Allsystems Go (D)
Allsystems Go (D)
Auto-Grafica Corp. (D)
CPS Technologies Inc. (D)
Duostat Co. (Affiliated with VGC Corp.) (D)
Durbin Associates (S)
Graphic Publishing Systems Inc. (M)
Penta Software Inc. (S)
Bob Weber Inc. (D)

Typesetters: Laser
Ad Vantage Computer Systems Inc. (S)
Allsystems Go (D)

Dynaric NP-2's: Keeping Newspapers Bundled All Across America

We Guarantee Customer Satisfaction. Period!

dynaric, inc.
Glenpointe Centre West,
500 Frank W. Burr Blvd. Teaneck, NJ 07666
800-526-0827 • Fax: 201-692-7757

"The Downtime Eliminators"

Copyright ©1996 by the Editor & Publisher Co.

VI-44 Equipment, supplies, services

Auto-Grafica Corp. (D)
Autologic Inc. (Subsidiary of Volt Info. Svc.) (M)
Autologic Information International Inc. (M)
Axelrod, Norman N., Assoc./Optical, Laser & Vision Systems (S)
Berkshire/Westwood Graphics Group Inc. (D)
Bidco Manufacturing Corp. (M)
CNI Corp. (D)
CPS Technologies Inc. (D)
Duostat Co. (Affiliated with VGC Corp.) (D)
Durbin Associates (S)
Foley, Torregiani & Associates, Inc. (S)
Freedom System Integrators (D)
Graphic Enterprises of Ohio Inc. (M)
Graphic Publishing Systems Inc. (M)
GraphLine Inc. (D)
IC Systems Solutions (M,D,S)
Konica Imaging USA Inc. (M)
Linotype-Hell Co. (M)
Mantis Computer Parts Inc. (D)
Monotype Systems Inc. (M,D,S)
National Graphic Supply Corp. (M)
Newstech Co. (Div. of Rovinter Inc.) (D)
NGCP/Laser Concepts (D)
Penta Software Inc. (S)
PrePRESS DIRECT (D)
PrePRESS SOLUTIONS (M)
Software Consulting Services (D)
Systems Oasis (Div. of Graphic Enterprises of Ohio Inc.) (M,D)
Three Sigma (S)
Bob Weber Inc. (D)
Wedge Computer Systems (S)
Xitron Inc. (D)

Typesetters: Photo
GraphLine Inc. (D)
National Graphic Supply Corp. (M)
Newstech Co. (Div. of Rovinter Inc.) (D)

Typesetting Programs
Adobe Systems Inc. (M,D)
Advanced Technical Solutions (D)
Allsystems Go (D)
Auto-Grafica Corp. (D)
Computer Services Group Inc. (S)
Computer Tree (D)
Concept Publishing Systems (M)
CPS Technologies Inc. (D)
Durbin Associates (S)
Foley, Torregiani & Associates, Inc. (S)
Linotype-Hell Co. (M)
Monotype Systems Inc. (M,D,S)
Newstech Co. (Div. of Rovinter Inc.) (D)
NGCP/Laser Concepts (D)
Software Consulting Services (D)
System Facilities Inc. (D)
Total Systems Engineering Inc. (S)
Bob Weber Inc. (D)
Wedge Computer Systems (S)

Vacuum Frames
Allpress Equipment Inc. (D)
Berkshire/Westwood Graphics Group Inc. (D)
BESCO Graphic Systems Corp. (D)

Burgess Industries Inc. (M)
ByChrome Co. (M)
Consolidated International Corp. (M)
Douthitt Corp. (M)
Duostat Co. (Affiliated with VGC Corp.) (D)
GraphLine Inc. (D)
Konica Imaging USA Inc. (M)
Mid Atlantic Lighting (D)
Midwest Publishers Supply Co. (D)
National Graphic Supply Corp. (M)
Newstech Co. (Div. of Rovinter Inc.) (D)
NuArc Co. Inc. (M)
Pitman Co. (D)
Richmond/Graphic Products Inc. (M)
Roconex Corp. (M)
Stoesser Register Systems (M)
Western LithoTech (D)

Visual Display Terminals
American Data Voice Systems (D,S)
Arri Systems Inc. (D)
AT & T Information Systems (GCBS) (D)
Crosfield Electronic Ltd. (M)
Digital Equipment Corp. (M)
DuPont Co. (D)
Durbin Associates (S)
Falco Data Products Inc. (M)
Graphline (D)
Harris Corp. (Corporate Headquaters) (D)
IC Systems Solutions (M,D,S)
Krypton Systems (S)
Linotype-Hell Co. (D)
Megadata Computer & Communications Corp. (S)
Midwest Publishers Supply Co. (D)
Newstech Co. (Div. of Rovinter Inc.) (D)
Nortec Imaging (M)
PrePRESS DIRECT (D)
Rasterops (M)
Support Systems International Corp. (M)
Sysdeco U.S. (D,S)
Bob Weber Inc. (D)
West Coast Computer Systems/Newspaper Technologies (M,D)

Wastewater Treatment
Beckart Environmental Inc. (M,D)
Dario Designs Inc. (S)
Drew Products (M,D,S)
Hart Industries (D)
Konica Imaging USA Inc. (D)
Master Flo Technology (M)
MGI International Inc. (M,D,S)
Mid Atlantic Lighting (D)
Pressroom Products Inc. (D)
Semler Industries Inc. (Graphic Arts Products Div.) (M)
STI - Separation Technologies Inc. (M)
U.S. Petrolon Industrial (S)
Western LithoTech (M)

Water Management Systems
Allpress Equipment Inc. (D)
Frank Drazan (M)
MGI International Inc. (M,D,S)
National Graphic Supply Corp. (M)
Pressroom Products Inc. (M)

Web Break Detector
Allpress Equipment Inc. (D)
Arco Engineering Inc. (Newspaper Div.) (M)
Baldwin Web Controls (Div./Subsidiary Baldwin Technology) (M)
Continental Printing Machinery (S)
The Electric Tachometer Corp. (M,D)
M. Golda Engineering (S)
Grafitek International (M)
Heidelberg Harris Inc. (D)
Jardis Industries Inc. (Cary Equipment Div.) (M)
Kaim & Associates Int'l. Marketing Inc. (D)
Manassy Precision Corp. (M)
Miracle Industries Inc. (M)
Newstech Co. (Div. of Rovinter Inc.) (D)
Offset Web Sales Inc. (D)
Oxy-Dry Corp. (M)
Quad/Tech Int'l. (M)
Moss Reck & Associates Inc. (D)
R T P Technical Specialists (S)
William C. Spells (RTP Technical Specialists) (D,S)
Star International Corp. (D)
Tech-Energy Co. (D,S)
Web Printing Controls/WPC Machinery Corp. (M)
World Net & Associates Inc. (S)

Web Cleaners
MGI International Inc. (M,D,S)
Newstech Co. (Div. of Rovinter Inc.) (D)
Oxy-Dry Corp. (M)
Ryco Graphic Manufacturing Inc. (M)
Tech-Energy Co. (D,S)
Western Printing Machinery (D)
World Net & Associates Inc. (S)

Web Guides (See also Reel & Tensions, Tension & Web Controls
Kaim & Associates Int'l. Marketing Inc. (D)
MAH Machine Co. Inc. (S)

Web Guides (See also Reel & Tensions; Tension & Web Controls
ARC/Doyle Machinery Corp. (M)
Baldwin Web Controls (Div./Subsidiary Baldwin Technology) (M)
Ebway Industries Inc. (Div. of Jardis Industries Inc.) (M)
Enkel Corp. (A Baldwin Technology Co.) (M)
M. Golda Engineering (S)
Grafica Worldwide Inc. (D,S)
Grafitek International (M)
Heidelberg Harris Inc. (D)
Jardis Industries Inc. (Cary Equipment Div.) (M)
Martin Automatic Inc. (M)
M E G (US) Inc. (M)
Offset Web Sales Inc. (S)
Perretta Graphics Corp. (M)
Quad/Tech Int'l. (M)
R T P Technical Specialists (S)
William C. Spells (RTP Technical Specialists) (M,D,S)
Tech-Energy Co. (M,D,S)
Web Printing Controls/WPC Machinery Corp. (M)
Will-Pemco Inc. (M)
World Net & Associates Inc. (S)

Web Offset Remoisturizers
D & R Engineering (Graybar Int'l.) (M,D)
Dahlgren USA Inc. (M)
Grafitek International (M)
M E G (US) Inc. (M)
Newstech Co. (Div. of Rovinter Inc.) (D)
Pressroom Products Inc. (M)
Printing Equipment Specialists Inc. (S)
Vapo Systems Co. (M)

Web Preconditioners & Pretreaters
Printing Equipment Specialists Inc. (S)
Vapo Systems Co. (M)

Web Press - Special Equipment
Advance Graphics Equipment of York Inc. (M,D)
ALTA Graphics Inc. (S)
Baldwin Web Controls (Div./Subsidiary Baldwin Technology) (M)
Bell Camp Inc. (S)
Continental Printing Machinery (S)
D & R Engineering (Graybar Int'l.) (M,D)
Florida Printing Equipment and Supply (D)
Flynn Burner Corp. (M,D)
Grace Tec/W.R. Grace & Co. (M)
Grafica Worldwide Inc. (S)
Grafitek International (M)
Graphic System Services (M,D,S)
H&M Paster Sales & Service Inc. (M)
Heidelberg Harris Inc. (D)
Inter-Continental Web Inc. (D)
Kaim & Associates Int'l. Marketing Inc. (D)
KBA-Motter Corp. (Koenig & Bauer-Albert Group) (M)
Koenig & Bauer- Albert AG (KBA) (M)
MAH Machine Co. Inc. (M,S)
Manassy Precision Corp. (M)
Master Flo Technology (M)
M E G (US) Inc. (M)
Miracle Industries Inc. (M)
Newstech Co. (Div. of Rovinter Inc.) (D)
Offset Web Sales Inc. (S)
ONE Corp. (M)
Printing Equipment Specialists Inc. (S)
Printing Press Services Inc. (M,D)
Robertson Press Machinery Co. Inc. (M)
R T P Technical Specialists (S)
Solna Web USA Inc. (M)
William C. Spells (RTP Technical Specialists) (M,D,S)
Tech-Energy Co. (M,D,S)
Tidland Corp. (M)
Tolerans-Ingol Inc. (M,D)
Western Printing Machinery (M)
Western Roller Corp. (M)
World Net & Associates Inc. (S)
WPC Machinery Corp. (M)

Web Press-Special Equipment
Graphic Enterprises (M,D,S)
Wesco Graphics (S)

Web Width Changer
Global Press Sales Inc. (M)
George R Hall Inc. (M)
Newstech Co. (Div. of Rovinter Inc.) (D)
Northeast Industries Inc. (M)
Pressroom Products Inc. (M,D)
World Net & Associates Inc. (M)

Word Processing System
Advanced Publishing Technology (M)
Auto-Grafica Corp. (D)
CNI Corp. (D)
Computer Services Group Inc. (S)
Computer Tree (D)
CompuText Inc. (D)
CPS Technologies Inc. (D)
Cybergraphic Inc. (M,D)
Derus Media Service Inc./Editorial Pace (S)
Durbin Associates (S)
IC Systems Solutions (M,D,S)
International Memory Products of Illinois Inc. (D)
Krypton Systems (S)
Lazer-fare Media Services Ltd. (D,S)
Linotype-Hell Co. (D)
Mantis Computer Parts Inc. (D)
Newstech Co. (Div. of Rovinter Inc.) (D)
NGCP/Laser Concepts (D)
Nisus Software Inc. (M)
North Atlantic Publishing Systems Inc. (M)
PrePRESS DIRECT (D)
Scandinavian PC Systems Inc. (M,D)
Software Consulting Services (M,D)
The Software Development Group Inc. (S)
Starlite Software Corp. (M)
Support Systems International Corp. (M)
Syntactics (M)
The Technology Group (M)
West Coast Computer Systems/Newspaper Technologies (M,D)
Word Mark International Corp. (M,D)

WHEN YOU WANT THE LATEST NEWSPAPER PRODUCTION NEWS, SEE

Jim Rosenberg

ONLY IN E&P!

No one covers newspaper production news like E&P. And Associate Editor Jim Rosenberg is a big part of that. Jim has been covering tech news for E&P for more than eight years. Experience, knowledge and an enthusiasm for this dynamic part of the newspaper business all add up to the best coverage around.

Editor & Publisher

TO SUBSCRIBE: Look for the convenient order card bound in this Year Book or call the E&P Circulation Department at (212) 675-4380.

Copyright ©1996 by the Editor & Publisher Co.

INTERACTIVE PRODUCTS AND SERVICES COMPANIES SERVING THE NEWSPAPER INDUSTRY

A

A+ Network Inc.
1700 California St., Ste. 430
San Francisco, CA 94109
tel (415) 346-0079; fax (415) 346-5053
e-mail 73074.3062@compuserve.com
President — John Armstrong
Director-Production — Robin Solis

AccuWeather Inc.
619 W. College Ave.
State College, PA 16801
tel (814) 237-0309; fax (814) 231-0621
e-mail intermail@accuwx.com
Executive Director-Sales —
Sheldon E. Levine
President — Dr. Joel N. Myers
Director-Sales & Marketing —
Andrew Hoover
Senior Vice President — Michael Steinberg
Manager Perfect Data Voice Personals —
Phil Gelenburg
Regional Sales Manager — Fred Standridge

Aces Research Inc.
46750 Fremont Blvd., #107
Fremont, CA 94538
tel (510) 683-8855; fax (510) 683-8875
e-mail acesxprt@aol.com
Contact — Davis Chen
Managing Director — Sherry Hsu

Ad National Yellow Pages
12510 Prosperity Dr., Ste. 230
Silver Spring, MD 20904
tel (800) 722-2559; fax (301) 680-0652
Vice President — Alan Klaff
President — Dick Kravitz

Ad One Classified Network
75 Varick St., Ste. 1400
New York, NY 10013
tel (212) 431-3303; fax (212) 226-5842
e-mail http://www.adone.com
Director — Roddy de la Garza
President — Stephen Brotman

Adams and Associates
80 Gilman Ave., Ste. 2-D
Campbell, CA 95008
tel (408) 370-5390; fax (408) 370-5392
e-mail jaadams@ix.netcom.com
Contact — Jim Adams

Adams Consulting Group Inc.
3952 Western Ave.
Western Springs, IL 60550
tel (708) 246-0766; fax (708) 246-0971
e-mail ninaa@mcs.com
Contact — Nina Adams
Associate — Olaf Westgaard
Associate — Jaymie Esch

Adaptive Optics Associates Inc., A United Technologies Co.
54 Cambridge Park Dr.
Cambridge, MA 02140
tel (617) 864-0201; fax (617) 864-5855
e-mail info@aoainc.com
Contact — J.A. Maddocks
SII Manager — Dean Wormell

Adeptsoft
3465 N.W. 27th Ave.
Boca Raton, FL 33434
tel (407) 483-1146; fax (407) 483-2480
e-mail adeptsoft.com,
BBS: (407) 477-6310
CEO — John Lawlor

Admakers Multimedia Marketing
106 1/2 N. Walnut
Champaign, IL 61820
tel (217) 359-8484; fax (217) 359-8484
Contact — Robin C. Peters
Technical Director — Shehzad Najmi
Creative Director — Lenore Gray
Account Executive — Christopher Warnes

Adobe
1585 Charleston Rd.
Mountain View, CA 94039
tel (415) 961-4400; fax (415) 961-3761
Vice President-Marketing & Advertising —
Linda Clarke

ADTRAN
901 Explorer Blvd.
Huntsville, AL 35806-2807
tel (205) 971-8000; fax (205) 971-8699
e-mail gfree@adtran.com
http://www.adtran.com
Director-Sales/Marketing —
Danny Windham
President — Mark Smith

Advanced Communication Design Inc.
7901 12th Ave. S.
Bloomington, MN 55425
tel (612) 854-4000; fax (612) 854-4000, ext. 123
President — Marco Scibora
Vice President — Brian Follett

Advanced Interactive Systems
1377 Main St.
Waltham, MA 02154
tel (617) 899-4700; fax (617) 899-1186
General Manager — Dave Paterson

Advanced Multi-Point Conferencing
320 March Rd., Ste. 102
Kanata, ON K2K 2E3 Canada
tel (613) 592-5752; fax (613) 592-7688
e-mail mkelly@resudox.net
President — Wendy Threader
Vice President-Technology — Mark Kelly
Vice President-Business Development —
Roger Harbord

Advanced Publishing Technology
826 S. Victory Blvd.
Burbank, CA 91502
tel (818) 557-3035; fax (818) 557-1281
e-mail 74541.3353@compuserve.com
Vice President — Jeff Sie
President — David Kraai

Advanced Telecom Services Inc.
996 Old Eagle School Rd., Ste. 1105
Wayne, PA 19087
tel (610) 688-6000; fax (610) 964-9117
Marketing Director — Robert Jay Bentz
President — Tom Coffey
Newspaper Voice Services Director —
David Sawyer
CFO — Bret Dunlap
Marketing Information Director — Kim Leasure

Advanced Telecom Services Inc.-Canada
1505 Barrington St.
Halifax, NS B3J 2W3 Canada
tel (800) 247-1287; fax (610) 964-9117
Senior Account Executive — Brad Bierman
Marketing Director — Robert Jay Bentz

Advanced Telecom Services Inc.-U.K.
162 Queen Victoria St.
London, EC4V 4BS England
tel (44-171) 246-8242; fax (44-171) 236-8244
U.K. Sales Manager — Paul Gregson
U.S. Marketing Director — Robert Jay Bentz
Newspaper Voice Services Director —
David Sawyer

Advanced Voice Technologies
369 Lexington Ave.
New York, NY 10017
tel (212) 599-2062; fax (212) 697-9236
Contact — Ann Armstrong

Advertising Age
220 E. 42nd St.
New York, NY 10017
tel (212) 210-0287; fax (212) 210-0440
Publisher — Ed Erhardt
Marketing Director — Sam Uretsky

Advertising Research Corp.
77 Brant Ave.
Clark, NJ 07066-1540
tel (908) 388-5955; fax (908) 388-5645
Vice President — Harold Bragen

Agency for Interactive Television
13 Eno Ln.
Westport, CT 06880
tel (203) 227-0653; fax (203) 221-0987
e-mail quigly@aol.com
Contact — John S. Warwick

Agis/net.99
22015 W. Outer Dr.
Dearborn, MI 48124
tel (313) 730-1130; fax (313) 563-6119
e-mail george@agis.net
http://www.agis.net
Director-Sales & Marketing — George Kelley
Director-Sales & Marketing — Eric Jensen
President — Phil Lawlor

AI Multimedia
2340 Stanley Hills Dr.
Los Angeles, CA 90046
tel (213) 656-2185/Voice Mail: (213) 960-4303; fax (213) 656-6194
Contact — Mark Hanav
Vice President — Tom Wood
Techinical Director — John McNair

Aldea Communications
2380 Camino Vida Roble, Ste. A
Carlsbad, CA 92009
tel (619) 929-1100; fax (619) 929-0580
e-mail info@aldea.com
http://www.aldea.com
Contact — Glen Sorensen

Allied Digital Technologies
1301 Avenue of Americas, 14th Fl.
New York, NY 10019
tel (212) 757-6800
Vice President-Marketing — Steven Granat

AltaVista Technology Inc.
1671 Dell Ave., Suite 209
Campbell, CA 95008
tel (408) 364-8777; fax (408) 364-8778
e-mail altavista.com/altavista
Director-Marketing — Karin Vogel
President — Jack Marshall
Engineering Vice President — Chris McConn
Vice President-Technology — Keith Queeney

Altimedia Inc.
11278 James Swart Circle, Ste. 125
Fairfax, VA 22030
tel (703) 648-0300/(800) 524-7272
fax (703) 648-0345
e-mail info@mail.wwmedia.com
Vice President — Monica Palmer

America Online
8615 Westwood Center Dr.
Vienna, VA 22182-2285
tel (703) 448-8700; fax (703) 918-2002
Chief of Staff/General Manager — Jack Daggitt
President/CEO — Steve Case
President — Ted Leonsis

American Banking Systems Corp.
8000 S. Orange Ave., Ste. 102
Orlando, FL 32809
tel (407) 888-9091; fax (407) 888-9092
e-mail abs@innet.com
http://www.inet.com/~abs
BBS: (407) 888-9093
COO — Helena Santos
CEO — Darren Humay

American Voice Mail Inc.
327 Vienna Ave., Ste. 2
Niles, OH 44446-2627
tel (216) 544-8505; fax (216) 544-9098
President — William Hunter

Amerikids USA
14010 Captain's Row
Marina del Rey, CA 90292-7504
tel (310) 823-5880; fax (310) 823-8780
e-mail amerikids@aol.com
Media Producer — Mark Tabashnick
Administrator — Harriet Kottick
CFO — Stan Kottick
Programmer — Tom Carr

Ameritech Corp.
225 W. Randolph St.
Chicago, IL 60606
tel (312) 727-9411; fax (312) 207-1594
Senior Vice President-Market Development
— Gary G. Drook
Chairman/President/CEO — Richard C. Notebaert
Vice Chairman — Richard H. Brown

AmEuro Direct Marketing
PO Box 2523
Hyannis, MA 02601
tel (508) 778-6247; fax (508) 775-1901
Contact — E. Pendergast-Waasdorp

Ampersand
11 W. 19th St.
New York, NY 10011
tel (212) 675-4380; fax (212) 929-1894
e-mail martinr@mediainfo.com
Vice President-Business Development —
Martin Radelfinger
Vice President-Operations — Dennis O'Neill

AMUSE, Interactive Learning Environments
PO Box 534
Tiburon, CA 94920-0534
tel (415) 435-7791; fax (415) 435-7782
e-mail 71551.3305@compuserve.com
Contact — Roberto Pfeil Von Der Heyde

Analysis & Technology Inc.
Route 2; PO Box 220
North Stonington, CT 06359
tel (203) 599-3910; fax (203) 599-8907
e-mail marketing@cc.atinc.com
Contact — Suzanne Cattanach

And Software Inc.
300 Madison Ave., Ste. 200
New York, NY 10017
tel (212) 490-0181; fax (212) 490-0185
e-mail andinc@ix.netcom.com
Contact — Tony Ferraro
Project Director — Sander Raaymakers

Animated Software Co.
PO Box 188006
Carlsbad, CA 92009
tel (619) 720-7261
e-mail 71333.721@cis.com
Contact — Russell Hoffman

The Answer Team-A PE Co.
PO Box 64
New York, NY 10159-0064
tel (212) 686-5264
Executive Coordinator — Emmett T. (Pick) Pickett

APCO Associates Inc.
1615 L St., N.W., Ste. 900
Washington, DC 20036
tel (202) 778-1000; fax (202) 466-6002
e-mail jhausrath@apco.mhs.compuserve.com
Senior Vice President-Media Relations —
Jan Hausrath
President/CEO — Margery Kraus

APDI-Application Programming & Development Inc.
6805 Coolridge Dr., 2nd Fl.
Camp Springs, MD 20748
tel (800) 785-APDI/(301) 449-1400
fax (301) 449-1224
e-mail BBS: (301) 449-6100
Director-Marketing & Product Development
— Lee Havner
President — Mark Burnett
General Manager — Suradee Burnett

Apostrophe Publishing
1666 Liberty Rd., # 10; PO Box 202
Sykesville, MD 21784
tel (410) 795-6490; fax (410) 795-6490
Contact — Alisa M. Hoffman

Apple Computer
1877 Broadway
Boulder, CO 80302
tel (303) 820-3450
Research Development — Dennis Dube

Apple E-World
1 Infinite Loop
Cupertino, CA 95014
tel (800) 775-4556
Contact — Peter Scott

AppleTree Multimedia
1706 Northeast Expressway
Atlanta, GA 30329
tel (404) 235-3515; fax (404) 235-3518
e-mail 75767.2440@compuserve.com
Contact — Mardi Forman

Copyright ©1996 by the Editor & Publisher Co.

Interactive products and services

Applied Optical Media
1450 E. Boot Rd., Bldg. 400A
West Chester, PA 19380
tel (610) 429-3701; fax (610) 429-3810
President — John Brown
Vice President — Paul Dellivigne

Applied Segmentation Technology
1624 Market St., Ste. 300A
Denver, CO 80202
tel (303) 446-2525; fax (303) 446-2901
President — Tom Ratkovich
Vice President — Rick Matsumoto

Arbitron Newmedia
142 W. 57th St.
New York, NY 10019
tel (212) 887-1545; fax (212) 887-1390
e-mail 71732.643@compuserve.com
National Sales Manager — Holly Williams
General Manager — Marshall Snyder
Sales & Marketing Vice President — Kevin Smith
Senior Account Manager — Robert Bourquard
Marketing Management — Carol Edwards

ARC Studios International Inc.
137 E. 25th St.
New York, NY 10010
tel (212) 447-0001; fax (212) 447-0083
e-mail arcstudio@aol.com
Senior Vice President — Frank Coppola
President — Nicholas D'Antona
Executive V.P.-Production & Design — Edward Rapp
Vice President-Creative — Paul Hollett

Arch Communications Inc.
1327 Hampton Ave.
St. Louis, MO 63139-3113
tel (314) 645-8000
President — David Brandstetter

Arena Marketing Group
4717 Central
Kansas City, MO 64112
tel (816) 561-8120; fax (816) 561-8087
President — Jeffrey Dillon

Arlen Communications Inc.
7315 Wisconsin Ave., #600E
Bethesda, MD 20814
tel (301) 656-7940
e-mail gaha@prodigy.com
President — Gary H. Arlen

Assignment Desk
351 W. Hubbard, Ste. 801
Chicago, IL 60610
tel (312) 464-8600; fax (312) 464-8605
Director-Sales — Brian McCourt
President — Bill Scheer

Associated Press
50 Rockefeller Plaza
New York, NY 10020
tel (800) AP-CALL-1; fax (212) 621-5488
Director-Informantion Services — Chris Pederson
Manager-Distributor Development — Ted Mendelsohn
Manager-Marketing & Production — Julie Denny
Sales Manager — Jack Szluka

Atlantic Communication Resources Inc.
1 Natalie Dr.
West Caldwell, NJ 07006
tel (201) 403-0331; fax (201) 403-1003
Contact — David Snyder

AT&S Inc./Voice Magic
3402 Fernandina Road, Ste. C
Columbia, SC 29210
tel (803) 750-7279; fax (803) 798-0351
Partner — Steve Rogers
Partner — Dave Swetnam

AT&T Interchange Online Network
25 First St.
Cambridge, MA 02141
tel (617) 252-5000; fax (617) 252-5551
Public Relations Specialist — Jennifer Christensen

Audio Communications Inc.
3110 Polaris St., Ste. 24
Las Vegas, NV 89102
tel (702) 227-4999; fax (702) 251-7743
General Manager — John Wennstrom
Operations Coordinator — Mark Lepire
West Coast Sales Manager — Charles DeNatale
Customer Service Manager — Barbara Corrado

Audio Service America
15303 Ventura Blvd., Ste. 675
Sherman Oaks, CA 91403
tel (818) 788-3344; fax (818) 788-3443
e-mail voice@earthlink.net
President — Mr. Childs
Director-Sales — T. Raymound Gruno

Audionet-A Division of ADP
175 Jackson Plaza
Ann Arbor, MI 48106
tel (800) 829-2206; fax (313) 995-6458
e-mail http://www.adpnet.com
Marketing Manager — Andy Vasher

Audiotex News
2362 Hempstead Tpke., 2nd Fl.
East Meadow, NY 11554
tel (516) 735-3398/(800) 735-3398; fax (516) 735-3682
e-mail cmgaudiot@aol.com
Contact — Carol Morse Ginsburg
Associate Editor — Dory Doering
Assistant — Kimberly Tennant

Automated Graphic Systems Inc.
4950 Graphics Dr.
White Plains, MD 20695
tel (301) 834-1800/(800) 678-8760
fax (301) 843-6339
e-mail admin@ags.com
Contact — Eileen Bok
Co-Chairman/Co-CEO — Mark Edgar
Manager (One-Off CD Shop) — Mark Czajka

Automatrix Inc.
PO Box 196
Rexford, NY 12148-0196
tel (518) 885-4317; fax (518) 885-0271
e-mail rct@automatrix.com
Contact — Robert C. Tatar
Software Development Manager — Skip Montanaro

Automedia Inc.
1521 Alton Rd., Ste. 310
Miami Beach, FL 33139
tel (305) 531-9000; fax (305) 538-0663
Contact — Stephanie Sladon
Vice President-Marketing — George Onik

B

B-Linked Inc.
Murray Hill Station; PO Box 1951
New York, NY 10156
tel (800) B-Linked; fax (800) 74-Faxed
e-mail blink.tm@eworld.com
Contact — Todd Melet

Baby Mogul Interactive
1711 Purdue Ave., Ste. 11
Los Angeles, CA 90025
tel (310) 478-3886; fax (310) 478-2907
e-mail babymogul@aol.com
Partner — Paul Angles
Partner — Brian Buel

Ballantine & Co. Inc.
1 River Rd.; PO Box 805
Carlisle, MA 01741-0805
tel (508) 369-1772; fax (508) 369-9179
e-mail 74170.2306@compuserve.com
Vice President — Richard Medley
President — Ann Ballantine

Banana Programing
1916 Brook, #205
Missoula, MT 59801
tel (406) 549-1928; fax (406) 549-3522
e-mail banana@montana.com, BBS: (406) 543-8234
Director-Operations — Chad Payne
President — Paul Wheaton

Beda Design
26179 Tarvin Ln.
Ingleside, IL 60041
tel (708) 973-1719; fax (708) 973-1719
Contact — Lynn Beda
Public Relations — Sandy Wiszowaty
Electronic Publishing — Alan Buttela

BEI Communication
701 East Bay St., Mail Stop 1308
Charleston, SC 29403
tel (803) 724-3570/(800) 673-6356
fax (803) 577-5908/(800) 414-2329
Contact — Frank R. Borghetti
Administrative Assistant — Laurie Casey
Developer-Business Developement — Spencer Chen

Belden
3102 Oak Lawn Ave., #500
Dallas, TX 75219
tel (214) 522-8630; fax (214) 522-0926
President — Deanne Termini

Bruce Bell & Associates
425 Main St., Ste. 10
Canon City, CO 81212
tel (719) 275-1661; fax (719) 275-1664
Chairman — Bruce Bell
President — Jim Parnau

Bell Atlantic Video Services Co.
1880 Campus Commons Dr.
Reston, VA 22091
tel (703) 708-4429; fax (703) 708-4352
Media Ventures — Juan Veiga

Bell South
Room 314-C, 125 Perimeter Center West
Atlanta, GA 30346
tel (404) 529-8611
Senior Project Manager — Bonnie Reeves

Benchmark Kiosk Enclosures
775 Brookside Dr.
Richmond, CA 94801
tel (707) 544-9895; fax (707) 544-9896
Contact — David R. Millar

Bender, Goldman & Helper
11500 W. Olympic Blvd., # 655
Los Angeles, CA 90064
tel (310) 473-4147; fax (310) 478-7914
e-mail bghhe@aol.com
Contact — Dean Bender
Vice President — Shawna Lynch
Director — Jenny Roelle

Berkeley Software Design Inc.
212 Centenial St.
Santa Cruz, CA 95060
tel (408) 425-1581; fax (408) 425-1368
e-mail steven@bsdi.com
Director-Advertising — Steven Beedle
President — Rob Kolstad

Bersearch Information Services
26160 Edelweiss Circle
Evergreen, CO 80439
tel (303) 674-8875/(800) 851-0289; fax (303) 674-1850
e-mail bersearch@mcimail.com
President — Tom Bernard

Big Hand Inc.
4514 Travis St., Ste. 220
Dallas, TX 75205-4315
tel (214) 526-2888; fax (214) 526-2889
e-mail kathleen@bighand.com
Marketing Manager — Kathleen Thielen
President/Creative Director — Jay Wolff
COO — Steve O'Brien

Bigio Concepts
216 Marin St., Ste. 304
San Rafael, CA 94901
tel (415) 455-0514; fax (415) 455-0560
President — Terry Bigio
Sr. Account Executive — Kimberly Hathaway
Account Executive — Jeannette Bitz
Account Executive — Tanya Eckert

Bizcomm
539 Sheridan
Evanston, IL 60202-3128
tel (708) 866-9095; fax (708) 866-9095
Contact — Will Turbow

BKJ Productions
402 Rutherford Ave., #2
Charlestown, MA 02129
tel (617) 242-0660; fax (617) 242-2611
e-mail bkj productions@bmugbos.org
Contact — Brian K. Johnson

BKR Studio Inc.
55685 Current Rd.
Mishawaka, IN 46545
tel (219) 259-9576; fax (219) 259-9577
President — Brian Rideout
Graphic Designer — Michael Prout

Black Star Link
116 E. 27th St.
New York, NY 10016
tel (212) 679-3288; fax (212) 889-2052
e-mail sales@blackstar.com,
http://www.blackstar.com
Contact — John P. Chapnick
Director-National Business Development — Edward Healy

Black Swan Graphics
3100 Carlisle, Ste. 222
Dallas, TX 75204
tel (214) 922-8161; fax (214) 871-8899
Contact — Mark Kaiser

Blender
25 W. 39th St., Ste. 1103
New York, NY 10018
tel (212) 302-2626 ext. 3006; fax (212) 302-2635
e-mail lestrange@aol.com
Editor — Howard Stringer
Publisher — Jenny Von Feldt
Vice President-Advertising — Gary Gonya
Creative Director — Jason Pearson
Programmer — David Cherry

Block Interactive
5150 El Camino Real, Ste. A-32
Los Altos, CA 94022
tel (415) 254-7600; fax (415) 254-7601
e-mail info@blockinteractive.com
Contact — Danny Shapiro
Principal — Miriam Block
Principal — Lance Thornswood

BMC Group Inc.
PO Box 429
Lilburn, GA 30226
tel (770) 923-8602, ext. 155
fax (404) 923-8579
e-mail bmcmktg@america.net;
http://www.America.net/com/bmc/bmc.html
Marketing — Jill Riedl
President — Richard Farmer
Vice President-Technical Services — Mark Farmer
National Sales Manager — Sandy Walsh
Director — William Valles

BNDC Interactive
3400 W. MacArthur Blvd., Ste. L
Santa Ana, CA 92704
tel (714) 751-9675; fax (714) 751-1329
e-mail bianco@aol.com
Executive Producer — Bianco Nikki
Management — Kimberly Nikki
Staff — Rico Nikki
Staff — Sebastian Nikki

Books That Work
2300 Geng Rd., Bldg. 3, Ste. 100
Palo Alto, CA 94303
tel (415) 326-4280; fax (415) 812-9700
e-mail grams@btw.com
Contact — Laura Grams
CEO — Stuart Gannes
Vice President-Sales — Bob Citelli
CFO — Eric Levin
President — Dan Levin

Boston Technology
100 Quannapowitt Pkwy.
Wakefield, MA 01880
tel (617) 246-9000; fax (617) 246-4510
Executive Vice President-World Sales — Frank Girard
President/CEO — Dr. John Taylor
Investor Relations — Nancy Barnes

Branch Internet Services Inc.
2901 Hubbard
Ann Arbor, MI 48105
tel (313) 741-4442; fax (313) 995-1931
e-mail info@branch.com
Contact — Beth O'Connor

Branfman & Associates
12750 High Bluff Dr., Ste. 100
San Diego, CA 92130
tel (619) 481-5800; fax (619) 481-3709
e-mail dpbranfman@aol.com
Owner — David Branfman
Of Counsel — Devon Goldberg

Breze Inc.
PO Box 904
Dayton, NJ 08810-0904
tel (908) 329-3742; fax (908) 329-1108
Vice President — S. Patel

Brite
7309 E. 21st N.
Wichita, KS 67206
tel (316) 652-6500; fax (316) 652-6800
President, CEO — Stan Brannan
National Sales Director — R.D. (Bud) Calvert
Senior Product Manager — Dan Weatherford
Market Manager — Kyle Rogg

Brockway Direct Response Television
755 New York Ave.
Huntington, NY 11743
tel (516) 673-4400; fax (516) 673-4468
Chairman — Richard Brockway
President — William Maier

BSI Technologies Inc.
10030 Griffin Rd.
Fort Lauderdale, FL 33328
tel (305) 434-0189; fax (305) 434-7116

Copyright ©1996 by the Editor & Publisher Co.

Interactive products and services

e-mail 77117.1520@compuserve.com
BBS: (305) 434-5619
Project Manager — George J. Romano
President — Mike Julson

Bureau of Electronic Publishing Inc.
141 New Rd.
Parsippany, NJ 07054
tel (201) 808-2700; fax (201) 808-2676
President — Larry Shiller
Controller — Brent Subkowsky
Vice President-Sales & Marketing —
Coleen Brady
Director-New Business — Marcelle Souiero

Bureaucom Corp.
921 14th Ave.
Longview, WA 98632
tel (800) 321-8384; fax (360) 636-0016
National Sales Manager — Jim Spotts
President — Jay Shepard

The Business BBS
2531 Sawtelle Blvd., Ste. 109
Los Angeles, CA 90064-3163
tel (310) 477-0593; fax (310) 477-9475
Vice President — Susan Bloom
Presidemt — Jim Appleby
General Manager — Julia Bagnall

C

Cable Online Inc.
607 10th St., #103
Golden, CO 80401
tel (303) 271-9960; fax (303) 271-9965
e-mail cble00a@prodigy.com
General Manager — Gail Colbert
President — Paul Maxwell

Cable Vision Systems Corp.
1 Media Crossways
Woodbury, NY 11797
tel (516) 364-8450; fax (516) 496-2830
Vice President-Community Affairs —
Charles Schuler
Vice President-Sales & Marketing —
Patricia Salece

Call Interactive
2301 N. 117th Ave.
Omaha, NE 68164
tel (800) 428-2400/(402) 498-7000; fax
(402) 498-7530
Director-Sales Development — Rich Nelson
President — Eric Huff

Captured Images Inc.
31200 Via Colinas, #102
Westlake Village, CA 91362
tel (818) 707-9491; fax (818) 707-9783
President — William Grimm
Vice President — Laura Grimm
Production Manager — Leslie Shiotani

Cascade Technologies Inc.
333 Thornall St., Ste. 7
Edison, NJ 08837-2220
tel (908) 906-2020; fax (908) 906-2018
President — Vigdis Austad
Vice President-Technology — Frank Joicy

CD Technology
764 San Aleso Ave.
Sunnyvale, CA 94086
tel (408) 752-8500; fax (408) 752-8501
Contact — Bill Liu

CEC Corp. (CyCube)
271 City Island Ave.
City Island, NY 10464
tel (800) 477-0791/(718) 885-0791; fax
(718) 885-3101
BBS: (718) 885-0990
President — Gus Pedersen

Century Desing
530 15th Ave. S.
Hopkins, MN 55343
tel (612) 939-3120; fax (612) 939-3020
Vice President-Marketing — Larry Erickson

Centigram Communications Corp.
91 E. Tasman Dr.
San Jose, CA 95134
tel (408) 944-0250; fax (408) 428-3737
President/CEO — George Sollman
Vice President-Sales — Rene Thibault
Vice President-Sales — John Ver Meulen
Vice President-Sales — John McCarthy

Chase-Bobko
431 N. 34th
Seattle, WA 98103
tel (206) 547-4310; fax (206) 548-0749
e-mail chase@netquest.com
Contact — Patricia Chase
Vice President — Bob Boiko
Vice President — Jayson Antonoff

Cheersoft
457 Highway 79
Morganville, NJ 07751
tel (908) 591-1234; fax (908) 591-8652
BBS: (908) 591-1171
President — Ian Rintell

Chelsea IVR
329 W. 6th St.; PO Box 369
Chelsea, OK 74016
tel (918) 789-5503; fax (918) 789-3645
President — Rick Clark
Vice President — James Duke

The Chronicle of Higher Education
1255 23rd St., N.W., Ste. 700
Washington, DC 20037
tel (202) 466-1000; fax (202) 296-2691
e-mail joyce.guisto@chronicle.com,
http://www.chronicle.merit.edu,
http://www.chronicle.com
Director-Strategic Planning — Joyce A.
Giusto
Publisher — Robinette Ross
Associate Editor — Edward R. Weldlein
Director-Electronic Projects — Judith Axler
Turner
Associate Director-Electroinic Projects —
Richard G. Schmalgameir

Cimarron International Inc.
3131 S. Vaughn Way, Ste. 134
Aurora, CO 80014
tel (303) 368-0988; fax (303) 695-8238
e-mail cimarronco.com
President — Michael Theis
Vice President — Sam Brennan
Producer — Andrew McGrath

CKS/Interactive
10260 Bandley Dr.
Cupertino, CA 95014
tel (408) 366-5100; fax (408) 777-4242
Vice President/General Manager — Pete
Snell

Cinecom Corp.
15621 Neath Dr.
Woodbridge, VA 22193
tel (703) 680-4733; fax (703) 680-1697
e-mail spotter@sincom.com
BBS: (703) 730-1420
Office Manager — Annie Potter
President — Skip Potter

Clark Development Company Inc.
3950 S. 700 E, Ste. 303
Murray, UT 84107
tel (801) 261-1686/(800) 356-1686
fax (801) 261-8987
e-mail sales@saltair.com
BBS: (801) 261-8976
Sales Manager — Joe Robinson
President — Fred Clark
General Manager — Steve Klingler

Clark Internet Services Inc. (ClarkNet)
10600 Clarksville Pike
Ellicott City, MD 21046
tel (410) 254-3900; fax (410) 254-2745
e-mail info@clark.net, sales@clark.net,
drew@clark.net
Vice President-Sales & Support — Drew
Janssen
President/CEO — James H. Clark Jr.
Vice President-Technical — Stephen
Balbach
CFO — Sunil Cheetoo

ClassAct
1121 S. Orem Blvd.
Orem, UT 84058
tel (801) 221-9400; fax (801) 221-9942
e-mail tcrowell@softone.com
Corporate Communications — Teresa
Crowell
Marketing — Mickey Cochran
Marketing — Scott Johnson
Marketing — Dale Hales

Classifacts
2821 S. Parker Rd., Ste. 305
Aurora, CO 80014
tel (303) 745-1011; fax (303) 745-1122
e-mail jdale@classifacts.com
Vice President-Sales & Marketing — Jack
Dale
President — Don Golden

Classroom Connect
1866 Colonial Village Ln.; PO Box 10488
Lancaster, PA 17605-0488
tel (717) 393-1000; fax (717) 393-5752
e-mail jgg@wentworth.com
Contact — Greg Giagnocauo
Editor — Chris Sturm

Clement Mok Designs
600 Townsend St., Penthouse
San Francisco, CA 94103
tel (415) 703-9900; fax (415) 703-9901
e-mail info@cmdesigns.com
Marketing Director — Ann Burgraff
Creative Director/Information Architect —
Clement Mok
Vice President-New Media — Brad Husick
Vice President-Operations — Shel Perkins
Marketing & Strategy Consultant —
Amanda Pike
Creative Director — Mark Crumpacker
Associate Creative Director — Claire Barry

Cobbey & Associates Marketing Research
1 Sansome St., Ste. 2000
San Francisco, CA 94104
tel (415) 951-1001; fax (707) 433-4225
e-mail cobbey@aol.com
Contact — Robin Cobbey

Cobotyx
20 Miry Brook Rd.
Danbury, CT 06810
tel (203) 830-4880; fax (203) 830-4886
Sales Manager — Eileen Nolan

Coe-Truman Technologies Inc.
206 Burwash Ave.
Savoy, IL 61874
tel (217) 398-8594; fax (217) 355-0101
e-mail pj@cttmwoc.mhs.compuserve.com
Director-Multimedia Services — Patrick
Patterson
Vice President — Tom Russell
Multimedia Consultant — Whitney Proffitt

Cognitronics Corp.
3 Corporate Dr.
Danbury, CT 06810-4130
tel (203) 830-3400; fax (203) 830-
3405/(203) 830-3554
Director-Marketing — John Stanley
President — Brian Kelley
Vice President-Sales — Ken Brix

Rapp Collins Communications
901 Marquette Ave., 17th Fl.
Minneapolis, MN 55424
tel (612) 373-3000; fax (612) 373-3062
e-mail rcc mpls@aol.com,
76020.3627@compuserve.com
Senior Vice Pres.-Business Development —
Victoria S. Leavitt

Colorite Film
117 E. 31st St.
New York, NY 10016
tel (212) 532-2116; fax (212) 686-1006
Contact — Sal Nasca

CommGraphics
126 N. 11th St., Ste. 10
Lincoln, NE 68508
tel (402) 438-1919; fax (402) 438-5352
Contact — Don Albrecht
General Manager — Jean Albrecht

Commotion New Media Inc.
1424 4th St., #604
Santa Monica, CA 90401
tel (310) 451-6240; fax (310) 451-6243
e-mail info@commotion.com
Business Development/Line Producer —
Joseph Nuccio
President — Philip van Allen
Creative Director — Martha Swetzoff
Director-Art/Music — Jonathan Abarbanel
Software Engineer — Mark Rudholm

Communication Design
1604 Hodges Ct.
Marina, CA 93933
tel (408) 883-1361; fax (408) 883-1463
e-mail john ittelson@monterey.edu
Contact — John Ittelson

Communications Management Service Inc.
720 Barnum Ave. Cutoff
Stratford, CT 06497
tel (800) 233-7785; fax (203) 377-2632
President — John F. Roy
Vice President — Daniel F. Rindos

Communique Interactive Solutions Inc.
PO Box 4814
Richmond, VA 23220-8814
tel (804) 355-6400/(800) FOCUS-12; fax
(804) 354-9625
e-mail cisinc1@aol.com
Contact — Cheryl Spencer
Media Director — Marguerite Bardone

CommuniTech Inc.
321 Bond St.
Elk Grove Village, IL 60007
tel (708) 439-4333; fax (708) 439-3456
Marketing Manager — Dale R. Haring

Competence Software
RRI Box 24, Jct. Rts. 28 & 107; PO Box 66
Pittsfield, NH 03263
tel (603) 435-5098; fax (603) 435-7864
e-mail competence@aol.com
Vice President-Market Development —
Larry Brennan
CEO/President — Larry Byrnes
Vice President-Marketing — Jessica Byrnes
Vice President-Operations — Tom Hardy

Compudoc Inc.
50 Mount Bethel Rd.
Warren, NJ 07059
tel (908) 561-7000; fax (908) 757-4550
e-mail !compudoc@at&tmail.com,
76600.1517.compuserve.com
Contact — David A. Fuhrman

Compuserve
5000 Arlington Center Blvd.
Columbus, OH 43220
tel (614) 457-8600; fax (614) 457-0348
e-mail 70006.101@compuserve.com,
70006#.101@compuserve.com
Public Relations Manager — Russ Robinson
President/CEO — Robert Massey

CompuTalk Inc.
100 Park Dr., Ste. 108; PO Box 12335
Research Triangle Park, NC 27709
tel (919) 549-8444; fax (919) 549-0066
President — Jerry Grant

Computer Communications Specialists
6529 Jimmy Carter Blvd.
Norcross, GA 30071
tel (770) 441-3114; fax (770) 263-0487
Marketing Specialist — Theresa Wiltman
President — Lynda Richter

Computer Talk Technology
225 E. Beaver Creek, Ste. 310
Richmond Hill, ON L4B 3P4 Canada
tel (905) 882-5000; fax (905) 882-5501
President/CEO — Mandle Cheung
Director-Sales — Jenny Cooper

COMSAT Entertainment Group
6560 Rock Spring Dr.
Bethesda, MD 20817
tel (301) 214-3000; fax (301) 214-7100
e-mail paul.e.jacobson@comsat.com
Director-Communications — Paul Jacobson
President — Charlie Lyons
President-On Command Video — Bob Snyder

Comsys International B.V.
Huis ter Heldeweg 6
Zeist, LZ 3705 The Netherlands
tel (31-3404) 32323; fax (31-3404) 22920
Contact — A. Borm

Comtex Scientific Corp.
4900 Seminary Rd.
Alexandria, VA 22311
tel (703) 820-2000; fax (703) 820-2005
Vice President-Sales — Deborah Ikins
President — Charles W. Terry
Senior Vice President — A.J. Germek
Director-Technical Operations — Brad Fraley
Director-Marketing & Product Development
— Jill Falci

Congressional Quarterly Inc.
1414 22nd Street N.W.
Washington, DC 20007
tel (202) 887-8500; fax (202) 728-1863
e-mail jjenings@cqalert.com
Marketing Manager — Jeanne S. Jennings
Media Relations — Loretta Salici
National Sales Manager — Bettie Ann Wise

Connect
515 Ellis St.
Mountain View, CA 94043
tel (800) 262-2638; fax (415) 254-4800
President — Thomas P. Kehler

Convergent Media Systems
25 Porter Rd.
Littleton, MA 01460
tel (508) 486-3030; fax (508) 952-4630
New Media Business Development — John
B. Rice
Manager-Business Development Services
— Jennifer Sorenti
President — Murray Holland

VI-48 Interactive products and services

Conxtion
3311 B Broadriver Rd.
Columbia, SC 29201
tel (803) 772-4044; fax (803) 750-3299
BBS: (803) 772-4624
Owner — Edward Rothschild

Coolware Inc.
1330 Harker Ave.
Palo Alto, CA 94301
tel (415) 322-4722
e-mail mcooley@coolware.com
Vice President-Public Relations & Marketing — Margaret Cooley
President — Keith Cooley
Art Director — Stan Young
Sales Director — Chuck Gneer

Coopers & Lybrand
101 E. Kennedy Blvd., Ste. 1500
Tampa, FL 33602
tel (813) 229-0221; fax (813) 229-3646
Contact — Madonna Carey

Copia International Ltd.
1342 Avalon Ct.
Wheaton, IL 60187
tel (800) 689-8898; fax (708) 665-3911
e-mail copia@copia.com
Vice President-Marketing — Dorothy Gaden
President — Steve Hersee
Vice President-Engineering — Terry Flanagan

Corporate Creative Services Inc.
33 Parkway
Maywood, NJ 07607
tel (201) 368-2296; fax (201) 368-1489
Contact — Ken Petretti

Corporate Disk Co.
1226 Michael Dr.
Wood Dale, IL 60191
tel (708) 616-0700; fax (708) 616-9170
e-mail http://www.disk.com
Vice President — William Mahoney
President — Alan Gault
General Manager — Joseph Foley
Marketing Manager — Steve Steeves

Cortex Communications Inc.
1010 Rio Grande, Ste. B (78701)
PO Box 33448
Austin, TX 78764
tel (512) 472-1213; fax (512) 472-5767
e-mail cortexcom@aol.com
Partner — Debby Kalk
Partner — Brenda Fondren

Cosmos Communications Inc.
11-05 44th Dr.
Long Island City, NY 11101-9615
tel (718) 482-1800 ext. 250
fax (718) 482-1968
Contact — Heather Weiss
President — Gerald Weiss
Sales Representative — Michael Feniello
Vice President-Operations — Steven Brauner

Costello & Assoc.
4210 S. 33rd St.
Lincoln, NE 68506
tel (402) 483-7611; fax (402) 483-6847
e-mail COSTO@Gallup.com
Contact — Donald F. Costello
Vice President-Marketing — Richard Henry
Vice President-Finance — Daniel Costello
Vice President-Systems — Thomas Costello

Cramp & Associates Inc.
1500 Walnut St.
Philadelphia, PA 19102
tel (215) 893-0500; fax (215) 893-0543
e-mail jcramp@pond.com
Contact — A. Jeffrey Cramp
Vice President-Research — Curtis Johnson
Vice President/Director-Public Relations — Barbara Moss

Creative Associates Inc.
1180 Lexington Ave.
Mansfield, OH 44907
tel (419) 756-6526; fax (419) 756-3126
e-mail caonline@aol.com
Contact — Jeff Davidson
President — Peter Dignan
Copy Writer — Amy Hochstetler

Creative Audio Enterprises (On Hold Productions)
266 Harristown Rd., Ste. 203
Glen Rock, NH 07452
tel (201) 444-6488; fax (201) 445-4653
Director-Sales — Neil Fishman

Creative Communications
7 The Pines Ct., Ste. C
St. Louis, MO 63141
tel (314) 434-6688; fax (314) 469-5539
President — David Hammond
Director-Graphics — Sherry Hannick
Administration — Linda Hammond
Sales — Greg Kirkpatrick

Creative Syndication SUS
PO Box 40
Eureka, MO 63025
tel (314) 587-7126; fax (314) 938-4486
Contact — Ed Baldwin
Vice President — Nadya Klepatskaya
Editor — Debbie Holly

CRIT Inc.
PO Box 18808
Baltimore, MD 21206
tel (410) 426-1478/(800) 410-CRIT (2748); fax (410) 426-7768
e-mail crit@charm.net
President — Carl Schuetz

Customer Communications Group
12600 W. Cedar Dr.
Denver, CO 80228
tel (303) 986-3000; fax (303) 989-4805
e-mail markr@customer.com
Contact — Mark Richtermeyer
CEO — Thad Peterson
Online Account Manager — Dan Murray
Account Executive — Kelly Dunn

Cyber Sales One (Div. of CMS)
9 E. 38th St., Ste. 802
New York, NY 10016
tel (212) 213-0233; fax (212) 213-4757
e-mail albert-cms@interramp.com
President/CEO — Albert H. Crane III

Cyberdreams Inc.
23586 Calabasas Rd., Ste. 102
Calabasas, CA 91302
tel (818) 223-9990; fax (818) 222-9346
Director-Sales & Marketing — Andrew Balzer
President — Paul Licari
CFO — John Kojima
Director-Operations — Michael Buscher

The CyberMedia Group
10410 San Fernando Ave.
Cupertino, CA 95014-2833
tel (408) 255-5007; fax (408) 255-5730
e-mail cybrmdagrp@aol.com
Chairman/Chief Futurist — Kenneth T. Lim
Executive Vice President/Director-Research — Peter Teige

Cyberspace Information Systems
10000 Canoga Ave., #C4
Chatsworth, CA 91311
tel (818) 709-8492; fax (818) 709-6793
e-mail info@cyberinfo.com,
http://www.webcom/~cyberspc
BBS: (818) 709-8492
Director-Sales — John Peterson
Owner — Michael C. Kovnick

Cybertech Inc.
935 Horsham Rd.
Horsham, PA 19044
tel (215) 957-6220; fax (215) 674-8515
New Business Mgr. — Gil Gindhart
President — Harry Schmidt
Vice President — Ronald Schimdt
Secretary/Treasurer — Lloyd Barnett
Sales Manager — Joe Foulke

CYCO International Inc.
1908 Cliff Valley Way
Atlanta, GA 30329
tel (404) 634-3302; fax (404) 633-4604
e-mail 102003.750@compuserve.com
Vice President-Marketing — Kenneth S. Shain
Vice President-Sales — Jewell Smokes
Manager-Customer Service — Chris Tsallgarides

D

D & H Information Services
1519 Wagontrain Dr. (87123)
PO Box 3201
Albuquerque, NM 87190-3201
tel (505) 298-0838/(800) 460-0388
fax (505) 298-1557
e-mail dhinfo@rt66.com
Contact — Debby Dolan
Vice President-Technology — Tony Holderith

D & S Associates
19 Carroll Ave.
Westwood, MA 02090
tel (617) 329-1344; fax (617) 329-1344
e-mail dsalitser@aol.com
Contact — Dan Petitpas
Partner — Susan Gellerman
Writer — Paul Angelosanto

DAC Systems
60 Todd Rd., Ste. 1B
Shelton, CT 06484
tel (203) 924-7000; fax (203) 944-1618
President — Mark Nickson

Dana Communications
2 E. Broad St.
Hopewell, NJ 08525
tel (609) 466-9187; fax (609) 466-0285
President — Thos Paine
Chairman — Michael Prewitt

Data Voice Systems
1150 Logan St.
Louisville, KY 40204
tel (502) 636-2700; fax (502) 636-3317
President — Don Fleming

Database Network Services
10801 Wayzata Blvd., #350
Minnetonka, MN 55305-1533
tel (612) 544-1920
CEO — Bill Erickson

Datasafe Publications Inc.
3301 Juan Tabo Rd. N.E., Ste. 113 (87111);
PO Box 16032
Albuquerque, NM 87191-6032
tel (505) 294-4980; fax (505) 294-8225
e-mail sysop@dump.com
BBS: (505) 294-1574
President — Dean Kerl

DataTimes Corp.
14000 Quail Springs Pkwy.
Oklahoma City, OK 73134
tel (405) 751-6400; fax (405) 755-8028
Training — Brad Watson

Datavoice Technology
2825 Wilcrest, Ste. 311
Houston, TX 77042
tel (713) 783-0123; fax (713) 783-9538
President — Ralph Hayes

DDB Needham Interactive Communications
200 Crescent Ct.
Dallas, TX 75201
tel (214) 855-2929; fax (214) 855-2298
Executive Director — David King
CFO — Mark O'Brien
Manager-Multimedia Product Services — Karen King
Manager-Communication Technologies — Mark Landrum

Deloayza Associates Productions
3034 Deakin St.
Berkeley, CA 94705
tel (510) 704-0545; fax (510) 704-0252
e-mail daprod@aol.com
Contact — Hugh deLoayza
CEO — Winifred M. deLoayza

Delphi Internet
620 Ave. of the Americas, 6th Fl.
New York, NY 10011
tel (212) 462-5000
e-mail evanrud@newscorp.com
Newspaper Partners/Program Manager — Evan Rudowski
Business Development Vice President — Bruce Thurlby

Delrina
895 Don Mills Rd., 500-2 Park Center
Toronto, ON M3C 1W3 Canada
tel (416) 446-8174; fax (416) 443-1633/(800) 642-9167
e-mail mikebr@delrina.com
Internet Product Manager — Mike Brookbank

DemoSource Inc.
8502 E. Via de Ventura, Ste. 220
Scottsdale, AZ 85258
tel (800) 283-4759/(602) 922-5500
fax (602) 922-5572
President — Brian L. Berman

Design Collaborative
1 Simms, Ste. 150
San Rafael, CA 94901
tel (415) 456-0252
Principal — Bob Ford
Art Director — Joyce Mueller
Illustrator — Glenn Cavalli

Design Media Inc.
2235 Harrison St.
San Francisco, CA 94110
tel (415) 641-4848; fax (415) 641-5245
e-mail desmedia@ix.netcom.com
Contact — Norman Kurtin
Producer — Howard Steinman
Producer — Wallace Murray
Producer — Robert Russo

Design O'Saurs
67-71 Yellowstone Blvd., #6D
Forest Hills, NY 11375
tel (718) 268-1493; fax (718) 268-1493
Contact — Harry Widoff

Design Tekneka
PO Box 2510
Decatur, GA 30031-2510
tel (404) 378-7900; fax (404) 378-9139
e-mail blanden2@aol.com
Contact — Dennis A. Blanchard
Office Manager — Jill Kaminski

dh design
415 15th St., #18
Huntington Beach, CA 92648
tel (714) 960-6085; fax (714) 960-0556
e-mail dlhefner@aol.com
Contact — Donna Hefner

DH Design
186 Riverside Dr., Ste. 4B
New York, NY 10024
tel (212) 721-6721; fax (212) 721-6721
e-mail hurstdc.@aol.com
Contact — Deborah Hurst

Dialogic Communications Corp.
1106 Harpeth Industrial Ct.
Franklin, TN 37064
tel (615) 790-2882; fax (615) 790-1329
Sales Representative — Bill Carman

Dialogic Corp.
1515 Rte. 10
Parsippany, NJ 07054
tel (201) 993-3000; fax (201) 993-3093
President — Howard Bubb
Vice President-Marketing — John Landau

Dictaphone Corp.
3191 Broadbridge Ave.
Stratford, CT 06497-2559
tel (203) 381-7000; fax (203) 386-8597
Vice President-Commercial Marketing — Mary Haislip
President — John Duerden

Digicom Systems Inc.
188 Topaz St.
Milpitas, CA 95035
tel (408) 262-1277; fax (408) 262-1390
Director-Sales — Cliff Gard
President — Gwong Yih Lee

Digital Audio Information Systems Inc.
P.O. Box 5605
Katy, TX 77491
tel (713) 224-4000; fax (713) 224-4000 ext. 200
Contact — Maurice Collins

Digital Cinema Corp.
600 Townsend, Ste. 415W
San Francisco, CA 94103
tel (415) 626-2060
e-mail 72360.2727@compuserve.com
Contact — Joe Asady

Digital Consulting Services Inc.
PO Box 2142
Secaucus, NJ 07094
tel (800) 899-2002/(212) 697-7340
fax (201) 865-4820
e-mail mehrmann@digiconsult.com
BBS: (201) 865-1783
President — Michael Ehrmann

Digital Design Group Ltd.
955 Milton St.
Pittsburgh, PA 15218
tel (412) 243-9119; fax (412) 243-9119
e-mail robdill@interact.lm.com
Contact — Rob Dillon

Digital Express Group Inc.
6800 Virginia Manor Rd.
Beltsville, MD 20705
tel (800) 99-DIGEX; fax (301) 847-5215
e-mail info@digex.net
Inside Sales — Brett Davis

Digital Information
PO Box 110235
Stamford, CT 06911-0235
tel (203) 348-2751; fax (203) 977-8310
Editor & Publisher — Jeff Silverstein
President — Maureen Fleming

Copyright ©1996 by the Editor & Publisher Co.

Interactive products and services VI-49

Digital Media Arts
460 Market St., Ste. 103
Williamsport, PA 17701
tel (717) 327-8314; fax (717) 327-9106
e-mail matman@pipline.com
Contact — John E. Young
Program Manager — Eric Haines

Digital Post & Graphics
1921 Minor Ave.
Seattle, WA 98101
tel (206) 623-3444; fax (206) 340-1548
e-mail design@dpg.com
Producer — Edwin Stone

Digital Solutions Inc.
899 Western Ave. N. Ste. 1
St. Paul, MN 55117
tel (612) 488-1740; fax (612) 488-4014
e-mail info@solon.com, http://www.solon.com
VP-Commercial Services — Ben Tucker
CFO — Michael Alexander
Vice President-Technology — Peter Seebach
Vice President-WWW Services — Tim Sauve
CEO — Corrie Bergeron

Digital Speech Systems Inc.
1735 Analog
Richardson, TX 75081
tel (214) 235-2999; fax (214) 235-3036
CEO/President — Lev Frenkel
Vice President-Operations — Dina Frenkel

Digital Stock Corp.
400 S. Sierra Ave., Ste. 100
Solana Beach, CA 92075
tel (619) 794-4040/(800) 545-4514
(Sales); fax (619) 794-4041
Contact — Charles J. Smith
Sales — Harriet Davey

Digital United
18 Briggs Ln.
Croton-on-Hudson, NY 10520
tel (914) 271-4959; fax (914) 271-4787
e-mail markmagel@aol.com
Contact — Mark Magel
Producer — Nina Romanoff
Audio Design — James Welsh

Digitcom Multimedia Corp.
2190 Colorado Ave., Ste. B
Santa Monica, CA 90404
tel (310) 584-0750; fax (310) 584-0759
Director-Marketing — Roger Templeton
President — Jim Chin
Manager-Sales — Chuck Greenberg

Dirad Technologies
14 Computer Dr. E.
Albany, NY 12205
tel (518) 438-6000; fax (518) 458-2782
Regional Sales Manager — Richard Marine

Direct Images
14020 Outrigger Dr. (San Leandro, 94577); PO Box 29392
Oakland, CA 94604
tel (510) 614-9783; fax (510) 614-9286
e-mail dimages@aol.com
Producer/Director — Bill Knowland
Art Director — Beverly Knowland

Diskalog Inc.
247 E. Chestnut St.; PO Box 2302
Chicago, IL 60611-2415
tel (312) 944-4384; fax (312) 649-0970
e-mail diskalog@aol.com
President — Steven Slomka
Vice President-Operations — Maxine Rosen
VP-Technical Services — Dave McCue

Distributed Processing Technology
140 Candace Dr.
Maitland, FL 32751
tel (800) 322-4378; fax (407) 260-5366
e-mail sales@dpt.com
Inside Sales Manager — Zelda Kuszmaul
President — Steve Goldman

Reuben H. Donnelley
287 Bowman Ave.
Purchase, NY 10577-2596
tel (914) 933-6461; fax (914) 933-6680
e-mail cooperbj@ix.netcom.com
Asst. Vice Pres.-Communications —
Barbara J. Cooper
Chairman — Frank R. Noonan
Sr. Vice Pres.-Strategic Marketing &
Business Development — Michael D. Cole
Sr. VP-HR — Michael J. Koeller
Vice Pres.-New Client Development —
Joseph A. DeBlasio
Vice Pres.-Interactive Voice Services —
Michael A. Soriano
Asst. Vice Pres.-Interactive Voice Services
— Thomas Fabry

Dow Jones & Co. Inc.
P.O. Box 300
Princeton, NJ 08543-0300
tel (617) 536-2772; fax (617) 526-0470
Public Relations — Michael Bayer

Dream Theater
2727 Main St.
Santa Monica, CA 90405
tel (310) 319-1111; fax (310) 396-5113
e-mail dchuckry@aol.com
Contact — Darren Chuckry

D3 Inc.
112 W. 9th St., Ste. 400
Kansas City, MO 64105
tel (816) 471-7373; fax (816) 471-4223
e-mail marks@d3
Contact — Mark R. Mourm
Partner — Mark Schraad
Partner — Mark Porter
Partner — David Suet

Ken D'Urso & Associates
698 S. 13th St.
San Jose, CA 95112
tel (408) 277-0783; fax (408) 277-0783
e-mail kdurso@aol.com
Owner — Ken D'Urso
Office Manager — Diana Miller
Production Manager — Paula Lianza

Dynacom Inc.
1512 N. Fremont, Ste. 101
Chicago, IL 60622
tel (312) 951-5510; fax (312) 951-5562
President — Jerry Sullivan
Asst. to the President — Jamey Brumfield

Dynamic Fax
5301 E. State St., Ste. 305
Rockford, IL 61108
tel (815) 398-9009; fax (815) 398-5123
Director-Marketing — Gail Fischer
Vice President-Sales — James Hughes

DYNEX Digital Publishing
610 Des Moines St.
Des Moines, IA 50309
tel (515) 246-1250; fax (515) 246-8612
e-mail dynexdp@aol.com
Partner — Wes Ritchie
Partner — Jean Jorgensen
Partner — Steve Vickery

Dytel Inc.
160 Hansen Ct., Ste. 100
Wood Dale, IL 60191
tel (708) 350-9700; fax (708) 350-9683
President — John L. Baugh

E

E and E Display Group
910 E. 29th St.
Lawrence, KS 66046
tel (800) 456-7679; fax (913) 843-9288
CEO — Edward White
President — Daryl Morgison
Vice President Research — Keith White
Vice President Finance — Brian Iverson

Editor & Publisher Co.
11 W. 19th St.
New York, NY 10011
tel (212) 675-4380; fax (212) 929-1259
e-mail edpub@mediainfo.com
Co-Publisher — Colin Phillips
Co-Publisher — Chris Phillips
Advertising Director — Steve Townsley
Vice President-Operations — Dennis O'Neill
Vice President-Business Development —
Martin Radelfinger

Edmonton Telephones Corp.
10044 108th St., #286
Edmonton, AB T5J 3S7 Canada
tel (403) 441-2000; fax (403) 426-1871
Marketing Manager Level Two —
Edward Burchmore

EDR Media
23330 Commerce Park Rd.
Beachwood, OH 44122
tel (216) 292-7300; fax (216) 292-0545
e-mail staff@edr.com, http://www.edr.com
VP-Business Development — Marc J. Ricker
Senior Account Manager — John Martin

EDR Systems
23330 Commerce Park Rd.
Beachwood, OH 44122
tel (216) 292-1700; fax (216) 292-1779
e-mail staff@edr.com, http://www.edr.com
Vice President-Interactive Marketing Group
— Nick Mussulin
VP-Interactive Kiosks — Matt Handler

EDS (Electronic Data Systems)
1251 Avenue of the Americas, 41st Fl.
New York, NY 10020
tel (212) 403-6029; fax (212) 403-6010
e-mail http://www.eds.com
Director-Marketing — Linda E. Penrod
VP-Sales & Publishing — Sean Dolan

E-fax Communications Inc.
1611 Telegraph Ave., Ste. 555
Oakland, CA 94612
tel (510) 836-6000; fax (510) 836-8935
Vice President-Marketing — William S. Perell
President — Joseph Karwat

EFE News Services (US) Inc.
1252 National Press Building
Washington, DC 20045
tel (202) 745-7692; fax (202) 393-4119
Bureau Chief — Fernando Pajares

EIS International
555 Herndon Pkwy.
Herndon, VA 22070
tel (703) 478-9808; fax (703) 787-6720
Exec Vice President-Sales & Marketing —
Robert F. Kelly
President — Kevin Dahill

Electric Classifieds Inc.
340 Brannan St., Ste. 203
San Francisco, CA 94107
tel (415) 284-5300; fax (415) 284-5315
e-mail gary@match.com
Marketing Director — Fran Maier
President/CEO — Gary Kremen
General Manager-Technology & Solutions
— Sterling Hutto
Business Development VP — Dave Witherow

Electronic Book Technologies Inc. (EBT)
1 Richmond Sq.
Providence, RI 02906
tel (401) 421-9550; fax (401) 421-9551
e-mail info@ebt.com, http://www.ebt.com
Contact — Stacey Gottfried
President/CEO — Louis Reynolds
VP-North American Sales — Yvonne Dahl
Director-Marketing — Kent Summers
Public Relations Manager — Paul Lamoureux

The Electronic Newsstand
1225 19th St. N.W. Ste. 650
Washington, DC 20036
tel (202) 466-8688; fax (202) 466-2565
e-mail tspalmer@enews.com
Contact — Tom Palmer
President — Paul Vizza
Advertising — Larry Everling
Technical — Lisa Losito
Assistant — Sara Aducci

Electronic Press Inc.
101 Rogers St.
Cambridge, MA 02142
tel (617) 225-9023; fax (617) 225-7983
e-mail info@ep.cursci.com
Contact — Anna Sabasteanski
Dir-Business Development — Jeff Coutu

Electronic Publishing & Licensing Group
1725 K St. N.W., Ste. 700
Washington, DC 20006
tel (202) 872-4000; fax (202) 739-9578
e-mail sfk@access.digex.net,
msk@access.digex.net
Editor — Meg House
Editor — Nick Shears

Electronic Tele-Communications Inc.
3605 Clearview Pl.
Atlanta, GA 30340
tel (404) 457-5600; fax (404) 455-3822
Vice President — R.W. Johns Jr.
National Sales Manager — Roy Daniel

Electronic Vision Inc.
5 Depot St.
Athens, OH 45701
tel (614) 592-2433; fax (614) 592-2650
Marketing Communications Manager —
Kristin R. Hatem
President — David Burke
CEO — Dan Krivicich

Electronic World Communications Inc.
8916 Reading Rd., #4
Cincinnati, OH 45215
tel (513) 563-7424; fax (513) 769-3296
e-mail ewcnews@tso.uc.edu,
israelfaxx@pol.com
Contact — Don Canaan

ElectoPix Inc.
28729 S. Western Ave., #209
Rancho Palos Verdes, CA 90275-0800
tel (310) 831-6227
Producer — Kristen Simmons
Creative Director — S. Simmons
Programing Manager — L. Andersen
Sound Manager — D. Nienaltowski
Accounting — N. Beccerra

ELF Works 3D Construction Co.
1421 Page St.; PO Box 459
Alameda, CA 94501
tel (510) 769-9391; fax (510) 769-0895
e-mail elfwork@aol.com
Contact — Erik Flom

Elite of America Inc.
1190 Saratoga Ave., Ste. 210
San Jose, CA 95129
tel (408) 236-3266; fax (408) 236-3267
e-mail elite'rus@aol.com
Contant — Linda Huffman
Vice President — Norman Evangelista
Director-National Sales — Jae Chang

Emerging Technology Consultants Inc.
2819 Hamline Ave., N.
St. Paul, MN 55113-7118
tel (612) 639-3973; fax (612) 639-0110
e-mail 72717.2252@compuserve.com
CEO — Richard A. Pollak
President — Rubyanna R. Pollak
Marketing Coordinator — Chris Pihlstrom
Customer Service — Kelly Kern

Empire Information Services
PO Box 742
Schenectady, NY 12301
tel (518) 372-0785; fax (518) 372-0787
e-mail peter@eisinc.com
President — Peter G. Pollak

E-NEPH
7628 Densmore Ave.
Van Nuys, CA 91406
tel (818) 782-7328; fax (818) 782-7450
e-mail 74737.1367@compuserve.com
Contact — Doug Lynner

En Technology Corp.
310 Marlboro St.
Keene, NH 03431
tel (603) 355-1111; fax (603) 355-4388
Director-Administration — Matt Cookson
President — Patricia Gallup
Chairman of the Board — David Hall

Enhanced Systems Inc.
6961 Peacetree Industrial
Norcross, GA 30092
tel (770) 662-1503; fax (770) 242-1630
Vice President-Marketing — Mike Mittel

Enigma Information Systems Ltd.
10 Kishon St.
Brei-Brak, 51203 Israel
tel (972-3) 579-7061; fax (972-3) 579-7062
e-mail shai@enigma.co.il
Vice President-Marketing & Sales — Shai Onn
President — Johathan Yaron
Product Manager — Asher Amir
VP-Research & Development—Ronnen Armon

EPI Communications
6116 Executive Blvd., Ste. 210
Rockville, MD 20852
tel (301) 230-2023; fax (301) 468-2060
e-mail @epi-net.com
Director-Video Multimedia — Tom Bentz
Marketing Manager — Joe Criscuoli
General Manager — Jim Moore

E.P.I.C. Software Group Inc.
5 Grogans Park Dr.
The Woodlands, TX 77380
tel (713) 363-EPIC; fax (713) 292-9700
President — Vic Cherubini

Epsilon
50 Cambridge St.
Burlington, MA 01803
tel (617) 273-0250; fax (617) 270-4162
Manager-Marketing Communictations —
Natasha Lopoukhine
President/CEO — Robert Drummond

eSoft
15200 E. Girard Ave., Ste. 3000
Aurora, CO 80014
tel (303) 699-6565; fax (303) 699-6872
BBS: (303) 699-8222
Director-Marketing — Alan D. Bryant
President — Phil Becker

Copyright ©1996 by the Editor & Publisher Co.

VI-50 Interactive products and services

ESPN/SportsTicker
Harborside Financial Center-600 Plaza Two
Jersey City, NJ 07311-3992
tel (201) 309-1200; fax (201) 860-9742/
(800) 336-0383
Director-Marketing Services — Lou Monaco
President — Peter Bavasi
Vice President — Rick Alessandri
General Manager-News Operations —
John Mastroberardino
Managing Editor — Joe Carnicelli

ET Srl Elettronica Telecomunicazioni
Viale Veneto 4
Cinisello Balsamo, Milano 20092 Italy
tel (39-02) 66033.1;
fax (39-02) 66033.316
Contact — Sandro Sciaky
Commercial Manager — Massimo Fiocchi
Project Manager — Alberto Donzelli
SW Development Manager — Marco Prandi

Evans Michaels & Jaymes Inc.
Caputo Rd.; PO Box 659
North Branford, CT 06471-0659
tel (203) 484-4191; fax (203) 484-4519
Publisher/CEO — D. Trevor Michaels
CAO — Jason D. Roberts
Director — K.C. Michaels
Director — Edward H. Konesky Jr.

Excalibur Communications Inc.
2530 E. 71st St., Ste. E
Tulsa, OK 74136
tel (918) 488-9801; fax (918) 491-0033
e-mail excalibur@excalbbs.com
Operations Manager — Russell King
President — Eric Weber

Expert Systems Inc.
1301 Hightower Trail, Ste. 201
Atlanta, GA 30350
tel (770) 642-7575; fax (770) 587-5547
Director-Sales — Alan Hansen
President — Carlton Carden

F

Fabulous Footage Inc.
19 Mercer St., 4th Fl.
Toronto, ON M5V 1H2 Canada
tel (416) 591-6955; fax (416) 591-1666
e-mail sgarson@fabfootage.com
Business Manager — Julie Kovacs
Head of Research — Patricia Harvey
Researcher — Steve Race

FAR Systems Inc.
7898 High Ridge Rd.
Fort Atkinson, WI 53538
tel (414) 563-2221; fax (414) 563-1865
General Manager — Helen M. Rose

Fax Resources Inc.
2351 W. Northwest Hwy., Ste. 2115, LB 108
Dallas, TX 75220
tel (214) 353-0553; fax (214) 353-0686
e-mail faxresc@onramp.net
Marketing Director — Mike McKinney
President/CEO — Henry Rosen
Publisher — David Vaughn
Technical Director — Scott Williams

The Findlay Group
12575 Broadmoor
Overland Park, KS 66209
tel (913) 491-4353
e-mail tfindlay@unicom.net
President — Ted Findlay

fine.com Corp.
1109 First Ave., Ste. 212
Seattle, WA 98101-2945
tel (206) 292-2888; fax (206) 292-3889
e-mail info@fine.com
Contact — Dan Fine
Systems Administrator — Troy Muljat
Content Director — Jay Christensen
Sales Coordinator — Tricia Iboshi
Microsoft Network Developer —
Robin Sherwood

Fisher Photography
2234 Cathedrel Ave. N.W.
Washington, DC 20008
tel (202) 232-3181
Contact — Wayne W. Fisher
Owner — Patricia Fisher

First Alliance
PO Box 2352
Neptune, NJ 07754
tel (800) 480-6694; fax (908) 449-6291

e-mail 75720.1154@compuserve.com
Sales Manager — Dave Dauer

FLI Inc.
11900 Olympic Blvd., Ste. 530
Los Angeles, CA 90064-1151
tel (310) 820-2040; fax (310) 820-2341
Vice President — Peter F. Gastaldi
President — John Wills

Focus Interactive Technology Inc.
1223 Peoples Ave.
Troy, NY 12180
tel (518) 276-8276; fax (518) 276-6380
e-mail granda@focusweb.com
President — Leonard V. Granda
VP-Tech. Development — John W. Woods

Fonahome Corp.
6224 Bury Dr.
Minneapolis, MN 55346-1718
tel (612) 975-6102; fax (612) 934-5792
e-mail ntb@fona.com
CEO — Nick T. Boosalis

Four Palms Inc.
11260 Roger Bacon Dr.
Reston, VA 22090
tel (703) 834-0200; fax (703) 834-0219
Sales — Scott Santucci
President — Pat Buteux
Vice President — Ken Santucci
Marketing Services Manager — Judy Ballou

Frederiksen Television Inc.
2735 Hartland Rd., Ste. 300
Falls Church, VA 22043
tel (703) 560-8290; fax (703) 560-8292
Marketing Manager — Nancy Whalen
President — Lee Frederiksen
Media Director — Diane Parker

Freemyers Design
575 Nelson Ave.
Oroville, CA 95965
tel (916) 533-9365
Contact — Don Freemyers

Frontier Interactive Multimedia Communications
117 Great Valley Parkway
Malvern, PA 19355
tel (610) 647-5535, ext. 116;
fax (610) 647-0174
e-mail 70304.2565@compuserve.com
President — Robert T. Cooper

Fujitsu Systems Business of America Inc.
5200 Patrick Henry
Santa Clara, CA 95054
tel (800) 446-4736; fax (203) 964-1007
e-mail andyb@fsba.com
Product Manager — Carol Higgins
President — Takashi Matsutani

Future Light
153 E. Hartsdale Ave., #2A
Hartsdale, NY 10530
tel (914) 723-0592
e-mail futurel@aol.com
Contact — Marsha Waldman
President — William Waldman

FutureVideo
23 Argonaut
Aliso Viejo, CA 92656
tel (714) 770-4416; fax (714) 770-4667
Vice President — Stephen E. Godfrey
President/CEO — Robert A. Cohen
Sales Manager — Stuart Brenner

G

Galacticomm Inc.
4101 S.W. 47th Ave., Ste. 101
Fort Lauderdale, FL 33314
tel (305) 583-5990/(800) 328-1128
(Sales);fax (305) 583-7846
e-mail sales@gcomm.com
Contact — Michele Rodieu
President/CEO — Scott Brinker
Marketing Vice-President — Linda Haury
Communications Manager — Dihan Rosenburg

Galileo Inc.
6055 Barfield Rd., Ste. 200
Atlanta, GA 30328
tel (404) 255-6377; fax (404) 255-6301
e-mail http://www.galileoinc.com
Contact — Mike Wittenstein
Co-President — Jackie Goldstein
Producer — Kelly Wingate
Office Manager — Kelly Powlay

GammaLink
1314 Cheasapeake Ter.
Sunnyvale, CA 94089
tel (408) 744-1400; fax (408) 744-1900
North American Sales Mgr — Bob Green

Gannett Digital XPRESS
1000 Wilson Blvd.
Arlington, VA 22229
tel (703) 276-5900; fax (703) 558-3870
e-mail candrew@usatoday.gannett.com
Executive Vice President — Blake Barker
Dir.-Infomation Services — Thomas Turco
Dir.-Technical Services — Wayne Nugent
Operations Chef — Christopher Andrew

Gannett Media Technology International
151 W. 4th St., Ste. 201
Cincinnati, OH 45202
tel (513) 665-3777; fax (513) 241-7219
President/CEO — Daniel Zito

Gannett/USA Today Information Center
1000 Wilson Blvd.
Arlington, VA 22066
tel (703) 276-5900; fax (703) 558-3870
Executive Vice President-Information
Center — M. Blake Barker
Systems Coordinator — Chris Andrew

GE Information Services
570 Lexington Ave., 17th Fl.
New York, NY 10022
tel (212) 836-3100; fax (212) 836-3376
Pubnet® Community Manager —
Nadine Rosenbaum

GEN Inc.
141 W. Foothill Blvd.
Monrovia, CA 91016
tel (818) 932-1338; fax (818) 932-1342
e-mail richard@genine.com
President — Richard Madock
Executive Vice President — Robert Helm

General Fax Inc.
Continental Business Center, Ste. 103
Bridgeport, PA 19405
tel (610) 277-1722; fax (610) 277-1748
Contact — Christopher Stephano
System Engineer — Jeffrey Gross
Sales Manager — Theresa Mack

Glas News
12412 S.E. 26th Pl.
Bellevue, WA 98005
tel (206) 957-0219; fax (206) 957-0219
e-mail glasnews@eskimo.com,
http://www.solar.ptd.uti.edu/~aboyle/glasnews/master.html
Managing Editor — Alan Boyle
Chairman — David Endicott
Vice Chairman — Marina Orlova

Glenayre Electronics
4800 Rivergreen Pkwy
Atlanta, GA 30136
tel (770) 623-4900; fax (770) 497-3990
Senior VP/General Manager — Dan Case
President — Ray Aridizzona

Godfrey Advertising
2890 Hempland Rd.
Lancaster, PA 17601
tel (717) 393-3831; fax (717) 393-1403
e-mail denny@godfrey.com
Contact — Denny Miller
Creative Director — Jim Everhart
Internet Specialist — Harry Furness
Interactive Design Specialist —
Catharine Oakes

The Gourley Group
1621 W. 25th St., Ste. 204
San Pedro, CA 90732
tel (310) 519-1324; fax (310) 519-9323
President — Bob Gourley

GP Productions
362 3rd Ave., Ste. 1B
New York, NY 10016-9012
tel (212) 686-5267
President — Gill R. Pessoa

Grafica Multimedia Inc.
1777 Borel Pl., Ste. 500
San Mateo, CA 94402
tel (415) 358-5555; fax (415) 358-5556
e-mail grafica@netcom.com
CEO — Mike McGrath
Business Manager — Gabriella Martino
Director-Engineering — Wallace Rutherford

Gralin Associates Inc.
5525 Swamp Rd.
Fountainville, PA 18923
tel (215) 249-4980; fax (215) 249-4985
President — Graeme P. Watson
Vice President — Tim Watson

Graphic Systems
440 9th Ave., 17th Fl.
New York, NY 10001
tel (212) 947-2996; fax (212) 947-3089
e-mail 72570.1766@compuserve.com
Contact — Jean-Paul Peretz

Graphics Syndicate
1000 Gerard St. E.; PO Box 98098
Toronto, ON M4M 2Z3 Canada
tel (416) 463-3824; fax (416) 463-7854
e-mail info@hotgraphics.com
http://www.hotgraphics.com
Editorial Manager — Catherine Farley
General Manager — Michael Lea

Great!
3527 Knollhaven N.E.
Atlanta, GA 30319-1908
tel (404) 303-7311; fax (404) 252-0697
e-mail smigrod@greattv.com,
http://www.greattv.com
Marketing Director — Dan Smigrod
Account Executive — Mark Lawson
Promotion Manager — Shelley King
Promotion Manager — Elizabeth LaBar
Promotion Coordinator — Angela Carpenter

Grey Direct
875 3rd Ave.
New York, NY 10022
tel (212) 303-2300; fax (212) 303-2333
President — George Weidemann
Vice President — Emilie Schaum

Griffin & Boyle
445 E. Illinois, Ste. 345
Chicago, IL 60611
tel (312) 836-5900; fax (312) 836-5920
e-mail orgelbau@aol.com
Contact — W. Dennis Boyle
Vice President — William R. Milligan

G.T.E. Directories
5601 Executive Dr. (75063);
PO Box 165008
Irving, TX 75016-5008
tel (214) 518-2810; fax (214) 518-0150
Contact — Harris Johnson
Manager-Voice Product Operations —
Patricia Clark
Product Analyst — Lori Murray

GTEK
399 Highway 90 (39520); PO Box 2310
Bay St. Louis, MS 39521-2310
tel (601) 467-8048; fax (601) 467-0935
BBS: (601) 452-0058
Sales Manager — Deb Sogard
President — Bill Groves

GW Associates
1 Regency Dr.; PO Box 6606
Holliston, MA 01746
tel (508) 429-6227; fax (508) 429-3859
e-mail petewhite@gwabbs.com
BBS: (508) 429-8385
Owner — Pete White

H

Ha! Design Inc.
6112 Misty Pine Ct.
Crystal Lake, IL 60012
tel (815) 363-1964; fax (815) 363-0095
e-mail ktee1964@aol.com
Contact — Katie Hayden

Hands-On Interactive Publishing Inc.
611 N. 10th St., 6th Fl.
St. Louis, MO 63101
tel (314) 241-6966; fax (314) 241-4026
President — Christopher P. Ruess

Harris Publishing Systems
PO Box 8700
Melbourne, FL 32902
tel (407) 242-4065; fax (407) 242-4074
Vice President-Sales — Tony Perry
VP/General Manager — Stan Padgett

Haukom Associates
10 Lombard, #250
San Francisco, CA 94111
tel (415) 658-2820
Partner — Richard Haukom
Partner — Rita Winkler

Hearing Voices—Voice Overs
123 Bay Place, #107
Oakland, CA 94610-4445
tel (510) 452-9274
e-mail stophocles@aol.com
Contact — Christopher P. Sullivan

HEC Software Inc.
3471 S. 550 W.; (450 E. 1000 N., North
Salt Lake, 84150)
Bountiful, UT 84101

Copyright ©1996 by the Editor & Publisher Co.

Interactive products and services VI-51

tel (801) 295-7054/(800) 333-0054;
fax (801) 295-7088
Vice President — Leonard Eversole
President — Linda Eversole
Accounts Receivable — Marie Christiansen

Hemsing Advertising Inc.
755 W. Big Beaver, Ste. 416
Troy, MI 48084
tel (810) 362-0448; fax (810) 362-3884
e-mail jabourque@mcimail.com
President — Jeffrey A. Bourque
Vice President — Ken Wasvary

Hennig Productions
504 W. 7th St.; PO Box 2111
Austin, TX 78701
tel (512) 477-4917; fax (512) 477-4918
Contact — Tom Hennig
Producer — Steve Ross

Hewlett-Packard
5301 Stevens Creek Blvd. MS 53UGF
Santa Clara, CA 95052
tel (408) 553-2948; fax (408) 553-2945
e-mail casey
sheldon@hp4200.desk.hp.com
Contact — Casey Sheldon
General Manager-Home Products Division — Webb McKinney
Sales Manger — Joe Kail

High Velocity Software
PO Box 33455
Phoenix, AZ 85067-3455
tel (800) 572-5582
e-mail support@mail.hvs.com
http://www.hvs.com
Director-Sales — Rob Palsma
President — Jeff Moriarty

Highlighted Data Inc.
3901 Indian School Rd. N.E., Ste. C405
Albuquerque, NM 87110-3845
tel (505) 255-7701; fax (505) 255-7841
President — David Drake
Vice President-Marketing — Anne-Maria Barker

Hinckley & Slade Inc.
4 Chelsea Pl.
Houston, TX 77006
tel (713) 520-1515; fax (713) 520-7509
President — Joe Slade

HintonWells Communications Inc.
2727 Paces Ferry Rd. N.W., Ste. 1-1260
Atlanta, GA 30339
tel (404) 436-1400; fax (404) 436-3358
Contact — Michael E. Wells

Hitchcock Fleming & Associates Inc.
500 Wolf Ledges Pkwy.
Akron, OH 44311
tel (216) 376-2111; fax (216) 376-2220
President — Jack S. DeLeo
Chairman — R. Cyrus Hitchcock
Asst. VP/Acct. Supv. — Shirley Shriver
Production Manager — Tina Purnell

Hollywood Online Inc.
3015 Main St., Ste. 400
Santa Monica, CA 90405
tel (310) 581-4488; fax (310) 581-4499
e-mail hollywoodc@aol.com
Executive Vice President-Marketing — Stuart Halperin
CEO — Steven Katinsky
President — Anthony Farwell
Executive VP/CFO — Bruce Cameron
Dir.-Product Development — Curtis Beck

Hometown Video Productions
1200 Artesia Blvd., Ste. 300
Hermosa Beach, CA 90254-2755
tel (310) 798-1500; fax (310) 798-1511
e-mail fkilpatrick@stanford-media.com,
http://www.hometowntv.com
President — Frank S. Kilpatrick
Vice President-Sales — Linda H. Kilpatrick
Producer — Anne Hulegard
Director — Philip Earl

HorizonMedia
145 Wood Rd.
Braintree, MA 02184
tel (617) 848-1201; fax (617) 843-3665
e-mail twoten210@aol.com
Contact — Peter Huston
Editor — Jeff Rhind
Software Engineer — John Capellupo

Hot Sheet Publishing
114 Sansome St., Ste. 1224
San Francisco, CA 94104
tel (415) 421-6220; fax (415) 421-6225
e-mail agarcia@aol.com
Editor/Publisher — Art Garcia
Principal — Thomas A. Pelandini

Hotwax Interactive
16 Stoneybrook Ct.
Ramsey, NJ 07446
tel (201) 818-0001; fax (201) 818-0108
Contact — David R. Huber

HTI Voice Solutions Inc.
333 Turnpike Rd.
Southborough, MA 01772
tel (508) 485-8400; fax (508) 485-9584
Vice President-Sales — Peter B. Keenan

Hummingbird Studios Inc.
887 W. Marietta St., N.W. N-105
Atlanta, GA 30318
tel (404) 724-0021; fax (404) 249-7813
e-mail jharne@mindspring.com
Contact — Gina Winchester

I

IBM
590 Madison Ave.
New York, NY 10022
Media Business Unit Executive — Peter O'Sullivan
Media Solutions Mgr — Stephen Ehrlich

Idealdial Corp.
910 15th St., Ste. 900
Denver, CO 80202
tel (303) 534-0300; fax (303) 595-8707
VP-Sales & Marketing — Ronald P. Kubicki
President — Michael G. Payne
CFO — Michael A. Scata
Senior Vice President — Mark J. Payne

IICS: International Interactive Communications Society
14657 S.W. Teal Blvd., Ste. 119
Beaverton, OR 97007
tel (503) 579-4427; fax (503) 579-6272
e-mail iicshq@aol.com,
70274.1075@compuserve.com
Managing Director — Debra Palm

ILIO Entertainment
PO Box 3772
Chatsworth, CA 91311
tel (818) 883-4546; fax (818) 883-4361
Contact — Shelly Williams
Co-Owner — Mark Hiskey

Image Communications
1420 Springhill Rd., Ste. 400
McLean, VA 22102
tel (703) 848-2700; fax (703) 848-0770
Contact — Mary Sasser

Image Communications Group
5151 Beltline Rd., Ste. 804
Dallas, TX 75240
tel (214) 404-1234
Contact — Wayne Richard
Vice President-Marketing — Pat Sullivan
Project Manager — Susan Hutchinson

Image Technologies Inc.
12425 28th St. N., Ste. 101
St. Petersburg, FL 33716
tel (813) 573-5268; fax (813) 573-0431
e-mail imagetech@applelink.apple.com
President/Founder — Bruce Bennett
Director-Marketing Communications — Florine Mackay
Director-Production — Don Gillespie
Director-Development — Steve Kos
Creative Director — Dan Mackay

Image Technology Inc.
5605 Roanne Way
Greensboro, NC 27409
tel (910) 299-2452; fax (910) 292-3096
Vice Pres.-Marketing & Sales — Jody Tester
President — Douglas Young

Imagen Inc.
2200 N. Lamar, Ste. 104
Dallas, TX 75202
tel (214) 871-2747; fax (214) 871-2748
e-mail imageninc@aol.com
Contact — Al Schmidt
Contact — Ruben Esquivel

Imagetects
PO Box 4
Saratoga, CA 95071
tel (408) 252-5487; fax (408) 252-7409
e-mail imagetects@aol.com
President — Alan Reed

Imagine That Creative Services
1331 Union Ave., Ste. 709
Memphis, TN 38104
tel (901) 276-8828; fax (901) 276-0227
e-mail imagethat@aol.com
Contact — Scott Stalcup
Partner — Tami Oglesby

Imergy
12 South Main St.
South Norwalk, CT 06854
tel (203) 853-6200; fax (203) 831-9090
e-mail imergy@aol.com
Executive Vice President — Tom Weisz
President — Flora W. Perskie
VP-Media Integration — Peter Mackey
Senior Creative Director — Debra Leeds
Director-Multimedia Productions — Richard Spitalny
Director-Administration & Human Resources — Suzanne Mason

IMMediacy
5753 Uplander Way
Culver City, CA 90230
tel (310) 642-4995; fax (310) 642-4998
e-mail immedcy@primenet.com
COO — Paul Atkinson
President — Lloyd Pentecost

Impact Media Group
1920 Franklin St., Ste. 7
San Francisco, CA 94109
tel (415) 563-9083; fax (415) 563-7637
e-mail impactmg@slip.net
impactmg@aol.com
http://www.slip.net/~impactmg
Senior Partner — Garner M. Moss
Senior Partner — Greg Munson
Marketing Director — Trey Roski

InContext Systems
2 St. Clair Ave W., 16th Fl.
Toronto, ON M4V 1L5 Canada
tel (416) 922-0087; fax (416) 922-6489
e-mail david@InContext.ca
Product Manager — David J. Turner
President — Robert Arn

Index Inc.
6030 E. Alabama Rd., Ste. 114
Woodstock, GA 30188
tel (770) 924-8667; fax (770) 924-3323
e-mail info@index.com,
BBS: (770) 924-Index
Office Manager — Debbie St. Angelo
President — Rodney Aloia

InfiNet, Landmark Communications
150 W. Brambleton Ave.
Norfolk, VA 23501
tel (804) 628-1020; fax (804) 628-1050
VP-Affiliate Marketing — Peter III

Infinity Promotions Inc.
1024 N. Corona
Colorado Springs, CO 80903
tel (719) 475-8380; fax (719) 475-2839
Contact — Steven A. Suslow
Founding Partner — Jeff Voss

INFO-CONNECT (J.H. Zerby Newspapers Inc.)
111 Mahontongo St.
Pottsville, PA 17901
tel (717) 628-6067/(717) 628-6016;
fax (717) 621-3308
e-mail sesmith@ricnet.pottsville.com
Dir-Sales & Marketing — Sharon Smith
Director — Jim Dible

InfoAccess Inc.
2800 156th Ave. S.E., Ste. 205
Bellevue, WA 98007-6548
tel (206) 747-3203; fax (206) 641-9367
e-mail infoaccess@infoaccess.com
Contact — Frances Bigley
Director-Sales — Brian Pavicik
Director-Marketing — Michael New

The InfoCenter Group Inc.
3302 Enterprise Rd.
Fort Pierce, FL 34982
tel (407) 465-8388; fax (407) 461-3115
e-mail infogrp@aol.com
President — Don Mullins
Director-Marketing — Don Urschalitz
Director-System Support — Debbie Rudd

InfoMotion
1370 Filbert St., #2
San Francisco, CA 94109-1735
tel (415) 474-5194; fax (415) 474-5194
e-mail 74077.554@compuserve.com
Principal — W. Leake Little
Principal — Frank Trozzo

Information Command Inc.
444 N. Wells
Chicago, IL 60610-4513
tel (312) 245-1111; fax (312) 245-1128
President — Donald Young

Information Handling Services
15 Inverness Way E.; PO Box 1154
Englewood, CO 80150
tel (303) 790-0600/(800) 525-7052/(800) 716-1447
fax (303) 754-3940
VP-U.S. Marketing — Terry Erdle
Mgr-Corp Communications — Chris McGary

Information Highways Inc.
PO Box 612287
Dallas/Fort Worth Airport, TX 75261-2287
tel (817) 379-5178; fax (817) 431-1011
e-mail holbein@onramp.net
President — Thomas J. Holbein

Information Presentation Tech.
555 Chorro St.
San Luis Obispo, CA 93405
tel (805) 541-3000; fax (805) 541-3037
e-mail info@iptech.com
President — Jonathan Simonds

Information Technologies Corps.
1004 N. Thompson St., Ste. 205
Richmond, VA 23230
tel (804) 342-1200; fax (804) 342-1209
President — Frank E. Butler
Vice President-Marketing — Doug Blue
Marketing Services — Lisa Gibbs

Infornonics Inc.
550 Newtown Rd.
Littleton, MA 01460
tel (508) 486-8976; fax (508) 486-0027
e-mail info@infor.com
Contact — Robin Humes
President — Laurence Buckland
Executive VP — Bruce Buckland

InfoUse
2560 9th St., Ste. 216
Berkeley, CA 94710
tel (510) 549-6520; fax (510) 549-6512
e-mail lewiskraus@aol.com
Vice President — Lewis Kraus
President — Susan Stoddard
Project Manager — Paul Shain
Operations Officer — Tessa David

Ingels Inc.
7080 Hollywood Blvd., 11th Fl.
Hollywood, CA 90028
tel (213) 464-0800; fax (213) 464-0047
CEO — Rusty Schreiber
President — Deborah R. Getson
Vice President — Ed Adler

Innovative Systems Design Inc.
16025 Pierrefonds Blvd.
Pierrefonds, QC H9H 3X6 Canada
tel (514) 696-8377; fax (514) 696-9016
Sales Manager — Jeff Tierney
Sales Rep. — Laurie Scott

Innovative Telecom Corp.
2 Harrison St., PO Box 3231
Nashua, NH 03060
tel (603) 889-8411; fax (603) 598-5590
Vice President — Arthur Butt
President — Mark Tubinis
CFO — Jack Mead
Vice President-Engineering — Larry Ferns

Inpho Inc.
225 5th St.
Cambridge, MA 02142
tel (617) 868-7050; fax (617) 868-5476
e-mail skropper@mcimail.com
Contact — Steve Kropper
CFO — Fran Rivkin
Director-Customer Service — Mike Greco

Insider Magazine
4124 Oakton St.
Skokie, IL 60076
tel (847) 673-3703; fax (847) 329-0358
e-mail spinetwork@aol.com
Publisher — Mark Jansen
Editorial Director — Alex Gordon
Senior Editor — Rob Bernstein

Instant Information Inc.
5 Broad St.
Boston, MA 02109
tel (617) 523-7636; fax (617) 723-6522
President — Joe Kolawczyk
Mgr-Business Development — Steve Rankel

Intecom
5057 Keller Springs Rd.
Dallas, TX 75248
tel (214) 447-9000; fax (214) 447-8329
President — George Platt

Copyright ©1996 by the Editor & Publisher Co.

VI-52 Interactive products and services

Integra IMA GmbH
Will-Brandt-Platz 2
Bielefeld, 33602 Germany
tel (49-521) 9620-0; fax (49-521)9620-190
e-mail info@integra.de
Contact — Dirk Sasse
Sales Manager — Noelle Le Blanc

Intelligent Media
1350 Abbot Kinney Blvd., Ste. 203
Venice, CA 90291
tel (310) 581-8840; fax (310) 581-8844
e-mail magoc@netcom.com,
http://www.smartworld.com/intmedia.
imedia.html
Executive Producer — John Hughes
President — Ronnie A. Margolis
Vice President — Zeke Margolis

IntelliPro Inc.
120 Jersey Ave.
New Brunswick, NJ 08901
tel (908) 220-1766; fax (908) 846-4887
e-mail ipro@cnj.digex.net
Contact — Rick Clinton
Vice President — Philippe Marchal

Intellisystems Inc.
6490 S. McCarran Blvd., #33
Reno, NV 89509
tel (702) 828-2800; fax (702) 828-2828
Contact — Boris Hallerbach
Director-Operations — Michael Beare
Office Administration — Lisa Tintle

Interactive Arts
3200 Airport Ave., #16
Santa Monica, CA 90405
tel (310) 390-9466; fax (310) 390-7525
e-mail psbloc@aol.com
CEO — Peter Bloch
Vice President — David Schwartz
Creative Director — Mary Jo Reutter

Interactive Business Communications
570 Beatty Rd.
Monroeville, PA 15146-1334
tel (412) 373-2902; fax (412) 372-2161
e-mail ibc94@aol.com
Contact — Robert J. DiGioia
Art Director — Matthew Smerbeck
Director-Management Information Systems
— Sanjay Akut
Animation Director — Dave Hopson

Interactive CARDnet Telephone Co.
PO Box 15272
Las Vegas, NV 89114-5272
tel (702) 477-0200; fax (702) 375-0033
e-mail spmm39a@prodigy.com
Contact — Stuart Ervin

Interactive Catalog Corp.
1420 5th Ave., #1800
Seattle, WA 98101
tel (206) 623-0977; fax (206) 623-0477
Contact — Dan Merrill
Contact — Bob Nelson
President — Craig Danuloff
CFO — Jamie Miller
VP-Corp Communications — Elaine Rickman
Public Relations Manager — Jeanne Miller

Interactive Conferencing Network
42 Oak Ave.
Tuckahoe, NY 10707
tel (914) 961-0700; fax (914) 961-8234
Contact — Steve Campus

Interactive Consulting
11 Victor Ave.
Glen Ridge, NJ 07028
tel (201) 743-5640; fax (201) 743-5640
Contact — Kathy Berni
Executive Producer — Jeff Atlas

Interactive Design
37 Brooks Ave.
Venice, CA 90291
tel (310) 392-9204; fax (310) 392-2568
e-mail jaryl lane@aol.com
Contact — Jaryl Lane

Interactive Educational Systems Design Inc.
310 W. 106th St.
New York, NY 10025
tel (212) 769-1715; fax (212) 769-0909
e-mail 71541.1541@compuserve.com,
iesdinc@aol.com
Contact — Ellen Bialo
Vice President — Jay Sivin-Kachala

Interactive International Inc.
290 West End Ave.
New York, NY 10023-8106
tel (212) 580-5015; fax (212) 580-5017
President — George M. Bulow

Interactive Marketing News
1201 Seven Locks Rd., Ste. 300
Potomac, MD 20854
tel (301) 340-1520; fax (301) 340-1451
Marketing Manager — Angela Duff
Managing Editor — Donna Englegau
Publisher — Kismet Toksu-Gould

Interactive Media Associates
11 Eagle Nest Rd.
Morristown, NJ 07960
tel (201) 539-5255; fax (201) 539-5711
Managing Director — Len Muscarella

Interactive Media Group
12540 Beatrice St.
Los Angeles, CA 90066
tel (310) 574-4400; fax (310) 574-4404
Contact — Richard Dorfman
Vice President — Ronnie Shrira
VP Sales & Marketing — Charles Acquisto

Interactive Media Inc.
500 3rd Ave. SE
Cedar Rapids, IA 52401
tel (319) 398-8421; fax (319) 368-8538
e-mail imi@netims.net
Vice Pres./General Manager — Jim Debth
Product Development Manager —
Mark McCoid
Online Coordinator — Lisa Wilson

Interactive Multimedia Project
3700 Southridge, Ste. 100
Austin, TX 78704
tel (512) 326-8858; fax (512) 326-8859
Vice President — Shelley Runyan
President — Sjon Veckert

Interactive Newspaper Network
Times Information Services; 720 Olive
Way, Ste. 500
Seattle, WA 98101
tel (206) 464-2608; fax (206) 464-8322
e-mail lstt-tis@ctimes.com
Chairperson — Linda Stlzner

Interactive Productions
610 Thimble Shoals Blvd.
Newport News, VA 23606
tel (804) 873-3635; fax (804) 873-3626
e-mail fairman@infi.net
President — Richard Fairman

interActive Publishing
33 Lake Front Rd.
Putnam Valley, NY 10579-2226
tel (914) 528-4117/(212) 751-4141
fax (914) 528-7184
Contact — Tom O'Reilly
CEO — Victor Milt
Chief Programmer — Cynthia Romano
Editor — Chris Apa
Graphics — Eric Reinfeld

Interactive Publishing Alert
1124 Harrison St.
Hollywood, FL 33019
tel (305) 920-5326; fax (305) 926-7655
e-mail rosalind@harrison.win.net
Editor/Publisher — Rosalind Resnick

Interactive Services Association
8403 Colesville Rd., Ste. 865
Silver Spring, MD 20910
tel (301) 495-4955; fax (301) 495-4959
e-mail sarafitz@aol.com
Contact — Sara Fitzgerald
Executive Director — Robert L. Smith
Director-Conferences — Patti McKnight

Interactive Television Association
1030 15th St. N.W., Ste. 1053
Washington, DC 20005
tel (202) 408-0008; fax (202) 408-0111
CEO — Peter C. Waldheim
President — Andrew L. Sernovitz
Director-Membership — Yasha M. Harari
Director-Member Services —
Matthew J. Laurencelle

Interactive Video Solutions
70 State Rd.; PO Box 1280
Media, PA 19063
tel (610) 891-6777; fax (610) 891-8529
President — Jim Pitts
Vice President-Sales — Tom Pitts
Consultant — Al Pitts

Interactive Visuals Inc.
5230 N. Wayne Ave.
Chicago, IL 60640-2223
tel (312) 275-5039; fax (312) 275-3830
e-mail interact@ripco.com
Technical Director — Mark Weber
Creative Director — Julie Weber
Producer/Designer — Amy Ezop
Producer/Designer — Michele Craig

Interactivity Magazine
411 Borel Ave., Ste. 100
San Mateo, CA 94402
tel (415) 655-4321; fax (415) 655-4360
e-mail interactivity@mfi.com
Associate Publisher — Thomas M. Edwards
Advertising Director — Carol Robinson
Editor — Dominic Milano

Interalia Communications
10340 Viking Dr., #135
Eden Prairie, MN 55344-7231
tel (612) 942-6088; fax (612) 942-6172
Sales Manager — Tom Peterson
Vice President-Marketing — John Trester

Interaxx Television Network Inc.
10800 Biscayne Blvd. #800
Miami, FL 33161
tel (305) 893-9911; fax (305) 891-9498
Contact — Roberta Miller
Vice President-Direct Marketing — Ken Angel
President/CEO — Donald Rhoades

InterCom
3 Grogan's Park Dr., Ste. 100
The Woodlands, TX 77380
tel (800) 298-7070; fax (713) 364-7032
GM-Marketing Services — Jeanne
O'Connor-Green
Chairman/CEO — C.E. (Gene) Hahne
President — Bob Yeager
General Manager — Margo Pearson

Interface
747 Pacific Ave.
Salt Lake City, UT 84104
tel (801) 521-4600 ext. 9638
fax (801) 359-2800
Systems Manager — Phil Pearl
General Manager — Ron Thornton

Interface Builder
208 Spruce; PO Box 5987
Ketchum, ID 83340
tel (208) 726-5232; fax (208) 726-5350
e-mail intbuild@well.sf.ca.us
BBS: (208) 726-9360
President — Lee Chubb

Interleaf Inc.
Prospect Pl., 9 Hillside Ave.
Waltham, MA 02154
tel (617) 290-0710 ext. 2277
fax (617) 290-4966
e-mail i-direct@ileaf.com
Product Manager — Mary Beth Smartt

International Connectivity Consortium
3872 Grove Ave.
Palo Alto, CA 94303
tel (415) 265-8843; fax (415) 493-8415
e-mail phillum@aol.com
Contact — Philip Lumish
Vice President — Greg Schatzel

International Information Technologies Ltd.
Sunnehaldenstr. 7
Bruetten, 8311 Switzerland
tel (41-52) 347-1011; fax (41-52) 347-1012
e-mail drwier@pax.eunet.ch
Contact — Dennis Wier

International Software Service Inc.
1560 Tilco Dr.
Frederick, MD 21701
tel (301) 695-6300/(800) 368-9900; fax
(301) 662-0402
e-mail johnmagruder@ichange.com
Contact — John Magruder

International Teleprogrpms Inc.
10 Dell Glen Ave., Ste. 5
Lodi, NJ 07644
tel (201) 340-7799; fax (201) 546-8012
President — David Lapidus

Internet Distribution Services Inc.
665 Wellsbury Way
Palo Alto, CA 94306
tel (415) 856-8265; fax (415) 856-8165
e-mail marc@service.com
Contact — Marc Fleischmann

Internet Research Inc.
1212 Boylston St., Ste. 120
Chestnut Hill, MA 02167
tel (617) 527-2771; fax (617) 928-1514

e-mail jonathan@gis.net
Director-Marketing — Jonathan Horblitt
President — Robert Carp

The Internet Unplugged
104 Carnegie Center, CN 5302
Princeton, NJ 08543
tel (800) 242-7675; fax (609) 452-1288
e-mail ken@planet.net
Director-Training — Ken Musiak

InterVoice Inc.
17811 Waterview Pkwy.
Dallas, TX 75252
tel (214) 497-8862; fax (214) 497-8905
Marketing Manager — Tom Anderson

Intra-Active Designs
PO Box 4022
Minneapolis, MN 55343
tel (612) 938-1473
e-mail corrie@sown.com
CEO — Corrie Bergeron

The Investext Group
22 Pittsburgh St.
Boston, MA 02210
tel (617) 345-2704/(800) 662-7878
(Customer Support); fax (617) 330-1986
Marketing Communications Manager —
John Webber

IPA The Editing House
1208 W. Webster
Chicago, IL 60614
tel (312) 871-6033; fax (312) 871-5463
e-mail ipascott@aol.com
Director-Sales & Marketing — Evie Silvers
President — Scott Jacobs
VP/General Manager — Deb Cottie
President — Stan Sutherland
Vice-President — Scott Jacobs

Iron Design
1137 E. Shore Dr.
Ithaca, NY 14850
tel (800) 304-4766; fax (607) 275-0370
e-mail irondzign@aol.com
Contact — Todd Edmonds
Designer — Ted Skibinski

It Network/Source Media
8140 Walnut Hill Ln., Ste. 1000
Dallas, TX 75231
tel (214) 890-9050; fax (214) 890-9014
Contact — John Reed
CEO — Tim Peters
COO — Scott Bedford
Exec. VP/Pres-"Interactive Channel" —
John Reed

i3 Information & Imagination Inc.
325 Riverside Ave.
Westport, CT 06880
tel (203) 227-2030; fax (203) 227-2218
e-mail i3spark@aol.com
Contact — Stuart Park
VP/Creative Director — James Fabry

iTV1 Multimedia Inc.
305 E. 46th St., 10th Fl.
New York, NY 10017
tel (212) 644-7108; fax (212) 644-7995
e-mail itv1@panix.com
Contact — Juliana Park
Account Manager — Mark Fiducia
Creative Director — Abraham Ku
Consultant — Jane Pirone
Technical Director — Glenn White

Ivy Hill Packaging
375 Hudson St.
New York, NY 10014
tel (212) 741-1404; fax (212) 691-9737
VP-Marketing — Herbert Friedman
Executive Vice President — Arthur Kern
Vice President-Sales — Anthony Adamoli
Manager-Marketing Services — Sandra Olson

J

Jackson Graphics Inc.
W141 N9314 Fountain Blvd.
Menomonee Falls, WI 53051
tel (414) 251-5657; fax (414) 251-7230
e-mail jgi@execpc.com
http:\\www.execpc.com\jgi
Contact — Gary Zaffke

Jordan Whitney Inc.
17300 17th St., Ste. J-111
Tustin, CA 92680
tel (714) 832-2432; fax (714) 832-3053
e-mail greensheet@aol.com
President — Clare Kogler
Publisher/COO — John Kogler
Executive Assistant — Monica Cantrell

Interactive products and services VI-53

Joyce Communications
1714 Sanborn Ave.
Los Angeles, CA 90027
tel (213) 661-5225; fax (213) 661-4999
Contact — Joyce A. Schwarz

Judson Rosebush Co.
154 W. 57th St., Studio 826
New York, NY 10019
tel (212) 581-3000; fax (212) 757-8283
e-mail rosebush@applelink.apple.com
boo@panix.com
Contact — Sanford Streim
President — Judson Rosebush

Just Softworks Inc.
15419 127th St.; PO Box 552
Lemont, IL 60439
tel (708) 257-7616; fax (708) 257-9678
Vice President-Sales & Marketing —
John Williams
CEO — Steve Peskaitis
CFO — Stan Peskaitis
Shipping Manager — Jim Jones

K

Kallisto Productions Inc.
2173 E. Francisco Blvd., Ste. E
San Rafael, CA 94901
tel (415) 257-4777; fax (415) 257-4770
e-mail kallisto.pro@applelink.apple.com
kallisto@aol.com
Director-Marketing — Vince Datolli
Senior Partner — Alan Weiler
Senior Partner — John de Lorimier

Kan Image Inc.
11-05 44th Dr.
Long Island City, NY 11101
tel (718) 482-1800 ext. 250
fax (718) 482-1968
e-mail cosmosinc@aol.com
Contact — Heather Weiss
Vice President-Marketing —
Dr. Jerome Skapof
President — Gerald Weiss
Vice President-Operations — Steven Brauner
Photographer — Terrance McGuiness

Keller Production
4305 Gunderson Ct.
Sebastopol, CA 95472
tel (707) 829-9129; fax (707) 829-8331
e-mail kelprod@earthlink.net
Contact — Steve Keller

The Kelsey Group
600 Executive Dr.
Princeton, NJ 08540
tel (609) 921-7200; fax (609) 921-2112
e-mail tkg@ix.netcom.com
Contact — Natalie Kaye
Vice President — Marsha Stoltman

Kinetic Corp.
240 Distillery Commons
Louisville, KY 40206-1990
tel (502) 583-1679; fax (502) 583-1104
e-mail kinetic@win.net
Contact — G. Raymond Schuhmann
Creative Director — Denise Mitchell

King Features Syndicate
235 E. 45th St.
New York, NY 10017
tel (212) 455-4000; fax (212) 682-9763
Sales Manager — Paul Eberhart

Kiosk Information Systems
2745 Industrial Ln. #101
Broomfield, CO 80020
tel (303) 466-5471; fax (303) 466-6730
Sales Manager — Karla Guarino

Walter J. Klein Company Ltd.
6311 Carmel Rd.; PO Box 472087
Charlotte, NC 28247-2087
tel (704) 542-1403; fax (704) 542-0735
Contact — Richard A. Klein
Executive Producer — Arny Pickholtz
Manager — Julie Lipes

Knight Mediacom
780 Piermont Ave
Piermont, NY 10968
tel (914) 398-1922; fax (914) 398-1923
e-mail 74547.2740@compuserve.com
knighter@aol.com, knimediaco@aol.com
Contact — Ron Knight
Marketing Coordinator-Audio
Communication — Susan Berkley
Designer-Graphic Imaging —
Lawrence Mitchell
Business Affairs-Europe-EEC Markets —
Alain Collant

Knight-Ridder Information Inc.
2440 El Camino Real
Mountain View, CA 94040
tel (415) 254-8145; fax (415) 254-8486
e-mail regan senkarik@corp.dialog.com
General Manager-CD-ROM Division —
Regan Senkarik
Sr Marketing Manager — Sharon Guldner

The Law Offices of Clayton Knowles
770 Lexington Ave., 6th Fl.
New York, NY 10021-8165
tel (212) 888-1200; fax (212) 935-4865
Attorney — Clayton Knowles

Kobie Marketing Inc.
270 1st Ave. S., Ste. 203
St. Petersburg, FL 33704
tel (813) 822-5353; fax (813) 822-5265
e-mail jaredhech@aol.com
Contact — Jared Hechtkopf
Executive Vice President — Tal Bratton

Komenar Production & Marketing Group
2143 Centro East
Tiburon, CA 94920-1906
tel (415) 435-9470; fax (415) 435-6143
e-mail komenar@aol.com
Contact — Margo Komenar

Kreutler
Brauerstr 50
Karlsruhe, 76137 Germany
tel (43-721) 824-1540
fax (43-721) 824-1519
Contact — Youcef Hamadache

Kudosoft Inc.
11320 Chandler Blvd., #G
North Hollywood, CA 91601
tel (818) 766-2958; fax (818) 766-7616
e-mail s.szymk@ix.netcom.com
President — Scott Szymkowski
Vice President — Dan Kessler

L

Landels, Ripley & Diamond
350 Steuart St.
San Francisco, CA 94105
tel (415) 788-5000; fax (415) 788-7550
Contact — Curtis E.A. Karnow

The Lantz Foundation
2002 Ellington Dr.
Wilson, NC 27896
tel (919) 243-7691
Contact — John Lantz

Lazer-fare Media Services Ltd.
916 Grosvenor Ave.
Winnipeg, MB R3B ON4 CN
tel (204) 452-5023; fax (204) 452-5061
Contact — C. Murray Burt

Legi-Tech
1029 J St., Ste. 450
Sacramento, CA 95814
tel (916) 447-1886; fax (916) 447-1109
President/General Manager — Ann M. Job

Lenel Systems International
290 Woodcliff Office Park
Fairport, NY 14450-4212
tel (716) 248-9720; fax (716) 258-9185
Contact — Michelle Stone
Marketing Specialist — Bill Muscato
President — Elena Prokupets
Vice President-Research & Development —
Rudy Prokupets

LEXIS-NEXIS
9443 Springboro Pike; PO Box 933
Dayton, OH 45401
tel (800) 227-9597 ext. 6044
fax (513) 865-1350
e-mail stevee@lexis-nexis.com
Senior. Public Relations Specialist —
Steve Edwards
CEO/President — Ira Siegel
Media Product Manager — Julia Vance

Liberty Communications
P.O. Box 348
Presto, PA 15142
tel (412) 221-8810; fax (412) 221-1161
Owner/President — Steve Wood
Sales — Greg Thomas

Lieberman Research West
1900 Avenue of the Stars
Los Angeles, CA 90067
tel (310) 553-0550; fax (310) 553-4607
President — Dave Sackman
Senior Vice President — Tim McPartlin
Vice President — Kevin Gentry
Vice President — Melissa Russel
Chairman — Arnie Fishman

The Listening Chair
3015B Canton St.
Dallas, TX 75226
tel (214) 748-8846; fax (214) 741-3530
Contact — Brain Flores
President — Steve Gerik

Live Wire Productions
28729 S. Western Ave., Ste. 209
Rancho Palos Verdes, CA 90275
tel (310) 831-6227
Producer — Kristen Simmons

LO/AD Communications
200 S. Los Robles Ave., Ste. 525
Pasadena, CA 91101
tel (818) 304-7750; fax (818) 304-2716
Director-Sales & Marketing — Kris Flynn

Logica Inc.
32 Hartwell Ave.
Lexington, MA 02173-3103
tel (617) 476-8000; fax (617) 476-8010
e-mail karenm@corp.logica.com
Contact — Karen McPhillips
CEO — Jim Yates
President — Bill Engel
Exec. Vice Pres.-Professional Services
Group — Frank Winters
Vice Pres./Gen. Mgr.-Interactive
Multimedia — Joel Ginsparg
Vice Pres.-Mktg. Interactive Multimedia —
Jeanne Friedgen

Logical Design Solutions
571 Central Ave.
Murray Hill, NJ 07974
tel (908) 771-9221
e-mail http://www.lds.com
VP-Marketing & Sales — Thom Shea
President — Mimi Brooks
Vice President — Darren Bryden

Logicom Inc.
5701 Pine Island Rd., Ste. 350
Tamarac, FL 33321
tel (305) 726-3868; fax (305) 726-3748
e-mail kmiller@logicom.com
72706.3541@compuserve.com
BBS: (305) 726-3849
Sales Manager — Keith A. Miller
President — Donald M. Arnel

Luckman Interactive
6430 Sunset Blvd., Ste. 518
Hollywood, CA 90028
tel (213) 468-8881; fax (213) 468-8884
e-mail stan@rezn8.com
CFO/Director — Stan Goldin

Luminare
2 Bryant St., Ste. 150
San Francisco, CA 94105
tel (415) 882-9372; fax (415) 882-9375
VP-Strategic Development — David Leventhal

Lyon & Associates Creative Services Inc.
2187 Newcastle Ave., Ste. 102
Cardiff-by-the-Sea, CA 92007
tel (619) 634-1886; fax (619) 634-0896
e-mail pretentious ad@lyonassoc.com
Owner — Susan Lyon
Production Manager — Heidi Temple
Designer — Mark Lyon
Designer — Karen Abrams
Designer — Jennifer Weissman

M

The MacDonald Classified Service
14 N. 2nd St.
Lafayette, IN 47901-1204
tel (800) 237-9075/(317) 742-9012
fax (317) 742-2843
e-mail mcsxpres@gibson.cioe.com
mcsonline@aol.com
Contact — Sharon Bardonner
Press — Michael Kaiser

Macromedia Corp.
600 Townsend St., Ste. 310 W.
San Francisco, CA 94103
tel (415) 252-2000/(800) 288-4797
fax (415) 626-0554
e-mail http://www.macromedia.com
President — John (Bud) C. Colligan
Vice President-Marketing — Miles Walsh
VP-World Wide Sales — Susan Gordon Bird

MAGELLAN Geographix
6464 Hollister Ave.
Santa Barbara, CA 93117
tel (800) 929-4MAPS/(805) 685-3100;
fax (805) 685-3330
e-mail info@magellangeo.com
gomagellan@compuserve.com
gomgmaps@compuserve.com
President/CEO — J. Douglas Crawford
Vice President-Development — Chris Baker

Magibox Inc.
1873 Hidden Oaks Dr.
Germantown, TN 38138
tel (901) 752-7835; fax (901) 753-3814
e-mail imarcus@magibox.net
Contact — Louis Marcus
Systems Administration — Ken McCleaft

Frank Magid & Associates
1 Research Center
Marion, IA 52302
tel (319) 377-7345; fax (319) 377-5861
Manager-Publishing — Dale Pearson
President — Bruce Norchott
Vice President/CFO — Daniel Bormann

Maginnis Inc.
1440 N. Dayton
Chicago, IL 60622
tel (312) 915-0592; fax (312) 915-0454
Contact — Kevin Maginnis
Production Manager — Jim Julien

Magnum Software Corp.
21115 Devonshire, #337
Chatsworth, CA 91311
tel (818) 701-5051; fax (818) 701-5459
e-mail magnum@primenet.com
http://www.primenet.com/~magnum/
President — Robert McTyre

MainStream Data Inc.
420 Chipeta Way, Ste. 200
Salt Lake City, UT 84108
tel (801) 584-2800; fax (801) 581-2831
Executive Director-Sales — B.J. Warnick
CEO — Scott Calder
President — Mo Gardener

Malhotra & Associates Inc.
379 Princeton-Hightstown
Cranbury, NJ 08512
tel (609) 426-3700; fax (609) 443-5777
General Manager — Barbara Wayman
Shareholder — Raj Malhotra

Mall Marketing Media
344 E. 100 South, Ste. 300
Salt Lake City, UT 84111
tel (801) 355-9034; fax (801) 355-9957
e-mail BBS: (801) 530-7207
Executive Vice President — William A.
McIntyre
VP-Marketing — Debbie Reverman
Business Manager — Julie Yost
Sales Director — Kayla Vigil

Mammoth Enterprise Productions
6140 Canterbury Dr., #102
Culver City, CA 90230
tel (310) 348-1326; fax (310) 348-1326
Contact — Andre Alporter
Video Production Operator — Rudy Gerren
Chief Engineer — Arnol Tolbert

MarCole Enterprises Inc.
2920 Camino Diablo, Ste. 200
Walnut Creek, CA 94596
tel (510) 933-9792; fax (510) 933-9795
e-mail marcole@cenet.com
Contact — Jim Brennan
President/CEO — Ron Coleman
VP-Mktg & Development — Jane Burton
Vice President-Information Services —
Elsie Mallonee
Director-Sales — David Pava

Aaron Marcus and Associates Inc.
1144 65th St., Ste. F
Emeryville, CA 94608-1109
tel (510) 601-0994; fax (510) 547-6125
e-mail marcus.1@applelink.apple.com
Business Development Mgr — Lynne Ching
President — Aaron Marcus
Projects Director — John Armitage

Marcus Technology Inc.
243 Riverside Dr., Ste. 103
New York, NY 10025
tel (212) 678-0406; fax (212) 222-7322
President — Irwin Marcus
Technology Sales Manager — Edward Fleiss
Director-Research & Development —
Todd Eckler

Copyright ©1996 by the Editor & Publisher Co.

VI-54 Interactive products and services

Marke Communications Inc.
105 Madison Ave.
New York, NY 10016
tel (800) 829-0065; fax (212) 213-0785
e-mail markecomm@aol.com
President — Klaus Merkle
VP-Creative Services — Sandra Cooper
Vice President-Marketing — Chuck Orlowski
Senior Partner-Sales — Allen Rosenberg
Director-Computer Technology — Bob Aiese
CFO — Irwin Katz

Market Opinion
31700 Middlebelt Rd.
Farmington Hills, MI 48334
tel (810) 737-5300; fax (810) 737-5326
Vice President — Peter Haag
President — Francis Ward

Marketing Messages
72-B Rowe St.
Newton, MA 02166
tel (617) 527-3023; fax (617) 527-3728
President — Richard Snider

The Marketing Trust Inc.
611 Riverside Ave.
Westport, CT 06880
tel (203) 454-1540; fax (203) 221-9176
e-mail nmay@mktrust.com
Managing Partner — Nancy May
Partner — Robert Antonion

MarketLink
10340 Viking Drive, Ste. 150
Eden Prairie, MN 55344-7231
tel (612) 996-9000; fax (612) 942-9424
Dir-Sales & Marketing — Cathy Gronfield
Senior Marketing Manager — Kristin Goltz
VP-Customer Service — Greg Mohn

MarketTrac
5568 Fremont St.
Oakland, CA 95608
tel (510) 658-4635; fax (510) 658-7051
e-mail markettrac@aol.com
Contact — David A. Barrett

Match.Com
340 Brannan St., Ste. 203
San Francisco, CA 94107
tel (415) 284-5300; fax (415) 284-5315
e-mail gkremen@match.com
Marketing Director — Fran Maier
President/CEO — Gary Kremen
General Manager-Technology & Solutions — Sterling Hutto
Business Development VP — Dave Witherow

MCCommunications
8131 LBJ Frwy., Ste. 275
Dallas, TX 75251
tel (214) 480-8383; fax (214) 669-8447
e-mail info@mccom.com
Contact — Kyle Holmes
President — Mike Crawford
Director of Accounting Services — Bridget Stevens
PR Director — Mary Nell Westbrook
Creative Director — Celia Hilton

MCI Telecommunications Corp.
3 Ravinia Dr.
Atlanta, GA 30346
tel (770) 668-6000; fax (770) 668-6474
Advertising Manager — William Pate

Mecklermedia Corp.
20 Ketchum St.
Westport, CT 06880
tel (203) 341-2842; fax (203) 454-5840
e-mail tanya@meklermedia.com
Director-PR — Tanya F. Mazarowski
President — Jeffery Dearth
CEO — Alan M. Meckler

MED.I.A. Inc.
3011 North I.H. 35 Ste. 100
Austin, TX 78722
tel (512) 328-7422; fax (512) 479-8292
e-mail media92@aol.com
Executive VP — Darrel L. Burnett
President — Emory Clark

Media Circus LLC
17 W. 17th St.
New York, NY 10011
tel (212) 645-9113; fax (212) 645-3082
e-mail mcircus@interport.net
New Business Development — Jason Port
Vice President — Joe Butt

Media Design Group
1133 W. Morse Blvd.
Winter Park, FL 32789
tel (407) 628-1755; fax (407) 647-4071
Contact — John D. Slack
President — Anthony Huesca

Media Direct Inc.
PO Box 302
Tenafly, NJ 07670
tel (201) 894-1551; fax (201) 894-5586
e-mail dpkaplan@aol.com
Technical Director — David Kaplan
Editorial Dir — Bette Weinstein Kaplan

Media House Software Inc.
32 Eardley Rd.
Aylmer, QC J9H 7A3 Canada
tel (819) 682-9737; fax (819) 685-0994
Sales Representive — Serge Vadeboncoeur
President — Seth Hamilton

Media Learning Systems
1492 W. Colorado Blvd.
Pasadena, CA 91105
tel (818) 791-7187; fax (818) 798-3666
e-mail jimgrif@aol.com
President/CEO — James F. Griffith

Media Marketing
5749 Arapahoe Ave.
Boulder, CO 80303
tel (800) 874-8798; fax (303) 440-8035
e-mail jamest28@aol.com
VP-Marketing — Charles Mauldin
CEO — James Theall
Director-Sales — Allyn Hallisey
VP-Customer Support — Chris Browne

Media Productions Inc.
11212 River Dr.
Warren, MI 48093
tel (810) 979-3344
e-mail mjnewton@aol.com
Contact — Michael Newton

The Media Shop Inc.
PO Box 13524
Research Triangle Park, NC 27709-3524
tel (919) 981-7467; fax (919) 981-0120
e-mail tmshop!@aol.com
Contact — Chuck Rueben
President — Patrick Miller
Senior Developer — Ken Hubbel

Media Synergy
300 Brannan St., Ste. 501
San Francisco, CA 94107
e-mail m synergy@sirius.com
Contact — Cory Smith
Products — Bob Fitzpatrick
Sales Director — Patrice Whilson

MediaNet International Inc.
130 E. 59th St.
New York, NY 10022
tel (212) 888-6610; fax (212) 371-2851
e-mail m.a.@ix.netcom.com
President — Don Middleberg
Account Executive — Isabelle Fymatt

Mediaweave Inc.
2 N. 1st St., 3rd Fl.
San Jose, CA 95113
tel (408) 279-3970; fax (408) 279-3617
e-mail mediaweave@aol.com
President — Gary L. McDaniel
Director-Art — Chris Swetlin

Media X
325A River St.
Santa Cruz, CA 95062
tel (408) 457-2783; fax (408) 457-2985
e-mail max92@aol.com
CEO — Matthew MacLaurin
Art Director — Gaben Chancellor
Producer — Chris Culp

Medio Multimedia
2617 151st St. N.E.
Redmond, WA 98052-5562
tel (206) 867-5500 ext. 202
fax (206) 885-4142
e-mail bobwyman@medio.com
VP-Emerging Technologies — Bob Wyman
Marketing — Rick Witham

Megadrive
489 S. Robertson Blvd.
Beverly Hills, CA 90211
tel (310) 247-8118; fax (310) 247-0006
e-mail sales@uu1201.megadrive.com
President — Paul Bloch

The Meeting Works!
957 Park Ave.
New York, NY 10028
tel (212) 737-8910; fax (212) 737-8910
e-mail johnmac@gcomm.com
Contact — John K. MacKenzie

Mercury Center
750 Ridder Park Dr.
San Jose, CA 95190
tel (408) 920-5494; fax (408) 271-3718
e-mail merc.center@sjmercury.com
Director-Mercury Center — Bob Ryan
Product Development Mgr — Barry Parr
Managing Editor — Bruce Koon
Advertising Manager — Jean Edwards

Mercury Telemedia Inc.
42 Woodward Ave.
Gloucester, MA 01930
tel (800) 999-2329; fax (508) 281-4117
Contact — Tom Spalding
Vice President-Engineering — David Dion
West Coast Sales Mgr — John Bogdanoff
Administration — Barb Russell

Meridian Creative Group
5178 Station Rd.
Erie, PA 16510
tel (814) 898-2612; fax (814) 898-0683
Contact — Michael Moulton
President/CEO — R. Scott O'Neil
Senior Vice President — Linda Kifer

Meteoquest Inc.
57 Catesby Ln.; PO Box 10360
Bedford, NH 03110-0360
tel (603) 471-1802; fax (603) 471-1803
President — Jimmie Smith

Micro Interactive
1123 Broadway, Ste. 1200
New York, NY 10010
tel (212) 366-1391; fax (212) 366-1393
Director-Marketing — Gary Exelbert
President — Steve Baum
Exec. VP/Creative Director — Eric Freedman
Senior Programmer — Derrick Shriver

Microlog Corp.
20270 Goldenrod Ln.
Germantown, MD 20876
tel (301) 428-3227; fax (301) 916-2475
President — Richard Thompson
CFO — Steve Delmar

MicroMall Inc.
1501 42nd St., Ste. 501
West Des Moines, IA 50266
tel (515) 224-9655; fax (515) 224-9620
e-mail bob@micromall.com
Contact — Robert Sorensen
President — Charles Spong
VP-Advanced Systems Development — Rich Ketcham

Micronet Technologies Inc.
80 Technology
Irvine, CA 92718
tel (714) 453-6100; fax (714) 453-6101
e-mail micronettech.com
Public Relations Manager — Meryl Cook
President/CEO — Morris Taradalsky
Vice President-Marketing — Alex Grossman

MicroVoice Applications Inc.
100 S. 5th St.
Minneapolis, MN 55402
tel (612) 373-9300; fax (612) 373-9779
e-mail mjames@mva.com
National Sales Manager — Rich Berg
Int'l Sales Mg. — Damien Chadwick
Marketing Dir. — Ken Shore
VP-Operations — Catherine Clary

Microsoft Corp.
1 Microsoft Way
Redmond, WA 98052-6399
tel (206) 882-8080; fax (206) 936-7329
Public Relations — Waggener Edstrom

MicroTouch Systems Inc.
300 Griffen Park
Methuen, MA 01844
tel (508) 659-9000; fax (508) 659-9100
e-mail touch@mts.mhs.compuserve.com
President/CEO — James Logan
Vice President-Operations — Ted Miller
Vice President-Finance — Geoffrey Clear
Vice President-Sales — Jay Waldron

Microware Systems Corp.
1900 N.W. 114th St.
Des Moines, IA 50325-7077
tel (515) 224-1929; fax (515) 224-1352
e-mail info@microware.com

Mktg. Communications Specialist-New Media — Deb Fry
President/CEO — Kenneth B. Kaplan
Exec. Vice Pres./Gen. Mgr.-New Media — Steven L. Johnson
Strategic Marketing Manager-New Media — Arthur Orduna
Mktg Mgr-New Media — Kristi Kramersmeier

Larry Miller Productions
1 Thompson Sq.
Charlestown, MA 02129
tel (617) 242-4242; fax (617) 242-9259
e-mail lmppg.aol.com
VP-Marketing & Sales — Robert B. Kiel
President — Jeff Janer
Creative Director — Curtiss Butler
VP-Project Manager — Janet Ahlgren

Millstar Electronic Publishing Group
1170 Wheeler Way
Langhorne, PA 19047
tel (215) 752-2900; fax (215) 752-9454
e-mail 74634.42@compuserve.com
National Sales Director — Al Kernan
President — Matthew Cohn
Project Manager — Star Pittman
Director-Development — Dave Bulken

M!ND GAMES new media
1806 Palisades Dr.
Carlsbad, CA 92008
tel (619) 434-2196; fax (619) 434-5366
e-mail 71531.2026@compuserve.com
Contact — Paul Unterweiser

Mindshare
11011 Anderson Lakes Pkwy., #103
Eden Prairie, MN 55344
tel (612) 941-9323; fax (612) 941-2121
e-mail outofbox@maroon.tc.umn.edu
Contact — Bob Brosch

MMB Development Corp.
904 Manhattan Ave.
Manhattan Beach, CA 90266
tel (310) 318-1322; fax (310) 318-2162
e-mail bob@mmb.com
President — Bob Baskerville

Modern BBS
744 Walnut Ave., Unit 1C
Bensalem, PA 19020
tel (215) 638-1424; fax (215) 244-9214
e-mail BBS: (215) 638-1299
Owner — Rick Kosick

Montage Group Ltd.
1 W 85th St., Ste. 3D
New York, NY 10024
tel (212) 769-4100; fax (212) 496-5547
e-mail jennie.mgl.com
Sales & Marketing — Jennifer Benepe
President — Seth Haberman
Sales Assistant — Owen Stein

Montage Multimedia Communications
320 San Francisco Blvd.
San Anselmo, CA 94960
tel (415) 868-9819
e-mail gisellemb@aol.com
gnelle@well.com
Marketing Communications Director — Giselle Bisson
Creative Director — Leigh Rosser

Morning Star Technologies
3518 Riverside Dr.
Columbus, OH 43221-1715
tel (800) 558-7827; fax (614) 459-5054
Audiotex Manager — Bob Sutterfield
President — Dave Ford

Mortgage Market Information Services
53 E. St. Charles Rd.
Villa Park, IL 60181
tel (708) 782-4359/(312) 771-0191
fax (708) 834-7283
e-mail robert.sturino@mmis.com
Dir.-National Media/Interactive Mktg. Mgr. — Robert A. Sturino
President — Jim DeBoth
Director-Marketing — Keith Kubik
Interactive Media Manager — Dan Eaton
Sales Supervisor — Krystyna Lewandowski

Motion City Films
1847 Centinela Ave.
Santa Monica, CA 90404
tel (310) 264-4870; fax (310) 264-4871
e-mail mcfilms@aol.com
Producing Director — Jerry Witt
Producing Director — David Beedon
Lead Animator — Jim McVay
Composer/Audio Engineer — Marty Blasick
Production Manager — Dennis Domingo

Copyright ©1996 by the Editor & Publisher Co.

Interactive products and services — VI-55

Motorola Paging
1500 Gateway Blvd., #25
Boynton Beach, FL 33426
tel (407) 739-2762; fax (407) 364-2225
Marketing Manager — Julie Greene

Moving Graphics
10331 Almayo Ave., Ste. 3
Los Angeles, CA 90064
tel (310) 286-0969; fax (310) 286-0969
e-mail 70451.243@is
President — Tom Bunzel

Moxie Media Inc.
PO Box 10203
New Orleans, LA 70181
tel (504) 733-6907; fax (504) 733-4892
Contact — Martin Glenday
Senior Editor — Julius Evans
Senior Graphic Designer — Robert Racine
Marketing Manager — Lucy Glenday
Sales Representative — Sharron Webb

MP Music Previews
6 Piedmont Center, Ste. 240
Atlanta, GA 30305
tel (404) 237-7825; fax (404) 237-5259
President — Wayne Parker

MPI Multimedia
16101 S. 108th Ave.
Orland Park, IL 60462
tel (708) 460-0555; fax (708) 873-3177
President — Matthew White
Creative Director — Jeff Martin

MPS Media Phone Service KGF
Liesegangstrasse 10; PO Box 24 02 12
Duesseldorf, D-40091 Germany
tel (49-211) 17450;
fax (49-211) 174511
Contact — Hans-Joachim Kruse
Marketing Manager — Klaus Schmitt

M/S Database Marketing
10982 Roebling Ave.
Los Angeles, CA 90024
tel (310) 208-2024; fax (310) 208-5681
e-mail 70243.3452@compuserve.com
Consultant — Robert McKim
Partner-Data Solutions — Evelyn Schlaphoff

Multimedia Computer Solution Inc.
400 Union Ave., Unit #4
Haskell, NJ 07420
tel (201) 839-3300; fax (201) 839-8890
Production Marketing Mgr — Jeff Cirilis
President — Edward G. Harmon

Multimedia Ink Designs
14544 High Pine St.
Poway, CA 92064
tel (619) 679-8317; fax (619) 679-1536
e-mail rdegel@mmink
Contact — Rick Degelsmith
Vice President — Lisa Degelsmith

Multimedia Journeys
5117 47th Ave. S.
Seattle, WA 98118
tel (206) 722-0393
Producer/Performer — Joyce Yarrow
Producer — Gary Gorland

Multimedia Productions
2280 N. Bechelli Ln.; PO Box 494155
Redding, CA 96002
tel (916) 222-5354; fax (916) 222-2528
e-mail rzakhari@interserv.com
Vice President-Marketing —
Claudette Zakhariya
President — Ramiz Zakhariya
Director-Marketing — Kristina Rogers
Director-Operations — Laurie Leiser

Multimedia Research Group
499 S. Sunnyvale Ave.
Sunnyvale, CA 94086
tel (408) 524-9767; fax (408) 524-9770
e-mail mrgi@eworld.com
Principal Analyst/President — Gary Schultz
Research Analyst — Norma Schroeder
Account Services Supervisor —
Annette Ruder

MultiMedia Resources
14 Mark Dr.
Rye Brook, NY 10573-1410
tel (914) 937-1344; fax (914) 934-0069
e-mail heilbrunn@aol.com
Contact — Henry Heilbrunn
Managing Partner — Lynn J. Branigan

Multimedia Resources Inc.
1631 S.W. Columbia
Portland, OR 97201
tel (503) 241-9315; fax (503) 223-7528
e-mail mail@mmresources.com
Contact — Jeff Dowell

Multimedia Strategies
3720 Millswood Dr.
Irving, TX 75062
tel (214) 650-1986; fax (214) 650-1622
e-mail 71563.144@compuserve.com, boothdfw@delphi.com
Contact — Doris Booth

The Multimedia Studies Program
San Francisco State University
425 Market St., 2nd Fl.
San Francisco, CA 94115
tel (415) 904-7741; fax (415) 904-7760
e-mail drago@sfsu.edu
Contact — Beth Rogozinski
Director — Randall Packer
Captain of Technology — Robert Todd
Program Advisor — Robert Martin
Technical Coordinator — Patrick Clancy

Murk Works Inc.
PO Box 610
Potsdam, NY 13676
tel (315) 268-1000; fax (315) 268-9812
e-mail info@murkworks.com
BBS: (315) 268-6875
General Manager — Marsha Farr
President — Brad Clements

Muse Presentation Technologies
3415 W. Lake Center Dr.
Santa Ana, CA 92704-6925
tel (714) 850-1008; fax (714) 850-1018
e-mail jimmuse@ix.netcom.com
Contact — Jim Muse
General Manager — Wil Bigelow
Marketing — Joyce Logan

Music Access Inc.
90 5th Ave.
Brooklyn, NY 11217
tel (718) 398-2146; fax (718) 230-5539
e-mail mabar@pipeline.com
Contact — Bar Biszick
Public Relations — Rachel Davenport
Advertising — Danny Nelson

Mustang Software Inc.
6200 Lake Ming Rd. (93306)
PO Box 2264
Bakersfield, CA 93303
tel (805) 873-2500; fax (805) 873-2599
e-mail sales@mustang.com
BBS: (805) 873-2400
Marketing Representative — Bob Allman
President/CEO — Jim Harrer

N

Navisoft
8619 Westwood, Center Dr.
Vienna, VA 22182
tel (800) 879-6882/(703) 918-2136
fax (703) 918-1106
Contact — Chris Brooks

Neptune Interactive Design
600 Essex Rd.
Neptune, NJ 07754
tel (908) 922-0770; fax (908) 922-0783
e-mail cneal@injersey.com
Marketing Coordinator — Christine Neal
Multimedia Strategist — Marie Mitchell
Director — Diane Burley

Netcom
3031 Tisch Way
San Jose, CA 95128
tel (408) 556-3272; fax (408) 241-9145
Contact — Scott Sorochak

Netscape Communications Corp.
501 E. Middlefield Rd.
Mountian View, CA 94043
tel (415) 528-2555; fax (415) 428-4124
e-mail info@netscape.com
sales@netscape.com
Director-Sales — Annette Shotter
President/CEO — Jim Barksdale
Chairman — Jim Clark

Network Long Distance Inc.
525 Florida St.; PO Box 1947
Baton Rouge, LA 70821-1947
tel (504) 343-3125/(800) 349-1111
fax (504) 343-2444/(800) 349-1112
President — Michael M. Ross
Vice President-Sales — David Rosenfeld
Financial — Lou Resweber
Reseller-Agent Program — Mike Simmons

Network Telephone Services
6233 Variel Ave.
Woodland Hills, CA 91367
tel (800) 727-6874; fax (818) 992-8415
Marketing Manager — Mark Buchler

The Networks
20 W. Market St.
York, PA 17401
tel (717) 849-0600; fax (717) 849-0620
e-mail http://www.net works.net
Director-Administrative & Customer Services — Patti Chaterdon
President — David Dreyer

New Art Communications
200 W. 79th St., Ste. 8H
New York, NY 10024
tel (212) 362-0559; fax (212) 873-8231
e-mail newart@panix.com
Contact — Jessica Keyes
Director — Rebecca Lacser
Administration — Debra Nencel

New Cool Media (Publishing Inc.)
66 Madrone Ave. (Moss Beach, 94038);
PO Box 305
Half Moon Bay, CA 94019
tel (415) 728-0190; fax (415) 728-0192
e-mail paulb1021863@eworld.com
Contact — Paul B. Bader
CFO — Debby Bader
Vice President-International Development — Joseph DeMaria

New Horizons Group/Pottsville Republican
111 Mahantongo St.
Pottsville, PA 17901
tel (717) 628-6016/(717) 628-6067; fax (717) 621-3308
e-mail nhg@ricnet.pottsville.com, sesmith@ricnet.pottsville.com
Dir-Sales & Marketing — Sharon E. Smith
Director — Jim Dible
Research Manager — Edward Scheetz
Training & Services — Julian Milewski
Sales Representative — Ed Costick
Sales Representative — Kevin Hoppes
Sales Representative — Mark Osburn
Sales Representative — Jim Burke

New [Media] Directions
808 Broadway, 3rd Fl.
Nashville, TN 37203
tel (615) 742-1490; fax (615) 742-1487
e-mail nmd@edge.ercnet.com
Vice President-Sales & Marketing — Dianne Naff
President — Mark Magnuson
Executive Producer — Michael McGraw
Creative Director/Interactive Services — Chris Lee

New Media Hollywood
1433 N. Cole Pl.
Hollywood, CA 90028
tel (213) 957-5000; fax (213) 957-8500
e-mail info@nmh.com
Contact — Travis Berkley

Newman Brothers
112 E. Pecan St., Ste. 1725
San Antonio, TX 78205
tel (210) 226-0371; fax (210) 226-6506
Owner — John Newman

NewOrder Media Inc.
209 10th Ave. S., Ste. 450
Nashville, TN 37203
tel (615) 248-4848; fax (615) 248-6833
Director-Marketing — Mae Hardcastle

News USA
8300 Boone Blvd., Ste. 810
Vienna, VA 22182
tel (800) 355-9500; fax (703) 827-5814
e-mail vpmedia@newsusa.com
VP-Media Services — William H. Watson
Media Services Specialist — Victoria Jancek

Newscom
2801 Ponce De Leon
Coral Gables, FL 33134
tel (305) 448-8411; fax (305) 443-6538
e-mail peter@newscom.com
Managing Director — Peter Eisner
Director-Sales — Geoff Biddulph

Newsday Direct
235 Pinelawn Rd.
Melville, NY 11747
tel (516) 843-2677; fax (516) 843-4186
e-mail yxgk09a@prodigy.com
Marketing Manager — Susan Brandt
General Manager — Fred Tuccillo

NewsNet Inc.
945 Haverford Rd.
Bryn Mawr, PA 19010
tel (610) 527-8030/(800) 345-1301
fax (610) 527-0338
Contact — Ellen S. Keech
President — Andrew S. Elston
VP-Marketing — Robert Hunsicker

Newspaper Voice Services Inc.
1150 Wehrle Dr.
Williamsville, NY 14221
tel (716) 626-0100; fax (716) 626-1592
Contact — Reginald V. Williams III
Vice President — Jonathan Ewert
VP-Promotion Sales — Cindy Sterner

New Tech Telemedia
444 N. Wells St.
Chicago, IL 60610
tel (312) 245-1111; fax (312) 245-1128
e-mail donyoung@ix.netcom.com
President — Donald Young

NewsView Solutions
9443 Springboro Pike; PO Box 933
Dayton, OH 45401
tel (800) 227-9597; fax (573) 865-1948
Contact — Betsy Ashton
Product Analyst — Todd Stowe
Product Analyst — Steve Brooke

Next Vision Graphics Inc.
PO Box 612077
North Miami, FL 33261-2077
tel (305) 926-5467; fax (305) 926-5467
Contact — Manuel Vicnansky

The Next Wave
100 Bonner St.
Dayton, OH 45410
tel (513) 228-4433; fax (513) 228-4111
e-mail nextwavead@aol.com
Contact — David Esrati

Tom Nicholson & Associates
295 Lafayette St., Ste. 805
New York, NY 10012
tel (212) 274-0470; fax (212) 274-0380
President — Tom Nicholson

Nicollet Technologies
7901 12th Ave. S.
Minneapolis, MN 55425-1017
tel (612) 854-3336; fax (612) 854-5774
Vice President — Brian Follet
President — Marco Scibora

Nitsuko America Corp.
4 Forest Pkwy.
Shelton, CT 06484
tel (203) 926-5400; fax (203) 926-5458
(Sales)/(203) 929-0535
Vice President-Sales — Albert F. Kelly
President — Naoki Kiyomine

NKH & W Inc.
600 Broadway; PO Box 410977
Kansas City, MO 64105
tel (816) 842-8881; fax (816) 842-6340
e-mail @nkhw.com
President/CEO — F. Peter Kovac
Executive Vice President — Nick Nicholson
Senior Vice President — Sheree Johnson
Marketing Director — Jan Ray
PR Management Super. — Vicki Cummiskey

Nortel
2920 Matheson Blvd.
East Mississang, ON L4W 4M7 Canada
tel (905) 238-7000/(800) 667-8437
(Customer Service); fax (905) 238-7350
Marketing Manager — Adrian Horwood

North Valley Diver Publications
585 Royal Oaks Dr.
Redding, CA 96001
tel (916) 246-7755; fax (916) 246-0587
Contact — Dan Bailey

NorthCoast Interactive
1201 W. Chase Ave., #2A
Chicago, IL 60626
tel (312) 973-2858; fax (312) 973-2859
e-mail nrthcoast@aol.com
Principal — Lorelei F. Ermentrout
Principal — Josh Ermentrout

Northern Telecom
97 Humboldt St.
Rochester, NY 14609
tel (716) 482-5000; fax (716) 654-2180
Marketing — Greg Gilinas

Copyright ©1996 by the Editor & Publisher Co.

VI-56 Interactive products and services

Northwest Nexus Inc.
10800 N.E. 8th St., Ste. 802
Bellevue, WA 98004
tel (206) 455-3505; fax (206) 455-4672
e-mail info@nwnexus.wa.com
Vice President — Ralph Sims
President — Ed Morin

Novell
1555 N. Technology
Orem, UT 84052-2399
tel (800) 451-5151
e-mail http://www.novell.com
Market Communications Coordinator —
Bethanne Field
President — Bob Frankenberg

NTN Communications Inc.
2121 Palomar Airport Rd., Ste. 205
Carlsbad, CA 92009
tel (619) 438-7400; fax (619) 438-7470
Senior VP-Marketing — Jerry Petrie
Chairman — Patrick J. Downs
President — Daniel Downs

NYNEX Corp.
1095 Ave. of Americas
New York, NY 10036
tel (212) 395-6352
e-mail
notes.prenner@a5ovmi.trg.nynex.com
Business Plan Development —
Pete Renner

O

Octel Communications
2 Ravinia Dr., Ste. 790
Atlanta, GA 30346-3104
tel (770) 390-3300; fax (770) 395-1557
Region Manager — Bill Dumont

O'Halloran Advertising Inc.
116 Danbury Rd.
Wilton, CT 06897
tel (203) 762-0054; fax (203) 834-2664
Senior Vice President-Client Services —
Mark O'Halloran
President — James O'Halloran

O'Keefe Interactive
700 E. Franklin St., Ste. 700
Richmond, VA 23219
tel (804) 643-4415; fax (804) 649-1816
Contact — Delina Papit
Programming Director — Josh Stella
Network Administrator — Mike Davis
Interactive Content Developer —
Brad Freeman

On Target Inc.
123 South St.
Boston, MA 02111
tel (617) 482-3707; fax (617) 482-9333
e-mail ontargge@aol.com
Contact — Glenn Engman

OpenNet Technologies Inc.
1100 Cleveland St., Ste. 803
Clearwater, FL 34615
tel (813) 446-6558; fax (813) 446-6456
e-mail rdorsey@opennet.com,
http://www.opennet.com
Director-Marketing — Randy Dorsey
President — Kurt Long

Open Text Corp.
180 Columbia St.
Waterloo, ON N2L 3L3 Canada
tel (519) 888-9910; fax (519) 888-0677
e-mail opentext.com
Executive Vice President — Mike Farrell

OptImage
7185 Vista Dr.
West Des Moines, IA 50266
tel (515) 225-7000; fax (515) 225-0252
e-mail info@optimage.com
President/CEO — Terry Smail
VP-Marketing & Sales — Gail Wellington
Vice President/CTO — Tim Wahlers

Origin Systems Inc.
3630 Sinton Rd., Ste. 300
Colorado Springs, CO 80907
tel (719) 630-3384; fax (719) 630-8537
e-mail mrbuddy@usa.net
Account Services — Eric Beteille
Media Director — Jil Goebel
Creative Director — Randel Castleberry
Art Director — Todd Jones

Tom O'Toole Communications Group
115 W. 79th St.
Burr Ridge, IL 60521
tel (708) 789-8666/(800) 789-8666
Contact — Tom O'Toole

Owen Associates Inc.
1450 Sheridan St., E17
Hollywood, FL 33020
tel (305) 921-8580
Contact — Edward H. Owen

Oza Communications Corp.
150 Aero Camino
Santa Barbara, CA 93117
tel (805) 685-1880; fax (805) 685-3060
President — Kandarp Oza

P

Pace Design Group
665 3rd St., Ste. 250
San Francisco, CA 94107
tel (415) 495-3600; fax (415) 495-3155
e-mail pdg@sirius.com
Contact — Cliff Gerrish
Creative Director — Joel Blum
Design Director — Laura Christensen
Art Director — David Ice

Pacific Gold Coast Corp.
15 Glen St., Ste. 201
Glen Cove, NY 11542
tel (516) 759-3011; fax (516) 759-3014
Contact — Janine Avedisian

Pacific Video Resources/PVR Labs
2331 3rd St.
San Francisco, CA 94107
tel (415) 864-5679; fax (415) 864-2059
VP-Strategic Media — Bentley Nelson
Director-Production — Steve Kotton
Account Manager-Video Compression
Studios — James Santanorea
Chief Engineer — Bob Frey
Operations Manager — Greg Pellitteri

PAGE
998 Old Eagle School Rd., Ste. 1202
Wayne, PA 19087
tel (610) 687-3778; fax (610) 687-2147
e-mail pagewayne@aol.com
General Manager — H. Charles Berkey

Page Systems Inc.
1 Eva Rd., Ste. 416
Toronto, ON M9C 4Z5 Canada
tel (416) 695-2288; fax (416) 695-2290
President — Michael Clark
Vice President — Terence Bower
Vice President — Russ Thaim

Palm Beach Post
2751 S. Dixie Hwy.
W. Palm Beach, FL 33405
tel (407) 820-4462; fax (407) 820-2039
e-mail dsfxo2a@prodigy.com
Contact — Dan Shorter

Panic Pink
140 E. 28th St., Penthouse B
New York, NY 10016
tel (212) 725-5059; fax (212) 725-5059
e-mail thessy@escape.com
Contact — Thessy Mehrain

Pantheon
1415 Western Ave., Ste. 505
Seattle, WA 98101
tel (206) 628-3411; fax (206) 628-3412
e-mail jeffs@pantheoninc.com
Contact — Jeffrey Schrock
Executive Manager — Joseph Snell
Engineering Manager — Daren Tsui

Parrish Wickersham & Partners
420 Boylston St.
Boston, MA 02116
tel (617) 424-0316; fax (617) 424-0399
Senior Vice President — Jim Graves

Party-Line Israel, Audio Communication Ltd.
7 Yirmiyahu St., 2nd Fl.
Tel Aviv, Israel
tel (972-3) 6042211
fax (972-3) 5469517
Contact — Mrs. Frances Harazi
Manager — Zohar Shalit

PC Catalog
120 W. Harvest Dr. (68521);
PO Box 82523
Lincoln, NE 68501-2523
tel (800) 544-1296/(402) 479-2142
fax (402) 479-2120
e-mail market@pccatalog.peed.com,
http://www.peed.com/pccataolg.html
Circulation Coordinator — Anne Herman
President — Thomas J. Peed
Circulation Manager — Jerry Fike

PDM Creative
1623 3rd Ave.
New York, NY 10128
tel (212) 534-3695; fax (212) 427-8587
e-mail montypm@aol.com
Contact — Paul De Monterice

Peeke Voice Mail Personals
188 Crossbow Ln.
Gaithersburg, MD 20878
tel (301) 840-5752/(800) 886-4636
fax (301) 670-2881
Vice President — Linda Parkhill
President — Victor J. Peeke

Pegasus Telesis Group
2525 Thames St.
Los Angeles, CA 90046
tel (213) 656-3899; fax (213) 654-9594
e-mail pegasustel@aol.com
Contact — Joann Leonard

Peirce-Phelps Inc.
2000 N. 59th St.
Philadelphia, PA 19131-3099
tel (215) 879-7243; fax (215) 878-5252
e-mail dss@peirce-phelps.ccmail.
compuserve.com
Director-Marketing — David Schwartz
Senior Vice President — Henry Grove III
Consulting Services Mgr — Jonathan Morton
Gen Mgr-Technical Operations — Don Leith

Performance Resources International
10 Libertyship, #263; PO Box 337
Sausalito, CA 94966
tel (415) 332-5211; fax (415) 332-6911
e-mail pek@well.com
Contact — Phillip Know Hon
Technology Director — David Chang
Web Master — J. Oberman

Performance Software Inc.
100 Shield St.
West Hartford, CT 06110
tel (203) 953-4040; fax (203) 953-7407
e-mail 71621.351@compuserve.com
Contact — Michael T. Ganci
Director-Development — Audra Wade

Periphonics Corp.
4000 Veterans Memorial Hwy.
Bohemia, NY 11716
tel (516) 467-0500; fax (516) 737-8520
President — Peter J. Cohen

Peters Video Productions
305 5th St.
Pacific Grove, CA 93950
tel (408) 655-4800; fax (408) 655-4800
e-mail 73162.561@compuserve.com
Contact — Jesse Peters
Manager-Operation — Brian Ross
Director-Marketing — Kathy Gardener

Philips Media
825 8th Ave.
New York, NY 10019
tel (212) 333-6767; fax (212) 333-6706
President/CEO — Scott C. Marden
Senior VP-Planning — Susan Caulo
CTO — Michael Whelan

Phone Masters
1022 S. La Cienega Blvd.
Los Angeles, CA 90035
tel (310) 289-0222; fax (310) 289-0776
Operations Manager — David Hajian

Phone Works
146 2nd St. N.
St. Petersburg, FL 33701
tel (813) 823-7144; fax (813) 823-6523
Vice President — Kathy Montgomery
President — Brad Wenkos

Pierian Spring Software
5200 S.W. Macadam Ave., Ste. 570
Portland, OR 97201
tel (503) 222-2044; fax (503) 222-0771
Contact — Jerry Dawson
Marketing Coordinator — Angie Maddox
Dealer Advocate — Jennifer Davis

The Pinnacle Group Media Consultants Ltd.
23 E. 17th St., 5th Fl.
New York, NY 10003-1916
tel (212) 229-1001; fax (212) 229-0825
e-mail pinnacleny@aol.com
Contact — Berry Brunk
Executive Vice President — Susan Brunk
Vice President-Finance — Gerald Brunk
Controller — Sheldon Kleeger
Sales Director — John McCarthy

PixelDance Communications Inc.
336 Baker Ave.
Concord, MA 01742
tel (508) 287-1400; fax (508) 287-1411
e-mail info@pixeldance.com
President — Jim Levinger
Creative Director — Steven Todd

Pixel Touch
1840 Carlos Ave., 15-A
Ontario, CA 91761
tel (909) 923-6124; fax (909) 923-6126
President — Jim Stewart
Vice President — Holly Zul Zubillaga

PixelWorks Corp.
8611 Botts Ln.
San Antonio, TX 78217
tel (210) 826-5375; fax (210) 826-2856
Contact — Mike Gaffney
Vice President — Rob Simons

Planetary News LLC
3420 Berkley Ave.
Boulder, CO 80303
tel (303) 543-7810; fax (303) 543-8550
e-mail outings@netcom.com
President — Steve Outing

Poppe Tyson
707 California St.
Mountain View, CA 94041
tel (415) 969-6800; fax (415) 969-6137
e-mail klewis@poppe.com
Contact — Nick Buck
CEO — Fergus O'Daly
Director-Strategic Consulting —
Geoff Watters
Partner-Strategic Consulting —
Andreas Panayi
Senior Vice President/General Manager —
David Carlick

Power BBS Computing
35 Fox Ct.
Hicksville, NY 11801
tel (516) 938-0506; fax (516) 681-3226
President — Russell Frey

PR Marketing & Communications Inc.
448 Gurney Ave.
Lake Bluff, IL 60044
tel (708) 295-9568; fax (708) 295-2168
Contact — Pam Russell

PR Newswire
810 7th Ave., 35th Fl.
New York, NY 10019
tel (800) 832-5522; fax (800) 793-9313
e-mail http://www.prnewswire.com
Electronic Markets Mgr — Ashley T. Suhler
Senior Vice President — John Williams
Vice President-Marketing — Ira Krawitz

Prairie Systems Inc.
7200 World Communications Dr.;
PO Box 34960
Omaha, NE 68134-0960
tel (402) 398-4100; fax (402) 398-4855
V.P. Strategy & Marketing Communications
— Jeff Finn
President — J. Richard Abramson
Vice President — Dale Ratliff

Precision Systems Inc.
11800 30th Ct. N.
St. Petersburg, FL 33716
tel (813) 572-9300; fax (813) 573-9195
President/CEO — Russ Pillar
Sales — Michael Felix

Premiere Audiotex
06 391 S.R. 576
Bryan, OH 43506
tel (419) 636-7293/(800) 982-1592
fax (419) 636-9022
e-mail 76260.756@compuserve.com
paudiotex@aol.com
President — Todd A. Rhoades
Service Bureau Operations — John Hughes
Custom Programming — Mark Snyder
Sales Manager — Paul Taylor

Copyright ©1996 by the Editor & Publisher Co.

Interactive products and services VI-57

Premiere Interactive Media LLC
150 Fifth Ave., Ste. 817
New York, NY 10011
tel (212) 929-1800; fax (212) 929-1807
e-mail premiere5@aol.com
Contact — Mark Cohen
Partner — D.J. Hacker
Partner — Jerome LoMonaco

Presscom Technologies Corp. (P.T.C.)
Church St. Station; PO Box 3228
New York, NY 10008-3228
tel (718) 768-7681; fax (718) 768-5099
President — Lawrence Fischer
Vice President — William Carroll
Vice President — Sean Donahue

PressLink Inc.
11800 Sunrise Valley Dr., Ste. 1130
Reston, VA 22091-5339
tel (703) 758-1740; fax (703) 758-8368
e-mail presslink@plink.geis.com
presslink@presslink.com
Director-Sales & Marketing —
Michael Martucci
President — Rich Cates
Director-Operations — Tom Priddy

Princeton Interactive Communications
5 Vaughn Dr., #119
Princeton, NJ 08540
tel (609) 520-1325; fax (609) 520-0695
e-mail picdirect@btb.com
74710.2272@compuserve.com
picdirect@aol.com, picdirect@eword.com
Principal — Larry Trink
Executive Vice President — Jeff Friedman
Principal — Robert Zyantz

Print Marketing Concepts
10590 W. Office Dr., Ste. 250
Houston, TX 77042
tel (713) 780-7055; fax (713) 780-9731
Vice President Newspaper Relations —
Edward R. Bryant
Sales Manager — Johnna Bryant

Print Media Marketing Group
1525 Wilson Blvd., Ste. 1000
Arlington, VA 22234
tel (703) 812-2887; fax (703) 812-2701
e-mail slchemaly@aol.com
Marketing Director — Soraya L. Cheonaly
President — Lawrence B. Sackett
Vice President — Keith Satter

Process Software
959 Concord St.
Framingham, MA 01701
tel (508) 879-6994; fax (508) 879-0342
e-mail info@process.com,
hppt://www.process.com,
Contact — David Rosenlund

Prodigy Services Co.
445 Hamilton Ave.
White Plains, NY 10601
tel (914) 448-8000; fax (914) 448-3400
Contact — Brain Ek
President/CEO — Edward Bennett

Profound
655 Madison Ave.
New York, NY 10022
tel (212) 750-6900; fax (212) 750-0660
Marketing Director — John O'Brien

Projects In Knowledge Inc.
1 Harmon Plaza
Secaucus, NJ 07094
tel (201) 617-9700; fax (201) 617-5606
Contact — Robert Stren
VP-New Business — Patricia Peterson
Vice President-Program Management —
Susan Hostetler
VP-Design Services — Adrian Holmes

Proline-Bib
PO Box 27682
Denver, CO 80227
tel (303) 761-3999; fax (303) 761-1818
President — Tony Marcon
Director-Operations — John Frisk

Proxima
9440 Carroll Park Dr.
San Diego, CA 92121
tel (619) 457-5500; fax (619) 457-9014
Contact — Lois Peterman
Public Relations Manager — George Wilson
Vice President — Mary Zoeller

PSINet
510 Huntmar Park Dr.
Herndon, VA 22070
tel (703) 709-0300/(800) 82 psi 82
(Sales); fax (800) Faxpsi1 (PsiNet fax server)
e-mail info@psi.com
Pres/CEO/Chairman — William Schraeder
Senior VP/CTO — Martin Schoffstall
VP-Finance — Daniel Cunningham

Publitech Inc.
211 Farm Rd.; PO Box 840
Sherborn, MA 01770
tel (508) 651-3932; fax (508) 653-7214
e-mail cshedd@adcom.net,
72405.26@compuserve.com
President/Publisher — Carl Shedd
Editor — Michael Pogopzinski

Pulse Interactive
9999 S.W. Wilshire St. (97225);
PO Box 230693
Portland, OR 97281
tel (503) 292-1146; fax (503) 292-0144
e-mail marling&@pulse-research.com
http://www.pulse-research.com
BBS: (503) 292-3708
President — John W. Marling
CIO — John Bertoglio
Vice President-Marketing — Paul McGilvra

R

The Radio Response Co.
12620 War Admiral Way
North Potomac, MD 20878-3738
President — Steve P. Korn

Radius
215 Mojete Park Dr.
Sunnyvale, CA 94089
tel (408) 541-6100
Contact — Gaylen Wells

Rancho Park Publishing
11766 Wilshire Blvd.; PO Box 310
Los Angeles, CA 90025
tel (310) 479-6326; fax (310) 479-4024
e-mail ranchopark@aol.com
Contact — Stan Cheren

Alan Rand Multimedia Group Inc.
764 Shady Ln.; PO Box 400
Dayton, IN 47941-0400
tel (317) 449-1000; fax (317) 449-1727
e-mail alanrand@indy.net
CEO — David Leininger
Vice President — Gary Christie
Art Director — John Metzinger

Random Access
62 Birdsall St.
Greene, NY 13778
tel (607) 656-7584
Marketing Manager — William Marsland

Real Time Strategies
960 S. Broadway, Ste. 118C
Hicksville, NY 11801
tel (516) 939-6655; fax (516) 939-6189
President — Jay Moskowitz
Vice President — Spencer Kravitz

Red Hill Studios
761 Sir Francis Drake Blvd.
San Anselmo, CA 94960
tel (415) 485-6855; fax (415) 485-6874
e-mail redhill1@aol.com
Producer — Dana Bishop
Executive Producer — Robert Hone
Art Director — Todd Reamon

Red Sky Interactive
60 Green St.
San Francisco, CA 94111
tel (415) 421-7332; fax (415) 397-9523
Director-Sales — Sandra Susilovich
President — Tim Smith
Director-Marketing — April Minnich
Creative Director — Joel Hladecek

Renaissance Computer
29 W. 38th St.
New York, NY 10018
tel (212) 575-6100
e-mail www.reac.com
Contact — Anthony Del Monte

ResNova Software Inc.
5011 Argosy Dr., Ste. 13
Huntington Beach, CA 92649
tel (714) 379-9000; fax (714) 379-9014
e-mail sales@resnova.com
http://www.resnova.com

BBS: (714) 379-9004
Account Executive — Mike Myers
President — Alex Hopmann
CEO — Jon Kantor
Vice President-Sales — Daniel Link

Rezn8
6430 Sunset Blvd., Ste. 100
Hollywood, CA 90028
tel (213) 957-2161; fax (213) 464-8912
e-mail stan@rezn8.com
Vice President — Stan Goldin
Business Manager — Jake Klejna

RG Creations Inc.
1660 S. Amphlett Blvd., Ste. 109
San Mateo, CA 94402
tel (415) 571-5177; fax (415) 571-5259
Contact — Robert G. Fuller
Corporate Representative — Tim Fuller
Accounts Manager — Mitch Goodman
Accounts Manager — Michelle Fuller

Ribit Productions Inc.
14951 N. Dallas Pkwy., Ste. 220
Dallas, TX 75240
tel (214) 239-8866; fax (214) 239-8788
e-mail robin@ribit.com
President — Robin Moss
Senior Multimedia Developer — Ronda Bailey
Multimedia Developer — Scott Lumley
Creative Director — Danna Stuart

Richardson, Myers & Donofrio Inc.
120 W. Fayette St.
Baltimore, MD 21201
tel (410) 576-9000; fax (410) 528-8809
e-mail rmd@rmd.com
President — Chuck Donofrio

Risdall Linnihan Advertising Interactive
2475 15th St.
New Brighton, MN 55112
tel (612) 631-1098; fax (612) 631-2561
e-mail ted risdall@rladvert.com
President-Interactive — Ted Risdall
Chairman — John Risdall
President — Neal Linnihan

R.R. Donnelley & Sons Co./Database Technology Services
99 Park Ave., 14th Fl.
New York, NY 10016
tel (212) 503-1246; fax (212) 503-1307
e-mail predmon@rrddts.donnelley.com
Marketing Manager — Patricia Redmon
Development Manager — Mark Steinborn

RSP Inc.
1840 E. River Rd., Ste. 100
Tucson, AZ 85718
tel (520) 577-0321; fax (520) 577-8670
e-mail vdesire@rspinc.com
Contact — Vince Desiderio
Chairman — Eugene J. Lipkin
President — Michael J. Riedel

S

Sage Marcom Inc.
717 Erie Blvd. W.
Syracuse, NY 13204
tel (315) 478-6612; fax (315) 475-9723
e-mail http://www.sagemarcom.com/delta
Contact — Mark Lesselroth

Sandbox Digital Playground
203 N. Wabash, Ste. 1602
Chicago, IL 60601
tel (312) 372-1170; fax (312) 372-6480
e-mail sandboxdp@aol.com
Contact — Sandy L. Ostroff
Animation — Ted Gordon

Santronics Software
30034 S.W. 153 Ct.
Leisure City, FL 33033
tel (305) 248-3204; fax (305) 248-7815
e-mail hsantos@santronics.com
FidoNet: 1:135/382
BBS: (305) 248-7815
Director-Marketing — Andrea Santos
President — Hector Santos

Scala Inc.
2323 Horse Pen Rd., Ste. 202
Herndon, VA 22071
tel (703) 713-0900; fax (703) 713-1960
Contact — Edward Larese
Executive Vice President — Tom Hillman

Scherers Communications Inc.
575 Scherers Ct.
Worthington, OH 43085
tel (800) 356-6161; fax (614) 847-2395
President/CEO — Gordon Scherer
Div. Mgr./Voice Technologies Group & Nat'l
Sales — Greg Garrett

Science Dynamics
1919 Springdale Rd.
Cherry Hill, NJ 08003-1619
tel (609) 424-0068; fax (609) 751-7631
Marketing Administrator — Joe Lawless

Scrambl-Gram Inc.
1772 State Rd.
Cuyahoga Falls, OH 44223
tel (216) 923-2397; fax (216) 923-4346
Marketing Director — Mary L. Elum
President — Charles R. Elum

The Screen House
55 Temple Pl., 3rd Fl.
Boston, MA 02111
tel (617) 542-2050; fax (617) 542-2050
Partner — Adain Prince
Partner — Drake Roberts
Graphic Design — Jason Prince
Graphic Design — Angelia Geyer
Digital Audio Specialist — Josh Greco

Sealander & Co.
611 N. Buckner Blvd.
Dallas, TX 75218
tel (214) 321-8612; fax (214) 321-8612
e-mail sealand@onramp.net,
http://rampages.onramp.net/~sealand/
Contact — John Sealander

Searchlight Software Inc.
6516 Detriot Ave.
Cleveland, OH 44102
tel (216) 631-9290/(800) 988-LITE
(Orders); fax (216) 631-9289
e-mail info@searchlight.com
BBS: (216) 631-9285
Vice President — Tim Rossiter
President — Frank LaRosa

R. Seide & Associates International
7660 Beverly Blvd., Ste. 446
Los Angeles, CA 90036
tel (213) 938-9408; fax (213) 938-5150
Contact — Ray Seide
Creative Director — Vittoria Lera
Copy Writer — Jean Hester

Sentinel
375 6th St.; PO Box 588
Lewiston, PA 17044
tel (717) 248-6741; fax (717) 248-8317
Publisher — Bart Leath

Seybold Publications
428 E. Baltimore Pike
Media, PA 19063
tel (610) 565-2480; fax (610) 565-4659
Editor — Steven Edwards

Sigma Communications Services Inc.
350 Springfield Ave.; PO Box 675
Summit, NJ 07901
tel (908) 277-2122; fax (908) 277-1998
Contact — Michael Rogers

Silicon Graphics
PO Box 7311
Mountain View, CA 94039
tel (415) 960-1980
Contact — Harry Pforzheimer

Silver Oaks Communications
PO Box 8445
Moline, IL 61265
tel (309) 797-9898
Contact — Charles Dostale

SIMBA Information Inc.
213 Danbury Rd.; PO Box 7430
Wilton, CT 06897-7430
tel (203) 834-0033; fax (203) 834-1771
e-mail simba99@aol.com
Contact — Patti J. Devine
Director Electronic Products & Services —
Gordon Joseloff
Editor Media Daily — Andy Torgan

Simon & Schuster Interactive
1230 Avenue of the Americas
New York, NY 10020
tel (212) 698-7000; fax (212) 698-7555

Copyright ©1996 by the Editor & Publisher Co.

VI-58 Interactive products and services

VP/Dir.-Marketing — Walter W.J. Walker
President — Peter Yunich
Senior Producer — Jeff Siegel
Executive Producer — Keith Halper
Director-Business Development — Ted Hill

Singer Consulting Inc.
1533 Cambridge Ct.; PO Box 628
Palmyra, PA 17078-0628
tel (717) 838-6906
e-mail singerw@iia.org
Vice President — William H. Singer
President/CEO — Nanette Singer

Smart and Friendly
16539 Saticoy St.; PO Box 9277
Van Nuys, CA 91409-9277
tel (818) 994-8001; fax (818) 988-6581
President — Perry Solomon
Vice President — Marie Solomon
Technical Manager — Michael Forman
Purchasing Manager — Steve Matsuyama
Marketing Manager — Jeremy Gerber

Smart Phone Communications
Metro Center, 1 Station Plaza
Stamford, CT 06902
tel (203) 353-5950; fax (203) 353-5962
e-mail http://www.custserv@
smartphone.com
President — Steve Francesco
Chairman/CEO — Sam Cassetta

Smartalk
76 Clipper St.; PO Box 460404
San Francisco, CA 94114
tel (415) 821-7722; fax (415) 821-4007
Creative Director — Beth Kaufman

Laura Smith/Graphic Design
237 1/2 9th St.
West Palm Beach, FL 33401
tel (407) 833-6037; fax (407) 659-4886
Contact — Laura Smith

Soft-Com Inc.
140 W. 22nd St., Ste. 7A
New York, NY 10011-2420
tel (212) 242-9595; fax (212) 694-6223
President — John J. Perri
Vice President-Sales & Marketing Voice
Processing Division — Jim Cadigan

SoftKey International Inc.
201 Broadway
Cambridge, MA 01239
tel (800) 227-5609 (Consumer)/(617)
494-1200 (Customer Service)/(800) 323-
8088 (Dealers); fax (617) 494-1219
Contact — Kristin Keyes
President — Kevin O'Leary
Executive VP Sales & Marketing —
David Patrick
Vice President-Sales — Jack Dolan
Vice President/General Manager ZSoft —
Alexander Hoag
Director-Public Relations — Kathleen
Baum

SoftMagic Corp.
72 Mallard Way
Waltham, MA 02154
tel (617) 899-9966/(800) 672-9999
(Sales); fax (617) 899-1458
e-mail softmagic.com
Contact — Jennifer Sant'Anna

SoftQuad Inc.
56 Aberfoyle Crescent
Toronto, ON M8X 2W4 Canada
tel (416) 239-4801; fax (416) 239-7105
e-mail linda@sq.com
Director-Marketing — Linda Hazzan

Software Consulting Services
3162 Bath Pike
Nazareth, PA 18064
tel (610) 837-8484; fax (610) 837-8080
e-mail sales@nscs.fast.net
http://nscs.fast.net
Technical Writer — Becky Schnur

Software Publisher Association
1730 M St., N.W. #700
Washington, DC 20036-4510
tel (202) 452-1600; fax (202) 223-8756
e-mail mbstrum@spa.org
http://www.spa.org
Contact — Mandy Braun Strum
President — Ken Wasch
Vice President — Glenn Ochsenreiter

Solo Photography Inc.
3503 N.W. 15th St.
Miami, FL 33125
tel (305) 634-8820; fax (305) 634-8820
e-mail spinc@magic.winnet.net
Contact — Raul Pedroso

Sony Electronic Publishing
3181 N. Fruitridge Ave.
Terre Haute, IN 47804
tel (812) 462-8799; fax (812) 462-8886
e-mail gary_wesley@sepc.sony.com
Contact — Gary L. Wesley
VP-Software Services — Don Willis
VP-Software Services — Bob Marsh
Director-Sales — Steve Gunning

Source Digital Systems
1420 Springhill Rd., Ste. 400
McLean, VA 22102
tel (703) 821-6800; fax (703) 821-7785
Contact — Mary Sasser

Spafax Inflight Media
112 E. 36th St., Ste. 3
New York, NY 10016
tel (212) 447-0390; fax (212) 447-0405
Contact — David Bannister
Regional Director — Dick Dee
National Director — Jack Tolbert

Spanlink Communications
1 Main St. S.E., 4th Fl.
Minneapolis, MN 55414
tel (612) 362-8000; fax (612) 362-8351
e-mail http://www.spanlink.com
Sales Director — Kevin Avery
President — Pat Irestone
Product Manager — Ellen Ratchye

Spar Associates Inc.
927 West St.
Annapolis, MD 21401
tel (410) 263-8593; fax (410) 267-0503
e-mail spar@spar.nsnet.com
Contact — Laurent C. Deschamps

Specialty Systems
2301 Industrial Way S.
Toms River, NJ 08755
tel (908) 341-1011; fax (908) 341-0655
Vice President — Bill Cabey

SpectraFax Corp.
3050 N. Horseshoe Dr., Ste. 100
Naples, FL 33942
tel (813) 643-5060; fax (813) 643-5070
National Sales Director — Kent Conwell
Marketing Asst. — Suzanne P. Giddings

SpectraLink
1650 38th St., Ste. 202 E.
Boulder, CO 80301
tel (303) 440-5330; fax (303) 440-5331
Marketing Director — Thomas Ohlsson

Spectrum Universal
PO Box 341169
Arleta, CA 91334
tel (818) 834-8220; fax (818) 834-8221
e-mail aware@netcom.com
Contact — Richard De A'Morelli

Spectrumedia Inc.
11 Center St.
Middletown, NY 10940
tel (914) 294-7106; fax (914) 344-0642
e-mail spctrmda@los.com
spctrmda@aol.com
President — Erik Unhjem

Spin Interactive
350 Townsend, #308
San Francisco, CA 94107
tel (415) 284-0490; fax (415) 284-0493
e-mail spininto@aol.com
Executive Director — Irene Graff
Technical Director — Peter Wolf
Art Director — Barbara Mehlman

The Sports Network
701 Mason's Mill Business Park
Huntingdon Valley, PA 19006
tel (215) 947-2400; fax (215) 938-8466
Director-Marketing — Stacy B. Tucker
President/CEO — Mickey Charles
National Sales Manager — Ken Zajac
Media Sales Manager — Kevin Spiegel
Dir-Technical Operations — Bruce Michaels

Sprint TeleMedia
6600 College Ave., Ste. 310
Overland Park, KS 66211-1522
tel (800) 735-5900; fax (913) 661-8008
Vice President/GM — Gerry Euston
Marketing Director — Dianna DeSmet
National Sales Director — Nick Sample
National Sales Director — Tom Murphy
PR & Trade Show Mgr — Sharon Lundeen

Spry
316 Occidental Ave. S., #200
Seattle, WA 98104
tel (206) 515-2813
Vice President-Marketing — Lisa Thorell

Stanford Multimedia Technology Group
1219 Morningside Dr., #500
Manhattan Beach, CA 90266
tel (310) 376-8070; fax (310) 374-0530
e-mail fkilpatrick@Stanford-media.com
Contact — Frank S. Kilpatrick
Design Director — Charles Larson
Advisor — R. Teren Dunlap
Advisor — Robert Flynn

Stauffer Media Systems
3316 E. 32nd St.; PO Box 1330
Joplin, MO 64802
tel (417) 782-0280; fax (417) 782-1282
Sales Manager — Keith Wood
Product Development Manager —
Lynn Grantham
Dir-Audiotex Technical — Harry Stewart
Sales Representative — Kim Sexton

Stein Educational Marketing Group
2161 Monroe Dr., N.E.
Atlanta, GA 30324
tel (404) 875-0421; fax (404) 875-4916
e-mail edmarkgrp@intergate.net
Contact — Jay Williams
Senior Account Executive — Rob Glass
Associate Director-Creative Services —
Ingrid Krein

Stella Interactive Inc.
2185 Faraday Av., Ste. 100
Carlsbad, CA 92008-7206
tel (619) 431-8221; fax (619) 431-8108
e-mail benpadnos@aol.com
Director-Marketing — Benjamin L. Padnos
President/CEO — Richard B. Beedon
COO — David W. Wogahn
VP/General Counsel — Michael R. Shea

Stockalert Inc.
7000 Boulevard E.
West New York, NJ 07093
tel (201) 854-0499; fax (201) 854-4971
VP-International Sales — Mala Bawer
President — James Teicher

Stok Software Inc.
92-30 56th Ave., Ste. LC
Elmhurst, NY 11373
tel (718) 699-9393; fax (718) 271-4404
President — Glenn Stok

Stoneman Law Offices Ltd.
1606 W. Indian School Rd.
Phoenix, AZ 85012
tel (602) 263-9200; fax (602) 274-7752
e-mail marty@indirect.com
Lawyer — Marty Stoneman

Storage Comm
5004 W. 92nd Ave., Ste. 110
Westminster, CO 80030
tel (303) 420-3472; fax (303) 456-9775
President — Henry Lubbe

Stormfront Studios
4000 Civic Center Dr., Ste. A
San Rafael, CA 94903
tel (415) 479-2800
Vice President-Marketing — Latricia Turner
President/CEO — Don Daglow
Vice President — David Bunnett

Strategic Images
9807 Woodland View Ln.
Cordova, TN 38018
tel (901) 753-0998; fax (901) 759-5203
e-mail regshoots@aol.com
Contact — Ed Griffith
Creative Director — Cathie Griffith

Strategic Systems Inc.
460 Totten Pond Rd.
Waltham, MA 02154
tel (617) 487-0055; fax (617) 487-0056
Executive VP — Mark Krentzman
President — Ray Noveck

Strategic Telemedia Inc.
PO Box 1162, Old Chelsea Station
New York, NY 10011
tel (212) 366-0895; fax (212) 366-0897
Managing Director — Mark Plakias
Vice President — Daniel M. Miller

StrayLight
150 Mount Bethel Rd.
Warren, NJ 07059
tel (908) 580-0086; fax (908) 580-0092
Contact — Victoria Massulli
President — Tony Asch
Director-Engineering — Scott Lavender

Studio Interactive
650 N. Brenson Ave. #223
Hollywood, CA 90004
tel (213) 856-8048; fax (213) 461-4202
Partner — Steve Soffer
Partner — Jerry Weinstock
Partner — Jay Jacoby

Studio One Multimedia
1107 Fribourg St. (36608); PO Box 6466
Mobile, AL 36660
tel (334) 460-0400; fax (334) 344-8586
e-mail awhitman@learn.com
Contact — Alan Whitman

Sumeria Inc.
329 Bryant St., Ste. 3D
San Francisco, CA 94107
tel (415) 904-0800; fax (415) 904-0888
e-mail sumeria@applelink.apple.com
Contact — Janine Lee
President — Jerry Borrell
Director-Operations — Sandy Butler

Summit Business Systems
PO Box 92768
Long Beach, CA 90809-2768
tel (310) 498-8006; fax (310) 498-8668
e-mail 74407.533@compuserve.com
Contact — Joe Nicassio

Sun Microsystems Computer Co.
2550 Garcia Ave.
Mountain View, CA 94043-1100
tel (415) 960-1300; fax (415) 856-2114
e-mail http://www.sun.com
Contact — Katherrine L. Parker

Sunbelt Video Inc.
4205-K Stuart Andrew Blvd.
Charlotte, NC 28217
tel (704) 527-4152; fax (704) 523-8459
Contact — Tim Bulter

SunMedia Inc.
PO Box 1753
Englewood Cliffs, NJ 07632-0753
tel (201) 330-3229; fax (201) 865-0282
e-mail 74357.101@compuserve.com
Contact — Harley J. Sun

Super Mosaic
6430 Sunset Blvd.
Hollywood, CA 90028
tel (818) 243-4411
Contact — Stan Goldin

Supra
312 S.E. Stone Mill Dr., Ste. 150
Vancouver, WA 98684
tel (503) 967-2410; fax (360) 604-1401
e-mail sales@supra.com
President — John Wiley
Vice President — Frank Hausmann

Symmetry Development Systems Inc.
330 Townsend St., #202
San Francisco, CA 94107
tel (415) 512-0595; fax (415) 512-0295
e-mail ssres@aol.com
Partner — Amy Margowsky Bellin
Partner — Alicia Sebastian

Syntellect
160 Hansen Ct., Ste. 100
Wood Dale, IL 60191
tel (708) 238-0650, ext. 5360
fax (708) 238-0670
e-mail krisz@syntellect.com
Contact — Kristine Zeigler
Sales Manager — John McIntire

Syracomp Inc.
201 S. Main St., Ste. 310
North Syracuse, NY 13212
tel (315) 458-0098; fax (315) 458-0782
e-mail syracomp@dreamscape.com,
http://www.syracomp.dreamscape.com
Executive Vice President — Jeffrey Berezin
President — Joanne Berezin
Vice President-Sales — Nathan Diniro

Copyright ©1996 by the Editor & Publisher Co.

Interactive products and services　　VI-59

Syracuse Language Systems Inc.
719 E. Genesee St.
Syracuse, NY 13210
tel (315) 478-6729; fax (315) 478-6902
Marketing Manager — Sarah Vaivoda
President — Dr. Martin Rothenberg
VP-Marketing & Sales — Larry Rothenberg
VP-Technical Development — Roy Thomas

Sysdeco US
15 Crosby Dr.
Bedford, MA 01730-1418
tel (617) 275-2323; fax (617) 276-1253
Director-Sales — Jerome Riley
COO — Clive Segal
CFO — Debra Behanger

System Guides
31 Sandpiper Strand
Coronado, CA 92118
tel (619) 575-6974
Marketing Director — James G. Root

Systems Integrators Inc.
1300 National Dr.
Sacramento, CA 95834
tel (916) 929-9481; fax (916) 928-0319
Vice President-Publishing Products —
John Cook
President/CEO — William Aaronson

T

Tadiran Electronic Industries Inc.
5733 Myerlake Circle
Clearwater, FL 34620
tel (813) 523-0000; fax (813) 523-0010
VP/Gen Manager-Telecommunications —
Pinchas Just
Vice President/Marketing & Planning —
John Dabnor

Law Offices of James Talbot
6234 Cavalleri Rd.
Malibu, CA 90265-4017
tel (310) 457-1387
Contact — James Talbot

TALX Corp.
1633 Des Peres Rd.
St. Louis, MO 63131-1800
tel (314) 984-8200; fax (314) 984-8233
e-mail fmoroni@talx.com
Contact — Fred Moroni
District Sales Manager — Sal Salgado
District Sales Manager — Rudy Brynac
District Sales Manager — Tina Maas
Operations Manager — Tom Werner

Tam Communications
160 W. Santa Clara St., Ste. 703
San Jose, CA 95113
tel (408) 279-2400; fax (408) 279-2562
e-mail michele
bertolone@tamcomm.globalcenter.net
Contact — Michele Bertolone
Vice President-Creative Affairs —
Susan O'Connor Fraser
Director-Multimedia Development —
Sandra Silva

Tape House Interactive
222 E. 44th St.
New York, NY 10017
tel (212) 953-1784; fax (212) 953-1787
Contact — Marylyn Dintenfass

Target Computer Inc.
94 Medford Ave.
Patchogue, NY 11772
tel (516) 475-5600; fax (516) 475-5683
President — Clifford A. Leventhal
Office Manager — Karen Areg
Sales Manager — Fred Williams
Internet Consultant — Bob O'Brien

Targetbase Marketing
7850 N. Beltline Rd.; PO Box 650083
Irving, TX 75063
tel (214) 506-3719; fax (214) 506-3898
e-mail mmcquown@metronet.com
Director — Maggie McQuown
President — Jack Wolf
Vice President — Beth Kuykendall
Vice President — George Williams

TeamDesign
1809 7th Ave., Ste. 500
Seattle, WA 98101
tel (206) 623-1044
Business Development — Alice Boytz
Director-Multimedia & Online Services —
Dale Carlson

Tech Image Ltd.
334 E. Colfax St., Ste. E2
Palatine, IL 60067-5343
tel (708) 705-0040; fax (708) 776-3444
e-mail techimage@interaccess.com
Contact — Mike Nikolich
Account Manager — Jean Wright Medina
Account Manager — Michael B. Young
Account Executive — Scott Jackman
Account Executive — Heather Gillison

Technicolor Optical Media Services
3301 Mission Oaks Blvd.
Camarillo, CA 93012
tel (805) 445-4270; fax (805) 388-0389
e-mail pierre loubet@technicolor.com
Contact — Pierre Loubet
President — Ram Nomula
Plant Manager — Steve Glaza

Technidisc
20251 Sealpoint Cr. 104
Huntington Beach, CA 92646
tel (714) 536-0025; fax (714) 536-1700
Contact — Deborah Janus
President — Ron Balousek
General Manager — Jeff Blackwell

Techware Corp.
PO Box 151085
Altamonte Springs, FL 32715-1085
tel (407) 695-9000/(800) 347-3224
fax (407) 695-9014
Contact — Dan Lampert
Customer Service Manager — James Heidrich

Telcom Technologies
981 Corporate Ctr. Dr.
Pomona, CA 91768
tel (909) 620-7711; fax (909) 620-9438
Marketing Manager — Jeanne Michelson

Tele-Publishing Inc.
126 Brookline Ave.
Boston, MA 02215
tel (800) 874-2340; fax (617) 536-7977
President — Andrew Sutcliffe
Vice President — David Dinnage
National Sales Director — David Miller
National Director-Client Development —
Cheryl DiMeo
Marketing Director — Nancilee Franklyn

Telecide Productions Inc.
37 Circle Dr.
Circle Pines, MN 55014
tel (612) 785-0351; fax (612) 783-9280
e-mail 74163.54@compuserve.com
Contact — Larry Hutchinson
Consultant/Producer — Lisa Hutchinson

Telecompute Corp.
1275 K St., N.W. G-9
Washington, DC 20005
tel (202) 371-8195; fax (202) 371-8193
e-mail warren@telecompute.com
Contact — Warren Miller

TeleGrafix Communications Inc.
16458 Bolsa Chica, #15
Huntington Beach, CA 92649
tel (714) 379-2140; fax (714) 379-2132
Contact — Patrick Clawson

Telemedia
63 Ave. Marceau
Paris, F-75116 France
tel (33 1) 42 01 01 01
fax (33 1) 42 01 01 02
President — Pierre Guillermo

Telephone Doctor Inc.
30 Hollenberg Ct.
St. Louis, MO 63044
tel (314) 291-1012; fax (314) 291-3710
General Manager — David Friedman
President — Nancy Friedman
Sales Manager — Meg Hegeman

TeleQuest
1250 E. Copeland Rd., Ste. 850
Arlington, TX 76011
tel (817) 460-5700; fax (817) 460-1287
VP-Sales & Marketing — Jody Novacek
National Sales Director — Mark Merrill

Telescan Inc.
10550 Richmond, Ste. 250
Houston, TX 77042
tel (713) 952-1060; fax (713) 952-7138
e-mail http://www.telescan.com
Chairman/CEO — David L. Brown
Vice President — Jeffrey Brown
Media Communications — Richard Ames

TeleSystems Marketing Inc.
11320 Random Hills Rd., Ste. 200
Fairfax, VA 22030
tel (703) 385-1212; fax (703) 385-2091
President — Jan Poort
Sales/Marketing — Tim Hall

Teletutor
104 Congress St.; PO Box 6667
Portsmouth, NH 03802-6667
tel (800) 542-2242/(603) 433-2242; fax
(603) 433-2260
e-mail mail@teletutor.com
Contact — Tom McCarron
President — James Cooper

Televation Telecommunication Systems Inc.
2723 Curtis St.
Downers Grove, IL 60515
tel (708) 852-9695; fax (708) 971-3246
Contact — Bob Groetzenbach

TelSpan Inc.
National City Center; 115 W. Washington
St., Ste. 200
Indianapolis, IN 46204
tel (317) 687-1655; fax (317) 687-1656
Vice President/General Manager — Keith
E. Locke
President — J. Bruce Laughrey
Finance Director — Larry Flaten

Templeton George
1308 Ocean Park Blvd., #12
Santa Monica, CA 90405
tel (310) 450-1045
President — Roger Templeton
Vice President/Creative Director — David
George
Software Engineer — Conrad Van De Bud

TFSnet Inc.
5700 Broadmoor
Mission, KS 66202
tel (913) 262-INET (4638); fax (913)
262-INET (4638)
e-mail http://www.fileshop.com
BBS: (913) 262-7000
Internet Specialist — John Howard
President — Walt Lane

Thinc. Engineering
Westerlaan 10, 3016 CK; PO Box 1015
Rotterdam, 3000 BA Netherlands
tel (31 10) 4642850; fax (31 10)
4367453
Contact — Wim Tuijl

Thomas & Daniels Inc.
3900 Veterans Memorial Hwy., Ste. 171
Bohemia, NY 11716
tel (516) 471-4659; fax (516) 471-4202
e-mail keyboarder@aol.com
President — Thomas R. Gabrielli

J. Walter Thompson/OnLine
500 Woodward Ave.
Detroit, MI 48226
tel (313) 964-2923; fax (313) 964-2315
e-mail jwt-online@aol.com
Manager — Brad Carse
Creative Director — Randy Campbell
Art Director — Doug Tocco
Production Manager — Scott Lawrence

Thunderstone Software
11115 Edgewater Dr.
Cleveland, OH 44102
tel (216) 631-8544; fax (216) 281-0828
e-mail info@thunderstone.com
http://www.thunderstone.com
General Manager — Bart Richards

Time Communications Ltd.
1600 Laperriere Ave.
Ottawa, ON K1Z 8P5 Canada
tel (613) 725-9111; fax (613) 725-2053
VP-Voice Processing — P.J. Mackie

Toshiba America Information Systems Inc.
9740 Irvine Blvd.
Irvine, CA 92718
tel (714) 583-3700; fax (714) 583-3896
Director-Sales Support — David Rafsky

Total Media Inc.
3015 Main St.
Santa Monica, CA 90405
tel (310) 450-1315; fax (310) 450-8270

e-mail totalmedia.com
President — Paul Rother

Touchscreen Media Group Inc.
1674 Broadway
New York, NY 10019
tel (212) 262-7014; fax (212) 262-6764
e-mail cheryl@touchscreen.com
President — Dennis McCole
Executive Producer — Cheryl Moellenbeck
Technical Director — John Tabbone

Tower Software Development
9 Tower Dr.
Mill Valley, CA 94941
tel (415) 388-8613; fax (415) 381-4412
Contact — Egidio Sponza
Director-Marketing — Joshua Dimondstein

Traders Connnections
PO Box 19817
Indianapolis, IN 46219-0817
tel (800) 753-4223; fax (317) 322-4310
Director-Marketing — Brent Jordon
President — Steve Edsall

Tradewinds Publishing Co.
3901 West End Ave., Ste. 706;
PO Box 90363
Nashville, TN 37209-0363
tel (615) 383-0042; fax (615) 297-1174
e-mail trade@telalink.net
Contact — William Gray

Transformation Group
8744 Landmark Rd.
Richmond, VA 23228
tel (804) 266-7345; fax (804) 266-7362
e-mail transgt@richmond.infi.net
Contact — Gayle Turner
Managing Director — Tom Laughon
Creative Director — Aimee Noonan
Education Director — Beverly Stewart

Travel Bank Systems
8760 E. Yale Ave., Unit-D; PO Box 371762
Denver, CO 80237
tel (303) 745-8586
e-mail jmelnick@travelbank.com
Contact — H. Jay Melnick

Treehouse Computer Services
40310 Three Forks Rd.
Magnolia, TX 77355
tel (713) 356-7926; fax (713) 356-8256
e-mail treehouse1@aol.com
76054.1723@compuserve.com
Contact — Brian K. Hecht
Graphics Design — Heidi Miller
Systems Engineer — Liz Hecht
Administration — Terry Gaines
Marketing — Mike Beeman

Tribune Media Services
435 N. Michigan Ave., Ste. 1500
Chicago, IL 60611
tel (312) 222-4444/(800) 245-6536;
fax (312) 222-3334/(312) 222-5038
e-mail tms@tribune.com
GM-Electronic Information Services —
Jay Fehnel
VP-Editorial & Development — Michael Silver
Senior Account Exec — Kris Stenstrom
Account Executive — Susan Alton
Vice President-Sales — Walter Mahoney

Trimark Interactive
2644 30th St.
Santa Monica, CA 90405
tel (310) 314-2000; fax (310) 392-8170
e-mail trimark@aol.com
VP-Sales & Marketing — David Localio
Director of Acquisitions & Business Affairs
— Gary Rosenfeld
Director of Marketing — Erica Montolfo
Director of Development — Kevin Hunt

triMedia Interactive
1024 Logan St.
Louisville, KY 40204
tel (502) 635-6920; fax (502) 634-3127
e-mail trimedia@iglou.com
Vice President-Marketing — Hal Park
President — C.J. Pressma
Vice President-Finance — Anita Selch
Producer — Marilyn Whitesell
Product Engineer — Steve Scherdin

Copyright ©1996 by the Editor & Publisher Co.

VI-60 Interactive products and services

TRX Corp.
160 E. 56th St., 11th Fl.
New York, NY 10022
tel (212) 644-0370; fax (212) 752-4260
President — Gary Glicker
Chairman — Eric Fuchs

TRX Interactive Communications Inc.
588 Broadway, Ste. 810
New York, NY 10012
tel (212) 431-9300; fax (212) 925-5204
e-mail trx@interport.net
President/Principal — Tony Lulling
CEO/Principal — Roger James

Tsang Seymour Design
197 10th Ave., Ste. 3
New York, NY 10011
tel (212) 727-8768; fax (212) 807-9196
Principal — Patrick Seymour
Principal — Catarina Tsang

The Tucker Group
19 Edgewood Rd.; PO Box 55
Sharon, MA 02067
tel (617) 784-0901; fax (617) 784-0930
e-mail mctttg@sri.kbt.com
Partner — Michael Tucker
Partner — Hank Tucker
Vice President — Natania Mlawer
Director — Janice Halpern

TV Data
Northway Plaza
Queensbury, NY 12804
tel (800) 338-TVDT (8838)
fax (800) 755-6786
e-mail tvdata@tvdata.com
Vice President-Marketing & Product Development — Michael Laddin
Online Services Product Mgr — Kevin Joyce
Vice President-Sales — Kathleen Wern

Twelve Point Rule Ltd.
35 W. 20th St.
New York, NY 10011
tel (212) 929-7644; fax (212) 929-7947
e-mail bryan@fusebox.com
Contact — Bryan Thatcher

Twin Stars Inc.
1824 Valley Park Ave.
Hermosa Beach, CA 90254
tel (310) 318-5511; fax (310) 318-2487
e-mail twinstars@aol.com
President — Mark Pavlakovich
Vice President — Katie Pavlakovich

2-Lane Media
1575 Westwood Blvd., Ste. 301
Los Angeles, CA 90024
tel (310) 473-3706; fax (310) 473-6736
e-mail tlanemedia@aol.com
Executive Vice President — Jonathan Pajion
President — David Lane
General Manager — Jonathan Lane

Two Twelve Associates Inc.
596 Broadway, Ste. 1212
New York, NY 10012
tel (212) 925-6885; fax (212) 925-6988
e-mail staff@212.com
Associate — David Peters
Designer — David Reinfurt
Principal — David Gibson

Twosprings Productions
432 Broadway
Saratoga Springs, NY 12866
tel (518) 583-3465
Contact — Seth Merrow

TyJill Enterprises Inc.
413 Superior St.
Rossford, OH 43460
tel (419) 666-7400; fax (419) 666-3245
e-mail jappt@aol.com
President — John J. Appt
Digital Media Designer — Tom Person
Digital Media Designer — Brett Baker

U

U-Graph Inc.
1275 Westtown Thounton Rd.;
PO Box 105
Westtown, PA 19395
tel (610) 399-1521/(800) 406-3048
e-mail u graph@novalink.com
Contact — Robert Morris

Ulead Systems Inc.
970 W. 190th St., Ste. 520
Torrance, CA 90502
tel (310) 523-9393/(800) 858-5323;
fax (310) 523-9399
e-mail support@ulead.com
Ulead Systems Inc.
Sales Associate — Debby Eddy
President — Liming Chen Ph.D.
Director-Sales — Steve Stautzenbach
Marketing Communications Manager — Gary Kervorkian

Ultimate Symbol Inc.
31 Wilderness Dr.
Stony Point, NY 10980
tel (914) 942-8083; fax (914) 942-0004
Contact — Sabrina Joy

UltiTech Inc.
Foot of Broad St., Ste. 204
Stratford, CT 06497
tel (203) 375-7300; fax (203) 375-6699
e-mail ultitech@meds.com
President — William J. Comcowich
Operations Manager — Ann Dunn

UMAX Technologies Inc.
3353 Gateway Blvd.
Fremont, CA 94538
tel (510) 651-8883/(510) 651-4000;
fax (510) 651-8834

Unet 2 Corp.
80 E. 11th St., Rm. 212
New York, NY 10003
tel (212) 777-5463; fax (212) 777-5534
Vice President — Harlan S. Levinson
President — James Monaco
Vice President — E. Holley Atkinson

Unisys
PO Box 500
Blue Bell, PA 19424
tel (215) 986-3501; fax (215) 986-6850
e-mail solutions@unisys.com
Executive Vice President — Alan G. Lutz
Vice President-Public Relations & Advertising — Bob O'Leary

United Media
200 Madison Ave.
New York, NY 10016
tel (800) 221-4816; fax (212) 293-8600
Vice President-Sales — Lisa Klem Wilson
Director of New Media — Alma Derricks
Manager-New Media Projects — Jonathan Young

Universal Press Syndicate & Cos.
4900 Main St.
Kansas City, MO 64112
tel (816) 932-6600; fax (816) 932-6648
Director-Information Technology — Lisa Schmidt
Director-Human Resources — Mickey Stewart

US Audiotex Inc.
18 Crow Canyon Ct., Ste. 300
San Ramon, CA 94583
tel (510) 838-7996; fax (510) 838-4395
e-mail http://www.usaudiotex.com
Contact — Jane B. Lawrence
President — Kenneth Stern
Executive Vice President — Bud Bauer
Sales-Media — Jim Herbst

U.S. Telecom International Inc.
211 Main St., Ste. 401
Joplin, MO 64801
tel (417) 781-7000 ext. 1127/(800) 835-7788; fax (417) 623-2963
Vice President-Sales — Kim Cooke

US West Marketing Resources Group
198 Inverness Dr. W.
Englewood, CO 80112
tel (303) 784-2349; fax (303) 784-1322
Contact — Tom Thompson

USA 800 Inc.
6616 Raytown Rd.
Kansas City, MO 64133
tel (800) 821-7539; fax (816) 358-3101

CEO — Ron White Sr.
Executive Vice President — Tom Davis
General Manager — Sue Hofmann
National Director-Sales & Marketing — Jerry Smutzler

UUNET Technologies Inc.
3060 Williams Dr.
Fairfax, VA 22031-4648
tel (703) 206-5600; fax (703) 206-5601
e-mail info@uu.net
Director-Sales — Clint Heiden
Western Regional Sales Mgr — Rob Lewis
Eastern Regional Sales Manager — Steve Evans

V

V-Channel
3080 Olcott St., #135C
Santa Clara, CA 95054-3217
tel (408) 980-9999 ext. 102
fax (408) 492-9999
e-mail vicix.netcom.com
Contact — Alan S. Yatagai

V Communications
6201 Haney Dr.; PO Box 49036
Austin, TX 78765-9036
tel (512) 929-7317; fax (512) 929-9106
e-mail vcomm@vcomm.com
http://www.eden.com/~vcomm
Contact — Christopher D. Brown
Managing Partner — Virginia Brown

Vartec, L.P., A TCI Co.
12835 E. Arapaho Rd., Tower 2
Englewood, CO 80112
tel (800) VARTEC1; fax (303) 705-7719
e-mail terry@vartec.com
Director-Marketing — Terry Thompson

Verbex Voice Systems Inc.
1090 King George Post Rd., Bldg. 107
Edison, NJ 08837
tel (908) 225-5225/(800) ASK-VRBX
fax (908) 225-7764
VP-Marketing & Sales — E.R. Nahm

Vicorp Interactive Systems
399 Boylston St.
Boston, MA 02116-3305
tel (617) 536-1200; fax (617) 536-6647
Director-Marketing — Laurie Gooding
Managing Dir-Sales — Stuart Patterson
Managing Dir-Technical — Mark Holthouse

Video Pipeline Inc.
16 Haddon Ave.
Haddonfield, NJ 08033
tel (609) 427-9799
e-mail vpipeline@aol.com
President — Jed Horovitz
Technical Services — Dan Lomas
Program Design — Dan Horovitz
Production Manager — Anne Green

Video Symphony
1492 W. Colorado St.
Pasadena, CA 91105
tel (818) 449-0118
Contact — Michael Flanagan

Videoactv
1487 Chain Bridge Rd., Ste. 105
McLean, VA 22101
tel (703) 998-8800; fax (703) 866-4839
e-mail videoactv@aol.com,
75202.2664@compuserve.com
Contact — Moe Benesch
VP-Marketing & Sales — Mike Castle
Vice President-Promotions — Troy Benesch
VP-Production — Brad Holcombe
Vice President-Operations — Mitch Shack

Videodata Inc.
3346 Walnut Bend
Houston, TX 77042-4712
tel (800) 544-1681; fax (713) 977-2515
e-mail vdata@netropolis.net
Director-Marketing — Van Sanders
Director-Technical Services — Gene Robinson
Director-Program Services — Brian Roberts
Technical Services — Julia Kassay

Virtual Valley Inc.
550 S. First St.
San Jose, CA 95113
tel (408) 885-8840; fax (408) 777-8701
e-mail online@vval.com
Contact — David Lea
President — Dan Pulcrano
Technical Manager — Michael Larsen

VIS
5 French Creek Pl.
San Mateo, CA 94402
tel (415) 312-9008; fax (209) 499-6928
President — Paul Meek Jr.

Visionary Media Inc.
180 Harbor Dr., Ste. 205
Sausalito, CA 94965
tel (415) 332-9201; fax (415) 332-9268
President — Kelly Jones
Associate Producer — Steve Cowan

Visionix
931 N. State Rt. 434, Ste. 1201-321
Altamonte Springs, FL 32714
tel (407) 332-1379
Business Manager — Amy Schiff
President — Jon R. Taylor

Visionautics Inc.
703 S. Dearborn St.
Chicago, IL 60606-1837
tel (312) 986-0321; fax (312) 986-0322/13129860322
e-mail vision@visionautics.com
President — Jay Goudelman
Vice President — Steven D. Hausheer
Director-Operations — Christina Robinson

Visualize Interactive
625 Arizona Ave.
Santa Monica, CA 90401
tel (310) 458-8000; fax (310) 458-1485
e-mail dmangone@pacopost.com
Executive Vice President/Creative Director — David Mangone
Director — Jerry Kramer
Executive Producer — Sandra Hay
Project Manager — Michele Panzarella
Senior Vice President — Rick Hassen

Vivid Details
8228 Sulphur Mtn. Rd.
Ojai, CA 93023
tel USA (800) 948-4843/(805) 646-0217 (International); fax (805) 646-0021
Contact — Kirk Lyford

Vivid Images Press Inc.
10530 Darkroom Dr., Ste. 100
Wise, VA 24293
tel (540) 328-2223; fax (540) 328-6915
e-mail 71141.716@compuserve.com
Contact — David Allio

VLH Communications
1607 Alta Vista Ave.
Austin, TX 78704
tel (512) 416-8018; fax (512) 416-8018
Contact — Vince Hollister

VoCal Telecommunications
77 W. Las Tunas Dr. 202
Arcadia, CA 91007
tel (818) 447-9425; fax (818) 447-2115
e-mail 73142.2547@compuserve.com
President — Ron Emerling

Voice FX Corp.
1100 E. Hector St., 4th Fl.
Conshohocken, PA 19428
tel (610) 941-1000; fax (610) 941-9844
President — Marc Cohen
COO — Jeffrey Cohen
Vice President-Sales — Elizabeth Oettinger

Voice Power Review
P.O. Box 313
Don Mills, ON M3C 2S7 Canada
tel (800) 267-6937/(416) 449-7229
fax (407) 362-4375
Publisher/Editor — Jacob Gordon

Voice Technologies Group Inc.
2350 N. Forest Rd.
Buffalo, NY 14068-1296
tel (716) 689-6700; fax (716) 689-6800
e-mail info@vtg.com
Director-Sales — John Alexander
Manager-Marketing Service — Cathryn Apenowich

Voicetek Corp.
19 Alpha Rd.
Chelmsford, MA 01824-4175
tel (508) 250-9393; fax (508) 250-9378
Director-Marketing Communications — Catherine Jaspersohn
President — Sheldon Dinkes
Vice President-Sales — Scott Ganson

Copyright ©1996 by the Editor & Publisher Co.

Interactive products and services VI-61

VoiceText Interactive
702 Colorado, Ste. 125
Austin, TX 78701
tel (512) 404-2300; fax (512) 404-2343
National Marketing Director —
Paul Cohen
President — Eileen Williams

Volt Information Sciences
1 Sentry Pkwy., Ste. 1000
Blue Bell, PA 19422
tel (610) 825-0999; fax (610) 941-6874
Contact — John Stewart
Production — Edward D. Valentine
President — Gerard Dipippo

Votan
7020 Koll Ctr. Pkwy., Ste. 142
Pleasanton, CA 94566
tel (510) 426-5600; fax (510) 426-6767
Sr Product Manager-Voice Technology —
Graeme Kinsey
General Manager — Dick Vail

VuCom Graphicsystems
1256 Kirts Blvd., Ste. 300
Troy, MI 48084
tel (810) 362-4212; fax (810) 362-3212
e-mail afhetzel@netcom.com
Contact — Andrew Hetzel
Sales Manager — Chris Wilson
General Manager — Robin Danek

W

Bill Wadsworth Productions
1913 W. 37th St.
Austin, TX 78731-6012
tel (512) 452-4243
Contact — Bill Wadsworth

WAIS (Wide Area Information Servers) Inc.
690 Fifth St.
San Francisco, CA 94107
tel (415) 356-5413; fax (415) 356-5444
e-mail dia@wais.com, http://www.wais.com
Marketing — Dia Cheney
Vice President-Business Development —
John Duhring

Walnut Creek CDROM
4041 Pike Ln., Ste. D (Concord, 94520);
PO Box 260
Walnut Creek, CA 94596
tel (800) 786-9907/(510) 674-0783
fax (510) 674-0821
e-mail info@cdrom.com
Media Contact — Carsie McCarthy
President — Bob Bruce
Vice President — Jack Velte

Carl Waltzer Digital Services Inc.
873 Broadway
New York, NY 10003
tel (212) 475-8748; fax (212) 475-9359
President — Carl Waltzer
Photographer — Bill Waltzer
Designer — Valerie English

The Washington Times Corp.
3600 New York Ave., N.E.
Washington, DC 20002
tel (202) 636-8811; fax (202) 526-8826
e-mail natletr@mcimail.com
Vice President/General Manager —
Geoffrey H. Edwards

Waters Design Associates Inc.
3 W. 18th St.
New York, NY 10011
tel (212) 807-0717; fax (212) 627-8818
e-mail wda94@aol.com
Contact — John Waters
Senior Designer — Colleen Syron
Senior Designer — Michelle Novak

Weather Services Corp.
420 Bedford St.
Lexington, MA 02173
tel (617) 676-1000; fax (617) 676-1001
e-mail @wx.com
National Sales Manager —
Deborah L. Gambell
Graphics Manager — Julie Quinn
President — Michael Leavitt

Welcome to the Future Inc.
10451 Twin Rivers Rd., Ste 413;
PO Box 755
Columbia, MD 21045
tel (410) 964-9590; fax (410) 964-9591
CEO — Brandon Calder
President — Hamid Qayyum
COO — Gerald Williams
Executive Vice President — John Shin

Wessan Interactive
3033 N. 93rd St.
Omaha, NE 68134
tel (402) 572-8200; fax (402) 572-7244
Contact — Terry Sanford
President — Karen Westerfield

West End Post Interactive
2211 N. Lamar, Ste. 100
Dallas, TX 75202
tel (214) 720-8660; fax (214) 720-8600
e-mail robspaul@aol.com
Sales & Marketing Manager — Paul Roberts
Group Manager — Carolyn Carmines
Designer/Developer — James Marzano
Designer/Developer — Bill Marcus
Network Manager — Darrin Woods

West Interactive Corp.
9223 Bedford Ave.
Omaha, NE 68134
tel (402) 573-1000; fax (402) 573-8952
e-mail dubuc@ix.netcom.com
Contact — Danielle Pedersen
Executive Vice President —
Nancee Berger
VP-Sales & Marketing — Mike Sturgeon

West Publishing
620 Opperman Dr.
Eagan, MN 55123
tel (612) 687-7000; fax (612) 687-7302
Contact — Ruth Stanoch

WideCom Group Inc.
55 City Ctr. Dr., #500
Mississauga, ON L5B 1M3 Canada
tel (905) 566-0180; fax (905) 556-0181
Vice President — Suneet Tuli

Willow Bend Communications
16479 Dallas Pkwy., #770 (75248)
PO Box 797485
Dallas, TX 75379-7485
tel (214) 248-0451; fax (214) 732-8807
President — Steve Thompson

Winkler McManuas Advertising
150 Spear St., 16th Fl.
San Francisco, CA 94105
tel (415) 957-0242; fax (415) 495-7118
e-mail tom@winklermcmanus.com
Senior Vice Pres./Dir.-Business
Development — Tom Henry
President/CEO — Agnieszka Winkler
Sr VP/Creative Director — Mike Duvall
VP/Media Director — Steve Davison
VP-Strategic Resources — Bill Green

Wireless Cable Association International
1140 Connecticut Ave. N.W., Ste. 810
Washington, DC 20036
tel (202) 452-7823; fax (202) 452-1468
e-mail wca@cais.com
Communications Associates — William Ray
President — Robert L. Schmidt
VP/Communications Dir — Andrew T. Kreig
Asst. to the Pres/Office Mgr — Lisa Maffei
Membership Dir — Michael MacPherson

WolfBayne Communications
PO Box 50287
Colorado Springs, CO 80949
tel (719) 593-8032
e-mail kimmik@bayne.com,
http://www.bayne.com/wolfbayne
Contact — Kim M. Bayne

Woodward Communications
801 8th & Bluff St.; PO Box 688
Dubuque, IA 52001
tel (319) 588-5687; fax (319) 588-5745
Vice President-Shopping News Division —
Craig L. Trongaard

World Data Delivery Systems Inc.
19992 Kelly Rd.
Harper Woods, MI 48225
tel (313) 527-7000; fax (313) 527-1100
COO — Rick Jaffey

World Interactive Network
200 Haven Ave., Ste. 5B
New York, NY 10033-5303
tel (212) 795-0148; fax (212) 795-8553
e-mail win@2inglobal.com
VP/General Manager — Claudia Soifer
Executive Producer — Charles Padro
Senior Project Manager — Russell Stoll
Account Management — Trish Lewin
Senior Animator — Paul Johnson

Worthington Voice Services Inc.
740 E. Lake View Plz. Blvd., Ste. E.
Worthington, OH 43085
tel (614) 431-9710; fax (614) 431-5792
Sales Rep. — Tricia Barnes

The Writers Alliance Inc.
12008 Golden Twig Ct.
Gaithersburg, MD 20878
tel (301) 926-4447; fax (301) 948-8028
e-mail makulow@trainer.com
Contact — John Makulowich

WTS Bureau Systems
14850 Venture Dr.
Dallas, TX 75234
tel (214) 353-5000; fax (214) 353-5025
Owner — J.L. Summers
Vice President — Dave Harmon

X

Xpedite Systems Inc.
446 Highway 35 S.
Eatontown, NJ 07724
tel (800) 546-1541/(908) 389-3900;
fax (908) 542-9436
e-mail http://www.xpedite.com
President/CEO — Roy B. Anderson
VP-Sales & Marketing — Max Slifer
Marketing Manager — Kathleen Peters

Y

Gay Young Agency Inc.
700 Washington St., Ste. 3 Upper
New York, NY 10014
tel (212) 691-3124; fax (212) 807-9772
e-mail gyaency@aol.com,
73352.372@compuserve.com
Contact — Gay Young
Executive VP — Richard Weisman

Z

Z Creek
197 Wells St.
Felton, CA 95218
tel (408) 335-7412; fax (408) 335-7412
e-mail sheiman@netcom.com
CEO — Michelle Sheiman
Business Development Mgr.—
Jim Phillips
Technical Manager — Rich Rasmussen
Senior Programmer — Pat True
Talent Management — Jeanie Golino

Zane Publishing Inc.
1950 Stemmons Fwy., Ste. 4044
Dallas, TX 75207-3109
tel (214) 746-5555; fax (214) 746-5560
e-mail zane@zane.com
Vice President/COO — Reed Bilbray
CEO — Andrew Preston

Zelos Digital Learning
98 Battery St., Ste. 300
San Francisco, CA 94111
tel (415) 788-0566; fax (415) 788-0562
President/CEO — Randall Stickrod
VP-Development — Suzanne Dunn
VP-Sales & Marketing — Sarah Scharf
Director-Acquisitions — Susan Lynch

Zimmers Interactive
4250 Ferguson Dr.
Cincinnati, OH 45248
tel (513) 943-9000; fax (513) 943-0822
e-mail zimmers@iac.net
President — Louis E. Zimmers
Vice President — Steven L. Zimmers
Vice President — Gregory P. Zimmers
Dir-Interactive Media — Richard Casey
Dir-Interactive Media — Sonna L. Whitney

Zuma Group Inc.
6733 N. Black Canyon Hwy.
Phoenix, AZ 85015-1050
tel (602) 246-4238; fax (602) 246-6708
e-mail jbitt@primenet.com
Vice President — Copper Bittner
President — John Bittner

PRIMARY CATEGORIES OF INTERACTIVE PRODUCTS AND SERVICES

Advertising/Marketing Agency
Ad National Yellow Pages
Adams and Associates
Advertising Research Corp.
The Answer Team-A PE Co.
Arena Marketing Group
Ballantine & Co. Inc.
Belden
Bender, Goldman & Helper
Bigio Concepts
Black Star Link
Block Interactive
CKS/Interactive
Rapp Collins Communications
Colorite Film

Compudoc Inc.
Cramp & Associates Inc.
Cyber Sales One (Div. of CMS)
Dana Communications
DDB Needham Interactive Communications
Diskalog Inc.
Epsilon
fine.com Corp.
Frederiksen Television Inc.
Frontier Interactive Multimedia Communications
Godfrey Advertising
The Gourley Group
GP Productions
Grey Direct

Griffin & Boyle
Hemsing Advertising Inc.
Hinckley & Slade Inc.
Hitchcock Fleming & Associates Inc.
Hometown Video Productions
Image Communications
Interactive Consulting
Interactive Media Group
Joyce Communications
Lieberman Research West
Lyon & Associates Creative Services Inc.
Mall Marketing Media
Marke Communications Inc.
MCCommunications
M/S Database Marketing

New Art Communications
The Next Wave
NKH & W Inc.
O'Halloran Advertising Inc.
O'Keefe Interactive
Origin Systems Inc.
Tom O'Toole Communications Group
Parrish Wickersham & Partners
Performance Resources International
Peters Video Productions
Phone Works
Poppe Tyson
PR Marketing & Communications Inc.
Premiere Interactive Media LLC
Print Media Marketing Group

Copyright ©1996 by the Editor & Publisher Co.

Interactive products and services

Richardson, Myers & Donofrio, Inc.
Risdall Linnihan Advertising Interactive
Sage Marcom Inc.
Sealander & Co.
R. Seide & Associates International
Stein Educational Marketing Group
Tam Communications
Targetbase Marketing
Tech Image Ltd.
Templeton George
Thomas & Daniels Inc.
J. Walter Thompson/OnLine
Transformation Group
The Tucker Group
Twin Stars Inc.
Winkler McManuas Advertising

CD-ROM Designer/Manufacturer
Aces Research Inc.
Allied Digital Technologies
Amerikids USA
AMUSE, Interactive Learning Environments
And Software Inc.
Automated Graphic Systems Inc.
Blender
Bureau of Electronic Publishing Inc.
CD Technology
Cimarron International Inc.
ClassAct
Commotion New Media Inc.
Corporate Disk Co.
Cortex Communications Inc.
Digital Post & Graphics
ElectoPix Inc.
Elite of America Inc.
Enigma Information Systems Ltd.
Galileo Inc.
Grafica Multimedia Inc.
Hands-On Interactive Publishing Inc.
Highlighted Data Inc.
Information Handling Services
Interactive Arts
Interactive Multimedia Project
interActive Publishing
International Software Service Inc.
Ivy Hill Packaging
Just Softworks Inc.
The Listening Chair
Luminare
Media Design Group
Media Learning Systems
Media X
Moving Graphics
Moxie Media Inc.
MPI Multimedia
Next Vision Graphics Inc.
Performance Software Inc.
Alan Rand Multimedia Group Inc.
R.R. Donnelley & Sons Co./Database Technology Services
RSP Inc.
Silver Oaks Communications
Simon & Schuster Interactive
SoftKey International Inc.
Sony Electronic Publishing
Stormfront Studios
Sumeria Inc.
SunMedia Inc.
Technicolor Optical Media Services
Technidisc
Visionary Media Inc.
Walnut Creek CDROM
Zane Publishing Inc.
Zelos Digital Learning

Consultants
Adams Consulting Group Inc.
Agency for Interactive Television
Altimedia Inc.
AmEuro Direct Marketing
Ampersand
Analysis & Technology Inc.
APCO Associates Inc.
Applied Segmentation Technology
Arlen Communications Inc.
Atlantic Communication Resources Inc.
Automedia Inc.
Bizcomm
Branfman & Associates
Cobbey & Associates Marketing Research
Coopers & Lybrand
The CyberMedia Group
D & H Information Services
D & S Associates
Digital Consulting Services Inc.
Emerging Technology Consultants Inc.
The Findlay Group
First Alliance
FLI Inc.
Index Inc.
Information Highways Inc.
Ingels Inc.
Interactive Educational Systems Design Inc.
Interactive Media Associates
Interactive Productions
International Connectivity Consortium
Intra-Active Designs
i3 Information & Imagination Inc.
The Law Offices of Clayton Knowles
Kobie Marketing Inc.
Komenar Production & Marketing Group
Landels, Ripley & Diamond
The Lantz Foundation
Logica Inc.
Frank Magid & Associates
Market Opinion
Meteoquest Inc.
Multimedia Research Group
MultiMedia Resources
New Cool Media (Publishing Inc.)
Owen Associates Inc.
The Pinnacle Group Media Consultants Ltd.
Planetary News LLC
Singer Consulting Inc.
Solo Photography Inc.
Stoneman Law Offices Ltd.
Strategic Systems Inc.
Symmetry Development Systems Inc.
Law Offices of James Talbot
Visionix
VLH Communications
WolfBayne Communications
Gay Young Agency Inc.

Graphic/Design Firm
Beda Design
Bersearch Information Services
BKJ Productions
Black Swan Graphics
Clement Mok Designs
Cosmos Communications Inc.
Design Collaborative
DH Design
Direct Images
D3 Inc.
Dynacom Inc.
ELF Works 3D Construction Co.
Fisher Photography
Ha! Design Inc.
Hennig Productions
Image Technology Inc.
Imagen Inc.
Imagine That Creative Services
Impact Media Group
Interactive Visuals Inc.
Iron Design
Keller Production
Maginnis Inc.
Aaron Marcus and Associates Inc.
On Target Inc.
Pace Design Group
PixelWorks Corp.
RG Creations Inc.
Sandbox Digital Playground
Laura Smith/Graphic Design
Spectrumedia Inc.
TeamDesign
Tsang Seymour Design
Twelve Point Rule Ltd.
Two Twelve Associates Inc.
V Communications
Video Symphony
Waters Design Associates Inc.

Hardware/Software Supplier
Adaptive Optics Associates Inc., A United Technologies Co.
Adeptsoft
Adobe
ADTRAN
Advanced Publishing Technology
American Banking Systems Corp.
Apple Computer
Banana Programing
Bruce Bell & Associates
Berkeley Software Design Inc.
BSI Technologies Inc.
The Business BBS
CEC Corp. (CyCube)
Cheersoft
Cinecom Corp.
Clark Development Company Inc.
Competence Software
Computer Talk Technology
Copia International Ltd.
Cyberspace Information Systems
Cybertech Inc.
CYCO International Inc.
Datasafe Publications Inc.
Digicom Systems Inc.
Digital Audio Information Systems Inc.
Distributed Processing Technology
EDR Media
Electronic Book Technologies Inc. (EBT)
Enhanced Systems Inc.
eSoft
ET Srl Elettronica Telecomunicazioni
Excalibur Communications Inc.
Expert Systems Inc.
Freemyers Design
FutureVideo
Gannett Media Technology International
GTEK
GW Associates
Harris Publishing Systems
Hewlett-Packard
High Velocity Software
IBM
ILIO Entertainment
InContext Systems
The InfoCenter Group Inc.
Information Presentation Tech.
Intellisystems Inc.
Interactive International Inc.
Interface
Interleaf Inc.
International Information Technologies Ltd.
Kan Image Inc.
Lenel Systems International
Liberty Communications
Logicom Inc.
Luckman Interactive
Magnum Software Corp.
Marcus Technology Inc.
Media House Software Inc.
Media Marketing
Megadrive
Microlog Corp.
Micronet Technologies Inc.
Microsoft Corp.
MicroTouch Systems Inc.
Microware Systems Corp.
MMB Development Corp.
Modern BBS
Montage Group Ltd.
Morning Star Technologies
Multimedia Computer Solution Inc.
Murk Works Inc.
Muse Presentation Technologies
Navisoft
Netscape Communications Corp.
New Media Hollywood
Newscom
NewsView Solutions
Nicollet Technologies
Novell
Open Text Corp.
OptImage
Pacific Gold Coast Corp.
Pantheon
Peirce-Phelps Inc.
Pierian Spring Software
Pixel Touch
Precision Systems Inc.
Process Software
Proline-Bib
Proxima
Pulse Interactive
Radius
ResNova Software Inc.
Santronics Software
Scala Inc.
Searchlight Software Inc.
Silicon Graphics
Smart and Friendly
SoftMagic Corp.
SoftQuad Inc.
Software Consulting Services
Software Publisher Association
Source Digital Systems
Spar Associates Inc.
Specialty Systems
Stauffer Media Systems
Storage Comm
Summit Business Systems
Sun Microsystems Computer Co.
Super Mosaic
Syracomp Inc.
Sysdeco US
System Guides
Systems Integrators Inc.
Target Computer Inc.
TeleGrafix Communications Inc.
Televation Telecommunication Systems Inc.
Thinc. Engineering
Thunderstone Software
U-Graph Inc.
UMAX Technologies Inc.
Unisys
Vartec, L.P., A TCI Co.
Vivid Details
WAIS (Wide Area Information Servers) Inc.
Zuma Group Inc.

Multimedia/Interactive Products
A+ Network Inc.
AccuWeather Inc.
Admakers Multimedia Marketing
Advanced Communication Design Inc.
Advanced Multi-Point Conferencing
AltaVista Technology Inc.
Animated Software Co.
AppleTree Multimedia
Applied Optical Media
ARC Studios International Inc.
Assignment Desk
Baby Mogul Interactive
Big Hand Inc.
BKR Studio Inc.
BNDC Interactive
Breze Inc.
Brockway Direct Response Television
Century Desing
Chase-Bobko
Chelsea IVR
CommGraphics
Communication Design
Communique Interactive Solutions Inc.
CompuTalk Inc.
Computer Communications Specialists
COMSAT Entertainment Group
Connect
Convergent Media Systems
Corporate Creative Services Inc.
Creative Associates Inc.
Creative Communications
CRIT Inc.
Cyberdreams Inc.
Deloayza Associates Productions
Design Media Inc.
Design O'Saurs
Design Tekneka
dh design
Dictaphone Corp.
Digital Cinema Corp.
Digital Design Group Ltd.
Digital Media Arts
Digital Stock Corp.
Digital United
Digitcom Multimedia Corp.
Dow Jones & Co. Inc.
Dream Theater
Ken D'Urso & Associates
Dynamic Fax
DYNEX Digital Publishing
EDR Systems
Electronic Vision Inc.
EPI Communications
E.P.I.C. Software Group Inc.
ESPN/SportsTicker
Focus Interactive Technology Inc.
Fonahome Corp.
Four Palms Inc.
Fujitsu Systems Business of America Inc.
Future Light
Graphic Systems
G.T.E. Directories
Haukom Associates
Hearing Voices—Voice Overs
HintonWells Communications Inc.
HorizonMedia
Hotwax Interactive
Hummingbird Studios Inc.
Idealdial Corp.
Image Communications Group
Image Technologies Inc.
Imergy
IMMediacy
INFO-CONNECT (J.H. Zerby Newspapers Inc.)
InfoAccess Inc.
InfoMotion
Information Technologies Corps.
InfoUse
Inpho Inc.
Integra IMA GmbH
Intelligent Media
IntelliPro Inc.
Interactive Business Communications
Interactive Catalog Corp.
Interactive Design
Interactive Television Association
Interactive Video Solutions
Interalia Communications
Interaxx Television Network Inc.
InterCom
The Internet Unplugged
IPA The Editing House
It Network/Source Media
iTV1 Multimedia Inc.

Copyright ©1996 by the Editor & Publisher Co.

Interactive products and services   VI-63

Judson Rosebush Co.
Kallisto Productions Inc.
Walter J. Klein Company Ltd.
Kreutler
Kudosoft Inc.
Live Wire Productions
Logical Design Solutions
Macromedia Corp.
MAGELLAN Geographix
Mammoth Enterprise Productions
MarCole Enterprises Inc.
The Marketing Trust Inc.
MarketLink
MED.I.A. Inc.
Media Circus LLC
Media Direct Inc.
Media Productions Inc.
The Media Shop Inc.
Mediaweave Inc.
The Meeting Works!
Meridian Creative Group
Micro Interactive
MicroMall Inc.
Larry Miller Productions
Millstar Electronic Publishing Group
M!ND GAMES new media
Mindshare
Mortgage Market Information Services
Motion City Films
MP Music Previews
Multimedia Journeys
Multimedia Productions
Multimedia Resources Inc.
Multimedia Strategies
The Multimedia Studies Program
Music Access Inc.
Neptune Interactive Design
New [Media] Directions
Newman Brothers
NewOrder Media Inc.
Newspaper Voice Services Inc.
Tom Nicholson & Associates
NorthCoast Interactive
NTN Communications Inc.
Pacific Video Resources/PVR Labs
Page Systems Inc.
Panic Pink
PDM Creative
Pegasus Telesis Group
Philips Media
PixelDance Communications Inc.
PR Newswire
Presscom Technologies Corp. (P.T.C.)
Profound
Projects In Knowledge Inc.
The Radio Response Co.
Random Access
Red Hill Studios
Red Sky Interactive
Renaissance Computer
Ribit Productions Inc.
Scrambl-Gram Inc.
The Screen House
Smartalk
Spin Interactive
The Sports Network
Stella Interactive Inc.
Stockalert Inc.
Strategic Images
Strategic Telemedia Inc.
StrayLight
Studio Interactive
Studio One Multimedia
Sunbelt Video Inc.
Syracuse Language Systems Inc.
Tape House Interactive
Techware Corp.
Telecide Productions Inc.
Telecompute Corp.
Teletutor
Total Media Inc.
Touchscreen Media Group Inc.
Tower Software Development
Treehouse Computer Services
Tribune Media Services
triMedia Interactive
TRX Corp.
TRX Interactive Communications Inc.
2-Lane Media
Twosprings Productions
TyJill Enterprises Inc.
Ulead Systems Inc.
UltiTech Inc.
Unet 2 Corp.
US Audiotex Inc.
US West Marketing Resources Group
Verbex Voice Systems Inc.
Vicorp Interactive Systems
Videoactv
Videodata Inc.
Visionautics Inc.
Visualize Interactive
Voicetek Corp.
Volt Information Sciences
VuCom Graphicsystems
Bill Wadsworth Productions
Welcome to the Future Inc.
West End Post Interactive
West Interactive Corp.
Willow Bend Communications
World Interactive Network
Zimmers Interactive

Online Service Provider and Internet Hosts
Ad One Classified Network
Agis/net.99
AI Multimedia
America Online
Apple E-World
AT&T Interchange Online Network
Automatrix Inc.
Branch Internet Services Inc.
Cable Online Inc.
Clark Internet Services Inc. (ClarkNet)
Classifacts
Coe-Truman Technologies Inc.
Communications Management Service Inc.
Compuserve
Comtex Scientific Corp.
Conxtion
Coolware Inc.
Customer Communications Group
DataTimes Corp.
Delphi Internet
Delrina
Digital Express Group Inc.
Digital Solutions Inc.
Electric Classifieds Inc.
The Electronic Newsstand
Empire Information Services
E-NEPH
Galacticomm Inc.
GEN Inc.
Hollywood Online Inc.
InfiNet, Landmark Communications
Internet Distribution Services Inc.
Internet Research Inc.
The Investext Group
Kinetic Corp.
Knight-Ridder Information Inc.
Legi-Tech
LEXIS-NEXIS
Magibox Inc.
Match.Com
Media Synergy
MediaNet International Inc.
Mercury Center
Multimedia Ink Designs
Netcom
The Networks
NewsNet Inc.
Northwest Nexus Inc.
OpenNet Technologies Inc.
Palm Beach Post
Power BBS Computing
PressLink Inc.
Princeton Interactive Communications
Prodigy Services Co.
PSINet
Publitech Inc.
Rezn8
Smart Phone Communications
Spry
Stanford Multimedia Technology Group
Tele-Publishing Inc.
Telemedia
Telephone Doctor Inc.
Telescan Inc.
TFSnet Inc.
Traders Connnections
Travel Bank Systems
TV Data
UUNET Technologies Inc.
Virtual Valley Inc.
VIS
Weather Services Corp.
West Publishing
The Writers Alliance Inc.

POP/Kiosk Designer
Benchmark Kiosk Enclosures
E and E Display Group
Infinity Promotions Inc.
Inforonics Inc.
Kiosk Information Systems
Montage Multimedia Communciations
Video Pipeline Inc.

Publisher/Media
Advertising Age
Aldea Communications
Apostrophe Publishing
Associated Press
Audiotex News
Books That Work
Cable Vision Systems Corp.
The Chronicle of Higher Education
Classroom Connect
Congressional Quarterly Inc.
Creative Syndication SUS
Digital Information
Reuben H. Donnelley
Editor & Publisher Co.
EDS (Electronic Data Systems)
EFE News Services (US) Inc.
Electronic Press Inc.
Electronic Publishing & Licensing Group
Electronic World Communications Inc.
Evans Michaels & Jaymes Inc.
Fabulous Footage Inc.
Gannett Digital XPRESS
Gannett/USA Today Information Center
Glas News
Graphics Syndicate
HEC Software Inc.
Hot Sheet Publishing
Imagetects
Insider Magazine
Interactive Marketing News
Interactive Media Inc.
Interactive Publishing Alert
Interactivity Magazine
Jackson Graphics Inc.
Jordan Whitney Inc.
The Kelsey Group
King Features Syndicate
Knight Mediacom
The MacDonald Classified Service
MarketTrac
Mecklermedia Corp.
Medio Multimedia
New Horizons Group/Pottsville Republican
News USA
Newsday Direct
North Valley Diver Publications
PC Catalog
Print Marketing Concepts
Rancho Park Publishing
Sentinel
Seybold Publications
SIMBA Information Inc.
Spafax Inflight Media
Spectrum Universal
Tradewinds Publishing Co.
Trimark Interactive
Ultimate Symbol Inc.
United Media
Universal Press Syndicate & Cos.
The Washington Times Corp.
Woodward Communications

Telecommunications/Service Bureaus
Advanced Interactive Systems
Advanced Telecom Services Inc.
Advanced Telecom Services Inc.-Canada
Advanced Telecom Services Inc.-U.K.
Advanced Voice Technologies
American Voice Mail Inc.
Ameritech Corp.
APDI-Application Programming & Development Inc.
Arbitron Newmedia
Arch Communications Inc.
AT&S Inc./Voice Magic
Audio Communications Inc.
Audio Service America
Audionet-A Division of ADP
B-Linked Inc.
BEI Communication
Bell Atlantic Video Services Co.
Bell South
BMC Group Inc.
Boston Technology
Brite
Bureaucom Corp.
Call Interactive
Captured Images Inc.
Cascade Technologies Inc.
Centigram Communications Corp.
Cobotyx
Cognitronics Corp.
CommuniTech Inc.
Comsys International B.V.
Creative Audio Enterprises (On Hold Productions)
DAC Systems
Data Voice Systems
Database Network Services
Datavoice Technology
DemoSource Inc.
Dialogic Communications Corp.
Dialogic Corp.
Digital Speech Systems Inc.
Dirad Technologies
Dytel Inc.
Edmonton Telephones Corp.
E-fax Communications Inc.
EIS International
Electronic Tele-Communications Inc.
En Technology Corp.
FAR Systems Inc.
Fax Resources Inc.
GammaLink
GE Information Services
General Fax Inc.
Glenayre Electronics
Gralin Associates Inc.
Great!
HTI Voice Solutions Inc.
Information Command Inc.
Innovative Systems Design Inc.
Innovative Telecom Corp.
Instant Information Inc.
Intecom
Interactive CARDnet Telephone Co.
Interactive Conferencing Network
International Teleprograpms Inc.
InterVoice Inc.
Lazer-fare Media Services Ltd.
LO/AD Communications
MainStream Data Inc.
Malhotra & Associates Inc.
Marketing Messages
MCI Telecommunications Corp.
Mercury Telemedia Inc.
MicroVoice Applications Inc.
Motorola Paging
MPS Media Phone Service KGF
Mustang Software Inc.
Network Long Distance Inc.
Network Telephone Services
New Tech Telemedia
Nitsuko America Corp.
Nortel
Northern Telecom
NYNEX Corp.
Octel Communications
Oza Communications Corp.
PAGE
Party-Line Israel, Audio Communication Ltd.
Peeke Voice Mail Personals
Periphonics Corp.
Phone Masters
Prairie Systems Inc.
Premiere Audiotex
Real Time Strategies
Scherers Communications Inc.
Science Dynamics
Sigma Communications Services Inc.
Soft-Com Inc.
Spanlink Communications
SpectraFax Corp.
SpectraLink
Sprint TeleMedia
Stok Software Inc.
Supra
Syntellect
Tadiran Electronic Industries Inc.
TALX Corp.
Telcom Technologies
TeleQuest
TeleSystems Marketing Inc.
TelSpan Inc.
Time Communications Ltd.
Toshiba America Information Systems Inc.
U.S. Telecom International Inc.
USA 800 Inc.
V-Channel
Vivid Images Press Inc.
VoCal Telecommunications
Voice FX Corp.
Voice Power Review
Voice Technologies Group Inc.
VoiceText Interactive
Votan
Carl Waltzer Digital Services Inc.
Wessan Interactive
WideCom Group Inc.
World Data Delivery Systems Inc.
Worthington Voice Services Inc.
WTS Bureau Systems
Xpedite Systems Inc.
Z Creek

Trade Association
IICS: International Interactive Communications Society
Interactive Newspaper Network
Interactive Services Association
Wireless Cable Association International

Copyright ©1996 by the Editor & Publisher Co.

MECHANICAL FORCES PAY SCALES
January 1, 1996 — PRINCIPAL CITIES IN THE U.S. AND CANADA
(Compiled by Communications Workers of America)

COMPOSING ROOM

	Day Work Hours	Wkly Rate	Night Work Hours	Wkly Rate	Effective Date
ALABAMA					
Birmingham (News)	37½	617.12	37½	625.55	04-01-95
	37½	633.12	37½	641.55	04-01-96
	37½	649.12	37½	657.55	04-01-97
CALIFORNIA					
Bakersfield (Californian)	35	605.95	35	615.95	07-22-95
Long Beach (Press-Telegram)	35	627.50	35	639.50	03-04-95
Palmdale (Antelope Valley Press)	35	593.63	35	604.50	08-01-95
	35	585.00	35	595.50	08-01-95
San Francisco (Examiner)	35	723.75	35	733.00	07-01-95
	35	733.75	35	743.00	01-01-96
	35	743.75	35	753.00	07-01-96
	35	753.75	35	763.00	01-01-97
	35	768.75	35	778.00	07-01-97
	35	786.75	35	796.00	01-01-98
	35	806.75	35	816.00	07-01-98
San Jose (Mercury News)	35	734.75	35	712.00	12-04-95
	35	743.75	35	753.00	07-01-96
	35	754.75	35	764.00	12-30-96
	35	765.75	35	775.00	06-30-97
	35	783.75	35	793.00	12-29-97
	35	803.75	35	813.00	06-29-98
Santa Rosa (Press Democrat)	35	647.26	35	656.50	01-01-95
	35	640.95	35	650.19	07-02-95
	35	665.95	35	681.50	12-29-96
	35	652.95	35	668.50	12-31-96
	35	679.95	35	695.50	12-28-97
	35	694.95	35	710.50	12-27-98
	35	710.36	35	725.91	12-26-99
Torrance (Breeze)	35	702.87	35	707.87	05-01-95
	35	723.96	35	728.96	05-01-96
COLORADO					
Denver (Post)	36	650.58	36	660.98	06-04-95
	36	659.58	36	669.98	12-03-95
	36	673.58	36	683.98	06-02-96
	36	683.58	36	693.98	12-01-96
	36	698.58	36	708.98	03-30-97
	36	708.58	36	718.98	09-28-97
Denver (Rocky Mnt. News)	36	713.50	36	718.50	04-01-97
CONNECTICUT					
Middletown (Press)	37½	426.75	37½	456.62	03-15-95
	37½	439.64	37½	470.41	03-15-96
	37½	375.95	37½	402.27	03-15-95
	37½	387.30	37½	414.41	03-15-96
New Britain (Herald)	37½	583.14	—	—	03-01-95
Stamford (Advocate)	36¼	659.89	36¼	686.29	01-01-95
Waterbury (Republican-American)	37½	622.22	37½	640.52	05-01-95
DISTRICT OF COLUMBIA					
Washington (Post)	35	919.15	35	925.15	10-01-95
	35	949.15	35	955.15	09-29-96
GEORGIA					
Atlanta (Constitution, Journal)	37½	713.00	37½	718.00	09-25-95
	37½	739.00	37½	744.00	09-23-96
	37½	765.00	37½	770.00	09-22-97
	37½	570.40	37½	574.40	09-25-95
	37½	591.20	37½	595.20	09-23-96
	37½	612.00	37½	616.00	09-22-97
HAWAII					
Hawaii Newspaper Agency (Advertiser, Star-Bulletin)	35	933.50	35	943.50	06-12-95
Hilo (Hawaii Tribune-Herald)	35	711.15	35	720.30	05-14-95
	35	732.48	35	741.91	05-19-96
IDAHO					
Boise (Idaho Statesman)	35	497.53	35	517.44	05-15-95
ILLINOIS					
B.F. Shaw Printing (Crystal Lake Northwest Herald, Dixon Telegraph, Morris Herald, Geneva Kane County Chronicle, Creston (IA) News Advertiser, Newton (IA) Daily News)	40	429.00	37½	459.60	01-13-98
Belleville (News-Democrat)	40	623.20	—	—	01-01-95

COMPOSING ROOM

	Day Work Hours	Wkly Rate	Night Work Hours	Wkly Rate	Effective Date
Champaign (News-Gazette)	37½	695.63	37½	716.25	05-15-95
	37½	714.38	37½	725.00	05-15-96
	37½	733.13	37½	753.75	05-15-97
Chicago (Sun-Times)	35	638.05	35	665.12	01-01-95
	35	654.05	35	681.76	01-01-96
	35	670.05	35	698.40	01-01-97
	35	687.05	35	716.08	01-01-98
	35	707.05	35	735.33	01-01-99
	35	727.05	35	756.13	01-01-00
	35	747.05	35	776.93	01-01-01
	35	767.05	35	797.13	01-01-02
	35	787.05	35	818.53	01-01-03
	35	807.05	35	839.33	01-01-04
Chicago (Tribune)	35	674.65	35	700.52	08-02-95
	35	674.65	35	700.52	08-02-96
Danville (Commercial-News)	37½	454.38	37½	463.88	05-29-95
	37½	465.74	37½	475.24	05-29-96
Edwardsville (Intelligencer)	35	351.49	32½	351.49	06-06-95
	35	351.49	32½	351.49	06-06-96
	35	363.65	32½	363.65	06-06-97
	35	377.65	32½	377.65	06-06-98
Jacksonville (Journal Courier)	37½	480.00	36¼	505.00	01-01-95
Joliet (Herald-News)	37	724.55	37	744.55	01-01-95
	37	745.55	37	765.55	01-01-96
Kankakee (Journal)	38¾	567.69	38¾	577.38	01-02-95
	38¾	582.02	38¾	591.71	01-02-96
	38¾	596.75	38¾	606.44	01-02-97
	38¾	611.48	38¾	621.63	01-02-98
Peoria (Journal Star)	37½	695.54	37½	737.27	06-11-95
	37½	716.40	37½	759.39	06-11-96
	37½	737.89	37½	782.17	06-11-97
Springfield (State Journal-Register)	37½	615.94	37½	630.94	02-13-95
INDIANA					
Gary (Post-Tribune)	40	618.20	40	618.20	11-26-95
	40	618.20	40	618.20	11-26-96
	40	618.20	40	618.20	11-26-97
Indianapolis (Star, News)	36¼	798.83	36¼	805.73	10-01-95
	36¼	813.62	36¼	820.52	10-01-96
	36¼	828.41	36¼	835.32	10-01-97
	36¼	843.21	36¼	850.11	10-01-98
	36¼	858.00	36¼	864.90	10-01-99
	36¼	872.79	36¼	879.70	10-01-00
	36¼	887.59	36¼	894.49	10-01-01
	36¼	902.37	36¼	909.28	10-01-02
	36¼	917.17	36¼	924.08	10-01-03
South Bend (Tribune)	37½	560.63	37½	570.01	07-01-95
	37½	571.88	37½	581.26	07-01-96
	37½	583.13	37½	592.51	07-01-97
	37½	594.75	37½	604.13	07-01-98
	37½	606.75	37½	616.13	07-01-99
	37½	618.75	37½	628.13	07-01-00
	37½	633.00	37½	642.38	07-01-01
Vincennes (Sun-Commercial)	37½	591.21	37½	620.77	01-01-95
	37½	611.90	37½	642.50	01-01-96
	37½	633.32	37½	664.99	01-01-97
	37½	655.49	37½	688.26	01-01-98
	37½	681.71	37½	715.80	01-01-99
(hired after 1-1-88)	37½	247.05	37½	259.40	01-01-95
	37½	255.70	37½	268.49	01-01-96
	37½	264.65	37½	277.88	01-01-97
	37½	273.91	37½	287.61	01-01-98
	37½	284.87	37½	299.11	01-01-99
IOWA					
Council Bluffs (Nonpareil)	38¾	457.64	38¾	465.39	05-01-95
	38¾	468.10	38¾	475.85	05-01-96
	38¾	478.56	38¾	486.31	05-01-97
	38¾	489.41	38¾	497.16	05-01-98
	38¾	500.26	38¾	508.01	05-01-99
	38¾	511.50	38¾	519.25	05-01-00
Des Moines (Register)	37½	567.38	37½	584.62	11-27-95
	37½	576.00	37½	593.25	11-27-96
	37½	584.62	37½	602.25	11-27-97
KANSAS					
Hutchinson (News)	37½	498.00	37½	498.00	03-02-95
Wichita (Eagle)	37½	668.33	37½	675.34	11-05-95
KENTUCKY					
Ashland (Daily Independent)	37½	580.00	37½	617.50	09-01-95
	37½	594.00	37½	631.50	09-01-96

Copyright ©1996 by the Editor & Publisher Co.

VI-65 Mechanical forces pay scales

COMPOSING ROOM

	DAY WORK Hours	Wkly Rate	NIGHT WORK Hours	Wkly Rate	Effective Date
MAINE					
Augusta (Kennebec Journal)	37½	529.64	37½	541.64	01-29-95
Bangor (News)	36¼	615.00	35	621.50	01-01-95
Waterville (Central Maine Morning Sentinel)	37½	654.00	—	—	06-01-96
	37½	670.00	—	—	06-01-99
	37½	686.00	—	—	06-01-02
MARYLAND					
Baltimore (Record)	37½	668.26	37½	715.04	11-01-95
Baltimore (Sun)	36¼	772.72	36¼	777.72	01-01-95
MASSACHUSETTS					
Boston (Globe)	37½	904.82	37½	911.69	01-01-95
Boston (Wall Street Journal)	36¼	838.05	36¼	843.05	06-01-95
	36¼	863.05	36¼	868.05	06-01-96
Fall River (Herald News)	37½	703.33	37½	760.37	09-21-95
Fitchburg (Sentinel & Enterprise)	37½	495.75	37½	505.88	05-01-95
Hyannis (Cape Cod Times)	37½	592.51	37½	598.88	12-01-95
Lawrence (Eagle-Tribune)	37½	708.00	37½	723.00	11-05-95
	37½	725.00	37½	740.00	11-03-96
Lowell (Sun)	37½	700.70	37½	738.20	01-02-95
	37½	714.71	37½	757.21	01-01-96
MICHIGAN					
Benton Harbor/St. Joseph (Herald-Palladium)	37½	485.63	37½	495.63	06-01-95
	37½	495.38	37½	505.38	06-01-96
	37½	505.13	37½	515.13	06-01-97
Escanaba (Press)	37½	485.62	37½	485.62	04-01-95
	37½	497.25	37½	497.25	04-01-96
	37½	508.87	37½	508.87	04-01-97
	37½	520.87	37½	520.87	04-01-98
	37½	522.25	37½	522.25	04-01-99
Lansing (State Journal)	37½	664.16	37½	697.39	10-03-95
	37½	684.07	37½	718.28	10-03-96
Port Huron (Times Herald)	37½	577.16	37½	593.66	11-01-95
	37½	594.49	37½	610.99	11-01-96
Traverse City (Record-Eagle)	37½	572.50	37½	597.50	05-01-95
	37½	586.50	37½	611.50	05-01-96
MINNESOTA					
Austin (Herald)	40	442.00	40	445.75	09-16-95
	40	450.00	40	453.75	09-16-96
	40	460.75	40	463.75	09-16-97
Duluth (News-Tribune)	35	633.61	35	643.50	02-01-95
Mankato (Free Press)	37½	532.50	37½	537.50	10-30-95
Minneapolis (Star Tribune)	35	801.26	35	811.76	01-01-95
	35	822.26	35	832.76	01-01-96
	35	843.26	35	853.76	01-01-97
	35	864.26	35	874.76	01-01-98
	35	885.26	35	895.76	01-01-99
St. Paul (Pioneer Press)	35	778.75	35	792.75	12-01-95
	35	796.25	35	810.25	12-01-96
Virginia (Mesabi Daily News)	35	423.50	—	—	09-29-95
	35	434.00	—	—	09-29-96
MISSOURI					
Kansas City (Star)	40	584.85	40	591.85	10-10-95
	40	596.75	40	603.75	10-10-96
St. Louis (Post-Dispatch)	36¼	821.47	35	833.64	03-01-95
	36¼	845.47	35	857.64	03-01-96
	36¼	869.47	35	881.64	03-01-97
	36¼	886.47	35	898.64	03-01-98
	36¼	903.47	35	915.64	03-01-99
Sedalia (Democrat)	37½	410.00	37½	416.23	03-20-95
	37½	421.00	37½	427.23	03-25-96
MONTANA					
Billings (Times)	40	572.00	40	582.00	07-01-95
Havre (News)	37½	418.88	37½	430.13	02-12-97
NEW HAMPSHIRE					
Nashua (Telegraph)	40	601.32	40	606.80	01-01-95
	40	619.35	40	625.00	01-01-96
NEW JERSEY					
Cherry Hill (Courier-Post)	37½	867.00	37½	878.00	07-23-95
	37½	907.00	37½	918.00	07-23-96

COMPOSING ROOM

	DAY WORK Hours	Wkly Rate	NIGHT WORK Hours	Wkly Rate	Effective Date
Morristown (Record)	35	679.99	35	693.72	01-01-95
	35	700.39	35	714.53	01-01-96
	35	721.40	35	735.97	01-01-97
	35	743.04	35	758.05	01-01-98
	35	765.33	35	780.79	01-01-99
	35	788.29	35	804.21	01-01-00
	35	811.94	35	828.34	01-01-01
Newark (Star-Ledger)	36¼	974.47	36¼	1023.19	07-01-95
	36¼	998.83	36¼	1048.77	07-01-96
	36¼	1049.38	36¼	1101.24	07-01-97
	36¼	1075.61	36¼	1183.17	07-01-98
	36¼	1102.50	36¼	1157.63	07-01-99
	36¼	1130.06	36¼	1186.56	07-01-00
	36¼	1158.31	36¼	1216.23	07-01-01
	36¼	1187.27	36¼	1246.63	07-01-02
	36¼	1248.12	36¼	1310.53	07-01-03
	36¼	1279.32	36¼	1343.29	07-01-04
	36¼	1344.89	36¼	1412.13	07-01-05
	36¼	1378.51	36¼	1447.44	07-01-06
	36¼	1412.97	36¼	1483.62	07-01-07
Passaic (North Jersey Herald-News)	36¼	631.98	36¼	640.52	08-01-95
	36¼	644.62	36¼	653.33	08-01-96
	36¼	660.74	36¼	669.66	08-01-97
(hired after 1-1-88)	36¼	557.44	36¼	565.24	08-01-95
	36¼	568.58	36¼	576.54	08-01-96
	36¼	582.79	36¼	590.95	08-01-97
Trenton (Trentonian)	37½	681.63	37½	687.63	11-01-95
	37½	698.67	37½	704.67	11-01-96
NEW YORK					
Albany (Times Union)	38¾	657.30	38¾	665.90	05-01-95
	38¾	674.30	38¾	682.90	05-01-96
Long Island (Newsday)	35	996.00	35	1011.94	03-01-95
	35	954.00	35	968.94	05-01-95
Plattsburgh (Press Republican)	37½	441.25	37½	449.75	05-01-95
	37½	441.25	37½	449.75	05-01-96
Schenectady (Gazette)	36¼	636.00	36¼	645.00	11-01-95
Troy (Record)	36¼	560.36	36¼	568.60	05-01-95
OHIO					
Canton (Repository)	37½	553.70	37½	573.08	11-15-95
	37½	567.54	37½	587.40	11-15-96
	37½	581.73	37½	602.09	11-15-97
Hamilton (Journal-News)	35	590.14	35	610.14	07-25-95
Massillon (Independent)	37½	506.25	35	521.25	01-01-95
Newark (Advocate)	37½	462.75	37½	468.38	07-01-95
	37½	475.88	37½	481.51	07-01-96
Toledo (Blade)	36½	765.96	36½	784.90	03-22-95
	36½	775.96	36½	794.90	09-22-95
	36½	785.96	36½	804.90	03-22-96
	36½	795.96	36½	814.90	09-22-96
	36½	805.96	36½	825.90	03-22-97
	36½	815.96	36½	834.90	08-22-97
Youngstown (Vindicator)	37½	535.98	36¼	540.98	05-16-95
	37½	541.85	36¼	546.85	11-16-95
	37½	547.72	36¼	552.72	05-16-96
	37½	553.59	36¼	558.59	11-16-96
	37½	557.78	36¼	562.78	05-16-97
OKLAHOMA					
Enid (News and Eagle)	40	492.00	40	504.64	01-13-95
OREGON					
Eugene (Register-Guard)	35	616.00	35	632.25	02-15-00
PENNSYLVANIA					
Bradford (Era)	37½	465.19	37½	477.19	10-01-95
Chester (Delaware County Daily Times)	37½	695.14	37½	736.14	06-15-95
	37½	711.84	37½	752.84	06-15-96
Clearfield (Progress)	40	460.00	40	462.40	07-01-95
DuBois (Courier-Express)	37½	537.38	37½	567.38	04-01-95
	37½	556.13	37½	586.13	04-01-96
Greensburg (Tribune-Review)	37½	510.00	37½	519.38	04-17-95
	37½	525.00	37½	534.38	04-17-96
Hazleton (Standard-Speaker)	37½	533.21	37½	543.21	01-01-95
Johnstown (Tribune-Democrat)	37½	561.38	37½	580.88	05-01-95
	37½	578.25	37½	598.50	05-01-96
	37½	595.50	37½	616.50	05-01-97
Kittanning (Leader-Times)	37½	408.75	37½	412.50	03-01-95
	37½	416.63	37½	420.38	03-01-96
	37½	424.50	37½	428.25	03-01-97
Lancaster (Intelligencer Journal, New Era)	37½	583.88	37½	600.76	03-01-95
Latrobe (Bulletin)	35	290.50	—	—	01-01-95
New Castle (News)	37½	517.50	37½	543.38	01-01-95
Norristown (Times Herald)	37½	679.13	—	—	10-01-95

Copyright ©1996 by the Editor & Publisher Co.

Mechanical forces pay scales

COMPOSING ROOM

	DAY WORK Hours	Wkly Rate	NIGHT WORK Hours	Wkly Rate	Effective Date
Philadelphia (Inquirer, News)	37½	841.50	37½	849.50	09-01-95
	37½	856.50	37½	864.50	09-01-96
	37½	886.50	37½	894.50	09-01-97
	37½	936.50	37½	944.50	09-01-98
Pottstown (Mercury)	35	632.85	35	641.13	10-13-95
	35	652.39	35	660.92	10-13-96
Reading (Eagle, Times)	37½	709.00	37½	711.00	01-01-95
	37½	732.04	37½	734.04	01-01-96
	37½	755.83	37½	757.83	01-01-97
	37½	780.39	37½	782.39	01-01-98
	37½	805.75	37½	807.75	01-01-99
	37½	831.94	37½	833.94	01-01-00
	37½	858.98	37½	860.96	01-01-01
	37½	914.81	37½	916.81	01-01-02
	37½	944.54	37½	946.54	01-01-03
	37½	976.24	37½	978.24	01-01-04
	37½	1007.97	37½	1009.97	01-01-05
	37½	1040.73	37½	1042.73	01-01-06
	37½	1074.55	37½	1076.55	01-01-07
	37½	1109.47	37½	1111.47	01-01-08
Sharon (Herald)	37½	519.00	37½	526.50	01-01-95
State College (Centre Daily Times)	37½	494.28	37½	510.03	11-02-95
Wilkes-Barre (Citizens' Voice)	35	450.00	35	460.00	07-02-95
York (Dispatch)	37½	572.99	37½	582.99	01-23-95
	37½	595.91	37½	605.91	01-23-96
	37½	616.77	37½	626.77	01-23-97
	37½	638.36	37½	648.36	01-23-98
	37½	660.70	37½	670.70	01-23-99
	37½	683.82	37½	693.82	01-23-00
TENNESSEE					
Kingsport (Times-News)	37½	513.75	37½	519.38	01-02-95
	37½	534.38	37½	540.00	01-02-96
	37½	555.00	37½	560.63	01-02-97
Memphis (Commercial Appeal)	40	577.00	40	582.00	03-12-95
	40	592.00	40	597.00	03-10-96
	40	607.00	40	612.00	03-09-97
TEXAS					
Dallas (Wall Street Journal)	35	779.50	35	804.50	01-01-95
	35	825.00	35	828.00	01-01-96
UTAH					
Salt Lake City (Tribune, Deseret News)	36¼	525.35	36¼	531.57	09-01-95
	36¼	525.35	36¼	531.57	09-01-96
	36¼	525.35	36¼	531.57	09-01-97
	36¼	525.35	36¼	531.57	09-01-98
	36¼	525.35	36¼	531.57	09-01-99
VIRGINIA					
Petersburg (Progress-Index)	37½	442.70	37½	447.70	01-01-95
	37½	453.70	37½	458.70	01-01-96
WASHINGTON					
Bremerton (Sun)	35	585.50	35	596.00	01-01-95
	35	600.15	35	610.90	01-01-96
	35	615.15	35	626.15	01-01-97
	35	630.55	35	641.80	01-01-98
Everett (Herald)	35	593.60	35	601.65	11-01-95
	35	607.60	35	616.00	11-01-96
	35	623.35	35	631.75	11-01-97
Yakima (Herald-Republic)	35	582.45	35	605.75	10-14-95
WEST VIRGINIA					
Wheeling (Intelligencer, News-Register)	37½	334.00	37½	340.00	03-07-95
WISCONSIN					
Milwaukee (Journal-Sentinel)	36¼	678.49	36¼	688.49	03-03-96
Sheboygan (Press)	36¼	696.49	36¼	706.49	03-02-37
	37½	597.00	37½	615.75	10-01-95
Superior (Telegram)	35	435.75	35	446.95	01-01-95

COMPOSING ROOM — CANADA

	DAY WORK Hours	Wkly Rate	NIGHT WORK Hours	Wkly Rate	Effective Date
ALBERTA					
Lethbridge (Herald)	37½	742.13	37½	789.00	08-01-95
	37½	757.13	37½	804.00	08-01-96
Red Deer (Advocate)	37½	741.38	35	815.52	01-01-95
MANITOBA					
Brandon (Sun)	37½	783.38	35	779.45	07-01-94
NEW BRUNSWICK					
Fredericton (Gleanor)	36¼	724.19	36¼	832.82	11-01-95
	36¼	731.43	36¼	841.15	11-01-96
	36¼	746.06	36¼	857.97	11-01-97

COMPOSING ROOM

	DAY WORK Hours	Wkly Rate	NIGHT WORK Hours	Wkly Rate	Effective Date
NOVA SCOTIA					
Halifax (Chronicle-Herald, Mail-Star)	37½	988.00	35	1006.00	01-01-95
ONTARIO					
Stratford (Beacon Herald)	37½	652.88	35	718.17	01-01-95
	37½	666.00	35	732.60	01-01-96
SASKATCHEWAN					
Prince Albert (Herald)	38¾	578.93	—	—	12-01-95
	38¾	590.55	—	—	12-01-96
	38¾	605.28	—	—	12-01-97

MAILROOM

	DAY WORK Hours	Wkly Rate	NIGHT WORK Hours	Wkly Rate	Effective Date
CALIFORNIA					
Bakersfield (Californian)	35	583.69	35	593.69	07-22-95
DISTRICT OF COLUMBIA					
Washington (Post)	35	842.75	35	850.75	06-11-95
	35	875.75	35	883.75	06-16-96
GEORGIA					
Atlanta (Journal, Constitution)	37½	640.00	37½	645.00	06-26-95
ILLINOIS					
Champaign (News-Gazette)	40	577.20	40	599.20	03-01-95
	40	593.20	40	615.20	03-01-96
	40	609.20	40	631.20	03-01-97
Chicago (Sun-Times)	36¼	611.50	—	—	01-01-95
	36¼	611.50	—	—	09-01-95
Chicago (Wall Street Journal)	36¼	765.50	36¼	771.50	07-15-95
Springfield (State Journal-Register)	37½	598.68	37½	613.68	03-20-95
	37½	616.64	37½	631.64	03-18-96
	37½	635.14	37½	650.14	03-17-97
INDIANA					
Muncie (Star)	37½	653.50	37½	663.50	05-01-95
MAINE					
Bangor (News)	36¼	597.50	36¼	603.50	04-15-94
MASSACHUSETTS					
Boston (Wall Street Journal)	36¼	825.20	36¼	830.20	06-01-95
	36¼	850.20	36¼	855.20	06-01-96
New Bedford (Standard Times)	37½	481.80	37½	487.80	06-14-95
	37½	493.80	37½	499.80	12-01-95
	37½	505.80	37½	511.80	12-01-96
MICHIGAN					
Lansing (State Journal)	37½	664.16	37½	697.39	10-03-95
	37½	684.07	37½	718.28	10-03-96
MISSOURI					
St. Louis (Post-Dispatch)	36¼	762.76	33¾	767.00	01-15-95
	36¼	785.64	33¾	790.01	01-15-96
	36¼	809.21	33¾	813.71	01-15-97
	36¼	825.39	33¾	829.98	01-15-98
NEW YORK					
Buffalo (News)	35	727.52	35	732.52	11-11-95
New York (Post)	39½	716.35	35	729.30	06-07-95
	39½	730.68	35	743.89	09-07-96
New York (Times)	39½	1018.75	36½	1018.75	03-31-95
PENNSYLVANIA					
Norristown (Times Herald)	37½	591.51	—	—	10-01-95
Pittsburgh (Post-Gazette)	35	721.14	35	682.14	01-01-95
	35	735.14	35	740.14	07-01-95
	35	749.14	35	754.14	01-01-96
TEXAS					
Waco (Tribune-Herald)	37½	461.63	37½	467.63	10-01-95
	37½	470.63	37½	477.00	10-01-96

MAILROOM — CANADA

	DAY WORK Hours	Wkly Rate	NIGHT WORK Hours	Wkly Rate	Effective Date
BRITISH COLUMBIA					
Vancouver (Province, Sun)	37½	1108.70	36¼	1219.57	12-01-95
	37½	1130.87	36¼	1243.96	12-01-96
	37½	1153.49	36¼	1268.84	12-01-97

Copyright ©1996 by the Editor & Publisher Co.

Reporter and Photographer
Top Minimums as of December 1, 1995
Compiled by the Newspaper Guild (AFL-CIO, CLC)

Newspaper Name	Minimum	After
New York Times	$1283.33	2 yrs
Montreal Gazette	$1129.00	5 yrs
Boston Globe	$1087.10	5 yrs
Victoria (British Columbia) Times-Colonist	$1084.46	5 yrs
Philadelphia Inquirer, Daily News	$1060.00	5 yrs
Ottawa (Ontario) Citizen	$1023.64	5 yrs
Chicago Sun-Times	$1015.19	5 yrs
St. Louis Post-Dispatch	$978.76	5 yrs
Honolulu Advertiser, Star-Bulletin	$971.90	5 yrs
Minneapolis Star Tribune	$961.25	5 yrs
Baltimore Sun	$958.00	5 yrs
Washington Post	$956.60	4 yrs
Pittsburgh Post-Gazette	$954.00	6 yrs
St. Paul Pioneer Press	$950.56	5 yrs
Cleveland Plain Dealer	$931.51	4 yrs
San Jose Mercury-News	$917.71	6 yrs
Toledo (Ohio) Blade	$915.92	4 yrs
Buffalo News	$902.67	5 yrs
San Francisco Chronicle, Examiner	$900.08	6 yrs
Denver Post	$889.00	5 yrs
Denver Rocky Mountain News	$889.00	5 yrs
gSan Mateo (Calif.) Times	$887.44	3 yrs
Providence Journal-Bulletin	$877.46	4 yrs
Santa Rosa (Calif.) Press Democrat	$874.37	6 yrs
Maui (Hawaii) News	$864.99	5 yrs
San Diego Union-Tribune	$832.76	6 yrs
Eugene (Ore.) Register Guard	$827.80	5 yrs
Akron (Ohio) Beacon Journal	$820.00	4 yrs
Long Beach (Calif.) Press-Telegram	$817.48	5 yrs
Boston Herald	$815.09	4 yrs
Indianapolis Star	$801.25	6 yrs
Seattle Times	$796.90	5 yrs
Seattle Post-Intelligencer	$796.88	4 yrs
Kenosha (Wis.) News	$794.00	5½ yrs
Memphis (Tenn.) Commercial Appeal	$792.69	5 yrs
Delaware County (Pa.) Times	$791.74	5 yrs
Manchester (N.H.) Union Leader	a$791.68	3 yrs
Cincinnati Post, Kentucky Post	$775.00	5 yrs
Erie (Pa.) News, Times	$775.00	5 yrs
Allentown (Pa.) Call	b$771.35	4 yrs
Monterey (Calif.) Herald	$769.00	6 yrs
Detroit News	$750.54	4 yrs
Portland (Maine) Press Herald	$750.25	4 yrs
Detroit Free Press	$749.84	4 yrs
Sudbury (Ontario) Star	$741.94	6 yrs
Hilo (Hawaii) Tribune-Herald	$732.28	5 yrs
North Bay (Ontario) Nugget	$727.65	5 yrs
Pottstown (Pa.) Mercury	$720.10	5 yrs
Joliet (Ill.) Herald-News	$720.00	4 yrs
Fall River (Mass.) Herald-News	$719.12	4 yrs
Scranton (Pa.) Times-Tribune	$699.10	3 yrs
Sheboygan (Wis.) Press	$695.67	5 yrs
New York El Diario-La Prensa	$694.37	4 yrs
Norristown (Pa.) Times Herald	$683.44	5 yrs
Peoria (Ill.) Journal Star	$680.00	5 yrs
Albany (N.Y.) Times-Union	$678.22	4 yrs
Duluth (Minn.) News-Tribune	$675.30	5 yrs
Lowell (Mass.) Sun	$664.29	4 yrs
Dayton (Ohio) Daily News	$660.50	5 yrs
Mt. Clemens (Mich.) Macomb Daily, Daily Tribune	$660.37	5 yrs
Los Angeles Daily News	$659.75	6 yrs
Fresno (Calif.) Bee	$654.77	6 yrs
Waukegan (Ill.) News-Sun	$653.56	5 yrs
Milwaukee Journal, Sentinel	d$651.00	e4 yrs
Jersey City (N.J.) Jersey Journal	$650.03	4 yrs
Sacramento (Calif.) Bee	$649.00	6 yrs
Lynn (Mass.) Item	$644.00	4 yrs
Youngstown (Ohio) Vindicator	$646.35	5 yrs
Canton (Ohio) Repository	$642.94	5 yrs
Gary (Ind.) Post-Tribune	$638.18	5 yrs
gHarrisburg (Pa.) Patriot, News	$631.90	4 yrs
Brockton (Mass.) Enterprise	$630.78	4 yrs
Pawtucket (R.I.) Times	$625.25	4 yrs
Kingston (N.Y.) Daily Freeman	$620.61	4 yrs
Knoxville (Tenn.) News-Sentinel	$617.50	4 yrs
Salem (Mass.) News	c$610.61	4 yrs
Sioux City (Iowa) Journal	$605.44	4 yrs
York (Pa.) Dispatch	$600.14	4 yrs
Lansing (Mich.) State Journal	$579.27	5 yrs

Newspaper Name	Minimum	After
York (Pa.) Daily Record	$578.00	4 yrs
Woonsocket (R.I.) Call	$571.27	4 yrs
Yakima (Wash.) Herald-Republic	$556.80	4 yrs
Pueblo (Colo.) Chieftain	$543.33	5 yrs
Waterville (Maine) Sentinel	$540.40	5 yrs
Bakersfield (Calif.) Californian	f$535.00	5 yrs
Hazelton (Pa.) Standard Speaker	$535.00	4 yrs
Bellevue (Wash.) Journal-American	$528.10	5 yrs
Lexington (Ky.) Herald-Leader	$525.00	4 yrs
Malden (Mass.) Daily News-Mercury	$514.25	3 yrs
Monessen (Pa.) Valley Independent	$511.00	5 yrs
Wilkes-Barre (Pa.) Citizens' Voice	$489.00	4 yrs
San Juan Star	$484.00	6 yrs
San Juan El Vocero	$470.00	5 yrs
Terre Haute (Ind.) Tribune-Star	$438.02	5 yrs
Massillon (Ohio) Independent	$426.92	4 yrs
Rochester (N.Y.) Democrat & Chronicle, Times Union	$419.00	4 yrs
New York Noticias del Mundo	$412.25	4 yrs
Utica (N.Y.) Observer-Dispatch	$387.50	5 yrs
Norwalk (Conn.) Hour	$360.00	2 yrs
Chattanooga (Tenn.) Times	$351.52	4 yrs
Battle Creek (Mich.) Enquirer	$346.00	5 yrs

a - $826.03 for Senior reporter

b - Plus 2% after 10 years and at five year intervals to 10% after 30 years, up to $20.00/wk to $791.35

c - Photographers scale, $639.47, for work week three and a half hours longer than reporter. Editorial district reporter scale, $702.00, for work week three and a half hours longer than reporter.

d - $714.00 for senior journalist.

e - After three years for fully qualified practioner.

f - $606.40 if hired before 1/1/90 and at top minimum.

g - Contracts do not cover photographers.

Deferred Increases

Bellevue (Wash.) Journal-American — (12/22/96) $4.00, (12/21/97) $4.00
Boston Herald — (2/14/96) $28.53, (5/14/97) $33.76, (8/14/98) $39.50
Buffalo News — (8/1/96) $19.53
Canton (Ohio) Repository — (9/6/96) $16.07, (9/6/97) $16.48, (9/6/98) $18.23
Chicago Sun-Times — (10/1/96) $20.69
Cincinnati Post, Kentucky Post — (1/1/96) $12.50
Denver Post — (1/1/96) $34.22, (1/1/97) $35.59
Denver Rocky Mountain News — (12/29/96) $36.00
Duluth (Minn.) News-Tribune — (1/1/98) $20.25
Erie (Pa.) News, Times — (3/2/96) $22.00
Hilo (Hawaii) Tribune-Herald — (5/1/96) $21.97
Kingston (N.Y.) Daily Freeman — (6/11/96) $15.52, (10/26/97) $15.90, (611/98) $13.04
Manchester (N.H.) Union Leader — (1/1/96) $23.75, (1/1/97) $24.46, (1/1/98) $29.40
Minneapolis Star Tribune — (8/1/96) $28.75, (8/1/97) $29.75
North Bay (Ontario) Nugget — $10.91, $18.46
Norwalk (Conn.) Hour — (1/1/96) $10.80
Ottawa (Ontario) Citizen — (7/1/96) $20.47
Peoria (Ill.) Journal Star — (8/31/96) $20.00, (8/31/97) $21.00
Philadelphia Inquirer, Daily News — (9/1/96) $47.70
Pittsburgh Post-Gazette — (1/1/96) $15.00, (7/1/96) $15.00, (1/1/97) $15.00, (7/1/97) $15.00
Providence Journal-Bulletin — (1/1/96) $17.55
St. Louis Post-Dispatch — (1/1/96) $24.14, (1/1/97) $25.00, (1/1/98) $26.00
St. Paul Pioneer Press — (2/3/97) $28.52, (1/5/98) $39.16
San Francisco Chronicle, Examiner — (1/1/96) $12.65, (7/1/96) $6.32, (12/30/96) $12.65, (6/30/97) $12.65, (12/29/97) $17.70, (6/29/98) $18.97
San Jose Mercury News — (6/30/96) $7.72, (12/29/96) $14.07, (6/29/97) $7.26, (1/4/98) $17.79, (6/28/98) $19.05
Sheboygan (Wis.) Press — (2/1/96) $16.98
Toledo (Ohio) Blade — (3/22/96) $11.81, (9/22/96) $11.78, (3/22/97) $11.83, (9/22/97) $11.97
Washington Post — (11/11/96) $11.40, (11/11/97) $11.40
Woonsocket (R.I.) Call— (10/20/96) $11.43, (10/20/97) $11.65
Yakima (Wash.) Herald-Republic — (9/23/96) $18.00
York (Pa.) Dispatch — (10/17/96) $18.00
Youngstown (Ohio) Vindicator — (11/16/96) $7.00, (6/16/97) $5.00

Copyright ©1996 by the Editor & Publisher Co.

Reporter and Photographer
Starting Minimums as of December 1, 1995
Compiled by the Newspaper Guild (AFL-CIO, CLC)

Newspaper Name	Minimum
New York Times	$1254.00
Washington Post	$775.40
Honolulu Advertiser, Star-Bulletin	$742.04
Montreal Gazette	$713.00
Ottawa (Ontario) Citizen	$704.80
Chicago Sun-Times	$687.53
Victoria (British Columbia) Times-Colonist	$684.13
Pittsburgh Post-Gazette	$668.00
Boston Herald	$659.77
Philadelphia Inquirer, Daily News	$655.22
Maui (Hawaii) News	$649.69
Boston Globe	$648.33
Hilo (Hawaii) Tribune-Herald	$643.97
St. Louis Post-Dispatch	$612.84
Toledo Blade	$593.59
Manchester (N.H.) Union Leader	$584.51
San Mateo (Calif.) Times	$572.81
Cleveland Plain Dealer	$566.79
San Francisco Chronicle, Examiner	$566.42
San Jose Mercury-News	$557.98
Seattle Post-Intelligencer	$548.22
Seattle Times	$538.45
Detroit News	$529.84
Detroit Free Press	$529.14
Eugene (Ore.) Register Guard	$527.89
New York El Diario-La Prensa	$527.15
Denver Rocky Mountain News	$522.00
Indianapolis Star	$520.75
Portland (Maine) Press Herald	$518.03
Mineapolis Star Tribune	$510.75
Los Angeles Daily News	$506.51
St. Paul Pioneer Press	$503.02
Santa Rosa (Calif.) Press Democrat	$500.94
Delaware County (Pa.) Times	$497.44
Providence Journal-Bulletin	$492.81
Buffalo News	$484.05
Milwaukee Journal, Sentinel	$482.00
Memphis (Tenn.) Commercial Appeal	$480.93
Denver Post	$469.88
Mt. Clemens (Mich.) Macomb Daily, Daily Tribune	$467.52
Pottstown (Pa.) Mercury	$461.02
Monterey (Calif.) Herald	$455.00
Fall River (Mass.) Herald-News	$453.71
Joliet (Ill.) Herald-News	$446.40
York (Pa.) Daily Record	$445.50
Jersey City (N.J.) Jersey Journal	$445.17
Norristown (Pa.) Times Herald	$443.89
Allentown (Pa.) Call	$442.58
North Bay (Ontario) Nugget	$441.00
Sheboygan (Wis.) Press	$438.00
Woonsocket (R.I.) Call	$434.93
San Diego Union-Tribune	$433.95
Long Beach (Calif.) Press-Telegram	$432.81
Knoxville (Tenn.) News-Sentinel	$432.00
Erie (Pa.) News, Times	$430.00
York (Pa.) Dispatch	$423.74
Lowell (Mass.) Sun	$420.47
Bakersfield (Calif.) Californian	$417.77
Canton (Ohio) Repository	$417.28
Lynn (Mass.) Item	$414.54
Kenosha (Wis.) News	$411.96
Waukegan (Ill.) News-Sun	$410.21
Sudbury (Ontario) Star	$409.81
Sacramento (Calif.) Bee	$400.18
Akron (Ohio) Beacon Journal	$400.00
Fresno (Calif.) Bee	$398.79
Kingston (N.Y.) Daily Freeman	$398.48
San Juan El Vocero	$395.00
Malden (Mass.) Daily News-Mercury	$392.46
Peoria (Ill.) Journal Star	$390.66
Bellevue (Wash.) Journal-American	$388.00
Youngstown (Ohio) Vindicator	$387.80

Newspaper Name	Minimum
Cincinnati Post, Kentucky Post	$385.00
Albany (N.Y.) Times-Union	$384.20
Pawtucket (R.I.) Times	$381.82
Harrisburg (Pa.) Patriot, News	$379.60
Salem (Mass.) News	$374.17
Baltimore Sun	$370.00
San Juan Star	$370.00
Waterville (Maine) Sentinel	$364.00
Rochester (N.Y.) Democrat & Chronicle, Times Union	$362.00
Scranton (Pa.) Times, Tribune	$360.91
Gary (Ind.) Post-Tribune	$357.07
Wilkes-Barre (Pa.) Citizens' Voice	$352.24
Dayton (Ohio) Daily News	$351.00
Yakima (Wash.) Herald-Republic	$346.76
Norwkalk (Conn.) Hour	$340.00
Hazleton (Pa.) Standard-Speaker	$334.06
Lexington (Ky.) Herald-Leader	$330.00
Brockton (Mass.) Enterprise	$328.21
Chattanooga (Tenn.) Times	$325.00
Monessen (Pa.) Valley Independent	$319.00
Duluth (Minn.) News-Tribune	$306.38
Lansing (Mich.) State Journal	$289.95
Pueblo (Colo.) Chieftain	$272.83
Terre Haute (Ind.) Tribune-Star	$263.88
Massillon (Ohio) Independent	$262.09
Utica (N.Y.) Observer-Dispatch	$245.00
Battle Creek (Mich.) Enquirer	$184.00

Deferred Increases

Allentown (Pa.) Call — (8/1/96) $13.28, (8/1/97) $13.68
Bellevue (Wash.) Journal-American — (12/1/96) $4.00, (12/1/97) $4.00
Boston Herald — (2/14/96) $23.09, (5/14/97) $27.31, (8/14/98) $31.96
Canton (Oh.) — (9/6/97) $10.23, (9/6/98) $11.32
Chicago Sun-Times — (10/1/96) $13.49
Denver Post — (1/1/96) $18.80, (1/1/97) $19.55
Denver Rocky Mountain News — (12/29/96) $21.00
Duluth (Minn.) News-Tribune — (2/1/97) $9.19, (1/1/98) $9.46
Erie (Pa.) News, Times — (3/2/96) $12.00
Hilo (Hawaii) Tribune-Herald — (5/1/96) $19.32
Indianapolis Star — (10/27/96) $9.75, (10/26/97) $9.75, (10/25/98) $9.75, (10/24/99) $9.75
Kingston (N.Y.) — Daily Freeman — (6/11/96) $9.96, (6/11/97) $10.21, (6/11/98) $8.37
Manchester (N.H.) Union Leader — (1/1/96) $17.53, (1/1/97) $18.06, (1/1/98) $21.70
Minneapolis Star Tribune — (8/1/96) $15.50, (8/1/97) $15.75
North Bay (Ontario) Nugget — $6.62, $11.19
Ottawa (Ontario) Citizen — (7/1/96) $14.10
Peoria (Ill.) Journal Star (8/31/96) $11.72, (8/31/97) $12.07
Philadelphia Inquirer, Daily News — (9/1/96) $29.48
Pittsburgh Post-Gazette — (1/1/96) $14.00, (7/1/96) $15.00, (1/1/97) $15.00, (7/1/97) $15.00
Providence Journal Bulletin — (1/1/96) $10.13
St. Louis Post Dispatch — (1/18/96) $15.16, (1/1/97) $15.00, (1/1/98) $16.00
St. Paul Pioneer Press — (2/3/97) $15.09, (1/5/98) $20.72
San Francisco Chronicle, Examiner — (1/1/96) $8.93, (7/1/96) $4.53, (12/30/96) $9.14, (6/30/97) $9.28, (10/29/97) $13.20, (6/29/98) $14.45
San Jose (Calif.) Mercury News — (6/30/96) $5.17, (12/29/96) $9.17
Sheboygan (Wis.) Press — (2/1/96) $10.44
Toledo (Oh.) Blade — (7/22/96) $7.65, (9/22/96) $7.63, (3/22/96) $7.67, (9/22/97) $7.64
Washington D.C. Post — (11/11/96) $9.30, (11/10/97) $9.30
Woonsocket Call — (10/20/96) $8.70, (10/20/97) $8.87
Yakima (Wash.) Herald-Republic — (9/23/95) $10.00, (9/23/96) $10.00
York (Pa.) Dispatch — (10/7/96) $12.69
Youngstown (Ohio) Vindicator — (5/16/96) $4.20, (11/16/97) $4.20, (5/16/97) $3.00

Copyright ©1996 by the Editor & Publisher Co.

SECTION VII

Other Organizations and Industry Services

Advertising/Circulation newspaper promotion services	1
Association of American Correspondents in London	1-2
Associations and clubs – national and international	3-6
Associations and clubs – city, state and regional	6-11
Clip art services	11
Clipping bureaus	12
Electronic clipping bureaus	12
Foreign newspaper representatives	12-13
Foreign press and radio-TV correspondents in the United States	
New York based correspondents	13-21
Washington, DC based correspondents	21-28
California based correspondents	28-31
Chicago based correspondents	31
Foreign Press Association membership directory	32-34
National newspaper representatives	34-40
Newspaper Association of America membership roster	40-44
Newspaper brokers and appraisers	45
Organization of News Ombudsmen	46
Schools and departments of journalism	47-64
State newspaper representatives	65
Trade unions in the newspaper field	65
United Nations Correspondents Association	66
Index to 1996 International Year Book	67-68
Index to 1996 International Year Book Advertisers	68

ADVERTISING/CIRCULATION NEWSPAPER PROMOTION SERVICES

CIRCULATION

Church Rickards, Whitlock & Co. Inc. — 10001 Roosevelt Rd., Westchester, IL 60154; tel (800) 323-0227; fax (708) 345-1166
President — E H Powell
Vice Pres./Gen. Mgr. — Fred Hohnke
Vice Pres. — Dan Marcquenski
Sales Mgr. — Jack Estlow

Circulation Specialists Inc. — 4840 Fox Rd., House Springs, MO 63051; tel (314) 942-2285; fax (314) 942-3769
President — Frank J Helderle

Communications Services Co. — PO Drawer 2956, Naples, FL 33939; tel (813) 649-0013
President — John A Mehaffey

Creative Marketing Associates Inc. — 3100 Broadway, Ste. 227, Kansas City, MO 64111; tel (816) 474-1400
President — Maynard Small

McCarthy, Francis X & Gladys T — 2850 Brairwood Dr., San Jose, CA 95125; tel (408) 448-4274
Pres./Publisher — Francis X McCarthy

New Haven Register — 40 Sargent Dr., New Haven, CT 06511; tel (203) 789-5200/(203) 789-5440
Research Manager — Tina Goodwin

Normandy — 24 Mendota Rd., Toronto, ON M8Y 1E8; tel (416) 252-7177
President — J G Brown

Pro Starts — 1691 Georgetown Rd., Ste. I, Hudson, OH 44236; tel (216) 650-5678
President — Tom Zgonc

Scrambl-Gram Inc. — 1772 State Rd., Cuyahoga Falls, OH 44223; tel (216) 923-2397
President — Chic Elum

CONTESTS

Coupon Bingo & Coupon Ringo Creative Mktg. Associates Inc. — 3100 Broadway, Ste. 227, Kansas City, MO 64111; tel (816) 474-1400
President — Maynard Small

Eastman Kodak Co. — 343 State St., Dept. 841, Rochester, NY 14650; tel (716) 724-4000
Coordinator — Charlotte Fischer

Marden-Kane Inc. — 36 Maple Pl., Manhasset, NY 11030; tel (516) 365-3999; fax (516) 365-5250
Exec. Vice Pres. — Paul Goldman

Name Game Co. Inc., The — 401 S.W. 54th Ave., Plantation, FL 33317; tel (305) 321-0032; fax (305) 321-8617
President — Melodye Hecht Icart

Satco Marketing Inc. — 1100 Ponce de Leon Blvd., Coral Gables, FL 33134; tel (305) 441-2526/(800) 535-5844; fax (305) 443-2176
President — Scott Thompson

COUPON INSERTS

Farago & Associates — 3240 Coolidge, Berkley, MI 48072; tel (810) 546-7070; fax (810) 546-7521
President — Peter Farago
Director of Operations — Scott Schofding
Creative Director — Bob Folster
Director of Finance — Bruce MacDonald
Computer Graphics Consultant — Sharon Jonah

News America FSI — 1211 Ave. of the Americas, 5th Fl., New York, NY 10036; tel (212) 782-8000; fax (212) 575-5847
President — Al Ovadia
Exec. Vice Pres./National Sales Manager — Dominick Porco
Senior Vice Pres./Marketing — Joseph Traynor
Vice Pres./Media Director — Celeste Lavezzari
Director of Marketing Services — Hope Bader
Atlanta, GA
1530 Dunwoody Village Pkwy., Ste. 115, Atlanta, GA 30338; tel (770) 668-9321; fax (770) 395-6835
Detroit, MI
5745 W. Maple Rd., Ste. 209, West Bloomfield, MI 48322; tel (810) 855-9180; fax (810) 855-2354
Chicago, IL
205 N. Michigan Ave., Ste. 2200, Chicago, IL 60601; tel (312) 540-4100; fax (312) 938-5456
Minneapolis, MN
100 S. 5th St., Ste. 490, Minneapolis, MN 55402; tel (612) 376-0875; fax (612) 376-0990
Los Angeles, CA
5750 Wilshire Blvd., Ste. 375, Los Angeles, CA 90036; tel (213) 549-2350; fax (213) 938-4158
Dallas, TX
2811 McKinney Ave., Ste. 303, Dallas, TX 75204-2530; tel (214) 953-3113; fax (214) 953-3090

Valassis Communications Inc. — 36111 Schoolcraft Rd., Livonia, MI 48150; tel (800) 437-0479
President — David A Brandon
Sales offices in Atlanta (404) 956-1445; Boston (508) 238-4808; Wilton, CT (800) 445-2904; Chicago (708) 330-0111; Dallas (800) 677-6282; Seal Beach, CA (310) 799-6001; Minneapolis (612) 338-3566

EDUCATIONAL SERVICES

Knowledge Unlimited — PO Box 52, Madison, WI 53701; tel (800) 356-2303
President — Judith Laitman

PROMOTIONAL MERCHANDISE

Atlas Flags Inc. — 2010 Weems Rd., Tucker, GA 30084; tel (404) 938-0003
President — Faryl Rosenthal

Hot Off The Press Promotions — 2441 Bellevue Ave., Daytona Beach, FL 32114; tel (904) 257-2500 ext. 1237/(817) 329-0648
President — Harry Campbell

Lester A Stone Inc. — PO Box 590, Holyoke, MA 01041
President — Lillian C Stone

RESEARCH

E&P Research Inc. — 7615 Brigham Dr., Dunwoody, GA 30350; tel (404) 391-0224; fax (404) 391-0319
Research Director — Francisco Vasquez

Marketing Research Associates Inc. — 4901 W. 77th St., Ste. 125, Minneapolis, MN 55435; tel (612) 835-2676
Marketing Director — Adam Scott Day

Simmons Market Research Bureau — 420 Lexington Ave., 8th Fl., New York, NY 10170; tel (212) 916-8900
President/CEO — Rebecca McPheters

SERVICES

Classified Internaitional Advertising Services — 1439 Presidio Dr., Ft. Lauderdale, FL 33327; tel (954) 349-8455
Contact — Ray J Greene

Frank W Pierson & Associates — 2718 Westshire Dr. (Hollywood, 90068), PO Box 8363, Universal City, CA 91608; tel (213) 467-7011; fax (213) 466-4762

Vendor Plus Inc. — 250 Catalonia Ave., Ste. 801, Coral Gables, FL 33134; tel (305) 441-8100; fax (305) 445-8646
President — Carol Brock
Vice Pres. — T J Eagen
Offices in Houston; Hartford, CT; San Francisco

MISCELLANEOUS

Community Club Awards Inc. — PO Box 151, Westport, CT 06881; tel (203) 226-3377; fax (203) 222-0779
President — John C Gilmore
Exec. Vice Pres. — Bess Gilmore
Exec. Vice Pres./Mktg. Sales — Tom Boone
Vice Pres./Corporate — Douglas Gilmore

Lyon Enterprises — 7 W. 41st Ave., Ste. 505, San Mateo, CA 94403; tel (800) 243-1144; fax (415) 345-8861
President — Ray Lyon

THE ASSOCIATION OF AMERICAN CORRESPONDENTS IN LONDON

OFFICERS-1995

President—Barry Hillenbrand, Time Magazine
Vice President—Lawrence Ingrassia, Wall Street Journal
Treasurer—Sandra Marshall, Associated Press
Secretary—Sandra Marshall, Associated Press

EXECUTIVE COMMITTEE

John Darnton, New York Times; Paula Dwyer, Business Week; Carla Rapoport, Fortune Magazine; Al Ortiz, CBS News; Myron Belkind, Associated Press; Daniel Pedersen, Newsweek; Robin Knight, U.S. News and World Report

EX. OFFICIAL

David Feingold, Cable News Network

ABC NEWS INTERCONTINENTAL INC.
8 Carburton St., London W1P 7DT; tel (0171) 637-9222; fax (0171) 631-5084
NED WARWICK (Director of News Coverage for Europe, Middle East and Africa), Linda Albin (Radio), Ron Allen (Correspondent), Janet Aquino (Senior Program Controller), Baruch Ben-Chorin (Producer), Jenny Dow (GME Producer), Jim Laurie, Deanna Lee (Nightline Assoc. Producer), John Boylan (Producer), Paul Cleveland (Operations Manager), Joyce Cooksey (Manager of Administration), Mark Foley (Assistant Manager), Richard Gizbert (Correspondent), Mike Lee (Correspondent), Laura Logan (WNT Producer), Sheila MacVicar (Correspondent for Day One), Parlo Marenghi (Correspondent), Kevin O'Hare (Finance and Administration Director), Fiona Turner (Producer), Barbara Rafaeli (Weekend Shows Producer), Steve Schnee (Producer), Kathryn Seaton-Reid (PTL Producer), Julie Sertel (Producer), Garrick Utley (Chief Foreign Correspondent), Hal Walker (Correspondent), Marcus Wilford (Producer), Terry Wrong (Producer for Day One), Clark Bentson (Producer)

AP RADIO
12 Norwich St., EC4A 1BP; tel (0171) 353-3692; fax (0171) 353-8118
KAREN SLOAN (European Coordinator)

AP-DOW JONES News Services (Editorial)
Newsroom
10 Fleet Pl., Limeburner Ln., London EC4M 7RB; tel (0171) 832-9105; fax (0171) 832-9101, Energy (0171) 832-9106, fax (0171) 832-9103, Capital (0171) 832-9107, Markets fax (0171) 832-9102

AP-DOW JONES (Marketing)
12 Norwich St., EC4A 1BP; tel (0171) 832-9105;
ARJEN BONGARD (Managing Editor for Information Services, EMEA), Andrew Atkinson (Correspondent), Jim Washburn (London Bureau Chief), Jonathan Birt (Correspondent), Paul Beckett (Correspondent), Adam Bradbery (Correspondent), Gene Colter (Correspondent), Peter Dowling (Correspondent), Nick Elliott (News Editor, CMR Europe), Edna Fernandes (Correspondent), Rob Fisher (Editor, European Corporate Report), Dee Gill (Correspondent), Nicholas Hastings (Correspondent), Martine Hogarty (Correspondent), Stephen Jack (Correspondent), Belinda Keheyan (Correspondent), Liz Main (Correspondent), Suzanne Miller (Correspondent), Chui-Ling Tam (Correspondent), Lloyd Vassell (Correspondent), Peter Greiff (News Editor)

AP-DOW JONES (Telerate Energy Service)
10 Fleet Place, Limeburner Lane, London EC4M 7RB; tel (0171) 832-9106/832-9520; fax (0171) 832-9103/832-9893
JAN BOUCEK (Managing Editor), Louise Anderson (Reporter), Joanne Barton (Reporter), Kam Foroohar (Reporter), Gordon Geddes (Reporter), Ronan Kavanagh (Reporter), Adrian Kerr (Reporter), Debra Marks (Reporter), Hazel Marlow (Reporter), Guy Welch (Reporter), Paul Young (Reporter)

APTV
12 Norwich St., EC4A 1BP; tel (0171) 427-4000; fax (0171) 583-0207
STEPHEN CLAYPOLE (Managing Director), Nigel Hancock (Editor, APTV News)

ASSOCIATED PRESS
12 Norwich St., London EC4A 1BP; tel (0171) 353-1515, (0171) 353-6323 (News), (0171) 353-4731 (Photos); fax (0171) 353-8118
MYRON L BELKIND (Chief of Bureau/Managing Director AP Limited), Bob Barr (News Editor), Dirk Beveridge, Karin Davies, Horst Faas (Senior Photo Editor-Operations in Europe, Africa & Middle East), Michael Feldman (Senior Photo Editor-News for Europe, Africa & Middle East), Maureen Johnson, Edie Lederer, Ron Kampeas, Shawn Pogatchnik, Sue Leeman, Robert Millward (Sports), Steve Wilson (European Sports Editor) Michael West, Joseph White (Sports), Matt Wolf, Audrey Woods

AVIATION WEEK & SPACE TECHNOLOGY
34 Dover St., London W1X 4BR; tel (0171) 409-1482; fax (0171) 493-9896
CAROLE A SHIFRIN (London Bureau Chief)

BALTIMORE SUN
10 Bolt Ct., Fleet St., London EC4A 3DB; tel (0171) 353-3531; fax (0171) 353-5331
BILL GLAUBER (Bureau Chief), Michèle Nevard

BLOCK NEWS ALLIANCE
33 Gloucester Walk, London W8 4HY; tel (0171) 938-2172
FERNAND AUBERJONOIS (Bureau Chief)

Copyright ©1996 by the Editor & Publisher Co.

VII-2 American correspondents in London

BLOOMBERG BUSINESS NEWS
City Gate House, 39-45 Finsbury Sq., London EC2A 1PX; tel (0171) 256-7500, fax (0171) 374-6138, News (0171) 374-7668
DOUGLAS McGILL (*European Bureau Chief*), James Ludden (*Editor*), Rebecca Anderson (*Correspondent*), Richard Baum (*Markets Editor*), Charles Birch (*Correspondent*), Gerard Bray (*Senior Company Editor*), Thom Calandra (*Markets Editor*), Eilis Brennan (*Correspondent*), David Callaway (*Correspondent*), David Clarke (*Correspondent*), Martin Cej (*Correspondent*), Conrad de Aenelle (*Company Editor*), Mike Dolan (*Correspondent*), Laura Frost (*Correspondent*), Pat Gerber (*Forum Editor, London & Europe*), Mark Gilbert (*Correspondent*), Daniella Gluck (*Coreespondent*), Ray Goff (*Markets Editor*), James Gomez (*Company Editor*), Dane Hamilton (*Correspondent*), Jerry Hart (*Senior Markets Editor*), Dawn Hayes (*Correspondent*), Peter Joseph Hegarty (*Company Editor*), David Holmes (*Correspondent*), Lauren Hoffman (*Correspondent*), Beth Karlin (*Correspondent*), Kate Lee Butler (*Features Editor*), Joanne Mason (*Markets Editor*), Rob McLeod (*Correspondent*), Craig Meyer (*Correspondent*), Richard Morrissey (*Correspondent*), Swaha Pattanaik (*Correspondent*), Alan Purkiss (*Company Editor*), Sheldon Reback (*Company Editor*), Paul Sillitoe (*European News Editor*), John Sims (*Company Editor*), Mark Stein (*Page One Editor*), Steve Stroth (*Correspondent*), Neil Thapar (*Correspondent*), Peter Torday (*Correspondent*), Isabel Unsworth (*Markets Editor*), Stephen Voss (*Correspondent*), Ivanna Wong (*Editor*), Samantha Zee (*Correspondent*).

BUSINESS WEEK
34 Dover St., London W1; tel (0171) 491-8985; fax (0171) 409-7152
PAULA DWYER (*Bureau Manager*), Julia Flynn (*Correspondent*)

CABLE NEWS INTERNATIONAL INC. (CNN)
CNN House, 19-22 Rathbone Pl., London W1P 1DF; tel (0171) 637-6800; fax (0171) 637-6868, (0171) 637-6878
DAVID FEINGOLD (*Bureau Chief*), Charles Hoff (*Deputy Bureau Chief/Assignment Manager*), Kieran Baker (*Assignment Editor*), Tom Bogdanowicz (*Producer/Business News*), Vicki Barker (*Producer "World News"*), Richard Blystone (*Senior Correspondent Europe*), Hilary Bowker (*Anchor, "World News," "International Hour"*), Debra Kocher (*Executive Producer/Business News*), Edith Chapin (*Field Producer*), Ingrid Formanek (*Field Producer*), Felice Hawley (*Producer/Business News*), John Defterios (*Correspondent/Business News*), Anders Edenhom (*Field Producer/Business News*), Dagmar Sauder (*Producer/Business News*), Todd Benjamin (*Correspondent/Business-News*), Leora Kapelus (*Associate Producer/Business News*), Kira Grishkoff (*News Feed Producer*), Rod Huntress (*Producer "International Hour"*), Rosalind Jackman (*Office Manager*), Alison Kee (*Associate Producer*), Mandy Kibel (*Associate Producer*), Margaret Lowrie (*Correspondent*), Jim Clancy (*Correspondent*), Blair Thompson (*Editor*), Arbelaez Maria (*News Feed Producer*), Chris Niles (*News Feed Producer*), Robert Reynolds (*Producer-Correspondent*), Nic Robertson (*Field Producer*), Kimberly Safford (*News Feed Producer*), Craig Vermay (*Producer*), Emma Hasler (*Administration Assistant*)

CBC TELEVISION
43/51 Great Titchfield St., London W1P 8DD; tel (0171) 412-9200; fax (0171) 631-3095
JOHN OWEN (*Bureau Chief*), Wivina Belmonte (*Producer*), Nancy Durham (*Correspondent*), Ann MacMillan (*Correspondent*), Brian Denike (*Producer*), Anna Maria Tremonti (*Correspondent*), Rick MacInnes-Rae (*Correspondent*), Valma Glenn (*Producer*)

CBS NEWS
68 Knightsbridge, London SW1X 7LL; tel (0171) 581-4801; fax (0171) 581-4431
AL ORTIZ (*Bureau Chief*), Marcy McGinnis (*Asst. Bureau Chief*), Mark Phillips (*Correspondent*), Barry Petersen (*Correspondent*), Cinny Kennard (*Correspondent*), Joe Halderman (*Producer*), Deborah Thomson (*Producer*), Adam Raphael (*Correspondent Radio*), Andrew Clarke (*Producer*), Yvonne Simpson (*Director, News Assignments*), Peter Bluff (*Producer*), Linda Karas (*Producer*), William McClure (*Producer 60 Minutes*), Jeanne Solomon Langley (*Producer 60 Minutes*), John Tiffin (*Producer 60 Minutes*), Michael Gavshon (*Producer 60 Minutes*), Francois Bringer (*Researcher*)

CHICAGO TRIBUNE PRESS SERVICE
169 Piccadilly, W1V 9DD; tel (0171) 499-8769; fax (0171) 499-8781
RAY MOSELEY (*Chief European Correspondent*)

CHRISTIAN SCIENCE MONITOR
49 Chartfield Ave., London SW15 6HW; tel (0181) 543-9393; fax (0181) 545-0392
ALEXANDER MacLEOD (*British Isles Correspondent*)

CNBC
8 Bedford Ave., London, WC1B 3NQ; tel (0171) 927-6759; tel (0171) 636-2628
SISSEL McCARTHY

COX NEWSPAPERS
Atlanta Journal-Constitution, Flat 5, Belsize Park House, 59/60 Belsize Park, London NW3 4EJ; tel (0171) 586-7743; fax (0171) 586-7742
LOU SALOME (*European Correspondent*)

C-SPAN
70 De Beauvoir Rd., London NI 5AT; tel (0171) 254-3648/(0171) 254-7801; fax (0171) 241-5153/923-0699
BERNARD TATE (*European Representative*)

DOW JONES (Telerate-Commodities & France)
10 Fleet Place, Limeburner Lane, London EC4M 7RB; tel (0171)832-9522, fax (0171) 832-9894
JAMES DYSON (*Managing Editor*), Graham Barnes (*Assistant Editor*), Fergal Duffy (*Reporter*), Melissa Score (*Reporter*), Sarah Miller (*Reporter*), Jennie Harris (*Reporter*), Helen Ubels (*Reporter*), Peter Nurse (*Reporter*), Mara Lemos-Webb (*Reporter*)

DOW JONES (Telerate-UK Markets Report)
10 Fleet Place, Limeburner Lane, London EC4M 7RB; tel (0171) 832-9234, fax (0171) 832-9895
IAIN MACDONALD (*Managing Editor*), Jeremy Clark (*Analyst*), Helen Donnelan (*Reporter*), Elizabeth Fosler (*Analyst*), Judith Huntley (*Assistant Editor*), William McIntosh (*Analyst*)

DOW JONES (Telerate-Emerging Markets)
10 Fleet Place, Limeburner Lane, London EC4M 7RB; tel (0171) 832-9513, fax (0171) 832-9102
PAUL HANNON (*Reporter*)

FAIRCHILD PUBLICATIONS OF NEW YORK (Div. of Capital Cities Media Inc.)
121 Kingsway, London WC2B 6PA; tel (0171) 831-3607; fax (0171) 831-6485
JAMES FALLON (*Bureau Chief*), Gloria La Rue (*London Correspondent*)

FORBES MAGAZINE
51 Charles St., London W1X 7PA; tel (0171) 465-0120; fax (0171) 465-0121
PETER FUHRMAN (*European Bureau Manager*), Richard C Morais (*Contributing Editor*)

FORTUNE MAGAZINE
Brettenham House, Lancaster Place, London WC2E 7TL; tel (0171) 499-4080
CARLA RAPOPORT (*European Editor*)

FUTURES WORLD NEWS
2 Royal Mint Court, Dexter House, London EC3N 4QN; tel (0171) 867-8867, fax (0171) 867-1368
TERRY WOOTEN (*Editor-In Chief & European Editor*), Barbara Kollmeyer

GLOBE & MAIL
The Quadrangle; PO Box 4YG, 180 Wardour St., London W1A 4YG; tel (0171) 396-4116; fax (0171) 734-0561
PAUL KORING (*European Correspondent*)

INTERNATIONAL HERALD TRIBUNE
63 Long Acre, London WC2E 9JH; tel (0171) 836-4802; fax (0171) 240-2254
ERIK IPSEN (*London Correspondent*)

JOURNAL OF COMMERCE
Totara Park House, 3rd Fl., 34/36 Grays Inn Rd., London WC1X 8HR; tel (0171) 430-2495; fax (0171) 837-2168
JANET PORTER (*Chief European Correspondent*), Keith Rockwell (*European Bureau Chief*)

KNIGHT-RIDDER FINANCIAL NEWS
K.R. House, 78 Fleet St., EC4Y 1HY; tel (0171) 842-4000; fax (0171) 583-5032
BARRY SCHNEIDER (*Editor for Europe, Middle East and Africa*), Abby Deveney (*Europe Chief Copy Editor*), Patty Buchanan (*Copy Editor*), Timothy Penn (*London Bureau Chief*), Jenifer Otwell (*News Editor Europe, Middle East and Africa*), Al Webb (*Copy Editor*), Mark Hillier (*Slot Editor*), Thor Valdmanis (*Copy Editor*), Emma Farrington (*Copy Editor*), Janine Ogier (*Copy Editor*), Paul Francis (*Copy Editor*), Jackie Cowhig (*Chief Energy Reporter*), Paolo Berbotto (*Energy Reporter*), Rose Farrell (*Energy Price Reporter*), Chris Davidson (*Energy Price Reporter*), Vicky Fox (*Govt. Reporter*), Mona Megalli (*Middle East Correspondent*), Christopher Lyddon (*Senior Grains Reporter/ Europe*), Irena Guzelova (*Financial Reporter*), David Thomas (*Financial Reporter*), Randy Walerius (*Financial Reporter*), Karen Lane (*Financial Reporter*), David Robinson (*Financial Reporter*), Pat Jones (*Chief Commodities/Shipping Reporter*), Janet Govan (*Reporter*), Lucy Hine (*Reporter*), Andy Home (*Reporter*), Sonia Kolensnikov (*Reporter*), David Townsend (*Reporter*)

LIFE MAGAZINE
Brettenham House, Lancaster Pl., London, WC2E 7TL; tel (0171) 499-4080; fax (0171) 322-1021
GAIL RIDGWELL

LOS ANGELES TIMES
150 Brompton Rd., London SW3 1HX; tel (0171) 823-7315; fax (0171) 823-7308
DAN FISHER (*Bureau Chief*)

MACLEAN'S MAGAZINE
60/62 Great Titchfield St., London W1P 7FL; tel (0171) 637-7410; fax (0171) 637-7195
BRUCE WALLACE (*London Bureau Chief*)

MARKET NEWS SERVICE INC.
Wheatsheaf House, 4 Carmelite St., London EC4Y 0BN; tel (0171) 353-4462; fax (0171) 353-9122
JOHN HURDLE (*Bureau Chief*), Eamon Quinn (*Editor*), Tom Burroughes (*Reporter*), Jeremy Carvell (*Correspondent*)

McGRAW HILL
34 Dover St., London W1X 4BR; tel (0171) 493-0538; fax (0171) 493-9896
DAVID BREZOVEC

NBC NEWS WORLDWIDE INC. (NBC NEWS)
8 Bedford Ave., London WC1B 2NQ; tel (0171) 637-8655; fax (0171) 636-2628
KAREN CURRY (*Bureau Chief*), David Philips (*Producer*), Truus Bos (*News Editor*), Steffi Fields (*News Editor*), Victor Solis (*Producer*), Dale Curran (*Producer*), Walter Millis (*Producer*), Charles Sabine (*Producer*), Justin Balding (*Producer*), Lynne Edwards (*Producer*), Lucy Muccini (*Bureau Coordinator*), Keith Miller (*Correspondent*), Richard Roth (*Correspondent*), Linda Vester (*Correspondent*), Alan Harding (*Manager Technical Services*), Nigel Hoare (*Director Financial Affairs*), Yuka Tachibana (*Desk Editor*)

NATIONAL PUBLIC RADIO
Bush House, Room G-10 East Wing, The Strand, London WC2B 4PH; tel (0171) 257-8086; fax (0171) 379-6486
ANDREW BOWERS (*London Bureau Chief*), Michael Goldfarb (*Reporter*)

NEWSWEEK
18 Park St., London W1Y 4HH; tel (0171) 629-8361; fax (0171) 408-1403
DANIEL PEDERSEN (*Bureau Chief*), Bill Burger (*European Economics Editor*), Deborah Curran (*Bureau Manager*), Bija Bociek (*Photo Editor*)

NEW YORK TIMES
66 Buckingham Gate, London SW1E 6AU; tel (0171) 799-5050; fax (0171) 799-2962
JOHN DARNTON (*Chief Correspondent*), William Schmidt (*Correspondent*), Richard W. Stevenson (*Correspondent*), Marion Underhill (*Office Manager*), Pam Kent (*Features*), R A (Tony) Beard (*Telecommunications Manager*)

PEOPLE MAGAZINE
Brettenham House, Lancaster Pl., London WC2E 7TL; tel (0171) 499-4080; fax (0171) 322-1125
JERENE JONES (*Special Correspondent*)

PHILADELPHIA INQUIRER
14 Queen's Grove, London NW8 6EL; tel (0171) 483-3766; fax (0171) 483-3766
DICK POLMAN

PUBLIC BROADCASTING
33 Bryanston Sq., Flat 7, London W1H 7LR; tel (0171) 262-2524
PAUL DUKE (*Senior Commentator*)

READER'S DIGEST ASSOCIATION LIMITED
Berkeley Sq. House, London W1X 6AB; tel (0171) 629-8144; fax (0171) 408-0748
RUSSELL TWISK (*Editor-In-Chief, British Edition*)

ROTOR & WING MAGAZINE
Rosemont House, Rosemont Ave., West Byfleet, Surrey, KT14 6NP; tel (093) 235-5515; fax (093) 235-5962
BILL CAREY (*European Bureau Chief*)

TIME-LIFE NEWS SERVICE
Brettenham House, Lancaster Pl., London WC2E 7TL; tel (0171) 499-4080; fax (0171) 322-1230

TIME MAGAZINE
Brettenham House, Lancaster Pl., London WC2E 7TL; tel (0171) 499-4080; fax (0171) 322-1230
BARRY HILLENBRAND (*Bureau Chief*), Frank Melville (*Correspondent*), Helen Gibson (*Correspondent*), Paul Durrant (*Picture Editor*)

UNITED PRESS INTERNATIONAL
408 Strand, London WC2R ONE; tel (0171) 333-0999 (News Dept.)/(0171) 333-1666 (Sports)/(0171) 333-0990 (Admin./Accounts)/(0171) 333-1665 (Communications), Telex: 28829/8811443; fax (0171) 333-1690
MICHAEL COLLINS (*Bureau Chief*), Simona de Logu (*Correspondent*), Paul Gould (*Correspondent*), Michael Rawlinson (*Sales Representative*), Morley Myers (*International Sports Editor*), Julian Linden (*Sports Correspondent*), Mitch Phillips (*Sports Correspondent*), David Alexander (*Regional Editor*)

US NEWS & WORLD REPORT
169 Piccadilly, London W1V 9DD; tel (0171) 493-4643; fax (0171) 493-8308
ROBIN KNIGHT (*Senior European Editor*), Jennifer Fisher (*London Correspondent*)

VOICE OF AMERICA
International Press Centre, 76 Shoe Ln., London EC4A 3JB; tel (0171) 410-0960; fax (0171) 410-0966
MARK HOPKINS (*Senior Editor*), Sally Hodgson (*Deputy Editor*), Andre de Nesnera (*London Correspondent*), Mike Batho (*Chief Engineer*)

WALL ST. JOURNAL
10 Fleet Pl., London EC4M 7RB; tel (0171) 832-9200; fax (0171) 832-9201
LAWRENCE INGRASSIA (*London Bureau Chief*), Nicholas Bray (*Correspondent*), Janet Guyon (*Correspondent*), Richard Hudson (*Correspondent*), Dana Milbank (*Correspondent*), Barry Newman (*Correspondent*), Michael Sesit (*Correspondent*), Kyle Pope (*Correspondent*), Tara Parker-Pope (*Correspondent*), Glenn Whitney (*Correspondent*), Diana Edwards (*News Assistant*), Julia Dennis (*News Assistant*)

WASHINGTON POST
18 Park St., London W1Y 4HH; tel (0171) 629-8958; fax (0171) 629-0050
FRED BARBASH (*Bureau Chief*), Steve Coll (*Correspondent*)

WTN (Television Newsfilm Agency of ABC, ITN and Channel 9 Sydney)
The Interchange, Oval Road, Camden Lock, London NW1; tel (0171) 410-5200; fax (0171) 413-8302
KENNETH A COYTE (*Chairman*), Lowndes Lipscomb (*VP & Managing Editor*), Jeff Coote (*Manager Special Coverage*)

Copyright ©1996 by the Editor & Publisher Co.

ASSOCIATIONS, CLUBS & PRESS CLUBS— NATIONAL & INTERNATIONAL

A

AAF COLLEGE CHAPTERS — 1101 Vermont Ave. NW, Ste. 500, Washington, DC 20005; tel (202) 898-0089
President — Wallace Snyder; Chmn. of Acad. Div. — Ronald Lane (Univ. of Georgia); Vice Pres./Ed. Serv. — Mary Ellen Woolley; Editor of Communicator — Stefanie Ganz
Elections held in June.

ACCREDITING COUNCIL ON EDUCATION IN JOURNALISM AND MASS COMMUNICATIONS — Univ. of Kansas, School of Journalism, Stauffer-Flint Hall, Lawrence, KS 66045; tel (913) 864-3973
Pres. (Representing ASNE) — Robert Giles; Vice Pres. — Richard Cole; Exec. Dir. — Susanne Shaw

ADVERTISING COUNCIL INC. — 261 Madison Ave., New York, NY 10016-2303; tel (212) 922-1500
President — Ruth A Wooden; Chairman — Phil Geier; Secretary — Dewit F Helm Jr; Manager/PR — Paula Veale
Elections held in May.

ADVERTISING MEDIA CREDIT EXECUTIVES ASSN. INT'L — PO Box 167249, Irving, TX 75016-7249; tel (214) 506-0175
Pres. — Kerry O Kelly (Baltimore Sun Co.); 1st Vice Pres. — Kim Walter (Los Angeles Daily News); Exec. Dir. — Gail B Chapman
Elections held in Oct.

ADVERTISING RESEARCH FOUNDATION — 641 Lexington Ave., New York, NY 10022; tel (212) 751-5656
Pres. — Michael J Naples; Man. Ed. Journal of Adv. Research — Kathryn Kucharski Grubb
Elections held in Jan.

AGRICULTURAL PUBLISHERS ASSOCIATION — 401 N. Michigan Ave., Chicago, IL 60611-4267; tel (312) 644-6610
Pres. — Gary L Vorpahl; Exec. Dir. — Walter G Purcell; Vice Pres. — Gary T Fitzgerald; Sec. — Ed Dickinson; Treas. — Ronald Sorensen
Elections held in Oct./Nov.

AMERICAN ADVERTISING FEDERATION — 1101 Vermont Ave. NW, 5th Fl., Washington, DC 20005; tel (202) 898-0089
President — Wallace Snyder

AMERICAN AGRICULTURAL EDITORS ASSOCIATION — 612 W. 22nd St., Austin, TX 78705; tel (512) 474-2041; fax (512) 474-7787
Pres. — Joe Dan Boyd; Exec. Sec./Treas. — Denise Clarke
Elections held in Oct.

AMERICAN ASSN. OF ADVERTISING AGENCIES — 666 3rd Ave., New York, NY 10017; tel (212) 682-2500
President — John O'Toole; Chairman — Roy Bostock; Sec./Treas. — Eric Mower
Elections held in April.

AMERICAN ASSN. OF SUNDAY AND FEATURE EDITORS — 11600 Surnise Valley Dr., Reston, VA 22091; tel (703) 648-1286
President — Michael Smith (Knight-Ridder); 1st Vice Pres. — Janet Grimley (Seattle Post-Intelligencer); 2nd Vice Pres. — Marcia Judson (Lakeland (FL) Ledger); Sec. — Betsy Cantler (Charleston (SC) Post & Courier); Treas. — Jane Marshall (Houston Chronicle)
Elections held in Oct.

AMERICAN BUSINESS PRESS — 675 3rd Ave., Ste. 400, New York, NY 10017; tel (212) 661-6360
Chmn.— J Roger Friedman (Lebhar-Friedman Inc., Pres.); Vice Chmn.— Keith E Crain (Crain Communications Inc., Vice Chmn.); President— Scott A Smith (Argus Inc., Treasurer); Sr. Vice Pres. — Terilyn McGovern
Elections held in April/May.

AMERICAN COURT & COMMERICAL NEWSPAPERS INC. — PO Box 430209, Pontiac, MI 48343-0209; tel (810) 334-4329; fax (810) 334-2226
Pres. — Bradley L Thompson II; VP/Sec. — Debra J Quaal; VP/Treas. — Richard H Groves; Exec. Dir. — Sheila R Ashcraft
Elections at annual meeting in fall.

AMERICAN FOREST & PAPER ASSOCIATION INC. — 1111 19th St. NW, Ste. 800, Washington, DC 20036; tel (202) 463-2700; fax (202) 463-2785
Chairman — Frank C Breese III; President — Red Cavaney; Vice Pres. — Virgil K Horton Jr; Mgr./Media Relations — Barry Polsky; Public Information Coordinator — Karen L Moore
Elections held in March.

AMERICAN INSTITUTE OF GRAPHIC ARTS — 164 5th Ave., New York, NY 10010; tel (212) 752-0813
Pres. — William Drenttel; Dir. — Caroline Hightower; Assoc. Dir. — Irene Bareis
Elections held in June.

AMERICAN JEWISH PRESS ASSN. — 12703 Research Blvd., Ste. 220, Austin, TX 78759; tel (512) 250-2409
Pres. — Debra Rubin; 1st Vice Pres. — Fredda Sacharow; 2nd Vice Pres. — Nova Contini; Exec. Dir. — L Malcolm Rodman; Treas. — Richard Waloff; Recording Sec. — Mollie Collins
Elections held at annual spring conference.

AMERICAN MARKETING ASSOCIATION — 250 S. Wacker Dr., Ste. 200, Chicago, IL 60606; tel (312) 648-0536; fax (312) 993-7540
COO — Dennis Jorgensen; Chairperson — Rosann Spiro; Chairperson-Elect — David E Gordon; Immed. Past Chmn. — J Berry Mason; VP Finance/Sec. — Margery Steinberg
Elections held in Feb.

AMERICAN NEWS WOMEN'S CLUB INC. — 1607 22nd St. NW, Washington, DC 20008; tel (202) 332-6770; fax (202) 265-6477
President — Helen R G White; Vice Pres. — Alison Duquette; Secretary — Nikkola Whitlock
Elections held in May.

AMERICAN PRESS INSTITUTE — 11690 Sunrise Valley Dr., Reston, VA 22091; tel (703) 620-3611; fax (703) 620-5814
Pres./Exec. Dir. — William L Winter; Dir. Admin. — John Finneman; Assoc. Dir. — Jeff Cowart; Assoc. Dir. — Evelyn Hsu; Assoc. Dir. — Carol Ann Riordan; Assoc. Dir. — Robert Secundy

AMERICAN SOCIETY OF NEWSPAPER EDITORS — 11600 Sunrise Valley Dr. (22091), PO Box 4090, Reston, VA 22090-1700; tel (703) 648-1144; fax (703) 476-6125
President — Robert Giles (Detroit News); Vice Pres. — Sandra Mims Rowe (Portland Oregonian); Secretary — Edward Seaton (Manhattan (KS) Mercury); Treas. — N Christian Anderson (Colorado Springs (CO) Gazette Telegraph); Exec. Dir. — Lee Stinnett
Elections held in April.

ANGLO-AMERICAN PRESS ASSOCIATION OF PARIS — International Herald Tribune, 181 ave. Charles de Gaulle, Cedex Neuilly, 92521; France; tel (33-1) 41439426; fax (33-1) 41439393
President — Tom Sancton (Time Magazine); British Vice Pres. — Barry James (Int'l. Herald Tribune); American Vice Pres. — Michael Balter (Science Magazine)

ASIAN-AMERICAN JOURNALISTS ASSOCIATION — 1765 Sutter St., Ste. 1000, San Francisco, CA 94115; tel (415) 346-2051; fax (415) 931-4671
President — Dinah Eng; Vice Pres./Print — Benjamin Seto; Vice Pres./Broadcast — Linda Yu; Secretary — Catalina Camia; Treasurer — Dickson Louie

ASSOCIATED PRESS MANAGING EDITORS ASSN. — 50 Rockefeller Plz., New York, NY 10020; tel (212) 621-1552
Immed. Past Pres. — Robert Ritter (Gannett News Service); Pres. — Rich Archbold (Long Beach (CA) Press-Telegram); Treas. — Kathy Kozdemba (Pittsburg (PA) North Hills News Record)
Elections held in Oct.

ASSOCIATION FOR EDUCATION IN JOURNALISM AND MASS COMM. — University of South Carolina, 1621 College St., Columbia, SC 29208-0251; tel (803) 777-2005; fax (803) 777-4728
Past Pres. — Judy VanSlyke Turk; Pres. — Pamela Shoemaker; Pres.-Elect — Alex Tan; Exec. Dir. — Jennifer H McGill
Elections held in March.

ASSOCIATION OF ALTERNATIVE NEWSWEEKLIES — 1001 Connecticut Ave. NW, Ste. 822, Washington, DC 20036-4104; tel (202) 822-1955; fax (202) 822-0929
Pres. — Jeff Vonkaenel (Sacramento News & Review); Vice Pres. — Jane Levine (Chicago Reader); Sec. — Bradley Zeve (Seaside (CA) Coast Weekly); Treas. — Michael Crystal (Seattle Weekly)
Elections held annually in June.

ASSOCIATION OF ALTERNATIVE POSTAL SYSTEMS — 112 E. 6th St., PO Box 1331, Gaylord, MI 49734; tel (517) 731-2988; fax (517) 732-8300
Pres. — Robert A Leach Sr (Independent Delivery Service); Vice Pres./Sec. — Dwayne L Lien (Direct Market Media); Treas./Exec. Dir. — Ken Bradsheet
Elections held at annual conference in Feb.

ASSOCIATION OF AMERICAN EDITORIAL CARTOONISTS — 4101 Lake Boone Trail, Ste. 201, Raleigh, NC 27607; tel (919) 787-5181
Pres. — Jim Larrick (Columbus Dispatch); Past Pres. — Brian Basset (Seattle Times); Pres.-Elect — Kevin Kallaugher (Baltimore Sun); Vice Pres. — Signe Wilkinson (Philadelphia Daily News); Dir. — Vance Rodewatt (Calgary Herald); Dir. — John Trever (Albuquerque Journal); Dir. — Joel Pett (Lexington Herald-Leader); Sec.— Bruce Beattie (Wilmington (DE) The News Journal, Sec./Treas.); Gen. Mgr. — Susan Rexer
Elections held in June.

ASSOCIATION OF CANADIAN ADVERTISERS INC. — 175 Bloor St. E., South Tower, Ste. 307, Toronto, ON M4W 3R8 Canada; tel (416) 964-3805; fax (416) 964-0771
Pres. — Patrick McDougall; Sr. Vice Pres. — Maurice Brisebois; Vice Pres. — Joan Curran
Elections held in Nov.

ASSOCIATION OF FOOD JOURNALISTS INC. — 38309 Genesee Lake Rd., Oconomowoc, WI 53066; tel (414) 965-3251
Pres. — Dale Curry (New Orleans Times-Picayune); Vice Pres. — Julian Armstrong (Montreal Gazette); Sec. — Michael Bauer (San Francisco Chronicle); Treas. — Tommy C Simmons (Baton Rouge Advocate)
Election held in summer of even years.

ASSOCIATION OF FREE COMMUNITY PAPERS — 401 N. Michigan Ave., Chicago, IL 60601; tel (312) 644-6610; fax (312) 321-6869
Immed. Past Pres. — LeeAnne Borkowski; President — Dick Mandt; Vice Pres. of Admin. — Bill Welsh; Vice Pres. of Industry Promotions — Pete Gorman; Vice Pres. of Member Services — Craig Trongaard; Assoc. Dir. — Deirdre Flynn
Elections held in June.

ASSOCIATION OF NATIONAL ADVERTISERS INC. — 155 E. 44th St., New York, NY 10017; tel (212) 697-5950
Pres. — Harry Davis;Senior VP— Robin Webster (Weight Watchers International GM of New Products and Services)

ASSOCIATION OF SCHOOLS OF JOURNALISM AND MASS COMM. — University of South Carolina, 1621 College St., Columbia, SC 29208-0251; tel (803) 777-2005; fax (803) 777-4728
Past Pres. — Willard Rowland; Pres. — Douglas Anderson; Pres.-Elect — Robert Ruggles; Exec. Dir. — Jennifer H McGill
Elections held in April.

AUDIT BUREAU OF CIRCULATIONS — 900 N. Meacham Rd., Schaumburg, IL 60173-4968; tel (708) 605-0909
Pres./Man. Dir. — M David Keil;Initiative Media— Hugh F Dow (COB); Exec. Vice Pres.— Michael J Lavery (Auditing Services); Sr. Vice Pres.— John R Payne (Member Services); Sr. Vice Pres.— Michael K Moran (Field Auditing); Vice Chmn. — Anthony M Gasparro (The Great Atlantic & Pacific Tea Co.); Vice Chmn. — Lance R Primis (New York Times Co.); Vice Chmn. — Michael D Moore (DMB&B); Vice Chmn. — Dennis Stoakes (Hiram Walker Group); Secretary — Karen M Vereb (AT&T); Treasurer — R David Threshie (Santa Ana (CA) Orange County Register)
Elections held in Nov.

AVIATIONS/SPACE WRITERS ASSN. — 6540 50th St. N., Oakdale, MN 55128-1708; tel (612) 779-9390; fax (612) 779-9573
Pres. — William Sweetman; Sec./Treas. — Dwight E Weber
Elections held at annual conference.

B

BANK MARKETING ASSN. — 1120 Connecticut Ave. NW, Washington, DC 20036; tel (202) 663-5049
Pres. — Jeffrey M Westergren; Pres.-Elect — Faye E Cannon; Exec. Vice Pres. — Douglas Adamson; Admn. Mgr. — Cynthia Werthman

BASEBALL WRITERS ASSN. OF AMERICA — 36 Brookfield Rd., Ft. Salonga, NY 11768, 78 Olive St., Lake Grove, NY 11755; tel (516) 757-0562/(516) 981-7938; fax (516) 585-4669
President — Paul Meyer (Pittsburgh Post Gazette); Vice Pres. — Jerome Holtzman (Chicago Tribune); Sec./Treas. — Jack O'Connell (Hartford Courant); Asst. Sec./Treas. — Jack Lang (SportsTicker)
Elections held in Oct.

BBM BUREAU OF MEASUREMENT — 1500 Don Mills Rd., Ste. 305, Don Mills, ON M3B 3L7 Canada; tel (416) 445-9800; fax (416) 445-8644
Pres./CEO — Owen A Charlebois;Sr. Vice Pres.— Rodger Hone (Global Television Network, Chmn.); Exec. Vice Pres.— Jim MacLeod (Radiocorp Inc., Radio Exec. Committee Chmn.); Vice Pres./Gen. Mgr. — Greg Mudry (ATV, Halifax, TV Exec. Committee Chmn.); Vice Pres.— John Snow (ComQuest, Vice Pres.); Vice Pres.— Brian Parish(Mgr./Radio); Vice Pres.— Ken Purdye (Mgr. TV); Vice Pres.— David Chambers (Finance/Administration); Vice Pres. — Robert Langlois (Quebec Services); Sr. Vice Pres./CFO — Glen Shipp

BPA INTERNATIONAL — 270 Madison Ave., 2nd Fl., New York, NY 10016-0699; tel (212) 779-3200
Pres./CEO — Michael Marchesano
Elections held in May.

BRITISH TOURIST AUTHORITY — 551 5th Ave., 7th Fl., New York, NY 10176; tel (212) 986-2200; fax (212) 986-1188
Exec. Vice Pres. — Jeff Hamblin (The Americas); Dir./Pub. Relations — Bedford Pace; Mktg. Dir. — Craig Robertson

BUSINESS MARKETING ASSOCIATION — 150 N. Wacker Dr., Ste. 1760, Chicago, IL 60606-1607; tel (312) 409-4262; fax (312) 409-4266
Chairman — Paul Sherrington (EquiFax Inc.); Immed. Past Chmn.— Robert Lauterborn (Univ. of North Carolina, CBC); Vice Chmn. — Mark Semmelmayer (Kimberly-Clark Corp.); Sec. — Marlah Rose-Asch (Gardner Publications); Treas. — Roberta Emerson (Tencor Instruments)
Elections held in June.

C

CANADIAN BUSINESS PRESS — 40 Shields Ct., Ste. 201, Markham, ON L3R 0M5 Canada; tel (905) 946-8889
Chmn. — James O Hall; Pres. — Brandon Jones
Elections held in June.

CANADIAN CIRCULATION MANAGEMENT ASSN. — 298 Highfield St., Moncton, NB E1C 5R6 Canada; tel (506) 854-7091; fax (506) 855-1334

Copyright ©1996 by the Editor & Publisher Co.

President — Ron Keith (Winnepeg Sun); 1st Vice Pres. — Rupert Fry (Toronto Star); 2nd Vice Pres. — George Ritchot (Calgary Herald); Sec./Treas. — Dave Dorman
Elections held in June.

CANADIAN CIRCULATIONS AUDIT BOARD (CCAB INC.) — 188 Eglinton Ave. E., Ste. 304, Toronto, ON M4P 2X7 Canada; tel (416) 487-2418; fax (416) 487-6405
Chmn. — Scott A Warne; Vice Chmn. — Peter W Little; Pres./Gen. Mgr. — Patrick Sweeney; Treas. — David McClung
Elections held in April.

CANADIAN COMMUNITY NEWSPAPERS ASSN. — 90 Eglinton Ave. E., Ste. 206, Toronto, ON M4P 2Y3 Canada; tel (416) 482-1090; fax (416) 482-1908
Chmn. — Joyce Carlson; Pres. — Duff Jamison; Corp. Sec. — Sharon McCully
Elections held in July.

CANADIAN DAILY NEWSPAPER ASSN. — 890 Yonge St., Ste. 1100, Toronto, ON M4W 3P4 Canada; tel (416) 923-3567; fax (416) 923-7206
President — John E Foy;Chairman— Kevin B Peterson (Calgary Herald, Pres./Pub.); Chairman-elect— Hunter S Grant (Brockville (ON) Recorder & Times, Co-Pub./Pres./GM); Vice Chairman/Treas.— Gilbert Lacasse (Quebec Le Soleil, Pres./Pub.); Past Chairman— Roger D Landry (Montreal La Presse, Pres./Pub.)
Elections held in April.

CANADIAN MANAGING EDITORS CONFERENCE — PO Box 5020, Ottawa, ON K2C 3M4 Canada; tel (613) 829-9100
Past Pres. — Sharon Burnside (Ottawa Citizen); Pres. — Mike Strobel (Toronto Sun); 1st Vice Pres. — Bill Turpin (Halifax Daily News); 2nd Vice Pres. — Neil Graham (Vancouver Province); Sec./Treas. — Chris Nelson (Calgary Sun)
Elections held in June.

THE CANADIAN PRESS — 36 King St. E., Toronto, ON M5C 2L9 Canada; tel (416) 364-0321
Chmn. — Roger D Landry; Pres. — Keith Kincaid; Sec. — Donald Jarrett
Elections held in April.

CANADIAN PRINTING INK MFRS. ASSN. — 304 The East Mall, Ste. 320, Etobicoke, ON M9B 6E2 Canada; tel (416) 236-3733
Pres. — Ralph Marshall; Sec./Treas. — John A Nace
Elections held in Jan. for a two year term.

CANADIAN RADIO-TELEVISION NEWS DIRECTORS ASSOCIATION — 2175 Sheppard Ave. E., Ste. 110, Willowdale, ON M2J 1W8 Canada; tel (416) 756-2213; fax (416) 491-1670
President — Gary Ennett (CFPL London Press); Vice Pres./Radio — Tom Mark (CJJR FM/CHRX Vancouver); Vice Pres./TV — Dave McGinn (CJOH Ottawa); Treasurer — Al Gibson (Broadcast News, Toronto); Administrator — Jennifer Rogers
Elections held in June.

CATHOLIC PRESS ASSOCIATION — 3555 Veterans Hwy., Unit O, Ronkonkoma, NY 11779; tel (516) 471-4730; fax (516) 471-4804
Pres. — Anthony Spence; Vice Pres. — Margaret Gabriel; Exec. Dir. — Owen P McGovern; Sec. — Robert Zyskowski; Treas. — Mary Lou Darnell
Elections held in April.

CENTER FOR FOREIGN JOURNALISTS — 11690-A Sunrise Valley Dr., Reston, VA 22091; tel (703) 620-5984; fax (703) 620-6790
Chmn. — Thomas Winship; Vice Chmn./Treas. — James D Ewing; Pres. — George A Krimsky; Vice Pres./Exec. Dir. — Whayne Dillehay

COLLEGE MEDIA ADVISERS — University of Memphis, Department of Journalism, Memphis, TN 38152; tel (901) 678-2403; fax (901) 678-4798
Immd. Past Pres. — Ron Johnson (Kansas State Univ., Manhattan); Pres. — Jan T Childress (Texas Tech University, Lubbock); Vice Pres. — Linda Owens Whitlaw (Univ. of South Carolina, Aiken); Treas. — Kathy Lawrence (University of Texas, Austin); Vice Pres. Member Services — Mark Witherspoon (Southern Methodist Univ., Dallas); Sec. — Mona Cravens (Univ. of So. California, Los Angeles); Headquarters Mgr. — Ronald Spielberger (University of Memphis)
Elections held in Oct.

COUNCIL FOR THE ADVANCEMENT OF SCIENCE WRITING INC. — PO Box 404, Greenlawn, NY 11740; tel (516) 757-5664
President — Joann Rodgers; Vice Pres. — Jerry Bishop; Vice Pres. — Dr Robert F Murray; Exec. Dir. — Ben Patrusky; Admin. Sec. — Diana McGurgan; Treas. — Paul Raeburn
Elections held in May.

COUNCIL FOR ADVANCEMENT AND SUPPORT OF EDUCATION — 11 Dupont Cir., Ste. 400, Washington, DC 20036; tel (202) 328-5900
President — Peter Buchanan; VP/External Affairs — Sarah Hardesty Bray; Editor-In-Chief — Karla Taylor
Elections held in July.

COUNCIL OF BETTER BUSINESS BUREAUS INC. — 4200 Wilson Blvd., Ste. 800, Arlington, VA 22203; tel (703) 276-0100
Pres. — James H McIlhenny;Exec. Vice Pres.— Russell Bodoff (Corporate Sec.); Vice Pres.— George Wolcott (CFO)
Elections held in Oct.

D

DIRECT MARKETING ASSN. INC. — 11 W. 42nd St., New York, NY 10036-8096; tel (212) 768-7277
President— Jonah Gitlitz (CFO); Chairman — John Cleary (Donnelley Marketing Inc.); Exec. Vice Pres. — Walter A Deehring;Sr. Vice Pres./PR— Connie Heatley (Communications); Sec. — Sheila Martin (Triplex Direct Mktg. Corp.); Treas.— Jerome W Pickholz (Ogilvy & Mather Direct, Chmn.-Elect)
Elections held in Oct.

DOG WRITERS' ASSN. OF AMERICA — 55 Bethune St., Ste. C-614, New York, NY 10014; tel (212) 929-2015
Pres. — Mordecai Siegal; Vice Pres. — Chris Walkowicz; Sec. — Salley W Cooper
Elections held in Feb.

E

EDUCATION COUNCIL OF THE GRAPHIC ARTS INDUSTRY INC. — 1899 Preston White Dr., Reston, VA 22091-4367; tel (703) 648-1768; fax (703) 620-0994
Chmn. — Randolph Camp; Administrator — Carol J Hurlburt

F

FEDERATION INTERNATIONALE DES EDITEURS DE JOURNAUX — 25 rue d'Astorg, Paris, 75008; France; tel 47 428500; fax 47 424948
Pres./Pub. — K Prescott Low (Quincy (MA) Patriot-Ledger); 1st Vice Pres.— Jayme Sirotsky (Porto Alegre (Brazil) Zero Hora, 1st Vice Pres.); Dir. Gen. — Timothy Balding
Elections held in May every two years.

FOOTBALL WRITERS ASSN. OF AMERICA — PO Box 1022, Edmond, OK 73083; tel (405) 341-4731
Pres. — Ed Sherman (Chicago Tribune); 1st Vice Pres. — Ivan Maisel (Long Island (NY) Newsday); Exec. Dir. — Volney Meece
Elections held in June.

FOREIGN PRESS ASSN. — 110 E. 59th St., New York, NY 10022; tel (212) 826-4452; fax (212) 826-4657
Pres. — Santi Visalli; Vice Pres. — Gabriel Plesea; Dir. — Suzanne Adams; Treas. — Victor Peicinow; Asst. Treas. — Gianni Capra; Gen. Sec. — Gabrielle Barth; Asst. Gen. Sec. — Yolanda Gerritsen
Elections held in Dec.

FREE PRESS ASSOCIATION — PO Box 63, Port Hadlock, WA 98339; tel (206) 385-5097; fax (206) 385-3704
Board Member — Bill Bradford; Board Member — Michael Grossberg; Board Member — Paula Brookmire; Director — Jesse Walker

FREEDOM FORUM — 1101 Wilson Blvd., Arlington, VA 22209; tel (703) 528-0800; fax (703) 522-4831
Chairman — Allen H Neuharth; Dep. Chairman — John C Quinn; Pres./CEO — Charles L Overby; Exec. VP — Gerald M Sass; Sr. VP/Exec. Dir. — Everette E Dennis (Freedom Forum Media Studies Center); Sr. VP/Exec. Dir. — Peter Prichard (Newseum); Sr. VP/Int'l. Oper. — Chris Wells; VP/Finance/Treas. — Harvey S Cotter; VP/Gen. Services — Pamela Galloway-Tab; VP/Exec. Dir. — Felix F Gutierrez (Freedom Forum Pacific Coast Center); VP/Broadcasting — Jack A Hurley; VP — Tracy A Quinn (Freedom Forum New York City Conference Center); VP/News & Public Info. — Rod Sandeen

G

GRAPHIC ARTS TECHNICAL FOUNDATION INC. — 4615 Forbes Ave., Pittsburgh, PA 15213; tel (412) 621-6941; fax (412) 621-3049
Chmn. — Donald N Reeves; Vice Chmn. — John A Young; Communications Mgr. — Maria Harris; Sec. — Lawrence G Tapp; Treas. — Mark Jorgensen; Pres. — John A Burgess
Elections held in Oct.

GRAPHIC COMMUNICATIONS INTERNATIONAL UNION — 1900 L St. NW, Washington, DC 20036-5080; tel (202) 462-1400
President — James J Norton; Sec./Treas. — Guy DeVito
Elections held quadrennially.

GRAVURE ASSOCIATION OF AMERICA — 1200-A Scottsville Rd., Rochester, NY 14624; tel (716) 436-2150; fax (716) 436-7689
Pres. — William E Martin; Exec. Vice Pres. — Cheryl L Kasunich
Elections held in April.

I

IFRA (INCA-FIEJ) RESEARCH ASSOCIATION — Washingtonplatz 1, Darmstadt, D-64287; Germany; tel 06151/7005-0
Pres. — M Ringier; Man. Dir. — G W Boettcher; Documentalist — Heike Appel

INDEPENDENT FREE PAPERS OF AMERICA — 395 S. High St., PO Box 69, Covington, OH 45318; tel (800) 441-4372; fax (513) 473-3299
Immed. Past Pres. — Carol Hoheisel (Little Falls (MN) Morrison Co. Record); Pres. — John Jacobs (J-Ad Corp., Marshall, MI); Vice Pres. — Joe Nicastro (Pompton Lakes (NJ) Independent News); Sec./Treas. — Gary L Godfrey (Arens Publications & Printing Corp., Covington, OH); Director — Tom Aird (Martinsburg (PA) Buyers Guide); Director — Blain Fowler (Camrose (AB) Booster); Director — Valerie Stokes (Lebanon (PA) Merchandiser); Director — Joe Green (Banner Publications, Pekin, IN); Director — Bill Gibbon (Crown Point (IN) Shopping News); Sergeant at Arms — Mary Nelson (West Fargo (ND) Midweek)
Elections held in Sept.

INTER AMERICAN PRESS ASSOCIATION — 2911 N.W. 39th St., Miami, FL 33142; tel (305) 634-2466
President — Alejandro Junco De la Vega (El Norte, Canada); 1st Vice Pres. — A Roy Megarry (The Globe and Mail); 2nd Vice Pres. — Raul E Kraiselburd (El Dia, La Plata, Argentina); Treasurer — Andres Garcia Gamboa (Novedades, Merida, Mexico); Secretary — Hector Davalos (Novedades, Mexico, D.F.); Exec. Dir. — W P Williamson Jr

INTERMARKET ASSOCIATION OF ADVERTISING AGENCIES — Communications Ctr., 1605 N. Main St., Dayton, OH 45405; tel (513) 278-0681; fax (513) 277-1723
Pres. — Walter Ohlmann

INTERNATIONAL ADVERTISING ASSN. INC. — 342 Madison Ave., Ste. 2000, New York, NY 10173; tel (212) 557-1133
World Pres.— Louis C Mendiola Codina (Group PMP, Mexico City, CEO); Sr. VP/World Pres.-Elect for 1996-98— Senyon Kim (Sonyon Communications, Seoul, Korea, Chmn./CEO); Sec.— Michael Reinarz (Visual Communications, Nestle S.A. Verey, Switzerland, Dir.); Treas.— Leon Hertz (News Corp., New York, Exec. VP); VP/Area Dir. Asia/Pacific— Gohei Kogure (Dentsu, Tokyo, CEO); VP/Area Dir. Europe— Ed Wessing (Mktg. Communications, ABN AMRO Bank, The Netherlands, VP); VP/Area Dir. Latin America— Geraldo Alonso Filho (Norton Publicidade, Sao Pablo, Brazil, Pres.); VP/Area Dir. Middle East/Africa — Talal Dhulaymi (Arab Radio and TV, Jeddah, Saudi Arabia); VP/Area Dir. USA/Canada— Les Margulis (BBDO New York, Sr. VP/Int'l. Media Dir.); Dir./Gen. — Norman Vale (Int'l. Adv. Assn. New York); Exec. Dir. — Richard M Corner (Int'l. Adv. Assn.)
Elections held every two years at the IAA World-Advertising Congress. The next World Congress will take place June 9-12, 1996 in Seoul, Korea.

Note: The IAA is the only global partnership of advertisers, agencies and media. The Association has 3,400 members in 86 countries, 99 corporate members, 53 organizational members and 59 chapters in 58 countries.

INTERNATIONAL ASSOCIATION OF BUSINESS COMMUNICATORS (IABC) — 1 Hallidie Plz., Ste. 600, San Francisco, CA 94102; tel (415) 433-3400
Pres./CEO — Elizabeth Allan (ABC, CAE); Chairman Exec. Board — Mike Heron
Elections held at international conference.

INTERNATIONAL LABOR COMMUNICATIONS ASSN. AFL-CIO-CLC — AFL-CIO Bldg., 815 16th St. NW, Ste. 4, Washington, DC 20006; tel (202) 637-5068
President — Leo Canty; Sec./Treas. — Susan L Phillips
Elections held biennially.

INTERNATIONAL NEWS AGENCY — 2445 Pine Tree Dr., Ste. 20, Miami Beach, FL 33140-4611; tel (305) 674-9746; fax (305) 674-1939
Editor-In-Chief — T M Mosberg; Exec. Ed. — C H Garvey; Mng. Ed. — Mary Quinn

INTERNATIONAL NEWSPAPER FINANCIAL EXECUTIVES — 11600 Sunrise Valley Dr., Reston, VA 22091; tel (703) 648-1160; fax (703) 476-5961
Past Pres. — R Scott Messer (A H Belo); President — Brian A Storey (Edmonton Journal); Vice Pres. — Dianna Williams (St. Petersburg (FL) Times); Vice Pres./Exec. Dir. — Robert J Kasabian (INFE); Treasurer — Robert D Carothers (Home News Enterprises); Secretary — James Filiggi (Billings (MT) Gazette)
Elections held in June.

INTERNATIONAL NEWSPAPER MARKETING ASSOCIATION INC. — 12770 Merit Dr., Ste. 330, Dallas, TX 75251; tel (214) 991-5900; fax (214) 991-3151
Exec. Dir. — Earl J Wilkinson; Membership Mgr. — Cathy Siegismund Olsson
Elections held in May.

INTERNATIONAL PREPRESS ASSOCIATION — 7200 France Ave. S., Ste. 327, Edina, MN 55435; tel (612) 896-1908
Pres. — Lowell Carlson; 1st Vice Pres. — Kim Kozel; 2nd Vice Pres. — Bernard Cote; Exec. Dir. — Henry Hatch; Tech. Dir. — Paul F Borth; Treas. — Robert Swan; Ed. — Bessie Halfacre
Elections held in Oct.

INTERNATIONAL PRESS CLUB OF CHICAGO (IPCC) — 222 W. Ontario, Ste. 502, Chicago, IL 60610-3695; tel (312) 787-2679; fax (312) 787-2680
President — Arnie Matanky (Near North News); Vice Pres. — Dr Jerry J Field; Treasurer — Gera-Lind Kolarik (Avon Books)

INTERNATIONAL PRESS INSTITUTE — Spiegelgasse 2, Vienna, A-1010; Austria; tel (431) 512-9011; fax (431) 512-9014
Dir. — Johann P Fritz; Chmn. American Committee — Andrew Barnes; Int'l. Chmn. — Peter Preston (UK)
Elections held every year on a rotation basis.

INTERNATIONAL SOCIETY OF WEEKLY NEWSPAPER EDITORS — South Dakota State Univ., Dept. of Journalism, Brookings, SD 57007; tel (605) 688-4171; fax (605) 688-4271
Pres. — Brian Mazza (Rocky Mountain House (AB) The Mountaineer); Vice Pres. — Vickie Canfield Peters (Albion (PA) News); Exec. Sec. — Richard W Lee
Elections held in July.

INVESTIGATIVE REPORTERS AND EDITORS — PO Box 838, Columbia, MO 65205; tel (314) 882-2042
Pres. — Deborah Nelson; Vice Pres. — Judy Miller; Sec. — Edward Delaney; Treas. — John Lindsay
Elections held in June.

J

JAPAN NEWSPAPER PUBLISHERS & EDITORS ASSOCIATION — The Newspaper Ctr., 11600 Sunrise Valley, Reston, VA 22091; tel (703) 648-1135; fax (703) 620-4557
North American Representative — Naoshi Hashimoto

K

KAPPA ALPHA MU HONORARY SOCIETY IN PHOTO JOURNALISM — School of Journalism, Neff Annex, Rm. 27, Columbia, MO 65201; tel (314) 882-8074/(314) 882-4882

Founder — Clifton C Edom (Univ. of Missouri); Pres. — Michael Hamtil; KAM Adviser — Loup Langton
An affiliate of the National Press Photographers Association.

KAPPA TAU ALPHA NATIONAL HONOR SOCIETY FOR JOURNALISM AND MASS COMMUNICATIONS — Univ. of Missouri, School of Journalism, 100 Neff Hall, Columbia, MO 65211; tel (573) 882-7685; fax (573) 882-4823
President — William Ryan; Vice Pres. — Karen List; Exec. Dir./Treas. — Dr Keith Sanders
Elections held every two years.

L

LEAGUE OF ADVERTISING AGENCIES INC. — 2 South End Ave., Ste. 4-C, New York, NY 10280; tel (212) 945-4990
President — Richard Lipman; Vice Pres. — Wendell Pope; Vice Pres. — Norma Vavolizza; Exec. Dir. — Mary C Boland; Treasurer — Lori Fabisiak; Secretary — Joan Sloser
Elections held in May.

LES HEBDOS REGIONAUX — 110 de la Barre, Bureau 212, Longueuil, QC J4K 1A3 Canada; tel (514) 651-2181
Pres. — Alain Guilbert; Vice Pres. — Gilles A Cerat; Gen. Dir. — Jean Longval; Sec. — Andree Wright
Elections held in June.

M

MEDIA CREDIT ASSOCIATION — 919 3rd Ave., New York, NY 10022; tel (212) 752-0055
Pres. — James R Guthrie; Chmn. — Peter D Jones; Vice Pres. — James E Van Meter; Treas. — Nancy Shapiro; Sec. — John Van de Merien
Elections held in March.

MUTUAL ADVERTISING AGENCY NETWORK — Landmark Ctr., 25700 Science Park Dr., Cleveland, OH 44122-7308; tel (216) 292-6609; fax (216) 292-6780
Pres. — Peter Langmack; 1st Vice Pres. — David Littlefield; 2nd Vice Pres. — David Lane; 3rd Vice Pres. — Robert Cook; Treas. — Kim Martiny
Elections held in Oct.

N

NATIONAL ADVERTISING AGENCY NETWORK — 245 5th Ave., Ste. 2103, New York, NY 10016; tel (212) 481-3022
Chmn. — William Loeffler; Pres. — Robert Purcell
Elections held in May.

NATIONAL ASSN. OF AGRICULTURAL JOURNALISTS — 312 Valley View Dr., Huron, OH 44839; tel (419) 433-5412
Pres. — Tim White; Exec. Sec./Treas. — Audrey Mackiewicz
Elections held in April.

NATIONAL ASSOCIATION OF BLACK JOURNALISTS — 11600 Sunrise Valley Dr., Reston, VA 22091; tel (703) 648-1270
Pres. — Dorothy Butler Gilliam; Past Pres. — Sidmel Estes-Sumpter; Vice Pres./Print — Jackie Jones; Vice Pres./Broadcast — Sheila Stainback; Sec. — Vanessa Williams; Treas. — Jackie Greene; Exec. Dir. — Walterene Swanston; Parliamentarian — Angelo Henderson

NATIONAL ASSOCIATION OF BROADCASTERS — 1771 N St. NW, Washington, DC 20036; tel (202) 429-5350; fax (202) 429-5406
Pres./CEO — Edward O Fritts; Exec. Vice Pres./CFO — Kenneth D Almgren; Sr. Vice Pres./Public Affairs — Walt Wurfel
Elections held in March.

NATIONAL ASSN. OF CREDIT MANAGEMENT — 8815 Ctr. Park Dr., Ste. 200, Columbia, MO 21045-2158; tel (410) 740-5560; fax (410) 740-5574
President— Paul J Mignini Jr(CAE); Ed. & Pub. — Cindy Tursman; VP/Education — Robin D Schauseil; Treas./CPA — James E Vanghel
Elections held in May.

NATIONAL ASSOCIATION OF HISPANIC JOURNALISTS — 1193 National Press Building, 529 14th St. NW, Washington, DC 20045; tel (202) 662-7145; fax (202) 662-7144
President — Gilbert Bailon (Dallas Morning News); Vice Pres./Print — Carol Castaneda (USA Today); Vice Pres./Broadcast — Rodrigo Sierra (WGN-Radio); Financial Officer — Rick Martinez (Sacramento Bee); Secretary — Sylvia Martinez (Dallas Morning News)

NATIONAL ASSN. OF PRINTERS AND LITHOGRAPHERS — 780 Palisade Ave., Teaneck, NJ 07666; tel (201) 342-0700
Chmn. — William E Mullins (CME, CFME); Vice Chmn. — Donald Duncanson (CBPE, CFME); Pres. — I Gregg Van Wert;Exec. Vice Pres.— Joseph P Truncale(CAE); Marketing Dir. — Rhona Bronson
Elections held in Oct.

NATIONAL ASSN. OF REAL ESTATE EDITORS (NAREE) — 1003 N.W. 6th Terrace, Boca Raton, FL 33486; tel (407) 391-3599; fax (407) 391-0099
Pres. — Glen Fischer (MetroAmerica Publishing); 1st VP — Corrie Anders (San Francisco Examiner); 2nd VP — Patty Doyle (Patty Doyle Public Relations); Treas. — Ellen James Martin (Universal Press Syndicate/Baltimore Sun); Sec. — James McAlexander (Landmark Designs Inc.); COB — Mary Doyle-Kimball (Self-Syndicated Columnist)

NATIONAL ASSOCIATION OF SCIENCE WRITERS — PO Box 294, Greenlawn, NY 11740; tel (516) 757-5664
President — Laurie Garrett (Long Island Newsday); Admn. Sec. — Diane McGurgan; VP/Pres.-Elect — Richard Harris (NPR); Secretary— Paul Raeburn (AP); Treasurer — Joe Palca (NPR)
Elections held every two years in October.

NATIONAL CONFERENCE OF EDITORIAL WRITERS — 6223 Executive Blvd., Rockville, MD 20852; tel (301) 984-3015
Pres. — Rena Pederson (Dallas Morning News); Vice Pres. — Sue Ryon (Milwaukee Journal); Treas. — Morgan McGinley (New London (CT) The Day); Sec. — Susan Albright (Minneapolis Star Tribune)

NATIONAL FEDERATION OF HISPANIC OWNED NEWSPAPERS — 685 S. Hwy. 427, Longwood, FL 32750-6403; tel (407) 767-0561; fax (407) 767-5478
President — Manuel A Toro

NATIONAL FEDERATION OF PRESS WOMEN — 4510 W. 89th St., Ste. 110, Prairie Village, KS 66207-2282; tel (913) 341-0165; fax (913) 341-6912
Pres. — Ruth Neil Anna; 1st Vice Pres. — Linnea K Rounds; 2nd Vice Pres. — Donna Hunt; 3rd Vice Pres. — Ella Wright; Treas. — Donna Douglas Penticuff; Sec. — Catherine Petrini
Elections held odd years in June.

NATIONAL NEWSPAPER ASSOCIATION — 1525 Wilson Blvd., Ste. 550, Arlington, VA 22209; tel (703) 907-7900
Pres. — R Jack Fishman (Lakeway Publishers); Past President — Michael A Parta (New York Mills (MN Herald); Vice Chmn. — Roy J Eaton (Decatur (TX) Wise County Messenger); Treas. — Dalton C Wright (Lebanon Publishing Co.)
Elections held in Sept.

NATIONAL NEWSPAPER PUBLISHERS ASSN. BLACK PRESS OF AMERICA — 3200 13th St. NW, Washington, DC 20010; tel (202) 588-8764
President — Dorothy Leavell (Chicago Crusader); 1st Vice Pres. — Hardy Brown (Black Voice News); 2nd Vice Pres. — Terry Jones (Data News Weekly); Secretary — Jane Woods-Miller (St. Louis Sentinel); Treasurer — Janis Ware (Atlanta Voice)
Elections held every two years in June.

NATIONAL PAPER TRADE ASSN. INC. — 111 Great Neck Rd., Great Neck, NY 11021; tel (516) 829-3070
Vice Chmn. — Rolf Turnquist; Pres. — John J Buckely; Chmn. — Tucker Jones
Elections held in Oct.

NATIONAL PRESS CLUB — National Press Building, 14th and F St., Washington, DC 20045; tel (202) 662-7500
President — Monroe (Bud) Karmin (Bloomberg Business News); Vice Pres. — Sonja Hillgren (Farm Journal); Secretary — Wendy Koch (Gannett News Service); Treasurer — Mick Rood (Freelance); Gen. Mgr. — William O Vose; Library Dir. — Barbara Vandegrift; Membership Sec. — Christopher Rosche (Scripps League Newspapers)
Elections held in Dec.

NATIONAL PRESS PHOTOGRAPHERS ASSN. INC. — 3200 Croasdaile Dr., Ste. 306, Durham, NC 27705; tel (919) 383-7246; fax (919) 383-7261
Pres. — Steve Sweitzer; Past Pres. — Joe Traver; Vice Pres. — Jim McNay; Exec. Dir. — Charles H Cooper; Sec. — David Lutman
Elections held in June.

NATIONAL RETAIL FEDERATION — 325 7th St. NW, Liberty Pl., Ste. 1000, Washington, DC 20004; tel (202) 783-7971
President — Tracy Mullin
Elections held in Jan.

NATIONAL SCHOLASTIC PRESS ASSOCIATION — Univ. of Minnesota, 330 21st Ave. S., Minneapolis, MN 55455-0478; tel (612) 625-8335; fax (612) 626-0720
Pres. — Daniel Wackman; Exec. Dir. — Tom E Rolnicki; Assoc. Dir. — Annie Christman

NATIONAL WRITERS CLUB — 1450 S. Havana St., Ste. 424, Aurora, CO 80012; tel (303) 751-7844
Pres. — Carole Williams; Exec. Dir. — Sandy Whelchel

NATIVE AMERICAN JOURNALISTS ASSOCIATION — 1433 Franklin Ave. E., Ste. 11, Minneapolis, MN 55404; tel (612) 874-8833; fax (612) 874-9007
Pres./Board of Dir. — Karen Lincoln-Michel; Exec. Dir. — Gordon Regguinti; Vice Pres. — Ruth Denny; Treas. — Nancy Butterfield

NEWSPAPER ADVERTISING SALES ASSOC. — Newhouse Newspapers, 140 E. 45th St., New York, NY 10017; tel (212) 697-8020
President — Robert Schoenbacher (Newhouse Newspapers); Exec. Vice Pres. — Sheldon Lyons (Gannett Advertising Sales); Vice Pres. — Wayne Kuhn (Chicago Sun Times); Treasurer — Gary Tozzi (Papert Companies); Secretary — Jarvis Coffin (NAM LA Times)
Elections held in June.

NEWSPAPER ASSOCIATION OF AMERICA — The Newspaper Center, 11600 Sunrise Valley Dr., Reston, VA 22091-1412; tel (703) 648-1000; fax (703) 620-4557
Pres./CEO — Cathleen P Black; Immed. Past Chmn. — Charles T Brumback (Tribune Co.); Chairman — Uzal H Martz Jr; Vice Chmn. — John J Curley (Gannett Co.); Sr. VP/Communications — Debra Shriver; Dir./Public Relations — Paul Luthringer; CFO — Mary Anne Kanter; Chief Marketing Officer — Nick Cannistro; Secretary — David C Cox (Cowles Media); Treasurer — Richard D Gottlieb (Lee Enterprises); Dir./Membership Svcs. — Kimberly Lysik; Dir./Advanced Computer Science — John W Iobst, Ph D
Elections held in April/May.

NEWSPAPER ASSOCIATION MANAGERS INC. — PO Box 28875, Atlanta, GA 30358; tel (404) 256-0444; fax (404) 252-9135
Pres. — David L Bennett (Illinois Press Assn.); Immed. Past Pres. — Linda I Falkman (Minnesota Newspaper Assn.); Vice Pres. — J LeRoy Yorgason
Elections held in Aug.

NEWSPAPER GUILD (AFL-CIO-CLC) — 8611 Second Ave., Silver Spring, MD 20910; tel (301) 585-2990
Int'l. Chairperson — Carol D Rothman; Pres. — Linda Foley; Sec./Treas. — Bernie Lunzer

NEWSPAPER PERSONNEL RELATIONS ASSN. — c/o Society for Human Resource Management, 606 N. Washington St., Alexandria, VA 22314; tel (703) 548-3440 Ext. 4710
President — James P Spangler; Sec./Treas. — Robert E Carlquist; Board Members ; Mgr. Workforce Mgmt. — Gerald Alcantar (Times-Mirror Co.); Human Resources Director (SPHR) — Edith Auslander (TNI Partners); Corporate HR Director — Patricia Houck (Shaw Newspapers); VP Human Resources — Timothy Hughes (Cox Enterprises); VP/Director HR — Frank McDonald (Richmond (VA) Newspapers); Dir. Employee Relations — Catherine Paffenroth (Ottaway Newspapers); Dir. HR — Steven Robinson (Tacoma (WA) News-Tribune); Employee & Industrial Labor Relations Dir. — J Hector Rodriguez (Thomson Newspapers); Asst. Dir. HR — Donald Zimmerman (Providence (RI) Journal Co.)
Elections held in June.

NEWSPAPER PURCHASING MANAGEMENT ASSN. INC. — 401 N. Wabash Ave., Chicago, IL 60611; tel (312) 321-2264
Pres.— Sharon Hite (Scripps Howard Supply Co., Cincinnati, OH); Pres. Elect — Theresa Sinner (Denver (CO) Rocky Mountain News); Vice Pres.— Mark Grunlund (Median Supply Co., Staten Island, NY); Sec. — Dennis Radtke (Minneapolis Star Tribune); Treas. — Joan Salter (Louisville (KY) Courier-Journal)
Elections held in April.

NPES, THE ASSOCIATION FOR SUPPLIERS OF PRINTING AND PUBLISHING TECHNOLOGIES — 1899 Preston White Dr., Reston, VA 22091-4367; tel (703) 264-7200; fax (703) 620-0994
Chairman — Richard Stevens; President — Regis J Delmontagne; Dir. Commun. — Carol J Hurlburt
Elections held at fall meeting.

O

ORGANIZATION OF NEWS OMBUDSMEN — PO Box 15779, Sacramento, CA 95852; tel (916) 442-8050; fax (916) 321-1996
Pres. — Lynne Glaser (Fresno (CA) Bee); Vice Pres.— Phil Record (Fort Worth Star-Telegram); Sec./Treas. — Art Nauman (Sacramento Bee); Ex Officio — John Sweeney (Wilmington (DE) News Journal)
Elections held in May.

OUTDOOR ADVERTISING ASSN. OF AMERICA — 1850 M St. NW, Ste. 1040, Washington, DC 20036; tel (202) 371-5566
Chairman — Bill Nassau; President — Nancy Fletcher

OUTDOOR WRITERS ASSN. OF AMERICA INC. — 2017 Cato Ave., Ste. 101, State College, PA 16801; tel (814) 234-1011
COB — Glenn Sapir; Pres. — Mark LaBarbera; Pres.-Elect — Judd Cooney; 2nd Vice Pres. — Betty Lou Fegely; 3rd Vice Pres. — Tom Wharton
Elections held in June.

OVERSEAS PRESS CLUB OF AMERICA INC. — 320 E. 42nd St., Mezzanine, New York, NY 10017; tel (212) 983-4655; fax (212) 983-4692
President — William J Holstein; 1st Vice Pres. — Norman Schorr; 2nd Vice Pres. — Janice Castro; 3rd Vice Pres. — John Corporon; Secretary — Felice Levin; Treasurer — George Burns
Elections held in the spring.

OVERSEAS WRITERS — 2071 National Press Bldg., Washington, DC 20045; tel (301) 229-2387
Pres.— Don Oberdorfer (Distinguished Journalist in Residence, Johns Hopkins University); Vice Pres. — Carol Giacomo (Reuters); Sec. — Carlotta Anderson

P

PRINTING, PUBLISHING & MEDIA WORKERS SECTOR, COMMUNICATION WORKERS OF AMERICA — 501 3rd St. NW, Washington, DC 20001-2760; tel (202) 434-1238
President — William J Boarman
Elections will be held at CWA convention in 1996.

PROFESSIONAL FOOTBALL WRITERS OF AMERICA (PFWA) — 12154 Fahrpark Ln., St. Louis, MO 63146; tel (314) 991-2791
Pres. — Len Pasquarelli (Atlanta Journal-Constitution); Vice Pres. — Steve Schoenfeld (Arizona Republic); Vice Pres. — John Clayton (Tacoma (WA) News Tribune); Sec./ Treas. — Howard Balzer (Pro Football Weekly)
Elections held in Jan.

PROMOTION MARKETING ASSN. OF AMERICA — 275 Park Ave. S., 11th Fl., New York, NY 10010; tel (212) 420-1100; fax (212) 533-7622
Chmn. Emeritus — H Pierce Pelouze III; Chairman — Frances Caci; Exec. Dir. — John A Kalemkerian; Secretary — N Jean Washington; Treasurer — Robert E Balzer
Elections held in June.

Assns., national, international

PROMOTIONAL PRODUCTS ASSOCIATION INT'L. — 3125 Skyway Cir. N., Irving, TX 75038; tel (214) 252-0404
President — H Ted Olson; Vice Pres. — Lindsay Schieffelin

PUBLIC RELATIONS SOCIETY OF AMERICA INC. — 33 Irving Pl., New York, NY 10003-2376; tel (212) 995-2230; fax (212) 995-0757
Past Pres. — John R Beardsley (APR); Pres. — Luis W Morales (APR); Pres. Elect — Debra A Miller, Ed D (APR); Treas. — Mary Lynn Cusick (APR); Sec. — Samuel L Waltz Jr (APR); COO — Ray Gaulke
Elections held during the fall assembly.

Q

QUILL AND SCROLL SOCIETY — School of Journalism and Mass Comm., University of Iowa, Iowa City, IA 52242-1528; tel (319) 335-5795; fax (319) 335-5210
Chmn. — George H Gallup Jr (The Gallup Poll, Princeton); Exec. Dir. — Richard P Johns (School of Journalism, Univ. of Iowa)

R

RADIO TELEVISION NEWS DIRECTORS ASSN. — 1000 Connecticut Ave. NW, Ste. 615, Washington, DC 20036; tel (202) 659-6510
Chairman — Marci Burdick; Chmn.-Elect — Bill Yeager
Elections held in Sept.

REGIONAL REPORTERS ASSOCIATION — 1092 National Press Building, Washington, DC 20045; tel (202) 879-6710; fax (202) 879-6712
President — Sylvia Smith (Fort Wayne (IN) Journal-Gazette); Vice Pres. — Ellyn Ferguson (Gannett News Service); Treasurer — Maureen Groppe (Thomson News Service); Secretary — Randy Wynn (Thomson News Service)

RELIGION NEWSWRITERS ASSOCIATION — Fort Worth Star-Telegram, 400 W. 7th St., Fort Worth, TX 76102; tel (817) 390-7707
Pres. — Jim W Jones (Fort Worth Star-Telegram); 1st Vice Pres. — Richard Dujardin (Providence (RI) Journal-Bulletin); 2nd Vice Pres. — Cecile Holmes White (Houston Chronicle); Treas. — Judy Weidman (Religious News Service); Sec. — Joan Connell (Newhouse News Service)

REPORTERS COMMITTEE FOR FREEDOM OF THE PRESS — 1101 Wilson Blvd., Ste. 1910, Arlington, VA 22209; tel (800) 336-4243/(703) 807-2100; fax (703) 807-2109
Exec. Dir. — Jane E Kirtley; Exec. Committee — Jack Nelson; Exec. Committee — Diane Camper; Exec. Committee — Hodding Carter

S

SALES AND MARKETING EXECUTIVES INTERNATIONAL — Statler Office Tower, Ste. 458, Cleveland, OH 44115; tel (216) 771-6650
CME, Pres. — John C Lennon Jr; CSE, Exec. Dir. — L Bryant Barry; CSE, Exec. Dir. — Jack I Criswell
Elections held in June.

SOCIETY OF AMERICAN BUSINESS EDITORS AND WRITERS — Univeristy of Missouri, 76 Gannett Hall, Columbia, MO 65211; tel (314) 882-7862; fax (314) 882-9002
Pres. — Jodi Schneider; Vice Pres. — Myron Kandel; Treas. — Janine Latus Musick; Treas. — Henry Dubroff; Sec. — Susan Wells
Elections held in May.

SOCIETY OF AMERICAN TRAVEL WRITERS INC. — 4101 Lake Boone Trail, Ste. 201, Raleigh, NC 27607; tel (919) 787-5181
Pres. — Barbara Gillam (New York Travel Writer/Photographer); Travel Editor — Jack Schnedler (Chicago Sun Times); Sec./Treas. — Joyce Martin (Hill & Knowlton); Admin. Coordinator — Susan Rexer

SOCIETY OF ENVIRONMENTAL JOURNALISTS — PO Box 27280, Philadelphia, PA 19118; tel (215) 247-9710; fax (215) 247-9712
Pres. — Emila Askari (Detroit Free Press); Vice Pres. — Rae Tyson (USA Today); Vice Pres. — Tom Meersman (Minneapolis Star Tribune); Sec. — Kevin Carmody (Chicago Daily Southtown); Treas. — Steve Cuwood (NPR's Living on Earth); Exec. Dir. — Beth Parke
Elections held in Oct.

SOCIETY OF NEWSPAPER DESIGN — The Newspaper Center, PO Box 4075, Reston, VA 22090; tel (703) 620-1083; fax (703) 620-4557
Pres. — Jim Jennings (Newspaper Consultant); 1st Vice Pres. — Neal Pattison (Albuquerque Tribune); 2nd Vice Pres. — Lynn Staley (Newsweek); Treas. — Ed Kohorst (Dallas Morning News); Sec. — Jean Moxam (Kansas City Star); Exec. Dir. — Ray Chattman
Elections held in Oct.

SOCIETY OF PROFESSIONAL JOURNALISTS — 16 S. Jackson St., PO Box 77, Greencastle, IN 46135; tel (317) 653-3333; fax (317) 653-4631
National Pres. — Reginald Stuart; Exec. Dir. — Gregory Christopher; Dir. Communications — Julie Grimes

SOCIETY OF THE SILURIANS — c/o Paul Buiar Assoc., 155 E. 31st St., Ste. 8-F, New York, NY 10016; tel (212) 532-0887
Pres. — Martin J Steadman; 1st Vice Pres. — Myron Kandel; Sec. — Bernard Stengren; Treas. — Leo Meindl
Elections held in April.

T

TECHNICAL ASSN. OF THE GRAPHIC ARTS — 68 Lomb Memorial Dr., Rochester, NY 14623-5604; tel (716) 475-7470; fax (716) 475-2250
Pres. — Richard Fisch; Exec. Vice Pres. — John Long; Tech. Vice Pres. — Richard Holub; Membership Vice Pres. — Jeannette Truncellito; Managing Dir. — Karen E Lawrence; Sec./Treas. — Miles Southworth
Elections held in April.

TRANS-CANADIAN ADVERTISING AGENCY NETWORK — 3390 N. York, Toronto, ON M2M 3S3 Canada; tel (416) 221-8883; fax (416) 221-8260
Past Pres. — David Hawkins (Hawk Communications Inc.); Dir. — Roald Thomas (Palmer Jarvis); Sr. Vice VP — Cam Cooper (Cooper Quine & Fraser Inc.); Sr. Exec. VP — I B Wallace (Ian B Wallace Marketing Inc.); Exec. VP — Al Albania (Acart Comm.); Exec. VP — Bruce Smith (Smith Radimer Communications); VP — Dan LeBrun (Great River Advertising & Design); Man. Dir.— W S H Whitehead (Whitehead Inc., Treas.); Chairman — L Foley, I.A.A.A. — B Sefton (Video Impact Inc.); Dir. — P Bleau (Bleau & Assoc. Inc.); Dir. — B Brooks (Brooks Mktg. Resources Inc.); Dir. — B A Chadwick (Kelley Advertising Inc.); Pres. — T M Harris (Harris Mktg. Communications Inc.); Dir. — J R Michener (Campbell & Michener Ltd.); Dir. — J P Mallon (Mallon, Hudolin & Assoc.); Affiliation — T H Mills, MTD Communications Inc.; Affiliation — The Newlands Partnership; Affiliation — MacMillan Advertising Ltd.; Affiliation — Shinwa International Inc.; Affiliation — Intermarket Association of Advertising Agencies; Affiliation — R A Quarry, Quarry Advertising Agency Ltd.; Affiliation — H Lowry, The Quarto Group; Affiliation — Laykin Communications

TYPOGRAPHERS INTERNATIONAL ASSOCIATION — 84 Park Ave., Flemington, NJ 08822; tel (908) 782-4635; fax (908) 782-4671
President — Jacques Cangelose; Treasurer — Carmen Gutierrez-Bolger; Ed./Adv. Mgr. — David Fort
Elections held in Oct.

U

UNITED NATIONS CORRESPONDENTS ASSOCIATION — United Nations, Rm. 486, New York, NY 10017; tel (212) 593-3407; fax (212) 371-4054
Pres. — Ian Williams (Tribune & New York Observer); 1st Vice Pres. — J Tuyet Nguyen (UPI); 2nd Vice Pres. — Masood Haider (Dawn, Academic File); 3rd Vice Pres. — Zhaolong Xia (Xinhua); Sec. — Ted Morello (Far East Economic Review); Treas. — Behzat Baris (IKA News Agency); Exec. Cmte. Mem. at Large — Judith Aita (USIA Press Service); Exec. Cmte. Mem. at Large — Ricardo Alday (Mexican News Agency); Exec. Cmte. Mem. at Large — Louis Foy (France Soir); Exec. Cmte. Mem. at Large — Azim Mian (The News, Daily Jang); Exec. Cmte. Mem. at Large — Frances Mourani (BBC); Exec. Cmte. Mem. at Large — Julia Preston (Washington Post); Exec. Cmte. Mem. at Large — Ruth Pearson (Business Week); Exec. Cmte. Mem. at Large — Rene Slama (Agence France-Press); Exec. Cmte. Mem. at Large — Norberto L Svarzman (Televisa)
Elections held in Dec.

W

WINNIPEG PRESS CLUB — Marlborough Hotel, 331 Smith St., Winnipeg, MB R3B 2G9 Canada; tel (204) 957-1188
Past Pres. — Lionel Ditz; Pres. — Kelly Dehn; Vice Pres./Admin. — Kelly Taylor; Treas. — Don Wilkie; Sec. — Carolyn Rickey
Elections held in Feb.

WOMEN IN COMMUNICATIONS INC. — 3717 Columbia Pike, Ste. 310, Arlington, VA 22201; tel (703) 920-5555
Pres.-Elect — Carol Fenstermacher; Immed. Past Pres. — Anne Greenberg; President — Jennifer Engle; Vice Pres. — Hale Sheikerz (Student Affairs); Vice Pres. — Wendy Bishop (Membership); Vice Pres. — Cathy Coers Frank (Programs); Vice Pres.— Ann Taylor (Professional Development)
Elections held at national annual business meeting in Sept

ASSOCIATIONS, CLUBS & PRESS CLUBS—CITY, STATE & REGIONAL

A

ADVERTISING CLUB OF GREATER BOSTON — 38 Newbury St., Boston, MA 02116; tel (617) 262-1100
Exec. Dir. — Elizabeth G Cook; Assoc. Dir. — Anne Bear

ADVERTISING CLUB OF NEW YORK — 235 Park Ave. S., New York, NY 10003; tel (212) 533-8080
President — Ronald S Fierman; Vice Pres. — R Jeffrey Petersen
Elections held in June.

ALABAMA ASSOCIATED PRESS ASSOCIATION — 116 S. McDonough St., Montgomery, AL 36104; tel (334) 262-5947; fax (334) 265-7177
Pres. — Joe Distelhein (Huntsville Times); Secretary — Kendal Weaver (AP)
Elections held at spring awards convention.

ALABAMA PRESS ASSOCIATION — 3324 Independence Dr., Ste. 200, Birmingham, AL 35209; tel (205) 871-7737; fax (205) 871-7740
President — Linda Breedlove; 1st Vice Pres. — Doug Pearson; 2nd Vice Pres. — Mike Kelley
Elections held in Feb.

ALASKA NEWSPAPER ASSOCIATION — PO Box 7900, Ketchikan, AK 99901; tel (907) 225-3157
President — Teena Williams (Ketchikan Daily News); Secretary — Dorothy Williams
Elections held in May.

ALBERTA WEEKLY NEWSPAPER ASSOCIATION — 4445 Calgary Trail S., Ste. 360, Edmonton, AB T6H 5R7, Canada; tel (800) 282-6903/(403) 434-8746; fax (403) 438-8356
President — Gordon Scott; 1st Vice Pres. — Richard Holmes; 2nd Vice Pres. — Joan Plaxton; Sec. — Frank McTighe

ALLIED DAILY NEWSPAPERS OF WASHINGTON — PO Box 29, Olympia, WA 98507-0029; tel (360) 943-9960; fax (360) 943-9962
Exec. Dir. — Rowland Thompson

ARIZONA ASSOCIATED PRESS MANAGING EDITORS ASSOCIATION — 500 N. Third St., Ste. 120, Phoenix, AZ 85004; tel (602) 258-8934
Chairman — Bobbie Jo Buel (Arizona Daily Star); Chief of Bureau — Charlotte Porter
Elections held in the summer.

ARIZONA NEWSPAPERS ASSOCIATION — 1001 N. Central Ave., Phoenix, AZ 85004; tel (602) 261-7655; fax (602) 261-7525
President — Don Hatfield (Tuscon Citizen); 1st Vice Pres. — Alan Cruikshank (Times of Fountain Hills); 2nd Vice Pres. — Blake DeWitt (Western Newspapers Inc.); Sec./Treas. — Bret McKeann (Sun City Independent); Exec. Dir. — John F Fearing
Elections held in Nov.

ARKANSAS ASSOCIATED PRESS — Associated Press, 1101 W. Second, Little Rock, AR 72201-2003; tel (501) 374-5536
Chief of Bureau — Bill Simmons

ARKANSAS PRESS ASSOCIATION — 1701 Broadway, Little Rock, AR 72206; tel (501) 374-1500; fax (501) 374-7509
President — Ron Wylie (Clarksville); Exec. Dir. — Dennis Schick
Elections held in Feb.

ARKANSAS PRESS WOMEN ASSOCIATION INC. — 21 Helen Cir., Batesville, AR 72501; tel (501) 698-1673/(501) 793-2383
President — Debbie Miller; 1st Vice Pres. — Carol S Reiner
Elections held in the fall of even numbered years.

ASSOCIATED COLLEGIATE PRESS — University of Minnesota, 330 21st Ave. S., Minneapolis, MN 55455-0478; tel (612) 625-8335; fax (612) 626-0720
President — Daniel Wackman; Exec. Dir. — Tom E Rolnicki; Assoc. Dir. — Annie Christman

ASSOCIATED PRESS ASSOCIATION OF CALIFORNIA-HAWAII-NEVADA — 221 S. Figueroa St., Ste. 300, Los Angeles, CA 90012; tel (213) 626-1200
New York Pres. — Lou Boccardi; Bureau Chief — Andrew Lippman; News Ed. — Steve Loeper

ASSOCIATED PRESS/CALIFORNIA-NEVADA NEWS EXECUTIVES — 221 S. Figueroa St., Ste. 300, Los Angeles, CA 90012; tel (213) 626-1200
Chairman — Frank Daniels Jr; Bureau Chief — Andrew Lippman; San Francisco Bureau Chief — Dan Day
Elections held in May.

ASSOCIATED PRESS/OKLAHOMA NEWS EXECUTIVES — 525 Central Park Dr., Ste. 202, Oklahoma City, OK 73105; tel (405) 525-2121
President — Gene Triplett (Oklahoma City Daily Oklahoman); Past Pres. — Mike McCormick (Shawnee News-Star); Bureau Chief/Sec./Treas. — Lindel Hutson
Elections held in May.

B

BRITISH COLUMBIA & YUKON COMMUNITY NEWSPAPERS ASSOCIATION — 230-1380 Burrard St., Vancouver, BC V6Z 2B7, Canada; tel (604) 669-9222; fax (604) 684-4713
President — Steve Houston (Royal City Record Now); 1st Vice Pres. — Penny Graham (Revelstoke Times Review); 2nd Vice Pres. — Duane Geddes (Surrey North Delta Leader); Sec./Treas. — Tom Siba (Delta Optimist); Exec. Dir. — Allan Treleaven

Assns. city, state, regional VII-7

C

CALIFORNIA NEWSPAPER ADVERTISING EXECUTIVES ASSOCIATION (SOUTHERN DIV.) — PO Box 440, Bakersfield, CA 93302; tel (805) 395-7227
President — Bartley C Green (San Francisco Newspaper Agency); Vice Pres. — John Bennett (San Bernardino Sun); Treasurer — John Wells (Bakersfield Californian); Secretary — Bob Hess (North County Blade Citizen)

CALIFORNIA NEWSPAPER PUBLISHERS ASSOCIATION INC. — 1225 8th St., Ste. 260, Sacramento, CA 95814; tel (916) 443-5991; fax (916) 443-6447
President — Richard Wallace; Pres.-Elect — Roy Herburger; Vice Pres. — Frank Whittaker; Exec. Dir. — Jack B Bates
Changes effective in Feb.

CALIFORNIA PRESS ASSOCIATION — 657 Mission St., Ste. 602, San Francisco, CA 94105; tel (415) 777-6761; fax (415) 362-6208
President — R David Threshie Jr (Orange County Register); 1st Vice Pres. — James L Lyons (Porterville Recorder); 2nd Vice Pres. — John H Clinton Jr (San Mateo Times); Sec./Treas. — Anthony Newhall (San Francisco Chronicle)
Elections held in Dec.

CALIFORNIA PRESS PHOTOGRAPHERS ASSOCIATION INC. — 3512 14th St., Riverside, CA 92501-3878; tel (909) 684-1200
President — Steve Medd; 1st Vice Pres. — Dave Nielsen; 2nd Vice Pres. — Joel Zwink; Sec./Treas. — Craig Kohlross
Elections held in June every two years.

CAL WESTERN CIRCULATION MANAGERS ASSOCIATION — PO Box 338, Chester, CA 96020; tel (916) 259-2346
President — Lauren Flynn (Los Angeles (CA) Wall Street Journal); Pres.-Elect — John Reichard (Sierra Vista (AZ) Herald); 1st Vice Pres. — Rovert Perona (Riverside (CA) Press-Enterprise); 2nd Vice Pres. — Leslie Smith (Los Angeles (CA) La Opinion)
Elections held in Oct.

CENTRAL STATES CIRCULATION MANAGERS ASSOCIATION — PO Box 1686, Cedar Rapids, IA 52406-1686; tel (319) 366-0959; fax (319) 366-0959
Chairman — Don Michel (Cedar Rapids (IA) Gazette); President — Nick Nicks (La Crosse (WI) Tribune); 1st Vice Pres. — Geoffrey Vanderlin (Dixon (IL) Telegraph); 2nd Vice Pres. — Larry Gray (Louisville (KY) Courier-Journal)
Elections held in March.

COLORADO ASSOCIATED PRESS EDITORS AND REPORTERS — 1444 Wazee St., Ste. 130, Denver, CO 80202-1395; tel (303) 825-0123
President — Gary Burns (Boulder Daily Camera); Vice Pres. — Bill Spencer (Fort Morgan Times); Sec./Treas. — Joe McGowan Jr (AP)
Elections held in Feb.

COLORADO PRESS ASSOCIATION — The Press Bldg., 1336 Glenarm Pl., Denver, CO 80204; tel (303) 571-5117
Chairman — Jean Gray; President — Bill Kezziah; Secretary — Jacque Scott; Exec. Dir. — Ed Otte
Elections held in Feb.

CONNECTICUT ASSOCIATED PRESS MANAGING EDITORS ASSOCIATION — Associated Press, 55 Farmington Ave., Ste. 402, Hartford, CT 06105; tel (203) 246-6876
President — Judith W Brown (New Britain Herald); Vice Pres. — James Smith (Meriden Record Journal); Sec./Treas. — Mary Anne Rhyne (AP)

CONNECTICUT DAILY NEWSPAPERS ASSOCIATION — 24 Bailey Ave., Ste. 1, Ridgefield, CT 06877; tel (203) 438-4434; fax (203) 438-0158
President — Richard H King (Hartford Courant); 1st Vice Pres. — B J Frazier (Norwalk Hour); 2nd Vice Pres. — William J Rush (New Haven Register); Sec./Treas. — Wayne Shephard (Danbury News-Times); Gen. Counsel — Eileen McGann
Elections held in April.

CONNECTICUT PRESS CLUB — 4 Forest Dr., Westport, CT 06880; tel (203) 259-2618
President — Lori Moody; 1st Vice Pres. — Doris Skutch; Treasurer — Wilma Lauricella; Secretary — Kristi Vaughan
Elections held annually.

D

DELAWARE PRESS ASSOCIATION — See Maryland-DC Listing.

DELAWARE PRESS WOMEN — 105 Front St., Wyoming, DE 19934; tel (302) 697-1025
President — Kay Bailey
Elections held in Nov. of odd numbered years.

DISTRICT OF COLUMBIA PRESS ASSOCIATION — See Maryland-DC Listing.

E

EASTERN SKI WRITERS ASSOCIATION — PO Box 608, Bedford, MA 01730; tel (617) 275-0977
President — Richard Muello; 1st Vice Pres. — Tommy Hine; 2nd Vice Pres. — Phil Johnson

F

FLORIDA NEWSPAPER ADVERTISING & MARKETING EXECUTIVES — 8759 Baypointe Dr., Tampa, FL 33615; tel (813) 882-4979
Immed. Past Pres. — Joe Gess (Tampa Tribune); Exec. Sec. — Sandy Osteen; President — Andy Kohot (Creative Newspaper Concepts); 1st Vice Pres. — Lucy Talley (Lakeland Ledger); 2nd Vice Pres. — Eric Moody (The Newspaper Network); Secretary — Dale Bowen (Citrus County Chronicle); Treasurer — Greg Anderson (Stuart News)

FLORIDA PRESS ASSOCIATION — 336 E. College Ave., Ste. 103, Tallahassee, FL 32301-1554; tel (904) 222-5790; fax (904) 222-4498
Chairman — Bob Vedder; Pres. — Tom Giuffrida; Vice Pres. — Richard Hitt; Treas. — Gerry Mulligan; Exec. Dir. — Dick Shelton
Elections held in June.

FLORIDA PRESS WOMEN — 606 Faulkner St., New Smyrna Beach, FL 32168; tel (904) 427-1087/(904) 428-9001
President — Cathy J Vaughn; Vice Pres. — Jeanne Tonkin; Treasurer — Jane Lepley
Elections held in April.

FLORIDA SOCIETY OF NEWSPAPER EDITORS — 336 E. College Ave., Ste. 103, Tallahassee, FL 32301; tel (813) 953-7755
Pres. — Diane McFarlin (Sarasota Herald-Tribune); Vice Pres. — Lawrence McConnell
Elections held at June convention.

FREEDOM OF INFORMATION FOUNDATION OF TEXAS — 400 S. Record St., 6th Fl., Dallas, TX 75202; tel (214) 977-6658
President — Cathy Martindale (Amarillo Globe); Vice Pres. — Paul Watler (Jenkens & Gilchrist, Attorney); Treas.— Laura Peterson Elkend (Locke Purnell Rain Harrell, Attorney); Sec. — Keith Shelton (University of North Texas, Journalist in Residence); Immed. Past Pres. — Thomas Leatherbury (Vinson & Elkins, Attorney); Past Pres. — Jack Loftis (Houston Chronicle); Past Pres. — Ralph Langer (Dallas Morning News); Exec. Dir. — Nancy E Monson
Elections held in Dec.

G

GEORGIA PRESS ASSOCIATION — 3066 Mercer Univ. Dr., Ste. 200, Atlanta, GA 30341-4137; tel (770) 454-6776
Exec. Dir. — Robin Rhodes; Pres. — Mike Buffington (Jefferson Jackson Herald); Vice Pres. — Billy Fleming (Blakely Early County News); Treas. — Rick Thomas (Macon Telegraph)
Elections held at annual convention in June.

GREAT LAKES NEWSPAPER PRODUCTION CONFERENCE INC. — 7737 U.S. 6, Bremen, IN 46506; tel (219) 546-3703
President— Art Vogel (Columbus (OH) Dispatch, 34 S. 3rd St., Columbus, OH 43215, (614) 461-5000); Bus. Mgr. & Sec./Treas. — Tom Boyer (South Bend (IN) Tribune)
Elections held in March.

GREATER LOS ANGELES PRESS CLUB — Hollywood Roosevelt Hotel, 7000 Hollywood Blvd., Cabana 3, Hollywood, CA 90028; tel (213) 469-8180; fax (213) 469-8183
President — Dusty Brandel; Treasurer — Virginia Depew
Elections held in Dec.

H

HOLLYWOOD FOREIGN PRESS ASSOCIATION — 292 S. La Cienega Blvd., Ste. 316, Beverly Hills, CA 90211-3055; tel (310) 657-1731; fax (310) 657-5576
President — Mirjana Van Blarcicom; P.R. Officer — Michael Russell

HOOSIER STATE PRESS ASSOCIATION INC. — 1 Virginia Ave., Ste. 701, Indianapolis, IN 46204; tel (317) 637-3966; fax (317) 624-4428
President — Gary Blackburn; Vice Pres. — Robert Hansen; Treasurer — Jeffrey B Rogers (Indianapolis Star & News); Secretary — Roger Huntzinger
Elections held in July.

I

IDAHO NEWSPAPER ASSOCIATION INC. — 6560 Emerald, Ste. 124, Boise, ID 83704; tel (208) 375-0733; fax (208) 375-0914
President — Jim Simpson; Vice Pres. — Pam Morris; Exec. Dir. — Bob C Hall
Elections held in July.

IDAHO PRESS CLUB — PO Box 2221, Boise, ID 83701; tel (208) 389-2879
Pres. — Kevin Richert; Sec. — Dan Morris; Treas. — David Woolsey; Admin. Asst. — Martha Borchers
Elections and awards ceremony held in April. Annual seminar in Sept.

ILLINOIS ASSOCIATED PRESS EDITORS ASSOCIATION — Associated Press, 230 N. Michigan Ave., Chicago, IL 60601; tel (312) 781-0500
President — John Foreman (Champaign News-Gazette); Vice Pres. — Linda Kleczewski (LaSalle News-Tribune); Sec./Treas. — James Wilson
Elections held in Sept.

ILLINOIS PRESS ASSOCIATION — 701 S. Grand Ave. W., Springfield, IL 62704; tel (217) 523-5092; fax (217) 523-5103
President — William Garth; Vice Pres. — John Foreman
Elections held in Nov.

ILLINOIS PRESS PHOTOGRAPHERS ASSOCIATION — Pioneer Press, 3701 W. Lake Ave., Glenview, IL 60025; tel (708) 486-7364
President — Bill Oakes (Pioneer Press); Vice Pres. — Bob Davis (Chicago Sun-Times); Secretary — Jean Lachat (Chicago Daily Southtown)
Elections held in Nov. Education Conference and Pictures of the Year contest is held in combination with the Wisconsin News Photographers Assoc., April 19, 1996, in Gurnee, IL. Newsletter "ClipNotes" published monthly.

ILLINOIS WOMEN'S PRESS ASSOCIATION INC. — 17208 Greenwood Ave., South Holland, IL 60473; tel (708) 339-2744
President — Cecila Green
Elections held in May.

INDEPENDENT FREE PAPERS OF AMERICA — 210 Washington St., PO Box 208, Chardon, OH 44024; tel (216) 285-2218
Immed. Past Pres. — H Wayne Cox (Denison (TX) Grayson County Shopper); Vice Pres. — Brian Kovsky (Desert Mailer Inc., Lancaster, CA); Sec./Treas. — Chalmers E Bennett (Chardon (OH) Free Enterprise); Director— Milton T Helmer (Shopper Publications, Beldenville, WI); Director — Carlene Phelps (The Douglas (GA) Shopper); Director — Joe Duval (Willimantic (CT) Broadcaster); Director — Carol Hoheisel (Little Falls (MN) Morrison County Record)
Elections held in Sept.

INDIANA ASSOCIATED PRESS MANAGING EDITORS ASSOCIATION — PO Box 1950, Indianapolis, IN 46206; tel (317) 639-5501; fax (317) 638-4611
President — Frank Caperton (Indianapolis Star); Secretary — Robert Shaw (AP)
Elections held in Oct.

INDIANA REPUBLIC EDITORIAL ASSOCIATION — 200 S. Meridian St., Ste. 400, Indianapolis, IN 46225; tel (317) 635-7561
President — Norm Grissom (Mitchell Tribune); 1st Vice Pres. — Howard (Bud) Herron (Franklin Daily Journal); 2nd Vice Pres. — Nancy Thomas (Salem Leader); Secretary — Arden Draeger (Kokomo Tribune); Treasurer — John Klingenberger (Four Corners Courier)
Elections held in Sept.

INDIANAPOLIS PRESS CLUB — ISTA Center, 150 W. Market St., Indianapolis, IN 46204; tel (317) 237-6222
President — Donna Imus; Vice Pres. — Gary Miller; Secretary — Bob Lugar; Treasurer — Bryce Bennett
Elections held in Oct.

INLAND PRESS ASSOCIATION — 777 Busse Hwy., Park Ridge, IL 60068; tel (708) 696-1140; fax (708) 696-2463
Board Chmn. — Sonja Sorensen Craig; Assn. Pres. — Daniel E Baumann; Assn. Pres.-Elect — Malcolm W Applegate; Assn. Vice Pres. — Joe Richter; Foundation Pres. — John Mathew; Foundation Vice Pres. — William Block Jr; Exec. Dir./Sec./Treas. — Ray Carlsen
Elections held in Oct.

INNER CIRCLE — Rm. 9, City Hall, New York, NY 10007; tel (212) 210-1664/(212) 210-1550
President — Jim Ryan (WNYW-TV); Vice Pres. — Larry Sutton (New York Daily News); Treasurer — Gabe Pressman (WNBC-TV); Secretary — Carl Pelleck (New York Post)

INTER AMERICAN PRESS ASSOCIATION SCHOLARSHIP FUND — 2911 N.W. 39th St., Miami, FL 33142; tel (305) 634-2466
President — Alejandro Aguirre (Diario Las Americas); Vice Pres. — Hilda O'Farrill (The News, Mexico); Treasurer — Jim Hampton (Miami Herald); Secretary — Bartolome Mitre (La Nacion, Buenos Aires, Argentina); Exec. Dir. — Bill Williamson
Up to ten scholarships awarded in Oct. Deadline is Aug. 1.
Elections held in Oct.

INTER STATE CIRCULATION MANAGERS ASSOCIATION — Baltimore Sun Co., 501 Calvert St., Baltimore, MD 21278
President — Richard Forgay (Allentown (PA) Morning Call); 1st. Vice Pres. — Tom McGeehan (Harrisburg (PA) Patriot); Sec./Treas. — Bruce C McEntee (Baltimore Sun)
Elections held in Oct.

IOWA ASSOCIATED PRESS MANAGING EDITORS ASSOCIATION — Associated Press, PO Box 1741, Des Moines, IA 50306; tel (515) 243-3281
Chairman — Brian Cooper
Elections held in June.

IOWA NEWSPAPER ASSOCIATION INC. — 319 E. Fifth St., Des Moines, IA 50309; tel (515) 244-2145; fax (515) 244-4855
Pres. — Carolyn Gage (Villisca); Vice Pres. — Mike Lyon (Mapleton); Exec. Dir. — Bill Monroe
Elections held in May.

IOWA PRESS PHOTOGRAPHERS ASSOCIATION INC. — 715 Locust St., Des Moines, IA 50309; tel (515) 284-8000
Pres. — Jeff Carney; Vice Pres. — John Gaps (AP); Sec. — Doug Wells (Des Moines Register); Treas. — Mark Davitt (Ames Daily Tribune)
Elections held in April.

K

KANSAS ASSOCIATED PRESS MANAGING EDITORS ASSOCIATION — Associated Press, 215 W. Pershing, Ste. 221, Kansas City, MO 64108; tel (816) 421-4844
President — Scott Seirer (Salina Journal); Vice Pres. — Carol Crupper (Garden City Telegram); Chief of Bureau — Paul Stevens
Elections held in May.

KANSAS ASSOCIATED PRESS PUBLISHERS AND EDITORS — Associated Press, 215 W. Pershing, Ste. 221, Kansas City, MO 64108; tel (816) 421-4844
Chmn. — Peter Stauffer; Vice Chair. — Vivien Sadowski; Chief of Bureau — Paul Stevens
Elections held in Dec.

KANSAS PRESS ASSOCIATION — 5423 S.W. 7th St., Topeka, KS 66606; tel (913) 271-5304; fax (913) 271-7341
Pres. — Vivien Sadowski (Abilene Reflector-Chronicle); 1st Vice Pres. — Lee Anderson (Ark Valley News); Exec. Dir. — David Furnas
Elections held in April.

KANSAS PRESS WOMEN INC. — 1824 S.W. Crest Dr., Topeka, KS 66604; tel (913) 272-4383

Copyright ©1996 by the Editor & Publisher Co.

VII-8 Assns. city, state, regional

President — Linnie Norsworthy; 1st Vice Pres./Membership — Donna Lamm; 2nd Vice Pres./Bylaws — Joy Deaver; Secretary — Rebecca Funke; Treasurer — Vivien Sadowski
Elections held in April of even numbered years.

KENTUCKY ASSOCIATED PRESS EDITORS ASSOCIATION — 525 W. Broadway, Louisville, KY 40202; tel (502) 583-7718
Pres. — Karl Harrison (Paducah Sun); Sec. — Ed Staats (AP)
Elections held in Oct.

KENTUCKY PRESS ASSOCIATION INC. — 101 Consumer Ln., Frankfort, KY 40601; tel (502) 223-8821; fax (502) 875-2624
Pres. — John Del Santo; Exec. Dir. — David T Thompson
Elections held in Jan.

L

LEGISLATIVE CORRESPONDENTS ASSOCIATION — State Capitol Bldg., PO Box 7340, Albany, NY 12224; tel (518) 455-2388
President— Jay Gallagher (Gannett News, Albany Bureau Chief); 1st Vice Pres. — Dave Bauder (AP); Secretary — Sylvia Saunders (Ottaway News Service); Treasurer — Cathy Woodruff (Schenectady Gazette); Press Room Superviser — Paula Van Leweven
Elections held in May.

LOUISIANA DAILY NEWSPAPER PUBLISHER ASSOCIATION — 680 N. Fifth St., Baton Rouge, LA 70802; tel (504) 344-9309; fax (504) 336-9921
President — Miles Forrest; Sec. — Will Chapman; Exec. Dir. — Pam Mitchell-Wagner
Elections held in March.

LOUISIANA-MISSISSIPPI ASSOCIATED PRESS MANAGING EDITORS ASSN — 1001 Howard Ave., Ste. 200-A, New Orleans, LA 70113; tel (504) 523-3931; fax (504) 586-0531
Chief of Bureau — Charlotte M Porter

LOUISIANA PRESS ASSOCIATION — 680 N. Fifth St., Baton Rouge, LA 70802; tel (504) 344-9309; fax (504) 336-9921
Pres. — Bob Barton; Vice Pres. — Keenan Gingles; Vice Pres. — David Manship; Sec. — Lou Major Jr; Dir. — Pamela Mitchell-Wagner
Elections held in March/April.

LOUISIANA PRESS WOMEN INC. — Baton Rouge Advocate, PO Box 588, Baton Rouge, LA 70821; tel (504) 383-1111
President — Tommy Simmons
Elections held even years.

M

MAINE DAILY NEWSPAPER PUBLISHERS ASSOCIATION — Industry Rd., PO Box 10, Brunswick, ME 04011; tel (207) 729-3311
President — Campbell Niven (Brunswick Times Record)
Elections held in June.

MAINE PRESS ASSOCIATION — University of Maine at Orono, 5743 Lord Hall, Orono, ME 04469; tel (207) 772-2954
President — Sheila Tenggren (Lincoln News); 1st Vice Pres. — Earl Breeklin (Bar Harbor Times); 2nd Vice Pres. — Janet Warner (Franklin Journal); Treasurer — Abbie Roberts (Lincoln County News); Exec. Sec. — Steve Riley
Elections held in Sept.

MANITOBA COMMUNITY NEWSPAPERS ASSOCIATION — 310-275 Portage Ave., Winnipeg, MB R3B 2B3, Canada; tel (204) 947-1691; fax (204) 947-1919
President — Gerald Dorge (Canadian Publishers); 1st Vice Pres. — Shelley Ross (Souris Plaindealer); 2nd Vice Pres. — Garry Struth (Killarney Guide); Sec./Treas./Exec. Dir. — Emily Boitson-Murray
Elections held at annual April convention.

MARYLAND-DELAWARE-DC PRESS ASSOCIATION — 275 W St., Ste. 310, Annapolis, MD 21401; tel (410) 263-7878; fax (410) 263-7825
President — Jean C Halle; Pres.-Elect — Larry Effingham; Exec. Dir. — James E Donahue
Elections held in Feb.

MASSACHUSETTS MEDIA WOMEN — 32 Lawrence St., Canton, MA 02021; tel (617) 828-7481
President — Marilyn Roache; Vice Pres./Programming — Judith Ingram; Vice Pres./Membership — Nina Belsan; Treasurer — Maura Renehan
Elections held bi-annually in the spring.

MASSACHUSETTS NEWSPAPER PUBLISHERS ASSOCIATION — 70 Washington St., Ste. 214, Salem, MA 01970; tel (508) 465-7539; fax (508) 465-4796
President — Bruce Bennett (Worcester Telegram & Gazette); 1st Vice Pres. — Charles N Fuller (Brockton Enterprise); 2nd Vice Pres. — John P Kinney (Essex Co. Newspapers, Beverly); Sec. — Sheila Smith (Memorial Press Group, Plymouth); Treas. — William Barrett (Suburban World Newspapers, Needham); Exec. Dir. — William L Plante Jr

MASSACHUSETTS PRESS ASSOCIATION — 640 Commonwealth Ave., Boston University, School of Journalism, Boston, MA 02215; tel (617) 353-3484
President — Jane Lopes (Middleboro Gazette); 1st Vice Pres. — Charles Bennett (Independent Journalist); Treasurer — Joanne Root (Holden Landmark); Secretary — David Anable (Boston University)
Elections held in May.

MICHIGAN ASSOCIATED PRESS EDITORIAL ASSOCIATION — 300 River Pl., Ste. 2400, Detroit, MI 48207; tel (313) 259-0650
President — Ken Winter (Petoskey News-Review); Secretary— Charles C Hill. (AP, Detroit Bureau Chief)
Elections held in June.

MICHIGAN PRESS ASSOCIATION — 827 N. Washington Ave., Lansing, MI 48906; tel (517) 372-2424
President — Karen Spang; Vice Pres. — David Jackson; Pres.-Elect — Stephen Gray; Exec. Dir. — Warren M Hoyt; Treasurer — Dirk Milliman
Elections held in Jan.

MID-ATLANTIC CIRCULATION MANAGERS ASSOCIATION — News & Advance, PO Box 10129, Lynchburg, VA 24506; tel (804) 385-5400
President — Nelson Mitchell; 1st Vice Pres. — Carol Mosely; 2nd Vice Pres. — Gary Anderson; Convention Secretary — Tim Eddins
Elections held in Oct.

MID-ATLANTIC NEWSPAPER ADVERTISING MARKETING EXECUTIVES — 4101 Lake Boone Trail, Ste. 201, Raleigh, NC 27607; tel (919) 787-5181; fax (919) 787-4916
President — Judy Perfater; Exec. Vice Pres. — Don Freeman; 1st Vice Pres. — Melanie Arney; Exec. Dir. — Banner Huggins
Elections held in March.

MIDWEST TRAVEL WRITERS ASSOCIATION — 8911 Raven Oaks Dr., Omaha, NE 68152; tel (402) 571-4097
President — Barc Wade (Omaha Home & Away Magazine); Vice Pres. — Mike Whye (Freelance Writer/Photographer); Secretary — Elizabeth Jacobson (Freelance Writer); Treasurer — Ruth Chin (Freelance Photographer/Writer); Assoc. Vice Pres. — Nicky Stratton
Elections held in May.

MINNESOTA ASSOCIATED PRESS ASSOCIATION — 511 11th Ave. S., Ste. 404, Minneapolis, MN 55415; tel (612) 332-2727
Pres. — Jon Losness; 1st Vice Pres. — Kathy Vos; 2nd Vice Pres. — Steve Ronald; 3rd Vice Pres. — Holly Gruber; Bureau Chief — Dave Pyle
Elections held in May.

MINNESOTA NEWS COUNCIL — 822 Marquette Ave., Ste. 200, Minneapolis, MN 55402; tel (612) 341-9357
Chairman — Justice John E Simonett; Exec. Dir. — Gary Gilson

MINNESOTA NEWSPAPER ASSOCIATION — 12 S. Sixth St., Ste. 1120, Minneapolis, MN 55402; tel (612) 332-8844
President — Chuck Wann (New Parque Times); Immed. Past Pres. — Bob Bradford (Northfield News); 1st Vice Pres. — Carolynn Allen-Evans (Owatonna People's Press); 2nd Vice Pres. — Bill Ramige (Glencoe McLeod Co. Chronicle); 3rd Vice Pres. — Julie Gillie (Minnesota Northern Light); Treasurer — Richard Norlander; Adv. Dir. — Lisa Hills
Elections held in Jan.

MISSISSIPPI ASSOCIATED PRESS ASSOCIATION — See Louisiana-Mississippi listing.

MISSISSIPPI PRESS ASSOCIATION — 351 Edgewood Terrace, Jackson, MS 39206-6217; tel (601) 981-3060; fax (601) 981-3676
Past Pres. — Sid Salter (Scott County Times); President — Tom Pittman (NE Mississippi Daily Journal); Vice Pres.-Weeklies — Jim Lambert (Copiah County Courier); Sec./Exec. Dir. — Carolyn Wilson; Adv. Coord. — Marsha Burton; Mem. Serv. Coord. — Susan Massey; Adv. Asst. — Reba Butler; Adv./Mktg. Dir. — Jeff Ashley; Sec./Classified Network — Marte Lawrence; Bookkeeper — Julia Lambert
Elections held in June.

MISSISSIPPI VALLEY CLASSIFIED ADVERTISING MANAGERS ASSOCIATION — Vincennes Sun-Commercial, 702 Main St., PO Box 396, Vincennes, IN 47591; tel (812) 886-9955
President — Carol Smith (South Bend (IN) Tribune); 1st Vice Pres. — Jack Pate (Evansville (IN) Courier-Press); General Manager — Veronica Kopp
Elections held in March.

MISSOURI ASSOCIATED DAILIES — 802 Locust, Columbia, MO 65201; tel (314) 449-4167
President — John Goossen (Hannibal Courier-Post); 1st Vice Pres. — Jules Molenda (Sedalia Democrat); Secretary — Roman Patten (Jefferson City News Tribune); Treasurer — Doug Crews (Missouri Press Association)
Elections held in Oct.

MISSOURI ASSOCIATED PRESS MANAGING EDITORS — Associated Press, 215 W. Pershing, Ste. 221, Kansas City, MO 64108
Pres. — Jim Robertson (Columbia Daily Tribune); Vice Pres. — Mark Snow (Macon Chronicle-Herald)
Elections held in April.

MISSOURI ASSOCIATED PRESS PUBLISHERS AND EDITORS — Associated Press, 215 W. Pershing, Ste. 221, Kansas City, MO 64108; tel (816) 421-4844
Chairman — Ken Newton (St. Joseph News-Press); Vice Chair. — Patti Hoddinott (Columbia Missourian)
Elections held in Dec.

MISSOURI PRESS ASSOCIATION — 802 Locust, Columbia, MO 65201; tel (314) 449-4167
President — Harold Ellinghouse (Piedmont Wayne County Journal Banner); 1st Vice Pres. — David Lipman (Pulitzer 2000); 2nd Vice Pres. — William E James (Harrisonville Cass County Democrat-Missourian); Secretary — W Ferrell Shuck (Lee's Summit Journal); Treasurer — William W Farmer (Rock Port Atchison County Mail); Exec. Dir. — Doug Crews
Elections held in Oct.

MISSOURI PRESS WOMEN — 9607 Hayes, Overland Park, KS 66212; tel (913) 341-0165/ (913) 642-9421; fax (913) 341-6912
Pres. — Priscilla Owings-Chansky; 1st Vice Pres. — Allison Stein Best; 2nd Vice Pres. — Julie Edison; Treas. — Karen Zarky; Dir. Outreach — Anita DeZego; Dir. Mktg. — Leanna Hafften; Dir. Mktg. — Pam Soetart; Dir. Dist./Northeast — Nona Bauer; Dir. Dist./Northwest — Carol Conrow; Dir. Dist./Central — Annette Sanders; Dir. Dist./Southwest — Susan Wade

MONTANA ASSOCIATED PRESS ASSOCIATION — PO Box 5810, Helena, MT 59604; tel (406) 442-7440
Chairman — Drew Van Fossen (Butte Montana Standard); Chief of Bureau — John W Kuglin
Elections held in May or June.

MONTANA NEWSPAPER ASSOCIATION — 534 N. Main, Ste. 202, Helena, MT 59601; tel (406) 443-2850; fax (406) 443-2860
President — John Watson (Miles City Star); Exec. Dir. — James R Fall
Elections held in June.

N

NEBRASKA ASSOCIATED PRESS ASSOCIATION — Associated Press, 232 World-Herald B, Omaha, NE 68102-1122; tel (402) 341-4963
President — Larry Hauraner (Hastings Tribune); Secretary — Paul Simon
Elections held in Sept.

NEBRASKA PRESS ASSOCIATION — 1120 K St., Lincoln, NE 68508; tel (402) 476-2851/ (800) 369-2850; fax (402) 476-2942
President — Ron (Butch) Furse (Aurora News-Register); Vice Pres. — Don Russell (Sutton Clay County News); Exec. Dir. — Allen Beermann; Sales Mgr. — Rob James
Elections held in April.

NEVADA STATE PRESS ASSOCIATION INC. — 1502 N. Carson, Ste. 10, PO Box 1030, Carson City, NV 89702; tel (702) 885-0866; fax (702) 885-8233
Pres. — Sherman Frederick (Las Vegas Review-Journal); 1st Vice Pres. — Bill Kunerth; 2nd Vice Pres. — Susan Brockus; Exec. Dir. — Kent Lauer
Elections held in Oct.

NEW ENGLAND ASSOCIATION OF CIRCULATION EXECUTIVES — 4 Trotting Rd., Chelmsford, MA 01824; tel (508) 256-0691/(508) 459-4076
Pres. — David Jameson (Brockton (MA) Enterprise); Sec. — William H Hoar (Lowell (MA) Sun); Treas. — James Baldis (Hartford Courant)
Elections held in April/May.

NEW ENGLAND ASSOCIATED PRESS NEWS EXECUTIVES ASSOCIATION — Associated Press, 184 High St., Boston, MA 02110; tel (617) 357-8100
Pres. — Terry Williams (Nashua (NH) Telegraph); Sec./Treas.— Michael Short (AP, Boston Bureau Chief)
Elections held in Oct.

NEW ENGLAND NEWSPAPER ASSOCIATION INC. — 70 Washington St., Ste. 214, Salem, MA 01970; tel (508) 744-8940; fax (508) 744-0333
Immed. Past Pres.— Andrew T Bickford (Independent Publications Inc., Bryn Mawr, PA); President — Judith V Brown (New Britain (CT) Herald); 1st Vice Pres. — Peter H Gamage (Lynn (MA) Daily Evening Item); 2nd Vice Pres. — Howard G Sutton (Providence (RI) Journal Co.); Sec./Treas. — Mark Smith (St. Johnsbury (VT) Caldonian-Record); Exec. Dir. — Morley L Piper
Elections held in March.

NEW ENGLAND NEWSPAPER ADVERTISING EXECUTIVES ASSOCIATION — 70 Washington St., Salem, MA 01970; tel (508) 744-8940
President — John Ebbets (Northampton (MA) Daily Hampshire Gazette); 1st Vice Pres. — Gracie E Johnston (Rutland (VT) Herald); 2nd Vice Pres. — William A Taylor (New Britain (CT) Herald); Secretary — Patrick J Cox (Waterbury (CT) Republican-American); Treasurer — Morley L Piper (New England Newspaper Association Inc.); Asst. Treas. — George F White (Quincy (MA) Patriot Ledger)
Elections held in Oct.

NEW ENGLAND PRESS ASSOCIATION — 360 Huntington Ave., 428 CP, Boston, MA 02115; tel (617) 373-5610; fax (617) 373-5615
Pres. — Ross Connelly (Hardwick (VT) Gazette); 1st Vice Pres. — Linda Lemmon (Putnam (MA) Town Crier & Northeast Ledger); 2nd Vice Pres. — Dan Warner (Lawrence (MA) Eagle-Tribune); Exec. Dir. — John Coykendall
Elections held at annual winter convention.

NEW ENGLAND SOCIETY OF NEWSPAPER EDITORS — PO Box 3030, Worcester, MA 01602; tel (508) 754-5131
President — Thomas F Kearney (Keene (NH) Sentinel); Vice Pres. — Ann Gibbons (Barre-Montpelier (VT) Times Argus); Treas. — John H Howe (Laconia (NH) Citizen); Sec. — Tom Ferriter (Portland (ME) Press Herald); Exec. Asst. — Jeanne M Fassett; Bd. Member — Bernard W Caughey (Quincy (MA) Patriot Ledger); Bd. Member — Larry McDermott (Springfield (MA) Union-News); Bd. Member — Jeff Rivers (Hartford Courant); Bd. Member — Leonard L Levin (Providence (RI) Journal-Bulletin); Bd. Member — Ronald S Hutson (Boston Globe); Bd. Member — Tom Ferriter (Portland (ME) Press Herald); Bd. Member — Morgan McGinley (New London (CT) Day)
Elections held in Nov.

NEW JERSEY ASSOCIATED PRESS MANAGING EDITORS ASSOCIATION — 50 W. State St., Ste. 1114, Trenton, NJ 08608; tel (201) 642-0151
Chief of Bureau — Mark Mittelstadt

Copyright ©1996 by the Editor & Publisher Co.

Assns. city, state, regional VII-9

NEW JERSEY LEGISLATIVE CORRESPONDENTS CLUB — Asbury Park Press Inc., 3601 Hwy. 66, PO Box 1550, Neptune, NJ 07754; tel (908) 922-6000
President — Karen De Masters; Vice Pres. — Robert Schwaneberg (Newark Star-Ledger); Vice Pres. — Joseph W Donohue (Atlantic City Press); Sec./Treas. — John O Davies Jr

NEW JERSEY PRESS ASSOCIATION — 840 Bear Tavern Rd., West Trenton, NJ 08628-1019; tel (609) 406-0600; fax (609) 406-0300
Chairman — Patricia Haughey (Medford Central Record); Pres. — Robert Mawhinney (Press of Atlantic City); Exec. Vice Pres.— E Christopher Cone (West Essex Tribune); Vice Pres.-Dailies — John V R Bull (Philadelphia Inquirer); Vice Pres.-Weeklies — David Worrall (Worrall Newspapers); Treas. — Charles Bryant (Press of Atlantic City); Exec. Dir. — John O'Brien; General Counsel — Thomas Cafferty

NEW JERSEY PRESS PHOTOGRAPHERS ASSOCIATION — 150 River St., Hackensack, NJ 07601; tel (201) 646-4131
President — Linda M Cataffo (Bergen Co. Record); 1st Vice Pres. — John Decker (Bergen Co. Record); 2nd Vice Pres. — Thomas Costello (Asbury Park Press); Secretary — Najlah Feanny (Freelance, Saba Agency)

NEW MEXICO PRESS ASSOCIATION — 2531 Wyoming N.E., Albuquerque, NM 87112; tel (505) 275-1377
President — Kent Walz (Albuquerque Journal); Immed. Past Pres. — Morrow Hall (Estancia Valley Citizen); 1st Vice Pres. — Robert B Trapp (Espanola Rio Grande Sun); Treas. — Nick Payton (Clayton Union Co. Leader)
Elections held in Oct.

NEW MEXICO PRESS WOMEN — 2200 Lester Dr. N.E., Ste. 261, Albuquerque, NM 87112; tel (505) 292-4329
President — Jean Jordan; Vice Pres. — Denise Tessier; Secretary — Kathy Cordova; Treasurer — Rita Popp
Elections held in spring of even numbered years.

NEW ORLEANS PRESS CLUB — 150 Barrone St., Ste. 513, New Orleans, LA 70112; tel (504) 523-1010
President — S Lee Alexander; 1st Vice Pres. — Matt Scallan; 2nd Vice Pres. — Jay Handleman
Elections held in May.

NEWS LIMITED OF AUSTRALIA — 1211 Ave. of the Americas, 2nd Fl., New York, NY 10036; tel (212) 852-7600
Bureau Chief — Peter Atkinson; Correspondent — Marcus Casey; Weekend Australian — Susan Wyndham

NEWSPAPER ADVERTISING SALES ASSOCIATION (NASA)/NEW YORK CHAPTER — 405 Lexington Ave., New York, NY 10174; tel (212) 661-10174
President — Chris Avery (Los Angeles Times); Treasurer — Pam Bender (CWO&O); Secretary — Elliott Huron (Gannett); 1st Year Dir.— Kevin O'Brien (Sawyer Ferguson Walker); 2nd Year Dir. — Dick Tushingham (New York Times); 3rd Year Dir. — Otis Henderson (Newspapers First)
Elections held in June.

NEWSPAPER ADVERTISING SALES ASSOCIATION (NASA)/SAN FRANCISCO CHAPTER — 501 Second St., Ste. 406, San Francisco, CA 94107; tel (415) 957-9490
Vice Pres. — Linda Bowers (CWO&O); Treas. — Ron O'Neal (Sawyer Ferguson Walker)
Elections held in Aug.

NEWSPAPER ASSOCIATION OF AMERICA — 11600 Sunrise Valley Dr., Reston, VA 22091-1412; tel (703) 648-1000; fax (703) 620-4557
Dir./Membership Svcs. — Kimberly Lysik; Chief Mktg. Officer — Nick Cannistraro; Dir./Advanced Computer Science — John W Iobst, Ph D; CEO — Cathie Black; CFO — Mary Anne Kanter; Sr. Vice Pres./Comm. — Debra Shriver

NEWSPAPER CREDIT MANAGERS ASSOCIATION OF NEW YORK/NEW JERSEY — 950 Fingerboard Rd., Staten Island, NY 10305; tel (718) 981-1234 ext. 2490
President — James Benedict (Newark Star-Ledger); Treasurer — James Grasso (New York Times); Vice Pres. — Peter Gallo (USA Today); Secretary — Marcel E Crampon (Staten Island Advance)
Election held in Nov.

NEWSPAPER FEATURES COUNCIL INC. — 37 Arch St., Greenwich, CT 06830; tel (203) 661-3386; fax (203) 661-7337
Pres. — Ron Patel (Assoc. Man. Ed./Features); 1st Vice Pres.— Richard S Newscombe(Pres./CEO); 2nd Vice Pres. — Jane Amari (Man. Ed./Design & Features); Sec./Treas. — Steve Christensen (Vice Pres./GM); Exec. Dir. — Corinta Kotula
Elections held every two years.

NEW YORK ASSOCIATED DAILIES — 8-10 E. 2nd St., Dunkirk, NY 14048; tel (716) 366-3000
President — Richard J Anthony (Oneonta Daily Star); Sec./Treas.— Mike Williams (Dunkirk Evening Observer, Vice President)
Election held in June.

NEW YORK CHAPTER BASEBALL WRITERS ASSOCIATION OF AMERICA — 36 Brookfield Rd., Ft. Salonga, NY 11768; tel (516) 757-0562; fax (516) 757-6817
Chmn. — Claire Smith (New York Times); Vice Chmn. — Joel Sherman (New York Post); Exec. Sec./Treas. — Jack Lang (Sports Ticker)
Elections held every two years in Nov.

NEW YORK FAIR TRIAL FREE PRESS CONFERENCE — Syracuse University, Newhouse Communications Ctr., Syracuse, NY 13244-2100; tel (315) 443-2381; fax (315) 443-3946
Chairman— Judith S Kaye (New York State Court of Appeals, Chief Judge); Vice Chmn. — Harry Rosenfeld (Albany Times Union); Sec./Treas. — Angelo T Cometa (Tenzer Greenblatt LLP, NYC); Exec. Dir. — Jay B Wright (Syracuse University, Newhouse Commun. Ctr.)
Elections held in May.

NEW YORK FINANCIAL WRITERS ASSOCIATION INC. — 28 Robert Cir., Syosset, NY 11791; tel (516) 921-7766; fax (516) 921-5762
Pres. — Terri Thompson (Knight-Bagehot Fellowship); Vice Pres. — Marvin Mack (Knight-Ridder Financial News); Treas. — Stan Strachan (National Mortgage News); Board Member — Martin Cherrin (Reuters); Exec. Sec. — Joyce Spartonos
Elections held on fourth Wed. of Jan.

NEW YORK FOOTBALL WRITERS ASSOCIATION — Montclair State University, Upper Montclair, NJ 07043; tel (201) 655-5249
Pres. — Lenn Robbins (Bergen Co. (NJ) Record); Sec./Treas.— Al Langer(Administrator)

NEW YORK NEWSPAPER PUBLISHERS ASSOCIATION — The Carriage House, 8 Thurlow Terrace, Albany, NY 12203; tel (518) 449-1667; fax (518) 449-5053
Pres. — Diane Kennedy; Chmn. — E Pat Thompson Frantz (Elmira Star-Gazette); Vice Chmn. — James Marshall (Glens Falls Post-Star); Sec./Treas. — Karen Messineo (New York Times)

NEW YORK NEWSPAPERS ADVERTISING AND MARKETING EXECUTIVES — The Carriage House, 8 Thurlow Terrace, Albany, NY 12203; tel (518) 449-1667; fax (518) 449-5053
Pres. — Christine Zovistoski (Middletown Times Herald-Record); 1st Vice Pres. — Robert Provost (Albany Times Union); Treas. — Sean McNamara (Plattsburgh Press Republican)
Elections held in June.

NEW YORK PRESS ASSOCIATION — 1681 Western Ave., Albany, NY 12203; tel (518) 464-6483
Immed. Past Pres. — Carl J Aiello (Wallkill Valley Times and Mid-Huson Times); Pres. — Trey Measer (Bee Newspapers); Pres.-Elect — Victoria Simons (Columbia County Independent); Vice Pres. — Grant Hamilton (East Aurora Advertiser and Elma Review); Sec./Treas. — Clifford Richner (Richner Publications); Exec. Dir. — Michelle K Rea
Elections held in Sept.

NEW YORK PRESS PHOTOGRAPHERS ASSOCIATION INC. — 225 E. 36th St., New York, NY 10016; tel (212) 889-6633; fax (212) 889-3099
Pres. — Bill Turnbull; 1st Vice Pres. — Richard Lee; Sec. — Tom Middlemiss
Elections held every other year.

NEW YORK SOCIETY OF NEWSPAPER EDITORS — 215 University Pl., Syracuse, NY 13244; tel (315) 443-2305
President — A J Cartez (Long Island Newsday); Vice Pres. — Joann M Crupi (Albany Times Union)

NEW YORK STATE ASSOCIATED PRESS ASSOCIATION — PO Box 11010, Albany, NY 12211; tel (518) 458-7821
Past Pres. — Donald C Hadley (Finger Lakes Times); Pres. — Timothy Atseff (Syracuse Herald-Journal); 1st Vice Pres. — Dan Lynch (Albany Times Union); 2nd Vice Pres. — James Dynko (Plattsburg Press Republican); Sec.— Lew Wheaton (AP, Chief of Bureau)
Elections held in Sept.

NEW YORK STATE CIRCULATION MANAGERS ASSOCIATION — 40 Mulberry St., Middletown, NY 10940; tel (914) 343-2181
Chmn. — Chester Valiante (Middletown Times Herald-Record)
Elections held in May.

NORTH CAROLINA ASSOCIATED PRESS NEWS COUNCIL — Associated Press, 4020 Westchase Blvd., Raleigh, NC 27607-3933; tel (919) 833-8687
Pres. — Al Clark (Greenville Daily Reflector); 1st Vice Pres. — Marion Gregory (Raleigh News & Observer); Bureau Chief — Ambrose B Dudley
Elections held in Sept.

NORTH CAROLINA ASSOCIATION OF AFTERNOON NEWSPAPERS INC. — PO Box 1309, Raleigh, NC 27602
President — Mike Rouse; Vice Pres. — David Wiggings (West Jefferson); Columnist — Paul T O'Connor
Elections held in Jan.

NORTH CAROLINA PRESS ASSOCIATION — 4101 Lake Boone Trail, Ste. 202, Raleigh, NC 27607; tel (919) 787-7443; fax (919) 787-5302
Pres. — Fred Crisp (Raleigh News & Observer); Vice Pres. — Ron Paris (Forest City Daily Courier); Sec./Treas. — Dennis Tharrington (Communication Resources); Sec./Treas. — Gayle Smith (Charlotte Observer); Exec. Dir.— Teri Saylor (CAE)
Elections held in July.

NORTH CAROLINA PRESS CLUB — 506 Northwood Rd., Washington, NC 27889; tel (919) 975-3640; fax (919) 975-3640
COB — Blue Greenburg; Pres. — Peggy Pond; 1st Vice Pres. — Linda Thearell; 2nd Vice Pres. — Flo Johnston; 3rd Vice Pres. — Kathryn Dalton; Sec. — Betty Neff; Treas. — Lib Swindell
Elections held in March.

NORTH DAKOTA ASSOCIATED PRESS — PO Box 1018, Bismarck, ND 58502; tel (701) 223-8450
Pres. — Sharon Ditz (Dickinson Press); Vice Pres. — Wayne Nelson
Elections held in Sept.

NORTH DAKOTA NEWSPAPER ASSOCIATION — 1435 Interstate Loop, Bismarck, ND 58501; tel (701) 223-NEWS
President — Robert Denison; Exec. Vice Pres. — Jill Denning; 1st Vice Pres. — Duane Schatz; 2nd Vice Pres. — Mark Carlson; 3rd Vice Pres. — Allen Stock
Elections held in April.

NORTH JERSEY PRESS CLUB — PO Box 612, Scotch Plains, NJ 07076; tel (908) 322-8343
Attn: — Charles Horner
Elections held in April.

NORTHERN ILLINOIS NEWSPAPER ASSOCIATION — Journalism Dept., Northern Illinois Univ., DeKalb, IL 60115; tel (815) 753-1925
Pres. — Bob Nelander; Vice Pres. — Jane Rio; Exec. Sec. — Daniel Riffe
Elections held in April.

NORTHERN STATES CIRCULATION MANAGERS ASSOCIATION — 425 Portland St., Minneapolis, MN 55488; tel (612) 673-4304
Pres. — Ron Oleheiser (Grand Rapids (MN) Herald Review); Sec./Treas. — Paul Holland (Minneapolis Star-Tribune)
Elections held in Sept.

NORTHWEST INTERNATIONAL CIRCULATION EXECUTIVES — 8002 N.E. Hwy. 99, Ste. 267, Vancouver, WA 98665; tel (360) 694-2312; fax (360) 737-4074
Chairman — Jim Thomas (Yakima (WA) Herald-Republic); Pres. — Chris Blaser (Pasco (WA) Tri-City Herald); 1st Vice Pres. — Dale Irvine (Mt. Vernon (WA) Skagit Valley Herald); 2nd Vice Pres. — Alan Fisco (Seattle Times); Sec./Treas. — Steve Schurkey (Vancouver (WA) Columbian)
Management seminars sponsored in Oct.
Elections held at annual conference in May.

O

OHIO CIRCULATION MANAGERS ASSOCIATION — PO Box 4210, Athens, OH 45701; tel (614) 592-6612
Pres. — David Hoskin (Ravenna Record Courier); Vice Pres. — Mark Keller (Cambridge Jeffersonian); Sec./Treas. — Fred W Weber II (Athens Messenger)
Elections held in Oct.

OHIO NEWSPAPER ADVERTISING EXECUTIVES — 1335 Dublin Rd. S., Columbus, OH 43215; tel (614) 486-6677
Pres. — Walling Gray (Sandusky Register); Vice Pres. — Gary Merrell (Columbus Dispatch); Sec. — Randy Guthrie (Athens Messenger); Treas. — Jeni Wehrmeyer (Cincinnati Enquirer)
Elections held in Oct.

OHIO NEWSPAPER ASSOCIATION — 1335 Dublin Rd., Ste. 216-B, Columbus, OH 43215; tel (614) 486-6677
Chairman — Harold Douthit (Douthit Communications Inc.); Pres. — Tom Thomson (Delaware Gazette); Exec. Dir./Sec. — Frank E Deaner
Elections held in Feb.

OHIO NEWSPAPER WOMEN'S ASSOCIATION — 202 N. Limestone St., Springfield, OH 45501; tel (513) 328-0368
Pres. — Lynn Hulsey (Springfield News-Sun); Sec. — Linda Martz (Mansfield News-Journal); Treas. — Jan Centa (Wooster Daily Record)
Elections held in Oct. of odd numbered years.

OKLAHOMA PRESS ASSOCIATION — 3601 N. Lincoln, Oklahoma City, OK 73105-5499; tel (405) 524-4421
Pres. — Al Hruby; Exec. VP/Sec. — Mark Thomas; Treas. — Ted Phillips
Elections held in Feb.

OKLAHOMA PRESS WOMEN — 10020 Mahler Pl., Oklahoma City, OK 73120; tel (405) 751-5962
Pres. — Nina G Smith; Pres.-Elect. — Edna Hennessee
Elections held in spring of even numbered years.

ONTARIO COMMUNITY NEWSPAPERS ASSOCIATION — 1184 Speers Rd., Oakville, ON L6J 5A8, Canada; tel (905) 844-0184; fax (905) 844-2769
President — Paul Winkler (Fairway Group); 1st Vice Pres. — Carol Helfenstein (Teeswater News); 2nd Vice Pres. — Len Pizzey (Haliburton County Echo); Sec./Treas. — Tom Flynn (Signal-Star Publishing); Manager-Member Services — Anne Lannan

OREGON ASSOCIATED PRESS NEWSPAPER EXECUTIVES ASSOCIATION — Associated Press, 121 S.W. Salmon, Ste. 1450, Portland, OR 97204; tel (503) 228-2169
Bureau Chief — Eva Parziale
Elections held every year.

OREGON NEWSPAPER PUBLISHERS ASSOCIATION/OREGON NEWSPAPER ADVERTISING CO. — 7150 S.W. Hampton St., Ste. 111, Portland, OR 97223; tel (503) 624-6397; fax (503) 639-9009
Pres. — Judy Zelmer Smith (Brookings Curry Coastal Pilot); Pres.-Elect — Michael O'Brien (Ashland Daily Tidings); Past Pres. — Robert Moody (La Grande Observer); Exec. Dir. — Leonard W Lanfranco
Elections held in July.

OVERSEAS PRESS CLUB OF PUERTO RICO — PO Box 12326, Santurce, PR 00914-0326
President — Mayra Acevedo Orta; Vice Pres. — Yolanda Zavala; Secretary — Nidzy Ortiz; Treasurer — Mary McHale Wood; Administrative — Gail Arenas
Elections held in March.

P

PACIFIC NORTHWEST NEWSPAPER ASSOCIATION — PO Box 11128, Tacoma, WA 98411; tel (206) 272-3611; fax (206) 272-9081

VII-10 Assns. city, state, regional

President — Scott Campbell; Exec. Dir./Sec. — Evonne Agnello
Elections held in the fall.

PENNSYLVANIA LEGISLATIVE CORRESPONDENTS ASSOCIATION — Capitol News Room, PO Box 1287, Harrisburg, PA 17108; tel (717) 787-6183
Pres. — Russ Eshleman; Sec./Treas. — Jack Nagle (Newsroom Supt.)
Elections held in July of odd numbered years.

PENNSYLVANIA NEWSPAPER PUBLISHERS ASSOCIATION — 2717 N. Front St., Harrisburg, PA 17110; tel (717) 234-4067; fax (717) 234-4067
Pres. — William B Northrop (Washington Observer-Reporter); VP/Dailies — Pamela J Mayer (Johnston Tribune-Democrat); VP/Weeklies — Coulston S Henry (Philadelphia News Gleaner Publication); Sec./Treas. — Wanda Reid (Reid Newspapers); Exec. Dir. — Timothy M Williams
Elections held in Sept.

PENNSYLVANIA SOCIETY OF NEWSPAPER EDITORS — 2717 N. Front St., Harrisburg, PA 17110; tel (717) 234-4067
Pres. — James Sachetti (Bloomsburg Press-Enterprise); 1st Vice Pres. — James Kevlin (Pottsville Republican); 2nd Vice Pres. — Woodene Merriman (Pittsburgh Post-Gazette); Sec./Treas. — Wade Fowler (Swank-Fowler Publications, New Bloomfield)
Elections held in May.

PENNSYLVANIA WOMEN'S PRESS ASSOCIATION — PO Box 426, Grove City, PA 16127; tel (412) 981-66100
Pres. — Natalie Love (Lewistown Sentinel); Vice Pres. — Marigrace Heyer (Leighton Times News); Treas. — Sharon Santus (Greensburg Tribune Review); Sec. — Katherine Reinhard (Allentown Morning Call)
Elections held in May.

PITTSBURGH BASEBALL WRITERS ASSOCIATION OF AMERICA — Associated Press, 6 Gateway Ctr., Pittsburgh, PA 15222; tel (412) 281-3747; fax (412) 281-1869
Pres. — Alan Robinson (AP)
Elections held in Sept.

PRESS CLUB OF OHIO — 50 W. Broad St., Ste. 1622, Columbus, OH 43215; tel (614) 464-1856
Pres. — John Tanoury; Vice Pres. — Bill Vance; Sec./Treas. — Scott Elias
Elections for trustees held in Feb., officers in March.

PUBLISHERS BUREAU OF NEW JERSEY INC. — 34 South Terrace, Short Hills, NJ 07078; tel (201) 379-5259
Mgr. — David J Winkworth

R

RHODE ISLAND PRESS ASSOCIATION — Journalism Dept., Kingston, RI 02881; tel (401) 792-2195
Pres. — Rudolph Hempe; Vice Pres. — Mary Harrington; Sec. — Linda Lotridge Levin; Treas. — Frederick Wilson III
Elections held in Jan.

S

SALES AND MARKETING EXECUTIVES INTERNATIONAL — Statler Office Tower, Ste. 977, Cleveland, OH 44115; tel (216) 771-6650; fax (216) 771-6652
Exec. Dir.— Jack I Criswell (CSE)
Elections held in June.

SASKATCHEWAN WEEKLY NEWSWPAPER ASSOCIATION — 4-2155 Airport Dr., Saskatoon, SK S7L 6M5, Canada; tel (306) 382-9683; fax (306) 382-9421
President— Bruce Penton (Moosomin World Spectator); Past Pres.— Lyle Emmons (Last Mountain Times); Vice Pres.— Daryl Hasein (Biggar Independent); Sec./Treas. — Linda Bobowski

SOCIETY OF PROFESSIONAL JOURNALISTS — 16 S. Jackson, PO Box 77, Greencastle, IN 46135; tel (317) 653-3333; fax (317) 653-4631
Pres. — Reginald Stuart; Exec. Dir. — Greg Christopher

SOUTH CAROLINA ASSOCIATIED PRESS NEWS COUNCIL — 1311 Marion St., Columbia, SC 29201; tel (803) 799-5510; fax (803) 252-2913
Pres. — Graham Osteen; Vice Pres. — Sue Deans; Board Member — David Lauderdale; Board Member — Paula Ellis; Bureau Chief — John Shurr
Elections held in Feb.

SOUTH CAROLINA NEWS PHOTOGRAPHERS ASSOCIATION — The State, 1401 Shop Rd., PO Box 1333, Columbia, SC 29202; tel (803) 771-8420; fax (803) 771-8430
Pres. — Renee Ittner-McManus (Columbia (SC) The State); Vice Pres. — Travis Bell (Rock Hill Herald); Clip — Jeff Otto (Florence Morning News); Sec. — Jonathan Tedder (Myrtle Beach Sun News); Treas. — Andy Burris (Rock Hill Herald)
Elections held in Jan.

SOUTH CAROLINA PRESS ASSOCIATION — PO Box 11429, Columbia, SC 29211; tel (803) 750-9561; fax (803) 551-0903
Pres. — Scott Hunter (Aiken Standard); Exec. Dir. — William C Rogers
Elections held in Feb.

SOUTH DAKOTA NEWSPAPER ASSOCIATION — South Dakota State Univ., Communications Center, PO Box 2230, Brookings, SD 57007; tel (605) 692-4300
Pres. — Kathy Snyder Nelson; 1st Vice Pres. — Jon Hunter; 2nd Vice Pres. — Nelson Miller; GM — Keith M Jensen
Elections held in May.

SOUTHERN BAPTIST PRESS ASSOCIATION — PO Box 10289, Jacksonville, FL 32247; tel (904) 396-2351
Pres. — Jack E Brymer; Sec. — Bob Terry
Elections held in Feb.

SOUTHERN CIRCULATION MANAGERS ASSOCIATION — PO Box A, LaGrange, GA 30241; tel (706) 845-9053
COB — Rob Kearley (Daytona Beach (FL) News-Journal); Pres. — Marshall Andrews (Hattiesburg (MS) American); 1st Vice Pres. — Don Cunningham (Morristown (TN) Citizen Tribune); 2nd Vice Pres. — Robert Eickfoff (Orlando Sentinel); 3rd Vice Pres. — Tom Sheppard (Atlanta Journal-Constitution); Sec./Treas. — Linnie Pride (Savannah (GA) News-Press)
Elections held in Sept.

SOUTHERN CLASSIFIED ADVERTISING MANAGERS ASSOCIATION — PO Box 14634, Savannah, GA 31416; tel (912) 354-5650; fax (912) 354-9801
Exec. Officer— Geraldine Provence(CAE); Pres. — JoAnn Chiasson (New Orleans Times-Picayune); 1st Vice Pres. — Andy Bass (Rock Hill (SC) Herald); 2nd Vice Pres. — Jim Hollenbeck; Sec./Treas. — Carl Bates
Elections held in Feb.

SOUTHERN NEWSPAPER PUBLISHERS ASSOCIATION — PO Box 28875, Atlanta, GA 30358; tel (404) 256-0444
Chmn. — David E Easterly; Pres. — Frank McDonald (Chattanooga (TN) Free Press); Pres.-Elect — Lissa Walls Vahldiek (Southern Newspapers Inc., Houston); Exec. Dir. — Reg Ivory; Treas. — H Graham Woodlief (Media General Inc., Richmond, VA); Asst. Exec. Dir. — Edward VanHorn;
Elections held in fall.

SOUTHWEST KANSAS EDITORIAL ASSOCIATION — Ness County News, PO Box C, Ness City, KS 67560; tel (913) 798-2213
District Dir. — Luke Brown (Hoisington)
Elections held at annual meeting.

SPECIAL LIBRARIES ASSOCIATION, NEWSPAPER DIVISION — 1700 18th St. NW, Washington, DC 20009-2508; tel (202) 234-4700
Chair — Charles Campo (Bangor (ME) Daily News); Bulletin Editor — Linda Henderson (Providence (RI) Journal)

STATE HISTORICAL SOCIETY OF WISCONSIN — 816 State St., Madison, WI 53711; tel (608) 264-6461
Ed. — Paul H Hass (Wisconsin Magazine of History); Assoc. Ed. — William C Marten; Assoc. Ed. — John O Holzhueter

SUBURBAN NEWSPAPERS OF AMERICA — 401 N. Michigan Ave., Chicago, IL 60611; tel (312) 644-6610; fax (312) 321-6869
Pres. — Wayne Toske (Community Newspapers Inc., WI); 1st Vice Pres. — Larry Randa (Life Printing & Publishing, IL); 2nd Vice Pres. — Jim Toms (Suburban News Publications/CM Newspapers, OH); Sec./Treas. — Tom Bradlee; Exec. Dir. — Larry Fleischman
Elections held in June.

T

TENNESSEE ASSOCIATED PRESS MANAGING EDITORS — PO Box 22990, Nashville, TN 37202; tel (423) 244-2205
Pres. — Frank Trexler (Maryville Daily Times); Pres.-Elect — Douglas Ray (Clarksville Leaf-Chronicle); Chief of Bureau — Kent Flanagan

TENNESSEE PRESS ASSOCIATION INC. — 6915 Office Park Cir., Knoxville, TN 37909-1162; tel (423) 584-5761
Pres. — Bobby Buckner (Lenoir City News-Herald); Vice Pres. — William R Fryar (Murfreesboro Daily News Journal); Vice Pres. — Scott Whaley (Henderson Chester County Independent); Treas. — Bob Childress (Sevierville Mountain Press); Exec. Dir. — Don G Campbell
Elections held in June.

TENNESSEE PRESS SERVICE INC. — 6915 Office Park Cir., Knoxville, TN 37909-1162; tel (615) 584-5761
Pres. — William R Fryar (Murfreesboro Daily News Journal); Vice Pres. — George T Whitley (Covington Leader); Exec. VP — Don G Campbell
Elections held in June.

TEXAS ASSOCIATED PRESS MANAGING EDITORS — PO Box 1792, Longview, TX 75606; tel (214) 745-0362
Pres. — Terry Scott Bertling (El Paso Herald-Post); 1st Vice Pres. — Tony Pederson (Houston Chronicle)
Elections held in March.

TEXAS CIRCULATION MANAGEMENT ASSOCIATION — PO Box 1870, Fort Worth, TX 76101; tel (817) 551-2201
Chmn. — Joe Ducote (Amarillo Globe); Pres. — Hollis Price (Houston Chronicle); Sec. — Weldon Whiteman (Fort Worth Star Telegram)
Elections held in Oct.

TEXAS DAILY NEWSPAPER ASSOCIATION — 98 San Jacinto Blvd., Ste. 1250, Austin, TX 78701-4039; tel (512) 476-4351; fax (512) 476-0515
Chmn. Exec. Cmte. — Dolph Tillotson (Galveston County Daily News); Pres. — Aubrey L Webb (Beaumont Enterprise); Vice Pres. — Richard L Connor (Fort Worth Star-Telegram); Treasurer — Garet Von Netzer (Amarillo Daily News); Exec. VP — Philip A Berkebile
Elections held in Nov.

TEXAS PRESS ASSOCIATION — 718 W. 5th St., Austin, TX 78701; tel (512) 477-6755; fax (512) 477-6755
Board Chariman — Dick Richards (Arkansas Pass Progress); Pres. — Sarah Greene (Gilmer Mirror); 1st VP — Jerry Tidwell (Granbury Hood County News); 2nd VP — Rollie Hyde (Plainview Daily Herald); Treas. — Larry Jackson (Wharton Journal-Spectator); Exec. VP — Lyndell Williams (TPA Central Office)
Elections held in June.

TUCSON PRESS CLUB — PO Box 1469, Tucson, AZ 85702-1469; tel (520) 690-1708
Pres. — David Fitzsimmons; Vice Pres. — Jack Sheaffer; Sec. — Y Z Painter-Demonte; Treas. — John Bort
Elections held in Jan.

U

UNIVERSITY PRESS OF KENTUCKY — 663 S. Limestone, Lexington, KY 40508-4008; tel (606) 257-2951; fax (606) 257-2984
Dir. — Kenneth Cherry
Elections held in spring/fall of odd numbered years.

UTAH-IDAHO-SPOKANE ASSOCIATED PRESS ASSOCIATION — 161 Regent St., Salt Lake City, UT 84111; tel (801) 322-3405; fax (801) 322-0051
Pres. — Jerry Brady (Idaho Falls (ID) Post Register); Sec. — William R Beecham
Elections held in June.

UTAH PRESS ASSOCIATION INC. — 307 W. 200 S., Ste. 5005, Salt Lake City, UT 84101-1212; tel (801) 328-8678; fax (801) 328-2226
Pres. — Lane Henderson; Vice Pres. — Steve Wallis; Treas. — Kevin Ashby; Exec. Dir. — Janice Keller
Elections held in March.

UTAH PRESS WOMEN — Box Elder News Journal, 625 W. 600 S., PO Box 370, Brigham City, UT 84302; tel (801) 723-3853; fax (801) 723-5247
Pres. — Sarah Yates (Brigham City Box Elder News Journal)
Elections held in April.

V

VALLEY PRESS CLUB INC. — PO Box 2901, Springfield, MA 01101; tel (413) 788-1287; fax (413) 788-1136
Pres. — Nancy Piccin; Vice Pres. — Trudy Tynan; Sec. — Derek Jarvis; Treas. — John S Mullen
Elections held in March.

VERMONT PRESS ASSOCIATION — St Michael's College, Journalism Dept., Colchester, VT 05439; tel (802) 654-2442
Pres. — Steve Costello (Barre-Montpelier Times Argus); Vice Pres. — Julie Metzger (Burlington Free Press); Sec. — Mary Jane Alexander (St. Michael's College); Treas. — M Dicky Drysdale (Herald Of Randolph); Exec. Dir. — Mike Donoghue (St. Michael's College)
Elections held in June.

VIRGINIA ASSOCIATED PRESS NEWSPAPERS ASSOCIATION — Associated Press, 700 E. Main St. S., Richmond, VA 23219; tel (804) 643-6646; fax (804) 643-6223
Member Ex-Officer — Dorothy Abernathy

VIRGINIA PRESS ASSOCIATION INC. — PO Box 85613, Richmond, VA 23285-5613; tel (804) 550-2361
Pres. — Harry Nanney; Pres.-Elect — Dick Morin
Elections held in July.

VIRGINIA PRESS WOMEN INC. — 218 Lakewood Park Dr., Newport News, VA 23602; tel (804) 247-4790
Pres. — Carolyn West; 1st Vice Pres. — Katherine Calos; 2nd Vice Pres. — Louise Seals; Sec. — Rebecca Whyley; Treas. — Mary Ann Johnson
Elections held in Sept. of even numbered years.

W

WASHINGTON ASSOCIATED PRESS NEWSPAPER EXECUTIVES ASSOCIATION — 201 Boren Ave. N., Seattle, WA 98109; tel (206) 682-1812
Pres. — Ken Robertson; Sec./Treas. — Dan Day (AP)
Elections held in Oct./Nov.

WASHINGTON NEWSPAPER PUBLISHERS ASSOCIATION INC. — 3838 Stone Way N., Seattle, WA 98103; tel (206) 634-3838
Pres. — Brown Maloney; 1st Vice Pres. — Fred Willenbrock
Elections held in July; officers installed in Sept.

WASHINGTON PRESS ASSOCIATION — 14243 156th Ave. S.E., Renton, WA 98059; tel (206) 654-5100/(206) 228-5903; fax (206) 277-8584

WASHINGTON WOMEN IN PUBLIC RELATIONS — Washington Sq., PO Box 65297, Washington, DC 20035-5297; tel (202) 310-1027; fax (202) 296-3727
Pres. Emerita — Pam Jenkins; Past Pres. — Kate Perrin; Bd. Member — Jackie Marquis; Mktg. Dir. — Shelly Caplan
Elections held every Jan.

WEST TEXAS PRESS ASSOCIATION — 2502 Ivanhoe Ln., Abilene, TX 79605; tel (915) 692-1087; fax (915) 692-1086
Pres. — Jim Lowe; 1st Vice Pres. — Mark Jordan; 2nd Vice Pres. — Russel Skiles; Sec./Treas. — Barbara Craig Kelly
Election held at annual convention in July.

WEST VIRGINIA NEWS PHOTOGRAPHERS ASSOCIATION — 1001 Virginia St., Charleston, WV 25301; tel (304) 348-1234

Copyright ©1996 by the Editor & Publisher Co.

Pres. — Craig Cunningham; Vice Pres. — Dale Sparks; Sec./Treas. — Kenneth Kemp
Elections held in Feb.

WEST VIRGINIA PRESS ASSOCIATION INC. — 3422 Pennsylvania Ave., Charleston, WV 25302; tel (304) 342-1011; fax (304) 343-5879
Pres. — Robert Nutting; VP/Weeklies — Jim McGoldrick; VP/Dailies — Terry Horne; Treas. — George Wallace
Elections held in Aug.

WESTERN CLASSIFIED ADVERTISING ASSOCIATION — News Press, 722 Dela Guerra Plz., Santa Barbara, CA 93102; tel (415) 777-7415
Pres. — Larry Kline (Los Angeles Times); 1st Vice Pres. — Rebecca Bradner; 2nd Vice Pres. — Nancy Stimac (Los Angeles Daily News); Treas. — Joyce Brede (Spokane (WA) Spokesman Review)
Elections held in Oct.

WESTERN STATES ADVERTISING AGENCIES ASSOCIATION — 6404 Wilshire Blvd., Ste. 1111, Los Angeles, CA 90048; tel (213) 387-7432
Exec. Dir. — Ruth Oreck

WHITE HOUSE CORRESPONDENTS ASSOCIATION — 1067 National Press Bldg., Washington, DC 20045; tel (202) 737-2934; fax (202) 783-0841
Pres. — Carl P Leubsdorf (Dallas Morning News); Treas. — Larry McQuillan (Reuters); Sec. — Mike McKee (Conus)
Elections held in March.

WHITE HOUSE NEWS PHOTOGRAPHERS ASSOCIATION — 7119 Ben Franklin Sta., Washington, DC 20044-7119; tel (202) 785-5230; fax (301) 428-4904
Pres. — Kenneth L Blaylock; Vice Pres. — Kevin Gilbert; Sec. — Steve Affens; Treas. — J David Ake

WISCONSIN ASSOCIATED PRESS ASSOCIATION — 918 N. Fourth St., Milwaukee, WI 53203; tel (414) 225-3580
Pres. — Debbie Bradley (Stevens Point Journal); Chief of Bureau — T Lee Hughes
Elections held in May.

WISCONSIN NEWSPAPER ASSOCIATION — 3822 Mineral Point Rd., PO Box 5580, Madison, WI 53705; tel (608) 238-7171
Pres. — David Johnson; 1st Vice Pres. — Mike Mathes; 2nd Vice Pres. — David Gentry; 3rd Vice Pres. — Bill Haupt; Sec. — Mary Kunasch; Treas. — Diane Everson
Elections held in June.

WISCONSIN OUTDOOR COMMUNICATORS ASSOCIATION (WOCA) — 917 N. Glendale Ave., Tomah, WI 54660; tel (608) 372-2640
Pres. — Gene Cooper; Vice Pres. — Pat Durkin; Newsletter Ed. — Kevin Naze
Elections held in Aug.

WOMEN'S PRESS CLUB OF INDIANA — 240 S. Main St., Sullivan, IN 47882; tel (812) 268-5588
Pres. — Ellen Sparks; 1st Vice Pres. — Jackie Davis; 2nd Vice Pres. — Marty Heline; 3rd Vice Pres. — Ann Weldy; Recording Sec. — Judi Turpen; Corresponding Sec. — Ann Hubbard; Treas. — Dana Cline; Historian — Joan Bey
Elections held in Mar. of even numbered years.

WORLD PRESS FREEDOM COMMITTEE — The Newspaper Center, 11600 Sunrise Valley Dr., Reston, VA 22091; tel (703) 648-1000; fax (703) 620-4557
Chmn. — Harold W Andersen; Treas. — Leonard H Marks; Exec. Dir. — Dana R Bullen
Elections held every two years in May.

WYOMING ASSOCIATED PRESS ASSOCIATION — PO Box 1323, Cheyenne, WY 82003; tel (307) 632-9351
Pres. — Dave Perry
Elections held in Jan.

WYOMING MEDIA PROFESSIONALS INC. — 4606 E. 13th St., Cheyenne, WY 82001; tel (307) 634-1744/(307) 777-7014
President — Linda Rollins; 1st Vice Pres. — Denice Wheeler; 2nd Vice Pres. — Leslie Blythe; Secretary — Sandra Hansen; Treasurer — Janet Kolb
Elections held in Jan. of odd numbered years.

WYOMING PRESS ASSOCIATION — 1369 N. Fourth, Laramie, WY 82070; tel (307) 745-8144
Pres. — Ron Franscell (Gillette News-Record)
Elections held in Jan.

CLIP ART SERVICES

This listing includes services that furnish ready-made art work, as well as complete advertisements or suggestions that can be used to sell prospective advertisers in either mat form or in the form of offset reproduction proofs; some are available on contractual basis, while others are sold as a complete package.

Advertisers Exchange Inc. — 36 Forest Rd., PO Box 74, Tranquility, NJ 07879; tel (908) 852-2186; fax (908) 852-8863
Malcolm G Smith
Super Market Ad Service — For markets using medium or space layouts. Includes headings, copy, decorative boxes. Monthly.

Associated Release Service Inc. — 2 N. Riverside Plz., Chicago, IL 60606; tel (312) 726-8693; fax (312) 726-8596
Mat and offset service — Free publicity features to editors including individual mat releases and themed pages (two or more features mailed together).

Banker & Brisebois Co. — 200 E. Long Lake Rd., Ste. 145, Bloomfield Hills, MI 48304-2361; tel (810) 540-1033; fax (810) 540-4379
Furniture Ad Idea Services — Two different monthly services for low to medium grade and medium to medium-high grade furniture stores. New each month, no repeats. Monthly issues feature ready-to-run ads, direct mail pieces and radio scripts for promoting various store-wide events and departments.
Continental Furniture Ad Idea Service — Medium to medium-high priced lines with distinctive quality approach (monthly).

B.A.S.I.C.-Bedell Advertising Selling Improvement Corp. — 600 Ward Dr., Ste. H, Santa Barbara, CA 93111; tel (805) 863-5857
Instant Inches Copy Library — Individual ads and campaign series covering virtually all retail categories from auto service and beauty salons to pharmacies, real estate and many more, including food markets. Show and sell copy written by the nation's top retail response specialists. Many with working layouts and repro art.

Century Features Inc. — PO Box 597, Pittsburgh, PA 15230; tel (412) 471-6533
Charles Reichblum
I Bet You Didn't Know — Series of sports columns leased exclusively to automobile dealers, tire dealers, men's stores, etc.
Calling All Home Makers — Series of furniture columns leased to furniture stores.
Interesting Facts — Leased exclusively to one sponsor in each community.
Thoughts for the Week — Leased exclusively to one sponsor in each community.

Coleman Advertising Inc. — 6000 S. Padre Island Dr., Ste. 202, PO Box 271316, Corpus Christi, TX 78427; tel (512) 992-6499
General Manager — Zack Coleman
Everyone in The Church and Support America — Advertising—Selling Programs—local weekly sponsorships; 3 X 4 col. SA6 proof series.

Derus Media Service Inc. — 500 N. Dearborn St., Chicago, IL 60610; tel (312) 644-4360
Matt McGawn
Production and Mass Distribution Service — Offset repro proofs on regular basis to newspapers, company publications, etc. Publishers, Editorial Pace Magazine. Features available in English and Spanish.

Dynamic Graphics Inc. — 6000 N. Forest Park Dr., Peoria, IL 61614; tel (309) 688-8800
Chairman — John L Rush
Co-Pres. — Jayme Mueller
Co-Pres. — Nancy Ruenzel
VP-Mktg./Sales — Peter Force
All-Purpose Art and Idea Service

Family Features Editorial Services Inc. — 8309 Melrose Dr., Shawnee Mission, KS 66214; tel (913) 888-3800; fax (913) 888-3503
President — Dianne Selders Hogerty
Director of Marketing — Nancy Parsons
Mgr. of Media & Member Services — Ken Glaser
Family Features Editorial Service Inc. — Provides editors with reproduction materials of pre-designed color features for food, lifestyle, home, garden, travel and entertainment. These industry sponsored features are free-of-charge for exclusive publication by editors whose orders are confirmed by Family Features. Materials provided include: 85-line film for the entire page; film separations for the photography only; transparencies, black-and-white glossies and disks. Also available free-of-charge are non-exclusive feature infographics provided as transparencies and black & white slicks. Editors wanting to review samples of available features may call (800) 800-5579 and ask for Media and Member Services.

Jobson Publishing Corp. — 100 Ave. of the Americas, 9th Fl., New York, NY 10013; tel (212) 274-7000; fax (212) 431-0500
Package Power Retail Advertising Services — Published semiannually for each of the following classifications: Drug/Mass Merchandise, Liquor, Wine & Beer, Supermarket/Non-Food and Grocery Product Editions. All editions contain camera-ready product illustrations (line art) for retailers and newspapers for use in retail advertisements, circulars, handbills, coupon promotion, catalogs, etc. Product illustrations are available in B&W and four-color.

Keister-Williams Newspaper Services Inc. — 1807 Emmet St., PO Box 8005, Charlottesville, VA 22906; tel (800) 293-4709; fax (804) 293-4884
President — Walton G Lindsay
Mktg. Dir. — Meta Noy
Sales Mgr. — Ky Lindsay
Support the Church — Weekly series; Two, three or four column glossy form. Solicitation of sponsorship available through Keister in most states or by newspaper staff.

Macdonald Classified Service Inc. — 14 N. Second Ave., Lafayette, IN 47901-1204; tel (800) 237-9075; fax (317) 742-2843
MacDonald Classified Service — A monthly information/art/idea service for classified advertising departments of newspapers.

Marktime Advertisers Inc. — PO Box 66, Indian Hills, CO 80454; tel (303) 986-5656; fax (303) 986-5657
Syndicated cartoons for editorial and feature use. Cartoons and ad copy for display advertising. Specializing in bank and auto dealers.

Metro Creative Graphics Inc. — 33 W. 34th St., New York, NY 10001; tel (800) 223-1600/(212) 947-5100; fax (212) 967-4602
Metro Newspaper Service — Art, ideas and color in a monthly subscription. Cost-effective way to enhance creative, production and sales staffs.
Classified Dynamics — A service of promotional ideas and tie-ins geared toward automotive, real estate and classified advertisers.
Sales Spectaculars — Themed spec ads targeted toward smaller advertisers.
Metro Publicity Services — Generic and advertorial section features in tabloid formats.
Holiday Advertising Service — Holiday greetings service with color and content.
Plus Business — Monthly journal of ideas and case histories.
AdCreation Toolkit — New QuarkXTension that enhances ability of QuarkXPress to create, track and paginate ads.

Mosaic Arts Co. (Estab. 1956) — 43288 Happy Woods Rd., Hammond, LA 70403; tel (504) 542-8311
Gina Matticari

Multi-Ad Services Inc. — 1720 W. Detweiller Dr., Peoria, IL 61615-1695; tel (800) 447-1950/(309) 692-1530; fax (309) 693-1648
Marketing Manager — Marc Radosevic
Ad-Builder — Monthly publication geared at increasing size and effectiveness of retail advertising.
SCAN (Selective Classified Advertising for Newspapers) — Monthly publication specifically designed to build classified display advertising.

News USA Inc. — 8300 Boone Blvd., Ste. 810, Vienna, VA 22182; tel (703) 827-5800/(800) 355-9500; fax (703) 827-5814
Media Relations Director — William H Watson
Features — From non-profit national associations and federal government agencies free to newspapers on request. Attribution to News USA as source is requested.
Health — Your Medicines.
Consumer Issues — Around the House by Jeff Keller.
Car Care Tips — From the Car Care Council.
Photos-Food-TV-Seniors-Holiday Gifts — Written by top journalist formerly with the Associated Press and the Washington Post.

North American Precis Syndicate Inc. — 201 E. 42nd St., New York, NY 10017; tel (212) 867-9000; fax (212) 983-0970
President — Ronald N Levy
Editor-In-Chief — Candace Leiberman
Service Manager — Steve Seeman
Featurettes (free filler/feature service) — Free repro proofs or diskettes of cartoons, features and fillers from PR sources mailed twice a week; free on behalf of 700 non-profit organizations, trade associations and government agencies to newspapers on request. Not copyrighted. Background on Business, Fancy That, Family Health, Car Care Corner, Good Citizenship, News of Food, America's Leaders, Quick Quiz, Exterior Decorating, Understanding Our Economy, News of Travel, Inflation Fighting Ideas, Facts & Figures, Voter Information Department, Hints For Homeowners, Good News Department, News For Senior Citizens and Holiday Hints.

Reilly Graphics Chicago — 160 E. Illinois, Chicago, IL 60611; tel (312) 337-5500; (800) 621-8314; fax (312) 337-3724
Creative and Production — Service in preparation and distribution of full color and B&W ROP publicity and feature releases for food companies and related associations (direct or through their agencies). All printing materials for editorial features (such as food pages in color) are offered free to newspapers in U.S. by the sponsoring source.

Retail Reporting Bureau, Div. Of Milton B Conhaim Inc. — 302 5th Ave., New York, NY 10001; tel (212) 279-7000; fax (212) 279-7014
Retail Ad Week — Weekly reprints of department & specialty store advertising culled from over 255 newspapers published in U.S. & Canada.

Syndicated Ad Features Inc. — 19 Needham St., Newton Highlands, MA 02161; tel (617) 965-7333; fax (617) 527-4501
A specialized advertising agency established in 1967. Ghostwrites feature columns and personalized concluding paragraphs for 35 businesses and medical professions that appear under a client's picture and by-line in a local newspaper on an exclusive basis. The program consists of a 52-week supply of informative, fresh, topical articles run as display ads. Each column covers a different aspect of the particular subject, prepared in a manner that is not too technical and well within the easy understanding of the average newspaper reader.

CLIPPING BUREAUS

Allen's Press Clipping Bureau — 657 Mission St., Rm. 602, San Francisco, CA 94105; tel (415) 392-2353; fax (415) 362-6208
Gen. Mgr. — John N McCombs
Portland, OR 97205-3620 — 621 S.W. Alder, Rm. 540; tel (503) 223-7824;
Seattle, WA 98101 — 1218 3rd Ave., Rm. 1010; tel (206) 622-8312;
Los Angeles, CA 90014 — 215 W. 6th St., Rm. 1100; tel (213) 628-4214
Bacon's Clipping Bureau — 332 S. Michigan Ave., Chicago, IL 60604; tel (312) 922-2400/(800) 621-0561; fax (312) 922-3127
Marketing Manager — Steve Pattengale
Bowdens MH Media Monitoring — 2206 Eglinton Ave., Ste. 190, Scarborough, ON M1L 4T5 Canada; tel (416) 750-2220
Burrelle's Press Clipping Bureau — 75 E. Northfield Ave., Livingston, NJ 07039; tel (201) 992-6600/(800) 631-1160
President — Robert C Waggoner
Canadian Press Clipping Services — 2206 Eglinton Ave. E., Ste. 190, Scarborough, ON M1L 4T5 Canada; tel (416) 750-2220 ext. 203; fax (416) 750-2233
Manager — S Petrykewycz
Colorado Press Clipping Service — 1336 Glenarm Pl., Denver, CO 80204; tel (303) 571-5117; fax (303) 571-1803
Director of Advertising — Gregory V Appel
Illinois Press Clip — 701 S. Grand West, Springfield, IL 62704; tel (217) 523-5095; fax (217) 523-5134
Asst. Exec. Dir. — Kathy Galloway
International Press Clipping Bureau Inc. — (See Burrelle's Press Clipping Bureau)
International Press Cutting Bureau — 224/236 Walworth Rd., London, SE17 1JE; England; tel (0171) 708-2113; fax (0171) 701-4489
Partner — Robert Podro
Luce Press Clippings Inc. — 420 Lexington Ave., Ste. 203, New York, NY 10170; tel (212) 889-6711/(800) 628-0376; fax (212) 481-0105
Nat'l. Sales Dir. — Arnold B Knepper
Mutual Press Clipping Service Inc. — 1930 Chestnut St., Philadelphia, PA 19103; tel (215) 569-4257; fax (215) 557-9120
Vice Pres./Gen. Mgr. — Sharon L Redcay
New England Newsclip Agency Inc. — 5 Auburn St., PO Box 9128, Farmingham, MA 01701-9128; tel (508) 879-4460
Vice Pres./Gen. Mgr. — Gail E Milligan
New Jersey Clipping Service — 99 E. Northfield Rd., Livingston, NJ 07039; tel (201) 994-3333
Vice Pres. — Ruth Booth
New Mexico Press Clipping Bureau — 2531 Wyoming N.E., Albuquerque, NM 87112; tel (505) 275-1241; fax (505) 275-1241
Manager — Holly Mote
New York State Clipping Service — 200 Central Park Ave., Hartsdale, NY 10530; tel (800) 772-5477; fax (914) 948-3534
General Manager — Rick Melchers
Oklahoma Press Association — 3601 N. Lincoln, Oklahoma City, OK 73105-5499; tel (405) 524-4421
President — Marshall Settle
Clipping Bureau Mgr. — Chris Johnson
Romeike & Curtice Ltd. — Hale House, 290-296 Green Lanes, London, N13 5TP; England; tel (0181) 882-0155; fax (0181) 882-6716
Managing Dir. — Simon H Lanyon
Sales & Mktg. Mgr. — Angela D Webb
South Carolina Press Services Inc. — PO Box 11429, Columbia, SC 29211; tel (803) 750-9561; fax (803) 551-0903
Exec. Dir. — William C Rogers
Manager — Jill Bettendorf
South Dakota Newspaper Association — South Dakota State Univ., PO Box 2230, Brookings, SD 57007; tel (605) 692-4300
Clipping Bureau Mgr. — Judy Raines
Virginia Press Services Inc. — PO Box 85613, Richmond, VA 23285-5613; tel (804) 550-2361; fax (804) 550-2407
Exec. Mgr. — Ginger Stanley
West Virginia Press Services Inc. — 3422 Pennsylvania Ave., Charleston, WV 25302; tel (304) 342-6908; fax (304) 343-8879
Manager — W F Childress

ELECTRONIC CLIPPING BUREAUS

Associated Press Information Services/*News-Desk Software* — 50 Rockefeller Plz., New York, NY 10020; tel (212) 621-1585/(800) 272-2551; fax (212) 621-5488
Sales Manager/AP Information Services — Jack Szluka
Business Wire/*BW NewsClips* — 1185 Ave. of the Americas, 3rd Fl., New York, NY 10036; tel (212) 575-8822;
Customer Service: New York Office (800) 221-2462
San Francisco Office (800) 227-0845
Clarinet Communications Corp./*Clarinet e.News* — 4880 Stevens Creek Blvd., Ste. 206, San Jose, CA 95129-1034; tel (408) 296-0366/(800) 873-6387
Vice Pres./Sales & Mktg. — Simon Clephan
Data Times/*PASSPort fax product* — 14000 Quail Springs Pkwy., Ste. 450, Oklahoma City, OK 73134; tel (800) 419-1329
Exec. Services Mgr. — Dan Cavallo
Dialog Information Services Inc./*DIALOG Alert* — 3460 Hillview Ave., Palo Alto, CA 94304; tel (415) 858-3785/(800) 334-2564
Genie Information Services/*Quick News* — 401 N. Washington St., Rockville, MD 20850; tel (301) 340-4184
Sr. Product Manager — Jackie Isreal
Individual Inc./*Heads Up - Personalized Daily News Service* — 8 New England/Executive Park W., Burlington, MA 01803; tel (617) 354-2230/(800) 414-1000
Product Manager — James F Leightheiser
Luce Online 8096 N. 85 Way, Scottsdale, AZ 85258; tel (800) 518-0088; fax (602) 922-3174
President — John P French
Nat'l. Sales Mgr. — Kelly Schmitt
Mainstream Data Inc./*Eclipse* (LEXIS/Nexis electronic clipping service) — 420 Chipeta Way, Salt Lake City, UT 84108; tel (801) 584-2800
Director of Marketing — Tim Bruske
NewsNet/*NewsFlash* — 945 Haverford Rd., Bryn Mawr, PA 19010; tel (610) 527-8030; fax (610) 527-0338
President — Andrew Elston
VP/Marketing — Robert M Hunsicker
VP/Systems Services — Tom Scott
VP/Software Development — Mike Stein
Dir. Customer Support — Susan Volk
Mgr./Publisher Services — Sandra McLean
Southam Electronic Publishing/*Infomart Custom Search* — 1450 Don Mills Rd., Don Mills, ON M38 2X7; tel (800) 668-9215; fax (416) 442-2126
National Sales Manager — Gino Sette

FOREIGN NEWSPAPER REPRESENTATIVES

ASSOCIATED NEWSPAPERS (USA) LTD.
500 5th Ave., Rm. 312, New York, NY 10110; tel (212) 869-2570
Chief of Bureau — George Gordon
Columnist — Dermot Purgavie
Manager — Linda Pacheco
Correspondent — Tony Gallagher
England — Daily Mail, Mail on Sunday, Evening Standard

AXEL SPRINGER GROUP INC.
565 5th Ave., New York, NY 10017-2413; tel (212) 972-1720; fax (212) 972-1724
e-mail: asginc@aol.com
Vice President — Dieter Bruhn
Asst. Account Exec. — Petra Gerstenberger
Germany — Bild, Bild am Sonntag, Die Welt, Welt am Sonntag, Hamburger Abendblatt, Berliner Morgenpost, BZ, BZ am Sonntag, Bergedorfer Zeitung, Elmshorner Nachrichten, Harburger Anzeigen und Nachrichten, Kieler Nachrichten, Leipziger Volkszeitung, LÅbecker Nachrichten, Ostsee-Zeitung, Pinneberger Tageblatt, Spandauer Volksblatt

THE N DE FILIPPES CORP.
310 Madison Ave., Ste. 1012, New York, NY 10017-6009; tel (212) 697-6868; fax (212) 697-6770
Mgr.-International Group — Veronica Shea

Argentina — Ambito Financiero, Buenos Aires Herald, Clarin, El Cronista Comercial, Prensa Economica., La Nacion
Bahamas — Freeport News, Nassau Guardian
Bolivia — El Diario
Brazil — Correio Brasilense, Diario Catarinense, Diario da Manha, Diario do Comercio, Gazeta Mercantil, El Diario, Jornal do Brasil, Jornal da Tarde, O Estado de Minas, O Estado de Sao Paulo, O Globo, Zero Hora
Chile — El Diario, El Mercurio, La Tercera
Colombia — El Colombiano, El Espectador, El Pais, El Tiempo
Costa Rica — La Nacion, Tico Times
Curacao — La Prensa
Dominican Republic — El Nacional, La Informacion, Listen Diario
Ecuador — El Comercio, El Universo
Germany — Borseri-Zeitung
Guam — Pacific Daily News, La Prensa
Honduras — El Heraldo, El Tiempo, La Prensa, La Tribuna
Hong Kong — South China Morning Post
Mexico — El Economista, El Excelsior, Al Riyadh, Arrayah, El Financiero, El Heraldo, El Informador, El Norte, El Universal, The News, Novedades, Reforma
Middle East — Al Qabas, Al Ra'i, Al Riyadh, Arrayah, Jordan Times, Khaleej Times, Okaz, Riyadh Daily, Saudi Gazette
Panama — La Estrella de Panama, La Prensa
Paraguay — El Diario Noticias, Hoy
Peru — Correo, El Comercio, Expreso, Gestion
Philippines — Manila Bulletin
Puerto Rico — El Vocero
St. Maarten — Chronicle
Tortola — Island Sun
Uruguay — El Pais
Venezuela — Caracas Daily Journal, Economia Hoy, El Mundo, El Nacional, El Universal, Reporte de la Economia, Ultimas Noticias
Virgin Islands — Daily News, St. Croix Avis

DOW JONES INTERNATIONAL MARKETING SERVICES
420 Lexington Ave., New York, NY 10170; tel (212) 808-6618
Managing Director — Jim Friedlich
Sales Director — Lawrence J Dill
Administrative Manager — Pat Carrino
Advertising Mgr.-Latin America/Caribbean — Michele Evenson
Asia — Far Eastern Economic Review
Hong Kong — South China Morning Post
Japan — Nihon Keizai Shimbun
Singapore — Straits Times

INTERCONTINENTAL SERVICES LTD.
347 5th Ave., Ste. 1007, New York, NY 10016; tel (212) 679-3910; fax (212) 679-3912
Sales Representative — Mercedes M Amundsen
SAN JUAN, PUERTO RICO 00910
1605 Ponce de Leon Ave.
Santurce, Puerto Rico 00910
tel (809) 722-5665
Antigua — Outlet, Nation
Aruba — Aruba Today, Bon Dia Aruba
Curacao — Business Journal, Extra, La Prensa
Grenada — Voice, Informer, Times
Guyana — Guyana Chronicle
Jamaica — The Observer
St. Kitts — Democrat, Labour Spokesman
St. Lucia — Voice of St. Lucia
St. Maarten — Chronicle
Trinidad — Trinidad Express, Weekend Sun, Tobago News, Junior Express

INTERNATIONAL SUBSCRIPTIONS INC.
30 Montgomery St., 7th Fl., Jersey City, NJ 07302; tel (800) 544-6784/(201) 451-9420; fax (201) 451-5745
Operations Manager — Barbara Errico

LATIN ADMERICA INC.
1260 S.W. 1st St., Miami, FL 33135; tel (305) 649-2005; fax (305) 649-7733
President — Omar Pinto
Argentina — Buenos Aires-Buenos Aires Herald, El Clarin
Bolivia — La Paz-Presencia
Brazil — Rio De Janeiro-Jornal Do Brasil, O Globo, Sao Paulo-Folha De Sao Paulo
Chile — Santiago-El Mercurio, La Segunda, La Tercera
Colombia — Bogota-El Tiempo, Cali-El Pais, Medellin-El Colombiano
Costa Rica — San Jose-La Nacion
Dominican Republic — Santo Domingo-El Caribe, Listin Diario
Ecuador — Guayaquil-El Telegrafo, Quito-El Comercio
El Salvador — San Salvador-El Mundo, La Prensa Grafica
Guatemala — Guatemala City-Prensa Libra

Copyright ©1996 by the Editor & Publisher Co.

Honduras — San Pedro-La Sula Prensa
Mexico — CD Juarez-El Fronterizo, Larado-El Diario, Mexico City-Excelsior, El Universal, Monterey-El Norte, Saltillo-El Heraldo De Saltillo, Tijuana-El Heraldo De Baja California, Netherlands Antilles-Willemstad-La Prensa
Nicaragua — Managua-La Prensa
Panama — Panama City-La Estrella De Panama, La Prensa
Paraguay — Asuncion-Ultima Hora
Uruguay — Montevideo-El Pais
Venezuela — Caracas-Diario De Caracas, El Mundo, El Universal

LEE & STEEL INC.

415 Madison Ave., New York, NY 10017; tel (212) 754-0800; fax (212) 421-4419
Adelaide — The Advertiser
Brisbane — Courier Mail, Sunday Mail
Europe — European
Fiji — Times
Japan — Asahi Shimbun, Asahi Evening News
Perth — Western Australian
Scotland — Scotsman, Scotland on Sunday, Evening News
Spain — Diario 16
England — Illustrated London News

MARSTON WEBB INTERNATIONAL

60 Madison Ave., Ste. 1101, New York, NY 10010; tel (212) 684-6601; fax (212) 725-4709
President — Victor Webb
Vice President — Madiene Olson
Australia — Australian Financial Review, Sydney Morning Herald, Melbourne Age, Business Review Weekly
Germany — Top Business
Japan — Yomiuri Shimbun

MULTIMEDIA INC.

7061 Grand National Dr., Ste. 127, Orlando, FL 32819-8377; tel (407) 363-1555/(800) 985-8588; fax (407) 363-9809
President — Fernando Mariano
Vice President — Wanderley Pucci
Director — Suely Mariano
Brazil — O Globo

PUBLICITAS INC.

220 5th Ave., New York, NY 10001; tel (212) 689-1888; fax (212) 689-1717
Pres./US Adv. Rep. For Foreign Publications — Anthony R Wight
Australia — Australian, National; Sunday Telegraph, Sydney; Daily Telegraph Mirror, Sydney; Herald-Sun News Pictorial, Melbourne
Austria — Die Presse, Vienna; Kurier, Vienna; Der Standard, Vienna; Neue Kronen Zeitung, Vienna
Belgium — Le Soir, Brussels; L'Echo, Brussels; Le Soir Illustre, Brussels; De Standaard, Brussels; De Financieel Ekonomische TITD, Antwerp
Denmark — Berlingske Tidende, Copenhagen; Morgenavisen/Jyllands Posten, Aarhus
Dubai — Khaleej Times
Egypt — Al Ahram, Cairo
Finland — Helsingin Sanomat, Helsinki; Ilta-Sanomat, Helsinki; Aamulehti, Tampere; Turun Sanomat, Turku
France — La Tribune Desfosses, Paris; L'Agefi, Paris
Germany — Frankfurter Allgemeine, Zeitung; Rheinische Post, Duesseldorf; Der Tagesspiegel, Berlin; Die Zeit, Hamburg; Sueddeutsche Zietung
Greece — Naftemboriki, Athens; Akropolis, Athens
Hong Kong — Hong Kong Standard, Sing Tao Jih Pao, Sing Tao Wan Pao
Indonesia — Indonesian Observer, Jakarta; Merdeka, Jakarta
Ireland — Irish Times, Dublin
Israel — Jerusalem Post; Ha'Aretz, Tel Aviv
Italy — Il Sole 24 Ore, Milan; Giornale, Milan; Il Messaggero, Rome; La Repubblica, Rome; Il Venerdi, Rome; Il Secolo XIX, Genoa; La Stampa, Turin
Japan — Japan Times, Tokyo; Mainichi Shimbun, Tokyo; Nikkan Kogyo Shimbun, Tokyo
Korea — Korean Economic Daily, Seoul
Kuwait — Al Seyassah, Al Qabas, Arab Times
Luxembourg — Luxemburger Wort
Netherlands — De Telegraaf, Amsterdam; De Courant Nieuws Van de Dag, Amsterdam; Weekeinde, Amsterdam; De Volkskrant, Amsterdam; Het Financieele Dagblad, Amsterdam; Nrc Handelsblad, Rotterdam; Algemeen Dagblad, Rotterdam
New Zealand — New Zealand Herald, Aukland

Foreign correspondents VII-13

Norway — Aftenposten, Oslo; Bergens Tidende, Bergen; Adresseavisen, Trondheim
Pakistan — Dawn, Karachi
Philippines — Manila Bulletin
Portugal — Diario de Noticias, Lisbon; Expresso, Lisbon
Russia — Izvestia, Moscow; Kommersant
Scotland — Glasgow Herald, Glasgow, Evening Times
Spain — La Vanguardia, Barcelona; ABC, Madrid; El Pais, Madrid; Cinco Dias, Madrid; ABC, Seville
Sweden — Svenska Dagbladet, Stockholm; Dagens Dyheter, Stockholm; Expressen, Stockholm; Gotesborgs-Posten, Gothenburg; GT, Gothenburg; Sydsvenska Dagbladet; Malmo, Kvaellsposten, Malmo
Switzerland — Neue Zuercher Zeitung, Zurich; Tages Anzeiger, Zurich; Finanz und Wirtschaft, Zurich; Schweizerische Handelszeitung, Zurich; Basler Zeitung, Basel; Der Bund, Berne; Journal de Geneve, Geneva; Tribune de Geneve, Geneva; Le Nouveau Quotidien, Lausanne; 24 Heures, Lausanne; Corriere del Ticino, Lugano
United Kingdom — Independent, London; Independent on Sunday, London
Yorkshire — Yorkshire on Sunday

SYDNEY MORNING HERALD LTD. (JOHN FAIRFAX U.S. LIMITED)

1500 Broadway, Rm. 1002, New York, NY 10036; tel (212) 398-9494; fax (212) 819-1745
Editor/Manager — Philip McCarthy
Australia — Sydney Morning Herald, Sun-Herald, Melbourne, Age, Australian Financial Review

T.L.I. INTERNATIONAL CORP.

680 N. Lake Shore Dr., Ste. 1220, Chicago, IL 60611; tel (312) 944-7800; fax (312) 944-7674
President — Lyric Hughes

People's Republic of China, Hong Kong, Taiwan, — Renmin Ribao (The People's Daily), Beijing, Jinhji Ribao (Economic Daily), Beijing, China Daily, Beijing, Beijing Market, Beijing, Weh Hui Bao, Shanghai, Yangcheng Wanbao (Yangcheng Evening Post), Guangzhou (Canton), Guangzhou Ribao, Nanfang Daily, Guangzhou, Liaoning Daily, Shenyang, Science and Technology Daily, Beijing, Economic Daily, Beijing and a host of trade, journals in telecommunications, electric, power, construction, machinery building and other, industries.

TRADE MEDIA INTERNATIONAL CORP.

1328 Broadway, New York, NY 10001-2190; tel (212) 5643380
Account Supervisor — Gabrielle Lefer
Thailand — Bangkok Post
TMI deals in several hundred trade and industrial publications in approximately 40 Standard Industry code categories in Wetern Europe, Japan, Australia & the Pacific Rim.

U.S. BUREAU OF NEWS LTD. & TIMES NEWSPAPER

1211 Ave. of the Americas, New York, NY 10036; tel (212) 852-7600; fax (212) 852-7671
Bureau Chief & Chief U.S. Correspondent — Peter Atkinson
London Times Correspondent — Ben McIntyre
London Sunday Times Correspondent — Sean McCartaigh
London Sun Correspondent — Caroline Graham
London — London Times, London Sunday Times, London Sun London Today
Australia — Australian, Weekend Australian, Adelaide, Advertiser, Sun Mail, Brisbane, Courier-Mail, Sydney, Telegraph Mirror, Perth, Sunday Times Melbourne, Courier-London Mail, Mercury Sunday Tasmanian

---

FOREIGN PRESS & RADIO-TV CORRESPONDENTS IN THE UNITED STATES

NEW YORK CORRESPONDENTS

ARGENTINA

Avante Premier — 209 E. 60th St., Ste. D-1, New York, NY 10022; tel (212) 963-1608; fax (212) 832-8744
Correspondent — Jacqueline Aidenbaum
Cablevision — 382 3rd Ave., Ste. 15-A, New York, NY 10016; tel (212) 696-4767; fax (212) 213-9631
Correspondent — Claudio Bevilacqua
Correspondent — Carlos Alberto Marino
DYN-Diarios Y Noticias S A — PO Box 357, Prince St. Sta., New York, NY 10012; tel (212) 925-4889
Photographer — Marcelo Javier Duek
Editorial Atlantida — 847-A 2nd Ave., Ste. 161, New York, NY 10017; tel (212) 682-3011; fax (212) 682-2943
Bureau Chief — Alberto Oliva
Correspondent — Adriana Siero
El Cronista Comercial — 382 3rd Ave., Ste. 15-A, New York, NY 10016; tel (212) 696-4767; fax (212) 213-9631
Correspondent — Claudio Bevilacqua
Correspondent — Carlos Alberto Marino
Gente — 847-A 2nd Ave., Ste. 161, New York, NY 10017; tel (212) 682-3011; fax (212) 682-2943
Bureau Chief — Alberto Oliva
Correspondent — Adriana Siero

Interco Press Agency — PO Box 4463, Grand Central Sta., New York, NY 10163; tel (718) 896-6736; fax (718) 996-6736
Correspondent — Juan Fercsey
La Nacion — 285 Central Park West, New York, NY 10024; tel (212) 866-0248
Correspondent — Roberto E Socas
La Prensa — PO Box 4463, Grand Central Sta., New York, NY 10163; tel (718) 896-6736; fax (718) 996-6736
Correspondent — Juan Fercsey
La Verdad — PO Box 1196, Triborough Sta., New York, NY 10035; tel (212) 722-5061
Correspondent — Jose Otero
Noticias — PO Box 210, Prince St. Sta., New York, NY 10012; tel (212) 732-1647; fax (201) 792-4230
Correspondent — Charles Torrini
Perfil Editorial — 200 E. 58th St., Ste. 8-A, New York, NY 10022; tel (212) 888-6453; fax (212) 421-9344
Correspondent — Carlos Lauria

ARMENIA

Armenian News Agency — PO Box 228, Murray Hill Sta., New York, NY 10156-0228
Correspondent — Florence Avakian

AUSTRALIA

Australian — 305 W. 98th St., Ste. 4-ES, New York, NY 10025; tel (212) 852-7644; fax (212) 852-7671
Correspondent — Susan Wyndham
Australian Age — 209 E. 10th St., Ste. 11, New York, NY 10003; tel (212) 254-8117; fax (212) 254-8117
Correspondent — Anthony Perrottet

Australian Broadcasting Corp. — 630 5th Ave., Ste. 2260, New York, NY 10111; tel (212) 332-2542; fax (212) 332-2546
Correspondent — Phillip Lasker
Australian Consolidated Press — 209 E. 10th St., Ste. 11, New York, NY 10003; tel (212) 254-8117; fax (212) 254-8117
Correspondent — Anthony Perrottet
40 1/2 St. Marks Pl., Ste. 2, New York, NY 10003; tel (212) 505-0384
Photographer — Alexander Towle
Australian Financial Review — 1500 Broadway, Ste. 1002, New York, NY 10036; tel (212) 398-9494; fax (212) 819-1745
Correspondent — Brian Hale
Australian Geo — 209 E. 10th St., Ste. 11, New York, NY 10003; tel (212) 254-8117; fax (212) 254-8117
Correspondent — Anthony Perrottet
Channel 9 Australia — 524 W. 57th St., Ste. 4800, New York, NY 10019; tel (212) 975-3618; fax (212) 975-8468
Producer — Richard Andrews
National Publishing Group — 206 W. 79th St., Ste. 3-F, New York, NY 10024; tel (212) 721-4553; fax (212) 265-3519
Correspondent — Kerry Wren
News Ltd. & Times Newspapers — 1211 Ave. of the Americas, 4th Fl., New York, NY 10036; tel (212) 852-7600; fax (212) 852-7671
Bureau Chief — Peter Atkinson
Correspondent — Sharon Krum
524 E. 79th St., Ste. 6-A, New York, NY 10021; tel (212) 472-7433; fax (212) 819-3312
Correspondent — Peter Simunovich
Sydney Morning Herald — 1500 Broadway, Ste. 1002, New York, NY 10036; tel (212) 398-9494; fax (212) 354-4796
Bureau Chief — Phillip McCarthy

40 1/2 St. Marks Pl., Ste. 2, New York, NY 10003; tel (212) 505-0384
Photojournalist — Alexander Towle
The Sunday Age — 364 W. 51st St., Ste. 3-E, New York, NY 10019; tel (212) 262-5002; fax (212) 262-5002
Correspondent — Suzy Freeman-Greene

AUSTRIA

Austria Presse-Agentur — 405 E. 42nd St., Ste. C-320, New York, NY 10017; tel (212) 888-6440; fax (212) 486-8122
Correspondent — Walter Pfaeffle
Austrian Radio & Television (ORF) — 1206 Eton Ct. N.W., Washington, DC 20007; tel (202) 822-9569
Bureau Chief — Franz Koessler
Basta — 112 Christopher St., Ste. 3, New York, NY 10014; tel (212) 645-3037; fax (212) 925-1531
Photographer — Ashkan Sahihi
Buchkultur — 203 W. 107th St., Ste. 9-B, New York, NY 10025; tel (212) 864-5452
Photographer — Nathalie Schuller
Daily Standard — 971 Highland Ave., Pelham, NY 10803; tel (914) 738-9002
Correspondent — Karin Bratone
Der Standard — 63 Emerson Ave., Croton-on-Hudson, NY 10520; tel (914) 271-5060; fax (914) 271-2329
Correspondent — Susanne Schneider
Parnass — 971 Highland Ave., Pelham, NY 10803; tel (914) 738-9002
Correspondent — Karin Bratone
Profil — 70/72 Laight St., New York, NY 10013; tel (212) 431-0421
Correspondent — Irene Jancsy
Correspondent — Ernst Schmiederer

Copyright ©1996 by the Editor & Publisher Co.

VII-14 Foreign correspondents

Tanz Affiche — 54 Bleecker St., Ste. 8-A, New York, NY 10012; tel (212) 966-2284; fax (212) 966-1612
Photojournalist — Anja Hitzenberger
Wirtschaftswoche — 971 Highland Ave., Pelham, NY 10803; tel (914) 738-9002
Freelance — Karin Bratone

AZERBAIJAN

Azertac — 43-25 43rd St., Ste. 5-J, Queens, NY 11104; tel (718) 729-1962
Correspondent — Fasil Aliev

BAHAMAS

Goombay Magazine — 788 Columbus Ave., Ste. 5-G, New York, NY 10025; tel (212) 662-9013
Correspondent — T Peter Davis

BANGLADESH

Khabar Group of Publications — PO Box 5702, Astoria, NY 11105; tel (718) 626-0323; fax (718) 626-1970
Correspondent — Nazmul Haque Helal

BARBADOS

Barbados Advocate News — 1206 Bergen St., Ste. 3-G, Brooklyn, NY 11213
Correspondent — Clyde Jones

BELGIUM

BRTN-Television — 54 Clinton St., Staten Island, NY 10304; tel (718) 727-9019; fax (718) 816-3092
Correspondent — Jacqueline Goossens
De Financieel Ekonomische — 162 W. 13th St., Ste. 42, New York, NY 10011; tel (212) 929-5349; fax (212) 929-5349
Correspondent — Peter Vanderbruggen
De Morgen — 54 Clinton St., Staten Island, NY 10304; tel (718) 727-9019
Correspondent — Jacqueline Goossens
Correspondent — Thomas Ronse
Kunst & Cultuur — 451 Broome St., Ste. 7-W, New York, NY 10013; tel (212) 226-0857
Correspondent — Batia Adith
Panorama — 54 Clinton St., Staten Island, NY 10304; tel (718) 816-8681; fax (718) 816-3092
Correspondent — Thomas Ronse

BRAZIL

Bandeirantes TV — 15 W. 53rd St., Ste. 9-E, New York, NY 10019; tel (212) 245-3035
Correspondent — Beatriz Duarte
Bandeirantes TV & Radio — 30 Park Ave. S., Ste. 3-J, New York, NY 10016; tel (212) 889-2910
Correspondent — Patricia Macruz
Bloch Editores (Manchete) — 37 Carmine St., Ste. 308, New York, NY 10014; tel (212) 206-8256; fax (212) 229-0530
Bureau Chief — Arnaldo Dines
203 7th Ave., Ste. 7, Brooklyn, NY 11215; tel (718) 499-3805; fax (718) 499-3805
Photographer — Alcir Da Silva
The Brazilians — 345 W. 86th St., Ste. 1111, New York, NY 10024; tel (212) 873-9600
Producer-Writer — Laura Giannoni
Claudia — 20 River Rd., Ste. 9-A, Roosevelt Island, NY 10044; tel (212) 980-3933
Correspondent — Katia Zero
Correio De Noticias — 73-75 E. 7th St., Ste. 5-E, New York, NY 10003; tel (212) 387-8368; fax (212) 387-8368
Correspondent — Andrea Lerner
Cosmopolitan — 20 River Rd., Ste. 9-A, Roosevelt Island, NY 10044; tel (212) 980-3933
Correspondent — Katia Zero
Eco Press — 116 Pinehurst Ave., Ste. M-22, New York, NY 10033; tel (212) 923-7800
Correspondent — Nira Worcman
Editora Abril — 60 E. 42nd St., Ste. 3403, New York, NY 10017; tel (212) 557-5990; fax (212) 983-0972
Bureau Chief — Grace Da Souza
Editora Referencia Ltd. — 3270 Linda Ct., Yorktown, NY 10598; tel (914) 962-7109
Correspondent — Joseph Magnoli
Elle Brasil — 20 River Rd., Ste. 9-A, Roosevelt Island, NY 10044; tel (212) 980-3933
Correspondent — Katia Zero
Estado De Minas — 44 N. Broadway, Ste. 6-AN, White Plains, NY 10603; tel (914) 761-2080; fax (914) 761-2080
Correspondent — Argemiro Ferreira
Folha De Sao Paola — 306 E. 52nd St., Ste. 2-S, New York, NY 10022; tel (212) 371-9668; fax (212) 753-2369
Correspondent — Daniella Costa
231 W. 25th St., Ste. 3-D, New York, NY 10001; tel (212) 741-2753; fax (212) 741-2753
Correspondent — Fernando Da Silva
Gazeta De Noticias — 975 Park Ave., Ste. 6-D, New York, NY 10028; tel (212) 879-5318
Correspondent — Hylde Marye Munson
Gazeta Mercantil — 333 9th Ave., Pelham, NY 10803; tel (914) 738-0557; fax (914) 738-1540
Correspondent — Getulio Bittencourt
Globo Radio — 45 5th Ave., Ste. 2-D, New York, NY 10003; tel (212) 475-4402
Correspondent — Maria Cristina Ruiz
Globo Television Network — 909 3rd Ave., 21st Fl., New York, NY 10022; tel (212) 446-3000
Bureau Chief — Paulo H Amorin
Correspondent — David Presas
Editor — Fernando Baccarin
Producer — Orlando Moreira Da Silva
Producer — Siomara Tauster
Globosat — 270 Park Ave. S., Ste. 10-F, New York, NY 10010; tel (212) 420-6027; fax (212) 254-9456
Correspondent — Nelson Motta
Info — 217 E. 25th St., Ste. 6-D, New York, NY 10010; tel (212) 477-5077; fax (212) 473-0830
Correspondent — Vera Franco
Istoe — 3240 Henry Hudson Pkwy., Ste. 7-R, Bronx, NY 10463; tel (718) 549-5068; fax (718) 549-5068
Correspondent — Osmar S Freitas
Istoe/Senhor — 456 Broome St., New York, NY 10013; tel (212) 219-8619
Correspondent — Claudio Edinger
Jornal Da Tarde — 301 E. 47th St., Ste. 21-J, New York, NY 10017; tel (212) 826-2839; fax (212) 759-9075
Correspondent — Sonia Nolasco
64 E. 86th St., Ste. 9-C, New York, NY 10028; tel (212) 472-1295
Correspondent — Nessia Leonsini Pope
Jornal Do Brasil — 217 E. 25th St., Ste. 6-D, New York, NY 10010; tel (212) 477-5077; fax (212) 473-0830
Correspondent — Vera Franco
211 E. 17th St., Ste. 8, New York, NY 10003; tel (212) 473-7783; fax (212) 473-7783
Photojournalist — Maria Jose Lessa
346 E. 10th St., Ste. 3, New York, NY 10009; tel (212) 388-9088; fax (212) 388-9088
Correspondent — Marcia Fortes
635 E. 9th St., Ste. 20, New York, NY 10009; tel (212) 674-6672
Photographer — Fabio Ghivelder
Jornal Do Economista — 175 W. 87th St., Ste. 12-D, New York, NY 10024; tel (212) 724-2094
Correspondent — Jennifer Gonzales
Moda Brasil — 231 W. 25th St., Ste. 3-D, New York, NY 10001; tel (718) 923-2294; fax (718) 923-2294
Correspondent — Liza Papi
News From Brazil — 37 W. 54th St., New York, NY 10019; tel (212) 586-6280; fax (212) 333-0111
Correspondent — Marilyn Barnell
O Estado De Sao Paulo — United Nations, Rm. 344-B, New York, NY 10017; tel (212) 963-7141; fax (212) 371-9020
Correspondent — Sonia Nolasco
O Globo — 690 Greenwich St., Ste. 4-F, New York, NY 10014
Correspondent — Edney Silvestre
240 W. 64th St., Ste. 6-G, New York, NY 10023; tel (212) 721-8149; fax (800) 685-4580
Correspondent — Leila Sterenberg
909 3rd Ave., 21st Fl., New York, NY 10022; tel (212) 754-0400; fax (212) 255-6890
Corr. — Heloisa Maria Villela De Castro
Radio Eldorado — 3240 Henry Hudson Pkwy., Ste. 7-R, Bronx, NY 10463; tel (718) 549-5068; fax (718) 549-5068
Correspondent — Osmar S Freitas
338 W. 46th St., Ste. 4-R, New York, NY 10036; tel (212) 956-3988
Correspondent — Tulio Reis-Leite
Radio Gaucha — 154 Nyac Ave., Pelham, NY 10803-1906; tel (212) 989-5572
Correspondent — Maria Beatriz Guimaraes
Record Television — 220 E. 23rd St., Ste. 1005, New York, NY 10010; tel (212) 447-7833; fax (212) 447-7920
Bureau Chief — Julio Sobral
Correspondent — Tiberio Romulo Fietosa
630 5th Ave., Ste. 2607, New York, NY 10111; tel (212) 262-0522
Correspondent — Miriam Araujo
Super Interesante — 116 Pinehurst Ave., Ste. M-22, New York, NY 10033; tel (212) 923-7800
Correspondent — Nira Worcman
Telework — 31 W. 8th St., Ste. 8, New York, NY 10011; tel (212) 979-6969
Correspondent — Sergio Ricardo Cesario
Tribuna Da Bahia — 108 E. 66th St., Ste. 2-B, New York, NY 10021; tel (212) 472-2725
Correspondent — Diva Possati Barranqueiros
Tribuna Da Imprensa — 44 N. Broadway, Ste. 6-AN, White Plains, NY 10603; tel (914) 761-2080; fax (914) 761-2080
Correspondent — Argemiro Ferreira
TV Cultura — 747 3rd Ave., 29th Fl., New York, NY 10017; tel (212) 833-9301; fax (212) 752-8301
Bureau Chief — Lucas Mendes
Correspondent — Lucia Guimaraes
Editor — Angelica Vieira
Vogue Brasil — 20 River Rd., Ste. 9-A, Roosevelt Island, NY 10044
Correspondent — Katia Zero
245 E. 25th St., Ste. 10-B, New York, NY 10010; tel (212) 481-9185; fax (212) 481-9185
Correspondent — Ana Luiza Nascimento

BULGARIA

Bulgarian Studio 2 (News) — 1255 Park Ave., New York, NY 10029-7204; fax (212) 308-3899
Correspondent — Victor Peicinow
Xepmec 5 — 41-43 39th Pl., Ste. 1-D, New York, NY 11104
Correspondent — Robert Tsanev

CANADA

Can-Am Communications — 135 Central Park West, PH-South, New York, NY 10023; tel (212) 877-7440
Correspondent — Valerie Jennings
Canadian Broadcasting Corp. — 747 3rd Ave., Ste. 8-C, New York, NY 10017; tel (212) 546-0507; fax (212) 759-1305
Correspondent — Estelle Fournier
747 3rd Ave., 8th Fl., New York, NY 10017; tel (212) 546-0500
Producer —Linda Perry
United Nations, Rm. S-394, New York, NY 10017; tel (212) 546-0510
Producer —Genevieve Ast
Canadian Television Network — PO Box 135, New York, NY 10159; tel (212) 388-9552; fax (212) 388-9552
Correspondent — Michael Reubens
Charhdi Kala — 97-07 116th St., Richmond Hill, NY 11419; tel (718) 849-0910; fax (718) 849-0910
Correspondent — Balwinder Pal Singh
Financial Post — 14 E. 60th St., PH, New York, NY 10022; tel (212) 371-3088; fax (212) 753-4814
Correspondent — Eric Reguly
Globe & Mail — c/o WSJ, 200 Liberty St., New York, NY 10281; tel (212) 416-3246; fax (212) 416-3672
Correspondent — Brian Milner
Polish Voice Publishing — 120 E. 62nd St., Ste. 1-A, New York, NY 10021; tel (212) 753-0403
Correspondent — Wieslaw Cyprys
Toronto Star — 163 W. 88th St., Apt. 1, New York, NY 10024; tel (212) 873-5593; fax (212) 787-3943
Correspondent — Stephen Handelman

CHILE

Channel 13 TV — 626 West End Ave., Ste. A, New York, NY 10024; tel (212) 799-4198; fax (212) 799-4198
Correspondent — Carmen Lopez
Cameraman — Ralf Oberti
Chilean National TV — 190 Garfield Pl., Apt. 3-E, Brooklyn, NY 11215; tel (718) 499-7401
Correspondent — Cecilia Valdez
Cosas — 117 E. 57th St., Ste. 47-G, New York, NY 10022; tel (212) 838-1066
Correspondent — Karen Poniachik
213 E. 25th St., Ste. 5-C, New York, NY 10010; tel (212) 697-3367
Correspondent — Manuel Santelices
Estrategia — 126-B Cedar Ln., Highland Park, NJ 08904; tel (908) 247-4155; fax (908) 247-4155
Correspondent — Sandra Radic
La Estrella — 303 E. 60th St., Ste. 4-S, New York, NY 10022; tel (212) 758-5006; fax (212) 758-4625
Correspondent — Rogelio Ferrada

CHINA

Economic Daily — 40 River Rd., Ste. 15-H, Roosevelt Island, NY 10044; tel (212) 755-6113; fax (212) 752-2237
Bureau Chief — Zhinian Zhang
People's Daily — 320 E. 46th St., Ste. 31-E, New York, NY 10017; tel (212) 986-0322; fax (212) 986-0322
Bureau Chief — Shiquan Xu
Correspondent — Shi Guanggiu
Correspondent — Hongze He
Science & Technology Daily — 324 Casper Rd., Englewood Cliffs, NJ 07632; tel (201) 569-6855; fax (201) 569-2609
Correspondent — Yadong Liu
Shanghai Wenhuibao Daily — 447 Golf Course Dr., Leonia, NJ 07605; tel (201) 346-1328; fax (201) 346-1297
Bureau Chief — Huanpei Zhang
Xinhua News Agency — 40-35 72nd St., Woodside, NY 11377; tel (718) 335-8388; fax (718) 335-8778
Bureau Chief — Zhaolong Xia
Correspondent — Jian Gao
Correspondent — Pingxing Wang
Correspondent — Zhenhua Wang
Correspondent — Renfang Zhao
Editor — Chengzhi Yu

COLOMBIA

El Colombiano — 82-16 166th St., Jamaica, NY 11432; tel (718) 380-2116; fax (718) 380-2116
Correspondent — Elizabeth Mora-Mass
El Tiempo — 924 3rd Ave., Ste. 3-A, New York, NY 10022; tel (212) 832-3541; fax (212) 223-4540
Correspondent — Andreas Cavelier
PO Box 1155, New York, NY 10001; tel (212) 889-1356; fax (212) 889-1356
Correspondent — Jose Hernandez
Globo Television LTDA — 423 W. 120th St., Ste. 72, New York, NY 10027; tel (212) 222-8734; fax (212) 222-8735
Correspondent — Juan Carlos Velasquez
Producer — Andi Vaida
Programar Television — 8707 35th Ave., Ste. 4-C, Jackson Heights, NY 11372; tel (718) 478-9862
Correspondent — Luis Ramirez
Qap Noticias — 51 Sheldon Terrace, New Haven, CT 06511; tel (203) 785-8677; fax (203) 785-8677
Correspondent — Adriana Saldarriaga

CROATIA

Globus — 158 Engert Ave., Brooklyn, NY 11222; tel (718) 389-3783; fax (718) 349-7038
Correspondent — Dean Dujmovic
Monitor — 236 E. 36th St., Ste. 3-E, New York, NY 10016; tel (212) 779-8240
Correspondent — Milka Tadic
Novi List — 158 Engert Ave., Brooklyn, NY 11222; tel (718) 389-3783; fax (718) 349-7038
Correspondent — Dean Dujmovic
Start — 517 E. 77th St., Ste. 2-M, New York, NY 10021; tel (212) 517-6838; fax (212) 517-3077
Correspondent — Larenz Ferich

CZECH REPUBLIC

Czech News Agency — 40 River Rd., Ste. 19-C, New York, NY 10044; tel (212) 888-2992; fax (212) 888-3067
Correspondent — Jiri Majstr
Pop Life — PO Box 59, New York, NY 10028; tel (212) 861-5520; fax (212) 861-5520
Photographer — Zsolt Savary
Svobodne-Slovo — 549 Riverside Dr., New York, NY 10027; tel (212) 663-3987
Correspondent — Josef Schrabel

DENMARK

Borsen — 306 E. 11th St., Ste. 3-A, New York, NY 10003; tel (212) 260-3753; fax (212) 475-6926
Correspondent — Vibeke Hjortlund
BT — 235 W. 56th St., Ste. 22-H, New York, NY 10019; tel (212) 333-5332; fax (212) 333-5462
Correspondent — Peter Juul Jensen

Foreign correspondents VII-15

Extra Bladet — c/o Cabret, 226 W. 75th St., Ste. 42, New York, NY 10023; tel (212) 874-8306
Photojournalist — Henry Arvidsson

Information — 200 E. 94th St., Ste. 2212, New York, NY 10128; tel (212) 427-0500; fax (212) 427-0505
Correspondent — Niklas Von Daehne

Jydske Vestkysten — 200 E. 94th St., Ste. 2212, New York, NY 10128; tel (212) 427-0500; fax (212) 427-0505
Correspondent — Niklas Von Daehne

Jyllands Posten — 330 E. 38th St., Ste. 42-L, New York, NY 10016; tel (212) 297-1775; fax (212) 949-6365
Correspondent — Jan Lund

Nordfoto — 425 Park Ave. S., Ste. 17-B, New York, NY 10016; tel (212) 889-7191; fax (212) 889-7239
Photographer — Finn Petersen Foens

Kristeligt Dagblad — 200 E. 94th St., Ste. 2212, New York, NY 10128; tel (212) 427-0500; fax (212) 427-0505
Correspondent — Niklas Von Daehne

DOMINICAN REPUBLIC

Editora Hoy C Por A — 545 E. 5th St., Ste. 6, New York, NY 10009; tel (212) 343-2539; fax (212) 343-2659
Correspondent — Sully Saneaux

ECUADOR

El Expresso — 26-45 9th St., Ste. 605, Astoria, NY 11102; tel (718) 777-0830
Correspondent — John Iturralde

Gamavision Television Network — 4601 39th Ave., Ste. 606, Sunnyside, NY 11104; tel (718) 392-3816
Correspondent — Edwin Almeida

Teleamazonas Ch 4 — 67 E. 3rd St., Ste. 4-B, New York, NY 10003; tel (212) 533-1133
Correspondent — Malena Marchan

Telesistema — 26-45 9th St., Ste. 605, Astoria, NY 11102; tel (718) 777-0830
Correspondent — John Iturralde

EGYPT

Al Comhouria — 31-60 41st St., Ste. 2, Astoria, NY 11103; tel (718) 278-7153; fax (718) 278-7153
Correspondent — Safie Eldin Deyab

Al-Ahram — 405 Lexington Ave., 39th Fl., New York, NY 10174; tel (212) 972-6440; fax (212) 286-0285
Correspondent — Mohamed Ezzat Mousa

Al-Akhbar — United Nations, Rm. S-301, New York, NY 10017; tel (212) 688-8910
Correspondent — Sanaa Youssef

Radio Cairo — 64 Greenwood Rd., Bay Shore, NY 11706; tel (212) 963-6511; fax (212) 968-0488
Correspondent — Essam El Badry

FIJI

Fiji Times — United Nations, TCC-Booth 22, New York, NY 10017; tel (212) 963-0085; fax (212) 688-8302
Correspondent — Mere Momoivalu

Pacnews — United Nations, TCC-Booth 22, New York, NY 10017; tel (212) 963-0085; fax (212) 688-8302
Correspondent — Mere Momoivalu

FINLAND

Aamulehti — 570 44th St., Ste. 10, Brooklyn, NY 11220; tel (718) 851-1462; fax (718) 851-1462
Correspondent — Varpu Sihvonen

Anna — 240 E. 27th St., Ste. 10-L, New York, NY 10016; tel (212) 213-8438
Correspondent — Tarja Tuppurainen

Ilta Lehti — 310 E. 44th St., Ste. 419, New York, NY 10017; tel (212) 983-6959; fax (212) 867-5807
Correspondent — Dan Steinbock

Ilta-Sanomat — 240 E. 27th St., Ste. 10-L, New York, NY 10016; tel (212) 213-8438
Correspondent — Tarja Tuppurainen
570 44th St., Ste. 10, Brooklyn, NY 11220; tel (718) 851-1462; fax (718) 851-1462
Correspondent — Matti Jappinen

Kaleva — 72 Barrow St., Ste. 4-I, New York, NY 10014; tel (212) 243-3252; fax (212) 243-3252
Correspondent — Antti Korkeakivi

Kauppalehti — 55 Herbert St., Brooklyn, NY 11222; tel (718) 383-5938; fax (718) 383-5938
Correspondent — Markku Huusko
600 Warren Rd., Ste. 3-1A, Ithaca, NY 14850; tel (607) 257-9851; fax (607) 257-9851
Correspondent — Eljas Repo

Mainosuutiset — 310 E. 44th St., Ste. 419, New York, NY 10017; tel (212) 983-6959; fax (212) 867-5807
Correspondent — Dan Steinbock

Uusi Suomi — 310 E. 44th St., Ste. 419, New York, NY 10017; tel (212) 983-6959; fax (212) 867-5807
Correspondent — Dan Steinbock

FRANCE

Africa I — 314 E. 41st St., Ste. 605, New York, NY 10017; tel (212) 963-7576; fax (212) 697-6579
Correspondent — Michele De Rosset

Agence Angeli — 320 E. 22nd St., Ste. 37-D, New York, NY 10010; tel (212) 260-3345; fax (212) 260-3442
Bureau Chief — Jean-Jacques Dousset

Agence France Presse — 747 3rd Ave., 31st Fl., New York, NY 10017; tel (212) 755-1750; fax (212) 755-1928
Bureau Chief — Frederic Bichon
Correspondent — Pablo Ruelas Nunez
55 Broadway, 7th Fl., New York, NY 10006; tel (212) 785-1983; fax (212) 785-2168
Correspondent — Vincent Baby

Agence Press Economique — 100 Beekman St., New York, NY 10038; tel (212) 571-1957
Correspondent — David Levin

Amina — 220 W. 13th St., New York, NY 10011; tel (212) 645-9824
Correspondent — Patricia Lebaud

Atlas Air France — 95 Grand St., New York, NY 10013; tel (212) 925-8494
Correspondent — Giles Larrain

ATS — 223 2nd Ave., Ste. 4-D, New York, NY 10003; tel (212) 982-0813
Correspondent — Maria-Pia Mascaro

Canal Plus — 333 E. 69th St., Ste. 12-C, New York, NY 10021; tel (212) 975-2316; fax (212) 888-0755
Producer — Allison Black
c/o CBS, 524 W. 57th St., Ste. 6313, New York, NY 10019; tel (212) 975-2315; fax (212) 633-2698
Bureau Chief-Laura Haim

Colombus News Agency — 233 E. 4th St., Ste. 5-E, New York, NY 10009; tel (212) 529-1086; fax (212) 995-5228
Correspondent — Francois Cusset
Correspondent — Laurent Mauriac

Elle Magazine — 222 W. 14th St., Ste. 14-C, New York, NY 10011; tel (212) 929-5634; fax (212) 366-5569
Correspondent — Natalie D'Harcourt

France 2 Television — 1290 Ave. of the Americas, Ste. 2720, New York, NY 10104; tel (212) 571-1771; fax (212) 541-4309
Bureau Chief — Nicole Devilaine
Correspondent — Aubreri Edler
Correspondent — Alexandre Gunuey
Correspondent — Alexander Marshall

France Amerique — 1560 Broadway, Ste. 511, New York, NY 10036; tel (212) 221-6700; fax (212) 221-6997
Bureau Chief — Jean-Louis Turlin
333 E. 68th St., New York, NY 10021; tel (212) 963-7611
Correspondent — Louis Foy

France Soir — 20-31 42nd St., Long Island City, NY 11105; tel (718) 721-3838; fax (718) 204-8120
Correspondent — Judith Weiner

France-Radio — 210 W. 89th St., New York, NY 10024; tel (212) 873-4735; fax (212) 873-4735
Correspondent — Jean Gallia

French Vogue — 163 3rd Ave., Ste. 255, New York, NY 10003; tel (212) 533-3035; fax (212) 533-4033
Correspondent — Martine Trittoleno

Gamma Presse Images Inc. — 11 E. 26th St., New York, NY 10011; tel (212) 447-2520; fax (212) 447-0284
Photographer — Michel Bernard

Hebdomadaire De Paris — 34 Hillside Ave., Ste. 2-AA, New York, NY 10040; tel (212) 567-6099
Correspondent — Marek Ruszczynski

Hugo Press — 36 W. 20th St., New York, NY 10011; tel (212) 645-8227; fax (212) 691-9304
Correspondent — Daniel Teboul

Jeune Afrique — 1435 York Ave., Ste. 7-D, New York, NY 10021; tel (212) 570-6845; fax (212) 371-9020
Correspondent — Celia De Lavarene

L'Express — 138 W. 73rd St., Ste. 3, New York, NY 10023; tel (212) 595-8586; fax (212) 595-8683
Correspondent — Philippe Coste

L'Industrie Textile — 333 E. 54th St., Ste. 2-B, New York, NY 10022; tel (212) 755-3421; fax (201) 533-1756
Correspondent — Marie Munck

La Derniere Heure/Les Sport — 230 Central Park West, Ste. 7-G, New York, NY 10024; tel (212) 769-9580; fax (212) 956-8077
Correspondent — Patrice Bertrand

Le Figaro — 1560 Broadway, Ste. 511, New York, NY 10036; tel (212) 221-6700; fax (212) 221-6997
Correspondent — Jean-Louis Turlin

Le Journal Du Dimanche — 230 Central Park West, Ste. 7-G, New York, NY 10024; tel (212) 769-9580; fax (212) 956-8077
Correspondent — Patrice Bertrand

Le Monde — 138 W. Houston St., Ste. 3, New York, NY 10012; tel (212) 777-7383; fax (212) 777-7383
Correspondent — Henri Behar
476 Broadway, Ste. 9-F, New York, NY 10013; tel (212) 593-2954; fax (212) 532-6226
Correspondent — Afsane Bassir-Pour

Le Nouvel Economiste — 245 E. 93rd St., Ste. 2-J, New York, NY 10128; tel (212) 427-8528; fax (212) 427-4722
Correspondent — Veronique Dumont

Le Parisien — 301 W. 53rd St., Ste. 19-C, New York, NY 10019; tel (212) 315-0615; fax (212) 956-8077
Correspondent — Marc Chalamet

Le Point — 421 Hudson St., Ste. 812, New York, NY 10014; tel (212) 807-6162; fax (212) 807-1265
Bureau Chief — Jerome Godard-Godefroy
14 E. 60th St., PH, New York, NY 10022; tel (212) 874-8586
Correspondent — Francoise D'Avout
1435 York Ave., Ste. 7-D, New York, NY 10021; tel (212) 570-6845; fax (212) 371-9020
Correspondent — Celia De Lavarene

Le Quotidien Du Medicin — 67 Vestry St., Ste. 4-C, New York, NY 10013; tel (212) 941-7874; fax (212) 219-8432
Correspondent — Dr Veronique Nguyen

Les Cles De L'Actualite — 2601 Henry Hudson Pkwy., Ste. 6-E, Bronx, NY 10463; tel (718) 796-3571; fax (718) 796-6094
Correspondent — Caroline Crosdale

Les Echos — 14 E. 60th St., PH, New York, NY 10022; tel (212) 750-2983; fax (212) 750-4293
Correspondent — Jacques Hubert-Rodier

Max Magazine — 222 W. 14th St., Ste. 14-C, New York, NY 10011; tel (212) 929-5634; fax (212) 366-5569
Correspondent — Natalie D'Harcourt

Paris Match — 1633 Broadway, 45th Fl., New York, NY 10019; tel (212) 767-6328; fax (212) 767-5621
Bureau Chief — Olivier Royant
Correspondent — Francoise Joyes
Correspondent — Jean-Jacques Naudet
Photographer — Yann Gamblin

Press Sportive Internationale — 400 E. 70th St., Ste. 3502, New York, NY 10021; tel (212) 288-3295
Correspondent — Pascal Silvestre

Radio Classique — 424 E. 11th St., Ste. 17, New York, NY 10009; tel (212) 963-9480; fax (212) 963-1307
Correspondent — Helene Caux

Radio France Internationale — 210 W. 16th St., Ste. 2-B, New York, NY 10011; tel (212) 989-5572; fax (212) 645-3781
Corr. — Marie Beatriz Guimaraes Ball
314 E. 41st St., Ste. 605, New York, NY 10017; tel (212) 963-7576
Correspondent — Michele De Rosset
540 E. 20th St., Ste. 5-B, New York, NY 10009; tel (212) 979-6550; fax (212) 979-6550
Correspondent — Alexandre Geneste

RTL French Radio — 421 Hudson St., Ste. 821, New York, NY 10014; tel (212) 807-6162; fax (212) 807-1265
Correspondent — Jerome Godard-Godefroy

Sante Magazine — c/o Brohy, 45 E. 3rd St., Basement, New York, NY 10003; tel (212) 533-9236; fax (212) 675-7900
Correspondent — Gerard L Ungerman

Sipa Press — 30 W. 21st St., 6th Fl., New York, NY 10010; tel (212) 463-0150
Bureau Chief — James Colton

Sphinx Agence De Presse — 90 Prince St., New York, NY 10012
Photojournalist — Jacques Cochin

Sudoueste — 540 E. 20th St., Ste. 5-B, New York, NY 10009; tel (212) 979-6550; fax (212) 979-6550
Correspondent — Alexandra Geneste

Sygma Photo News — 322 8th Ave., 11th Fl., New York, NY 10001; tel (212) 675-7900
Photographer — Jean Pierre Laffont

GERMANY

Ambiente — 225 Lafayette St., Ste. 1114, New York, NY 10012; tel (212) 343-1520; fax (212) 343-1522
Correspondent — Brigitte Knauf

Amica — 229 E. 5th St., Ste. 9, New York, NY 10003; tel (212) 995-1340; fax (212) 995-9139
Freelance — Ilona Weoeres

Art De Vivre Magazine — 230 Central Park West, Ste. 14-H, New York, NY 10024; tel (212) 875-0177; fax (212) 496-0887
Correspondent — Heike Wipperfuerth

Avanti TV GBR — 495 Broome St., New York, NY 10013; tel (212) 226-5588; fax (212) 206-5164
Correspondent — Edda Baumann

Bayerischer Rundfunk — 355 Bleecker St., New York, NY 10014; tel (212) 463-9510; fax (212) 463-9441
Correspondent — Martin Ebbing
334 W. 89th St., Ste. 3, New York, NY 10025; tel (212) 787-0840
Freelance —Andrea Bockmann-Mohr

Berlin Radio — 11 Jones St., Ste. 18, New York, NY 10014; fax (212) 989-6286
Correspondent — Claudia Hamboch

Boersen-Zeitung — 15 Boulderol Rd., Stamford, CT 06903; tel (203) 329-0642
Correspondent — Karl Grun

Brigitte — 229 E. 5th St., Ste. 9, New York, NY 10003; tel (212) 995-1340; fax (212) 995-9139
Freelance — Ilona Weoeres

Bunte (Burda) — 147 W. 75th St., Ste. 1-B, New York, NY 10023; tel (212) 721-0490; fax (212) 721-2191
Correspondent — Jurgen Kalwa

Burda Publications — 1270 Ave. of the Americas, Ste. 1918, New York, NY 10020; tel (212) 757-1100; fax (212) 397-0822
Bureau Chief — Fritz Blumenberg
Correspondent — Gunther Krumminga
200 E. 16th St., Ste. 18-B, New York, NY 10003; tel (212) 254-1852; fax (212) 260-3651
Correspondent — Michael Baumann
179-55 80th Rd., Jamaica Estates, NY 11432; tel (718) 380-4007; fax (718) 969-2318
Correspondent — Ursula Besch
322 W. 57th St., Ste. 31-T, New York, NY 10019; tel (212) 757-1100; fax (212) 397-0822
Correspondent — Tina Schulz-Roos
147 W. 75th St., Ste. 2-A, New York, NY 10023; tel (212) 724-6040; fax (212) 724-3251
Photographer — Tobias Everke

Conde Nast Verlag — 632 Broadway, 5th Fl., New York, NY 10012; tel (212) 387-7610; fax (212) 387-7608
Editor — Anja Schaefer

Decor (Burda) — 1270 Ave. of the Americas, Ste. 1918, New York, NY 10020; tel (212) 757-1100; fax (212) 397-0822
Correspondent — Doris Chevron

Der Spiegel — 516 5th Ave., PH, New York, NY 10036; tel (212) 221-7583; fax (212) 302-6258
Bureau Chief — Matthias Matussek
Correspondent — Angelika Wrubel
243 E. 14th St., 4th Fl., New York, NY 10003; tel (212) 674-4811; fax (212) 677-0319
Photojournalist — Andreas Sterzing

Deutsche Welle — 531-33 W. 112th St., Ste. 2-C, New York, NY 10025; tel (212) 222-4257; fax (212) 222-4257
Correspondent — Karin Oehlenschlaeger

Deutschlandfunk — 143 Ave. B, Ste. 12-E, New York, NY 10009; tel (212) 420-8839; fax (212) 420-1514
Correspondent — Dr Ulrike Heider

Die Abendzeitung — 200 W. 108th St., Ste. 12-A, New York, NY 10025; tel (212) 222-1341
Correspondent — Susanne Lingemann

Die Woche — 156 W. 15th St., Ste. 3-B, New York, NY 10011; tel (212) 645-6211; fax (212) 645-6943
Correspondent — Marc Pitzke
229 E. 5th St., Ste. 9, New York, NY 10003; tel (212) 995-1340
Freelance — Ilona Weoeres
329 E. 10th St., Ste. 1, New York, NY 10009; tel (212) 673-0024; fax (212) 673-5499
Freelance — Ute Thon

Die Zeit — 143 Ave. B, Ste. 12-E, New York, NY 10009; tel (212) 420-8839; fax (212) 420-1514
Correspondent — Dr Ulrike Heider
51 W. 81st St., New York, NY 10024; tel (212) 874-6598
Correspondent — Jes Rau
846 Rte. 121, North Salem, NY 10560; tel (914) 669-8148
Correspondent — Christian Tenbrock
630 Ft. Washington Ave., New York, NY 10040; tel (212) 740-1496; fax (212) 740-1497
Correspondent — Guenter Knop

Elle — 1270 Ave. of the Americas, Ste. 1918, New York, NY 10020; tel (212) 757-1100; fax (212) 397-0822
Correspondent — Doris Chevron

Ergo — 11 Prince St., Ste. 3-B, New York, NY 10012; tel (212) 431-1006; fax (212) 431-8595
Correspondent — Steffan Heuer

Frankfurter Allgemeine Zeitung — PO Box 615, Old Greenwich, CT 06870; tel (203) 698-0856
Correspondent — Benedikt Fehr
2109 Broadway, Ste 1770, New York, NY 10023
Correspondent — Verena Lueken

Frankfurter Rundschau — 143 Ave. B, Ste. 12-E, New York, NY 10009; tel (212) 420-8839; fax (212) 420-1514
Correspondent — Dr Ulrike Heider

Frau Im Spiegel Magazine — 83 Gibbspond Rd., Nesconset, NY 11767; tel (516) 360-7713
Photographer — Max Jochen Stein

Gabi Suren TV Productions — 225 W. 80th St., Ste. 3-C, New York, NY 10024; tel (212) 873-4937; fax (212) 873-4937
Producer — Rene Bastian

Gala — 225 Lafayette St., Ste. 1002, New York, NY 10012; tel (212) 343-0790
Photographer — Christiana Dittman

German Press Agency-DPA — United Nations, Rm. S-352, New York, NY 10017; tel (212) 319-6626; fax (212) 753-6168
Bureau Chief — Helmut Raether
Correspondent — Gabriela Sala-Rigler
Correspondent — Joe Lauria
Correspondent — Gisela Ostwald
30 Garry Rd., Closter, NJ 07624; tel (202) 767-3835; fax (201) 767-6841
Correspondent — Peter Bauer

German Radio Newtork-ARD — 420 E. 50th St., Ste. 3, New York, NY 10022; tel (212) 752-9642; fax (212) 752-4155
Correspondent — Hermann Denecke
48 W. 11th St., New York, NY 10011; tel (212) 529-3343
Correspondent — Tilman Rascher

German Television Network-ARD — 251 W. 57th St., Ste. 2420, New York, NY 10019; tel (212) 307-0242; fax (212) 262-5089
Bureau Chief — Dr Petra Lidschreiber
Producer — Annamarie G Kammerlander
Producer — Maria Scarvalone
200 W. 60th St., Ste. 35-D, New York, NY 10023; tel (212) 265-1210; fax (212) 265-5644
Correspondent — Yoash Tatari

German Television-ZDF — 20 Beekman Pl., Ste. 3-G, New York, NY 10022; tel (212) 980-9566; fax (212) 980-9566
Correspondent — Patricia Naggiar
322 W. 14th St., PH, New York, NY 10014; tel (212) 645-8922
Correspondent — Marianne Schaefer

German Vogue — 8 Gramercy Park S., Ste. 4-H, New York, NY 10003; tel (212) 473-1123; fax (212) 473-4804
Correspondent — Claudia Steinberg
632 Broadway, 5th Fl., New York, NY 10012; tel (212) 387-7610; fax (212) 387-7608
Editor — Anja Schaefer

Gong — 295 Lafayette St., Ste. 910, New York, NY 10012; tel (212) 925-1877; fax (212) 925-1944
Correspondent — Josephine Mechseper

Gruner & Jahr TV — 4 Sound View Terrace, Greenwich, CT 06830; tel (203) 862-8976; fax (203) 862-8977
Correspondent — Renata Kurowski Cardello

Hamburger Morgenpost — 241 E. 14th St., Ste. 2-A, New York, NY 10003; tel (212) 677-8014; fax (212) 677-8962
Correspondent — Roger Kunsemueller

Handelsblatt — 26 Puddingstone Rd., Morris Plains, NJ 07950; tel (201) 539-8197
Correspondent — Jens Eckhardt

Holiday (Burda) — 1270 Ave. of the Americas, Ste. 1918, New York, NY 10020; tel (212) 757-1100; fax (212) 397-0822
Correspondent — Doris Chevron
147 W. 75th St., Ste 1-B, New York, NY 10023; tel (212) 721-0490; fax (212) 721-2191
Correspondent — Jurgen Kalwa

Inter Topics — 78 Franklin St., New York, NY 10013; tel (212) 925-6082
Correspondent — Waring Abbott

Jetzt — 229 E. 5th St., Ste. 9, New York, NY 10003; tel (212) 995-1340; fax (212) 995-9139
Freelance — Ilona Weoeres

Maenner Vogue — 259 Three Mile Harbor Rd., East Hampton, NY 11937; tel (516) 329-0026; fax (516) 329-0026
Correspondent — Simon Worrall

Marie Claire — 241 E. 14th St., Ste. 2-A, New York, NY 10003; tel (212) 677-8014; fax (212) 677-8962
Correspondent — Roger Kunsemueller

Max — 225 W. 78th St., Ste. 8, New York, NY 10024-6639; tel (212) 877-9034; fax (212) 877-0092
Correspondent — Christiane Visbeck

Media Access — 7 Crows Nest Ln., Sandy Hook, CT 06482; tel (212) 832-2744; fax (212) 832-3766
Correspondent — Silke Haladjian

NDR German Television (Hamburg) — 322 W. 14th St., PH, New York, NY 10014; tel (212) 645-8922; fax (212) 645-8987
Correspondent — Marianne Schaefer

Network Press — 495 Broome St., New York, NY 10013; tel (212) 226-5588; fax (212) 206-5164
Correspondent — Edda Baumann

Neue Bildende Kunst — 212 Ave. B, Ste. 15, New York, NY 10009; tel (212) 420-9761; fax (212) 420-9761
Correspondent — Gabriele Stellbaum

Newmag — 1965 Broadway, New York, NY 10019; tel (212) 682-2824; fax (212) 682-2824
Correspondent — Gabrielle Barth

Oskar's — 60 Ave. B, Ste. 4-C, New York, NY 10009; tel (212) 979-8619; fax (212) 979-6352
Correspondent — Anja Hinrichsen
Photojournalist — Christian Oth

Penthouse Magazine — 1965 Broadway, New York, NY 10019; tel (212) 682-2824; fax (212) 682-2824
Correspondent — Gabrielle Barth

PM Science Magazine — 48 W. 11th St., New York, NY 10011; tel (212) 529-3343; fax (212) 473-6903
Correspondent — Tilman Rascher

Popcorn — 62 Ave. C, Ste. 04, New York, NY 10009; tel (212) 475-5235; fax (212) 475-5235
Photojournalist — Annette Eggerath

Premier TV — 8 Gramercy Park S., Ste. 4-H, New York, NY 10003; tel (212) 473-1123; fax (212) 473-4804
Correspondent — Claudia Steinberg

Rheinischer Merkur — 11 Jones St., Ste. 18, New York, NY 10014; tel (212) 989-1444; fax (212) 989-6286
Correspondent — Claudia Hamboch

RTL Television — 524 W. 57th St., Ste. IFF-G1, New York, NY 10019; tel (212) 975-7441; fax (212) 975-7448
Bureau Chief — Peter Kleim
38 W. 94th St., Ste. 3, New York, NY 10025; tel (212) 316-7647; fax (212) 316-7690
Correspondent — Barbara Biemann
Correspondent — Ralf Hoogestraat
99 Ave. B, Ste. 5-BC, New York, NY 10009; tel (212) 353-8435; fax (212) 353-8435
Correspondent — Peter Meffert

Schrift — 89 Bowery, Ste. 5, New York, NY 10002
Correspondent — Isolde Kille

Sports — 147 W. 75th St., Ste. 1-B, New York, NY 10023; tel (212) 721-0490; fax (212) 721-2191
Correspondent — Jurgen Kalwa

Springer Foreign News Service — 565 5th Ave., 8th Fl., New York, NY 10017-2413; tel (212) 983-1983; fax (212) 983-2464
Correspondent — Holger H Hoetzel
Correspondent — Irmie Jost
Correspondent — Jens Wiegmann

Stern Magazine — 685 3rd Ave., 23rd Fl., New York, NY 10017-4024; tel (212) 949-0404; fax (212) 949-1227
Bureau Chief — Deiter Steiner
Correspondent — Teja Fiedler
241 E. 14th St., Ste. 2-A, New York, NY 10003; tel (212) 677-8014; fax (212) 677-8962
Correspondent — Roger Kunsemueller

Stern Television — 4 Sound View Terrace, Greenwich, CT 06830; tel (203) 862-8976; fax (203) 862-8977
Correspondent — Renata Kurowski Cardello

Suddeutsche Zeitung — 5 Tudor Place City, New York, NY 10017; tel (212) 370-9379; fax (212) 370-9379
Correspondent — Thomas Schuler

Tempo — 115 Hester St., New York, NY 10002; tel (212) 941-8163
Correspondent — Andrian Kreye
8 Gramercy Park S., Ste. 4-H, New York, NY 10003; tel (212) 473-1123; fax (212) 473-4804
Correspondent — Claudia Steinberg

Textil-Wirtschaft — tel (718) 846-1990
Correspondent — Ingeborg Ledermann

Time Zone — 325 W. 71st St., Ste. 6-B, New York, NY 10023
Correspondent — Silke Gondolf

Tip Magazine — 495 Broome St., New York, NY 10013; tel (212) 226-5588; fax (212) 206-5164
Correspondent — Edda Baumann

Transglobe Agency — 11 W. 17th St., 12th Fl., New York, NY 10011; tel (212) 807-1762; fax (212) 807-1763
Photographer — Douglas Rice
40 E. 12th St., Ste. 2-C, New York, NY 10003; tel (212) 420-9105
Photographer — Charlyn Zlotnick

Trebitsch Production/Bertelsmann — 225 W. 78th St., Ste. 8, New York, NY 10024-6639; tel (212) 877-9034; fax (212) 877-0092
Correspondent — Christiane Visbeck

Verlag W Wachter — 13 Mansfield Ln., East Northport, NY 11731
Correspondent — Hans Peter Wiedemann

VWD-German Economic News — 200 Liberty St., 12th Fl., New York, NY 10281; tel (212) 838-7440; fax (212) 752-9435
Correspondent — Gabrielle Gutscher

Welthandel — 846 Rte. 121, North Salem, NY 10560; tel (914) 669-8148
Correspondent — Christian Tenbrock

Wochenpost — 5 Tudor Place City, New York, NY 10017; tel (212) 370-9379; fax (212) 370-9379
Correspondent — Thomas Schuler

ZDF German Television — 747 3rd Ave., 34th Fl., New York, NY 10017; tel (212) 833-9247; fax (212) 752-8432
Producer — Christiane Von Der Goltz

Zeitmagazin — 112 Christopher St., Ste. 3, New York, NY 10014
Photographer — Ashkan Sahihi

GREECE

A102 — 208 W. 29th St., Ste. 315, New York, NY 10001; tel (718) 463-1623; fax (718) 274-5302
Correspondent — Fotis Papagermanos

Antenna TV — 286 Engle St., Tenafly, NJ 07670; tel (201) 871-8620; fax (201) 567-0799
Correspondent — Alexandra Spyridaki

The Athenian — 405 E. 54th St., Ste. 11-D, New York, NY 10022
Correspondent — Robert Bartholomew

Athens News Agency — 131 Purchase St., Rye, NY 10580; tel (914) 921-4034
Correspondent — Mirella Georgiadou

Athens Radio — 245 E. 93rd St., Ste. 9-A, New York, NY 10128; tel (212) 963-0925; fax (718) 421-7024
Correspondent — Michalis Ignatiou

Eleftherotypia — 67 Thompson St., Ste. 2-D, New York, NY 10012; tel (212) 219-2473
Correspondent — Yiannis Kanellakis

Ena — 286 Engle St., Tenafly, NJ 07670; tel (201) 871-8620; fax (201) 567-0799
Correspondent — Alexandra Spyridaki

Ethnos — 245 E. 93rd St., Ste. 9-A, New York, NY 10128; tel (212) 963-0925; fax (718) 421-7024
Correspondent — Michalis Ignatiou

Hellenic Broadcasting Corp. (ERT) — 21-40 78th St., Ste. B-2, Flushing, NY 11357; tel (718) 278-1813; fax (718) 278-1813
Correspondent — Thomas Ellis

Ikones — 304 E. 62nd St., Ste. 18, New York, NY 10021; tel (212) 758-5149
Correspondent — John Mavrogiannopulos

Istos — 125 Mulberry St., Ste. 2-N, New York, NY 10013; tel (212) 431-3848; fax (212) 431-3848
Correspondent — John Kyriazis

Kathimerini — 286 Engle St., Tenafly, NJ 07670; tel (201) 871-8620; fax (201) 567-0799
Correspondent — Alexandra Spyridaki
551 5th Ave., Ste. 1910, New York, NY 10017; tel (212) 245-2338
Photographer — Costa Hayden

Klik — 138 Duane St., Ste. 4-S, New York, NY 10013; tel (212) 285-7016; fax (212) 285-7016
Corr. — Maria-Stefania Vavylopoulou

Mia — 286 Engle St., Tenafly, NJ 07670; tel (201) 871-8620; fax (201) 567-0799
Correspondent — Alexandra Spyridaki

New Channel — 208 W. 29th St., Ste. 315, New York, NY 10001; tel (718) 463-1623; fax (718) 274-5302
Correspondent — Fotis Papagermanos

Radio City — 311 76th St., Brooklyn, NY 11209-3105; tel (718) 748-6516; fax (212) 661-1575
Correspondent — Lambros Lambracos

Tele-City — 551 5th Ave., Ste. 1910, New York, NY 10176; tel (212) 661-1177; fax (212) 661-1575
Correspondent — Lambros Lambracos

HAITI

Caribbean Network System — United Nations, Rm. S-301, New York, NY 10017; tel (212) 888-1745; fax (212) 496-0829
Correspondent — Serge Beaulieu
Producer — Sondra Singer Beaulieu

Cosmopolitique — PO Box 3480, Rock Center Sta., New York, NY 10185; tel (718) 763-9263; fax (718) 763-1911
Correspondent — Frantz Israel

Le Nouvelliste — 596 N.W. 79th Ave., Plantation, FL 33324
Correspondent — Jean-Claude Sanon

HONG KONG

Asia Week — 34 Burgher Ave., Staten Island, NY 10304; tel (212) 963-6156; fax (212) 888-6099
Correspondent — Thalif Deen

Asian Business Magazine — 275 W. 96th St., Ste. 31-A, New York, NY 10025; tel (212) 866-9820; fax (212) 866-9820
Correspondent — Greg Dalton

Chinese Television Network (CTN) — 1995 Broadway, Ste. 602, New York, NY 10023; tel (212) 501-8088; fax (212) 501-7533
Producer — Peter Yung-Teh Hsu

Hong Kong Standard — 39 Bowery, Ste. 213, New York, NY 10002; tel (212) 219-1859; fax (212) 966-0645
Correspondent — Chi-Hon Tam

Radio Television Hong Kong (RTHK) — 39 Bowery, Ste. 213, New York, NY 10002; tel (212) 219-1859; fax (212) 966-0645
Correspondent — Chi-Hon Tam

South China Morning Post — 915 West End Ave., Ste. 3-E, New York, NY 10025; tel (212) 865-3404; fax (212) 865-1520
Correspondent — Alexis Sinclair-Krimstein

Ta Kung Pao — 15 Mercer St., Ste. 406, New York, NY 10013; tel (212) 431-9270; fax (718) 237-2850
Bureau Chief — Sui-Wai Cheung

Television Broadcasts Ltd. — 275 W. 96th St., Ste. 31-A, New York, NY 10025; tel (212) 866-9820; fax (212) 866-9820
Correspondent — Greg Dalton

HUNGARY

Blikk — 139-09 84th Dr., Briarwood, NY 11435; tel (718) 739-6483; fax (718) 739-6483
Correspondent — Agnes Niemetz

Hungarian Radio/TV — 175 E. 96th St., Ste. 28-G, New York, NY 10128; tel (212) 427-4530; fax (212) 427-4671
Bureau Chief — Miklos Martin-Kovacs
Correspondent — Julia Torda

Kurir — 67-30 Clyde St., Ste. 5-K, Forest Hills, NY 11375; tel (718) 261-4558; fax (718) 268-5418
Correspondent — Dr Peter Regos

Operaelet — 443 78th St., Ste. 58, New York, NY 10021; tel (212) 517-5637
Correspondent — Zita Vilmanyi

ICELAND

Icelandic National Broadcasting Service — 437 E. 80th St., Ste. 32, New York, NY 10021; tel (212) 249-9287
Correspondent — Kristinn Hrafnsson

INDIA

Dinkaran — 43-27 Elbertson St., Elmhurst, NY 11373; tel (718) 803-3408; fax (718) 803-3408
Bureau Chief — Joseph D Aranha

Foreign correspondents VII-17

The Hindu — 521 E. 14th St., Ste. 8-D, New York, NY 10009; tel (212) 260-7344; fax (212) 260-7219
Correspondent — Raghavendra Chakrapani
India Today — 6 Peter Cooper Rd., Ste. 7-F, New York, NY 10010; tel (212) 445-4273; fax (212) 445-4120
Correspondent — Vibhuti Patel
One Nation Chronicle — PO Box 207, Orangeburg, NY 10962; tel (914) 359-8800; fax (914) 359-1585
Correspondent — Sumbul A Ahmad
Press Trust of India — 318 Edgewood Ave., Teaneck, NJ 07666; tel (201) 833-1881; fax (201) 833-1835
Correspondent — Bhaskar Menon
United Nations, Rm. S-301, New York, NY 10017; tel (212) 751-0850; fax (202) 260-7525
Correspondent — Dharam Shourie
Times of India — 318 Edgewood Ave., Teaneck, NJ 07666; tel (201) 833-1881; fax (201) 833-1835
Correspondent — Bhaskar Menon
Vasuki — 43-27 Elbertson St., Elmhurst, NY 11373; tel (718) 803-3408; fax (718) 803-3408
Correspondent — Joseph D Aranha
The Week — 30-85 48th St., 3rd Fl., Astoria, NY 11103; tel (718) 626-4002; fax (718) 626-0465
Freelance — O P Malik

INDONESIA

Berita Buana — 53-11 90th St., Apt. 3-B, Elmhurst, NY 11373; tel (718) 699-7138; fax (718) 699-7138
Correspondent — Hidajat Supangkat
Bola — Indonesian Consulate General, 5 E. 68th St., New York, NY 10021; tel (212) 879-0600; fax (212) 570-6206
Correspondent — Hasani Abdulgani
Media Indonesia Daily — 110-33 72nd Ave., Forest Hills, NY 11375; tel (718) 261-9369; fax (718) 261-9369
Correspondent — Muchlis Hasyim

INTERNATIONAL

European Broadcasting Union (EBU) — 524 W. 57th St., Ste. 4330, New York, NY 10019; tel (212) 265-3288; fax (212) 956-7930
Deputy Bureau Chief — Kevin Kellogg
524 W. 57th St., Ste. 4390, New York, NY 10019; tel (212) 265-3288; fax (212) 956-7930
Producer — Linh Ong
Inter Press Service News Agency — 34 Burgher Ave., Staten Island, NY 10304; tel (212) 963-6156; fax (212) 888-6099
Correspondent — Thalif Deen
Middle East Magazine — United Nations, Rm. C-321, New York, NY 10017; tel (212) 963-7619
Correspondent — Raghida Dergham

IRELAND

Irish Independent — 540 E. 20th St., New York, NY 10009; tel (212) 460-5147
Correspondent — John O'Mahony
Irish Press — 19 Independence Pl., Ossining, NY 10562; tel (212) 686-1266; fax (212) 686-1756
Correspondent — Ray O'Hanlon
Sunday World — 47-25 44th St., Ste. 3-F, Woodside, NY 11377; tel (718) 361-8167
Freelance — John Byrne

ISRAEL

At Magazine — 838 Greenwich St., Ste. 4-B, New York, NY 10014; tel (212) 727-3811; fax (212) 727-3811
Correspondent — Zina Segev
Channel 2 TV — 714 9th Ave., Ste. 501, New York, NY 10019; tel (212) 247-8549; fax (212) 247-8549
Producer — Michal Lebowitsch
Globes — 108 82nd Rd., Kew Gardens, NY 11415; tel (718) 261-5755; fax (718) 261-5755
Correspondent — Jacob Shargal
150 West End Ave., Apt. 27-H, New York, NY 10023; tel (212) 724-3254; fax (212) 501-8357
Correspondent — Mary Sagi
Ha'aretz — 24 Tehama St., Brooklyn, NY 11218; tel (718) 436-5969
Correspondent — Shlomo Shamir
161 W. 61st St., New York, NY 10023; tel (212) 957-2876; fax (212) 581-2924
Correspondent — Haim Handwerker
Ha'ir — 511 6th Ave., PO Box 299, New York, NY 10011; tel (212) 929-7484; fax (212) 924-4121
Correspondent — Ronen Tal
Haolam Hazeh — 55 Bethune St., Ste. A-412, New York, NY 10014; tel (212) 675-7133
Correspondent — Yigal Mann
Israel Broadcasting Authority — 110-46 72nd Rd., Forest Hills, NY 11375; tel (718) 544-6408
Correspondent — Gideon Katzan
19 W. 69th St., Ste. 703, New York, NY 10023; fax (212) 595-0470
Correspondent — Amalie Rosenblum
Israel Television — 88 Lexington Ave., Ste. 5-E, New York, NY 10016; tel (212) 684-5292; fax (212) 477-5072
Producer — Ori Hod
Jerusalem Post — 211 E. 43rd St., Ste. 601, New York, NY 10017; tel (212) 599-3666; fax (212) 599-4743
Correspondent — Susan Fishkoff
Correspondent — Marilyn Henry
160 Central Park South, New York, NY 10019; tel (212) 599-3666; fax (212) 599-4743
Correspondent — Samuel Segev
Kol Ha'ir — 333 W. 19th St., Ste. 3-N, New York, NY 10011; tel (212) 243-4417; fax (212) 243-4417
Correspondent — Max Levitte
Kol Israel — 545 W. 111th St., Ste. 81, New York, NY 10025; tel (212) 666-2144
Correspondent — Jonathan Schachter
Maariv — 104-40 Queens Blvd., Apt. 3-J, Forest Hills, NY 11375; tel (718) 459-3644; fax (718) 459-3643
Bureau Chief — Yitzhak Ben-Horin
286 E. 10th St., Ste. 2-W, New York, NY 10009; tel (212) 982-5152; fax (212) 982-5152
Correspondent — Avi Alcalay
40 E. 80th St., New York, NY 10021; tel (212) 737-5843
Correspondent — Mira Weingarten
Shishy — 150 West End Ave., Apt. 27-H, New York, NY 10023; tel (212) 724-3254; fax (212) 501-8357
Correspondent — Mary Sagi
Yediot Ahronot — 235 E. 95th St., Ste. 8-J, New York, NY 10128; tel (212) 722-3021; fax (212) 722-3021
Bureau Chief — Tsadok Yecheskeli
254 Manhattan Ave., Ste. 3-D, New York, NY 10026; tel (212) 316-5169; fax (212) 864-3605
Correspondent — Roee Rosen
54 W. 16th St., Ste. 14-C, New York, NY 10011
Correspondent — Rebecca Rass

ITALY

Agenzia Giornali Locali (AGL) — 444 Madison Ave., 36th Fl., New York, NY 10022; tel (212) 755-0091; fax (212) 644-0753
Correspondent — Andrew Visconti
Ansa — 866 U.N. Plaza, Ste. 476, New York, NY 10017; tel (212) 319-6802; fax (212) 644-8798
Bureau Chief — Allessandra Baldini
Editor — Vincenzo Ficile
245 E. 44th St., Ste. 32-C, New York, NY 10017; tel (212) 838-1431
Freelance — Horacio Sofi
Antina Photo Agency — 214 W. 17th St., Ste. 31-B, New York, NY 10011; tel (212) 691-8355
Photographer — Claude Rolo
Aviazione — 225 E. 36th St., New York, NY 10016; fax (212) 481-9878
Correspondent — Gian Carlo Treggi
Avvenire — 3 E. 63rd St., Ste. 1-A, New York, NY 10021; tel (212) 223-0007
Correspondent — Paolo Mastrolilli
Casa Editrice Ance — PO Box 885, Lenox Hill Sta., New York, NY 10021; tel (212) 988-0322; fax (212) 488-0064
Correspondent — Piero Piccardi
Class Magazine — c/o Dow Jones, 200 Liberty St., New York, NY 10281; tel (212) 416-4106; fax (212) 416-2658
Correspondent — Andrea Fiano
Corriere Della Sera — 31 W. 57th St., 5th Fl., New York, NY 10019; tel (212) 308-2000; fax (212) 308-3719
Bureau Chief — Gianni Riotta
Correspondent — Alessandra Farkas
DOC — 109 W. 26th St., Ste 11-A, New York, NY 10001; tel (212) 255-9838; fax (212) 645-3799
Photojournalist — Patrizia Bordoni
Difesa Oggi — 225 E. 36th St., New York, NY 10016; tel (212) 481-3973; fax (212) 481-9878
Correspondent — Gian Carlo Treggi
Dove — 36 Gramercy Park E., New York, NY 10003; tel (212) 260-0692; fax (212) 308-3718
Correspondent — Patrizia Banas
Editoriale Comunicare — 257 Church St., New York, NY 10013; tel (212) 343-0151; fax (212) 343-1486
Correspondent — Francesca Monari
Editoriale Moda — 488 7th Ave., Ste. 12-C, New York, NY 10018; tel (212) 736-1537; fax (212) 465-1134
Freelance — Marianne Cassone
Gazetta Del Mezzogiorno — 531 Main St., Ste. 919, Roosevelt Island, NY 10044; tel (212) 963-0937; fax (212) 758-1349
Correspondent — Gianna Pontecorboli
Gazzetta Di Parma — 225 E. 36th St., New York, NY 10016; fax (212) 481-9878
Correspondent — Gian Carlo Treggi
Grazia — 740 Broadway, 6th Fl., New York, NY 10003; tel (212) 505-7900; fax (212) 420-9721
Bureau Chief — Sandy Auriti
Grazia Neri — 184 E. 3rd St., New York, NY 10009; tel (212) 228-0399; fax (212) 228-0399
Photographer — Lina Pallotta
GRTV Roma — 1728 Bay Ridge Ave., Brooklyn, NY 11204; tel (718) 232-2762
Correspondent — Giuseppe Guglielmo
Gulliver — 36 Gramercy Park E., New York, NY 10003; tel (212) 260-0692; fax (212) 308-3718
Correspondent — Patrizia Banas
Il Giornale — 150 W. 56th St., Ste. 3702, New York, NY 10019; tel (212) 644-8798; fax (212) 644-8798
Correspondent — Luca Ciarrocca
Il Giornale Di Napoli — 88 Bleecker St., New York, NY 10012-1514; tel (212) 982-1690
Photographer — Stefania Zamparelli
Il Manifesto — 44 Morton St., New York, NY 10014; tel (212) 633-8167
Correspondent — Giulia D'Agnolo Vallan
Il Mattino — 531 Main St., Ste. 919, Roosevelt Island, NY 10044; tel (212) 963-0937; fax (212) 758-1349
Freelance — Gianna Pontecorboli
Il Mattino Di Padova — 418 Central Park West, Ste. 74, New York, NY 10025; tel (212) 243-7404
Freelance — Raffaella Bertucci
Il Messaggero — 375 Park Ave., Ste. 2709, New York, NY 10152; tel (212) 421-6210; fax (212) 421-6547
Bureau Chief — Roberto Carlo Pesenti
Correspondent — Anna Guaita
Correspondent — Stefano Trincia
Il Mondo — 31 W. 57th St., 4th Fl., New York, NY 10019; tel (212) 308-2000; fax (212) 308-3718
Correspondent — Pietro Banas
Il Resto Del Carlino — 300 E. 40th St., Ste. 15-D, New York, NY 10016; tel (212) 758-5920; fax (212) 371-1099
Correspondent — Giampaolo Pioli
Il Secolo XIX — 151 E. 31st St., Ste. 23-F, New York, NY 10016; tel (212) 308-3510
Correspondent — Franco Pantarelli
Il Sole 24 Ore — 10 E. 53rd St., 28th Fl., New York, NY 10022; tel (212) 755-7766; fax (212) 755-8825
Bureau Chief — Mario Platero
Correspondent — Giovanni Padula
Correspondent — Stefania Pensabene
Correspondent — Marco Valsania
121 W. 72nd St., PH, New York, NY 10023; tel (212) 874-4661; fax (212) 787-1669
Correspondent — Mauro Calamandrei
Image Bank Milano — 319 E. 50th St., Ste. 10-D, New York, NY 10022; tel (212) 688-5140
Photojournalist — Santi Visalli
Impresa Italia — PO Box 885, Lenox Hill Sta., New York, NY 10021; tel (212) 988-0322; fax (212) 488-0064
Correspondent — Piero Piccardi
Intimo Pui Mare — 488 7th Ave., Ste. 12-C, New York, NY 10018; tel (212) 736-1537; fax (212) 465-1134
Freelance — Marianne Cassone
Italia Radio — 343 E. 76th St., Ste. 6-B, New York, NY 10021; tel (212) 249-5693; fax (212) 888-7335
Correspondent — Attilio Moro
Italian Elle — 13 Commerce St., New York, NY 10014; tel (212) 691-7531; fax (212) 691-7531
Freelance — Cristina Lazzati
Italian Esquire — 44 Morton St., New York, NY 10014; tel (212) 633-8167
Correspondent — Guilia D'Agnolo Vallan
L'Eco Notizie — 375 Park Ave., Ste. 3307, New York, NY 10152; tel (212) 949-8721; fax (212) 949-8723
Correspondent — Maria Grazia Galati
L'Espresso — 444 Madison Ave., 36th Fl., New York, NY 10022; tel (212) 755-0091; fax (212) 644-0753
Correspondent — Andrew Visconti
L'Unita — 473 Hudson St., New York, NY 10024; tel (212) 243-4472; fax (212) 633-0366
Correspondent — Pietro Sansonetti
Freelance — Annalisa Riccobono
La Gazzetta Dello Sport — 31 W. 57th St., 4th Fl., New York, NY 10019; tel (212) 308-2000
Correspondent — Massimo Lopes Pegna
La Nuova Venizia — 418 Central Park West, Ste. 74, New York, NY 10025; tel (212) 243-7404
Freelance — Raffaella Bertucci
La Repubblica — 444 Madison Ave., Ste. 2105, New York, NY 10022; tel (212) 826-6234; fax (212) 838-5672
Bureau Chief — Arturo Zampaglione
Correspondent — Furio Colombo
221 N. Salem Rd., Katonah, NY 10536; tel (914) 232-1422; fax (914) 232-7708
Correspondent — Romano Giachetti
La Sicilia — 531 Main St., Ste. 919, Roosevelt Island, NY 10044; tel (212) 963-0937
Correspondent — Gianna Pontecorboli
La Tribuna Di Treviso — 418 Central Park West, Ste. 74, New York, NY 10025; tel (212) 243-7404
Freelance — Raffaella Bertucci
Lo Spettacolo — 156 E. 79th St., New York, NY 10021; tel (212) 628-5643
Freelance — Mauro Lucentini
Maglieria Italian — 488 7th Ave., Ste. 12-C, New York, NY 10018; tel (212) 736-1537; fax (212) 465-1134
Freelance — Marianne Cassone
Marie Claire — 740 Broadway, 6th Fl., New York, NY 10003; tel (212) 505-7900; fax (212) 420-9721
Bureau Chief — Sandy Auriti
Marka Photo Agency — 876 Broadway, 4th Fl., New York, NY 10003; tel (212) 254-7273
Photographer — Albano Ballerini
Milano Finance — c/o Dow Jones, 200 Liberty St., New York, NY 10281; tel (212) 416-4106; fax (212) 416-2658
Correspondent — Andrea Fiano
Multimedia — 74 Reade St., Ste. 5-E, New York, NY 10007; tel (212) 566-3590
Correspondent — Maria Paola Sutto
No Limits World — 375 Park Ave., Ste. 3307, New York, NY 10152; tel (212) 949-8721; fax (212) 949-8723
Correspondent — Maria Grazia Galati
Nuovo Corso — PO Box 885, Lenox Hill Sta., New York, NY 10021; tel (212) 988-0322; fax (212) 488-0064
Correspondent — Piero Piccardi
Oggi — 31 W. 57th St., 4th Fl., New York, NY 10025; tel (212) 308-2000; fax (212) 308-3718
Correspondent — Luca Dini
Panorama — 44 Morton St., New York, NY 10014; tel (212) 633-8167
Freelance — Guilia D'Agnolo Vallan
740 Broadway, 6th Fl., New York, NY 10003; tel (212) 420-9700
Correspondent — Sandro Ottolenghi
Prisma Fotogiornalismo — 426 E. 86th St., Ste. 2-E, New York, NY 10028
Photojournalist — Piero Pomponi
RAI — 1350 Ave. of the Americas, 21st Fl., New York, NY 10019; tel (212) 468-2500; fax (212) 765-1956
Bureau Chief — Giuseppe Lugato
Correspondent — Paolo Aleotti
Correspondent — Antonio Di Bella
Correspondent — Paolo Longo
Correspondent — Fernando Masullo
Correspondent — Raffaello Siniscalco
Producer — Marina DiTommaso
Producer — Susan Fisher
Producer — Francesca Leoni
Producer — Malina Mannarino
Producer — Mia Rowan
Producer — Angela Treglia
Rassegna Dell'Ambiente — 175 5th Ave., Ste. 2215, New York, NY 10010; tel (212) 254-0562; fax (212) 254-0562
Correspondent — Giuseppe Buscemi
Reti Televisive Italiane (RTI) — 524 W. 57th St., Ste. 4360, New York, NY 10019
Correspondent — Francesca Forcella

Copyright ©1996 by the Editor & Publisher Co.

VII-18 Foreign correspondents

Rizzoli Magazines — 319 E. 50th St., Ste. 10-D, New York, NY 10022; tel (212) 688-5140
Photojournalist — Santi Visalli
Tensione — 175 5th Ave., Ste. 2215, New York, NY 10010; tel (212) 254-0562; fax (212) 254-0562
Correspondent — Giuseppe Buscemi
Trend Discotec — 109 W. 26th St., Ste. 11-A, New York, NY 10001; tel (212) 255-9838; fax (212) 645-3799
Photojournalist — Patrizia Bordoni
Tutto Disco — 109 W. 26th St., Ste. 11-A, New York, NY 10001; tel (212) 255-9838; fax (212) 645-3799
Photojournalist — Patrizia Bordoni
Viaggi Vacanze — 375 Park Ave., Ste. 3307, New York, NY 10152; tel (212) 949-8721; fax (212) 949-8723
Correspondent — Maria Grazia Galati

JAPAN

ALC Press — 55 W. 14th St., Ste. 9-F, New York, NY 10011; tel (212) 647-0809
Correspondent — Michie Yamakawa
Asahi Broadcasting Network — 875 3rd Ave., 3rd Fl., New York, NY 10022; tel (212) 644-6300; fax (212) 644-0003
Bureau Chief — Tamoo Tama
Asahi Broadcasting Network-TV Asahi — 630 5th Ave., Ste. 2707, New York, NY 10111; tel (212) 489-7928; fax (212) 489-6872
Bureau Chief — Toshio Fukuda
Correspondent — Kazuyoshi Imohara
Correspondent — Madoka Murakami
Producer — Michael Cucek
Producer — Fumiko Miyamoto
Producer — Haruo Nakamura
Producer — Christopher Poston
875 3rd Ave., 3rd Fl., New York, NY 10022; tel (212) 644-6300; fax (212) 644-0003
Correspondent — Hiroshi Shinozuka
Correspondent — Tadao Uchida
Correspondent — Tetsuhiro Yamada
Producer — Greg Fleischmann
Producer — Kenzo Hashimoto
Producer — James Kennedy
Asahi Shimbun — 229 W. 43rd St., Ste. 961, New York, NY 10036; tel (212) 398-0257; fax (212) 221-1734
Bureau Chief — Takahiro Oda
Correspondent — Roger Dilworth
Correspondent — Brian Kenety
Correspondent — Hideo Kotoku
Correspondent — Yoshio Sato
Correspondent — Shingo Uegi
Asahi Shimbun International — 35-27 28th St., Ste. B-2, Long Island City, NY 11106; tel (718) 472-4061; fax (718) 472-4061
Correspondent — Masaki Shiomi
Bungei Shunju Ltd. — 153 E. 18th St., Ste. 5, New York, NY 10003; tel (212) 387-8930; fax (212) 387-8930
Correspondent — Kinuyo Hagiwara
Cadet — 212 W. 17th St., Ste. 1-C, New York, NY 10011; tel (212) 255-3324; fax (212) 727-2747
Correspondent — Michiyo Shibahara
Chubu Nippon Broadcasting — 1270 Ave. of the Americas, Ste. 1907, New York, NY 10020
Correspondent — Hisashi Kawakita
Chunichi Shimbun — 1270 Ave. of the Americas, Ste. 1902, New York, NY 10020; tel (212) 969-1870; fax (212) 969-1843
Correspondent — Judith Wallace
Cosmopolitan — 280 Park Ave. S., Ste. 9-B, New York, NY 10010; tel (212) 598-0252; fax (212) 598-0346
Freelance — Misao Itoh
Diamond Inc. — 310 E. 44th St., Ste. 1404, New York, NY 10017; tel (212) 949-0868; fax (212) 983-0546
Correspondent — Norio Murai
Dire Magazine — 72 E. 86th St., Ste. 4-R, New York, NY 10028; tel (212) 772-8964
Correspondent — Junko Tamaoki
East-West Television — 280 Park Ave. S., Ste. 20-B, New York, NY 10010; tel (212) 673-6800; fax (212) 673-5482
Producer — Shizuko Amano
Correspondent — Keith R Vyse
English Journal — 55 W. 14th St., Ste. 9-F, New York, NY 10011; tel (212) 647-0809; fax (212) 647-0981
Correspondent — Michie Yamakawa
Femina — 90-57 51st Ave., Elmhurst, NY 11373; tel (718) 699-1897; fax (718) 699-1897
Correspondent — Reiko Isago
Forbes Nihonban — Forbes Bldg., 60 5th Ave., New York, NY 10011; tel (212) 206-5149; fax (212) 206-5127
Correspondent — Yuji Anezaki
Fujifotos — 470 Flushing Ave., Brooklyn, NY 11205; tel (718) 625-3043
Photographer — Meredith Davenport
Fujisankei Communications-Fuji TV — 150 E. 52nd St., 34th Fl., New York, NY 10022; tel (212) 753-8100; fax (212) 688-0392
Bureau Chief — Yuji Sawa
Bureau Chief — Masanobu Takada
Cameraman — Scott Guido
Correspondent — Keiko Aoki
Correspondent — Yuko Jogasaki
Correspondent — Yoichi Koizumi
Correspondent — Tracy Steinmetz
Correspondent — Tetsuo Suda
Producer — Albert Bronander
Producer — Martha Carlucci
Producer — Kazumi Iseno
Producer — Alexander Kuenstler
Producer — Leigh Mackall
Producer — Sawaka Nagano
Producer — Richard Shirley
Producer — Jessica Slepian
Producer — Naoto Suzuki
Producer — Taro Takeo
Producer — Makiko Wakabayashi
Producer — Toru Wananabe
Global Business — 530 West End Ave., Ste. 3-A, New York, NY 10024; tel (212) 877-6430; fax (212) 877-6471
Correspondent — Richard Katz
Home Economic — 601 W. 110th St., Ste. 555, New York, NY 10025; tel (212) 505-1969; fax (212) 505-1030
Correspondent — Tatsushi Tahara
Intervista Communications Inc. — 80 St. Marks Pl., New York, NY 10003; tel (212) 254-2845
Correspondent — Taku Nishimae
Producer — Noriaki Kaneko
Producer — Marti Louw
Producer — Tom Nagae
Producer — Hiroshi Noguchi
Producer — Yutaka Sato
Producer — Ann Yamamoto
Producer — Takuo Yasuda
Jiji Press — 120 W. 45th St., 14th Fl., New York, NY 10036; tel (212) 575-5830; fax (212) 764-3950
Bureau Chief — Suguru Sasaki
Correspondent — Yumi Hagio
Correspondent — Takayuki Nagahama
Correspondent — Yoshito Okubo
Editor — Kuniji Oguro
Kobunsya Publishers Ltd. — 36 E. 36th St., New York, NY 10016; tel (212) 725-1072
Correspondent — Shizue Fujita
Kyodo News Service — 50 Rockefeller Plaza, Ste. 816, New York, NY 10020; tel (212) 586-0152; fax (212) 603-6621
Bureau Chief — Kunihiko Suzuki
Deputy Bureau Chief — Masaru Imai
Correspondent — Heather Harlan
Correspondent — Toru Maruyama
Photographer — Meg Maruyama
Mainichi Broadcasting System (MBS) — 1271 Ave. of the Americas, Ste. 4659, New York, NY 10020; tel (212) 581-1960
Bureau Chief — Kunio Hiramatsu
Bureau Chief — Toshiaki Yasue
Mainichi Shimbun — 630 5th Ave., Ste. 2114, New York, NY 10111; tel (212) 765-1240; fax (212) 765-1243
Bureau Chief — Yoshiyuki Wantanbe
Correspondent — Mori Tawara
Marco Polo — 153 E. 18th St., Ste. 5, New York, NY 10003; tel (212) 387-8930; fax (212) 387-8930
Correspondent — Kinuyo Hagiwara
Nara Nichinichi Newspaper — 100 U.N. Plaza, Ste. 16-F, New York, NY 10017; tel (212) 223-3186; fax (212) 223-2962
Bureau Chief — Kosei Kamazaki
Correspondent — Teruko Ninomiya
Newsweek Japan Magazine — 251 W. 57th St., 15th Fl., New York, NY 10019; tel (212) 445-5005; fax (212) 445-5138
Bureau Chief — Valerie Burch-Abrahams
NHK-Japan Broadcasting Corp. — 1177 Ave. of the Americas, 33rd Fl., New York, NY 10036; tel (212) 704-9898; fax (212) 704-4075
Bureau Chief — Tadashi Sonoda
Deputy Bureau Chief — Akira Ogawa
Correspondent — Koki Morinaga
Correspondent — Yoshio Nishikawa
Correspondent — Emiko Tate
Producer — Hiromu Fukase
Producer — David Liebowitz
Producer — Bill Love
Producer — Setsu Mikumo
Producer — Haruo Sakitsu
Nihon Keizai Shimbun — 1325 Ave. of the Americas, Ste. 2400, New York, NY 10019; tel (212) 261-6333; fax (212) 261-6398
Correspondent — Maho Kawachi
Correspondent — Akihiko Nishiyama
Correspondent — Yuka Obayashi
Correspondent — Sadaharu Shimizu
Nihon Short Wave Broadcasting — 1325 Ave. of the Americas, Ste. 2403, New York, NY 10019; tel (212) 261-6440; fax (212) 261-6440
Bureau Chief — Yasuhiro Matsuzaki
Nikkan Gendai — 80-50 Baxter Ave., Ste. 384, Elmhurst, NY 11373; tel (718) 729-1251; fax (718) 729-6426
Correspondent — Takeo Kaji
Nikkan Kogyo Shimbun — 60 E. 42nd St., Ste. 1411, New York, NY 10165; tel (212) 697-4372; fax (212) 697-4269
Bureau Chief — Joji Ito
Nikkei Business Publications — 1325 Ave. of the Americas, Ste. 2400, New York, NY 10019; tel (212) 261-6450; fax (212) 261-6459
Bureau Chief — Kenichi Hanioka
Correspondent — Hidehiko Koguchi
Correspondent — Hideyuki Konaka
Correspondent — Hideyuki Mitsuhashi
Correspondent — Maho Kawachi
Nikkei Trendy Home Publishing Inc. — 341 E. 90th St., New York, NY 10128; tel (212) 534-7576; fax (212) 534-7576
Photographer — Junichi Takahashi
Nippas Inc. — 320 E. 39th St., New York, NY 10016; tel (212) 972-5557; fax (212) 661-1759
Producer — Izumi Sakamoto
Nippon Television Network (NTV) — 50 Rockefeller Plaza, Ste. 940, New York, NY 10020; tel (212) 765-5076; fax (212) 265-8495
Bureau Chief — Jusaburo Hayashi
Correspondent — Setsuko Inaki
Correspondent — Jun Kawakama
Correspondent — Saburo Kawakami
Correspondent — Hiromitsu Tokunaga
Producer — Jin Nakamura
Producer — Takashi Tanatusgu
NTI Broadcasting — 320 E. 39th St., New York, NY 10016; tel (212) 972-5557; fax (212) 986-2173
Bureau Chief — Masashi Miyama
Producer — Mike Nichoson
Producer — Kaoru Emura
Producer — Tracy Roberts
Producer — Noboru Sato
Producer — Kazuko Shingyoku
Orient News Agency — 212-A E. 26th St., 2nd Fl., New York, NY 10010; tel (212) 683-3734; fax (212) 683-7315
Correspondent — Young C Kim
Preseez — 152 W. 57th St., 10th Fl., New York, NY 10019; tel (212) 757-5577; fax (212) 757-5557
Photographer — Hisashi Tsumura
Radio Nippon Ltd. — 333 E. 30th St., New York, NY 10016; tel (212) 889-1763; fax (212) 889-1763
Correspondent — Kiyoshi Nasu
Ryuko-Tsushin — 319 E. 5th St., Ste. 14, New York, NY 10003; tel (212) 674-8684
Correspondent — Hideko Otake
Sankei Shimbun — 150 E. 52nd St., 34th Fl., New York, NY 10022; tel (212) 753-0350; fax (212) 688-0392
Bureau Chief — Kazuo Miyata
Sekai Nippo — 333 E. 30th St., New York, NY 10016; tel (212) 889-1763; fax (212) 889-1763
Correspondent — Kiyoshi Nasu
Senken Shimbun — 280 Park Ave. S., Ste. 9-B, New York, NY 10010
Bureau Chief — Misao Itoh
Correspondent — Yoshiko Sugimoto
Seven Seas — 55 W. 14th St., Ste. 9-F, New York, NY 10011; tel (212) 647-0809; fax (212) 647-0981
Correspondent — Michie Yamakawa
Shogakukan — 72 E. 86th St., Ste. 4-R, New York, NY 10028; fax (212) 772-3750
Correspondent — Junko Tamaoki
Shukan Bunshun — 153 E. 18th St., Ste. 5, New York, NY 10003; tel (212) 387-8930; fax (212) 387-8930
Correspondent — Kinuyo Hagiwara
Sugi Production Inc. — 5 Bentley Rd., Great Neck, NY 11023; tel (516) 487-2675; fax (516) 487-2915
Producer — Motomi Sugita
Tak Inagaki Productions Inc. — 670 Broadway, 2nd Fl., New York, NY 10012-2318; tel (212) 254-3840; fax (212) 254-3874
Producer — Tak Inagaki
Tank Inc. — PO Box 5996, Grand Central Sta., New York, NY 10163; tel (212) 840-1234
Photographer — Bruno Zehnder
Telecom Japan International — 80 St. Marks Pl., New York, NY 10003; tel (212) 254-2845; fax (212) 254-7845
Correspondent — Taku Nishimae
Television Tokyo Channel 12 — 1325 Ave. of the Americas, Ste. 2402, New York, NY 10019; tel (212) 261-6430; fax (212) 261-6439
Bureau Chief — Hiroya Konishi
Correspondent — Meguru Akao
Correspondent — Jun Ito
Correspondent — Mariko Okamoto
Correspondent — Osamu Taniguchi
Producer — Beth Blatt
Producer — Midori Matsumoto
Cameraman — Robert Haley
Tokyo Broadcasting System (TBS) — 524 W. 57th St., Ste. 4350, New York, NY 10019; tel (212) 975-8446; fax (212) 757-8193
Bureau Chief — Ichiro Nobukuni
Bureau Chief — Hirotoshi Yamanaka
Correspondent — Michiro Ohara
Correspondent — Toshio Suzuki
Correspondent — Shinsuke Tanaka
Producer — Javier Bajana
Producer — Kim Maurer
Producer — Lucy Seham Malatesta
Producer — Stafford Smith
Producer — Shoichiro Watanabe
Tokyo Business Today — 380 Lexington Ave., Ste. 4505, New York, NY 10168; tel (212) 949-6758; fax (212) 949-6648
Correspondent — Peter Ennis
Tokyo Shimbun — 1270 Ave. of the Americas, Ste. 1902, New York, NY 10020; tel (212) 969-1870
Correspondent — Yoshiharu Muto
Trendsetter — 280 Park Ave. S., Ste. 9-B, New York, NY 10010; tel (212) 598-0252; fax (212) 598-0244
Correspondent — Yoshiko Sugimoto
US Frontline News — 211 W. 56th St., Ste. 31-B, New York, NY 10019; tel (212) 957-4023; fax (212) 957-4023
Correspondent — Toshiko Tanaka
Urban Network/JR West Communications — 35-27 28th St., Ste. B-2, Long Island City, NY 11106; tel (718) 472-4061; fax (718) 472-4061
Correspondent — Masaki Shiomi
Vision Quest International — 72 E. 86th St., Ste. 4-R, New York, NY 10028; fax (212) 772-3750
Correspondent — Junko Tamaoki
Weekly Bunshun — 145 W. 67th St., Ste. 26-E, New York, NY 10023; tel (212) 877-2550; fax (212) 595-4634
Photographer — Kazumoto Ohno
Weekly Post — 222 W. 83rd St., Ste. 7-A, New York, NY 10024; tel (212) 362-9885; fax (212) 362-9857
Correspondent — Yoshikazu Demura
Weekly Shincho — 153 W. 27th St., New York, NY 10001; tel (212) 645-2684; fax (212) 645-1539
Photojournalist — Toshiro Kan
Yomiuri Shimbun — 50 Rockefeller Plaza, Ste. 825, New York, NY 10020; tel (212) 582-5827; fax (212) 957-9693
Bureau Chief — Shigeo Masui
Bureau Chief — Toshio Mizushima
Correspondent — Debbie Lau
Correspondent — Jacob Margolies
Correspondent — Lisa Schwartz
Correspondent — Kunihiko Yamaoko
Editor — Kikuro Takagi
Photographer — Don Pollardu
Wind — 127 E. 30th St., Ste. 9-C, New York, NY 10016; tel (212) 779-4420
Correspondent — Yasuko Nagasawa
Zoho 110 Inc. — 110 Greene St., Ste. 404, New York, NY 10012; tel (212) 274-8138; fax (212) 274-8137
Correspondent — Tomoko Sasaki

JORDAN

PETRA (Jordan News Agency) — PO Box 964, New York, NY 10021; tel (718) 956-0405
Correspondent — Mohammed Al Damamseh

KAZAKHSTAN

Panorama — 150 S. 2nd St., Brooklyn, NY 11211; tel (718) 388-7311
Correspondent — Gulzada Bafina

KOREA

Auditorium — 410 Broad Ave., Ste. 203, Palisades Park, NJ 07650; fax (201) 461-6630
Correspondent — Young Kee Kim

Copyright ©1996 by the Editor & Publisher Co.

Foreign correspondents VII-19

Chosen Ilbo — 23 Princeton St., Closter, NJ 07624; tel (201) 784-9669; fax (201) 784-1173
Correspondent — Hee Young Youn
The Economic Daily — 29 W. 30th St., Ste. 1003, New York, NY 10001; tel (212) 594-0493; fax (212) 643-0479
Bureau Chief — Kuhyun Yune
Hankook Ilbo — 420 Lexington Ave., Ste. 638, New York, NY 10170; tel (212) 986-6060; fax (201) 986-8131
Bureau Chief — Kook Byung Yoon
Correspondent — Jae Yong Cho
Correspondent — Heegon Hong
Joong-Ang Daily News — 35 Churchill Rd., Cresskill, NJ 07626; tel (201) 894-5721; fax (201) 894-5897
Correspondent — Chang-kyu Lee
Korean Broadcasting System — 1926 Broadway, Ste. 602, New York, NY 10023; tel (212) 501-0335; fax (212) 501-0437
Correspondent — Jaeha Baek
Correspondent — Kung-sub Song
Munhwa Broadcasting Corp. — 150 W. 51st St., Ste. 722, New York, NY 10019; tel (212) 489-0973; fax (212) 765-2083
Bureau Chief — Sung-man Cheung
Correspondent — Yung-chul Shin
Naeway Economic Daily — 2458 Rossett St., Fort Lee, NY 07024; tel (201) 944-5260; fax (201) 944-0245
Correspondent — Yoon-sub Shin
Segye Ilbo — 74 Dewey Ave., Little Falls, NJ 07424; tel (201) 785-8665; fax (201) 785-3072
Correspondent — Hyeju Kim
Seoul Broadcasting System — 51 E. 42nd St., Ste. 1401, New York, NY 10017; tel (212) 986-6801; fax (212) 986-6047
Correspondent — Byung Lee
Seoul Shimbun — 407 Jane St., Fort Lee, NJ 07024; tel (201) 585-2407; fax (201) 585-7281
Correspondent — Kun-Yung Lee

KUWAIT

Kuwait News Agency — 405 E. 42nd St., Ste. C-320, New York, NY 10017; tel (212) 888-6440; fax (212) 486-8122
Correspondent — Walter Pfaeffle

LEBANON

L'Orient Le Jour — 5 E. 22nd St., Ste. 25-C, New York, NY 10010; tel (212) 529-9136; fax (212) 333-4028
Correspondent — Sylviane Zehil

MEXICO

Activa — 871 7th Ave. Ste. 89, New York, NY 10019; tel (212) 974-7460; fax (212) 974-7462
Photographer — Eva Norvind
Agencia Mexicana De Informacion — 535 W. 111th St., Ste. 51, New York, NY 10025; tel (212) 678-2307
Correspondent — Karina Paladin
Corresponsales Y Directores De La Prensa — 415 E. 54th St., Ste. 4-D, New York, NY 10022; tel (212) 486-3098
Correspondent — Marta Solano
Eco Television — 767 5th Ave., Ste. 1200, New York, NY 10153; tel (212) 826-5383; fax (212) 754-4873
Bureau Chief — Victor Fuentes
Correspondent — Lucrecia Botin
Correspondent — Maria Gonzalez-Sieira
Correspondent — Philip Klint
El Diario De Monterrey — East Lake Stable Rd., Tuxedo Park, NY 10987; tel (212) 439-1799; fax (914) 351-5451
Correspondent — Jaime Pena-Verde
Excelsior — 501 W. 28th St., New York, NY 10001; tel (212) 736-0622
Correspondent — Beryl Sokoloff
Foro — 90-60 Union Tpk., Glendale, NY 11385; tel (718) 849-9838; fax (718) 849-9838
Correspondent — Irwin Friedland
Grupo Acir — 4901 Henry Hudson Pkwy., Ste. 10-C, Bronx, NY 10471; tel (718) 884-1978; fax (914) 476-1431
Correspondent — Anna Hernandes
Infored — 212 E. 47th St., Ste. 18-F, New York, NY 10017; tel (212) 758-5642; fax (212) 757-4642
Corr. — Marie Carmen Boue Guignard
Notimex — 155 E. 31st St., Ste. 19-D, New York, NY 10016; tel (212) 371-1289; fax (212) 754-0296
Bureau Chief — Ricardo Alday
Televisa — United Nations, Rm. C-322, New York, NY 10017; tel (212) 750-6477; fax (212) 963-6860
Correspondent — Norberto L Svarzman

NETHERLANDS

Algemeen Dagblad — 6 Beresford Ln., Larchmont, NY 10538; tel (914) 834-6793
Correspondent — Tonko Rodolf Dop
Avro Radio/Television — 5 E. 22nd St., Ste. 24-P, New York, NY 10010; tel (212) 228-1041
Correspondent — Monique Martens
De Groene Amsterdammer — 500 Ellsworth Ave., New Haven, CT 06511; tel (203) 789-2227
Correspondent — Hans Koning
De Telegraaf — 49 Drake Rd., Scarsdale, NY 10583; tel (914) 723-2904; fax (914) 725-8707
Corr. — Marcella Barron Van Der Wiel
De Volkskrant — 250 E. 90th St., Ste. 2-N, New York, NY 10128; tel (212) 860-0195; fax (212) 860-0195
Correspondent — Meindert Van Der Kaaij
335 Bloomfield St., Ste. 1, Hoboken, NJ 07031; tel (201) 222-0799
Correspondent — Tim Overdiek
Elsevier — PO Box 857, Chappaqua, NY 10514-0857; tel (914) 747-1880; fax (914) 747-1480
Correspondent — John Van Rosendaal
European Business Magazine — 50 Pine St., Apt. 4-L, Montclair, NJ 07042; tel (201) 744-2360; fax (201) 744-2410
Correspondent — Yashoda Jordan
Evangelische Omroep Broadcasting — 92 Glenwood Ave., Leonia, NJ 07605; tel (201) 944-3241
Correspondent — Peter S Mecca
792 Columbus Ave., Ste. 2-C, New York, NY 10025; tel (212) 866-8957
Correspondent — Jacob Van Rossum
Financieel Economisch Magazine — 30 W. 95th St., New York, NY 10025; tel (212) 663-0202; fax (212) 663-0101
Correspondent — Anton Foek
Het Financieele — PO Box 857, Chappaqua, NY 10514-0857; tel (914) 747-1880; fax (914) 747-1480
Correspondent — John Van Rosendaal
Het Parool — 212 W. 17th St., Ste. 2-A, New York, NY 10011; tel (212) 989-8692; fax (212) 691-6640
Correspondent — Frans Kotterer
219 Bowery, Ste. 4, New York, NY 10002; tel (212) 995-0289
Photographer — Dana Lixenberg
KRO Dutch TV — 6 Beresford Ln., Larchmont, NY 10538; tel (914) 834-4991; fax (914) 834-4331
Producer — David Hammelburg
KRO Radio & Television — 618-A 3rd St., Brooklyn, NY 11215; tel (718) 499-2428; fax (718) 965-3551
Correspondent — Yolanda Gerritsen
NCRV-TV — 6 Beresford Ln., Larchmont, NY 10538; tel (914) 834-6793
Correspondent — Tonko Rodolf Dop
Correspondent — Bernard Hammelburg
Netherland American Trade — PO Box 862, Montclair, NJ 07042
Correspondent — Martin J Bakels
Netherlands Press Association — 250 E. 90th St., Ste. 2-N, New York, NY 10128; tel (212) 860-0195; fax (212) 860-0195
Correspondent — Meindert Van Der Kaaij
Nieuwe Revu — 250 E. 90th St., Ste. 2-N, New York, NY 10128; tel (212) 860-0195; fax (212) 860-0195
Correspondent — Meindert Van Der Kaaij
Nieuws Tribune — 7004 Louise Terrace, Bay Ridge, NY 11209; tel (718) 748-2158; fax (718) 680-1226
Correspondent — Marcel Van Tuyn
NOS Dutch Radio & TV — 6 Beresford Ln., Larchmont, NY 10538; tel (914) 834-6793; fax (914) 834-4331
Correspondent — Bernard Hammelburg
NOS-TV — 76 Degraw St., Brooklyn, NY 11231; tel (718) 875-2104
Correspondent — Ben Van Meerendonk
NCR Handelsblad — 376 Broadway, Ste. 14-F, New York, NY 10013-3943; tel (212) 267-7407; fax (212) 267-3042
Correspondent — Lucas M Ligtenberg
87-50 204th St., Ste. A-65, Hollis, NY 11423; tel (718) 464-8431; fax (718) 464-8431
Correspondent — Arnon Grunberg
Opzij — 165 W. 4th St., Ste. 12, New York, NY 10014; tel (212) 242-8795
Producer-Writer — Shirley Barenholz
Panorama — 5 E. 22nd St., Apt. 24-P, New York, NY 10010; tel (212) 228-1041
Correspondent — Jim Schilder
Persbelangen Associatie — 34 Sherrill Rd., East Hampton, NY 11937; tel (516) 324-9130
Correspondent — Fred Vaz Dias
RTL Dutch Television — 524 W. 57th St., Ste. 6360, New York, NY 10019; tel (212) 975-6484; fax (212) 975-7448
Producer — Bregtje Van Der Haakk
524 W. 57th St., Ste. IFF-G1, New York, NY 10019; tel (212) 975-6484
Correspondent — Max Westerman
Sante — 250 E. 90th St., Ste. 2-N, New York, NY 10128; tel (212) 860-0195; fax (212) 860-0195
Correspondent — Janet Van Dijk
Strictly — 36 W. 17th St., 4th Fl., New York, NY 10011-5701; tel (212) 260-5570; fax (212) 260-5570
Correspondent — Sebastian Bremer
Striptur — 245 E. 63rd St. Ste. 111, New York, NY 10021; tel (212) 688-4152
Correspondent — Nathan Serphos
Vara Television — PO Box 250327, New York, NY 10025; tel (212) 316-3376; fax (212) 316-3564
Correspondent — Ton Vriens
Vaz Dias International — 34 Sherrill Rd., East Hampton, NY 11937; tel (516) 324-9130
Correspondent — Fred Vaz Dias
Veronica Broadcasting — 314 Main St., Ste. 7, Great Barrington, MA 01230; tel (413) 528-5760
Correspondent — Reinout Van Wagtendonk
VPRO Television — 25 Washington Sq. N., New York, NY 10011; tel (212) 254-5559
Correspondent — Frederikus Lieshout

NEW ZEALAND

DX News Systems — 2 Karin Ct., New Paltz, NY 12561; tel (914) 883-9142; fax (914) 883-9142
Correspondent — Rodney Bicknell
Radio New Zealand — 1422 Beverly Rd., Brooklyn, NY 11226; tel (718) 469-2767; fax (718) 469-2808
Correspondent — Judy Lessing
Television New Zealand — PO Box 1956, Rockefeller Ctr., New York, NY 10185; tel (718) 965-0214; fax (718) 768-2718
Freelance — Roy Murphy

NIGERIA

News Agency of Nigeria — United Nations, Rm. S-367, New York, NY 10017; tel (212) 688-4588; fax (212) 826-6158
Correspondent — Olusegun Adeyemi

NORWAY

Aftenposten — 25 Sutton Pl. S., New York, NY 10022; tel (212) 752-2642; fax (212) 888-7673
Correspondent — Else Hvistendahl
Arbeiderbladet — 30 River Rd., Ste. 9-D, Roosevelt Island, NY 10044; tel (212) 935-9078; fax (212) 935-9122
Correspondent — John Arne Markussen
Dagbladet — 30 River Rd., Ste. 22-C, Roosevelt Island, NY 10044; tel (212) 355-2567; fax (212) 355-2567
Correspondent — Halvor Elvik
200 Clermont Ave., Ste. 2, Brooklyn, NY 11205; tel (718) 858-0593
Photographer — Anders Lindkvist
Dagens Naeringsliv — 102-14 Russell St., Howard Beach, NY 11414; tel (718) 738-3008; fax (718) 835-0069
Correspondent — Geir Aakhus
Norsk Ukeblad — 25 Sutton Pl. S., New York, NY 10022; tel (212) 752-2642; fax (212) 888-7673
Correspondent — Else Hvistendahl
Radio P4 — 102-14 Russell St., Howard Beach, NY 11414; tel (718) 738-3008; fax (718) 835-0069
Freelance — Geir Aakhus
TV 3 — 200 E. 94th St., Ste. 2212, New York, NY 10128; tel (212) 427-0500; fax (212) 427-0505
Producer — Cecilie Holter
Verdens Gang — 45 Larchmont Ave., Larchmont, NY 10538; fax (914) 833-2136
Correspondent — Frode Holst
190-A Duane St., New York, NY 10013; tel (212) 343-0492; fax (212) 343-0496
Photographer — Per Fronth Nygaard
Vi Menn — 30 River Rd., Ste. 9-D, Roosevelt Island, NY 10044; tel (212) 935-9078; fax (212) 935-9122
Correspondent — John Arne Markussen

PAKISTAN

Associated Press of Pakistan — United Nations, Rm. S-344-A, New York, NY 10017; tel (212) 688-0860; fax (212) 371-9020
Bureau Chief — Saleem Baig
Jang — PO Box 2884, Grand Central Sta., New York, NY 10163-2884; tel (212) 963-7142; fax (908) 495-3756
Correspondent — Azim Mian
The News International — 17 5th Ave., Ste. 14, Pelham, NY 10803; tel (914) 738-1102; fax (914) 738-1150
Correspondent — Javed Malik
PO Box 2884, Grand Central Sta., New York, NY 10163-2884; tel (212) 963-7142; fax (908) 495-3756
Correspondent — Azim Mian

PANAMA

La Republica — 601 W. 149th St., Ste. 57, New York, NY 10031; tel (212) 368-7365
Correspondent — Luis Franco

PHILIPPINES

Depth News — United Nations, Rm. S-301, New York, NY 10017; tel (212) 421-4966
Correspondent — Ian Steele
Philippine Daily Express — 15 LaGuardia Ave., Staten Island, NY 10314; tel (718) 370-9268
Correspondent — Wilfredo Paderon
Press Foundation of Asia — United Nations, Rm. S-301, New York, NY 10017; tel (212) 421-4966
Correspondent — Ian Steele

POLAND

Agencja Informacyjna — 227 Riverside Dr., New York, NY 10025; tel (212) 749-4001; fax (212) 768-4829
Correspondent — Kazimierz Bilanow
Polish Press Agency — 42-10 82nd St., Ste. 3-O, Elmhurst, NY 11373; tel (212) 371-6147; fax (212) 355-4390
Correspondent — Anna Rogozinska-Wickers
Radio Zet — 5725 Van Horn St., Ste. 4-A, Elmhurst, NY 11343; tel (718) 898-8209; fax (718) 898-8209
Correspondent — Malgazata Zawadka
Rzeczpospolita — 331 W. 43rd St., Ste. 4-D, New York, NY 10036; tel (212) 594-2266; fax (212) 594-2383
Correspondent — Sylwester Walczak
Sportowiec-Polpress — 48-20 44th St., Ste. 4-C, Woodside, NY 11377; tel (718) 361-2316; fax (718) 361-2316
Correspondent — Leszek Sibilski
Teleexpress — tel (718) 898-8209; fax (718) 898-8209
Correspondent — Malgazata Zawadka

PORTUGAL

Casa & Jardim — 1116 Richmond Terrace, Staten Island, NY 10310; tel (718) 448-0622
Correspondent — Theresa Lobo
Coleccoes — 237 Lafayette St., Ste. 8, New York, NY 10012; tel (212) 226-5460; fax (212) 226-5460
Correspondent — Ana Gil Costa
Expresso — United Nations, Rm. S-360, New York, NY 10017; tel (212) 832-1232
Correspondent — Anthony Jenkins
222 W. 23rd St., Ste. 1008, New York, NY 10011; tel (212) 255-9427; fax (212) 727-8718
Photographer — Rita Barros
Gazeta Das Aldeias — 75 Riverside Dr., Ste. 4-F, New York, NY 10024; tel (212) 877-0543
Photographer — Manuel Bruges
Jornal De Noticias — 44 N. Broadway, Ste. 6-AN, White Plains, NY 10603; tel (914) 761-2080; fax (914) 761-2080
Correspondent — Argemiro Ferreira
Moda E Moda — 1116 Richmond Terrace, Staten Island, NY 10310; tel (718) 448-0622
Correspondent — Theresa Lobo
Portuguese Television (RTP) — 96 Wilson Ave., Newark, NJ 07105; tel (201) 578-8230; fax (201) 578-8297
Bureau Chief — Luis Pires
Cameraman — Jose Da Silva
Publico — 341 W. 11th St., PH-A, New York, NY 10014; tel (212) 614-0151; fax (212) 614-0151
Correspondent — Barbara Reis

ROMANIA

Dreptatea — 25-10 30th Rd., Ste. 6-L, Astoria, NY 11102; tel (718) 204-4980; fax (718) 204-4980
Correspondent — Silvia Dutchevici

Copyright ©1996 by the Editor & Publisher Co.

VII-20 Foreign correspondents

Romania Libera — 92-40 Queens Blvd., Ste. 2-D, Rego Park, NY 11374; tel (212) 224-1278
Correspondent — Gabriel Plesea

RUSSIA

Express Newspaper — 1858 W. 4th St., Ste. 1-R, Brooklyn, NY 11223; tel (718) 339-1840
Correspondent — Andre Sharapov
Inter Vip — 6197 Spencer Terrace, 2nd Fl., Riverdale, NY 10471; tel (718) 549-7318
Correspondent — Larissa Olchanetskaya
Komsolmoskaya Pravda — 5712 Mosholu Ave., Bronx, NY 10471; tel (718) 884-9702; fax (718) 543-0177
Correspondent — Sergei Ivanov
Literary Gazette — 35 Sea Coast Terrace, Apt. 12-P, Brooklyn, NY 11235; tel (718) 934-6944; fax (718) 934-7961
Correspondent — Edgar Tcheporov
Moscow News — 250 W. 100th St., Ste. 1009, New York, NY 10025; tel (212) 749-0391; fax (212) 749-0391
Correspondent — Dmitry Radyshevsky
New Times — 415 E. 37th St., Ste. 16-J, New York, NY 10016; tel (212) 725-7416; fax (212) 725-7416
Correspondent — Evgueni Rusakov
Novosti News Agency — 35 Sea Coast Terrace, Apt. 12-P, Brooklyn, NY 11235; tel (718) 934-6944; fax (718) 934-7961
Correspondent — Edgar Tcheporov
Robotchaya Tribuna — 415 E. 37th St., Ste. 16-J, New York, NY 10016; tel (212) 725-7416; fax (212) 725-7416
Correspondent — Evgueni Rusakov
Russian Radio/TV — 3059 Henry Hudson Pkwy., Riverdale, NY 10463; tel (718) 549-0062; fax (718) 549-0062
Bureau Chief — Yuri Rostov
Tass — 50 Rockefeller Plaza, Ste. 501, New York, NY 10020; tel (212) 245-4250; fax (212) 245-4258
Bureau Chief — Alexey Berezhkov
Correspondent — Sergei Babitch
Correspondent — Sergey Baybakov
Correspondent — Yuri Kirilchenko
Correspondent — Mikail Kolesnichenko
Correspondent — Sergei Kouznetsov
Correspondent — Alexander Pakhomov
Correspondent — Leonid Raitsin
Tass (UN Bureau) — United Nations, Rm. 312, New York, NY 10017; tel (212) 688-6764
Correspondent — Mikail Kochetkov
Zavtra — 45 John St., Ste. 411, New York, NY 10038; tel (212) 227-5993; fax (212) 227-8296
Correspondent — Nickolaj Von Freitor

SAUDI ARABIA

Al Jazeerah — 83-55 Lefferts Blvd., Kew Gardens, NY 11415; tel (718) 805-7937; fax (718) 805-7937
Correspondent — Adly Elzoheary
Saudi Press Agency — 4 Martine Ave., White Plains, NY 10606; tel (914) 428-8448; fax (914) 428-8448
Correspondent — George Dfouni

SERBIA & MONTENEGRO

Nin — 319 E. 78th St., Apt. 3-A, New York, NY 10001; tel (212) 213-1625; fax (212) 750-2802
Correspondent — Svetlana Kalusevic
Radio Free Europe-Serbian Service — 20 W. 84th St., Ste. 2-A, New York, NY 10024; tel (212) 370-1440; fax (212) 867-9882
Correspondent — Milorad Boskovic
Politika — 210 W. 103rd St., Ste. 4-G, New York, NY 10025; tel (212) 316-4057; fax (212) 213-1660
Correspondent — Lale Nenadovic
401 E. 80th St., Ste. 17-G, New York, NY 10021; tel (212) 517-7085; fax (212) 879-3368
Correspondent — Dusan Pesic
Radio B-92 — 575 Main St., Ste. 903, New York, NY 10044; tel (212) 371-6348; fax (212) 371-6348
Correspondent — Marina Komarecki

SLOVENIA

RTV Ljubljana — 330 E. 39th St., Ste. 25-L, New York, NY 10016; tel (212) 949-8603; fax (212) 949-8603
Correspondent — Uros Lipuscek

SOUTH AFRICA

Femme Magazine — 88 Charles St., New York, NY 10014; tel (212) 242-2933
Photographer — Rose Hartman
Independent Newspaper Group — 1010 Pine Island Tpk., Pine Island, NY 10969; tel (914) 258-4952; fax (914) 258-4617
Correspondent — Cheetah Haysom
Mnet — 1010 Pine Island Tpk., Pine Island, NY 10969; tel (914) 258-4952; fax (914) 258-4617
Correspondent — Cheetah Haysom

SPAIN

ABC Newspapers — 170 Montrose Ave., South Orange, NJ 07079; tel (212) 935-1964; fax (201) 762-1794
Correspondent — Juan Boo
190 E. Moshulu Pkwy. S., Ste. 6-F, Bronx, NY 10458; tel (718) 733-9841; fax (718) 733-9841
Correspondent — Inigo Javaloyes Ruiz
Actualidad Economica — 14 E. 60th St., PH, New York, NY 10022; tel (212) 319-0707; fax (212) 319-0704
Correspondent — Marti Saballs
Antena 3 De Radio S A (24 Hour News) — 429 E. 52nd St., Ste. 21-D, New York, NY 10022; tel (212) 421-6781; fax (212) 421-6781
Correspondent — Emmanuela Roig
Antena 3 TV — 220 E. 42nd St., Ste. 1404, New York, NY 10017; tel (212) 682-0571; fax (212) 682-0571
Correspondent — Alejandro Duenas
Avui — 224 Sullivan St., Ste. A-32, New York, NY 10012; tel (212) 982-2499; fax (212) 982-2499
Correspondent — Montserrat Vendrell
132 Summit Ave., Cliffside Park, NJ 07010; tel (201) 941-5870; fax (201) 941-5870
Correspondent — Raphael Corbalan
Cinevideo 20 — 12 Sterling Pl., Ste. 2, Brooklyn, NY 11217; tel (718) 398-1326
Correspondent — Jose Valencia
Cover Press Agency — 452 W. 57th St., Ste. 2, New York, NY 10019; tel (212) 307-9010
Photogrpaher — Gerardo Somoza
Diario Medico — 145 W. 67th St., Ste. 14-A, New York, NY 10023; fax (212) 319-0704
Correspondent — Nerea Prieto
Ecologia International — 76 Jewel St., Ste. 1, Brooklyn, NY 11222; tel (718) 349-0165
Correspondent — Jaime Gonzalez
Economia Y Finanzas — 792 Columbus Ave., Ste. 90, New York, NY 10025; tel (212) 666-0571; fax (212) 666-0571
Correspondent — Jaime A Gomez
EFE Spanish News Agency — 220 E. 42nd St., Ste. 1404, New York, NY 10017; tel (212) 867-5757; fax (212) 867-9074
Bureau Chief — Anne Leroux
Correspondent — Pilar Dominguez
Correspondent — Juan Velazquez
Correspondent — Jose Sobrino
Photographer — Gerardo Dominguez
El Economista — 305 Henry St., Brooklyn, NY 11201; tel (718) 624-5210; fax (718) 624-4808
Correspondent — Julio Pastor Bayon
El Mundo — 155 E. 31st St., Ste. 24-C, New York, NY 10016; tel (212) 889-6115; fax (212) 951-4467
Correspondent — Ana Romero
300 Mercer St., Ste. 15-M, New York, NY 10003; tel (212) 539-1843; fax (212) 539-1845
Correspondent — Carlos Fresneda
El Nuevo Lunes — 345 E. 52nd St., Ste. 4-G, New York, NY 10022; tel (212) 832-1876; fax (212) 832-1876
Correspondent — Carmen Gea
c/o Camino, 330 E. 39th St., Ste. 5-F, New York, NY 10016; tel (212) 867-6085; fax (212) 867-5490
Correspondent — Sergio De La Serna
El Observador — 224 Sullivan St., Ste. A-32, New York, NY 10012; tel (212) 982-2499; fax (212) 982-2499
Correspondent — Montserrat Vendrell
El Pais — 155 W. 68th St., Apt. 1110, New York, NY 10023; tel (212) 873-9146
Correspondent — Juan Cavestany
Elle — 102 W. 85th St., Apt. 8-F, New York, NY 10024; tel (212) 724-3696; fax (212) 724-3696
Correspondent — Jane Folpe
Euskadi Irratia — 124 W. 60th St., Ste. 27-C, New York, NY 10023; tel (212) 262-0292
Correspondent — Joseba A Basurto Lasarte
Expansion — 14 E. 60th St., PH, New York, NY 10022; tel (212) 319-0707; fax (212) 319-0704
Correspondent — Marti Saballs
Gaceta De Negocios — 253 Newark Ave., Ste. 5-L, Jersey City, NJ 07302; tel (201) 653-6067; fax (201) 653-6067
Correspondent — Elena Ruiz
Grupo Zeta — 253 Newark Ave., Ste. 5-L, Jersey City, NJ 07302; tel (201) 653-6067; fax (201) 653-6067
Correspondent — Elena Ruiz
Hachette Filipacchi — 523 E. 83rd St., Ste. 5-E, New York, NY 10028; tel (212) 249-4548; fax (212) 249-4548
Correspondent — Inaki (Jose) Escudero
Hola — 555 Park Ave., Ste. 3-E, New York, NY 10021; fax (212) 838-1681
Correspondent — Gaetana Enders
Iconica/The Spanish Link — 117 Sullivan St., Ste. 2-C, New York, NY 10012; tel (212) 941-9137; fax (212) 941-9137
Correspondent — Inma Guiu
La Vanguardia — 216 E. 29th St., Ste. 4-C, New York, NY 10016; tel (212) 685-4268
Correspondent — Candy Rodo
La Voz De Galicia — 84 1/2 Morris St., Ste. 3-L, Jersey City, NJ 07302; tel (201) 434-2128
Correspondent — Jaime Meilan
Multimedia Capital S L — 565 61st St., West New York, NJ 07093; tel (212) 286-0123; fax (212) 818-9249
Correspondent — Elena Herrero
Onda Cero Radio — 235 E. 95th St., Ste. 21-K, New York, NY 10128; tel (212) 427-7587; fax (212) 427-7587
Correspondent — Agustin de Frutos
Penta Press — 7 Secretariat Ct., Tinton Falls, NJ 07724; tel (908) 389-2774; fax (908) 389-3779
Photographer — Andres Palomino
Quipus Press — 400 W. 23rd St., Ste. 5-K, New York, NY 10011; tel (212) 989-0413; fax (212) 989-0413
Correspondent — Nicanor Cardenosa
Ragazza — 151 Lexington Ave., Ste. 10-F, New York, NY 10016; tel (212) 447-0894; fax (212) 447-0894
Photographer — Jose Escudero
Revistaturia — PO Box 8520, FDR Sta., New York, NY 10150; tel (212) 979-6244
Correspondent — Emilio Mayorga Calabuig
Techniarte — 3 W. 102nd St., Ste. 5-B, New York, NY 10025
Correspondent — Mara Mahia
Television of Spain — 501 Madison Ave., Ste. 604, New York, NY 10022; tel (212) 371-5112; fax (212) 758-7390
Bureau Chief — Jose Martinez Soler
Correspondent — Christina Carrion
Correspondent — Guillermo De Mulder
Correspondent — Nuria Ribo
Producer — Miguel Moreno
Tiempo — 425 E. 51st St., Ste. 8-A, New York, NY 10022; tel (212) 888-2996; fax (212) 319-8330
Correspondent — Gustavo Valverde
Tribuna De Actualidad — 141 Beach Ave., Mamaroneck, NY 10543; tel (914) 381-2465; fax (914) 381-2465
Correspondent — Christina Mella
TV-3/Televisio De Catalunya — 34 King St., New York, NY 10014
Correspondent — Carlos Bosch
Woman — 145 W. 67th St., Ste. 14-A, New York, NY 10023; tel (212) 721-1421; fax (212) 319-0704
Correspondent — Nerea Prieto
Yate — PO Box 1614, Madison Sq. Sta., New York, NY 10159; tel (212) 366-5093; fax (212) 366-5093
Correspondent — Helena Medina

SWEDEN

Aftonbladet — 71 Park Ave., Ste. 9-B, New York, NY 10016; tel (212) 213-8450
Correspondent — Leif-Ake Josefsson
Arbetet — 170 E. 94th St., Ste. 6-A, New York, NY 10128-2572; tel (212) 423-0157; fax (212) 423-1056
Correspondent — Gunilla Perez Faringer
Dagens Industri — 12 Sherwood Farms Ln., Westport, CT 06880; tel (203) 226-3994; fax (203) 226-3998
Correspondent — Hans-Inge Olsson
Dagens Medicin — 118 W. 3rd St., Ste. 3-A, New York, NY 10012; tel (212) 387-9002; fax (212) 387-8955
Freelance — Peter Svensson
Dagens Nyheter — 352 W. 12th St., Ste. 12-D, New York, NY 10014; tel (212) 627-5379; fax (212) 627-5379
Correspondent — Peter Borgstrom
c/o Cabret, 226 W. 75th St., Ste. 42, New York, NY 10023; tel (212) 874-8306
Photojournalist — Henry Arvidsson
Expressen — 245 E. 93rd St., Apt. 12-H, New York, NY 10128; tel (212) 996-5026; fax (212) 996-5028
Correspondent — Staffan Thorsell
1775 York Ave., Ste. 25-A, New York, NY 10128
Photographer — Stefan Hyttfors
FTL Press Agency — 230 Riverside Dr., Ste. 12-L, New York, NY 10025; tel (212) 866-3313; fax (212) 866-1711
Correspondent — Nils Horner
320 W. 56th St., Ste. 4-D, New York, NY 10019; tel (212) 956-4094
Freelance — Leif Bergstrom
Gefle Dagblad — 209 W. 108th St., Ste. 9, New York, NY 10025; tel (212) 678-7801
Correspondent — Monika Gutestam
Goteborgs-Posten — 75 West End Ave., Ste. Park 31-D, New York, NY 10023; tel (212) 957-9202; fax (212) 974-0701
Correspondent — Bengt Hansson
Gotesborgs Posten — 209 W. 108th St., Ste. 9, New York, NY 10025; tel (212) 678-7801
Freelance — Monika Gutestam
Hufvudstadsbladet — 209 W. 108th St., Ste. 9, New York, NY 10025; tel (212) 678-7801
Correspondent — Monika Gutestam
Idag — 161 W. 4th St., Ste. 3-F, New York, NY 10014; tel (212) 206-8516
Photographer — Christina Sjogren
530 E. 84th St., Ste. 5-A, New York, NY 10028; tel (212) 439-6857
Photographer — Per-Anders Pettersson
Info — 118 W. 3rd St., Ste. 3-A, New York, NY 10012; tel (212) 387-9002; fax (212) 387-8955
Freelance — Peter Svensson
Kemisk Tidskrift — 118 W. 3rd St., Ste. 3-A, New York, NY 10012; tel (212) 387-9002; fax (212) 387-8955
Freelance — Peter Svennson
Lakartidningen — 1826 2nd Ave., Ste. 107, New York, NY 10128; tel (212) 721-1092; fax (212) 987-0883
Freelance — Gregory-Zvi Wirschubsky
Landstings Varlden — 118 W. 3rd St., Ste. 3-A, New York, NY 10012; tel (212) 387-9002; fax (212) 387-8955
Freelance — Peter Svensson
Res Guide — 160 Barry St., Brooklyn, NY 11211; tel (718) 387-7610; fax (718) 387-7610
Photographer — Peter Norrman
Saf — 320 W. 56th St., Ste. 4-D, New York, NY 10019; tel (212) 956-4094
Freelance — Leif Bergstrom
Svenska Dagbladet — 170 E. 94th St., Ste. 6-A, New York, NY 10128-2575; tel (212) 423-0157; fax (212) 423-1056
Correspondent — Gunilla Perez Faringer
Svenska Nyhetsbyran — 720 Saunders Ave., Westfield, NJ 07090; tel (908) 233-0806
Correspondent — E Elizabeth Precht
Swedish National Radio — 212 E. 47th St., Ste. 30-F, New York, NY 10017; tel (212) 888-6469; fax (212) 758-6989
Correspondent — Lars Asgard
1826 2nd Ave., Ste. 107, New York, NY 10128; tel (212) 721-1092; fax (212) 987-0883
Correspondent — Gregory-Zvi Wirschubsky
Swedish News Agency — 14 Wildwood Rd., Larchmont, NY 10538; tel (914) 834-3243; fax (914) 833-3685
Correspondent — Thomas Hogeberg
Sydsvenska Dagbladet — 215 W. 88th St., Ste. 7-G, New York, NY 10024; tel (212) 721-7370; fax (212) 721-7370
Correspondent — Lennart Pehrson
Upsala Nya Tidning — 207 Walton St., Ste. B, Ridgewood, NJ 07450; tel (201) 251-8291; fax (718) 858-0593
Correspondent — Erling Hoh
Vasterbottens Kuriren — 161 W. 4th St., Ste. 3-F, New York, NY 10014; tel (212) 206-8516
Photographer — Christina Sjogren

SWITZERLAND

Annabelle — PO Box 343, New Suffolk, NY 11956; tel (516) 734-4147; fax (516) 734-6937
Correspondent — Walter Werthmueller
Aramis — 156 Prince St., Ste. 5-B, New York, NY 10012; tel (212) 925-7273
Correspondent — Philip Rust

Foreign correspondents VII-21

Azzurro Matto — 208 E. 7th St., Ste. 20, New York, NY 10009; tel (212) 330-0466
Photographer — Frederic Ruegg
Cash TV — 365 W. 20th St., New York, NY 10011; tel (212) 924-3664; fax (212) 924-3664
Photographer — Michael Dames
Finanz Und Wirtschaft — 365 W. 20th St., New York, NY 10011; tel (212) 924-3664
Photographer — Michael Dames
40 River Rd., Ste. 14-K, Roosevelt Island, NY 10044; tel (212) 758-6411; fax (212) 758-3684
Correspondent — Giorgio V Mueller
Illustrated Press Agency — 485 5th Ave., 5th Fl., New York, NY 10017; tel (212) 490-3995; fax (212) 490-6061
Correspondent — Helen Marchel
461 5th Ave., 4th Fl., New York, NY 10017; tel (212) 561-2951
Correspondent — Sieglinde Uetzfeld
Le Nouveau Quotidien — 33 Gold St., Apt. 619, New York, NY
Corr. — Anne-Frederique Widmann
Neue Zuercher Zeitung — 15 Boulderol Rd., Stamford, CT 06903; tel (203) 329-0642; fax (203) 968-2927
Correspondent — Karl Grun
343 E. 78th St., Ste. 6, New York, NY 10021; tel (212) 773-8456
Correspondent — Armin Kunz
Penthouse — PO Box 343, New Suffolk, NY 11956; tel (516) 734-4147; fax (516) 734-6937
Photographer — Walter Werthmueller
Radio Lac — 239 E. 33rd St., Ste. 2-B, New York, NY 10016; tel (212) 679-0197
Correspondent — Etienne Roch
Republican Press Ltd. — 292 Hardenburgh Ave., Demarest, NJ 07627; tel (201) 767-7667; fax (201) 767-3450
Correspondent — George Simor
Rhone International Informations — 300 E. 57th St., Ste. 18-F, New York, NY 10022; tel (212) 355-4432
Correspondent — Andre De Beauharnais
Sonntags Blick — 20 Canal Rd., Easton, PA 18042; tel (212) 258-9556; fax (212) 258-2825
Correspondent — Rico Carisch
Sonntags Zeitung — 356 Bowery, 5th Fl., New York, NY 10012; tel (212) 353-2697; fax (212) 353-2972
Correspondent — Martin Suter
Tages-Anzeiger — 310 E. 46th St., Ste. 26-A, New York, NY 10017; tel (212) 986-1167; fax (212) 986-9298
Correspondent — Monica Hegglin
TR7/Switzerland — 1965 Broadway, New York, NY 10019; tel (212) 682-2824; fax (212) 682-2824
Correspondent — Gabrielle Barth
Walter Greminger Press AG — PO Box 343, New Suffolk, NY 11956; tel (516) 734-4147; fax (516) 734-6937
Correspondent — Walter Werthmueller

TAIWAN

Central News Agency — c/o UPI, 2 Penn Plaza, 18th Fl., New York, NY 10001-1803; tel (212) 643-9332; fax (212) 643-9334
Correspondent — Kwang-chun Huang
Correspondent — Ranan Huang
Correspondent — David Y C Wang
China Economic News Service (CENS) — 102 Bedford St., New York, NY 10014; tel (212) 684-3770; fax (212) 684-3858
Freelance — Ava Chien
China News Service — 58 White St., New York, NY 10013; tel (212) 966-2681; fax (212) 219-9696
Correspondent — Dianwei Tang
China Television Co. (CTV) — 875 Ave. of the Americas, Ste. 2111, New York, NY 10001; tel (212) 244-2102; fax (212) 244-2105
Correspondent — Anni Shih
Chinese Television System — 408 8th Ave., Ste. 6-C, New York, NY 10001; tel (212) 947-0851; fax (212) 967-2567
Correspondent — Kuanyuh Tony Lin
Economic Daily News — 141-07 20th Ave., College Point, NY 11357; tel (718) 746-9423; fax (718) 746-9434
Correspondent — I Chieh Fu
Taiwan Television Enterprises Ltd. — 50 W. 34th St., Ste. 25-C8, New York, NY 10001; tel (212) 695-4377; fax (212) 695-4287
Correspondent — Yueh Chiou
United Daily News Group — 141-07 20th Ave., College Point, NY 11357; tel (718) 746-9423; fax (718) 746-9434
Correspondent — I Chieh Fu

TURKEY

ATV — 37-B Crosby St., Ste. 3, New York, NY 10013; tel (212) 925-8147; fax (212) 752-5028
Correspondent — Sebnem Senyener
Dunya — 39-06 62nd St., Ste. B-I, Woodside, NY 11377; tel (718) 533-8384
Freelance — Garbis Kesisoglu
Hurriyet — 500 5th Ave., Ste. 1021, New York, NY 10110; tel (212) 921-8880; fax (212) 391-4017
Correspondent — Dogan Uluc
Kanal 6 — 333 E. 45th St., Ste. 14-S, New York, NY 10017; tel (212) 818-0716; fax (212) 818-0716
Correspondent — Nilay Karaelmas
Karadeniz — 412 E. 16th St., Brooklyn, NY 11226; tel (718) 282-9091; fax (718) 941-7186
Correspondent — Salih Zeki Gungor
Milliyet — 245 Beverly Rd., Douglaston, NY 11363; tel (718) 279-9140; fax (718) 631-1218
Freelance — Iskender Songur
Sabah — 37-B Crosby St., Ste. 3, New York, NY 10013; tel (212) 925-8147; fax (212) 752-5028
Correspondent — Sebnem Senyener
Turkiye — 337 Clifton Ave., Clifton, NJ 07011; tel (201) 777-0699
Correspondent — Murat Yesil
Zaman — tel (718) 899-7401; fax (718) 899-7814
Correspondent — Musa Aydemir
Correspondent — Halim Daglar

UKRAINE

Nezavisimost — 36-85 Shore Pkwy., Ste. 2-D, Brooklyn, NY 11235; tel (718) 648-7586; fax (718) 252-5386
Correspondent — Aleksander Budnitskiy

UNITED ARAB EMIRATES

UAE News Agency — United Nations, Rm. 453-A, New York, NY 10017; tel (212) 752-9466
Correspondent — Anita Sunukjian

UNITED KINGDOM

AFX News — 1 Broadway Plaza, 55 Broadway, New York, NY 10006; tel (212) 514-9559; fax (212) 514-9605
Correspondent — Victoria Thieberger
British Broadcasting Corp. (BBC) — 1995 Broadway, Ste. 505, New York, NY 10023; tel (212) 501-1500; fax (212) 501-0040
Bureau Chief — Mark McDonald
Correspondent — Juli Steadman
Producer — Heather Maclean
United Nations, Rm. C-309, New York, NY 10017; tel (212) 688-6266; fax (212) 421-4841
Correspondent — Rob Watson
Camera Press Ltd. — 529 E. 88th St., Ste. 2-A, New York, NY 10028; tel (212) 737-1225
Photographer — Carol Haggerty
Daily Express — 220 E. 42nd St., Ste. 500, New York, NY 10017; tel (212) 682-4111
Bureau Chief — Philip Finn
Daily Mail — 500 5th Ave., Ste. 312, New York, NY 10110; tel (212) 869-2570; fax (212) 302-3902
Bureau Chief — George Gordon
United Nations, Rm. S-352, New York, NY 10017; tel (212) 319-6626; fax (212) 753-6168
Correspondent — Joe Lauria
RD 2, Box 210, Titusville, NJ 08560; tel (609) 737-6992; fax (609) 737-9687
Correspondent — Dermont Purgavie
92 Cranford Pl., Teaneck, NJ 07666; tel (201) 833-4080; fax (201) 833-4026
Photographer — Malcolm Clarke
420 E. 81st St., 1st Fl., New York, NY 10028; tel (212) 535-6900; fax (212) 535-7077
Photographer — Michael Brennan
Daily Mirror — 25 Tudor City Pl., Ste. 1704, New York, NY 10017; tel (212) 490-0294; fax (212) 661-9344
Correspondent — Stewart Dickson
The European — 31 Union Sq. W., Ste. 9-B, New York, NY 10003; tel (212) 691-5644; fax (212) 691-5832
Correspondent — Edward Helmore
235 E. 49th St., Ste. 1-A, New York, NY 10017; tel (212) 593-3407; fax (212) 371-4054
Correspondent — Ian Williams
Evening Standard — 170 John St., Ste. 3-D, New York, NY 10038; tel (212) 361-2452; fax (212) 361-2457
Correspondent — Susana Antunes
Correspondent — Lawrence Black
The Guardian — 275 Greenwich St., Ste. 4-K, New York, NY 10007; tel (212) 406-8551
Correspondent — Mark Tran
19 W. 44th St., Ste. 1613, New York, NY 10036; tel (212) 391-1602; fax (212) 391-1613
Correspondent — Ian Katz
The Independent — 444 Madison Ave., Ste. 2105, New York, NY 10036; tel (212) 308-4656; fax (212) 308-4539
Correspondent — David Usborne
95 Greene St., Ste. 4-E, New York, NY 10012; tel (212) 431-9843
Freelance — Reggie Nadelson
Independent Radio News (IRN) — 98 Chambers St., New York, NY 10007; tel (212) 385-2974; fax (212) 732-4896
Correspondent — Paul Woodley
Independent Television News — PO Box 135, New York, NY 10159; tel (212) 388-9552; fax (212) 388-9552
Correspondent — Michael Reubens
Investor Relations — 235 E. 49th St., Ste. 1-A, New York, NY 10017; tel (212) 593-3407; fax (212) 371-4054
Correspondent — Ian Williams
Mail On Sunday — 845 West End Ave., Ste. 7-E, New York, NY 10025; tel (212) 932-8808; fax (212) 932-8460
Freelance — Adrianne Pielou
The Observer — 135 Greenway S., Forest Hills, NY 11375; tel (718) 263-4667
Freelance — Joyce Egginton
Reuters — 1700 Broadway, 31st Fl., New York, NY 10019; tel (212) 603-3300; fax (212) 603-3368
Correspondent — Arthur Spiegelman
Reuters Radio — 41-42 50th St., Apt. 1-G, Woodside, NY 11377; tel (718) 458-6929
Correspondent — Gavin Walker
Reuters TV — 747 3rd Ave., 29th Fl., New York, NY 10017; tel (212) 833-9220; fax (212) 752-1363
Producer — Helen Sahin
Producer — Chris Turque
Producer — Cynthia Wallace
Scotland On Sunday — 559 17th St., Ste. 1-F, Brooklyn, NY 11215; tel (718) 965-9700; fax (718) 965-9700
Correspondent — James Cruickshank
Sourakia — 230 W. 55th St., Ste. 17-F, New York, NY 10019; tel (212) 769-7792; fax (212) 333-2574
Correspondent — Michael James Gazelle
Sunday Times — 80 N. Moore St., Ste. 37-G, New York, NY 10013; tel (212) 732-2458; fax (212) 732-2458
Photographer — Carl Glassman
The Times — United Nations, Rm. C-135, New York, NY 10017; tel (212) 308-3390; fax (212) 308-3390
Correspondent — James Bone
Transworld News — 255 Chatterton Pkwy., White Plains, NY 10606; tel (212) 504-9000; fax (212) 504-9000
Correspondent — Richard S Grayson
West Africa — 710 West End Ave., Ste. 11-B, New York, NY 10025; tel (212) 678-2237; fax (212) 678-2237
Correspondent — Tunji Lardner
WTN Worldwide Television News — 82 Horatio St., Ste. 5-B, New York, NY 10014; tel (212) 741-0301; fax (212) 741-0304
Producer — Fiona MacKenzie

URUGUAY

Estediario — 875 5th Ave., Ste. 18-G, New York, NY 10021; tel (212) 744-0620; fax (212) 744-0620
Correspondent — Joseph Novoa
Guia Financiera — 120 7th Ave., Ste. 2-F, Brooklyn, NY 11215; tel (718) 398-9232; fax (718) 398-9232
Correspondent — Jose Real
La Republica — 666 Broadway, Ste. 625, New York, NY 10012; tel (212) 645-8896; fax (212) 674-6190
Correspondent — Gabriela Fried

VENEZUELA

El Nuevo Pais — 531 E. 13th St., Ste. 9, New York, NY 10009; tel (212) 876-7804; fax (212) 876-7804
Correspondent — Edmundo Bracho Polanco
Numero — 10 W. 66th St., Ste. 12-G, New York, NY 10023; tel (212) 769-4727; fax (212) 769-4727
Correspondent — Marisela Le Foust
Venpress — United Nations, Rm. S-360, New York, NY 10017; tel (212) 759-9039; fax (212) 371-9020
Correspondent — Lisette Gonzalez

WASHINGTON CORRESPONDENTS

AFRICA

Intro Communications Inc. — 6908 Strata St., McLean, VA 22101; tel (703) 847-6405; fax (703) 356-4357
Correspondent — Neil Lurssen
West Africa (London) — PO Box 29161, Washington, DC 20017; tel (301) 779-1382; fax (301) 779-1382
Correspondent — James Butty

ALGERIA

Algerian News Agency — 2441 46th St. N.W., Washington, DC 20007; tel (202) 338-3058; fax (202) 338-3286
Bureau Chief — Nacer Mehal
Algerian Television — 2241 46th St. N.W., Washington, DC 20007; tel (202) 338-3058; fax (202) 338-3286
Bureau Chief — Nacer Mehal
Algerie-Actualite — 1591 Kimblewick Rd., Potomac, MD 20854-6165; tel (301) 309-9734; fax (301) 309-9734
Correspondent — Mouny Berrah

ARGENTINA

Diario Clarin — 1260 21st St. N.W., Ste. 310, Washington, DC 20036; tel (202) 331-1274
Correspondent — Maria Luisa Mackay
El Cronista — 1114 Brentfield Dr., McLean, VA 22101; tel (703) 893-5485; fax (703) 448-0537
Correspondent — Mario Federico Del Carril
La Nacion — 220 National Press Bldg., Washington, DC 20045; tel (202) 628-7907; fax (202) 333-1053
Correspondent — Fernan Saguier
Somos — 3271 Prospect St. N.W., Washington, DC 20007; tel (202) 223-7982; fax (202) 337-2242
Correspondent — Ana Baron-Supervielle

AUSTRALIA

The Australian — 1040 National Press Bldg., Washington, DC 20045; tel (202) 628-6269; fax (202) 393-3892
Correspondent — Peter J Wilson
Australian Associated Press (AAP) — 1731 P St. N.W., Washington, DC 20036; tel (202) 332-0311; fax (202) 483-4327
Correspondent — Sophie Scott
Australian Broadcasting (ABC) — 2030 M St. N.W., Ste. 504, Washington, DC 20036; tel (202) 466-8575; fax (202) 775-9308
Correspondent — Michael Gleeson
Correspondent — Tony Jones
Correspondent (TV) — Peter Ryan
Australian Financial Review — 1331 Pennsylvania Ave. N.W., Ste. 904, Washington, DC 20004; tel (202) 639-8084; fax (202) 639-8036
Correspondent — Michael Stutchbury
Australian Radio News — 3622 Stanford Cir., Falls Church, VA 22041; tel (703) 354-6795; fax (703) 354-6371
Correspondent — Connie Lawn
Canberra Times — 1901 Columbia Rd. N.W., Ste. 703, Washington, DC 20009; tel (202) 462-8232; fax (202) 462-8232
Correspondent — Jamie Dettmer
Daily Telegraph Mirror — 1731 P St. N.W., Washington, DC 20036; tel (202) 332-0311; fax (202) 483-4327
Correspondent — Sophie Scott
Freelance-Various Radio/TV — 6451 Lee Hwy., Ste. 918, Fairfax, VA 22031; tel (703) 385-7216
Correspondent — Paul Hodges
Melbourne Age — 1331 Pennsylvania Ave. N.W., Ste. 904, Washington, DC 20004; tel (202) 737-6360; fax (202) 639-8036
Correspondent — Pilita Clark
Sydney Morning Herald — 1331 Pennsylvania Ave. N.W., Ste. 904, Washington, DC 20004; tel (202) 737-6360; fax (202) 639-8036
Correspondent — Pilita Clark

Copyright ©1996 by the Editor & Publisher Co.

AUSTRIA

Die Presse — 3121 33rd Pl., N.W., Washington, DC 20008; tel (202) 362-4045; fax (202) 686-2092
Correspondent — Monica Riedler

ORF-Austrian Radio/Television — 1206 Eton Ct., N.W., Washington, DC 20007; tel (202) 822-9570; fax (202) 822-9569
Bureau Chief — Franz Koessler
Correspondent — Raimund Loew
Freelance — Michael Nothnagl

West-Ost Jornal — 3733 Massachusetts Ave. N.W., Washington, DC 20016; tel (202) 966-7433
Correspondent — Robert Bauer

BAHRAIN

Sada Al-Usbou — 5550 Columbia Pike, Ste. 751, Arlington, VA 22204; tel (202) 298-8865; fax (703) 998-5163
Correspondent — Mohamed Maaty

BANGLADESH

The Telegraph — 11235 Oakleaf Dr., Ste. 1020, Silver Spring, MD 20901; tel (301) 681-6360; fax (301) 681-6360
Bureau Chief — Golam Arshad

BELARUS

Zwiazda — 1511 P St. N.W., Washington, DC 20005; tel (202) 332-7545
Correspondent — Vassilli Siltchuk

BELGIUM

Belga-Belgian News Agency — 2030 M St. N.W., Ste. 400, Washington, DC 20036; tel (202) 775-0894; fax (202) 293-7204
Correspondent — Odile Isralson

BRTN-Belgium TV — 2030 M St. N.W., Washington, DC 20036; tel (202) 466-8781; fax (202) 828-4146
Bureau Chief — Anna Maria Nysters

L'Echo — PO Box 6613, Arlington, VA 22206; tel (202) 667-8308; fax (202) 667-3465
Correspondent — Yve Janssens Laudy

La Libre Belgique — PO Box 6613, Arlington, VA 22206; tel (202) 667-8308; fax (202) 667-3465
Correspondent — Yve Janssens Laudy

Le Soir — 3217 Volta Pl. N.W., Washington, DC 20007; tel (202) 333-4119; fax (202) 337-2898
Correspondent — Nathalie Annette Mattheiem

Talent — 6501 Majory Ln., Bethesda, MD 20817; tel (301) 229-6217; fax (301) 229-6217
Correspondent — Catherine Antoine

Trends-Tendances — 6501 Majory Ln., Bethesda, MD 20817; tel (301) 229-6217; fax (301) 229-6217
Correspondent — Catherine Antoine

BOLIVIA

El Diario — PO Box 817, McLean, VA 22101; tel (703) 847-0810; fax (703) 790-2755
Correspondent — Julio Cesar Duran

Horizonte — 4406 Forest Glen Ct., Annandale, VA 22003; tel (703) 642-1256; fax (703) 642-6660
Bureau Chief — Juan Bernardo Davila
Correspondent — Johnny Arnez
Correspondent — Marco Antonio Decker

Primera Plana/Radio Fides — 4600 S. Four Mile Run Dr., Ste. 115, Arlington, VA 22204; tel (703) 998-0035; fax (703) 998-0035
Bureau Chief — Francisco Juan Roque
Correspondent — Francisco Roque-Higorre

BRAZIL

Correio Brazilense — 3726 S. 12th St., Arlington, VA 22204; tel (703) 521-7396
Correspondent — Jose Ribamar De Carvalho

Folha De Sao Paulo — 3409 Glemore Dr., Chevy Chase, MD 20815; tel (301) 656-0347; fax (301) 656-2019
Correspondent — Carlos Eduardo Lins-Da Silva

Gazeta Mercantil — 1194 National Press Bldg., Washington, DC 20045; tel (202) 783-4129; fax (202) 783-4128
Correspondent — Paulo Totti

Jornal Do Brasil — 1286 National Press Bldg., Washington, DC 20045; tel (202) 628-2978; fax (202) 628-2977
Correspondent — Ana Maria Goncalves Mandim

Jornal Do Commercio — 3705 S. George Mason Dr., Ste. 217, Falls Church, VA 22041; tel (703) 845-3472; fax (703) 845-3472
Correspondent — Jose R D Leme

Manchete — 4505 Cortland Rd., Chevy Chase, MD 20815; tel (301) 652-4205; fax (301) 652-5217
Stringer — Haroldo De Faria Castro

O Estado De Sao Paulo — 1225 I St. N.W., Ste. 810, Washington, DC 20005; tel (202) 682-3752; fax (202) 289-5475
Correspondent — Paulo Sotero

O Globo — 1251 National Press Bldg., Washington, DC 20045; tel (202) 628-3313; fax (202) 347-6481
Correspondent — Jose Meirelles Passos

TV Globo — 2030 M St. N.W., Ste. 400, Washington, DC 20036; tel (202) 429-2525; fax (202) 429-1713
Correspondent — Laura Downhower

Veja — 1153 National Press Bldg., Washington, DC 20045; tel (202) 393-7252; fax (202) 393-2563
Correspondent — Flavia Sekles

BULGARIA

Maritza — 2400 Clarendon Blvd., Ste. 316, Arlington, VA 22201; tel (703) 358-9562
Correspondent — Norbert J Yasharoff

CAMEROON

Cameroon Herald — 6731 New Hampshire Ave., Ste. 513, Takoma Park, MD 20912; tel (301) 270-6651; fax (301) 270-6651
Correspondent — Philip A Tazi

CANADA

Broadcast News Ltd. — 1825 K St. N.W., Ste. 615, Washington, DC 20006; tel (202) 223-8813; fax (202) 728-0348
Correspondent — Brian Kennedy

Canadian Broadcasting Corp. (CBC) — 500 National Press Bldg., Washington, DC 20045; tel (202) 638-3286; fax (202) 783-9321
Dir.-US Operations — Jean-Louis Arcand
Deputy Dir. — Andre Gascon
News Bureau Mgr. — George Hoff
Producer-French — Jessica Armstrong
Producer-English — Marion Barbar
Producer — Ian O Cameron
Producer — Helene Parenteau
Assoc. Producer — Sarah Wolfe
Assoc. Producer — Joanne Elgart
Assoc. Producer — Lisa Gabriele
Correspondent — Karine M Fossou Briand
Correspondent — David Halton
Correspondent — Pierre-Leon LaFrance
Correspondent — Jennifer Lee Westaway
Corr./English (TV) — Terry Milewski
Corr./English (Radio) — Susan M Murray
Corr./French (Radio) — Hugues Poulin
E.N.G. Editor — Louis Saint-Cyr
Prog. Rep./Eng. — Michael H C McDowell

Canadian Jewish News — 1263 National Press Bldg., Washington, DC 20045; tel (202) 628-0030
Correspondent — Joseph Polakoff

Canadian Press — 1825 K St. N.W., Ste. 615, Washington, DC 20006; tel (202) 223-4837; fax (202) 728-0348
Correspondent — Laura Eggertson
Correspondent — Christine Morris

CTV Television News — 2030 M St. N.W., Ste. 602, Washington, DC 20036; tel (202) 466-3595; fax (202) 296-2025
Bureau Chief — James O'Connell

Financial Post — 1225 I St. N.W., Ste. 810, Washington, DC 20005; tel (202) 842-1190; fax (202) 842-4441
Bureau Chief — Peter Morton

Freelance — 1508 33rd St. N.W., Washington, DC 20007; tel (202) 338-0759; fax (202) 338-0759
Correspondent — Hilary J D Mackenzie
2933 28th St. N.W., Washington, DC 20008; tel (202) 797-8467
Correspondent — David Macdonald

Globe & Mail — 1331 Pennsylvania Ave. N.W., Ste. 524, Washington, DC 20004; tel (202) 662-7165; fax (202) 662-7112
Bureau Chief — Graham Fraser
Correspondent — Drew Fagan

Kipling News Service — 12611 Farnell Dr., Silver Spring, MD 20906; tel (301) 929-0760; fax (301) 949-8519
Correspondent — Bogdan Kipling

Latin Trade Magazine — PO Box 523176, Springfield, VA 22152; tel (202) 597-1524
Correspondent — Vincent Fernando Arraya

Maclean's — 994 National Press Bldg., Washington, DC 20045; tel (202) 662-7321; fax (202) 662-7341
Correspondent — Carl Mollins
5309 Slipper Ct., Columbia, MD 21045; tel (301) 596-5306; fax (301) 997-0017
Freelance — William Lowther

Thompson News Service — 1331 Pennsylvania Ave. N.W., Ste. 524, Washington, DC 20004; tel (202) 628-2157; fax (202) 347-5017
Correspondent — Paul Andrew Bagnell

Toronto Star — 928 National Press Bldg., Washington, DC 20045; tel (202) 662-7390; fax (202) 662-7388
Correspondent — Linda L Diebel
News Aide — Donna Barne

Toronto Sun — 8202 Excalibur Ct., Annandale, VA 22003-1343; tel (703) 876-0594; fax (703) 849-9069
Bureau Chief — Patrick Harden

CHILE

Channel 13-TV Chile — 6819 Tennyson Dr., McLean, VA 22101; tel (703) 356-9427; fax (703) 506-0643
Correspondent — Cecilia Domeyko

Contacto-Channel 13 TV-Chile — 1534 N. 16th Rd., Ste. 8, Arlington, VA 22209; tel (301) 277-4919; fax (301) 277-4919
Journalist — Carmen Lopez
Producer — Ralf Oberti

Television Nacional De Chile — 3435 R St. N.W., Ste. 22, Washington, DC 20007; tel (202) 333-6032
Correspondent — Monica Perez

CHINA

Beijing Daily/Beijing Evening News — 3003 Van Ness St. N.W., Apt. S-901, Washington, DC 20008; tel (202) 363-7188; fax (202) 363-7188
Bureau Chief — Xianxu Ning

China Central Television — 4601 Connecticut Ave. N.W., Ste. 713, Washington, DC 20008; tel (202) 362-7383; fax (202) 362-7572
Correspondent — Weichang Lu
Correspondent — Chunquan Wang

China News Service — 1400 S. Joyce St., Ste. 1519, Arlington, VA 22202; tel (703) 920-6223; fax (703) 271-0513
Correspondent — Liping Liu

China Radio International — 2401 Calvert St. N.W., Ste. 1012, Washington, DC 20008; tel (202) 387-6860; fax (202) 387-0459
Bureau Chief — Minguo Tang
Correspondent — Hongfeng Dai
Correspondent — Qiao Luo

China Youth Daily — 4647-C S. 28th Rd., Arlington, VA 22206; tel (703) 671-3591; fax (703) 671-3591
Bureau Chief — Zhengxin Li
Correspondent — Xiang Weng

Guangming Daily — 4816 Butterworth Pl. N.W., Washington, DC 20016; tel (202) 363-0628; fax (202) 244-5956
Bureau Chief — Fengyi Gao

International Trade News — 700 New Hampshire Ave. N.W., Ste. 1120, Washington, DC 20037; tel (202) 337-5270; fax (202) 337-5850
Correspondent — Alice Tian

People's Daily — 3706 Massachusetts Ave. N.W., Washington, DC 20016; tel (202) 966-2285; fax (202) 966-8693
Correspondent — Ai-cheng Liu

Science & Technology Daily — 4701 Willard Ave., Ste. 518, Chevy Chase, MD 20815; tel (301) 652-4151; fax (301) 652-4151
Bureau Chief — Hongkai Wei
Correspondent — Shukun Zhong

Wen Hui Bao — 1600 S. Eads St., Ste. 935-N., Arlington, VA 22202; tel (703) 521-2371; fax (703) 521-2371
Bureau Chief — Xingfu Zhu
Correspondent — Yansong Yang

Xinhua News Agency — 1740 N. 14th St., Arlington, VA 22209; tel (703) 875-0080; fax (703) 875-0086
Bureau Chief — Qian Ying
Economic/Statistics — Xiren Guo
Entertainment/Sports — Jiuyue Si
U.S. Politics — Jinhe Wang
Economic Policy — Nan Wang
Foreign Relations — Zhiqiang Wu
Foreign Relations — Changyin Xu
Science/Technology — Yong Xu

COLOMBIA

CMI Television — 1401 N. Taft St., Ste. 1122, Arlington, VA 22201; tel (703) 527-2036
Correspondent — Gilberto Cabrera

El Tiempo/Colmundo Radio — 7300 Riggs Rd., Ste. 102, Hyattsville, MD 20783; tel (202) 445-4768
Correspondent — Marino Perez Murcia

CROATIA

Croatian News Agency — 2122 Massachusetts Ave. N.W., Ste. 36, Washington, DC 20008; tel (202) 785-8390; fax (202) 785-8390
Correspondent — Zvonko Lerotic

Freelance — 5101 River Rd., Ste. 1106, Bethesda, MD 20816; tel (301) 951-3369; fax (301) 951-3369
Correspondent — Zorz Crmaric

Slobodna Dalmacija — 370 L'Enfant Promenade S.W., Ste. 704, Washington, DC 20024; tel (202) 287-3000; fax (202) 287-3772
Correspondent — Mislav Kukoc

CYPRUS

Cyprus News Agency — PO Box 2391, Washington, DC 20013; tel (202) 388-0355
Bureau Chief — Lambros Papantoniou

CZECH REPUBLIC

Czech News Agency (CTK) — 3231-A Sutton Pl. N.W., Washington, DC 20016; tel (202) 362-2002; fax (202) 362-2003
Correspondent — Stanislav Mundil

Czech Radio & Television — 4849 Connecticut Ave. N.W., Ste. 204, Washington, DC 20008; tel (202) 244-6020; fax (202) 362-3183
Correspondent — Jan Smid

DENMARK

Berlingske Tidende — 1331 Pennsylvania Ave. N.W., Ste. 506, Washington, DC 20004; tel (202) 347-1744; fax (202) 347-2158
Bureau Chief — Michael Kuttner
1600 30th St. N.W., Washington, DC 20007; tel (202) 338-9137; fax (202) 342-2463
Freelance/Art/Life — Susanne Bernth

Danish Broadcasting Corp. — 3001 Q St. N.W., Washington, DC 20007; tel (202) 342-2454; fax (202) 342-2463
Bureau Chief/TV — Frank Esmann-Jensen
PO Box 15523, Washington, DC 20003-0523; tel (703) 415-0632; fax (703) 415-0723
Bureau Chief/Radio — Torben Rasmussen

Erhvers-Bladet — 7313 Blair Rd. N.W., Washington, DC 20009; tel (202) 726-1003; fax (202) 726-1004
Trade — Mette Horlyck

Jyllands-Posten — 8607 Burdeite Rd., Bethesda, MD 20817; tel (301) 299-4429; fax (301) 469-0988
Bureau Chief — Klaus Justsen

Monday Morning — 4425 Westover Pl. N.W., Washington, DC 20016; tel (202) 244-7876; fax (202) 244-2704
Correspondent — Samuel Rachlin

Politiken — 1257 National Press Bldg., Washington, DC 20045; tel (202) 347-9696; fax (301) 469-0277
Correspondent — Jacob Moller

TV 2 Denmark — 2030 M St. N.W., Ste. 506, Washington, DC 20036; tel (202) 828-4555; fax (202) 828-8367
Bureau Chief — Ulla Pors Nielsen

EGYPT

Akher Saa — 4701 Willard Ave., Ste. 1002, Chevy Chase, MD 20815; tel (301) 654-5610; fax (301) 654-5675
Correspondent — Maha Adbel Fattah

Al Ahram — 1258 National Press Bldg., Washington, DC 20045; tel (202) 737-2121; fax (202) 737-2122
Correspondent — Osiris Hamdi Fouad Makkar

Al Akhbar — 4701 Willard Ave., Ste. 1002, Chevy Chase, MD 20815; tel (301) 654-5610; fax (301) 654-5675
Correspondent — Maha Abdel Fattah

Al Gumhouriuya — 1258 National Press Bldg., Washington, DC 20045; tel (202) 393-0546
Correspondent — Hoda Tawfik

Al Hadarah — PO Box 7148, Fairfax Station, VA 22039; tel (703) 764-0942
Correspondent — Aly R Abuzaakouk

Al Wafd — 408 Independence Ave. S.E., Ste. 204, Washington, DC 20003; tel (202) 544-5982; fax (202) 544-6203
Correspondent — Thomas K Gorguissian

Al-Mussawar — 2148 Kings Garden Way, Falls Church, VA 22043; tel (202) 338-5749; fax (703) 749-9380
Bureau Chief — Mohammed Wahby

Middle East News Agency — 9418 Wareham Ct., Vienna, VA 22180; tel (703) 281-2314; fax (703) 281-2179
Bureau Chief — Mahmoud Abdel Aziz Ahmed

Sabeh El Kheir — 1350 Beverly Rd., McLean, VA 22101; tel (703) 790-1142; fax (703) 790-1142
Correspondent — Ahmed Nasr Said

FINLAND

Finnish Broadcasting Co. — 2030 M St. N.W., Ste. 700, Washington, DC 20036; tel (202) 785-1054; fax (202) 785-5834
Bureau Chief — Aarne Tanninen
Correspondent — Risto Anders Johnson
Correspondent — Kjell Lindroos

Helsingin Sanomat — 915 National Press Bldg., Washington, DC 20045; tel (202) 662-7555; fax (202) 662-7554
Correspondent — Kyosti Kalervo Karvonen

FRANCE

AFP-Agence France Presse — 1612 K St. N.W., Ste. 400, Washington, DC 20006; tel (202) 861-8585; fax (202) 861-8524
Bureau Chief — Pierre LeSourd
Chief Editor — Jean-Loup Sense
Business Editor — Isabel T G Parenthoen
Lat. America Corr. — Gilbert E Guzman
White House Corr. — Christian Chaise
State Dept. Correspondent — Andre Viollaz
Sports Corr. — Stephane Ghazarian
Correspondent — Souksaveui Chanthalangsy
Correspondent — Nicole Deshayes
Correspondent — Susan Kendall-Bilicki
Correspondent — Robert Koch
Economic Reporter — Bruno Rossignol
Economics Corr. — Jean-Louis Santini

Al-Muharer Weekly Newspaper — 2102-D Gallows Rd., 2nd Fl., Vienna, VA 22182; tel (703) 591-0677; fax (703) 591-0678
Correspondent — Abdulsalam Y Massarueh

Europe One Radio — 5205 Abingdon Rd., Bethesda, MD 20816-1834; tel (301) 229-9064; fax (301) 229-9062
Correspondent — Beniot LaPorte

France 2-French Broadcasting System — 2030 M St. N.W., Ste. 502, Washington, DC 20036; tel (202) 833-1818; fax (202) 833-2777
Bureau Chief — Jean-Marc Illouz

Jacques Tiziou News Service — 5152 Linnean Terrace N.W., Washington, DC 20008; tel (202) 966-6960; fax (202) 537-3054
Correspondent — Jacques Tiziou

L'Agefi — 9424 Byeforde Rd., Kensington, MD 20895; tel (301) 942-4592; fax (301) 942-4459
Bureau Chief — Pierre-Yves Dugua

La Croix — 10233 Farnham Dr., Bethesda, MD 20814; tel (301) 493-4824; fax (301) 564-1633
Correspondent — Marie-Christine Ray

La Lettre de L'Expansion — 6501 Majory Ln., Bethesda, MD 20817; tel (301) 229-6217; fax (301) 229-6217
Correspondent — Catherine Antoine

La Tribune de L'Expansion — 1025 Connecticut Ave. N.W., Ste. 800, Washington, DC 20036; tel (202) 862-6613; fax (202) 862-9266
Bureau Chief — Jean-Marie Macabrey

Le Figaro — 4426 Lowell St. N.W., Washington, DC 20016; tel (202) 686-4119; fax (202) 686-4120
Bureau Chief — Stephane Marchand
4745 Massachusetts Ave. N.W., Washington, DC 20016; tel (202) 966-5071; fax (202) 966-0478
Economics — Jacqueline Grapin

Le Monde — 2230 Cathedral Ave. N.W., Washington, DC 20008; tel (202) 483-7776; fax (202) 483-0035
Correspondent — Sylvie Kauffmann
6012 Kennedy Dr., Chevy Chase, MD 20815; tel (301) 986-8606; fax (301) 986-8554
Correspondent — Laurent Zecchini

Le Point — 5205 Abingdon Rd., Bethesda, MD 20816-1834; tel (301) 229-9064; fax (301) 229-9062
Correspondent — Benoit LaPorte

Liberation — 5005 Brookdale Rd., Bethesda, MD 20816; tel (301) 657-9649; fax (301) 657-9676
Bureau Chief — Pierre Briancon

Madame Figaro — 2138 California St., Washington, DC 20008; tel (202) 265-3183; fax (202) 265-3904
Correspondent — Marie-Helene Tisa

Radio France — 4940 Catherdral Ave. N.W., Washington, DC 20016; tel (202) 686-0963; fax (202) 686-1485
Correspondent — Philippe Reltien

Radio Tele Luxemborg (RTL) — 421 Hudson St., Ste. 812, New York, NY 10014; tel (212) 807-6162; fax (212) 807-1265
Correspondent — Jerome Godard

TF-1 French Television — 2100 M St. N.W., Ste. 302, Washington, DC 20037; tel (202) 223-3642; fax (202) 223-2196
Bureau Chief — Ulysse Gosset
Producer — Lisa Draine

2407 — 1612 K St. N.W., Ste. 400, Washington, DC 20006; tel (202) 861-8585
Pentagon Correspondent — Emmanuel Serot

GERMANY

ARD-German Television — 3132 M St. N.W., Washington, DC 20007; tel (202) 298-6535; fax (202) 298-5933
Bureau Chief — Jochen Schweizer
Producer — Thea Rosenbaum

Bavarian Broadcasting Corp. — 3142 Q St. N.W., Washington, DC 20007; tel (202) 625-6555; fax (202) 625-6556
Correspondent — Johannes C Tschech

Bayerischer Rundfunk — 2331 Ontario Rd. N.W., Apt. 37, Washington, DC 20009; tel (202) 543-2701; fax (202) 543-2701
Correspondent — Christina Eck
2555 Pennsylvania Ave. N.W., Apt. 703, Washington, DC 20037; tel (202) 872-0422; fax (202) 296-4183
Correspondent — Andrea Theresia Eimer

Bleidorns Wirthscaftsdienst — 15321 Jones Ln., North Potomac, MD 20878; tel (301) 926-2336; fax (301) 926-2379
Economics — Heide Gabriel

Bremer Nachrichten — 4100 Massachusetts Ave. N.W., Washington, DC 20016; tel (202) 244-7013; fax (202) 244-7069
Bureau Chief — Peter Schroeder
Corr. — Dagmar Schroeder-Hildebrand
Correspondent — Bjorn Ole Schroeder

Der Spiegel — 1202 National Press Bldg., Washington, DC 20045; tel (202) 347-5222; fax (202) 347-3194
Bureau Chief — Siegesmund Von Ilsemann
Correspondent — Karl-Heinz Bueschemann
Correspondent — Gisela Leske

Deutsche Welle — PO Box 50641, Washington, DC 20091-0641; tel (202) 393-7427; fax (202) 393-7434
Bureau Chief — Volker Strobel
Producer — Wolf Soete
Correspondent — Robert Burdy
8221 Larry Pl., Chevy Chase, Washington, MD 20815; tel (301) 652-3736
Correspondent — David Walsh

Deutchland Radio — 972 National Press Bldg., Washington, DC 20045; tel (202) 393-1966; fax (202) 393-1967
Bureau Chief — Siegfried A Buschsluter
3810 Candlelight Ct., Alexandria, VA 22310; tel (703) 960-1186; fax (703) 960-5487
Correspondent — Eckhard Fritz Tollkuhn

DFA/GTA German TV Agency — 1199 National Press Bldg., Washington, DC 20045; tel (202) 393-7571; fax (202) 393-8554
Bureau Chief — Roger Horne

Die Tageszeitung — 1915 Kalorama Rd., Ste. 302, Washington, DC 20009; tel (202) 986-5042; fax (202) 588-1969
Correspondent — Andrea Bohm

Die Welt — 11148 Powder Horn Dr., Potomac, MD 20854; tel (301) 983-4177; fax (301) 299-7928
Correspondent — Gerd Bruggemann

Die Zeit — 8205 Beechtree Rd., Bethesda, MD 20817; tel (301) 365-8812; fax (301) 365-8829
Correspondent — Ulrich Schiller

DPA-German News Agency — 939 National Press Bldg., Washington, DC 20045; tel (202) 783-8726; fax (202) 786-4116
Photographer — Michael Stephen Pladeck

DPA-German Press Agency — 969 National Press Bldg., Washington, DC 20045; tel (202) 783-8726; fax (202) 783-4116
Bureau Chief — Herbert Winkler
Correspondent — James Anderson
Correspondent — Hans-Jochen Kaffsack
Correspondent — Thomas Maier
Correspondent — Anke Wienand
Latin America — Agostino Della Porta
Reporter — David Thomas McIntyre
Editor — Richard James Tomkins

DPA Photo Report — 8910 Moreland Ln., Annandale, VA 22003; tel (703) 978-8073; fax (703) 878-8073
Photographer — Mehmet Biber

Focus — 4527 Windom Pl. N.W., Washington, DC 20016; tel (202) 363-2397; fax (202) 363-2397
Correspondent — Peter Michael Gruber

Frankfurter Allgemeine Zeitung — 9413 Copenhaven Dr., Potomac, MD 20854; tel (301) 294-2345; fax (301) 294-0102
Bureau Chief — Leo Wieland
1093 National Press Bldg., Washington, DC 20045; tel (202) 662-7255; fax (202) 337-2950
Economics — Carola Kaps

Frankfurter Rundschau — 1755 Seaton Pl. N.W., Washington, DC 20009; tel (202) 265-7240; fax (202) 265-7259
Bureau Chief — Rolf Paasch

German Broadcasting-ARD — 1000 Wilson Blvd., Ste. 916, Arlington, VA 22209; tel (703) 524-0706; fax (703) 524-8147
Bureau Chief — Ingolf Karnahl
2200 Wyoming Ave. N.W., Washington, DC 22208; tel (202) 332-3482; fax (202) 332-3511
Correspondent — Joachim Lenz

German Broadcasting-ARD Radio — 1000 Wilson Blvd., Ste. 916, Arlington, VA 22209; tel (703) 524-8617; fax (202) 524-8147
Correspondent — Gunnar Schultz-Burkel

German Broadcasting-NDR/WDR — 3132 M St. N.W., Washington, DC 20007; tel (202) 342-1730; fax (202) 337-3889
Producer — Heidi Jacobi-Mandel
Correspondent — Udo Koelsch
Correspondent — Sabine Reifenberg

German Broadcasting Systems (ARD) — 1824 S St. N.W., Ste. 404, Washington, DC 20009; tel (202) 265-7001; fax (202) 265-7001
Correspondent — Sophie Gudrun Alf

German Radio NDR/WDR — 3132 M St. N.W., Washington, DC 20007; tel (202) 342-1730; fax (202) 337-3889
Correspondent — Ruediger Paulert

German Radio News Agency — PO Box 3849, Reston, VA 22090; tel (703) 742-3933; fax (703) 742-3934
Correspondent — Peter De Thier

German Television News Agency — 901 National Press Bldg., Washington, DC 20045; tel (202) 393-7577; fax (202) 393-8554
Cameraman — David Sunderhauf

German TV Agency — 901 National Press Bldg., Washington, DC 20045; tel (202) 393-7571; fax (202) 393-8554
Correspondent — Joerg Rositzke
Producer — Hans-Peter Otto

Handelsblatt — 3206 Q St. N.W., Washington, DC 20007; tel (301) 965-0563; fax (301) 333-1394
Correspondent — Viola Herms-Drath

Hannoversche Allgemeine Zeitung — 11204 Powder Horn Dr., Potomac, MD 20854; tel (301) 983-0735; fax (301) 983-2716
Correspondent — Juergen Koar

Koelner Stadtanzeiger — 11204 Powder Horn Dr., Potomac, MD 20854; tel (301) 983-0735; fax (301) 983-2716
Correspondent — Juergen Koar

Nachrichten Fuer Aussenhandel — 412 National Press Bldg., Washington, DC 20045; tel (202) 662-7415; fax (202) 662-7419
Bureau Chief — Rainer Lindberg

Neue Osnabruecker Zeitung — 4100 Massachusetts Ave. N.W., Washington, DC 20016; tel (202) 244-7013; fax (202) 244-7069
Correspondent — Peter Schroeder
Corr. — Dagmar Schroeder-Hildebrand

Neue Presse-Hanover — PO Box 814, Washington, DC 20044-0814; tel (202) 332-9675
Correspondent — Israel Rafalovich

Norddeutscher Rundfunk — 704-A Little St., Alexandria, VA 22301; tel (703) 684-0448; fax (703) 684-2118
Correspondent — Georg F Hirsch

Nurnberger Nachrichten — 624 G St. N.E., Washington, DC 20002; tel (202) 546-7090; fax (202) 546-7125
Correspondent — Klaus D Lucas

Radioropa-Info — 314 12th St. N.E., Washington, DC 20002; tel (202) 544-6849; fax (202) 544-6892
Correspondent — Susanne G Sperling

Rheinische Post — 1979 Lancashire Dr., Potomac, MD 20854; tel (301) 251-2367; fax (301) 251-2364
Correspondent — Peter Rzeznitzeck

SAT-1 German Television — 1620 I St. N.W., Ste. 200, Washington, DC 20006; tel (202) 331-9400; fax (202) 331-9508
Bureau Chief — Dieter Kronzucker
Correspondent — Stephan Strothe
Producer — Angela C Strothe
Producer — Sabine Ulbrich

Schweizer Handelszeitung — PO Box 19437, Alexandria, VA 22314; tel (703) 684-9213
Correspondent — Jan Hoehn

Springer Foreign News Service — 4830 Brandywine St. N.W., Washington, DC 20016; tel (202) 342-3103; fax (202) 342-3104
Correspondent — Frauke Beyer
Correspondent — Cornel Faltin

Stern — 3127 38th St. N.W., Washington, DC 20016; tel (202) 462-2223; fax (202) 462-1208
Correspondent — Birgit Klare

Stern Magazine — 3127 38th St., PO Box 39119, Washington, DC 20016; tel (202) 462-2223; fax (202) 462-1208
Bureau Chief — Teja Fiedler

Stuttgarter Nachrichten — 4100 Massachusetts Ave. N.W., Washington, DC 200016; tel (202) 244-7013; fax (202) 244-7069
Correspondent — Peter Schroeder
Corr. — Dagmar Schroeder-Hildebrand

Stuttgarter Zeitung — 11204 Powder Horn Dr., Potomac, MD 20854; tel (301) 983-0735; fax (301) 983-2716
Correspondent — Juergen Koar

Sueddeutsche Zeitung — 2555 Pennsylvania Ave. N.W., Ste. 703, Washington, DC 20037; tel (202) 872-0422; fax (202) 296-4183
Correspondent — Kurt Kister

Westdeutsche Allgemeine Zeitung — 8204 Hamilton Spring Ct., Bethesda, MD 20817-2729; tel (301) 469-8933; fax (301) 469-8934
Correspondent — Uwe Knuepfer

Wirtschaftswoche — 8515 Longfellow Pl., Chevy Chase, MD 20815; tel (301) 907-9036; fax (301) 907-0185
Bureau Chief — Christian Deysson

Women Magazine — 3127 38th St. N.W., Washington, DC 20016; tel (202) 462-2463; fax (202) 462-1208
Correspondent — Swantje Strieder

ZDF-German Television — 1077 31st St. N.W., Washington, DC 20007; tel (202) 333-3909; fax (202) 333-9814
Bureau Chief — Gerd Helbig
Correspondent — Karin Storch
Producer — Lanny Johnson
Producer — Alice Kelly

Zeitungspring — 3019 Cambridge Pl. N.W., Washington, DC 20007; tel (202) 338-6583
Correspondent — Marlene Manthey

GREECE

Athens News Agency — 2045 National Press Bldg., Washington, DC 20045; tel (202) 466-3846; fax (202) 466-3858
Bureau Chief — Dimitri Dimas

Avriani — PO Box 2391, Washington, DC 20013; tel (202) 388-0355
Correspondent — Lambros Papantoniou

Eleftheri Ora — 6914 Selkirk Dr., Bethesda, MD 20817; tel (301) 907-3812; fax (301) 907-3814
Correspondent — John Perdikis

Eleftheria — 10201 Haywood Dr., Silver Spring, MD 20902; tel (301) 593-5115; fax (301) 593-4763
Correspondent — Theodore Kariotis

Kathimerini — 2415 20th St. N.W., Ste. 36, Washington, DC 20009; tel (202) 234-1312; fax (202) 667-2378
Bureau Chief — Alexis Papachelas

Macedonian Press Agency — PO Box 2391, Washington, DC 20013; tel (202) 388-0355
Correspondent — Lambros Papantoniou

Mega Channel — 2415 20th St. N.W., Ste. 36, Washington, DC 20009; tel (202) 234-1312; fax (202) 667-2378
Correspondent — Alexis Papachelas

Radio Flash — 2500 Q St. N.W., Washington, DC 20007; tel (202) 965-1194; fax (202) 338-4832
Correspondent — John Liveris

GUATEMALA

Nuevo Mundo Network — 7213 Grubby Thicket Way, Bethesda, MD 20817; tel (301) 365-8224
Bureau Chief — Oscar E Padilla-Vidaurre

Copyright ©1996 by the Editor & Publisher Co.

HONDURAS

HRN Radio — 1069 National Press Bldg., Washington, DC 20045; tel (202) 737-5349
Bureau Chief — Jacobo Goldstein
La Tribuna — 1069 National Press Bldg., Washington, DC 20045; tel (202) 737-5349
Bureau Chief — Jacobo Goldstein
Telesistema Hondureno Channels 3 & 5 — 1069 National Press Bldg., Washington, DC 20045; tel (202) 737-5349
Bureau Chief — Jacobo Goldstein

HONG KONG

Asian Business — 2106 National Press Bldg., Washington, DC 20045; tel (202) 338-4864; fax (202) 337-9096
Correspondent — Kristin Knauth
Asian Wall Street Journal — 1025 Connecticut Ave., Ste. 800, Washington, DC 20036; tel (202) 862-9274; fax (202) 862-9266
Bureau Chief — Eduardo Lachica
Asia Week — 2039 National Press Bldg., Washington, DC 20045; tel (202) 527-8950
Correspondent — Jeffery Ubois
Eastern Express — 850 N. Randolph St., Ste. 617, Arlington, VA 22203; tel (703) 527-3667; fax (202) 527-3668
Correspondent — Paul Godfrey
Far Eastern Economic Review — 1025 Connecticut Ave. N.W., Ste. 800, Washington, DC 20815; tel (202) 862-9286; fax (202) 728-0624
Correspondent — Nigel Robert Holloway
Hong Kong Standard — 4228 Military Rd. N.W., Washington, DC 20015; tel (202) 244-4082; fax (202) 244-4082
Correspondent — Sheila C Y Tang
Sing Tao Daily — 4228 Military Rd. N.W., Washington, DC 20015; tel (202) 244-4082; fax (202) 244-4082
Correspondent — Sheila C Y Tang
South China Morning Post — 1758 N. Troy St., Apt. 667, Arlington, VA 22201; tel (703) 528-7784; fax (703) 528-7784
Correspondent — Simon Beck

HUNGARY

Budapest Sun — 2901 Connecticut Ave. N.W., Ste. 108, Washington, DC 20008; tel (202) 986-5509; fax (202) 986-5509
Correspondent — Les L Gapay
Duna — 4849 Connecticut Ave. N.W. Ste. 504, Washington, DC 20008; tel (202) 362-3058; fax (202) 966-8015
Correspondent — Tibor Purger
Magyar Nemzet — 4515 Willard Ave., Ste. 1409-S, Chevy Chase, MD 20815; tel (301) 986-5516; fax (301) 951-0371
Correspondent — Miklos Blaho
MTI-Hungarian News Agency — 8515 Farrell Dr., Chevy Chase, MD 20815; tel (301) 565-2221; fax (301) 589-6907
Correspondent — Peter Racz
Nepszabadsag — 4701 Willard Ave., Ste. 1603, Chevy Chase, MD 20815; tel (301) 986-5267; fax (301) 986-5267
Correspondent — Oszkar L Fuzes

INDIA

Aras News — 1331 Pennsylvania Ave., Ste. 920, Washington, DC 20004-1703; tel (202) 638-7183; fax (202) 638-1887
Correspondent — Afshin Molavi
Asia Today International/ATN News — 2020 National Press Bldg., Washington, DC 20045; tel (202) 597-1565; fax (703) 978-7572
Correspondent — Raghubir Goyal
Business & Political Observer — 13106 Collingwood Terrace, Silver Spring, MD 20904; tel (301) 384-1297
Correspondent — Vinod Ghildiyal
Business Standard — 5070 Linnean Ave. N.W., Washington, DC 20008; tel (202) 833-4505; fax (202) 833-4505
Correspondent — Sujatha Shenoy
Economic Times — 4318 Puller Dr., Kensington, MD 20895; tel (301) 564-0425; fax (301) 493-4977
Correspondent — Sundaram Sankaran
Hindu — 4701 Willard Ave., Ste. 1531, Chevy Chase, MD 20815; tel (301) 654-9038; fax (301) 907-3493
Correspondent — Chilamkuri Raja Mohan
Hindustan Times — 5597 Seminary Rd., Ste. 2217-S, Fall Church, VA 22041; tel (703) 931-9038; fax (703) 931-9087
Correspondent — Nambalat C Menon
India Abroad News Service — 2046 National Press Bldg., Washington, DC 20045; tel (202) 818-1733; fax (202) 818-7490
Bureau Chief — Aziz Haniffa
Correspondent — Ela Dutt
India Press Agency — 7400 Colshire Dr., Ste. 3, McLean, VA 22102; tel (703) 893-1715; fax (703) 893-6022
Bureau Chief — Batuk Vora
India Globe — 2020 National Press Bldg., Washington, DC 20045; tel (202) 597-1565; fax (703) 978-7572
Correspondent — Raghubir Goyal
Indo-American Business Times — PO Box 33364, Farragut Sta., Washington, DC 20033; tel (301) 572-6067; fax (301) 572-7233
Publisher — Hasmukh Shah
Malayalam Pathram — 762 Smylie Rd., Philadelphia, PA 19124; tel (215) 289-3783; fax (215) 744-3565
Correspondent — Joby George
News India Times — 18704 Nathans Pl., Gaithersburg, MD 20879; tel (301) 869-0531; fax (301) 869-0531
Bureau Chief — Ranganathan Murali
NRI Today — 2 Joppawood Ct., Ste. A-1, Baltimore, MD 21236; tel (410) 256-8665; fax (410) 256-4631
Bureau Chief — Kewal Kapoor
Observer News Service — 13106 Collingwood Terrace, Silver Spring, MD 20904; tel (301) 384-1297
Correspondent — Vinod Ghildiyal
Pioneer — 1701 K St. N.W., Ste. 805, Washington, DC 20006; tel (202) 223-8299; fax (202) 223-8298
Correspondent — Sunil Adam
Press Trust of India — 4450 S. Park Ave., Ste. 1719, Chevy Chase, MD 20815; tel (301) 951-8657; fax (301) 951-8657
Corr. — Tattamangalam V Parasuram
The Tribune — 4455 Greenwich Pkwy. N.W., Washington, DC 20007; tel (202) 965-0439; fax (202) 965-0439
Correspondent — Amir C Tuteja
United News of India — 1600 S. Eads St., Ste. 1126-N, Arlington, VA 22202; tel (703) 486-2696; fax (703) 486-2693
Correspondent — Chandra K Arora
Correspondent — Vasantha Arora
USA India Monitor — 2 Joppawood Ct., Ste. A-1, Baltimore, MD 21236; tel (410) 256-8665; fax (410) 256-4631
Correspondent — Kewal Kapoor
Views & News Agency (VANA) — 1255 New Hampshire Ave. N.W., Ste. 631, Washington, DC 20036; tel (202) 452-1462; fax (202) 857-0619
Freelance — Ludwina A Joseph

INDONESIA

Suara Pembaruan — 4806 Ertter Dr., Rockville, MD 20852-2202; tel (301) 881-8173; fax (301) 881-8174
Bureau Chief — Albert P Kuhon
Correspondent — Harry Ponto
SWA Sembada (Business Monthly) — 4806 Ertter Dr., Rockville, MD 20852; tel (301) 881-8240; fax (301) 881-8174
Correspondent — Saraswati Kuhon

INTERNATIONAL

AP World Service — 2021 K St. N.W., Washington, DC 20006; tel (202) 828-6400; fax (202) 828-9663
Correspondent — David Briscoe
Correspondent — Carl Hartman
Correspondent — Gene Kramer
Elet Es Irodalom — 358 N St. S.W., Washington, DC 20024; tel (202) 863-1972
Correspondent — Magda Zalan
European Broadcasting Union (EBU) — 2030 M St. N.W., Ste. 500, Washington, DC 20036; tel (202) 775-1295; fax (202) 887-0337
Producer — Katrien Everaert
Producer — Susan Henderson
Producer — Lorraine Mottola
General News Service — 2026 National Press Bldg., Washington, DC 20045; tel (202) 546-8993
Correspondent — Stuart M Silverstone
Inter Press Service — 1293 National Press Bldg., Washington, DC 20045; tel (202) 662-7160; fax (202) 662-7164
Bureau Chief — James R Lobe
Correspondent — Marco Antonio Sibaja
Correspondent — Yvette Jenipher Collymore
Editor — Pratap Kumar Chatierjee
Knight-Ridder Financial News — 740 National Press Bldg., Washington, DC 20045; tel (202) 383-6150; fax (202) 383-6198
Correspondent — Edward S Kean
Correspondent — Catherine E Kristiansen
Mai Photo News Agency — 6601 Ashmere Ln., Centreville, VA 22020; tel (703) 968-0030; fax (703) 968-0040
Correspondent — Greg E Mathieson
Radio Free Europe/Radio Liberty — 1201 Connecticut Ave. N.W., Washington, DC 20036; tel (202) 457-6967; fax (202) 457-6997
Correspondent — Constatine Alexander
Correspondent — Tibor Csipan
Correspondent — Kevin Foley
Correspondent — Robert Lyle
Correspondent — Miroslav Neovesky
Correspondent — Nestor Ratesh
Correspondent — Mort Von Duyke
Correspondent — Sonia Winter
Correspondent — Ilza Zvirgzdins
Reuters — 1333 H St. N.W., Ste. 410, Washington, DC 20005; tel (202) 898-8300; fax (202) 898-8383
News Editor — Robert Doherty
State Dept. Correspondent — Alan Elsner
State Dept. Correspondent — Carol Giacomo
State Dept. Corr. — Deborah Zabarenko
Reuters TV — 1333 H St. N.W., 5th Fl., Washington, DC 20005; tel (202) 898-0056; fax (202) 898-1237
Exec. Producer — Paolo Prado Machado
Producer — George Tamerlani
World Wide TV News — 1705 DeSales St. N.W., Ste. 300, Washington, DC 20036; tel (202) 835-0705; fax (202) 887-7978
Bureau Chief — Paul Sisco

IRAN

Washington-Tehran Post — 9701 Fields Rd., Ste. 1600, Gaithersburg, MD 20878; tel (301) 840-9444; fax (301) 990-0678
Editor — Khosrow Afshar

IRELAND

Irish Sunday Independent — 1901 Columbia Rd. N.W., Ste. 703, Washington, DC 20009; tel (202) 462-8232; fax (202) 462-8232
Correspondent — Jamie Dettmer
Irish Times — 6221 Redwing Rd., Bethesda, MD 20817; tel (301) 320-2308; fax (301) 229-1036
Bureau Chief — Conor O'Clery

ISRAEL

Al Mujtama — 5524 Hempstead Way, N. Springfield, VA 22151; tel (703) 750-9011; fax (703) 750-9010
Bureau Chief — Yousef Ahmed Saleh
Davar — 112 Shaw Ave., Silver Spring, MD 20904; tel (301) 662-1591; fax (301) 662-7910
Correspondent — Drora Perl
Ha'aretz — 5821 Tudor Ln., Rockville, MD 20852; tel (301) 816-2427; fax (301) 770-4911
Correspondent — Akiva Eldar
Israel Radio — 1722 Wilmart St., Rockville, MD 20852; tel (301) 881-4049; fax (301) 881-4167
Bureau Chief — Arie Golan
Israeli Broadcasting Authority — 1620 I St. N.W., Washington, DC 20006; tel (202) 331-2859; fax (202) 331-9064
Bureau Chief — Jacob Shlomo Ahimeir
Israeli Defense Force Radio — 112 Shaw Ave., Silver Spring, MD 20904; tel (301) 622-1591; fax (301) 622-7910
Correspondent — Drora Perl
Jerusalem Post — 2813 Lee Oaks Ct., Apt. 204, Falls Church, VA 22046; tel (703) 573-6031; fax (703) 573-6031
Correspondent — Hillel Kuttler
Jerusalem Report — 6339 31st St. N.W., Washington, DC 20015; tel (202) 364-1913; fax (202) 364-0366
Correspondent — Jonathan Broder
Maariv — 5821 Tudor Ln., Rockville, MD 20852; tel (301) 468-6160; fax (301) 468-6250
Bureau Chief — Avinoham Bar-Yosef
Telegraph — 21 Chantilly Ct., Rockville, MD 20850; tel (301) 217-9178; fax (301) 217-9369
Correspondent — Ran Dagony
Yedioth Aronoth — 12 Dairyfield Ct., Rockville, MD 20852; tel (301) 816-0989; fax (301) 816-9820
Bureau Chief — Haim Shibi

ITALY

ANSA-Italian News Agency — 1285 National Press Bldg., Washington, DC 20045; tel (202) 628-3317; fax (202) 638-1792
Bureau Chief — Bruno Marolo
Dep. Bureau Chief — Christiano Del Riccio
Correspondent — Margery Friesner
Correspondent — Luigi Mayer
Correspondent — Gaetano Stellacci
Avvenire — 510 2nd St. S.E., Ste. 2, Washington, DC 20003; tel (202) 543-2920; fax (202) 543-2932
Correspondent — Paolo Guietti
Corriere Della Sera — 450 National Press Bldg., Washington, DC 20045; tel (202) 879-6733; fax (202) 879-6735
Bureau Chief — Ennio Caretto
Il Corriere Salute — 1234 34th St. N.W., Ste. 7, Washington, DC 20007; tel (202) 298-8306; fax (202) 298-8306
Freelance — Ilaria Caputi
Il Giornale — 1331 Pennsylvania Ave. N.W., Washington, DC 20004; tel (202) 393-0509
Correspondent — Alberto Pasolini Zanelli
Il Manifesto — 1420 33rd St. N.W., Washington, DC 20007; tel (202) 625-0308; fax (202) 625-0308
Correspondent — Elisabetta Castellani
Il Mattino — 1234 34th St. N.W., Ste. 7, Washington, DC 20007; tel (202) 298-8306; fax (202) 298-8306
Correspondent — Ilaria Caputi
4609 Foxhall Crescent, Washington, DC; tel (202) 338-4226; fax (202) 338-4226
Correspondent — Mariuccia Chiantaretto
Il Resto Del Carlino — 916 National Press Bldg., Washington, DC 20045; tel (202) 347-0245; fax (202) 362-2377
Bureau Chief — Cesare De Carlo
Il Sole 24 Ore — 4371 Westover Pl. N.W., Washington, DC 20016-5555; tel (202) 363-6153; fax (202) 363-6153
Correspondent — Francesca P Mengarelli
Il Tempo — 916 National Press Bldg., Washington, DC 20045; tel (202) 347-0245; fax (202) 362-2377
Bureau Chief — Cesare De Carlo
L'Informazione — 1600 N. Oak St., Ste. 1818, Arlington, VA 22209-2770; tel (703) 276-9055; fax (703) 465-4085
Editor — Marino De Medici
La Nazione — 916 National Press Bldg., Washington, DC 20045; tel (202) 347-0245; fax (202) 362-2377
Bureau Chief — Cesare De Carlo
La Repubblica — 1726 M St. N.W., Ste. 700, Washington, DC 20036; tel (202) 737-6447; fax (202) 838-5672
Bureau Chief — Arturo Zambaglione
La Stampa — 916 National Press Bldg., Washington, DC 20045; tel (202) 347-5233; fax (202) 347-5691
Bureau Chief — Paolo Passarini
Mondo Economico — 4371 Westover Pl. N.W., Washington, DC 20016-5555; tel (202) 363-6153; fax (202) 363-6153
Correspondent — Francesca P Mengarelli
RAI-Italian Televison — 1234 34th St. N.W., Ste. 7, Washington, DC 20007; tel (202) 298-8306; fax (202) 298-8306
Correspondent — Ilaria Caputi

JAPAN

Akahata — 978 National Press Bldg., Washington, DC 20045; tel (202) 393-5238; fax (202) 393-5239
Bureau Chief — Norio Okada
Correspondent — Shinji Yamasaki
Asahi Broadcasting Network-TV Asahi — 670 National Press Bldg., Washington, DC 20045; tel (202) 347-2933; fax (202) 347-6558
Bureau Chief — Junichi Kitasei
Correspondent — Hideaki Saito
Correspondent — Kyoko Altman
Assistant Producer — Eiko Toda
Assistant Producer — Brian Robert Walker
Asahi Shimbun — 1022 National Press Bldg., Washington, DC 20045; tel (202) 783-1000; fax (202) 783-0039
Bureau Chief — Yoichi Funabashi
Diplomatic — Koji Igarashi
Ecomonics — Hiroaki Ito
Science/Technology — Takashi Otsuka
Diplomatic — Eiichi Murano
Politics — Tadakazu Kimura
Chunichi Shimbun — 1230 National Press Bldg., Washington, DC 20045; tel (202) 783-9479; fax (202) 628-9622
Bureau Chief — Hiroshi Sekiguchi
Politics — Yoshikarzu Imazato
Economics — Maroru Ohnoki

Copyright ©1996 by the Editor & Publisher Co.

Focus Magazine — 1020 N. Quincy St., Ste. 808, Arlington, VA 22201; tel (703) 243-1569; fax (703) 243-3545
Photographer — Yasushi Takeda
Fuji Sankei Communication-Fuji TV — 530 National Press Bldg., Washington, DC 20045; tel (202) 347-6070; fax (202) 347-0724
Bureau Chief — Seitaro Murao
Politics/Economics — Fumio Hirai
Correspondent — Amy Margolius
Hokkaido Shimbun — 1232 National Press Bldg., Washington, DC 20045; tel (202) 783-9479; fax (202) 783-3944
Bureau Chief — Tsukasa Ejiri
Correspondent — Yuji Tamura
Japan Digest (Newsletter) — 5510 Columbia Pike, Ste. 207, Arlington, VA 22204; tel (703) 931-2500; fax (703) 931-2504
Correspondent — Ayako Doi
Jiji Press — 550 National Press Bldg., Washington, DC 20045; tel (202) 783-4330; fax (703) 783-6093
Bureau Chief — Ikuo Taniguchi
Economics — Kensuke Karube
Economics — Katsumi Matsubara
Economics — Tomohiro Sugita
Politics — Kiyotaka Kato
Diplomatic — Yoshiaki Okuma
Research Asst. — Melanie Ram
Kodansha Ltd. — 2001 N. Adams St., Ste. 214, Arlington, VA 22201; tel (703) 525-0576; fax (703) 525-4249
Correspondent — Yoshio Hotta
Kyodo News Service — 400 National Press Bldg., Washington, DC 20045; tel (202) 347-5767; fax (202) 393-2342
Bureau Chief — Mikio Haruna
Dep. Bureau Chief — Masamichi Fujitsuka
Ecomonics — Hayato Ishii
Economics — Hiroshi Matsumoto
Economics — Tsuneo Yamahiro
Pol./Econ.,Eng. Lang. — Antonio Kamiya
Science — Nobuyuki Mori
Diplomatic — Masatoshi Nagata
White House Corr. — Yuji Nakaya
Pentagon Corr. — Shigeyuki Yoshida
Politics/Military — Tsuyoshi Yamazaki
Research Asst. — Monta Monaco
Mainichi Shimbun — 540 National Press Bldg., Washington, DC 20045; tel (202) 737-2817; fax (202) 638-5188
Bureau Chief — Yoshinori Kando
Science/Technology — Toshifumo Kawano
Politics — Hiroshi Komatsu
Foreign Relations — Akio Takahata
Economics — Michio Ushioda
Newsweek Japan — 1750 Pennsylvania Ave. N.W., Ste. 1220, Washington, DC 20006; tel (202) 626-2044; fax (202) 626-2010
Bureau Chief — Dana M Lewis
NHL-Japan Broadcasting Corp. — 2030 M St. N.W., Ste. 706, Washington, DC 20036; tel (202) 828-5180; fax (202) 828-4571
Bureau Chief — Hidetoshi Fujisawa
Producer — Rosalynn Frank
Producer — Izumi Okubo
Producer — Michael Viqueira
Producer — Shinichiro Yoshikai
Politics — Tamaki Imai
Politics — Junko Tanaka
Economics — Nobuyuki Itagaki
Correspondent — Kei Tamura
Nihon Hoso Kyokai — 7855 Enola St., Ste. TA-1, McLean, VA 22102; tel (703) 893-9017; fax (703) 893-9017
Correspondent — Hiroko Kiriishi
Nihon Keizai Shimbun — 636 National Press Bldg., Washington, DC 20045; tel (202) 393-1388; fax (202) 737-0170
Bureau Chief — Hirotsugu Koike
Economics/Currency — Shigeru Komago
Economics/Notes/Bank — Yasuhiro Ota
Economics/Ind./Agr. — Masanori Matsui
Economics/Trade/USTR — Satoru Tsugawa
General — Yoshiko Onuki
Politics — Tsuyoshi Sunohara
Politics — Hideo Kawai
Politics — Keiko Ono
Nohon Shimbun Kyokai — 11600 Sunrise Valley Dr., Reston, VA 22091; tel (703) 648-1135; fax (703) 834-8716
Correspondent — Yoshio Sato
Nippon Television Network (NTV) — 1036 National Press Bldg., Washington, DC 20045; tel (202) 638-0890; fax (202) 638-0308
Bureau Chief — Hisao Adachi
Correspondent — Naoto Kambe
Correspondent — Genichiro Shoriki
Producer — Shannon Lauterbach
Asst. Field Producer — Thad A Behrens
Nishi Nippon Shimbun — 1226 National Press Bldg., Washington, DC 20045; tel (202) 393-5812; fax (202) 628-9622
Correspondent — Tamio Shibuta
Sam Sara (Monthly) — 1920 N St., Ste. 750, Washington, DC 20036; tel (202) 463-8035; fax (202) 463-0997
Correspondent — Mitchell Eisen
Sankei Shimbun — 530 National Press Bldg., Washington, DC 20045; tel (202) 347-2015; fax (202) 662-7518
Bureau Chief — Takamitsu Kumasaka
Pentagon Corr. — Tsutomu Saito
Economics — Seiji Yajima
Editor-at-Large — Yoshihisa Komori
Research Asst. — Scott Stewart
Sekai Nippo — 924 National Press Bldg., Washington, DC 20045; tel (202) 879-6785; fax (202) 879-6789
Bureau Chief — Yuji Yokoyama
Correspondent — Seisaku Morita
Shakai Shimpo — PO Box 562, Garrett Park, MD 20896; tel (301) 942-0547; fax (301) 942-0547
Correspondent — Yasu Nakada
Tokyo Broadcasting System (TBS) — 1088 National Press Bldg., Washington, DC 20045; tel (202) 393-3800; fax (202) 393-3809
Bureau Chief — Michio Saito
Correspondent — Takushi Harima
Producer — Yae Katsumura
Production Asst. — Lani Asato
Production Asst. — Grier Patterson
Tokyo Shimbun — 1230 National Press Bldg., Washington, DC 20045; tel (202) 783-9479; fax (202) 628-9622
Bureau Chief — Hiroshi Sekiguchi
Politics — Yoshikazu Imazato
Economics Corr. — Mamoru Ohnoki
TV Tokyo-Television Tokyo Channel 12 — 803 National Press Bldg., Washington, DC 20045; tel (202) 662-8925; fax (202) 662-8955
Bureau Chief — Masaji Oshida
Producer — Stephen G Holowesko
Yomiuri Shimbun — 802 National Press Bldg., Washington, DC 20045; tel (202) 783-0363; fax (202) 737-2050
Bureau Chief — Akira Saito
Science/Foreign Rel. — Mikio Ikuma
Politics — Makoto Kito
Correspondent — Lani Christine Cossette
Correspondent — Jeremy Lechtman Milk
Correspondent — Amelia Ames Newcomb
Correspondent — Masaichi Nosaka
General — Saki Ouchi
Defense — Tsutomu Yamaguchi

JERUSALEM

Al-Quds — 2988 Paddock Wood Ct., Oakton, VA 22124; tel (202) 785-8394; fax (202) 887-5337
Correspondent — Abdellatif Rayan
Arab-American Media Service — 2102-D Gallows Rd., 2nd Fl., Vienna, VA 22182; tel (703) 591-0677; fax (703) 591-0678
Bureau Chief — Abdulsalam Y Massarueh
Jerusalem Press Service — 2102-D Gallows Rd., 2nd Fl., Vienna, VA 22182; tel (703) 591-0677; fax (703) 591-0678
Editor — Abdulsalam Y Massarueh

JORDAN

Al Rai Daily Newspaper — 2102-D Gallows Rd., 2nd Fl., Vienna, VA 22182; tel (703) 591-0677; fax (703) 591-0678
Bureau Chief — Abdulsalam Y Massarueh
Al-Muslimoon — 4406 Brevard Ct., Alexandria, VA 22309; tel (703) 780-9591; fax (703) 750-9010
Correspondent — Jawad M El-Hamad

KOREA

Chosen Ilbo — 1171 National Press Bldg., Washington, DC 20045; tel (202) 783-4236; fax (202) 783-5382
Bureau Chief — Hae young Jung
Correspondent — Changkyoon Kim
Christian Broadcasting System (CBS) — 1257-A National Press Bldg., Washington, DC 20045; tel (202) 737-6031; fax (202) 737-6821
Bureau Chief — Jung-sik Lee
Dong-A Ilbo — 974 National Press Bldg., Washington, DC 20045; tel (202) 347-4097; fax (202) 393-1866
Bureau Chief — Chan Soon Nam
Economic Daily — 909 National Press Bldg., Washington, DC 20045; tel (202) 637-3258; fax (202) 393-1866
Bureau Chief — Dae-Ho (Grace) Kim
Han-Kyoreh Shinmun — 1259 National Press Bldg., Washington, DC 20045; tel (202) 662-7185; fax (202) 662-7186
Bureau Chief — Yun Joo Jung
Hankook Ilbo/Korea Times — 1143 National Press Bldg., Washington, DC 20045; tel (202) 783-2674; fax (202) 783-0484
Bureau Chief — Sang Seok Leewhite
Correspondent — Jin-suk Chung
Joong-Ang Daily News — 1294 National Press Bldg., Washington, DC 20045; tel (202) 347-0121; fax (202) 628-2719
Bureau Chief — Chang-ook Jin
Correspondent — Yong Yil Kim
Kookman Daily — 923 National Press Bldg., Washington, Dc 20045; tel (202) 662-7441; fax (202) 662-7442
Bureau Chief — Young Jin Kim
Korean Broadcasting System (KBS) — 1076 National Press Bldg., Washington, DC 20045; tel (202) 662-7348; fax (202) 662-7347
Bureau Chief — Chung Soo Lee
Correspondent — Soon-yong Cho
Kyung Hyang Daily News — 839 National Press Bldg., Washington, DC 20045; tel (202) 737-3459; fax (202) 737-5320
Bureau Chief — Jong-Yon Lee
Munhwa Broadcasting Co. (MBC) — 414 National Press Bldg., Washington, DC 20045; tel (202) 347-4013; fax (202) 347-1611
Bureau Chief — Sung-Dai Noh
Correspondent — Jae-Ki Ahn
Correspondent — Ki Cheol Lee
Correspondent — In-Yong Rhee
Pusan Daily News/Pusan Economic News — 905 National Press Bldg., Washington, DC 20045; tel (202) 347-8816; fax (202) 347-8817
Correspondent — Jong Hwan Kim
Pusan Ilbo — 1115 National Press Bldg., Washington, DC 20045; tel (202) 638-1628; fax (202) 638-5422
Bureau Chief — Seo Hwan Chung
SBS-Seoul Broadcasting System — 979 National Press Bldg., Washington, DC 20045; tel (202) 662-1260; fax (202) 662-1261
Bureau Chief — Nak-cheon Baek
Production Asst. — Hyon Sok Chang
Segye Times — 1160 National Press Bldg., Washington, DC 20045; tel (202) 879-6790; fax (202) 879-6791
Correspondent — Sangin Shin
Seoul Shinmun — 1262-A National Press Bldg., Washington, DC 20045; tel (202) 662-7335; fax (202) 662-7337
Bureau Chief — Kyung-Hyung Lee
Sisa Journal — 990 National Press Bldg., Washington, DC 20045; tel (202) 638-2090; fax (202) 638-2089
Bureau Chief — Seung-woong Kim
Yonhap News Agency — 1299 National Press Bldg., Washington, DC 20045; tel (202) 783-5539; fax (202) 393-3460
Bureau Chief — Young-sup Chang
Correspondent — Jai-Kyu Sun

KUWAIT

Dar Al Watan — 3606 Paramount Rd., Fairfax, VA 22033; tel (703) 715-0948; fax (703) 715-0948
Bureau Chief — Mahmud A Shammam
Kuwait News Agency — 906 National Press Bldg., Washington, DC 20045; tel (202) 347-5554; fax (202) 347-6837
Bureau Chief — Faisal S M Alzaid
Correspondent — Saleh Al-Tabeekh
Correspondent — James C Flanigan

LATIN AMERICA

Agence France Presse (AFP) — 1612 K St. N.W., Ste. 400, Washington, DC 20006; tel (202) 861-8585; fax (202) 861-8524
Correspondent — Jose Antonio Puertas
ANSA-Italian News Agency — 1285 National Press Bldg., Washington, DC 20045; tel (202) 628-3317; fax (202) 638-1792
Correspondent — Alejandro Rodrigo
Caribbean News Agency — c/o OAS, 17th St. & Constitution Ave. N.W., Washington, DC 20006; tel (202) 458-3754; fax (202) 458-6421
Correspondent — Brian Wesley Kirton
Caribbean Sun — c/o OAS, 17th St. & Constitution Ave. N.W., Washington, DC 20006; tel (202) 458-3754; fax (202) 458-6421
Correspondent — Brian Wesley Kirton

LEBANON

Ad-Diyar — 5501 N. 11th St., Arlington, VA 22205; tel (703) 533-0541; fax (703) 533-0556
Correspondent — Samir N Nader
Al-Anwar — 9200 Chanute Dr., Bethesda, MD 20814; tel (301) 564-0374; fax (301) 564-0973
Correspondent — Farid El Khatib
Al-Hewar — PO Box 2104, Vienna, VA 22180; tel (703) 281-2641; fax (703) 281-0528
Correspondent — Laura Ghandour Dorn
Editor — Sobhi Ghandour
Al-Kifah Al-Arabi — 3501 Stringfellow Ct., Fairfax, VA 22033; tel (703) 471-5125; fax (703) 471-4421
Bureau Chief — Samir Karam
An Nahar — 1185 National Press Bldg., Washington, DC 20045; tel (202) 783-5544; fax (703) 783-0471
Correspondent — Rafic Maalouf
Correspondent — Dana H Sandarusi
Assayad — 9200 Chanute Dr., Bethesda, MD 20814; tel (301) 564-0374; fax (301) 564-0973
Correspondent — Farid El Khatib
La Revue De Liban — 2109 Greenery Ln., Ste. 301, Wheaton, MD 20906; tel (301) 933-4748
Correspondent — Samia Abboud

MALAYSIA

Bernama — 7700 Tremayne Pl., Apt. 307, McLean, VA 22102; tel (703) 356-2087; fax (703) 760-7671
Bureau Chief — Salmy Mohd-Hashim
TV-3 Malaysia — RR 1, Box 13, Aldie, VA 22001; tel (703) 779-7690; fax (703) 779-7691
Correspondent — Zulkafly Baharuddin

MALI

The Continent — 1221 Massachusetts Ave., Ste. 402, Washington, DC 20005; tel (202) 347-3353; fax (202) 393-0787
Correspondent — Adam Ouologuem
Nouvel Horizon — PO Box 3469, Washington, DC 20043-4696; tel (202) 347-3353; fax (202) 393-0787
Correspondent — Chouaidou Traore
Radio-Television Du Mali — 1221 Massachusetts Ave., Ste. 402, Washington, DC 20005; tel (202) 347-3353; fax (202) 393-0787
Correspondent — Adam Ouologuem

MAURITIUS

Le Mauricien — 1084 Pipestem Pl., Potomac, MD 20854; tel (301) 424-3884; fax (301) 424-0199
Correspondent — Pamela Glass

MEXICO

El Financiero — PO Box 65392, Washington, DC 20035; tel (703) 707-0236; fax (703) 707-0237
Correspondent — Dolia Estevez
El Norte — 1265 National Press Bldg., Washington, DC 20045; tel (202) 628-0031; fax (202) 628-0131
Correspondent — Maria Isabel Gonzalez
El Universal — 801 National Press Bldg., Washington, DC 20045; tel (202) 662-7190; fax (202) 662-7189
Correspondent — Jose Carreno
Epoca — 8316 Beech Tree Rd., Bethesda, MD 20817; tel (301) 229-8003; fax (301) 469-9548
Correspondent — Dora Cruz
Excelsior — 2321 1st St. N.W., Washington, DC 20001; tel (202) 265-3400; fax (202) 265-2066
Correspondent — Jose Manuel Nava
La Jornada — 132 North Carolina Ave. S.E., Washington, DC 20003; tel (202) 547-5852; fax (202) 546-7776
Correspondent — James W Cason
Notimex — 425 National Press Bldg., Washington, DC 20045; tel (202) 347-5227; fax (202) 347-5126
Bureau Chief — Ignacio Basauri
Correspondent — Horacio Chavez
Correspondent — Jesus Esquivel
Correspondent — Alfonso Gonzalez
Correspondent — Jacqueline Lerma
Correspondent — Jose Lopez
Correspondent — Irma Martinez

Proceso — 972 National Press Bldg., Washington, DC 20045; tel (202) 393-1966; fax (202) 393-1967
Bureau Chief — Pascal Beltran-Del-Rio
Radio Acir Sat — 99 S. Bragg St., Alexandria, VA 22312; tel (703) 354-6300; fax (703) 354-6300
Correspondent — Miguel Eduardo Valle
Reforma — 1265 National Press Bldg., Washington, DC 20045; tel (202) 628-0031; fax (202) 628-0131
Correspondent — Maria Isabel Gonzalez
Televisa TV Network — 1199 National Press Bldg., Washington, DC 20045; tel (202) 638-4282; fax (202) 737-0207
Bureau Chief — Yolanda Sanchez
Correspondent — Jack Kasofsky
Cameraman — Luis F Pacheco-Mendez
Unomasuno — 1069 National Press Bldg., Washington, DC 20045; tel (202) 628-2724; fax (202) 628-2718
Correspondent — Rodolfo Medina-Palomino
Viva — 205 E. Duncan Ave., Alexandria, VA 22301; tel (703) 836-0320
Correspondent — Jose Luis Avendano

MIDDLE EAST

Al Hayat — 1185 National Press Bldg., Washington, DC 20045; tel (202) 783-5544; fax (202) 783-0471
Bureau Chief — Rafic Maalouf
Correspondent — Dana H Sandarusi
Almajalla — 1331 Pennsylvania Ave. N.W., Ste.920, Washington, DC 20004; tel (202) 638-7183; fax (202) 638-1887
Correspondent — Mohammad A Salih
Dar Al Watan — 20020 Hoffstead Ln., Gaithersburg, MD 20879-1416; tel (202) 429-1670; fax (301) 590-9358
Bureau Chief — Muhammed Dalbah
Future Television — 1884 Columbia Rd. N.W., Ste. 710, Washington, DC 20009; tel (202) 232-2011; fax (202) 783-0326
Correspondent — Amal Mudallali
Middle East Broadcasting Center — 2030 M St. N.W., Ste. 400, Washington, DC 20036; tel (202) 775-0894; fax (202) 223-7997
Correspondent — Hanan El-Badry
Correspondent — Aziz Fahmy Farag
Middle East Reporter — 3313 Wessynton Way, Alexandria, VA 22309; tel (703) 780-2256; fax (703) 780-1046
Correspondent — David Hume
Radio Monte Carlo — 2000 S. Eads St., Ste. 723, Arlington, VA 22202; tel (703) 892-3415; fax (703) 892-3415
Correspondent — Nouhad Hayek

MOROCCO

Maghreb Arabe Presse — 1119 Waverly Way, McLean, VA 22101; tel (703) 790-3277; fax (703) 790-3279
Bureau Chief — Mostafa Chtaini
Correspondent — Alem Azzam
Correspondent — Farid Bernoussi

NEPAL

Kantipur Dailes — PO Box 13542, Silver Spring, MD 20910; tel (301) 587-0454
Correspondent — Puru Ghimire
Kathmandu Post — PO Box 13542, Silver Spring, MD 20910; tel (301) 587-0454
Correspondent — Puru Ghimire
Spotlight — 7315 Essex Ave., Springfield, VA 22150; tel (202) 289-0100; fax (202) 289-7601
Correspondent — Arun Banskota

NETHERLANDS

ANP-Dutch News Agency — 11903 Renwood Ln., Rockville, MD 20852; tel (301) 468-6863; fax (301) 816-9173
Bureau Chief — Jaap Van Wesel
De Volkstrant — 8209 Beech Tree Rd., Bethesda, MD 20817; tel (301) 469-6153; fax (301) 469-6827
Bureau Chief — Oscar Garschagen
Elsevier — PO Box 857, Chappaqua, NY 15014-0857; tel (914) 747-1880; fax (914) 747-1480
Correspondent — John Van Rosendaal
Het Financieele Dagblad — PO Box 857, Chappaqua, NY 15014-0857; tel (914) 747-1880; fax (914) 747-1480
Correspondent — John Van Rosendaal
Netherlands Press Association — 520 Woodland Ct., Vienna, VA 22180; tel (703) 938-7715; fax (703) 938-2846
Correspondent — Hans De Bruijn
Nos Television (Netherlands) — 2030 M St. N.W., Ste. 400, Washington, DC 20036; tel (202) 466-8793; fax (202) 828-4146
Bureau Chief — Paul Sneyder
NRC Handelsblad — 3007 Albemarle St. N.W., Washington, DC 20008; tel (202) 363-6944; fax (202) 537-2959
Correspondent — Maarten Huygen
Radio Netherlands/Arabic Service — 2031-A Florida Ave. N.W., Ste. 104, Washington, DC 20009; tel (202) 467-6253; fax (202) 467-6254
Correspondent — Mohamed El Faith Saeed
Staatscourant — 7207 Barnett Rd., Bethesda, MD 20817; tel (301) 469-9019; fax (301) 469-5930
Freelance — Henk Kolb
Trouw Daily — 11903 Renwood Ln., Rockville, MD 20852; tel (301) 468-6863; fax (301) 816-9173
Bureau Chief — Jaap Van Wesel
United Dutch Newspapers — 10404 Holbrook Dr., Potomac, MD 20854; tel (301) 983-0071; fax (301) 983-3134
Correspondent — Marc De Koninck

NIGERIA

Nigerian Tide — 6813 Riggs Rd., Ste. 204, Hyattsville, MD 20783; tel (301) 442-0270; fax (301) 345-4187
Correspondent — Wolaebi Fidelis Iyebote

NORWAY

Aftenposten — 2030 M St. N.W., Ste. 700, Washington, DC 20036; tel (202) 785-0658; fax (202) 785-1546
Correspondent — Per Christiansen
Norwegian Broadcasting Corp. (NRK) — 2030 M St. N.W., Ste. 700, Washington, DC 20036; tel (202) 785-1460; fax (202) 785-5834
Bureau Manager — Grethe Winther
Correspondent — Bjorn Hansen
Correspondent — Gunnar Myklebust
Scandinavian News Agency — 1257-C National Press Bldg., Washington, DC 20045; tel (202) 628-0653
Correspondent — Helge Ogrim

PAKISTAN

Dawn — 301 G St. S.W., Apt. 130, Washington, DC 20024; tel (202) 488-7840; fax (202) 488-7840
Bureau Chief — Muhammad ali Siddiqi
Ibrat Group of Papers — 6518 Democracy Blvd., Bethesda, MD 20817; tel (301) 530-9022; fax (301) 530-9022
Bureau Chief — Asghar Abbasit
Frontier Post — PO Box 7111, Washington, DC 20044-7111; tel (202) 660-6060; fax (202) 660-6060
Correspondent — Syed Adeeb
Jang — 12776 Captain's Cove, Woodbridge, VA 22192; tel (703) 643-1668; fax (703) 643-1668
Bureau Chief — Nayyar Zaidi
The Nation — 1426 H St. N.W., Ste. 1104, Washington, DC 20005; tel (202) 638-5394; fax (202) 638-5395
Bureau Chief — Khalid Hasan
The News — 12776 Captain's Cove, Woodbridge, VA 22192; tel (703) 643-1668; fax (703) 643-1668
Correspondent — Nayyar Zaidi
Pakistan Link — 10178 Portsmouth Rd., Ste. 1, Manassas, VA 22110; tel (703) 257-9514; fax (703) 257-9514
Correspondent — Syed Mussarat Shah
Pakistan Television Corp. — 1426 H St. N.W., Ste. 1104, Washington, DC 20005; tel (202) 638-5394; fax (202) 638-5395
Bureau Chief — Khalid Hasan

PANAMA

Diario Libre De Panama — 7729 Brookville Rd., Chevy Chase, MD 20815; tel (301) 652-0629; fax (301) 652-0629
Correspondent — Elizabeth Brannan
La Prensa — 7729 Brookville Rd., Chevy Chase, MD 20815; tel (301) 652-0629; fax (301) 652-0629
Correspondent — Elizabeth Brannan

PERU

Express/Extra — 3333 University Blvd. W., Ste. 811, Kensington, MD 20895; tel (301) 942-0614; fax (301) 942-0614
Correspondent — Edgar Triveri
Gestion — 13600 Glen Mill Rd., Rockville, MD 20850; tel (301) 279-7954; fax (301) 279-7954
Correspondent — Vladimir Kocerha

PHILIPPINES

Business World — 2873 Seminole Rd., Lake Ridge, VA 22192; tel (703) 643-9716; fax (703) 491-2516
Correspondent — Mercedes Tira Andrei
Philippines News Agency — 2873 Seminole Rd., Lake Ridge, VA 22192; tel (703) 643-9716; fax (703) 491-2516
Bureau Chief — Mercedes Tira Andrei

POLAND

Gazeta Gdanska — 840 National Press Bldg., Washington, DC 20045; tel (202) 393-3511; fax (202) 393-2511
Correspondent — Tomasz Wroblewski
Gazeta Wyborcza — 6003 Coral Sea Ave., Rockville, MD 20851-1722; tel (301) 279-9427; fax (301) 309-3774
Correspondent — Jacek Kalabinski
Correspondent — Bartosz Weglarozyk
PAP-Polish Press Agency — 7505 Democracy Blvd., Ste. 413-A, Bethesda, MD 20817; tel (301) 365-1099; fax (301) 365-8124
Correspondent — Wifold Tomasz Zalewski
Polish Radio & Television — 4515 Willard Ave., Ste. S-2201, Chevy Chase, MD 20815; tel (301) 718-9824; fax (301) 718-9619
Bureau Chief — Tomasz Lis
Radio Wolna Europe — 1201 Connecticut Ave. N.W., Ste. 1111, Washington, DC 20036; tel (202) 457-6927; fax (202) 457-6998
Correspondent — Tadeusz K Zachurski
RMF FM Poland — 840 National Press Bldg., Washington, DC 20045; tel (202) 393-3511; fax (202) 393-2511
Correspondent — Marcin Wrona
Rzeczpospolita — 5103 Alta Vista Rd., Bethesda, MD 20814; tel (301) 530-8172; fax (301) 530-4711
Correspondent — Ewa Szymanska-Wierzynska
Warsaw Voice — 1201 S. Barton St., Ste. 177, Arlington, VA 22204; tel (202) 828-0814; fax (202) 828-4136
Correspondent — Krystyna Anna Stachowiak
Zycie Warszawy — 840 National Press Bldg., Washington, DC 20045; tel (202) 393-3511; fax (202) 393-2511
Correspondent — Tomasz Wroblewski

PORTUGAL

Lusa — 4942 Americana Dr., Annandale, VA 22003; tel (703) 914-0681; fax (703) 914-0438
Correspondent — Jose M Ricardo
Publico — 3801 Connecticut Ave. N.W., Ste. 436, Washington, DC 20008; tel (202) 686-5413
Correspondent — Paulo Moura
Radio Renascenca — 5301 Westbard Cir., Ste. 416, Bethesda, MD 20816; tel (301) 907-7969; fax (301) 907-7969
Correspondent — Paulo G A Oliveira
RTP-Portuguese Radio/Television — 2030 M St. N.W., Ste. 538, Washington, DC 20036; tel (202) 775-2969; fax (202) 775-2938
Bureau Chief — Mario Crespo

ROMANIA

Central Mass Media (Evenimentul) — 1237 4th St. S.W., Washington, DC 20024; tel (202) 554-0740; fax (202) 554-0740
Freelance — William Edwards
Evenimentul Zilei — PO Box 3085, Oakton, VA 22124; tel (703) 352-0898; fax (703) 352-0898
Correspondent — Liviu Turcu
Rompres-Romanian News Agency — 2301 S. Jefferson Davis Hwy., Ste. 1306, Arlington, VA 22202; tel (703) 418-1730; fax (703) 418-1730
Correspondent — Mircea Podina

RUSSIA

Commersant Daily — 131 11th St. S.E., Washington, DC 20003; tel (202) 546-5217
Correspondent — Andrey Edemsky
European — 2615 42nd St., Apt. 101, Washington, DC 20007; tel (202) 338-1270; fax (202) 336-8425
Correspondent — Yevgeny A Slivkin
Itar-Tass-Russian News Agency — 1004 National Press Bldg., Washington, DC 20045; tel (202) 662-7080; fax (202) 393-6495
Bureau Chief — Vitaly Yakovlevich Chukaseev
Correspondent — Igor Barsukov
Correspondent — Igor Borisenko
Correspondent — Vladimir Ivanovich Kikilo
Correspondent — Andrew A Loschilin
Correspondent — Mikhail Mzarevlov
Correspondent — Arkadi Sidoruk
Izvestia — 1601 Kirby Rd., McLean, VA 22101; tel (703) 917-0517; fax (703) 917-0518
Correspondent — Vladimir D Nadeine
NTV Russia — 1705 DeSales St. N.W., Ste. 300, Washington, DC 20036; tel (202) 833-0750; fax (202) 222-7898
Bureau Chief — Peter Orlov
Correspondent — Nickolai Federov
Rossiya — 4500 S. Four Mile Run Dr., Arlington, VA 22204; tel (703) 931-4482; fax (703) 931-4482
Correspondent — Evgueni Berezin
Russian TV & Radio Co. (Ostankino) — 4500 S. Mile Run Dr., Ste. 323, Arlington, VA 22204; tel (703) 824-9066; fax (703) 998-8382
Bureau Chief — Sergei Goryachev
Segodnia — 1601 Kirby Rd., McLean, VA 22101; tel (301) 648-6747
Correspondent — Nickolay I Zimin
Trud — 4701 Willard Ave., Apt. 904, Chevy Chase, MD 20815; tel (301) 656-3744; fax (301) 656-3744
Correspondent — Vissarion Sisnev

SAUDI ARABIA

Al-Riyadh — 1155 15th St. N.W., Ste. 606, Washington, DC 20005; tel (202) 822-0814; fax (202) 882-0806
Columnist — Fouzi El-Asmar
1884 Columbia Rd. N.W., Ste. 710, Washington, DC 20009; tel (202) 232-2011; fax (202) 783-0326
Freelance — Amal Mudallali
Al-Sharq Al-Awsat — 1331 Pennsylvania Ave. N.W., Washington, DC 20004; tel (202) 638-7183
Correspondent — Mohammed Sadeq
Arab News — 1331 Pennsylvania Ave. N.W., Washington, DC 20004; tel (202) 638-7138
Correspondent — Mohammed Sadeq
Okaz Newspapers — 1145 National Press Bldg., Washington, DC 20045; tel (202) 393-0433; fax (202) 393-0421
Bureau Chief — Mohamed Hakki
Correspondent — Mohamed El-Maddah
Correspondent — Ahmed El-Bashari
Correspondent — Mahassen Hanna
Correspondent — Maysarah Hasanain
Saudi Arabian TV — 1215 Jefferson Davis Hwy., Ste. 302, Arlington, VA 22202; tel (703) 416-6800; fax (703) 416-6805
Asst. Bureau Chief — Faisal Abordaif
Director — Saleh A Al-Said
Producer — Abdelgader Dawad
Correspondent — Rashid Dhere
Correspondent — Mohammad Ghalib
Corr./Announcer — Magda Kamal Radwan
Asst. Producer — Abdullah Al-Douh
Saudi Gazette — 1145 National Press Bldg., Washington, DC 20045; tel (202) 347-6469; fax (202) 393-0421
Bureau Chief — Barbara G Ferguson
Correspondent — Timothy Kennedy
Correspondent — Geoffrey Schad
Saudi Press Agency — 1155 15th St. N.W., Ste. 1111, Washington, DC 20005; tel (202) 861-0324; fax (202) 872-1405
Bureau Chief — Naila Al-Sowayel
Correspondent — Thomas Canahuatez

SERBIA & MONTENEGRO

Borba — 3414 Manor Rd., Chevy Chase, MD 20815; tel (301) 656-6535; fax (301) 718-7891
Correspondent — Slobodan Pavlovic
Decye Novine — 5214 Wissioming Rd., Bethesda, MD 20816; tel (301) 229-4860
Correspondent — Milovan Misic
Magyar Szo — 4849 Connecticut Ave. N.W., Ste. 504, Washington, DC 20008; tel (202) 362-3058; fax (202) 966-8015
Correspondent — Tibor Purger

Copyright ©1996 by the Editor & Publisher Co.

Foreign correspondents VII-27

Tanjug-Yugoslav News Agency — 4601 N. Park Ave., Ste. 207, Chevy Chase, MD 20815; tel (301) 656-6365; fax (301) 656-6365
Bureau Chief — Dejan Lukic
Vreme — c/o Getleins, 915 Prince St., Alexandria, VA 22314; tel (703) 549-5181
Columnist — Cvijeto Job

SINGAPORE

Business Times — 4701 Willard Ave., Ste. 1024, Chevy Chase, MD 20815; tel (301) 654-2389; fax (301) 654-2295
Correspondent — Leon Hadar

SLOVAK REPUBLIC

Slovak Radio — 2501 Porter St. N.W., Washington, DC 20008; tel (202) 537-3101
Correspondent — Peter Susko
Tasr-Press Agency of Slovak Republic — 4501 Connecticut Ave. N.W., Ste. 713, Washington, DC 20008; tel (202) 686-4710; fax (202) 537-0574
Correspondent — Otakar Korinek

SLOVENIA

Slovenian Press Agency — 1701 Andy Holt Ave., Ste. D-52, Knoxville, TN 37916; tel (615) 595-6797; fax (615) 974-3121
Correspondent — Rok Klancnik

SOUTH AFRICA

Argus South African Newspapers — 960-C National Press Bldg., Washington, DC 20045; tel (202) 662-8722; fax (202) 662-8723
Bureau Chief — Peter Albert Fabricius
Business Day — 960-B National Press Bldg., Washington, DC 20045; tel (202) 662-8760; fax (202) 662-8761
Correspondent — Simon Barber
National Media Ltd. — 1060-D National Press Bldg., Washington, DC 20045; tel (202) 638-0399; fax (202) 393-5647
Bureau Chief — Arrie Jordaan Rossouw
South African Broadcasting Corp./Radio — PO Box 954, Rockville, MD 20848; tel (301) 686-5885; fax (301) 816-2028
Correspondent — Mike Kellerman

SPAIN

ABC — 1401 N. Taft St., Ste. 1224, Arlington, VA 22201; tel (703) 841-7368; fax (703) 841-7368
Correspondent — Pedro J Rodriquez
Antenna-3 Television — 4666 S. 34th St., Arlington, VA 22206; tel (703) 931-6398; fax (703) 931-1012
Producer — Isabel Garcia
Cambio 16 — 5603 Surrey St., Chevy Chase, MD 20815; tel (301) 961-5232; fax (301) 961-5111
Bureau Chief — Carlos Enrique Bayo
Cope — 11924 Sloan Ct., Reston, VA 22091; tel (703) 715-9405; fax (703) 715-9525
Correspondent — Manuel A Gomez
Diario 16 — 5603 Surrey St., Chevy Chase, MD 20815; tel (301) 961-5232; fax (301) 961-5111
Bureau Chief — Carlos Enrique Bayo
EFE-Spanish News Agency — 1252 National Press Bldg., Washington, DC 20045; tel (202) 745-7692; fax (202) 393-4119
Bureau Chief — Fernando Pajares
Dep. Bureau Chief — Emilio Sanchez
Lat. America Corr. — Maria Luisa Azpiazu
Correspondent — Ester Borrell
Correspondent — Nicolas Dulanto
Correspondent — Rosendo Majano
Correspondent — Hernan Martin
Correspondent — Enrique M Merino
Correspondent — Delia A Millan
Correspondent — Rafael Moreno
El Correo Espanol — 1057-D National Press Bldg., Washington, DC 20045; tel (202) 662-7183; fax (202) 907-6881
Correspondent — Beatriz Iraburu
El Pais — 1134 National Press Bldg., Washington, DC 20045; tel (202) 638-1533; fax (202) 628-4788
Bureau Chief — Antonio Cano
Europa Press Reportajes — 10519 Apple Ridge Rd., Gaithersburg, MD 20879; tel (301) 921-8289; fax (301) 821-8289
Correspondent — Montserrat Doval
Illacrua — 4531 Everett St., Kensington, MD 20895; tel (301) 493-4328
Correspondent — Eduard Vinyamata
La Vanguardia — 4343 Massachusetts Ave. N.W., Washington, DC 20016; tel (202) 362-6785; fax (202) 362-6705
Correspondent — Joaquin Luna
Onda Regional De Murcia — 11924 Sloane Ct., Reston, VA 22091; tel (703) 715-9525; fax (703) 715-9405
Correspondent — Ana Maria Diaz
Radio Nacional De Espana — 1288 National Press Bldg., Washington, DC 20045; tel (202) 783-0768; fax (202) 347-0147
Bureau Chief — Luz Maria Rodriguez
SER-Sociedad Espanola De RadioDifusion — 1134 National Press Bldg., Washington, DC 20045; tel (202) 628-2522; fax (202) 628-4788
Bureau Chief — Jose M Calvo
Tribuna — 6923 Tyndale St., McLean, VA 22101; tel (703) 893-7880; fax (202) 393-4119
Correspondent — Rosana Ubanell
TV-3 Televiso De Catalunya — 1620 I St. N.W., Ste. 650, Washington, DC 20001; tel (202) 785-0580; fax (202) 331-9064
Bureau Chief — Joan Nogues
Woman — 5603 Surrey St., Chevy Chase, MD 20046; tel (301) 961-5232; fax (301) 961-5113
Correspondent — Pilar Casanova

SUDAN

Al Nasr Daily Newspaper — 5550 Columbia Pike, Ste. 572, Arlington, VA 22204; tel (703) 671-4482
Correspondent — Gorashi Yasir
Freelance — 2813 S. 8th St., Ste. 402-A, Arlington, VA 22204; tel (703) 685-6383
Correspondent — Awatif M Sidahmed
Sudan House — 2210 Massachusetts Ave. N.W., Washington, DC 20008; tel (202) 466-6280; fax (202) 745-2615
Correspondent — Atif Badri
Sudan News Agency — 2210 Massachusetts Ave. N.W., Washington, DC 20008; tel (202) 466-6280; fax (202) 745-2615
Correspondent — Safwat Hassan Siddiq

SWEDEN

Dagens Nyheter — 1726 M St. N.W., Ste. 700, Washington, DC 20036; tel (202) 429-0134; fax (202) 429-0136
Bureau Chief — Kurt Malarstedt
Svenska Dagbladet — PO Box 11816, Washington, DC 20008; tel (202) 362-8253; fax (202) 362-9338
Correspondent — Karin Henriksson
1800 K St. N.W., Ste. 400, Washington, DC 20006; tel (202) 775-3317
Editorial Writer — Gudrun Persson
SVT 2-Swedish Broadcasting Corp. — 2030 M St. N.W., Ste. 700, Washington, DC 20036; tel (202) 785-1779; fax (202) 785-5834
Correspondent — Folke Ryden
SVT 4-Swedish Broadcasting Corp. — 1034 31st St. N.W., Washington, DC 20007; tel (202) 333-5351; fax (202) 333-5357
Correspondent — Lennart Lundh
Swedish Broadcasting Corp. — 3929 Morrison St. N.W., Washington, DC 20015; tel (202) 362-5138; fax (202) 362-3758
Bureau Chief — Anders B G Lindquist

SWITZERLAND

Aarguer Tagblatt (Freelance) — 103 G St. S.W., Ste. B-203, Washington, DC 20024; tel (202) 646-1870; fax (202) 484-8812
Correspondent — Richard G Anderegg
Agence Telegraphique Suisse — 5235 Baltimore Ave., Bethesda, MD 20816; tel (301) 654-1009
Correspondent — Steven Golob
Basler Zeitung — 980 National Press Bldg., Washington, DC 20045; tel (202) 393-0434; fax (202) 363-8305
Bureau Chief — Johann Aeschlimann
3008 1/2 R St. N.W., Washington, DC 20007; tel (202) 338-4569; fax (202) 337-6132
Economic Correspondent — Luzian Caspar
Berner Zietung — 4140 Widebrance Ln., Woodbridge, VA 22193; tel (703) 878-6808; fax (703) 878-4452
Correspondent — Stefan Georg Ragaz
Der Bund — 7502 Arden Rd., Cabin John, MD 20818; tel (301) 229-1570; fax (301) 229-1570
Correspondent — Dieter Arnold
Die Weltwoche & NZZ-Folio — 1601 30th St. N.W., Washington, DC 20007; tel (202) 342-3189; fax (202) 337-4635
Correspondent — Kathrin Meier-Rust
Judische Rundschau — 1263 National Press Bldg., Washington, DC 20045; tel (202) 628-0030
Correspondent — Joseph Polakoff
Le Nouveau Quotiden — 4935 Albemarle St. N.W., Washington, DC 20016; tel (202) 537-7189; fax (202) 537-7213
Correspondent — Jeanclaude Buffle
Neue Zurcher Zeitung — 1093 National Press Bldg., Washington, DC 20045; tel (202) 662-7235; fax (202) 662-7274
Political Correspondent — Reinhard Meier
Solothurner Zeitung — 103 G St. S.W., Ste. B-203, Washington, DC 20024; tel (202) 646-1870; fax (202) 484-8812
Correspondent — Richard G Anderegg
SRG-Swiss German TV — 2030 M St. N.W., Ste. 400, Washington, DC 20036; tel (202) 785-1121; fax (202) 293-7204
Correspondent — Peter Achten
Editor — Monique Silberstein
German Service — Christoph Heri
Producer — Odile Isralson
Tages Anzeiger — 3147 Tennyson St. N.W., Washington, DC 20015; tel (202) 686-1665; fax (202) 686-1715
Bureau Chief — Thomas Ruest
Tribune De Geneve — 103 G St. S.W., Ste. B-203, Washington, DC 20024; tel (202) 646-1870; fax (202) 484-8812
Correspondent — Richard G Anderegg
24 Heures — 103 G St. S.W., Ste. B-203, Washington, DC 20024; tel (202) 646-1870; fax (202) 484-8812
Correspondent — Richard G Anderegg

SYRIA

Free Syria Newsletter — Rte. 2, PO Box 220-L, Gretna, VA 24557; tel (804) 335-5055; fax (804) 335-5055
Correspondent — Tammam Al-Barazi

TAIWAN

Central Daily News — 1 Lawngate Ct., Potomac, MD 20854; tel (301) 871-6732; fax (301) 871-1715
Correspondent — Brice Wang
Central News Agency — 1173 National Press Bldg., Washington, DC 20045; tel (202) 628-2738; fax (202) 637-6788
Bureau Chief — Wan-li Wang
Correspondent — Edward Han
Correspondent — Herman Y C Pan
China Television Co. (CTV) — 400 N. Capitol St., Ste. 177, Washington, DC 20001; tel (202) 393-3604; fax (703) 393-3605
Correspondent — Gary Chun Jung Tsai
China Television System (CTS) — 1273 National Press Bldg., Washington, DC 20045; tel (202) 662-8950; fax (202) 662-8865
Bureau Chief — Tina Chung
China Times — 952 National Press Bldg., Washington, DC 20045; tel (202) 662-7570; fax (202) 662-7573
Bureau Chief — Norman C Fu
Correspondent — Ping Lu
Commercial Times — 3420 Annandale Rd., Falls Church, VA 22402; tel (703) 573-4376; fax (703) 876-0662
Correspondent — Louise Ran Costich
Liberty Times — 12911 Winterthur Ln., Silver Spring, MD 20904; tel (301) 384-2908; fax (301) 989-8712
Correspondent — Manfried Changlien Hsu
14431 Pebble Hill Ln., North Potomac, MD 20878; tel (301) 279-0917; fax (301) 279-0871
Correspondent — Paul T P Tsai
Ming Sheng Pao — 1099 National Press Bldg., Washington, DC 20045; tel (202) 737-6426
Correspondent — Lisa Lee-Yuan Cheng
Taiwan Daily News — 8600 Aqueduct Rd., Potomac, MD 20854; tel (301) 251-0852; fax (301) 294-2516
Correspondent — Benedict S Hsu
TTV-Taiwan Television — 1705 DeSales St. N.W., Ste. 302, Washington, DC 20036; tel (202) 223-6642; fax (202) 452-8692
Bureau Chief — Linda Lin
United Daily News — 1099 National Press Bldg., Washington, DC 20045; tel (202) 737-6426; fax (202) 737-3732
Bureau Chief — James C Wang
Correspondent — Betty Lin
Youth Daily News — 7654 Westlake Terrace, Bethesda, MD 20817; tel (301) 469-6534; fax (301) 469-7253
Correspondent — Nelson N K Liu

TUNISIA

L'Observateur — 4601 Harvard Rd., College Park, MD 20740; tel (301) 779-0421; fax (301) 779-4727
Correspondent — Anouar Moalla

TURKEY

Anatolia News Agency — 4450 S. Park Ave., Ste. 1614, Chevy Chase, MD 20815; tel (301) 718-7966; fax (301) 718-3691
Bureau Chief — Mehmet Kasim Cindemir
ATV — 5432 Midship Ct., Burke, VA 22015; tel (703) 425-3846; fax (703) 425-3453
Correspondent — Savas Suzal
Cumhuriyet — 4401 Lee Hwy., Ste. 56, Arlington, VA 22207; tel (703) 527-8356; fax (703) 527-8382
Correspondent — Fuat Kozluklu
Hurriyet Newspaper — 2727 29th St., Apt. 332, Washington, DC 20008; tel (202) 328-3747; fax (202) 328-3747
Bureau Chief — Serdar Turgut
Milliyet — 8607 Jones Mill Rd., Chevy Chase, MD 20815; tel (301) 654-5183
Correspondent — Turan Yavuz
Correspondent — Ayda Yavuz
Sabha — 5432 Midship Ct., Burke, VA 22015; tel (703) 425-3846; fax (703) 425-3453
Bureau Chief — Savas Suzal
Tercuman — 9430 Clover Dale Ct., Burke, VA 22015; tel (703) 455-9636
Correspondent — Ahmet Ali Arslan
TGRT TV — 495 National Press Bldg., Washington, DC 20045; tel (202) 737-7800; fax (202) 737-7509
Correspondent — Hasan Mesut Hazar
TRT-Turkish TV — 4401 Lee Hwy., Ste. 56, Arlington, VA 22207; tel (703) 527-8356; fax (703) 527-8382
Correspondent — Fuat Kozluklu
Turkish Daily News — 18222 Flower Hill Way, Ste. 191, Gaithersburg, MD 20879; tel (301) 963-6234; fax (301) 948-8961
Bureau Chief — A Ugur Akinci
Turkish Probe — 18222 Flower Hill Way, Ste. 191, Gaithersburg, MD 20879; tel (301) 963-6234; fax (301) 948-8961
Bureau Chief — A Ugur Akinci
Turkiye Daily — 495 National Press Bldg., Washington, DC 20045; tel (202) 737-7800; fax (202) 737-7509
Bureau Chief — Hasan Mesut Hazar

UKRAINE

Dialogue — 3918 W St. N.W., Washington, DC 20007; tel (202) 338-8163; fax (202) 337-9096
Correspondent — Misha Knight

UNITED ARAB EMIRATES

UAE News Agency — 1155 15th St. N.W., Ste. 606, Washington, DC 20005; tel (202) 822-0814; fax (202) 822-0806
Bureau Chief — Fouzi El-Asmar

UNITED KINGDOM

AFX News — 835 National Press Bldg., Washington, DC 20045; tel (202) 347-3237; fax (202) 347-6241
Bureau Chief — Gregory Robb
Corr. — Alkman Nikolaos Granitsas
Belfast Telegraph — 1901 Columbia Rd. N.W., Ste. 703, Washington, DC 20009; tel (202) 462-8232; fax (202) 462-8232
Correspondent — Jamie Dettmer
British Broadcasting Corp. (BBC) — 2030 M St. N.W., Ste. 607, Washington, DC 20036; tel (202) 223-2050; fax (202) 775-1395
Bureau Chief — Steve Selman
Chief US Corr. — Gavin Esler
Radio Corr. — Jeremy Harris
Radio Producer — Beth Miller
World Service Corr. — Chris Nuttall
World Service Corr. — Jan Ziff
Producer — Sharon Blanchet
Producer — David Taylor
Compass News Features — 3521 30th St. N.W., Washington, DC 20008; tel (202) 686-5189; fax (202) 686-5189
Correspondent — Mark Milstein
Daily Express — 5516 Charlcote Rd., Bethesda, MD 20817-3736; tel (301) 951-6130
Correspondent — Peter J Hitchens

Daily Telegraph — 1331 Pennsylvania Ave. N.W., Ste. 904, Washington, DC 20004; tel (202) 393-5195; fax (202) 393-1335
Bureau Chief — Stephen Robinson
Correspondent — Hugh Davies
Economist — 1331 Pennsylvania Ave. N.W., Ste. 510, Washington, DC 20004; tel (202) 783-5753; fax (202) 737-1035
Bureau Chief — Daniel Franklin
Correspondent — John Heilemann
Evening Standard — 4312 Fessenden St. N.W., Washington, DC 20016; tel (202) 966-9423; fax (202) 362-2956
Correspondent — Jeremy Campbell
Financial Times of London — 1225 I St. N.W., Ste. 810, Washington, DC 20005; tel (202) 289-5474; fax (202) 289-5475
Bureau Chief — Jurek Martin
Correspondent — Nancy Dunne
Correspondent — George Graham
Correspondent — Michael Prowse
Glasgow Herald — 1730 Rhode Island Ave. N.W., Ste. 502, Washington, DC 20036; tel (202) 223-2910; fax (202) 223-1764
Correspondent — Patrick Brogan
GM TV — 1333 H St. N.W., Ste. 505, Washington, DC 20005; tel (202) 371-2011; fax (202) 371-2015
Bureau Chief — Maxine Mawhinney
Guardian — 1730 Rhode Island Ave. N.W., Ste. 502, Washington, DC 20036; tel (202) 223-2486; fax (202) 233-1764
Bureau Chief — Martin Walker
Correspondent — Jonathan Freedland
Independent TV News of London (ITN) — 1726 M St. N.W., Ste. 703, Washington, DC 20036; tel (202) 429-9080; fax (202) 429-8948
Bureau Chief — Bill Neely
Channel 4 News — David Smith
Independent/Independent on Sunday — 1726 M St. N.W., Ste. 700, Washington, DC 20036; tel (202) 467-4460; fax (202) 467-4458
Bureau Chief — Rupert Cornwell
Correspondent — John Carlin
London Broadcasting Co. — 6416 79th St., Bethesda, MD 20818; tel (301) 320-0707; fax (301) 320-5802
Correspondent — Nick Peters
Mail On Sunday — 5309 Slipper Ct., Columbia, MD 21045; tel (301) 596-5306; fax (410) 997-0017
Correspondent — William Lowther
Nature — 1234 National Press Bldg., Washington, DC 20045; tel (202) 737-2355; fax (202) 628-1609
Bureau Chief — Barbara J Culliton
New Scientist — 1350 Connecticut Ave. N.W., Ste. 403, Washington, DC 20036; tel (202) 331-2080; fax (202) 331-2082
Correspondent — Vincent Kiernan
Correspondent — Kurt Kleiner
Observer — 1730 Rhode Island Ave. N.W., Ste. 502, Washington, DC 20036; tel (202) 223-2910; fax (202) 223-1764
Bureau Chief — Edward Vulliamy
1726 M St. N.W., Ste. 700, Washington, DC 20036; tel (202) 467-4460; fax (202) 467-4458
Freelance — Timothy Cornwell
Scotland On Sunday — 1901 Columbia Rd. N.W., Ste. 703, Washington, DC 20009; tel (202) 462-8232; fax (202) 462-8232
Correspondent — Jamie Dettmer
Scotsman Publications — PO Box 25521, Washington, DC 20007-8521; tel (202) 363-4850; fax (202) 364-1070
Correspondent — Colin Waugh
The Sun — 2039 New Hampshire Ave. N.W., Ste. 103, Washington, DC 20009; tel (202) 289-1632
Correspondent — Ross Mark
Sunday Telegraph — 1331 Pennsylvania Ave. N.W., Ste. 904, Washington, DC 20004; tel (202) 628-4823; fax (202) 393-1335
Bureau Chief — Ambrose Evans-Prichard
1010 Vermont Ave. N.W., Ste. 721, Washington, DC 20005; tel (202) 393-5130
Financial Correspondent — James Srodes
Sunday Times of London — 6524 79th St., Cabin John, MD 20818; tel (301) 320-4138; fax (301) 320-3746
Bureau Chief — James Adams
Researcher — Jaimie Seaton
The Times-London — 1040 National Press Bldg., Washington, DC 20045; tel (202) 347-7659; fax (202) 393-3892
Bureau Chief — Martin Fletcher
Correspondent — Ian Brodie
Correspondent — Thomas Rhodes
Today — 414 10th St. S.E., Ste. 512, Washington, DC 20003; tel (202) 546-7231; fax (202) 546-2767
Correspondent — Maggie Hall
Yorkshire Post — 5309 Slipper Ct., Columbia, MD 21045; tel (301) 596-5306; fax (410) 997-0017
Correspondent — William Lowther

URUGUAY

CX8 Radio Sarandi — 5601 Seminary Rd., Ste. 806-N, Falls Church, VA 22041; tel (703) 820-9367; fax (703) 820-3323
Correspondent — Carlos A Banales-Marino

VENEZUELA

El Universal — 4293 Embassy Park Dr. N.W., Washington, DC 20016; tel (202) 966-1024; fax (202) 898-8047
Correspondent — Everett A Bauman
Venpress — 960-A National Press Bldg., Washington, DC 20045; tel (202) 347-5505; fax (202) 347-8327
Correspondent — Delia Linares
Correspondent — Aida Raygada
Welcome — 4319 Ellicott St. N.W., Washington, DC 20016; tel (202) 364-5985; fax (301) 907-9443
Corr. — Jose-Luis Figarotti Jimenez

YEMEN

Al-Thawrah — 2600 Virginia Ave. N.W., Ste. 705, Washington, DC 20037; tel (202) 965-4760; fax (202) 337-2017
Correspondent — Hussein Al-Awadhi

ZAIRE

Le Potentiel — 1511 K St. N.W., Ste. 925, Washington, DC 20005; tel (202) 783-2777; fax (202) 783-2776
Correspondent — Deogratias J Symba

CALIFORNIA CORRESPONDENTS

AUSTRALIA

The Age — 2256 El Contento Dr., Los Angeles, CA 90068; tel (213) 465-8498; fax (213) 654-0863
Correspondent — David Hay
Australian Associated Press — 124 Corbett St., San Francisco, CA 94109; tel (415) 626-2238; fax (415) 553-8679
Correspondent — Andrew Kruger
2168 Carol View Dr., Ste. 114-B, Cardiff, CA 92007; tel (619) 634-1869; fax (619) 634-1869
Correspondent — Dale Paget
Australian Broadcasting Co. — 1941 Lyon St., San Francisco, CA 94115; tel (415) 928-7385; fax (415) 928-7385
Bureau Chief — Phil Hay
Australian Broadcasting Corp. — 124 Corbett St., San Francisco, CA 94109; tel (415) 626-2238; fax (415) 553-8679
Correspondent — Andrew Kruger
Australian Financial Review — 1941 Lyon St., San Francisco, CA 94115; tel (415) 928-7385; fax (415) 928-7385
Bureau Chief — Phil Hay
Australian Women's Day — PO Box 5137, Sherman Oaks, CA 91403; tel (818) 986-3248
Correspondent — Peter McDonald
Bulletin — 2256 El Contento Dr., Los Angeles, CA 90068; tel (213) 465-8498; fax (213) 654-0863
Correspondent — David Hay
Channel 7 Australia — 10100 Santa Monica Blvd., Ste. 2060, Los Angeles, CA 90067; tel (310) 553-3345; fax (310) 553-4812
Bureau Chief — Paul Marshall
3440 Motor Ave., Los Angeles, CA 90034; tel (310) 287-3800; fax (310) 287-3808
Correspondent — Tony Coghlan
Channel 9 Australia — 6255 Sunset Blvd., Ste. 1500, Los Angeles, CA 90028; tel (213) 461-3853; fax (213) 462-4849
Bureau Chief — Mark Burrows
Correspondent — Nick McCallum
Currie News Network — PO Box 4096, Glendale, CA 91222; tel (818) 243-7770; fax (818) 240-2222
Correspondent — Gordon Currie
Elle/Blitz — 465 S. Detroit St., Apt. 306, Los Angeles, CA 90036; tel (213) 939-6770; fax (213) 938-8380
Correspondent — Alexander McGregor
International Features — PO Box 987, Malibu, CA 90265; tel (310) 457-2996
Correspondent — Colin Dangaard
MacQuarie Network — 68140 Alva Ct., Cathedral City, CA 92234; tel (619) 325-6675
Correspondent — Richard Arnold
Melbourne Age — 1941 Lyon St., San Francisco, CA 94115; tel (415) 928-7385; fax (415) 928-7385
Bureau Chief — Phil Hay
Melbourne Herald — 2256 El Contento Dr., Los Angeles, CA 90068; tel (213) 465-8498; fax (213) 654-0863
Correspondent — David Hay
Network 10 Australia — 3440 Motor Ave., Los Angeles, CA 90034; tel (310) 287-3800; fax (310) 287-3808
Correspondent — Andrew Warne
Correspondent — Ken Burslem
News Limited & Times Newspapers — 938 18th St., Hermosa Beach, CA 90254; tel (310) 376-8041; fax (310) 372-9070
Bureau Chief — Dan McDonnell
Radio Central News — 866 Oneonta Dr., Los Angeles, CA 90065; tel (213) 256-3625
News Director — James Thompson
Southdown Press — 3640 Cardiff Ave., Ste. 107, Los Angeles, CA 90034; tel (310) 842-9450
Correspondent — Jenny Cooney
Sydney Herald/Time Out — 465 S. Detroit Ave., Ste. 306, Los Angeles, CA 90036; tel (213) 939-6775; fax (213) 938-8380
Correspondent — Alexander McGregor
TV Week — 3640 Cardiff Ave., Ste. 107, Los Angeles, CA 90034; tel (310) 842-9450
Correspondent — Jenny Cooney

AUSTRIA

ORF Austrian Radio & Television — 7100 Hillside Ave., Apt. 602, Hollywood, CA 90046; tel (213) 876-8591; fax (213) 874-3334
Correspondent — Thomas Aigner
Skip/Rex Kurier — 7100 Hillside Ave., Apt. 602, Hollywood, CA 90046; tel (213) 876-8591; fax (213) 874-3334
Correspondent — Thomas Aigner

BANGLADESH

Ananda Bichitra — 11250 Morrison St., Ste. 203, North Hollywood, CA 91601; tel (818) 985-2624; fax (818) 788-9844
Correspondent — Munawar Hosain
Weekly Bichitra — 11250 Morrison St., Ste. 203, North Hollywood, CA 91601; tel (818) 985-2624; fax (818) 788-9844
Correspondent — Munawar Hosain

BELIZE

Beacon — 1769 N. El Cerrito Pl., Ste. 309, Hollywood, CA 90028; tel (213) 876-6098; fax (213) 657-5576
Correspondent — Lowell Staine
Youth Advocate — 1769 N. El Cerrito Pl., Ste. 309, Hollywood, CA 90028; tel (213) 876-6098; fax (213) 657-5576
Correspondent — Lowell Staine

BRAZIL

Corpo 2 Assessoria De Comunicado — 3301 Ocean Park Blvd., Ste. 108, Santa Monica, CA 90405; tel (310) 450-0906; fax (310) 399-1126
Correspondent — Sergio Junqueira Do Lago
Eldorado Radio — 2039 N. Ave. 52, Los Angeles, CA 90042; tel (213) 255-8062; fax (213) 257-3487
Correspondent — Rodney Neves De Mello
Folha De Sao Paulo — 3770 Keystone, Apt. 305, Los Angeles, CA 90034; tel (310) 839-1544; fax (310) 839-1544
Correspondent — Angela Marsiaj
Correspondent — Arthur Ribiero Neto
O Estado De Sao Paulo — 2039 N. Ave. 52, Los Angeles, CA 90042; tel (213) 255-8062; fax (213) 257-3487
Correspondent — Rodney Neves De Mello
TV Gazeta & Radio Sidade — 1010 Spaulding Ave., Ste. 3, West Hollywood, CA 90046; tel (213) 650-2824; fax (213) 650-7425
Correspondent — Roberto Lestinge

BULGARIA

Demokratsia — 18333 Algiers St., Northridge, CA 91324; tel (818) 360-5200; fax (818) 360-5200
Correspondent — Marin V Pundeff

CANADA

Canadian Broadcasting Corp. — 2016 Redesdale Ave., Los Angeles, CA 90039; tel (213) 662-0253
Correspondent — Ann Gregor
PO Box 34219, Los Angeles, CA 90034; tel (310) 204-2262; fax (310) 204-0329
Correspondent — Michael Binstock
Macleans Magazine — 2016 Redesdale Ave., Los Angeles, CA 90039; tel (213) 662-0253
Correspondent — Ann Gregor
Vancouver Sun — 632 1/2 Naranja Dr., Glendale, CA 91205; tel (310) 276-9882
Correspondent — Tom Unger

CHINA

China Television Corp. — 2500 Wilshire Blvd., Ste. 506, Los Angeles, CA 90057; tel (213) 383-9922; fax (213) 383-9875
Correspondent — Xu Chuang Cheng

CROATIA

Slobodna Dalmacija (Split, Croatia) — 1050 Crestview Dr., Ste. 218, Mountain View, CA 94040; tel (415) 969-3707; fax (415) 969-3707
Correspondent — Tomislav Perica

DENMARK

Jyllands-Posten — 9645 Farralone Ave., Chatsworth, CA 91311; tel (818) 718-0460; fax (818) 718-0689
Correspondent — Arne Myggen
Morgenvisen — 9645 Farralone Ave., Chatsworth, CA 91311; tel (818) 718-0460; fax (818) 718-0689
Correspondent — Arne Myggen
Politiken — 813 Rim Crest Dr., Westlake Village, CA 91361; tel (805) 495-3633; fax (805) 495-4173
Correspondent — Ole Grunbaum

EGYPT

Al Ahram — 600 S. Curson St., Ste. 402, Los Angeles, CA 90036; tel (213) 857-0941; fax (213) 857-7084
Correspondent — Soraya Aboul Seoud
El Kawakeb — 12665 Venice Blvd., Ste. 7, Los Angeles, CA 90066
Correspondent — Ibrahim Hassanen
Sabah Bi Khier — 700 E. Harvard St., Ste. 204, Glendale, CA 91205; tel (818) 547-5979
Correspondent — Gamil Youssef
Watani Weekly — 12335 Gorham Ave., Los Angeles, CA 90049; tel (310) 826-3388; fax (310) 820-8480
Correspondent — Mahfouz Doss

FINLAND

Aamulehti/Finnish Broadcasting — 2745 Machado St., Simi Valley, CA 93065; tel (805) 584-9639; fax (805) 584-9749
Photojournalist — Ilona Kanto
Producer — Erkki Kanto
Erkki Kanto Productions — 2745 Machado St., Simi Valley, CA 93065; tel (805) 584-9639; fax (805) 584-9749
Photojournalist — Ilona Kanto
Producer — Erkki Kanto

FRANCE

Agence France Presse — 1543 W. Olympic Blvd., Ste. 525, Los Angeles, CA 90015; tel (213) 383-1744; fax (213) 383-1745
Bureau Chief — Carlos Schiebeck
Photojournalist — Mike Nelson
Air Action — 10338 Eastborne Ave., Westwood, CA 90024; tel (310) 477-4576; fax (310) 477-4576
Photojournalist — Philippe Aimar
Angeli America Inc. — 15000 Burbank Blvd., Ste. 205, Van Nuys, CA 91411; tel (818) 785-7647
Photojournalist — Pablo Grosby
Antenne-2 — 7551 Sunset Blvd., Ste. 202, Los Angeles, CA 90046; tel (213) 969-0113; fax (213) 969-0217
Correspondent — Claude Gaignaire

Copyright ©1996 by the Editor & Publisher Co.

French TV — 1123 N. Flores, Ste. 16, West Hollywood, CA 90069; tel (213) 654-5070; fax (213) 654-5073
Correspondent — Claudine P Mulard

Gamma Liasion — 6606 Sunset Blvd., Ste. 201, Los Angeles, CA 90028; tel (213) 469-2242; fax (213) 469-4924
Bureau Chief — Dia Collins
Photojournalist — Chris Delmas

Impact — 6224 Rockcliff Dr., Los Angeles, CA 90068; tel (213) 466-6060
Correspondent — Jack Tewksbury

Input/Output Productions — 7551 Sunset Blvd., Ste. 202, Los Angeles, CA 90046; tel (213) 969-0113; fax (213) 969-0217
Correspondent — Claude Gaignaire

La Tribune De L'Expansion — 238 Francisco St., San Francisco, CA 94133; tel (415) 391-1489
Correspondent — Jacques Gauchey

Lavaud News Agency — 6224 Rockcliff Dr., Los Angeles, CA 90068; tel (213) 466-6060
Correspondent — Jack Tewksbury

Le Figaro/Le Point — 802 Franklin, Santa Monica, CA 90403; tel (310) 828-2174
Correspondent — Catherine Delapree

Le Journal Francais — PO Box 433, Vista, CA 92083; tel (619) 758-8631
Correspondent — Kitty Morse

Le Monde — 540 Landfair Ave., Ste. 7, Los Angeles, CA 90024; tel (310) 208-8607; fax (310) 208-8607
Correspondent — Regis Navarre

Le Monde/Archi-Cree/Geo — 1123 N. Flores, Ste. 16, West Hollywood, CA 90069; tel (213) 654-5070; fax (213) 654-5073
Correspondent — Claudine P Mulard

Le Parisien — PO Box 433, Vista, CA 92083; tel (619) 758-8631
Correspondent — Kitty Morse

Maison et Jardin — 1123 N. Flores, Ste. 16, West Hollywood, CA 90069; tel (213) 654-5070; fax (213) 654-5073
Correspondent — Claudine P Mulard

Quotidien de Paris — 25414 Malibu Rd., Malibu, CA 90265; tel (310) 456-6536
Correspondent — Pierre Jovanovic

Sipa Press — 10338 Eastborne Ave., Westwood, CA 90024; tel (310) 477-4576; fax (310) 477-4576
Photojournalist — Philippe Aimar
1800 Camden Ave., Los Angeles, CA 90025; tel (310) 444-9010; fax (310) 444-9010
Photojournalist — Catherine LeRoy

Stills Press Agency — 11028 Blix St., Toluca Lake, CA 91602; tel (818) 752-6446; fax (818) 752-4114
Correspondent — Michel Bourguard

Sygma — 213321 Pacific Coast Hwy., Malibu, CA 90265; tel (310) 854-1838; fax (310) 854-1838
Correspondent — Guy-Pierre Bennet
745 N. Genessee, Los Angeles, CA 90046; tel (213) 656-5205; fax (213) 656-5207
Correspondent — Keline Howard
1441 Queens Rd., Los Angeles, CA 90069; tel (213) 656-0453; fax (213) 656-1862
Photojournalist — Christian Simonpietri
1526 Rosalia Rd., Ste. 1, Los Angeles, CA 90027; tel (213) 664-3062; fax (213) 913-0701
Photojournalist — Frank Trapper

Tele K-7 — 12106 Herbert St., Los Angeles, CA 90066; tel (310) 398-7443; fax (310) 398-6774
Correspondent — Laurent Triqueneaux

Tele Loiseur — 12106 Herbert St., Los Angeles, CA 90066; tel (310) 398-7443; fax (310) 398-6774
Correspondent — Laurent Triqueneaux

TF 1/Canal Plus — 7551 Sunset Blvd., Ste. 202, Los Angeles, CA 90046; tel (213) 969-0113; fax (213) 969-0217
Correspondent — Claude Gaignaire

GERMANY

American Television Network Inc. — 8550 Rudnick Ave., West Hills, CA 91304; tel (818) 888-8673; fax (818) 888-2029
Correspondent — Pierre Kandorfer

ARD TV/Radio — 21821 Castlewood Dr., Malibu, CA 90265; tel (310) 456-2298; fax (310) 456-3214
Bureau Chief — Armin Amler
2354 N. Canyon Dr., Los Angeles, CA 90068; tel (213) 467-6664; fax (213) 462-1520
Correspondent — Alexander Von Wechmar
Editorial Asst. — Daniel Dermitzel
460 Greencraig Rd., Los Angeles, CA 90049; tel (310) 476-0305; fax (310) 476-2997
Correspondent — Andrea Von Troschke
68 Lloyd St., San Francisco, CA 94117; tel (415) 864-1740; fax (415) 552-9651
Correspondent — Ingrid Koehler

Austrian Radio & TV — 21821 Castlewood Dr., Malibu, CA 90265; tel (310) 456-2298; fax (310) 456-3214
Bureau Chief — Armin Amler

Bauer Publishing — 15300 Ventura Blvd., Ste. 505, Sherman Oaks, CA 91403; tel (818) 907-1185; fax (818) 907-1565
Correspondent — Edmund A Brettschneider

Bavarian Radio — 7164 Macapa Dr., Hollywood, CA 90068; tel (213) 876-9422; fax (213) 851-9867
Correspondent — Frances Schoenberger

CDF Network — 7164 Macapa Dr., Hollywood, CA 90068; tel (213) 876-9422; fax (213) 851-9867
Correspondent — Frances Schoenberger

Cosmopolitan — 3111 3rd St., Apt. 8, Santa Monica, CA 90405; tel (310) 396-6113; fax (310) 396-6113
Correspondent — Sonja Kochius

CSF Productions Inc. — 5332 Strohm Ave., North Hollywood, CA 91601; tel (818) 509-7999
Correspondent — Christian Sebaldt

Der Spiegel — 7164 Macapa Dr., Hollywood, CA 90068; tel (213) 876-9422; fax (213) 851-9867
Correspondent — Frances Schoenberger

Der Tagespiegel — 1149 S. Sherbourne Dr., Los Angeles, CA 90035; tel (310) 274-5727; fax (310) 285-9728
Correspondent — Christa Piotrowski

Die Bunte — 3797 Lavell Dr., Los Angeles, CA 90065; tel (213) 255-3336; fax (213) 258-0882
Photojournalist — Volker Corell

Die Ganze Woche — 933 Westholme Ave., Los Angeles, CA 90024; tel (310) 279-1468; fax (310) 475-9951
Correspondent — Lisa Trumpler

Enterpress — 4880 Corbin Ave., Tarzana, CA 91356; tel (818) 342-9357; fax (818) 342-0518
Correspondent — Dierk Sinderman

Fernsehwoche (TV Week) — 15300 Ventura Blvd., Ste. 505, Sherman Oaks, CA 91403; tel (818) 907-1185; fax (818) 907-1565
Correspondent — Edmund A Brettschneider

Flug Revue International — 57 Overhill Rd., Orinda, CA 94563; tel (510) 254-0569
Correspondent — Peggy Hillweg

Frankfurter Allgemeine Zeitung — 57 Overhill Rd., Orinda, CA 94563; tel (510) 254-0569
Correspondent — Horst Rademacher

Frankfurter Rundschau — 1149 S. Sherbourne Dr., Los Angeles, CA 90035; tel (310) 274-5727; fax (310) 285-9728
Correspondent — Christa Piotrowski
5432 Janisann St., Culver City, CA 90230
Correspondent — Angela Thomson

Fuer Sie — 933 Westholme Ave., Los Angeles, CA 90024; tel (310) 279-1468; fax (310) 475-9951
Correspondent — Lisa Trumpler

German Bazaar & Vogue — 7164 Macapa Dr., Hollywood, CA 90068; tel (213) 876-9422; fax (213) 851-9867
Correspondent — Frances Schoenberger

German Press Agency-DPA — 1341 Church St., San Francisco, CA 94114; tel (415) 550-8215; fax (415) 550-8758
Correspondent — Gabriele Chwallek

German Radio — PO Box 6427, Beverly Hills, CA 90212; tel (310) 288-1137; fax (310) 843-1478
Correspondent — Henri Zix

Kino Film — 933 Westholme Ave., Los Angeles, CA 90024; tel (310) 279-1468; fax (310) 475-9951
Correspondent — Lisa Trumpler

Neue Presse — 2324 Grenich St., San Francisco, CA 94124; tel (415) 775-7800; fax (415) 775-5009
Correspondent — Werner Kraus

Neue Zuercher Zeitung — 1149 S. Sherbourne Dr., Los Angeles, CA 90035; tel (310) 274-5727; fax (310) 285-9728
Correspondent — Christa Piotrowski

One — 2354 N. Canyon Dr., Los Angeles, CA 90068; tel (213) 467-6664; fax (213) 462-1520
Correspondent — Alexander Von Wechmar

RLI Television — 8550 Rudnick Ave., West Hills, CA 91304; tel (818) 888-8673; fax (818) 888-2029
Correspondent — Pierre Kandorfer

Rufa — 638 Belvedere St., San Francisco, CA 94117; tel (415) 665-1656; fax (415) 665-1659
Correspondent — Barbara Munker

Sat — 2354 N. Canyon Dr., Los Angeles, CA 90068; tel (213) 467-6664; fax (213) 462-1520
Correspondent — Alexander Von Wechmar

Springer Foreign News Service — 1015 Gayley Ave., Ste. 203, Los Angeles, CA 90024; tel (310) 208-5846; fax (310) 824-1898
Bureau Chief — Helmut Voss

Stern — 7164 Macapa Dr., Hollywood, CA 90068; tel (213) 876-9422; fax (213) 851-9867
Correspondent — Frances Schoenberger

Stuttgarter Zeitung — 68 Lloyd St., San Francisco, CA 94117; tel (415) 964-1740; fax (415) 552-9651
Correspondent — Ingrid Koehler

West German Television — 4517 Mary Ellen Ave., Sherman Oaks, CA 91423; tel (818) 985-3838
Correspondent — Manford Lasting

World Media Press Agency — 400 S. Beverly Dr., Ste. 214, Beverly Hills, CA 90212; tel (310) 659-2872; fax (310) 652-5070
Correspondent — John Harris

ZDF-TV — 2354 N. Canyon Dr., Los Angeles, CA 90068; tel (213) 467-6664; fax (213) 462-1520
Correspondent — Alexander Von Wechmar

HONG KONG

Asia Week — PO Box 5385, Beverly Hills, CA 90209; tel (310) 275-2630
Correspondent — Norman Sklarewitz

Cosmorama Cultural Enterprise Co. Ltd. — 2805 Lawndale Dr., Los Angeles, CA 90065; tel (213) 256-8747
Correspondent — William Loh

Imperial Press — PO Box 5385, Beverly Hills, CA 90209; tel (310) 275-2630
Correspondent — Norman Sklarewitz

South China Morning Post — PO Box 49808, Los Angeles, CA 90049; tel (310) 451-1110
Correspondent — Dodi Fromson

INDIA

First Serve Entertainment (FSE) — 5228 Andasol Ave., Encino, CA 91316; tel (818) 907-8481; fax (818) 501-8921
Correspondent — Munish Gupta

Organizer Weekly — 1724 N. Edgemont St., Ste. 311, Los Angeles, CA 90027; tel (213) 663-6397; fax (213) 663-6397
Correspondent — Probir Sarkar

View & News Agency (VANA) — 5228 Andasol Ave., Encino, CA 91316; tel (818) 907-8481; fax (818) 501-8921
Correspondent — Munish Gupta

INTERNATIONAL

Fotos International — 4230 Ben Ave., Studio City, CA 91604; tel (818) 508-6400; fax (818) 762-2181
Photographer — Max Miller

HDTV News — 917 S. Tremaine Ave., Los Angeles, CA 90119; tel (213) 939-2345
Correspondent — Syd Cassyd

IRELAND

Irish Times — 115 Andover, San Francisco, CA 94110; tel (415) 824-3549; fax (415) 824-3422
Correspondent — Elgy Gillespie

ISRAEL

Ha'aretz — 913 S. Holt Ave., Los Angeles, CA 90035; tel (310) 659-5860
Correspondent — Benjamin Landau

Jerusalem Post — 3700 Beverly Ridge Dr., Sherman Oaks, CA 91423; tel (818) 783-4135; fax (818) 783-4135
Correspondent — Tom Tugend

ITALY

Amica — 3654 Wasatch Ave., Los Angeles, CA 90066; tel (310) 313-0802; fax (310) 391-1232
Correspondent — Silvia Bizio
Correspondent — Carlo Bizio

Cesare Photography — 1018 N. Martel Ave., Los Angeles, CA 90046; tel (310) 842-9914; fax (310) 842-9334
Photojournalist — Cesare Bonazza

Ciak — 2614 Halm Ave., Los Angeles, CA 90034; tel (310) 559-1761; fax (310) 559-2860
Photojournalist — Elisa Leonelli

Corriere Della Sera — 3654 Wasatch Ave., Los Angeles, CA 90066; tel (310) 313-0802; fax (310) 391-1232
Correspondent — Silvia Bizio
Correspondent — Carlo Bizio
9454 Wilshire Blvd., Ste. M-7, Los Angeles, CA 90212; tel (310) 273-1454; fax (310) 273-5349
Correspondent — Claudio Castellacci

Donna Moderna — 6321 S. Mecham Way, Los Angeles, CA 90043; tel (213) 296-4962; fax (213) 296-6815
Correspondent — Alessandra Venezia

Epoca — 2614 Halm Ave., Los Angeles, CA 90034; tel (310) 559-1761; fax (310) 559-2860
Photojournalist — Elisa Leonelli

Il Manifesto — 2343 Selby Ave., Los Angeles, CA 90064; tel (310) 474-9911; fax (310) 474-1136
Correspondent — Andrea Rocco

Il Sole/24 Ore — 10568 Blythe Ave., Los Angeles, CA 90064; tel (310) 836-4200; fax (310) 836-8189
Correspondent — Daniela Roveda

Italian News Agency (ANSA) — 10568 Blythe Ave., Los Angeles, CA 90064; tel (310) 836-4200; fax (310) 836-8189
Correspondent — Daniela Roveda
1264 N. Ozeta Terrace, Ste. 101, West Hollywood, CA 90069; tel (310) 652-7120
Correspondent — Ivan Rojas
1890 Clay St., Ste. 1203, San Francisco, CA 90028; tel (415) 775-8094; fax (415) 563-7178
Correspondent — Jorge Brignole

L'Espresso — 3654 Wasatch Ave., Los Angeles, CA 90066; tel (310) 313-0802; fax (310) 391-1232
Correspondent — Silvia Bizio
Correspondent — Carlo Bizio
600 N. Sweetzer, Los Angeles, CA 90048; tel (213) 653-4323; fax (213) 653-3737
Correspondent — Lorenzo Soria

L'Unita — 6321 S. Mecham Way, Los Angeles, CA 90043; tel (213) 296-4962; fax (213) 296-6815
Correspondent — Alessandra Venezia

Man — 3654 Wasatch Ave., Los Angeles, CA 90066; tel (310) 313-0802; fax (310) 391-1232
Correspondent — Silvia Bizio
Correspondent — Carlo Bizio

Marie Claire — 2614 Halm Ave., Los Angeles, CA 90034; tel (310) 559-1761; fax (310) 559-2860
Photojournalist — Elisa Leonelli

Max — 9454 Wilshire Blvd., Ste. M-7, Los Angeles, CA 90212; tel (310) 273-1454; fax (310) 273-5349
Correspondent — Claudio Castellacci

Mega Agency — 1714 N. Wilton Pl., Los Angeles, CA 90028; tel (213) 462-6342; fax (213) 462-7572
Correspondent — Michelle Mattei

Mondo Economico — 10568 Blythe Ave., Los Angeles, CA 90064; tel (310) 836-4200; fax (310) 836-8189
Correspondent — Daniela Roveda

Note — 11550 Kling St., North Hollywood, CA 91602; tel (818) 769-1172
Correspondent — William Donati

Panorama — 6321 S. Mecham Way, Los Angeles, CA 90043; tel (213) 296-4962; fax (213) 296-6815
Correspondent — Alessandra Venezia

Quita Communications — 1925 Century Park E., Ste. 13, Los Angeles, CA 90067; tel (310) 282-8427
Bureau Chief — Silvio Muraglia

Rai Corp. — 1925 Century Park E., Ste. 13, Los Angeles, CA 90067; tel (310) 282-8427; fax (310) 282-8005
Correspondent — Luca Celada
VP/Co-Production — Guido Corso

2001 — 11550 Kling St., North Hollywood, CA 91602; tel (818) 769-1172
Correspondent — William Donati

JAPAN

Asahi Shimbun — 3435 Wilshire Blvd., Ste. 1750, Los Angeles, CA 90010; tel (213) 381-1514; fax (213) 381-1535
Bureau Chief — Hiroshi Sugimoto

VII-30 Foreign correspondents

PO Box 10556, Honolulu, HI 96816; tel (808) 845-2255; fax (808) 737-7702
Correspondent — Koichi Dai
Asahi TV — 11400 W. Olympic Blvd., Ste. 500, Los Angeles, CA 90064; tel (310) 575-8655; fax (310) 575-8806
Bureau Chief — Akira Kawanishi
5031 Pacific Coast Hwy., Ste. 131, Torrance, CA 90505; tel (310) 377-0488; fax (310) 377-7035
Producer — Masahiro Kimura
Asahi Weekly — PO Box 930, Beverly Hills, CA 90213; tel (310) 276-8884; fax (310) 276-5349
Photographer — Chika Kujiraoka
26710 Menominee Pl., Palos Verdes, CA 97274; tel (310) 378-3791; fax (310) 378-5451
Photojournalist — Tatsuo Kurihara
Focus — 12021 Wilshire Blvd., Ste. 421, Los Angeles, CA 90025; tel (310) 474-6348; fax (310) 474-6378
Correspondent — Alan Shadrake
1621 Via Zurita, Palos Verdes, CA 90274; tel (310) 375-6514; fax (310) 375-7406
Correspondent — Naonori Kohira
1031 Leavenworth St., Apt. 10, San Francisco, CA 94109; tel (415) 474-3854; fax (415) 474-1264
Photojournalist — Marie Ueda
Fujisankei Communications Int'l. Inc. — 2049 Century Park E., Ste. 2720, Los Angeles, CA 90067; tel (310) 553-2202; fax (310) 553-2042
Correspondent — Katsuyoshi Shoji
Exec. VP — Masaru Kakutani
Hotai Video Productions Inc. — 1106 Goodman Ave., Redondo Beach, CA 90278; tel (310) 798-5159; fax (310) 798-9175
Correspondent — Kazumi Hotai
Japan International Network — 5031 Pacific Coast Hwy., Ste. 131, Torrance, CA 90505; tel (310) 377-0488; fax (310) 377-7035
Producer — Masahiro Kimura
Japan Magazines — 635 Arden Ave., Glendale, CA 91202; tel (818) 507-0876; fax (818) 549-0440
Correspondent — Mitzi Fukuda
Japan Press Bureau — 244 S. San Pedro St., Ste. 303, Los Angeles, CA 90012; tel (213) 620-1512; fax (213) 620-1516
Correspondent — Yuji Toyama
Jiji Press-Los Angeles — 800 W. 6th St., Ste. 800, Los Angeles, CA 90017; tel (213) 488-0958; fax (213) 488-1319
Bureau Chief — Shigebumi Sato
14637 Bestor Blvd., Pacific Palisades, CA 90272; tel (310) 454-0735; fax (310) 454-3797
Correspondent — Foumiko Kometani
Jiji Press-San Francisco — 564 Market St., Ste. 418, San Francisco, CA 94104; tel (415) 986-3933; fax (415) 986-6192
Bureau Chief — Mikio Koike
Correspondent — Mike Ukawa
K Z Associates Inc. — 422 Pasadena Ave., Ste. A, Pasadena, CA 91105; tel (818) 793-9311; fax (818) 793-8278
Correspondent — Kaz Ueda
Kodansha — PO Box 930, Beverly Hills, CA 90213; tel (310) 276-8884; fax (310) 276-5349
Photographer — Chika Kujiraoka
Kyodo News Service — 250 E. 1st St., Ste. 1107, Los Angeles, CA 90012; tel (213) 680-9448; fax (213) 680-3547
Bureau Chief — Eiichi Sonobe
Correspondent — Sandy Usui
NHK — 12401 W. Olympic Blvd., Los Angeles, CA 90064; tel (310) 207-0075; fax (310) 207-1735
Bureau Chief — Kenji Kohno
News Director — Kazumi Fujita
438 Calle de Aragon, Redondo Beach, CA 90277; tel (310) 378-8899; fax (310) 378-9899
Correspondent — Eddie Shuji Noguchi
Nihon Keizai Shimbun — 725 S. Figueroa St., Ste. 1515, Los Angeles, CA 90017; tel (213) 955-7480/7482; fax (213) 955-7489
Bureau Chief — Susumu Takiyama
Correspondent — Makiko Ogihara
635 Arden Ave., Glendale, CA 91202; tel (818) 507-0876; fax (818) 549-0440
Correspondent — Mitzi Fukuda
Nikkan Kogyo Shimbun (Industrial News) — 611 W. 6th St., Ste. 3201, Los Angeles, CA 90017; tel (213) 623-2927; fax (213) 623-5898
Correspondent — Etsuji Nakamura
Nikkan Sports — PO Box 930, Beverly Hills, CA 90213; tel (310) 276-8884; fax (310) 276-5349
Photographer — Chika Kujiraoka
Nippon Television (NTVIC) — 3000 W. Alameda St., Ste. 4202, Burbank, CA 91523; tel (818) 954-0288; fax (818) 954-9281
Correspondent — Katsundo Enomoto
Pan Asian Newspaper Alliance — 707-B E. Elk St., Glendale, CA 91205; tel (818) 549-9591; fax (818) 549-9757
Correspondent — Kenjiro Kitamura
Sankei Shimbun — 2049 Century Park E., Ste. 2720, Los Angeles, CA 90067; tel (310) 553-2614; fax (310) 553-1014
Bureau Chief — Masayuki Takayama
Sekai Nippo — c/o One Way Productions, 432 Norton Ave., Ste. 110, Los Angeles, CA 90020; tel (213) 384-9790; fax (213) 384-9790
Correspondent — Takefumi Miyagi
Tokyo Broadcasting System — 6290 Sunset Blvd., Ste. 1414, Los Angeles, CA 90028; tel (213) 466-7155; fax (213) 466-7246
Bureau Chief — Shinsuke Tanaka
Editoral Asst. — Donna Glassford
707-B E. Elk St., Glendale, CA 91205; tel (818) 549-9591; fax (818) 549-9757
Correspondent — Kenjiro Kitamura
Tokyo Shimbun — 14637 Bestor Blvd., Pacific Palisades, CA 90272; tel (310) 454-0735; fax (310) 454-3797
Correspondent — Foumiko Kometani
US-Japan Business News — 256 S. Los Angeles St., Los Angeles, CA 90012; tel (213) 626-5001; fax (213) 613-1187
Correspondent — Mitsuko Yoshimoto
Weekly Shincho — 1621 Via Zurita, Palos Verdes, CA 90274; tel (310) 375-6514; fax (310) 375-7406
Correspondent — Naonori Kohira
Yomiuri Shimbun — 601 S. Figueroa St., Ste. 4650, Los Angeles, CA 90017; tel (213) 623-7699; fax (213) 623-5887
Bureau Chief — Itsuki Iwata
Correspondent — Takashi Hatano
Editorial Assistant — Martin Bernard

KOREA

Korea Herald Syndicated — 6245 Lindley Ave., Reseda, CA 91335; tel (818) 343-0668
Correspondent — Helena Mar-Elisa
Korean Broadcasting System — 625 S. Kingsley Dr., Los Angeles, CA 90005; tel (213) 382-6700; fax (213) 382-4265
Correspondent — Seung Lee
Korean Broadcasting System (Radio & TV) — 625 S. Kingsley Dr., Los Angeles, CA 90005; tel (213) 382-6759; fax (213) 382-6760
Bureau Chief — Young-Myung Seo
Munhwa Broadcasting System — 5757 Wilshire Blvd., Ste. 260, Los Angeles, CA 90036; tel (213) 934-1042; fax (213) 934-8194
Bureau Chief — Jaeki Ahn
Editorial Assistant — Mie Lee

LATIN AMERICA/ CARIBBEAN

Agencia Estado (Brazil) — 6561 Bluefield Pl., San Diego, CA 92120; tel (619) 265-8162; fax (619) 582-0966
Correspondent — Ivani Vassoler
America Economia (Chile) — 6561 Bluefield Pl., San Diego, CA 92120; tel (619) 265-8162; fax (619) 582-0966
Correspondent — Ivani Vassoler
Radio Eldorado (Brazil) — 6561 Bluefield Pl., San Diego, CA 92120; tel (619) 265-8162; fax (619) 582-0966
Correspondent — Ivani Vassoler

MEXICO

Eco — 2121 Ave. of the Stars, Ste. 2300, Los Angeles, CA 90067; tel (310) 552-6721; fax (310) 286-1716
Bureau Chief — Felix Cortez Camarillo
Correspondent — Rigoberto Cervantes
Correspondent — Mario Lechuga
El Universal — 411 W. 5th St., Ste. 704, Los Angeles, CA 90013; tel (213) 624-9636; fax (213) 629-2127
Corr. — Jose Carlos Ferreyra Hernandez
Excelsior — 721 N. La Brea Ave., Ste. 105, Los Angeles, CA 90038; tel (213) 938-2248; fax (213) 938-2249
Correspondent — Guillermo Espinosa
La Voz De Michoacan — 208 Mardina, West Covina, CA 91791; tel (818) 966-2112; fax (818) 966-1922
Bureau Chief — Alberto Aviles
Notimex News Agency — 523 W. 6th St., Ste. 352, Los Angeles, CA 90014-1004; tel (213) 891-1802; fax (213) 891-1805
Bureau Chief — Rafael Croda
Correspondent — Lourdes Cardenas
Editorial Asst. — Adriana Scheinbaum
Radio Red — 5429 Russell Ave., Ste. 31, Los Angeles, CA 90027; tel (213) 465-2970
Correspondent — Jose Luis Sierra
Stereo Rey — 513 S. Adams St., Ste. 202, Glendale, CA 91205; tel (818) 546-8534; fax (818) 546-8534
Correspondent — Zully Roman
Televiso — Apartado Postal 12, C P 22000, Tijuana, BC, Mexico tel (619) 540-7897; fax (619) 540-7897
News Manager — Gregorio Meraz
Uno Mas Uno — 5429 Russell Ave., Ste. 29, Los Angeles, CA 90027; tel (213) 466-7921
Correspondent — Francisco Mendoza
Xewt Channel 12 — Apartado Postal 12, C P 22000, Tijuana, BC, Mexico tel (619) 540-7897; fax (619) 540-7897
News Manager — Gregorio Meraz

MOROCCO

Le Liberal — PO Box 433, Vista, CA 92083; tel (619) 758-8631
Correspondent — Kitty Morse

NETHERLANDS

Daily Telegraph — 4410 Yosemite, Los Angeles, CA 90065; tel (213) 255-7246; fax (213) 255-7246
Photojournalist — Joe Freizer
International News Media — PO Box 436, Beverly Hills, CA 90213; tel (310) 472-8224
Photojournalist — Conrad Collette
Panorama — PO Box 436, Beverly Hills, CA 90213; tel (310) 472-8224
Photojournalist — Conrad Collette
Prive — 4410 Yosemite, Los Angeles, Ca 90065; tel (213) 255-7246; fax (213) 255-7246
Photojournalist — Joe Freizer
Veronica Broadcasting Organization — 2307 Ocean Ave., Ste. 208, Santa Monica, CA 90405; tel (310) 399-1101
Correspondent — Liliane Pelzman
Volkskrant — 4060 Tilden Ave., Culver City, CA 90232; tel (310) 836-0404; fax (310) 836-0101
Correspondent — Patricia Braun
VPRO-TV — 4060 Tilden Ave., Culver City, CA 90232; tel (310) 836-0404; fax (310) 836-0101
Correspondent — Patricia Braun
Weekend — PO Box 436, Beverly Hills, CA 90213; tel (310) 472-8224
Photojournalist — Conrad Collette

NEW ZEALAND

New Zealand Radio — 2168 Carol View Dr., Ste. 114-B, Cardiff, CA 92007; tel (619) 634-1869; fax (619) 634-1869
Correspondent — Dale Paget

NIGERIA

Network Nigeria (Freelance) — PO Box 8223, Los Angeles, CA 90008; tel (213) 734-9848
Correspondent — Stella Okereke
Newswatch — 19408 Leon Circle, Cerritos, CA 90701; tel (818) 982-1653
Correspondent — Ben Edokpayi

NORWAY

Verdens Gang — 9645 W. Olympic Blvd., Beverly Hills, CA 90212; tel (310) 557-3062; fax (310) 557-0131
Correspondent — Aud Berggren

PAKISTAN

Daily Jang — 7322 Rampart Ln., La Palma, CA 90623; tel (714) 994-4995; fax (310) 861-6468
Correspondent — Mohammad Asif

PHILIPPINES

Manila Globe/Star — 8055 Willow Glen Rd., Los Angeles, CA 90046; tel (213) 650-6328; fax (213) 650-7349
Correspondent — Henry Von Seyfried
Philippine Journal — 8055 Willow Glen Rd., Los Angeles, CA 90046; tel (213) 650-6328; fax (213) 650-7349
Correspondent — Henry Von Seyfried
Philippines News Agency (PNA) — 531 E. 238th St., Carson, CA 90745; tel (310) 522-0508; fax (310) 522-0170
Correspondent — Teddy Cecilio

PORTUGAL

K — 2029 1/2 Ivar Ave., Hollywood, CA 90068; tel (213) 962-7390
Correspondent — Rui Henriques Coimbra

RUSSIA

Itar-Russian News Agency (TASS) — 1390 Market St., 1224 Fox Plaza, San Francisco, CA 94102; tel (415) 626-1434; fax (415) 626-3774
Correspondent — Gennady Shishkin
Ostankino Broadcasting Co. — 531 Noriega St., San Francisco, CA 94122; tel (415) 731-1015; fax (415) 731-4164
Correspondent — Michael Taratuta

SERBIA & MONTENEGRO

Borba — 971 Pacific Ave., Ste. 3, San Francisco, CA 94133; tel (415) 391-7100; fax (415) 391-1913
Correspondent — Serge Vejvoda
Radio Beograd — 971 Pacific Ave., Ste. 3, San Francisco, CA 94133; tel (415) 391-7100; fax (415) 391-1913
Correspondent — Serge Vejvoda

SOUTH AFRICA

Argus — 6829 McLennan Ave., Van Nuys, CA 91406; tel (818) 782-6074; fax (213) 657-5576
Correspondent — Philip Berk
Argus Newspapers — 1416 Broadway, Ste. 2, San Francisco, CA 94109; tel (415) 775-1985; fax (415) 474-1985
Correspondent — Ros Davidson

SWEDEN

Aftenbladet — 930 Palm Ave., Ste. 420, Los Angeles, CA 90069; tel (310) 657-4687; fax (310) 659-8273
Correspondent — Annchi Erikes
Aftonbladet — 918 N. Hayvenhurst Dr., Ste. 211, West Hollywood, CA 90046; tel (213) 650-1870; fax (213) 650-1870
Correspondent — Magnus Sundholm
Elektronikvarlden — 1221 Horn Ave., West Hollywood, CA 90069; tel (310) 657-8686; fax (213) 851-1641
Correspondent — Thor-Bjorn Hansson
Expressen — 1221 Horn Ave., West Hollywood, CA 90069; tel (310) 657-8686; fax (213) 851-1641
Correspondent — Thor-Bjorn Hansson
930 Palm Ave., Ste. 420, Los Angeles, CA 90069; tel (310) 657-4687; fax (310) 659-8273
Correspondent — Annchi Erikes
3312 Montana Ave., Santa Monica, CA 90403; tel (310) 828-0619; fax (310) 828-2415
Photographer — Kenneth Johansson
Morra Vasterbotten — 1934 12th St., Ste. 6, Santa Monica, CA 90404; tel (213) 301-8046
Photographer — Anna Fuhrman
Radio Sweden — 529 Garfield Ave., South Pasadena, CA 91030; tel (818) 799-6784; fax (818) 441-6498
Correspondent — Claes Andreasson
Correspondent — Kristina Hjelmgren
Sanomat Corp. — 3312 Montana Ave., Santa Monica, CA 90403; tel (310) 828-0619; fax (310) 828-2415
Photographer — Kenneth Johansson
Swedish Television — 1221 Horn Ave., West Hollywood, CA 90069; tel (310) 657-8686; fax (213) 851-1641
Correspondent — Thor-Bjorn Hansson
815 Lachman Ln., Pacific Palisades, CA 90272; tel (310) 459-9326; fax (310) 459-9417
Correspondent — Jan-Olaf Fritze
Teknik — 529 Garfield Ave., South Pasadena, CA 91030; tel (818) 799-6784; fax (818) 441-6498
Correspondent — Claes Andreasson
Correspondent — Kristina Hjelmgren

Copyright ©1996 by the Editor & Publisher Co.

Veckorevyn — 2301 Roscomore Rd., Ste. 11, Los Angeles, CA 90077; tel (310) 476-1079
Correspondent — Vivi-Ann Anderson

SWITZERLAND

Cash — 9951 Robbins Dr., Ste. C, Beverly Hills, CA 90212; tel (310) 557-2648; fax (310) 557-9042
Correspondent — Helene Laube
Film Demnaethst — 933 Westholme Ave., Los Angeles, CA 90024; tel (310) 279-1468; fax (310) 475-9951
Correspondent — Lisa Trumpler
Gong Publishing Co. — 247 S. Beverly Dr., Ste. 201, Beverly Hills, CA 90212; tel (310) 859-7024; fax (310) 859-7257
Bureau Chief — Claus Preute
L'Illustre' Weekly — 9951 Robbins Dr., Ste. C, Beverly Hills, CA 90212; tel (310) 557-2648; fax (310) 557-9042
Correspondent — Christophe Rasch
Sonntagsblick — 446 S. Lapeer Dr., Beverly Hills, CA 90211; tel (310) 271-0371; fax (310) 271-0371
Photographer — Marcel Noecker
Swiss Broadcasting Corp. — 9951 Robbins Dr., Ste. C, Beverly Hills, CA 90212; tel (310) 557-2648; fax (310) 557-9042
Correspondent — Christophe Rasch
Swiss Radio/TV — 21821 Castlewood Dr., Malibu, CA 90265; tel (310) 456-2298; fax (310) 456-3214
Bureau Chief — Armin Amler

TAIWAN

Central News Agency — 209 San Miguel Dr., Arcadia, CA 91006; tel (818) 446-6756; fax (818) 446-9058
Correspondent — Chung-tze Liu

THAILAND

Thai International News Agency — 2730 W. Burbank Blvd., Burbank, CA 91505; tel (818) 567-0169; fax (818) 567-0169
Correspondent — Art Kruaprasert
Thai Rath News — 2730 W. Burbank Blvd., Burbank, CA 91505; tel (818) 567-0169; fax (818) 567-0169
Correspondent — Art Kruaprasert

UNITED KINGDOM

BBC — 3000 W. Alameda Ave., Ste. 4227, Burbank, CA 91523; tel (818) 840-2958; fax (818) 840-4693
Correspondent — Richard Wortmann
5070 Woodley Ave., Encino, CA 91436; tel (818) 905-1660; fax (818) 905-1662
Correspondent — Mandy Cunningham
BBC Publications — 3141 Ellington Dr., Hollywood, CA 90068; tel (213) 851-5715
Correspondent — Sylvia Norris
BBC Radio Scotland — 1416 Broadway, Ste. 2, San Francisco, CA 94109; tel (415) 775-1985; fax (415) 474-1985
Correspondent — Ros Davidson
British Weekly — 12021 Wilshire Blvd., Ste. 421, Los Angeles, CA 90025; tel (310) 474-6348; fax (310) 474-6378
Correspondent — Alan Shadrake
1235 Hayvenhurst Dr., Ste. 5, West Hollywood, CA 90046; tel (213) 654-6651
Correspondent — Brendan Bourne
21724 Ventura Blvd., Ste. 312, Woodland Hills, CA 91364; tel (818) 340-9572; fax (818) 340-9679
Correspondent — Ian Markham-Smith
3141 Ellington Dr., Hollywood, CA 90068; tel (213) 851-5715
Correspondent — Sylvia Norris
Daily Express — 18928 Pasadero Dr., Tarzana, CA 91356; tel (818) 996-0180; fax (818) 996-0250
Correspondent — Douglas Thompson
4601 Lakewood Ave., Woodland Hills, CA 91308; tel (818) 347-8294; fax (818) 884-2505
Photojournalist — Paul Harris
Daily Mirror-London — 107 N. Lucerne Blvd., Los Angeles, CA 90004; tel (213) 462-3342; fax (213) 462-3344
Correspondent — Paul Smith
Daily Star — Woodland Hills, CA 91364; tel (818) 999-2619; fax (818) 999-4579
Correspondent — Terry Willows
Daily Telegraph — 1330 Pine St., Santa Monica, CA 90405; tel (310) 450-4026; fax (310) 450-9703
Correspondent — John Hiscock

Economist — c/o Los Angeles Times, Times Mirror Sq., Los Angeles, CA 90053; tel (213) 237-4373; fax (310) 822-0974
Correspondent — Nick Valery
The European — 1743 Miramar Dr., Ventura, CA 93001; tel (805) 648-2182; fax (805) 648-3398
Correspondent — Ivor Davis
Financial Times — 1487 Tarrytown, San Mateo, CA 94402; tel (415) 574-4396; fax (415) 570-5164
Correspondent — Louise Kehoe
Guardian-London — 9612 Glacier Gulch Rd., Weldon, CA 93283; tel (619) 378-3183; fax (619) 378-2604
Correspondent — Christopher Reed
The Independent — 5070 Woodley Ave., Encino, CA 91436; tel (818) 905-1660; fax (818) 905-1662
Correspondent — Phil Reeves
IPC Magazine International — 1850 Camden Ave., Los Angeles, CA 90025; tel (310) 477-4870; fax (310) 657-5576
Photographer — Jean Cummings
London Evening Standard — PO Box 5137, Sherman Oaks, CA 91403; tel (818) 986-3248
Correspondent — Peter McDonald
The Mail On Sunday — 1235 Hayvenhurst Dr., Ste. 5, West Hollywood, CA 90046; tel (213) 654-6551
Correspondent — Brendan Bourne
National Daily — 7357 Woodrow Wilson Dr., Hollywood, CA 90046; tel (213) 851-8250
Correspondent — William Cash
Newswire — 1330 Pine St., Santa Monica, CA 90405; tel (310) 450-4026; fax (310) 450-9703
Correspondent — John Hiscock
Observer — 9612 Glacier Gulch Rd., Weldon, CA 93283; tel (619) 378-3183; fax (619) 378-2604
Correspondent — Christopher Reed
Option — 902 Palms Blvd., Venice, CA 90291; tel (310) 823-3268
Correspondent — Gabrielle Donnelly
Radio Time — 4601 Larkwood Ave., Woodland Hills, CA 91308; tel (818) 347-8294; fax (818) 884-2505
Photojournalist — Paul Harris
Reuters-Los Angeles — 445 S. Figueroa St., Ste. 450, Los Angeles, CA 90071; tel (213) 380-2014; fax (213) 622-0056
Bureau Chief — Matt Spetalnick
Correspondent — Mike Miller
Reuters-San Francisco — 153 Kearny St., Ste. 301, San Francisco, CA 94108; tel (415) 677-2541; fax (415) 986-5147
Bureau Chief — Adrian Croft
Correspondent — Russ Blinch
1416 Broadway, Ste. 2, San Francisco, CA 94109; tel (415) 775-1985; fax (415) 474-1985
Correspondent — Ros Davidson
3000 W. Alameda Ave., Ste. 4227, Burbank, CA 91523; tel (818) 840-2958; fax (818) 840-4693
Correspondent — Richard Wortmann
Scope — 3141 Ellington Dr., Hollywood, CA 90068; tel (213) 851-5715
Correspondent — Sylvia Norris
Scotsman — 401 Washington Ave., Apt. 201, Santa Monica, CA 90403; tel (310) 394-4025; fax (805) 965-4898
Correspondent — Sophia Wyatt
Spectator — 308 Westwood Plaza, Kerckhoff Hall, Los Angeles, CA 90024; tel (310) 825-2859; fax (310) 206-0906
Correspondent — Frances Fernandes
Sunday People — 21724 Ventura Blvd., Ste. 312, Woodland Hills, CA 91364; tel (818) 340-9572; fax (818) 340-9679
Correspondent — Ian Markham-Smith
Sunday Times — 820 S. Detroit St., Los Angeles, CA 90036; tel (213) 936-6347; fax (213) 939-1698
Bureau Chief — Sam Kiley
172 S. Sycamore St., Los Angeles, CA 90036; tel (213) 938-7038; fax (213) 938-1952
Correspondent — Sue Ellicott
The Times — 7357 Woodrow Wilson Dr., Hollywood, CA 90046; tel (213) 851-8250
Correspondent — William Cash
The Times of London — 1743 Miramar Dr., Ventura, CA 93001; tel (805) 648-2182; fax (805) 648-3398
Correspondent — Ivor Davis
2439 Chelsea Pl., Santa Monica, CA 90404; tel (310) 829-5216
Correspondent — Ian Kimbery
Transworld Syndicate — 3141 Ellington Dr., Hollywood, CA 90068; tel (213) 851-5715
Correspondent — Sylvia Norris

Visnews — 3000 W. Alameda Ave., Ste. 4227, Burbank, CA 91523; tel (818) 840-2958; fax (818) 840-4693
Correspondent — Richard Wortmann
Westmail — 401 Washington Ave., Apt. 201, Santa Monica, CA 90403; tel (310) 394-4025; fax (805) 965-4898
Correspondent — Sophia Wyatt
Women's Own — 4601 Larkwood Ave., Woodland Hills, CA 91308; tel (818) 347-8294; fax (818) 884-2505
Photojournalist — Paul Harris

CHICAGO CORRESPONDENTS

AUSTRALIA

BBC Freelance Radio — 3813 N. Alta Vista Terrace, Chicago, IL 60613; tel (312) 296-9590; fax (708) 491-8150
Correspondent — Judy Kampfner

CANADA

Canadian Press Wire Service — 700 Hinman Ave., Evanston, IL 60202; tel (708) 864-3183
Correspondent — Mathew C Carlson

CHINA

China Press — 535 W. 31st St., Ste. 101, Chicago, IL 60616; tel (312) 326-2223; fax (312) 326-2045
Correspondent — Sam Chin
China Times News — 1912 Chatfield Rd., Lisle, IL 60532; tel (708) 983-9166; fax (708) 416-0210
Columnist — Charles C S Yin
Mid-America Chinese TV — 1900 S. Michigan Ave., Chicago, IL 60616; tel (312) 949-0888; fax (312) 949-0800
Vice Editor-in-Chief — Wenbo Li

CZECH REPUBLIC

Czechoslovak Daily Herald — 6426 W. Cermak Rd., Berwyn, IL 60402; tel (708) 749-1891; fax (708) 749-1935
Midwest Bureau Chief — Denni Hlasatel

FRANCE

Agence France Presse (AFP) — 712 N. Wells St., Chicago, IL 60610; tel (312) 337-0909; fax (312) 337-0908
Midwest Bureau Chief — Chris Wilkins
Photographer — Eugene Garcia

GERMANY

German Media Group — 389 Duane St., Ste. 302, Glen Ellyn, IL 60137-4389; tel (708) 858-8085; fax (708) 858-3087
Managing Director — Bert Lachner

INDIA

New India — 6157 N. Sheridan Rd., Chicago, IL 60660; tel (312) 561-3876; fax (312) 338-5427
Bureau Chief — Nand Kapoor

ITALY

Manifesto — 5334 S. Greenwood Ave., Chicago, IL 60615; tel (312) 643-7481
Freelance — Anna Maria Torriglia

JAPAN

Chicago Tokyo Television — 225 N. Michigan Ave., Ste. 230, Chicago, IL 60601; tel (312) 565-0022
General Manager — Takako Yoshihara
Freelance — 3950 N. Lake Shore Dr., Ste. 1008, Chicago, IL 60613; tel (312) 935-1658; fax (312) 935-1658
Freelance — Koji Fukuma
Jiji Press — 175 W. Jackson Blvd., Ste. A-655, Chicago, IL 60604; tel (312) 427-5865
Correspondent — Naoto Takamura
Nihon Keizai Shimbun — 15 Wacker Dr., Chicago, IL 60606; tel (312) 726-9470; fax (312) 726-3610
Bureau Chief — Hiroshi Yamoto

Foreign correspondents VII-31

1 S. Wacker Dr., Ste. 2790, Chicago, IL 60606; tel (312) 726-9478; fax (312) 726-3610
Correspondent — Yoko Noge
Correspondent — Kyoko Imagawa
Yomiuri Shimbun — 435 N. Michigan Ave., Ste. 952, Rm. 930, Chicago, IL 60611; tel (312) 836-1046
Bureau Chief — Taiji Fujimura

MEXICO

Eco International News — 4306 N. Lincoln Ave., Chicago, IL 60618; tel (312) 463-7700; fax (312) 463-7720
President — Juan Gil
El Norte — 732 W. Bittersweet Pl., Chicago, IL 60613; tel (312) 296-1949
Correspondent — Martha Vigil
Correspondent — Norberto Zuarez
Notimex — 715 W. Belden 3-N, Chicago, IL 60614; tel (312) 975-6684; fax (312) 975-6687
Correspondent — Jose Luis Ruiz Zarate

NETHERLANDS

Tros Dutch Public TV — 6237 N. Wayne Ave., Chicago, IL 60660; tel (312) 937-6220
Correspondent — Richard Jansen

NORWAY

Norwegian Press — 882 Hillside Ave., Glen Ellyn, IL 60137; tel (708) 790-0805; fax (708) 790-0819
Correspondent — Henrik Faerevaag

PHILIPPINES

Philippine News — 2642 W. Foster B-3, Chicago, IL 60625; tel (312) 989-3618
Correspondent — Plaridel Seneris

POLAND

Pollvision/Morning Voice — 3656 W. Belmont Ave., Chicago, IL 60618; tel (312) 558-6300; fax (312) 267-4913
Correspondent — Mariola Waktor

SCANDINAVIA

The Sun/Scandinavia USA News — 637 S. Waukegan Rd., Lake Forest, IL 60045; tel (708) 295-5386; fax (708) 295-6402
Publisher — Karen Gagen

TAIWAN

Central News Agency Inc. — 2626 Laurel Ln., Wilmette, IL 60091; tel (708) 256-7225
Correspondent — Wan-Lai Lee
Taiwan News Agency — 180 N. Stetson Ave., 58th Fl., Chicago, IL 60601; tel (312) 616-0100
Correspondent — Raymond Mou

TURKEY

Hurriyet — 9205 N. Potter Rd., Ste. 2-A, Des Plaines, IL 60016; tel (312) 237-3855; fax (312) 237-4729
Correspondent — Canan Korkmaz-Donmez
Milliyet — 6140 N. Central Park Ave., Chicago, IL 60659; tel (312) 583-5559; fax (312) 583-0731
Correspondent — Kubilay Celik
Turkish Radio & TV — 2146 W. Windsor Ave., Chicago, IL 60625; tel (312) 728-1578; fax (312) 728-3614
Correspondent — Yucel Donmez

UNITED KINGDOM

Economist — 360 N. Michigan Ave., Ste. 801, Chicago, IL 60601; tel (312) 849-3115; fax (312) 704-0448
Correspondent — Edward Field
Financial Times of London — 1555 N. Dearborn Pkwy., Apt 20-D, Chicago, IL 60610; tel (312) 587-3325; fax (312) 587-3326
Journalist — Laurie Morse

Copyright ©1996 by the Editor & Publisher Co.

FOREIGN PRESS ASSOCIATION
DIRECTORY OF MEMBERS

OFFICERS
President — Santi Visalli, Italy
Vice Pres. — Maria Gonzalez-Sieira, Mexico
General Secretary — Gabrielle Barth, Germany
Asst. Gen. Sec. — Gabriel Plesea, Romania
Treasurer — Karl Grun, Germany
Asst. Treasurer — Gianni Capra, Italy

ACTIVE MEMBERS

ALBANIA
FINORA, JOSEPH (Illyria) — 2321 Hughes Ave., Bronx, NY 10458; Tel. (718) 220-2000

ARGENTINA
ABRAHAM-LARENA, JUAN ALBERTO (Radio America) — 55 E. 87th St., Apt. 8L, New York, NY 10128; Tel. (212) 772-8900
BEVILACQUA, CLAUDIO (Cablevision TV) — 382 3rd Ave., Apt. 15A, New York, NY 10016; Tel. (212) 696-4767
CHISTIK, GABRIELA J (Film Magazine) — 234 W. 27th St., Apt. 6, New York, NY 10001; Tel. (212) 924-1350
DOMINIKA, EWA (La Nacion Cronista) — Florida 1065 7b Capital Federal, Buenos Aires, Argentina 1005; Tel. (541) 790-5863
DUEK, MARCELO JAVIER (DYN) — PO Box 357, Prince St. Sta., New York, NY 10012; Tel. (212) 925-4889
FERCSEY, JOHN (La Presna) — PO Box 4463, Grand Central Sta., New York, NY 10163; Tel. (212) 963-0168
GABOR, ROBERT (Interco Press Group) — 815 16th St., NW, Rm. 705, Washington, DC 20006
MARINO, CARLOS A (America TV) — 382 3rd Ave., Ste. 15A, New York, NY 10016; Tel. (212) 695-4767
MASO, GEORGE (International Press Information Agency) — PO Box 7006, Boca Raton, FL 33431; Tel. (407) 995-9930
PELLECCHI, DR SERGIO (El Economista) — 29 E. 64th St., Ste. 7C New York, NY 10021; Tel. (212) 570-2813
RADONJIC, DUSAN (El Economista) — 29 E. 64th St., New York, NY 10021; Tel. (212) 570-2813
SLEZAK, STEPHAN (Interco Press) — 815 16th St., Ste. 705, Washington, DC 20006
SOCAS, ROBERTO E (La Nacion) — 285 Central Park West, New York, NY 10024; Tel. (212) 724-0760

AUSTRALIA
GILES, FIONA R (Channel Nine News) — 524 W. 57th St., Ste. 4800, New York, NY 10019; Tel. (212) 975-5618
HAVEKES, ANNA-MARYKE (Interiors Magazine) — 25 Mercer St., New York, NY 10013; Tel. (212) 334-1848
KRUGER, ANDREW (Australian Press Agency) — 124 Corbett Ave., San Francisco, CA 94114; Tel. (415) 626-2238
KRUM, SHARON L (News Ltd. of Australia) — 1211 Ave. of the Americas, 2nd Fl., New York, NY 10036; Tel. (212) 819-3310
MCKENNA, JOSEPHINE (News Limited of Australia) — 1211 Ave. of the Americas, 2nd Fl., New York, NY 10036; Tel. (212) 852-7641
SIMUNOVICH, PETER (Herald-Sun) — 524 E. 79th St., Apt. 6A, New York, NY 10021; Tel. (212) 472-7433
YOUNG, MARK GEOFFREY (Worldwide Press Service) — 21 South End Ave., Ste. 437, New York, NY 10280; Tel. (212) 355-5049

AUSTRIA
AMBERGER, MADELEINE H (Profil) — 115 W. 16th St., Rm. 225, New York, NY 10011; Tel. (212) 924-2241
SCHNEIDER, HANS E (Tourist Austria International) — 73 165 Segura Ct., Palm Desert, CA 92260; Tel. (619) 776-9498

BELGIUM
VAN VLIET, NICO J (Freelance) — 160 Florida Hill Rd., Ridgefield, CT 06877; Tel. (203) 431-9395

BRAZIL
BARRANQUEIROS, DIVA POSSATI (Journal Da Bahia) — 108 E. 66th St., Apt. 2B, New York, NY 10021; Tel. (212) 472-2725
FRANCO, VERA (Jornal Do Brasil) — 123 5th Ave., New York, NY 10003; Tel. (212) 799-8292

BULGARIA
CHILINGIROVA, NEDYALKA (Bulgarian Radio) — 241 Central Park West, Apt. 7D, New York, NY 10024; Tel. (212) 787- 3210
PEICINOW, VICTOR (Pressa) — 1255 Park Ave., New York, NY 10029; Tel. (212) 860-1494

CANADA
ALATON, SALEM (Toronto Globe & Mail) — 68 Hillside Dr., Ste. 205, Toronto, ON M4K 2M4; Tel. (416) 696-8555
ARNOLD, DENISE (DIA Communications) — 4154 Riverside Dr., Lilburn, GA 30247; Tel. (404) 717-5858
DORNER, ROBERT C (Dorcom International) — c/o Fischer, 171 E. 84th St., New York, NY 10028; Tel. (212) 570-1766
FARRELL, NAOMI (Freelance Radio) — 321 E. 48th St., Apt. 3A, New York, NY 10017; Tel. (212) 759-7285
FISCHLER, STANLEY I (Hockey News) — 520 W. 110th St., New York, NY 10025; Tel. (212) 749-4152

CARIBBEAN
BEAULIEU, SERGE (Caribbean Network System) — 405 E. 42nd St., Rm. 301, New York, NY 10017; Tel. (212) 888-1745

CHILE
FERRARA, ROGER E (La Estrella Daily) — 303 E. 60th St., Apt. 4S, New York, NY 10022; Tel. (212) 758-5006

CHINA
HONGZE, HE (Peoples Daily of China) — United Nations, C-322, New York, NY 10017; Tel. (212) 963-0511

COLOMBIA
MORA-MASS, ELIZABETH (El Colombiano) — 82-16 166th St., Jamaica, NY 11432; Tel. (718) 380-2116

CZECH REPUBLIC
MAJSTR, JIRI (Czech News Agency) — 40 River Rd., Apt. 19C, Roosevelt Island, NY 10044; Tel. (212) 888-2992
SCHRABAL, JOSEF (Svobodne Slovo) — 549 Riverside Dr., New York, NY 10027; Tel. (212) 663-3987

DENMARK
ALBRECTSEN, BENT (Weekendavisen) — 396 Iris Ln., Winchester, VA 22602; Tel. (703) 877-1881
NIELSEN, ELENA F (Danish Publications) — 1128 E. Lombardy Dr., Deltona, FL 32725; Tel. (407) 860-3569

DOMINICAN REPUBLIC
BASILIS, FEDERICO S (Channel 7 (CIBAO)) — PO Box 770, New York, NY 10036; Tel. (212) 247-1837
GERONIMO, ROBERTO (El Siglo) — 427 Fort Washington Ave., Apt. 6D, New York, NY 10033

EGYPT
EL-BADRY, ESSAM A (Radio Cairo) — Rm. 1760, United Nations, NY 10017; Tel. (212) 963-2059

EUROPE
RIUDAVETS-LEVAN, JEANNE (Freelance Broadcaster) — 301 E. 79th St., Apt. 19B, New York, NY 10021; Tel. (212) 288-4043

FINLAND
INKERI, ELVIA (Finland Publications) — 3500 S. Ocean Blvd., Palm Beach, FL 33480; Tel. (407) 588-4522

ROTHOVIUS-KORHONEN, ANITA (Kaivnuun Sanomat) — 826 43rd St. Apt. 14, Brooklyn, NY 11232; Tel. (718) 435-0500
SIMOLA, LIISA (Ilta Sanomat) — 39 E. 12th St., Apt. 206, New York, NY 10003; Tel. (212) 254-1123

FRANCE
BERNARD, MICHEL (Gamma Presse Images) — 11 E. 26th St., New York, NY 10010; Tel. (212) 447-2510
CARRIL, ANA (France Television) — 338 E. 55th St., Apt. 2B, New York, NY 10022; Tel. (212) 888-6227
DARGENT, MARIE C (Voici) — 39 Great Jones St., Ste. 2, New York, NY 10012; Tel. (212) 387-8321
GORCZYNSKI, RENATA (Kultura Magazine) — 960 Madison Ave., Apt. 5W, New York, NY 10021; Tel. (212) 570-0296
JACQUET-FRANCILLON, J (Le Figaro) — 37, rue du Louvre, Paris, Cedex 02, France 75081; Tel. (331) 233-4400
KAHLER-DANILEVSKY, CHARLOTTE (French Publications) — 165 E. 72nd St., Apt. 12G, New York, NY 10021; Tel. (212) 988-6945
LAFFONT, JEAN-PIERRE (Sygma Photo News) — 322 W. 72nd St., New York, NY 10023; Tel. (212) 787-7831
MILOSZ, CZESLAW (Kultura Magazine) — 978 Grizzly Peak Blvd., Berkeley, CA 94708; Tel. (510) 526-8062
VAN HASSELT, JOHN COPES (Sygma News Agency) — 95 MacDougal St., 3A, New York, NY 10012; Tel. (212) 777-7741

GERMANY
BARTH, GABRELLE (Penthouse Magazine, German Edition) — 1965 Broadway, New York, NY 10023; Tel. (212) 496-6100
BAUER, PETER (Deutsche Presse Agentur) — 30 Garry Rd., Closter, NJ 07624; Tel. (201) 767-3835
CHASEY-CZERNAK, BOHUMIR (German Economic News Service/VWD) — 866 United Nations Plz., Ste. 566, New York, NY 10017; Tel. (212) 838-7440
DITTMANN, CHRISTINA (Bauer Publishing Co.) — 307 Park Pl., Brooklyn, NY 11238; Tel. (718) 622-0065
ECKHARDT, JENS (Handelsblatt) — 26 Puddingstone Rd., Morris Plains, NJ 07950; Tel. (201) 539-8197
ERNST, THOMAS (German Bundeshehr) — Sterngasse 82, Griesheim, Germany 64347; Tel. (61-551-4117)
FEHR, BENEDIKT (Frankfurter Allgemeine Zeitung) — 48 Lockwood Ave., PO Box 615, Old Greenwich, CT 06870; Tel. (203) 698-0856
FOXX, JEFFREY JAY (Bauer Publishing Co.) — 307 Park Pl., Ste. 3, Brooklyn, NY 11238; Tel. (718) 783-2043
GERAGHTY, COLEEN L (German Economic News/VWD) — 866 United Nations Plz., Ste. 566, New York, NY 10017; Tel. (212) 838-7440
GRANITSAS, MARGOT (Hannoversche Allgemeine) — Box 140, RD1, Accord, NY 12404; Tel. (914) 626-3668
GRUN, KARL (Borsen-Zeitung) — 15 Boulderol Rd., Stamford, CT 06903; Tel. (203) 329-0642
GUTSCHER, GABRIELLE (German Economic News Service/VWD) — 866 United Nations Plz., Ste. 566, New York, NY 10017; Tel. (212) 838-7440
JOST, IRMIE M (Springer Foreign News Service) — 565 5th Ave., 8th Fl., New York, NY 10017; Tel. (212) 983-1983
KIND, MONIKA (Esquire Magazine) — 50 E. 42nd St., Ste. 506, New York, NY 10017; Tel. (212) 867-8616
KING, JEANNE (Quick Magazine) — 101-21 75th Rd., Forest Hills, NY 11375; Tel. (718) 261-2355
KOHL, WOLF D (Musik Express/Sounds Magazine) — 7 E. 14th St., Apt. 42D, New York, NY 10003; Tel. (212) 242-6996
LACHMANN, LOTTE B (Der Spiegel) — 115-30 Park Ln., Kew Gardens, NY 11418; Tel. (718) 847-8965
LEBENS-NACOS, BRIGITTE (Neue Ruhrzeitung) — 33 Bingham Cir., Manhasset, NY 11030; Tel. (516) 627-5316

LEDERMANN, INGEBORG (Textil-Wirtschaft) — 83-31 116th St., Kew Gardens, NY 11418; Tel. (718) 846-1990
LIETZMANN, SABINA (Frankfurter Allgemeine Zeitung) — 59 Pierce Ln., West Cornwall, CT 06796; Tel. (203) 672-6861
NISCHK, MICHAEL R A (News Int'l. Service Inc.) — 532 State St., Brooklyn, NY 11217; Tel. (718) 624-7866
RIEHLE, JURGEN (Burda Publications) — 231 E. 14th St., Rm. 4F, New York, NY 10003; Tel. (212) 777-7884
SCHATZSCHNEIDER, LENNART (Guitar World Germany) — 336 W. 17th St., Apt. 3C, New York, NY 10011; Tel. (212) 645-7953
SCHAUMBERGER, BEATRIX (MAX Magazine) — 6 Varick St., Ste. 7B, New York, NY 10013; Tel. (212) 925-1400
SCHIPPRACK, ANNETTE (Focus Magazine/Burda) — 1270 Ave. of the Americas, Ste. 1918, New York, NY 10020; Tel. (212) 757-1100
STEINER, DIETER (Stern Magazine) — 685 3rd Ave., 23rd Fl., New York, NY 10017; Tel. (212) 949-0404
STRICKER, WILLIAM (German Publications) — 131 Riverside Dr., New York, NY 10024; Tel. (212) 874-6949
WRUBEL, ANGELIKA (Der Spiegel) — 516 5th Ave., New York, NY 10036; Tel. (212) 221-7583

GREECE
GEORGIADOU, MIRELLA (Athens News Agency) — c/o Greek Press Office, 601 5th Ave., Ste. 566, New York, NY 10017; Tel. (21 751-8788

HAITI
SANON, JEAN-CLAUDE (Le Nouvelliste) — 596 NW 97th Ave., Plantation, FL 33324; Tel. (305) 476-0343

HONG KONG
MORELLO, TED (Far Eastern Economic Review) — Rm. 310, United Nations, NY 10017; Tel. (212) 963-7134

HUNGARY
CZANYO, ADRIAN (Uj Magyarorszag) — 3330 Esmeralda, Florida Buenos Aries, Argentina
DE SZEKELY, ANDRE (ABC-TV) — XII Hataror Utica 24, Budapest, Hungary
EGRI, GYORGY (Magyar Nemzet) — Uzsoki-Y3/A-4, Budapest, Hungary 1145
VARGA, LASZLO (Hungarian Guardian) — 62-60 99th St., Ste. 1721, Rego Park, NY 11374

INTERNATIONAL
MINTHORN, DAVID H (Associated Press) — 50 Rockefeller Plz., New York, NY 10020; Tel. (212) 621-1657
NIBLEY, ANDREW N (Reuters America) — 1700 Broadway, New York, NY 10019; Tel. (212) 603-3300
TOMPKINS, JOHN S (Reader's Digest Int'l.) — 149 E. 73rd St., New York, NY 10021; Tel. (212) 861-4896

IRELAND
BARRON, PATRICK E (Anner Films) — 49 Drake Rd., Scarsdale, NY 10583; Tel. (914) 725-2878
BYRNE, JOHN (Sunday World) — 47-25 44th St., Woodside, NY 11377; Tel. (718) 361-8167

ISRAEL
AVNI, BENNY (Hadashot) — 303 E. 37th St., Apt. 6K, New York, NY 10016; Tel. (212) 686-7353
BEREZ, ISAAC (Israel Press Photo Service) — 76-05 113th St., Apt. 6D, Forest Hills, NY 11375; Tel. (718) 268-5911
COOPER, ZEV (Freelance) — PO Box 750271, Flushing, NY 11375; Tel. (718) 897-4743
HOS-PELES, ADA (Yedioth Achronoth) — 402 E. 72nd St., Apt. 27, New York, NY 10021; Tel. (212) 517-4345
POKORNY, BRAD (One Country) — 866 United Nations Plz., Ste. 120, New York, NY 10017; Tel. (212) 486-0560

Copyright ©1996 by the Editor & Publisher Co.

WEINGARTEN, MIRIAM H (Ma'ariv Daily) — 40 E 80th St., Apt. 9B, New York, NY 10021; Tel. (212) 737-5843

WIESEL, ELIE (Yedioth Achronoth) — 745 Commonwealth Ave., Boston, MA 02215; Tel. (617) 353-4566

ITALY

BUSCEMI, GIUSEPPE (Notiziario dell'Ambiente) — PO Box 1148, New York, NY 10276; Tel. (212) 254-0562

CALAMANDREI, MAURO (Il Sole) — 121 W. 72nd St., New York, NY 10023; Tel. (212) 874-4661

CAPASSO, MICHELE (RAI Italian TV) — 1350 Ave. of the Americas, New York, NY 10019; Tel. (212) 468-2550

CAPPELLI, JOHN (Il Paese Sera) — Rm. 371, United Nations, NY 10017; Tel. (212) 963-7155

CAPRA, GIANNI (Parliament) — PO Box 455, Radio City Sta., New York, NY 10101

CAVALLINI, MASSIMO (L'Unita) — 424 West End Ave., Apt. 20E, New York, NY 10024; Tel. (212) 724-2625

CAZZANIGA, LUIGI (Tekros Magazine) — 393 W. Broadway, New York, NY 10012; Tel. (212) 219-8567

CERULLO, TONY (RAI Italian TV) — 1350 Ave. of the Americas, New York, NY 10019; Tel. (212) 468-2550

CIAMPA, VENANZIO (RAI Italian TV) — 1350 Ave. of the Americas, New York, NY 10019; Tel. (212) 468-2500

DI BELLA, ANTONIO (RAI) — 1350 Ave. of the Americas, New York, NY 10019; Tel. (212) 468-2566

FARKAS, ALESSANDRA (Corriere Della Sera) — 31 W. 57th St., 4th Fl., New York, NY 10019; Tel. (212) 308-2000

FERRETTI, ANTONIO (Il Gazzettino) — Rm. 360, United Nations, NY 10017; Tel. (212) 688-7334

FIANO, ANDREA (Milano Finanza Class/Dow Jones) — 200 Liberty St., New York, NY 10281; Tel. (212) 416-4106

FICILE, ENZO (Ansa News Agency) — 866 United Nations Plz., Ste. 476, New York, NY 10017; Tel. (212) 319-6802

GALATI, MARIA GRAZIA (Freelance Journalist) — 200 E. 61 St., Apt. 21C, New York, NY 10021; Tel. (212) 758-6708

GALLO, GIUSI (Italian American Multimedia) — 138 Wooster St., New York, NY 10012; Tel. (212) 674-4132

GATTI, CLAUDIO (Europeo Magazine) — 31 W. 57th St., 4th Fl., New York, NY 10019; tel. (212) 308-2000

GIACHETTI, ROMANO (La Republica) — AME Publishing, 740 Broadway, New York, NY 10003; Tel. (212) 470-9701

GINZBERG, SIEGMUND (L'Unita) — 473 Hudson St., New York, NY 10014; Tel. (212) 243-4472

GUAITA, ANNA (Il Messaggero) — 1114 Ave. of the Americas, 33rd Fl., New York, NY 10036; Tel. (212) 719-5340

GUGLIEMO, GIUSEPPE (GR TV) — 1728 Bay Ridge Ave., Brooklyn, NY 11204; Tel. (718) 232-3239

HORN, LEILA (Gambero Rosso) — 5 E. 22nd St., Apt. 30D, New York, NY 10010; Tel. (212) 388-9449

HOWE, ULRIKE (Sportswear International) — Via Forcella 13, Milano, Italy 1-20144

KRAMAR, SILVIA (RTI) — 524 W. 57th St., Ste. 4360, New York, NY 10019; Tel. (212) 246-7750

LEOTTA, IPPOLITO (RTI Italian TV) — 524 W. 57th St., Ste. 4360, New York, NY 10019; Tel. (212) 246-0400

LOCATELLI, STEFANIA (L'Unita) — 473 Hudson St., New York, NY 10014; Tel. (212) 633-0366

MANASSE, ERIC (America Magazine) — 903 Madison Ave., Apt. 3R, New York, NY 10021; Tel. (212) 772-3840

MARIANI, PAOLA (Avvenire) — 235 Lexington Ave., Apt. 9, New York, NY 10016; Tel. (212) 685-4451

MARINO, ALDO (RAI Italian TV & Radio) — 1350 Ave. of the Americas, New York, NY 10019; Tel. (212) 468-2550

MONETTI, NADIA (AREA Agency) — 429 E. 52 St., Apt. 31C, New York, NY 10022; Tel. (212) 371-7699

MORINI, SIMONA (Television Sorrisi e Canzoni) — 757 3rd Ave., Ste. 1906, New York, NY 10017; Tel. (212) 944-1509

OREFICE, GASTONE (RAI Radio & TV) — 1350 Ave. of the Americas, New York, NY 10019; Tel. (212) 468-2500

PACHETTI, RENATO M (RAI Radio & TV) — 1350 Ave. of the Americas, New York, NY 10019; Tel. 468-2501

PEGNA, MASSIMO LOPES (La Gazzetta Dello Sport) — 31 W. 57th St., New York, NY 10019; Tel. (212) 308-2000

PESENTI, ROBERTO (Il Messaggero) — 1114 Ave. of the Americas, 33rd Fl., New York, NY 10036; Tel. (212) 719-5340

PIOLI, GIANPAOLO (Il Resto del Carlino) — Rm. S306, United Nations, NY 10017; Tel. (212) 758-5920

POGLIANI, FRANCESCO (RAI Italian TV) — 1350 Ave. of the Americas, New York, NY 10019; Tel. (212) 468-2566

PONTECORBOLI, GIANNA (Quotidiani Associati) — Rm. 368, United Nations, NY 10017; Tel. (212) 963-0937

QUARANTA, PAOLO (RAI-TV) — 1350 Ave. of the Americas, New York, NY 10019; Tel. (212) 468-2550

RUGGERI, LUCIANO (RAI) — 1350 Ave. of the Americas, New York, NY 10019; Tel. (212) 468-2550

SANTALUCIA, REMO (RAI Italian TV) — 1350 Ave. of the Americas, New York, NY 10019; Tel. (212) 468-2550

SARCHIELLI, GRAZIANO (AGIP/Il Giorno) — 666 5th Ave., 5th Fl., New York, NY 10103; Tel. (212) 887-0439

SCARPA, ALDO (Freelance) — 769 Blvd. E, Weehawken, NJ 07087; Tel. (201) 865-6963

STIZZA, BRUNO (RAI Radiotelevisione) — 1350 Ave. of the Americas, New York, NY 10019; Tel. (212) 468-2500

TREGLIA, ANGELA (RAI Italian TV) — 1350 Ave. of the Americas, New York, NY 10019; Tel. (212) 468-2570

TRINCIA, STEFANO (Il Messaggero) — 1114 Ave. of the Americas, 33rd Fl., New York, NY 10036; Tel. (212) 719- 5340

VISALLI, SANTI (Publifoto) — 319 E. 50th St., Room 10D, New York, NY 10022; Tel. (212) 699-5140

VISCONTI, ANDREA ALBERTO (AGL Newspapers) — 444 Madison Ave., 36th Fl., New York, NY 10023; Tel. (212) 755-0091

ZAMPALIONE, ARTURO (La Repubblica Daily) — 444 Madison Ave., Rm. 2105, New York, NY 10022; Tel. (212) 692-9448

JAPAN

IJICHI, NOBUO (US Japan Publication NY, Inc.) — 211 E. 43rd St., Ste. 1600, New York, NY 10017; Tel. 697-3330

IMOHARA, KAZUYOSHI (TV Asahi) — 630 5th Ave., Ste. 2707, New York, NY 10111; tel. (212) 489-7928

ISHIHARA, MAKOTO (TV Asahi) — 630 5th Ave., Ste. 2707, New York, NY 10111; Tel. (212) 489-7928

JOJU, YASUHIDE (Shukan Gendai) — 800 3rd Ave., New York, NY 10022; Tel. (212) 308-1808

KAWACHI, MAHO (Nikon Keizai Shimbum) — 1325 Ave. of the Americas, Ste. 2400, New York, NY 10019; Tel. (212) 261-6333

KIM, YOUNG C (Orient News Agency) — 212A E. 26th St., 2nd Fl., New York, NY 10010; Tel. (212) 683-3734

MASUI, SHIGEO (Yomiruri Shimbun) — 50 Rockefeller Plz., Ste. 825, New York, NY 10020; Tel. (212) 582-5827

MATSUMOTO, HIROYUKI (Orion Press News Agency) — PO Box 242, Cooper Sta., New York, NY 10003

MORIIWA, HIROSHI (Kodansha Ltd.) — 2-12-21 Otowa, Bunkyo-ku, Tokyo; Tel. (03) 5395-3440

SEVILLE, KAEDE (Kaede Media, Inc.) — 300 E. 54th St., New York, NY 10022; Tel. (212) 759-1715

SHINOZUKA, HIROSHI (TV Asahi) — 630 5th Ave., Ste. 2707, New York, NY 10111; Tel. (212) 489-7928

UCHIDA, TADAO (TV Asahi) — 630 5th Ave., Ste. 2707, New York, NY 10111; Tel. (212) 489-7928

YAMADA, TETSUHIRO (TV Asahi) — 630 5th Ave., Ste. 2707, New York, NY 10111; Tel. (212) 489-7928

KOREA

KIM, CHIN WHA (Korea Broadcasting System) — 20 River Rd., Apt. 15B, Roosevelt Island, NY 10044; Tel. (212) 755- 8077

KOH, JUNG SOOK (Korea Broadcasting System) — 330 E. 46 St., Apt. 9-O, New York, NY 10017; Tel. (212) 286-0966

MEXICO

GONZALEZ-SIEIRA, MARIA (Eco News TV) — 767 5th Ave., 12th Fl., New York, NY 10153; Tel. (212) 826-5379

MULLIGAN, JOHN R (International Media Service) — 438 W. Broadway, New York, NY 10012; Tel. (212) 989-9154

SVARZMAN, NORBERTO L (Televisa, SA) — 109-14 Ascan Ave., Apt. 6E, Forest Hills, NY 11375; Tel. (212) 963- 6860

SWARTZ, DR. HARRY (Mundo Medico) — 126 Gristmill Ln., Chapel Hill, NC 27514, Tel. (919) 968-6681

NETHERLANDS

ASHTARY, KAMRAN (BTV Media) — 125 Saint Marks Pl., Brooklyn, NY 11217; Tel. (718) 857-5467

BRAUN, PATRICIA B (Dutch TV and Publications) — 4060 Tilden Ave., Culver City, CA 90232; Tel. (310) 836-0404

FOEK, ANTON (Financial Economic Magazine) — 30 W. 95th St., New York, NY 10025; Tel. (212) 663-0202

GERRITSEN, YOLANDA G H (VARA Radio & TV) — 618A 3rd St., Brooklyn, NY 11215; Tel. (718) 499-2428

GROENVELD, BENNO (Radio Netherlands) — 788 Osceola Ave., St. Paul, MN 55105; Tel. (612) 227-9603

HAMMELBURG, BERNARD E (NCRV Radio & TV) — 6 Beresford Ln. Larchmont, NY 10538; Tel. (914) 834-6793

HAMMELBURG, DAVID H (KRO Dutch TV) — 6 Beresford Ln., Larchmont, NY 10538; Tel. (914) 834-6793

MARTENS, MONIQUE (AVRO TV) — 5 E. 22nd St., Apt. 24P, New York, NY 10010; Tel. (212) 410-2451

RINGMA, E W (Nieuwe Revu) — 169 Ave. A, Rm. 11, New York, NY 10009; Tel. (212) 598-4591

VAN HASSELT, JOHN COPES (De Telegraaf) — 49 Drake Rd., Scarsdale, NY 10583; Tel. (914) 723-2904

VAN MEERENDONK, BEN (Televizier Magazine) — 76 Deghraw St., Brooklyn, NY 11231; Tel. (718) 875-2104

VAN VLIET, NICO J (Freelance) — 160 Florida Hill Rd., Ridgefield, CT 06877; Tel. (203) 431-9395

VAN WAGTENDONK, REINOUT (Veronica Broadcasting) — 6 Brainard Ave., Great Barrington, MA 01230; Tel. (413) 528-5760

NEW ZEALAND

LESSING, JUDY (Radio New Zealand) — 1422 Beverley Rd., Brooklyn, NY 11226; Tel. (718) 469-2767

MURPHY, ROY (Television New Zealand) — PO Box 1956, Rockefeller Center, New York, NY 10185; Tel. (718) 965-0214

NORWAY

AAKHUS, GEIRR (Dagans Naeringsliv) — 102-14 Russell St., Howard Beach, NY 11414; Tel. (718) 738-3008

HVISTENDAHL, ELSE (Aftenposten) — Rm. 310, United Nations, NY 10017; Tel. (212) 963-7134

ROREN, TOM (Norway Times) — 481 81st St., Brooklyn, NY 11209; Tel. (718) 921-9648

CHANG, RODRIGUEZ EUGENIO (La Tribuna Oriental) — 60 Sutton Pl. S., Apt. 12J, New York, NY 10022; Tel. (212) 751-3779

PERU

CHANG, RODRIGUEZ EUGENIO (La Tribuna Oriental) — 60 Sutton Pl. S., Apt. 12J, New York, NY 10022; Tel. (212) 751-3779

POLAND

CZAPLINSKI, CZESLAW (Kariera) — 107 Milton St., Brooklyn, NY 11222

KALUZA-MARCINIAK, MALGORZATA (Polish Radio) — 303 Beverly Rd., Apt. 8J, Brooklyn, NY 11218; Tel. (718) 436-5484

RINGER, ELZBIETA (Dziennik Polski) — 119-51 Metropolitan Ave., Apt. 4A, Kew Gardens, NY 11415; Tel. (718) 441-8372

SIBILSKI, KRYSTYNA (Sportowiec-Polpres Magazine) — 48-20 44th St., Apt. 4C, Woodside, NY 11377

SIBILSKI, LESZEK (Sportowiec-Polpres Magazine) — 48-20 44th St., Apt. 4C, Woodside, NY 11377

SWIATEK, DANUTA (PANI Magazine) — 207 E. 37th St., Apt. 4A, New York, NY 10016; Tel. (212) 949-1467

ROMANIA

MILHOVEN, DEAN (Dreptatea) — 1A Bonn Pl., Weehawken, NJ 07087; Tel. (201) 867-1678

NASTASE-BORIGA, AURELIA E (Evenimentul Zilei) — 9457 Somerset Ln., Cypress, CA 90630; Tel. (212) 603-3300

PLESEA, GABRIEL (Romania Libera) — 92-40 Queens Blvd., Apt. 2D, Rego Park, NY 11374; Tel. (718) 639-0003

RUSSIA

RUSAKOV, YEVGENIY M (News Times) — 415 E. 37th St., Apt. 16J, New York, NY 10016; Tel. (212) 725-7416

SLOVENIA

MERSOL, MITJA (Delo Daily) — 301 E. 64th St., Apt. 10H, New York, NY 10021; Tel. (212) 861-5931

SPAIN

AVENDANO, ALBERTO (Radio Galega) — 2510-25th St., Lubbock, TX 79410; Tel. (806) 744-3861

CARRION, CHRISTINA (Radio & TV of Spain) — 501 Madison Ave., Rm. 604, New York, NY 10022; Tel. (212) 371-5112

GARDNER, DANIELLE L (US Embassy) — US Embassy, Madrid PSC 61, APO AE, Spain 09642; Tel. (011) 34 1577 4000

GOMEZ-FUENTES, ANGEL (Radio & TV of Spain) — 501 Madison Ave., Rm. 604, New York, NY 10022; Tel. (212) 371-5112

HERVAS, MERCEDES (Ya Daily) — Rm. C320, United Nations, NY 10017; Tel. (212) 963-7617

HURTADO, JOSE (Interco Press) — Paseo de la Castellana, 266 IV izq., Madrid, Spain 28046

PORTA, FREDERIC (Radio & TV of Spain) — 501 Madison Ave., Rm. 604, New York, NY 10022; Tel. (212) 371-5112

PRAT, INES (TV of Spain) — 501 Madison Ave., Rm. 604, New York, NY 10022; Tel. (212) 371-5112

RIBO, NURIA (Radio & TV of Spain) — 501 Madison Ave., Rm. 604, New York, NY 10022; Tel. (212) 371-5112

RIOS, CARMEN (TV of Spain) — 501 Madison Ave., Rm. 604, New York, NY 10022; Tel. (212) 371-5112

RODRIGUEZ, FERNANDO (Radio & TV of Spain) — 501 Madison Ave., Rm. 604, New York, NY 10022; Tel. (212) 371-5112

VALVERDE-RUIZ, GUSTAVO (Ya Daily) — Rm. C320, United Nations. NY 10017; Tel. (212) 319-8330

SRI LANKA

DEEN, THALIF (Daily News) — Rm. 485, United Nations, NY 10017; Tel. (212) 963-6156

SWEDEN

JOSEFSSON, LEIF (Aftonbladet) — 71 Park Ave., Apt. 9B, New York, NY 10016; Tel. (212) 213-8450

MORLING, ULF (Sydsvenska Dagbladet Daily) — 70 Hickory Rd., Apt. 424, Naples, FL 33963; Tel. (813) 566-8548

PRECHT, ELISABETH (SNB) — 165 Harrison Ave., Westfield, NJ 07090; Tel. (908) 233-0806

SWITZERLAND

CORVINGTON, EDITH (Annabelle) — 6 Burbury Ln., Great Neck, NY 11023; Tel. (516) 466-9852

SPEISER, IRENE (Neue Zurcher Zeitung) — 334 W. 86th St., Apt. 7A, New York, NY 10024; Tel. (212) 496-5868

STEWART, BARBARA (UN Observer & Int'l. Report) — 527 Madison Ave., New York, NY 10022; Tel. (212) 223-1303

WECHSLER, BERT (Der Tanz der Dinge) — 215 E. 80th St., Ste. 6E, New York, NY 10021; Tel. (212) 744-6504

TAIWAN

CHIEN, AVA (China Economic News Service) — PO Box 7275, New York, NY 10150; Tel. (212) 754-4595

MA, JACOB KJ (United Daily News) — 141-07 20th Ave., Whitestone, NY 11357; Tel. (718) 445-8889

Copyright ©1996 by the Editor & Publisher Co.

VII-34 Foreign press association

TURKEY
BARIS, BEHZAT H (Ika Economic News Agency) — Rm. 362, United Nations, NY 10017; Tel. (212) 963-0935
KESISOGLU, GARBIS (Dunya Daily & Dunya Weekly) — Alpha Pub. 50-22 23rd St., Long Island City, 11101; Tel. (718) 729-3314
ULUC, DOGAN (Hurriyet Daily) — 500 5th Ave., Ste. 1021, New York, NY 10110; Tel. (212) 921-8880
ULUC, SIMAVI ULUTUG (Hurriyet Daily) — 500 5th Ave., Ste. 1021, New York, NY 10110; Tel. (212) 921-8880

UNITED KINGDOM
BLACK, LARRY (Independent) — 117 Beekman St., Apt 5B, New York, NY 10038; Tel. (212) 406-1033
BLYTH, JEFFREY (Sunday People) — 400 Madison Ave., New York, NY 10017; Tel. (212) 832-2839
BRUNTON, JOHN (The Observer) — 39 Great Jones St., Ste. 2, New York, NY 10012; Tel. (212) 387-8321
CAHAIL, EARL (Viscom International) — 1408 Newport Way, Seattle, WA 98122
EGGINTON, JOYCE (Observer) — 135 Greenway S., Forest Hills, NY 11375; Tel. (718) 263-4667
GORDON, GEORGE (London Daily Mail) — 500 5th Ave., Ste. 312, New York, NY 10110; Tel. (212) 869-2570
GRAYSON, RICHARD S (Glasgow Herald) — 255 Chatterton Pkwy., White Plains, NY 10606; Tel. (914) 948-5858
POLLARD, JEREMY (British Broadcasting Corp.) — 341 W. 11th St., Apt. 4B, New York, NY 10014; Tel. (212) 996- 7765
SULLIVAN, ROBERT (Worldwide Television News) — 1995 Broadway, New York, NY 10028; Tel. (212) 362-4400
TANTON, JOHN (United Kingdom Publications) — 180 West End Ave., Apt. 18A, New York, NY 10023; Tel. (212) 580-0480
TETLOW, EDWIN (Director) — PO Box 140, Esopus, NY 12429; (914) 384-6672
VERNON, RAY C (World Toy News) — 91 Hight St., Armonk, NY 10504; Tel. (914) 273-6658

UNITED NATIONS
DAVID HOROWITZ (World Press Union) — Rm. 373, United Nations, NY 10017; Tel. (212) 688-7557

VENEZUELA
OSORIO, PEDRO S (World Press Service) — PO Box 21027, Midtown Sta., New York, NY 10129; Tel. (212) 563-2252

NATIONAL NEWSPAPER REPRESENTATIVES
Representatives of daily and selected weekly newspapers published in the United States and Canada

---

AD REPS
BOSTON, MA
51 Church St., Boston, MA 02116; tel (617) 542-6913; fax (617) 542-7227
President — Steve Ganak
New Jersey — Newark Star-Ledger
New York — Gannett New York Travel Group, Syracuse Post-Standard, Syracuse Herald-Journal/Herald-American
New Brunswick — St. John Telegraph-Journal
Nova Scotia — Halifax Chronicle-Herald
Quebec — Montreal La Presse

AMALGAMATED PUBLISHERS INC.
NEW YORK, NY
45 W. 45th St., Ste. 500, New York, NY 10036; tel (212) 869-5220; fax (212) 302-9406
President/COO — Michael A House
CHICAGO, IL
350 W. Ontario, Ste. 3-E.
Chicago, IL 60610
tel (312) 943-2033; fax (312) 943-1478
LOS ANGELES, CA
3200 Wilshire Blvd., Ste. 606, North Tower, Los Angeles, CA 90010
tel (213) 292-2456; fax (213) 292-2034
Alabama — Birmingham Times, Birmingham World, Huntsville Speakin' Out News, Mobile Beacon, Mobile Inner City News, Mobile New Times
California — El Mundo, Los Angeles Metro Gazette Group (6), Los Angeles Sentinel, Post Newspaper Group (4), Reporter Publications, San Diego Voice & Viewpoint, San Jose La Voz Latina
Connecticut — New Haven/Waterbury Inner City News, Waterbury Brass-City Voice
Dist. of Columbia — Washington New Observer
Florida — Central Florida Advocate, Daytona Times, Ft. Lauderdale Westside Gazette, Ft. Myers Community Voice, Ft. Pierce Florida Courier, Jacksonville Advocate, Jacksonville Florida Star, Jacksonville Free Press, Jacksonville Northeast Florida Advocate, Miami Times, New Smyrna Beach Times-Herald, Orlando Times, Pensacola Voice, Pompano Beach Broward Times Inc., Tallahassee Capital Outlook, Tampa Florida Dollar Stretcher, Tampa Florida Sentinel Bulletin, West Palm Beach Florida Photo News
Georgia — Atlanta Daily World, Atlanta Tribune, Atlanta Voice, Augusta Focus, Augusta Metro County Courier, Columbus Times, Decatur Champion, Georgia Sentinel Bulletin, Savannah Herald
Illinois — Bloomington-Normal Voice, Chicago Crusader, Chicago Independent Bulletin, Chicago Westside Journal, Chicago Windy City Word, Decatur Voice, Illinois Tri-City Journal, Peoria Voice, Springfield Voice
Indiana — Gary Crusader, Indiana Herald, Indianapolis Recorder
Kentucky — Louisville Defender
Louisiana — Alexandria News Weekly, Baton Rouge Weekly Press, Baton Rouge Weekly Press, Shreveport Sun
Maryland — Baltimore Annapolis Times, Baltimore Shore Times
Massachusetts — Boston Bay State Banner
Michigan — Afro-American Gazette, Detroit/Pontiac Michigan Chronicle, Ecorse Telegram, Grand Rapids Times, Jackson Blazer News
Minnesota — Minneapolis Spokesman, St. Paul Recorder
Missouri — Kansas City Call, St. Louis American, St. Louis Argus, St. Louis Sentinel
New Jersey — Newark City News
New York — Brooklyn Network Journal, Buffalo Challenger, Buffalo Criterion, New York Amsterdam News, New York Beacon, Westchester County Press
North Carolina — Carolina Peacemaker, Charlotte Post, Raleigh Urban Journal, Raeford Public Post, Raleigh Carolinian, Raleigh Carolinian
Ohio — Cincinnati Call & Post, Cincinnati Herald, Cleveland Call & Post, Columbus Call & Post, Columbus Communicator News, Dayton Communicator News
Oklahoma — Oklahoma City Black Chronicle, Tulsa Oklahoma Eagle
Oregon — Portland Observer
Pennsylvania — Philadelphia News Observer, Philadelphia Tribune Group, Pittsburgh Courier Group, Pittsburgh Renaissance News
South Carolina — Charleston Chronicle, Pee Dee Times, South Carolina Media Group (7)
Tennessee — Jackson Metro Forum, Memphis Silver Star, Nashville Pride, Tri-State Defender
Texas — Dallas Examiner, Dallas/Ft. Worth Texas Times, Dallas Post Tribune, Ft. Worth La Vida News, Houston Forward Times Group, Houston Informer & Texas Freeman Group, San Antonio Register, South Texas Informer & Business Journal
Virginia — Alexandria Metro-Herald, Norfolk Journal & Guide Group, Hampton Roads Voice, Norfolk Journal & Guide Group, Richmond Free Press, Richmond Voice, Roanoke Tribune
West Virginia — West Virginia Beacon Digest
Wisconsin — Milwaukee Community Journal, Milwaukee Courier, Milwaukee Star

THE AMERICAMEDIA CO.
MIDDLESEX, ENGLAND
5 Woodhall Ave., Pinner, Middlesex HA5 3DY England; tel (071) 866-3328
Telex 268048, ext. LDNG
Chairman — Dan Yadin
VERT-LE-GRAND, FRANCE
6 rue des Acacias, Vert-le-Grand 91810 France; tel 456-0015
Minnesota — Minneapolis Star Tribune
Washington — Seattle Times/Post-Intelligencer

AMERICAN NEWSPAPER NETWORK
SEATTLE, WA
215 W. Harrison St., Seattle, WA 98119; tel (800) 426-5537/(206) 282-8111; fax (206) 282-1280
Chairman — Gilbert Scherer
President — Carleton W Bryant
Exec. Vice Pres. — G.Kingsley Anthony
CHICAGO, IL
Chicago, IL
tel (800) 676-2838
LOS ANGELES, CA
Los Angeles, CA
tel (800) 624-1496
NEW YORK, NY
529 5th Ave., 12th Fl.
New York, NY 10017
tel (800) 473-6474
SEATTLE, WA
Seattle, WA
tel (800) 359-6676

AMERICAN NEWSPAPER REPRESENTATIVES INC.
DETROIT, MI
1700 W. Big Beaver, Ste. 235, Troy, MI 48084; tel (810) 643-9910; fax (810) 643-9914
President — Hillary Howe
General Manager — Robert Sontag
MINNEAPOLIS, MN
1000 Shelard Pkwy., Ste. 360
Minneapolis, MN 55426
tel (612) 545-1116; fax (612) 545-1481
Sales Manager — Richard F Rummel
ANR represents over 7,000 weekly community newspapers nationwide.

AMERICAN PASSAGE MEDIA CORP.
SEATTLE, WA
215 W. Harrison St., Seattle, WA 98119; tel (800) 426-5537/(206) 282-8111; fax (206) 282-1280
President/COB — Gilbert Scherer
Exec. Vice Pres. — Carleton W Bryant
CHICAGO, IL
Chicago, IL
tel (800) 676-2838
LOS ANGELES, CA
Los Angeles, CA
tel (800) 624-1496
NEW YORK, NY
529 5th Ave., 12th Fl.
New York, NY 10017
tel (800) 473-6474
SEATTLE, WA
Seattle, WA
tel (800) 359-6676
Newspaper representative for the college market.

AMERICAN PUBLISHERS REPRESENTATIVES LTD.
TORONTO, ON
41 Britain St., Ste. 303, Toronto, ON M5A 1R7 Canada; tel (416) 363-4004/(416) 363-1388; fax (416) 363-2889
President/CEO — Garry Power
VP-Sales/Admin. — Alex Kinninmont
VP-Sales — Penny Dickenson
Account Exec. — Jeff Denberg
Sales Rep. — Linda Maceachern
Sales Rep. — Cyndy Fleming
Sales Rep. — Vince O'Meara
Connecticut — Hartford Courant
Dist. of Columbia — USA Today
Florida — St. Petersburg Times
Georgia — Atlanta Journal-Constitution
Illinois — Chicago Sun-Times
Indiana — Indianapolis Star & News
Maryland — Baltimore Sun
Massachusetts — Boston Globe
Michigan — Detroit News/Free Press
Minnesota — Minneapolis Star Tribune
Missouri — Kansas City Star
New Jersey — Newark Star-Ledger
New York — Buffalo News, Gannett Suburban Newspapers, Long Island Newsday, Rochester Democrat & Chronicle, Syracuse Herald American, Watertown Times
Nevada — Las Vegas Review-Journal & Sun
Ohio — Cincinnati Enquirer, Cleveland Plain Dealer, Toledo Blade
Pennsylvania — Erie Daily Times, Pittsburgh Post-Gazette

APC NATIONAL MARKETING (HOLLINGER)
CHICAGO, IL
111 S. Emma St., PO Box 1000, West Frankfort, IL 62896; tel (618) 937-6411; fax (618) 932-6155
President/CEO — Larry Perrotto
CFO — David Dodd
Dir. Mktg./Nat'l. Adv. — Phil Ballard
Arkansas — Fayetteville Northwest Arkansas Times, Harrison Daily Times, Helena-West Helena Daily World, Malvern Daily Record, Newport Independent, Stuttgart Daily Leader
California — Yreka Siskiyou Daily News
Colorado — Fort Morgan Times, Lamar Daily News, Sterling Journal Advocate
Connecticut — Naugatuck Daily News
Florida — New Smyrna Beach News & Observer
Idaho — Blackfoot Morning News
Illinois — Benton Evening News, Canton Daily Ledger, Carmi Times, Chicago Daily Southtown, Chicago Sun-Times, Du Quoin Evening Call, El Dorado Daily Journal, Flora Clay County Advocate, Harrisburg Daily Register, Marion Daily Republican, Monmouth Review Atlas, Olney Mail, Pontiac Daily Leader, West Frankfort Daily American
Indiana — Columbia City Post & Mail, Decatur Daily Democrat, Greensburg Daily News, Hartford City News-Times, New Albany Tribune, Rensselaer Republican, Rushville Republican, Winchester News-Gazette
Iowa — Atlantic News-Telegraph, Charles City Press
Kansas — Atchison Daily Globe, Augusta Daily Gazette, Derby Daily Reporter, El Dorado Times, Leavenworth Times, McPherson Sentinel
Kentucky — Corbin Times Tribune, Harlan Daily Enterprise, Middlesboro Daily News, Richmond Register
Massachusetts — North Adams Transcript
Michigan — Cheboygan Daily Tribune, Ionia Sentinel-Standard, Sault Ste. Marie Evening News, South Haven Daily Tribune
Minnesota — Crookston Times, Stillwater Gazette
Mississippi — Laurel Leader-Call, Meridian Star, Starkville Daily News, West Point Daily Times-Leader
Missouri — Boonville News Advertiser, Camdenton Lake Sun Leader, Carthage Press, Chillicothe Constitution-Tribune, Kirksville Daily Express, Macon Chronicle Herald, Mexico Ledger, Neosho Daily News, Rolla Daily News, Sikeston Standard Democrat, Waynesville Fort Gateway Guide

Copyright ©1996 by the Editor & Publisher Co.

Nebraska — Beatrice Daily Sun, Sidney Telegraph
New Jersey — Bridgeton Evening News, Millville News
New York — Herkimer Evening Telegram, Hornell Evening Tribune, North Tonawanda News, Olean Times Herald, Oswego Palladium-Times, Salamanca Reporter, Wellsville Reporter
North Carolina — Newton Observer-News-Enterprise, Tarboro Daily Southerner
North Dakota — Jamestown Sun, Valley City Times-Record
Ohio — Portsmouth Daily Times, St. Mary's Evening Leader, Wapakoneta Daily News
Oklahoma — Ada Evening News, Woodward News
Pennsylvania — Bradford Era, Corry Journal, Honesdale Daily Independent, Kane Republican, Lewisburg Union County Journal, Milton Standard, Punxsutawney Spirit, Ridgeway Record, St. Mary's Daily Press, Sayre Evening Times, Titusville Herald, Waynesboro Record Herald
Texas — Big Spring Herald, Corsicana Daily Sun, Del Rio News-Herald, Greenville Herald Banner, Huntsville Item, Marshall News Messenger, Mexia Daily News, Orange Leader, Port Arthur News, San Marcos Daily Record

BRYDSON MEDIA SALES INTERNATIONAL INC.
NEW YORK, NY
330 W. 56th. St., New York, NY 10019; tel (212) 586-7773; fax (212) 582-6353
President — David Brydson
Alberta — Calgary Sun, Edmonton Sun
Nova Scotia — Halifax Chronicle Herald/Mail Star
Ontario — Kitchener/Waterloo Record, Ottawa Sun, St. Catharines Standard, Toronto Sun
Quebec — Montreal La Presse
England — London Daily Mail, London Mail on Sunday, London Evening Standard

CALIFORNIA NEWSPAPER SERVICE BUREAU
LOS ANGELES, CA
915 E. 1st St. (90012), PO Box 54310, Los Angeles, CA 90054-0310; tel (213) 229-5530/(213) 229-5511; fax (213) 626-7183
President — Michael D Smith
Adv. Mgr. — Ari Gutierrez
CNSB places legally mandated advertising, including class action notices, in all U.S. newspapers.

CASS COMMUNICATIONS INC.
CHICAGO, IL
1800 Sherman Pl., Evanston, IL 60201-3769; tel (708) 475-8800; fax (708) 475-8807
Chairman — Alan M Weisman
Publisher/Nat'l. Sales Mgr. — Robert M Roen
Mktg. & Research Coord. — Tracy Anderson
LOS ANGELES, CA
6100 Wilshire Blvd.
Los Angeles, CA 90048
tel (213) 937-7070
NEW YORK, NY
369 Lexington Ave.
New York, NY 10017
tel (212) 986-6441
Vice Pres./Sales Mgr. — Mark Businski
Regional Sales Mgr. — Michael Callan
Newspaper representative for high school, college, military, Hispanic and other markets.

CRESMER, WOODWARD, O'MARA & ORMSBEE INC.
NEW YORK, NY
866 3rd Ave., 23rd Fl., New York, NY 10022; tel (212) 750-4040; fax (212) 935-9514
CEO — Michael Veitch
President/COO — Harlan Evans
Chairman — States D Tompkins
Exec. VP/Finance — Bernadette Soens
Eastern Reg. Mgr. — Harlan Evans
Sr. VP/Dir. Research & Mktg. — David Schuster
Sr. VP/Dir. Retail Sales & Mktg. — James F Boynton
New York Mgr. — Michael Druckman

ATLANTA, GA
4360 Georgetown Sq. II, Ste. 809
Atlanta, GA 30338
tel (707) 455-8446; fax (770) 455-1860
Manager — James Lavender
BOSTON, MA
105 Eastern Ave., Ste. 201
Dedham, MA 02026
tel (617) 326-8871; fax (617) 326-8429
New England Mgr. — David Harken
CHICAGO, IL
1 E. Wacker Dr., Ste. 2300
Chicago, IL 60601
tel (312) 321-6360; fax (312) 321-6364
Sr. VP/Central Region Mgr. — Richard A Mitchell
Asst. Mgr. — Pam Eisenberg
DALLAS, TX
13601 Preston Rd., Ste. 617-E
Dallas, TX 75240
tel (214) 960-7085; fax (214) 960-8986
Manager — Doug Olsson
DENVER, CO
3025 S. Parker Rd., Ste. 109
Aurora, CO 80014
tel (303) 337-5968; fax (303) 369-8803
Manager — Patrice Berry
DETROIT, MI
3331 W. Big Beaver Rd., Ste. 114
Troy, MI 48084
tel (810) 649-4030; fax (810) 649-3843
Manager — Richard G Knight
LOS ANGELES, CA
4929 Wilshire Blvd., Ste. 415
Los Angeles, CA 90010
tel (213) 936-2800; fax (213) 936-2828
Sr. VP/Western Reg. Mgr. — John Morrison
Manager — Molly Collins
MIAMI, FL
1550 N.E. Miami Garden Dr., Ste. 302
North Miami Beach, FL 33179
tel (305) 945-2266; fax (305) 947-2299
Florida/Caribbean Mgr. — Peter Evans
MID ATLANTIC OFFICE
5570 Sterret Pl., Ste. 300
Columbia, MD 21044
tel (410) 715-9444; fax (410) 715-9442
Manager — John Ryan
SAN FRANCISCO, CA
235 Montgomery St., Ste. 1020
San Francisco, CA 94104
tel (415) 981-2882; fax (415) 981-2730
Manager — Stuart Falk
Alaska — Anchorage Daily News, Fairbanks Daily News-Miner
California — Antioch Ledger Dispatch, Fresno Bee, Los Angeles Daily News, Modesto Bee, Monterey County Herald, Excelsior del Condado de Orange, Orange County Register, Pasadena Star-News, Pleasanton Valley Times, Richmond West County Times, Sacramento Bee, San Diego Union-Tribune, San Gabriel Valley Tribune, Santa Barbara News-Press, Stockton Record, Ventura County Star, Walnut Creek Contra Costa Times, Whittier News, Contra Costa Daily Group, Register News Network, Southern California Newspaper Network, Thomson LA News Group
Colorado — Colorado Springs Gazette Telegraph, Grand Junction Daily Sentinel, Pueblo Chieftain
Connecticut — Waterbury Republican-American
Florida — Miami Diario Las Americas, St. Petersburg Times
Illinois — Chicago Sun-Times, Galesburg Register-Mail, Peoria Journal Star
Indiana — South Bend Tribune
Kansas — Topeka Capital-Journal
Maryland — Baltimore Sun, Lanham Prince George's Journal, Rockville Montgomery Journal
Missouri — Kansas City Star
Nebraska — Omaha World-Herald
New Mexico — Santa Fe New Mexican
North Dakota — Fargo-Moorhead Forum
Pennsylvania — Reading Times/Eagle
Rhode Island — Providence Journal-Bulletin
Texas — Beaumont Enterprise, Dallas Morning News
Virginia — Alexandria Journal, Arlington Journal, Fairfax Journal, Journal Newspaper Network
Washington — Spokane Spokesman-Review, Tacoma News Tribune
West Virginia — Charleston Daily Mail, Charleston Gazette, Clarksburg Exponent-Telegram
Canada — Southam Newspapers
British Columbia — Victoria Times-Colonist
Manitoba — Winnipeg Free Press

GANNETT NATIONAL NEWSPAPER SALES
NEW YORK, NY
535 Madison Ave., New York, NY 10022; tel (212) 715-5300; fax (212) 935 9774
President — Sheldon Lyons
Exec. VP/Sales, VP/Sales Nat'l. Four Color Newsp. Network — Bette Ann Yarus
VP/Eastern Sales Director — Elliott Huron
VP/Mid West Sales Director — James Moore
VP/Western Sales Director — Charles Williams
CHICAGO, IL
444 N. Michigan Ave.
Chicago, IL 60611
tel (312) 527-0550; fax (312) 527-9089
Midwest Sales Director — Jim Moore
DETROIT, MI
340 E. Big Beaver Rd., Ste. 150
Detroit, MI 48083
tel (810) 680-9900; fax (810) 680-9905
LOS ANGELES, CA
1111 Santa Monica Blvd., Ste. 2100
Los Angeles, CA 90025
tel (310) 444-2100; fax (310) 479-2550
Western Sales Director — Charles Williams
Arizona — Tucson Citizen
California — Marin County Independent Journal, Palm Springs Desert Sun, Salinas Californian, San Bernardino County Sun, Stockton Record, Tulare Advance-Register, Visalia Times-Delta
Colorado — Ft. Collins Coloradoan
Connecticut — Norwich Bulletin
Delaware — Wilmington News-Journal
Florida — Brevard Florida Today, Ft. Myers News-Press, Pensacola News-Journal
Georgia — Gainesville Times
Guam — Pacific Daily News
Hawaii — Honolulu Advertiser
Idaho — Boise Idaho Statesman
Illinois — Danville Commercial News, Rockford Register Star
Indiana — Lafayette Journal & Courier, Marion Chronicle-Tribune, Richmond Palladium-Item
Iowa — Des Moines Register, Iowa City Press-Citizen
Louisiana — Monroe News-Star, Shreveport Times
Michigan — Battle Creek Enquirer, Detroit Free Press/News, Lansing State Journal, Port Huron Times-Herald
Minnesota — St. Cloud Times
Mississippi — Hattiesburg American, Jackson Clarion-Ledger
Missouri — Springfield News-Leader
Montana — Great Falls Tribune
Nevada — Reno Gazette-Journal
New Jersey — Bridgewater Courier-News, Camden Courier-Post, Vineland Journal
New York — Binghamton Press & Sun Bulletin, Elmira Star-Gazette, Gannett Suburban Newspapers, Ithaca Journal, Niagara Falls Gazette, Poughkeepsie Journal, Rochester Democrat & Chronicle Times-Union, Saratogain, Gannett Suburban Newspapers, Utica Observer Dispatch
Ohio — Chillicothe Gazette, Cincinnati Enquirer, Cincinnati Post, Dayton Daily News, Fremont News-Messenger, Marietta Times, Port Clinton News Herald
Oklahoma — Muskogee Phoenix & Times-Democrat
Oregon — Salem Statesman-Journal
Pennsylvania — Chambersburg Public Opinion, Lansdale Reporter, North Hills News Record, Tarentum Valley News Dispatch
South Dakota — Sioux Falls Argus Leader
Tennessee — Jackson Sun, Nashville Banner, Nashville Tennessean
Texas — El Paso Times, Herald-Post
Vermont — Burlington Free Press
Virgin Islands — St. Thomas Daily News
Washington — Bellingham Herald, Olympian
West Virginia — Huntington Herald-Dispatch
Wisconsin — Green Bay Press-Gazette, Wausau Daily Herald

THE GLOBE & MAIL (CANADA)
NEW YORK, NY
310 Madison Ave., Ste. 2106, New York, NY 10017; tel (212) 599-5057; fax (212) 599-8298
Manager — Joy DeSanto

National newspaper reps VII-35

CHICAGO, IL
333 N. Michigan Ave., Ste. 728
Chicago, IL 60601
tel (312) 201-9393; fax (312) 201-9398
Manager — Salvatore Zammuto
DALLAS, TX
15400 Knoll Trail Dr., Ste. 110
Dallas, TX 75248
tel (214) 980-8858; fax (214) 233-9819
Manager — Brad White
HONOLULU, HI
3615 Harding Ave., Ste. 402
Honolulu, HI 96816
tel (808) 735-9188; fax (808) 737-1426
Manager — Debbie Choy
LOS ANGELES, CA
3301 Barham Blvd., Ste. 300
Los Angeles, CA 90068
tel (213) 850-8339; fax (213) 851-1508
Manager — George Mackin
SAN FRANCISCO, CA
150 Greene St., PH-B, Ste. 306
San Francisco, CA 94111
tel (415) 362-8339; fax (415) 362-5474
Manager — Tamara Sims

GLOBE MEDIA
NEW YORK, NY
261 Madison Ave., 19th Fl., New York, NY 10016; tel (212) 599-5057; fax (212) 599-8298
President — Richard Fontana
LOS ANGELES, CA
11766 Wilshire Blvd., Ste. 1660
Los Angeles, CA 90025
tel (310) 478-7028; fax (310) 478-7257
CEO — George Mackin
California — Los Angeles Times, San Francisco Examiner & Chronicle
Florida — Miami Herald
New York — New York Times
Texas — Dallas Morning News
Ontario — Toronto Globe & Mail
Paris — International Herald Tribune

HARTE-HANKS COMMUNICATIONS INC.
SAN ANTONIO, TX
200 Concord Plz. Dr., Ste. 800 (78216), PO Box 269, San Antonio, TX 78291-0269; tel (210) 829-9000; fax (210) 829-9101
President/CEO — Larry Franklin
South Carolina — Anderson Independent-Mail
Texas — Abilene Reporter-News, Corpus Christi Caller-Times, Piano Star Courier, San Angelo Standard-Times, Wichita Falls Times Record News

HAWAIIAN MEDIA SALES
HONOLULU, HI
904 Ainapo St., Honolulu, HI 96825; tel (808) 396-5363; fax (808) 395-6685
President — Harry Schneider
California — Desert Sun, Los Angeles Daily News, Orange County Register, Sacramento Bee, San Jose Mercury News

ROBERT HITCHINGS & CO. INC.
WILKES-BARRE, PA
580 W. Germantown Pike, Ste. 108, Plymouth Plz., Plymouth Meeting, PA 19462; tel (610) 941-3555; fax (610) 941-1289
Manager — Robert Hitchings Jr
Manager — Eileen Adelsberger
Manager — Margaret Freels
Account Exec. — R Brian Hitchings
New Jersey — Bridgeton Evening News, Salem Today's Sunbeam, Toms River Daily Observer, Willingsboro Burlington County Times, Woodbury Gloucester County Times
Pennsylvania — Chester Delaware County Daily Times, Doylestown Daily Intelligencer, Lansdale Reporter, Levittown-Bucks County Courier Times, Montgomery County Record, Norristown Times Herald, Phoenixville Evening Phoenix, Pottstown Mercury, West Chester Daily Local News

JOSEPH JACOBS ORGANIZATION
NEW YORK, NY
60 E. 42nd St., New York, NY 10165; tel (212) 687-6234; fax (212) 687-9785

Copyright ©1996 by the Editor & Publisher Co.

Chairman — Richard A Jacobs
President — David Koch
Representing Jewish publications.

LANCASTER NEWSPAPERS INC.

LANCASTER, PA
8 W. King St., PO Box 1328, Lancaster, PA 17603; tel (717) 291-8800; fax (717) 399-6523
Vice Pres./Mktg. — Harold E Miller Jr
Nat'l. Advertising Mgr. — Melvin W Williams
Nat'l. Scheduling Coordinator — Peg Miller
Promotion Manager — James B McGrew
Pennsylvania — Intelligencer Journal, Lancaster New Era, Sunday News

LANDON ASSOCIATES INC.

NEW YORK, NY
750 3rd Ave., New York, NY 10017; tel (212) 867-1112; fax (212) 986-4398
Chairman/CEO — Owen E Landon Jr
President/COO — Robert Keim
Dir. Sales Development — Dorothy Wayner
ATLANTA, GA
4488 N. Shallowford Rd., Ste. 101
Dunwoody, GA 30338
tel (404) 399-6407; fax (404) 399-6574
Regional Mgr. — Kevin Kinney
BOSTON, MA
239 Causeway St.
Boston, MA 02114
tel (617) 742-0221; fax (617) 742-1236
VP/Finance — William T Anderson Jr
BOSTON, MA
1515 Washington St., Ste. 107
Braintree, MA 02184
tel (617) 356-2772; fax (617) 356-2837
Regional Mgr. — Frank Chicko
CHARLOTTE, NC
3820 Bon Rea Dr.
Charlotte, NC 28226
tel (704) 542-3202; fax (704) 542-8209
Manager — Gary Davis
CHICAGO, IL
435 N. Michigan Ave., Ste. 1317
Chicago, IL 60611
tel (312) 644-8270; fax (312) 644-9011
Dir. Sales & Mktg.-Central Region — Peter Stegner
CINCINNATI, OH
431 Ohio Pike, Ste. 109
Cincinnati, OH 45255
tel (513) 688-0050; fax (513) 688-0086
Manager — Scott Thibodeau
CLEVELAND, OH
6964 Promway St. N.W.
North Canton, OH 44720
tel (216) 966-8616; fax (216) 966-8717
DALLAS, TX
333 W. Campbell Rd., Ste. 210
Richardson, TX 75080
tel (214) 699-0766; fax (214) 699-0769
DETROIT, MI
11111 Hall Rd., Ste. 201
Utica, MI 48317
tel (810) 997-0767; fax (810) 997-0766
Manager — Beverly Smith
HARRISBURG, PA
523 Cherry St.
Martinsburg, PA 16662
tel (814) 793-4545; fax (814) 793-4965
KANSAS CITY, KS
8700 Monrovia, Ste. 310
Lenexa, KS 66215
tel (913) 492-0731; fax (913) 492-2745
LOS ANGELES, CA
222 N. Sepulveda Blvd., Ste. 1790
El Segundo, CA 90245
tel (310) 414-0022; fax (310) 414-0648
Regional Mgr. — Mark B Landon
MILWAUKEE, WI
707 Cheyenne Dr.
Waukesha, WI 53188
tel (414) 549-6835
Manager — John Hock
MINNEAPOLIS, MN
250 Prairie Ctr. Dr., Ste. 210
Eden Prairie, MN 55344
tel (612) 944-0245; fax (612) 944-0246
Manager — Kevin Sullivan
ORLANDO, FL
451 Melrose Ave.
Winter Park, FL 32789
tel (407) 645-5105; fax (407) 628-3769
Manager — Teri Holt
PHILADELPHIA, PA
998 Old Eagle School Rd., Ste. 1204
Wayne, PA 19087
tel (610) 688-5612; fax (610) 688-5615
Dir. Sales & Mktg.-Mid Atlantic Region — Kevin Griffin
PITTSBURGH, PA
234 Adams St.; PO Box 407
Rochester, PA 15074
tel (412) 774-4411; fax (412) 774-5743
VP/Dir. Sales & Mktg.-East Central Region — Don Devich
PORTLAND, ME
46 Winnock's Neck Rd.
Scarborough, ME 04074
tel (207) 883-2631; fax (207) 883-2631
Manager — Mark Sangster
SAN FRANCISCO, CA
14 Crow Canyon Ct., Ste. 110
San Francisco, CA 94583
tel (510) 855-1450; fax (510) 855-1454
Manager — Sonny Cordeiro
SEATTLE, WA
19707 44th Ave. W., Ste. 103
Lynwood, WA 98036
tel (206) 778-2180; fax (206) 778-2758
Manager — Ron Anderson

Alabama — Alexander City Outlook, Decatur Daily, Florence Times Daily, Gadsden Times, Jasper Mountain Eagle, Lanett Valley Times-News, Montgomery Advertiser-Journal, Selma Times Journal, Troy Messenger, Huntsville/Decatur/Florence DMA Network, Select Alabama Markets
Arizona — Casa Grande Dispatch, Lake Havasu City Today's News
Arkansas — Mountain Home Baxter Bulletin
California — Auburn Journal, Bakersfield Californian, El Cajon Daily Californian, Palos Verdes Penisula News
Colorado — Boulder Daily Camera
Connecticut — Bristol Press, Danbury News-Times, Greenwich Time, Manchester Journal Inquirer, Middletown Press, Naugatuck Daily News, New Britain Herald, New Haven Register, New London Day, Norwalk Hour, Stamford Advocate, Torrington Register Citizen, Willimantic Chronicle, Central Connecticut Newspaper Network, Fairfield County Dailies, Southern Connecticut Newspapers Inc.
District of Columbia — Greater Capital Newspaper Network
Florida — Boca Raton News, Bradenton Herald, Cape Coral Breeze, Charlotte Harbor Sun Herald, Crystal River Citrus County Chronicle, Gainesville Sun, Homestead South Dade News Leader, Lake City Reporter, Leesburg Commercial, Ocala Star-Banner, Palatka Daily News, Sanford Herald, Tallahasse Democrat, Central Florida Golden Markets Group
Georgia — Athens Banner-Herald, Augusta Chronicle, Columbus Ledger-Enquirer, Dublin Courier Herald, La Grange News, Macon Telegraph, Milledgeville Union-Recorder, Moultrie Observer, Savannah News-Press, Statesboro Herald, Mid-Georgia Newspaper Network, The Georgia Group
Idaho — Blackfoot News, Burley South Idaho Press, Hailey Wood River Journal
Illinois — Beardstown Illinoian-Star, Belvidere Republican, Carbondale Southern Illinoisan, Clinton Journal, Decatur Herald & Review, Dekalb Chronicle, Jacksonville Journal-Courier, Kankakee Journal, Kewanee Star-Courier, Macomb Journal, Mattoon Journal-Gazette, Ottawa Daily Times, Paris Beacon-News, Pekin Times, Quincy Herald-Whig, Sterling-Rock Falls Gazette, Streator Times-Press, Taylorville Breeze-Courier, Chicago DMA Plus Network, Mid-Illinois Newspapers, Quad Cities DMA Newspaper Network, Quincy/Hannibal DMA BUY, Rockford Area Newspaper Network
Indiana — Bedford Times-Mail, Bloomington Herald-Times, Connersville News-Examiner, Ft. Wayne News-Sentinel, Gary Post-Tribune, Goshen News, Jeffersonville News, Logansport Pharos-Tribune, Valparaiso Vidette-Messenger, Michiana Newspaper Network, South Bend DMA Network
Iowa — Davenport Quad City Times, Mason City Globe-Gazette, Muscatine Journal, Ottumwa Courier, Sioux City Journal, Central Iowa Unit, Metro Iowa Plus Network
Kansas — Beloit Call, Clay Center Dispatch, Kansas City Kansan, Manhattan Mercury, Ottawa Herald, Parsons Sun, Russell News, Wellington News, Winfield Courier
Kentucky — Ashland Independent, Corbin Times-Enterprise, Elizabethtown News-Enterprise, Frankfort State Journal, Harlan Enterprise, Maysville Ledger Independent, Middlesboro News, Owensboro Messenger-Inquirer, Richmond Register, The Kentucky Group
Maine — Augusta Kennebec Journal, Biddeford Journal Tribune, Brunswick Times Record, Lewiston-Auburn Sun-Journal, Portland Press-Herald/Telegram, Waterville Sentinel, Central Maine Newspaper Network, Maine Newspaper Network
Maryland — Annapolis Capital, Easton Star-Democrat, Elkton Cecil Whig, Frederick News-Post, Salisbury Times, Westminster Carroll County Times
Massachusetts — Attleboro Sun-Chronicle, Brockton Enterprise, Clinton Item, Dedham Transcript, Fall River Herald News, Fitchburg Sentinel-Enterprise, Framingham Middlesex News, Gardner News, Greenfield Recorder, Haverhill Gazette, Hyannis Cape Cod Times, Lawrence Eagle-Tribune, Lynn Item, Malden Mercury, Milford News, North Adams Transcript, Northampton Hampshire Gazette, Pittsfield Berkshire Eagle, Quincy Patriot Ledger, Salem News, Taunton Gazette, Waltham News-Tribune, Westfield News, Boston Area Newspaper Dailies, Essex County Community Newspapers, North Shore Network, Springfield DMA Newspaper Network, Western Massachusetts Network
Michigan — Adrian Telegram, Alpena News, Benton Harbor Herald-Palladium, Cheboygan Daily Tribune, Escanaba Press, Grand Haven Tribune, Houghton Mining Gazette, Iron Mountain News, Ironwood Globe, Marquette Mining Journal, Menominee Herald-Leader, Mount Pleasant-Alma Sun, Sault Ste. Marie News, Michigan Upper Peninsula Newspaper Network, Sault Ste. Marie/Cheboygan Newspaper Group
Minnesota — Duluth News-Tribune, Willmar West Central Tribune, Winona Daily News, Best of Minnesota, La Crosse Winona Newspaper Unit
Mississippi — Biloxi Sun Herald, Brookhaven Leader, Natchez Democrat, Tupelo Northeast Mississippi Journal, Jackson DMA Newspaper Network
Missouri — Chillicothe Constitution-Tribune, Hannibal Courier-Post, Mexico Ledger, Sedalia Democrat, St. Louis Suburban Journals, Kansas City DMA Network Plus
Montana — Billings Gazette, Butte Montana Standard, Glendive Ranger-Review, Helena Independent-Record, Livingston Enterprise, Miles City Star, Missoula Missoulian, Montana Group, Yellowstone Newspapers
Nebraska — Lincoln Journal Star
New Hampshire — Claremont Eagle-Times, Concord Monitor, Dover Foster's Democrat, Keene Sentinel, Laconia Citizen, Lebanon Valley News, Nashua Telegraph, Portsmouth Herald, Band New Hampshire
New Jersey — Atlantic City Press, Bridgeton News, Morristown Record, Newton New Jersey Herald, Toms River Ocean County Observer, Trenton Trentonian, Salem Today's Sunbeam, Woodbury Gloucester County Times, Newark Metro Unit, Southern Jersey Newspaper Network
New Mexico — Los Alamos Monitor
New York — Amsterdam Recorder, Batavia News, Catskill Mail, Cortland Standard, Dunkirk-Fredonia Observer, Glens Falls Post-Star, Gloversville Leader-Herald, Herkimer Telegram, Hornell Evening Tribune, Hudson Register-Star, Jamestown Post-Journal, Little Falls Times, Lockport Union Sun & Journal, Medina Journal-Register, Middletown Times Herald-Record, North Tonawanda News, Norwich Sun, Ogdensburg Journal/Advance-News, Oswego Palladium-Times, Oneida Dispatch, Port Jervis Tri-State Gazette, Salamanca Press, Saranac Lake Adirondack Enterprise, Troy Record, Albany DMA Newspaper Network, Buffalo DMA Newspaper Network, Buffalo Plus Newspaper Network, Greater Buffalo Newspaper Network, Middletown/Port Jervis Unit, New York DMA Suburban Ring-North, Niagara County Newspaper Network, Southern Tier Daily Newspaper Network
North Carolina — Asheville Citizen Times, Clinton Sampson Independent, Dunn Daily Record, Durham Herald Sun, Elizabeth City Advance, Fayetteville Times/Observer, Gastonia Gaston Gazette, Goldsboro News-Argus, Greensboro News & Record, Henderson Dispatch, Hendersonville Times-News, High Point Enterprise, Kinston Free Press, Lenoir News-Topic, Lexington Dispatch, Morganton News-Herald, New Bern Sun-Journal, Reidsville Review, Roanoke Rapids Herald, Rocky Mount Telegram, Sanford Herald, Tarboro Southerner, Wilson Times, Charlotte DMA Newspaper Network, Eastern North Carolina Newspaper Network, Greater Hickory Newspaper Group, Greensboro/Winston-Salem/High Point DMA Newspaper Network, Piedmont Area Newspaper Group, Raleigh/Durham DMA Plus Newspaper Network
North Dakota — Bismarck Tribune, Dickinson Press, Grand Forks Herald, Jamestown Sun, Minot News, Williston Herald
Ohio — Alliance Review, Ashland Times-Gazette, Ashtabula Star-Beacon, Bellefontaine Examiner, Bowling Green Sentinel-Tribune, Cambridge Jeffersonian, Canton Repository, Coshocton Tribune, Dover-New Philadelphia Times Reporter, East Liverpool Evening Review, Fairborn Herald, Gallipolis Tribune, Greenville Advocate, Hamilton Journal-News, Kent-Ravenna Record-Courier, Lake County News-Herald, Lancaster Eagle-Gazette, Lisbon Morning Journal, Lorain Morning Journal, Mansfield News Journal, Marion Star, Massillon Independent, Middletown Journal, Mount Vernon News, Newark Advocate, Norwalk Reflector, Piqua Call, Pomeroy-Middleport Sentinel/Times-Sentinel, Sandusky Register, Steubenville Herald-Star, Troy News, Warren Tribune Chronicle, Wooster Daily Record, Xenia Daily Gazette, Zanesville Times Recorder, Bi-Cleveland Network, Canton MSA Newspaper Network, Cleveland DMA Newspaper Network, Greater Columbus Newspaper Network, Southwest Ohio Newspaper Network, Toledo DMA Newspaper Group, Tri-Ohio Network, Youngstown DMA Newspaper Network
Oklahoma — Ardmore Daily Ardmoreite, Enid News-Eagle, Lawton Constitution, McAlester News-Capital & Democrat, Ponca City News, Shawnee News-Star, Stillwater News Press
Oregon — Bend Bulletin, Corvallis Gazette-Times, Eugene Register-Guard, Ontario Argus Observer, Pendleton East Oregonian
Pennsylvania — Altoona Mirror, Beaver County Times, Bedford Gazette, Bradford Era, Butler Eagle, Carlisle Sentinel, Clearfield Progress, Connellsville Daily Courier, Danville News, DuBois Courier-Express, Ellwood City Ledger, Erie Morning News/Daily Times/Times-News, Gettysburg Times, Greensburg Tribune-Review, Hanover Evening Sun, Huntingdon-Mt. Union Daily News, Johnstown Tribune-Democrat, Irwin Standard Observer, Kane Republican, Kittanning Leader-Times, Latrobe Bulletin, Lebanon Daily News, Lewistown Sentinel, Lock Haven Express, McKeesport Daily News, Meadville Tribune, Monessen Valley Independent, Oil City News Herald, New Castle News, Pottsville Republican, Oil City News Herald, Pottstown Mercury, Pottsville Republican, Punxsutawney Spirit, Ridgway Record, Sayre-Athens Evening Times, Shenandoah Herald, St. Marys Daily Press, Shamokin-Mt. Carmel News-Item, Somerset Daily American, Sharon Herald, State College Centre Daily Times, Sunbury Daily Item, Towanda Daily Review, Tyrone Daily Herald, Uniontown Herald-Standard, Warren Times-Observer, Washington Observer-Reporter, Waynesboro Record Herald, West Chester Daily Local News, Wilkes-Barre Times Leader, Williamsport Sun-Gazette, York Daily Record/Dispatch/News, Central Penn Newspaper Network, Erie DMA Newspaper Network, Mason/Dixon Newspaper Network, Philadelphia DMA Newspaper Network, Pittsburgh DMA Newspaper Network, Suburban Philadelphia Area Newspapers, Suburban Philadelphia Plus Network, Wilkes-Barre/Scranton DMA Network
Rhode Island — Pawtucket Times, West Warwick Kent County Times, Westerly Sun, Woonsocket Call, Rhode Island/S.E. Massachusetts Network
South Carolina — Aiken Standard, Anderson Independent-Mail, Columbia State, Florence Morning News, Greenville News-Piedmont, Myrtle Beach Sun News, Spartanburg Herald-Journal, Greenville/Spartanburg/Anderson Newspaper Network, South Carolina Metro Plus Network
South Dakota — Aberdeen American News, Rapid City Journal, Spearfish Black Hills Pioneer
Tennessee — Athens Daily Post-Athenian, Chattanooga Free Press/Times, Clarksville Leaf-Chronicle, Greeneville Sun, Johnson City Press, Kingsport Times-News, Morristown Citizen Tribune, Tri-Cities Group, Tennessee East Newspaper Network, Tri-Cities Group

Texas — Clute-Freeport Brazosport Facts, Mount Pleasant Daily Tribune, Sulphur Springs News-Telegram
Vermont — Bennington Banner, Brattleboro Reformer, St. Johnsbury Caledonian-Record
Virginia — Alexandria Gazette Packet, Bristol Herald-Courier Virginia Tennessean, Covington Virginian Review, Danville Register & Bee, Fredericksburg Free Lance-Star, Harrisonburg Daily News-Record, Hopewell News, Martinsville Bulletin, Petersburg Progress-Index, Staunton Daily News Leader, Strasburg Northern Virginia Daily, Waynesboro News-Virginian, Winchester Star, Shenandoah Valley Newspaper Network, Tri-Cities Group, Tri-Cities Group
Washington — Pasco Tri-City Herald, Walla Walla Union-Bulletin, Wenatchee World, Yakima Herald-Republic, Central Washington Network
West Virginia — Beckley Register-Herald, Bluefield Daily Telegraph, Clarksburg Exponent-Telegram, Elkins Inter-Mountain, Logan Banner, Martinsburg Journal, Morgantown Dominion Post, Parkersburg News/Sentinel, Weirton Daily Times, Welch Daily News, Wheeling Intelligencer/News-Register, Williamson Daily News, Bluefield-Beckley DMA Network, Charleston-Huntington DMA Network, Northern West Virginia Network, Ogden Newspaper Network, West Virginia Newspaper Network, Wheeling/Belmont Newspaper Unit, Wheeling/Steubenville DMA Network
Wisconsin — Appleton Post-Crescent, Beloit Daily News, Eau Claire Leader-Telegram, Fond du Lac Reporter, Green Bay News-Chronicle, Kenosha News, La Crosse Tribune, Madison Capital Times/Wisconsin State Journal, Manitowoc Herald Times Reporter, Marinette Eagle-Star, Oshkosh Northwestern, Racine Journal Times, Shawano Leader, Sheboygan Press, Waukesha County Freeman, West Bend Daily News, Janesville/Beloit Metro Unit, Kenrac, LaCrosse/Eau Claire DMA Network, Madison DMA Network, Marinette/Menominee Newspaper Network, Milwaukee DMA Network, Wausau/Rhineland DMA Network

LEE NATIONAL SALES GROUP
DAVENPORT, IA
400 Putnam Bldg., 215 N. Main St., Davenport, IA 52801-1924; tel (319) 383-2100; fax (319) 383-2104
Director of Sales — Mike Kament
Regional Acct. Exec. — Jody Andruss
Regional Acct. Exec. — Abby Hatfield
Regional Acct. Exec. — Eugene Uehling
Illinois — Carbondale-Herrin-Murphysboro Southern Illinoisan, Decatur Herald & Review, Kewanee Star-Courier
Iowa — Davenport Quad City Times, Mason City Globe-Gazette, Muscatine Journal, Ottumwa Courier
Minnesota — Winona Daily News
Montana — Billings Gazette, Butte-Anaconda Montana Standard, Helena Independent Record, Missoula Missoulian
Nebraska — Lincoln Journal-Star
North Dakota — Bismarck Tribune
Oregon — Corvallis Gazette-Times
South Dakota — Rapid City Journal
Wisconsin — La Crosse Tribune, Madison Capital Times/Wisconsin State Journal, Racine Journal Times

THE LEONARD CO.
HOLLYWOOD, FL
5740 Hollywood Blvd., Ste. 500, Hollywood, FL 33021; tel (305) 961-5664; fax (305) 966-1779
President/COB — Leonard Adler
Exec. Financial Officer — Illene Gross
Sales Director — Beth Adler
Office Manager — Bernice Feierstadt
ORLANDO, FL
PO Box 677699, Orlando, FL 32867-7699 tel (407) 671-2226; fax (407) 671-2226
California — San Francisco Chronicle/Examiner (Caribbean only)
Florida — Jacksonville Florida Times-Union, St. Petersburg Times
Pennsylvania — Pittsburgh Post Gazette
Tennessee — Memphis Commercial Appeal
Virginia — Journal Newspapers
Ontario — Toronto Sun, Travel Courier
Quebec — Quebec City Le Soleil
England — London Mail on Sunday
Germany — Reiseburo Bulletin

LINGUA ADS SERVICE
TORONTO, ON
7 Belmont St., Toronto, ON M5R 1P9 Canada; tel (416) 922-5258; fax (416) 922-5562
President — Greta Ram

LONG & ASSOCIATES
SAN FRANCISCO, CA
1575 Old Bayshore Hwy., Burlingame, CA 94010; tel (415) 692-8236; fax (415) 692-3802
President — Daniel J Long
CHICAGO, IL
5311 N. Oak Park Ave.
Chicago, IL 60656
tel (312) 775-0871
NEW YORK, NY
420 Lexington Ave., Ste. 300
New York, NY 10170
tel (212) 297-6152; fax (212) 986-1952
California — Golden Gate Group, Marin Independent Journal, Napa Valley Register, San Mateo Times, Santa Rosa Press Democrat

MARKET PLACE MEDIA
SANTA BARBARA, CA
26 Castilian Dr., Santa Barbara, CA 93117; tel (805) 968-8000; fax (805) 968-8003
Sales Mgr. — Diana Stoddard
MPM specializes in the military, college, Hispanic, African- American, ethnic and senior markets.

MCGOWN/INTERMAC
MONTREAL, QC
8250 Decarie Blvd., Ste. 205, Montreal, QC H4P 2P5 Canada; tel (514) 735-5191; fax (514) 342-9406
President — John McGown
McGown/Intermac represents 25 U.S. daily newspapers.

METROLAND PRINTING/PUBLISHING/ DISTRIBUTING
TORONTO, ON
10 Tempo Ave., Willowdale, ON M2H 2N8 Canada; tel (416) 493-1300
National Sales Rep. — Dal Browne

METROPOLITAN PUBLISHERS REPRESENTATIVES INC.
MIAMI, FL
2500 S. Dixie Hwy., Miami, FL 33133; tel (305) 856-8326; fax (305) 856-2133
President — Joel Meltzer
TAMPA, FL
3016 Mason Pl.
Tampa, FL 33629
tel (813) 837-5618; fax (813) 839-8834
TORONTO, ON
3 Church St., Ste. 503
Toronto, ON M5E 1M2 Canada
tel (416) 862-7157; fax (416) 862-0603
Vice Pres./Gen. Mgr. — Beverly Maloney
Minnesota — St. Paul Pioneer Press

METROPOLITAN SUNDAY NEWSPAPER INC.
NEW YORK, NY
260 Madison Ave., New York, NY 10016; tel (212) 689-8200; fax (212) 779-9795
President — Phyllis Cavaliere
Vice Pres. — Nellie DeBono
Dir. Newspaper Relations — Francis Bee
Sales Rep. — William Huck
MSN places advertising for represented newspapers through its Sunday Magazine Network and Metro-Puck Comics Network. Please see these entries in Section V of the Year Book.

MORRIS NEWSPAPER CORP.
SAVANNAH, GA
PO Box 8167, Savannah, GA 31412; tel (912) 233-1281
President — Charles H Morris
California — Manteca Bulletin, Newhall Signal
Georgia — Statesboro Herald
Kansas — Great Bend Tribune
Tennessee — Daily News Journal

NEWHOUSE NEWSPAPERS METRO SUBURBIA
NEW YORK, NY
140 E. 45th St., New York, NY 10017; tel (212) 697-8020; fax (212) 972-3146
President — Edwin F Russell
VP/Sales Mktg. Dir. — Robert N Schoenbacher
ATLANTA, GA
2000 River Edge Pkwy., Ste. 650
Atlanta, GA 30328
tel (770) 955-2335; fax (770) 955-6564
Southern Adv. Sales Mgr. — Robert E Rowland
BOCA RATON, FL
6001 Broken Sound Pkwy. N.W., Ste. 422
Boca Raton, FL 33487
tel (407) 998-0944; fax (407) 998-0953
Adv. Sales Mgr. — Brenda Goodwin
CHICAGO, IL
221 E. Ontario St.
Chicago, IL 60611
tel (312) 337-6242; fax (312) 337-7129
Mid-Western Adv. Sales Mgr. — David W Feldman
DETROIT, MI
3250 W. Big Beaver Rd., Ste. 223
Detroit, MI 48084
tel (810) 643-8417; fax (810) 643-8754
LOS ANGELES, CA
6300 Wilshire Blvd.
Los Angeles, CA 90048
tel (213) 965-3677; fax (213) 965-4962
Adv. Sales Mgr. — George R Broadhead
Alabama — The Alabama Group, Birmingham News/Post Herald, Huntsville Times/News, Mobile Press-Register
Louisiana — New Orleans Times-Picayune
Massachusetts — Springfield Sunday Republican, Springfield Union-News
Michigan — Ann Arbor News, Bay City Times, Flint Journal, Grand Rapids Press, Jackson Citizen Patriot, Kalamazoo Gazette, Muskegon Chronicle, Saginaw News (Booth 8 Paper group)
Mississippi — Pascagoula Press
Missouri — St. Louis Post-Dispatch
New Jersey — Jersey City Journal (UNYT), Star-Ledger (UNYT), Trenton Times
New York — Staten Island Advance (UNYT), Syracuse Herald-Journal/American/Post-Standard, (UNYT (NY Metro Area)
Ohio — Cleveland Plain Dealer
Oregon — Portland Oregonian
Pennsylvania — Harrisburg Patriot-News

NEWSPAPER MARKETING BUREAU INC.
TORONTO, ON
10 Bay St., Water Park Pl., Ste. 201, Toronto, ON MJ5 2R8 Canada; tel (416) 364-3744; fax (416) 363-2568
President — John A Finneran
Central Sales Mgr. — Meling Johnston
Exec. Asst. to the President — Lois Juscenko
MONTREAL, QC
2020 rue Universite Bureau 1328
Montreal, QC H3A 2A5 Canada
tel (514) 282-1542; fax (514) 843-4354
Eastern Sales Mgr. — Maurice LeClerc
VANCOUVER, BC
1166 Alberni St., Ste. 1005
Vancouver, BC V6E 3Z3 Canada
tel (604) 669-8796; fax (604) 683-1240
Western Sales Mgr. — Paul McGeachie
Alberta — Calgary Herald, Calgary Sun, Edmonton Journal, Edmonton Sun, Lethbridge Herald, Medicine Hat News, Red Deer Advocate
British Columbia — Cranbrook Daily Townsman, Kamloops Daily News, Kelowna Daily Courier, Nelson Daily News, Prince George Citizen, Vancouver Province, Victoria Times-Colonist
Manitoba — Winnipeg Free Press, Winnipeg Sun
News Brunswick — St. John Telegraph-Journal/Evening Times-Globe
Nova Scotia — Halifax Daily News
Ontario — Brantford Expositor, Brockville Recorder & Times, Hamilton-Burlington Spectator, Kingston Whig-Standard, Kitchener-Waterloo Record, London Free Press, North Bay Nugget, Ottawa Citizen, Ottawa Le Droit, Ottawa Sun, Owen Sound Sun Times, St. Catharines Standard, Sault Ste. Marie Sault Star, Stratford Beacon-Herald, Toronto Globe & Mail, Toronto Star, Toronto Sun, Windsor Star
Quebec — Chicoutimi Le Quotidien, Granby La Voix de l'Est, Montreal Gazette, Le Journal de Montreal, Montreal Le Presse, Le Journal de Quebec, Quebec Le Soleil, Sherbrooke Record, Sherbrooke La Tribune, Trois Rivieres Le Nouvelliste
Saskatchewan — Regina Leader Post, Saskatoon Star-Phoenix

NEWSPAPER NATIONAL NETWORK
NEW YORK, NY
711 3rd Ave., 6th Fl., New York, NY 10017; tel (212) 856-6383; fax (212) 856-6343
Vice Pres/GM — Patricia Haegele
Media Director — Carol Karasick
Marketing Director — Nancy Weber
NNN represents every newspaper in the U.S.

THE NEWSPAPER NETWORK (TNN)
HEADQUARTERS OFFICE
2001 21st St., Ste. 100, Sacramento, CA 95818; tel (916) 737-3700; fax (916) 737-3707
President — Jerry Grilly
Sr. Vice Pres. — Gary Moore
Sr. Vice Pres. — Glenn Powers
CFO — Rod Acosta
Mktg. Dir. — Karen Hardison
Exec. Asst. to Pres. — Barbara Hoyt
MID-ATLANTIC REGION (CAROLINAS DIVISION)
131 Falls St., Ste. 201
Greenville, SC 29601
tel (803) 233-7208; fax (803) 241-0707
Reg. Sales Mgr. — Louisa Koken
Reg. Sales Exec. — Debra Jones
MIDWEST REGION (DAYTON)
5450 Far Hills Ave., Ste. 206
Kettering, OH 45429
tel (513) 433-6898; fax (513) 433-6930
Div. Network Sales Mgr. — Eric Brown
MIDWEST REGION (DETROIT)
43422 W. Oaks Dr., Ste. 313
Novi, MI 48377
tel (810) 291-4551; fax (810) 347-1890
Reg. Sales Mgr. — Kimberly Balentine-Garcia
MOUNTAIN REGION (COLORADO)
3801 E. Florida Ave., Ste. 400
Denver, CO 80210
tel (303) 782-9557; fax (303) 782-9572
Div. Sales Mgr. — Tim Collum
MOUNTAIN REGION (UTAH)
699 E. South Temple, Ste. 120
Salt Lake City, UT 84102
tel (801) 521-4636; fax (801) 521-3345
Div. Sales Mgr. — Joe Conaty
NORTHWEST REGION
18270 S.W. Boones Ferry Rd., Ste. 1
Portland, OR 97223
tel (503) 684-8265; fax (503) 968-2378
Reg. Sales Mgr. — Dianne McGill
SOUTHWEST REGION
5025 Arapaho Rd., Ste. 345
Dallas, TX 75248
tel (214) 770-0032; fax (214) 770-0040
Reg. Sales Mgr. — Dick Mathauer
Div. Sales Mgr. — Brad Blakemore
Reg. Sales Exec. — Byron Morriss
SOUTHERN REGION
400 Interstate N. Pkwy., Ste. 620
Atlanta, GA
tel (404) 988-1750; fax (404) 988-1756
Sales Mgr. — Jeff Deitz
Reg. Automotive Sales Mgr. — June Holmes
WESTERN REGION (NORTHERN CALIFORNIA DIVISION)
2001 21st St., Ste. 100
Sacramento, CA 95818
tel (916) 737-3700; fax (916) 737-3733
Reg. Sales Exec. — Bob Badgley
Reg. Sales Exec. — Jim Paquette
Reg. Sales Exec. — Marie Miller
WESTERN REGION (SOUTHERN CALIFORNIA DIVISION)
10401 S. Vermont Ave., Ste. B-200
Torrance, CA 90502
tel (310) 380-4535; fax (310) 527-7002
Sales Mgr. — John Bennett
Reg. Sales Exec. — Donald Borucki
TNN represents over one-third of US dailies and places business in nearly 1,500 daily and weekly newspapers.

NEWSPAPERS FIRST

NEW YORK, NY
711 3rd Ave., New York, NY 10017; tel (212) 692-7100; fax (212) 986-9592
President/CEO — Jay T Zitz
Sr. VP/National Sales — James R Lytle
Sr. VP/Mktg. — Joseph E Maschio
VP/Eastern Region — Keith Flinn
Mktg. Systems Mgr. — Mark Mattison
Mktg. Research Mgr. — Larry Lynch
Classified Sales Mgr. — Beth Williams

FLORIDA REGION
4601 Sheridan St., Ste. 317
Hollywood, FL 33021
tel (305) 987-8666; fax (305) 963-0921
Vice Pres./Sales Mgr. — Lawrence J Malloy

MIDWEST REGION
444 N. Michigan Ave., Ste. 1100
Chicago, IL 60611
tel (312) 822-8666; fax (312) 822-9835
Vice Pres./Sales Mgr. — Geoffrey Welch

SOUTHERN REGION
5956 Sherry Ln., Ste. 610
Dallas, TX 75225
tel (214) 696-8666; fax (214) 696-3416
Vice Pres./Sales Mgr. — Greg Wilson

WESTERN REGION
3701 Wilshire Blvd., Ste. 530
Los Angeles, CA 90010
tel (213) 252-8585; fax (213) 252-0511
Vice Pres./Sales Mgr. — Kay Schultz-Mount

Arizona — Arizona Republic & Phoenix Gazette
California — San Jose Mercury News, Walnut Creek Contra Costa Times
Colorado — Denver Post
Florida — El Nuevo Herald, Miami Herald
Georgia — Atlanta Journal-Constitution
Indiana — Indianapolis Star & News
Kansas — Wichita Eagle
Kentucky — Lexington Herald-Leader
Massachusetts — Boston Globe
Michigan — Detroit News & Free Press
Minnesota — Saint Paul Pioneer Press
North Carolina — Charlotte Observer
Ohio — Akron Beacon Journal
Pennsylvania — Philadelphia Inquirer/Daily News, Pittsburgh Post-Gazette
South Carolina — Columbia State
Texas — Houston Chronicle
Washington — Seattle Times-Post Intelligencer
Wisconsin — Milwaukee Journal & Sentinel

NIXON NEWSPAPERS INC.

PERU, IN
35 W. 3rd St., PO Box 1149, Peru, IN 46970; tel (317) 473-3091; fax (317) 473-8428
President — John R Nixon
Exec. Vice President — Ken Bronson
Vice President/Finance — John Stackhouse
Controller — Deborah Huff

Illinois — Hoopeston Chronicle, Watseka Times-Republic
Indiana — Brazil Times, Connersville News-Examiner, Fountain County Neighbor, Frankfort Times, Michigan City News Dispatch, New Castle Courier-Times, Newton County Enterprise, Wabash Plain Dealer
Louisiana — Hammond Daily Star

THE PAPERT COMPANIES

DALLAS, TX
400 N. St. Paul, Ste. 1300, Dallas, TX 75201-31199; tel (214) 969-0000; fax (214) 754-0421
President — S W Papert Jr

BOSTON, MA
85 Constitution Ln., Ste. 3-D
Danvers, MA 01923
tel (508) 762-0570; fax (508) 762-6298

CHICAGO, IL
400 N. Michigan Ave., Ste. 1010
Chicago, IL 60611
tel (312) 822-9116; fax (312) 822-9119

DENVER, CO
274 Union Blvd., Ste. 350
Denver, CO 80228
tel (303) 987-8288; fax (303) 987-8286

DETROIT, MI
31201 Chicago Rd., Ste. C-201
Warren, MI 48093
tel (810) 977-7706

KANSAS CITY, KS
2200 W. 75th St., Ste. 202
Prairie Village, KS 66208
tel (913) 432-6600; fax (913) 432-6604

LOS ANGELES, CA
19730 Ventura Blvd., Ste. 16
Woodland Hills, CA 91364
tel (818) 888-5793; fax (818) 888-5859

MEMPHIS, TN
5050 Poplar Ave., Ste. 1702
Memphis, TN 38157
tel (901) 767-6572; fax (901) 761-3071

MINNEAPOLIS, MN
33 S. 6th St., Ste. 3980, Multifoods Tower
Minneapolis, MN 55402
tel (612) 338-1958; fax (612) 336-4420

NEW YORK, NY
60 E. 42nd St., Ste. 2544
New York, NY 10165
tel (212) 687-4750; fax (212) 687-5082

SAN FRANCISCO, CA
501 2nd St., Ste. 406
San Francisco, CA 94107-1431
tel (415) 957-9490; fax (415) 957 9014
Manager — Jon Edwards

SEATTLE, WA
33305 1st Way S., Ste. B-207
Federal Way, WA 98003
tel (206) 661-3748; fax (206) 661-3175

Alabama — Anniston Star, Dothan Eagle, Enterprise Ledger, Opelika-Auburn News, Tuscaloosa News
Alaska — Juneau Empire, Kenai Peninsula Clarion, Ketchikan Daily News, Sitka Sentinel
Arizona — Kingman Daily Miner, Mesa Tribune, Prescott Daily Courier, Scottsdale Progress Tribune, Sun City Daily News-Sun, Yuma Daily Sun
Arkansas — Arkadelphia Siftings Herald, Batesville Guard, Benton Courier, Camden News, Conway Log Cabin Democrat, Fayetteville Northwest Arkansas Times, Fort Smith Southwest Times Record, Harrison Daily Times, Helena-West Helena Daily World, Hope Star, Hot Springs Sentinel-Record, Jacksonville Patriot, Jonesboro Sun, Magnolia Banner-News, Malvern Daily Record, Newport Daily Independent, Paragould Daily Press, Pine Bluff Commercial, Russelville Courier-Democrat, Springdale-Rogers Morning News of Northwest Arkansas, Stuttgart Daily Leader
California — Barstow Desert Dispatch, Benicia Herald, Crescent City Triplicate, Davis Enterprise, El Centro Imperial Valley Press, Eureka Times-Standard, Fairfield Daily Republic, Gilroy Dispatch, Glendale News-Press, Hemet News, Hollister Free Lance, Lakeport Lake County Record-Bee, Lodi News-Sentinel, Lompoc Record, Madera Tribune, Manteca Bulletin, Marysville Appeal-Democrat, Monterey County Herald, Ontario Inland Valley Daily Bulletin, Orange County-Costa Mesa Daily Pilot, Oroville Mercury-Register, Placerville Mountain Democrat, Porterville Recorder, Red Bluff Daily News, Redding Record Searchlight, Redlands Daily Facts, Roseville Press Tribune, San Luis Obispo Telegram-Tribune, Santa Clarita Signal, Santa Cruz County Sentinel, Turlock Journal, Ukiah Daily Journal, Vacaville Reporter, Vallejo Times-Herald, Ventura County Star, Victorville Daily Press, Watsonville Register-Pajaronian, Woodland Daily Democrat
Colorado — Boulder Daily Camera, Canon City Daily Record, Craig Northwest Colorado Press, Durango Herald, Fort Collins Coloradoan, Fort Morgan Times, Glenwood Springs Glenwood Post, Greeley Tribune, La Junta Tribune-Democrat, Longmont Daily Times-Call, Loveland Daily Reporter-Herald, Montrose Daily Press, Salida Mountain Mail, Sterling Journal-Advocate
Connecticut — Meriden Record Journal, Norwich Bulletin
Delaware — Dover Delaware State News, Lewes Daily Whale
District of Columbia — Washington Times
Florida — Ft. Pierce-Port St. Lucie Tribune, Ft. Walton Beach Northwest Florida Daily News, Key West Citizen, Marianna Jackson County Floridan, Okeechobee News, Panama City News-Herald, Stuart News, Vero Beach Press-Journal, Winter Haven News Chief
Georgia — Albany Herald, Americus Times-Recorder, Carrollton Times-Georgian, Cartersville Daily Tribune News, Conyers Rockdale Citizen, Cordele Dispatch, Dalton Daily Citizen-News, Griffin Daily News, Marietta Daily Journal, Moultrie Observer, Thomasville Times-Enterprise, Tifton Gazette, Valdosta Daily Times, Warner Robins Daily Sun
Hawaii — Hilo Hawaii Tribune-Herald, Kailua-Kona West Hawaii Today, Lihue Garden Island, Wailuku Maui News
Idaho — Idaho Falls Post-Register, Lewiston Morning Tribune, Moscow-Pullman Daily News, Pocatello Idaho State Journal, Twin Falls Times-News
Illinois — Alton Telegraph, Centralia Sentinel, Chicago Daily Herald, Chicago Daily Southtown, Dixon Telegraph, Edwardsville Intelligencer, Freeport Journal-Standard, Moline Dispatch, Rock Island Argus
Indiana — Anderson Herald-Bulletin, Crawfordsville Journal Review, Kokomo Tribune, Madison Courier, New Albany Ledger & Tribune, Seymour Daily Tribune, Shelbyville News, Terre Haute Tribune-Star, Vincennes Sun-Commercial, Washington Times-Herald
Iowa — Ames Daily Tribune, Atlantic News-Telegraph, Burlington Hawk Eye, Clinton Herald, Council Bluffs Daily NonPareil, Dubuque Telegraph Herald, Fort Dodge Messenger, LeMars Daily Sentinel, Marshalltown Times-Republican, Oskaloosa Herald, Webster City Daily Freeman-Journal
Kansas — Arkansas City Traveler, Chanute Tribune, Coffeyville Journal, Fort Scott Tribune, Great Bend Tribune, Independence Daily Reporter, Junction City Daily Union, Lawrence Journal-World, Liberal Southwest Daily Times, Newton Kansan, Pittsburgh Morning Sun, Pratt Tribune
Kentucky — Bowling Green Daily News, Danville Advocate-Messenger, Glasgow Daily Times, Henderson Gleaner, Hopkinsville Kentucky New Era, Madisonville Messenger, Mayfield Messenger, Murray Ledger & Times, Paducah Sun, Somerset Commonwealth-Journal, Winchester Sun
Louisiana — Alexandria Daily Town Talk, Hammond Daily Star, Houma Courier, Lafayette Advertiser, Lake Charles American Press, New Iberia Daily Iberian, Opelousas Daily World, Thibodaux Daily Comet
Maryland — Cambridge Daily Banner, Cumberland Times-News, Hagerstown Herald Mail
Massachusetts — New Bedford Standard Times, Northampton Daily Hampshire Gazette
Michigan — Bad Axe Huron Daily Tribune, Cadillac News, Hillsdale Daily News, Holland Sentinel, Ludington Daily News, Midland Daily News, Mount Clemens Macomb Daily, Owosso Argus-Press, Royal Oak Daily Tribune
Minnesota — Albert Lea Tribune, Austin Daily Herald, Bemidji Daily Pioneer, Brainerd Daily Dispatch, Crookston Daily Times, Fairmont Sentinel, Fergus Falls Daily Journal, Hibbing Daily Tribune, International Falls Daily Journal, Marshall Independent, New Ulm Journal, Red Wing Republican Eagle, Rochester Post-Bulletin, Stillwater Evening Gazette, Virginia Mesabi Daily News, Worthington Daily Globe
Mississippi — Clarksdale Press Register, Cleveland Bolivar Commercial, Columbus Commercial Dispatch, Corinth Daily Corinthian, Greenville Delta Democrat-Times, Greenwood Commonwealth, Grenada Daily Sentinel-Star, McComb Enterprise-Journal, Meridian Star, Oxford Eagle, Picayune Item, Vicksburg Evening Post, West Point Daily Times Leader
Missouri — Branson Tri-Lakes Daily News, Cape Girardeau Southwest Missourian, Dexter Statesman, Fulton Sun, Joplin Globe, Kennett Daily Dunklin Democrat, Macon Chronicle-Herald, Marshall Democrat-News, Maryville Daily Forum, Moberly Monitor-Index & Democrat, Nevada Daily Mail/Herald, Poplar Bluff Daily American Republican, Sikeston Standard-Democrat
Nebraska — Alliance Times-Herald, Beatrice Daily Sun, Columbus Telegram, Fremont Tribune, Grand Island Independent, Hastings Tribune, Holdrege Daily Citizen, Kearney Hub, McCook Daily Gazette, Nebraska City News-Press, Norfolk Daily News, North Platte Independent, Scottsbluff Star-Herald, Sidney Telegraph, York News-Times
Nevada — Carson City Nevada Appeal, Ely Daily Times, Las Vegas Review-Journal/Sun
New Mexico — Alamogordo Daily News, Carlsbad Current-Argus, Clovis News Journal, Farmington Daily Times, Las Cruces Sun-News, Las Vegas Optic, Portales News-Tribune, Roswell Daily Record
New York — Amsterdam Recorder, Canandaigua Daily Messenger, Corning Leader, Geneva Finger Lakes Times, Kingston Daily Freeman, Oneida Daily Dispatch, Oneonta Daily Star, Plattsburgh Press-Republican
North Carolina — Aberdeen Citizen News-Record, Asheboro Courier-Tribune, Burlington Times-News, Concord Tribune, Gastonia Gaston Gazette, Greenville Daily Reflector, Hickory Daily Record, Jacksonville Daily News, Kannapolis Daily Independent, Monroe Enquirer-Journal, Mount Airy News, Newton Observer-News-Enterprise, Rockingham Richmond County Daily Journal, Salisbury-Spencer Post, Shelby Star, Statesville Record & Landmark, Washington Daily News
North Dakota — Devils Lake Daily Journal
Ohio — Athens Messenger, Bellevue Gazette, Bucyrus Telegraph-Forum, Celina Daily Standard, Circleville Herald, Delaware Gazette, Delphos Daily Herald, Elyria Chronicle-Telegram, Fostoria Review-Times, Galion Inquirer, Greenfield Daily Times, Ironton Tribune, Kenton Times, Logan Daily News, London Madison Press, Marysville Journal-Tribune, Medina County Gazette, Mount Vernon News, Napoleon Northwest Signal, St. Marys Evening Leader, Shelby Daily Globe, Sidney Daily News, Tiffin Advertiser-Tribune, Upper Sandusky Daily Chief-Union, Urbana Daily Citizen, Van Wert Times-Bulletin, Wapakoneta Daily News, Washington Court House Record Herald, Wilmington News Journal
Oklahoma — Ada Evening News, Altus Times, Anadarko Daily News, Bartlesville Examiner-Enterprise, Blackwell Journal-Tribune, Claremore Daily Progress, Clinton Daily News, Cushing Daily Citizen, Duncan Banner, Durant Daily Democrat, Edmond Evening Sun, Elk City Daily News, Frederick Leader, Guthrie Daily Leader, Guymon Daily Herald, Henryetta Daily Free-Lance, Holdenville Daily News, Hugo Daily News, Idabel McCurtain Daily Gazette, Miami News-Record, Norman Transcript, Okmulgee Daily Times, Pauls Valley Daily Democrat, Pryor Daily Times, Seminole Producer, Tahlequah Daily Press, Vinita Daily Journal, Weatherford Daily News, Wewoka Daily Times, Woodward News
Oregon — Albany Democrat-Herald, Astoria Daily Astorian, Baker City Herald, Bend Bulletin, Klamath Falls Herald & News, La Grande Observer, Medford Mail Tribune
Pennsylvania — Bloomsburg Press-Enterprise, Easton Express-Times, Johnstown Tribune-Democrat, Lehighton Times News, Wilkes-Barre Citizens' Voice
South Carolina — Beaufort Gazette, Greenwood Index-Journal, Hilton Head Island Packet, Orangeburg Times & Democrat, Sumter Item
South Dakota — Brookings Register, Huron Plainsman, Watertown Public Opinion, Yankton Daily Press & Dakotan
Tennessee — Cleveland Daily Banner, Columbia Daily Herald, Cookeville Herald-Citizen, Dyersburg State Gazette, Elizabethton Star, Lebanon Democrat, Maryville-Alcoa Daily Times, Murfreesboro Daily News Journal, Paris Post-Intelligencer, Sevierville Mountain Press, Shelbyville Times-Gazette, Union City Daily Messenger
Texas — Abilene Reporter-News, Alice Echo-News, Amarillo Daily News/Globe Times, Athens Daily Review, Big Spring Herald, Bonham Favorite, Borger News-Herald, Brownsville El Heraldo, Brownsville Herald, Brownwood Bulletin, Bryan-College Station Eagle, Cleburne Times-Review, Corpus Christi Caller-Times, Corsicana Daily Sun, Dalhart Daily Texan, Del Rio News-Herald, Denison Herald, Gainesville Daily Register, Galveston County Daily News, Greenville Herald Banner, Harlingen Valley Morning Star, Jacksonville Daily Progress, Kerrville Daily Times, Kilgore News Herald, Killeen Daily Herald, Laredo Morning Times, Longview News-Journal, Lubbock Avalanche-Journal, Marshall News Messenger, McAllen Monitor, Mexia Daily News, Midland Reporter-Telegram, Odessa American, Orange Leader, Pampa News, Paris News, Plainview Daily Herald, Plano Star Courier, San Angelo Standard-Times, Stephenville Empire-Tribune, Sweetwater Reporter, Taylor Daily Press, Temple Daily Telegram, Texarkana Gazette, Texas City Sun, Victoria Advocate, Waco Tribune-Herald, Wichita Falls Times Record News
Utah — St. George Spectrum
Vermont — Barre-Montpelier Times Argus, Rutland Herald
Virginia — Woodbridge Potomac News
Washington — Aberdeen Daily World, Bellevue Journal American, Bremerton Sun, Centralia-Chehalis Chronicle, Ellensburg Daily Record, Kent Valley Daily News, Mount Vernon Skagit Valley Herald, Port Angeles Peninsula Daily News

Copyright ©1996 by the Editor & Publisher Co.

West Virginia — Fairmont Times-West Virginian
Wisconsin — Ashland Daily Press, Marshfield News-Herald, Monroe Evening Times, Stevens Point Journal, Superior Daily Telegram, Wausau Daily Herald
Wyoming — Casper Star-Tribune, Cheyenne Wyoming Tribune-Eagle, Laramie Daily Boomerang, Rawlins Daily Times, Riverton Ranger, Sheridan Press, Worland Northern Wyoming Daily News

PUBLICATIONS REPRESENTATIVES INTERNATIONAL INC.

FORT WORTH, TX
8228-B Woodvale Dr., Fort Worth, TX 76136; tel (817) 332-1990; fax (817) 877-1888

MEXICO CITY, MEXICO
Londres 177 Primer Piso, Colonia Juarez Mexico City, 06600 Mexico
tel (011) 52 52 084518; fax (011) 52 52 084269

California — San Jose Mercury News
Colorado — Denver Rocky Mountain News
District of Columbia — USA Today
Florida — Ft. Lauderdale Sun-Sentinel
Illinois — Chicago Sun Times
New York — New York Times
Texas — Dallas Morning News, San Antonio Express News
Washington — Seattle Times/Post Intelligencer

PUBLISHERS REPRESENTATIVES OF FLORIDA INC.

JACKSONVILLE, FL
4700 San Jose Manor Dr. W., Jacksonville, FL 32217; tel (904) 730-9903; fax (904) 730-7781
President — Martin Steinburg

MIAMI, FL
285 N.W. 199th St., Ste. 202
Miami, FL 33169
tel (305) 652-8510; fax (305) 652-0796
Manager — Vern Goff

ORLANDO, FL
455 Douglas Ave., Ste. 2255-M
Altamonte Spring, FL 32714 US
tel (407) 862-0024; fax (407) 862-0024
Manager — Lee Knox

TAMPA, FL
4601 W. Kennedy Blvd., Ste. 227
Tampa, FL 33609
tel (813) 286-8299; fax (813) 286-8299
Manager — Jim Gundry

Florida — Bradenton Herald, Central Florida Golden Markets Groups, Clearwater Sun, Daytona Beach News Journal, Ft. Lauderdale News/Sun, Jacksonville Times-Union, Lake City Reporter, Lakeland Ledger, Leesburg Commercial, Naples News, Ocala Star-Banner, Orlando Sentinel, Palatka Daily News, Palm Beach Post, Sarasota, Herald-Tribune, St. Augustine Record, Stuart News, Tallahassee Democrat, Tampa Tribune, Vero Beach Press-Journal
New Jersey — Bergen Record, Middlesex Home News & Tribune
New York — Albany Times-Union, Gannett New York Travel Group, Westchester/Rockland Newspaper
North Carolina — Asheville Citizen-Times, Charlotte Observer
South Carolina — Charleston Courier Post, Columbia State, Greenville News Piedmont, Spartanburg Herald Journal
Tennessee — Knoxville News Sentinel

C.M. SAVAGE ASSOCIATES

BROOKLYN, NY
510 E. 16th. St., Brooklyn, NY 11226; tel (718) 287-2057
President — Carey Savage
Vice President/Sales — Michael C Savage
New York — Staten Island Advance

SAWYER-FERGUSON-WALKER CO. INC.

NEW YORK, NY
90 Park Ave., New York, NY 10016-1301; tel (212) 661-6262; fax (212) 808-5434
Chmn./CEO — D S Tomlinson Jr
President — J A Thompson
Exec. VP/Gen. Sales Mgr. — Chas McKeown
Sr. Vice Pres. — B P Zangara
VP/Dir. Retail Mktg.-Sales — M De Robertis

Asst. NY Sales Mgr./Supv. — J D McCabe
Retail Supv. — E N Kessler
Supervisor — P W Mueller
Exec. VP/Dir. Research & Mktg. — S Seraita
Assoc. Dir. Research & Mktg. — L J Crossin
Art Dir. — F Reyes

ATLANTA, GA
3390 Peachtree Rd. N.E., Lenox Towers
Atlanta, GA 30326
tel (404) 261-1362
Sr. Vice President/Mgr. — R G Huthwaite

BOSTON, MA
209 W. Central St.
Natick, MA 01760
tel (508) 655-7544; fax (508) 655-1919
Vice President/Mgr. — Grenville Willis

CHICAGO, IL
500 N. Michigan Ave., Ste. 500
Chicago, IL 60611
tel (312) 329-1780; fax (312) 329-1787
Vice President/Mgr. — D P Stephenson

DALLAS, TX
12201 Merit Dr., Ste. 430, Two Forest Plz.
Dallas, TX 75251
tel (214) 960-8900; fax (214) 387-8114
Vice President/Mgr. — Joseph Roddy

DETROIT, MI
26877 Northwestern Hwy., Ste. 407
Southfield, MI 48034
tel (810) 352-9810; fax (810) 352-5866
Vice President/Regional Mgr. — D W Stemmermann

LOS ANGELES, CA
5757 Wilshire Blvd., Ste. 448
Los Angeles, CA 90036
tel (213) 936-1069; fax (213) 936-0955
Vice President/Regional Mgr. — J M Kephart

MIAMI, FL
3050 Biscayne Blvd., Ste. 410
Miami, FL 33137
tel (305) 573-6768; fax (305) 571-9313
Vice President/Mgr. — Ronald M Simpson

PHILADELPHIA, PA
495 Virginia Ave.
Paoli, PA 19087
tel (610) 640-4140; fax (610) 640-9711
Vice President/Mgr. — G R Ervin

SAN FRANCISCO, CA
560 Mills Tower, 220 Bush St.
San Francisco, CA 94104
tel (415) 421-5707; fax (415) 421-5730
Manager — Leonora Plizga

Arkansas — Little Rock Arkansas Democrat-Gazette
California — Copley Los Angeles Newspapers, Long Beach Press-Telegram, Riverside Press-Enterprise, San Diego Union-Tribune
Colorado — Denver Rocky Mountain News
Dist of Columbia — Washington Post
Florida — Daytona Beach News-Journal, Naples Daily News, Tampa Tribune, Jacksonville Florida Times-Union
Illinois — Chicago Newspapers, Aurora Beacon-News, Copley Belleville News Democrat, Elgin Courier-News, Joliet Herald-News, Waukegan News Sun
Indiana — Evansville Courier-Press
Louisiana — Baton Rouge Advocate
Maine — Bangor Daily News
Massachusetts — Boston Herald
Michigan — Oakland Press
Minnesota — Minneapolis Star Tribune
New Hampshire — Manchester Union Leader
New Jersey — Asbury Park Press, Bergen Record, Burlington County Times, Middlesex Home News & Tribune
New Mexico — Albuquerque Journal & Tribune
New York — Albany Times Union, Buffalo News, Schenectady Daily Gazette
North Carolina — Winston-Salem Journal
Ohio — Columbus Dispatch, Toledo Blade, Youngstown Vindicator
Oklahoma — Oklahoma City Oklahoman
Pennsylvania — Doylestown Intelligencer, Levittown Bucks County Courier Times, Greater Philadelphia Newspapers, Levittown Bucks County Courier Times, Scranton Times
Tennessee — Knoxville News-Sentinel, Memphis Commercial Appeal
Texas — Fort Worth Star-Telegram, San Antonio Express News
Virginia — Richmond News Leader & Times Dispatch
Washington — Tacoma News-Tribune, Everett Herald

SOUTHAM NEWSPAPER GROUP MARKETING DIVISION

TORONTO, ON
1450 Don Mills Rd., Don Mills, ON M3B 2X7 Canada; tel (416) 445-6641; fax (416) 442-3378

National newspaper reps VII-39

Vice President — R D Munro
Vice President — S J Short
Mgr./Nat'l. Sales — Greg Varga
Mgr./Nat'l. Sales — Don Fisher

MONTREAL, QC
231 St. Jacques St. W.
Montreal, QC H2Y 1M6 Canada
tel (514) 849-9987; fax (514) 849-3422
Manager — Phil Pannenton

VANCOUVER, BC
4285 Canada Way
Burnaby, BC V5G 1H2 Canada
tel (604) 433-6125; fax (604) 433-9549
Nat'l. Sales Mgr. — Glen Sayers

Alberta — Calgary Herald, Edmonton Journal, Medicine Hat News
British Columbia — Kamloops Daily News, Prince George Citizen, Vancouver Province, Kamloops News
Ontario — Brantford Expositor, Hamilton Spectator, North Bay Nugget, Ottawa Citizen, Owen Sound Sun Times, Sault Ste. Marie Daily Star, Windsor Star
Quebec — Montreal Gazette

SOUTHERN CROSS ADVERTISING AGENCY LTD.

NEW YORK, NY
301 W. 57th St., Ste. 48-C, New York, NY 10019; tel (212) 581-9237/(917) 881-8412; fax (212) 865-4528
Chairman/CEO — Mario Mieli
President/CFO — Andre Aleradique
Newspaper representative for the ethnic market.

THOMSON NEWSPAPERS INC.

CHICAGO, IL
3150 Des Plaines Ave., Des Plaines, IL 60018; tel (708) 299-5544; fax (708) 299-5929
Sr. Vice Pres./COO — Don P Hicks

KANSAS CITY, MO
11020 Ambassador Dr., Ste. 400
Kansas City, MO 64153
tel (816) 891-7582; fax (816) 891-7078

PITTSBURGH, PA
345 Rouser Rd., Airport Office Park Bldg., Ste. 5
Coraopolis, PA 15108
tel (412) 262-7870; fax (412) 262-7891

TAMPA, FL
600 N. Westshore Blvd., Ste. 400
Tampa, FL 33631
tel (813) 289-4455; fax (813) 287-2137

Alabama — Dothan Eagle, Enterprise Ledger, Opelika-Auburn News
California — Eureka Times-Standard, Pasadena Star-News, West Covina San Gabriel Valley Tribune, Whittier Daily News
Connecticut — Fairfield County-Bridgeport Connecticut Post
Florida — Key West Citizen, Marianna Jackson County Floridan
Georgia — Americus Times-Recorder, Cordele Dispatch, Dalton Daily Citizen-News, Griffin Daily News, Thomasville Times-Enterprise, Tifton Gazette, Valdosta Daily Times
Illinois — Mount Vernon Register-News
Indiana — Anderson Herald-Bulletin, Kokomo Tribune, Logansport Pharos-Tribune, Terre Haute Tribune-Star
Iowa — Council Bluffs Daily Nonpareil
Louisiana — Lafayette Advertiser
Maryland — Cumberland Times-News, Salisbury Daily Times
Massachusetts — Fitchburg Sentinel & Enterprise, Taunton Daily Gazette
Michigan — Adrian Daily Telegram, Benton Harbor-St. Joseph Herald-Palladium, Escanaba Daily Press, Houghton Daily Mining Gazette, Iron Mountain-Kingsford Daily News, Marquette Mining Journal
New Hampshire — Portsmouth Herald
North Carolina — Elizabeth City Daily Advance, Monroe Enquirer-Journal, Rocky Mount Telegram, Shelby Star
Ohio — Ashtabula Star Beacon, Bucyrus Telegraph-Forum, Canton Repository, Coshocton Tribune, East Liverpool Evening Review, Greenville Daily Advocate, Hamilton Journal-News, Lancaster Eagle-Gazette, Mansfield News Journal, Marion Star, Middletown Journal, Newark Advocate, Piqua Daily Call, Steubenville Herald-Star, Warren Tribune Chronicle, Xenia Daily Gazette, Zanesville Times Recorder

Oklahoma — Enid News & Eagle
Pennsylvania — Altoona Mirror, Connellsville Daily Courier, Hanover Evening Sun, Kittanning Leader Times, Lebanon Daily News, Lock Heaven Express, Meadville Tribune, Monessen Valley Independent, New Castle News, Shamokin-Mt. Carmel News-Item
South Carolina — Florence Morning News
Utah — St. George Spectrum
Virginia — Petersburg Progress-Index
West Virginia — Beckley Register-Herald, Bluefield Daily Telegram, Charleston Daily Mail, Fairmont Times-West Virginian, Weirton Daily Times
Wisconsin — Appleton Post-Crescent, Fond du Lac Reporter, Manitowoc Herald Times Reporter, Sheboygan Press, Waukesha County Freeman, West Bend Daily News, Wisconsin Rapids Daily Tribune
Alberta — Lethbridge Herald
British Columbia — Kelowna Daily Courier, Nanaimo Daily Free Press, Penticton Herald, Vernon Daily News, Victoria Times-Colonist
Manitoba — Brandon Sun, Winnipeg Free Press
Newfoundland — Corner Brook Western Star, St. John's Evening Telegram
Nova Scotia — New Glasgow Evening News, Sydney Cape Breton Post, Truro Daily News
Ontario — Chatham Daily News, Cornwall Standard-Freeholder, Kirkland Lake Northern Daily News, Sarnia Observer, Sudbury Star, Thunder Bay Times-News/Chronicle-Journal, Timmins Daily Press, Toronto Globe & Mail
Prince Edward Island — Charlottetown Guardian

TOWMAR

MEXICO CITY, MEXICO
Presa de la Angostura 8, Mexico City, 11500 Mexico; tel 52 53 955888; fax 52 53 954985
Telex: 1763128

MIAMI, FL
1111 Lincoln Rd., Ste. 340
Miami, FL 33139
tel (305) 532-0726; fax (305) 531-7616
California — Los Angeles Daily News, Orange County Register, Sacramento Bee, San Francisco Chronicle/Examiner
Colorado — Denver Post
Florida — St. Petersburg Times, Tampa Tribune
Georgia — Atlanta Journal/Constitution
Illinois — Chicago Tribune
Massachusetts — Boston Globe
New Jersey — Newark Star-Ledger, Trenton Times
Texas — Fort Worth Star-Telegram, Houston Chronicle
Canada — Financial Post
Quebec — Montreal La Presse
England — Financial Times

TRADE UNION ADVERTISING

NEW YORK, NY
114 E. 32nd St., Ste. 906, New York, NY 10016; tel (212) 683-7905; fax (212) 447-6628
Pres./Labor Newspapers — Alex Smith
California — Union Reporter, Oakland-East Bay Labor Journal, Sacramento Union Labor Bulletin, San Jose Construction Labor News, Santa Barbara Labor News
Connecticut — Government News, AFL-CIO News
Colorado — Labor Adv.
Illinois — Chicago Fed. News, DuPage Co. Labor Record, Fox Valley Labor Record, Grundy Co. Labor News, Kankakee Labor Record, Lake Co. Labor News, No. LaSalle Labor News, Dekalb Co. Labor News, Will Co. Labor Record, Peoria Labor News, Quincy Labor News, Streator Labor News, So. Illinois & St. Louis Labor Tribune, McHenry Co. Labor Record
Indiana — AFL-CIO News
Iowa — Dubuque Leader
Kansas — Wichita Plain Dealer
Kentucky — Labor News
Maine — Labor Record
Michigan — Detroit Bldg. Tradesman, Detroit Labor News, Grand Valley Labor News, Lansing Labor News, Grand Valley Labor News
Minnesota — Duluth Labor World, Minneapolis Labor Review, St. Paul Union Advocate
Missouri — Kansas City Union Beacon, St. Louis & So. Illinois Labor Tribune, State News
New York — Rochester Allegro Labor News

VII-40   National newspaper reps

Ohio — Cincinnati Union Builder, Cleveland Citizen, Labor Citizen, Labor Citizen, Toledo Union Journal
Oregon — Northwest Labor Press, Union Register
Pennsylvania — Hershey Labor News
Texas — Dallas Craftsman
Washington — King Co. Scanner, Olympia Sentinel
Wisconsin — Kenosha Labor, Madison Union Labor News, Milwaukee Labor Press, Racine Labor

TRIBUNE NEWSPAPER NETWORK

NEW YORK, NY
220 E. 42nd St., Ste. 1402, New York, NY 10017; tel (212) 210-5956; fax (212) 210-5963
President — Gerald McCarthy
Sales Manager — Milan Chilla
Mgr. Branch Operations — Ted Sheldon
Network Account Mgr. — Andreas Drosie

ATLANTA, GA
2839 Paces Ferry Rd., Ste. 1105
Atlanta, GA 30339
tel (770) 433-9554; fax (770) 433-1927
Atlanta Manager — Gail Brinkman

CHICAGO, IL
435 N. Michigan Ave.
Chicago, IL 60611
tel (312) 222-3909; fax (312) 222-3935
Midwest Manager — Janet Cassello

DALLAS, TX
8350 N. Central Expy., Ste. 660
Dallas, TX 75206
tel (214) 363-5044; fax (214) 368-8253
Southwestern Regional Mgr. — Tom Stansfield

DETROIT, MI
4000 Town Center, Ste. 710
Southfield, MI 48075
tel (810) 352-1630; fax (810) 352-5926
Detroit Manager — Mark Barrons

HOLLYWOOD, FL
4651 Sheridan St., Ste. 410
Hollywood, CA 33021
tel (305) 989-8833; fax (305) 963-3395
Florida Manager — Barry Werblow

LOS ANGELES, CA
4601 Wilshire Blvd., Ste. 110
Los Angeles, CA 90010
tel (213) 933-5623; fax (213) 938-3486
Pres./Western States — Norm Branchflower
Exec. VP/Western States — Rick Gables

SAN FRANCISCO, CA
101 California St., Ste. 930
San Francisco, CA 94111
tel (415) 421-7946; fax (415) 421-0827
Vice Pres./Western States — Ron DeCook
Florida — Ft. Lauderdale Sun-Sentinel, Orlando Sentinel
Illinois — Chicago Tribune
Virginia — Newport News Daily Press

THE COLIN TURNER GROUP

LONDON, ENGLAND
188-196 Old St., City Cloisters, London, EC1V 9BX England; tel (011) 171 490-5551 (National)/44-171-490-5551 (International); fax (011) 171 490-2271
Telex: 261140 Turner G
Chairman/Managing Director — Anthony Turner
Finance Director — Ken Ball

U.S. SUBURBAN PRESS INC.

SCHAUMBURG, IL
500 E. Remington Rd., Ste. 104, Schaumburg, IL 60173; tel (708) 490-6000; fax (708) 843-9058
President — Robert Noga
VP/Research — Donald R Garrabrant

CHICAGO, IL
203 N. Wabash Ave., Ste. 2219
Chicago, IL 60601
tel (312) 578-1700; fax (312) 578-0908

DETROIT, MI
200 E. Big Beaver Rd., Ste. 122
Troy, MI 48083
tel (313) 680-4626; fax (313) 524-4914

NEW YORK, NY
420 Lexington Ave., Ste. 453
New York, NY 10170
tel (212) 687-8425; fax (212) 986-8033
Anaheim — Orange County Daily Pilot
Atlanta — Gainesville Times, Marietta Daily Journal
Baltimore — Carroll County Times, Cecil Whig, Easton Star-Democrat
Boston — Brockton Enterprise, Dedham Daily Transcript, Gloucester Daily Times, Haverhill Gazette, Lowell Sun, Lynn Daily Evening Item, Malden Daily News-Mercury, Middlesex News, Newburyport Daily News, Salem Evening News, Waltham News Tribune, Woburn Daily Times Chronicle
Bridgeport — Danbury News-Times, Milford Citizen, Norwalk Hour
Buffalo — Niagara Gazette, Tonawanda News
Charlotte — Monroe Enquirer-Journal, Salisbury Post, Statesville Record & Landmark
Chicago — Daily Herald, Daily Southtown, McHenry County Northwest Herald
Cincinnati — Hamilton Journal News, Middletown Journal
Columbus — Circleville Herald, Delaware Gazette, London Madion Press, Marysville Journal-Tribune
Dallas — McKinney Courier-Gazette, Plano Star Courier, Terrell Tribune
Dayton — Beavercreek News-Current, Fairborn Daily Camera, Troy Daily News
Denver — Boulder Daily Camera, Longmont Times-Call, Loveland Reporter-Herald
Detroit — Monroe Evening News, Mt. Clements Macon Daily, Port Huron Times Herald, Royal Oak Daily Tribune
Hartford — Bristol Press, Manchester Journal Inquirer, Middletown Press, New Britain Herald
Hawaii — Lihue Garden Island, Maui News
Houston — Baytown Sun, Brenham Banner Press, Conroe Courier, Galveston Daily News, Martinsville Reporter, Rosenberg Herald Coaster
Indianapolis — Martinsville Reporter, Noblesville Daily Ledger, Shelbyville News
Kansas City — Blue Springs Examiner, Independence Examiner
Los Angeles — Glendale News-Press, Pasadena Star News, San Gabriel Valley Daily Tribune, Santa Monica Outlook, Whitter Daily News
Northern Michigan — Ludington Daily News, Midland Daily News, Mt. Pleasant Morning Sun, Petoskey News-Review
Nashville — Murfreesboro Daily News-Journal, Bridgewater Courier-News
New Jersey — Bridgewater Courier-News, Toms River Ocean County Observer
New Orleans — Slidell Sentry-News
Oklahoma City — Edmond Evening News
Philadelphia — Bucks County Courier Times, Bucks County Intelligencer, Burlington County Times, Delaware County Daily & Sunday Times, Lansdale Reporter, Norristown Times Herald, Pottstown Mercury, Salem Today's Sunbeam, Woodbury Gloucester County Times
Phoenix — Sun City News-Sun
Pittsburgh — Beaver County Times, Ellwood City Ledger, Greensburg Tribune-Review, Irwin Standard Observer, New Kensington-Tarentum Valley News Dispatch, North Hills News Record, Uniontown Herald-Standard, Washington Observer Reporter
Palm Springs — Desert Sun
Sacramento — Auburn Journal, Daily Democrat, Davis Enterprise, Fairfield Daily Republic
San Diego — Daily Californian, Escondido Times-Advocate, North City Blade-Citizen, Temecula Californian
San Francisco — Antioch Daily Ledger/Post Dispatch, Benicia Herald, Pinole West County Times, Pleasanton Valley Times, Walnut Creek Contra Costa Times
Seattle — Bellevue Journal-American, Kent Valley Daily News
Washington DC — Frederick News-Post, Fredericksburg Free Lance-Star, Prince William County Potomac News
Wilkes-Barre — Citizens' Voice

WESTERN STATES ASSOCIATES INC.

LOS ANGELES, CA
4601 Wilshire Blvd., Ste. 110, Los Angeles, CA 90010; tel (213) 933-5623; fax (213) 938-3486
President — Norm Branchflower

SAN FRANCISCO, CA
101 California St., Ste. 930
San Francisco, CA 94111
tel (415) 421-7946; fax (415) 421-0827
Manager — Ron DeCook
Florida — Ft. Lauderdale Sun-Sentinel, Orlando Sentinel
Illinois — Chicago Tribune
New York — Daily News
Virginia — Newport News Daily Press

RICHARD H. WITT

TRENTON, NJ
10 Lake Dr., PO Box 1015, Hightstown, NJ 08520; tel (609) 448-9100; fax (609) 448-4828
Dir. Advertising — Richard H Witt
Arizona — Phoenix Daily Racing Form

NEWSPAPER ASSOCIATION OF AMERICA
MEMBERSHIP ROSTER — December 1, 1995

ALABAMA
Anniston Star
Birmingham News
Birmingham Post-Herald
Cleburne News
Decatur Daily
Dothan Eagle
Enterprise Ledger
Florence-Sheffield Times Daily
Gadsden Times
Huntsville Times/News
Jacksonville News
Mobile Press/Register
Montgomery Advertiser
Opelika-Auburn News
Prattville Progress
Talladega Daily Home
Tuscaloosa News

ALASKA
Anchorage Daily News
Fairbanks Daily News-Miner
Juneau Empire
Kenai Peninsula Clarion
Ketchikan Daily News
Matanuska Frontiersman

ARIZONA
Arizona Business Gazette
Arizona Range News
Arizona Republic/Phoenix Gazette
Bisbee Daily Review
Casa Grande Dispatch
Cavecreek-North Scottsdale Foothills Sentinel
Chandler Arizonan Tribune
Douglas Daily Dispatch
Gilbert Tribune
Grahm Eastern Arizona Courier
Green Valley News & Sun
Kingman Daily Miner
Lake Havasu Today's News-Herald
Mesa Tribune
Nogales International
Parker Pioneer
Payson Roundup
Prescott Daily Courier
San Pedro Valley News-Sun
Scottsdale Progress Tribune
Sierra Vista Herald
Sun City Daily News-Sun
Tempe Daily News Tribune
Tucson Citizen
Tucson Daily Territorial
Verde Independent
Williams-Grand Canyon News
Yuma Daily Sun

ARKANSAS
Arkadelphia Daily Siftings Herald
Benton Courier
Bentonville County Daily Record
Blytheville Courier-News
Booneville Democrat
Camden News
Conway Log Cabin Democrat
Corning Clay County Courier
El Dorado News-Times
Ft. Smith Southwest Times Record
Hot Springs Sentinel-Record
Jonesboro Sun
Little Rock Arkansas Democrat-Gazette
Magnolia Banner-News
Mountain Home Baxter Bulletin
Searcy Daily Citizen
Springdale-Rogers Morning News of Northwest Arkansas
Osceola Times
Paragould Daily Press
Pine Bluff Commercial
West Memphis Evening Times

CALIFORNIA
Alameda Times-Star
Amador Ledger-Dispatch
Antioch Ledger Dispatch
Bakersfield Californian
Barstow Desert Dispatch
Brentwood News
Calexico La Cronica
Cambria Cambrian
Chico Enterprise-Record
Clovis Independent
Colusa County Sun Herald
Contra Costa Sun
Crescent City Triplicate
Davis Enterprise
El Cajon Daily Californian
El Centro Imperial Valley Press
Escondido Times Advocate
Eureka Times-Standard
Fairfield Daily Republic
Fort Bragg Advocate News
Fremont-Newark Argus
Fresno Bee
Gilray Dispatch
Glendale News-Press
Grass Valley Union
Half Moon Bay Review
Hayward Daily Review
Hemet News
Hollister Free Lance
Lake County Record-Bee
Lake Elsinore Valley Sun-Tribune
Lincoln News Messenger
Lompoc Record
Long Beach Press-Telegram
Los Angeles Daily Journal
Los Angeles Daily News
Los Angeles Korea Central Daily
Los Angeles Times
Manteca Bulletin
Marin Independent Journal
Marysville-Yuba City Appeal-Democrat
Modesto Bee
Monterey County Herald
Moreno Valley Times
Morgan Hill Times
Oakland Tribune
Oceanside North County Blade-Citizen
Ojai Valley News
Ontario-Upland Inland Valley Daily Bulletin
Orange County-Costa Mesa Daily Pilot
Oroville Mercury Register
Pacific Palisades Post
Palm Springs-Palm Desert Sun
Palmdale Antelope Valley Press
Palo Verde Valley Times
Paradise Post
Pasadena Star-News
Pleasanton Tri-Valley Herald
Pleasanton Valley Times
Porterville Recorder
Red Bluff Daily News

Copyright ©1996 by the Editor & Publisher Co.

NAA members VII-41

Redding Record Searchlight
Redlands Daily Facts
Richmond West County Times
Ridgecrest Daily Independent
Sacramento Bee
Salinas Californian
San Bernardino Sun
San Diego Daily Transcript
San Diego Union-Tribune
San Francisco Chronicle
San Francisco Examiner
San Gabriel Valley Daily Tribune
San Jose Mercury News
San Luis Obispo Telegram-Tribune
San Mateo Times
San Pedro News-Pilot
Santa Ana Orange County Register
Santa Ana Press Democrat
Santa Barbara News-Press
Santa Clarita Signal
Santa Cruz County Sentinel
Santa Monica Outlook
Simi Valley Star & Enterprise
South Lake Tahoe Daily Tribune
Stockon Record
Sun City News
Thousand Oaks Star
Torrance Daily Breeze
Tracy Press
Tulare Advance-Register
Turlock Journal
Ukiah Daily Journal
Vallejo Times-Herald
Ventura County Star
Victorville Daily Press
Visalia Times-Delta
Walnut Creek Contra Costa Times
Whittier Daily News
Woodland Daily Democrat

COLORADO

Boulder Daily Camera
Canon City Daily Record
Canyon Courier
Castle Rock News-Press
Colorado Springs Gazette Telegraph
Craig Northwest Colorado Daily Press
Denver Post
Denver Rocky Mountain News
Durango Herald
Fort Collins Coloradoan
Glenwood Post
Grand Junction Daily Sentinel
Greeley Tribune
Longmont Daily Times-Call
Loveland Daily Reporter-Herald
Pueblo Chieftain
Steamboat Springs Steamboat Pilot
Telluride Times-Journal
Trinidad Chronicle-News

CONNECTICUT

Avon News
Bloomfield Journal
Branford Review
Bristol Press
Clinton Recorder
Colchester Regional Standard
Danbury News-Times
East Haven Advertiser
Fairfield Co.-Bridgeport Connecticut Post
Farmington News
Greenwich Time
Guilford Shore Line Times
Hartford Courant
Litchfield County Times
Meridan Record-Journal
Middletown Press
New Britain Herald
New Haven Register
New London Day
Newington Town Crier
Norwalk Hour
Norwich Bulletin
Old Saybrook Pictorial-Gazette
Rocky Hill Post
Simsbury News
Stamford Advocate
Torrington Register Citizen
Waterbury Republican-American
West Hartford News
Wethersfield Post
Windsor Journal
Windsor Locks Journal

DELAWARE

Wilmington News Journal

DISTRICT OF COLUMBIA

China Times Weekly
Stars and Stripes

Washington Informer
Washington Post
Washington Times

FLORIDA

Amelia Island News-Leader
Apalachicola Times
Apopka Chief
Boca Raton News
Bradenton Herald
Charlotte Sun Herald
Crystal River Citrus County Chronicle
Daytona Beach News-Journal
Destin Log
Ft. Lauderdale Sun-Sentinel
Ft. Myers News-Press
Ft. Pierce/Port St. Lucie Tribune
Ft. Walton Beach Northwest Florida Daily News
Gainesville Sun
Jacksonville Beaches Leader
Jacksonville Florida Times-Union
Jupiter Journal Courier
Key West Citizen
Lake City Reporter
Lakeland Ledger
Marco Island Eagle
Marianna Jackson County Floridan
Melbourne Florida Today
Miami Diario Las Americas
Miami El Nuevo Herald
Miami Herald
Miami Times
Naples Daily News
Ocala Star-Banner
Orlando Sentinel
Palatka Daily News
Palm Beach Daily News
Palm Beach Post
Panama City News Herald
Pasco News
Pensacola News Journal
Perry News Herald
St. Augustine Record
St. Petersburg Times
Sanford Herald
Sarasota Herald-Tribune
Sebrias News-Sun
South Dade News-Leader
Stuart News
Sumter County Times
Taco Times
Tallahassee Democrat
Tampa Tribune
Venice Gondolier
Winter Haven News Chief

GEORGIA

Albany Herald
Americus Times-Recorder
Athens Daily News/Banner-Herald
Atlanta Journal & Constitution
Augusta Chronicle
Bainbridge Post-Searchlight
Bowdon Bulletin
Carrollton Times-Georgian
Columbus Ledger-Enquirer
Conyers Rockdale Citizen
Cordele Dispatch
Cumming Forsyth County News
Dublin Courier Herald
Dalton Daily Citizen-News
Douglasville Douglas County Sentinel
Gainesville Times
Griffin Daily News
Haralson Gateway Beacon
La Grange Daily News
Lawrenceville Gwinnett Post-Tribune
Macon Telegraph
Marietta Daily Journal
Milledgeville Union-Recorder
Moultrie Observer
Newnan Times-Herald
Rome News-Tribune
Savannah News-Press
Statesboro Herald
Thomasville Times-Enterprise
Tifton Gazette
Valdosta Daily Times
Villa Rica Villa Rican
Warner Robins Daily Sun

HAWAII

Hilo Hawaii Tribune-Herald
Honolulu Advertiser
Kailua-Kona West Hawaii Today
Wailuku Maui News

IDAHO

Boise Idaho Statesman
Bonners Ferry Herald
Burley South Idaho Press

Coeur d'Alene Press
Fremont County Herald-Chronicle
Jefferson Star
Kellogg Shoshone News-Press
Minidoka County News
Nampa-Caldwell Idaho Press-Tribune
Payette Co. Independent Enterprise
Pocatello Idaho State Journal
Post Falls Tribune
Priest River Times
Rexburg Standard-Journal
Sandpoint Bonner County Daily Bee
Twin Falls Times-News
Wallace Miner

ILLINOIS

Alton Telegraph
Aurora Beacon-News
Belleville News-Democrat
Belvidere Daily Republican
Bloomington-Normal Pantagraph
Bolingbrook Sun
Carbondale Southern Illinoisan
Cass County Illinoian-Star
Centralia Sentinel
Champaign Daily Illini
Charleston Coles County Daily Times-Courier
Chicago Advertising Age
Chicago Tribune
Crystal Lake Northwest Herald
Danville Commercial-News
Decatur Herald & Review
Dixon Telegraph
Edwardsville Intelligencer
Effingham Daily News
Elgin Daily Courier-News
Fox Valley Sun
Freeport Journal-Standard
Galesburg Register-Mail
Geneva Kane County Chronicle
Highland News Leader
Jacksonville Journal-Courier
Joliet Herald-News
Juneau County Star-Times
Kankakee Daily Journal
Kewanee Star-Courier
La Crosse County Countryman
Lincoln Courier
Lisle Sun
Litchfield News-Herald
Macomb Journal
Marissa Journal-Messenger
Mattoon Journal-Gazette
McLeansboro Times-Leader
Moline Dispatch
Morris Herald
Mount Vernon Register-News
Naperville Sun
O'Fallon Progress
Ottawa Daily Times
Pekin Daily Times
Peoria Journal Star
Pinckneyville Democrat
Princeton Bureau County Republican
Quincy Herald-Whig
Rock Island Argus
Rockford Register Star
Romeoville Sun
Sparta News-Plaindealer
Springfield State Journal-Register
Streator Times-Press
Taylorville Daily Breeze-Courier
Vandalia Leader-Union
Waterloo Republic-Times
Waukegan-North Chicago News-Sun
Wheaton Sun
Zion Benton News

INDIANA

Anderson Herald-Bulletin
Angola Herald-Republican
Auburn Evening Star
Bedford Times-Mail
Bloomington Herald-Times
Bluffton News Banner
Bourbon News-Mirror
Bremen Enquirer
Chesterton Tribune
Columbus Republic
Crawfordsville Journal Review
Dearborn County Register
Evansville Courier
Evansville Press
Fort Wayne Journal-Gazette
Fort Wayne News-Sentinel
Franklin Daily Journal
Gary Post-Tribune

Goshen News
Greenfield Daily Reporter
Indianapolis North Side Topics
Indianapolis Sheridan News
Indianapolis Star/News
Jasper Herald
Jeffersonville Evening News
Kendall News-Sun
Kokomo Tribune
La Porte Herald-Argus
Lafayette Journal and Courier
Lawrenceburg Journal-Press
Ligonier Advance-Leader
Logansport Pharos-Tribune
Marion Chronicle-Tribune
Monticello Herald-Journal
Mount Vernon Democrat
Muncie Star/Muncie Evening Press
Munster Times
Nappanee Advance-News
Noblesville Daily Ledger
Perry County News
Plymouth Pilot-News
Portland Commercial-Review
Richmond Palladium-Item
Seymour Daily Tribune
Shelbyville News
South Bend Tribune
Spencer County Journal-Democrat
Terre Haute Tribune-Star
Valparaiso Vidette-Messenger
Vincennes Sun-Commercial
Washington Times-Herald

IOWA

Ames Daily Tribune
Carroll Times-Herald
Cedar Rapids Gazette
Clinton Herald
Council Bluffs Daily Nonpareil
Creston News Advertiser
Davenport Quad-City Times
Des Moines Register
Fairfield Ledger
Glenwood Opinion-Tribune
Iowa City Press-Citizen
Mason City Globe-Gazette
Mount Pleasant News
Muscatine Journal
Newton Daily News
Oskaloosa Herald
Ottumwa Courier
Red Oak Express
Sioux City Journal
Vinton Cedar Valley Daily Times
Washington Evening Journal
Waterloo Courier

KANSAS

Arkansas City Traveler
Dodge City Daily Globe
Great Bend Tribune
Independence Daily Reporter
Junction City Daily Union
Kansas City Kansan
Lawrence Journal-World
Manhattan Mercury
Newton Kansan
Pittsburg Morning Sun
Topeka Capital-Journal
Wellington Daily News
Wichita Eagle
Winfield Daily Courier

KENTUCKY

Ashland Daily Independent
Bardstown Kentucky Standard
Bedford Trimble Banner Democrat
Bowling Green Daily News
Campbellsville Central Kentucky News-Journal
Carlisle Mercury
Carrollton News-Democrat
Covington Kentucky Post
Cynthiana Democrat
Danville Advocate-Messenger
Elizabethtown News-Enterprise
Glasgow Daily Times
Grant County News
Grayson County News Gazette
Grayson Journal-Enquirer
Greenup News
Henderson Gleaner
Hogderville LaRue County Herald News
Laurel County Sentinel-Echo
Lawrenceburg Anderson News
Lebanon Enterprise

Copyright ©1996 by the Editor & Publisher Co.

NAA members

Lexington Herald-Leader
Liberty Casey County News
Louisville Courier-Journal
Madisonville Messenger
Mayfield Messenger
Maysville Ledger-Independent
McCreary County Record
Menifee County News
Morehead News
New Castle Henry County Local
Oldham Era
Olive Hill Times
Owensboro Messenger-Inquirer
Owerton News-Herald
Paducah Sun
Richmond Register
Russellville News-Democrat & Leader
Shelbyville Sentinel-News
Somerset Commonwealth-Journal
Spencer Magnet
Springfield Sun
Winchester Sun

LOUISIANA

Alexandria Daily Town Talk
Baton Rouge Advocate
Bogalusa Daily News
Crowley Post-Signal
Houma Courier
Jennings Daily News
Lafayette Advertiser
Lake Charles American Press
Minden Press-Herald
Monroe News-Star
New Iberia Daily Iberian
New Orleans Times-Picayune
Opelousas Daily World
Ruston Daily Leader
Shreveport Times
Slidell Daily Sentry-News
Thibodaux Daily Comet

MAINE

Augusta Kennebec Journal
Bangor Daily News
Courier Publications
Kennebunk York County Coast Star
Portland Press Herald
Waterville Central Maine Morning Sentinel

MARYLAND

Annapolis Capital
Baltimore Afro-American
Baltimore Jewish Times
Baltimore Sun
Bel Air Aegis
Bowie Blade-News
Cumberland Times-News
Frederick Post/News
Gazette Newspapers
Glen Burnie Maryland Gazette
Hagerstown Morning Herald/Daily Mail
Salisbury Daily Times
Westminster Carroll County Times

MASSACHUSETTS

Acton Citizen
Attleboro Sun Chronicle
Boston Globe
Boston Phoenix Inc.
Cape Cod Times
Edgartown Vineyard Gazette
Fairhaven Advocate
Fall River Herald News
Fitchburg Sentinel & Enterprise
Foxboro Reporter
Gloucester Times
Greenfield Recorder
Halifax Reporter
Hello Holyoke
Lowell Sun
Marion Sentinel
Mildford Daily News
Nantucket Inquirer and Mirror
New Bedford Standard-Times
Northampton Daily Hampshire Gazette
Pembroke Reporter
Pittsfield Berkshire Eagle
Plymouth Old Colony Memorial
Quincy Patriot Ledger
Revere Journal
Salem Evening News
Springfield Union-News
Taunton Daily Gazette
Wareham Courier
Worcester Telegram & Gazette

MICHIGAN

Adrian Daily Telegram
Ann Arbor News
Armada Times
Bad Axe Huron Daily Tribune
Battle Creek Enquirer
Bay City Times
Benton Harbor-St. Joseph Herald-Palladium
Brown City Banner
Cadillac News
Coldwater Daily Reporter
Detroit Free Press
Detroit News
Escanaba Daily Press
Flint Journal
Grand Haven Tribune
Grand Rapids Press
Greenville Daily News
Hillsdale Daily News
Holland Sentinel
Houghton Daily Mining Gazette
Iron Mountain-Kingsford Daily News
Ironwood Daily Globe
Jackson Citizen Patriot
Kalamazoo Gazette
Lansing State Journal
Lapeer County Press
Livonia Observer & Eccentric Newspapers
Ludington Daily News
Marlette Leader
Marquette Mining Journal
Midland Daily News
Mount Pleasant Morning Sun
Muskegon Chronicle
Pidgeon Newsweekly
Pontiac Oakland Press
Port Huron Times Herald
Saginaw News
Southgate News-Herald
Traverse City Record-Eagle
Vassar Pioneer Times

MINNESOTA

Alexandria Echo-Press
Anoka County Union & Shopper
Bemidji Daily Pioneer
Black Duck American
Brainerd Daily Dispatch
Cambridge Isanti County News
Detroit Lakes Tribune
Duluth News-Tribune
Faribault Daily News
Hastings Star Gazette
International Falls Daily Journal
Mankato Free Press
Milaca Mille Lacs County Times
Minneapollis Star Tribune
New Brighton Bulletin
North St. Paul Ramsey County Review
Northfield News
Owatonna People's Press
Park Rapids Enterprise
Princeton Union-Eagle
Red Wing Republican Eagle
Rochester Post-Bulletin
Rural Minnesota News
St. Cloud Times
St. Paul Pioneer Press
Wadena Pioneer Journal
Willmar West Central Tribune
Winona Daily News
Worthington Daily Globe

MISSISSIPPI

Biloxi-Gulfport Sun Herald
Booneville Banner Independent
Clarksdale Press Register
Corinth Daily Corinthian
Greenville Delta Democrat-Times
Greenwood Commonwealth
Grenada Daily Sentinel-Star
Hattiesburg American
Jackson Clarion-Ledger
Magee Courier
McComb Enterprise-Journal
Pascagoula Mississippi Press
Picayune Item
Vicksburg Evening Post

MISSOURI

Bollinger County Banner Press
Bloomfield Vindicator
Blue Springs Examiner
Cape Girardeau Southeast Missourian
Caruthersville Democrat-Argus
Columbia Daily Tribune
Dexter Daily Statesman
Doniphan Prospect-News
Excelsior Springs Daily Standard
Fulton Sun Gazette
Hannibal Courier-Post
Independence Examiner
Joplin Globe
Kansas City American City Business Journals
Kansas City Star
Kennett Daily Dunklin Democrat
Maryville Daily Forum
Moberly Monitor-Index & Democrat
Moniteau County California Democrat
Poplar Bluff Daily American Republic
Richmond Daily News
St. Joseph News-Press
St. Louis Post-Dispatch
Sedalia Democrat
Springfield News-Leader
Trenton Republican-Times
Warrensburg Daily Star-Journal
Washington Missourian

MONTANA

Billings Gazette
Bozeman Daily Chronicle
Butte-Anaconda Montana Standard
Dillon Tribune Examiner
Glendive Ranger Review
Great Falls Tribune
Havre Daily News
Helena Independent Record
Kalispell Daily Inter Lake
Livingston Enterprise
Miles City Star
Missoula Missoulian
Sidney Herald
Terry Tribune

NEBRASKA

Alliance Times-Herald
Columbus Telegram
Grand Island Independent
Hastings Tribune
Kearney Hub
Lexington Clipper-Herald
Lincoln Journal-Star
Norfolk Daily News
North Platte Telegraph
Omaha World-Herald
Papillion Times
Scottsbluff Star-Herald
York News-Times

NEVADA

Ely Daily Times
Lahontan Valley News & Fallon Eagle Standard Fallon
Las Vegas Review-Journal
Las Vegas Sun
Reno Gazette-Journal

NEW HAMPSHIRE

Concord Monitor
Claremont Eagle Times
Dover Foster's Daily Democrat
Exeter News-Letter
Hampton Union
Keene Sentinel
Kingston Kingstonian
Laconia Citizen
Nashua Telegraph
New London Argus-Champion
Peterborough Monadnock Ledger
Plaistow Hampstead-News
Portsmouth Herald
Raymond Times

NEW JERSEY

Belvidere News
Bergen County Record
Bernardsville News
Blairstown Press
Bloomfield Glen Ridge Paper
Bridgewater Courier-News
Caldwell Progress
Camden-Cherry Hill Courier-Post
Clifton Beacon
Cranbury Press
Dayton Central Post
Delaware Valley News
East Orange Record
Hackettstown Star-Gazette
Highstown Windsor-Hights Herald
Hillsborough Beacon
Hopewell Valley News
Hunterdon Review
Jersey City Jersey Journal
Lacey Beacon
Lambertville Beacon
Lawrence Ledger
Ledgewood Star Journal
Manville News
Mendham-Chester Observer-Tribune
Middlesex County Home News & Tribune
Monmouth County Messenger-Press
Morris County Suburban Trends
Morristown Daily Record
Netcong News-Leader
Newark Star-Ledger
New Providence Independent Press
News-Record
Newton New Jersey Herald
North Brunswick Post
Orange Transcript
Passaic-Clifton North Jersey Herald & News
Phillipsburg Free Press
Press of Atlantic City
Princeton Packet
Randolph Reporter
Ridgewood News
Roxbury Register
Salem Today's Sunbeam
Sterling Echoes-Sentinel
Summit Herald-Dispatch
Sussex County Chronicle
Teaneck-Fort Lee Sun-Bulletin
Toms River-Bricktown Ocean County Observer
Trenton Times
Trenton Trentonian
Tuckerton Beacon
Vineland Daily Journal
West Orange Chronicle
Willingboro Burlington County Times
Woodbury Gloucester County Times

NEW MEXICO

Alamogordo Daily News
Albuquerque Journal
Albuquerque Tribune
Artesia Daily Press
Belen News-Bulletin
Carlsbad Current-Argus
Clovis News Journal
Defensor Chieftain
Deming Headlight
Farmington Daily Times
Gallup Independent
Hobbs Daily News-Sun
Las Cruces Sun-News
Las Vegas Optic
Los Alamos Monitor
Los Lunas Villager
Santa Fe New Mexican
Roswell Daily Record
Ruidoso News
Taos News
Truth or Consequences Herald

NEW YORK

Albany Times Union
Albion Advertiser
Auburn Citizen
Baldwin Buy-Lines Press
Batvia Daily News
Binghamton Press & Sun-Bulletin
Buffalo News
Canandaigua Daily Messenger
Carthage Republican Tribune
Catskill Daily Mail
Chatham Courier-Rough Notes
Corning Leader
Cortland Standard
Elmira Star-Gazette
Geneva Finger Lakes Times
Glens Falls Post-Star
Hudson Register-Star
Ithaca Journal
Kingstown Daily Freeman
Livingston County News
Lockport Union-Sun & Journal
Long Island Newsday
Long Island Suffolk Life Newspapers
Lowville Journal & Republican
Malone Telegram
Mamaroneck Daily Times
Massena Courier-Observer
Medina Journal-Register
Middletown Times Herald-Record
Mount Vernon Daily Argus
New Rochelle Standard-Star
New York Editor & Publisher
New York Financial Times
New York Forward
New York France-Amerique
New York Jewish Week
New York Parade Publications Inc.
New York Securities Industry Daily
New York Times
New York USA Weekend
New York Village Voice
New York Wall Street Journal
Niagara Gazette
Nyack Rockland Journal-News

Copyright ©1996 by the Editor & Publisher Co.

NAA members

VII-43

Ogdensburg Advance-News
Ogdensburg Journal
Oneida Daily Dispatch
Oneonta Daily Star
Ossining Citizen Register
Peekskill Star
Plattsburgh Press-Republican
Port Chester Daily Item
Port Jervis Gazette
Poughkeepsie Journal
Rome Daily Sentinel
St. Lawrence Plaindealer
Saratoga Springs Saratogian
Setauket Beach Haven Times
Staten Island Advance
Syracuse Post-Standard/Herald-Journal
Tarrytown Daily News
Troy Record
Utica Observer-Dispatch
Watertown Daily Times
White Plains Gannett Rochester Newspapers
White Plains Reporter Dispatch
Windham Journal
Yonkers Herald Statesman
Yorktown Heights North County News

NORTH CAROLINA

Aberdeen Citizen News-Record
Asheboro Courier-Tribune
Asheville Citizen-Times
Burlington Times-News
Canton Enterprise
Carteret County News
Cary News
Charlotte Observer
Clinton Sampson Independent
Concord Tribune
Durham Herald-Sun
Eden Daily News
Elizabeth City Daily Advance
Elizabethtown Bladen Journal
Fayetteville Observer-Times
Gaston Gazette
Gates County Index
Goldsboro News-Argus
Greensboro News & Record
Greenville Daily Reflector
Henderson Daily Dispatch
Hendersonville Times-News
Hertford County News-Herald
Hickory Daily Record
High Point Enterprise
Jacksonville Daily News
Kannapolis Daily Independent
Kinston Free Press
Laurinburg Exchange
Lenoir News-Topic
Lexington Dispatch
Lumberton Robesonian
Marshall News Record
McDowell News
Mecklenburg Gazette
Monroe Enquirer-Journal
Mooresville Tribune
Morganton News Herald
Mount Airy News
Mount Olive Tribune
New Bern Sun Journal
Northampton News
Perquimans Weekly
Raeford News-Journal
Raleigh News & Observer
Roanoke Rapids Daily Herald
Rockingham Richmond County Daily Journal
Rocky Mount Telegram
Salisbury Post
Shelby Star
Smithfield Herald
Statesville Record & Landmark
Thomasville Times
Washington Daily News
Waynesville Mountaineer
Wendell Gold Leaf Farmer
Wilmington Morning Star
Wilson Daily Times
Winston-Salem Journal
Zebulon Record

NORTH DAKOTA

Bismarck Tribune
Devils Lake Daily Journal
Dickinson Press
Fargo-Moorhead Forum
Grand Forks Herald
Mandan News
Wahpeton-Breckenridge Daily News
Williston Daily Herald

OHIO

Akron Beacon Journal
Ashtabula Star-Beacon
Beavercreek News-Current
Bowling Green Sentinel-Tribune
Bucyrus Telegraph-Forum
Canton Repository
Carrollton Free Press Standard
Chillicothe Gazette
Cincinnati Enquirer
Cincinnati Post
Cleveland Plain Dealer
Coshocton Tribune
Dayton Daily News
Delaware Gazette
Delphos Daily Herald
Dover-New Philadelphia Times-Reporter
East Liverpool Evening Review
Elyria Chronicle-Telegram
Fairborn Daily Herald
Findlay Courier
Fostoria Review Times
Fremont News-Messenger
Gallipolis Daily Tribune
Greenville Daily Advocate
Hamilton Journal-News
Lake County News-Herald
Lancaster Eagle-Gazette
Lima News
Lisbon Morning Journal
Lorain Morning Journal
Mansfield News Journal
Marietta Times
Marion Star
Massillon Independent
Medina County Gazette
Middletown Journal
Newark Advocate
Norwalk Reflector
Oxford Press
Piqua Daily Call
Pomeroy-Middleport Daily Sentinel
Port Clinton News-Herald
Portsmouth Daily Times
Salem News
Sandusky Register
Sidney Daily News
Springfield News-Sun
Steubenville Herald-Star
Toledo Blade
Troy Daily News
Warren Tribune Chronicle
Xenia Daily Gazette
Youngstown Vindicator
Zanesville Times Recorder

OKLAHOMA

Altus Times
Ardmore Daily Ardmoreite
Bartlesville Examiner-Enterprise
Blackwell Journal-Tribune
Chickasha Daily Express
Claremore Daily Progress
Durant Daily Democrat
Enid News & Eagle
Guthrie Daily Leader
Guymon Daily Herald
Hartshorne Sun
Henryetta Daily Free-Lance
Lawton Constitution
McAlester News-Capital & Democrat
Muskogee Phoenix & Times-Democrat
Norman Transcript
Oklahoma City Daily Oklahoman
Okmulgee Daily Times
Pauls Valley Daily Democrat
Pawhuska Journal-Capital
Ponca City News
Sapulpa Daily Herald
Shawnee News-Star
Stillwater News Press

OREGON

Albany Democrat-Herald
Ashland Daily Tidings
Baker City Herald
Bend Bulletin
Corvallis Gazette-Times
Cottage Grove Sentinel
Curry Coastal Pilot
Eugene Register-Guard
Gresham Outlook
Hermiston Herald
Hillsboro Argus
Klamath Falls Herald and News
La Grande Observer
Lebanon Express
Medford Mail Tribune
Newport News-Times
Ontario Argus Observer
Portland Oregonian
Redmond Spokesman
Roseburg News-Review
Salem Statesman Journal
Sandy Post
Springfield News

PENNSYLVANIA

Allentown Morning Call
Altoona Mirror
Beaver County Times
Brookville Jeffersonian Democrat
Butler Eagle
Carlisle Sentinel
Chambersburg Public Opinion
Chester Delaware County Daily Times
Clearfield-Curwensville Progress
Connellsville Daily Courier
Delaware County News of Delaware County
Doylestown Intelligencer/Record
Du Bois Courier-Express
Easton-Bethlehem Express-Times
Edensburg Traders Guide
Erie Daily Times/Morning News
Gettysburg Times
Greensburg Tribune-Review
Grove City Allied News
Hanover Evening Sun
Harrisburg Patriot/Evening News
Indiana Gazette
Irwin Standard Observer
Johnstown Tribune-Democrat
Kittanning Leader-Times
Lancaster Intelligencer Journal/New Era
Lansdale Reporter
Lebanon Daily News
Levittown-Bristol Bucks County Courier Times
Lock Haven-Jersey Shore Express
McKeesport Daily News
Meadville Tribune
Monessen Valley Independent
New Castle News
New Kensington-Tarentum Valley News Dispatch
Norristown Times Herald
Northwest Washington County Record-Enterprise
Philadelphia Jewish Exponent
Philadelphia Inquirer/Daily News
Phoenixville Phoenix
Pittsburgh North Hills News Record
Pittsburgh Post-Gazette
Pittston Sunday Dispatch
Pottstown Mercury
Pottsville Republican
Radnor Twp-Lower Merion Main Line Times
Reading Times/Reading Eagle
Scranton Times/Tribune
Shamokin-Mount Carmel News-Item
Sharon-Farrell Herald
Somerset Daily American
State College Centre Daily Times
Stroudsburg Pocono Record
Sunbury Daily Item
Towanda Daily Review
Uniontown Herald-Standard
Valley View Citizens Standard
Warren Times-Observer
West Chester Daily Local News
Wilkes-Barre Times Leader
York Daily Record
York Dispatch

RHODE ISLAND

Chariho Times
East Greenwich Pendulum
Narragansett Times
Newport Daily News
Pawtucket-Central Falls Times
Providence Journal-Bulletin
Standard-Times
West Warwick Kent County Daily Times
Westerly Sun
Woonsocket Call

SOUTH CAROLINA

Anderson Independent-Mail
Beaufort Gazette
Camden Chronicle-Independent
Charleston Post and Courier
Chester News & Reporter
Clover Herald
Columbia State
Florence Morning News
Fountain Inn Tribune Times
Greenville News
Hilton Head Island Packet
Lancaster News
Myrtle Beach Sun News
Orangeburg Times and Democrat
Rock Hill Herald
Spartanburg Herald-Journal
Sumter Item
Union Daily Times
Yorkville Enquirer

SOUTH DAKOTA

Aberdeen American News
Brookings Register
Huron Plainsman
Mitchell Daily Republic
Mobridge Tribune
Pierre Capital Journal
Rapid City Indian Country Today
Rapid City Journal
Sioux Falls Argus Leader
Spearfish Black Hills Pioneer
Yankton Daily Press & Dakotan

TENNESSEE

Ashland City Times
Athens Daily Post-Athenian
Chattanooga Free Press
Chattanooga Times
Clarksville Leaf-Chronicle
Columbia Daily Herald
Dickson Herald
Dyersburg State Gazette
Gallatin News-Examiner
Greeneville Sun
Harriman Record
Jackson Sun
Johnson City Press
Kingsport Times-News
Kingston Roane County News
Knoxville News-Sentinel
La Follette Press
Lebanon Democrat
Maryville-Alcoa Daily Times
Memphis Commercial Appeal
Morristown Citizen Tribune
Murfreesboro Daily News Journal
Nashville Banner
Nashville Tennessean
Oak Ridge Oak Ridger
Rockwood Times
Sevierville Mountain Press
Springfield Robertson County Times
Stewart-Houston Times
Warburg Morgan County News

TEXAS

Abilene Reporter-News
Allen American
Amarillo Globe-News
Arlington News
Athens Daily Review
Austin American-Statesman
Beaumont Enterprise
Borger News-Herald
Brownsville Herald
Cedar Creek Pilot
Clear Lake Citizen
Cleburne Times-Review
Conroe Courier
Corpus Christi Caller-Times
Dallas Morning News
Denison Herald
Denton Record-Chronicle
Diario de Juarez
El Campo Leader-News
El Paso Herald-Post
El Paso Times
Fort Worth Star-Telegram
Gainesville Daily Register
Garland News
Graham Leader
Grand Prairie News
Harlingen Valley Morning Star
Houston Chronicle
Houston Defender
Hurst Mid-Cities News
Irving News
Jacksboro Gazette
Jacksonville Daily Progress
Jefferson Jimplecute
Kilgore News Herald
Laredo Morning Times
Longview News-Journal
Lubbock Avalanche-Journal
Lufkin Daily News
McAllen Monitor
Midland Reporter-Telegram
Nacogdoches Daily Sentinel
Odessa American
Palestine Herald-Press
Pampa News
Panola Watchman
Pasadena Citizen
Pecos Enterprise
Plainview Daily Herald
Plano Star Courier
Port Isabel/South Padre Press
Richardson News

Copyright ©1996 by the Editor & Publisher Co.

NAA members

Round Rock Leader
San Angelo Standard-Times
San Antonio Express-News
San Benito News
Sherman Democrat
Sweetwater Reporter
Temple Daily Telegram
Texarkana Gazette
Victoria Advocate
Waco Tribune-Herald
Weatherford Democrat
Wichita Falls Times Record News

UTAH
Logan Herald Journal
Ogden Standard-Examiner
Saint George Spectrum
Summit County Park Record

VERMONT
Barre-Montpelier Times Argus
Bennington Banner
Brattleboro Reformer
Burlington Free Press
Manchester Journal
Rutland Herald
St. Johnsbury Caledonian-Record
Wilmington-Dover Deerfield Valley News

VIRGINIA
Arlington USA Today
Bedford Bulletin
Berryville Clarke Courier
Charlottesville Daily Progress
Culpeper Star-Exponent
Fauquier Times-Democrat
Fredericksburg Free Lance-Star
Galax Gazette
Greene County Record
Harrisonburg Daily News-Record
Loudoun Times-Mirror
Lynchburg News & Advance
Madison County Eagle
Manassas Journal Messenger
Newport News-Hampton Daily Press
Norfolk Virginian-Pilot
Orange County Review
Poquoson Post
Petersburg Progress-Index
Rappahannock News
Reston Times-Mirror
Richlands News-Press
Richmond Times-Dispatch
Roanoke Times
Stauton Daily News Leader
Suffolk News-Herald
Tazewell Clinch Valley News
Warren Sentinel
Waynesboro News-Virginian
Winchester Star
Woodbridge Potomac News

WASHINGTON
Aberdeen Daily World
Bellevue Journal American
Bellingham Herald
Bremerton Sun
Burien Des Moines News
Burien Highline Times
Ellensburg Daily Record
Everett Herald
Federal Way News
Kent Valley Daily News
Longview Daily News
Mercer Island Reporter
Moses Lake Columbia Basin Herald
Mount Vernon Skagit Valley Herald
Olympia Olympian
Pasco Tri-City Herald
Peninsula Gateway
Pierce County Herald
Port Angeles Peninsula Daily News
Seattle Daily Journal of Commerce
Seattle Post-Intelligencer
Seattle Times
Snoqualmie Valley Record
Spokane Spokesman-Review
Sunnyside Daily Sun News
Tacoma News Tribune
Vancouver Columbian
Walla Walla Union-Bulletin
Yakima Herald-Republic

WEST VIRGINIA
Beckley Register-Herald
Bluefield Daily Telegraph
Charleston Daily Mail
Charleston Gazette

Clarksburg Exponent/Telegram
Fairmont Times-West Virginian
Fayette Tribune
Huntington Herald-Dispatch
Keyser Mineral Daily News-Tribune
Montgomery Herald
Morgantown Dominion Post
Point Pleasant Register
Princeton Times
Weirton Daily Times
Williamson Daily News

WISCONSIN
Appleton Post-Crescent
Baraboo News-Republic/South Central Wisconsin News
Beaver Dam Daily Citizen
Beloit Daily News
Chippewa Falls Chippewa Herald
Delavan Enterprise
Eau Claire Leader-Telegram
Edgerton Reporter
Elroy Tribune-Keystone
Fond du Lac Reporter
Fort Atkinson Daily Jefferson County Union
Green Bay Press-Gazette
Janesville Gazette
Kenosha News
La Crosse Tribune
Lakeshore Chronicle
Madison Newspapers Inc.
Manitowoc-Two Rivers Herald Times Reporter
Marinette Eagle Herald
Menomonie Dunn County News
Milwaukee Journal Sentinel
Monroe Evening Times
Oconomowoc Enterprise
Portage Daily Register
Racine Journal Times
Reedsburg Times-Press
Shawano Leader
Sheboygan Press
Watertown Daily Times
Waukesha County Freeman
Wausau Daily Herald
West Bend Daily News
Wisconsin Dells Events
Wisconsin Rapids Daily Tribune
Wonewoc Reporter

WYOMING
Casper Star-Tribune
Cheyenne Wyoming Tribune-Eagle
Laramie Daily Boomerang
Sheridan Press

PUERTO RICO
San Juan El Nuevo Dia
San Juan El Vocero de Puerto Rico

CANADA

ALBERTA
Bashaw Star
Calgary Sun
Castor Advance
Edmonton Examiner
Edmonton Sun
Fort McMurray Today
Grand Prairie Daily Herald-Tribune
Lethbridge Herald
Red Deer Advocate
St. Albert Gazette
Stettler Independent
Taber Times
Vegreville News-Advertiser
Vermilion Standard

BRITISH COLUMBIA
Abbotsford News
Campell River Courier/Islander
Chilliwack Progress
Hope Standard
Kelowna Daily Courier
Mission Fraser Valley Record
Nanaimo Daily Free Press
North Vancouver North Shore News
Penticton Herald
Vernon Daily News
Victoria Times-Colonist

MANITOBA
Brandon Sun
Dauphin Herald
Portage La Prairie Daily Graphic
Winnipeg Free Press

NEW BRUNSWICK
Choleur Region Northern Light
Fredericton Daily Gleaner
Moncton Times-Transcript
St. John Telegraph-Journal/Times-Globe

NEWFOUNDLAND
Corner Brook Western Star
St. John's Evening Telegram

NOVA SCOTIA
Halifax Chronicle-Herald/Mail-Star
New Glasgow Evening News
Sydney Cape Breton Post
Truro Daily News

ONTARIO
Aurora/Newmarket Era-Banner
Bolton Enterprise
Brockville Recorder & Times
Chatham Daily News
Cobourg Daily Star
Cornwall Standard-Freeholder
Don Mills Hockey News
Elliot Lake Standard
Georgetown Independent
Kenora Daily Miner & News
Kirkland Lake Northern Daily News
London Free Press
Markham Economist & Sun
Milton Canadian Champion
North York Mirror
Oakville Beaver
Ottawa Le Droit
Ottawa Sun
Pembroke Observer
Port Hope Guide
Rexdale Etobicoke Guardian
Richmond Hill Liberal
Richmond Hill Woodbridge & Vaughn News
St. Catharines Standard
St. Thomas Times-Journal
Scarborough Mirror
Stratford Beacon-Herald
Sudbury Star
Thunder Bay Times-News/Chronicle-Journal
Timmins Daily Press
Toronto Financial Post
Toronto Globe and Mail
Toronto Sun

PRINCE EDWARD ISLAND
Charlottetown Guardian

QUEBEC
Chicoutimi Le Progres Du Saguenay
Granby La Voix de l'Est
Montreal Journal Les Affaires
Montreal La Presse
Quebec City Le Soleil
Sherbrooke La Tribune
Trois-Rivieres Le Nouvelliste

SASKATCHEWAN
Regina Leader-Post
Saskatoon StarPhoenix
Saskatoon Western Producer
Yorkton This Week & Enterprise

YUKON TERRITORY
Whitehorse Yukon News

INTERNATIONAL

ARGENTINA
Buenos Aires Diario Clarin

AUSTRALIA
Hobart Mercury/Sunday Tasmanian
Kalgoorlie Miner
Perth Daily News
South Melbourne Regional Dailies of Australia
Townsville Bulletin
Tweed Daily News/Gold Coaster

BARBADOS
Bridgetown Daily Nation

BERMUDA
Hamilton Bermuda Sun
Hamilton Royal Gazette Ltd.

BRAZIL
Cutitiba Industria & Comercio
Porto Alegre Zero Hora
Rio de Janeiro O Globo
Sao Paulo O Estado De Sao Paulo

COLOMBIA
Bogotá El Tiempo
Medellín El Colombiano

COSTA RICA
San José La Nacion

ECUADOR
Guayaquil El Universo
Quito Diario Hoy

EL SALVADOR
San Salvador El Diario De Hoy

ENGLAND
Leeds Yorkshire Evening Post

FINLAND
Tampere Aamulehti Group

GERMANY
Hamburg Hamburger Abendblatt

GUAM
Pacific Daily News
TV Guam

GUATEMALA
Guatemala City Prensa Libre

HONDURAS
San Pedro Siela Diario La Prensa

ICELAND
Reykjavik Dagbladid-Visir
Reykjavik Morgunbladid

INDIA
Bhopal Dainik Bhaskar

JAMAICA
Kingston Gleaner Co.

MALAYSIA
Petating Java Star

MEXICO
Cia Periodística Meridiano S.A D
Ciudad Juárez Norte de Ciudad Juárez
Monterrey El Norte

NETHERLANDS
Amsterdam De Telegraaf

NEW ZEALAND
Christchurch Press
Ivercargill Southland Times
Napier Daily Telegraph
Nelson Evening Mail
Newspaper Advertising Bureau
Oamaru Mail
Palmerston North Evening Standard
Timaru Herald
Wellington Evening Post
Wellington Newspapers Ltd.
Whangarei Northern Advocate

PANAMA
Editora Panama America, S.A.
La Prensa

SINGAPORE
SBC Enterprises Pte. Ltd.
Straits Times Press

SOUTH AFRICA
Capetown Nasionale Pers Capetown
Greyville Natal Newspaper Group Greyville
Johannesburg Star
Johannesburg Times Media Limited

TRINIDAD & TOBAGO
Port of Spain Trinidad Publishing Co. Ltd.

UNITED ARAB EMIRATES
Dubai Gulf News

URUGUAY
Montevideo Diario El Pais

VENEZUELA
Maracaibo Diario Panorama

VIRGIN ISLANDS
Daily News of the Virgin Islands

NEWSPAPER BROKERS AND APPRAISERS

American Newspaper Consultants Ltd. — PO Box 411731, Kansas City, MO 64141-1731; tel (800) 554-3091
Dane S Claussen, Pres. & Principal

Apex Realty — 200 W. Vine St., Ste. 320, Lexington, KY 40507-1620; tel (606) 233-1000; fax (606) 233-0001
P Steve Hupman, Pres. & Principal

Apex Valuation Group Inc. — 200 W. Vine St., Ste. 320, Lexington, KY 40507-1620; tel (606) 233-1000; fax (606) 233-0001
Seth Gakpo, President
Dennis Badger, Vice President

Associated Texas Newspapers Inc. — 1801 Exposition Blvd., Austin, TX 78703; tel (512) 476-3950; fax (512) 476-6356
Bill Berger, President
Jeff Berger, Vice President

Beckerman Associates Inc. — 14001 Miramar Ave., Madeira Beach, FL 33708; tel (813) 391-2824
Lincoln A Mayo
Tampa, FL 33682; PO Box 82784; tel (813) 971-2061

Berky C & Associates Inc. — 123 N.W. 13th St., Ste. 214-7, Boca Raton, FL 33432; tel (407) 368-4352; fax (407) 391-2178
H Charles Berky, President

Blackburn & Co. Inc. — 201 N. Union St., Ste. 340, Alexandria, VA 22314; tel (703) 519-3703
James W Blackburn Jr
Richard F Blackburn
Jack V Harvey
Joseph M Sitrick
Tony Rizzo
Susan K Byers
Richard L Sharpe
Neil Rockoff
Joseph P Rapchak

Bolitho-Cribb & Associates — PO Box 3008, Palm Beach, FL 33480; tel (407) 820-8530; fax (407) 820-8531
John T Cribb, President
Bozeman, MT 59715 — 1 Annette Park Dr.; tel (406) 586-6621; fax (406) 586-6774
Robert N Bolitho, Chairman

Briggs, Richard & Assoc. — 207 Turner St., PO Box 579, Landrum, SC 29356; tel (803) 457-3846; fax (803) 457-3847
Dick Briggs, Owner

Brydon Media Services — PO Box 8197, New York, NY 10150; tel (718) 997-7561; fax (718) 997-7561
Donald J Brydon, Owner

Dirks Van Essen & Associates — 123 E. Marcy St., Ste. 207, Santa Fe, NM 87501; tel (505) 820-2700; fax (505) 850-2900
Lee E Dirks, Pres.
Owen D Van Essen, Vice Pres.
Victoria L Hall, Office Mgr.

Ford, Milton Q & Assoc. Inc. — 4006 Baronne Way, Memphis, TN 38117; tel (901) 763-2570
Milton Q Ford, President

Fournier Media Services Inc. — PO Box 5789, Prosser, WA 99350; tel (509) 786-4470; fax (509) 786-1779
John L Fournier Jr, President

French, L Barry — Ashland Rd., Assonet, MA 02702; tel (508) 644-5772
L Barry French

Gomm, R Gary & Co. Inc. — 27025 Smithson Valley Rd., San Antonio, TX 78216; tel (512) 366-9366; fax (210) 438-4325
R Gary Gomm, President
R Greg Gomm, Vice Pres.

Grimes, W B & Co. — PO Box 442, Clarksburg, MD 20871; tel (301) 540-0636; fax (301) 540-0686
Larry Grimes, President

Dane S Claussen, Midwest Manager (913) 395-3694
Tom Sexton, Northeast Associate (617) 545-6175
Wren Barnett, Southeast Associate (704) 698-0021
Bruce Lantz, Canadian Operations (604) 785-2385
Ronald Holla, Canadian Operations (613) 525-1666

Gruntal & Co. Inc. — 717 5th Ave., 13th Fl., New York, NY 10022; tel (212) 872-3928; fax (212) 826-3440
William J McCluskey, Managing Director

Hall, Jim Media Services — 410 Elm St., PO Box 1088, Troy, AL 36081-1088; tel (334) 566-7198; fax (334) 566-0170
James W Hall Jr, Owner

Hare Associates Inc. — 62 Black Walnut Dr., Rochester, NY 14615; tel (716) 621-6873
Richard L Hare, President

Harvey, Faye — PO Box 1410, Lebanon, MO 65536; tel (417) 532-4809; fax (417) 532-4809
Faye Ellingsworth Harvey, Owner

Hempstead & Co. Inc. — 807 Haddon Ave., Haddonfield, NJ 08033; tel (609) 795-6026
John E Hempstead, President

Henry Associates — 3051 N.E. 55th Ln., Ft. Lauderdale, FL 33308; tel (305) 771-8280; fax (305) 771-6053; e-mail idgray@aol.com
Maurice Henry, President
Gray R Henry, Associate

Hicks, J F Media Service — 336 Hwy. 16 E., Buffalo, WY 82834; tel (307) 684-9407; fax (307) 684-7431
Jim Hicks

Hodell, Mel Media Broker Inc. — 5196 Benito St., Ste. 11, Montclair, CA 91763-2891; tel (909) 626-6440; fax (909) 624-8852
Mel Hodell, President

Holding-Kramer & Associates — PO Box 472, Gibson City, IL 60936; tel (217) 784-4736
David Kramer, Owner

Lewis, Alan G Associates — Ridge Rd., PO Box 73, Hardwick, MA 01037; tel (413) 477-6009
Alan G Lewis

Management Planning Inc. — 101 Poor Farm Rd., PO Box 611, Princeton, NJ 08542; tel (609) 924-4200
James O Roberts, President
Scott A Richards, Sr. Analyst

Martin, James & Associates — 3061 Cranston Dr., PO Box 798, Dublin, OH 43017; tel (614) 889-9747; fax (614) 889-2659
Jim Martin, President

Matthew, Bill Co. — PO Box 3364, Clearwater Beach, FL 34630; tel (813) 733-8053
William L Matthew, President
Timothy Matthew, Vice Pres.
Bob Grimm, Vice Pres.

Media America Brokers — Lenox Towers, Ste. 1000, 3390 Peachtree Rd. N.E., Atlanta, GA 30326; tel (404) 364-6554; fax (404) 233-2318
Lon W Williams

Media Consultants & Associates — 36 Monarch Hill Rd., Tunbridge, VT 05077; tel (802) 889-5600; fax (802) 889-5627
C Peter Jorgensen, Managing Partner

Media Consultants Inc. — PO Box 556, Lingle, WY 82223; tel (307) 837-2748
Michael D Lindsey

Gilbert, AZ 85234 — 1221 N. Kingston St.; tel (602) 813-9344.

Newspaper Service Co. Inc. — 2005 N. Pt. Alexis Dr., Tarpon Spring, FL 34689; tel (813) 942-2883
R H Fackelman, Chmn. of Board
Ann Nixon, President
Marc A Richard, VPO
Broward E Ratliff, Treas.
David H Davis, Assistant

Northwest Publishers Inc. — 710 Lake St., PO Box 275, Spirit Lake, IA 51360-0275; tel (712) 336-2805; fax (712) 336-0611
John E van der Linden, Broker
Thomas J van der Linden, Assoc. Broker

Paine, Abbott E. (Paine, Paine & Miller) — PO Box 6267, Orange, CA 92613-6267; tel (714) 998-1091
Abbott Paine, Newspaper Broker

Park Jr, John A & Co. — 202 Springmoor Dr., Raleigh, NC 27615; tel (919) 848-7202; fax (919) 848-7148
John A Park Jr, President
S Leigh Park, Vice Pres.

Phillips Media Services Inc. — 2720 Prosperity Ave. (Fairfax, 22124-1000), PO Box 3308, Merrifield, VA 22116-3308; tel (703) 846-8410; fax (703) 846-8406
Rupert Phillips

Price Waterhouse Valuation Services — 200 E. Randolph Dr., Chicago, IL 60601; tel (312) 540-2690; fax (312) 565-1458
Stephen M Carr, Dir. Media Services

Reilly, Gerald D — 12 Taconic Rd., Greenwich, CT 06830; tel (203) 622-0599
Gerald D Reilly

Rickenbacher Media Co. — 3828 Mockingbird Ln., Dallas, TX 75205; tel (214) 520-7025
Ted Rickenbacher, President

Romano, George Ltd. — 6165 Via de La Tortola, Tucson, AZ 85718; tel (602) 229-5292
George Romano, President

Veronis, Suhler & Associates Inc. — 350 Park Ave., New York, NY 10022; tel (212) 935-4990; fax (212) 935-0877
John S Suhler, President/Co-CEO
John J Veronis, Chairman/Co-CEO
Kevin M Lavalla, Managing Director

Wells, J N & Co. Inc. — 21 W. 075 Monticello Rd., Lombard, IL 60148; tel (708) 916-6491; fax (708) 627-1233
Joseph N Wells, President
Joseph P Tito, Vice Pres.
Jonathan (Scott) Wells, Vice Pres.

Whitesmith Publication Services — PO Box 4487, Vancouver, WA 98662; tel (206) 892-7196
Rod Whitesmith, Newspaper Broker

John A. Park, Jr. & Associates

Expertise and reliability for owners considering the sale of their *newspapers*.

(919) 848-7202
Fax: (919) 848-7148
202 Springmoor Drive
Raleigh, NC 27615

Available for private, confidential consultation

Nationwide Personal Service

DIRKS, VAN ESSEN & ASSOCIATES

Lee E. Dirks

We specialize in assisting owners in exploring, negotiating, and consummating the sale of their daily newspapers or newspaper groups.

Owen Van Essen

123 E. Marcy St., Suite 207, Santa Fe, New Mexico 87501
Phone (505) 820-2700 • Fax (505) 820-2900

Copyright ©1996 by the Editor & Publisher Co.

ORGANIZATION OF OMBUDSMEN

CALIFORNIA
Fresno — Fresno Bee
Ombudsman, Lynne E Glaser
Sacramento — Sacramento Bee
Ombudsman, Arthur C Nauman
San Diego — San Diego Union-Tribune
Reader Representative, Gina Lubrano
Santa Ana — Orange County Register
Ombudsman, Pat Riley

COLORADO
Denver — Rocky Mountain News
Reader Representative, Jean Otto

CONNECTICUT
Hartford — Hartford Courant
Assoc. Ed./Reader Rep., Elissa Papirno

DELAWARE
Wilmington — News-Journal
Public Editor, John Sweeney

DISTRICT OF COLUMBIA
Washington — Washington Post
Ombudsman, Geneva Overholser

FLORIDA
West Palm Beach — Palm Beach Post
Listening Post Editor, C B Hanif
Bradenton — Bradenton Herald
Reader Representative, Paul W Bartley
Jacksonville — Florida Times-Union
Reader Advocate, Mike Clark

ILLINOIS
Chicago — Chicago Tribune
Public Editor, George Langford

INDIANA
Fort Wayne — News-Sentinel
Reader Representative, Joseph F Sheibley

KENTUCKY
Louisville — The Courier-Journal
Ombudsman, John C Long

MAINE
Lewiston — Sun-Journal/Sunday Sun-Journal
Reader Representative, David W Ehrenfried

MASSACHUSETTS
Boston — Boston Globe
Ombudsman, Mark M Jurkowitz
Quincy — Patriot Ledger
Assoc. Ed./Reader Rep., William Flynn

MICHIGAN
Ann Arbor — Ann Arbor News
Ombudsman, David Bishop
Detroit — Free Press
Reader Representative, Anne L Musial
Detroit — Detroit News
Ombudsman, Chuck Theisen

MINNESOTA
Minneapolis — Star Tribune
Reader Representative, Louis I Gelfand
Rochester — Post-Bulletin
Executive Editor, Robert Retzlaff

MISSOURI
Kansas City — Kansas City Star
Reader Representative, Miriam Pepper

NEW YORK
White Plains — Gannett Suburban Newspapers
Reader Editor, Gail Williams

New York — NBC News
Sr. Producer, Broadcast Standards, David G McCormick

PENNSYLVANIA
Philadelphia — Philadelphia Inquirer
Asst. to the Editor, John V R Bull

TEXAS
Amarillo — Amarillo Globe-News
Reader Representative, Jeff Langley
Fort Worth — Fort Worth Star-Telegram
Ombudsman, Phil Record

UTAH
Salt Lake City — Salt Lake Tribune
Reader Advocate, Shinika Sykes

VIRGINIA
Alexandria — Stars & Stripes Newspapers
Ombudsman, Phillip Robbins
Norfolk — Virginian-Pilot and Ledger-Star
Public Editor, Lynn Feigenbaum
Richmond — Richmond Times-Dispatch
Ombudsman, Jerald A Finch

BRAZIL
Florianopolis/Sc — AN Capital
Ombudsman, Mario Xavier
Fortaleza/Ce — O Povo
Ombudsman, Adisia Sa
Sao Paulo — Folha da Tarde
Ombudsman, Antenor Braidor
Sao Paulo — Folha De S Paulo
Ombudsman, Marcelo Nogueira Leite

CANADA
Montreal — The Gazette
Ombudsman, Robert Walker

Montreal — Maison de Radio-Canada
L'Ombudsman-SRC, Mario Cardinal
Nova Scotia — Chronicle-Herald
Ombudsman, Roger Edge
Toronto — Canadian Broadcasting Corp.
Office of Journalistic Policy & Practices
Ombudsman, William Morgan
Office for English Service
Ombudsman, David Bazay
Toronto — Toronto Star
Ombudsman, Don Sellar

COLOMBIA
Bogota — El Tiempo
Ombudsman, Leopoldo Villar Borda

ECUADOR
Quito — Diario Hoy
Defensor del Lector, Diego Araujo

ISRAEL
Tel Aviv — Maariv
Ombudsman, Avraham Tirosh

JAPAN
Tokyo — Yomiyuri Shimbun
Sr. Staff Ombudsmen Cmte., Takeshi Ito

PARAGUAY
Asuncion — Diario Hoy
Ombudsman, Jose Luis Simon

SPAIN
Barcelona — La Vanguardia
Defensor del Lector, Roger Jimenez
Madrid — El Pais
Ombudsman, Juan Arias

TAKE A LOOK AT THE NEW E&P

• MORE NEWS • MORE SECTIONS • MORE DEPTH • MORE ENERGY

E&P, the "bible of the newspaper business, has positioned itself to respond to new readers, new technologies, new opportunities — to bring you the news and information you need, in a new, easier-to-read format that fits E&P into your busy schedule.

Take a look at the NEW Editor & Publisher. You'll find details about an exciting, vibrant industry within the pages of a fresh, more colorful, journal that will help make you more effective working within the industry, or working with the industry. **Order today!**

Complete coverage in these sections:
• News Tech • Interactive Communications • Advertising/Promotion
• Circulation • Syndicates/News Services • Newspeople in the News
• Campus Journalism • Financial • Legal

Editor & Publisher Guarantee:
If at any time after becoming a paid subscriber to Editor & Publisher you find E&P does not measure up to your expectations, you are guaranteed a refund for the balance of your subscription payment.

TO SUBSCRIBE: Look for the convenient order card bound in this Year Book or call the E&P Circulation Department at (212) 675-4380.

Editor & Publisher
THE FOURTH ESTATE

Copyright ©1996 by the Editor & Publisher Co.

SCHOOLS AND DEPARTMENTS OF JOURNALISM

Reprinted with permission from the Journalism Directory, published by the Association for Education in Journalism and Mass Communication. Mailing lists of the Association for Education in Journalism, the American Society of Journalism School Administrators and the Association of Schools of Journalism and Mass Communication are available from: Jennifer McGill, Executive, University of South Carolina, College of Journalism, Columbia, SC 29208; tel (803) 777-2005; fax (803) 777-4700

Schools and departments listed here offer undergraduate and/or graduate programs in journalism and mass communications. Information for each school or department includes major sequences or programs in which students may concentrate.

In addition, faculty and educational facilities are listed for schools and departments affiliated with the Association of Schools of Journalism and Mass Communication (ASJMC) and/or the American Society of Journalism School Administrators (ASJSA), both cofounding affiliates of the Association for Education in Journalism and Mass Communication (AEJMC).

Information for these listings was provided by the respective schools and departments; neither Journalism Directory, the AEJMC nor E&P, can vouch for the accuracy or authenticity of the listings.

KEY TO LISTINGS

The most commonly used abbreviations in this directory are:

Association Affiliations:
ASJMC—Association of Schools of Journalism and Mass Communication.
ASJSA—American Society of Journalism School Administrators.

ACEJ Accreditation—The American Council on Education for Journalism and Mass Communication, representing both educational and professional media organizations, is the agency formally recognized by the Council on Postsecondary Accreditation and H.E.W. for accreditation of programs for professional education in journalism and mass communications in institutions of higher learning in the United States. Accreditation means that the overall unit and the program or programs to which that term is applied have been evaluated by a team of educators, media and industry professionals; and that the evaluation team, the Accreditation Committee and the Council have agreed that the overall unit and the program(s) meet the Accreditation Standards published by the American Council on Education for Journalism. Courses accredited by ACEJ are indicated following the school's course sequence listing.

Student and Professional Organizations:
ACT—Agricultural Communicators of Tomorrow.
AAF—American Advertising Federation campus affiliate.
AER—Alpha Epsilon Rho.
BPG—Beta Phi Gamma.
IABC—International Association of Business Communicators.
KAM—Kappa Alpha Mu.
KTA—Kappa Tau Alpha.
NABJ—National Association of Black Jounalists campus affiliate.
NPPA—National Press Photographers Association student chapter.
NATAS—National Academy of Television Arts and Sciences campus affiliate.
PRSSA—Public Relations Student Society of America.
SCJ—Society for Collegiate Journalists.
SPJ/SDX—Society of Professional Journalists, Sigma Delta Chi.
WICI—Women in Communications Inc.

Abbreviations for Facilities:
AP—Associated Press.
CP—Canadian Press.
NYTS—New York Times Service.
RNA—Reuters News Agency.
UPI—United Press International.
AM/FM—Radio station operated by educational institution.
AdA—Advertising agency or department provides work experience for students as part of academic program.
CATV—Local community antenna TV channel used by students in presenting work as part of academic program.
CCTV—Closed circuit TV facility for laboratory and classroom use.
CN—Campus newspaper, published independently of school or department, utilize academic program.
ComN—Local commercial newspaper provides work experience for students as part of academic program.
ComR—Local commercial radio station used by students in presenting work as part of academic program.
DR—Darkroom facilities for photography.
ETV—Educational institution owns TV facility; broadcasts extend to general public.
JM—Journalism school or department produces magazine.
JN—Journalism school or department produces newspaper.
PRA—Public relations agency or department provides work experience for students as part of academic program.
VDT—Electronic news and data processing equipment used in class.

Year Programs Began:
Given in most listings before affiliations.

ALABAMA

Alabama, University of
Tuscaloosa, AL 35487-0172; tel (205) 348-5520. College of Communication, 1927. KTA, AER, AAF, NPPA, PRSSA, SPJ. Edward Mullins, dean.
FACULTY: *Profs.*: Arnold Barban (chair, Adv. and Public Relations), Jennings Bryant (Reagan chair, Brdct. and dir., Institute for Comm. Research), Frank Deaver, John Eighmey, Eva McMahan, Edward Mullins (dean), Loy Singleton (chair, Telecomm. and Film), David Sloan, James Stovall, Dolf Zillmann (sr. assoc. dean, Grad. Studies and Research); *Assoc. Profs.*: James A Brown, Jeremy Butler, Raymond C Carroll, Karen J Cartee (assoc. dean, undergrad. studies), Gary Copeland, George Frangoulis, Tom Harris, George Katz, Leah Lievrouw, William F O'Connor, Yorgo Pasadeos, David Perry, Bruce Roche; *Asst. Profs.*: Matthew Bunker, Diane M Burns, Pamela Doyle, William Gonzenbach, Marylynn Hanily, Kuen-Hee Ju, Joseph Phelps, David Roskos-Ewoldsen; *Instrs.*: Dwight Cameron, Mary Clark (Reading Room/Instructional Materials Specialist), Brent Davis, Alan Dennis, Marilyn Mancini, Dan Messiner, Jim Oakley (placement dir.), Marie Parsons (Minorities), Tom Rieland (dir., Center for Public Television), Glenda Williams.
DEPARTMENTS: Advertising and Public Relations, Telecommunication and Film, Journalism, Speech Communication.
FACILITIES: AP, CN, DR, ETV, JM, JN, FM, VDT.
DEGREES: BA, MA, PhD.

Alabama State University
Montgomery, AL 36101-0271; tel (334) 229-4493. Department of Communications Media. David Okeowo, PhD, acting chairperson.
Journalism Program: Students emphasize print journalism, radio/TV or public relations. Offers training program in telecommunications.

Auburn University
Auburn, AL 36849-5206; tel (205) 844-4607; fax (205) 844-2378. Department of Journalism, 1974. (Major offered before 1974 by English Dept.) SPJ. Jerry E Brown, head.

Jacksonville State University
700 Pelham Rd. N., Jacksonville, AL 36265-9982; tel (205) 782-5300; fax (205) 782-5645. Department of Communication. ASJMC, ACA, BEA, SPJ. Ralph E Carmode, head.
FACULTY: *Prof.*: Ralph E Carmode; *Assoc. Profs.*: Robyn L Eoff, Marian Huttenstine; *Asst. Prof.*: Jerry Chandler; *Instrs.*: Joe Langston (manager of student media).
FACILITIES: TV, FM, VDT.
DEGREE: BA, major in communication, minor in communication.

Samford University
Birmingham, AL 35229; tel (205) 870-2465. Department of Journalism/Mass Communication, 1985. SPJ. Jon Clemmensen, chair.
FACULTY: *Assoc. Profs.*: Jon Clemmensen, Dennis Jones; *Asst. Profs.*: Mark Baggett, David Shipley; *Instrs.*: Melissa Tate, Julie Williams; *Adjunct Instrs.*: George Elliott, Art Meripol, Lynn Sampson, Glenn Stephens.
SEQUENCES: Broadcast, News/Editorial, Public Relations/Advertising.
FACILITIES: AP, FM, CN, DR, VDT.
DEGREES: BA.

South Alabama, University of
Mobile, AL 36688; tel (205) 380-2800; fax (205) 380-2850. Department of Communication, 1964. Gerald L Wilson, acting chair.
FACULTY: *Profs.*: Michael S Hanna, Michael B Hesse, Gerald L Wilson, Donald K Wright; *Assoc. Profs.*: Louise W Hermanson, J Clifton Trimble; *Asst. Profs.*: James L Aucoin, W A (Kelly) Huff, James M Rosene, Craig R Scott; *Instrs.*: Graham Heath, Donna L Robinson, George D Smith, Julie Zink; *Senior Lectrs.*: Linda J Busby, John F Pettibone; *Lectrs.*: Carolyn Combs, Barbara Carter, Jerry Hough, Catherine Lehocky, Linda Pereira, RayLin Snowden, Thresa White.
SEQUENCES: Broadcast News, Communication Studies, Print Journalism, Organizational Communication, Public Relations, Radio-TV.
FACILITIES: CATV, CCTV, CN, ComN, ComR, ComTV, JN, PRA, VDT.
DEGREES: BA, MA.

Spring Hill College
Mobile, AL 36608; tel (205) 460-2392; fax (205) 460-2095. Discipline of Communication Arts, 1971. Varnell Lee, dir.
Journalism Program: BA with concentrations in journalism and media writing, advertising and public relations, and radio/TV.

Troy State University
Troy, AL 36082; tel (334) 670-3289; fax (334) 670-7707. Hall School of Journalism. Merrill Bankester, dean.
Journalism Program: Professionally oriented programs to prepare students for entry-level positions in print and broadcast journalism.

ALASKA

Alaska Anchorage, University of
3211 Providence Dr., Anchorage, AK 99508; tel (907) 786-4180; fax (907) 786-4190. e-mail AFLEC@orion.alaka.edu. Department of Journalism and Public Communications, 1976. AAF, PRSSA. Larry Campbell, chair.
FACULTY: *Profs.*: Jim Avery, Larry Pearson; *Asst. Profs.*: Edgar Blatchford, Larry Campbell, Frederick W Pearce; *Atwood Prof.*: Tad Bartimus; *Writer-in-Residence*: John Strohmeyer; *Professor Emeritus*: Sylvia Broady.
SEQUENCES: News-Editorial, Advertising, Public Relations, Telecommunications, Photography.
FACILITIES: AdA, AM, CATV, CN, ComN, ComTV, DR, JM, NACB, PRA, VDT.
DEGREE: BA.

Alaska at Fairbanks, University of
Fairbanks, AK 99775-6120; tel (907) 474-7761, E-mail: FYJNB or FFLM; fax (907) 474-6369. Department of Journalism Broadcasting, 1966. SPJ, KAM. Lael Morgan, head.
Journalism Program: The department offers two sequences: news/editorial and broadcasting. Campus facilities include two radio stations, a TV station, campus newspaper, computer writing lab, audio/video editing labs, print production lab, darkroom facilities, 24-hour student resource center.

ARIZONA

Arizona, University of
Tucson, AZ 85721; tel (602) 621-7556; fax (602) 621-7557; e-mail jourdept@ccit.arizona.edu. Department of Journalism, 1947. SPJ, Investigative Reporters & Editors, NNA, AZ Newspaper Assn. Jim Patten, head.
FACULTY: *Profs.*: Donald W Carson, Philip Mangelsdorf (grad. adviser), George W Ridge, Jacqueline E Sharkey; *Assoc. Profs.*: Ford N Burkhart, William F Greer, James W Johnson, Jim Patten; *Lectr.*: C Bickford Lucas (undergrad. adviser); *Instrs.*: Anita Caldwell, Lawrence W Cheek, Joseph Garcia, Larry R Ketchum, Mark S Kimble, Susan Knight, Robert E Mackle, Jane B Marcellus, Janet R Mitchell, Peter W Sibley, Robert E Zucker.
SEQUENCE: News-Editorial.
FACILITIES: AP, Arizona Community News Service, CN, CATV, DR, ETV, ComN, ComTV, JM (*The Pretentious Idea-Media Review*), JN (*The Tombstone Epitaph*), Bilingual JN (*The South Tucson El Independiente*), laboratory bureaus in Tombstone, Phoenix, Mexico.
DEGREES: BA, MA.

Arizona State University
Tempe, AZ 85287-1305; tel (602) 965-5011; fax (602) 965-7041; e-mail icdaaaasuvm.inre.asu.edu. Walter Cronkite School of Journalism and Telecommunication, 1957. NPPA, NATAS, PRSSA, RTNDA, SPJ, WICI. Douglas A Anderson, dir.
FACULTY: *Profs.*: Douglas A Anderson (Cronkite Endowment Board of Trustees Prof.), ElDean Bennett, John E Craft (dir., Grad. Studies), Donald G Godfrey, Roy K Halverson, Bruce D Merrill (dir., Media Research Program), Edward J Sylvester; *Assoc. Profs.*: Craig Allen,

Copyright ©1996 by the Editor & Publisher Co.

Mary-Lou Galician, Frank P Hoy, Richard Lentz, Fran Matera, Sharon Bramlett-Solomon, George Watson, Kyu Ho Youm; *Asst. Profs.:* Marianne Barrett, Eric K Gormly, Dennis E Russell, Joseph A Russomanno; *Clinical Assoc. Profs.:* Bruce D Itule, Frederic A Leigh (deputy dir.); *Instrs.:* Michael D Casavantes, Renea Nash; *Fac. Assocs.:* Alan Baker, David Bodney, Carol Osman Brown, James Brown, David Cannella, Andy Czarnecki, Matt S DeJesus, James P Dove, John Genzale, Mary L Gilmore, Norman S Ginsburg, Jeff Halberg, David A Howell Jr., David Hume, Julie M Knapp, John Leach, Mark Lodato, Larry L Martel, Tyrone Meighan, Eldon Phillips, Larry N Phillips, Grace Provenzano, Paul J Schatt, Judith P Smith, Lee Whitehead, Mike Wong; *Profs. Emer.:* Donald E Brown, Troy F Crowder, Joe W Milner, W Parkman Rankin (special asst. to the dir.), Benjamin Silver, Stanley E Smith.
SEQUENCES: Journalism, Broadcasting, Photojournalism, Public Relations, Journalism Education.
FACILITIES: AP, FM, CATV, CCTV, CN, ComN, ComTV, DR, ETV, PRA, VDT.
DEGREES: BA, MMC.

Northern Arizona University
Flagstaff, AZ 86011-5619; tel (602) 523-2232; fax (602) 523-1505. School of Communication, 1966. AAF, AER, AZ Newspapers Assn., KTA, NPPA, PAD, PRSSA, RMCPA, SCA, SPJ, SWECJMC, WICI, WSCA, BEA. Sharon Porter, dir.
Communication Program: The school offers sequences in Advertising, Broadcast Journalism, Communication Studies, Electronic Media Management, Electronic Media Production, Family and Interpersonal Communication, Journalism Education, Journalism-Political Science, Mass Communication, News-Editorial, Organizational Communication, Photography, Photojournalism, Pre-Law, Public Relations, Speech Communication, and Speech Communication Education.

ARKANSAS

Arkansas, University of
Fayetteville, AR 72701; tel (501) 575-3601. Walter J Lemke Department of Journalism, 1930. AAF, KTA, PRSSA, SPJ, UAABJ, NPPA. Patsy Watkins, chair.
FACULTY: *Profs.:* Hoyt Purvis, Roy Reed; *Assoc. Profs.:* Robert Carey, Larry Foley, Phyllis Miller, Louise Montgomery, Rick Stockdell, Patsy Watkins; *Asst. Profs.:* Dale Carpenter, Robbie Morganfield, Jan Wicks; *Instr.:* Gary Lundgren.
SEQUENCES: News/Magazine, Advertising/Public Relations, Broadcasting.
FACILITIES: AP, FM, CATV, CN, ComN, ComR, ComTV, DR, JM, VDT.
DEGREES: BA, MA.

Arkansas at Little Rock, University of
Little Rock, AR 72204; tel (501) 569-3250. Department of Journalism, 1971. AER, KTA, PRSSA, SPJ.
FACULTY: *Prof.:* Luther W Sanders; *Assoc. Profs.:* Bruce L Plopper, Jeanne Rollberg; *Asst. Prof.:* Jeff Boone; *Instr.:* Tim Edwards; *Adjunct Assoc. Prof.:* William K Rutherford; *Part-Time Lectrs.:* Frank Fellone, Paul Greenberg, Craig Rains.
SEQUENCES: News-Editorial, Broadcast Journalism, Professional and Technical Writing, Public Information.
FACILITIES: AM/FM, AP, CATV, CN, ComN, ComR, ComTV, DR, JM, PRA, VDT, departmental statewide weekly news service, semi-annual research publication, *Journal of Arkansas Journalism Studies.*
DEGREES: BA, MA.

Arkansas State University
State University, AR 72467; tel (501) 972-2468; fax (501) 972-3828. College of Communications, 1936. AAF, AER, KTA, PRSSA, SPJ, ABC, BEA, INAME, WICI. Russell E Shain, dean.
FACULTY: *Profs.:* Gilbert L Fowler Jr., Russell E Shain; *Assoc. Profs.:* Joel T Gambill (chair, Dept. of Jour. and Printing), J Marlin Shipman; *Asst. Profs.:* Osa Amienyi, Beverly Bailey, Richard A Carvell (chair, Dept. of Radio-TV), Gregory G Pitts; *Instrs.:* Richard Bundsgaard (dir., Printing Plant), James L Cathey, Michael B Doyle, Lillie Fears, Laura Deen Johnson, Kenneth R Lane, Mary Jackson Pitts, Jennifer Engles Rogers, Bonnie Thrasher, Pat Tinnin, Jennifer Winningham, John B Zibluk.
SEQUENCES: General Radio-Television, Broadcast News, Radio-TV Production and Performance, Radio-TV Management and Sales, Cable and Alternative Technologies, News-Editorial, Community Journalism, Advertising, Public Relations, Photojournalism, Printing Management, Printing Technology.
FACILITIES: AP, UPI, FM, CATV, DR, JR, VDT, NPR, UPI, AdA, JN, PRA.
DEGREES: BS in Journalism, Radio-TV, Printing; MSMC in Journalism, Radio-TV.

Arkansas Tech University
Russellville, AR 72801; tel (501) 968-0640; fax (501) 964-0504; e-mail SJVT@ATUVM.ATU.EDU. Department of Speech, Theatre and Journalism. Van A Tyson, head.
Journalism Program: General journalism degree, with emphasis in print, broadcast or public relations.

Central Arkansas, University of
Conway, AR 72035; tel (501) 450-3162; fax (501) 450-5678; e-mail bobw@cci.uca.edu. Department of Speech, Theatre and Mass Communication, 1943. AER. Bob Willenbrink, chair.
Mass Communication Program: BA and BS degrees with emphasis in Telecommunications or Journalism. Courses offered in magazine/newspaper writing, photography, TV/radio production, desktop publishing/video, media theory/ethics/law.

Harding University
Searcy, AR 72149-0001; tel (501) 279-4445; fax (501) 279-4600; e-mail james@harding.edu. Department of Communication, 1983. BEA, AER, SCA. Michael L James, chair.
FACULTY: *Profs.:* Louis F Butterfield, Steven N Frye, Michael L James; *Assoc. Profs.:* Kay Gowen, Jack R Shock.
SEQUENCES: Print Journalism, Public Relations, Radio-Television, Communication Management.
FACILITIES: TV studio, Cable TV Channel, AM/FM.
DEGREE: BA

Henderson State University
1100 Henderson St., Arkadelphia, AR 71999-0001; tel (501) 230-5042; fax (501) 230-5144; e-mail DUNCANR@HOLLY.HSU.EDU. Communication and Theatre Arts Department, 1989. Randy Duncan, chair.
SEQUENCES: News-Editorial, Mass Media, Communication, Theater.
DEGREES: BA.

John Brown University
Siloam Springs, AR 72761; tel (501) 524-3131; fax (501) 524-9548. Department of Journalism, Division of Communication, 1983. Mike T Flynn, chair.
Journalism Program: A full program leading to a BS in Journalism, Broadcasting, Graphic Design or PR.

CALIFORNIA

California at Berkeley, University of
Berkeley, CA 94720; tel (510) 642-3383; fax (510) 643-9136. Graduate School of Journalism, 1968 (as school). Tom Goldstein, dean.
FACULTY: *Profs.:* William J Drummond, Timothy Ferris, Tom Goldstein, Thomas Leonard, David Littlejohn, A Kent Mac Dougall, Marlon T Riggs; *Acting Assoc. Prof.:* Lydia Chavez, Neil Henry, Susan Rasky; *Asst. Prof.:* Carolyn Wakeman; *Senior Lectr.:* Joan Bieder; *Lectrs.:* Vincent Cosgrove, Barbara Erickson, Jane Gross, Phil Hager, Jane Kay, Kenneth Light, Raul Ramirez, Richard Reinhardt, Linda Schacht, Peter Schrag, William B Turner, David Weir, Lance Williams; *Profs. Emer.:* Ben H Bagdikian, Edwin Bayley, Albert G Pickerell; *Senior Lectr. Emer.:* James C Spalding, Andrew A Stern.
SEQUENCES: News-Editorial, Radio News, Television News.
DEGREE: MJ.

California Lutheran University
60 W. Olsen Rd., Thousand Oaks, CA 91360-2787; tel (805) 493-3366; fax (805) 493-3479. e-mail kelley@robles.callutheran.edu. Department of Communication Arts, 1981. Beverly Kelley, chair; Steven Ames, Journalism Concentration.
Journalism Program: The Communication Arts Department offers a BA in Communication Arts along with concentrations in journalism, advertising/public relations and media production; also, the department offers a BA in marketing communication in conjunction with the business school.

California Polytechnic State University
San Luis Obispo, CA 93407; tel (805) 756-2508; fax (805) 756-5744. Journalism Department, 1953. ACT, SPJ, California Newspaper Publishers Association, California Intercollegiate Press Association, Nishan Havandjian, head.
FACULTY: *Profs.:* Nishan Havandjian (head), Randall L Murray; *Assoc. Prof.:* Clay Carter, Victor Valle; *Lect.:* LaMonte Summers.
SEQUENCES: Agricultural Journalism, Broadcast Journalism, News-Editorial, Public Relations.
FACILITIES: AP, FM, ComN, ComR, ComTV, DR, JN, VDT.
DEGREE: BS.

California State Polytechnic University, Pomona
Pomona, CA 91768-4007; tel (909) 869-3520; fax (909) 869-4823; internet JAKaufman@CSUPomona.Edu. Communication Department, 1968. ASJSA, PRSSA, SPJ, WICI. J.A. Kaufman, acting chair.
Journalism Program: Majors offered in journ., telecomm., public relations/org. and communication studies.

California State University, Chico
Tehama Hall, Chico, CA 95929-0145; tel (916) 898-4015; fax (916) 898-4345. College of Communication, 1969. SPJ, IABC. Forensics, Designers in Progress, Organizational Communication Club, Instructional Technology Club. Stephen King, dean.
FACULTY: Dept. of Communication Design: *Profs.:* John G Berryman, Aaron M Bor, Kevin Cahill, Terry D Curtis, Fleet R Irvine, John C Ittelson, John Long, Robert G Main (chair), George Rogers (intern adviser); *Assoc. Profs.:* Dolores T Blalock, Richard Hannemann; *Prof. Emer.:* James Babcock.
Department of Communication Arts and Sciences: *Profs.:* Steven R Brydon (chair), Gary G Collier, Samuel M Edelman, Ruth M Guzley, Madeline M Keaveney, W Marc Porter, Michael D Scott, William R Todd-Mancillas; *Prof. Emer.:* Allan Forbes.
Department of Journalism: *Profs.* Peter Gross, Katherine Milo (chair); *Assoc. Profs.:* Kurt Nordstrom (intern adviser), Sharon Yoder; *Asst. Prof.:* Glen Bleske; *Prof. Emer.:* John Sutthoff; *Professional in Residence:* Bob Vivian.
SEQUENCES: Department of Communication Design: Media Arts, Visual Communications (Graphic Arts, Graphic Design), Instructional Technology, Information and Communication Systems. Dept. of Communication Arts and Sciences: Speech Communication, Organizational Communication. Department of Journalism: News-Editorial, Public Relations.
FACILITIES: AP, Ada, UPI, NPR-FM, CCTV, DR, EVT, JM, PRA, JN, VDT.
DEGREES: BA, MA.

California State University, Dominguez Hills
Carson, CA 90747; tel (310) 516-3313; fax (310) 516-3779. Department of Communications, 1973. PRSSA, SPJ. Leonard Lee, chair.
Communication Program: Offers BA degree in communications; also minor in advertising.

California State University, Fresno
2225 E. San Ramon Ave., Fresno, CA 93740-0010; tel (209) 278-2087; fax (209) 278-4995. Department of Mass Communication and Journalism, 1952. ADS, NPPA, SPJ. R.C. Adams, chair.
FACULTY: *Profs.:* Paul D Adams, R C Adams, Roberta R Asahina, Rita A Atwood, Russell A Hart, Philip J Lane, D Gregory Lewis, William N Monson, B Schyler Rehart, James B Tucker, James R Wilson, John D Zelezny; *Assoc. Profs.:* George A Flynn; *Asst. Profs.:* Muriel Jackson; *Lectr.:* Donald M Priest; *Profs. Emer.:* Lee Alden, Merlyn Burriss, John Highlander, Dayle H Molen.
FACILITIES: AP, AM, FM, AdA, CN, ComTV, DR, JN, PRA, VDT.
DEGREES: BA, MA.

California State University, Fullerton
Fullerton, CA 92634; tel (714) 773-3517; fax (714) 773-2209; internet rpicard@fullerton.edu. Department of Communications, 1961. AAF, BEA, IABC, KTA, NPPA, PRSSA, SPJ, WICI. Robert G Picard, chair.
FACULTY: *Profs:* Wendell C Crow, (coord., PR), David DeVries (coord., Photocommunications), Ron Dyas (coord., TV/Film), Anthony Fellow (vice chair and coord., Journalism), Norman Nager, Coral Ohl, Wayne Overbeck, Robert Picard, David Pincus, Rick D Pullen, Anthony Rimmer, Edgar P Trotter, Larry W Ward, Fred Zandpour (coord., Grad.); *Assoc. Profs.:* Carolyn E Johnson (coord., Internships), Paul Lester, George Manross, Shay Sayre; *Asst. Profs.:* Edward Fink, Cheryl Harris, Kuentlee Ju-Pak, Hazel Warlaumont; *Full-Time Lectrs.:* Jeff Brody (adviser, *Daily Titan*), Ava Caposela, Debra Conkey, Robert Davis, Dennis Gascher; *Part-Time Lectrs.:* Suzanne Adelson, J Jeffrey Brazil, Tom Clanin, Mike Cozzens, Thomas Dale, Dennis Gaschen, Ivan Goldman, Alfred Hewitt, Allison Hill, Shelly Jenkins, Debbi Schultz Manross, Robert Neill, Mark Platte, Robert Quezada, Russell Romain, Sue Schenkel, Miki Turner, Robert Whittenburg; *Profs. Emer.:* James Alexander, Fenton Calhoun, Terry Hynes, J William Maxwell, Robert Rayfield, Ted C Smythe, Don Sunoo.
SEQUENCES: Advertising, Journalism, Photocommunications, Public Relations, Television/Film.
FACILITIES: AdA, CCTV, ComN, ComTV, DR, JN, PRA, VDT, CATV.
DEGREES: BA, MA in Communications.

California State University, Hayward
Hayward, CA 94542; tel (510) 881-3292; fax (510) 885-4099. Department of Mass Communication, 1973. SPJ. Thomas S McCoy, chair.
FACULTY: *Profs.:* Thomas S McCoy, Robert L Terrell, Mary E Trapp; *Assoc. Profs.:* Gregory MacGregor; *Asst. Profs.:* Mohammed Osman Elsayed; *Prof. Emer.:* John Cambus, David Sanders; *Instrs.:* Larry Bensky, Paul Chutkow, Quintin Doroquez, Reese Erlich, Tom Ferentz, Marsha Ginsburg, Peter Graumann, Nancy Green, Cedric Puleston, Eric Ronning, Valerie Sue, Rick Tejada-Flores.
SEQUENCE: Mass Communication, with options in Advertising, Broadcasting, Journalism and Public Relations; Minor in Mass Communication, a Mass Communication Option in the Liberal Studies Major, and a Mass Communication emphasis in the waiver program for the Single Subject English, approved by the State Commission on Teacher Credentialing. Related minors are available in Advertising, Communication Skills, and Photography.
FACILITIES: AM/FM, CATV, DR, JM, JN, VDT.
DEGREE: BA (also special major).

California State University, Long Beach
1250 Bellflower Bl., Long Beach, CA 90815; tel (310) 985-4981; fax (310) 985-1740. Department of Journalism, 1966. KTA, PRSSA, WICI, SPJ, NPPA, IABC. William Mulligan, chair.
FACULTY: *Profs.:* Daniel Garvey, Wayne Kelly, Whitney Mandel, William Mulligan; *Lectr.:* Emma Daugherty; *Instrs.:* Gerald M Bush, Nick Roman, Robert Sykes, Tom Vasich, Philip Reed.
SEQUENCES: Broadcast, Education, Print, Public Relations, Photojournalism.
FACILITIES: AP, CATV, FM, DR, JM, JN, VDT.
DEGREE: BA.

California State University, Los Angeles
Los Angeles, CA 90032; tel (213) 343-4200; fax (213) 343-6467. Department of Communication Studies, Music 104, 5151 State University Dr., 1965.
Communication Program: Program sequences in Public Relations, Professional Communication and Broadcast Journalism.

California State University, Northridge
Northridge, CA 91330-8311; tel (818) 885-3135; fax (818) 885-3638. Department of Journalism, 1958. KTA, PRSSA, SPJ, RTNDA, Student Assn. of Black Communicators. Tom Reilly, chair.
FACULTY: *Profs.:* Michael Emery, Susan Henry, Tom Reilly, Maureen Rubin, Lawrence Schneider; *Assoc. Profs.:* Kent Kirkton, Cynthia Rawitch; *Asst. Profs.:* Rick Marks, Roberto Soto; *Lects.:* Henrietta Charles; *Prof. Emer.:* Kenneth S Devol, Sam Feldman, Jerry Jacobs, DeWayne B Johnson: *Part-Time Fac.:* Lori Baker-Schena, Barbara Eisenstock, Daniel Foster, Keith Goldstein, Kim Hunter, Douglas Kilian, Wynona Majied Muhammad, Kathleen Neumeyer, Barbara Osborn, Barbara Palermo, Paul Pringle, James Ruebsamen, Ezra Shapiro, Patricia Smith, Sally Turner, Manley Witten, Mari Womack.
SEQUENCE: News-Editorial.
FACILITIES: CNN, AP, UPI, FM, ComTV, ComN, ComR, DR, JM, JN, PRA, VDT.
DEGREES: BA, MA.

California State University, Sacramento
Sacramento, CA 95819; tel (916) 278-6353, 278-6354. Department of Journalism, 1947. SPJ. Michael Fitzgerald, chair.

Copyright ©1996 by the Editor & Publisher Co.

FACULTY: *Profs.:* Gwen Amos, Shirley Biagi, Miguel Blanco, William A Dorman, Michael Fitzgerald, Robert Humphrey, Leigh Stephens, Ralph E Talbert; *Asst. Profs.:* Jeanne Abbott, Sylvia Fox, Audrey Moore: *Part-Time Lectrs.:* Sigrid Bathen, Sharmon Goff.
SEQUENCES: News-Editorial, Graphic Design, Government Journalism.
FACILITIES: AM, FM, AdA, CATV, CN, ComN, ComR, ComTV, DR, JM, JN, PRA, VDT (IBM and Macintosh labs).
DEGREES: BA-Journalism, BA-Government/Journalism.

Humboldt State University
Arcata, CA 95521; tel (707) 826-4475; fax (707) 826-5419. Department of Journalism, 1960. SPJ. Mark A. Larson, chair.
FACULTY: *Profs.:* Sherilyn C Bennion, Mark A Larson, Maclyn H McClary, Howard L Seemann.
SEQUENCES: News-Editorial, Public Relations, Broadcast News, Media Studies.
FACILITIES: AP, FM, ComN, DR, JM, JN, PRA, VDT.
DEGREE: BA.

Menlo College
1000 El Camino Real, Atherton, CA 94027-4185; tel (415) 323-6141; fax (415) 324-4937. Department of Mass Communication. Susanna Barber, chair.
Communication Program: Offers three areas of concentration: Corporate Media, Print and Broadcast Journalism, and Creative Expression. Classes integrate theory and practice – using state-of-the-art production facilities – and focus on evaluating, managing, writing and producing media content.

Pacific, University of the
3601 Pacific Ave., Stockton, CA 95211; tel (209) 946-2505; fax (209) 946-3046. Department of Communication. Kenneth D Day, chair. Internet kday@uop.edu.
Communication Program: Offers BA in Communication with an emphasis on one of three tracks: Communication Studies, Public Relations and Organizational Communication, and Media Studies. MA degree offered with concentration in Communication Theory, Interpersonal Communication, Mass Communication, Organizational Communication, Public Relations, or Rhetoric and Public Address.

Pacific Union College
Angwin (Napa County), CA 94508; tel (707) 965-6437. Communication Department, 1945. James David Chase, chair.
Journalism Program: Emphases: newspaper; magazine; broadcasting; public relations for local, regional and national media. Includes internships, practicums. Majors: Journalism, Public Relations, Communication, International Communication and Speech Pathology.

Pepperdine University
Malibu, CA 90263; tel (310) 456-4211; fax (310) 456-3083; e-mail shores@pepperdine.edu. Communication Division, 1972. AAF, AERho, PRSSA, SPJ, WICI. Donald L Shores, chair.
FACULTY: *Profs.:* Bert Ardoin, Fred L Casmir, Dwayne VanRheenen, David Lowry, Don Shores, Ron Whittaker; *Assoc. Profs.:* Kyu Chang, Mike Jordan (dir., Student Publications), Milton Shatzer, (Grad. coord.), Ken Waters, Robert Woodroof; *Asst. Profs.:* Louella Benson-Garcia; *Staff:* William Dawson (chief brdct. engineer), Adam Thompson (mgr., Broadcast Services), Tammy Clarke, (asst. Publications adviser); *Visiting Prof.:* Lynne Gross; *Adjunct Profs.:* James Ruebsamen, Kathleen Shores, Ginger Rosencranz.
MAJORS: Advertising, Journalism (News Editorial), Public Relations, Telecommunications.
FACILITIES: AdA, AP, FM, CCTV, CATV, ComN, ComTV, JN, JM, DR, PRA, UDT.
DEGREES: BA, MA.

Point Loma Nazarene College
San Diego, CA 92106; tel (619) 221-2297/2260; fax (619) 221-2566; e-mail hesterll@oa.ptloma. edu. Journalism and Mass Communications majors. SPJ satellite chapter with San Diego State U. Vicki Hesterman, Dean Nelson, Journalism co-directors; Mark Hamilton, Mass Communications director.
BA Programs: Journalism major with emphasis in Newspaper/Magazine, Broadcast Journalism, or Linguistics. Mass Communications major in TV-Radio producing. Campus newspaper, magazine and radio station; access to television facilities.

Saint Mary's College of California
Moraga, CA 94575; tel (510) 631-4000; fax (510) 631-0938. Department of Communications, 1987. Michael A Russo, PhD, chair.
Journalism Program: A comprehensive Liberal Arts program including communications theory and practice in audio, video and print media.

San Diego State University
San Diego, CA 92182; tel (619) 594-5450; fax (619) 594-6246. School of Communications, 1951. AAF, ADS, KTA, PRSSA, SPJ. John Pavlik, dir.
FACULTY: *Profs.:* Glen M Broom, James K Buckalew, David M Dozier, Barbara W Hartung, K Tim Wulfemeyer (head, Radio-TV emphasis); *Assoc. Profs.:* Joel J Davis (grad. adviser), Martha Lauzen (head, Pubic Relations emphasis), Barbara Mueller (head, Advertising emphasis); *Asst. Prof.:* Joseph E Spevak; *Lectrs.:* Allen Center (distinguished resident lectr.), David Feldman, Jonathan Freeman, Syd Love, Sue Lussa, January Riddle (undergrad. adviser), Joseph Schneider.
SEQUENCES: Advertising, News-Editorial, Public Relations, Radio-TV News.
FACILITIES: AP, CATV, CCTV, ComN, ComR, ComTV, DR, ETV, AM, FM, JM, PRA, VDT.
DEGREES: BA, MS.

San Francisco, University of
2130 Fulton St., San Francisco, CA 94117-1080; tel (415) 666-6680; fax (415) 666-2772; e-mail RUNYON@USFCA.EDU. Media Studies Program, Journalism emphasis, 1974. Steven C Runyon, dir.
Journalism Program: Program combines traditional academic foundation and professional internship orientation in San Francisco at Jesuit University. Emphases: Journalism, Electronic Media, and Media and Society.

San Francisco State University
1600 Holloway Ave., San Francisco, CA 94132; tel (415) 338-1689; fax (415) 338-3111; e-mail journal@ceres.sfsu.edu. Department of Journalism, 1961. SPJ. Erna Smith, acting chair.
FACULTY: *Profs.:* John Burks, John T Johnson, Kenneth Kobre, Leonard Sellers; *Assoc. Profs.:* Austin Long-Scott, Vernon Thompson; *Profs. Emer.:* William Chapin, B H Liebes, Jerrold Werthimer, Leo V Young; *Lectrs.:* Michael Collier, Roland DeWolk, Angelo Figueroa, Jon Funabiki, Vicki Haddock, Gregory Lewis, Elizabeth Mangelsdorf, Raul Ramirez, Dick Rogers, Carol Urzi, Jeff Vendsel, James Wagstaffe, William Wong.
SEQUENCES: News-Editorial, Magazine, Photojournalism.
FACILITIES: DR, JM, JN, VDT.
DEGREES: BA, Interdisciplinary master's degree.

San Jose State University
San Jose, CA 95121-0055; tel (408) 924-3240; fax (408) 924-3229. School of Journalism and Mass Communications, 1934. AAA, AAF, CNAEA, CNPA, NCCPA, KTA, SPJ, PRSSA, WICI, NPPA. Kenneth W Blase, director.
FACULTY: *Profs.:* Ken Blase, William Briggs, Harvey Gotliffe, Stephen Greene, David L Grey, Thomas Jordan, Clyde E Lawrence, James E Noah, Marshall L Raines, Diana Stover-Tillinghast (coord. Grad. Studies), William A Tillinghast, Dennis Wilcox; *Assoc. Profs.:* Cecelia Baldwin, Kathleen Martinelli, James McNay, Bob Rucker; *Asst. Prof.:* Zhou He, Kenneth Plowman; *Lectrs.:* Darla Belshe, Elias Castillo, DeAnna DeRosa, Denise Franklin, Joseph Gilbert, Lynn Louie, C Mack Lundstrum, Colleen Martell, Bob McDermand, Jane McMillan, Robert Nelson, Jack C Quinton, Antionette Saylor, Jan Shaw, Jane Wertz.
SEQUENCES: Magazine, News-Editorial, Radio-TV News, Photojournalism, Advertising, Public Relations, Mass Communication.
FACILITIES: AP, FM, AdA, CCTV, ComN, ComR, ComTV, DR, JN, PRA, VDT.
DEGREES: BS, MS.

Santa Clara University
Santa Clara, CA 95053; tel (408) 554-2798; fax (408) 554-4913; e-mail psoukup@sluacc.scu.edu. Department of Communication. Paul Soukup, PhD.
Journalism Program: Department offers BA in Communication, Print and Broadcast Journalism emphases. Courses include newswriting, editing, design, etc.

Southern California, University of
University Park, Los Angeles, CA 90089-1695; tel (213) 740-3914; fax (213) 740-8624. School of Journalism, 1929. AER, PRSSA, SPJ. Murray Fromson, interim dir.
FACULTY: *Profs.:* Murray Fromson (dir., Center for International Journalism), A Jack Langguth, Bryce Nelson, Joe Saltzman, Clancy Sigal; *Assoc. Profs.:* Ed Cray, William Faith (head, PR), Jon Kotler, Sherrie Mazingo (head, Brdct.); *Adj. Profs.:* Carolyn Cline, Norman Corwin, Ed Guthman (head, Print).
SEQUENCES: Print, Broadcast, Public Relations.
FACILITIES: AP, AM, CN, ComN, ComTV, JM, PRA.
DEGREES: BA, MA.

Stanford University
Stanford, CA 94305-2050; tel (415) 723-1941; fax (415) 725-2472. Department of Communication. Donald F Roberts, chair.
FACULTY: *Profs.:* Henry Breitrose (dir., Grad. Program in Documentary Film), Steven H Chaffee (Peck Professor and dir. Institute for Communication Research), Marion Lewenstein, Byron Reeves, James Risser (dir., Knight Fellowship program), Donald Roberts (chair), Kristine Samuelson; *Assoc. Profs.:* Theodore L Glasser (dir., Grad. Program in Jour.), Jan Krawitz, Clifford Nass; *Asst. Prof.:* June Flora; *Lectrs.:* James Bettinger, Benjamin H Detenber, Dennis Kinsey, Dale Maharidge; *Profs. (by courtesy):* Richard Brody (Political Science), Michael Ray (Business), Eugene Webb (Business); *Profs. Emer.:* Elie Abel (Chandler Professor), Lyle Nelson (Storke Professor).
SEQUENCES: Communication, (BA), Journalism, (MA), Documentary Film, (MA), Media Studies, (MA),Communication Research, (PhD).
FACILITIES: CCTV, FM, RNA, UPI, VDT.
DEGREES: BA, MA, PhD.

COLORADO

Adams State College
Alamosa, CO 81101; tel (303) 589-7427; fax (719) 589-7522. English/Journalism Program, Communications Dept. Dr. Joseph Kolupke (Communications Dept. chair) and John Morris (Journalism instr.).
Journalism Program: Emphasis on print news-editorial, with practical experience in both print and radio broadcasting offered.

Colorado, University of
Macky Auditorium 201, Campus Box 287, Boulder, CO 80309-0287; tel (303) 492-5007; fax (303) 492-0969. School of Journalism and Mass Communication, 1922. AAF, KTA, SPJ, WICI. Willard D Rowland, Jr., dean.
FACULTY: *Profs.:* Sandra Moriarty, Willard D Rowland Jr., Michael Tracey (dir., Center for Mass Media Research), Robert Trager (dir., Grad. Studies): *Assoc. Profs.:* Len Ackland, (dir., Center for Environmental Journalism), Andrew Calabrese, William Celis III, Ray Chávez, (dir., Office of Student Diversity), Thomas Duncan, (dir., Integrated Marketing Communications prog.), Stewart Hoover, (head, Media Studies seq.), Frank Kaplan (head, News-Editorial), Polly McLean, Marguerite Moritz (fac. assoc. and head, Electronic Media seq.), Janice Peck, Patricia Raybon, Brett Robbs, Lawrence Weisberg (head, Advertising seq.); *Asst. Profs.:* Shu-Ling Everett, Stephen Everett, Anders Groustedt, Jan Whitt; *Instrs.:* Don Heider, Bruce Henderson, (adv., *Campus Press*) Stephen Jones (asst. dean); *Lectrs.:* Joann Dennett, Elizabeth Gaeddert, (dir., Master's Newsgathering prog. and dir., Internship and Placement prog.), Fred Hobbs, Carl Kay, Douglas Looney, Paul Moloney, Walt Perls, Bert Quint.; *Profs. Emer.:* Sam Archibald, Joanne Arnold, James Brinton, Malcolm Deans, Harold Hill, William McReynolds, Robert Rhode, Don Somerville, Gayle Waldrop; *Instr. Emer.:* Don Ridgway (exec. dir., Colorado High School Press Association).
SEQUENCES: Advertising, Electronic Media (Broadcast News & Broadcast Production/Management), Media Studies News-Editorial.
FACILITIES: AdA, AP, CATV, ComN, ComR, ComTV, DR, JN, PRA, VDT.
DEGREES: BS, MA, PhD.

Colorado State University
Fort Collins, CO 80523; tel (303) 491-6310, 491-6319; fax (303) 491-2908. Department of Technical Journalism, 1958. PRSSA, SPJ, RTNDA. James K VanLeuven, chair.
FACULTY: *Profs:* Fred Shook, James VanLeuven, Don Zimmerman; *Assoc. Profs.:* Judith Buddenbaum, Dan Hilleman, Garrett Ray, Donna Rouner, Michael Slater, Marty Tharp; *Asst. Profs.:* Marilee Long, Gregory Luft, David Morrissey; *Instrs.:* Gary Ferguson, Amy Gaddes, Sara Hoffman, Johnieann Pearson, Ed Otte, Roger Lipken, Timothy Sandsmark, Marty Traynor, Donna Uchida; *Profs. Emer.:* David G Clark, Derry Eynon, Stephen Lamoreux, Delbert McGuire.
SEQUENCES: Electronic Reporting, News-Editorial, Public Relations, Technical-Specialized Communication.
FACILITIES: AM/FM, CCTV, CN, ComN, DR, PRA, VDT.
DEGREES: BA-Agricultural Journalism, BA-Technical Journalism, MS-Technical Communication.

Denver, University of
Denver, CO 80208; tel (303) 871-2166; fax (303) 871-4949. Department of Mass Communications and Journalism Studies, 1956. IABC. Michael O Wirth, chair.
FACULTY: *Prof.:* Michael O Wirth; *Assoc. Prof.:* Linda Cobb-Reiley, Diane Waldman; *Asst. Profs.:* Jeff Rutenbeck (dir., Undergrad. Studies), Laurie Schulze, Phillip Stephens, Margaret Thompson (dir., IIC Grad. Program), Michael Basil; *Lectr.:* Rodney Buxton (dir., Grad. Studies), Catherine A Grieve (dir., Internships); *Profs. Emer.:* Noel Jordan, Harold Mendelsohn.
SEQUENCE:Communications, Journalism Studies, Mass Communications.
FACILITIES: AdA, CN, CCTV, PRA, VDT, ComN.
DEGREES: BA, MA, MS.

Mesa State College
Grand Junction, CO 81502; PO Box 2647; tel (303) 248-1687, ext. 1287. Mass Communications Dept., 1981. Byron Evers, dir.
Communications Program: The department offers a Mass Communications bachelor's degree with emphasis in Print Media, News-Editorial, Public Relations, Radio/Television.

Metropolitan State College of Denver
PO Box 173362, Denver, CO 80217-3362; tel (303) 556-3485, Department of Journalism, 1987. Deborah C Hurley, chair.
Journalism Program: The journalism department his three sequences: news/editorial, photojournalism and public relations. The department uses a hands-on approach to teach reporting an editing. All faculty are current or former reporters/editors. The department sponsors an internship newspaper that covers the Colorado legislature.

Northern Colorado, University of
Greeley, CO 80639; tel (303) 351-2726; fax (303) 351-2983. Department of Journalism and Mass Communications, 1970. IABC, SPJ. Charles Ingold, chair.
FACULTY: *Assoc. Profs.:* David L Anderson, John Bromley, Charles Ingold; *Asst. Profs.:* Robert A Hess, Patrick McCarthy; *Instrs.:* Michael Applegate, William Woodward.
SEQUENCES: Public Relations and Advertising Media, News-Editorial, Telecommunications.
FACILITIES: FM, CN, DR, CATV, 20 VDTs and 3 printers in news lab.
DEGREES: BA.

Southern Colorado, University of
Pueblo, CO 81001; tel (719) 549-2818, 549-2835; fax (719) 549-2120. Department of Mass Communications. Patricia Bowie Orman, head.
Communications Program: Integrated umbrella program provides emphases in News-Editorial Journalism, Public Relations, Telecommunications and Advertising.

CONNECTICUT

Bridgeport, University of
Bridgeport, CT 06601; tel (203) 576-4705; e-mail CARVETHR@CSUSYS.CTSTATEU.EDU Department of Mass Communication, 1948. AAF, IABC, SPJ, WICI. Rod Carveth, chair.
Journalism Program: The department offers sequences in news-editorial, advertising, and communication studies.

Connecticut, University of
Storrs, CT 06269; tel (203) 486-4221, 486-4222; fax (203) 486-3294. Journalism Department, 1948. New England Newspaper Association. Maureen Croteau, head.
FACULTY: *Profs.:* Maureen Croteau, Wayne Worcester; *Assoc. Prof.:* John J Breen; *Asst. Prof.:* Marcel Dufresne; *Visiting Asst. Prof.:* Peggy McCarthy; *Lectrs.:* John Bailey, Constance Chambers, Laurence Cohen, Garret Condon, Bob Hamilton, Terese Karmel, Bryant Michaud, Joseph Nunes, Daryl Perch, John Peterson, Jon Sandberg.
SEQUENCE: News-Editorial.
FACILITIES: AP, CN. ComN, ComTV, PRA, AM, FM, JN, VDT.
DEGREE: BA.

Hartford, University of
200 Bloomfield Ave., West Hartford, CT 06117; tel (860) 768-4633; fax (860) 768-4096; e-mail jassem@uhavax.hartford.edu. School of Communication, 1956. Harvey C Jassem, dir.

Copyright ©1996 by the Editor & Publisher Co.

Journalism Program: Offers BA and MA in Communication with emphasis in Journalism, Mass Communication, Advertising, Public Relations.

Quinnipiac College
275 Mt. Carmel Ave., Hamden, CT 06518; tel (203) 281-8974; fax (203) 281-8931. Mass Communications Department, Ed McMahon Center, 1993. Raymond Foery, chair.
FACULTY: *Profs:* James W Ferguson, John M. Gourlie, Grace F Levine; *Assoc. Profs.:* Mira Bindford, Raymond A Foery, Louis C. Adler; Bill McLaughlin.
DEGREES: BA.

Southern Connecticut State University
New Haven, CT 06515; tel (203) 397-4311; fax (203) 397-4154. Journalism Department, 1976. SPJ. Jerry Dunklee, chair.
FACULTY: *Prof.:* Robin Glassman, Jane Hamilton-Merritt; *Assoc. Profs.:* Jerry Dunklee, Joseph Manzella; *Asst. Profs.:* Frank Harris III; *Adjunct Fac.:* George Grande, Richard Odermatt, William Seymour, Cynthia Simoneau, Dorothy Torres, Melinda Tuhus, Ken Warren.
SEQUENCES: News-Editorial, Magazine, Broadcast, Public Relations.
FACILITIES: AM, AdA, AP, CATV, CCTV, CN, ComN, ComR, ComTV, DR, PRA, VDT.
DEGREES: BA, BS.

DELAWARE

Delaware, University of
Newark, DE 19716; tel (302) 451-2361. Journalism Program.
Journalism Program: Offers 21 hours of news writing, magazine writing, opinion writing and copy editing-layout courses, as well as extensive internship program with newspapers, magazines, electronic media and public relations offices.

DISTRICT OF COLUMBIA

The American University
Washington, DC 20016; tel (202) 885-2060; fax (202) 885-2099. School of Communication, 1966. KTA, NATAS, PRSSA, SPJ, WICI. Sanford J Ungar, dean.
FACULTY: *Profs.:* Laird B Anderson, Dom Bonafede, Glenn Harnden, Jerry Hendrix, Jack Orwant (div. dir., Public Communication), Richard Stout, Ronald Sutton, Sanford Ungar, Lewis Wolfson, Joanne Yamauchi; *Assoc. Profs.:* John C Doolittle (div. dir., Journalism), John Douglass (div. dir., Visual Media), Lincoln Furber, Donald Moore, J C Seigle, Rodger Streitmatter, Ann Zelle; *Asst. Profs.:* Patricia Aufderheide, Barbara Diggs-Brown, Pat Ellis, Robert Goald, S Kendall, Josef Lustig, Jill Olmsted, Susanne Roschwalb (dir., Grad. Public Communication Weekend Program), Linda Searing, Chris Simpson, Joe Spear, Richard Stack, Wendy Swallow Williams (dir., Grad. Journalism Weekend Program), Rhonda Zaharna; *Visiting Scholar:* John Trattner; *Instrs.:* Karen Howze; *Part-Time Instrs.:* George Arnold, Randall Blair, Jean Marie Bunton, William Burns, Francis Carpousis, Wendell Cochran, Eddie Cockrell, Maria Cooper, Robert Cuccia, Libby Cullen, Janet Darsie, Barbara Davis, Olifed Dukes, Jonathan Eig, Jeff Finn, Jane Frank, Peter Gamba, Darrell Hayes, Marge Holtz, Desmon Howe, David Hyatt, Yeshi Imagnu, Claire Johnson, Frank Johnson, Jane Kirtley, Christine Lawrence, David Lightman, Mary Beth Marklein, Judy Miller, Leigh Mosley, Jed Nitzberg, Lynne Olson, Paul Orgel, Joan Pryde, Jane Putman, Rosemayr Reed, Jon Ross, Elizabeth Rose, Vivian Shayne, Michael Sheward, Paul Siegel, Nan Siemer, Allison Silberberg, Sue Ann Staake, Dianne Sutton, David Swanston, John Tarpey, Steve Taylor, Vincent Tocci, Susan Trento, Debra Wall, Ken Walsh, Larry Waltman, Susan Watters, Al Way, Raymond White, Bonnie Willette, Andrew Wolvin.
PROGRAMS: Broadcast Journalism, Print Journalism, Public Communication, Visual Media, Graduate Journalism and Public Affairs, Graduate Film and Video, Graduate Public Communication.
FACILITIES: AP, UPI, AM, FM, CCTV, ComN, DR, ComR, ComTV, PRA, VDT.
DEGREES: BA, MA.

Catholic University School of Law
Washington, DC 20064; tel (202) 319-5140; fax (202) 319-4459. Institute for Communications Law Studies. Harvey L Zuckman, dir.
Communications Program: Specialized legal training in communications law for JD degree candidates with journalism or telecommunications backgrounds.

George Washington University
Washington, DC 20052; tel (202) 994-6227; fax (202) 994-5806; e-mail NCCS1@GWUVM. Journalism Program (National Center for Communication Studies), 1947. SPJ. Philip Robbins, dir.
FACULTY: *Prof. Lectr.:* Lawrence B Laurent; *Profs.:* Jean Folkerts, Haynes Johnson, Jarol Manheim, Philip Robbins; *Assoc. Profs.:* C W Puffenbarger; *Assoc. Prof. Lectrs:* Robert Becker, Charlotte Blount, Theodore Cron, John Echave, John Fogarty, Judith Marden, Paige McMahon, Michael Sheward, Daniel Smith.
SEQUENCE: News-Editorial.
FACILITIES: AP, ComN, DR, ComR, ComTV, VDT.
DEGREE: BA.

Howard University
Washington, DC 20059; tel (202) 806-7855; fax (202) 806-9227. Department of Journalism, 1972. SPJ, NABJ, PRSSA, AAF, BCCA. Barbara Bealor Hines, chair.
FACULTY: *Prof.:* Lawrence Kaggwa; *Assoc. Profs.:* Anju Chaudhary, Barbara Hines, Anne Nunamaker, Lee Thornton, Clint C Wilson, II; *Asst. Profs.:* Sandra Wills Hannon; *Lectrs.:* Robert Asher, Connie Frazier, Marcia Freeman, Lori George, Dash Parham, Otis Thomas, Mike Tucker, Pat Wheeler-Holmes.
SEQUENCES: News-Editorial, Broadcast Journalism, Advertising, Public Relations.
FACILITIES: AM, AdA, RNA, FM, CN, ComN, ComR, ComTV, ETV, JN, PRA, VDT.
DEGREE: BA.

Mount Vernon College
Washington, DC 20007; tel (202) 625-4652; fax (202) 337-0259. Communications Department. Dr. Maria E Carrington, chair.
Communications Program: Offers BA in Communications to women in all mass communications areas.

FLORIDA

Central Florida, University of
Orlando, FL 32816; tel (407) 823-2681; fax (407) 823-5156. School of Communication, 1964. James W Welke, dir.; Fred Fedler, div. head, Journalism; Milan Meeske, div. head, RTV.
Journalism Program: Offers majors in News/Editorial, Advertising/Public Relations and Radio TV: General.

Edward Waters College
Jacksonville, FL 32218; tel (904) 366-2502, ext. 502. Mass Communications Program, 1982/83. Emmanuel C Alozie, coord.
SEQUENCES: Radio/TV, Journalism.
DEGREE: BA.

Florida, University of
Gainesville, FL 32611-8400; tel (904) 392-0466; fax (904) 392-3919. College of Journalism and Communications, 1948. AAF, AER, KTA, PRSSA, SPJ, NAEB, BEA, Florida Press Assn., Florida Public Relations Assn., Florida Assn. of Broadcasters, Florida Magazine Assn. Terry Hynes, dean.
FACULTY: *Profs.:* James W Anderson, Glenn A Butler, Bill F Chamberlin (eminent scholar), John S Detweiler, Mary Ann Ferguson (asst. dean, research), John L Griffith, Robert Kendall, Kurt Kent, Kent Lancaster, David L Malickson, David Ostroff, Robert N Pierce, Joseph R Pisani (chair, Dept. of Adv.), Jon A Roosenraad (dir., Student Services), Paul Smeyak (chair, Dept. of Telecomm.), F Leslie Smith, John C Sutherland, James L Terhune (assoc. dean), Leonard Tipton, Elaine Wagner, John Wright (asst. dean, Grad. Studies); *Assoc. Profs.:* Laurence B Alexander (chair, Dept. of Jour.), Charles Burke, Les M Carson, Jean C Chance, H H (Hank) Conner, Julie Dodd (exec. dir., Florida Scholastic Press Association), Marilyn S Fregly, Frankie A Hammond (acting chair, Dept. of Public Relations), Jon D Morris, H Sidney Pactor, Benton R Patterson, Edward G Weston; *Asst. Profs.:* James Babanikos, Sandra Chance, Frank S Counts, John Freeman, Thomas Krynski (news dir., WRUF), Michael Leslie, Milagros Rivera-Sanchez, Kim Walsh-Childers, Linda Childers Hon, Marilyn Roberts, Michael Weigold, Edward L Wells, Julian Williams (on leave); *Lectrs.:* Helen E Aller (dir., Scholarship/Placement Center), C J Harris (dir., Minority Programs Office), Kevin Allen (news dir., WUFT-FM), Catherine Harwood (news dir., WUFT-TV); *Deans Emer.:* John Paul Jones, Ralph L Lowenstein, Rae O Weimer; *Profs. Emer.:* Kenneth A Christiansen, Hugh W Cunningham, H G (Buddy) Davis, Mickie Edwardson, Harry H Griggs, Arthur J Jacobs, Frank N Pierce, Jo Anne Smith, Charles G Wellborn Jr., Edward D Yates; *Part-Time Lectrs.:* Kay Ford, Gregory Ling, Roy Mays, Marshall Prine, Judy Tipton, John Walther.
SEQUENCES: *Undergraduate:* Advertising, Telecommunication (news and public affairs, production, operations/management), News Editorial (reporting, editing, photojournalism), Magazines, Public Relations, Technical Communication.
Graduate: Advertising, Communication Research, International Communication, Journalism, Political Campaigning, Public Relations, Telecommunication.
FACILITIES: AP, UPI, AM, FM, AdA, CATV, CCTV, CN, ComN, ComR, DR, ETV, JM, PRA, VDT.
DEGREES: BS in Advertising, BS in Journalism, BS in Public Relations, BS in Telecommunication, MA in Mass Communication, PhD in Mass Communication.

Florida A&M University
Tallahassee, FL 32307; tel (904) 599-3379; fax (904) 561-2399. School of Journalism, Media and Graphic Arts, 1974. Black College Communication Assn., SPJ, PRSSA, Florida Public Relations Assn., WICI (tri-campus chapter), Florida Society of Newspaper Editors, Florida Assn. of Broadcasters, Florida Press Assn., Graphic Arts Education Assn., American Assn. of University Printers, Graphic Arts Technical Foundation. Robert M Ruggles, dean.
FACULTY: *Profs.:* Michael E Abrams, F Todd Bertolaet, Gerald O Grow, James W Haskins Jr., James E Hawkins (dir., Div. of Jour.), James P Jeter (dir., Grad. Studies), Phillip O Keirstead, Arvid Mukes (acting dir., Div. of Graphic Arts), Ronald L Norvelle, Joe Ritchie (Knight chair), Robert M Ruggles, Gale Workman; *Assoc. Profs.:* Vincent Blyden, Thomas Rasheed, Louise Ritchie (newspaper adviser), Roosevelt Wilson; *Asst. Profs.:* Gerald M Gee, M Diane Hall (dir., School Information Services), Gloria Horning, Joseph Ippolito, John O Omachonu (dir., University Broadcast Services), Lucinda Stiff (dir., JOU Placement/Internships); *Instrs.:* Archie V Hannon, Ernest Jones, Melvin L Lamb; *Adjunct Instr.:* Michael Nathan.
SEQUENCES: Newspaper Journalism, Magazine Production, Broadcast Journalism, Public Relations, Printing Production, Photography, Graphic Design, Printing Management.
FACILITIES: UPI, FM, DR, JN, VDT, CCTV, ComN, JM, Printing Plant.
DEGREES: BSJ, BS in Magazine Production, BS in Graphic Arts Technology, BS in Graphic Design, MS in Journalism.

Florida International University
North Miami Campus, N.E. 151st St. & Biscayne Blvd., North Miami, FL 33181; tel (305) 940-5625; fax (305) 956-5203. School of Journalism and Mass Communication, 1978. AAF, PRSSA, WICI, SPJ, Video Club. J Arthur Heise, dean.
FACULTY: *Profs.:* J Arthur Heise, Lillian Lodge Kopenhaver (assoc. dean), David Martinson; Mary Alice Shaver (chair, Dept. Journ. and Broadcasting) *Assoc. Profs.:* Bill Adams, William Biglow, Humberto Delgado, Charles Fair, Patricia Rose (chair, Dept. of Adv. & PR), Robert Ruttenberg; *Asst. Profs.:* Margo Berman (visiting), Hernando Gonzalez, Michael Huber (visiting), Laura Kelly, Debra Miller (asst. dean), Lorna Veraldi; *Editor-in-Residence:* Kevin Hall; *Spanish Professional Journalist-in-Residence:* Mario Diament; *Instrs:* Barry Nemcoff (visiting); *Latin American Journalism Program:* Charles H Green (exec. dir.), Gerardo Bolanos (dep. exec. dir.), Roy Carter (visiting), Lisa Gross (visiting), Ruth Merino, Agatha Ogazon (project coord.), Jack Virtue, Ana Cecelia With; *Adjunct Profs.:* Holly Anderson, Robert Brechner, Yves Colon, Sue Greer, Rick Hirsch, Jeff King, Mike McQueen, Blair Somberg, Juan Vasques, Carlos Verdecia, Richard Westlund, Joe Williams, Barbara Walsh, Sherri Winston.
SEQUENCES: News-Editorial, Advertising, Public Relations, Broadcasting.
FACILITIES: DR, VDT, AdA, PRA, Graphics Lab, EDIT, DESK, EFP, PR Newswire, ENG.
DEGREES: BS, MS.

Florida Southern College
111 Lake Hollingsworth Dr., Lakeland, FL 33801-5698; tel (813) 680-4168; fax (813) 680-4126. Mass Communications Department. David F Snodgrass, chairman.
Journalism Program: BA in Mass Communications with emphases in Advertising, Public Relations and Journalism.

Jacksonville University
Jacksonville, FL 32211; tel (904) 744-3950. Department of Mass Communication Studies. Dennis Stouse, dir.
Journalism Program: JU's program blends the arts and sciences with a skills-oriented communications curriculum. Sequences available are Newspaper/Magazine, PR/Advertising, Radio/TV/Film. Media include weekly newspaper, college magazine, yearbook, radio station, cable television access, and national film studies journal. Many internship opportunities are available including a summer internship experience in Los Angeles. SCJ and Florida Public Relations Association.

Miami, University of
5202 University Dr., Coral Gables, FL 33124; tel (305) 284-2265; fax (305) 284-3648; internet epfister@ umiamivm.ir.miami.edu. School of Communication, 1985. AAF, AER, BEA, KTA, NATAS, SPJ, PRSSA, 4-A Ad Club, WICI, RTNDA, FL Assoc. of Brdct., Edward Pfister, dean.
FACULTY: *Profs.:* Anthony Allegro, Stephen Bowles, Michael Carlebach, Bruce Garrison, Josephine Johnson, John Masterson, Edward Pfister, Lemuel Schofield, Mitchell Shapiro (asst. dean), Don Stacks, Tom Steinfatt (program dir., Speech); *Assoc. Profs.:* Paul Driscoll (program dir., Brdct.), Stanley Harrison (program dir., Public Relations & Adv.), Robert Hosmon (assoc. dean and dir. of development), Paul Lazarus (program dir., Motion Pictures), William Rothman, Michael Salwen, John Soliday, Gonzalo Soruco; *Asst. Profs.:* Marie-Helene Bourgoignie, Sanjeev Chatterjee, Diane Christophel, Christine Davidson, Michel Dupagne, Leonardo Ferreira, Peter Hutcheson, Janet Meyer, Cynthia Servidio, Sigman Splichal, Donn Tilson, Ludmilla Wells; *Instrs.:* Grace Barnes, Kathleen Roberts; *Lectrs.:* George Capewell, Carolyn Cefalo, Louise Gainey, Valerie Giroux, Alan Prince, David Steinberg, Tsitsi Wakhisi; *Adjunct Assoc.:* Paul Steinle (program dir., Journalism and Photo.); *Part-Time Lectrs:* Kathy Bensen, Cynthia Capewell, Sara Castany, Jay Gladwell, Fred Goldberg, Elaine Goncalves, C W Griffin, Mimi Kelly, Ray McPhee, Alexis Moore, Paul Nagel, Sondra Pierce, Cornelia Splichal, Alexander Stuart, Jane Swanko; *Visiting Scholar:* Allan Casebier; *Knight Chair:* James Goodsell, Randy Stano; *Comm. Studies Chair:* Joseph Angotti.
MAJORS: Advertising, Public Relations, Journalism, Photography, Motion Pictures, Video/Film, Speech Communication, Organizational Communication, Broadcasting, Broadcast Journalism.
FACILITIES: AP, FM, CN, CATV, ComN, ComR, ComTV, DR, AdA, PRA, VDT.
DEGREES: BS, BFA, MA, MFA.

North Florida, University of
4567 St. Johns Bluff Rd. S., Jacksonville, FL 32246-2645; tel (904) 646-2650; fax (904) 646-2652; e-mail rbohle@unf6.unf.edu. Department of Communications and Visual Arts, 1987. PRSSA, AdFed. Robert H Bohle, PhD, chairman.
FACULTY: *Prof.:* Robert Cocanougher, Louise F Brown, Robert H Bohle, (chairman); *Assoc. Profs.:* Charles Charles, Paul Ladnier, Ken McMillan, David Porter; *Asst. Prof.:* Ed Grimm, Paula Horvath-Neimeyer, Joe Lesem, Debra Murphy-Livingston; *Prof. Emer.:* William Roach; *Visiting Asst. Profs.:* Helena Angell, Marsha Leidendorff; *Visiting Instr.:* Gary Warner; *Collateral Profs.:* Paul Karabinis, Jack Funkhouser.
SEQUENCES: Communications: News-Editorial, Advertising, Public Relations, Broadcasting. Visual Arts: Computer Graphics, Graphic Design, Photography, Painting, Drawing, Ceramics, Art History.
FACILITIES: CATV, CCTV, CN, ComN, DR, PRA, AdA.
DEGREES: BA, BFA.

South Florida, University of
Tampa, FL 33620-7800; tel (813) 974-2591; fax (813) 974-2592. School of Mass Communications, CIS 1040, 1970. BEA, FPA, FSNE, AAF, KTA, PRSSA, SPJ. Edward Jay Friedlander, dir.
FACULTY: *Profs.:* Jay Black, Donna Dickerson, Edward Jay Friedlander, George M Killenberg, Manny Lucoff, Arthur M Sanderson (emeritus); *Assoc. Profs.:* Dan Bagley, Tilden Counts (head, Telecomm. seq.), Robert Dardenne, William G Fudge (head, Adv. seq.); *Asst. Profs.:* Karen Brown, Scott Liu, Randy Miller (head, News-Ed seq.), Barbara Petersen, (grad. dir.); *Lectrs.:* David Togie, Gary Werner, (head, PR seq.), Rick Wilber; *Advising Coord.:* Cathy D'Azzo; *Adjunct Fac.;* Mary Floyd, Mark Gould, Lowell Harris, Bert Price, Neil Vicino.
SEQUENCES: Advertising, Telecommunications, Journalism (news-editorial and magazine), Public Relations, Visual Communications.

FACILITIES: AM/FM, AdA, CATV, CCTV, CN, ComN, ComR, ComTV, DR, ETV, PRA, computer and graphics labs.
DEGREES: BA, MA.

West Florida, University of
Pensacola, FL 32514; tel (904) 474-2874; fax (904) 474-3337. BITNET CRoberts@UWF. Communication Arts, 1967. BEA, SPJ, PRSSA, FPRA, AAF. Churchill L Roberts, chair.
FACULTY: *Profs.:* J Laurence Day, Tom Groth, Ralph T Eubanks (emeritus), Churchill L Roberts (chair); *Assoc. Profs.:* Sandra H Dickson (fac. adviser, *Nautilus News*), Amir M Karimi, Martha Saunders (coord., PRSSA), W Stuart Towns; *Asst. Profs.:* Jamie Comstock, Peter Gershon, Hugh Merrill, Kartik Pashupati; *Instrs.:* Cynthia Hill, Cara Parks, Eileen Perrigo, Toni Whitfield; *Part-Time and Adjunct Fac.:* J Earle Bowden, William Clark, Jean-Marie McDonnell (fac. adviser, *Voyager*), Barbara Regan, John Teelin.
SEQUENCES: Journalism (broadcast and print), Advertising & Public Relations, Radio/Television/Film, Communication Studies, Graduate Mass Communication.
FACILITIES: AP, FM, AdA, CCTV, ComN, ComTV, DR, JN, PRA, VDT.
DEGREES: BA, MA.

GEORGIA

Berry College
5022 Berry College, Mt. Berry, GA 30149-5022; tel (706) 232-5374; Fax (706) 236-9004. Department of Communication Arts, 1986. BEA, KAM, KTA, KPPA, SCJ. Robert L Frank, coord.
FACULTY: *Assoc. Prof.:* Bob Frank (Coord.); *Asst. Prof.:* Kathy McKee, Dan Panici (Broadcasting adviser), Randy Richardson; *Instrs.:* Kevin Kleine (Publication adviser).
SEQUENCES: Journalism, Public Relations, Speech-Broadcasting.
FACILITIES: CATV, CCTV, ComN, DR, JM, PRA.
DEGREES: BA.

Brenau University
One Central Circle, Gainesville, GA 30501; tel (404) 534-6179, 718-0555; fax (404) 534-6114. Department of Humanities and Communication Arts. James Southerland, dept. chair; Carrie Chrisco, dir.
Mass Media Program: Two-year BA degree program in Journalism, Electronic Media, Public Relations, Business Communications, and Broadcast News follows the lower-division Liberal Arts core curriculum.

Clark Atlanta University
Atlanta, GA 30314; tel (404) 880-8304. Mass Media Arts Department, 1977. James McJunkins, chair.
SEQUENCES: Journalism, Public Relations, Radio/Tv/Film.
DEGREE: BA in Mass Media Arts.

Georgia, University of
Athens, GA 30602; tel (706) 542-1704; fax (706) 542-4785. Henry W Grady College of Journalism and Mass Communication, 1915. ADS, NABJ, PRSSA, IABC, SPJ, Di Gamma Kappa, AAF, KTA. J Thomas Russell, dean.
FACULTY: *Profs.:* Alison Alexander (head, Telecomm. Dept.), Joseph R Dominick (dir. of grad. studies), Wallace B Eberhard, John W. English, Conrad C Fink, James E Fletcher, Albert L Hester, Ernest C Hynds (head, Jour. Dept.), Dean M Krugman, W Ronald Lane, William E Lee, Leonard N Reid (head, Ad/PR Dept.), J Thomas Russell (dean), Barry L Sherman (dir., Peabody Awards program); *Assoc. Profs.:* William F Griswold Jr., David C Hazinski, Karen W King, Peggy J Kreshel, Ruth Ann Lariscy, Allen E MacLeod, Kent R Middleton, Scott A Shamp, Otto W Smith, Spencer F Tinkham, Leila S Wenthe, Robert W Willett, Alfred Wise; *Asst. Profs.:* Louise M Benjamin, Glen T Cameron, Katrina K Covington-Whitmore, Barry A Hollander, Andy P Kavoori, Elli Lester, Karen S Miller, Glen J Nowak, Leara D Rhodes, Lynne M Sallot; *Instrs.:* Margaret M Johnston (coord., GSPA); *Lectrs:* G Stephen Dozier.
DEPARTMENTS: Advertising/Public Relations, Journalism, Telecommunications.
FACILITIES: AP, FM, CCTV, CN, ComN, DR, JM, PRA, VDT, Satellite downlink.
DEGREES: ABJ (BA in Journ.), MA, MMC, PhD.

Georgia Southern University
Statesboro, GA 30460; tel (912) 681-5138; fax (912) 681-0822; e-mail DADDINGT@GSVMS2.CC.GASOU.EDU. Journalism Program in Department of Communication Arts. Ernest T Wyatt, program head.
Journalism Program: A B.S. degree program of practical news-editorial orientation. Curriculum emphasizes liberal arts, esp. History. Internships optional. Journalism is one of five disciplines in Communication Arts. Others are Broadcasting (Radio-TV-Film), Public Relations, Speech and Theatre. The PR program has an active PRSSA chapter. Students also can major in Communication Arts, with curriculum from combining disciplines. Broadcasting and PR require internships.

Georgia State University
Atlanta, GA 30303; tel (404) 651-3200; fax (404) 651-1409. Department of Communication, 1963. SPJ, PRSSA, WICI. Carol Winkler, chair.
FACULTY: *Assoc. Profs.:* Theodora K Beck, Jack Boozer, Carol Lieber, Greg Lisbly, Ray Miller, Lawrence J Rifkind, Mary Ann Romski, Leonard Teel, Frank Tomasulo; *Asst. Profs.:* Gayle Austin, Douglas Barthlow, Jane Bick, Kent Colbert, Janis Edwards, Shirlene Holmes, Frank Johnson, Marion Meyers, Jimmie Moomaw; *Adjunct Fac.:* Carolyn Crimmins, Gary Moss, Ed Ploy.
SEQUENCES: Print, Broadcast, Public Relations, Film/Video, Speech, Theatre.
FACILITIES: AP, FM, CCTV, CN.
DEGREES: BA, MA.

Mercer University at Macon
Macon, GA 31207; tel (912) 744-2700. Communication Concentration Program, 1976. L Kenneth Hammond, Jour., and John Chalfa, Broadcast/Film.
Communication Program: Administered by English and Speech-Dramatic Arts Departments. Students may emphasize print journalism or broadcasting and film.

Toccoa Falls College
Toccoa Falls, GA 30598; tel (706) 886-6831; fax (706) 886-6412. School of Communication. Donald T Williams, acting dir.
Communication Program: Offers BA, BS degrees with sequences in Broadcasting, Interpersonal/Organizational, Journalism.

HAWAII

Chaminade, University of Honolulu
Honolulu HI 96816-1578; tel (808) 739-4642. Department of Communication, 1985. SCA. Jude Yablonsky, PhD, chair.
SEQUENCES: Advertising, Broadcasting, General Communication, Journalism, Public Relations.
FACILITIES: CN, DR, JN, PRA
DEGREE: BA.

Hawaii at Manoa, University of
2550 Campus Rd., CR208, Honolulu, HI 96822; tel (808) 956-8881; fax (808) 956-5396; e-mail Lowell@uhunix.uhcc.Hawaii.Edu. Department of Journalism, 1963. KTA, PRSSA, SPJ, WICI. Lowell Frazier, chair.
FACULTY: *Prof.:* John Luter; *Assoc. Profs.:* Thomas J Brislin, Jane Evinger, Lowell D Frazier, Beverly Deepe Keever; *Asst. Profs.:* Ann E Auman, Gerald Kato, Craig Miyamoto; *Lectrs.:* Robin Gould, Patricia Hartwell, Ray Lovell, Ruth Lucas, Jeffrey Portnoy; *Prof. Emer.:* Robert L Scott, Bonnie Wiley.
SEQUENCES: News-Editorial, Broadcast Journalism, Public Relations.
FACILITIES: AP, FM, CN, ComN, ComR, ComTV, DR, PRA, VDT.
DEGREE: BA.

IDAHO

Boise State University
Boise, ID 83725; tel (208) 385-3320. BITNET: RCNMORRI@IDBSU. Department of Communication, Journalism Emphasis Area. Dan Morris, head.
Journalism Program: Offers mass communication/journalism emphasis degree, with practical skills courses in reporting and news writing, editing, editorial and feature writing, photocommu-nication, and ethics and law. Instruction also in radio and television.

Idaho, University of
Moscow, ID 83844-1072; tel (208) 885-6458; fax (208) 885-6450. School of Communication. PRSSA. Peter Haggart, dir.
FACULTY: *Profs.:* Don H Coombs, Tom Jenness, Paul Miles, Bill Woolston; *Assoc. Profs.:* Roy Atwood, Stephen Banks, Sandra Haarsager, Alan Lifton; *Asst. Profs.:* Anna Banks, Martha Einerson, Mark Secrist; *Lectrs.:* Dennis Deccio, Patricia Hart, Jane Pritchett.
SEQUENCES: Editorial, Radio-TV News, Public Relations, Advertising.
FACILITIES: FM, CN, DR, ETV, JN, ComN.
DEGREES: BA, BS.

Idaho State University
880 S. 5th, Box 8242, Pocatello, ID 83209; tel (208) 236-3295; fax (208) 236-4000. Mass Communication Program. Janet House, assoc. prof.
Mass Communication Program: Five areas of emphases: Journalism, Photography, Television, Media Studies, Advertising/PR. Facilities include CATV, DR, VDT, ETV.

ILLINOIS

Bradley University
Peoria, IL 61625; tel (309) 677-2354; fax (309) 677-3750; internet jcs@bradley.bradley.edu. Department of Communication, 1947. AER, AAF, PRSSA, SPJ, WICI, KTA, NPPA. John Schweitzer, chair.
FACULTY: *Prof.:* E Neal Claussen, John C Schweitzer; *Assoc. Profs.:* Jack Fought, Howard Goldbaum, Paul Gullifor, Bob Jacobs, Ron Koperski, Ed Lamoureux; *Asst. Profs.:* William Bender, Hong Cheng, Larry Elliott, Teresa Holder, Chris Kasch, Diane Pacetti, Betty Parker, Dan Smith; *Lectrs.:* B J Lawrence, David Moscowitz, Linda Strasma, Karni Tiernan; *Part-time Instrs:* Rob Bertram, Mark Butzow, Sondra Craft, Phil Supple, Frank Thomas, Jon Yoder.
SEQUENCES: Advertising, Journalism, Photo Journalism, Public Relations, Radio/TV, Speech Communication.
FACILITIES: CCTV, FM, CN, ETV, DR, VDT.
DEGREES: BA, BS.

College of St. Francis
Joliet, IL 60435; tel (815) 740-3696; fax (815) 740-4285; e-mail VAX.COLSF.EDU Department of Journalism/Communications, 1976. Richard Lorenc, chair.
Journalism Program: Concentrations in News/Editorial, Graphic Design, Advertising/Public Relations, Broadcasting. Internships in all areas.

Columbia College Chicago
Chicago, IL 60605-1996; tel (312) 663-1600; fax (312) 986-8784. Department of Journalism. Nat Lehrman, chair.
Journalism Program: Curriculum concentrates on reporting, writing, editing news for print. Separate magazine publishing and broadcast journalism programs. All courses taught by working professionals. Master of Arts degree in Public Affairs Journalism offered.

DePaul University
Chicago, IL 60614; tel (312) 325-7585; fax (312) 325-7584; internet dmartin@wppost.depaul.edu. Department of Communication, 2320 N. Kenmore. Dr. Donald R Martin, chair.
Journalism Program: Complete undergraduate course offerings in journalism, radio, advertising/PR and film studies.

Eastern Illinois University
Charleston, IL 61920; tel (217) 581-6003; internet cflrh@bgu.edu. Department of Journalism, 1978. KTA, NABJ, PRSSA, SCJ, WICI, CMA. Les Hyder, chair.
FACULTY: *Profs.:* Evelyn Goodrick, John David Reed (dir., student pubs. coord.), Daniel E Thornburgh (emeritus), James Tidwell, Peter M Voelz, (adviser minority nwsp.); *Assoc. Profs.:* Susan Kaufman, Marta Ladd, (adviser, PRSSA), Glenn Robinson (business mgr., stud. pubs.), John Ryan (adviser, nwsp.); *Asst. Profs.:* Brian Poulter, (adviser, mag.), Howard Price; *Instrs.:* Ron Claxton, William Lair, Lola McElwee, (adviser yearbook), Carl Walworth.
SEQUENCE: News-Editorial.
FACILITIES: AP, FM, CN, ComN, DR, ETV, HS (sponsors high school press assn. and hosts state high school journalism assn.), JM, PRA, VDT.
DEGREE: BA.

Illinois College
Jacksonville, IL 62650; tel (217) 245-3000. Journalism, 1970. Donna Metcalf, dir.
Journalism Program: Students interested in a career in journalism may major in communications. The college offers two journalism courses and various internships. Local newspapers also employ students.

Illinois, University of
Urbana, IL 61801; tel (217) 333-2350; fax (217) 333-9882; e-mail ccomm@uiuc.edu. URL: http://www.uiuc.edu/providers/comm/. College of Communications, 1927. SPJ, WICI, KTA. Kim B Rotzoll, dean.
FACULTY: *Profs.:* William F Brewer, Clifford Christians (dir., Inst. Comm. Res.), Jesse G Delia, Norman Denzin, James Evans, Martin Fishbein, Larry Grossberg, Thomas H Guback, Thomas B Littlewood, Howard S Maclay, Richard Merritt, Kim B Rotzoll (dean), Thomas Srull (Sandage Professorship); *Assoc. Profs.:* Bill Berry (asst. dean, media studies), James S Haefner (head, Adv.), Robert Hays, Steve Helle (head, Jour.), Jerry Landay, Louis Liebovich, John Nerone, Thomas O'Guinn, Andrea Press, Robert Reid, Sharon Shavitt, Josephine Thomas, Paula Treichler, Bruce Williams; *Asst. Profs.:* Aida Barrera, Sandra Braman, Matthew Ehrlich, Terrence Finnegan, George Gladney, Brian Johnson, Sunder Narayanan, Cele Otnes (dir. grad. studies, adv.), Lisa Peñaloza, Michal Strahilevitz, Angharad Valdivia; *Teaching Assoc.:* Mitchell Kazel; *Lectrs.:* Dana Ewell, Jennifer Follis, Fred Mohn, Donald P Mullally; *Visiting Lectrs.:* Bonnie Bellew, Larry Bernard, Holly Grisham, Jean McDonald; *Adjunct Lectrs.:* Robin Kaler; *Profs. Emer.:* Eleanor Blum, James Carey, Gene Gilmore, Glenn Hanson, Richard Hildwein, Jay W Jensen, L W McClure, Theodore Peterson, C H Sandage, Nugent Wedding, Gordon White.
SEQUENCES: Advertising, Broadcast Journalism, News-Editorial, Media Studies.
FACILITIES: AP, FM, CATV, DR, CN, VDT, ETV.
DEGREES: BS, MS, PhD.

Illinois State University
4480 Communication, Normal, IL 61790-4480; tel (309) 438-3671; fax (309) 438-3048. Department of Communication. Mass Communication Program. Catherine Konsky, chair.
Journalism Program: Majors in Mass Communication, Public Relations and Speech Communication. Concentrations in Print Journalism, Broadcast Journalism, Broadcast Production, International Communication, Media Management, Visual Communication. Television and radio stations, daily newspaper, computer labs and photography studios and darkroom facilities.

Loyola University of Chicago
6525 N. Sheridan, Chicago, IL 60626; tel (312) 508-8891; fax (312) 508-8492. Department of Communication, 1968. Bren A O Murphy, chair.
Journalism Program: Within an integrated communication curriculum, Loyola offers participatory learning in journalism as well as administrative and critical analyses of mass communication.

MacMurray College
Jacksonville, IL 62650; tel (217) 479-7049; Fax (217) 245-0405. Journalism Program. Allan Metcalf, dir.
Journalism Program: Undergraduate major with required field experience. Program publishes a daily student newspaper.

Northern Illinois University
DeKalb, IL 60115; tel (815) 753-1563; fax (815) 753-7109. Department of Communication, Journalism Area, 1959. KTA, PRSSA, SPJ, WICI. Richard Johannesen, chair.
FACULTY: *Assoc. Prof.:* Abraham Bass, Anthony Scantlen; *Asst. Profs.:* Richard Digby-Junger, Russell Elder, Orayb Najjar, Angela Powers; *Instr.:* Karen Flowers.
SEQUENCES: Journalism; students select courses in news-editorial, broadcast news, photojournalism, and public relations.
FACILITIES: AP, AM, CATV, CCTV, CN, DR, FM, PRA, VDT.
DEGREES: BA, BS.

Northwestern University
Evanston, IL 60208-2101; tel (708) 491-5091; fax Admin. & Editorial (708) 491-3956, Advertising (708) 491-5925, Magazine Programs (708) 491-5907, Newspaper Management Center (708) 491-4900, Washington Programs (202) 662-1814. Medill School of Journalism, 1920. KTA, SPJ. Michael C Janeway, dean.
FACULTY: *Profs.:* Charles Alexander (dir., Washington programs), Martin Block, Richard Christian (assoc. dean), Michael Janeway (dean), John Lavine (dir., Newspaper Management Center), Robert Mulholland (chair, Brdct. News programs), Raymond Nelson, Don Schultz, Richard Schwarzlose (assoc. dean), Jack Sissors; *Assoc. Profs.:* Jack Doppelt, Robert Entman, George Harmon (chair, Newspaper), Ronald Kaatz, Paul Lavrakas, Donna Leff, David Nelson, Abe Peck (chair, Magazine), Louis Prato, David Protess, Edward Spiegel (dir., Direct Marketing), Stanley Tannenbaum (chair, Integrated Adv./Marketing Comms. program); *Asst. Profs.:* John Bace, Brenda Boudreaux, Roger Boye (dir., Undergrad. Studies), Tamara Brezen, Clarke Caywood, Patrick Clinton, Patricia Dean, Jack Holley, Linda Jones, John Kupetz (dir., Student Placement), Robert McClory, Michael O'Don-

nell, Leland Ryan, Paul Wang, Mary Ann Weston, Jonathan Ziomek (dir., Grad. Editorial programs); *Profs. Emer.:* Benjamin H Baldwin, I W Cole, Richard W Hainey, Jack Sissors.
FACILITIES: JM, AP.
DEGREES: BSJ, MSA, MSJ.

Roosevelt University
Chicago, IL 60605; tel (312) 341-3715; fax (312) 341-6362. Faculty of Journalism and Communication Studies, Linda Jones, head.
Journalism Program: Print and broadcast news, public relations, marketing communications; campuses downtown and suburbs. All faculty professionals in their fields.

Southern Illinois University
Carbondale, IL 62901; tel (618) 453-4308; fax (618) 453-7714; e-mail mcma@siu.edu. College of Mass Communication and Media Arts, 1993. Joe S Foote, dean. AAF, BEA, BICA, ITVA, KTA, NAEB, NBS, SINBA, SIRIS, SPJ, WICI
FACULTY: *Profs:* Richard M Blumenberg, Joe S Foote (dean), Dennis T.Lowry (acting director, journalism), K S Sitaram, Gerald C Stone, Charles A Swedlund; *Assoc. Profs:* Roya Akhavan-Majid, (head, graduate studies, journalism), Lilly A Boruszkowski, William R Elliott, (associate dean), David A Gilmore, Scott Hodgson, Walter B Jaehnig, Jr.,Thomas Johnson, Gary Kolb (chair, dir. grad. studies, cinema & photography), Michael H Murrie, Jyotika Ramaprasad, Jan Patterson Roddy, Robert L Spellman, Michael F Starr,(chair, dir. graduate studies, radio-television); *Asst. Profs.:* Thomas A Birk, Loren D Cocking, Larry Collette, Mike Covell, Susan Duhig, Phylis Johnson, Barbara Kowalewski Kaye, James D Kelly, Haeryon Kim, Fern Logan, Judith McCray, Daniel Overturf, Anna R Paddon, Stephen P Phelps, Jon A Shidler; *Lecturers:* John Philbin; *Profs. Emer.:* George C Brown, William E Brown, Homer E Dybig, James L C Ford, Jim Allee Hart, Ralph E McCoy, John Mercer, Frank Paine, Manion Rice, Buren Robbins, Charles W Shipley, Harry W Stonecipher.
SEQUENCES: Cinema and Photography (cinema production, cinema studies, fine arts photography, professional photography), Journalism (Advertising, News Editorial), Radio-Television (Management and Sales, Production).
FACILITIES: AdA, UPI, ComN, CCTV, ETV, JN, JM, VDT.
DEGREES: BA in Cinema & Photography, BA in Radio-Television, BS in Journalism, MA in Journalism, MA in Telecommunications, MS in Journalism, MFA in Cinema & Photography, PhD in Journalism.

Southern Illinois University
Edwardsville, IL 62026; tel (618) 692-2230; fax (618) 692-3716. Department of Mass Communications, 1969. SPJ, ITVA. Peter J Bukalski, acting chair.
FACULTY: *Profs.:* Peter J Bukalski (dir., grad. studies and acting chair), John A Regnell (emeritus), John R Rider (emeritus), Jack Shaheen, (emeritus), William G Ward (dir., Jour.), Kamil Winter (emeritus); *Assoc. Profs.:* Barbara C Regnell, Riley Maynard; *Asst. Profs.:* Nora Baker, Cynthia Cooper, Robert Murphy; *Instrs:* Judy Landers, Patrick Murphy; *Lectrs.:* Courtney Barrett, Richard Collotin, Mary Leonard.
SEQUENCES: Television and Radio, Journalism.
FACILITIES: FM, AdA, CCTV, CN, ComN, ComTV, DR, JM VDT, ComR, UPI.
DEGREES: BA, BS, MS.

Western Illinois University
Macomb, IL 61455; tel (309) 298-1424, 298-1103; fax (309) 298-2974; internet mfjh@uxa.ecn.bgu. edu. Department of English & Journalism, Journalism Program. Jai Hyon Lee, dir. of Journ.
Journalism Program: BA in Journalism with News-Editorial, PR and Advertising emphases.

INDIANA

Anderson University
Anderson, IN 46012; tel (317) 641-4340. Department of Communications, 1978. Donald G Boggs, chair.
Journalism Program: Fifty-two hour interdisciplinary Mass Communications major with specializations in Journalism, Broadcasting and Public Relations. SCJ, BEA.

Ball State University
Muncie, IN 47306; tel (317) 285-8200; fax (317) 285-7997; e-mail DOOOJOURN@ BSUVAX1BIT NET. Department of Journalism. KTA, NABJ, NPPA, PRSSA, SND, SPJ, WICI. Earl L. Conn, chair.
FACULTY: *Profs.:* Earl L Conn, Beverley J Pitts, Mark Popovich, Melvin Sharpe (coord., Public Relations sequence); *Assoc. Profs.:* Richard Ware (coord., Photojourn. sequence), Marilyn Weaver (dir., High School Journalism Workshop, admin. asst. and coord., Secondary Education sequence); *Asst. Profs.:* Robert Gustafson (coord., Adv. sequence), Robert W Heintzelman, David Knott (coord., Daily News Operations), Tendayi Kumbula (coord., News-Ed sequence), Alfredo Marin-Carle (coord., Jour. Graphics sequence), Becky McDonald, David E Sumner (coord., Magazine sequence), Steven Thomsen; *Instrs.:* Walter Baker, Pamela Farmen-Leidig, Patricia Mills, Michael Price, Deborah Reed, Larry Riley, Howard Snider, Sheryl Swingley, Dan Waechter (curricular advising and grad. adviser), Gardi Ipema Wilks; *Part-Time Instrs.:* Ray Begovich, Rebecca Clock, John Disher, William Holbrook, Dawna Kemper, Mark Kornmann, Larry Lough, Charmaine Schmitt, Larry Shores; *Profs. Emer.:* Kenneth Atwell, Louis E Ingelhart, Frank Wellnitz, Fred Woodress.
SEQUENCES: Journalism Graphics, News-Editorial, Public Relations, Advertising, Magazine, Photojour., Secondary Ed.
FACILITIES: AdA, AP, FM, JM, JN, ComN, DR, ETV, PRA, VDT.
DEGREES: AA, BA, BS, BAEd, BSEd, MA.

Butler University
4600 Sunset Ave., Indianapolis, IN 46208; tel (317) 940-9708; fax (317) 940-9252. Department of Journalism, Arthur Levin, chair.
Journalism Program: A six-member staff offers a complete journalism curriculum with emphases on news-editorial and public relations/advertising.

Calumet College
Whiting, IN 46394; tel (219) 473-7700. Division of Communication and Fine Arts. Robert Anderson, chair.
Journalism Program: News-Editorial sequence. BA in Communication Arts with journalism emphasis.

DePauw University
Greencastle, IN 46135; tel (317) 658-4473, 658-4495; fax (317) 653-4830. Department of English and Department of Communication Arts and Sciences. Richard J Roth and Jeffrey M McCall, dirs.
Journalism Program: Coursework offered in news writing and editing, magazine writing, broadcast journalism, media law and organizational communication.

Evansville, University of
1800 Lincoln Avenue, Evansville, IN 47722; tel (812) 479-2377; fax (812) 479-2320; internet ms47@evansville.edu; Web Page: www.evansville.edu. Department of Mass Communication, 1955. AAF, NACB, SPJ. Michael J Stankey, chair.
FACULTY: *Prof.:* Michael J Stankey; *Assoc. Profs.:* Douglas C Covert, Caroline Dow (Journalism Coordinator, ASJMC rep.); *Asst. Profs.:* Larry G Burkum, Lynne Y Edwards.
SEQUENCES: Advertising, Public Relations, Journalism, Telecommunication
FACILITIES: FM, AP, CN, DR, VDT
DEGREES: BA, BS.

Franklin College
Franklin, IN 46131; tel (317) 738-8200; fax (317) 738-8234. Pulliam School of Journalism, 1940. WICI, SCJ. John Ellerbach, chair.
FACULTY: *Profs.:* William A Bridges (Eugene C and Nina Mason Pulliam Chair of Jour.); *Assoc. Profs.:* Joel Cramer, Jerry Miller; *Asst. Profs.:* Dennis Cripe (exec. dir., Indiana High School Press Assn.), John Ellerbach, Susan Fleck; *Prof. Emer.:* Robert F Chupp. *Editor in Residence:* Harvey Jacobs.
SEQUENCES: News/Editorial, Advertising/Public Relations, Broadcast Journalism.
FACILITIES: AdA, AP, FM, DR, JM, JN, PRA, VDT.
DEGREE: BA.

Goshen College
Goshen, IN 46526-4798; tel (219) 535-7587; fax (219) 535-7660; e-mail stuarts@ cedar.goshen. edu. Department of Communication. Stuart W Showalter, chair.
Journalism Program: Communication major includes courses in broadcasting, journalism, public relations, photography and film. Internship required.

Indiana State University
Terre Haute, IN 47809; tel (812) 237-3027; fax (812) 237-3217. Department of Communication, 1952. SPJ.
FACULTY: *Assoc. Profs.:* Warren E Barnard, David Bennett, Michael O Buchholz, Paul D Hightower.
SEQUENCES: News/Editorial, Photojournalism and Magazine Writing.
FACILITIES: AP, FM, CCTV, JN, DR, VDT.
DEGREES: BA, BS.

Indiana University
Seventh and Woodlawn Sts., Bloomington, IN 47405; tel (812) 855-9247; fax (812) 855-0901. School of Journalism, 1911. NPPA, SPJ, WICI. Trevor R Brown, dean.
FACULTY: *Profs.:* I Wilmer Counts, Dan G Drew, Peter P Jacobi, David P Nord, Christine L Ogan (dir., Grad. Studies), David H Weaver (Roy W Howard Research Prof.), G Cleveland Wilhoit; *Assoc. Profs.:* David E Boeyink, Trevor R Brown (dean), Bonnie J Brownlee, Jon P Dilts (assoc. dean for regional campuses), John E Dvorak (dir., High School Jour. Institute), Owen V Johnson, Carol C. Polsgrove, S Holly Stocking; *Asst. Profs.:* Randal A Beam, Claude H Cookman, Linda Lawson, Jane Rhodes, Andrew Rojecki; *Adjunct Prof.:* David L. Adams (publisher, *Indiana Daily Student); Lectr.:* Paul S Voakes; *Adjunct Lectr.:* Edward Gubar; *Part-Time Asst. Prof.:* Frances G Wilhoit; *Profs. Emer.:* John W Ahlhauser, Mary I. Benedict, Ralph L Holsinger, Richard D. Yoakam; *Librarian:* Frances G Wilhoit.
INDIANAPOLIS CAMPUS: 902 W. New York St., Indianapolis, IN 46223; tel (317) 274-2773; fax (317) 274-2786.
FACULTY: *Prof.:* James W Brown (assoc. dean); *Assoc. Prof.:* Jonas Bjork; *Asst. Profs.:* Sherry Ricchiardi, Jeff Springston; *Adjunct Prof.:* Patrick McKeand (publisher, *The Sagamore).*
SEQUENCES: News-Editorial, Broadcast News, Photojournalism, Advertising, PR, Magazine, Media Management, Journalism Education.
FACILITIES: AP, AM, FM, CATV, CCTV, CN, DR, ETV, JM, VDT.
DEGREES: BAJ, MA Prof., MA Res., PhD.

Indianapolis, University of
Indianapolis, IN 46227; tel (317) 788-3445; fax (317) 788-3490. Department of Communication, 1985. Bonnie R Kingsbury, instr.
Communication Program: Program includes skills and theory courses in journalism in a liberal arts college, at a Methodist University, bimonthly tabloid newspaper, with computer generated layout and design.

Notre Dame, University of
Notre Dame, IN 46556; tel (219) 631-7316; fax (219) 631-4268. Department of American Studies. Robert Schmuhl, chair and dir. of grad. studies.
Journalism Program: Students take courses on journalism and the media, as well as writing courses, within the context of American Studies.

Purdue University
West Lafayette, IN 47907-1366; tel (317) 494-3429; fax (317) 496-1394; internet cstewart@ plato.sla.purdue.edu. Department of Communication. Charles J Stewart, head.
Journalism Program: Undergraduate majors in Journalism, Telecommunication, Public Relations and Mass Communication. MA and PhD programs in Mass Communication.

Saint Mary-of-the-Woods College
Saint Mary-of-the-Woods, IN 47876; tel (812) 535-5209. Department of English, Journalism and Languages. Janice Dukes, chair.
Journalism Program: Stresses professional preparation in liberal arts context. News/Editorial, Advertising/Public Relations.

Southern Indiana, University of
8600 University Blvd., Evansville, IN 47712; tel (812) 464-1734; fax (812) 465-7152; internet dherring.ucs@smtp.usi.edu. Department of Communications, 1985. Dal M. Herring, chair. SPJ, AAF.
Journalism Program: The department offers BA, BS, AA and AS in Advertising, Journalism (print and broadcast), Public Relations, Radio-TV, Interpersonal-Organizational and Theatre Arts sequences.

Valparaiso University
Valparaiso, IN 46383; tel (219) 464-5271; fax (219) 464-6742; internet dkocher@exodus. valpo. edu. Department of Communication. Douglas J Kocher, chair.
Communication Program: Three sequences – Print Journalism, PR, Broadcast Journalism. Practical experience stressed; internship required; co-op education available.

Vincennes University
Vincennes, IN 47591-5201; tel (812) 888-4551/4554. The Journalism Program. Fred Walker Jr., dir. and prof. of Journ.
Journalism Program: Newspaper-oriented curriculum with two sequences, news-editorial and print media advertising. Five lecture courses, production laboratories for each sequence, and two inter-departmental photography courses. Weekly laboratory newspaper.

IOWA

Clarke College
Dubuque, IA 52001; tel (319) 588-6306; fax (319) 588-6789. Communication Department. Michael R Acton, chair.
Journalism Program: Corporate Communication Major – print journalism, video production, advertising and PR combined with business studies.

Drake University
Des Moines, IA 50311; tel (515) 271-3194/2838; fax (515) 271-2798. School of Journalism and Mass Communication, 1920. AAF, KTA, NABJ, PRSSA, SPJ. Janet Hill Keefer, dean; Henry Milam, dir., Grad. program.
FACULTY: *Profs.:* John Lytle, Henry Milam, Herbert Strentz, Louis J Wolter, Robert D Woodward; *Assoc. Profs.:* Todd Evans (asst. dean), Barry Foskit, Patricia Prijatel, Gary Wade; *Asst. Profs.:* Ronda Menke, Michael Perkins, David Wright; *Instr:* Sheree Curry; *Lectrs.:* Barbara Boose, Pat Denato, Polly Flug, Donna Kubis, Tom Mahoney, Carol McGarvey, Dale Woolery; *Profs. Emer.:* William E Francois, Frank Mathews, Joe R Patrick.
SEQUENCES: Advertising, Broadcast News, Journalism Teaching, Magazines, News-Editorial, Public Relations, Radio/TV.
FACILITIES: AdA, CATV, CCTV, CN, ComN, ComR, ComTV, DR, JM, PRA, VDT.
DEGREES: BA, MA.

Grand View College
Des Moines, IA 50316; tel (515) 263-2931; fax (515) 263-2998. Communication Department, 1974. Stephen Winzenburg, chair.
Journalism Program: GVC has around 120 majors earning bachelor of arts degrees in Mass Communication, Journalism and Radio/TV.

Iowa, University of
Iowa City, IA 52242; tel (319) 335-5821; fax (319) 335-5210; internet journalism-admin@ uiowa.edu. School of Journalism and Mass Communication, 1924. KTA, PRSSA, SPJ, NABJ, WICI. Ken Starck, dir.
FACULTY: *Profs.:* Kay Amert (assoc. dir.), Joseph Ascroft, Carolyn Stewart Dyer, Hanno Hardt (adviser, *Journal of Communication Inquiry*), Don D Smith, Jeffery A Smith, (coord., Iowa Center for Comm. Study), John Soloski (head, grad. studies), Ken Starck, Albert Talbott; *Assoc. Profs.:* Dan Berkowitz, Stephen Bloom, John Erickson, Judy Polumbaum; *Asst. Profs.:* John Bennett (head, undergrad. studies), Venise Berry, John Kimmich Javier, Sue Lafky; *Instr.:* Richard Johns; *Gallup Prof.:* Gilbert Cranberg; *Adjunct Asst. Profs.:* Mary Arnold, Gerald Carroll, Dan Lind; *Adjunct Instr:* Doug Allaire; *Assoc. Prof. Emer.:* William Zima.
FACILITIES: AP, AM, FM, CN, DR, ComN, PRA, VDT, LEXIS/NEXIS.
DEGREES: BA, BS, MA, PhD.

Iowa State University
Ames, IA 50011-1180; tel (515) 294-4340; fax (515) 294-5108. Department of Journalism and Mass Communication, 1905. ACT, AER, IABC, KTA, PRSSA, SPJ, AAF. Jane W Peterson, interim chair.
FACULTY: *Profs.:* Eric A Abbott, Thomas L Beell (coord. Undergrad. Studies), J Thomas Emmerson, Willard E Gillette, Kim A Smith; *Assoc. Profs.:* Stephen C Coon, Giles M Fowler, Veryl L Fritz, Joel Geske (coord., Adv.), Richard H Haws (coord., Nwsp.), Walter E Niebauer (coord., Grad. Studies and PR), Jane W Peterson (coord., Science Comm.), Marcia R Prior-Miller (coord., Mag.); *Asst. Profs.:* Dominic Caristi (coord. Electr. Media Studies), Olan Farnall, Robert L McConnell, Bonney L Rega, Lula Rodriguez; *Instrs.:* Maureen Deisinger, Wayne P Davis, Jeffrey Stein; *Profs. Emer.:* Edmund G Blinn, Dale E Boyd, Richard L Disney, Karl H Friederich, J K Hvistendahl, William F Kunerth, James W Schwartz, John D (Jack) Shelley, Lorraine Wechsler.
SEQUENCES: Advertising, Electronic Media Studies, Magazine, Newspaper, Public Relations/Corporate Communication, Science Communication, Visual Communication.
FACILITIES: AP, AM/FM, AdA, CATV, CN, ComN, DR, JM, LEXIS/NEXIS.
DEGREES: BA, BS, MS.

Marycrest College
Davenport, IA 52804; tel (319) 326-9343. Dept. of Communications and Performing Arts, 1976. J T Jacobs, chair.
Journalism Program: Communication theory with a hands-on specialization in Newspaper/Mag., Radio/TV, PR/Adv. and Organizational Communication.

Northern Iowa, University of
Cedar Falls, IA 50614; tel (319) 273-2821. Department of English Language and Literature— Mary Rohrberger, head.
Journalism Minor: Christian Ogbondah, coord. Newspaper-oriented minor emphasizing writing, editing, reporting; includes magazine and feature writing and advising student publications.
Tel (319) 273-2217. Department of Theatre and Communication Arts. Jon Hall, head.
Communications/Public Relations Major: Dean Kruckeberg, coord. A comprehensive program including courses in oral and written communication, graphic arts and design, and business (accounting, marketing, and management).
Communications/Broadcast Major: J C Turner, coord. Emphases available: (a) production, performance, and writing; (b) broadcast journalism; (c) broadcast business.

KANSAS

Baker University
PO Box 65, Baldwin City, KS 66006-0065; tel (913) 594-6451; fax (913) 594-2522. Department of Communication, 1976. Richard A Bayha, chair and assoc. prof.
Journalism Program: Program is news-editorial oriented, emphasizing writing, editing, reporting and production skills.
Mass Communication Program: Program is theory and production oriented emphasizing radio and television production, and post production skills as well as social implications of the media.

Fort Hays State University
Hays, KS 67601; tel (913) 628-4411; fax (913) 628-4087. Department of Communication, Area of Journalism. Linn Ann Huntington, dir.
Journalism Program: Coursework in journalism, mass communications, public relations, advertising, photography, radio-television-film, desktop publishing and other journalism-related areas. In addition, experience in student newspaper and yearbook stressed.

Kansas, University of
200 Stauffer-Flint Hall, Lawrence, KS 66045; tel (913) 864-4755; fax (913) 864-5318. William Allen White School of Journalism and Mass Communications, 1911 (Dept.), 1944 (School). AAF, ADS, KTA, PRSSA, SPJ. Mike Kautsch, dean.
FACULTY: *Profs.:* Del Brinkman (on leave), Ted Frederickson, John Ginn, Paul Jess (associate dean), Richard Musser, Susanne Shaw, Bruce Swain (head, News); *Assoc. Profs.:* Sam Adams, Robert Basow, Sharon Bass (head, Mag.), Timothy Bengtson (head, Adv.), John Broholm, John Katich, (head, Radio-TV), Carole Rich, Adrienne Rivers, Max Utsler; *Asst. Profs.:* Mike Cuenca, David Guth, Carol Holstead, Denise Linville, Charles Marsh, Arlo Oviatt, Tom Volek (grad. program), Paul Wenske; *Instrs.:* Tom Hedrick, Diane Lazzarino; *Lectrs.:* Len Alfano, Bill Dickinson, Tom Eblen, John Hudnall, Tim Janicke, John Leifer, Bill Snead; *Retired and Profs. Emer.:* Mel Adams, Bruce Linton, Calder Pickett, Lee Young.
SEQUENCES: News, Advertising, Radio-TV, Magazine.
FACILITIES: AdA, AP, CATV, CCTV, DR, FM, JM, JN, PRA, VDT.
DEGREES: BS, MS.

Kansas State University
Manhattan, KS 66506-1501; tel (913) 532-6890; fax (913) 532-7309; e-mailCEO@KSUVM.KSU. EDU. A Q Miller School of Journalism and Mass Communications, 1910. AAF, ITVA, PRSSA, SCJ, SPJ, WICI. Carol Oukrop, dir.
FACULTY: *Profs.:* Carol Oukrop (dir.), Harry Marsh (head, Jour.), Paul Parsons (assoc. dir.); *Assoc. Profs.:* William J Adams, Rob Daly, Tom Grimes (Ross Beach Prof.), David MacFarland, R Charles Pearce (head, Adv.), Paul Prince (head, Grad. Studies and RTV): *Asst. Profs.:* Lori Bergen, Douglass Daniel, Ali Kanso El-Ghori, Gloria Freeland (assoc. dir., Student Publications Inc.), Ron Johnson, (dir., Student Publications Inc.), David Kamerer, Charles Lubbers, Beverly McLean-Murray, Carol Pardun, Linda Puntney (exec. dir., Jour. Ed. Assn.); *Instr.:* Larry Lamb; *Visiting Prof.:* John Neibergall (R M Seaton Prof.).
SEQUENCES: Jour., Adv., PR, Radio/TV.
FACILITIES: AP, FM, AdA, CN, DR, JM, PRA, VDT.
DEGREES: BS, BA, MS.

Pittsburg State University
Pittsburg, KS 66762; tel (316) 235-4715; fax (316) 232-2430. Department of Communication. Peter K Hamilton, chair.
Communication Program: A Communication major with seqences in Advertising, Communication Studies, Communication Education, Journalism, Public Relations, Radio and Television, and Theatre (BA Degree). MA in Communication with specialized emphasis in applied communication or communication theory. Graduate assistantships available.

Washburn University
Topeka, KS 66621; tel (913) 231-1010 ext. 1380; internet zzchor@acc.wuacc.edu. Dr. Frank J Chorba, chair.
Speech Communications: Major concentrations include organizational communication, political communication ,a nd interpersonal communications. Mass Media: Major areas of concentration include broadcasting, journalism, and PR. For Journal of Radio Studies contact Frank Chorba.

Wichita State University
Wichita, KS 67260-0031; tel (316) 689-3185; fax (316) 689-3006; Bitnet KEEL@TWSUVM. Elliott School of Communication, 1927/1989. SPJ, WICI, Ad Club, AAF. Vernon A Keel, dir.
FACULTY: *Prof.:* Vernon A Keel; *Assoc. Profs.:* Phillip Gaunt, Charles Pearson (emer.); *Asst. Profs.:* Les Anderson, Rick Armstrong, Denise Wigginton Cecil, Susan Huxman, Sharon Iorio, Frank Kelly,Chris Leland, Keith Williamson; *Instrs.:* Thane Chastain, Dan Close, Jesse Huxman, Connie Morris, Maggie Chamberlin Ryan; *Lectrs.:* Randy Brown, Janis Friesen, Bonnie Garber, Brenda Gray, Rebecca Nordyke, Vada Snider.
SEQUENCES: Advertising, Broadcasting, Journalism, Public Relations, Speech Communication.
FACILITIES: DR, CATV, CN, FM, ComN, ComTV, AdA, PRA, VDT.
DEGREES: BA, MA.

KENTUCKY

Asbury College
1 Macklem Dr., Wilmore KY 40390-1198; tel (606) 858-3511. Department of Journalism. Marcia L Hurlow, dir.
Broadcast Communications Program: BA degrees in Journalism or Broadcast Communications within liberal arts; performance and theory courses form media emphases; extracurricular newspaper, yearbook, literary magazine, cable tv, radio.

Eastern Kentucky University
Richmond, KY 40475-3103; tel (606) 622-1871; fax (606) 622-2354. Department of Mass Communications, 1973. AAF, KTA, PRSSA, SPJ. Ron G Wolfe, chair.
FACULTY: *Profs.:* Donald R Cain, Dean C Cannon, Elizabeth Fraas, Jack Hillwig, Jerry P Perry, Ron G Wolfe; *Assoc. Profs.:* Renee Everett, John Taylor; *Asst. Profs.:* Elizabeth Hansen, Linda Henson, Fred Kolloff, Doug Rogers, Ferrell Wellman, Dave Woolverton; *Part-Time Instrs.:* Mark Daniels, Gwenn French, Jay Nolan, Sharon Reynolds, Chris Swindell, Kit Wagar.
SEQUENCES: Broadcasting, Journalism, PR.
FACILITIES: AP, AM/FM, CATV, CCTV, JN, DR, ETV, VDT, ComN, ComR, ComTV, PRA.
DEGREE: BA.

Kentucky, University of
Lexington, KY 40506-0042; tel (606) 257-2786; fax (606) 257-7818; e-mail MOORE@UKCC. School of Journalism and Telecommunications, 1914. AAF, NABJ, NPPA, PRSSA, SPJ. Roy L Moore, acting dir.
FACULTY: *Profs.:* David B Dick, Roy L Moore (acting dir.); *Assoc. Profs.:* Maria Braden, Thomas Lindlof, Robert Orndorff, Scott Whitlow; *Asst. Profs.:* Steve Dozier, James Hertog, Haeryon Kim, Greg Lowe, Carmen Manning Miller, Nancy Reynolds, Rick Roth, Edward Scheiner; *Profs. Emer.:* William Moore, Joseph Ripley, John Wild.
SEQUENCES: General Editorial, Advertising, and Telecommunications.
FACILITIES: AP, FM, CN, DR, JN, VDT.
DEGREES: BA, BGS, BS.

Louisville, University of
Louisville, KY 40292; tel (505) 588-6976; fax (502) 588-8166. Department of Communication, 1971. Charles A Willard, chair.
Communication Program: Bachelor's degree with major in Communication and concentrations in Communication Studies, Advertising and Public Relations, and Mass Media (Print or Broadcast).

Morehead State University
Morehead, KY 40351; tel (606) 783-5312; fax (606) 783-2678. Journalism Area, BR 101-C, Department of Communications. Dr. Serjit Kasior and Joan Atkins, journ. coords.
Journalism Program: Undergraduate and master's programs in News-Editorial, Photojournalism and Advertising-Public Relations sequences. Journalism labs equipped for computer pagination and electronic photo-imaging. University-owned FM radio station and television facilities which provide daily broadcasts by cable to the community.

Murray State University
Murray, KY 42071; tel (502) 762-2387; fax (502) 762-3175. Department of Journalism and Radio-TV, 1975. SPJ, AER, AAF, PRSSA. Robert H McGaughey III, chair.
FACULTY: *Profs.:* Roger Haney, Gary Hunt (dean), Robert McGaughey (chair); *Assoc. Profs.:* John Dillon, Ann Landini, Bob Lochte, Allen White (grad. coord.); *Instrs.:* Cynthia Hopson, Gill Welsch; *Part-Time Instrs.:* Joe Hedges, Dwain McIntosh, Bob Valentine, Karen Welch, Mark Welch, Bill Williams; *Prof. Emer.:* W Ray Mofield; *Staff:* Larry Albert, Orville Herndon, Barry Johnson.
MAJORS: Journ., Advertising, PR, Radio/TV.
FACILITIES: AP,FM,CATV,DR, ETV, JN, PRA, VDT.
DEGREES: BS, BA, MS, MA.

Northern Kentucky University
Highland Heights, KY 41076; tel (606) 572-5435. Communications Department, 1972. AAF, BEA, PRSSA. Michael L Turney, PhD, ABC, chair.
FACULTY: *Profs.:* Stephen D Boyd, Robert W Mullen, Michael L Turney (chair); *Assoc. Profs.:* J Gaut Ragsdale (coordinator of speech communication), Penelope B Summers, David S Thomson (coord., Radio/TV); *Asst. Profs.:* Joyce Adams, Michael Adee, Durell Hamm (dir., forensics),Yasue Kuwahara, Patrick Moynahan; *Lectrs.:* Vicki Abney-Ragsdale (dir., speech lab), Karen P Slawter; *Prof. Emer.:* Lois O Sutherland.
JOURNALISM SEQUENCES: Advertising, General Editorial, Public Relations, Photojournalism.
RADIO/TELEVISION SEQUENCES: Business, Engineering, Programming.
SPEECH COMMUNICATION SEQUENCES: Organizational Communication, Rhetorical Theory, Speech/Theatre Arts.
FACILITIES: AM/FM, CATV, CCTV, CN, ComN, ComTV, DR, PRA, VDT.
DEGREE: BA.

Western Kentucky University
Bowling Green, KY 42101; tel (502) 745-4143, 745-2653; fax (502) 745-5387. Department of Journalism, 1970. AAF, KTA, NPPA, PRSSA, SPJ, NABJ. Jo-Ann Huff Albers, dept. head.
FACULTY: *Profs.:* James L Highland (coord., Print Journalism sequence), Michael L Morse (coord., Photojour. sequence); *Assoc. Profs.:* Robert R Adams (coord., Jour. Education), Jo-Ann Huff Albers, Harry L Allen (dir., Job Placement and Professional Relations), John Barnum (coord., PR sequence), Robert L Blann, Corban Goble, Paula Quinn, Carolyn F Stringer (coord., Adv. sequence); *Asst. Profs.:* Wilma King-Jones, Cliff Shaluta; *Adv. Professional-in-Residence:* Gilbert Stengel; *Photojournalists-in-Residence:* Jack Corn, James Kenney; *Part-Time Instrs.:* David Bauer, Kevin Corbett, Larry Craig, Fred Hensley, Al Jolly, Terry Jones, Robert Skipper.
SEQUENCES: News-Editorial, Photojournalism, PR, Advertising, Journalism Education.
FACILITIES: FM, AdA, CCTV, CN, ComR, ComTV, DR, ETV, PRA, VDT.
DEGREE: BA.

LOUISIANA

Grambling State University
PO Box 45, Grambling, LA 71245; tel (318) 274-2189/2403; fax (318) 274-3194. Department of Mass Communication,1988. PRSSA, NABJ, AERho, SND, WICI. Rama M Tunuguntla, head.
FACULTY: *Prof.:* Rama M Tunuguntla; *Assoc. Prof.:* Reginald Owens (dir., *The Gramblinite*), *Asst. Profs.:* Martin Edu, Sharon Ford, Pamela Fridie, Charles Hoy, Bonnie Jackson, Parvin Lalehparvaran, Gaylon Murray, James E Penny; *Instrs.:* Edrene Frazier, Sandra Lee; *Part-Time Instr.:* Michael Pitts; *University Editor:* Joice Dunn; *Acting Director, TV Center:* Grover Brown.
SEQUENCES: News-Editorial, Public Relations, Advertising, Visual Communication, Technical Communication and Broadcasting.
FACILITIES: FM, AP, CATV, DR, JN, VDT.
DEGREE: BA in Mass Communication.

Louisiana State University
Baton Rouge, LA 70803-7202; tel (504) 388-2336; fax (504) 388-2125. Manship School of Mass Communication, 1925. AAF, SPJ, WICI, KTA, NABJ, RTNDA. John M Hamilton, dean.; Ronald G Garay, assoc. dean; Richard A Nelson, assoc. dean.
FACULTY: *Profs.:* Louis A Day, Alan D Fletcher, Ronald G Garay, John M Hamilton, Elsie S Hebert, Richard A Nelson, John W Windhauser; *Assoc. Profs.:* A Robert McMullen, Whitney R Mundt; *Asst. Profs.:* LeAnne Daniels, Jules A d'Hemecourt, Charles M Mayo, Jay L Perkins, Judith L Sylvester, Dale Thorn; *Instrs.:* Laura Berthelot, Phil Ward; *Manship Chair Prof.:* Peter Kohler; *Distinguished Profs.:* Sig Mickelson, Billy I Ross.
AREAS: Advertising, Journalism, Political Communication, Public Relations, Electronic Media.
FACILITIES: AdA, CCTV, FM, CN, ComN, ComTV, DR, PRA.
DEGREES: BMC, MMC.

Louisiana State University in Shreveport
Shreveport, LA 71115; tel (318) 797-5374. Department of Communications. Jack Nolan, chair.
FACULTY: *Profs.:* Dalton Cloud, Ida Anne Torrans; *Assoc. Profs.:* Robert Critcher, Charlene Handford, Jack Nolan; *Instrs.:* Suzzanne Bright, Mary Jarzabek, Linda Martin, John R Tabor.
SEQUENCES: Journalism, Public Relations, Speech, Speech Pathology.
FACILITIES: Typing, desktop publishing labs.
DEGREES: BA.

Louisiana Tech University
152 Keeny, PO Box 10258, Ruston, LA 71272-0045; tel (318) 257-4427; fax (318) 257-4558; e-mail ronwhite@vm.cc.latech.edu Journalism Department, 1928. Wiley W Hilburn Jr., head.
FACULTY: *Prof:* Wiley W Hilburn Jr.; *Assoc. Profs.:* Sallie Rose Hollis, Ron White; *Asst. Prof.:* Thomas Edward Blick Jr.
SEQUENCE: News-Editorial.
FACILITIES: FM, AdA, ComN, ComR, DR, JN, VDT.
DEGREE: BA.

Loyola University
6363 St. Charles Ave., New Orleans, LA 70118; tel (504) 865-3430; fax (504) 865-2666; internet elcmall@music.loyno.edu. Department of Communications. William M Hammel, chair.
FACULTY: *Profs.:* Ralph T Bell, Mary I Blue,William M Hammel, A L Lorenz, David M Myers (dir., grad. program), John H Pennybacker, Raymond A Schroth; *Asst. Profs.:* S L Alexander, Michael L Braden, Nancy M Dupont, Teri Kline Henley, Leslie G Parr, J Cathy Rogers, Gerald M Schuppert, Elizabeth B Scott.
SEQUENCES: Advertising, Broadcast Journalism, Broadcast Production, Communications Studies, Film Studies, Photojournalism, Print Journalism, Public Relations.
FACILITIES: AdA, AP, CATV, CCTV, CN, ComN, ComTV, DR, PRA, VDT, Carrier Current Radio Station.
DEGREES: BA, MA, MA/JD.

McNeese State University
PO Box 90335, Lake Charles, LA 70609-0335; tel (318) 475-5290; fax (318) 475-5122; internet mcnmcom@aol.com. Department of Mass Communication, 1990. Peter Dart, acting head.
FACULTY: *Prof.:* Peter Dart (acting head), Barbara Ellis; *Assoc. Prof.:* David Rigney; *Asst. Profs.:* Carrie Chrisco, Steven Dick, Pam Mathews.
SEQUENCES: Broadcast Journalism, Broadcasting, Print Journalism.
FACILITIES: Broadcast Studios (TV and Radio), Computer Writing Lab.
DEGREE: BS.

Copyright ©1996 by the Editor & Publisher Co.

New Orleans, University of
New Orleans, LA 70148; tel (504) 286-6273, (504) 286-6378 (student newspaper). Journalism Area, English Department. Ralph Adamo, coord.
Journalism Program: Three-person journalism faculty offers coursework and minor in print journalism.

Nicholls State University
Thibodaux, LA 70310; tel (504) 448-4586; internet maco-ejb@nich/nsunet.nich.edu. Department of Mass Communication. 1957. E. Joseph Broussard, PhD, head.
FACULTY: *Profs.:* E Joseph Broussard, (head), Lloyd Chiasson; *Asst. Prof.:* Rickey Duet, Erik A Stilling; *Instrs.:* Joye C Gordon, James Stewart; *Prof. Emer.:* Alfred Delahaye.
SEQUENCES: Broadcast Journalism, Print Journalism, Public Relations.
FACILITIES; AdA, FM, CATV, CN, ComN, ComTV, DR, PRA, VDT.
DEGREE: BA.

Northeast Louisiana University
Monroe, LA 71209-0320; tel (318) 342-1390; fax (318) 342-1369; internet cnrambin@alpha.nlu.edu. School of Communication, Department of Journalism/Department of Radio-TV-Film. 1989. AER, KTA, PRAL, PRSSA, SPJ. William R Rambin, dir.
FACULTY: *Assoc. Profs.:* Richard L Baxter, Jeffrey M Gibson, (acting head, RTVF), James D Whitfield (head, Jour.); *Asst. Profs.:* Ginger Carter, Robert E Lewis, Belle Malone, Tim Walters, Joel R Willer; *Part-Time Adjunct Fac.:* Susan C Allain, Ray Davidson, Sunny Meriwether, Mark Simmons.
SEQUENCES: Broadcast News, Film-Making, News-Editorial, Photojournalism, PR, RTVF Management and Marketing, RTVF Production.
FACILITIES: AP, CCTV, CN, ComN, ComR, ComTV, DR, FM (2), PRA, VDT.
DEGREES: BA, MA.

Northwestern State University of Louisiana
Natchitoches, LA 71497; tel (318) 357-4425; fax (318) 357-4434. Department of Journalism and Telecommunications, 1957. Ron McBride, head.
Journalism Program: The Journalism degree offers three areas of emphases – Public Relations, News/Editorial and Broadcasting.

Southeastern Louisiana University
Hammond, LA 70402-0428; tel (504) 549-2100; fax (504) 549-5021; internet FENG1678@ SELU.EDU. Dept. of English. Joseph A Mirando (jour. program coord), Suzanne Campbell (instr.), Vic Couvillion (stud. pub. dir.).
Journalism Program: Offers a print journalism sequence within majors in liberal arts studies and general studies and secondary school teaching certification in journalism through a major in English education.

Southwestern Louisiana, University of
Lafayette, LA 70504-3650; tel (318) 482-6103; fax (318) 482-6104. Department of Communication, 1981. AAF, PRSSA, SPJ, SGM, SNPA, LPA, SCA, ICE, PIMS, LBEA, NAB, ASJMC, Hearst Awards Program. Paul A Barefield, head.
FACULTY: *Profs.:* Paul A Barefield (dept. head), Gerald V Flannery, (Grad. coord.); *Assoc. Profs.:* Janet A Bridges, (grad. advisor), Kathleen S Kelly, (Hubert J Bourgeois Prof.), Jung-Sook Lee, (grad. advisor), Russell A Mann, (internship coord.), Laura V. Rouzan, (interpersonal seq.); *Asst. Profs.:* Robert T Buckman, (journ. coord.), William R Davie, (mass comm. coord.), Timothy R Dee, Mike Maher, Ronald S Rich, (mass comm. advtg.), Patricia A Rockwell, (speech & debate team dir.); *Instr.:* Wesley S Sandel, Kathleen Valdetero, (grad. asst. coord.).
SEQUENCES: Interpersonal and Public Communication, Journalism, Mass Communication (Broadcasting or Advertising seq.) and Public Relations.
FACILITIES: AM/FM, CATV, CCTV, ComN, DR, ETV, VDT.
DEGREES: BA, MA.

Xavier University of Louisiana
909 S. Jefferson Davis Pkwy. (mailing address: 7325 Palmetto) New Orleans, LA 70125; tel (504) 486-7411 or 483-7510 (ext. 3224/3215); fax (504) 486-2108. Mass Communication Program, 1982. Joe A Melcher, chair (ext. 3667).
Communications Program: Undergraduate liberal arts based program; Public Relations, Radio, TV or Print emphases available; houses student newspaper, *Xavier Herald*.

MAINE

Maine, University of
Orono, ME 04469-5743; tel (207) 581-1283; fax (207) 581-1286; Bitnet Bullion@Maine. Department of Communication and Journalism, 1948. AAF, BEA, SPJ. Stuart J Bullion, chair.
FACULTY: *Prof.:* Steve Craig; *Assoc. Profs.:* Stuart Bullion, Kathryn Olmstead; *Asst. Profs.:* Patricia Dooley, Paul Grosswiler, John Weispfenning; *Instrs.:* Carole Bombard, Marie Tessier; *Profs. Emer.:* Arthur Guesman, Brooks Hamilton, Alan Miller.
SEQUENCES: News-Editorial, Broadcast Journalism, Advertising, Mass Communication.
FACILITIES: AP, CCTV, CN, ETV, FM, VDT.
DEGREE: BA.

MARYLAND

Bowie State College
Bowie, MD 20715; tel (301) 464-7253; fax (301) 464-7723. Department of Communications, 1978. Elaine Bourne Heath, chair.
Journalism Program: The Journalism program prepares students for careers in news, broadcasting, public relations and advertising.

Defense Information School
8362 Dutt Rd., Ft. George G. Meade, MD 20755-5600; tel (301) 677-4263; fax (301) 677-4263. Journalism, Broadcasting and Public Affairs Departments, 1965. MPI, NAGC, NCACS, PRSA (CEPR). Col. Ronald A Grubb (commandant), CDR Jeffrey P Smallwood (dir., Public Affairs/ Journalism), LTC Dick David (dir., Brdct. Dept.).
Journalism Program: Eighteen journalism programs with emphases on News-Editorial, Photojournalism, Public Affairs, Broadcast Writing, Radio/TV Production, Newspaper Production, Media Management and Video Production.
AFRTS-BC(AP), CCTV, DR, JN, VDT.

Hood College
Frederick, MD 21701; tel (301) 663-3131. Communication Arts Program. Al Weinberg, co-dir., assoc. prof. of journalism.
Communication Program: BA in communication arts offered. Program requires a core of basic courses and then divides into the print track, emphasizing journalism, the visual track, emphasizing graphic and visual arts, and the public relations track.

Loyola College
4501 N. Charles St., Baltimore, MD 21210; tel (410) 617-2528; fax (410) 323-2768; internet KING@LOYOLA.EDU Writing and Media Department. Andrew Ciofalo, media program coord.
Communications Program: BA, professional program: journalism, advertising/PR, creative writing. Internships, international study, graphics, computer lab. Majors: 350.

Maryland, University of
College Park, MD 20742; tel (301) 405-2399 (Main Office), 405-2383 (Dean's Office); fax (301) 314-9166; internet Rcleghorn @ JOUR.UMD.EDU. College of Journalism, 1947. KTA, PRSSA, SPJ, NABJ, RTNDA, Ad Club. Reese Cleghorn, dean; Greig M Stewart, asst. dean for administration; Christopher Callahan, asst. dean.
FACULTY: *Profs.:* Maurine H Beasley, Jay G Blumler, Reese Cleghorn, Douglas Gomery, James E Grunig, Michael Gurevitch, Ray E Hiebert (dir., American Journalism Center, Budapest), Benjamin F Holman, Mark R Levy, Eugene L Roberts; *Assoc. Profs.:* Steve M Barkin, Marjorie Ferguson, Larissa Grunig, Carl Sessions Stepp, Eric Zanot; *Asst. Profs.:* Kevin Keenan, Katherine C McAdams, John Newhagen, Judith Paterson, James Roche; *Instrs.:* Linda Fibich (dir., Annapolis Bureau), Christine Harvey (dir., Washington Bureau), Charles C Rhodes, Carol Rogers; *Dir. of Development:* Frank Quine; *Dir. of Business Adm.:* Carroll Volchko; *Dir. of Undergraduate Studies:* Olive Reid; *Eugene L. Roberts Visiting Professor:* Nan Robertson; *Faculty Assocs.:* Rem Rieder (editor), *American Journalism Review;* Howard Bray (dir., Knight Center for Specialized Journalism), Cathy Trust (dir., Casey Journalism Center for Children and Families); *Prof. Emer.:* L John Martin; *Adjunct Fac.:* Marlon Allen, Jeffrey Barker, Charles Bussey, Carol Burnett, William J Eaton (curator, Hubert H Humphrey Fellowship Program),Andy Ellis, Jay Goldman, Sharon O'Malley, James Plumb, Cindy Pohoryles, Rem Reider, David Runkel, Larry Sanders, Jeffery Sheler, Mike Sullivan.
SEQUENCES: Advertising, Broadcast News, News-Editorial (with magazine and news specializations), Public Relations.
FACILITIES: AP, AM/FM, AdA, CATV, CCTV, CN, ComN, ComR, ComTV, DR, ETV, JM, PRA, Reuters, VDT.
DEGREES: BA, MA, PhD.

Towson State University
Towson, MD 21204; tel (410) 830-2891/2448; fax (410) 830-3656. Speech and Mass Communication Department. Ronald J Matlon, chair.
Mass Communication Program: 1200 BA, BS and MA students (25 full-time and 50 part-time faculty). Sequences in Communication Studies, General Mass Communication, Journalism, Film, Television, Broadcast Journalism, Radio, Advertising, Public Relations.

MASSACHUSETTS

Boston University
640 Commonwealth Ave., Boston, MA 02215; tel (617) 353-3450; fax (617) 353-3405; internet com@bw.edu College of Communication, 1947. PRSSA, SPJ, WICI, B/PAA, BEA. Brent Baker, dean.
Communication Program: Undergraduate: Broadcasting and Film (Television and Film Programs), Communication (Mass Communication, Advertising and Public Relations), Journalism (News-Editorial, Magazine, Photojournalism, Broadcast Journalism). Graduate: Broadcast Journalism, Broadcast Administration, Broadcasting, Business and Economic Journalism, Film, Journalism, Mass Communication, Public Relations, Science Journalism. Dual-Degree Programs: Mass Communication/Law (MS/JD), Broadcasting Administration/Business Administration (MS/MBA). Joint Degree: International Relations and International Communication (MA).

Emerson College
Boston, MA 02116; tel (617) 578-8800; fax (617) 578-8804. Mass Communication Division, 1953. SPJ, BEA AER, NATAS, RTNDA. Donald L Fry, chair.
SEQUENCES: Video, Film, Audio, Print and Broadcast Journalism.
FACILITIES: FM, AP, UPI, TV Studios, VDT, CATV, CN, ComN, ComTV, DR.
DEGREES: BA, BFA, BS, MA.

Hampshire College
Amherst, MA 01002; tel (413) 549-4600, ext. 501. School of Communications and Cognitive Science. Richard Muller, dean.
Journalism Program: Interdisciplinary program in communication study; TV and print journalism; mass communication emphasis on liberal arts background.

Massachusetts, University of
Amherst, MA 01003-0520; tel (413) 545-1376; fax (413) 545-3880. Department of Journalism, 1971. KTA.
FACULTY: *Prof:* Madeleine H Blais, David DuBois, Sara Grimes, Karen List, Norman H Sims, Ralph Whitehead, Howard M Ziff (chair); *Assoc. Prof:* Nicholas C McBride; *Part-Time Fac.:* Thomas Mitchell, B J Roche, Rhonda Swan, Stephen Simurda.
SEQUENCES: News-editorial, Non-Fiction writing.
FACILITIES: FM, AP, CN, DR, VDT.
DEGREE: BA.

Northeastern University
Boston, MA 02115; tel (617) 373-3236; fax (617) 373-8773. School of Journalism, 1964. SPJ, Advertising Club, PRSSA. KTA, New England Press Association. Nicholas Daniloff, dir.
FACULTY: *Assoc. Profs.:* Charles Fountain, William Kirtz, James Ross (coord., Grad. Program); *Asst. Profs.:* Jerome Berger, Lisa Cantwell (coord., Cooperative Education Placement), Kelley Chunn (coord., PR concentration), Linda Conway-Tompkins (coord., Adv. concentration), Andrew Jones (coord., Radio-TV News concentration), Kellianne Murphy (coord., Cooperative Education Placement), Bill Smith; *Part-Time Fac.:* Vincent Catania, William Coulter, Susan Davis, Valerie Elmore, Marilyn Jackson, Maria Karagianis, Lincoln McKie, William Mungo, Laura White, Deidre Wilson.
SEQUENCES: News-Editorial, Radio-Television News, Advertising, Public Relations.
FACILITIES: CATV, CN, AdA, ComN, ComR, ComTV, DR, PRA, VDT, FM.
DEGREES: BA, BS, MA.

Simmons College
Boston, MA 02115; tel (617) 521-2838; fax (617) 521-3199; internet JCORCORAN@ VMSVAX. SIMMONS.EDU. Department of Communications. James Corcoran, chair.
Journalism Program: Writing for news media. Reporting, features, interviews, editorials, reviews. Emphasis is on the practical, with students encouraged to supplement classroom experience and instruction through work on campus publications and supervised professional internships off campus.

Suffolk University
41 Temple St., Boston, MA 02114; tel (617) 573-8500. Department of Communications and Journalism. Robert Rosenthal, acting chair.
Journalism Programs: Print Media, Broadcast Media, Public Relations, Film, Advertising and Communication Law.

MICHIGAN

Alma College
Alma, MI 48801; tel (517) 463-7132. Journalism program. Eugene H Pattison, coord.
Journalism Program: Core of writing and journalistic studies courses augmented by practicums and liberal arts courses.

Calvin College
3201 Burton S.E., Grand Rapids, MI 49546; tel (616) 957-6283; fax (616) 957-6601; internet forr@calvin.edu. Department of Communication Arts and Sciences. Randall Bytwerk, chair.
Communication Programs: BA degree with liberal-arts emphases in critical studies, popular culture, and international communication. Department of English (Journalism concentration). Don Hettinga, chair, (616) 957-6520. Interdisciplinary liberal-arts program with strong writing component.

Central Michigan University
Mt. Pleasant, MI 48859; tel (517) 774-3196; fax (517) 774-7106/7805. Department of Journalism, 1959. AER, AAF, PRSSA, SPJ. John Palen, chair.
FACULTY: *Profs.:* John Hartman, Dennis Jeffers, Michael Petrick; *Assoc. Profs.:* Guy Meiss, Elliott Parker, Alice Tait, James Wieghart; *Asst. Profs.:* Jerome Fitzhenry, John Palen; *Instr.:* James Bow; *Part-Time Instrs.:* Peggy Brisbane, Steven Griffin, Ronald Marmarelli, James Wojcik.
SEQUENCES: Advertising, General Journalism, News-Editorial, Photojournalism, Public Relations.
FACILITIES: AP, CATV, CN, ComN, DR, ETV, FM, PRA, VDT.
DEGREES: BA, BS.

Detroit Mercy, University of
PO Box 19900, 4001 W. McNichols, Detroit, MI 48219-0900; tel (313) 993-1173; fax (313) 993-1120. Communication Studies Department, 1956. Vivian I Dicks, chair.
Journalism Program: One of the most popular majors of the university, the department features emphases in broadcasting, public speaking, public relations/advertising and journalism.

Eastern Michigan University
Ypsilanti, MI 48197-2210; tel (313) 487-0147; Univ. Publications fax (313) 481-1095. Department of English Language and Literature. Marcia Dalbey, head.
Journalism Program: Offers a major and minor in Journalism and an interdisciplinary major in Public Relations. Journalism courses cover news/feature writing, copyediting, editorial procedures of layout and design, history of journalism, law and contemporary problems of journalism. Public Relations courses cover writing for public relations, principles of public relations, case studies in public relations, radio-TV-film production and continuity writing, organizational communications, graphic communications, copyediting, public speaking and persuasion. Internships available and recommended in both fields.

Grand Valley State University
Allendale, MI 49401; tel (616) 895-3668; fax (616) 895-3106. School of Communications. Alex Nesterenko, dir.
Journalism Program: BA, BS degrees offered in Journalism, Advertising/PR, Photography, Broadcasting, Film/Video, Communication Studies, Theatre, and Health Communication. Master's program (MS) in Communication Management.
FACILITIES: WGVU-TV (PBS station) and WGVU-FM (NPR station).

Madonna University
36600 Schoolcraft, Livonia, MI 48150; tel (313) 591-7556; fax (313) 591-0156. Journalism-Public Relations Program, 1947. Neal Haldane, dir.
Journalism Program: Program is broadly based to include aspects of newspaper, magazine, publicity, graphics, television, photography and advertising production.
Video Communications: Aimed at those interested in writing, producing and directing for single-camera productions and/or business videos.

Michigan, University of
Ann Arbor, MI 48109-1285; tel (313) 764-0420; fax (313) 764-3288. Department of Communication, 1926. KTA, SPJ, WICI.
SEQUENCES: BA, Communication; MA, Journ., Telecommunication Arts; PhD Mass Comm.
FACILITIES: AM/FM, AP, CCTV, CN, JN, VDT.
DEGREES: BA, MA, PhD.

Michigan State University
East Lansing, MI 48824-1212; tel (517) 353-6430; fax (517) 432-1244; e-mail 2141MGR@MSU.edu School of Journalism, 1910. IABC, KTA, SPJ, WICI, PRSSA. Stanley I. Soffin, dir.
FACULTY: *Profs.:* Mary A Gardner (emer.), Frederick Fico (chair, Grad. Studies), Robert V Hudson (coord., Mag.), Todd Simon, Stanley I Soffin; *Assoc. Profs.:* Howard Bossen (coord., Visual Jour.), William Cote (coord., Capital News Service), Lucinda Davenport (Asst. Dir.), Darcy Drew-Greene, Stephen Lacy, Boyd Miller (emer.); *Asst. Profs.:* L Susan Carter (coord., Brdct. News), Folu Ogundimu; *Instr.:* Carole Eberley; *Specialists:* Cheryl Pell (dir. Michigan Interscholastic Press Assoc.), Keith Greenwood (coord., Placement & Internships); *Adjunct Fac.:* Yolanda Alvarado (coord., Hispanics in Jrn program), Frank Ochberg (prof.), Berl Swartzell (lectr. and gen. mgr., *The State News).*
SEQUENCES: News-Editorial (including Broadcast News, Newspapers, Magazines, Visual-Journalism), Journalism Education.
FACILITIES: AP, AM, FM, CCTV, COMN, CN, DR, ETV, VDT.
DEGREES: BA, MA, PhD.

Oakland University
Rochester, MI 48309-4401; tel (313) 370-4120/4121; fax (313) 370-4208. Journalism Program, 1978. Jane Briggs-Bunting, dir.
Journalism Program: Professional approach, designed to educate and train reporters, with emphases on print, public relations, broadcast and advertising. Mandatory internship.

Wayne State University
Detroit, MI 48202; tel (313) 577-2627; fax (313) 577-6300. Journalism Program, Department of Communication, 1948. SPJ. Ben Burns, dir.
Journalism Program: Two computer labs. One has 18 Power Mac 6100's and the other has 18 Mac-LCII's. Each has a laser printer and a scanner is available. Basic Journalism Desk-Top Publishing is taught. Degree offered is a Bachelor of Arts with a major in Journalism.

Western Michigan University
Kalamazoo, MI 49008; tel (616) 387-2572. Journalism Program, English Department. Thomas W Minehart, asst. prof. of English.
Journalism Program: Major and minor offered in journ.; internships available for advanced students.

MINNESOTA

Bemidji State University
Bemidji, MN 56601; tel (218) 755-2915. Department of Mass Communication. Lee Hawk, chair.
Mass Communication Program: Offers BS in Mass Communication, with concentrations in print, public relations, and broadcast media.

Mankato State University
Mankato, MN 56002-8400; tel (507) 389-6417; fax (507) 389-5887. Mass Communications Department, 1968. SPJ. Marshel Rossow, chair.
FACULTY: *Assoc. Profs.:* Ellen M. Mrja, Marshel Rossow; *Asst. Profs.:* John Gaterud, Charles Lewis; *Part-Time Instrs.:* John Cross, Mary Effertz, Dale Ericson; *Profs. Emer.:* Gladys B Olson, Robert O Shipman.
SEQUENCES: News Editorial, Public Relations.
FACILITIES: CN, DR, FM, VDT.
DEGREES: BA, BS.

Minnesota, University of
111 Murphy Hall, 206 Church St. S.E., Minneapolis, MN 55455-0418; tel (612) 625-9824; fax (612) 626-8251. School of Journalism and Mass Communication, 1924. AAF, KTA, NABJ, NPPA, PRSSA, SPJ, WICI. Daniel B Wackman, dir .
FACULTY: *Profs.:* Hazel Dicken-Garcia (Grad. Studies), Ronald Faber, Irving Fang, Donald M Gillmor (Silha Prof.), Chin Chuan Lee, Daniel B Wackman, Jean W Ward, William Wells (Mithun Land-Grant Chair); *Assoc. Profs.:* William Babcock, John Busterna, Tsan-Kuo Chang, Kenneth Doyle, Kathleen Hansen, Nancy Roberts, Dona Schwartz, Albert Tims (Undergrad. Studies); *Asst. Profs.:* Michael Griffin, Leola Johnson; *Profs. Emer.:* Roy E Carter, J Edward Gerald, Virginia A Harris, Robert L Jones, Raymond B Nixon, Willard H Thompson, Philip J Tichenor.
FACILITIES: AP, CCTV, CN, DR, JM, AM/FM, AdA, VDT, ComN, ComR, ComTV, PRA.
DEGREES: BA, MA, PhD.

Moorhead State University
Moorhead, MN 56563; tel (218) 236-2983/2984; fax (218) 236-2168; internet 355DLS@MHD5. MOORHEAD.MSUS.EDU. Mass Communications Department, 1967. AAF, PRSSA. SPJ. Martin Grindeland, chair.
FACULTY: *Prof.:* Martin Grindeland, Shelton Gunaratne, C T Hanson, Dean Hustuft; *Assoc. Profs.:* Marvin Bossart, Wayne Gudmundson, Melva Moline; *Asst. Profs.:* William B Hall, Mark Strand; *Instrs.:* Nancy Edmonds Hanson, David Howland; *Profs. Emer.:* Allen E Carter, Roger G Hamilton.
SEQUENCES: Advertising, Broadcast Journalism, Photojournalism, Print Journalism, PR, Dual Major in English/Mass Communications.
FACILITIES: AP, AM, AdA, CATV, CCTV, CN, ComN, ComR, ComTV, DR, PRA, VDT.
DEGREES: BS, BA.

St. Cloud State University
St. Cloud, MN 56301; tel (612) 255-3293; fax (612) 255-3126. Department of Mass Communications, 1972. AAF, Minn. Newspaper Assoc., PRSSA, SPJ, WICI. Dick Hill, chair.
FACULTY: *Profs.:* E Scott Bryce (coord., Broadcast), Marjorie Fish, Amde-Michael Habte, Dick Hill, Michael Vadnie (coord., News Editorial); *Assoc. Prof.:* Gretchen Tiberghien (coord., Public Relations); *Asst. Profs.:* Niaz Ahmed, Amy Heebner, Lisa Heinrich, Mark Mills, Peter Przytula, Roger Rudolph (coord. Adv.); *Adjunct Profs.:* Rebecca Beyers, Charles Czech, Michael Knaak, J Allen Neff, Michael Nistler, Tony Parker; *Prof. Emer.:* Francis Voelker.
SEQUENCES: Advertising, Broadcast, News Editorial, Public Relations.
FACILITIES: AdA, AP, FM, CATV, CN, ComN, DR, PRA, VDT, JN.
DEGREE: BS, MS.

St. Mary's University
Winona, MN 55987; tel (507) 452-4430; fax (507) 457-1633; e-mail sschild@smumn.edu. Media Communications Department, 1977. Steven Schild, chair.
Journalism Program: Liberal Arts program with emphases in public relations and electronic publishing.

St. Thomas, University of
St. Paul, MN 55105; tel (612) 962-5251; fax (612) 962-6360; internet tbconnery@STThomas.edu. Department of Journalism and Mass Communications, 1958. SPJ, PRSSA, Ad Fed. Thomas B Connery, chair.
FACULTY: *Assoc. Prof.:* Thomas B Connery, Robert L Craig; *Asst. Profs.:* Jim Hutton, Norman W Larson, Mark Neuzil, Dave Nimmer, Kris Bunton, James W Whalen; *Part-Time Instrs.:* Bruce Benidt, Michael Carroll, Jack Coffman, Robert Franklin, Dan Haag, John Jarvis, Al Maleson, Elgin Manhard, Theresa Palmerscheim, Reggie Radniecki, Michael Zerby.
SEQUENCES: Advertising, Broadcasting, International, News/Editorial, Public Relations.
FACILITIES: AM, CATV, CCTV, CN, ComN, DR, PRA, VDT.
DEGREE: BA.

Winona State University
Winona, MN 55987; tel (507) 457-5474. Department of Mass Communication, 1981. AER, IABC, SCJ. Dennis H Pack, chair.
FACULTY: *Profs.:* Dennis H Pack, John H Vivian; *Assoc. Profs.:* Donald Cramer, Ajit Daniel, Terry Schwarze; *Asst. Profs.:* William Withers; *Instrs.:* Ronald Elcombe, Cindy Killion.
SEQUENCES: Advertising, Broadcast, Journalism, Photojournalism, Public Relations.
FACILITIES: AP, FM, CATV, CN, ComN, DR, ETV, JN, VDT.
DEGREE: BA.

MISSISSIPPI

Alcorn State University
Lorman, MS 39096-9402; tel (601) 877-6612, 6613. Department of Communications, 1990. BCCA, PBS-ALSS. Shafiqur Rahman, chair.
FACULTY: *Profs.:* David L Crosby (Seniors Adviser/Internship Coord.); *Asst. Profs:* Shafiqur Rahman (Chair, Title III Activity Dir., General Mngr. WPRL-FM); *Instrs.:* Hatti Jones (Newsletter Adviser), Elvin Jenkins (Video Supervisor), Patrick Stearns (News Director WPRL-FM).
SEQUENCES: Print, Broadcast.
FACILITIES: FM, Video Production Editing facilities, Satellite TVRO, Electronic Newsroom/Layout Design Lab.
DEGREE: BA.

Jackson State University
Jackson, MS 39217; tel (601) 968-2151; fax (601) 974-5800. Department of Mass Communications, 1974. NABJ, SPJ AER, BEA. Doris Saunders, chair.
FACULTY: *Prof.:* Doris E Saunders (adviser, NABJ); *Assoc. Prof.:* Robert N List (chair, Curriculum), Joseph C Enos; *Asst. Profs.:* O "Dare" Aworuwa, Arnold Crump (adviser, AER), Reginald Franklin, Samuel O Otitgbe; *Instr.:* Gail Chadwick; *Prof. Emer.:* Gloria B Evans.
SEQUENCES: News-Editorial, News-Editorial (Public Relations), Broadcast Journalism, Broadcast Production, Advertising.
FACILITIES: TV Production Center, Radio Production Lab, Computer/Reporting Lab, Journalism Center.
DEGREES: BS, MS.

Mississippi, University of
University, MS 38677; tel (601) 232-7147; fax (601) 232-7765. Department of Journalism, 1947. BEA, KTA, MSPA, RTNDA, SPJ, WICI. Samir Husni, acting chair.
FACULTY: *Profs.:* Jack Bass, Don Sneed; *Assoc. Profs.:* S. Gale Denley, Samir A Husni, Edwin Meek; *Asst. Profs.:* Jeanni Atkins, Joe Atkins, Ralph Braseth, Gerald Donnelly, Flora Caldwell, Bob Oesterling, Charles Raiteri, Judy Wall; *Instr.:* Robin Street (dir., MS Scholastic Press); *Prof. Emer.:* Jere Hoar, Jim Pratt (assoc. prof. emer.).
SEQUENCES: Print, Radio/TV (PR, magazine, advertising emphases available in both).
FACILITIES: AP, CATV, CN, DR, FM, JM, VDT.
DEGREES: BA, MA, BSJ.

Mississippi State University
Mississippi State, MS 39762; tel (601) 325-3320; fax (601) 325-3210. Department of Communication. Sidney R Hill Jr, prof. and head.
Journalism Program: Offers major in Communication with emphasis in print journalism, broadcast or public relations.

Mississippi University for Women
PO Box W-1340, Columbus, MS 39701; tel (601) 329-7249. Division of Communication. Barbara A Hanners, PhD, head.
Journalism and Broadcasting Programs: Seek to provide students with a strong foundation for careers in mass media.

Rust College
Holly Springs, MS 38635; tel (601) 252-4661. Division of Mass Communication, 1981. Sylvester W Oliver Jr., chair.
Journalism and Mass Communication Programs: Major coursework in news-editorial, radio/TV, recording. Also public relaions and advertising courses.

Southern Mississippi, University of
Hattiesburg, MS 39406-5158; tel (601) 266-5650; fax (601) 266-4263. School of Communication, 1983. AAF, NPPA, PRSSA, SPJ. R Gene Wiggins, dir.
Department of Journalism, 1957. ACP, NPPA, PRSSA, SPJ. Arthur J Kaul, chair, (601) 266-4258; fax (601) 266-4263.
FACULTY: *Prof.:* R Gene Wiggins (dir., School of Communication); *Assoc. Profs.:* Arthur J Kaul (chair, Journalism), Kathryn L Theus, Ed Wheeler; *Asst. Profs.:* David R Davies, Barbara R Shoemake, Tommy V Smith, Johan Yssel; *Part-Time Instrs.:* Allyn Boone, M E Williams.
EMPHASIS AREAS: Advertising, News/Editorial, Public Relations.
Department of Radio, Television and Film, 1975. SBA, Southern Cinema. David H Goff, chair, (601) 266-4281; fax (601) 266-4263.
FACULTY: *Prof.:* S M Mazharul Haque; *Assoc. Profs.:* Robert B Cade, David H Goff (chair, Radio, Television, Film), James L Hall, S Dixon McDowell; *Asst. Profs.:* Phillip Gentile, Lawrence N Strout, Dennis B Webster (dir., Div. Broadcast Services).
EMPHASIS AREAS: Broadcast Journalism, Film, Radio-Television Production.
Department of Speech Communication, 1977. SCA. Keith Erickson, chair, (601) 266-4271; fax (601) 266-4263.
FACULTY: *Profs.:* Richard L Conville, Keith V Erickson (chair, Speech Communication), Stanford P Gwin, Lawrence A Hosman, Susan A Siltanen, Charles H Tardy; *Assoc. Profs.:* Linda D Goff; *Asst. Prof.:* John Meyer.
EMPHASIS AREAS: Speech Communication, Speech Communication Education, Organizational Communication.
Advertising Program, 1972. AAF. Communication Program,1964. R.Gene Wiggins, dir.
FACILITIES: FM, AdA, DR, JN, PRA, VDT.
DEGREES: BA in Advertising, Communication, Journalism, Radio-Television-Film, Speech Communication; MA, MS in Communication; MS in Public Relations; PhD in Communication.

Tougaloo College
Tougaloo, MS 39174; tel (601) 977-6159. Freda Lewis, dir., Journalism program.
Journalism Program: Course offerings represent a solid foundation in journalistic study in keeping with a liberal arts education.

MISSOURI

Central Missouri State University
Warrensburg, MO 64093; tel (816) 543-4840; fax (816) 543-8006. Department of Communication, 1972. AER, BEA, KTA, NPPA, PRSSA, SPJ, Missouri Broadcasters Assoc., Missouri Press Assoc., UFVA. Daniel B Curtis, chair.
FACULTY: *Profs.:* Kuldip Rampal, John Smead; *Assoc. Prof.:* A John Graves; *Asst. Profs.:* Carol Mills-Atkinson, Ralph Bardgett, Jason Berger, Olin Briggs, Suzanne Heck, Jeffrey Neal-Lunsford, Keith Mehlinger; *Instr.:* Barbara Lach-Smith (Supervisor JN); *JN Managing Editor:* Mark Arbuckle; *JN Business Manager:* Adam Estrup.
SEQUENCES: Mass Communication, Broadcasting and Film, PR, Journalism (News Editorial).
FACILITIES: FM, CATV, ComN, ComR, ComTV, DR, ETV, JM, JN, PRA, VDT.
DEGREES: BA, BS, BSE (teacher certification), MA.

Culver-Stockton College
Canton, MO 63435; tel (314) 288-5221; fax (314) 288-3984. Communication Department. Steve Wiegenstein, jour. and PR head.
Communication Program: A general communication education in a liberal arts setting. Students may choose between three interdisciplinary tracks which include interpersonal communication, journalism, and public relations.

Evangel College
1111 N. Glenstone, Springfield, MO 65802; tel (417) 865-2811 (ext. 7383); fax (417) 865-9599. Department of Communication (with an emphasis either in journalism or broadcasting). Shirley Shedd, chair.
Journalism Program: Includes a major, minor and concentration in the field.

Lincoln University
Jefferson City, MO 65101; tel (314) 681-5437; fax (314) 681-5438. Department of Communications, Journalism: 1942. Eddie L Madison, Jr., dept. head.
Journalism Program: Offers BA and BS degrees.

Lindenwood College
209 S. Kings Hwy., St. Charles, MO 63301; tel (314) 949-4835; fax (314) 949-4910. Communications Department, 1948. Jim Wilson, chair.
Journalism Program: Majors offered in Corporate Communication and Mass Communication (emphases in radio/TV, PR or journalism).

Maryville University
St. Louis, MO 63141; tel (314) 576-9300; fax (314) 542-9085. Department of Communications. Nancy Wahonick McGormleg, dir.
Journalism Program: Students may specialize in one of three areas offered through the department: Print Journalism, Business Comm. or Broadcasting.

Missouri, University of
Columbia, MO 65205; tel (314) 882-4821; fax (314) 882-4823. School of Journalism, 1908. AAF, KAM, KTA, PRSSA, SPJ, WICI. Dean Mills, dean.
FACULTY: *Profs.:* James Atwater, Won Ho Chang, Roger Gafke, Edmund Lambeth, Robert Logan, Dean Mills, Daryl Moen, Don Ranly, Keith Sanders, Byron Scott, Esther Thorson, Lee Wilkins, Betty Winfield; *Assoc. Profs.:* Rosemary Armao (adjunct), Brian Brooks, Phillips Brooks, George Kennedy, Bill Kuykendall, Mike McKean, Wes Pippert, Zoe Smith (chair, Editorial Dept.), Charles Warner, Birgit Wassmuth, Stephen Weinberg, Dwight Williams, Jean Gaddy Wilson (adjunct); *Asst. Profs.:* Ann Brill, Jan Colbert, Kent Collins, Lillian Dunlap, Tim Gallimore, Suzette Heiman, Brant Houston (adjunct), Lee Jolliffe, Glenn Leshner, Richard Mullins, Ron Naeger, David Rees, Anna Romero, Sandra Scott, Kurt Wildemuth, Gail Baker Woods (chair, Advertising Dept.); *Instrs.:* Phyllis Gilchrist, Sharon Harl, Cecil Hickman, Sherri Hildebrandt, Lynda Kraxberger, Greeley Kyle, Loup Langton, Lorraine Orlandi, Ernest Perry, Mike Sappington, Bill Silcock, Jack Swartz, Stacey Woelfel, Barbara Zang; *Asst. Instrs.:* Patricia Atwater, Dianna Borsi, Lisa Brown, Tom Brooks, Fritz Cropp,Janine Latus-Musick, Karen Pautz, Steve Twitchell, Takuga Yoskimaura; *Grad. Instrs.:* Chris Allen, Fred Blevens, Kyle Cole, Stanley Ketterer, Cathy Roan, Matthew Reavy, Jane Singer, Ginny Whitehouse; *Lectr.:* Robert Woods; *Profs. Emer.:* Donald Brenner, Jane Clark, Rod Gelatt, Henry Hager, Bob Humphreys, John Merrill, Vernon Stone.
SEQUENCES: Advertising, Broadcast News, Magazine, News-Editorial, Photojournalism.
FACILITIES: AdA, AP, ComN, ComTV, Cox Ns, DR, ETV, FM, JM, JN, NYTS, VDT, Washington Post Ns.
DEGREES: BJ, MA, PhD.

Missouri-Kansas City, University of
Kansas City, MO 64110; tel (816) 276-1337; fax (816) 235-5539. Department of Communication Studies, 1972. SCA, PRSA. Gregory D Black, chair.
FACULTY: *Prof.:* Gregory D Black (chair, Communication Studies), Walter Bodine; *Assoc. Profs.:* Larry Ehrlich, Greg Gutenko, Gaylord Marr, Michael Neer; *Asst. Profs.:* Joan Aitken, Linda Collier, Carol Koehler, Thomas Poe, Pierre Rener (undergrad. adviser), Jae Slim.
FACILITIES: AM/FM, CCTV, CN, DR, AdA, PRA.
DEGREE: BA, MA.

Missouri-St Louis, University of
590 Lucas Hall, 8001 Natural Bridge Rd., St. Louis, MO 63121; tel (314) 516-5485; fax (314) 516-5415; internet smdmurr@umslv-ma.umsl.edu. Department of Communication. Michael D Murray, chair.
Journalism Program: Undergraduate program with emphasis in Mass Communication. Minor in Public Affairs Reporting.

Missouri Western State College
St. Joseph, MO 64507; tel (816) 271-4310; fax (816) 271-4543; internet frick@acad.mwsc.edu. Department of English, Foreign Languages, and Journalism, 1973. Jane Frick, chair.
Journalism Program: We offer a journalism minor, and three BAs in English, with emphases in public relations, writing, and technical communications. We produce a weekly newspaper, a yearbook and an annual literary publication.

Northeast Missouri State University
Kirksville, MO 63501; tel (816) 785-4000, ext. 4481; fax (816) 785-7486. Communication Department, 1974. ASJMC, IABC, SPJ. Edwin C Carpenter.
FACULTY: *Prof.:* Edwin C Carpenter; *Instrs.:* Amanda Crane, David Fortney, Gary Jones, John Langley, Neil Ralston.
SEQUENCES: Journalism, Speech Communication.
FACILITIES: AP, CCTV, CN, ComN, ComR, ComTV, DR, PRA, VDT.
DEGREE: BA.

Northwest Missouri State University
Maryville, MO 64468; tel (816) 562-1617; fax (816) 562-1900. Department of Mass Communiction. Fred C Lamer, chair.
Journalism Program: Programs in Mass Media, Broadcast Journalism, Media Advertising, Public Relations and Print Journalism.

Saint Louis University
St. Louis, MO 63108; tel (314) 658-3191; fax (314) 658-2999; internet paulyjj@sluvca.slu.edu Department of Communication, 1973. John Pauly, chair.
FACULTY: *Profs.:* Rob Anderson (Grad. Dir.), John Pauly (Chair); *Assoc. Prof:* Avis Meyer (Dir., Political Jour.), William Tyler; *Asst. Profs.:* Peggy Bowers, James Connor, Robert Krizek, Karla Scott, Vivian Sheer, Robert Stahl, Robert Strain.
SEQUENCES: Journalism and Mass Communication, Communication Studies, Promotion.
FACILITIES: CN.
DEGREES: BA, MA, MA (Research)

Southeast Missouri State University
Cape Girardeau, MO 63701; tel (314) 651-2241; fax (314) 651-5967. Department of Mass Communication, 1983. AAF, PRSSA, SCJ, ITVA, Missouri Broadcasters Assoc., Missouri Press Assoc. R Ferrell Ervin, chair.
FACULTY: *Prof.:* R Ferrell Ervin; *Assoc. Profs.:* Gordon Holland; *Asst. Profs.:* Tamara Baldwin, James Dufek, Roy Keller, Robert Poteet; *Instrs.:* Cynthia App, Susan Gonders, Bruce Mims; *Adjunct Fac.:* Nancy Bray, Kari Hollerbach, Bryan Uptain.
SEQUENCES: Advertising, Journalism, Journalism Education, Media Studies, PR, Radio and Corporate Video.
FACILITIES: FM, CATV, CCTV, DR, JM, JN.
DEGREES: BA, BS, BSE (teacher certification).

Southwest Missouri State University
Springfield, MO 65804; tel (417) 836-4423; fax (417) 836-6940. Department of Communications, 1971. AER, IABC, PR Club. Donal Stanton, head; Jim Sneegas, Mass Media Program coord..
Mass Media Program: Journalism, Film Studies, Media Operations, and Media Prodiction. Facilities include FM, CN, ComN, ComTV, DR, PRA, VDT. Degrees include: BA, BS, MS.

Stephens College
Columbia, MO 65215; tel (314) 872-7104; fax (314) 876-7248. Mass Communication Department (TV-Radio-Journalism-Public Relations). John S Blakemore, APR, chair.
Journalism Program: Mass Communication major with choice of three emphases: Broadcast Media Production, Journalism or Public Relations. Mass Communication minors in Broadcast Media Production, Journalism, Public Relations.

Webster University
470 E. Lockwood Ave., St. Louis, MO 63119; tel (314) 968-6975; fax (314) 968-7077. Department of Journalism/Media Communications Dept., 1977. Don Corrigan, journalism sequence.
Journalism Program: Department is heavy on print/community newspaper orientation. Media program offers photojournalism, audio recording, video production, radio, and cable television access. Also offers media courses on Vienna and Leiden campuses.Graduate school program is for evening media students.

MONTANA

Montana, University of
Missoula, MT 59812; tel (406) 243-4001. School of Journalism, 1914. Frank Edward Allen,dean.
FACULTY: *Profs.:* Sharon Barrett, Joseph Durso Jr., Charles Hood, Bill Knowles, Gregory MacDonald; *Assoc. Profs.:* Patty Reksten, Carol Van Valkenburg, Clem Work; *Asst. Prof.:* Dennis Swibold; *Instrs.:* John Talbot, Sheri Venema; *Profs. Emer.:* Nathaniel Blumberg, Edward Dugan, Robert McGiffert; *Telecomm. Instrs.:* Gus Chambers, Terry Conrad, Ray Ekness, William Marcus, Sally Mauk.
SEQUENCES: Print, Broadcast.
FACILITIES: AP, FM, CN, ComN, DR, JM, VDT.
DEGREES: BA, MA.

NEBRASKA

Creighton University
2500 California Plaza, Omaha, NE 68178-0119; tel (402) 280-2825; fax (402) 280-4730; internet jflanery@bluejay.creighton.edu. 1924. Department of Journalism and Mass Communication, 1924. AAF, AER, PRSSA, SPJ. James A. Flanery, chair.
FACULTY: *Prof.:* David Haberman; *Assoc. Prof.:* James A Flanery, Lynette M Lashley; *Asst. Profs.:* Bruce Hough, Mary Hart, Eileen M Wirth; *Charles and Mary Heider Endowed Jesuit Chair:* Father Don Doll, S J; *Lectrs.:* Stuart Bay, Louise Donahue, Robert Ericson, Holly Herman, Mark Hughes, Susan Cleary Johnson, Steven K Jordon, Mike Larsen, David Luebke, Joan Lukas, Cathleen Solarana, Donald Summerside, Dennis Wilden.
SEQUENCES: News, Broadcast, PR, Advertising.
FACILITIES: AdA, CCTV, CN, ComN, ComR, ComTV, DR, PRA, VDT.
DEGREES: BA, BS.

Hastings College
Hastings, NE 68902; tel (402) 461-7460; fax (402) 463-3002. Department of Communication Arts/Business and Economics. Roger Doerr, chair.
Journalism Program: Communication Arts major with four possible emphases: advertising and public relations, broadcasting, print journalism and information services.

Midland Lutheran College
900 N. Clarkson, Fremont, NE 68025; tel (402) 721-5480; fax (402) 727-6223. Communication Arts/Journalism. Richard Northcutt, chair.
Journalism Program: Four sequences are offered in the major: News-Editorial, Black and White Photography and Color Photography, Advertising and Public Relations, and Radio and Television. The Dunklau Journalism Center is a state-of-the-art complex, professionally designed. Publications and people are recognized as national leaders in the media field. Complete Desktop Publishing Department.

Nebraska-Kearney, University of
Kearney, NE 68849; tel (308) 865-8249; fax (308) 865-8157. Department of Journalism and Mass Communication. Keith Terry, chair.
Broadcast Program: Specializations offered in broadcast producation management, sales/management and broadcast journalism.
Journalism Program: Specializations offered in News-Editorial, Advertising, Public Relations, Journalism Education and Sports Communication.

Nebraska-Lincoln, University of
12th St. and Stadium Dr., Lincoln, NE 68588-0127; tel (402) 472-3041; fax (402) 472-8597; e-mail WNORTON@UNL.edu. College of Journalism and Mass Communications, 1917. AAF, AER, APME, ASNE, KTA, NAB, NAMA, NBA, NPA, SPJ. Will Norton Jr., dean.
FACULTY: *Profs.:* Peter Mayeux, Will Norton Jr., Linda Shipley (assoc. dean), Michael Stricklin, George Tuck, Larry Walklin; *Assoc. Profs.:* Daryl Frazell, Stacy James, Wayne Melanson, Al Pagel (dept. chair, News-Ed.), Charles Piper, Tom Spann (dept. chair, Broadcast), Richard Streckfuss; *Asst. Profs.:* John Bender, Hubert Brown, Laurie Thomas Lee, Nancy Mitchell, Charles Pinzon, Jerry Renaud; *Lectrs.:* Richard Thien; *Instr.:* Rick Alloway; *Prof. Emer.:* Albert Book, Jack Botts, Neale Copple, Wilma Crumley; *Assoc. Prof. Emer.:* Jim Neal.
DEPARTMENTS: Advertising, Broadcasting, News-Editorial.
FACILITIES: AP, AM/FM, PR, VDT, JN.
DEGREES: BJ, MA.

Nebraska at Omaha, University of
Omaha, NE 68182; tel (402) 554-2600; fax (402) 554-3296, VAX mail CW15: WHITSELL. Department of Communication, 1951. PRSSA, SPJ, BEA. Hugh P Cowdin, chair.
FACULTY: *Profs.:* Hugh Cowdin, Warren Francke, Bruce Johansen, Michael Sherer; *Assoc. Prof.:* Michael Hilt; *Asst. Profs.:* Jeremy Lipschultz, Susan Pendleton, Deborah Smith-Howell; *Instr.:* Karen Weber; *Lectrs.:* Barry Anderson, Corraine Boyd, Jim Ferguson, Mark Ford, Jeff Gauger, Dave Hamer, Jeff Heineman, Mary Heng, Heidi Hess, Mike Kohler, Cydney Koukol, Mike Krainak, Sandy Lipschultz, Jill Lynch, Joe McCartney, Bob Reilly, Gary Repair, Anne Steinhoff, Kerin, Warneke, Tim Winters.
SEQUENCES: News-Editorial, Broadcasting, PR/Advertising.
FACILITIES: FM, AdA, CATV, CN, ComN, ComR, ComTV, DR, ETV, PRA, VDT.
DEGREES: BA, BS, MA.

NEVADA

Nevada, Las Vegas, University of
Las Vegas, NV 89154-5007; tel (702) 895-3325; fax (702) 895-4805. Greenspun School of Communication, 1976. SCA, ICA, WSCA, AEJMC. Gary L Kreps, dir.
FACULTY: *Profs.:* Hugh Branigan, Barbara Cloud, Richard Jensen (grad. advisor), Gary L Kreps, (exec. dir.); *Assoc. Profs.:* Evan Blythin, Gage Chapel, Steve Duffy, (undergrad. advisor), Anthony J Ferri, Stephen Nielsen, (assoc. dir.), Allan Padderud: *Asst. Profs.:* Leesa Dillman, Erika Engstrom, (scholarship coord.), Mary Hausch, Vicki L Holmes, (dir. ELC), Lawrence Mullen, Barbara A Pickering, (dir. Debate & Forensics); *Instrs.:* Frank Barnas, Laurel Fruth, Margaret L Hoppe, Helena Rose Mays, Edna Zhuo; *Adjunct Fac.:* Mark Andrews, Joseph Bauer, Richard Benoit, Robert Boyd, David Clayton, Diane Cody, James Day, Jennifer Ell, April Hebert, Chris Horak, Teresa Horvath, Karla Huntsman, Ira Kimball, Rom Kirsh, James Lapp, James Leavitt, Jayde Leonard, Christine Mason, Joan McSweeney, Stephanie Myers, John Przybys, Gene Redden, Roberta Sabbath, Carrie Schmidt, Steve Schorr, Steve Sebelius, Diane Sjoberg, Gary Thompson, Rick Velotta, Larry White, Charles Zobell.
SEQUENCES: Advertising, Communication Theory, Broadcast Journalism, Print Journalism, Media Studies, Rhetorical Theory, Public Relations, Telecommunications Production, Telecommunications Management.
FACILITIES: AdA, FM, CN, ComN, ComTV, DR, PRA, VDT. Computerized Writing Labs, (Mac & PC), TV Studios, Cable Channel.
DEGREES: BA, MA.

Nevada-Reno, University of
Reno, NV 89557-0040. MS #310. CompuServe 76117, 2012; tel (702) 784-6531; fax (702) 784-6656; internet unrjourn@scs.unr.edu; Dean's Internet: jgentry@equinox.unr.edu; Web Site: http://www.unr.edu/unr/journalism/Reynolds School of Journalism, 1921. IABC, SPJ, RTNDA, PRSSA. James K Gentry, dean.
FACULTY: *Profs.:* David C Coulson, (Grad. Dir.), Jake Highton, Warren Lerude, Travis Linn, Bourne Morris; *Asst. Profs.:* James Ellis, Jean Trumbo; *Visiting Profs.:* Randy Cox, Robert Laxalt; *Profs. Emer.:* Theodore Convover, Joseph Howland, Myrick Land; *Adjunct Fac.:* Larry Baden, Stanley Burroway, Jacquie Ewing-Taylor, Susan Hill, Lynnae Hornbarger, Craig Sailor; *Adm. Fac.:* Paul Mitchell (coordinator of recruiting and retention).
SEQUENCES: Print Journalism, Broadcast Journalism, Advertising, Public Relations, Graduate.
FACILITIES: AP, FM, AdA, CN, ComN, ComTV, DR, JM, PRA, VDT.
DEGREES: BA, MA.

NEW HAMPSHIRE

Keene State College of the University System of New Hampshire
Keene, NH 03431-4183; tel (603) 352-1909, 358-2405, 358-2411, 358-2404; fax (603) 358-2257. Journalism Major (in Division of Arts and Humanities), 1975. S M Smallman, prof. coord.
FACULTY: *Assoc. Profs.:* Shirley Smallman, Rose Kundanis.
SEQUENCES: Journalism with courses in print and broadcast journalism.
FACILITIES: AP, FM, CCTV, CN, ComN, DR. JM, VDT.
DEGREE: BA.

New Hampshire, University of
Durham, NH 03824; tel (603) 862-3968; fax (603) 862-3563. English/Journalism major. Jane Harrigan, dir.
Journalism Program: Newswriting, editing, magazine writing, internships taught and supervised by journalists on English Department faculty.

NEW JERSEY

Fairleigh Dickinson University
Teaneck, NJ 07666; tel (201) 692-2415; fax (201) 692-2081. Department of Communications and Speech. 1973. Donald W Jugenheimer, chair.
Communication Program: BA Sequences in Advertising/Public Relations, Journalism, Film and Television; MA in Corporate and Organizational Communication.

Glassboro State College
Glassboro, NJ 08028; tel (609) 256-4626, 256-4627; fax (609) 256-4920. Communications Department, 1966. David Cromie, chair; Richard Ambacher, Toni Libro, Journalism Program coords.
Journalism Program: The Communications major offers specializations in journalism/news editorial, advertising, radio/TV/film, PR and liberal arts.

Rider University
Lawrenceville, NJ 08648; tel (609) 896-5089; fax (609) 896-8029. Department of Communications, 1934. VDT, FM, AP, Microcomputer, SPJ, RTV. Howard Schwartz, chair.
Journalism Program: News-editorial, PR; emphasis on internships.

Rutgers University
4 Huntington St., New Brunswick, NJ 08903; tel (908) 932-8567; fax (908) 932-1523. Department of Journalism and Mass Media, 1925. Roger Cohen, chair.
FACULTY: *Profs.:* Jerome Aumente (dir., Journalism Resources Institute), Richard F Hixson; *Assoc. Prof.:* Roger Cohen, Barbara Straus Reed, William Solomon; *Asst. Profs.:* H Montague Kern, Shannon Martin, Linda Steiner; *Instr.:* Steven Miller; *Prof. Emer.:* Thomas B Hartmann; *Univ. Prof.:* Richard Heffner; *Adjunct Fac.:* Robert Comstock, Tim Espar, Elizabeth Y Fuerst, Ronald Miskoff, Bruce Reynolds, Daniel Weissman.
SEQUENCES: News-Editorial, Broadcast Journalism, Mass Media and Government, Media Studies.
FACILITIES: FM, CN, ComN, VDT, ETV, AdA.
DEGREE: BA.

Rutgers University-Newark
Newark, NJ 07102; tel (201) 648-5431. Rutgers Newark Journalism Program, 1975. Allan Wolper, dir. of Journalism.
FACULTY: *Prof.:* John A Williams; *Assoc. Profs.:* George Davis, Allan Wolper; *Instrs.:* Rose Marie Aree (*New York Newsday*); Guy Baehr, Robert Braun, Leonard Fisher (*The Star Ledger*); Jody Calendar, Susan DeSantis, Steve Giegrich (*Asbury Park Press*); Dianne Doctor (WWOR-TV); Richard Eittreim (McCarter & English); Rachelle Garbarine, Jerry Gray, Albert Parisi (*New York Times*); Janet Gardner (freelance writer); Deborah Gichon (*Hoboken Weekly*); William Jobes, Sandra King (*New Jersey Network*); David Levine (*Hudson Dispatch*); Edward Martone (*NJ Civil Liberties Union*); Albert Porro, Jeff Weingrad (*DailyNews*); RobertRodriguez (*Gannett Westchester Papers*); John Watson (*Jersey City Journal*).

Seton Hall University
South Orange, NJ 07079; tel (201) 761-9474. Department of Communication. Will H Rockett, assoc. prof., chair.
Journalism Program: BA program with News/Editorial sequence. Courses in broadcasting, print graphics, computer graphics and public relations.

William Paterson College
Wayne, NJ 07470; tel (201) 595-3358. Department of Communication. Anthony Maltese, prof., and chair.

NEW MEXICO

Eastern New Mexico University
Portales, NM 88130; tel (505) 562-2130; fax (505) 562-2130; internet AshmoreT@Email.enmu.edu Department of Communicative Arts and Sciences, 1972. Timothy M Ashmore, chair.
Journalism Program: Offers a major and a minor degree in journalism. Stresses editorials, reporting, editing, feature writing and photojournalism.

New Mexico, University of
Albuquerque, NM 87131; tel (505) 277-5305; fax (505) 277-4206. Department of Communication and Journalism, 1948. SPJ, KTA. Everett M Rogers, chair.
FACULTY: *Profs.:* Jean M Civikly, John C Condon, Wayne Eubank, Kenneth D Frandsen, Anthony G Hillerman (emer.), L L Jermain (emer.), Everett M Rogers, Janice E Schuetz; *Assoc. Profs.:* Fred V Bales, Charles K Coates, Karen Foss, Diane Furno-Lamude,Bob Gassaway, Diane Lamb, Robert H Lawrence (emer.), Henry L Trewhitt, W Gill Woodall, Estelle M Zannes; *Asst. Prof.:* James Barker, Miguel A Gandert, Brad Hall, Nagesh Rao (visiting), Diana Rios, LaVonne Wahl (visiting); *Lectr.:* Thomas E Jewell.
SEQUENCES: Broadcast Journalism, Broadcast/Cable Management, Print Journalism, PR.
FACILITIES: CN, ComN, ComR, ComTV, DR, VDT, FM, ETV, AdA, AP.
DEGREE: BA.

New Mexico Highlands University
Las Vegas, NM 87701; tel (505) 425-7511. Department of English, Speech and Journalism of the Humanities Div. Richard J Panofsky, chair, Division of Humanities.
Journalism Program: Offers major course work with emphasis on news-editorial.

New Mexico State University
Las Cruces, NM 88003; tel (505) 646-1034; fax (505) 646-1924. Department of Journalism and Mass Communications, Box 30001, 1963. NAB, BEA, NPR, PBS, NMPA, AAF, NMBA, SPJ. Steve Pasternack, head.
FACULTY: *Prof.:* J Sean McCleneghan; *Assoc. Profs.:* Don R Martin, Steve Pasternack, Bob Worthington; *Asst. Profs.:* Rob Sitz, Frank Thayer; *Instrs.:* David Brower, James Ficklin, Ken Fischer, Colin Gromatzky, J D Jarvis, Bob Nosbisch, Ron Salak, Ricardo Trusillo, Gary Worth.
SEQUENCES: Advertising, News-Editorial, Public Relations, Broadcasting.
FACILITIES: AP, NPR-FM, PBS-TV, CN, ComN, DR, VDT.
DEGREE: BA.

NEW YORK

Albany, State University of New York at
Albany, NY 12222; tel (518) 442-4065; fax (518) 442-4599. Department of English. 1973. Carolyn Yalkut, dir. of Journalism program.
Journalism Program: Interdisciplinary minor emphasizing print reporting and editing, nonfiction writing, law, ethics, etc. (Application pending for major within Department of Communication.) Maintains very active internship program.

Buffalo, State University College at
Buffalo, NY 14222; tel (716) 878-6008; fax (716) 878-6914; internet netzhaec@snybufaa.cs.snybuf.edu. Department of Communication, 1975. PRSSA, SPJ. Emile C Netzhammer, III, chair.
FACULTY: *Profs.:* Robert J Elmes, Janet Ramsey, W Richard Whitaker; *Assoc. Profs.:* Charles Y Adair, Bruce Bryski, Marian Deutschman, Emile C Netzhammer III, Ron Rabin, Kerran Sanger; *Asst. Profs.:* Paul DeWald, Tom McCray, Ronald Smith; *Lectr.:* Judith Cramer; *Part-Time Lectrs.:* Robert Brady, Cathalena Burch, Rose Ciotta, Annemarie Franczyk, Vastye Gillespie, Deborah Hadley-Bush, David Harrington, Barbara Lattanzi, Brian Meyer, Robert Orrange, Joseph Roland, Dwight Rountree.
SEQUENCES: Journalism, Broadcast Journalism, Broadcast Production & Management, Public Communication.
FACILITIES: FM, AdA, CCTV, CN, ComN, ComR, ComTV, PRA, VDT.
DEGREE: BA

Canisius College
Buffalo, NY 14208; tel (716) 883-7000; fax (716) 888-2525. Department of Communication. Marilyn G S Watt, PhD, chair.
Journalism Program: Eight courses (in print and broadcast) form one component in the Communication major; other sequences include Telecommunication, Organizational Communication (Adv. & PR), Interpersonal/Intercultural.

Columbia University
New York, NY 10027; tel (212) 854-4150; fax (212) 854-7837; internet admissions@jrn.columbia.edu; info@jrn.columbia.edu. Graduate School of Journalism, 1912. NABJ, SPJ. Joan Konner, dean.
FACULTY: *Profs.:* Barbara Belford, James W. Carey, Phyllis T. Garland, (dir., Pew Fellowships), Kenneth K Goldstein, Stephen Isaacs, Joan Konner, Seymour Topping; *Assoc. Prof.:* Helen Benedict, Sigvard Gissler, Peter M Herford, David Klatell, (coord., brdct. progs.), Sandy Padwe, (assoc. dean), Steven S Ross; *Asst. Profs.:* Samuel G Freedman, Ari Goldman, Jane Tillman Irving, Derwin Johnson, David J Krajicek, Rhoda Lipton, Robin Reisig, Michael Shapiro, E R Shipp, Sreenath Sreenivasan, Wayne Svoboda, Craig Wolff; *Visiting Profs.:* Floyd Abrams, Vincent A Blasi, Anthony Lewis; *Prof. Emers.:* W Phillips Davison, Osborn Elliott, John Foster Jr., Fred W Friendly, John Hohenberg, Luther Jackson, Penn T Kimball, Melvin Mencher, Donald Shanor, Frederick T C Yu; *Adjunct Fac.:* Stephanie Abarbanel, Carol Agus, Sarah Barrett, Mervin Block, Steven Brill, Maurice Carroll, Ray Cave, Philip Chin, Samme Chittum, Daniel Cohen, Judith Crist, Jerry Dantzic, Tony DeStefano, Joshua Friedman, Robert Friedman, Joseph A Gambardello, Martin Gottlieb, Samuel S Graff, Timothy Healy, Michael Hoyt, Andrea Kannappell, Suzanne Braun Levine (ed., *Columbia Journalism Review*), Andrew Lih, Wendy Lin, William B Logan, Michel Marriott, David McCormick, Roland Miller, Joshua B Mills, Mary Jo Murphy, Mireya Navarro, Sara Nelson, Nancy Novick, Roberta Oster, Carol Pauli, Bruce Porter, Michael H Powell, Joshua Quittner, Roger Rosenblatt, Trevor Rowe, Joshua Schroeter, Leslie Seifert, Joyce Young Shelby, Lloyd Siegel, James B Stewart, Thomas Sullivan, Jeffrey Szmulewicz, David Tereschuk, Marilyn Webb, Howard Weinberg, Chapin Wright, Jon Zonderman.
SEQUENCES: Newspaper Journalism, Electronic Journalism, Magazine Journalism, New Media
EACILITIES: AP, JM, JN, CCTV, VDT.
DEGREE: MSJ.

Cornell University
Ithaca, NY 14853-4203. Kennedy Hall; tel (607) 255-2111; fax (607) 255-7905. Department of Communication, 1945. PRSSA, WICI. Carroll J Glynn, chair.
FACULTY: *Profs:* Royal D Colle, Ronald E Ostman, Donald F Schwartz, Shirley A White, J Paul Yarborough; *Assoc. Profs.:* Geraldine Gay, Carroll J Glynn (chair), Bruce Lewenstein, Daniel G McDonald, Clifford Scherer, Michael A Shapiro (GFR); *Asst. Profs.:* Alicia Marshall, James E Shanahan, Pamela L Stepp; *Senior Lectrs.:* Brian O Earle, Ralph B Thompson; *Lectrs.:* Dale Grossman, Toni M Russo, Marcelle L Toor, Linda P VanBuskirk; *Ajunct Fac.:* Daryl Bem, James Maas.
Journalism Program: Comprehensive communication program with emphases in publications, public communication, interpersonal communication and communication planning/strategy.
DEGREES: BS, MS, MPS, PhD.

Empire State College of SUNY
Rochester, NY 14607; tel (716) 244-3641. Circulation Marketing and Management Program.
Journalism Program: Management study in newspaper circulation through directed independent study, cross-registered study at other colleges, industry internships, executive tutorials and annual seminars of the Circulation Management Institute leading to a BS in Business, Management and Economics: Circulation Marketing and Management.

Fordham University
Bronx, NY 10458; tel (212) 579-2533; fax (212) 579-2708. Department of Communications. Donald Matthews, chair.
Journalism Program: A comprehensive Liberal Arts program including communications theory and practice, leading to undergraduate and graduate degrees (MA).

Hofstra University
Hempstead, NY 11550; tel (516) 463-5424; fax (516) 564-4296. Communication Arts Dept.: Journalism Concentration, 1972. BEA, UNFV, ICA, SCA, ECA, ACA, AER, WICI, SPJ. Peter L Haratonik, chair and Journalism coord.
FACULTY: *Prof.:* Frank Iezzi; *Assoc. Profs.:* Jerome Delamater (Film coord.), Sybil Delgaudio, Peter L Haratonik (chair and dir., T.V. Institute), William Renn (Broadcast Coord.), Sondra Rubenstein; *Asst. Profs.:* Stewart Bird, Nancy Kaplan, Vern LeCount, Fred Rosen.
SEQUENCES: Broadcasting, Journalism, Film, General Communication Studies.
FACILITIES: CCTV, VDT, FM, CN, JM, AP.
DEGREES: BA, BS.

Iona College
New Rochelle, NY 10801; tel (914) 633-2230. Department of Mass Communication. Orly Shachar, chair.
FACULTY: *Profs.:* John Darretta, Stanley Solomon; *Assoc. Prof.:* George Thottam; *Asst. Profs.:* George Cohen, Orly Schachar, Ray Smith, Kenneth Weiss, Elizabeth Wissner-Gross; *Instr.:* Thomas Gencarelli; *Adjunct Fac.:* Tony Adolfi, Alice Agoos, Martin Arnold, William Corbett, Frank Carr, Colleen Duffy, Michael Iachetta, Patricia Keegan, Nancy Krizmorton, Drew Kulakovich, Allison Lapetino, Michael Marraffino, Kevin McCabe, Evelyn McCormick, Michael McDormett, Berton Miller, Joseph McCarski, Richard Palladino, Joseph Rees, William Shambroom, Susan Stacey, Joanne Steele.
SEQUENCES: Journalism, Advertising, Public Relations, Film, Broadcast.
FACILITIES: Film/Video Tape Library, Film Theater, Radio Lab, Ad&PR Resource Library, Television Studio, Computer Lab.
DEGREES: BA, BS, MS.

Ithaca College
Ithaca, New York 14850; tel (607) 274-1021. Roy H Park School of Communications, 1948. Thomas W Bohn, dean.
FACULTY: *Profs.:* Sandra Herndon, (Graduate chair), John Keshishoglou, Wenmouth Williams (TV-Radio chair); *Assoc. Profs.:* Howard Cogan, Ben Crane, Diane Gayeski (Corporate Communication Chair), Raymond Gozzi, Danny Guthrie, John Hess, John Hochheimer, Peter Klinge, Janice Levy, Barbara Morgenstern, Megan Roberts, John Rosenbaum, R William Rowley (Cinema/Photography Chair), Steven Seidman, Jonathan Tankel, James Treble, W Williams, (Television-Radio Chair), Patricia Zimmermann; *Asst. Profs.:* Cynthia Baughman, Julia Biegler, Pierre Desir, Marty Hansen, Christine Iacobucci, Robert Harris, Curt Louison, Frank Marra, Sharon Mazzarella, Karen Norton, Marcelle Pecot, Gordon Rowland, Alan Schroeder, David Shapiro, Stephen Skopik, Michael Steele, Jocelyn Steinke, Jill Swenson, Stephen Tropiano (Director/LA Program); *Instrs:* John Efroymson, Sheree Galpert, Robert Gearhart, Mary Lou Kish, Gossa Tsegaye, Gordon Webb; *Lectrs.:* Don Ellis, Jon Hilton, Susan Johnston, Barbara Steinwachs; *Prof. Emer.:* Palmer Dyer, Ron Niloson.
SEQUENCES: TV-Radio, Journalism, Media Studies, Corporate Communication, Telecommunications Management, Cinema & Photography, Film, Photography, & Visual Arts.
FACILITIES: Gannett Journalism lab, DEC Media Research lab, Multi-Media lab, three video studios, 20 video and film editing suites, a film soundstage with adjoining mixing facility, motion picture and still photography processing facilities, a sound mixing and recording studio, still photo lighting studio and a 210-seat auditorium.
DEGREES: BS, BA, BFA, MS.

Long Island University—The Brooklyn Campus
University Plaza, Brooklyn, NY 11201-9926; tel (718) 403-1053, 834-6000, ext. 3292; fax (718) 403-1088, BITNET JOU LIU@LIUVAX. Department of Journalism, 1945. KTA, SPJ, WICI. Ralph Engelman, chair.
FACULTY: *George Polk Journalist-in-Residence:* Kalman Seigel: *Assoc. Profs.:* Donald Allport Bird, Ralph Engelman; *Adjunct Profs.:* Claudia Caruana, Jerry Dantzic, Edward Hershey, Sherman Robbins; *Adjunct Assoc. Profs.:* Stephen J Berch, M.D., Olivia Delgado de Torres, Jane Hanson, David Liu, Diana Lore, Samori Marksman, Alex Oliver, Ernie Palladino, Edye Tadox; *Adjunct Asst. Profs.:* Gerald Seymour, Sabrina White; *Prof. Emer.:* Jacob H Jaffe.
SEQUENCES: Newspaper, Advertising, Magazine, Public Relations, Radio-Television.
FACILITIES: AM, AdA, CATV, ComN, ComR, ComTV, PRA, DR, AM, CCTV, CN, VDT.
DEGREE: BA.

Marist College
North Rd., Poughkeepsie, NY 12601; tel (914) 575-3650; fax (914) 575-3645. Electronic Mail Address: HMDA on Marist A Division of Communication and the Arts, Lowell Thomas Communications Center. Augustine Nolan, chair.
Journalism Program: BA in Communication. Concentration in print and broadcast journalism.

New York University
New York, NY 10003; tel (212) 998-7980; fax (212) 995-4148. Department of Journalism and Mass Communication, 10 Washington Place, 1909. PRSSA, KTA, SPJ. Mitchell Stephens, chair.
FACULTY: *Profs.:* William E Burrows (head, Science and Environmental Reporting program), Edwin Diamond, Richard Petrow; *Assoc. Profs.:* Richard Cunningham, Michael Norman, Marcia Rock (head, Broadcast), William Serrin, Stephen Solomon, Carol Sternhell (dir., Undergrad. Studies), Ellen Willis; *Visiting Prof.:* Carl Bernstein; *Asst. Profs.:* David Dent, Michael Ludlum, Mary W. Quigley, Jay Rosen (dir., Grad. Stud.); *Adjunct Fac.:* David Abrahamson, Ilene Barth, Samme Chittum, Donna Hanover, John Garcia, Jonathan Kaufman, Caroline Kitch, Arlene Krebs, Frank LePore, Barbara Lovenheim, Margery Mandell, Daniel Meltzer, Pamela Newkirk, Mary Perot Nichols, Sonia Robbins, Suzanne Rothenberg, Marlene Sanders, Ruth Bayard Smith, Jane Stone, Dennis Sullivan; *Prof. Emer.:* John Tebbel.
SEQUENCES: Newspaper, Magazine, Broadcast News, Public Relations, Media Criticism.
FACILITIES: AP, FM, CCTV, CN, DR, broadcast studios and editing facilities, computer labs, news service, desktop publishing, student mag.
DEGREES: BA, MA.

Niagara University
Niagara University, NY 14109; tel (716) 286-8577; internet jwitt@eagle.niagara.edu. Communication Studies Program, 1973. ASJMC, ICA. James H Wittebols, chair.
FACULTY: *Assoc. Profs.:* Robert F Crawford, James H Wittebols; *Asst. Prof.:* Mark R Barner; *Instr.:* Lynette Miller; *Part-Time Instrs.:* Kevin Collison, Lyn Hamister (adviser, Photo Exhibition and Graphics), Lisa Stephens.
SEQUENCES: Print Journalism, Mass Communication, Broadcasting.
FACILITIES: CCTV, CN, DR.
DEGREE: BA.

Pace University (College of White Plains)
78 N. Broadway, White Plains, NY 10603; tel (914) 422-4134. Department of Journalism, 1975. Allen Oren, chair.
FACULTY: *Assoc. Prof.:* Allen Oren; *Asst. Prof.:* Denis Hurley; *Instrs.:* Robin Bergstrom, Mary Dolan, Karen Johnson, Pat Vingo, Bob Wolff.
SEQUENCES: Special sequences in Print Journalism, Broadcast Journalism, Photography. Journalism major and minor.
FACILITIES: AP, CN, ComN, DR, JM, JN, VDT.
DEGREE: BA.

Rochester Institute of Technology
Rochester, NY 14623; tel (716) 475-2720. Photojournalism—Applied Photography Department. Kathy Collins, chair.
Photojournalism Program: Third and fourth year concentration in Narrative/Documentary/Editorial program leading to BFA degree.

St. Bonaventure University
St. Bonaventure, NY 14778-2289; tel (716) 375-2520; fax (716) 375-2588; internet mhamilton@sbu.edu. Russell J Jandoli Department of Journalism and Mass Communication, 1949. BEA, IRE, KTA, NYSSE, PCWNY, SPJ, WICI. Mary A Hamilton, acting chair.
FACULTY: *Assoc. Profs.:* Mary A Hamilton; *Asst. Profs.:* Steven D Koski, (coord. Macintosh lab), Penny Williams Cardinale (coord., brdct); *Adjuncts.:* John Bartimole, Sean Brennan, Anthony Cardinale, Renee Caya, Jean Trevarton Ehman, Richard Gates (Photography), Carole McNall, Patrick Vecchio; *Bristish Vstg. Profs.:* Alan MacKenzie, Barbara MacKenzie.
SEQUENCES: News-Editorial.
FACILITIES: AM/FM, AP, CN ComN, ComR, DR, JM, PRA, VDT.
DEGREE: BA.

St. John Fisher College
3690 East Ave., Rochester, NY 14618; tel (716) 385-8191; fax (716) 385-8289. Communication/Journalism, 1975. James Seward, chair.
Journalism Program: A liberal arts orientation to the study of communication, journalism, broadcasting and advertising/public relations.

SUNY College at New Paltz
Faculty Tower 214, New Paltz, NY 12561; tel (914) 257-2720, 257-2743; fax (914) 257-3459. Communication & Media Department. Robert Miraldi, coordinator.
SEQUENCES: Journalism Program with wide range of practical and theoretical courses. Requires: one-semester, full-time paid internship at weekly newspaper in state capitol. Radio-TV Production Program with advanced television and radio production courses. Facilities include: JN, VDT, AM/FM.

Syracuse University
Syracuse, NY 13244-2100; tel (315) 443-2301; fax (315)443-3946; e-mail dmrubin@suadmin.syr.edu S.I. Newhouse School of Public Communications, 1934. KTA, NATAS, NPPA, PRSSA, SPJ, WICI. David Rubin, dean.
FACULTY: *Profs.:* Richard L Breyer, George A Comstock, Sheldon F Gilbert, William A Glavin, Sharon R Hollenback, J T W Hubbard, John P Jones, Lawrence Mason Jr., Thomas A Richards, David M Rubin (dean), William D Ryan, Nancy W Sharp, Pamela J Shoemaker, Vernone M Sparkes, Jay B Wright; *Assoc. Profs.:* Stanley R Alten, Kevin G Barnhurst, Lois Bianchi, Fiona Chew, Constantin Cotzias, Michael E Cremedas, Joan A Deppa, Donald Edwards, Elizabeth L Flocke, Anthony R Golden, Dona Hayes, W John Hottenstein, Ron Javers, Samuel V Kennedy III, Gerald F Lanson, E Robert Lissit, Carla V Lloyd, C Marshall Matlock, Peter K Moller, Frances F Plude, Maria P Russell, Holli A Semetko, David C Sutherland, Robert J Thompson, Elizabeth L Toth, Francis Ward, Roosevelt R Wright Jr.; *Asst. Profs.:* Barbara C Fought, Joel K Kaplan, Donald H Singletary, Catherine A Steele, Donald C Torrance; *Non-Tenure Track Faculty.:* Ron Hastings, Thomas Herling, Carol Liebler, Michael Schoonmaker, Sherri Taylor, Randy Wenner; *Profs. Emer.:* Richard B Barnhill, Philip Ward Burton, Frederic A Demarest Jr., William P Ehling, Andre Fontaine, John C Keats, Cleve L Mathews, John D Mitchell, Lawrence Myers Jr., David Norton, Roland E Wolseley.
SEQUENCES: *Undergraduate:* Advertising, Broadcast Journalism, Magazine, Newspaper, Photography, Public Relations, Television/Radio/Film. *Graduate:* Advertising, Magazine, Media Administration, Newspaper, PhD in Mass Communications, Photography, Public Communications Studies, Public Relations, Television/Radio.
FACILITIES: FM, CCTV, VDT, DR, PRA, ComN, CN, AP.
DEGREES: BS, MA, MS, MPS, PhD.

Utica College of Syracuse University
1600 Burrstone Rd., Utica, NY 13502; tel (315) 792-3093; fax (315) 792-3173; internet kbl@ucsu.ucl.edu. Department of Journalism & Public Relations, 1949. PRSSA. Kim Landon, dir.
FACULTY: *Prof.:* John Behrens; *Assoc. Prof.:* Cecillia Friend, Kim Landon; *Asst. Profs.:* Marjorie Marable, Joseph Zappala; *Prof. Emer.:* Raymond Simon.
SEQUENCES: Journalism, Public Relations, Public Relations-Journalism.
FACILITIES: Internet, CCTV, CN, ComN, ComR, DR, FM, JM, PRSSA, VDT.
DEGREES: BA, BS.

NORTH CAROLINA

Appalachian State University
Boone, NC 28608; tel (704) 262-2221, 262-2405; fax (704) 262-2511. Department of Communication. Terry Cole, chair.
Journalism Program: Offered as a concentration in the communication media sequence, along with concentrations in broadcasting, advertising and public relations (BA and BS).

Campbell University
Buies Creek, NC 27506; tel (919) 893-1520. Department of Mass Communication, PO Box 130, 1980. Daniel R Ensley, chair.
Mass Communication: Department offers BA degrees in Broadcast Production, Performance and Management, Journalism, Public Relations and Advertising. Facilities include FM radio station, desktop publishing/graphic design computer labs, radio and television studios, photography labs, and ENG equipment.

East Carolina University
Greenville, NC 27858-4353; tel (919) 328-4227; fax (919) 328-6458. Journalism Program. T H Allen, chair.
Journalism Program: Offers program that leads to a BA in Communication with a concentration in journalism and public relations. Facilities include VDT, CN.

Elon College
Elon College, NC 27244; tel (919) 584-9711 (main switchboard), (919) 584-2522 (journalism). Journalism-Mass Communication major in Department of Literature, Languages and Communication, 1977. D A Grady, chair, Department of Journalism and Communications.
Journalism Program: Journalism and Communications majors combine pre-professional work (writing, editing, practical experience) with liberal arts approach to media (history, law and ethics, international communication). Facilities include FM, CATV, CCTV, CN, ComN, DR.

Johnson C. Smith University
Charlotte, NC 28216; tel (704) 378-1062, 378-1173. Department of Communication Arts. Diane J Cody, head.
Journalism Program: Sequences of course work and internships in journalism, public relations and telecommunications.

Lenoir-Rhyne College
Hickory, NC 28303; tel (704) 328-7176. Department of Art, Theater Arts and Communication. Arthur G Barnes, chair.
Communication Program: Offers mass comm., journalism, television, speech, law, internship, PR and integrated liberal arts courses leading to an AB in Communication. Facilities include FM, CCTV, CN, DR, ITVA, SPJ, VDT.

North Carolina, University of
Chapel Hill, NC 27599-3365; tel (919) 962-1204; fax (919) 962-0620; internet richard_cole@unc.edu. School of Journalism and Mass Communication, 1950. AAF, IABC, ETA, SPJ, NPPA, WICI. Richard R Cole, dean.
FACULTY: *Profs.:* Margaret Blanchard (William Rand Kenan Jr. Prof. and Dir. Grad. Program, 962-4072), John R Bittner (962-2555), Thomas A Bowers (assoc. dean and James L Knight prof., 962-1204), Jane Delano Brown (962-4089), Richard R Cole (dean, 962-1204), A Richard Elam (962-5624), Robert F Lauterborn (James L Knight prof. of Adv., 962-0282), Philip Meyer (Knight Chair in Jour., 962-4085), Carol Reuss (962-4091), Donald L Shaw (Kenan prof. and dir. Honors Program, 962-4087): James H Shumaker (962-4092), Richard Simpson (962-5177), Robert L Stevenson (Kenan prof., 962-4082), Chuck Stone (Walter Spearman Prof., 962-0547), Ruth Walden (coord., PhD Prog., 962-4088); *Assoc. Profs.:* Harry Amana (962-4080), Jay Anthony (962-4076), Richard J Beckman (962-4081), Frank A Biocca (dir., Center for Research in Jour. and Mass Comm., 962-7024), George W Cloud (962-4070), Jan Elliott (962-4083), Anne Johnston (962-4286), Raleigh C Mann (962-4071), Cathy Packer (Coord. MA Program, 962-4077), Mary Alice Shaver (962-6421), Dulcie Straughan (962-9003), John Sweeney (962-4074); *Asst. Profs.:* Deb Aikat (962-4090), Lucila Vargas (962-4075), Michael Williams (962-4073), Xinshu Zhao (962-1465); *Lectr.:* Sally Walters (962-0025); *Part-Time Lectrs.:* Val Lauder (962-4078), Paul O'Connor (962-4075), Kathleen Phillips (Dir., NC Scholastic Press Assoc., 962-4639), Don Seaver (962-4075); *Profs. Emer.:* John B Adams, Kenneth R Byerly, James J Mullen, Vermont Royster (William Rand Kenan Jr. Prof. of Jour. and Public Affairs), Stuart Sechriest.
SEQUENCES: News-Editorial, Electronic Communication, Public Relations, Visual Comm., Advertising.
FACILITIES: AP, CN, DR, ETV, JN, VDT.
DEGREES: AB, MA, PhD.

North Carolina—Asheville, University of
One University Heights, Asheville, NC 28804; tel (704) 251-6227; fax (704) 251-6614. Department of Mass Communication, 1980. Catherine C Mitchell, chair.
Mass Communication Program: A Liberal Arts program focusing on the functions of print and electronic media in society. The program emphasizes clear writing, critical thinking and creative visual production.

Wingate College
Wingate, NC 28174; tel (704) 233-8089; fax (704) 233-8192. Communication Studies. Leon Smith, coord.
Journalism Program: Interdisciplinary, focusing on communication theories and techniques. Emphasis in journalism, public relations, speech communication and media arts.

NORTH DAKOTA

North Dakota, University of
Grand Forks, ND 58202; tel (701) 777-2159; fax (701) 777-3090; e-mail UD191185 @ NDSUVM1. School of Communication, Box 7169. AAF, KTA, PRSSA, SPJ. Lana Rakow, dir.
FACULTY: *Profs.:* Alvin E Austin (emer.), Dennis Davis, Raymond Fischer, Lana Rakow; *Assoc. Profs.:* Heather O'Keefe, Stephen Rendahl; *Asst. Profs.:* Lucy Ganje, Kirk Hallahan, Victoria Holden, William Holden, Neil McCutchan; *Instrs.:* Mary Haslerud Opp, Patti-Jean Hooper.
SEQUENCES: Journalism, Broadcasting, Public Relations, Advertising Communication Studies.
FACILITIES: AM, FM, CATV, CCTV, CN, ComN, ComTV, DR, ETV, JN, VDT.
DEGREES: BA, BS Ed., MA, MS Ed.

North Dakota State University
Fargo, ND 58105-5075; tel (701) 237-7705; fax (701) 237-7784; internet sellnow@badlands.nodak.edu. Department of Communication, Box 5075. PRSSA, SPJ. Timothy Sellnow, chair.
Mass Communication Program: Concentrations in Public Relations, Broadcast and Print Media.

OHIO

Akron, University of
Akron, OH 44325-1003; tel (216) 972-7954; fax (216) 972-8045. School of Communication. John D Bee, dir.
Journalism Program: Twelve journalism and public relations courses plus internships are part of the Mass Media-Communication degree.

Bowling Green State University
Bowling Green, OH 43403; tel (419) 372-2076; fax (419) 372-0202. Department of Journalism, 1941. IABC, KTA, NPPA, PRSSA, Radio-TV News Assn., KTA, NPPA, PRESSA, RTNDA, SPJ, WICI. Nancy Brendlinger, chair.
FACULTY: *Profs.:* Dennis Hale; *Assoc. Profs.:* James Bissland, Laurence Jankowski, Raymond Laakaniemi; *Asst. Profs.:* Nancy Brendlinger, Catherine Cassara, James Foust, Debbie Owens, Sam Winch; *Instrs.:* Terry Rentner; *Parttime Instrs.:* Caren Goldman, Paul Obringer, Kristine Pilliod; *Prof. Emer.:* Joseph Delporto, Harold Fisher, James Gordon, John Huffman.
SEQUENCES: Broadcast, Magazine, News-Editorial, Photography, Public Relations.
FACILITIES: AP, AM, FM, CCTV, CN, CNN, DR, ETV, JM, PRA, VDT, Leaf Picture Desk.
DEGREES: BS in Journalism, MA, PhD in Mass Communication.

Cincinnati, University of
Cincinnati, OH 45221-0003; tel (513) 556-4394, 556-9491; fax (513) 556-0202; internet WOLFRAM@UC.EDUC Division of Electronic Media. Manfred K Wolfram, chair; Marjorie Fox, jour. coord.
Journalism Program: Degree is in Electronic Media; students may concentrate in electronic journalism. Journalism courses offered include Broadcast News Writing, Broadcast News Production, Independent Study sequences which involve work on Uptown, a televised campus news program; in addition Introduction to Broadcast Journalism, Introduction to Broadcast Writing, and Ethics of Mass Media are required of all Electronic Media majors. A variety of related courses in Audio and Television Production are offered. Internships with local television and radio news operations are widely available. Students interested in journalism are encouraged to earn a Writing Certificate through the Department of English.

Cleveland State University
Cleveland, OH 44115; tel (216) 687-4630; fax (216) 687-9366; telex (810) 421-8252. Department of Communication. Victor D Wall, Jr., chair.
Journalism Program: Mass Communication area offers Journalism, Political Communication, Promotional Communication and Broadcasting sequences. Journalism sequence focuses on reporting public affairs in an urban context.

Dayton, University of
Dayton, OH 45469-1410; tel (513) 229-2028, BITNET SKILL@DAYTON. Department of Communication. Thomas Skill, chair.
Journalism Program: Undergraduate concentration areas include news-editorial, broadcasting, PR and communication management. Largest department at university.

Franciscan University of Steubenville
G-8 Egan Hall, University Blvd., Steubenville, OH 43952; tel (614) 283-6386; fax (614) 283-6452; e-mail 74305.263@ compuserve.com Communication Arts Department. James E Coyle, Jr., chair.
Communication Program: BA degree in Mass Communications with concentrations in Journalism and Radio/TV.

John Carroll University
University Heights, OH 44118; tel (216) 397-4378; fax (216) 397-4256. Department of Communications. Jacqueline J Schmidt, chair.
FACULTY: *Assoc. Profs.:* Mary Beadle, Alan Stephenson; *Asst. Profs.:* Mary Ann Flannery, Marianne Salcetti, Craig Sanders; *Instrs.:* Bob Noll David Reese; *Part-time Instrs.:* Fred Buchstein, Marcia Goldberg.
FACILITIES: Electronic newsroom, international journalism library, television studio, editing booths, screening rooms, audio production booth, satellite downlink, graphics laboratory. Department members advise student newspaper, FM station.
DEGREE: BA.

Kent State University
Kent, OH 44242; tel (216) 672-2572; fax (216) 672-4064. School of Journalism and Mass Communication, 1932. AAF, AER, BEA, PRSSA, SPJ, WICI. Pamela J Creedon, dir.
FACULTY: *Profs.:* Fredric Endres, Joseph Harper, Thomas Olson, Timothy Smith; *Assoc. Profs.:* Barbara Hipsman, Ann Schierhorn (coord., Mag.), Gene Stebbins (coord., Radio/TV), Stanley Wearden (coord., Grad); *Asst. Profs.:* Greg Blase (coord., Adv.), Frances Collins, LuEtt Hanson, E Zoe McCathrin (coord., PR), Greg Moore (coord., Photo.), Carl Schierhorn, William Sledzik, Robert West, Bennett Whaley, Evonne Whitmore; *Instrs.:* Nona Bowes, Dale Dengerd, Kathleen Fraze, Chris Howey, Roy Jones, David McCoy, Keith McKnight; *Asst. to the Dir.:* Nona Bowes.
SEQUENCES: News/Editorial, Advertising, Public Relations, Photography, Broadcast News and Radio/TV.
FACILITIES: AP, AdA, CCTV, CN, ComN, ComTV, DR, ETV, FM, JM, JN, PRA, VDT.
DEGREES: BA, BS, MA.

Marietta College
Marietta OH 45750; tel (614) 374- 4802; fax (614) 374-4896. Mass Media Department, 1975. Joseph H Berman, chair.

Journalism Program: Department offers majors in Radio/TV, Journalism, Public Relations and Advertising.

Ohio State University
Columbus, OH 43210; tel (614) 292-6291; fax (614) 292-3809. School of Journalism, 1914. AAF, ACT, KTA, NABJ, PRSSA, RTNDA, SND, SPJ. Lee B Becker, interim dir.
FACULTY: *Profs.:* Lee B Becker, James Neff (Kiplinger Prof.), Pamela J Shoemaker; *Assoc. Profs.:* Eric Fredin, Jiri Hochman, Thomas Hubbard, Gerald Kosicki, Joseph McKerns, David Richter, Thomas Schwartz, Conrad Smith, Sharon C West; *Asst. Profs.:* Sharon S Brock, Prabu David, Felecia Jones, Geetu Melwani, Kasisomayajula Viswanath; *Thurber Writer:* Will Haygood; *Lectr.:* Paula Dix, Cathleen Carey Treyens, Dave Golowenski (Lantern adviser); *Lantern Bus. Mgr.:* Raymond Catalino; *Part-Time Fac.:* Don Alexandre, Rose Hume, Cynthia Rickman, John Sanchez; *Profs. Emer.:* Llyle Barker, Walter K Bunge, John J Clarke, Robert Holsinger, Paul V Peterson, Walter W Seifert, William B Toran.
SEQUENCES: Broadcast, News-Editorial, Public Relations.
FACILITIES: AdA, AP, CATV, DR, ETV, JN, VDT, PRA, AM, FM.
DEGREES: BA. MA.

Ohio University
Athens, OH 45701; tel (614) 593-2590; fax (614) 593-2592; e-mail JOURDEPT@OUVAXA.CATS. OHIOU.EDU. E.W. Scripps School of Journalism. 1924. AAF, KTA, PRSSA, RTNDA, SPJ, WICI. Ralph Izard. dir.; Paul Nelson, dean, College of Communication.
FACULTY: *Profs.:* Michael Bugeja, Dru Riley Evarts, Melvin Helitzer, Ralph Izard, Donald Lambert, Jerry Sloan, Guido H Stempel III (distinguished prof.), Patrick Washburn (asst. dir.); *Assoc. Profs.:* Anne Cooper Chen, Marilyn Greenwald, Sandra Haggerty, Thomas Hodges, Thomas Peters (assoc. dir.), Ronald Pittman, Robert Stewart, Patricia Westfall; *Asst. Profs.:* Joseph Bernt, Eddith Dashiell (dir., High School Jour. Workshop), Larry Levin, Cassandra Reese (asst. dean, College of Communication); *Profs. Emer.:* James Alsbrook, Russell Baird, Robert Baker, Hugh Culbertson, Norman Dohn, Ralph Kliesch, Robert Richardson; *Asst. Instrs.:* Richard Bean (dir., Graphics Lab.), Douglas Nohl (mgr., Broadcast Studio); *Part-Time Instrs.:* Nancy Burton (news dir., WOUB), Thomas Hodson, Roger Watson; *Scripps Howard Visiting Professional.:* Walter Friedenberg; *Grad. Teaching/Research Assocs.:* Debashis Aikat, Nil Bardhan, Peggy Dillon, Adam Music, Jacqueline Nash, Bill O'Connell, Sarah Plaster, Katrin Pomper, Virginia Mansfield-Richardson, Kevin Robbins, Kevin Sanders, Ute Sartorius, Lara Simms, Teresa Smith, Yixio Sun, Michael Sweeney, Dawn Timbario, Christine Winderlin, Xinlu Yu, Dale Zacher; *Adjunct Fac.:* Herb Amey, Raymond Frye, Ellen Gerl, Carol James, Kathy Pittman, Karl Runser.
SEQUENCES: Advertising, Magazine, Newswriting and Editing, Public Relations, Broadcast News.
FACILITIES: AP, NYTS, UPI, AM, FM, AdA, CATV, CCTV, CN, CNN, ComN, ComR, DR, ETV, JM, PRA, VDT.
DEGREES: BSJ, MSJ, PhD.

Ohio Wesleyan University
Delaware, OH 43015; tel (614) 368-3650; fax (614) 368-3314. Department of Journalism, 1945. Trace Regan, chair.
FACULTY: *Profs.:* Trace Regan; *Asst. Prof.:* Paul Kostyu; *Lectr.:* Richard McClure, Jim Underwood.
SEQUENCES: News-Editorial, Broadcast News.
FACILITIES: AP, FM, CATV, CN, VDT.
DEGREE: BA.

Otterbein College
Westerville, OH 43081; tel (614) 823-1760. Department of English. PRSSA. Norman Chaney, chair.
Journalism Program: BA program in news-editorial sequence. Interdisciplinary BA in PR and in Broadcasting. Courses in media writing, news writing, broadcast production, public relations, desktop publishing, advanced reporting, media ethics and regulations. Facilities include CN, FM, CATV, DR, VDT.

Toledo, University of
403 Libby Hall, Toledo, OH 43606; tel (419) 530-2005. Department of Communication, 1945. PRSSA, SPJ. Richard Knecht, chair; Paul Many and Ralph Frasca, Journalism Coords.
Communication Program: Offers BA in communication with concentrations in journalism, broadcasting, and public relations. Journalism concentration combines professional skills approach (writing, reporting, editing) with liberal-arts approach (law, history, ethics).

Wright State University
Dayton, OH 45435; tel (513) 873-2145. Department of Communication, 1966. James Sayer, chair.
Journalism Program: Offers coursework and experience in broadcast and print journalism and public relations.

Xavier University
Cincinnati, OH 45207-5171; tel (513) 745-3087; fax (513) 745-3705. Communication Arts Department. William Daily, chair.
Journalism Program: Multi-track program with 36 hour majors in Public Relations, Advertising, Electronic Media and Organizational Communication leading to a BA in Communication Arts.

Youngstown State University
Youngstown, OH 44555; tel (216) 742-3415. Department of English (journalism offered as a minor in the English Dept.). Barbara Brothers, chair, English; Carolyn Martindale, dir., Journalism.
Journalism Program: Offers a Journalism minor through writing courses and lab experience in basic newspaper journalism. Students may combine journalism with other communications-related courses for an individualized curriculum journalism degree. Students also may study journalism as part of a Professional Writing and Editing major in the English Dept.

OKLAHOMA

Central Oklahoma, University of
Edmond, OK 73034; tel (405) 341-2980 (ext. 5122); fax (405) 341-4964. Journalism Department. Terry M Clark, chair.
Journalism Program: BA degree with emphasis in newspaper, magazine, photography, advertising, public relations, professional writing, business and economics journalism. Also BA Education, Master of Education.

East Central University (Oklahoma)
Ada, OK 74820; tel (405) 332-8000 (ext. 482); fax (405) 332-1623. Communication Department. Robert A Payne, chair.
Journalism Program: Major in Mass Communication. Concentration in Electronic and Print Media, and Advertising/Public Relations.

Northeastern State University (Oklahoma)
Tahlequah, OK 74464; tel (918) 456-5511, ext. 2891. Department of Mass Communications. Dana Eversole, coord.
Mass Communications Program: Approximately 250 students, half are majors. Courses offered in all areas of print, broadcast, public relations, advertising and photography.

Oklahoma, University of
Norman, OK 73019; tel (405) 325-2721; fax (405) 325-7565; internet kadams@aardvark.ucs. uoknor.edu. H.H. Herbert School of Journalism and Mass Communication, 1913. AAF, KTA, NABJ, PRSSA, SPJ, WICI, NACB. David Dary, dir.
FACULTY: *Profs.:* David Dary, J Madison Davis; *Assoc. Profs.:* Deborah Chester; Bruce H Hinson, Timothy Hudson (assoc. dir), David Jaffe, Roy Kelsey, Linda Morton, Shirley Ramsey; *Asst. Profs.:* Fred Beard, David Goodloe, Gerald Howard, Baohua Jin, Bill Loving, Jim McCluskey, Ken McMillen, Mary Marcus, Misha Nedeljkovich, Laura Schaub; *Instrs.:* Alice Klement (McMahon Centennial Prof.), Linda duBuclet (Visiting Asst. Prof.).
SEQUENCES: Advertising, News-Communication, Professional Writing, Public Relations, Broadcasting and Electronic Media.
FACILITIES: AP, FM, CATV, CN, ComR, DR, JM, PRA, VDT.
DEGREES: BAJ, MA.

Oklahoma Baptist University
Shawnee, OK 74801; tel (405) 275-2850. Department of Journalism, Michael D Chute, dept. chair.
Journalism Program: Offers BA degree in Journalism (news-editorial sequence) and Public Relations. Minor: Broadcast News, Journalism and Public Relations.

Oklahoma Christian University of Science and Arts
2501 E. Memorial Rd., Oklahoma City, OK 73136; tel (405) 425-5520; fax (405) 425-5316. Department of Communication, 1970. Philip D Patterson, chair.
Communication Program: BA degrees in journalism, advertising/public relations, radio/TV. Weekly student newspaper housed in state-of-the-art laboratory; student-run FM station.

Oklahoma City University
Oklahoma City, OK 73116; tel (405) 521-5252. Department of Mass Communications. Karlie Harmon, chair.
Mass Communications Program: Multi-track system with sequences of study in Advertising, Broadcast, Public Relations, Print.

Oklahoma State University
Stillwater, OK 74078-0195; tel (405) 744-6354; fax (405) 744-7104. School of Journalism and Broadcasting, 1927. ACT, AAF, AER, KTA, PRSSA, RTNDA, SPJ, WICI. Marlan D Nelson, dir.
FACULTY: *Prof.:* Charles Fleming, Marlan Nelson; *Assoc. Profs.:* Marshall E Allen, Brooks Garner, Thomas E Hartley, Maureen Nemecek, Edward Welch Jr.; *Asst. Profs.:* Anita Caldwell, John R Catsis, Donald Forbes, William Hickman, Jack Hodgson, Rose Mary Mercer, Steve Smethers, Fritz Wirt; *Instr.:* Shelly Peper-Sitton; *Profs. Emer.:* Harry E Heath Jr., Harry M. Hix, Frederick Kolch, Charles Overstreet, P E Paulin, D U Reed; *Lectrs.:* David Bennett, Doug Drummond; *Adj. Instr.:* Susan Geisert.
SPECIALIZATIONS: Advertising and Sales, News-Editorial, Public Relations, Broadcast News, Broadcast Sales and Management.
FACILITIES: AP, FM, CATV, CCTV, CN, ComN, ComR, DR, ETV, JN, PRA, Mac labs.
DEGREES: BS, BA, MS, EdD (jointly with College of Education).

Southern Nazarene University
Bethany, OK 73008; tel (405) 789-6400. Mass Communication/Journalism Degree. Pam Broyles (Speech Communication Department), Marcia Feisal (Speech Communication Department), Jim Wilcox (English Department).
Journalism Program: A Liberal Arts degree offered in cooperation with the departments of Speech Communication and English. Emphasis in either print or electronic media.

Tulsa, University of
Tulsa, OK 74104; tel (918) 631-3805. Faculty of Communication. Steve Jones, chair.
Mass Communication Program: One seven-course emphasis with applied electives in journalism and video production. Part of a comprehensive Communication major.

OREGON

Linfield College
McMinnville, OR 97128; tel (503) 472-4121. Dept. of Comm. William M Lingle, head.
Journalism Program: BA degree. Offers Mass Communication major with Journalism, Radio-Video and Public Relations sequences. Required internships.

Oregon, University of
Eugene, OR 97403-1275; tel (503) 346-3738; fax (503) 346-0682. School of Journalism and Communication, 1912. KTA, Ad Club, PRSSA, SPJ, WICI. Duncan McDonald, dean.
FACULTY: *Profs.:* Thomas H Bivins, Jon Franklin, Charles F Frazer, Arnold H Ismach, Lauren J Kessler (dir., Grad Studies), James B Lemert, Duncan L McDonald (dean), Karl J Nestvold, Deanna M Robinson, Ronald E Sherriffs, James Upshaw, Janet Wasko; *Assoc. Profs.:* Carl R Bybee, Timothy W Gleason (assoc. dean), Gregory J Kerber (asst. dean), Roger M Lavery, Stephen E Ponder, William E Ryan II, H Leslie Steeves, Wayne Wanta, Thomas H Wheeler, William Willingham; *Asst. Profs.:* Karen C Alman, Cynthia-Lou Coleman, Jennifer L King, Debra Merskin, John Russial, Alan G Stavitsky; *Senior Instruc.:* Ann K Maxwell; *Profs. Emer.:* Charles T Duncan, Jack E Ewan, John L Hulteng, Kenneth Metzler, Roy Paul Nelson, R Max Wales, Carl C Webb, Willis Winter.
SEQUENCES: News-Editorial, Advertising, Communication Studies, Electronic Media, Radio-TV News, Public Relations, Magazine.
FACILITIES: AP, AM, FM, CCTV, CN, DR, ETC, VDT.
DEGREES: BA, BS, MA, MS, PhD

Portland, University of
5000 N. Willamette Blvd., Portland, OR 97203-5798; tel (503) 283-7229; fax (503) 283-7399. Department of Communication Studies, Steven A Ward, chair.
Communication Program: BA degree. Offers broad preparation for graduate study or professional careers.
Organizational Communication Program: BS degree. For students seeking careers in organizational communication, public relations or personnel. Offered in cooperation with the School of Business Administration.
Journalism Program: BS degree. Emphasizes preparation for careers in print journalism. Program has a strong liberal arts and professional writing orientation. Internships available.
Masters Programs: MA sequences are offered in Communication. An MS degree in Management Communication is granted in conjunction with the School of Business Administration.

Southern Oregon State College
Ashland, OR 97520; tel (503) 552-6674; fax (503) 552-6429; e-mail pyle@wpo.sosc.osshe.edu Department of Communication/Journalism emphasis. Thomas W Pyle, chair and assoc. prof., Journalism.
Journalism Program: News-editorial, photojournalism, public relations, sports information and secondary teaching concentrations available under Communication: Journalism major; radio/TV announcing and production concentrations available under Communication: Broadcasting major; strong practicum, internship program in all areas.

PENNSYLVANIA

Bloomsburg University
Bloomsburg, PA 17815; tel (717) 389-4633. Department of Mass Communications, 1986. Dana Ulloth, chair.
Mass Communications Program: Mass Communications program centered on Journalism, PR/Advertising, Telecommunications, with support from TV/studio, FM radio station, award winning student newspaper and magazine, weekly TV news program.

Cabrini College
610 King of Prussia Rd., Radnor, PA 19087-3698; tel (610) 902-8360; fax (610) 902-8309; Compuserve 70701,1751; internet zrurk@hslc. org. Department of English and Communications, 1973. SCJ. Jerome Zurek, chair.
FACULTY: *Profs.:* Marice Bezdek, Marilyn L Johnson, Arthur E Young, Jerome Zurek (chair); *Asst. Prof.:* Don Dempsey, Donnalyn Pompper, Jean Ritzke Rutherford, Catherine Yungmann; *Instr.:* Neal Newman; *Lectrs.:* Valerie Ward Hollis, Anne V Iskrant, Melissa Reich, Demetra Takes; *Prof. Emer.:* Carter Craigie.
SEQUENCES: Journalism & Writing, Theater, Television, Radio, Photography, & New Communication Technologies, Professional Communication, Advertising, Public Relations, Business Communication.
FACILITIES: Ada, CATV, CCTV, CN, ComN, ComTV, DR, JM, PRA, VDT, ComR, FM.
DEGREE: BA.

Duquesne University
Pittsburgh, PA 15282; tel (412) 396-6460; fax (412) 396-4792. Department of Communication, 1948. KTA, PRSSA, SPJ. Ronald C Arnett, chair.
FACULTY: *Prof.:* Ronald C Arnett ; *Assoc. Profs.:* Robert V Bellamy, D Clark Edwards, Margaret Patterson, Richard H Thames, Francis Thornton, Paul Traudt; *Asst. Profs.:* Robert E Frank, Geoffrey Gurd, Janie M H Frittz, Maureen Williams; *Instr.:* Tracy Irani; *Prof. Emer.:* Paul Krakowski, Eva Robotti.
SEQUENCES: Major: Communication Studies (Organizational/Professional Communication, Rhetoric, Human Communication); Major: Media Studies; Major: Journalism (News-Editorial, News Production and Management, Advertising, Public Relations, Broadcast Journalism.)
DEGREES: BA, MA.

Elizabethtown College
Elizabethtown, PA 17022; tel (717) 361-1262; fax (717) 361-1180; internet wennberg @vax.etown. edu. Department of Communications, 1975. BEA, IABC, SCJ, NACB, IRTS, IBS, WICI, DSR-TKA. Hans-Erik Wennberg, chair.
FACULTY: *Profs.:* Robert C Moore; *Assoc. Profs.:* Donald E Smith (dir., WWEC Radio), Hans-Erik Wennberg (chair, Dept. of Comm.); *Asst. Profs.:* Leota E Dye (dir., Forensics); *Instrs.:* Tamara L Gillis (dir., student pubs.), Martin Thomson (dir. Television); *Adjunct Instrs.:* Floyd B Lawrence, William M Sloane.
SEQUENCES: Corporate Media, Public Relations, Mass Communication (Radio, TV, Journalism).
FACILITIES: FM, AdA, CATV, CCTV, CN, ComN, DR, JN, JM, PRA, VDT.
DEGREE: BA.

Indiana University of Pennsylvania
Indiana, PA 15705; tel (412) 357-4411; fax (412) 357-7845. Department of Journalism. Patricia I Heilman, chair.
Journalism Program: Practical approach, interdisciplinary program (with internships) for careers in news-editorial and public relations.

La Salle University
1900 Olney Ave., Philadelphia, PA 19141-1199; tel (215) 951-1844; fax (215) 951-5043; e-mail Molyneaux@LaSalle.Edu. Department of Communication, 1985. Gerard F Molyneaux, chair.
Communication Program: The program provides a core of courses then invites students to track in human communication, mass communication, public relations and/or writing.
Masters Degree Program: Professional Communication. Richard J Goedkoop, dir; tel (215) 951-1155.

Lehigh University
Bethlehem, PA 18015; tel (610) 758-4180; fax (610) 758-6198; e-mail SMF6@Lehigh.edu. Department of Journalism and Communication. Sharon Friedman, head.
Journalism Program: Undergraduate degree programs in Newspaper Practice and Science Writing; minors in Public Relations, Journalism, Science Writing and Communication.

Lock Haven University
Lock Haven, PA 17745. Department of Journalism and Mass Communication. Douglas S Campbell, chair.

Lycoming College
Academy St., Williamsport, PA 17701; tel (717) 321-4000, 321-4295; fax (717) 321-4337. Department of Mass Communication, 1976. Brad Nason, chair.
Mass Communication Major: The program emphasizes the liberal arts through an interdisciplinary component and professional tracks in news and persuasive media.

Pennsylvania, University of (Annenberg School for Communication)
Philadelphia, PA 19104-6220; tel (215) 898-7041; fax (215) 898-2024; e-mail admin@asc.upenn.edu. Program in Communication. Kathleen Hall Jamieson, dean.
Communication Program: Graduate program in Communication Codes, Behavior, Systems, Institutions and Policies; Health and Development.
FACILITIES: FM, AdA, CATV, CCTV, CN, ComN, DR, JN, JM, PRA, VDT.
DEGREE: BA, MA, PhD

Pennsylvania State University, The
201 Carnegie Building, University Park, PA 16802; tel (814) 865-6597; fax (814) 863-8044. College of Communications, 1930. AER, KTA, NABJ, SPJ, WICI. Terri Brooks, dean.
FACULTY: *Profs.:* R Thomas Berner (head, Journ.), Terri Brooks (dean), Jeremy Cohen (assoc. dean), Daniel W Pfaff; *Palmer Prof.:* E Stratford Smith, Jorge Schement (assoc. dean), Richard D Taylor; *Assoc. Profs.:* Jim Avery, Richard L Barton, Robert A Baukus, Robert Frieden, Katherine T Frith, R Dorn Hetzel III, Cliff Jernigan, Mary S Mander, John S Nichols, Patrick R Parsons (head, telecomm.), Robert D Richards, Virginia Richardson; *Asst. Profs.:* Maria Cabrera-Baukus, Ronald Bettig, Sandra Ellis, Edward E Faust, Jacqueline Frost, David Goodman, David Griffiths, Jeanne Hall, Ann Jabro, Christopher Jordon, Bette Kauffman, Thomas E Keiter, Jock Lauterer, Ann Marie Major, Marea A Mannion, Anthony Olorunnisola, Michael Podolski, E Deidre Pribram, (head, Film), J Ford Risley, Trina Sego, Shari Roberts, Subir Sengupta, Shyam S Sethuraman, Susan M Strohm, Richard Wexler, Russell Williams; *Instr.:* Krishna Kishorde.
SEQUENCES: Advertising, Film and Video, Journalism, Media Studies, Telecommunications.
FACILITIES: AP, FM, DR, JM, CCTV, VDT.
DEGREES: BA, MA, MJ, MFA, PhD.

Pittsburgh, University of
526 Cathedral of Learning, Pittsburgh, PA 15260; tel (412) 624-6631; fax (412) 624-6639; e-mail patsy1@pitt.edu Department of English, Non-Fiction Writing (newspaper or magazine). Patsy Sims, Coordinator
Journalism Program: Undergraduate writing major in Newspaper and Magazine tracts, MFA in Creative Non-Fiction. Publish *Creative Nonfiction* Journal, Gut Kind, editor.

Point Park College
Pittsburgh, PA 15222-1984; tel (412) 392-4730; fax (412) 391-1980. Department of Journalism and Communications, 1960. Ad Club, SPJ, PRSSA,
NPPA, CSB (College Students in Brdct. – AWRT affiliation), TV Club. Nancy C Jones, chair.
FACULTY: *Profs.:* David M Jones, Nancy C Jones (dir., grad. prog.), Joan Williams-Givliani; *Assoc. Prof.:* Helen Fallon; *Asst. Profs.:* Kathleen Donnelly, David J Fabilli, John Leahey; *Instrs.:* Joseph Knupsky, Mark Vehec; *Visiting Prof.:* Robert O'Gara; *Adjunct Profs.:* Marvin Jacobson, Steven Segal, Susan Ryberg, Michael Walsh.
SEQUENCES: Advertising, Broadcasting (radio &TV), Print, Public Relations, Photojournalism.
FACILITIES: AdA, CCTV, CN, ComN, ComTV, DR, FM, JM, JN, PRA, UPI, VDT.
DEGREES: AA, BA, MA.

Shippensburg University
Shippensburg, PA 17257; tel (717) 532-1521. Communications/Journalism Department. C Lynne Nash, chair.
FACULTY: *Profs.:* John D Magaro, Audun J Olsen; *Assoc. Profs.:* Jeffrey T Bitzer, Richard W. Gibbs, Albert Mason, C Lynne Nash, Stephen Shenton; *Asst. Profs.:* Edward Carlin, Pat Waltermyer, Richard Warner.
SEQUENCES: News Editorial, Public Relations, Radio/Television.
FACILITIES: DR, CCTV, CN, ComN, PRA, VDT, AM/FM, AP.
DEGREES: BA in Communications/Journalism, MS in Communication Studies.

Temple University
Philadelphia, PA 19122; tel (215) 204-7433; fax (215) 204-1974; internet womack@astro.ocis. temple.edu. Department of Journalism, Public Relations & Advertising, 1927. KTA, PRSSA, SPJ, WICI. David L Womack, chair.
FACULTY: *Profs.:* Thomas Eveslage, James Marra (assoc. chair and dir. of special projects), Eugene Shaw, James Shea, Edward Trayes (dir., Photography sequence), Hiley Ward, David Womack (chair); *Assoc. Profs.:* Patricia Bradley, Jean Brodey, William Donnelly, Flordelindo Marquez (dir., Adv. sequence), Priscilla Murphy (dir., PR sequence), Kathryn News (dir., Mag. sequence); *Asst. Profs.:* Michael Maynard, Karen Turner; *Academic Professionals:* John Center, Robert Roberts, Libby Rosof; *Lectrs.:* William Alnor, Pete Boal, Diane Bones, Yvonne Dennis, Nancy Eshelman, Gerald Etter, Vincent Hill, Michael Incitti, Lauren Lipton, Paul Maryniak, Edward McFall, Noel Miles, Charles Newman, Rusty Pray, Carol Ritch, Howard Shapiro, Elmer Smith, Melvin Sussman, Ralph Vigoda.
SEQUENCES: Advertising, Broadcast Journalism, Magazine, Mass Media Photography, News-Editorial, Public Relations.
FACILITIES: AP, FM, CN, JM, DR, VDT, Dept. Library, AdA.
DEGREES: BA, MA, MJ, PhD.

Ursinus College
Collegeville PA 19426-1000; tel (610) 409-3603. Department of Communication Arts., 1987. Jay K Miller, chair.
Communication Program: established on liberal arts principles, critical thinking, and ethics, the communication arts program is designed to provide students with a comprehensive understanding of the communication processes in our contemporary society. Students examine communication concepts and apply communication principles in public, business, personal, and artistic contexts. Three tracks are available: (1) rhetorical/human, (2) mass, and (3) theatre.

RHODE ISLAND

Rhode Island, University of
Kingston, RI 02881; tel (401) 792-2195, 792-2196; fax (401) 792-4450; e-mail bfluebke@uriacc.uri. edu. Department of Journalism, 1960. RTNDA, SPJ. Barbara F Luebke, chair.
FACULTY: *Prof.:* Barbara F Luebke; *Assoc. Profs.:* Linda Levin, Tony Silvia; *Asst. Prof.:* David deHoyos.
SEQUENCES: News-Editorial, Broadcast Journalism, Public Relations.
FACILITIES: VDT, AM, FM, CCTV, CN, ComN, DR, ComR, ComTV, PRA.
DEGREE: BA.

SOUTH CAROLINA

Benedict College
Columbia, SC 29204; tel (803) 253-5256. Media Arts Department. Scott Blanks, acting chair.
Media Arts Program: Offers specialized training in Broadcasting, News Editorial and Public Communications/Marketing.

College of Charleston
66 George St., Charleston, SC 29424-0001; tel (803) 953-5664. Department English-Communication. 1994.
Communication Program: The bachelor of arts degree in communication has three concentrations: media studies (focus on newspaper, radio and television reporting,); corporate communication (public relations and advertising); and communication studies (speech and rhetorical studies).
DEGREES: BA

South Carolina, University of
Columbia, SC 29208; tel (803) 777-4102 (information), 777-5166 (grad. program), 777-6973 (continuing educ.), 777-8528 (undergrad. program), 777-4105 (dean's office); fax (803) 777-4103. College of Journalism and Mass Communications, 1923. AAF, AER, KTA, NPPA, PRSSA, SPJ. Judy VanSlyke Turk, dean.
FACULTY: *Profs.:* Ronald T Farrar, (assoc. dean, grad. studies and research), A Jerome Jewler, Patricia G McNeely (assoc. dean, continuing educ. and support service), Henry T Price (assoc. dean, undergrad. studies), M Kent Sidel (dir., develop.), Lowndes F Stephens, Judy VanSlyke Turk (dean), Richard M Uray; *Assoc. Profs.:* Lewis G Brierley, Mary P Caldwell, Kenneth Campbell, Erik L Collins, Elizabeth B Dickey, Keith Kenney, Bruce E Konkle, Jarvis H Latham, John Lopiccolo, (dir., electronic and print journ. seq.), Ralph T Morgan, Jon P Wardrip, (dir., advtg./PR seq.); *Asst. Profs.:* Bonnie Drewniany, Sonya F Duhé, Alan Fried, Van Kornegay, David Thompson, Lauren R Tucker, Ernest Wiggins, Lynn Zoch; *Profs. Deans Emer.:* Albert T Scroggins, Joseph W Shoquist; *Profs. Emer.:* Perry Ashley, Lloyd Brown, Lee Dudek, William Goodrich, Bryce Rucker.
SEQUENCES: Advertising/Public Relations, Electronic and Print Journalism.
FACILITIES: AP, AM, FM, AdA, CCTV, DR, ETV, JN, VDT.
DEGREES: BA, MA, MMC, PhD.

Winthrop University
Rock Hill, SC 29733-0001; tel (803) 323-2121; fax (803) 323-2464; internet mass-comm@ winthrop.edu. Department of Mass Communication, 1925. AER, BEA, KTA, SCJ, SPJ, WICI. J. William Click, chair.
FACULTY: *Profs.:* J William Click (chair), William A Fisher (part-time); *Assoc. Profs.:* Stewart Haas, Lawrence C Timbs, Jr.; *Asst. Profs.:* Haney Howell, Robert A Pyle, Marilyn S Sarow.
SEQUENCES: Broadcasting, Journalism.
FACILITIES: CCTV, CN, VDT.
DEGREE: BA.

SOUTH DAKOTA

Black Hills State University
Spearfish, SD 57783; tel (605) 642-6420, 642-6861; fax (605) 642-6214. College of Arts and Humanities. Richard Boyd, dean.
Journalism Program: Offers course work in print and broadcast journalism. Four-year undergraduate degree program with emphasis on mass communications. Also 2-year program in radio and television operations.

Mount Marty College
Yankton, SD 57078; tel (605) 668-1506. Mass Communications Program. Jerry W Wilson, dir.
Mass Communications Program: We offer the BA in Mass Communications with three emphases: Print Journalism, Broadcasting, and Advertising/Public Relations. Liberal Arts background and extensive applied experience instill comprehensive mass communications skills.

South Dakota, University of
414 E. Clark St., Vermillion, SD 57069; tel (605) 677-5477; fax (605) 677-5073. Department of Mass Communication, 1913. AAF, PRSSA. Bruce L Smith, chair.
PROGRAMS: Advertising, Broadcast Journalism and Print Journalism, Broadcast Production, Corporate Communications, Public Relations, Desktop Publishing.
DEGREES: BA, BS, MA.

South Dakota State University
Brookings, SD 57007-0596; tel (605) 688-4171; fax (605) 688-4271. Department of Journalism and Mass Communication, 1924. AAF, ACT, KTA, SPJ. Richard W Lee, head.
FACULTY: *Prof.:* Richard W Lee; *Assoc. Prof.:* Mary J Perpich, Lyle D Olson; *Asst. Profs.:* Karen L Buckley, John E Getz, Doris J Giago, Roxanne Neuberger Lucchesi, James L Paulson; *Instr.:* Frank A Klock; *Part-Time Instrs.:* Gene Chamberlin, James Smorada, Elizabeth Williams.
SEQUENCES: News-Editorial, Advertising, Broadcast Journalism, Agricultural Journalism.
FACILITIES: AP, CCTV, CN, ComN, ComR, DR, ETV, JN, VDT.
DEGREES: BS, BA, MS.

TENNESSEE

Austin Peay State University
Clarksville, TN 37044; tel (615) 648-7378; fax (615) 648-5992; e-mail kanervoe@lynx.apsu.edu. Department of Speech, Communication and Theatre, 1986. Ellen Kanervo, chair.
FACULTY: *Profs.:* Ellen Kanervo (dept. chair), Paul Shaffer; *Assoc. Profs.:* Mike Gotcher, David von Palko; *Asst. Profs.:* Margaret Duffy, Yvonne Prather, Ted Jones; *Instr.:* Patricia Ferrier.
SEQUENCES: Public Relations, Print Journalism, Radio-TV.
FACILITIES: AM, CN, TV studio, campus magazine.
DEGREES: BA, BS, MA.

Christian Brothers University
Memphis, TN 38104; tel (901) 722-0386; fax (901) 722-0494. Journalism Option (in Department of Communication and Performing Arts), 1986. Dr. Joseph Ajami, head.
FACULTY: *Assoc. Prof.:* Susan-Lynn Johns (coord., Performing Arts option); *Asst. Profs.:* Joseph Ajami (chair, Dept. of Comm. and Performing Arts), John Harwick, Matthew Szatkowski; *Instrs.:* Lisa Coleman, Kevin Griffin, Anthony Williams.
FACILITIES: AdA, CN, ComN, ComTV, DR, VDT.
DEGREE: BA.

East Tennessee State University
Johnson City, TN 37614; tel (615) 929-4308; e-mail Robertsc@ETSU.EAST-TENN-St.Edu Department of Communication, 1968. Charles Roberts, chair.
Communication Program: The Department of Communication has these objectives: to provide professional preparation for persons seeking careers in communication, to provide leadership for professionals now engaged in the practice of communication, to provide professional programs and supporting course work for students completing programs in other fields, and to increase public understanding of the value of freedom of communication in a democratic society. The Department of Communication offers a BS/BA with a major in mass communications with four division options — advertising, broadcasting (sequences in management, news and production/performance), journalism and public relations.

Memphis, University of
Memphis, TN 38152; tel (901) 678-2401; fax (901) 678-4287; internet dlattimore@cc.memphis. edu. Journalism Department, 1956. AAF, KTA, NABJ, PRSSA, SPJ. Dan Lattimore, chair.
FACULTY: *Profs.:* E W "Bill" Brody, Dan Lattimore, John Lee (head, News-Ed sequence), Jim Willis (chair of excellence); *Assoc. Profs.:* Rick Fischer (head, public relations), Elinor Grusin (head news ed., & grad. coord.), Jim Redmond, (head, Brdct. News), Ronald Spielberger (head, Adv. sequence), Art Terry, Sandra Utt; *Asst. Profs.:* David Arant, Cynthia Hopson, Candy Justice; *Instr.:* Kathy Wickham; *Adjunct Fac.:* Christy Bailey Byars, Robert Carey, Richard Jensen, Guy Reel, Sonja Whiteman, Jerome Wright, Emily Yellin; *Profs. Emer.:* John DeMott, Herbert Williams.
SEQUENCES: Advertising, Broadcast News, News-Editorial, Public Relations.
FACILITIES: FM, AdA, CATV, CN, ComN, ComR, ComTV, DR, ETV, JN, VDT, PRA.
DEGREES: BA, MA.

Middle Tennessee State University
Murfreesboro, TN 37132; tel (615) 898-2813; fax (615) 898-5682; internet sneely@al.mtsu.edu. College of Mass Communication, 1972. AAF, AER, KTA, NABJ, PRSSA, SPJ. Deryl R Leaming, dean.
FACULTY: *Profs.:* Richard Barnet (chair, Recording Industry Mgmt.), David Eason (dir. grad. studies), Glenn Himebaugh, Geoffrey Hull, Edward M Kimbrell, Deryl R Leaming, Alex Nagy, Elliott Pood, Robert O Wyatt (dir., Research Institute); *Assoc. Profs.:* Edward C Applegate, David P Badger, Marc Barr, Thomas R Berg, Larry Burriss, Christian Haseleu, John

Hill, Tom Jimison, E Albert Moffett, James R Norton III, Dennis J Oneal, Donald Parente, Momo Rogers Sr., Jan A Quarles (chair, journalism), Sharon Smith, Robert Spires, Robert S Wood, Ray Wong; *Asst. Profs.:* Julie Andsager, John Bodle, Robert Garfrerick, Christopher R Harris, Rush Hicks, Ann Haugland, Rush Hicks, Thomas Hutchison, Coreen D Jackson, Beverly Keel, Cosette Kennedy, Don McComb, Douglas Mitchell, Mary Lynn Nichols, (interim chair, Radio-TV/Photography), Matthew O'Brien, Daniel P Pfeifer, Jim Piekarski, Sharon Smith, Marilyn Wood; *Instrs.:* Jennifer Bailey, Jacqueline Heigle, Michael Johnson; *Adjunct Instrs.:* Tracy Blair, James Brown, A J Buse, John Egly, Walt Gunster, Wayne Halper, Will Higgins, Chris Hughes,Shawn Jacobs, Eric Leach, Kelly Lockhart, Lisa Marchesoni, Randy O'Brien, Craig Pulley, Denise Parker, Tony Stinnett, Mike West, William Williams, Wayne Wood; *Audio Engineers:* Dale Brown, Alton Dellinger; *WMOT:* Gary Brown, John Egly, John High, Greg Lee Hunt, Shawn Jacobs, Laura McComb, Randy O'Brien; *Video Maint. Engineers:* Raymond Pegg, Marc Parrish.
DEPARTMENTS: Journ., Radio-TV/Photography, Recording Industry Mgmt., Research Inst.
FACILITIES: AP, FM, CATV, CN, CNN, ComR, DR. VDT, Digital Imaging Lab, Mobile Production Lab, MIDI Lab, Electronic News Room.
DEGREES: BS, MS.

Southern College of Seventh-day Adventists
Collegedale, TN 37315-0370; tel (615) 238-2730; fax (615) 238-3001. Department of Journalism and Communication, 1959. R Lynn Sauls, chair.
Journalism Program: Offers BA degrees in News Editorial, Broadcast Journalism and Public Relations. Facilities include FM, CN, ComN, ComTV, DR, PRA, VDT.

Tennessee, University of
Knoxville, TN 37996-0332; tel (615) 974-3031; fax (615) 974-3896; internet teeter@utkvx.utk. edu. College of Communications, 1969; School of Journalism, 1947. ABC, AAF, AERho, KTA, PRSSA, SPJ. Dwight L Teeter Jr, dean.
FACULTY: *Profs.:* Paul G Ashdown, Dorothy A Bowles, James A Crook (dir., School of Jour.), Charles E Caudill, George A Everett, Herbert H Howard (assoc. dean, Grad. Studies), Mark E Littmann (Chair of Excellence-Jour.), M Mark Miller, Barbara A Moore (acting head, Brdct.), Michael W Singletary, Norman R Swan, Ronald Taylor (head, Adv.), Dhyana Ziegler; *Assoc. Profs.:* Robert B Heller, Mariea G Hoy, Roxanne Hovland (acting assoc. dean, Undergrad. Studies), Susan M Lucarelli, Jerry L Morrow; *Asst. Profs.:* Benjamin J Bates, Daniel J Foley, Eric Haley, Evelyn K Jackson, Candace L White, Jeffrey S Wilkinson; *Instrs.:* Bonnie L Hufford Margaret A Morrison; *Grad. Teaching Assocs.:* Elizabeth Atwood-Gailey, Dwight J Brady, Bryan E Denham, Kenneth C Killebrew, John J Lombardi, Kim E Sheehan, Patrick S Sullivan, James G Thornton, M Carol Zuegner; *Part-time Instrs.:* Samuel J Bass, Jeffrey D Gary, Edgar H Miller, Shyrl L Plum, Wanda H Richart, Susan R Siler, Larry K Smith, John L Williams; *Advising Coord.:* Gail Palmer; *Profs. Emer.:* June N Adamson, Dozier C Cade, Jack B Haskins, Darrel W Holt, Richard Joel, John M Lain, Frank B Thornburg, Willis C Tucker; *Assoc. Prof. Emer.:* DeForrest Jackson; *Dean Emer.:* Kelly Leiter.
SEQUENCES: Advertising, Broadcasting, Journalism (News-Editorial and Public Relations).
FACILITIES: AM, FM, AdA, CATV, CN, ComN, ComR, ComTV, DR, ETV, JM, PRA, VDT.
DEGREES: BS, MS, PhD in Communications.

Tennessee at Chattanooga, University of
Chattanooga, TN 37403-2598; tel (615) 755-4400; fax (615) 755-4695; internet krushing@utcvm. utc.edu; Communication Department, 1978. SPJ, BEA, PRSSA, AAF, S Kittrell Rushing, head.
FACULTY: *Profs.:* Peter K Pringle (Luther Masingill Professor), David B Sachsman (West Chair of Excellence in Comm.); *Assoc. Prof.:* Betsy B Alderman (UC Foundation Professor), S Kittrell Rushing; *Asst. Profs.:* Sarah M Regan, Joseph V Trahan III (APR); *Lectr.:* Stephynie Chapman; *Part-Time Instrs.:* Dan Alderman, Mark Kennedy, John McCormack, (dir., WUTC/ Jazz 88), Arlene Strickland, Mike Wadel.
SEQUENCES: Communication.
FACILITIES: FM, AdA, CCTV, CN, ComN, PRA, VDT, AP, CATV.
DEGREE: BA.

Tennessee at Martin, University of
Martin, TN 38238; tel (901) 587-7550; fax (901) 587-7205. Department of Communications, 1971. Newspaper, SPJ, PRSSA, Broadcasting Guild, yearbook. Ralph Donald, chair.
FACULTY: *Profs.:* Ralph Donald (chair), Dorotha Norton, Gary Steinke; *Asst. Profs.:* Paul Anderson, Rustin Greene, Robert Nanney, Jerald Ogg. *Instrs.:* Teresa Collard, Carla Gesell, Barbara Malinauskas.
SEQUENCES: Broadcasting, News Editorial, PR.
FACILITIES: AM/FM, DR, JN, CableTV, TV, AP, VDT, Audio/Video editing lab.
DEGREES: BA, BS.

Tennessee Technological University
Cookeville, TN 38505; tel (615) 372-3060; fax (615) 372-6138. Journalism Curriculum. Earl Hutchison, journ. prof.
Journalism Program: News-editorial work stressed along with experience on the campus newspaper, radio and public TV station. BS degree.

TEXAS

Abilene Christian University
Abilene, TX 79699; tel (915) 674-2298; fax (915) 674-2417; e-mail cmarler@acuvax. acu.edu Journalism and Mass Communication Department, 1969. AAF, AER, KTA, PRSSA, SPJ. Charles H Marler, chair.
FACULTY: *Profs.:* Larry Bradshaw (dir., Telecomm.), Charles H Marler, Jeff Warr (dir., Adv.); *Assoc. Prof.:* Cheryl Bacon (dir., PR); *Asst. Profs.:* , Merle "Dutch" Hoggatt, Keith McMillin (dir., Photojour.), Merlin Mann (dir., News-Ed).
SEQUENCES: Advertising, Public Relations, Journalism, News-Editorial, Broadcast Journalism, Broadcast Production, Corporate Video, Religious Journalism, Photojournalism.
FACILITIES: AP, AM/FM, AdA, CATV, ComN, ComTV, DR, ETV, JN, PRA, VDT, Lexis/Nexis.
DEGREES: BS, MA.

Angelo State University
San Angelo, TX 76909; tel (915) 942-2031. Department of Communications, Drama and Journalism, 1965. AAF, TIPA, TJEC. Jack C Eli, prof. and head.
Journalism Program: Offers courses in news editorial, advertising/public relations and broadcasting.

Angelo State University
San Angelo, TX 76909; tel (915) 942-2031. Department of Communications, Drama and Journalism, 1965. AAF, TIPA, TJEC. Jack C Eli, prof. and head.
Journalism Program: Offers courses in news editorial, advertising/public relations and broadcasting.

Baylor University
Waco, TX 76798; tel (817) 755-3261; fax (817) 755-1321. Department of Journalism, 1927. PRSSA, SPJ. Michael E Bishop, chair.
FACULTY: *Profs.:* Michael Bishop, Sara Stone; *Assoc. Prof.:* Douglas Ferdon; *Asst. Profs.:* Clark Baker, Kyle Cole, Lianne Fridriksson (dir., Grad. Studies); *Instrs.:* Judy Jopling, Keith Randall, John Tisdale; *Prof. Emer.:* Basil Raffety.
SEQUENCES: News-Editorial, Public Relations, International Journalism, Photojournalism.
FACILITIES: AP, FM, DR, JM, JN, PRA, VDT, CCTV.
DEGREES: BA, MA, MIJ.

East Texas State University
Commerce, TX 75429-4104; tel (903) 886-5239, 886-5229; fax (903) 886-5230. Journalism and Printing Department, 1948. Junior Litho Club.
FACULTY: *Prof.:* Lamar W Bridges; *Assoc. Prof.:* Hendrik Overduin (head); *Instrs.:* Lyndal Burnett, Steve Davis, Fred Stewart, Lonnie Visage; *Profs. Emer.:* W J "Jack" Bell, Otha C Spencer.
SEQUENCES: Journalism (majors in News/Ed., Adv./PR, Photojournalism, Agriculture/Journalism and Teaching emphases), Printing.
FACILITIES: FM, ComN, DR, JM, JN, Adlab, Photo Studios, Instructional Printing Facilities.
DEGREES: BA, BS, MA, MS.

Hardin-Simmons University
Abilene, TX 79698; tel (915) 670-1409. Dept. of Communication. Mary Evelyn Collins, chair.
Journalism Program: Forty-eight-hour composite in Public Communication and 60-hour PR program.

Houston, University of
Houston, TX 77204-3786; tel (713) 743-3002; fax (713) 743-5384, 743-2876; e-mail BBrown@UH.EDU. (Journalism Program, 1963), School of Communication, 1978. AAF, BEA, NABJ, PRSSA, SPJ, SMPTE, ITVA, UFVA, WICI. Robert B Musburger, dir., Les Switzer, area head.
FACULTY: *Profs:* Kenneth Harwood, William Hawes, Robert Heath (dir., grad studies), Garth Jowett, William A Linsley, Mike Ryan, Kenneth R M Short (area head RTV), Ted Stanton, Les Switzer (area head JOUR), Campbell Titchener; *Assoc. Profs.:* William Douglas, Larry Judd, Robert Musburger (dir.); *Asst. Profs.:* Mary Banski, Yvonne Becerra, Karen Kay Carter, David Donnelly, Martha Haun (area head SPCM), Moya Luckett, Richard Morgan, Jay Mower, Beth Olson, Fred Schiff; *Lectrs.:* Richard Carson, Ann Economou-Clarke, Tony Fuller, Janet Goforth, Kathy Hargrave, Jan Lockett, Nancy Mathis, Philip Morabito, Juan Palomo.
SEQUENCES: Advertising, Corporate/Organizational Communications, Editorial, Media Production, Public Relations, Telecommunications.
FACILITIES: FM, TV, CCTV, CN, ComN, ComTV, DR, ETV.
DEGREES: BA, MA.

Houston Baptist University
Houston, TX 77074-3298; tel (713) 995-3337. Department of Communications, 1979. James S Taylor, chair.
FACULTY: *Prof.:* James S Taylor (chair); *Asst. Prof.:* Alice Rowlands (Adviser, *Collegian*); *Instrs.:* Clay Porter (Program Manager, Instructional TV), Isaac Simpson (Operations Manager, Instructional TV); *Adjunct Profs.:* Janice Gibson, Paula Hutchinson, Dan O'Rourke, Tom Overton.
SEQUENCES: Newswriting/reporting, TV production, advertising/PR, photojournalism.
FACILITIES: TV studio, Newspaper lab, DR.
DEGREES: BA, BS.

Lamar University-Beaumont
PO Box 10050, Beaumont, TX 77710; tel (409) 880-8153. Dept. of Communication. Patrick Harrigan, director of communication.
Communication Program: The department offers a broad-based major in communication with concentrations in coporate communication studies, media/broadcast studies and journalism studies.
DEGREES: BS.

Midwestern State University
Wichita Falls, TX 76308; tel (817) 689-4243; fax (817) 689-4511. Mass Communications Program, 1985. BEA, TIPA. Carla P Bennett, coord.
FACULTY: *Prof.:* June Kable (emer.), *Assoc. Prof.:* Dencil R Taylor; *Asst. Profs.:* Carla P Bennett (coord.), Pamela Cope, James Sernoe, Brian Thornton.
FACILITIES: TV studios, visual arts lab, Macintosh labs.
DEGREE: BA.

North Texas, University of
Denton, TX 76201; tel (817) 565-2205; fax (817) 565-4659. Department of Journalism, 1945. AAF, KTA, NABJ, NAHJ, PRSSA, SPJ, WICI. Richard Wells, chair.
FACULTY: *Profs.:* James L Rogers Jr., Reg Westmoreland; *Assoc. Profs.:* Jim Albright, Roy K Busby, Ernestine Farr (coord., Adv. sequence), Tae Guk Kim, Mitchell Land, Richard Wells; *Asst. Profs.:* Meta G Carstarphen (coord. Public Relations sequence), Smith Kiker, J Roy Moses, Bradley Owens, Susan Zavoina (coord., Photojour. sequence); Jour. in Residence: Keith Shelton (coord. News-Editorial sequence); *Lectrs.:* Bridget Barry, Krispen Spencer, Marshall Surratt, Susan Woodley.
SEQUENCES: News Writing-Editorial, Advertising, Public Relations, Photojournalism, Broadcast News, Business Journalism, Teaching.
FACILITIES: AP, DR, JM, JN, FM, VDT, PRA, AdA.
DEGREES: BA, BS, MA, MJ.

Prairie View A&M University
PO Box 0156, Prairie View, TX 77446-0156; tel (409) 857-2229, 857-4511; fax (409) 857-2729. Department of Communications, 1974. ACA, NAB, NABJ, AAF, SCA, SPJ, SSCA, TSCA. Millard F Eiland, head.
Journalism Program: The department, a part of the College of Arts and Sciences, includes major options in Journalism, Radio-TV, Speech Communication and Communications (a combination of courses in the other three options). The degree offered is the BA. The department operates KPVU-FM, an educational broadcast facility, has four professional-quality television studios and was given status as an NPR affiliate.

Sam Houston State University
Huntsville, TX 77341; tel (409) 294-1497; fax (409) 294-3996. Department of Public Communication. Journalism Program (Division of Public Communication) Ruth M Pate, co-ordinator.
Journalism Program: Offers specialties in news/editorial, advertising, public relations.

Southern Methodist University
Dallas, TX 75275; tel (214) 768-3607; fax (214) 768-2784. Center for Communication Arts, 1982. AAF, AER, IABC, KTA, Press Club of Dallas, PRSSA, SPJ, WICI, Zeta Phi Eta. John Gartley, dir.

Southwest Texas State University
San Marcos, TX 78666; tel (512) 245-2656; fax (512) 245-3708. Department of Journalism. Roger Bennett, chair.
Journalism Program: Seven concentrations. Laboratory newspaper, magazine, yearbook, and radio station. Television facilities and strong internships available.

Stephen F. Austin State University
Nacogdoches, TX 75962; tel (409) 568-4001; fax (409) 568-1331; e-mail RamseyRT@Titan. SFASU.EDU Department of Communication. Robert Ramsey, chair.
Journalism Program: Broadcasting and journalism, with journalism courses grouped into news-editorial, photojournalism, advertising, and public relations emphases (also has a speech division).

Texas A&I University
Kingsville, TX 78363; tel (512) 595-3499; fax (512) 595-3500. Department of Communications and Theatre Arts. J R Jenson, head.
Journalism Program: SWECJMC, UIL, TIPA. BA in Communication; Journalism sequences: News-Ed and Radio-TV. Minor at master's level.

Texas A&M University
College Station, TX 77843-4111; tel (409) 845-4649; fax (409) 845-5408; internet c-self@acs. tamu.edu; Department of Journalism, 1948. ACT, AAF, BEA, IABC, KTA, NABJ, NAHJ, PRSSA, RTNDA, SPJ, WICI, SWECJMC. Charles C Self, head.
FACULTY: *Profs.:* Charles C Self, Douglas P Starr; *Assoc. Profs.:* Howard F Eilers, Barbara Gastel (asst. head, grad. coord.), Marilyn Kern-Foxworth, Susanna Hornig Priest, Edward J Smith, Don Tomlinson, Lynne Masel Walters; *Asst. Profs.:* Fred Blevens, Deborah Dunsford, Richard Schaefer, Richard Shafer; *Lectrs.:* Gene Charleton, John Mark Dempsey, Pamela Gerhardt, Donna Hajash, Rodger Lewis, Rae-Lynn Mitchell, Rodney Rather, Ed Walraven, Robert Wegener, Rod Zent.
SEQUENCES: Journalism, Agricultural Journalism, Science & Technology Journalism.
FACILITIES: AP, CCTV, CN, ComN, DR, ETV, FM, JN, JM, NYIS, PRA, VDT.
DEGREES: BA, BS, BS in Agricultural Journalism, MS in Science & Technology Journalism.

Texas at Arlington, University of
Arlington, TX 76019; tel (817) 273-2163; fax (817) 273-2857. Department of Communication, 1972. AAF, IABC, KTA, PRSSA, SPJ, WICI. Earl R Andresen, chair.
FACULTY: *Prof.:* Earl R Andresen; *Assoc. Profs.:* Nita Cox, Larry Elwell, Roy Hamric, Tom Ingram, Karin McCallum, George Rhoades, Chapin Ross, William J Stone Jr.; *Asst. Profs.:* Carroll Hickey, Charla Markham-Shaw, Robert Pennington, Tom Shuford, Marilyn Woods; *Lectrs:* Clint Bourland, Barbara Hickey, Sandra Idziak, Dawn Jacobs, D J Janes, Leiland Jaynes, Marjorie Lewis, Susan Linden, J D Mosley, Diona Nace, Rita Parson, Austin Robinson, Laura Sanders, Broc Sears, Karin Schwanbeck, Allen Sheffield, Margaret Smith, Charlotte Sullivan, Juandalyn Taylor; *Adjunct Prof.:* William McCorkle; *Adjunct Assoc. Prof.:* Tom Doron; *Adjunct Asst. Profs.:* Marian Haber, Alex Mwakikoti, Susan Rogers.
SEQUENCES: Advertising, News-Editorial, Broadcast, News and Public Affairs, Photojournalism, Public Relations and Comm. Theory.
FACILITIES: AdA, AP, CATV, ComN, ComR, ComTV, DN, DR, PRA, VDT.
DEGREE: BA.

Texas at Austin, University of
Austin, TX 78712. Tel. (512) 471-1845; fax (512) 471-7979; internet jdept@www. utexas.edu; Department of Journalism, 1914. KTA, PRSSA, SPJ, WICI. Russell G Todd, chair.
FACULTY: *Profs.:* Wayne A Danielson, Frank Kalupa, William Korbus (head, mag.), Maxwell E McCombs, Marvin Olasky, J Michael Quinn, Stephen D Reese (assoc. chair and grad. adviser), James W Tankard Jr., Russell G Todd (head, media studies and media skills), D Charles Whitney; *Assoc. Profs.:* Gene Burd, Mercedes L deUriarte, Dominic Lasorsa, Paula Poindexter, Werner J Severin, Gale F Wiley (acting head,

broadcast); *Asst. Profs.:* Ron Anderson (head, PR), Gigi Durham, Robert Jensen, Julianne Newton (head, photojour.), Marilyn Schultz, George Sylvie; *Asst. Instrs.:* Jane Ballinger, John Beatty, Bob Buckalew, Lori Eason, Pamela McQuesten, Randy Sumpter, Chris Williams; *Sr. Lect.:* Dave Garlock, Doris Schleuse, S Griffin Singer (head, news and public affairs); *Lectrs.:* Bob Buckalew, Frank Durham, Chuck Halloran, Rick Williams, Terry Wilson; *Profs. Emer.:* Al Anderson, Alan Scott, Ernest Sharpe.
SEQUENCE: Broadcast News, Magazine Journalism, News and Public Affairs Reporting, PR, Photojournalism, Media Skills, Media Studies.
FACILITIES: AP, AM, CCTV, CN, ComN, ComR, ComTV, DR, ETV, FM, JM, NYTS, PRA.
DEGREES: BJ, MA, PhD.

Texas at El Paso, University of
El Paso, TX 79968; tel (915) 747-5129; fax (915) 747-5641. Department of Communication. Henry Ingle, chair.
FACULTY: *Prof.:* Ray Small, Henry Ingle; *Assoc. Profs.:* Samuel C Riccillo, Barthy Byrd; *Asst. Profs.:* Jim Adams, Eduardo Barrera, Ronald Bassett, Connie Kubo Della-Piana, Louis Falk, Robert Jones, Patricia Lawrence, Gerard Power, Mary C Trejo; *Lectrs.:* Patrisia Gonzales; *Academic Student Advising:* Ofelia Aguilar; *Student Internship Coord.:* Beverly Linker.
SEQUENCES: Communication; Electronic Media; Media Analysis & Advertising; Print Media; Public Relations & Organizational Communication.
FACILITIES: AdA, AM, CN, DR, FM, JM, PRA, UPI, VDT.
DEGREES: BA, MA in Communication.

Texas Christian University
Fort Worth, TX 76129; tel (817) 921-7425; fax (817) 921-7133; internet babbili@gamuna.is.tcu. edu; Department of Journalism, 1927. AAF, IABC, KTA, NABJ, PRSSA, SPJ, WICI. Anantha S Babbili, chair.
FACULTY: *Prof.:* Douglas Ann Newsom; *Assoc. Profs.:* Anantha Babbili, (chair), Gerald L Grotta, Frederick John Raskopf, Tommy Thomason (cood., media studies); *Asst. Profs.:* Larry Lauer, Maggie Thomas; *Instrs..:* Mercedes Olivera, Eva Rumpf; *Adjunct Fac.:* Libby Afflerbach, Doug Clarke, Tommy Denton, Carol Glover, Jeff Guinn, Gary Kromer, Joe Norton, James Peipert, Katherine Roberts, Jim Peipert, Eugenia Trinkle, Thomas Williams, Brian Wilson.
SEQUENCES: News-Editorial (BA); News-Editorial, Broadcast Journalism, PR/Advertising (BS); Teaching Certification; Media Studies (MS).
FACILITIES: AP, AM, FM, Ad/PR A, ComN, DR, JM, JN, VDT, PhotoLab.
DEGREES: BA, BS, MS (Media Studies).

Texas Lutheran College
Seguin, TX 78155; tel (210) 372-8000; fax (210) 372-8096. Department of Communication Arts and Theatre-Areas of Speech; Media Studies; Theatre. Donna L Clevinger, dept. chair.
Media Program: Mixed with radio, TV, film and general media offerings. Specific journalism courses focus on history, methods and mass communication areas.

Texas-Pan American, University of
1201 University Dr., Edinburg, TX 78539-2999; tel (512) 381-3583. Communications Department. Bob Rollins, coord.
Journalism Programs: Advertising, Broadcast Journalism, Print Journalism, Public Relations.

Texas of The Permian Basin, University of
Odessa, TX 79762; tel (915) 552-2323; fax (915) 552-2374. Faculty of Communication. Robert N Rothstein, chair.
Journalism Program: Emphasizes preparation for professional work in radio, TV or print media.

Texas Southern University
Houston, TX 77004; tel (713) 527-7360. School of Communications, 1947. Clarice P Lowe, chair.
Journalism Program: The program offers bachelor's and master's degrees with concentrations in News/Editorial, Advertising/PR and Broadcast Journ.

Texas Tech University
Lubbock, TX 79409-3082; tel (806) 742-3385; fax (806) 742-1085. School of Mass Communications, Main and Broadway. PO Box 43082. AAF, AER, KTA, PRSSA, SPJ, TABJ, WICI. Roger C. Saathoff, dir.
FACULTY: *Profs.:* Jerry C Hudson; *Assoc. Profs.:* William F Dean, Barbare DeSanto, John Fryman, Mark Harmon, Dennis A Harp, Wayne Melanson, Jimmy Reeves, Roger C Saathoff, Ashton Thornhill; *Asst. Profs.:* J J Jaw, Keith Johnson, Judy Oskam, Randy Reddick, Elizabeth Watts, Hershel Womack; *Instrs./Lectrs.:* John DeSanto, Clive Kinghorn (dir., KTXT-FM and KOHM), Freda McVay; *Profs. Emer.:* Hower J Hsia, Billy I Ross; *Assoc. Profs. Emer.:* Louis Allen, Harmon L Morgan.
SEQUENCES: News-Editorial, Advertising, Telecomm., Broadcast Journalism, PR, Photocomm., Corporate Telecomm.
FACILITIES: AP, FM, AdA, CN, DR, ETV, JM, JN, PRA, VDT.
DEGREES: BA, MA.

Texas Wesleyan University
Fort Worth, TX 76105; tel (817) 531-4927; fax (817) 531-4814. Department of Mass Communication. Michael Sewell, chair.
Journalism Program: Undergraduate programs in three emphases: ad/PR, journalism and radio-TV.

Texas Woman's University
Denton, TX 76204-1866; tel (817) 898-2181; fax (817) 898-2188. Mass Communications Program, 1925. SPJ, WICI, NABJ. Ruth Ann Ragland, dir.
FACULTY: *Assoc. Prof.:* Mary Kahl Sparks; *Instr.:* Ruth Ragland; *Lectr.:* Charley E Orbison; *Adjunct Fac.:* Bob Carrell, Carol Dickie, Bob Ray Sanders.
SEQUENCES: News-Editorial, Advertising, Broadcast News.
FACILITIES: AP, CATV, DR, JN, VDT.
DEGREES: BS, BA.

Trinity University
San Antonio, TX 78212-7200; tel (210) 736-8113; fax (210) 736-8355. Department of Communication, 1930. ACA, ICA, BEA. Robert O Blanchard, chair.
FACULTY: *Profs.:* Robert O Blanchard, William G Christ, Sammye L Johnson; *Assoc. Prof.:* Harry W Haines, Suzanne Williams; *Asst. Profs.:* Gerald J Davey, Edward Lenert, Rob Huesca; *Part-Time Instrs.:* James Bynum (operations mgr.), Comm. Center), Scott Sowards (radio station mgr.).
FACILITIES: AP, FM, CATV, CCTV, ComN (Promotions Center), ComR, ComTV, DR, VDT.
DEGREE: BA.

West Texas A&M University
Canyon, TX 79016; tel (806) 656-2410; fax (806) 656-2818. Department of Art, Communication, and Theatre.
Journalism Program: Well-rounded program leading to BA or BS in Journalism with any one of the following emphases: news-ed, photojournalism, agricultural comm., ad/PR or electronic media.

UTAH

Brigham Young University
Provo, UT 84602; tel (801) 378-2997; fax (801) 378-6016. Department of Communications, 1933. AAF, AER, BEA, KTA, PRSSA, RTNDA, SPJ, WICI. David P Forsyth, chair.
FACULTY: *Profs.:* Ralph D Barney, M Dallas Burnett, David P Forsyth, Brad E Hainsworth , R John Hughes, Dennis G Martin, Paul Alfred Pratte, Joseph D Straubhaar, JoAnn M Valenti, Gordon C Whiting (head, Comms Studies Div.); *Assoc. Profs.:* Leonard L Bartlett (head, Adv. Div.), Kathryn S Egan, Larrie E Gale (head, Brdct./Media Mgmt. Div.), Richard I Kagel, Russell H Mouritsen, Jack A Nelson (head, Jour. Div.), William C Porter, J R Rush, Laurie Wilson (head, PR Div.); *Asst. Profs.:* Dale L Cressman, Patricia Paystrup, Daniel A Stout; *Special Lect.:* Allen Palmer; *Special Instrs.:* John Gholdston, Roger Gunn, Ted C Hindmarsh, Larry Macfarlane, Duane Roberts, R Melvin Rogers, Robert H Sink, JoLynne Van-Valkenburg.
SEQUENCES: Advertising, Broadcast/Media Sales Management, Communication Studies, Journalism, Public Relations.
FACILITIES: AP, UPI, NPR wire, AM, FM, AdA, CATV, CCTV, ComN, ComR, ComTV, DR, ETV, JN, PRA, VDT.
DEGREES: BA, MA.

Utah, University of
Salt Lake City, UT 84112; tel (801) 581-6888; fax (801) 585-6255. Department of Communication, 1948. AER, KTA, PRSSA, SPJ, WICI, UAF. James A Anderson, chair.
FACULTY: *Profs.:* James A Anderson, Robert K Avery, Milton Hollstein, Jerilyn S McIntyre, Robert K Tiemens; *Assoc. Profs.:* Douglas Birkhead, Craig Denton, Nickieann Fleener, Timothy L Larson; *Asst. Profs.:* Louise Degn, DeAnn Evans, David Vergobbi; *Adjunct Profs.:* Bruce Christensen, Borge Andersen, Fred Esplin, Kenneth Foster, Stephen Hess, Paul Rose, Don Woodward;*Prof. Emer.:* Parry D Sorensen, Quintus C Wilson.
SEQUENCES: PR, Broadcast Journalism, News-Ed, Radio-TV-Film.
FACILITIES: AP, AM, FM, CCTV, CN, ComN, ComR, ComTV, DR, ETV, PRA, VDT.
DEGREES: BS, BA, MS, MA PhD.

Utah State University
Logan, UT 84322-4605; tel (801) 797-3292; fax (801) 797-3973; internet tpease@wpo. hass. usu.edu; Department of Communication. SPJ, PNNA. Edward C Pease, head.
FACULTY: *Prof.:* Edward C Pease; *Assoc. Profs.:* Penny Byrne, Scott Chisholm, Donald Cundy, James Derry; *Asst. Profs.:* Steven Anderson, Brenda Cooper, Nancy Williams; *Instr.:* William J Sedivy (professional-in-residence); *Profs. Emer.:* Burrell F Hansen, Nelson B Wadsworth; *Assoc. Prof. Emer.:* Gerald L Allen; *Adjunct Prof:* Alan Hofmeister; *Adjunct Assoc. Profs.:* R Brent Ballow, Tim Henney; Lee Roderick, Bruce Smith, Michael L Zinser; *Adjunct Asst. Prof.:* Andrew Giarelli.
SEQUENCES: News-Editorial; Broadcast/Electronic Journalism, Public Relations/Corporate Communication.
FACILITIES: AP, FM, CCTV, CN, ComN, ComTV, DR, ETV, CATV, VDT.
DEGREES: BA, BS, MA, MS.

Weber State University
Ogden, UT 84408-1903; tel (801) 626-6426; fax (801) 626-7975; e-mail LStahle@cc. weber.edu; Department of Communication. Randolph J Scott, chair.
Journalism Program: Separate emphases in Journalism, Public Relations and Broadcasting leading to bachelor's degrees.

VERMONT

St. Michael's College
Winooski Park, Colchester, VT 05439; tel (802) 654-2206, 2257; fax (802) 655-3680; BITNET name@SMCVAX. Department of Journalism, 1975. New England Newspaper Assn., New England Press Assn., Vermont Press Assn., WICI. Dianne Lynch, chair.
FACULTY: *Assoc. Prof.:* Gifford Hart; *Asst. Profs.:* Jack Barry, Ken Burris, Tom Hacker, Betsy Liley, Dianne Lynch, David Payson; *Instrs.:* Mike Donoghue, Nick Monsarrat, Tom Slayton, Becky Stayner, Owen Stayner.
SEQUENCES: News-Editorial, Broadcast News, Public Relations/Advertising.
FACILITIES: AM/FM, AP, ComN, DR, JM, JN, PRA, VDT.
DEGREE: BA.

VIRGINIA

Emory and Henry College
Emory, VA 24327; tel (703) 944-4121 ext. 3243; fax (703) 944-5938. Mass Communications Department, 1975. Teresa Keller, chair.
Program: For students considering careers in print journalism, broadcasting, advertising or public relations. Strong liberal arts emphasis.

Hampton University
Hampton, VA 23668; tel (804) 727-5405; fax (804) 727-5047. Mass Media Arts, 1967. KTA, NABJ, WICI. Vanessa Moody Coombs, chair.
FACULTY: *Prof.:* Finis Schneider; *Assoc. Profs.:* Vanessa Moody Coombs, John Haydock, Emmanuel Onyedike, Gene Rebcook, Frank Render, Glanel Webb; *Asst. Profs.:* Samuel Adeleye, Sherilee Beam, Shannon Jackson; *Adjunct Prof.:* Felicia Mason.
SEQUENCES: Broadcast Journalism/Cinema Studies; Public Relations/Advertising; Print Journalism.
FACILITIES: AP, FM, CATV, CN, ComN, DR, ETV, VDT.
DEGREE: BA.

James Madison University
Harrisonburg, VA 22807; tel (703) 568-7007; fax (703) 568-6920. Department of Mass Communication. George Johnson, acting head.
Programs: Concentrations in corporate media, journalism, electronic media production and visual communication toward 30-hour undergraduate degree.

Liberty University
Box 20000, Lynchburg, VA 24506; tel (804) 582-2128. Department of Journalism, 1983. Albert W Snyder, chair.
Journalism Program: Offers concentrations in news-editorial, magazine, advertising, public relations and graphics.

Lynchburg College
1500 Lakeside Dr., Lynchburg VA 24501; tel (804) 522-8544; fax (804) 522-8499; internet Greenberg@ACAVAX.Lynchburg.edu Department of Communication Studies. 1980. Heywood L Greenberg, chair and assoc. prof., journalism.
Journalism Program: offers print and broadcast and speech communication. Students produce cable video program and weekly newspaper. Emphasis on experiential education as well as theory.

Mary Baldwin College
Staunton, VA 24401; tel (703) 887-7000. Mass Communications Program. William L DeLeeuw, dir.
Mass Communications Program: Concentrations in Media Writing, Broadcasting, Advertising/Public Relations. Independent campus newspaper, state of the arts radio studio, closed circuit radio station, TV studio (1/2" and 3/4" editing systems), application for LPTV pending, Staunton News Bureau for WHSV-TV in Harrisonburg,
Desktop Publishing System, independent Communications Institute for in-house and business print, video, and audio productions.

Norfolk State University
Norfolk, VA 23504. Department of Mass Communications and Journalism, 1994. (Formerly Dept. of Journalism, 1975 and Dept. of Mass Communications, 1975); tel (804) 683-8330, 683-8594; fax (804) 683-9119. NABJ, PRSSA, AAF, AER. Shirley Staples Carter, chair, internet sscarter@vger.nsu.edu.
FACULTY: *Profs.:* Shirley Staples Carter (chair), Wilbert Edgerton, Grady James, Stan Tickton, Erwin K Thomas (Grad. Coord.); *Asst. Profs.:* Paula Briggs, Wanda Brockington, Francis McDonald, Emeka Okoli, Obie Smith; *Instr.:* Carlton Edwards, Steve Opfer, Angela L Robertson.
SEQUENCES: Advertising, General Broadcasting, News-Editorial, Photojournalism, Public Relations.
FACILITIES: AP, AM/FM, AdA, CATV, CCTV, CN, ComN, ComTV, DR, JM, PRA, VDT.
DEGREES: BA, BS, MS.

Radford University
Radford, VA 24142; tel (703) 831-5282. Department of Communication, 1968. AER, IABC, SCJ. David H Dobkins, chair.
FACULTY: *Prof.:* Clayland H Waite; *Assoc. Prof.:* Charles D Millsaps (Journalism Coord.); *Asst. Profs.:* E Clayton Braddock, Carolyn M Byerly, William J Kovarik; *Temp. Asst. Prof.:* Donatus A Uzomah.
SEQUENCES: News-Editorial, PR.
FACILITIES: FM, CATV, CCTV, CN, ComN, VDT.
DEGREES: BS, BA in Journ., MS in Corporate PR.

Regent University
1000 Regent University Dr., Virginia Beach, VA 23464-9800; tel (804) 579-4247; fax (804) 424-7051. School of Journalism. J Douglas Tarpley, chair.
Journalism Program: The school offers a MA in Journalism with sequences in news-editorial, broadcast journalism, public relations, magazine, photojournalism, professional writing and journalism education.

Richmond, University of
Richmond, VA 23173; tel (804) 289-8324; fax (804) 289-8313; e-mail spear@urvax. urich.edu; Major and minor in Journalism (in Department of English). Mike Spear, journalism coord.
Journalism Program: Emphases on news gathering and news writing. Has broad liberal arts requirements. Facilities include: AP, FM, CN, DR.

Virginia Commonwealth University
Richmond, VA 23284-2034; tel (804) 367-2660; fax (804) 367-9175; internet jdodd@ cabell.vcu. edu; School of Mass Communications, 1950. AAF, KTA, PRSSA, SPJ. Joyce Wise Dodd, dir.
FACULTY: *Profs.:* George T Crutchfield, Thomas Donohue; *Assoc. Profs.:* Diane Cook-Tench, Joyce Wise Dodd, Robert L Hughes, J David Kennamer, James R Looney, June O Nicholson, Ted Smith, Wilma Wirt; *Asst. Profs.:*

John Campbell, Clarence Thomas; *Instructors:* Andrew Adams, Marianne Duprey, Jerry Torchia; *Adjunct Fac.:* Patricia Ferguson, Nancy Lampert, Valerie O'Brien, Terri Walker, Michael Paul Williams; *Prof. Emer.:* Edmund A Arnold.
SEQUENCES: Advertising, Broadcasting, News-Editorial, Public Relations.
FACILITIES: AP, AM, FM, AdA, CATV, CN, ComR, ComTV, JN, PRA, VDT.
DEGREES: BS, MS.

Virginia Polytechnic Institute and State University
Blacksburg, VA 24061; tel (703) 231-7136; fax (703) 231-7417; internet rdenton@vt.edu; Communications Studies, 1980. AERho, KTA, PRSSA, SPJ. Robert E Denton Jr., head.
FACULTY: *Profs.:* Robert E Denton, Jr., Marshall M Fishwick, Sam G Riley, Kenneth F Rystrom; *Assoc. Profs.:* Elizabeth C Fine, Louis M Gwin, Wayne E Hensley, Rachel Holloway, W. Wat Hopkins, Stephen Prince, Edward H Sewell, Beth M Waggenspack; *Asst. Profs.:* Detine L Bowers, Rebekah Bromley, Matthew P McAllister, Mary Beth Oliver, Scott Patterson; *Instrs.:* Aasha Blakely, Sonya Dye, Betty L Kennan, Shirley Hayden Mitchell, Gayle K Noyes; *Adjunct Prof:.* Gerald N Scheeler.
SEQUENCES: Speech, Print Journ., Broadcasting, PR, Film.
FACILITIES: FM, CATV, CCTV, CN, ComN, ComTV, DR, ETV, PRA, VDT.
DEGREE: BA in Communication Studies.

Virginia Union University
1500 N. Lombardy St., Richmond, VA 23220; tel (804) 257-5655; fax (804) 257-5818. Department of Journalism, 1974. Archibald H Benson, head.
Journalism Department: Offers Broadcast and News-Editorial sequences with internship programs in local news media.

Washington and Lee University
Lexington, VA 24450; tel (540) 463-8432; fax (540) 463-8045; internet smith.h@wlu.edu; Department of Journalism and Mass Communications, 1925. BEA, SPJ. Hampden H Smith III, head.
FACULTY: *Profs.:* Robert J deMaria, John K Jennings, Louis W Hodges, R H MacDonald, Hampden H Smith III, Edwin M Yoder Jr.; *Assoc. Prof.:* Brian E Richardson; *Prof. Emer.:* O W Riegel.
SEQUENCE: Broadcast prof., Print prof., Comm.
FACILITIES: AP, FM, CATV, CCTV, CN, ComN, DR, VDT.
DEGREE: BA.

WASHINGTON

Central Washington University
Ellensburg, WA 98926; tel (509) 963-1066. Department of Communication, 1947. L Gilbert Neal, chair.
Journalism Program: The Mass Communication major includes specializations in both print and broadcast journalism.

Gonzaga University
Spokane, WA 99258; tel (509) 328-4220, ext. 3253. Department of Communication Arts/ Journalism Program. Michael Kirkhorn, dir.
Journalism Program: BA combines historical, legal, ethical and theoretical perspectives with strong writing and editing component and professional practice and criticism. Special emphasis on sports and environmental reporting and reporting on religion, and moral and ethical topics.

Pacific Lutheran University
Tacoma, WA 98447; tel (206) 535-7762; fax (206) 536-5063. Department of Communication & Theatre (Journalism emphasis), 1980. Michael Bartanen, chair; Clifford Rowe, area head.
Journalism Program: PLU offers strong liberal arts education combined with excellent technical training in journalism and broadcasting.

Seattle University
Seattle, WA 98122; tel (206) 296-5340; fax (206) 296-5997. Communication Department. Gary Atkins, chair.
Journalism Program: News-Ed, Broadcast and PR. Seeks to produce graduates who can become responsible professionals or undertake specialized graduate study.
Communication Studies: Liberal arts study of communication, including speech, interpersonal and organizational communication.

Walla Walla College
College Place, WA 99324; tel (509) 527-2832. Communications Department, 1988. Loren Dickinson, chair.
Communication Program: BA in Mass Communication with concentrations in: Journalism and Public Relations, Media (includes broadcasting, video/audio production, performance).

Washington, University of
Seattle, WA 98195; tel (206) 543-2660; fax (206) 543-9285; e-mail kellus@ u. washington.edu. School of Communications, 1907. AAF, BEA, SPJ, PRSA, WICI. Edward P Bassett, dir.
FACULTY: *Profs.:* Edward P Bassett, Richard F Carter, C Anthony Giffard, Don R Pember, Keith R Stamm; *Assoc. Profs.:* Gerald J Baldasty, Lawrence Bowen, John E Bowes, Anthony Chan, Richard Kielbowicz, Richard Labunski, Roger A Simpson, Douglas M Underwood; *Asst. Profs.:* Kathleen Fearn-Banks, Diane Gromala, Katharine Heintz-Knowles, Martha N Matthews, Nancy K Rivenburgh; *Lectrs.:* W Baker, J Collins, J Hucka, A Sampson, R Simmons.
SEQUENCES: Advertising, Broadcast Journalism, Media Studies, Editorial Journalism, Public Relations.
FACILITIES: AP, AM/FM, AdA, CATV, CCTV, DR, ETV, VDT.
DEGREES: BA, MA, MC, PhD.

Washington State University
Pullman, WA 99164-2520; tel (509) 335-1556; fax (509) 335-1555. Edward R Murrow School of Communication, 1964. AERho, PRSSA, Ad Club, WICI, SPJ, IABC. Alexis S Tan, dir., (509) 335-1557.
FACULTY: *Profs.:* Joe Ayres (Grad. Prog. Coord.), Tom Heuterman, Tim Hopf, Alexis Tan; *Assoc. Profs.:* Erica Austin, (head, PR seq.), Bob Hilliard, (head, journ. seq.), Lincoln James (Adv. seq. Head), Glenn Johnson (Cable 8 News Exec. Producer), Betsy Krueger, Val Limburg, (head, brdctg. seq.), Bob Nofinger (Speech Comm. Sequence Head), Joey Reagan, Mike Salvador, Neal Robison; *Asst. Profs.:* Mary Cronin (Journalism Sequence Head), Bruce Pinkleton, Patricia Sias, Steve Thomsen, Elizabeth Wilson, Kak Yoon; *Instrs.:* Roberta Kelly, Tiffany Luginbill, Marvin Marcelo, Dan Petek, Joe Poire, Richard Taflinger, Randy Thompson, Peter Vincent; *Vstg. Profs.:* Fred Davis, Issam Mousa; *Profs. Emer.:* Maynard Hicks, Jan Miller, David Strother; *Teaching Assistants:* Tim Ball, Kyla Bloomfield, Paul Bolls, Elissa Braico, Kelly Brennan, Stan Carder, Patty Chantrill, Noelle Colby-Rotell, Bob Condotta, Noah Cooper, Michelle Dishong, Qingwen Dong, Pat Edwards, Jason Engelbertson, Mary Jo Gonzales, Michael Hazel, Howard Hecht, Brian Heuett, Heather Hibbs, Kristine Johnson, Karlyn Kawahara, Darrell Keim, Kyoung Joo Kim, Jim McPherson, Christie Odden, Patricia Opong, Jason Quan, Jeanne Ratliff, Kay Rutherford, Terry Schliesman, Richelle Scott-Dowdell, Ann Thornsen, Mark Wadleigh, Wendy Welch, Kathie Wilcox, Tony Will, Trinette Zawadzki.
SEQUENCES: Advertising, Broadcasting, Public Relations, Journalism Speech Communication.
FACILITIES: AAF, AM, FM, CATV, CN, VDT, DR, ETV, AP, CCTV, ComN.
DEGREES: BA, MA, Interdisciplinary PhD with Communication emphasis.

Western Washington University
Bellingham, WA 98225-9101; tel (206) 650-3252; fax (206) 650-2848; internet fmckay@cc.wwu. edu; Department of Journalism, 1967. SPJ. Floyd J McKay, chair.
FACULTY: *Profs.:* Lyle E Harris, Pete S Steffens; *Assoc. Prof.:* Carolyn Dale, Floyd McKay, Tim Pilgram.
SEQUENCES: News-Editorial, Public Relations.
FACILITIES: FM, CATV, CCTV, CN, ComN, ComR, ComTV, DR, ETV, JM, PRA, VDT.
DEGREE: BA in Journalism.

Whitworth College
Spokane, WA 99251; tel (509) 466-1000; fax (509) 466-3221. Department of Communication Studies. Gordon Jackson, head, journalism sequence.
Journalism Program: The Journalism track in the Communication Studies program offers 11 courses toward a broad-based Liberal Arts major.

WEST VIRGINIA

Bethany College
Bethany, WV 26032; tel (304) 829-7716; fax (304) 829-7223; e-mail j.keegan@mail. bethany. wvnet.edu; Department of Communication, 1965. SCJ, ABC, AAF, WICI, PRSSA. James Keegan, chair.
FACULTY: *Prof.:* James Keegan, Walter L Kornowski; *Assoc. Prof.:* Russell J Cook, (TV advisor); *Asst. Profs.:* Jon Gordon, (yearbook advisor) Nicholas Neupauer, (print advisor), January Riddle, (print advisor), Patrick J Sutherland, (radio advisor).
SEQUENCES: Advertising, Audio-Video, Graphics, Print, Public Relations.
FACILITIES: CATV, JM, JN, VDT, PRA, AdA, FM, AP, DR.
DEGREE: BA.

Marshall University
Huntington, WV 25755-2622; tel (304) 696-2360; fax (304) 696-3232; internet behrman @muvms6. mu.wvnet.edu; W Page Pitt School of Journalism and Mass Communications, 1926. AAF, AER, NABJ, PRSSA, SPJ. Harold C Shaver, dir.
FACULTY: *Profs.:* George T Arnold, Harold C Shaver, Ralph J Turner; *Assoc. Profs.:* Charles G Bailey, Carl P Burrows, Corley F Dennison III, Janet L Dooley, Dwight W Jensen, Rebecca J Johnson, Edward C Scheiner; *Asst. Profs.:* W Randy Bobbitt, Marilyn McClure; *Instr.:* Dennis C Lebec, Ruth Sullivan; *Part-Time Instrs.:* Mark Timney.
SEQUENCES: Advertising, Broadcast Journalism, Journalism Education, Print Journalism, Public Relations, Radio-Television.
FACILITIES: AP, FM, CATV, CCTV, CN, DR, ETV, JM, PRA, VDT.
DEGREES: BA, MAJ.

West Virginia University
Morgantown, WV 26506-6010; tel (304) 293-3505; fax (304) 293-3072. Perley Isaac Reed School of Journalism, 1939. AAF, KTA, PRSSA, RTNDA, SPJ. William T Slater, dean.
FACULTY: *Profs.:* John H Boyer (dir., Grad. Studies), Robert M Ours (head, News-Ed. sequence), William T Slater, William O Seymour; *Assoc. Profs.:* Mel Elbaum, Lynn Hinds (head, Brdct. News sequence), Richard A. Schreiber (head, Adv. sequence), Pamela D Yagle; *Asst. Profs.:* Ralph E Hanson, Ancella Livers, Theodore Lustig, Christine Martin, R Ivan Pinnell (assoc. dean and head, PR sequence), Maryanne Reed, Ron Schie; *Lect.:* Susan Bahna; *Profs. Emer.:* Paul A Atkins, Donovan H Bond, Charles F Cremer, Guy H Stewart (dean emer.), William R Summers; *Assoc. Prof. Emer.:* Harry W Elwood; *Adjunct Fac.:* Dennis R Godfrey, Jack M Johns, Ed Rabel.
SEQUENCES: Advertising, Broadcast News, Graduate Program, News-Editorial, Public Relations.
FACILITIES: AdA, AM/FM, AP, CN, DR, ETV, JN, PRA, VDT.
DEGREES: BSJ, MSJ.

WISCONSIN

Marquette University
Milwaukee, WI 53233; tel (414) 288-7133; fax (414) 288-3300. College of Communication, 1988. AAF, BEA, IABC, KTA, SPJ, PRSSA, WICI. Michael J Price, interim dean.
FACULTY: (Journalism and Mass Communication): *Profs.:* James W Arnold (dir., Film program), Bill Baxter (emer.), Clifford L Helbert (emer.), George Reedy (emer.), Lucas G Staudacher (emer.); *Assoc. Profs.:* Claire Badaracco, John Crowley (chair, Adv. and PR), John A Grams, Robert J Griffin, Michael J Havice, Kenneth Ksobiech, Judine Mayerle (chair, Broadcast & Electronic Comm.), James V Pokrywczynski, Gregory S Porter, James F Scotton (chair, Jour.), William J Thorn; *Asst. Profs.:* August Gribbin, Richard Leonard (Lucius Nieman Prof. of Jour.), Patrick O'Neill, Chude Okunkwor, Carl Schrank, Karen Slattery; *Adjunct Asst. Prof.:* Eva Rumpf; *Part-Time Instrs.:* Richard Feyrer, Bruce Gill, Eric Meyer, Gail Perlick, Paul E Salsini, Sandra Whitehead.
SEQUENCES: Advertising, Broadcast and Electronic Communication, Journalism, Public Relations, Film minor.
FACILITIES: AP, AM, CCTV, CN, DR, JM, JN, VDT.
DEGREES: BA, BAJ, MA.

Wisconsin—Eau Claire, University of
Eau Claire, WI 54702; tel (715) 836-2528; fax (715) 836-2380. Department of Communication and Journalism, 1953. AAF, ABC, IABC, KTA, SPJ. W Robert Sampson, chair.
FACULTY: *Profs.:* Henry W Lippold, Daniel J Perkins, W Robert Sampson, Sally A Webb, Wayne R Wolfert (emeritus); *Assoc. Profs.:* Terry L Chmielewski, Gerald L Conner, David Ford Hansen, Alice A Ridge; *Asst. Profs.:* Joseph Giordano, John S Gribas, Karen Kremer, Jan Larson, Timothy Leutwiler, Kenneth D Loomis, Judy R Sims, John H Ullmann; *Instr.:* Thomas A Glauner, Joan Rohr Myers, Kelly Jo Wright; *Part-Time Fac.:* Merritt Christensen, Janet Driever, Karin Menzel Sampson.
FACILITIES: FM, CATV, CCTV, CN, JM, DR, VDT.
Communication Program: BA, BS in Communication available with emphases in Organizational Communication, PR, Electronic Media, Public Communication, or Communication Studies.
Journalism Program: BA, BS in Journalism available with emphases in News-Editorial, Broadcast Journalism, Advertising. ACEJMC accredited.

Wisconsin—La Crosse, University of
La Crosse, WI 54601; tel (608) 785-8368; fax (608) 782-5575. Mass Communications, 1964. AAF, SPJ. Roger Grant, chair.
FACULTY: *Profs.:* Roger Grant, John Jenks; *Assoc. Profs.:* Gary Mac Donald, Patricia Muller, David Piehl, Joseph Zobin; *Asst. Prof.:* John Kristoff, Patricia Turner; *Instr.:* Bob Seaquist.
SEQUENCES: Mass Comm., minor-Photography.
FACILITIES: AP, FM, CATV, CCTV, CN, ComR, ComTV, DR, JM.
DEGREES: BA, BS.

Wisconsin—Madison, University of
821 University Ave., Madison, WI 53706-1497; tel (608) 262-3691; fax (608) 262-1361. School of Journalism and Mass Communication, 1905. AAF, PRSSA, SPJ, WICI. Robert E Drechsel, dir.
FACULTY: *Profs.:* Raymond Anderson, James L Baughman, William B Blankenburg (head, News-Ed and co-chair, Frank Thayer Center), Robert E Drechsel (dir. and co-chair, Frank Thayer Center), Sharon L Dunwoody (Evjue-Bascom Prof., chair, Center for Environmental Comm. and Educ. Studies and head, Grad. Studies), Robert P Hawkins (head, Mass Comm.), James L Hoyt, Jack M McLeod (Maier-Bascom Prof. and chair, Mass Comm. Research Center), Michael W Pfau (head, PR), Ivan L Preston (Journal Communications/ Warren Heyse-Bascom Prof.; head, Adv.), Stephen L Vaughn; *Assoc. Profs.:* Robert W McChesney, Diana C Mutz, Donald H Stoffels (adj.); *Asst. Profs.:* Jo Ellen Fair, Lewis Friedland (head, Brdct. News), Jacqueline Hitchon, Shiela Reaves, Hemant Shah; *Sr. Lectr.:* Roger Rathke; *Profs. Emer.:* James A Fosdick, William A Hachten, Charles E Higbie, Hartley E Howe, John T McNelly, Harold L Nelson, Wilmott Ragsdale, Clay Schoenfeld, Robert Taylor.
SEQUENCES: News-Editorial, Broadcast News, Advertising, Public Relations, Mass Communication.
FACILITIES: AP, AM, FM, CATV, ComR, ComTV, DR, VDT.
DEGREES: BA, BS, MA, PhD.

Wisconsin-Madison, University of
Madison, WI 53706; tel (608) 262-1464; fax (608) 265-3042. Department of Agricultural Journalism, 1908. AAF, NAMA, PRSSA, SPJ, WICI. Garrett J O'Keefe, chair.
FACULTY: *Profs.:* Margaret C Andreasen, Marion R Brown, John H Fett, Larry R Meiller, Garrett J O'Keefe , Suzanne Pingree, William Thiesenhusen; *Assoc. Profs.:* Albert C Gunther, Thomas P Schomisch; *Asst. Profs.:* Jeanne M Meadowcroft; *Adj. Assoc. Prof.:* Jacob G Stockinger; *Lectr.:* B Wolfgang Hoffmann; *Part-Time Lectrs.:* Michael Flaherty, Brian Howell, Ellen A Maurer, Christine Mlot, Ron Seely, Susan Lampert-Smith, Mary Ellen Spoerke; *Profs. Emer.:* Fritz A Albert, Lloyd R Bostian, Claron Burnett, Harold King, Nellie R McCannon, John E Ross, Maurice E White.
SEQUENCES: Print, Broadcast, Advertising, Public Relations, Science Reporting in Mass Communication, Agriculture, Natural Resources/ Environment, Family/Consumer Sciences.
FACILITIES: AdA, AM/FM, AP, CN, ComN, ComTV, DR, ETV, PRA, VDT.
DEGREES: BS, MS, PhD.

Wisconsin, Division of University Outreach
Madison, WI 53703; tel (608) 262-3888; fax (608) 265-2329. Communication Programs Department. Marshall Cook, chair.
Journalism Program: Continuing education and professional development programs in news-editorial, public relations, advertising, circulation, broadcasting, film/photography, telecommunications.

Wisconsin—Milwaukee, University of
Milwaukee, WI 53201; tel (414) 229-4436. Department of Mass Communication, 1970. IABC, NABJ, SPJ, WICI. Don Le Duc, chair.
FACULTY: *Profs.:* David Berkman, Don R Le Duc; *Assoc. Profs.:* George Bailey (grad. adviser), David J Backes, Genevieve G McBride, Earl S Grow (undergrad. adviser), David Pritchard; *Asst. Prof.:* Karen Riggs; *Lectrs.:* Patricia Hastings, Gregg Hoffmann, Kay Magowan; *Part-Time Lectrs.:* Dennis R Getto, Paul G Hayes, Elizabeth Hill, Eldon Knoche, Douglas Mitchell, Ronald M Overdahl, Kris Radish, James P Romanesko.
SEQUENCES: Telecommunications, Broadcast Journalism, Journalism, Public Relations.

Wisconsin—Oshkosh, University of
Oshkosh, WI 54901-8696; tel (414) 424-1042; fax (414) 424-7317. Department of Journalism, 1966. AAF, KTA, PRSSA, SPJ, Wisconsin Newspaper Association. Gene W Hintz, chair.
FACULTY: *Prof.:* Leroy L Zacher; *Assoc. Profs.:* F William Biglow, Gary R Coll, Margaret G Davidson, Gene W Hintz; *Asst. Profs.:* Julie K Henderson, Jean Matheson, James C Tsao.
SEQUENCES: News-Editorial, Ad/PR.
FACILITIES: AM/FM, CCTV, CN, ComN, DR, PRA, AdA, VDT.
DEGREES: BA, BS.

Wisconsin—River Falls, University of
River Falls, WI 54022; tel (715) 425-3169. Department of Journalism, 1963. Michael Norman, chair.
Journalism Program: The Department of Journalism offers a BS/BA in journalism with an emphasis in broadcast news or print. Special programs are also available in secondary education and agricultural journalism. ACEJMC accredited.

Wisconsin—Stevens Point, University of
Stevens Point, WI 54481; tel (751) 346-3409. Division of Communication, 1968. James Moe, assoc. dean and head.
Communication Program: Broadbased major in Communication with emphases in Interpersonal, Organizational, Broadcasting, Journalism, Film, Public Relations/Advertising, Individually Planned.

Wisconsin—Whitewater, University of
Whitewater, WI 53190; tel (414) 472-1634, 472-5259. Journalism Office, Department of Communication. Contact Rae Miller.
Journalism Program: Offers a comprehensive program in print and broadcast media. Majors and minors offered in College of Arts.

WYOMING

Wyoming, University of
Laramie, WY 82071-3904; tel (307) 766-3122/6277; fax (307) 766-3812; e-mail FMillar@UWYO. EDU. Department of Communication and Mass Media, 1948. AAF, SPJ, SCJ, Wyoming Press Assoc., Wyoming Assoc. of Broadcasters. Frank E Millar, chair.
FACULTY: *Profs.:* William C Donaghy, Frank E Millar, John W Ravage; *Assoc. Prof.:* Pam Kalbfleisch; *Asst. Profs.:* Peggy Bieber-Roberts, Michael Brown, Kent Drummond, George Gladney, Ken Smith; *Instrs.:* Bob Beck, Terry Buchanan, Mike McElreath, Tony Pedersen, Carol Tarantola, Eric Wiltse, Don Woods; *Prof. Emer.:* B Wayne Callaway, William J Roepke.
SEQUENCES: General Communication Studies, Advertising, Broadcasting, Print Journalism, PR.
FACILITIES: AdA, CATV, CCTV, CN, ComN, DESK, DR, EDIT, FM, JN, PRA, VID, VDT.
DEGREES: BA, BS, MA.

PUERTO RICO

Puerto Rico, University of
PO Box 21880, UPR Sta., San Juan, Puerto Rico 00931; tel (809) 764-0000, ext. 5036; fax (809) 763-5390. School of Public Communication. Federico C Iglesias, dir.
Journalism Program: BA and MA in Communication with journalism, radio, TV, cinema, PR and advertising, and theory and research as areas of interest.

University of the Sacred Heart
PO Box 12383, San Juan, Puerto Rico 00914-0383; tel (809) 728-1515 (ext. 2326, 2359); fax (809) 727-1250; internet A_ESTRADA%USCAC1@ UPR1.UPR.CLU.EDU. Department of Communication, 1981. Aileen Estrada-Fernández, dir.
Journalism Program: Department offers BA in Communication: major in advertising, media writing, telecommunications and visual arts. MA in Communication with major in Public Relations.

CANADA

Calgary, University of
2500 University Dr. N.W., Social Sciences 320, Calgary, Alberta T2N IN4 Canada. Communication Studies Programme, 1982; fax (403) 282-6716; e-mail 22052@UCDASVM1.
Communication Program: Graduate program (only) offering masters in Communication Studies (course-based) and MA in Communications. Specialties: Marketing Communications, Organizational Communications, Law and Communications Policy, International Communications.

Carleton University
1125 Colonel By Dr., Ottawa, Ontario K1S 5B6 Canada; tel (613) 788-7404; fax (613) 788-6690. School of Journalism and Communication, 1945. Peter Johansen, dir.
FACULTY: *Profs.:* G Stuart Adam, Vincent Mosco, T Joseph Scanlon; *Assoc. Profs.:* Elly Alboim, Paul Attallah, Roger Bird, Peter Bruck, Christopher Doman, Ross Eaman, George Frajkor, Alan Frizzell, Peter Johansen, Lionel Lumb, Patrick MacFadden, Catherine McKercher, Brian Nolan, Klaus Pohle, Daniel Pottier, Robert Rupert, Eileen Saunders, David Van Praagh, John R Weston; *Asst. Profs.:* Michael Dorland, Shelly Easton, Barbara Freeman, Joanne Marshall, Mary McGuire, David Tait, Lynne Van Luven; *Visiting Assoc. Prof.:* Cameron Graham; *Prof. Emer.:* Wilfred Kesterton.
FACILITIES: AM/FM, CATV, CCTV, CN, ComN, ComR, CP, DR, JN, VDT.
DEGREES: BJ, BA, MJ, MA.

Concordia University
7141 Sherbrooke St. W., Montreal, Quebec H4B 1R6 Canada; tel (514) 848-2465. Journalism Dept., 1975. Enn Raudsepp, chair.
Journalism Program: Oriented toward professional training within an academic framework. Offers three-year undergraduate and one-year graduate programs in broadcasting and print.
Communication Studies Department, 1965. Brian Lewis, chair.
Communication Studies Program: Offers BA, MA and PhD level programs in mass comm. theory and practice (excluding news and editorial seqs.).

King's College, University of
Halifax, Nova Scotia B3H 2A1 Canada; tel (902) 422-1271; fax (902) 423-3357. School of Journalism, Michael Cobden, dir.
Journalism Program: A four year program leading to a Bachelor of Journalism (Honours) and a one year program for students with a previous degree leading to a Bachelor of Journalism.

Regina, University of
Regina, Saskatchewan S4S OA2 Canada; tel (306) 585-4420; fax (306) 585-4867. School of Journalism and Communications, 1980.
Journalism Program: A four-year program leading to a Bachelor of Arts in Journalism and Communications or a two-year degree for students with a previous degree leading to a Bachelor of Journ.

Ryerson Polytechnic University
Toronto, Ontario M5B 2K3 Canada; tel (416) 979-5319; fax (416) 979-5216. School of Journalism, 1948. John Miller, chair.
FACULTY: *Profs.:* Joyce Douglas, Kathy English, Don Gibb, Mike Goodenough, Jennifer Hunter, Suanne Kelman, Loren Lind, Stuart McLean, Paul Nowack, Don Obe, Dale Ratcliffe, Paul Rush, Dean Tudor; *Instrs.:* Howard Bernstein, Mark Bulgutch, Robert Culbert, Cecil Foster, Hamlin Grange, David Hayes, Kevin Newman, Mark Nusca, Peter Robertson, Shelley Robertson; *Endowed Chair:* Rick Salutin.
FACILITIES: CP, CCTV, DR, JM, JN.
DEGREE: Bachelor of Applied Arts in Journ.

St. Clair College of Applied Arts and Technology
Windsor, Ontario N9A 6S4; Canada; tel (519) 966-1656; fax (519) 966-2737. Journalism Department. Susan MacKenzie, coord.
Journalism Program: Three-year print journalism (writing, editing, photography) and one-year diploma course for university graduates.

Western Ontario, University of
London, Ontario N6A 5B7; Canada; tel (519) 661-3377, 661-3383; fax (519) 661-3848; e-mail PETER@GSOJ.UWO.CA Graduate School of Journalism. Peter Desbarats, dean.
Journalism Program: A one-year, three-term program leading to a Master of Arts degree in Jour.

Windsor, University of
Windsor, Ontario N9B 3P4; Canada; tel (519) 253-4232, ext. 2896; fax (519) 971-3642; e-mail MGGOLD@UWINDSOR.CA Department of Communication Studies, 1969. Mary Gold, chair.
Journalism Program: Media production processes, media studies, and communication theory and research at undergraduate and master's levels.

AUSTRALIA

Bond University
Gold Coast, Queensland, Australia 4229; tel 61-75-95-1111; fax 61-75-95-1747; e-mail Mark_Pearson@Bond.edu.au. Communication and Media Studies, 1990. Journalism Education Association, Public Relations Institute of Australia. Mark Pearson, Assoc. Prof.
Programs: Two year (six semester) program leading to BA with major in journalism, public relations or media studies and producation or double major in communication studies. Coursework MA in journalism, PR or media studies and production — one year.

Charles Sturt University
Bathurst, NSW, Australia, 2795; tel Intl Access+61 63 38 4539; fax Intl Access+61 63 38 4409; e-mail Wblood@mit.csu.ed.au. School of Communication, 1974. Journalism Educ. Assoc., PR Institute of Aust., International Advertising Assoc. Warwick Blood, Assoc. Prof.
Programs: Print and Broadcast Journalism, PR and Organizational Communication, Advertising, Media Production.BA, MA, MA (Hons), PhD.

Southern Queensland, University of
Toowoomba, Queensland, Australia 4350; tel (076) 31 2100; fax (076) 31 2598; e-mail S97571@DDSCU.DDIAE.OZ.AU.
Journalism Program: Three-year course leading to a BA with a double major in journalism. All journalism units, except those for advanced broadcast, are available to external students.

Queensland, University of
Brisbane, Queensland, Australia 4072; tel 61-7-365-2060; fax 61-7-365-1377. Journalism, 1921. Bruce Grundy, dept. head; John P Henningham, journalism prof.
Journalism Program: A three-year program leading to BA with major or double major in Journalism. Fourth year honors program. Coursework Master of Journalism (MJ)–2 years. Supervision of Research MA and PhD degrees.

AUSTRIA

Salzburg, University of
PO Box 505, A-5010 Salzburg, Austria; tel (662) 8044-4150; fax (662) 8044-413; internet FABRIS@EDVZ. SBG.AC.AT. Dept. of Journ. and Comms., 1968. OeGPuK, DGPuK, IAMCR. Hans H Fabris, chair.
Communications Program: Offers a MA and PhD with sequences in journalism, PR and AV media.

FRANCE

Universite Partheon-Assas (Paris II)
Institut Français De Presse, Sciences De L'Information, 92 rue d'Assas 75006 Paris; tel (44) 41 57 93; fax (44) 41 57 04. Remy Rieffel, chair.
Journalism Program: For third-year (BA) students, at MA and PhD levels.

GERMANY

University for Music and Theater Hannover
Hannover, Hohenzollernstr.47, Germany D-W-30161; tel (511) 31 00-280; fax (511) 66 12 98; internet Klaus.Schoenbach@JOURNALISTIK. HMT-HANNOVER.D400.DE. Department of Journalism and Communication Research, 1985. Klaus Schoenbach, chair.
FACULTY: *Profs.:* Bernd Schmidt, Beate Schneider, Klaus Schoenbach; *Assoc. Prof.:* Gunter Reus; *Asst. Profs.:* Romy Froehlich, Lutz Goertz, Kurt Neubert, Wolfram Peiser, Dieter Stuerzebecher, Christa Wehner; *Honorary Prof.:* Ivo Frenzel.
FACILITIES: AM/FM, CCTV, VDT, media library.
DEGREES: Diploma Journalist, Diploma Media Scientist.

MALAYSIA

Universiti Kebangsaan Malaysia (National University of Malaysia)
43600 UKM Bangi, Malaysia; tel 03-8256796/03-8292456; fax 03-8256484. Department of Communication, Faculty of Social Sciences & Humanities, 1976. Samsudin Abdul Rahim, PhD and department head.
Communication Program: Sequences in PR, Jour., Film, Adv., Dev. Comm., Broadcasting; BA, MA and PhD degrees.

SCOTLAND

Strathclyde/Glasgow Caledonian, Universities of
Scottish Centre for Journalism Studies, Strathclyde University, Glasgow, G1 1XH Scotland; tel 041-553 4166; fax 041-552 3493; telex 7742. Scottish Centre for Journalism Studies, 1993. Jennifer McKay, course coord.
FACULTY: *Profs.:* Simon Frith (Dept. of English Studies), Bill Scott (Dept. of Comm.); *Lectrs.:* Jennifer McKay (course coord.), Mark Meredith.
SEQUENCES: Print Journalism, Broadcasting, Law, Government, Shorthand, Information Management, Journalism and Society.
DEGREES: Postgraduate Diploma in Journalism Studies, M.Litt Journalism Studies and M.Litt Journalism Research.

SOUTH AFRICA, REPUBLIC OF

Potchefstroom University
Private Bag X6001, 2520 Potchefstroom, Republic of South Africa; tel (0148)99-1642; tel Add. PUK telex 3-46019; telefax (0148) 99-1651. Department of Communication. Arnold S de Beer, head.
Communication Program: A three/four year program leading to BA (Comm.) or B.Com (Comm.), also: MA and PhD Offers a comprehensive program in print and broadcasting media, advertising and public relations, as well as intercultural communication, organizational communication, political communication, speech communication and graphic design. Institute for Communication Research: prof. Arnold S de Beer, dir. Publishes, *inter alia, Ecquid Novi*, the only refereed journal for journalism and mass media in South Africa.

UNITED KINGDOM

London College of Printing and Distributive Trades
Elephant and Castle, London SEI 6SB, England; tel (071) 735 9100; fax (071) 587 5297.
Journalism Program: The college offers various courses in Journalism including a Postgraduate Diploma in Radio Journalism.

University of Wales, Cardiff
Cardiff, Wales CF1 3 AS United Kingdom; tel 222-874786. Centre for Journalism Studies. 1970. Brian Winston, dir., prof.
FACULTY: *Prof.:* Brian Winston; *Sr. Lectr.:* Geoff Mungham (dir., research); *Lectrs.:* Bob Atkins, Gill Branston, Cynthia Carter, Jeff Daniels, David English (Deputy Dir.), John Foscolo, Marie Gillespie, Colin Larcombe, Jean Silvan-Evans, Mike Smith, John Thompson, Mike Ungesma; *Honorary Prof.:* Tim Traverse-Healy, OBE
SEQUENCES: Newspaper, Magazine, Broadcasting, Public Relations, Photojournalism, Documentary Film Production, Independent Film Production, European Journalism Studies.
FACILITIES: CCTV, CN, ComTV, PRA, RNA, VDT
DEGREES: BA, Diploma in Journalism Studies, Diploma in Film Production Studies, MA, MPhil, PhD.

STATE NEWSPAPER REPRESENTATIVES

ANA AD SERVICES INC. (ARIZONA NEWSPAPER ASSOCIATION) — 1001 N. Central, Phoenix, AZ 85004; tel (602) 261-7655; fax (602) 261-7525
Director of Sales — Anita Tamboli
Billing Manager — Nancy Burns
Represents daily and weekly newspapers in Arizona.

ARKANSAS PRESS SERVICES — 1701 Broadway, Little Rock, AR 72206; tel (501) 374-1500; fax (501) 374-7509
Advertising Manager — David Brown
Represents daily and weekly newspapers in Arkansas.

ALABAMA NEWSPAPERADVERTISING SERVICE INC. — 3324 Independence Dr., Ste. 200, Birmingham, AL 35209; tel (205) 871-7737; fax (205) 871-7740
Advertising Manager — Felicia Mason
Represents daily and weekly newspapers in Alabama.

CALIFORNIA NEWSPAPER NETWORK — 1225 8th St., Ste. 260, Sacramento, CA 95814; tel (916) 443-5991; fax (916) 449-6007
Manager — Sharla Trillo
Placement Service Specialist — Kari Sorenson
Placement Service Specialist — Cary Migret
Account Supervisor — Bev Schmit
Sales Representative — Frank Flood
Sales Representative — Doug Mayberry
Represents daily and weekly newspapers in California.

COLORADO PRESS SERVICE — 1336 Glenarm Pl., Denver, CO 80204; tel (303) 571-5117; fax (303) 571-1803
Director of Advertising — Gregory V Appel
Account Executive — Russell Sealy
Account Coordinator — Sarah Nell
Represents daily and weekly newspapers in Colorado.

FLORIDA PRESS SERVICE INC. — 336 E. College Ave., Ste. 103, Tallahassee, FL 32301-1554; tel (904) 222-6401; fax (904) 222-4498
Manager — Lesley Radius
Advertising Coordinator — Brad M Ray
Advertising Support Coordinator — Scott Harding
Represents daily and weekly newspapers in Florida.

GEORGIA NEWSPAPER SERVICE INC. — 3066 Mercer University Dr., Ste. 200, Atlanta, GA 30341-4137; tel (404) 454-6776; fax (404) 454-6778
Executive Director — Robin Rhodes
Represents daily and weekly newspapers in Georgia.

INDIANA DISPLAY ADVERTISING SERVICE — 1 Virginia Ave., Ste. 701, Indianapolis, IN 46204; tel (317) 637-3966; fax (317) 624-4428
Advertising Director — Lindsay Schafer
Account Manager — Sharon Martin
Represents daily and weekly newspapers in Indiana.

IDAHO'S COMPLETE ADVERTISING NEWSPAPER NETWORK (ICANN) — 6560 Emerald, Ste. 124, Boise, ID 83704; tel (208) 375-0733; fax (208) 375-0914
Executive Director/Manager ICANN — Bob Hall
Represents daily and weekly newspapers in Idaho.

ILLINOIS PRESS ADVERTISING SERVICE — 701 S. Grand Ave. W., Springfield, IL 62704; tel (217) 523-5092; fax (217) 523-5103
Assistant Executive Director — Kathy Galloway
Represents daily and weekly newspapers in Illinois.

CUSTOMIZED NEWSPAPER ADVERTISING (IOWA) — 319 E. Fifth St., Des Moines, IA 50309; tel (515) 244-2145; fax (515) 244-4855
Executive Director — Bill Monroe
Assistant Director — Chris Mudge
Advertising Director — Stacy Collins
Represents 344 daily and weekly newspapers in Iowa.

KANSAS PRESS ASSOCIATION — 5423 S.W. 7th St., PO Box 1773, Topeka, KS 66606; tel (913) 271-5304; fax (913) 271-7341
Executive Director — David L Furnas
Sales Representative — Kathleen Falk
Represents daily and weekly newspapers in Kansas.

KENTUCKY PRESS SERVICE INC. — 101 Consumer Ln., Frankfort, KY 40601; tel (502) 223-8821; fax (502) 875-2624
Executive Director — David Thompson
Advertising Director — Gloria Davis
Represents daily and weekly newspapers in Kentucky.

LOUISIANA PRESS ASSOCIATION — 680 N. Fifth St., Baton Rouge, LA 70802; tel (504) 344-9309; fax (504) 336-9921
Advertising Director — Gary Miller
Advertising Coordinator — Linda Boudreaux
Represents daily and weekly newspapers in Louisiana.

MICHIGAN NEWSPAPERS INC. — 827 N. Washington Ave., Lansing, MI 48906-5199; tel (517) 372-2424; fax (517) 372-2429
General Manager — Walter Dozier
Advertising Assistant — Linda Dancer
Represents daily and weekly newspapers in Michigan.

MID-ATLANTIC NEWSPAPER SERVICES INC. — 2717 N. Front St., Harrisburg, PA 17110; tel (717) 234-4067 ext. 239; fax (717) 234-8267
Director of Advertising — Sue Kelly
Sales Representative — Ed Boito
Sales Representative — Rick Pelak
Sales Representative — Anne Ryder
Represents daily and weekly newspapers in the Mid-Atlantic region of the U.S.

MINNESOTA NEWSPAPER ASSOCIATION — 12 S. 6th St., Ste. 1120, Minneapolis, MN 55402; tel (612) 332-8844; fax (612) 342-2958
Advertising Sales Director — Lisa Hills
Advertising Sales Rep. — Scott Lotts
Represents daily and weekly newspapers in Minnesota. In addition, the Fargo-Moorhead (ND) Forum and Wahpeton-Breckenridge (ND) News are members of MNA.

MISSISSIPPI PRESS SERVICE INC. — 351 Edgewood Terrace, Jackson, MS 39206-6217; tel (601) 981-3060; fax (601) 981-3676
Advertising Director — Sandy Blalock
Represents daily and weekly newspapers in Mississippi.

MISSOURI PRESS SERVICE INC. — 802 Locust St., Columbia, MO 65201; tel (314) 449-4167; fax (314) 874-5894
General Manager — Doug Crews
Sales Manager — Mike Sell
Represents daily and weekly newspapers in Missouri.

MONTANA NEWSPAPER ADVERTISING SERVICE INC. — 534 N. Main St., Ste. 202, Helena, MT 59601; tel (406) 443-850; fax (406) 443-2860
Advertising Coordinator — Linda Fromm
Represents daily and weekly newspapers in Montana.

NEBRASKA PRESS ADVERTISING SERVICE — 1120 K St., Lincoln, NE 68508; tel (800) 369-2850/(402) 476-2851; fax (402) 476-2942
Executive Director — Allan Beerman
Sales Director — Robert James
Advertising Manager — Carolyn Bowman
Represents daily and weekly newspapers in Nebraska.

NENA AD NETWORK (NEW ENGLAND NEWSPAPER ASSOCIATION) — 70 Washington St., Ste. 214, Salem, MA 01970; tel (508) 744-8940; fax (508) 744-0333
Executive Director — Morley L Piper
Advertising Representative — Patricia Baigle
Represents daily and weekly newspapers in New England.

NEW JERSEY NEWSPAPER NETWORK (NJNN) — 840 Bear Tavern Rd., Ste. 305, West Trenton, NJ 08628-1019; tel (609) 406-0600; fax (609) 406-0399
Director — George White
Assistant Director — Amy Lear
Coordinator — Christine Riley
Represents daily and weekly newspapers in New Jersey.

NEW MEXICO PRESS SERVICE INC. — 2531 Wyoming N.E., Albuquerque, NM 87112; tel (505) 293-0411; fax (505) 275-1449
Manager — Bill Johnson
Represents daily and weekly newspapers in New Mexico.

NEW YORK NEWSPAPER ADVERTISING SERVICE INC. — The Carriage House, 8 Thurlow Terrace, Albany, NY 12203; tel (518) 449-1667; fax (518) 449-5053
Display Manager — Pamela Stevens
Marketing Director — Stephen C Schaeffer
Represents daily newspapers in New York.

NEW YORK PRESS SERVICE — 1681 Western Ave., Albany, NY 12203; tel (518) 464-6483; fax (518) 464-6489
Executive Director — Michelle K Rea
Senior Sales Executive — David Van Dusen
Represents weekly newspapers in New York.

NORTH CAROLINA PRESS SERVICE INC. — 4101 Lake Boone Trail, Ste. 202, Raleigh, NC 27607; tel (919) 787-7443; fax (919) 787-5302
Marketing Director — Kathy Vitale
Account Services Administrator — Lindsay Jones
Represents daily and weekly newspapers in North Carolina.

NORTH DAKOTA ADVERTISING SERVICE — 1435 Interstate Loop, Bismarck, ND 58501; tel (701) 223-6397; tel (800) 223-8185
Executive Vice President — Denise Bjornson
Advertising/Sales Manager — Jim Hewitson
Represents daily and weekly newspapers in North Dakota.

OHIO NEWSPAPER SERVICES INC. — 1335 Dublin Rd., Ste. 216-B, Columbus, OH 43215; tel (614) 486-6677; fax (614) 486-4940
Exec. Dir./Secretary — Frank E Deaner
Manager — Mark Henry
Represents 86 daily and 88 weekly Ohio newspapers.

OKLAHOMA PRESS SERVICE — 3601 N. Lincoln, Oklahoma City, OK 73105-5499; tel (405) 524-4421; fax (405) 524-2201
Exec. Vice President — Ben Blackstock
Vice President — Ray Hibbard
Sales Manager — Bob Stacy
Represents daily and weekly newspapers in Oklahoma.

PENNSYLVANIA NEWSPAPERS PUBLISHERS ASSOCIATION — 2717 N. Front St., Harrisburg, PA 17110; tel (717) 234-4067; fax (717) 234-8267
Director of Advertising — Sue Kelly
Sales Representative — Ed Boito
Sales Representative — Rick Pelak
Sales Representative — Anne Ryder
Represents daily and weekly newspapers in Pennsylvania.

WISCONSIN NEWSPAPER ASSOCIATION — 702 N. Midvale Blvd., Ste. B-17, PO Box 5580, Madison, WI 53705; tel (608) 238-7171/ (800) 261-4242; fax (608) 238-4771
Executive Director — J LeRoy Yorgason
Advertising Manager — Jill Weigel
Represents daily and weekly newspapers in Wisconsin.

TRADE UNIONS IN THE NEWSPAPER FIELD

COMMUNICATIONS WORKERS OF AMERICA — 501 3rd St. NW, Washington, DC 20001-2797; tel (202) 434-1100
President — Morton Bahr
Sec./Treas. — Barbara J Easterling

GRAPHIC COMMUNICATIONS INTERNATIONAL UNION — 1900 L St. NW, Washington, DC 20036; tel (202) 462-1400; fax (202) 331-9516
President — James J Norton
Sec./Treas. — Guy DeVito

INTERNATIONAL ASSOCIATION OF MACHINISTS & AEROSPACE WORKERS — 9000 Machinists Pl., Upper Marlboro, MD 20772; tel (301) 967-4500

INTERNATIONAL BROTHERHOOD OF ELECTRICAL WORKERS — 1125 15th St. NW, Washington, DC 20005; tel (202) 728-6131; fax (202) 728-7664
Int'l. President — John J Barry
Int'l. Sec. — Jack F Moore

INTERNATIONAL BROTHERHOOD OF TEAMSTERS — 25 Louisiana Ave. NW, Washington, DC 20001-2198; tel (202) 624-6800; fax (202) 624-6918
Gen. Pres. — Ron Carey
Gen. Sec./Treas. — Tom Sever
Dir.-Communications — Matt Witt

INTERNATIONAL UNION OF OPERATING ENGINEERS — 1125 17th St. NW, Washington, DC 20036; tel (202) 429-9100
Gen. Pres. — Frank Hanley
Gen. Sec./Treas. — Budd Coutts

LABORERS' INTERNATIONAL UNION OF NORTH AMERICA — 905 16th St. NW, Washington, DC 20006; tel (202) 737-8320
Gen. Pres. — Arthur A Coia

THE NEWSPAPER GUILD — 8611 Second Ave., Silver Spring, MD 20910; tel (301) 585-2990
Int'l. Chairperson — Carol D Rothman
President — Charles Dale
Sec./Treas. — Linda Foley

(NEWSPAPER PERIODICAL) DRIVERS, CHAUFFEURS & HELPERS UNION — 3100 Amers Pl. NE, Washington, DC 20018; tel (202) 636-8170; fax (202) 259-9382
President — Philip Feaster

OFFICE & PROFESSIONAL EMPLOYEES INTERNATIONAL UNION — 815 16th St. NW, Ste. 606, Washington, DC 20006; tel (202) 393-4464; fax (202) 347-0649
Sec./Treas. — Gilles Beauregard

OIL, CHEMICAL & ATOMIC WORKERS INTERNATIONAL UNION — PO Box 281200, Lakewood, CO 80228-8200; tel (303) 987-2229; fax (303) 987-5370
Sec./Treas. — Bernie Rousselle

SERVICE EMPLOYEES INTERNATIONAL UNION — 1313 L St. NW, Washington, DC 20005; tel (202) 898-3200; fax (202) 898-3304
Int'l. Pres. — John Sweeney

UNITED PAPERWORKERS INTERNATIONAL UNION — 3340 Parameter Hill Dr. (37211), PO Box 1475, Nashville, TN 37202; tel (615) 834-8590; fax (615) 834-7741
Int'l. Pres. — Wayne Glenn

Copyright ©1996 by the Editor & Publisher Co.

UNITED NATIONS CORRESPONDENTS ASSOCIATION

UNITED NATIONS, NEW YORK CITY

The United Nations Correspondents Association was organized at a constitutent meeting of accredited United Nations correspondents in the Security Council Chamber at Lake Success on June 30, 1948. Its aims and purposes as stated in its Constitution are as follows:
1. To maintain and protect the freedom and prestige of Press, Radio and Television correspondents in all their relations with the United Nations.
2. To promote the interest of its members and to facilitate their personal and professional relationships.
3. To take whatever measures possible to protect the rights of bona fide correspondents to secure accreditation and unhindered access to the United Nations headquarters or regional offices and to their normally available facilities, without discrimination.
4. To undertake any other action, when required, on behalf of Press, Radio and Television correspondents accredited to the United Nations, either at its headquarters or at any of its regional offices.
5. To facilitate social contact between its members, delegates from member nations of the United Nations, officials of the Secretariat and distinguished personalities connected with international affairs.

UNCA EXECUTIVE COMMITTEE

President — Ian Williams (Tribune, London; New York Observer, New York)

First Vice President — J Tuyet Nguyen (UPI, Washington)

Second Vice President — Masood Haider (Dawn, Pakistan; Academic File, London)

Third Vice President — Zhaolong Xia (Xinhua News Agency, Beijing)

Secretary — Ted Morello (Far East Economic Review, Hong Kong)

Treasurer — Behzat Baris (IKA News Agency, Ankara)

EXECUTIVE COMMITTEE MEMBERS-AT-LARGE

Judith Aita (USIA Press Service, Washington)
Ricardo Alday (Mexican News Agency, Mexico City)
Louis Foy (France Soir, Paris)
Azim Mian (The News International, Pakistan; Daily Jang, Pakistan)
Frances Mourani (BBC, London)
Ruth Pearson (Business Week, New York)
Julia Preston (Washington Post, Washington)
Rene Slama (Agence France-Press, Paris)
Norberto L. Svarzman (Televisa, Mexico City)

REGULAR MEMBERS

Adeyemi, Olusegun A (News Agency of Nigeria, Lagos)
Aita, Judith (USIA Press Service, Washington)
Alday, Ricardo (Mexican News Agency/Notimex, Mexico City)
Alius, John A (Servico Universal de Noticias, Mexico; El Universal, Mexico)
Ast, Genevieve (Canadian Broadcasting Corp./Societe Radio-Canada, Ottawa)
Avdovic, Erol (Radio Televizija Bosne i Hercegovine, Sarajevo; BiH Exlusive, Sarajevo)
Baig, Saleem (Associated Press of Pakistan, Islamabad; National News Agency)
Baris, Behzat H (Barometre, Istanbul; IKA News Agency, Ankara; Interstar (TV), Istanbul; Barometre, Istanbul; Yeni Gunaydid, Istanbul)
Bassir Pour, Afsane (Le Monde, Paris; Voice of America (Freelance), Washington)
Berkand, Necdet (ABC Press Agency)
Boo, Juan-Vicente (ABC, Madrid)
Boulal, Abdelali (Maghreb Arabe Presse Agency/MAP, Morocco)
Brooks, Geraldine (Wall Street Journal, New York)
Burtis, Farida (World News Link Inc, London)
Cahill, Michael (Christian Science Monitor Radio, Boston)
Capra, Giovanni (The Parliament, Rome)
Cesar-Proenza, Gerardo (Presna Latina, Havana)
Chakrapani, Raghavendra (The Hindu, Madras)
Chishti, Syed T (Pakistan Business Report; Pakistan Observer)
Crossette, Barbara (New York Times, New York)
Darakjian, Vahe (Emirates News Agency, Abu Dhabi)
Deen, Thalif (Inter Press Service, Rome; Asiaweek, Hong Kong; Jane's Defense Weekly, London; Daily News, Sri Lanka)
de Lavarene, Celhia (Jeune Afrique; Afrique Magazine)
Demille, Arnold C (Chicago Daily Defender, Chicago; Pittsburgh Courier, Pittsburgh; Michigan Chronicle, Detroit; Tri-State Defender, Memphis)
Denecke, Hermann (ARD-German Radio Network)
Dergham, Raghida (Al-Hayat, London; Radio Orient, Paris)
Dominguez, Pilar (Spanish News Agency-EFE, Madrid)
Dwyer, Aubrey (Southern African Business News, Johannesburg)
Ebbing, Martin (Bayerischer Rundfunk, Munich)
Elliott, Joy (Reuters America Inc., New York)
Emiroglu, Sema (Milliyet, Istanbul; TRT, Turkish Radio/TV Corp., Ankara; BBC World Service, London; Deutsche Welle & WDR Koln, Cologne; Radio Netherlands, Hilversum)
Endrst, Elsa B (Northern Tier Publishing Corp., Yorktown Heights, NY; North County News, Yorktown Heights, NY; This Week Magazine, Yorktown Heights, NY)
Farrell, Naomi (New Middle East Magazine, Israel; New Lebanese American Journal-Al Hoda, New York; Freelance Canadian Media)
Fasulo, Linda M (NBC News, New York; US News & World Report, Washington)
Fercsey, John (Interco Press Inc., Washington; La Presna, Buenos Aires)
Ferreira, Argemiro (Correio Braziliense, Brasilia; Tribuna da Imprensa, Rio de Janeiro)
Ferretti, Antonio (Il Gazzettino, Venice; Il Giorno, Milan; Il Dovere, Switzerland)
Finora, Joseph (Illyria-Albanian-American News, Bronx, NY)
Foy, Louis (France Soir, Paris; Europe No.1, Paris)
Friedman, Joshua M (Newsday, Long Island, NY)
Fruchtbaum, Harold (Interalia Review, New York; The Nation, New York)
Gao Jian (Xinhua News Agency, Beijing)
Georgiadou, Mirella-Maria (Athens News Agency-ANA, Athens)
Ghani, Mian Zahid (Independent News Agency of Pakistan)
Goodman, Anthony R (Reuters Information Services Inc., New York)
Gungor, Salih Zeki (Karadeniz, Trabzon)
Haider, Masood (Dawn, Pakistan; Academic File, London)
Handelman, Stephen (Toronto Star, Toronto)
He Hongze (People's Daily, Beijing)
Helal, Reda (Al-Alam Al-Yom, Cairo)
Hervas, Mercedes (El Periodico, Barcelona)
Horowitz, David (World Union Press, New York)
Hottelet, Richard C (Writer, lecturer, broadcaster, CT)
Hudson, Richard (Global Report, New York)
Hung, Nguyen Thai (Vietnam News Agency, Hanoi)
Hvistendahl, Else (Aftenposten, Oslo)
Ignatiov, Michael (Ethnos Greece, Athens; 9.84 Athens Radio, Athens; Eikones, Athens)
Ilkhan, Mahmood (Islamic Republic News Agency/IRNA, Teheran)
Jendoubi, Salwa Amri (Kuwait News Agency-KUNA, Kuwait)
Jenkins, Tony (Expresso, Portugal)
Jimenez, Antonio E (German Press Agency-DPA, Hamburg)
Johanson, Elaine (Voice of America, Washington)
Kaneliakus, Yiannis (Eleftheerotypia)
Karaelmas, Nilay (Cyprus Newspaper, Lefkosa)
Kim, Seyng Young (The Chosun Ilbo, Seoul)
Kim, Tae-ung (Hankook Ilbo-Korea Times, Seoul)
Kins, Gloria Starr (Diplomatic World Bulletin, New York)
Krauss, Mitchell (CBS, New York)
Kuhon, Albert (Suara Pembaruan, Jakarta)
Lauria, Joe (German Press Agency, Hamburg; Southam Newspapers, Ottawa)
Leopold, Evelyn R (Reuters Information Services, New York)
Leroux, Anne (Spanish News Agency-EFE, Madrid)
Lessing, Judy M (Radio New Zealand News Ltd., Wellington)
Lidscreiber, Petra (ARD German TV)
Liggett, Thomas (World Peace News, New York)
Li Jianxiong (Xinhua, Beijing)
Littlejohns, Michael (Financial Times, London; The Economist Foreign Report, London)
Liu Hui (China Radio International, Beijing)
Love, Lee Morse (World Broadcasting News, New York)
Lyons, Richard (New York Times, New York)
Majstr, Jiri (Czech News Agency, Prague)
Malik, Javed A (News International, Pakistan; OPECNA, Austria)
Maslov, Nikolai D (Ukrinform, Kiev)
Matar, Khalil (Asharq al-Awsat, London; Radio Orient, Paris)
Meisler, Stanley (Los Angeles Times, Los Angeles)
Menon, Bhaskar P (International Documents Review, New York; Times of India, New Delhi)
Metzler, John J (USA Radio Network, Dallas, Texas; Worldwatch Column)
Mian, Azim M (News International, Pakistan; Jang, Pakistan; Akhbar-e-Jehan)
Miklas, Kestutis K (Lithuanian Press, New York)
Morello, Ted (Far Eastern Economic Review, Hong Kong; UN Observer & International Report, New York)
Moro, Attilio (Italia Radio, Rome; L'Unita, Rome)
Morsi, Ahmed (Middle East News Agency, Cairo)
Mouat, Lucia (Christian Science Monitor, Boston)
Mourani, Frances Jane (British Broadcasting Corp./BBC, London)
Narkeliunaite, Salomeja (Argentinos Lietuviu Balsas, Buenos Aires)
Nguyen, J Tuyet (United Press International-UPI, Washington)
Nguyen, Long Ba (Vietnam News Agency, Hanoi)
Nicolopoulos, Chris (Rizospastis, Athens)
Nolasco, Sonia (O Estado de Sao Paulo, Sao Paulo)
Osborne, Thomas (ABC News, New York)
Pearson, Ruth (Business Week Magazine, New York)
Pfaeffle, Walter (Kuwait News Agency-KUNA, Kuwait)
Pioli, Giampaolo (Il Resto del Carlino, Bologna; La Nazione, Florence; Il Piccolo, Trieste; Poligrafici Editoriale News Agency, Bologna; Il Tempo, Rome)
Pontecorboli, Gianna (Quotidiani Associati, Rome)
Posseme, Gwenola (Marches Tropicaux, Paris)
Preston, Julia (Washington Post, Washington)
Radovic, Vjekoslav (Tanjung, Belgrade)
Raether, Helmut H (German Press Agency/DPA, Hamburg)
Razzouki, Salah Awad (British Broadcasting Corp./BBC Arabic Service, London; Jana News Agency, Tripoli)
Rees, John H (International Reports, Washington)
Rogozinska-Wickers, Anna (Polish Press Agency, Warsaw)
Roren, Tom (Norway Times, Oslo)
Roth, Richard (CNN, Atlanta)
Rowe, Trevor M (National Public Radio, Washington; Canadian Broadcasting Corp., Toronto)
Ruottinen, Elvi (Gemini News Service, London; UN Observer & International Report, New York)
Rusakov, Yevgeniy M (New Times, Moscow)
Safaat, Aat Surya (Antara News Agency, Jakarta)
Saharkhiz, Isa (Islamic Republic News Agency/IRNA, Teheran, Iran)
Samuels, Gertrude (The News Leader, New York)
Schonfeld, Moses (CBS Radio Network, U.S.; Fairchild Broadcast News, U.S.; Standard Broadcast, Toronto)
Schuler, Thomas (Suddeustsche Zeitung, Germany)
Senyener, Sebnem (Sabah, Istanbul)
Shelley, Sally Swing (Deutsche Welle, Cologne; AP (Radio) Special Assignment; Maryknoll Radio Network)
Shourie, Dharam (Press Trust of India, New Delhi)
Shukur, Malih Salih (Iraqi News Agency, Baghdad)
Sitrin, Gregg M (World Union Press, New York)
Slama, Rene (Agence France-Presse/AFP, Paris)
Sobrino, Jose (EFE News Service, Madrid)
Sofi, Horacio (ANSA/Italian News Agency)
Songur, Iskender (Milliyet, Istanbul)
Spyridaki, Alexandra (Kathimerini, Athens; Antenna TV, Athens)
Stelle, Ian (Press Foundation of Asia-PFA, Manila)
Stewart, Barbara (UN Observer & International Report, New York)
Stroehle, Barbara (Diplomatic World Bulletin)
Sugita, Hiroki (Kyodo News Service, Tokyo)
Supangkat, Hidayat S (Berita Buana, Harian Indonesia)
Svarzman, Norberto L (Televisa, Mexico City)
Tate, Emiko (NHK-Japan Broadcasting Corp., Tokyo)
Tawfik, Hoda (Al-Gomhoria, Cairo; Al-Ittihad, Abu Dhabi)
Torres, Luis (Agence France-Presse/AFP, Paris)
Toups, Catherine (Washington Times, Washington)
Truchan, Barbara (Polish Horyzonty, Stevens Point, WI)
Tuan, Nguyen Minh (Vietnam News Agency, Hanoi)
Ucciardo, Frank J (WPIX-TV/Standard News Network, New York)
Uluc, Dogan (Hurriyet, Istanbul)
Valverde-Ruiz, Gustavo (El Independiente, Madrid)
Vourvouli, Galatia (Messimvrini, Athens)
Wakita, Tetsushi (NHK-Japan Broadcasting Corp., Tokyo)
Wang Pingxing (Xinhua News Agency, Beijing)
Wierzbianski, Boleslaw (Polish American Daily News "Nowy Dziennik", New York)
Williams, Ian G (Tribune, London; New York Observer, New York; Pacific Islands Monthly, Fiji; Al-Wasat, London)
Wolff, Uwe (Focus News Magazine, Munich)
Wurst, James H (Disarmament Times, New York)
Xu Shiquan (People's Daily, Beijing)
Yamazaki, Shinji (Jiji Press, Tokyo)
Youssef, Sanaa (Al-Akhbar, Cairo; Akhbar El-Yom, Cairo; Akher Saa, Cairo)
Zadeh, Akram (Islamedia, Brooklyn, NY; Arab Television of America Inc., New York; American Middle East Television Inc., New York)
Zhang Huangpei (Shanghai Wen Hui Bao, Shanghai)
Zhaolong Xia (Xinhua News Agency, Beijing)

Copyright ©1996 by the Editor & Publisher Co.

REF PN 4700 .E42 1996 c.2

Mongolia, People's Republic of IV-78	Northwest territories.................................... III-29	St. Pierre and Miquelon IV-87
Montana............................ I-235 / 238; II-46 / 47	Norway .... IV-36 / 38	San Marino IV-42
Montserrat, B.W.I. IV-86	Nova Scotia .... III-9 / 11; III-29	Saskatchewan .... III-24 / 25; III-34
Morocco, Kingdom of IV-56	Ohio .... I-302 / 325; II-59 / 63	Saudi Arabia.............................. IV-102 / 103
Mozambique IV-56	Oklahoma .... I-325 / 336; II-63 / 65	Schools of journalism..........................VII-47 / 64
Myanmar, Union of (Burma) IV-78	Oman IV-102	Scotland.. IV-5 / 6
Namibia IV-56	Ombudsmen VII-46	Senegal IV-57
National newspapers I-454	Ontario .... III-11 / 21; III-29 / 32	Seychelles IV-57
National newspaper representatives........VII-34 / 40	Oregon .... I-336 / 342; II-65 / 66	Sierra Leone IV-57
Nebraska .... I-238 / 243; II-47 / 49	Pacific Ocean territories IV-124	Singapore, Republic of IV-82
Nepal IV-78	Pakistan .... IV-78 / 81	Slovak Republic IV-42
Netherlands, The .... IV-35 / 36	Panama IV-100	Slovenia, Republic of IV-42
Netherlands Antilles IV-86	Papua New Guinea IV-124	Solomon Islands IV-124
Networks, magazine sections .... V-13 / 16	Paraguay IV-116	Somalia IV-57
Nevada .... I-243 / 246; II-49	Pay scales ....VI-64 / 66	South Africa, Republic of .... IV-57 / 58
Nevis .... IV-86 / 87	Pennsylvania .... I-342 / 367; II-66 / 68	South America.. IV-105 / 120
New Brunswick .... III-8 / 9; III-29	Peru .... IV-116 / 117	South Carolina .... I-370 / 376; II-68 / 69
New Caledonia IV-124	Philippines .... IV-81 / 82	South Dakota .... I-376 / 379; II-69 / 71
New daily newspapers xxiv	Picture services..V-1 / 11	South Pacific .... IV-120 / 124
New Hampshire .... I-246 / 250; II-49 / 50	Poland .... IV-38 / 40	Spain .... IV-42 / 46
New Jersey .... I-250 / 257; II-50 / 52	Population/Ready Reckoner .... vii / xi	Special service dailies .... I-466 / 471
New Mexico .... I-258 / 263; II-52 / 53	Portugal, Republic of................................... IV-40	Sports dailies.. I-471
New York .... I-263 / 285; II-53 / 57	Press associations & clubs ....VII-3 / 11	Sri Lanka... IV-82
New Zealand .... IV-122 / 124	Press services .... V-1 / 11	Standard advertising invoice xx
Newfoundland.................................. III-9; III-29	Prince Edward Island III-21; III-32	Starting minimums VI-68
Newspaper advertising networks xiv	Professional/special dailies .... I-466 / 471	State newspaper representatives VII-65
Newspaper Association of America ....VII-40 / 44	Promotion services - advertising/circulation VII-1	Sudan IV-58
Newspaper expanded SAU™ system xviii	Puerto Rico IV-86	Suppliers
Newspaper representatives	Qatar IV-102	of interactive equipment.................... VI-45 / 63
Foreign newspaper representatives ......VII-12 / 13	Quebec .... III-21 / 24; III-32 / 34	of newspaper equipment........................ VI-1 / 44
National newspaper representatives.....VII-34 / 40	Ready Reckoner .... vii / xi	Suriname IV-117
State newspaper representatives VII-65	Real estate dailies... I-471	Suspensions, daily newspapers xxiv
News services .... V-1 / 11	Religious newspapers .... II-98 / 100	Swaziland IV-58
Newsprint statistics — 1995 .... I-454	Reporters' starting minimums VI-68	Sweden .... IV-46 / 49
Nicaragua IV-100	Reporters' top minimums VI-67	Switzerland .... IV-49 / 52
Niger, Republic of IV-56	Reunion IV-57	Syndicated features....................................... V-1 / 11
Nigeria, Federal Republic of .... IV-56 / 57	Rhode Island .... I-367 / 370; II-68	Syndicated TMC products VI-16
Niue.. IV-124	Romania .... IV-40 / 41	Syria IV-103
Norfolk Island IV-124	Russia .... IV-41 / 42	Tabloid newspapers I-454; III-35
North Carolina .... I-285 / 299; II-57 / 59	Rwanda IV-57	Tahiti.................................. see French Polynesia
North Dakota .... I-299 / 302; II-59	St. Helena IV-58	Taiwan (Republic of China).............................. IV-83
Northern Ireland IV-5	St. Kitts-Nevis .... IV-86 / 87	Tajikistan IV-52
Northern Mariana Islands IV-124	St. Lucia IV-87	Tanzania IV-58
		Tennessee .... I-379 / 387; II-71 / 72
		Texas .... I-387 / 411; II-72 / 78
		Textiles/clothing dailies I-466
		Thailand .... IV-83 / 84
		Tobago IV-87
		Togo, Republic of IV-58

INDEX TO 1996
INTERNATIONAL YEAR BOOK

ARCHITECTS AND ENGINEERS	**INSURANCE**	Tonga IV-124
Dario Designs Inc. VI-23	Deane Weinberg Insurance	Top minimums VI-67
	Agency Inc. VI-33	Top 100 daily newspapers worldwide xii
CIRCULATION CONSULTANTS		Top 100 U.S. daily newspapers xiii
Kamen & Co. VI-462	**LEGAL SERVICES**	Top 10 Canadian daily newspapers xiii
	Genova, Burns, Trimboli & Vernoia ... I-464	Trade unions VII-65
EQUIPMENT AND SUPPLIES		Trinidad and Tobago IV-87
ALTA Graphics Inc. VI-34	**NEWSPAPER BROKERS AND APPRAISERS**	Tunisia IV-58
Sheridan Sytems .... Cover 2	AdMedia Corporate Advisors I-465	Turkey.. IV-103 / 104
Bulbtronics VI-26	Bolitho-Cribb & Associates I-456	Turks and Caicos Islands IV-87
D.Y.C. Supply Company VI-25	Dirks, Van Essen	Tuvalu IV-124
Dynaric Inc. VI-43	& Associates I-457, VII-45	Uganda IV-58
Ewert America	Hare Associates Inc. I-460	Ukraine IV-52
Electronics Ltd. VI-8	John A. Park, Jr. &	Unions, trade..VII-65
Ferag iii	Associates I-461, VII-45	United Arab Emirates IV-104
Franklin Wire Works Inc. VI-9	Gerald D. Reilly I-458	United Kingdom .... IV-2 / 6
GMA .... Divider I	George Romano I-455	United Nations correspondents VII-66
Industrial Noise Control Inc. VI-36	Veronis, Suhler & Associates Inc. I-459	University newspapers......................... II-101 / 112
Machine Design Service Inc. VI-29		Uruguay .... IV-117 / 118
MAN Roland .... Divider VI	**NEWSPAPERS OF THE UNITED STATES**	Utah .... I-411 / 414; II-78
Masthead International Inc. VI-31	New England Newspapers v	Uzbekistan IV-52
Mid-America Graphics Inc. VI-35	Scripps League Newspapers .... Cover 3	Vanuatu, Republic of................................... IV-124
Pitman Photo Supply VI-37		Vatican City IV-52
PressLink .... Divider V	**NEWS SERVICES AND SYNDICATED FEATURES**	Venezuela.. IV-118 / 120
Printing Press Services .... Divider VI	AFP .... Cover 4	Vermont............................. I-414 / 417; II-78
RRA, Inc. VI-24	Scrambl-Gram Inc. i	Vietnam.. IV-84
Bob Ray & Associates Inc. VI-30		Virgin Islands (British) IV-87
Sitma U.S.A. Inc. .... Divider II	**PERSONNEL AGENCIES**	Virgin Islands (U.S.) IV-87
Stauffer Media Systems VI-27	Gordon Wahls Executive Search I-463	Virginia............................. I-417 / 425; II-78 / 80
Tech-Energy Co. VI-20		Wage scales, mechanical forces .... VI-64 / 68
		Wales IV-6
		Washington (state) .... I-426 / 434; II-80 / 81
		Weekly newspapers .... II-1 / 85; III-26 / 34
		West Virginia..................... I-434 / 440; II-81 / 82
		Wire services .... V-1 / 11
		Wisconsin .... I-440 / 451; II-82 / 85
		Wyoming .... I-451 / 453; II-85
		Yemen, Republic of IV-104
		Yugoslavia IV-52
		Yukon Territory III-25; III-34
		Zaire, Republic of IV-59
		Zambia IV-59
		Zimbabwe IV-59

Copyright ©1996 by the Editor & Publisher Co.

INDEX TO 1996 INTERNATIONAL YEAR BOOK

Advertising/Circulation newspaper
   promotion services VII-1
Advertising/rates/basic data vii
Advertising representatives
   Foreign newspaper representatives ....VII-12 / 13
   National newspaper representatives .....VII-34 / 40
   State newspaper representatives VII-65
Afghanistan IV-59
Africa ....IV-53 / 59
Agricultural dailies I-466
Alabama ....I-1 / 8; II-1 / 2
Alaska ....I-8 / 11; II-2
Albania IV-6
Alberta ....III-1 / 3; III-26 / 27
Algeria IV-53
Alternative newspapers II-86
American Correspondents in London ....VII-1 / 2
American Samoa IV-124
Andorra IV-6
Angola IV-53
Anguilla, B.W.I. IV-84
Antigua and Barbuda IV-84
Apparel/clothing/textile dailies I-466
Argentina ....IV-105 / 108
Armenia IV-6
Arizona ....I-11 / 18; II-2 / 3
Arkansas ....I-18 / 26; II-3 / 4
Aruba ....IV-84 / 85
Asia & Far East ....IV-59 / 84
Associations, Clubs & Press Clubs
   City, State & Regional ....VII-6 / 11
   National & International ....VII-3 / 6
Australia ....IV-120 / 122
Austria ....IV-6 / 7
Azerbaijan IV-7
Azores ....see Portugal
Bahamas IV-85
Bahrain IV-101
Balearic Islands ....see Spain
Bangladesh, People's Republic of ....IV-59 / 60
Barbados IV-85
Barbuda IV-84
Belarus IV-7
Belgium ....IV-7 / 9
Belize IV-87
Benin IV-53
Bermuda IV-85
Bhutan IV-60
Black newspapers in U.S. ....II-87 / 90
Bolivia, Republic of IV-108
Botswana IV-53
Brazil ....IV-108 / 113
Britain ....see United Kingdom
British Columbia ....III-3 / 7; III-27 / 28
British press IV-1
Brokers & appraisers VII-45
Brunei Darussalam IV-60
Building and construction dailies I-466
Bulgaria IV-9
Burkina Faso IV-53
Burma ....see Myanmar
Burundi IV-53
Business special service dailies ....I-466 / 471
Caicos Island IV-87
California ....I-26 / 58; II-4 / 9
Cameroon, Republic of IV-53
Canadian newspaper unit (CNU) xix
Canadian newspapers
   Daily newspapers ....III-1 / 25
   Ethnic newspapers III-35
   Groups, daily newspapers III-36
   Tabloid newspapers III-35
   Weekly newspapers ....III-26 / 34
Canary Islands ....see Spain
Cape Verde IV-53
Caribbean region ....IV-84 / 87
Cayman Islands IV-85
Ceased publication, newspapers xxiv
Central African Republic IV-53
Central America ....IV-87 / 100
Chad IV-53
Channel Islands IV-2
Chile ....IV-113 / 115
China, People's Republic of ....IV-60 / 61

Circulation newspaper promotion services VII-1
Circulation/Ready Reckoner ....vii / xi
Clipping bureaus VII-12
Clip art services VII-11
Clothing/textile dailies I-466
Clubs, newspaper and press ....VII-3 / 11
College newspapers ....II-101 / 112
Colombia ....IV-115 / 116
Colorado ....I-58 / 65; II-9 / 10
Comic section ....V-12 / 13
Commercial dailies ....I-466 / 471
Composing room pay scales ....VI-64 / 66
Congo, Republic of ....IV-53 / 54
Connecticut ....I-65 / 73; II-10 / 11
Construction dailies I-466
Conversions, daily newspapers xxiv
Cook Islands IV-124
Correspondents
   American correspondents in London ....VII-1 / 2
   Foreign correspondents in the U.S. .....VII-13 / 31
   United Nations correspondents VII-66
Costa Rica IV-87
Court & commercial dailies ....I-466 / 471
Cuba IV-85
Curacao ....see Netherlands Antilles
Croatia, Republic of IV-9
Cyprus, Republic of IV-9
Czech Republic ....IV-9 / 10
Daily newspapers ....I-1 / 453; III-1 / 25
   in Canada ....III-1 / 25
   in the United States ....I-1 / 453
Delaware ....I-73 / 74; II-11
Denmark ....IV-10 / 11
District of Columbia ....I-74 / 75
Djibouti IV-54
Dominica IV-85
Dominican Republic ....IV-85 / 86
Ecuador IV-116
Egypt IV-54
Electronic clipping bureaus VII-12
El Salvador IV-88
Engineering dailies I-466
England ....IV-2 / 5
Entertainment dailies I-471
Equatorial Guinea, Republic of IV-54
Equipment ....VI-1 / 44
Estonia IV-11
Ethiopia IV-54
Ethnic newspapers II-90/92; III-35
Europe ....IV-6 / 52
Faeroe Islands ....VI-11 / 12
Far East, Asia ....IV-59 / 84
Feature syndicates ....V-1 / 11
Fiji, Republic of IV-124
Financial dailies ....I-466 / 471
Finland IV-13
Florida ....I-75 / 89; II-11 / 13
Foreign correspondents
   California based correspondents ....VII-28 / 31
   Chicago based correspondents VII-31
   New York based correspondents ....VII-13 / 21
   Washington, DC
     based correspondents ....VII-21 / 28
Foreign newspaper reps. in the U.S. ....VII-12 / 13
Foreign press association ....VII-32 / 34
France ....IV-13 / 15
French Guiana IV-116
French Polynesia IV-124
Gabon Republic IV-54
Gambia IV-54
Gay & lesbian newspapers ....II-92 / 93
Georgia (country) IV-15
Georgia (state) ....I-89 / 98; II-13 / 16
Germany, Federal Republic of ....IV-15 / 27
Ghana IV-54
Gibraltar IV-27
Greece ....IV-27 / 30
Grenada IV-86
Groups, magazine ....V-13 / 16
Groups, daily newspapers ....I-455 / 465; III-36
Guadeloupe IV-86
Guam IV-124
Guatemala IV-88
Guyana IV-116

Guinea, Republic of IV-54
Guinea-Bissau IV-55
Haiti IV-86
Hawaii ....I-98 / 100; II-16
Hispanic newspapers in the U.S. ....II-93 / 95
Honduras IV-88
Hong Kong ....IV-61 / 62
Hungary ....IV-30 / 31
Iceland IV-31
Idaho ....I-100 / 104; II-16
Illinois ....I-104 / 123; II-16 / 22
India ....IV-62 / 69
Indiana ....I-123 / 141; II-22 / 24
Indonesia ....IV-69 / 70
Interactive products and services ....VI-45 / 63
Iowa ....I-141 / 151; II-24 / 27
Iran IV-101
Iraq IV-101
Ireland (Irish Republic) IV-5
Israel ....IV-101 / 102
Italy ....IV-31 / 34
Ivory Coast (Cote D'Ivoire) IV-54
Jamaica IV-86
Japan ....IV-70 / 75
Jewish newspapers in the U.S. ....II-95 / 96
Jordan IV-102
Journalism schools ....VII-47 / 64
Kansas ....I-151 / 162; II-27 / 29
Kazakhstan IV-34
Kentucky ....I-162 / 169; II-29 / 31
Kenya, Republic of IV-55
Korea, North IV-75
Korea, Republic of South ....IV-75 / 76
Kuwait IV-102
Kyrgyzstan IV-34
Labor organizations VII-65
Laos IV-76
Latvia IV-34
Lebanon IV-102
Legal dailies ....I-466 / 471
Lesbian & gay newspapers ....II-92 / 93
Lesotho IV-55
Liberia IV-55
Libya IV-55
Liechtenstein IV-34
Linage, annual advertising vi
Lithuania IV-34
Louisiana ....I-169 / 176; II-31 / 32
Luxembourg IV-34
Macao IV-76
Madagascar IV-55
Magazine sections ....V-13 / 16
Mailroom pay scales VI-66
Maine ....I-176 / 180; II-32 / 33
Malawi IV-55
Malaysia ....IV-76 / 77
Maldives, Republic of IV-78
Mali, Republic of IV-55
Malta IV-34
Manitoba ....III-7 / 8; III-28 / 29
Manufacturers
   of interactive equipment ....VI-45 / 63
   of newspaper equipment ....VI-1 / 44
Marshall Islands IV-124
Martinique IV-86
Maryland ....I-180 / 184; II-33
Massachusetts ....I-184 / 195; II-33 / 36
Mauritania IV-55
Mauritius ....IV-55 / 56
Mayotte Island IV-56
Mechanical equipment — abbreviations xxiii
Mechanical personnel wages ....VI-64 / 66
Mergers, daily newspaper xxiv
Mexico ....IV-88 / 100
Michigan ....I-195 / 210; II-36 / 39
Middle East ....IV-101 / 104
Military newspapers in the U.S. ....II-96 / 98
Milline rates vi
Minnesota ....I-210 / 218; II-39 / 42
Miquelon IV-87
Mississippi ....I-218 / 224; II-42 / 43
Missouri ....I-224 / 235; II-43 / 46
Moldova IV-34
Monaco IV-35

Copyright ©1996 by the Editor & Publisher Co.